American Film Institute

**AMERICAN
FILM
INSTITUTE
CATALOG**

WITHIN OUR GATES:
ETHNICITY IN AMERICAN
FEATURE FILMS, 1911-1960

American Film Institute

Previously published *AFI Catalog* volumes:

Film Beginnings, 1893-1910
Feature Films, 1911-1920
Feature Films, 1921-1930
Feature Films, 1931-1940
Feature Films, 1941-1950, *Forthcoming*
Feature Films, 1951-1960, *In progress*
Feature Films, 1961-1970

American Film Institute

AMERICAN
FILM
INSTITUTE
CATALOG

WITHIN OUR GATES:
ETHNICITY IN AMERICAN
FEATURE FILMS, 1911-1960

ALAN GEVINSON
Editor

University of California Press
Berkeley Los Angeles London

University of California Press
Berkeley and Los Angeles, California

University of California Press, Ltd.
London, England

Published by arrangement with the American Film Institute

Copyright ©1997 by the American Film Institute

Cataloging-in-Publication data is on file with the Library of Congress

ISBN 0-520-20964-8 (cloth)

Printed in the United States of America

9   8   7   6   5   4   3   2   1

The paper used in this publication meets the minimum requirements of
American National Standard for Information Sciences—Permanence of
Paper for Printed Library Materials, ANSI Z39.48-1984.

AMERICAN FILM INSTITUTE

THE NATIONAL CENTER FOR FILM AND VIDEO PRESERVATION

CONTENTS

Foreword   ix

Preface   xi

Sponsor's Page   xii

Introduction   xiii

Acknowledgments   xvi

List of Abbreviations   xviii

Film Entries   1

Introduction to the Indexes   1177

Chronological Index   1179

Personal Name Index   1187

Subject Index   1427

Ethnic Category Index   1553

Foreign Language Index   1565

Bibliography   1569

FOREWORD

★ In the late 1960s, James Earl Jones and I acted together in a film called *The Great White Hope*, which told the story of an African-American champion boxer and his lover at the beginning of the twentieth century. Some people hated it for positing the notion that a black man and a white woman could be in love at all. Times, I hope, have changed.

Prejudice and discrimination are nothing new, and film, like all of the arts, has evolved in its treatment of these social ills. *Within Our Gates: Ethnicity in American Feature Films, 1911-1960* will help shed light on that evolution and on the extraordinary history of ethnic groups that make up our nation. Along with the films that played to stereotypes, there is an almost secret history of movies that take pride in the unique heritage of many ethnic communities. Yiddish films, Chinese films, Italian films, African-American films, Native American films—all tell the American story from a unique angle and perspective. This book will be invaluable to both students of film and anyone intersted in our progress toward respect and understanding.

The American Film Institute has done a remarkable job in researching and cataloging U.S. feature films. *Within Our Gates* is among the more important research tools for filmographers, and I hope it spurs and inspires historians and artists to take a look at the way film has reflected our changing notions of race and ethnicity through both stereotypes and celebration.

The National Endowments for the Arts is proud to have helped support this project and the work of the American Film Institute, which does so much to advance and preserve the art of the moving image.

Jane Alexander
Chairman
National Endowment for the Arts

FOREWORD

★ For anyone seeking to understand America's cultural diversity, the corpus of American feature films about the ethnic experience in the United States is a major resource. In its new catalog titled *Within Our Gates: Ethnicity in American Feature Films, 1911-1960*, the American Film Institute has provided an indispensible service by compiling detailed information about 2,464 films made between 1911 and 1960 that portray the experiences and perspectives of the many ethnic groups comprising America's rich cultural fabric.

Here you will fund plot summaries, the names and roles of actors, production information, and much more about African American films such as *The Homesteader* (1919) and *Harlem on the Prairie* (1938), about foreign-language films made by and for immigrant populations, such as *Senza mamma o innamorata* (1931, Italian), *Mazel Tov* (1932, Yiddish), and *Golden Gate Girl* (1941, Cantonese), and about Hollywood-produced foreign-language films such as *The Trial of Mary Dugan* (1929), *One Hour With You* (1932), and *Folies èBergère* (1934). There are entries for social-problem films of the late 1940s such as *Gentleman's Agreement* (1947), *Pinky* (1949) and *Intruder in the Dust* (1950), and for 1950s films exploring ethnic stereotypes such as *Broken Arrow* (1950), *Marty* (1955) and *The World, the Flesh and the Devil* (1959).

Many of these films are rare, and each is a treasure. *Within our Gates* makes a magnificent contribution, not just in the area of film studies but also to our national cultural heritage, by providing a comprehensive source of information about every known American feature film made from 1911 to 1960 relating to ethnicity. It is an enormous accomplishment.

For more than a decade, the National Endowment for the Humanities has provided funding for volumes in AFI's Catalog of Motion Pictures Produced in the United States. They are the *AFI Catalog of Feature Films* from 1911-1920, 1931-1940, 1941-1950 and 1951-1960. *Within Our Gates* includes all of the entries on ethnic films from these volumes, and much more as well.

Through our support of the earlier volumes, NEH is proud to have helped AFI bring *Within Our Gates* to fruition. It is a resource that will serve the American people—professional scholars and curious citizens alike—far into the future.

> Sheldon Hackney
> Chairman
> National Endowment for the Humanities

PREFACE

★ The American Film Institute has sought to advance and preserve the art of the moving image since it was established in 1967. As one of the cornerstones of AFI's preservation activities, the *AFI Catalog of Motion Pictures Produced in the United States* is an ongoing project which, upon completion, will catalog all American films. To create *Within Our Gates*, new and previously published entries have been culled from the extensive *AFI Catalog* database, which contains filmographic information on over 45,000 films and continues to grow every day.

Unlike the decade-by-decade volumes of the *AFI Catalog of Feature Films* series, *Within Our Gates* covers the entire history of American feature films from 1911 through 1960. Moreover, the volume highlights defining aspects of American social history that have both reflected and were influenced by contemporary motion pictures. Alongside entries for traditional Hollywood studio films, are ones for independently produced films, films made by ethnic groups to entertain and enlighten specific audiences and films made for non-English speaking people throughout the world.

The pages of *Within Our Gates* show both the good and the bad aspects of ethnic film characterizations and, as such, show us as Americans just how we changed through the first half of the century. That fifty-year-period in American history saw two world wars, women's suffrage, the Great Depression, extensive immigration and the start of the Civil Rights movement. Films that explore ethnicity offer great insights into the era, with particular interest provided by comparisons of the various versions of certain films such as *Show Boat* and *Imitation of Life*. To see how sensitive topics of race and society were portrayed in similar situations in different decades helps to illuminate how the nation had or had not changed.

The *AFI Catalog* project has been funded in large part by the National Endowment for the Humanities, the National Endowment for the Arts, the David and Lucile Packard Foundation and the Ahmanson Foundation. Additional funding for *Within Our Gates* was provided by a Challenge Grant from the National Endowment for the Arts. Typesetting costs were obtained from the Bank of America's Specialized Communications and Heritage Programs Foundation.

It is with great pleasure that AFI presents this groundbreaking catalog of films highlighting the ethnic American experience in the United States.

Jean Picker Firstenberg
Director
American Film Institute

SPONSOR'S PAGE

★ In the late 1800s, waves of immigrants came to America hoping to make a better life for themselves and their families. While some settled in the established cities of the East Coast, many saw the new American West as a place of opportunity where one could get ahead with hard work, brains, and character.

Bank of Italy (later Bank of America) was founded in 1904 expressly to help fulfill the dreams of immigrants and working people— those who weren't welcome in most banks of the day. Our founder A.P. Giannini was himself the son of Italian immigrants and he opened his bank in San Francisco's North Beach "International Quarter." He asked employees to treat customers with human warmth and make them feel valued, regardless of their country of origin or size of their accounts. A.P. created special departments to serve different ethnic groups—Chinese, Russian, Italian, Greek, Spanish, Portuguese, Slavonian—staffed with people who spoke their language and knew their needs. In 1921, after women gained the right to vote, he opened a Women's Banking Department with all female staff to help this underserved group achieve financial independence.

In 1908, a young man named Sol Lesser had come to A.P. Giannini for a loan. He owned a share in a local nickelodeon and needed $500 to pick up a new film. Since Lesser was underage, A.P. lent him the money out of his own pocket. Thus began the long-term relationship between Bank of America and the motion picture industry. In the early years, most banks did not see "movies" as a legitimate business and producers had to borrow at high interest from "bonus sharks." But A.P. and his brother Doc Giannini came to believe in this new industry. They made loans at normal rates and developed new forms of collateral.

In 1919, when Doc went to New York to run an affiliate bank, Sol Lesser introduced him to his friends—other hardworking entrepreneurs from immigrant families—people like Carl Laemmle, Marcus Loew, Joseph Schenck, and Lewis Selznick. They became customers and Bank of America went on to back such luminaries as Cecil B. DeMille, Sam Goldwyn, Frank Capra, Walt Disney, and David O. Selznick. In 1947, the bank financed *Boy! What a Girl!*, one of the first post-war films with an all black cast to be shot at a major movie studio with a relatively large budget. Bank of America backed other groundbreaking films with ethnic themes including *Showboat* (1936), *Home of the Brave*, (1949) and *Porgy and Bess* (1959).

Within Our Gates makes available information on hundreds of such films, many included for the first time in an American film history. This volume provides a unique and helpful perspective, presenting both films that stereotype ethnic groups and others that celebrate the human spirit. By studying these contrasts, we expand our own understanding and gain a deeper acceptance and appreciation of others. We at Bank of America feel privileged to support this publication.

David A. Coulter
Chairman and CEO
BankAmerica Corporation

INTRODUCTION

★Almost since the first film was exhibited over one hundred years ago, writers have debated the relationship between motion pictures and the people who enjoy them, often wrestling with issues of whether film influences life and society or merely reflects it. During the same period, the examination of ethnicity in American life also has expanded in fields such as sociology, ehtnic history and ethnic studies.

In this volume we have selected nearly 2,500 feature films in which a significant focus has been on the depiction of members of American ethnic groups. A small, yet significant number of films have been made from within ethnic communities. Countless other films contain ethnic characters in minor roles.

In light of this abundance of material and the growing interest in popular culture and ethnic studies, the staff of the *American Film Institute Catalog of Motion Pictures Produced in the United States* undertook a reference work to collect in one place relevant information on ethnic films. Aiming for authoritative and comprehensive documentation and listings, we have included Hollywood studio films and those made by independent producers; dramatic films and documentaries; films made by ethnic groups for ethnic audiences, and those that depict ethnic groups for the wider American and world screens.

The documentation and portrayal of ethnic groups on film offer unique avenues of exploration into the character of American society and cultures, past and present. Studying films concerning ethnic groups can facilitate understanding the heritage, lifestyle, shared experiences and customs of the many ethnic communities in this country. The documentation of stereotypical filmic portrayals can be useful in the study of societal prejudices. This volume includes films dealing with such topics as the assimilation experiences of immigrants; the maintenance of ethnic identity; generational conflicts within ethnic groups; transformations in ethnic identity; racial prejudice, discrimination and tolerance; xenophobia; experiences and reactions to interracial love and intermarriage; conflicts of ethnic identity, including 'passing' and the experiences of children from mixed marriages; and the fight of ethnic groups for respect and acceptance within the larger framework of American society.

A number of conceptual and definitional decisions have guided our efforts in this volume. For purposes of this project, we have defined an ethnic group as a group of people who by birth share a common culture, social structure, and/or physical appearance differing from those of other groups. Groups defined solely by reason of region, class, gender, age, sexual orientation or political preference were not included as "ethnic."

We decided to orient the volume toward those films in which a major or significant focus (though not necessarily the main focus) was on American ethnic identity. Determining whether ethnic identity was a major or significant focus of a film was our next task. Inclusion of a film in this project, based on our notion of focus, was justified by at least one of the following criteria: a protagonist's American ethnic identity was of thematic importance or colored the film significantly; issues of ethnic identity were dealt with explicitly, even if they were not the film's major focus; aspects of ethnic life, heritage or atmosphere were centered on for significant periods of screen time; conflicts concerning an ethnic group were a major focus, regardless of whether the protagonists were members of ethnic groups; the film was made by an ethnic organization or group explicitly representing an ethnic group; the film was in a foreign language and was exhibited in the U.S. (and thus was produced, at least partially, for an ethnic audience); the film dealt with peoples living in areas that later would become part of the U.S., whose descendants would later make up American ethnic groups; the film dealt with immigration.

In determining whether characters were members of American ethnic groups, citizenship made no difference, but residency did. Films were excluded if characters representing members of ethnic groups played only marginal roles; if the ethnic identity of characters was not focused on; if ethnic conflicts existed in the film, but were not major themes and were not dealt with explicitly; or if characters representing members of ethnic groups did not live in the U.S. Some films were included if they were made elsewhere, but were based on American ethnic literature. Some foreign- language films made in Hollywood for export only were not included, as they were not made for ethnic audiences in the United States.

In addition to these limits based on content, we soon recognized that additional determining restrictions regarding film length and time period of release would be necessary to allow the project to be completed in its alloted time, and so we chose to include only feature-length films released before 1961. These qualifications were chosen for practical reasons: *AFI Catalog* volumes had already published covering features made between 1911 and 1940 and work was in progress on the 1941-50 volume; thus, the only new group of films to be included would be features from the 1950s. Although these limitations were set to make the project manageable, the boundaries forced us to exclude many films that are relevant for the study of ethnicity in popular culture.

For *Within Our Gates*, we have relied heavily on research previously published in *AFI Catalog* volumes. Since its inception in 1969, the *AFI Catalog's* aim has been to provide comprehensive filmic information for all American theatrically released films. As the project has evolved over the years since 1969, cataloguing procedures have changed significantly in areas of plot summary length and the extent of note material and credit information. Readers will find that films included in this volume from the 1920s generally have far less material than films from later periods. In additon, beginning with the 1931-40 volumes, we made the decision to attempt to view films for cataloguing purposes, rather than to rely solely on secondary sources. Notations that a film has been viewed thus appear in many of the 1931-1960 entries. Entries for films produced between 1911-1930 that are notated "print viewed" have been viewed and revised specifically for *Within Our Gates*.

We selected films for inclusion by first examining relevant entries in the *AFI Catalog* volumes previously published, covering 1911-40. For the period 1941-60, we chose two film journals that either listed or reviewed nearly all theatrically-released features and analyzed plot descriptions of all films reviewed during this period: *Harrison's Reports* and *The Exhibitor*. In addition, we checked databases and catalogs at major American film archives; specialized published sources on ethnic films; educational film catalogs; and ethnic newspapers from periods in which we had reason to believe that relevant films were produced. Finally, we consulted and took advantage of our network of colleagues in the fields of film scholarship and archiving.

Decisions regarding inclusion or exclusion of films in certain categories proved to be extremely difficult to make. In films dealing with the two world wars, it was often unclear if "enemy" characters were ethnic Americans or spies sent from enemy countries. Films set in the Mexican-American border region had characters for which it was impossible to determine if they were Mexican Americans or Mexicans visiting the U.S. temporarily. In these and other questionable areas, we included films only if it appeared likely that our conditions for inclusion were fulfilled.

Once selection was made, we reviewed previously published cataloging from the decades 1911-40 and updated some of those records based on newly researched information. Much new material was added to African-American cast films from the 1920s after we viewed films that were previously unavailable and following a methodical perusal of certain African-American newspapers. For films newly cataloged from the decades 1941-60, we obtained a print or videotape of each film if this was possible. Otherwise, we attempted to find dialogue continuities taken from the screen

available from a number of sources, including studio records, U.S. Copyright Office records and New York State censorship records. Where relevant, studio records and those of the Production Code Administration, the motion picture industry's agency of self-regulation, were consulted. Reviews were sought for all films, and in many cases, news items in trade journals pertaining to production were researched. Our goal, as always, has been to provide accurate and comprehensive information regarding the production, distribution and exhibition of these films.

The entries in *Within Our Gates* are arranged alphabetically by title. A number of indexes are included following the entries, which list film titles in the main section according to relevant indexed features, among them the Ethnic Category Index, which arranges film titles according to ethnic group, the Personal Name Index, which provides filmographies for producers, directors, writers and actors, and a Subject Index that provides access to films through relevant subject headings of major or minor significance within the films.

All information presented in the main body of a *Catalog* entry is taken from onscreen credits or from sources contemporaneous to the film's production. Additionally, many sources from later periods have been consulted. Material coming solely from these later sources is given in the Note section of the entry and identified as being based on modern sources. When an entry indicates that a print has been viewed, credit listings appearing without brackets match onscreen credits; listings in brackets were not credited onscreen, but found in sources contemporaneous to the film's production, such as studio records and reviews.

A source for cast information that we used heavily, the Call Bureau Cast Service (CBCS), a service provided by the Association of Motion Picture Producers to their members, contains listings compiled during production for cast members, including 'bit' players. Although we have sometimes found that names included on the CBCS listings are not 100% reflective of the cast at the time of a film's release, due to changes in production following the compiling of the CBCS listings, we have nevertheless felt it to be a significant source of information. Whenever possible, the staff verified names on the often lengthy CBCS, but readers should be aware that some cast members listed may not have appeared in the released film.

Release dates given without qualification are national release dates. When we have found listings for multiple running times, we have included the various listings without selecting any one as authoritative. We have tried, where possible, to provide information regarding footage given by the releasing company. Plot summaries are intended to represent the stories of the films clearly, concisely and without bias. Subject indexing based on the plot summaries has been organized according to whether specific subject terms were of major or minor importance. The Note section includes relevant material relating to the film's production history. [In some cases, a note may refer the reader to the "Series Index." Due to space limitations, there is no Series Index within this volume, thus the reader should consult the Series Indexes in previously published *AFI Catalog* volumes.]

Foreign-language versions of films are listed following the Note section. In some cases, these versions have been included because they were made for ethnic audiences, not because of their specific ethnic content, which may be absent. In some specified cases, plot summaries have been based on the more accessible English-language versions, even though credit information pertains to the foreign-language versions.

Our title, *Within Our Gates*, comes from Oscar Micheaux's 1919 film, the earliest surviving feature made by an African American. That film has been viewed by some film historians as an attempt to challenge and correct the depiction of African Americans as portrayed in earlier, more widely seen productions. We dedicate this volume, which we hope also will challenge and correct, to those filmmakers like Micheaux whose independence, drive and struggles resulted in films that provided alternative views of the peoples of their time and to us, their descendants.

ACKNOWLEDGMENTS

★ This project was funded in part by a Challenge Grant awarded by the National Endowment for the Arts. Typesetting costs were provided by the Bank of America Specialized Communications and Heritage Foundation.

Thanks and acknowledgments are also extended to Twentieth Century-Fox for permission to use material in their Produced Scripts Collection and Records of the Legal Department at the UCLA Arts—Special Collections Library. Prints and videotapes of films were graciously provided for research purposes by Turner Entertainment, Republic Pictures, Sony Pictures, MCA, Kit Parker Films and Eddie Brandt's Saturday Matinee Video Emporium.

Many people gave generous assistance with consultation, research and production. The members of the advisory committee supplied needed help and encouragement during the early phases. Juan Heinink and Robert G. Dickson again allowed us to use material on Spanish-language films from their award-winning book *Cita en Hollywood: Antologia de las peliculas norteamericanas habladas en ñespañol* (Bilbao, Spain: Ediciones Mensajero, 1990) and additional unpublished material related to foreign-language films made in Hollywood and France. D. Richard Baer of Hollywood Film Archives supplied us with complete runs of the invaluable journals *The Exhibitor* and *Harrison's Report*.

Felicia Ho and Jen-Feng Lee researched and translated Chinese-language newspapers and other material. Berit Engen provided translations of Swedish material. Anna Dassonville translated articles from Polish-language newspapers. Pam Harris and Paige Harding assisted with research in Los Angeles. Nancy Seeger and Sam Brylawski of the Library of Congress Motion Picture, Broadcasting, and Recorded Sound Division provided help and work above and beyond the call of duty and friendship. The exemplary work and much appreciated advice of Marsha Maguire, a consultant and cataloger during the first half of the project, gave us direction and a strong foundation.

Within Our Gates would not have been finished were it not for the dedication of Pat Hanson, who oversaw the project through its final stages, and Amy Dunkleberger, Laura Lee McKay, Karl Rathcke, Cathy Root, Bob Dickson, Torene Svitil, Melanie Watkins, Howie Davidson, Lisa Wasserman, Shannon Kaussen, Valerie Kaussen and Dianna Ippolito, who labored to see it through to completion. If this volume is of importance to the study of ethnicity and film, it is to them and their efforts that indebtedness is owed.

Thanks is also extended to those project directors, editors and researchers who labored on the various volumes of the *AFI Catalogs*: Project Directors Audrey E. Kupferberg, Stephen Gong and Michael Friend; Editor Kenneth W. Munden; Researchers Lee Atwell, Patricia Ann Bledsoe, Virginia M. Clark, Harvey R. Deneroff, Harold Blanchard Grenwood, Barbara Humphrys, Francis L. Jones, Bridget O'Reilly, David Parket, Barry Sabath, Dan Sallitt, Eric Smoodin, Brian Taves and Stephen Francis Zito.

The following additional institutions and individuals have assisted the project instrumentally:

Bishop Museum Archives, Honolulu
Chinese Historical Society, San Francisco
CityLore
Cuadra Associates, Inc.
Dual Graphics
The Evangelical Lutheran Church in America
Hong Kong Film Archive
J. Pilsudski Institute
Library of Congress Motion Picture, Broadcasting, and Recorded Sound Division
The Louis B. Mayer Library at the American Film Institute
The Margaret Herrick Library at the Academy of Motion Picture Arts & Sciences
Museum of Modern Art
National Archives and Records Service
The National Center for Jewish Film
New York State Archives and Records Administration
UCLA Arts—Special Collections Library
UCLA Film and Television Archive
USC Cinema-Television Library & Archive of the Performing Arts
The Walt Disney Archives
Wisconsin Center for Film and Theater Research

Zachary Joseph Balian
Trudy Goodwin Barnes
Donovan Brandt
Alan Braun
DeSoto Brown
Margaret Byrne
Marie Capasso
Janet Carter
Kathleen Condon
Grover Crisp
Anthony Crouch
Susan Dalton
Sam Gill
Robert Gitt
William P. Gorman
Jere Guldin
Rosemary C. Hanes
Gladys B. Irvis
Kim Jacobson
Eric John
Lorrayne R. Jurist
Andrea Kalas
Christopher D. Kamyszew
J. B. Kaufman
Kevin Klages
Duncan Knowles
Lou Ellen Kramer

Miriam Saul Krant
Brigitte Kueppers
Barbara Kundanis
Him Mark Lai
Todd McCarthy
Henry Mattoon
Madeline F. Matz
Dick May
William Motley
David Parker
Rich Pontius
Howard Prouty
Steven Ricci
Ariane Ulmer Seitz
Patrick J. Sheehan
Wayne Shirley
Scott Simmon
David R. Smith
Michelle Tam
Faye Thompson
Shirley Ulmer
Chi Wang
Maureen O'Brien Will
Lubomyr R. Wynar
Judy Yung
Kathleen Zielinski

LIST OF ABBREVIATIONS

TERMS

Addl:	Additional	Gen:	General
Adpt:	Adapted by, Adaptor, Adaption	Int:	Interior
Adv:	Advisor	Loc:	Location, Locations
Anim:	Animated by, Animation, Animator	Mgr:	Manager
Arr:	Arranged by, Arrangement, Arranger	Mus:	Music, Musical
App:	Appendix	Narr:	Narration, Narrator
Assoc:	Associate	Op:	Operator
Asst:	Assistant	Orch:	Orchestra, Orchestration
Bus:	Business	Orig:	Original
Cam:	Camera, Cameraman	Photog:	Photographed by, Photographer, Photograpy
Cine:	Cinematographer, Cinematography by	Pres:	Presented by, Presenter
Col:	Color	Prod:	Produced by, Producer, Production
Comm:	Commentary by, Commentator	Prol:	Prologue
Comp:	Composed by, Composer	Prop:	Properties, Props
Cond:	Conducted by, Conductor	Pub:	Publicist, Publicity
Const:	Construction	Rec:	Recorded by, Recorder, Recording
Cont:	Continuity	Scen:	Senario, Scenarist
Contr:	Contributor, Contributing	Scr:	Screen, Screenplay, Script
Cost:	Costumes, Costumer	Sd:	Sound
Dec:	Decorations, Decorator	Secy:	Secretary
Des:	Design, Designed by, Designer	Seq:	Sequence, Sequences
Dial:	Dialogue	Si:	Silent
Dir:	Directed by, Director, Direction	Spec:	Special
Dist:	Distribution, Distributor	Spons:	Sponsor
Ed:	Edited by, Editor	Supv:	Supervised by, Supervisor
Eff:	Effects	Tech:	Technical, Technician
Elec:	Electrial, Electrician	Trmt:	Treatment
Eng:	Engineer	Ward:	Wardrobe
Exec:	Executive	Wrt:	Writer, Written by

PERIODICALS AND ORGANIZATIONS

AmCin:	American Cinematographer	MPA:	Motion Picture Almanac
AFI:	American Film Institute	MPAA:	Motion Picture Assoc of America
AMPAS:	Acad of Motion Pic Arts & Sciences	MPC:	Motion Picture Classic
AMPP:	Assoc of Motion Picture Prods	MPD:	Motion Picture Daily
AtlC:	Atlanta Constitution	MPH:	Motion Picture Herald
AtlJ:	Atlanta Journal	MPHPD:	Motion Picture Herald Prod Digest
BHCN:	Beverly Hills Citizen News	MPN:	Motion Picture News
BIO:	The Bioscope	MPNBG:	Motion Picture News Booking Guide
BFI:	British Film Institute	MPSI:	Motion Picture Studio Insider
Box:	Box Office	MPW:	Moving Picture World
CBCS:	Call Bureau Cast Service	NCJF:	The National Center for Jewish Film
ChiDef:	Chicago Defender	NYDN:	New York Daily News
CM:	Cine Mundial	NYDM:	New York Dramatic Mirror
Cinl:	Cinelandia	NYHT:	New York Herald Tribune
DV:	Daily Variety	NYMirror	New York Mirror
DW:	Daily Worker	NYMT:	New York Morning Telegraph
EHW:	Exhibitors Herald-World	NYN:	New York News
EK:	Edison Kinetogram	NYP:	New York Post
ETR:	Exhibitor's Trade Review	NYR:	New York Review
Exh:	The Exhibitor	NYSA:	New York State Archives
FD:	Film Daily	NYT:	New York Times
FDYB:	Film Daily Year Book	NYTr:	New York Tribune
FIR:	Films in Review	NYWorld:	New York World
Har:	Harrrison's Reports	PCA:	Production Code Administration
HCN:	Hollywood Citizen-News	Photo:	Photoplay
HF:	Hollywood Filmograph	PittsC:	Pittsburgh Courier
HH:	Hollywood Herald	PM:	PM (Journal)
HR:	Hollywood Reporter	SFChron:	San Francisco Chronicle
HS:	Hollywood Spectator	SatRev:	Saturday Review (of Literature)
IFJ:	Independent Film Journal	SAB:	Screen Achievements Bulletin
IP:	International Photographer	SEP:	The Saturday Evening Post
KW:	Kinematograph Weekly	STR:	Showmen's Trade Reviews
LADN:	Los Angeles Daily News	S&S:	Sight and Sound
LAEx:	Los Angeles Examiner	UCLA:	University of California at LA
LAHE:	Los Angeles Herald Express	USC:	University of Southern California
LAMirror	Los Angeles Mirror	Var:	Variety
LAMirror	News: Los Angeles Mirror-News	VarB:	Variety Bulletin
LASent:	Los Angeles Sentinel	VLP:	Vitagraph Life Portrayals
LAT:	Los Angeles Times	Wid's:	Wid's Daily
Motog:	Motography	Wid'sY:	Wid's Yearbook

American Film Institute

**AMERICAN
FILM
INSTITUTE
CATALOG**

WITHIN OUR GATES:
ETHNICITY IN AMERICAN
FEATURE FILMS, 1911-1960

FILM ENTRIES

WITHIN OUR GATES: ETHNICITY IN AMERICAN FEATURE FILMS, 1911-1960

ABIE'S IMPORTED BRIDE (Jewish Americans)

Temple Theater Amusement Co. *Dist* Trio Productions. **1925** [©Temple Theater Amusement Co.; 15 Jun 1925; LP21570]. Si; b&w. 7 reels.

Dir Roy Calnek. *Wrt* Roy Calnek.

Comedy. When Abie Lavinsky, the son of the owner of the prosperous Lavinsky woolen mills, learns of the plight of Jews starving in Russia, he sets out to collect money to help alleviate their hunger and suffering. He asks the workers at his father's factory to contribute and then, at the sarcastic urging of his father, arranges a charity ball at which he raises $100,000 from his jazz-minded friends. Abie is then elected to go to Russia with the money, and he makes plans to depart immediately. Max Rosenthal, a professional matchmaker, interests the elder Lavinsky in a young girl in Russia, and Abie violently opposes the match. His father is unmoved by Abie's pleas to be reasonable, and Abie is delegated to make the arrangements to bring the young girl to the United States to be wed to the elder Lavinsky. Abie falls in love with her himself, and they decide to be married, fully expecting Abie to be disinherited by his father. When they return to the United States, however, the elder Lavinsky greets them with love, showing Abie a telegram from Max, "Your plan worked fine. Abie swallowed it hook, line and sinker; no danger from flappers now; Abie safely married and on way home." After a few minutes of chagrin, Abie is reconciled with his father. *Charity. Family relationships. Famines. Jews. Matchmakers. Mills. Russia. Woolen mills.*

Note: This film was produced in Philadelphia in October and November of 1924.

ABIE'S IRISH ROSE (Jewish Americans)

Paramount Famous Lasky Corp. 5 Jan **1929** [©Paramount Famous Lasky Corp.; 8 Jan 1929; LP25986]. Talking sequences, sound effects, & music score (Movietone); b&w. 12 reels, 10471 ft. [Length also listed at 10,187 ft.].

Assoc prod B. P. Schulberg. *Dir* Victor Fleming. *Adpt* Jules Furthman. *Titles* Anne Nichols, Herman Mankiewicz and Julian Johnson. *Photog* Harold Rosson. *Film ed* Eda Warren.

Song(s): "Rosemary" and "Little Irish Rose," music by J. S. Zamecnik, lyrics by Anne Nichols.

Source: Based on the play *Abie's Irish Rose* by Anne Nichols (New York, 23 May 1922).

Cast: Charles Rogers (*Abie Levy*), Nancy Carroll (*Rosemary Murphy*), Jean Hersholt (*Solomon Levy*), J. Farrell MacDonald (*Patrick Murphy*), Bernard Gorcey (*Isaac Cohen*), Ida Kramer (*Mrs. Isaac Cohen*), Nick Cogley (*Father Whalen*), Camillus Pretal (*Rabbi Jacob Samuels*), Rosa Rosanova (*Sarah*).

Drama. During World War I, Abie Levy, a soldier in the A. E. F., is wounded in combat. While recovering in a hospital, he meets Rosemary Murphy, an entertainer. They fall in love, return to the United States, and get married in an Episcopal church in Jersey City. Abie takes Rosemary to his home and introduces her as his sweetheart, Rosie Murpheski; they are then married by a rabbi. Mr. Murphy arrives with a priest and, amid discord and discontent, the young people are married again, this time by the priest. Disowned by both families, Rosemary and Abie are befriended only by the Cohens. On Christmas Eve, the Cohens and their rabbi persuade Solomon to see his son and his new grandchildren; the priest urges Mr. Murphy to do the same. This surprise visit begins in acrimony, but ends peacefully as Rosemary presents her newborn twins: Patrick Joseph, named for her father, and Rebecca, named for Abie's dead mother. *Bigotry. Entertainers. Irish. Jersey City (NJ). Jews. Marriage–Mixed. Priests. Protestantism. Rabbis. Soldiers. Veterans. Weddings. World War I.*

FD 22 Apr 1928. *NYT* 20 Apr 1928, p. 26. *Var* 26 Dec 1928, p. 27.

ABIE'S IRISH ROSE (Jewish Americans, Irish Americans)

Bing Crosby Producers, Inc. *Dist* United Artists Corp. 27 Dec **1946**; New York opening: 21 Dec 1946; Prod: began 15 Apr 1946 [©Bing Crosby Producers, Inc.; 27 Dec 1946; LP820]. Sd (Western Electric Sound System); b&w. 8,693 ft. 96-96.5 or 98 min. PCA cert no. 11615.

Prod A. Edward Sutherland. *Dir* A. Edward Sutherland. *Asst dir* Barton Adams. *Scr* Anne Nichols. *Adpt* Anne Wigton and Rip Van Ronkel. *Photog* William C. Mellor. *Photog eff* Roy W. Seawright. *Prod des* William E. Flannery. *Supv film ed* William H. Ziegler. *Film ed* Harvey Manger. *Set dec* Victor A. Gangelin. *Cos des* Michael Woulfe. *Ward* Robert Martien. *Mus supv* Perry Botkin. *Mus* John Scott Trotter. *Sd rec* Roy Meadows. *Makeup supv* Paul Malcolm. *Hair stylist* Lillian Burkhart. *Prod mgr* Harold Schwartz.

Song(s): "Abie's Irish Rose," music and lyrics by Robert Wells and Mel Tormé.

Source: Based on the play *Abie's Irish Rose* by Anne Nichols (New York, 23 May 1922).

Cast: MICHAEL CHEKHOV (*Solomon Levy*), And introducing Joanne Dru By arrangement with Howard Hawks (*Rosemary Murphy* [*Levy*]), Richard Norris (*Abie Levy*), J. M. Kerrigan (*Patrick Murphy*), George E. Stone (*Isaac Cohen*), Vera Gordon (*Mrs. Cohen*), Emory Parnell (*Father [John] Whelan*), Art Baker (*Dr. [Jacob] Samuels*), Eric Blore (*Assistant manager [Mr. Stubbins]*), Bruce Merritt (*Rev. [Tom] Stevens*), Roy Atwell ([*Dick*] *Saunders*), Eddie Parks (*Gilchrist*), Vera Marshe (*Mrs. [Edna] Gilchrist*), James Nolan (*Policeman*), [Charles Hall (*Hotel porter*)], [Harry Hays Morgan (*Hotel clerk*)], [Walter Soderling (*Herman*)], [Ella Mae Brown (*Sarah, the maid*)], [Steve Olsen (*Airport clerk*)], [Louis Jean Heydt (*Priest*)], [Oscar O'Shea (*Bishop*)], [Larry Wheat (*Doctor*)], [Frances Morris, Helen Deverell (*Nurses*)], [Jimmy Aubrey (*Waiter*)], [Wilbur Mack (*Jewelry salesman*)], [Betty Gregory, Kay Jewell, Lucille Noble, Jean Herbers, Shirley Winters, Virginia Ellsworth (*Bridesmaids*)], [James Farley (*American general*)], [Patricia Kory, Maureen Kory (*Twins*)].

Domestic, Comedy-drama. [*Print viewed*]. On V-E Day in London, American soldier Abie Levy falls in love with U.S.O. entertainer Rosemary Murphy, and shortly after, they are married by an Army chaplain, Rev. Tom Stevens. When Abie returns home, however, he keeps his marriage a secret, knowing that his father Solomon would not approve of his marrying an Irish Catholic woman. A few months later, Rosemary returns to the United States, prompting Abie to reveal to Solomon that he met a woman overseas and intends to bring her to dinner. That evening, Abie introduces Rosemary as Rosie Murphiski, allowing Solomon to infer that she is Jewish. Although Rosemary privately protests to Abie, he insists that the deception is necessary until Solomon has time to know and love her. Delighted with Rosemary's beauty and sweetness, Solomon enlists the family rabbi, Dr. Jacob Samuels, to help plan a Jewish wedding for the couple. On the day of the wedding, Rosemary's father Patrick flies in from California with his friend, Father John Whelan, but arrives just after the vows have been uttered. Because Patrick dislikes Jews as much as Solomon dislikes the Irish, Rosemary has told him she is marrying a man named Michael McGee. When Patrick and Solomon finally learn about their children's deception, they engage in a fierce argument, while Solomon's friends, Isaac Cohen and his wife, side with Rosemary and Abie. Patrick insists that the Jewish marriage is not legal, and Father Whelan gets a special dispensation to allow him to perform a Catholic wedding ceremony. Abie and Rosemary are wed three times, but their fathers refuse to have anything to do with the couple or with each other. The Cohens stand by the newlyweds,

however, offering them both friendship and financial help, and a year later, they arrive at Abie and Rosemary's apartment to help them decorate a Christmas tree. Rosemary has given birth, but neither grandparent has visited or offered congratulations, until Father Whelan arrives with a reluctant Patrick, who is pleased to see the Christmas tree. Patrick brings presents for a girl, hoping that the baby is not a boy because he does not want his grandchild to bear the name Levy all of his life. Soon after, Dr. Samuels arrives with Solomon, who carries a menorah and presents for a boy, and the two grandfathers again become embroiled in a loud, endless argument. Father Whelan and Dr. Samuels are joined by Rev. Stevens, and the three theologians intervene and bring out a baby boy named Patrick Joseph Levy. Patrick loves the name as much as Solomon hates it, and Solomon declares that he will call the baby "Mr. Levy." Little Pat's twin sister is then brought out and when Solomon learns that she is named Rebecca for Abie's dead mother, his heart is softened. The joy of holding the babies brings the grandfathers together, but their happiness is temporarily interrupted when baby Pat swallows a hook from a Christmas tree ornament. A doctor saves the boy, much to the relief of the grandfathers, who immediately start to argue over who gets to hold Pat. A passing policeman stops by to investigate the doctor's badly parked car, and upon hearing the twins cry, assures Abie and Rosemary that he has a foolproof system for getting babies to sleep. Holding the twins close, the policeman sings both an Irish lullaby and a Jewish song, soothing them to sleep and proving to the grandfathers that their separate cultures can be satisfactorily intertwined. Patrick and Solomon then shake hands, and everyone enjoys a happy holiday. *Catholics. Intolerance. Irish Americans. Jews. Marriage–Mixed. Chaplains. Christmas. Fathers and daughters. Fathers and sons. Infants. London (England). Marriage–Secret. Physicians. Police. Priests. Rabbis. Twins. United Service Organizations. Veterans. Weddings.*

Note: In the opening title card, Anne Nichols' name appears above the title. Nichols' play ran for six years on Broadway, according to a 30 Dec 1946 article in *Time*. Later it served as the basis for a radio comedy serial, but the program was canceled in 1945 because of listener protests about its stereotyped ethnic portrayals. Although the play was an all-time box-office champion, the *Var* reviewer expressed doubts that the film would find an audience at a time when "minorities become political footballs, when all the energies of postwar rehabilitation seem to focus on an effort for better understanding...the story has become a topical misfit." The *NYT* reviewer agreed, stating, "it is downright embarrassing to see characters upon the screen insulting each other because one happens to be a Jew and the other an Irish Catholic." In a 6 Nov 1946 article, *DV* quotes members of the National Conference of Christians and Jews, who deemed the film, "the worst sort of caricature of both Jews and Catholics." A 22 Dec 1946 *NYT* article reported that after objections from the Anti-Defamation League, which complained about the use of Jewish characters for comedy relief, some of the gags referring to "Jewish parsimony" were cut.

In a 3 Feb 1947 article, *HR* noted that Rabbi Max Nussbaum defended the picture's intent to promote racial tolerance. Although he stated that "qualitatively the picture could have been much better," and that certain scenes and characters did not accurately reflect real Jewish life, Rabbi Nussbaum pointed to other films, such as *The Jolson Story*, which presented realistic portrayals of Jews and lauded producer Bing Crosby's service to Jewish and minority causes. A 6 May 1947 *HR* news item noted that despite a "whispering campaign" against the film, theaters that played the picture made a profit, and additional exhibitors were gradually booking the film. The news item added that the picture had been cleared by the Anti-Defamation League, the Legion of Decency and the Production Code Administration.

This film marked the motion picture debuts of Joanne Dru and Richard Norris. Anne Nichols' play also was the basis for the 1929 Paramount film of the same title, which starred Charles Rogers and Nancy Carroll (see below).

Box 30 Nov 1946. *Cue* 21 Dec 1946. *DV* 6 Nov 1946. *DV* 25 Nov 1946, p. 3, 10. *FD* 29 Nov 1946, p. 7. *Har* 30 Nov 1946, p. 190. *Har* 21 Dec 1946, p. 201. *HR* 15 Apr 1946, p. 10. *HR* 25 Nov 1946, p. 3. *HR* 27 Dec 1946, p. 6. *HR* 3 Feb 1947, p. 1, 18. *HR* 6 May 1947, p. 3. *MPHPD* 29 Jun 1946, p. 3066. *MPHPD* 30 Nov 1946, p. 3334. *NYT* 22 Dec 1946. *NYT* 23 Dec 1946, p. 19. *Time* 30 Dec 1946. *Var* 27 Nov 1946 p. 14.

ABRAHAM LINCOLN (African Americans)

Feature Productions, Inc. *Dist* United Artists Corp. 8 Nov **1930**; New York premiere: 25 Aug 1930 [©Feature Productions, Inc.; 1 Sep 1930; LP1585]. Sd (Movietone); b&w. 10 reels, 8,704 ft.

Pres Joseph M. Schenck. *Story and prod adv* John W. Considine, Jr. *Dir* D. W. Griffith. *Assoc dial dir* Harry Stubbs. *Adpt, cont and dial* Stephen Vincent Benét. *Cont and dial* Gerrit Lloyd. *Photog* Karl Struss. *Art dir* William Cameron Menzies and Park French. *Film ed* James Smith and Hal C. Kern. *Cost* Walter J. Israel. *Mus arr* Hugo Riesenfeld. *Sd rec* Harold Witt. *Prod mgr* Orville O. Dull. *Prod staff* Raymond A. Klune and Herbet Sutch.

Cast: Lucille La Verne (*Mid-Wife*), W. L. Thorne (*Tom Lincoln*), Helen Freeman (*Nancy Hanks Lincoln*), Otto Hoffman (*Offut*),

Walter Huston (*Abraham Lincoln*), Edgar Deering (*Armstrong*), Una Merkel (*Ann Rutledge*), Russell Simpson (*Lincoln's employer*), Charles Crockett (*Sheriff*), Kay Hammond (*Mary Todd Lincoln*), Helen Ware (*Mrs. Edwards*), E. Alyn Warren (*Stephen A. Douglas*), Jason Robards (*Herndon*), Gordon Thorpe (*Tad Lincoln*), Ian Keith (*John Wilkes Booth*), Cameron Prudhomme (*John Hay, Secretary to Lincoln*), James Bradbury, Sr. (*General Scott*), James Eagle (*Young Soldier*), Fred Warren (*General Grant*), Oscar Apfel (*Secretary of War*), Frank Campeau (*General Sheridan*), Hobart Bosworth (*General Lee*), Henry B. Walthall (*Colonel Marshall*), Hank Bell, Carl Stockdale, Ralph Lewis, George MacQuarrie, Robert Brower.

Historical, **Drama**. After a brief scene depicting the circumstances of Lincoln's birth in 1809, we find him at the age of twenty-two, "the ugliest and smartest man in New Salem, Ill." and a clerk in D. Offut's general store. In the spring of 1834, Abe is courting Ann Rutledge when she dies abruptly of fever, causing him great suffering. After three years of fighting in the Indian war as Captain of Volunteers, Abe begins his law practice. At a ball given by former governor Edwards, the awkward lawyer meets Mary Todd and later, despite misgivings, marries her. His reputation as a debater wins him the Republican nomination to the presidency, and he is elected. John Brown and the Abolitionists capture the armory at Harper's Ferry, and John Wilkes Booth, a fanatic exhorter, cries out for volunteers to avenge the act; thus the Civil War is launched. Following hostilities at Fort Sumter and Bull Run, Washington itself is threatened. Lincoln makes a personal visit to a battlefield and comes upon a court-martial in progress; he asks the defendant to explain his actions, pardons him, and orders him back to his regiment. The signing of the Emancipation Proclamation intensifies the struggle, and Lincoln is encouraged by Congress to end the war. Lincoln selects Grant to lead Union forces. While conferring with Stanton, the President receives word of Sheridan's defeat; he tells Stanton of his vision of a ship with white sails before each victory.... The last of the Confederate forces under Lee are defeated, and the war is over. On the night of 14 Apr 1865, Lincoln speaks from a box at Ford's Theatre, and just after the play has begun, he is shot by John Wilkes Booth; the resulting uproar gives way to the sobbing of an unseen multitude, and a voice calls out: "Now he belongs to the ages." *Abolitionists. John Wilkes Booth. John Brown. Courtship. Stephen Douglas. Elections. Emancipation Proclamation. Ford's Theatre (Washington, DC). Ulysses Simpson Grant. John Milton Hay. Illinois. Lawyers. Robert E. Lee. Abraham Lincoln. Mary Todd Lincoln. Rural life. Ann Rutledge. Winfield Scott. General Philip Henry Sheridan. Edwin McMasters Stanton. United States–History–Civil War, 1861-1865.*

FD 31 Aug 1930. *NYT* 26 Aug 1930, p. 24. *Var* 27 Aug 1930, p. 21.

ABSENT (African Americans)

Rosebud Film Corp. **1928**; World premiere in Los Angeles: 28 Aug 1928. Si; b&w. 6 reels, 5,046 ft.

Supv Harry A. Gant. *Dir* Harry A. Gant. *Photog* Harry A. Gant.

Cast: Clarence Brooks (*Soldier*), George Reed (*Miner*), Virgil Owens (*Villain*), Rosa Lee Lincoln, Floyd Shackelford, Clarence Williams.

Melodrama, **African American**. A shell-shocked African-American veteran drifts into a mining camp and is given sustenance by an old miner and his daughter. He later regains his memory in a fight and is given a fresh start by the American Legion. *African Americans. American Legion. Amnesia. Miners. Shell shock. Veterans.*

Note: According to an article in *California Eagle*, this was the first production of Rosebud Film Corp., a Hollywood production company. However, a news item in the same paper by the Associated Negro Press states that the film is owned and controlled by the Lincoln Motion Picture Co. Director Harry Gant and star Clarence Brooks had both been associated with Lincoln.

California Eagle 17 Aug 1928.

ACCENT ON LOVE (Portuguese Americans)

Twentieth Century-Fox Film Corp. *Dist* Twentieth Century-Fox Film Corp. 11 Jul **1941**; Prod: 31 Mar–22 Apr 1941; retakes 14 May 1941 [©Twentieth Century-Fox Film Corp.; 11 Jul 1941; LP10588]. Sd (Western Electric Mirrophonic Recording); b&w. 6 reels, 5,560 ft. 61 min. PCA cert no. 7274.

Assoc prod Walter Morosco and Ralph Dietrich. *Dir* Ray McCarey. [*Asst dir* William Eckhardt and Sam Schneider]. *Scr* John Larkin. *Orig story* Dalton Trumbo. *Dir of photog* Charles Clarke. *Art dir* Richard Day and Lewis Creber. *Film ed* Harry Reynolds. *Set dec* Thomas Little.

Cost Herschel. *Mus dir* Emil Newman. *Sd* George Leverett and Harry M. Leonard.

Cast: George Montgomery (*John Worth Hyndman* [*also known as John Worthymer*]), Osa Massen (*Osa*), J. Carrol Naish (*Manuel Lombroso*), Cobina Wright, Jr. (*Linda Hyndman*), Stanley Clements (*Patrick Henry Lombroso*), Minerva Urecal (*Teresa Lombroso*), Thurston Hall (*T. J. Triton*), Irving Bacon (*Mr. Smedley*), Leonard Carey (*Flowers*), Oscar O'Shea (*Magistrate*), John T. Murray (*Wardman*), [Hector Sarno (*Pedro*)], [Patricia Maier (*Miss Fanchette*)], [Monica Bannister (*Secretary*)], [Harold Goodwin, Dick Rich, Ralph Dunn (*Policemen*)], [Cecil Weston, Leila McIntyre (*Elderly women*)], [William Halligan (*Drunk*)], [Jack Chefe (*French barber*)], [William Haade (*Court attendant*)], [Cyril Ring (*Court clerk*)], [Mantan Moreland (*Prisoner*)], [John Banner], [Lee Tung-Foo].

Social, Comedy-drama. [*Print viewed*]. John Worth Hyndman grows restless in his job as first vice-president of Triton Corporation, which is owned by his father-in-law, T. J. Triton. T. J. complains when John omits Triton Realty from an important ad and refuses to listen to John's explanation that the realty company has received many complaints because of the high rents T. J. charges for run-down tenements. John is then confronted by his wife Linda, who is as dissatisfied with him as he is with her. For appearances's sake, however, she refuses to give him a divorce, and tells him that he could not even get a job digging ditches were it not for her father. Tired of his meaningless work and boring life, John roams the streets, where he sees a group of W.P.A. workers digging a ditch. The Portuguese foreman, Manuel Lombroso, tells John to see the W.P.A. wardman for a job, but the wardman, suspicious about why John would leave a $21,000-a-year job to dig ditches, turns him down. John returns to the site, where Manuel's pretty neighbor, Osa, tells him that only a shovel separates him from the other men. John then pawns his suit, buys work clothes and a shovel and jumps into the ditch. Despite the wardman's insistence that he stop, the crowd and a policeman support him, and Manuel lets him continue. The kind-hearted Manuel takes him home, and after introducing him to his wife Teresa and son Patrick Henry, promises John that he will get him a W.P.A. card. John allows the Lombrosos and Osa to think that he is a Lithuanian named John Worthymer and has not yet applied for U.S. citizenship. As six weeks pass, John revels in his physical labor, his friendship with the Lombrosos and a romance with Osa. One day, the Lombrosos and their friends, tired of their living conditions, decide to confront their landlord, who is T. J. They persuade John to be their spokesman, but when he goes to T. J.'s office, T. J. refuses to listen to his demands. John engineers his and T. J.'s arrests, and when he tries to tell the judge about the shameful state of T. J.'s rental properties, T. J. gets the trial postponed and bails them both out. John agrees to behave himself at the trial if T. J. follows his orders for the next twenty-four hours, and so, after outfitting T. J. in work clothes, John takes him to the Lombrosos' apartment. The immigrants welcome T. J., who they think is named Joe, and declare that Osa and John are engaged when Manuel sees them kissing. After spending the night in the apartment, T. J. returns to his office, where he is surprised by the Lombrosos and their friends. T. J. reveals his true identity, then tells them that John is his son-in-law. The disillusioned immigrants believe that John has been working behind their backs, and the devastated Osa refuses to listen to his explanations. When he sees the trouble he has caused, T. J. has a change of heart and orders Linda to get a divorce. He then follows John to the Lombrosos' apartment, where John is being accused of treachery. T. J. tells them that, thanks to John, his eyes have been opened, and that John now has control over Triton Realty. He also tells them that Linda is going to Reno, and after the Lombrosos forgive John, he and Osa are reconciled with a kiss. *Portuguese Americans. Romance. Transformation. Tycoons. Citizenship. Disillusionment. Divorce. Fathers-in-law. Friendship. Letters. Patriotism. Police. Snobs and snobbishness. Tenement-houses. United States. Work Projects Administration. Wives.*

Note: The working titles of this film were *Man with a Shovel* and *Man with the Shovel.* The title of Dalton Trumbo's original story was "Man with a Shovel (Return to Life)." Although the Twentieth Century-Fox Produced Scripts Collection at the UCLA Arts—Special Collections Library contains screenplays for the film written by Ben Grauman Kohn and Walter Bullock, the extent of their contributions to the released picture has not been determined. According to a 12 Nov 1940 *HR* news item, Harry Lachman was originally scheduled to direct the picture, and a 21 Nov 1940 *LAT* news item reported that the studio was considering Henry Fonda for the leading role.

Box 12 Jul 1941. *DV* 2 Jul 1941. *FD* 9 Jul 1941, p. 5. *HR* 13 Apr 1940, p. 1. *HR* 30 Oct 1940, p. 1. *HR* 12 Nov 1940, p. 4. *HR* 21 Mar 1941, p. 5. *HR* 28 Mar 1941, p. 15. *HR* 18 Apr 1941, p. 11. *HR* 22 Apr 1941, p. 5. *HR* 13 May 1941, p. 1. *HR* 2 Jul 1941, p. 3. *LAT* 21 Sep 1940. *MPD* 3 Jul 1941. *MPH* 5 Jul 1941, p. 37. *MPHPD* 17 May 1941, p. 137.

ACES AND EIGHTS (Latino)

Excelsior Pictures Corp. *Dist* State Rights; Puritan Pictures Corp. 6 Jun **1936**. Sd; b&w. 62 min. PCA cert no. 2116.

[*Prod* Sam Newfield and Leslie Simmonds]. *Dir* Sam Newfield. *Asst dir* William O'Connor. *Orig story and cont* Arthur Durlam. *Story ed* Joseph O'Donnell. *Photog* Jack Greenhalgh. *Film ed* Jack English. *Sd rec* Hans Weeren.

Cast: Tim McCoy (*Gentleman Tim Madigan* [*/Wild Bill Hickok*]), Luana Walters (*Juanita Hernandez*), Rex Lease (*Jose Hernandez*), Wheeler Oakman (*Ace Morgan*), Frank Glendon (*Amos Harden*), Charles Stevens (*Captain* [*Felipe*] *de Lopez*), Earl Hodgins (*Marshal*), Jimmy Aubrey (*Lucky*), Joseph Girard (*Don Juillo Hernandez*), [John Merton (*Gambler*)].

Western. [*Print viewed*]. In a prologue, Wild Bill Hickok is assassinated during a poker game in which he holds two pair, aces and eights, which comes to be known in the West as the "death hand." Gentleman gambler Tim Madigan is then introduced as Hickok's successor. During a poker game, Madigan, a notorious cardsharp who does not carry a gun, accuses a fellow professional of cheating. Overhearing Madigan's accusation, Jose Hernandez, a young Spaniard who had earlier lost heavily to the gambler, pulls his gun on the man, demanding his money. Although Madigan is nowhere in sight when the gambler is killed by a bullet emanating from a nearby tree, the marshal assumes Madigan's guilt and goes after him. They meet at the state border, but Madigan outwits the marshal and crosses into freedom. Once in Roaring Gulch, California, Madigan meets Jose, who offers his father's hacienda as a resting-place. There Madigan discovers that Don Juillo and his daughter Juanita are in danger of losing their property to gambler Ace Morgan and Amos Harden, the owner of the Gold Dollar saloon. By extending credit to Jose, they are plotting to drive Don Juillo into debt. Although Madigan has renounced gambling, he "borrows" the gold from the Hernandez *coupa d'ore* and wins the Gold Dollar from Harden with a hand of aces and eights, forcing him to relinquish Jose's debts. Morgan tries to take the ranch by force, but Madigan arrives with the money. They are fighting when the marshal arrives and proves that it was a bullet from Morgan's gun that killed the gambler. Finally, Madigan and Jose are cleared, Lucky, Madigan's sidekick, takes over the saloon, and the ranch is restored to the family. *Cardsharping. Latino. Murder. Poker (Game). Ranchers. Saloon keepers. Spaniards. California. Debt. False accusations. Haciendas. Wild Bill Hickok. Sheriffs.*

Note: Press materials, reviews, and the 1937 *FDYB* erroneously credit George Stevens with the role of "Captain Felipe" instead of Charles Stevens. Modern sources add the following credits to the cast: Frank Ellis (*Deputy*), Jack Evans and Tom Smith (*Spectators*), Fred Parker (*Gambler*), Karl Hackett, Jack Kirk, Oscar Gahan, Milburn Morante, Artie Ortego, Clyde McClary and Robert Walker. Frank Glendon is listed as J. Frank Glendon in modern sources. For information about the real Wild Bill Hickok, please see the entry below for *The Plainsman.*

Exb 1 Jul 1936. *FD* 8 Aug 1936 p. 3. *MPH* 22 Aug 1936, p. 51. *Var* 12 Aug 1936, p. 19.

ACROSS THE BORDER *see* A CALIFORNIA ROMANCE

ACROSS THE DIVIDE (Native Americans)

G. & J. Photoplay Co. *Dist* Playgoers Pictures, Inc. 9 Oct **1921** [©Playgoers Pictures, Inc.; 12 Oct 1921; LU17077]. Si; b&w. 6 reels, 5,500 ft.

Dir John Holloway. *Scen* Beatrice Frederick. *Photog* A. Quarrier Thompson.

Cast: Rex Ballard (*Kenneth* [*Buck*] *Layson*), Rosemary Theby (*Rosa*), Ralph Fee McCullough (*Wallace Layson*), Thomas Delmar (*Dago*), Gilbert Clayton (*Newton*), Dorothy Manners (*Helen*), Flora Hollister (*White Flower*).

Western. Wallace Layson, left by his dying mother in the care of Buck, a half-breed, has no knowledge of his true identity. Layson's father returns to cheat his own son out of a ranch, which he will inherit on his twenty-first birthday, and induces Rosa, a dancehall girl, to marry young Layson, who is in love with Helen. Buck tells him that the real heir has died and persuades him to pose as the heir, thus foiling the plans of his father and securing a home for young Layson and Helen. Buck then reveals the boy's identity and departs without revealing that he is the boy's half brother. *Brothers. Dance hall girls. Fatherhood. Impersonation and imposture. Indians of North America. Indians of North America–Mixed blood. Parentage.*

Note: This film was licensed in New York State as *Across the Great Divide*.

ACROSS THE GREAT DIVIDE *see* **ACROSS THE DIVIDE**

ACROSS THE PACIFIC (Japanese Americans)
Warner Bros. Pictures, Inc.; A Warner Bros.—First National Picture. *Dist* Warner Bros. Pictures, Inc. 5 Sep **1942**; New York opening: 4 Sep 1942; Prod: 2 Mar–1 May 1942; retakes 2 May 1942 [©Warner Bros. Pictures, Inc.; 5 Sep 1942; LP11564]. Sd (RCA Sound System); b&w. 10 reels, 8,709 ft. 86 or 97 min.

Prod Jerry Wald and Jack Saper. *Dir* John Huston and [Vincent Sherman]. *Dial dir* Edward Blatt. [*Asst dir* Lee Katz]. [*2nd asst dir* George Tobin]. [*Dir of retakes* Jo Graham]. *Scr* Richard Macaulay. *Dir of photog* Arthur Edeson. [*2nd cam* Mike Joyce]. [*Asst cam* Wally Meinardus]. [*Stills* Jack Woods]. [*Gaffer* William Conger]. *Spec eff* Byron Haskin and Willard Van Enger. *Mont* Don Siegel. *Art dir* Robert Haas and Hugh Reticker. [*Set dresser* Casey Roberts]. *Film ed* Frank Magee. [*Prop man* Armor Marlowe]. *Gowns* Milo Anderson. [*Ward* Hal Dunn and Janet Storck]. *Mus* Adolph Deutsch. *Mus dir* Leo F. Forbstein. *Sd* Everett A. Brown. *Makeup artist* Perc Westmore. [*Makeup* Gordon Bau]. [*Hair* Jean Burt]. [*Unit mgr* Chuck Hanson]. [*Scr clerk* Alma Dwight]. [*Grip* E. F. Dexter]. [*Best boy* William Studman]. [*Tech adv* Colonel J. G. Taylor and Dan Fujiwara]. [*Stand-in for Humphrey Bogart* Russ Lewellyn]. [*Stand-in for Mary Astor* Elaine Waters]. [*Stand-in for Sydney Greenstreet* George Becker].

Source: Based on the short story "Aloha Means Good-by" by Robert Garson in *The Saturday Evening Post* (28 Jun–26 Jul 1941).

Cast: HUMPHREY BOGART (*Rick Leland*), Mary Astor (*Alberta Marlow*), Sydney Greenstreet (*Dr. Lorenz*), Charles Halton (*A. V. Smith*), Sen Young (*Joe Totsuiko*), Roland Got (*Sugi*), Lee Tung Foo (*Sam Wing On*), Frank Wilcox (*Captain Morrison*), Paul Stanton (*Colonel Hart*), Lester Matthews (*Canadian major*), John Hamilton (*Court martial president*), Tom Stevenson (*Unidentified man*), Roland Drew (*Captain Harkness*), Monte Blue (*Dan Morton*), Chester Gan (*Captain Higoto*), Richard Loo (*First Officer Miyuma*), Keye Luke (*Steamship office clerk*), Kam Tong (*T. Oki*), Spencer Chan (*Chief engineer Mitsuko*), Rudy Robles (*A Filipino assassin*), [William Hopper (*Orderly*)], [Frank Mayo (*Trial judge advocate*)], [Garland Smith, Dick French, Charles Drake, Will Morgan (*Officers*)], [Jack Mower (*Major*)], [Frank Faylen (*Barker*)], [Ruth Ford (*Secretary*)], [Eddie Lee (*Chinese clerk*)], [Dick Botiller (*Waiter*)], [Beal Wong (*Usher*)], [Philip Ahn (*Man in theater*)], [Anthony Caruso (*Driver*)], [James Leong (*Nura*)], [Paul Fung (*Japanese radio operator*)], [Eddie Dew].

Espionage, **World War II**, **Drama.** [*Print viewed*]. Rick Leland, a captain in the United States Coast Auxiliary Army, is found guilty of stealing regimental funds and is dishonorably discharged from the service. He subsequently tries to enlist in the Canadian artillery but is turned down because of his record. Disillusioned, Rick buys passage on the Japanese freighter, the *Genoa Maru*, intending to offer his services to the Chinese. Traveling on the same ship is Alberta Marlow, who is heading for Panama, and Dr. Lorenz and his Japanese servant, T. Oki. Lorenz is a student of Japanese culture and is interested to learn that if war broke out in the Pacific, Rick would not participate. Over drinks, Lorenz quizzes Rick about his experience in the artillery in Panama. Rick also spends some time flirting with Alberta, who returns his interest. When the ship docks in New York City, Rick visits a man who turns out to be his undercover contact. Rick, whose dishonorable discharge was faked to cover his investigation of Lorenz, asks his contact to inquire into Alberta's background, as well. When Rick rejoins the ship, another passenger, Joe Totsuiko, a Nisei, joins the company. On board, Rick prevents a Filipino man from shooting Lorenz, who explains that some Filipinos resent his ties with the Japanese. Alberta later calls Rick's attention to the fact that Lorenz has a new servant who is using the same name as his former servant. Eventually Lorenz offers Rick money to disclose military information and Rick agrees. In Panama, the passengers learn that the ship will not be allowed to travel through the canal. After disembarking, they all check into a hotel. Lorenz demands that Rick find out the schedule of airplanes flying over the area in return for the money he paid him earlier. Rick also learns that Alberta is not who she is pretending to be and confronts her, but just as she is about to explain, she is called to the telephone. Rick then searches her room, where he finds that Lorenz has earlier done the same. Lorenz warns Rick about Alberta before knocking him unconscious. When Rick

comes to, he alerts his contact about Lorenz' plans, but the man is killed before he can act on the warning. Sam, the hotel keeper and an old friend of Rick's, puts him in touch with a man who advises him to travel quickly to a nearby plantation. There, workers are loading a bomber under cover of darkness. Rick is captured and taken inside, where he discovers Alberta and Joe. The owner of the plantation is Alberta's father, who has been forced to provide a cover for the Japanese. Lorenz's servant turns out to be a bomber pilot. Now the Japanese, supported by Joe and Lorenz, plan to bomb the canal's locks. Hearing the plane start its engines, Rick initiates a fight, during which Alberta's father is killed. Rick escapes and shoots down the plane, killing the Japanese pilot. His plan a failure, Lorenz tries to kill himself, but cannot go through with it. Rick captures him and takes him in for questioning. Alberta, who has been loyal all along, accompanies Rick. *Panama Canal (Panama). Spies. Undercover agents. World War II. Air pilots. Courts-martial and courts of inquiry. Fathers and daughters. Fights. Filipinos. Japanese. Plantations. Romance. Seasickness. Servants. Ships.*

Note: A Warner Bros. press release for this film dated Dec 1941 included in the file on the film in the AMPAS Library announced that Dennis Morgan and Ann Sheridan were to star. In her autobiography, Mary Astor notes that the original script was about a Japanese invasion of Hawaii, but after the Japanese bombed Pearl Harbor, the location was hastily changed to Panama. The *Var* review points out that the title is thus a "misnomer" as none of the action takes place in the Pacific. Production began shortly before the bombing and was closed down and restarted in Mar 1942. On 3 Mar 1942, President Franklin D. Roosevelt authorized the internment of Japanese Americans on the West Coast. At that time, Astor reports, the film kept losing its Japanese actors as they were rounded up by the United States government and sent to relocation camps. According to information in the file on the film at the USC Cinema-Television Library, however, Chinese actors were cast as Japanese from the beginning and with the exception of technical adviser Dan Fujiwara and a few bit players, no Japanese participated in the making of the film. As evidenced by the cast credits and as noted by the *New Yorker* review, Chinese actors played the roles of Japanese spies. Colonel J. G. Taylor acted as technical adviser on the court-martial scenes.

Before the picture was finished, director John Huston was summoned to report to the department of Special Services, and on 22 Apr 1942 Vincent Sherman took over as director, according to information at USC. In a modern interview, Huston relates that when he knew he was leaving, he filmed a scene in which he tied Humphrey Bogart to a chair with Japanese guards at every window and door and left Sherman to figure out a way to get Bogart's character out of his dilemma. Sherman managed to figure out a solution, but the resulting ending is somewhat implausible. The production finished ten days over schedule. This film marked the reunion of stars Bogart, Greenstreet and Astor and director Huston, who worked together in Warner Bros.' hit film *The Maltese Falcon*.

Box 22 Aug 1942. *DV* 14 Aug 1942, p. 3. *FD* 18 Aug 1942, p. 6. *HR* 2 Mar 1942, p. 9. *HR* 24 Apr 1942, p. 1. *HR* 1 May 1942, p. 4. *HR* 14 May 1942, p. 3. *MPHPD* 22 Aug 1942, p. 853. *NYT* 5 Sep 1942, p. 9. *Var* 19 Aug 1942, p. 8.

ACROSS THE RIVER *see* **DAUGHTER OF SHANGHAI**

ACROSS THE WIDE MISSOURI (Native Americans, Siksika)
Metro-Goldwyn-Mayer Corp.; controlled by Loew's Inc. *Dist* Loew's Inc. 23 Oct **1951**; Prod: late Jul–mid-Sep 1950 [©Loew's Inc.; 17 Sep 1951; LP1193]. Sd (Western Electric Sound System); col (Technicolor). 8 reels, 7,047 ft. 78 min. Passed by the National Board of Review. PCA cert no. 14912.

Prod Robert Sisk. *Dir* William Wellman. [*Asst dir* Howard Koch]. [*Dial dir* Jackson Halliday]. *Scr* Talbot Jennings. *Story* Talbot Jennings and Frank Cavett. *Dir of photog* William Mellor. *Spec eff* Warren Newcombe. *Technicolor col consultant* Henri Jaffa and James Gooch. *Art dir* Cedric Gibbons and James Basevi. *Film ed* John Dunning. *Set dec* Edwin B. Willis and Ralph S. Hurst. *Cost des* Walter Plunkett. *Mus dir* David Raskin. *Rec supv* Douglas Shearer. [*Sd* Conrad Kahn]. *Hair styles des by* Sydney Guilaroff. *Makeup created by* William Tuttle. *Indian tech adv* Nipo T. Strongheart. [*Stunt double for María Elena Marqués* Evelyn Finley]. [*Stunts* Edward Jauegui, Slim Talbot, Rocky Shanan, Fred McDougall, Ray Thomas, Henry Willis, Jimmy Van Horn, Clint Sharp and Archie Butler].

Song(s): "Skip to My Lou" and "Alouette, Pretty Alouette," traditionals; "Indian Lullaby," words and music by Alberto Colombo, Indian lyrics by Nipo T. Strongheart.

Source: Based on the novel *Across the Wide Missouri* by Bernard DeVoto (Boston, 1947).

Cast: CLARK GABLE [(*Flint Mitchell*)], Ricardo Montalban [(*Ironshirt*)], John Hodiak [(*Brecan*)], Adolphe Menjou [(*Pierre*)], J. Carrol Naish [(*Looking Glass*)], Jack Holt [(*Bear Ghost*)], Alan Napier [(*Captain Humberstone Lyon*)], George Chandler [(*Gowie*)],

Richard Anderson [(*Dick Richardson*)], and introducing María Elena Marqués [(*Kamiah*)], [Howard Keel (*Narrator, Chip Mitchell as an adult*)], [James Whitmore (*Old Bill*)], [John Hartmann (*Chip Mitchell*)], [Henri Letondal (*Lucien Chennault*)], [Douglas Fowley (*Tin Cup Owens*)], [Louis Nicoletti (*Roy DuNord*)], [Ben Watson (*Markhead*)], [Russell Simpson (*Hoback*)], [Frankie Darro (*Cadet*)], [Frank Richards (*Tige Shannon*)], [Michael Dugan (*Gordon*)], [John McKee (*Killbuck*)], [Bert LeBaron (*LeBonte*)], [Elmer Napier (*Shad Skeggs*)], [Tex Holden (*Peg Leg Smith*)], [Elaine Naish (*Indian girl*)], [Edith Mills, Talzumbie Dupea (*Indian women*)], [Bobby Barber (*Gardipe*)], [Gene Coogan (*Marcelline*)], [Fred Graham (*Brown*)], [Fred Gillman (*Harris*)], [Nipo T. Strongheart (*Indian crier*)], [Andrew Knife (*Yellow Plume*)], [Donald House (*Luke*)], [Jack Sterling (*Davis*)], [Albert Pollet, Albert Pettit, Manuel Paris, Maurice Brierre (*French trappers*)].

Historical, Northwest, Adventure, with songs. [*Print viewed*]. In the rugged northern Rocky Mountains of the 1830s, mountain man and fur trapper Flint Mitchell is planning a hunting trek into the beaver-rich Blackhawk Territory, despite protests from his Indian friend, Brecan, who tells him that the land belongs to Indians. After narrowly escaping an attack by Ironshirt, a young Indian war chief, Flint finds himself imperiled by a pack of wolves. He is rescued by Pierre, a French Canadian fur trapper, and Captain Humberstone Lyon, a bumbling Scottish hunter who fought in the Battle of Waterloo. While Pierre and Humberstone decide to join Flint on the dangerous expedition into Blackfoot territory, Flint, hoping to ensure the group's safe passage, buys and marries Kamiah, the granddaughter of Blackfoot chief Bear Ghost. Though he marries Kamiah for reasons other than love, Flint eventually becomes smitten with her. Kamiah successfully guides Flint and his men on their trek through rough terrain and crippling snow drifts and finally delivers them to beaver country. As Flint and Kamiah's marriage takes an unexpected romantic turn, Flint and Bear Ghost become good friends. Bear Ghost keeps the warring Ironshirt from harming Flint and his men, but tragedy strikes when Roy DuNord, one of Flint's men, kills Bear Ghost to avenge his brother's death at the hands of Indians. Brecan then kills Roy, and Flint sinks into a grieving depression over the death of Bear Ghost. Soon after replacing Bear Ghost as chief of the tribe, Ironshirt resumes his campaign of terror against the white trappers. The attacks begin in earnest in the spring, when Kamiah, who had recently given birth to a boy, Chip, is killed in an ambush by Ironshirt and his men. With Chip strapped to its back, Kamiah's horse then bolts and heads for the Blackfoot camp. Flint manages to get his son back, however, in a counterattack, during which Ironshirt is killed. Years pass, and Flint takes Chip, who is now six years old, to live in the Blackfoot camp, where, Flint believes, Kamiah would have wanted him. With the menacing Ironshirt no longer a threat, the Blackfoot gladly take Chip and Flint into their fold. *Miscegenation. Rocky Mountains. Siksika Indians. Trappers. United States–History–19th century. Chases. Christmas. Drunkenness. English. Escapes. Fathers and sons. Fistfights. French Canadians. Funerals. Gunfights. Infants. Marriage–Arranged. Murder. Pregnancy. Revenge. Scottish Americans. Snow. Spanking. Tribal chiefs. Wagon trains. Weddings. Widowers.*

Note: Voice-over narration, spoken by Howard Keel as the adult "Chip Mitchell," is heard intermittently throughout the film. According to modern sources, the narration was added after principal photography was completed at the suggestion of M-G-M producer Sam Zimbalist. María Elena Marqués made her Hollywood screen debut in the picture. Modern sources note that except for a small amount of studio interiors, the film was shot entirely on location in the Rocky Mountains, mostly at altitudes between 9,000 and 14,000 feet. According to *HR* production charts, Durango, CO, was the main location site. To cope with fast-changing weather conditions, the crew prepared two stand-by set-ups for each scene, and were aided by a four-wheel drive camera car with a front-mounted hydrolic. Despite the lush location shooting, *Across the Wide Missouri* did not do well at the box office, according to modern sources.

AmCin May 1951, pp. 178-79, 199. *DV* 18 Sep 1951, p. 3. *FD* 24 Sep 1951, p. 20. *HR* 28 Jul 1950, p. 12. *HR* 15 Sep 1950, p. 10. *HR* 18 Sep 1951, p. 3. *MPHPD* 29 Sep 1951, pp. 1041-42. *NYT* 6 Aug 1950. *NYT* 7 Nov 1951, p. 35. *Var* 19 Sep 1951, p. 6.

ACTION IN THE NORTH ATLANTIC (Jewish Americans, Multi-ethnic)
Warner Bros. Pictures, Inc.; A Warner Bros.—First National Picture. *Dist* Warner Bros. Pictures, Inc. 12 Jun **1943**; *Prod*: 3 Sep–late Nov 1942 [©Warner Bros. Pictures, Inc; 12 Jun 1943; LP12095]. Sd (RCA Sound System); b&w. 11,455 ft. 126 min.
Prod Jerry Wald. *Exec prod* Jack L. Warner. *Dir* Lloyd Bacon. *Dial dir* Harold Winston. [*Asst dir* Reggie Callow]. *Scr* John Howard Lawson. *Story* Guy Gilpatric. *Addl dial* A. I. Bezzerides and W. R. Burnett. *Dir of photog* Ted McCord. *Mont* Don Siegel and James Leichester. *Dir spec eff* Jack Cosgrove. *Spec eff* Edwin B. Du Par. *Art dir* Ted Smith. *Film ed* George Amy. *Set dec* Clarence Steensen. *Mus dir* Leo F. Forbstein. *Mus* Adolph Deutsch. *Sd* C. A. Riggs. *Makeup artist* Perc Westmore. [*Tech adv* Richard Sullivan].
Song(s): "Night and Day," music and lyrics by Cole Porter.
Cast: HUMPHREY BOGART [(*Joe Rossi*)], Raymond Massey [(*Captain Steve Jarvis*)], Alan Hale [("*Boats*" *O'Hara*)], Julie Bishop [(*Pearl O'Neill*)], Ruth Gordon [(*Sarah Jarvis*)], Sam Levene [("*Chips*" *Abrams*)], Dane Clark [(*Johnny Pulaski*)], Peter Whitney [(*Whitey Lara*)], Dick Hogan [(*Cadet Robert Parker*)], [Minor Watson (*Hartridge*)], [J. M. Kerrigan (*Cavier Jinks*)], [Kane Richmond (*Ensign Wright*)], [Art Foster (*Pete Larson*)], [Chic Chandler (*Goldberg*)], [George Offerman, Jr. (*Cecil*)], [Ray Montgomery (*Ahearn*)], [Glen Strange (*Tex Mathews*)], [Elliott Sullivan (*Hennessey*)], [Ralph Dunn (*Quartermaster*)], [Creighton Hale (*Sparks*)], [Syd Saylor (*Jim*)], [Lew Kelly (*Tony Gonzales*)], [Dick Wessel (*Cherub*)], [Russ Powell ("*Slops*" *Denton*)], [Alec Craig (*McGonigle*)], [Frederick Giermann (*German submarine captain*)], [Walter Soderling (*Pop*)], [Bill Crago (*Newsreel man*)], [Joseph Bernard (*Ed*)], [Virginia Christine (*Pebbles*)], [Irving Bacon (*Bartender*)], [Harry Seymour (*Piano player*)], [Leah Baird (*Mother*)], [Jack Mower (*Dispatcher*)], [Iris Adrian (*Jenny O'Hara*)], [George Kirby (*Pilot Johnson*)], [Victor Kendall (*Lieutenant McIntosh*)], [Frank Puglia (*Captain Carpolis*)], [Ludwig Stossel (*Captain Ziemer*)], [Jean Del Val (*Captain La Pricor*)], [Charles Trowbridge (*Rear Admiral Williams*)], [Roland Varno (*Gunnery captain*)], [Daniel De Jonghe (*Lookout*)], [Bill Nind (*Limey*)], [Sven-Hugo Borg (*Norwegian seaman*)], [Rudolf Myset (*Russian seaman*)], [Arthur Dulac (*French seaman*)], [Carl Ekberg (*Dutch seaman*)], [Edward Foster (*American seaman*)], [Carlos Barbé (*Brazilian seaman*)], [Manuel Lopez (*Mexican seaman*)], [Archie Got (*Chinese seaman*)], [Pedro Regas (*Greek seaman*)], [Henry Guttman (*Nazi submarine officer*)], [Tom Miller (*Boy*)], [William Haade (*Customer*)], [DeWolfe Hopper (*Canadian soldier*)], [George Neise, Al Winters (*German lieutenants*)], [Sigurd Tor (*Helmsman*)], [Nari Drevjen (*Norwegian gun captain*)], [Tony Marsh (*English gun captain*)], [Gordon Hayes (*American gun captain*)], [Kirk Alyn (*Brazilian gun captain*)], [Juan Varro (*Greek captain*)], [George Blagoi (*Russian sergeant*)], [Sam Waagenaar (*Steward*)], [William Yetter (*German Air Force captain*)], [Peter Auerbach (*German Air Force N.C.O.*)], [George Adrian (*German naval officer*)], [Stanley Blystone (*U.S. commander*)], [Edwin Mills (*Naval radio operator*)], [Alan Robert (*German gunner*)], [George Sorel (*German bombardier*)], [Arno Frey (*German pilot*)], [Bob Thom (*Man on bow of boat*)], [Bob Duncan (*Signal man*)], [Horace Brown (*Semaphore signal*)], [Carl Roth (*German naval N.C.O.*)], [Anthony Marlowe (*German N.C.O.*)], [Richard Woodruff (*Squadron leader*)], [Walter Rode (*Russian Air Force captain*)], [Dennis Moore, Eddie Coke (*Signal men*)], [Richard Abbott (*Officer on Dutch boat*)], [William Castello (*Sailor on Dutch boat*)], [Louis Arco (*Submarine commander*)], [James Flavin (*Lieutenant-commander of Merchant Marine school*)], [Kurt Kreuger (*Submarine lieutenant*)], [Fred Wolff (*N.C.O.*)], [Hans Furburg (*German officer*)], [Rolf Lindau (*Radio operator on submarine*)], [Frank Mayo (*Major*)], [Hugh Prosser, Gene O'Donnell, Edward Dow, Lee Phelps, Don Douglas, Hooper Atchley, William Forrest, Hans Schumm, Grandon Rhodes (*Lieutenant-commanders*)], [Monte Blue, Bill Edwards, Frank Mills, Herschel Graham, Paul Panzer, Bob Kimball, Cliff Saum, Gordon Murray, Bill Phillips, Frank Mayo, Eddy Chandler, Allen Mathews, Charles Sullivan, Harry McKee (*Seamen*)], [George Davis, Albert d'Arno, Joe Ploski, Walter Thiele (*German sailors*)], [Peter Pohlenz, Peter Van Eyck, Louis Adlon, John Royce, Ernst Hausserman (*German ensigns*)], [David Willock, John Estes, Gary Bruce, Robert Kent, Ross Ford (*Ensigns*)], [Earl Kent, Bob Stevenson, Paul Gilbert, Hans von Morhart, Hans Heilbronne, Edward Goedeck, Kurt Neumann, Charles Flynn, George Sherwood, Peter Michael, Peter Dunne, Ferdinand Schumann-Heink, Frank Alten (*Germans*)], [Sam Wren, Bill Hunter (*Chief petty officers*)], [Warren Ashe, John Whitney (*U.S. sailors*)], [Ted Jacques, Hal Craig (*Ship's officers*)], [William Vaughn, John Epper (*German lieutenant-commanders*)], [Otto Reichow, Hans Moebus (*German petty officers*)], [George O'Hanlon, Warren Douglas (*Navy pilots*)], [David Gaylord, Maurice Murphy (*1st lieutenants*)], [Joe Allen, Jr., Victor Kilian, Jr. (*U.S. naval petty officers*)], [Howard Mitchell], [Jana deLoos], [Vera Richkova], [Christine Gordon].

Sea, World War II, Drama. [Print viewed]. Joe Rossi is chief executive officer on the Merchant Marine vessel captained by Steve Jarvis. When their ship is torpedoed by the Germans while traveling in the North Atlantic, Steve vows retribution. After Joe, Steve and the other survivors are rescued, they return home to wait for assignment to another ship. Steve's wife Sarah is glad to have him back, although she knows that waiting and worrying are part of being married to a seaman. Joe heads for his favorite bar, where he meets singer Pearl O'Neill, whom he marries shortly before he is recalled to sea. The men learn that their new ship, the Sea Witch, is to be part of an international convoy bringing supplies to Murmansk in the Soviet Union. As the convoy heads into the open sea, it is attacked by several German submarines. United States naval destroyers engage the submarines in battle, but one singles out the Sea Witch. Steve orders his men to lure the submarine away from the convoy. The submarine follows the Sea Witch just out of range of its guns, waiting for its chance to attack. Joe suggests that they cut the engines and maintain complete silence, hoping that the submarine's sound sensors will not be able to track them. The ruse works, but the captain of the submarine is able to determine where the ship is headed and radios a request for airborne bombers. The airplanes and the ship engage in a battle, during which Steve is seriously wounded and several other sailors are killed. When the submarine torpedoes the ship, Joe, who has been named acting captain, orders the men to start a fire, hoping to lure the submarine to the surface, where the ship's guns can hit them. After the submarine surfaces, Joe orders the ship to ram it, and the submarine is destroyed just before Russian airplanes appear overhead to welcome the Sea Witch and her crew. Merchant Marine. Sailors. Ships. Submarine boats. World War II. Airplanes. Atlantic Ocean. Bombs. Cats. Dogs. Escapes. Explosions. Fires. Germany. Navy. Lifeboats. Reporters. Russians. Sea captains. Tankers. Torpedoes.

Note: The film's working title was Heroes Without Uniforms. An undated press release included in the file on the film at the AMPAS Library notes that twenty-three-year-old technical adviser Richard Sullivan was one of two cadets to survive a U-Boat attack on his Merchant Marine vessel. Another press release announces that Edward G. Robinson and George Raft were to star in the picture. According to a 24 Jun 1943 HR news item, this film was used in Merchant Marine schools as a part of their training sessions, because the War Shipping Administration believed that the film contained technical and educational material that would "aid considerably the training program." The studio donated three prints for official use at the Merchant Marine Academy in Kings Point, NY and at cadet basic schools in San Mateo, CA and Pass Christians, MI. According to a 26 Sep 1942 article in the PittsC, Humphrey Bogart wanted to includ a black Merchant Marine captain in the film, stating: "In the world of the theatre or any other phase of American life, the color of a man's skin should have nothing to do with his rights in a land built upon the self-evident fact that all men are created equal." This character did not appear in the film, however. Writer Guy Gilpatric was nominated for an Oscar for Best Original Screenplay. Modern sources add the following information about the production: Warner Bros. had originally intended to make a two-reel documentary about the Merchant Marine, but this idea was discarded as the war progressed, providing more opportunities for dramatic action footage. The film was shot entirely on the Warner Bros. backlot using special effects to provide the maritime atmosphere. Raymond Massey and Julie Bishop reprised their roles in a Lux Radio Theatre broadcast on 15 May 1944, co-starring George Raft.

AmCin Jun 1943, p. 215. Box 22 May 1943. DV 17 May 1943, p. 3. FD 17 May 1943, p. 6. HR 3 Sep 1942, p. 2. HR 17 May 1943, p. 3. HR 25 May 1943, p. 4. HR 24 Jun 1943, p. 3. MPH 22 May 1943. MPHPD 22 May 1943, p. 1325. NYT 22 May 1943, p. 10. NYT 30 May 1943, p. 2 (sec 2). PittsC 26 Sep 1942. Var 19 May 1943, p. 8.

ADAM HAD FOUR SONS (Immigrants)
Robert Sherwood Productions. Dist Columbia Pictures Corp. 18 Feb 1941; Prod: 2 Oct—14 Nov 1940 [©Columbia Pictures Corp.; 18 Feb 1941; LP10451]. Sd (Western Electric Mirrophonic Recording); b&w. 7,201 ft. 80-81 min.
Prod Robert Sherwood. Assoc prod Gordon Griffith. Dir Gregory Ratoff. Asst dir Norman Deming. Scr William Hurlbut and Michael Blankfort. Dir of photog Peverell Marley. Art dir Rudolph Sternad. Film ed Francis D. Lyon. Set dec Howard Bristol. Gowns des by David Kidd. Executed by Coyla. Orig score W. Franke Harling. Mus dir C. Bakaleinikoff. [Mus supv Morris Stoloff].
Source: Based on the novel Legacy by Charles Bonner (New York, 1940).
Cast: INGRID BERGMAN (Emilie Gallatin), WARNER BAXTER (Adam Stoddard), Susan Hayward (Hester [Stoddard]), Fay Wray (Molly [Stoddard]), Older Boys: Richard Denning (Jack [Stoddard]), Johnny Downs (David [Stoddard]), Robert Shaw (Chris [Stoddard]), Charles Lind (Phillip [Stoddard]), Younger Boys: Billy Ray (Jack [Stoddard]), Steven Muller (David [Stoddard]), Wallace Chadwell

(Chris [Stoddard]), Bobby Walberg (Phillip [Stoddard]), Helen Westley (Cousin Philippa), June Lockhart (Vance), Pietro Sosso (Otto), Gilbert Emery (Dr. Lane), Renie Riano (Photographer), [Clarence Muse (Sam)].
Domestic, Drama. [Print viewed]. In 1907, the Stoddard family anxiously awaits the arrival of their new European governess, Emilie Gallatin. Emilie and her four charges—Jack, David, Chris and Phillip Stoddard—share an instant rapport, and the boys are delighted when Emilie intuits the layout of their stately house, Stonehenge. As the year unfolds, the fortunes of Adam Stoddard, the head of the house and a prominent stockbrocker, begin to fall as the stock market plunges. Despondent, Adam returns home from work early one afternoon to find his wife Molly sick in bed. When Molly faints at Thanksgiving dinner, the doctor prescribes immediate surgery. Too sick to be moved to the hospital, Molly must be operated on at home, and before the procedure begins, she extracts a promise from Emilie to take care of her boys. When Molly dies during surgery, Emilie consoles Adam with the idea that his legacy lies in his four sons. After the stock market plummets, Adam is forced to sell Stonehenge and send his sons away to school. Adam's crusty old cousin Philippa advises him to send Emilie home, and he reluctantly agrees. As Emilie bids the family a tearful farewell, Adam promises to send for her as soon as his fortunes improve. The advent of World War I stimulates the economy, and ten years later, Stoddard and Company has regained its former glory. After buying back Stonehenge, Adam sends for Emilie, who returns to find her four charges fully grown. Jack and Chris, now soldiers, joyfully salute her homecoming. David arrives later with a surprise, his new bride Hester. Knowing that he is to be shipped overseas soon, David, a fighter pilot, asks that Hester be allowed to move in with his family. Desiring to be the only woman in the household, Hester lashes out at Emilie and accuses her of having designs on Adam. Upon meeting Hester, cousin Philippa questions her motives for marrying David. While at the house, Philippa suffers a fatal heart attack and with her dying breath warns Emilie about Hester. After David, Phillip and Chris are assigned overseas, Hester becomes bored and lonely and begins to drink. When Jack unexpectedly comes home for a two-day leave, he and Hester consume a bottle of scotch together, and then Hester begins to make romantic advances, declaring that she prefers him to David. Succumbing to Hester's charms, Jack kisses her just as Emilie enters the room. After the household retires that evening, Hester sneaks into Jack's room, and Adam sees a silhouette of them embracing at the window. As Adam pounds at Jack's door, Emilie, awakened by the commotion, slips into Jack's room through the back door and switches places with Hester to preserve Jack's honor. When Jack opens the door, Adam sees only Emilie in his son's bedroom. After Armistice is declared, Chris and Phillip come home, and when Hester tries to seduce Chris, Jack warns her to stay away from his brothers. The night of David's homecoming, Hester gets drunk as Jack watches in disgust. Later, Jack begs Emilie to tell Adam the truth, but she refuses, choosing to sacrifice her own honor to protect that of Adam and David. After retiring to their bedroom, the drunken Hester slips and calls David by Jack's name, thus arousing his suspicions. In defense, Hester threatens the family with scandal if David tries to divorce her. The next morning, David is discovered missing, and when the family is notified that he has been hospitalized after crashing his plane, Jack and Adam hurry to his bedside. Realizing that Hester has driven David to attempt suicide, Emilie orders her to leave the house. As Emilie shoves Hester toward the door, Adam returns, and Hester claims that Emilie resents her presence and is trying to get rid of her. Although Emilie stands mute to Hester's accusations, Adam begins to suspect that Hester is the cause of David's unhappiness. When Jack arrives, he assesses the situation and finally tells Adam the truth about Hester. As Emilie packs her suitcases, Adam knocks at her door, and after confessing that he loves her, he asks her to share his legacy. In reply, Emilie addresses him as "Adam" rather than "monsieur." Brothers. Family honor. Fathers and sons. Financial crisis. Governesses. Infidelity. Self-sacrifice. Air pilots, Military. Attempted suicide. Cousins. Drunkenness. Operations, Surgical. Physicians. Seduction. Thanksgiving Day. Widowers. World War I.

Note: The working title of this film was Legacy. This picture marked former radio announcer Robert Sherwood's (not to be confused with Robert Sherwood the playwright) debut as a film producer. According to the Var review, Sherwood bought the rights to Charles Bonner's novel and then used the property to orchestrate a production deal with Columbia. Var incorrectly lists

the picture's running time as 108 minutes. Ingrid Bergman was borrowed from David O. Selznick Productions to appear in the film. Gregory Ratoff also directed Bergman's American screen debut in the 1939 Selznick film *Intermezzo* (see *AFI Catalog of Feature Films, 1931–40*; F3.2140). On 4 Apr 1957, *Lux Video Theatre* broadcast a televised version of this film script titled *Adam Had Four Sons* and starring Leon Ames and Valentina Cortesa.

AmCin Mar 1941, p. 128. *Box* 22 Feb 1941. *DV* 17 Feb 1941. *FD* 24 Feb 1941, p. 5. *HR* 17 Feb 1941, p. 3. *MPH* 22 Feb 1941. *MPHPD* 11 Jan 1941, p. 38. *NYT* 28 Mar 1941, p. 26. *Var* 19 Feb 1941, p. 16.

ADDRESS UNKNOWN (Jewish Americans, German Americans)
Address Unknown, Inc. *Dist* Columbia Pictures Corp. 1 Jun 1944; New York opening: week of 15 Apr 1944; Prod: 22 Nov 1943–13 Jan 1944; addl scenes week of 25 Jan 1944 [©Columbia Pictures Corp.; 1 Jun 1944; LP12703]. Sd (Western Electric Mirrophonic Recording); b&w. 70 or 72 min.

Prod William Cameron Menzies. *Asst prod* Lonnie D'Orsay. *Dir* William Cameron Menzies. *Asst dir* John Sherwood. *Scr* Herbert Dalmas. *Dir of photog* Rudolph Mate. *Cam op* Victor Scheurich. *Art dir* Lionel Banks and Walter Holscher. *Film ed* Al Clark. *Set dec* Joseph Kish. *Cost* John Hambledon. *Ward* Henry West. *Mus score and arr* Ernst Toch. *Mus dir* M. W. Stoloff.

Source: Based on the novel *Address Unknown* by Kressmann Taylor (New York, 1939).

Cast: Paul Lukas [(*Martin Schulz*)], Carl Esmond [(*Baron von Friesche*)], Peter Van Eyck [(*Heinrich Schulz*)], Mady Christians [(*Elsa Schulz*)], Morris Carnovsky [(*Max Eisenstein*)], introducing K. T. Stevens [(*Griselle Eisenstein*)], Emory Parnell [(*Postman*)], Mary Young [(*Mrs. Delancey*)], Frank Faylen [(*Jimmie Blake*)], Charles Halton [(*Pip-Squeak*)], Erwin Kalser [(*Stage director*)], Frank Reicher [(*Professor Schmidt*)], Dale Cornell [(*Carl*)], Peter Newmeyer [(*Wilhelm*)], Larry Joe Olsen [(*Youngest*)], Gary Gray [(*Hugo*)], [Peter Helmers, Louis Arco, John Merton, Arno Frey, Sven-Hugo Borg, Otto Reichow (*Germans*)], [Dorothy Vernon (*Cook*)], [Ernest Golm (*Franz*)], [Hans Furburg, Anatole Frikin (*Footmen*)], [Carl Ekberg (*Chauffeur*)], [Tina Blagoi, Margarete Ries (*Maids*)], [Martha Bamattre (*Cook*)], [Major Fred Farrell (*Gateman*)], [Fred Easler (*Minister*)], [Hilda Tanzler, Lucy Von Boden (*Guests*)], [Robert Lawrence Powell (*Child*)], [Robert L. Stephenson (*Postman*)], [Vernon Dent, Dick Jensen, Bert Le Baron, Ralph Linn, Paul Kruger (*Party members*)], [Kurt Furberg (*Party member and guest*)], [Harry Hayes (*Waiter*)], [Frederick Giermann (*Bank clerk*)].

World War II, Drama. [*Print viewed*]. In the early 1930s, Martin Schulz, who owns a San Francisco art gallery with fellow German Max Eisenstein, leaves San Francisco with his wife Elsa and their sons for a buying trip in Germany. Remaining behind to run the business is Max and Martin's son Heinrich, who is engaged to Max's daughter Griselle. Griselle, an aspiring young actress, decides to postpone the marriage for one year while she pursues a stage career in Europe. In Germany, meanwhile, Martin meets Baron von Friesche, a cultivated nobleman and advocate of the recently spawned Nazi doctrine. Swayed by the baron's charms, Martin begins to embrace his assertion that Hitler is Germany's destiny. Back in San Francisco, Max and Heinrich become concerned when Martin begins penning letters in praise of Hitler. One night, Griselle, who had gone to Vienna to study acting, visits Martin to tell him that she has won a role in a play to be performed in Berlin. When the baron learns that Griselle's last name is Eisenstein and that her father is Martin's partner, he warns Martin that he must choose between his loyalty to Germany and his friendship with the Jews. Accepting the baron's ultimatum, Martin writes his partner that they must cease all communication because of Max's "race." Certain that Martin's sentiments are motivated by fear of the German censors, Max asks a friend who is traveling to Germany to deliver a message to Martin. When Martin reads the missive, which asks him to signify his affirmation of democratic values with the word "yes," Martin responds "no." One day, during the rehearsal of Griselle's play, a representative from the office of censorship appears at the theater and demands the deletion of several lines extolling the virtues of the meek. Defiant, Griselle speaks the lines during her performance, and when the audience learns that she is a Jew, they hurl racial epithets at her and storm the stage. Narrowly escaping the angry mob, Griselle plods through the countryside to seek refuge with Martin. Learning of his daughter's danger, Max sends Martin a plea to help Griselle. As the police close in on her, Griselle reaches Martin's door and knocks. In response, Martin slams the door in her face, leaving her at the mercy of her pursuers, who shoot and kill her.

Furious at her husband for allowing Griselle's death, Elsa decides to leave the country for Switzerland. When Martin sends Max a callous note informing him of Griselle's fate, Max cables back a cryptic message. Soon after, a messenger delivers a letter from Max to Martin, written in code. Martin notices that the censors have deleted part of the document and becomes worried. Martin's concern turns to panic when more coded letters arrive. After writing Heinrich a plea to stop Max's letters, Martin is visited by the baron, who informs him that it is illegal to send or receive coded documents. Desperate to stop the incriminating letters, Martin asks Elsa, who is leaving for Switzerland, to mail a final appeal to Max. Soon after Elsa's departure, the baron visits Martin and informs him that Elsa was stopped at the border and destroyed a letter written in Martin's hand. Although Martin protests his innocence, the baron refuses to believe him and abandons him. That night, Martin is tormented by imaginary voices calling Griselle's name. As he runs downstairs into his study, he hears the footsteps of soldiers coming to arrest him. Back in San Francisco, the mailman returns Max's letter to Martin, stamped "address unknown." When Max insists that he ceased all correspondence with Martin long ago, Heinrich steps from the shadows, and Max realizes that the incriminating letters were penned by Martin's own son. *Antisemitism. Betrayal. Frame-ups. Germans. Letters. Nazis. Partnership.* Actors and actresses. Art dealers. Censorship. Fathers and daughters. Fathers and sons. Germany. Jews. Mobs. Murder. Nobility. San Francisco (CA). Wives.

Note: Kressmann Taylor's novel originally appeared in *Story Magazine* in Sep–Oct 1938. Although onscreen credits read "introducing K. T. Stevens," Stevens, who was the daughter of director Sam Woods, had previously appeared in films as Katherine Stevens. This was the first time that she was billed as "K. T. Stevens." According to an Oct 1943 pre-production *HR* news item, this film was to be the first joint venture of Wood's independent production unit and Columbia. The *DV* review notes that although the project was originally slated as a Woods production, William Cameron Menzies, the film's director and Wood's associate, took over the producing chores. A 1 Feb 1944 *HR* news item added that Menzies rewrote sequences to expand the role of Carl Esmond, who was borrowed from Paramount to appear in the film. According to Columbia publicity materials contained in the production files for this film at the AMPAS Library, the beer hall seen in the picture was an exact replica of the beer hall frequented by Adolf Hitler. This film was nominated for an Academy Award for Best Art Direction and Best Score.

Box 22 Apr 1944. *DV* 17 Apr 1944, p. 3, 6. *FD* 24 Apr 1944, p. 12. *HR* 25 Oct 1943, p. 7. *HR* 25 Jan 1944, p. 3. *HR* 1 Feb 1944, p. 8. *HR* 17 Apr 1944, p. 3. *HR* 24 Apr 1944, p. 12. *MPHPD* 1 Jan 1944, p. 1695. *MPHPD* 29 Apr 1944, pp. 1866-67. *NYT* 17 Apr 1944, p. 20. *Var* 19 Apr 1944, p. 12.

ADIÓS *see* **THE LASH**

ADOBE WALLS *see* **ARROWHEAD**

THE ADVENTURER *see* **THE CISCO KID AND THE LADY**

THE ADVENTURES OF A MADCAP (Gypsies)
Balboa Amusement Producing Co. *Dist* Pathé Exchange, Inc. 3 Nov 1915. Si; b&w. 4 reels.

Cast: Jackie Saunders (*Jean*), Frank Mayo (*Jack Aubrey*), Corinne Grant (*Carmio*), Philo McCullough (*Carlos*).

Comedy-drama. A little waif named Jean is adopted by Jason, an old flower grower, and for several years sells his flowers by the roadside. Jack Aubrey, a country lad, loves Jean but hesitates to ask for her hand in marriage. When her foster father suddenly dies, Jean is adopted by the Gordons, a wealthy, childless couple from the city. Jean soon comes to dislike life among the well-to-do and, longing for the freedom of the countryside, runs away to join a band of gypsies. To escape the unwelcome attentions of Carlos, the son of the gypsy king and lover of Carmio, Jean hides in a deserted shack, but the eager gypsy finds her. Carmio alerts the camp to Jean's predicament, and she, Jack and the Gordons arrive in time to save the young girl from disgrace. Adoption. City-country contrast. Gypsies. Runaways. Waifs. Country boys. Flower vendors. Foster parents. Upper classes.

Note: According to news items, this film was hand-colored by the Pathé process in Vincennes, France.

MPN 6 Nov 1915, p. 79. *MPN* 13 Nov 1915, p. 10. *MPW* 6 Nov 1915, p. 1204. *MPW* 13 Nov 1915, p. 1318. *Motog* 27 Nov 1915, p. 1106. *NYDM* 13 Nov 1915, p. 32.

THE ADVENTURES OF BUFFALO BILL (Native Americans)
Essanay Film Mfg Co. *Dist* K-E-S-E Service. 29 Jan 1917 [©Essanay Film Mfg. Co.; 23 Jan 1917; LP10056]. Si; b&w. 5 reels.

Cast: William Frederick Cody, Nelson Appleton Miles, Jesse M. Lee, Frank D. Baldwin, Marion P. Maus, Chief Yellow Hand, Chief Tall Bull, Chief Sitting Bull, Chief Short Bull, Charles A. King, H. G. Sickles.

Biography, Documentary. This film is a review of the adventurous life of Col. William F. Cody, popularly known as "Buffalo Bill." During his early career in the West, Cody rode with the Pony Express and hunted buffalo before becoming the chief Indian scout for the U.S. Cavalry. Generals Nelson A. Miles, James M. Lee, Frank D. Baldwin, and Marion P. Maus, and 5,000 U.S. troops and Indians recreate battles at Summit Springs and Warbonnet. Also seen are Cody's fight with Chief Tall Bull and his knife duel with Chief Yellow Hand. Another side of the plainsman is illustrated by scenes of Cody and his family at home. The film concludes with picturizations of great hunting expeditions in the Rocky Mountains, including one during which Cody served as guide for the Prince of Monaco. *Buffalo Bill Cody. Indians of North America. Rocky Mountains. Summit Springs, Battle of, 1869. United States–History–Indian Campaigns. Warbonnet Creek, Battle of, 1876. Pony express. Chief Tall Bull. Chief Yellow Hand.*

Note: In 1914, Wm. F. Cody Historical Picture Co. and Essanay Film Mfg. Co. released a film called *The Indian Wars*, which was a recreation of four major Indian battles of the late 1800's. Footage for both films was shot in late 1913 in the Bad Lands of South Dakota, the Black Hills of Wyoming, and Nebraska. According to contemporary sources, Essanay re-edited and added material for the 1917 production, which was released shortly after Cody's death on 10 Jan 1917. The 1914 film, also known as *The Wars of Civilization* and various other titles, was made with the cooperation of the U.S. Government and was intended to be an educational, historically accurate document. The government, however, shelved the 1914 film before it had much distribution. As an homage, the 1917 version highlighted Cody's participation in the battles. Contemporary sources claim that two copies of the 1917 film were submitted to the U.S. Government in Washington, D.C. for posterity, although modern sources report that both copies decomposed in the 1920's. A pre-release title for the film was *The Life of Buffalo Bill.* The 1914 film was directed by Theodore Wharton, photographed by D. T. Hargan and, according to modern sources, Conrad Luperti. Modern sources also credit Charles King with the scenario of both versions. Another 1917 film, *The Buffalo Bill Show,* may also have used some footage from the 1914 production, but was made and distributed by different companies (see below). For more historical information about Cody, please see the entry below for *Buffalo Bill.*

ETR 27 Jan 1917, p. 563. *ETR* 10 Feb 1917, p. 703. *Motog* 10 Feb 1917, p. 317. *MPW* 27 Jan 1917, p. 527. *MPW* 10 Feb 1917, p. 910. *NYDM* 1 Oct 1913, p. 27. *NYDM* 27 Jan 1917, p. 60. *NYDM* 3 Feb 1917, p. 28.

ADVENTURES OF CAPTAIN FABIAN (Creoles)

Silver Films Productions; A William Marshall Production. *Dist* Republic Pictures Corp. 6 Oct **1951**; Prod: early Aug—late Oct 1950 in France [©Republic Pictures Corp.; 27 Jul 1951; LP1304]. Sd (Western Electric Recording); b&w. 8,997 ft. 97 or 100-101 min. Passed by the National Board of Review. PCA cert no. 15394. *Country of origin* France—U.S.

Prod William Marshall. *Pres by* HERBERT J. YATES. *Assoc prod* Robert Dorfmann. *Dir* William Marshall and [Robert Florey]. [*Asst dir* Marc Maurettz]. *Scr* Errol Flynn. *Cam* Marcel Grignon. *Film ed* Henri Taverna. *Sets* Eugene Lourie and Max Douy. *Cost* Arlington Valles. *Mus* Rene Cloerec. *Sd* Roger Cosson. *Prod supv* R. E. Marshall. *Tech adv* Marc Maurettz. *Prod mgr* Sacha Kamenka. *Tech collaborator* Guy Seitz. *Asst prod mgr* Jean Rossi.

Cast: ERROL FLYNN [(*Capt. Michael Fabian*)], MICHELINE PRELLE [(*Léa Marriotte*)], Vincent Price [(*George Brissac*)], Agnes Moorehead [(*Jesebel Marriotte*)], Victor Francen [(*Henri Brissac*)], Jim Gerald [(*Constable Gilpin*)], Helena Manson [(*Madame Pirot*)], Howard Vernon [(*Emil*)], Roger Blin [(*Phillipe*)], Valentine Camax [(*Housekeeper*)], Georges Flateau [(*Judge Brissac*)], Zanie Campan [(*Cynthia Winthrop*)], Reggie Nalder [(*Constant*)], Marcel Journet, Gilles Queant, Charles Fawcett [(*Defense attorney*)], Aubrey Bower [(*Mate*)].

Historical, Melodrama. [*Print viewed*]. In 1860, Léa Marriotte, a French Creole maid in the home of spoiled New Orleans socialite Cynthia Winthrop, smashes a vase in response to her mistress' cruel reference to the young woman's mother, who was hanged some years earlier. Jesebel, Léa's aunt and constant companion, fuels the girl's rage by reminding her that it is the Marriottes who possess the good blood, while families like the Winthrops' now enjoy power purely because of their wealth. In the Winthrops' absence, Léa and Jesebel throw a wild party for their Creole friends, but the revelry is interrupted by George Brissac, who, although once Léa's lover, is engaged to marry Cynthia. Still attracted to Léa, George kisses her, whereupon Phillipe, the Winthrop's footman, who has been courting Léa, attacks his wealthy rival in a jealous rage. Horrified, Léa strikes Phillipe with a cane until he is dead. George assures Léa that all will

be well, but when he soon afterward arrives at the Winthrop home with Constable Gilpin, he declares that Léa murdered the footman. Léa is arrested, but later, George's uncle, Henri Brissac, who runs a profitable mercantile business once owned by the Fabian family, threatens that if his brainless nephew causes a scandal, he will be disowned. On that same night, Michael Fabian, who has captained a ship since his family lost their business to the Brissacs, arrives and learns about the arrest. After the captain promises to ship a supply of Emil's gunpowder to the North, Emil, an employee of the Brissacs, reveals to Fabian what really happened. During Léa's trial, Fabian tells the judge, another Brissac, that he will implicate the family in the crime unless she is released. Fabian then purchases the Pierrot tavern for Léa, using money he blackmailed from George. Although attracted to Fabian, Léa rejects his attentions and even steals his watch, and while Fabian is away, she lures George to "Chez Léa" on the eve of his marriage to Cynthia. Léa persuades George to take her to his room, and when Uncle Henri bursts in and discovers her there, she assumes she now has her revenge. George, however, strangles his uncle to death, a development that allows Léa to attain her fondest wish. She and George bury the body, after which she threatens to have George arrested unless he agrees to marry her. The two are wed, and Léa becomes mistress of the elegant Brissac mansion, but George's hatred, her continued rejection by New Orleans society, and Fabian's anger bring her nothing but unhappiness. Léa visits Fabian on his ship, and although he at first threatens to throw her over the side, he soon kisses her passionately. George, meanwhile, finds Fabian's gold watch in Léa's room. At George's prompting, Constable Gilpin searches the grounds for signs of the missing uncle, and when the grave is opened, Fabian's watch is found by the body. Fabian is arrested, but because George fears the captain will be released, he hires some local cutthroats to break into the jail and lynch his enemy. Remembering that there is an old tunnel under the jail, Léa sends Jesebel to free her lover while she makes her way to Fabian's ship. Fabian is released just as the mob breaks down the door, but Jesebel is shot and killed. The mob pursues Fabian to the ship, and George convinces them to throw their torches at the captain's explosive cargo. Fabian and George fight, and George is drowned. Just then Léa runs toward the ship shouting Fabian's name, but the gunpowder explodes, and she dies in his arms. *Class distinction. Creoles. Family honor. New Orleans (LA). Pride and vanity. Revenge. Social climbers. Aunts. Blackmail. Constables. Corruption. Evidence. Exhumation. Explosions. False accusations. Idle rich. Lynching. Marriage–Forced. Mobs. Murder. Rescues. Saloons. Sea captains. Trials. Uncles.*

Note: The working titles of this film were *The Bargain* and *New Orleans Adventure.* It was released in France as *La Taverne de N.O.* In MPAA/PCA files contained in the AMPAS Library, the production company is listed variously as Marshall Productions and Flynn-Marshall Productions as well as Silver Films Productions. According to a *Var* news item, the picture was filmed in France by an independent company formed by Errol Flynn and William Marshall, who at the time was married to the film's star, Micheline Prelle. The news item notes that Flynn, who had never written a screenplay, provided some of the financing, and the French company Corona Pictures put up $350,000 on the basis of the Republic distribution deal. Marshall, who was directing for the first time, reportedly violated French government regulations by starting the film without a permit and by ignoring the rule that states every English language film produced in France must also be made in a French language version. According the *Var* item, Warner Bros. considered Flynn's appearance in this film as a breach of contract.

Materials contained in the MPAA/PCA files add that in May 1950, Marshall entered into negotiations with Twentieth-Century Fox to distribute the picture. An Aug 1950 *HR* news item stated that Robert Florey was initially signed to direct the film. Florey's name is listed as director in the production charts until 22 Sep 1950. Modern sources add that Marshall, who had no previous experience directing, hired Florey initially as a co-director and then as the full director of a separate French version. Marshall's lack of experience led him to keep Florey on as an uncredited directorial consultant. Florey was on the set every day during production, on location at the Villefrance harbor in Nice and at La Victorine, Billancourt and Boulogne studios. This was the last feature-length production on which Florey worked. According to a *LAT* news item, Princess Irene Ghika refused an offer to play the role of "Cynthia Winthrop." According to a 1955 unidentified source contained in the AMPAS Library production files, Flynn and Marshall were sued by Charles Gross, Jr., who claimed that he was hired in Jun 1950 to adapt the story to the screen. The outcome of that suit is unknown.

Box 29 Sep 1951. *DV* 21 Sep 1951, p. 3. *Exb* 26 Sep 1951, p. 3162. *FD* 1 Oct 1951, p. 6. *Har* 29 Sep 1951, p. 154. *HR* 1 Aug 1950. *HR* 11 Aug 1950, p. 8. *HR* 27 Oct 1950, p. 4. *HR* 21 Sep 1951, p. 4. *LAT* 14 Oct 1950. *MPHPD* 29 Sep 1951, p. 1042. *NYT* 14 Dec 1951, p. 36. *Var* 16 Jun 1950. *Var* 26 Sep 1951, p. 6.

THE ADVENTURES OF CAROL (Italian Americans)

World Film Corp. *Dist* World Film Corp. 12 Nov 1917 [©World Film Corp.; 2 Nov 1917; LU11655]. Si; b&w. 5 reels, 5,200 ft.

Pres William A. Brady. *Dir* Harley Knoles. *Story* Julia Burnham. *Cam* René Guissart.

Cast: Madge Evans (*Carol Montgomery*), George MacQuarrie (*Col. Montgomery*), Rosina Henley (*Mrs. Montgomery*), Carl Axzell (*James*), Nicholas Long (*Beppo*), Kate Lester (*Mme. Fairfax*), Jack Drumier (*Mr. Fairfax*), Frances Miller (*Mammy Lou*).

Drama. When little Carol Montgomery's father, a navy commander, discovers a spy in the house, he earnestly counsels the family not to answer questions regarding themselves. Later, while attempting to follow her mother, Carol becomes lost on the subway, and, taking her father's words to heart, refuses to tell a police officer who she is. Eluding the officer, Carol falls asleep in a tenement hallway where she is found by Beppo, an Italian organ grinder who decides to add her to his show. They travel south, where, becoming separated from Beppo, Carol seeks refuge at the Fairfax plantation. Mrs. Fairfax, estranged from her husband because he had disowned their daughter years earlier when she eloped without his permission, refuses to speak to anyone. However, under Carol's winning influence, the Fairfaxes are reconciled and send for their long-lost daughter, who turns out to be Carol's mother. *Children. Disinheritance. Parentage. Italians. Officers (Military). Organ grinders. Plantations. Police. Spies. Subways. Tenement-houses.*

Note: The title of this film was changed from *When Carol Took the Subway.* *Motog* 17 Nov 1917, p. 1054. *MPW* 10 Nov 1917, p. 879. *MPW* 17 Nov 1917, p. 1073. *NYDM* 10 Nov 1917, p. 18. *Var* 2 Nov 1917, p. 49.

ADVENTURES OF COSMO JONES see **CRIME SMASHER**

ADVENTURES OF DANIEL BOONE see **DANIEL BOONE, TRAIL BLAZER**

THE ADVENTURES OF DON COYOTE (Latino)

Comet Productions, Inc. *Dist* United Artists Corp. 9 May 1947; Prod: Aug 1946 [©Comet Productions, Inc.; 9 May 1947; LP1446]. Sd (RCA); col (Cinecolor). 7 reels, 5,889 ft. 64-65 min. PCA cert no. 11996.

Prod Buddy Rogers and Ralph Cohn. *Assoc prod* Selmer L. Chalif. *Dir* Reginald LeBorg. *Asst dir* Louis Germonprez. *Scr* Bob Williams and Harold Tarshis. *Orig story* Bob Williams. *Dir of photog* Fred Jackman. *Col dir* Wilton Holm. *Art dir* George Van Marter. *Film ed* Lynn Harrison. *Mus score* David Chudnow. *Songs* Rene Touzet. *Sd rec* Hugh McDowell. *Prod mgr* Robert M. Beche.

Cast: Richard Martin (*Don Coyote*), Frances Rafferty [(*Maggie Riley*)], Val Carlo [(*Sancho*)], Benny Bartlett [(*Ted Riley*)], Marc Cramer [(*Sheriff Dave Sherman*)], Frank Fenton [("*Big Foot*" *Ferguson*)], Byron Foulger [(*Henry Felton*)], [Edwin Parker (*Joe*)], [Pierce Lyden (*Jeff*)], [Frank McCarroll (*Steve*)], [Ed Ingram (*Frank*)].

Western, with songs. [*Print viewed*]. Near the town of Border Flats, cowboys Don Coyote and his guitar-playing friend, Sancho, who are on their way from Mexico to Santa Barbara, witness a fight between two outlaws and a cowboy. When tomboyish ranch owner Maggie Riley arrives on the scene and tries unsuccessfully to help the cowboy, who is her ranch hand, Sancho and the gentlemanly Coyote intercede on the cowboy's behalf. Maggie, who has lost a string of ranchhands after similar attacks, offers jobs to the sharpshooting Mexicans, but is refused. Maggie is determined to hire the pair, however, and after planting a gold locket in Coyote's saddlebag, has Sheriff Dave Sherman arrest them for theft. Once Coyote and Sancho have been jailed, Maggie offers to drop the charges if they agree to work for her. Reluctantly, Sancho and Coyote go to Maggie's dilapidated ranch, which she runs with her surly, adolescent brother Ted. That night, Coyote and Sancho sneak away from the ranch, but are ambushed by the two outlaws and taken to their hideout in an abandoned mine. There the outlaws' leader, "Big Foot" Ferguson, warns them "It ain't healthy to work for Maggie Riley" and prepares to whip the bound Sancho. As Big Foot raises his whip, however, Coyote tosses some bullets into the hideout's fire, causing a noisy explosion. In the ensuing chaos, the outlaws flee, and Coyote frees Sancho. Outraged by Big Foot's brutality, Coyote returns with Sancho to Maggie's ranch, bent on revenge. The next morning, Coyote and Sancho clean up the ranch house, while Maggie, who is attracted to Coyote, sheds her scruffy clothes in favor of a dress. Maggie then reveals that she has been trying to get her cattle to market in order to

repay a bank loan, but has been thwarted by the repeated attacks on her cowhands. Later, while Coyote and Ted, who disdains the "fancy pants" Mexican, are riding toward Border Flats, they are attacked by two of Big Foot's men. Coyote kills one and chases off the other, and his sharp shooting and skillful riding changes Ted's mind about him. Ted shows his new hero a surveyor's plumb marked "United Pacific Railroad," explaining he found it near the ranch house. In Border Flats, while Ted gets his first shave from jovial barber Henry Felton, Coyote goes to see the sheriff. Coyote tells Dave of his suspicions that Big Foot's gang is trying to drive Maggie off her land in order to sell it to the railroad, which has been surreptitiously surveying her property. After Ted's shave, Felton, who is the secret head of the outlaws, meets in private with Big Foot. When Coyote and Ted return to the ranch, they discover that two of Big Foot's outlaws have tied up Maggie and Sancho and are about to set fire to the house. During the ensuing fight, Sancho is untied, and he, Coyote and Ted knock out the two thugs. That night, Maggie dons a frilly gown, and she and Coyote flirt and dance together. When Coyote, Ted, Maggie, the sheriff and his deputies try to herd Maggie's cattle to Border Flats the next day, they are attacked in a pass by Big Foot and his men. Sancho arrives at the pass with reinforcements in time to save his friend, who then pursues Big Foot to Felton's barbershop. After a fierce fistfight, Coyote bests Big Foot and Felton, and the two are arrested. With peace and honor restored, Coyote and Sancho bid goodbye to Ted and Maggie, who sadly heads toward her ranch. Before Maggie has gone far, she is stopped by the sheriff, who tells her Coyote has accused her of stealing his watch. Coyote and Sancho ride up just after the planted watch is pulled from her saddlebag, and Maggie asks if Coyote plans to press charges. "Thieves should always remain together," replies Coyote, who then accompanies Maggie back to her ranch, with Ted and Sancho following. *Cowboys. Duplicity. Land rights. Mexicans. Outlaws. Ranchers. Adolescents. Arrests. Barbers and barbershops. Brothers and sisters. Chases. Clothes. English language. Explosions. Fights. Gunfights. Hideouts. Honor. Loans. Mexican-American border region. Rescues. Romance. Sheriffs. Tomboys. Transformation.*

Note: Richard Martin's credit appears last in the onscreen cast list as "and presenting Richard Martin as Don Coyote." Although Martin was a regular in RKO's Tim Holt westerns, appearing as Holt's Mexican-American sidekick, *The Adventures of Don Coyote* marked his first starring role. The *Var* review commented about the film: "By a remarkable 180-degree switch, the forces of virtue are embodied in two hard-riding Mexicans (one of whom is also the romantic lead) whereas villainy is played Yankee across the board." According to the *Var* review, "a brace of Spanish songs" is sung in the picture, but their titles have not been determined. A *HR* news item adds that some scenes in the film were filmed in Lone Pine, CA.

Box 3 May 1947. *DV* 28 Apr 1947. *HR* 11 Jul 1946, p. 1. *HR* 2 Aug 1946, p. 19. *HR* 23 Aug 1946, p. 21. *HR* 28 Apr 1947, p. 3. *MPHPD* 3 May 1947. *Var* 30 Apr 1947, p. 10.

THE ADVENTURES OF HUCKLEBERRY FINN (African Americans)

Metro-Goldwyn-Mayer Corp.; controlled by Loew's Inc. *Dist* Loew's Inc. 10 Feb 1939; Prod: 19 Nov 1938—early Jan 1939 [©Loew's Inc.; 10 Feb 1939; LP8644]. Sd (Western Electric Sound System); b&w. 10 reels. 85, 88 or 92 min. Passed by the National Board of Review. PCA cert no. 5021.

Prod Joseph L. Mankiewicz. *Dir* Richard Thorpe. [*2d unit dir* Charles Dorian]. [*Asst dir* Tom Andre]. *Scr* Hugo Butler. [*Contr to dial* Waldo Salt]. *Photog* John Seitz. *Art dir* Cedric Gibbons. *Art dir assoc* Randall Duell. *Film ed* Frank E. Hull. *Set dec* Edwin B. Willis. *Mus score* Franz Waxman. *Rec dir* Douglas Shearer. *Makeup created by* Jack Dawn. *Prod mgr* Art Smith. [*Still photog* Durwood "Bud" Graybill].

Source: Based on the novel *The Adventures of Huckleberry Finn* by Mark Twain (New York, 1884).

Cast: Mickey Rooney (*Huckleberry Finn*), Walter Connolly (*The "King"*), William Frawley (*The "Duke"*), Rex Ingram (*Jim*), Lynne Carver (*Mary Jane*), Jo Ann Sayers (*Susan*), Minor Watson (*Captain Brandy*), Elizabeth Risdon (*Widow Douglas*), Victor Kilian ("*Pap*" *Finn*), Clara Blandick (*Miss Watson*), [Anne O'Neal (*Miss Bartlett*)], [Harlan Briggs (*Mr. Bucker*)], [Sarah Edwards (*Mrs. Bucker*)], [Janice Chambers (*Mary Adams*)], [Harry Watson (*Ben Donaldson*)], [Billy Watson (*Eliot*)], [Johnny Walsh (*Sam*)], [Delmar Watson (*Joe*)], [Wade Boteler (*Captain*)], [Irving Bacon (*Tad*)], [Robert Emmett Keane (*Lawyer*)], [Roger Imhof (*Judge*)], [Arthur Aylesworth (*Pilot*)], [George Guhl (*Engineer*)], [Erville Alderson (*Sheriff*)], [E. Alyn Warren (*Mr. Shackleford*)], [Nora Cecil (*Mrs. Shackleford*)], [Jessie Graves (*Black butler*)], [Mickey Rentschler (*Harry*)], [Leni Lynn

(*School girl*)], [Frank Darien (*Old man in jail*)], [Alonzo Price (*Deputy*)], [Lew Kelly (*Pilot*)], [Sarah Padden], [Harry Cording], [Roger Gray], [John Ince], [Edwin J. Brady], [Joe Bernard].

Youth, Historical, Drama. [*Print viewed*]. In the mid-eighteenth century, along the Mississippi River, young Huckleberry Finn, the son of the loutish drunk "Pap" Finn, lives with the Widow Douglas and her sister, Miss Watson. Though the widow loves Huck and he is fond of her, he finds it difficult to behave like the gentleman she wants, preferring loafing to going to school and going barefoot to wearing shoes. One night, when Pap goes to the widow and demands eight hundred dollars from her to keep his son, Huck overhears and decides to leave to prevent her from impoverishing herself for him. Huck then leaves, but is caught by his father, who confines him in a shack across the river. When Pap leaves him alone, Huck escapes and makes it appear as if he has been murdered and dumped into the river. He then goes upstream, and sometime later runs into his friend Jim, the widow's slave. Jim has run away from the widow because she was planning to sell him to raise money to keep Huck. Unknown to either Jim or Huck, when evidence of Huck's apparent murder was discovered, Jim's disappearance led authorities to believe that he was the murderer. Jim is now trying to get to a free state and join his wife, so Huck decides to help him. Farther upstream they encounter "The King" and "The Duke," two conmen who have been set adrift from a riverboat for bilking passengers, and who try to convince Huck and Jim that they are the "Lost Dauphin of France" and "The Duke of Bridgewater." Though the King and the Duke know that Jim is a runaway slave and plan to collect a reward for his return, they pretend to help him and Huck. Trying to finance their trip, the group stops at a small town along the river and advertises a theatrical production of *Romeo and Juliet*, starring famous actors David Garrick and Mrs. Siddons. The town gathers for the performance, but when the King dresses as Romeo and Huck dresses as Juliet, the audience chases them out of town. They are able to get away with two hundred dollars, but during the confusion Huck finds a handbill in the Duke's pocket offering a large reward for Jim. At the next town, Pikesville, the King and the Duke plan to impersonate two men who have not been seen by their rich brother for many years. By the time they reach the man's house, they learn that he has just died, but decide to continue their ruse in order to take over the estate from the man's two daughters, Mary Jane and Susan. When Captain Brandy of the paddleboat *The River Queen* comes to the house, he becomes suspicous and, after Huck tells the captain about the King and the Duke, they are prevented from carrying out their greedy plans. Meanwhile, a posse has been formed to look for Jim, and when it arrives at Pikesville, Huck and Jim hide out in the woods. When a rattlesnake bites Huck, however, Jim carries the boy back to town, and he is arrested. Huck awakens from his delirium several days later and learns from the captain that he sent Jim home because of the murder charge. Almost hysterical, Huck then tells the captain that the murder for which Jim is being charged is his. Huck and the captain board *The River Queen* and race back home, braving a serious storm, and arrive just in time to prevent Jim from being lynched. After being re-united with the happy widow, Huck decides to change his ways and go to school like a good boy, and the widow sets Jim free to join his wife. *Adolescents. Confidence men. False accusations. Friendship. Mississippi River. Murder.* Actors and actresses. African Americans. Alcoholics. Battered children. Escapes. Fathers and sons. Female impersonation. Financial crisis. Foster parents. David Garrick. *Romeo and Juliet* (Play). Mrs. Sarah Kemble Siddons. Slaves–Runaway. Steamboats. United States–History– Social life and customs.

Note: The opening credits read, "Metro-Goldwyn-Mayer presents *Mark Twain's The Adventures of Huckleberry Finn*." According to contemporary news items, M-G-M purchased the rights to Mark Twain's novel from Paramount in Apr 1938 in order to produce a new version of the story especially for Mickey Rooney. Portions of the picture were filmed on location in Alabama and in Isleton, CA. The final steamboat sequence was filmed on the Sacramento River in Northern California. English Actors David Garrick and Mrs. Siddons, who are advertised as the "stars" of the production of *Romeo and Juliet* in the film, were two of the most famous actors of the nineteenth century. For information on other filmed adaptations of Twain's novel, consult the entry below for the 1960 M-G-M release *The Adventurs of Huckelberry Finn*.

DV 13 Dec 1938. DV 8 Feb 1939, p. 3. FD 17 Feb 1939, p. 6. HR 29 Apr 1938, p. 1. HR 16 Jul 1938, p. 2. HR 18 Nov 1938, p. 7. HR 5 Jan 1939, p. 3. HR 8 Feb 1939, p. 2. IP Jan 1939. MPD 16 Feb 1939, p. 15. MPH 24 Dec 1938, p. 33. MPH 11 Feb 1939, p. 35, 38. NYT 3 Mar 1939, p. 21. Var 15 Feb 1939, p. 12.

THE ADVENTURES OF HUCKLEBERRY FINN (African Americans)
Metro-Goldwyn-Mayer Corp.; controlled by Loew's Inc.; Formosa Productions, Inc.; Samuel Goldwyn Jr.'s Production. *Dist* Loew's Inc. May **1960**; Prod: early Oct–late Nov 1959 [©Loew's Inc. & Formosa Productions, Inc.; 7 Mar 1960; LP15872]. Sd (Westrex Recording System); col (Metrocolor); CinemaScope; Photographic Lenses by Panavision. 12 reels, 9,617 ft. 107 or 109 min. PCA cert no. 19461.
Dir Michael Curtiz. *Asst dir* L. V. McCardle, Jr. *Scr* James Lee. *Dir of photog* Ted McCord. *Spec eff* A. Arnold Gillespie. *Color consultant* Charles K. Hagedon. *Art dir* George W. Davis and McClure Capps. *Film ed* Fredric Steinkamp. *Set dec* Henry Grace and Robert Priestley. *Men's cost* Jack Martell. *Mus score comp and cond* Jerome Moross. *Rec supv* Franklin Milton. *Makeup created by* William Tuttle. [*Scr girl* Cleo Anton].

Source: Based on the novel *The Adventures of Huckleberry Finn* by Mark Twain (New York, 1884).

Cast: Tony Randall [(*The King*)], Patty McCormack [(*Joanna Wilkes*)], Neville Brand [(*Pap*)], Mickey Shaughnessy [(*The Duke*)], Judy Canova [(*Sheriff's wife*)], Andy Devine [(*Mr. Carmody*)], Sherry Jackson [(*Mary Jane Wilkes*)], Buster Keaton [(*Lion tamer*)], Finlay Currie [(*Capt. Sellers*)], Josephine Hutchinson [(*Widow Douglas*)], Parley Baer [(*Grangerford man*)], John Carradine [(*Slave catcher*)], Royal Dano [(*Sheriff*)], [Dolores Hawkins (*River boat singer*)], Sterling Holloway [(*Barber*)], Dean Stanton [(*Slave catcher*)], Presenting Archie Moore (*Jim*), And also starring Eddie Hodges (*Huckleberry Finn*), [Minerva Urecal (*Miss Watson*)], [Roy Glenn (*Drayman*)], [Rickey Murray (*Cabin boy*)], [Tony Merrill (*Gambler*)], [Miles Stephens (*Foreman*)], [Fred Kohler, Henry Corden (*Mates*)], [James Horan (*Clerk*)], [Eddie Fetherston (*Townsman*)], [Burt Mustin (*Old farmer*)], [Sam McDaniel (*Servant*)], [Patrick Whyte (*Uncle Harvey Wilkes*)], [Owen McGiveney (*Second uncle*)], [Haldane Zajic (*Percy*)], [Fred Coby (*Sheriff*)], [Virginia Rose, Anne Kunde (*Women at circus*)], [Mack Chandler (*Man at circus*)], [Jack Younger].

Historical, Rural, Comedy-drama. [*Print viewed*]. In the summer of 1851, young Huckleberry Finn watches excitedly as a huge steamboat docks in his town of Hannibal, Missouri. Huck's daydream of continuing down the Mississippi to New Orleans, and from there to South America, is interrupted by Jim, a slave whose master, the kindly widow Douglas, has looked after Huck since the disappearance of his widowed, alcoholic father. Jim worriedly reports that Huck's father, a brutal man whom Huck calls "Pap," has come looking for his son, and sure enough, Pap appears in Huck's room that night and drags the child to his shack near the river. Pap declares that if the widow gives him $5,000, he will return Huck to her care, and when she considers selling Jim in order to secure the money, the slave runs away. After Pap nearly kills Huck in a drunken rage, the boy makes it appear that he has been murdered and then paddles away in a stolen canoe. The townspeople assume that it is Jim, the runaway slave, who has killed Huck, and this prompts the boy to join forces with Jim in an attempt to reach the free state of Illinois. The two use Jim's raft to put some distance between them and Hannibal, but eventually, they go ashore in search of food. There they meet with two grifters, who introduce themselves as the King of France and the Duke of Bilgewater. The swindlers want Huck to join them in a scheme to impersonate the long-lost English relatives of the recently deceased Peter Wilkes, a wealthy businessman whose daughters live in nearby Packsville. Jim is against the plan, but Huck is intrigued, and soon the King, impersonating "Uncle Harvey" Wilkes, is introducing his little nephew "Percy" to the grieving Wilkes daughters, Mary Jane and Joanna. The younger girl immediately suspects that her visitors are impostors, but the gullible Mary Jane offers the King $3,000 as his part of the Wilkes inheritance. Huck finally tells the Wilkes sisters the truth, or something close to the truth, and the sheriff arrests the two con men. Huck then returns to the river with Jim, whose dreams of life as a free man include finding a job, saving his money, and someday buying the freedom of his wife and children. After seeing Pap's murdered corpse in a wrecked houseboat, a fact Jim hides from Huck, Jim is nearly caught by slave hunters. He and Huck are taken aboard a steamboat, but because the King and the Duke are also on board, they are forced to escape into the river as the boat approaches Cairo. Once on shore, Huck and Jim try to masquerade as performers in the Carmody circus, but the King appears and has Jim arrested. As he awaits the $200 reward for Jim's capture, however, Huck,

impersonating a young girl, manages to obtain the keys and free Jim, even though Jim has revealed that Pap is dead. Jim swims to freedom, and after the two friends bid each other a heartfelt goodbye, the now former slave heads north while Huck paddles toward a New Orleans-bound steamboat. *Children. Confidence men. Friendship. Impersonation and imposture. Mississippi River. Runaways. Slaves. United States–History–19th century. Alcoholics. Bounty hunters. Chases. Circuses. Escapes. Fathers and sons. Female impersonation. Liars. Missouri. Rafts. Rural life. Steamboats. Widows.*

Note: In the onscreen credits, the film's title reads "Mark Twain's *The Adventures of Huckleberry Finn.* While most sources list the running time as 107 minutes, *Var* mistakenly lists it as 90 minutes. According to a 1958 *DV* news item, M-G-M originally planned this picture as a musical to be produced by Arthur Freed. The article states that in 1953, Alan J. Lerner and Burton Lane wrote a score for the film, which M-G-M hoped would star Gene Kelly and Danny Kaye. The production was later shelved because of casting difficulties. According to the pressbook materials contained in the film's production files at the AMPAS Library, this picture was shot on location on the Mississippi River and along the Sacramento River Delta. The boat that served as the *Natchez Queen* was the same boat used in the 1951 version of *Showboat.*

Archie Moore, a light heavyweight boxing champion, made his acting debut in the film. According to a Oct 1958 *DV* news item, although the rights to Twain's story had passed into the public domain, M-G-M claimed it owned the world copyright and sole international rights to the film under a deal the company made with the Twain estate in 1952, which was renewed in 1956. The fact that the property was in the public domain in the United States led several companies, including Warner Bros., to plan productions in 1958 based on Twain's story. One version was to be shot in Mexico using unknowns. Only M-G-M's version made it to the screen, however. 1960 marked the fiftieth anniversary of Twain's death.

Twain's novel has been the basis of many films. Among the versions are a 1920 Famous Players-Lasky release, *Huckleberry Finn,* directed by William Desmond Taylor and starring Lewis Sergeant and Katherine Griffith (see below); a 1939 M-G-M version entitled *The Adventures of Huckleberry Finn,* starring Mickey Rooney and Walter Connolly and directed by Richard Thorpe (see above); a 1939 Paramount version titled *Huckleberry Finn,* starring Jackie Coogan and Junior Durkin and directed by Norman Taurog (see below); a 1974 United Artists release under the same title starring Jeff East and directed by F. Lee Thompson; and a 1995 Walt Disney Company release entitled *Tom and Huck,* directed by Peter Hewitt and starring Jonathan Taylor Thomas and Brad Renford.

Box 9 May 1960. *DV* 28 Oct 1958. *DV* Jan 30 1959. *DV* 3 May 1960, p. 3. *Exb* 11 May 1960, p. 4701. *FD* 3 May 1960, p. 6. *Har* 7 May 1960, p. 74. *HR* 24 Feb 1959. *HR* 2 Oct 1959, p. 12. *HR* 20 Nov 1959, p. 14. *HR* 3 May 1960, p. 3. *LAT* 14 Oct 1958. *MPHPD* 7 May 1960, p. 684. *NYT* 4 Aug 1960, p. 17. *Var* 11 May 1960, p. 6.

THE ADVENTURES OF LIEUTENANT PETROSINO (Italian Americans)

Feature Photoplay Co. *Dist* State Rights. Nov **1912** [©Feature Photoplay Co.; 14 Nov 1912; LU129]. Si; b&w. 4 reels.

Detective, Drama. Lieutenant Joseph Petrosino, an Italian-American police detective, is assigned to a murder case involving the Black Hand Society. Soon afterwards, a ragpicker is sent to murder banker Antonio Lorenzo, who has threatened to expose the criminals' blackmail schemes. Lieutenant Petrosino ingeniously traces the crime to the ragpicker but is knocked unconscious in the process. Later, two Black Hand members flee the country, pursued to Sicily by Lieutenant Petrosino, who impresses the local police with his heroic methods of pursuit. Eventually, however, Petrosino is killed by Black Hand assassins in Palermo. His body is returned to the United States, where he is proclaimed a martyr of law and order. *Black Hand (United States). Detectives. Murder. Sicily. Blackmail. Italian Americans. Palermo (Sicily). Joseph Petrosino. Police. Ragpickers.*

Note: The picture was also known as *The Life and Death of Lieutenant Petrosino.* Sidney M. Goldin, listed as "author" in the copyright statement, was a producer and director. It is possible that he produced and directed this film. It was made with the "special permission of Madame Petrosino," and is based on the adventures of Italian-American detective Joseph Petrosino. For further information on Petrosino and his investigation of the Black Hand, see the entry below for the 1960 film *Pay or Die,* a fictional film about the Italian police detective.

MPW 16 Nov 1912, p. 668. *MPW* 23 Nov 1912, p. 821.

ADVENTURES OF THE CISCO KID *see* **THE GAY AMIGO**

THE ADVENTURES OF TOM SAWYER (Native Americans)

Selznick International Pictures, Inc. *Dist* United Artists Corp. 11 Feb **1938**; Prod: 18 Jul–5 Oct 1937; retakes and addl scenes filmed beginning early Dec 1937 [©Selznick International Pictures, Inc.; 4 Mar 1938; LP7894]. Sd (Western Electric Sound System); col (Technicolor). 10 reels. 91-93 min. Passed by the National Board of Review. PCA cert no. 3745.

Prod David O. Selznick. *Dir* Norman Taurog. *Asst dir* Eric Stacey and [Jack Roberts]. [*Dir of retakes and addl scenes* William Wellman and George Cukor]. *Scr* John V. A. Weaver. *Cont* Barbara Keon. [*Contr to trmt* Marshall Neilan]. *Photog* James Wong Howe. *Assoc photog* Wilfrid M. Cline. *Spec eff* Jack Cosgrove. [*Asst cam* Roy Clark and Ben Cohen]. *Col supv for the Technicolor company* Natalie Kalmus. *Art dir* Lyle Wheeler. *Film ed* Margaret Clancey. *Supv film ed* Hal C. Kern. *Int dec* Casey Roberts. *Cave seq des by* William Cameron Menzies. *Cost* Walter Plunkett. *Mus dir* Lou Forbes. *Sd rec* William Fox. [*Chief elec* Neil McDonald]. [*Chief grip* Charles Rose]. *Asst to prod* William H. Wright. [*Props* Arden Cripe]. [*Research* Lillian K. Deighton].

Source: Based on the novel *The Adventures of Tom Sawyer* by Mark Twain (San Francisco, 1876).

Cast: Tommy Kelly (*Tom Sawyer*), Jackie Moran (*Huckleberry Finn*), Ann Gillis (*Becky Thatcher*), May Robson [(*Aunt Polly*)], Walter Brennan [(*Muff Potter*)], Victor Jory [(*Injun Joe*)], David Holt [(*Sid Sawyer*)], Nana Bryant [(*Mrs. Thatcher*)], Victor Kilian [(*Sheriff*)], Olin Howland [(*Schoolmaster*)], Donald Meek [(*Sunday school superintendent*)], Charles Richman [(*Judge Thatcher*)], Margaret Hamilton [(*Mrs. Harper*)], Marcia Mae Jones [(*Mary Sawyer*)], Mickey Rentschler [(*Joe Harper*)], Cora Sue Collins [(*Amy Lawrence*)], Philip Hurlic [(*Jim*)], [Spring Byington (*Widow Douglas*)], [George Billings (*Ben Rogers*)], [Byron Armstrong (*Billy Fisher*)], [Betsy Gay (*Susie Harper*)], [Luke Cosgrove (*Old soldier*)], [Frank McGlynn (*Minister*)], [Bob McKenzie (*River authority*)], [Roland Drew (*Dr. Robinson*)], [Erville Alderson (*District attorney*)], [Arthur Aylesworth (*Defense attorney*)], [Eric Alden (*Defense attorney's assistant*)], [Bob Murphy (*Bailiff*)], [Bruce Mitchell, Dan Wolheim (*Deputies*)], [Frank Darien (*Storekeeper*)], [Frank O'Connor (*Mr. Harper*)].

Youth, Comedy-drama. [*Print viewed*]. Freckle-faced schoolboy Tom Sawyer, his cousin Mary, his aunt Polly and his smug half brother Sid live in a small town on the banks of the Mississippi River. Tom often gets into trouble with his strict but good-hearted aunt when Sid snitches on him or sets him up for punishment. One day, when Tom is caught playing hookey from school, Aunt Polly punishes him by giving him the tedious chore of whitewashing their fence. Tom, however, cleverly manages to convince his friends that painting is pleasurable, and they soon pay him with marbles, fishhooks and other valuables for the privilege of doing it for him. When Tom first casts his eyes upon Becky Thatcher, he falls instantly in love with her and spurns his first love, Amy Lawrence. While trying to impress Becky with his collection of "Bible tickets," which are earned for memorizing passages from Scripture, Tom purchases the tickets from his schoolmates and is exposed when he is unable to answer a simple Biblical question at the award ceremony. Later, when Mr. Dobbins, the schoolteacher, discovers an unflattering caricature of himself, drawn by someone in his class, Tom takes the blame in order to save Becky from punishment. As a result, Tom wins Becky's admiration. That evening, Tom and his half-caste friend, Huckleberry Finn, go to the local cemetery with a dead cat in order to test Huck's cure for warts. Soon after they arrive, however, they witness three townsmen, Dr. Robinson, Injun Joe and Muff Potter, the town drunk, robbing a grave. During the robbery, a dispute between the men erupts, and Injun Joe stabs and kills Dr. Robinson. In an attempt to pin the murder on the unconscious Muff, Injun Joe plants the bloodied knife in his hand and flees. Terrified by the murder they witnessed, Tom and Huck take an oath of silence and return home. After Tom is spurned by Becky and wrongly accused of spilling sugar at home, he and Huck, whose mother has forced him to wear shoes against his will, decide to run away to play pirates on Jackson Island. Tom and Huck, along with their friend, Joe Harper, dress up as pirates and play along the river, but soon learn that a search party has been dispatched to find their presumed drowned bodies following the discovery of their clothes along the riverbank. The boys camp out for three days until Tom becomes homesick and decides to sneak home in the middle of the night to spy on the grieving mothers. Tom writes a note to Aunt Polly in which he assures her of his safety and his love for her, but pockets it when he learns that his funeral services are scheduled for the following day. Tom, Huck and Joe witness their own funeral service while hiding in the church, but emerge when they become overcome with emotion. Later, at Dr. Robinson's murder trial, Huck and Tom overhear the defense attorney state that there are no

witnesses to testify on Muff's behalf, which prompts the guilt-ridden Tom to come forward and tell the truth about the murder. Just as Tom is about to name Injun Joe as the real murderer, Injun Joe hurls a knife at him and flees the courtroom. Tom escapes injury, and during a school picnic at a nearby cavern, Tom, having won Becky's respect anew, takes his sweetheart on a walk through the labyrinth of underground passageways. After they find a treasure chest filled with gold in one of the corridors, Tom and Becky become lost in the cavern. While searching for an exit, Tom and Becky happen upon Injun Joe, who has been hiding in the caves, and run away from him. Meanwhile, a search party is sent into the caves when it is discovered that Tom and Becky are missing. A rockslide blocks efforts to rescue Tom and Becky, but they manage to escape death by sending Injun Joe off the side of a cliff to his death. After Tom and Becky find their way out of the caves, they meet up with the search party and are taken back to town, where they are celebrated as heroes. *Brothers. Caves. Children. False accusations. Frame-ups. Funerals. Murder. Runaways. Small town life. African Americans–Mixed blood. Aunts. Bible. Cemeteries. Courtship. Cures. Falls from heights. Heroes. Indians of North America. Missing persons, Assumed dead. Mississippi River. Schools. Self-sacrifice. Treasure. Trials.*

Note: According to *HR* news items, producer David O. Selznick made two unsuccessful attempts to film this picture before production commenced for the third and final time on 18 Jul 1937. The first round of filming, which began on 27 Mar 1937, was suspended and then begun again on 24 Jun, only to be halted for a second time shortly thereafter. H. C. Potter directed the first two production attempts, and although it is not clear why the first two rounds of filming did not succeed, a modern source claims that Potter walked off the picture because of "Selznickian interference." *HR* also notes that when Norman Taurog, who directed Paramount's 1931 *Huckleberry Finn*, took over the direction of the film, he discarded the footage that had already been shot (in black and white), and began production on the film in Technicolor. John Weaver was assigned to refurbish the script to "meet color demands."

Following Taurog's assignment as director of the picture, Ted Limes was replaced by Jackie Moran as "Huckleberry Finn," and Beulah Bondi supplanted Elizabeth Patterson as "Aunt Polly." Bondi was later replaced by May Robson. A 28 Jun 1937 *HR* production chart lists A. W. Sweatt, Hugh Chapman, Jimmie Swisher, and Hollis Jewell in the cast, but their appearance in the released film is doubtful. The same production chart included Tommy Bupp in the cast but, according to an interview with Bupp, he was originally cast in the role of Tom, but when the role of Huck was given to Jackie Moran, Bupp was replaced by Tommy Kelly because Bupp was considered too tall. *HR* news items also note that William Wellman, who was originally announced as the director of the picture, but who could not take the assignment at the time due to a schedule conflict with his work on *A Star Is Born*, directed two days of retakes in Dec 1937 while Taurog was busy with *Mad About Music*. George Cukor also directed some retakes and added scenes. Hundreds of boys were reportedly tested for the title role, which Selznick (according to a modern source printing of a memo he wrote on the subject) wanted to cast with an orphan who was unknown to film audiences. Selznick was unable to find a qualified orphan, but settled instead for the inexperienced Tommy Kelly, the son of an East Bronx fireman. The film marked Kelly's screen debut.

Contemporary sources note that an exhibit called "The Making of a Contemporary Film," sponsored by the Museum of Modern Art in New York, featured material that attested to the exhaustive research efforts that went into making the picture. For example, the studio's research department was said to have consulted over one hundred sources in order to insure the authenticity of the setting and the characters in the film. Among the many experts who were consulted were Bernard De Voto, H. L. Mencken and Albert Bigelow Paine. Late 19th century American school books and Missouri newspapers were also used for research purposes, as was Mark Twain's book, *Life on the Mississippi*. According to a Feb 1938 *Photoplay* study guide, some filming took place at Malibu Lake, CA, where a school for the twelve children who were featured in the film was run by Fletcher Clark. A *HR* news item notes that Culver City proclaimed a "Tom Sawyer Day" in honor of this picture.

As noted in a biography of photographer James Wong Howe, many disputes arose between Howe and Technicolor cameraman Wilfred Cline over which colors should be used in the wardrobe and sets. Cline suggested brilliant primary colors, while Howe insisted that the film maintain its true Southern and rural flavor by using only subdued earth tones. Howe prevailed, but by the end of the first week of production, the two were reportedly no longer on speaking terms. The biography also notes that while shooting the cave sequences, Howe overcame lighting difficulties by strapping Kelly to a harness that carried a 10,000 watt globe of light with an electrical cord running down the actor's leg. The device created the desired effect of Kelly lighting his path with a giant candle. In addition, Howe's biography notes that the Technicolor company, which had a virtual monopoly on color production, banned Howe from shooting subsequent pictures in color due to his poor rapport with their company. (Howe did not film another color production until 1949).

According to a *HR* news item, Selznick International made a separate print of the film for release in Great Britain. William Hamilton Burnside, an English sales consultant, helped the studio eliminate "American colloquialisms, dialogue and situations in the Missouri boy story that might not be understood by a British audience." The *NYT* review of the film ends with the reviewer stating: "...get busy [Mr. Selznick] on *Gone With the Wind*, will you, before we

begin throwing tomatoes." Lyle Wheeler was nominated for an Academy Award for Best Art Decoration for his work on the film.

Other films based on Twain's novel include: the 1917 Paramount film *Tom Sawyer*, directed by William D. Taylor and starring Jack Pickford and George Hackathorne (see *AFI Catalog of Feature Films, 1911-20*; F1.4513); the 1930 Paramount-Publix film of the same title, directed by John Cromwell and starring Jackie Coogan and Junior Durkin (see below); the 1938 Paramount film *Tom Sawyer, Detective* (see *AFI Catalog of Feature Films, 1931-40*; F3.4677); the 1973 Universal TV—Hal Roach Productions telefilm, directed by James Neilson and starring Jane Wyatt and Buddy Ebsen, which aired on the CBS television network on 23 Mar 1973; the 1973 United Artists musical film *Tom Sawyer*, directed by Don Taylor; and, the 1995 Walt Disney Company film entitled *Tom and Huck*, directed by Peter Hewitt and starring Jonathan Taylor Thomas and Brad Renfro.

DV 11 Feb 1938, p. 3. *FD* 15 Feb 1938, p. 8. *HR* 14 Dec 1936, p. 4. *HR* 28 Jun 1937, p. 23. *HR* 15 Jul 1937, p. 1. *HR* 19 Jul 1937, p. 15. *HR* 4 Oct 1937, p. 11. *HR* 5 Oct 1937, p. 6. *HR* 11 Dec 1937, p. 3. *HR* 14 Dec 1937, p. 3. *HR* 11 Feb 1938, p. 3. *HR* 10 Mar 1938, p. 18. *MPD* 14 Feb 1938, p. 2. *MPH* 9 Oct 1937, pp. 16-17. *MPH* 19 Feb 1938, p. 38. *NYT* 18 Feb 1938, p. 23. *Var* 16 Feb 1938, p. 15.

AFLAME IN THE SKY (Latino)

R-C Pictures Corp. *Dist* Film Booking Offices of America. 28 Nov 1927 [©R-C Pictures Corp.; 28 Nov 1927; LP24689]. Si; b&w. 6 reels, 6,034 ft.

Pres Joseph P. Kennedy. *Dir* J. P. McGowan. *Asst dir* James Dugan. *Story* Mary Roberts Rinehart. *Cont* Ewart Adamson. *Cam* Joe Walker.

Cast: Sharon Lynn (*Inez Carillo*), Jack Luden (*Terry Owen*), William Humphreys (*Major Savage*), Robert McKim (*Joseph Murdoch*), Billy Scott (*Saunders*), Charles A. Stevenson (*Grandfather*), Bill Franey (*Cookie*), Mark Hamilton (*Slim*), Walter Ackerman (*Desert Rat*), Jane Keckley (*Cordelia Murdoch*), Ranger (*Himself, a dog*).

Aviation, Drama. Aviators Terry Owen and Major Savage meet in the New Mexico desert to experiment with gas for night skywriting, and there they rescue Inez Carillo, who is being pursued by horsemen. She tells them of her grandfather, who is chronically ill, and of Murdoch, a renegade foreman who wants to marry her to gain control of their hacienda and is actually poisoning her grandfather. Upon returning home, she agrees to marry Murdoch to prolong her grandfather's life. When she overhears a plan to poison Terry's water, she sends him a warning. Terry signals Savage, who gets aid from border police. Murdoch's men are captured; Murdock escapes into the desert but dies of thirst. Free again to wed, Inez accepts Terry. *Air pilots. Border patrols. Deserts. Dogs. Grandfathers. Mexican Americans. New Mexico. Ranch foremen. Skywriting. Thirst.*

Var 2 Nov 1927, p. 24.

AFTER FIVE (Japanese Americans)

Jesse L. Lasky Feature Play Co. *Dist* Paramount Pictures Corp. 28 Jan 1915 [©Jesse L. Lasky Feature Play Co., Inc.; 25 Jan 1915; LU4276]. Si; b&w. 5 reels.

Pres Jesse L. Lasky. *Dir* Oscar Apfel and Cecil B. DeMille. *Scen* William C. de Mille. *Cam* Alfredo Gondolfi.

Source: Based on the play *After Five* by William C. de Mille and Cecil B. DeMille (New York, 29 Oct 1913).

Cast: Edward Abeles (*Ted Ewing*), Sessue Hayakawa (*Oki, his valet*), Betty Schade (*Nora Hildreth*), Jane Darwell (*Mrs. Russell, "Aunt Diddy"*), Theodore Roberts (*Bruno Schwartz*), Monroe Salisbury (*Sam Parker*), James Neil, Ernest Joy, Jode Mullally, Ernest Garcia.

Comedy. Ted Ewing entrusts $50,000 belonging to his ward Nora Hildreth, whom he loves, and $50,000 of his own, to broker Sam Parker to invest in Potash preferred stock on Parker's advice. After Parker disappears, Ted takes out a $50,000 life insurance policy payable to Nora. Because it contains a clause disallowing payment for suicide, Ted tries to arrange to die "accidentally." After a few misguided attempts, Ted pays his Japanese valet Oki a sum to deliver to Bruno Schwartz, the leader of a black hand organization, if they will kill him after five that afternoon. While Ted waits in terror for his "accident," Parker notifies him that his disappearance caused other brokers to sell, and that now the stock has doubled. Rather than go back on his word, Oki attempts hara-kiri. After Ted proposes to Nora's doting Aunt Diddy, to get money from her to pay off Schwartz, the gang is called off. Ted and Nora marry as Aunt Diddy smiles in resignation. *Accidents. Life insurance. Stock market. Suicide. Aunts. Black Hand (United States). Hara-kiri. Japanese. Stockbrokers. Valets. Wards and guardians.*

Note: Some scenes in this film were shot at Bear Lake Valley, CA. Famous

Players-Lasky released another film based on the same source in 1925 entitled *The Night Club*, starring Raymond Griffith. (See *AFI Catalog of Feature Films, 1921-30*; F2.3825.).

Motog 6 Feb 1915, pp. 229-30. *MPN* 30 Jan 1915, p. 43. *MPW* 13 Feb 1915, p. 987, 1048. *NYDM* 3 Feb 1915, p. 26. *Var* 5 Feb 1915, p. 23.

AFTER THE THIN MAN (Chinese Americans)

Metro-Goldwyn-Mayer Corp.; controlled by Lowe's Inc. *Dist* Metro-Goldwyn-Mayer Corp. **25 Dec 1936**; Prod: late Sep—31 Oct 1936 [©Metro-Goldwyn-Mayer Corp.; 21 Dec 1936; LP 6821]. Sd (Western Electric Sound System); b&w. 12 reels. 107 or 112 min. Passed by the National Board of Review. PCA cert no. 2889.

Series: The Thin Man.

Prod Hunt Stromberg. *Dir* W. S. Van Dyke. [*Asst dir* Charles Dorian]. *Scr* Frances Goodrich and Albert Hackett. *Story* Dashiell Hammett. *Photog* Oliver T. Marsh. *Art dir* Cedric Gibbons. *Art dir assoc* Harry McAfee and Edwin B. Willis. *Film ed* Robert J. Kern. *Ward* Dolly Tree. *Mus score* Herbert Stothart and Edward Ward. *Dances staged by* Seymour Felix. *Rec dir* Douglas Shearer. [*Still photog* Eddie Croninworth].

Song(s): "Smoke Dreams," music by Nacio Herb Brown, lyrics by Arthur Freed; "Blow That Horn," music by Walter Donaldson, lyrics by Chet Forrest and Bob Wright.

Cast: WILLIAM POWELL (*Nick Charles*), MYRNA LOY (*Nora [Charles]*), James Stewart (*David [Graham]*), Elissa Landi (*Selma [Landis]*), Joseph Calleia (*"Dancer"*), Jessie Ralph (*Aunt Katherine [Forrest]*), Alan Marshall (*Robert [Landis]*), Teddy Hart (*Casper*), Sam Levene (*[Lieutenant] Abrams*), Dorothy McNulty (*Polly [Byrnes]*), William Law (*Lum Kee*), George Zucco (*Dr. Kammer*), Paul Fix (*Phil*), Asta, Mrs. Asta, [Dorothy Vaughn (*Charlotte*)], [Maude Turner Gordon (*Helen*)], [William Burress (*Lucius*)], [Tom Ricketts (*Henry, the butler*)], [Joe Caits (*Joe*)], [Joe Phillips (*Willie*)], [Edith Kingdon (*Hattie*)], [John T. Murray (*Jerry*)], [John Kelly (*Harold*)], [Clarence Kolb (*General*)], [Zeffie Tilbury (*Lucy*)], [Donald Briggs, Jack Norton, Fredric Santly (*Reporters*)], [Baldwin Cooke, Sherry Hall, Jack Raymond (*Photographers*)], [Ed Dearing (*Bill, Policeman*)], [Dick Rush (*S.F. Detective*)], [Mary Gordon (*Rose the cook*)], [Heinie Conklin (*Trainman*)], [Dick Cramer (*Iceman*)], [Ben Hall (*Butcher boy*)], [George H. Reed (*Black porter*)], [Billy Benedict (*Newsboy*)], [Vince Barnett (*Wrestler's manager*)], [Ethel Jackson (*Girl with fireman*)], [Arthur Housman (*Man rehearsing welcome speech*)], [Jack Daley (*Bartender*)], [Bert Scott (*Man at piano*)], [George Guhl (*S.F. Police captain*)], [Norman Willis (*Fireman*)], [Edith Craig (*Girl with fireman*)], [Kewpie Martin (*Boyfriend of girl standing on hands*)], [Bert Lindley (*Station agent*)], [James Blaine (*S.F. Policeman*)], [Guy Usher (*Chief of detectives*)], [Bob Murphy (*Arresting detective*)], [Harry Tyler (*Fingers*)], [Bobby Watson (*Leader of late crowd*)], [Eric Wilton (*Butler*)], [Henry Roquemore (*Actor's agent*)], [Constantine Romanoff (*Wrestler*)], [Sam McDaniel (*Pullman porter*)], [Ernie Alexander (*Filing clerk in morgue*)], [John Butler, Louis Natheaux (*Race track touts*)], [Jonathan Hale (*Night city editor*)], [Jeanie Roberts (*Girl who works with Jerry*)], [Charles Arnt (*Drunk*)], [Harvey Perry (*Man who stands on hands*)], [Jesse Graves (*Red cap*)], [Alice H. Smith (*Emily*)], [Richard Powell (*Surprised policeman*)], [Cecil Elliott, Phillis Coghlan (*Servants*)], [Frank Otto (*Taxi driver*)], [Jack Adair (*Escort of dizzy blonde*)], [Irene Coleman, Claire Rochelle, Jean Barry, Jane Tallant (*Chorus girls*)], [Sue Moore (*Sexy blonde*)], [Edith Trivers (*Hat check girl*)], [George Taylor (*Eddie*)], [Lee Phelps (*Proprietor of Flop House*)], [Chester Gan, Richard Loo (*Chinese waiters*)], [Lew Harvey, Jimmy Brewster (*Thugs*)], [Harlan Briggs (*Burton Forrest*)], [Jimmy Blair, Marion Shelton (*Specialty dancers*)], [William Howard Gould], [Monte Vandergrift], [Jimmy Lucas].

Detective, Comedy. [*Print viewed*]. On New Year's Eve, Nick and Nora Charles arrive back home in San Francisco after Nick successfully solved the "Thin Man" murder case in New York. Exhausted from their trip, Nick and Nora want a quiet evening at home, but discover that their house has been taken over by a group of revelers they don't even know. When Nora's Great Aunt Katherine Forrest invites them to dinner, Nick doesn't want to go, but agrees when Nora's cousin, Selma Landis, pleads with Nora. At Katherine's house, they discover that Selma's husband Robert has been missing for three days. Katherine asks Nick to quietly find Robert, and, although he is reluctant, he takes Nora to the Lichee, a Chinese nightclub that Robert frequents. Robert has been at the Lichee, drinking and waiting for the club's entertainer, Polly Byrnes. Polly and "Dancer," one of the club's owners, are expecting to get money from Robert and Dancer tells Polly to take Robert home. A few days previously, Robert had approached David Graham, Selma's former fiancée, for $25,000 to leave for good. David meets Robert a short time later to give him negotiable bonds, then, after cruelly bidding Selma goodbye, Robert walks out into the fog and is shot. When David's car drives up to Robert's body, Selma is standing over it with a gun. Dazed, Selma gives David the weapon and he tells her not to say anything. Despite their efforts to protect Selma, Nick and Nora are unable to prevent her arrest by Lieutenant Abrams. Though Selma says that she had not fired her gun, David reveals that he threw it into the bay, thinking that Selma actually had killed her husband. The next day, Nick goes to the hotel room of Phil Byrnes, a man posing as Polly's brother, but actually her husband. Upon his arrival, Nick discovers Phil's dead body. Later, he also discovers that someone had been listening to Polly's apartment through a device in the apartment above. Suspicious when he hears Dancer enter Polly's apartment, Nick follows him to the basement and finds the body of the janitor. When Nora arrives at the apartment building and hears the janitor's name, Pedro, she reveals that Pedro used to be her father's gardener. Nick then asks Abrams to have all of the suspects congregate at Polly's. Though Dancer and Polly admit their plan to use a check forged with Robert's name, each claims to be innocent of the murders. During questioning, David says that he remembers Pedro, a man with a long white moustache, but hasn't seen him recently. When Nick looks at a picture of Pedro taken years before and sees that Pedro then had a small black moustache, he knows that David must be lying. Nick then says that the murderer has finally made a slip and reconstructs the evidence to reveal that David killed Robert out of revenge, then killed Phil when Phil tried to blackmail him. Finally, when Pedro recognized him, David was forced to kill him as well. Now cornered, David reveals that he had been planning to frame Selma for her husbands murder. He draws a gun and threatens to shoot Selma and then himself, but Lum Kee, Dancer's partner in the club, knocks the gun out of David's hand and David is overpowered. A short time later, Nick and Nora leave San Francisco on the train, accompanied by Selma, who plans to start a new life. Finally, when he is alone with Nora, Nick sees that she is crocheting a baby's sock and is shocked when she says "And you call yourself a detective." Detectives. Frame-ups. Marriage. Murder. San Francisco (CA). Chinese Americans. Dogs. Family relationships. Infidelity. New Year's Eve. Nightclubs. Parties. Reporters. San Francisco (CA)–Chinatown. Trains.

Note: According to contemporary news items, portions of the film were shot on location in San Francisco, and the base of the city's Coit Tower was used as the exterior of the Charles home. According to a news item in *HR* on 30 Oct 1934, author Dashiell Hammett was to have a small part in the picture, however, when the film went into production almost two years later, his name was not mentioned and the possibility of his acting in the picture was apparently dropped. The nightclub featured in the film was loosely modelled on the famous Forbidden City, a popular San Francisco night spot from the late 1930s through the 1950s.

This was the first film in more than five years made by actress Dorothy McNulty, who had been appearing on Broadway during the early 1930s. She changed her name in 1938 to Penny Singleton, and became more familiar under that name when she played the lead in Columbia's *Blondie* series (see below). A modern source credits Henry Grace with set decoration. This was the second of M-G-M's *Thin Man* pictures. For additional information on the series, please consult the Series Index and see the entry for *The Thin Man* in *AFI Catalog of Feature Films, 1931-40*; F3.4572.

DV 28 Sep 1936, p. 6. *DV* 3 Dec 1936, p. 3. *FD* 7 Dec 1936, p. 11. *HR* 30 Oct 1934, p. 4. *HR* 23 Sep 1936, p. 2. *HR* 29 Sep 1936, p. 14. *HR* 3 Dec 1936, p. 3. *MPD* 4 Dec 1936, p. 10. *MPH* 12 Dec 1936, p. 52. *NYT* 25 Dec 1936, p. 19. *Var* 30 Dec 1936, p. 1.

AGAINST THE CURRENT *see* **CONTRA LA CORRIENTE**

AIR FORCE (Japanese Americans, Multi-ethnic)

Warner Bros. Pictures, Inc.; A Howard Hawks Production; A Warner Bros.—First National Picture. *Dist* Warner Bros. Pictures, Inc. **20 Mar 1943**; New York premiere: 3 Feb 1943; Prod: 18 Jun—26 Oct 1942 [©Warner Bros. Pictures, Inc.; 20 Mar 1943; LP11920]. Sd (RCA Sound System); b&w. 11,179 ft. 124-125 min.

Exec prod JACK L. WARNER. *Prod* Hal B. Wallis. *Dir* Howard Hawks. [*Asst dir* Jack Sullivan]. *Orig scr* Dudley Nichols. [*Contr to scr* Arthur Horman]. *Dir of photog* James Wong Howe. *Aerial photog* Elmer Dyer and Charles Marshall. *Spec eff dir* Roy Davidson. *Spec eff* Rex Wimpy and H. F. Koenekamp. *Art dir* John Hughes. *Film ed* George Amy. *Set dec* Walter F. Tilford. *Gowns* Milo Anderson. *Mus*

Franz Waxman. *Mus dir* Leo F. Forbstein. *Sd* Oliver S. Garretson. *Makeup artist* Perc Westmore. *Chief pilot for Warner Bros.* Paul Mantz. [*Tech adv* Major Sam Triffy and Major Theron Coulter].

Cast: Members of the crew of the ''Mary Ann'' B-17 plane no. 05564 John Ridgely (*Pilot [Irish Quincannon]*), Gig Young (*Co-pilot [Bill Williams]*), Arthur Kennedy (*Bombardier [Tommy McMartin]*), Charles Drake (*Navigator [Monk Hauser]*), Harry Carey (*Crew chief [Robbie White]*), George Tobias (*Asst. crew chief [Cpl. Weinberg]*), Ward Wood (*Radio operator [Peterson]*), Ray Montgomery (*Asst. radio operator [Chester]*), John Garfield (*Aerial gunner [Joe Winocki]*), James Brown (*Pursuit pilot [Tex Rader]*), Stanley Ridges [(*Mallory*)], Willard Robertson [(*Colonel*)], Moroni Olsen [(*Commanding officer*)], Edward S. Brophy [(*Callahan*)], Richard Lane [(*Major Roberts*)], Bill Crago [(*Lieutenant Moran*)], Faye Emerson [(*Susan McMartin*)], Addison Richards [(*Major Daniels*)], James Flavin [(*Major Bagley*)], [Ann Doran (*Mary Quincannon*)], [Dorothy Peterson (*Mrs. Chester*)], [William Forrest (*Group commander*)], [Maurice Murphy (*Co-pilot*)], [Henry Blair (*Quincannon's son*)], [Warren Douglas (*Control officer*)], [Ruth Ford, Lynne Baggett, Marjorie Hoschelle, Leah Baird (*Nurses*)], [George Neise (*Radio operator*)], [William Hopper, Sol Gorss, Charles Flynn, Walter Sande (*Sergeants*)], [Victor Zimmerman, Pat Gleason (*Marines*)], [Edward Soo Hoo, Walter Soo Hoo (*Chinese*)], [Bill Edwards, Charles Lang (*Soldiers*)], [James Bush (*Control officer*)], [George Offerman, Jr. (*Ground crew man*)], [Murray Alper (*Corporal*)], [Warren Mace, John Estes (*Orderlies*)], [Hal Welling (*Officer*)], [Theodor Von Eltz (*First lieutenant*)], [Ross Ford (*Second lieutenant*)], [Edwin Stanley (*Physician*)], [Rand Brooks (*Co-pilot*)], [James Millican, Bill Hunter, Allan Lane, Bill Kennedy, Tom Neal, David Alison (*Marines*)], [Charles Sullivan], [Pat West], [Fred Steele], [Frank Marlowe], [Harry Lewis].

Aviation, World War II, Drama. [*Print viewed*]. At a San Francisco Air Force base, the crew of a B-17 Flying Fortress, nicknamed the ''Mary Ann,'' prepares for a routine flight to Hawaii. The crew, consisting of Captain Irish Quincannon, co-pilot Bill Williams, bombardier Tommy McMartin, navigator Monk Hauser, crew chief Robbie White, assistant crew chief Corporal Weinberg and radio operator Peterson, are joined by two new soldiers, assistant radio operator Chester and aerial gunner Joe Winocki. This is Chester's first flight and he is enthusiastic about it. Winocki, on the other hand, had wanted to be a pilot, but failed flight school and now, bitter about his disappointment, is counting the days until his enlistment is over. As the Mary Ann flies over the Pacific on 7 December 1941, the crew hears Japanese voices over their radio and soon learns that Hickam Air Field in Pearl Harbor is under attack. The news turns Winocki's cynicism around, and he announces that he is now in the air force for the duration of the war. The flight is diverted to an emergency air field on Maui, where the crew finishes emergency repairs just before fifth columnist snipers advance toward the plane. Despite the danger, the Mary Ann heads for Hickam. When the crew lands, they learn that McMartin's sister was wounded during the bombing. They have time to visit her briefly in the hospital before they are sent out, fully armed, to Manila, which has also been devastated by Japanese bombers. Flying along with the crew is pursuit pilot Tex Rader. Before a fuel stop on Wake Island, they receive a shortwave communication reporting that McMartin's sister will recover. The Marines on Wake, knowing that they are facing almost certain annihilation, hand the Mary Ann's crew letters to mail to their families and also persuade them to take their little dog Tripoli along with them when they leave for Manila. White is eager to reach Manila because his son is a pilot with the air force there. Upon landing at Clark Air Force Base, however, he receives the sad news that his son was killed during the first Japanese strike. The Mary Ann is loaded with bombs and when the Japanese return, the crew engages in a fierce battle during which Quincannon is fatally wounded, and Chester is also killed. Back on the ground, the crew hurriedly salvages parts from other planes to rebuild the badly damaged Mary Ann. When Manila falls to the Japanese, the Mary Ann heads for Australia with Rader as their new co-pilot and a former Marine as assistant radio operator. On the way they spot a Japanese fleet and radio their position to the Allied fleet. During the ensuing battle, the Japanese are routed. Later, the men prepare to lead an attack on Tokyo. Aerial combat. Airplanes. Bombing, Aerial. Flight crews, Military. Japan. Air Force. United States. Army Air Corps. Brothers and sisters. Coral Sea,

Battle of, 1942. Dogs. Explosions. Fathers and sons. Gunfights. Japan. Navy. Manila (Philippines). Parachuting. Patriotism. Pearl Harbor (HI), Attack on, 1941. Franklin Delano Roosevelt. United States. Marine Corps. Wake Island, Battle of, 1941.

Note: The film begins with the following written foreword: ''It is for us the living....to be dedicated here to the unfinished work which they who fought here have thus far so nobly advanced....It is...for us to be here dedicated to the great task remaining before us...that this nation, under God, shall have a new birth of freedom and that government of the people, by the people, for the people, shall not perish from the earth.''—Abraham Lincoln. The film ends with the following written statement: ''This story has a conclusion but not an end—for its real end will be the victory for which Americans—on land, on sea and in the air—have fought, are fighting now and will continue to fight until peace has been won. Grateful acknowledgement is given to the United States Army Air Force, without whose assistance this record could not have been filmed.''

HR news items add the following information about the production: Warner Bros. tried to borrow Alan Ladd from Paramount for a role in the film and cinematographer James Wong Howe replaced Tony Gaudio when the latter became ill. Because people on the West Coast were concerned about a Japanese invasion, the studio was unable to shoot locally any scenes with planes dressed to appear Japanese. For this reason, the aerial scenes were filmed at Drew Field, FL and Randolph Field, TX. Several international airports were recreated for the film, including Hickam Air Force base in Honolulu, HI; Wake Air Force Base and Clark Field in Manila. Warner Bros. showed the film starting at 9:00 AM to accommodate defense workers on the graveyard shift. According to a press release included in the file on the film at the AMPAS Library, twenty-seven-year-old Captain Hewitt Wheless, whom modern sources say acted as a technical adviser, was commended by president Franklin D. Roosevelt after his B-17 was attacked by eighteen Japanese planes. Even though one of his crew members was killed and another wounded, Wheless completed his mission and returned to base. According to contemporary sources, the film was made at the suggestion of General H. H. (Hap) Arnold, Commander of the U.S. Air Forces.

According to information in the Warner Bros. Collection at the USC Cinema-Television Library, Major Sam Triffy and Major Theron Coulter were assigned by the Army Air Force to act as technical advisers. A letter from the YMCA at the University of California, Berkeley, included in the Warner Bros. Collection, protests the film's portrayal of sabotage by Hawaiian Japanese on 7 Dec 1941. The letter states that reports of this activity were denied by director J. Edgar Hoover and Honolulu police chief William Gabrielson. Modern sources add the following information about the production: Major Triffy spent eight weeks assisting director Howard Hawks and writer Dudley Nichols in developing the story and dialogue and also did some of the stunt flying. Triffy was joined as technical adviser by Wheless during location shooting. The surface water combat sequences were shot on Santa Monica Bay before the screenplay was completed; although reviewers assumed the sea battle in the film was a recreation of the Battle of the Coral Sea, the miniature shooting had been completed before that battle took place. One modern source adds, however, that some real combat footage was included, probably from the Battle of the Coral Sea or Midway. (According to daily production reports in the Warner Bros. Collection, much of the miniature footage was shot in May and June of 1942. The first of several battles that comprised the battle of the Coral Sea began in early May 1942.) Modern sources also add that William Faulkner contributed to the screenplay. John O. Watson and Dudley Nichols wrote a novelization of the film that was published in 1943. George Amy received the Oscar for Best Editing. Dudley Nichols's screenplay was nominated for an Oscar; James Wong Howe, Elmer Dyer and Charles Marshall were nominated for the Academy Award for Best Black-and-White Cinematography; and Hans Koenekamp, Rex Wimpy and Nathan Levinson were nominated for Best Special Effects. Harry Carey reprised his role in a *Lux Radio Theatre* broadcast on 12 Jul 1943, co-starring George Raft.

AmCin Apr 1943, p. 135. *Box* 6 Feb 1943. *DV* 3 Feb 1943, p. 3. *FD* 3 Feb 1943, p. 6. *HR* 28 May 1942, p. 6. *HR* 9 Jun 1942, p. 3. *HR* 17 Jun 1942, p. 7. *HR* 1 Jul 1942, p. 6. *HR* 24 Jul 1942, p. 3. *HR* 26 Jan 1943, p. 7. *HR* 3 Feb 1943, p. 3. *HR* 18 Mar 1943, p. 2. *HR* 22 Mar 1943, p. 9. *MPH* 6 Feb 1943. *MPHPD* 6 Feb 1943, p. 1145. *NYT* 4 Feb 1943, p. 29. *Var* 3 Feb 1943, p. 14.

AL CAPONE (Irish Americans, Italian Americans)
Burrows-Ackerman Productions. *Dist* Allied Artists Pictures Corp. Feb 1959; Prod: 16 Sep–mid-Oct 1958 [©Allied Artists Pictures Corp.; 24 Feb 1959; LP12787]. Sd (RCA Sound Recording); b&w. 9,500 ft. 104-105 min. Passed by the National Board of Review. PCA cert no. 19216.

Prod John H. Burrows and Leonard Ackerman. *Dir* Richard Wilson. *Asst dir* Lindsley Parsons, Jr. and [Phil Rawlins]. *Wrt* Malvin Wald and Henry Greenberg. *Dir of photog* Lucien Ballard. [*Cam op* Bud Martino]. *Mont ed* Neil Brunnenkant. *Spec eff* Dave Koehler. *Prod des* Hilyard Brown. *Film ed* Walter Hannemann. *Set dec* Joe Kish. *Prop master* Max Frankel. [*Asst props* Teddy Mossman]. *Ward master* Russell Hanlin. *Ward mistress* Sabine Manela. [*Cost* Forrest T. Butler]. *Mus* David Raksin. *Mus ed* Harry Eisen. *Sd ed* Charles Schelling. *Sd mixer* Tom Lambert. [*Sd rec* Joe Keener]. *Makeup artist* Dave Grayson. *Prod mgr* Lonnie D'Orsa. *Dial supv* Joe Sargent. *Scr supv* Stanley Scheuer. *Gaffer* Lloyd Garnell. *Construction supv* George Troast. [*Key grip* Frank R. Lambers, Jr.].

Cast: Rod Steiger [(*Al Capone*)], Fay Spain [(*Maureen Flannery*)], James Gregory [(*Sgt. Schaefer*)], Martin Balsam [(*Mac Keely*)], Nehemiah Persoff [(*Johnny Torrio*)], Murvyn Vye [(*George "Bugs" Moran*)], Robert Gist [(*Dion "Dini" O'Banion*)], Lewis Charles [(*Earl "Hymie" Weiss*)], Joe DeSantis [(*"Big Jim" Colosimo*)], Sandy Kenyon [(*"Bones" Corelli*)], Raymond Bailey [(*Mr. Brancato*)], Al Ruscio [(*Tony Genaro*)], Louis Quinn [(*Joe Lorenzo*)], Ron Soble [(*Scalisi*)], Steve Gravers [(*Anselmo*)], Ben Ari [(*Ben Hoffman*)], [Peter Dane (*Pete Flannery*)], [Patricia Donahue (*Gladys*)], [Roy Jenson (*Customer*)], [Allen Jaffe (*Bodyguard*)], [Donald Foster (*Stevens*)], [Paul Bryar (*Police inspector*)], [Erskine Johnson, Lee Weaver, Jim Bacon (*Reporters*)], [Jim Healy (*Announcer at racetrack*)], [Russ Whiteman (*Judge*)], [Joseph D. Sargent (*Buell*)], [Ernest Molinari (*Tall man*)], [Clegg Hoyt (*Lefty*)], [Mason Curry (*Tailor*)], [Bobby Gilbert (*Herman*)], [Sally Todd (*Beautiful girl*)], [Elizabeth Harrower (*Proprietress*)], [Richard Norris (*Sergeant*)], [John Duke (*Pulaski*)], [Jack Orrison (*Police clerk*)], [Dan Riss (*Radio announcer's voice*)], [Craig Duncan, George Riley (*Detectives*)], [Jack Harris (*Leader of group*)], [Bennie Goldberg, Frank Stanlow (*Prisoners*)], [Larry Chance (*Vincent*)], [Norman Nazarr, Mauritz Hugo, Bru Danger, Mitchell Kowal, John Lomma (*Hoods*)], [Marlyn Gladstone (*Mrs. Torrio*)], [Cappy Carey (*Mrs. Schaefer*)], [Cindy Ames Salerno (*Nurse*)], [William Janssen, John Close (*Plainclothesmen*)], [Ralph Gamble (*Salesman*)], [Ralph Volkie (*Clerk*)], [Morgan Windbeil (*Motorcyclist*)], [Sidney Lassick (*Hot dog attendant*)], [Sam Scar (*Louie*)], [John Mitchum (*Photographer*)], [Aldo Silvani (*Waiter*)], [Robert Christopher], [Charles D. Campbell].

Gangster, Biography. [*Print viewed*]. It is 1919 and Brooklyn-born gangster Al Capone has just arrived in Chicago to become a bodyguard for Johnny Torrio, a mobster whose "emporium" offers "booze, gambling, and broads" to anyone willing to pay for them. Capone soon meets "Big Jim" Colosimo, who controls the First Ward and promises to introduce the young tough to famous Italian opera singer Enrico Caruso. After Prohibition is enacted in 1920, Capone devises ways to capitalize on the public's thirst for liquor, and helps to make Colosimo and Torrio rich and powerful. Nevertheless, gang leaders Dion "Dini" O'Banion, George "Bugs" Moran, and Earl Weiss ("Hymie the Pole"), complain that Colosimo is too old and soft, and O'Banion mocks the gangster's Italian accent and mannerisms. Secretly, Capone advises Torrio to get rid of Colosimo, but after the old man and his guards are shot, Torrio's guilt at betraying a member of his family gets the better of him, and he begins to drink heavily. Capone romances Maureen Flannery, the widow of one of Colosimo's murdered men, and although she at first rejects him, she eventually succumbs to his advances. In the meantime, Capone "kills like a crazy man," eliminating any underworld leaders who resist his plan to run the crime syndicate "like a business." When Chicago elects a reform mayor, one who accepts no bribes from Capone, the gangster moves his beer-brewing and other illegal operations to the nearby town of Cicero, and the money continues to roll in. Torrio is arrested for brewing beer, and Capone, believing O'Banion had him framed, kills the Irishman. Weiss and Moran then try to have Torrio executed, whereupon the latter, weary of the endless killing, serves a short prison sentence and enters into a quiet retirement. Capone has Weiss killed, while Schaefer, a police sergeant who for years bemoaned Capone's ownership of city hall, becomes captain of the force. Mac Keely, a dishonest reporter who works for Capone, attempts to bribe Schaefer, but the latter throws him out. Because Schaefer is unable to secure a single conviction against the criminals, however, a crooked mayor again assumes power, and Capone sets up shop in the center of Chicago's financial district. Capone now forces payments from every business owner in the South Side, terrorizing anyone who refuses to pay for his "protection." Worried about attempts by "the feds" to indict Capone, Keely suggests that the gangster leave town for a few months, and Capone settles into a comfortable home in Dade County, Florida. From there he orchestrates the St. Valentine's Day Massacre, in which many of Moran's men are killed. Although the crime rocks the nation, the police, as usual, are unable to unearth any evidence that implicates Capone. Moran and Capone finally negotiate a truce, but Keely learns that Moran intends to kill Capone, and the latter takes refuge in a Philadelphia jail for a year. Just before Capone's release, Moran persuades Keely to betray his old employer, and when Capone learns that the reporter now works for his enemy, he has Keely killed. The newspaperman's death sends Chicago into an uproar, and Schaefer publicly accuses Capone of having ordered the murders of many people, including Maureen's husband. Capone finally admits his guilt to Maureen, who hysterically begs him to kill her. Schaefer secures Capone's account books, and the evidence he finds in them leads to Capone's conviction on tax evasion charges and an eleven-year sentence at Alcatraz. While he is incarcerated, a mob of prisoners attack him mercilessly. Ambition. Al Capone. Chicago (IL). Gangsters. Italian Americans. Murder. Rivalry. Alcatraz Federal Penitentiary. Bodyguards. Bribery. Dissipation. Evidence. Extortion. Gambling. Guilt. Irish Americans. Police. Polish Americans. Political corruption. Prohibition. Raids. Reporters. Revenge. Scars. Shootings. St. Valentine's Day Massacre, 1929.

Note: The working title of this film was *The Al Capone Story*. As noted in the film, Alphonse Capone was born in Brooklyn, NY in 1899, and began his career as a petty criminal there. He acquired the name "Scarface Al" because of a scar left by a razor slash. While still a young man, he moved to Chicago and worked his way up the crime syndicates, eventually taking over the bootleg liquor business. As depicted in the film, Capone facilitated his rise by murdering his rivals, including "Big Jim" Colosimo in 1920, and Dion O'Bannion in 1924. By the end of the 1920s, Capone was earning more than $20 million a year. On Valentine's Day, 1929, Capone's gunmen, dressed as policemen, shot and killed seven members of the rival "Bugs" Moran gang. Capone was convicted of income-tax evasion and sent to Alcatraz Federal Penitentiary in Oct 1931. He was released in Nov 1939, ill with syphilis. Capone died on his Florida estate on 25 Jan 1947 from complications of syphilis. For more information about Capone's life, see entry below for *Scarface*.

According to a Nov 1957 *NYT* news item, *Al Capone* initially was to be made by independent producers John H. Burrows and Lindsley Parsons, and was to be financed as well as distributed by Allied Artists. Jack DeWitt was hired to write the screenplay at this time, but his contribution to the completed film has not been confirmed. Parsons later left the project and was replaced by Leonard J. Ackerman. According to a *DV* news item, second-unit photography was done in Chicago, and M-G-M's "Chicago Street" lot was used for a week of shooting.

Because of restrictions imposed during the 1930s and early 1940s by Will H. Hays, president of the MPPDA, and Joseph I. Breen, director of the PCA, screen biographies of notorious criminals like Capone and John Dillinger were impossible to make. By the mid-1940s, however, the restrictions were somewhat relaxed, and in 1945, Monogram released *Dillinger*, the first screen depiction of John Dillinger. In late 1947, Capone was announced as the subject of a proposed United Artists release, but, according to news items, Westbrook Pegler and Jack Moffitt's screenplay was rejected by the PCA. According to information in the MPAA/PCA collection at the AMPAS Library, in Jul 1958, the PCA rejected the first draft of the script for *Al Capone*, deeming it "unacceptable" because it contained "too much glorification" of Capone, an "overemphasis on evil," a lack of "counterbalancing good" and an "overemphasis on violence and slaughter." A revised script was approved, with eliminations, in Sep 1958. According to a 5 Feb 1959 letter to the PCA from U.S. Senator John L. McClellan, the U.S. Senate Select Committee on Improper Activities in the Labor or Management Field had a special screening of *Al Capone*. McClellan declared that the "picture should be shown throughout the land. Every citizen of this country should have the opportunity to see it. In my judgment it will have a potent influence for the maintenance of law and order and for the preservation of decent society in our country."

Although *Al Capone* marked the first time that the gangster was openly depicted in a film, many earlier pictures featured characters who were presumed based on him, including Columbia's 1931 picture *The Guilty Generation*, directed by Rowland V. Lee and starring Leo Carrillo; the 1932 United Artists release *Scarface*, directed by Howard Hawks and starring Paul Muni; and the 1949 Columbia film *The Undercover Man*, directed by Joseph H. Lewis and starring Glenn Ford (see entries below). In Apr 1959, Phil Karlson directed Neville Brand as Capone in a Desilu Production *The Scarface Mob*, which led to the popular ABC television series *The Untouchables*. That series ran from Oct 1959 through Sep 1963, starred Robert Stack as FBI agent Eliot Ness and occasionally featured Brand as Capone. The teleplay was released theatrically in 1962. In 1967, Roger Corman directed Jason Robards, Jr. in the Twentieth Century-Fox Film release *The St. Valentine's Day Massacre* (see *AFI Catalog of Feature Films, 1961-70*; F6.4205 and F6.4273). In 1987, Robert De Niro appeared as the gangster in Brian DePalma's *The Untouchables*, and in 1995, F. Murray Abraham portrayed Capone in Concorde-New Horizons' *Dillinger and Capone*.

Box 16 Feb 1959. *DV* 13 Nov 1947. *DV* 5 Sep 1958. *DV* 9 Feb 1959, p. 3. *Exh* 25 Feb 1959, p. 4561. *FD* 10 Feb 1959, p. 11. *Har* 14 Feb 1959, p. 27. *HR* 19 Sep 1958, p. 10. *HR* 17 Oct 1958, p. 10. *HR* 9 Feb 1959, p. 3. *LAT* 8 Nov 1947. *LAT* 10 Nov 1947. *MPHPD* 21 Feb 1959, p. 164. *NYT* 9 Nov 1957. *NYT* 26 Mar 1959, p. 27. *Var* 11 Feb 1959, p. 6.

THE AL CAPONE STORY see **AL CAPONE**

THE AL JOLSON STORY see **THE JOLSON STORY**

ALAMO see **THE LAST COMMAND**

ALAS SOBRE EL CHACO (Spanish language)
Universal Pictures Corp.; A Maurice Pivar Production. *Dist* Universal Pictures Corp. **1935**; San Juan, Puerto Rico opening: 15 Nov 1935; New York opening: 22 Nov 1935; Prod: Jun—Jul 1935, simultaneously with the original version. Sd; b&w. 82 min. Spanish language.

Prod Paul Kohner. *Assoc prod* Maurice Pivar. *Dir* Christy Cabanne. *Dial dir* Enrique Tovar Avalos. *Asst dir* Carlos F. Borcosque. *Scr* Albert DeMond, Frank Wead and Eve Greene. *Story* Elliott Gibbons and Laclade Christy. *Spanish version* René Borgia. *Photog* Charles Stumar. *Aerial photog* Ray Fernstrom. *Photog eff* John P. Fulton. *Art dir* Harrison Wiley and Thomas F. O'Neill. *Sd* William Hitchcock. *Tech asst* Rubí Gutiérrez de Marvin. *Secretary* Gertrude Frye.

Cast: José Crespo (*Capitán Roberto Kent*), Lupita Tovar (*Teresa*), Antonio Moreno (*Comandante Manuel Tovar*), Romualdo Tirado ("*Cracker*"), Julio Peña (*Mitchell*), Barry Norton (*Pablo Díaz*), Juanita Garfias (*Pepita*), Juan Torena (*Teniente Milano*), José Rubio ("*El Zorro*"), Luis Díaz Flores (*Silvers*), Francisco Marán (*El general*), Anita Camargo (*Juanita*), Paco Moreno (*León*), George Lewis (*El operador de la radio*), José Caraballo (*Teniente Cabello*), Lucio Villegas (*El doctor*), Hans von Twardowski (*Oberto*), Alma Real (*La enfermera*).

Aviation, War, Drama. [*Not viewed*]. [The following plot summary is based on the English-language version of this film, *Storm over the Andes*; character names refer to that version. For further information regarding the English-language version, please see the note below and the entry for *Storm over the Andes* in the *AFI Catalog of Feature Films, 1931-40*.] Cynical pilot Captain Robert Kent has hired on as a mercenary soldier on the Bolivian side in their war with Paraguay. Major Manuel Tovar is in charge of the men at Entre Rios where Kent is assigned. Kent's daredevil flying angers Tovar, who grounds him. Kent also makes an enemy of Mitchell, another flyer, when he flirts with Mitchell's girl Juanita, giving her a distinctive snake ring. He has given out many of these rings, not believing in love any more than he believes in patriotism. Tovar tells him that he is wrong; nothing is more wonderful, he says, than giving your love to one woman forever. When Paraguayan bombers fly over Entre Rios, everyone except Kent prepares to attack. Determined to fly, Kent knocks out Mitchell and takes his place. His flying is so good, that Tovar forgives him for the deception. Kent is slightly wounded in the attack, and he is sent to the hospital in La Paz to recuperate. Against his nurse's orders, he leaves the hospital to take part in a fiesta, where he meets a beautiful and mysterious woman named Teresa. They have a chocolate together, and Kent gives her one of the snake rings. This time, things are different for Kent. Because he has fallen in love, he tries to take back the ring, but Teresa begs to keep it as a momento. She slips off before he can learn where she lives. The next day, Tovar arrives in La Paz to celebrate his wedding anniversary and bring Kent back to Entre Rios. At the anniversary party, Kent learns that Teresa is Tovar's wife. While he is packing, Tovar finds the snake ring that Kent gave Teresa. Then he overhears the two of them talking on the balcony and assumes that they had an affair. He refuses to listen to Teresa's explanations and hurries off with Kent. On the way back, he tries to kill them both, plunging their airplane toward earth before Kent wrestles the controls away from him. On the ground, he too tries to convince Tovar that nothing happened between him and Teresa. Remaining unconvinced, Tovar flies a suicide mission and is shot down behind enemy lines. In the meantime, Teresa has flown into Entre Rios to try to save her marriage. She begs Kent to save her husband. Kent parachutes into the jungle and helps Tovar to safety. They happen upon a Paraguayan airstrip, where flying ace El Zorro is warming up his bomber. They steal the plane and capture El Zorro, but instead of returning immediately, Tovar decides to bomb the Paraguayan ammunition warehouse. When that is destroyed, they turn the plane toward home, but Mitchell, who has vowed to destroy El Zorro, attacks them, not knowing his own men are inside the airplane. The plane lands safely, but Kent is badly wounded. Tovar and Teresa, now reconciled, rush Kent to La Paz where it appears that he will recover. *Air pilots. Chaco War, 1932-1935. Cynics. Friendship. Jealousy. Marriage. Philanderers. Soldiers of fortune. Aerial combat. Airplanes. Attempted murder. Attempted suicide. Bolivia–History–1879-1938. Bombing, Aerial. Crocodiles. Festivals. Fidelity. Hospitals. Jungles. La Paz (Bolivia). Officers (Military). Paraguay. Parties. Romance. War. Wedding anniversaries.*

Note: For information on the English-language version, *Storm over the Andes*, which was directed by Christy Cabanne and starred Jack Holt, Mona Barrie and Antonio Moreno, please see the entry for that film in the *AFI Catalog of Feature Films, 1931-40*; F3.4326.

CM Dec 1935, p. 748. *DV* 8 Jul 1935, p. 3. *DV* 19 Jul 1935, p. 4. *DV* 31 Aug 1935, p. 3. *FD* 25 Sep 1935, p. 4. *HR* 31 Aug 1935, p. 3. *MPH* 19 Oct 1935, p. 86. *NYT* 28 Mar 1939, p. 20. *Var* 2 Oct 1935, p. 16.

ALASKA (Native Americans, Native Alaskans)
Dist Richard Suratt? 1919?. Si; b&w. 5 reels.
Documentary. The film examines the Alaskan fur industry and the customs of Alaskan Eskimos. [No other information concerning the film's content has been discovered.]. *Alaska. Fur industry. Native Alaskans.*

Note: It is unclear whether this film was ever released to theaters under this or another title. The records of the Community Motion Picture Bureau list Richard Suratt as the film's distributor, but it is unclear whether he distributed the film theatrically.

ALASKA BOUND *see* **TUNDRA**

ALASKA IN MOTION *see* **ALASKA WONDERS IN MOTION**

THE ALASKA-SIBERIAN EXPEDITION (Native Americans, Native Alaskans)
Alaskan-Siberian Motion Pictures. *Dist* State Rights. 20 May **1912.** Si; b&w. 6 reels.
Cam Frank E. Kleinschmidt.
Cast: Frank E. Kleinschmidt (*Himself*).
Documentary. The film records the Carnegie Museum expedition to the Arctic regions of Alaska and Siberia which was led by Captain Frank E. Kleinschmidt. Explorers study the environment and habits of Eskimos, polar bears, walruses, sheep, moose, reindeer and caribou, while hunters capture and kill game animals. *Alaska. Arctic regions. Expeditions. Explorers. Frank E. Kleinschmidt. Native Alaskans. Siberia. Wild animals. Carnegie Museum (New York City).*

Note: The film, also known as *The Carnegie Museum Alaska-Siberian Expedition*, was made "under the patronage" of the Carnegie Museum. Captain Kleinschmidt delivered a lecture to accompany the film at its New York opening, while a Mr. Clark, who was a member of the expedition, lectured at the Philadelphia showing.

MPW 4 May 1912, pp. 464-65. *MPW* 18 May 1912, insert between pp. 650 and 651. *MPW* 1 Jun 1912, p. 838. *NYDM* 3 Jul 1912, p. 23.

ALASKA WONDERS IN MOTION (Native Americans, Native Alaskans)
Smith Films. *Dist* State Rights; Smith Films; Educational Films Corp. of American. **1917** [©Al. I. Smith, W. A. Hillis, A. J. Buzard and W. E. Wright; 11 Jan 1917; MU819]. Si; b&w. 4-5 reels.
Cam Al. I. Smith.
Documentary. In southern Alaska, an Eskimo woman fishes and displays her raincoat of walrus intestines trimmed with the heads of sea parrots. A trip is taken along the government railway through timber lands and facilities to large copper deposits where a Blow Hole is built across a glacier. The greatest Bore in the world, a water wall, travels inland at 35 m.p.h. and reaches a height of 30 feet. Ore is loaded at a gold mine. Views are shown of the town of Roosevelt, a moving glacier near Valdez, Kenai Lake, and the village of Kenai, founded 160 years earlier by the Kenai tribe, some of whom are also shown. Many of the Kenai tribe go blind because they have only three months of daylight each year. Masses of ice drop off Miles Glacier. The Million Dollar span on the Copper River between Miles and Childs Glacier is shown. Hunters on Kodiak Island climb a mountain and spot a Kodiak bear and her two cubs eating clams on the beach. Later they shoot a large bear who escapes to the hills. After five shots, the bear is felled. The hunters exhibit its corpse, eat bear steak, and stretch the hide. Bear cubs play as the hunters return home. *Alaska. Copper River (AK). Glaciers. Kodiak Island (AK). Native Alaskans. Roosevelt (AK). Valdez (AK). Hunters.*

Note: This film was also reviewed under the titles *Alaskan Wonders in Motion* and *Alaska in Motion*. It was prepared for showing by Al. I. Smith and W. A. Hillis. According to a news item, after the film was projected at Slipper's Accessory Store, T. L. Tally, a major Los Angeles exhibitor, booked the film and ran it in Nov 1916 in one reel segments with features. Smith Films planned to release the film either as a feature production or as a series of travelogues. It is possible that the film was never shown commercially as a feature. Educational Films Corp. of America released the film as a four-part series in 1917: part one was released 6 Jun 1917, part two on 27 Jun 1917, part three on 18 Jul 1917, and part four on 8 Aug 1917. According to the Community Motion Picture Bureau files, a three reel version of the film was shown in May 1919. According to news items, the original negative ran over 10,000 feet. Cameraman Al. I. Smith was known for his documentaries. His partner, W. A. Hillis was a nationally known American sportsman.

Los Angeles Evening Express 15 Nov 1916. *MPN* 23 Dec 1916, p. 4019. *MPN* 30 Dec 1916, p. 4140. *MPW* 30 Jun 1917, p. 2082. *MPW* 14 Jul 1917, p. 247. *MPW* 18 Aug 1917, p. 1065. *MPW* 15 Sep 1917, p. 1687.

ALIAS MARC FURY see GAMBLING HOUSE

ALIAS MIKE FURY see GAMBLING HOUSE

ALIAS THE DOCTOR (foreign version) see LE CAS DU DOCTEUR BRENNER

THE ALIBI see BROKEN TIES

THE ALIEN (Italian Americans)
New York Motion Picture Corp. *Dist* Select Film Booking Agency, Inc., by arrangement with Kessel and Baumann. Jul 1915 [©New York Motion Picture Corp.; 2 Aug 1915; LU5992]. Si; b&w. 8-9 reels.

Supv Thomas H. Ince. *Prod* Thomas H. Ince. *Dir* Thomas H. Ince. *Asst dir* Raymond B. West. *Cam* Ned Van Buren. *Lab work supv* Alfred Brandt.

Source: Based on the play *The Sign of the Rose* by George Beban and Charles T. Dazey (New York, 11 Oct 1911).

Cast: George Beban (*Pietro Massena*), Blanche Schwed (*Rosina Massena*), Edward Gillespie (*Inspector Lynch*), Jack Nelson (*Phil Griswold*), Hayward Ginn (*William Griswold*), Andrea Lynne (*Mrs. William Griswold*), Thelma Salter (*Dorothy Griswold*), Jack Davidson (*Robbins*), Edith MacBride (*The cashier of the flower shop*), J. Frank Burke (*The proprietor*), William J. Kane (*Coogan*), Ida Lewis (*The nurse*), Fanny Midgley (*The maid*), Maude Gilbert, Claire Hillier, Nona Thomas.

Melodrama. Pietro Massena, a poor Italian ditch-digger, lovingly raises his motherless daughter Rosina. Phil Griswold, in order to throw a party to celebrate his expected inheritance, induces his friend Robbins to rob the flower shop where he works. After the inheritance goes to Phil's brother William, who refuses Phil money to return to the flower shop, Phil kidnaps William's daughter Dorothy and sends a "Black Hand" ransom demand to throw suspicion onto Pietro, who earlier frightened Dorothy when he delivered a Christmas tree to William's house. William drives into the slums looking for Pietro and accidentally runs down Rosina. The grieving Pietro goes to the flower shop on Christmas morning to buy a rose for Rosina's coffin and is accused of the kidnapping, because Phil arranged to have a man known by "the sign of the rose" pick up the ransom money there. Pietro threatens to kill the arresting detective so that he can return to his "bambino," when William arrives with news that Dorothy has been found. William offers Pietro compensation, but he refuses and sorrowfully returns home. *Fathers and daughters. Frame-ups. Italian Americans. Kidnapping.* Automobile accidents. Black Hand (United States). Brothers. Ditch diggers. Florists. Inheritance. Ransom. Robbery.

Note: *The Sign of the Rose* was originally a vaudeville piece in which Beban starred for five years, playing around the world. Klaw and Erlanger produced the subsequent four-act play from which the film was based. The film opened in Los Angeles on 12 Apr 1915 in nine reels under the name *The Sign of the Rose*, at Clune's Auditorium, where *The Birth of a Nation* had just finished its nine-week run. The film opened under the title *The Alien* in New York on 31 May 1915. In both of these showings, and in subsequent showings in large theaters around the country, the film ended as the character Pietro enters the flower shop to buy a rose for his daughter's coffin. The curtain then rose and lights came up on a stage set of the flower shop. The actors from the film then appeared live and enacted the denouement, which lasted for approximately thirty minutes. The film was released nationally in Jul 1915 in eight reels, with a filmed ending replacing the staged one. The Los Angeles showing had a musical score by Lloyd Brown and Carli D. Elinor, which included vocal selections. Some sources call the character played by Blanche Schwed "Rosa" rather than "Rosina." Some scenes in this film were shot at Mt. Baldy, CA. Some reviews refer to the film's title as *An Alien*. In 1922 George Beban Productions produced a film from the same source entitled *The Sign of the Rose*, which in its pre-release showings included live action mixed with filmed action during the last two reels (see below).

Motog 10 Apr 1915, p. 572. *Motog* 1 May 1915, p. 691. *Motog* 12 Jun 1915, p. 957. *Motog* 19 Jun 1915, p. 1035. *MPN* 6 Feb 1915, p. 35. *MPN* 27 Feb 1915, p. 41. *MPN* 6 Mar 1915, p. 42. *MPN* 27 Mar 1915, p. 45. *MPN* 3 Apr 1915, p. 150. *MPN* 1 May 1915, p. 43. *MPW* 27 Feb 1915, p. 1300. *MPW* 24 Apr 1915, p. 535, 561. *MPW* 1 May 1915, pp. 740-41. *MPW* 12 Jun 1915, p. 1789. *MPW* 24 Jul 1915, p. 732. *NYDM* 2 Jun 1915, p. 28. *NYDM* 30 Jun 1915, p. 24. *Var* 4 Jun 1915, p. 18.

AN ALIEN ENEMY (German Americans)
Paralta Plays, Inc. *Dist* W. W. Hodkinson Corp. 1 Apr 1918. Si; b&w. 7 reels.

Dir Wallace Worsley. *Story and scen* Monte M. Katterjohn. *Cam* L. Guy Wilky.

Cast: Louise Glaum (*Neysa von Igel/Frau Meyer*), Mary Jane Irving (*Fraulein Bertha Meyer*), Thurston Hall (*David J. Hale*), Albert Allardt (*Emil Koenig*), Charles Hammond (*Adolph Schmidt*), Jay Morley (*Mayor Samuel J. Putnam*), Roy Laidlaw (*Lewis Meyer*), Joseph J. Dowling (*Baron von Mecklin*), Clifford Alexander (*Wireless operator*).

World War I, Drama. After Emil Koenig, a brutal Prussian officer, kills Neysa Meyer's American parents, the little girl is adopted by Adolph Schmidt and given the surname von Igel. Having grown up ignorant of her past, Neysa is recruited for German espionage work at the outbreak of World War I, but the work soon proves distasteful to her. Later she falls in love with American David Hale, and after they marry, she abandons her intelligence activities. When Hale is sent to France as a member of the War Board, however, Koenig warns Neysa that she must resume her spying or he will tell her husband of her past. Even though she furnishes Koenig with false information, her actions arouse David's suspicions, and he leaves her. On his deathbed, Adolph Schmidt reveals that Koenig murdered Neysa's parents, and so apprised, she confronts the German agent. As Hale secretly watches, she informs Koenig that her reports have been false and then stabs him, thus avenging her parents' deaths. Sure of Neysa's love and patriotism, David embraces her. *Espionage. German Americans. Germans. Murder. Revenge. Spies. World War I.* Desertion (Marital). Foster parents. Marriage. Orphans. Patriotism.

Note: Working titles of the film were *Intelligence* and *The Iron Beast*. Three hundred members of the California National Guard took part in the war scenes.

ETR 30 Mar 1918, p. 1385. *ETR* 27 Apr 1918, p. 1691. *MPN* 27 Apr 1918, p. 2556. *MPW* 27 Apr 1918, p. 586. *MPW* 4 May 1918, p. 750. *NYDM* 27 Apr 1918, p. 596. *Var* 5 Apr 1918, p. 46. *Var* 19 Apr 1918, p. 41. *Wid's* 25 Apr 1918, p. 1103.

ALIEN SOULS (Japanese Americans)
Jesse L. Lasky Feature Play Co. *Dist* Paramount Pictures Corp. 11 May 1916 [©Jesse L. Lasky Feature Play Co.; 3 May 1916; LP8206]. Si; b&w. 5 reels.

Pres Jesse L. Lasky. *Dir* Frank Reicher. *Scen* Margaret Turnbull. *Story* Hector Turnbull. *Cam* Walter Stradling.

Cast: Sessue Hayakawa (*Sakata*), Tsuru Aoki (*Yuri Chan*), Earle Foxe (*Aleck Lindsay*), Grace Benham (*Mrs. Conway*), J. Parks Jones (*Jack Holloway*), Violet Malone (*Gertrude Van Ness*), Dorothy Abril (*Geraldine Smythe*).

Drama. Yuri Chan, a Japanese girl attending school in the United States, believes that she is very wealthy when in fact she has been supported by Sakata, a Japanese importer, since the death of her father. Although Yuri Chan is to marry Sakata upon her graduation, the young woman longs to enter American society, and to that end, she becomes involved with Aleck Lindsay, a society idler attracted only to her fortune. Despite Sakata's efforts to win Yuri Chan's heart, she decides to elope with Aleck, but Sakata catches them and tells the American the source of the girl's wealth. The fortune hunter immediately abandons Yuri Chan, and in disgrace, she tries to commit suicide, but the gun misfires and she faints. Awakening in Sakata's arms, Yuri Chan gratefully accedes to the wishes of her loving benefactor. *Fidelity. Fortune hunters. Japanese Americans. Unrequited love.* Attempted suicide. Cultural conflict. Elopement. Importers. Students.

Motog 20 May 1916, p. 1168. *MPN* 20 May 1916, p. 3091. *MPW* 20 May 1916, p. 1353. *NYDM* 13 May 1916, p. 29. *NYT* 15 May 1916, p. 7. *Var* 5 May 1916, p. 23. *Wid's* 11 May 1916, p. 572.

THE ALL-AMERICAN see JIM THORPE—ALL-AMERICAN

ALL GOD'S CHILDREN see THIS REBEL BREED

ALL GOD'S STEPCHILDREN see GOD'S STEP CHILDREN

ALL MINE TO GIVE (Scottish Americans)
RKO Radio Pictures. *Dist* Universal Pictures Co., Inc. Jan 1957; Great Britain world premiere: Apr 1957; Prod: late Jun–late Aug 1956 [©RKO Teleradio Pictures, Inc.; 28 Oct 1957; LP10317]. Sd (RCA Sound Recording); col (Technicolor). 9,154 ft. 100 or 102-103 min. PCA cert no. 18170.

Prod Sam Wiesenthal. *Dir* Allen Reisner. *Asst dir* Russell Llewellyn. *Scr* Dale Eunson and Katherine Eunson. *Dir of photog* William Skall. *Art dir* Albert S. D'Agostino and Frank T. Smith. *Ed supv* Alan Crosland, Jr. *Film ed* Bettie Mosher. *Set dec* Glen Daniels. *Cost* Bernice Pontrelli. *Mus* Max Steiner. *Orch* Murray Cutter. *Sd* James S. Thompson and Terry Kellum. *Makeup supv* Harry Maret, Jr. *Hair stylist* Larry Germain. [*Unit mgr* Ed Killy]. [*Unit pub* Ned Moss].

Source: Based on the novel *The Day They Gave Babies Away* by Dale Eunson (New York, 1946) and his short story of the same name in *Cosmopolitan* (Dec 1946).

Cast: Glynis Johns [(*Mamie Eunson*)], Cameron Mitchell [(*Robert Eunson*)], Rex Thompson [(*Robbie Eunson*)], Patty McCormack [(*Annabelle Eunson*)], Ernest Truex [(*Dr. Delbert*)], Hope Emerson [(*Mrs. Pugmeister*)], Alan Hale [(*Tom Cullen*)], Sylvia Field [(*Dela Delbert*)], Royal Dano [(*Howard Tyler*)], Reta Shaw [(*Mrs. Runyon*)], Stephen Wootton [(*Jimmie Eunson*)], Butch Bernard [(*Kirk* Eunson)], Yolanda White [(*Elizabeth Eunson*)], Rita Johnson [(*Katie Tyler*)], Ellen Corby [(*Mrs. Raiden*)], Rosalyn Boulter [(*Mrs. Stephens*)], Francis DeSales [(*Mr. Stephens*)], Jon Provost [(*Robbie, age 6*)], [Terry Ann Ross (*Jane Eunson*)], [Roy Engel (*Mr. Harry Bradley*)], [Margaret Brayton (*Mrs. Cecilia Bradley*)], [Ralph Sanford (*Mr. Raiden*)], [Mary Adams (*Mrs. Roscoe*)], [Dorothy Brody, Penny Brody (*The Raiden Twins*)], [Mark Easton, Paul Easton, Gloria Elaine Harris, Darleen Marie Harris, Karen D. Hartman, Vicki L. Hartman, Jeff Coyne (*Babies*)], [Madge Blake (*Mrs. Clary*)], [Norman Ollestad (*Boy*)], [Henry Kulky (*Drunk*)], [Dabbs Greer (*Clendenning*)], [Lida Piazza (*Passerby*)], [Frank Mitchell (*Painless Paine*)], [Peter Michael (*Dutch Fischer*)], [Frank Marlowe (*Hanson*)].

Domestic, Historical, Drama. [*Print viewed*]. While hauling his crying sister on a small sled through the freezing snow, young Robbie Eunson recalls how their situation came about: In September 1856, Robbie's father Robert and his pregnant wife Mamie arrive in backwoods Wisconsin from the Shetland Islands in Scotland. Shocked to discover that Mamie's uncle, who had invited them, died in a fire three weeks earlier, the couple is deeply touched when their neighbors take them in and then help them to build a cabin on the site of the burned home. Robbie is born on 12 October, the day on which, as proud father Rob exclaims, Columbus "discovered America for us." On that same night, Rob, whose money is now exhausted, walks to a logging camp located twenty-five miles from the cabin. The Irish-American boss, Tom Cullen, gives Rob a job as a cutter, but when Cullen calls him a "Nordsky," Rob replies that although the Scandinavians are a fine race, he happens to be Scottish. Rob visits Mamie and the baby when he can, but Cullen, who continues to call him "Nordsky," rarely allows him to go home. Exasperated with Cullen's insults, Rob finally challenges his boss to a fight. When Rob defeats Cullen, the Irishman laughs, begins calling him "Scotty" and becomes his fast friend. Rob returns to his own trade of boatbuilding following the birth of his son Jimmie. Mamie, who has noticed that most of the ladies in the nearby village of Eureka know how to read, attends school with little Robbie. During the next few years, she and Rob have four more children—Kirk, Annabelle, Elizabeth and Jane. One day, Dr. Delbert informs the Eunsons that Kirk has contracted diphtheria. While Rob and the other children stay in an abandoned cabin in the woods, Mamie nurses Kirk. Robbie, now eleven, tells his worried father that when he is a man, he hopes to be just like him, and soon afterward, Mamie tells Rob that Kirk has recovered. At this news, Rob breaks down and weeps. When Rob and the children return home, the family happily reunites, but to Mamie's distress, Rob begins coughing almost immediately. Mamie tenderly cares for Rob until his death and then takes in sewing to support her family. Robbie offers to quit school and work for Cullen, but Mamie insists that he complete his education. Winter comes, and Mamie, exhausted, contracts typhoid fever. Robbie takes charge of the household, but several days before Christmas, Mamie calls him to her side and asks him to find good homes for the children. After praising her son for having truly been the man of the house, Mamie dies. During her funeral, the haughty Mrs. Runyon loudly asks what the villagers are to do with six orphans. Robbie asks that the children be allowed to spend Christmas together before being sent to the state orphanage, and Dr. Delbert consents to the request. After the smaller children have fallen asleep, Robbie and Jimmie make plans for distributing the children among the village families, and on Christmas Day, Robbie visits each of the chosen families. The Tylers, just sitting down to Christmas dinner, happily agree to take Annabelle, but because the family Robbie has chosen for Lizzie is away, he offers her to the childless couple who teach in the village school. Back at the cabin, Robbie and Jimmie are distressed to see Mrs. Runyon trying to leave with little Jane. The brothers bar the door, but Mrs. Runyon threatens to return for Jane after speaking with "the council." Explaining that there is now no time to send Kirk to the family he had in mind, Robbie gruffly orders the tearful boy to report to another family. Tired and sad, Robbie collapses, but he soon regains his composure and bids

Jimmie farewell. As Jimmie knocks on the door of Mrs. Raiden, whose daughters have always considered him "cute," Robbie bundles Jane into a small sled and hauls her through the darkness to Berlin, ten miles away. A kindly woman agrees to take Jane, inviting Robbie to come and visit her sometime. Robbie hesitates for a moment and then continues through the snow to Cullen's logging camp. *Family life. Family relationships. Homesteaders. Immigrants. Orphans. Rural life. Boats. Brothers and sisters. Cabins. Christmas. Diphtheria. Education. Fistfights. Irish Americans. Lumber camp foremen. Lumberjacks. Midwives. Neighbors. Physicians. Quarantine. Scottish Americans. Snow storms. Typhoid fever. United States–History–19th century. Wisconsin.*

Note: The working title of this film was *The Day They Gave Babies Away*. The *MPH* notes that the film was based on incidents derived from the family background of writer Dale Eunson, who wrote the original story and collaborated with his wife Katherine on the screenplay. According to a news item in *HR*, RKO bought the property in 1947, at which time Walter Wanger was slated to produce. An 1952 news item in the AMPAS Library production files announced Edmund Grainger as producer. Although the film had its premiere in Great Britain in Apr 1957, it was not released in the United States until Jan 1958. The distribution of this film was taken over by Universal after the demise of RKO. *All Mine to Give* marked television director Allen Reisner's debut as as feature film director. On 24 Dec 1951, a radio version of Eunson's story was broadcast on NBC's *Cavalcade of America* program, starring Bobby Driscoll.

Box 9 Nov 1957. *DV* 29 Oct 1957, p. 3. *Exh* 30 Oct 1957, p. 4397. *FD* 13 Nov 1957, p. 8. *Har* 2 Nov 1957, p. 176. *HR* 22 Jun 1956, p. 8. *HR* 31 Aug 1956, p. 12. *HR* 29 Jan 1947. *HR* 14 Feb 1957, p. 3. *MPHPD* 2 Nov 1957, p. 586. *NYT* 4 Aug 1959, p. 32. *Var* 6 Nov 1957, p. 6.

ALL SOULS' EVE (Irish Americans)

Realart Pictures Corp. Feb **1921** [©Realart Pictures Corp.; 10 Jan 1921; LP16013]. Si; b&w. 5-6 reels, 5,778 ft.

Dir Chester Franklin. *Asst dir* Fred J. Robinson. *Scen* Elmer Harris. *Photog* Faxon Dean.

Source: Based on the play *All Souls' Eve* by Anne Crawford Flexner (New York, 12 May 1920).

Cast: Mary Miles Minter (*Alice Heath/Nora O'Hallaban*), Jack Holt (*Roger Heath*), Carmen Phillips (*Olivia Larkin*), Clarence Geldert (*Dr. Sandy McAllister*), Mickey Moore (*Peter Heath*), Fanny Midgley (*Mrs. O'Hallaban*), Lottie Williams (*Belle Emerson*).

Melodrama. Olivia Larkin, out of unrequited love for sculptor Roger Heath, urges a lunatic to kill his beautiful young wife and tries unsuccessfully to regain his affection. Meanwhile, Nora O'Hallahan, an Irish immigrant girl, has taken a position as nursemaid in Heath's household. After a period of severe depression, Heath realizes that the soul of his departed wife has returned to him in the person of Nora, who rekindles his inspiration. She consents to become his wife and the mother of his little son, Peter. *Immigrants. Irish Americans. Lunatics. Reincarnation. Sculptors. Widowers.*

ETR 26 Feb 1921, p. 1235. *FD* 20 Feb 1921. *Var* 18 Feb 1921, p. 41.

ALL THE FINE YOUNG CANNIBALS (African Americans)

Metro-Goldwyn-Mayer Corp.; controlled by Loew's Inc.; Avon Productions, Inc.; A Pandro S. Berman Production. *Dist* Loew's Inc. **1960**; Los Angeles opening: 19 Aug 1960; New York opening: 22 Sep 1960; Prod: early Nov—mid Dec 1959 [©Loew's Inc. & Avon Productions, Inc.; 9 Mar 1960; LP15831]. Sd (Westrex Recording System); col (Metrocolor); Photographic lenses by Panavision. 14 reels, 10,971 ft. 112 min. Passed by the National Board of Review. PCA cert no. 19515.

Assoc prod Kathryn Hereford. *Dir* Michael Anderson. *Asst dir* Al Jennings. *Scr* Robert Thom. *Dir of photog* William H. Daniels. *Col consultant* Charles K. Hagedon. *Art dir* George W. Davis and Edward Carfagno. *Film ed* John McSweeney, Jr. *Set dec* Henry Grace and Rudy Butler. *Cost des* Helen Rose. *Mus score comp and adpt* Jeff Alexander. *Rec supv* Franklin Milton. *Hair styles* Sydney Guilaroff. *Makeup* William Tuttle.

Song(s): "God Bless the Child," words and music by Arthur Herzog, Jr. and Billie Holiday; "Beep Beep," words and music by Donald Claps and Carl Cicchetti; "Happiness Is a Thing Called Joe," words by E. Y. Harburg, music by Harold Arlen; "I Thank God I'm Free at Last," spiritual.

Source: Suggested by the novel *The Bixby Girls* by Rosamond Marshall (Garden City, NY, 1957).

Cast: ROBERT WAGNER [(*Chad Bixby*)], NATALIE WOOD [(*Sara "Salome" Davis McDowall*)], Susan Kohner [(*Catherine McDowall Bixby*)], George Hamilton [(*Tony McDowall*)], Pearl Bailey (*Ruby [Jones]*), Jack Mullaney [(*Putney Tinker*)], Anne Seymour [(*Mrs. Bixby*)], Mabel Albertson [(*Mrs. McDowall*)], Onslow Stevens

[(*Joshua Davis*)], Virginia Gregg [(*Ada Davis*)], Louise Beavers [(*Rose Jones*)], [Addison Richards (*Mr. McDowall*)], [Davis Roberts (*Darl*)], [Don Towers (*Samuel*)], [Ricky Allen (*Saul*)], [Joey Scott (*Ezra*)], [Casey Peters (*Timothy*)], [Katie Sweet (*Esther*)], [Debbie Megowan (*Ruth*)], [Emerson Treacy, George Selk, Carl Christian (*Ministers*)], [Ken Christy (*Conductor*)], [Jay Adler (*Sammy Trist*)], [Mary Alan Hokanson (*Mrs. Macklederry*)], [Rusty Polan (*Little boy*)], [Ralph Montgomery (*Man in park*)], [Queenie Leonard, Pauline Myers (*Nurses*)], [Jesslyn Fox, Ruth Perrott (*Old ladies*)], [Zina Provendie (*Drunk lady*)], [George Cisar (*Policeman*)], [Irene Tedrow (*Supervisor*)], [Lucile Curtis (*Minister's wife*)], [Charles Calvert (*Deacon*)], [Ken Walker, Mark Houston, Frank Gardner (*Students*)], [John Frank (*Tailor*)], [Dick Winslow (*Orchestra leader*)].

Melodrama, with songs. [*Print viewed*]. Sara Davis, who prefers to be called "Salome," is a beautiful seventeen-year-old who helps her poor father to care for his many children in the rural community of Pine Alley, Texas. Salome is deeply in love with musician Chad Bixby, whose father, the local minister, has just died. In defiance of her father, Salome runs out of the house and attends a dance with Chad, who bitterly confesses that his father had beat him for hanging around with "niggers" in nearby Deep Elm. Later, Chad takes Salome and a black friend to a Deep Elm honky-tonk, where Rose Jones, the owner of the club, asks the young man to "play what he feels" on the trumpet. Chad picks up his instrument and plays a mournful tune, saying, "This is the love I had for my father and couldn't tell him about." While he performs, wealthy young Tony McDowall descends the stairs and approaches Salome, assuming that she is one of the club's "hostesses." Salome avoids him and spends the rest of the night with Chad, who declares that he is frightened of the dark. Some time later, Salome tells Chad that she is pregnant. Although he offers to marry her, she refuses, saying that despite their mutual love, she knows they would be miserable together. Uncertain of where to go, Salome boards a train, where she again meets Tony. Strongly attracted to her, Tony offers to take her to Connecticut, where he attends Yale University. There the two are secretly married. Meanwhile, Chad returns to Deep Elm and becomes acquainted with Rose's sister, Ruby Jones, a celebrated jazz singer who, since being abandoned by her trumpet-playing sweetheart, has settled into a drunken depression and swears she will never sing again. Ruby is impressed with Chad's playing, but when he asks her to take him to New York, she exclaims, "I don't carry on with no white boys!" Nevertheless, she and Chad eventually move into a New York apartment, and Ruby persuades her agent to get the young musician a job. At Yale, Tony and Salome receive a visit from Tony's attractive but spoiled sister Catherine, who frequently complains that she is bored. In the spring, Salome has her baby, but when she one night hears Chad's trumpet playing on a record, she becomes agitated and suggests that they all make a visit to New York City. At the nightclub at which Chad performs, Ruby agrees to sing a selection of blues laments to please the trumpet player, but afterward, she mutters, "I've sung for you, Chad, but that's it." Chad is overjoyed to see Salome in the audience, but Catherine also finds herself attracted to him and soon persuades him to leave with her. The next morning, Catherine triumphantly announces that she and Chad are mad about each other, whereupon Salome, consumed with jealousy, secretly visits her old flame. Chad asks Salome to leave Tony, and when she explains that her husband believes the child is his and that she is unable to leave him, Chad becomes enraged. Soon after this exchange, Catherine marries Chad and moves into the apartment he shares with Ruby, who is now dying. Catherine declares that she loves Chad, but sensing that his feelings for her are lukewarm, she becomes restless and exclaims, "There's nothing but niggers around here!" Although Chad slaps her, the couple moves into a separate apartment, leaving Ruby alone. Catherine next angers her husband by beating her horse with a riding whip. Furious, Chad reveals that he, not Tony, is the father of Salome's baby and only married her to hurt Salome. Dismayed, Catherine slashes her wrists. Realizing that he does care for his wife, Chad rushes her to the hospital and prays fervently for her recovery. When Tony asks Salome if she loves Chad, she finally confesses that she did, and that the child is the musician's son. Shaken by this news, Tony leaves her, whereupon she gets drunk and admits to Chad that she now loves Tony. In reply, Chad writes a message on the wall for Catherine: "Chad loves Catherine. I'm sorry." Having learned that

Ruby is dead, Chad then takes her body back to Deep Elm for burial. After returning to New York, Chad declares his love for Catherine and the two embrace. Salome, having returned to her father's small Texas house, is surprised when Tony enters and announces that he wants her back. *Blues music. Jazz music. Jealousy. Marriage. Musicians. Romantic rivalry. African Americans. Alcoholics. Attempted suicide. Family relationships. Funerals. Idle rich. Love affairs. New York City. Nightclubs. Pregnancy. Premarital sex. Racism. Reconciliation. Revenge. Rural life. Singers. Talent agents. Texas. Trumpets. Unrequited love.*

Note: The film's working titles were *Ever for Each Other* and *The Young Years*. A studio pressbook lists the film's title as *The Rebel Generation* (formerly *All the Fine Young Cannibals*). According to information in the MPAA/PCA files at the AMPAS Library, the PCA objected to the title *All the Fine Young Cannibals* and pressured producer Pandro Berman and director Michael Anderson to change it. Alhough Berman and Anderson refused, it is possible that the studio considered changing the title to appease the PCA. The MPAA/PCA file also indicates that a Jun 1959 draft of the film's script was rejected by the PCA because it contained too many illicit affairs, whorehouse scenes and blasphemous dialogue. The PCA also objected to the inclusion of the word "nigger" in the dialogue, noting that "even when legitimately used, it has caused fierce resentment among many members of the audience." Although the script was revised according to some of the PCA's suggestions, it was again rejected in Oct 1959, primarily because the affairs had not been eliminated. In the final film, Robert Wagner's and Pearl Bailey's characters are seen living together, but the relationship is portrayed as Platonic. The *HR* reviewer commented that Wagner's character "has a vague relationship with Pearl Bailey that introduces some superfluous notes of Negro-white tolerance."

According to an Apr 1957 *HR* news item, Jimmy Stewart and Lauren Bacall were first considered for the leads in the film. *All the Fine Young Cannibals* marked the first and only time in which Wagner and then-wife Natalie Wood appeared together in a feature film. The couple married in 1957 and divorced in 1963, then remarried seven years later. Although modern sources claim that this film was inspired by the life of jazz trumpeter Chet Baker, little of the film's story corresponds with Baker's life. The British rock group Fine Young Cannibals took its name from the picture.

Box 18 Jul 1960. *DV* 14 Jul 1960, p. 3. *Exh* 20 Jul 1960, p. 4721. *FD* 15 Jul 1960, p. 6. *Har* 16 Jul 1960, p. 114. *HR* 1 Apr 1957. *HR* 6 Nov 1959, p. 14. *HR* 18 Dec 1959, p. 20. *HR* 14 Jul 1960, p. 3. *MPHPD* 16 Jul 1960, p. 771. *NYT* 23 Sep 1960, p. 33. *Var* 20 Jul 1960, p. 6.

ALL THE YOUNG MEN (African Americans, Native Americans, Navajo, Swedish Americans)

Hall Bartlett Productions, Inc.; Jaguar Productions, Inc. *Dist* Columbia Pictures Corp. Sep 1960; New York opening: 26 Aug 1960; Prod: 10 Oct—12 Dec 1959 [©Hall Bartlett Productions, Inc. & Ladd Enterprises, Inc.; 1 Aug 1960; LP17509]. Sd (RCA Sound Recording); b&w. 10 reels, 7,740 ft. 86-87 min. PCA cert no. 19625.

Prod Hall Bartlett. *Assoc prod* Newton Arnold. *Dir* Hall Bartlett. *Asst dir* Lee Lukather. *Wrt* Hall Bartlett. *Dir of photog* Daniel Fapp. *Art dir* Carl Anderson. *Film ed* Al Clark. *Set dec* Bill Calvert. *Mus* George Duning. *Orch* Arthur Morton. *Sd supv* Charles J. Rice. *Sd supv* James Flaster. *Makeup supv* Ben Lane. *Mr. Ladd's makeup* Emile Lavigne. *Hair styles* Helen Hunt. *Asst to the prod* Ben Mantz. *Tech adv* Lt. Col. C. J. Stadler, U.S.M.C.

Song(s): "All the Young Men," music by George Duning, lyrics by Stanley Styne.

Cast: Charles Quinlivan (*The Lieutenant* [*Earl D. Toland*]), ALAN LADD (*Kincaid*), introducing Ingemar Johansson (*Torgil*), SIDNEY POITIER [(*Sgt. Eddie*) *Towler*], Mort Sahl ([*Cpl.*] *Crane*), Paul Richards (*Bracken*), Glenn Corbett (*Wade*), James Darren (*Cotton*), Lee Kinsolving (*Dean*), Joe Gallison (*Jackson*), Ana St. Clair [(*Maya*)], Dick Davalos [(*Casey*)], Paul Baxley [(*Lazitech*)], Michael Davis [(*Cho*)], [Mario Alcalde (*Hunter, "The Chief"*)], [Maria Tsien (*Korean woman*)], [Chris Seitz, William St. John, Jack McCall, Steve Drexel, Pat Colby (*Marines*)], [Morgan Roberts].

Social, War, Drama. [*Print viewed*]. In October 1950, shortly after U.S. forces invade Korea, an advance Marine unit is sent to find and hold a farmhouse that is situated in a strategic mountain pass. As the Marines make their way down a snow-covered mountainside, they are attacked by waiting Chinese troops. Just before he dies, Lieutenant Earl D. Toland orders Sgt. Eddie Towler, the unit's only black man, to take charge of the few surviving Marines, even though Towler suggests that Sgt. Kincaid, a veteran who has been with the outfit for eleven years, is better prepared to direct the unit. Towler guides the men across the slippery, heavily mined slopes, and during the trek, Kincaid rescues one of the men when he slips and lands among the mines. When they reach the farmhouse, one of the men panics and throws a grenade inside the courtyard walls, seriously injuring a Korean woman who lives there with her part-French daughter and

grandson. Once inside, the men begin to worry that the numerous Chinese troops in the area will kill them all before the advancing Marine battalion can reach them, but Towler orders the men to hold their position at all costs. Bracken, a Southern bigot, claims that black men are unsuited to be leaders. Kincaid, who thinks the men should be moved even though it would mean losing the pass to the enemy and thereby endangering their entire battalion, suggests that Towler wants to remain in the farmhouse merely to prove himself. Determined to carry out Toland's commands, Towler claims that he will kill any man who refuses to act like a Marine and defend the farmhouse. That night, as Towler contemplates their difficult situation, the men reminisce about home. A recent immigrant from Sweden named Torgil, who wants to become a citizen and bring his family to the U.S., sings a song from his native land. Crane, a cynical corporal, tells amusingly irreverent stories about high-ranking officers, and a young soldier named Cotton sings and accompanies himself on a Korean stringed instrument. Before long, an enemy patrol unit advances on the house and the shooting begins. The Marines repulse these troops, and Hunter, a Navajo from Arizona nicknamed "The Chief," volunteers to scout the area for other enemy soldiers. The Chinese capture Hunter and accompany him back to the farmhouse. To save his unit, Hunter refrains from giving the password and dies with his Chinese captors when Towler and Kincaid fire on the intruders. After Hunter's burial, the Eurasian woman living in the house thanks Towler for helping her, telling him that one day, his color will make no difference to the others. Bracken gets drunk and attacks the woman, whereupon Towler fights him and after enduring Bracken's racist insults and epithets, threatens to kill him if he touches the woman again. After another battle with Chinese troops that costs the life of one of the men, Towler and Kincaid come to blows, but their fight is interrupted by the sound of an approaching tank. Towler and Kincaid sneak onto the tank and set it ablaze, but Kincaid's leg is crushed as he tries to get out of the way, and it must be amputated by the medic, who is unsure of his ability. Encouraged by Towler, the medic continues with the operation, and Towler donates his own blood to keep Kincaid alive despite Bracken's objections. As a line of Chinese tanks approaches, Towler orders the Marines to safer ground and protects Kincaid during an explosion, then carries him out of the farmhouse. The enemy is about to reach the two men when U.S. planes appear overhead and blast the Chinese troops. Greatly relieved, Towler and Kincaid wish each other a merry Christmas. *African Americans. Korean War, 1950-1953. Racism. Soldiers. United States. Marine Corps. Amputation. Attempted rape. Battles. Blood–Transfusion. Chinese. Drunkenness. Fear. Homesickness. Insubordination. Koreans. Mines. Military. Mountains. Navajo Indians. Rescues. Self-sacrifice. Snow. Swedish Americans. Tanks (Military science). War heroes. War victims.*

Note: The opening credits differ from the end credits: In the opening credits, Alan Ladd and Sidney Poitier's names are listed first, above the title and are then followed by James Darren, Glen Corbett and the others. Ingemar Johansson is listed last in the opening credits. Onscreen credits note that exterior scenes were filmed at Glacier National Park through courtesy of the Dept. of the Interior. According to news items and an article about the production in *mCin*, a crew of seventy traveled to St. Mary's, Montana, an Eastern gateway to Glacier National Park, seventeen miles from the Canadian border, but because of warm weather, fog, blizzard conditions and a gale that destroyed the Korean farmhouse set, filming was continued on a Hollywood sound stage covered with silicate to simulate snow. Later, the company moved to Mt. Hood, Oregon, where the weather caused further problems. The scene in which two Marines set fire to a tank was shot in a parking lot at a lodge to avoid having ski-lifts appear in the frame. Because of delays, shooting was not completed until 54 days after it began, although the original schedule called for 28 days.

According to news items, the start date of the production was determined by Sidney Poitier's schedule in the Broadway play *A Raisin in the Sun*; Poitier left the role to be in the film, then returned to the play following shooting. Although Hall Bartlett's onscreen credit reads "written, produced and directed by Hall Bartlett," a Mar 1959 *HR* news item noted that the original story was to be written by Bartlett and Gene Coon. Coon's contribution to the story has not been verified, however. The news item added that Bartlett initially planned to produce this picture in partnership with John Champion, but later decided to make it as a solo venture. Jaguar Productions, Inc. was Alan Ladd's company, and Ladd Enterprises, Inc. was a co-copyright claimant. According to a *DV* news item, Jeffrey Hunter was sought for the co-starring role, and Stuart Whitman was also considered for a role, possibly for the same part. This picture marked the screen debut of Swedish world heavy weight boxing champion Ingemar Johansson. According to a *HR* news item, topical comedian Mort Sahl's contract had "the unusual stipulation that Sahl write all his own dialogue....[Bartlett] handed Sahl the story outline and told him to put in his own words for his role." The *HR* review noted, "Sahl's monologue on some of life's incongruities is

deftly inserted and brightly played."

According to the *AmCin* article, director of photography Daniel Fapp "violated a theory of exposure long held by most photographers" and opened up one stop above the exposure indicated on his light meter when he shot snow scenes, rather than decreasing exposure one stop. Fapp also shot so as to use the sun's light as a cross-light or back-light, rather than the key source, for which he used arc booster lights. Fapp shot night sequences "day-for-night."

According to letters in the MPAA/PCA Collection at the AMPAS Library, the PCA advised Bartlett and Columbia officials to drop the word "nigger" from the script; however, in the final film, the character "Bracken" uses the word in a verbal attack on "Towler." Many reviews commented that this picture presented a non-stereotypical portrayal of a black man.

AmCin Sep 1960, pp. 550-51, 568-70. *Box* 8 Aug 1960. *Cue* 27 Aug 1960. *DV* 24 Apr 1959. *DV* 4 Aug 1960, p. 3. *Exh* 3 Aug 1960, p. 4725. *FD* 4 Aug 1960, p. 7. *Har* 13 Aug 1960, p. 131. *HCN* 8 Sep 1960. *HR* 4 Mar 1959. *HR* 29 Sep 1959. *HR* 13 Oct 1959. *HR* 3 Aug 1960, p. 3. *LAEx* 8 Nov 1959, p. 7, 11. *LAT* 12 Nov 1959. *LAT* 8 Sep 1960. *Life* 14 Dec 1959. *MPD* 3 Aug 1960. *MPHPD* 6 Aug 1960, p. 796. *NYT* 27 Aug 1960, p. 8. *SatRev* 20 Aug 1960. *Time* 29 Aug 1960. *Var* 3 Aug 1960, p. 6.

ALL THROUGH THE NIGHT (German Americans)

Warner Bros. Pictures, Inc.; A Warner Bros.—First National Picture. *Dist* Warner Bros. Pictures, Inc. 10 Jan **1942**; New York opening: 23 Jan 1942; Prod: early Aug-early Oct 1941 [©Warner Bros. Pictures, Inc.; 10 Jan 1942; LP10951]. Sd (RCA Sound System); b&w. 107 min.

Exec prod Hal B. Wallis. *Assoc prod* Jerry Wald. *Dir* Vincent Sherman. [*Asst dir* Bill Kissell]. *Scr* Leonard Spigelgass and Edwin Gilbert. *Story* Leonard Q. Ross and Leonard Spigelgass. *Dir of photog* Sid Hickox. *Spec eff* Edwin A. DuPar. *Art dir* Max Parker. *Film ed* Rudi Fehr. *Gowns* Howard Shoup. *Mus* Adolph Deutsch. *Mus dir* Leo F. Forbstein. *Sd* Oliver S. Garretson. *Makeup artist* Perc Westmore.

Song(s): "All Through the Night," music by Arthur Schwartz, lyrics by Johnny Mercer; "Cherie, I Love You," music and lyrics by Lillian Goodman.

Cast: HUMPHREY BOGART (*Gloves Donahue*), CONRAD VEIDT ([*Hall*] *Ebbing*), KAAREN VERNE (*Leda Hamilton*), Jane Darwell (*Mrs. Donahue*), Frank McHugh (*Barney*), Peter Lorre (*Pepi*), Judith Anderson (*Madame*), William Demarest (*Sunshine*), Jackie C. Gleason (*Starchy*), Phil Silvers (*Waiter*), Wally Ford (*Spats Hunter*), Barton MacLane (*Marty Callahan*), Edward Brophy (*Joe Denning*), Martin Kosleck (*Steindorff*), Jean Ames (*Annabelle*), Ludwig Stossel (*Mr. Miller*), Irene Seidner (*Mrs. Miller*), James Burke (*Forbes*), Ben Welden (*Smitty*), Hans Schumm (*Anton*), Charles Cane (*Sage*), Frank Sully (*Spence*), Sam McDaniel (*Deacon*), [Leo White, Billy Wayne (*Chefs*)], [Al Eben (*Pastry chef*)], [Lottie Williams (*Flower woman*)], [Louis Arco, Wolfgang Zilzer, John Sinclair, John Stark, Bob Kimball, Charles Sherlock (*Gestapo*)], [Don Turner, Emory Parnell, Clancy Cooper (*Policemen*)], [Gertrude Carr (*Mrs. Novak*)], [Vera Lewis (*Mrs. Fogarty*)], [Charles Wilson (*Lieutenant*)], [Creighton Hale (*Waiter*)], [Dick Elliott (*Husband*)], [Mira McKinney (*Wife*)], [Philip Van Zandt (*Assistant auctioneer*)], [Hans Joby, Egon Brecher (*Watchmen*)], [Chester Clute (*Hotel clerk*)], [Charles Sullivan, Bob Perry, Main Bud Geary, Dutch Hendrian (*Henchmen*)], [Lee Phelps (*Jailer*)], [Eddy Chandler (*Sergeant*)], [Henry Victor, Otto Reichow (*Guards*)], [Fred Vogeding (*Doctor*)], [Carl Ottmar (*Lichtig*)], [Chester Gan (*Chinese laundryman*)], [George Meeker, Roland Drew, Ray Montgomery, De Wolfe Hopper, Walter Brooke (*Reporters*)], [Regina Wallace], [Leah Baird], [Stuart Holmes], [Mary Servoss].

Espionage, Comedy-drama. [*Print viewed*]. Former New York City mobster Gloves Donahue, now a professional gambler, will eat only cheesecake baked by his mother's neighbor, Mr. Miller. When Miller is murdered, Gloves is urged by his mother, to whom he always listens, to investigate, and although he is reluctant at first, his interest is piqued when an attractive young woman comes looking for Miller and disappears as soon as she learns he is dead. That night, nightclub owner Marty Callahan telephones Gloves to demand that he retrieve Mrs. Donahue, who has discovered Leda Hamilton, the mysterious woman from that morning, singing at Callahan's club. When Gloves questions Leda, she provides simple explanations for each of his questions, and before long, she is dragged away by her sinister accompanist Pepi. Curious when a man runs outside and speeds away in a taxi, Gloves rushes inside just in time to see fatally wounded Joe Denning, one of Callahan's men, stagger from a dressing room. Before he dies, Denning tells Gloves that Leda has been kidnapped. Through his contacts, Gloves, who is mistakenly accused of Denning's murder, traces the taxi to a warehouse. Leaving his driver Barney behind, Gloves and Sunshine, one of his cronies, sneak inside. While Gloves looks around, Sunshine is knocked out and carried away, and when

Gloves tries to find him, he is driven away by gunshots. Gloves suspects that the warehouse is connected to an exclusive auction house around the corner, where an auction is being conducted. Gloves bids on a piece in order to take a look at the offices, but once inside, he is spotted by Pepi and Leda, who knocks him unconscious. Gloves awakens in the warehouse, tied up next to the missing Sunshine. To Gloves's surprise, Leda helps free them from their bonds, and later, Gloves and Sunshine overpower their captors. Inside the auction house, the pair find evidence that the mysterious group consists of German spies and fifth columnists, as well as a notebook that indicates that Leda's father has died in Dachau. When Gloves tries to take Hall Ebbing, the leader of the spies, to the police, however, Ebbing summons the others, and Gloves barely escapes with an unconscious Leda during the ensuing gunfight. While they run from the Germans, Leda explains that Miller was forced to work for them against his will. She also reveals that she must work for them or they will kill her father, but when Gloves tells her that her father is dead, she readily agrees to help him. The police do not believe Leda's testimony, however, and Gloves is forced to call on Callahan for help in avenging Denning's death. Gloves and Sunshine infiltrate a meeting, where they learn that the Germans plan to blow up a ship docked in the Brooklyn shipyard. They keep the group distracted long enough for Callahan's men to arrive. Ebbing escapes, determined to blow up the ship by himself, and Gloves follows him. At gunpoint, Ebbing forces Gloves to drive a small boat toward the ship, but at the last minute, Gloves turns the boat sharply and knocks Ebbing overboard. Gloves is declared a hero and charges against him and Leda are dropped. *False accusations. Gamblers. Murder. Spies. Auctions. Boats. Cheesecake. Explosions. Fathers and daughters. German Americans. Gunfights. Mothers and sons. New York City. Police. Reporters. Sabotage. Shipyards. Singers. Taxicab drivers. Warehouses.*

Note: A press release dated 14 May 1941 included in the file on the film at the AMPAS Library announced that George Raft and Olivia De Havilland were to star in the film. When Raft turned down the part, Humphrey Bogart was cast instead. A 10 Apr 1941 *HR* news item notes that Marlene Dietrich was also considered as Raft's co-star. Conrad Veidt was borrowed from M-G-M for the part of "Ebbing." Some reviews erroneously list Barton MacLane's role as "Max Calucci" instead of "Marty Callahan." In 1991, some colorized shots of Bogart, taken from this film, were used in a Diet Coca Cola commercial, integrated with newly shot footage of singer Elton John. *Box* 6 Dec 1941. *FD* 28 Jan 1942, p. 13. *HR* 10 Apr 1941, p. 3. *HR* 28 May 1941, p. 6. *HR* 15 Jul 1941, p. 1. *HR* 1 Aug 1941, p. 4. *MPHPD* 6 Dec 1941, p. 394. *NYT* 24 Jan 1942, p. 13. *Var* 3 Dec 1941, p. 8.

ALLEGHENY UPRISING (Native Americans)

RKO Radio Pictures, Inc.; Pandro S. Berman in charge of production. *Dist* RKO Radio Pictures, Inc. 10 Nov **1939**; Prod: began 10 Jul 1939 [©RKO Radio Pictures, Inc.; 10 Nov 1939; LP9293]. Sd (RCA Victor System); b&w. 8 reels. 81 min. PCA cert no. 5538.

Prod P. J. Wolfson. *Dir* William A. Seiter. *Asst dir* Kenneth Holmes. *Scr* P. J. Wolfson. *Dir of photog* Nicholas Musuraca. *Art dir* Van Nest Polglase. *Art dir assoc* Albert D'Agostino. *Ed* George Crone. *Set dec* Darrell Silvera. *Miss Trevor's wardrobe* Walter Plunkett. *Mus score* Anthony Collins. *Dance dir* David Robel. *Rec* Earl A. Wolcott. [*Tech adv* Bob Watson].

Source: Based on the novel *The First Rebel* by Neil Harmon Swanson (New York, 1937).

Cast: Claire Trevor (*Janie MacDougall*), John Wayne (*Jim Smith*), George Sanders (*Capt. Swanson*), Brian Donlevy (*Callendar*), Wilfrid Lawson (*MacDougall*), Robert Barrat (*Duncan*), John F. Hamilton (*Professor*), Moroni Olsen (*Calhoun*), Eddie Quillan (*Anderson*), [Chill Wills (*McCammon*)], [Ian Wolfe (*Poole*)], [Wallis Clark (*McGlashan*)], Monte Montague (*Morris*), [Olaf Hytten (*General Gage*)], [Clay Clement (*John Smith*)], [Eddy Waller (*Jailer*)], [Carl Knowles, Ethan Laidlaw, Forrest Dillon, Earl Askam, Bud Osborne (*Jim's men*)], [Charles Middleton (*Doctor*)], [Clive Morgan (*English sergeant*)], [Jess Caven (*Colonial farmer*)].

Historical, Adventure. [*Print viewed*]. In 1759, Jim Smith and his friends, MacDougall and the Professor, return from fighting the Indian wars in Quebec to their home in Pennsylvania's Allegheny Valley. There they are welcomed by MacDougall's fiery daughter Janie. That night, Indians attack a nearby settlement, and Jim leads a contingent of settlers disguised as Indians to rout the marauders. Realizing that the Indians are acquiring their weapons from local traders, Jim rides to Philadelphia to request that the British governor order a trade ban with the Indians. General Gage consents to Jim's request, thus infuriating Callendar, a crooked trader who circumvents the ban by persuading an army clerk to issue permits to him. When Captain Swanson, the smug British officer in charge of the territory, refuses to believe Jim's accusation that Callendar is continuing to supply the Indians with rum and munitions, Jim and his men, once again disguised as Indians, attack the wagon and destroy the contraband. The wily Callendar, however, outsmarts Jim by destroying the army wagons and accusing the settlers of treason. When Swanson believes Callendar's accusations, Jim decides that the only way to prove the trader's treachery is to allow the contraband laden wagons safe passage to the fort, then seize the fort and send a wagon of trade goods to General Gage as proof. To eliminate Jim, Callendar frames him for murder, but his trial comes to an abrupt halt when General Gage arrives, orders Callendar's arrest and sends Swanson back to England. *Indians of North America. Pennsylvania. Settlers. Traders. Treason. United States–History–Colonial period, ca. 1600-1775. Fathers and daughters. Forts. Frame-ups. Impersonation and imposture. Murder. Soldiers. Traps. Trials.*

Note: The working titles of this film were *Pennsylvania Uprising* and *Allegheny Frontier*, and it was released in Britain as *The First Rebel*. According to a pre-production news item in *HR*, actor Bob Burns was slated to appear in this picture but withdrew over a disagreement about the story. Another news item in *HR* notes that George Sanders replaced Sir Cedric Hardwicke in the role of Capt. Swanson when Hardwicke left the film to fill the spot intended for Basil Rathbone in *The Hunchback of Notre Dame*. Other news items in *HR* add that the film was shot on location at Lake Sherwood and Sherwood Forest, CA. This was the second of three films that John Wayne and Claire Trevor made in 1939 and 1940. The first was *Stagecoach* and the third was *The Dark Command*. *DV* 21 Oct 1939, p. 3. *FD* 24 Oct 1939, p. 10. *HR* 12 Jun 1939, p. 4. *HR* 28 Jun 1939, p. 1. *HR* 8 Jul 1939, pp. 5-6. *HR* 10 Jul 1939, p. 1, 2, 3. *HR* 15 Jul 1939, p. 5. *HR* 21 Oct 1939, p. 3. *MPD* 24 Oct 1939, p. 8. *MPH* 7 Oct 1939, p. 45. *MPH* 28 Oct 1939, p. 43. *NYT* 10 Nov 1939, p. 29. *Var* 8 Nov 1939, p. 14.

ALMA DE GAUCHO (Spanish language)

Chris Phillis Productions. *Dist* Edward L. Klein Corporation. Jun **1930**; World Premiere in Los Angeles: 7 Jun 1930; Prod: Mar 1930 at Telefilm Studios with exteriors filmed at Universal Studios. Sd; b&w. 6 reels, 5,325 ft. 59 min. Spanish language.

Prod Chris Phillis. *Dir* Henry Otto. *Scr* Paul Ellis. *Story* Benjamín Ingénito Paralupi. *Photog* Leon Shamroy. *Mus comp* Benjamín Ingénito Paralupi. *Sd* Ralph M. Like.

Cast: Manuel Granado (*Antonio*), Mona Rico (*Elsa*), Francisco Amerise (*Don Alfredo*), Christina Montt (*Doña Cristina*), Humberto Bonavia (*Arturo*), George Rigas (*Don Casimiro*), Alberto Mendoza (*Carlos*), Emma Mora (*Monona*).

Romance, Drama, with songs. [*Not viewed*]. Elsa, a young girl from Buenos Aires, visits her aunt and uncle, Don Alfredo and Doña Cristina, at their ranch. While playing golf, Elsa meets a gaucho, Antonio, and is enchanted by his exquisite singing voice. When she loses a golf ball, she explains the game to the gaucho. Elsa, Don Alfredo, Doña Cristina, and two other rich visitors, Carlos and Arturo, attend a a rodeo, where Elsa dares one of the gauchos to ride a wild, unbroken colt named Moro. Antonio takes the challenge, and after he succeeds in breaking the horse, Don Alfredo gives it to Elsa. She grows fond of Antonio, and when she teaches him to play golf, Doña Cristina decides to intercede, but before she arrives, she and the gaucho agree to meet in the garden that night. During the evening card game, Cristina becomes angry that Elsa is preoccupied. Elsa meets Antonio as planned and he sings for her. Cristina takes Elsa away from her lover. Later, at a family tea, Doña Cristina argues that Antonio is too uncultured and uneducated for the girl. Elsa assures her that she is only carrying on an innocent flirtation with Antonio. Believing Elsa is sincere in this claim, Antonio is broken-hearted, and Don Casimiro tries to comfort him. At a fiesta, couples dance the Argentinian national dance, the Pericon. Elsa convinces the sorrowful Antonio to sing a song, and when she tries to flee the fiesta, he carries her off into the night. Arturo tells Alfredo and Casimiro what has occurred and they chase the pair on horseback. Antonio tells Elsa that despite his lack of education, he is a man with feelings and dignity. He chides her for playing with him, and then lets her go, telling her that he did not avenge his wrongs to prove to her the nobility of the gauchos. Elsa returns to her aunt and uncle, and falls into a delirium, calling incessantly for Antonio. Antonio finally comes to her and they embrace, reunited. *Argentina. Class distinction. Gauchos. Romance. Courtship. Fiestas. Flirts. Golf. Rodeos. Uncles.*

Note: The plot summary was based on a dialogue continuity deposited at the NYSA of a dubbed Italian version of this film, entitled *Povero cuore (Poor Heart)*. Newsreel footage of the premiere of *Alma de gaucho*, in the AMPAS

archive, reveals that director Henry Otto was not Spanish-speaking. Paul Ellis and Manuel Granado were pseudonyms used by Argentine-born Benjamín Ingenito Paralupi. The dubbed Italian version, which was also advertised under the title *Poor Heart*, contained the following written foreward, translated from the Italian: "Italians in Italy and outside, we sincerely dedicate this first work to you, without pretense but animated with great enthusiasm for our faraway country and with the firm will to make some more pictures. This typical drama of Argentine life comes to you from Hollywood, and we hope you will accept it as a start for taking the Italian language all over the world."

Cinl Sep 1930, p. 30.

ALOHA (Polynesian Americans)

Rogell Productions, Ltd. *Dist* Tiffany Productions, Inc. 27 Apr **1931** [©Tiffany Productions, Inc.; 4 Feb 1931; LP1962]. Sd; b&w. 9 reels. 85, 87 or 90 min.

Dir Albert Rogell. [*Asst dir* Edgar G. Ulmer]. *Story and scr* Thomas H. Ince and J. G. Hawks. [*Adpt* Adele Buffington]. *Dial* W. Totman and Leslie Mason. *Photog* Charles Stumar. *Film ed* Richard Cahoon. *Rec eng* H. R. Hobson. *Prod mgr* Rudolph Flothow.

Source: Based on the film *Aloha Oe* by J. G. Hawks and Thomas H. Ince (New York Motion Picture Corp.; Kay-Bee, 1915).

Cast: Ben Lyon [(*Jimmy Bradford*)], Raquel Torres [(*Ilanu*)], Robert Edeson [(*James Bradford, Jr.*)], Alan Hale [(*Stevens*)], Thelma Todd [(*Winifred Bradford*)], Marian Douglas [(*Elaine Marvin*)], Otis Harlan [(*Old Ben*)], T. Roy Barnes [(*Johnny Marvin*)], Robert Ellis [(*Larry Leavitt*)], Donald Reed [(*Kahea*)], Al St. John [(*A sailor*)], Dickie Moore [(*Junior Bradford*)], Marcia Harris [(*Governess*)], Addie McPhail [(*Rosalie*)], Phyllis Crane [(*Dixie*)], Rita Rey [(*Native girl*)].

Island, Melodrama. [*Viewed print incomplete*]. On a South Sea island, Ilanu, a half-caste, does not want to marry Kahea, a man of her tribe, but instead desires American Jimmy Bradford, who has been on the island for nearly a year overseeing his father's copra interests. After rebuking Kahea, Ilanu finds Jimmy sulking because he hungers for the life he has left. When she finds he exhibits no interest in her, she leaves him in tears. Old Ben, who brags he once earned three degrees at Harvard, warns Jimmy not to get involved with a native girl by pointing to his six half-caste children and quoting Kipling. Jimmy writes to his sweetheart Elaine Marvin back in America. That night, Ilanu tearfully begins the Dance of Love, a ceremony her grandfather, the chief, has ordered her to dance. She soon stops, however, tears her lei off and refuses to continue, despite her grandfather's reminder that her mother found only trouble marrying a white man and finally was driven to the arms of the volcanic Fire Goddess. Ilanu is then told to go and never return to her people. Just then a boat comes, but Jimmy is disappointed to find that his father still has not sent for him. When Ilanu comes into the bar and a sailor grabs her, Jimmy slugs him and tells Ilanu to go home. She follows him to his room and tells her she now has no home. He almost kisses her, but when a lustful onlooker chides them, Jimmy kicks Ilanu out. Feeling remorseful, Jimmy follows Ilanu to the beach, and they declare their love for each other. They marry and Jimmy brings Ilanu back to San Francisco. During a party in Jimmy's honor, Jimmy's sister Winnie gets Ilanu to do an island dance, which the Parkers, possible investors in Bradford's company, find vulgar. Bradford, greatly upset, orders Jimmy to send Ilanu back and says he will get the marriage annulled, but Jimmy stands firm and leaves with Ilanu for the islands. Jimmy works in a stock room, and he and Ilanu live in poverty. When Kahea visits to tell Ilanu that her grandfather forgave her as he died and bequeathed her some pearls, Jimmy sees them together and mistakenly thinks they are lovers. After Ilanu calms Jimmy with the truth, Elaine visits and tells him that his father is gravely ill. Jimmy returns home and lets his dying father think he has left Ilanu. Jimmy takes over the family business, but after three years, Ilanu and Winnie, who lives with them, battle after Winnie fires the governess whom Ilanu had hired to care for her and Jimmy's child Junior and hires her own. To calm things, Jimmy takes them all back to the islands on a vacation cruise. Winnie gets Ilanu drunk, and Junior, trying to wake his mother, falls into the ocean and is rescued by Elaine. Upset by the incident, Jimmy orders Ilanu to keep away from Junior. Ilanu then overhears guests say she will ruin Junior's life, and as the yacht nears the island, she sees the bubbling volcano and cries. She kisses Junior through the glass that separates them, then rows to the volcano. Jimmy, who has been persuaded by Elaine to apologize to Ilanu, sees her in the boat and hears Kahea sing "Aloha Oe." Kahea says the song means farewell and tells Jimmy that Ilanu is going to join her mother. Jimmy chases Ilanu

in a motorboat, but she jumps into the volcano before he can reach her. Junior asks for his mother, then asks Elaine to play. Elaine holds him and cries, while Jimmy stands on the beach in distress. *Cultural conflict. Marriage. Miscegenation. Mothers and sons. Polynesians. Americans in foreign countries. Bars. Brothers and sisters. Dancing. Governesses. Grandfathers. Islands. Parties. Poverty. Rites and ceremonies. Sailors. San Francisco (CA). South Seas. Suicide. Tribal chiefs. Volcanoes. Wealth. Yachts and yachting.*

Note: According to *FD*, the *Sultana*, one of the most famous yachts of the time, was used in some of the scenes. At the time of filming, the yacht belonged to John P. Mills, noted capitalist and turfman. Previously it belonged to E. H. Harriman. This film was based on the 1915 film *Aloha Oe*, produced by Thomas Ince, directed by Richard Stanton and Charles Swickard and starring Willard Mack and Enid Markey (see *AFI Catalog of Feature Films, 1911-20*; F1.0073).

FD 1 Feb 1931, p. 10. *HR* 20 Dec 1930, p. 4. *Var* 29 Apr 1931, p. 37.

ALWAYS SWEETHEARTS see THE STORY OF SEABISCUIT

AM I GUILTY? (African Americans)

Supreme Pictures Corp. *Dist* Supreme Pictures Corp. **1940**; Harlem opening: 27 Sep 1940. Sd; b&w. 70-71 min. PCA cert no. 6366.

Prod A. W. Hackel. *Dir* Samuel Neufeld. *Orig scr* Sherman Lowe. *Adpt* George Sayre and Earl Snell. *Cam* Robert Cline. *Film ed* S. Roy Luby. *Sd eng* Clifford Ruberg.

Cast: Ralph Cooper (*Dr. James Dunbar*), Sybil Lewis (*Joan Freeman*), Sam McDaniel (*John D. Jones*), Lawrence Criner ("*Trigger*" *Bennett*), Marcella Moreland (*Marcella*), Arthur Ray (*Dr. Freeman*), Reginald Fenderson (*Slick*), Monte Hawley (*Tracy*), "Tia Juana" Matthew Jones (*Monk*), "Pigmeat" Markham (*Proprietor*), Jesse Brooks (*Dr. Fairchild*), Napoleon Simpson (*John Parks*), Clarence Brooks (*Lieutenant Harris*), Cleo Desmond (*Mrs. Thompson*), Ida Coffin (*Mrs. Smith*), Lillian Randolph (*Mrs. Jones*), Vernon McCalla (*Judge*), Eddie Thompson (*Lawyer Henry Stafford*), Mae Turner (*Dunbar's mother*), Alfred Grant (*Intern*), Guernsey Morrow (*Pete*).

African American, Medical, Crime, Drama. [*Not viewed*]. As a fire rages through the Parks Manufacturing Company, injured workmen are taken to the company clinic, which is run by Dr. James Dunbar and his nurse, Joan Freeman. The clinic receives a visit by the notorious Dr. Fairchild, who is so impressed with James's surgical skills, that he offers him work at his clinic when Mr. Parks announces the closure of the company. James rejects Fairchild's generous offer, however, and tells him that he prefers to start his own clinic in the poor part of town, where people are without basic medical care. Time passes, and James and Joan, with whom he has fallen in love, are running their own clinic in a poor neighborhood. Although the clinic has a hard time paying its bills, James hires John D. Jones to work for him. The clinic soon becomes a regular haunt for Marcella, a young girl who is constantly getting injured. When one of gangster "Trigger" Bennett's men is injured in a payroll robbery, Bennett seeks the services of Dr. Freeman, Joan's father, who is in town for a visit. Because Dr. Freeman is drunk and cannot attend to the gangster's injury, Bennett forces James to accompany him to the gangster's hideout to administer aid. Although he refuses Bennett's payment for completing a successful operation on the injured man, James later receives a gift of $5,000 from an anonymous donor through his attorney, Henry Stafford. James and Joan use the money to make improvements on their clinic. Soon after learning that the money came from Bennett, James is abducted by the gangsters and forced to accompany them on robberies in other towns. After his stint as the gangsters' personal physician, James returns to his clinic, but he is unhappy about his association with the thugs. Just as James is about to operate on Marcella's fractured skull, the gangsters appear again and demand that he operate on Bennett, who has been shot. Bennett dies during the operation, but James rushes back to his clinic in time to save Marcella's life. In the meantime, Bennett's men are arrested and sentenced to prison. James turns himself in, and because of his connection to the gangsters, he is sentenced to one to ten years in prison, along with Stafford and Dr. Freeman. *Abduction. African Americans. Clinics. Gangsters. Physicians. Drunkenness. Ethics. Fathers and daughters. Fires. Hideouts. Jails. Lawyers. Nurses. Poverty. Robbery. Romance. Trials.*

Note: A working title for this film was *Free Clinic*. According to the *Var* review, this film marked "an entirely new concept" in black films in its use of an adult story rather than a "low" comedy, and because its production was on a par with the "B product" of the major studios. Although the picture was well-

received by the Harlem audiences, *Var* speculated that it might not perform well with the "more poorly educated negros of the South." *Am I Guilty?* marked Supreme Pictures' entry into the field of black-cast films; the company was previously associated with westerns. According to modern sources, Supreme planned to film four black-cast pictures annually. Six-year-old Marcella Moreland was the daughter of prominent black comedian Mantan Moreland. According to modern sources, the film was re-released in the late 1940s by Toddy Pictures under the title *Racket Doctor*.

DV 12 Jun 1940, p. 3. *Exb* 16 Oct 1940, p. 621. *Var* 2 Oct 1940, p. 25.

AMANTE Y TRAIDORA see DOS NOCHES

AMARILLY OF CLOTHES-LINE ALLEY (Irish Americans)
Mary Pickford Film Corp.; An Artcraft Picture. *Dist* Famous Players-Lasky Corp. 11 Mar **1918** [©Famous Players-Lasky Corp.; 2 Mar 1918; LP12142]. Si; b&w. 5 reels.

Pres Adolph Zukor. *Dir* Marshall A. Neilan. *Asst dir* Nat Deverich. *Adpt* Frances Marion. *Cam* Walter Stradling. *Art dir* Wilfred Buckland.

Source: Based on the novel *Amarilly of Clothes-Line Alley* by Belle K. Maniates (Boston, 1915).

Cast: Mary Pickford (*Amarilly Jenkins*), William Scott (*Terry McGowen*), Norman Kerry (*Gordon Phillips*), Ida Waterman (*Mrs. Stuyvesant Phillips*), Margaret Landis (*Colette King*), Kate Price (*Mrs. Jenkins*), Tom Wilson (*Boscoe McCarty*), Fred Goodwins (*Johnny Walker*), Herbert Standing (*Father Riordan*), Wesley Barry, Frank Butterworth, Antrim Short, George Hackathorne (*Amarilly's brothers*), Gertrude Short.

Comedy. In the tenements of Clothes-Line Alley, bartender Terry McGowan courts cigarette girl Amarilly Jenkins. When wealthy sculptor Gordon Phillips is injured in a brawl at her café, Amarilly takes him to her flat where her mother, an Irish laundress, tends his wounds. In gratitude, he hires Amarilly to clean his studio. Gordon's aunt, Mrs. Stuyvesant Phillips, hoping to make Amarilly the subject of a social experiment, takes the girl into her palatial home. To her consternation, Mrs. Phillips realizes that Gordon is falling in love with Amarilly. To illustrate the folly of such an alliance, Mrs. Phillips invites the entire Jenkins family to tea, where Mrs. Jenkins performs a lively jig with the butler. Amarilly and Gordon discover that they are not made for each other, and Amarilly returns to Terry and true happiness. *Aunts. Cigarette girls. Class distinction. Irish Americans. Sculptors. Tenement-houses. Bartenders. Butlers. Dancing. Experiments. Laundresses. Nursing back to health.*

ETR 2 Feb 1918, p. 761. *ETR* 16 Mar 1918, p. 1229. *MPN* 23 Mar 1918, p. 1299, 1762. *MPW* 9 Mar 1918, p. 1412. *MPW* 23 Mar 1918, p. 1703. *NYDM* 16 Mar 1918, p. 22, 25. *Var* 8 Mar 1918, p. 41. *Wid's* 21 Mar 1918, pp. 1018-19.

THE AMAZING MRS. HOLLIDAY (Chinese Americans, Refugees)
Universal Pictures Co., Inc.; A Bruce Manning Production. *Dist* Universal Pictures Co., Inc. 19 Feb **1943**; Prod: 11 Jun–30 Sep 1942; 19 Oct–mid-Dec 1942 [©Universal Pictures Co., Inc.; 24 Feb 1943; LP11882]. Sd (Western Electric Recording); b&w. 8,781 ft. 97-98 min.

Prod Bruce Manning. *Assoc prod* Frank Shaw. *Dir* Bruce Manning and [Jean Renoir]. [*Asst dir* Joseph McDonough]. *Scr* Frank Ryan and John Jacoby. *Adpt* Boris Ingster and Leo Townsend. *Orig story* Sonya Levien. *Dir of photog* Woody Bredell. *Art dir* Jack Otterson. *Assoc* Martin Obzina. *Film ed* Ted Kent. *Set dec* R. A. Gausman. *Assoc* T. F. Offenbecker. *Gowns* Vera West. *Mus dir* Charles Previn. *Mus score* Frank Skinner and H. J. Salter. *Vocal coach* Andres de Segurola. *Sd dir* Bernard B. Brown. [*Sd*] *tech* William Hedgcock. [*Tech adv* Madame Rosalyda Chang and Tom Gubbins].

Song(s): "Mong Djang Nu (A Chinese Lullaby)," traditional, English translation by Madame Rosalyda Chang; "The Old Refrain," words and music by Fritz Kreisler and Alice Mattullath; "Mighty Lak' a Rose," words and music by Ethelbert Nevin and Frank Stanton; "Visi d'Arte," from the opera *Tosca*, music by Giacomo Puccini, libretto by Giuseppe Giacosa and Luigi Illica; "Rock-a-bye Baby," traditional, Chinese translation by Madame Rosalyda Chang.

Cast: DEANNA DURBIN (*Ruth Kirke [Holliday]*), Edmond O'Brien ([*Thomas*] *Tom* [*Spencer Holliday III*]), Barry Fitzgerald (*Timothy [Blake]*), Arthur Treacher (*Henderson*), Harry Davenport (*Commodore* [*Thomas Spencer Holliday*]), Grant Mitchell (*Edgar [Holliday]*), Frieda Inescort (*Karen [Holliday]*), Elisabeth Risdon (*Louise [Holliday]*), Jonathan Hale (*Ferguson*), Esther Dale (*Lucy*), Gus Schilling (*Jeff [Adams]*), J. Frank Hamilton (*Dr. [Donald] Kirke*), The Children: Christopher Severn [(*Rodney*)], Yvonne Severn

[(*Elizabeth*)], Vido Rich [(*Vido*)], Mila Rich [(*Anna*)], Teddy Infuhr [(*Teddy*)], Linda Bieber [(*Winifred*)], Diane DuBois [(*Mari*)], Billy Ward [(*Pepe*)], and [Michael Chan] (*The Chinese baby*), [Douglas Wood (*Chairman*)], [Philip Ahn (*Major Ching*)], [Roland Got (*Dr. Ku*)], [Iris Wong (*Martha*)], [Bo Ching (*Bo Ching*)], [Eleanor Soo Hoo (*Bo Ming*)], [Paul Fung (*Old farmer*)], [Irving Bacon (*Ticket agent*)], [Joseph Crehan, Robert Homans (*Shipbuilding executives*)], [Charles Trowbridge, Wade Boteler (*Immigration officers*)], [Richard Loo (*General Chan*)], [Eddie Dunn (*Eddie*)], [Tom Dugan (*Gus*)], [Harold Minjir (*Hairdresser*)], [Dorothy Vaughan, Dorothy Granger (*Maids*)], [Ray Walker (*Chauffeur*)], [George Chandler (*Butler*)], [Joseph King (*Captain*)], [Chester Gan (*Young farmer*)], [Richard Davies, Jack Mulhall, Eddie Coke, Pat Gleason, Charles Sherlock, Bess Flowers, Bobby Barber (*Reporters*)], [George Guhl (*Captain Anderson*)], [Olaf Hytten (*Clerk*)], [Gene O'Donnell (*Announcer*)], [Leslie Denison (*Lt. Wilson*)], [Bruce Wong (*Soldier*)], [Polly Bailey (*Julie, the cook*)], [Shirley Lew (*Girl*)], [Eddie Burns], [Vangie Beilby].

Drama, with songs. [*Print viewed*]. Young schoolteacher Ruth Kirke is transporting a group of war orphans from South China to San Francisco when their cargo ship is torpedoed and sunk in the mid-Pacific. Along with sailor Timothy Blake, they are the only known survivors of the enemy attack. Upon arriving in San Francisco, Ruth is told by immigration officials that the undocumented children will be held unless someone posts a $500 bond for each child, guaranteeing that they will "not become public charges." Ruth and Timothy go to the home of Commodore Thomas Holliday, the wealthy owner of their sunken ship, to ask for his family's help. When they refuse, Timothy states that Ruth and the commodore were married aboard ship. For the good of the children, Ruth goes along with the deception, and she, Timothy and the war orphans move into the Holliday estate. They are later joined by the commodore's grandson, Thomas Spencer Holliday III. Ruth tells Tom how her father's mission was destroyed in a Japanese bombing raid, and she was sent south on the Burma Road with the European children. Along the way, they found a dying Chinese woman, and Ruth agreed to take care of her child as well. After Ruth learns that she is to inherit the commodore's vast shipping fortune, she and the children try to sneak out of the mansion in the middle of the night, but they are caught by Tom. She then confesses all, telling Tom that she smuggled the children aboard the commodore's ship, thinking that it was going to Calcutta. Once at sea, the commodore then promised to help her get the children into the United States, even if it meant adopting them. After their ship was torpedoed, Ruth and Timothy put the children into a lifeboat, but once they were away from the sinking ship, they discovered that one child, Pepe, had been left behind. The angry Tom insists that Ruth stay and continue the charade until the publicity about her "marriage" dies down, but agrees to care for the orphans at the Holliday estate once she leaves. Later, the children's immigration papers arrive, and Ruth, as promised, prepares to leave for her hometown of Philadelphia, despite the fact that she has fallen in love with Tom. As she waits for her train, Timothy tells Tom that Ruth is engaged to the man sitting next to her. The two are then forced to leave the train station when the innocent man, Jeff Adams, accuses them of a marriage "shake down." Later, a China relief ball is held at the Holliday estate, at which Ruth and Tom finally admit their true feelings for each other. The commodore and Pepe are also at the ball, having been rescued themselves, and knowing of the children's plight, the commodore continues the ruse. He then tells Ruth that he plans to marry her for real and raise the orphans as his own children. The commodore's plans are dashed when his brother Edgar, his sister Louise and his sister-in-law Karen tell him about the romance between Ruth and Tom. The commodore then announces that he and Ruth were never really married, but she is about to become Mrs. Holliday, as she and Tom are to be married in the Holliday estate in a few days. *Grandsons. Impersonation and imposture. Orphans. Schoolteachers. War refugees. Americans in foreign countries. Brothers and sisters. Butlers. Charity balls. China–History–Sino-Japanese Conflict, 1937-1945. China. Army. Deception. Housekeepers. Irish Americans. Lifeboats. Mansions. Missing persons, Assumed dead. Missionaries. Reporters. Sailors. San Francisco (CA). Shipping magnates. Shipwrecks. Stowaways. Torpedoes. Train stations. Uncles.*

Note: The working titles of this film were *The Divine Young Lady*, *Call Me Yours* and *Forever Yours*. The onscreen end credits do not list child actor Michael Chan, but only his character name, "The Chinese Baby."
In Jul 1941, Universal announced that actress Deanna Durbin's next film

would be *They Live Alone*, based on an original screenplay by Sonya Levien and directed by William Seiter. Later that month, *HR* stated that *They Live Alone* would begin production on 15 Sep 1941; however, on 13 Oct 1941, *HR* announced that Durbin had refused to attend a press conference announcing the production of the film, and was, in fact, meeting in New York City with Universal president Nate Blumberg to demand more control over her films. On 17 Oct 1941, Durbin was suspended by the studio for her refusal to appear in *They Live Alone*. *HR* later stated that Durbin was continuing her suspension indefinitely, as she wanted permission to work for studios other than Universal, specifically M-G-M, where the producer of her previous Universal films, Joe Pasternak, had moved. In Dec 1941, *HR* speculated that Durbin's suspension had cost Universal over $200,000, as both *They Live Alone* and *Marriage of Inconvenience*, a second project designated for director Seiter, had been canceled due to their failure to find an appropriate female lead. Finally, on 30 Jan 1942, Durbin and Universal settled their dispute, and the actress was given story and director approval on all her films. *HR* announced on 3 Feb 1941 that *They Live Alone* was once again being put back into the production schedule at Universal, with Durbin in the lead role. On 18 Mar 1942, however, Universal announced that *Three Smart Girls Join Up*, a second follow-up to Durbin's debut film, *Three Smart Girls* (see *AFI Catalog of Feature Films, 1931-40*; F3.4623) and based on a story by RAF pilot Derek Bolton, was replacing *They Lived Alone* on the Universal production schedule and would begin shooting in May 1942. *HR* then stated on 15 Apr 1942 that all previously announced Durbin films had been replaced on the Universal production schedule by *The Divine Young Lady*, the initial working title of this film.

In May 1942, the title of the film was changed to *Forever Yours* and noted French director Jean Renoir, who had signed a one-picture deal with Universal in Feb 1942, was assigned to the film. Later that month, *HR* stated that editor Ted Kent was being assigned to the film, replacing Bernard W. Burton, the editor on Durbin's previous films, who had been promoted to associate producer at Universal. On 7 Aug 1942, *HR* announced that Renoir was being removed from the film after forty-seven days of shooting. According to the trade journal, the French director was fired due to his slow filming pace. *Forever Yours* had a forty-nine day shooting schedule, and Renoir was reportedly ten weeks behind schedule. Renoir, however, stated that he was leaving the film due to recurring pain caused an old World War I leg injury. Durbin requested that producer Bruce Manning assume the directorial reigns, and it was projected that the film would complete shooting in seven weeks. In early Sep 1942, after seventeen weeks of filming, writer Robert White was brought in to re-write the film's finale. It has not been determined, however, if any of his work was used in the released film. In Sep 1942, Universal announced that it was suspending principal photography on the film for at least one week for script revisions and the shooting of shipyards and street scene backgrounds in San Francisco. *HR* reported that producer-director Manning was being forced to direct this second unit work in San Francisco himself, as some of the selected sites were considered military backgrounds and would require special clearances. Universal requested SAG permission to pay half-salaries to the players during this lay-off period. *HR* then announced that principal photography had resumed on 19 Oct 1942, after significant re-writing on the screenplay by Manning and Frank M. Ryan.

A Universal plot synopsis based on a working draft of the screenplay suggests that numerous plot changes were made before the final draft was completed. In the earlier draft, Commodore Holliday attempts to run the Japanese blockade of China; Ruth and the children sneak onto the cargo ship without the help or knowledge of Timothy; when the commodore safely returns to San Francisco and his "bride," the heartbroken Tom decides to head back to sea himself; the commodore is told of Tom and Ruth's romance by Timothy, not his relatives; Ruth and Tom are married and the commodore adopts the children; and after his marriage, Tom does go to sea, but when Ruth discovers Pepe missing once again, Tom finds the young stowaway on his ship and a raft is lowered to send Pepe back to the Holliday estate. Universal press materials state that the musical numbers "Carmean," "Kashmiri Song" and "The Recessional March" were recorded by Deanna Durbin for this film, but they were not heard in the viewed print. For "The Recessional March," Durbin was accompanied by a 285 member male chorus, according to press materials. Technical adviser and lyric translator Madame Rosalyda Chang was a noted Chinese author, lecturer and diplomat at the time of this film's production, and her husband was a former Chinese ambassador to Portugal, Poland and Czechoslovakia.

HR production charts include Kim Wong in the cast, but her participation in the released film has not been determined. Frank Skinner and H. J. Salter were nominated for an Academy Award for their musical score to this film, but lost to Alfred Newman's score for *The Song of Bernadette*. In 1955, Levien's story was presented on television under the same title as part of the *Lux Video Theatre*, starring Barbara Rush and Grant Williams, and directed by Richard Goode.

AmCin Mar 1943, p. 95. *Box* 13 Feb 1943. *DV* 5 Feb 1943, pp. 3, 6. *FD* 10 Feb 1943, p. 5. *HR* 7 Jul 1941, p. 1. *HR* 29 Jul 1941, p. 16. *HR* 13 Oct 1941, pp. 1-2. *HR* 17 Oct 1941, p. 3. *HR* 20 Oct 1941, p. 9. *HR* 3 Dec 1941, pp. 1-2. *HR* 2 Feb 1942, p. 1. *HR* 3 Feb 1942, p. 1. *HR* 18 Mar 1942, p. 2. *HR* 15 Apr 1942, p. 7. *HR* 22 May 1942, p. 6. *HR* 28 May 1942, p. 2. *HR* 29 May 1942, p. 2. *HR* 11 Jun 1942, p. 2. *HR* 12 Jun 1942, p. 7. *HR* 17 Jul 1942, p. 9. *HR* 7 Aug 1942, pp. 1-2. *HR* 4 Sep 1942, p. 1. *HR* 30 Sep 1942, p. 1. *HR* 1 Oct 1942, pp. 1-2. *HR* 20 Oct 1942, p. 5. *HR* 9 Nov 1942, p. 24. *HR* 12 Jan 1943, p. 1. *HR* 5 Feb 1943, p. 1. *MPHPD* 3 Oct 1942, p. 936. *MPHPD* 6 Feb 1943, p. 1145. *NYT* 22 Feb 1943, p. 20. *Var* 10 Feb 1943, p. 8.

AMBROSIA *see* **THE LOVE GIRL**

AMBUSH (Native Americans, Apache)
Metro-Goldwyn-Mayer Corp.; controlled by Loew's Inc.; A Sam Wood Production. *Dist* Loew's Inc. 13 Jan **1950**; Prod: 2 Jun—early Aug 1949; added scenes late Aug 1949. [©Loew's Inc.; 12 Dec 1949; LP2727]. Sd (Western Electric Sound System); b&w. 7,972 ft. 88-89 min. Passed by the National Board of Review. PCA cert no. 14027.

Prod Armand Deutsch. *Dir* Sam Wood. [*Asst dir* John Waters]. *Scr* Marguerite Roberts. *Dir of photog* Harold Lipstein. *Art dir* Cedric Gibbons and Malcolm Brown. *Film ed* Ben Lewis. *Set dec* Edwin B. Willis. *Assoc* Ralph S. Hurst. *Women's cost* Walter Plunkett. *Mus score* Rudolph G. Kopp. *Rec supv* Douglas Shearer. *Hair styles des* by Sydney Guilaroff. *Makeup created by* Jack Dawn. *Tech adv* Col. Charles E. Morrison, U.S.A. (Ret.). [*Unit mgr* David Friedman].

Source: Based on the short story "Ambush" by Luke Short in *The Saturday Evening Post* (25 Dec 1948—12 Feb 1949).

Cast: Robert Taylor (*Ward Kinsman*), John Hodiak (*Captain Ben Lorrison*), Arlene Dahl (*Ann Duverall*), Don Taylor (*Lt. Linus Delaney*), Jean Hagen (*Martha Conovan*), Bruce Cowling (*Tom Conovan*), Leon Ames (*Major [C. E.] Breverly*), John McIntire (*Frank Holly*), Pat Moriarty (*Sgt. Mack*), Charles Stevens (*Diablito*), Chief Thundercloud (*Tana*), Ray Teal (*Capt. J. R. Wolverson*), Robin Short (*Lt. Storrow*), Richard Bailey (*Lt. Tremaine*), [Cliff Clark (*Capt. Harcourt*)], [Lane Chandler (*Doc Horton*)], [Marta Mitrovich (*Mary Carlyle*)], [Flora Nez (*Indian girl*)], [Florence Lake (*Mrs. Wolverson*)], [Charles Cane (*Fat trooper*)], [Ray Bennett (*Headquarters orderly*)], [Archie Butler, Tom Forman, "Doc" George Meyers, Robert Hoy, Carol Henry, Bill Hale, Fred McDougal, James Van Horn, Reed Howes, Walter La Rue, Lynn Farr, Phil Schumacher, Arthur Loew, Jr. (*Troopers*)], [Hank Mann (*Barber*)], [Heinie Conklin (*Quartermaster*)], [Fred Somers (*Sutler*)], [Peter Prouse (*Corp. Evans*)], [James Harrison (*Sgt. Isaacs*)], [William Haade (*Joe, a guard*)], [Pat O'Malley (*Officer of the day*)].

Western. [*Print viewed*]. In 1878, at the foot of Bailey Mountain, Arizona Territory, Ward Kinsman, a prospector and Indian guide, is asked by Major C. E. Breverly of the U.S. Cavalry to help him find Mary Carlyle, the daughter of a general who was abducted during an Indian raid. Fearing a heavy loss of life if he carries out the mission, Ward refuses the Major's request, but later accepts the assignment when Ann Duverall, Mary's attractive sister, asks him to help. Before leaving the cavalry headquarters on a preliminary expedition, Ward punches Tom Conovan, an alcoholic cavalryman who falsely accuses him of being a horse thief. Tom's wife Martha, who has suffered many abuses by her husband, is having an affair with Lt. Linus Delaney. Accompanied by a small group of cavalrymen, Ward follows the trail of Mary's abductors to an Indian encampment. After raiding the camp, Ward learns from an Indian woman that Mary is still alive and is with Diablito's band of Indians, who are directly ahead of them on the trail. While reporting the discovery to Captain Ben Lorrison, Ann's former sweetheart, Ward learns that Breverly has been injured in an attack by Conovan and that Lorrison is now in command. The expedition returns to the fort with an Apache prisoner, Tana, and preparations are made for a full-scale attack on Diablito's caravan. When Lorrison falsely accuses Delaney of causing Conovan's attack on Breverly and orders the lieutenant's transfer, Ward, who dislikes the new commander, challenges him to a fistfight. Though Ward receives a beating from Lorrison, the two eventually put aside their differences and make final preparations for the ambush. On the eve of the ambush, Lorrison proposes to Ann, who later tells Ward that she plans to accept the proposal. Ward balks at the news, and insists that Ann is really in love with him. Soon, after the expedition sets out to find Diablito, Ward kills Tana in self-defense when the Indian double-crosses the squadron and attacks him. The Cavalry squadron eventually finds the Apaches and, after stampeding their horses, engages them in bloody gun battle. As the battle nears its conclusion, Captain Jim R. Wolverson's reinforcements arrive and Ward rescues Mary. Although Ward is satisfied with the outcome of the ambush, Lorrison, determined to effect a complete routing of the Apaches, takes some men with him and goes after a small band of escaping Indians. Ward, realizing that Lorrison and his men are in great danger without a scout, follows them. He arrives too late, however, and discovers that the Indians have killed Lorrison and his men in an ambush. When the expedition returns to the fort, Ann is reunited with her sister and stands at Ward's side as the United States flag is raised to honor the dead. *Abduction. Ambushes. Apache Indians. Expeditions.*

Rescues. Scouts (Frontier). United States. Army. Cavalry. Alcoholics. Arizona. Battered women. False accusations. Fistfights. Forts. Gunfights. Indians of North America. Infidelity. Officers (Military). Romance. Sisters.

Note: Luke Short's short story was published in novel form, under the same title, in 1950. According to *HR* news items, Sergei Petschnikoff was originally to have been the film's unit manager, Robert Planck was to have been the director of photography and Keogh Gleason was to have been the set decorator. This picture marked the final film of director Sam Wood, who died on 22 Sep 1949. Some location shooting took place in and around Gallup and Lupton, New Mexico.

Box 24 Dec 1949. *DV* 10 Jun 1949, p. 11. *DV* 21 Dec 1949, p. 3, 18. *FD* 29 Dec 1949, p. 6. *HR* 18 Apr 1949, p. 12. *HR* 13 Apr 1949, p. 8. *HR* 26 Apr 1949, p. 9. *HR* 3 May 1949, p. 15. *HR* 3 Jun 1949, p. 8. *HR* 8 Jun 1949, p. 11. *HR* 27 Jun 1949, p. 11. *HR* 14 Jul 1949, p. 8. *HR* 5 Aug 1949, p. 12. *HR* 23 Aug 1949, p. 7. *HR* 21 Dec 1949, p. 4. *MPHPD* 24 Dec 1949, p. 129-30. *NYT* 19 Jan 1950, p. 35. *Var* 21 Dec 1949, p. 8.

AMBUSH AT CIMARRON PASS (Twentieth Century-Fox, Jan 1958) *see* ESCAPE FROM RED ROCK

AMBUSH AT CIMARRON PASS (Native Americans, Apache, Latino)

Regal Films, Inc. *Dist* Twentieth Century-Fox Film Corp. Mar **1958**; Prod: mid-Sep 1957 [©Twentieth Century-Fox Film Corp.; 2 Feb 1958; LP10327]. Sd (RCA Sound Recording); b&w; RegalScope. 8 reels, 6,543 ft. 73 min. PCA cert no. 18791.

Prod Herbert E. Mendelson. *Dir* Jodie Copelan. *Asst dir* Jack McEdward and Leonard J. Shapiro. *Scr* Richard G. Taylor and John K. Butler. *Story* Robert A. Reeds and Robert W. Woods. *Dir of photog* John M. Nickolaus, Jr. *Art dir* John Mansbridge. *Supv ed* Carl L. Pierson. *Mus ed* Harry Eisen. *Ward* Clark Ross. *Mus* Paul Sawtell and Bert Shefter. *Sd* Harold Hanks and Harry M. Leonard. *Makeup* John Chambers. *Hair stylist* Fritzy LaBar. *Asst prod* Jack Eringer. *Scr supv* Joan Eremin. *Prop master* William F. Sittel, Jr. [*Stunts* Joe Yrigoyen and Bob Morgan].

Cast: Scott Brady (Sgt. [*Matthew*] *Blake*), Margia Dean (*Teresa* [*Santos*]), Clint Eastwood [(*Keith Williams*)], Irving Bacon [(*Judge Stanfield*)], Frank Gerstle [(*Sam Prescott*)], Dirk London [(*Johnny Willows*)], Baynes Barron [(*Corbin*)], William Vaughan [(*Henry*)], Ken Mayer [(*Cpl. Schwitzer*)], John Damler [(*Private Zach*)], Keith Richards [(*Private Lasky*)], John Merrick [(*Private Nathan*)], [Desmond Slattery (*Cob*)].

Western. [*Print viewed*]. Sgt. Matt Blake of the Seventh Cavalry, on a detail from Fort Revelry, leads his men through Apache territory during the period of the Indian Wars. As they come through a pass, they find that a group of former Confederate soldiers have them covered with their rifles. The southerners are suspicious because Apaches in Union uniforms have attacked them and taken their herd. Blake relates that Apaches have killed all his men except four and their scout; the Union soldiers have been escorting Corbin, a prisoner under arrest for selling guns to the Apaches, to Fort Waverly and are carrying thirty-six repeating rifles that Corbin planned to sell. Blake and the Confederate leader, Capt. Sam Prescott, decide to join forces despite the disapproval of Keith Williams, who hates Yankees because his mother and sister were killed in the war. When Blake taunts him, Keith is about to shoot in response, but Prescott stops him. At night, Apaches drop a bound woman near the white men, and as the soldiers go to help her, the Indians steal their horses and apprehend Cob, the soldier who was guarding them. The woman, Teresa Santos, a Mexican American, relates that the Apaches burned her rancho, killing her father and brother. After raping and killing her sister, they brought Teresa to the soldiers to give them a message that they can have their horses back in exchange for the rifles. Although Keith wants to trade, Blake refuses, saying they'll never see Cob again if they give up the rifles. Keith pulls out his gun, but Prescott again prevails. After the whites do not respond to the Apaches' offer, two Indians ride up and leave Cob's body; this proves to Blake that whites cannot deal with Indians. Blake suggests they walk, even though it will take six or seven days and they don't have enough water, because he knows the Indians will not attack as long as they keep the rifles. When Blake reprimands Teresa for wearing a low-cut blouse around the men, she bites his hand. As the men head to Cimarron Pass, Keith walks with Teresa. Judge Stanfield, who has been traveling with the southerners, encourages Keith to lead a revolt, as the southerners are carrying sixteen rifles. The judge earlier survived an Indian attack that killed everyone else on his wagon train by cowardly feigning death. After the scout is killed by the Apaches, the judge and Keith plan to take

command when it gets dark, with the help of Teresa and Corbin, whom they will free. At night, Keith is about to shoot Blake when the Indians attack. Blake protects Teresa from danger, and Prescott suffers a head wound. Keith now begins to change his mind about Stanfield's plan, but when Blake orders the group to break camp, Keith stubbornly refuses to leave until he gets his horse back from the Apaches. He hits Blake, who then thrashes him. Teresa comforts Keith, but Prescott angrily rebukes him. When a corporal, upset that his friend has been killed, attacks an Apache who has been riding near the group, the corporal is killed by a flurry of arrows. At a waterhole, the men find a dead man hanging upside down in the water from a tree, put there to scare them into giving up the rifles. When the judge balks at drinking the water, Blake fills his canteen and drinks, demonstrating that the water is safe. Keith, who now has begun to respect Blake and is getting annoyed with the judge, hits him when he is about to shoot three Indians in the distance. At Cimarron Pass, two days from Fort Waverly, Teresa apologizes to Blake for biting his hand and kisses him. When a small raiding party attacks, Blake tells the men to hold their fire, as he knows that the Indians want them to waste ammunition. The judge cuts Corbin loose, but Corbin kills the judge and gets some rifles to take to the Indians. On his way, he is killed with a spear. Blake kills an Indian who tries to get the rifles, and Prescott kills the next. When the Indians ride off, the rifles are retrieved. Aware that the Indians will attack again, Blake decides to steal the horses back, a plan which he does not think the Indians will be prepared to stop. During the raid on the Indian camp, a horse's neigh wakens the Indians, who then battle the soldiers. When Teresa is attacked, Blake rescues her. During the battle, the Indians are driven off and the horses stampede away. Realizing that the rifles are too heavy for the survivors to carry, Blake orders them burned. As they burn, Keith acknowledges that sometimes one has to lose before finally winning, and soon they make it to the fort. *Apache Indians. Mexican Americans. Southerners. United States–History–Indian campaigns. United States. Army. Cavalry. Bigotry. Confederate States of America. Army. Gunrunners. Horse thieves. Judges. Murder. Officers (Military). Prisoners. Rifles.*

Note: According to reviews, this was Jodie Copelan's first film as director. A film of the same name was announced in Mar 1955 as the first film of Tower Productions, with Arthur Hiller as director, but there is no indication that the Tower project was related to this film.

Box 24 Feb 1958. *DV* 12 Feb 1958, p. 3. *Exh* 19 Feb 1958, p. 4438. *FD* 27 Feb 1958, p. 6. *Har* 22 Feb 1958, pp. 30-31. *HR* 10 Mar 1955. *HR* 6 Sep 1957, p. 15. *HR* 13 Sep 1957, p. 17. *HR* 12 Feb 1958, p. 3. *MPHPD* 8 Mar 1958, p. 749. *Var* 19 Feb 1958, p. 6.

AMBUSH AT TOMAHAWK GAP (Native Americans, Apache, Navajo)

Columbia Pictures Corp. *Dist* Columbia Pictures Corp. May **1953**; Prod: 8 Jul–23 Jul 1952 [©Columbia Pictures Corp.; 6 Apr 1953; LP2481]. Sd (Western Electric Recording); col (Technicolor). 6,570 ft. 73 min. PCA cert no. 16105.

Prod Wallace MacDonald. *Dir* Fred F. Sears. *Asst dir* James Nicholson. *Story and scr* David Lang. *Dir of photog* Henry Freulich. *Technicolor color consultant* Francis Cugat. *Art dir* Walter Holscher. *Film ed* Aaron Stell. *Set dec* Louis Diage. *Mus dir* Ross DiMaggio. *Sd eng* George Cooper. [*Pub dir* George Lait].

Cast: JOHN HODIAK [(*McCord*)], JOHN DEREK [(*Kid*)], DAVID BRIAN [(*Egan*)], MARIA ELENA MARQUES [(*Indian girl*)], Ray Teal [(*Doc*)], John Qualen [(*Jonas P. Travis*)], Otto Hulett [(*Stranton*)], Percy Helton [(*Marlowe*)], Trevor Bardette [(*Sheriff*)], [Steve Clark (*Driver*)], [Harry Cording (*Blacksmith*)], [John War Eagle (*Apache chief*)], [Gail Robinson].

Western. [*Print viewed*]. Four outlaws—McCord, Kid, Egan and Doc—are released from the Yuma Territorial Prison and dropped off in the town of Twin Forks, Arizona. The outlaws immediately go into the saloon, where McCord, who was framed by the other three, gets into a fight with Kid. The sheriff throws Egan, Kid and Doc out of town after they knock McCord out, and when he reawakens, the bartender demands money for damages. McCord asks for buyers for his fancy Mexican saddle, and Stranton, a stranger, takes him up on the offer, paying off the bartender and giving McCord a horse and gun in exchange. McCord recognizes the horse's saddle as having belonged to Egan's brother Frank, but Stranton claims to have won it in a card game the night Frank was killed. McCord rides out of town and catches up with his cohorts, who are in the midst of a gun battle with Apache Indians. On McCord's suggestion, they all pretend that they have been killed, then attack and kill the Apaches as they come

for their scalps. McCord, who was framed after Egan, Frank, Doc and Kid robbed a stagecoach carrying cavalry payroll money, then holds his prisoners at gunpoint and delivers the news about Egan's brother. McCord demands $1,800 in reparations for the ranch wages he lost by going to prison in Frank's place. The four outlaws ride to Tomahawk Gap, where they had planned to meet Frank and recover the stolen money. As they get underway, they notice an Apache in the underbrush and prepare for an ambush. However, the Indian is a woman, who shoots Kid in self-defense when he attacks her. Kid demands that she be killed, but Egan takes her hostage. That night when they make camp, Kid becomes delirious because of his wound, and is tended to by the Indian woman, while Doc, a sympathetic older man, urges Kid to go straight and discover that it has become a ghost town. Doc insists on cutting Kid's arm open to remove the bullet. The next morning, Egan attacks the Indian woman by the well, but he is knocked out by Jonas P. Travis, the sole resident of Tomahawk Gap, who takes care of the cemetery, and is surprised to see a Navajo woman in Apache territory. Travis is distraught when the outlaws dig up a grave in which they had buried the stolen strongbox. However, they discover the strongbox is empty, prompting Kid to recall how they came to bury it: Frank has the strongbox when the outlaws split up after the robbery, agreeing to meet in Tomahawk Gap. Frank gets to town before anyone else, and as a posse is close behind, gives Kid the strongbox and suggests they meet in the graveyard and bury the money there. Frank does not show up until after they have buried the strongbox, and this is the last time they see him. The outlaws now realize that Frank must have emptied the strongbox before he gave it to them, and they proceed to look for the money by tearing up the town board by board. Stranton, a government agent, unexpectedly shows up at Tomahawk Gap and takes the gang hostage. His partner, Marlowe, is making contact at a nearby fort, and they intend to return the money to the Army. The Indian woman, who has already warned the outlaws about Apache smoke signals rising from the mountain ridges, knocks Stranton out with a blow to the head, and he and Jonas are tied up together. While the outlaws continue their destructive search, Stranton manages to get near a window and flash a signal with a piece of mirror, hoping it will be seen by a patrol. The Indian woman tries to warn Kid, but Egan claims it was she who sent the signal and attacks her. Kid starts to come to her defense, but the Apaches launch an attack and kill Egan as they invade the town. Although Kid has fallen in love with the Indian woman, he believes that she signaled the Apaches and sends her away. Doc is then killed by an Apache while trying to save Kid. In the saloon, Stranton admits to having signaled with the mirror and tells Kid that the woman is not an Apache, but was the Apaches' prisoner when she was kidnapped by the outlaws. After Jonas runs out of the saloon to protect his graveyard and is killed, Stranton is brutally murdered when Apaches drop through the ceiling of the saloon. During a lull in the fighting, McCord conceives of a plan to drop a keg of gunpowder into the gully in which the Apaches have gathered to nurse their wounded and ignite the powder with flaming arrows. McCord, Kid and the Indian woman leave the saloon to get the gunpowder, but McCord is stabbed by an Apache. Kid shoots McCord's assailant, and the woman shoots another attacker. McCord stumbles over to the gully with the keg and is immediately assaulted by the Indians. The gunpowder ignites, and McCord is killed in the explosion along with the Apaches. Later, Kid and the woman leave the ghost town together, headed for Sonora, and fail to notice the stolen money fluttering in the wind. *Ambushes. Apache Indians. Ex-convicts. Ghost towns. Kidnapping. Money. Aged men. Arizona. Attempted rape. Brothers. Caretakers. Cemeteries. Explosions. Fistfights. Frame-ups. Government agents. Gun powder. Gunfights. Gunshot wounds. Navajo Indians. Saloons. Wind storms.*

Note: Reviews mistakenly mention that the film includes an amputation, however, the only operation scene involves "Doc" removing a bullet from "Kid's" arm, which is left intact.

Box 2 May 1953. *DV* 21 Apr 1953, p. 3. *Exb* 6 May 1953, p. 3513. *Har* 25 Apr 1953, p. 66. *HR* 21 Apr 1953, p. 3. *MPHPD* 9 May 1953, p. 1829. *Var* 6 May 1953, p. 6.

AMEN CORNER *see* **THE BOND BETWEEN**

AMERICA *see* **AN AMERICAN ROMANCE**

AMERICA WAS RIGHT (German Americans)
Dist Hiram Abrams? 1919?. Si; b&w. 6 reels.

World War I, Drama. August Holtz, a wealthy German-American baker, contributes money to Germany in the early days of World War I and refuses to let his son George fight for the Allies. While George works on a new explosive for America, his sister Minna becomes a nurse for the Allies, and his friend Ned, Minna's sweetheart, joins the Canadian army. Ned is killed and Minna raped by German soldiers, and Ned's sister Jean joins the American Secret Service to avenge Ned's death. Meanwhile, German agents in America, failing to buy George's explosives formula, steal some of the explosives and blow up a factory. Jean discovers that George's explosives were used for the job, and George, believing that his father gave the explosives to the Germans, leaves home and joins the Marines. When Minna returns home with her illegitimate child, Holtz finally embraces the Allied cause and is reunited with George before the boy marches to war. *Explosives. Family relationships. German Americans. Germany. Army. Transformation. World War I. Bakers and bakeries. Canada. Army. Foreign agents. Illegitimacy. Nurses. Rape. Revenge. Secret Service. United States. Marine Corps. War victims.*

Note: It is unclear whether this film was ever released to theaters under this or any other title. Information about the film comes from the Community Motion Picture Bureau's records, which state that the film's battle scenes were badly edited from earlier footage.

THE AMERICAN *see* **THE MAN WHO DARED: AN IMAGINATIVE BIOGRAPHY**

AMERICAN EMPIRE (Creoles)
Harry Sherman Productions, Inc.; Paramount Pictures, Inc. *Dist* United Artists Productions, Inc. 11 Dec 1942; Prod: 21 Nov—late Dec 1941 [©United Artists Productions, Inc.; 30 Dec 1942; LP11767]. Sd (Western Electric Wide Range System); b&w. 8 reels, 7,359 ft. 81 min. Passed by the National Board of Review. PCA cert no. 8112.

Prod Harry Sherman and [Dick Dickson]. *Assoc prod* Lewis J. Rachmil. *Dir* William McGann. [*Asst dir* Glenn Cook]. [*Dir of fire barricade scene* B. Reeves Eason]. *Scr* J. Robert Bren, Gladys Atwater and Ben Grauman Kohn. *Orig story* J. Robert Bren and Gladys Atwater. *Dir of photog* Russell Harlan. [*2d unit cam* Archie Stout]. *Art dir* Ralph Berger. [*Artist for wave effects on lake* John Powers]. *Supv ed* Sherman A. Rose. *Ed* Carrol Lewis. *Set dec* Emile Kuri. *Ward* Earl Moser. *Mus dir* Irvin Talbot. *Mus score* Gerard Carbonara. *Sd* William Wilmarth. *Sd rec* General Service Studios. [*Stand-in for Leo Carrillo* Earl Spainard].

Song(s): "Little Pal," music and lyrics by Lew Pollack.

Cast: Richard Dix (*Dan Taylor*), Leo Carrillo (*Dominique Beauchard*), Preston Foster (*Paxton Bryce*), Frances Gifford (*Abby Taylor*), Robert H. Barrat (*Crowder*), Jack La Rue (*Pierre*), Guinn Williams (*Sailaway*), Cliff Edwards (*Runty*), Merrill Guy Rodin (*Paxton Bryce, Jr.*), Chris Pin Martin (*Augustin*), Richard Webb (*Crane*), William Farnum (*Louisiana judge*), Etta McDaniel (*Willa May*), Hal Taliaferro (*Malone*), [Jean Ann Rose Guthrie], [Earl Spainard], [Jim Ferrara], [Jack Trent].

Historical, Western. [*Print viewed*]. At the close of the Civil War, business partners Dan Taylor and Paxton Bryce work as riverboat captains, but Paxton yearns to earn more money. When the ferry accidentally runs aground, Creole cattle rustler Dominique Beauchard herds his cattle into the river and makes a deal with Dan and Paxton to transport his cattle on the ferry. Dan and Paxton throw Beauchard overboard and keep his cattle when they learn that he has no intention of paying the fare. Paxton convinces Dan to sell the ferry and cattle, buy land with the proceeds and take up Beauchard's business of rounding up loose cattle, which have strayed from their home ranges during the confusion of the war. Eventually, Paxton falls in love with and marries Dan's sister Abigail, and after a year of hard work, the three have accumulated vast ranch lands. They are still plagued by Beauchard, however, who rustles their herds because he resents the fact that they have taken his business. Shortly after a successful cattle drive, Dan has a run-in with Beauchard and believes that he has killed him. Beauchard's men rescue him, however, and he lays low while he plans his revenge. Seven years pass and Paxton and Abby's son Junior grows up carefree under the influence of Paxton's former riverboat mates, Sailaway and Runty, who now work as ranch hands. Paxton, having successfully built his own empire in Texas, has become obsessed with money and blames neighboring ranchers for the slow disappearance of 3,000 head of cattle. He insists on posting

"no trespassing" signs to prevent the ranchers from herding their cattle across his land, and refuses to sell any property to a proposed railroad which would improve local business. When neighboring rancher Crowder forces his herd onto Paxton property, Paxton, Jr. tries to defend his father's land and is killed in a stampede. Paxton refuses to accept responsibility for creating the situation which killed his son, so a disgusted Dan dissolves their partnership. Even Abby has grown disillusioned with her husband and plans to leave with Dan. Paxton has Beauchard arrested when he learns that he is responsible for his disappearing cattle. Although Beauchard is found guilty of theft, among other offenses, he escapes from jail, and he and his gang then ransack the town. The ranchers, meanwhile, gather forces to lynch Paxton because the barbed wire, which he bought to protect his land, will mutilate their cattle. Dan returns to the ranch to help Paxton, and when Abby comes to warn them of Beauchard's treachery, she appeals to Paxton to help his neighbors defend themselves against Beauchard. Dan, Paxton and the ranch hands set a firetrap with barbed wire at Bottleneck Pass, through which Beauchard and his men are headed, while Runty tries to forestall the angry ranchers. Beauchard's gang is trapped in the pass and a gunfight ensues amid the flames. The ranchers hear the gunfire and arrive to help Paxton and Dan. Beauchard eventually breaks through the barricades and shoots Paxton, who then kills the rustler. Peace is restored when Paxton recovers from his gunshot wound and compromises with Crowder by allowing the railroad on his land, in exchange for building fences with plenty of gates that allow free passage. *Greed. Land barons. Ranchers. Revenge. Rustlers. United States–History–Reconstruction, 1865-1898. Accidental death. Children. Creoles. Gunfights. Land sales. Marriage. Moral reformation. Partnership. Railroads. Ranchhands. River boats. Texas.*

Note: According to a *HR* news item, David Buttolph collaborated on the music score with Gerard Carbonara, and Adrian Scott contributed to the screenplay, but their contributions to the final film have not been confirmed. A *HR* news item also reported that Montie Montana, Jr. was tested for a role, and that Frances Farmer was considered for the female lead. However, the reference to Frances Farmer was probably a mistaken reference to Frances Gifford, who stars in the film. Some scenes were filmed on location in Kernville, CA. In 1942, Paramount sold the distribution rights to this film as part of a package deal with United Artists.

Box 19 Dec 1942. *DV* 26 Dec 1941. *DV* 4 Dec 1942, p. 3. *FD* 11 Dec 1942, p. 4. *HR* 2 Nov 1941. *HR* 10 Nov 1941, p. 2. *HR* 12 Nov 1941, p. 2, 3. *HR* 9 Dec 1941, p. 2. *HR* 20 Feb 1942, p. 4. *HR* 4 Dec 1942, p. 11. *MPHPD* 12 Dec 1942, p. 1053. *NYT* 14 Jan 1943, p. 25. *Paramount News* 17 Aug 1942. *Var* 9 Dec 1942.

AMERICAN FAMILY see DAUGHTERS COURAGEOUS

AN AMERICAN GENTLEMAN (Gypsies)

Liberty Motion Picture Co. *Dist* State Rights. 15 Sep **1915**. Si; b&w. 5 reels.

Dir John Gorman.

Source: Based on the play *An American Gentleman* by William Bonelli (New York, 27 Mar 1900).

Cast: William Bonelli (*George Hathaway*), Grace Lowell (*Helen Davis, later known as Corina*), Charles Graham (*Zeppo, the gypsy chief*), Virginia Fairfax (*Zara, the old gypsy queen*), Douglas Sibole (*A villain*), Martha Illington (*A villainess*), Wilbur Hudson, George W. Middleton.

Adventure. Four-year-old Helen Davis is run down by a reckless driver who carries her limp body into the woods. A band of gypsies find her and attempt to return her to her parents, but they are driven from the Davis estate. Fourteen years later, after having traveled across the world, the child, now named Corina, and the gypsies return to her childhood home. Accused of stealing a horse, the gypsies are forced by an unscrupulous lawyer to steal a map detailing the location of the buried fortune belonging to an elderly eccentric named Hathaway. While the gypsies rob the house, Hathaway is murdered. George Hathaway, who has been in Europe, undergoes a series of tribulations while attempting to avenge his father's death and recover the family fortune. During his exploits, he falls in love with Corina, who is also loved by Zeppo, the gypsy chief. After the gypsy leaders plunge to their deaths from a broken bridge, George restores Corina to her father, who consents to her marriage. *Children. Gypsies. Impersonation and imposture. Revenge. Automobile accidents. Buried treasure. Falls from heights. Horse thieves. Maps. Murder. Reunions. Robbery.*

Note: This was the first release of the Liberty Motion Picture Co., which also developed and printed film for the open market. William Bonelli toured North America in this play for eight years.

MPN 25 Sep 1915, p. 60. *MPN* 9 Oct 1915, p. 87. *MPW* 25 Sep 1915, p. 2254.

AMERICAN MATCHMAKER see AMERICANER SCHADCHEN

THE AMERICAN MIRACLE see AN AMERICAN ROMANCE

AN AMERICAN ROMANCE (Czech Americans, Irish Americans)

Metro-Goldwyn-Mayer Corp.; controlled by Loew's Inc.; King Vidor's Production. *Dist* Loew's Inc. **1944**; World premiere in Cincinnati, OH: 11 Oct 1944; New York opening: 23 Nov 1944; Los Angeles opening: 14 Dec 1944; Prod: 1 Apr–mid-Aug 1943; addl scenes mid-Oct–late Oct 1943; 27 Nov 1943 [©Loew's Inc.; 6 Jul 1944; LP169]. Sd (Western Electric Sound System); col (Technicolor). 16 reels, 13,545 ft. 150-151 min. Passed by the National Board of Review. PCA cert no. 9740.

Prod King Vidor. *Dir* King Vidor. [*Asst dir* Bert Spurlin and Jack MacKenzie]. [*2d unit dir* Al Kelley]. [*2d unit asst dir* Al Jennings]. *Scr* Herbert Dalmas and William Ludwig. *Based upon a story by* King Vidor. *Dir of photog* Harold Rosson. [*Cam op* Bob Martin]. [*2d unit dir of photog* Charles Boyle]. [*Stills* James Minette]. *Spec eff* Arnold Gillespie. *Technicolor color dir* Natalie Kalmus. *Assoc* Henri Jaffa. [*Technicolor tech* Henry Inius]. [*Technicolor maintenance* Adolph Crautsh]. *Art dir* Cedric Gibbons. *Assoc* Urie McCleary and [Malcolm Brown]. *Film ed* Conrad A. Nervig. *Set dec* Edwin B. Willis. *Assoc* Richard Pefferle. [*Props* Hal Sausser, Ray O'Brien and Walter Brown]. *Cost supv* Irene. [*Ward* William Beatty]. *Mus score* Louis Gruenberg. [*Cond* Nathaniel Shilkret]. *Rec dir* Douglas Shearer. [*Sd mixer* Ted Raymond]. [*Sd rec* John Dullan]. *Makeup created by* Jack Dawn. [*Makeup* Ben Libizer]. [*Unit mgr* Walter Strohm]. [*Scr clerk* Russ Haverick]. [*Stage man* Tom Edwards]. [*Pub* Greg Dickson and Edward Lawrence]. [*Electrician* A. W. Brown, John Cooney, Bill Linahan, James Carmichael, Tolliver Scheffield, Frank Leonetti, William Keily and Alvis Campbell]. [*Grip* Lloyd Isabel, Ford Clark, Harold Saunders and Wally Whittington]. [*Painter* John Venclik]. [*Cashier* Byron Ellerbrock]. [*Stand-in for Brian Donlevy* Byron Fitzpatrick].

Song(s): "Lo! Hear the Gentle Lark," words by William Shakespeare, music by Sir Henry Rowley Bishop.

Cast: Brian Donlevy (*Steve Dangos [previously known as Stefan Dangosbiblichek]*), Ann Richards (*Anna [O'Rourke Dangos]*), Walter Abel (*Howard Clinton*), John Qualen (*Anton Dubschek*), Horace McNally (*Teddy [Roosevelt] Dangos*), Mary McLeod (*Tina Dangos*), Bob Lowell (*George [Washington] Dangos*), [Fred Brady (*Abraham Lincoln Dangos*)], [Billy Lechner (*Joe Chandler, Jr.*)], [Jerry Shane (*Bob Chandler*)], [Harold Landon (*Joe*)], [J. M. Kerrigan (*Charlie O'Rourke*)], [Erville Alderson (*Olsen*)], [Robert Middlemass (*Carson Jennings*)], [Howard Freeman (*Humphries*)], [Roy Gordon (*MacLane*)], [Bobby Rich (*George Washington Dangos, age 14*)], [Richard Hall (*George Washington Dangos, age 5*)], [Bobby Winkler (*Thomas Jefferson Dangos, age 14*)], [Jackie "Butch" Jenkins (*Thomas Jefferson Dangos, age 6*)], [Andrew Warrocks (*Thomas Jefferson Dangos, age 10*)], [Carol Combs (*Tina Dangos, age 6*)], [Richard Hirsch (*Teddy Roosevelt Dangos, age 2*)], [Charles Bates (*Teddy Roosevelt Dangos, age 8*)], [Jimmy Griffin (*Teddy Roosevelt Dangos, age 15*)], [Bobby Larsen (*Abraham Lincoln Dangos, age 8*)], [Drew Roddy (*Abraham Lincoln Dangos, age 11*)], [Bryn Davis (*Danish mother*)], [Preston Peterson (*Danish father*)], [Axel Anderson, Molio Sheron (*Immigrants*)], [Edward Hearn (*Chief customs man*)], [Art Berry, Sr. (*Customs man*)], [D. H. Turner (*Customs guard*)], [Alex Davidoff, Rudolph Myzet (*Interpreters*)], [Michael Visaroff (*Yasha*)], [Wacklaw Reckwart (*Polish miner*)], [Ray Teal (*Paymaster*)], [Kay Medford (*Yulka*)], [Charles Wagenheim (*Merchant*)], [Rita Gould (*Merchant's wife*)], [Robert Emmet O'Connor (*Irish foreman*)], [Art Belasco (*Drowsy miner*)], [Ed O'Neill (*Brakeman*)], [Bill Borzage (*Miner with accordion*)], [Ed Hennerty (*Man with flag*)], [Dick Wessel (*Lumberjack*)], [George Meader (*Politician*)], [Dell Henderson (*Timothy Mulveen*)], [Leon Warwick (*Black singer*)], [Marty Faust (*Ship's officer*)], [Howard Mitchell (*Gateman*)], [John Sheehan (*Irish workman*)], [George Bunny, William Haade, Mitchell Lewis, Nolan Leary (*Workmen*)], [Frank Faylen (*Bartender*)], [Barbara Pepper (*Streetwalker*)], [Richard Ryen (*Papa Hartzler*)], [Greta Meyer (*Mama Hartzler*)], [Leon Belasco (*Cigar clerk*)], [Ilka Gruning (*Mrs. Vronsky*)], [June Pickrell (*McGregor's secretary*)], [Charles Irwin (*McGregor*)], [Jerry O'Neil (*Doctor*)], [Paul Porcasi (*Prof. Cantaloni*)], [Jack George (*Photographer*)], [Anna Marie Biggs (*Girl soprano*)], [Byron Foulger (*School principal*)], [Joseph Crehan (*Judge*)], [Tom Martin

(*Chauffeur*)], [Eddie Waller (*Constable*)], [Ben Hall (*Abner*)], [Jack Mulhall (*Customer*)], [Ernie Adams (*Man and dog act*)], [Dick Elliott (*Fat man*)], [William Tannen (*Test driver*)], [Norman Nesbit (*Announcer*)], [Phyllis Kennedy (*Receptionist*)], [Johnny Walsh (*Boy*)], [Ethan Laidlaw, Harry Semels, Larry Grenier, George Magrill, John Merton, Duke York (*Steel workers*)], [Noreen Roth, Billy Engle (*Vaudeville act*)], [John Bohn, Charles Regan (*Stage hands*)], [Bob Thom (*Stage manager*)], [Ed Mortimer, Bert Howard, James Carlisle (*Corporation executives*)], [Snub Pollard (*Bearded messenger*)], [Paul Gordon (*Trick bicyclist*)], [George Sherwood (*Auto plant guard*)], [Emmet Vogan (*Committee chairman*)], [Elliott Sullivan, Harry Cording, Jimmie Dodd, Ivan Miller, Lee Phelps, Earle Hodgins (*Workmen in meeting*)], [Pat O'Malley, Tom Chatterton (*Board of Directors members*)].

Domestic, Historical, Drama. [*Print viewed*]. In 1898, immediately after disembarking at New York's Ellis Island, Czech-born Stefan Dangosbiblichek is marked for deportation because he doesn't have enough money to pay the entrance fee. When he realizes that he is about to be shipped back, Steve starts to protest loudly in Czech and convinces a sympathetic interpreter to sign his entrance papers. The nearly penniless Steve then walks from New York to the Mesabi Range in northeast Minnesota, where his cousin, Anton Dubschek, works in an iron ore mine. After the cousins happily reunite, Anton gets Steve a job as a miner and gives him tips on how to act and talk like an American. Now known as Steve Dangos, the ambitious immigrant then asks Anna O'Rourke, the local schoolteacher, to teach him how to read so that he can learn about the iron and steel industry. Steve and Anna soon fall in love, and during the warm months, while the miners dig ore above ground, Steve teaches himself how to operate a steam shovel. Later, when Steve offers to work indefinitely in the Mesabi mines to be near her, Anna reminds him of his ambitions and encourages him to seek his fortune elsewhere. The following autumn, Steve leaves Mesabi for Chicago and tricks his way into a job at a steel mill. Although he is quickly promoted to section foreman, Steve misses Anna and is depressed. He writes to her, asking her to come to Chicago, and to his delight, she appears on the next boat. Once married, Steve and Anna move into a modest but attractive house that Steve has bought, and soon become the parents of a baby girl named Tina. Over the next several years, Steve receives many promotions at the steel mill, and his family expands to include four sons—George Washington, Thomas Jefferson, Abraham Lincoln and Theodore Roosevelt Dangos. In 1917, the Dangos family attends George's high school graduation and proudly listen as he delivers a moving valedictorian speech. Soon after, Tina prepares to marry her childhood sweetheart, and George announces to Steve that he is enlisting in the Army. Before leaving, George makes his father promise he will take the U.S. citizenship test during his absence. On the day of the test, Steve and Anna are notified of George's death, and although grief-stricken, Steve goes through with the test and earns his citizenship. Later, Howard Clinton, one of George's teachers, drops by the Dangos house to give Steve some poems that George had written for his class. Touched by the gesture, Steve, who has dismantled and reassembled the family car in an attempt to improve it, offers to take Howard for a ride. Steve's "adjustments" to the car enable it to go eighty miles an hour, and the two are arrested for speeding. While in jail, Howard, who is also a car "buff," suggests that he and Steve race the car at Indianapolis. Although they crash during the race, their experience gives them the idea to start their own auto company and build safer, faster cars. Anna accepts the move to Detroit without complaint, and the Danton Auto Works is soon opened with Steve and Howard's savings. Using his knowledge of mechanics and steel production, Steve then undertakes to design a car with a steel top and a suspension-mounted engine. After a rough prototype is completed, Steve demonstrates the car to a representative of a large manufacturing company, who then presents the design to the company's board of directors. The board offers to buy the innovative design, but declare that the company will not put the car into production until forced to do so by the competition. Disgusted by the board's attitude, Steve refuses to sell the design, then convinces his devoted staff to build a polished prototype for an upcoming New York auto show in exchange for a partnership in the company. At that moment, Anton shows up at the factory and offers to invest his entire savings in the project. The car is the hit of the auto show, and Howard gleefully informs Steve that

various investors have offered five million dollars to manufacture it. Sometime later, college-educated Teddy, who wants to learn the auto industry from "the ground up," takes a low-level job at the company. Although thrilled to have his youngest at Danton, Steve becomes distressed when Teddy gets involved in a campaign to organize the workers. Maintaining that he has always taken good care of his employees, Steve is unsympathetic when they go on strike. During a meeting between a workers' group and Danton's board of directors, Teddy, Anton and Howard all vote to allow the workers to organize, and the defeated Steve condemns them as traitors. Anna then suggests that Steve retire and travel, and the couple eventually settles in California. Just after the bombing of Pearl Harbor, Steve, who has become bored and listless, learns that the government has asked Danton to build airplanes in San Diego. Putting aside his pride, Steve reconciles with Teddy, Howard and Anton, and together they figure out ways to increase Danton's productivity and turn out thousands of airplanes for the war effort. *Ambition. Family relationships. Immigrants. Marriage. Patriotism. United States–History–Social life and customs. Aircraft industry. Assimilation (Sociology). Automobile industry and trade. Automobile racing. Chicago (IL). Citizenship. Cousins. Czechoslovakian Americans. Detroit (MI). Employer-employee relations. English language. Fourth of July. Graduations. Grief. Indianapolis (IN). Innovations. Iron mines. Meetings. Mesabi Range (MN). Miners. New York City. New York City–Ellis Island. Partnership. Pledges. Promotions. Retirement. San Diego (CA). Schoolteachers. Speeches. Steel. Steel mills. Strikes and lockouts. Trade unions. Traffic violations. Translators. World War I. World War II.*

Note: The working titles of this film were *America, American Miracle, The Magic Land, This Is America* and *An American Story*. According to modern sources, *Man of Tomorrow* was also a working title. The character of "Teddy Dangos," as played by Horace McNally, provides intermittent offscreen narration throughout the film. The picture also includes several documentary sequences depicting the manufacture of steel, cars and planes. According to a late Oct 1944 *HR* news item, the film was cut from 151 to 122 minutes after exhibitors complained about its length. It is possible that some of the above-listed actors were cut out for the shortened version. According to records in the M-G-M Music Collection, the hymn "Lord Please Send Down Your Love" was performed in the film by black singer Leon Warrick. Warrick is also listed in the CBCS, but the song was not heard in the viewed print and was apparently cut for the shortened version. (Modern sources note that director-producer King Vidor wrote the song's lyrics.)

In his autobiography, Vidor related that he conceived of *An American Romance*, a picture that took him three years to complete, as the final part of his self-proclaimed "war, wheat, and steel" trilogy. "War" was represented by Vidor's 1925 epic *The Big Parade* (see *AFI Catalog of Feature Films, 1921-30*; F2.0405), and "wheat" by the 1934 independent production *Our Daily Bread* (see below). Vidor adds that at the time of the film's inception, he was considering joining the Army Air Corps motion-picture division, but finally concluded that making *An American Romance*, with its "arsenal-of-democracy" theme, would be the most effective way to serve his country.

In a modern interview, Vidor stated that he got the film's basic story line from a series of stories and recollections by Yugoslavian-born Louis Adamic, who had worked in the Minnesota iron ore mines around the turn-of-the-century. Vidor was also influenced by the lives of American industrialists Andrew Carnegie, Charles Steinmetz, William Knudsen and Walter Chrysler, according to his autobiography. According to a modern source, in 1941, Vidor wrote a three-page outline for the film and sent it to Adamic, who then wrote the first few sequences of the picture. *HR* announced in Mar 1942 that Adamic was collaborating on the script with Vidor. Adamic's contribution to the completed film, if any, has not been confirmed, however. In the modern interview, Vidor stated that he used the town of Hibbing, MN, as the model for his screen town, although Hibbing was not specifically mentioned in the film. Modern sources note that from Jul 1941 to Apr 1942, many writers, including Norman Foster, John Fante, James Hill, Tom Treanor, Wessel Smitter, Ross B. Wills and Renata Oppenheimer, worked on drafts of the film's treatment. Smitter, Gordon Kahn, Frances Marion and Vincent Lawrence made minor contributions to the screenplay, which Vidor initially co-wrote with credited scenarist Herbert Dalmas. In Apr 1943, credited writer William Ludwig worked on a full rewrite of the script with Dalmas and Vidor. Robert Andrews contributed dialogue to the added scenes, which were shot in Nov 1943, according to modern sources.

According to the modern interview, Vidor pitched the story of *An American Romance* directly to M-G-M vice-president and general manager Louis B. Mayer, who in turn told the story to M-G-M president Nicholas Schenck, who then gave the final go-ahead. Spencer Tracy was Vidor's first choice to play "Steve Dangos" and was announced as the film's star in Aug 1942. In his autobiography, Vidor comments that Tracy symbolized "all that the character of Stephan Danahos [sic] stood for." Because of scheduling conflicts, Vidor was forced to replace Tracy with Brian Donlevy. Vidor noted in the modern interview that he had hoped to cast Ingrid Bergman as Steve's wife and Joseph Cotten as "Howard Clinton," but both actors had previous commitments. *HR* reported in early 1943 that Ann Sothern and Frances Gifford were also under consideration for the female lead, and Philip Dorn, John Hodiak and John Craven were tested for top roles, but not cast. After a screen test, Vidor was

persuaded to cast Australian newcomer Ann Richards, who reportedly came to America on the last boat to leave Australia after Pearl Harbor, as "Anna." According to *HR*, Richards was not cast until after principal photography had begun in Apr 1943. *HR* news items add Richard Crane, Richard Derr and Edmond Breon to the cast, but their participation in the final film has not been confirmed. In addition, *HR* notes that Donlevy's six-week-old daughter Judith Ann was cast in the role of baby "Tina."

In the modern interview, Vidor stated that certain aspects of the film's visuals were inspired by the paintings of American artist Charles Burchfield. Vidor claimed that he designed the film's color scheme to "follow the same progressive uplifting refinement" as its story line. A *HR* news item noted that paintings and sketches used in the film were created by the Society of Illustrations and were featured in the 2 Oct 1944 issue of *Life* magazine. According to Vidor's autobiography, miniatures were first used for the final bomber assembly line sequence. Upon viewing the completed scenes, however, Vidor declared that they looked "unreal in contrast to the rest of the film" and arranged to reshoot "in an honest-to-goodness factory, using the actual detailed construction of a Flying Fortress."

According to Records of the War Department, Public Relations Division, dated 28 Sep 1942, Vidor requested and received permission to shoot footage at many different mines and factories in the Midwest, including the Ull-Rust mine in Hibbing, MN, the Duluth dock in Duluth, MN, and the Ford River A & O Rouge Plant in Dearborn, MI. 16mm background footage was shot at a blast furnace in Irontown, UT, according to the War Department records. *HR* notes that second unit atmospheric and background shots were taken at Lake Superior, MI. Scenes were also shot at two U.S. Steel Corporation subsidiaries—the Carnegie Illinois Steel Works in Chicago and the Indiana Steel Plant in Gary—as well as at the Chrysler auto factory in Detroit, the Douglas aircraft factory in Long Beach, CA, and the Consolidated plant in San Diego, CA. According to a *HR* news item, a steel mill in Hammond, IN, was also used as a location. The War Department records add that footage from an Army Air Force feature entitled *Memphis Belle* was to be used in the picture. According to an *IP* article about the film, other scenes were shot in the Mesabi Range, MN. In the modern interview, Vidor recalled that some exteriors were shot in Wilmington, CA, near Los Angeles, and that for those scenes, actor John Qualen doubled for Donlevy. Vidor also noted that footage was taken during the Indianapolis 500 car race and was used as background in the racing scene. War Department Records from Sep 1942 include a long list of scheduled second-unit crew members, including director Gunther V. Fritsch, but their participation in the completed film has not been confirmed.

Prior to the film's 11 Oct 1944 world premiere in Cincinnati, Vidor, Donlevy, Richards, Walter Abel and Horace McNally dedicated *An American Romance* airplane in Dayton, OH, and participated in ten days of personal appearances and parades. In his autobiography, Vidor noted that after its Cincinnati premiere, M-G-M's New York office ordered that thirty minutes be cut from the film. Although Vidor expected the time to be taken out of the documentary sections, which he himself felt were too long, most of the cut footage came out of the dramatic scenes because the documentary sequences were already married to the music track. Modern sources and the modern interview note that the edited footage included a scene at the Indianapolis Speedway and a scene depicting a confrontation between Steve and his workers. Vidor recalled in the modern interview that head M-G-M editor Margaret Booth made the final edits. Despite some favorable reviews, the film, which cost almost three million dollars to make, did not do well at the box office. Displeasure over the studio's handling of *An American Romance* eventually led to Vidor's departure from M-G-M, the studio at which he had worked for twenty years, according to the modern interview. In Mar 1943, *HR* noted that the Museum of Modern Art in New York was using the film's production as a subject for an exhibit about the making of a motion picture. Scripts, research material, shooting schedules and inter-office memos were among the materials presented.

Box 1 Jul 1944. *FD* 3 Jun 1944. *HCN* 15 Dec 1944. *HR* 9 Mar 1942, p. 3. *HR* 26 May 1942, p. 2. *HR* 3 Aug 1942, p. 1. *HR* 28 Aug 1942, p. 2. *HR* 28 Sep 1942, p. 7. *HR* 6 Oct 1942, p. 3. *HR* 29 Oct 1942, p. 2. *HR* 18 Nov 1942, p. 7. *HR* 15 Dec 1942, p. 1. *HR* 28 Jan 1943, p. 9. *HR* 1 Feb 1943, p. 2. *HR* 25 Feb 1943, p. 2. *HR* 3 Mar 1943, p. 3. *HR* 19 Mar 1943, p. 2. *HR* 30 Mar 1943, p. 7. *HR* 1 Apr 1943, p. 1. *HR* 2 Apr 1943, p. 12. *HR* 9 Apr 1943, p. 7. *HR* 12 Apr 1943, p. 7. *HR* 23 Apr 1943, p. 1. *HR* 26 Apr 1943, p. 10. *HR* 6 May 1943, p. 1. *HR* 18 May 1943, p. 8. *HR* 28 May 1943, p. 5. *HR* 11 Jun 1943, p. 7. *HR* 28 Jun 1943, p. 9. *HR* 13 Aug 1943, p. 14. *HR* 15 Oct 1943, p. 5. *HR* 25 Oct 1943, p. 3. *HR* 16 Nov 1943, p. 4. *HR* 23 Nov 1943, p. 6. *HR* 7 Mar 1944, p. 6. *HR* 27 Apr 1944, p. 4. *HR* 4 May 1944, p. 4. *HR* 27 Jun 1944, p. 3. *HR* 21 Sep 1944, p. 2. *HR* 28 Sep 1944, p. 4. *HR* 27 Oct 1944, p. 5. *HR* 28 Nov 1944, p. 12. *IP* Dec 1943. *Life* 2 Oct 1944, pp. 75-77. *MPHPD* 1 Jul 1944, p. 1969. *MPHPD* 31 Jul 1944, p. 1457. *NYT* 24 Nov 1944, p. 19. *Var* 28 Jun 1944, p. 16.

AN AMERICAN STORY (1943) *see* **GANGWAY FOR TOMORROW**

AN AMERICAN STORY (1944) *see* **AN AMERICAN ROMANCE**

AMERICANER SCHADCHEN (Jewish Americans, Yiddish language)
Fame Films, Inc.; An Edgar G. Ulmer Production. *Dist* Fame-Pictures Distributors. **1940**; New York opening: May 1940. Sd (Variray Blue Seal Recording); b&w. 9 reels, 7,680 ft. Passed by the National Board of Review. Yiddish language with English subtitles.
Dir Edgar G. Ulmer. *Asst dir* William Mercur and Anna Guskin. *Scr* S. Castle. *Orig story* G. Heimo. *English titles by* S. Rubinstein. *Dial* B. Ressler. *Dir of photog* J. Burgi Contner. *Cam* E. Hyland. *Art dir* W. Saulter. *Ed* Hans E. Mandl. *Int dec* W. Mack. *Gowns* E. Rosenthal. *Wedding gown* Mme. Berthé. *Mus score comp and cond by* Sam Morgenstern. *Sd* D. Cole. *Prod mgr* Gustav Horowitz. [*Scr supv* Shirley Ulmer].
Song(s): Lyrics by William Mercur, composer unknown.
Cast: LEO FUCHS (*Nat Silver*), Judith Abarbanel (*Judith Aarons*), Judel Dubinsky (*Maurice*), Anna Guskin (*Elvie [Silver]*), Celia Boodkin (*Nat's mother*), Rosetta Bialis (*Mrs. Aarons*), Abraham Lax (*Simon P. Schwalbenrock*), E. Adler, M. Henig, H. Appel, S. Krohner, I. Arco, M. Lerner, M. Boodkin, V. Luboff, Ch. Cohen, W. Mercur, B. Gailing, J. Mestel, S. Gold, M. Schwartz, A. Gross, A. Winters, M. Grossman, A. Ulmer.

Yiddish, Comedy, with songs. [*Print viewed*]. In New York, Nat Silver, who has become wealthy through hard work, is given a bachelor party two weeks before his planned wedding to his eighth bride-to-be. Although Nat is unsure why the previous weddings were all called off at the last minute, he wonders if it could be because of his lack of spunk or nerve, or that he does not want anyone to marry him for his money. He thinks, however, that this time there is real love. That night, a man visits Nat, and after pulling a gun, identifies himself as Joe Pinches, the childhood sweetheart of his bride-to-be Shirley. After Joe accuses Nat of stealing Shirley and threatens to shoot himself, Nat agrees to break the engagement. When Nat breaks the news to his mother and sister Elvie, his mother laments that broken engagements run in the family and tells about Uncle Shya, a matchmaker in Europe, who never married and thought that by helping others he might help himself. With his uncle in mind, Nat, who tells his mother and sister that he is going to Europe, secretly opens offices in the Bronx, under the name of Nat Gold, as an adviser in human relations. With the assistance of a doctor, psychiatrist, lawyer and rabbi, Nat attempts to "scientifically" examine all clients and, with an elaborate filing system, perfect the art of matchmaking. In addition, Nat, who refuses to accept money for his services, gives in to the entreaties of a persistent publicity man and allows him to run a campaign as long as Nat's photograph is not part of it. When pickets led by Simon P. Schwalbenrock protest that Nat is hurting the business of other *schadkens*, or matchmakers, Nat offers to hire the *schadkens* and pay their wages once they have proven themselves. As the business prospers, Nat is visited by Mrs. Aarons, who is worried because her daughter Judith is dating "all sorts of crackpots," including artists, actors and dancers. Judith is stubbornly set against having others make a match for her, but Nat, taking this as a challenge, offers to introduce her to worthy men from good families. Judith sees the sadness in Nat's life, and as he finds a match for her, she investigates him and learns that he has done a lot of good for others. At dinner in the city, Nat talks up his match for Judith, Milton Geller, an athlete and scholar. Judith tries to flirt with Nat, but when he says that he will be happy if she accepts Milton, she agrees in frustration. When Elvie comes to the office for advice about her brother, Nat, shrouded in darkness, listens as she confesses her love for him and her desire to see him happy. Nat then reveals himself and embraces his sister. As Judith prepares for the wedding to Milton, her mother realizes that she loves Nat, and that she is going through with the wedding only to make Nat happy. Before the wedding, Nat, the best man, brings Judith the ring to see if it fits, but when she pointedly asks him to put it on her finger, he refuses in embarrassment. He does put a bracelet on her wrist, but fails to realize or acknowledge that she loves him. At the wedding, Nat receives a telegram from Milton saying that he is unable to go through with it and is leaving for South America. Nat blames himself for ruining Judith's life, whereupon Judith pushes him into a chair, calls him an idiot and says he still has a chance to make good by marrying her himself. Shocked, Nat is further surprised when she kisses him. He kisses her back and they get married. *Bachelors. Impersonation and imposture. Jews. Matchmakers. Brothers and sisters. Engagements. Lawyers. Mothers and sons. New York City–Bronx. Physicians. Protest marches. Psychiatrists. Publicity. Rabbis. Romance. Threats. Uncles. Weddings.*

Note: The English language title of this film is *American Matchmaker*. According to *NYT*, it was shot in the Bronx. S. Castle is a pseudonym for Shirley Ulmer, the wife of the director.

NYT 7 May 1940, p. 31.

AMERICANISM (VERSUS BOLSHEVISM) *see* **DANGEROUS HOURS**

AMERICA'S CHILDREN *see* **THEY LIVE IN FEAR**

AMOR AUDAZ (Spanish language)

Paramount Famous Lasky Corp. *Dist* Paramount Famous Lasky Corp.. Jul **1930**; Mexico City opening: 10 Jul 1930; San Antonio (Texas) opening: 2 Aug 1930; Prod: April 1930. Sd; b&w. 9 reels, 7,577 ft. 84 min. Spanish language.

Supv Geoffrey Shurlock. *Dir* Louis Gasnier. *Dial dir* A. Washington Pezet. *Scr* Howard Estabrook and Joseph L. Mankiewicz. *Story* Percy Heath. *Spanish version* Josep Carner Ribalta. *Photog* Allen Siegler. *Sd* R. H. Quick.

Cast: Adolphe Menjou (*Albert D'Arlons*), Rosita Moreno (*Lucy Stavrin*), Ramón Pereda (*Malatroff*), Barry Norton (*Sandy Carlton*), Vicente Padula (*Silvestre Corbett*), María Calvo (*Sra. Corbett*), Carmen Guerrero (*Esther*), Carlos Villarías (*Inspector*), Paco Moreno (*Maurice*).

Crime, Melodrama. [*Not viewed*]. Malatroff, head of an international gang of jewel thieves, pressures Lucy Stavrin to pose as a countess and become friendly with the Corbetts, a *nouveau-riche* American couple residing on the Costa Azul. Lucy is to switch a valuable pearl necklace which the Corbetts have just acquired, accompanied by much publicity, for a false one. Flattered by the attention of a countess, the Corbetts regard her visit as a great honor and invite her to stay indefinitely. When Lucy is about to commit the robbery, the enigmatic Albert D'Arlons, who was a neighbor and fervent admirer of hers in Paris, shows up, drawn to Nice by the publicity surrounding the necklace. After realizing that they are both in the same "business," Lucy and Albert decide to abandon their criminal pasts and begin a new life together. However, Malatroff has been watching them, and in order to extricate themselves from the situation, they are forced to kill him. Although the local police inspector has doubts about the veracity of their tale, after receiving favorable testimony from the Corbetts, he declares the case against Lucy and Albert closed and congratulates them for having rid the world of a dangerous criminal. *Criminals–Rehabilitation. Impersonation and imposture. Jewel thieves. Socialites. Americans in foreign countries. France. Gangs. Investigations. Murder. Nouveaux riches. Pearls. Police.*

Note: *Amor audaz* is a Spanish-language version of the 1930 film *Slightly Scarlet* (see *AFI Catalog of Feature Films, 1921-30*; F2.5159), which was directed by Louis Gasnier and starred Clive Brook and Evelyn Brent. The French-language version of the film, entitled *L'enigmatique*, is listed directly below. Some sources suggest that *Slightly Scarlet* was based on the play *Blackbirds* (New York, 6 Jan 1913) by Harry James Smith, which was adapted as a motion picture in 1915 and 1920 (see *AFI Catalog of Feature Films, 1911-20*; F1.0366 and F1.0367).

Other language version(s):

L'énigmatique Monsieur Parkes (French language)

1930, New York opening: 30 Aug 1930; Paris opening: mid-Oct 1930. Sd; b&w. 6,402 ft. 71 min. French language.

Dir Louis Gasnier. *French adpt* Henri Bataille.

French-language cast: Adolphe Menjou (*Courtenay Parkes*), Claudette Colbert (*Lucy*), Emile Chautard (*H. Silvester Corbett*), Adrienne D'Ambricourt (*Mrs. Corbett*), Armand Kaliz (*Malatroff*), Sandra Ravel, Jacques Jou-Jerville, André Cheron, Frank O'Neill. [*French version not viewed*]

AMOR CONTRA AMOR *see* **LA LLAMA SAGRADA**

AMOR ENTRE RASCACIELOS *see* **EL TANGO EN BROADWAY**

AMOR IN MONTAGNA (Italian Americans, Italian language)

Alta Phonofilm Co. **1932**; World premiere in New York: 20 Mar 1932; Prod: at Sight and Sound Studios, New York. Sd; b&w. 5 reels, 4,400 ft. 49 min. Italian language.

Dir Raymond B. Lewis. *Photog* Lester Lang and Walter Lang. *Film ed* Raymond Lewis. *Rec eng* Harry B. Jones. [*Makeup* Bert Tucy].

Cast: Francesca Doria (*Selvaggia*), Silvio Castelli (*Tonio*), Giovanni Burrascano (*Piero*), Eole Gambarelli (*Eole*), Angela Amoroso (*Countessa Giraldi*), Michele Gianfredo (*Nardo*), Frank Manzione (*Carlo*), Clara Deane (*Gina*), Davide Pini (*Giovanni*), Teresa Gambaro (*Violetta*), Frances Dolombo (*Francesca*), Juliet Galanga (*Vera*), Alex Colonna (*Edoardo*), Luigi Donadio (*Luigi*).

Rural, Drama, with songs. [*Not viewed*]. In the Catskill mountains, Selvaggia must fight to see her sweetheart Piero, a dreamy young man of whom her father does not approve. Indeed, Piero loves singing in the fields but finds all forms of labor odious. One day, as Piero sings a song about the beauty of the natural world, he is overheard and praised by a young girl, Eola. Later on, Tonio, a sheepherder, Selvaggia, and a young woman named Gina sing together as they stroll home from work. When the others leave, Piero catches up with Selvaggia, kisses her, and tells her that he loves her. Soon after, Piero sees Eola again and confesses to her his sadness, that his father wants him to work as a farmer, but he only loves the earth in the springtime. Eola invites Piero to the home of her mother, the Countess Giraldi, where a birthday party will take place. The next time that Selvaggia sees Piero, she notices that he seems distracted, and she decides that he may be fickle. Later, Selvaggia and Tonio see Piero and Eola talking intimately in the fields. Selvaggia is upset, but, later, Tonio plays his violin for her, and she thanks him with a kiss. Tonio visits Selvaggia's house and brings her flowers, then tells her that she is as fascinating as a melody by Schubert. A group of peasants serenade Selvaggia and Tonio with a song, and then invite them to the countess's party. Selvaggia is worried about the state of her dress, torn while she was climbing, but Tonio surprises her with a new one. At the party, Eola introduces Piero, who begins to sing for the countess when his father, Nardo, suddenly enters in a fury, angry that his son is busy enjoying himself instead of working, and hits him. The countess chides Nardo for his ill treatment of his son, and the old man confesses that Piero is not in fact his offspring. Twenty-two years earlier, when the house by the church caught fire, Nardo and some other men rushed in and managed to save a baby boy. Because the parents had perished in the flames, Nardo decided to raise Piero as his own. Nardo then remembers that the woman who died was only caring for this child and that the baby was in fact the son of an aristocrat. Hearing the surrogate mother's name, Lucia Castiglia, the countess is shocked to realize that she has been reunited with the son that she thought had died years earlier. The countess tells the story of her illegitimate union with a poor but respectable man, and of the baby she was forced to give up. The reunited mother and son decide to forget the past, and Eola is a little perplexed to find that Piero is now her brother. Selvaggia returns home and tells all to her father. Tonio shows up and proposes to the girl, and she admits to having once loved Piero. Tonio assures the contrite Selvaggia that she is not sullied in his eyes, and the girl's father happily consents to their marriage. *Class conflict. Italian Americans. Nobility. Parentage. Peasantry. Brothers and sisters. Catskill Mountains (NY). Farmers. Fathers and sons. Long-lost relatives. Mothers and sons. Parties. Proposals (Marital). Sheepherders.*

Note: The film's English-language title is *Love in the Mountains*. The plot summary and onscreen credits were taken from a dialogue continuity contained in files at the NYSA. According to *FD*, the stars of the film appeared in a dramatic sketch at the film's premiere. A title card in the dialogue continuity states that all exterior scenes were filmed in the Catskill Mountains near Cairo, New York. According to information at NYSA, actor Giovanni Burrascano acquired the rights to the film in an auction sale in 1936 for $25.00. A new version of the film was sent to the New York State censors for approval for exhibition in that state in 1939 under the title *Il Mio Passato (My Past)*. That version, submitted by Venice Phonofilm, according to NYSA records, listed Luigi Martini as director, Roberto De Luca as photographer, Nat De Luca as editor, and credited John [i.e. Giovanni] Burrascano with continuity and direction. In Jun 1944, another new version was submitted to the New York State censors by The New Italian-American Film Co. under the title *The Martyred Mother*.

FD 21 Feb 1932, p. 5. *FD* 17 Mar 1932, p. 5. *FD* 29 Apr 1932, p. 2.

AMOR QUE VUELVE (Spanish language)

Latin American Pictures, Inc. *Dist* Kinematrade, Inc. **1936**; Los Angeles opening: 20 Mar 1936. Sd; b&w. 6 reels. 55 min. Spanish language.

Prod Frank Z. Clemente. *Dir* W. L. Griffith. *Spanish dial* René Borgia. *Mus* Carlos Molina.

Source: Based on a short story by Eustace Hale Ball.

Cast: Don Alvarado (*Antonio*), Renée Torres (*Rosario*), Juan Duval (*José*), José Botollo (*Basilio*), Julián Rivero.

Drama. [*Not viewed*]. Rosario, the daughter of a rancher, and Antonio, who comes from a poor family, have been friends since childhood. Before thinking of marriage, Antonio, ambitious and daring, leaves in search of his fortune and a social position which will please his loved one's family. Two years later, with Antonio away and her father dead, Rosario falls into a trap set by a rich suitor, the owner of a neighboring ranch, who, to facilitate a marriage between him and Rosario and combine the two properties, bribes the secretary to the court to alter the father's will. When Antonio returns, with a small amount of money saved, he exposes the crook and regains his sweetheart. *Class distinction. Deception. Ranchers. Romance. Bribery. Fathers and daughters. Wills.*

Note: According to a pre-production news item in Jan 1934 in *CM*, George Rigas was to be in the film. A Feb 1934 *FD* news item states that the film had been completed and that negotiations were under way for its release in the Latin American market. No information concerning any release before the Mar 1936 Los Angeles opening has been located. However, this film may have been a re-issue, or a new edition, of the 1930 film *La rosa de fuego*, (see below) which was produced by Tom White Productions. The films are based on the same story, have the same director and the same two leading cast members. *Amor que vuelve* may be a recut version with new dubbing, and newly-shot scenes.

CM Jan 1934. *FD* 27 Feb 1934, p. 2. *La Opinión* 1 Apr 1930.

AMOR Y SACRIFICIO see LAS CAMPANAS DE CAPISTRANO

AMOR Y VIDA (Latino)
Jan 1932; San Antonio (Texas) opening: 23 Jan 1932; Prod: 1931. Sd; b&w. Length undetermined. Spanish language.
Prod Giuseppe Lauro. *Dir* Leonard Poole. *Scr* Leonard Poole. *Translation* Eduardo Gómez Cantón. *Photog* Jack Britton. *Sd* Jamieson Laboratories.
Cast: Luisa Bonancini de Lauro, Alejandro Rosas, Bernardo Fougá, Adela Hidalgo, Lasca Beltran, Guadalupe Armendáriz, Manuel Cotera, Juan Suárez, Vicente X. Pascal, Ester Estrada, Juan Segovia, Luisa Topete, Teodoro Cruz, Francisco Becerra, Genaro Rodriguez and His Orchestra, Elodia Calvo, Marta Gallardo, Carmen Lozano, Berta Lozano, Polín Carreón, Goldie Ochoa, Carmen de la Vega, Nila de la Vega, Sofía Morales, Elisa Terán.
Drama, with songs. [*Not viewed*]. [Beyond the fact that the story dealt with episodes of Mexican life, no information concerning the plot of this film has been located.]. *Mexican Americans.*
Note: *Amor y vida*, which was also advertised under the title *El terror de Torreón*, was made in San Antonio, Texas in late 1931 and featured a cast of local performers. Although an exact length has not been determined, feature length is assumed. The film had its premiere at a midnight screening in the Texas theater on 23 Jan 1932, but apart from a short run at the Nacional in San Antonio, starting in late Jan 1932, no other screenings of this film have been located. In one article, *La Prensa*, the San Antonio Spanish newspaper, credited the script to Ada May Cord.
La Prensa 21 Jan 1932. *La Prensa* 24 Jan 1932. *La Prensa* 29 Jan 1932.

AMORE CHE NON TORNA (Italian language, Italian Americans)
Victoria Film Company. 1938?. Sd; b&w. 6 reels, 5,267 ft. Italian language.
Song(s): "Tell Her Rose" and "Night of Love," composers undetermined.
Melodrama, Musical. [*Not viewed*]. Composer Alberto Sabelli and singer Dria Dora meet when Alberto's three-thousand dollar car breaks down on a highway near San Francisco. Although Alberto has claimed to be a simple music teacher, Dria recognizes him as the composer of the popular song "Night of Love." Smitten with each other, the pair plan to meet some time in San Francisco, and Dria asks that Alberto help her to interpret his songs. Alberto replies that he will write a new one, just for her entitled "Kissed Mouth." Dria and Alberto practice music together and are happily in love until Dria receives a contract to tour around the world. She promises that upon her return she will be famous and they will find joy together, but Alberto is worried. Dria becomes a great success. One evening her promoter barges into her dressing room and tells her that he has promised her company to a much older oil baron named Giovanni Pignatelli. Pignatelli adores Dria, and invites the young girl to take her exercise in the beautiful garden pool at his home. He tries to kiss her, then proposes, but the innocent girl politely eludes his advances. Later, Dria becomes angry when the promoter asks her when she will marry Pignatelli, telling her that she must be modern and unscrupulous to be a successful artist. At a huge party at Pignatelli's home, at which Dria will be presented as a great singing star, Alberto arrives and greets Pignatelli as his father, and Dria and Alberto unexpectedly see each other. Alberto chides his father for his philandering and then, after Dria has sung Alberto's composition "Night of Love," Alberto confronts her and implies that she is the lowest of women. Dria protests her innocence, but the evidence of fine clothes, linens, and jewelry, all gifts from Pignatelli, is too incriminating. Dria departs, asking only that she be forgiven, then enters a convent, where she dies a short time later. When Pignatelli learns of the innocent girl's death, he sadly tells his son that Dria was cruelly wronged and had deserved to bear the family name. *Composers. Innocence. Italian Americans. Romance–Age difference. Singers. Convents. Fathers and sons. Music teachers. Oil magnates. Romantic rivalry. San Francisco (CA).*

Note: The title is translated into English as "Lost Love" or "The Love Who Does Not Return." The summary is based on a dialogue continuity deposited with the NYSA. Although the continuity includes several songs, only two of the titles and none of the composers have been determined. Although no reviews or credits were located for the film, information at the NYSA indicates that it was made in the U.S. and was approved for exhibition in New York state in 1938.

AMORE E MORTE (Italian language)
Aurora Film Corp. *Dist* Aurora Film Corp. Oct 1932; New York premiere: 1 Oct 1932; Prod: mid Apr—late Sep 1932 at Standard Sound Recording Studios, New York. Sd (Standard Sound Recording Corp.); b&w. 8 reels, 10,846 ft. 94 min. Italian (Sicilian dialect) language with English subtitles.
Artistic dir Rosario Romeo. *Tech dir* Alfred Gandolfi. *Author, scen and dial* Rosario Romeo. *Cam* Alfred Gandolfi and Nick Rogalli. *Mus comp* L. Aversano. *Sd rec* Alfred Gandolfi and Nick Rogalli.
Cast: Rosario Romeo (*Ruggiero De Agro'*), Carmelina Romeo (*Barbara*), Ada Ruggiero (*Lucia*), Nino Ruggiero (*Mauro*), Raffaele Bongini (*Silvestro*), Angelo Gloria (*Minicu*), Clara Diana (*Chiara De Agro'*), Pia Perez (*Comare*), Guglielmo Onofri (*Gennarino*), Giuseppe Perez (*Brigadiere*), Josephine Busacco (*Saridda*), Ignazio Uzzo (*Nuzzu*), Francesco Sanci (*Ntoni*), Frances Colombo (*Lucrezia*), Salvatore Bavuso (*Carabiniere*), Luigi Di Fede (*Bettoliere*), Michele Matachieri (*Nniria*), Violetta Di Parma (*Soprano*), Tina Napolino (*Soprano*), Paolo Dones (*Baritono*), A. Fratellone.
Rural, Melodrama, with songs. [*Not viewed*]. When Ruggiero De Agro', a patriarch and the wealthy owner of a bustling farm in Sicily at the turn of the century, seems concerned about the health of his beloved daughter Chiara, the august farmhand Sylvestro tells his fellow workers, Mauro, Ntoni, Filippo, Simuni and Nuzzo, the story of a curse that was placed upon the De Agro' family long ago. When an evil young rake of the otherwise Christian clan married a young girl only to stab her to death a few months later, her mother, who was practiced in the art of Saracen magic, placed upon the family a curse whereby all the De Agro' women have died terrible deaths, and the men have never been permitted to enjoy their wives and daughters. Ruggiero believes Chiara's illness to be part of this cruel destiny. Meanwhile, in town, Mauro's wife Lucia tells a friend that she has not seen her husband in two months and that she is unable to feed their two children. The philandering husband Mauro and Chiara sneak a kiss in the chicken coup but are interrupted by Barbara, a faithful servant to Ruggiero and a mother figure for Chiara, who warns Mauro to stay away from the master's innocent daughter. Mauro then threatens to reveal to Chiara that Ruggiero and Barbara are living in sin. Years earlier, Ruggiero saved Barbara from an abusive husband who continues to torment them by refusing to annul their marriage so that Ruggiero and Barbara can wed. Chiara and Mauro rendezvous in the stable, and Chiara admits to having seen Mauro ride through the storm on her father's white horse. The horse, Ruggiero's favorite, has fallen sick with pneumonia, and Mauro, who used the horse to visit his mistress, the innkeeper's daughter Saridda, fears that Ruggiero will discover that he kept the horse out all night. Mauro lies and tells Chiara that he took the horse in order to see a lawyer about annulling his marriage, for which he asks Chiara to procure one hundred lire to pay at the Court of Catania. The next day, Ruggiero takes Mauro to see Lucia and scolds him for his neglect, then gives him money to buy his children food and to pay the landlord. Upon Ruggiero's departure, Mauro threatens Lucia and then goes to a pub where he spends the money on drink and a dress for the Saridda. A gay celebration ensues, and Gennarino, a Neapolitan salesman who sells Saridda the dress, sings the customers a few songs, including a Tarantella. The next day, a feast is being lavishly organized for Chiara's sixteenth birthday. The farmhands congratulate Chiara, sing, drink wine and toast the adored girl's health, and Ruggiero plans a special surprise: a performance by the best musicians and singers in the land. During the party, a messenger arrives with a letter for Ruggiero, and Mauro asks Chiara to find out its contents. Barbara overhears their intimate words and confronts the girl. Upon discovering that Chiara has lost her virginity, Barbara decides that she herself must leave Ruggiero's house as she has failed to protect her master's prize possession. She tells Ruggiero, however, that she must go because Chiara has discovered they have been conducting an illicit union. Ruggiero finally reads the letter, which informs him that Lucia has been arrested for stealing to feed her children. He finds Mauro and whips him, as Chiara begs him to

stop. After sending Mauro away, Ruggiero perceives that Chiara is in love, and she finally admits that she is Mauro's wife "before God." Incensed, Ruggiero falls back stricken, and Chiara dies of grief as she prays before the Virgin. Ruggiero then chases Mauro into the fields, and as he is about to catch up to him, the young man is struck dead by lightning. Ruggiero, having now gone crazy, returns to his daughter's bed and tells Barbara not to wake the "sleeping" girl. *Curses. Farms. Fathers and daughters. Infidelity. Love affairs. Sicilians. Womanizers.* Attempted murder. Birthdays. Confession. Deception. Farm hands. Farmers. Festivals. Horses. Innkeepers. Insanity. Lightning. Mistresses. Neglected wives. Poverty. Prayer. Pregnancy. Revenge. Servants. Stables. Storms. Thieves. Virginity. Whips and whippings.

Note: Reviews and news items also refer to the film by its English-language title, *Love and Death*. The plot summary was based on a dialogue continuity deposited at NYSA. *FD* news item noted that the visiting Marchesa Iside Minnucci and Countess Mariani Doni were signed to appear in the film. Their appearance in the final film is undetermined. According to news items in *FD*, the film was edited at Craft Film Laboratory. Harry DeBelsch and his assistant, Harry Glass, both employed by the Standard Sound Recording Corp., corrected a sequence of the film that was out of synchronization.

Although Alfred Gandolfi and Nick Rogalli were generally known as cameramen, *FD* news items noted that they "handled the sound and camera work." The *NYT* review notes that many of the performers were part of an Italian acting troupe in New York known as Teatro d'Arte, headed by Commander Giuseppe Sterni. Further news items in *FD* note that the film was shot on location in Peekskill, NY, although the *NYT* review indicates that the location was in New Jersey, near the Watchung Mountains. A new "edition" of the film was submitted to the New York State censors for approval for exhibition in May 1939 under the title *Il trionfo dell'innocenza (The Triumph of Innocence)*. This version credited Joseph G. Sedita as technical editor and technical director, J. Lombardi for "Title," and Harry Bellock and H. E. Reeves as sound engineers. It is unclear from the correspondence at NYSA if this version was ever approved for exhibition.

FD 13 Aug 1931, p. 6. *FD* 18 Apr 1932, p. 2. *FD* 8 May 1932, p. 5. *FD* 15 May 1932, p. 5. *FD* 25 May 1932, p. 2. *FD* 25 Jun 1932, p. 6. *FD* 13 Aug 1932, p. 2. *FD* 21 Sep 1932, p. 7. *FD* 28 Sep 1932, p. 2. *FD* 25 Oct 1932, p. 2. *NYT* 4 Oct 1932, p. 26. *Var* 4 Oct 1932, p. 27.

L'AMOUR GUIDE (French language)

Paramount Productions, Inc. *Dist* Paramount Productions, Inc. 1933. Sd; b&w. Length undetermined. French language.

Supv Richard Blumenthal. *Dir* Norman Taurog and Jean Boyer. *Orig scr* Gene Fowler and Benjamin Glazer. *French dial adpt* Jean Boyer. *Photog* Charles Lang.

Song(s): French lyrics de André Hornez.

Cast: Maurice Chevalier (*François*), Jacqueline Francell (*Madeleine*), Marcel Vallée (*Gaston Bigoudin, dit Bibi*), Bruce Wyndham (*Monsieur Joe*), Germaine de Neel (*Suzanne*), Adrienne D'Ambricourt (*Rosalie Bibi*), Georges Renavent (*Marco*), Emile Chautard (*M. Prias*), Léonie Pray (*Annette*), George Hagen (*Wladek*), Fred Malatesta, Mutt, a dog (*Casanova*).

Musical comedy. [*Not viewed*]. [The following plot summary is based on the English-language version of this film, *The Way to Love*; character names refer to that version. For further information regarding the English-language version, please see the note below and the entry for *The Way to Love* in the *AFI Catalog of Feature Films, 1931–40*.] François, a cheerful Parisian bohemian, wants more than anything to be a tour guide in his beloved city. Presently, however, he is a walking advertisement for Professor Gaston Bibi, who is in the business of "l'amour." Bibi helps the adulterers of Paris deceive their spouses by making mock postcards of them in exotic places and administering suntans to those who are supposed to have been at the sea. While working the streets for Bibi, François meets Madeleine, who is the target for circus knife-thrower Pedro, her guardian. Pedro is brutally jealous of Madeleine's associations with other men, and when he sees her with François, he beats her. Later, François rescues a dog who is believed rabid and, while chasing it, finds Madeleine running away from Pedro for the ninth time and takes her home to his rooftop apartment, which he shares with American composer Joe and performer Suzanne. Madeleine's dream is to open her own puppet show at the circus, and she eagerly makes a puppet of François as a tour guide. He, however, does not behave romantically toward her, so Joe proposes, but she refuses. Although he denies his love, François skips a date with another woman to come home to Madeleine. Pedro then arrives with a policeman, and Madeleine is forced to return to him unless she marries. Although Joe offers, François gallantly insists he be her husband, but does not swear his love. François is finally hired as a guide and tells Bibi of his impending marriage. Bibi's wife Rosalie, however, wants François to marry her homely niece Annette

and convinces Madeleine that if she loves François, she will let him marry a decent woman with a dowry. When François arrives home that night, he swears his love to Madeleine, but she tells him there is another man and leaves him to return to Pedro. Bibi, meanwhile, discovers Rosalie's scheme and quarrels with her. After Bibi is kicked out of the house, he hires François as his guide and they get drunk together and go about Paris clipping men's ties. When François finds a fight promoter at the circus with Madeleine's tour guide puppet, he is tricked into fighting a professional and wins, then finds Madeleine back at her old job. François fights Pedro and wins, then rides the carousel with Madeleine. *Bohemians and bohemianism. Circus performers. Paris (France). Romance. Tour guides.* Americans in foreign countries. Battered women. Composers. Dogs. Drunkenness. Fights. Infidelity. Marriage–Arranged. Puppets. Romantic rivalry. Runaways. Self-sacrifice. Wards and guardians.

Note: According to *HR*, Paramount filmed this French version simultaneously with the English version. According to the Paramount Script Collection at the AMPAS Library, sequences "E" and "F" of the script for the English version (when François first takes Madeleine home and her first night on the rooftop) were altered for the French version: instead of François taking Madeleine home after Pedro throws a knife at her, he saves Madeleine after Pedro physically attacks her. A modern source states that "Mutt," who played François' dog "Casanova," was a famous film dog owned by Henry East. For information on the English-language version, *The Way to Love*, which was directed by Norman Taurog and starred Maurice Chevalier and Ann Dvorak, please see the entry for that film in the *AFI Catalog of Feature Films, 1931-40*, F3.4972.

ANDY HARDY'S BLONDE TROUBLE (Chinese Americans)

Metro-Goldwyn-Mayer Corp.; controlled by Loew's Inc. *Dist* Loew's Inc. May 1944; New York opening: 4 May 1944; *Prod*: mid-Jul—late Sep 1943 [©Loew's Inc.; 3 Apr 1944; LP171]. Sd (Western Electric Sound System); b&w. 11 reels, 9,637 ft. 104 or 107 min. Passed by the National Board of Review.

Series: The Hardy Family.

[*Prod* Carey Wilson]. *Dir* George B. Seitz. [*Asst dir* John Burch]. *Scr* Harry Ruskin, William Ludwig and Agnes Christine Johnston. *Dir of photog* Lester White. *Art dir* Cedric Gibbons. *Assoc* Harry McAfee and [Hal Ferrari]. *Film ed* George White. *Set dec* Edwin B. Willis. *Assoc* Helen Conway. *Cost supv* Irene. *Mus score* David Snell. *Rec dir* Douglas Shearer. [*Unit mgr* Art Smith].

Song(s): "Easy to Love," words and music by Cole Porter.

Source: Based on characters created by Aurania Rouverol.

Cast: Lewis Stone (*Judge [James K.] Hardy*), Mickey Rooney (*Andy Hardy*), Fay Holden (*Mrs. [Emily] Hardy*), Sara Haden (*Aunt Milly*), Herbert Marshall (*Dr. M. J. Standish*), Bonita Granville (*Kay Wilson*), Jean Porter (*Katy Anderson*), Keye Luke (*Dr. Lee [Wong How]*), Lee Wilde (*Lee Walker*), Lyn Wilde (*Lyn Walker*), Marta Linden (*Mrs. Townsend*), [Jackie Moran (*Spud*)], [Tommy Dix (*Mark*)], [Connie Gilchrist (*Mrs. Gordon*)], [Emory Parnell (*Conductor*)], [Sam McDaniel (*Pullman porter*)], [Nicodemus Stewart (*Dining car waiter*)], [William Norton Bailey (*Brakeman*)], [Cliff Clark (*Officer Shay*)], [Emmett Vogan (*Baggage man*)], [Eddie Acuff, Frank Faylen, Garry Owen (*Taxi drivers*)], [Barbara Bedford (*Secretary*)], [Frank Darien (*Watchman*)], [Claire McDowell (*Servant*)].

Domestic, Youth, Comedy. [*Print viewed*]. While on a train to Wainwright College, incoming freshman Andy Hardy vows to himself that he will not allow anything to interfere with his academic endeavors. No sooner does the girl-crazy Andy say this, however, than he meets two attractive young women. Andy is pleasantly surprised to learn that Wainwright is now admitting women, and that one of the two co-eds, the sophisticated Kay Wilson, will be his classmate. The other woman, Lee Walker, an uncontrollable flirt, is traveling surreptitiously with her conservative twin sister Lyn, who is also enrolled at Wainwright. With help from their sympathetic aunt, the sisters have tricked their father, who wants the twins to be separated so that they can develop their own identities, into believing that Lee is in Vermont, but now realize they only have enough money for food and lodging for Lyn. Lee quickly overcomes the problem by convincing Andy, who is unaware that she is a twin, that upperclassmen will humiliate him and steal his money if he is found with too much cash. After Andy gives Lee ten dollars for safekeeping, his father, Judge James K. Hardy, wires him some more money on the train, and Andy frantically passes it on to Lee. Andy then has to deal with his mounting jealousy of fellow passenger Dr. M. J. Standish, whose mature, eloquent ways are making a positive impression on

Kay. Although Dr. Standish assures him that his interest in Kay is strictly friendly, Andy becomes upset when he learns that Dr. Standish is driving Kay onto campus. Later, at Wainwright, Andy, whose father is an influential alumnus of the school, is sent to see his faculty adviser, a dean, and is shocked to discover he is Dr. Standish. While talking with the dean, Andy realizes he was hoodwinked by Lee, but assures Dr. Standish he will resolve the problem on his own. Andy then tracks Lee to a boardinghouse and demands his money back. Lee, who is still posing as Lyn, tearfully promises she will pay him back with money earned from her new singing job at a club called Joe's Place. Soon after, however, Lyn receives a concerned, cryptic telegram from her father and starts to cry in front of Andy. The still unsuspecting Andy comforts Lyn with a kiss, a gesture witnessed by Kay, and makes a date with her for that night. Andy then convinces the jealous Kay that he is serious about school and eagerly suggests they become study partners, beginning that night. Now wanting to break his date with Lyn, Andy rushes to the off-limits Joe's Place, where Lyn is rehearsing, and is startled to find both twins there. Unable to hide anymore, Lyn and Lee reveal their situation to Andy and tell him their suspicions that their father knows Lee is there and is calling that night to confront them. To avoid their father's wrath, Lee intends to take a train for Vermont, while Lyn fills in for her at Joe's Place. Andy endorses their scheme, but then hears from Dr. Standish that Mr. Walker called him earlier that day to talk about Lyn. Sure that Dr. Standish knows about the twins, Andy goes to their boardinghouse that night to telephone their father, but has to wait for his return call. Kay, meanwhile, surmises she has been stood up by Andy and gladly accompanies Dr. Standish on a tour of the campus. When they reach a romantic spot, Kay gives Dr. Standish an impulsive kiss, then apologizes and runs off. Back at the boardinghouse, Andy finally gets Mr. Walker on the phone. After determining that Mr. Walker is unaware of his daughters' subterfuge, Andy, posing as Dr. Standish, convinces him that the depressed Lyn needs to be temporarily reunited with her twin. Having solved the twins's immediate dilemma, Andy tries to sneak out of the women-only boardinghouse, but is caught by the landlady, Mrs. Gordon, who informs him that she will have to report him to Dr. Standish. Before class the next morning, Dr. Standish asks to see Andy later, and fearing the worst, Andy prepares to leave school. On his way out, however, Andy runs into his father, who has just recuperated from a tonsilectomy, and pretends all is well. Dr. Standish then joins the two, and begins to reminisce about his carefree days as a student at Wainwright, when Judge Hardy was his moral mentor. The judge and the dean confess that they had arranged to test Andy's character by giving him a "responsibility" in the form of a "lollapalooza" named Lyn. At that moment, a grateful Lee and Lyn show up to pay Andy back and surprise Dr. Standish, who never suspected that Lyn had a twin. Dr. Standish then assures Andy that all is forgiven. Later, Dr. Standish admits to Judge Hardy that he was, in fact, tempted by Kay, but that she wisely chose Andy instead. Months later, Judge and Mrs. Hardy are reunited with Andy at Thanksgiving, and are thrilled to discover that he has truly fallen in love with Kay. College life. College students. Fathers and sons. Maturation. Romance. Twins. Boardinghouses. Chinese Americans. College deans. Financial crisis. Flirts. Impersonation and imposture. Infatuation. Jealousy. Judges. Landladies. Letters. Nightclubs. Physicians. Singers. Sisters. Thanksgiving Day. Trains.

Note: The working title of this film was *Andy Hardy's Double Trouble*. The opening credits are preceded by a photograph of the "Hardy family," and the opening title card of the film reads: "Judge Hardy's Family in *Andy Hardy's Blonde Trouble.*" Although Harry McAfee is credited onscreen as an associate art director, Hal Ferrari is listed in *HR* production charts as art director through Aug 1943. Modern sources state that in the film's screenplay, "Judge Hardy" and his wife "Emily" discuss "Andy's" possible military enlistment, but that scene was not included in the viewed print. According to news items, the picture was shot at the University of Nevada at Reno. It was the first Hardy Family picture in which Andy is seen at college. (At the end of the previous Hardy Family film, *Andy Hardy's Double Life*, Andy boards the train to Wainwright.)

The sub-plot of *Andy Hardy's Blonde Trouble* involves a multi-talented doctor named "Lee Wong How," who, upon meeting the startled Hardys, reassures them that he is not Japanese, but a Chinese American from Brooklyn, New York. Keye Luke first played the character in M-G-M's *Dr. Gillespie's Criminal Case* and in subsequent entries in the "Dr. Gillespie" series (see Series Index). In Aug 1943, *HR* announced that Ann Rutherford, who had played Andy Hardy's girl friend, "Polly Bailey," in a dozen previous Hardy Family films, would no longer be borrowed from Fox for the series. Ruth Clark is listed as a cast member in an Aug 1943 *HR* news item, but her participation in the final film has not been confirmed. According to a Mar 1944 *HR* news

item, a 16mm print of the film was to be shown to troops overseas before its release in the U.S. For more information on the "Hardy Family" series, see entry for *A Family Affair* in *AFI Catalog of Feature Films, 1931-40* (F3.1269) and consult the Series Index.

Box 8 Apr 1944. *DV* 4 Apr 1944, pp. 3-4. *FD* 24 Apr 1944, p. 12. *HR* 15 Jun 1943, p. 6. *HR* 16 Jul 1943, p. 6. *HR* 13 Aug 1943, p. 12. *HR* 18 Aug 1943, p. 11. *HR* 17 Sep 1943, p. 8. *HR* 21 Sep 1943, p. 6. *HR* 30 Mar 1944, p. 1. *HR* 3 Apr 1944, p. 6. *HR* 4 Apr 1944, p. 4. *MPHPD* 8 Apr 1944, pp. 1833-34. *NYT* 5 May 1944, p. 17. *Var* 5 Apr 1944, p. 14.

ANDY HARDY'S DOUBLE TROUBLE *see* **ANDY HARDY'S BLONDE TROUBLE**

ANGEL IN EXILE (Latino)
Republic Pictures Corp. *Dist* Republic Pictures Corp. 1 Nov **1948**; Prod: mid-Mar—mid-Apr 1948 [©Republic Pictures Corp.; 2 Sep 1948; LP1788]. Sd (RCA Sound System); b&w. 90-91 min. Passed by the National Board of Review. PCA cert no. 13119.
[*Assoc prod* Allan Dwan]. *Dir* Allan Dwan and Philip Ford. [*Asst dir* Dick Moder]. *Orig scr* Charles Larson. [*Scr supv* Dorothy Yutzi]. *Dir of photog* Reggie Lanning. [*Op cam* Herb Kirkpatrick]. [*Stills* Don Keyes]. *Spec eff* Howard Lydecker and Theodore Lydecker. *Optical eff* Consolidated Film Industries. *Art dir* Frank Arrigo. *Film ed* Arthur Roberts. *Set dec* John McCarthy, Jr. and Charles Thompson. *Cost supv* Adele Palmer. *Mus* Nathan Scott. *Mus dir* Morton Scott. *Sd* Victor B. Appel. *Makeup supv* Bob Mark. *Hair stylist* Peggy Gray. *Prod mgr* Virgil Hart. *Grip* Nels Mathias.
Music: "Yo me alegro" (Traditional).
Cast: John Carroll [(*Charlie Dakin*)], Adele Mara [(*Raquel Chavez*)], Thomas Gomez [(*Dr. Esteban Chavez*)], Barton MacLane [(*Max Giorgo*)], Alfonso Bedoya [(*Ysidro Alvarez*)], Grant Withers [(*Sheriff*)], Howland Chamberlin [(*J. H. Higgins*)], Art Smith [(*Ernie Coons*)], Paul Fix [(*Carl Spitz*)], Tom Powers [(*Warden*)], Ian Wolfe [(*Health officer*)], Elsa Lorraine Zepeda [(*Carmencita*)], Mary Currier [(*Nurse*)], [Fernando Alvarado, Jose Alvarado, Henry Mirelez (*Mexican boys*)], Soledad Jiménez (*Old woman*)], Don Haggerty (*Deputy sheriff*)], [Charles Marsh (*Clerk*)], Mickey Simpson (*Prison guard*)], [Rose Marie Lopez (*Young girl*)], [Gloria Varela (*Maria*)], [Julia Montoya (*Maria's mother*)], [Zenda Westfall (*Patient*)], [Dimas Sotello (*Sleeping man*)], [Trini Varela (*Mexican woman*)], [Elias Gamboa (*Mexican man*)], [Conchita Reyes].
Religious, **Drama**. [*Print viewed*]. In California, as the spring of 1939 approaches, Warden Cramer of the state penitentiary offers discharged prisoner Charlie Dakin the address of his brother and he suggests that Charlie look for honest work at his brother's ranch in Billings, Montana. Outside the prison, Charlie meets his partner, Ernie Coons, and they leave the prison. They are followed by Max Giorgio and Carl Spitz, men Charlie cheated just before going to prison. Max and Carl follow Charlie to the county recorder's office, where a clerk named J. H. Higgins files a claim to the abandoned Durango Mine. At the mine, Charlie and Ernie meet a Mexican peasant girl named Raquel Chavez from the nearby village of San Gabriel. Later, Charlie retrieves the bags of stolen gold dust which he had hidden in the mine before going to prison. Having guessed that Charlie and Ernie have hidden gold inside the mine, Higgins arrives and asks for half of their profit in exchange for help in registering the gold as authentically from the earth. Because they have no other choice, Charlie and Ernie agree to the deal. At San Gabriel, Charlie asks a villager, Ysidro Alvarez, for a table in exchange for an hour's worth of panning for gold in the mine. When Ysidro discovers the gold, the townspeople think that the ghost of a three-hundred-year-old woman known as "the blue lady" has created a miracle by making gold appear in the mine. At the mine, Max and Carl are forced to let Charlie and Ernie go when the townspeople suddenly arrive at the cabin with their mining gear. Some time later, after all the gold has been mined, Higgins arrives demanding his share. He suggests that Max kill Charlie and Ernie in order to increase their own profit. Later, Higgins gives Ernie his pistol and tells him that Max is planning to kill them. As Charlie prepares to leave San Gabriel the next day, Raquel begs him to take her with him. Meanwhile, Raquel's father, Dr. Esteban Chavez, treats the villagers, who have contracted typhus from the ground water which had been tainted by mining activities. Charlie visits each of the sick villagers and describes a vision of the blue lady, which miraculously cures them of the disease. Despite his efforts, Charlie feels guilty for inadvertently poisoning the villagers and asks Dr. Chavez to bring the sheriff to the mine. When Higgins demands his share of the money, Max shoots and kills him. Charlie

borrows Dr. Chavez's gun for protection and arrives at the mine in time to see both Max and Ernie killed in the shootout. When the sheriff arrives moments later, Charlie turns over the money, asking that it go toward the betterment of San Gabriel. The sheriff arrests Charlie, who promises to return for Raquel. *Gold mines. Mexicans. Typhus fever. Villages. Betrayal. Billings (MT). Brothers. California. Clerks. Cures. Ex-convicts. Extortion. Ghosts. Miracles. Prison wardens. Shootouts. Villages.*

Note: A working title for the film was *The Blue Lady*; *Dark Violence* was used as the re-release title in 1954.

Box 1 Jan 1949. *DV* 24 Dec 1948, p. 4. *FD* 27 Dec 1948, p. 4. *HR* 19 Mar 1948, p. 14. *HR* 9 Apr 1948, p. 15. *HR* 24 Dec 1948, p. 4. *MPHPD* 21 Aug 1948, p. 4283. *MPHPD* 1 Jan 1949, p. 4442. *Var* 29 Dec 1948, p. 6.

ANGELINA O EL HONOR DE UN BRIGADIER (Spanish language)

Fox Film Corp. *Dist* Fox Film Corp. **1935**; New York opening: 6 Sep 1935; Madrid, Spain opening: 25 Sep 1935; Prod: 19 Jan—early Feb 1935 [©Fox Film Corp.; 2 Mar 1935; LP5509]. Sd (Western Electric Noiseless Recording); b&w. 8 reels, 7,102 ft. 79 min. Passed by the National Board of Review. PCA cert no. 652. Spanish language.

[*Prod* John Stone]. *Dirección de* [*Dir*] Louis King. [*Asst dir* Sam Schneider]. [*Dial dir* Miguel de Zárraga, Jr.]. *Adaptación cinematográfica* [*Scr*] Enrique Jardiel Poncela. [*Script* Betty Reinhardt]. *Fotografía* [*Photog*] Daniel Clark. [*Cam oper* Curt Fetters]. [*Art dir* Duncan Cramer]. [*Film ed* Ernest Nims]. *Trajes* [*Gowns*] Lillian. *Números musicales* [*Mus numbers*] Troy Sanders. *Dirección musical* [*Mus dir*] Edward Kilenyi. [*Sd* Al Protzman].

Song(s): "Los dos galanes," music by Troy Sanders, lyrics by Enrique Jardiel Poncela.

Source: Based on the play *Angelina, o el honor de un brigadier* by Enrique Jardiel Poncela (Madrid, 2 Mar 1934).

Cast: ROSITA DÍAZ (*Angelina* [*Ortiz*]), José Crespo (*Germán* [*Valderramas*]), Enrique de Rosas (*Don Marcial* [*Ortiz*], *el Brigadier*), Julio Peña (*Rodolfo* [*Alvarez de Castro*]), Rina de Liguoro (*Marcela* [*de Cattaro*]), Juan Torena (*Federico*), Andrés de Segurola (*Don Justo*), Romualdo Tirado (*Don Elías*), Ligia de Golconda (*Doña Calixta*), Paco Moreno (*El capellán*), José Peña "Pepet" (*El posadero*), María Calvo (*Madre Superiora*), Magdalena Molino (*Madre Sortilegio*), Antonio Vidal (*El fantasma del padre*), Aura de Silva (*El fantasma de la madre*), [Martín Garralaga (*Pedro, el cochero*)], [Raquel Ríos], [Rosa Elvira Alvarez].

Historical, Comedy. [*Print viewed*]. In 1880, Angelina Ortiz, a student at a Catholic girls school in Madrid, is expelled for showing the other teenagers a photograph of her sweetheart, an overly romantic poet named Rodolfo Alvarez de Castro. Meanwhile, Angelina's mother, Marcela de Cattaro, informs her lover, Germán Valderramas, that her husband is returning home. Angelina goes home with her mother and is showered with gifts by her father, the famed brigadier Don Marcial. Marcial approves of his daughter's love for Rodolfo, but insists that the couple wait a while to be married. The night of Marcial's homecoming, the family is visited by their friends, including Don Justo, Don Elías and Doña Calixta. Germán also comes by and is entranced by Angelina, whom he has not seen before. Unaware of Germán's feelings, Marcela arranges to meet him in her room later that night. Germán sneaks into Angelina's room, however, and there declares his love for her. Angelina flirts with him but does not take him seriously, and later agrees when Rodolfo suggests that they elope during an upcoming party. Germán overhears as the sweethearts make their plans and vows to thwart them. At the party, Marcela is upset by Germán's lack of attention, and he admits that he now loves another woman. Germán then begs Angelina to elope with him, and his sophistication and passion sway the girl into accepting. Rodolfo, who is waiting for Angelina, is shocked to see her leave in Germán's coach. Germán is annoyed by Angelina's childish insistence on taking all of her pets and prized possessions with her, but his troubles really begin when she repents her actions and starts crying. Rodolfo follows them to an inn and then returns to tell Marcial where Angelina has gone. Angelina's pouting prompts Germán to agree that she should go home, but before they can leave the inn, the furious Marcial appears. Germán states that nothing improper has happened, but Marciel challenges him to a duel. Rodolfo refuses to let Angelina explain and acts as Marcial's second the next morning. Angelina, who has disguised herself as a coachman, sneaks onto the duelling grounds and watches as her father shoots Germán. Marcela has also arrived and betrays her feelings for Germán when he is wounded. Marcial is again

outraged and orders that Germán be taken to the Ortiz home so that he can watch his rival die. Marcial camps out in the garden while Germán wavers between life and death, and despite Angelina's pleas, refuses to forgive Marcela. Angelina coaxes Rodolfo into forgiving her, and finally Germán dies. Marcial still refuses to forgive his wife, however, until the ghost of his father appears and tells him that his mother was once unfaithful. The ghost of Marcial's mother also appears and tells her son that she was always true after his father forgave her. Marcial's mother's words are proven false when Germán's ghost begins to flirt with her, but Marcial forgives Marcela nonetheless and helps celebrate Rodolfo and Angelina's wedding. *Elopement. Honor. Infidelity. Jealousy. Officers (Military). Romantic rivalry. Adolescence. Death and dying. Disguise. Dogs. Duels. Expulsion. Family life. Gardens. Ghosts. Girls' schools. Innkeepers. Madrid (Spain). Monkeys. Nuns. Parrots. Parties. Physicians. Poets. Womanizers.*

Note: This film was reviewed by *FD* and *NYT* as *Angelita*.

DV 19 Jan 1935, p. 3. *FD* 13 Sep 1935, p. 5. *HR* 4 Feb 1935, p. 6, 8. *HR* 28 Jan 1935, p. 10. *NYT* 11 Sep 1935, p. 19.

ANGELITA *see* **ANGELINA O EL HONOR DE UN BRIGADIER**

ANN ACUSHLA *see* **THE LITTLE RUNAWAY**

ANNA ASCENDS (Syrian Americans)

Famous Players-Lasky Corp. *Dist* Paramount Pictures. 19 Nov **1922** [©Famous Players-Lasky Corp.; 20 Nov 1922; LP18598]. Si; b&w. 6 reels, 5,959 ft.

Pres Adolph Zukor. *Dir* Victor Fleming. *Scen* Margaret Turnbull. *Photog* Gilbert Warrenton.

Source: Based on the play *Anna Ascends* by Harry Chapman Ford (New York, 22 Sep 1920).

Cast: Alice Brady (*Anna Ayyob*), Robert Ellis (*Howard Fisk*), David Powell (*The Baron*), Nita Naldi (*Countess Rostoff*), Charles Gerrard (*Count Rostoff*), Edward Durand (*Siad Coury*), Florence Dixon (*Bessie Fisk*), Grace Griswold (*Miss Fisk*), Frederick Burton (*Mr. Fisk*).

Melodrama. While working in a coffeehouse, Syrian immigrant Anna Ayyob falls in love with Howard Fisk and discovers that her employer ("The Baron") is involved with Count and Countess Rostoff in smuggling jewels. Anna has an encounter with the baron and, thinking she has killed him, disappears. Later, after writing a widely popular novel, Anna again meets Howard and, to save Howard's sister from marrying Count Rostoff, exposes the count and confesses to the baron's murder. Investigation discloses the baron to be alive; Anna and Howard marry. *Brothers and sisters. Cafes. Immigrants. Murder. Nobility. Novelists. Smuggling. Syrians.*

ETR 25 Nov 1922, p. 1657. *FD* 19 Nov 1922. *MPW* 25 Nov 1922. *Var* 17 Nov 1922, p. 41.

ANNA CHRISTIE (Swedish Americans)

Thomas H. Ince Corp. *Dist* Associated First National Pictures. 3 Dec **1923**; New York showing: 28 Nov 1923 [©Thomas H. Ince Corp.; 26 Nov 1923; LP19652]. Si; b&w. 8 reels, 7,631 ft.

Pres Thomas H. Ince. *Dir* John Griffith Wray. *Scen* Bradley King. *Photog* Henry Sharp.

Source: Based on the play *Anna Christie* by Eugene Gladstone O'Neill (New York, 1922).

Cast: Blanche Sweet (*Anna Christie*), William Russell (*Matt Burke*), George F. Marion (*"Chris" Christopherson*), Eugenie Besserer (*Marthy*), Ralph Yearsley (*The Brutal Cousin*), Chester Conklin (*Tommy*), George Siegmann (*Anna's uncle*), Victor Potel, Fred Kohler.

Melodrama. Chris Christopherson, an old skipper, is determined to keep his daughter, Anna, away from the sea. Brought up by cousins on a farm in Minnesota, Anna is treated badly by her relatives, and she runs away to Chicago where she soon becomes a streetwalker. Anna visits her father in New York City, hoping he will provide the peace and shelter she needs. The old man, ignorant of her previous life, invites Anna to live on the coal barge he commands. During one trip Anna meets a sailor and, to her father's regret, falls in love. The two men argue Anna's future. Finally, Anna reveals her past life and both men, angry and hurt, leave—to return several days later for a reconciliation. *Barges. Chicago (IL). New York City. Prostitution. Sailors. Sea captains. Swedish Americans.*

Note: In 1930, M-G-M released a film based on the same source, directed by Clarence Brown and starring Greta Garbo and Charles Bickford (see below).

NYT 10 Dec 1923, p. 20. *Var* 6 Dec 1923, p. 23.

ANNA CHRISTIE (Swedish Americans)
Metro-Goldwyn-Mayer Corp.; controlled by Loew's Inc.; Clarence Brown's Production. *Dist* Metro-Goldwyn-Mayer Distributing Corp. 21 Feb **1930**; Los Angeles opening: 22 Jan 1930 [©Metro-Goldwyn-Mayer Distributing Corp.; 10 Feb 1930; LP1062]. Sd (Western Electric System); b&w. 10 reels, 8,268 ft. 92 min. [also si.].

Dir Clarence Brown. *Adpt* Frances Marion. *Photog* William Daniels. *Art dir* Cedric Gibbons. *Film ed* Hugh Wynn. *Gowns* Adrian. *Rec dir* Douglas Shearer. [*Rec eng* G. A. Burns].

Source: Based on the play *Anna Christie* by Eugene Gladstone O'Neill (New York, 2 Nov 1921).

Cast: GRETA GARBO (*Anna*), Charles Bickford (*Matt*), George F. Marion (*Chris*), Marie Dressler (*Marthy*), James T. Mack (*Johnny, the Harp*), Lee Phelps (*Larry*).

Drama. [*Print viewed*]. When she was a child, Anna Christie's sailor father left her with cruel and abusive relatives on a farm. Leaving the place as a young woman, Anna drifted into prostitution in St. Paul, Minnesota. Her father, Chris, now captain of a coal barge based in New York, receives a letter from her indicating that she is coming to New York. Anna has been in a hospital and resents the fact that, over the years, her father has not attempted to locate and help her. Anna finds Chris in a waterfront bar where he has been keeping company with Marthy, an old souse. Although they have not seen each other for many years, Anna and her father eventually reconcile and she takes care of him on the barge. During a trip up the coast, they rescue a young sailor, Matt, who falls in love with Anna. Although she has grown to hate men, she is very attracted to Matt, but is unable to keep her previous life a secret. After she confesses her past to Matt and to her father, Matt leaves her. However, realising that he cannot live without her, Matt returns. Anna swears on his mother's crucifix that she loves only him and they are reunited. Anna is then content with the prospect of becoming Matt's wife and looking after her father. *Fathers and daughters. Prostitution. Romance. Sailors. Swedish Americans. Amusement parks. Barges. Bars. Catholics. Coal. Crucifixes. Drunkenness. Fog. Irish. Letters. Lutheran Church. New York City. Oaths. Rescues. Storms. Superstition. Waterfronts. Widowers.*

Note: In addition to the English and German-language versions of this film, a silent version, with titles by Madeleine Ruthven, was also made. *Anna Christie* was Greta Garbo's first talking picture. In the restored and subtitled German version, the scene in which Anna swears on the crucifix is missing, although it is included in the cutting continuity of the German version. In papers of Edgar G. Ulmer at the AMPAS Library, Ulmer states that he directed the German version. In addition, an affidavit by Fritz Feld testifies to this statement; however, Jacques Feyder is listed as director in the onscreen credits. Actress Salka Steuermann, who appears in the German version, was also known as Salka Stearman and Salka Viertel. John Griffith Wray directed an earlier version of the play in 1923, which starred Blanche Sweet, William Russell and George F. Marion (see above).

Other language version(s):
Anna Christie (German language)
1930; Cologne, Germany opening: 23 Dec 1930: New York opening: 2 Jan 1931: Chicago opening: 19 Mar 1931; Sd (Western Electric Sound System); b&w. 10 reels. 85 min. German language.

Regie [*Dir*] Jacques Feyder. *Bearbeiten von* [*Adpt*] Frances Marion. *Deutsches drehbuch* [*German adpt*] Frank Reicher. *Deutscher dialog* [*German dial*] Walter Hasenclever. *Photographie* [*Photog*] William Daniels. *Bauten* [*Art dir*] Cedric Gibbons. *Filmschnitt* [*Film ed*] Finn Ulback. *Kostüme* [*Ward*] Adrian. *Tontechniker* [*Sd tech*] Douglas Shearer.

German-language cast: :t add Greta Garbo (*Anna*), Theo Shall (*Matt*), Hans Junkermann (*Chris*), Salka Steuermann (*Marthy*), [Hermann Bing (*Larry*)]. [*German version viewed*].

FD 9 Feb 1930. *NYT* 15 Mar 1930, p. 22. *Var* 19 Mar 1930, p. 34.

ANNA LUCASTA (Polish Americans)
Security Pictures, Inc. *Dist* Columbia Pictures Corp. Aug **1949**; New York opening: 11 Aug 1949; Prod: 26 Jan—16 Mar 1949 [©Security Pictures, Inc.; 19 Aug 1949; LP2499]. Sd (Western Electric Recording); b&w. 84 or 86 min. PCA cert no. 13746.

Prod Philip Yordan. *Dir* Irving Rapper. *Asst dir* James Nicholson. *Scr* Philip Yordan and Arthur Laurents. *Dir of photog* Sol Polito. *Art dir* George Brooks. *Film ed* Charles Nelson. *Set dec* William Kiernan. *Gowns* Jean Louis. *Mus score* David Diamond. *Mus dir* Morris Stoloff. *Sd eng* George Cooper. *Makeup* Clay Campbell. *Hair styles* Helen Hunt.

Source: Based on the play *Anna Lucasta* by Philip Yordan, as presented by John J. Wildberg (New York, 8 Jun 1944).

Cast: Paulette Goddard [(*Anna Lucasta*)], William Bishop [(*Rudolf Strobel*)], John Ireland [(*Danny Johnson*)], Oscar Homolka [(*Joe Lucasta*)], Broderick Crawford [(*Frank*)], Will Geer [(*Noah*)], Gale Page [(*Katie*)], Mary Wickes [(*Stella*)], Whit Bissell [(*Stanley Lucasta*)], Lisa Golm [(*Theresa Lucasta*)], James Brown [(*Buster*)], Dennie Moore [(*Blanche*)], Anthony Caruso [(*Eddie*)], [Grayce Hampton (*Queenie*)], [Jean "Babe" London (*Woman in bar*)], [Joe McTurk, Olin Howlin (*Station masters*)], [Jean Andren (*Woman on street*)], [Harry Cheshire (*Minister*)], [William Cabanne (*Young man*)], [Esther Dale (*Mrs. Pulaski*)], [Joseph Ploski].

Melodrama. [*Print viewed*]. The Lucasta family—father Joe, mother Theresa, their two children Stanley and Stella and their spouses Frank and Katie—receives a letter from Joe's old friend Strobel, stating that his son Rudolf is coming to their city in Pennsylvania. The friend asks Joe to find a good wife for Rudolf and mentions that he will arrive with $4,000. In order to get the money for themselves, Theresa suggests that Anna, their "black sheep" daughter, be brought home as a prospective wife for Rudolf. Joe, who hates Anna, refuses to consider the idea until Frank beats him up. Anna, meanwhile, is working at a Brooklyn bar called the Noah's Ark when sailor Danny Johnson, a regular customer, tells her that he has saved enough money to go back to taxi driving. Contrary to Anna's expectations, Danny does not ask her to marry him. While Anna is dancing with Danny's friend Buster, Joe arrives and asks Anna to come home. Because she is broke and locked out of her apartment, Anna agrees to return, and quickly learns the reason for Joe's request. When Rudolf arrives, the family is surprised to learn that he is not a naïve man from the country, but a college graduate who plans to work the family farm in addition to teaching at the local school. After Stanley and Frank are fired from their jobs, they unsuccessfully try to con Rudolf out of his money. Rudolf is attracted to Anna, despite Joe's drunken warning to keep away from women like her. Insulted by her father, Anna escapes to the hotel bar for a drink. Rudolf follows, and the two dine together. The next day, Rudolf takes Anna on a tour of the farm and proposes marriage. Anna does not answer, however, and that night, recalls the event that caused her to leave home: Having been locked out of the house after a dance, she gets a spare key from the shed. There, her date kisses her, and they are found by her father, who angrily vows never to let her date again. This unpleasant memory compels Anna to leave town, but while she is waiting for the train, Rudolf arrives and persuades her to marry him. Before the wedding, Rudolf gives Anna his money, which is later stolen. While all the Lucastas except Joe are attending the wedding, Danny comes looking for Anna. Danny's presence convinces Joe of Anna's worthlessness, and when Anna and Rudolf return, Joe tells her that he took Rudolf's money and vows to expose her past to the school principal and ruin Rudolf unless she leaves immediately with Danny. Vowing never to see her jealous father again, Anna leaves with Danny. Some time later, Rudolf searches Brooklyn for Anna. He waits for her to return to Noah's Ark, but eventually gives up, leaving behind a letter that discloses Joe's death. When Anna arrives at the bar, Noah, the bartender, reads the letter to her and then dials the number of Rudolf's hotel. After learning that Rudolf has checked out of the hotel, Anna leaves for the night, believing that she has lost her chance for happiness. Rudolf is waiting outside, however, and calls her name. The two walk off together. *Family relationships. Fathers and daughters. Greed. Jealousy. Polish Americans. Bars. Bartenders. Dismissal (Employment). Farmers. Letters. Money. New York City–Brooklyn. Pennsylvania. Robbery. Sailors. Weddings.*

Note: Philip Yordan's stage play *Anna Lucasta* was written in 1936 about a Polish family, but failed to get a Broadway opening until 8 Jun 1944, when it was staged by the American Negro Theater in the basement of the 135th St. Library in Harlem with an all-black cast. For the film, the play's original Polish-American characters were reinstated. *HR* news items provide the following information about the production: The film was slated to begin production early in 1948, but the production was delayed several times due partly to Paulette Goddard's prior commitments. A 29 Sep 1948 *HR* news item reported that negotiations for Susan Hayward to star had been concluded. According to the same item, Linda Darnell and Rita Hayworth had also been considered for the lead. The film finally went into production in Jan 1949 with Goddard in the lead. Other news items note that Gig Young was tested for a role, and that William Dieterle was announced as the film's director.
Material included in the MPAA/PCA files at the AMPAS Library adds the following information about the production: In a 7 Nov 1944 letter to Paramount producer Hal Wallis, PCA director Joseph I. Breen stated that the

play would not be acceptable material for a film because of the "general, overall low tone and immoral flavor of the story," particularly its depiction of Anna's prostitution, frequent use of vulgarities and blasphemies, portrayal of one character as a pimp, and suggestion of an incestuous relationship or desire on the part of Joe toward Anna. In the original play, Anna is clearly portrayed as a prostitute and it is Joe's incestuous feelings toward his daughter that cause the split between them. The *HR* review states, "so much of the story has to be implied rather than stated, that it winds up resorting to melodramatic cliches." Subsequent to Paramount's inquiry, almost every studio in Hollywood submitted the play to the PCA and received a copy of the same letter.

In a 7 Jul 1947 letter to the MPAA, Philip Yordan made a plea for a film version of his play, stating that "the immoral elements of open prostitution, incest and the characterization of the pimp were completely absent from my original version. It is my full intent and purpose to eliminate these unwholesome elements from the screenplay." Despite Yordan's statements, the published play contains the elements proscribed by the MPAA. According to a 30 Jan 1949 *NYT* article, the PCA suggested to Yordan that if the screenplay stressed the "danger of a narrow-minded and repressive attitude toward children by foreign-born parents," it would be given "the widest possible latitude in telling the story." According to a *LAEx* article, the property was bought in Jul 1947 by producer Robert Kane as a 20th Century Fox release. Columbia then purchased the play's screen rights in Oct 1947, and subsequent submissions of Yordan and Arthur Laurent's screenplay were deemed acceptable by the MPAA with minor changes. Another adaptation of Yordan's play was made in 1958 by UA, featuring a black cast headed by Eartha Kitt and Sammy Davis, Jr. and was directed by Arnold Laven.

Box 16 Jul 1949. *DV* 5 Aug 1949, p. 3. *FD* 11 Jul 1949, p. 7. *HR* 20 Oct 1947, p. 3. *HR* 2 Mar 1948, p. 2. *HR* 9 Mar 1948, p. 3. *HR* 29 Sep 1948, p. 1. *HR* 21 Dec 1948, p. 3. *HR* 26 Jan 1949, p. 3. *HR* 11 Mar 1949, p. 10. *LAEx* 19 Jul 1947. *MPHPD* 16 Jul 1949, p. 4682. *NYT* 30 Jan 1949. *NYT* 12 Aug 1949, p. 13. *Var* 13 Jul 1949, p. 16.

ANNA LUCASTA (African Americans)

Longridge Enterprises, Inc. *Dist* United Artists Corp. Feb **1959**; World premiere in Chicago: 26 Nov 1958; New York opening: 14 Jan 1959; Prod: early May—early June 1958 at Samuel Goldwyn Studios [©Longridge Enterprises, Inc.; 26 Nov 1959; LP12448]. Sd (Westrex Recording System); b&w. 10 reels, 8,688 ft. 92 or 97 min. PCA cert no. 19104.

Prod Sidney Harmon. *Dir* Arnold Laven. *Assoc to the dir* Irving Lerner. *Asst dir* Eugene Anderson, Jr. *Scr* Philip Yordan. *Dir of photog* Lucien Ballard. *Spec photog eff* Jack Rabin and Louis DeWitt. *Montage conceived by* Irving Lerner. *Art dir* John S. Poplin, Jr. *Graphic art* Charles White. *Film ed* Richard C. Meyer and Robert Lawrence. *Mus ed* Lee Osborne. *Set dresser* Lyle B. Reifsnyder. *Prop master* Richard Rubin. *Ward stylist* Virginia Dey. *Men's ward* Norman Martien. *Women's ward* Sophia Stutz. *Mus* Elmer Bernstein. *Sd* Jack Solomon. *Makeup artist* Ted Cooley. *Hair stylist* Helene Parrish. *Prod supv* Leon Chooluck. *Scr supv* James Yarbrough.

Song(s): "That's Anna," words by Sammy Cahn, music by Elmer Bernstein, sung by Sammy Davis, Jr.

Source: Based on the play *Anna Lucasta* by Philip Yordan (Harlem, New York, 8 Jun 1944).

Cast: Eartha Kitt [(*Anna Lucasta*)], Frederick O'Neal [(*Frank*)], Henry Scott [(*Rudolph Slocum*)], Rex Ingram [(*Joe Lucasta*)], James Edwards [(*Eddie*)], Isabelle Cooley [(*Katie Lucasta*)], Rosetta Le Noire [(*Stella*)], Georgia Burke [(*Theresa Lucasta*)], Claire Leyba [(*Blanche*)], Alvin Childress [(*Noah*)], John Proctor [(*Stanley Lucasta*)], Charles Swain [(*Lester*)], Isaac Jones [(*Police officer*)], Eileen Harley, Sammy Davis, Jr. (*Danny* [*Johnson*]), [Wally Earl (*Secretary*)].

African American, Domestic, Psychological, Drama. [*Print viewed*]. Anna Lucasta is a wisecracking young beauty who supports herself on the streets near the San Diego naval station. As she sits in her friend Noah's waterfront café one evening, she suddenly looks lost and murmurs, "I wish someone would find me." Meanwhile, her parents, Joe and Theresa, who live in Los Angeles with their son Stanley, a mailman, his wife Katie, their daughter Stella, and her scheming husband Frank, receive a letter from an old friend in Alabama, Otis Slocum. Otis asks old Joe to find a wife for his son Rudolph, who has been given four thousand dollars and a train ticket to California. Theresa thinks a marriage to Rudolph would give their wayward daughter Anna a fresh start, but Joe, who kicked his daughter out of the house sometime earlier for reasons he has never explained to the others, angrily refuses even to mention her name. Pressured by his family, Joe finally agrees to fetch Anna from San Diego, but when he arrives at the café, he finds his daughter drinking with a sailor named Danny Johnson. The cocky young man has just asked Anna to live with him, but because his plans do not include marriage, Anna decides to return to her family. When Rudolph arrives from Alabama, he explains to the Lucasta family that what he really wants in

California is a job. An honors graduate of an agricultural college, Rudolph soon lands a teaching job at a junior college and falls deeply in love with Anna. When he confesses his feelings, Anna tells him why her father threw her out: On the night of her high school prom, Joe had found her holding hands with a young man he had forbidden her to see. Wild with anger, Joe had given his daughter twenty dollars and sent her away. She took a bus to San Diego, where she was forced to earn her living on the streets. Despite Anna's confession, Rudolph proposes, but during the wedding, Joe visits the college and tells the dean that Rudolph's new wife is a tramp. After the wedding, Danny arrives, determined to take Anna away with him. Anna wants to remain with Rudolph, but when Joe comes in and shouts that he plans to ruin all of Rudolph's future job prospects, Anna decides to go with Danny. The two carouse in San Diego for a week, and when Danny's bank account runs low, he suggests they use Anna's trousseau money to buy passage to Brazil. Danny and Anna sneak into the Lucasta home one Sunday to retrieve the money, but as they are leaving, they hear her father moaning in the next room. Calling Anna his little angel, Joe takes her hand and dies. Anna collapses in tears, and Danny leaves the house for good. As the rest of the family arrive home from church, Rudolph, seeing Danny drive away, realizes Anna must be in the house and happily runs up the stairs. *African Americans. Family life. Fathers and daughters. Forgiveness. Prostitution. Romance. African Americans. Alcoholism. Bars. Bartenders. Confidence men. Death and dying. Insanity. Jealousy. Junk trade. Los Angeles (CA). Postal workers. Sailors. San Diego (CA). Schoolteachers. Southerners. Weddings.*

Note: The opening credits read: "Philip Yordan's *Anna Lucasta*." Yordan's stage play was written in 1936 and originally was about a Polish family. The play failed at that time to get a Broadway opening, and on 8 Jun 1944, it was staged by the American Negro Theater in the basement of the 135th St. Library in Harlem, with an all-black cast. Frederick O'Neal, John Proctor and Alvin Childress, who appear in the film, were in the Harlem production. The play opened on Broadway on 30 Aug 1944 and ran for 959 performances, closing on 30 Nov 1946. In addition to O'Neal, Proctor and Childress, the following actors from the film were in the Broadway run or were on tour with it in the U.S. or England: Henry Scott, Rex Ingram, Isabelle Cooley, Rosetta Le Noire, Georgia Burke and Claire Leyba. The leading role of "Anna" was played by Hilda Simms on Broadway. For additional information about the play, please see entry above for the 1949 Columbia film *Anna Lucasta*.

Longridge Enterprises, Inc., was associated with Security Pictures, Inc., which produced the 1949 version, according to *LAT*. MPAA/PCA records at the AMPAS Library note that after the script was submitted in 1958, PCA officials replied, "we think it would be wise were some additional motivation to be attributed to the father which would not place the emphasis so unequivocally on the suggestion of incestuous desire. We believe it would be quite easily possible to say that he was 'possessive' in nature, and for this reason would not want to see anyone else get Anna." Reviews commented that the film was faithful to the play, although the *HR* review stated that the film's ending, "which cleans up both father and daughter, is more palatable than the one on the stage," and *S&S*, in comparing the film to the London stage production, noted, "It includes several aspects of racial stereotyping which were absent from the play."

Before the film's world premiere in Chicago in Nov 1958, the MPAA Advertising Code Administration refused to approve a number of ads for the film, claiming, according to *HR*, that the ads "blatantly portray the femme lead as a prostitute" and that "the art emphasizes her posterior." According to *DV*, United Artists informed the MPAA that they would run their ads without the Advertising Code Administration's approval, if necessary. *DV* reported that the MPAA might possibly withdraw their seal of approval from the film. United Artists then ran follow-up ads attempting to capitalize on the ad campaign controversy by using the slogan, "Why won't they let us tell you what sort of woman 'Anna Lucasta' is?" The Advertising Code Administration also refused to approve the follow-up ads, citing a regulation prohibiting publicity based on censorship. In Jan 1959, *MPH* noted that revised ad copy had finally been accepted. According to a Jan 1960 *HR* news item, Eartha Kitt and Sammy Davis, Jr., who both had "financial participation" in the film, sent letters on Longridge letterhead, to hundreds of exhibitors in the South requesting correspondence because they felt that many Southern theaters did not book the film on "racial grounds."

Anna Lucasta marked Sammy Davis, Jr.'s first dramatic film role. According to *LAT*, during filming, he was also performing two shows nightly in Las Vegas. A number of reviews commented on the film's portrayal of African Americans. *HR* stated, "The story has none of the so-called comic cliches usually associated with Afro-American drama but it is rich with the humor and common sense wisdom of the Negro point of view." *DV* commented, "There is no particular feeling that this is a 'Negro film.' The racial character dwindles as the human characters come through. The people are not humorously Negro or pitifully Negro, but people, funny and sad."

Box 24 Nov 1958. *Cue* 17 Jan 1959. *DV* 18 Nov 1958. *DV* 19 Nov 1958, p. 3. *DV* 20 Nov 1958. *Exb* 26 Nov 1958, p. 4535. *FD* 19 Nov 1958, p. 6. *Har* 22 Nov 1958, pp. 186-87. *HCN* 27 Nov 1958. *HR* 9 May 1958, p. 13. *HR* 6 Jun 1958, p. 8. *HR* 7 Nov 1958, p. 1. *HR* 19 Nov 1958, pp. 3-4. *HR* 19 Jan 1960. *LAEx* 27 Nov 1958. *LAT* 1 May 1958. *LAT* 15 Jun 1958, pt. V, p. 1, 4. *LAT* 9 Nov 1958. *MPD* 24 Nov 1958. *MPH* 31 Jan 1959. *MPHPD* 22 Nov 1958, p. 60. *New Yorker* 24 Jan 1959. *NYT* 8 Jun 1958. *NYT* 15 Jan 1959, p. 27. *S&S* Spr 1959, p. 91. *Time* 26 Jan 1959. *Var* 19 Nov 1958, p. 6.

ANNE NICHOLS' ABIE'S IRISH ROSE *see* ABIE'S IRISH ROSE
   (1946)

ANNE OF LITTLE SMOKY (Gypsies)
   Wistaria Productions. *Dist* Playgoers Pictures, Inc. 20 Nov **1921** [©Playgoers Pictures, Inc.; 6 Dec 1921; LU17300]. Si; b&w. 5 reels, 5,000 ft.
   Dir Edward Connor. *Scen* Frank Beresford. *Story* Edward Connor. *Photog* John S. Stumar.
   Cast: Winifred Westover (*Anne*), Dolores Cassinelli (*Gita*), Joe King (*Bob Hayne*), Frank Hagney (*Ed Brockton*), Ralph Faulkner (*Tom Brockton*), Harold Callahan (*Buddy*), Alice Chapin (*Mrs. Brockton*), Frank Sheridan (*"The" Brockton*), Edward Roseman (*Sam Ward*).
   Rural, Melodrama. The Brocktons claim the Little Smoky region as their own when the government turns it into a forest and game preserve and challenges their rights to use the area as they please. Bob Hayne, a forest ranger, loves Anne, daughter of the Brockton clan leader; but Anne is jealous when Bob defends Gita, a Gypsy princess, from unwelcome attentions and when the Gypsy later saves his life. Bob arrests Anne's father for breaking the game laws, but Brockton is acquitted when Anne steals the evidence. In a row following the trial, Bob is trailed by hounds when he is believed to have killed Ed Brockton. Anne dresses in Bob's clothes to mislead the hounds, and during a storm she finds Ed alive in Bob's cabin. Tom, Anne's brother who was shell-shocked in France, saves the Gypsy, whom he loves, from a renegade Indian, and both couples are happily united. *Brothers and sisters. Forest rangers. Game-preserves. Gypsies. Indians of North America. Land rights. Mountaineering. Veterans.*
   FD 15 Jan 1922. *Var* 13 Jan 1922, p. 42.

ANNIE GET YOUR GUN (Native Americans)
   Metro-Goldwyn-Mayer Corp.; controlled by Loews Inc. *Dist* Loew's Inc. 23 May **1950**; Prod: 10 Oct–17 Dec 1949; retakes 6 Feb 1950 [©Loew's Inc.; 21 Apr 1950; LP114]. Sd (Western Electric Sound System); col (Technicolor). 9,667 ft. 107 min. Passed by the National Board of Review. PCA cert no. 14293.
   Prod Arthur Freed. *Dir* George Sidney. [*Asst dir* George Rhein]. *Scr* Sidney Sheldon. *Dir of photog* Charles Rosher. [*Cam op* Jack Nickolaus, Jr.]. [*Stills* Edward Hubbell]. *Spec eff* A. Arnold Gillespie and Warren Newcombe. *Mont seq* Peter Ballbusch. *Technicolor col consultant* Henri Jaffa and James Gooch. *Art dir* Cedric Gibbons and Paul Groesse. *Film ed* James E. Newcom. *Set dec* Edwin B. Willis. *Assoc* Richard A. Pefferle. *Women's cost* Helen Rose. *Men's cost* Walter Plunkett. *Mus dir* Adolph Deutsch. *Mus numbers staged by* Robert Alton. *Rec supv* Douglas Shearer. [*Sd* Norwood A. Fenton]. *Hairstyles des by* Sydney Guilaroff. [*Hairstylist* Martha Acker]. *Makeup created by* Jack Dawn. [*Makeup* Ben Lane]. [*Prod mgr* Eddie Woehler]. [*Scr supv* Jack Aldworth]. [*Grip* Leo Monlon]. [*Gaffer* M. D. Cline]. [*Singing voice double for Keenan Wynn* Henry Kruse]. [*Singing voice double for Louis Calbern* Charles Schrouder].
   Song(s): "Colonel Buffalo Bill," "Doin' What Comes Natur'lly," "The Girl That I Marry," "You Can't Get a Man with a Gun," "There's No Business Like Show Business," "They Say It's Wonderful," "My Defenses Are Down," "I'm an Indian Too," "I Got the Sun in the Morning," "Anything You Can Do, I Can Do Better," music and lyrics by Irving Berlin.
   Source: Based on the musical *Annie Get Your Gun*, book by Herbert Fields and Dorothy Fields, music by Irving Berlin, as produced by Richard Rodgers and Oscar Hammerstein, II (New York, 16 May 1946).
   Cast: Betty Hutton [(*Annie Oakley*)], Howard Keel [(*Frank Butler*)], Louis Calhern [(*Buffalo Bill*)], J. Carrol Naish [(*Chief Sitting Bull*)], Edward Arnold [(*Pawnee Bill*)], Keenan Wynn [(*Charlie Davenport*)], Benay Venuta [(*Dolly Tate*)], Clinton Sundberg [(*Foster Wilson*)], [James H. Harrison (*Mac*)], [Bradley Mora (*Little Jake*)], [Diana Dick (*Nellie*)], [Susan Odin (*Jessie*)], [Eleanor Brown (*Minnie*)], [Chief Yowlachie (*Little Horse*)], [Sue Casey, Mary Ellen Gleason, Mary Jane French, Meredith Leeds, Helen Kimbell, Dorinda Clifton, Marietta Elliott, Judy Landon (*Cowgirls*)], [Jack Trent, Michael Dugan, Carl Sepulveda, Warren MacGregor, Carol Henry, Archie Butler, Fred Gillman (*Cowboys*)], [W. P. Wilkerson, Shooting Star, Charles Mauu, Riley Sunrise, Tom Humphreys, John War Eagle (*Indian braves*)], [Edith Mills, Dorothy Sky Eagle (*Indian women*)], [Bridget Carr, Bette Arlen, Sandra Spence, Dorothy Abbott (*Women in*

carriage*)], [Tony Taylor (*Little boy*)], [Edward Kilroy (*Guest*)], [Robert Malcolm (*Conductor*)], [Lee Tung Foo (*Waiter*)], [William Tannen, Al Rhein, Charles Regan (*Barkers*)], [Phil Dunham (*Cynical man*)], [Helen Dickson (*Sour-faced wife*)], [Anne O'Neal (*Miss Willoughby*)], [Evelyn Beresford (*Queen Victoria*)], [John Hamilton (*Ship captain*)], [Nolan Leary, Budd Fine (*Immigration officers*)], [William Bill Hall (*Tall man*)], [Edward Earle (*Footman*)], [Marjorie Wood (*Constance*)], [Elizabeth Flournoy (*Helen*)], [Mae Clarke Langdon (*Mrs. Adams*)], [Frank Wilcox (*Mr. Clay*)], [Andre Charlot (*President Loubet of France*)], [Nino Pipitone (*King Victor Emanuel*)], [John Mylong (*Kaiser Wilhelm 2d*)], [Carl Sklover], [Buddy Roosevelt], [Cameron Grant], [Polly Bailey], [Rhea Mitchell], [Margaret Bert], [Bunny Waters], [Sue Carleton], [Jackee Waldron], [Kerry O'Day], [Alice Wallace].
   Show business, Biography, Musical. [*Print viewed*]. When champion sharpshooter Frank Butler, his personal manager Charlie Davenport and Buffalo Bill Cody's Wild West troupe of headliners arrive in Cincinnati to put on a show, the town breaks out in celebration. The arrival of the troupe brings joy to everyone except Foster Wilson, a persnickety hotel owner who will be housing the troupe. Wilson later joins in the celebration, however, when Annie Oakley, a bedraggled sharp shooting tomboy, and her ragtag gang of children check into the hotel. Impressed by Annie's shooting abilities, Wilson quickly arranges a match between her and Frank, whom he calls a "swollen-headed stiff." Annie falls instantly in love with Frank, and the show gets underway when Buffalo Bill introduces the two sharpshooters. The crowd heckles Annie, believing that she is no match for Frank, but to everyone's astonishment, she outdraws her opponent and wins the contest. Angered by the defeat, Frank refuses to accept Buffalo Bill's suggestion that Annie join the touring show as his assistant. Annie eventually persuades Frank to let her join, and the two sharpshooters become a successful team. After shedding her country clothes and making herself more attractive, Annie tries to impress Frank by learning how to read. While a romance blossoms between Frank and Annie, Buffalo Bill grows increasingly concerned that his show is losing money and appeal. Realizing that his troubles stem from his competitor, Pawnee Bill, Buffalo Bill decides to spice up the show by giving Annie top billing. Annie does well in a solo performance, but her success prompts Frank to doubt his star status and long for the days when Annie was a "sweet, simple little girl." After the show, Annie is introduced to Sitting Bull, an Indian chief who decides to adopt Annie as his daughter and finance the show. Following her induction into Chief Sitting Bull's tribe, Annie receives a farewell letter from Frank, who believes that Annie has lost interest in him. A short time later, Buffalo Bill takes his cowboy and Indian show to Europe, where Annie and Chief Sitting Bull become an instant sensation. Frank, meanwhile, joins Pawnee Bill's troupe. Despite the show's critical success in Europe, Buffalo Bill continues to lose money. When Buffalo Bill realizes that his star is lovesick, he decides to pack up the show and return home. In New York, Annie learns that Frank is now consorting with debutantes, and she is certain that he will reject her. Buffalo Bill tries to rescue his show by negotiating a merger with Pawnee Bill and by selling Annie's valuable medals. Annie and Frank eventually reconcile, but when Frank sees all her awards, he becomes jealous of her success and they argue over who is the better shooter. Annie and Frank decide to settle their argument in a shooting match, but before the match, Chief Sitting Bull, hoping to forge a permanent reconciliation between the two sweethearts, persuades Annie to deliberately lose. The strategy works, and Frank, with his pride restored, finally proposes marriage to Annie. *Buffalo Bill Cody. Envy. Indians of North America. Annie Oakley. Romance. Sharpshooters. Sitting Bull. Wild West shows. Adoption. Children. Cincinnati (OH). Class distinction. Country girls. Cowboys. Debutantes. Hotel owners. Literacy. New York City. Prizes and trophies. Reconciliation. Rivalry. Show business. Singers. Theatrical backers. Theatrical producers. Tribal chiefs. Victoria, Queen of England, 1819-1901.*
   Note: As depicted in the film, Annie Oakley, born Phoebe Anne Oakley Moses in 1860, was a markswoman who first toured circus and vaudeville circuits, and from 1885 to 1902 was a star attraction in Buffalo Bill's Wild West Show. Her husband, Frank E. Butler, was a noted marksman who toured with her. For more biographical information on Buffalo Bill Cody, please see the entry below for *Buffalo Bill*. The stage musical *Annie Get Your Gun* was first performed on Broadway on 16 May 1946, directed by Joshua Logan and starring Ethel Merman and Ray Middleton.
   Contemporary sources add the following information about the production:

In late Feb 1947, M-G-M purchased the film rights to the Broadway show for a record $650,000, and immediately cast Judy Garland in the title role. Bing Crosby was considered to co-star with Garland in Apr 1948. Rehearsals on the film began in early Oct 1948, and Garland's daughter Liza Minnelli, who was three years old at the time, was set to portray Annie Oakley's young sister. Production on the film initially began on 4 Apr 1949, with Busby Berkeley directing and Al Jennings assisting. Harry Stradling was the film's photographer. In early May, Berkeley was replaced by fellow dance director Charles Walters. Although a 4 May 1949 *HR* news item stated that Berkeley asked to be removed from the film "after a difference of opinion with Freed," a modern source notes that producer Arthur Freed removed Berkeley from the picture because he thought Berkeley was directing the film in the manner of a stage play. In mid-May, according to a *LAT* article, studio executives suspended Garland for repeated failures to report to the set. The article also noted that studio executives in the East were "particularly irked by the temperament of stars under the strained economic circumstances" of the time, and that the footage that had already been shot for the film (at a cost of $1,250,000) might have to be scrapped. M-G-M shut down production on the film while searching for a replacement for Garland and re-writing parts of the script.

A 13 May 1949 *HR* news item stated that Betty Garrett was a "hot contender" for the role, and modern sources note Judy Canova and Doris Day were considered as possible replacements. According to records of the M-G-M legal department, as reproduced in a modern source, a $100,000 contract was drawn up on 21 Jun 1949 for the loan-out of Paramount actress Betty Hutton. Previously-shot footage of the film was discarded, and production on the film resumed on 10 Oct 1949 with George Sidney directing and George Rhein assisting. Charles Rosher replaced cameraman Harry Stradling, and James E. Newcom replaced editor Al Akst. Actor Louis Calhern replaced Frank Morgan, who was originally cast in the role of "Buffalo Bill" but who died on 18 Sep 1949. Geraldine Wall, originally cast in the role of "Dolly Tate," was replaced by Benay Venuta, although a 30 Sep 1949 *DV* news item noted that Marjorie Reynolds was also considered for the role. An 11 Apr 1949 *HR* news item included Evelyn Finley and Napoleon Whiting in the cast, but their participation in the completed film is doubtful. *DV* news items include Vance Henry and trick riders Sharon and Shirley Lucas in the cast, but their participation in the completed film has not been confirmed. Production on the film was completed on 16 Dec 1949, ahead of schedule, and at $61,000 over the $3,707,000 budget. A shooting match sequence was cut from the final film following a 29 Jan 1950 preview in Long Beach, CA.

According to information contained in the MPAA/PCA Collection at the AMPAS Library, M-G-M was warned by the Breen Office in late Mar 1949 that the "Secretary of the Interior has gotten very Indian-minded and will raise hell about your showing the Indians lousing up the train in *Annie Get Your Gun*." It is not known whether any changes were made regarding the portrayal of Native Americans in the script following the recommendations of the Breen Office. In a May 1950 *Daily News* column, screenwriter Sidney Sheldon noted that several changes in the adaptation of the story from stage to screen were "unavoidable." Among the changes noted by Sheldon were the cutting of some of Annie's "earthy" lines, the elimination of a romantic subplot involving an ingenue, the combining of some of the stage version's minor characters and the elimination of two Irving Berlin songs ("Moonshine Lullaby" and "I Got Lost in His Arms"). Unused film footage featuring Garland singing "Doin' What Comes Natur'lly" and "I'm an Indian Too" was shown publicly for the first time in Paris in Oct 1991. In 1978, according to modern sources, Irving Berlin, who retained the music rights, refused to allow the picture to be shown commercially.

Annie Get Your Gun marked the American screen debut of actor Howard Keel. The picture grossed more than eight million dollars following its May 1950 release and its 1956-57 re-release, and received an Academy Award for Best Musical Direction. The film was also nominated for Best Color Cinematography, Best Color Art Direction and Best Editing. The Annie Oakley story was featured in the non-musical 1935 RKO film *Annie Oakley*, directed by George Stevens and starring Barbara Stanwyck and Preston Foster (see entry below). Oakley's exploits were also portrayed in an ABC television series, which starred Gail Davis and ran from 1953-57. In 1957, Mary Martin and John Raitt appeared in a television adaptation of the musical, and on 19 Mar 1967, the NBC television network aired a second version of the musical starring Ethel Merman and Bruce Yarnell.

Box 15 Apr 1950. *Daily News* 8 May 1950. *DV* 30 Sep 1949, p. 2. *DV* 14 Oct 1949, p. 14. *DV* 25 Oct 1949, p. 4. *DV* 30 Nov 1949, p. 11. *DV* 5 Dec 1949, p. 1. *DV* 16 Dec 1949, p. 3. *DV* 31 Jan 1950, p. 2. *DV* 12 Apr 1950, p. 3. *FD* 12 Apr 1950, p. 4. *HR* 27 Feb 1947, p. 2. *HR* 28 Feb 1947, p. 4. *HR* 1 Apr 1948, p. 1. *HR* 8 Oct 1948, p. 3. *HR* 15 Mar 1949, p. 1. *HR* 8 Apr 1949, p. 10. *HR* 11 Apr 1949, p. 8. *HR* 4 May 1949, p. 1. *HR* 6 May 1949, p. 10. *HR* 11 May 1949, p. 2. *HR* 13 May 1949, p. 2. *HR* 20 May 1949, pp. 1-2. *HR* 23 May 1949, p. 2. *HR* 7 Oct 1949, p. 10. *HR* 12 Apr 1950, p. 3, 13. *HR* 12 Oct 1991. *LAT* 19 May 1949. *MPHPD* 15 Apr 1950, p. 261. *NYT* 18 May 1950, p. 37. *Var* 12 Apr 1950, p. 6.

ANNIE OAKLEY (Native Americans)

RKO Radio Pictures, Inc. *Dist* RKO Radio Pictures, Inc. 15 Nov 1935; *Prod:* 3 Aug—mid-Sep 1935 at Prudential Studios [©RKO Radio Pictures, Inc.; 15 Nov 1935; LP5984]. Sd (RCA Victor System); b&w. 10 reels. 79, 85, 88 or 90.5 min. PCA cert no. 1538.

Assoc prod Cliff Reid. *Prod* George Stevens. [*Asst dir*] James Hartnett. *Scr* Joel Sayre and John Twist. *Story* Joseph A. Fields and Ewart Adamson. *Photog* J. Roy Hunt and [Harold Wenstrom]. *Art dir* Van Nest Polglase. *Art dir assoc* Perry Ferguson. *Ed* Jack Hively. *Mus dir* Alberto Colombo. *Rec* John L. Cass. *Mus rec* P. J. Faulkner, Jr. [*Research* Elizabeth McGaffey].

Cast: BARBARA STANWYCK [(*Annie Oakley*)], Preston Foster [(*Toby Walker*)], Melvyn Douglas [(*Jeff Hogarth*)], Moroni Olsen [(*William "Buffalo Bill" Cody*)], Pert Kelton [(*Vera Delmar*)], Andy Clyde [(*MacIvor*)], Chief Thunderbird [(*Chief Sitting Bull*)], Margaret Armstrong [(*Mrs. Oakley*)], Delmar Watson [(*Wesley Oakley*)], Adeline Craig [(*Susan Oakley*)], [Willie Best (*Cook*)].

Drama, Historical, Biography. [*Print viewed*]. At the turn of the century, young Annie Oakley leaves her backwoods home to challenge the handsome New York vaudeville sharpshooter, Toby Walker, to a shooting contest in Cincinnati. Unknown to Toby, Annie is a crack shot who stuns the crowd with her sure-handed marksmanship. Attracted to Toby, Annie deliberately loses the contest, but her skills are noticed by Jeff Hogarth, a partner in Buffalo Bill Cody's Wild West Show, who convinces her to join the troupe as Toby's counterpart. After his initial skepticism, Cody and the others welcome Annie into the show. However, when Toby later overhears Cody questioning Annie's showmanship, he generously teaches her his shooting tricks, transforming her into such a star that during her first performance in Washington, D.C., she impresses Chief Sitting Bull into joining the troupe. Once polished, Annie bests the braggart Toby in the ring, which gives promoter Ned Buntline the idea of formalizing a feud between them. Although Toby confesses his love for Annie, he encourages her to play her part for the sake of the show. Soon after, while camped in Cincinnati, Toby saves Sitting Bull from an attack by a vengeful drunk but damages his eyesight in the process. Because he wants her to shine in front of her family, Toby says nothing about his eyes and ends up accidentally shooting Annie in the hand, an error that some of the troupe believes is deliberate and leads to his immediate dismissal. Although Annie makes a triumphant tour of Europe, she is unable to forget Toby, and when Hogarth, who also loves her, reluctantly shows her a newspaper article that vindicates Toby, she determines to find him. At the New York show, Sitting Bull spots Toby in the audience and, after a chase, returns Annie to his side. Buffalo Bill Cody. Annie Oakley. Rivalry. Romance. Sharpshooters. Show business. Cincinnati (OH). Contests. Cowboys. Europe. Eyes. Firearms. Indians of North America. Murphy beds. Ohio. Sitting Bull. Vaudevillians. Washington (D.C.).

Note: The working title of this film, in which Stanwyck made her western movie debut, was *Shooting Star*. As depicted in the film, Annie Oakley, born Phoebe Anne Oakley Moses in 1860, was a markswoman who first toured circus and vaudeville circuits, and from 1885 to 1902 was a star attraction in Buffalo Bill's Wild West Show. Unlike the film's depiction, however, Oakley married in 1876. Her husband, Frank E. Butler, was a noted marksman who toured with her. For more information about Buffalo Bill Cody, please see the entry below for *Buffalo Bill*.

Early *HR* production charts credit Joseph A. Fields and Robert Neville with the script. Fields is listed on screen as a co-story writer, but Neville's contribution to the final film has not been confirmed. Ray Mayer, Jack Mulhall, Dick Elliott, Eddie Borden, Otto Hoffman, Brooks Benedict, Pat Moriarity, Brandon Hurst, Will Stanton and George Lollier were listed as cast members in *HR* production charts, but their participation in the final film has not been confirmed. According to the production charts, at least part of the film was shot at the Prudential Studios. Harold Wenstrom, not J. Roy Hunt, is listed as photographer in all of the charts. Much of the sub-plot of the film involved Sitting Bull's encounters with modern "technology," such as Murphy beds and gas lighting.

In 1946, Irving Berlin presented a Broadway musical version of the Annie Oakley story called *Annie Get Your Gun*, which starred Ethel Merman. In 1950, George Sidney directed an M-G-M version of the stage musical, also titled *Annie Get Your Gun*, which starred Betty Hutton and Howard Keel. Annie Oakley was also featured in an ABC television series, which starred Gail Davis and ran from 1953-57.

DV 26 Oct 1935, p. 3. *FD* 29 Oct 1935, p. 6. *HR* 23 Apr 1935, p. 6. *HR* 2 Aug 1935, p. 6. *HR* 5 Aug 1935, p. 7. *HR* 12 Aug 1935, p. 7. *HR* 19 Aug 1935, p. 11. *HR* 3 Sep 1935, p. 10. *HR* 9 Sep 1935, p. 6. *HR* 26 Oct 1935, p. 3. *MPD* 28 Oct 1935, p. 9. *MPH* 31 Aug 1935, p. 54. *MPH* 9 Nov 1935, pp. 60-61. *NYT* 24 Dec 1935, p. 10. *Var* 25 Dec 1935, p. 15.

ANOUSH (Armenian language)

Crown Productions. 1945; New York opening: 27 Apr 1945. Sd; b&w. 4 reels. Armenian language.

Prod Charles Merjanian. *Dir* Setrag Vartian. *Dir of photog* Marcel LePicard. *Art dir* Kourken. *Film ed* John F. Link. *Arr and cond* Marshall Chashoudian. *Mus comp* Armen Dickranian. *English titles* Serene Kassapian.

Source: Based on the *Anoush* by Hovannes Toumanian, and the operetta of the same name by Armen Dickranian (Nineteenth century, publication and production undetermined).

Cast: Zaruhi Elmassian (*Anoush*), S. T. Vartian (*Saro*), Misak Frankian (*Mosi*), Satig Logian (*Zarnishan*), Krish Andikian (*Zakar*),

Haiyastan Baronian (*Fortune teller*), George Konjoian (*Devrish*), Hrach Amber (*Traveler*).

Melodrama, with songs. [*Not viewed*]. Deep in the Lori Mountains, a young girl named Anoush hears the song of the shepherd Saro as he sings beneath her window. Despite her mother's disapproval, Anoush goes to Saro, and, learning that the shepherd loves her as much as she loves him, hides with him while her mother desperately searches for her. Later, on the feast of the Ascension, the young girls of the village tell one another's fortunes, and when Anoush's turn arrives, the prediction is bleak: a dagger will one day pierce her lover's breast. The young girls try to comfort the distraught Anoush, but she insists that as an infant she was cursed when her mother refused to give alms to a wandering beggar. At a wedding celebration, Saro and Anoush's brother Mosi wrestle for the amusement of the assembled guests. Inspired by Anoush's presence, Saro squarely bests Mosi, and the latter vows eternal revenge for the humiliation. Mosi makes Anoush promise never to see Saro again, but Saro appears and the lovesick Anoush flees with him. Sheriff Zakar looks for the renegade couple, and, finding Saro, kills him. Weeping upon Saro's grave, Anoush dies of a broken heart and joins her lover as he walks to his eternal resting place. *Armenians. Brothers and sisters. Caucasus Mountains. Revenge. Romance. Runaways. Curses. Fortune-tellers. Holidays. Murder. Peasantry. Weddings. Wrestlers and wrestling.*

Note: The above credits and plot summary were based on a translated dialogue continuity and press materials deposited with the NYSA. The Lori Mountains, the film's setting, are located in the Caucasus Mountains. Press materials claim that *Anoush* was the first Armenian-language film made in Hollywood. Press notes also include the statement that the cast was "supported by hundreds of character players."

ANSWER FOR ANNE (Immigrants)

Caravel Films, Inc. *Dist* National Lutheran Council. **1949.** Sd; b&w. 40 min.

Pres Lutheran World Action.

Cast: Lenka Peterson (*Anne*), Will Geer (*Her father*), Harvey Stevens (*Pastor*).

Postwar life, Drama. [*Print viewed*]. Inside her bedroom, a small town girl named Anne sits at a desk gazing at a souvenir photograph of the Statue of Liberty. As she contemplates the inscription, "Give me your tired, your poor,/Your huddled masses yearning to breathe free,/The wretched refuse of your teeming shore,/Send these, the nameless, tempest-tost to me,/I lift my lamp beside the golden door!" Anne recalls the lesson she learned earlier that day in her civics class about "DPs," displaced persons who, because of the war, have lost their homes in Europe: The teacher tells the class that hundreds of thousands of DPs are currently living in former concentration camps in Germany. When the teacher calls on a student named Walker, he describes new legislation that would allow for the entry of 215,000 refugees, with priority being given to skilled workers. For that evening's homework, the teacher assigns an essay on the topic, "Why Our Town Should Take in Displaced Persons." After school, Anne, whose father is the editor of the local newspaper, sneaks into his office and raids his files for information about DPs. When Anne asks for help in writing the essay, her father advises her to take a poll of the local business owners to gauge their opinions. The town's cobbler tells Anne he is worried about housing and jobs for the DPs, while her classmate Wallie, who works at the drugstore, says he already knows what he will write for his essay. Wallie, facing graduation at the end of the term, says he does not want to have to compete against "foreigners" for a job. When she asks Ed, a policeman, for his opinion, he refers her to the mayor, who also expresses anxiety over housing and jobs. Anne reaches the conclusion that everyone in her town is selfish and goes to the local Lutheran church to seek solace. There she tells a kindly pastor her feelings, after which he explains that he has just been sent a short documentary film showing the plight of the DPs. Just before the pastor turns off the light switch, Anne's father sneaks into the room and watches from the back row. The film depicts the story of a man and his two starving children, who are taken in by an official of the Lutheran Church. The official delivers them to a converted concentration camp in Nuremberg, where they receive food and clothing. They are given a place to sleep, and as soon as the man is strong enough, he is assigned work around the camp. Given lessons in English and the Scriptures, the refugees pray that God will let them come to America. Sadly, the man is told that America is

accepting only childless single men. When the film ends, Anne sees her father, who tells her that he is writing an editorial about DPs for the newspaper. The pastor then tells Anne that if people would only follow Christ's example, they would not behave so selfishly. Back in her room, Anne looks again at the Statue of Liberty, prays silently for a moment, then begins her essay. *Immigrants. Lutheran Church. Small town life. Students. Concentration camps. Drugstores. Editors. Family relationships. Isolationism. Mayors. Nuremberg (Germany). Photographs. Police. Prayer. Reverends. Schools. Shoemakers. Small town life. Statue of Liberty National Monument (New York City). Teachers. War refugees. World War II. Xenophobia.*

Note: The credits on the viewed print reveal that the film was reissued in 1990 to commemorate the fiftieth anniversary of the Lutheran Immigration and Refugee Service. This entry is based on the reissued version, which appears to be the same as the 1949 version with the addition of a written statement about the reissue, which was made with the "financial assistance of Fraternal Benefits and Financial Services for Lutherans." *Exb* noted that "this fine production is available in 16mm. and 35mm. free to theatres and other interested parties." The opening credits also include the following note: "Overseas Sequence Filmed with the cooperation of International Refugee Organization and Lutheran World Federation Service to Refugees."

Exb 2 Feb 1949, p. 2556.

ANYBODY HERE SEEN KELLY? (French Americans, Irish Americans)

Universal Pictures Corp. 9 Sep 1928 [©Universal Pictures Corp.; 13 Apr 1928; LP25163]. Si; b&w. 6 or 7 reels, 6,243 ft.

Dir William Wyler. *Scen and adpt* John B. Clymer. *Adpt* Joseph Franklin Poland, James Gruen, Rob Wagner, Earl Snell and Samuel M. Pike. *Story* Leigh Jason. *Titles* Walter Anthony and Albert De Mond. *Photog* Charles Stumar. *Film ed* George McGuire.

Cast: Bessie Love (*Mitzi Lavelle*), Tom Moore (*Pat Kelly*), Kate Price (*Mrs. O'Grady*), Addie McPhail (*Mrs. Hickson*), Bruce Gordon (*Mr. Hickson*), Alfred Allen (*Sergeant Malloy*), Tom O'Brien (*Buck Johnson*), Wilson Benge (*Butler*), Rosa Gore (*French mother*), Dorothea Wolbert (*Slavey*).

Comedy-drama. Mitzi Lavelle, in love with carefree Pat Kelly, a member of the A. E. F. in France, follows him to America as a stewardess on a liner. Arriving in New York, Mitzi is met by Buck Johnson, once a rival for her hand, now a customs official. He promises to extend her leave if she will spend it with him. Mitzi rejects him, finds Kelly directing traffic at 42nd Street and Broadway (where he is stationed as a traffic policeman), and proceeds to settle down with him. Johnson attempts to have Mitzi deported while Kelly is held in jail for assaulting the customs official. Assisted by an Irish sergeant, Kelly claims Mitzi before the ship departs and marries her, thus forever thwarting Johnson's intentions to eject her. *American Expeditionary Force. Customs officials. Deportation. France. French Americans. Immigrants. Irish Americans. Police. World War I.*

Note: The following were not given screen credit for adaptation: Joseph Franklin Poland, James Gruen, John B. Clymer, Rob Wagner, Earl Snell, and Samuel M. Pike.

FD 21 Oct 1928.

ANYBODY'S WAR (African Americans)

Paramount-Publix Corp. 2 Aug **1930**; New York opening: 10 Jul 1930 [©Paramount-Publix Corp.; 1 Aug 1930; LP1460]. Sd (Movietone); b&w. 10 reels, 8,120 ft.

Dir Richard Wallace. *Scr* Lloyd Corrigan. *Adpt* Hector Turnbull. *Addl dial* Walter Weems. *Photog* Allen Siegler. *Film ed* Otto Levering. *Rec eng* M. M. Paggi.

Source: Based on the novel *The Two Black Crows in the A.E.F.* by Charles E. Mack (Indianapolis, 1928).

Cast: George Moran (*Willie*), Charles E. Mack (*Amos Crow*), Joan Peers (*Mary Jane Robinson*), Neil Hamilton (*Ted Reinhardt*), Walter Weems (*Sergeant Skipp*), Betty Farrington (*Camilla*), Walter McGrail (*Captain Davis*).

Comedy. At the time of the United States' entry into World War I, Amos Crow is dogcatcher in the little river town of Buford, Tennessee; he is so kind-hearted that he boards all his captive canines rather than kill them. His pal, Willie, decides to enlist after being chided for his lack of patriotism by Camilla, cook in the home of Mary Jane Robinson, daughter of an aristocratic family. Amos is rejected by the Army because of his feet, but manages to get in line with recruits bound for France, along with his dog, Deep Stuff. At a camp in France, Mary Jane, now a YMCA hostess, breaks off with Captain Davis, who is unmasked as a German spy, and Amos and Willie promise to find

Ted for her. In rescuing Ted from a dugout, they learn of a surprise attack; they send Deep Stuff back with a message, but he is missing upon their return. After the war, he returns with a dachshund "war bride" and six pups. *African Americans. Courtship. Dog-catchers. Dogs. France. Soldiers. Spies. Tennessee. United States. Army. World War I. Young Men's Christian Association.*

Note: For information about George Moran and Charles Mack, the vaudeville and burlesque black-faced comedians, please see the entry below for the 1932 film *Hypnotized*.

FD 13 Jul 1930. *NYT* 11 Jul 1930, p. 22. *Var* 16 Jul 1930, p. 15.

ANYTHING CAN HAPPEN (Russian Americans)

Paramount Pictures Corp.; The Perlberg—Seaton Production. *Dist* Paramount Pictures Corp. May **1952**; *Prod:* 21 Jun—10 Aug 1951 [©Paramount Pictures Corp.; 26 Feb 1952; LP1735]. Sd (Western Electric Recording); b&w. 11-12 reels, 9,552 or 9,595 ft. 105 or 107 min. PCA cert no. 15514.

Prod William Perlberg. *Dir* George Seaton. [*Asst dir* Chico Day and Alvin Ganzer]. [*2d asst dir* Danny McCauley and Al Mann]. [*Asst dir— New York* E. Fay]. *Wrt for the scr by* George Seaton and George Oppenheimer. *Dir of photog* Daniel L. Fapp. [*2d cam* Haskell Boggs]. [*Asst cam* James Grant and Harlowe Stengel]. [*1st cam—New York* Wallace Kelley]. [*1st cam—Gallup, NM* Rex Wimpy]. [*Stills* Jack Koffman]. [*Gaffer* Earl Crowell]. *Spec photog eff* Gordon Jennings. *Process photog* Farciot Edouart. *Art dir* Hal Pereira and Earl Hedrick. *Ed* Alma Macrorie. *Set dec* Sam Comer and Ross Dowd. *Cost* Edith Head. [*Ward—Ladies* Grace Harris]. [*Ward—Men* Eric Seelig]. *Mus score* Victor Young. *Sd rec* Harry Mills and Gene Garvin. [*Rec* Malon Boyce]. *Makeup supv* Wally Westmore. [*Makeup* Carl Silvera]. [*Hair* Lenore Weaver]. *Asst to the prod* [*and dir of roadshots*] Arthur Jacobson. [*Prod mgr* Frank Caffey]. [*Asst prod mgr* Hugh Brown]. [*Unit prod mgr* Charles Woolstenhulme and Edward J. Ralph]. [*Asst unit prod mgr* Donald A. Robb]. [*Dial coach* Ruth Roberts]. [*Balkan dial tutor* Wladimir Babishwili]. [*Guitar coach* Tiny Timbrell]. [*Turkish translations* Galip Aysay]. [*Casting* Bert McKay]. [*Scr supv* Claire Behnke]. [*Publ* Jack Hirshberg]. [*Stage engineer* Ray Cossar]. [*1st prop* Bob McCrillis]. [*2d prop* Dick Brandow]. [*Company grip* Irving Newmeyer]. [*Mike grip* Herb Welts]. [*Elec* Chet Stafford]. [*Casting secy* Olive Long].

Song(s): "Love Laughs at Kings," music by Victor Young, Georgian lyrics by Wladimir Babishwili, English lyrics by Jay Livingston and Ray Evans; "Pray Koonak," "Alla Verdi," "Souliko," "Goolem John" and "Niko, Niko (Chirime)," traditional Georgian folk songs; unidentified Turkish folk song.

Source: Based on the book *Anything Can Happen* by George and Helen Papashvily (New York, 1944).

Cast: JOSÉ FERRER [(*Giorgi Papashvily*)], Kim Hunter [(*Helen Watson*)], Kurt Kasznar [(*Nuri Bey*)], Eugenie Leontovich [(*Anna Godiedze*)], Oscar Karlweiss [(*Uncle Besso*)], Oscar Beregi [(*Uncle John*)], Mikhail Rasumny [(*Tariel Godiedze*)], Nick Dennis [(*Chancho*)], Gloria Marlowe [(*Luba Godiedze*)], Otto Waldis [(*Sandro*)], George Voskovec [(*Pavli*)], Alex Danaroff [(*Eliko*)], Natasha Lytess [(*Madame Greshkin*)], [Harry Clark (*Davit Routinian*)], [Mary Jackson (*Jane Shantz*)], [Jimmie Parnell (*Harry Shantz*)], [Wladimir Babishwili, Vladimir Strichevsky (*Georgians*)], [Billie Bird, Minerva Urecal, Mabel Smaney, Pauline Creasman (*Women on bus*)], [Tiny Timbrell (*Fat man on bus*)], [Will Orlean (*Card man*)], [Esther Zeitlin (*Polish immigrant woman*)], [William Kaufman, Albert d'Arno (*German immigrants*)], [Paul Cristo (*Greek immigrant*)], [Alan Harris (*Handy man*)], [Demetri Alexis (*Hotel clerk*)], [Richard Kipling, Vincent Neptune (*Swedish immigrants*)], [George Humbert, Dario Piazza, Gilda Oliva (*Italian immigrants*)], [Rev. Vasilios Markopoulos (*Minister*)], [Bert Freed, E. G. Marshall (*Immigration officers*)], [Anthony Blair (*Bailiff*)], [Thomas Chalmers (*Judge*)], [Lewis Charles (*The fixer*)], [Spencer Davis (*Custom officer*)], [Mary Love, Ruth Rickaby (*Landladies*)], [Charles McClelland (*Policeman*)], [George Papashvily (*Man on boat*)], [Samuel Schwartz (*Taxi driver*)], [Alexander Pulkaradse, P. Rochin (*Immigrants*)], [George Barton (*Mailman*)], [Eddie Laughton, Somer Albert (*Clerks*)], [Allan Douglas (*Immigration official*)], [Willis Bouchey (*Judge Gordon*)], [Nolan Leary (*Doctor*)], [John Miljan, Rus Conklin (*Indians*)], [Maxie Thrower (*Postman*)], [Mary Field (*Aunt Florence*)], [David Ormont (*Maitre d'*)], [Elspeth Dudgeon (*Grandma*)], [Sid Raymond (*Clerk in employment agency*)], [S. Prevore (*Attorney*)], [Jack Albertson (*Flower vendor*)], [Chuck

Hamilton, Lyle Moraine], [Waclaw Rekwart (*Steward*)], [Nicholas Conavaras], [Paul Manning].

Romance, Comedy. [*Print viewed*]. Giorgi Papashvily, an immigrant from Georgia in Russia, arrives in New York City on an ocean liner. Giorgi speaks no English, but his friend, Nuri Bey, a Turk, translates for him as he is interviewed by an immigration official. The official welcomes Giorgi, saying that all people are foreigners in America. Enthralled by the city, Giorgi gets a job tarring roofs, and as he gradually learns to speak English, he asks around town about his uncle John, a chef with whom he has communicated since 1936. When Pedras, one of his friends, picks some flowers in Central Park, Giorgi, Pedras and Nuri Bey are ticketed by an officer. They go to a "fixer" to take care of the ticket, but Giorgi refuses to pay him, saying he is not guilty. In court, while mangling the language, Giorgi convinces the judge that he did not pick the flowers. Helen Watson, the court transcriber, is pleased to learn that Giorgi is from Georgia, and after the judge dismisses the case, tells Giorgi that she is a collector of folk music. Learning that he can sing and play on the guitar songs from his village, she invites him to her apartment to sing and record for her and other folk song collectors. On one of the recordings, he recognizes the voice of Uncle John. He then locates Uncle John working at a restaurant, and Uncle John brings Giorgi to live at the boarding house of Anna Godiedze, home to immigrants from a number of different countries. Helen invites Giorgi and Nuri Bey to dinner, and after she twice calls Giorgi "a darling," he finds the meaning of the word in a dictionary as "dearly beloved." Striken with love, he invites her to the boarding house for dinner. During the meal, Giorgi, now five months in America, looks over his friends and comments that if a Georgian, Syrian, Turk and Armenian can eat together, then in America, "anything can happen." When Uncle John sadly tells Helen that he failed the citizenship test because he mixed up the names of presidents, she offers to coach him. Sometime later, the boarders, seeing that Giorgi is heartsick, decide he should propose to Helen; however, before he can ask her, she relates that her grandmother in Pasadena has had a stroke, and she must fly there for two weeks. She calls him "dear" and kisses him on the cheek before she leaves. Two months later, Giorgi is despondent, as Helen has reported that her grandmother has gotten neither better nor worse. Uncle John proposes that they go to California with money he has saved. To their dismay, the whole household wants to join them, except for Eliko Tornavily, who has tried to keep records on all Georgians living in the U.S. In the Southwest, the group gets stuck in a hole. Giorgi finds two American Indians to help, and Uncle John instructs the group to treat them with respect, as they were the first citizens of the country. As they approach Los Angeles, they decide to go first to Azusa, where Eliko's cousin Besso lives. When Giorgi expresses the wish to own a ranch like Besso's, where he could grow oranges, Besso offers to lend him money, saying he wants to move to Nevada, where the nearest neighbor would be fifty miles away, and Giorgi agrees. He visits Helen and her grandmother, who takes a liking to him. Seeing that he is humbled by their expensive house and vast acreage of orange trees, Helen's grandmother tells of the success of her husband, a poor man who emigrated from Scotland in 1903 when he was Giorgi's age. This incites Giorgi's determination, and he writes Eliko, who asks all the Georgians in California to come with their friends one Sunday to help overhaul the ranch. Uncle John, who plans to take the citizenship exam soon, reveals to Helen that once the ranch is in operation, Giorgi plans to marry her. Greatly shaken, Helen admits to Uncle John that she is not in love. She tries to tell Giorgi, but because of his great enthusiasm over his plans, she cannot. During a celebration for Besso, Uncle John suffers a heart attack. As he lies in bed dying, Helen brings a judge to his bedside, who, after questioning him on the reasons immigrants have come to the U.S., administers the oath and confers citizenship on the proud man. Uncle John dies holding Giorgi's and Helen's hands. At Christmas time, Helen's grandmother talks to her about Giorgi, reminding her that Helen's former husband didn't need her, while Georgi does. She advises Helen that the only basis for marriage is to be needed and wanted in everyday life, not the "chill up and down her spine" that Helen says she does not get from Giorgi. Just then, the radio broadcasts frost warnings. Helen is upset that Giorgi has not gotten expert help with his orange trees. She rushes to his groves and with irritation yells and instructs Giorgi, who has been using a book, that he is improperly placing the smudge pots. The next day, after most

of the trees have been saved, Giorgi proposes. She accepts, she says, because she now feels she needs him. *Citizenship. Immigrants. Romance. Russian Americans.* Armenians. Aunts. Azusa (CA). Boardinghouses. Chefs. Death and dying. Folk songs. Grandmothers. Heart disease. Hermits. Indians of North America. Misers. New York City. New York City–Central Park. Orange groves. Pasadena (CA). Syrian Americans. Trials. Turkish Americans.

Note: Parts of the best-selling book, *Anything Can Happen*, described as an autobiographical novel, appeared originally as short stories in the magazines *Direction* and *Common Ground*. Location shooting for the film was done in New York City; Gallup, New Mexico, at an Indian reservation; and in California in West Covina ("Besso's" farm), Pasadena ("Helen's" grandmother's house), Azusa, Saugas and Simi. The S.S. *Saturnia* was used in the opening scenes of the boat entering New York harbor. Author George Papashvily appeared as an extra on the boat. Other New York scenes were shot in Central Park, on a midtown bus and at 153 E 57 St. at the Magistrate's Court. According to publicity, the film marked the screen debuts of Oscar Beregi, who was a top Hungarian actor before the postwar Communist government; Otto Waldis, a producer from Austria who founded the drama department at the University of Alabama; George Voskovec, known as the Czech Charlie Chaplin; Alex Danaroff, a restaurateur; and stage actors Oscar Karlweiss and Gloria Marlowe. Natasha Lytess was loaned from Twentieth Century-Fox.

Tiny Timbrell, formerly a guitarist in Harry James's band, coached Jose Ferrer in playing a five-string guitar. Robert Merrill was originally to star in the film, according to a 27 Sep 1950 *HR* news item. In Feb 1951, Nancy Olson was signed to co-star. Producer William Perlberg saw Kim Hunter in a preview screening of *A Streetcar Names Desire* in Jun 1951 and gave her the role. Jack Albertson, who played the role of a flower vendor, was originally cast in the role of "The Fixer." Sources conflict concerning the roles played by Voskovec and Danaroff; while the Call Bureau Cast Service and reviews list Voskevec as "Pavli" and Danaroff as "Eliko," a studio cast list credits Voskevec as "Kortan" and Danaroff as "Pavli." In addition, the Call Bureau Cast Service and the studio cast list credit a second actor, Elia Louis Geladze, in the role of "Eliko." It is not known if Geladze was in the final film.

The film had a preview showing in Jan 1952 at Hunter College to 2,000 delegates attending the U.S. National Commission for Unesco, according to a *NYT* news item. A spokesman for Paramount stated, "Unesco officials feel that the picture, by showing the assimilation of immigrants into the American way of life and the opportunities available to all Americans, illustrates what Unesco is trying to accomplish." *LAEx*, in their review of the film commented, "I'm sure Messrs. William Perlberg and George Seaton, its producer-director-writer combination, didn't intend it to be American propaganda—but it is that, so completely and thoroughly, that I wish it could be shown in every city, town and hamlet behind the Iron Curtain." While most reviews were favorable, *New Yorker* called the film "somewhat superficial," and *NYT* opined that while the Papashvilys' tale of immigration twenty years earlier "was reasonable," the film's story was not, as "the prospect of such a young fellow arriving today is nigh absurd." *NYT* also criticized the depiction of the immigrant group Papashvily finds in New York: "that a strong and gregarious colony of South Georgians is currently thriving and being chauvinistic in this land is beyond the range of acceptance of all but the lovers of romance. Thus the cozy picture Mr. Seaton presents of a band of genial eccentrics singing songs and having feasts in old-country style, as of the present, is in the realm of myth."

The length of the version prepared for foreign distribution was 868 feet (or about ten minutes) shorter than the domestic version. According to a *NYT* news item, a theater in Baltimore showing the film was picketed on 21 May 1952 by members of a local American Legion post because Jose Ferrer had been questioned a year earlier by the House Un-American Activities Committee concerning membership in the Communist party. Ferrer denied ever having been a Communist.

Box 8 Mar 1952. *Cue* 5 Apr 1952. *DV* 27 Feb 1952, p.3 *Exb* 12 Mar 1952, p. 3254 *FD* 28 Feb 1952, p.10 *Har* 1 Mar 1952, p. 35 *HCN* 2 May 1952. *HR* 27 Sep 1950. *HR* 20 Jul 1951. *HR* 27 Feb 1951, p.4 *LADN* 2 May 1952. *LAEx* 17 Jan 1951. *LAEx* 2 May 1952. *LAT* 21 Jan 1951. *LAT* 23 Mar 1952. *LAT* 2 May 1952, pt. III, p. 9. *Look* 6 May 1952. *MPD* 27 Feb 1952. *MPHPD* 1 Mar 1952, p. 1253 *New Yorker* 12 Apr 1952. *NYT* 8 Jul 1951. *NYT* 27 Jan 1952. *NYT* 23 May 1952. *NYT* 4 Apr 1952, p. 21 *Paramount News* 9 Oct 1950. *Paramount News* 18 Jun 1951. *Paramount News* 2 Jul 1951. *Paramount News* 16 Jul 1951. *Paramount News* 17 Mar 1952. *Paramount News* 7 Apr 1952. *Paramount News* 21 Apr 1952. *Var* 27 Feb 1952, p.6

APACHE (Native Americans, Apache, Cherokee)

Norma Productions, Inc.; A Hecht-Lancaster Presentation. *Dist* United Artists Corp. Jul 1954; Chicago premiere: late Jun 1954; *Prod:* mid-Oct 1953—mid-Jan 1954 at Keywest Studio [©Linden Productions; 30 Jun 1954; LP4003]. Sd (Western Electric Recording); b&w (col); 1.85-1. 8,030 ft. 86, 87, 89 or min. PCA cert no. 16783.

Prod Harold Hecht. *Dir* Robert Aldrich. *Asst dir* Sid Sidman and [Leon Chooluck]. *Wrt for the scr by* James R. Webb. *Photog* Ernest Laszlo and [Stanley Cortez]. *Spec eff* Lee Zavitz. *Technicolor color consultant* Leonard Doss. *Prod des* Nicolai Remisoff. *Ed supv* Alan Crosland, Jr. [*Film ed* Edward Mann]. *Set dec* Joseph Kish. *Cost des* Norma. *Mus* David Raksin. *Orch* Maurice de Packh and Ruby Raksin. *Mus ed* W. Lloyd Young. *Sd eng* Jack Solomon. *Makeup* Robert Schiffer and Harry Maret. *Hair styles* Katherine Shea and Lillian Ugrin. *Prod mgr* Jack R. Berne. [*Stunts* Janie Statz].

Source: Based on the novel *Broncho Apache* by Paul I. Wellman (New York, 1936).

Cast: BURT LANCASTER [(*Massai*)], JEAN PETERS [(*Nalinle*)], John McIntire [(*Al Sieber*)], Charles Buchinsky [(*Hondo*)], John Dehner [(*Weddle*)], Paul Guilfoyle [(*Santos*)], Ian MacDonald [(*Clagg*)], Walter Sande [(*Lt. Col. Beck*)], Morris Ankrum [(*Dawson*)], Monte Blue [(*Geronimo*)], Ta-wah-yi.

Western. [*Print viewed*]. In 1886, Geronimo, chief of the Chiricahua Apaches, finally surrenders to the U.S. Cavalry. As he carries a white flag to the victors, however, Massai, a young warrior who refuses to accept surrender, shoots at both the flag and the assembled soldiers. Massai is soon subdued, and as cuffs are placed on his hands, Indian fighter Al Sieber scoffs, "You're not a warrior any more; you're just a whipped Injun." Geronimo, Massai, and the other warriors are separated from the women, children and old men of the tribe and herded onto a train bound for Florida. Near St. Louis, the train stops for water, and a photographer takes a picture of the Apaches. As the photographer focuses on Weddle, an Indian hater who falsely claims to have captured Geronimo, Massai quietly slips from the train and begins running. Massai is alternately baffled and fascinated by city life in St. Louis, but he is forced to flee when a group of citizens sees his handcuffs. Massai moves on until, in Oklahoma territory, he meets a Cherokee Indian who owns his own farm. When Massai angrily accuses him of living like a white man, the Cherokee explains that after years of fighting and running, his people finally realized that rather than living on a reservation, the Cherokee must grow their own food and live in peace with the white man. Massai looks skeptical, but as he works his way back to the mountains of New Mexico, the idea begins to take hold. The new chief, Santos, and his daughter Nalinle are surprised when Massai appears in their dwelling. After listening to his plan of negotiating a "warrior's peace" with the white man, as the Cherokee had done, Nalinle tells Santos that Massai will again breathe life into the tribe. Santos, disheartened and muddled from drinking too much aguardiente, binds and gags Nalinle and then turns Massai over to Sieber. Believing that Nalinle loves a traitorous Apache named Hondo, Massai assumes that she helped her father and vows revenge on them both. Weddle is again ordered to transport Massai and several other Apache men to Florida, but this time, Weddle gives his prisoners an opportunity to run away as an excuse to shoot them all. Massai catches him off guard, however, and the Indians escape. Consumed by hatred, Massai launches a private war against white civilization, destroying telegraph lines, causing cattle stampedes and damaging the fort. The Apache kidnaps Nalinle, forcing her to travel for days without food or water. When Sieber and the soldiers approach, Nalinle warns Massai and he lets her go. Nalinle wants to remain with Massai, but he angrily orders her to return to the reservation. Exhausted and bleeding, she crawls up a hillside after him, whereupon he finally accepts her love. Sieber and his soldiers later find signs of the couple's marriage: Nalinle's beads placed carefully on a rock pile. This deeply disappoints Hondo, who swears that she soon will be a widow. Some time later, Nalinle informs Massai that she is pregnant, and the two decide to spend the winter in the western mountains. Although the mountains offer them refuge from their pursuers, it is bitterly cold, and there is little food. Nalinle tries to persuade Massai to end his war and plant the Cherokee corn, but he protests that because he is the last remaining Apache warrior, he must continue to fight. In the spring, the couple moves to warmer ground, and Nalinle steals more seed corn from the nearby trading post. Angry at first, Massai finally joins her in planting the corn. By this time, the Cavalry wants to call off the search for Massai, but Sieber insists on tracking the Apache. When Sieber learns that an Indian stole seed corn from the local merchant, he contacts the fort for reinforcements. Massai sees the troops coming and returns to the hut just as Nalinle goes into labor. She urges him to go out and die a warrior's death, whereupon he leaves the hut and charges some of the soldiers. Shot in the side, Massai takes refuge among the corn stalks. Sieber crawls in after him, but Massai tricks him and points a gun at his head. Just then, a baby cries, and Massai is mesmerized by the sound. Slowly he returns to the hut, throws down his rifle, and goes in. The colonel remarks that no Apache has ever grown corn before, adding that the war has been called off. Regretfully, Sieber replies that "it was the only war we had." *Apache Indians. Escapes. Legendary characters. Massai. Revenge. Abduction. Agriculture. Alcoholics. Assimilation (Sociology). Battered women. Betrayal.*

Cherokee Indians. Childbirth. Corn. Fathers and daughters. Feats of strength. Geronimo. Hunger. New Mexico. Obsession. Prisoners. Racism. Rites and ceremonies. Romance. Romantic rivalry. St. Louis (MO). Trains. Tribal chiefs. United States. Army. Cavalry. Voyages and travel.

Note: The working title of this film was *Bronco Apache*. The picture opens with the following written prologue: "This is the story of Massai, the last Apache warrior. It has been told and re-told until it has become one of the great legends of the Southwest. It began in 1886 with Geronimo's surrender." The first part of the film is based on the historical surrender of Geronimo, chief of a band of Chiricahua Apaches, to U.S. Gen. Nelson Miles on 3 Sep 1886. Following the surrender, the U.S. government violated its agreement and transported nearly 450 Apache men, women, and children, some of whom had had no part in Geronimo's escape from the San Carlos Reservation, to Fort Marion and Fort Pickens in Florida.

Although a *HR* production chart lists Phil Van Zandt, Morris Ankrum, David Hoffman, John Dehner, Frank Ferguson and Johnny McGough in the cast, their participation in the released film has not been confirmed. According to a 16 Mar 1956 written by Robert Aldrich and contained in the Aldrich Collection of the DGA, Aldrich noted that a considerable amount of the social comment in the film was eliminated. According to a modern source, Aldrich wanted to end the film with the U.S. Cavalry shooting Massai in the back but United Artists, however, favored a more peaceful finale. Aldrich filmed both endings, but in the final print, Massai remains unharmed and lives happily ever after. According to a *NYT* news item, production was delayed for one month due to injuries suffered by Burt Lancaster in a riding accident while on location in Sonora, CA. Other location scenes were filmed in Sedona, AZ, along the CA-NV state border and at Burro Flats, Solemit Canyon, Vasquez Rocks and the Agoura Ranch in CA. Charles Buchinsky, who played the role of "Hondo," adopted the name Charles Bronson shortly after this film was released. According to a Nov 1960 *DV* news item describing a 1957 law suit filed on behalf of cinematographer Stanley Cortez, Cortez was fired from the picture and replaced by Leonard Doss. The court ruled that Cortez was entitled to partial pay for his work on the film. The film was ranked twenty-third in *Variety*'s list of "1954 Box Office Champs." For information about films featuring Al Sieber, a real-life Cavalry scout, see entry below for *Arrowhead*.

Box 3 Jul 1954. *DV* 30 Jun 1954, p. 3. *DV* 8 Nov 1960. *Exb* 14 Jul 1954, pp. 3786-87. *FD* 7 Jul 1954, p. 10. *Har* 3 Jul 1954, p. 107. *HR* 16 Oct 1953, p. 11. *HR* 8 Jan 1954. *HR* 28 Jun 1954. *HR* 30 Jun 1954, p. 3. *MPHPD* 3 Jul 1954, p. 49. *NYT* 27 Dec 1953. *NYT* 10 Jul 1954, p. 7. *Var* 30 Jun 1954, p. 6.

APACHE AGENT *see* WALK THE PROUD LAND

APACHE AMBUSH (Latino, Native Americans, Apache)

Columbia Pictures Corp. *Dist* Columbia Pictures Corp. Sep **1955**; Prod: 28 Mar–6 Apr 1955 [©Columbia Pictures Corp.; 26 Aug 1955; LP5311]. Sd (Western Electric Recording); b&w. 7 reels, 6,101 ft. 67-68 min. PCA cert no. 17513.

Prod Wallace MacDonald. *Dir* Fred F. Sears. *Asst dir* Charles S. Gould. *Story and scr* David Lang. *Dir of photog* Fred Jackman, Jr. *Art dir* Paul Palmentola. *Film ed* Jerome Thoms. *Set dec* Frank Tuttle. *Mus cond* Mischa Bakaleinikoff. *Sd* Don McKay.

Cast: Bill Williams [(*James Kingston*)], Richard Jaeckel [(*Lee Parker*)], Alex Montoya [(*Joaquin Jironza*)], Movita [(*Rosita*)], Adelle August [(*Ann Parker*)], Tex Ritter [(*Trager*)], Ray "Crash" Corrigan [(*Hank Calvin*)], Ray Teal [(*Sgt. Tim O'Roarke*)], Don C. Harvey [(*Tex McGuire*)], James Griffith [(*President Abraham Lincoln*)], James Flavin [(*Col. Marshall*)], George Chandler [(*Chandler*)], Forrest Lewis [(*Silas Parker*)], George Keymas [(*Tweedy*)], [Harry Lauter (*Bailey*)], [Henry Escalante (*Ramierz*)], [Bill Hale (*Bob Jennings*)], [Robert Foulk (*Red Jennings*)], [Victor Millan (*Manoel*)], [Clayton Moore (*Cameron*)], [John Zaremba (*Secretary*)], [Don Carlos (*Brigand*)], [Edmund Cobb (*Clinton*)], [Frank Sully (*Leslie*)], [Ed Hinton (*Husky pioneer*)], [Joseph Breen (*Sgt. Federman*)], [Robert B. Williams (*Drunk, Williams*)], [Leonard Geer (*Man of courage*)], [Lane Chandler (*Rider*)], [Jack Perrin (*Fraser*)], [Guy Teague (*Charlie*)], [Iron Eyes Cody (*Chief Mahmo*)], [Chris Alcaide (*Lt. Shaffin*)], [Steven Ritch (*Barnes*)], [J. W. Cody (*Indian*)], [Chuck Cason (*Smith*)], [Harry Strang].

Western. [*Print viewed*]. On the night of April 14, 1865, James Kingston, formerly an Apache Indian fighter and now a Union scout, and Sergeant Tim O'Roarke, who had been a cattleman prior to the Civil War, meet with President Abraham Lincoln in the White House. Now that the war has ended, Lincoln says, the thousands of cattle waiting to be sold in Texas must be moved at once to Abilene, Kansas to feed the starving people of the North. He warns, though, that lawless elements bent on keeping the Union apart may disrupt the planned 1,000-mile cattle drive. After Lincoln writes out orders for Colonel Marshall at San Arturo to supply soldiers to help guard against Apache attacks, the president leaves to go to Ford's Theatre. His assassination that night does not stop Jim and O'Roarke, who join a wagon train to San Arturo. As they approach Kearny Pass, Jim sends Bob Jennings to bring back soldiers for protection, but Bob is wounded and captured by Apaches. Meanwhile, Rosita, a spy for Mexican guerrilla leader Joaquin Jironza, locates money and a cache of repeating rifles hidden in the back of a wagon belonging to Hank Calvin, a San Arturo general store owner, whom she seduced in Abilene. Jironza hopes to recapture Texas and New Mexico for Mexico. Rosita rides to Jironza's cave hideout, where Jironza shoots Bob as he tries to escape. Jironza then makes a deal with the Apache leader to attack the wagons, saying he wants the rifles, but that everything else, horses, food and white women, will be left for the Apaches. When the Apaches and Jironza's raiders attack, Lee Parker, a bitter Confederate ex-soldier who lost an arm in the war, uses the repeating rifles. Hearing their sound, Jim sends men to the wagon to use them against the raiders. Although Jironza kills Calvin, his men and the Apaches are driven off. At San Arturo, the jailkeeper Manoel, a Mexican American who is loyal to the U.S. and hates Jironza, greets Jim. Colonel Marshall and Jim find that the rifles have disappeared from Calvin's wagon. Lee refuses to tell about the rifles, saying he hopes they will be used to run the "Yankees" out of town. Just then a dispatch rider arrives with a message from the Secretary of War ordering Marshall to abandon the post because of rioting and looting at the Mexican border. After the soldiers leave, to the jeers of the townspeople, Jim, with Silas Parker, the sheriff and father of Lee, interrupts a meeting of plotters, and a fight erupts. Jim stops it when he pulls his gun, then interrogates Lee, who refuses to cooperate. When the men with Jim begin to beat Lee, despite Jim's objection, Silas draws his gun and tells Lee to go. Rosita takes Lee to Jironza, who says he can help the South with the rifles. Lee offers to show him the location of the rifles if Jironza agrees to have the Apaches stop the cattle drive, as Lee is outraged that Texas cattle is going to feed Northerners, and also to refrain from shooting any of the Southerners or his father or sister Ann, who has fallen in love with Jim. Jironza agrees and sends a man to meet with the Apache chief. Jim locates the buried boxes of rifles as Jironza's band arrives, and a gun battle ensues. When Lee objects that Jironza is shooting Southerners, Jironza shoots Lee and says he will kill them all. Ann and Silas drag Lee to safety, but Silas also is shot. Lee admits to Ann that he was wrong and before dying warns her to tell Jim that Jironza is sending Apaches to stop the cattle at Kearny Pass. Manoel is shot, but just before dying, he throws dynamite at the raiders. Jironza tries to use Ann as a hostage to escape, but Jim jumps him and then shoots him dead as he approaches with a knife. Meanwhile, a scout for Jironza meets with the Apaches, who decide to attack to steal the cattle, as their people are starving. Jim meets up with O'Roarke, and during the Indian attack, they use the cattle to stampede and drive the Indians off. Jim kills Jironza's man, and seeing that the Apache chief is dead, says he does not think the Indians will come back. As the cattle return to the streets of San Arturo, Jim promises Ann that he will return after he takes them to Abilene, and she says she'll be waiting. *Mexican-American border region. Mexicans. Scouts (Frontier). Southerners. Texans. Uprisings. Apache Indians. Brothers and sisters. Cattle. Cattlemen. Dynamite. Fathers and sons. Fights. General stores. Gunrunners. Abraham Lincoln. Mexican Americans. Officers (Military). Rifles. Seduction. Sheriffs. Wagon trains. War injuries.*

Note: The working title of this film was *Renegade Roundup*. *HR*, in their review, commented, "You can nearly always learn something not found in your history books in these stock-shot westerns. This is stimulating, even though what you learn isn't true. This time the Apaches are being used by the Mexicans. (Actually, it was the other way around. The Apaches, by threats of torture, forced peons to raise crops and horses for them and to supply them with information.)" *MPD* pointed out, "The picture is notable for the fact that Ray Corrigan and Tex Ritter, those stalwarts of the Western format, appear as villains." According to modern sources, Kermit Maynard was in the cast.

Box 13 Aug 1955. *DV* 12 Aug 1955, p. 3. *Exb* 24 Aug 1955, p. 4013. *FD* 18 Aug 1955, p. 6. *Har* 13 Aug 1955, p. 131. *HR* 12 Aug 1955, p. 3. *LAT* 14 Oct 1955. *MPD* 19 Aug 1955. *MPHPD* 3 Sep 1955, p. 577. *Var* 10 Aug 1955, p. 15.

APACHE CHIEF (Native Americans, Apache)

Lippert Productions, Inc. *Dist* Screen Guild Productions, Inc. 4 Nov **1949**; Prod: late Jul–early Aug 1949 [©Apac Corp.; 28 Nov 1949; LP2667]. Sd (Glen Glenn Sound Company); sepia. 6 reels, 5,375 ft. 58-60 min. PCA cert no. 14024.

Pres ROBERT L. LIPPERT. *Prod* Leonard S. Picker. *Assoc prod* George D. Green. *Dir* Frank McDonald. *Asst dir* Ralph Black. *Orig scr* George D. Green and [Leonard S. Picker]. *Dir of photog* Benjamin H.

Kline. [*Cam op* Perry Finnerman]. [*Stills* Buddy Longworth]. *Film ed* Stanley Frazen. *Set dec* Robert Priestly. *Ward supv* Stanley Kufell. *Mus dir* Albert Glasser. *Sd eng* Harry Eckles and Earl Snyder. *Makeup supv* Ted Coodley. [*Hair stylist* Elaine Ramsey]. [*Grip* C. O. Morris]. [*Scr supv* Eleanor Donahoe].

Cast: Alan Curtis [(*Young Eagle*)], Tom Neal [(*Lt. Brown*)], Russell Hayden [(*Black Wolf*)], Carol Thurston [(*Watona*)], Fuzzy Knight [(*Nevada Smith*)], Trevor Bardette [(*Big Crow*)], Francis McDonald [(*Mohaska*)], Ted Hecht [(*Pani*)], Alan Wells [(*Lame Bull*)], Roy Gordon [(*Col. Martin*)], Billy Wilkerson [(*Grey Cloud*)], Roderic Redwing [(*Tewa*)], [Dale Blanchard (*Indian boy*)], [Hazel Nilsen (*White Faun*)], [Charles Soldani (*Councillor*)].

Western. [*Print viewed*]. Along a Western trail, Apache chief Grey Cloud, his son Black Wolf and two braves, Pani and Lame Bull, attack a wagon. In the ensuing shootout, all of the wagoners are killed, and Grey Cloud is fatally shot. Before dying, Grey Cloud begs his son to do everything he can to strike down the white man. At the village, Black Wolf and his men report Grey Cloud's death to his brother Big Crow, but claim that they were the innocent victims in the attack. Later, when speaking to his son Young Eagle, Big Crow claims the attack was in violation of the treaty the tribe recently signed with Col. Martin of the U.S. Army. When Lt. Brown and his cavalry platoon arrive at the Indians' village, Big Crow repeats Black Wolf's charges. Realizing that Black Wolf has lied, Brown asks to speak with him, but Big Crow says he has gone to nearby Sacred Mountain to pray. After she learns the truth from the lecherous Black Wolf, Young Eagle's sweetheart Watona reports to Big Crow. When Big Crow confronts Black Wolf, he arrogantly admits lying, so Big Crow asks village holy man Mohaska to communicate the spirits' decree of punishment. Mohaska then banishes Black Wolf to Sacred Mountain, where he must spend five days without food or weapons. After Big Crow confiscates Black Wolf's knife and orders him to leave, Watona feels guilty. She persuades Young Eagle to return the knife to him, and the next morning, Black Wolf stabs the driver of another wagon. After he steals the passengers' jewelry, Black Wolf finds Watona at a nearby river and gives her one of the stolen items: a gold pocket watch. Although Black Wolf tells Watona to keep the watch well hidden, she pins it to the front of her dress and returns to the village. When Martin and Brown arrive later, they notice the watch, which bears an inscription proving that it was stolen during the raid. Watona admits that Black Wolf gave her the watch, after which Big Crow begs Martin to delay his arrest so that Black Wolf can first be punished according to tribal law. Martin agrees and leaves, and later, Black Wolf is tried and sentenced to walk a gauntlet of stick-wielding maidens, who beat him on the head. Afterward, a pair of braves is escorting Black Wolf to Martin, when suddenly, Pani and Lame Bull free him. Later, at the scene of another wagon raid, Young Eagle tells Martin that he knows from the tracks left by his horse's crooked hoof that Black Wolf was involved. Young Eagle then tries to convince Black Wolf that he wants to join him, but Black Wolf suspects him immediately and ties him to a rock in the mountains. Planning to usurp the chieftainship, Black Wolf returns to the village and kills Big Crow. He then kidnaps Watona and takes her to his hideout in an attempt to force Mohaska, who is in charge of the tribe, to concede control. After Young Eagle struggles free from his ropes, he returns to the village, where Mohaska immediately installs him as chief. Then, Young Eagle tracks down Black Wolf at his hideout, kills him and rescues Watona. *Apache Indians. Family relationships. Officers (Military). Renegades. Rivalry. Tribal chiefs. Escapes. Gunshot wounds. Hideouts. Kidnapping. Lechery. Medicine men. Murder. Robbery. Stabbings. Treaties. United States. Army. Cavalry. Villages. Wagons. Watches.*

Note: The film's opening credits include the following onscreen statement: "Introducing the latest scientific achievement in motion picture photography, the Garutso Balanced Lens, a new optical principle which creates a three dimensional effect." George D. Green's onscreen credit reads: Original screenplay by Associate Producer George D. Green. The copyright claimant, Apac Corp., appears to have been created solely for the purpose of producing this film.

Box 22 Oct 1949. *DV* 12 Oct 1949, p. 3. *HR* 29 Jul 1949, p. 10. *HR* 12 Oct 1949, pp. 3-4. *MPHPD* 22 Oct 1949, p. 59. *Var* 19 Oct 1949, p. 8.

APACHE COUNTRY (Native Americans, Apache)
Gene Autry Productions. *Dist* Columbia Pictures Corp. May **1952**; Prod: 11 Nov–20 Nov 1951 [©Gene Autry Productions; 7 Apr 1952; LP1625]. Sd; b&w. 5,571 ft. 62 min.

Prod Armand Schaefer. *Dir* George Archainbaud. [*Asst dir* Paul Donnelly]. *Wrt* Norman S. Hall. *Dir of photog* William Bradford. *Art dir* Charles Clague. *Film ed* James Sweeney. *Set dec* Frank Tuttle. *Mus supv* Paul Mertz. *Mus dir* Mischa Bakaleinikoff. [*Sd eng* Russell Malmgren].

Song(s): "The Covered Wagon Rolled Right Along," words and music by Britt Wood and Hy Heath; "Crime Will Never Pay," words and music by Willard Robinson and Jack Pepper; "I Love to Yodel," words and music by Carolina Cotton; "Cold, Cold Heart," words and music by Hank Williams.

Cast: Gene Autry [(*Gene Autry*)], and Champion World's Wonder Horse, Carolina Cotton [(*Carolina Cotton*)], Harry Lauter [(*Dave Kilrain*)], Mary Scott [(*Laura Rayburn*)], Sydney Mason [(*Walter Rayburn*)], Francis X. Bushman [(*Commissioner Lathan*)], Cass County Boys, Tony Whitecloud's Jemez Indians, Pat Buttram [(*Pat Buttram*)], [Gregg Barton (*Luke Thorn*)], [Tom London (*Patches*)], [Byron Foulger (*Bartlett*)], [Frank Matts (*Steve*)], [Mickey Simpson (*Tom Ringo*)], [Kitty McHugh (*Sandwich woman*)], [Iron Eyes Cody (*Indian brave*)], [Edwin Parker (*Cowboy*)], [George Russell].

Western, with songs. [*Print viewed*]. When a rash of Indian raids plagues the Southwest territory, Gene Autry, chief scout for the Southwest Cavalry Command, is summoned to Washington, D.C., to meet with Commissioner Lathan of the Bureau of Indian Affairs. Lathan orders Gene to resign his post so that he can conduct an undercover investigation of the raids. Outside Lathan's office, Bartlett, the commisioner's secretary is conspiring with Laura Rayburn, the daughter of Apache Springs Indian Agent Walter Rayburn, and her fiancé, Dave Kilrain, to sabotage Gene's mission. After ostensibly resigning his post to go into ranching, Gene, accompanied by his friend, Pat Buttram, travels to Junction City and is about to board the stage bound for Apache Springs when Laura, a passenger on the stage, feigns a fear of guns and begs the men to remove theirs. After Gene and Pat oblige Laura and hand their guns over to the stage driver, Carolina Cotton, the sharpshooting proprietor of a medicine show, also boards the stage. Along the trail, Kilrain and his road agents wait for Laura's signal to attack the stage, thinking that Gene and Pat have been disarmed. When the outlaws appear, Gene and Pat extract their pistols from the lunch boxes in which they were hidden and start firing, sending Kilrain and his gang scurrying for cover. When the stage reaches Apache Springs, Laura reports to her father and Kilrain. The three have been inciting the Indians by providing them with liquor and guns, and the resulting raids have kept the Cavalry occupied, thus allowing the railroad bandits free reign of the territory. Laura warns Kilrain that Carolina, a friend of the Indians performing in her show, may endanger their operation and should be eliminated. After Kilrain disrupts the medicine show that evening, Carolina informs Gene that Kilrain is the leader of the bandit underground that has been engineering the Indian raids. The next day, Gene, posing as a would-be land buyer, visits Rayburn, who is also the government land agent. When Rayburn sends Gene and Pat to look at property in the isolated Bear Valley, Gene, anticipating an ambush, covers their horses' hooves with canvas bags, thereby covering their tracks and making it impossible for Rayburn's men to follow them. Doubling back to town, Pat and Gene listen outside Kilrain's office as Kilrain confers with notorious outlaw Tom Ringo about a railroad robbery. Bursting into the office, Gene and Pat arrest Kilrain, but he is soon released for lack of evidence. The next day, Carolina joins the wagon train bound for Fort Ballard, and Gene hands her a coded message to deliver to the commandant there. Witnessing the exchange, Rayburn and Kilrain decide to attack the wagon train and destroy the message. Soon after Carolina departs, Gene receives a message from Lathan, warning him that Barlett has divulged the code to Rayburn. Realizing that Carolina is in danger, Gene and Pat gallop after the wagon train, arriving just in time to join Carolina in fending off Kilrain's attack. After Carolina wounds both Kilrain and Rayburn, the bandit ring is smashed, and Gene, Pat and Carolina travel to Washington to be commended for their heroic efforts. *Apache Indians. Indian agents. Outlaws. Scouts (Frontier). Undercover operations. Fathers and daughters. Medicine shows. Raids. Secret codes. Secretaries. Sharpshooters. Stagecoach robberies. Train robberies. United States–Southwest. United States. Bureau of Indian Affairs. Washington (D.C.).*

Note: In the film, a group of Jemez Pueblo Apache Indians performs a war dance, an eagle dance and a buffalo dance while Gene Autry's character comments on the significance of the dancing.

Exb 4 Jun 1952, p. 3305. *Box* 24 May 1952. *DV* 14 May 1952, p. 6. *FD* 29 May 1952, p. 6. *HR* 14 May 1952, p. 3. *MPHPD* 24 May 1952, p. 1374. *Var* 21 May 1952, p. 6.

APACHE DRUMS (African Americans, Native Americans, Apache, Mescalero, Latino, Welsh Americans)

Universal-International Pictures Co., Inc. *Dist* Universal Pictures Co., Inc. Jun **1951**; New York opening: 5 May 1951; Prod: early Aug–early Sep 1950 [©Universal Pictures Co.; 18 Apr 1951; LP870]. Sd (Western Electric Recording); col (Technicolor). 8 reels, 6,774 ft. 74-75 min. PCA cert no. 14882.

Prod Val Lewton. *Dir* Hugo Fregonese. [*Asst dir* Bill Holland]. [*Dial dir* Irvin Berwick]. *Scr* David Chandler. *Story* Harry Brown. *Dir of photog* Charles P. Boyle. *Technicolor color consultant* William Fritzsche. *Art dir* Bernard Herzbrun and Robert Clatworthy. *Film ed* Milton Carruth. *Set dec* Russell A. Gausman and A. Roland Fields. *Cost* Bill Thomas. *Mus* Hans J. Salter. [*Supv of Apache traditional music* Dr. Chris Willowbird]. *Sd* Leslie I. Carey and Glenn E. Anderson. *Hair stylist* Joan St. Oegger. *Makeup* Bud Westmore. [*Unit prod mgr* Dewey Starkey].

Song(s): "The March of the Men of Harlech," traditional Welsh song; "Oranges and Lemons," "Evening," "Carmen Carmela" and "The Tisvin Song," composers undetermined.

Cast: STEPHEN McNALLY (*Sam Leeds*), COLEEN GRAY (*Sally [Barr]*), Willard Parker (*Joe Madden*), Arthur Shields (*Reverend Griffen*), James Griffith (*Lt. Glidden*), Armando Silvestre (*Pedro-Peter*), Georgia Backus (*Mrs. Keon*), Clarence Muse (*Jehu*), Ruthelma Stevens (*Betty Careless*), James Best (*Bert Keon*), Chinto Guzman (*Chacho*), Ray Bennett (*Mr. Keon*), [Irving Kane (*Mr. Franks*)], [Steve Dunhill (*Bob, a townsman*)], [Monte Montague (*Rancher*)], [John War Eagle (*Apache guard*)], [Maurice Jara (*Indian*)], [George Lynn (*Bartender*)], [James Parnell, Ian Murray (*Miners*)], [Josephine Parra (*Mexican girl*)], [Clem Fuller (*Out rider*)], [Sheb Wooley, Chuck Hayward, Dan Poore, Hal Bokor, Alex Sharp, Stanley Fraser, Harte Wayne, Buddy Roosevelt, Cliff Parkinson (*Townsmen*)], [Ann Lovelady, Gertrude Astor, Joy Hallward, Copper Johnson, Herberta Williams (*Townswomen*)], [Alan Dinehart III, Donna Corcoran, Sherry Jackson (*Children*)].

Western, with songs. [*Print viewed*]. In 1880, in the desert mining town of Spanish Boot, New Mexico, gambler Sam Leeds shoots and kills another man, claiming that he acted in self-defense. Mayor Joe Madden, who is also the town's blacksmith, orders the gambler to leave because he no longer wants men like Sam in his growing town. Reverend Griffen, a Welsh minister, convinces Madden that the dance hall should also be closed down. Happy to leave Spanish Boot, Betty Careless, the dance hall's earthy proprietor, sells her property and prepares her black assistant Jehu and her various female employees to catch the noon stagecoach to Silver Springs. Before he leaves town, Sam asks his sweetheart, Sally Barr, to go with him. Torn between her love for Sam and her desire for an honest and upright husband, Sally reluctantly decides to remain in Spanish Boot. Sam suspects that Madden plans to win Sally for himself. Along the trail to the next town, Sam discovers that the stagecoach has been attacked and the dance hall employees brutally killed. Just before he dies, Jehu tells Sam that hundreds of Mescalero Apaches have reappeared from across the border and begs him to warn the town. Frightened, Sam returns to Spanish Boot, but realizes to his horror that because of their distrust of him, neither Madden nor any of the other citizens believe his story. However, when a stagecoach full of arrows arrives, the citizens begin to worry and send a young man to the nearest fort for help. The next morning, a local resident named Chacho discovers the young man's mutilated body in the well, and the citizens, afraid to drink the tainted well water, wonder if they will all die of thirst. Their concern does not extend, however, to Pedro-Peter, a cavalry scout who, because he is an Apache, is forbidden by law to drink liquor. As the townspeople quaff beers in the local tavern, Sam enters and buys Pedro-Peter a beer. When Griffen reminds Sam of the law, Sam decides that because Madden refuses to act, he himself will lead a party of men to fetch water from the river. On the way home, the party is attacked, and Sam and the minister try to hold off the Indians while the others escape. When Sam's bullet strikes a chief, the Apaches withdraw, their voices joined in a keening that echoes across the desert. Trudging back to town, Sam and Reverend Griffen see horses approaching. Believing they are about to die, Sam confesses that he risked the lives of the other men in the party merely to shame Madden. The horsemen are actually cavalrymen, but after Lt. Glidden

congratulates Sam on having shot Chief Victorio, an Apache "prophet, priest, and war chief all in one," Madden arrests him for having given liquor to an Indian. Back in town, Sam bids Sally farewell one more time, but just then, a large party of Apaches attacks Spanish Boot. The townspeople take refuge inside the church, but Glidden points out that the Indians can easily complete their attack by scaling the church's many elevated windows. After a long wait, the terrified settlers hear the Apaches approaching with drums, flutes and song. Glidden explains that the Mescaleros are preparing to kill by drinking a potent whiskey, and that when the song changes, braves will jump through the windows and attack. Griffen maintains that the Indians are heathens, but Glidden argues that the Apaches are a dying people and that Chief Victorio gave them hope. The Mescaleros continue a cycle of attacking and singing, while the miners inside counter with their own Welsh fighting song. Sam fights heroically and is reconciled with Sally. To buy time, Madden claims he is a doctor and attempts to treat Chief Victorio, but when Victorio finally dies of Sam's gunshot wound, Madden is killed, and the Indians set fire to the church's wooden door. As the Apaches are about to enter the church, the cavalry arrives, and the townspeople are saved. Mescalero Indians. Moral reformation. Romantic rivalry. Uprisings. Apache Indians. Battles. Blacksmiths. Churches. Dance hall girls. Dances. Deserts. Gamblers. Massacres. Mayors. Mexican Americans. Miners. Mining towns. Ministers. New Mexico. Racism. Rescues. Rites and ceremonies. Romance. Scouts (Frontier). Settlers. Songs. Tribal chiefs. United States. Army. Cavalry. Victorio (Chiricahua Apache). Welsh Americans.

Note: The working title of this film was *War Dance*. Onscreen credits note that Harry Brown's story was titled "Stand at Spanish Boot." Although reviews refer to Brown's story as a novel, no publication information has been found to support that claim. Location shooting was done in the Mojave Desert in California, according to materials contained in the MPAA/PCA files at the AMPAS Library. An offscreen, presumably Mescalero Apache, narrator states as the film opens that his people can go neither north nor south. "The hunger wolf chews on our strengths. Soon the warriors will be too weak to fight. Then the white man will thrust us away from the earth, and only the empty sky will know the voices of the Mescalero." This is followed by an onscreen statement: "A hungry people rose to fight. Their fury fell upon settled places where peaceful Americans carried on trade and Welsh miners dug for silver. One of these places was the town of Spanish Boot." The historical Victorio was a Chiricahua Apache leader who led his people from the hated San Carlos Reservation to their homeland, the Black Mountains.

According to the pressbook for the film, Dr. Chris Willowbird, a "noted authority on Indian lore," supervised the recording of the authentic Apache music for the soundtrack. An orchestra of twenty Apache Indians was used for the recording, which was highlighted by an Apache religious chant sung in ceremonial preparation for going into battle. The soundtrack also includes Apache drinking songs and "several warpath numbers." The *LAEx* reviewer commented that the "Indian drum work, tribal music and primitive customs are particularly well handled in this film, and the sets for once seem real." The *DN* reviewer remarked, "The picture is also notable for portraying an Indian as an honorable person—not just as a man who says 'Ugh!' to your face and then scalps you from the rear."

Apache Drums marked Val Lewton's last film and his only Technicolor production. Lewton died of a heart attack on 14 Mar 1951; the film was released after his death. In 1956, the picture was reissued by Realart.

Box 28 Apr 1951. *DN* 21 Jun 1951. *DV* 20 Apr 1951, p. 3. *FD* 30 Apr 1951, p. 6. *HCN* 21 Jun 1951. *HR* 18 Jul 1950. *HR* 11 Aug 1950, p. 9. *HR* 1 Sep 1950, p. 11. *HR* 20 Apr 1951, p. 3. *LAEx* 21 Jun 1951. *LAT* 21 Jun 1951. *MPD* 24 Apr 1951. *MPHPD* 21 Apr 1951, p. 810. *NYT* 7 May 1951, p. 22. *Var* 25 Apr 1951, p. 6.

APACHE LANDING see **THE STAND AT APACHE RIVER**

THE APACHE OUTPOST see **THE LAST OUTPOST**

APACHE TERRITORY (Native Americans, Apache, Pima)

Rorvic Productions. *Dist* Columbia Pictures Corp. Oct **1958**; Prod: 10 Dec–23 Dec 1957 [©Calhoun-Orsatti Enterprises, Inc.; 8 Jul 1958; LP11206]. Sd; col (Eastman Color). 8 reels, 6,373 ft. 70, 72 or 75 min. PCA cert no. 18909.

Prod Rory Calhoun and Victor M. Orsatti. *Dir* Ray Nazarro. *Asst dir* Eddie Saeta. *Scr* Charles R. Marion and George W. George. *Adpt* Frank Moss. *Dir of photog* Irving Lippman. *Technicolor color consultant* Henri Jaffe. *Art dir* Cary Odell. *Film ed* Al Clark. *Mus cond* Mischa Bakaleinikoff. *Rec supv* John Livadary. *Sd* Josh Westmoreland.

Source: Based on the novel *Last Stand at Papago Wells* by Louis L'Amour (New York, 1957).

Cast: Rory Calhoun (*Logan Cates*), Barbara Bates (*Jennifer Fair*), John Dehner (*Grant Kimbrough*), Carolyn Craig (*Junie Hatchett*), Thomas Pittman (*Lonnie Foreman*), Leo Gordon (*Zimmerman*), Myron Healey (*Webb*), Francis De Sales (*Sgt. Sheehan*), Frank de Kova (*Lugo*), Reg Parton (*Conley*), Bob Woodward (*Graves*), Fred Krone (*Styles*).

Western. [*Not viewed*]. After the Civil War, Logan Cates, a drifter, travels through Apache desert lands on his way to Yuma, Arizona. When the Apaches attack a small wagon train, Logan routs them, then helps the only survivor, young Junie Hatchett. With little water left, they ride to the oasis of Apache Wells. At the wells, they find Lonnie Foreman, an eighteen-year-old whose friends had also been killed by the Apaches. They are soon joined by Grant Kimbrough and his fiancée, Jennifer Fair, on their way to Yuma to take the stage East. Kimbrough, who led a Confederate cavalry detachment during the war, bristles at following Logan's suggestion that they wait until dark before leaving. Logan and Jennifer had once been sweethearts, but he left her because he felt that the life of a drifter was not for a woman. She expresses frustration that he didn't let her decide for herself. The group is joined by six cavalry soldiers, Sgt. Sheehan and Pvts. Zimmerman, Graves, Conley, Styles and Webb, survivors of a Apache attack. Logan realizes that Churupati, a renegade chief, is on the loose again. The soldiers, having experienced their first Apache skirmish, question the wisdom of staying, but Sheehan, formerly a desk sergeant from St. Louis, adheres to Logan's advice. Soon Churupati and his men have the group boxed in. Rather than attack, the Indians fire and snipe at them. After Styles is killed with an arrow in his belly, Zimmerman, who had been busted to private, tries to foment dissent among the others. When Lugo, a half-Pima Indian, sneaks into the oasis on the run from the law, Zimmerman wants to kill him because he's an Indian, but Logan, knowing that the Pimas and Apaches are enemies, asks Lugo to stay and help fight. Sheehan objects that Lugo is wanted for the murder of a soldier, but Lugo claims that the killing was done in self-defense after the soldier tried to steal his gold. He then shows the group some of the gold that he has found in the hills. Lugo senses that a dust storm is approaching, which Logan thinks could serve as a cover for them to break out. Zimmerman challenges Logan saying they should leave tonight, and in their subsequent fight, Logan wins. After Sheehan is wounded, Zimmerman and Kimbrough decide to leave at night with Jennifer. Meanwhile, Lonnie, who plans to build a ranch house in California, nearly proposes to Junie, but his shyness prevents him. Zimmerman steals Lugo's saddlebags and breaks out alone, but he is shot and killed by the Apaches. Lugo then reveals that he had filled the bags with rocks and hidden the gold. Jennifer confesses to Logan that she and Kimbrough were planning to leave with Zimmerman and says she is glad that Logan is strong. As the group is low on food, Logan leaves and brings some back, suffering a flesh wound from the Apaches. Since the well is starting to dry up, they begin to ration water. As Webb worries that he'll never see his children again, Lonnie gets up the nerve to ask Junie to go to California with him. Logan explains to Jennifer that since no one cared about him, he learned not to care. He became a drifter, responsible only for himself, and always looking to the other side of the hill. He admits he loved her, but says he thought he would have hurt her had he stayed. Jennifer tells him she would have crossed the hills with him. When the storm begins, Graves is killed, and Webb, losing his control, runs out and dares the "heathens" to show themselves. He is dragged off and tortured to death slowly. His screams are unnerving to the group, especially Junie, who reveals that the Apaches also tortured her father. Logan determines to attack the Apaches during the storm. He and Sheehan prepare bombs, using four canteens filled with blasting powder and rocks, and four of the men, including Kimbrough, leave to hit the Apaches with the bombs. Kimbrough, however, returns, hoping to escape with Jennifer, but she refuses to go, saying she doesn't want to spend her life with a coward. Kimbrough attempts to leave alone, but Lugo refuses to let him take a horse and then kills him in self-defense. The canteen bombs kill most of the Apaches, and the rest scatter. Before leaving, Lugo gives Lonnie some gold for him and Junie to buy a house in California. Jennifer tells Logan good-bye and wishes him luck to find whatever he is looking for, but it seems likely they probably will start a life together. *Apache Indians. Arizona. Deserts. Oases. Sieges. Vagabonds. Cowardice. Dust storms. Engagements. Explosives. Fights. Gold. Indians of North America–Mixed blood. Pima Indians. Renegades. Robbery. Romance. Self-defense. Shyness. Torture. United States. Army. Cavalry. Wagon trains.*

Note: The working title of this film was *Papago Wells*. The plot summary was based on a dialogue continuity in the copyright descriptions and a summary in the MPAA/PCA Collection at the AMPAS Library. A pre-production news item called the film "a *Grand Hotel* of the desert."

Box 8 Sep 1958. *DV* 27 Aug 1958, p. 3. *Exb* 17 Sep 1958, p. 4513. *FD* 4 Sep 1958, p. 6. *Har* 6 Sep 1958, p. 142. *HR* 12 Jul 1957. *HR* 20 Dec 1957. *HR* 27 Aug 1958, p. 3. *LAT* 12 Jul 1957. *LAT* 5 Dec 1957. *MPD* 4 Sep 1958. *MPHPD* 6 Sep 1958, p. 967. *Var* 3 Sep 1958, p. 6.

APACHE TRAIL (Native Americans, Apache)
Metro-Goldwyn-Mayer Corp.; controlled by Loew's Inc. *Dist* Loew's Inc. Sep **1942**; Prod: early Mar—mid Apr 1942 [©Loew's Inc.; 23 Jun 1942; LP11435]. Sd (Western Electric Sound System); b&w. 7 reels, 5,907 ft. 66 min. Passed by the National Board of Review. PCA cert no. 8397.
Prod Samuel Marx. *Dir* Richard Thorpe and [Richard Rosson]. [*Asst dir* Bert Spurlin, Horace Hough and Stanley Goldsmith]. *Scr* Maurice Geraghty. [*Contr wrt* Gordon Kahn]. *Dir of photog* Sidney Wagner. *Art dir* Cedric Gibbons. *Assoc* Stan Rogers. *Film ed* Frank Sullivan. *Set dec* Edwin B. Willis. *Assoc* Hugh Hunt. *Mus score* Sol Kaplan. *Rec dir* Douglas Shearer. *Hair styles by* Sidney Guilaroff. [*Prod mgr* Charles Hunt].
Source: Based on the short story "Stage Station" by Ernest Haycox in *Colliers* (22 Apr 1939).
Cast: Lloyd Nolan (*"Trigger" Bill* [*Folliard*]), Donna Reed (*Rosalia Martinez*), William Lundigan (*Tom Folliard*), Ann Ayars (*Constance Selden*), Connie Gilchrist (*Señora Martinez*), Chill Wills (*"Pike" Skelton*), Miles Mander (*James V. Thorne*), Gloria Holden (*Mrs. James V. Thorne*), Ray Teal (*Ed Cotton*), Grant Withers (*Lestrade*), Fuzzy Knight (*"Juke"*), Trevor Bardette (*Amber*), Tito Renaldo (*Cochee*), Frank M. Thomas (*Major Lowden*), George Watts (*Judge Keely*), [Emory Parnell (*Mr. Walters*)], [Edgar Dearing (*Marshal*)], [Nora Cecil (*Passenger*)], [Mitchell Lewis (*Bolt Saunders*)], [Joe Bernard (*Tall man*)], [Arthur Hoyt (*Meredith*)], [Byron Foulger (*Clerk*)], [Al Hill (*Shotgun man*)].
Western. [*Print viewed*]. At a border town, stagecoach guard Tom Folliard is released from jail after serving time for consorting with criminals. When his brother, "Trigger" Bill, offers him a cut from a robbery, Tom says he wants nothing more to do with him, then tries to get his old job back. His boss decides instead to offer him a manager's post at the worst station on the line, Tonto Valley, in Apache territory. Tom is happy for the chance, and takes the next stage out. At the station, he is greeted by cook Señora Martinez and her daughter Rosalia, who is secretly in love with Tom. They are happy to have Tom as their new boss and, along with teenaged Indian Cochee, resolve to make Tonto Valley the best station on the line. Some weeks later, on the day that a coach carrying artist James V. Thorne and his wife and attractive, opportunistic widow Constance Selden arrives, distant smoke signals and Apache war drums concern Tom. That afternoon, U.S. Cavalry Major Lowden arrives to pick up supplies, and a short time later, Bill rides in, causing the wary Tom to lock up the company strongbox and confiscate Bill's guns. The next morning, when an Apache arrow is shot into the station, Tom rides out to investigate and gives the strongbox key to the stagecoach drivers. While Tom is gone, Constance indicates to Señora Martinez and Rosalia that she plans to marry him, even though Bill tells her that he is more her kind than Tom's. Despite the danger of an impending Apache attack, the major leaves for his fort and promises to send help. Out in the hills, Tom sees an Apache war party pulling a white man after them. He is able to free the wounded man, whose name is "Pike" Skelton, when the Apaches dismount to investigate a shot he fired. As they ride back to the station, Pike tells Tom that the Apaches are on the warpath because of an underhanded white man. Back at the station, Thorne paints a portrait of Cochee, then, on Bill's suggestion, paints him as well. When Bill says that the picture would be better with his guns, Thorne innocently gives him his, and Bill forces the other men to hand over the strongbox and all the weapons. He starts to ride off, forcing Constance to go with him, but when Cochee opens the station gates, Tom and Pike are there. Bill goads Tom into a gunfight and is shocked that Tom is able to outdraw him. Tom merely wounds Bill's hands, and while Bill and Pike are being treated, Pike reveals details about the white man whom the Apaches are seeking, and Bill is revealed to be the man. Later that night, when Constance tells Tom that she wants to spend the rest of her life with him, he kisses her, breaking Rosalia's heart. The next morning, the Apaches attack the station and Cochee is killed saving Tom's life. Mr. Thorne is also killed, after which a lone Apache rides to the station to warn that they must surrender Bill or be killed. When the Apache throws down the major's hat, they realize that the cavalry will not be coming. Tom insists that they vote on Bill's fate, and Tom breaks a tie by voting

to save him. As they prepare for the next attack, Rosalia confesses her love to Tom, then Bill chides his brother for saving him, while secretly admiring him. As the station is surrounded, Bill steals a horse and rides off, leading the Apaches away from Tonto Valley. The next day, Constance takes the stage out, but Señora Martinez and Rosalia stay when Tom asks for Rosalia's hand. Apache Indians. Brothers. Stagecoaches. Unrequited love. Artists. Cooks. Firearms. Gunfights. Jails. Mothers and daughters. Robbery. Self-sacrifice. Spanish Americans. United States. Army. Cavalry. Widows.

Note: The working titles of this film were *Stage Station* and *Desert Station*. According to a contemporary, but unidentified news item in the AMPAS Library file on the film, Ernest Haycox's story was originally sold to Samuel Goldwyn studios. On 1 Aug 1941, Goldwyn sold the rights to the story, for which Haycox had written a brief treatment, to M-G-M. At that time, Donald Hough and Houston Branch worked on a sixty-five page treatment. A 20 Aug 1941 *HR* news item noted that Cyril Hume was "scripting" the picture, which was to co-star John Carroll and Hedy Lamarr. Neither Hume, Hough nor Houston is credited onscreen, in the SAB or in reviews, and the extent of their contribution to the final film has not been determined. An *HR* news item on 29 Dec 1941 notes that Robert Taylor and Wallace Beery were to star in the film. According to *HR* news items and production charts, director Richard Rosson worked on the picture from the pre-production stage in late Dec 1941 through early Apr 1942, when thirty-one days of shooting had been completed. A *HR* news item on 6 Apr 1942 noted that Rosson was ill and was being replaced by Richard Thorpe, who would finish the picture. Only Richard Thorpe is given onscreen credit for direction of the film, which was completed by mid-Apr 1942. Other news items reveal the following information: exteriors for the film were shot on location in and around Tucson, AZ, where a "stage station" set was built especially for the production; following location shooting, production resumed at the studio on 27 Mar 1942; actors Eddie Dunn, Aubrey Mather, Grant Withers and Sarah Edwards were cast in the film, but none of them were in the released film; and, David Snell was at one time set to score the film.

According to information in the file on the film in the PCA/MPAA Collection at the AMPAS Library, the PCA advised M-G-M that the nationality of Rosalia and Señora Martinez should be changed to Spanish instead of Mexican, as they were in Ernest Haycox's short story. Correspondence in the file indicates that Addison Durland, the PCA's expert in Latin American matters, was concerned that certain aspects of the characterizations of the two women might be offensive to the Mexican people. A 18 Dec 1941 letter from Durland to M-G-M studio head Louis B. Mayer advised that, despite the change in Señora Martinez and Rosalia's nationality, the film should not "present them in such a manner that might make them appear grotesque, inferior or servile, in order to avoid the possibility of offending the great number of Latin American people of Spanish extraction." Additional information in the file indicates that the film contained stock shots originally shot for Walter Wanger's 1939 film *Stagecoach* (see *AFI Catalog of Feature Films, 1931-40*; F3.4284). M-G-M also adapted Haycox's story for the 1952 film entitled *Apache War Smoke* (see below), directed by Howard Kress, and starring Gilbert Roland and Robert Horton. That film used some footage from the 1942 film.

Box 27 Jun 1942, p. 3. *Exb* 1 Jul 1942. *FD* 25 Jun 1942, p. 5. *HR* 20 Aug 1941, p. 1. *HR* 29 Dec 1941, p. 1. *HR* 27 Jan 1942, p. 8. *HR* 5 Feb 1942, p. 4, 7. *HR* 19 Feb 1942, p. 11. *HR* 20 Feb 1942, p. 6. *HR* 3 Mar 1942, p. 4. *HR* 6 Mar 1942, p. 6. *HR* 27 Mar 1942, p. 2. *HR* 30 Mar 1942, p. 4, 7. *HR* 3 Apr 1942, p. 8. *HR* 6 Apr 1942, p. 1. *HR* 24 Jun 1942, p. 3. *MPD* 24 Jun 1942. *MPHPD* 27 Jun 1942, p. 737. *Var* 24 Jun 1942, p. 8.

APACHE WAR SMOKE (Native Americans, Apache)

Metro-Goldwyn-Mayer Corp.; controlled by Loew's Inc. *Dist* Loew's Inc. Oct 1952; *Prod*: late May—early Jun 1952 [©Loew's Inc.; 17 Sep 1952; LP1963]. Sd (Western Electric Sound System); b&w. 7 reels, 6,046 ft. 65 or 67 min. Passed by the National Board of Review. PCA cert no. 16039.

Prod Hayes Goetz. *Dir* Harold Kress. *Asst dir* Al Jennings. *Scr* Jerry Davis. *Dir of photog* John Alton. *Spec eff* A. Arnold Gillespie. *Art dir* Cedric Gibbons and Arthur Lonergan. *Film ed* Newell P. Kimlin. *Set dec* Edwin B. Willis and Ralph Hurst. *Mus dir* Alberto Colombo. *Rec supv* Douglas Shearer. *Hair styles* Sydney Guilaroff. *Makeup created by* William Tuttle.

Source: Based on the short story "Stage Station" by Ernest Haycox in *Collier's* (22 Apr 1939).

Cast: Gilbert Roland (*Peso [Herrera]*), Glenda Farrell (*Fanny Webson*), Robert Horton (*Tom Herrera*), Barbara Ruick (*Nancy Dekker*), Gene Lockhart (*Cyril R. Snowden*), Henry Morgan (*Ed Cotten*), Patricia Tiernan (*Lorraine Sayburn*), Hank Worden (*Amber*), Myron Healey (*Pike Curtis*), Emmett Lynn (*Les*), Argentina Brunetti (*Madre*), Bobby Blake (*Luis [Herrera]*), Douglas Dumbrille (*Major Dekker*), [Chubby Johnson (*Juke*)], [Charlita (*Maria*)], [Carlos Vera (*Juan*)], [Connie Vera (*Suzie*)], [Iron Eyes Cody (*Apache brave*)].

Western. [*Print viewed*]. During the 1870s, in New Mexico, the Tonto Valley Wells Fargo stagecoach station run by Tom Herrera is preparing to defend against an attack by an Apache war party seeking revenge for the cold-blooded slaughter of several Indians by an outsider. As distant smoke signals warn of the impending attack, a stagecoach arrives at the station with passengers Nancy Dekker, the daughter of a U.S. Cavalry major, Wells Fargo home office representative Cyril R. Snowden, Tom's old flame, Lorraine Sayburn, and Fanny Webson, a thrill-seeking gambling queen posing as a New England matron. The passengers, along with the stagecoach driver, become stranded at the station with Tom and his bandit father Peso. Peso, the "most sought after feller in the Southwest," is after gold contained in the casket of the stagecoach, and Tom, knowing this, takes his father's guns as a precaution. Tom is not pleased to see Lorraine, whom he no longer loves, but she manages to coax a kiss from him. Witnessing the kiss, Nancy, who has fallen instantly in love with Tom, becomes jealous. As the Apaches, under the command of Geronimo, begin their attack, suspicion is immediately cast on Peso as the source of the Apache rage. Tom and Fanny are the only ones at the station who come to Peso's defense when others suggest the bandit be turned over to the Indians to bring a speedy end to the conflict. Though Snowden threatens to report Tom's stubbornness, the station head eventually wins out, and Peso stays. With the help of Fanny, who idolizes the notorious bandit and gives him her guns to him, Peso holds up Tom and the others and demands that they hand over the casket. Tom, however, outdraws his father and shoots the gun out of his hand. Despite the robbery attempt, Tom continues to believe that his father is not responsible for the war party. A fierce battle ensues between the Apaches and those trapped inside the station, resulting in the death of Major Dekker. During a lull in the fighting, an Apache emissary tries to negotiate for the surrender of the murderer, but Tom again refuses to turn his father out, and the fighting resumes. During the battle, Peso knocks out Pike Curtis, a local man who Peso knows is the killer, and turns him over to the Indians. With all doubt about his father's trustworthiness removed, Tom bids Peso farewell as he joins Fanny on her journey to San Francisco. As the stagecoach fades into the horizon, Nancy, who has remained behind to marry Tom, informs him that the gold is not as secure as he thinks, because Luis, the young boy assigned to guard the treasure, is actually another one of Peso's sons. Apache Indians. Bandits. Fathers and sons. Mexican Americans. New Mexico. Romance. Stagecoach lines. False accusations. Gamblers. Geronimo. Gold. Gunfights. Horse owners. Impersonation and imposture. Mistaken identity. Revenge. Stagecoach robberies. Wells Fargo & Co..

Note: Some stock footage from the 1942 M-G-M film *Apache Trail* (see above), which was also based on the Ernest Haycox short story, was used in this picture. Richard Thorpe directed the earlier version, and Lloyd Nolan and Donna Reed starred in it.

Box 20 Sep 1952. *DV* 18 Sep 1952, p. 3. *FD* 25 Sep 1952, p. 10. *HR* 29 May 1952, p. 13. *HR* 6 Jun 1952, p. 14. *HR* 18 Sep 1952, p. 3. *MPHPD* 20 Sep 1952, p. 1533. *Var* 24 Sep 1952, p. 6.

APACHE WARRIOR (Native Americans, Apache)

Regal Films, Inc. *Dist* Twentieth Century-Fox Film Corp. 1957; *Prod*: mid-Mar—early Apr 1957 [©Twentieth Century-Fox Film Corp.; 17 Jul 1957; LP8803]. Sd (Westrex Recording System); b&w; RegalScope. 8 reels, 6,636 ft. 73-74 min. PCA cert no. 18558.

Prod Plato Skouras. *Dir* Elmo Williams. *Asst dir* H. E. Mendelson. *Scr* Carroll Young, Kurt Neumann and Eric Norden. *Story* Carroll Young and Kurt Neumann. *Dir of photog* John M. Nickolaus, Jr. *Spec eff* Bob Gray. *Art dir* John Ewing. *Film ed* Jodie Copelan. *Set dec* Walter M. Scott and Chester Bayhi. *Women's ward* Ollie Hughes. *Men's ward* Robert Olivas. *Mus* Paul Dunlap. *Sd* Alfred Bruzlin. *Makeup* Ernie Park. *Hair dressing* Madine Danks. *Prod mgr* H. E. Mendelson. *Prop master* Max Goldman. *Scr supv* Joan Buck.

Cast: Keith Larsen [(*Katawan, also known as The Apache Kid*)], Jim Davis [(*Ben Ziegler*)], Rodolfo Acosta [(*Mahteen*)], John Miljan [(*Chief Nantan*)], Damian O'Flynn [(*Major*)], George Keymas [(*Chato*)], Lane Bradford [(*Sgt Gaunt*)], Dehl Berti [(*Chikisin*)], Introducing Eugenia Paul [(*Liwana*)], with Nick Thompson [(*Horse trader*)], Eddie Little, Michael Carr [(*Apaches*)], Ray Kellogg, Karl Davis [(*Bounty men*)], David Carlile [(*Cavalry leader*)], Alan Nixon [(*Bounty man*)].

Western. [*Print viewed*]. In 1885, after the defeat of Geronimo, Katawan, an Apache Indian, also known as The Apache Kid, joins the U.S. Army in order to work for peace between Indians and whites. One day, Katawan and his friend, Ben Ziegler, discover a camp in which the men have been killed by Indians. Katawan recognizes the work of the infamous Indian renegade Mahteen, and he and Ben capture the criminal, who taunts Katawan for being a traitor to the Indian cause.

Later that evening, Katawan's brother, Chikisin, goes to see Chief Nantan in order to speak on behalf of Katawan, who wishes to marry the Chief's daughter, Liwana. Meanwhile, Katawan explains to Liwana why he is working for peace with the white man from whom, he believes, the Indians can learn a great deal. Liwana expresses her preference for the white man's marriage customs because the men do not beat their squaws and the women can buy all the calico that they want. Nantan tells Chikisin that he fears Katawan is a traitor to the Indians, but Chikisin assures him that his brother only fights bad Indians. Just then Chato, another suitor, arrives, and when he too calls his rival Katawan a traitor, Chikisin fights with him. Chato throws his knife into Chikisin's back, and when Katawan learns later that Chikisin has died, Nantan urges him to avenge his brother's death, following Apache law. Ben and an Army scout named Sergeant Gaunt witness Katawan killing Chato and are forced to arrest him. The major who heads the local Army unit sentences Katawan to seven years imprisonment at the territorial prison at Yuma, despite Ben's attempts to defend his friend. Nantan also defends Katawan, as he does not see why the white man's law prevails over that of the Apaches. Katawan is sent to Yuma with Mahteen and his gang, who have been sentenced to death by hanging. During the journey, Mahteen grabs an Army scout's gun and kills the guards. Katawan then attacks Ben, who had been following the group, knocking him unconscious. When Mahteen tells Katawan to shoot Ben as an expression of allegiance, Katawan pretends to do so, but in fact shoots at a rock. As the renegades ride away, Mahteen shoots Ben in the leg. When Ben returns to the reservation, the major chastises Ben for his faith in Katawan. Soon after, news arrives of an Indian raid on the Oliver ranch, where Mahteen and Katawan were spotted. Meanwhile, at Mahteen and Katawan's camp, Katawan angrily confronts Mahteen for his senseless killing of white men. While Katawan insists that he only raids ranches in order to get supplies so that he can escape, Mahteen admits that he is making war. The two fight, during which Mahteen carves a cross onto Katawan's arm, a sign of Indian hatred. After Mahteen and Katawan split up, the raids and killings continue, and the Major, believing that Katawan is behind the violence, decides to hire bounty hunters and offer a reward for the renegades' capture. Ben arrives at Army headquarters and offers to go himself, saying that he owes Katawan a bullet, because he believes it was his friend who shot him in the leg. The major decides to allow Nantan and Liwana, who have been under guard, to leave the reservation, reasoning that they will lead the Army to Katawan's whereabouts. As the father and daughter leave, Ben follows them. Meanwhile, a bounty hunter, who has been on Ben's trail, meets up with Army scouts who have Mahteen's dead body. When Nantan finds Katawan, he gives him ponies and offers him his daughter, telling him to settle far away, and assuring him that his descendants will respect the memory of Katawan. Liwana and Katawan reunite in a cave, unaware that Ben is waiting for them, gun in hand. When the couple emerge, Liwana attacks Ben, and Katawan gets the gun. Katawan convinces Ben that it was Mahteen who shot him, and just then three bounty hunters shoot from a rock above and demand that Katawan give himself up. Ben insists that Katawan fight for his life so that he might live to have a family. During the ensuing gunfight, all of the bounty hunters except the leader are killed. Finally free, the reunited friends and Liwana walk away and wave farewell to the now defeated bounty hunter. *Ambushes. Apache Indians. Renegades. Traitors. United States–History–Indian campaigns. United States. Army. Cavalry. Bounty hunters. False accusations. Fathers and daughters. Geronimo. Gunfights. Indians of North America–Reservations. Knife throwing. Officers (Military). Revenge. Romantic rivalry. Yuma (AZ).*

Note: The working titles for the film were *The Apache Kid*, *The Long Knives*, *Red Arrow*. The following written prologue appears in the onscreen credits: "This is the true story of the Apache Kid, who joined the U. S. Army in 1885, with the hope of helping his people. Today he is one of the great legends of the Southwest." According to the *HR* review, the film depicts the problems facing the Apaches after the defeat of Geronimo, when scattered war parties were still resisting U.S. seizure of their lands. Reviews in both *HR* and *Var* report that the real Katawan disappeared after the events depicted in the film. The *HR* reviewer states that the film's dialogue is old-fashioned and that it is "out of date" as a Western, as the characterizations are "stereotyped."

Box 27 Jul 1957. *DV* 16 Jul 1957, p. 3. *Exh* 7 Aug 1957, p. 4362. *FD* 30 Jul 1957, p. 9. *Har* 27 Jul 1957, p. 119. *HR* 22 Mar 1957, p. 17. *HR* 29 Mar 1957, p. 54. *HR* 16 Jul 1957, p. 3. *MPHPD* 27 Jul 1957, p. 465. *Var* 24 Jul 1957, p. 7.

APACHE WOMAN (Apache, Native Americans)
Golden State Productions. *Dist* American Releasing Corp. Oct **1955**; Los Angeles opening: 12 Oct 1955; Prod: mid-Jun—early Jul 1955 [©Golden State Productions; 12 Sep 1955; LP7780]. Sd (Ryder Sound Services); col (Pathecolor). 9 reels, 7,479 ft. 82-83 min. PCA cert no. 17650.
Prod Roger Corman. *Exec prod* Alex Gordon. *Prod supv* Bart Carre. *Dir* Roger Corman. *Story and scr* Lou Rusoff. *Photog* Floyd Crosby. *Film ed* Ronald Sinclair. *Set dec* Harold Rief. *Ward* George Herrington. *Mus comp and cond* Ronald Stein. *Sd* Herman Lewis. *Makeup* Curly Batson. *Scr supv* Barbara Bohren.
Cast: LLOYD BRIDGES [(*Rex Moffet*)], JOAN TAYLOR [(*Anne Libeau*)], LANCE FULLER [(*Armand Libeau*)], Morgan Jones [(*Macey*)], Paul Birch [(*Sheriff*)], Lou Place [(*Carrom Bentley*)], Paul Dubov [(*Ben*)], Jonathan Haze [(*Tom Chandler*)], Gene Marlowe [(*White Star*)], Dick Miller [(*Tall Tree*)], Chester Conklin [(*Dick Mooney*)], Jean Howell [(*Mrs. Chandler*)].
Western. [*Print viewed*]. In a turn-of-the-century Arizona town, cowboy Tom Chandler calls "half-breed" Anne Libeau a "dirty Apache squaw." Furious, she threatens to kill him, and the two engage in a knife fight. Rex Moffet, a government Indian expert called in to quell the growing unrest between the townspeople and the reservation Apaches, stops the fight, calling Anne "quite a fireball." After Anne leaves, the sheriff explains why the townspeople are so edgy: During the past several months, many white travelers have been ambushed, robbed, and even killed. Because Apache tokens have been found at attack sites, the townspeople believe the tribe is again gearing up for war. Rex reminds the men that the Indian wars are over, but a cowboy named Ben replies, "Not for us." Back at the Libeau ranch, Anne's brother Armand tries to convince her to move to the city, where the two of them can live in "oblivion." Their grandfather was an Apache chief, but because his daughter married a Frenchman, Anne and Armand became outcasts, accepted by neither the Apaches nor the white ranchers. Later that day, when Rex surprises Anne as she bathes in a stream, she explains the hatred and bitterness that possess her. Armand attended college, taking top honors in law school, but because of his mixed racial background, his career ended before it began. Struck by Anne's beauty and strength of character, Rex tries to persuade her that no thinking man would shun her because of her race. Rex's suspicion that the attackers may be outlaws, rather than Indians, is strengthened when he later witnesses an attack on town drunk Dick Mooney, who had ridden out of town carrying a large wad of bills. Rex tells Apache chief White Star that evening that some of the outlaws he saw from a distance appeared to be Apaches, whereupon the chief promises that renegades in his tribe will be punished. Nevertheless, the townspeople decide to launch an attack on the reservation on the following day. In order to increase their numbers, they send Chandler to the next town for more men, but Armand, secretly the leader of the outlaw gang, pursues and kills him. Worried about these events, and suspicious of her brother's meetings with a tough cowboy named Macey, Anne questions Armand, complaining that a wall has sprung up between them. Smilingly denying involvement in the murders, Armand tells her to let the wall stand. Torn between loyalty to her brother and her growing love for Rex, Anne follows Armand and finds him talking secretly with Macey. White Star also arrives, hinting that he knows the truth about Armand's role in the recent crimes. After White Star leaves, Armand orders Macey to kill him. Anne pursues White Star, approaching just in time to see Macey empty his gun into her Apache cousin. Back in town, Rex spreads the rumor that a large sum of money will be carried from the town bank to nearby Paiute on the following day. Meeting with a group of reluctant volunteers, Rex explains that they will "ambush the ambushers," when the men carrying the money are attacked by the outlaws. Rex then asks for information from Anne, but she refuses to implicate her brother in the killings. After his departure, however, Anne confronts Macey, who reveals that Armand had ordered him to kill White Star. When Armand himself confirms Macey's story, Anne begs him to begin a new life with her elsewhere, but he is anxious to rob the money that will be transported to Paiute. Anne reveals Rex's plans, but Armand and Macey tie her up and ride away. Working on her bindings throughout the night, Anne finally frees herself and rides to Rex's party with a warning: Armand and his men will rob the money in an unexpected location. Claiming at first that Apaches never betray their own people, she refuses to reveal

Armand's exact whereabouts, but Rex ultimately talks her into a confession. Riding swiftly, Rex's party arrives at Armand's location just as he begins shooting at the men from the bank. Armand realizes that his sister has betrayed him and takes a shot at her, and when Macey decides to surrender, Armand kills the outlaw and runs into the rocky heights. Rex chases him, and the two men fight. Leaping at Rex, Armand falls over a steep cliff, and although Rex tries to catch him, the outlaw falls to his death. Anne offers Rex her arm and helps him limp back down the hill. *Apache Indians. Brothers and sisters. Indians of North America–Mixed blood. Loyalty. Ambushes. Arizona. Betrayal. Falls from heights. Indian agents. Indians of North America. Knife fighting. Mobs. Murder. Outlaws. Racism. Revenge. Romance. Sheriffs. Small town life. Stagecoach robberies. Tribal chiefs.*

Note: Although a *HR* production chart places Tamar Cooper in the cast, her participation in the released film has not been confirmed. In a modern interview, Roger Corman noted that *Apache Woman* was "...the first time that I tried to deal with the subject of racial prejudice within the framework of a commercial movie."

Box 15 Oct 1955. *DV* 6 Oct 1955, p. 3. *Exb* 2 Nov 1955, p. 4056. *Har* 22 Oct 1955, pp. 170-71. *HR* 17 Jun 1955, p. 11. *HR* 24 Jun 1955, p. 7. *HR* 6 Oct 1955, p. 3. *MPHPD* 15 Oct 1955, p. 634. *Var* 12 Oct 1955, p. 22.

APPOINTMENT WITH A SHADOW *see* THE MIDNIGHT STORY

APRIL FOOL (Jewish Americans)

Chadwick Pictures Corp. 15 Nov **1926**. Si; b&w. 7 reels, 7,100 ft.

Dir Nat Ross. *Scen* Zion Myers. *Titles* James Madison. *Photog* L. William O'Connell.

Source: Based on the play *An April Shower* by Edgar Allan Woolf and Alexander Carr (ca 21 Aug 1915).

Cast: Alexander Carr (*Jacob Goodman*), Duane Thompson (*Irma Goodman*), Mary Alden (*Amelia Rosen*), Raymond Keane (*Leon Steinfield*), Edward Phillips (*Joseph Applebaum*), Snitz Edwards (*Mr. Applebaum*), Nat Carr (*Moisha Ginsburg*), Baby Peggy, Pat Moore, Leon Holmes (*The children*).

Comedy. A discharged pants-presser makes a fortune in the umbrella business. His daughter is to marry the nephew of a newly-rich neighbor, until her intended is accused by his uncle of stealing a sum of money that was, in fact, stolen by the man's own son. The marriage is called off until the former pants-presser gives up his fortune to assure his daughter's happiness. *Jews. Nouveaux riches. Pants-pressers. Robbery. Umbrellas.*

FD 7 Nov 1926. *Var* 3 Nov 1926, p. 17.

APRIL SHOWERS (Irish Americans)

Preferred Pictures, Inc. 21 Oct **1923** [©Preferred Pictures, Inc.; 4 Sep 1923; LP19377]. Si; b&w. 6 reels, 6,350 ft.

Pres B. P. Schulberg. *Prod* B. P. Schulberg. *Dir* Tom Forman. *Story and scen* Hope Loring and Louis D. Lighton. *Photog* Harry Perry.

Cast: Colleen Moore (*Maggie Muldoon*), Kenneth Harlan (*Danny O'Rourke*), Ruth Clifford (*Miriam Welton*), Priscilla Bonner (*Shannon O'Rourke*), Myrtle Vane (*Mrs. O'Rourke*), James Corrigan (*Matt Gallagher*), Jack Byron (*Flash Irwin*), Ralph Faulkner (*Champ Sullivan*), Tom McGuire (*Lieutenant Muldoon*), Kid McCoy, Danny Goodman (*The ring managers*).

Melodrama. Danny O'Rourke, the son of an Irish-American policeman who dies a hero, is training to join the force. His sweetheart, Maggie, is the daughter of a police lieutenant. When society girl Miriam Welton arrives in their slum neighborhood to do social work, she nearly causes a split between the two lovers. Danny takes his final examination and thinks he has failed. At the same time, Danny's sister Shannon is caught shoplifting. Danny enters a prizefighting contest to raise money to save his sister. He loses the fight but discovers that an error in the scoring of his examination makes him eligible to join the police force. *Boxers. Brothers and sisters. Irish Americans. Police. Shoplifting. Social workers.*

Note: Copyright material states that Al Lichtman Corp. was distributor, but the exact date of the merger between Preferred Pictures, Inc., and Al Lichtman Corp. has not been determined.

FD 11 Nov 1923. *MPW* 17 Nov 1923. *Var* 22 Nov 1923, p. 27.

ARAPAHO TRAIL *see* SIEGE AT RED RIVER

ARCILLA *see* DEL MISMO BARRO

ARCTIC FLIGHT (Native Americans, Native Alaskans)

Monogram Pictures Corp.; Lindsley Parsons Productions, Inc. *Dist* Monogram Pictures Corp. 19 Oct **1952**; Los Angeles opening: 8 Oct 1952; Prod: late Feb–early Apr 1952 [©Monogram Pictures Corp.; 23 Sep 1952; LP1936]. Sd; b&w. 7,055 ft. 78 min. PCA cert no. 15888.

Prod Lindsley Parsons. *Asst to prod* Wayne Morris. *Assoc prod* Ewing Scott. *Dir* Lew Landers and Ewing Scott. *Asst dir* Rex Bailey. *Scr* Robert Hill and George Bricker. *Story* Ewing Scott. *Photog* Jack Russell. *Art dir* Dave Milton. *Supv film ed* Leonard Herman. *Mus supv* Edward J. Kay. *Rec* Tom Lambert. *Makeup* Ted Larson. *Set cont* Moree Herring.

Cast: Wayne Morris (*Mike Maley*), Lola Albright (*Martha Raymond*), Alan Hale, Jr. (*Harold Wetherby*), Carol Thurston (*Saranna Koonuk*), Phil Tead (*Squid Tucker*), Tom Richards (*Dave Karluck*), Anthony Garson (*Miksook*), Kenneth McDonald (*Father François*), Paul Bryar (*Hogan*), Dale Van Sickle (*Dorgan*).

Espionage, Drama. [*Not viewed*]. Mike Maley, a bush pilot based at Kotzebue in the Arctic Circle, receives a U.S. government assignment to fly schoolteacher and nurse Martha Raymond to the U.S. island of Little Diomede, close to the Russian owned Big Diomede Island. Mike's next passenger, Harold Wetherby, whom he picks up in Nome, claims to be a wealthy Midwestern businessman on a polar bear hunt. Dave Karluck, an Eskimo reindeer herder, and his girl friend, Saranna Koonuk, who becomes infatuated with Mike, go along on the hunt. After they kill a bear and are in the process of skinning it, Wetherby's wallet falls out of his pocket, and Mike sees an identity card entitling Wetherby to enter Russian territory. Mike realizes that Wetherby is a Russian agent and has used the flight to take photographs of U.S. military installations. Mike forces Wetherby back into the plane and flies to Kotzebue, where he finds additional evidence and exposes Wetherby as a Russian spy. After wounding Mike in the arm, Wetherby escapes and heads for Big Diomede. In his haste, however, Wetherby drops his papers and fails to realize his loss until he reaches the Russian sentries, who shoot and kill him. Later, Martha helps Mike to recover from his wound. *Air pilots. Arctic regions. Native Alaskans. Russians. Spies. Bering Sea. Diomede Islands. Dogsledding. Espionage. Fights. Hunting. Infatuation. Microfilm. Nurses. Photographs. Polar bears. Reindeer. Rites and ceremonies. Teachers.*

Note: Studio production sheets deposited with copyright records and reviews indicate that Ewing Scott's screen story was titled "Shadow of the Curtain." Parts of this film were shot on Little Diomede Island in Alaska. According to the *Var* review, Scott directed most of the Alaskan footage, but was replaced by Lew Landers after a flare-up of an old leg injury. The *Har* review notes that the film includes footage of an Eskimo dance. Contemporary sources suggest that Raoul Kraushaar may have contributed to the music score.

Box 2 Aug 1952. *DV* 28 Jul 1952, p. 3. *Exb* 13 Aug 1952, p. 3346. *Har* 9 Aug 1952, p. 126. *HR* 29 Feb 1952, p. 16. *HR* 28 Jul 1952, p. 3. *MPD* 5 Aug 1952. *MPHPD* 2 Aug 1952, p. 1470. *Var* 30 Jul 1952, p. 6.

ARCTIC FURY (Native Alaskans, Native Americans)

Plymouth Productions, Inc. *Dist* RKO Radio Pictures, Inc. 1 Oct **1949**; Los Angeles opening: 4 May 1949 [©Plymouth Productions, Inc.; 10 May 1949; LP2353]. Sd (Western Electric Recording); b&w. 61-63 min. PCA cert no. 13809.

Prod Boris Petroff. *Dir* Norman Dawn and Fred R. Feitshans, Jr. *Asst dir* Glen Cook. *Story* Norman Cook. *Adpt* Charles F. Royal. *Dial* Robert Libbot [sic], Frank Burt and Norton S. Parker. *Photog* Norman Dawn, Jacob Hill, Edward Kull and William C. Thompson. *Art dir* Charles Clague. *Film ed* Fred R. Feitshans, Jr. *Rec eng* Frank Moran. *Sd eff* John Hall. *Prod supv* Fred R. Feitshans, Jr.

Cast: Del Cambre [(*Dr. Thomas Barlow*)], Eve Miller [(*Martha Barlow*)], Gloria Petroff [(*Emily Barlow*)], Dan Riss [(*Narrator*)], Merrill McCormick [(*Trapper Mack*)], Fred Smith [(*Uncle Jim Thompson*)].

Animal, Adventure, Biography. [*Print viewed*]. Dr. Thomas Barlow, a young physician living in Alaska, is called upon to come to the aid of a wandering tribe of Eskimos, who are spreading a plague of unknown origin in the far reaches of the Arctic Circle. Thomas learns that the Eskimos, having fled their encampment, traveled to Noonack, the nearest settlement, where, within two months, they infected the entire area. Tragedy strikes soon after Thomas sets out for the plague-ridden area, when his small airplane loses an engine. The plane crashes in a wilderness area hundreds of miles from human habitation. Although he manages to eject safely from his airplane before it crashes into an iceberg, Thomas suddenly finds himself stranded in one of nature's most brutal environments. Almost

immediately, Thomas is threatened by a polar bear attack and crashing icebergs. Surviving only on the fish he captures from the icy Arctic waters, Thomas, accompanied by two young polar bear cubs he has adopted, begins a desperate search for civilization. Two weeks pass, and Thomas, still wandering through the wilderness, barely survives an attack by musk oxen, which he calls the "most dangerous animal of the North." Meanwhile, Trapper Mack, a friend of Thomas', sadly tells Thomas' wife Martha that her husband never arrived in Noonack, and that pieces of his plane were found by an Eskimo in the Coleville River region. A search party is formed, but hope of finding the doctor lessens with every passing day. Thomas continues to travel in the direction he hopes will lead him to safety, but only finds himself in greater danger. A short time after a search plane flying above Thomas fails to spot him, Martha is told that the search is being called off. Refusing to believe that her husband is dead, Martha insists that the search continue, and her hopes are bolstered when some of Thomas' gear is found miles from the plane wreck. Three months pass, and the famished doctor, nearing Noonack, is attacked by a pack of wild dogs. Things look bad for Thomas until Trapper Mack, who has just arrived in the Noonack area, finds Thomas and scares away the dogs with rifle fire. Thomas makes a full recovery and settles with his family in Cape Fear, where his ordeal becomes a local legend. *Airplane accidents. Arctic regions. Missing persons. Native Alaskans. Plague. Search and rescue operations. Survival skills. Alaska. Bears. Burial. Dogs. Fires. Icebergs. Igloos. Marriage. Physicians. Polar bears. Snow storms. Starvation. Trappers.*

Note: The first of Fred R. Feitshans, Jr.'s two onscreen credits reads: "Production supervisor and film editor." Writer Robert Libott's name was misspelled as "Libbot" onscreen. The foreword to the film describes "that mighty wilderness known as the Alaskan tundra...abounding with life and sudden death," and dedicates the picture to "that dauntless brotherhood of mercy flyers [who] fly to remote settlements, annihilating time and space, carrying food, supplies, and precious medical aid to combat pestilence." The foreword also describes the film as a "photographic record of a dramatic chapter in the life of one of those heroic riders of the sky, a young physician known as the 'Flying Doctor' [Dr. Thomas Barlow]." Opening credits for the film note that "certain scenes and sequences of this photoplay are taken or adapted from the motion picture *Tundra*, a photographic record filmed within the Arctic Circle." Except for scenes involving "Barlow's" family, the plot of *Arctic Fury* follows that of *Tundra*, a 1936 Burroughs-Tarzan Picture, very closely. According to a 17 Jul 1949 *NYT* article, however, almost half of *Arctic Fury* was "fresh material," shot in Hollywood. In 1938, according to the article, producer Boris Petroff acquired 120,000 feet of *Tundra* footage from director Norman Dawn, re-edited it and briefly roadshowed it, but withdrew prints after a poor reception. Realizing that he had scenery but no story, he later shot narration and new scenes, some using the original actors, over a two-year period. Before RKO took over as national distributor, the picture was released by the Fox West Coast circuit. Wally Howe (*Trappers*), Earl Dwire (*Storekeeper*), Jack Santos (*Halfbreed*), Fraser Acosta (*Eskimo father*), Mrs. Elsie Duran and Bertha Maldanado (*Eskimos*) are listed in the cast of *Tundra*, but are not listed for *Arctic Fury*. It is possible, however, that all or some of these actors were included to some extent in the later film. In addition, while crew credits for *Arctic Fury* include most of the crew credits from *Tundra*, music director Abe Meyer and film editors Walter Thompson and Thomas Neff are not listed for the later picture. It is possible that some of these men's work was also utilized for *Arctic Fury*. Although copyright records indicate that, before RKO became the distributor for *Arctic Fury*, prints of the film contained a 1948 copyright statement, the viewed print contained a 1949 statement.

The following production information was taken from the entry for *Tundra* (see below): According to *HR*, *Tundra* was started by Carl Laemmle, but dropped by Universal when the studio passed to new owners. It was shot on location in Alaska for seven months, after which, according to a *HR* news item, Norman Dawn made a deal with Universal for the rights to the footage and took it to Burroughs-Tarzan for editing, who distributed it in Jul 1936 as a "roadshow special." A modern source states that *Tundra* contains large portions of stock shots from Universal's 1933 film *S.O.S. Iceberg* (see *AFI Catalog of Feature Films, 1931-40;* F3.5456) and other pictures.

Box 18 Jun 1949. DV 6 May 1949, p. 3. Exh 25 May 1949. Exh 8 Jun 1949. FD 10 May 1949, p. 7. HR 6 May 1949, p. 3. MPHPD 1 Oct 1949, p. 34. Var 11 May 1949, p. 18.

ARCTIC MANHUNT (Native Alaskans, Native Americans)
Universal-International Pictures Co., Inc. *Dist* Universal Pictures Co., Inc. 1949; New York opening: week of 18 Aug 1949; Prod: late 1947; late Nov—early Dec 1948 [©Universal Pictures Co., Inc.; 28 Apr 1949; LP2299]. Sd (Western Electric Recording); b&w. 61 or 69 min. PCA cert no. 13695.
Prod Leonard Goldstein. *Assoc prod* Billy Grady. *Dir* Ewing Scott. [*Asst dir* John Sherwood]. *Scr* Oscar Brodney and Joel Malone. *Story* Ewing Scott. *Dir of photog* Irving Glassberg. *Exterior photog* Kay Norton. *Spec photog* David S. Horsley. *Art dir* Bernard Herzbrun and Robert Boyle. *Film ed* Otto Ludwig. *Set dec* Russell A. Gausman and Al Fields. *Mus arr and dir by* Milton Schwarzwald. *Sd* Leslie I. Carey

and Joe Lapis. *Hair stylist* Carmen Dirigo. *Dir of makeup* Bud Westmore.
Cast: Mikel Conrad [(*Mike Jarvis, also known as Ed Johnson and Reverend John Douglas*)], Carol Thurston [(*Narana*)], Wally Cassell [(*Tooyuk*)], [Helen Brown (*Lois Jarvis*)], [Harry Harvey (*Carter*)], [Russ Conway (*Landers*)], [Paul E. Burns (*Hotel clerk*)], [Quianna (*Eskimo girl*)], [Chet Huntley (*Narrator*)], [Howard Negley (*Harry*)], [Michael Cisney (*Tourist*)], [Joe Bernard (*Clem Phillips*)], [Herbert Heywood (*Mailman*)], [Rosa Turich (*Nakuchluk*)], [Jack George (*Reverend John Douglas*)], [Iron Eyes Cody, Roque Ybarra (*Eskimos*)], [Charles Rivero (*Eskimo guide*)], [Jack Gargan (*Steward*)].

Crime, Drama. [*Print viewed*]. After being released from prison following a seven-year sentence for the $250,000 robbery of an armed truck, Mike Jarvis is continually hounded at his sister Lois's home in Greenport, Washington by Carter and Landers, two insurance investigators who are determined to retrieve the stolen money. Mike recovers the money from its hiding spot above his mother's grave, and heads for Nome, Alaska, to meet up with his partner-in-crime, Frank Hogg. Once there, a hotel clerk tells Mike that Frank is hiding from the police in a distant Eskimo village. Mike hires an Eskimo guide to take him to Frank, but the guide deserts him in the middle of the Alaskan wilderness after being whipped for overturning their dogsled. He is fortunate enough, however, to stumble across Reverend John Douglas, a missionary, who is on his way to the Eskimo village to treat Frank for diphtheria. When Douglas is killed in an accident on the way to the village, Mike is forced once again to struggle alone in the Arctic wasteland, and along the way, loses his bag of money. He miraculously makes his way to the Eskimo village just in time for Frank's funeral. Mike then assumes Douglas' identity and, with his money seemingly lost forever, takes up the missionary's work at the village. He soon becomes romantically involved with Narana, a Westernized Eskimo woman. Mike confesses his past to Narana, but she tells him that his good work for the village is all that matters to her. Meanwhile, Carter and Landers arrive in Nome in their continued search for Mike, and learn from the Eskimo guide that he is somewhere in the Alaskan wilderness. Later, in the spring, Tooyuk, Narana's ex-boyfriend, returns from a trip to Nome with the stolen money, having found Mike's bag along the trail. As soon as he is reunited with his riches, Mike prepares to return home, but Narana refuses to go with him. When Carter and Landers arrive at the village, Mike flees on his own, but is trapped when the ice starts to break around him. As Narana, Tooyuk, and the insurance investigators watch, Mike dies in the freezing Arctic waters. *Alaska. Ex-convicts. Impersonation and imposture. Missionaries. Mistaken identity. Money. Native Alaskans. Accidental death. Brothers and sisters. Cemeteries. Churches. Criminals–Rehabilitation. Dogsledding. Fights. Funerals. Greed. Hotels. Hunting. Insurance–Investigators. Love. Nome (AK). Polar bears. Searches. Walruses. Washington (State). Whales and whaling. Whips and whippings.*

Note: The film begins with the following written statement: "We gratefully acknowledge the assistance of the Alaskan Territorial Officials whose splendid cooperation made possible all exterior scenes actually photographed in Alaska." Onscreen credits list the title of Ewing Scott's original story as "Narana of the North." According to a *LAT* news item, Scott, along with cameraman Kay Norton and actor Mikel Conrad, spent four months in the winter of 1947 shooting footage on the north coast of Alaska. Universal then purchased the footage, and in late Nov 1948 shot additional footage at the studio, featuring actress Carol Thurston. According to a *DV* news item, actress Quianna was once a "Miss Alaska" beauty contest winner.

Box 17 Sep 1949. DV 26 Nov. 1948. DV 15 Sep 1949, p. 3. HR 26 Nov 1948, p. 17. HR 15 Sep 1949, p. 3. LAT 4 Nov 1948. NYT 19 Aug 1949, p. 12. Var 24 Aug 1949, p. 22.

ARIZONA AMBUSH see **RIDERS OF THE RANGE**

ARIZONA FRONTIER (Native Americans)
Boots and Saddles Pictures, Inc. *Dist* Monogram Pictures Corp. 19 Aug **1940** [©Monogram Pictures Corp.; 16 Aug 1940; LP9859]. Sd; b&w. 6 reels. 55 or 60 min. PCA cert no. 6511.
Prod Edward Finney. *Dir* Al Herman. *Scr* Robert Emmett. *Photog* Marcel A. LePicard. *Film ed* Fred Bain and Robert Golden. *Mus dir* Frank Sanucci. *Sd rec* Glen Glenn. *Tech dir* E. R. Hickson.
Cast: Tex Ritter (*Tex Whitedeer*), Slim Andrews (*Slim Chance*), Frank LaRue (*Captain Farley*), John Merton (*Lieutenant James*), Tristam Coffin (*Graham*), Gene Alsace (*Bisbee*), Jim Pierce (*Kansas*), Jim Thorpe (*Grey Cloud*), Hal Price (*Joe Lane*), Evelyn Finley (*Honey Lane*), and His Romaine Lowdermilk, Chick Hannon, White Flash, Dick Cramer, and His Art Wilcox.

Western, with songs. [*Not viewed*]. Tex Whitedeer, the agent appointed by the government to choose the spot where the East and West branches of the railroad will meet, is believed to be an Indian, but actually is a white man reared on the reservation from boyhood by the Indian Grey Cloud, a close friend of his father. Tex's heritage becomes an issue because Graham and his men have been raiding Joe Lane's freight lines and planting suspicion on the Indians. Upon investigating the circumstances, Tex is certain that white men are behind the raids, but Lieutenant James, an officer at the army post, accuses Tex of leading the Indians on the raids. To trap the villains, Tex lets James overhear a conversation that he has with Honey, Lane's daughter, in which he informs her that the railroad junction will be placed on her father's land. James and his cohorts then buy Lane's land, only to find that Tex has picked another section on which to build the junction. In revenge, Graham's men kidnap Honey and capture Tex when he rides to her rescue, but the pair escape in time to thwart Graham's attempt to rob the freight line again. The final confrontation occurs as Tex, aided by the soldiers and the Indians led by his old friend Grey Cloud, round up Graham's gang and prove that James had been working in conjunction with the outlaws. *False accusations. Indians of North America. Mistaken identity. Robbery. Kidnapping. Outlaws. Racial impersonation. Railroads. United States. Army. Cavalry.*

Note: Sources conflict over the credits of this film. Whereas the copyright records credit Robert Golden as editor, *MPH* credits Fred Bain. Although the copyright records credit John Merton with the role of James, *MPH* credits the role to Tristam Coffin; copyright records credit Coffin with the role of Graham, while *MPH* credits to Dick Cramer. Finally, *MPH* credits the singing group that appears in the film as Art Wilcox and His Arizona Rangers, whereas the copyright records list the group as Romaine Lowdermilk and His Ranchhouse Boys. Although the reviews indicate that the film contained some songs, their titles and composers have not been determined. According to the reviews, the picture was filmed on location in Arizona.

DV 25 Oct 1940, p. 3. *FD* 28 Oct 1940, p. 5. *HR* 24 Oct 1940, p. 3. *HR* 13 Jun 1940, p. 6. *MPH* 4 May 1940, p. 46. *MPH* 31 Aug 1940, p. 54. *Var* 12 Jun 1940, p. 16.

THE ARIZONA KID (Latino)

Fox Film Corp. *Dist* Fox Film Corp. 27 Apr **1930** [©Fox Film Corp.; 12 Apr 1930; LP1257]. Sd (Movietone); b&w. 9 reels, 7,902 ft. [Also si.].

Pres William Fox. *Dir* Alfred Santell. *Asst dir* Marty Santell. *Story, scen and dial* Ralph Block. *Photog* Glen MacWilliams. *Film ed* Paul Weatherwax. *Settings* Joseph Wright. *Ward* Sophie Wachner. *Sd eng* George Leverett.

Cast: Warner Baxter (*The Arizona Kid*), Mona Maris (*Lorita*), Carol Lombard (*Virginia Hoyt*), Theodore von Eltz (*Nick Hoyt*), Arthur Stone (*Snakebit Pete*), Solidad Jiminez (*Pulga*), Walter P. Lewis (*Sheriff Andrews*), Jack Herrick (*The Hoboken Hooker*), Wilfred Lucas (*His manager*), Hank Mann (*Bartender Bill*), James Gibson (*Stagedriver*), De Sacia Mooers (*Molly*), Larry McGrath (*Homer Snook*).

Western. Posing as a wealthy and carefree Mexican miner, The Arizona Kid is loved by many se'noritas, including Lorita, while carrying out his mission as bandit-hero. Their romance is interrupted, however, by the arrival of Virginia, an eastern girl accompanied presumably by her brother, Dick (actually her husband). While The Kid falls for the blonde and she makes a play for him, the sheriff becomes suspicious of his absence. Eventually, The Kid's mine, worked in secret, is raided and his two coworkers are killed. With the help of Lorita, The Kid learns that Dick and Virginia are the culprits; after a showdown in which Dick is killed, The Kid escapes with Lorita at his side. *Bandits. Courtship. Mexican Americans. Miners.*

FD 18 May 1930. *Var* 21 May 1930, p. 25.

THE ARIZONA RANGER (Latino)

RKO Radio Pictures, Inc. *Dist* RKO Radio Pictures, Inc. 23 Mar **1948**; Prod: 20 Oct–early Nov 1947 [©RKO Radio Pictures, Inc.; 4 Apr 1948; LP1652]. Sd (RCA Sound System); b&w. 5,646 ft. 63-64 min. PCA cert no. 12800.

Prod Herman Schlom. *Dir* John Rawlins. [*Asst dir* John Pommer]. *Orig scr* Norman Houston. *Dir of photog* J. Roy Hunt. *Art dir* Albert S. D'Agostino and Charles F. Pyke. *Film ed* Desmond Marquette. *Set dec* Darrell Silvera and Jack Mills. *Mus dir* C. Bakaleinikoff. *Mus* Paul Sawtell. *Sd* Garry Harris and Terry Kellum.

Cast: TIM HOLT [(*Bob Morgan*)], JACK HOLT [(*Rawhide Morgan*)], Nan Leslie [(*Laura Butler*)], Richard Martin [(*Chito Rafferty*)], Steve Brodie [(*Quirt Butler*)], Paul Hurst [(*Ben Riddle*)],

Jim Nolan [(*Nimino Welch*)], Robert Bray [(*Jasper Todd*)], Richard Benedict [(*Gil*)], William Phipps [(*Mac*)], Harry Harvey [(*Peyton*)], [Richard Foote (*Red*)], [Herman Nowlin (*Stage driver*)], [Lane Chandler (*Capt. McNeil*)].

Historical, Western. [*Print viewed*]. In 1898, just after Arizona rancher Rawhide Morgan learns that his son Bob, a recently discharged Rough Rider, will be returning home soon, the Morgan Ranch is besieged by a gang of cattle rustlers. Fearless Rawhide and devoted hand Ben Riddle chase the rustlers off the range but are unable to catch them. Although Rawhide is sure that the gang's leader, Quirt Butler, is hiding in the cabin he sometimes shares with his wife Laura, he finds nothing there. Apprised by Rawhide of Butler's illegal activities, Laura attempts to flee town on the next stage, but is spotted by Butler and dragged into the street. Seeing Laura thus abused, Bob and his fellow Rough Riders, Mac and Gil, who have just arrived in town, begin to brawl with Butler and his men. Rawhide breaks up the fight, but learns that his reunion with Bob is to be shortlived when Bob admits that he has accepted a commission from the governor to organize the Arizona Rangers and bring law and order to the territory. An outspoken believer in vigilante justice, Rawhide belittles Bob's choice and angrily parts with him. Bob's first assignment as a Ranger is to arrest Nimino Welch, one of Butler's men, who is wanted for armed robbery. Although Bob easily arrests Nimino, Butler ambushes the stagecoach that is carrying him to jail and frees him. In town, meanwhile, Bob tries to convince Laura to leave Butler, but she contends that she can never escape him and is resigned to her fate. Later, Butler, who was shot by Rawhide while fleeing the stagecoach, shows up at Laura's cabin. To protect Bob when he arrives looking for the gun-wielding Butler, Laura lies that he has come and gone. Butler's men then raid Rawhide's cattle and shoot and kill Ben. Sure that Butler is his friend's killer, Rawhide corners him at Laura's and prepares to lynch him. Explaining that Butler could not have murdered Ben because he was with her, Laura risks her own reputation to alert Bob to Rawhide's impending injustice. Bob forces his father to turn over the outlaw, but Butler's men later trick Laura into diverting Bob and a posse so that they can free Butler from jail. Ridiculed by his father and removed from his post, Bob becomes determined to recapture Butler and Nimino and stakes out Laura's cabin. Soon, Nimino and Jasper, another rustler, show up looking for Laura. Before the men can deliver her to Butler, however, Bob engages them in a fierce fight. During the mêlée, Laura shoots Nimino, but Jasper rides away to warn Butler. Bob pursues the rustler into a rocky enclave and soon finds himself pinned down by the gang. Laura, meanwhile, rides to Rawhide for help, but he rejects her entreaties. Outraged by the rancher's stubborn indifference, Laura accuses him of being a heartless old man. Laura's words cause a change of heart in Rawhide, who then rallies his men to rescue Bob. While Rawhide and his hands round up the gang, Bob fights Butler, who is eventually shot by Rawhide. Later, Rawhide asks the departing Laura to remain in Arizona, but she insists she must go. Rawhide is equally determined to make her stay, however, and rides out on the stage with her. Suddenly concerned for his romantic future, Bob chases after his father. *Animal traps. Arizona. Fathers and sons. Law and order. Rangers. Rustlers. United States–History–19th century. Battered women. Fistfights. Gunfights. Gunshot wounds. Mexican Americans. Rescues. Romance. Stagecoaches. Veterans.*

Note: The working title of this film was *Rawhide*. The reviews and CBCS list Jack and Tim Holt's characters' surname as "Wade," but they are called "Morgan" in the film. *HR* production charts add Jason Robards to the cast, but that actor did not appear in the final film. Modern sources add Bud Osborne to the cast.

Box 3 Apr 1948. *DV* 24 Mar 1948, p. 4. *FD* 31 Mar 1948, p. 10. *HR* 26 Sep 1947, p. 1. *HR* 17 Oct 1947, p. 15. *HR* 20 Oct 1947, p. 2. *HR* 31 Oct 1947, p. 29. *HR* 24 Mar 1948, p. 5. *MPHPD* 20 Mar 1948, p. 4103. *MPHPD* 3 Apr 1948, p. 4110. *Var* 24 Mar 1948, p. 8.

ARMENIA CRUCIFIED *see* **AUCTION OF SOULS**

ARMS AND THE WOMAN (Hungarian Americans)

Astra Film Corp.; Gold Rooster Plays. *Dist* Pathé Exchange, Inc. 26 Nov **1916** [©Pathé Exchange, Inc.; 17 Jul 1916; LU8717]. Si; b&w. 5 reels.

Dir George Fitzmaurice. *Scen* Ouida Bergère. *Cam* A. C. Miller.

Cast: Mary Nash (*Rozika*), Lumsden Hare (*David Trevor*), H. Cooper Cliffe (*Captain Halliday*), Robert Broderick (*Marcus*), Rosalind Ivan (*Marcus' wife*), Carl Harbaugh (*Carl*), Susanne Willa.

World War I, Drama. Rozika, a Hungarian girl with a beautiful voice, emigrates to America with her ne'er-do-well brother Carl. After she gets a job singing in a saloon in New York's Lower East Side, Rozika's street singing attracts David Trevor, the owner of a large steel works that manufactures munitions. Trevor pays for Rozika's lessons with a master, and after she becomes a famous opera singer, she marries him. When World War I breaks out in Europe, Rozika, realizing that Trevor's munitions will be used against her homeland, pleads with him to refuse the allies' orders, but he ignores her. Meanwhile, Carl, who returned to Hungary after killing a man in a brawl, is sent by an anarchist group to blow up Trevor's plant. Rozika learns of Carl's plans and locks him in a closet, but he breaks through and shoots Trevor. After chases, gunfights and killings, German spies explode the factory. The wounded and financially ruined Trevor, realizing that his marital conflict is now over, says of his factory's destruction, "It is better so." *Hungarian Americans. Munitions factories. Steel magnates. World War I. Anarchists. Brothers and sisters. Chases. Germans. Gunfights. Immigrants. Murder. New York City–Lower East Side. Sabotage. Singers. Spies.*

Note: According to reviews, this film included material from news weeklies. According to modern sources, Anton Grot was the art director.

MPN 25 Nov 1916, p. 3329. *MPW* 25 Nov 1916, ad following p. 1102, p. 1181, 1230. *NYDM* 18 Nov 1916, p. 26. *Var* 10 Nov 1916, p. 29. *Wid's* 16 Nov 1916, p. 1107.

ARMY BRAT *see* **LITTLE MISTER JIM**

AROUND THE CORNER (Jewish Americans)
Columbia Pictures Corp.; Columbia Pictures Corp. 25 Apr **1930** [©Columbia Pictures Corp.; 17 May 1930; LP1309]. Sd (Movietone); b&w. 7 reels, 6,419 ft.

Prod Harry Cohn. *Dir* Bert Glennon. *Asst dir* David Selman. *Dial dir* Patterson McNutt. *Story, cont and dial* Jo Swerling. *Photog* Joe Walker. *Art dir* Harrison Wiley. *Film ed* Gene Milford. *Sd eng* John Livadary. *Sd mixing eng* Harry Blanchard.

Cast: George Sidney (*Kaplan*), Charlie Murray (*O'Grady*), Joan Peers (*Rosie O'Grady*), Larry Kent (*Tommy Sinclair*), Charles Delaney (*Terry Callahan*), Jess Devorska (*Moe Levine*), Fred Sullivan (*Sinclair, Sr.*), Harry Strang (*Mac*).

Comedy-drama. O'Grady, an Irish policeman, and Kaplan, a Jewish pawnbroker, bring up a child found on their doorstep. Eighteen years later, Rosie is in love with prizefighter Terry Callahan, although her guardians prefer Moe Levine as a prospective match. A dispute is settled when Rosie declares that the rivals may both escort her to a dress ball; there she meets Tommy Sinclair, a young socialite. O'Grady and Kaplan, resenting Tommy's affections for the girl, pay Sinclair, Sr., a visit, and as a result Tommy chooses to leave home rather than give up Rosie. He arranges a match between himself and Terry, and, to everyone's surprise, he wins the fight. When Rosie's guardians see that she has won $25,000 for them, they welcome Tommy as their son-in-law. *Boxers. Courtship. Foundlings. Irish. Jews. Pawnbrokers. Police. Socialites. Wards and guardians.*

FD 4 May 1930.

¡ARRIBA EL TELÓN! *see* **GENTE ALEGRE**

ARROW *see* **BROKEN ARROW**

ARROW IN THE DUST (Native Americans, Apache, Pawnee)
Allied Artists Pictures Corp. *Dist* Monogram Pictures Corp. 25 Apr **1954**; Prod: mid-Sep—early Oct 1953 [©Allied Artists Pictures Corp.; 8 Apr 1954; LP3507]. Sd (Western Electric Recording); col (Technicolor). 1.85. 7,201 ft. 79 min.

Prod Hayes Goetz. *Assoc prod* Marvin Mirisch. *Dir* Lesley Selander. *Asst dir* Dick Mayberry. *Scr* Don Martin. *Photog* Ellis W. Carter. *Spec eff* Ray Mercer. *Technicolor color consultant* Robert Brower. *Art dir* David Milton. *Supv film ed* Lester A. Sansom. *Ed* William Austin. *Set dec* Robert Priestley. *Set cont* Ted Schilz. *Ward* Smoke Kring. *Mus* Marlin Skiles. *Rec* Virgil Smith. *Makeup* Norman Pringle. *Prod supv* Allen K. Wood.

Song(s): "The Weary Stranger," words and music by Jimmy Wakely.

Source: Based on the novel *Road to Jacinto* by L. L. Foreman (New York, 1943).

Cast: Sterling Hayden [(*Bart Laish*)], Coleen Gray [(*Christella Burke*)], Keith Larsen [(*Lt. Steve King*)], Tom Tully [(*Crowshaw*)], Jimmy Wakely [(*Carqueville*)], Tudor Owen [(*Tillotson*)], Lee Van Cleef [(*Crew boss*)], John Pickard [(*Sgt. Lybarger*)], Carleton Young [(*Major Andy Pepperis*)].

Western. [*Print viewed*]. After deserting his command, cavalry trooper Bart Laish comes upon the remnants of a wagon train bound for Oregon and discovers that its inhabitants have been massacred by Indians. The only survivor is Major Andy Pepperis, a distant cousin of Laish's who served with him at West Point. With his dying breath, Pepperis appeals to Laish's sense of honor and decency and begs him to find the main train up ahead and lead it to safety at Fort Laramie. Having fled the rigors of army life, Laish remains ambivalent to Pepperis' pleas until he reaches Fort Taylor and finds the men annhilated, the victims of another Indian raid. Finally acceeding to the major's dying wishes, Laish dons the dead man's uniform and catches up to the wagon train. Finding the settlers wounded and the troops decimated, Laish identifies himself as Major Pepperis and assumes command from Lt. Steve King. When King reports that the wagons have been beseiged by continual Indian raids, Laish decides to cross the mountain pass that night. Laish's command is challenged by Crowshaw, the frontier scout who had previously met Pepperis. When Laish explains that he is carrying out the major's final orders, the two men form an uneasy alliance. Crowshaw then warns Laish about Tillotson, the belligerent owner of the huge trade wagon. As the wagons charge through the pass, they are fired upon by Apaches, causing Crowshaw to wonder why Apache Chief Rasakura has singled out their train for attack. After the Indians are driven off, Christella Burke, one of the wagon owners, insists upon stopping to bury the dead. The train resumes its journey, and Laish and the other troopers are forced to fend off another Indian onslaught, during which Laish is wounded. As Christella tends to Laish's injuries, she apologizes for her earlier defiance. Soon after, two arrows are shot into the camp, symbolizing the banding together of the Apache and Pawnee tribes. Later, when Christella overhears Crowshaw and Laish discussing his true identity, Laish confesses that he is a deserter, but confides that he feels obligated to carry out Pepperis' dying wish. Resentful of Laish's authority, Tillotson's crew boss challenges him, causing Laish to shoot him. Laish then orders Tillotson to leave his cache of liquor behind as bait for the Indians. Laish's ploy works, and as the Indians wallow drunkenly, the wagons continue on in peace. As they near the hill country, Laish informs Crowshaw that he plans to head for Santa Fe, New Mexico, and Crowshaw vehemently denounces him for forsaking his responsibilities. Poised for attack in the hills, the Indians charge the wagons, and Laish sends Lt. King to Fort Laramie for reinforcements. Laish decides to lead the wagons onto the ridge for protection, and Christella, having come to admire Laish's courage, kisses him. That night, as the wagons climb onto the ridge, Laish instructs his men to collect rocks and brush. As the Indians converge on the plain, Laish sets fire to the brush and sends the burning embers spilling onto the Indians below. About to run out of wood, Laish orders that Tillotson's giant wagon be sacrificed for fuel. When Crowshaw approaches the wagon, Tillotson attacks him and Crowshaw slays him with his knife. Upon discovering that the wagon is loaded with guns and ammunition, Crowshaw and Laish realize that the Indians have been following them for the weapons, and they catapult the wagon over the ridge. With the guns' destruction, the Indians retreat. Finally safe, the wagons head for the fort and are met by Lt. King and a troop of reinforcements. Although he knows that he will be arrested for desertion, Laish elects to remain with the wagons. As he reaches the train, Lt. King greets Laish, and after promising to vouch for his loyalty and integrity, asks him to lead the wagons to the fort. *Apache Indians. Desertion, Military. Impersonation and imposture. Indians of North America. Pawnee Indians. Raids. United States. Army. Cavalry. Wagon trains. Duplicity. Forts. Pledges. Rifles. Romance. Scouts (Frontier). Transformation.*

Note: The working title of this film was *The Deserter*. This was Allied Artists' first domestically produced Technicolor picture.

Box 17 Apr 1954. *DV* 14 Apr 1954, p. 3. *Exh* 7 Apr 1954, p. 3725. *FD* 22 Apr 1954, p. 7. *Har* 17 Apr 1954, p. 62. *HR* 18 Sep 1953, p. 10. *HR* 2 Oct 1953, p. 18. *HR* 14 Apr 1954, p. 3. *MPHPD* 24 Apr 1954, p. 2269. *NYT* 1 May 1954, p. 13. *Var* 21 Apr 1954, p. 6.

ARROWHEAD (Native Americans, Apache, Chiricahua)
Paramount Pictures Corp. *Dist* Paramount Pictures Corp. Aug **1953**; Prod: 11 Nov—5 Dec 1952 [©Paramount Pictures Corp.; 1 Aug 1953; LP2891]. Sd (Western Electric Recording); col (Technicolor). 11 reels, 9,473 ft. 105 min. PCA cert no. 16336.

Prod Nat Holt. *Assoc to the prod* Harry Templeton. *Dir* Charles Marquis Warren. *Asst dir* Daniel McCauley. *Scr* Charles Marquis Warren. *Dir of photog* Ray Rennahan. *Technicolor col consultant*

Richard Mueller. *Art dir* Hal Pereira and Al Roelofs. *Ed* Frank Bracht. *Set dec* Sam Comer and Bertram Granger. *Cost* Edith Head. *Mus score* Paul Sawtell. *Sd rec* Harold Lewis and Gene Garvin. *Makeup supv* Wally Westmore.

Source: Based on the novel *Adobe Walls* by W. R. Burnett (New York, 1953).

Cast: CHARLTON HESTON [(*Ed Bannon*)], Jack Palance [(*Toriano*)], Katy Jurado [(*Nita*)], Brian Keith [(*Capt. North*)], Mary Sinclair [(*Lela Wilson*)], Milburn Stone [(*Sandy Mackinnon*)], Richard Shannon [(*Lt. Kirk*)], Lewis Martin [(*Col. Weybright*)], Frank de Kova [(*Chief Chattez*)], Robert Wilke [(*Sgt. Stone*)], Peter Coe [(*Spanish*)], Kyle James [(*Jerry August*)], John M. Pickard [(*John Gunther*)], Pat Hogan [(*Jim Eagle*)], [Judith Ames (*Mrs. Kirk*)], [Kathryn Grandstaff (*Miss Mason*)], [Richard Paxton (*Jordan*)], [Mike Ragan (*Corp. Ives*)], [Rus Conklin (*Wakamaza*)], [Eric Alden, James Burke, Frank Cordell, Don Dunning, Dick Farnsworth, Chick Hannon, Bryan Hightower, Leroy Johnson, Robert J. Miles, Bob Peoples, A. Guy Teague, Bob Templeton, Willard Willingham, Henry Wills (*Cavalrymen*)], [John S. Peters (*Dr. "Captain" Mason*)], [Paul Marion (*Kuni*)].

Historical, Biography, Western. [*Print viewed*]. In 1878, Ed Bannon, a civilian scout for Fort Clark, a U.S. Cavalry post in the heart of Texas Apache country, spoils the government's attempt at a peaceful reconciliation with the Indians when he and his pal, Sandy Mackinnon, kill three Chiracahua Apache go-betweens. Bannon warns Col. Weybright that Chief Chattez' agreement to move Apaches onto a Florida reservation is a dangerous Indian ploy and insists that Indians are not to be trusted. Having lived among the Apaches as a boy, Bannon claims to know the way Indians think, and when he learns that Chief Chattez' son Toriano will be arriving from the East Coast, he suspects a trick. Weybright fires Bannon and, soon after, is mortally wounded in an Apache ambush. Bannon returns to the post to resume his romance with widow Lela Wilson, but Lela, who is now being courted by Capt. North, rejects his advances. Sgt. Stone and other cavalrymen blame Bannon for creating trouble with the Indians and try to force him out of the post, but Bannon refuses to leave. Having been rejected by Lela, Bannon courts Nita, the half-Mexican, half-Apache laundress at the post. Toriano arrives at the post just as the Indians are being given identification tags and placed in a holding area. Bannon's suspicions about the Apaches prove justified when Toriano leads a group of rebellious Indians in a late-night raid of the post. The next day, Bannon and Sandy kill Nita's brother Spanish, who has shown his loyalty to Toriano. Bannon, in an impassioned speech to the cavalry officers, again warns of the dangers of believing that peace with the Indians can be attained. Later that night, Bannon catches Nita as she attempts to kill him, and accuses her of being a spy for Toriano. When Bannon orders Nita's imprisonment, she grabs his knife and kills herself. Toriano, meanwhile, has led the army into a trap, and the Apaches ambush North and his men on their way to negotiate a peace settlement with the Indians. A bloody gun battle ensues, during which half the men in North's command are killed. Realizing that Bannon has been right about the Apaches all along, North relinquishes his authority and lets Bannon lead an attack on Toriano. Bannon uses his knowledge of Indian fighting tactics to give the army the upper hand in the battle, and the Indians are defeated. Toriano is killed by Bannon in a hand-to-hand fight, and with his death, the Apaches denounce Toriano and his ways, and vow to seek peace with the whites. Apache Indians. Fort Clark (TX). Scouts (Frontier). United States–History–Indian campaigns. United States. Army. Cavalry. Adoption. Arson. Bigotry. Brothers and sisters. Dances. Drunkenness. Fathers and sons. Fistfights. Gunfights. Indians of North America–Mixed blood. Internment. Mexicans. Murder. Suicide. Texas. Traps. Treaties. Tribal chiefs.

Note: The working title of this film was *Adobe Walls*. The opening title card contains the following excerpted letter: "To: *The General of the Armies* regarding the subject of: *Recommendation of the Congressional Award....*and in my opinion this man—in constant disregard of his personal feelings and (as Chief of Scouts) repeatedly risking his life that others might be saved—deserves to have his name rank with Daniel Boone, Kit Carson, Wm. F. Cody and others whose unselfish service to this country can never be forgotten. Respectfully, George Crook, Brig. General, U.S. Army, May 7, 1886." The subject of the letter, Al Sieber, Chief of Scouts of the United States Army of the Southwest, is acknowledged in the closing credits as having provided, in part, the basis for the character of "Ed Bannon." Born in 1844, Sieber, a Civil War veteran, became chief of scouts for the U.S. Army at San Carlos Indian Reservation in 1870. Sieber participated in the hunt for Geronimo, aided by Apache trackers.

He reportedly survived twenty-nine gun and arrow wounds and died in 1907. Closing credits also acknowledge that *Arrowhead* was filmed entirely on location at Fort Clark, in Bracketville, TX. An Aug 1951 *Par News* article indicates that Paramount producer Pat Dugan was originally to produce the film, and that Sy Bartlett was to write the screenplay. Bartlett's contribution to the completed film has not been confirmed. In addition to *Arrowhead*, Al Sieber was a featured character in United Artists' 1954 film *Apache* (see above entry), and in *Mr. Horn*, a 1979 CBS television mini-series, directed by Jack Starrett and starring Richard Widmark as Sieber.

Box 27 Jun 1953. *DV* 17 Oct 1952. *DV* 15 Jun 1953, p. 3. *FD* 24 Jun 1953, p. 10. *HR* 18 Aug 1952. *HR* 15 Jun 1953, p. 3. *MPHPD* 20 Jun 1953, p. 1878. *NYT* 16 Sep 1953, p. 38. *Var* 17 Jun 1953, p. 6.

ARSHIN MAL ALAN (Armenian language)

Marana Films, Inc. *Dist* Marana Films, Inc. 5 Mar **1937**. Sd; b&w. Length undetermined. Armenian language with English titles.

Prod Setrag Vartian. *Dir* Setrag Vartian. *Mus dir* Serge Koushnareff.

Source: Based on the operetta *Arshin Mal Alan* by Uzeir Hajibeyov (production undetermined).

Cast: Setrag Vartian (*Askiar*), Louise Barsamian (*Gulchora*), Vart Ankin (*Asyia*), Setrag Sourabian (*Sultan Bey*), Roupen Stepanian (*Suleyman*), Gayoush Sinko (*Hallam*), Vram Sakayan (*Valey*), Masha Sourabian.

Romance, Musical. [*Not viewed*]. Askiar, son of a wealthy Persian merchant, returns home from Europe ready to marry. Askiar intends to marry for love, and go against his country's tradition of arranged marriages. He refuses a marriage arranged by his father, with a bride chosen, according to custom, by his mother. Askiar's friend Suleyman advises him to disguise himself as a peddler, as in his travels, he is bound to meet a woman and fall in love. Suleyman then proposes to ask for the woman's hand in marriage on Askiar's behalf. Askiar follows Suleyman's advice and soon falls in love with Hallam, the daughter of a Bey, who is also opposed to arranged marriages. Despite initial parental objections, Hallam and Askiar are married. *Impersonation and imposture. Marriage–Arranged. Peddlers and peddling. Persia. Persians. Romance. Aunts. Fathers and sons. Friendship. Merchants. Street vendors. Weddings.*

Note: According to contemporary sources, this film was the first Armenian-language sound film to be produced in the United States. Contemporary reviews translate the title into English as *The Vagabond Lover* and *The Peddler Lover*. Although *Var*'s listed running time of 37 min. is probably an error, no indication of the film's length has been found. According to modern sources, the songs from Azerbaijani composer Uzeir Hajibeyov's operetta *Arshin Mal Alan* were adopted as folk music by the Azerbaijan nation. A program for the film contained in the Special Collections in the Mayer Library at AFI lists the following song titles: "I'll Seek a Wife for You," "Come My Beloved," "Hearken My Voice" and "Power in Gold." It is assumed that these songs are performed in the film. According to *FD*, Setrag Vartian was a former Fox contract player and produced and directed Armenian stage plays. A 1945 Soviet film also based on his operetta, directed by Rza Takhmasib and Nikolai Leshchenko, and starring Rashid Beibutov and Leila Djavanshirova, was awarded the 1946 Stalin Prize for fictional films.

FD 15 Mar 1937, p. 18. *NYT* 8 Mar 1937, p. 22. *Var* 10 Mar 1937, p. 15.

THE ARYAN (Native Americans, Latino)

New York Motion Picture Corp.; Kay-Bee. *Dist* Triangle Film Corp. 19 Mar **1916** Si; b&w. 5 reels.

Supv Thomas H. Ince. *Prod* Thomas H. Ince. *Dir* William S. Hart. *Story and scen* C. Gardner Sullivan. *Cam* Joe August.

Cast: William S. Hart (*Steve Denton*), Bessie Love (*Mary Jane*), Louise Glaum (*Trixie*), Charles K. French ("*Ivory*" *Wells*), Swallow (full name unknown) (*Mexican Pete*), Gertrude Claire (*Steve's mother*), Herschel Mayall (*Trixie's lover*).

Western. After years of labor, miner Steve Denton gathers up his fortune and sets out to visit his ailing mother. He is detained, however, in the town of Yellow Ridge, where a dance hall girl named Trixie not only cheats him of his gold, but also conceals a message wired to him from his dying mother. Learning the next day that his mother is dead, Steve kills Trixie's lover and then drags the dance hall girl into the desert, where he assumes the leadership of a band of Indian and Mexican bandits. Two years later, a caravan of Mississippi farmers, lost in the desert, appeals to Steve for help, but he refuses. That night, one of the settlers, little Mary Jane, visits him secretly to plead their cause and express her belief that no white man would refuse to protect a woman in distress. Deeply moved, Steve guides the caravan out of the desert and then resumes his wanderings. *Bandits. Dance hall girls. Gold miners. Regeneration. Settlers. Children. Deserts. Indians of North America. Mexicans. Mothers and sons. Murder. Telegrams.*

Note: The picture was filmed in part in California's Mojave Desert. Modern sources list the actor Swallow as Ernest Swallow. *MPW* quoted the following intertitle as exemplifying the film's theme: "Oft written in letters of blood, deep carved in the face of destiny, that all men may read, runs the code of the Aryan race: 'Our women shall be guarded'; and a man of the white race may forget much—friends, duty, honor, but this he will not, he cannot forget."

Motog 1 Apr 1916, p. 766. *MPN* 8 Apr 1916, p. 2064. *MPW* 15 Apr 1916, pp. 368-69. *MPW* 29 Apr 1916, p. 868. *NYDM* 1 Apr 1916, p. 28. *Var* 24 Mar 1916, p. 28. *Wid's* 30 Mar 1916, p. 474.

AS A MAN THINKS (Jewish Americans)

Artco Productions, Inc.; Four Star Pictures. *Dist* W. W. Hodkinson Corp. through Pathé Exchange, Inc. 20 Apr **1919**. Si; b&w. 5 reels.

Pres Harry Raver. *Supv* Augustus Thomas. *Prod* Harry Raver. *Dir* George Irving. *Cam* A. A. Cadwell.

Source: Based on the play *As a Man Thinks* by Augustus Thomas (New York, 13 Mar 1911).

Cast: Leah Baird (*Elinor Clayton*), Henry Clive (*Frank Clayton*), Warburton Gamble (*Benjamin De Lota*), Charles C. Brandt (*Dr. Seelig*), Betty Howe (*Vedah Seelig*), Alexander Herbert (*Burrell*), Mlle. Elaine Amazar (*Mimi Chardenet*), Joseph Smiley (*Mr. Hoover*), Jane Jennings (*Mrs. Hoover*), Bobby Ward (*Dick Clayton*).

Social, Drama. Frank Clayton, a successful New York publisher, his wife Elinor, and their seven-year-old son Dick, visit Paris. Art critic Benjamin De Lota, who becomes a contributor to Clayton's magazine, introduces Frank to Mimi Chardenet, an artist's model, and they have an affair. While walking with Mimi, Frank encounters Elinor, and introduces Mimi as a newly engaged contributor to his journal. In New York, however, Elinor learns of the affair and embittered, flirts with De Lota. Frank, learning that De Lota and Elinor were once sweethearts and that Elinor's father rejected De Lota's suit because he is Jewish, questions his wife's fidelity and the paternity of his son. Piqued, Elinor visits De Lota's apartment, where Frank sees De Lota attempt to embrace her. Dissuaded by his father-in-law from killing De Lota, Frank initiates divorce proceedings. Elinor and Dick take refuge with Dr. Seelig, a Jewish physician, who uses his religious bond to learn from De Lota that he was imprisoned for two years prior to Dick's birth. Now assured of his wife's fidelity, Frank reconciles with Elinor. *Divorce. Fidelity. Infidelity. Jews. Paternity. Antisemitism. Critics. Duplicity. Flirtation. Models. New York City. Paris (France). Physicians. Publishers and publishing.*

Note: This film, shot at the Biograph studios, was the first Four Star Picture. Mlle. Elaine Amazar, a French grand opera singer, made her American motion picture debut in this picture. Some reviews state that Baby Ivy Ward, using the name "Bobby Ward," played the role of Dick Clayton.

ETR 26 Apr 1919, p. 1609. *MPN* 3 May 1919, p. 2893. *MPW* 3 May 1919, p. 711. *Var* 25 Apr 1919, p. 82. *Wid's* 20 Apr 1919, p. 25.

AS THE EARTH TURNS (Polish Americans)

Warner Bros. Pictures, Inc. *Dist* Warner Bros. Pictures, Inc.; The Vitaphone Corp. 14 Apr **1934**; Prod: began early Nov 1933 [©Warner Bros. Pictures, Inc.; 7 May 1934; LP4542]. Sd; b&w. 8 reels. 73 min. PCA cert no. 2629-R [3 Sep 1936].

[*Supv* Robert Lord]. *Dir* Alfred Green. *Scr* Ernest Pascal. *Photog* Byron Haskin. *Art dir* Robert M. Haas. *Ed* Herbert Levy. *Gowns* Orry-Kelly. *Vitaphone Orch cond* Leo F. Forbstein.

Source: Based on the novel *As the Earth Turns* by Gladys Hasty Carroll (New York, 1933).

Cast: Jean Muir (*Jen [Shaw]*), Donald Woods (*Stan [Janowski]*), Russell Hardie (*Ed [Shaw]*), Emily Lowry (*Margaret*), Arthur Hohl (*George [Shaw]*), Dorothy Peterson (*Mil [Shaw]*), David Landau (*Mark [Shaw]*), Clara Blandick (*Cora [Shaw]*), William Janney (*Ollie [Shaw]*), Dorothy Appleby (*Doris [Shaw]*), Sarah Padden (*Mrs. Janowski*), Egon Brecher (*Mr. Janowski*), David Durand [(*Manuel*)], Wally Albright [(*John*)], George Billings [(*Junior*)], Marilyn Knowlden (*Esther*), Jevere Gibbons [(*Betty*)], Gloria Fisher [(*Louisa*)], Joyce Kay [(*Sister*)], Cora Sue Collins [(*Marie*)], Dorothy Gray [(*Bunny*)], [Harry C. Bradley (*Elder*)], [Lloyd Neal (*Mail carrier*)], [John H. Elliott (*Country doctor*)].

Rural, Drama. [*Print viewed*]. During a severe Maine winter, the Polish-American Janowski family moves to a farm near the farms of Mark Shaw and his brother George. Mark, a hard working farmer, is used to aiding his lazy brother when things go badly, much to the disgust of his second wife Cora and her daughter Doris. Doris hates farm life, so she is disappointed when Mark gives George a cow that Cora had planned to sell to earn money to send her to secretarial school in the city. Jen, Mark's daughter from his first marriage, tries to comfort Doris, who responds bitterly. When Ollie Shaw, Jen's brother, returns from college, he makes friends with Stan Janowski, who has always wanted to be a farmer even though he is a talented violinist. When Stan and Jen finally meet, they realize they share a love of farming. Not everyone is as happy on the farm as Jen, however. Mil, George's wife, is tired of their poverty and hard work and confesses she is planning to leave her husband. Doris unsuccessfully tries to force Ollie to quit school and marry her. After Stan's tailor father collapses from exhaustion, the Janowski family, with the exception of Stan, returns to the city. Mil learns she is pregnant and decides to stay with her husband. Stan asks Jen to marry him, but she wants to be sure he really loves farming and is not staying just because he loves her. Having failed to marry Ollie, Doris flirts with Stan, convincing him to take her to the Halloween dance, and while they are there, Stan's house is hit by lightning and burns to the ground. Stan must return to the city to earn the money to start again, and Doris asks him to take her with him. She tells Jen they are planning to marry, but Jen learns otherwise from Stan's letters. The following spring, Stan returns to the farm and Jen finally agrees to marry him. *Family life. Farmers. Romance. Cattle. City-country contrast. Dances. Fires. Flirtation. Halloween. Letters. Lightning. Maine. Marriage. Polish Americans. Pregnancy. Tailors. Violinists.*

Note: According to *FD*, the rights to the Gladys Hasty Carroll novel were purchased for $25,000. *DV* reported that the film's world premiere was scheduled to be held in Bangor, ME.

DV 26 Jan 1934, p. 3. *DV* 12 Feb 1934, p. 8. *FD* 12 May 1933, p. 3. *FD* 15 Feb 1934, p. 11. *HR* 4 Nov 1933, p. 4. *HR* 3 Jan 1934, p. 3. *MPD* 15 Feb 1934, p. 10. *MPH* 10 Feb 1934, p. 42. *NYT* 12 Apr 1934, p. 27. *Var* 17 Apr 1934, p. 18.

AS THE RIVER RISES *see* WILD RIVER

AS THE WORLD ROLLS ON (African Americans)

Andlauer Productions. *Dist* Elk Photo Plays. 10 Sep **1921**. Si; b&w. 7 reels, 5,600 ft.

Photog W. A. Andlauer.

Cast: Jack Johnson (*Himself*), Blanche Thompson (*Molly Moran*), Reed Thomas (*Joe Walker*), Walter Simpson, Versia Rice, Sam Crawford, Bruce Petway, Rube Foster, Torrientti (*Themselves*).

African American, Drama. [*Not viewed*]. Joe Walker, an industrious yet sickly young man, and Tom Atkins, a ne'er-do-well, are rivals for the affection of Molly Moran, the tireless assistant of Dr. Saunders, a respected physician. Tom bullies and beats up the weaker Joe, after which a workplace heart attack forces the latter to seek medical advice. Dr. Saunders prescribes out-of-doors work, and Joe gets a new job with outside work after taking a night class. While going home from the new job through a park one night, Joe is jumped by Tom and his gang of ruffians. Meanwhile, former boxing champion Jack Johnson, a friend of Joe, Tom, Molly and Dr. Saunders, who has opened a business near the doctor's office, is in the park with his two nieces, telling them the story of Indian days when tribes roamed the hills. When Jack hears Joe's anguished cries for help, he goes to him and thrashes Tom and his gang. Jack then offers to give Joe boxing lessons and advises him on how to become a healthier, stronger person. A short time later, Joe has become a real athlete, and he goes to see the National Colored League baseball games. In a game between the Kansas City Monarchs and the Detroit Stars, Sam Crawford, captain of the Monarchs, injures his wrist. He spots Joe in the crowd, and, remembering him to be a good amateur pitcher, asks him to pitch the rest of the game. Joe does so and helps the Monarchs to win. At an Elks Lodge reception, Joe, a member, is the honored guest, and Nelson Crews, editor of a leading black publication, presents the Monarchs with silver monogrammed buckles. A few weeks later, after a Clover Leaf Club Masquerade Ball, Tom, in a jealous rage, has Joe beaten up and thrown over a precipice, but Molly overhears the plot, denounces Tom, and rescues Joe. Undaunted, Tom then frames both Molly and Joe for the robbery of some of Dr. Saunders' valuable papers and jewelry. Molly is arrested and tried, but at the trial, a small boy denounces Tom as the thief. Tom tries to escape, but Joe catches him and fights him to the ground. When Molly, the doctor and the police arrive, Molly begs the doctor to release the repentant Tom, which he does. Joe and Molly marry and visit Jack, who gives the newlyweds a check for $1,000. Six years later, Molly, Joe and their family live happily in a pleasant home. *African Americans. Baseball. Boxing. Chicago American Giants (Baseball team). Detroit Stars (Baseball team). Kansas City Monarchs (Baseball team). Manhood. Physical education and training. Romantic rivalry.*

Ruffians. Elks Club. Falls from heights. Fights. Frame-ups. Heart disease. Marriage. Parks. Rescues. Robbery. Trials.

Note: The working title of this film was *The Heart of Jack Johnson*. The film was advertised as featuring "a guaranteed all star colored cast." It starred ex-heavyweight champion Jack Johnson and included scenes of a baseball game between Colored National Baseball League teams the Kansas City Monarchs and the Detroit Stars featuring Sam Crawford and Bruce Petway, the respective captains of the Monarchs and the Stars. According to information in the George P. Johnson Collection at the UCLA Special Collections Library, Johnson was paid $7,500 for eighteen and one-half hours of work on the film. According to a letter in the Johnson collection from producer W. A. Andlauer, following the film's early showings, Andlauer added 500 feet of baseball footage and "made one reel all baseball and parades taking all of the shots pertaining to players and parades out of the story" to make a one-reel supplement. Andlauer wrote, "This makes the action better and we know improves the film."

An ad for the film stated that it included scenes of "Rube Foster and his celebrated Chicago American Giants, including Torrientti, the Babe Ruth of the Colored National League, playing for the League leadership in opposition to the Kansas City Monarchs" and had scenes of "the Elk's celebration, the Odd Fellow's (St. Joseph) encampment and the Knights of Pythias' National Conclave (Topeka)." According to *ChiDef*, prints were made by the Burton Holmes Co. of Chicago.

ChiDef 20 Aug 1921. *ChiDef* 9 Nov 1921, p. 7.

AS THOUSANDS CHEER *see* **WHILE THOUSANDS CHEER**

¡ASEGURE A SU MUJER! (Spanish language)

Fox Film Corp. *Dist* Fox Film Corp. **1935**; New York opening: 8 Mar 1935; Prod: late Oct-early Nov 1934 [©Fox Film Corp.; 20 Jan 1935; LP5273]. Sd; b&w. 9 reels, 7,427 ft. 83 min. Passed by the National Board of Review. Spanish language.

[*Prod* Sol M. Wurtzel and John Stone]. *Dirección de* [*Dir*] Lewis Seiler. [*Asst dir* Sam Schneider]. *Adaptación cinematográfica* [*Scr*] Enrique Jardiel Poncela, Robert Ellis and Helen Logan. [*Photog* Daniel Clark]. *Dirección musical de* [*Mus dir*] Sam Kaylin. [*Sd* Al Protzman].

Song(s): "Mientras dure la noche" and "Radiante," music by Ernesto Piedra, lyrics by Enrique Jardiel Poncela; "Sneezing Love," music by Raúl Roulien and Troy Sanders, lyrics by Enrique Jardiel Poncela.

Source: Based on the play *¡Asegure a su mujer!* by Julio Escobar (Buenos Aires, ca. 1934).

Cast: RAÚL ROULIEN (*Ricardo Randall*), Conchita Montenegro (*Camelia Cornell*), Antonio Moreno (*Eduardo Martin*), Mona Maris (*Rita Martin*), Luis Alberni (*Bernardo Perry*), Barbara Leonard (*Mona Perry*), Carlos Villarías (*Presidente*), José Peña Pepet (*Un secretario*), [Blanca Vischer], [Gloria Roy], [Carmen Bailey], [Julie Cabanne], [Margaret Strand], [Eve Reynolds], [Fay Estelle], [Alice Adair], [Antoinette Lees], [Elsie Larson].

Comedy. [*Not viewed*]. At Fidelity Insurance Company, the board of trustees await the arrival of Ricardo Randall, an "idea" man who, they hope, will lift the corporation out of financial ruin. Ricardo arrives at the meeting without an idea, and as he stalls, waiting for inspiration to strike him, his former mistress' husband, Bernardo Perry, walks in the room. Ricardo then gets the bright idea of "insurance for wives" and explains that the company will work hard to insure that a wife is faithful, but if they fail, the husbands will receive compensation. He redubs the company the (In)fidelity Insurance Company, and he is made vice-president. As scores of husbands scramble to buy into the new plan, Mona Perry arrives and warns Ricardo that he is ruining the wives' lives. Ricardo declares his devotion to his secretary, Camelia Cornell, but as he awaits her arrival in a restaurant, he runs into another former mistress, Rita Martin. Rita seduces Ricardo and feigns an ankle injury so that he is required to take her back to her home. Camelia witnesses their departure in Rita's limousine and, for revenge, calls Rita's husband Eduardo at his office and offers him wife insurance. Eduardo refuses, as he trusts his wife, but he goes home to check on her anyway, and Camelia meets him, claiming that her boss, Mr. Randall, will arrive any moment with corroborating evidence. When Ricardo tries to leave, Camelia makes it appear as if he's just arrived and stuffs Rita's monogrammed underwear into his pocket. He shows the evidence to Eduardo and then sells him the insurance, but refuses to divulge the name of his wife's lover. After the ruse, Camelia agrees to marry the contrite Ricardo. Bernardo, meanwhile, hopes that his wife will be unfaithful so that he can collect insurance money. He arranges to have Eduardo seduce her at the Hotel Merael Mar, where he plans to take pictures of the seduction for proof. Bernardo's secretary, an agent for the insurance company, tells Ricardo of the scam. Ricardo arrives at the

hotel, finds Bernardo on the fire escape, and kicks him as he's about to snap a picture of his wife and Eduardo. The two fall into the room, and Eduardo realizes that Ricardo was seeing his wife, as a familiar cigarette lighter falls from Ricardo's pocket onto the floor. Ricardo runs into his room, where Rita appears again, this time with an entourage of scantily-clad wives and photographers, who frame him in order to ruin (In)fidelity's wife insurance program. The plan works, as the policy collections ruin the company. Camelia, again estranged from Ricardo, finally reunites with her philandering employer after much hesitation. *Infidelity. Insurance. Marriage. Mistresses. Secretaries. Wives. Frame-ups. Hotels. Limousines. Photographers. Restaurants. Romance. Ruses. Seduction. Vamps.*

Note: The plot was based on a dialogue continuity in the Twentieth Century-Fox Produced Scripts Collection, and the onscreen credits were taken from a screen credit sheet in the Twentieth Century-Fox Records of the Legal Department, both of which are at the UCLA Theater Arts Library. The title was translated as *Insure Your Wife*. The running time was calculated based on the footage given in NYSA records. According to information in the legal records, Anthony Coldeway wrote a treatment based on the play, and Bernice Mason and Winifred Dunn wrote an outline and original dialogue, but it is not known if any of their material was used in the finished film. Contemporary sources indicate that L. William O'Connell may have photographed part of this film.

FD 13 Mar 1935, p. 7. *HR* 22 Oct 1934, p. 6. *NYT* 12 Mar 1935, p. 25.

ASÍ ES LA VIDA (Spanish language)

Sono-Art Productions, Inc. *Dist* Sono-Art World Wide Pictures, Inc. May **1930**; World premiere in Los Angeles: 3 May 1930.; Prod: Feb—Mar 1930 at Metropolitan Studios, Hollywood, CA. Sd (Western Electric); b&w. 7 reels. 72 min. Spanish language.

Pres by O. E. Goebel and George W. Weeks. *Personal supv by* O. E. Goebel. *Dir* George J. Crone. *Scr* Harvey Gates. *Adpt* Tom Gibson. *Span vers* Jorge Juan Crespo. *Photog* Arthur Todd. *Film ed* Arturo Tavares. *Mus dir* Carlos Molina. *Sd* J. G. Greger. *Tech dir* Charles Cadwallader. *Prod mgr* J. R. Crone. *Asst* A. S. Black.

Song(s): "Son cosas de la vida," "Que tienes en la mirada?" and "Mi princesita," music and lyrics by José Bohr and Eva Bohr.

Source: Based on the novel *The Dark Chapter* by E. J. Rath (New York, 1924) and the play *They All Want Something* by Courtenay Savage (New York, 1927).

Cast: José Bohr (*José Rolan*), Lolita Vendrell (*Blanca Franklyn*), Delia Magaña (*Luisa Franklyn*), Enrique Acosta (*Sr. Franklyn*), Tito Davison (*Jorge Franklyn*), César Vanoni (*Manuel, the butler*), Julián Rivero (*Calton*), Marcela Nivón (*Sra. Franklyn*), Myrta Bonillas (*Countess*), Ernesto Piedra ("*Sapo*"), Rosita Gil (*Cora*).

Comedy. [*Not viewed*]. When Señora Franklyn's car breaks down several miles outside the city, her haughty chauffeur is unable to repair it. She impatiently accepts the offer of a hobo, José Rolan, who assures her that he is a mechanic. After Rolan fixes the problem immediately, Señora Franklyn hires him as her new chauffeur, despite opposition from the rest of the family. Shaved, and with hair combed and shoes polished, Rolan no longer looks like a vagrant and more like a perfect gentleman capable of winning Blanca, the Franklyns' daughter. However, social class distinctions keep Rolan and Blanca apart. During a long weekend party at the Franklyn mansion, two bogus European counts infiltrate the ranks of the distinguished guests and plan to crack open the safe and steal the family's jewelry. Just as the thieves are about to strike, Rolan leaps into action and reveals that he is, in fact, an undercover detective. This also enables him to eliminate the only obstacle to his love for Blanca and he declares his love openly. *Class distinction. Hoboes. Impersonation and imposture. Safecrackers. Automobiles. Butlers. Chauffeurs. Mansions. Mothers and daughters. Parties. Romance. Undercover agents.*

Note: The working title of the film was *Cosas de la vida*. The picture was a simultaneously filmed, Spanish-language version of the 1930 film *What a Man* (see *AFI Catalog of Feature Films, 1921-30*; F2.6195), which was directed by George J. Crone and starred Reginald Denny and Miriam Seegar.

Cinl Jun 1930, p. 34.

AT PINEY RIDGE (African Americans)

Selig Polyscope Co.; A Selig Red Seal Play. *Dist* V-L-S-E, Inc. 1 May **1916** [©Selig Polyscope Co.; 8 Apr 1916; LP8049]. Si; b&w. 5 reels. *Dir* William Robert Daly. *Scen* Gilson Willets.

Source: Based on the play *At Piney Ridge* by David K. Higgins (New York, 22 Feb 1897).

Cast: Fritzi Brunette (*Cindy Lane*), Al W. Filson (*Zeb Lane*), Leo Pierson (*Jack Rose*), Edward J. Piel (*Mark Brierson*), Frank Clark (*General Deering*), Vivian Reed (*Azalia Deering*), James Bradbury

(*Major Jartree*), William Scott (*Rube Hollar*), Lillian Hayward (*Dagmar*).

Drama. When Cindy Lane becomes pregnant, Mark Brierson, the father, refuses to marry her. Instead, Brierson romances Azalia Deering, whose father, General Deering, owns the town bank. Brierson misuses bank funds, but the bank is saved by Jack Rose, a wealthy farmer. Cindy's father Zeb vows to kill her lover, but she refuses to reveal the man's identity. Brierson realizes that Azalia and Jack love each other, and so, to eliminate his rival, he tells Zeb that Jack is the child's father. To disgrace Jack further, Brierson convinces Dagmar, a black woman, to claim Jack as her son, but Zeb is told that Brierson is the father of Cindy's child and is also Dagmar's son. In the end, Zeb kills Brierson, who, before he dies, learns from Dagmar that although she is not his mother, he is black. Jack marries Azalia, and Cindy, whose child has died, goes back to the man she loved before Brierson. *Farmers. Liars. Philanderers. Revenge. Rivalry.* African Americans. African Americans–Mixed blood. Bankers. Embezzlement. Fathers and daughters. Illegitimacy. Murder. Officers (Military). Parentage.

Note: Contemporary reviews disagree on whether Cindy returns to a former lover at the film's end.

Motog 29 Apr 1916, p. 1000. *MPN* 29 Apr 1916, p. 2558. *MPW* 6 May 1916, p. 982, 1049. *NYDM* 29 Apr 1916, p. 29. *Var* 12 May 1916, p. 19. *Wid's* 27 Apr 1916, pp. 538-39.

AT THE CROSS ROADS (African Americans)

Select Photo Play Producing Co. *Dist* Alliance Films Corp. 26 Oct **1914**. Si; b&w. 5 reels.

Dir Frank L. Dear. *Scen* Frank L. Dear. *Adpt* Arthur C. Aiston.

Source: Based on the play *At the Old Cross Roads* by Hal Reid (New York, 12 May 1902).

Cast: Estha Williams (*Parepa Mendoza*), Rae Forde (*Annabelle Thornton*), Mrs. Stuart Robson (*Eliza Morton*), Arthur Morrison (*Dayton Thornton*), Master Martin (*Colonel Kerr*), Frank L. Dear (*James Martin*), Madge Loomis (*Menda Mendoza*), Jack Gordon (*Stanton Thornton*), Elmer Peterson (*Tom Martin*), Charles H. Streimer (*Tom Johnson*), Miss Harlan, Edward Thorne.

Drama. Parepa Mendoza, a former slave, is employed by the Reverend Thornton, a Southern clergyman whose son Dayton abuses her. When Dayton kills James Martin during a drunken brawl, he flees to the hills, taking Parepa as his mistress. He soon tires of her, however, and orders her from his cabin, even though she is pregnant with his child. Parepa confesses her transgressions to Thornton, who is shocked, and orders Dayton to marry her. Dayton and Parepa go North, after which the reverend dies of grief. As their daughter Annabelle grows up, Parepa has assumed the role of maid to Dayton, and the girl never knows of her background. When the family returns South, Tom Martin attacks his father's killer, but Annabelle intervenes. Later the two fall in love, but at their engagement party Dayton tells everyone that Parepa is Annabelle's mother. Parepa kills Dayton after he is pursued by a band of outraged blacks, but during her trial it is revealed by Colonel Kerr, a former suitor, that Parepa is actually a white woman of Spanish heritage, and she is released. *African Americans. Fathers and sons. Mistresses. Murder. Parentage. Racism. United States–South.* Clergy. Desertion (Marital). Revenge.

Note: Estha Williams recreated the role of Parepa from the well-known stage play.

Motog 24 Oct 1914, p. 577. *MPN* 17 Oct 1914, p. 63, 65, 67. *MPN* 9 Jan 1915, p. 57. *MPW* 15 Aug 1914, p. 1015. *MPW* 29 Aug 1914, p. 1290. *MPW* 17 Oct 1914, p. 351. *Var* 10 Oct 1914, p. 25.

AT THE RACE TRACK WITH CHARLIE CHAN *see* CHARLIE CHAN AT THE RACE TRACK

AT YALE *see* HOLD 'EM YALE

L'ATHLÈTE INCOMPLET (French language)

First National Pictures, Inc.; controlled by Warner Bros. Pictures, Inc. *Dist* First National Pictures, Inc. **1932**. Sd; b&w. 93 min. French language.

Dir Claude Autant-Lara. *Scr* Valentin Mandelstamm.

Source: Based on the play *The Poor Nut* by J. C. Nugent and Elliott Nugent (New York, 27 Apr 1925).

Cast: Douglas Fairbanks, Jr. (*Fred Miller*), Jeannette Ferney (*Evelyn Legrand*), Barbara Leonard (*Nina Granier*), Carrie Daumery (*Mlle. Schmoltz*), Mathilde Comont (*Eulalie*), George Davis (*Bavette*), Jean Delval (*Coach*), Jean Delmour (*Picard*), William Barry (*Lacour*), Arthur Hurni (*Bertrand*).

College, **Comedy**. [*Not viewed*]. [The following plot summary is based on the English-language version of this film, *Local Boy Makes Good*; character names refer to that version. For further information regarding the English-language version, please see the note below and the entry for *Local Boy Makes Good* in the *AFI Catalog of Feature Films, 1931-40*.] Ohio University student John Miller is too involved with his botanical experiments to participate in college life. He is not too busy, however, to develop a crush on Julia Winters, a beautiful student at a rival college. He writes her love letters in which he pretends to be a great athlete and top fraternity man, but has no intention of sending them. By accident, the chambermaid picks up one of them and drops it in the mail. Meanwhile, student librarian Marjorie Blake starts work at the same bookstore where John is employed. As they are both shy, they strike up a friendship. When John receives a letter from Julia announcing her imminent arrival on campus, he begs Marjorie for advice. Even though she is in love with John, she counsels him to try and become what he has pretended to be. To this end, John shows up at the track to practice javelin. He is terrible and one of his wild throws almost hits a runner, who chases him off the track. To everyone's surprise, John outruns the fastest runner on the team as he escapes. The coach tries to call John back to the track, but thinking he will be punished, John does not turn back. Later, he contemplates suicide. When Julia arrives at the bookstore looking for John, Marjorie, who is an old school friend, pretends that John is someone else. Soon Julia, who is a psychology student, learns the truth. As she is scolding him, the coach appears and asks John to run in the track meet. When he refuses, Julia decides he has an inferiority complex and offers to psychoanalyze him. She finally convinces him to run in the same two races as her boyfriend, Spike Hoyt. Spike's threats frighten John so much that he loses the first race. He refuses to run in the relay until Marjorie fills him full of grain alcohol and gives him a kiss. He wins the race and by the next day, has undergone a complete personality change. Emboldened by his success, he asks Marjorie to marry him. *Braggarts. College life. Inferiority complexes. Romance. Transformation.* Athletes. Athletic coaches. Booksellers and bookselling. Botanists. Cactus. Drunkenness. Jealousy. Letters. Psychoanalysis. Relay racing. Suicide.

Note: This French-language version was also known as *L'athlète malgre lui*. In 1927, Richard Wallace directed Jack Mulhall and Jean Arthur in a First National production of the Nugents' play, entitled *The Poor Nut* (see *AFI Catalog of Feature Films, 1921-30*; F2.4290). For information on the English-language version, *Local Boy Makes Good*, which was directed by Mervyn LeRoy and starred Joe E. Brown, please see the entry for that film in the *AFI Catalog of Feature Films, 1931-40*; F3.2549.

L'ATHLÈTE MALGRE LUI *see* L'ATHLÈTE INCOMPLET

ATOP OF THE WORLD IN MOTION (Native Americans, Native Alaskans)

Beverly B. Dobbs. *Dist* State Rights; Joseph Conoly. Nov **1912**. Si; b&w. 6 reels.

Cam Beverly B. Dobbs.

Documentary. This documentary, which is divided into several titled sections, covers life in the Arctic and in Siberia, including scenes of Eskimos in their daily routine of work, ritual and play. A cruise to the coast of Siberia in the trading schooner the *Sea Wolf* follows a segment called ''The Ice Parks in the Arctic,'' which shows streams of ice flowing across the Bering Strait. The United States mail dog team, pulling mail shipments across the arctic landscape, is feature in another segment; and in ''The Walrus Hunt,'' methods of killing and securing walrus hides and tusks are shown in detail. The final section focuses on gold mining in Nome, Alaska, particularly the hydraulic process of removing ore from river beds and ocean beaches. *Arctic regions. Expeditions.* Alaska. Bering Sea. Dogsledding. Gold mines. Hunting. Ice floes. Native Alaskans. Nome (AK). Postal service. Rites and ceremonies. Schooners. Siberia. Walruses.

Note: This film, which was first called *Beverly B. Dobbs Original Alaska-Siberia Motion Pictures*, opened in New York in Nov 1912 after playing a reported 330-350 performances in Chicago. Advertisements for Frank E. Kleinschmidt's *The Alaska-Siberia Expedition* (see above), which was released in May 1912, claim that Dobb's production was actually a re-issue of two-year-old ''tourographologs'' that had been shown in Y.M.C.A.'s, hotels, and other non-theatrical establishments. According to a Jan 1913 advertisement, *Atop of the World in Motion* was to be withdrawn from the state rights market on 15 Jan 1913. One source lists the film at seven reels.

MPW 2 Nov 1912, p. 442, 479. *MPW* 16 Nov 1912, p. 701. *MPW* 30 Nov 1912, p. 903. *MPW* 4 Jan 1913, p. 95.

AUCTION OF SOULS (Armenian Americans)

Selig Studios for the American Committee for Armenian and Syrian Relief. *Dist* First National Exhibitors Circuit. 19 Jan **1919** [©Associated First National Pictures, Inc.; 7 Feb 1922; LP17531]. Si; b&w. 8 reels, 7,820 ft.

Prod William N. Selig. *Dir* Oscar Apfel. *Scen* Nora Waln and /or Frederic Chapin.

Source: Based on the book *Ravished Armenia* by Aurora Mardiganian, interpreted by H. L. Gates (New York, 1918).

Cast: Aurora Mardiganian (*Herself*), Irving Cummings (*Andranik*), Anna Q. Nilsson (*Edith Graham*), Henry Morgenthau (*Himself*), Howard Davies, Hector Dion, Frank Clark, Miles McCarthy, Eugenie Besserer, Lillian West.

Drama. Aurora Mardiganian, a young Armenian girl who lives with her parents in the Turkish town of Harpout, falls in love with Andranik, a young shepherd. Passelt Pasha, the Turkish Governor of the province, demands Aurora's hand in marriage, but her father refuses, explaining that like other Armenians, she is Christian and does not want to change. In March 1915, despite pleas from American Ambassador Henry Morgenthau, the Turkish government orders the Armenians into the desert, where rampant atrocities occur. After her parents are killed, Aurora and other Armenian girls are taken by Turks from an English mission run by Edith Graham. Miss Graham disguises herself as an Armenian and with Aurora, escapes, aided by Andranik. They are captured by Kurds, however, after which they are raped, sold to a Mohammedan chieftain and later sold again at a slave market. With the help of Andranik they escape finally to an American Relief Home. Aurora comes to America and pleads for help for her people, who literally have been decimated. *Armenians. Christianity. Evacuations. Genocide. Edith Graham. Kurds. Muslims. Rape. Slavery. Turkey. Turks. Ambassadors. Americans in foreign countries. Disguise. Escapes. Governors. Missions. Henry Morgenthau. Rescues. Shepherds. Tribal chiefs.*

Note: Viscount Bryce's official report and Ex-Ambassador Henry Morgenthau's official story were additional sources for this film. The book was serialized in the Hearst publications. The film and the book are based on true incidents in the life of Aurora Mardiganian. The film's working titles were *Ravished Armenia* and *Armenia Crucified*. It may also have been known as *An Armenian Crucifixion* (see *AFI Catalog of Feature Films, 1911-20*; F1.0146). The film opened originally in various cities at $10 a seat, the proceeds going to the Committee for the Relief of the Near East and the Armenian War Relief Association. Sources disagree concerning the scenarist. Records from the Selig Collection credit Frederic Chapin, while publicity pamphlets produced by the Armenian War Relief Association credit both Chapin and Nora Waln, a member of the committee. Shots representing Mt. Ararat were actually filmed at Mt. Baldy, CA.

Bio 20 Nov 1919, p. 101.

THE AUCTIONEER (Jewish Americans)

Fox Film Corp. *Dist* Fox Film Corp. **1927** [©Fox Film Corp.; 16 Jan 1927; LP23669]. Si; b&w. 6 reels, 5,500 ft.

Pres William Fox. *Dir* Alfred E. Green. *Asst dir* Jack Boland. *Scen* L. G. Rigby and John Stone. *Photog* George Schneiderman.

Source: Based on the play *The Auctioneer* by Charles Klein, Lee Arthur (New York, 30 Sep 1913).

Cast: George Sidney (*Simon Levi*), Marion Nixon (*Ruth Levi*), Gareth Hughes (*Richard Eagan*), Doris Lloyd (*Esther Levi*), Ward Crane (*Paul Groode*), Sammy Cohen (*Mo*), Claire McDowell (*Mrs. Tim Eagan*).

Comedy-drama. Simon, a Jewish immigrant, adopts the child of a woman dying at sea, and later builds up a successful pawnbroking-auctioneering business on New York's East Side. The girl, Ruth, falls in love with Richard, who is admitted to a bond-brokerage firm when his prospective father-in-law invests his entire fortune in the firm. Owing to the evil machinations of broker Paul Groode, Simon loses everything and is forced to start over again as a peddler. Eventually he catches the crooked broker and regains his money. All ends happily with the lovers united. *Adoption. Auctions. Brokers. Courtship. Jews. New York City–East Side. Pawnbrokers. Peddlers and peddling.*

FD 23 Jan 1927. *MPW* 5 Feb 1927.

AULD JEREMIAH see **BONNIE, BONNIE LASSIE**

THE AVENGER (Latino)

Columbia Pictures Corp. *Dist* Columbia Pictures Corp. 6 Mar **1931**; Prod: 19 Dec—15 Jan 1931 [©Columbia Pictures Corp.; 11 Mar 1931; LP2843]. Sd; b&w. 5,865 ft. 58, 62, 65 or 72 min. PCA cert no. 202-R [29 Aug 1934].

Dir Roy William Neill. *Asst dir* Mack Wright. *Story* Jack Townley. *Adpt and dial* George Morgan. *Cam* Charles Van Enger. *Film ed* Ray Snyder. *Sd eng* Russell Malmgren.

Cast: Buck Jones (*Joaquin Murieta*), Dorothy Revier (*Helen Lake*), Edward Peil, Sr. (*Ike Mason*), Otto Hoffman (*Black Kelly*), Sidney Bracey (*Windy*), Edward Hearn (*Captain Lake*), Walter Percival (*Al Goss*).

Historical, Western. [*Not viewed*]. In 1849, Joaquin Murieta, son of a wealthy Spanish family, quarrels with three prospectors, Ike Mason, Black Kelly, and Al Goss. When Joaquin returns home, he finds that the house has been raided and his father is dying from wounds received during the raid. On his way to tell his brother Juan of the news, Joaquin meets Helen Lake and they begin a romance. Soon after Joaquin arrives at the camp, Mason and Goss kill Juan and knock Joaquin unconscious as they seize Juan's claim. The trio does not become wealthy, however, as the mysterious "Black Shadow," actually Joaquin in disguise, robs the stagecoach of their shipments. Although Helen's father, Captain Lake of the U.S. Army, offers a reward of $5,000 for the Black Shadow, Joaquin's disguise remains intact. After posting a notice at the saloon threatening Kelly, Mason and Goss with revenge, Joaquin arranges for their death by tricking the trio into shooting one another. Joaquin, however, is wounded in the process and seeks refuge with Helen, to whom he confesses the truth. Helen is unable to prevent his and Goss's arrest, and as a mob threatens to storm the jail, Joaquin convinces Goss to dress as the Black Shadow in order to escape. Goss is shot while fleeing, thus completing Joaquin's revenge. Helen tells her father the entire story, and he, convinced of the justice of Joaquin's case, gives them permission to marry. *California–History–1846-1850. Joaquin Murieta. Revenge. Vigilantes. Brothers. Disguise. Fathers and daughters. Gold rushes. Impersonation and imposture. Jailbreaks. Land claims. Marriage. Mexicans. Mines. Prospectors. Ranches. Romance. United States. Army.*

Note: A working title for this film was *Phantom Hoofs*. The film is loosely based on the exploits of legendary Mexican bandit Joaquin Murieta, who, in the mid-19th century, went to California and, according to the legend, swore vengeance against Americans and began a series of robberies in the mining country after being discriminated against by white men. Varying accounts of Murieta's exploits in the California Mother Lode exist, including one story claiming that he was seized and decapitated by a ranger who killed him for a reward. Other films about Murieta that were made in the 1930s are the 1936 M-G-M film *Robin Hood of El Dorado* and the 1937 Principal Productions film *The Californian* (see below). *MPH* lists Teddy Tetzlaff, rather than Charles Van Enger, as cameraman. According to modern sources, the cast also included Paul Fix, Frank Ellis, Al Taylor, Blackjack Ward and Slim Whitaker. Modern sources also list Sol Lesser as the producer. *The Avenger* was remade by Columbia in 1942 as *Vengeance of the West*, directed by Lambert Hillyer and starring Bill Elliott and Tex Ritter. Other films featuring a character identified with Murieta include the 1919 D. W. Griffith film *Scarlet Days*, starring Richard Barthelmess and Clarine Seymour (see below); the 1927 Paramount film *The Gay Defender*, directed by Gregory Le Cava and starring Richard Dix and Thelma Todd (see below) and the 1965 film *Murieta*, filmed in Spain and distributed by Warner Bros., which starred Jeffrey Hunter and Arthur Kennedy (see *AFI Catalog of Feature Films, 1961-70*; F6.3351).

FD 19 Apr 1931, p. 10. *MPH* 28 Mar 1931, p. 37. *Var* 22 Apr 1931, p. 19.

AVENGING ANGELS see **NATION AFLAME**

AVRUM OVENU see **THE ETERNAL JEW**

¡AY AMOR, CÓMO ME HAS PUESTO! see **LOCURAS DE AMOR**

AZ ORVOS TITKA see **EL SECRETO DEL DOCTOR**

BABY DOLL (Italian Americans, African Americans)

Warner Bros. Pictures, Inc.; Newtown Productions, Inc.; An Elia Kazan Production. *Dist* Warner Bros. Pictures, Inc. 29 Dec **1956**; New York opening: 18 Dec 1956; Los Angeles opening: 26 Dec 1956; Prod: late Dec 1955—late Feb 1956 [©Newtown Productions, Inc.; 29 Dec 1956; LP9720]. Sd; b&w. 114 min. PCA cert no. 18129.

Dir Elia Kazan. *Asst dir* Charles H. Maguire. *Orig scr* Tennessee Williams. *Dir of photog* Boris Kaufman. *Art dir* Richard Sylbert. *Assoc art dir* Paul Sylbert. *Film ed* Gene Milford. *Cost* Anna Hill Johnstone. *Ward* Florence Transfield. *Mus comp* Kenyon Hopkins. *Sd* Edward J. Johnstone. *Makeup* Robert E. Jiras. *Hairdresser* Willis Hanchett. *Mgr of prod* Forrest E. Johnston. *Script and cont* Roberta Hodes.

Song(s): "Shame, Shame, Shame," music by Kenyon Hopkins, lyrics by Ruby Fisher.

Source: Based on the play *27 Wagons Full of Cotton* by Tennessee Williams (New York, 19 Apr 1955).

Cast: Karl Malden [(*Archie Lee Meighan*)], Carroll Baker [(*Baby Doll Meighan*)], Eli Wallach [(*Silva Vacarro*)], Mildred Dunnock [(*Aunt Rose Comfort*)], Lonny Chapman [(*Rock*)], Eades Hogue [(*Town marshal*)], Noah Williamson [(*Deputy*)], And some people of Benoit, Mississippi.

Drama. [*Print viewed*]. In the Mississippi Delta region, nineteen-year-old Baby Doll lives unhappily with her husband, Archie Lee Meighan, a middle-aged, down-on-his-luck cotton gin owner. Archie cannot afford to repair the decrepit ante-bellum mansion, Fox Tail, that the couple inhabits, and the Ideal Pay-as-You-Go furniture company is threatening to repossess their meager household belongings, thus giving Baby Doll more and more reason to malign Archie's masculinity. When Baby Doll was betrothed to Archie on her father's death bed, the dying man made Archie promise not to deflower the girl until her twentieth birthday, and with her birthday just two days away, Archie is anxious to make Baby Doll his wife "for real." As the childlike Baby Doll sleeps in her crib sucking her thumb, Archie tries to drill a hole in the wall in order to spy on her. Baby Doll awakes furious, and later during her bath, she becomes even more enraged when Archie tries to grab her. The next day, in town, while Archie is seeing his doctor about his sexual troubles, Baby Doll, determined to get a job, flirts with a young dentist who is looking for a secretary. As the couple returns to Fox Tail, they see the furniture being taken away, prompting Baby Doll to announce her desire to leave Archie and move to the Cotton King Motel. Meanwhile, Silva Vacarro, a Sicilian immigrant and the owner of the new cotton gin that has taken away all of Archie's business, gives his employees a fish fry to celebrate their first successful crop. As the festivities, which include a speech by a senator, ensue, a drunken Archie sets fire to Vacarro's cotton gin, burning it to the ground. Vacarro tries to tell the police that he was a victim of arson, but they treat him as an outsider and refuse to investigate. The next morning, Vacarro brings his twenty-seven loads of cotton to Archie's gin, and Archie is overjoyed to have the business. As Archie tends to the cotton, however, Vacarro meets Baby Doll and flirts with her in order to get information about Archie's whereabouts the night before. After Baby Doll reveals that Archie had indeed left her alone in the house on the previous evening, she grows suspicious, but Vacarro tickles and flirts with her to coax her to talk. Baby Doll gets nervous and goes to the gin to find Archie, but he slaps her and tells her not to go "where niggers are working." Vacarro is disgusted at the state of Archie's equipment and is furious that the work has not yet been started. He orders Archie to find a new belt for the cotton gin, but when Archie leaves, he is chased by a hysterical Baby Doll, who does not want to be left alone with Vacarro. After Vacarro's assistant informs him that they already have the belt, Vacarro approaches a weeping Baby Doll, who is upset because her live-in aunt, Rose Comfort, has left the house to go to the county hospital, where she satisfies her passion for sweets by visiting dying patients and eating their chocolate candies. Baby Doll explains her marital situation to a surprised Vacarro and then declares that her "being ready" depends on whether or not the furniture comes back. Baby Doll goes to make lemonade, telling Vacarro to wait on the front porch, but he sneaks into the house and begins to make ghost noises to scare her. When she locks herself in her bedroom, he makes the lemonade himself. The pair then begins a riotous game of tag and hide-and-seek, and Baby Doll locks herself in the attic. Annoyed, Vacarro tells Baby Doll that he will break the door down unless she signs the affidavit that he has prepared regarding Archie's guilt. He breaks in, and Baby Doll screams, fearing that the rickety floor of the attic will cave in. She tearfully signs the paper, then as Vacarro is about to leave, she offers to let him take a nap in her baby crib. Archie, meanwhile, is treated badly at the parts shop because he has no money and has to pay for the part with his gold watch. After he hurries back to the cotton gin and discovers that the repair has already been made, he returns home, only to be accused of arson by Baby Doll. She announces that their agreement is over, then Vacarro appears. Baby Doll reveals that Vacarro has decided not to rebuild his gin, but will bring the cotton to Archie's gin and have Baby Doll entertain him while it is being processed. Archie, confused, tells Vacarro to stay for supper while he considers his proposal. While Archie is on the phone, Baby Doll and Vacarro kiss, and then Archie, suspicious and angry, begins to scream at Aunt Rose to bring in the food. Archie decides to fire Aunt Rose, whom he claims has overstayed her welcome, but he is perplexed when Vacarro hires the

teary-eyed old woman as his cook. Archie finally accuses the pair of having cheated on him, but Vacarro swears that he came for only one thing, the signed affidavit. Archie then calls Vacarro a "wop" and grabs his rifle. After Vacarro hides outside in a tree, Baby Doll calls the police and joins Vacarro in the tree. Archie, frustrated and exhausted after his rampage, finally breaks down in tears crying out Baby Doll's name. Once the police arrive and take the gun away from Archie, Vacarro emerges and shows them the affidavit, threatening to take it to the county sheriff. Before leaving, Vacarro promises to return the next day with more cotton. The town marshal then informs Archie that they must go through with his arrest for "appearance sake," and Archie watches Baby Doll go back to the house as midnight strikes, signaling her twentieth birthday. A transformed Baby Doll tells Aunt Rose that they will have to wait until the next day to see if they will be remembered or forgotten by the tall, dark stranger. *Business rivals. Infidelity. Italian Americans. Marriage. Mississippi. Sex.* African Americans. Arson. Cotton. Flirtation. Maturation. Police. Poverty. Romantic rivalry. Seduction. Virginity.

Note: The working titles of this film were *Twenty-Seven Wagon Loads of Cotton* and *Mississippi Woman*. The film's title card reads: "Tennessee Williams' *Baby Doll*. In her autobiography, Carroll Baker reports that on her last day of shooting, director Elia Kazan offered to change the film's title from *Mississippi Woman* to *Baby Doll*, her character's name, as a "present" to her. Kazan, in his autobiography, claims that Williams only "half-heartedly" contributed to the screenplay, and that it was, in fact, Kazan, himself, who wrote most of the script. He also reports that although he urged Williams to stay in Benoit, Mississippi, the film's location, for the duration of the shooting, Williams departed after only a few weeks because "he didn't like the way people looked at him on the streets." *HR* production charts add that the film was shot on location in Greenville, Mississippi and New York City. According to Kazan, the film's final bittersweet lines, uttered by "Baby Doll" to "Aunt Rose Comfort," were later sent by Williams "as a consolation" for his departure.

According to studio production notes, African Americans from the Benoit area were featured in bit roles. Production notes also state that Uncle Pleasant, purported to be 107 years old at the time of shooting, and Sam General were in the cast, and that Boll Weevil "served as both actor and utility man for nearly three months with the location unit." A plantation house, built in 1848 and known as "Old Burras Place," was used in the film. According to Baker's autobiography, Kazan had the actors choose props for the house to reflect their characters' personalities.

The film created controversy immediately upon its release. Although a Code seal for the film was granted, the Legion of Decency found the film to be "grievously offensive to Christian and traditional standards of morality and decency," and gave the film a "C," or condemned, rating. In an 8 Dec 1956 article, *MPH* complained about the picture: "Both the general principles of the Code and several specific stipulations thereof are tossed aside in granting the film a Code seal. Among these, the law is ridiculed, there are sexual implications, vulgarity, and the words 'wop' and 'nigger.'" A 28 Nov 1956 *Var* news item noted that *Baby Doll* marked the first time in years that the Legion of Decency had "nixed" a major American production, particularly one with the Code Seal.

The Legion of Decency's ruling set off a storm of debate in religious communities. The Roman Catholic Archbishop of New York, Cardinal Francis J. Spellman, forbade parisioners from viewing the film, calling it "sinful." According to a 24 Dec 1956 *LAT* article, Rev. Dr. James A. Pike, dean of the Protestant Episcopal Cathedral of St. John the Divine, devoted his entire Advent sermon responding to Spellman's attack on *Baby Doll*. Pike argued that the film *The Ten Commandments* contained a great deal more "sensuality" than *Baby Doll*, but had nonetheless been deemed "excellent" by "a leading New York prelate." A 7 Jan 1957 *LAT* article reported that the Roman Catholic authorities of the Paris Archdiocese, led by Cardinal Feltin, also disagreed with Spellman's attack, and that Father John Burke, head of Britain's Catholic Film Institute, had called the film "a powerful denunciation of social and racial intolerance and as such is something for thoughtful people to see." In addition, the ACLU complained that the Roman Catholic Bishop of Albany's motion to forbid Catholics to attend the local Strand Theatre for six months in protest of the film's opening there was a violation of the First Amendment. In his autobiography, Kazan writes that although Spellman made *Baby Doll* famous, his attack ultimately hurt the film, and that Kazan never made any money on it.

According to memos in the MPAA/PCA Collection at the AMPAS Library, the first rough script of *Baby Doll* was received by PCA director Joseph I. Breen on 1 Aug 1952. In a memo to the producers, Breen suggested rewriting the police roles, so that they would appear more decent and sympathetic to "Vacarro." Breen also worried about a scene (eventually cut) in which a "Negro girl" offers herself to Vacarro "for sex purposes," and the fact that Vacarro "deliberately and with malice" uses adultery to get back at "Archie." The latter, Breen wrote, is "impossible under the Code." On 24 Oct 1955, PCA official Geoffrey M. Shurlock wrote to studio head Jack Warner about the "serious Code violations" in the script, especially the suggestion of an adulterous affair between Vacarro and Baby Doll, which Kazan previously had promised to avoid. Shurlock also warned that "the element of Archie's sex frustration" was in violation of the Code and that this element would have to be removed if the film was to be approved. In a letter to Warner dated 15 Nov 1955, Kazan asked Warner to "assure Sherlock and Vizzard once more that both

Williams and I specifically do not want there to have been a 'sex-affair' between our two people." Kazan pointed out several places in the script where he had eliminated hints of sex between Baby Doll and Vacarro, but stated that, "I cannot reduce the element of Archie Lee's sex frustration. I will, you can be sure, handle it delicately and in good taste." In the same letter, Kazan argued passionately that in order for theatrical films to survive, their makers must offer viewers fare that cannot be seen on television. Kazan urged Warner to break taboos and "strike out for increasingly unusual material." On 25 Jul 1956, the PCA deemed the film's basic story acceptable, including the "sex frustration" element.

The film received the following Academy Award nominations: Carroll Baker for Best Actress, Mildred Dunnock for Best Supporting Actress, Boris Kaufman for Best Black and White Cinematography, Tennessee Williams for Best Writing (Screenplay-Adapted). *Baby Doll* marked the first screen appearance by Eli Wallach, who had played "Mangiacavallo" in Williams' *The Rose Tattoo* on Broadway. In her autobiography, Baker states that Marilyn Monroe was an important contender for the part of Baby Doll, and that the famous actress acted as an usherette at the film's New York premiere, which was a benefit for the Actors' Studio.

AmCin Jan 1956, p. 10. *AmCin* Feb 1957, pp. 92-93, 106-7. *BHCN* 20 Dec 1956. *BHCN* 8 Jan 1957. *Box* 8 Dec 1956. *Cue* 22 Dec 1956. *DV* 26 Nov 1956, p. 3. *DV* 28 Nov 1956. *DV* 5 Dec 1956. *DV* 7 Dec 1956. *DV* 13 Dec 1956. *DV* 17 Dec 1956. *DV* 20 Dec 1956. *DV* 24 Dec 1956. *DV* 31 Dec 1956. *DV* 30 Jan 1957. *DV* 4 Apr 1957. *DV* 27 May 1957. *FD* 5 Dec 1956, p. 6. *Har* 8 Dec 1956, p. 195. *HCN* 17 Dec 1956. *HCN* 27 Dec 1956. *HCN* 3 Jan 1957. *HR* 4 Feb 1952. *HR* 30 Dec 1955, p. 12. *HR* 24 Feb 1956, p. 16. *HR* 28 Nov 1956. *HR* 5 Dec 1956, p. 3. *HR* 12 Dec 1956. *HR* 4 Jan 1957. *LAEx* 27 Dec 1956. *LAHE* 27 Dec 1946. *LAMirror-News* 23 Nov 1956. *LAMirror-News* 17 Dec 1956. *LAMirror-News* 27 Dec 1956. *LAT* 25 Nov 1956. *LAT* 26 Nov 1956. *LAT* 8 Dec 1956. *LAT* 9 Dec 1956. *LAT* 24 Dec 1956. *LAT* 27 Dec 1956. *LAT* 7 Jan 1957. *LAT* 1 Apr 1957. *MPD* 5 Dec 1956. *MPHPD* 8 Dec 1956, p. 177. *Newsweek* 31 Dec 1956. *Newsweek* 31 Dec 1956. *New Yorker* 29 Dec 1956. *NYT* 19 Dec 1956, p. 40. *NYT* 30 Dec 1956. *NYT* 20 Jan 1957. *Var* 4 Feb 1952. *Var* 20 Nov 1956. *Var* 28 Nov 1956. *Var* 5 Dec 1956, p. 6. *Var* 26 Dec 1956. *Var* 16 Jan 1957. *Var* 6 Feb 1957. *Var* 1 May 1957.

BACHELOR FATHER (1939) *see* **PAPÁ SOLTERO**

THE BACHELOR FATHER (*foreign version*, 1931) *see* **LE PÈRE CÉLIBATAIRE**

BACHELOR MOTHER (*foreign verion*) *see* **TRES AMORES**

A BACHELOR'S WIFE (Irish Amricans)
American Film Co. *Dist* Pathé Exchange, Inc. 1 Jun **1919** [©American Film Co.; 8 May 1919; LP13737]. Si; b&w. 5 reels.
Dir Emmett J. Flynn. *Scen* Joseph Franklin Poland.
Cast: Mary Miles Minter (*Mary O'Rourke*), Alan Forrest (*John Stuyvesant*), Myrtle Reeves (*Norah Cavanagh*), Lydia Knott (*Mrs. Stuyvesant*), Charles Spere (*Fred Stuyvesant*), Margaret Shelby (*Genevieve Harbison*), Harry Holden (*Doctor Burt*).
Comedy. When Mary O'Rourke leaves Ireland to visit her cousin Norah in New York, she finds that Norah and her baby have been deserted by her husband, John Stuyvesant. Mary goes to the aristocratic home of the Stuyvesants, where Mrs. Stuyvesant, an invalid, mistakes her for her son's wife. Warned that the woman could die from shock, Mary reluctantly assumes the role of daughter-in-law and nurses her back to health. Meanwhile, John and his cousin Fred return from a trip, and Genevieve Harbison, John's fiancée, demands that they get married the following day to prove that he is not married already. At the church, Mary produces Norah's marriage certificate, which John notices is for "John Frederick," Fred's real name. Fred then explains that his inheritance requires that he not be married until the next day. Genevieve angrily leaves after John agrees to play Fred's role, but when Fred sees Norah, he acknowledges the marriage. Mary then confuses Fred's trustee with Irish blarney and wins the legacy for Fred. She then accepts John's proposal. *Desertion (Marital). Impersonation and imposture. Inheritance. Irish. Marriage. Cousins. Invalids. Marriage licenses. New York City. Nursing back to health.*
Note: The working title of the film was *Mary O'Rourke*.
ETR 31 May 1919, p. 2013. *MPW* 24 May 1919, p. 1235, 1237. *Var* 16 May 1919, p. 51. *Var* 6 Jun 1919, p. 57. *Wid's* 18 May 1919, p. 18.

BACK TO BATAAN *see* **BATAAN**

BACKBONE (French Americans)
Distinctive Pictures Corp. *Dist* Goldwyn Distributing Corp. 30 Apr **1923** [©Distinctive Pictures Corp.; 26 Apr 1923; LP18899]. Si; b&w. 7 reels, 6,821 ft.
Dir Edward Sloman. *Scen and adpt* Charles E. Whittaker. *Photog* Harry A. Fischbeck. *Art dir* Clark Robinson.
Source: Based on the short story "Backbone" by Clarence Budington Kelland in *The Saturday Evening Post* (30 Sep—4 Nov 1922).

Cast: Edith Roberts (*Yvonne de Mersay/Yvonne de Chausson*), Alfred Lunt (*John Thorne/André de Mersay*), William B. Mack (*Anthony Bracken*), Frankie Evans (*Doc Roper*), James D. Doyle (*Colonel Tip*), L. Emile La Croix (*André de Mersay*), Charles Fang (*The Chinaman*), Marion Abbot (*Mrs. Whidden*), Frank Hagney (*The Indian*), Sam J. Ryan (*Paddy*), George MacQuarrie (*The Constable of France*), William Walcott (*Count de Chausson*), J. W. Johnston (*Captain of the Guards*), Adolph Milar (*The Jailer*), Hugh Huntley (*King*).
Romance. As has his family for generations, André de Mersay rules the little town of St. Croix, Maine, and its surrounding lumber interests. While thinking of his granddaughter, Yvonne, who is returning from France, André recalls the story of his namesake ancestor who, in the time of Louis XV of France, was cruelly separated from his sweetheart, Yvonne de Chausson, and exiled to America. When Yvonne arrives she is told by Anthony Bracken, de Mersay's business manager, that her grandfather is seriously ill and may see no one. The arrival of John Thorne and his efforts to open up a tract of lumber long intended to be worked by the de Mersays further infuriate Yvonne. After much conflict and danger to Yvonne and John, it is revealed that de Mersay died sometime ago; that Bracken and his partner, Doc Roper, were embezzling de Mersay funds; and that John Thorne is descended from Yvonne de Chausson. Yvonne and John are united, thus fulfilling a promise centuries old. *Embezzlement. Exile. French Americans. Louis XV, King of France, 1710-1774. Lumber industry. Maine.*
FD 6 May 1923. *MPW* 7 Apr 1923. *MPW* 7 Jul 1923. *NYT* 30 Apr 1923, p. 11. *Var* 3 May 1923, p. 22.

BAD BASCOMB (Native Americans)
Metro-Goldwyn-Mayer Corp.; controlled by Loew's Inc. *Dist* Loew's Inc. **1946**; *Prod:* 16 Jul—mid-Oct 1945 [©Loew's Inc.; 4 Feb 1946; LP149]. Sd (Western Electric Sound System); b&w. 110 min. PCA cert no. 11263.
Prod O. O. Dull. *Dir* S. Sylvan Simon. [*Asst dir* Earl McAvoy]. *Scr* William Lipman and Grant Garrett. *Orig story* D. A. Loxle. *Dir of photog* Charles Schoenbaum. [*2d cam* Irving Glassberg]. *Spec eff* Warren Newcombe. [*Transparency projection shots* A. Arnold Gillespie]. *Art dir* Cedric Gibbons and Paul Youngblood. *Film ed* Ben Lewis. *Set dec* Edwin B. Willis. *Assoc* Jack Ahern. *Cost supv* Irene. *Men's cost* Valles. *Mus score* David Snell. *Orch* Wally Heglin. *Rec dir* Douglas Shearer. [*Unit mixer* Howard Fellows]. [*Re-rec and eff mixer* James Z. Flaster, Ralph A. Pender, Robert Shirley, Newell Sparks, William Steinkamp, Michael Steinore and Don T. Whitme]. [*Mus mixer* Earl Cates, Peter P. Decker and M. J. MacLaughlin]. [*Unit mgr* Art Smith]. [*Unit casting dir* Billy Selwyn]. [*Research dir* George Richelavie and Madge MacDonald]. *Matte paintings* Mark Davis.
Cast: WALLACE BEERY (*Zeb Bascomb*), MARGARET O'BRIEN (*Emmy*), Marjorie Main (*Abbey Hanks*), J. Carrol Naish (*Bart Yancey*), Frances Rafferty (*Dora*), Marshall Thompson (*Jimmy Holden*), Russell Simpson (*Elijah Walker*), Warner Anderson (*Luther Mason*), Donald Curtis (*John Fulton*), Connie Gilchrist (*Annie Fremont*), Sara Haden (*Tillie Lovejoy*), Renie Riano (*Lucy Lovejoy*), Jane Green (*Hannah*), Henry O'Neill (*Governor Winton*), Frank Darien (*Elder Moab McCabe*), [Wally Cassell (*Curley*)], [John Gallaudet (*Selkirk*)], [Joseph Crehan (*Governor Ames*)], [Clyde Fillmore (*Governor Clark*)], [Arthur Space (*Sheriff*)], [Eddie Acuff (*Corporal*)], [Stanley Andrews (*Colonel Cartwright*)].
Comedy-drama, Western. [*Print viewed*]. In the 1860s, governors from three territories east of the Rocky Mountains are joined by federal agents in their quest to find outlaw Zeb Bascomb and stop his gang of bandits. John Fulton, the head of the federal agents, and the governors know little about the elusive Zeb, except that he has a rope burn scar on the back of his neck. One day, when Elder Moab McCabe, a lone Mormon missionary, rides into Zeb's territory on horseback, Zeb's partner, Bart Yancey, a white renegade reared by Indians, kills him in cold blood. Zeb and Bart later learn that a federal manhunt is underway, and decide to split from the gang and take refuge with Elijah Walker's Mormon caravan. Posing as new converts, Zeb and Bart join the Mormons on their journey to Utah. Zeb and Emmy, the young granddaughter of missionary Abbey Hanks, become fast friends, and Zeb soon discovers the drawbacks of being a new convert when he and Bart are assigned to do heavy work for the unmarried women in the caravan. While Zeb chooses to work for Abbey and the widow Annie Fremont, Bart goes to work for sisters

Tillie and Lucy Lovejoy. One day, the caravan picks up Jimmy Holden, one of Zeb's gang, who has been shot and left for dead. Jimmy is nursed back to health by Dr. Luther Mason and his nurse Dora, who falls in love with the young outlaw. When Zeb discovers that the wagon train is carrying a cache of gold that the Mormons intend to use to build a hospital, he and Bart devise a plan to steal it. Ignoring Jimmy's warning to stay out of trouble, Zeb and Bart begin searching all the wagons for the hidden gold. While the wagon train attempts a dangerous river crossing, Emmy falls into the water and is rescued by Zeb, who has developed a fatherly love for the girl. Late that night, Emmy, believing that Zeb no longer loves her, runs away from the caravan camp. Zeb finds Emmy, but soon after he returns her to the wagon train, she becomes ill. Realizing that his love for Emmy is stronger than his determination to steal the gold, Zeb decides to forgo the theft and stay with Emmy. Bart, however, tries to steal the gold on his own, and shoots Elijah while fleeing the camp. In his dying words, Elijah appoints Zeb as the new leader of the Mormon group. Zeb's first challenge as the caravan leader is to protect it from an impending Indian attack that Bart has incited, and he succeeds in doing so by risking his life and riding his horse through Indian territory to get help from a nearby fort. Zeb returns to the camp with U.S. Cavalry reinforcements just in time to save the Mormons from an Indian massacre. Zeb kills Bart, but during their struggle, Fulton discovers Zeb's rope burn and arrests him. After bidding Emmy and the others farewell, Zeb leaves the caravan to serve his time in prison. *Bandits. Children. Criminals–Rehabilitation. Fugitives. Mormons. Wagon trains. Bank robberies. Caravans. Friendship. Gold. Governors. Gunfights. Gunshot wounds. Heroes. Indians of North America. Missionaries. Murder. Rescues. Romance. Special agents. Spinsters. United States. Army. Cavalry. The West. Widows.*

Note: An Apr 1944 *HR* news item indicates that actor Bruce Kellogg was originally set for the part played by Marshall Thompson. According to *HR*, production included six weeks of location shooting in Jackson Hole, Wyoming. Wallace Beery and Margaret O'Brien recreated their roles for a *Lux Radio Theatre* broadcast on 1 Mar 1948.

Box 9 Feb 1946. *DV* 5 Feb 1946, p. 3. *FD* 8 Feb 1946, p. 6. *HR* 27 Apr 1944, p. 15 *HR* 5 Jun 1945, p. 8. *HR* 16 Jul 1945, p. 11. *HR* 20 Jul 1945, p. 8. *HR* 10 Aug 1945, p. 10. *HR* 30 Aug 1945, p. 13. *HR* 12 Oct 1945, p. 18. *HR* 4 Feb 1946, p. 3. *HR* 28 May 1946, p. 6. *MPHPD* 9 Feb 1946, p. 2837. *NYT* 23 May 1946, p. 18.

BAD BOY *see* EAST OF THE RIVER

BAD DAY AT BLACK ROCK (Asian Americans, Japanese
   Americans)
Metro-Goldwyn-Mayer Corp.; controlled by Loew's Inc. *Dist* Loew's Inc. 7 Jan **1955**; Prod: mid-Jul—mid-Aug 1954 [©Loew's Inc.; 6 Dec 1954; LP4305]. Sd (Western Electric Sound System); col (Eastman Color). 7,329 ft. 81 min. Passed by the National Board of Review. PCA cert no. 17184.
   Prod Dore Schary. *Assoc prod* Herman Hoffman. *Dir* John Sturges. *Asst dir* Joel Freeman. *Scr* Millard Kaufman. *Adpt* Don McGuire. *Dir of photog* William C. Mellor. *Cor consultant* Alword Eiseman. *Art dir* Cedric Gibbons and Malcolm Brown. *Film ed* Newell P. Kimlin. *Set dec* Edwin B. Willis and Fred MacLean. *Mus* Andre Previn. *Rec supv* Wesley C. Miller.
   Source: Based on the short story "Bad Time at Honda" by Howard Breslin in *American Magazine* (Jan 1947).
   Cast: SPENCER TRACY (*John J. Macreedy*), ROBERT RYAN (*Reno Smith*), Anne Francis (*Liz Wirth*), Dean Jagger ([*Sheriff*] *Tim Horn*), Walter Brennan (*Doc Velie*), John Ericson (*Pete Wirth*), Ernest Borgnine (*Coley Trimble*), Lee Marvin (*Hector David*), Russell Collins (*Mr. Hastings*), Walter Sande (*Sam*), [Billy Dix (*Ron Bentham*)], [Francis McDonald (*Walt Murty*)], [Walter Beaver (*Franklin Krool*)], [Ken Smith (*Sterling Lenard*)], [Harry Harvey, Sr., Robert Griffin (*Conductors*)], [Mickey Little (*T. J.*)], [Bobby Johnson (*Porter*)].
   Social, Suspense, Drama. [*Print viewed*]. One hot summer day in 1945, when the Streamliner train stops at the remote desert town of Black Rock, Arizona, for the first time in four years, the townspeople greet the visiting stranger, a one-armed man named John J. Macreedy, with suspicion and hostility. Hastings, the telegraph agent, learns that Macreedy wants to visit nearby Adobe Flat, whereupon he immediately telephones Pete Wirth, the hotel keeper. Explaining that war restrictions make it impossible for him to let a room, Pete is flustered when Macreedy reminds him that World War II ended several months earlier. Macreedy finally settles into a room, but

cowboy Hector David soon enters and, for no apparent reason, challenges him to a fight. Macreedy is baffled by the town's hostility but remains calmly determined to reach his destination. As Macreedy tries unsuccessfully to rent a car, locals Reno Smith and Coley Trimble drive up. A group of men, some of them obviously jumpy, enter the hotel lobby and begin to talk. Doc Velie wonders aloud why Smith, Coley, Hector, Pete and Sam are so worried about the stranger, but Smith, silences Doc and orders Hastings to get information about Macreedy's identity from a private detective in Los Angeles. Macreedy visits the sheriff's office and finds the head lawman, Tim Horn, just waking up from a drink-induced sleep. When Macreedy mentions that he is looking for a farmer named Kumoko in Adobe Flat, Tim becomes hostile, too, and refuses to answer the stranger's questions. Smith approaches Macreedy in the street and explains that Kumoko, having arrived in Adobe Flat just before the Pearl Harbor attack in 1941, was soon shipped off to a relocation camp. Just then, Pete's sister Liz drives up in her jeep, and Macreedy rents the vehicle and heads for Adobe Flat. Smith is furious with Liz, but she insists that Macreedy will surely find nothing. Tim, protesting that he never really knew what happened to Kumoko, reminds Smith that he is still the law, but Smith only laughs at him. When the private detective telegraphs that there are no records available on Macreedy, Smith orders Coley to get rid of the stranger, adding that "these maimed guys are all troublemakers, do-gooders." Pete objects to this plan, and Doc tells Tim that the town, in blindly obeying Smith for so long, has lost its self-respect. At Adobe Flat, meanwhile, Macreedy finds nothing but a burned house, a deep well and some wildflowers growing in the dirt. As he returns to town, Coley races up behind him and rams him off of the road. Shaken but unhurt, Macreedy returns to Black Rock, where Coley calls him a roadhog. Macreedy finally decides to check out, but Pete informs him that the train will not arrive until the next morning. Liz refuses to take him to the next town, saying, "I don't want to get involved." Next, Smith drives up and asks why "a big man like you" would look for "a lousy Jap farmer." Macreedy remarks that because wildflowers were growing at Adobe Flat, he believes something is buried there. Convinced that Smith is going to kill him, he then tries to telephone the state police, but Pete refuses to put the call through. Doc, telling Macreedy that he is "consumed by apathy," nonetheless offers his hearse as an escape vehicle, but the wires have been tampered with and the car will not start. Macreedy then attempts to telegraph the state police about his "urgent and dangerous situation," after which he pays a visit to the local bar. Smith and Coley enter, and Coley tries repeatedly to goad Macreedy into a fight. When Coley calls Macreedy a "yellow-bellied Jap lover," Macreedy injures him with several swift judo slices to the throat and neck. He then turns to Smith and openly accuses him of having murdered Kumoko. Hastings shows Smith the wire he never sent, whereupon Macreedy accuses the telegraph agent of having committed a federal offense. Smiling, Smith leaves, and Doc exclaims that this is the town's last chance to redeem itself. Defeated, the sheriff departs, but Pete admits to Doc and Macreedy that he has never forgotten what happened four years earlier. Macreedy reveals that Kumoko's son Joe died in battle in Italy trying to save his life. He came to Black Rock to give Kumoko the young man's medal. Upon hearing this, Doc and Pete reveal Kumoko's fate: Smith leased Adobe Flat to Kumoko, promising good land and plenty of water. Soon realizing that Smith had cheated him, Kumoko dug a sixty-foot well, thereby infuriating Smith. When Smith was turned down by the Marine recruiting office, he returned to Black Rock and got "patriotic drunk" with Coley, Pete, Hector and Sam. The men decided to scare Kumoko, and when the farmer locked his door, Smith began shooting. Kumoko's clothes caught fire, and as he ran from the house, Smith shot him. Abruptly, Pete calls Liz and asks for her help in getting Macreedy out of town. At night, Doc and Pete knock the watchful Hector unconscious, and Macreedy jumps into Liz's waiting jeep. Liz drives Macreedy into the desert, but she soon delivers her passenger to Smith, who is waiting in the rocks with his rifle. Explaining that he wants no witnesses, Smith shoots Liz dead and then starts shooting at Macreedy as Macreedy hides behind the jeep. Macreedy fills a glass bottle with gasoline from the jeep, stuffs his tie into the neck and touches his lighter to the bottle. When he throws it at Smith, the bottle explodes, and Smith catches fire. Macreedy returns to town to find the four other murder witnesses locked in a cell. Later, as Macreedy walks to the train, Doc asks if Black Rock might have Kumoko's medal. Smiling, Macreedy gives Doc

this token of courage and climbs onto the train. *Bigotry. Conspiracy. Guilt. Moral reformation. Ruffians. Self-respect. Small town life. Alcoholics. Arizona. Attempted murder. Automobile chases. Citizenship. Deserts. Fear. Fires. Gas stations. Handicapped. Hotels. Japanese Americans. Japanese Americans–Evacuation and relocation, 1942-1945. Judo. Mobs. Murder. Sheriffs. Trains. Traps. Veterans. Veterinarians. War heroes. War injuries. World War II.*

Note: According to materials contained in the MPAA files on this film in the AMPAS Library, Joseph Breen, the Vice President of the Production Code Administration, suggested that the filmmakers reconsider their use of expressions such as "Jap-lover" and "lousy Jap." John Sturges received an Academy Award nomination for Best Director; Spencer Tracy for Best Actor; and Millard Kaufman for Best Writer. Spencer Tracy won a Golden Globe Award for acting. Modern critics have pointed to this film as a metaphor for the reaction to the House Un-American Activities Committee. The 1960 Metro-Goldwyn-Mayer film *Platinum High School*, directed by Charles Haas and starring Mickey Rooney and Terry Moore, was loosely based on Howard Breslin's story.

Box 18 Dec 1954, p. 6. *DV* 15 Dec 1954, p. 3. *Exb* 15 Dec 1954, pp. 3885-86. *FD* 15 Dec 1954, p. 6. *Har* 18 Dec 1954, p. 202. *HR* 23 Jul 1954, p. 20. *HR* 13 Aug 1954, p. 9. *HR* 15 Dec 1954, p. 3. *MPHPD* 18 Dec 1954, p. 249. *NYT* 2 Feb 1955, p. 22. *Var* 15 Dec 1954, p. 6.

BAD GIRL *(foreign version)* see **MARIDO Y MUJER**

BAD LANDS (Latino, Ntive Americans, Apache)
RKO Radio Pictures, Inc. *Dist* RKO Radio Pictures, Inc. 28 Aug **1939**; Prod: 15 May—late May 1939 [©RKO Radio Pictures, Inc.; 11 Aug 1939; LP9171]. Sd (RCA Victor System); b&w. 8 reels, 6,327 ft. 70 min. PCA cert no. 5402.
Prod Robert Sisk. *Dir* Lew Landers. [*Asst dir* Sam Ruman]. *Story and scr* Clarence Upson Young. *Photog* Frank Redman and [Russell Metty]. *Art dir* Van Nest Polglase. *Art dir assoc* Feild Gray. *Film ed* George Hively. *Mus score* Roy Webb. *Rec* Earl A. Wolcott. *Prod exec* Lee Marcus.
Cast: Robert Barrat (*Sheriff* [*Bill Cummings*]), Noah Beery, Jr. (*Chic Lyman*), Guinn Williams (*Billy Sweet*), Andy Clyde (*Cluff*), Paul Hurst (*Curley Tom*), Robert Coote [(*Eaton*)], Addison Richards [(*Rayburn*)], Douglas Walton [(*Mulford*)], Francis Ford [(*Garth*)], Francis McDonald [(*Manuel Lopez*)], [John Payne].
Western. [*Print viewed*]. In 1875, notorious outlaw Apache Jack flees into the Arizona desert after killing the bride of Manuel Lopez. Sheriff Bill Cummings sets out on Apache Jack's trail with a posse comprised of Manuel Lopez, who seeks to avenge his wife's murder; Westerners Rayburn and Chic Lyman; an Easterner named Mulford; frontiersman Kier; cowboy Billy Sweet; Eaton, an Englishman; and two prospectors, Cluff and Garth. Deep in the Arizona wastelands, the party discovers the body of an advance scout who was killed by Apache Jack. When the posse arrives at an oasis in a narrow wash, the men quench their thirst in the water, but are startled by the sight of several skeletons near the watering hole. While Cluff and Garth find indications of a rich silver deposit in the area, the posse sets up camp. Eaton is appointed to stand guard over the horses at night, but at daybreak the Sheriff awakens to find him, his horse and Cluff and Garth missing. No sooner are the men found at an adjoining wash, however, than Cluff is killed by a bullet fired by an unseen Apache sharpshooter on the ridge. Certain that they are surrounded by Apaches, the men play cards to determine who will be sent to get help. Garth and Billy are pressed into the dangerous mission, but before they go, a horse carrying Eaton's corpse rides in, reminding them of the Apaches' deadliness. The endless wait for help to arrive proves too much for Lopez, who takes off on a mad search for his dead wife. While attempting to stop Lopez, Kier is stabbed. The Sheriff, Mulford, and Rayburn are the only men left alive after the wounded Kier dies, and Lyman is shot from his horse by an Apache. Desperate, the three men devise a plan to create a diversion to allow two of them to flee unnoticed by the Apaches. Rayburn goes up the wash, while the Sheriff and Mulford hide in the rocks, but he is soon shot by the indians, who approach the watering hole thinking that they have killed off the last remaining man. As Apache Jack examines the graves of the murdered posse, the Sheriff and Mulford shoot and kill the outlaw and several indians. Believing that they have eliminated the Apache threats, the Sheriff and Mulford emerge, only to be fired upon by a wounded indian, who kills Mulford. The Sheriff, the sole survivor of the ambush, shoots the wounded Apache and is soon rescued by a passing cavalry party. *Apache Indians. Arizona. Deserts. Murder. Outlaws. Posses. Cards. English. Horses. Insanity. Prospectors. Rescues. Revenge. Sheriffs. Silver mines. Skeletons. United States. Army. Cavalry. Watchmen.*

Note: A working title for this film was *The Great Seizer*. According to a *HR* pre-production news item, *Bad Lands* was set for a two-week shoot on location at Victorville, California. A *HR* production chart lists Stanley Ridges in the cast, but his appearance in the released film has not been confirmed. Many contemporary reviews of the picture compare it to the 1934 RKO film *The Lost Patrol* (see *AFI Catalog of Feature Films, 1931-40*; F3.2580).

DV 21 Jul 1939, p. 3. *FD* 28 Aug 1939, p. 7. *HR* 12 May 1939, p. 4. *HR* 20 May 1939, p. 6. *HR* 21 Jul 1939, p. 3. *MPH* 3 Jun 1939, p. 35. *MPH* 19 Aug 1939, p. 54. *NYT* 9 Aug 1939, p. 15. *Var* 16 Aug 1939, p. 16.

THE BAD MAN (Spanish language, Latino)
First National Pictures, Inc. *Dist* First National Pictures, Inc. 13 Sep **1930** [©First National Pictures, Inc.; 1 Sep 1930; LP1576]. Sd (Vitaphone); b&w. 9 reels, 7,124 ft.
Supv Henry Blanke. *Dir* Clarence Badger. *Scr* Howard Estabrook. *Dial* Howard Estabrook. *Photog* John Seitz. *Film ed* Frank Ware. *Sd tech* Glenn E. Rominger.
Source: Based on the play *The Bad Man* by Porter Emerson Browne, presented by William Harris, Jr. (New York, 30 Sep 1920).
Cast: Walter Huston (*Pancho López*), Dorothy Revier (*Ruth Pell*), James Rennie (*Gilbert Jones*), O. P. Heggie (*Henry Taylor*), Sidney Blackmer (*Morgan Pell*), Marion Byron (*Angela Hardy*), Guinn Williams (*Red Giddings*), Arthur Stone (*Pedro*), Edward Lynch (*Bradley*), Harry Semels (*José*), Erville Alderson (*Hardy*).
Western. [*Not viewed*]. Notorious Mexican bandit Pancho López recognizes Gilbert Jones as the man who once saved his life; therefore, when Jones is in danger of losing his ranch for default of mortgage payment, López determines to help him. At the same time, Morgan Pell, intending to swindle Jones out of his potentially oil-rich property, offers him a sum of money, which Jones conditionally accepts. When López discovers that Jones and Mrs. Pell are in love he has Pell shot, then robs a local bank, pays the mortgage, and returns the cattle he has stolen. With Mr. Pell out of the way and the ranch secure, Jones and Mrs. Pell are free to marry. *Bandits. Mexicans. Murder. Oil. Ranches. Swindlers and swindling.*

Note: A Spanish-language version of this film, *El hombre malo*, was shot simultaneously with the English-language version. A French version, *López, le bandit* was also made in 1930, but no evidence of its U.S. exhibition has been found. The French version was directed by Jean Daumery and starred Geymond Votal, Jeanne Helbling, Gaston Glass and Suzy Vernon. Other adaptations of Porter Emerson Browne's play include a 1923 version (see *AFI Catalog of Feature Films, 1921-30*; F2.0237) and a 1941 M-G-M production, directed by Richard Thorpe and starring Wallace Beery.

Other language version(s):
El hombre malo (Spanish language)
1930; Los Angeles premiere: 28 Jun 1930. 8 reels, 6,204 ft. 69 min.; Sd. b&w. Spanish language.
Supv Henry Blanke. *Dir* William McGann. *Dial dir* Roberto E. Guzmán. *Spanish adpt and dial* Baltasar Fernández Cué. *Photog* Frank Kesson. *Film ed* Thomas Pratt.
Spanish-language cast: Antonio Moreno (*Pancho López*), Andrés de Segurola (*Taylor*), Juan Torena (*Alberto*), Rosita Ballesteros (*María*), Roberto Guzmán (*Morris*), Carlos Villarías (*Dobbs*), Conchita Ballesteros (*Angela*), Manuel Conesa (*Guillermo*), Delia Magaña (*Cocinera*), Martín Garralaga (*Bradley*), Carlos Ramos (*Pedro*), José Domínguez (*Luciano*), Daniel F. Rea. [*Spanish version not viewed*].

Cinl Sep 1930, p. 30. *CM* Sep 1930. *NYT* 27 Sep 1930, p. 21.

BAD MAN OF HARLEM see **HARLEM ON THE PRAIRIE**

BADGE OF EVIL see **TOUCH OF EVIL**

THE BADGE OF SHAME see **THE YELLOW PASSPORT**

THE BADLANDERS (Latino)
Arcola Pictures Corp. *Dist* Loew's Inc. Aug **1958**; New York opening: 3 Sep 1958; Prod: 3 Feb—19 Mar 1958 [©Loew's Inc. & Arcola Pictures Corp.; 14 Jul 1958; LP11545]. Sd (Westrex Recording System); col (Metrocolor). 8,090 ft. 83 or 85 min. Passed by the National Board of Review. PCA cert no. 19001.
Prod Aaron Rosenberg. *Dir* Delmer Daves. *Asst dir* Ridgeway Callow. *Scr* Richard Collins. *Dir of photog* John Seitz. *Col consultant* Charles K. Hagedon. *Art dir* William A. Horning and Daniel B. Cathcart. *Film ed* William H. Webb and James Baiotto. *Set dec* Henry Grace and Jack Mills. *Rec supv* Dr. Wesley C. Miller. *Hair styles* Sydney Guilaroff. *Makeup* William Tuttle. [*Unit mgr* Ruby Rosenberg]. [*Tech adv on gold mine scenes* Wilfred Babcock]. [*Stunts* Willard Willingham and Henry Wills].

Source: Based on the novel *The Asphalt Jungle* by W. R. Burnett (New York, 1949).

Cast: ALAN LADD [(*Peter Van Hoek*)], ERNEST BORGNINE [(*John McBain*)], Katy Jurado [(*Anita*)], Claire Kelly [(*Ada Winton*)], Kent Smith [(*Cyril Lounsberry*)], Nehemiah Persoff [(*Vincente*)], Robert Emhardt [(*Sample*)], Anthony Caruso [(*Comanche*)], Adam Williams [(*Leslie*)], Ford Rainey [(*Warden*)], John Day [(*Lee*)], [Karl Swenson (*Marshal*)], [Roberto Contreras (*Pepe*)], [Anna Navarro (*Raquel*)], [Richard Devon (*Guard*)], [Tex Terry (*Yard guard*)], [Sam Edwards (*Crazy*)], [Pat Lawless (*Irish guard*)], [Robert E. Griffin, Dick Bartell (*Bartenders*)], [Ann Doran, Almira Sessions (*Mothers*)], [Carol Nugent, Helen Jay (*Girls*)], [James McCallion (*Hotel clerk*)], [Jorge Moreno (*Pancho*)], [Vinnie DeCarlo (*Driver*)], [Gregg Barton (*Foreman*)], [Erwin Neal (*Powder man*)], [Joe Haworth (*Miner*)], [Robert Totten (*Young miner*)], [Joe Dominguez (*Mexican miner*)], [Annette Claudier], [Paul Baxley].

Western. [*Print viewed*]. In 1898, at the Arizona Territorial Prison in Yuma, convict John McBain saves several prisoners, including Peter Van Hoek, from drowning. Peter, also known as "the Dutchman," then prevents an enraged McBain from attacking a sadistic guard and is awarded an early release for this act. As he prepares to leave, Peter again asserts what he has claimed from the beginning: that he was framed for the gold robbery that landed him in prison. McBain, having served a ten-year sentence for the slaughter of Bascom, a man who swindled him out of his gold-rich land, is released on the same day, but while Peter seems outwardly amiable, McBain is consumed by an angry bitterness. After arriving in nearby Prescott, the marshal, the very man who Peter believes framed him, orders the Dutchman to leave town. Peter promises to go the following evening, and as he ascends to his room, he meets the lovely Ada Winton, whose "gentleman friend," the wealthy Cyril Lounsberry, has locked her in her suite. Later, Peter sneaks into an abandoned section of the Lisbon mine, his former property, and chips off a small chunk of gold. Meanwhile, McBain risks his life to defend a Mexican-American woman named Anita when she is attacked by roughnecks on the street. He then helps her to deliver the baby of a woman who, like every Mexican-American in town, is too poor to afford medical care. By the end of the day, McBain and Anita have fallen deeply in love. After flirting with Ada, Peter, meanwhile, visits the current owner of the Lisbon mine, who turns out to be Lounsberry, a Bostonian who acquired the mine by marrying Bascom's sister. Peter explains his proposal: having been cheated and framed by the manager of a mine he prospected, Peter, with the aid of Lounsberry's money and supplies, wants to remove a hidden but very rich deposit of gold from that mine and then sell the gold to Lounsberry. Although worth $200,000, the gold would cost Lounsberry only $100,000. Unaware that the mine in question is the Lisbon, the mine owner agrees to the plan. Sample, Lounsberry's henchman, warns Peter to avoid using Mexicans for the job, but Peter remarks that he trusts Mexicans. "I've even forgotten the Alamo," he remarks. Because the mine is on land once owned by McBain, Peter hires him to assist with the job and offers to share the money with him. Also hired is Vincente, a skilled "powder monkey," who worked with Peter years before. On the following afternoon, Peter, Vincente, and McBain enter the deserted mine shaft and begin setting caps of explosive powder near Peter's secret gold deposit. The explosion, timed to coincide with the daily blasting of the Lisbon, yields several huge bags of ore-rich rock, which the men quickly haul outside. Vincente is injured during a sudden cave-in, and it is only with great difficulty that the three escape to a waiting wagon. They then deliver the gold to Lounsberry, who has ordered the crooked deputy to seize the gold at gunpoint and return the men to prison. The deputy shoots McBain in the shoulder, but the three manage to escape to Anita's shack with the gold. Peter bids farewell to Anita and McBain and rides away, but Lounsberry and his thugs begin shooting at him just as an annual Mexican fiesta gets underway in the center of town. McBain rushes out to help his friend, but Lounsberry's men surround them. Anita quickly rallies the celebrants to their aid, and soon fireworks fill the plaza with smoke and confusion. The thugs are disarmed and captured by the mob, thereby enabling Anita to flee with McBain and Peter. After promising to meet them in Texas for his share of the money, Peter steps aboard the departing stagecoach, where he is greeted by the beautiful Ada.
Duplicity. Escapes. Gold miners. Mexican Americans. Mine owners. Revenge. Robbery. Arizona. Engineers. Ex-convicts. Explosives. Festivals. Fireworks. Gold mines. Laborers. Loyalty. Marshals. Mine accidents. Mistresses. Poverty. Prescott (AZ). Prostitution. Racism. Rescues. Yuma (AZ).

Note: According to information in the MPAA/PCA collection at the AMPAS Library, in Nov 1957, the PCA rejected the first draft of this film because it portrayed criminals in a sympathetic manner. In Feb 1958, a revised script was deemed acceptable, on condition that certain changes were made, including the elimination of any suggestion of prostitution. Despite these conditions, the finished film, which included identifiable prostitutes, received a PCA certificate. (The *Var* reviewer commented that "Katy Jurado and Claire Kelly...are ladies who are plainly of easy and saleable virtue, and there is none of the usual subterfuge about dance hall girls.") Although Fred Gerstle is credited in the role of the "hotel clerk" in the studio cast list, the CBCS list, which is dated eight months later than the studio's, credits James McCallion in the part. The studio cast list also indicates that Barbara Baxley and Zina Provendie were cut from the final film. *The Badlanders* marked Alan Ladd's only appearance in an M-G-M film. According to contemporary information contained at the AMPAS Library, exteriors were filmed on location at the Tennessee Mine in Kingman, AZ, the Elk Hart and Schulhill Mines near Kingman, the Yuma Prison, and a Mexican settlement in Tucson.
W. R. Burnett's novel was first adapted in 1950 as *The Asphalt Jungle*. John Huston directed Sterling Hayden and Louis Calhern in the M-G-M production. In 1963, Wolf Rilla directed George Sanders in another M-G-M version, titled *Cairo* (see *AFI Catalog of Feature Films, 1961-70*; F6.0625). In 1972, Barry Pollack directed a fourth version, M-G-M's *Cool Breeze*, starring Thalmus Rasulala and Judy Pace. A television series inspired by the book was broadcast on the ABC network during the 1961 season. Jack Warden and Arch Johnson starred in series, also titled *The Asphalt Jungle*. Ernest Borgnine and Katy Jurado were married from 1959 to 1964.
Box 21 Jul 1958. *DV* 16 Jul 1958, p. 3. *Exh* 23 Jul 1958, p. 4493. *FD* 18 Jul 1958, p. 6. *Har* 19 Jul 1958, pp. 114-15. *HR* 14 Mar 1958. *HR* 16 Jul 1958, p. 3. *MPHPD* 19 Jul 1958, p. 911. *NYT* 4 Sep 1958, p. 33. *Var* 16 Jul 1958, p. 6.

BAJO EL CIELO DE HOLLYWOOD see HOLLYWOOD, CIUDAD DE ENSUEÑO

THE BALLAD OF FURNACE CREEK see FURY AT FURNACE CREEK

BAND OF ANGELS (African Americans)

Warner Bros. Pictures, Inc.; A Warner Bros.—First National Picture. *Dist* Warner Bros. Pictures, Inc. 10 Jul 1957; Prod: early Jan—late Mar 1957; addl scene shot 28 Apr 1957 [©Warner Bros. Pictures, Inc.; 3 Aug 1957; LP12348]. Sd (RCA Sound System); col (Warnercolor); 1.85. 11,436 ft. 125 or 127 min. PCA cert no. 18433.

Dir Raoul Walsh. *Asst dir* Russ Saunders and Al Alleborn. *Scr* John Twist, Ivan Goff and Ben Roberts. *Dir of photog* Lucien Ballard. *Art dir* Franz Bachelin. *Film ed* Folmar Blangsted. *Set dec* William Wallace. *Cost des* Marjorie Best. *Mus* Max Steiner. *Orch* Murray Cutter. [*Vocal arr* Lester Hairston]. *Sd* Francis Stahl. *Makeup supv* Gordon Bau. *Dial supv* Lewis Smith.

Source: Based on the novel *Band of Angels* by Robert Penn Warren (New York, 1955).

Cast: CLARK GABLE [(*Hamish Bond*)], YVONNE DE CARLO [(*Amantha "Manty" Starr*)], Sidney Poitier [(*Rau-Ru*)], Efrem Zimbalist, Jr. [(*Ethan Sears*)], Patric Knowles [(*Charles de Marigny*)], Rex Reason [(*Seth Parton*)], Torin Thatcher [(*Capt. Canavan*)], Andrea King [(*Miss Idell*)], Ray Teal [(*Mr. Calloway*)], Russ Evans [(*Jimmee*)], Caroline Drake [(*Michele*)], Raymond Bailey [(*Mr. Stuart*)], Tommie Moore [(*Dollie*)], [William Forrest (*Aaron Starr*)], [Zelda Cleaver (*Sukie*)], [Joe Narcisse (*Shad*)], [Marshall Bradford (*General Benjamin Butler*)], [Noreen Corcoran (*Manty, as a child*)], [Juanita Moore (*Budge*)], [Jack Williams (*Runaway*)], [Charles Heard (*Helper*)], [Roy Barcroft (*Overseer, Gillespie*)], [Curtis Hamilton (*Jacob, a coachman*)], [Riza Royce (*Mrs. Hopewell*)], [Mayo Loizeaux, June-Ellen Anthony, Carla Merry (*Girls*)], [Jim Hayward (*Sheriff*)], [William Fawcett, Jean G. Harvey, Alfred Meissner, Dan White (*Mourners*)], [Guy Wilkerson (*Minister*)], [Larry Blake (*Crier-off*)], [Ewing Mitchell (*An old gentleman*)], [Forbes Murray (*A younger man*)], [Joe Gilbert, Robert Carson (*Bidders*)], [Robert Clarke (*Friend*)], [Maurice Marsac (*Young dandy*)], [Jeanine Grandel (*Proprietor*)], [Gizelle D'Arc (*Salesgirl*)], [Harry Fleer (*Aide*)], [Bob Steele, Zon Murray (*Privates*)], [Morgan Shaan (*Corporal*)], [X Brands, Paul McGuire, Martin Smith, William Hughes, Myron Cook, Charles Victor, Pete Dunn, William Hudson (*Officers*)], [Ann Doran (*Mrs. Morton*)], [Walter Smith (*Black soldier*)], [Carl Harbaugh (*Seaman*)], [William Schallert (*Lieutenant*)], [Charles Horvath (*Soldier*)], [Anthony Ghazlo (*Driver*)], [Robyn Faire (*Little girl*)], [Ann Staunton (*Mother*)], [Milas Clark, Jr. (*Black child*)], [Madame Sul-Te-Wan (*Flower vendor*)].

Historical, Psychological, Drama. [*Print viewed*]. In antebellum Kentucky, the beautiful Amantha "Manty" Starr arrives home from finishing school in Cincinnati just after the death of her father, kindly plantation owner Aaron Starr. During the funeral, it is revealed that Manty's mother was one of Starr's slaves and that Manty, now considered chattel of the estate, is to be sold by a slave trader to whom Starr had been deeply in debt. At a slave auction in New Orleans, a wealthy gentleman named Hamish Bond pays a huge sum for Manty, intending to treat her as a lady in his household. Because she assumes she is to be a kept woman, however, she rebuffs his offer of friendship. Michele, the head housekeeper, who is herself in love with Hamish, secretly gives Manty a ticket to Cincinnati, but Rau-Ru, an educated slave who helps Hamish manage his business affairs, prevents Manty from boarding the boat. Later Hamish confesses that he is tormented by his past, and Manty, who now sees another side of Hamish, kisses him. The next morning, Hamish takes Manty to his largest plantation and offers to free her. She hesitates but decides to remain with Hamish. Soon afterward, Hamish learns that war has been declared. While he visits another of his plantations, Manty accepts the attentions of her wealthy white neighbor, Charles de Marigny, which leads Rau-Ru to accuse her of betraying her people by attempting to live as a white woman. When de Marigny attacks Manty, however, Rau-Ru strikes him, and subsequently is forced to run away to the North. There he becomes a Union soldier under the command of Seth Parton, a self-righteous minister who had courted Manty when she was at finishing school. Hamish returns to the plantation and, in defiance of Union general Benjamin Butler's order, sets his own crops ablaze in order to keep them out of Yankee hands. As his fields burn, Hamish confesses to Manty that in his younger days, he had been a ruthless slave trader. With some reluctance, Manty leaves Hamish to begin a new life in New Orleans, and there she encounters Parton, who threatens to tell her new sweetheart, Ethan Sears, that she is black unless she makes love to him. Horrified, Manty returns to Hamish's New Orleans home, where she learns that he is on the run for burning his crops. Rau-Ru, who despises Hamish for having treated him with kindness, which he calls, "the worst kind of bondage," discovers where his old master is hiding and holds him at gunpoint. When Hamish tells Rau-Ru that he rescued him from a slave trader's bullet when he was an infant, however, Rau-Ru decides to let Hamish go. At that moment, Union troops arrive and Rau-Ru, while loudly proclaiming that he has captured Hamish, quietly slips his former owner the handcuff keys. Hamish escapes from the Union soldiers as Rau-Ru leads Manty to the cove where Hamish plans to rendezvous with an old seafaring friend. Bidding farewell to Rau-Ru, Hamish and Manty embrace and then board the boat that will take them to safety.
African Americans. African Americans–Mixed blood. Miscegenation. Plantation owners. Slave traders. Slavery. United States–History–Civil War, 1861-1865. Arson. Attempted rape. Benjamin Butler. Cincinnati (OH). Escapes. Finishing schools. Funerals. Jealousy. Kentucky. Louisiana. Love. Ministers. New Orleans (LA). Parentage. Plantations. Racial impersonation. Revenge. Slaves. Soldiers. Spirituals (Songs).

Note: According to *DV*, Warner Bros. acquired the rights to Robert Penn Warren's novel on 13 Sep 1955, a few months before its publication. *HR* stated that the title, *Band of Angels*, "referred to the short life expectancy of freed Negros who fought with Union troops during the war," but commented that the film dealt very little with this subject. Many of the reviews criticized the film's superficial and melodramatic treatment of racial issues. A number of reviews noted discrepancies between the novel and the film. *HR* stated that in the novel, "the story seems to have been of a girl torn between two worlds. In the picture there is only the vaguest hint of a potential romance between Miss De Carlo and Poitier....The screenwriters seem to have been held back from being more explicit in their delineation of the De Carlo-Poitier relationship." *New Yorker* commented, "What Mr. Warren was after in his novel was a description of Southern society when slavery was still the order of the day. What we are offered here is a spate of romantic hokum." *DV* predicted that the film would encounter opposition below the Mason-Dixon Line.

According to a memo dated 14 Nov 1956 in the MPAA/PCA Collection at the AMPAS Library, the story as originally presented to the PCA was "an unacceptable treatment of illicit sex between the leading characters" because of their master-slave relationship. A certificate of approval was granted only after the scenes containing illicit sex were removed. Location shooting took place near Baton Rouge, LA, on the banks of the Mississippi River, and on two antebellum plantations. A packet boat more than one hundred years old was also used in the film, according to an Aug 1957 *BHCN* item.

BHCN 7 Aug 1957. *Box* 20 Jul 1957. *Cue* 13 Jul 1957. *DV* 14 Sep 1955. *DV* 10 Jul 1957, p. 3. *Exb* 24 Jul 1957, pp. 4358-59. *FD* 10 Jul 1957, p. 8. *Har* 13 Jul 1957, p. 112. *HR* 11 Jan 1957, p. 14. *HR* 29 Mar 1957, p. 54. *HR* 10 Jul 1957, p. 3. *LAEx* 28 Apr 1957. *LAT* 8 Aug 1957. *MPD* 10 Jul 1957. *MPHPD* 13 Jul 1957, p. 449. *New Yorker* 20 Jul 1957. *NYT* 11 Jul 1957, p. 21. *Var* 10 Jul 1957, p. 6.

THE BAND PLAYED ON *see* **SYNCOPATION**

BANDIT QUEEN (Latino)

Lippert Productions, Inc. *Dist* Lippert Productions, Inc. 22 Dec **1950**; Prod: mid-Sep—late Sep 1950 [©Lippert Productions, Inc.; 18 Nov 1950; LP584]. Sd; b&w. 6285 ft. 68-70 min. Passed by the National Board of Review. PCA cert no. 14899.

Assoc exec Jack Leewood. *Exec prod* Murray Lerner. *Pres* Robert L. Lippert. [*Prod* William Berke]. [*Dir* William Berke]. *Asst dir* John Francis Murphy. *Story* Victor West. *Scr* Victor West and Budd Lesser. *Addl dial* Orville Hampton. *Dir of photog* Ernest Miller. *Spec eff* Ray Mercer. *Film ed* Carl Pierson. *Set dec* Vin Taylor. *Ward supv* Alfred Berke. *Mus comp and cond* Albert Glasser. *Eng* Glen Glenn and Bob Callan. *Makeup artist* Bob Cowan. *Prod mgr* William Magginetti. *Set continuity* Sam Freedle.

Cast: Barbara Britton [(*Lola Montalvo, also known as Zara*)], Willard Parker [(*Dan Hinsdale*)], Philip Reed [(*Carlos Murietta, also known as Joachim and Carlos Del Rio*)], Barton MacLane [(*Jim Harden*)], Martin Garralaga [(*Father Antonio*)], Victor Kilian [(*Jose Montalvo*)], Thurston Hall [(*Governor*)], Angie [(*Niño*)], Anna Demetrio [(*Maria*)], Paul Marion [(*Manuel*)], Mike Conrad [(*Capt. Gray*)], Margia Dean [(*Carol Grayson*)], Minna Phillips [(*Mrs. Grayson*)], John Merton [(*Hank*)], [Pepe Hern (*Rafael*)], [Lalo Rios (*Juan*)], [Cecil Weston (*Zara Montalvo*)], [Carl Pitti (*McWilliams*)], [Hugh Hooker (*Dawson*)], [Jack Ingram (*Barton*)], [Jack Perrin (*Mr. Grayson*)], [Felipe Turich (*Ortiz*)], [Joe Dominguez (*Mr. Morales*)], [Trina Varela (*Mrs. Morales*)], [Nancy Laurents (*Ann*)], [Roy Butler (*Guard*)], [Elias Gamboa (*Waiter*)], [Chuck Roberson (*Deputy*)].

Western. [*Print viewed*]. During the gold rush in California, young Lola Montalvo witnesses her parents, Jose and Zara, lynched by a gang when they try to oppose the state's inflated tax rates. Lola rushes to report the murders to her parents' friend, Father Antonio, at Mission San Sebastian. Later, she visits Sheriff Jim Harden in the nearby town of Madera, but she recognizes him as one of the murderers and decides not to make a complaint. When Lola meets attorney Dan Hinsdale, he explains that because the Montalvos owed taxes on their mine at the time of their death, the state took possession of it. The state, in turn, sold the mine for a fraction of its true value, and, Hinsdale says, he purchased it. Later, Harden and Hinsdale, who are planning to take over all of the gold mines in the area, plot to murder a miner named Dawson. At the mission, Carlos Murietta, also known as the bandit Joachim, introduces himself to Lola as Carlos Del Rio. With Carlos's encouragement, Lola begins her life of crime as a bandit called Zara. One day, Carlos, Lola and some townspeople, who are also angry about the high taxes, attack one of Harden's men who was assigned to guard the Montalvo mine. Later, Harden finds the corpse and a note from Zara nearby. At the mission, a cook named Maria tries to convince Lola to forsake her bandit ways, while a dwarf named Niño warns her that Harden's men are looking for her. Later, when another member of his gang, McWilliams, is found dead, Hinsdale realizes that those who lynched the Montalvos are being targeted. That evening, unaware that Lola is Zara, Hinsdale tells her that he will try to trap the bandit by staging a fake gold shipment. After Hank, another of Harden's men, tries to double-cross the gang, Harden kills him. At a party at Hinsdale's house, Hinsdale proposes to Lola, but asks for some time to consider her response. While dining, the guests are discussing the infamous Zara, when Hank's corpse is suddenly thrown through the window with a note attached threatening: "You're next." The next day, Father Antonio, who is aware of Lola's double life, warns her that the military has been called in to apprehend her. After Lola hijacks the real gold shipment, she escapes and visits the jail to see Carlos, who was captured by Harden's men. Once inside, Lola slips into the back room, quickly changes into her bandit clothes and forces Harden and his men into the cell at gunpoint. She allows Carlos to escape, changes back and then takes her time to release the men from the cell. At the mission, Carlos admits that he is Joachim, and Lola accepts his proposal of marriage. Harden and Hinsdale then ride to the mission and demand that Carlos return to jail, but Father Antonio explains that he has taken sanctuary at the mission. Later, Carlos and Lola are married, but must escape the festivities when Harden and Hinsdale arrive. When Hinsdale realizes that Zara is Lola, she shoots him. After Capt. Gray arrests Hinsdale and the gang, he promises to urge a pardon for Carlos and Lola, after which Maria presents them with their wedding cake. *Bandits. California–History–1846-1850. Impersonation and imposture. Lawyers.*

Murder. Priests. Dwarfs. Escapes. Firearms. Gangs. Gold mines. Gold rushes. Investigations. Lynching. Missions. Officers (Military). Pardons. Parties. Proposals (Marital). Threats. Traps. Weddings.

Note: According to a Jan 1950 *DV* news item, Lippert Productions purchased a story by Ken Bohn titled "The Bandit Queen." Victor West is credited onscreen as the film's story writer, however, and Bohn's contribution to the completed picture, if any, has not been determined.

Box 9 Dec 1950. *DV* 24 Jan 1950. *DV* 22 Nov 1950, p. 4. *FD* 4 Dec 1950, p. 4. *HR* 15 Sep 1950, p. 10. *HR* 29 Sep 1950, p. 12. *HR* 22 Nov 1950, p. 4. *MPHPD* 2 Dec 1950, p. 599. *Var* 29 Nov 1950, p. 22.

BAPTISM OF FIRE see THE GLORY BRIGADE

BAR-MITZVAH (Yiddish language)

S & L Film Co. *Dist* State Rights. **1935**; World premiere in New York City: 15 Mar 1935 [ⓒS & L Film Co.; 15 Mar 1935; LP5447]. Sd; b&w. 8 reels, 7,265 ft. 81 min. Yiddish language with English subtitles.

Dir Henry Lynn. *Scr* Henry Lynn. *Photog* Robert J. Marshall and George H. Wicke, Jr. *Ed* Jack Kemp. *Mus dir* Jack Stillman. *Sd eng* Jerry Barton.

Source: Based on the play *Bar-Mitzvah* by Boris Thomashefsky (production undetermined).

Cast: BORIS THOMASHEFSKY (*Israel*), Regina Zuckerberg (*Leah*), Anita Chayes (*Rosalie*), Peter Graf (*Yeruchim*), Gertrude Bulman (*Feigele*), Morris Strassberg (*Abraham*), Leah Naomi (*Sara*), Sam Colton (*Sam*), Morris Tarlowsky (*Alexander*), Benjamin Schechtman (*Yudele*).

Yiddish, Domestic, Melodrama, with songs. [*Print viewed*]. On the eve of his son Yudele's *bar mitvah*, Israel, whose wife Leah was reported to have died in a shipwreck ten years earlier when she left their European town to visit her mother in America, returns from Warsaw with a new wife, Rosalie. Unknown to Israel, Rosalie is conniving with a man whom she says is her brother to get Israel's money. Israel's family is not happy with his new bride. After Yudele falls asleep in front of his mother's portrait and dreams of her singing to him, Leah, who recovered slowly after being rescued ten years earlier, returns and learns from her in-laws about Israel's recent marriage. She stays with Yeruchim, the cantor, but comes to the *bar mitzvah* service to hear her son's speech. During the service, when Yudele says the *Kaddish*, the prayer for the dead, Leah cries. When Israel sees Rosalie and her "brother" embrace, the "brother" pulls a gun and demands Israel's money. Israel's daughter Feigele, who has just become engaged to Sam, an American Jew, calls the police. During a struggle, Sam gets the gun, and after the police identify Rosalie and her "brother" as an infamous husband and wife confidence team, Leah is reunited with her family. *Bar mitzvah. Confidence games. Jews. Long-lost relatives. Marriage. Missing persons, Assumed dead. Mothers and sons. Cantors, Jewish. Dreams. Fights. Impersonation and imposture. Prayer. Shipwrecks. Warsaw (Poland).*

Note: According to *FD*, *Bar Mitzvah* was produced in New York. In Nov 1938, proceeds from showings in Kansas City went to the B.M.B.G. Polish Aid society to provide funds for Polish Jews. Modern sources give the following information: *Bar Mitzvah* did well financially and was one of the first American Yiddish pictures to reach Europe; Jack Stillman and Henry Lyon were the producers; and it was the only sound film with Yiddish theater legend Boris Thomashefsky. Although the film includes various songs, no information concerning their titles has been located.

FD 13 Mar 1935, p. 6. *FD* 20 Mar 1935, p. 11. *Kansas City Jewish Chronicle* 11 Nov 1938.

THE BAR SINISTER (African Americans)

Edgar Lewis Productions. *Dist* State Rights; Abrams & Werner. Apr **1917**. Si; b&w. 8 reels.

Dir Edgar Lewis. *Scen* Anthony P. Kelly. *Cam* Edward C. Earle. *Mus accompaniment* Frederick O. Hanks and Sol Levy.

Cast: Preston Rollow (*Colonel George Stilliter*), Mary Doyle (*Annabel*), William Anderson (*Sam Davis*), Florence St. Leonard (*Lindy*), Hedda Nova (*Belle Davis*), Mitchell Lewis (*Ben Swift*), Frank Reilly (*Big Tom*), George Dangerfield (*Luke Waller*), J. R. Chamberlin (*Nick Benson*), Victor Sutherland (*Page Warren*), Jules Cowles (*Buck*), W. J. Gross, William A. Williams, Mack Wright.

Social, Drama. Lindy, the wife of a black man whose death resulted from the cruelty of his employer, Colonel George Stilliter, kidnaps the colonel's daughter and with her own child, escapes to another part of the South. Fifteen years later, Belle lives in a small town with Lindy, and though the latter insists that she is her daughter, it is difficult for Belle to believe that she is black, and she rebels against

the thought. Mulatto Ben Swift falls in love with Belle, but she loves Page Warren, a white man who hates blacks. Belle attempts to hide her origins from Page, but when he discovers that she is part black, he spurns her. Belle's instincts are finally proved correct when Lindy confesses that Belle is of white blood and the daughter of a distinguished man. *African Americans. African Americans–Mixed blood. Kidnapping. Revenge. Confession. Family life. Racism. United States–South.*

Note: This was the first film made by Edgar Lewis Productions. Frank G. Hall obtained the world rights. A private showing was given in New York on 18 Apr 1917.

ETR 28 Apr 1917, p. 1463. *Motog* 5 May 1917, p. 964. *MPN* 5 May 1917, p. 2855. *MPW* 7 Apr 1917, p. 44. *MPW* 28 Apr 1917, p. 554. *MPW* 5 May 1917, p. 751, 808, 854. *NYDM* 26 May 1917, p. 31. *Var* 20 Apr 1917, p. 25. *Wid's* 26 Apr 1917, pp. 257-58.

THE BARATARIANS see THE BUCCANEER

EL BARCO DEL AMOR see EAST IS WEST

BAREFOOT BATTALION (Greek language)

Peter Boudoures Film Co. *Dist* Leon L. Brandt Associates; Twentieth Century-Fox Film Corp. Original release **1954**; dubbed version Jul **1956** Sd; b&w. 10 [1954 version] or 8 [1956 version] reels. 89 [1954 version] or 63 [1956 version] min. 1954 version: Greek, with English subtitles; 1956 version: (Dubbed) English language.

Prod [*credit on 1954 version*]; *Exec prod* [*credit on 1956 version*] Peter Boudoures. *Prod* [*credit on 1956 version*] Gregg Tallas. *Dir* Gregg Tallas. *Orig story* Gregg G. Tallas and Nico Katsiotes. *Scr* Nico Katsiotes. [*Wrt of English subtitles*] Leo Katcher]. *Cam* Michel Gasiadis. *Asst cam* Giorgios Athanasiadis. *Gaffer* Kostas Karanasos. *Ed* Gregg Tallas. *Asst film ed* Despina Kontogiorgi. *Mus* Mikis Theodorakis. *conducting* The Athens Symphony Orchestra. *Sd rec* Mikias Damalas. *Mus rec* Vassilios Krondiras. *Sd eff* James Graham. *Re-rec* Glen Glenn. *Unit mgr* Kostas Doukas.

Cast: Nicos Fermas [(*Black marketeer, known as Captain Blackie*)], Vassilios Frakadakis [(*Andreas*)], Antonios Voulgaris [(*Niko*)], Stavros Krozos [(*Dimitri, as a boy*)], Kitty Keny [(*Martha*)], Manoles Regas [(*Professor*)], Evangelos Giotopoulos [(*Jacob*)], Giorgios Axiotis [(*Thanos*)], Christos Sokouroglou [(*Joe*)], Nikos Zaxarias, Apostolos Bekiaris [(*Dimitri, as a man*)], Elias Papadopoulos, Lola Xazexrestou, Introducing Maria Costi [(*Alexandra*)], [Chet Huntley (*Narrator of foreword*)].

Youth, War, Drama. [*Print viewed*]. In Salonika, Greece, in 1953, a barefoot boy named Stavros awakens from his slumbers on a boat and urinates in the sea. On shore, he attempts to steal a purse from a woman in a crowded market area, then runs off. Dimitri, a young man, follows the boy and catches him. He searches the boy and when Stavros begins to cry and says he has no family, Dimitri explains that he only wants to help and that he himself used to steal on the street for a living. Stavros refuses to believe him, so Dimitri steals a wallet from a man buying flowers, then returns it, saying the man dropped it. Stavros suggests they become partners, but Dimitri tells him he is a teacher now and relates the following story: In 1943, during the German occupation, as a war orphan, Dimitri lives with his young sister Martha in an abandoned wrecked boat, surviving on food rations. After the Red Cross dispensary runs out of food, Dimitri finds a group of boys passing bread in a line from a German supply truck into a house. When their lookout sees the German driver returning, the boys scatter. Spying a loaf left on the street, Dimitri picks it up. The German catches him with it and throws him to the ground calling him a "dirty Greek," then drives off. When Niko, one of the boys, learns that Dimitri's sister is hungry, he goes with Dimitri to the boat, and they bring her with some meager belongings to a ruined castle outside the gate of the city, where they enter a series of caves, which Niko says was a hiding place for Greek Christians when the Turks conquered their country. Niko explains that most of the parents of the boys disappeared when the Nazis took over in 1941. After the orphanages were used for arsenals, the boys fought each other for food, but have since joined together as "The Barefoot Battalion" to provide food for themselves and others, and to work with the underground. When Andreas, the battalion's leader, arrives, he objects that a cave is no place for a little girl, but relents when Martha cries. After Dimitri takes an oath to never betray the cause of liberty, to help the sick and helpless, and to defend and protect the oppressed of his country, he goes with Niko to deliver food to the needy. As they give milk and food to Mrs. Giorgas, whose grandchild is hungry, two

people enter her home in flight from the Nazis. The woman, Alexandra, who is working with the underground resistance, hides in bed with the grandchild and pretends to sleep while the Nazis search. The man, an American fighter pilot named Joe, who was shot down off the coast, is brought to the boys' hideout. Andreas learns from Alexandra that the underground, who rescued Joe from the Nazis, is trying to smuggle him to Egypt and have contacted a ship captain willing to help, but they need money. The boys steal an olive oil shipment from a black marketeer Nazi collaborator, whom they call "Captain Blackie," and hide it in the caves, planning to sell it for the money. When Blackie tells his Nazis partners about the theft, they interrogate him, using Alexandra as a translator. Thinking that Blackie is the thief, they give him a week to recover the oil or he will lose his boat. Blackie finds Niko and Dimitri trying to sell some of the oil, but a Greek officer sides with the boys. Later, Blackie locates some of the boys at a shadow show and then follows them through the streets. When Dimitri diverts the attention of a Nazi truck driver, while the others steal cans of food from the back of the truck, Blackie informs the driver, then beats and captures Dimitri. The boy is questioned by the Nazi captain, but released after Alexandra interprets Blackie's statements incorrectly. The collaborator follows Dimitri, who makes it to the caves unseen after an air raid siren sounds and the Nazis begin to fire at Allied planes. Meanwhile, Andreas arranges with Alexandra to bring Joe and the money to a waterfront café that night at nine, when the ship captain will be waiting. Blackie wanders outside the gate to the ruins and sees boys with a cart full of oil cans. After he tells the Nazis, Alexandra asks Dimitri to warn Andreas. Dimitri brings her to the caves, and Andreas sends Joe to another hiding place until nightfall. As the boys take the oil out to hide it, Blackie sees them and recognizes Alexandra. Blackie climbs the ruins chasing after Dimitri. When Dimitri slips, Blackie catches him and attempts to smash him with an oil can, but Dimitri moves out of the way after getting hit twice, and Blackie falls off the parapet. Before he dies, he mentions Alexandra's name to the Nazis. In the present, Dimitri tells Stavros that Alexandra paid with her life for Joe to escape. Stavros says that the poor pay for a lot in this world. Dimitri tells Stavros that although stealing was their weapon in the fight for liberty, now, no one must steal. They arrive at the orphans' trade school, where Dimitri teaches, and he invites Stavros to learn a trade. Stavros starts to leave, then tries to return the money that he stole, but Dimitri tells him to keep it. Stavros then walks with Dimitri into the school. Children. Greece–History. Greeks. Nazis. Orphans. Robbery. Self-sacrifice. War victims. World War II–Resistance movements. Accidental death. Air pilots. Americans in foreign countries. Attempted murder. Black market. Boats. Bombing, Aerial. Castles. Caves. Falls from heights. Interrogation. Oaths. Police. Red Cross. Teachers. Translators. Truck drivers.

Note: Peter Boudouras, producer of this film, was a Greek-American restaurateur in San Francisco, who had been the regional director of Greek War Relief on the West Coast from 1940-1949, according to *HCN*. This was his first film. Gregg Tallas, the film's director, co-writer and editor, also a Greek American, was a veteran editor when he made the film, according to a Jun 1953 *DV* news item. (The *DV* review of the film in Jun 1954 states that Tallas was a former cameraman, not an editor; further information concerning his earlier career has not been located.) Nico Katsiotes, who co-wrote the story with Tallas and alone was credited with the screenplay, had been with Twentieth Century-Fox for years, according to *Har*. Leo Katcher, who wrote the English subtitles, was the Hollywood correspondent for a number of Greek publications. Reviews state that an actual "Barefoot Battalion" did exist during the war. According to news items, the film was shot in Athens and Salonika with a cast of non-professionals, except for Maria Costi and Nicos Fermas. This was the first film for Costi, who was brought over from Hollywood. News items disagree concerning the origin of the actors playing the boys: while *DV* states that they came from an orphanage in Salonika, *HCN* asserts they were from a reform school. The film's production cost was $38,000. It was shot without sound, using a 1920s camera and minimal additional equipment. News broadcaster Chet Huntley recorded the foreword.

The film was shown in Los Angeles by invitation only at the Academy of Motion Picture Arts & Sciences in a 97-minute version on 8 Nov 1953. When it opened in New York on 28 May 1954, in a release by Leon Brandt, it had a running time of 89 minutes. The 1954 version was released in New York and four other U.S. cities; it was also released in Greece under the title *Xypoleto, Tagma* or *Xepolyto. Tagman*, according to letters submitted to the Library of Congress by Peter Boudoures. In 1956, Twentieth Century-Fox acquired the distribution rights and released a dubbed 63-minute version in Jul. According to *Har*, the film was acclaimed at the Edinburgh Film Festival. *Har*, reviewing the 1954 version, called the film, "One of the best foreign-made pictures brought to this country in some time" and praised Tallas' "outstanding directorial work." *Exh* noted that the film was designed "along the lines of post-war realistic films" and was a "conscious attempt to emulate past successes in this type of film making." *Var* commented that it "has a

documentary flavor and shapes up as an interesting entry for art house bookings," but cautioned it "is too downbeat and much too long to rate more than average bookings in the program market." *NYT* criticized the film, maintaining that "although director Gregg Tallas starts the picture with unflinching realism, it soon slips into lagging, melodramatic pantomime."

Cue 29 May 1954. *DV* 18 Jun 1953. *DV* 3 Jun 1954. *DV* 2 Jul 1956. *Exh* 16 Jun 1954, p. 3771. *Exh* 25 Jul 1956, p. 4190. *Har* 12 Jun 1954, p. 94. *Har* 14 Jul 1956, p. 110. *HCN* 26 Aug 1953. *HR* 3 Nov 1953. *HR* 3 Jun 1954. *LADN* 29 Oct 1953. *LADN* 12 Jun 1954. *LAEx* 12 Jun 1954. *LAT* 22 Nov 1953. *LAT* 12 Jun 1954. *NYT* 29 May 1954, p. 13. *Var* 7 Oct 1953. *Var* 9 Jun 1954, p. 20.

THE BARGAIN see **ADVENTURES OF CAPTAIN FABIAN**

BARGAIN WITH BULLETS (African Americans)
Million Dollar Productions, Inc. *Dist* Million Dollar Productions, Inc. **1937**; New York premiere: 17 Sep 1937. Sd; b&w. 8 ft. 72 min. PCA cert no. 3781.
Exec prod Harry M. Popkin. *Assoc prod* Leo C. Popkin. *Dir* Harry Fraser. *Asst dir* William Nolte. *Story* Lillian Powell. *Scr story* Phil Dunham. *Photog* Roland Price. *Ed* Arthur Brooks. *Sd eng* Glen Glenn. *Prod mgr* William Nolte.
Song(s): by International Publishing Co.
Cast: Ralph Cooper (*Ed "Mugsy" Moore*), Theresa Harris (*Grace Foster*), Edward Thompson (*Lieutenant Lester*), Francis Turham (*Kay Latour*), Lawrence Criner (*Charlie Bayley*), Sam McDaniel (*Captain Holmes*), Clarence Brooks (*Bill Pierce*), Reginald Fenderson (*Dave Ellis*), John Lester Johnson (*Samson*), Billy McClain (*Judge*), Al Duval (*Jack*), Elmer Fain (*Tom*), Ray Martin (*Lige*), Les Hite, and his Cotton Club Orchestra, Eddie Barfield's Trio, Covan Studio Dancers.
African American, Gangster, Drama, with songs. [*Not viewed*]. When Harlem gangster Ed "Mugsy" Moore kills a watchman during a robbery at Zemanski's Fur Loft, he is reprimanded by Bill Pierce, the bail-bond broker who promised to fence the stolen furs. Pierce then suggests that Mugsy go into hiding for awhile. Mugsy's moll, Kay Latour, is proud of the gangster when he he threatens to kill Pierce for refusing to purchase the stolen furs from him. Meanwhile, Police Captain Holmes, who is under pressure from the commissioner to solve the case, assigns Lieutenant Lester to investigate the robbery. When Mugsy encounters a childhood friend, singer Grace Foster, she reminds him that he wanted to become a doctor when he was young and that they were meant to be sweethearts. Grace, however, soon realizes that she has lost Mugsy to Kay when she learns that he is a gangster. As the police investigation progresses, Holmes begins to suspect Mugsy, whom he knows cannot afford Kay's expensive tastes. One evening, as Mugsy is about to take Kay to a nightclub, he gets a telephone call from one his men, Dave Ellis, who tips him off to another fur heist opportunity. Mugsy immediately cancels his plans with Kay and rushes to meet with his gang. The robbery, which is handled by Mugsy's men, takes place the following morning, while Mugsy meets with Grace. When Lester is informed of the heist, he immediately suspects Mugsy, but an officer trailing the gangster attests to the fact that Mugsy was with Grace at the time the crime was committed. Later, Mugsy and Charlie Bayley, one of his men, kill Dave shortly after he is interrogated by the police. Mugsy then kills Charlie for suggesting that they take a trip to Chicago. Lester goes to Kay's apartment hoping to find Mugsy, but Mugsy sees the police there and waits until they leave before he enters. After telling Kay that he is going to his hideout near Albany for a month, Mugsy leaves. Meanwhile, a ballistics expert at the police department discovers that the gun that was used to kill both the watchman and Charlie belongs to Mugsy. After interrogating Grace, Holmes brings in Kay for questioning and she tells him where Mugsy is hiding when the captain offers her money. After putting out a fake radio broadcast to fool Mugsy into thinking that he is safe in Albany, the police descend on his hideout and arrest him. Sometime later, Kay and her new boyfriend are listening to radio as a news bulletin announces Mugsy's execution in the electric chair. African Americans. Gangsters. Molls. Murder. Singers. Albany (NY). Executions. Explosions. Friendship. Fur. Investigations. New York City–Harlem. Police. Police chiefs. Radio broadcasting. Thieves.

Note: *Bargain with Bullets* was re-released in 1945 under the title *Gangsters on the Loose*. At the time of this film's release, Million Dollar Productions had announced its intentions to produce ten black-cast pictures annually, primarily for black audiences. According to modern sources, the screen story was authored by Phil Dunham and Ralph Cooper, with Cooper also directing, and the cast included Milton Shockley (*Doc*), Art Murray (*Tom*) and Halley Harding (*Halley*). In addition, modern sources note that the picture was

the first independently produced black-cast film purchased by Loew's theater chain for exhibition in two of their smaller theaters. According to the file for the film in the MPAA/PCA Collection at the AMPAS Library, in Jun 1937, the PCA rejected the story "in toto," citing gangster themes, detailed crimes, offensive sex in the "character and conduct of Kay" and undue glorification of the character "Mugsy" as the basis for its decision. The PCA objected to other details of the story, including the suggestion that "Kay" is being kept by "Mugsy"; the "bumping off" of "Doc"; the cold-blooded killing of three men by "Mugsy"; the suggestion of an electric chair; and the final scene, in which "Mugsy's" execution is juxtaposed with "Kay" continuing her "questionable career." In Sep 1937, the PCA reviewed the film and denied it certification for various reasons, but primarily because it showed "American gangsters armed and in violent conflict with the law." A number of scenes were cut from the film following the PCA preview, and in Oct 1937, the film was granted certification.

DV 18 Sep 1937, p. 3. *HS* 25 Sep 1937, pp. 12-13.

BARNABY LEE (English Americans)

Thomas A Edison, Inc. **1917?**. Si; b&w. 4 reels.
Dir Edward H. Griffith. *Scen* E. Clement d'Art.

Source: Based on the short story "Barnaby Lee" by John Bennett in *St. Nicholas Magazine* (Nov 1900—Apr 1902).

Cast: John Tansey (*Barnaby Lee*), Sam Niblack (*Harry Lee*), Hugh Thompson (*John King*), Charles Edwards (*Philip Calvert*), William Wadsworth (*Gunner Kregier*), John Ridgeway (*The Schout Fiskaal*), Norbert Wicke (*Mynheer Van Sweringen*), Peggy Adams (*Dorothy Van Sweringen*), Jessie Stevens (*Mevrouw Barbara Van Sweringen*), Joseph Burke (*Peter Stuyvesant*), Alexander Rene (*Charles Calvert*).

Historical, Drama. In 1644, as rebels are hanged by the British after their war with Scotland, Barnaby Lee and his father sail for America, but their ship is captured by pirates and Barnaby is led to believe that his father has been killed. At the Hudson River, the ship is stopped by the sheriff of New Amsterdam, Mynheer Van Sweringen, and ordered to leave, but the pirates continue in the boat toward a trading point. Barnaby escapes and meets the sheriff's daughter Dorothy, but he is not allowed to enter the city because of his British ancestry. After an investigation reveals that the leader of the pirates is the brother of the governor of Maryland, and that Barnaby's father, who was not killed but taken prisoner, owns an estate in Maryland, Barnaby invites Dorothy and her family to Maryland to live in his new home. *Exiles. Great Britain–History–17th century. Maryland. New York City–History. Pirates. Ships. United States–History–Colonial period, ca. 1600-1775. Brothers. Escapes. Fathers and sons. Governors. Hudson River (NY). Missing persons, Assumed dead. Revolutionaries. Sheriffs.*

Note: The only information located concerning this film was from the George Kleine Papers. It was included in a list of "Edison Unreleased Subjects," and a note from 1925 mentioned that it was never nationally released, although it had some distribution. The film was probably produced in 1917, as a title sheet is dated 15 Jun 1917.

THE BARON OF ARIZONA (Latino)

Deputy Corp. *Dist* Lippert Productions, Inc. 4 Mar 1950; World premiere in Phoenix, AZ: 1 Mar 1950; Prod: late Oct—late Nov 1949 at Nassour Studios [©Deputy Corp.; 12 Feb 1950; LP2925]. Sd (RCA Sound System); b&w. 10 reels, 8,677 or 8,709 ft. 96-97 min. PCA cert no. 14333.

Pres Robert L. Lippert. *Prod* Carl K. Hittleman. *Exec asst* Murray Lerner. *Dir* SAMUEL FULLER. *Asst dir* Frank Fox. *Wrt* Samuel Fuller. *Dir of photog* James Wong Howe. [*Cam op* Curt Fetters]. [*Gaffer* Roy Black]. [*Stills* Marty Crail]. *Spec eff* Ray Mercer and [Don Steward]. *Art dir* F. Paul Sylos. *Ed* Arthur Hilton. *Set dec* Otto Seigel and [Ray Robinson]. *Ward* Alfred Berke and Kitty Major. *Mus comp and cond* Paul Dunlap. *Sd eff* Harry Coswick. *Sd eng* Garry Harris. *Makeup* Vernon Murdoch. *Hair stylist* Loretta Franzel. *Casting* Yolanda Molinari. *Dial coach* Millie Winters. [*Scr supv* Dorothy B. Cormack]. [*Grip* Joe Carpenter].

Source: Based on the article "The Baron of Arizona" by Homer Croy in *American Weekly* (Jan 1949).

Cast: Vincent Price (*James Addison Reavis, "The Baron"* [*also known as "Brother Anthony"*]), Ellen Drew (*Sofia de Peralta-Reavis, "The Baroness"*), Vladimir Sokoloff (*Pepito* [*Alvarez*]), Beulah Bondi (*Loma* [*Morales*]), Reed Hadley ([*John*] *Griff*), Robert H. Barrat (*Judge*), Robin Short ([*Tom*] *Lansing*), Tina Rome (*Rita*), Karen Kester (*Sofia, as a child*), Margia Dean (*Marquesa* [*de Santella*]), Jonathan Hale (*Governor*), Edward Keene [(*Surveyor Miller*)], Barbara Woodell [(*Carry Lansing*)], I. Stanford Jolley [(*Secretary of Interior*)], Fred Kohler, Jr. [(*Demming*)], Tristram Coffin [(*McCleary*)], Gene Roth [(*Father Guardian*)], Angelo Rosito

[(*Angie*)], Ed East, Joe Greene [(*Gunther*)], [Terry Frost (*Morelle*)], [Zachary Yaconelli (*Greco*)], [Adolfo Ornelas (*Martinez*)], [Wheaton Chambers (*Brother Gregory*)], [Robert O'Neil (*Brother Paul*)], [Stephen Harrison (*Surveyor's assistant*)].

Historical, Drama. [*Print viewed*]. In 1912, during a party at the governor's mansion to celebrate Arizona's admission to the Union, John Griff, an employee of the Department of the Interior, tells the story of the notorious James Addison Reavis, a clerk working at the land office in Santa Fe, New Mexico, who almost "stole" Arizona: In 1872, Reavis visits the home of Pepito Alvarez, a Mexican living in Phoenix. After telling Pepito that he works in the federal land office, Reavis inquires about Sofia, an infant whom Reavis left with Pepito some years previous. When Reavis meets Sofia, now a shy young girl, he tells her that he is going to bring her to live with him in Santa Fe. Reavis, who is plotting to turn himself into a phony baron, wants Sofia as his baroness and hires governess Loma Morales to school her in proper etiquette. In the meantime, Reavis spends long hours chiseling his forged land grant into a stone tablet which he will use to establish the claim of Arizona's fictitious "first baron of Arizona," Miguel de Peralta. Later, Reavis purchases some headstones to establish the births and deaths of Sofia's "parents" and then sails to Europe to complete the forgery. In Spain, he joins a monastery at which the original land grant book of King Ferdinand VI is kept. Taking the name Brother Anthony, Reavis waits three years for an opportunity to be left alone in the library so that he can alter the grants record book, giving his baron the territory of Arizona. During this time, Reavis learns from the monastery's head, Father Guardian, that a second copy of the book is kept at the Madrid castle of the Marquis de Santella. When Reavis is finally able to commit the forgery, he is caught by Father Guardian and forced to flee. Reavis steals a horse-driven cart, but it overturns along the winding monastery road. He is rescued by a band of gypsies, then travels to Madrid, and after befriending the Marquesa, convinces her to invite him to the castle. There, Reavis alters the entry in Santella's book, returns to Arizona, marries Sofia and claims Arizona. Suspecting forgery, the surveyor general, Miller, investigates the claim, which is validated by the discovery of the tablets. When Reavis begins evicting the residents of Arizona, Griff, an expert in the art of forgery, is consulted. After the local newspaper criticizes Reavis, a displaced landowner, Tom Lansing, firebombs his office in town. Reavis then rejects a government offer to buy the territory for $25,000,000, and he and Sofia are summoned to federal court to defend their claim. Griff states that he cannot prove that Reavis' claim is false, but later, Pepito tells Reavis that he plans to break his silence and tell Griff about Sofia's real parents, who were Indians. Reavis attempts to flee the country, but Griff arranges for an immediate local trial. After Pepito is shot by an angry mob, Reavis is nearly lynched, but saves himself by reminding the displaced landowners that they need his testimony in order to reclaim their land. Years later, when Reavis is released from prison, he is surprised to see his faithful wife, a now recovered Pepito and Loma waiting to take him home. *Arizona. Forgers and forgery. Impersonation and imposture. Land rights. James Addison Reavis. United States–History– 19th century. Castles. Employment. Escapes. Eviction. Governesses. Graves. Gypsies. Libraries and librarians. Madrid (Spain). Mansions. Marriage. Mexican Americans. Mobs. Monks. Newspapers. Parties. Phoenix (AZ). Prisons. Riots. Santa Fe (NM). Ships. Shootings. Statehood (American politics). Surveyors.*

Note: Onscreen credits note that "the title of this Motion Picture appeared on an article published by: *The American Weekly*." The film's opening credits read: "Robert L. Lippert presents Samuel Fuller's *The Baron of Arizona*." Fuller's other screen credit reads: "Written and directed by Samuel Fuller." According to a 30 Aug 1949 *HR* news item, Fuller wrote a novel based on his research for the film, which he planned to publish following the picture's completion. James Addison Reavis was born in Missouri in 1843, and as depicted in the film, was found guilty of attempting to steal a major portion of Arizona. He served two years in a federal penitentiary and paid a fine of $5,000. He died in 1914. According to *HR*, the film was shot on location in Florence, AZ. According to a 24 Oct 1949 *HR* news item, a federal lawsuit was filed by producer-director Sam White against Hearst Publishing Co., publishers of *American Weekly*, over "alleged plagiarism of material later sold by the Hearst firm for the basis of [the film]." The report notes that the plagiarized article was originally published in a 1945 issue of *True*, and the disposition of the suit is not known. According to a 14 Feb 1950 *HR* news item, the studio arranged for a special screening of the film for Arizona's governor Dan E. Garvey, in conjunction with the 38th anniversary of the state's admission into the Union. Modern sources include the following in the cast: Stuart Holmes, Stanley Price, Sam Flint and Richard Cramer. A modern source notes that a short called *The Baron of Arizona* was produced for television in 1956.

Box 18 Feb 1950. *DN* 3 Mar 1950. *DV* 8 Feb 1950, p. 4. *FD* 14 Feb 1950, p. 6. *HR* 23 Aug 1949, p. 7. *HR* 30 Aug 1949, p. 4. *HR* 24 Oct 1949, p. 13. *HR* 4 Nov 1949, p. 14. *HR* 18 Nov 1949, p. 12. *HR* 22 Dec 1949, p. 18. *HR* 1 Feb 1950, p. 14. *HR* 8 Feb 1950, p. 3. *HR* 8 Feb 1950, p. 12. *HR* 14 Feb 1950, p. 10. *MPHPD* 18 Feb 1950, p. 198. *NYT* 23 Jun 1950, p. 29. *Var* 15 Feb 1950, p. 13.

BARRERAS SOCIALES see **DEL MISMO BARRO**

THE BARRICADE (Jewish Americans)

Robertson-Cole Co. *Dist* R-C Pictures. 2 Oct **1921** [©R-C Pictures; 2 Oct 1921; LP17108]. Si; b&w. 6 reels, 5,700 ft.

Dir William Christy Cabanne. *Story* Daniel Carson Goodman. *Photog* Philip Armond and William Tuers.

Cast: William H. Strauss (*Jacob Solomon*), Katherine Spencer (*Jane Stoddard*), Kenneth Harlan (*Robert Brennon*), Eugene Borden (*Sam Steiner*), Dorothy Richards (*Doris Solomon*), James Harrison (*Phillip Stoddard*), John O'Connor (*Tim*).

Melodrama. On New York's East Side, Jacob Solomon and Michael Brennon are partners in a cigar store. Michael dies, and his son, Robert, is adopted by Jacob and becomes a successful physician in the neighborhood. He meets and falls in love with Jane Stoddard, a wealthy society girl, and after their marriage she induces him to forsake his East Side friends and open a Fifth Avenue practice. Jacob is heartbroken when he is snubbed by Robert and does not reveal that he mortgaged his home to pay for Robert's education. Robert and his wife quarrel when her friends discover that Jacob is the young physician's foster father; returning to his home, Robert finds that Jacob has lost everything. There is a reconciliation between them, and Robert moves back to the East Side. His wife acknowledges the mistake she has made and is forgiven by Robert. *Class distinction. Irish. Jews. New York City–East Side. Physicians. Tobacconists.*

ETR 12 Nov 1921, p. 1703. *FD* 9 Oct 1921.

THE BARRIER (Native Americans)

Rex Beach Pictures Co. *Dist* State Rights. Feb **1917**. Si; b&w. 10 reels.

Supv Rex Beach and Benjamin B. Hampton. *Dir* Edgar Lewis. *Scen* Adrian Gil-Spear. *Cam* Edward Earle. *Film ed* Paul E. Maschke.

Source: Based on the novel *The Barrier* by Rex Beach (New York, 1907).

Cast: Mabel Julienne Scott (*Necia/Merridy*), Russell Simpson (*John Gaylord/John Gale*), Howard Hall (*Dan Bennett/Ben Stark*), Victor Sutherland (*Lieut. Meade Burrell*), Mitchell Lewis (*Poleon Doret*), Edward Roseman (*Runnion*), W. J. Gross (*"No Creek" Lee*), Mary Kennevan Carr (*Alluna*).

Drama. The barrier which stands between Lieutenant Meade Burrell and Necia, the daughter of Alaskan trader John Gale, has its origin in her Indian blood. Burrell, who has declared his love for Necia, is released from his proposal of marriage when she realizes what a sacrifice his marriage to a half-breed would be. The appearance of a gambler in the Alaskan town serves as a means of proving that Necia is actually white and not the daughter of Gale by his Indian woman, Alluna. Thus, the barrier is removed and the two lovers are united. *Indians of North America–Mixed blood. Mistaken identity. Racism. Self-sacrifice. Alaska. Fathers and daughters. Fur traders. Indians of North America. Marriage.*

Note: This was the first production of the Rex Beach Picture Company. According to contemporary news items, it was shot on location in the Alaskan Yukon in Aug 1916 using the Kinemacolor process. *Wid's* related that after the trade showing, scenes from the end were shortened and Rex Beach wrote a number of new titles. Metro-Goldwyn-Mayer Pictures released a film based on the same source on 8 Mar 1926. George Hill directed this version, which starred Norman Kerry, Henry B. Walthall and Lionel Barrymore (see below). Paramount released a film based on the same source in 1937, which starred Leo Carrillo, Jean Parker and James Ellison, and was directed by Leslie Selander (see below).

ETR 27 Jan 1917, p. 564. *Motog* 10 Feb 1917, p. 315. *MPN* 27 Jan 1917, p. 588. *MPW* 27 Jan 1917, p. 545. *NYDM* 26 Aug 1916, p. 33. *NYDM* 20 Jan 1917, p. 30. *Var* 2 Jun 1916, p. 14. *Wid's* 15 Feb 1917, pp. 101-02.

THE BARRIER (Native Americans)

Metro-Goldwyn-Mayer Corp.; controlled by Loew's Inc. *Dist* Metro-Goldwyn-Mayer Distributing Corp. 8 Mar **1926** [©Metro-Goldwyn-Mayer Corp.; 5 Apr 1926; LP22600]. Si; b&w. 7 reels, 6,480 ft.

Dir George Hill. *Scen* Harvey Gates. *Photog* Max Fabian and Ira H. Morgan.

Source: Based on the novel *The Barrier* by Rex Beach (New York, 1908).

Cast: Norman Kerry (*Meade Burrell*), Henry B. Walthall (*Gale* [*Gaylord*]), Lionel Barrymore (*Stark Bennett*), Marceline Day

(*Necia*), George Cooper (*Sergeant Murphy*), Bert Woodruff (*No Creek Lee*), Princess Neola (*Alluna*), Mario Carillo (*Poleon*), Pat Harmon (*First mate*), Shannon Day (*Necia's Indian mother*).

Northwest, Melodrama. During a storm off the coast of Alaska, Bennett, a brutal sea captain, forces his wife to assist his men, and she is fatally hurt in an accident. Seaman Gaylord thereupon agrees to take her child from the influence of its father. Seventeen years later, Gale (*i.e.,* Gaylord) is a storekeeper at Flambeau, Alaska. He has reared the child, Necia, as his daughter in ignorance of her half-caste parentage. Although she is loved by Poleon Doret, a half-breed, she falls under the influence of Lieut. Meade Burrell, a Virginia aristocrat stationed in the North. When Bennett's ship comes into the port, he reveals the truth about the girl's parentage, and Burrell is stunned. Necia resolves to leave with her brutish father without seeing Meade again. When their ship is ice-jammed, the crew deserts, but Burrell arrives over the ice, leaves the captain unconscious, and rescues Necia; Bennett is destroyed in an ice floe, and the lovers are happily united. *Alaska. Ice floes. Indians of North America–Mixed blood. Parentage. Sea captains. Traders. Virginians.*

Note: For other versions of *The Barrier*, see entries above and below.

FD 4 Apr 1926. *MPW* 3 Apr 1926. *NYT* 22 Mar 1926, p. 16. *Var* 24 Mar 1926, p. 39.

THE BARRIER (Native Americans, Native Alaskans)

Harry Sherman Productions, Inc. *Dist* Paramount Pictures, Inc. 12 Nov **1937**; *Prod:* early Jul—early Aug 1937 at General Service Studios [©Paramount Pictures, Inc.; 12 Nov 1937; LP7581]. Sd (Western Electric Wide Range System); b&w. 93 min. Passed by the National Board of Review. PCA cert no. 3751.

Pres ADOLPH ZUKOR. *Prod* Harry Sherman. *Dir* Lesley Selander. *Asst dir* Ralph Slosser, Joe Dill and V. O. Smith. *Scr* Bernard Schubert. *Add'l seq* Harrison Jacobs. *Add'l dial* Mordaunt Shairp. *Photog* George Barnes. *Operative cam* George Nogle. *Art dir* Lewis J. Rachmil. *Film ed* Thomas Neff and Robert Warwick, Jr. *Ward* Earl Moser. *Mus dir* Boris Morros. *Orig mus* Gerard Carbonara. [*Mus* Maurice Lawrence]. *Sd rec* Earl Sitar. *Prod mgr* Eugene Strong and [Jack Vorshell]. *Spec prop* Robert Lander.

Song(s): "Moonlit Paradise" and "Song of the Wild," words and music by Jack Stern and Harry Tobias.

Source: Based on the novel *The Barrier* by Rex Beach (New York, 1908).

Cast: Leo Carrillo (*Poleon* [*Doret*]), Jean Parker (*Necia*), James Ellison (*Lieutenant Burrell*), Otto Kruger ([*Ben*] *Stark*), Robert Barrat (*John Gale*), Andy Clyde (*"No Creek" Lee*), Addison Richards (*Runnion*), Sara Haden (*Alluna*), J. M. Kerrigan (*Sergeant Thomas*), [Fernando Alvarado (*Johnny*)], [Sally Martin (*Molly*)], [Alan Davis (*Sergeant Tobin*)].

Northwest, Drama, with songs. [*Print viewed*]. In the 1890s, among the residents of Flambeau, Alaska, a small mining town near the Canadian border, are gold prospectors John Gale and "No Creek" Lee (the only man in town who doesn't have a creek named after him), and a big-hearted, singing French fur trapper named Poleon Doret. Gale lives with an Indian woman, Alluna, and a young woman, Necia, whom he calls his daughter. In reality, she is the daughter of another Indian, Merridy, a woman Gale had loved, but who married another man, Bennett, who mistreated her. When Necia was three, Merridy summoned Gale for help and asked him to take care of Necia while she confronted Bennett about his abuse. Although Merridy planned to join Gale and Necia, she never came, and Gale was charged with kidnapping and murder. To save the child, Gale changed her name to Necia and became an outlaw. When the U.S. Army, led by Lieutenant Burrell, sets up a post in Flambeau, the town booms. Among the newcomers is Bennett, who is using the alias of Stark. He has been tracking Gale for fifteen years and plans to have him arrested and to steal Necia from him. Although Poleon, who has grown up with Necia, is deeply in love with her, she falls in love with Burrell. Alluna warns her that a white man will never marry a "half-breed," after which Necia confronts Burrell, who intimates that their parting would be the best thing for her. In a state of grief, Necia wanders off alone in the woods and Stark follows, sending her down the river to a mission. Meanwhile, in town, Gale has decided to confess all to Burrell in order to secure Necia's future with him. When Stark orders Burrell to arrest Gale, Gale confronts Stark and both men are wounded. As Stark lays dying, he tells Gale he has "Merridy," and Poleon runs to the river to rescue Necia. He arrives in time to stop her from being accosted by her oarsman. Burrell gets a signed confession

about Merridy's murder from Stark before he dies, and the Miners Committee clears Gale of blame in Stark's death. Poleon gallantly gives up Necia to Burrell and leaves Flambeau singing in a canoe. *Alaska. False accusations. Indians of North America–Mixed blood. Mining towns. Self-sacrifice. Trading posts. Battered women. Canada. Fathers and daughters. Gold rushes. Indians of North America. Justice. Kidnapping. Lynching. Murder. Officers (Military). Outlaws. Prospectors. Revenge. Romantic rivalry. Singers. United States. Army.*

Note: The title card for this film reads: "Rex Beach's *The Barrier*." The film was shot on location at Mount Baker National Park, WA. According to a *MPH* "Pictorial Preview" article about this film, it "does not include a single process shot." The article also states that producer Harry Sherman had hoped for seven years to make this film. In a location news item in *HR*, Jack Vorshell is listed as production manager and Joseph Pickle as assistant director. "Joseph Pickle" was apparently a nickname for Joe Dill. A 16 Feb 1937 news item in *HR* announced the departure the following week of Harry Sherman, Eugene Strong and Edward Ludwig (who was then set to direct) for location shooting in Alaska, although the location and production schedule later changed. Earlier versions of *The Barrier* include the 1917 Rex Beach Pictures Co. film, directed by Edgar Lewis and starring Russell Simpson and Mabel Julienne Scott and the 1926 M-G-M film, directed by George Hill and starring Norman Kerry, Henry B. Walthall, Lionel Barrymore and Marceline Day (see above).

DV 28 Oct 1937, p. 3. *HR* 16 Feb 1937, p. 3. *HR* 12 Jul 1937, p. 10. *HR* 9 Aug 1937, p. 3, 14. *HR* 28 Oct 1937, p. 3. *MPD* 29 Oct 1937, p. 13. *MPH* 18 Sep 1937, pp. 14-15. *MPH* 6 Nov 1937, p. 36. *NYT* 27 Nov 1937, p. 21. *Var* 3 Nov 1937, p. 14.

BATAAN (African Americans, Jewish Americans, Latino, Multi-ethnic)

Metro-Goldwyn-Mayer Corp.; controlled by Loew's Inc. *Dist* Loew's Inc. Jun—Aug 1943; New York opening: week of 3 Jun 1943; Prod: 30 Nov 1942—3 Feb 1943 [©Loew's Inc.; 25 May 1943; LP12096]. Sd (Western Electric Sound System); b&w. 10,275 ft. 110 or 113-114 min. Passed by the National Board of Review. PCA cert no. 9122.

Prod Irving Starr. *Dir* Tay Garnett. [*Asst dir* William Lewis]. *Orig scr* Robert D. Andrews. *Dir of photog* Sidney Wagner. [*Cam* George Bourne and Harry Downard]. *Spec eff* Arnold Gillespie and Warren Newcombe. *Art dir* Cedric Gibbons. *Assoc* Lyle Wheeler. *Film ed* George White. *Set dec* Edwin B. Willis. *Assoc* Glen Barner. *Mus score* Bronislau Kaper. [*Cond* Nat W. Finston]. *Rec dir* Douglas Shearer. *Makeup created by* Jack Dawn. *Tech adv* L. S. Chappelear. [*Unit mgr* Arch Smith].

Song(s): "St. Louis Blues," words and music by W. C. Handy.

Cast: Robert Taylor (*Sergeant Bill Dane*), George Murphy (*Lieut. Steve Bentley*), Thomas Mitchell (*Corp. Jake Feingold*), Lloyd Nolan (*Corp. Barney Todd [previously known as Danny Burns]*), Lee Bowman (*Capt. Henry Lassiter*), Robert Walker (*Leonard Purckett*), Desi Arnaz ([*Pvt.*] *Felix Ramirez*), Barry Nelson ([*Pvt.*] *F[rancis] X[avier] Matowski*), Phillip Terry ([*Pvt.*] *Matthew Hardy*), Roque Espiritu (*Corp. Juan Katigbak*), Kenneth Spencer ([*Pvt.*] *Wesley Eeps*), J. Alex Havier ([*Pvt.*] *Yankee Salazar*), Tom Dugan (*Sam Malloy*), Donald Curtis (*Lieutenant*), [Mary McLeod (*Nurse Elsie McAlister*)], [Bud Geary (*Infantry officer*)], [Ernie Alexander (*Wounded soldier*)], [Phil Schumacher (*Machine gunner*)], [Tom Yuen (*Filipino*)], [Beal Wong, Wing Foo, Bruce Wong, Luke Chan (*Japanese soldiers*)].

World War II, Drama. [*Print viewed*]. As civilians and American and Filipino forces are being driven out of Manila by the invading Japanese, Sgt. Bill Dane and Corp. Jake Feingold of the U.S. infantry are assigned to assist cavalry captain Henry Lassiter in destroying a bridge along the Bataan penisula. The bridge spans a mountainous jungle ravine, and Lassiter's unit is stationed on one side, abutting a cliff. In addition to Dane and Feingold, Lassiter's ragtag unit consists of eleven disenfranchised men: pilot Lieut. Steve Bentley and his disabled plane; Corp. Barney Todd of the signal battalion; young, naïve Leonard Purckett, until recently a musician in the Navy; Pvt. Felix Ramirez of the tank corps, a former member of the California National Guard; Matthew Hardy of the medical battalion; Corp. Juan Katigbak of the Philippine Army Air Force; engineer Pvt. Francis Xavier Matowski; demolitions expert Pvt. Wesley Eeps, a black man; former boxer Pvt. Yankee Salazar of the Philippine Scouts; and Sam Malloy, a cook from the motor transport crew. Dane, a no-nonsense career soldier, explains to the men that they are expected to destroy the bridge as many times as the Japanese rebuild it, in order to buy time for General Douglas MacArthur's troops to the south. Later, in private, Dane questions Todd about his past, noting that Todd resembles a soldier he once knew named Danny Burns. Dane states that, years before, Burns was arrested for killing a man in a gambling

dispute and when Dane, then an M.P., was assigned to guard him, took advantage of his trust and escaped. The recalcitrant Todd dismisses Dane's insinuations and advises him to "watch his back." Soon after, the men blow up the bridge, but their victory celebration is cut short when Capt. Lassiter is killed by a sniper. Although Dane discourages them from giving Lassiter a funeral, the men insist on a proper burial, and Eeps, an aspiring preacher, delivers a brief eulogy. Later, after Dane gives each man their assignment, which includes continuous manning of the unit's machine guns, he asks for a volunteer to climb a tree and scan for the enemy. Matowski volunteers and no sooner does he reach the top of the tree, than he is shot down and killed. With two men dead, Dane sends Felix and the multi-skilled Purckett to help Bentley repair his nearby plane. Dane and Todd then toss grenades at the bridge, which the Japanese have already begun to rebuild, and during their attack, Dane notices that Todd throws left-handed, just like Burns did. After Dane and Todd narrowly escape the Japanese's return fire, Salazar asks permission to search for more artillery. Dane denies his request, but Salazar sneaks off on his own, only to be found stabbed to death a short time later. At the same time, the jazz-loving Felix comes down with malaria and is ordered to bed. The Japanese then launch an aerial attack on the camp, and while Eeps and Malloy succeed in downing some planes, Malloy is killed. Afterward, through the jungle fog, the men see the slain, tortured body of Katigbak, who earlier had gone to work on the plane's carburetor, dangling by a rope from a tree. The next day, Felix, delirious with malarial fever, recites a Latin prayer in front of Hardy and Dane, then dies. Aware that their time is limited, Bentley announces he will attempt a takeoff that night and suggests that they all leave together. Dane refuses to give up the mission, but orders the feverish Hardy, a conscientious objector who gave the last dose of quinine to Felix, to accompany Bentley. When Todd threatens to leave with Bentley, Dane assures him that he will be shot if he deserts. That night, under heavy cover from Feingold, Todd, Purckett and Eeps, Dane helps Bentley to start the plane. Although Bentley's repair job proves successful, he is wounded by the Japanese before getting off the ground. Hardy stumbles back to camp and tells Dane that Bentley wants to load two boxes of dynamite on his plane. The dying Bentley then deliberately crashes his plane into the bridge, causing a huge explosion. Soon after, a delirious Hardy, feeling guilty about Bentley's sacrifice, runs madly into the jungle hurling a grenade, and is shot down. Later, at his machine gun, Purckett notices that the "foliage" is moving and alerts Kane. Dane waits until the camouflaged Japanese are close to their guns, then signals his men to begin firing. Although many Japanese are slain in the brutal, close attack, Eeps and Feingold are also killed. After narrowly escaping death, Purckett, whose only wish was to "kill a Jap," realizes his arm has been wounded, and Todd bandages the injury. At Dane's insistence, Todd then offers to help Purckett write an optimistic letter to his mother. Immediately after finishing, however, Purckett is killed by a sniper, and Dane deduces that the killer must be hiding among some Japanese corpses. While Dane and Todd inspect the bodies, Todd is shot in the back by the sniper. Dane finishes off the sniper, then takes Todd back to camp. Before dying, Todd admits that he is, in fact, Burns, but offers no apology to Dane, who earlier had offered to forget the past. Now alone, an exhausted Dane digs his own grave, then dozes off while waiting at his machine gun for the enemy. Suddenly realizing that the Japanese have surrounded him, Dane startles awake and, from his grave, opens fire on the swarming enemy, doing his duty to the deadly end. *Bataan (Philippines). Combat. Japan. Army. Self-sacrifice. Soldiers. United States. Army. African Americans. Air pilots, Military. Airplanes. Aliases. Bombing, Aerial. Bridges. Burial. Confession. Cooks. Duty. Engineers. Explosions. Fever. Filipinos. Graves. Latino. Jews. Jungles. Letters. Malaria. Mechanics. Musicians. Nurses. Pacifism and pacifists. Polish Americans. Prayer. Snipers. United States. Army. Medical personnel. War injuries.*

Note: The working titles of this film were *Back to Bataan, Bataan Patrol* and *Bataan's Last Stand*. The film's opening credits include the following written dedication: "When Japan struck, our desperate need was time—time to marshal our new armies. Ninety-six priceless days were bought for us—with their lives—by the defenders of Bataan, the Philippine army which formed the bulk of MacArthur's infantry fighting shoulder to shoulder with Americans. To those immortal dead, who heroically stayed the wave of barbaric conquest, this picture is reverently dedicated." The following written statement appears at the end of the picture: "So fought the heroes of Bataan. Their sacrifice made possible our victories in the Coral and Bismarck Seas, at Midway, on New Guinea and Guadalcanal. Their spirit will lead us back to Bataan!" According

to a *HR* news item, *Bataan* was to include a disclaimer that read: "Although the characters depicted in this photoplay are fictitious, its events are adapted without exaggeration from known fact." Only the standard disclaimer was used in the completed film, however.

As depicted in the film, for three months after being driven out of Manila, American and Filipino forces defended the mountainous Bataan penisula against Japanese attack. Along with thousands of refugees, the soldiers were crowded into a ten-mile square area and many suffered from beriberi and other deficiency diseases. On 9 Apr 1942, General Edward King, who took over command after General Douglas MacArthur was sent to Australia, surrendered Bataan to the Japanese. The prisoners were subsequently forced to march to captivity, and the long trek became known as the Bataan Death March after 25,000 soldiers and civilians died along the way from mistreatment and starvation. With no supplies coming in, Lt. Gen. Jonathan M. Wainwright surrendered nearby Corregidor Island on 6 May 1942, and 10,000 troops, medical personnel and civilians were taken prisoner. Manila, Bataan and Corregidor were not liberated from the Japanese until early 1945.

HR news items and M-G-M publicity items add the following information about the production: *HR* announced in Apr 1942 that M-G-M had hired Bill Lyons and Eddie Read to write the film's screenplay. The contribution of these writers, if any, to the finished film has not been determined. In Jul 1942, in an apparent attempt to stave off any copyright infringement suits, M-G-M paid RKO $6,500 for the right to use any part of RKO's 1934 war film *The Lost Patrol*. In that picture, which was directed by John Ford, Victor McLaglen heads a unit of British soldiers who become lost in the North African desert and are killed one-by-one by unseen Arab snipers. [In his autobiography, M-G-M executive producer Dore Schary referred to *Bataan* as a "remake" of the Ford film.] Walter Pidgeon was announced as the star of *Bataan* in Oct 1942 and was to play "Sgt. Bill Dever," a "new model sergeant" in the "new model United States Army." At that time, the story featured nineteen principals, including a Native American character, each representing separate arms of the service. In mid-Nov 1942, Robert Young was announced as George Murphy's co-star, and on the first day of shooting, Richard Whorf was announced in the role of "Barney Todd" and Richard Carlson in the role of "Matthew Hardy." William Gargan was to play an Army truck driver. Although Robert Walker, a former radio star, did not make his screen debut in the film, as some reviews contend, "Leonard Purckett" marked his first significant role. The *Var* review noted that Walker won the part after a previous "Hollywood brushoff" and predicted that he would prove "one of the top 'finds' of the year." Other reviewers praised Walker's performance as well, and the actor went on to star in M-G-M's 1944 comedic military film *See Here, Private Hargroves*, after appearing in a smaller part in *Madame Curie*.

Bataan also marked the first dramatic screen role for Desi Arnaz, and won him much praise. In his autobiography, Arnaz claimed that he suggested that his character utter the same Latin confessional prayer, *Mea Culpa*, he had learned as a boy in Cuba as part of his death scene. (The ethnicity of Arnaz' character is not clearly established in the film, though he describes himself as a Californian.) Richard Derr and Leigh Sterling are listed as cast members in *HR* news items, but their participation in the final film has not been confirmed. *HR* lists Mary Elliott as a nurse, "the only female in the film," but she was not seen in the viewed print. In addition, CBCS lists Lynne Carver and Dorothy Morris as "nurses," but they were not seen in the viewed print. According to *HR*, Tommy Dorsey and his orchestra are heard offscreen during a scene in which "Felix Ramirez" listens to a radio broadcast of a jazz number. Technical adviser Lewis C. Chappelear, Jr., was a member of the 45th Infantry, Philippine Scouts, according to *HR*.

Many film historians consider *Bataan* a seminal World War II combat film. According to modern sources, M-G-M and the OWI planned the film together, and the OWI enthusiastically endorsed the script, particularly its depiction of "Lassiter's" unit as "democratic" in nature. The OWI approved the inclusion of the African American soldier, but disapproved of the condescending way in which the Filipino soldiers were first drawn. Although not the first film to depict gritty World War II combat, real or fictional, *Bataan* was distinctive in that virtually all of its action takes place on the battlefield. It was also the first World War II picture to include a pointedly multi-ethnic, multi-racial cast of characters, a device that became relatively common in later World War II films. Reviewers commented on the film's graphic, realistic depiction of war. Bosley Crowther wrote about the film: "This time, at least, a studio hasn't purposely 'prettified' facts. This time it has made a picture about war in true and ugly detail....There is sickening filth and bloodshed in it." The *Var* reviewer stated that "*Bataan* graphically generates public hate of the Japs, and is the first picture of that kind in the high budget class since release of *Wake Island*."

The role of "Pvt. Wesley Eeps" was reportedly inspired by Pvt. Robert H. Brooks, the first American soldier killed in the Philippines, and the man for whom the parade grounds at Fort Knox were renamed. (It has not been determined whether Brooks was African American.) As all U.S. Armed Forces were segregated during World War II, the casting of African American actor Kenneth Spencer was notable. The *NYT* reviewer commented favorably on the Eeps character, noting that his "placement in the picture is one of the outstanding merits of it." The *HR* review stated that "the one Negro role included in the group is performed with distinction by Kenneth Spencer, and the note he sounds is an effective tribute to his race." In early Jun 1943, the NAACP awarded M-G-M a scroll of merit, congratulating the studio for the film's realism and for showing "how superfluous racial and religious problems are when common danger is faced." In Feb 1944, the Junior Council of NAACP gave M-G-M a special award for its sympathetic and intelligent portrayal of a black soldier. According to his autobiography, Schary deliberately did not tell writer Robert Andrews that he was going to cast a black actor in one of the roles because he did not want any race-conscious speeches in the script. *HR* reported

in May 1943 that the film had been pre-screened for a group of soldiers, press correspondents and dignitaries who were on Bataan during the siege, and all approved of the picture. In 1945, RKO produced *Back to Bataan*, a fact-based sequel to *Bataan*.

AmCin Jul 1943, p. 257. *Box* 29 May 1943. *DV* 26 May 1943, pp. 3-4 *FD* 28 May 1943, p. 7. *HR* 27 Apr 1942, p. 2. *HR* 6 Jul 1942, p. 2. *HR* 14 Oct 1942, p. 1. *HR* 6 Nov 1942, p. 3. *HR* 13 Nov 1942, p. 1. *HR* 23 Nov 1942, p. 3. *HR* 24 Nov 1942, p. 11. *HR* 30 Nov 1942, p. 4. *HR* 3 Dec 1942, p. 4. *HR* 4 Dec 1942, p. 2. *HR* 7 Dec 1942, p. 4. *HR* 9 Dec 1942, p. 4. *HR* 21 Dec 1942, p. 2. *HR* 22 Dec 1942, p. 7. *HR* 4 Jan 1943, p. 7. *HR* 5 Jan 1943, p. 2. *HR* 4 Feb 1943, p. 6. *HR* 15 Feb 1943, p. 9. *HR* 29 Apr 1943, p. 4. *HR* 5 May 1943, p. 2. *HR* 20 May 1943, p. 15. *HR* 26 May 1943, p. 3. *HR* 2 Jun 1943, p. 7. *HR* 7 Jun 1943, p. 4. *HR* 25 Apr 1944, p. 5. *MPH* 29 May 1943. *MPHPD* 29 May 1943, p. 1337. *NYT* 4 Jun 1943, p. 17. *Var* 26 May 1943, p. 8.

BATAAN PATROL *see* **BATAAN**

BATAAN'S LAST STAND *see* **BATAAN**

THE BATTLE AT APACHE PASS (Native Americans, Apache)
Universal-International Pictures Co., Inc. *Dist* Universal Pictures Co., Inc. Apr **1952**; Los Angeles opening: 5 Apr 1952; Prod: late Jun—late Jul 1951 [©Universal Pictures Co.; 18 Feb 1952; LP1504]. Sd (Western Electric Recording); col (Technicolor). 10 reels. 84-85 min. PCA cert no. 15477.

Prod Leonard Goldstein. *Assoc prod* Ross Hunter. *Dir* George Sherman. [*Asst dir* William Holland]. *Story and scr* Gerald Drayson Adams. *Dir of photog* Charles Boyle. **Technicolor color consultant** William Fritzsche. *Art dir* Bernard Herzbrun and Richard H. Riedel. *Film ed* Ted J. Kent. *Set dec* Russell A. Gausman and Oliver Emert. *Cost* Rosemary Odell. *Mus* Hans J. Salter. *Sd* Leslie I. Carey and Corson Jowett. *Hair stylist* Joan St. Oegger. *Makeup* Bud Westmore.

Cast: John Lund [(*Major Jim Colton*)], Jeff Chandler [(*Cochise*)], Susan Cabot [(*Nona*)], Bruce Cowling [(*Neil Baylor*)], Beverly Tyler [(*Mary Kearny*)], Richard Egan [(*Sgt. Reuben Bernard*)], Jay Silverheels [(*Geronimo*)], John Hudson [(*Lt. George Bascom*)], Jack Elam [(*Mescal Jack*)], Regis Toomey [(*Dr. Carter*)], Tommy Cook [(*Little Elk*)], Hugh O'Brian (*Lt. Robert Harley*), James Best [(*Corp. Hasset*)], Richard Garland [(*Culver*)], Palmer Lee [(*Joe Bent*)], William Reynolds [(*Lem Bent*)], Paul Smith [(*Trumpeter Ross*)], Jack Ingram [(*Johnny Ward*)], [John Baer (*Pvt. Bolin*)].

Western. [*Print viewed*]. In New Mexico Territory, Apache chief Cochise has forged a firm and peaceful friendship with Major Jim Colton, commander of Fort Buchanan. One day, Cochise and his pregnant wife Nona visit the fort, and Colton explains to Cochise that many soldiers are leaving the fort to fight in the Civil War in the East. Colton promises to stay in the Southwest near his Apache friends. Soon after, Neil Baylor, a government Indian agent, arrives with an untrustworthy scout named Mescal Jack and announces that reinforcements will be brought in to deal with the Indian problem. Much to Colton's anger, Baylor expresses his intent to move the Apaches to the San Carlos reservation away from the Butterfield Overland route, a stagecoach pass, even though peace treaties granting them land rights have already been signed. A short time later, a Butterfield Overland Stagecoach bound for Tucson is attacked by Geronimo, chief of the Mogollon Apaches, and all the women and children are mutilated. Colton and Baylor go to see Cochise, and Baylor declares that if the killers are not found, the Chiricahua, Cochise's Apache tribe, will be sent to San Carlos. Cochise responds that his tribe will not leave their lands, but that at the Indian's council he will vote to send the bad Apaches away from the area. At the council, Geronimo tries to persuade the Chiricahua to fight the whites, but the council chiefs vote to banish him. When Cochise tells Geronimo and his men that they must leave behind Mary Kearney, a young schoolteacher whom the renegades kidnapped at the time of the Butterfield stage massacre, another brave, Niga, challenges him to fight for her. Cochise wins the battle, and Nona thinks that he is in love with the white girl. Cochise assures Nona that he only has eyes for her, and then brings Mary to Fort Buchanan, telling Colton that she would make a good wife. Meanwhile, Baylor and Mescal meet with Geronimo, and offer to sell him guns and ammunition in exchange for raiding a ranch and making it look as if Cochise were responsible. Geronimo agrees, kills the rancher's wife, kidnaps his son, and leaves behind the emblem of Cochise's tribe, a thunderbird pendant. While Colton is away investigating the attack, Baylor approaches Lt. George Bascom and says he will be promoted if he can get the kidnapped boy back from Cochise. At the meeting between Cochise and Bascom, Cochise tells Bascom that Geronimo perpetrated the attack, but Bascom accuses him of lying, and as he is about to arrest him, Cochise

escapes. Bascom takes Nona and three braves hostage. Sgt. Reuben Bernard, Colton's ally, demands that he release Nona, but Bascom insists that the three hostages will not be released until the boy and the guilty Indians are turned over. Cochise takes a military man hostage, and when Bascom calls him a liar, he kills him. In retaliation, Bascom hangs the three braves, one of whom is Little Elk, Cochise's brother. Cochise and the Chiricahuas go into mourning and then vow to avenge the deaths of their braves by joining forces with Geronimo and declaring war on the whites. Meanwhile, Colton returns and learns from Bernard that Baylor masterminded the conflict between Cochise and Bascom. He arrests Bascom, and just then the Indians attack. Mescal goes to Cochise and says that troops are arriving to drive the villagers from their lands. Cochise accuses him of lying and has him shot. Eventually, Colton decides to abandon Fort Buchanan, and the entire population of the fort, including Mary, moves to Fort Sheridan. As the wagon train travels through Apache Pass, the Indian warriors, including Cochise, watch from the rocks above and then shoot. Baylor is shot, and then runs to the Indians claiming to be their friend, but Geronimo kills him. Colton and Bernard decide that they must use cannons in order to win the battle, and when they begin to shell the area, the warriors scatter. Cochise finds Nona, who has been injured, and then approaches the wagon train in order to get medical attention from Dr. Carter. Geronimo tells the remaining braves that Cochise is no longer their leader as he only thinks of his squaw, and then he attacks. Cochise rides with a white flag to Geronimo, who challenges Cochise to a fight to the death. Cochise wins but decides not to kill Geronimo, declaring instead that he is an outcast and no longer an Apache warrior. Later, Nona gives birth to a boy, and then gives Mary, who has cared for her, a bracelet that will protect her from Apaches. Mary and Nona say goodbye, and Cochise and Colton, who is in love with Mary, agree to speak again about peace sometime soon. *Apache Indians. Cochise. Geronimo. Indian agents. New Mexico. United States–History–Indian campaigns. Ambushes. Brothers. Cannons. Childbirth. Duplicity. Fights. Forts. Frame-ups. Gunfights. Hanging. Indians of North America–Reservations. Kidnapping. Marriage. Officers (Military). Scouts (Frontier). Stagecoaches. United States–History–Civil War, 1861-1865.*

Note: The opening credits state that the film's battle scenes were photographed at Arches National Monument Park and include a written acknowledgement commending the National Park Service of the United States Department of the Interior "whose splendid cooperation made these scenes possible." The film's remaining exteriors were shot in Professor Valley, near Moab, Utah. According to the *LAEx* review, Professor Valley was the actual site of Apache Pass. The events depicted in the film are based on a true incident which occurred in 1861 when a rancher wrongfully accused Cochise of kidnapping his children and stealing his cattle. At a meeting between Cochise and Lt. George Bascom from Fort Buchanan, Bascom tried to arrest Cochise, who escaped, and each side took and murdered hostages. Most of the forts in Chiricahua country were indeed abandoned due to the need for troops to fight the Civil War. When reinforcements were sent in to protect the routes to California, a battle took place in Apache Pass between Cochise and troops led by Colonel James Carleton. Carleton claimed victory over the attackers by using howitzers and repeater rifles. The incident is credited with instigating twenty-five years of Apache unrest. Apparently Geronimo was not actually involved in this battle, and the character "Major Colton" is fictional. Contemporary reviews praised the film for its sympathetic, honest and authentic depiction of Indians. The *Var* review applauded, in particular, Cochise's kindly treatment of his pregnant wife and the scenes of authentic Indian wrestling. Jeff Chandler also played Cochise in Twentieth Century-Fox's 1950 film, *Broken Arrow* (see entry below).

Box 5 Apr 1952. *DV* 2 Apr 1952, p. 3. *Exh* 9 Apr 1952, p. 3272. *FD* 9 Apr 1952, p. 6. *Har* 5 Apr 1952, p. 54. *HR* 22 Jun 1951, p. 11. *HR* 20 Jul 1951, p. 13. *HR* 2 Apr 1952, p. 3. *LAEx* 7 Apr 1952. *MPD* Apr 2 1952. *MPHPD* 5 Apr 1952, p. 1306. *NYT* 10 May 1952, p. 16. *Var* 2 Apr 1952, p. 6.

BATTLE OF ROGUE RIVER (Native Americans, Tututni)

Esskay Pictures Co. *Dist* Columbia Pictures Corp. Mar **1954**; Prod: 20 Aug–29 Aug 1953 [©Columbia Pictures Corp.; 1 Mar 1954; LP3505]. Sd (Western Electric Recording); col (Technicolor). 6,338 ft. 70-71 min. PCA cert no. 16767.

Prod Sam Katzman. *Dir* William Castle. *Asst dir* Charles S. Gould. *Story and scr* Douglas Heyes. *Dir of photog* Henry Freulich. *Spec eff* Jack Erickson. *Technicolor color consultant* Francis Cugat. *Art dir* Paul Palmentola. *Film ed* Charles Nelson. *Set dec* Sidney Clifford. *Mus dir* Mischa Bakaleinikoff. *Sd eng* Josh Westmoreland. *Unit mgr* Herbert Leonard.

Cast: George Montgomery [(*Major Frank Archer*)], Richard Denning [(*Stacey Wyatt*)], Martha Hyer [(*Brett McClain*)], John Crawford [(*Capt. Richard Hillman*)], Emory Parnell [(*Sergeant McClain*)], Michael Granger [(*Chief Mike*)], Freeman Morse [(*Private*

Reed)], Bill Bryant [(*Corporal*)], Charles Evans [(*Matt Parish*)], Lee Roberts [(*Lt. Keith Ryan*)], Frank Sully [(*Kohler*)], Steve Ritch [(*Brave*)], [Bill Hale (*Henry*)], [Wes Hudman (*Roy*)], [Jimmy Lloyd (*Hamley*)], [Willis Bouchey (*Major Wallich*)].

Historical, Western. [*Print viewed*]. In the 1850s, in the Rogue River Valley area of the Oregon territory, Indian tribes resist the encroachment of white settlers. After Army captain Richard Hillman reports to Major Wallich that they have lost another battle against Indian Chief Mike's warriors, he learns that Wallich is being replaced by Major Frank Archer, a renowned disciplinarian. As Archer and his reinforcements approach the fort, they scare off Indian ambushers with a round of cannon fire. Archer finds the fort in the midst of a recruitment campaign, during which rum is served to entice the civilian volunteers known as "Irregulars," who are led by Stacey Wyatt. Archer is appalled by the festivities and insists that Wyatt and his men follow military decorum. Archer also reprimands Hillman, and orders him to take command of the pack mules until he learns military discipline. Already unpopular with his troops, Archer also earns the resentment of Brett McClain, the sergeant's daughter, when he prevents his men from attending her social. Later, Chief Mike sends emissaries to the fort requesting a conference, but Archer initially refuses because he has been ordered to attack. After receiving new orders, however, Archer meets with Chief Mike, and the Indian chief assesses his honesty. Chief Mike agrees to a thirty-day truce during which the Indians will stay on one side of the river, and the whites will stay on the other. Their talk is disrupted when two dead Indians are brought in, reportedly the victims of an unprovoked attack. Chief Mike angrily attacks Archer, but Archer overpowers him and insists that they stick to their agreement. To protect his men, Archer takes Chief Mike back to the fort and guarantees his safety. The civilians demand that Chief Mike be hanged, but Archer stands by his word and releases the tribal leader, thereby earning his respect. Later, Brett also calls a truce with Archer and finds that she has grown fond of the stern soldier. After several peaceful days, Archer sends out a patrol led by McClain and Hillman. Wyatt is then sent out to obtain McClain's report, but when Wyatt encounters the troop, he tells McClain that the settlers' camp has been brutally attacked by Indians and that Brett has been taken hostage. Dutifully observing his strict orders, McClain refuses to cross the river even to save Brett, until Wyatt tells him that Archer has sent new orders. Wyatt accompanies McClain to the edge of the Indian village, and watches as McClain and his troops attack the unsuspecting villagers. Many Indians are slaughtered, but another faction of the tribe attacks the Army and massacres them. Later, Wyatt meets with Matt Parish and other members of the Irregulars to reveal how he has deceived McClain on their behalf. Wyatt has been secretly working against the peace process so that he, Parish and others can gain control of the territory's riches before Oregon becomes a state. After Wyatt reports that the truce is over, Archer leads a unit to search for survivors and discovers that Brett has followed him. With no evidence of survivors, Brett angrily lashes out at Archer and rides away. Archer orders Hillman, who has gained his confidence, to return to the fort and then follows Brett. Archer is forced to kill three Indians to protect Brett, but after spending the night in the open, they are captured and taken to Chief Mike. Archer says that the peace was broken against his will, but Chief Mike declares war and releases his hostages to repay his debt to Archer. Archer sends his troops to set up for a heavy artillery attack and instructs them to begin their barrage at nine the next morning. He then leaves Wyatt in charge of the fort and forms a post at the river. The Indians attack, and while Archer and his men are fighting them off, Brett and the settlers are surprised to see McClain, severely wounded, stumble into the fort. Brett learns the truth about Wyatt and Parish's subterfuge and takes them both to Archer. Archer forces Wyatt to accompany him to meet with Chief Mike and warns the Indian leader that he is unable to alert his men in time to stop the artillery barrage. However, Wyatt discounts Archer's story, and in an effort to decide the matter, Chief Mike suggests that he and Wyatt engage in hand-to-hand combat. Archer reluctantly agrees and is the victor. Wyatt finally admits the truth but is killed when he tries to attack Chief Mike. Chief Mike then agrees to lead his people across the river to safer ground. Parish is arrested, and everyone watches as the artillery fires away. No one is injured during the barrage, and afterward, Chief Mike agrees to lasting peace. Having discovered his true nature, Brett embraces Archer. *Duplicity. Oregon. Peace conferences. Rogue River Indian War, 1855-1856. Traitors. Tututni*

Indians. United States. Army. Drunkenness. Fathers and daughters. Fistfights. Forts. Hostages. Military discipline. Militia. Settlers. Statehood (American politics). Tribal chiefs. War injuries.

Note: The film opens with the following spoken narration: "In the 1850s savage Indian wars were the prime issue preventing the rich young Oregon territory from becoming a state. Though many tribes had retreated to the reservations, fierce resistance was still felt in the Rogue River Valley, where proud red men sworn to drive the white invaders from the land continued their defiance. Neither red men nor white could foretell the ending of the decisive battle which was yet to come." The film closes with the following narration: "In 1859, by act of Congress, the territory of Oregon was officially admitted into the Union of the United States of America." Although Esskay Pictures Co., headed by producer Sam Katzman, was listed as the production company in SAB, Katzman's company had changed its name to Clover Productions, Inc. by the time the picture was released.

The Rogue River Valley in Oregon was so-named by whites due to the "rogue" attacks made on settlers by the Takelma and Tututni Indians who inhabited the region. In 1855, Capt. Andrew Jackson Smith invited the Indian population to settle within the confines of the fort. However, his attempt at a peaceful solution to the hostilities between settlers and Indians was thwarted when civilian militia ambushed a Native American village. Retaliations ensued for a year until the Indian leaders in the area notified Smith that they would surrender. Smith was warned by informers that it was a trap, resulting in a battle between the Cavalry and the Indians. After several weeks of fighting, the battered Takelma and Tututni surrendered.

Box 27 Feb 1954. *DV* 26 Feb 1954, p. 3. *FD* 1 Mar 1954, p. 6. *Exb* 10 Mar 1954, p. 3709. *Har* 27 Feb 1954, pp. 34-35. *HR* 26 Feb 1954, p. 3. *MPHPD* 6 Mar 1954, p. 2206. *Var* 3 Mar 1954, p. 6.

BATTLE STATIONS *see* THE NAVY COMES THROUGH

BATTLEGROUND (Latino, Jewish Americans, Multi-ethnic)

Metro-Goldwyn-Mayer Corp.; controlled by Loew's Inc. *Dist* Loew's Inc. 20 Jan **1950**; Washington, D.C. premiere: 9 Nov 1949; Los Angeles premiere: 1 Dec 1949; Prod: 5 Apr–3 Jun 1949 [©Loew's Inc.; 19 Oct 1949; LP2594]. Sd (Western Electric Sound System); b&w. 10,988 ft. 118 min. Passed by the National Board of Review. PCA cert no. 13886.

Prod Dore Schary. *Assoc prod* Robert Pirosh. *Dir* William Wellman. [*Asst dir* Sid Sidman]. *Story and scr* Robert Pirosh. *Dir of photog* Paul C. Vogel. [*Cam op* James Harper]. [*Stills* Edwin Hubbell and Jimmy Manatt]. *Mont seq* Peter Ballbusch. *Art dir* Cedric Gibbons and Hans Peters. *Film ed* John Dunning. *Set dec* Edwin B. Willis. *Assoc* Alfred E. Spencer. *Mus score* Lennie Hayton. *Rec supv* Douglas Shearer. [*Sd* Conrad Kahn]. *Make-up created by* Jack Dawn. *Tech adv* H. W. O. Kinnard, Lt. Col. Inf. [*Scr supv* John Banse]. [*Grip* Henry Forrester]. [*Unit mgr* William Kaplan].

Cast: Van Johnson (*Holley*), John Hodiak (*Jarvess*), Ricardo Montalban (*Roderigues*), George Murphy (*"Pop" Stazak*), Marshall Thompson (*Jim Layton*), Jerome Courtland (*Abner Spudler*), Don Taylor (*Standiferd*), Bruce Cowling (*Wolowicz*), James Whitmore (*Kinnie*), Douglas Fowley (*"Kipp" Kippton*), Leon Ames (*The Chaplain*), Guy Anderson (*Hansan*), Thomas E. Breen (*Doc*), Denise Darcel (*Denise*), Richard Jaeckel (*Bettis*), Jim Arness (*Garby*), Scotty Beckett (*William J. Hooper*), Brett King (*Lt. Teiss*), and the original The "Screaming Eagles" of the 101st Airborne Division, who play themselves, [Roland Varno (*German lieutenant*)], [John Royce, Peter Michael, Robert Boon, Tony Christian, Eugene Gericke, Fred Zendar (*German soldiers*)], [Edmon Ryan (*Major*)], [Michael Browne (*Levenstein*)], [William Erwin (*Warrant officer*)], [Arthur Walsh, George Offerman, Jr., William Self, John Riffel, Robert N. Porter, Ted Eckelberry, Martin Lowell, Victor Paul, Nelson Scott, John Gardner, John Dutra (*G. I.'s*)], [Jim Drum (*Supply sergeant*)], [Nadine Ashdown, Janine Perreau (*Little girls*)], [Dewey Martin, Tom Noonan, David Holt (*G. I. stragglers*)], [Steve Pendleton (*Sergeant*)], [William R. Murphy, Phillip Pine, Sam Resnick (*Non-coms*)], [Jerry Paris (*German sergeant*)], [Tommy Bond, Billy Lechner (*Runners*)], [Nan Boardman (*Belgian volunteer*)], [Ivan Triesault (*German captain*)], [Henry Rowland (*German*)], [John Mylong (*German major*)], [Ian MacDonald (*American colonel*)], [William F. Leicester (*Tank destroyer man*)], [George Chandler (*Mess sergeant*)], [Charles B. Smith (*Clerk*)], [Tommy Walker (*Mechanic*)], [Dan Foster (*Gunner*)], [Roger McGee, Dick Jones (*Tankers*)], [Joel Allen, James Horne (*Transportation captains*)], [George Dee (*Frenchman*)], [Bert Davidson, Carl Saxe (*101st Battalion officers*)], [Irene Seidner, Martha Bamattre, Gertl Dupont, Louise Colombet (*French peasant women*)], [Jean Del Val, Albert Pollet (*French peasant men*)], [Lilian Clays (*Old woman*)], [Chris Drake (*Medic private*)], [Raymond C. Bowsher, Harry Mackin, John Mansfield, Richard Bartlett, Tommy

Kelly, Peter Rankin (*Casualties*)], [Norman Budd (*Crying casualty*)], [Otto Reichow (*German platoon leader*)], [Gene Coogan (*G. I. scout*)], [Victor Desny (*Wounded German soldier*)], [Robert Ward Wood (*Replacement*)], [Jim Martin (*G. I. from the South*)], [Edmund Glover (*G. I. from Maine*)], [Richard Irving (*G. I. from New York*)].

World War II, Drama. [*Print viewed*]. In December of 1944, only days before Christmas, battle-weary soldiers of the U.S. 101st Airborne Division, stationed at an Army base in France, eagerly await their long-promised leave in Paris. Their hopes of a rest are dashed, however, when they are given orders to go to the Belgian town of Bastogne and hold back the 47th German Panzer Corps, which is advancing through Allied lines. Among those sent to defend the French town are Jarvess, a small town newspaper columnist; Holley, a girl crazy soldier; Roderigues, a Mexican American enlistee; "Pop" Stazak, an older serviceman from Wichita, Kansas; Jim Layton, a new recruit; and Kinnie, the platoon leader. Soon after the men arrive in Bastogne, they meet Denise, an attractive French woman who provides them with lodging. While patrolling the fog-shrouded woods near Bastogne, the American soldiers come under intense enemy fire and realize that they have been surrounded and trapped by the Germans. The American soldiers, fighting without air support, soon find themselves engaged in a long battle to keep the Nazis out of Bastogne. The stand-off exacts its first American casualty when Roderigues is struck by an enemy bullet. Unable to carry the wounded Roderigues through the snow to safety, his fellow soldiers hide him under an abandoned jeep and promise to return for him. A short time later, Holley and a small rescue party return for Roderigues, only to find that he has died. As the fighting in the woods near Bastogne intensifies, the American casualties continue to mount. Following a late night surprise attack on the division by a Nazi patrol, the Americans capture a number of Nazi prisoners and take them back to Bastogne. Greatly outnumbered by the Nazis, the men of the 101st Airborne believe their situation to be near hopeless. One day, Nazi officers attempt to negotiate an American surrender, but General A. C. McAuliffe, the highest ranking officer in charge of the operation, responds with just a single word: "Nuts!" A short time later, the Lutheran chaplain delivers a moving sermon to the defenders of Bastogne and reminds them of the importance of their mission. As the fog lifts around Bastogne for the first time since the Nazis began their counterattack, American bombers and relief planes are seen flying overhead. The men of the 101st Airborne Division rejoice at the sight of the planes, and the arrival of the reinforcements make it possible for the Americans to quickly defeat the Nazis. With their mission accomplished, the men of the 101st Airborne Division march out of Bastogne. Military invasion. Military life. Nazis. United States. Army. World War II. Bastogne (Belgium). Battles. Bulge, Battle of the, 1944-1945. Death and dying. Dentures. Fog. French. Mexican Americans. Military leave. Officers (Military). Prisoners of war. Rescues. War injuries.

Note: The following written prologue appears in the onscreen credits: "This story is about, and dedicated to, those Americans who met General Heinrich von Luttwitz and his 47 Panzer Corps and won for themselves the honored and immortal name 'The Battered Bastards of Bastogne.' " Robert Pirosh's credit appears onscreen as "Story and screenplay by Robert Pirosh, Associate Producer." The film is based, in part, on actual events that took place in the Ardennes Forest in December of 1944. The Nazi counterattack and the overwhelming Allied resistance with which it was met is commonly referred to as the "Battle of the Bulge." According to the onscreen credits, members of one of the original resistance forces, the "Screaming Eagles" of the 101st Airborne Division, appear in the film. Lt. Col. Harry W. O. Kinnard, the technical adviser on this film, served as a World War II intelligence officer at the Battle of The Bulge, according to a Mar 1949 *DV* news item. . An Aug 1948 *HR* news item indicates that former RKO production head Dore Schary purchased the rights to the *Battleground* script from RKO following his move to M-G-M. According to the news item, the film, which was one of several projects at RKO that were shelved when Schary resigned, was to have been made by Jesse Lasky and Walter MacEwan. The news item also noted that RKO had already invested approximately $100,000 in the film before it was shelved.

In Oct 1948, following M-G-M's acquisition of the property, a *HR* news item noted that Robert Taylor, Van Johnson John Hodiak, Ricardo Montalban and Keenan Wynn were set to star, and that the picture was given a $2,000,000 budget. An Oct 1948 *HR* news item noted that Pandro S. Berman was set to produce the film, but his contribution to the released film has not been determined. A *HR* production chart lists actor Jim Mitchell in the cast, but he did not appear in the released film. A pre-production news item in *HR* noted that half of the picture was to be filmed in Northern California, Oregon and Washington. A May 1949 *HR* news item adds that Fort Lewis, WA served as the background for the tank sequence depicting the relief of Bastogne. According to a May 1949 *HR* news item, Shary instituted a system of dubbing and cutting during production which made it possible to preview the film within forty-

eight hours of the scenes being filmed. Each day's film was processed as it was shot, reducing the average time between completion and preview by several weeks.

Schary completed the film twenty days under its original shooting schedule by instituting several other innovations. He also ordered twenty-five sets built on one sound stage, and then had art director Hans Peters map out in detail the terrain, action and possible camera angles. Copies of these drawings were then given to director William Wellman and cinematographer Paul Vogel. Some of the sets were used several times over as the film's actions shifted, according to a Jun 1949 *HR* news item.

The Washington, D.C. premiere was attended by Brig. Gen. A. C. McAuliffe, the defender of Bastogne, according to an Oct 1949 *DV* news item. Robert Pirosh, who himself fought in the Battle of the Bulge, received an Academy Award for Best Story and Screenplay, and Paul C. Vogel received an Academy Award in the category of Best Black-and-White Cinematography. The film also received the following Academy Award nominations: Best Picture, Best Director, Best Supporting Actor (James Whitmore); and Best Editing. *Battleground* was listed as the Best Picture of the Year by *Photoplay*. According to a *DV* news item, the film took in $3,750,000 at the box office and was M-G-M's largest grossing film in five years. In 1951, Van Johnson starred in M-G-M's follow-up film to this picture, entitled *Go for Broke*, which was written and directed by Robert Pirosh.

AmCin Dec 1949, p. 436-37, 448. *Box* 8 Oct 1949. *DV* 10 Mar 1949, p. 10. *DV* 5 Apr 1949, p. 8. *DV* 28 Sep 1949, p. 3, 6. *DV* 26 Oct 1949, p. 3. *DV* 17 Nov 1949, p. 1. *DV* 20 Feb 1950, p. 1. *FD* 28 Sep 1949, p. 7. *HR* 5 Aug 1948, p. 2. *HR* 6 Oct 1948, p. 2. *HR* 12 Oct 1948, p. 1. *HR* 14 Oct 1948, p. 13. *HR* 18 Mar 1949 p. 7. *HR* 29 Mar 1949 p. 10. *HR* 8 Apr 1949, p. 10. *HR* 5 May 1949, p. 12. *HR* 9 May 1949, p. 4. *HR* 2 Jun 1949, p. 4. *HR* 3 Jun 1949, p. 10 *HR* 6 Jun 1949, p. 4. *HR* 28 Sep 1949, p. 3. *MPHPD* 1 Oct 1949, p. 33. *NYT* 12 Nov 1949, p. 8. *Var* 28 Sep 1949, p. 6.

BATTLES OF CHIEF PONTIAC (Native Americans, Ottawa)

Jack Broder Productions. *Dist* Realart Pictures, Inc. Dec **1952**; Prod: late Jul—early Aug 1952. Sd; b&w. 6,549 ft. 71-72 or 74 min.

Prod Irving Starr. *Assoc prod* Herman Cohen. *Dir* Felix Feist. *Asst dir* Richard Dixon. *Scr* Jack DeWitt. *Dir of photog* Charles Van Enger. *Art dir* Boris Leven. *Ed supv* Philip Cahn. *Set dec* Charles Thompson. *Men's ward* Isidore Berne. *Women's ward* Florence Hayes. *Mus comp and dir* Elmer Bernstein. *Sd* Hugh McDowell. *Hairdresser* Lillian Shore. *Makeup* William Woods. *Scr supv* Dan Alexander.

Cast: LEX BARKER [(*Kent McIntire*)], HELEN WESTCOTT [(*Winifred Lancaster*)], LON CHANEY [(*Chief Pontiac*)], Berry Kroeger [(*Colonel von Weber*)], Roy Roberts [(*Major Gladwin*)], Larry Chance [(*Hawkbill*)], Katharine Warren [(*Cbia*)], Ramsey Hill [(*General Jeffrey Amherst*)], Guy Teague [(*Von Weber's aide*)], James Fairfax [(*Sentry*)], Abner George [(*Doctor*)].

Historical, Western. [*Print viewed*]. In the late 1700s, after British troops have driven the French out of the northern American territory, the British hire Hessian soldiers as reinforcements in their war against the Indians. Notoriously brutal Hessian commander von Weber launches surprise raids against Indian villages, ruthlessly killing men, women and children. Near Fort Detroit, Chief Pontiac, a spiritual and tribal leader, declares war against the whites because of the harsh new British rule. British general Jeffrey Amherst, meanwhile, congratulates von Weber on his successful campaign against the Indians. Amherst instructs von Weber, who hates all Indians because he was once captured and tortured by a tribe, to continue until the British can gain control of the Great Lakes region. While they are talking, Ranger Lieutenant Kent McIntyre comes in and demands that Amherst put a halt to the butchery. Amherst, however, refuses to rein in von Weber and orders him to take command of Ft. Detroit away from Major Gladwin, who is sympathetic to the Indians. While returning to Ft. Detroit through the wilderness, Kent secretly speaks with Winifred Lancaster, the daughter of a British officer recently killed by the Indians, who is among a group of women taken hostage by Pontiac's warrior Hawkbill. Hawkbill captures Kent and takes him to Pontiac, who is Kent's "blood brother." Kent tells Pontiac about the British campaign against his tribe and warns him that Hessian reinforcements are being brought to the fort. Although Pontiac is committed to fighting the whites, he agrees to meet with Gladwin to discuss the possibility of peace. When Hawkbill starts to court Winifred, Kent claims her as his wife, pointing out a gold ring he had secretly given her as proof, and after a makeshift tribal wedding ceremony insisted upon by Pontiac, Winifred is accepted as family. Hawkbill, however, holds a grudge against Kent. Kent reports to Gladwin about his progress with Pontiac, but when von Weber takes over, he refuses to confer with Pontiac and threatens to arrest Gladwin when he insists that von Weber maintain the truce. Instead, von Weber sends a "gift" of clothing and blankets infested with smallpox to Pontiac's tribe, and plans to attack as soon as they are stricken by the illness. Kent revolts against von Weber and is arrested,

but Gladwin helps him escape unharmed. At Pontiac's village, Winifred, who previously hated the Indians, has developed a newfound respect for them, and is distraught when her new friends become mortally ill with smallpox. Kent tells Pontiac that the disease is von Weber's doing, and Pontiac suggests that he and Winifred flee before the warriors find out. Kent and Winifred leave after they help boil the blankets and clothing to rid them of the disease. That night, they declare their love for each other and return to the fort after seeing von Weber march out with his troops. When Kent tells Gladwin that Pontiac is massing for war, Gladwin orders him to warn von Weber, who expects to ambush the Indians. Kent does not catch up to von Weber and his troops until after the Indians have made their initial attack. During a pause in the battle, Kent warns von Weber and his men to retreat, but von Weber shoots him. Pontiac and his men slaughter the soldiers and capture von Weber alive. At the Indian village, von Weber is tied to a post and covered in pestilence-ridden blankets, and in time, he becomes ill and dies. Gladwin and Winifred ride to the village bearing a white flag, and Pontiac agrees to consider peace, although the Great Spirit has advised him that all Indians will soon be overwhelmed by the whites. As Gladwin and Pontiac smoke a peace pipe, Winifred runs to embrace the wounded Kent. *Biological warfare. English. Fort Detroit (IL). Hessians. Pontiac. United States–History–Colonial period, ca. 1600-1775. Ambushes. Jeffrey Amherst. Battles. Bigotry. Blood brotherhood. Courtship. Death and dying. Escapes. Imprisonment. Marriage–Forced by circumstances. Ottawa Indians. Peace conferences. Peace pipes. Prisoners of war. Revenge. Romance. Smallpox. Spiritualism. Treaties.*

Note: This film opens with the following spoken foreword: "This is the city of Detroit. Where this teeming industrial metropolis now stands, there was some two hundred years back, a small guarded fort, protecting a handful of white settlers. Fort Detroit was surrounded by many Indian tribes. The most prominent of these was the Ottawas, a proud people who in the period from 1763 to 1769, was ruled over by Chief Pontiac. Pontiac was a great warrior, a man of faith, who believed the Indian and white man could live together. The English who controlled his territory, hired professional German soldiers known as Hessians, to help patrol the area. One of the Hessian officers, a Colonel von Weber, did not share Pontiac's point of view. He was ambitious, ruthless and greedy for power." As depicted in the film, after the French surrendered the northern territories to the British, Hessian troops were hired as reinforcements. Modern historical sources also recount that the British instituted more regulations to control the Native Americans than the French and planned to take over the territories completely. Chief Pontiac waged several attacks against Fort Detroit, which was under the command of Major Henry Gladwin, but Gladwin forestalled the attacks after being forewarned by informers. At Fort Pitt, Captain Simeon Ecuyer was also under attack by local tribes, and followed orders from Lord Jeffrey Amherst, then British commander-in-chief of the Americas, to send smallpox-ridden blankets to the tribes. Many Native Americans died from the resulting smallpox epidemic. After the French were compelled to withdraw their support of the Native Americans when the Treaty of Paris was signed, Pontiac called a truce.

A 1950 *Var* news item noted that an original story titled "Chief Pontiac," written by credited writer Jack DeWitt and Woodruff Smith, was purchased by Jack Schwarz Productions. Smith's contribution to the final screenplay has not been confirmed, and Schwarz's connection to the final film is also unknown..

Box 20 Dec 1952. *DV* 9 Dec 1952. *Exb* 19 Nov 1952, p. 3417. *Har* 20 Dec 1952, p. 203. *HR* 25 Jul 1952, p. 11. *HR* 1 Aug 1952, p. 11. *HR* 9 Dec 1952, p. 3. *Var* 28 Mar 1950. *Var* 17 Dec 1952, p. 18.

THE BATTLING BUCKAROO (Latino)

Willis Kent Productions. *Dist* State Rights. Apr **1934**. Sd (International Sound Engineers); b&w. 6 reels.

Pres BERNARD SMITH. *Prod* Willis Kent. *Dir* Oliver Drake. *Asst dir* Bartlett Carre. *Photog* James Diamond. *Ed* S. Roy Luby. *Rec eng* Terry Kellum.

Cast: LANE CHANDLER [(*Blackjack, alias of Driftin' Slim Stanley*)], Doris Hill [(*Tonia Mendoza*)], Yakima Canutt [(*Sheriff Hank Jones*)], Lafe McKee [(*Don Felipe Mendoza*)], Bill Patton [(*Duke Lawson*)], Ted Adams [(*Pedro*)], Olin Francis [(*Bull*)], Joe Dellacruz.

Western. [*Viewed print incomplete*]. While a gang of outlaws attempts to rob the pack train of Tonia Mendoza and her father, Don Felipe, who are the owners of a valuable gold mine, Blackjack, a notorious bandit, watches from a distance. When the bandits discover the gold bags are empty, Tonia and Don Felipe are kidnapped but, to their surprise, are soon rescued by Blackjack. Later, Blackjack rides into the town of Rawlins, where he is recognized and arrested by Sheriff Hank Jones. Before the sheriff jails him, however, Blackjack escapes with the help of wealthy rancher Duke Lawson and rides to the sheriff's home. There, he is met by Tonia, who has come to speak

with the sheriff. Although she denounces him as an outlaw, Tonia hides Blackjack in the house and then engages the sheriff and Duke in conversation long enough to facilitate his escape. Blackjack heads for Duke's ranch, where he overhears Duke and his foreman, Butch, discussing the earlier raid and abduction and their plans for a second raid on the Mendoza gold mine. Before Blackjack can get away, he is caught by two of Duke's men and is sent into the Badlands on a wild horse. Blackjack's faithful horse Raven, however, follows the wild horse and eventually rescues his master. While Raven rides to town with a note for the sheriff, Blackjack walks to the Mendoza gold mine. When Blackjack arrives at the mine, he discovers that Duke and his men are holding Tonia and Don Felipe prisoner, while laying siege to the mine. Blackjack battles the gang and, with help from the sheriff and his posse, kills Duke and rescues the Mendozas. After the bandits are rounded up, Blackjack reveals that he is actually a United States marshal named Driftin' Slim Stanley. His reputation cleared, Blackjack embraces Tonia. *Bandits. Gold mines. Mexican Americans. Undercover operations. United States. Marshals. Fathers and daughters. Horses. Imprisonment. Kidnapping. Posses. Ranch foremen. Ranchers. Rescues. Romance. Sheriffs. Thieves.*

Note: Publicity material for this film notes that the picture was based on a story titled "Driftin' Slim." It is not known if this story was a screen original; no author is cited. Although a print of this film was not viewed, the above credits were taken from a British release print. That print was titled *His Last Adventure*. Modern sources claim that this film was a 1932 release, and that Armand Schaefer, not Oliver Drake, directed the picture. Oliver Drake is listed in modern sources as screenwriter. Herman Hack and Bartlett Carre (the film's assistant director) are included in the cast by modern sources. In addition, modern sources claim that actor Bill Patton actually played the part of "Pedro," while Ted Adams played "Duke Lawson."

MPD 21 Apr 1934, p. 4.

BAYOU (Cajuns)

American National Films, Inc. *Dist* United Artists Corp. Jun **1957** [©American National Films, Inc.; 14 Jun 1957; LP8607]. Sd; b&w. 88 min. PCA cert no. 18405.

Prod M. A. Ripps. *Dir* Harold Daniels. *Asst dir* Harold Templeton and George Templeton. *Story and scr* Edward I. Fessler. *Dir of photog* Ted Saizis and Vincent Saizis. *Film ed* Maury Wright. *Ward* Leone K. Zainey. *Mus score comp and cond* Gerald Fried. *Sd* Don McKay. *Makeup* Jack Byron. *Scr supv* Joe Cannon.

Song(s): "Bayou" and "Hold Me Close," words and music by Edward I. Fessler.

Cast: Peter Graves (*Martin*), Lita Milan (*Marie*), Douglas Fowley (*Herbert*), Jonathan Haze (*Bos*), Edwin Nelson (*Etienne*), Eugene Sondfield (*Jean Titho*), Evelyn Hendrickson (*Doucette*), Milton Schneider (*Cousine*), Michael Romano (*Felician*), Tim Carey (*Ulysses*).

Melodrama. [*Not viewed*]. Martin, an insecure, young architect, comes to New Orleans from the north to compete against a local architect for the design of a new civic center. On a visit to a carnival in the Cajun country of Southern Louisiana, Martin meets Marie, a sensual Cajun girl of seventeen, who works crabbing in the bayou in order to support herself and her senile father, Herbert. Marie has already aroused the lustful instincts of the local store-keeper, Ulysses, a sadistic, illiterate bully, who resents Martin's attentions to her. As Ulysses and Martin compete against each other in a race using pirogues, primitive canoes hollowed out of tree trunks, Ulysses deliberately crashes into Martin's boat causing him to lose. Martin and Marie find themselves falling in love. Ulysses visits her one evening and attempts to rape her, but is scared off by her father. Later, at a frenetic wedding celebration of a young couple, Ulysses performs a strange, gyrating dance that horrifies Martin. At the climax of this dance, a hurricane sweeps through the area causing much devastation. Herbert, alone in his house, goes berserk and is killed by a falling tree. After the hurricane has subsided and Herbert's body is found, Martin decides to take Marie back north with him. At Herbert's funeral, Ulysses makes a final effort to win Marie and taunts Martin into a brutal fight. Martin is victorious, and later he and Marie leave the bayou to begin a new life together. *Bayous (LA). Cajuns. Fathers and daughters. Rivalry. Romance. Accidental death. Architects. Attempted rape. Axes. Bullies. Canoes and canoeing. Carnivals. Cultural conflict. Dances. Fights. Funerals. Hurricanes. New Orleans (LA). Northerners. Racing. Shivarees. Weddings.*

Note: According to this film's press book, except for two brief scenes shot in New Orleans, the entire picture was filmed in Louisiana's Cajun country. The

Var review noted that *Bayou* was the first producing effort by Southern exhibitors M.A. Ripps and Edward I. Fessler. According to *Var*, Douglas Fowley played two roles, "Herbert" and a contractor friend of "Martin." *Bayou* was reissued with added footage in 1962, under the title *Poor White Trash*.

AmCin Jun 1957, p. 362. *Box* 15 Jun 1957. *DV* 31 May 1957, p. 3. *Exh* 26 Jun 1957, p. 4343. *FD* 31 May 1957, p. 6. *Har* 8 Jun 1957, p. 90. *HR* 31 May 1957, p. 3. *MPHPD* 1 Jun 1957, p. 403. *Var* 5 Jun 1957, p. 6.

BE BIG (*foreign version*) *see* **LOS CALAVERAS**

BE IT EVER SO HUMBLE *see* **HI, BEAUTIFUL**

THE BEACHCOMBER (Hawaiians)

Bosworth, Inc. **1915**? [©Bosworth, Inc.; 4 Jan 1915; LU4098]. Si; b&w. Length undetermined.

Prod Hobart Bosworth. *Story* Hobart Bosworth. *Cam* Gus C. Peterson.

Cast: Hobart Bosworth (*The sailor*), Helen Wolcott (*Taleaa*), Mr. Rahawanaku (*Kane Pili*), Mrs. Drew (*Mother*), John Weiss (*Maukaa*), W. F. Harrison (*Nalu*), J. Harvey (*Ka'alebai*), Dan Waid (*Waonokiki*), Rhea Haines (*Palikii*), Mr. Stedman (*Mate of the Edith/Missionary*).

Drama. Raised by a religious mother, a boy grows up at sea and, after growing to adulthood, is washed overboard one day in a storm. He is rescued by a Hawaiian named Kane Pili, whose blood brother the sailor becomes after the islanders nurse him back to health. Tempted by the love of Kane Pili's sister Taleaa and by the easy life on the island, the sailor is about to abandon the ways of civilization and become a beachcomber when a message in a bottle from a lost whaling ship revives his childhood religiosity. Taleaa, angry at the sailor's rejection of her advances, frames him for the desecration of an idol but intervenes to save his life at the last minute. The sailor leaves the island and takes up residence in a Christian community, eventually returning to bring Kane Pili and Taleaa back with him and to marry Taleaa. *Castaways. Hawaii. Religion. Sailors. Tribal life. Beachcombing. Brothers and sisters. Christianity. Executions. Frame-ups. Nursing back to health. Storms.*

Note: Bosworth, Inc. began production on this project, but it is unclear whether the film was ever completed or exhibited. Cast credits have been taken from handwritten notes on a production sheet in the Paramount studio records, and exact spellings for some of the names, particularly Mr. Rahawanaku, cannot be determined. Mrs. Drew is probably the actress Cora Drew, who worked for Bosworth, and Mr. Stedman is probably Marshall Stedman. The production notes give the name of the actor playing the sailor as a child as "Antrim," which is possibly a reference to the child actor Antrim Short. A modern source credits Phil Rosen, not Gus C. Peterson, as the film's cinematographer. No contemporary reviews or news items for the film have been located.

AmCin 1 Feb 1922, p. 19.

BEALE STREET MAMA (African Americans)

Sack Attractions. *Dist* Sack Amusement Enterprises. **1946**?. Sd (RCA Sound Recording); b&w. 5,611 ft. 62-63 min.

Pres Alfred N. Sack. *Entire prod supv and prod by* Bert Goldberg. *Dir* Spencer Williams. *Scr* Sam Elljay. *Dir of photog* H. Arthur Smith. *Set const* Hiram Benson. *Cost* Eve Lavere. *Mus dir* Vincent Valentini. *Sd eng* George Whiting. *Makeup* Andre Marteen.

Song(s): "Beale Street Mama" and "Don't Put Your Hands on Me," music and lyrics by Vincent Valentini.

Cast: July Jones (*July Jones*), Spencer Williams (*Bad News Johnson*), Rosalie Larrimore (*Mathilda Mae Grimes*), Howard Galloway (*Pretty Boy Brown*), J. W. Hemmings (*Chief of Police*), Montyne McCormick (*Hazel Smith*), Mary Louise Stevens (*Rosie Scott*), George Sutton (*Detective*), Allen and Allen, Joyce McElrath (*Entertainers*), *Music by* Don Albert and His Orchestra.

African American, Show business, Comedy, with songs. [*Print viewed*]. On Memphis' famed Beale Street, the home of Memphis Blues and St. Louis Blues, a birthday party for Pretty Boy Brown, given by golddigger Mathilda, is underway. When Mathilda's old flame July Jones, whom she took for everything he was worth, crashes the party, she tells Pretty Boy that July was merely her "policy writer." Later, Mathilda notices that the penniless July has taken a job as a street sweeper and tries to make him jealous by having Pretty Boy kiss her in his view. Shortly after a newspaper story about Mathilda riding around town with Bad News Johnson in a car paid for by July appears in the *Beale Street Bugle*, a parcel filled with money is thrown out a window and lands at July's feet. Believing that his luck has finally changed, and unaware that the money he found is counterfeit, July celebrates his newly-found wealth by throwing money into a crowd of people along Beale Street. To get back at Mathilda, July buys a new

suit and takes a pretty date with him to a nightclub, where he tries to make Mathilda jealous. Although July's plan works, his luck runs out when detectives enter the club and arrest him on charges of passing counterfeit money. July winds up in jail but is released when the real counterfeiters are captured. Back on the streets, July encounters some of his friends, who jump on him for passing fake money on to them and steal his clothes. *African Americans. Gold diggers. Jazz music. Memphis (TN). Romance.* Bands (Music). Counterfeiters and counterfeiting. Dancers. Detectives. Gambling. Jails. Jealousy. Nightclubs. Parties. Poverty. Reporters. Robbery. Singers.

Note: Although the onscreen credits include a copyright statement for Sack Amusement Enterprises, the film was not registered for copyright. No reviews have been located for the film, but it was evaluated for release by New York censors in 1946 and was accepted without eliminations for exhibition in the state. A modern source states that this film was made in Texas.

BEAU JAMES (Irish Americans)

Paramount Pictures Corp.; Hope Enterprises, Inc.; Scribe Productions. *Dist* Paramount Pictures Corp. Jul **1957**; Los Angeles premiere: 2 Jul 1957; *Prod*: 23 Jul—14 Sep 1956 [©Hope Enterprises, Inc. and Scribe Productions; 1 Jul 1957; LP8639]. Sd (Westrex Recording System); col (Technicolor); VistaVision Motion Picture High Fidelity. 9,411 ft. 105 min. PCA cert no. 18340.

Prod Jack Rose. *Dir* Melville Shavelson. *Asst dir* Michael D. Moore. [*2d asst dir* Clem Jones]. [*3rd asst dir* Al Mann]. *Scr* Jack Rose and Melville Shavelson. *Dir of photog* John F. Warren. *2d unit photog* Wallace Kelley. *Spec photog eff* John P. Fulton. *Process photog* Farciot Edouart. *Technicolor color consultant* Richard Mueller. *Art dir* Hal Pereira and John Goodman. *Ed* Floyd Knudtson. *Set dec* Sam Comer and Frank McKelvy. [*Props* Tommy Plews]. *Cost* Edith Head. [*Ward* Glenita Dineen]. *Mus arr and cond by* Joseph J. Lilley. *Dances and mus numbers staged by* Jack Baker. *Sd rec* Hugo Grenzbach and Charles Grenzbach. *Makeup supv* Wally Westmore. *Hair style supv* Nellie Manley. *Prod assoc* Hal C. Kern. [*Unit prod mgr* Charles Woolstenhulme]. [*Scr supv* Stanley Scheuer]. [*Casting dir* Bert McKay]. [*Tech adv* Harold Melnicker].

Song(s): "Will You Love Me in December," music and lyrics by Ernest J. Ball and James J. Walker; "Manhattan," music by Richard Rodgers, lyrics by Lorenz Hart; "Blossoms on Broadway," music and lyrics by Ralph Rainger and Leo Robin; "Someone to Watch Over Me," music by George Gershwin, lyrics by Ira Gershwin; "When We're Alone" ("Penthouse Serenade") music and lyrics by Will Jason and Val Burton; "His Honor the Mayor of New York," music and lyrics by Joseph J. Lilley and Sammy Cahn; "Sidewalks of New York," music and lyrics by James W. Blake and Charles B. Lawlor; "Happy Days Are Here Again," music by Milton Ager, lyrics by Jack Yellen.

Source: Based on the book *Beau James* by Gene Fowler (New York, 1949).

Cast: Bob Hope [(*James J. "Jimmy" Walker*)], Vera Miles [(*Betty Compton*)], Paul Douglas [(*Chris Nolan*)], Alexis Smith [(*Allie Walker*)], Darren McGavin [(*Charley Hand*)], Joe Mantell [(*Bernie Williams*)], Horace McMahon [(*Prosecutor*)], Richard Shannon [(*Dick Jackson*)], Willis Bouchey [(*Arthur Julian*)], Sid Melton [(*Sid Nasb*)], George Jessel [(*Himself*)], Walter Catlett [(*Gov. Al Smith*)], Walter Winchell (*Narrator*), [Jack Benny, Jimmy Durante (*Themselves*)], [Rhubarb, a cat (*Tom*)], [Richard B. Fitzgerald (*Police secretary*)], [Babette Bain (*Puerto Rican child*)], [Sammy Cahn (*Arranger*)], [Charles Meredith (*Judge Harrison*)], [Charles Irwin (*Capt. O'Shea*)], [William Forrest (*Attorney*)], James Flavin (*Capt. Dennis*)], [Sandra Gould (*Secretary*)], [Joe McTurk (*Speakeasy owner*)], [Jack Pepper, Richard Keene (*Walker's friends*)], [George Pat Collins, Charles Keane, Dick Ryan, Mickey Finn, James Hyland (*Policemen*)], [Harlan Warde, Larry Blake, Philip Van Zandt, Gordon Wynn, Hy Anzel, Bing Russell, Johnny Grant, Russ Bender, Joseph Turkel, George Lynn, Paul Gary, Don Brodie, Eric Alden, Bill Meader (*Reporters*)], [Leonard Bremen (*Building inspector*)], [Tim Ryan (*Police captain*)], [James E. McNally, Joel Smith (*Governor's secretaries*)], [Sidney Marion, Danny Davenport, Len Hendry, Llorna Jordan (*New Yorkers*)], [James Joseph O'Neill (*Patrolman*)], [Vilis Lapenieks (*Latvian ambassador*)], [Dick Nelson (*Franklin D. Roosevelt*)], [Mike Mahoney (*Intern*)], [Joseph Donte, Ralph Brooks, John Benson, Robert Strong (*Photographers*)], [Lyle Moraine, James Davies (*Spectators*)], [Edgar Murray (*Doctor*)], [Hazel Boyne (*Flower woman*)], Pat Moran (*Court clerk*).

Political, Biography, Romance, with songs. [*Print viewed*]. In the spring of 1925, New York State Senator James "Jimmy" Walker is summoned to the office of Gov. Al Smith, who makes a personal request that the popular Jimmy run for mayor of New York City. Smith and his associates in the Democratic Party are certain that Jimmy can easily win the election, thereby consolidating the Party's power in the state of New York. However, Jimmy, an Irish Catholic, is reluctant because he is estranged from his wife Allie, who tired of his womanizing and irresponsibility. Smith soon removes this obstacle to Jimmy's campaign when he reveals that Allie is waiting nearby, ready to lend her support and attempt a reconciliation. With his political mentor, Chris Nolan, and Allie at his side, Jimmy begins his campaign, taking his message to the streets of New York. Visiting the city's various ethnic neighborhoods, Jimmy delights the assembled crowds with his own composition, "Will You Love Me in December," which he sings in Yiddish, Polish and Italian. After winning the election by a landslide, Jimmy sets himself to the task of appointing his staff. The politically savvy Chris hands Jimmy a list of job candidates who are owed "favors," but Jimmy insists on hiring staff members on their own merits. At home, Allie rebuffs Jimmy's advances, informing him that his election to mayor has not restored his full marital privileges. That night, Jimmy visits a nightclub and later passes out drunk on a park bench, where he is discovered by young nightclub singer Betty Compton, a Canadian emigre with a fondness for stray cats. Unaware that Jimmy is the mayor, Betty attempts to help him home. Shortly after, upon learning of Jimmy's identity, Betty angrily denounces his behavior as unbecoming to public office, and Jimmy finds himself smitten by her spunk. Using his power as mayor, Jimmy forces Broadway producer Bernie Williams to hire Betty for his new show. At first angry at Jimmy for his machinations on her behalf, Betty is eventually won over by his charm and sincerity. Back at City Hall, Jimmy proclaims that he will wipe out corruption in the city government. Chris, angry that Jimmy has not consulted Tammany Hall about his plans, condemns him as hopelessly naïve. As his first term comes to a close, Jimmy finally realizes that he will have to play the political game if he is to stay in office and fulfill his promises to the electorate. In the fall of 1929, Jimmy and Chris prepare for Jimmy's reelection campaign against Congressman Fiorello LaGuardia, who has released newsreels dismissing Jimmy as the "musical comedy mayor" and accusing him of spending one third of his term on vacation while giving himself a hefty salary hike. Although LaGuardia's accusations are not without foundation, Jimmy's charisma overshadows his weaknesses as mayor and he is reelected in another landslide victory. Now broke as a result of the stock market crash, Jimmy retains his happy go lucky attitude, but Betty, tired of being hidden from public view, is bitterly disappointed by his reelection and the prospect of four more years of secrecy. Jimmy, who cannot persuade Allie to divorce him, then takes Betty to his victory party over the protests of his handlers. Soon after, the committee of Judge Samuel Seabury begins investigating allegations of graft and corruption in Jimmy's government. Chris and Charley Hand, Jimmy's loyal secretary, beg Jimmy to give up Betty so that he won't lose the Church's support, but Jimmy refuses, leading Charley to resign. With much dignity, the long suffering Allie warns Betty not to cast her lot with Jimmy, who will never be happy out of the public eye. That evening, at a boisterous roast in Jimmy's honor, Betty realizes that Jimmy will never give her the stable home life of which she dreams and she tearfully breaks off their relationship. After Betty attempts suicide, Chris hustles her onto a boat headed for Havana, and she later marries a young suitor. Jimmy, heartbroken over the loss of Betty, is summoned by the Seabury Committee and Gov. Franklin D. Roosevelt to testify about stocks and bonds he accepted from various political associates, and, in August 1932, he travels to Albany with Allie and Chris. Speaking in his own defense, Jimmy admits that he accepted monetary gifts, but claims that he never intended any wrongdoing and was guilty only of stupidity. After reciting the tale of "Susanna and the Elders," Jimmy goes on to proclaim that if he is guilty, then so are all of the politicians present. On the train back to New York City, Allie and Chris praise Jimmy for his honesty, but Charley, who now works for Roosevelt, denounces Jimmy for causing a split in the Party vote which may damage Roosevelt's chances in the Presidential election. Jimmy, sure that he still has the support of his constituents, attends a Yankees game, but is loudly booed by the spectators. From the field, Jimmy makes a resignation speech in which he apologizes for any

wrongdoing he may have committed, but he also reminds the spectators that they bear some of the responsibility by electing him in the first place. After saying goodbye to a tearful Allie, who still loves him and refuses to divorce, Jimmy boards a boat bound for Europe. As he gazes at the skyline of his beloved New York, Betty, who has gotten a quick divorce, arrives and declares her intention to spend her life with him, no matter where the boat should take them. *Infidelity. Mayors. New York City. Politics. Jimmy Walker. Ambition. Banquets. Baseball. Canadians. Catholic Church. Democratic Party. Divorce. Irish Americans. Marriage. Nightclubs. Parades. Political alliances. Political campaigns. Political corruption. Franklin Delano Roosevelt. Secretaries. Singers. Alfred E. Smith. Songs. Theatrical producers. Womanizers.*

Note: This film is subtitled "The Life and Times of Jimmy Walker." *Beau James* opens with a prologue, narrated by Walter Winchell, in which New York City is compared to a seductive woman, a metaphor which is used throughout the film in Winchell's intermittent voice-overs and in the lyrics of its theme song, "Will You Love Me in December." The voice-over epilogue by Winchell consists of the final paragraph from Gene Fowler's biography of Walker. James "Jimmy" Walker (1881-1946) was the one-hundredth mayor of New York City. The son of a man active in New York City political circles, Walker entered politics after a brief stint on Tin Pan Alley during which he wrote the 1908 hit song "Will You Love Me in December." Walker was elected mayor in 1925 and reelected in 1929. Judge Samuel Seabury began his investigation of Walker's administration in 1930, calling Walker to testify in the summer of 1932. Walker was not formally charged with wrongdoing and was still popular with his constituents, but resigned his office in August 1932 to avoid further scandal. Soon after, he left the United States to live in Europe. Although the film ends with Allie and Jimmy deciding not to divorce, the Walkers did divorce in 1933, after which Walker married singer Betty Compton, his mistress of six years. Compton did not marry another man during Walker's troubles with the Seabury Commission, as the film suggests, but was married briefly prior to meeting Walker. In 1935, Walker returned with Compton to the United States, where he was greeted by crowds of cheering New Yorkers. Compton divorced Walker in 1941 and remarried shortly after, but she and Walker remained close until her early death at age 40 from cancer. Walker died two years later, in 1946. According to Fowler's biography, Walker returned to the Catholic Church, from which he had long been estranged, following his divorce from Compton.

A *HR* news item dated Aug 1947 reported that Fowler, then in the process of writing Walker's biography, was turning down offers of up to $500,000 for the screen rights to his forthcoming book because he wanted to produce the film himself. There is no indication, however, that Fowler was involved in the production of this film, which was made ten years after the publication of his book. According to a *LAT* article published in Aug 1956, in order to ensure accuracy and avoid lawsuits, the producers paid clearance fees of up to $7,500 to a number of individuals, including Janet Allen ("Allie") Walker, Betty Compton's mother and Charley Hand's widow. Mrs. Walker reportedly approved of the story, asking only that a reference to her as "brittle" be removed and that Walker be treated more sympathetically in one particular scene. A modern source indicates that Melville Shavelson and Jack Rose paid clearance fees totaling $50,000, while a biography of Bob Hope notes that Florence Compton stipulated that her daughter's real name be used in the film and requested that the actress chosen to play the role bear a physical resemblance to her.

According to publicity material contained in the AMPAS Library file on this film, Shavelson and Rose went location scouting in New York City, but discovered that the only places frequented by Walker still standing were Yankee Stadium and City Hall. Although background footage was shot of New York City streets and of the crowds at Yankee Stadium and the St. Patrick's Day Parade, the majority of the film was shot on a soundstage. The technical adviser on the film, Harold Melnicker, had been an aide to Judge Seabury and participated in the legal proceedings against Walker. Vera Miles was given permission to appear in *Beau James* by Alfred Hitchcock, to whom she was under contract. Hitchcock required that Miles be dressed in white, black or gray, and, save for one scene in which she sings in a pale pink period costume, Miles wears nothing but these shades in the film.

Correspondence dated Jul 1956 and contained in the MPAA/PCA Collection at the AMPAS Library indicates that the PCA was highly critical of the script's depiction of the relationship between Walker and Compton. The PCA asked the producers to "preserve some regard for the institution of marriage" by eradicating "any aura of romanticization" of the affair and went on to suggest that since the marriage of Walker and Compton "ended in dire tragedy," the producers might solve the problem by "introduc[ing] a note of strong foreboding" in the liaison. The script's happy ending, the PCA declared, "is a false note both historically and from the Code point of view." The Catholic Legion of Decency gave *Beau James* a "B" rating because the film did not depict Walker's return to his faith in his later years. According to a *DV* news item published in Nov 1957, Paramount paid a $1,500 settlement to Marion Sunshine, a vaudeville performer who recognized one of her songs in the sketch "His Honor, the Mayor of New York," which is performed in the film by Jimmy Durante. Paramount held the option on a Sunshine composition entitled "Little Jimmy, the Mayor of New York."

Although reviewers felt that *Beau James* was entertaining and captured the tone of Walker's era, the film was not viewed as particularly factual. *Films in Review* denounced the picture as a "whitewash of a lax and tainted public official," while *Time* magazine stated that its affectionate portrayal of a

"whoopee-making clown" was "just as irresponsible as its taxpayer-take-the-hindmost hero." Following Shavelson's and Rose's *The Seven Little Foys* (1955), *Beau James* marked Bob Hope's second appearance in a role with strong dramatic elements. Although Hope received generally favorable reviews for his performance, his biographers have noted that he was disappointed that his work in this film did not garner more critical attention; he never again attempted a dramatic role.

Box 15 Jun 1957. *DV* 7 Jun 1957, p. 3. *FD* 7 Jun 1957, p. 8. *FIR* Jun-Jul 1957. *Har* 8 Jun 1957, p. 92. *HR* 28 Aug 1947. *HR* 14 Sep 1956. *HR* 7 Jun 1957, p. 3. *LAT* 9 Jun 1957. *MPD* 7 Jun 1957. *MPHPD* 15 Jun 1957, p. 417. *NYT* 27 Jun 1957, p. 21. *Time* 1 Jul 1957. *Var* 12 Jun 1957, p. 6.

THE BEAUTIFUL CITY (Italian Americans, Irish Americans)

Inspiration Pictures, Inc. *Dist* First National Pictures, Inc. 25 Oct 1925 [©Inspiration Pictures, Inc.; 26 Oct 1925; LP21930]. Si; b&w. 7 reels, 6,466 ft.

Dir Kenneth Webb. *Scen and titles* Don Bartlett and C. Graham Baker. *Adpt* Violet E. Powell. *Wrt* Edmund Goulding. *Photog* Roy Overbaugh and Stuart Kelson. *Art titles* H. E. R. Studios. *Film ed* William Hamilton. *Sett* Tec-Art Studios.

Cast: Richard Barthelmess (*Tony Gillardi*), Dorothy Gish (*Mollie*), William Powell (*Nick Di Silva*), Frank Puglia (*Carlo Gillardi*), Florence Auer (*Mamma Gillardi*), Lassie Bronte (*The dog*).

Melodrama. Tony Gillardi, a young Italian flower vendor, makes a poor living when compared by his mother with her favorite, his brother Carlo. Only Mollie O'Connor, his little Irish sweetheart, believes in him. Carlo's source of income, however, is not within the law, for he is dominated by gangster Nick Di Silva, who operates a Chinese theater as a front. Rather than hurt his mother's feelings, Tony takes the blame for a robbery Nick and Carlo committed. After serving a term "up the river," Tony finds out that Carlo is still under Nick's domination and sets out to get him. In a fight between Nick and Tony, Nick accidentally shoots Mamma Gillardi. Nick falls to his death while escaping, the mother recovers, and Tony and Mollie marry. While making a trip around the Battery to Coney Island with Mollie, Tony comes to see, once again, the beauty of his city. *Dogs. Family life. Flower vendors. Gangsters. Irish Americans. Italian Americans. New York City. Scapegoats. Theater.*

FD 1 Nov 1925. *NYT* 23 Nov 1925, p. 25. *Var* 25 Nov 1925, p. 38.

BEAUTY AND THE BANDIT (Latino)

Monogram Pictures Corp. *Dist* Monogram Pictures Corp. 9 Nov 1946; Prod: mid-Jul—early Aug 1946 [©Monogram Pictures Corp.; 28 Oct 1946; LP654]. Sd (Western Electric Mirrophonic Sound); b&w. 69 min.

Series: The Cisco Kid.

Prod Scott R. Dunlap. *Dir* William Nigh. *Asst dir* Eddie Davis. *Tech dir* Ernest Hickson. *Orig story and scr* Charles S. Belden. *Dir of photog* Harry Neumann. *Film ed* Frank Maguire. *Set des* Vin Taylor. *Ward* Harry Bourne. *Mus dir* Edward J. Kay. *Rec eng* Franklin Hansen. *Makeup* Harry Ross. *Prod mgr* Charles J. Bigelow.

Song(s): "Viens, Cherche Ton Baiser," music and lyrics by Gordon Clark; "Ride, Amigos, Ride!" music by Charles Rosoff, lyrics by Eddie Cherkose.

Source: Based on the character created by O. Henry.

Cast: Gilbert Roland [(*The Cisco Kid*)], Martin Garralaga (*Valegra*), Frank Yaconelli (*Baby*), Ramsay Ames (*Jeanne [Du Bois]*), Vida Aldana (*Rosita*), George J. Lewis (*Captain*), William Gould (*Doc Walsh*), Dimas Sotello (*Farmer*), Felipe Turich (*Sick farmer*), Antonio Damas (*Luis*), Alex Montoya.

Western. [*Print viewed*]. Outlaw The Cisco Kid learns from a former member of his band that a rich, young Frenchman named Du Bois has recently landed at a California port and will travel with a chest of silver to the town of San Marino. Pretending to be a policeman, Cisco meets Du Bois and offers the services of himself and several of his men as escorts. Unknown to Cisco, Du Bois is actually a woman named Jeanne, who has disguised herself as a man. Along the way, Cisco's men remove the silver from the chest and replace it with stones. Meanwhile, in San Marino, Doc Walsh and his associate, Valegra, quarrel when Valegra frets about his part in Walsh's scheme to drive the farmers off their land by poisoning their grain. Walsh plans to use the silver that Jeanne is bringing to town to buy the land and sell it at a high price in Europe. After Cisco and Jeanne arrive, Jeanne reveals her true identity to Walsh, who had been a business associate of her dead father. When Walsh tells Jeanne that there is no silver in the chest, she lies that she has hidden the silver in a safe place. The next morning, Jeanne drops her male disguise, and Cisco

offers to give her a riding lesson. In the middle of the lesson, Cisco is summoned by his sidekick, Baby, who informs him that the real police chief has arrived and has arrested several of Cisco's men. Followed by Jeanne, Cisco rescues his men and then heads for his hideout. At the camp, Jeanne reveals that she knows Cisco stole her money, but did not tell Walsh because she has fallen in love with him. When Cisco learns what Jeanne plans to do with the money, he scolds her for the ugliness in her heart and spanks her. He adds that he has dedicated his life to helping the poor and does not want to settle down with any woman. When they all return to town, they find that the starving farmers have eaten the poisoned grain and are dying. While Cisco and his men demand the antidote from Valegra, a reformed Jeanne pays Walsh for the deed and then burns it. Walsh then locks Jeanne in one of the rooms, intending to lure Cisco to the house and kill him. Despite Walsh's attempts to confuse Cisco with ventriloquism, however, Cisco kills him. The next day, the police arrest Cisco, who has a criminal record, but Cisco escapes and rejoins his men, who will continue to fight for the poor. *Bandits. Land rights. Poisoning.* California. Farmers. Fathers and daughters. Male impersonation. Moral reformation. Murder. Silver. Ventriloquists and ventriloquism.

Note: According to modern sources, star Gilbert Roland wrote additional dialogue for this film. For more information about "The Cisco Kid" series, consult Series Index and see the entry below for *The Cisco Kid.*

HR 19 Jul 1946, p. 22. *HR* 2 Aug 1946, p. 18. *MPHPD* 16 Nov 1946, p. 3312. *MPHPD* 7 Dec 1946, p. 3347.

BEEHRT SICH VORZUFAEHREN see DON JUAN DIPLOMáTICO

BEFORE THE WHITE MAN CAME (Native Americans)

Northwestern Film Corp. *Dist* State Rights; Northwestern Film Corp.; Arrow Film Corp. **1920.** Si; b&w. 5-7 reels.

Dir John E. Maple. *Story and scen* William E. Wing. *Cam* John W. Fuqua and Emil B. Sonntag.

Western. Big Elk and Che-wee-na, both of the Great Bear tribe, are engaged to be married. White Wolf, the son of the chief of another tribe, offers to buy Che-wee-na; when her father refuses, Little Wolf challenges Big Elk to a physical contest that Big Elk wins. Embittered, Little Wolf provokes a war between the tribes, kidnapping Che-wee-na while Big Elk and the other Great Bear warriors are away from their camp. Che-wee-na feigns insanity among Little Wolf's people, who think that she is in communication with the great spirits. She wins the gratitude of the tribe when she nurses a sick child to health, but in so doing incurs the jealousy of the tribe's medicine man, who accuses her of poisoning the tribe's water supply. Che-wee-na is about to be burned at the stake when Big Elk and his warriors rescue her. The lovers are united among their people. *Indians of North America. Rivalry. Abduction. Medicine men. Rescues. War.*

Note: The film was shot in the Big Horn Mountains in Montana and Wyoming, and the cast was composed entirely of Crow and Cheyenne Indians. Northwestern advertised the film as ready for the state rights market in Dec 1919 and Jan 1920, and some reviews appeared in early 1920. Arrow acquired the film for distribution in the spring of 1920, announcing its release on 10 May 1920; the film may not have been released on that date, as Arrow later announced a 1 Sep 1920 release. The film seems to have been cut, first from seven reels to six, then from six reels to five over the course of 1920. One modern source speculates that certain shots from the film were borrowed from Maple's 1918 documentary *Indian Life* (see below).

ETR 7 Feb 1920, p. 1003. *ETR* 23 Oct 1920, p. 2208. *MPN* 6 Mar 1920, p. 2390. *MPN* 3 Apr 1920, p. 3122. *MPN* 1 May 1920, p. 3908. *MPN* 24 Jul 1920, p. 806. *MPN* 31 Jul 1920, p. 973. *MPW* 27 Dec 1919, p. 1046. *MPW* 31 Jan 1920, p. 779.

BEHIND THE DOOR (German Americans)

Thomas H. Ince Productions. *Dist* Famous Players-Lasky Corp.; Paramount-Artcraft Pictures. 14 Dec **1919** [©Thomas H. Ince; 5 Nov 1919; LP14413]. Si; b&w. 7 reels.

Supv Thomas H. Ince. *Dir* Irvin V. Willat. *Scen* Luther Reed. *Cam* J. O. Taylor and Frank M. Blount. *Tech dir* Harold G. Oliver.

Source: Based on the short story "Behind the Door" by Gouverneur Morris in *McClure's Magazine* (Jul 1918).

Cast: Hobart Bosworth (*Oscar Krug*), Jane Novak (*Alice Morse*), Wallace Beery (*Lieutenant Brandt*), James Gordon (*Bill Tavish*), Dick Wain (*McQuestion*), J. P. Lockney (*Matthew Morse*), Gibson Gowland (*Gideon Blank*), Otto Hoffman (*Mark Arnold*).

Drama. Oscar Krug, an old sea-faring man, returns to his village in Maine after a long absence and reminisces. In a flashback, he is seen as a middle-aged German American who faces anti-German sentiment when the United States enters World War I. He enlists as a navy

captain to prove his loyalty, then secretly marries Alice Morse who follows him on his boat after being thrown out by her father who objects to the marriage. A German submarine sinks their vessel, and Oscar and Alice are the sole survivors. Days later, a German U-boat appears and takes Alice aboard, but abandons Oscar, who vows revenge after being rescued. A year later Oscar takes Lieutenant Brandt, the U-boat commander, prisoner. When Oscar learns the sad fate of his wife who was brutalized by Germans, he retaliates by killing the man, attempting to skin him alive behind a closed door. Back in Maine, the broken old man has a vision of his bride. His soul rises and embraces her. *German Americans. Germans. Revenge. Sea captains. Submarine boats. World War I.* Maine. Marriage–Secret. Murder. Rape. Rescues. United States. Navy. Visions.

Note: According to Paramount studio records, this film was produced independently by Thomas H. Ince.

ETR 17 Jan 1920, p. 711. *MPN* 20 Dec 1919, p. 4466. *MPN* 3 Jan 1920, pp. 314-15, 418. *MPN* 10 Jan 1920, p. 683. *MPN* 17 Jan 1920, p. 915. *MPN* 10 Jul 1920, p. 416. *MPW* 10 Jan 1920, p. 300. *NYT* 5 Jan 1920, p. 15. *Var* 31 Jan 1920, p. 56. *Wid's* 4 Jan 1920, p. 11.

BEHIND THE MAKE-UP (French Americans, Italian Americans)

Paramount Famous Lasky Corp. *Dist* Paramount Famous Lasky Corp. 11 Jan **1930** [©Paramount Famous Lasky Corp.; 8 Jan 1930; LP981]. Sd (Movietone); b&w. 8 reels, 6,364 ft.

Dir Robert Milton. *Adpt and dial* George Manker Watters and Howard Estabrook. *Photog* Charles Lang. *Film ed* Doris Drought. *Rec eng* Harry D. Mills.

Song(s): "My Pals," "Say It with Your Feet" and "I'll Remember, You'll Forget," music and lyrics by Leo Robin, Sam Coslow and Newell Chase.

Source: Based on the short story "The Feeder" by Mildred Cram in *Red Book* (May 1926).

Cast: Hal Skelly (*Hap Brown*), William Powell (*Gardoni*), Fay Wray (*Marie*), Kay Francis (*Kitty Parker*), E. H. Calvert (*Dawson*), Paul Lukas (*Boris*), Agostino Borgato (*Chef*), Jacques Vanaire (*Valet*), Jean De Briac (*Sculptor*).

Romance, Drama. Hap Brown, an easygoing, happy-go-lucky actor, falls in love with Marie, a waitress in the French Quarter of New Orleans, and befriends Gardoni, a fallen actor with whom he forms a partnership. They fall out, however, when Gardoni insists on dominating the act, and Hap takes a job in the café where Marie works. When he and Gardoni team up again, Marie is taken with the Italian and they are soon married, leaving Hap hurt and rejected. Overwhelmed by a brilliant Broadway reception, Gardoni neglects his wife for adventuress Kitty Parker; though Hap knows of it, he does not tell Marie. Scorned by Kitty, Gardoni dies tragically. Hap turns to Marie for moral support, and under her guidance he proves himself to be a brilliant comedian. *Actors and actresses. Adventuresses. Italian Americans. Jealousy. Marriage.* New Orleans (LA). New York City–Broadway. Vaudeville. Waitresses.

FD 19 Jan 1930. *NYT* 18 Jan 1930, p. 21. *Var* 15 Jan 1930, p. 22.

BEHIND THE NEWS (Latino)

Republic Pictures Corp. *Dist* Republic Pictures Corp. 20 Dec **1940**; Prod: 22 Oct–8 Nov 1940 [©Republic Pictures Corp.; 20 Dec 1940; LP10173]. Sd (RCA Sound System); b&w. 8 reels, 6,607 ft. 75 min. Passed by the National Board of Review. PCA cert no. 6841.

Assoc prod Robert North. *Dir* Joseph Santley. [*Asst dir* George Blair]. *Scr* Isabel Dawn and Boyce De Gaw. *Orig story* Dore Schary and Allen Rivkin. *Photog* Jack Marta. *Art dir* John Victor Mackay. *Film ed* Ernest Nims and [Eddie Mann]. *Supv ed* Murray Seldeen. *Ward* Adele Palmer. *Mus dir* Cy Feuer. *Prod mgr* Al Wilson.

Cast: Lloyd Nolan [(*Stuart Woodrow*)], Doris Davenport [(*Barbara Shaw*)], Frank Albertson [(*Jeff Flavin*)], Robert Armstrong [(*Vic Archer*)], Paul Harvey [(*Hardin S. Kelly*)], Charles Halton [(*Neil Saunders*)], Eddie Conrad [(*Enrico*)], Harry Tyler [(*Monroe*)], Dick Elliott [(*Foster*)], Archie Twitchell [(*Reporter*)], Veda Ann Borg [(*Bessie*)], Milton Parsons [(*Eddie*)], [Frank Puglia (*Tomas Olmedo*)], [Charles Stevens].

Newspaper, Drama. [*Print viewed*]. Jeff Flavin, an idealistic journalism school graduate, wins a scholarship entitling him to six months employment as a cub reporter on the *Enquirer.* On the day Jeff arrives, managing editor Vic Archer is ranting against his star reporter, Stuart Woodrow, whose cynicism and laziness are destroying his reputation as a great writer. Archer assigns Jeff to Stu in hopes of resuscitating Stu's interest in his career, but because Stu loathes cubs, he treats Jeff badly. Stu is covering the arrest of

notorious racketeer Harry "Face" Houseman, who is to be prosecuted by district attorney Hardin S. Kelly. The reporters accuse Kelly of going after Houseman merely because he is up for re-election, and indeed the case secures the election for Kelly. Meanwhile, Jeff investigates a rash of food poisonings at the local home for elderly people. Jeff gets himself and Stu arrested while trying to obtain evidence, causing Stu to miss an important date with his fiancée, Barbara Shaw, who is Kelly's secretary. Soon after, Stu gets drunk and tells Jeff off, but Jeff nonetheless helps Stu out when he is too drunk to cover Houseman's escape from prison. Jeff goes to the apartment of Houseman's sister and watches in horror as Houseman is gunned down and an innocent child, killed. Jeff writes the story under Stu's byline, which prompts Stu's gratitude but makes him more determined to get Jeff out of the newspaper racket, as he thinks he is too decent for it. He gives Jeff a false story about the mayor's divorce, and an infuriated Archer demotes Jeff to reading the funny pages on the radio. Later, Jeff goes to court to aid one of his young listeners and afterward watches the trial of Carlos Marquez, a Mexican accused of killing Houseman. Jeff, who speaks Spanish, hears translator Tomas Olmedo falsely state that Carlos confessed to the murder. Carlos is convicted, and when Jeff tries to convince Archer and the others of his innocence, they refuse to listen to him because of the fake story. Barbara finally convinces Stu to give Jeff a break, and the trio searches Kelly's office for clues. They discover that Olmedo was paid off by Kelly and also that Kelly had been receiving graft from Houseman and other racketeers for years. Speculating that Kelly was behind Houseman's escape and murder, they then find Olmedo and secure his testimony. Kelly is arrested and convicted, Carlos is freed, and Jeff, now a full-fledged reporter, is the best man at Stu and Barbara's wedding. *Disillusionment. Frame-ups. Political corruption. Reporters. Transformation. Bribery. Deception. District Attorneys. Drunkenness. Editors. Engagements. Mexican Americans. Murder. Racketeers. Radio broadcasting. Scholarships. Translators. Trials.*

Note: The working title for this film was *A Flagpole Needs a Flag.* HR production charts include Carol Adams in the cast, but her participation in the completed film has not been confirmed. This film was remade in 1955 by Republic under the title *Headline Hunters,* directed by William Whitney and starring Rod Cameron (see below).

Box 21 Dec 1940. *DV* 11 Dec 1940, p. 3. *FD* 23 Dec 1940, p. 6. *HR* 21 Oct 1940, p. 6. *HR* 25 Oct 1940, p. 8. *HR* 8 Nov 1940, p. 2, 8. *HR* 11 Dec 1940, p. 4. *MPD* 16 Dec 1940, p. 9. *MPH* 14 Dec 1940, p. 41. *NYT* 16 Jan 1941, p. 25. *Var* 25 Dec 1940, p. 18.

BEHOLD MY WIFE! (Native Americans)

Paramount Productions, Inc.; A B. P. Schulberg Production. *Dist* Paramount Productions, Inc. 7 Dec **1934** [©Paramount Productions, Inc.; 10 Dec 1934; LP5154]. Sd (Western Electric Noiseless Recording); b&w. 9 reels, 7,104 ft. 78-79 min. Passed by the National Board of Review. PCA cert no. 372.

Pres ADOLPH ZUKOR. [*Exec prod* Emanuel Cohen]. *Dir* Mitchell Leisen. *Scr* Vincent Lawrence and Grover Jones. *Adpt* William R. Lipman and Oliver La Farge. [*Contr to trmt* Ainsworth Morgan, Gladys Lehman, Charles Brackett and Frank Partos]. *Photog* Leon Shamroy. [*Art dir* Hans Dreier and Bernard Herzbrun].

Source: Based on the novel *The Translation of a Savage* by Sir Gilbert Parker (New York, 1893).

Cast: SYLVIA SIDNEY (*Tonita Storm Cloud*), Gene Raymond (*Michael Carter*), Laura Hope Crews (*Mrs. Carter*), H. B. Warner (*Mr. Carter*), Juliette Compton (*Diana Curzon*), Monroe Owsley (*Bob Prentice*), Ann Sheridan (*Mary White*), Charlotte Granville (*Mrs. Sykes*), Kenneth Thomson (*Jim Curzon*), Dean Jagger (*Pete*), Eric Blore (*Benson*), Charles Middleton (*Juan Storm Cloud*), [Ralph Remley (*Jenkins*)], [Cecil Weston (*Gibson*)], [Dewey Robinson (*Bryan*)], [Charles C. Wilson (*Police captain*)], [Edward Gargan (*Connolly*)], [Olin Howland (*Mattingly*)], [Greg Whitespear (*Medicine man*)], [Jim Thorpe (*Indian chief*)], [Otto Hoffman (*Minister*)], [Evelyn Selbie (*Neighbor woman # 1*)], [Raymond Turner (*Porter*)], [Ferdinand Munier (*Arthur*)], [Nella Walker (*Mrs. Copperwaithe*)], [Countess Rina De Liguoro (*Countess Slavotski*)], [Virginia Hammond (*Mrs. Lawson*)], [Lillianne Leighton (*Neighbor woman #2*)], [Fuzzy Knight (*First news photographer*)], [Jack Mulhall, Martin Malone, Pat O'Malley, Neal Burns (*Reporters at train*)], [Phillips Smalley (*Society man*)], [Celeste Ford (*Society girl*)], [Edmund Mortimer (*First society man*)], [Mabel Forrest (*Society dowager*)], [Cyril Ring (*Second society man*)], [Rhea Mitchell (*Woman reporter*)], [Phil Tead (*First chauffeur*)], [Eddie Anderson (*Second chauffeur*)], [Matt McHugh (*Chunky, third chauffeur*)], [Rafael Storm (*Fourth chauffeur*)], [Cosmo Kyrle Bellew

(*Mr. Lawson*)], [Gwenllian Gill (*Miss Copperwaithe*)], [Frank Dunn (*Footman*)], [Arnold Korff (*Mr. Lawson's companion*)], [Joseph Sauers (*Morton, Michael's chauffeur*)], [Joan Standing (*Miss Smith*)], [Kate Price (*Mrs. MacGregor*)], [Mike Morita (*Fuji*)], [Charles Stevens (*Apache herder*)], [Whitedove Clemens (*Indian girl at meal*)], [Billy Lee (*Indian boy at meal*)], [Howling Wolf (*Indian father at meal*)], [Mrs. Choree (*Indian mother at meal*)].

Comedy-drama. [*Print viewed*]. After Michael Carter's wealthy family sabotages his marriage to Mary White, a stenographer, and she commits suicide, Michael angrily drives across the country vowing vengeance. He crashes his car and ends up in a saloon, where he buys drinks for Pete, an Indian. Pete becomes irrational and pulling out his gun, accidentally shoots Michael. Pete's girl friend, Tonita Storm Cloud, wants to keep Pete out of jail and falls in love with Michael while treating his injury. After her Indian tribe excommunicates her for staying alone with a white man, Michael proposes marriage to her, seeing this as a way to get even with his prejudiced, status-seeking family. He apprises them of his marriage via a telegram to New York, in which he states that they will approve of her because she is from one of America's "first families." Michael does not consummate his marriage with Tonita, who is confused by his abstention and lack of affection. On their arrival in New York, he insists she wear her customary Indian garb, and his family is horrified by her appearance. The press and society have great fun mocking the Carters for their new family member, and seeking to save face, Diana Curzon, Michael's sister, convinces the family to have a coming-out party for Tonita, for which Diana will have her immaculately dressed in "modern" clothes. Although the guests are all ready to humiliate Tonita, she overcomes their prejudice and reveals their pettiness, becomes a big hit at the party. Michael is furious, however, for even in this, he feels, his family has won. Tonita finally becomes aware of the reason that Michael married her, and in defiance, she leaves with Bob Prentice, a notorious home wrecker. At his apartment, Bob is about to seduce Tonita, when Diana, with whom he has been having an affair, rushes in and says she has left her husband for him. She shoots him when he refuses to reconcile with her. Tonita takes the blame for the murder, believing she no longer has a life worth living, and also that this is an excellent way to revenge herself on Michael. While the police investigate Bob's apartment, Michael hides in the closet, having come to find Tonita. He overhears the discussion about Tonita's arrest and allows himself to be arrested instead to save his wife, whom he now realizes he loves. At the police station, Michael is allowed a few moments alone with Tonita, during which she confesses that his sister really killed Bob. The police listen in on their conversation, and the true killer revealed, Michael and Tonita are free to pursue their love without further familial interference. *Class distinction. Cultural conflict. Family relationships. Indians of North America. Miscegenation. Self-sacrifice. Automobile accidents. Confession. Drunkenness. Excommunication. False arrests. Gunshot wounds. Infidelity. Jumps from heights. Marriage. Murder. Nursing back to health. Parties. Racism. Revenge. Saloons. Seduction. Snobs and snobbishness. Suicide. Trains. Transformation.*

Note: An early story by Oliver LaFarge in the Paramount story files at the AMPAS Library is titled "Redskin Girl," and an early script was called *Red Woman.* Ann Sheridan changed her name from Clara Lou Sheridan during production. In 1920, Famous Players-Lasky Corp. produced *Behold My Wife,* based on the same source, directed by George Melford, and starring Mabel Julienne Scott and Milton Sills (see *AFI Catalog of Feature Films, 1911-20;* F1.0268).

DV 22 Nov 1934, p. 3. *FD* 16 Feb 1935, p. 7. *LAT* 3 Oct 1934. *MPH* 23 Feb 1935, p. 59. *NYT* 18 Feb 1935, p. 19. *Var* 20 Feb 1935, p. 15.

BELLE OF OLD MEXICO (Latino)

Republic Pictures Corp. *Dist* Republic Pictures Corp. 1 Mar **1950;** Prod: mid-Aug—early Sep 1949 [©Republic Pictures Corp.; 20 Jan 1950; LP2896]. Sd (RCA Sound System); col (Trucolor). 6,302 ft. 70 min. Passed by the National Board of Review. PCA cert no. 14110.

Assoc prod Edward J. White. *Dir* R. G. Springsteen. [*Asst dir* Art Vitarelli]. *Wrt* Bradford Ropes and Francis Swann. *Dir of photog* Jack Marta. [*Cam op* Joe Novak]. [*Gaffer* Ozzie Herie]. [*Stills* Mickey Marigold]. *Spec eff* Howard Lydecker and Theodore Lydecker. *Optical eff* Consolidated Film Industries. *Art dir* Frank Hotaling. *Film ed* Harold Minter. *Set dec* John McCarthy, Jr. and James Redd. *Cost de* Adele Palmer. *Mus* Stanley Wilson. *Sd* Frank T. Dyke. *Makeup supv* Bob Mark. *Hair stylist* Peggy Gray. [*Scr supv* Joan Eremin]. [*Grip* Gary Lambrecht].

Song(s): "Lost Now," "Oh, That Rhythm," "I'll Forget You" and "Making with the Conversation," music and lyrics by Walter Kent and Walton Farrar; "Yoyo Yaya," music and lyrics by Antonio C. Martins.

Cast: Estelita Rodriguez [(*Rosita*)], Robert Rockwell [(*Kip Armitage III*)], Dorothy Patrick [(*Deborah Chatfield*)], Florence Bates [(*Nellie Chatfield*)], Dave Willock [(*Tommy Mayberry*)], Gordon Jones [(*Tex Barnett*)], Thurston Hall [(*Horatio Huntington*)], Fritz Feld [(*Dr. Quincy*)], Anne O'Neal [(*Mrs. Ambercrombie*)], Nacho Galindo [(*Pico*)], Joe Venuti [(*Himself*)], Edward Gargan [(*Sam*)], Carlos Molina and Orchestra [], [Gerald Oliver Smith (*Matthews*)], [Julian Rivero (*Papa Dominez*)], [Rosa Turich (*Mama Dominez*)], [Claire Meade (*Aunt Cornelia*)], [Paul Scardon (*Mr. Ambercrombie*)], [George Davis (*Headwaiter*)], [Jean Andren (*Miss Brewster*)], [Bert King (*Al*)], [Robert Jellison (*Gregory*)], [Dick Elliott (*Captain Winslow*)], [Mary Alice Valles, David Garcia (*Rumba dancers*)].

Domestic, Comedy, with songs. [*Print viewed*]. Honoring a promise he made to José, an old army pal, Kip Armitage III, the president of an American university, goes to Mexico to adopt José's sister Rosita. En route to Mexico, Kip tells his attorney, Tommy Mayberry, that his gold-digging, social-climbing fiancée, Deborah Chatfield, does not know about the adoption. Kip assumes that he is adopting a little girl, but he soon discovers that José's daughter is a flirtatious young woman with a beautiful singing voice. When Kip tell Rosita that she cannot live with him because he must keep up proper appearances, she throws her arms around him and pushes him into a fountain. A photographer snaps a picture of the couple apparently embracing in the fountain, which later appears in American newspapers. Infuriated by the picture, Deborah vows to end Kip's association with the young Mexican woman. Soon after returning home with Rosita, Kip begins to worry that Horatio Huntington, the chairman of the university's board of trustees, will disapprove of the unorthodox adoption. Dressed in new clothes, Rosita is introduced to Kip's aunt Cornelia, Deborah and Deborah's mother Nellie. Later, Huntington tells Kip that the Ambercrombies, who have offered to endow the university's science department, will be accompanying him to Kip's party for the board of trustees. At the party, Deborah cajoles Dr. Quincy, a psychoanalyst, into giving an impromptu analysis of Rosita, hoping that an unfavorable report will hasten the young woman's departure. Quincy begins his analysis of Rosita but is interrupted by the arrival of Tex Barnett, a member of Kip's Air Corps unit, who has also promised José that he would adopt Rosita. When Tex defends Rosita against Quincy's aggressive manner, a fistfight ensues, and the incident is reported in the newspapers. Rosita, who has fallen in love with Kip, eventually becomes jealous of Deborah, and when Deborah sends her to boarding school, she vows to break up their marriage plans. Rosita is further angered when she learns that Deborah arranged her session with Quincy, and, before leaving for boarding school, decides to get even with Deborah by sending two bill collectors to her house. Rosita's plan works, and Deborah is thoroughly humiliated before her friends. Later, Tex and Tommy, certain that Kip and Rosita are made for each other, decide to take Rosita away from her boarding school and reunite her with Kip. Tex, Tommy and Rosita hurry to board a cruise ship, where they intrude upon Kip and Deborah, who are about to take their marriage vows. Kip rejects Deborah when he realizes that she is only interested in him for his money, and takes Rosita into his arms. *Adoption. Class distinction. College presidents. Mexicans. Singers. Social climbers. Americans in foreign countries. Aunts. Automobile chases. Boarding schools. Brothers and sisters. Butlers. Engagements. Female impersonation. Frame-ups. Jealousy. Lawyers. Parties. Photographs. Psychologists. Texans. Veterans.*

Note: Although the viewed print was in black and white, all reviews list Trucolor as the film process. Another song was performed in the film, but its title and composer have not been determined. *Belle of Old Mexico* marked Estelita Rodriguez's first starring role.

Box 4 Feb 1950. *FD* 10 Feb 1950, p. 10. *HR* 19 Aug 1949, p. 23. *HR* 26 Aug 1949, p. 13. *HR* 25 Jan 1950, p. 3. *MPHPD* 11 Feb 1950, p. 189. *Var* 8 Feb 1950, p. 18.

BELLE OF THE BOWERY see **SUNBONNET SUE**

BELLE STARR (African Americans)

Twentieth Century-Fox Film Corp. *Dist* Twentieth Century-Fox Film Corp. 12 Sep **1941**; World premiere in St. Louis, MO: 5 Sep 1941; Prod: 7 Apr—late May 1941; retakes and added scenes mid-Jun 1941 [©Twentieth Century-Fox Film Corp.; 12 Sep 1941; LP10790].

Sd (Western Electric Mirrophonic Recording); col (Technicolor). 9 reels, 7,809 ft. 87 min. PCA cert no. 7275.

Prod Kenneth Macgowan. [*Asst prod* Len Hammond]. *Dir* Irving Cummings. [*Asst dir* Saul Wurtzel]. [*2d unit dir in Missouri* Otto Brower]. *Scr* Lamar Trotti. *Story* Niven Busch and Cameron Rogers. *Dir of photog* Ernest Palmer and Ray Rennahan. *Technicolor dir* Natalie Kalmus. *Art dir* Richard Day and Nathan Juran. *Film ed* Robert Simpson. *Set dec* Thomas Little. *Cost* Travis Banton. *Mus* Alfred Newman. *Sd* E. Clayton Ward and Roger Heman. [*Pub dir* Harry Brand]. [*Prod mgr* William Koenig].

Cast: Randolph Scott (*Sam Starr*), Gene Tierney (*Belle Starr*), Dana Andrews (*Major Thomas Crail*), John Shepperd (*Ed Shirley*), Elizabeth Patterson (*Sarah*), Chill Wills (*Blue Duck*), Louise Beavers (*Mammy Lou*), Olin Howland (*Jasper Tench*), Paul Burns (*Sergeant*), Joseph Sawyer (*John Cole*), Joseph Downing (*Jim Cole*), Howard Hickman (*Colonel Thornton*), Charles Trowbridge (*Colonel Bright*), James Flavin (*Sergeant*), Charles Middleton (*Carpetbagger*), [Hugh Chapman (*Young Tench*)], [Stymie Beard (*Young Jake*)], [Michael Morris (*Fat orderly*)], [Dolores Hurlic (*Black girl*)], [Clarence Muse, Clinton Rosemond (*Black men*)], [George Melford (*Preacher*)], [Mae Marsh (*Preacher's wife*)], [Herbert Ashley (*Jailer*)], [Davison Clark (*Bartender*)], [George Reed (*Old Jake*)], [Norman Willis (*Corporal*)], [Billy Wayne (*Soldier*)], [Dick Rich].

Biography. [*Print viewed*]. Soon after the Civil War, Confederate soldier Ed Shirley returns to Missouri and is greeted by his headstrong, beautiful sister Belle, who has been managing their plantation on her own. Belle furiously rejects Ed's assertion that the South has lost the war, and is cold to Union major Thomas Crail, who was Belle's sweetheart before the war. Crail has returned to Missouri to stop the Confederate guerrillas who are plaguing Union soldiers. Wanting to restore his friendship with Crail, Ed invites him to dinner, although Belle declares that she would prefer the company of Sam Starr, one of the bandits whom Crail has been ordered to capture. One of Sam's compatriots overhears Belle's remarks, and Sam joins the dinner party that evening. Sam and Belle are attracted to each other, and later that night, after Sam is wounded while trying to escape from Crail's men, Belle hides him in her room. Crail finds Sam, however, and is also forced to arrest Ed, as he is the head of the household, and to burn the Shirley mansion, as punishment for aiding the renegades. Belle then accompanies Sam's right-hand man, Blue Duck, to Sam's hideout, and the next night, Belle and Blue Duck engineer the jailbreak of Sam and Ed. While Ed maintains that they must return, Belle announces her intention to join Sam's outfit. Ed tries to persuade Belle that Sam is fighting purely for the love of fighting, but Belle, honestly believing that Sam is trying to preserve the South she loves, orders her brother to leave. As time passes, Belle is branded an outlaw for participating in Sam's raids, but their love for each other grows. On the night they are married, Sam makes a speech to his men that makes Belle wonder about his motives, and when he invites Jim and John Cole to join the group, she becomes even more worried. One afternoon, while the Coles and Sam are leading a train robbery, Ed visits Belle and tells her that Sam's actions are tearing Missouri apart. Explaining that the Coles are hurting innocent people, Ed makes Belle promise to question Sam about their activities. As he is leaving, Ed is shot by Jim Cole, and a tearful Belle confronts Sam, who promises to give up his bandit lifestyle after one more job. Sam plans to kidnap Missouri governor Johnson, who will be speaking in town, so that he can dictate his terms to him. Unhappy with the plan, which was orchestrated by the Coles to get ransom money, Belle returns her wedding ring to Sam and tells him that she cannot wear it if they no longer think alike. Intending to turn herself in, Belle goes to her faithful servant, Mammy Lou, for help. Mammy Lou goes to town, and there learns that the governor's appearance is a trap to capture Sam. Hoping that giving herself up will save Sam, Belle rides to town, but on the way, she is shot by Jasper Tench, a horse thief who holds a grudge against her. Tench takes her body to Crail to claim the reward offered for her, but when Sam and Mammy Lou arrive, they state that the corpse is not Belle's so that Tench cannot receive the money. Sam and Mammy Lou then bid Belle a last farewell, after which Sam turns himself in to Crail. As Sam and Crail discuss Belle, they overhear two black men state that Belle can never be killed because she is a legend. *Bandits. Idealists. Romance. Southerners. Belle Starr. Sam Starr. United States–History–Reconstruction, 1865-1898. African Americans. Ambushes.*

Brothers and sisters. Carpetbaggers. Disillusionment. Bluford "Blue" Duck. Fires. Hideouts. Horse thieves. Jailbreaks. Missouri. Officers (Military). Rewards. Servants. Ed Shirley.

Note: The film's title card reads, "Twentieth Century-Fox presents Belle Starr 'The Bandit Queen,'" followed by a listing of players Randolph Scott, Dana Andrews, John Shepperd, Louise Beavers, Chill Wills, Elizabeth Patterson, and a separate card listing "Gene Tierney as Miss Belle." Belle Starr was born Myra Maybelle Shirley on 5 Feb 1848 near Medoc, MO. Accounts of her exploits and association with outlaws such as the Younger Brothers and Jesse James vary widely, but little in these accounts resembles events depicted in the film. She was killed in early Feb 1889, allegedly by Edgar Watson, whom she had refused to accept as a tenant on some farm land that she owned. Sam Starr was three-quarters Cherokee and was born in 1857. Sam and Belle were married in the summer of 1880, but biographical sources disagree as to whether Sam was Belle's second or third husband. Belle's criminal career apparently did not begin until after her marriage to Sam, and was not politically motivated. Sam was killed in late 1887 during an argument with an old enemy, Frank West.

According to the Twentieth Century-Fox Records of the Legal Department and the studio's Produced Scripts Collection, located at the UCLA Arts—Special Collections Library, biographical material on Belle Starr was obtained from a chapter in Cameron Rogers' book *Gallant Ladies* (New York, 1928). This chapter was first published in *Pictorial Review* as "Gay and Gallant Ladies: Belle Starr, the Gadfly of the South" (Feb 1927). According to the studio records, Harvey F. Thew (in collaboration with Rogers), John L. Balderston and Sonya Levien worked on treatments or story outlines for the picture. The extent of their contributions to the completed film has not been confirmed, however. An 11 Jun 1941 *HR* news item asserted that there was a "hushed-up battle over the original screen credit" for the picture but that the problem had "just been settled with the Screen Writers' guild as intermediary." Rogers and Niven Busch received story credit in the final film.

Studio records, material publicity and *HR* news items provide the following information about the production: Roy Del Ruth was originally set as the picture's director. Alice Faye was first cast as "Belle Starr," but was reassigned to Twentieth Century-Fox's *The Great American Broadcast*. At least "48 top feminine figures" were also tested by director Irving Cummings for the title role. Among those actresses who were considered for the part were Carole Landis, Ida Lupino, Arleen Whelan, Joan Crawford, Barbara Stanwyck, Ann Sheridan, Paulette Goddard and June Adams, "a completely unknown player." Henry Fonda was scheduled to play "Ed Shirley," and Tyrone Power was to make a brief, unbilled appearance as "Jesse James," recreating his title role from the 1939 Twentieth Century-Fox film. Actor Chill Wills was borrowed from M-G-M for the production. From approximately 17 Apr to 5 May 1941, Cummings had to shoot around actress Gene Tierney, who was afflicted by severe eye infections and allergies. An 11 Jul 1941 *HR* news item noted that Len Hammond, assistant to producer Kenneth Macgowan, took over post-production duties on the picture when Macgowan left the studio to work for the Latin-American Amity Committee. Studio publicity and legal records noted that backgrounds were shot on location near Joplin and Noel, MO, and in Sherwood Forest, the Santa Susannah Mountains, and the Iverson Ranch in Chatsworth, all of which are located in Southern California. According to *HR* news items, the studio considered filming the entire picture in the Ozark Mountains or near Tucson, AZ.

The legal records note that a trailer entitled "Three of a Kind," for the 1941 Twentieth Century-Fox picture *Charley's Aunt*, also advertised this picture. In the trailer, Jack Benny, the star of *Charley's Aunt*, Tyrone Power, the star of *A Yank in the R.A.F.*, and Randolph Scott meet to discuss "the merits of his individual picture." No actual scenes of the three films were shown. A similar trailer, featuring Gene Tierney, Don Ameche of *Confirm or Deny* and Anne Baxter of *Swamp Water*, was planned but not made. This was the first film in which actor Shepperd Strudwick was billed as John Shepperd. According to studio publicity, Twentieth Century-Fox executives changed his name because they felt it was "too long for a marquee and too hard to remember." The actor changed his name back to Strudwick in 1948. The legal records contain letters from Flossie E. Hutton, Belle Starr's granddaughter, in which she alternately offers information and threatens legal suit if the studio did not compensate her and her sisters for the depiction of their grandmother's story. The legal records do not list any actions taken by the studio in respect to Hutton's claims.

Other films based on the legend of Belle Starr include Twentieth Century-Fox's 1948 picture *Belle Starr's Daughter*, directed by Lesley Selander and starring George Montgomery, Ruth Roman and Isabel Jewell as "Belle." In 1952 RKO released *Montana Belle*, which was directed by Allan Dwan and starred George Brent and Jane Russell as "Belle." According to studio records, in 1957, Twentieth Century-Fox considered producing a television series about Belle. Pamela Reed played "Belle" in the 1980 United Artists release *The Long Riders*, which was directed by Walter Hill.

AmCin Oct 1941, p. 475. *Box* 23 Aug 1941. *DV* 22 Aug 1941, p. 3, 15. *FD* 22 Aug 1941, p. 5. *HR* 4 Oct 1940, p. 10. *HR* 24 Oct 1940, p. 1. *HR* 9 Dec 1940, p. 5. *HR* 6 Jan 1941, p. 4. *HR* 8 Jan 1941, p. 2. *HR* 19 Feb 1941, p. 4. *HR* 4 Mar 1941, p. 9. *HR* 21 Mar 1941, p. 6. *HR* 26 Mar 1941, p. 2. *HR* 27 Mar 1941, p. 2. *HR* 4 Apr 1941, p. 4, 11. *HR* 18 Apr 1941, p. 4. *HR* 25 Apr 1941, p. 2. *HR* 5 May 1941, p. 6. *HR* 30 May 1941, p. 13. *HR* 2 Jun 1941, p. 2. *HR* 11 Jun 1941, p. 2. *HR* 11 Jul 1941, p. 4. *HR* 20 Aug 1941, p. 4. *HR* 22 Aug 1941, pp. 3-4. *HR* 29 Aug 1941, p. 3. *HR* 5 Sep 1941, p. 2. *MPD* 22 Aug 1941. *MPH* 23 Aug 1941. *MPHPD* 14 Jun 1941, p. 161. *MPHPD* 6 Sep 1941, p. 250. *NYT* 1 Nov 1941, p. 20. *Var* 27 Aug 1941, p. 8.

THE BELLS OF ST. MARY'S (Irish Americans)

Rainbow Productions, Inc. *Dist* RKO Radio Pictures, Inc. **1945**; New York opening: 7 Dec 1945; *Prod*: 1 Mar—14 May 1945; retakes late Jun 1945 [©Rainbow Productions, Inc.; 7 May 1945; LP1000]. Sd (RCA Sound System); b&w. 7 reels, 11,330 ft. 126 min. PCA cert no. 10824.

Prod LEO McCAREY. *Dir* Leo McCarey. *Asst dir* Harry Scott. *Scr* Dudley Nichols. *Story* Leo McCarey. *Dir of photog* George Barnes. [*2d cam* Jack Warren]. *Spec eff* Vernon L. Walker. *Art dir* William Flannery. [*Supv art dir* Albert D'Agostino]. *Ed* Harry Marker. *Set dec* Darrell Silvera. *Des of the costs* Edith Head. *Mus score* Robert Emmett Dolan. *Sd* Richard Van Hessen and James G. Stewart.

Song(s): "The Bells of St. Mary's" by Douglas Furber and A. Emmett Adams; "Aren't You Glad You're You?" words and music by Johnny Burke and James Van Heusen; "In the Land of Beginning Again," words and music by George W. Meyer and Grant Clarke; "Varvindar friska," English words by Eddie Lisbona and Bob Musel; "Adeste Fideles," words and music by John Francis Wade and "O Sanctissima," traditional hymn.

Cast: BING CROSBY [(*Father O'Malley*)], INGRID BERGMAN *by arrangement with David O. Selznick* [(*Sister Mary Benedict*)], Henry Travers [(*Horace P. Bogardus*)], William Gargan [(*Joe Gallagher*)], Ruth Donnelly [(*Sister Michael*)], Joan Carroll [(*Patsy Gallagher*)], Martha Sleeper [(*Mrs. Gallagher*)], Rhys Williams [(*Dr. McKay*)], Dickie Tyler [(*Eddie*)], Una O'Connor [(*Mrs. Breen*)], [Bobby Frasco (*Tommy*)], [Aina Constant, Gwen Crawford, Eva Novak (*Nuns*)], [Matt McHugh (*Clerk in store*)], [Edna Wonacott (*Delphine*)], [Jimmy Crane (*Luther*)], [Tim Hawkins, George Noakes, Bobby Dolan, Michael Orr (*Children*)], [Dewey Robinson (*Truck driver*)], [Jimmy Dundee (*Taxi driver*)], [Joseph Palma (*Workman*)], [Minerva Urecal (*Landlady*)], [Peter Sasso (*Blind man*)], [Cora Shannon (*Elderly woman*)].

Religious, Drama. [*Print viewed*]. When Father O'Malley is designated priest of St. Mary's church and its concomitant elementary school, he is warned that the strong-willed nuns drove the previous priest into a rest home. Unfamiliar with the precepts of running a school, O'Malley incurs the disapproval of Swedish American Sister Mary Benedict, the Mother Superior and school principal, when as his first official act, he grants the students a holiday. As Sister Benedict escorts O'Malley on a tour of the dilapidated school building, she points to the building under construction across the way and confesses that it is her dream to have its owner, wealthy, old curmudgeon Horace P. Bogardus, donate his building to the church. Later, O'Malley meets Bogardus when he complains about the children playing on the fence surrounding his building. Bogardus warns O'Malley that unless the church agrees to sell him the school to use as a parking lot, he will ensure that the city council will condemn it. After leaving Bogardus, O'Malley is approached by a desperate woman, who begs the priest to allow her little daughter Patsy to attend the school. The woman, full of self-recrimination, relates the sad story of how her husband, a musician named Joe Gallagher, deserted her soon after the birth of their child and how she has had to depend on the generosity of men to support her young daughter. Sympathetic, O'Malley agrees to care for the troubled Patsy, who experiences difficulty adjusting to the school. As the office building nears completion, Sister Benedict visits Bogardus in his new quarters and envisions a modern classroom and gymnasium there. Overworked and aggravated, Bogardus is then paid a housecall by his physician, Dr. McKay. As the doctor is recommending relaxation and rest, Bogardus recoils at the sound of the school choir across the schoolyard and slams the window shut, causing it to shatter. One day, O'Malley visits Patsy's mother with news that he has located her husband, who is now anxiously waiting to meet her in the hallway. Mrs. Gallagher runs into the hall, and the couple is reunited after being separated for many years. At the same time, Patsy, excited at the thought of her upcoming graduation, goes to visit her mother to show off her commencement dress. Spotting her mother speaking to Gallagher, Patsy believes that he is one of her mother's clients and flees the building. Patsy fails her exams, but O'Malley urges Sister Benedict to pass the girl in order to boost her confidence. The sister adamantly refuses, however, arguing that the school must maintain its standards. Informed that she has failed her courses, Patsy somberly returns her graduation dress. Soon after, Sister Benedict becomes ill and O'Malley sends for Dr. McKay. As they await the doctor's arrival,

Sister Benedict chides O'Malley for writing to the Mother General about Patsy. Although Sister Benedict protests that she is just tired and demoralized by her inability to save St. Mary's, the doctor insists on examining her in his office the next day. On the doctor's way out, O'Malley questions him about Bogardus' heart condition and suggests that good deeds can cure a bad heart. The next day, O'Malley meets Bogardus after he has just visited his physician. Bogardus is preoccupied by the doctor's diagnosis of his condition, but is consoled by O'Malley, who encourages him to perform good deeds. Taking the priest's advice, Bogardus dashes into the street to save a stray dog. After ushering an elderly woman onto her bus, Bogardus then proceeds to the church. Astonished by the sight of Bogardus bowed in prayer, Sister Benedict approaches him and, after confessing that he has acted selfishly, he offers the nun his new building to use as a school, making her giddy with happiness. The good news is soon clouded by Dr. McKay's diagnosis that Sister Benedict is suffering from the early stages of tuberculosis and should be sent to a dry climate and relieved of all strenuous duties. Although the doctor cautions O'Malley to keep the sister's condition secret from her, the priest fears that sending her away without an explanation will lead her to believe that she was transferred at his behest. As the sister arranges the furniture in the new classroom, O'Malley notifies her that she is being transferred, causing her to react with disbelief and sorrow that she will no longer be working with children. Soon after, the girls prepare for their commencement ceremony as Patsy watches longingly in the distance. Upon seeing her mother and her male escort enter the schoolyard, she ducks behind a post to hide, and when Sister Benedict observes her actions, she realizes that Patsy never told her mother that she has failed. Anguished, Patsy asks for the nun's help and admits that she deliberately failed so that she could remain at the school. When O'Malley introduces Patsy's parents to Sister Benedict, Patsy is dumbfounded to learn that the stranger is actually her father. After Mrs. Gallagher promises Patsy a real home and a new life, O'Malley remarks that the couple has come to watch their daughter graduate. Finally comprehending the enormous handicap under which Patsy has suffered, Sister Benedict relents and allows the girl to graduate. After the ceremony, Sister Benedict visits the chapel one last time to pray for guidance. When she departs, bent in sorrow, O'Malley, overwhelmed with compassion, tells her the truth about her condition. Immensely relieved, the sister fills with joy as she bids farewell to the priest. *Churches. Faith. Nuns. Priests. Schools. Swedish Americans. Transformation. Businessmen. Graduations. Heart disease. Irish Americans. Mothers and daughters. Physicians. Reconciliation. Students. Tuberculosis.*

Note: According to a 1945 *NYT* news item, David O. Selznick was paid $175,000 to lend Ingrid Bergman to RKO. As part of the deal, Selznick also acquired the screen rights to *Little Women* and *A Bill of Divorcement.* This was the first effort of Rainbow Productions, Inc., an independent production company owned by Leo McCarey, Bing Crosby, B. G. DeSylva, David Butler and Hal Roach, Jr. According to a 1944 news item in *NYT*, in 1942, McCarey, who was at the time under contract to RKO, outlined the story to Crosby, who was intrigued but unavailable because of his contract with Paramount. Crosby was freed to make the picture when DeSylva, then an executive producer at Paramount, agreed to lend Crosby to RKO in exchange for a commitment with McCarey, who then wrote and directed *Going My Way* for Paramount (see below). Crosby first played the role of "Father O'Malley" in *Going My Way*, which was released prior to *The Bells of St. Mary's* and won an Academy Award for his performance in *Going My Way.* The *HR* review adds that McCarey based Bergman's character on his aunt, Sister Mary Benedict of the Immaculate Heart Convent in Hollywood, CA.

HR news items yield the following information: In Feb 1945, Anna Q. Nilsson was tested for one of the leads. The closing street scene was shot on Paramount's New York street set. Although an Apr 1945 news item places Myra Nelson and Marion Lessing in the cast, their participation in the released film has not been confirmed. Bobby Dolan, the little boy who narrated the nativity scene in the film, was the son of Robert Emmett Dolan, the film's musical director. The film was nominated for the following Academy Awards: Best Picture, Best Actor, Best Actress, Best Director, Best Film Editor, Best Score and Best Song ("Aren't You Glad You're You"). It won the Academy Award for Best Sound Recording. According to a modern source, the film became the year's top box-office picture and was the biggest hit in RKO history. In the 1950s, Republic acquired the picture for its film library and re-issued it in 1959. On 7 Oct 1959, CBS broadcast a televised version of the story, starring Claudette Colbert, Robert Preston and Glenda Farrell.

Box 1 Dec 1945. *DV* 23 Nov 1945, p. 3. *FD* 23 Nov 1945. *HR* 21 Feb 1945, p. 2. *HR* 23 Feb 1945, p. 13. *HR* 26 Feb 1945, p. 10. *HR* 1 Mar 1945, p. 6. *HR* 4 Apr 1945, p. 10. *HR* 11 Apr 1945, p. 9, 11. *HR* 4 May 1945, p. 14. *HR* 27 Jun 1945, p. 1. *HR* 23 Nov 1945, p. 3. *HR* 10 Dec 1945, p. 6. *MPHPD* 5 May 1945, p. 2434. *MPHPD* 1 Dec 1945, p. 2734. *NYT* 1 Apr 1944. *NYT* 4 Mar 1945. *NYT* 7 Dec 1945, p. 26. *Var* 28 Nov 1945, p. 10.

BELLS OF SAN FERNANDO (Latino)
Hillcrest Productions, Inc. *Dist* Screen Guild Productions, Inc. 1 Mar **1947**; Prod: mid-Nov—late Nov 1946 [©Screen Guild Productions, Inc.; 1 Mar 1947; LP893]. Sd (RCA Sound System); b&w. 74 min. PCA cert no. 12199.
Pres S. K. DECKER and B. J. LEAVITT. *Prod* James S. Burkett. *Assoc prod* Renault Duncan. *Dir* Terry Morse. *Asst dir* Willard Sheldon. *Orig story and scr* Jack DeWitt and Renault Duncan. *Dir of photog* Robert Pittack. *Art dir* Frank Dexter. *Supv ed* George McGuire. *Set dresser* Tommy Thomson. *Mus dir* Albert Deano. *Mus score* Rudy DeSaxe. *Dance dir* Antonio Triana. *Sd rec* Perc Townsend. *Makeup* Fred T. Walker. *Prod mgr* Wm. Strohbach.
Song(s): "Land of My Dreams," music by Marian Boyle, lyrics by Don Roland.
Cast: Donald Woods (*Michael O'Brien*), Gloria Warren (*Maria Garcia*), Byron Foulger (*Francisco Garcia*), Shirley O'Hara (*Nita*), Anthony Warde (*Juan Mendoza*), Paul Newlan (*Gueyon*), David Leonard (*Father Xavier*), Monte Blue (*Don Sebastian Fernando*), Gordon Clark (*Enrico*), Frank Cody (*Junipero*), Luisa Triana (*Spanish dancer*), Felipe Turich (*Pablo*), Claire Du Brey (*Manta*), Drew Allen (*Secretary*), Ray Dolciame (*First clerk*), John Parker (*Second clerk*), [Gilbert Galvan (*Perdido*)].
Historical, Drama. [*Print viewed*]. For five years, Paradise Valley in Spanish-controlled California has been overseen by the cruel, greedy Juan Mendoza, who keeps guards posted at the isolated valley's only pass in order to prevent his subjects from leaving and reporting his actions to the outside world. One day, Mendoza informs pious blacksmith Francisco Garcia that he is hosting a fiesta at his hacienda and demands that he and his daughter Maria, whom he has long coveted, attend. Although Garcia despises Mendoza and wants Maria to marry tile maker Michael O'Brien, an Irish seaman who years before wandered into the valley, he is compelled to accept the invitation. When Garcia, who forges church bells, learns that his enormous assistant, Gueyon, has discovered gold in the ground near the valley's mission, he goes to see Father Xavier to ask permission to secretly mine the lode. Aware that Garcia desires the gold so that he can forge his bells with it as a way of repenting for past sins, Father Xavier reluctantly allows Gueyon to continue prospecting. Later, at the fiesta, Mendoza announces that he is marrying Maria, even though Garcia had earlier refused him permission. Mendoza's presumptuousness infuriates Michael, who then challenges Mendoza to a duel. The cowardly Mendoza refuses to fight, however, prompting feisty Michael to knock him down. Enraged with humiliation, Mendoza orders his men to arrest Michael, but the Irishman escapes the hacienda and hides at the mission. While waiting for his opportunity to flee the valley, Michael helps Gueyon mine for gold, which is then smelted and poured into Garcia's bell casts. As Mendoza's wedding to Maria is fast approaching, Michael becomes anxious to make his escape and agrees to Gueyon's plan to sneak past Mendoza's guards while hiding in the tile wagon. Garcia and Gueyon send Perdido, an Indian under Father Xavier's charge, with information regarding the tile wagon rendezvous point. Before reaching Michael, however, Perdido is shot and killed by Mendoza's men, who then find a gold nugget in his pouch, which was to have been used to bribe Pablo, the wagon driver. Excited, the men turn the nugget over to Mendoza, who questions Father Xavier about it without success. Gueyon, meanwhile, gives Michael more gold and leads him to Pablo's wagon. Michael is thrilled to discover Maria already hidden in the wagon and gives Pablo some gold to get them through the pass. While stopped at the guards' post, Pablo quietly alerts the men about the fugitive's presence, but Michael and Maria sense his betrayal and dash off on Pablo's horses. Eventually, Michael and Maria reach Monterey, and are received by the governor, the kindly Don Sebastian Fernando. After telling Don Sebastian about Mendoza, he agrees to go with them to Paradise Valley to confront the overseer. At Mendoza's hacienda, meanwhile, Nita, his ambitious half-Indian lover, informs him that Maria is in the village, grieving over Michael. When Mendoza reacts to the news with anger, Nita is filled with jealousy, but is placated when Mendoza promises to take her to Spain with him. Later, however, after she tells him about Garcia's gold, Nita realizes that he was feigning his love in order to extract information from her. Aware that Mendoza is planning to torture and kill Garcia to get the gold, a vengeful Nita rushes to warn the blacksmith but is killed by Mendoza's men. Mendoza then captures

Garcia, Gueyon and Father Xavier and threatens to put out the priest's eyes unless the gold's whereabouts is revealed. Gueyon finally agrees to take Mendoza to the gold and, at the church, points to the bells. Sure that he is stalling, Mendoza starts to whip Gueyon, who then grabs the bell posts and yanks them to the ground, killing Mendoza. Michael and Maria, who have rescued Garcia and Father Xavier, arrive at the church in time to see the brave Gueyon die. Later, Don Sebastian gives his official blessing to Michael and Maria's marriage and decrees that Michael, now a citizen of Spain, will be the valley's new overseer. Bells. California–History. Gold. Greed. Overseers. Romance. Spanish Americans. Betrayal. Blacksmiths. Escapes. Fiestas. Giants. Governors. Guards. Indians of North America. Irish Americans. Jealousy. Missions. Monterey (CA). Murder. Priests. Self-sacrifice. Unrequited love. Whips and whippings.

Note: The film's opening scene includes a brief narration, in which the history of Paradise Valley is discussed. Modern sources add Angelo Rossitto to the cast.

Box 5 Apr 1947. DV 27 Mar 1947. FD 4 Apr 1947, p. 6. FD 4 May 1947. HR 22 Nov 1946, p. 27. HR 29 Nov 1946, p. 15. HR 27 Mar 1947, p. 3. IFJ 4 Jan 1947, p. 35. MPHPD 5 Apr 1947. Var 2 Apr 1947, p. 16.

BELOVED (Austrian Americans)

Universal Pictures Corp.; Carl Laemmle, President; A B. F. Zeidman Production. Dist Universal Pictures Corp. 22 Jan **1934**; Prod: completed 21 Oct 1933 [©Universal Pictures Corp.; 12 Jan 1934; LP4407]. Sd (Western Electric Noiseless Recording Sound System); b&w. 9 reels. 80 or 82 min. PCA cert no. 4321-R [14 May 1938].

Pres CARL LAEMMLE. [Prod Carl Laemmle, Jr.]. [Assoc prod B. F. Zeidman]. Dir Victor Schertzinger. Scr Paul Gangelin and George O'Neil. Orig story Paul Gangelin. Cam Merritt Gerstad. Art dir Charles D. Hall. Film ed Edward Curtiss. [Ed supv Maurice Pivar]. Mus score Victor Schertzinger and Howard Jackson. Orch cond S. K. Wineland. [Rec eng Gilbert Kurland].

Song(s): "Beloved" and "Forget," music and lyrics by Victor Schertzinger; "Roaming in the Gloaming," Civil War traditional.

Cast: John Boles [(Carl Hausmann)], Gloria Stuart [(Lucy Tarrant Hausmann)], Morgan Farley [(Eric Hausmann)], Ruth Hall [(Patricia Sedley)], Albert Conti [(Baron Franz Von Hausmann)], Dorothy Peterson [(Baroness Irene Von Hausmann)], Edmund Breese [(Major Tarrant)], Louise Carter [(Mrs. Tarrant)], Anderson Lawler [(Tom Rountree)], Richard Carle [(Judge B. T. Belden)], Lucile Webster Gleason [(The Duchess)], Mae Busch [(Marie)], Jimmy Butler [(Charles Hausmann, as a youngster)], Edward Woods [(Charles Hausmann)], Oscar Apfel [(Henry Burrows)], Jane Mercer [(Helen)], [Lester Lee (Carl, age 10)], [Mickey Rooney (Tommy, a violin student)], [Holmes Herbert (Lord Landslake)], [Lucille La Verne (Mrs. Briggs)], [Mary Gordon (Mrs. O'Leary)], [Wallis Clark (Yates)], [Joseph Swickard (Revolutionist leader)], [James Flavin (Wilcox)], [Bessie Barriscale (Mrs. Watkins)], [Bobbie Arnst (The dancer)], [Fred Kelsey (Mulvaney)], [Otto Hoffman (Mr. Dietrick)], [George Ernest (Eric, as a youngster)], [Cosmo Kyrle Bellew (Doctor)], [King Baggot (Second doctor)], [Sherwood Bailey (Tom, as a boy)], [William Strauss (Jewish father)], [Neysa Nourse (Laurette)], [Peggy Terry (Alice)], [Clara Blandick (Miss Murfee)], [Margaret Mann (Countess Von Brandenburg)], [Montague Shaw (Alexander Talbot)], [Walter Brennan (Stuttering boarder)].

Musical, Romance, Melodrama. [Print viewed]. In his aristocratic castle in Vienna in 1838, Baron Franz Von Hausmann cultivates a love of classical music in his infant son Carl. Ten years later, Carl performs his first composition before an audience as lead violin in a string ensemble. When revolution strikes and his father is killed, Carl and his mother flee to Charleston, South Carolina. Carl becomes enlightened of the music sung by the slaves, which he likens to his first waltz composition. In January, 1861, twenty-three-year-old Carl defends his right to be called a Southern gentleman in a scuffle with the arrogant Wilcox, impressing his friend, Tom Rountree, and a woman he soon learns is named Lucy Tarrant, a prospective piano student of his mother. After Lucy convinces her mother to hire Carl to teach her piano, he falls in love with his student, but Major Tarrant, Lucy's father, refuses the couple permission to marry. During the Civil War, Carl survives a hero, but his mother dies while he is fighting for the Confederacy, and Lucy's father is killed at the Battle of Shiloh. The Tarrants' estate is ruined by the war's end, so Carl and Lucy marry and move to New York, where he gives music lessons and they live in happy poverty. While Carl dreams of creating a musical composition embodying the spirit of America, he runs into Tom, his friend from Charleston, who introduces him to Judge B. T. Belden, a show promoter known for his publicity stunts, whose axiom is "the public loves to be fooled." Belden's exploitation of Carl's violin abilities borders on impropriety, as Carl agrees to personify an eccentric artist with a foreign accent who is popular with the ladies. In the fall of 1867, Carl is enthusiastically received, until Lucy convinces him his reputation as a serious musician is at stake when the press labels him Belden's freakish creation. The couple moves into Mrs. Briggs's boardinghouse, where Carl composes as Lucy supports them. When the nosy proprietress and Miss Murfee scoff at Carl for making his wife support him, he gets a job playing piano at the Duchess Palace Saloon in the Bowery. Meanwhile, the pregnant Lucy is forced to quit work and six months later gives birth to a boy, Charles. Nearly ten years pass, and Carl, now a teacher of piano and violin, is unable to instill his love of music in his son. While working on his "American Symphony," Carl reluctantly agrees to sell some of his songs to an advertising agent, who is interested in using them to promote his patent medicine. Charles grows into a profligate young man and impregnantes Helen Burrows. Learning of the girl's condition from her father, Carl orders his son to marry Helen immediately. In an attempt to reform, Charles enlists to fight in the Spanish-American War, where he dies. Helen dies giving birth to a son, Eric, who, at seven, is "borrowing" his grandfather's waltz and changing it to suit the more modern style. In 1918, Eric, after fighting in World War I, returns home and adapts the themes of Carl's classical Negro spirituals into jazz and publishes the song "My Beloved," which Carl claims he has plagiarized. More songs follow and are made successful in hit stage comedies as sung by Patricia Sedley, whom Eric marries. Informed by Carl that Lucy has had a stroke, Eric grants her last request by playing his grandfather's music the old-fashioned way. Later, Carl visits Eric's publisher, Mr. Yates, who insults the elderly man by saying his music lacks distinction and is a poor imitation of Eric's. Enraged, Carl accuses Eric of stealing his melodies and moves out of Eric's luxurious house into his own small apartment. Alexander Talbot of the Metropolitan Symphony Society, encouraged by a donation from Eric to an unemployed musicians' fund, then offers to feature Carl's symphony in the society's next season. Examining the "American Symphony," Talbot is astounded by its greatness. Eric and Carl are reconciled and attend opening night, where Lucy's ghost smiles as Carl's music is finally performed. As he listens from his box seat, Carl dies, satisfied that his composing genius is at last recognized. Ambition. Austrian Americans. Composers. Family relationships. Marriage. Violinists. Aristocrats. Austria–History. Boardinghouses. Family life. Ghosts. Grandsons. Immigrants. Loyalty. Marriage–Forced. Music teachers. New York City–Bowery. Plagiarism. Poverty. Pregnancy. Publicity stunts. Saloons. Self-sacrifice. Southerners. Stroke. United States–History–Civil War, 1861-1865. United States–History–War of 1898. Working wives. World War I.

Note: The title card on the viewed print read: "Beloved A Musical Romance." The DV Los Angeles preview length for this film was 90 minutes, suggesting that at least eight minutes were cut for the final film.

DV 6 Dec 1933, p. 3. FD 27 Jan 1934, p. 4. HR 23 Oct 1933, p. 2. MPH 23 Dec 1933, p. 43, 46. NYT 27 Jan 1934, p. 9. Var 30 Jan 1934, p. 12.

THE BELOVED BRAT (African Americans)

Warner Bros. Pictures, Inc.; A First National Picture. Dist Warner Bros. Pictures, Inc. 30 Apr **1938**; Prod: began mid-Sep 1937 [©Warner Bros. Pictures, Inc.; 27 Jan 1938; LP7935]. Sd; b&w. 6 reels. 62 min. PCA cert no. 3789.

[Exec prod Jack L. Warner and Hal B. Wallis]. [Assoc prod Bryan Foy]. Dir Arthur Lubin. Dial dir Frank Beckwith. [Asst dir Arthur Lueker]. Scr Lawrence Kimble. Orig story Jean Negulesco. [Contr scr const Wally Klein]. Photog George Barnes. Art dir Stanley Fleischer. Film ed Frederick Richards. Gowns Howard Shoup. Sd Francis J. Scheid.

Cast: Bonita Granville (Roberta [Morgan]), Dolores Costello (Helen Cosgrove), Donald Crisp (Mr. Morgan), Natalie Moorhead (Mrs. Morgan), Lucille Gleason (Miss Brewster), Donald Briggs (Williams), Emmett Vogan (Jenkins), Loia Cheaney [(Mrs. Jenkins)], Leo Gorcey [(Spike)], Ellen Lowe [(Anna)], Mary Doyle [(Miss Mitchell)], Paul Everton [(Judge Harris)], Bernice Pilot [(Mrs. White)], Stymie Beard [(Pinkie White)], Meredith White [(Arabella White)], Gloria Fischer [(Boots)], [Carmencita Johnson (Estella)], [Priscilla Lyon (Sylvia)], [Doris Brenn (Jackie)], [Patsy Mitchell (Betty

Mae)], [Betty Compson (*Eleanor Sparks*)], [Victor Wong (*Gardener*)], [Al Duval (*Cab driver*)], [Glen Cavender, Jack Mower, Cliff Saum (*Firemen*)], [John Harron (*Driver*)], [Monte Vandergrift (*Officer*)], [Jessie Arnold (*Nurse*)], [Gordon Hart (*Judge*)], [Mary Avery (*Teacher*)], [Sarah Edwards (*Miss Brundage*)], [Douglas Wood (*Mr. Butler*)], [Isabelle La Mal (*Teacher*)], [William Worthington (*Dr. Reynolds*)], [Ottola Nesmith (*Mrs. Higgins*)], [Lottie Williams (*Maid*)], [Evelyn Mulhall], [Louise Bates], [Maybelle Palmer].

Drama. [*Print viewed*]. Although Roberta Morgan's parents give her everything money can buy, she is an unhappy child. Her parents are too busy for her, and her bratty behavior, which is actually an unspoken cry for love, only alienates them further. The only person to take any notice of her thirteenth birthday is her father's secretary, Williams. Roberta's only friends are a little black boy, Pinkie White, and his sister Arabella. When they take Roberta home with them, she is charmed by the warmth and love of their mother, Mrs. White, who unlike Mrs. Morgan, gives her children first priority. When Roberta tries to reciprocate by inviting Pinkie for dinner, however, Jenkins, the butler, angrily throws Pinkie out. Furious, Roberta acts even brattier, and after her parents leave for Europe, Jenkins locks her in her room. She runs away, but Jenkins tracks her to Pinkie's house. On the way home, Roberta and Jenkins argue and Roberta grabs the steering wheel causing the car to swerve into an oncoming car and kill the driver. At first, out of revenge, Roberta insists that Jenkins was drinking and the accident was all his fault, but after he is sentenced to prison, she confesses and is sent by the court to a special girls' school run by the enlightened Helen Cosgrove. Helen tries every method to reach Roberta and is about to give up when a talk with Williams convinces her to ask for Roberta's help with the younger students. Roberta loves her new duties and is delighted when she makes friends. By the time her parents return from Europe, Roberta has changed, but when Helen tells her that she will be allowed to go home, Roberta cries that her parents never loved her and refuses to go. The Morgans overhear her protests and, chastened, change their ways. At Roberta's next birthday party, they attend with all her new friends, including Pinkie, Arabella and Mrs. White, who has baked a beautiful cake. *Brats. Family relationships. Neglected children. Transformation. African Americans. Automobile accidents. Birthdays. Butlers. Confession (Law). Dogs. Girls' schools. Governesses. Juvenile delinquents. Runaways. Secretaries. Teachers.*

Note: The film's pre-release titles were *Girls on Probation*, not to be confused with the 1938 Warner Bros. film of the same name, and *Too Much of Everything*.

DV 10 Feb 1938. p. 3. *FD* 5 May 1938, p. 6. *HR* 10 Feb 1938, p. 2. *MPD* 11 Feb 1938, p. 2. *MPH* 19 Feb 1938, p. 39. *NYT* 2 May 1938, p. 13.

THE BELOVED ROGUE *see* **THE BOLD CABALLERO**

BELOW THE BORDER (Latino)
Monogram Pictures Corp. *Dist* Monogram Pictures Corp. 30 Jan **1942**; Prod: 8 Dec–late Dec 1941 [©Monogram Pictures Corp.; 30 Jan 1942; LP11177]. Sd (Western Electric); b&w. 6 reels, 5,148 ft. 57 or 60 min. PCA cert no. 8039.
Series: The Rough Riders.
Prod Scott R. Dunlap. *Dir* Howard P. Bretherton. *Asst dir* Mack V. Wright. *Orig scr* Jess Bowers. *Film ed* Carl Pierson. *Mus dir* Edward Kay. *Rec eng* Karl Zint. *Tech dir* E. R. Hickson. *Prod mgr* Allen Wood.
Cast: Buck Jones [(*Buck Roberts*)], Tim McCoy [(*Tim McCall*)], Raymond Hatton [(*Sandy*)], Linda Brent [(*Rosita*)], Dennis Moore [(*Joe Collins*)], Charles King [(*Slade*)], Eva Puig [(*Aunt Maria Garcia*)], Roy Barcroft [(*Ed Scully*)], Bud Osborne [(*Al*)], [Merrill McCormick (*Gus*)], [Ted Mapes (*Max*)], [Silver, a horse].
Western. [*Print viewed*]. Using a pseudonym, Buck Roberts, one of three U.S. Marshals known as the Rough Riders, rides into Border City near the Mexican border to determine who killed one of his fellow Marshals. Buck cooperates with the robbers who attack his stagecoach and kill its drivers, and induces his fellow passengers, Rosita and Maria Garcia, to turn over their family jewels. His partner, Tim McCall, in the meantime, has arrived in Border City and makes contact with their third partner, Sandy, who has been working undercover in the saloon pushing a mop. Buck and Tim meet to discuss their suspicion that someone at the Garcia ranch is working with the robbers, and, based on Sandy's information, that the saloon owner, Ed Scully, may also be involved. Buck impersonates a well-known "fence" and lets it be known that the robbers will have to deal

with him if they plan to sell the Garcia jewels. Tim, meanwhile, represents a cattle buyer and stays at the Garcia ranch. Unknown to the Rough Riders, the Garcia ranch foreman, Joe Collins, who is in love with Rosita, has been working with the robbers, who also rustle cattle, and, with Joe's help, hides the robbers on a corner of the Garcia ranch. When he tries to pull out because of the jewel theft, Slade, who murdered the Marshal and runs the thieving gang with Scully, shoots Joe. That same night, Buck is arrested by the sheriff when he is caught rustling some cattle with the gang, but Scully escapes and learns Buck's true identity. Buck, who is working with the sheriff, pretends to break out of jail and shoots Slade during a confrontation. He then goes after Scully, while Tim joins Sandy to capture the rest of the bandits. After the outlaws are brought to justice, the jewels are restored to the Garcia ranch, and Joe recovers and reforms. The Rough Riders then leave for their separate ranches. *Rustlers. Stagecoach robberies. Undercover operations. United States. Marshals. Fences (Criminal). Gunshot wounds. Jewelry. Mexican-American border region. Murder. Ranches. Saloon keepers. Sheriffs.*

Note: For additional information on "The Rough Riders" series, consult the Series Index.

Box 21 Feb 1942. *DV* 20 Feb 1942, p. 3. *MPHPD* 28 Feb 1942, p. 525. *Var* 25 Feb 1942, p. 8.

BELOW THE DEADLINE (Irish Americans)
Chesterfield Motion Pictures Corp. *Dist* Chesterfield Motion Pictures Corp. 1 Jun **1936** [©Chesterfield Motion Pictures Corp.; 5 Jun 1936; LP6396]. Sd (RCA Victor High Fidelity Recording System); b&w. 8 reels. 65 or 69-70 min. PCA cert no. 2270.
Prod George R. Batcheller. *Prod exec* Lon Young. *Dir* Charles Lamont. *Asst dir* Melville Shyer. *Story and scr* Ewart Adamson. *Photog* M. A. Anderson. *Art dir* Edward C. Jewell. *Film ed* Roland D. Reed. *Rec eng* Richard Tyler.
Cast: Cecilia Parker (*Molly Fitzgerald*), Russell Hopton (*Terry Mulvaney*), Theodore Von Eltz (*Flash Ackroyd*), Thomas Jackson (*Pearson*), Warner Richmond (*Diamond Dutch*), John St. Polis (*Abrams*), Katherine Sheldon (*Aunt Mary Tibbett*), Robert Homans (*Captain Symonds*), Jack Gardner (*Spike*), Al Thompson, Charles Delaney (*Artie Nolan*), Sidney Payne, [Robert Frazer (*Palmer*)], [Edward Le Saint].
Crime, Drama. [*Print viewed*]. In a section of New York called "below the deadline," where there are more diamonds per square foot than in any other part of the world, gangster Flash Ackroyd schemes to steal an incoming diamond shipment from Abrams and Co. by seducing secretary Molly Fitzgerald. One night, as Molly leaves work, Flash's henchman, Spike, tries to pick her up, but is forced to drive off when he sees Molly's boyfriend, police officer Terry Mulvaney, approach. Flash then bets Spike and his partner, Diamond Dutch, $500 each that, by the following evening, he can get Molly to tell him when the diamonds will arrive. Impersonating a buyer, Flash learns from Abrams that more stones will be coming on Thursday and then gives Molly a ride home, where he meets Terry. Returning to Diamond Dutch and Spike, Flash collects on their bet and announces his plans to "pin the rap" on the diamond heist on Terry. Tricked into meeting Molly at the office on Thursday night, Terry, who is known as "brick-top" because of his conspicuous red hair, is seen by two officers on his way to Abrams' office. Flash's henchman, Al, knocks him out, ties him up, and leaves him in an alley. Meanwhile, Spike, Flash and Diamond Dutch rob the office with handkerchiefs over their faces. After Flash kills a guard, Molly hears him use an Irish brogue similar to Terry's and, lifting his hat to reveal red hair, thinks Terry is one of the robbers and faints. After Al cuts Terry's ropes and leaves, Terry revives and stops a police car for help, but is arrested. Terry escapes and boards a train, which crashes, and he is again knocked out. When he revives, he places his wallet in the pocket of a dead man whose face is unrecognizable, and is assumed dead. He then has plastic surgery performed on his nose, dyes his hair, and assumes a new identity. Meanwhile, Molly is suspected of being in on the heist by the police and the insurance investigator, Pearson. Because of the allegations against her, Molly is unable to find work, so Flash offers a job as a cashier in his club, the Alhambra. Terry, meanwhile, introduces himself to Pearson as Terry's brother Ed from Colorado who is in town to clear Terry's name. Pearson procures Terry's fingerprints, however, and determines his real identity. Believing he was framed, Pearson offers to help Terry investigate, but warns him not to let Molly know, lest she inadvertently give him away to the

police. To ease Molly's mind, Terry visits her as Ed and tells her that Terry is back in Colorado. Overcome with passion, Terry kisses her forcefully, which troubles her, as she realizes she is attracted to him. Flash, seeing Molly with another man, becomes jealous and, as an insult to "Ed," mimics an Irish brogue. He then orders Al to shadow "Ed," and Al follows Terry to Artie Nolan's gym, where he works out as a boxer. Terry hears Al whistle the same Irish tune he heard when Al knocked him out in the alley and tells Pearson about his discovery. When he learns that Al is Flash's chauffeur, Pearson realizes it was Flash who framed Terry. Molly, meanwhile, finally realizes that Ed is Terry. She acts indignant at first, but then makes up with him in a taxi. However, the taxi driver works for Flash and brings them to him. As Flash sends Molly and Terry to be killed by Al and the driver, the police invade and capture the gang. Terry fights Flash, and Pearson shoots Al. The jewels are returned, and Terry is promoted to detective, while Abrams gives Molly a wedding ring on the house. *Frame-ups. Gangsters. Impersonation and imposture. New York City. Robbery. Boxing. Diamonds. Escapes. False accusations. Gymnasiums. Insurance-Agents. Irish Americans. Missing persons, Assumed dead. Plastic surgery. Romance. Taxicab drivers. Train wrecks. Wagers.*

Note: According to the screen credits, actress Cecilia Parker appeared courtesy of M-G-M..

Exb 15 Jun 1936. *FD* 6 Jun 1936, p. 7. *HR* 17 Aug 1936, p. 3. *MPD* 26 Jun 1936, p. 14. *Var* 10 Jun 1936, p. 18.

BENEATH THE SEAS *see* **DOWN TO THE SEA**

BENEATH THE 12-MILE REEF (Greek Americans)
Twentieth Century-Fox Film Corp. *Dist* Twentieth Century-Fox Film Corp. Dec **1953**; Los Angeles opening: 25 Dec 1953; Prod: 6 Apr—late May 1953 [©Twentieth Century-Fox Film Corp.; 17 Dec 1953; LP3394]. Sd (Western Electric Recording); col (Technicolor). 12 reels, 9,145 ft. 102 min. PCA cert no. 16484.
[*Exec prod* Darryl F. Zanuck]. *Prod* Robert Bassler. *Dir* Robert D. Webb. *Asst dir* Joseph E. Rickards. [*2nd asst dir* Jack Sonntag and Paul Wurtzel]. *Wrt by* A. I. Bezzerides. *Dir of photog* Edward Cronjager. *Underwater photog* Till Gabbani. *Spec photog eff* Ray Kellogg. *Technicolor color consultant* Leonard Doss. *Art dir* Lyle Wheeler and George Patrick. *Film ed* William Reynolds. *Set dec* Fred J. Rode. *Ward dir* Charles LeMaire. *Cost des by* Dorothy Jeakins. *Mus* Bernard Herrmann. [*Mus arr* Urban Thielman]. *Sd* W. D. Flick and Roger Heman. *Makeup artist* Ben Nye. [*Unit mgr* Gene Bryant]. [*Loc adv* Howard Lightbourn]. [*Miniatures* Jack Shafton].
Song(s): "Yiati Yiati," music and lyrics by James Harakas and Andrew Ladas.
Cast: ROBERT WAGNER [(*Tony Petrakis*)], TERRY MOORE [(*Gwyneth Rhys*)], GILBERT ROLAND [(*Mike Petrakis*)], J. Carrol Naish [(*Socrates "Soak" Houlis*)], Richard Boone [(*Thomas Rhys*)], Angela Clarke [(*Mama Petrakis*)], Peter Graves [(*Arnold Dix*)], Jay Novello [(*Sinan*)], Jacques Aubuchon [(*Demetrios Sofotes*)], Gloria Gordon [(*Penny Petrakis*)], Harry Carey, Jr. [(*Griff Rhys*)], [James Harakas (*Card*)], [Charles Wagenheim (*Paul*)], [Marc Krah (*Fat George*)], [Rush Williams (*Davis Rhys*)], [John Gonatos (*Jemmy*)], [C. P.O. Eugene Halpin (*Long Arm*)], [Jonathan Jackson (*Lt. Bryant*)], [James McLaughlin (*Ambulance attendant*)], [Jack English (*Doctor*)], [Guy Carleton (*Jamison*)], [George Tsourakis (*Young priest*)], [Wm. Llewellyn Johnstone (*Crewman of "Snapper"*)], [Frank Joyner (*Capt. of "Snapper"*)], [Milton B. Wright (*Buyer at sponge market*)], [John George Gladakis (*Auctioneer*)], [Jack Pappas, Demetrios J. Mitsoras (*Deckhands on the "Helios"*)], [Michael Pappas (*Sailor on the "Helios"*)], [Jack Burke, Ski Skewis, John Lehman (*Conchs*)].
Sea, Drama. [*Print viewed*]. Following another disappointing fishing expedition off the Florida coast, Greek American sponge fisherman Mike Petrakis, his son Tony and the rest of the crew on board the *Aegli* return home to Tarpon Springs, where they are greeted by Mama Petrakis and Tony's sister Penny. Also waiting for them at the dock is money-lender Demetrios Sofotes, who is eager to get a payment toward the money that he invested in the *Aegli*. Mike and his crew are further disappointed when they learn that another boat, the *Helios*, brings in a profitable catch after sponge-fishing the dangerous Twelve Mile Reef. At a Greek Orthodox Church Epiphany festival, held on boats anchored at Tarpon Springs, Tony receives a special blessing for himself and his family after winning an underwater diving contest. Tony uses the victory to extract a promise from his father to let him dive on the next expedition. Believing that

the waters around Tarpon Springs are no longer good for sponge fishing, Mike decides to break with tradition and take his boat out to Key West, a region unofficially designated off-limits to Greeks. In the keys, as the *Aegli* crew brings in a great catch of sponges, two American sponge fishermen, Arnold Dix and Griff Rhys, approach in their small boat, grab Mike's air line and threaten to cut off his air unless the Greeks give them their sponge catch. Tony and the others comply with the demand, but later seek out the thieves at Key West. There, Mike and the rest of the *Aegli* crew go to a café and make believe that they are joining in the celebration of the day's great sponge catch. Meanwhile, Tony falls in love with Gwyneth Rhys, Arnold's sweetheart, and shares a dance with her. Arnold becomes jealous, and during an ensuing brawl, Tony and Gwyneth sneak off to a nearby park, where they embrace in a kiss. The *Aegli* crew eventually gets its revenge when Mike subdues Arnold and forces him to eat a cigar. For the next expedition, Mike takes the *Aegli* to the Twelve Mile Reef, but tragedy strikes during a dive when Mike slips on the reef, loses compression and is propelled to the water's surface too fast. Mike gets "the bends" from coming up too fast, and later dies. While Tony wanders off to mourn, Arnold and Griff loot the *Aegli*, and another group of American fishermen scuffles with Tony's uncle Socrates "Soak" Houlis, and set the boat ablaze, nearly destroying it. Gwyneth then takes Tony to see her father, Thomas, a fair man who orders Arnold and his gang to pay Tony for the stolen sponges. Furious at Thomas' order, Arnold goes after Tony and gives him a beating. The injured Tony makes his way back to the dock, where he and Gwyneth steal a boat, the "Conch," and head out to sea. Gwyneth, more in love with Tony than ever, gets an idea to turn the "Conch" into a deep sea diving boat, and they get to work sponge fishing at the Twelve Mile Reef. Arnold and his compatriots eventually find Tony and Gwyneth and engage them in a bruising fistfight. The struggle forces Tony and Arnold into the water, and when Arnold becomes entangled in kelp, Tony rescues him. Arnold is grateful to Tony for saving his life and the two adversaries make amends. Gwyneth decides to marry Tony, and the her family and Tony's join together to put on a festive wedding. *Divers and diving. Fishermen. Florida. Greek Americans. Rivalry. Romance. Sponges. Death and dying. Debt. Decompression sickness. Fathers and sons. Fires. Fishing boats. Fishing villages. Fistfights. Grief. Key West (FL). Marriage-Mixed. Octopi. Orthodox Eastern Church. Priests. Rescues. Revenge. Robbery. Tarpon Springs (FL).*

Note: The working title of the film was *12 Mile Reef*. Within the film, the Greek American fishermen refer to their rivals as "English," even though they are American. Puppeteer Jack Shafton created miniature diving figures that were used in underwater sequences in the film. According to studio production records in the AMPAS Library file on the film, while filming at Tarpon Springs, FL, Robert Wagner "nearly drowned" when he was accidentally kicked in the stomach by another swimmer. According to *HR*, the film was shot entirely on location at Tarpon Springs and Key West, Florida. Underwater scenes were shot with the use of a specially designed French underwater camera called the Aquaflex. Cameraman Edward Cronjager was nominated for an Academy Award for color cinematography for the film.

Box 19 Dec 1953. *DV* 16 Dec 1953, p. 3. *FD* 16 Dec 1953, p. 10. *HR* 7 Dec 1953. *HR* 16 Dec 1953, p. 3. *LADN* 9 Feb 1954. *MPHPD* 19 Dec 1953, p. 2109. *NYT* 20 Dec 1953, p. 52. *Var* 16 Dec 1953, p. 6.

THE BENNY GOODMAN STORY (African Americans, Jewish Americans)
Universal-International Pictures Co., Inc. *Dist* Universal Pictures Co., Inc. Feb **1956**; New York opening: 21 Feb 1956; Prod: 1 Jul—20 Aug 1955 [©Universal Pictures Co.; 28 Nov 1955; LP5688]. Sd (Western Electric Recording); col (Technicolor). 10,463 ft. 115-116 min. PCA cert no. 17731.
Prod Aaron Rosenberg. *Dir* Valentine Davies. *Asst dir* Phil Bowles and [Terry Nelson]. [*Dial dir* Leon Charles]. *Wrt* Valentine Davies. *Dir of photog* William Daniels. [*Cam op* William Dodds]. [*Asst cam* Walter Williams]. [*Stills* Roland Lane]. *Technicolor color consultant* William Fritzsche. *Art dir* Alexander Golitzen and Robert Clatworthy. *Film ed* Russell Schoengarth. [*Asst cutter* Berna MacCurran]. *Set dec* Russell A. Gausman and Julia Heron. [*Props* Robert Laszlo]. [*Asst props* Roy Neal]. *Gowns* Bill Thomas. [*Ward women* Nerada Penn]. [*Ward man* Truman Eli]. [*Asst ward* Rydo Loshak]. *Mus supv* Joseph Gershenson. *Addl mus* Henry Mancini. *Instrumental coach* Sol Yaged, Alan Harding and Harold Brown. *Sd* Leslie I. Carey and Robert Pritchard. [*Rec* William Sostello]. [*Mike man* Frank Gorback]. *Hair stylist* Joan St. Oegger. *Makeup* Bud Westmore and [Mark Reedall]. [*Body makeup* Fay Cheney]. [*Unit mgr* Edward Dodds]. [*Scr clerk*

Adele Cannon]. [*Gaffer* Lloyd Hill]. [*Best boy* Julius Madison]. [*Cable man* Jim Rogers]. [*Coordinator* Charles Bagueta]. [*Pub* Don Morgan]. [*Sync man* Edward Frasier]. [*Clarinet coach* Al Harding]. [*Painter* Jim Cole]. [*Laborer* Jim Barrett]. [*Playback op* Frank Moorehead]. [*Crane operator* Kenneth Smith and Ollie Hensel]. [*Grip* Ed Jones]. [*Co-grip* Fred Buckley, Marion Pierce and James Ryan]. [*Lamp op* Harold Haselbusch, Ben Graves, Lawrence McCarthy, Arthur Shadur, Pierce Nippell and Frederic Dorr]. [*Stand-in* Harold Lockwood, Lloyd Dawson, Walter Lawrence and Francis Haldoran].

Music: *Concerto for Clarinet* by Wolfgang Amadeus Mozart; "Stompin' at the Savoy" by Benny Goodman, Edgar Sampson and Chick Webb, arranged by Fletcher Henderson; "Memories of You" by Eubie Blake; "One O'Clock Jump" by Count Basie and Harry James; "Don't Be That Way" by Benny Goodman and Edgar Sampson; "Shine" by Ford Dabney; "Sing, Sing, Sing" by Louis Prima; "Let's Dance," based on "Invitation to Dance" by Carl Maria von Weber; "Avalon" by B. G. DeSylva and Vincent Rose; "Moonglow" by Will Hudson, Eddie De Lange and Irving Mills; "Jersey Bounce" by Bobby Plater, Tiny Bradshaw, Edward Johnson and Robert B. Wright; "Dixieland One-Step," "Waitin for Katie" and "Twenty Years of Jazz," composers undetermined.

Song(s): "And the Angels Sing," words by Johnny Mercer, music by Ziggy Elman.

Cast: Steve Allen (*Benny Goodman*), Donna Reed (*Alice Hammond*), Berta Gersten (*Dora Goodman*), Barry Truex (*Benny Goodman, age 14*), Herbert Anderson (*John Hammond*), Robert F. Simon (*Dave Goodman*), Hy Averback (*Willard Alexander*), Sammy Davis, Sr. (*Fletcher Henderson*), Dick Winslow (*Gil Rodin*), Shepard Menken (*Harry Goodman*), Jack Kruschen (*Murph Podolsky*), Wilton Graff (*Mr. Hammond*), Fred Essler (*Prof. Schepp*), David Kasday (*Benny Goodman, age 10*), John M. Erman (*Harry Goodman, age 16*), George Givot ([*Little*] *Jake Primo*), Lionel Hampton, Gene Krupa, Teddy Wilson, Ben Pollack, Edward "Kid" Ory, Urbie Green, Buck Clayton, Stan Getz, Guest appearances Harry James, Martha Tilton, Ziggy Elman, Benny Goodman and His Orchestra:, Teddy Wilson (*Piano*), Hymie Schertzer, Blake Reynolds, Stan Getz, Babe Russin (*Saxophones*), Urbie Green, Murray McEachern, James Priddy (*Trombones*), Gene Krupa (*Drums*), Buck Clayton, Chris Griffin, Conrad Gozzo, Irving Goodman (*Trumpets*), George Duvivier (*Bass*), Allan Reuss (*Guitar*), and Clarinet played by Benny Goodman, [Louise Lorimer (*Mrs. Vanderbilt*)], [Douglas Evans (*Kel Murray*)], [Richard Kapp (*Freddie*)], [Betty Howard (*Girl*)], [Cynthia Patrick (*Jane Kruger*)], [Robert Clarke (*Roger Gillsepie*)], [Charles Tannen (*Stewart*)], [George Ramsey (*Joe Soldcrown*)], [Benny Rubin (*Mr. Strauss*)], [Hal K. Dawson (*Mr. McHenshey*)], [Jack Lomas (*Clark*)], [Antonio Filauri (*Headwaiter*)], [Bob Crosson (*Stage manager*)], [Ralph Neff, Ben Welden (*Gangsters*)], [Ned LeFevre (*Announcer*)], [John McGovern (*Dick Reiner*)], [Chris Alcaide, Jack Richardson (*Boatmen*)], [Diane Jergens (*Velma Kruger*)], [Arthur Lovejoy (*Butler*)], [Dick Ames, Jimmy Hayes (*Ushers*)], [Cosmo Sardo (*Barber*)], [Carli D. Elinor (*Concertmeister*)], [Ralph Montgomery (*Waiter*)], [Smoki Whitfield (*Taxi driver*)], [Steve Allen, Jr., Don Gordon, Whitey Haupt (*Tough boys in gang*)], [Audrey Dineen (*Lena*)], [Brian Allen (*Boy at Hull House*)], [John Herrin, John Yates (*Teenagers*)], [Jack Richardson (*Boatman*)], [Dick Ryan], [Sara Taft], [Helen Spring].

Biography, **Musical**. [*Print viewed*]. Poor though they are, Dave and Dora Goodman are determined to secure a good education for their sons. In 1919, Prof. Schepp offers music classes to Chicago's tenement dwellers at Hull House, and although young Benny Goodman dislikes the instrument at first, he becomes an excellent clarinetist by the time he is fourteen. Benny practices his Mozart passages, but when an opportunity to play in a ragtime band arises, he joins the musicians' union and begins his performance career. During a break, Benny listens with awe to the New Orleans jazz band of Edward "Kid" Ory, who advises him to play the way he feels and invites him to sit in. Later Benny, still two years away from high school graduation, joins the Ben Pollack band and plays for dances throughout the country. On his first visit back home, Benny is dismayed to learn that his father, who always supported his musical aspirations, has been killed in an accident on the way to the train station. The Pollack band secures a job in the speakeasy of Benny's former neighbor, Little Jake Primo, who is now a gangster. There he meets the wealthy John Hammond, a jazz lover and music critic, and

John's sister Alice, who prefers classical to "hot" music and is uncomfortable in Benny's presence. Pollack's band flops in New York, and Benny, full of ideas but worried that there is no audience for his kind of music, is forced to perform with more traditional dance bands in order to earn a meager living. Still impressed with Benny's talent, Hammond invites him to perform a Mozart clarinet concerto before an audience of blue bloods in the Hammond mansion. Alice is pleasantly surprised by Benny's performance and remarks that although he seems calm and quiet, "all this emotion comes pouring out" when he plays. Benny forms a band and begins to perform on an NBC Saturday night radio program. Admired jazz musician Fletcher Henderson hears the program from his home base in Harlem and is so impressed that he begins to contribute musical arrangements to the band. After the show is canceled, Benny's orchestra goes on tour, but before he leaves, he and Alice declare their strong but confusing feelings for each other. The tour is a failure until the orchestra reaches Palomar, California, where, the group, having won a large following of young fans on the West Coast, is a tremendous success. Benny sees Alice in the audience and plays "Memories of You" for her, and after the show, the two kiss. Benny forms a quartet that includes Lionel Hampton, Teddy Wilson and Gene Krupa, and by the time Benny, his orchestra and his quartet return to Chicago, they are making headlines in *Variety*. Alice attends the orchestra's New York debut, where a surging crowd dances in the aisles, and later that day, she is relieved to learn that her father approves of the romance. Benny's mother, however, informs her son that his love for Alice is "like a knife in my heart." Worried, Alice visits Mrs. Goodman, who declares that "you don't mix caviar with bagels." Benny is booked into Carnegie Hall, but he wonders why Alice is not planning to attend and worries that "a hall full of longhairs" will disapprove of the orchestra's music. Finally realizing how much Benny loves Alice, Mrs. Goodman secretly invites her to attend the concert, which will feature the orchestra and guest performers Harry James, Ziggy Elman and Martha Tilton. Travel delays nearly cause Alice to miss Benny's triumphant performance, but she arrives in time for a standing ovation and an encore performance of "Memories of You." *Band leaders. Bands (Music). Benny Goodman. Jazz music. Mothers and sons. Musicians. Swing music. African Americans. Brothers and sisters. California. Carnegie Hall (New York City). Chicago (IL). Clarinets. Cultural conflict. Cultural elitism. Family relationships. Jews. Music teachers. New York City. Poverty. Radio programs. Shyness. Socialites.*

Note: Valentine Davies' onscreen credit reads "written and directed by Valentine Davies." According to a 1954 *HR* news item, the tremendous success of his 1954 Universal film *The Glenn Miller* story prompted producer Aaron Rosenberg to make this film. When Rosenberg asked Davies, the writer of the 1954 production, to script this film, Davies expressed an interest in directing it, and Rosenberg acceded to his demands. This was the only film that Davies directed. According to materials contained in the Valentine Davies' Collection at the AMPAS Library, Benny Goodman was paid $25,000 for the rights to his story, plus an additional $10,000 for consulting. Ludwig Stoessell was originally to play the role of "Professor Schepp," according to the Davies' files.

Although the events depicted in the film were inspired by real incidents, their chronology has been altered. Benny Goodman (1909-1986) began playing professionally at the age of twelve, and while still a teenager, joined Ben Pollack's band. In the early 1930's, Goodman's band, which at the time included Teddy Wilson and Lionel Hampton, was the first interracial jazz ensemble to appear in public. From 1936 on, Goodman was known as "The King of Swing," and his 1938 Carnegie Hall appearance marked the first time that a jazz band performed in that venerable institution. Materials contained in the production files on the film in the AMPAS Library note that Sol Yagel spent two months teaching Steve Allen to play the clarinet. According to the *Har* review, Goodman newly recorded all the songs on the film's soundtrack. In addition to the music listed above, a number of Benny Goodman's well-known pieces, including "Goody Goody," were heard briefly on the soundtrack. Although the Davies' files indicate that Martha Tilton recorded several songs for the film, none were heard on the sound track. The film was shot on location in Chicago, according to the Davies' files. A joint memo issued by the American Jewish Committee and the Anti-Defamation League of B'nai B'rith praised this film for its "sympathy and dignity in handling Jewish family life, and because it is symbolic of the contributions of Jews to America's artistic and cultural life." The film was also commended for its "handling of the integration of white and negro musicians in Goodman's orchestra. The subject is never raised, but it is quite plain that the test for Goodman was always the competence of the man and never his color."

Box 17 Dec 1955. *DV* 15 Dec 1955, p. 3. *Exh* 28 Dec 1955, p. 4080. *FD* 15 Dec 1955, p. 6. *Har* 17 Dec 1955, p. 204. *HR* 3 Feb 1954. *HR* 15 Dec 1955, p. 3. *MPHPD* 24 Dec 1955, p. 713. *NYT* 22 Feb 1956, p. 22. *Var* 21 Dec 1955, p. 6.

BENNY'S MEDAL *see* A MEDAL FOR BENNY

THE BENSON MURDER CASE *(foreign version) see* EL CUERPO DEL DELITO

UN BESO APASIONADO *see* EL PRECIODE UN BESO

UN BESO DE PASIÓN *see* EL PRECIO DE UN BESO

BEST OF ENEMIES (German Americans)

Fox Film Corp. *Dist* Fox Film Corp. 23 Jun **1933**; Prod: 20 Mar–mid-Apr 1933; retakes and added scenes May 1933 [©Fox Film Corp.; 9 Jun 1933; LP3952]. Sd (Western Electric Noiseless Recording); b&w. 8 reels, 6,800 ft. 71-72 min. Passed by the National Board of Review. PCA cert no. 3323-R [15 Apr 1937].

Dir Rian James and [Frank Craven]. [*Asst dir* Percy Ikerd]. [*Dir of retakes and added scenes* James Cruze]. *Scr* Sam Mintz and [Frank Craven]. *Dial* Rian James. *Photog* L. W. O'Connell. [*Cam op* Harry Daw and Russell Hoover]. [*2d cam* Don Anderson]. *Settings* William Darling. [*Ed* Margaret Clancy]. *Frocks* Joe Strassner. *Mus dir* Arthur Lange. *Dance dir* Sammy Lee. *Sd* A. L. Von Kirbach.

Song(s): "All American Girls," "Hans and Gretchen" and "We Belong to Alma," words and music by Val Burton and Will Jason; "Bier Hir" and "Ein Prosit," composer unknown; "Oh You Beautiful Doll," music by Nat D. Ayer, lyrics by Seymour Brown.

Cast: Buddy Rogers (*Jimmie Hartman*), Marian Nixon (*Lena Schneider*), Frank Morgan (*Wm. H. Hartman*), Joseph Cawthorn (*Gus Schneider*), Greta Nissen (*The blonde*), Arno Frey (*Emil*), William Lawrence (*August*), Anders Van Haden (*Professor Herman*).

Comedy, with songs. [*Print viewed*]. William H. Hartman, an American businessman who has contributed a lot of money to help bring about prohibition, visits the beer garden of his German-American neighbor, Gus Schneider, hoping to buy Schneider's lease. Schneider, who hates Hartman, refuses. Hartman, whose young son Jimmie is a playmate of Schneider's daughter Lena, orders Jimmie not to play with Lena, after which he imbibes from a hidden bottle of whiskey. After prohibition takes effect, Schneider's converted restaurant draws few customers. Hartman now refuses Schneider's offer to sell the lease, and soon Schneider is dispossessed. He moves back to Germany, although he keeps his American citizenship. Meanwhile, Hartman builds a forty-story office building on the spot of Schneider's former beer garden. Twelve years later, Jimmie is devoting more time to music than to his studies. Although Hartman would like his son to become a financier, he agrees to send him to a conservatory in Germany. There he meets Lena, who is also studying music. Their initial attraction is furthered when they have dinner together and realize their identities. Because Schneider hates the name of Hartman, Jimmie suggests that Lena introduce him as "Jim Harty." Hartman, after purusing a girly magazine from Europe, decides to take a trip to visit his son. When Jimmie sees that his roommate August, a cellist, cannot afford to eat lunch everyday, he visits Schneider in his hofbrau and convinces Schneider to hire him and his fellow students to play jazz for food and beer. On the night of Lena's music competition, after which Jimmie plans to sail home, Lena tells him in German, which he does not understand, that she would like more than anything for him to stay. When Lena does not win, because a professor whose name is Hartman breaks a tie vote and chooses her competitor, Schneider vows to choke the next Hartman who comes into his life. Jimmie, who has now learned what Lena told him in German, comforts her and, after telling her that he loves her, gets a job in a brewery and moves in with a friend. He writes a tune based on the rhythm he hears at the brewery and on Lena's music, and soon after he performs the song with his band, he has a hit which makes the hofbrau one of the busiest places in town. Hartman, with a blonde date, drinks beer there, not knowing that Schneider is the owner, but when he sees Jimmie, he goes backstage and orders him to give up the band. When Schneider interrupts and learns Jimmie's identity, he fires the band and objects to Jimmie marrying his daughter because, he says, he does not want to be the grandfather of little Hartmans. Jimmie and Lena elope on an ocean liner bound for America, and the two fathers follow. When Jimmie learns that they are on the boat, he delivers messages to both, supposedly from the other, urging a reconciliatory meeting. Hartman and Schneider drink beer together and sing, and decide to open a brewery together, when Jimmie and Lena interrupt them and reveal that they have married. A final argument about which father gave in and wrote the first note is

never settled because in the midst of their bickering, the notes are blown overboard. *Fathers and daughters. Fathers and sons. Feuds. Germans. Germany. Music students. Romance. Beer. Brewers and breweries. Businessmen. Deception. German Americans. Hypocrisy. Jazz music. Music schools. Ocean liners. Prohibition. Restaurants. Roommates. Songwriters.*

Note: The working title of this film was *Five Cents a Glass*. *Var* stated, "Coast reports are that at least three directors had a hand in the making of the subject....The finished work has a patchy look that easily could have been the result of changing direction, and new ideas imposed upon an unsatisfactory original in an effort to make it jell." According to news items and information in the Twentieth Century-Fox Records of the Legal Department at the UCLA Theater Arts Library, Frank Craven, who was co-author with Sam Mintz of the original screenplay, was also the original director of this film. According to a letter dated 21 Apr 1933, in the legal files, Craven and Fox came to a mutual understanding that his name, both as a writer and director, would be eliminated from the screen credits and publicity. On 24 Apr 1933, Rian James, who was under contract to Fox as a writer, was removed from his then-present assignment and assigned "to do certain work" on this film. He continued with the film until 1 Jun. On 10 May 1933, Fox executed a contract with James Cruze to direct retakes and added scenes, with the proviso that his name would not be included in the screen credits or publicity. Cruze's contract ended on 1 Jun 1933, and James, subsequently received screen credit for direction. Also according to the legal records, Dan Jarrett was originally cast for the role of "William H. Hartman," and Walter Thiele was original cast as "August." *Var* noted that the film marked "the screen come-back attempt of Buddy Rogers."

FD 13 Jan 1933, p. 5. *FD* 28 Feb 1933, p. 4. *FD* 16 Mar 1933, p. 2. *FD* 17 Jul 1933, p. 7. *HF* 25 Mar 1933, p. 12. *HF* 15 Apr 1933, p. 8. *HR* 17 Mar 1933, p. 3. *IP* Apr 1933, p. 20. *MPD* 5 Jul 1933, p. 9. *MPH* 22 Jul 1933, pp. 56-57. *NYT* 17 Jul 1933, p. 19. *Var* 18 Jul 1933, p. 37.

THE BETRAYAL (African Americans)

Astor Pictures Corp. *Dist* Astor Pictures Corp. Jun **1948**; New York opening: week of 24 Jun 1948. Sd; b&w. 17,276 ft. 183 min.

Prod Oscar Micheaux. *Dir* Oscar Micheaux. *Scr* Oscar Micheaux. *Photog* N. Spoor.

Source: Based on the novel *Wind from Nowhere* by Oscar Micheaux (New York, 1944).

Cast: Lou Vernon (*Ned Washington*), Edward Fraction (*Nelson Boudreaux*), Leroy Collins (*Martin Eden*), Jessie Johnson (*Preble*), William Byrd (*Jack Stewart*), Myra Stanton (*Deborah Stewart*), Frances DeYoung (*Mrs. [Hattie] Bowles*), Arthur McCoo (*Joe Bowles*), Vernetties Moore (*Eunice*), Barbara Lee (*Jessie*), Verlie Cowan (*Linda Lee*), Alice B. Russell (*Aunt Mary*), Yvonne Maehen (*Terry*), Gladys Williams (*Mrs. Dewey*), Richard Lawrence (*Broyle*), Harris Gaines (*Dr. Lee*), David Jones (*Crook*), Vernon B. Duncan (*Duval*), Curley Ellison (*Glavis*), Sue McBride (*Bernadine*), Harold Mers (*Richards*).

African American, Romance. [*Not viewed*]. Martin Eden, a successful black farmer in South Dakota, hires the Stewart family to manage his ranch while he vacations in Chicago. Martin is attracted to Deborah, the Stewarts' daughter, but believes that because she is white, he stands little chance of marrying her. Deborah, however, is actually half black, and has been kept ignorant of her mixed-race descent all her life. Soon after Martin arrives in Chicago, his friends, Hattie and Joe Bowles, suggest that he marry a white woman who will understand his rugged lifestyle. Despite their suggestion, the Bowleses introduce Martin to Eunice, a black cabaret performer, who is definitely not the marrying kind. Martin later reunites with Jessie, a former sweetheart, and meets her friend, Linda Lee. When Martin returns to his ranch and tells Deborah that he intends to marry Linda, Deborah breaks down in tears and confesses that she is in love with him. Martin tries to explain to Deborah the impossibility of a mixed-race marriage, and tells her stories about several doomed mixed marriages to illustrate his point. Linda accepts Martin's marriage proposal, but before they wed, Linda files a land claim to help Martin acquire more land. Though Linda's dishonest father believes that Martin is only interested in Linda for her money, he eventually gives them his blessing. Linda and Martin marry, and Linda later gives birth to a baby boy, whom she names Martin Eden, Jr. One day, while Martin is away on a business trip, Linda is convinced by her father that Martin is planning to kill her for her money. Linda returns to Chicago with her family, who successfully prevent Linda from receiving any letters from Martin. After a year of being estranged from his wife, Martin goes to Chicago and tricks Linda into meeting him at a theater. Martin insists that he has always loved Linda, and Linda agrees to spend the rest of the night with him. When Linda tries to telephone her father to tell him her plans, Martin demands that her whereabouts be kept

a secret and pulls out a gun to force Linda into agreement. A struggle ensues, during which a shot is accidentally fired into Martin. Only slightly wounded, Martin returns to his ranch alone and offers Linda's share of the property to Deborah. Deborah later plans a trip to Indiana to visit her family, and tells Martin that she will be stopping in Chicago to visit her grandfather, whom she has never met. Martin is surprised when Deborah tells him her grandfather's address, as his home is located in a black neighborhood. Deborah soon discovers the truth about her parentage, and immediately feels that she is responsible for Martin's ill-fated association with the Lee family. To assuage her guilt, Deborah sets out to find Linda and convince her that Martin had no evil designs upon her or her family. Realizing that she was wrong about Martin and that Deborah would make a better wife than she, Linda asks Deborah to marry Martin and rear their child. Linda then kills her father out of revenge for destroying her marriage. Deborah returns to South Dakota, where she foils a scheme by Duval and Crook, two thieves who planned to grab Linda's parcel of land. After Deborah tells Martin about her parentage, the two embrace and look forward to a happy future together. *African Americans. African Americans–Mixed blood. Desertion (Marital). Homesteaders. Marriage. Miscegenation. Secrets. Chicago (IL). False accusations. Farms. Fathers and daughters. Gangsters. Grandfathers. Gunshot wounds. Land claims. Marriage. Murder. Racism. Revenge. Self-sacrifice. South Dakota.*

Note: The above credits and plot synopsis were taken from contemporary reviews and a dialogue script contained in the NYSA. Although the film is based on Oscar Micheaux's novel *Wind from Nowhere*, it has sometimes been described as a loose remake of Micheaux's first film, *The Homesteader*, which was released in 1919 (see entry below). *The Betrayal* was the first all-black film to have a Broadway premiere. According to the *Var* review, the film was cut down from approximately 195 minutes to its release length of 183 minutes. Reviewers strongly criticized the film, calling it amateurish and overly long. The *NYHT* reviewer, as quoted in an article about the picture in the *LASent*, stated: "The fact that the movie is aimed at Negro audiences is an afront to that large minority of moviegoers." Regional censorship reports contained in the MPAA/PCA Collection at the AMPAS Library indicate that some portions of the dialogue were cut from prints of the film shown in Ohio and Maryland. In Maryland, censors deleted the sequence early in the film in which "Eden" discusses the suicide of a mixed-race Army draftee. Micheaux died in 1951; *The Betrayal* was his final picture.

Box 28 Aug 1948. *LASent* 8 Jul 1948. *MPD* 30 Jun 1948. *MPHPD* 10 Jul 1948, p. 4233. *NYT* 26 Jun 1948, p. 10. *Var* 30 Jun 1948.

BETRAYAL FROM THE EAST (Japanese Americans)

RKO Radio Pictures, Inc. *Dist* RKO Radio Pictures, Inc. **1945**; New York opening: week of 24 Apr 1945; *Prod:* early Jul—early Aug 1944 [©RKO Radio Pictures, Inc.; 22 Mar 1945; LP13283]. Sd (RCA Sound System); b&w. 7,404 ft. 82-83 min. PCA cert no. 10313.

Prod Herman Schlom. *Exec prod* Sid Rogell. *Dir* William Berke. *Asst dir* Sam Ruman. *Dial dir* Ben Bard. *Scr* Kenneth Gamet and Aubrey Wisberg. *Adp* Aubrey Wisberg. *Dir of photog* Russell Metty. *Spec eff* Vernon L. Walker. *Art dir* Albert S. D'Agostino and Ralph Berger. *Ed* Duncan Mansfield. *Set dec* Darrell Silvera and William Stevens. *Gowns* Edward Stevenson. *Mus dir* C. Bakaleinikoff. *Mus* Roy Webb. *Rec* Jean L. Speak. *Re-rec* Terry Kellum.

Source: Based on the novel *Betrayal from the East* by Alan Hynd (New York, 1943).

Cast: Lee Tracy [(*Eddie Carter*)], Nancy Kelly [(*Peggy Harrison*)], Richard Loo [(*Tanni*)], Abner Biberman [(*Yamato*)], Regis Toomey [(*Jimmy Scott*)], Philip Ahn [(*Kato*)], Addison Richards [(*Capt. Bates*)], Bruce Edwards [(*Purdy*)], Hugh Hoo [(*Araki*)], Sen Young [(*Omaya*)], Roland Varno [(*Kurt Gunther*)], Louis Jean Heydt [(*Jack Marsden*)], Jason Robards [(*C. H. Hildebrand*)], [Drew Pearson (*Narrator*)], [Rosemary La Planche (*American girl*)], [Steve Winston (*First American boy*)], Chris Drake (*Second American boy*), [Harold Fong (*Purser*)], [Fred Carpenter (*Newsie*)], [Jean Wong (*Miss Morita*)], [Spencer Chan (*Japanese agent*)], [Mary Halsey (*Gloria*)], [Patti Brill (*Peg*)], [Margie Stewart (*Jeanne*)], [Virginia Belmont (*Girl*)], [Sammy Blum (*Drunk*)], [Victor Wong (*Joe*)], [Alfred Song (*Ito*)], [Early Cantrell (*Waitress*)], [Key H. Chang (*Japanese consul*)], [Peter Chong (*Capt. Yasuda*)], [Alan Ward (*Police officer*)], [Henry Victor (*Brunzman*)], [Erick Hanson (*Holtzig*)], [Weaver Levy (*Taxi driver*)], [Paul Fung (*Dr. Kabeneshki*)], [Grace Lem (*Fortune teller*)], [Fay Wall (*Helga*)], [Hermine Sterler (*Keller*)], [Howard Johnson (*Wilheim*)], [George Lee (*Bellhop*)], [Lee Phelps (*Immigration officer*)], [Manuel Lopez (*Waiter*)], [Guy Zanett (*Desk clerk*)], [Manuel Paris (*Travel desk clerk*)], [Edmund Glover], [Isabelle La Mal], [Chester Conklin], [Sherry Hall], [Russell Hopton], [Bryant Washburn].

Espionage. [*Print viewed*]. Journalist Drew Pearson relates the following story, cautioning that it must never happen again: In 1941, as Emperor Hirohito preaches peace, the armed forces of Japan prepare to sabotage strategic defense sites in the western United States. When reporter Jack Marsden informs C. H. Hildebrand, the chief of the foreign press service in Tokyo, that he has stumbled upon a list of Japanese espionage agents operating in the United States, Hildebrand directs him to deliver the information to Army intelligence in San Francisco. When the U.S. agents meet Marsden's boat in San Francisco, however, they are informed by Tanni, the cabin boy, that the reporter fell overboard during a storm. Marsden's death is followed by the news that Hildebrand has plunged to his death from a Tokyo hotel room window. Meanwhile, at the Japanese Consulate in San Francisco, saboteurs Yamato and Kato arrange a meeting in Los Angeles to discuss obtaining information about the defense system of the Panama Canal. Kato then contacts Eddie Carter, an ex-soldier who likes easy money, to offer him the job of acquiring the plans. Eddie, who is now working as a carnival barker, feigns knowledge about the canal and agrees to meet Kato in a Los Angeles nightclub the following week. On the train to Los Angeles, Eddie meets Peggy Harrison, who pleads with him to give up his compartment so that she will have somewhere to sleep. Eddie obliges, and after he vacates his room, Peggy searches his luggage. Upon arriving in Los Angeles, Eddie asks Peggy to join him at the nightclub. There he is greeted by Kato, who escorts him into a darkened room filled with saboteurs. Although he is unable to see their faces, Eddie notices a pin worn by the ringleader. After lying that his old army friend, Jimmy Scott, is an ordnance worker in Panama, Eddie is hired by the Japanese to buy plans of the canal from Jimmy. Upon returning home, Eddie is about to telephone army intelligence when he notices that he is being watched by Omaya, the apartment handyman. To avoid detection, Eddie proceeds to headquarters to confer in person. After telling the intelligence officers about the fictitious Jimmy Scott, Eddie agrees to infiltrate the ring. On his way home, he is picked up and taken to see Yamato, who shows him a flim clip of Omaya and Peggy searching his apartment. After declaring Omaya and Peggy to be American spies, Yamato tortures Omaya and orders Eddie to deliver Peggy to his office later that afternoon. Although Peggy, who is aware of Eddie's cover, insists that he follow Yamato's orders, Eddie refuses, and as they begin to argue, Peggy steps out into the street and is run down and apparently killed by a passing car. That night, Kato presents Eddie with a ticket to Panama and tells him that he will be contacted by Araki once he arrives. In his hotel room, Eddie is visited by a fellow spy calling himself Jimmy Scott, who warns him that a dictaphone and camera have been planted in the room. As Nazi agents listen to their conversation over the dictaphone, Eddie offers Jimmy money in exchange for military information. When Jimmy asks for time to consider the proposition, they agree to meet the following evening. The next night, as they drive in Jimmy's car, Jimmy gives Eddie obsolete plans of the canal and warns him that Araki intends to kill him once he has gained possession of the plans. Jimmy instructs Eddie to stall until his safe transportation to the U.S. can be arranged, and informs him that he will be signalled by a telegram from his "sister". Their discussion completed, Eddie and Jimmy proceed to an exclusive nightclub, where Jimmy sees Peggy, who is alive and posing as a Danish socialite. Overhearing her make a date to meet her escort, Kurt Gunther, a beauty salon owner and Nazi agent, at the beach the next day, Eddie follows her there and swims out to the raft on which she is sunning herself. There, Peggy explains that her accident was staged to fool Yamato and that she is in Panama to investigate Nazi relations with the Japanese. Their meeting is reported to Yamato by Nazi spies. Soon after, Eddie receives a telegram from his "sister", notifying him that their "mother" is near death. Feigning grief, Eddie informs Araki that he must return home immediately and books passage on a ship leaving that afternoon. Araki instructs the Nazis to kill Eddie on his way to the ship, but the Department of Immigration arrests them for improper documentation before they can complete their mission. While visiting Kurt's salon, Peggy overhears Araki tell Kurt that he has ordered Eddie to be killed. When a call notifies him of the arrest of the Nazi assassins, Araki decides to drive to the harbor and kill Eddie himself. To warn Eddie, Peggy borrows Kurt's car and, pretending to have car trouble, flags down his cab and directs him to the airport rather than the harbor. Upon returning to the beauty salon, Peggy is imprisoned in a steam room and interrogated by Araki and

Kurt. Rather than betray her country, she perishes from suffocation. Upon arriving at the Los Angeles airport, Eddie is met by Kato, who takes him to a Japanese ship. Recognizing the pin worn by Tanni, the cabin boy, Eddie realizes that he has uncovered the identity of the spies' ringleader. As Tanni examines the plans, Eddie sneaks into his cabin and discovers a trunk filled with the plans of the saboteurs' targets. After affirming that he is a lieutenant commander in the Japanese Navy, Tanni taunts Eddie with news of Peggy's death. Enraged, Eddie attacks Tanni, and in a furious struggle, seizes the Japanese's gun and shoots him, only to be then shot by Tanni's men. Returning to the present, Drew Pearson concludes that "Eddie died in an undeclared war...a war against underground enemies that never begins and never ends." *Espionage. Japanese. Panama Canal (Panama). Sabotage. Barkers (Carnival). Beauty shops. Cabin boys. Impersonation and imposture. Los Angeles (CA). Murder. Nightclubs. Reporters. San Francisco (CA). Self-sacrifice. Ships. Surveillance devices. Trains.*

Note: According to a pre-production news item in *HR*, Bonita Granville was originally slated to play the female lead in this picture. Although a *HR* production chart places Kurt Krueger in the cast, his participation in the released film has not been confirmed. A news item in *NYT* notes that this was Lee Tracy's first screen appearance since his two-year stint in the Military Police. A *HR* news item adds that Tracy's performance in this picture won him a contract with RKO. Although noted news commentator Drew Pearson's name is not included in the onscreen credits, Pearson does appear as the narrator in the film.

Box 3 Mar 1945. *DV* 15 Feb 1945, p. 3. *FD* 20 Feb 1945, p. 8. *HR* 5 Jun 1944, p. 3. *HR* 10 Jul 1944, p. 1. *HR* 11 Aug 1944, p. 1. *HR* 15 Feb 1945, p. 8. *HR* 30 Apr 1945, p. 8. *MPHPD* 16 Dec 1944, p. 2230. *MPHPD* 17 Feb 1945, pp. 2318-19. *NYT* 30 Jul 1944. *NYT* 25 Apr 1945, p. 27. *Var* 25 Apr 1945, p. 14.

BETRAYED (Native Americans)

Thanhouser Film Corp.; Mutual Masterpicture De Luxe Edition. *Dist* Mutual Film Corp. 29 Jan 1916. Si; b&w. 5 reels.

Pres Edwin Thanhouser. *Dir* Howard M. Mitchell. *Scen* Philip Lonergan.

Cast: Grace De Carlton (*Little Fawn*), Robert Whittier (*Heart of Oak*), Roy Pilcher (*Granville Wingham*), Gladys Leslie (*Carolyn Wingham*).

Drama. Heart of Oak leaves the reservation and attends an Eastern college, where he becomes best friends with the wealthy Granville Wingham. A year later, Little Fawn, Heart of Oak's sister, joins him at the school. She and Granville fall in love, but Heart of Oak tells her that she must not even think of marrying a white man. Nevertheless, Granville and Little Fawn spend the night together in a cabin, where Heart of Oak finds them the next morning. Enraged, Heart of Oak threatens to kill Granville, but then Little Fawn kills herself, and a stunned Heart of Oak sends Granville away so he can be alone with his dead sister. *Brothers and sisters. Indians of North America. Miscegenation. Racism. College life. Friendship. Students. Suicide.*

Note: Some scenes in this film were shot on Indian reservations in New York.

Motog 12 Feb 1916, p. 370. *MPN* 29 Jan 1916, p. 554. *MPW* 22 Jan 1916, p. 544, 625. *MPW* 5 Feb 1916, p. 837.

BETTY SMITH'S A TREE GROWS IN BROOKLYN *see* **A TREE GROWS IN BROOKLYN**

BETWEEN THE THUNDER AND THE SUN *see* **THUNDER IN THE SUN**

BETWEEN TWO WOMEN (Chinese Americans)

Metro-Goldwyn-Mayer Corp.; controlled by Loew's Inc. *Dist* Loew's Inc. Mar **1945**; New York opening: 28 Mar 1945; *Prod:* early Aug—early Sep 1944; added scenes 22 Oct—23 Oct 1944 [©Loew's Inc.; 19 Dec 1944; LP13053]. Sd (Western Electric Sound System); b&w. 8 reels, 7,296 ft. 82-83 min. Passed by the National Board of Review. PCA cert no. 10434.

Series: Dr. Gillespie.

[*Prod* Carey Wilson]. *Dir* Willis Goldbeck. [*Asst dir* Al Raboch]. *Orig scr* Harry Ruskin. *Dir of photog* Harold Rosson. [*2d cam* Robert Martin*]. *Art dir* Cedric Gibbons and Edward Carfagno. *Film ed* Adrienne Fazan. *Set dec* Edwin B. Willis. *Assoc* Ralph S. Hurst. [*Props* Aaron Masure]. *Cost supv* Irene. *Assoc* Marion Herwood. *Mus score* David Snell. *Dance dir* Jeannette Bate. *Rec dir* Douglas Shearer. [*Unit mixer* Thomas Edwards]. [*Re-rec and eff mixer* Standish J. Lambert, Robert W. Shirley, Newell Sparks, William Steinkamp and Michael Steinore]. [*Mus mixer* Edward Baravalle and M. J. McLaughlin]. [*Unit mgr* Walter Strohm].

Song(s): "Look at Me," words and music by Earl Brent; "I'm in the Mood for Love," words and music by Dorothy Fields and Jimmy McHugh.

Source: Based on characters created by Max Brand.

Cast: Van Johnson (*Dr. [Randall] "Red" Adams*), Lionel Barrymore (*Dr. Leonard [B.] Gillespie*), Gloria DeHaven (*Edna*), Keenan Wynn (*Tobey*), Marilyn Maxwell (*Ruth Edley*), Alma Kruger (*Molly Byrd*), Marie Blake (*Sally*), Keye Luke (*Dr. Lee*), Nell Craig (*Nurse Parker*), Edna Holland (*Nurse Morgan*), Lorraine Miller (*Marian*), Walter Kingsford (*Dr. Walter Carew*), Tom Trout (*Eddie Smith*), Shirley Patterson (*Nurse Thorsen*), [Henry O'Neill (*Goff*)], [George H. Reed (*Conover*)].

Medical, Drama, with songs. [*Print viewed*]. When his wheelchair-bound, irascible boss, Dr. Leonard B. Gillespie, insists that he take his place at a gala war bond event, hard-working, young physician Randall "Red" Adams reluctantly agrees. To Red's surprise, Dr. Gillespie's wealthy "date" turns out to be Ruth Edley, a sincere socialite whose determination to marry Red is the cause of much gossip at his New York hospital, Blair General. After Red informs Ruth that, although he loves her, he cannot marry her because of her money, his attention is caught by Edna, a singer at the nightclub. Red tells the jealous Ruth that he senses something "peculiar" about Edna, and shortly after, Edna falls unconscious in her dressing room and is rushed to Blair by Red. The next morning, Red questions the revived Edna about her life, and she reveals that she has been unable to eat anything for four days. Red diagnoses Edna with neuropsychiatric self-starvation, but cannot say why she has developed a sudden loathing for food. At the same time, Sally, the hospital's beloved switchboard operator, falls ill after complaining for days about feeling tired and sick. Red diagnoses Sally with Bright's disease, an incurable but controllable urinary condition. Red then returns to Edna's nightclub to question her co-workers about recent events that may have contributed to her illness. Red does his best to uncover useful information about Edna, but learns nothing. Ruth, however, smugly tells Red that he is not asking the right questions and has a chat with Edna's dancer friend Marian. Based on their conversation, Ruth then suggests to Red that Edna's problems may be connected to her boyfriend's former admirer, Sylvia. Following Ruth's lead, Red returns to the hospital with Sylvia's theatrical agent, Goff, and drills Edna about her relationship with Sylvia, a dancer at the club. Edna states that after she became involved with her boyfriend, she and a jealous Sylvia began to fight, and Sylvia was eventually fired. Sometime later, Sylvia, a known drinker, died from starvation, and after hearing the news, Edna stopped eating. At Red's urging, the agent then reveals that Sylvia was fired after giving the stage manager an ultimatum, and did not starve because she lacked money, but because she was drinking too much. Convinced now that she was in no way responsible for Sylvia's death, Edna declares herself cured and looks forward to her next meal. Sally, meanwhile, is experiencing great pain, and Red is forced to reconsider his diagnosis. Upon examining some X-rays, Red concludes that she has a blocked kidney and requires emergency surgery. Sally, who feared she had cancer, is relieved by the diagnosis but insists that Red, on whom she has a crush, perform the operation. Despite some life-threatening complications, the operation is successful, and Sally makes a full recovery. Later, Red, Ruth, Sally, Dr. Gillespie and Red's fellow physician Dr. Lee attend another war bond event at the nightclub, and this time, Red eagerly kisses Ruth in exchange for war bonds. *Hospitals. Physicians. Singers. Telephone operators. Chinese Americans. Fund-raising. Gossip. Guilt. Handicapped. Jealousy. New York City. Nightclubs. Nurses. Operations, Surgical. Psychosomatic illness. Romance. Starvation. Theatrical agents. Unrequited love. War bonds. X-rays.*

Note: The working title of this film was *Dr. Red Adams*. Although reviewers speculated that following this film, M-G-M's "Dr. Kildare/Dr. Gillespie" series would be retitled the "Dr. Red Adams" series, Van Johnson, who played Adams, actually left the series after this film. In his *NYHT* review of the picture, Bert McCord wrote about Johnson's apparent take-over of the series: "...there is one more 'Dr. Kildare' sequel I would like to see M-G-M make, and it is a story out of their own backyard. They should put one of their screen writers to work on the tribulations of a brilliant young actor whose religious beliefs were misinterpreted as cowardice, who endured internment and public scorn rather than join a combatant unit and who went on to become a medical aide in the front lines. Van Johnson could play it. Or better still, let Lew Ayres himself play it when he returns from service in the South Pacific." Although twins Lee and Lyn Wilde and Peggy O'Neill were announced as cast members, they did not

appear in the completed film. In addition, a M-G-M news item announced Patricia Dane in the role of "Muriel," but that part was played by Ruthe Brady. According to an Oct 1944 *HR* news item, scenes featuring Gloria DeHaven were added after she received good notices during a sneak preview of the film. For additionl information on the "Dr. Kildare" and "Dr. Gillespie" series, consult the Series Index and see entry for the 1938 film *Young Dr. Kildare* in *AFI Catalog of Feature Films, 1931-40* (F3.5251).

Box 13 Jan 1945. *DV* 20 Dec 1944, p. 3. *FD* 18 Dec 1944, p. 8. *HR* 29 May 1944, p. 14. *HR* 19 Jul 1944, p. 9. *HR* 4 Aug 1944, p. 46. *HR* 14 Aug 1944, p. 4. *HR* 25 Aug 1944, p. 3. *HR* 1 Sep 1944, p. 12. *HR* 24 Oct 1944, p. 15. *HR* 20 Dec 1944, p. 3. *MPHPD* 14 Oct 1944, p. 2142. *MPHPD* 23 Dec 1944, p. 2238. *NYHT* 29 Mar 1945. *NYT* 29 Mar 1945, p. 18. *Var* 20 Dec 1944, p. 17.

BEVERLY B. DOBBS ORIGINAL ALASKA-SIBERIA MOTION PICTURES *see* ATOP OF THE WORLD IN MOTION

BEWARE (African Americans)

Astor Pictures Corp. *Dist* Astor Film Corp. Jul **1946**; New York premiere: 14 Jun 1946; Prod: Dec 1945 at Filmcraft Studios, N.Y.. Sd; b&w. 4,978 ft. 55 or 64 min.

Pres BERLE ADAMS and R. M. SAVINI. *Exec prod* R. M. Savini. *Prod* Bud Pollard. *Dir* Bud Pollard. *Asst dir* Ed Kelly. *Orig scr story* John E. Gordon. *Photog* Don Malkames. *Mont* Fred Barber. *Settings* Frank Nemczy. *Film ed* Bud Pollard. *Cost* Variety. *Orig mus arr* Louis Jordan. *Sd rec* Walter Hicks. *Makeup* Fred Ryle. *Lighting* Arthur Burns. *Prod mgr* John Doran.

Song(s): "Beware, Brother, Beware," music and lyrics by Morry Lasco, Dick Adams and Fleecie Moore; "Don't Worry 'Bout that Mule," music and lyrics by William Davis, Duke Groner and Charles Stewart; "Salt Pork, West Virginia," music and lyrics by Bill Tennyson Jr.; "Good Morning, Heartache," music and lyrics by Irene Higginbotham, Ervin Drake and Dan Fisher; "In the Land of the Buffalo Nickel," music and lyrics by Bob Hilliard and Dick Miles; "Long Legged Lizzie," music and lyrics by Herman Fairbanks and Deek Watson; "How Long Must I Wait," "Hold On," "You Got to Have a Beat," "Old Fashioned Passion," composers undetermined.

Cast: Frank Wilson (*Professor Drury*), Emory Richardson (*Dean Hargraves*), Valerie Black (*Miss Annabelle Brown*), Milton Woods (*Benjamin Ware, 3rd*), Joseph Hilliard (*Harry, schoolboy*), Tommy Hix (*Donald, schoolboy*), Charles Johnson (*Robert, schoolboy*), John Grant (*Joe, schoolboy*), Walter Earle (*Porter*), Ernest Calloway (*Stranger*), Dimples Daniels (*Long Legg'd Lizzie*), The "Aristo-Genes" Girls Club, LOUIS JORDAN AND HIS TYMPANY BAND: (*Himself* [*Lucius Brokenshire Jordan*]), William Davis (*Piano*), Joshua W. Jackson (*Sax*), Aaron Izenhall (*Trumpet*), Carl Hogan (*Guitar*), Jesse Simpkins (*Bass*), Eddie Byrd (*Drums*).

African American, College, Musical. [*Print viewed*]. Ware College, a prestigious black university in Ohio founded by Benjamin Ware in 1867, is on the brink of financial collapse following a decision by Benjamin Ware, III, the greedy grandson of the late founder, to cut off the school's revenues. In a meeting, Dean Hargraves, Professor Drury and Annabelle Brown, a former student who is now a physical education instructor, agree that the young Ware has a complete disregard for the welfare of the school. Although Hargraves and Drury remind Annabelle that Ware may acting out of revenge for her refusal to marry him when they were classmates, neither blames her for the current troubles they face. Instead, they devise a plan to raise money for the school by holding a reception for graduates of the college to solicit them for donations. While poring over the roster of former students, Hargraves and Drury come across the name of Lucius Brokenshire Jordan, a student they both thought would surely not amount to anything. They also recall that Lucius was smitten with Annabelle and that the jealous Benjamin drove him out of town. Unknown to Hargraves and Drury, Lucius has become an American jazz sensation and is presently on a concert tour across the country. By coincidence, Lucius' train is delayed at Ware College, and he arrives at the school just as the reception gets underway. While the former students pour in from all over the country, Lucius and his band play music for them in one of the classrooms. The festive mood is soon broken, however, when Ware declares that their revenue-raising scheme is against the school rules. Ware then fires Hargraves and tries to blackmail Annabelle into marrying him. When Lucius learns of the situation, he quickly works to reverse the school's misfortune by holding a benefit concert. Lucius succeeds in raising the money needed to keep the school open and does so in time to prevent Annabelle's marriage to Ware. Lucius also exposes Ware's scheme to defraud the school of its rightful funds. Lucius leads the school in a

musical celebration and then leaves town with Annabelle at his side. *African Americans. Band leaders. Colleges. Jazz music. Musicians. Romance.* Benefit performances. Blackmail. College deans. Concerts. Embezzlement. Financial crisis. Jealousy. Marriage–Forced. Professors. Revenge.

Note: Although the viewed print of this film contained a copyright statement for Astor Pictures, Inc., no record of such a copyright has been found. This film marked Louis Jordan's first starring role in a feature film. The film's credit titles include Claude Demetrius and Louis Jordan as composers. The *Var* review lists the following additional credits for music and lyrics: Lucky Millinder and Jerry Black. According to modern sources, women protested Louis Jordan's title song, "Beware, Brother, Beware," because of its sexist lyrics. Louis Jordan offered an apology to women in the title song of his next film, *Lookout Sister* (see below).

Exh 26 Jun 1946. *FD* 27 Jun 1946, p. 12. *MPHPD* 22 Jun 1946, p. 3054. *Var* 19 Jun 1946, p. 8.

BEWARE THE WOMAN *see* UNTAMED YOUTH

BEYOND THE BLUE HORIZON *see* THE FAR HORIZONS

BEYOND THE CALL *see* HELL TO ETERNITY

BEYOND THE CALL OF DUTY *see* HELL TO ETERNITY

BEYOND VICTORY (German Americans)

RKO Pathé Pictures, Inc.; C. E. Sullivan, Vice-President Pathé Studios, Inc. *Dist* RKO Pathé Distributing Corp. 12 Apr **1931** [©RKO-Pathé Distributing Corp.; 12 Apr 1931; LP2140]. Sd (RCA Photophone System); b&w. 8 reels, 6,581 ft. 70-71 or 73 min. Passed by the National Board of Review.

Prod E. B. Derr. *Dir* John Robertson. *Wrt* Horace Jackson and James Gleason. *Photog* Norbert Brodine. *Prelude eff* William Dietz. *Art dir* Carroll Clark. *Film ed* Daniel Mandell. *Cost* Gwen Wakeling. *Mus dir* Francis Groman. *Prelude mus* Arthur Alexander. *Sd eng* Ben Winkler, Harold Stine, [Charles O'Loughlin and Tom Carman].

Cast: Bill Boyd [(*Sergeant Bill Thatcher*)], James Gleason [(*Private Jim Mobley*)], Lew Cody [(*Lew Cavanaugh*)], ZaSu Pitts [(*"Mlle." Fritzi*)], Marion Shilling [(*Ina*)], Russell Gleason [(*Russell "Bud"*)], Lissi Arna [(*Katherine*)], Mary Carr [(*Mother*)], Fred Scott [(*Fred*)], Theodore Von Eltz [(*Major Sparks*)], Frank Reicher, [(*Wade Boteler*)], [E. H. Calvert], [Charles Coleman], [Max Barwyn], [Hedwiga Reicher].

War, Drama. [*Print viewed*]. As the remnants of an American battalion fights the German army for control of a French village, four soldiers recall how they came to the battlefields of World War I. The first young wounded soldier, Russell, called "Bud," begs his commanding officer, Sergeant Bill Thatcher, to tell his mother that he had been selfish and then recalls the following scene: Although his mother pleads with him to stay on the farm and not jeopardize his life in a faraway war, he ignores her and enlists. After telling his story, Bud dies in Bill's arms. Soon after, in France, another dying soldier, Lew Cavanaugh, recounts to Bill how he came to enlist: A wealthy New York playboy, Lew invites Ina, his latest conquest, to his apartment. When his former mistress telephones, Lew puts her off by telling her that he has enlisted in the army. Ina, overhearing the lie, proudly throws her arms around Lew and, assuming that he will be shipped out the next morning, promises to give him a night to remember. In France, after he is nicked in the ear by a passing bullet, "K-P" private Jim Mobley remembers his wife, "Mlle." Fritzi, a vaudeville knife thrower who doesn't understand why men wage war, and who becomes very upset when her housekeeping husband announces his intention to enlist. Back on the battle grounds, Jim finds Bill at the machine gun and listens as he tells the story of his fiancée in New Orleans: On the day before their wedding, Bill informs German-born Katherine that he would rather fight Germans overseas than marry a German in America. Despite her impassioned call to reason, Katherine cannot convince Bill that war is meaningless. Before blowing up a German-controlled bridge, Bill confesses to Jim that Katherine was wiser than he. After Jim and Bill are shelled, they are taken to a Red Cross hospital, where Katherine finds them and convinces the German doctors to allow her to donate blood for Bill's life-saving transfusion. Armistice is declared, and generously decorated, Bill and Jim toast to peace with Katherine. *Combat. Pacifism and pacifists. Soldiers. War. World War I.* Blood–Transfusion. Farmers. France. German Americans. Germany. Army. Hospitals. Military service, Voluntary. Mothers and sons. New Orleans (LA). New York City. Playboys. United States. Army. Vaudevillians. War injuries.

Note: Hedwiga Reicher was Frank Reicher's sister, and Russell Gleason was James Gleason's son. According to modern sources, director Edward H. Griffith

was brought in to shoot retakes. Modern sources also note that scenes featuring Helen Twelvetrees and June Collyer were edited out of the final film.

FD 12 Apr 1931, p. 32. *HR* 10 Apr 1931, p. 6. *MPH* 18 Apr 1931, p. 40. *NYT* 6 Apr 1931, p. 24. *Var* 8 Apr 1931, p. 19.

BIG BOY (African Americans)

Warner Bros. Pictures, Inc. *Dist* Warner Bros. Pictures, Inc. 6 Sep **1930** [©Warner Bros. Pictures, Inc.; 5 Aug 1930; LP1465]. Sd (Vitaphone); b&w. 9 reels, 6,275 ft.

Dir Alan Crosland. *Scr and dial* William K. Wells, Perry Vekroff and Rex Taylor. *Photog* Hal Mohr. *Film ed* Ralph Dawson. *Rec eng* Hal Bumbaugh.

Song(s): "What Will I Do Without You?" music by Joe Burke, lyrics by Al Subin; "Liza Lee" and "Tomorrow Is Another Day," by Bud Green and Sammy Stept; "Down South," music by William H. Myddleton, lyrics by Sigmund Spaeth; "The Handicap March," by Dave Reed, Jr. and George Rosey.

Source: Based on the play *Big Boy* by Harold Atteridge (New York, 7 Jan 1925).

Cast: Al Jolson (*Gus*), Claudia Dell (*Annabel*), Louise Closser Hale (*Mrs. Bedford*), Lloyd Hughes (*Jack*), Eddie Phillips (*Coley Reed*), Lew Harvey (*Doc Wilbur*), Franklin Batie (*Jim*), John Harron (*Joe*), Tom Wilson (*Tucker*), Carl White (*Song director*), Colin Campbell (*Steve Leslie*), Noah Beery (*Bagley*), The Monroe Singers.

Musical, Comedy-drama. Hoping to recoup the family fortune, the Bedfords stake their hopes on Big Boy, a horse trained for the Kentucky Derby by the ever-singing Gus, their faithful black jockey. Shortly before the race, Jack and Annabel return from eastern schools, bringing with them Coley Reid, his confidant Doc Wilbur, and Steve Leslie, an English jockey. Reid persuades Jack to urge Mrs. Bedford to entrust the race to Steve, but she declines, saying Gus has served the family for generations and telling them a story (incorporated in the film and providing the opportunity for the singing of Negro spirituals) of how Gus's grandfather saved Annabel's grandmother from kidnappers in 1870. Threatening Jack with a forged check, Reid forces him to have Gus break training rules, and the trainer is dismissed. Joe becomes suspicious and learns that Dolly, Reid's wife, is plotting against Annabel, of whom she is jealous, and that Steve plans to "throw" the race. Gus then appears, outsmarts the crooks, and wins the race. Jolson appears without blackface at the end of the film to sing "Tomorrow Is Another Day." *African Americans. Courtship. Forgers and forgery. Horse trainers. Horseracing. Horses. Jockeys. Kentucky Derby. Motion pictures.*

FD 14 Sep 1930. *NYT* 13 Sep 1930, p. 9. *Var* 17 Sep 1930, p. 21.

BIG CITY (Russian Americans)

Metro-Goldwyn-Mayer Corp.; controlled by Loew's Inc.; A Frank Borzage Production. *Dist* Loew's Inc. 3 Sep **1937**; Prod: mid-Jun—28 Jul 1937 [©Metro-Goldwyn-Mayer Corp.; 27 Aug 1937; LP7387]. Sd (Western Electric Sound System); b&w. 8 reels. 75 or 80 min. Passed by the National Board of Review. PCA cert no. 3613.

Prod Norman Krasna. *Dir* Frank Borzage. [*Jack Dempsey seq dir* George B. Seitz]. [*Asst dir* Lew Borzage]. *Scr* Dore Schary and Hugo Butler. *Orig story* Norman Krasna. *Photog* Joseph Ruttenberg. [*Jack Demsey seq photog* Clyde De Vinna]. *Art dir* Cedric Gibbons. *Art dir assoc* Stan Rogers and Edwin B. Willis. *Film ed* Fredrick Y. Smith. *Ward* Dolly Tree. *Mus score* William Axt. [*Vocal coach for Russian chorus* Leon Stewart]. *Rec dir* Douglas Shearer. [*Prod mgr* Jay Marchand].

Cast: LUISE RAINER (*Anna Benton*), SPENCER TRACY (*Joe Benton*), Charley Grapewin (*The mayor*), Janet Beecher (*Sophie Sloan*), Eddie Quillan (*Mike Edwards*), Victor Varconi (*Paul Roya*), Oscar O'Shea (*John C. Anderson*), Helen Troy (*Lola Johnson*), William Demarest (*Beecher*), John Arledge (*Buddy*), Irving Bacon (*Jim Sloane*), Guinn Williams (*Danny Devlin*), Regis Toomey (*Fred Hawkins*), Edgar Dearing (*Tom Reilley*), Paul Harvey (*District Attorney Gilbert*), Andrew J. Tombes (*Inspector Matthews*), Clem Bevans (*Grandpa Sloan*), Grace Ford (*Mary Reilley*), Alice White (*Peggy Devlin*), Jack Dempsey, James J. Jeffries, Jimmy McLarin, Maxie Rosenbloom, Jim Thorpe, Frank Wykoff, Jackie Fields, Man Mountain Dean, Gus Sonnenberg, George Godfrey, Joe Rivers, Cotton Warburton, Bull Montana, Snowy Baker, Taski Hagio (*Themselves*), [Edward James Flanagan (*Stanley, cab driver*)], [Russell Hopton (*Buddy*)], [Ray Walker (*Eddie Donogan*)], [Helen Brown (*Nora*)], [Natalie Garson], [Robert McKenzie (*Frank Turner*)], [Joseph King (*Jackson*)], [Dewey Robinson (*Fuller*)], [Stanley Andrews (*Detective Bennett*)], [Joseph Crehan (*Curtis*)], [Edward Gargan (*Dumb cop*)], [Eddie Gribbon (*Dumb detective*)], [Mitchell Lewis (*Detective Haley*)], [Alonzo Price (*Detective Meyers*)], [Richard Tucker (*Dr. Franklin*)], [George Skultesky (*Priest*)], [Landers Stevens (*Ship captain*)], [Herbert Ashley (*First detective*)], [Eadie Adams (*Eddie's wife*)], [Matt McHugh (*Cab driver*)], [Harry Woods (*Miller*)], [Paul Fix (*Night watchman*)], [Jules Cowles (*Janitor*)], [Mahlon Hamilton, Dick Rush, Ralph Bushman (*Doormen*)], [Will Stanton], [Dick Rich, Jack Pennick, Robert O'Connor, Robert Brister, James Flavin, Frank S. Hagney, Lew Harvey, Orville Caldwell, Paul Newman (*Comet cab drivers*)], [Sam Ash (*Man who gets punched*)], [Maine Geary (*Independent cab driver*)], [Jack Dougherty (*Started*)], [Barbara Bedford (*Screaming woman*)], [Jack Daley (*Mounted policeman*)], [Gladden James, Ruth March (*Mayor's secretaries*)], [Lowden Adams, Eric Wilton (*Butlers*)], [Lee Phelps (*Adams, immigration officer*)], [Frank DuFrane (*Purser*)], [Charles McMurphy (*Heller*)], [Leigh DeLacy (*Landlady*)], [Lester Dorr (*Petty officer*)], [Nick Thompson, Harry Semels (*Counter men*)], [Matty Roubert (*Newsboy*)], [Tom Dugan (*Policeman*)], [Larry Wheat (*Minor official*)], [Jack C. Grey (*Detective*)], [Jack Hutchinson (*Clerk*)], [Lillian Nicholson, Lillian Worth (*Immigrants*)], [George Chandler (*Mr. Briggs*)], [Don Sugai Matsuda, Neal Glisby (*Athletes*)], [Monya Andre], [Abdullah Abbas].

Drama. [*Print viewed*]. New York cabbie Joe Benton and his Russian-born wife Anna have a loving marriage, despite their constant teasing. Joe and Anna's brother, Paul Roya, are both independent cab drivers who are at odds with the large Comet Cab Company. After Paul is beaten up by some Comet cabbies, he decides to be a "double agent" and infiltrate the company. Beecher, a labor agitator, is hired by Comet to foment trouble among the independents and secretly works with Buddy, a friend of Joe and Paul's. On the night of Anna's birthday, Anna, who is pregnant, asks Buddy to take a raincoat to Paul, who is working late. When Buddy turns up at the garage, Beecher is angry with him for being there, then takes the box with the raincoat from him. Meanwhile, the night watchman finds a bomb in the garage and, seeing Paul there, thinks that he is the bomber. He then shoots and kills Paul just before the bomb goes off, terrifying Buddy, who did not know that he would be involved in serious violence. At the inquest, Beecher accuses Anna of transporting the bomb to Paul in the box with the raincoat. Though District Attorney Gilbert does not believe that Anna is involved in the bombing, he feels that Beecher will use the incident to his political advantage, and so decides that Anna should be deported. At Paul's funeral, government men try to take her away, but she escapes, aided by her friends. Because they do not want her to be deported, all of her friends decide to take turns hiding her from the authorities. After some time, the district attorney, supported by the mayor, decides to offer amnesty to cabbies if they voluntarily turn Anna in. No one takes advantage of the offer, but soon detectives follow Joe to the home of Jim and Sophie Sloan, who are currently hiding Anna. Though the detectives only find Grandpa Sloan in the house, they know that Anna has been there, and the district attorney decides that he will arrest all of the cabbies for the bombing. Anna cannot stand to think of her friends suffering to protect her, so she calls the mayor to see if his amnesty offer is still available. When he says yes, she tells him where she is staying and waits for the authorities. At the boat that will take her back to Europe, Joe comes to visit Anna and promises to meet her there, but she tells him that she wants him to stay in America. When he leaves, he and his friend, Mike Edwards, find Buddy and discover that he is being paid to keep quiet about the bombing. They then force him to come with them while they look for the mayor and the district attorney. They track the mayor down at Jack Dempsey's restaurant, where he and the district attorney are attending a banquet with a number of famous athletes. After Joe and Mike force Buddy to confess in front of the dignitaries, Joe pleads with the mayor to do something quickly to save Anna. Everyone at the banquet then rushes to the pier, where they arrive just before the boat is about to sail. As Anna is being taken away from the boat, she says that she is about to give birth and an ambulance is summoned. While she is giving birth, the Comet cabbies decide to teach the independent cabbies a lesson, and a fight breaks out in which the mayor, Dempsey and other athletes join Joe in teaching the Comet cabbies a lesson. A few days later, when Joe and Anna christen their baby, he is given dozens of names to honor all of their friends. *Deportation. Immigrants. Marriage. New York City. Russian Americans. Taxicab drivers. Athletes. Banquets. Birthdays. Brothers and sisters.*

Childbirth. Confession (Law). Detectives. District Attorneys. Escapes. Fistfights. Funerals. Impersonation and imposture. Labor agitators. Mayors. Rescues. Steamboats.

Note: According to a news item in *HR*, the "Jack Dempsey Sequence," was filmed by Clyde De Vinna in New York, under George Seitz's direction. The sequence featured many popular sports figures of the day portraying themselves. Jack Dempsey's restaurant was a popular New York restaurant in the 1930s. This was the first film of actress Ruth Hussey, who was billed in the CBCS as Ruth March, and portrayed one of the mayor's secretaries. Hussey used the name March for a short period of time in 1937, but she was never billed onscreen as Ruth March, and this was apparently the only film for which she received any credit under that name. Her first onscreen credit was in *Madame X*, released on 1 Oct 1937 (see FI Catalog of Feature Films, 1931-40; F3.2649).

DV 25 Aug 1937, p. 3. FD 17 Jun 1937, p. 7. FD 30 Aug 1937, p. 9. HR 19 Jun 1937, p. 2. HR 21 Jun 1937, p. 6. HR 25 Aug 1937, p. 3. MPD 26 Aug 1937, p. 3. MPH 14 Aug 1937, p. 33. MPH 4 Sep 1937, p. 40, 43. NYT 17 Sep 1937, p. 29. Var 15 Sep 1937, p. 13.

BIG CITY (Irish Americans, Jewish Americans)

Metro-Goldwyn-Mayer Corp.; controlled by Loew's Inc. *Dist* Loew's Inc. 23 Mar **1948**; Prod: 15 Oct—early Dec 1947; retakes completed 30 Dec 1947 [©Loew's Inc.; 3 Mar 1948; LP1528]. Sd (Western Electric Sound System); b&w. 9,265 ft. 103 min. Passed by the National Board of Review. PCA cert no. 12898.

Prod Joe Pasternak. *Dir* Norman Taurog. [*Asst dir* Sid Sidman]. *Scr* Whitfield Cook and Anne Morrison Chapin. *Addl dial* Aben Kandel. *Adpt* Nanette Kutner. *Story* Miklos Laszlo. *Dir of photog* Robert Surtees. *Art dir* Cedric Gibbons and Preston Ames. *Film ed* Gene Ruggiero. *Set dec* Edwin B. Willis. *Assoc* Alfred E. Spencer. *Women's cost* Helen Rose. *Mus dir* Georgie Stoll. *Orch arr* Leo Arnaud. *Dance dir* Stanley Donen. *Rec dir* Douglas Shearer. *Hair styles des by* Sydney Guilaroff. *Makeup created by* Jack Dawn. *Dubbed "Kol Nidre" and "Ok'l Baby Dok'l" for Margaret O'Brien* Frankie Day. *Dubbed "What'll I Do" for Karen Booth* Marsha Norman. *Dubbed for Robert Preston* Charles Prescott. *Dubbed for Edward Arnold* Charles Schrouder.

Song(s): "God Bless America" and "What'll I Do," music and lyrics by Irving Berlin; "Ok'l Baby Dok'l," music and lyrics by Inez James and Sidney Miller; "The Kerry Dance," music and lyrics by James Lyman Molloy; "Don't Blame Me," music by Jimmy McHugh, lyrics by Dorothy Fields; "Lullaby," by Johannes Brahms; "Yippee-o, Yippie-ai," music and lyrics by Walter Popp and Jerry Seelen; "I'm Gonna See a Lot of You," music and lyrics by Fred Spielman and Janice Torre; "Kol Nidre" and "Sholem Aleichem," traditional hymns.

Cast: Margaret O'Brien (*Midge [also known as Mary Ellen Rachel O'Donnell Andrews Feldman]*), Robert Preston (*Reverend Phillip Y. Andrews*), Danny Thomas (*Cantor David Irwin Feldman*), George Murphy (*Patrick O'Donnell*), Karin Booth (*Florence Bartlett*), Edward Arnold (*Judge Martin O. Abercrombie*), Butch Jenkins (*Lewis Keller*), and introducing to the screen Betty Garrett (*"Shoo Shoo" Grady*), and Lotte Lehmann (*"Mama" Feldman*), Page Cavanaugh Trio (*Song specialties*), Connie Gilchrist (*Martha*), [Marles Noie (*Little girl*)], [Peter Roman (*Stooge*)], [Brick Sullivan, Jack Worth (*Cops*)], [Hank Mann, Heinie Conklin (*Drunks*)], [Ben Moselle, Bobby Barber, Sailor Vincent, Clarence Hennecke (*Fighters*)], [Charles Sullivan (*Brawler*)], [Stanley Blystone (*Bartender*)], [David Leonard (*Rudy*)], [Lotte Stein (*Rudy's wife*)], [Arthur Walsh (*Jitterbug boy*)], [Joy Ames (*Jitterbug girl*)], [George Davis (*Florist*)], [Skeets Noyes (*Cleaning man*)], [Patricia Vaniver (*Bride*)], [Maynard Holmes (*Groom*)], [Wilson Wood (*Best man*)], [Doris Kemper (*Mrs. Crouse*)], [Jerry Michelson, David Bair (*Boys' voices*)], [Frank Mayo, Colin Kenny (*Lawyers*)], [Sherry Hall (*Court clerk*)], [Irene Seidner (*Woman guardian*)], [George Calliga (*Rabbi*)], [Robert Emmett Keane], [Don Gordon].

Domestic, Religious, Drama, with songs. [*Print viewed*]. One day, in New York City's East Side, cantor David Irwin Feldman rescues an abandoned infant girl he has found on an apartment building stoop. After caring for the girl for a few days, David and his friends, Phillip Y. Andrews, a Protestant minister, and Patrick O'Donnell, an Irish American Catholic police officer, decide to adopt the girl jointly. Judge Martin O. Abercrombie consents to the adoption in the hopes that it will bring together the East Side Jewish, Protestant and Catholic communities. As part of the agreement, however, the judge stipulates that the first of the three men to marry shall become the sole and permanent foster father. After naming the girl Midge, the three bachelors take up the responsibility of rearing the girl. Time passes, and Midge, now a grade school student, suffers the taunts of her schoolmates when she tries to explain her "family" situation.

When one of Midge's classmates, Lewis Keller, pelts her with a tomato, Midge loses her confidence and tells Phillip that she is ashamed that she has no mother. Later, Midge's teacher, Florence Bartlett, tells Phillip that she is opposed to their parenting "experiment" because it makes Midge "different" and mixes Midge up in three different faiths. Phillip, however, argues that the three faiths have a "common denominator," and that Midge is learning manners from Pat and singing from David. Realizing that he has not convinced Florence of the success he, Pat and David have had in rearing Midge, Phillip invites Florence to visit their home and see the results for herself. Phillip's plan works, and Midge changes her opinion about the unconventional family. While David falls in love with Florence, Pat begins courting "Shoo-Shoo" Grady, a street-smart singer at Bernie's Bar. Midge and Shoo-Shoo become fast friends, but their friendship is soon questioned by David when he sees Midge imitating the singer's sultry style. While David and Phillip prohibit Midge from spending time with Shoo-Shoo, Pat makes an unsuccessful attempt to persuade them that the singer is actually a good influence. Pat and Shoo-Shoo secretly marry, but soon after Shoo-Shoo learns of David and Phillip's decision, she leaves town. An outraged Pat takes his case to court, but Phillip and David refuse to give up custody of Midge without a fight. When Judge Abercrombie asks Midge to decide her fate, the girl says that she loves all three men and believes the only way to resolve the dispute is to put herself in the custody of an orphanage. Abercrombie agrees with Midge's suggestion, but the decision is protested by all three foster fathers, who tell the judge that they are willing to relinquish custody rather than see Midge sent to an orphanage. Realizing that the three men, Florence and Shoo-Shoo all love Midge, Abercrombie decides to return Midge to them and discard the stipulation he made about marriage. *Adoption. Foster parents. Foundlings. New York City–East Side. Religion. Trials. Cantors, Jewish. Catholics. Child custody. Irish Americans. Jews. Judges. Marriage. Marriage–Forced by circumstances. Mothers and sons. New York City–Coney Island. Ostracism. Police. Protestantism. Self-confidence. Self-sacrifice. Singers. Synagogues. Teachers.*

Note: The working title for this film was *Brothers of the East Side*. A Feb 1947 *HR* news item noted that actor Van Heflin was "penciled in" for the part played by Robert Preston. Preston was loaned to M-G-M from Paramount for this film. Jul 1947 *HR* news items indicate that producer Joe Pasternak purchased the rights to the film story in 1937, and that M-G-M writer Leslie Kardos was orginally set to make his directorial debut with this film. The picture marked the screen debut of Broadway actress Betty Garrett and opera star Lotte Lehmann. Although a Nov 1947 *M-G-M News* item noted that former Keystone Kop players Hank Mann and Heinie Conklin appear in the film as police officers, they actually played "drunks." According to a 1953 *HCN* article, writer Walter Abbott received a "very good settlement" from M-G-M following his $100,000 plagiarism suit against the company. Abbott claimed in the suit that the studio based *Big City* on his story entitled "Choir Boy."

Box 27 Mar 1948. DV 23 Mar 1948, p. 3, 11. FD 29 Mar 1948, p. 6. HCN 11 Feb 1953. HR 11 Feb 1947, p. 1. HR 1 Jul 1947, p. 13. HR 16 Jul 1947, p. 1. HR 6 Oct 1947, p. 10. HR 17 Oct 1947, p. 14. HR 5 Dec 1947, p. 12. HR 30 Dec 1947, p. 13. HR 23 Mar 1948, p. 3. HR 20 May 1948, p. 9. MGM News 7 Nov 1947. MPHPD 20 Mar 1948, p. 4103. MPHPD 3 Apr 1948, p. 4111. NYT 17 May 1948, p. 23. Var 24 Mar 1948, p. 8.

BIG COUNTRY *see* **IT'S A BIG COUNTRY: AN AMERICAN ANTHOLOGY**

BIG DAN *see* **NIGHT WIND**

THE BIG FIGHT (*foreign version*) *see* **LA FUERZA DEL QUERER**

THE BIG HANGOVER (ChineseAmericans)

Metro-Goldwyn-Mayer Corp.; controlled by Loew's Inc. *Dist* Loew's Inc. 26 May **1950**; Prod: early Aug—late Sep 1949 [©Loew's Inc.; 13 Mar 1950; LP2945]. Sd (Western Electric Sound System); b&w. 7,380 ft. 82 min. Passed by the National Board of Review. PCA cert no. 14167.

Prod Norman Krasna. *Dir* Norman Krasna. [*Asst dir* Marvin Stuart]. *Wrt* Norman Krasna. *Dir of photog* George Folsey and [Joseph Ruttenberg]. *Spec eff* Warren Newcombe. *Art dir* Cedric Gibbons and Paul Groesse. *Film ed* Fredrick Y. Smith. *Set dec* Edwin B. Willis. *Assoc* Henry W. Grace. *Women's cost* Helen Rose. *Mus score* Adolph Deutsch. *Rec supv* Douglas Shearer. *Makeup created by* Jack Dawn.

Song(s): "At Sundown," music and lyrics by Walter Donaldson; "Sleepy Time Gal," music by Ange Lorenzo and Richard Whiting, lyrics by Joseph R. Aldem and Raymond B. Egan.

Cast: VAN JOHNSON (*David Maldon*), ELIZABETH TAYLOR (*Mary Belney*), Percy Waram (*John Belney*), Fay Holden (*Martha Belney*), Leon Ames (*Carl Bellcap*), Edgar Buchanan (*Uncle Fred Mahoney*),

Selena Royle (*Kate Mahoney*), Gene Lockhart (*Charles Parkford*), Rosemary De Camp (*Claire Bellcap*), Phillip Ahn (*Dr. Lee*), Gordon Richards (*Williams*), Matt Moore (*Mr. Rumlie*), Pierre Watkin (*Samuel C. Lang*), Russell Hicks (*Steve Hughes*), [Kathleen Lockhart (*Mrs. Parkford*)], [Gayne Whitman, Bert Moorhouse, Stuart Holmes, Philo McCullough, Harold Miller, Cameron Grant, Jay Eaton (*Associates*)], [Cliff Clark (*Albert Johnson*)], [Anna Q. Nilsson (*Helen Lang*)], [Bess Flowers (*Mrs. Hughes*)], [Tristram Coffin (*Jenkins*)], [Lester Dorr, Cosmo Sardo, Dino Bolognese (*Waiters*)], [John Valentine (*Thomas*)], [Elsa Peterson (*Miss Dowling*)], [Everett Glass (*Attendant*)], [Louise Lorimer (*Mrs. Johnson*)], [Peter Thompson (*Phil*)], [Charles Evans (*Dean Hardwick*)], [Brett King (*Intern*)], [Mickey McCardle, Fred Shellac, Bert Davidson, Jonn Rosser, Bob Davis, Lew Smith, Lyle Clark (*Veterans*)], [The Country Gentlemen (*Singers*)], [Loulie Jean Norman (*Soloist in "Sleepy Time Gal" and "At Sundown" numbers*)].

Comedy-drama, with songs. [*Print viewed*]. While attending law school, honor student David Maldon is awarded a job at the prestigious law firm of Belney, Parkford, Evans and Hughes. One day, at a birthday cocktail party for the law firm's senior partner, John Belney, David behaves in an erratic manner. His behavior catches the notice of John's daughter Mary, an attractive psychoanalyst, who accuses John of being drunk. John denies the accusation and explains that he suffers from "liquor recoil," a condition he developed during World War II, when he nearly drowned in a vat of brandy at a French monastery. Realizing that David gets drunk at the mere mention of alcohol, Mary saves him from further humiliation by sending him home. In the hope of curing himself of his sensitivity to alcohol, David decides to take a teaspoonful of brandy every night before going to bed. The experiment appears doomed to failure, however, when David begins imagining that his dog is talking to him. The day after John's birthday party, Mary, who has fallen in love with David, offers to help David overcome his problem. Intrigued by David's claim that his dog talks to him, Mary offers him a glass of brandy and observes him conversing with his dog. One day, at the law office, David is present when Carl Bellcap, the city attorney, threatens to sue John if he allows one of his clients, the manager of a luxury apartment building, to evict the Lees, a Chinese couple. Carl also warns John that if the pregnant wife of the Chinese doctor loses her child, he will charge the law firm with causing her undue trauma and will hold it responsible. When Dr. Lee's wife loses her child in childbirth, David, working without the consent of the attorneys at his firm, contacts the management company and insists that the Lees be returned to their apartment. Later, at an alumni dinner, Charles Parkford, the partner at the law firm who is responsible for the eviction of the Chinese couple, learns that David is allergic to alcohol and decides to take revenge on his initiative by secretly slipping some wine into his soup. The wine makes David drunk, and he embarrasses himself by singing with the band. When David regains his sobriety, he accuses Bellcap of compromising his responsibilities as a public servant to gain favor with the partners at the law firm. Bellcap admits that he is seeking a job at the law firm, but tells David that he has been stymied in his efforts to fight rich and powerful law firms like John's because few talented lawyers are willing to work for the city. Convinced that Bellcap has done the best he could to fight the many injustices in the city, David apologizes to him. At his law school graduation ceremony, David announces his resignation from John's law firm, and accepts a job with the city attorney's office. Though Mary prefers that David remain with her father's firm, she respects his principles and plans to marry him. *Alcoholism. Allergy. Business ethics. Employer-employee relations. Lawyers. Psychoanalysts. Public defenders. Aunts. Birthdays. Chinese Americans. Dogs. Duplicity. Eviction. Fathers and daughters. Graduations. Hallucinations. Idealists. Law students. Racism. Romance. Uncles. Universities and colleges-Alumni. Veterans.*

Note: The working title of this film was *Drink to Me Only*. Norman Krasna's onscreen credit reads: "Written, directed and produced by Norman Krasna." The opening cast list differs slightly in order from the end credits. *HR* production charts list Joseph Ruttenberg as the film's photographer, while onscreen credits list George Folsey.

Box 18 Mar 1950. *DV* 15 Mar 1950, p. 4. *FD* 22 May 1950, p. 8. *HR* 12 Aug 1949, p. 12. *HR* 19 Sep 1949, p. 16. *HR* 14 Mar 1950, p. 3. *MPHPD* 18 Mar 1950, p. 229. *NYT* 26 May 1950, p. 20. *Var* 14 Oct 1949. *Var* 15 Mar 1950, p. 12.

THE BIG HOUSE (*foreign version*) *see* **EL PRESIDIO**

THE BIG POND (French Amercans)
Paramount-Publix Corp. *Dist* Paramount-Publix Corp. 3 May **1930** [©Paramount Publix Corp.; 6 May 1930; LP1278]. Sd (Movietone); b&w. 8 reels, 6,984 ft.
Prod Monta Bell. *Dir* Hobart Henley. *Stage dir* Bertram Harrison. *Scen* Robert Presnell and Garrett Fort. *Dial* Preston Sturges. *Cam* George Folsey. *Film ed* Emma Hill. *Mus arr* John W. Green. *Rec eng* Ernest F. Zatorsky.
Song(s): "Livin' in the Sunlight, Lovin' in the Moonlight," music and lyrics by Al Lewis and Al Sherman; "This Is My Lucky Day," music and lyrics by Lew Brown, B. G. De Sylva and Ray Henderson; "Mia Cara" and "You Brought a New Kind of Love to Me," music and lyrics by Irving Kahal, Pierre Norman and Sammy Fain.
Source: Based on the play *The Big Pond* by George Middleton and A. E. Thomas (New York, 21 Aug 1928).
Cast: Maurice Chevalier (*Pierre Mirande*), Claudette Colbert (*Barbara Billings*), George Barbier (*Mr. Billings*), Marion Ballou (*Mrs. Billings*), Andrée Corday (*Toinette*), Frank Lyon (*Ronnie*), Nat Pendleton (*Pat O'Day*), Elaine Koch (*Jennie*).
Comedy-drama. [*Not viewed*]. Pierre Mirande, son of an impoverished French family, makes a living by acting as guide to Mrs. Billings and her daughter, Barbara, tourists in Venice. Although Barbara falls in love with him, her suitor, Ronnie, and her father see him as a fortune-hunting foreigner, and accordingly offer him a job in Mr. Billings' chewing gum factory in New York. Forced to live in a dingy boardinghouse, Pierre is given the toughest work in the plant, but Barbara assures him that bluff and fast thinking are necessities in American business. With his humorous songs, he captivates his landlady, Toinette, and the maid, Jennie, but falls asleep on the night he is expected to attend Barbara's party. Wrongfully accused of spilling rum on some chewing gum samples, Pierre is discharged; he is later reinstated and promoted when he sells the idea of rum-flavored chewing gum with his own advertising lyrics. Insulted, Barbara plans to marry Ronnie, but Pierre kidnaps her aboard a speedboat. *Boardinghouses. Business managers. Chewing gum. Courtship. Fortune hunters. French. Guides. Landladies. Tourists. Venice (Italy).*
Note: A French version of *The Big Pond*, *La grande mare*, was filmed simultaneously to the English-Language film. Maurice Chevalier sings "You Brought a New Kind of Love to Me" and "Livin' in the Sunlight, Lovin' in the Moonlight" in both versions.
Other language version(s):
La grande mare (French language)
1930. World premiere in New Orleans: 9 Jun 1930, New York opening: 16 Aug 1930; Sd. b&w. 7,784 ft. 78 or 86 min.;. French language.
Prod Monta Bell. *Dir* Hobart Henley. *Supv French vers and addl dial* Jacques Bataille-Henri. *Editor* Barney Rogan.
French-language cast: Maurice Chevalier (*Pierre Mirande*), Claudette Colbert (*Barbara Billings*), Andrée Corday (*Toinette*), Lorraine Jaillet (*Jennie*), Maude Allen (*Mrs. Billings*), Henry Mortimer (*Mr. Billings*), William Williams (*Ronnie*). [*French version not viewed*].
FD 13 Apr 1930. *NYT* 19 May 1930, p. 21. *Var* 20 Aug 1930.

THE BIG SHOWDOWN *see* **THE LAWLESS**

THE BIG SKY (Native Americans, Blackfoot, Siksika)
Winchester Pictures Corp. *Dist* RKO Radio Pictures, Inc. Aug **1952**; Prod: late Jul—mid-Nov 1951 [©RKO Radio Pictures, Inc.; 29 Jul 1952; LP1938]. Sd (RCA Sound System); b&w. 16 reels, 10,975 ft. 122 min. PCA cert no. 15447.
Prod HOWARD HAWKS. *Assoc prod* Edward Lasker. *Dir* Howard Hawks. *Asst dir* William McGarry. *Unit dir* Arthur Rosson. *Scr* Dudley Nichols. *Dir of photog* Russell Harlan. *Spec eff* Donald Steward. *Sd eff* Walter G. Elliott. *Art dir* Albert S. D'Agostino and Perry Ferguson. *Film ed* Christian Nyby. *Set dec* Darrell Silvera and William Stevens. *Cost des* Dorothy Jeakins. *Mus comp and dir* Dimitri Tiomkin. *Mus coordination* C. Bakaleinikoff. *Mus ed* Richard Harris. *Sd* Phil Brigandi and Clem Portman. *Makeup artist* Mel Berns and Don Cash. *Hair stylist* Larry Germain. *Unit mgr* Arthur Siteman. *Casting asst* Harvey Clermont.
Song(s): "The Big Sky," words by Stan Jones, music by Dimitri Tiomkin; "Oh Brandy Leave Me Alone," words and music by Josef

Marias; "Buffalo Gal," words by Gordon Clark, music by Dimitri Tiomkin; "Charlotte," French lyrics by Gordon Clark, music by Dimitri Tiomkin.

Source: Based on the novel *The Big Sky* by A. B. Guthrie, Jr. (Cleveland, 1949).

Cast: KIRK DOUGLAS [*Jim Deakins*)], DEWEY MARTIN [(*Boone Claudel*)], ELIZABETH THREATT [(*Teal Eye*)], Arthur Hunnicutt [(*Zeb Calloway*)], Buddy Baer [(*Romaine*)], Steven Geray [(*Jourdonnais*)], Henri Letondal [(*Labadie*)], Hank Worden [(*Poordevil*)], Jim Davis [(*Streak*)], [Robert Hunter (*Chouquette*)], [Booth Colman (*Pascal*)], [Paul Frees (*MacMasters*)], [Frank de Kova (*Moleface*)], [Guy Wilkerson (*Longface*)], [Cliff Clark (*Jailer*)], [Fred Graham (*Sam Eggleston*)], [George Wallace, Max Wagner, Charles Regan (*Friends*)], [Sam Ash, Abe Dinovitch (*Singers*)], [Don Beddoe (*Horse trader*)], [Jim Hayward, Anthony Jochim, Jay Novello, Bill Self (*Trappers*)], [Frank Lackteen (*Indian*)], [Nolan Leary (*Storekeeper*)], [Sherman Sanders (*Dance caller*)], [Ray Hyke (*Bartender*)], [Eugene Borden (*Proprietor of tavern*)], [Viola Vonn (*Bar maid*)], [Pete Vigue, Dan Carson, Ernest Altmiller, Albert d'Arno, Gordon Clark, Peter Camlin, Ben Larson, John McKee (*Rivermen*)], [Crane Whitley (*Henchman*)], [Dennis Dengate, Ray Bennett, Rory Mallinson, Gil Warren], [Theodore Last Star (*Chief Red Horse*)].

Historical, Adventure, with songs. [*Print viewed*]. In 1832, trapper Jim Deakins leaves his Kentucky home to look for work in St. Louis. En route, Jim meets Boone Claudel, a quick-fisted fugitive who has been falsely accused of a crime. Boone and Jim become fast friends, and Boone joins Jim on his journey. Soon after the two arrive in St. Louis, Boone strikes an innocent Indian crossing his path and tells Jim that he dislikes all Indians. It eventually becomes clear to Jim that Boone's prejudice against Indians stems from the poor opinion he holds of his alcoholic uncle, Zeb Calloway, who is half Indian. While searching for his uncle, Boone meets Sam Eggleston, the ill-tempered owner of the Missouri River Co., who tells Boone that Zeb owes him money for a missing delivery of whiskey. Later, Boone and Jim are thrown in jail for starting a barroom brawl with Eggleston and his men. To their astonishment, Boone and Jim discover that their cellmate is none other than Zeb. Zeb tells Jim and Boone that Eggleston and his company dislike him and that they killed his partner because as a free trader he was too much competition for the Missouri River Company. Following their release from jail, Boone and Jim decide to join Zeb on a keelboat expedition up the Missouri River and into dangerous Montana Indian territory. The head of the expedition, Jourdonnais, warns his men that they are about to embark on a 2,000-mile journey into the heart of the Blackfoot Indian territory, a region that has never been traversed by white men. To quell the trappers' fears, Jourdonnais explains that their safety will be ensured by the presence of Teal Eye, a young Indian woman, whom they will be escorting to her Blackfoot chief. Once the expedition gets underway, Zeb tells Jim and Boone that the Indians fear the white man's presence in their territory because of what they call the "grab," the white man's habit of grabbing everything in sight. Many months into the journey, the expedition, having survived the perils of white water rapids and Indian attacks, is beset upon by a group of white men, who attack their camp and abduct Teal Eye. The attackers, who are all in the employ of rival fur trader MacMasters, then try to sabotage the traders' effort to reach the Blackfoot territory by setting fire to their ship. The ship is saved just in time, and two of the saboteurs are captured by the traders and later confess to working for MacMasters. Teal Eye is eventually rescued and rejoins the expedition as it enters Blackfoot territory. Once the traders reach their destination and pick up their furs, Boone announces that he has decided to marry Teal Eye and live among the Blackfoot. *Business competition. Expeditions. Fur trappers. Montana. Siksika Indians. Abduction. Alcoholics. Arson. Cooks. Creoles. Fistfights. Indians of North America. Indians of North America–Mixed blood. Jails. Marriage. Miscegenation. Racism. Rescues. Rivers. Sabotage. Snakes. St. Louis (MO). Uncles.*

Note: The following acknowledgment appears onscreen after the opening credits: "Grateful acknowledgment is made to The National Park Service, United States Department of the Interior for their assistance in photographing the natural beauty of Grand Teton National Park." According to contemporary news items, the film rights to the A. B. Guthrie, Jr. novel on which this picture is based were purchased by Howard Hawks in Mar 1950 for approximately $40,000. A *NYT* article noted that Guthrie retained the film rights to the unused portions of his novel for a possible sequel. Although news items published at the time of the purchase noted that production on the film was set to start in Aug 1950, filming did not begin until Jul 1951. According to information contained in the MPAA/PCA Collection at the AMPAS Library, the PCA, in Aug 1950, raised objections to "three major items" in the script. In addition to scenes depicting what the PCA believed to be gratuitous "brutality and gruesomeness," it criticized the excessive drinking in the script and "the suggestion that one of the principals, Boone, sleeps with the Indian girl, Teal Eye, only to wake up the next morning and find that he has married her." The PCA called this sequence "unacceptable under the [Production] Code," and demanded that the script be re-written to have "Boone" married to "Teal Eye" in a way that "does not involve his having pre-marital experience with her."

Although the film's preview running time was 140 minutes, the picture was cut to 122 minutes before its general release. According to an 11 Nov 1951 *HR* news item, *The Big Sky* marked the first time in Hollywood history that a "$2,000,000 outdoor drama has been completed without using a single frame of process photography." The news item also noted that nine weeks of shooting by the first unit was followed by twelve weeks of second unit shooting at Jackson Hole, WY, and eight weeks of interior shooting at the RKO Pathe lot. *The Big Sky* was nominated for an Academy Award for Best Cinematography, and Arthur Hunnicutt was nominated for Best Supporting Actor. Modern sources add Cactus Mack to the cast.

Box 12 Jul 1952. *Box* 19 Jul 1952. *DV* 9 Jul 1952, p. 3. *FD* 14 Jul 1952, p. 6. *HR* 27 Jul 1951, p. 11. *HR* 9 Nov 1951, p. 14. *HR* 9 Jul 1952, p. 3. *MPHPD* 12 Jul 1952, p. 1441. *NYT* 20 Aug 1952, p. 21. *Var* 13 Mar 1950. *Var* 9 Jul 1952, p. 6.

BIG STAKES (Latino)
Metropolitan Pictures. *Dist* East Coast Productions. 15 Aug **1922.** Si; b&w. 5 reels, 4,650 ft.

Pres Franklyn E. Backer. *Dir* Clifford S. Elfelt. *Scen* Frank Howard Clark.

Source: Based on the short story "High Stakes" by Earl Wayland Bowman in *American Magazine* (Sep 1920).

Cast: J. B. Warner (*Jim Gregory*), Elinor Fair (*Señorita Mercedes Aloyez*), Les Bates (*"Bully" Brand*), Willie May Carson (*Mary*), H. S. Karr (*Skinny Fargo*), Robert Grey (*El áCapitán Montaya*).

Western. Although she is betrothed to Captain Montaya, Mercedes Aloyez, the daughter of a wealthy Mexican rancher, shows an interest in newcomer Jim Gregory. The feeling is mutual, and Gregory earns Montaya's enmity. The captain surprises Mercedes and Gregory in a rendezvous, threatens to loose a dangerous reptile on the cowboy, but instead finds himself wagering his life against Gregory's with jumping beans. A victorious Gregory spares Montaya but passes to Mercedes the choice of who will live. This situation is interrupted by a request for help from Mary, a waitress, who has been captured by night riders. Gregory leaves Mercedes and Montaya to rescue and find happiness with Mary. *Cowboys. Mexican Americans. Waitresses.*

MPW 30 Sep 1922.

THE BIG TRAIL (*foreign version*) see **LA GRAN JORNADA**

BILLIONS (Russian Americas)
The Nazimova Productions. *Dist* Metro Pictures Corp. 6 Dec **1920** [©Metro Pictures Corp.; 22 Nov 1920; LP15826]. Si; b&w. 6 reels.

Dir Ray C. Smallwood. *Scen* Charles Bryant. *Adpt* Charles E. Whittaker. *Titles* Nazimova. *Cam* Rudolph J. Bergquist. *Ed* Nazimova. *Set design* Nazimova.

Source: Based on the play *L'Homme riche* by Jean Jose Frappa and Henry Dupuy-Mazuel (Paris, Jun 1914).

Cast: Nazimova (*Princess Triloff*), Charles Bryant (*Krakerfeller/ Owen Carey*), William J. Irving (*Frank Manners*), Victor Potel (*Pushkin*), John Steppling (*Isaac Colben*), Marian Skinner (*Mrs. Colben*), Bonnie Hill (*Mazie Colben*), Emmett King (*John Blanchard*), Eugene H. Klum (*Bellboy*).

Comedy. Princess Triloff, an emigrée from Czarist Russia, escapes to America where she becomes a patron of the arts. She falls in love with the verses of impoverished poet Owen Carey and becomes his anonymous benefactor. When Owen inherits a fortune from his rich Uncle Krakerfeller, he assumes his uncle's identity and confers his own upon an impoverished friend, Frank Manners. At a resort, Owen meets the princess and falls in love with her, but is chagrined to discover that she is enamored with Manners. The princess finally discovers Owen's real identity and the two fall in love. However, when a later will rescinds Owen's inheritance, he becomes intimidated by the princess' wealth and sulks away to his garret. The princess follows him and they are happily reunited in poverty when she discovers that her fortune has been confiscated in the revolution. *Impersonation and imposture. Nobility. Poets. Russian Americans. Charity. Inheritance. Resorts. Russia–History–Revolution, 1917-1921.*

Note: According to a news item, in addition to starring in the film, designing

the sets, and cutting, titling and assembling the film, Nazimova supervised the execution of the sets and gave her personal attention to the lighting effects.

ETR 11 Dec 1920, p. 110. *MPN* 11 Dec 1920, p. 4503. *MPW* 10 Jul 1920, p. 216. *MPW* 11 Dec 1920, p. 912. *Var* 10 Dec 1920, p. 35. *Wid's* 5 Dec 1920, p. 13.

THE BIRTH OF A NATION (African Americans)

David W. Griffith Corp.; Griffith Feature Films. *Dist* Epoch Producing Corp. 8 Feb **1915** Si; b&w. 12 reels.

Prod D. W. Griffith. *Prod under the personal direction of* D. W. Griffith. [*Asst dir* Thomas E. O'Brien and George Andre Beranger]. *Story arr by* D. W. Griffith. [*Scen* Frank E. Woods]. *Photog* G. W. Bitzer. [*Cost* Goldstein Co., Los Angeles]. [*Mus accompaniment comp* Joseph Carl Breil].

Source: Based on the novel *The Clansman: An Historical Romance of the Ku Klux Klan* by Thomas Dixon (New York, 1905) and his play of the same name (New York, 8 Jan 1906).

Cast: Lillian Gish (*Elsie, Stoneman's daughter*), Mae Marsh (*Flora Cameron, the pet sister*), Henry Walthall (*Col. Ben Cameron*), Miriam Cooper (*Margaret Cameron, elder sister*), Mary Alden (*Lydia, [Brown] Stoneman's mulatto housekeeper*), Ralph Lewis (*Hon. Austin Stoneman, leader of the house*), George Siegmann (*Silas Lynch, mulatto Lieut. Governor*), Walter Long (*Gus, a renegade negro*), Wallace Reid (*Jeff, the blacksmith*), Jos. Henabery (*Abraham Lincoln*), Elmer Clifton (*Phil, Stoneman's elder son*), Josephine Crowell (*Mrs. Cameron*), Spottiswoode Aitken (*Dr. Cameron*), J. A. Beringer (*Wade Cameron, second son*), Maxfield Stanley (*Duke Cameron, youngest son*), Jennie Lee (*Mammy, the faithful servant*), Donald Crisp (*Gen. U.S. Grant*), Howard Gaye (*Gen. Robert E. Lee*), [Raoul Walsh (*John Wilkes Booth*)], [Sam de Grasse (*Charles Sumner*)], [William DeVaull (*Nelse*)], [William Freeman (*Jake*)], [Thomas Wilson (*Stoneman's servant*)], [Fred Burns], [Allan Sears], [Elmo Lincoln].

Historical, War, Drama. [*Print viewed*]. Many years after Africans are brought in chains to America, the nineteenth century abolitionists demand that the Africans' descendants be freed. Phil and Tod Stoneman, sons of abolitionist leader and congressman Austin Stoneman, visit Phil's school friend, Ben Cameron, and his family in Piedmont, South Carolina. Phil courts Ben's sister Margaret, while Tod and Ben's young brother Duke become friends. When President Abraham Lincoln calls for volunteers, Phil and Tod return, but first, Ben playfully steals Phil's locket which contains a portrait of Phil's sister Elsie. During the war, Duke and Tod die in each others' arms. Northern guerrillas raid Piedmont and devastate the Cameron home. After Atlanta is burned and General Sherman marches to the sea, Ben, leading an heroic, but unsuccessful counterattack against General Grant's campaign on Petersburg, is wounded and rescued by Phil. At a Washington hospital, Ben meets Elsie, now a nurse. Ben's mother visits and successfully pleads to Lincoln for Ben's pardon from an unfounded charge. After Lee's surrender and Lincoln's assassination, Stoneman assumes great power in Congress. He sends his protégé, the mulatto Silas Lynch, to Piedmont, where the whites are disenfranchised. Lynch is elected lieutenant governor, and illiterate blacks gain control of the legislature and courts. To oversee Lynch's progress, Stoneman travels to Piedmont with Phil and Elsie. Ben and Elsie become engaged, but Margaret, prideful over the South's loss, is cold to Phil. To respond to the injustice which he feels, Ben forms the Ku Klux Klan. When Elsie learns that Ben is a clansman, she breaks their engagement. After Gus, a black soldier who becomes one of Lynch's followers, finds Flora, Ben's youngest sister, alone in the woods, he asks her to marry him. She runs in fright, and jumps off a cliff because she thinks that Gus will rape her. After she dies in Ben's arms, Gus is captured and hanged by the Klan. Dr. Cameron is arrested for having Klan costumes in his house, and although Phil and the Cameron's black servants rescue him, they become entrapped, with Margaret and Mrs. Cameron, in a country cabin. As black militia troops invade the streets of Piedmont, Lynch asks Elsie to be the queen of his black empire. Repelled, Elsie barely fends off Lynch. Her father arrives and is also horrified by Lynch's proposal, but he is powerless to prevent a forced marriage. After Ben leads the Klan's ride to rescue Elsie and Stoneman—and afterward, the Camerons—the blacks are disenfranchised. Margaret and Phil honeymoon with Ben and Elsie. In an allegorical epilogue the millenium is depicted wherein Christ's resurrection binds nations with brotherhood and love. *Abolitionists. African Americans. African Americans–Mixed blood. Carpetbaggers. Friendship. Ku Klux Klan. Lynching. Miscegenation. Piedmont (SC). Rape. Rescues. Southerners. United States–History–Civil War, 1861-1865. United States–History–Reconstruction, 1865-1898. Assassination. Atlanta (GA). Brothers. Brothers and sisters. Combat. Falls from heights. Fathers and daughters. Ulysses Simpson Grant. Honeymoons. Hospitals. Jesus Christ. Jewelry. Robert E. Lee. Abraham Lincoln. Literacy. Marriage–Forced. Military service, Voluntary. Mothers and sons. Nurses. Pardons. Petersburg (VA). Physicians. Servants. William Tecumseh Sherman. Slavery. Soldiers. Suicide. United States. Congress. United States. National Guard. War injuries. Washington (D.C.).*

Note: [Onscreen credits were taken from a 1921 reissue print of the film.] The opening title card reads, "Griffith Feature Films produced exclusively by D. W. Griffith," followed by a title card that bears the following written statement below "DG," Griffith's trademark: "This is the trade mark of the Griffith feature films. All pictures made under the personal direction of D. W. Griffith have the name 'Griffith' in the border line, with the initials 'DG' at bottom of captions. There is *no exception* to this rule. DW Griffith." Another written statement appears after the production credits: "A PLEA FOR THE ART OF THE MOTION PICTURE. We do not fear censorship, for we have no wish to offend with improprieties or obscenities, but we do demand, as a right, the liberty to show the dark side of wrong, that we may illuminate the bright side of virtue—the same liberty that is conceded to the art of the written word—that art to which we owe the Bible and the works of Shakespeare." Prior to the film's action, the following written prologue appears: "If in this work we have conveyed to the mind the ravages of war to the end that *war may be held in abhorrence*, this effort will not have been in vain."

The David W. Griffith Corp. copyrighted the film under the title *The Birth of the Nation: Or The Clansman*. According to modern sources, in addition to having Dixon's *The Clansman* as its literary source, the film also used material from Dixon's novel *The Leopard's Spots* (New York, 1902). Modern sources indicate that the film previewed in Riverside, CA on 1-2 Jan 1915 under the title *The Clansman*. The film was produced by the David W. Griffith Corp. under the auspices of the Majestic Motion Picture Co. It was financed by D. W. Griffith and Harry E. Aitken representing various investors. According to contemporary sources, the film opened under the title *The Clansman* in Los Angeles on 8 Feb 1915. Showings in Los Angeles later in the year retained that title. The film received a preview showing in New York on 1 Mar 1915, and had its premiere under the title *The Birth of a Nation* [which was on the viewed print] on 3 Mar 1915 in New York at the Liberty Theatre. The top ticket prices there were $2. On opening night, after the first act, Thomas Dixon appeared on stage and introduced D. W. Griffith to the audience. According to a letter dated 3 Mar 1915 in the NAACP Papers, African Americans were not allowed into the theater for the performance, but the organization hoped to get in at least two "very fair colored people."

A *NYDM* news item relates that the film was shown to President Woodrow Wilson in the East Room of the White House in Feb 1915, and that Griffith came from the West Coast especially to attend to the details of the presentation. Modern sources reveal that the date of the White House showing was 18 Feb 1915, that it was arranged to comply with the request of author Thomas Dixon, who knew Wilson from college, and that in addition to President Wilson, members of his cabinet and staff and their families attended the screening. Wilson reportedly commented about the film, "It is like writing history with lightning, and my only regret is that it is all so terribly true." The next night, according to modern sources, the film was shown to an invited audience in Washington, including Chief Justice Edward White and members of Congress.

The following information regarding protests against the film by the NAACP and others is taken from information in the NAACP Papers at the Library of Congress and from news stories: Prior to the first showings of the film in Los Angeles, a committee consisting of members of the L.A. branch of the NAACP, the Ministers' Alliance and a local organization called the Forum, were given a screening on 29 Jan 1915, as arranged by the local censor board. The group filed a protest with the censor board, which passed the film nonetheless, after which the local branch of the NAACP appealed to the mayor and chief of police, but both said that the censor board had jurisdiction. The NAACP subsequently registered a protest with the L.A. City Council urging that the film not be shown in the city. They stated that the film made "an appeal to violence and outrage" and was designed to "excuse the lynchings and other deeds of violence committed against the Negro and to make him in the public mind a hideous monster." They cited some specific scenes they objected to, including one that was subsequently cut from the film: "The little black boy who typified slavery at the abolitionist meeting, is taken in the arms of a saintly and very portly Puritan woman; but she drops him very suddenly and decisively and displays her disgust at his offensive odor by holding her nose and turning her head." They complained, "The Negro is made to look hideous and is invested with most repulsive habits and depraved passions." The secretary of the local group, E. Burton Ceruti, however, praised the film's artistic merits in a letter to NAACP national secretary May Childs Nerney, stating, "it is a masterpiece ... and, from an artistic point of view, the finest thing of its kind I have ever witnessed." By late Feb, Nerney had succeeded in getting the support of the chairman of the National Board of Censorship's executive committee, Frederick C. Howe, and his wife. After the Board approved the film, Howe requested that the Board's General Committee review it. According to W. D. McGuire, Jr., the executive director of the Board, they viewed the film on 1 Mar 1915 and decided that certain changes should be made; McGuire wrote that they met with officers and owners of Epoch Producing Corp., who "at once offered to modify certain scenes." The General Committee met again on 12 Mar and voted 12-9 to pass the film with the requirement that two additional changes be made, and the producers agreed. (Nerney reported that after the vote, the committee members

"cheered the author [i.e. D. W. Griffith] when he came into the room.")

Following the Board's decision, a number of members resigned, including Howe. According to Nerney, the two most objectionable parts, the "attack of a colored man upon a white girl ending in his lynching, and the attempt of a mulatto leader of the blacks who had been educated by a white Northern man, to force the latter's daughter to marry him," remained in the film. A letter dated 13 Apr 1915 lists deletions that were made for showings in New York. In Part I, only "The smell incident" (the scene mentioned above taking place during the abolitionist meeting) was the only cut. In Part II, the letter continues, the deletions were, "The beating of a little white child in the presence of her mother by an old colored man who meets them on the street and who is annoyed because the child accidentally gets in his path. The showing of the dead body of 'Gus' after his murder by the Ku Klux Klan. A saloon brawl showing most degraded types of Negroes in a drunken fight. The incident in the South Carolina Legislature where a colored member takes off his shoes." (A number of these scenes are in surviving prints of the film.) In addition, the letter lists the scenes in Part II that were modified: "The incident of the Southern Colonel's refusal to shake hands with the mulatto politician in the North which is cut short. When 'Gus' approaches the white girl whom he afterwards pursues he originally said, 'Missy, I'm a captain now.' This has been changed to 'Missy, I'm a captain now and I will marry -' At the beginning of the second part a new legend has been introduced reading, 'This is an historical presentation of Reconstruction and is not meant to reflect upon any race or people of today.'

An expansion of this sentiment is also introduced in a long legend which is run at the beginning of the performance inviting censorship. The two rape scenes have not been omitted though the first one has been shortened." The added set of introductory titles, called "A Plea for the Art of the Motion Picture," was signed by Griffith. Correspondence from Sep 1915 indicates that scenes had been inserted at the end of the film "purporting to show the advance of Negroes since the War"; these scenes showed Hampton Institute and other African-American schools. According to a letter dated 20 Sep 1915, "There was so much criticism of Hampton having lent its name that the Secretary was sent to New York to see what could be done to have these pictures cut out." A letter to a Buffalo newspaper in Feb 1916 states that the Hampton Institute scenes received the heartiest applause at a screening.

The NAACP got the support of a number of influential people to try to get the film banned, including social reformers Lilian D. Ward, Jane Addams and Rabbi Stephen S. Wise. In addition, they tried to get financier Otto Kahn to influence his brother Felix, who had invested money in the Mutual Motion Picture Corp. Addams wrote about the film, "it appeals to race prejudice upon the basis of conditions of half a century ago, which have nothing to do with the facts we have to consider today. It is both unjust and untrue. The producer seems to have followed the principle of gathering the most vicious and grotesque individuals he could find among colored people, and showing them as representatives of the truth about the entire race. The same method could be followed to smirch the reputation of any race."

In an article dated 13 May 1915, *The Congregationalist and Christian World* describes a visit that author Thomas Dixon paid to the newspaper's offices the day before the first showing of the film in Boston. When asked what he hoped to accomplish with the film, Dixon "expressed his desire to teach his version of the Reconstruction Period and urged at considerable length the virtues of the Ku Klux Klan.... He further emphasized his desire to create a feeling of abhorrence for colored men in the hearts of white people, especially white women, in order to stop intermarriage.... Finally, Mr. Dixon proceeded from the inference of white supremacy to argue his desire to secure the removal of all the Negroes from the United States. In order to strengthen his argument he quoted from President Lincoln, who in the last days of the war advocated colonization schemes for the ignorant slaves recently enfranchised and those about to be discharged from the Union Army."

On 24 Apr 1916, the *Chicago American* reported a murder that occurred following a showing of the film in Lafayette, IN. After seeing the film, Henry Brocj, who had arrived from Kentucky five weeks earlier, "walked out on the main street of the city and fired 3 bullets into the body of Edward Manson, a Negro high school student, 15 years old. The boy died tonight. There was no provocation for the tragedy and Brocj is in jail under a charge of murder." No further information regarding the crime has been located.

According to documents in the NAACP Papers, from the time of the film's first release until the end of 1931, the following governmental actions were taken either to ban the film or to cut it; some of these actions pertained to re-issues of the film, including the 1930 version with an added soundtrack: In Alaska, on 8 Oct 1918, the mayor of Juneau stopped the showing of the film; in California, in Jun 1921, the film was taken off the market, and in 1922, it was prohibited from exhibition by an ordinance passed by the City Council of Sacramento; in Connecticut, in Dec 1915 in New Haven, substantial cuts were made, on 21 Aug 1924, the exhibition of the film was canceled in New Britain, and in Mar 1925, the mayor of Hartford ordered two theaters to show another picture instead; in Illinois, on 15 May 1915, the mayor of Chicago refused to permit a license for the film; in Indiana, in Sep 1915, the film was banned in Gary; in Kansas, in Jan 1916, the film was banned; in Kentucky, on 20 Nov 1918, the mayor of Louisville stopped the exhibition of the film using an executive order; in Massachusetts, in 1915 in Boston, the rape scene involving "Gus" was nearly all cut out, in May 1921, the mayor of Boston suspended the license of a theater owner who planned to show the film, and in Jul 1924, in West Newton, the mayor made a request to a theater not to show the film; in Michigan, on 14 Feb 1931, the mayor of Detroit issued an order prohibiting the film's exhibition; in Minnesota, in Aug 1921, the mayor of Minneapolis refused to allow its exhibition, and on 30 Dec 1930, the City Council of St. Paul passed a resolution ordering the chief of police to stop the film's exhibition; in Nebraska, on 30 Mar 1931, the mayor of Omaha prohibited the showing of the film; in New Jersey, on 15 Dec 1923, the film was withdrawn in Camden, in Jul 1924, the Board of Commissioners of Montclair passed a resolution directing that the film not be shown, in Nov 1931, officials in Roselle deleted portions of the film, and on 4 Sep 1931, the deputy director of public safety in Jersey City forbid a theater from continuing to exhibit the film; in New York, on 13 Oct 1931, the mayor of Glen Cove, Long Island stopped the showing of the film; in Ohio, in Oct 1916, the film was banned, on 2 Jun 1925, the Supreme Court refused to license the film in the state, and on 4 Mar 1926, the attorney general ruled that the Ku Klux Klan could not show the film privately; in Oregon, in Mar 1931, the city council of Portland prohibited the showing; in Pennsylvania, on 2 Sep 1931, the mayor of Philadelphia ordered the film barred from the screen; in Rhode Island, in Sep 1915, the police commissioner of Providence refused to give the producers a license to show the film; and in West Virginia, in Feb 1919, the legislature passed a bill barring the film from the state. Many of these actions came in response to protests organized by local branches of the NAACP, which also organized protests in other jurisdictions. Protests also occurred in the cities of Morristown, NJ, Norfolk, VA, Springfield, IL, Vancouver, Canada, Atlanta, Atlantic City, Baltimore, Cleveland, Dallas, Milwaukee, Nashville, Pittsburgh, St. Louis, San Francisco, Spokane and Toronto.

When the film was re-issued in May 1921 in New York, two black ex-servicemen and three black women who served in France as canteen workers were arrested for distributing a circular put out by the NAACP called "Stop the KKK Propaganda in New York." The protesters carried signs reading, "We represented America in France, why should *The Birth of a Nation* misrepresent us here?" They were charged with violating a city ordinance prohibiting the distribution of hand bills, circulars, or other advertising materials. The NAACP appealed a guilty verdict to make it a test case on whether "educational material" could be distributed in public in New York City, and on 3 Nov 1921, Judge Alfred Talley of the Court of General Sessions ruled in their favor, stating that the ordinance was designed to prevent littering of advertising matter. After the arrests, D. W. Griffith issued the following statement, which was quoted in *NYT*: "It is a source of regret to me that poorly advised people are endeavoring to stir up animosity against *The Birth of a Nation*. The opposition is misguided, and was misguided and laid away many years ago. The leading villain in the story is a white man, who leads a misguided following into conflicts which do not reflect upon the negro. If there were the slightest ground for protest against the film it seems to me that white men would have more claim to it than negroes."

The film was revived again in New York for one week beginning 4 Dec 1922. At that time, the NAACP protested to the Motion Picture Commission of the State of New York, stating, "it is our firm belief that it is being reproduced in New York City again as a part of the campaign of the Ku Klux Klan to recruit members. Much color is lent to this statement by reason of the announcements made in today's New York papers coming from the Rev. Dr. Oscar Haywood, admittedly a national organizer for the Klan to inaugurate during this week a drive for membership in New York City." The Motion Picture Commission voted to disregard the complaint. *New York World* reported that at the first night, the "audience seemed to be composed largely of modern Klansmen, to judge by the cheers every time a Clansman appeared on the screen."

During this period, W. E. B. Du Bois, Director of Publications and Research for NAACP, sent a memo to Walter White, the organization's assistant secretary of the NAACP, concerning their fight to get the film banned, which he wrote "illustrates the peculiar contradictions into which the Negro problem often forces this organization," as the NAACP "stands for liberty: physical liberty, political liberty, and particularly liberty in artistic expression." After documenting that the number of lynchings of blacks per year, from 1915 until 1922, was greater than one per week, and that, "The chief alleged excuse for this lynching was the attacks upon white women by colored men," he reasoned, regarding liberty in artistic expression, that *The Birth of a Nation* presented "a special case. A new art was used, deliberately, to slander and vilify a race. There was no chance to reply. We had neither the money nor the influence.... What were we to do? We decided to try to make the authorities stop the picture on the ground that it was a public menace; that it was not art, but vicious propaganda." He ended the memo with the statement, "We are aware now as then that it is dangerous to limit expression, and yet, without some limitations civilization could not endure."

The stand that the NAACP took in trying to get the film banned was criticized by the American Civil Liberties Union. In a letter dated 25 Apr 1939, Director Roger N. Baldwin wrote to Walter White, now Executive Secretary of the NAACP, that efforts to ban the film "are inevitably a boomerang. The precedent established will work against films favorable to Negroes, opposed by the other side.... Of course there can be no objection to protests to motion picture distributors nor to picketing. But when appeal is made to the public authorities to take action, it crosses the line of legitimate pressure, and invades the field of censorship." In a letter dated 5 May 1939, Baldwin argued, "public officials should not use their discretion in permitting or banning films because of their content. If one film can be banned on that ground, any film can be." In a letter dated 17 Jun 1939, Baldwin wrote, "Any exception from the general principles of freedom for all forms of expression opens the door to official censorship." He asked White, "Can't your Board of Directors be persuaded to take a line drawing that distinction?"

The issue was brought up again in 1950 when the film was revived again and picketed again at a New York theater. In a letter dated 19 May 1950, Thurgood Marshall, chief of the legal-defense section of NAACP, wrote to Roy Wilkins, editor of the organization's journal *The Crisis*, "As I understand it, we are opposed to southern cities and states banning pictures which place the Negro in a favorable light. Do we continue to take that position and at the same time take the position that pictures such as *Birth of a Nation* should be censured by

governmental authorities? You will note that this question does not in any wise interfere with the question of picketing such pictures as the *Birth of a Nation* which we have always done and which I am thoroughly in favor of. When we get to the question of governmental censorship, we get into an awfully tough problem. At any rate, I think it should be passed on by the Committee on Administration."

In late 1932, Walter White met with William H. Short, Director of the Motion Picture Research Council to discuss the Payne Fund Studies, a psychological survey Short's organization had undertaken to gather and assess information on "attitudes as affected by motion pictures." In a memo about the meeting, White noted that the study had determined that *The Birth of a Nation* "produced an increase in unfavorable attitude toward the negro among the children examined." Short expressed the hope that evidence from the study could be used in the NAACP's fight to have the film banned, but no indication that the study's findings were actually used by NAACP has been located.

The original programs and reviews list George Andre Beranger as J. A. Beringer, the character of "Mammy" as "Cyndy," and actor John French as the character "Duke Cameron." Wallace Reid's name was spelled "Reed" in original programs and reviews. Some programs and reviews omit the character "Nelse" and list William De Vaull as the character "Jake." A news item credits scenarist Frank E. Woods with "intricate work in assembling in the cutting room." A broadsheet notes that G.A.R. vets who took part in the battle at Petersburg, VA assisted Griffith in laying out trenches. Listings in the *MPSD* credit J. A. Barry as executive and producing assistant to Griffith, and Henry I. McMahon as press representative.

According to a news item in Feb 1916, Southern Amusement Corp. sued Epoch Producing Corp. in the Supreme Court for $500,000 because, they claimed, on 6 May 1906 Thomas Dixon gave them the sole dramatic rights to *The Clansman*. No additional information has been located concerning this suit. According to the 21 Oct 1916 *MPSD*, Samuel De Vall, who worked in films as a superintendent of art departments and technical director, and F. B. Good, a cinematographer, worked in some capacity on this film. In Jan 1938, the *Washington Herald* reported that the film was going to be remade in New York by D. W. Griffith, with Wallace Ford in the role of "The Little Colonel." A 13 Mar 1940 *Washington Times-Herald* article stated that Harry E. Aitken, president of Epoch Producing Co., was planning to remake the film with a new director, although Griffith would supervise.

Modern sources indicate the following additional credits: *Chief asst dir* George Siegmann; *Asst dir* Monte Blue, William Christy Cabanne, Elmer Clifton, Donald Crisp, Howard Gaye, Fred Hamer, Erich von Stroheim, Herbert Sutch, Tom Wilson, Baron von Winther; *Asst cam* Karl Brown; *Mus* D. W. Griffith and Joseph Carl Briel; *Film ed* James and Rose Smith; *Master carpenter* Frank "Huck" Wortman; *Spec eff* "Fireworks" Wilson; *Cast* Violet Wilkey (*Flora Cameron as a child*), Elmo Lincoln (*White-arm Joe* and eight other roles), Alberta Lee (*Mrs. Lincoln*), William Freeman (*Sentry at hospital*), Olga Grey (*Laura Keene*), Eugene Pallette (*Union soldier*), Mme. Sul-te-Wan, Erich von Stroheim, and Gibson Gowland. John Ford, in interviews, claimed that he played one of the clansmen. Modern sources note that battle scenes were shot at a location which later became the Universal studio lot, and other scenes were shot at Calexico, CA.

Baltimore Herald 18 Apr 1925. *Boston Herald* 15 Apr 1915. *Boston Post* 11 Apr 1915. *Chicago American* 24 Apr 1916. *Chicago Sunday Tribune* 16 May 1915. *Cleveland Herald* 6 Jun 1925. *Columbus Citizen* 24 Oct 1916. *Congregationalist and Christian World* 22 Apr 1915. *Congregationalist and Christian World* 13 May 1915. *Des Moines News* 11 May 1916. *ETR* 27 Jan 1917, p. 559. *ETR* 10 May 1919, p. 1766. *HR* 23 Oct 1942. *Kansas City Call* 16 Jul 1938. *Kansas City Star* 7 Jun 1923. *Michigan State News (Grand Rapids)* 19 May 1921. *Motog* 20 Feb 1915, p. 272. *Motog* 20 Mar 1915, pp. 431-32. *Motog* 19 Jun 1915, p. 1009. *Motog* 17 Jul 1915, p. 123. *MPN* 2 Jan 1915, p. 33. *MPN* 9 Jan 1915, p. 37. *MPN* 30 Jan 1915, p. 26. *MPN* 6 Feb 1915, p. 74. *MPN* 13 Feb 1915, p. 34. *MPN* 20 Feb 1915, p. 74. *MPN* 13 Mar 1915, pp. 49-50. *MPN* 27 Mar 1915, p. 32. *MPN* 1 May 1915, p. 57. *MPN* 15 May 1915, p. 51. *MPN* 12 Jun 1915, p. 55. *MPN* 19 Jun 1915, p. 57, 60. *MPN* 26 Jun 1915, p. 56. *MPN* 24 Jul 1915, p. 40. *MPN* 7 Aug 1915, p. 56. *MPN* 14 Aug 1915, p. 56. *MPN* 4 Sep 1915, p. 37, 59. *MPN* 11 Sep 1915, p. 69. *MPN* 9 Oct 1915, p. 70. *MPN* 6 Nov 1915, p. 77. *MPN* 13 Nov 1915, p. 68, 69. *MPN* 4 Dec 1915, p. 83. *MPN* 11 Dec 1915, p. 74. *MPN* 22 Jan 1916, p. 369, 370. *MPN* 12 Feb 1916, p. 852. *MPN* 26 Feb 1916, p. 1153. *MPN* 28 Apr 1917, p. 2674. *MPW* 20 Feb 1915, p. 1121. *MPW* 13 Mar 1915, pp. 1586-87. *MPW* 10 Apr 1915, p. 219. *MPW* 29 May 1915, p. 1416. *MPW* 5 Jun 1915, p. 1649. *MPW* 12 Jun 1915, pp. 1758-59. *MPW* 9 Oct 1915, p. 296. *MPW* 1 Apr 1916, p. 120. *NYCall* 13 May 1921. *NYP* 5 Oct 1937. *NYDM* 24 Feb 1915, p. 24, 33. *NYDM* 10 Mar 1915, p. 28. *NYDM* 15 Jan 1916, p. 24. *NYDM* 5 Feb 1916, p. 26. *NYHT* 2 Dec 1954. *NYT* 4 Mar 1915, p. 9. *NYT* 7 May 1921. *NYT* 9 May 1921. *NYTr* 7 May 1921. *NYTr* 17 May 1921. *NYWorld* 5 Dec 1922. *Topeka Capital* 25 Jan 1916. *Topeka Capital* 6 Dec 1923. *Topeka Capital* 12 Dec 1923. *Topeka Capital* 1 Jan 1924. *Topeka Capital* 20 Jan 1924. *Topeka Journal* 25 Jan 1916. *Topeka Journal* 26 Jan 1916. *Topeka Journal* 7 Feb 1916. *Topeka Journal* 26 Feb 1916. *Topeka Journal* 13 Mar 1916. *Topeka Journal* 16 Jun 1916. *Topeka Journal* 22 Jun 1916. *Topeka Journal* 4 Dec 1923. *Topeka Journal* 7 Mar 1951. *Traveler* 27 Apr 1915. *Var* 12 Mar 1915, p. 23. *Var* 3 Dec 1954. *Var* 6 Dec 1954. *Var* 8 Dec 1954. *Washington Herald* 4 Jan 1938. *Washington Times-Herald* 13 Mar 1940. *Wichita Beacon* 3 Dec 1923.

THE BIRTH OF A RACE (German Americans, African Americans)

Birth of a Race Photoplay Corp.; Frohman Amusement Corp. *Dist* State Rights. 1 Dec **1918**. Si; b&w. 10 reels.

Supv John W. Noble. *Dir* John W. Noble. *Asst dir* Charles Horan, Arthur Vaughan and Ralph Dean. *Scen* George F. Wheeler, Rudolph De Cordova, John W. Noble and Anthony P. Kelly. *Titles* Tom Bret. *Cam* Herbert O. Carleton. *Technique* W. Bruce Bradley. *Art titles* Ferdinand Pinney Earle. *Mus accompaniment comp* Joseph Carl Breil.

Cast: Louis Dean (*The Kaiser*), Harry Dumont (*Crown Prince*), Carter B. Harkness (*Adam*), Doris Doscher (*Eve*), Charles Graham (*Noah*), Ben Hendricks (*Fritz Schmidt*), Alice Gale (*Frau Schmidt*), John Reinhardt (*Oscar Schmidt*), Gertrude Braun (*Louisa Schmidt*), Stephen Gratton (*Pat O'Brien*), Mary K. Carr (*Mrs. O'Brien*), Jane Grey (*Jane O'Brien*), Edward Elkas (*Herr Von H.*), Anna Lehr, Philip Van Loan, George Le Guere, Warren Chandler, Anita Cortez, Edwin Boring, Dick Lee, David Wall, Belle Seacombe.

Drama. After a biblical and historical prologue detailing the evolution of the idea of democracy through the creation of the world, the flood, the crucifixion of Christ, the discovery of America, the signing of the Declaration of Independence and the Civil War, the present-day threat to this idea by autocratic powers is dramatized. Fritz Schmidt, a German-American steel plant owner, and his son Oscar remain loyal to the Kaiser, while son George fights for the Allies. When the American army hospital where Louisa Schmidt works as a nurse is attacked by the Germans, Oscar, now a German soldier, assaults her, not recognizing his sister in the confusion. George, recovering in the hospital, kills his brother and then returns home to find his mother and a German spy struggling for some secret papers. George kills the spy, Fritz realigns his loyalty to the American cause, and the family is reunited. Democracy. Loyalty. Soldiers. United States–Defenses. World War I. Biblical characters. Brothers and sisters. German Americans. Germany. Army. Hospitals. Mill owners. Nurses. Rape. Secret documents. Spies. Steel mills. United States–History. United States. Army.

Note: Although this film is not listed in the *Cumulative Copyright Catalog of Motion Pictures, 1912-1939*, information on an existing print states that it was copyrighted in 1918. The Birth of a Race Photoplay Corp., located in Chicago and organized on 12 Jul 1916, contracted with the Selig Polyscope Co. to produce this film. According to *Motog* 17 Mar 1917, the late Booker T. Washington was interested in the possibility of portraying "the race story of the negro" in a sympathetic manner, but by the beginning of World War I, the original idea had been expanded to trace "all the factors in the life of America which have contributed to making the American people almost a race in themselves." The theme by then had been changed to the development of the idea of democracy and the threat to that idea by the autocratic powers of Europe. The prologue, which includes nudity in several scenes, may have been added at this point. According to *Var*, an executive of the Selig company stated that the film originally was intended "as an answer to alleged racial prejudice said to have been created by [D. W.] Griffith's *The Birth of a Nation*." The Selig executive asserted that the contract was canceled before production began because the Birth of a Race Photoplay Corp. failed to raise enough money by an agreed upon time. In another *Var* article, the Birth of a Race Photoplay Corp. claimed that the contract was canceled because Selig's studios were inadequate to make the film. The Frohman Amusement Corp. then agreed to produce the film in their Tampa, FL studios. More than half of it was made by Feb 1918, when officials of the fiscal agents for the Birth of a Race Photoplay Corp. were arrested and charged with violations of the "blue sky" law for failing to take out a state license to sell stock. According to *Var*, most of the stock was sold to blacks in Chicago. Although the fine was paid, Frohman canceled the agreement to produce the film in Mar 1918. Their staff, including director-in-chief John W. Noble, and their facilities in Tampa were turned over to the promoters to finish the film. According to *Var*, after the armistice, the film was to be called *The Story of a Great Peace*, but the original title was retained. The film had its premiere at Chicago's Blackstone Theatre on 1 Dec 1918. In addition to the filming in Tampa, some scenes were shot in Chicago and New York. According to *Var*, George Le Guerre played the role of Oscar Schmidt. Joseph Carl Breil, who scored *The Birth of a Nation*, composed the music for this film. Modern sources note that the idea for a film about the black race originated at the New York office of the National Association for the Advancement of Colored People in the spring of 1915 after the premiere of the Griffith film. This idea was changed by the white-owned Birth of a Race Photoplay Corp. because of the need to attract backers other than blacks, and because of the United States' entrance into the war. Modern sources also state that the film, as originally intended, was to have been called *Lincoln's Dream*.

ETR 10 May 1919, p. 1761. *Motog* 17 Mar 1917, p. 584. *Motog* 2 Mar 1918, p. 435. *MPN* 3 May 1919, p. 2891. *MPW* 23 Feb 1918, p. 1111. *MPW* 9 Mar 1918, p. 1353. *MPW* 10 May 1919, p. 938. *NYDM* 16 Feb 1918, p. 17. *NYDM* 23 Nov 1918, p. 776. *Var* 12 Oct 1917, p. 29. *Var* 8 Feb 1918, p. 45. *Var* 22 Feb 1918, p. 48. *Var* 22 Mar 1918, p. 58. *Var* 6 Dec 1918, p. 38. *Var* 25 Apr 1919, p. 82.

BIRTH OF THE BLUES (African Americans)

Paramount Pictures, Inc. *Dist* Paramount Pictures, Inc. 7 Nov **1941**; Memphis, TN and New Orleans, LA premieres: 31 Oct 1941; Prod: 21 Apr—4 Jun 1941 [©Paramount Pictures, Inc.; 7 Nov 1941; LP10985]. Sd (Western Electric Mirrophonic Recording); b&w. 7,686 ft. 80 or 87 min. Passed by the National Board of Review. PCA cert no. 7330.

[*Prod* B. G. DeSylva]. *Assoc prod* Monta Bell. *Dir* Victor Schertzinger. [*Asst dir* Hal Walker and Harry Tugend]. [*Dial dir* J. Vincent]. *Scr* Harry Tugend and Walter De Leon. *Story* Harry Tugend. [*Contr wrt* Erwin Gelsey and Wilkie Mahoney]. [*Comedy gags by* Bert

Lawrence]. *Dir of photog* William C. Mellor. [*2d cam* N. Beckner]. [*Asst to 2d cam* S. Sanford]. *Art dir* Hans Dreier and Ernst Fegté. *Ed* Paul Weatherwax. [*Film ed asst* F. Bracht]. [*2d asst dir* A. Ganzer]. [*Set dresser supv* S. Comer]. [*Set dresser* S. Seymour]. [*Props* R. Krueger and J. Cottrell]. *Cost* Edith Head. [*Ward woman* M. Cohn]. [*Ward woman* Gladys Baxter]. *Mus supv and dir* Robert Emmett Dolan. *Mus adv* Arthur Franklin. [*Dixieland arr* Joe Glover]. [*Dance dir* E. Prinz]. *Sd rec* Earl Hayman and John Cope. [*Hairdresser supv* Lenore Sabine]. [*Hairdresser* Mary Ann Jones]. [*Makeup supv* Wally Westmore]. [*Makeup artist* R. Ewing]. [*Prod mgr* George Bertholon]. [*Prod control mgr* Ed Ebele]. [*Unit mgr* Harold Schwartz]. [*Livestock supv* W. Hurley]. [*Dial coach* Eda Edson]. [*Scr clerk* Lee Fredricks]. [*Secy* Eleanor Edwards]. *Stand-in* Leo Lynn, Jerry Donovan, Dan Wyler and Byron Fitzpatrick. [*Clarinet double for Bing Crosby* Danny Polo]. [*Cornet double for Brian Donlevy* "Pokey" Carriere].

Music: "Minuet in G" from *6 Humoresques de Concert* by Ignacy Jan Paderewski.

Song(s): "The Waiter, the Porter and the Upstairs Maid," music and lyrics by Johnny Mercer; "After the Ball," music and lyrics by Charles K. Harris; "At a Georgia Camp Meeting," music by Kerry Mills; "The Birth of the Blues," music by Ray Henderson, lyrics by B. G. De Sylva and Lew Brown; "By the Light of the Silvery Moon," music by Gus Edwards, lyrics by Edward Madden; "Carnival of Venice," music by Nicolò Paganini, lyrics by Barclay Gray; "Cuddle Up a Little Closer," music by Karl Hoschna, lyrics by Otto Harbach; "The Memphis Blues" and "St. Louis Blues," music and lyrics by W. C. Handy; "My Melancholy Baby," music by Ernie Burnett, lyrics by George A. Norton and Maybelle E. Watson; "St. James Infirmary," music and lyrics by Joe Primrose; "Tiger Rag," music by Original Dixieland Jazz Band, lyrics by Harry DeCosta; "Wait 'Til the Sun Shines, Nellie," music by Harry Von Tilzer, lyrics by Andrew B. Sterling; "Waiting at the Church," music by Henry E. Pether, lyrics by Fred W. Leigh; "That's Why They Call Me 'Shine'," music by Ford Dabney, lyrics by Cecil Mack.

Cast: Bing Crosby (*Jeff Lambert*), Mary Martin (*Betty Lou Cobb*), Brian Donlevy (*Memphis*), Carolyn Lee (*Aunt Phoebe Cobb*), Rochester (*Louey*), J. Carrol Naish (*Blackie*), Warren Hymer (*Limpy*), Horace MacMahon (*Wolf*), Ruby Elzy (*Ruby*), Jack Teagarden (*Pepper*), Danny Beck (*Deek*), Harry Barris (*Suds*), Perry Botkin (*Leo*), Minor Watson (*Henri Lambert*), Harry Rosenthal (*Piano player*), Donald Kerr (*Skeeter*), Barbara Pepper (*Maizie*), Cecil Kellaway (*Granet*), Ronnie Cosbey (*Jeff, as a boy*), [Victor Potel (*Trumpet player in beer garden*)], [Jimmie Dundee (*Jake, "thug"*)], [Hayden Stevenson (*Stagehand*)], [Jeni LeGon (*Black girl in jail*)], [Jimmie Lucas, Guy Wilkerson (*Men outside of jail*)], [Grace Hayle (*Fat woman in cafe*)], [Edward Emerson (*Mayor's son in cafe*)], [John Miller (*Skinny man in cafe*)], [Sarah Edwards (*Dowager in cafe*)], [Brandon Hurst (*Headwaiter, Lafayette Cafe*)], [Roscoe Ates (*Hack driver*)], [Bert Roach (*Fat man in theater*)], [Nell Craig, Alice Keating, Betty Farrington, Besse Wade, Bertha Carlisle, Kathryn Bates, Pearl Early, Rose Allen, Evelyn West (*Women in theater*)], [Payne Johnson (*Boy in theater*)], [Mary Thomas (*Child in theater*)], [Charles Lane (*Theater manager*)], [Richard Keene (*Stage man*)], [Ernest Whitman (*Fancy-pants*)], [John Gallaudet (*Dude in pool parlor*)], [Pat West (*Proprietor of pool hall*)], [Wade Boteler (*Desk sergeant*)], [Mantan Moreland (*Black trumpet player*)], [Sam McDaniel (*Black clarinet player*)], [George Guhl (*Cop*)], [Keith Richards (*Man in illustrated slides*)], [Yvonne Jungquist (*Girl in illustrated slides*)], [James T. Mack].

Musical. [*Print viewed*]. As a young boy in 1890s New Orleans, Jeff Lambert instinctively leans toward the jazz music of the local black musicians, despite the severe beatings he gets from his conservative father for associating with them. As an adult, Jeff bails renowned white coronet player Memphis out of jail and forms a Dixieland-style jazz band. The band, billed as the Basin Street Hotshots, is thrown out of a movie theater for playing "black" music and is thereafter rejected from every nightclub and café for the same reason. They finally get a break when Betty Lou Cobb, who has befriended Jeff and is the cause of rivalry between him and Memphis, gets a job singing at the mob-owned Black-Tie Café and insists that she be backed only by Jeff's band. Although the audience is initially resistant to the jazz music, Betty Lou encourages people to dance, and everyone becomes enthusiastic for the "new" style of jazz. As the band brings renown and acclaim to itself and the club, Memphis and Jeff have a falling out

over Betty Lou, who rejected Memphis' marriage proposal because she loves Jeff, who is only interested in his music. Jeff insists that the band move on to a better engagement at the Lafayette Café, but Blackie, the owner of the Black-Tie Café, makes good on his threats and raids the Lafayette, where he beats up the band members and severely injures their close friend Louey, who was trying to deliver to Jeff a telegram informing him of an engagement in Chicago. After seeing that Louey will recover, the band members prepare to leave for Chicago, but Blackie's thugs trap them in their apartment. By putting on a record while the thugs wait outside, the band pretends to rehearse and the members sneak out one by one. Finally, only Jeff and Memphis remain and when the record skips, the thugs run in shooting. After they unintentionally shoot their boss, Blackie, the thugs run, but not before Jeff saves Memphis from their attack. Memphis admits to Jeff that he is not a one-woman man, and so when they reach the boat, Jeff and Betty Lou profess their love for each other. *African Americans. Cultural conflict. Jazz music. Musicians. New Orleans (LA). Romantic rivalry. Singers. Bigotry. Cafés. Children. Fathers and sons. Fistfights. Gangsters. Motion picture theaters. Murder. Ostracism. Ruses.*

Note: The following written prologue appears in the onscreen credits of the film: "Dedicated to the musical pioneers of Memphis and New Orleans who favored the 'hot' over the 'sweet'—those early jazz men who took American music out of the rut and put it 'in the groove'." A photographic montage closing the film features Ted Lewis, Duke Ellington, Louis Armstrong, Tommy Dorsey, Jimmy Dorsey, Benny Goodman, George Gershwin and Paul Whiteman. A *St. Louis Post-Dispatch* review mistakenly stated that W. C. Handy appears in the montage. A scene from Paramount's 1925 release *The Golden Princess*, starring Betty Bronson and Neil Hamilton, is featured in this film (see *AFI Catalog of Feature Films, 1921-30; F2.2171*). According to information in *Life* magazine, the film is loosely based on the Original Dixieland Jazz Band, "one of the first white bands to play in respectable quarters," and the band that young "Jeff" encounters as a boy is loosely based on the Razzy Dazzy Spasm Band, a black group that played along Basin Street in New Orleans. Director Victor Schertzinger died approximately two weeks before the film was released, on 26 Oct 1941.

The following information derives from the Paramount Collection at the AMPAS Library: The film finished four days ahead of schedule and came in $15,000 under budget at a final cost of $857,283; Douglas Gardner and Harry Harvey, Jr. tested for the part of "Jeff" as a young boy. The contractual agreement attached to the main title billing shows that Paramount had the right to bill actor Eddie Anderson as "Rochester," the name of the character for which he was renowned, but could not address him as such in the film. This film marked trombonist Jack Teagarden's feature film debut. Bassist Harry Barris previously played with Bing Crosby in his Rhythm Boys group. *HR* news items indicate that Constance Moore, Lillian Cornell and Virginia Dale were teamed to star in the film; Eddie Bracken was initially signed for a comedy role; Ben Holmes was signed to work on the script; Mark Sandrich was originally enlisted to produce and direct; and Monta Bell took over producing when producer A. M. Botsford left Paramount studios.

The MPAA/PCA files at the AMPAS Library reveal the following information: The initial plot synopsis, dated 21 Mar 1941, includes the death of the character "Louey," who is killed by a gunshot wound. (In the film he survives a blow to the head.) One day later, PCA director Joseph I. Breen reported to Paramount, "While the basic story is satisfactory...the present script cannot be approved for the reason that it contains many unacceptable scenes of the 'red light district' of New Orleans, prostitutes, unacceptable dialogue and the business of two murderers escaping all punishment." Paramount subsequently submitted a revised script and Breen added some other suggestions regarding specific scenes in the script: "We regard it as unnecessary for the proper telling of this story that the colored man, who is thrown out of the saloon, be shown *drunk*. This...should be omitted"; "Care must be exercised as to the costuming and the dancing of these Negroes if the scenes are to be approved by us"; "It is very questionable as to how the people of the South will react to these scenes showing a white boy playing with the Negro band"; "Any suggestion that the colored girl is acting 'flirtatiously' toward Jeff, a white man, should be avoided. Her speech 'Anything in Memphis that Chattanooga ain't got?' must be read without sexual suggestiveness." Some later suggestions as the script was developed are as follows: "Phoebe's use of the word 'panties' may be deleted by some political censor boards." "The business of Phoebe putting panties on the doll should be handled carefully."

John Seitz was listed as photographer in the first *HR* production chart listing for this film, but the extent of his contribution to the final film has not been determined. According to the press book, trumpet player "Pokey" Carrier coached Brian Donlevy for this film. A trailer advertising the film featured band leaders Freddy Martin, John Scott Trotter, Ray Noble and Bob Crosby. The Paramount press department cooked up a "feud" between the cities of Memphis and New Orleans to determine which city was the true originator of "the blues" and thus would rightfully premiere the film, resulting in a double premiere in both Memphis and New Orleans. Robert Emmett Dolan was nominated for an Academy Award for Music (Scoring of a Musical Picture) for this film.

In 1942, a *HR* news item reported that the British music publishing house of Campbell, Connelly and Co., Ltd., was suing Paramount over the rights to W. C. Handy's song "Memphis Blues." According to the news item, Paramount

obtained rights to the song from the owners, listed as Mercer and Morris, despite the fact that Campbell, Connelly and Co. previously bought the rights. The outcome of the lawsuit has not been determined.

AmCin Dec 1941, p. 570. *Box* 6 Sep 1941. *DV* 3 Sep 1941. *FD* 3 Sep 1941, p. 6. *HR* 31 Jan 1941. *HR* 18 Feb 1941, p. 4. *HR* 27 Feb 1941, p. 1. *HR* 18 Apr 1941, p. 10. *HR* 21 Apr 1941, p. 3. *HR* 9 May 1941, p. 6. *HR* 3 Sep 1941, p. 3. *HR* 18 Sep 1941, p. 7. *HR* 22 Oct 1941, p. 7. *HR* 27 Oct 1941, p. 2. *Life* 17 Nov 1941. *Look* 16 Dec 1941. *MPH* 6 Sep 1941. *MPHPD* 13 Sep 1941, p. 261. *NYT* 11 Dec 1941, p. 39. *NYHT* 7 Dec 1941. *New Yorker* 13 Dec 1941. *St. Louis Post-Dispatch* 4 Jan 1942. *Var* 3 Sep 1941, p. 8.

BIRTHRIGHT (African Americans)

Micheaux Film Corp. **1924**; Harlem, NY opening: 14 Jan 1924. Si; b&w. 10 reels, 9,500 ft.

Prod Oscar Micheaux. *Dir* Oscar Micheaux. *Adpt* Oscar Micheaux.

Source: Based on the novel *Birthright* by T. S. Stribling (New York, 1922).

Cast: J. Homer Tutt (*Peter Siner*), Evelyn Preer (*Cissie Deldine*), Salem Tutt Whitney (*Tump Pack*), Lawrence Chenault, W. B. F. Crowell, E. G. Tatum, Callie Mines, Ed Elkas, Alma Sewall.

African American, Drama. [*Not viewed*]. After graduating from Harvard, Peter Siner, a black man, travels to the South by train, planning to set up a school for black children in his hometown. At the town of Cairo, he is ordered to leave his Pullman car and get into the "Jim Crow" car for blacks. At the platform of his destination, he meets Tump Pack, a burly, loud-mouthed black man, who is returning home from fighting overseas, after receiving the Distinguished Service badge. When Tump arrives at his home on the Tennessee River, he is given a warm welcome, but during the celebration, the white constable, Dawson Bobbs, arrests him on a four-year-old charge of shooting craps. A few days later, Bobbs raids Peter's village, searching for a stolen turkey roaster, and ransacks the house where Peter and his mother live. When the roaster turns up after Bobbs leaves, Peter is embarrassed. Peter meets and falls in love with Cissie Dildine, but then learns that she is Tump's girl friend. A local lodge raises one hundred dollars for Peter's school, and he purchases land on which to build it. He soon learns, however, that the deed for the land has a clause in it that prohibits blacks from occupying the land. The black townfolk now ridicule Peter and his education, but Cissie stands by him. Tump, released from jail, beats Peter up after seeing him and Cissie together, which further adds to Peter's humiliation in the eyes of the townfolk. Some time later, Tump goes to shoot Peter, but he is apprehended and sent to work on a chain gang. Peter and Cissie now become engaged. Peter's mother dies, and after a strange, elderly white man named Captain Renfrew visits Peter, he goes to live with the man. On the night before their wedding is to take place, Cissie, feeling that Peter is too far above her intellectually, tells him that she is an immoral woman and unfit to marry him. Peter leaves her, and afterwards, Cissie, goaded by ambition, struggles to rise up and be someone, but the townfolks' accusations against her contribute to her downfall. When she goes to visit Peter, Bobbs, tipped off by a black informant known as "The Persimmon," waits outside. He arrests her for grand larceny as she leaves Peter, but it is uncertain whether she is actually guilty, or has been framed because she has refused to give her body to a seducer. [No information has been located concerning the conclusion of this plot]. African Americans. Bigotry. Bullies. Class distinction. Segregation. Small town life. United States–South. Chain gangs. Constables. Deeds. Engagements. Harvard University. Informers. Mothers and sons. Police raids. Trains–Pullman cars. Veterans.

Note: According to *New York Age*, in adapting the novel by T. S. Stribling, Oscar Micheaux was "following the book very closely, even using in the headlines the identical language contained therein." *New York Age* called the film "a sort of colored *Main Street*. All of the ignorance, prejudice and many of the crimes of both races in this town is graphically depicted." *Billboard* stated, "It was apparently not intended for colored audiences alone. It's brutal frankness hurts, and some of the titles put a sting into the evening's entertainment."

In an article by Micheaux published in *PittsC* on 13 Dec 1924 (the text of which is similar to a talk given by Micheaux to a motion picture audience on 7 Dec 1924, as reported in *Billboard* on 27 Dec 1924), he addressed critics of this film and states his some of his intentions in filmmaking: "I have been informed that my last production, *Birthright*, has occasioned much adverse criticism, during its exhibition in Philadelphia. Newspapermen have denounce me as a colored Judas, merely because they were either unaware of my aims, or were not in sympathy with them. What then, are my aims, to which such critics have taken exception? I have always tried to make my photoplays present the truth, to lay before the race a cross section of its own life to view the colored heart from close range. My results might have been narrow at times, due perhaps to certain limited situations, which I endeavored to portray, but in those limited situations, the truth was the predominant characteristic. It is only by presenting those portions of the race portrayed in my pictures, in the light

and background of their true state, that we can raise our people to greater heights. I am too much imbued with the spirit of Booker T. Washington to engraft false virtues upon ourselves, to make ourselves that which we are not. Nothing could be a greater blow to our own progress. The recognition of our true situation, will react in itself as a stimulus for self-advancement. It is these ideals that I have injected into my pictures, and which are now being criticized. Possibly my aims have been misunderstood, but criticism arising from such misunderstanding, only doubles the already overburdening labors of the colored producer." Micheaux remade this film in 1938 (see below).

Billboard 25 Jan 1924, p. 52. *Billboard* 27 Dec 1924, p. 49. *ChiDef* 15 Mar 1924, p. 7. *New York Age* 19 Jan 1924. *PittsC* 13 Dec 1924, p. 10.

BIRTHRIGHT (African Americans)

Micheaux Pictures Corp. *Dist* Micheaux Pictures Corp. **1938**. Sd (Wickmar Noiseless Recording); b&w. 9 reels.

Pres Burton Russell. *Prod* Oscar Micheaux. *Dir* Oscar Micheaux. *Adpt* Oscar Micheaux. *Photog* Robert Marshall. *Sd eng* George Wicker.

Song(s): "Caravan," music and lyrics by Juan Tizol; "That's How Rhythm Was Born," music by J. C. Johnson, lyrics by George Whiting and Nat Schwartz; "I Never Knew," music by Ted Fiorito, lyrics by Gus Kahn; "All God's Children Got Rhythm," music by Bronislau Kaper and Walter Jurmann, lyrics by Gus Kahn.

Source: Based on the novel *Birthright* by T. S. Stribling (New York, 1922).

Cast: Carman Newsome, S. O. Moses, Alec Lovejoy, Trixie Smith, Hazel Lisz, W. Herbert Jelly, Ida Forsyne, John Ward, C. R. Chace, Alice B. Russell, H. E. Knight, George Lessey, Columbus Jackson, Harry Moses, Tom Dillon, Allen Lee, Robert Alderdice.

African American, Social, Drama, with songs. [*Viewed print incomplete*]. Harvard University graduate Peter Siner is trying to raise money to start a school for blacks. On his way to Hookers Bend, his hometown in the South, Peter encounters his friend Tump Pack, a decorated war hero and a gambler. While Tump is charged under an old town ordinance forbidding gambling, Peter becomes the object of attention from every eligible girl in town, including Cissie Dildane. Although Cissie pledges a contribution to fund Peter's school, she tells him that she disagrees with his approach to bettering the condition of blacks through industrial training, and instead favors literacy education. Soon after purchasing an old building from the unscrupulous white banker Henry Hooker, to house his school, Peter learns that Hooker has been conniving against him and trying to thwart his efforts to establish a black school in the area. When Peter takes a closer look at the contract he signed, he realizes that it contains a "stopper clause" preventing blacks from having anything to do with the property. He complains to Hooker, who only offers to buy back the deed at a fraction of the original purchase price. As word of Hooker's act of treachery spreads through the town, Cissie sends a letter to her sister Ida May, in which she writes that "the whole dirty little town" has turned its back on Peter because he is a college graduate who has been duped by a white man. Even Peter's mother berates him for being taken in by a white man. When Cissie goes to Peter to comfort him, she is met with his mother's scorn and she and Peter leave together. Following the death of his mother, Peter goes to work for the town's richest man, Captain Renfrew. Renfrew's maid resents having to serve Peter as if he were a white man and lies to Renfrew, by telling him that Peter plans to marry Cissie, who, she claims, is a suspected thief. Although Peter denies the maid's charges and defends Cissie's innocence, the sheriff arrests Cissie for grand larceny. Soon after being arrested, however, Cissie escapes and goes to a nightclub, where Ida May is singing. There, Cissie tells her sister that it was Tump's brother who brought her to the nightclub, and that she witnessed him kill the jailer's assistant, known as "The Persimmon." When Peter shows up at the nightclub, he reads a telegram stating that Renfrew has died and left everything to him, including ninety percent of his ownership of the bank where Hooker works. He also reads that charges against Cissie have been dropped. As Peter develops plans to turn Renfrew's mansion into an industrial training school for black youths, he tries to encourage enrollment in his school by suggesting a law making it illegal to loiter near a popular meeting place. After having successfully established his school, Peter marries Cissie, and the couple drive to Chicago, where they will honeymoon. African Americans. Education. Racism. Schools. United States–South. Bankers. Deeds. Evangelists. Fugitives. Gamblers. Harvard University. Honeymoons. Jailbreaks. Land rights. Maids. Mansions. Marriage. Mothers and sons. Murder. Nightclubs. Segregation. Singers. Sisters. Thieves. Trains. Truck drivers. Wealth. Wills.

Note: The film's subtitle is, "A story of the Negro and the South." Oscar Micheaux made an earlier film based on the same source in 1924 (see above).

BITS OF LIFE (Chinese Americans)

Marshall Neilan Productions. *Dist* Associated First National Pictures. 26 Sep **1921** [©Marshall Neilan Productions; 25 Oct 1921; LP17129]. Si; b&w. 6 reels, 6,339 ft.

Pres Marshall Neilan. *Dir* Marshall Neilan. *Asst dir* James Flood and William Scully. *Scen* Lucita Squier. *Addl story* Marshall Neilan. *Photog* David Kesson.

Source: Based on the short story "Hop" by Hugh Wiley in *Jade and Other Stories* (New York, 1921) and the short story "The Man Who Heard Everything" by Walter Trumbull in *Smart Set* (Apr 1921).

Cast: Wesley Barry (*Tom Levitt, a boy*), Rockliffe Fellowes (*Tom Levitt*), Lon Chaney (*Chin Gow*), Noah Beery (*Hindoo*), Anna May Wong (*Chin Gow's wife*), John Bowers (*Dentist's patient*), Teddy Sampson, Dorothy Mackaill, Edythe Chapman, Frederick Burton, James Bradbury, Jr., Tammany Young, Harriet Hammond, James Neill, Scott Welsh.

Melodrama. *Episode 1: The Bad Samaritan.* Tom Levitt, half-breed son of a Chinese and a white woman, is the victim of brutality during his boyhood and becomes a criminal. A friend, released from jail, tells Tom he is going straight and asks for money to leave town; Tom takes a stolen wallet from another boy. After hearing a preacher tell the story of the Good Samaritan, he goes to aid a man who has been assaulted; facing a ten-year sentence for robbery, he reflects on the irony of his downfall. *Episode 2: The Man Who Heard Everything.* Ed Johnson, who barely makes a living from barbering, is deaf, but he is happy in the belief that the world is good and that he is loved by his wife. Coming into possession of an instrument that restores his hearing, he learns that the persons he has idolized are not to be trusted and that his wife is unfaithful; in despair, he destroys the instrument. *Episode 3: Hop.* As a boy in China, Chin Gow learns that girl infants are undesirable. When a man, he becomes proprietor of several San Francisco opium dens and weds Toy Sing, who bears him a baby girl. Chin Gow beats his wife and vows to slay the child. His wife's friend brings in a crucifix sent by the priest, and as he nails it to the wall, the spike penetrates the skull of Chin Gow lying in a bunk on the other side of the wall and kills him. *Episode 4: The Intrigue.* On a yachting tour of the world, Reginald Vandebrook, reaching a foreign country, falls in love with a girl he has never seen before; he hears her called Princess and follows her into a building. There he is surrounded by East Indians who are about to murder him. He awakens to find himself in a dentist's chair having a tooth extracted. *Barbers and barbershops. Chinese. Chinese Americans. Deafness. Dentists. Dreams. Good Samaritans. Half-castes. Opium. San Francisco (CA)–Chinatown.*

Note: The film was prefaced by a message from Mr. Neilan explaining the reasons for producing it and introducing the characters of each story. Some sources also attribute "The Bad Samaritan," by Thomas McMorrow as an additional literary source, however, its relation to the film has not been established.

ETR 29 Oct 1921, p. 1557. *FD* 4 Sep 1921. *NYT* 17 Oct 1921, p. 18. *Var* 21 Oct 1921, p. 35.

BITTER APPLES (Italian Americans)

Warner Bros. Pictures, Inc. *Dist* Warner Bros. Pictures, Inc. 23 Apr **1927** [©Warner Bros. Pictures, Inc.; 9 Apr 1927; LP23844]. Si; b&w. 6 reels, 5,463 ft.

Dir Harry O. Hoyt. *Asst dir* Ross Lederman. *Scen* Harry O. Hoyt. *Cam* Hal Mohr.

Source: Based on the short story "Bitter Apples" by Harold MacGrath in *Red Book* (Jul–Oct 1925).

Cast: Monte Blue (*John Wyncote*), Myrna Loy (*Belinda White*), Paul Ellis (*Stefani Blanco*), Charles Hill Mailes (*Cyrus Thornden*), Sidney De Grey (*Joseph Blanco*), Ruby Blaine (*Mrs. Channing*), Patricia Grey (*Wyncote's secretary*).

Melodrama. Following the demise of his father, John Wyncote, finding himself with a bankrupt business, instructs attorney Thornden to sell all interests. One of the depositors, Joseph Blanco, unable to face financial ruin, commits suicide, leaving a daughter, Belinda, and a son, Stefani. Stefani takes the Sicilian oath to avenge his father's death along with his sister; Belinda agrees to take an assumed name and make John fall in love with her and marry him. After the ceremony, aboard an ocean liner, she denounces him. The ship crashes onto a reef, and the crew is overpowered by rum-runners. Wyncote rescues

Belinda from the drunken captain's advances, and they are reconciled after being saved by a U. S. destroyer. *Bankruptcy. Brothers and sisters. Businessmen. Courtship. Italian Americans. Ocean liners. Revenge. Shipwrecks. Sicilians. Suicide. United States. Navy.*

FD 5 Jun 1927. *MPW* 7 May 1927. *Var* 27 Apr 1927, p. 21.

BITTER IS THE RIDE see **GUN FEVER**

THE BITTERNESS OF SWEETS see **LOOK YOUR BEST**

THE BLACK BOOMERANG (African Americans)

William H. Clifford Photoplay Co. **1925**. Si; b&w. Length undetermined. [Feature length assumed.].

Prod William H. Clifford. *Wrt* William H. Clifford.

Melodrama (?), African American. No information about the precise nature of this film has been found. *African Americans.*

Note: The indicated year of release is approximate.

THE BLACK CAMEL (Chinese Americans)

Fox Film Corp.; Hamilton MacFadden Production. *Dist* Fox Film Corp. 7 **1931**; Prod: mid-Apr—early May 1931 [©Fox Film Corp.; 27 May 1931; LP2301]. Sd (Western Electric System); b&w. 8 reels, 6,560 ft. 67 or 71 min. Passed by the National Board of Review.

Series: Charlie Chan.

Pres WM. FOX. *Assoc prod* William Sistrom. *Dir* Hamilton MacFadden. [*Asst dir* Sam Wurtzel]. *Scr and dial* Barry Conners and Philip Klein. *Adpt* Hugh Stange. [*Contr wrt* Dudley Nichols]. *Photog* Joseph August and Daniel Clark. *Art dir* Ben Carré. [*Film ed* Al De Gaetano]. [*Cost* Dolly Tree]. *Sd rec* W. W. Lindsay, Jr. [*Bus mgr* W. F. Fitzgerald].

Song(s): "Uheuhene" and "Na Lei O Hawaii," words and music by Charles E. King; "I Have a Thought in My Heart for You," words and music by Sol Hoopii, Jr.; "Aloha Oe," words and music by Queen Liliuokalani.

Source: Based on the novel *The Black Camel* by Earl Derr Biggers (Indianapolis, 1929).

Cast: Warner Oland [(*Charlie Chan*)], Sally Eilers [(*Julie O'Neill*)], Bela Lugosi [(*Tarneverro, also known as Arthur Mayo*)], Dorothy Revier [(*Shelah Fane*)], Victor Varconi [(*Robert Fyfe*)], Murray Kinnell [(*Smith*)], William Post, Jr. [(*Alan Jaynes*)], Robert Young [(*Jimmy Bradshaw*)], Violet Dunn [(*Anna, also known as Mrs. Denny Mayo*)], J. M. Kerrigan [(*MacMasters*)], Mary Gordon [(*Mrs. MacMasters*)], Rita Rozelle [(*Native girl*)], Otto Yamaoka [(*Kashimo*)], [Dwight Frye (*Jessop*)], [Richard Tucker (*Ballou*)], [Marjorie White (*Rita Ballou*)], [C. Henry Gordon (*Von Horn*)], [Robert Homans (*Chief of police*)], [Louise Mackintosh (*Housekeeper*)].

Detective, Drama. [*Print viewed*]. Shelah Fane, a motion picture star filming in Honolulu, consults the mystic Tarneverro, her spiritual adviser, to decide if she should marry Alan Jaynes, a wealthy globetrotter she met on the boat to Hawaii. During a crystal ball session, Shelah confesses that three years earlier she fell in love with her co-star, Denny Mayo, and that she was in his house the night he was murdered. Agitated after the consultation, Shelah tells Julie O'Neill, her protegée, that she cannot marry Alan. Anna, Shelah's maid, is greatly upset when, as she brings Shelah some orchids from stage actor Robert Fyfe, who is appearing in town, she sees Shelah tearing a photograph of Denny Mayo. That evening, just before a dinner party Shelah is giving, Julie and Jimmy Bradshaw, a tourist bureau employee who wants to marry Julie, find Shelah stabbed to death in her pavillion. Julie removes Shelah's emerald ring. During his investigation, Inspector Charlie Chan of the Honolulu police finds the orchids crushed next to Shelah's body with their pin missing. He also notices in the sand outside the pavillion a footprint made by a shoe with a hole in it. Chan gathers the guests, who were all in Hollywood at the time of Mayo's murder, and relates an old saying: "Death is a black camel that kneels unbidden at every gate." After Chan's blundering assistant Kashimo finds the ripped photograph of Mayo, both Tarneverro and Julie secrete pieces of it. When Kashimo brings in a beach bum, who calls himself Smith, and whose shoes match the footprints found outside the pavillion, Fyfe, Shelah's ex-husband, confesses that he killed her. Alan, greatly upset, wants to leave immediately to catch a boat to the mainland, but Chan deduces that Fyfe could not have been at the pavillion when the murder took place, and warns the guests not to leave the island. Needing money, Smith, an artist, threatens Fyfe that he will tell what he overheard

Shelah say in the pavillion unless Fyfe buys one of his paintings. After Fyfe gives him $100 and promises to pay $200 more, an unseen assailant shoots Smith on the beach. At Jimmy's urging, Julie confesses to Chan that she took the emerald ring because it contains an inscription from Mayo; Shelah, she says, wanted to keep their relationship a secret. Chan learns from an Australian couple that Tarneverro is really Denny Mayo's brother Arthur. Before Smith dies from his gunshot wound, he reveals to Chan that he heard Shelah tell Fyfe that she confessed killing Mayo to Tarneverro. Fyfe confirms this and says that after Shelah had found out that Mayo had a wife in England, she shot him during a quarrel. Fyfe says he confessed to her murder because he loved her and wanted to protect her memory. Smith also reveals that he took a diamond pin from the pavillion, which Chan notices, has a part missing. As Chan finds a scratch mark on the floor under the dinner table in Shelah's house that he believes was made by the shoe in which the missing piece of the pin is probably still lodged, a knife is thrown at him. Chan deduces that Shelah's murderer must have sat in the chair nearest the scratch. Meanwhile, Julie accepts Jimmy's proposal and agrees to remain with him in Hawaii. Chan has the suspects sit where they sat the previous night. Tarneverro sits in the chair next to the scratch, but Chan, investigating further, learns that later the previous night, the maid Anna sat in the same chair. When Chan finds the piece of the diamond pin in the heel of her shoe, she reveals that she is really Mrs. Denny Mayo and admits killing Shelah. Tarneverro confesses that he came to Hollywood to find his brother's murderer, and says that when Shelah confessed to him, he told Anna. He asks to share Anna's fate. As Chan goes to arrest Anna, Jessop, the butler, who loves her, pulls a gun, but after a struggle, Chan disarms him. Jessop admits he shot Smith because he knew too much and that he threw the knife at Chan. Just then, Kashimo enters with a clue, but Chan instructs him to save it for the next case. *Chinese Americans. Detectives. Honolulu (HI). Motion picture actors and actresses. Murder. Mystics. Artists. Australians. Beachcombing. Blackmail. Brothers. Butlers. Confession (Law). Crystal balls. Engagements. Evidence. Ex-spouses. Hawaiians. Impersonation and imposture. Japanese Americans. Maids. Mistresses. Photographs. Rings. Self-sacrifice.*

Note: The novel was originally published serially in *The Saturday Evening Post*, 18 May-22 Jun 1929. Sources conflict concerning the release date. According to information in the Twentieth Century-Fox Records of the Legal Department at the UCLA Theater Arts Library, some scenes were shot in Honolulu, where some of the film's music was also recorded. For more information regarding the series, please consult the Series Index and see entry below for *Charlie Chan Carries On*.

FD 5 Jul 1931, p. 10. HF 11 Apr 1931, p. 24. HF 2 May 1931, p. 24. MPH 16 May 1931, p. 34. NYT 4 Jul 1931, p. 11. Var 7 Jul 1931, p. 34.

THE BLACK CHAMBER see **RENDEZVOUS**

THE BLACK DAKOTAS (Native Americans, Dakota)
Columbia Pictures Corp. *Dist* Columbia Pictures Corp. Sep **1954**; Prod: 16 Mar—27 Mar 1954 [©Columbia Pictures Corp.; 1 Sep 1954; LP4061]. Sd (Western Electric Recording); col (Technicolor). 7 reels. 65 min. PCA cert no. 17017.
Prod Wallace MacDonald. *Dir* Ray Nazarro. *Asst dir* Wilbur McGaugh. *Scr* Ray Buffum and DeVallon Scott. *Story* Ray Buffum. *Dir of photog* Ellis W. Carter. *Technicolor color consultant* Francis Cugat. *Art dir* Edward Ilou. *Film ed* Aaron Stell. *Set dec* James Crowe. *Mus cond* Mischa Bakaleinikoff. *Rec supv* John Livadary.
Cast: Gary Merrill [(*Brock Marsh, also known as Zachary Paige*)], Wanda Hendrix [(*Ruth Lawrence*)], John Bromfield [(*Mike Daugherty*)], Noah Beery, Jr. (*"Gimpy" Joe Woods*), Fay Roope [(*John Lawrence*)], Howard Wendell [(*Judge Horatio Baker*)], Robert Simon [(*Marshal Whit Collins*)], James Griffith [(*Warren*)], Richard Webb [(*Frank Gibbs*)], Peter Whitney [(*Grimes*)], John War Eagle [(*War Cloud*)], Jay Silverheels [(*Black Buffalo*)], [George Keymas (*Spotted Deer*)], [Robert Griffin (*Boggs*)], [Clayton Moore (*Stone*)], [Chris Alcaide (*Burke*)], [Frank Wilcox (*Zachary Paige*)], [Shooting Star (*Indian brave*)], [William P. Wilkerson (*Medicine man*)], [Rankin Mansfield (*Sherwood "Undertaker"*)].
Western. [*Print viewed*]. During the Civil War, John Lawrence, a Southern sympathizer, and his men hold up a stagecoach carrying Brock Marsh, who is posing as a businessman but is actually another sympathizer, and Zachary Paige, who is conveying documents signed by President Lincoln that promise a peace offering to the Sioux tribe. Lawrence has concocted a scheme to steal government gold earmarked for the Sioux and send it back to Jefferson Davis' treasury. To pull off the plot, Marsh plans to pose as Paige so that they can more easily steal the gold when it arrives. Lawrence intends to keep the real Paige in hiding until the heist has been performed, but Marsh unexpectedly pulls out a gun and shoots him, much to Lawrence's surprise and indignation. When Marsh, now posing as Paige, rides into town, he reports that the coach was attacked by Indians, and the crowd, led by loudmouth Grimes, uses the raid as an example of how the government is neglecting the frontiers in favor of the Southern war. Meanwhile, Lawrence, who has been caught negotiating with another Indian tribe on behalf of the Southern rebels, is brought in as a traitor. At his quick trial, Lawrence admits that he is not from Boston, as everyone thought, but is a Virginian. As he is about to be hanged from a makeshift gallows, his daughter Ruth arrives and is horrified at the scene. "Gimpy" Joe Woods, another of Lawrence's men, whispers to Marsh that, as a government man, he could stop the hanging. Nevertheless, Lawrence is hanged, and Mike Daugherty, Ruth's sweetheart, who speaks the Sioux language and is friends with their chief, War Cloud, takes Ruth to the jailhouse for safety. When Grimes's angry mob shows up to run Ruth out of town, Mike fights Grimes and takes Ruth back to her ranch. Gimpy goes to Marsh's hotel to offer his help, and Marsh accepts the offer but insists that he is now the boss. Mike then arrives at the hotel to take Marsh to see War Cloud and explains that the old chief's authority is being challenged by a younger, white-hating leader named Black Buffalo. While riding through Sioux territory, the pair is attacked by Black Buffalo's renegades and Marsh is captured. A messenger arrives and reports that in the skirmish, Mike killed Black Buffalo's brother and that Marsh will have to die. Mike negotiates Marsh's release, however, and Marsh makes a speech promising that there will be no more white aggression against the Indians. Back in town, Paige's body is brought in, and as Marshal Whit Collins and Judge Horatio Baker examine the body, they discover the name "Zachary Paige" monogrammed on the coat. Just as they are about to accuse Marsh, Gimpy, who has been watching from the window, shoots them both dead. When Mike, Grimes and the mob arrive, Grimes insists that Ruth is responsible for the murders, and Mike rides out to warn Ruth. The Southern rebels also ride to the ranch, knock Mike out, and take the couple to their hiding place, a nearby cave. Gimpy and Marsh then go to see War Cloud and offer him the terms of Lincoln's peace treaty: hunting grounds, no white settlers and $100,000 in gold. War Cloud warns that if the whites are lying, his braves will kill everyone in the town. At the cave, Ruth is apprised of the Southerners' plan and, in order to gain more information, pretends to join their cause. As the men prepare for the gold heist, Ruth and Mike fake an argument so she can cut his ropes. Mike escapes and as the men pursue him, Marsh shoots two of his fellow rebels, hoping to eventually claim the gold for himself. Marsh, Gimpy and the remaining rebels wait for the stage, and when it approaches, they kill the guards. All the rebels are killed in the ensuing fight, except Gimpy and Marsh. Ruth sees them unloading the gold, and when she holds her rifle on them, Marsh grabs his own gun, but Gimpy convinces him just to tie her up. Just as Ruth tries to warn Gimpy that Marsh will kill him, Marsh shoots Gimpy dead. Marsh rides away with the gold, but the Indians and Mike pursue him, and he drops the booty. Mike and Marsh fight, and Mike wins. Back in town, Mike gives a speech and presents the gold and Lincoln's original peace treaty to War Cloud. As Mike and Ruth embrace, War Cloud promises to keep the peace, and the crowd cheers. *Dakota Indians. Impersonation and imposture. Southerners. Stagecoach robberies. Treaties. United States–History–Civil War, 1861-1865. Ambushes. Betrayal. Caves. Fathers and daughters. Gold. Gunfights. Hanging. Hideouts. Judges. Marshals. Mobs. Murder. Peace. Ranches. Trials. Tribal chiefs.*

Note: The following written prologue appears in the onscreen credits: "During the Civil War, Southern sympathizers made desperate efforts to aid the Confederacy by inciting Indian uprisings against defenseless towns along the Western frontier. The objective was to force large withdrawals of Northern troops from the main battlefronts, leaving them more vulnerable to Southern attack. This is the story of one such attempt that took place in Dakota territory in the year 1864."

Box 11 Sep 1954. DV 8 Sep 1954, p. 6 Exb 22 Sep 1954, p. 3837. FD 27 Sep 1954, p. 6. Har 11 Sep 1954, p. 146. MPD 13 Sep 1954. MPHPD 11 Sep 1954, p. 137. NYT 2 Oct 1954, p. 21. Var 8 Sep 1954, p. 6.

BLACK FURY (Immigrants)

First National Productions Corp.; controlled by Warner Bros. Pictures, Inc. *Dist* First National Pictures, Inc.; The Vitaphone Corp. 18 May **1935**; Prod: began 20 Oct 1934 [©First National Pictures, Inc.; 24 Apr 1935; LP5494]. Sd; b&w. 10 reels. 90, 95 or 97 min. PCA cert no. 579.

[*Exec prod* Jack L. Warner and Hal B. Wallis]. [*Supv* Robert Lord]. *Dir* Michael Curtiz. *Dial dir* Frank McDonald. [*Asst dir* Russ Saunders]. [*Second asst dir* Carroll Sax]. *Scr* Abem Finkel and Carl Erickson. *Photog* Byron Haskin. [*Asst cam* Ted Hayes]. *Art dir* John Hughes. *Ed* Thomas Richards. [*Wardrobe man* Dan Brown]. [*Asst wardrobe man* Hugh Blair]. [*Wardrobe woman* Mary Dery]. *Vitaphone Orch cond* Leo F. Forbstein. [*Hair* Emily Moore]. [*Unit mgr* Frank Mattison]. [*Grip* Harry Barnhouse]. [*Props* Emmet Emmerson]. [*Script asst* Fred Applegate]. [*Gaffer* Charles Alexander]. [*Still photog* John Ellis]. [*Stand in* Harry Raven].

Source: Based on the short story "Jan Volkanik" by Judge M. A. Musmanno and the play *Bohunk* by Harry R. Irving (publication and production undetermined).

Cast: PAUL MUNI (*Joe Radek*), Karen Morley (*Anna Novak*), William Gargan (*Slim [Johnson]*), Barton MacLane (*McGee*), John Qualen (*Mike [Shemanski]*), J. Carrol Naish (*Steve [Croner]*), Vince Barnett (*Kubanda*), Tully Marshall ([*Tommy*] *Poole*), Henry O'Neill ([*John W.*] *Hendricks*), Joe Crehan ([*Johnny*] *Farrell*), Mae Marsh [(*Mrs. Novak*)], Sarah Haden [(*Sophie Shemanski*)], Willard Robertson [(*J. J. Welsh*)], Effie Ellsler [(*Bubitchka*)], Wade Boteler [(*Mulligan*)], Egon Brecher [(*Alec Novak*)], George Pat Collins [(*Lefty*)], Ward Bond [(*Mac*)], Akim Tamiroff [(*Sokolsky*)], Purnell Pratt [(*Henry B. Jenkins*)], Eddie Shubert [(*Butch*)], [George Offerman, Jr. (*Pete Novak*)], [John M. Bleifer (*Ivan*)], [Harry Hastings (*Mose*)], [Harry Tyler (*Johnny*)], [Mitchell Ingraham (*Lawyer*)], [Herbert Heywood (*Bartender*)], [Samuel S. Hinds (*Judge*)], [Katherine Clare Ward (*Mrs. Clancy*)], [Pedro Regas (*Tony*)], [Patrick Moriarity (*Bill*)], [Harry Curdins (*Louie*)], [Nick Copeland (*Waiter*)], [Mary Russell (*Lefty's girl*)], [Claire McDowell (*Nurse*)], [Christian Rub (*Miner*)], [Ferike Boros (*Wife*)], [Dick French (*Orderly*)], [William H. Turner (*Watchman*)], [Addison Richards (*Government man*)], [Don Brodie (*Newsreel Man*)], [June Eberling (*Tessie Novak*)], [Edith Fellows (*Agnes Shemanski*)], [Bobby Nelson (*Johnny Novak*)], [Wally Albright, Jr. (*Willie Novak*)], [Dorothy Gray (*Mary*)], [Charles C. Wilson (*Welch*)], [Mickey Rentschler (*Chris Shemanski*)].

Social, Drama. [*Print viewed*]. Joe Radek, a simple, well-liked, Eastern European immigrant, is in love with Anna Novak. He dreams of quitting his job as a miner, buying a farm, and marrying Anna. Anna likes Joe, but longs for a different life, and runs away with Slim Johnson. Joe falls apart, gets drunk, and during a union meeting joins a dissenter named Steve Croner in a rebellion against the coal company. Joe's good friend Mike Shemanski, the local union leader, unsuccessfully begs Joe to trust the union. Joe is fired and the company brings in a private police force, headed by a thug named McGee. The union is forced to strike, scabs are sent in to work the mine, and Croner, who turns out to be a company agent, leaves town. One night, McGee and his police pick a fight with Mike; Joe comes to his rescue, but it is too late. McGee kills Mike and Joe is seriously wounded. In the hospital, Anna visits Joe and asks his forgiveness. At first he refuses her offer for support, but after a change of heart, he leaves the hospital and, with Anna's help, enters the mine, threatening to dynamite the shaft if the company doesn't negotiate with the union. McGee goes in after Joe, but after a brutal fight, McGee becomes Joe's hostage. Finally, after days of holding his position, the company agrees to Joe's terms. A federal investigation proves that the coal company instigated the strike, and Joe and Anna are redeemed in the eyes of the townspeople. *Coal miners. Immigrants. Strikes and lockouts. Trade unions.* Labor violence. Police. Romance. Strikebreakers.

Note: The film's working title was *Black Hell*. A second unit shot footage in Pennsylvania for the film and a full-scale mine shaft was dug on the Warner Ranch. Scenes were also shot on the stages at the Burbank studio and at the old Warner lot on Sunset Blvd. in Hollywood. According to a news item in *DV*, a complaint against the movie was brought by an east coast coal mine operators group. MPPDA President Will H. Hays was asked to stop the production because it dealt with "certain capital-labor relations which the complainants consider against the best public policy at this time." The MPAA/PCA collection at the AMPAS Library contains a letter from J. D. Battle, the executive secretary of the National Coal Association to the Hays office, expressing his concern that the film would prove harmful to the coal industry, and claiming that bad conditions

had been eliminated and that the industry currently enjoyed good relations with its workers. Modern sources report New York censorship board demands that the scene depicting the brutal murder of Mike Shemanski be cut, but files in the MPAA/PCA Collection at the AMPAS Library indicate that they passed it without objection. The scene was based on an actual strike case in which John Barkowski, a coal miner, was murdered by three company policemen. MPPDA files reveal that the entire film was banned in Chicago, Guatamala, Spain, Peru, Venezuela and Trinidad, and several other states and countries demanded cuts in the scenes portraying police brutality, Mike's murder, and the mine explosion. The film was passed without objection in Pennsylvannia, which might have been expected to raise the most objections because of its dependence on the coal industry. Some objections were raised because Joe's criminal activities in setting off explosions in the mine remain unpunished, but Director of Studio Relations for AMPP Joseph Breen addressed this problem in a letter to Hays stating, "Joe is not a criminal. Rather is he an infuriated, stupid fellow gone temporarily mad because of his high emotionalism. ... [W]hile the audience is certain to understand the forces which motivated Joe to commit the criminal act, there is not likely to be any disposition to sympathize with his crime." Breen requested that some of the dialogue refer to the fact "that while the miners may not have ideal working conditions, nevertheless working conditions of the coal industry have vastly improved and are getting better all the time." The studio was also asked to strengthen the fact that Croner is promoting strife as an agent of a firm of professional strikebreakers masquerading as coal and iron police, to develop the love story and to delete any suggestion that Anna is pregnant when she runs away with Slim. In a letter to Jack L. Warner, Breen notes that care should be taken in showing "serious conflict between employer and employee" as censor boards throughout the country were cutting similar scenes from newsreels. The fact that the strike is settled by the NRA was considered a mitigating factor in the strike story. John Qualen, variously billed as John M. Qualen is here billed as John T. Qualen. Modern sources credit Perc Westmore for makeup. According to modern sources, *Bohunk* was an unproduced play.

DV 20 Oct 1934, p. 2. *DV* 25 Oct 1934, p. 1. *DV* 22 Nov 1934, p. 1. *DV* 26 Mar 1935, p. 3. *FD* 28 Mar 1935, p. 4. *HR* 22 Oct 1934, p. 11. *HR* 26 Mar 1935, p. 3. *HR* 19 Apr 1935, p. 2. *MPD* 26 Mar 1935, p. 8. *MPH* 19 Jan 1935, p. 67. *MPH* 3 Apr 1935, p. 50. *NYT* 11 Apr 1935, p. 27. *Var* 17 Apr 1935, p. 14.

BLACK GOLD (African Americans)

Norman Film Mfg. Co. **1928**; New York showing: 4 Jul 1928. Si; b&w. 6 reels, 5,600 ft.

Cast: Lawrence Criner, Kathryn Boyd, Steve Reynolds, United States Marshal L. B. Tatums, and the entire All-Colored City of Tatums, Oklahoma.

Drama, African American. Advertising material for this film indicated that it was "a stirring epic of the oil fields" and that it was "one of the true stories of living colored examples." *African Americans. Oil prospectors.*

Note: The Norman Film Mfg. Co. was located in Arlington, FL.

BLACK GOLD (Native Americans, Chinese Americans)

Allied Artists Productions, Inc. *Dist* Monogram Pictures Corp. 16 Aug **1947**; Prod: late Nov 1946—late Jan 1947 [©Allied Artists Productions, Inc.; 6 Sep 1947; LP1189]. Sd (Western Electric Recording); col (Cinecolor). 90-92 min. Passed by the National Board of Review.

Prod Jerry Bernerd. *Dir* Phil Karlson. [*Asst dir* Bob Farfan and Harry Jones]. *Racing seq dir by* B. Reaves Eason. *Scr* Agnes Christine Johnston. *Orig story by* Caryl Coleman. *Photog* Harry Neumann. *Cam tech* Leonard Jones. *Spec eff* A. J. Lohman. *Cinecolor supv* Wilton Holm. *Art dir* E. R. Hickson. *Asst art dir* Dave Milton. *Supv film ed* Otho Lovering. *Film ed* Roy Livingston. *Set dec* Vin Taylor. *Ward* Harry Bourne. *Cost supv* Lorraine MacLean. *Mus dir* Edward J. Kay. *Orch by* Laurence A. Russell. *Rec* Tom Lambert. *Makeup* Harry Ross. *Commentary on the Kentucky Derby by* Clem McCarthy. *Scenes of the Kentucky Derby photog courtesy of* Colonel Matt J. Winn. *Prod mgr* Glenn Cook. *Tech adv* Ralph McCutcheon. *Indian history and ethnology* Nipo T. Strongheart. [*Prod mgr* William Calihan]. [*Commentary of the Tijuana race* Joe Hernandez].

Cast: ANTHONY QUINN [(*Charley Eagle*)], Katherine De Mille [(*Sarah Eagle*)], Ducky Louie [(*Davey*)], Raymond Hatton [(*Buckey*)], Kane Richmond [(*Stanley Lowell*)], Thurston Hall [(*Colonel Caldwell*)], Moroni Olsen [(*Dan Toland*)], Jonathan Hale, Darryl Hickman [(*Schoolboy*)], Charles Trowbridge [(*Senator Watkins*)], Elyse Knox [(*Ruth Fraser*)], [Alan Bridge (*Jones*)], [H. T. Tsiang (*Davey's father*)], [Jack Norman (*Monty*)].

Horse race, Drama. [*Print viewed*]. South of the Mexican border, Davey, a Chinese boy, is orphaned when his father, whom he only recently met, is killed by thieving white men. The boy is befriended by an Indian named Charley Eagle, whose father was also killed by white men. Charley enters his thoroughbred mare, Black Hope, in a race south of the border and is tricked by Dan Toland, a crooked

American, into selling Black Hope to him after she wins the race. Charley returns Toland's money in the night, retrieves Black Hope and returns to his humble ranch in Oklahoma with Davey. Charley's wife Sarah, who is well-educated, insists that Davey attend school, but when the schoolboys tease him because of his yellow skin, Davey refuses to go. Finally, Sarah decides to adopt Davey, and he agrees to begin school. After an oilman gives the Eagles an advance for allowing him to drill on their land, Charley pays for a thoroughbred stud owned by Colonel Caldwell to impregnate Black Hope. The mare is unable to walk following the birth of her male colt, however, and Charley must shoot her. Within months, the Eagles strike oil, and Charley names the colt Black Gold. After the now-rich Charley is hit by a beam at the oil rig, he is forced to walk with a cane. Charley is nonetheless determined to win the Kentucky Derby and arranges for his old friend Buckey to train Black Gold, with Davey as his jockey. One day while training, Buckey's pet goat, Beautiful, crosses Black Gold's path on the racetrack, causing Davey to fall. He is not hurt, but Charley has a heart attack. Charley has often left Sarah unannounced when he has had a yen for the great outdoors, but now he leaves her for good to die alone. She, Davey and Black Gold visit Charley as he camps and hear his last words, "She won." At the Kentucky Derby, Black Gold competes with Toland's favored horse, Corsair, and wins. As Sarah accepts the gold cup from Colonel Caldwell on behalf of all Indians, she repeats her husband's dying words, "She won." *Adoption. Chinese Americans. Horseracing. Indians of North America. Kentucky Derby. Orphans. Racism.* Adolescents. Horse owners. Horse trainers. Horses. Jockeys. Marriage. Mexican-American border region. Murder. Oil wells. Oklahoma. Orphans. Schoolteachers. Swindlers and swindling.

Note: This was the first Monogram film made in color. Contemporary reviews note that the film was based on the real-life adventures of Black Gold, the longshot winner of the 1924 Kentucky Derby. *HR* news items provide the following information about the production: Some background footage was filmed at the Kentucky Derby race at Churchill Downs in Louisville, KY, on 4 May 1946, and at a Tijuana racetrack. Other scenes were shot at Vasquez Rocks, CA, and Hollywood Park, in Los Angeles. A 1 Apr 1946 *HR* news item stated that because the black colt that played "Black Gold," which Monogram purchased and named Black Gold, was born on the last weekend of Mar 1946, the film would take almost a year to complete. In Nov 1946, principal photography was delayed for two weeks because of a shutdown at the Cinecolor plant. After seeing some of the dailies, Monogram increased the film's budget to $100,000. Clem McCarthy, a professional racetrack commentator, was assigned to make a special trailer for the film in May 1947. In mid-Jun 1947, American Indians from nine tribes were invited to attend a special screening of the film in Los Angeles, as well as a "powwow" at Farmer's Market, which was proclaimed a temporary "Indian reservation." To promote the film in Los Angeles, an Indian village with five teepees and twelve Indians was set up at a drugstore near Beverly Hills. *HR* news items list Harry Woods, Carmen D'Antonio and Bob Patten as cast members, but their participation in the final film has not been confirmed. Anthony Quinn and Katherine De Mille were married at the time of this production. *Black Gold* marked the only time they appeared on screen together. They divorced in 1965.

Box 28 Jun 1947. *DV* 23 Jun 1947. *FD* 26 Jun 1947, p. 5. *HR* 18 Jan 1946, p. 2. *HR* 1 Apr 1946, p. 8. *HR* 5 Nov 1946, p. 15. *HR* 22 Nov 1946, p. 19. *HR* 2 Dec 1946, p. 9. *HR* 3 Dec 1946, p. 11. *HR* 6 Dec 1946, p. 16. *HR* 16 Dec 1946, p. 20. *HR* 18 Dec 1946, p. 19. *HR* 24 Jan 1947, p. 18. *HR* 8 May 1947, p. 10. *HR* 19 Jun 1947, p. 9. *HR* 23 Jun 1947, p. 3. *HR* 25 Sep 1947. p. 13. *IFJ* 4 Jan 1947, p. 34. *MPHPD* 28 Jun 1947. *NYT* 5 Sep 1947, p. 16. *Var* 25 Jun 1947, p. 8.

BLACK HAND (Italian Americans)

Metro-Goldwyn-Mayer Corp.; controlled by Loew's Inc. *Dist* Loew's Inc. 17 Mar **1950**; Prod: late Jul–late Aug 1949 [©Loew's Inc.; 18 Jan 1950; LP2805]. Sd (Western Electric Sound System); b&w. 9 reels, 8,304 or 8,323 ft. 92 min. Passed by the National Board of Review. PCA cert no. 14100.

Prod William H. Wright. *Dir* Richard Thorpe. [*Asst dir* Al Jennings]. [*2d unit dir* John Walters]. *Scr* Luther Davis. *From a story by* Leo Townsend. *Dir of photog* Paul C. Vogel. *Spec eff* Warren Newcombe. *Art dir* Cedric Gibbons and Gabriel Scognamillo. *Film ed* Irvine Warburton. *Set dec* Edwin B. Willis. *Assoc* Charles de Crof. *Cost* Walter Plunkett. *Mus score* Alberto Colombo. *Rec supv* Douglas Shearer. *Hair styles des by* Sydney Guilaroff. *Makeup created by* Jack Dawn.

Cast: Gene Kelly (*Johnny Columbo*), J. Carrol Naish (*Louis Lorelli*), Teresa Celli (*Isabella Gomboli*), Marc Lawrence (*Caesar Xavier Serpi*), Frank Puglia (*Carlo Sabballera*), Barry Kelley (*Captain Thompson*), Mario Siletti (*Benny Danetta*), Carl Milletaire (*George Allani* [previously known as George Tomasino]), Peter Brocco (*Roberto Columbo*), Eleonora Mendelssohn (*Maria Columbo*), Grazia Narciso (*Mrs. Danetta*), Maurice Samuels

(*Moriani*), Burk Symon (*Judge*), Bert Freed (*Prosecutor*), Mimi Aguglia (*Mrs. Sabballera*), Baldo Minuti (*Bettini*), Carlo Tricoli (*Pietro Riago*), Marc Krah (*Lombardi*), Jimmy Lagano (*Rudi Gomboli*), Phyllis Morris (*Mary the Shamrock*), [Alfred Linder (*Rat type*)], [Frank Richards (*Semi-moron*)], [Felix Romano (*Hunchback*)], [Tony Barrett (*Defense attorney*)], [Jean Hartelle (*Sestini*)], [Raymond Malkin (*Johnny Columbo, age 14*)], [Vincent Renno (*Editor*)], [Anthony Dante (*Alfredo*)], [Angi O. Poulos (*Hurdy-gurdy man*)], [Michele Ventrella (*Mr. Abanase*)], [Joseph De Angelo (*Man on boat*)], [Theresa Testa (*Signora Di Palma*)], [Anna Demetrio (*Manageress*)], [Richard Richonne (*Businessman*)], [Adolpho Romeo, Eugene Borden (*Laborers*)], [Ernesto Morelli (*Hokey-pokey man*)], [John Marlin, Manuel Alda (*Customers*)], [Maria Genardi (*Signora Bernadoni*)], [Doug Williams (*Signor Taricco*)], [George Restivo (*Sexton*)], [John Ardizoni (*Mr. Larti*)], [Rosario Ardizoni (*Mrs. Larti*)], [Ray Bennett, Thomas P. Dillon, John McGuire, Mario Roselle (*Policemen*)], [Sid Tomack (*Handwriting expert*)], [Jim Pierce (*Bailiff*)], [Don Orlando, Carlo Schipa, Dino Bolognese, Pete Cusanelli (*Translators*)], [John Carboni (*Don Giuseppe*)], [Kenneth Garcia (*Officer of boat*)], [Michael Vallon (*Cartman*)], [Lillian Bronson, Almira Sessions (*Tourists*)], [David Bond (*Saturnine*)], [Guido Di Capua (*Waiter*)], [Bobby Blake (*Pasquale, a bus boy*)], [Louis Nicoletti (*Headwaiter*)], [John Good (*Assistant consul*)], [Bob Evans, Ott George, Marc Snow, John Bagni (*Footpads*)], [Antonio Filauri (*Official*)], [Robert Malcolm (*Firechief*)], [Fernanda Elison].

Gangster, **Historical**, **Drama**. [*Print viewed*]. Late one night, in the year 1900, Roberto Columbo, an Italian lawyer living in New York's Little Italy neighborhood, secretly meets with police at the Carey Street Hotel to show them a threatening letter he received from the notorious Black Hand extortion gang. The letter indicates that the Black Hand is demanding that Roberto pay them protection money or face death. No sooner does Roberto begin to describe some of the gang members to the police than two mobsters enter the station and kill him. The murder devastates Roberto's wife Maria, who decides to return to Italy with her son Johnny. Eight years later, following the death of his mother, Johnny returns to New York vowing to avenge his father's death and end the Black Hand's operations. While looking for Black Hand gangsters, Johnny has a reunion with Isabella Gomboli, a childhood friend, who warns him that the mob is unstoppable and that he will be in great danger. Although Isabella's parents were killed by the Black Hand, she suggests that Johnny drop "La Vendetta" and form a citizen's league instead. Johnny rejects Isabella's suggestion, though, and insists on meeting with Moriani, former owner of the Carey Street Hotel, who was with his father the night he was killed. Shortly after Johnny's meeting with Moriani, Moriani is found dead in his hotel room. Hoping to steer Johnny away from trouble, police officer Louis Lorelli, a friend of Johnny's father, offers him a job in New Jersey and advises him to make a success of himself. Johnny eventually decides to take Isabella's advice and form a citizen's league when he discovers that Francesco, the son of tailor Benny Danetta, has been kidnapped by the Black Hand. Francesco is released soon after the first citizen's league meeting is convened, but Johnny is punished by the Black Hand for organizing the group and is given a severe beating. Later, a bomb is found on the steps of Carlo Sabballera's dry goods store. Johnny's investigation into the Black Hand leads to the arrest of George Allani, who is accused of placing the bomb in front of Sabballera's store. At Allani's trial, Carlo is about to identify the gangster as the culprit when he is given the death sign by some Black Hand men. The frightened store owner refuses to identify Allani, and, as a result, it appears that Allani will go free. At the last moment, however, it is revealed that Allani is using an assumed name, and that he is really George Tomasino, an Italian fugitive. The judge orders Tomasino's deportation, which gives Lorelli the idea to go to Italy to check Italian police records against his list of suspects. In Naples, Italy, Lorelli is shot and killed by Black Hand gangsters right after he mails a list of Italian criminals to Johnny. Back in New York, the Black Hand has kidnapped Isabella's younger brother Rudi, and is demanding the list of names as ransom. While attempting to rescue Rudi, Johnny is captured by the Black Hand. Johnny manages to escape by setting off a time bomb that kills everyone in the Black Hand headquarters except Caesar Xavier Serpi. Serpi later engages Johnny in a fight with a pickax, but Johnny kills him with a knife. With Lorelli's list safely delivered to the police, Johnny is confident that he has put an end to the Black Hand

operations in New York. *Black Hand (United States). Italian Americans. Mafia. Murder. New York City–Little Italy. Revenge. Aliases. Bartenders. Bombings. Detectives. Fathers and sons. Hotelkeepers. Immigrants. Italy. Kidnapping. Lawyers. Naples (Italy). Police. Romance. Tenement-houses. Trials.*

Note: A working title for this film was *The Knife.* The film opens with the following written foreword: "At the turn of the century, there were more Italians living in New York than in Rome. Many had hurried here seeking fortune and freedom. Some of them found only failure and fear. From all these Italian immigrants came no truer American names than Di Maggio, Pecora, Giannini, La Guardia and Basilone. This story deals with the hard, angry days when these new citizens began to place their stake in the American dream—when they purged the Old World terror of the Black Hand from their ranks and gave bright dignity to their people and to this nation." A Sep 1948 *HR* news item notes that although the picture is fictional, it is based on factual material about the Black Hand organized crime syndicate. The Black Hand crime syndicate originated in Italy and operated in the United States in the late 19th century and the early part of the 20th century. A biography of Gene Kelly notes that Robert Taylor was originally slated for the starring role, and that M-G-M had changed the picture's ranking from a "B" picture to a "programmer" when its potential for success was fully realized. An Aug 1949 *HR* news item notes that John Waters directed the second unit on location in Naples, Italy. Other *HR* news items add that actor Carlo Tricoli was a former San Francisco District Attorney and that Marc Snow was a UCLA drama professor.

Box 21 Jan 1950. *DV* 19 Jan 1950, p. 3. *FD* 19 Jan 1950, p. 12. *HR* 21 Sep 1948. *HR* 22 Jul 1949, p. 12. *HR* 19 Aug 1949, p. 22. *HR* 24 Aug 1949, p. 2. *HR* 25 Aug 1949, p. 1. *HR* 1 Sep 1949, p. 3. *HR* 19 Jan 1950, p. 3. *MPHPD* 21 Jan 1950, p. 161. *NYT* 13 Mar 1950, p. 15. *Var* 25 Jan 1950, p. 18.

BLACK HEART *see* **FLAMING STAR**

BLACK HELL *see* **BLACK FURY**

THE BLACK HILLS (1951) *see* **OH! SUSANNA**

THE BLACK HILLS (1960) *see* **WALK TALL**

BLACK IRISH *see* **THE LADY FROM SHANGHAI**

THE BLACK KING (African Americans)

Southland Pictures Corp. *Dist* Southland Pictures Corp. **1932**; New York opening: week of 9 Jul 1932; Prod: completed late Apr 1932 at Metropolitan Studios, Fort Lee, NJ. Sd (Victor Recording; Western Electric System); b&w. 9 reels. 72 min.

Prod supv Charles P. Nasca. *Dir* Bud Pollard. *Asst dir* Jos. A. Bannon. *Adpt* Morris M. Levinson. *Dial* Donald Heywood. *Cine* Dal Clawson. *Asst by* Lester Lang. *Art dir* Anthony Continer. *Ed* Morris M. Levinson. *Cost* Brooks. *Rec eng* Gerre Barton and Armand Schettini. *Tech dir* Marc S. Asch.

Song(s): "Swing Low, Sweet Chariot," traditional, arranged by Henry Thacker Burleigh; and other songs.

Cast: A. B. Comethiere (*Deacon Charcoal Johnson*), Vivianne Baber (*Mary Lou Lawton*), Knolly Mitchell (*Sug [Jackson]*), Dan Michaels (*Brother Longtree*), Mike Jackson (*Brother Lawton*), Mary Jane Watkins (*Mrs. Bottoms*), Harry Gray (*Deacon Jones*), Lorenzo Tucker ([*Stephen*] *Carmichael*), Freeman Fairley (*Mob leader*), Ismay Andrews (*Mrs. Ashfoot*), Trixie Smith (*Delia*).

African American, Social, Drama, with songs. [*Print viewed*]. Soon after being forced out of the Rise and Shine Baptist Church in Logan, Mississippi, by newcomer Deacon Charcoal Johnson, the kindhearted, old Deacon Jones dies of a broken heart. Troubled by the takeover, Mary Lou Lawton, one of the parishoners, tells her boyfriend, Sug Jackson, that Johnson is nothing but a crooked backslider. When Johnson holds a meeting at the Masonic Hall to lead the "Back to Africa Movement," promising his parishoners great fortune on the African continent, Sug informs white judge Allan Lee that Johnson is planning to take workers off the plantations. The judge orders the sheriff to raid the meeting, and in the confusion, Johnson flees with the parishoners' money. He takes refuge at Mary Lou's house, where he proposes marriage to her. Sug tries to help Mary Lou, but she resents his forceful manner and takes the side of the desperate Johnson. Soon, a crowd of angry parishoners gathers at Mary Lou's demanding a return of their money, and when they storm her bedroom, they find that Johnson has fled. Time passes, and Johnson and Mary Lou turn up in Tulsa, Oklahoma, where Johnson has established himself as a reigning religious sovereign, calling himself the Emperor of the United States of Africa, and Mary Lou is his queen. Johnson and Mary Lou expand their empire and travel to Kansas City and Chicago, where they are feted by the city's social elite. Meanwhile, attorney Stephen Carmichael and his associates decide that Johnson is gaining too much influence in the black community

and vow to put a stop to his movement. After failing in his attempt to lure Mary Lou away from Johnson by disrupting a parade in his honor, Sug pleads with her not to board the ship bound for Africa and tells her that he loves her. A grand farewell ceremony for those about to depart to Africa is stormed by Sug and his pals, who threaten to explode the place unless he is heard. When the room falls silent, Sug exposes Johnson's lies, telling the crowd that no country has agreed to accept them. The crowd then turns on Johnson, who is immediately deposed, and Sug and Mary Lou embrace in a kiss. *African Americans. Charlatans. Fraud. Ministers. Religious cults. Africa. Chicago (IL). Churches. Deacons. Editors. Freemasons. Judges. Lawyers. Mississippi. New York City–Harlem. Romantic rivalry. Tulsa (OK). Uniforms.*

Note: A working title for this film was *Empire, Inc.* The viewed print bore the title *Harlem Big Shot,* which may have been a theatrical re-release title. The actor portraying Judge Lee was the only white member of the cast. The film was billed as a satirical portrayal of Marcus Garvey, founder of the Universal Negro Improvement Association, who was convicted of fraud in 1925 and was deported to his native Jamaica following the commutation of his sentence by President Calvin Coolidge. Stars A. B. Comethiere and Vivianne Baker were well-known stage players. According to contemporary sources, the movie was produced by the white-run Southland Pictures Corp. as the first in a series of films with "all-colored casts." The company made no further pictures following the failure of *The Black King.*

FD 24 Apr 1932, p. 5. *FD* 1 May 1932, p. 5. *FD* 8 May 1932, p. 5. *FD* 15 Jul 1932, p. 7. *Var* 19 Jul 1932, p. 25.

BLACK LEGION (Immigrants)

Warner Bros. Pictures, Inc. *Dist* Warner Bros. Pictures, Inc. 30 Jan **1937**; Prod: began late Aug 1936 [©Warner Bros. Pictures, Inc. & The Vitaphone Corp.; 29 Jan 1936; LP6843]. Sd; b&w. 10 reels. 83 min. PCA cert no. 2507.

Prod Robert Lord. [*Exec prod* Jack L. Warner and Hal B. Wallis]. *Dir* Archie L. Mayo. [*Asst dir* Jack Sullivan]. *Scr* Abem Finkel and William Wister Haines. *Story* Robert Lord. *Photog* George Barnes. [*2d cam* George Nogle]. [*Asst cam* Gene Davenport]. [*Spec eff* Fred Jackman, Jr. and H. F. Koenekamp]. *Art dir* Robert Haas. *Film ed* Owen Marks. *Gowns* Milo Anderson. [*Mus* Bernhard Kaun]. [*Sd* C. A. Riggs]. [*Unit mgr* Frank Mattison].

Cast: Humphrey Bogart (*Frank Taylor*), Dick Foran (*Ed Jackson*), Erin O'Brien-Moore (*Ruth Taylor*), Ann Sheridan (*Betty Grogan*), Helen Flint (*Pearl Davis [Danvers]*), Joseph Sawyer (*Cliff Moore [Summers]*), Clifford Soubier (*Mike Gorgan*), Alonzo Price (*Alf Hargrave*), Paul Harvey (*Billings*), Dickie Jones (*Buddy Taylor*), Samuel Hinds (*Judge*), Addison Richards (*Prosecuting attorney*), Eddie Acuff (*Metcalf*), Dorothy Vaughan (*Mrs. Grogan*), John Litel (*Tommy Smith*), Henry Brandon (*Joe Dombrowski*), Charles Halton (*Osgood*), Pat C. Flick (*Nick Strumpas*), Francis Sayles (*Charlie*), Paul Stanton (*Barham*), Harry Hayden (*Jones*), Egon Brecher (*Dombrowski*), [Robert Barrat (*Brown*)], [Ed Chandler, Robert E. Homans (*Policemen*)], [William Wayne (*Counterman*)], [Frederick Lindsley ("*March of Time*" *voice*)], [Fred MacKaye, Frank Nelson, John Hiestand, Ted Bliss (*Radio announcers*)], [Larry Emmons (*Man in drugstore*)], [Don Barclay (*Drunk*)], [Emmett Vogan (*News commentator*)], [John Butler (*Salesman*)], [Frank Sully (*Helper*)], [Max Wagner (*Truck driver*)], [Carlyle Moore, Jr., Dennis Moore, Milt Kibbee (*Reporters*)], [Lee Phelps (*Guard*)], [Wilfred Lucas (*Bailiff*)], [Jack Mower (*County clerk*)].

Drama. [*Print viewed*]. At a midwestern factory, workers speculate about who will fill the opening for plant foreman. Most agree that the job will go to Frank Taylor, who has seniority. That night Frank and his family celebrate, but in the morning, he learns that the job has gone to Joe Dombrowski, a younger man who has invented a time saving device for the plant. When Cliff Summers, another worker, sees how angry Frank is about losing his job to a "foreigner," he suggests that Frank join the Black Legion, a secret organization dedicated to eliminating foreigners from the country. Their first action is to burn down Dombrowski's chicken farm and chase the Dombrowskis out of town. After this, Frank is made foreman, but pressure from the founders of the Legion force him to spend time recruiting new members and he is demoted in favor of his neighbor Mike Grogan. That night, the gang attacks Grogan. Co-worker Ed Jackson, who is married to Grogan's daughter Betty, starts to suspect Frank's connection to all the trouble. He says something to Frank's wife Ruth and when she confronts Frank, his violent reaction drives her away. Frank continues to drink. He loses his job and associates with Pearl Davis, a woman with a bad reputation. When Ed threatens to go to the police, he becomes the next victim of the Legion. Unlike the other

victims, though, Ed is not afraid, and when he tries to escape, a panicky Frank shoots him. Frank is then arrested for the murder and Ruth returns from her parents' house to stand by him. The lawyer for the Legion threatens Frank's wife and son in order to stop him from implicating the Legion, but finally, filled with self-loathing, Frank tells the truth. The entire Black Legion is sentenced to life in prison for Ed's murder. *Factory workers. Secret societies. Terrorism. Xenophobia. Drunkenness. False accusations. Immigrants. Murder. Reputation. Trials.*

Note: Actor Clifford Soubier, who portrays Mike Grogan in the film, had been an NBC broadcaster working out of Chicago. According to the Warner Bros. Collection in the USC Cinema-Television Library, Robert Homans was at one time considered for the part of "Grogan." Memos in the files note that executive producer Hal B. Wallis had suggested Edward G. Robinson for the lead, but producer Robert Lord objected on the grounds that Robinson looked too foreign. He felt they needed a "distinctly American looking actor to play this part." According to a memo dated 10 August 1936, Paul Graetz and Joseph Crehan were signed for roles, but their participation in the final film has not been determined. A memo from Lord to Wallis indicates that Glenda Farrell was considered for the part of "Pearl." Outdoor scenes were shot at the Warner Ranch in Calabasas and the Providencia Ranch. The Taylor and Grogan homes were shot on location in Hollywood. The film, which was made for a total cost of $235,000, was inspired by an actual case involving the Black Legion in Michigan, where Charles Poole, a WPA worker, was killed, and Dayton Dean, Legion executioner, turned state's evidence at the trial. According to a *NYT* article about the film, the Legion's "stock in trade is blatant 'Americanism' coupled with persecution of those differing in economics and racial viewpoints....a sort of 'America for Americans' jehad in which native-born labor was to carry the banner—and take the risks." According to *HR*, The Ku Klux Klan sued Warner Bros. for patent infringement for alleged use of the Klan's patented insignia of a white cross on a background of red with a black square. On screen credits list Helen Flint's character as "Pearl Davis," but some contemporary reviews call her "Danvers," the name which she is called in the film. Onscreen credits and contemporary reviews call Joseph Sawyer's character "Cliff Moore," but he is called "Cliff Summers" in the film. Robert Lord received an Academy Award nomination for original story and the National Board of Review chose it as best film for 1937 and named Humphrey Bogart best actor. In 1936, Columbia made *Legion of Terror*, the first film to be based on the Black Legion killing (see *AFI Catalog of Feature Films, 1931-40* F3.2450).

FD 30 Dec 1936, p. 11. *HR* 5 Jan 1937, p. 3. *HR* 11 Aug 1937, p. 2. *MPD* 11 Jan 1937, pp. 6-7. *MPH* 10 Oct 1936, p. 42. *MPH* 9 Jan 1937, p. 44. *NYT* 17 Jan 1937. *NYT* 18 Jan 1937, p. 21. *Time* 25 Jan 1937, p. 46. *Var* 20 Jan 1937, p. 14.

BLACK MAGIC (Chinese Americans, African Americans)

Monogram Pictures Corp. *Dist* Monogram Pictures Corp. 9 Sep 1944; Prod: 3 May—mid-May 1944 [©Monogram Pictures Corp.; 15 Jul 1944; LP12737]. Sd (Western Electric Mirrophonic Recording); b&w, 5,822 ft. 64-65 min.

Series: Charlie Chan.

Prod Philip N. Krasne and James S. Burkett. *Dir* Phil Rosen. *Asst dir* Bobby Ray. *Orig scr* George Callahan. *Dir of photog* Arthur Martinelli. [*Cam op* Dave Smith]. [*Asst* Monty Steadman]. [*Still photog* Earl Crowley]. [*Spec eff* M. B. Kinne]. *Art dir* Dave Milton. *Film ed* John Link. *Set dec* Al Greenwood. [*Ward* Harry Bourne]. *Mus dir* David Chudnow. *Mus score* Alexander Laszlo. *Sd rec* Max Hutchinson. *Prod mgr* Dick L'Estrange. [*Script girl* Marie Messinger]. [*Props* Sammy Gordon and Ralph Martin]. [*Grip* Lew Dow and George Booker]. [*Gaffer* Joe Wharton].

Source: Based on characters created by Earl Derr Biggers.

Cast: Sidney Toler [(*Charlie Chan*)], Mantan Moreland [(*Birmingham Brown*)], Frances Chan [(*Frances Chan*)], Joseph Crehan [(*Inspector Matthews*)], Helen Beverley [(*Norma Duncan, also known as Nancy Wood*)], Jacqueline de Wit [(*Justine Bonner*)], Geraldine Wall [(*Harriett Green*)], Ralph Peters [(*Rafferty*)], Frank Jaquet [(*Paul Hamlin, also known as Chardo*)], Edward Earle, Claudia Dell [(*Vera Starkey*)], Harry Depp, Charles Jordan [(*Tom Starkey*)], Richard Gordon, [Byron Foulger (*Charles Edwards*)], Joe Whitehead [(*Dawson*)], [Crane Whitley (*W. Bonner*)], [Darby Jones (*Johnson*)].

Detective, Drama. [*Print viewed*]. While holding a séance at his home, psychic W. Bonner asks for questions from those present. After a voice asks what happened in London on 5 Oct 1935, the lights are extinguished, a gunshot rings out and Bonner is found murdered. As Bonner's wife Justine summons Inspector Matthews of the homicide bureau, Bonner's assistants, Tom and Vera Starkey, who operate from a hidden chamber, panic and flee. Matthews orders all those present at the Bonner house to headquarters for questioning. Among the suspects are seance particpants Harriett Green, Paul Hamlin, Charles Edwards, Nancy Wood, newly hired valet Birmingham Brown and Frances Chan, the daughter of famed Honolulu detective Charlie

Chan, who had been alerted to the séance by her old friend Brown. When the coroner notifies Mathews that the bullet has disappeared in Bonner's body, the inspector coerces Chan into joining the investigation. After studying the interviews with the suspects, Chan asks to speak to Nancy Wood and informs the inspector that she must be using an alias because the monogram on her purse reads "ND". A conversation with the hotel clerk reveals that Nancy's real name is Norma Duncan. Confronted with her lie, Norma claims that she used the alias to infiltrate Bonner's séance and prove that the psychic drove her father to commit suicide. At the Bonner house, meanwhile, Mrs. Bonner communicates to Tom and Vera through an intercom linked to their hidden chamber. When Frances, who has come to visit Brown, overhears the conversation, she alerts her father. Hurrying to the house, Chan discovers the secret chamber hidden behind a cabinet in the séance room. After reassembling the suspects at police headquarters, Chan reveals that Mr. Hamilton and Mrs. Green were both being blackmailed by Bonner and that Mrs. Bonner had threatened to kill her husband because of his infidelity. Chan then asks if anyone can identify the speaker at the séance who framed the question about London. Later, Norma sends Chan a message to come to her hotel, but when Chan enters her room, he finds her in a trance. Just then, the lights go out, a gun is fired and the assailant runs out the door. Awakened from her trance, Norma is unable to remember what happened to her, and Chan entrusts her to Rafferty, Mathew's assistant, while he goes to send a cable to Scotland Yard. Later, at the Bonner house, Frances and Birmingham overhear Mrs. Bonner asking the unseen Tom and Vera for their help, and Frances decides to follow her. Soon after, Norma phones the inspector to inform him that Edwards is acting strangely on the second floor of the Berekley building. Following Mrs. Bonner to the Berekely building, Frances meets her father and the inspector there and finds Mrs. Bonner's glove outside a closed door. Mrs. Bonner, in a trance, ascends to the rooftop where a voice coaxes her to jump from the ledge. After she plunges to her death, Chan notices a peculiar stain on her coat and takes it to the lab for analysis. The coroner identifies it as the residue of a powerful mind-altering drug that renders its victims helpless. He then gives Chan several pills that contain the antidote to the drug. Announcing that Mrs. Bonner committed suicide out of remorse for murdering her husband, the inspector declares the case closed. Dissatisfied with the inspector's conclusion, Chan returns to search the room in front of which Mrs. Bonner's glove was found. There Chan is manacled and hypnotized by an unseen assailant who orders him to climb to the roof and jump. After swallowing one of the pills, Chan proceeds to the roof. Meanwhile, becoming concerned when she is unable to locate her father, Frances notifies Rafferty. Together they hurry to the Berekley building and trace Chan to the roof. As Chan totters precariously on the ledge, the antidote begins to work and he comes out of his trance just as Frances and Rafferty appear. When Rafferty hands Chan the response from Scotland Yard, Chan reconvenes a séance at the Bonner house. That night, Chan exposes Tom and Vera in their secret chamber and then challenges the séance participants to answer a series of word association questions. After the lights go out and another gunshot is fired, Chan produces a cable from Scotland Yard imparting the information that on 5 Oct 1935, Chardo, a famous magician, was gravely injured in a car accident. Chan continues that Chardo's wife, Justine, had just run away with his assistant, Bonner. After undergoing plastic surgery to alter his appearance, Chardo determined to make Justine and Bonner pay for their betrayal. Chan then extracts a bullet made from frozen blood from his chair, thus explaining the disappearing bullet that killed Bonner. Addressing Hamlin as Chardo, Chan seizes the cigar case in which is hidden the spring gun used to kill Bonner. *Detectives. Fathers and daughters. Hypnotists. Magicians. Murder. Séances. Trance. African Americans. Blackmail. Blood. Chinese Americans. Coroners. Falls from heights. Impersonation and imposture. Infidelity. Revenge. Servants. Suicide. Telegrams.*

Note: The working titles of this film were *Murder Chamber* and *Charlie Chan in the Murder Chamber*. It was also reviewed as *Charlie Chan in Black Magic*. The film was reissued as *Murder at Midnight*. Although a *HR* news item lists Trevor Bardette in the cast, his participation in the released film has not been confirmed. For additional information on the series, please consult the Series Index and see the entry below for *Charlie Chan Carries On*.

Box 9 Sep 1944. *DV* 31 Aug 1944, p. 3. *Exb* 26 Jul 1944, p. 1543. *FD* 26 Jul 1944, p. 11. *HR* 1 May 1944, p. 14. *HR* 10 May 1944, p. 8. *HR* 12 May 1944, p. 22. *HR* 31 Aug 1944, p. 3. *MPHPD* 22 Jul 1944, p. 2007. *MPHPD* 12 Aug 1944, p. 2042.

THE BLACK ORCHID (Italian Americans)

Paramount Pictures Corp. *Dist* Paramount Pictures Corp. Mar **1959**; New York opening: 12 Feb 1959; Prod: early Feb—late Mar 1958 [©Paramount Pictures Corp.; 30 Dec 1958; LP12870]. Sd (Westrex Recording System); b&w; VistaVision. 94-96 min. PCA cert no. 19016.

Prod Carlo Ponti and Marcello Girosi. *Dir* Martin Ritt. *Asst dir* Richard Caffey. *Wrt* Joseph Stefano. *Dir of photog* Robert Burks. *Spec photog eff* John P. Fulton. *Process photog* Farciot Edouart. *Art dir* Hal Pereira and Roland Anderson. *Ed* Howard Smith. *Set dec* Sam Comer. *Set dec* Robert Benton. *Cost* Edith Head. *Mus score* Alessandro Cicognini. *Sd rec* Hugo Grenzbach and Winston Leverett. *Makeup supv* Wally Westmore. *Hair style supv* Nellie Manley. [*Prod mgr* Harry Caplan].

Cast: SOPHIA LOREN [(*Rose Bianco*)], ANTHONY QUINN [(*Frank Valente*)], Mark Richman [(*Noble*)], Virginia Vincent [(*Alma Gallo*)], Frank Puglia [(*Henry Gallo*)], Jimmy Baird [(*Ralphie Bianco*)], Naomi Stevens [(*Giulia Gallo*)], Whit Bissell [(*Mr. Harmon*)], Robert Carricart [(*Priest*)], Joe di Reda [(*Joe*)], Jack Washburn [(*Tony Bianco*)], and introducing Ina Balin [(*Mary Valente*)], [Vito Scotti (*Paul*)], [Majel Barrett (*Luisa*)], [Victor Romito, Nick Borgani, Bruno Della Santina, Henry DarBoggia, Felix Romano, Eddie Scarpa (*Bocce players*)], [Florine Carlan (*Bridesmaid*)], [David Fresco, Frank Richards, Steve Conte, John Indrisano (*Hoods*)], [Hugh Lawrence (*Policeman*)], [Hans Moebus (*Undertaker*)], [Grazia Narciso (*Aunt Catherine*)], [Lili Valenty (*Aunt Agnes*)], [Nina Varela (*Aunt Millie*)], [Zolya Talma (*Consuelo*)], [Frank Yaconelli (*Uncle Angelo*)], [Don Orlando (*Cousin Peter*)], [Angela Austin (*Blondie*)], [Rosa Barbato (*Flower woman*)], [Irene Seidner (*Old lady in mourning*)], [Danny Lewis, William Sattaneo (*Men at party*)], [Martine Gari (*Younger daughter*)], [Mary Andre (*Aunt Millie's daughter*)], [John Giovanni (*Uncle Mike*)], [Helen Thayler (*Maid of honor*)], [Saverio Lo Medico (*Best man*)], [Frederic Roberto (*Man at reception*)], [Jacques Gallo (*Usher*)], [Martin Dean (*Young nephew*)], [Barbara Aler, Alix Nagy, Gaylen McClure, Rosemarie Meyers, Francesca Bellini (*Girls at wedding shower*)], [Courtland Shepard (*Guard*)], [Howard Joslin (*Prison guard*)], [Murray Parker (*Waiter*)], [Stewart East (*Bus driver*)], [Hope Monroe (*Luisa, age twelve*)], [Randie Stevens (*Alma, age eight*)], [Steven Jay (*Boy*)], [Kay Colominas (*Girl*)], [Ida Smeraldo], [Diana Roberti], [Oreste Seragnoli], [Agnes Marc].

Domestic, Drama. [*Print viewed*]. After her husband Tony is murdered by gangsters for his role in a bank robbery, Rose Bianco, having emigrated from Italy to marry Tony, recalls their wedding day when she danced gaily with him and told him about the beautiful house she wanted. With Tony now dead, Rose takes a job making imitation flowers. One evening, while wrapping flower stems at home, Rose is interrupted by her nosy neighbor, Giulia Gallo. Giulia invites Rose over to meet Frank Valente, a widowed family friend who has become enamored of Rose and comments that she reminds him of black orchids in her mourning attire. Distraught over her son Ralphie, who was caught robbing parking meters and placed in a state work farm, a bitter and withdrawn Rose rejects the invitation. Frank, whose daughter Mary is preparing to marry and move to Atlantic City, is undeterred and begins speaking to her as she works on her back porch, but Rose ignores him. Later that night, Frank brings her some food from Giulia and asks to accompany her when she goes to visit her son on Sunday. During the visit to the work farm, an official named Harmon warns Rose that if Ralphie attempts to run away again, he will be sent to a reform school. While Frank waits outside, Ralphie makes Rose cry by saying that he hates the work farm and implying that she is responsible for his unhappy situation and his father's death. The following weekend, Frank takes Mary to a surprise wedding shower given by her friend Alma, after which he meets Rose for ice cream. Frank tells Rose that after Mary's birth, his wife became mentally ill, then later died. Next, he mentions that he would like to buy a little house near his business in Somerville and asks her to marry him. To his great surprise and joy, Rose accepts, but Mary, who is worried about her father marrying a gangster's widow, rushes home and confronts him, whereupon Frank assures Mary that nothing can threaten his love for Rose. At the work farm, Frank takes a walk with Ralphie and asks for his mother's hand in marriage. Ralphie is pleased at the news, but when he learns that he will be allowed to live with the couple, he is overjoyed. Although Mary and her fiancé Noble have plans to live in Atlantic City, Mary insists that they move in with

Frank. It was his loneliness, she maintains, that drove him to be with Rose. Exasperated, Noble sends Mary home, where she finds Frank and Rose kissing. In a fit of pique, Mary locks herself in her room for several days, just as her mother had done. Insisting that Frank stay with his daughter, Rose breaks off their engagement. Later, Rose learns that Ralphie has again escaped from the work farm. On Sunday, Frank goes to church to pray for Mary and Ralphie, while Mary decides to stay home to wait for Ralphie's call. During mass, Ralphie enters the church and is surprised to learn that Frank's problems, not Rose's, have ended their engagement. Meanwhile, Rose visits Mary and admits that her greed led to her husband's demise and begs her to allow Frank some happiness. Eventually, Mary relents and invites her to stay for coffee. Soon, they begin cooking breakfast, and when Frank enters the kitchen, he is thrilled to see them getting along. He informs Rose that he returned Ralphie to the state farm and talked Harmon out of sending him to reform school. When Noble enters, the two couples sit down to breakfast. Sometime later, Frank and Rose fetch Ralphie from the work farm, and the three set out for their new home. *Fathers and daughters. Guilt. Italian Americans. Love. Mothers and sons. Churches. Engagements. Family relationships. Flowers. Funerals. Gangsters. Greed. Immigrants. Juvenile delinquents. Loneliness. Mental illness. Murder. Neighbors. Proposals (Marital). Remarriage. Rivalry. Runaways. Self-sacrifice. Showers (Parties). Urban life.*

Note: According to contemporary news item, Joseph Stefano's screenplay was based on his own unproduced television script. According to a pre-release *HR* news item, Jane Rose appeared in the cast, but her participation in the released film has not been confirmed. According to modern sources, director Martin Ritt hoped to enhance the film's realism by asking costume designer Edith Head to design only Sophia Loren's costumes, while the rest of the cast wore their own clothing. Because of limited shooting time in St. Paul's Catholic Church in Los Angeles, modern sources add, Martin Ritt performed a wedding scene and a funeral scene on the same day. Danny Lewis, Jerry Lewis's father, appears in the cast as a party guest. Jack Washburn, a Broadway star, made his only film appearance in *The Black Orchid*, playing the role of "Tony Bianco." Most reviews praised the film, calling it similar to *Marty*. The *Time* reviewer, however, blasted the script: "The Hollywood sociologists have also investigated a specific minority group, the Italian-Americans, and have reached some unshakable conclusions: 1) many of them speak broken English, 2) most of them eat spaghetti, 3) some of them grow up to be gangsters." *The Black Orchid* marked producer Carlo Ponti's first Hollywood picture and the first of many American films he and Sophia Loren, his wife, made together.

Box 2 Feb 1959. *DV* 22 Jan 1959, p. 3. *Exh* 28 Jan 1959, p. 4553. *FD* 22 Jan 1959, p. 6. *Har* 24 Jan 1959, p. 16. *HR* 7 Feb 1958, p. 16. *HR* 21 Mar 1958, p. 12. *HR* 22 Jan 1959, p. 3. *MPHPD* 24 Jan 1959, p. 124. *NYT* 13 Feb 1959, p. 33. *Time* 2 Mar 1959. *Var* 28 Jan 1959, p. 6.

BLACK ROSES (Japanese Americans)

Hayakawa Feature Play Co. *Dist* Robertson-Cole Distributing Corp. 22 May **1921** [©Robertson-Cole Co.; 22 May 1921; LP16700]. Si; b&w. 6 reels, 5,700 ft.

Dir Colin Campbell. *Story and scen* E. Richard Schayer. *Photog* Frank D. Williams. *Art dir* Robert Ellis.

Cast: Sessue Hayakawa (*Yoda*), Myrtle Stedman (*Blanche De Vore*), Tsura Aoki (*Blossom*), Andrew Robson (*Benson Burleigh*), Toyo Fujita (*Wong Fu*), Henry Hebert ("*Monocle*" *Harry*), Harold Holland ("*Detective*" *Cleary*), Carrie Clark Ward (*Bridget*).

Crime, Drama. Yoda, a Japanese architect, takes a job as gardener of the estate of retired criminal Benson Burleigh. Members of Burleigh's former gang—"Monocle" Harry, Blanche De Vore, and Wong Fu—murder Burleigh, frame Yoda for the crime, and kidnap Yoda's wife, Blossom. In prison, a former member of the gang who was betrayed by Blanche aids Yoda's escape and his plot of revenge. Reappearing as a Japanese nobleman, Yoda pretends to be in search of a Japanese girl to impersonate the daughter of a rich merchant and is led to his wife's hiding place. There he entraps the gang, proves that Blanche and Harry were the murderers, and is himself absolved of the charge. *Architects. Disguise. Gangs. Gardeners. Japanese Americans. Murder. Revenge.*

ETR 23 Apr 1921, p. 1868. *FD* 17 Apr 1921. *Var* 13 May 1921, p. 43.

BLACK STAR *see* **FLAMING STAR**

BLACKBOARD JUNGLE (African Americans)

Metro-Goldwyn-Mayer Corp.; controlled by Loew's Inc. *Dist* Loew's Inc. 25 Mar **1955**; New York opening: 20 Mar 1955; Prod: early Nov—late Dec 1954 [©Loew's Inc.; 4 Mar 1955; LP4496]. Sd (Western Electric Sound System); b&w; 1.75. 11 reels, 9,040 ft. 100-102 min. Passed by the National Board of Review. PCA cert no. 17376.

Prod Pandro S. Berman. *Dir* Richard Brooks. *Asst dir* Joel Freeman. *Scr* Richard Brooks. *Dir of photog* Russell Harlan. *Art dir* Cedric Gibbons and Randall Duell. *Film ed* Ferris Webster. *Set dec* Edwin B. Willis and Henry Grace. *Mus adpt* Charles Wolcott. *Rec supv* Wesley C. Miller. [*Sd* Conrad Kahn]. *Makeup* William Tuttle. [*Dial coach* Harold Clifton]. [*Unit mgr* Al Shenberg].

Music: "Invention for Guitar and Trumpet" by Bill Holman, performed by Stan Kenton and His Orchestra, Courtesy of Capitol Records, Inc.; "The Jazz Me Blues" by Tom Delaney, played by Bix Beiderbecke and His Gang, Courtesy of Columbia Records.

Song(s): "Rock Around the Clock," words and music by Max C. Freedman and Jimmy DeKnight, performed by Bill Haley and His Comets, Courtesy of Decca Records, Inc.

Source: Based on the novel *The Blackboard Jungle* by Evan Hunter (New York, 1954).

Cast: Glenn Ford (*Richard Dadier*), Anne Francis (*Anne Dadier*), Louis Calhern (*Jim Murdock*), Margaret Hayes (*Lois Judby Hammond*), John Hoyt (*Mr. Warnecke*), Richard Kiley (*Joshua Y. Edwards*), Emile Meyer (*Mr. Halloran*), Warner Anderson (*Dr. Bradley*), Basil Ruysdael (*Prof. A. R. Kraal*), Sidney Poitier (*Gregory W. Miller*), Vic Morrow (*Artie West*), Dan Terranova (*Belazi*), Rafael Campos (*Pete V. Morales*), Paul Mazursky (*Emmanuel Stoker*), Horace McMahon (*Detective*), Jameel Farah (*Santini*), Danny Dennis (*De Lica*), [David Alpert (*Lou Savoldi*)], [Chris Randall (*Levy*)], [Yoshi Tomita (*Tomita*)], [Gerald Phillips (*Carter*)], [Dorothy Neumann (*Miss Panucci*)], [Joan Danton (*Irate mother*)], [Gary Diamond (*Child*)], [Henny Backus (*Miss Brady*)], [Paul Hoffman (*Mr. Lefkowitz*)], [Tom McKee (*Manners*)], [Robert Foulk (*Mr. Katz*)], [Manuel Paris (*Italian proprietor*)], [Jim Murphy (*Frank Adams*)], [Tommy Ivo (*Crying boy*)], [Peter Miller (*Joey*)], [Benny Burt (*Bartender*)], [Teddy Infuhr (*Needles*)], [Carl Kress (*PeeWee*)], [Tony Garr (*News vendor*)], [Richard Deacon (*Mr. Stanley*)], [Martha Wentworth (*Mrs. Brophy*)], [Isaac Jones (*Black mechanic*)], [Isaac Palacios (*Speranza*)], [Rod Bauman (*Finlay*)], [Jerry Michelsen (*Krauss*)], [John Erman (*Daly*)], [Jerry Wynne (*Murphy*)], [Doyle Baker (*Wilson*)], [James Shumpert (*Davidson*)], [Emil Sitka (*Father*)], [James Drury (*Hospital attendant*)], [Willard Sage (*Radio voice*)], [Roger Blank (*Jerry*)], [Jack Gargan (*Electrician*)], [Dwayne Avery, Gerald King, Willard Wissner, Del Erickson, Albert Shubert, Ben Avila, Ben Sandefure, Boyd Bilbo, Bob Beaudry (*Students*)], [Skip Torgerson, Mickey Little, Steve Roberts (*Boys on bus*)], [Jim Ames], [William Rhinehart], [Nikki Juston].

Social, Drama. [*Print viewed*]. As Richard Dadier, a soft-spoken ex-serviceman, accepts his first teaching job in a tough New York City high school, he asks Mr. Warnecke, the principal, about the discipline problem and is assured that at North Manual High, "there is no discipline problem." The other teachers, particularly the cynical Jim Murdock, who calls the all-male school a "garbage can" and cautions Dadier not to turn his back on the students, do not lessen his anxiety. That evening, Dadier celebrates his new job with his wife Anne, who, although deeply in love with her husband, worries not only that her pregnancy will make her unattractive to him, but that she will miscarry as she had once before. Dadier's first day teaching English is discouraging. The pupils, mostly lower-class juvenile delinquents, ignore his requests and call him "Daddy-o," and when he asks Gregory W. Miller, a bright but alienated black student, to use his leadership abilities to promote cooperation in the classroom, the young man just shakes his head. That afternoon, Lois Judby Hammond, another new teacher who seems attracted to Dadier, is nearly raped by one of the students. Dadier severely beats the boy, and the next day, the students greet him with threatening glares and angry silence. After work, Dadier accompanies Joshua Y. Edwards, a new math teacher who passionately loves jazz and swing, to a bar, where they have a drink too many and bemoan the students' hostility. While cutting through an alley to the bus stop, both teachers are brutally beaten by Dadier's student Artie West and his gang of hoodlums. Anne urges Dadier to leave the school, but he declares, "I've been beaten up, but I'm not beaten." While recuperating, Dadier visits his former professor, who assures him that students do want to learn, but that urban schools need more instructors who care. Dadier returns to school, and when the police question him, he refuses to identify his attackers. In class, Artie calls fellow student Pete Morales a "spic," whereupon Dadier remarks that calling one another names, like "spic, mick, and nigger," can lead to big trouble. Later the principal,

acting on a confidential student complaint, accuses Dadier of bigotry, but Dadier angrily defends himself. Warnecke finally apologizes and puts Dadier in charge of the Christmas play. Soon afterward, West destroys Josh's prized record collection while his class looks on, leading the discouraged math teacher to resign. Meanwhile, Anne begins receiving anonymous letters and phone calls accusing her husband of infidelity. Unaware of Anne's growing suspicion, Dadier concentrates on his students. He convinces Miller and his singing group to perform their version of "Go Down, Moses" in the Christmas play, and he stimulates an animated class discussion by showing a "Jack and the Beanstalk" cartoon in class. Summarizing the discussion, Dadier encourages the young men to consider the real meaning of what they hear and to think for themselves. Miller later tells Dadier that because black people have limited options, he will drop out of school at term's end, but Dadier maintains that blacks can succeed in the modern world and that some teachers do care. At Christmas, Anne, tormented by the letters, gives birth prematurely, and when Dadier learns what has happened, he assumes the students are guilty and decides to resign. Defeated, Dadier claims that, regardless of everything a teacher must endure, even a cook makes a higher salary than an instructor. Murdock, cured of his cynicism by Dadier's dedication, and Anne, admitting that she should not have doubted her husband, encourage Dadier to remain, and he does take heart when the doctor says his baby son is out of danger. Back at school, Dadier orders West to see the principal when the gang leader flagrantly cheats in class. West threatens him with a knife, ordering the other gang members to jump the teacher. To West's surprise, only Belazi obeys his orders. Following a scuffle, Dadier accuses West of having sent the anonymous letters and then drags him and Belazi to Warnecke's office. Later that day, Miller, having heard that Dadier plans to quit, promises to remain in school if Dadier will do the same. *African Americans. High schools. Juvenile delinquents. Marriage. Teachers. Attempted rape. Boys schools. Cynics. Fistfights. Gangs. Infants (Premature). Irish Americans. Italian Americans. Jealousy. Jews. Knife fighting. New York City. Pregnancy. Puerto Ricans. Racism. School life. School superintendents and principals. Spirituals (Songs).*

Note: Before the opening credits are given, a rolling written introduction to the film states: "We, in the United States, are fortunate to have a school system that is a tribute to our communities and to our faith in American youth. Today we are concerned with juvenile delinquency—its causes—and its effects. We are especially concerned when this delinquency boils over into our schools. The scenes and incidents depicted here are fictional. However, we believe that public awareness is a first step toward a remedy for any problem. It is in this spirit and with this faith that *Blackboard Jungle* was produced."

Evan Hunter's novel was serialized beginning with the Oct 1954 issue of *Ladies Home Journal*. According to an Apr 1954 *NYT* news item, M-G-M paid Hunter $95,000 for the rights to his novel. In May 1962, a *HR* news item reported that writers Murray Burnett and Frederick Stephani accused Hunter of plagiarizing their work, but their suit was dismissed. According to a modern source, director Richard Brooks was originally hired to direct M-G-M's *Ben Hur* and William Wyler to direct *Blackboard Jungle*. Brooks convinced Wyler to switch assignments with him, and completed *Blackboard Jungle* on a low budget and one-month shooting schedule. In a 1983 *NYT* interview, Brooks recalled that M-G-M wanted one of their contract players, either Mickey Rooney or Robert Taylor, to play schoolteacher "Mr. Dadier." Brooks insisted upon casting new, unknown faces, and as a result, hired unpolished actors with little camera experience, thus infusing a raw realism into their performances. Among the actors making their screen debut in this picture were Vic Morrow, Rafael Campos, Dan Terrnaova, Danny Dennis and Jameel Farah, who later changed his name to Jamie Farr. Although the studio wanted the film shot in color, Brooks insisted upon black and white because he feared that "color would beautify everything," according to the interview.

Upon its release, the film was greeted by controversy. According to an Apr 1955 *DV* news item, the school authorities of New Brunswick, NJ, objected to the depiction of school conditions in the film. As a result, the theater circuit was forced to add a disclaimer stating: "To our patrons, the school and situations you have just seen are NOT to be found in this area. We should all be proud of the facilities provided OUR youth by the Public School of New Brunswick..." A Jun 1955 news item in *Var* reported that the film was banned in Atlanta because it was deemed "immoral, obscene, licentious and will adversely affect the peace, health, morals and good order of the city." Claire Boothe Luce, at the time the U.S. Ambassador to Italy, prevented the film's screening at the Venice Film Festival by threatening to walk out if it was shown. Luce claimed that "if she attended a performance of the film, she would be giving ammunition to Italian Communist and anti-U.S. propaganda." The picture's soundtrack also created a stir. According to Brooks's *NYT* interview, a Boston theater ran the first reel in silence for fear that the rock and roll music on the soundtrack would over-stimulate the audience. "Rock Around the Clock," the song played beneath the film's credits, was one of the top ten songs of the year and played an important part in expanding the rock and roll market. The film was nominated for the following Academy Awards: Best Screenplay, Best Film Editing, Best Cinematography (Black and White) and Best Art Direction.

AmCin Jun 1955, pp. 334-35, 358-59. *Box* 5 Mar 1955. *DV* 28 Feb 1955, p. 3. *DV* 20 Apr 1955. *DV* 21 Apr 1955. *DV* 29 Aug 1955. *DV* 22 Sep 1955. *FD* 28 Feb 1955, p. 6. *HR* 12 Nov 1954, p. 6. *HR* 17 Dec 1954, p. 8. *HR* 28 Feb 1955, p. 3. *HR* 4 May 1962. *MPHPD* 5 Mar 1955, p. 345. *NYT* 13 Apr 1954. *NYT* 21 Mar 1955. *NYT* 15 Jan 1983. *Var* 2 Mar 1955, p. 8. *Var* 8 Jun 1955.

BLARNEY (Irish Americans)

Metro-Goldwyn-Mayer Corp.; controlled by Loew's Inc. *Dist* Metro-Goldwyn-Mayer Distributing Corp. 26 Sep **1926** [©Metro-Goldwyn-Mayer Corp.; 23 Sep 1926; LP23165]. Si; b&w. 6 reels, 6,055 ft.

Dir Marcel De Sano. *Adpt* Albert Lewin and Marcel De Sano. *Titles* Joe Farnham. *Photog* Ben Reynolds. *Film ed* Lloyd Nosler. *Settings* Cedric Gibbons and Sidney Ullman. *Ward* André-ani.

Source: Based on the short story "In Praise of John Carabine" by Brian Oswald Donn-Byrne in *The Saturday Evening Post* (9 May 1925).

Cast: Renée Adorée (*Peggy Nolan*), Ralph Graves (*James Carabine*), Paulette Duval (*Marcolina*), Malcolm Waite (*Blanco Johnson*), Margaret Seddon (*Peggy's aunt*).

Melodrama. James Carabine comes to New York from Ireland, his fare paid by Peggy Nolan, a girl from his hometown who harbors an affection for the fighting Irishman. However, he falls for Marcolina, who leaves with him when her husband loses a match as the result of scheming by friends of Blanco Johnson. Then Peggy takes him in and, with the aid of an Irish relative, brings him back to form, enabling him to get even with Johnson in a knockout fight. Marcolina is united with Johnson and Carabine with Peggy. *Boxers. Flattery. Immigrants. Irish Americans. New York City. Vamps.*

FD 10 Oct 1926. *Var* 20 Oct 1926, p. 62.

BLAZE O' GLORY (*foreign version*) see **SOMBRAS DE GLORIA**

BLAZING ARROWS (Native Ameicans)

Doubleday Productions. *Dist* Western Pictures Exploitation Co. **1922**; New York premiere: 18 Oct 1922. Si; b&w. 5 reels.

Supv Charles W. Mack. *Dir* Henry McCarty. *Story and scen* Henry McCarty.

Cast: Lester Cuneo (*Sky Fire*), Francelia Billington (*Martha Randolph*), Clark Comstock (*Gray Eagle*), Laura Howard (*Mocking Bird*), Lafayette McKee (*Elias Thornby*), Lew Meehan (*Bart McDermott*), Jim O'Neill (*Scarface*).

Western. Sky Fire, a student at Columbia, falls in love with Martha Randolph, but their engagement is broken when a disappointed suitor reveals Sky Fire's Indian identity. The hero returns west, only to have another run-in with the villain, who murders Martha's guardian. Martha seeks Sky Fire's protection, which leads to a long chase and a general cleanup of numerous scoundrels. Finally, Sky Fire learns that he is really a white man who was adopted and brought up by an Indian. *Columbia University. Indians of North America. Murder. Racism. Students.*

Note: The working title of this film was *Skyfire*.

MPW 4 Nov 1922. *Var* 27 Oct 1922, p. 62.

BLIND ALLEYS (Latino)

Famous Players-Lasky Corp. *Dist* Paramount Pictures. 12 Mar **1927**; New York showing: 26 Feb 1927 [©Famous Players-Lasky Corp.; 12 Mar 1927; LP23760]. Si; b&w. 6 reels, 5,597 ft.

Pres Adolph Zukor and Jesse L. Lasky. *Assoc prod* William Le Baron. *Dir* Frank Tuttle. *Scr* Emmet Crozier. *Story* Owen Davis. *Photog* Alvin Wyckoff.

Cast: Thomas Meighan (*Capt. Dan Kirby*), Evelyn Brent (*Sally Ray*), Greta Nissen (*María d'Álvarez Kirby*), Hugh Miller (*Julio Lachados*), Thomas Chalmers (*Dr. Webster*), Tammany Young (*Gang leader*).

Melodrama. Captain Dan Kirby of the merchant marine arrives in New York with his Cuban bride, María. Leaving his hotel to buy flowers, Dan forgets his billfold but meets Julio Lachados, a former admirer of María's. As Dan crosses the street, he is knocked unconscious by an automobile, and the owner, Dr. Webster, has him taken to a private hospital. Failing to find her husband and learning that an unidentified man has been hospitalized, María becomes innocently involved with two jewel thieves, who kidnap her. Dan, regaining consciousness, leaves the hospital and is nursed by Sally Ray. Freed from her captors, María turns to Julio for help and learns of Dan's relationship with Sally, but Dan perceives Sally's duplicity and is reunited with his bride. *Cuban Americans. Kidnapping. Merchant marine. New York City. Sea captains. Thieves.*

MPW 15 Mar 1927. *NYT* 1 Mar 1927, p. 31. *Var* 2 Mar 1927, p. 16.

BLIND JUSTICE see **THE TELL-TALE STEP**

BLOCK BUSTERS (French Americans)

Banner Productions. *Dist* Monogram Pictures Corp. 16 Sep **1944**; Prod: mid Dec—late Dec 1943 [©Monogram Pictures Corp.; 22 Jul 1944; LP12749]. Sd; b&w. 5,432 ft. 60 min. PCA cert no. 9913.

Series: The East Side Kids.

Prod Sam Katzman and Jack Dietz. *Assoc prod* Barney Sarecky. *Dir* Wallace Fox. *Asst dir* Arthur Hammond. *Orig story and scr* Houston Branch. *Photog* Marcel LePicard. *Film ed* Carl Pierson. *Set des* David Milton. *Mus dir* Edward Kay. *Sd eng* Glen Glenn. [*Sd rec* Harold McNiff].

Cast: The East Side Kids: LEO GORCEY (*Muggs* [*McGuiness*]), HUNTZ HALL (*Glimpy*), GABRIEL DELL (*Skinny*), BILLY BENEDICT (*Butch*), with Frederick Pressel (*Jean*), Jimmy Strand (*Danny*), Bill Chaney (*Tobey* [*Dunn*]), Roberta Smith (*Jinx*), Noah Beery (*Judge*), Harry Langdon (*Higgins*), Minerva Urecal (*Amelia* [*Norton*]), Kay Marvis (*Irma* [*Treadwell*]), Tom Herbert (*Meyer*), Bernard Gorcey (*Lippman*), Jimmie Noone and his orchestra, with The Ashburns, [Jack Gilman (*Batter*)], [Charles Murray, Jr. (*Umpire*)].

Youth, Drama. [*Print viewed*]. After an afternoon of playing baseball, Muggs McGinnis and his East Side Kids gang arrive at the door of their clubhouse, where a man named Higgins is removing their "East Side Club" sign. Higgins explains that the owner of the place plans to rent it to some "respectable" tenants. When Muggs learns that the new tenants are due to examine the place at noon the following day, he plans to frighten them away by picking a fight with Butch and the Five Pointers, a rival gang. The next day, Glimpy and Skinny, two East Side Kids, scribble a challenge to the Five Pointers on the sidewalk. When Butch and his gang read the message, "The East Siders dare you to fight," they seek out their challengers. Meanwhile, Muggs and the gang see Higgins supervising the delivery of some window boxes that he ordered to replace the weather-beaten pots that are lining the street. Pretending to be helpful, the gang offers to dispose of the old pots, but instead, stack them against a nearby wall. Soon, the prospective tenants, an elderly woman named Amelia Norton and her French-born grandson Jean arrive, and Higgins greets them. Just then, Butch and his gang show up and take the bait, hurling the empty pots at Muggs and his gang, while a shocked Amelia looks on. When Jean critiques Muggs's fighting style, Muggs begins to brawl with him. After they are both arrested, the judge tells Muggs that he will hold each one accountable for the other's behavior. Later, Jean goes to the clubhouse to make sure that Muggs is staying out of trouble, and the gang teaches him some American games. Afterward, Jean invites the gang over for tea, and they meet snobby Irma Treadwell and her mother Virginia. When Muggs and Glimpy see a black sedan pick up Jean, who is dressed like Count Dracula, they decide to follow him. The car takes Jean to a costume party at a chic club, where Muggs wins best costume for being dressed as a Bowery tough. Meanwhile Tobey Dunn, an ailing member of Muggs's baseball team, is told by his doctor that a stay in the country will cure him, but unfortunately, Tobey's family cannot afford the trip. Later, one of Muggs's friends, Danny, sees his girl friend Jinx dancing with Jean at a party, so the gang decides to crash it. When Glimpy tells Danny that he saw Jinx riding on the back of Jean's bicycle, Danny tries to fight with his rival, but Muggs intervenes. The gang then goes to the field to play baseball, and Jean quickly learns the game. At the clubhouse, Amelia thanks the gang for allowing Jean to play with them. During the team's next game, Lippman, the team's sponsor, tells the gang that if they win, he will send them all to summer camp in the Catskill Mountains. With the bases loaded, Jean hits a home run and wins the game, and Tobey is awarded his much-needed trip to the country. *Baseball. Class distinction. French Americans. Gangs. New York City–East Side. Arrests. Assimilation (Sociology). Baseball–Umpires. Bicycles. Clubhouses. Disease. Fights. Games. Judges. New York City. Nightclubs. Parties. Physicians. Rivalry. Romantic rivalry. Set-ups. Tea.*

Note: Although a *HR* news item places Betty Sinclair in the cast, her participation in the released film has not been confirmed. A 10 1943 Dec *HR* production chart lists Lukas Tello (a pseudonym for Lou Costello) as director, but it is doubtful that he worked on this film. For additional information on the series, please consult the Series Index and see the entries for *Crime School* and *Little Tough Guy* in *AFI Catalog of Feature Films, 1931-40*; F3.0873 and F3.2534.

Box 19 Aug 1944. DV 27 Sep 1944, p. 3. FD 15 Aug 1944, p. 6. HR 10 Dec 1943, p. 12. HR 16 Dec 1943, p. 11. HR 24 Dec 1943, p. 8. HR 27 Sep 1944, p. 3. MPHPD 22 Jul 1944, p. 2007. MPHPD 19 Aug 1944, p. 2054. Var 16 Aug 1944, p. 16.

BLOCK PARTY see **VERBENA TRÁGICA**

BLONDE COUNTESS see **RENDEZVOUS**

BLOOD ARROW (Native Americans, Blackfoot, Siksika)

Regal Films, Inc.; An Emirau Production. *Dist* Twentieth Century-Fox Film Corp. Sep **1958**; Prod: mid-Aug—late Aug 1957 [©Twentieth Century-Fox Film Corp.; 29 Dec 1957; LP12720]. Sd (Westrex Recording System); b&w; Regalscope. 8 reels, 6,712 ft. 73-76 min. PCA cert no. 18805.

Exec prod Charles Marquis Warren. *Prod* Robert Stabler. *Dir* Charles Marquis Warren. *Asst dir* Nathan R. Barrager. *Wrt* Fred Freiberger. *Dir of photog* Fleet Southcott. *Spec photog eff* Jack Rabin and Louis DeWitt. *Art dir* James W. Sullivan. *Supv ed* Fred W. Berger. *Ed* Michael Luciano. *Set dec* Raymond Boltz, Jr. *Ward* Joseph Dimmitt and Vou Lee Giokaris. *Mus comp and cond by* Raoul Kraushaar. *Sd* Hugh McDowell. *Sd facilities* Roderick Sound, Inc. *Makeup* Jack Dusick. *Prod mgr* Nathan R. Barrager. *Scr supv* Mary Chaffee. *Prop master* Ted Cooper.

Cast: Scott Brady [(*Dan Kree*)], Paul Richards [(*Brill*)], Phyllis Coates [(*Bess Johnson*)], Don Haggerty [(*Gabe*)], Diana Darrin [(*Lennie*)], Jeanne Bates [(*Aimee*)], Rocky Shahan [(*Taslatch*)], John Dierkes [(*Ez*)], Richard Gilden [(*Little Otter*)], Patrick O'Moore [(*McKenzie*)], Desmond Slattery [(*Ceppi*)], Bill McGraw [(*Norm*)].

Western. [*Print viewed*]. When Ceppi's Overland freight from St. Louis arrives at McKenzie's trading post in Wyoming, McKenzie refuses to give Bess Johnson, a Mormon who arrived two weeks earlier, the medicine Ceppi has brought to fight an epidemic of smallpox at her valley settlement three days away. McKenzie explains that Little Otter, the new chief of the Blackfeet, has threatened to burn the post down if he lets her have the medicine. Unlike the old chief, Bear Paw, Little Otter wants to wipe out all the whites in his territory, and has refused to allow hunting or trapping. To escort her to the valley, Bess enlists the aid of gunfighter Dan Kree, who has just arrived with the freighters on his way to Oregon, hoping to get away from people. With them go Taslatch, an Indian whose tongue has been cut out by the Blackfeet for telling the Mormons about the valley; Gabe, a trapper trying to locate his partner Ez; and Brill, a gambler who is attracted to Bess and believes that the Mormons have a secret gold mine in the valley. At moonrise, they make off with the medicine. After riding all night, they set up camp while Gabe goes to look for signs of Ez. Gabe returns with ominous news that he has found an animal in Ez's trap, dead for three or four days, but no sign of Ez. As they sleep, Dan, despite Bess's entreaties of friendship, refuses to sleep near the group, saying he doesn't like people around when his eyes are closed. The next day, Brill tries to talk Dan into joining him in his scheme to get the Mormons' mine, but Dan rebuffs him, saying he wouldn't trust him. After they move on, Little Otter and his people find the warm stones of the group's campfire. When the group is one day away from the valley, the Blackfeet pass nearby, and the party hides behind rocks. Dan is attacked by a poisonous snake, and Bess cuts the wound from his arm and sucks out the poison. When she sees a scar on the side of his chest, he explains that he got it from his own brother, who shot him in the back during an argument. After he killed his brother, his own wife took a shot at him. He says he hasn't trusted anyone since. At night, Bess relates that after the Mormons settled in the valley, the Blackfeet tried to burn them out, but the wind changed and caught the Blackfeet on the valley floor. They escaped, but Bear Paw, sure that the spirits were angry, made a treaty with the Mormons and declared that the Blackfeet would not enter the valley again. When Dan walks away after Bess entreats him to stay near, Brill tries to talk her into taking the gold from the valley and going with him to New Orleans. When he grabs her, Taslatch intercedes, and after Bess has Taslatch release him, Brill is about to fire at the Indian when Dan stops him. She tries to thank Dan, but he says he acted in his own interest, as a shot would bring the Blackfeet. They soon come upon Ez, wandering about in hysterics, his eyes burned out by Little Otter and his people, who took his pelts and said no white eyes shall look on Blackfeet land again. When Brill suggests they give Gabe and Ez enough food to return to McKenzie's, Dan objects that alone they would never make it past Little Otter. Although Gabe volunteers to go back, knowing of Bess's concern to

return soon with the medicine, she painfully decides to wait until nightfall and try to make it to the valley together. As she sobs, Dan comforts her. Bess tells him her belief that every human being is responsible for every other human being, and says that the twenty families waiting for the medicine would rather lose it than turn their backs on a man in need, even if it meant their lives. After Taslatch is shot and killed with an arrow, a battle ensues. Dan rescues Bess, and following a hand-to-hand fight, the Indians retreat. They begin to chant in the distance, asking help from the spirits. As they wait, Dan reveals to Bess that his wife had their marriage set aside and has taken up with a riverboat owner. Little Otter comes to talk and offers them safe passage if they will give up the medicine. Although Brill wants to make the deal, Dan proposes they stall until after nightfall. Little Otter is told that they have to ask their own spirits' advice after the full moon. Because the Blackfeet never make a move without consulting spirits, Little Otter agrees. At night, the group slips away, but the next day as they near the last mountain before the valley, Little Otter and his people block their path and demand the medicine. The whites take cover in the rocks, and during the subsequent battle, Ez goes into hysterics, and when Gabe goes to help, Little Otter shoots them both. Dan then shoots Little Otter. When the other Indians come to take their chief's body away, Dan prevents Brill from shooting them. Brill now asks Bess to point out the mine. She reveals that it is near Tombstone and that she and her people worked it and asked to be paid in nuggets. Exasperated, Brill plans to sell the medicine to McKenzie or the Blackfeet and starts off with it. Bess shoots a rifle, but Dan deflects the shot. Dan then traps Brill from behind and shoots him as he draws. As Bess and Dan ride toward the valley, she asks him if he'll stay, and he says maybe he will. *Cynics. Gunfighters. Medicine. Mormons. Personality change. Religiosity. Siksika Indians. Tribal chiefs. Blindness. Freight lines. Gamblers. Gold mines. Indians of North America. Mutes. Partnership. Romance. Smallpox. Snake bites. Trading posts. Trappers. Treaties. Wyoming.*

Note: *MPH* noted that the film's success might be tied to the popularity of Scott Brady, Paul Richards and Don Haggerty, who all had recent starring assignments on major network television productions, and that Phyllis Coates was also featured on television. *Exb*, however, complained, "The value of such western entertainment [as this] has been diminished by the fact that entertainment equally as good is available free on television."

Box 5 May 1958. DV 24 Apr 1958, p. 3. Exb 19 Feb 1958, p. 4439. FD 23 May 1958, p. 7. Har 3 May 1958, p. 71. HR 16 Aug 1957, p. 11. HR 30 Aug 1957, p. 13. HR 24 Apr 1958, p. 3. MPD 11 Apr 1958. MPHPD 12 Apr 1958, p. 792. Var 7 May 1958, p. 23.

BLOOD BROTHERS see **BROKEN ARROW**

THE BLOOD OF JESUS (African Americans)

Amegro Films. *Dist* Sack Amusement Enterprises. **1941?**. Sd; b&w. Length undetermined.

Dir Spencer Williams. *Wrt* Spencer Williams. *Cine* Jack Whitman. *Sd rec* R. E. Byers.

Song(s): "Good News!" "Go Down, Moses," "Amazing Grace," "Were You There When They Crucified My Lord?" "Swing Low, Sweet Chariot," "I've Heard of a City Called Heaven," "Run, Child, Run," "All God's Children Got Shoes," "On Jordan's Stormy Banks I Stand," spirituals; "Weary Blues," composer undetermined.

Cast: CATHRYN CAVINESS [(*Sister Martha Ann Jackson*)], SPENCER WILLIAMS [(*Ras Jackson*)], Juanita Riley (*Sister Jenkins*), Reather Hardeman (*Sister Ellerby*), Rogenia Goldthwaite (*The angel*), Jas. B. Jones (*Satan*), Frank H. McClennan (*Judas Green*), Eddie DeBase (*Rufus Brown*), Alva Fuller (*Luke Willows*), Rev. R. L. Robertson and The Heavenly Choir.

African American, Fantasy, Religious, Drama, with songs. [*Print viewed*]. At the riverside baptism of Sister Martha Ann Jackson, two members of a Southern black church congregation, Sister Ellerby and Sister Jenkins, discuss Martha's three-month-old marriage to the godless Ras Jackson and agree that, because of his wayward behavior, she is not ready for religion. After the baptism, Sister Jenkins escorts Martha home and advises her to get some rest. As she is leaving, Sister Jenkins encounters Ras, who missed the baptism and is returning home from a hunting trip. When Ras's wife presses him with questions about his hunting trip and the hog he captured, he confesses that it was a neighbor's hog that he killed. Ras begrudgingly joins his wife in prayer and then sets down his rifle, which falls to the ground and fires a bullet. The bullet strikes Martha, passes through her and hits a picture of Jesus Christ. On her deathbed, Martha is visited by a heavenly angel, who takes her spirit to a mystical

graveyard where those whose lives have been cut short by the sins of others walk in silence. The angel tells Martha that this is not the place for her yet, and sends her on a journey down the highway of life to the crossroads of life and death. No sooner does the angel warn Martha to beware of hypocrites and false prophets, than she is tempted by Judas Green, Satan's emissary, who dresses her in fancy clothes and takes her to a nightclub in the city. While Martha is entertained by an acrobat and a jazz singer, Judas makes arrangements with sleazy roadhouse operator Rufus Brown to hire her as one of his "girls." Martha is tempted with the promise of abundant wealth for little work, but she changes her mind just before she is to begin her job. Claiming that he invested money in her clothing, Brown ignores her pleas and insists that she go to work immediately. Martha eventually takes the advice of the angel and flees the roadhouse, only to be chased by a customer who mistakes her for the escort who picked his pocket. The man and his friends chase Martha to the crossroads of eternal life and death, where Satan and a jazz band assembled on the back of a flatbed truck are waiting for her. Martha collapses at the crossroads but is saved by the angel, who sends away the men who have been chasing her. As the crossroads sign lands on a crucifix and drops of Jesus Christ's blood land on Martha's forehead, she is revived and returned to life. Ras is amazed at Martha's miraculous recovery, and they fall into an embrace under the watchful eye of the angel. *Accidental death. Death and dying. The Devil. Religion. Revivification. Acrobats. Angels. Baptism. Cemeteries. Chases. Churches. Crucifixes. Heaven. Jazz music. Jesus Christ. Ne'er-do-wells. Nightclubs. Pickpockets. Regeneration. Snakes.*

Note: The viewed print of the film bore the title *The Blood of Jesus*, but information contained in the file on the film in the MPAA/PCA Collection at the AMPAS Library indicates that in 1941 a censored version, running 57 minutes, was exhibited in New York State under the title *The Glory Road*. It has not been determined when the title of the film was changed. Modern sources list the running time of the film at 68 minutes, and the length at 6,065 feet; however, the print viewed ran only 57 minutes. Modern sources also note that as a result of the film's success, producer Alfred Sack offered director Spencer Williams a ten-year contract with his company to produce eight more films.

BLOSSOM TIME (Chinese language, Chinese Americans)
Grandview Film Company. 1934. Sd; b&w. Length undetermined. Chinese language.
Dir Joseph Sunn.
Cast: Sin Lang Dew (*Chin Quai Fong, the hero*), Wu Dip Ying (*Mui Far Ying, the heroine*), Lim Yah On (*Wong Ting, the villain*), Yong Sin Lon (*Wong Lai Ying, the cabaret singer*), Jow Sil Ying (*Mother*), Lee (*Innkeeper*), Wong Gum (*Cigarette girl*), Jung Quai Lung (*Cabaret owner*), Yip Quon Ping (*Theatre manager*).
Melodrama, Musical. [*Not viewed*]. Lom Won and Fei Ying, members of a Chinese opera troupe, take some off to tour California and look at wild flowers. As they stroll in the countryside near San Francisco, Ying notices the beautiful voice of Chin Quai Fong, a farmer, as he sings a traditional Chinese song. Fong's mother offers the touring artists a cup of tea, but Wong, anxious and jealous of Ying's attention to Fong, insists that they return to San Francisco. Ying promises to leave Fong and his mother tickets for her upcoming performance in the city. Later, during an intermission of the performance, Fong visits Ying, but Wong enters the dressing room and intimidates him. Fong is about to leave, but Ying reappears and tells him her wish that he audition for the show. Fong's only worry is his mother, but Ying convinces the kindly matriarch that Fong is a great talent and that she would support the family in the event that he failed on the stage. Chin, the director of the show, is hesitant to hire Fong, but after hearing his lovely singing voice and witnessing the reaction of female members of the audience to Fong's handsome face, he offers Fong a six-month contract. Soon Fong and Ying begin to fall in love, and Wong grows jealous of Fong for stealing his fame and the woman he loves. One night, at a restaurant, Spanish caberet performer Yong Sho Lum, whom Wong has hired to rupture the relationship between Fong and Ying, flirts with Fong, and when Ying goes to take a phone call from Wong, Lum slips Fong her phone number. A few days later, Fong tells Ying that he is sick and then goes to Lum's apartment. Worried about Fong, Ying goes to his home, finds the dancer's note, then follows Fong to his *rendez-vous*. Furious and hurt, Ying leaves Fong and in her sorrow begins to spend more time with Wong, fixing his stage makeup as she once did for Fong. Meanwhile, Fong's performances grow sloppy, and he spends so much time with Lum that he frequently arrives late to the theater. On

one such occasion, Chin fires Fong, who then seeks comfort with Lum. Lum, meanwhile, has gone to see Wong to demand her payment for ruining Fong and Ying's love affair, but Wong slaps her and laughs in her face and the teary-eyed dancer returns to Fong and tells him of Wong's treachery. Fong goes to see Wong, punches him in the face, then goes to another town, where he struggles to find work. Meanwhile, Fong's mother and niece have not heard from him, and Ying sends them money for their support. One day, as they drive through a town near San Francisco, Ying and Wong get a flat tire. While taking a walk they hear the voice of Fong singing in a Chinese restaurant. Ying forgives Fong, and Wong storms out. Then Ying tells Fong that together they will restore his career and the pair go for a reunion with Fong's overjoyed mother. *Actors and actresses. Chinese Americans. Deception. Opera. Romantic rivalry. San Francisco (CA). Singers. Cabarets. Chinese restaurants. City-country contrast. Dancers. Farmers. Jealousy. Mothers and sons. Theatrical directors.*

Note: The Mandarin transliteration of the title is "Guh Lu Chin Chow," and the Cantonese transliteration is "Go Lui Qing Qiu." The above credits and plot summary are based on a translated dialogue continuity deposited with the NYSA. Although the film included several songs, none of the titles or composers could be verified. Correspondence deposited with the cutting continuity indicates that the Grandview Film Company was located in San Francisco, and that the film was approved for exhibition in New York state in May 1934. According to a 1947 article in *East Wind*, director Joseph Sunn, also known as Joseph Sunn Jue, organized the company in San Francisco in 1933. Following this film, the company opened a studio in Kowloon, Kwangtung, where they made over ninety films until 1939, when production was halted because of the war. The company returned to San Francisco at that time and resumed production there during the war.

East Wind Dec 1947, pp. 18-20.

BLUE HORIZONS *see* **THE FAR HORIZONS**

THE BLUE LADY *see* **ANGEL IN EXILE**

LE BLUFFEUR (French language)
Warner Bros. Pictures, Inc. *Dist* Warner Bros. Pictures, Inc.; The Vitaphone Corp. 1932. Sd; b&w. Length undetermined. French language.
Prod Henry Blanke. *Dir* Andre Luget. *Adpt and dial* Andre Luget.
Source: Based on the play *Hot Money* by Aben Kandel (New York, 7 Nov 1931).
Cast: Jeannette Freney (*Elaine*), Lucienne Radisse (*Francine*), Andre Luget (*Evans*), Émile Chautard (*Brown*), Turben Mayer (*Ginsberg*), Jacques Jou-Jerville (*Mike*), Andre Cheron (*Clifford Gray*), Christian Rub (*L'inventeur*), George Renavent (*Banks*), Jean Delmour, Pierre De Ramey, Carrie Daumery, Alice Ardelle.
Comedy. [*Not viewed*]. [The following plot summary is based on the English-language version of this film, *High Pressure*; character names refer to that version. For further information regarding the English-language version, please see the note below and the entry for *High Pressure* in the *AFI Catalog of Feature Films, 1931-40*.] With the help of Mike Donoghey, wealthy Mr. Ginsberg searches for promoter Gar Evans. Ginsberg owns a process for making rubber out of sewage, and Donoghey has convinced him that Gar is the best promoter in the world. After Gar sobers up, he agrees to take on the project. He arranges a good deal on a prestigious building for company headquarters, hires an impressive looking man to act as the company president and starts to sell stock. The only thing missing is the presence of Gar's girl friend, Francine Dell. Although he considers her his good luck charm, she is fed up with his schemes and plans to marry a wealthy South American. Eventually, she succumbs to Gar's entreaties and signs on as his secretary. While Gar holds inspirational meetings for salesmen, the company stock sells rapidly and everything looks good until the rubber industry sends an investigator. Gar must prove that they can really make rubber from sewage, but the inventor of the process is missing. In the meantime, to prove that he really loves Francine, Gar turns over his shares in the company to her. Ginsberg finds the inventor, who is not only a fake, but crazy as well. Gar refuses to run out on the company, however, and plans to return at least a portion of the invested money until a lawyer from the rubber company offers to buy them out. In order to sell, Gar must get the stock certificate back from Francine, who is leaving town to marry her South American. He finds her in time and obtains the certificate. Then he begs her not to leave. She agrees to marry him, but as they leave, Donoghey proposes another new deal. At first Gar resists, but as Francine listens resignedly, he starts to plan his new campaign. *Confidence men. Fraud. Promoters. Stocks.*

Chemical formulas. Drunkenness. Insanity. Inventions. Lawyers. Rubber. Salesmen. Secretaries. Steam rooms.

Note: The play *High Pressure* was also the basis for the 1936 Warner Bros. film *Hot Money* (see *AFI Catalog of Feature Films, 1931-40*; F3.1998). For information on the English-language version, *High Pressure*, which was directed by Mervyn LeRoy and starred William Powell and Evelyn Brent, please see the entry for that film in the *AFI Catalog of Feature Films, 1931-40*; F3.1909.

BOARDING HOUSE BLUES (African Americans)

All American News, Inc. *Dist* State Rights. **1948?**. Sd (RCA Sound System); b&w. 9 reels, 7,790 ft. 87 min.

Prod E. M. Glucksman. *Dir* Josh Binney. *Asst dir* Salvatore Scappa, Jr. *Orig story* Hal Seeger. *Dir of photog* Sid Zucker. *Cam* Frank La Follette and George Stoetzel. *Art dir* Sam Corso. [*Mus arr* Henry B. Glover]. *Sd eng* Harold Vivian. *Makeup artist* Doc Liszt.

Song(s): "I Love You, Yes I Do," words and music by Sally Nix and Henry B. Glover; "You Never Know If an Apple Is Ripe Before You Bite It," "Throw It Outta Your Mind," "It Ain't Like That," "I Will Hold You in My Arms Again Tonight," and "Let It Roll," composers undetermined.

Cast: Dusty Fletcher (*Dusty*), Jackie Mabley (*Mom* [*s*]), John Mason & Co. (*Boarders*), John D. Lee, Jr. (*Stanley*), Marcellus Wilson (*Jerry* [*Lewis*]), Marie Cooke (*Lila* [*Foster*]), Emory Richardson (*Simon*), Harold Cromer (*Moofty*), Sid Easton (*Boo Boo*), Freddie Robinson (*Freddie*), Augustus Smith (*Norman Norman*), Edgar Martin (*Joe*), John Riano (*Steggy*), Lucky Millinder and his Band, Una Mae Carlisle, Bull Moose Jackson, Berry Brothers, Lewis and White, Anistine Allen, Paul Breckenridge, Stump & Stumpy, Lee Norman Trio, "Crip" Heard (*Specialty acts*), [Vivian Harris].

African American, Show business, Comedy-drama, with songs. [*Print viewed*]. When Dusty, an irresponsible tenant at Moms's theatrical boardinghouse, tries to sneak Steggy, a man in an ape suit, into his room, Moms scolds him and reminds him to pay his overdue rent. Later, after singer Lila Foster arrives looking for a room, Boo Boo, an alcoholic tenant, enters Dusty's room to drink his gin, is startled by the apeman and runs off. When Moms is told that she has until midnight to pay the money she owes the landlord, her boarders, including Lila, who has taken over the room vacated by Boo Boo, band together and decide to pool their money. They soon realize that they do not have enough money, but the landlord sees the pretty Lila and offers to postpone Moms's debt if Lila consents to marry him. He then gives Lila twenty-four hours to make a decision. Moms and the boarders pin their hopes on Lila to save them, but she is in love with singer and fellow boarder Jerry Lewis. Lila and Jerry try to save Moms's boardinghouse by putting on a show with their fellow boarders, however, Lila's producer friend, Norman Norman, has been spooked out of show business by a fortune-teller's warning. Desperate to keep the show from being canceled, Jerry and Lila arrange a second fortune reading, with Moms impersonating a fortune-teller, and succeed in dispelling Norman's fears. The show is a great success, and when the landlord returns, Moms pays him with the money her boarders have earned. With the boardinghouse no longer threatened, Lila and Joe become engaged, and Moms resumes her harassment of Dusty. *African Americans. Boardinghouse mistresses. Boardinghouses. Debt. Landlords. Romance. Singers. Alcoholics. Amputees. Costumes. Dancers. Engagements. Fortune-tellers. Irresponsibility. Rabbits. Stuttering. Theatrical producers.*

Note: The viewed print of this film contained a 1948 copyright statement for All American News, Inc., but the film was not in the copyright registry. Although billed in the onscreen credits as "Mom," Jackie Mabley's character is referred to as "Moms" in the film, and she was known throughout her career as Jackie "Moms" Mabley. No information regarding the film's release date was found, but the picture was approved for exhibition in New York in 1948, and was subsequently reviewed in *Exh* on 8 Jun 1949. "Crip" Heard, who performs in the film, was a one-legged, one-armed dancer.

Exh 8 Jun 1949, p. 2633.

BODY AND SOUL (African Americans)

Micheaux Film Corp. **1925**; Harlem, NY opening: 15 Nov 1925. Si; b&w. 9 reels.

[*Dir* Oscar Micheaux].

Cast: Paul Robeson (*The Rt. Reverend Isiaah Jenkins alias "Jeremiah the Deliverer" still posing as a man of God* [*/Sylvester*]), Marshall Rodgers (*The Negro in Business*), Lawrence Chenault (*Yellow-Curley Hinds of Atlanta*), Chester A. Alexander (*Deacon Simpkins*), Walter Conick (*Brother Amos*), Lillian Johnson (*Sis Ca'line*), Madame Robinson (*Sis Lucy, District Grand Matron of the*

Household of Ruth), [Julia Theresa Russell], [Tom Fletcher], [Mercedes Gilbert].

African American, Melodrama. [*Print viewed*]. In Tatesville, Georgia, a prisoner being transported to the North for extradition to Britain, escapes and takes on the disguise of the Rt. Reverend Isiaah T. Jenkins. With his fiery sermons, Pastor Jenkins gains many followers in the small town, in particular, Sister Martha Jane, the hard-working mother of a young daughter named Isabelle. Jenkins is joined in Tatesville by Yellow-Curley Hinds, another criminal whom he knew in jail, and together they plan to swindle Jenkins' congregation by selling liquor at inflated prices and taking the parish's contributions. Martha Jane has been saving her hard-earned money, which she hides in a Bible, so that Isabelle and Pastor Jenkins can marry and buy a house, even though Isabelle is in love with a young man named Sylvester. When Isabelle learns of her mother's plans, she is horrified and calls Jenkins a drunk and a sinner. Angry at her daughter, Martha Jane leaves Isabelle alone in the house with Jenkins, despite the young girl's sobs, so that he can save her soul. Jenkins steals Martha Jane's money, then suggests that Isabelle take the blame and flee to Atlanta, as her mother would never believe that her dear pastor was the culprit. Isabelle does as Jenkins tells her, and after Martha Jane finds her daughter's note of confession, she forgives her in her heart and follows her to Atlanta where she finds her ill and living in poverty. Isabelle tells her mother the whole truth about the pastor, including the fact that he took advantage of her in a deserted cabin during a storm and forced her to reveal where the money was hidden, then take the blame for the theft. Martha Jane cradles her daughter in forgiveness, and shortly thereafter, Isabelle dies. Returning to Tatesville, Martha Jane goes to the church where a drunken Jenkins is giving his "Dry Bones in the Valley" sermon to the congregation. Martha Jane publicly accuses Jenkins of being her daughter's murderer, and the congregation turns upon him. That night, Jenkins, hunted by bloodhounds, arrives at Martha Jane's parlor and tells her that her pampering ruined him. When two church ladies, Sis Ca'line and Sis Lucy, arrive to offer help to Martha Jane, she hides Jenkins in the kitchen and sends them away. Forgiven by his accuser, but unrepentant, Jenkins takes refuge in the woods. When he encounters one of his pursuers, Jenkins knocks him unconscious and brutally kills the man. The next morning, Martha Jane awakens from her slumber to realize that the events she thought transpired the night before were actually part of a dream. Isabelle tells her that Sylvester has earned a handsome sum of money on a discovery that he has made. Although earlier Martha Jane had refused Sylvester's proposal to her daughter on the grounds that he was too poor, she now offers to give the couple the money in the Bible so that they can marry right away. A short time later, the happy newlyweds return from their honeymoon to Martha Jane's house, which the changed woman has redecorated and made fit for her dear daughter and new son-in-law. *African Americans. Dreams. Forgiveness. Impersonation and imposture. Mothers and daughters. Reverends. Small town life. Atlanta (GA). Cabins. Escapes. Georgia. Murder. Newlyweds. Proposals (Marital). Rape. Robbery. Sermons. Swindlers and swindling.*

New York Age 14 Nov 1925, p. 9. *PittsC* 14 Feb 1925, p. 3. *Var* 9 Nov 1927, p. 24.

BODY AND SOUL (*foreign version*, 1931) see CUERPO Y ALMA

BODY AND SOUL (Multi-ethic, African Americans)

Enterprise Productions, Inc.; Roberts Productions, Inc. *Dist* United Artists Corp. 22 Aug **1947**; Prod: 9 Jan—late Mar 1947; late Apr 1947 [©Roberts Productions, Inc.; 22 Aug 1947; LP1279]. Sd (Western Electric Wide Range System); b&w. 12 reels. 103-104 min. Passed by the National Board of Review. PCA cert no. 12435.

Prod Bob Roberts. *Dir* Robert Rossen. *Asst dir* Robert Aldrich. *Orig scr* Abraham Polonsky. *Dir of photog* James Wong Howe. [*Stills* Durward B. Graybill]. *Montages dir* Gunther V. Fritsch. *Art dir* Nathan Juran. *Film ed* Robert Parrish. *Supv ed* Francis D. Lyon. *Set dec* Edward J. Boyle. *Ward des* Marion Herwood Keyes. *Mus comp* Hugo Friedhofer. *Cond* Emil Newman. *Mus dir* Rudolph Polk. *Sd eng* Frank Webster. *Sd rec* Sound Services, Inc. *Makeup supv* Gustaf M. Norin. *Exec prod mgr* Joseph C. Gilpin.

Song(s): "Body and Soul," music by Johnny Green, lyrics by Edward Heyman, Robert Sour and Frank Eyton.

Cast: JOHN GARFIELD [(*Charley Davis*)], LILLI PALMER [(*Peg Born*)], and introducing Hazel Brooks (*Alice*), Anne Revere [(*Anna Davis*)], William Conrad [(*Quinn*)], Joseph Pevney [(*Shorty Polaski*)], Lloyd Goff [(*Roberts*)], Canada Lee [(*Ben Chaplin*)], [Art

110

Smith (*David Davis*)], [James Burke (*Arnold*)], [Virginia Gregg (*Irma*)], [Peter Virgo (*Drummer*)], [Joe Devlin (*Prince*)], [Shimen Ruskin (*Grocer*)], [Mary Currier (*Miss Tedder*)], [Milton Kibbee (*Dan*)], [Tim Ryan (*Shelton*)], [Artie Dorrell (*Jackie Marlowe*)], [Cy Ring (*Victor*)], [Glen Lee (*Marine*)], [John Indrisano (*Referee*)], [Dan Tobey (*Announcer*)].

Boxing, Film Noir. [*Print viewed*]. In New York City, Charley Davis, the middleweight champion of the world, wakes up from a nightmare screaming the name "Ben," then visits his mother, telling her that Ben died that day. After his mother bitterly tells Charley to leave, Charley sees Peg Born, his ex-girl friend, and although he kisses her, he falls limp, weeping on her bed. Charley, who is scheduled to fight an important match the next day, enters a nightclub where singer Alice performs, and gets drunk. Charley's manager, Roberts, tells Charley he must go fifteen rounds and win the fight by a decision. Charley then recalls his early days as a boxer: After winning his first amateur bout, Charley meets Peg, a beautiful, free-spirited painter living in Greenwich Village, and they fall in love. Charley's father, who owns a candy store, is killed when a bomb is thrown into a nearby speakeasy. Although Charley's mother hopes he will get an education, he is determined to be a fighter, and Peg encourages him. Promoter Quinn arranges a series of bouts for Charley, which he wins. After a year on the road, Charley, who has become cocky and is driven by money, returns to a swank apartment in New York and affectionately greets Peg. Roberts, who runs the fighting racket in New York, decides to set up a fixed fight between Charley and the black "champ," Ben Chaplin, who is suffering from a blood clot in the brain. Roberts' scheme is to tell Ben that he and Charley will go fifteen rounds and that the bout will end in a decision, rather than a knockout. Charley is not told that Ben is ill, and Roberts cruelly says that the audience loves a killing. Later, Roberts goes to see Charley at his apartment, where Mrs. Davis is waiting for the boxer with Quinn and his girl friend, Alice. When Charley shows up with Peg, she is wearing a new dress and mink coat, having spent the afternoon drinking champagne. Although Charley's manager, Shorty Polaski, warns Peg to marry Charley immediately before he becomes a pawn of the mob, Roberts offers to help Charley win the championship and make him a wealthy man if he gives Roberts fifty percent of his take, fires Shorty, and postpones marriage. Shorty is suspicious of Roberts' conniving ways, but Peg lovingly agrees to put off her wedding. The night of the fight, Charley beats Ben repeatedly in the head and wins the title. After the fight, Ben's manager, Arnold, whom Roberts had double-crossed, protests to Roberts that Ben will undoubtedly die, but Roberts merely comments that "everybody dies." Later, as Peg and Charley celebrate in a bar with Roberts, Shorty tells Charley that he did not win fair, but foul, and that Roberts is the only one who won the fight. When Shorty then quits in disgust, Roberts coldly informs him that he had been getting only a handout from Charley. Shorty exits the bar, and Peg runs after him, but one of Roberts' thugs beats him up, and Peg runs for Charley's help. Charley rescues Shorty, but dazed, Shorty walks into an oncoming car and is killed. Peg then gives Charley an ultimatum: stop boxing or lose her. Charley breaks his engagement with Peg and wins a series of fights, becoming both richer and more careless. He begins dating Alice and buying her expensive gifts, then gambles away the rest of his winnings. Ben recovers, and Charley makes him his trainer. After years of holding the title, Charley is set to fight newcomer Jackie Marlowe, in a fixed fight: fifteen rounds and a decision. Jackie will win, and Charley will get $60,000, money he will use to bet against himself in the match. Alice, meanwhile, is hoping to share in Charley's fortune. Charley, however, visits Peg and, telling her he is about to fight his last fight, asks her to marry him. While Charley sleeps, Peg deposits his $60,000 in her bank account, unaware that he needs it to bet on the fight. At his mother's apartment, a grocer tells Charley that while the Nazis are killing Jews in Europe, Charley's old neighborhood is proudly placing money on Charley, whom they look up to with pride. Charley bitterly tells his mother and Peg that the fight is fixed, then demands his money back from Peg, accusing her of loving him for his money like everybody else. Hurt and enraged, Peg slaps Charley and leaves. While Ben trains Charley, he tries to convince him not to throw the fight. Roberts overhears and fires Ben, but Ben resists Roberts' orders and, in a frenzy of rage, pummels the air and falls dead. During the big match, after several rounds in which neither Charley nor Jackie are displaying any effort to fight, Jackie starts beating on Charley, and

he realizes he has been set up by Roberts, just as Ben was. Charley fights back and wins the bout with a knockout. As he exits the ring, Roberts tries to warn Charley he will not get away with double-crossing him, but Charley says, "What are you gonna do, kill me? Everybody dies." Peg then rushes into his arms. *African Americans. Betrayal. Boxers. Boxing managers. Fixed fights. Racketeers. Blood. Boxing trainers. Dismissal (Employment). Gold diggers. Grocery stores. Jews. Marriage. Mothers and sons. New York City–East Side. Painters (Of paintings). Poverty. Romantic rivalry. Wagers. Wealth.*

Note: The working title of this film was *The Burning Journey*. According to the *HR* review, the picture was based on an original story by Barney Ross, which star John Garfield had purchased in 1945. The reviewer commented that Ross's story was "practically thrown out the window." Ross's contribution to the final film, if any, has not been confirmed. Although some modern sources identify Garfield's character, "Charley Davis," as Jewish, in the film his character is never identified as such. The neighborhood in which Charley and his mother "Anna Davis" live is multi-ethnic, but at one point in the film, the grocer says that while Nazis are "killing Jews in Europe," the neighborhood is betting on Charley, of whom they are proud.

Body and Soul marked Garfield's first independent picture, and according to modern sources, he was greatly involved in all aspects of the production. Contemporary news items in *HR* add the following information about the production: Professional boxers Mickey Walker, Benny Leonard and Jack Dempsey were sought for roles, and actors Caryl Lincoln, Ethelreda Leopold, Forbes Murray and Al Eben were cast, but their appearance in the released film has not been confirmed. Frank Gaskin Fields was hired to write two songs and background music for the film, but his contribution to the final film also has not been confirmed. Three film crews were sent to fight arenas in twenty-six cities around the country to shoot boxing footage for the picture.

Cinematographer James Wong Howe used eight cameras to film the fight sequences: three placed on cranes for bird's-eye shots of the ring, three mounted on dollies and two hand-held cameras to provide a newsreel effect. Some location filming was done in New York City. Modern sources add that Garfield took sparring lessons from boxer Mushy Callahan to prepare for his role and performed all his own fight scenes. Garfield was knocked out and injured during the filming of one of his fight scenes, according to modern sources.

An early Dec 1946 *HR* news item noted that production on the film was held up for two weeks due to censorship problems. Information contained in the MPAA/PCA Collection at the AMPAS Library indicates that early drafts of the script were deemed "unacceptable" under the provisions of the Production Code due to, among other things, excessive violence and the inclusion of a suicide, which was later removed from the script. A letter contained in the PCA file, dated 4 Jan 1947, indicates that the Breen Office demanded an entire sequence in which a white boxer fights an African American boxer be cut from the script. The stated reason for the deletion was that the Production Code did "not permit any scenes showing the social intermingling of white and colored people or of a boxing contest between two people of these opposite colors."

The film garnered much critical praise, with the boxing sequences receiving particular notice. The *DV* review commented that "seldom has the camera caught such exciting ring sequences," while the *New Yorker* reviewer proclaimed the fight scenes "marvellously realistic." The casting of African American actor Canada Lee, who had been a middleweight boxing champion in the 1930s, was also lauded. Reviewers noted the timeliness of the film's subject matter. In appraising the picture's earning potential, the *Var* review commented that the "widely-ballyhooed N.Y. State Boxing Commission probe of bribery last winter, gives 'Body' a strong boxoffice chance." In Sep 1947, according to a *HR* article, Charles Johnson, president of the Boxing Managers' Guild, petitioned Enterprise Pictures, Inc. to withdraw the film from distribution, claiming that it was "slanderous" in its depiction of boxing managers, and that it characterized managers as "thieves, gangsters, fixers, contrivers [and] doublecrossers." According to the *HR* article, David Loew, president of Enterprise, refused to withdraw the film or make any changes to it.

According to a 1953 *DV* article, Bank of America, a Roberts Productions creditor, assumed control of this and Roberts' next film, *Force of Evil*, after Roberts failed to repay outstanding loans. According to *DV*, Roberts borrowed $1,000,000 from Bank of America to make this film. In Oct 1947, shortly after the release of this film, Garfield was accused by California State Senator Jack Tenny of being a Communist sympathizer. Garfield later refused to supply the House Un-American Activities Committee (HUAC) with a list of suspected Communists, and was subsequently blacklisted. Director Robert Rossen, actors Anne Revere and Canada Lee, and screenwriter Abraham Polonsky were also blacklisted in the 1950s for their political views. (For more information on the HUAC hearings, see the entry below for *Crossfire*.)

Francis Lyon and Robert Parrish received an Academy Award for Best Editing for their work on the picture. Garfield was nominated for Best Actor, and Polonsky was nominated for Best Original Screenplay. Some modern critics describe *Body and Soul* as the quintessential boxing film. Garfield reprised his screen role in a *Lux Radio Theatre* broadcast version of the story, which aired on 15 Nov 1948. In 1981, George Bowers directed Leon Isaac Kennedy, Jayne Kennedy and Muhammed Ali in *Body and Soul*, a Golan-Globus Productions film that was loosely based on Polonsky's screenplay.

Box 16 Aug 1947. *DV* 13 Aug 1947. *DV* 9 Oct 1953. *FD* 13 Aug 1947, p. 6. *HCN* 25 Feb 1953. *HR* 12 Nov 1946, p. 30. *HR* 22 Nov 1946, p. 20. *HR* 6 Dec 1946, p. 4. *HR* 24 Dec 1946, p. 2. *HR* 9 Jan 1947, p. 11. *HR* 17 Jan 1947, p. 8. *HR* 3 Mar 1947, p. 10. *HR* 11 Mar 1947, p. 8. *HR* 12 Mar 1947, p. 11. *HR* 18 Mar 1947, p. 6. *HR* 21 Mar 1947, p. 18. *HR* 3 Apr 1947, p. 6. *HR* 18 Apr 1947, p. 10. *HR* 13 Aug 1947, p. 3, 4. *HR*

14 Aug 1947, p. 2. *HR* 17 Sep 1947, p. 1. *HR* 18 Sep 1947. *HR* 24 Sep 1947, pp. 1-2. *HR* 13 Nov 1947, p. 14. *IFJ* 1 Feb 1947, p. 46. *Life* 29 Sep 1947, pp. 141-42. *MPHPD* 16 Aug 1947, p. 3781. *NYT* 10 Nov 1947, p. 21. *New Yorker* 15 Nov 1947. *Var* 13 Aug 1947, p. 15.

THE BOLD CABALLERO (Latino)

Republic Pictures Corp.; A Nat Levine Production. *Dist* Republic Pictures Corp. 1 Dec **1936**; Prod: began 15 Sep 1936 [©Republic Pictures Corp.; 4 Jan 1937; LP6831]. Sd; col (Magnacolor). 8 reels. 56, 60 or 71-72 min. Passed by the National Board of Review. PCA cert no. 2681.

Assoc prod Albert E. Levoy. *Dir* Wells Root. *Orig scr* Wells Root. *Idea by* Johnston McCulley. *Photog* Alvin Wycoff and Jack Marta. *Film ed* Lester Orlebeck. *Supv ed* Murray Seldeen. [*Cost* Eloise]. *Mus supv* Harry Grey. *Mus settings* Carlos Hajos. *Sd eng* Harry Jones.

Cast: Robert Livingston (*Zorro* [*also known as Don Diego Vega*]), Heather Angel (*Isabella* [*Palma*]), Sig Rumann (*Commandante* [*Sebastian Golle*]), Ian Wolfe (*Priest*), Robert Warwick (*Governor* [*General Palma*]), Emily Fitzroy (*Duenna*), Charles Stevens (*Vargas*), Walter Long (*Chate*), Ferdinand Munier (*Landlord*), Chris King Martin [(*Pedro*)], Carlos de Valdez [(*Alcalda*)], Soledad Jimenez, [*Slim Whitaker*].

Historical, Adventure, Drama. [*Print viewed*]. Zorro, the masked deliverer of Indians of Spanish-ruled California, is about to be hanged when General Palma is declared governor of Santa Cruz. Palma is to replace the tyrannical commandante, Sebastian Golle, who has been pilfering King Charles' tax money and terrorizing the natives. With the help of the Indians, Zorro escapes and, posing as Don Diego Vega, a gentleman pauper from Mexico, offers his services to Palma and his lovely daughter Isabella. Palma, however, refuses Diego and unwittingly sends him out as bait for Zorro. But as Palma chases the elusive hero, he is killed by a bandit who leaves Zorro's "Z" mark on his dead body. After Isabella is made governor, Golle plans to marry her and receive Santa Cruz as her dowery, and Diego agrees to do his wooing for him. Golle, meanwhile, has been taxing the Indians beyond their means and enslaving the sons of those who cannot pay. When Golle's soldiers herd the slaves into the public square, their mothers cry for Zorro to deliver them. Hoping to expose Golle's barbarism, Diego brings Isabella to the square, where she promises to free the slaves once information on Zorro's whereabouts is brought to her and offers a public bounty of two hundred pieces of gold for the outlaw. Zorro, however, steals the gold and buys the slaves' freedom himself. Then, on Isabella's birthday, Golle stages a burlesque bullfight in which a child is placed in the ring, hoping to lure Zorro out of hiding. When Isabella pleads with the foppish Diego to save the child, he fights the bull bravely and adeptly, revealing his true virility and love for Isabella. Seeing them kiss, Golle accuses Diego of betraying him, and Diego bends off Golle and his soldiers and escapes. When Zorro's mark is found on Golle's wounded body, Isabella finally realizes Diego is Zorro and escapes from Golle's clutches to capture him, still determined to avenge her father's murder. Golle captures them both, however, and fatally whips Isabella's female companion, planning to blame her death on Zorro. When Zorro finds the woman marred with the same backwards "Z" found on Palma, Isabella finally realizes it was Golle who killed her father. Just as Zorro is about to be hanged, the natives stage an uprising and help him defeat Golle. Zorro's loyal priest then blesses Isabella and Zorro, and the couple falls through the gallows box and kisses. *California-History–To 1846. Impersonation and imposture. Masked bandits. Murder. Outlaws. Territorial governors. Aristocracy. Birthdays. Bullfighters and bullfighting. Dictators. Duplicity. Escapes. Executions. Fathers and daughters. Fops. Frame-ups. Heroes. Imperialism. Imprisonment. Indians of North America. Mexicans. Officers (Military). Rescues. Revenge. Rewards. Romance. Slavery–Emancipation. Spaniards. Taxation. Thieves. Traps. Uprisings.*

Note: The working titles for this film were *The Mask of Zorro* and *The Beloved Rogue*. This film was based on Johnston McCulley's character of Zorro, which first appeared in McCulley's story "The Curse of Capistrano" in *All-Story Weekly* (9 Aug-6 Sep 1919). Although onscreen credits state "Idea by Johnston McCulley"—suggesting that he contributed only to the screen treatment—and credit Wells Root with an original screenplay, a modern source credits McCulley and Root as co-screenwriters. Another modern source says this film is based on McCulley's story "The Return of Zorro." *The Bold Caballero* was Republic's first all-color feature. The film was screened in Lincoln, NE, the week of 8 Mar 1937 at a length of 60 minutes, as compared to the original length of 71-72 minutes. "The Curse of Capistrano" was published in book form under the title *The Mark of Zorro* in 1924. Among adaptations of

McCulley's story is the 1920 film *The Mark of Zorro*, which was produced by Douglas Fairbanks Picture Corp., directed by Fred Niblo, and starred Douglas Fairbanks (see below); for a list of other "Zorro" films consult that entry. In 1974, 20th Century-Fox Television produced a version of *The Mark of Zorro*, directed by Don McDougall and starring Frank Langella and Ricardo Montalbon. Modern sources list the following additional cast members: John Merton, Jack Kirk, Vinegar Roan, George Plues, Henry Morris, Chief Thunder Cloud, Pascale Perry, Jack Roberts, William Emile, Gurdial Singh, Steve Clark, Herman Hack, Rube Dalroy, Bill Wolfe, Si Jenks, Harrison Greene, Jimmy Aubrey, Jack Rockwell, Artie Ortego, Dick Botiller, Wally West, Ed Phillips, Sherry Tansey, Henry Hall, Ben Corbett and Bud McClure.

DV 23 Nov 1936, p. 3. *Exb* 15 Dec 1936. *FD* 3 Dec 1936, p. 6. *HR* 15 Sep 1936, p. 8. *HR* 2 Nov 1936, p. 13. *HR* 23 Nov 1936, p. 4. *MPD* 24 Nov 1936, p. 20. *MPH* 24 Oct 1936, p. 44. *MPH* 5 Dec 1936, p. 46. *Var* 23 Nov 1936, p. 3. *Var* 17 Mar 1937, p. 15.

BONANZA *see* LUST FOR GOLD

THE BOND BETWEEN (French Americans)

Pallas Pictures. *Dist* Paramount Pictures Corp. 2 Apr **1917** [©J. C. Ivers; 13 Mar 1917; LP10407]. Si; b&w. 5 reels.

Dir Donald Crisp. *Scen* George Beban. *Cam* J. O. Taylor.

Cast: George Beban (*Pierre Duval*), John Burton (*Hans von Meyernick*), Nigel De Brullier (*Feole Zelnar*), Paul Weigel (*Carl Riminoss*), Colin Chase (*Jacques Duval*), Eugene Pallette (*Raoul Vaux*), W. H. Bainbridge (*John Fownes*), Vola Vale (*Ellen Ingram*), Signor Buzzi (*M. Lorillard*), Mrs. Buehler (*Mme. Lorillard*).

Drama. Pierre Duval, a poor Frenchman living in a New York boardinghouse, is barely able to support his son Jacques's studies in a Parisian art school. When war breaks out, Jacques returns home, unaware that a disreputable art dealer named Raoul Vaux has tricked him into smuggling stolen paintings into the United States, hidden among his own works. The Secret Service suspects that Jacques is Vaux and send their agent, Ellen Ingram, to entrap him. She goes to live at the same boardinghouse as Pierre and Jacques and soon becomes friendly with them. To support himself and his son, Pierre takes on an extra job as a nightwatchman at a museum. When Jacques learns through Ellen that "Vaux" is an art thief who plans to steal some paintings from the museum where Pierre works, he tries to prevent the theft, but is arrested himself instead. Finally, the real Vaux is captured, and Pierre and Jacques receive a reward from the French government for helping to recover stolen paintings. Financially secure, Jacques is now able to marry Ellen, with whom he has fallen in love. *Fathers and sons. French Americans. Secret agents. Smuggling. Thieves. Art dealers. Art students. Boardinghouses. Museums. New York City. Paintings.*

Note: Signor Buzzi, who plays the part of M. Lorillard, is probably Pietro Buzzi. The original title of the scenario was *Amen Corner*.

ETR 7 Apr 1917, p. 1251. *MPN* 14 Apr 1917, p. 2364. *MPW* 14 Apr 1917, p. 283. *MPW* 21 Apr 1917, p. 494. *NYDM* 7 Apr 1917, p. 26. *Var* 6 Apr 1917, p. 23. *Wid's* 5 Apr 1917, p. 215.

LA BONNE VIE *see* QUAND ON EST BELLE

BONNIE, BONNIE LASSIE (Scottish Americans)

Universal Film Mfg. Co. *Dist* Universal Film Mfg. Co. 5 Oct **1919** [©Universal Film Mfg. Co.; 1 Oct 1919; LP14258]. Si; b&w. 6 reels.

Dir Tod Browning. *Asst dir* Fred Tyler. *Scen* Violet Clark, Tod Browning and Waldemar Young. *Cam* William Fildew.

Source: Based on the short story "Auld Jeremiah" by Henry C. Rowland in *Ainslee's Magazine* (publication date undetermined).

Cast: Mary MacLaren (*Alisa Graeme*), Spottiswoode Aitken (*Jeremiah Wishart*), David Butler (*David*), Arthur Carewe (*Archibald Loveday*), Fred Turner, Clarissa Selwyn, Eugenie Forde.

Comedy. Alisa Graeme journeys from Scotland to America to visit Jeremiah Wishart, an old wealthy friend of her grandfather. The invalid Jeremiah is charmed by Alisa and decides she would make a good wife for his favorite nephew David. Without meeting Alisa, David refuses the arrangement and runs away. Later, Alisa also runs away rather than wed another of Jeremiah's nephews and meets a young billboard painter in the country. The two form a partnership, travel the countryside together painting billboards and gradually fall in love. When the painter tells Alisa that he won't marry until his finances are secure, she leaves him in anger and heads for Jeremiah's house. From his wheelchair, Jeremiah sees first his wayward nephew painting a nearby billboard, then a young woman stopping to help him. Jeremiah's initial fury at David softens when he recognizes the woman as Alisa. Once Alisa and David realize the other's identity, they blissfully reunite. *Marriage–Arranged. Painters (Of paintings). Runaways. Scottish Americans. Billboards. Fathers and sons. Invalids.*

Note: This film's working title was *Auld Jeremiah*. Trade articles during the first weeks of production credited Waldemar Young with the scenario, but later trade notices credit Violet Clark, and the copyright register credits Clark and Browning.

Camera 13 Jul 1919, p. 5. *Camera* 27 Jul 1919. *MPN* 8 Nov 1919, p. 3506. *MPW* 19 Jul 1919, p. 379. *MPW* 9 Aug 1919, p. 839. *MPW* 23 Aug 1919, p. 1121. *MPW* 8 Nov 1919, p. 246. *Var* 31 Oct 1919, p. 56.

BOOTS AND SADDLES (English Americans)

Republic Pictures Corp. *Dist* Republic Pictures Corp. 4 Oct **1937**; Prod: late Jul—early Aug 1937 [©Republic Pictures Corp.; 4 Oct 1937; LP7557]. Sd (RCA Victor High Fidelity Sound System); b&w. 6 reels, 5,221 ft. 58 min. Passed by the National Board of Review. PCA cert no. 3649.

Assoc prod Sol C. Siegel. *Dir* Joe Kane. [*Asst dir* William O'Connor]. *Scr* Jack Natteford and Oliver Drake. *Orig story* Jack Natteford. *Photog* William Nobles. *Film ed* Lester Orlebeck. *Mus dir* Raoul Kraushaar.

Song(s): "Take Me Back to My Boots and Saddle," words and music by Walter G. Samuels, Leonard Whitcup and Teddy Powell; "Ridin' the Range," words and music by Gene Autry, Fleming Allan and Nelson Shawn; "The One Rose (That's Left in My Heart)," words and music by Lani McIntire and Del Lyon; "Dusty Roads," words and music by Smiley Burnette; "Oh, Why Did He Get Married?" words and music by Carson Robison; "Cielito lindo," traditional.

Cast: GENE AUTRY [(*Gene Autry*)], Smiley Burnette [(*Frog Millhouse*)], Judith Allen [(*Bernice Allen*)], Ra Hould [(*Edward, Earl of Granville, also known as Spud*)], Guy Usher [(*Colonel Allen*)], Gordon Elliott [(*Jim Neale*)], John Ward [(*Henry Wyndham*)], Frankie Marvin [(*Shorty*)], Chris Martin [(*Juan*)], Stanley Blystone [(*Sergeant*)], Bud Osborne [(*Joe Larkins*)], [Merrill McCormack (*Neale's benchman*)], [Champion].

Western, with songs. [*Print viewed*]. After his father dies, Edward, the young Earl of Granville, travels from England with his solicitor, Henry Wyndham, to his father's ranch in the western United States. Edward is greeted by ranch foreman Gene Autry and Gene's pal, Frog Millhouse. Gene and Frog, who promised their late friend that they would make a real Westerner of his son, are dismayed by Edward's arrogant demeanor and Wyndham's assertion that the ranch, which is deeply in debt, will be sold at once. Gene rescues Edward from a runaway horse, and Edward's apology for his earlier attitude proves to Gene that he is a "regular fellow." Gene and Frog christen him "Spud," which was also his father's nickname, and encourage him to keep the ranch open. They are approached about buying the ranch by Jim Neale, a wealthy rancher to whom the late earl owed money. Neale inadvertently gives them the idea to save the ranch by selling their feisty cow ponies to the Army, but he warns them that if they do not pay him his money in sixty days he will sue. A few days later, Edward has proven his mettle by helping round up the horses, and the cowboys drive them back to the ranch. On the way to nearby Fort Wayne, where Gene intends to offer his horses for sale to Colonel Allen, Gene, Frog and the others insult the passengers of a buggy by deliberately overwhelming them with the dust raised by their wagons. Unknown to Gene, the passengers are Neale, Allen and his daughter Bernice. Bernice recognizes Gene when he comes to the colonel's quarters and pretends to be a maidservant in order to ridicule him later. She falsely advises that Allen is hard of hearing, and so the next day Allen is put off by Gene's yelling at him during the horse auction. Allen refuses to consider Gene's cow horses until he sees Gene's own horse, the magnificent "Champion," in action. Gene and Neale's bids are the same, so Allen proposes that they each race twelve horses the next morning and that the winner will receive the contract. That night, Gene eludes Neale's henchmen, who have been ordered to get him out of the way, while Edward locks up a process server attempting to serve a summons claiming all their property for Neale. Gene then gets the upper hand on Bernice and reveals that he knows who she is. They are quarreling when Gene spots a fire in the barn where his horses are being kept. While the horses are being saved, Frog reveals that he does not know who knocked him out and started the blaze, but that he was able to grab hold of the man's watch and can use it to discover the arsonist's identity. The next morning, Gene determines to carry on even though he has only five horses left, and the race begins. Edward tells Bernice what a fine fellow Gene is for helping him, and Frog discovers that the watch belongs to Neale's henchman, Joe Larkins. Despite Neale's dirty tricks, Gene wins the race, and Edward's ranch is awarded the

contract. Larkins reveals Neales's underhanded schemes, and Gene and Bernice make up. *English. Horses. Officers (Military). Ranch foremen. Ranchers. Arson. Cowboys. Debt. Fires. Forts. Horseracing. Impersonation and imposture. Lawyers. Maturation. Nobility. Process servers. Snobs and snobbishness. Soldiers.*

Note: The film's titles credit Aaron Gonzalez, Jr. as an additional song writer, but his contribution to the released film has not been determined. Modern sources add the following actors to the cast: Max Terhune, Jerry Frank, Bob Reeves, Nelson McDowell and Al Taylor.

DV 3 Nov 1937, p. 3. *FD* 26 Oct 1937, p. 6. *HR* 2 Aug 1937, p. 14. *HR* 9 Aug 1937, p. 14. *HR* 3 Nov 1937, p. 3. *MPD* 18 Oct 1937, p. 6. *MPH* 13 Nov 1937, p. 46. *NYT* 8 Nov 1937, p. 19. *Var* 13 Oct 1937, p. 16.

BORDER BANDITS (Latino)

Great Western Productions, Inc. *Dist* Monogram Pictures Corp. 12 Jan **1946**; Prod: early Aug—mid Aug 1945 [©Monogram Pictures Corp.; 5 Dec 1945; LP20]. Sd; b&w. 57-58 min. PCA cert no. 10964. [*Prod* Scott R. Dunlap]. *Supv* Charles J. Bigelow. *Dir* Lambert Hillyer. *Asst dir* Eddie Davis. *Scr* Frank H. Young. *Dir of photog* William A. Sickner. *Settings* Vin Taylor. *Film ed* Carrol Lewis. *Mus dir* Frank Sanucci. *Rec eng* Glen Glenn.

Cast: JOHNNY MACK BROWN [(*Nevada*)], Raymond Hatton [(*Sandy Hopkins*)], Riley Hill [(*Steve Halliday*)], Rosa del Rosario [(*Celia*)], John Merton [(*Spike*)], Tom Quinn [(*Pepper*)], Frank La Rue [(*John Halliday*)], Steve Clark [(*Doc Bowles*)], Charles Stevens [(*José*)], Lucio Villegas [(*Gonzales*)], Bud Osborne [(*Dutch*)], Pat R. McGee [(*Cupid*)].

Western. [*Print viewed*]. Steve Halliday proposes to Celia, but she is afraid that her grandfather, rancher Gonzales, will not approve of the marriage. After Gonzales receives a threatening note demanding the family jewels, his friend, Sandy Hopkins, sends for Nevada, a U.S. Marshal. Sandy and Nevada wait for the sheriff at Sandy's cabin, and there, they discover the sheriff's body. Back at the ranch, three masked men, Dutch and his partners, Pepper and deputy sheriff Spike, demand that Gonzales give them the jewels. Before he can reveal their hiding place, Gonzales is murdered by Dutch. Steve chases the killers, but they escape after shooting him. Celia and José, a ranch hand, then take Steve to town for medical care. Meanwhile, Nevada befriends Doc Bowles, who has been thrown out of the saloon. Elsewhere in the saloon, Dutch, Pepper and Spike report to their boss, Steve's uncle, John Halliday, the owner of the land and water company. Then Celia and José bring the unconscious Steve into the saloon, so that Doc can take care of his wounds. Meanwhile, at the ranch, Sandy discovers that Gonzales has been killed. After Steve regains consciousness, Spike arrests Nevada for the murders. Later, Doc helps Nevada escape from jail. Nevada then rides out to the hacienda and arrives in time to stop Halliday's men from killing José and Sandy. Nevada forces Spike to jail Pepper for trying to kill him, and suggests that Sandy should be jailed for murdering Gonzales. In jail, Sandy pretends to be an outlaw and befriends Pepper, but before Pepper can reveal the name of the gang leader, he is killed. Steve, who does not know that his uncle is the head of the gang, tells Halliday that Nevada is a U.S. Marshal. Later, José brings the jewels to Halliday for safekeeping. Halliday kills him, but is unable to get rid of the body before Nevada arrives and arrests him. With the jewels safe, Celia marries a recovered Steve. *Gems. Murder. Robbery. Undercover operations. United States. Marshals. Bankers. Grandfathers. Gunshot wounds. Jailbreaks. Mexican Americans. Physicians. Proposals (Marital). Romance. Saloons. Servants. Uncles.*

DV 15 Feb 1946, p. 3. *HR* 3 Aug 1945, p. 12. *HR* 10 Aug 1945, p. 10. *HR* 15 Feb 1946, p. 3. *MPHPD* 5 Jan 1946, p. 2792. *MPHPD* 23 Feb 1946, p. 2859. *Var* 3 Apr 1946, p. 12.

BORDER CAFE (Latino)

RKO Radio Pictures, Inc. *Dist* RKO Radio Pictures, Inc. 4 Jun **1937**; Prod: early Apr—mid-Apr 1937 [©RKO Radio Pictures, Inc.; 4 Jun 1937; LP7208]. Sd (RCA Victor System); b&w. 7 reels. 65 or 67 min. PCA cert no. 3264.

Prod Robert Sisk. [*Exec prod* Samuel J. Briskin]. *Dir* Lew Landers. [*Asst dir* Bob Barnes]. *Scr* Lionel Houser. *Photog* Nicholas Musuraca. *Art dir* Van Nest Polglase. *Art dir assoc* Al Herman. *Ed* Jack Hively. *Mus dir* Nathaniel Shilkret. *Rec* Denzil A. Cutler.

Source: Based on the short story "In the Mexican Quarter" by Tom Gill in *Hearst's International-Cosmopolitan* (Jun 1930).

Cast: HARRY CAREY [(*Tex Stevens*)], JOHN BEAL [(*Keith Whitney*)], Armida [(*Dominga*)], George Irving [(*Senator Henry Whitney*)], Leona Roberts [(*Emma Whitney*)], J. Carrol Naish [(*Rocky*

Alton)], Marjorie Lord [(*Janet Barry*)], Lee Patrick [(*Ellie*)], Paul Fix [(*Dolson*)], Max Wagner [(*Shakey*)], Walter Miller [(*Evans*)].

Western. [*Print viewed*]. After bailing his irresponsible, alcoholic son Keith out of jail, Senator Henry Whitney announces that Keith must join the family law firm in Boston or lose his allowance. Keith, however, chooses to seek his fortune elsewhere and winds up in Verde, Texas, a small town on the Mexican border. Free from his father's scrutiny, Keith spends his time drinking in a café, where he meets Dominga, a pretty Mexican singer. He also wrangles a job playing piano in exchange for bar credit and a bed in Dominga's room. Down to his last dollar, Keith wires his father for a $2,000 loan, telling him that he needs the money to buy a ranch. When Keith, who has spent the loan on alcohol and gambling, later receives word that his parents are on their way to Texas to visit him, he turns to veteran rancher Tex Stevens for aid. Tex, grateful for Keith's life-saving help in a bar fight, agrees to let him work on his ranch and tell the senator that they are partners. At the same time, Dominga, who has witnessed the aftermath of a murder committed by an ardent admirer, Eastern gangster Rocky Alton, quits her café job out of fear and begs for a job cooking on Tex's ranch. Soon after, Rocky visits Tex and "invites" him to join his Cattlemen's Protection Agency, but Tex, wise to Rocky's highly organized cattle rustling business, refuses the offer and later suffers the loss of several cattle. When Henry, his wife Emma, and Janet Barry, Keith's Boston fiancée, arrive at the ranch, they are greeted by a reformed Keith. Although satisfied with his son's transformation, Henry disapproves of his romance with Dominga and his future as a rancher. While Keith, Tex and Henry argue the point, Rocky and his men, who are now wanted for murder, burst in and take Dominga and Henry hostage. After a fierce gun battle in the hills, Rocky is defeated and Dominga is reunited with Keith, who finally receives his father's complete blessing. *Alcoholics. Fathers and sons. Gangsters. Irresponsibility. Ranchers. Regeneration. Boston (MA). Cafés. Cattlemen's associations. Cowboys. Gunfights. Kidnapping. Mexican Americans. Mexican-American border region. Rustlers. Senators. Singers. Texas.*

Note: The working titles of this film were *In the Mexican Quarter* and *Mexican Quarter*. Marjorie Lord made her screen debut in this film. *MPH*'s "In the Cutting Room" adds Dudley Clements to the cast, while *HR* production charts and news items add Alec Craig and Hooper Atchley. Their participation in the final film has not been confirmed.
DV 21 May 1937, p. 3. *FD* 9 Jun 1937, p. 12. *HR* 5 Apr 1937, p. 7. *HR* 12 Apr 1937, p. 11. *HR* 14 Apr 1937, p. 6. *HR* 21 May 1937, p. 3. *MPD* 25 May 1937, p. 4. *MPH* 1 May 1937, p. 38. *MPH* 29 May 1937, p. 48, 50. *NYT* 8 Jun 1937, p. 30. *Var* 9 Jun 1937, p. 15.

BORDER DEVILS (Chinese Americans)
Supreme Features, Inc.; Alfred T. Mannon, President. *Dist* State Rights; Weiss Bros.; Artclass Pictures Corp. 4 Apr **1932**. Sd; b&w. 63 or 65 min.
Pres LOUIS WEISS. *Assoc prod* Geo. M. Merrick. *Dir* William Nigh. *Asst dir* Harry P. Crist. *Cont and dial* Harry P. Crist. *Cine* William H. Dietz. *Settings* Tec-Art Studios, Inc. *Film ed* Holbrook Todd. *Rec* General Sound Corp. Ltd. *Sd eng* B. J. Kroger. *Prod mgr* Geo. M. Merrick.
Source: Based on a novel by Murray Leinster (publication undetermined).
Cast: HARRY CAREY (*Jim Gray*), Kathleen Collins (*Marcia Brandon*), George F. Hayes (*"Squint" Sanders*), Niles Welch (*Tom Hope*), Olive Fuller Golden (*Ethel Denham*), Albert Smith (*Inspector Bell* [*later known as Burt Dorgan*]), Merrill McCormick (*Jose Lopez*), Art Mix (*Bud Brandon*), Tetsu Komai (*"The General"*), Jack Gallagher (*Neil Denham*), [Maston Williams (*"The Hawk"*)].
Western. [*Print viewed*]. Two friends, Jim Gray and Bud Brandon, drink drugged water after a long ride and pass out. While Bud is unconscious, someone kills him and frames Jim for the murder. Jim is arrested, but escapes with the help of Neil Denham of the Cattlemen's Association. "The General," a mysterious Chinese leader of a gang of bandits, wants to control all the surrounding ranchland. He has Neil killed, but exchanges Neil's personal possessions with those of Burt Dorgan, who works for him. Jim impersonates Neil and intervenes in a feud between ranchers Marcia Brandon, Bud's sister who runs the Hermosa, and Tom Hope of the Piñon ranch. Jim reveals that the vandalism to their livestock has been caused by The General, who hopes to cause dissent so he can take dynamite over the border unnoticed. "Squint" Sanders, an elderly ranch hand working for Marcia, becomes Jim's sidekick, trusting Jim's sincerity even though

he knows he is not really Neil. Inspector Bell, of the border patrol, works with Tom and tries to arrest Jim, but is unsuccessful. Bell identifies Jim, but Jim and Squint are captured by The General. Jim is forced to prove his loyalty to The General by shooting Squint. Fortunately, his gun is loaded with blanks. Meanwhile, Marcia, who has fallen in love with Jim, is reassured by Neil's widow that although Jim falsified his identity, he is a trustworthy friend. As Jim and Squint escape, Squint is shot. Bell turns out to be Burt Dorgan, who is the real leader of The General's gang. Jim forces him to write a confession, but afterward Squint kills Dorgan and The General. Squint recovers and Jim and Marcia marry. *Bandits. Impersonation and imposture. Murder. Ranchers. Cattlemen's associations. Chinese Americans. Confession (Law). Drugging. Dynamite. Escapes. Feuds. Frame-ups. Jails. Loyalty. Mexican-American border region.*

Note: Several contemporary sources list Albert Smith's character as "Inspector Bell," or "Patrolman Bell." *MPH* calls Jack Gallagher "Ray Gallagher." According to a news item in *FD*, some scenes were filmed near Palm Springs, CA. A modern source includes Murdock MacQuarrie in the cast.
FD 19 Feb 1932, p. 4. *FD* 20 Mar 1932, p. 11. *MPH* 9 Apr 1932, p. 25. *Var* 17 May 1932, p. 15.

BORDER INCIDENT (Latino)
Metro-Goldwyn-Mayer Corp.; controlled by Loew's Inc. *Dist* Loew's Inc. 28 Oct **1949**; *Prod:* 26 Jan—early Mar 1949 [©Loew's Inc.; 25 Aug 1949; LP2505]. Sd (Western Electric Sound System); b&w. 10 reels, 8,563 ft. 92 or 95-96 min. Passed by the National Board of Review. PCA cert no. 13741.
Prod Nicholas Nayfack. *Dir* Anthony Mann. [*Asst dir* Howard Koch]. *Scr* John C. Higgins. *Story* John C. Higgins and George Zuckerman. *Dir of photog* John Alton. *Art dir* Cedric Gibbons and Hans Peters. *Film ed* Conrad A. Nervig. *Set dec* Edwin B. Willis. *Assoc* Ralph S. Hurst. *Mus dir* André Previn. *Rec supv* Douglas Shearer. *Makeup created by* Jack Dawn.
Cast: Ricardo Montalban (*Pablo Rodriguez*), George Murphy (*Jack Bearnes*), Howard da Silva (*Owen Parkson*), James Mitchell (*Juan Garcia*), Arnold Moss (*Zopilote*), Alfonso Bedoya (*Cuchillo*), Teresa Celli (*Maria*), Charles McGraw (*Jeff Amboy*), Jose Torvay (*Pocoloco*), John Ridgely (*Mr. Neley*), Arthur Hunnicutt (*Clayton Nordell*), Sig Ruman (*Hugo Wolfgang Ulrich*), Otto Waldis (*Fritz*), [Harry Antrim (*John Boyd*)], [Tony Barr (*Inis*)], [Rozene Jones (*Senora*)], [John McGuire (*Norson*)], [Jack Lambert (*Chuck*)], [Nedrick Young (*Happy*)], [Fred Graham (*Leathercoat*)], [Lynn Whitney (*Bella Amboy*)], [José Dominguez, Roque Ybarra, George Derrick, Charles Rivero, Albert Haskell, Samuel Herrera, Jerry Riggio, David Cota, Danilo Valente, Mitchell Lewis, Robert Cabal, Elias Gamboa, Miguel Contreras (*Braceros*)], [Martin Garralaga (*Colonel Alvarado*)], [Paul Marion (*One-armed man*)], [Gerald Echeverria (*Padre Ignacio*)], [Manuel Lopez (*Mexican lieutenant*)], [Enrique Escalante (*Mexican sergeant*)], [William "Bill" Phillips (*Jim*)], [Lita Baron (*Rosita*)], [Frank Conlan (*Elderly postal clerk*)], [Ed Max (*Doc Kelso*)], [Gordon Harris, Riley Sunrise (*Bandits*)].
Film noir. [*Print viewed*]. At the All-American Canal, along the California-Mexico border, hundreds of Mexican farm workers, known as "braceros," wait to make their daily crossing into California. Some of the workers cross into the United States legally, while many others enter illegally. Many of the workers are robbed and sometimes stabbed by bandits, who ambush the braceros on their way home. Hoping to end the often deadly ambushes, the Mexican and American governments send officials to meet and discuss a possible solution to the problem. Soon after immigration investigators Pablo Rodriguez, a Mexican, and Jack Bearnes, an American, are assigned to the case by their respective countries, Pablo volunteers to disguise himself as a bracero and investigate the well-organized bandit operation. As part of their plan, Jack will follow Pablo and monitor all the contacts he makes on the Mexican side. After finding Owen Parkson, an American bracero broker posing as a rancher, Pablo tries to win his trust by telling him that he is running from the police. Though reluctant to believe Pablo's story, Parkson agrees to transport him across the border, and directs him to a truck filled with farm workers. Jack, meanwhile, loses his trail and falls into the hands of Parkson, who holds him prisoner in his camp, demanding the "stolen" immigration papers that Jack has offered him. Pablo sees Jack there, but does not offer him help for fear that he might expose their identities. Parkson eventually discovers the trap when he intercepts a telegram that Jack has sent to the immigration authorities. After ordering Jack killed,

Parkson, realizing that he is the target of an investigation and is about to be arrested, decides to hide the evidence of his operation by sending the braceros back to Mexico. Pablo, who is among the men who are to be sent back, spurs the braceros to riot, and a bloody fight ensues. Parkson and many of his henchmen are killed in the battle, but a border patrol unit arrives in time to bring order and arrest the remaining crooks. *Mexican-American border region. Mexicans. Migrant workers. Ranchers. Smuggling. Undercover operations. United States. Dept. of Immigration.* Aliens, Illegal. Bandits. Border patrols. California. Disguise. Fistfights. Gunfights. Mexico. Murder. Prisoners. Quicksand. Torture. Traps.

Note: The working title of this film was *Border Patrol*. *HR* news items in Nov and Dec 1948 indicate that this film was originally to be produced by Aubrey Schenck and William Katzell for Eagle-Lion Films, and that production on the Eagle-Lion film was set to begin in late Oct 1948 at the United States-Mexican border. In Nov 1948, according to *HR*, M-G-M paid Eagle-Lion $100,000 for the completed screenplay and the services of director Anthony Mann. A Dec 1948 *NYT* news item put the amount paid by M-G-M for the screenplay at $50,000, and noted that it was originally entitled *Wetbacks*. According to a Nov 1948 *V* news item, Eagle-Lion sold the story to M-G-M because the projected $650,000 budget was too expensive for the independent studio. *Border Incident* marked the screen debut of Italian opera singer Teresa Celli. Actress and dancer Lita Barron was formerly known as *Isabelita*. According to the *NYT* news item, the picture was filmed in the border region of Mexico and California. Studio publicity materials indicate that some filming took place in the border towns of Mexicali, Mexico, and in Calexico and El Centro, CA.

Box 27 Aug 1949. *DV* 26 Aug 1949, p. 3. *FD* 26 Aug 1949, p. 12. *HR* 20 Nov 1948, p.9. *HR* 30 Nov 1948. *HR* 26 Jan 1949, p. 13. *HR* 28 Jan 1949, p. 14. *HR* 25 Feb 1949, p. 16. *HR* 26 Aug 1949, p. 4. *MPHPD* 27 Aug 1949, p. 4730. *NYT* 1 Dec 1948. *NYT* 21 Nov 1949, p. 29. *Var* 29 Nov 1948. *Var* 30 Nov 1948. *Var* 31 Aug 1949, p. 8.

BORDER PATROL (1949) *see* **BORDER INCIDENT**

BORDER PATROL (Latino)

Harry Sherman Productions. *Dist* United Artists Productions, Inc. 2 Apr **1943**; Prod: 11 Jun—late Jun 1942 [©United Artists Productions, Inc.; 11 Dec 1942; LP12293]. Sd (Western Electric Wide Range System); b&w. 5,928 ft. 63-65 min. Passed by the National Board of Review. PCA cert no. 8665.

Series: Hopalong Cassidy.

Assoc prod Lewis J. Rachmil. *Prod* Harry Sherman. *Dir* Lesley Selander. *Asst dir* Glenn Cook. *Scr* Michael Wilson. *Photog* Russell Harlan. *Art dir* Ralph Berger. *Ed* Sherman A. Rose. *Set dec* Emile Kuri. *Ward* Earl Moser. *Mus dir* Irvin Talbot. *Sd* William Wilmarth. *Sd rec* Sound Services, Inc.

Source: Based on characters created by Clarence E. Mulford.

Cast: William Boyd (*Hopalong Cassidy*), Andy Clyde (*California*), Jay Kirby (*Johnny*), Russell Simpson (*Orestes Krebs*), Claudia Drake (*Inez La Barca*), George Reeves (*Don Enrique Perez*), Duncan Renaldo (*Commandant [La Barca]*), Pierce Lyden (*Loren*), Bob Mitchum (*Quinn*), Cliff Parkinson (*Barton*).

Western. [*Print viewed*]. Texas Rangers Hopalong Cassidy, California and Johnny are assigned to the border patrol, and cross into Mexico to consult with Mexican authorities about a murder. La Barca, the Mexican commandant, explains that the Silver Bullet Mine in the U.S. has been recruiting Mexican workers, but the men have never returned or contacted their families. The commandant's friend, Don Enrique Perez, disappeared during his investigation and his vaquero returned with his horse, but was mysteriously shot before he could talk. La Barca's daughter Inez distrusts the Rangers, although they have papers proving their commission, and follows them across the border to investigate the Silver Bullet Mine herself. As soon as the Rangers arrive, they are shot at and captured by Orestes Krebs, the self-appointed mayor, sheriff and judge of Silver Bullet City. Krebs charges the Rangers with trespassing and with the murder of Enrique and his vaquero, even though one of Krebs's guards has already confessed to Hoppy. When Inez rides into the town, Krebs convinces her that the Rangers are guilty and holds a kangaroo court, in which the jury is comprised of his outlaw confederates. Inez testifies against the Rangers, who are then found guilty and sentenced to hang. Before going to jail, Hoppy advises Inez to check out the mines, and Krebs gives her a tour after making sure that the Mexican workers whom he has enslaved are out of sight. During the tour, however, Enrique purposely drops his hat for Inez to see, and calls to her from within the mine shaft. Inez pretends she did not hear his call and offers to make dinner for Krebs and his gang. After Inez slips a gun and ammunition into the food that is being served to the prisoners, Hoppy, California and Johnny escape just before they are to be

hanged. During the ensuing gunfight, several of Krebs's outlaws are shot, and the Rangers and Inez escape to the mines. The disgruntled Mexican workers aid the Rangers in capturing Krebs's guards at the mine, and Inez is reunited with her beloved Enrique. Hoppy uses Krebs's own equipment against him, and with the help of the Mexican workers, the Rangers encircle Krebs and his gang with wagons and exchange gunfire until the gang surrenders. Krebs, however, escapes, only to be captured and arrested by Hopalong. Krebs insists that he has done nothing illegal, as he is the law in Silver Bullet City, but Hoppy reminds him that he is still in the United States, where contract labor and peonage are illegal. The Rangers force Krebs at gunpoint to pay the Mexican workers, and Johnny is disappointed to learn that Inez is engaged to Enrique. *Border patrols. Kidnapping. Mexican Americans. Mexican-American border region. Mock trials. Texas Rangers. Trials.* Fathers and daughters. Gunfights. Judges. Mayors. Mines. Missing persons. Murder. Outlaws. Sheriffs.

Note: The working title of this film was *Missing Men*. A modern source adds Merrill McCormack to the cast. For additional information on the series, consult the Series Index and see entry for *Hop-Along Cassidy* in *AFI Catalog of Feature Films, 1931-40*; F3.1990.

Box 6 Feb 1943. *DV* 19 Jun 1942. *DV* 26 Jan 1943, p. 3. *FD* 10 Jun 1943, p. 14. *HR* 12 Jun 1942. *HR* 26 Jan 1943, p. 3. *MPH* 20 Jan 1943. *MPHPD* 20 Jan 1943, p. 1137. *Var* 27 Jan 43, p. 8.

BORDER PHANTOM (Chinese Americans)

Republic Pictures Corp. *Dist* Republic Pictures Corp. 28 Dec **1936** [©Republic Pictures Corp.; 28 Dec 1936; LP6830]. Sd; b&w. 6 reels. 58 or 60 min. Passed by the National Board of Review. PCA cert no. 2891.

Prod A. W. Hackel. *Dir* S. Roy Luby. *Orig story and scr* Fred Myton. *Photog* Jack Greenhalgh. *Film ed* Roy Claire. *Sd eng* Clifford Ruberg.

Cast: BOB STEELE (*Larry O'Day*), Harley Wood (*Barbara*), Don Barclay (*Lucky Smith*), Karl Hackett (*Obed Young*), Horace Murphy (*Sheriff*), Miki Morita (*Chon Lee*), Perry Murdock (*Jim Barton*), John Peters (*Dr. Von Kurtz*), Frank Ball (*Prof. [Andrew] Hartwell*).

Drama. [*Print viewed*]. When Professor Andrew Hartwell, an entomologist, camps near the Mexican border in search of a new bug, he is murdered and his niece Barbara is held hostage at their hacienda by ranch hand Jim Barton. Travelling cowboys Larry O'Day and his partner, Lucky Smith, decide to camp at the deserted hacienda, where they discover Barbara. After Lucky is nearly strangled by an elusive assailant, Larry finds Dr. Von Kurtz attempting to steal specimens from Hartwell's lab. Next, a Chinese man arrives at the door looking for pig farmer Obed Young, who has been threatening the Hartwells to leave their hacienda. When the sheriff arrives for Hartwell's autopsy, he arrests Barbara on suspicion of murder, claiming the bullet came from her gun. An anonymous man then helps Barbara escape, but hands her over to Barton, who tries to force her to marry him. As she tries to escape, she falls off her horse and is knocked unconscious. Lucky, meanwhile, sees young Chinese women disappearing inside the house and, finding a movable wall, lands in the middle of a smuggling ring run by Chon Lee, who has been selling the women as brides to wealthy Americans. Upon discovering Von Kurtz stealing from the lab, Larry is knocked out. Barton then places Barbara in Lee's care until she revives. After overhearing Barton's plans to have Young smuggle her across the border, Lucky finds a letter written by Hartwell saying Lee threatened to kill him. Larry finally finds Lucky and races to rescue Barbara, but the sheriff intervenes and chases the couple back to the hacienda. There, Lucky names Lee as Hartwell's killer, and Barbara is free to marry Larry. *Brides. Chinese Americans. Hostages. Marriage—Forced. Murder. Smuggling.* Abduction. Attempted murder. Deserts. Entomologists. Evidence. False arrests. Farmers. Jailbreaks. Mexican-American border region. Proposals (Marital). Sheriffs. Thieves. Uncles.

Note: *Var* and copyright records refer to Miki Morita's character as "Chang Lu" and Perry Murdock's character as "Slim Barton." Two contemporary reviews and the copyright material credit Hans Joby with the part of Dr. Von Kurtz, although John Peters is credited on the film. Modern sources add Budd Buster, Clyde McClary and Horace B. Carpenter to the cast.

FD 7 Jun 1937, p. 9. *MPD* 7 Jun 1937, p. 4. *Var* 17 Feb 1937, p. 23.

THE BORDER RAIDERS (Chinese Americans)

Diando Film Corp.; A Pathé Program Feature. *Dist* Pathé Exchange, Inc. 6 Oct **1918** [©Pathé Exchange, Inc.; 27 Sep 1918; LU12902]. Si; b&w. 5 reels, 4,882 ft.

Dir Stuart Paton. *Story* Frank Beresford and Jack Cunningham. *Cam* William H. Thornley.

Cast: Betty Compson (*Rose Hardy*), George Larkin (*John Smith*), Frank Deshon (*Mock Sing*), H. C. Carpenter (*John Hardy*), Claire Du Brey (*Cleo Dade*), Howard Crampton (*Emanuel Riggs*), Fred M. Malatesta (*"Square Deal" Dixon*).

Western. Ranch owner John Hardy marries Cleo Dade, not realizing she belongs to a gang planning to use the ranch as headquarters for Mock Sing's opium smuggling operations. When Hardy suddenly disappears, Cleo takes charge of the ranch, usurping the place of Hardy's daughter, Rose. Suspecting her father is still alive, Rose visits Mock Sing's cabin. John Smith, a card dealer for Mock Sing who is attracted to Rose, saves her from Mock Sing's assault and frees Hardy, who has been held prisoner. Soon after, Hardy's ranch hands attack and kill Mock Sing, Cleo is revealed as the wife of gang member "Square Deal" Dixon, and the ranch is restored to Hardy. John Smith, actually a government agent sent to curb opium trafficking on the border, marries Rose. *Chinese Americans. Gangs. Opium. Ranchers. Ranches. Smuggling. Attempted rape. Bigamy. Cards. Cowboys. Government agents. Imprisonment.*

ETR 5 Oct 1918, p. 1517. *ETR* 12 Oct 1918, p. 1623. *MPN* 5 Oct 1918, p. 2079, 2260. *MPW* 28 Sep 1918, p. 1920. *MPW* 5 Oct 1918, p. 129. *Var* 4 Oct 1918, p. 47. *Wid's* 22 Sep 1918, p. 21.

BORDER TREASURE (Latino)

RKO Radio Pictures, Inc. *Dist* RKO Radio Pictures, Inc. 8 Jan **1950**; Prod: 27 Mar—early Apr 1950 [©RKO Radio Pictures, Inc.; 11 Aug 1950; LP367]. Sd (RCA Sound System); b&w. 5,418 ft. 60 min. PCA cert no. 14181.

Prod Herman Schlom. *Dir* George Archainbaud. [*Asst dir* John E. Pommer]. *Wrt* Norman Houston. *Dir of photog* J. Roy Hunt. [*Stills* George Hammell]. *Art dir* Albert S. D'Agostino and Charles F. Pyke. *Film ed* Desmond Marquette. *Set dec* Darrell Silvera and Harley Miller. *Mus dir* C. Bakaleinikoff. *Mus* Paul Sawtell. *Sd* John Cass and Clem Portman. [*Makeup* Mel Berns and Gene Hibbs]. [*Hair stylist* Vera Peterson]. [*Scr supv* Arnold Laven]. [*Grip* Henry Burton].

Song(s): "When I'm Walking Arm and Arm with Jim," words by Harry Harris, music by Lew Pollack; "Up in a Balloon," words and music by H. B. Farnie.

Cast: TIM HOLT [(*Ed Porter*)], Jane Nigh [(*Stella*)], John Doucette [(*Bat*)], House Peters, Jr. [(*Rod*)], Inez Cooper [(*Anita Castro*)], Julian Rivero [(*Felipe*)], Ken MacDonald [(*Sheriff Kerrigan*)], Vince Barnett [(*Pokey*)], Robert Peyton [(*Del*)], David Leonard [(*Padre*)], Tom Monroe [(*Dimmick*)], Richard Martin [(*Chito Rafferty*)], [Alex Montoya (*Manuel*)], [Charles Rivero (*Luis*)].

Western, with songs. [*Print viewed*]. After an earthquake devastates northern Mexico, a relief expedition, consisting of goods, jewels and money, is organized in Arizona by wealthy Mexican-American rancher Anita Castro. Just before the expedition is to leave, Rod, a slick outlaw, poses as a concerned contributor in order to gather information about Anita's plans. Rod reports his findings to saloon owner Bat, who plots to rob the expedition before it crosses the border. At the same time, cowboys Ed Porter and Chito Rafferty ride into town looking for work. After ladies man Chito is snubbed by Rod's girl friend, saloon singer Stella, he and Ed are hired to mend fences on the range. Anita and her major domo, Felipe, meanwhile, see Dimmick, one of Bat's henchmen, spying on the expedition's mule train and fire warning shots at him. Chito hears the gunshots and rides to investigate, while Dimmick races back to town to tell Bat the train's location. Later, on the range, a masked Bat mistakes the passing Chito for an expedition member and holds him at gunpoint until Rod, who has spotted the mule train, corrects his error. To protect the train, which is now hiding among some rocks, Felipe deliberately rides by the gang, who shoot and capture him. As Bat tries to whip Felipe into revealing the train's hiding place, Chito and Ed ride up and begin firing on the gang. After the cowboys drive off the outlaws and deliver the wounded Felipe to a nearby mission, they go to town to find Sheriff Kerrigan. Unable to locate the sheriff, Ed and Chito visit the saloon, where Chito recognizes a ring on Bat's finger and accuses him of the attack. Bat then engages Ed in a fistfight, which finally ends with the arrival of the sheriff. Bat is arrested, and Rod assumes control of the gang. Ed and Chito, meanwhile, return to the range to hunt for the mule train and are fired upon by Anita. Ed soon out-manuevers Anita and convinces her to keep the train hidden until the next morning. Ed then instructs Chito, who is smitten with Anita, to ride to town and tell the sheriff where the train is hiding. The sheriff is unavailable, however, so Chito writes the location down for

Pokey, the dimwitted deputy, unaware that Stella is watching him. The next morning, Stella, who stole the paper away from Pokey, Rod and his gang, wait near the rocks for the expedition to pass. To draw Ed and Chito away from the train, Stella pretends to lose control of her buggy and races by, screaming for help. Then, while the cowboys are busy rescuing her, Rod and his men rob the train, causing Anita to accuse Ed and Chito of betraying her. Eager to clear themselves, Ed and Chito go to town to question Stella. Just outside the saloon, Chito overhears Stella and Rod discussing a diamond necklace that was part of the relief package. Ed then sneaks into Stella's room to search for the necklace and becomes entangled in a fight when she unexpectedly returns. As Bat and his men fire on them, Ed and Chito flee the saloon with the necklace and return it to Anita at the mission. Having convinced Anita of their innocence, Ed and Chito connive to have Bat escape from jail and follow him to the gang's hideout. While Chito rides back to town to alert the sheriff, Ed stays at the hideout. There Bat confronts Rod at gunpoint and demands his cut. As he is collecting the booty, however, Stella sees Ed outside and warns the gang. Ed and the gang exchange gunfire, and during the confusion, Rod tries to escape with Stella but is shot down by Bat. After the sheriff and his posse arrive with Chito, Bat and his gang are apprehended, and Ed outdraws Stella. Later, at the border, Ed and Chito say goodbye to Anita and return to their cowboy existence. *Cowboys. Mexican Americans. Outlaws. Robbery. Betrayal. Deputies. Earthquakes. False accusations. Fistfights. Gunfights. Hideouts. Jailbreaks. Mexican-American border region. Missions. Necklaces. Posses. Saloon keepers. Sheriffs. Singers.*

Note: The working title of this film was *Treasure of Los Alamos*. According to a *HR* news item, exteriors were filmed in Lone Pine, CA.

Box 2 Sep 1950. *DV* 24 Aug 1950, p. 3. *FD* 25 Aug 1950, p. 6. *HR* 24 Mar 1950, p. 2, 3. *HR* 31 Mar 1950, p. 11. *HR* 24 Aug 1950, p. 3. *MPHPD* 9 Sep 1950, p. 478. *Var* 30 Aug 1950, p. 6.

BORDERTOWN (Latino)

Warner Bros. Productions Corp. *Dist* Warner Bros. Pictures, Inc.; The Vitaphone Corp. 23 Jan **1935**; Prod: began 17 Aug 1934 [©Warner Bros. Pictures, Inc.; 15 Dec 1934; LP5174]. Sd; b&w. 89 min. PCA cert no. 399.

[*Exec prod* Jack L. Warner and Hal B. Wallis]. [*Supv* Robert Lord]. *Dir* Archie Mayo. *Scr* Laird Doyle and Wallace Smith. *Story* Robert Lord. *Photog* Tony Gaudio. *Art dir* Jack Okey. *Ed* Thomas Richards. *Gowns* Orry-Kelly. [*Mus comp* Bernhard Kaun]. *Vitaphone Orch cond* Leo F. Forbstein.

Source: Based on the novel *Border Town* by Carroll Graham (New York, 1934).

Cast: Paul Muni (*Johnny [Juanito] Ramirez*), Bette Davis (*Marie Roark*), Margaret Lindsay (*Dale Elwell*), Eugene Pallette (*Charlie Roark*), Robert Barrat (*Padre*), Soledad Jimenez (*Mrs. Ramirez*), Hobart Cavanaugh [(*The Drunk*)], Gavin Gordon [(*Brook Manville*)], William Davidson [(*Dr. Carter*)], Arthur Stone [(*Manuel Diego*)], Vivian Tobin [(*Dale's friend*)], [Henry O'Neill (*Mr. Elwell*)], [Nella Walker (*Mrs. Elwell*)], [George Regas].

Drama. [*Print viewed*]. In Los Angeles, Johnny Ramirez, a poor Mexican, graduates from Pacific Night Law School, having worked days as a mechanic. Although Johnny is convinced that he will be a great lawyer, earning lots of money, his clients are all poor people from the neighborhood. When he loses his first court case against socialite Dale Elwell because he's poorly prepared, he angrily punches the opposing lawyer, Brook Manville, thinking he has been patronized and discriminated against. As a result, Johnny is disbarred. His dreams of being the Mexican-American Abe Lincoln shattered, Johnny leaves behind his adoring mother and hitchhikes to a border town in Mexico, determined to return as a rich man. He does very well, working his way into a partnership in a successful night club, whose owner, Charlie Roark, admires Johnny, as does his wife Marie. Thinking that her husband is all that stands between her and Johnny, Marie locks a drunken Charlie in the garage, leaving the car motor running. Johnny, in partnership with Marie, remodels the club into a stylish night club designed to attract the wealthy. One night Dale visits the club with some friends. She playfully starts a flirtation with Johnny, who, misunderstanding, falls in love with her. Sick with jealousy, Marie publicly accuses Johnny of murdering Charlie, but at his trial, she breaks down on the witness stand, having gone insane with guilt. Free at last, Johnny drives to Los Angeles to propose to Dale, who tells him their differences make any marriage impossible.

To escape Johnny's anger, she runs into the street, where she is hit by a car. Once again, Johnny must reassess his life. He sells his club, endows a law school with the money, and returns to Los Angeles to live with his own people. *Class distinction. Jealousy. Mexican Americans. Moral reformation. Mothers and sons. Poverty. Racism. Carbon monoxide. Catholic Church. Insanity. Lawyers. Los Angeles (CA). Mechanics. Murder. Nightclubs. Priests. Socialites. Trials.*

Note: The film's pre-release title was *New Bordertown. FD* notes that Miriam Hopkins was considered for the lead opposite Muni. According to *DV*, the studio did not intend to credit Carroll Graham because they felt the script was so different from the book. Although credited to different writers, portions of the 1940 Warner Bros. film *They Drive By Night* closely resemble scenes in this film. Modern sources note that the opening scenes were shot in Los Angeles' Olvera St. According to modern sources, Muni hired a Mexican chauffeur named Manuel and studied his accent and gestures as part of his preparation for the role.

DV 13 Aug 1934, p. 1. DV 17 Aug 1934, p. 2. DV 23 Aug 1934, p. 3. DV 14 Jan 1935, p. 3. FD 18 Jun 1934, p. 8. FD 24 Jan 1935, p. 3. HR 14 Jan 1935, p. 3. HR 30 Jan 1935, p. 2 MPD 15 Jan 1935, p. 8. MPH 29 Sep 1934, p. 51. MPH 2 Feb 1935, p. 58. NYT 24 Jan 1935, p. 22. Var 29 Jan 1935, p. 14.

BORN TO DIE *see* **ROBIN HOOD OF EL DORADO**

BORN TO KISS *see* **LJUBAV I STRAST**

BORSHT BELT FOLLIES *see* **MONTICELLO, HERE WE COME!**

BOSTON BLACKIE'S CHINESE VENTURE (Chinese Americans)
Columbia Pictures Corp. *Dist* Columbia Pictures Corp. 2 Mar **1949**; Prod: 18 May–5 June 1948 [©Columbia Pictures Corp.; 3 Mar 1949; LP2155]. Sd (Western Electric Recording); b&w. 5,335 ft. 59 min.
Series: Boston Blackie.
Prod Rudolph C. Flothow. *Dir* Seymour Friedman. [*Asst dir* James Nicholson]. *Orig scr* Maurice Tombragel. *Dir of photog* Vincent Farrar. *Art dir* Paul Palmentola. *Film ed* Richard Fantl. *Set dec* James Crowe. *Mus dir* Mischa Bakaleinikoff. [*Sd* George Cooper].
Source: Based on the character created by Jack Boyle.
Cast: Chester Morris [(*Boston Blackie*)], Maylia [(*Mei Ling*)], Richard Lane [(*Inspector Farraday*)], Don McGuire [(*Bus guide*)], Joan Woodbury [(*Red*)], Sid Tomack [(*Runt*)], Frank Sully [(*Sergeant Matthews*)], Charles Arnt [(*Pop Gerard*)], Louis Van Rooten [(*Bill Craddock*)], Philip Ahn [(*Wong*)], [Peter Brocco (*Rolfe*)], [Benson Fong (*Ab Hing*)], [Edgar Dearing (*Reiber*)], [Fred Sears (*Chemist*)], [Pat O'Malley (*Jim*)], [Victor Sen Yung (*Chinese lad*)], [Bob Williams (*Cynical tourist*)], [George Lloyd (*Bartender*)], [Harry Strang (*Mac*)], [Celeste Savoi (*Tourist*)], [James Leong (*Chinese hatchet man*)], [Harold Fong (*Chinese victim*)], [William Yip, Eddie Lee, George Lee (*Fantan players*)], [Ottola Nesmith (*Solicitous tourist*)], [Aen Ling Chow (*Cashier*)], [Marya Marco (*Chinese girl*)].
Mystery. [*Print viewed*]. After Mei Ling discovers the body of her uncle, Charley Wu, in the Chinese laundry he owned, the police question reformed safe cracker Boston Blackie and his sidekick Runt. Blackie admits that he was at the laundry and, because Charley was not there, wrote his name on a piece of paper and attached it to his laundry. Then Mei Ling informs the police that Charley had telephoned Bill Craddock, the owner of the Club Cathay where she works, after he discovered a strange package in the club's laundry delivery. Craddock tells the police that he did not know what the package contained and adds that Charley objected to Mei Ling working at the club. Later, Mei Ling asks Blackie to watch Craddock, because she suspects that he knows more than he will admit. At the club, Blackie sits in the bar, pretending to be drunk, while Runt watches outside. Blackie overhears a conversation between Craddock and his girl friend Red, and when she leaves the club, Blackie follows her to a movie theater in Chinatown, which is owned by Pop Gerard. From there, Runt follows her to her job working as a shill for a Chinatown tour. While the guide takes the tourists along some corridors, where they witness staged "scenes" with fantan players, Chinese slave girls and an attack by a hatchet man, Red slips away for a few minutes to speak with Reiber, a Dutch jewel cutter, who has been forced to work with her. The tour ends at Wong's Curio Shop, where the guide is given a package of tea by the clerk. After observing the exchange, Blackie also buys some tea and switches packages with the guide. Later, Blackie and Runt examine the tea and discover cut diamonds among the leaves. The next morning Blackie and Runt ask Craddock to cut them in on his jewel racket, but at first he professes not to know what they are talking about. When he is about to give Blackie some information, someone throws a knife in his back. During

the next Chinatown tour, Blackie and Runt then kidnap the guide, with Mei Ling's help, and question him. The guide reveals nothing, and Blackie and Runt are forced to run from the police, who want to question them about Craddock's murder. While hiding at the movies, Blackie and Runt see Red enter a closet and follow her through a secret door into Reiber's laboratory. There, after Reiber reveals that Gerard committed the murders, Gerard tries to kill Blackie and Runt. His shots attract the attention of the police. Following Red, Blackie then leads them all to Wong's Curio Shop. In order to prove that Red and Gerard are recutting stolen jewels, Blackie proceeds to examine all the packages of tea. The jewels are found in the very last package, and Runt suggests that they use the opened tea for the Boston Blackie Tea Party. *Amateur detectives. Chinatowns. Chinese Americans. Jewel thieves. Murder. Diamonds. Kidnapping. Laundries. Motion picture theaters. Nightclubs. Police. Tea. Tour guides.*

Note: The film's working titles were *Boston Blackie's Honor* and *Boston Blackie's Chinese Adventure*. For more information on the "Boston Blackie" series, consult the Series Index.

Box 26 Mar 1949. DV 31 Dec 1948, p. 3. HR 18 Jun 1948, p. 20. HR 25 Jun 1948, p. 20. HR 4 Jan 1949, p. 3. MPHPD 15 Jan 1949, p. 4462.

BOSTON BLACKIE'S HONOR *see* **BOSTON BLACKIE'S CHINESE VENTURE**

THE BOTTLE IMP (Hawaiians)
Jesse L. Lasky Feature Play Co. *Dist* Paramount Pictures Corp. 26 Mar **1917** [©Jesse L. Lasky Feature Play Co.; 22 Mar 1917; LP10420]. Si; b&w. 5 reels.
Dir Marshall Neilan. *Asst dir* William Horwitz. *Scen* Charles Maigne. *Cam* Walter Stradling.
Source: Based on the novel *The Bottle Imp* by Robert Louis Stevenson (London, 1891).
Cast: Sessue Hayakawa (*Lopaka*), Lehua Waipahu (*Kokua*), H. Komshi (*Keano*), George Kuwa (*Makale*), Guy Oliver (*Rollins*), James Neill (*A priest*).
Fantasy, Drama. When Lopaka, a poor Hawaiian fisherman, falls in love with Kokua, a young girl of royal blood, her father refuses her hand until Lopaka can bring him two feather cloaks from a rare bird. While searching the mountains for the bird, Lopaka encounters a dying priest of Pele who sells him a wishing bottle in which Kono, the god of the volcanos, is confined. He is warned that the possessor of the bottle who dies still owning it will be damned and that the only way to rid oneself of the bottle is by selling it for a sum less than it was bought. Made rich by Kono, Lopaka marries Kokua and sells the bottle. He later finds himself in a terrible dilemma when, as a victim of leprosy, he is forced to buy the bottle back for the smallest coin of the realm. To save her husband from damnation, Kokua sacrifices herself by buying the bottle for a smaller French coin, but luckily a base and wicked sailor appears with a still smaller Chinese coin and becomes its final owner when the bottle is lost at sea. The wealth of Lopaka vanishes with the bottle, but he is content with Kokua by his side. *Genies. Hawaiians. Magic. Mythical characters. Self-sacrifice. Wishes. Fishermen. Leprosy. Marriage. Royalty.*

Note: This picture was shot in Hawaii according to press releases. The original title of the scenario was "The Mountain Devil." The continuity for this film included in the studio records states that the film begins with Robert Louis Stevenson, played by James Neill, reading the story of *The Bottle Imp* to a little boy and girl.

ETR 31 Mar 1917, p. 1180. Motog 14 Apr 1917, p. 796. MPN 7 Apr 1917, p. 2194. MPW 7 Apr 1917, p. 113, 162. NYDM 31 Mar 1917, p. 26. Wid's 29 Mar 1917, p. 202.

BOU YU LEI FA *see* **BOW YU LEE HUA**

BOUDOIR DIPLOMATIQUE *see* **DON JUAN DIPLOMÁTICO**

BOW YU LEE HUA (Chinese language)
Grandview Film Co. **1947**?; Hong Kong showing: 1947? Sd; b&w. Length undetermined. Chinese language. [*Not viewed*]. [No information concerning the plot of this film has been located.].
Note: The Cantonese transliterated title is *Bou Yu Lei Fa*. This film was probably made in the U.S.

BOWERY BUCKAROOS (Native Americans)
Monogram Pictures Corp.; A Jan Grippo Production. *Dist* Monogram Pictures Corp. 22 Nov **1947**; New York opening: week of 8 Oct 1947 [©Monogram Pictures Corp.; 22 Nov 1947; LP1285]. 12527 (Western Electric Recording); b&w. 65-66 min.

Series: The Bowery Boys.

Prod Jan Grippo. *Dir* William Beaudine. [*Asst dir* Frank Fox]. *Orig scr* Edmond Seward, Tim Ryan and Jerry Warner. *Photog* Marcel LePicard. [*Spec eff* Augie Lohman]. *Art dir* Dave Milton. *Supv film ed* Otho Lovering. *Set dec* Raymond Boltz, Jr. *Mus dir* Edward J. Kay. *Rec* John Carter.

Song(s): "Louie, the Lout," words and music by Eddie Maxwell; "Two-Gun Tillie," words by Eddie Maxwell, music by Edward J. Kay.

Cast: LEO GORCEY [(*Slip, also known as "Dead Eye" Dan McGurke*)], Huntz Hall [(*Sach*)], Bobby Jordan [(*Bobby*)], Gabriel Dell [(*Gabe*)], Billy Benedict [(*Whitey*)], David Gorcey [(*Chuck*)], Julie Gibson [(*Carolyn Briggs, previously known as Kathryn Briggs*)], Russell Simpson [(*Luke Barlow*)], Minerva Urecal [(*Kate T. Barlow*)], Jack Norman [(*Blackjack*)], Iron Eyes Cody [(*Indian Joe*)], Bernard Gorcey [(*Louie*)], Rosa Turich [(*Ramona*)], Chief Yowlachi [(*Chief Hi-Octane*)], Sherman Sanders [(*Rufe*)], Billy Wilkerson [(*Moose*)], Jack O'Shea [(*Jose*)], Cathy Carter, [Bud Osborne (*Spike*)].

Comedy, Western, with songs. [*Print viewed*]. In Louie's Sweet Shop, in New York's Bowery, Sach, a member of the Bowery Boys gang, is reading a comic book called "Western Yarns" when Sheriff Luke Barlow, of Hangman's Hollow, New Mexico, enters the shop on his horse. Barlow has traveled 3,000 miles to arrest Louie for the twenty-year-old murder of Pete Briggs, his partner in a gold mine. After Barlow leaves, Louie explains to the boys and to Slip that he was framed by saloon owner Blackjack, who killed Pete for the gold, but never found it. The map to the treasure, which he hopes to restore to Pete's daughter Kathryn, is painted on Louie's back. Slip sends his friend Gabe, a cardsharp, to Hangman's Hollow to acquaint himself with Blackjack, and Slip and the boys—Whitey, Chuck, Bobby and Sach—follow Gabe after painting a copy of the map on Sach's back. As they near Hangman's Hollow, they are met by a band of Indians, who are dressed in war regalia for their annual heritage celebration. Sach shows the map to Joe, one of the Indians, and Indian Joe reports to Blackjack, who in turn orders his men to shoot at the boys when they arrive in town. The local marshal is Kate T. Barlow, Luke's wife, who lives with Carolyn Briggs, a performing sharpshooter at Blackjack's saloon. Slip and the boys tell Kate they are looking for a baby named Kathryn Briggs, and show her a photograph of an infant that Louie had given them, which matches one in her scrapbook. While sleeping outdoors, Sach is taken hostage by Indian Joe and brought to Blackjack. Enroute, however, they go through a pond, and the map is washed off. In Blackjack's Plugged Dollar Saloon, Gabe introduces Slip to Blackjack as sharpshooting outlaw "Dead Eye" Dan McGurke, and Slip fools Blackjack into believing he is a perfect shot by apparently hitting the center of an ace of spades, which Carolyn has actually shot. After Carolyn performs in the saloon, she matches her childhood photo with Slip's, and he realizes she is Pete's grown daughter. Sach, meanwhile, has told Blackjack that there is another map, and, thinking it is on the back of one of the boys, Blackjack's men stage a hoedown in which they try to pull off the boy's shirts. Slip holds up Blackjack and brings him to the Barlow ranch. By stringing him up in a bull pen, Slip and the boys force Blackjack to confess to murdering Pete and framing Louie. Louie arrives with Luke for his hanging, but is exonerated, and Sach follows with Blackjack's men as his captives. Back in Louie's Sweet Shop, Sach tells Louie, Slip and the boys about his Western dream. *Cardsharping. Frame-ups. Gold. New York City–Bowery. The West. Bulls. Confession (Law). Dreams. Impersonation and imposture. Indians of North America. Mothers and daughters. Murder. New Mexico. Saloon keepers. Sharpshooters. Sheriffs. United States. Marshals.*

Note: The title card of the opening credits reads: "Leo Gorcey and The Bowery Boys in *Bowery Buckaroos*." The *Var* review lists actress Julie Gibson as Julie Briggs, by which name she was also known. This film was part of the Bowery Boys series. For more information about the Bowery Boys series, consult the Series Index and the entries for *Crime School* and *Little Tough Guy* (see *AFI Catalog of Feature Films, 1931-40*; F3.0873 and F3.2534.).

DV 26 Nov 1947. *HR* 26 Nov 1947. *MPHPD* 25 Oct 1947. *Var* 15 Oct 1947, p. 10.

THE BOWERY PRINCESS *see* **DIMPLES**

THE BOWIE KNIFE *see* **COMANCHE TERRITORY**

A BOY AND THE LAW (Jewish Americans)

Youth Photo Play Co. *Dist* Pan-American Film Mfg Co. Mar **1914**? [©Willis Brown & William Wesley Young; 17 Nov 1913; LU1593]. Si; b&w. 4-5 reels.

Cast: Willis Brown (*Himself*), William Eckstein (*Himself*).

Social, Drama. In Czarist Russia, William ("Willie") Eckstein, persecuted for being a Jew, faces imprisonment when school officials discover his membership in a secret society. Willie soon escapes and flees to America, making his way to Salt Lake City, Utah, where his uncle lives. Willie starts his new life as a newspaper boy but soon ends up in the hands of truancy officers. Summoned to the court of Judge Willis Brown, Willie at first defies the law, but later, he realizes that the judge sincerely wishes to help him. Judge Brown is instrumental in purchasing a farm for wayward boys, which he hopes will serve as a substitute for jail. A village called "Boy Town" is built on the farm, and Willie is elected mayor. At Boy Town, the youths practice discipline and self-government, and consequently, many of them grow into successful and law-abiding adults. Willie attends college and later becomes the manager of a large farm owned by the judge. *Antisemitism. Willis Brown. Criminals–Rehabilitation. William Eckstein. Immigrants. Jews. Judges. Juvenile delinquents. Escapes. Farms. Newsboys. Reformatories. Religious persecution. Russia. Salt Lake City (UT). Secret societies.*

Note: The story is said to reflect William Eckstein's own experiences. *Var* 3 Apr 1914, p. 21. *MPW* 14 Mar 1914, p. 1418.

BOY OF THE STREETS (Irish Americans)

Monogram Pictures Corp.; Scott R. Dunlap in Charge of Production. *Dist* Monogram Pictures Corp. 8 Dec **1937**; Prod: mid-Oct—31 Oct 1937 [©Monogram Pictures Corp.; 29 Nov 1937; LP7660]. Sd (Western Electric Mirrophonic Recording); b&w. 9 reels, 6,852 ft. 76 min. PCA cert no. 3858.

[*Prod* George Kann]. *Dir* William Nigh. *Asst dir* W. B. Eason. *Orig story* Rowland Brown. *Adpt and dial* Gilson Brown and Scott Darling. *Dir of photog* Gilbert Warrenton. *Film ed* Russell Schoengarth. [*Mus* Abe Meyer]. *Rec eng* W. C. Smith. *Tech dir* E. R. Hickson. *Prod mgr* George E. Kann.

Cast: JACKIE COOPER [(*Chuck Brennan*)], Maureen O'Connor [(*Norah*)], Kathleen Burke [(*Julie Stone*)], Robert Emmett O'Connor [(*Rourke*)], Marjorie Main [(*Mary Brennan*)], Matty Fain [(*Blackie Davis*)], George Cleveland [(*Tim Farley*)], Gordon Elliott [(*Dr. Allan*)], Guy Usher [(*Fog Horn Brennan*)], Paul White [(*Spike*)], [Don Latorre (*Tony*)], [Edwin Brian (*Chuck's lieutenant*)], [Hollis Jewell], [Wesley Giraud], [Robert Tucker], [Kent Rogers], [Johnny Morris], [Frank Malo], [Mortimer Kurt], [Henry Caruso], [Al Frazer], [Frank Bishell], [Freddie Jackson].

Social, Drama. [*Print viewed*]. In a predominantly Irish slum in New York, sixteen-year-old Chuck Brennan has become the leader of a gang, in emulation of his father, who, Chuck believes, has become an important leader in ward politics without working at a job. To help Norah, a neighbor whose mother is taken to a sanitarium for tuberculosis, Chuck arranges for her to sing at a nightclub, but because she is underage, women from the Children's Aid Society arrive to take her to an orphanage. Julie Stone has recently inherited the tenement in which Norah and Chuck's family live, and with the help of the neighborhood doctor, she is trying to fix it up. Julie pays to send Norah to a private girls' school. During a fight between Chuck's gang and a rival Italian gang, Spike, a young black shoeshine boy, is killed when he tries to save Chuck from getting hit by a truck. After Chuck's mother blames him for Spike's death, he goes to ward boss Olden's office looking for work, but sees that his father is only Olden's stooge. Chuck then goes to work for gambler Blackie Davis, who is trying to shake down establishments in Chuck's neighborhood, but during a break-in at a laundry warehouse, Chuck tries to prevent Blackie from shooting the neighborhood cop Rourke, and both he and Rourke are shot. In the hospital, Chuck realizes that Blackie used him for a stooge and fought unfairly without giving Rourke a chance. He tells Rourke that he feels bad for calling his father a stooge and gives Blackie's address. After he turns seventeen, Chuck says goodbye to his parents, Julie and Norah, whom he hesitatingly kisses, and ships out with the Navy. *Fathers and sons. Gangs. Irish Americans. Juvenile delinquents. Maturation. Moral reformation. Slums. African Americans. Automobile accidents. Fights. Good Samaritans. Gunshot wounds. Halloween. Inheritance. Nightclubs. Physicians. Police. Political bosses. Racketeers. Reformers. Singers. Tenement-houses. Tuberculosis. United States. Navy.*

Note: *Var* called this film Monogram's most ambitious production to date. Some reviews noted similarities to Samuel Goldwyn's *Dead End* (see *AFI Catalog of Feature Films, 1931-40*; F3.0981), which was released a few

months earlier. *Har* commented, "It is a sort of *Dead End*, in which George Kann, the producer, and William Nigh, the old reliable director, have been able to accomplish almost what Sam Goldwyn accomplished with more than twenty times the amount of money they had at their disposal....The moral is the same in the story of this picture as it is in the story of *Dead End*—that poverty and environment in the tenement districts of the big cities breed criminals, and that the same young boys and girls, reared in a better environment, would turn out good citizens." According to *NYT*, this film was awarded the *Parents' Magazine* medal for the best movie of the month. According to *NYT*, Jackie Cooper, whose contract a year earlier was not renewed by M-G-M, was signed by Monogram for two more films because of his performance in this film. This was the first film of Maureen O'Connor, a fourteen-year-old radio singer. Doris Rankin is listed as a cast member in a *HR* production chart, but her participation in the final film has not been confirmed.

Box 11 Dec 1937. *DV* 2 Dec 1937, p. 3. *FD* 2 Dec 1937, p. 7. *Har* 11 Dec 1937, p. 198. *HR* 18 Oct 1937, p. 11. *HR* 1 Nov 1937, p. 9. *HR* 2 Dec 1937, p. 3. *MPD* 2 Dec 1937, p. 6. *MPH* 11 Dec 1937, pp. 40-41. *NYT* 31 Dec 1937, sect. II, p. 162. *NYT* 9 Jan 1938. *NYT* 24 Jan 1938, p. 17. *Var* 1 Dec 1937, p. 14.

BOY! WHAT A GIRL! (African Americans)

Herald Pictures, Inc. *Dist* Screen Guild Productions, Inc. 20 Sep **1947**; New York opening: 21 May, 1947; Prod: began mid-Sep 1946 at Fox Movietone Studios, New York [©Herald Pictures, Inc.; 6 Apr 1947; LP194]. Sd (RCA Sound Recording); b&w. 7 reels, 6,408 ft. 73 min. Passed by the National Board of Review. PCA cert no. 04317.

Prod Jack Goldberg and Arthur Leonard. *Dir* Arthur Leonard. *Orig scr* Vincent Valentini. *Dir of photog* George Webber. *Art dir* Sam Corso. *Film ed* Jack Kemp. *Cost* Ann Blazier. *Mus supv* John Gluskin. *Sd eng* Mac Williams. *Makeup* Morgan Jones. *Casting dir* Billy Shaw. *Tech dir* J. M. Lehrfeld.

Music: "Slamboree," music by Slam Stewart; "Just a Riff" and "Whuss Happenin'," performed by Big Sid Catlett and Band.

Song(s): "Satchel Mouth Baby," words and music by Mary Lou Williams; "Just in Case You Change Your Mind," words and music by Harry Patterson, Melvin Bell and Deek Watson; "Oh Me, Oh My, Oh Gosh," words and music by Slam Stewart; "I Just Refuse to Sing the Blues," words and music by Walter Bishop; "Crazy Riffin'," words and music by Walter Fuller and Robert Brown.

Cast: Betti Mays [(*Cristola Cummings*)], Elwood Smith [(*Jim Walton*)], Duke Williams [(*Harry Diggs*)], Sheila Guyse [(*Francine Cummings*)], Warren Patterson [(*Mr. Donaldson*)], Al Jackson [(*Mr. Cummings*)], Sybil Lewis [(*Madame Deborah*)], Tim Moore [(*Bumpsie*)], Milton Wood [(*Gaston*)], Slam Stewart, Trio, [Beryl Booker (*Piano*)], [John Collins (*Guitar*)], Big Sid Catlett and Band, Basil Spears, Ann Cornell, Harlemaniacs, and introducing Deek Watson and The Brown Dots, Guest Artist Gene Krupa, [Jimmy Fuller], [Lorenzo Tucker], [Ram Ramirez], [Al Gluster], [The International Jitterbugs].

African American, Comedy, with songs. [*Print viewed*]. In a Harlem apartment building, Jim Walton listens to Slam Stewart and his band, which he plans to feature in his new show along with female impersonator Bumpsie. Jim is in love with Cristola Cummings, whose wealthy father, believing that Jim is a successful producer, has promised to put up half the money for the new show if Parisian Madame Deborah will supply the rest of the funds. Cummings arrives unexpectedly from Chicago with Cristola and her sister Francine, hoping to meet Madame Deborah. Attempting to maintain a pretense of wealth, Jim and his partner, Harry Diggs, ask one of their actors to impersonate a butler. Their ruse is almost exposed when their landlord, Mr. Donaldson, demands that they pay their back rent, but Jim manages to convince Cummings that Donaldson is an actor in a play called "I Want My Room Rent." Learning that Madame Deborah will not arrive for a few days, Harry persuades Bumpsie to impersonate her by promising to star him in the new show. Later, when she is alone with Jim, Cristola scolds him for not writing, but embraces him when he honestly admits he does not have the Long Island mansion he claimed. While Francine gets to know Harry, Cummings converses with Bumpsie. Cummings, who is attracted to Bumpsie, hints that he would like to marry again for the sake of his daughters. Meanwhile, the real Madame Deborah arrives and introduces herself as "Mrs. Martin." Seeing that she is wealthy, Donaldson is pleased to rent a room to her. From Gaston, who has followed her from Paris, Donaldson learns that Madame Deborah has "oodles of money" and suddenly takes an interest in Bumpsie, who he thinks is Madame Deborah. Donaldson then plans a garden party in Madame Deborah's honor and offers his actor residents free rent for a week, plus ten dollars, for providing the entertainment. When Cummings learns that his daughters want to marry Jim and Harry, he

objects at first, but later agrees to give his consent if Madame Deborah approves, as he will announce his engagement to her that night. Coincidentally, both Gaston and Donaldson also intend to announce their engagements to Madame Deborah that night. During the garden party, Bumpsie invites his two suitors to a rent party for Jim and Harry, explaining it is a rehearsal of a show titled "The Rent Party." When Bumpsie dances in a scanty ballet costume, Cummings, thinking that "Madame Deborah" is exposing herself to other men, jealously stalks out. Escaping from pranksters, Bumpsie encounters the real Madame Deborah, who hides him in her room, where he falls asleep. Outraged because he thinks that the whole building is being lured by Bumpsie's charms, Cummings decides to return to Chicago with his daughters. When Cristola confesses that she knows Jim is broke, but admires the way he has kept up his courage, the real Madame Deborah vows to intercede with Cummings. Although he has sworn to avoid women, Cummings is immediately attracted by Madame Deborah's flirtations. Meanwhile, two French thugs kidnap Bumpsie after they, too, mistake him for Madame Deborah. When Gaston removes the cover over Bumpsie's head, in preparation for a kiss, he recoils in horror. Bumpsie challenges him to a fight and then, still dressed in a ballet costume, runs away. When a dropped handkerchief is found in Madame Deborah's room, Cummings and Donaldson think she has been kidnapped. Meanwhile, the rent party erupts in a fight. Gaston threatens Madame Deborah and Cummings, and Jim punches him. Later Bumpsie reappears without his disguise, and Madame Deborah reveals her true identity. Cummings and Madame Deborah decide to marry, and all ends happily when they agree to back Jim's show. *African Americans. Female impersonation. New York City—Harlem. Romantic rivalry. Theatrical backers. Theatrical producers. Bands (Music). Cigars. Dances. Drugging. Fathers and daughters. Fights. French. Kidnapping. Landlords. Parties. Romance. Wealth.*

Note: In the opening credits, following a standard indemnification clause (in which it is stated that the story, names, incidents and characters are fictitious), the following parenthetical statement was included: "Our lawyer, Mr. Hemindinger of Callahan, Callahan, & Callahan told us we had to say this." *Boy! What a Girl!* was the first production of Herald Pictures, which, according to the film's pressbook, planned to produce eleven more films and release one per month. The pressbook claimed that "the production cost of the picture is at least four times that spent on any all-Negro feature to date." Praising producer Jack Goldberg as a "successful pioneer in Negro stage and screen attractions," the pressbook stated, "For over twenty years he has fought slip-shod methods in all-Negro productions, and with each of his releases he has forced other producers to raise the standard of their pictures to meet his competition. This time they will be forced to jump their production cost to $50,000 on each picture if they expect to compete." Herald, which apparently hoped to widen the audience for their films, asserted in the pressbook that, "an all-Negro motion picture can be produced to play any theater in the country and, not merely confined to the some 600 odd playhouses that cater strictly to an all-Negro audience." The *Var* reviewer commented, "The several hundred Negro film houses in this country have long been faced with a product shortage on race-films, and the newly formed Herald pictures will do something to alleviate the numerical relief." The pressbook claimed that this film was the first black-cast film to be made "under modern Hollywood conditions." It was produced at Fox Movietone Studios in New York City, where, according to the pressbook, they shared a studio floor with the production of *Carnegie Hall* (see below). Some location shooting was done in Harlem.

A *HR* news item from Aug 1946 stated that Marva Louis, the ex-wife of heavyweight champion Joe Louis, had been signed to appear in the film, which was to be her first, but, her appearance in the released film has not been confirmed. According to the pressbook, Big Sid Catlett played at Carnegie Hall the previous year as the drummer in an all-American jazz band; the Harlemaniacs were winners in "Lindy hopping" at the Harvest Moon Ball held at Madison Square Garden; and the noted drummer Gene Krupa was invited to appear in the film by director Arthur Leonard after Krupa came to the set to visit Catlett. According to *Var*, Warren Patterson and Al Jackson, who played "Donaldson" and "Cummings," respectively, were a vaudeville comedy team.

Box 15 Feb 1947. *FD* 4 Feb 1947, p. 12. *HR* 29 Aug 1946. *HR* 13 Aug 1947, p. 4. *MPHPD* 8 Feb 1947. *Var* 5 Feb 1947, p. 20.

THE BOY WITH GREEN HAIR (Irish Americans)

RKO Radio Pictures, Inc.; A Dore Schary Presentation. *Dist* RKO Radio Pictures, Inc. 27 Dec **1948**; Prod: 9 Feb—mid-Mar 1948 [©RKO Radio Pictures, Inc.; 24 Nov 1948; LP2012]. Sd (RCA Sound System); col (Technicolor). 7,373 ft. 82 min. PCA cert no. 13015.

Prod Stephen Ames. *Dir* Joseph Losey. *Asst dir* James Lane. *Scr* Ben Barzman and Alfred Lewis Levitt. *Dir of photog* George Barnes. [*Cam op* Eddie Pyle]. [*Stills* Rod Tolmie]. *Technicolor color dir* Natalie Kalmus. *Assoc* Morgan Padelford. *Art dir* Albert S. D'Agostino and Ralph Berger. *Film ed* Frank Doyle. *Set dec* Darrell Silvera and William Stevens. *Gowns* Adele Balkan. *Mus dir* C. Bakaleinikoff. *Mus* Leigh Harline. *Orch arr* Gil Grau. *Sd* Earl Wolcott and Clem Portman.

Makeup supv Gordon Bau. [*Hair stylist* Hazel Rogers]. [*Prod mgr* Ruby Rosenberg]. [*Script supv* Richard Kinon]. [*Grip* Ralph Wildman].

Song(s): "Nature Boy," words and music by eden ahbez; "Tail of the Coat" and "Gyp, Gyp, My Little Horse," composers unknown.

Source: Based on the short story "The Boy with Green Hair" by Betsy Beaton in *This Week* (29 Dec 1946).

Cast: Pat O'Brien (*Gramp [Frye]*), Robert Ryan (*Dr. Evans*), Barbara Hale (*Miss Brand*), Dean Stockwell (*Peter [Frye]*), Richard Lyon (*Michael*), Walter Catlett (*"The King"*), Samuel S. Hinds (*Dr. Knudson*), Regis Toomey (*Mr. Davis*), Charles Meredith (*Mr. Piper*), David Clarke (*Mr. Davis*), Billy Sheffield (*Red*), John Calkins (*Danny*), Teddy Infuhr (*Timmy*), Dwayne Hickman (*Joey*), Eilene Janssen (*Peggy*), Curtis Jackson (*Classmate*), Charles Arnt (*Mr. Hammond*), [Don Pietro (*Newsboy*)], [Patricia Byrnes, Carol Coombs, Cynthia Robichaux, Georgette Crooks, Donna Jo Gribble (*Girls*)], [Billy White, Rusty Tamblyn, Baron White, Spear Martin, Michael Losey (*Boys*)], [Al Murphy (*Janitor*)], [Anna Q. Nilsson, Lynn Whitney (*Townswomen*)], [Eula Guy (*Mrs. Fisher*)], [Brick Sullivan, Kenneth Patterson, Dayle Robertson (*Policemen*)], [Carl Saxe (*Plainclothesman*)], [Sharon McManus (*Girl who cries*)], [Ann Carter (*Eva*)], [Howard Brody (*Eva's brother*)], [Ray Burkett, Warren Shannon (*Little old men*)], [Diane Graeff (*Tiny girl*)], [Roger Perry (*Small boy*)], [Wendy Oser (*Frail girl*)], [Charles Lane (*Passerby*)], [Max Rose].

Fantasy, Social, Youth, Drama. [*Print viewed*]. In a police station, a sad, bald-headed boy, who has refused to reveal his name or utter a word, is questioned by Dr. Evans, an expert on "boys." Coaxed by Dr. Evans, the boy, Peter Frye, finally relates his story: After his parents are killed while doing relief work in war-torn Europe, Peter is shipped from relative to relative, until he is taken in by family friend Gramp Frye, an Irish-born widower living in a small town. Although at first wary of his new home, Peter soon comes to trust and respect the understanding Gramp, a former vaudevillian and magician who works nights as a singing waiter. Peter is unaware that his parents are dead, and Gramp, afraid to upset the boy, allows him to believe that they will someday return for him. At his new school, Peter makes friends quickly; he later gets a job delivering groceries and joins in a clothing drive for war victims. Peter's newfound happiness ends abruptly, however, when a classmate unwittingly tells him that he is an orphan and compares him to a pathetic-looking boy in a war orphan poster on display at the school. Peter pretends to shrug off the painful news, but is filled with confused feelings about his parents' death. That night, he questions Gramp about death and war, and during their discussion, Gramp mentions that his wife loved to grow green plants, which she felt symbolized the hope of spring. Gramp then promises Peter he will have a surprise waiting for him in the morning. The next day, after Peter takes his bath, he discovers that his hair has turned green and assumes that Gramp is behind the "trick." Gramp, however, tells Peter that his surprise was a magician's scarf and takes Peter to see Dr. Knudson. When the baffled doctor suggests that Peter either dye his hair or cut it off, the boy refuses to consider either option and asks Gramp if he can stay at home until his hair returns to its former color. Eventually, a bored and lonely Peter dares to venture outside and, as he and Gramp walk to school, draws the stares of curious passersby. Although Gramp challenges the hysterical attitudes of his neighbors, some of whom believe Peter's green hair is the result of tainted milk, Peter remains the target of speculation and is ridiculed and ostracized by his schoolmates. Even after Miss Brand, Peter's kindhearted teacher, tries to ease the other children's fears by pointing out that only one child in the class has red hair, Peter feels rejected. That night, Peter tears in two a letter that his father had left for him to read on his sixteenth birthday and runs away to some nearby woods. There, after Peter gives in to his pent-up tears, he hears a young voice calling his name. To his amazement, Peter discovers all of the children from the war orphan posters standing, alive, in the woods. When Michael, the frail poster boy to whom Peter was once compared, suggests that his green hair is the "mark of something good," Peter bristles with sarcasm. Michael soon changes Peter's feelings, however, and advises him to use his unusual hair to call attention to the horrors of war. Following the boy's instructions, the now-inspired Peter goes from adult to adult, explaining to them that his hair is green because he is a war orphan. Peter's words fail to soothe the town's fears, and he is told that he is ruining the milkman's business because the people are convinced that his hair is the result

of contaminated milk. When Peter is asked by various adults to cut off his hair, he once again refuses, stating that it has "meaning." He then returns to the woods, hoping to find the poster children there, but instead is chased by his male classmates, who are determined to cut off his hair. Peter escapes from the woods, but when he returns home, Gramp, who wants his foster son to be happy and carefree, suggests that shaving his hair might be the only remedy to his problems. Reluctantly Peter agrees to have his hair cut, but cries silent tears as the barber shaves his head in front of Gramp and a crowd of onlookers. Peter's brave tears cause Gramp and the crowd to grow suddenly ashamed of themselves. Although Gramp later apologizes to Peter for not supporting him, Peter runs away from home. Back in the police station, Dr. Evans gently chides Peter for not having more faith in himself and then returns him to Gramp, who is waiting outside with Dr. Knudson and Miss Brand. Feeling that Peter is now mature enough, Gramp reads from his father's torn letter. Written shortly before his father's death, the letter reassures Peter of his parents' love and asks him to remind people who might otherwise forget about the terrible price of war. Moved by the letter, Peter declares that he hopes his hair will grow back green and returns home with his proud foster father. *Children. Hair. Intolerance. Ostracism. Pacifism and pacifists. Barbers and barbershops. Forests. Foster parents. Irish Americans. Letters. Milkmen. Orphans. Physicians. Runaways. Schoolteachers. Small town life. Vaudevillians. Visions.*

Note: In the opening credits, Dean Stockwell's character name is listed as "The Boy." eden ahbez' name is spelled entirely in lower case letters onscreen; according to modern sources, the composer preferred this spelling for religious reasons. "Nature Boy" was the only song he ever wrote. In addition to the indicated flashbacks, the film also used voice-over narration delivered by Stockwell. In mid-Nov 1947, Adrian Scott, who had just produced RKO's successful social film *Crossfire* (see entry below), was announced as this picture's producer. By late Nov 1947, however, Scott and his frequent collaborator Edward Dmytryk were fired by RKO for violating the morality clause of their contract because they had refused to "name names" during the House Un-American Activity Committee (HUAC) hearings. Scott and Dmytryk became the first two members of the "Hollywood Ten," a group of filmmakers charged with contempt of Congress and subsequently blacklisted by the movie industry because of reputed connections to the Communist Party. In 1951, Scott was sentenced to a year of imprisonment after Dmytryk finally identified him as a Communist. Director Joseph Losey was also blacklisted in 1951, and this film is frequently cited as contributing to his image as a Communist subversive. For more information on the HUAC hearings, see entry for *Crossfire*.

LAT reported in its *This Week* section that after RKO bought Betsy Beaton's story, it shelved the project for almost a year because of story problems. In a modern interview, Losey, who made his feature-directing debut with this film, recalled that he and Scott worked on the script with the screenwriters. Losey added that the original story was a fantasy about racial discrimination, but that its thrust was changed because he and his collaborators felt that a film about peace would be more timely and important. RKO production head Dore Schary said in a Jan 1948 *NYT* article that, contrary to declarations by "the leftists" and pressures from the right, the story was to be made as a "pro-peace picture" with "no change in subject-matter." According to *HR*, after Scott's departure from the project, the script was completely revamped for producer Stephen Ames. *HR* notes that *The Boy with Green Hair* was made as part of RKO's "experiment" with modestly budgeted quality pictures, the first of which was the highly successful *Crossfire*. In the modern interview, Losey stated that when Scott was still involved in the project, he wanted to shoot it in 16mm Eastmancolor stock to save money. Because Ames was a major stockholder in Technicolor, Losey added, he could obtain color stock cheaply, thereby making it possible to produce the picture on a relatively modest budget. (Contemporary sources give the film's budget as between $850,000 and $900,000.) Losey also claimed that Ames's status at Technicolor helped to overcome some of the company's artistic restrictions, such as not using dark browns or low-key lighting while shooting.

RKO borrowed Stockwell from M-G-M for this production. Albert Sharpe, who played "Finian" in the Broadway production of *Finian's Rainbow*, was to make his screen debut in the picture, according to *HR*. Losey recalled in the modern interview that the part of Gramp was written with Sharpe in mind, but that RKO insisted that O'Brien, who was a contract star, be cast. Rusty Tamblyn and Dale Robertson made their screen debuts in the production. The CBCS lists Robertson's first name with its original spelling, "Dayle." In the CBCS, Peter Brocco is credited in the role of "Mr. Hammond #1," but it unclear whether he actually appeared in the film, as Charles Arnt is also listed as "Mr. Hammond." Losey stated that he used two cameras to shoot the hair cutting scene and had Stockwell wear three different wigs during the sequence. According to *LAT*, Stockwell wore wigs throughout the picture because the studio feared that he would be ridiculed in his private life if his hair were dyed green. *NYT* notes that to save money, primary sets from *I Remember Mama* were used.

According to the *Var* review, Howard Hughes, who acquired RKO in the spring of 1948, demanded that this film be re-edited to remove the "tolerance theme," which he felt detracted from the entertainment value of the picture. A *DV* news item claims that Floyd Odlum, who was the chairman of RKO's board, actually ordered the re-editing and insisted that the only acceptable "message" was one for "preparedness." According to a 3 Aug 1948 *DV* article,

new footage was to be shot to stress the fantasy elements of the picture. On 30 Aug 1948, *DV* announced that after RKO executive vice-president Ned Depinet and two members of the RKO board viewed the revised picture, Depinet decided to restore the original cut. The disputed footage, which cost $150,000 to produce, included new background music as well as new scenes. Losey added in the modern interview that "a few extra lines off screen were stuck in in an attempt to soften the message." Despite Schary's desire to release the film in mid-1948, Hughes delayed the release for six months, according to Losey. (Protesting Hughes's interference with this and other films, Schary left RKO in Jul 1948.) *DV* also notes that "Nature Boy," which is sung by an offscreen group, cost RKO $10,000 and was almost cut from the picture. As used, "Nature Boy," which was popularized by Nat King Cole in 1947, is an early example of a credit sequence theme song. The Irish folk song "Tail of My Coat" is performed by Pat O'Brien and Walter Catlett as part of a brief fantasy sequence.

Box 20 Nov 1948. *DV* 28 Apr 1948. *DV* 3 Aug 1948. *DV* 30 Aug 1948, p. 1. *DV* 16 Nov 1948, p. 3. *FD* 16 Nov 1948, p. 5. *HR* 25 Aug 1947, p. 2. *HR* 29 Sep 1947, p. 4. *HR* 12 Nov 1947, p. 12. *HR* 28 Nov 1947, p. 1, 9. *HR* 5 Jan 1948, p. 1. *HR* 9 Feb 1948, p. 2. *HR* 19 Mar 1948, p. 14. *HR* 16 Nov 1948, p. 3. *HR* 17 Jan 1949, p. 6. *MPHPD* 23 Oct 1948, p. 4358. *MPHPD* 20 Nov 1948, p. 4389. *NYT* 25 Jan 1948. *NYT* 30 May 1948. *NYT* 13 Jan 1949, p. 26. *Var* 17 Nov 1948, p. 13.

BRADY'S BUNCH *see* **WAR ARROW**

BRAND OF COWARDICE (Latino)

Phil Goldstone Productions. *Dist* Truart Film Corp. **1925**; New York premiere: 30 Jun 1925. Si; b&w. 5 reels, 4,250 or 4,600 ft.

Dir John P. McCarthy. *Story* Roger Pocock and John P. McCarthy.

Cast: Bruce Gordon, Carmelita Geraghty, Cuyler Supplee, Ligio De Colconda, Harry Lonsdale, Charles McHugh, Mark Fenton, Sidney De Grey.

Western. A stranger arrives on Don Luis Alvarado's ranch in Southern California for work, only to discover that the Don's daughter, Senorita Carmelita, is involved with a gang of robbers who are after her father's jewels. The stranger is arrested along with the thieves, but his true identity is revealed in court when he reveals that he is a U.S. marshal who infiltrated the gang of thieves to obtain a conviction. He brings the gang to justice and marries the rancher's beautiful daughter. *Bandits. Mexican Americans. Ranchers. Thieves. United States. Marshals.*

The Film Renter and Moving Picture News 24 Oct 1925. *FD* 5 Jul 1925. *Var* 29 Jul 1925, p. 36.

THE BRAND OF JUDAS (African Americans)

1919? [©Lillian Howarth; 18 Apr 1919; LU13610]. Si; b&w. Length undetermined.

Story Lillian Howarth.

Historical, Drama. After eight-year-old Gazelle Pasca's mother is killed during a saloon brawl, and her father goes to prison for killing her murderer, Gazelle is selected to be educated at a fashionable seminary in Maryland. Ten years later, when Gazelle's endowment runs out, her inseparable companion Edith Austin, an orphaned heiress to a Maryland estate, finances Gazelle's education. After Edith marries her guardian, Robert Granger, he falls in love with Gazelle. Aware of his social position, Gazelle encourages Granger's attentions. When Edith dies from hemorrhaging, Granger, now a U.S. Senator, burns papers Edith prepared to free her slaves. After the housekeeper's little nephew dies because Gazelle refuses to get a competent doctor, the slaves storm the house. Gazelle, holding Edith's baby, escapes on Edith's horse. After order is restored, she and Granger marry. Their subsequent quarrels climax with Gazelle's non-fatal shooting of Granger. Later in Paris, Gazelle frames a French officer who would not elope with her. When the revolution breaks out, she and her new lover, a grand duke, are taken prisoner. As Gazelle is taken to the guillotine, Granger witnesses lightning strike her and embraces her. *France–History–Revolution, 1789-1799. Guillotine. Infidelity. Lightning. Maryland. Slaves. Betrayal. Fights. Frame-ups. Heiresses. Infants. Nobility. Officers (Military). Paris (France). Saloons. Theological seminaries. Wards and guardians.*

Note: Although still photographs from this film housed with the copyright deposits at the Library of Congress indicate that the film was produced, no reviews were found and no information was located concerning its release.

BRAVE WARRIOR (Native Americans, Shawnee)

Esskay Pictures Co. *Dist* Columbia Pictures Corp. Jun **1952**; Prod: early—mid-Aug 1951 [©Columbia Pictures Corp.; 31 Mar 1952; LP1613]. Sd (RCA Sound System); col (Technicolor). 6,532 ft. 72-75 min.

Prod Sam Katzman. *Dir* Spencer G. Bennet. *Asst dir* Charles S. Gould. *Wrt for the scr by* Robert E. Kent. *Dir of photog* William V. Skall. *Spec eff* Jack Erickson. *Technicolor color consultant* Francis

Cugat. *Art dir* Paul Palmentola. *Film ed* Aaron Stell. *Set dec* Sidney Clifford. *Mus dir* Mischa Bakaleinikoff. *Sd eng* Josh Westmoreland. *Unit mgr* Herbert Leonard.

Cast: Jon Hall [(*Steve Ruddell*)], Christine Larson [(*Laura Macgregor*)], Jay Silverheels [(*Chief Tecumseh*)], Michael Ansara [(*The Prophet*)], Harry Cording [(*Shayne Macgregor*)], James Seay [(*Gov. Harrison*)], George Eldredge [(*Barney Demming*)], Leslie Denison [(*Gen. Proctor, also known as Bancroft*)], Rory Mallinson [(*Barker*)], Rusty Wescoatt [(*Standish*)], [Bert Davidson (*Gilbert*)], [William P. Wilkerson (*Chief Little Cloud*)], [Gilbert V. Perkins (*English lieutenant*)].

Western. [*Print viewed*]. In the days before the War of 1812, a band of outlaws led by British sympathizer Barney Demming attack a flatboat carrying a shipment of salt from Vincennes, Indiana, to the Kishpoco band of Shawnee Indians living on the Tippecanoe River. At a village powwow, the tribe's shaman, "The Prophet," vows revenge against the white man, but Prophet's brother, Chief Tecumseh, decides to discuss the attack with Gov. Harrison. At Vincennes, Tecumseh warns Harrison of Prophet's threat, and after Prophet and his braves ride into town and raid the general store, Harrison promises to pay the Kishpoco for any of their land already occupied by white settlers. Later, Harrison announces the land sale at a dinner party attended by Tecumseh and the secret leader of the outlaws, fur trader Shayne Macgregor. When the guests leave, government emissary Steven Buddell, who has been eavesdropping in the next room, says that if the gang attacks Tecumseh's tribe now, they will know that Macgregor, who does not want the tribe to sell land to the United States, is somehow involved. Later, at his fur trading shop, Macgregor and his daughter Laura, who is unaware of her father's illegal dealings, greet the traitorous Gen. Proctor, who is working under the name Bancroft. Proctor informs them of the plan to place cannons along the trail between Tippecanoe and Vincennes, hoping that their attacks will incite war between the United States and England. When he learns about the land sales, Macgregor sends Prophet to kill Tecumseh as a warning to other local chiefs not to sell their land. Later, at Tippecanoe, Prophet is banished after he loses a tomahawk fight against Tecumseh. Tecumseh tells Steve about his plans to build houses and schools for his people, and Harrison pledges the men and supplies for the job. When Demming goes to Macgregor's shop to report that Steve has arrived in town, Proctor, who is afraid of being recognized, rushes downstairs to the basement. Laura goes down to look for him, and when she returns, she tells Steve that "Bancroft" dropped his snuff box. When Steve notices the military insignia on it, he offers to return it to Proctor at his hotel. There, Demming knocks Steve out, and when he wakes up, Steve goes to Macgregor's shop and accuses him of being involved with the gang. Macgregor, however, maintains his innocence, and invites Steve to dinner. After Steve leaves, Macgregor tells Prophet and his braves to attack his home that evening and kill Steve. After dinner that evening, Steve and Laura are talking downstairs, while from his bedroom window upstairs, Macgregor signals to Prophet to begin the attack. Laura and Steve hear the attacking Indians outside, and Laura manages to escape in a horse and carriage. Later, Macgregor tells Prophet to take over the tribe, hoping to lure Harrison into battle so that war would be openly declared. When Tecumseh and Steve find the hidden cannons, Harrison calls every able-bodied male in Vincennes to battle. After Laura confesses her love for him, Steve disguises himself as one of Proctor's soldiers, then finds Macgregor sneaking behind enemy lines. When he tries to escape, Macgregor is shot by some Indians whom Demming has armed with muskets. Demming orders them to attack, but they retreat when the townsmen fight back. After Prophet and his braves burn Tecumseh's settlement to the ground, Macgregor is killed. Later, Tecumseh returns to his village. *Government agents. Medicine men. Shawnee Indians. Traitors. Tribal life. Aliases. Arson. Boats. Cannons. Eavesdropping. Escapes. Family relationships. Firearms. Fur traders. Governors. Hotels. Indiana. Land sales. Officers (Military). Outlaws. Parties. Pledges. Raids. Rivers. Salt. Undercover operations. War.*

Note: This film opens with offscreen narration that briefly describes the story's setting.

Box 17 May 1952. *DV* 14 May 1952, p. 6. *Exb* 21 May 1952, p. 3297. *FD* 5 Jun 1952, p. 6. *Har* 17 May 1952, p. 80. *HR* 10 Aug 1951, p. 10. *HR* 14 May 1952, p. 4. *MPHPD* 17 May 1952, p. 1366. *NYT* 14 May 1952, p. 6. *Var* 14 May 1952, p. 6.

BRAVEHEART (Native Americans)

Cinema Corp. of America. *Dist* Producers Distributing Corp. 27 Dec **1925** [©Cinema Corp. of America; 28 Dec 1925; LP22170]. Si; b&w. 7 reels, 7,256 ft.

Pres Cecil B. De Mille. *Dir* Alan Hale. *Adpt* Mary O'Hara. *Photog* Faxon M. Dean.

Source: Based on the short story "Braveheart" by William Churchill De Mille (publication undetermined).

Cast: Rod La Rocque (*Braveheart*), Lillian Rich (*Dorothy Nelson*), Robert Edeson (*Hobart Nelson*), Arthur Housman (*Frank Nelson*), Frank Hagney (*Ki-Yote*), Jean Acker (*Sky-Arrow*), [Frederick] Tyrone Power (*Standing Rock*), Sally Rand (*Sally Vernon*), Henry Victor (*Sam Harris*).

Western. Braveheart, a young Indian brave, is sent east to study law in order to prepare himself to defend the tribe's hereditary fishing rights, which are endangered by Hobart Nelson, the avaricious president of a fish-canning combine. While at college, Braveheart becomes an outstanding scholar and an All-American football player, but his work there comes to nothing, for, in order to save his friend Frank Nelson from disgrace, he confesses to selling football signals to an opposing team and is expelled. He is an outcast from his tribe as well, but goes into court and wins the fishing rights for his people. Ki-Yote, a troublemaker, incites the tribe to kidnap Nelson and his daughter, Dorothy, with whom Braveheart is in love. Braveheart rescues the Nelsons, but he denies his love for the white girl and marries one of red blood instead. *Businessmen. College life. Fishing rights. Football. Indians of North America. Lawyers.*

THE BRAVEST WAY (Japanese Americans)

Famous Players-Lasky Corp. *Dist* Famous Players-Lasky Corp.; Paramount Pictures. 16 Jun **1918** [©Famous Players-Lasky Corp.; 25 May 1918; LP12464]. Si; b&w. 5 reels.

Pres Jesse L. Lasky. *Dir* George H. Melford. *Asst dir* Claude Mitchell. *Scen* Edith Kennedy. *Cam* Paul Perry.

Cast: Sessue Hayakawa (*Kara Tamura*), Florence Vidor (*Nume Rogers*), Tsuru Aoki (*Sat-Su*), U Aoyama (*Shiro Watana*), Jane Wolff (*Miss Tompkins*), Winter Hall (*Moreby Nason*), Tom Kurahara (*Sam Orson*), Josephine Crowell (*Janitress*), Goro Kino (*Motoyoshi*), Clarence Geldart (*The minister*), Guy Oliver (*The lawyer*), Billy Elmer.

Drama. Tamura, a Japanese landscape gardener living in America, is saving to marry his Japanese American sweetheart, Nume Rogers, while his friend, Watana, works for a Japanese merchant named Motoyoshi so that he can bring his wife and children to America. Watana is murdered on the day his wife Sat-Su arrives, and Tamura, having promised to take care of her and the children, marries her, despite his love for Nume. Heartbroken, Nume accepts money from Nason to study voice, but when she debuts successfully, Nason attacks her. Tamura rescues Nume and takes her to visit the dying Sat-Su, who explains Tamura's sacrifice. After Sat-Su's death, Tamura and Nume are reunited. *Japanese. Japanese Americans. Marriage–Forced by circumstances. Self-sacrifice. Singers. Attempted rape. Gardeners. Immigrants. Merchants. Murder. Rescues.*

Note: The original title of the scenario was "The Desire of Tamura".

ETR 11 May 1918, p. 1843. *ETR* 15 Jun 1918, p. 126. *MPN* 15 Jun 1918, p. 3548. *MPW* 15 Jun 1918, p. 1615. *MPW* 22 Jun 1918, p. 1759. *NYDM* 15 Jun 1918, p. 852. *NYDM* 29 Jun 1918, p. 925. *Var* 7 Jun 1918, p. 32. *Wid's* 9 Jun 1918, pp. 23-24.

BREAD, BUTTER AND RHYTHM see **HAPPY LANDING**

THE BREAK UP (Native Americans, Native Alaskans)

Dist Talking Picture Epics. **1930**; New York showing: 29 Jul 1930. Sd; b&w. 5 reels, 4,761 ft.

Dir Capt. Jack Robertson. *Mus cond* Nathaniel Shilkret.

Travelogue. Capt. Jack Robertson, his dog Skooter, and several others journey to Alaska in winter by steamship via the Inside Passage and Prince William Sound. A smaller boat takes them past Harvard Glacier, Chugash Range, and the Great Divide. Continuing by canoe, raft, and dogsled, the group heads northward past Mt. McKinley. In the spring, the breakup of the frozen river permits a 1,200-mile trip on the Tanana and Yukon Rivers to the Bering Sea, visiting Eskimos along the way. The next destination is the Alaska Peninsula, with its Valley of Ten Thousand Smokes and spawning salmon, followed by a last stop on the Kenai peninsula before the coming of winter and a turn toward home. *Alaska. Bering Sea. Dogs. McKinley, Mount (AK). Native Alaskans. Rivers. Salmon. Yukon Territory.*

NYT 29 Nov 1930, p. 21. *Var* 6 Aug 1930, p. 38.

BREAKING HOME TIES (Jewish Americans)

Dist Associated Exhibitors, Inc. 12 Nov **1922** [©Associated Exhibitors, Inc.; 11 Nov 1922; LU18390]. Si; b&w. 6 reels, 5,622 ft.

Pres E. S. Manheimer. *Dir* Frank N. Seltzer and George K. Rolands. *Wrt* Frank N. Seltzer and George K. Rolands.

Cast: Lee Kohlmar (*Father Bergman*), Rebecca Weintraub (*Mother Bergman*), Richard Farrell (*David Bergman*), Arthur Ashley (*Paul Zeidman*), Betty Howe (*Esther*), Jane Thomas (*Rose Neuman*), Henry B. Schaffer (*J. B. Martin*), Maude Hill (*Mrs. Martin*), Robert Maxmillian (*Moskowitz*).

Drama. Thinking he has killed his friend Paul Zeidman in a jealous rage, David Bergman flees his native Russia; becomes a successful lawyer in New York; and loses touch with his penniless family, who have followed him to America. At his wedding to Rose, which takes place in a home for the aged to which they have contributed, David recognizes Paul among the musicians; and when the Bergmans, who live in the home, hear Paul's rendition of *Eili, Eili* all are reunited. *Jews. Lawyers. Musicians. Retirement homes. Russians.*

FD 26 Nov 1922. *MPW* 2 Dec 1922. *Var* 17 May 1923, p. 26.

BREAKING INTO SOCIETY (Irish Americans)

Hunt-Stromberg Productions. *Dist* Film Booking Offices of America. 30 Sep **1923** [©Hunt-Stromberg Productions; 30 Aug 1923; LP19362]. Si; b&w. 5 reels, 4,112 ft.

Prod Hunt Stromberg. *Dir* Hunt Stromberg. *Wrt* Hunt Stromberg. *Photog* Irving Reis.

Cast: Carrie Clark Ward (*Mrs. Pat O'Toole*), Bull Montana (*Tim O'Toole*), Kalla Pasha (*Pat O'Toole*), Francis Trebaol (*Marty O'Toole*), Florence Gilbert (*Yvonne*), Leo White (*A barber*), Tiny Sanford (*A chiropractor*), Stanhope Wheatcroft (*A man of wealth*), Chuck Reisner (*The "Pittsburgh Kid"*), Gertrude Short (*Sally*), Rags (*Marty O'Toole's dog*).

Comedy. The O'Tooles inherit a fortune and move to Pasadena where they try to break into society by having lavish dinner parties. The guests are shocked by the O'Tooles' manners, and they leave when the "Pittsburgh Kid" and his Bowery wife, Yvonne, uninvited guests, arrive. *Barbers and barbershops. Chiropractors. Dogs. High society. Irish Americans. Pasadena (CA). Social climbers.*

MPW 29 Dec 1923. *Var* 20 Dec 1923, p. 26.

THE BREAKING POINT (African Americans, Chinese Americans)

Warner Bros. Pictures, Inc.; A Warner Bros.—First National Picture. *Dist* Warner Bros. Pictures, Inc. 30 Sep **1950**; Prod: 28 Mar—10 May 1950 [©Warner Bros. Pictures, Inc.; 15 Sep 1950; LP337]. Sd (RCA Sound System); b&w. 8,754 ft. 97 min. PCA cert no. 14521.

Prod Jerry Wald. *Dir* Michael Curtiz. *Dial dir* Norman Stuart. *Asst dir* Sherry Shourds. *2d unit dir* David C. Gardner. *Scr* Ranald MacDougall. *Dir of photog* Ted McCord. *Art dir* Edward Carrere. *Film ed* Alan Crosland, Jr. *Set dec* George James Hopkins. *Ward* Leah Rhodes. *Mus dir* Ray Heindorf. *Sd* Leslie G. Hewitt.

Source: Based on the novel *To Have and Have Not* by Ernest Hemingway (New York, 1937).

Cast: John Garfield (*Harry Morgan*), Patricia Neal (*Leona Charles*), Phyllis Thaxter (*Lucy Morgan*), Juano Hernandez (*Wesley Park*), Wallace Ford (*Duncan*), Edmon Ryan (*Rogers*), Ralph Dumke (*Hannagan*), Guy Thomajan (*Danny*), William Campbell (*Concho*), Sherry Jackson (*Amelia*), Donna Jo Boyce (*Connie*), Victor Sen Yung (*Mr. Sing*), Peter Brocco (*Macho*), John Doucette (*Gotch*), James Griffith (*Charlie*), Norman Fields (*Dock attendant*), Juan Hernandez (*Joseph*), Juan Duval, Benny Long (*Bartenders*), Paul Vierro (*Hernandez*), Spencer Chan (*Chinese man*), Helene Hatch (*Mrs. Cooley*), Donna Gibson, George Hoagland, Bob MacLean (*Leona's friends*), Beverly Mook (*Freckle-faced kid*), John Close (*Deputy*), Alex Gerry (*Mr. Phillips*), Mary Carroll (*Girl at bar*), Glen Turnbull (*Taxi driver*), John Morgan, John Alvin (*Reporters*), Dave McMahon (*Coast guard cop*), Paul McGuire (*Leona's escort*), Gregg Rhinelander (*Intern*), Bob Williams (*Doctor*), Len Hendry (*Boatswain*).

Drama. [*Print viewed*]. From his home in Newport Beach, California, former P.T. boat operator Harry Morgan rents out his private boat, the *Sea Queen*, to fishing parties. Harry barely manages to make enough money to support his wife Lucy and their two children, and tired of the financial struggle, Lucy continually begs him to give up the boat and move to her father's farm. One day, Harry

is hired to take Hannagan and Leona Charles, Hannagan's attractive blonde friend, fishing off the Mexican coast. While in Mexico, Hannagan abandons Leona and leaves without paying Harry. Desperate, Harry makes a deal with Duncan, a shady lawyer, to transport illegal Chinese laborers into California. In order to prevent his mate, Wesley Park, from becoming involved in the illicit activity, Harry tries to send him back to the United States on the bus, but Wesley and Leona both sneak aboard the boat. Later, Harry docks the boat in a deserted cove to pick up the laborers, but when Mr. Sing, the smuggler, tries to shortchange Harry, a fight breaks out, and Sing is killed. Harry throws his body overboard and returns the Chinese men to the shore. Unknown to Harry, the Chinese, one of whom remembers the boat's name, are picked up by the border patrol, and when Harry reaches San Diego, his boat is confiscated. Later, both Leona and Duncan turn up in Newport Beach. Learning of Leona's presence, Lucy becomes jealous and, deciding that Harry prefers blondes, dyes her hair. Meanwhile, Harry almost succumbs to Leona's seductive attentions, but finally decides to be faithful to Lucy. After Duncan arranges for the "Sea Queen" to be returned, the boat is repossessed by the bank, and Harry is again forced to ask for Duncan's help. Duncan arranges for him to take two gangsters to an offshore boat after they commit a robbery. With money coming in again, Harry is able to get his boat back, and he now concocts a plan to double-cross the gangsters. When he sees him loading a gun, Lucy announces that she is planning to leave him. Nonetheless, Harry goes ahead with his plans, but Wesley becomes involved when he happens by the boat just before the gangsters arrive. After the boat is at sea, the gangsters kill Wesley and throw his body overboard. Harry uses the diversion to get rid of some of the gangsters' guns. He then fakes engine trouble, grabs the gun he has hidden aboard, and attacks the gangsters. During the ensuing fight, Harry is badly wounded. Later, the Coast Guard finds the "Sea Queen." Harry is barely alive, and a doctor asks Lucy for permission to amputate his arm. Lucy, who still loves her husband, convinces Harry to have the operation and save his life. As they leave, Joseph, Wesley's child, waits futilely on the dock for his father's return. *Debt. Fishing boats. Gangsters. Sailors. Vocational obsession. African Americans. Amputation. Chinese. Firearms. Fishermen. Gunfights. Gunshot wounds. Jealousy. Lawyers. Marriage. Mexico. Murder. Newport Beach (CA). Physicians. Seduction. Smuggling.*

Note: Credits were obtained from copyright records and reviews. "Wesley's" child "Joseph" was played by Juano Hernandez' real-life son, Juan. News items in *HR* add the following information about the production: Jack Webb was tested for the second lead. Scenes were shot on location at Balboa and Newport Beach, CA, and at Santa Anita racetrack in Arcadia, CA. Ernest Hemingway's novel also served as the inspiration for Warner Bros. 1945 film *To Have and Have Not* and the 1958 United Artists film *The Gun Runners*, directed by Don Siegel and starring Audie Murphy.

Box 9 Sep 1950. *DV* 11 Sep 1950, p. 3. *FD* 12 Sep 1950, p. 8. *HR* 24 Mar 1950, p. 53. *HR* 28 Mar 1950, p. 9. *HR* 19 Apr 1950, p. 3. *HR* 20 Apr 1950, p. 6. *HR* 11 May 1950, p. 1. *HR* 11 Sep 1950, p. 3. *MPHPD* 16 Sep 1950, p. 486. *NYT* 7 Oct 1950, p. 10. *Var* 13 Sep 1950, p. 6.

BREAKING THE ICE (Mennonites)
Principal Productions, Inc.; Bobby Breen Productions, Inc. *Dist* RKO Radio Pictures, Inc. 26 Aug **1938**; Prod: late May—late Jun 1937. Sd (RCA Victor System); b&w. 80-81 min. PCA cert no. 4393.
Prod Sol Lesser and [Barney Briskin]. [*Dir* Edward F. Cline]. *Asst dir* George Hippard. [*Scr* Mary McCall, Jr., Manuel Seff and Bernard Schubert]. [*Story* Fritz Falkenstein and N. Brewster Morse]. *Photog* Jack McKenzie. *Art dir* Lewis J. Rachmil. *Film ed* Arthur Hilton. *Cost* Helène. *Mus dir* Victor Young. *Ice numbers staged by* Dave Gould. *Sd tech* Richard Van Hessen.
Song(s): "Happy as a Lark," "Put Your Heart in a Song" and "The Sunny Side of Things," words and music by Frank Churchill and Paul F. Webster; "Tellin' My Troubles to a Mule" and "Goodbye My Dreams, Goodbye," words and music by Victor Young and Paul F. Webster.
Cast: Bobby Breen (*Tommy Martin*), Charles Ruggles (*Samuel* [*"Swapping Sam"*] *Terwilliger*), Dolores Costello (*Martha Martin*), Irene Dare (*Herself*), Robert Barrat (*William Decker*), Dorothy Peterson (*Annie Decker*), John King (*Henry Johnson*), Billy Gilbert (*Mr. Small*), Margaret Hamilton (*Mrs. Small*), Charles Murray (*Janitor*), Jonathan Hale (*Kane*), Delmar Watson (*Reuben Johnson*), Spencer Charters (*Farmer Smith*), Cy Kendall (*Judd*), [Maurice Cass (*Mr. Jones*)].

Drama, with songs. [*Print viewed*]. Although Pennsylvanian Mennonite Martha Martin longs to move to Goshen, Kansas to be near widower Henry Johnson, William Decker, her brother-in-law, refuses to lend her $92 for the train trip and writes a letter to Henry stating that if Henry wants to marry widow Martha, he should send the train fare himself. Embarrassed for his mother, little Tommy Martin tears up the letter and offers his collection of old newspapers to Samuel "Swapping Sam" Terwilliger, a wily, cheap "antique" dealer who gives the boy a dollar and, as a gift, a harmonica. That evening, the pious William punishes Tommy severely for accepting Sam's harmonica without earning it. Frustrated, Tommy runs away and convinces Sam to bring him to Philadelphia, where he hopes to earn the needed money. The next day, William discovers that a twenty-dollar bill, which had blown off a table and into Tommy's newspapers, is missing from his crop payment and denounces Tommy as a thief to Martha. In Philadelphia, Tommy lands a job as an ice skate boy in the rink that neighbors Sam's antique shop and later impresses the rink's owner, Mr. Kane, with his singing talents. Billed with six-year-old skater Irene Dare, Tommy is given a $25-per-week salary, of which Sam secretly takes twenty. When Tommy, who has been sending his earnings home, learns of Sam's deceit, he is crushed but returns home with all of his money. Scorned and branded as a thief by William, Tommy vows to prove his innocence before moving to Kansas. With help from a contrite Sam, Tommy, having determined that the ink-stained bill blew off the table, tracks the newspapers, which Sam had used as "antique" chair stuffing, to a museum in Washington, D.C. Vindicated, Tommy says goodbye to Sam and his singing career and happily leaves for Kansas. *Antique dealers. Children. False accusations. Mennonites. Pennsylvania. Antique shops. Duplicity. Farms. Greed. Ice skaters and ice skating. Money. Museums. Philadelphia (PA). Singers. Thieves. Washington (D.C.).*

Note: The working titles of this film were *Keep Moving* and *Easy Street*. The viewed print lacked directing and writing credits. Six-year-old Irene Dare was billed as the world's youngest ice skater.

DV 23 Aug 1938, p. 3. *FD* 1 Sep 1938, p. 7. *HR* 15 Apr 1938, p. 9. *HR* 23 May 1938, p. 11. *HR* 27 Jun 1938, pp. 6-7. *HR* 23 Aug 1938, p. 3. *MPH* 2 Jul 1938, p. 29. *MPH* 27 Aug 1938, p. 53. *NYT* 23 Sep 1938, p. 35. *Var* 7 Sep 1938, p. 12.

BREED OF THE SUNSETS (Latino)
FBO Pictures. 1 Apr **1928** [©F.B.O. Productions, Inc.; 5 Mar 1928; LP25039]. Si; b&w. 5 reels, 4,869 ft.
Dir Wallace W. Fox. *Asst dir* Sam Nelson. *Adpt and cont* Oliver Drake. *Story* S. E. V. Taylor. *Titles* Randolph Bartlett. *Photog* Robert De Grasse. *Film ed* Della M. King.
Cast: Bob Steele (*Jim Collins*), Nancy Drexel (*The Spanish girl*), George Bunny (*Don Alvaro*), Dorothy Kitchen (*Marie Alvaro*), Leo White (*Señor Diego Valdez*), Larry Fisher (*Hank Scully*).
Western. Jim, a young cowboy, is in love with a Spanish girl promised to an unlikely suitor. On the eve of her wedding, he disguises himself as a Mexican and abducts the girl. Her father and a posse give chase, but the father, being sympathetic and admiring the cowboy's courage, consents to their marriage. *Abduction. Cowboys. Latino.*

Var 13 Jun 1928, p. 27.

BREVITIES OF 1955 (African Americans)
Dist Union Films. **1955.** Sd; b&w. 52 or 56 min.
Prod Joseph Tuller. *Dir* William Alexander. *Photog* G. G. Leontough and Vide Martino. *Film ed* Nathan Cy Braunstein and Sheldon Nemeyer. *Cost* Betty Taylor. *Sd* J. Suacure. *Tech adv* Dewitt Jackson.
Song(s): "Fat Man Blues," "I Like the Hucklebuck," "It Takes a Dark Brown," "He's Knocking, But He Can't Get In," "Juice Head Baby," "I Love It" and "Doing the Best I Can," composers undetermined.
Cast: Dewey "Pigmeat" Markham, *Supported by* George Wilshire [sic], Vivian Harris, Dick Barrow (*Master of ceremonies*), Jo Jo Adams, Mabel Hunter, Gertrude "Baby" Banks, Luella Owens, Princess D'Orsey, Gloria Howard (*"Atomic Bomb"*), Slip and Slide, Tarza Young, *Supported by* The Betty Taylor Taylorettes, Olive Sayles, Maria Rout, Adella Gross, Ezella Lester, Marion L. Greene, Dorothy McCarty, Fannie Thornton, Griffen Trixie Terry, Rose Marie Foster, Gwendolyn Shaklett.
Exploitation, with songs. [*Print viewed*]. After master of ceremonies Dick Barrow welcomes the audience to "bronze burlesque," a parade of strip-tease dancers, singers and comedians

perform. Dancers Slip and Slide do a soft-shoe routine, while Dewey "Pigmeat" Markham appears in a comedy sketch about a love-making bureau. *African Americans. Burlesque. Comedians. Singers. Strip-tease. Brassieres. Chorus girls. Dancers.*

Note: The print viewed was titled *Burlesque in Harlem.* Performer George Wiltshire's surname was mistakenly spelled "Wilshire" in the onscreen credits. In the strip-tease sequences, the dancers only disrobe to brassieres and G-strings.

Exb 10 Aug 1955, p. 4008.

THE BRICK FOXHOLE see CROSSFIRE

THE BRIDE OF HATE (African Americans)

New York Motion Picture Corp.; Kay-Bee. *Dist* Triangle Distributing Corp. 14 Jan **1917.** Si; b&w. 5 reels, 4,714 ft.

Supv Thomas H. Ince. *Prod* Thomas H. Ince. *Dir* Walter Edwards. *Asst dir* David M. Hartford. *Scen* Monte Katterjohn. *Picturized by* J. G. Hawks. *Story* John Lynch. *Cam* Charles Kaufman. *Art dir* Robert Brunton.

Cast: Frank Keenan (*Dr. Dudley Duprez*), Margery Wilson (*Mercedes Mendoza*), Jerome Storm (*Paul Crenshaw*), David M. Hartford (*Judge Shone*), Elvira Weil (*Rose Duprez*), Mrs. J. Hunt (*Mammy Lou*), J. P. Lockney (*Don Ramon Alvarez*), Nona Thomas (*Don Ramon's daughter*), Jack Gilbert (*Dr. Duprez's son*).

Historical, Drama. In the antebellum South, the respected Louisiana physician Dr. Dudley Duprez wins the beautiful slave Mercedes during a riverboat poker game on his way home from St. Louis. At his plantation, Duprez discovers that his beloved niece Rose has poisoned herself rather than face him after she had been seduced by the doctor's young friend Paul Crenshaw. Overcoming an urge to kill Crenshaw, Duprez instead trains Mercedes, who supposedly has only a trace of Negro blood, to impersonate a wealthy Spanish girl and win Crenshaw's affection, after threatening to send her to the cotton fields if she does not comply. After the wedding, Duprez announces to the guests that because Crenshaw betrayed Rose, Duprez tricked him into marrying a "nigger." Crenshaw is ostracized and later is shot attempting to evade a yellow fever quarantine. After a dying overseer from Mercedes' plantation confesses that Mercedes is really the legitimate daughter of Duprez' son and an aristocratic Spanish girl, whose father, objecting to her marrying an American, had her enslaved, Duprez makes amends and Mercedes forgives him. *African Americans. Impersonation and imposture. Louisiana. Parentage. Physicians. Plantations. Revenge. Seduction. Slaves. Southerners. United States–South. Cards. Nieces. Ostracism. Overseers. Poisoning. Poker (Game). Quarantine. Racism. River boats. Spaniards. Suicide. Weddings. Yellow fever.*

Note: The working title of this film was *His Slave.* It was re-issued by Tri-Stone Pictures in 1922 under the title *Wanted for Murder, Or Bride of Hate.* It was copyrighted by Tri-Stone Pictures under the title *The Bride of Hate;* 12 Jun 1924; LP20306.

ETR 30 Dec 1916, p. 276. *MPN* 6 Jan 1917, pp. 115-16. *MPW* 6 Jan 1917, pp. 99-100. *MPW* 13 Jan 1917, p. 170. *MPW* 27 Jan 1917, p. 589. *Wid's* 25 Jan 1917, p. 57.

BRIDE OF THE BAYOU see LAZY RIVER

BRIDE OF THE VAMPIRE see CRY OF THE WEREWOLF

THE BRIDGE see THE GIRL ON THE BRIDGE

BRIGHT ROAD (African Americans)

Metro-Goldwyn-Mayer Corp.; controlled by Loew's Inc. *Dist* Loew's Inc. 17 Apr **1953**; Prod: mid-Aug—early Sep 1952 [©Loew's Inc.; 24 Mar 1953; LP2457]. Sd (Western Electric Sound System); b&w. 7 reels, 6,141 ft. 68 min. Passed by the National Board of Review. PCA cert no. 16176.

Prod Sol Baer Fielding. *Dir* Gerald Mayer. *Asst dir* George Rhein. *Scr* Emmet Lavery. *Dir of photog* Alfred Gilks. [*Spec eff* A. Arnold Gillespie]. *Art dir* Cedric Gibbons and Eddie Imazu. *Film ed* Joseph Dervin. *Set dec* Edwin B. Willis and Jacque Mapes. *Mus* David Rose. *Rec supv* Douglas Shearer. *Hair stylist* Sydney Guilaroff. [*Hair dresser* Vivian Dandridge]. *Makeup* William Tuttle. [*Props* Aaron Masure].

Source: Based on the short story "See How They Run" by Mary Elizabeth Vroman in *Ladies' Home Journal* (Jun 1951).

Cast: Dorothy Dandridge (*Jane Richards*), Philip Hepburn (*C. T. Young*), Harry Belafonte (*School principal* [*Mr. Williams*]), Barbara Ann Sanders (*Tanya* [*Hamilton*]), Robert Horton (*Dr. Mitchell*), Madie Norman (*Tanya's mother*), *C. T.'s Classmates:* Renee Beard (*Booker T. Jones*), Howard McNeely (*Boyd*), Robert McNeely

(*Lloyd*), Patti Marie Ellis (*Rachel Smith*), Joy Jackson (*Sarablene Babcock*), Fred Moultrie (*Roger*), James Moultrie (*George*), Carolyn Ann Jackson (*Mary Louise*), [William Walker (*C. T.'s father, Mr. Young*)], [Willa Pearl Curtis (*Mrs. Young*)], [Clifford Jackson (*Brother Young, 7 years*)], [Theron Jackson (*Brother Young, 10 years*)], [Michael Jackson (*Brother Young*)], [James Ellis Smith (*Brother Young*)], [Patricia Hoddison (*Sister Young, 9 years*)], [Janet Heard (*Sister Young, 17 years*)], [Moneta Peters (*Sister Young, 14 years*)], [Vivian Dandridge (*Miss Nelson*)], [Libby Taylor (*Miss Winthrop*)], [Louise Franklin (*Marilyn Meadows*)], [Jeni LeGon (*Martha Swife*)].

African American, **Youth**, **Drama.** [*Print viewed*]. On her first day at a small black elementary school in the South, Jane Richards, a fourth grade schoolteacher, takes a particular interest in C. T. Young, a polite but bored child, who has consistently taken two years to get through each grade. After class, Jane asks C. T. about his family and learns that he has eight brothers and sisters. Although C. T. also claims that his father has a big job at the mill, Jane sees in her records that Mr. Young is a part-time laborer. Later, Jane realizes that C. T. does not have money for lunch and arranges for him to get a free one through the school. After school, C. T. walks hand-in-hand with his friend, Tanya Hamilton, and warns him not to catch any birds, noting that they, too, have a right to live. Tanya convinces C. T. to attend Sunday school, which Jane also teaches, and after Jane states that God created everyone in His image, C. T. asks what color God is. Jane skirts the question by declaring that all men are brothers, but when C. T. wonders why they do not act like brothers, she explains that God is always willing to help mankind when asked. During a multiplication lesson, Jane sees that C. T. is drawing instead of listening, but nonetheless compliments him on his picture. Although Jane gives C. T. his first passing grade, a "C" for "Desire to Learn," he takes the report card without opening it. Outside, the children taunt C. T. and Tanya, and a fight ensues. Jane separates the children, and after she rebukes C. T. for fighting on the same day he received his first good mark, he looks at the report card with pride. At Christmas, C. T. gives his adoring mother a jar of honey he collected from the beehive he tends, and she is grateful, knowing that he keeps the bees to raise money. After New Year's, C. T. further impresses Jane when, unlike the other children who brag about their Christmas gifts, he describes the good acts he did for his family and others. Soon after, during dress rehearsal for a performance of *The Sleeping Beauty*, Tanya becomes ill and is diagnosed with viral pneumonia. Jane comforts C. T., who cries that if there is a God, he won't let Tanya die. Tanya does die and C. T. stays away from school for a time. When he finally returns to the playground, he becomes embroiled in a confrontation with a group of boys and brawls with one of them until the principal, Mr. Williams, intervenes. As punishment Jane orders C. T. to sit in the front of the classroom and instructs the other children not to speak to him until he says he is sorry, but he vows never to apologize. In the third quarter, C. T.'s performance deteriorates drastically. When he helps another boy work out multiplication problems on the blackboard, however, Jane changes his "F" to an "A." Later, classmate Booker T. Jones asks C. T. to go to the circus with him, but C. T. still refuses to tell Jane that he is sorry and insists that he does not care about the circus, prompting Jane to conclude that she has failed C. T. During a rest period, however, C. T. again proves himself after a swarm of bees flies into the classroom window and causes the other children to panic. C. T. puts the queen bee into a jar and, while covered with the other bees, takes her to a hollow tree in the woods. He then presents Jane with a butterfly cocoon that he had been saving for Tanya. As the class watches, the butterfly emerges from its cocoon, inspiring Jane to comment that everyone they know and love will be born again. Later, while alone with Jane, C. T. tells her that he loves her, then runs off with his dog as she watches from her window. *African Americans. Children. Schoolteachers. Bees. Butterflies. Christmas. Death and dying. Fights. Obstinacy. Poverty. Religion. School superintendents and principals. Sleeping Beauty* (Play).

Note: The film's working title was *See How They Run.* The opening credits state that the story "See How They Run" won the Christopher Award. According to the film's pressbook and news items, first-time author Mary Elizabeth Vroman, based her story on her personal experiences and wrote it in while teaching in Montgomery, AL. Vroman, born in Antigua, West Indies, sent her story to *Ladies' Home Journal* along with a pleading letter, and the magazine printed both. After M-G-M purchased the rights to her story, Vroman spent six weeks working with scriptwriter Emmet Lavery. The film was shot completely

on the M-G-M lot.

Reviewers noted that *Bright Road* was the first non-musical film made by a major studio to feature a predominately black cast. (The only non-black actor was Robert Horton, who played the doctor.) Producer Sol Baer Fielding, in a *HCN* interview, stated about the story, "It could take place anyplace and to a boy of any race. But some of the events have more significance because they happen in a Negro community." In a *LADN* interview, Vroman stated, "Love solves more problems than anger. That is why this isn't an angry story. I didn't want to prove anything, I didn't want to agitate anything. I merely thought—if people could know these children as I do, they would be certain to love them all." *NYT* praised the film as "an honorable endeavor to say something fair and meaningful about the emotional maladjustment of children who sense the sting of hardship and bigotry," but criticized it for its "caution and reluctance to come out bluntly and say the dismal things about racial and economic pressures that are vaguely and overtly implied in the theme and the contour of the story." *SatRev* called the film "a syrupy piece that manages to beg a good many questions" and noted that "by so narrowly focusing the range on the 'do-good' and by seeing so little evil there is an occasional air of unreality."

Bright Road marked the screen debuts of Harry Belafonte and eleven-year-old Philip Hepburn, who had six years of stage experience and had acted on Broadway. Dorothy Dandridge, better known at the time as a café singer, stated in the film's pressbook, "When M-G-M first offered me this part, I hesitated. I didn't think I could do it. It didn't seem to be me. But then I realized that this story would do more to promote understanding between people than any picture Hollywood has made, and I determined to accept the challenge." According to the pressbook, Dandridge's sister Vivian visited the set and then stayed on as a hairdresser, before being asked to replace an actress unable to report for work. Barbara Ann Sanders, who played "Tanya," was the daughter of actress Lillian Randolph. The film won an Urban League award for "contribution towards interracial cooperation," and Fielding was awarded the George Washington Carver Institute Merit Plaque. According to *DV*, the film had a limited exhibition in 1953. The film was re-released in 1957 after Dandridge and Belafonte became more well-known. According to modern sources, the song "Suzanne" was a revision of an old folk ballad known as "Every Night When the Sun Goes Down." Belafonte wrote the song with Millard Thomas and recorded it for Victor.

Box 11 Apr 1953. *Cue* 2 May 1953. *DV* 3 Apr 1953, pp. 3-4. *DV* 12 Feb 1954. *DV* 11 Sep 1957. *Exh* 22 Apr 1953, p. 3502. *FD* 28 Apr 1953, p. 6. *Har* 4 Apr 1953, p. 55. *HCN* 28 Aug 1952, p. 18. *HR* 6 Mar 1952. *HR* 8 Aug 1952, p. 10. *HR* 29 Aug 1952, p. 8. *HR* 3 Apr 1953, p. 3. *HR* 23 Apr 1953. *IP* Dec 1952, pp. 11-12. *LADN* 21 Aug 1952. *LADN* 4 Jun 1953. *LAT* 11 May 1953. *LAT* 18 May 1953. *LAT* 4 Jun 1953. *MPD* 7 Apr 1953. *MPHPD* 11 Apr 1953, p. 1790. *Newsweek* 27 Apr 1953, p. 33. *NYT* 29 Apr 1953, p. 33. *SatRev* 25 Apr 1953. *Time* 20 Apr 1953. *Var* 25 Mar 1953. *Var* 8 Apr 1953, p. 6.

BRIGHT VICTORY (African Americans)

Universal-International Pictures Co., Inc. *Dist* Universal Pictures Co., Inc. Jan **1952**; World premiere in Los Angeles: 16 Jul 1951; New York opening: 31 Jul 1951; pre-release engagements in selected cities: Aug 1951; Prod: mid-Aug—late Sep 1950 [©Universal Pictures Co.; 25 Sep 1951; LP1173]. Sd (Western Electric Recording); b&w. 11 reels. 96-97 min. PCA cert no. 14932.

Prod Robert Buckner. *Dir* Mark Robson. [*Asst dir* John Sherwood, Les Warner and George Lollier]. *Scr* Robert Buckner. *Dir of photog* William Daniels. *Art dir* Bernard Herzbrun and Nathan Juran. [*Supv art dir* Bert Tuttle]. *Film ed* Russell Schoengarth and [Milton Carruth]. *Set dec* Russell A. Gausman and John Austin. *Gowns* Rosemary Odell. *Mus* Frank Skinner. *Sd* Leslie I. Carey and Corson Jowett. *Hair stylist* Joan St. Oegger. *Makeup* Bud Westmore. [*Unit prod mgr* Edward Dodds]. [*Tech adv* Howard Burton].

Source: Based on the novel *Lights Out* by Baynard Kendrick (New York, 1945).

Cast: Arthur Kennedy (*Larry Nevins*), Peggy Dow (*Judy Greene*), Julia Adams (*Chris Paterson*), James Edwards (*Joe Morgan*), Will Geer (*Mr. Nevins*), Nana Bryant (*Mrs. Nevins*), Jim Backus (*Bill Grayson*), Minor Watson (*Mr. Paterson*), Joan Banks (*Janet Grayson*), Richard Egan (*Sergeant John Masterson*), John Hudson (*Corporal John Flagg*), Marjorie Crossland (*Mrs. Paterson*), Donald Miele (*"Moose" Garvey*), Murray Hamilton (*Pete Hamilton*), Larry Keating (*Jess Coe*), Hugh Reilly (*Captain Phelan*), Mary Cooper (*Nurse Bailey*), Rock Hudson (*Dudek*), Ken Harvey (*Scanlon*), Russell Dennis (*Private Fred Tyler*), Phil Faversham (*Lt. Atkins*), Robert F. Simon (*Psychiatrist*), Virginia Mullen (*Mrs. Coe*), Ruth Esherick (*Nurse*), [Jerry Paris (*Reynolds*)], [Bernard Hamilton (*Negro soldier*)], [Robert Anderson (*M.P.*)], [June Whitley (*Nurse at Oran*)], [Sydney Mason (*Dr. Bannerman*)], [Richard Karlan, Billy Newell (*Bartenders*)], [Glen Charles Gordon (*Lt. Conklin*)], [Ted Jordan (*Soldier*)], [Chester Jones (*Butler*)], [Thaddeus Jones (*Pullman porter*)], [Paul Hoffman, Larry Winter (*German soldiers*)], [Dee Carroll (*Nurse*)], [Terry Terrell (*Officer*)], [Grace Richey (*Barmaid*)], [Paul Robinson (*Bank teller*)], [J. Raymond Shipp (*Third soldier, O'Brien*)], [Robert Myers (*First soldier, Neymeyer*)], [Louis Morsbach (*Sergeant*)], [Freddie Marcellino (*Fourth soldier, Myers*)], [William

Friedborn (*Bus driver*)], [William J. Drohan (*Gateman*)], [Alvin Busch (*Second soldier, Campanella*)], [Richard Houser, John M. Robinson (*Medical orderlies*)], [J. Walter Burns (*Civilian*)], [Alice Richey], [Sara Taft], [Scotty Beal].

Social, Drama. [*Print viewed*]. In 1943, during World War II, Sergeant Larry Nevins is hit by German sniper fire in North Africa. He regains consciousness after he has been rescued to find that his eyes are enclosed in a head dressing. He is sent back to the U.S. so that the damage to his eyes can be assessed. On the plane, Larry, a Southerner from the small town of Semolina in the northern part of Florida, chats amicably with a soldier from Atlanta, until he realizes that the other soldier is black. Larry then abruptly ends the conversation. At the Valley Forge General Hospital in Pennsylvania, where 2,000 blind soldiers learn to adjust to their condition, Larry is told that his optic nerve was destroyed and that he will never see again. He makes his way to the bathroom in his ward, intending to cut his wrists, but is stopped by Corporal John Flagg. Lt. Atkins, Larry's superior officer, demands that he inform his parents of his condition, and when Larry refuses, threatens to tell them himself. Humiliated, Larry lets his mother know he is blind. Atkins then reveals that he, too, is blind, and Larry apologizes. During an obstacle test, Larry learns that he can sense a wall ahead of him before he reaches it. Excited about this newfound ability, he calls his mother to boast. Larry becomes friends with Joe Morgan, a soldier from New Orleans, who, unknown to Larry, is black. At a dance, he meets Judy Greene, whom he earlier insulted in a bar when he thought she was trying to pick him up. They spend an enjoyable evening together, but he admits that he has a girl friend, Chris Paterson, in Florida. The day before Joe is to leave for home on furlough, Larry comments that among the new men arriving the next day are three "niggers," whereupon Joe, offended by Larry's bigotry, reveals that he is black. After Joe leaves, the other men in his ward stop speaking to Larry. When Larry complains that Joe should have told him he was black, Flagg asks if, for the rest of his life, he will want to ask the race or religion of those he meets before he decides whether he likes them, and advises Larry to learn to trust what he feels about people. Two days before he is to visit his home, Larry spends a weekend at a cabin with Judy, her sister Janet, and Janet's husband, Bill Grayson. Bill, a Philadelphia lawyer, encourages Larry to study law, telling him of a colleague, Jess Coe, who has been blind since World War I and is one of the best trial lawyers in the city. Larry is unsure of his own capabilities, however. That night, Larry discovers for the first time that Judy loves him. When she kisses him, he pulls away, saying he still loves Chris and that he needs the security of a life with Chris, the daughter of a wealthy barrel manufacturer. In Seminola, he rebukes his mother when she makes a disparaging remark about "our nigras." Alone with his father, Larry talks about his broken friendship with Joe and complains that his mother taught him her way of thinking about blacks. His father explains that she herself was taught by others to think that way and expresses gratitude to his son for fighting in the war and helping to change the world. The next night, at Chris's party for him, Larry becomes upset when a clergyman suggests that a miracle may allow him to see. When he is alone with Chris, he asks that they take things slow and not talk about his blindness and their plans yet. During the month at home, Larry finds his small town less hospitable than Valley Forge, where the people are used to living with the blind. Although he plans to marry Chris at Christmas, he does not want to accept a job in the Paterson barrel factory that Chris's father plans to give him for his daughter's sake. A few days before he is to leave for Avon, Connecticut to learn an occupation, Larry tries to convince Chris that he would rather get his own job than accept one offered out of charity. After thinking about their situation, Chris says she is not strong enough for what he has in mind, and they break their engagement. On his way to Avon, Larry stops at the train station in Philadelphia, where Bill, to whom Larry sent a telegram, meets him and takes him to Coe's home. Coe tells Larry that he succeeded in law school because he was able to concentrate better than the other students, and because his dedicated wife read the law books, which were not available in Braille, aloud to him. Back at the station, Larry is disheartened that Judy, to whom he also sent a telegram, is not there, but she arrives just before the train leaves, and they hug. Larry admits he looked for security in the wrong place and realizes now that he has to make it for himself. They decide that they will find their way together, and that he will become a lawyer. At the train, Larry hears Joe's name. The two men agree to

be friends, and sit together during the train trip to Avon. *Blind–Rehabilitation. Engagements. Hospitals. Racism. Romance. Southerners. Valley Forge (PA). Veterans. War injuries. Africa, North. African Americans. Attempted suicide. Barrels. Dances. Factories. Family relationships. Florida. Friendship. Lawyers. Officers (Military). Pennsylvania. Philadelphia (PA). Train stations. World War II.*

Note: The working title of this film was *Lights Out*. According to a *HR* news item, in Mar 1946, David W. Siegel and producer-director Robert Thoeren considered forming a partnership to make a film based on the novel, which was a best-seller. The author, Baynard Kendrick, had earlier written a detective series, featuring "sightless detective" Duncan McClain. The accuracy of that portrayal led Kendrick to be recommended to the War Department to help in the rehabilitation of blind veterans, and that work led to his writing *Lights Out*. *LAT* reported in Aug 1946, that the novel was "as good as bought" by M-G-M, although the studio denied the deal. According to *NYT*, the screen rights to the novel were bought in 1946 by Clarence Brown for $10,000. Brown then sold it the next year for $50,000 to Robert Montgomery, who had recently become associated with Universal-International. Montgomery planned to direct and star in the film, with Joan Harrison writing the screenplay and producing. In Mar 1947, *NYT* reported, "The color problem will not loom as large on the screen as it did in the novel, according to Miss Harrison, since the love story will be the primary subject in the screen treatment. On the other hand, she declared, sectional prejudice in the United States will not prevent the studio from facing the Negro question on the screen, although box-office dictates have previously blocked all examination of the subject." Subsequently the film was produced and written by Robert Buckner, who, according to *NYT*, said he found it necessary to change certain aspects of the book, but author Kendrick praised the resulting film. According to information in the MPAA/PCA Collection at the AMPAS Library, in May 1950, PCA director Joseph I. Breen, after examining a draft of the screenplay, advised, "The two uses of the word 'niggers' are likely to prove offensive, and we seriously recommend that you substitute the word 'Negroes.' " The studio, however, kept the word in the film.

Extensive filming was done at the United States Army General Hospital at Valley Forge, PA, which, according to *NYT*, Kendrick had in mind when he wrote the novel. Ten blind World War II veterans at the hospital appeared as extras and advised the actors. *NYT* stated that Arthur Kennedy, like director Mark Robson, was "devoted to realism" and noted that Kennedy acted the role wearing contact lenses that had been dyed black. Scenes were also shot on location in Florida. *Cue* praised the film as "one of the year's most distinguished." Reviews were mixed concerning the film's treatment of racism. *Time* wrote, "Not content with solving the problems of the blind hero so easily, *Bright Victory* is even more superficial in an over-tricky subplot that as glibly poses and solves the Negro problem." *HCN* commented, "*Bright Victory* would have been stronger, story-wise, and boast greater unity if Negro discrimination... had not been touched upon." However, *LAT* praised the film, stating, "The racial issue that arises... is very ably depicted and is an important component of the plot." *SatRev* praised the acting of James Edwards, saying he "gives the role dignity and dimension." Concerning the realism of the film's hospital scenes, *NYT* applauded the "fine documentation of the techniques by which blinded veterans are treated and trained at an Army hospital." The film received a number of awards and citations, including the Distinguished Service Award of the President's Committee for Employment of the Physically Handicapped and the Veteran of Foreign War's National Citation.

Box 28 Jul 1951. *Cue* 4 Aug 1951. *DN* 9 Oct 1950. *DV* 20 Jul 1951, p. 3, 8. *Exh* 1 Aug 1951, p. 3119. *FD* 23 Jul 1951, p. 6. *Har* 21 Jul 1951, p. 115. *HCN* 17 Jan 1951. *HCN* 1 Dec 1951. *HCN* 5 Dec 1951. *HR* 18 Aug 1950, p. 13. *HR* 9 22 Sep 1950, p. 9. *HR* 20 Jul 1951, p. 3. *HR* 18 Oct 1951. *HR* 18 Apr 1952. *LADN* 7 Jul 1951. *LADN* 17 Jul 1951. *LADN* 1 Dec 1951. *LAEx* 1 Dec 1951. *LAEx* 19 Jul 1951. *LAT* 10 Aug 1946. *LAT* 12 Mar 1947. *LAT* 28 Jan 1951. *LAT* 17 Jul 1951. *LAT* 1 Dec 1951. *LAT* 14 Oct 1952. *Life* 3 Sep 1951. *MPD* 20 Jul 1951. *MPHPD* 28 Jul 1951, pp. 946-47. *Newsweek* 23 Jul 1951. *New Yorker* 4 Aug 1951. *NYT* 16 Mar 1947. *NYT* 3 Sep 1950. *NYT* 1 Aug 1951, p. 19. *SatRev* 21 Jul 1951. *Time* 13 Aug 1951. *Var* 2 May 1951. *Var* 25 Jul 1951, p. 6.

BRINGING UP FATHER (Irish Americans)
Monogram Pictures Corp. *Dist* Monogram Pictures Corp. 23 Nov 1946; New York premiere: 20 Nov 1946; Prod: 20 Jun—early Jul 1946 [©Monogram Pictures Corp.; 27 Oct 1946; LP657]. Sd (Western Electric Mirrophonic Recording); b&w. 8 reels. 68 min. PCA cert no. 11859.

Series: Jiggs and Maggie.

Prod Barney Gerard. *Dir* Eddie Cline. [*Asst dir* Frank Fox]. *Scr* Jerry Warner. *Orig story* Barney Gerard and Eddie Cline. *Photog* L. W. O'Connell. *Film ed* Ralph Dixon. *Ward* Harry Bourne. *Mus dir* Edward J. Kay. *Recordist* Elden Ruberg. *Makeup* Harry Ross. *Hair dresser* Carla Hadley. *Prod mgr* Glenn Cook. *Tech dir* David Milton.

Song(s): "When the Mush Begins to Rush Down Father's Vest," music and lyrics by Barney Gerard; "Corned Beef and Cabbage," music by Edward J. Kay, lyrics by Eddie Cline.

Source: Based on the comic strip "Bringing Up Father" by George McManus, owned and copyrighted by King Features Syndicate, Inc. (12 Jan 1913—).

Cast: Joe Yule [(*Jiggs*)], Renie Riano [(*Maggie*)], Tim Ryan [(*Dinty Moore*)], June Harrison [(*Nora*)], Wallace Chadwell [(*Danny*)], Tom Kennedy [(*Murphy*)], Laura Treadwell [(*Mrs. Kermishaw*)], William

Frambes [(*Junior Kermishaw*)], Pat Goldin [(*Dugan*)], Jack Norton [(*Norton*)], Ferris Taylor [(*Mr. F. Newson Kermishaw*)], Tom Dugan [(*Hod Carrier*)], Joe Devlin [(*Casy*)], Fred Kelsey [(*Tom*)], Charles Wilson [(*Frank*)], Herbert Evans [(*Jenkins*)], Dick Ryan [(*Grogharty*)], Mike Pat Donovan [(*Jerry*)], Bob Carleton [(*Pianist*)], George Hickman [(*Fogarty*)], Featuring the famous international cartoonist George McManus [(*Himself*)], [Jimmy Aubrey (*McGurk*)], [Ralph Peters (*Goofy*)], [Stanley Blystone, Joe Weston (*Deputies*)], [Jasper Palmer (*Delivery man*)], [Walden Boyle (*Father O'Malley*)], [Bryn Davis (*Mrs.Grogharty*)], [Polly Bailey (*Mrs. Norton*)], [Daun Kennedy (*Secretary*)], [Bill Haade (*Leader*)], [Frank Marlowe (*Pugugly*)], [Bert Roach (*Calendar man*)], [Sailor Vincent (*Jim*)], [Tiny Lipson (*Fat man*)].

Domestic, Society, Comedy, with songs. [*Print viewed*]. Construction contractor Jiggs and his overbearing, social-climbing wife Maggie are visited in their posh Park Avenue, New York apartment by the snobbish Mrs. Kermishaw, who, unaware that Jiggs is Maggie's husband, tells her that Jiggs is a "hybrid" and that she wants him removed from the building. Jiggs makes his presence known during Mrs. Kermishaw's visit and embarrasses Maggie, who then punches her husband for ruining her chances to get into the society *Blue Book*. When Jiggs stumbles down the stairs of his building and into a parked car, he happens upon his daughter Nora, who introduces her to date, Junior Kermishaw, son of F. Newson Kermishaw, a dishonest developer who is planning to tear down Dinty Moore's Tenth Avenue saloon. Dinty's nephew Danny, an architect, is in the employ of Kermishaw but is unaware that he plans to welch on his promise to Dinty that he will modernize the building and let the saloon stand. Kermishaw's neighborhood improvement plan is nothing more than a front that he plans to use to take over the neighborhood. As part of his scheme, Kermishaw begins circulating a petition containing a clause in small print that turns over ownership of Dinty's saloon to him. The petition is soon signed by Maggie and all the patrons of Dinty's saloon. Meanwhile, Junior proposes to Nora and asks Jiggs for his blessing to marry his daughter, even though Danny is in love with Nora. When two men present Dinty with an injunction ordering the closure of his saloon, Dinty realizes that he made a terrible mistake in ignoring the small print of the petition, which also stipulates that its patrons refrain from drinking at any establishment. Jiggs is blamed for the fiasco by Dinty and all of the saloon's patrons, and is banished from the bar. Distraught, Jiggs wanders the streets and happens upon Danny, who is also upset because he knows that he has been had by the Kermishaws. Danny decides to fight back, though, and begins circulating a "counter petition" and goes to the Kermishaw Holding Company to slug Junior. Danny succeeds in reopening Dinty's saloon, and he is reunited with Nora. Later, an attempt by Kermishaw's thugs to "rough up" the patrons of the saloon is called off when the leader of the thugs recognizes Murphy, a regular habitué of the saloon, as an old friend. *New York City–Park Avenue. Real estate magnates. Snobs and snobbishness. Social climbers. Tycoons. Alcoholism. Irish Americans. Marriage. Petitions. Proposals (Marital). Romantic rivalry. Saloon keepers. Saloons. Unrequited love.*

Note: The opening credits read: "Jiggs and Maggie in Bringing Up Father." *Bringing Up Father* was the first of five Monogram films between 1946 and 1950 based on the George McManus cartoon strip of the same title. The "Jiggs and Maggie" films all starred Joe Yule (actor Mickey Rooney's father) and Renie Riano and, with the exception of the first film, were all directed by William Beaudine. The series ended following the death of Yule in 1950. According to contemporary sources, Barney Gerard acquired the screen rights to the comic strip in May 1940, at which time it was announced that he would produce two "Jiggs and Maggie" films annually. A Jun 1946 *LAEx* article indicates that the final decision as to who would play the role of Jiggs was made just prior to the start of production. According to the article, the choice was narrowed down to either McManus or Yule, but McManus rejected the role because it required that he shave his head. The *Var* review notes that this film marked Barney Gerard's "first attempt as a single producer." An article in *Look* magazine in Jul 1947 featured comic strip cells from McManus' "Bringing Up Father" newspaper series placed side-by-side with film frames from corresponding scenes in the movie, to illustrate how the filmmakers created settings, costumes and facial expressions that were nearly identical to those in the cartoon. For additional titles in the series, consult the Series Index.

Box 19 Oct 1946. *DV* 11 Oct 1946, p. 3. *FD* 16 Oct 1946, p. 11. *HR* 21 Jun 1946, p. 16. *HR* 5 Jul 1946, p. 14. *HR* 11 Oct 1946, p. 3. *LAEx* 13 Jun 1946. *Look* 8 Jul 1947. *MPD* 6 May 1940. *MPHPD* 7 Sep 1946, p. 3186. *MPHPD* 19 Oct 1946, p. 3262. *NYT* 22 Nov 1946, p. 27. *Var* 27 Nov 1946, p. 28.

BRITTON OF THE SEVENTH (Native Americans)

Vitagraph Co. of America. *Dist* V-L-S-E, Inc. 8 May **1916** [©The Vitagraph Co. of America; 8 Dec 1915; LP7643]. Si; b&w. 4 reels.

Dir Lionel Belmore. *Scen* Jasper Ewing Brady.

Source: Based on the novel *Britton of the Seventh: A Romance of Custer and the Great Northwest* by Cyrus Townsend Brady (Chicago, 1914).

Cast: Darwin Karr (*Lieut. Tony Britton, age 30*), Charles Kent (*Lieut. Tony Britton, age 70*), Bobby Connelly (*Bobby*), Eleanor Woodruff (*Barbara Manning*), Ned Finley (*General Custer*), Harry Northrup (*Captain Granson*), Eulalie Jensen (*Frances Granson*), Logan Paul (*Rain-in-the-Face*), Marion Henry (*Otanowah*), Rose E. Tapley (*Madge Eversly*).

Historical, Drama. Lieutenant Tony Britton explains to his grandson that things were different back in 1876, when General George Armstrong Custer's Seventh Cavalry used muskets, and cavalry scouts did the work that airplanes do today. In 1876, Britton loves Barbara Manning. When Indian warrior Rain-in-the-Face scalps two soldiers of the Seventh to show his bravery to Indian maiden Otanowah, Britton is sent to arrest him. The tribe offers any three other Indians, but Britton captures Rain-in-the-Face and he is jailed. Meanwhile, Captain Granson's wife implores Britton to run away with her. He writes a note of refusal, but Captain Granson, learning of the affair, makes trouble. Rain-in-the-Face escapes and issues a threat against Captain Granson. To prove his innocence in the matter of the captain's wife, Tony cites the note, but Mrs. Granson refuses to acknowledge its existence, and so Tony is forced to resign his commission. He becomes an Indian scout and learns that the Indians are planning to attack. Britton tries to notify Custer, but his message arrives late, and Custer and his men are massacred. Rain-in-the-Face mutilates Captain Granson; however, before he dies, Granson finds the note clearing Tony and gives it to Custer. When the note turns up among Custer's effects, the cavalry re-admits Tony, and he and Barbara plan their marriage. *Letters. Officers (Military). Reputation. Scouts (Frontier). Unrequited love. General George Armstrong Custer. Grandfathers. Indians of North America. Infidelity. Little Big Horn, Battle of the, 1876. Massacres. United States. Army. Cavalry.*

Note: According to a news item, this film was shot along the U.S.-Mexican border, and Indians from Oklahoma reservations and United States troops appeared in the film. Logan Paul may be the same as the actor Paul Logan.

MPN 22 Jan 1916, p. 391. *MPW* 15 Jan 1916, p. 439, 470. *MPW* 20 May 1916, p. 1406. *NYDM* 29 Apr 1916, p. 26. *Var* 5 May 1916, p. 23. *Wid's* 11 May 1916, p. 566.

A BRIVELE DER MAMEN (Jewish Americans, Yiddish language)

Green-Film. *Dist* Sphinx Films Corp. 14 Sep **1939**. Sd; b&w. 11 reels, 9,799 ft. 105-106 min. *Country of origin* Poland. Yiddish language with English subtitles.

Assoc prod Benjamin J. Weinberg. *Dir* Joseph Green. *Asst dir* Leo Tristan. *Story* Mendel Osherowitz. [*Scenario* Mendel Osherowitz and Joseph Green]. *Literary assistance* J. M. Neuman. *English titles* Julian Leigh. *Photog* Seweryn Steinwurtcel. *Mus* Abe Ellstein.

Song(s): "Deep as the Night" and "To Mother, Write a Letter," by Abe Ellstein.

Cast: LUCY GEHRMAN [(*Dobrish Berdichevski*)], MISHA GEHRMAN [(*Mr. Shein*)], Max Bozyk [(*Shimen*)], Edmund Zayenda [(*Irving Bird*)], Gertrude Bulman [(*Miriam Berdichevsky*)], Alexander Stein [(*David Berdichevsky*)], Samuel Landau [(*Hersh Leyb*)], Simche Fostel [(*A cantor*)], Chana Levin [(*Shimen's wife Malka*)], Icchok Grudberg [(*Meyer Berdichevsky*)], [Irving Bruner (*Arele Berdichevsky*)].

Yiddish, Domestic, Melodrama, with songs. [*Print viewed*]. In Lubomil, a town in the Ukraine, in 1912, David and Arele Berdichevsky, a father and son, listen to a beautiful shepherd's song together. David, a kind-hearted man, then composes a tune from the shepherd's song. Because he devotes his time to composing songs, David cannot support his family, which is in disarray. Miriam, David's daughter, is betrothed to Yudke, the son of Shimen the tailor, a family friend; however, while Yudke is away studying engineering in Odessa, Miriam is courted by her dancing teacher, Solomon. Meyer, David's other son, has decided to leave his job in a pharmacy to go to Odessa and be a dentist. When he berates his father, who is depressed, for not working, Dobrish, David's wife, who supports the family through her work in a fabric shop, slaps him. David wanders through the town and overhears gossip about him. Feeling lost where he is, he decides, for his family's sake, to go to America and gets money for the

trip from Shimen. At the Passover *seder*, the whole family cries over David's departure. Miriam secretly joins Solomon when he leaves town for Balta and sadly leaves a note for her mother. Ashamed of her daughter's action, Dobrish tells others that she sent Miriam to live with an aunt. Sometime later, Dobrish receives a letter from America with money and a steamship ticket, and the family and friends prepare Arele to leave to live in America with his father, as rumors grow that David has amassed a fortune. David, however, is now a pushcart salesman hawking ties and socks. As Arele's train pulls out, Dobrish asks him to write a letter when he arrives in America. Miriam returns, looking forlorn, and asks her mother's forgiveness, revealing reveals that Solomon has a wife and child. Dobrish relates that Yudke has returned and talks her daughter into marrying him. After the wedding, the couple goes to Odessa. World War I erupts, and Meyer leaves to fight. The town of Lubomil is destroyed, and Dobrish goes to a big city with Shimen and his wife Malka, where she has to stand in a bread line. When a former creditor, Hersh Leyb, who earlier harassed Dobrish, is unable to get bread, Dobrish gives him half of her loaf. After the war ends, a soldier visits Dobrish with a medal from Meyer and relates that he was killed in action, as she had dreamed, and that his dying word was "Mother." After the Versailles Treaty, Mr. Shein, the American director of HIAS, the Hebrew Immigrant Aid Society, visits a Jewish displaced persons headquarters and, after deploring the formalities, witnesses an official rebuke Dobrish when she asks about her husband and son in America. Shein then writes his wife in America about David. Meanwhile, Shimen's brother in America sends tickets for him and his wife to come. Unfortunately, Shein learns that David has died and that Arele cannot be found. Dobrish faints at this news. Seeing that Dobrish cries at the thought of being alone now, Shimen refuses to go to America without her. Shein then offers to take Dobrish with him on the next boat. Dobrish cries in the hope of seeing her Arele again. In America, Arele, now the famous singer Irving Bird, and his wife go to see Shein because they are planning to travel to Europe to try to find his family. Dobrish sees them leave Shein's office, but doesn't recognize Arele. The next day, Dobrish attends Arele's concert for Jewish refugees and hears him sing the Hebrew song his father composed from the shepherd's tune. She cries and tries to approach him, but he doesn't recognize her and gets into a limousine with his wife. In a daze, Dobrish is hit by a car. Arele gets out of the limousine and holds her. In the hospital room, Arele recognizes her, and Dobrish sees scenes of him as a boy as she looks at his face. She says his name and they hug. *Family life. Immigrants. Jews. Long-lost relatives. Singers. Small town life. Songwriters. Ukraine. Automobile accidents. Bread lines. Concerts. Dance teachers. Engagements. Hebrew Immigrant Aid Society. Rumors. Seder (Jewish holiday). Seduction. Tailors. World War I.*

Note: The English translation of the title of this film is *A Letter to Mama*. This was the fourth and last film made in Poland by Joseph Green, an American, who, beginning in 1936, produced Yiddish language films there. For more information on Green, please see the entry below for *Yiddle with His Fiddle*. *NYT* called this "the last Yiddish movie made in Poland before the Nazi invasion put an end, at least temporarily, to such activities." Although this film is not listed in the book of copyright entries, the scenario by Mendel Osherowitz and Joseph Green was copyrighted as an unpublished dramatic work and registered in the name of Joseph Green on 23 Apr 1938, number D56550. According to Joseph Green's personal papers at NCJF, the film cost 302.040 zlotys to produce. In an oral history conducted by the Hebrew University Oral History Department, Joseph Green stated that the film was shot in parts of the Ukraine, ending up in Lemberg and that box office receipts were higher for this film than his first Polish film *Yiddle with His Fiddle*, which also was successful. This film was re-released in 1949 under the title *The Eternal Song*.

FD 21 Sep 1939, p. 7. *MPD* 22 Sep 1939. *NYT* 15 Sep 1939, p. 26. *Var* 20 Sep 1939, p. 27.

BROADWAY BILL (African Americans)

Columbia Pictures Corp.; Harry Cohn, President; A Frank Capra Production. *Dist* Columbia Pictures Corp. 27 Dec **1934**; New York opening: week of 30 Nov 1934; Prod: 18 Jun–16 Aug 1934 [©Columbia Pictures Corp.; 24 Jan 1934; LP5123]. Sd (Western Electric Noiseless Recording); b&w. 11 reels, 9,407 ft. 90 or 103 min. PCA cert no. 390.

[*Assoc prod* Samuel J. Briskin]. *Dir* Frank Capra. [*Asst dir* C. C. Coleman]. [*2d unit dir* Ray Davidson]. *Scr* Robert Riskin. *Story* Mark Hellinger. *Contr to scr construction* Sidney Buchman. *Photog* Joseph Walker. [*Cam op* Vic Scheurich and George Kelly]. [*Cam crew* James Goss, Jack Andersen and Walter Lackey]. *Stills* Irving Lippman. *Film ed* Gene Havlick. *Sd eng* Edward Bernds. *Lab tech* Marty Crail.

Stand-in for Warner Baxter Frank McGrath. *Stand-in for Myrna Loy* Melrose Hooper. *Stand-in for Walter Connolly* Joe Lynch.

Cast: WARNER BAXTER (*Dan Brooks*), MYRNA LOY (*The Princess [Alice Higgins]*), Walter Connolly (*J. L. Higgins*), Helen Vinson (*Margaret [Brooks]*), Douglas Dumbrille (*Eddie Morgan*), Raymond Walburn (*Colonel Pettigrew*), Lynne Overman ([*Oscar*] *Happy McGuire*), Clarence Muse (*Whitey*), Margaret Hamilton (*Edna*), Frankie Darro (*Ted Williams*), George Cooper (*Joe*), George Meeker (*Henry Early*), Jason Robards (*Arthur Winslow*), Edward Tucker (*Jimmy Baker*), Edmund Breese (*Presiding judge*), [Broadway Bill (*Dan's horse*)], [Helen Flint (*Mrs. Early*)], [Helene Millard (*Mrs. Winslow*)], [Harry Holman (*Rube*)], [Charles Levinson, Ward Bond (*Morgan's benchmen*)], [Harry Todd (*Pop Jones*)], [Charles C. Wilson (*Collins*)], [Paul Harvey (*James Whiteball*)], [Claude Gillingwater, Sr. (*J. P. Chase*)], [Inez Courtney (*Mae*)], [Lucille Ball (*Switchboard operator*)], [Clara Blandick (*Mrs. Peterson, secretary*)], [Alan Hale (*Orchestra leader*)], [Bob Tansill (*Whiteball's jockey*)], [Robert Allen, Dick Sumner, Frank O'Connor (*Reporters*)], [James Blakely (*Interne*)], [Forrester Harvey (*Horse trainer*)], [Charles B. Middleton (*Veterinarian*)], [Herman Bing (*Waiter*)], [Eddie Kane (*Assistant judge*)], [Irving Bacon (*Hot dog stand owner*)], [Edward Keane (*Head waiter*)], [Tom Ricketts (*Johnson*)], [Harrison Greene (*Auctioneer*)], [A. R. Haysel (*Mike*)], [Sam Flint (*Race track judge*)], [Pat Moriarity (*Policeman*)], [Joan Standing (*Secretary*)], [Frank Yaconelli (*Spaniard*)], [Ky Robinson, Frank Holliday (*Deputy sheriffs*)], [Christian Frank (*Sheriff*)], [William H. Strauss (*Pawnbroker*)], [Spec O'Donnell (*Office boy*)], [Fred Walton, Sidney Bracy (*Butlers*)], [Alfred James (*Mel*)], [Gladys Hale (*Head nurse*)], [Ara Haswell, Betty May, Helene Caverly, Rita Ross, Irene Coleman, Ila Lee (*Nurses*)], [P. H. Levy (*Bearded man*)], [Stanley Blystone (*Jailer*)], [Kit Guard (*Cab driver*)], [John Ince (*Mayor*)], [Henry Barrows (*Governor*)], [Otto Fries (*Waiter*)], [Bess Flowers (*Secretary*)], [Ernie Adams (*Patient*)], [Bruce Galbraith (*Jockey*)], [Kernan Cripps (*Policeman*)], [Stanley Mack (*Tout*)], [Charles Brinley (*Horseman*)], [Jack Mulhall], [Richard Heming], [Arthur Rankin], [Patricia Caron], [Harry C. Bradley], [Eddy Chandler], [Louis Natheaux], [Pat O'Malley], [Sydney de Grey], [Edmund Burns], [Bud Flanagan], [Babe Lawrence], [Harry Dunkinson], [Gino Corrado], [Philo McCollough], [Mert La Varr], [John Webb Dillion], [Dick Kipling], [Bert Morehouse], [Reginald Simpson], [Matty Roubert], [Eddie Sturgis], [Harry Keaton], [Marvin Loback], [Kay McCoy], [Bert Starkey], [Kay Sherris], [John Irwin], [Phyllis Crane], [Bill Irving], [Eris Norman], [Joe Bordeaux], [Dixie Russell], [Bobby Dunn], [Janet Harper], [Herbert Ashley], [Alice Lake], [Dick Pritchard], [Evelyn Pierce], [Dutch Hendrian], [Elinor Fair], [Brooks Benedict], [Edith Craig], [Frank Mills], [Beatrice Curtis], [Jack Kenny], [Anita Pike], [Don Roberts], [Ethel Sykes], [Larry McGrath], [Catherine Wallace], [Tom Costello], [Maurine Gray], [Bond Davis], [Lillian West], [Dick Gordon], [Peggy Leon], [Lee Willard], [Ruth Hiatt], [Bob Ryan], [Janet Eastman], [Gunnis Davis], [Ruth Milo], [Tony Martelli], [Blanche Churchill], [Gene McKay], [Symona Boniface], [Sammy Blum], [Margaret Morgan], [Harry Hume], [Sue Stevens], [Herman Marks], [Anna Chandler], [Paul Irving], [Violet Carlton], [George Morrell], [Adelyn Hall], [Ethel Bryant], [Billee Van Every].

Horse race, Comedy-drama. [*Print viewed*]. Businessman J. L. Higgins, president of the Higgins National Bank in Higginsville, announces a board of directors' dinner meeting for his four daughters and three sons-in-law, each of whom presides over one of Higgins' subsidiaries. All are reached quickly except for Dan Brooks, who is attending to his thoroughbred, "Broadway Bill," with the help of Alice, J. L.'s unwed daughter. Dan hates running his Aather-in-law's paper box factory, and is urged by Alice and stablehand Whitey to devote himself to racing Bill. While preparing for dinner that night, Dan's wife Margaret refuses to sympathize with Dan's misery over his job or share his excitement about his first love, horseracing. She informs him that he could someday own the vast Higgins financial empire, and they then attend the dinner, during which J. L. informs his family of his acquisition that morning of the Acme Lumber Co. He says that its presidency will be left vacant until Alice's future husband takes the post, but free-willed Alice insists she would never marry a man who would walk into such a job. Following dinner, J. L. reports that sales are dangerously off in Dan's paper box division due to his inattention to work. When J. L. orders Dan to sell Broadway Bill and return full time to the office, Dan quits instead and leaves Higginsville without

Margaret, who refuses to go with him. Alice cries in happiness for Dan's "escape," while also hiding her attraction to him. At the Imperial Race Track, Dan rejoins his friends as he enters Broadway Bill in the $25,000 Imperial Derby, which is to be held in two weeks. Dan scrapes together the entry fee, then sets about finding the five hundred dollar nominating fee. He convinces Pop Jones to give him feed and shelter on credit, but is unable to get money from his old friend Colonel Pettigrew, who is also penniless. At a preliminary race the next day, Bill is disqualified when he bolts the starting gate. Dan writes to Margaret, asking her to send Bill's friend "Skeeter," a pet rooster, but it is Alice who delivers Skeeter. Alice stays to help, despite the protests of Dan, who is unaware of her feelings for him, and also that Margaret expects him to return home to apologize. Alice's presence proves fortunate when Bill gets a serious cold from being soaked by rain pouring through the leaky barn. She nurses Bill back to health, then pawns her fur coat and jewelry to raise money when Whitey is discovered to be using loaded dice while shooting craps to raise the nominating fee. On the eve of the derby, Pop Jones, angry that he has not been paid, has Bill seized and Dan thrown in jail. When a two-dollar bet placed on Bill by J. P. Chase, a bored, bedridden millionaire, is misinterpreted as a $200,000 bet, bookmaker Eddie Morgan, who is backing "Sun Up," is pleased because the odds on his horse go up as Bill's decline. To prevent Bill from being scratched, Eddie bails Dan out and pays his bills. Meanwhile, Eddie has bribed Ted Williams, Bill's jockey, and the jockey riding favorite "Gallant Lady," to throw the race. Eddie's plan is partially crippled, however, when Gallant Lady's jockey is suspended. On the day of the race, Williams reigns Bill in, but Bill ignores his instructions and sprints to victory, only to collapse and die of a burst heart. The following day, Bill is buried at the track, after which J. L. takes Alice home, and Dan leaves with Whitey. Two years pass and J. L. calls another dinner meeting. He announces that since Dan and Margaret's divorce, he has sold his subsidiaries, and that the bank will be next. He hopes his remaining sons-in-law will become independent men, not spineless parasites. Just then, a honking car horn and a shattered window announce Dan's demand that J. L. "release the Princess (Alice) from the dark tower." She runs to join Dan, Whitey and their two new horses, "Broadway Bill II" and "Princess." J. L. then leaves behind his shocked family and escapes with Alice. *Debt. Horseracing. Horses. Marriage. Romance. African Americans. Barns. Bookies. Businessmen. Dice. Fathers and daughters. Fixed horse races. Friendship. Funerals. Gamblers. Hospitals. In-laws. Jockeys. Nursing back to health. Wagers.*

Note: According to the SAB, Mark Hellinger's story was entitled "On the Nose." A *HR* news item, however, gives the name of the story as "Strictly Confidential." No publication information for Hellinger's story has been found. According to *HR* news items, Louis Calhern was briefly assigned to the part played by Douglas Dumbrille, Sidney Skolsky was set to play a jockey, and Frank Capra sought to borrow Lewis Stone from M-G-M for an unspecified role. Contemporary sources also state that Osgood Perkins, Sterling Holloway, Samuel S. Hinds, Barbara Read and Mary McGrath were included in the cast, but their participation in the final film has not been verified. Location shooting was done at Tanforan Racetrack, which was located in San Mateo County, the Warner Ranch and Pacific Coast Steel Mills. According to contemporary sources, the film was 125 minutes long when it was previewed on 24 Oct 1934. *FD* states that another preview was held on 21 Nov 1934. In his autobiography, photographer Joseph Walker states that Capra originally tried to get Clark Gable for the part of Dan Brooks, but he was not available. On 24 Apr 1939, Robert Taylor performed in a radio verson of Broadway Bill for *Lux Radio Theatre*.

Modern sources list the following additional crew members: *Microphone op* Irving Libbott; *Elec* Bob Charlesworth; *Props* George Rhein; *Gaffer* George Hager; *Best Boy* Al Later; and *Head grip* Jimmy Lloyd. Modern sources also include Harry Semels *Conductor* in the cast, and complete the character identifications for Harry C. Bradley (*Bookkeeper*) and Eddy Chandler (*Onlooker*). *Broadway Bill* was remade by Capra as *Riding High*, a 1950 release starring Bing Crosby and Colleen Grey. Capra states in his autobiography that he traded the script for *A Woman of Distinction* for the rights to *Broadway Bill* and its negative. He made *Broadway Bill* for Paramount, and in order to save money, cut in approximately twenty minutes of racing and dialogue footage from the original film. Among the actors reprising their original roles were Clarence Muse, Douglas Dumbrille, Margaret Hamilton, Frankie Darro, Ward Bond, Raymond Walburn and Irving Bacon.

Box 17 Nov 1934. *DV* 25 Oct 1934, p. 3. *FD* 9 Nov 1934, p. 7. *FD* 22 Nov 1934, p. 10. *FD* 14 Dec 1934, p. 2. *HR* 19 Feb 1934, p. 3. *HR* 28 Apr 1934, p. 1. *HR* 6 Jun 1934, p. 2. *HR* 11 Jun 1934, p. 3, 6, 8. *HR* 14 Jun 1934, p. 3, 4. *HR* 10 Jul 1934, p. 3. *HR* 20 Jul 1934, p. 3. *HR* 16 Aug 1934, p. 1. *HR* 25 Oct 1934, p. 3. *IP MPD* 26 Oct 1934, p. 8. *MPH* 14 Jul 1934, p. 48. *MPH* 10 Nov 1934, p. 38. *NYT* 30 Nov 1934, p. 22. *Var* 4 Dec 1934, p. 12.

A BROADWAY SCANDAL (French Americans)

Bluebird Photoplays, Inc. *Dist* Bluebird Photoplays, Inc. 1 Jun **1918** [©Bluebird Photoplays, Inc.; 18 May 1918; LP12435]. Si; b&w. 5 reels, 4,400 ft.

Dir Joseph De Grasse. *Story* Harvey Gates. *Cam* Edward Ullman.

Cast: Carmel Myers (*Nenette Bisson*), W. H. Bainbridge (*Dr. Kendall*), Edwin August (*David Kendall*), Lon Chaney (*"Kink" Colby*), Andrew Robson (*Armande Bisson*), S. K. Shilling (*Paul Caval*), Frederick Gamble (*Falkner*).

Comedy-drama. Nenette Bisson, who dances in her father's French restaurant in New York, takes a joy ride with "Kink" Colby in a stolen car, and is shot in the shoulder by a pursuing policeman. The driver leaves her at the hospital of David Kendall, with whom she falls in love, but he, believing French women to be frivolous, does not return her affections. Nenette's parents turn her out when they learn of her trouble with the police, after which she becomes a success on the stage. David serves overseas for two years during World War I and there learns to appreciate the valiance of French women. On his return, he proclaims his love for Nenette and helps her achieve a reconciliation with her parents. *Dancers. Family relationships. French Americans. Hospitals. Reputation. Automobiles. Gunshot wounds. New York City. Police. Restaurants. Robbery. World War I.*

    MPW 1 Jun 1918, p. 1338. *MPW* 15 Jun 1918, p. 1613. *NYDM* 8 Jun 1918, p. 812. *Wid's* 6 Jun 1918, pp. 29-30.

BROKEN ARROW (Native Americans, Apache)

Twentieth Century-Fox Film Corp. *Dist* Twentieth Century-Fox Film Corp. Aug **1950**; World premieres in New York, Tulsa, OK and Broken Arrow, OK: 21 Jul 1950; Prod: 3 Jun—2 Aug 1949 [©Twentieth Century-Fox Film Corp.; 21 Jul 1950; LP440]. Sd (Western Electric Recording); col (Technicolor). 10 reels, 8,333 or 8,406 ft. 92-93 min. PCA cert no. 13926.

Prod Julian Blaustein. *Dir* Delmer Daves. [*Asst dir* Jasper Blystone]. [*Scr (uncredited)* Albert Maltz]. *Scr* [*("front" for Albert Maltz)*] Michael Blankfort. *Dir of photog* Ernest Palmer. [*Cam op* Curt Fetters]. [*Stills* Al St. Hilaire]. *Spec photog eff* Fred Sersen. *Technicolor color consultant* Leonard Doss. *Art dir* Lyle Wheeler and Albert Hogsett. *Film ed* J. Watson Webb, Jr. *Set dec* Thomas Little and Fred J. Rode. *Ward dir* Charles Le Maire. *Cost des* Rene Hubert. *Mus dir* Alfred Newman. *Mus* Hugo Friedhofer. *Orch* Edward Powell. *Sd* Bernard Freericks and Harry M. Leonard. *Makeup artist* Ben Nye. [*Hair stylist* Stephanie Garland]. [*Unit prod mgr* Stanley Goldsmith]. [*Tech adv* Jennifer Chatfield and Richard von Opel]. [*Scr supv* Marvin Weldon]. [*Archery expert* Al Leman]. [*Dir of publ* Harry Brand]. [*Speaking voice double for Argentina Brunetti* Eleanor Audley].

Source: Based on the novel *Blood Brother* by Elliott Arnold (New York, 1947).

Cast: JAMES STEWART [(*Tom Jeffords*)], Jeff Chandler [(*Cochise*)], Debra Paget [(*Sonseeahray*)], Basil Ruysdael [(*General Oliver Howard*)], Will Geer [(*Ben Slade*)], Joyce MacKenzie [(*Terry*)], Arthur Hunnicutt [(*Milt Duffield*)], [Raymond Bramley (*Col. Bernall*)], [Jay Silverheels (*Goklia*)], [Argentina Brunetti (*Nalikadeya*)], [Jack Lee (*Boucher*)], [Robert Adler (*Lonergan*)], [Robert Griffin (*Lowrie*)], [Bill Wilkerson (*Juan*)], [Mickey Kuhn (*Chip Slade*)], [John War Eagle (*Nahilzay*)], [Robert Foster Dover (*Machogee*)], [Harry Carter (*Miner*)], [Chris Willow Bird (*Nochalo*)], [J. W. Cody (*Pionsenay*)], [Charles Soldani (*Skinyea*)], [Iron Eyes Cody (*Teese*)], [John Marston (*Maury*)], [Edwin Rand (*Sergeant*)], [John Doucette (*Mule driver*)], [Richard von Opel (*Adjutant*)], [Nacho Galindo (*Barber*)], [Julian Rivero (*Diaz*)], [Fred Marlowe], [Charles Conrad], [Peter Brocco], [Chet Brandenburg], [Al Kunde].

Western. [*Print viewed*]. In 1870, prospector Tom Jeffords, a former soldier in the Union Army, is summoned to Tucson by Colonel Bernall. Riding through the Arizona territory of the Chiricahua Apache, who have been fighting with the white settlers for ten years, Tom finds an injured fourteen-year-old Chiricahua youth. Tom easily dodges the boy's weak attempt to stab him, then removes some bullets from the boy, who is named Machogee. When Machogee is well enough to travel, he gives Tom a necklace to ward off sickness and explains that he must return because he knows his mother misses him. Then Machogee's father, Pionsenay, accompanied by other warriors, finds them. The warriors interrogate and taunt Tom, then release him as a reward for helping Machogee. At first, Tom is impressed with their sense of fair play, but changes his mind when they tie him to a tree and gag him to prevent him from warning an

approaching party of miners, who are then slaughtered by the Indians. In Tucson, Tom refuses to be Bernall's scout. Bernall is convinced that he can win the war against the Apache leader Cochise in six months, but Tom believes that Cochise, who now commands the entire Apache nation, will prevail. After Ben Slade, a rancher whose wife was killed in an Apache raid, questions Tom's loyalty, Tom decides to negotiate with Cochise to allow the mail to pass safely through Apache territory. After studying Chiricahua language and customs with Juan, a friendly Apache, Tom travels three days to Cochise's stronghold in the mountains. During his meeting with Cochise, Tom admits that the Americans have done the Apache much harm, but adds that maybe they can live together as brothers. Cochise invites Tom to stay the night, and later, during a ceremonial dance, is surprised by Tom's knowledge of the sunrise ceremony. Pleased with the respect that Tom has for his people, Cochise introduces Tom to the beautiful Sonseeahray, in whose honor the sunrise ceremony will be held. The next morning, while shaving, Tom sees Sonseeahray watching him with interest. When he gives her his mirror, she refuses it uneasily, explaining that she can only talk to young men at ceremonies or dances. Later Tom finds her and confesses his feelings for her, but Sonseeahray runs off when Cochise approaches. Cochise announces that he will let the mail riders pass through his territory in order to demonstrate his power over his people. Back in Tucson, Tom presents the agreement to the skeptical townsfolk, one of whom bets Tom $300 that five riders in succession cannot go through unharmed. Milt Duffield, who is in charge of the mail service, volunteers to be the first rider. Milt returns safely, as do the second, third and fourth riders. Then Bernall escorts a wagon train through Apache territory hoping to be ambushed, as he has secretly armed the wagons. Despite his precautions, Cochise and his men destroy the train. A survivor reports the attack, just as the fifth mail rider arrives safely. Some of the townsfolk think that Cochise knew about the colonel's plan and accuse Tom of spying. A fight breaks out, and General Howard narrowly prevents Tom from being hanged. Howard then asks Tom to help negotiate a fair treaty with Cochise, which will grant the Apaches equality and the right to remain free on their own land. Tom takes the offer to Cochise and renews his romance with Sonseeahray. During a ceremony, Cochise notices Tom looking at Sonseeahray and explains that she is promised to Nahilzay, but she chooses to dance with Tom anyway. When Cochise catches them meeting secretly, Tom says that he wants to marry Sonseeahray, who insists that she will refuse Nahilzay as she has in the past. Cochise advises them that no matter where they live, they will face prejudice from both whites and Apaches. Even though Cochise is against the marriage, he broaches the subject to Sonseeahray's parents, who consent to the wedding. Cochise then instructs Tom to set up a meeting between Howard and representatives of the Apache tribes. That night, Nahilzay sneaks into Tom's wickiup and tries to kill him. Tom fights him off, and Cochise, aroused by the noise, shoots Nahilzay, one of his most trusted warriors. At the peace conference, when Tom explains the details of the treaty, Goklia, an Apache leader, proclaims that Cochise has lost his taste for battle and demands a new chief. Cochise encourages his people to learn new ways, saying that the Americans are now stronger than the Apache. He proposes a trial lasting three "moons" to see if the treaty will be kept and breaks an arrow as a symbol of peace. Those who stay with him must promise to follow the way of peace. If more walk than stay, he will no longer be their chief. Only a small number join Goklia, who says he is ashamed to be a Chiricahua and will now be known by his Mexican name, "Geronimo." Soon after, Tom is riding with the first stage to leave Tucson when the stage is attacked by Apaches. Tom realizes that they are Geronimo's warriors and sends a smoke signal for help, after which the renegades are driven off by Apaches. On the twelfth day of the peace, Tom and Sonseeahray are married. When Cochise is told about the attack on the stage, he orders his men to protect all whites in the future. While Cochise visits Tom and Sonseeahray, Slade's son Chip is found in the stronghold. Chip claims that Apaches stole two colts from his ranch, and Tom convinces Cochise to investigate. When they arrive at the river, Chip signals his father, who is waiting with some other men on the rocks above. During the ensuing battle, Tom is shot, Sonseeahray is killed, and Cochise kills Chip and Slade. Seeing that their plan has failed, the others head for Mexico. When Tom revives and finds Sonseeahray dead, he asks Cochise for a knife to kill her murderer, but Cochise reminds him that peace will not come

easily and vows that no one on his territory will start a war again. Later, Tom and Cochise learn that the men who attacked them were executed. Tom rides off, knowing that his wife, whose death sealed the peace, will always be with him. *Apache Indians. Cochise. Courage. Thomas Jeffords. Peace. Racism. Treaties.* Ambushes. Death and dying. False accusations. Fathers and sons. Geronimo. Honeymoons. General Oliver Otis Howard. Lynching. Mobs. Murder. Officers (Military). Peace conferences. Postal service. Ranchers. Renegades. Revenge. Rites and ceremonies. Romance. Stagecoaches. Tests of character. Torture. Tucson (AZ). Wagers. Wagon trains.

Note: The working titles of this film were *Blood Brother*, *Arrow* and *War Paint*. In an author's note to the novel *Blood Brother*, Elliott Arnold states that "the main events in the book are entirely true.... Thomas Jeffords ran the mail, went up alone to see Cochise, became his friend and later his blood brother, and then led General Howard to Cochise's camp to make the final peace." While noting that Jeffords "confided in a number of close American friends that he was intimate with a lovely Indian girl," Arnold points out, however, that "the entire story of Jeffords and Sonseeahray is pure fiction and every detail in it was invented, against a known historical background." The novel covers a longer period of history than the film. Cochise died in 1874 and Jeffords in 1914.

According to information in news items and the Twentieth Century-Fox Records of the Legal Department at the UCLA Arts—Special Collections Library, Norma Productions, Inc., of which Burt Lancaster and Harold Hecht were the principals, bought the screen rights to *Blood Brother* in 1948, planning to make the film in the spring of 1949 with Julian Blaustein producing. On 30 Jul 1948, Norma Productions signed a contract with Michael Blankfort to write the screenplay. In 1991, it was publicly revealed that Blaustein had actually asked blacklisted writer Albert Maltz to write the screenplay. After several writers turned down his request to "front" for him, Maltz asked Blankfort, a close friend, who accepted and allowed his name to be used for free. A 29 Jun 1991 *LAT* article reproduces a contract dated 21 Aug 1948 in which Blankfort engages Maltz to do "the major portion of the work."

In Apr 1949, Twentieth Century-Fox purchased the rights to the novel from Music Corporation of America, which then owned the rights, according to a *NYT* news item. The deal included the stipulation that James Stewart (a client of MCA) would star in the film, that Blaustein would produce (as his first assignment under a seven-year optional contract with the studio) and that Twentieth Century-Fox would own the rights to the story treatments and scripts, supposedly written by Blankfort, but which in reality were by Maltz. The rights had previously been offered to Warner Bros., also with a stipulation that Stewart would star. In an "Author's Foreward" to a script dated 11 Apr 1949, in the Twentieth Century-Fox Produced Scripts Collection, also at the UCLA Arts—Special Collections Library, Maltz, writing under Blankfort's name, listed a number of concerns dealing with retaining the screenplay's accuracy and authenticity in the filming. He emphasized that "the drama is based upon fact. The main events of the story, which occurred in the years 1870-1872, happened as they are related here." Noting that "it would be regrettable if the film did not convey the quality of authenticity present in a documentary and the fascination always contained in the facts of history," Maltz stated that in his screenplay, "the style of the narrative and the selection of background detail have been directed to achieve these ends." He assumed that "all exterior scenes will be photographed in the magnificent and neglected section of Arizona, in which the events occurred," and encouraged the studio to use Apache Indians as cast members: "The Apaches are today, as they were yesterday, a vigorous and handsome people. It is both practical and advisable that they be used in the cast." In a pre-release *LAT* article of 21 May 1950, Blaustein stated, "We have treated [the Indians] as people, not savages, have tried to show that the only real 'heavies' are ignorance, misunderstanding and intolerance. In short, none of our Indians say 'Ugh!'" In the narrated opening of the film, the character of "Tom Jeffords" declares, "what I have to tell happened exactly as you'll see it. The only change will be that when the Apaches speak—they will speak in our language."

After reviewing the final script draft of 20 May 1949, Darryl F. Zanuck, Vice-President in charge of production, complained that Jeffords was too "noble and untainted, so uncompromisingly lofty in his ideals" and that it was unclear what "motivated him to go to Cochise in the first place." Zanuck commented that in recent films, a "too noble hero is doomed at the box office." Jeffords, Zanuck cautioned, "is never wrong about anything. He is perfection itself, and this worries me greatly." In a meeting between Zanuck, Blaustein, Blankfort and director Delmer Daves, it was decided to have Jeffords, in the opening narration, state that he came to Apache country to look for gold and that when he met up with the Indian boy, he was on his way back to Tucson to take a job as a scout. In the narration, Jeffords explains that he saved the boy's life because "some crazy impulse made me do it." After the revised final script of 11 Jun 1949, the scene of the attempted lynching of Jeffords was added following a meeting with Zanuck, Blaustein and Blankfort.

In the 1991 *LAT* article, Blaustein stated that he showed Blankfort's changes secretly to Maltz. The article states that Maltz was in prison when *Broken Arrow* was released, serving time for failing to cooperate with the House Committee on Un-American Activities (HUAC), and that in 1952, after Blankfort testified before HUAC and mentioned names of his ex-wife and cousin, while stating that he had no knowledge that they had been members of the Communist party, Maltz refused ever to speak to Blankfort again. Before he died, Blankfort wrote a letter to the Writers Guild of America acknowledging that Maltz wrote *Broken Arrow*, but died before he mailed it. Blaustein related that Maltz preferred that the letter not be sent, but changed his mind a year after Blankfort's death and authorized writer Larry Ceplair to make his role known. Maltz died in 1985, and in Jul 1991, the Writers Guild voted to correct the screen credit for the film to reflect that Maltz wrote the screenplay and to issue "a strong statement of appreciation for the courage of screenwriter Michael Blankfort," who by "fronting" risked being blacklisted himself. Alfred Levitt, a blacklisted writer, brought the issue before the board based on information received by Ceplair, following talks with the wives of both writers and other principals. In 1992, the Writers Guild posthumously awarded Maltz the award that had been given to Blankfort in 1950 for the best-written American western of that year.

In correspondence included in the Records of the Twentieth Century-Fox Legal Department (concerning a lawsuit filed on behalf of author Robert Gessner, who had used the title *Broken Arrow* for his 1933 novel about an Indian boy), the origination of the title for the film is described: Blaustein stated that Zanuck did not like the title of the novel, *Blood Brother*. *Arrow* was selected as a temporary title. Sometime later, *War Paint*, which Blaustein did not like, was suggested by the studio's New York office. During shooting in Arizona, a local Indian told director Daves a story concerning his father, who had "engaged in a number of battles" with Cochise, and mentioned that the breaking of an arrow was the symbol for peace being made. Daves related the story to Blaustein, who came up with the title *Broken Arrow*, "a wonderful title for our picture, and in fact the only title that would symbolically represent our entire story." In Feb 1952, Fox agreed to settle with Gessner for $1,000 to dispose of litigation regarding the title.

Location shooting for the film was done during a six week period near the Apache White River Reservation and in the Coconino National Forest in Arizona. According to publicity for *Broken Arrow*, the film was shot in the locations where the story actually took place, and 375 Apache Indians appeared in the film. Jeff Chandler was under contract to Universal-International at the time. This was the film debut of Raymond Bramley, a New York stage actor. The Governor of Oklahoma invited the studio to hold their premiere there. According to an unidentified news item in the file for the film at the AMPAS Library, *Broken Arrow* was cited by the film committee of the Association on American Indian Affairs "as one of the first films since *The Vanishing American* (see below) to attempt a serious portrayal of the Indian side of American history and to show the Indian as a real human being the same as a white man." The film was nominated for Academy Awards for Best Screenplay, Supporting Actor (Jeff Chandler), and Cinematography (color).

Reviews generally praised the film's effort to depict the Apaches in a more sympathetic and well-rounded manner than most of Hollywood's previous portrayals; however, some reviewers criticized the film for its "romantic" characterization of Native Americans. *HR* commented that the film "accomplishes the miracle of portraying the American Indian as a person much more than the stereotyped rug peddler or vicious savage. Instead he is presented as a member of an ancient and honorable race whose primitive intelligence is the match of any civilized culture, not merely in matters of conflict but in social organization, community service and morality." *HR noted further that the wars between Apaches and settlers had been "covered many, many times before on the screen but never from the angle of the Apaches. This is the plot point that sets Broken Arrow* apart." *Fortnight* wrote, "It chides the canard that the warlike Apaches were a murderous lot, presenting them as a nation fighting honorably for survival. While this theory undoubtedly has historical fact behind it, *Broken Arrow* substitutes earnestness for profundity and romance in lieu of honest drama." Bosley Crowther of *NYT* complained, "The misfortune here is that a purpose and an idea have been submerged in a typical rush of prettification and over-emphasis. Sure, the American Indian has been most cruelly maligned and his plight as a 'minorities' person has not yet been fully clarified. But in trying to disabuse the public of a traditional stereotype, the producers have here portrayed the Indian in an equally false, romantic white ideal. Why couldn't the Indians in this picture be as natural, inelegant and unkempt as Mr. Stewart and the other white men?"

Screen Directors' Playhouse presented a radio broadcast of *Broken Arrow* on 5 Sep 1951, starring James Stewart, Jeff Chandler and Debra Paget. On 2 May 1956, the *20th Century-Fox Hour* presented a broadcast of a television version of *Broken Arrow*, starring Ricardo Montalban, John Lupton and Rita Moreno, and directed by Robert Stevenson. This became the pilot for the *Broken Arrow* television series, starring Lupton and Michael Ansara, which began on 25 Sep 1956 and ran through the 1958 season, with re-runs lasting through the summer of 1960. Author Elliott Arnold was the story editor of the television series. According to modern sources, Trevor Bardette was also in the cast.

Box 17 Jun 1950. *Cue* 22 Jul 1950. *DV* 12 Jun 1950, p. 3. *DV* 3 Jul 1991, p. 3, 10. *Exh* 21 Jun 1950, pp. 2871-72. *FD* 14 Jun 1950, p. 12. *Fortnight* 9 Jun 1950. *Har* 17 Jun 1950, p. 94. *HCN* 22 Aug 1950. *HR* 8 Sep 1948. *HR* 12 Apr 1949. *HR* 3 Jun 1949, p. 3. *HR* 29 Jul 1949, p. 11. *HR* 12 Jun 1950, p. 3. *HR* 21 Jul 1950. *HR* 3 Jul 1991, pp. 1-2. *LAT* 21 May 1950. *LAT* 19 Aug 1950. *LAT* 29 Jun 1991, p. F1, F16. *LAT* 3 Jul 1991. *LAT* 24 Mar 1992. *MPHPD* 17 Jun 1950, p. 345. *NYT* 8 Sep 1948. *NYT* 13 Apr 1949. *NYT* 21 Jul 1950, p. 15. *NYT* 23 Jul 1950. *SatRev* 5 Aug 1950. *Var* 14 Jun 1950, p. 8. *Var* 19 Jul 1950.

BROKEN CHAINS (African Americans)

William A. Brady Picture Plays, Inc. *Dist* World Film Corp. 11 Dec **1916** [©World Film Corporation; 6 Dec 1916; LU9673]. Si; b&w. 5 reels.

Dir Robert Thornby. *Scen* Mrs. E. M. Ingleton. *Story* Joseph R. Grismer and Clay M. Greene. *Cam* Lucien Andriot.

Cast: John Tansy (*Harry Ford, as a boy*), Carlyle Blackwell (*Harry Ford, as an adult*), Herbert Barrington (*General Gwynne*), Stanhope Wheatcroft (*Paul Fitzhugh*), Herbert Delmore (*Dr. Tom Lincoln*), Henry West (*Sampson*), Louis Grisel (*Moses*), William Sherwood

(*Jefferson*), Madge Evans (*Georgia Gwynne, as a girl*), Ethel Clayton (*Georgia Gwynne, as an adult*), Jessie Lewis (*Bessie Fitzhugh*).

Drama. The federal government sends Captain Harry Ford south to round up some moonshiners, and while there he falls in love with Georgia Gwynne, whose brother Jefferson accuses Harry of aiding black agitators in their political fight against whites. The two men quarrel, then, later, Jefferson is found murdered. Authorities throw Harry in jail for the crime, but Sampson, a black leader, talks in his sleep and is overheard by an elderly black man, whom Harry had befriended, confessing to the murder of Gwynne. This clears Harry and allows him and Georgia to plan their marriage. *African Americans. Government agents. Murder. United States–South. Brothers. Confession (Law). False accusations. False arrests. Moonshiners.*

Note: The film was originally entitled *The New South. MPW* commented concerning the depiction of African Americans in the film: "Viewed as a peculiarly venomous stimulant of race hatred, the mischief-creating possibilities contained in *Broken Chains* cannot be denied.... It requires no unnatural amount of perspicacity to visualize the sort of reception a Southern audience would accord to the production.... But even in other sections of the country, we doubt if the sight of a blood-lustful negro murdering a white man, or the lashing of a Caucasian with a whip by a colored convict, acting under orders from an overseer of the Simon Legree type, will win public approval, to say nothing of injury to the feelings of Afro-Americans who form no small portion of the smaller theatres' patronage. Nor is the stealing of a ballot-box during an election by the colored hosts and the precipitation of a race riot especially alluring to the average citizen. It is just such pictures as this that feed ammunition to the censorship advocates, with which to bombard the citadels of filmland." *MPN*, in their review, commented, "The black villain... is tortured by a third degree of remorse and superstition easily imagined in a negro."

MPN 16 Dec 1916, p. 3741. *MPW* 16 Dec 1916, p. 1654, 1696. *NYDM* 9 Dec 1916, p. 26. *Var* 1 Dec 1916, p. 28. *Wid's* 7 Dec 1916, p. 1151.

BROKEN DREAMS (German Americans)

Monogram Pictures Corp.; Trem Carr, Vice-President in Charge of Production; a Ben Verschleiser Production. *Dist* Monogram Pictures Corp. 20 Oct **1933**; Prod: late Aug—mid-Sep 1933 [©Monogram Pictures Corp.; 15 Jan 1934; LP4797]. Sd (Balsley and Phillips Recording System); b&w. 7 reels, 6,066 ft. 68 min. Passed by the National Board of Review.

Dir Robert Vignola. [*Asst dir* Robert Parkinson]. *Scr* Maude Fulton. *Story* Olga Printzlau. *Photog* Robert Planck. *Film ed* Carl Pierson. *Rec* John Stransky, Jr. *Tech dir* E. R. Hickson.

Cast: Randolph Scott [(*Dr. Robert Morley*)], Martha Sleeper [(*Martha Morley*)], Joseph Cawthorn [(*Pop, John Miller*)], Beryl Mercer [(*Mom, Hilda Miller*)], Buster Phelps [(*Billy Morley*)], Charlotte Merriam [(*Grace*)], Martin Burton [(*Paul*)], Adele St. Maur [(*Mam'selle*)], Sidney Bracey [(*Hopkins*)], Phyllis Lee [(*Nurse*)], Clarence Geldert [(*Dr. Fleming*)], E. J. Le Saint [(*Judge Harvey E. Blake*)], [Finis Barton (*Gladys*)], [Sam Flint (*Dr. Greenwood*)], [George Nash], [Bradley Page].

Domestic, Melodrama. [*Print viewed*]. When his wife dies during childbirth, intern Bob Morley becomes disconsolate and disappears for ten days before returning to his worried Aunt Hilda and angry Uncle John Miller, a German-American pet shop owner, to tell them he is going away. The Millers offer to rear the boy, whom Bob refuses to see. Bob goes to Vienna for four years of intensive study with a leading surgeon. Two years later, when Hilda reads that Bob, now a child specialist, is about to be married, she brings his son Billy to his office. Bob is quite moved and breaks a lunch date with his fiancée Martha to attend Billy's sixth birthday party. When he is late for a reception, Martha finds him at the Miller's pet shop. Upset at what she calls the "horrible neighborhood" and "common people," Martha leaves in a huff after Billy expresses displeasure at her interference. When Bob explains that Billy is his son, they reconcile. After they marry, Martha suggests that they get Billy to live with them. John angrily refuses, but a judge rules in Bob's favor because the Millers never legally adopted the boy. Although Billy cries profusely in Hilda's arms and refuses to go with Bob, when Hilda insists, he obeys. Billy's initial days at the Morley home are trying for all concerned. Billy is uneasy with the servants and his domineering French tutor, Mam'selle, while Martha, upset at Billy's lack of table manners, also fears that Bob loves Billy more than her. When Bob encourages her to endear herself to Billy, she agrees to try and sends Mam'selle to buy Billy a dog, but when he sees the small "prize" dog she selects, he calls it a rat and cries. After the Millers visit with Beans, the mutt Billy loved when he lived with them, and Jiggs, a chimpanzee, Billy hides Beans in his bedroom closet. That night, after Bob is called out of

town for an operation, Martha's friends, Paul, Gladys and Frank, visit for bridge, while Jiggs comes to Billy's window and joins Billy and Beans in devouring a cake Hilda baked. Although Martha does not get angry, Mam'selle yells at Billy. After Gladys and Frank leave, Paul flirts with Martha and encourages her to leave Bob. He attempts to kiss her when Billy, running away, sees them and tries to help Martha. Paul pushes him down and his head hits the floor hard, which causes him to go into a deep coma. When Bob returns, Martha, who has given Billy a lot of blood and attended to him day and night, packs because she feels that the incident was her fault. However, as Billy starts to revive, he calls Martha "mother," which moves her deeply and she embraces Bob. Sometime later, they happily celebrate Billy's birthday with the Millers and Billy's friends and animals. *Child custody. Children. Class distinction. Family relationships. Parenthood. Physicians. Aunts. Birthdays. Cads. Chimpanzees. Coma. Death in childbirth. Dogs. German Americans. Judges. Nursing back to health. Parties. Pet shops. Servants. Tutors and tutoring. Widowers.*

Note: The film's length at a preview early in Oct 1933 was 72 minutes. According to a pressbook in the copyright descriptions, Randolph Scott was borrowed from Paramount for this film. Director Robert Vignola and actor Sidney Bracey appeared together in the 1910 film *White Man's Gold*, according to the pressbook. The pressbook also contains ads which link this film in theme and audience appeal to the earlier hit *The Champ* (see *AFI Catalog of Feature Films, 1931-1940*; F3.0645) and claims that "Buster Phelps...and Randolph Scott...rival [Jackie] Cooper and [Wallace] Beery in their appeal...." The song "Broken Dreams," lyrics by Harry D. Kerr, music by Maurice Spitalny, while not in the film, was advertised as being "inspiration for the Monogram picture."

DV 4 Oct 1933, p. 3. *FD* 8 Nov 1933, p. 6. *Har* 11 Nov 1933, p. 179. *HF* 26 Aug 1933, p. 7. *HF* 9 Sep 1933, p. 8. *MPD* 22 Nov 1933, p. 11. *MPH* 4 Nov 1933, p. 38. *NYT* 21 Nov 1933, p. 23. *Var* 28 Nov 1933, p. 43.

BROKEN FETTERS (Chinese Americans)

Bluebird Photoplays, Inc. *Dist* Bluebird Photoplays, Inc. 3 Jul **1916** [©Bluebird Photoplays, Inc.; 3 Jun 1916; LP8422]. Si; b&w. 5 reels.

Dir Rex Ingram. *Scen* Rex Ingram. *Cam* Stanley Sinclair.

Cast: Kittens Reichert (*Mignon, as a child*), Violet Mersereau (*Mignon, grown up*), Charles Francis (*Kong Hee*), Earl Simmons (*Bruce King*), Frank Smith (*Foo Shai*), William Dyer (*The Captain*), Paul Panzer (*Carleton Demarest*), Isabel Patterson (*His wife*), William Garwood (*Lawrence Demarest*), Paddy Sullivan (*Mike*), Guy Morville (*The Detective*), Charles Fang (*Chang*), Charles Tang (*Hop Sing Toi*).

Drama. After an American diplomat in China is murdered, a Mandarin friend of the family raises Mignon, his orphaned daughter. Mignon yearns to return to America, making her easy prey for the slave trader Foo Shai, who promises to take her to New York and then brutally mistreats her once they arrive. A young artist, Lawrence Demarest, uses Mignon as a model and falls in love with her but is unable to free her from Foo Shai. Finally, finding Foo Shai abusing Mignon, the girl's friend, Chang, kills the slave trader. Lawrence and Mignon can now plan their marriage, and they are also welcomed back by Lawrence's businessman father, who, several years before, had severed relations with his son for his refusal to make a living in the commercial world. *Artists. Chinese. Chinese Americans. New York City. Orphans. White-slave traffic. Businessmen. China. Fathers and sons. Foster parents. Justifiable homicide. Models. Murder. United States. Diplomatic and Consular Service.*

Note: The plot of *Broken Fetters* is similar to that of the 1915 film *Mignon* which stars Beatriz Michelena. The working title for the film was *Yellow and White*. According to a modern source, the cameraman was B. C. "Duke" Hayward.

Motog Jul 1916, p. 111. *MPN* 1 Jul 1916, p. 4079. *MPW* 27 May 1916, p. 1543. *MPW* 1 Jul 1916, p. 103. *MPW* 8 Jul 1916, p. 307. *NYDM* 24 Jun 1916, p. 32. *Var* 23 Jun 1916, p. 20. *Wid's* 22 Jun 1916, p. 662.

BROKEN HEARTS (1932) see THE UNFORTUNATE BRIDE

BROKEN HEARTS (African Americans, Gypsies)

Dist State Rights; Tyrad Pictures, Inc. **1920?**. Si; b&w. 5 reels.

Cast: Lucille De Tar, Florence Hackett, Charles Eldridge, Mabel Young, Alex Rene.

Drama. A young woman, adopted by a wealthy family, is distressed when an octoroon maid claims that the young woman is her daughter. Running away with a band of gypsies, the young woman falls in love with the son of a wealthy family while fending off the advances of a gypsy man. After she encounters the husband of the maid, she returns home and obtains her adoption papers, which lead her to the discovery that her parents were both white. The young woman and

the boy she loves are married. *Adoption. Gypsies. Parentage. Racism. African Americans–Mixed blood. Maids. Orphans. Runaways.*

Note: When purchased by Tyrad in 1919 or early 1920, this film was called *Scar of Shame* or *The Scar of Shame*; articles announcing the title change appeared in trade journals in mid-1920. A Tyrad film called *Broken Hearts*, however, is on the *MPN* release charts from the beginning of 1920. Early 1920 *MPN* charts list Gareth Hughes as its star, while later ones credit Lucille De Tar and Florence Hackett. Records of the Community Motion Picture Bureau make reference to a film entitled *Scar of Shame* with the same plot as the Tyrad picture, produced by the Helen Gardner Film Co., controlled in Oct 1919 by one Mr. Spitz, and viewed by the Community Motion Picture Bureau at the time. Given the other films presented by Mr. Spitz to the Community Motion Picture Board at the same time, it seems likely that *Scar of Shame* was made much earlier, possibly during the existence of the Helen Gardner Picture Players in 1912-14. The Bureau's plot synopsis gives Hester Powers as the name of the film's principal character.

ETR 27 Mar 1920, p. 1912. *ETR* 29 May 1920, p. 2981. *MPN* 3 Jan 1920, p. 488. *MPN* 7 Feb 1920, p. 1541. *MPN* 12 Jun 1920, p. 4796. *MPN* 19 Jun 1920, p. 5010. *MPW* 3 Apr 1920, p. 74.

BROKEN HEARTS (Jewish Americans)
Jaffe Art Films. **1926**; New York State license: 16 Feb 1926. Si; b&w. 8 reels, 8,200 ft.

Pres Louis N. Jaffe. *Dir* Maurice Schwartz. *Adpt* Frances Taylor Patterson. *Photog* Frank Zucker.

Source: Based on the play *Di Gebrokhene Hertser oder Libe un Flikht* by Zalmen Libin (New York, 1903).

Cast: Maurice Schwartz (*Benjamin Rezanov*), Lila Lee ·(*Ruth Esterin*), Wolf Goldfaden (*Cantor Esterin*), Bina Abramowitz (*Mama Esterin*), Isidor Cashier (*Victor Kaplin*), Anna Appel (*Shprintze*), Charles Nathanson (*Mr. Kruger*), Liza Silbert (*Mrs. Kruger*), Theodore Silbert (*Milton Kruger*), Miriam Ellias (*Miriam*), Morris Strassberg (*Marriage broker*), Henrietta Schnitzer (*Esther*), Betty Ferkauf (*Benjamin's mother*), Louis Lyman (*Mishka*), Leonid Snegoff (*Cossack captain*), Julius Adler (*David Adler*).

Domestic, Drama. A Russian writer is forced to flee his homeland when the government finds his writings objectionable. He goes to New York, where he hears from a friend that his wife, whom he was forced to leave behind in Russia, has died. The writer later meets and marries the daughter of the cantor of an East Side congregation. He is rejected by the girl's family, however, who had wanted her to marry the dumbbell son of a rich cloak-and-suitor. The writer then learns that his first wife is still alive, and he sadly returns to Russia, only to find that while he was on his way to Russia she did die in a government hospital. The writer returns to the United States and is happily reunited with his wife on Yom Kippur. *Authors. Bigamy. Cantors, Jewish. Immigrants. Jews. New York City. Russia. Russians. Yom Kippur.*

Note: This film was re-released in 1932 in a new version entitled *The Unfortunate Bride* (see below) with talking sequences and a synchonized score.

FD 7 Mar 1926. *MPW* 20 Mar 1926. *NYT* 3 Mar 1926, p. 26.

BROKEN LANCE (Native Americans)
Twentieth Century-Fox Film Corp. *Dist* Twentieth Century-Fox Film Corp. Aug **1954**; *Prod:* 2 Mar—1 May 1954 [©Twentieth Century-Fox Film Corp.; 29 Jul 1954; LP4080]. Sd (Western Electric Recording); col (De Luxe). 11 reels, 8,648 or 8,659 ft. 96 min. PCA cert no. 16964.

[*Exec prod* Darryl F. Zanuck]. *Prod* Sol C. Siegel. *Dir* Edward Dmytryk. *Asst dir* Henry Weinberger. *Scr* Richard Murphy. *Based on a story by* Philip Yordan. *Dir of photog* Joe MacDonald. *Art dir* Lyle Wheeler and Maurice Ransford. *Film ed* Dorothy Spencer. *Set dec* Walter M. Scott and Stuart Reiss. *Ward dir* Charles LeMaire. *Cost des by* Travilla. *Mus* Leigh Harline. *Mus cond* Lionel Newman. *Orch* Edward B. Powell. *Sd* W. D. Flick and Roger Heman. *Makeup artist* Ben Nye. *Hair styling by* Helen Turpin. *Spec photog eff* Ray Kellogg. [*Unit mgr* Richard McWhorter].

Cast: SPENCER TRACY [(*Matt Devereaux*)], ROBERT WAGNER [(*Joe Devereaux*)], JEAN PETERS [(*Barbara*)], RICHARD WIDMARK [(*Ben Devereaux*)], Katy Jurado [(*Senora Devereaux*)], Hugh O'Brian [(*Mike Devereaux*)], Eduard Franz [(*Two Moons*)], Earl Holliman [(*Denny Devereaux*)], E. G. Marshall [(*The governor*)], Carl Benton Reid [(*Clem Lawton*)], Philip Ober [(*Van Cleve*)], Robert Burton [(*McAndrews*)], [Robert Adler (*O'Reilly*)], [Robert Grandin (*Capitol clerk*)], [Harry Carter (*Prison guard*)], [Nacho Galindo (*Cook*)], [Julian Rivero (*Manuel*)], [Edmund Cobb (*Court clerk*)], [Russell Simpson (*Judge*)], [King Donovan (*Clerk*)], [Jack Mather (*Gateman*)],

[George E. Stone (*Paymaster*)], [John Eppers (*Ranger*)], [Paul Kruger (*Bailiff*)], [James F. Stone (*Stable owner*)], [Arthur Q. Bryan (*Man in capitol rotunda*)], [Chief Geronimo Kuthlee], [Anthony Marsh, Al Hill (*Miners*)], [Clint Sharp (*Ranger*)], [Roy Jenson (*Bailiff*)], [Steve Raines, Frosty Royce (*Cowboys*)], [Jack Low], [Bill Wallace].

Western. [*Print viewed*]. In the 1880s, soon after being paroled from a Southwest prison, rancher Joe Devereaux, a half-breed, is taken to see the governor, an old friend of Joe's father Matt, who has arranged a meeting between Joe and his three white half-brothers, Ben, Denny and Mike. Determined to take over the ranch now that their father is dead, the brothers offer Joe $10,000 to move to Oregon and forget the place. Joe refuses the offer, throwing the money into a spittoon, and then goes to the deserted, neglected Devereaux ranch house. While staring at a portrait of Matt, Joe's thoughts go back to a time when his father was still alive: One day, Matt discovers that his sons Mike and Denny are part of a gang of rustlers who are stealing cattle from him. Matt strikes Mike when he tries to justify the rustling by complaining about his father's low wages. Ben also demands higher wages and sides with his two rebellious brothers, and only Joe remains loyal to his father. As punishment, Matt banishes Ben, Mike and Denny, giving them only a few stolen cattle to support themselves. Days later, Matt is upset to find that Joe has brought home Mike and Denny, and that his exiled sons are mingling with his dinner guests. The guests include the governor and his young daughter Barbara, with whom Joe is smitten. Soon after discovering that his cattle are dying, Matt learns that his herd has been poisoned by waste in the river coming from the Associated Western Copper Mine. Matt and his sons demand that the owner of the mine, McAndrews, stop polluting the river, and when the miner rejects that demand, Matt vows to get an injunction against him. Before leaving the mine, Matt punches McAndrews and destroys the mining company's refinery. Later, Barbara tells Joe that she is not concerned about his Indian roots, but her father, who is prejudiced against Indians, wants the couple separated. When Matt discovers the governor's prejudice, he angrily vows to have him removed from office. A trial concerning Matt and the mining company gets underway with Van Cleve, McAndrews' lawyer, making the case that Matt never sought to use the proper legal channels to handle his dispute with the miners, and that his attack was premeditated. During the trial, Matt's lawyer makes a deal with Van Cleve, in which McAndrews agrees to drop his charges in exchange for a promise by Matt to repair the damage from the attack on the mine. Matt reluctantly accepts the deal but is troubled by the part of the bargain that requires Joe to take the blame for the attack and be jailed. The court defeat, along with the defeat he suffers when Ben, Mike and Denny refuse to abide by the provisions of the deal, causes Matt to have a stroke. After making a partial recovery, Matt tries to get Joe out of prison by asking Ben to sacrifice his share of the ranch, but Ben refuses. Matt dies while following Ben on a horse. Joe is permitted leave prison to attend his father's funeral, during which he formally severs his ties with his brothers and proclaims a blood feud. As Joe comes out of his reverie, his mother enters the house and persuades him to forget revenge and leave the country. Joe takes her advice, but when Ben intercepts him with the intent to kill him, the two half-brothers engage in a hand-to-hand battle that ends when Two Moons, the Indian ranch foreman, shoots Ben dead. Time passes, and Joe and Barbara, now married, visit Matt's grave. There, Joe sees the down-turned lance, the Indian symbol for a blood feud, and breaks it in half, thus ending the fight forever. *Fathers and sons. Feuds. Half brothers. Indians of North America. Indians of North America–Mixed blood. Miscegenation. Ranchers. Romance. Bigotry. Copper mines. Deputies. Ex-convicts. Exiles. Fistfights. Funerals. Governors. Lawsuits. Lawyers. Prisons. Ranch foremen. Rustlers. Self-sacrifice. Snakes. Stroke. Trials. Water-rights.*

Note: According to information in the Twentieth Century-Fox Legal Files at the UCLA Arts–Special Collections Library, Richard Murphy's screenplay for *Broken Lance* was based on Philip Yordan's screenplay for the 1949 Twentieth Century-Fox film *House of Strangers* (see below). Yordan's screenplay, in turn, was based on Jerome Weidman's 1941 novel *I'll Never Go There Any More*. According to the *SAB*, Yordan was given sole screen credit for the story of *Broken Lance*, even though it was based on a "slight story line" from Weidman's novel. The Legal Files add that Dolores Del Rio was originally contracted for the role of "Señora Devereaux" and that Fox borrowed Spencer Tracy from M-G-M for the production. According to studio publicity material contained in the AMPAS Library file on the film, Chief Geronimo Kuthlee, grandson of the legendary Geronimo, appeared in the film in a small role. The publicity material also notes that ninety percent of the picture was filmed in

Arizona's Santa Cruz Valley.

Legal files list Elgin and Nogales, AZ, as specific location sites. Yordan won an Academy Award for Best Original Story for his work on the film. In addition to the 1948 film, which was directed by Joseph Mankiewicz and starred Edward G. Robinson, Richard Conte and Susan Hayward, Weidman's novel and Yordan's screenplay were the basis of a 30 Nov 1956 network television broadcast on the *20th Century Fox Hour*, entitled "The Last Patriarch," starring Walter Slezak, John Cassavetes and Vince Edwards. In 1961, James B. Clark directed Esther Williams and Cliff Robertson in *The Big Show*, a Fox production that is considered by some modern sources to be a remake of *Broken Lance*. In 1975, according to the legal files, the Folger Shakespeare Library in Washington, D.C. requested a 16mm print of *Broken Lance* because it had been deemed an adaptation of Shakespeare's play *King Lear*.

Box 31 Jul 1954, p. 50. *Box* 7 Aug 1954, p. 50. *DV* 23 Jul 1954, p. 3. *FD* 23 Jul 1954, p. 10. *HR* 9 Apr 1954. *HR* 23 Jul 1954, p. 3. *MPHPD* 31 Jul 1954, p. 89. *NYT* 30 Jul 1954, p. 9. *Var* 29 Jul 1954, p. 6.

THE BROKEN LAW (Native Americans)

Ermine Productions, Inc. *Dist* Usla Co. 1924 [©Ermine Productions, Inc.; 29 Dec 1924; LU20999]. Si; b&w. 5 reels.

Supv Bernard D. Russell. *Scen* George Hively.

Western. Losing his last dime at poker, Burt Morgan sets out to find a job. When his horse bolts, Burt is thrown and knocked unconscious. His dog is shot by an Indian, who later regrets the action and gives Burt a bag of gold nuggets as a token of his sorrow. Steve and Hal subsequently beat the Indian and steal his treasure map, leaving him for dead. Burt finds work on the cattle ranch of a woman named Sally, with whom he falls in love. Hal is the foreman of the ranch and informs the sheriff that Burt killed the Indian. The sheriff does not arrest Burt, for Burt has hidden the Indian's nuggets and the body of the Indian has mysteriously disappeared. Hal and Steve attempt to kill Burt, but Sally intervenes and chases them off. Hal and Steve then ride into the desert in search of the Indian's hidden gold hoard. While the badly wounded Indian watches, the two men go to their deaths in a booby-trapped mine. The Indian tells the sheriff that Hal and Steve beat him, and then dies. Sally and Burt are married. *Cowboys. Dogs. Indians of North America. Ranch foremen. Sheriffs. Treasure.*

Note: The film was announced by Ermine as one of a series of six westerns, three others of which starred Jack Meehan.

THE BROKEN MASK (Latino)

Morris R. Schlank Productions. *Dist* Anchor Film Distributors. Jan 1928. Si; b&w. 6 reels, 5,600 ft.

Pres Morris R. Schlank. *Dir* James P. Hogan. *Scen* Adele Buffington. *Story* Francis Fenton. *Titles* De Leon Anthony. *Photog* Edward Gheller and Shirley Williams. *Film ed* Roy Eiler.

Cast: Cullen Landis (*Pertio*), Barbara Bedford (*Caricia*), William V. Mong (*Santo Bendito*), Wheeler Oakman (*Dr. Gordon White*), James Marcus (*Maurice Armato*), Philippe De Lacy (*Pertio, as a boy*), Ina Anson (*Delores*), Nanci Price (*Caricia, as a girl*), Pat Harmon.

Drama. Unsuccessful in his career because of facial scars, Pertio, an Argentine dancer living in New Orleans, undergoes plastic surgery at the urging of an Argentine girl, Caricia, whose dancing has made her a star. The dancers team up, enjoy success, and fall in love. However, the surgeon, who also has fallen in love with the girl, gives the hero a treatment that causes the scars to reappear. The heroine remains faithful, and the hero punishes the doctor with a whip. *Argentines. Dancers. Disfiguration. New Orleans (LA). Plastic surgery. Surgeons. Whips and whippings.*

Var 21 Mar 1928, p. 26.

BROKEN SOIL see THE WEDDING NIGHT

THE BROKEN STAR (Native Americans, Apache, Latino)

Bel-Air Productions. *Dist* United Artists Corp. 1956; Prod: early Oct—mid-Oct 1955 [©Northridge Productions, Inc.; 19 Apr 1956; LP6407]. Sd (Western Electric Recording by Sound Services, Inc.); b&w. 1.85. 7,384 ft. 81-82 min. PCA cert no. 17819.

Exec prod Aubrey Schenck. *Prod* Howard W. Koch. *Dir* Lesley Selander. *Asst dir* Paul Wurtzel. *Wrt* John C. Higgins. *Photog* William Margulies. *Op cam* Ben Colman. *Photog eff* Jack Rabin and Louis DeWitt. *Ed* John F. Schreyer. *Sd ed* B. Richard Connors. *Mus ed* Lester Morris. *Set des* Bob Kinoshita. *Prop master* Arden Colman. *Ward* Wesley V. Jeffries and Angela Alexander. *Mus* Paul Dunlap. *Sd mixer* Joe Edmonson. *Hair stylist* Mary Westmoreland. *Casting supv* Nina Vine. *Lighting tech* Joe Edesa. *Key grip* Martin Kashuk.

Song(s): "I Hate You," lyrics by John C. Higgins, music by Paul Dunlap; cowboy songs called by Lloyd Shaw.

Cast: Howard Duff [(*Deputy Marshal Frank Smead*)], Lita Baron [(*Conchita Alvarado*)], Bill Williams [(*Deputy Bill Gentry*)], Douglas Fowley [(*Hiram Charleton*)], Henry Calvin [(*Thornton Wills*)], Addison Richards [(*U.S. Marshal Wayne Forrester*)], Joel Ashley [(*Messendyke*)], John Pickard [(*Van Horn*)], Wm. "Bill" Phillips [(*Doc Mott*)], Joe Dominguez [(*Nachez*)], [Dorothy Adams (*Mrs. Trail*)].

Western. [*Print viewed*]. Arizona deputy marshal Frank Smead watches from a distance as a rancher delivers a water-rights payment to Carlos Alvarado, who works for land baron Thornton Wills. As Frank rides off, he discovers a dead cow and drags it away, then rides back to Alvarado's house and, unaware that Apache handyman Nachez is watching, shoots Alvarado to death and steals a bag of money. Back in town, Frank tells U.S. Marshal Wayne Forrester and Deputy Bill Gentry that he caught Alvarado rustling and shot him in self-defense, producing the hide from the dead cow as evidence. At Alvarado's place, Bill tells Doc Mott, the town's coroner and undertaker, that Alvarado's next of kin is his cousin Conchita, who sings at the local saloon and is engaged to Bill. Bill and Doc enter the house, where they encounter two armed men, Messendyke and Van Horn, who demand to know who killed Alvarado. The men claim that Alvarado worked for them, that they work for someone much higher up and that something valuable is missing. At the saloon, Frank is watching Conchita perform when Messendyke and Van Horn come in and order him to come to a meeting at Wills's ranch. Later, at her rooming house, Conchita is ambushed by Messendyke and Van Horn, who demand information on Alvarado's activities. Her screams attract Bill, who comes to her rescue and arrests the men. Frank goes to Wills's ranch, where a square dance is taking place. Wills tells him that $8,000 in gold pieces is missing from Alvarado's home, and pride demands that he get the cash back. However, Frank denies any knowledge of the money. At the marshal's office, where corrupt Indian agent Hiram Charleton has just posted bail for Messendyke and Van Horn, Forrester reminds Bill that they should wait until Frank's story is checked before assuming it is true. Bill explains that, two years ago, when he was involved in a controversial shooting, Frank stopped a mob from lynching him and gathered evidence to exonerate him. Meanwhile, Wills tells Messendyke and Van Horn that he suspects Conchita of engineering the theft of his money, in cahoots with Frank. Nachez comes to the marshal's office to give his account of the shooting, but because he speaks only Spanish, he writes out his statement, then identifies Frank from a picture. Nachez then meets Conchita on the street and tells her in Spanish what happened to her cousin. Forrester asks Bill to take the note to a Spanish-speaking judge for a translation. On his way, Bill is intercepted by Mrs. Trail, Conchita's landlady, who takes him to Conchita, who has been badly beaten by Messendyke and Van Horn. Conchita begs Bill to stay, saying she has something to tell him about Frank, but Bill storms out in search of her assailants. Bill finds Messendyke and Van Horn in a saloon, where he disarms them and, after a lengthy fistfight, defeats them. Back at Conchita's, Bill expresses disbelief at the news of Frank's deeds. Conchita translates Nachez's statement, which indicates that Alvarado was unarmed, and tells Bill that Nachez said he followed Frank to the old mine. Meanwhile, outside the Apache reservation, Frank waylays Nachez, who tells him in Spanish that Conchita knows everything. Frank takes Nachez to the mine and kills him, but is discovered by Bill. Frank disarms Bill and takes him into the mine, but he cannot bring himself to shoot Bill in the back, so he knocks him out and ties him up. The marshal and his posse chase Frank onto the reservation, where Frank offers to pay Charleton if he will hide him and help him escape. Charleton lies to the marshal, and when the posse rides off, he informs Frank that Nachez told him everything and demands $4,000 for his assistance. Frank agrees to meet Charleton's representative later on to exchange money for horses. When Frank shows up for his appointment, Messendyke and Van Horn are waiting. Frank has attempted to swindle Charleton, and a gunfight breaks out in which Van Horn is killed. Frank escapes and returns to the mine for the rest of his money. With the posse closing in on him, Frank searches for Bill, who has managed to untie himself and hide. The two lawmen have a showdown in the mine shaft, and Bill kills Frank. Later, Bill and Conchita get married and leave for Bill's new job as marshal of the northern territory. *Corruption. Deputies. Friendship. Mexican Americans. United States. Marshals. Apache Indians. Arizona. Cattle. Coroners. Cousins. Evidence. Extortion.*

False accusations. Fistfights. Gunfights. Indian agents. Land barons. Landladies. Law and order. Mines. Murder. Posses. Revenge. Robbery. Saloons. Singers. Square dances. Water-rights. Witnesses.

Note: According to the *HR* review, some of the filming took place at "Old Tucson," an open-air museum operated by the government.

Box 11 Feb 1956. *DV* 1 Feb 1956, p. 4. *Exb* 22 Feb 1956, p. 4112. *FD* 7 Feb 1956, p. 6. *Har* 4 Feb 1956, p. 19. *HR* 7 Oct 1955, p. 17. *HR* 14 Oct 1955, p. 13. *HR* 1 Feb 1956, p. 3. *MPHPD* 4 Feb 1956, p. 770. *Var* 1 Feb 1956, p. 18.

BROKEN STRINGS (African Americans)

Goldport Productions; L. C. Borden Productions. *Dist* International Road Shows, Inc. **1940**; Prod: began: 12 Feb 1940. Sd; b&w. 6 reels, 5,470 ft. 60 min. PCA cert no. 6123.

[*Prod* L. C. Borden]. *Dir* Bernard B. Ray. *Story* Bernard B. Ray. *Cont and dial* Carl Krusada. *Addl dial* Clarence Muse and David Arlen. *Photog* Max Stengler. *Art dir* Fred Preble. *Film ed* Fredric Bean. *Mus arr* Elliott Carpenter. *Sd tech* Hans Weeren. *Make-up artist* Harry Ross. *Prod mgr* Bobby Ray.

Song(s): "Kentucky Babe," music by Adam Geibel, lyrics by Richard Buck.

Cast: Clarence Muse (*Arthur Williams*), Sybil Lewis (*Grace Williams*), William Washington (*John Williams*), Tommiwatta Moore (*Mary*), Stymie Beard (*Dickey Morley*), Pete Webster (*Gus Stevens*), Edward Thompson (*Sam Stilton*), Buck Woods (*Fred Stilton*), Darby Jones (*Stringbeans [Johnson]*), Jess Lee Brooks (*Dr. [Charles] Matson*), Earl Morris (*Earl Wells*), The Stevens Sisters (*Themselves*), Elliott Carpenter (*Himself*).

African American, Domestic, Drama. [*Print viewed*]. After playing a concert, violinist Arthur Williams and his business manager, Earl Wells, are injured in an automobile accident. As a result of the accident, Arthur's fingers become paralyzed and he is unable to play the violin, which leads him to become a music instructor. Arthur's favorite student, Dickie Morley, aspires to classical music, while John, Arthur's twelve-year-old son, prefers "wild" swing music. Arthur's daughter Grace, who works as a secretary for James Stilton hair products, is in love with Gus Stevens, a fellow employee at the company. When Grace arranges an appointment for her father with Dr. Charles Matson, a famous nerve specialist visiting the city, Matson agrees to forgo his usual $1,000 fee and allow Johnny to raise the money at a later date. Meanwhile, Stilton's son Sam, who is jealous of Gus's romance with Grace, refuses to give her an advance and then tries to frame Gus and get him fired for mishandling a cash deposit. After the two men fight, both Gus and Grace quit. Meanwhile, Johnny becomes a hit playing at the Miller Café, a nightclub. Arthur, however, is furious when he finds out and, as punishment, forces his son to play until he drops from exhaustion. Arthur soon learns from Grace that Johnny was only trying to raise money for the operation and to supplement the family income during her unemployment. Johnny and Grace enter a radio talent contest, and their act is scheduled to follow banjo player Stringbeans Johnson and the Stevens Sisters, who dance and sing "Kentucky Babe." Johnny takes the stage, but his act is a disaster when first one violin string, then another, snaps. Johnny realizes that with only two strings remaining on the violin, he can only play a swing number and the entire orchestra joins in. Johnny wins the contest, and in his enthusiasm, Arthur is able to applaud his son, regaining the use of his fingers. Dickie then confesses to sabotaging the violin and apologizes, and Arthur resumes his career as a premier violinist. *Family relationships. Fathers and sons. Jazz music. Music. Violinists. Automobile accidents. Banjos. Business managers. Contests. Dances. Frame-ups. Jealousy. Nightclubs. Paralysis. Physicians. Radio broadcasting. Romantic rivalry. Secretaries. Show business.*

Note: The opening title card bears a copyright statement, listing L. C. Borden as the claimant in 1940, however no copyright registration has been found. According to modern sources, Goldport productions was organized in 1939 by Bert Goldberg and Mabel Port. The company only produced this picture and *Mystery in Swing* (see below). Some contemporary sources list Elliott Carpenter as Alec Carpenter and film editor Fred Bean as Freddie Bain. Modern sources also list Curtis Mosby and his Orchestra in the cast.

DV 13 Mar 1940, p. 3. *FD* 18 Mar 1940, p. 4. *HR* 8 Feb 1940, p. 4. *HR* 13 Mar 1940, p. 4. *MPD* 19 Mar 1940, p. 3. *MPH* 23 Mar 1940, p. 44.

BROKEN TIES (African Americans)

World Film Corp. *Dist* World Film Corp. 18 Feb **1918** [©World Film Corp.; 31 Jan 1918; LU12013]. Si; b&w. 5 reels.

Pres William A. Brady. *Dir* Arthur Ashley. *Story* Woodbridge Clapp. *Cam* Jacques Monteran.

Cast: June Elvidge (*Marcia Fleming*), Montagu Love (*John Fleming*), Arthur Ashley (*Arnold Curtis*), Pinna Nesbit (*Corinne La Force*), Alec B. Francis (*Henry Hasbrook*), Kate Lester (*Mrs. Fleming*), Arthur Matthews (*Mr. La Force*), Frances Miller (*Mammy Liza*).

Drama. Corinne La Force, who is half-black, as her father had been shipwrecked on a West Indian island inhabitated by blacks, is raised by Henry Hasbrook after her father's death. Corinne loves Hasbrook's nephew, Arnold Curtis, and murders Hasbrook when he tries, because of her mixed blood, to prevent the match. Marcia Fleming, a married woman with whom Arnold was having an affair, and her mother-in-law are suspects, although Arnold is arrested for the murder. John Fleming, hired to defend Arnold, renounces his wife when he learns of her involvement with Arnold. Just as Arnold is about to confess to the crime in hopes of saving Marcia's reputation, Corinne admits her guilt and stabs herself. Fleming decides to pay more attention to Marcia, and the two are reconciled. *African Americans–Mixed blood. False arrests. Infidelity. Murder. Self-sacrifice. Confession (Law). Foster parents. Lawyers. Racism. Reputation. Suicide. Trials.*

Note: The working title of the film was *The Alibi.*

ETR 9 Feb 1918, pp. 833, 835. *MPW* 16 Feb 1918, pp. 1001-02. *NYDM* 9 Feb 1918, p. 19. *Wid's* 28 Feb 1918, pp. 97-98.

THE BROKEN VIOLIN (African Americans)

Micheaux Film Corp. **1927**. Si; b&w. 7 reels.

Pres Frank G. Kirby. *Dir* Oscar Micheaux.

Source: Based on the short story "House of Mystery" by Oscar Micheaux (publication undetermined).

Cast: J. Homer Tutt, Ardelle Dabney, Alice B. Russell, Ike Paul, Daisy Foster, Gertrude Snelson, Boots Hope, Ethel Smith, W. Hill.

African American, Melodrama. [*Not viewed*]. Lelia Cooper, a beautiful African-American violin prodigy, is the daughter of a washerwoman and a drunkard. One day, after having lost his pay gambling, Lelia's father arrives home intoxicated. When her mother refuses to give him the money he has demanded, he smashes his daughter's violin over the hard-working woman's head. Lelia's younger brother intervenes and he, too, is severely beaten. When the boy, whose pay the father also tries to take, flees and the father chases him, the father is run over and killed by a speeding truck. Lelia eventually triumphs over her surroundings and finds love and success. *African Americans. Alcoholism. Battered children. Battered women. Family life. Poverty. Prodigies. Violinists. Accidental death. Automobile accidents.*

PittsC 25 Aug 1928.

BRONCO APACHE *see* APACHE

THE BRONZE BRIDE (Native Americans)

Universal Film Mfg. Co.; Red Feather Photoplays. *Dist* Universal Film Mfg. Co. 2 Apr **1917** [©Universal Film Mfg. Co.; 21 Mar 1917; LP10428]. Si; b&w. 5 reels.

Dir Henry McRae. *Scen* Maud Grange and W. B. Pearson. *Story* J. R. Burkey.

Cast: Claire McDowell (*A-Che-Chee*), Frank Mayo (*Harvey Ogden*), Edward Clark (*William Ogden*), Charles Hill Mailes (*Joe Dubois*), Eddie Polo (*White Feather*), Harry Archer (*Black Lynx*), Winter Hall (*Mr. Carter*), Betty Schade (*His daughter*), Frankie Lee (*A-Che-Chee's child*).

Northwest, Drama. Disgusted with his son Harvey's attitude since his return from college, wealthy William Ogden turns the boy out to make his own way in the world. Harvey finally lands in the Canadian North Woods, where he goes into business with Joe Dubois, a hunter and trapper. One day while Harvey is trapping, his leg is caught in a steel trap. He is rescued by A-Che-Chee, the daughter of Black Lynx the Indian Chief. A-Che-Chee takes Harvey to her cabin, where she dresses his wound. When her father and brother discover Harvey there, they insist upon an immediate marriage. Harvey protests, but finally agrees in order to maintain the good will of the Indians. Three years pass and Harvey is content with his wife and child until receiving a letter from his father. Drawn back to civilization, Harvey steals away with his son one night, leaving his wife behind. Upon discovering their flight, A-Che-Chee is overcome with grief, but Joe persuades her to follow her husband and try to win him back. He takes her to the home of his rich aunt and uncle, the Carters, who compassionately coach her in the ways of white society. Making her debut at a reception given by Harvey's father, A-Che-Chee is joyously

recognized by her son and remorsefully embraced by her husband. *Canada. Cultural conflict. Desertion (Marital). Family relationships. Indians of North America. Miscegenation. Animal traps. Hunters. Nursing back to health. Parties. Rescues. Trappers. Tribal chiefs.*

ETR 31 Mar 1917, p. 1182. *MPN* 7 Apr 1917, p. 2192. *MPW* 7 Apr 1917, p. 113, 153. *Wid's* 29 Mar 1917, p. 199.

THE BRONZE BUCKAROO (African Americans)

Hollywood Productions. *Dist* Sack Amusement Enterprises, Inc. 1 Jan **1939**. Sd; b&w. 6 reels, 5,212 ft. 60 min.

Dir Richard C. Kahn. *Wrt* Richard C. Kahn. *Photog* Roland Price and Clark Ramsey. *Art dir* Vin Taylor. *Mus* Lew Porter. *Sd eng* Cliff Ruberg. *Prod mgr* Dick L'Estrange.

Cast: Herbert Jeffrey (*Bob Blake*), Lucius Brooks (*"Dusty"*), Artie Young (*Betty Jackson*), F. E. Miller (*Jim Pecklat*), Spencer Williams, Jr. (*Pete*), Clarence Brooks (*Gus*), Lee Calmer (*Bartender*), Earl J. Morris, The Four Tones, [Rellie Hardin].

African American, Western, with songs. [*Print viewed*]. Five cowboys led by Bob Blake ride from Texas to help their friend, Joe Jackson, who has moved to Arizona for his health. At the Jackson ranch, his sly assistant, Slim Perkins, throws his voice, using ventriloquism to convince foolish "Dusty" that the mule "Gabriel" talks. Bob learns from Joe's sister Betty that Joe disappeared three weeks before and is reminded that her father had vanished in a similar manner and later had turned up dead. The cowboys drift into town to learn what they can. Dusty and a companion enter a saloon, where brutish cowhand Pete shoots his partner in a card game and then forces Dusty to smoke four cigars at once. Bob enters to interrupt the bully and the two have a fistfight. Dusty, who has purchased Gabriel for twelve dollars, is angry that the mule does not talk for him, but finds Slim's book on ventriloquism. Later, Dusty tells Slim that he is teaching Gabriel to recite poetry, then loses his clothes in a crooked poker game with Slim. Bob visits Buck Thorn, a neighbor of the Jacksons' who has offered to buy their ranch, and employs Pete and some other tough cowhands. While riding together, Bob and Betty encounter Uncle, a codger who informs them that he mailed a letter from Joe to Bob a few weeks earlier, a letter he found unstamped and lying on the ground underneath a window of the saloon. Bob enters the saloon, pretending to be drunk. Upstairs, Buck, Pete and their henchmen try to force Joe to sign a deed to his land over to them because it contains a mine worth one million dollars in gold. Bob finds them and pulls a gun but is knocked over the head by the bartender. A shootout breaks out downstairs when his friends come to his rescue. Returning to the ranch, they discover that Betty is gone. She has left to follow Pete, who carries a message that Joe is hurt, and is captured. Buck has Joe branded with a hot iron, and Betty is threatened with the same treatment. Meanwhile, Betty's horse returns to the ranch and Bob and his friends follow the animal's tracks. They are caught by Pete, but escape when Slim throws his voice to make them think others have arrived. During a gunfight among the rocks, the sheriff and his men are led to the scene by Dusty riding Gabriel, and Dusty shoots Pete. Dusty then wins back his clothes and twelve dollars from Slim by using ventriloquism to impersonate Gabriel reciting a satirical poem, while Bob and Betty ride off together. *African Americans. Cowboys. Extortion. Kidnapping. Land rights. Ranches. Branding. Brothers and sisters. Bullies. Cards. Friendship. Gold. Gullibility. Loyalty. Mines. Mules. Poetry. Prisoners. Saloons. Ventriloquists and ventriloquism.*

Note: According to the onscreen credits, the film was copyrighted, but no record of copyright registration has been found. No song titles for this film were found. According to modern sources, Earl Morris was drama editor of the *Pittsburgh Courier*. The picture was filmed at N. B. Murray's dude ranch near Victorville, CA. The ranch catered to African-American guests. According to modern sources, and Jed Buell was producer.

Exb 15 May 1940, p. 528. *FD* 23 Jan 1939, p. 10.

THE BRONZE VENUS *see* THE DUKE IS TOPS

BROTHER AND SISTER *see* COSÌ È LA VITA

BROTHER VAN *see* THE LAWLESS EIGHTIES

BROTHERS IN THE SADDLE (Latino)

RKO Radio Pictures, Inc. *Dist* RKO Radio Pictures, Inc. 8 Feb **1949**; Prod: mid-Jun—late Jun 1948 [©RKO Radio Pictures, Inc.; 18 Feb 1949; LP2167]. Sd (RCA Sound System); b&w. 5,421 ft. 60 min. PCA cert no. 13257.

Prod Herman Schlom. *Dir* Lesley Selander. [*Asst dir* John Pommer and Harry Templeton]. *Orig scr* Norman Houston. *Dir of photog* J. Roy Hunt. [*Cam op* James Daly and Edwin Pyle]. [*Gaffer* R. L. Buddie]. [*Stills* Alex Kahle]. *Art dir* Albert S. D'Agostino and Feild Gray. *Film ed* Samuel E. Beetley. *Set dec* Darrell Silvera and James Altwies. *Mus* Paul Sawtell. *Mus dir* C. Bakaleinikoff. *Sd* Richard Van Hessen and Roy Granville. [*Makeup* Jack Barron]. [*Hair stylist* Kay Shea]. [*Scr supv* Mercy Weireter]. *Grip* Tom Clement].

Cast: TIM HOLT [(*Tim Taylor*)], Richard Martin [(*Chito Rafferty*)], Steve Brodie [(*Steve Taylor*)], Virginia Cox [(*Nancy Austin*)], Carol Forman [(*Flora Trigby*)], Richard Powers [(*Nash Prescott*)], Stanley Andrews [(*Sheriff Oakley*)], Robert Bray [(*Poke Lynch*)], Francis McDonald [(*Hoyt Parker*)], Emmett Vogan [(*Judge Coulter*)], Monte Montague [(*Stage driver*)], [Ted Adams (*House player*)], [Juan Duval].

Western. [*Print viewed*]. When ranch owner Nancy Austin arrives home from a pre-nuptial Tucson shopping spree and discovers that her fiancé and ranch hand, Steve Taylor, is absent, she sends his brother Tim to find him. Tim discovers Steve losing at poker in the Lordsburg saloon and, after accusing saloon owner Nash Prescott of cheating his brother, starts a brawl. Later, Tim chastises Steve for gambling with Nancy's money, but Steve smugly maintains that he needs a big payoff in order to leave his cowboy life behind. Steve's condescending words anger Tim, who then announces that he is quitting his job as Nancy's foreman. That night, Steve borrows more money from Nancy to play poker with Prescott and his crooked partner, Hoyt Parker. At the saloon, Steve accuses Parker of dealing from the bottom of the deck, and Parker reaches for his gun, but is outdrawn and killed by Steve. The next day, Tim finds Steve hiding in the hills and persuades him to turn himself in to Sheriff Oakley. Because Prescott and his associates have threatened saloon girl Flora Trigby, the shooting's only honest witness, Steve is found guilty by a circuit judge and is sentenced to hang. Steve condemns his brother for his plight, and out of guilt, Tim and his best friend, Chito Rafferty, help Steve to escape. While the now-fugitive brothers hide in the hills, Chito travels to Mexico to find Flora. When Chito later reports that Flora is in Mexico but is refusing to testify out of fear for her life, Tim instructs Steve to stay put in the hills and goes to Mexico himself. With Chito's help, Tim frees Flora from Prescott's guard and brings her back to Lordsburg. Before Flora can testify, however, Steve, having become impatient for his brother, holds up a stagecoach and murders Prescott, who happens to be traveling on the coach. Disgusted by Steve's coldbloodedness, Tim confronts him at the hideout and demands that he return the stolen money. Steve refuses, however, and the two men fight until Steve pushes Tim down a ravine to his apparent death. Steve then heads for Nancy's ranch, unaware that Tim has survived with help from his horse. At the ranch, Steve asks Nancy to flee East with him, but she refuses, finally seeing through his manipulations. When the sheriff's posse rides up, Steve shoots Chito and takes Nancy hostage, escaping back to the hills. There a bruised and battered Tim surprises his brother and, condemning him as morally corrupt, fights him to a deadly draw. Later, Nancy leaves for the East, while a recuperating Chito and Tim vow to wait for her return. *Brothers. Cowboys. False arrests. Fugitives. Moral corruption. Murder. Arizona. Cheating. Dance hall girls. Engagements. Escapes. Fights. Hideouts. Horses. Hostages. Judges. Mexican Americans. Mexico. Poker (Game). Ranchers. Saloon keepers. Sheriffs. Stagecoach robberies. Trials.*

Note: According to a pre-production *HR* news item, exteriors for the film were to be shot in Kernville, CA.

Box 5 Mar 1949. *DV* 9 Feb 1949, p. 3, 11. *FD* 11 Feb 1949, p. 6. *HR* 2 Apr 1948, p. 5. *HR* 11 Jun 1948, p. 4, 13. *HR* 18 Jun 1948, p. 21. *HR* 9 Feb 1949, p. 4. *MPHPD* 26 Feb 1949, p. 4514. *Var* 9 Feb 1949, p. 13.

THE BROTHERS OF BROKEN LANCE *see* FLAMING STAR

THE BROTHERS OF FLAMING ARROW *see* FLAMING STAR

BROTHERS OF THE EAST SIDE *see* BIG CITY

THE BROTHERS RICO (Italian Americans)

William Goetz Productions, Inc.; Columbia Pictures Corp. *Dist* Columbia Pictures Corp. Sep **1957**; Prod: 23 Nov—27 Dec 1956 [©Columbia Pictures Corp.; 1 Jun 1957; LP8438]. Sd (Westrex Recording System); b&w. 10 reels, 8,228 or 8,231 ft. 90-91 min. PCA cert no. 18275.

Prod Lewis J. Rachmil. *Dir* Phil Karlson. *Asst dir* Jack Berne. *Scr* Lewis Meltzer and Ben Perry. *Dir of photog* Burnett Guffey. *Art dir*

Robert Boyle. *Film ed* Charles Nelson. *Set dec* William Kiernan and Darrell Silvera. *Gowns* Jean Louis. *Mus comp* George Dunning. *Cond* Morris Stoloff. *Orch* Arthur Morton. *Rec supv* John Livadary. *Sd* Lambert Day. *Makeup* Clay Campbell. *Hair styles by* Helen Hunt.

Source: Based on the novel *Les frères Rico* by Georges Simenon (Paris, 1952).

Cast: Richard Conte [(*Eddie Rico*)], Dianne Foster [(*Alice Rico*)], Kathryn Grant [(*Norah Rico*)], Larry Gates [(*Sid Kubik*)], James Darren [(*Johnny Rico*)], Argentina Brunetti (*Mama Rico*)], Lamont Johnson [(*Peter Malaks*)], Harry Bellaver [(*Mike Lamotta*)], Paul Picerni [(*Gino Rico*)], Paul Dubov [(*Phil*)], Rudy Bond [(*Gonzales*)], Richard Bakalyan [(*Vic Tucci*)], William Phipps [(*Joe Wesson*)], [Mimi Aguglia (*Julia Rico*)], [Maggie O'Byrne (*Mrs. Felici*)], [George Cisar (*Dude cowboy*)], [Peggy Maley (*Jean*)], [Jane Easton (*Nellie*)], [James Waters (*Laundry truck driver*)], [Patricia Donahue (*Miss Van Ness*)], [Estelle Lawrence (*Counter girl*)], [Darren Dublin (*El Camino bellboy*)], [George Lewis (*El Camino desk clerk*)], [Don Orlando (*El Camino cabbie*)], [Mimi Gibson (*Felici, little girl*)], [Marvin Bryan (*Phoenix ticket clerk*)], [Samuel Finn (*Cabbie*)], [Ernesto Morelli (*Pizza maker*)], [Jerry Summers (*Bellboy*)], [Bonnie Bolding (*Stewardess*)], [Dean Cromer (*Marco Felici*)], [Nesdon Booth (*Phoenix burly man*)], [Pepe Hern (*New York bank clerk*)], [Robert Malcolm (*New York bank guard*)], [Rankin Mansfield (*New York bank official*)], [Betsy Jones Moreland (*Looping voice*)].

Gangster, Drama. [*Print viewed*]. Eddie Rico, owner of a prosperous laundry company in Bayshore, Florida, is awakened early one morning by a phone call from Phil, a member of the crime syndicate for which he had been the accountant three years earlier. Phil only asks for a small favor, but the call upsets Eddie's wife Alice, who worries that Eddie will revive his association with the syndicate. A letter from Eddie's mother, stating that his two brothers, Gino and Johnny, have disappeared, causes further concern for the couple, who hope soon to adopt a child. Gino meets with Eddie and asks his help with leaving the country, as he was the gunman for a gang killing, for which Johnny was the driver, and believes that the organization is after them. Eddie, who does not believe that the organization is out to get them, suggests that he cooperate with them. Ordered to Miami to meet with Uncle Sid Kubik, the syndicate's head, Eddie leaves despite his wife's objections that he will miss an adoption interview. In Miami, Kubik tells Eddie of his concern that Johnny has now disappeared and that Johnny's wife's brother has made a deal with the New York district attorney not to charge Johnny if he cooperates. Kubik professes to believe that Johnny would not squeal, but he insists that Eddie find Johnny and give him money to leave the country. After Eddie goes, Kubik enters another room, where he watches as Gino is tortured. Eddie flies to New York and visits his mother, who once took a bullet in the leg protecting Kubik. She now distrusts Kubik and does not want to tell Eddie the location from which Johnny last wrote; however, when Eddie warns that she will be the cause of Johnny's death, she breaks down and prays before a statue of the Virgin, then says that Johnny last wrote from El Camino, California at a farm belonging to Marco Felici. Eddie finds Johnny there and tries to convince him to leave the country. Johnny's wife Norah, who is pregnant, faints at the commotion and Johnny angrily orders Eddie to leave. At his hotel, when Eddie learns from Mike Lamotta, the organization's boss in the area, that Kubik has ordered Johnny killed, he realizes Kubik used him to locate Johnny. Mike asks Eddie to call Johnny to tell him to go quietly into one of their cars, but when Eddie calls and learns that Norah has given birth and that Johnny has named the boy after their father, Eddie instead advises him to run. Eddie is knocked out, and Lamotta picks up the phone and instructs Johnny for Norah's good to come quietly. After Johnny is killed, Lamotta's hood, Gonzales, is sent to accompany Eddie east by plane. Eddie learns that Gino also has been killed by the syndicate. In a men's room during a layover in Arizona, Eddie knocks out Gonzales and takes his gun. When Kubik learns that Eddie has escaped, an all-out search is launched. In New York, Eddie meets Alice at a rendezvous. He blames himself for his brothers' deaths and realizes he has to fight against the syndicate using his knowledge of their operations. He meets with Johnny's brother-in-law, Peter Malaks, and convinces him to meet him at a bank the next day, where he will withdraw money for Johnny's son, for his mother and for Alice. He plans to have Malaks set up an appointment with the district attorney, and hopes Malaks will see that Alice gets out of the country safely. At

the bank, Eddie puts his money into three envelopes and give one to Alice and one to Malaks. That night, Eddie gives his mother the last envelope. Thinking that Johnny's death is her fault, Mama Rico asks for a reason to live. Eddie tells her about Johnny's newborn son, whom he hopes can live without fear like a decent human being. Kubik arrives and Mama Rico, in a rage, rushes at him and calls him an animal. One of Kubik's men pushes her away and Eddie shoots him. Kubik then shoots Eddie in the stomach, but Eddie kills Kubik. With Eddie's help, the district attorney triumphs over the crime syndicate. Eddie and Alice, armed with a letter from the district attorney, now go to a children's home hoping to adopt a child. *Brothers. Gangsters. Italian Americans. Marriage. Mothers and sons. Murder. Accountants. Adoption. Arizona. Banks. Bathrooms. Brothers-in-law. California. District Attorneys. Escapes. Farms. Florida. Guilt. Hotels. Infants. Laundries. Miami (FL). New York City. Religious articles. Torture.*

Note: The novel, translated as *The Brothers Rico*, was published in the U.S. in a collection of three works by Georges Simenon, entitled *The Tidal Wave* (Garden City, NY, 1954). According to news items, the rights to the book, which was a best-seller, was purchased by Goetz Productions in Sep 1954. Peter Viertel was scheduled at that time to write the screenplay. A television remake, entitled *The Family Rico*, was broadcast in 1973. It was directed by Paul Wendkos and starred Ben Gazzara.

Box 24 Aug 1957. *DV* 24 Sep 1954. *DV* 1 Nov 1956. *DV* 21 Aug 1957, p. 3. *Exh* 4 Sep 1957, pp. 4373-74. *FD* 26 Aug 1957, p. 6. *Har* 24 Aug 1957, p. 136. *HR* 21 Aug 1957, p. 3. *LAT* 26 Sep 1957. *MPD* 26 Aug 1957. *MPHPD* 24 Aug 1957, p. 506. *Newsweek* 16 Sep 1957. *NYT* 3 Jul 1955. *Time* 16 Sep 1957. *Var* 21 Aug 1957, p. 18.

THE BRUTE (African Americans)
Micheaux Film Corp. *Dist* Micheaux Film Corp. Aug **1920**. Si; b&w. 7-8 reels.

Prod Oscar Micheaux. *Dir* Oscar Micheaux. *Scen* Oscar Micheaux. *Cam* "Whitie" [full name unknown].

Cast: Evelyn Preer (*Mildred Carrison*), A. B. DeComathiere ("*Bull*" *Magee*), Sam Langford ("*Tug*" *Wilson*), Susie Sutton (*Aunt Clara*), Lawrence Chenault (*Herbert Lanyon*), Laura Bowman (*Mrs. Carrison*), Mattie Edwards (*A guest in "The Hole"*), Alice Gorgas (*Margaret Pendleton*), Virgil Williams (*Referee*), Marty Cutler (*Sidney Kirkwood*), Foy Clements (*Irene Lanyon*), Louis Schooler ("*Klondike*"), Harry Plater, E. G. Tatum, Al Gaines.

African American, Drama. Herbert Lanyon is thought to be dead after a shipwreck, and his fiancée Mildred Carrison is forced by her money-minded Aunt Clara into marriage with "Bull" Magee, a gambler and underworld boss who mistreats Mildred. After Herbert returns, Magee undergoes financial difficulties that he blames on Mildred and Herbert, and seeks revenge. Herbert and a repentant Aunt Clara, however, free Mildred from Magee, and the lovers are able to marry. [A subplot involves boxer "Tug" Wilson, who is ordered by his manager Magee to lay down in the seventeenth round of a prizefight at the film's climax. No other information concerning the plot has been discovered.]. *African Americans. Aunts. Battered women. Boxing. Marriage–Forced. Boxers. Fixed fights. Gamblers. Gangsters. Revenge. Shipwrecks.*

Note: One contemporary source states that this black independent film was based on a play, but no evidence to support this statement has been located. Another contemporary source states that the film's length was 8,000 feet, not seven reels. The film may have been cut to six reels sometime after it opened. In the records of the George P. Johnson Negro Film Collection, the cameraman was identified only as "Whitie." Foy Clements may actually be the actress Flo Clements.

ChiDef 28 Aug 1920, p. 4. *ChiDef* 4 Sep 1920, p. 4. *New York Age* 18 Sep 1920, p. 6.

THE BUCCANEER (Creoles, Dutch Americans)
Paramount Pictures, Inc.; A Cecil B. DeMille Production. *Dist* Paramount Pictures, Inc. 4 Feb **1938**; New Orleans premiere: 7 Jan 1938; Prod: 12 Aug–late Oct 1937 [©Paramount Pictures, Inc.; 4 Feb 1938; LP7794]. Sd (Western Electric Mirrophonic Sound System); b&w. 13 reels. 124 or 126 min. Passed by the National Board of Review. PCA cert no. 3654.

Pres ADOLPH ZUKOR. *Assoc prod* William H. Pine. *Dir* Cecil B. DeMille. *2d unit dir* Arthur Rosson. [*Asst dir* Richard Harlan]. *Dial supv* Edwin Maxwell. *Scr* Edwin Justus Mayer, Harold Lamb and C. Gardner Sullivan. [*Contr to scr const and dial* Grover Jones]. *Adpt* Jeanie Macpherson. *Photog* Victor Milner. *Spec photog eff* Farciot Edouart and Dewey Wrigley. *Art dir* Hans Dreier and Roland Anderson. *Ed* Anne Bauchens. *Asst ed* Hans Lubitsch. [*Set des* Dan Sayre Groesbeck]. *Int dec* A. E. Freudeman. [*Cost manufactured by* Western Costume Co.]. *Cost des* [Natalie] Visart, Dwight Franklin and Dan Sayre Groesbeck. *Mus dir* Boris Morros. *Orig mus* George

Antheil. *Sd rec* Harry Lindgren and Louis Mesenkop. [*Franciska Gaal's hair and makeup* Nellie Manley]. [*Makeup supv* Wally Westmore]. [*Loc dir* Arthur Rosson]. [*Loc scout* Frank Calvin]. [*Bus mgr* Gene Hornbostel]. [*Still photog* G. E. Richardson, Don English, Malcolm Bullock, Kenneth Lobben, Eugene Robert Ritchie, William Walling, Jr., Hurrell, Jack Lubin and Hyman Fink].

Source: Based on the novel *Lafitte the Pirate* by Lyle Saxon (New York, 1930).

Cast: FREDRIC MARCH (*Jean Lafitte*), Franciska Gaal (*Gretchen*), Akim Tamiroff (*Dominique You*), Margot Grahame (*Annette [de Remy]*), Walter Brennan (*Ezra Peavey*), Ian Keith ([*Senator*] *Crawford*), Spring Byington (*Dolly Madison*), Douglass Dumbrille (*Governor Claiborne*), Robert Barrat (*Captain Brown*), Hugh Sothern (*Andrew Jackson*), Beulah Bondi (*Aunt Charlotte*), Anthony Quinn (*Beluche*), Louise Campbell (*Marie de Remy*), Montagu Love (*Admiral Cockburn*), Eric Stanley (*General Ross*), Fred Kohler, [Sr.] (*Gramby*), Gilbert Emery (*Captain Lockyer*), Holmes Herbert (*Captain McWilliams*), Evelyn Keyes (*Madeleine*), Francis McDonald (*Camden Blount*), Frank Melton (*Lieutenant Shreve*), Stanley Andrews (*Collector of port*), Jack Hubbard (*Charles*), Richard Denning (*Captain Reid*), [John Rogers (*Mouse*)], [Hans Steinke (*Tarrus*)], [Evan Thomas (*Sir Harry Smith*)], [Michael Brooke (*Mr. Rogers*)], [Thaddeus Jones (*John Freeman*)], [Reginald Sheffield (*Ship's surgeon*)], [Eugene Jackson (*James Smith*)], [Davison Clark (*Colonel Butler*)], [Ivan Miller (*Commodore*)], [Lina Basquette (*Roxane*)], [Luana Walters (*Suzette*)], [J. P. McGowan (*Jailer*)], [Barry Norton (*Villere*)], [Charles Trowbridge (*Daniel Carroll*)], [Alex Hill (*Scipio*)], [George Reed (*Nicodemus*)], [Mert La Varr (*Major Latour*)], [Melville Ruick (*Pirate with violin*)], [Philo McCullough (*Assistant jailer*)], [Jim Dundee (*Stunt pirate*)], [Pearl Adams (*Praline seller*)], [John Patterson (*Young blade*)], [Lee Prather (*Legislator*)], [Loulette LaPlante (*French woman*)], [Edward Brady, Robert Terry, Buddy Roosevelt (*Officers*)], [J. M. Sullivan (*Colonel*)], [Lita Marty (*French woman*)], [Roy Flynn (*Major Hinds*)], [Harry Woods (*American sergeant*)], [Jack Rutherford (*Orderly*)], [Carey Harrison (*Courier*)], [Charles Brokaw (*Vincent Nolte*)], [Paul Fix (*Dying pirate*)], [Leyland Hodgson (*Naval lieutenant*)], [James Flavin (*British sergeant*)], [Sidney Newman, Ray Hanford, John Naxboro, Tom Burke, Floyd Criswell, Cy Schindell, Al Downing, Victor Delinsky, Baron Lichter, Frank Abbot, Bob St. Angelo, James Burke, Monte Montague, Maston Williams, Stanley Blystone, Richard Cramer, Philip Morris, Ben Hendricks, Anthony Patorno, Vic Demourelle, Carl Lindbom, Pete Rasch (*Pirates*)], [Bessie Wade, Dorothy Rodgers, Natalie Finley, Ione Reed, Tiny Jones, Jane Keckley, Maude Fealy, Carmelita Meek, Rita Owin, Lupe Gonzales, Margaret Martin, Yvonne Pelletier, Gertrude Simpson (*Wives*)], [Curt von Fuerberg, Olga Borget, Albert Petit, Rosita Granada (*Passengers*)], [Ralph Lewis, Louis Natheaux, J. C. Fowler (*Prominent gentlemen*)], [Foy Van Dolsen, Jack Clifford (*Mountaineers*)], [Carl LeViness, Edwin Stanley (*Male guests*)], [Grace Goodall, Ottola Nesmith, Helen Littrell (*Women guests*)], [Ethel Clayton], [Gloria Williams], [Alexander Leftwich], [Demetrius Alexis], [Leon Novello], [George Calliga], [César Vanoni], [Ed Cecil], [Ernesto Morelli], [Walter Shumway], [Lillian Harmer], [Blanche Begon], [Ruth Robinson].

Historical, Adventure, Drama. [*Print viewed*]. In August, 1814, as the British seize and burn the President's Palace in Washington, D.C., Senator Crawford of Louisiana plots with British naval officers to attack New Orleans. Meanwhile, the *Corinthian* sets sail from New Orleans carrying Marie de Remy, whose sister Annette loves privateer Jean Lafitte, who is wanted by Governor Claiborne. Lafitte and his thousand pirates hold Barataria, a territory of bayous which separates the ocean from New Orleans and claims allegiance to no nation. When pirate Captain Brown sinks the *Corinthian*, breaking Lafitte's rule never to attack an American ship, the sole survivor is a Dutch girl, Gretchen, who falls in love with Lafitte. On the advice of Crawford, the British bribe Lafitte to lead them through the bayous to attack General Andrew Jackson's army at New Orleans. Lafitte, however, convinces his men to fight for "the only shore that has let [them] stay" and turns the letters of conspiracy over to Claiborne. Now a man of honor, Lafitte proposes to Annette. Crawford, however, convinces Claiborne that Lafitte's letters were forged and when Lafitte's men greet the American ships, they are met with cannon fire and taken prisoner. Lafitte escapes, however, and when General Jackson learns of Crawford's demands for surrender, Lafitte offers his army of pirates

in exchange for their pardon and a head start of one hour for his own escape. Behind bales of cotton, aided by Dominique You, ex-cannoneer for Napoleon, Lafitte defeats the Scottish army, while Jackson fights the British. That night at the victory ball, when Annette sees Gretchen wearing Marie's dress and the miniature of her mother, she demands to know the whereabouts of the *Corinthian*. As leader of his men, Lafitte takes responsibility for Brown's crime and is about to be hanged when Jackson fulfills his promise of Lafitte's escape. As Lafitte's ship sails, Gretchen, at his side, swears her loyalty to him. *Barataria Bay (LA). Chalmette (LA). Dutch Americans. False accusations. Great Britain. Navy. Andrew Jackson. Jean Lafitte. New Orleans (LA). New Orleans, Battle of, 1815. Patriotism. Pirates. Privateering. Sieges. Teche Bayou (LA). United States–History–War of 1812. Balls (Parties). Bladensburg, Battle of, 1814. William Charles Coles Claiborne. Class distinction. Creoles. Foreign agents. Gulf of Mexico. Honor. Dolly Madison. Outlaws. Proposals (Marital). Scots. Self-sacrifice. Ship fires. Ships. Sisters.*

Note: Early titles for this film were *Lafitte the Pirate* and *The Baratarians.* The film's opening credits appear on a simulated parchment scroll being removed from a treasure chest. The film's opening narrative includes the "immortal words" that George Byron wrote about Jean Lafitte, the "Last of the Buccaneers"—"He left a Corsair's name/to other times/Linked with one virtue and a thousand crimes." This film was promoted as Cecil B. DeMille's 25th anniversary film and marked his 64th personal production. According to a news item in *HR* on 28 May 1934, Charles Laughton was originally slated to star in this film. On 4 Dec 1935, *HR* reported that British writer C. S. Forrester was set to write the script for the film, although he receives no credit on the film or in any reviews. A 11 Feb 1937 news item in *HR* stated that DeMille visited New Orleans with his technical staff to research the life of Lafitte. On 5 Jun 1937, *HR* reported that William de Mille returned to Hollywood after an absence of several years and conferred with Cecil DeMille on the film's script. Shooting began on DeMille's 56th birthday, 12 Aug 1937. According to *HR*, 350 guests attended DeMille's birthday party in the Paramount commissary. Creole food was served and the cake was sent by the Governor of Louisiana.

The preview length for this film was 115 min. The premiere at the New Orleans Saenger Theatre drew a crowd of 15,000 people. Traffic was so heavy, authorities made announcements over local radio stations asking that no one attempt to go downtown for the second showing. The onscreen credits acknowledge the assistance of the Louisiana State Museum. An early pictorial review in *MPH* listed Preston Sturges among the several writers who "checked in" early on in the writing stages of the film; however, it is unclear whether he actually contributed to the final script. Locations for the film include the Mississippi bayous near New Iberia, LA and Catalina Island and Baldwin Oaks, CA, where 450 actors recreated the Battle of New Orleans. According to press material, Barataria was recreated on a seven-acre settlement at White's Landing, Catalina. The Battle of New Orleans was staged using parapets of cotton bales, furniture and sandbags on four acres of the Baldwin Oaks area because of its resemblance to Chalmette Field, east of New Orleans, where the original battle was fought on 8 Jan 1815. A news item in *HR* on 24 Aug 1937 reported that fifty actors hired to play pirates, of the 450 encamped at Catalina, left their tents in search of hotel rooms and, finding no vacancies, were barred from returning to camp and were forced to sleep on the beach. The following day, they had to present DeMille with a formal apology in order to readmitted to the camp. According to a *DV* news item, assistant director Richard Harlan testified at a National Labor Relations Board investigation that he directed three weeks of battle scenes off Catalina; the investigation was concerned with the question of whether assistant directors were ever called on to direct scenes.

Press material includes the following information on the production: the interior of Lafitte's home was furnished with pieces of the famous Mario Ramirez collection of silver valued at $250,000. Dan Sayre Groesbeck made 173 sketches to create a visual impression of costumes and sets for DeMille; and sculptor Dwight Franklin made miniature wax figures of all the principal characters. Groesbeck also painted the brooch miniature of "Mrs. de Remy." Paramount chartered and re-designed two square-rigged warships and three gunboats from the period of 1814. Editors Anne Bauchens and Hans Lubitsch worked throughout the film's shooting and for three months following. The 700 stills and 3,000 negatives shot totaled nearly ten times that of the average film production at the time, and the cast and crew totaled almost 10,000. Sixty-three functional cast iron cannons were manufactured by Paramount's property shop for the film. The character of "Dominique You" was based on the real-life cannoneer of Napoleon. Numerous contemporary reviews applauded Tamiroff's comic performance as superior to that of March, who was reportedly paid $150,000 in cash for the role. After seeing her in a foreign film, DeMille hand-picked Hungarian actress Franciska Gaal for her American debut as "Gretchen." According to the file on the film in the Paramount Script Collection, a short personality sketch tentatively titled "Star Bright" was written for Gaal depicting DeMille calling her in Budapest, her trip to the United States, her preparing for the role and shooting a couple of scenes, as well as DeMille introducing her to American audiences at her debut and Gaal asking to stay in America.

Early scripts list Porter Hall in the role of "Mouse" and Barton MacLane as "Gramby," although they were later replaced. Judith Allen and Richard Loo were cast in Aug 1937, according to *HR*, but their appearance in the final film has not been confirmed. In the middle of shooting, actor Hugh Sothern was given a contract by Paramount. A modern source credits William LeBaron as executive producer on the film. Cecil B. DeMille remade *The Buccaneer* in

1958 with Anthony Quinn directing and Yul Brynner, Claire Bloom, Charlton Heston and Charles Boyer starring. The 1958 version was DeMille's last film.

DV 8 Jan 1938, p. 3. *DV* 5 Oct 1938, p. 7. *FD* 4 Feb 1938, p. 10. *HR* 28 May 1934, p. 1. *HR* 4 Dec 1935, p. 2. *HR* 21 Dec 1936, p. 2. *HR* 11 Feb 1937, p. 3. *HR* 5 Jun 1937, p. 2. *HR* 23 Jun 1937, p. 3. *HR* 5 Aug 1937, p. 1. *HR* 13 Aug 1937, p. 7. *HR* 17 Aug 1937, p. 18. *HR* 18 Aug 1937, p. 3, 11. *HR* 24 Aug 1937, p. 15. *HR* 25 Aug 1937, p. 2, 3. *HR* 2 Sep 1937, p. 2. *HR* 18 Oct 1937, p. 10. *HR* 22 Oct 1937, p. 8. *HR* 8 Jan 1938, p. 3, 5. *HR* 24 Jan 1938, p. 2. *MPD* 8 Jan 1938, p. 3. *MPH* 23 Oct 1937, pp. 14-15. *MPH* 15 Jan 1938, p. 47, 50. *NYT* 17 Feb 1938, p. 17. *Var* 12 Jan 1938, p. 14.

BUCCANEER'S GIRL (French Americans)

Universal-International Pictures Co., Inc. *Dist* Universal Pictures Co., Inc. Mar **1950**; Prod: early Jul—mid-Aug 1949 [©Universal Pictures Co., Inc.; 17 Mar 1950; LP18]. Sd (Western Electric Recording); col (Technicolor). 6,910 ft. 77 min.

Prod Robert Arthur. *Assoc prod* John W. Rogers. *Dir* Frederick de Cordova. [*Asst dir* Fred Frank]. *Scr* Harold Shumate and Joseph Hoffman. *Adpt from a story by* Joe May and Samuel R. Golding. *Dir of photog* Russell Metty. *Spec photog* David S. Horsley. *Technicolor color dir* William Fritzsche. *Art dir* Bernard Herzbrun and Robert F. Boyle. *Film ed* Otto Ludwig. *Set dec* Russell A. Gausman and John Austin. *Cost* Yvonne Wood. *Choreographer* Harold Belfer. *Sd* Leslie I. Carey and Corson Jowett. *Hair stylist* Joan St. Oegger. *Makeup* Bud Westmore.

Song(s): "A Sailor Sails the Seven Seas," "Monsieur" and "Because You're in Love," music by Walter Scharf, lyrics by Jack Brooks.

Cast: Yvonne de Carlo (*Deborah McCoy*), Philip Friend (*Frederic Baptiste [also known as Captain Robert Kingston]*), Robert Douglas (*[Alexander] Narbonne*), Elsa Lanchester (*Mme. Brizar*), Andrea King (*Arlene Villon*), Norman Lloyd (*Patout*), Jay C. Flippen (*Jared Hawkins*), Henry Daniell (*Captain Duval*), Douglas Dumbrille (*Captain Martos*), Verna Felton (*Dowager*), John Qualen (*Vegetable man*), Connie Gilchrist (*Vegetable woman*), Ben Welden (*Tom*), Dewey Robinson (*Kryl*), Peggie Castle (*Cleo*).

Adventure, with songs. [*Print viewed*]. Frederic Baptiste, a gentleman pirate, captures yet another ship belonging to Alexander Narbonne, the wealthy New Orleans shipping magnate, not realizing that among his booty is a stowaway from Boston named Deborah McCoy, who is disguised as a cabin boy. Rather than being put on a lifeboat with the other passengers, Deborah is kept aboard the pirate ship, where she soon attracts Baptiste's attention. When the pirate threatens to maroon her on a small island, Deborah slips ashore while his ship is docked in New Orleans, and is soon hired as an entertainer by Mme. Brizar, the proprietor of a "School for Genteel Young Ladies." After months of training, Deborah is finally sent out on her first assignment, a party held by Captain Robert Kingston, the head of the Seaman's Fund. Deborah is surprised to discover that Robert and Baptiste are one and the same, but she agrees to keep his secret when she learns that Robert has been using his plunder from Narbonne's ships to support the local seamen. In actuality, Robert killed the real Baptiste, who had been hired by Narbonne to destroy the competition, and now pretends to be the pirate in order to raise money to rebuild the local fleet. Robert's ruse is discovered by Narbonne when his thugs steal the sea captain's ring. With the help of Patout, his secretary, Narbonne sets a trap for Robert, not knowing that Deborah has overheard their plotting. Later, Deborah gets into a fight with Robert's fiancée, Arlene Villon, the governor's niece, and becomes a fugitive when Villon files assault charges against her. Later, Robert returns to his ship and sets sail, unaware that Deborah is aboard, waiting for him. When Deborah tells Robert what she overheard between Narbonne and Patout, he recognizes Narbonne's deception and changes course in order to attack the French ships that are actually carrying the shipping magnate's riches. After months at sea, Robert successfully sinks Narbonne's three remaining ships, then heads back to New Orleans. Deborah proclaims her love to Robert, but, as a man of honor, he rejects her, having already promised himself to Arlene. Upon arriving in New Orleans, however, Robert learns that Arlene wed Narbonne during his absence, and is further shocked to learn that she sees her marriage merely as a convenience that should not interfere with their romance. When Robert rejects her adulterous proposal, the infuriated Arlene agrees to help prosecute her ex-fiancé for piracy. After Robert and his crew are arrested, the sea captain mistakenly believes that Deborah betrayed him. Later, Narbonne offers Robert clemency if he agrees to sign a statement stating that all the money raised by the Seaman's Fund was from his looted ships, but the pirate refuses. He then learns from

Patout that it was Arlene who betrayed. Robert and his men are then broken out of jail by Deborah and the local seamen, and the pirates set sail for distant waters, with Robert and Deborah happily united. *Impersonation and imposture. Pirates. Revenge. Romantic rivalry. Sea captains. Singers. Engagements. Escapes. Fights. Jailbreaks. Jealousy. Male impersonation. Marriage of convenience. New Orleans (LA). Police. Priests. Prison escapes. Sea battles. Secretaries. Snobs and snobbishness. Stowaways. Sword fights.*

Note: The working titles of this film were *No Other Woman*, *Debbie's Escape* and *Mme. McCoy and the Pirate*. As noted in a *NYT* news item, Elsa Lanchester's character "Madame Brizar," while presented as the headmistress of a girl's finishing school in order to comply with PCA code regulations, is clearly meant to be the madam of an upper-class New Orleans bordello.

Box 4 Mar 1950. *DV* 1 Mar 1950, p. 3, 6. *FD* 6 Mar 1950, p. 6. *HR* 8 Jul 1949, p. 9. *HR* 1 Mar 1950, pp. 3-4. *MPHPD* 4 Mar 1950, p. 213. *NYT* 27 Mar 1950, p. 19. *NYT* 2 Apr 1950. *Var* 1 Mar 1950, p. 6.

BUCK PRIVATES COME HOME (French Americans, Immigrants)

Universal-International Pictures Co., Inc. *Dist* Universal Pictures Co., Inc. **1947** Sd (Western Electric Recording); b&w. 75 or 77-78 min. PCA cert no. 12264.

Prod Robert Arthur. *Dir* Charles T. Barton. *Asst dir* Joseph E. Kenney. *Scr* John Grant, Frederic I. Rinaldo and Robert Lees. *Based on a story by* Richard Mucaulay and Bradford Ropes. *Dir of photog* Charles Van Enger. *Spec photog* David S. Horsley. *Art dir* Bernard Herzbrun and Frank A. Richards. *Film ed* Edward Curtiss. *Set dec* Russell A. Gausman and Charles Wyrick. *Gowns* Yvonne Wood. *Mus* Walter Schumann. *Orch* David Tamkin. *Sd* Charles Felstead. [*Sd*] *tech* Robert Pritchard. *Hair stylist* Carmen Dirigo. *Makeup* Jack P. Pierce.

Song(s): "Goin' Home," music based on "Largo" from his symphany No. 9, Op. 85 in E minor, "The New World," by Antonín Dvorák, words by William Arms Fisher.

Cast: BUD ABBOTT (*Slicker Smith*), LOU COSTELLO (*Herbie Brown*), Tom Brown (*Bill Gregory*), Joan Fulton (*Sylvia Hunter*), Nat Pendleton (*Sgt. Collins*), Beverly Simmons ([*Yvonne*] *Evey LeBrec*), Don Porter (*Captain Christie*), Donald MacBride (*Police captain*), Don Beddoe (*Mr. Roberts*), Charles Trowbridge (*Mr. Quince*), Russell Hicks (*Mr. [Walter] Appleby*), Joe Kirk (*Real estate salesman*), Knox Manning (*Commentator*), Milburn Stone (*Announcer*), [Lane Watson, William Ching (*Lieutenants*)], [Peter Thompson (*Steve*)], [George Beban, Jr. (*Cal*)], [Jimmie Dodd (*Whitey*)], [Lennie Bremen (*Hank*)], [Al Murphy (*Murphy*)], [Bob Wilke (*Stan*)], [William Haade (*Husband*)], [Janna deLoos (*Wife*)], [Buddy Roosevelt, Chuck Hamilton (*New York policemen*)], [Patricia Alphin (*Young girl*)], [Ralph Dunn (*Ed*)], [John Sheehan (*Drew*)], [Cliff Clark (*Quentin*)], [Jean Del Val (*Duprez*)], [Harlan Warde, Lyle Latell, Myron Healy, Ralph Brooks, Eddie Coke, Clarence Straight, Russell Conway, Thomas M. Skinner, Bob Bacon (*Medics*)], [Eddie Acuff, Milton Kibbee (*Passengers*)], [Frank Marlowe, Tony Merrill, Ernie Adams, Donald Kerr (*Tie buyers*)], [Ottola Nesmith (*French matron*)], [Eddie Dunn (*Mulroney*)], [Charles Sullivan (*Harry*)], [Billy Curtis (*Man with baby*)], [Betty Alexander (*Juliet*)], [Jerry Farber (*Boy*)], [Doris Kemper (*Matron*)], [James Farley, Lee Shumway (*Bank guards*)], [Rex Lease (*Chauffeur*)], [Frank Mayo (*Colonel*)], [John Michaels, Dick Dickerson (*Rookie soldiers*)], [George Barton (*Painter*)].

Comedy, Postwar life. [*Print viewed*]. Upon the conclusion of World War II, old friends Slicker Smith and Herbie Brown head home from Europe aboard a troop ship. When Captain Christie orders an inspection of the soldiers' belongings, Herbie nearly blows up the ship with a contraband German booby trap. Slicker and Sgt. Collins then learn that Herbie has also smuggled Yvonne "Evey" LeBru, a French war orphan, aboard the ship. Evey is soon discovered by Christie and is put into the custody of Lt. Sylvia Hunter, a nurse who quickly becomes attached to the little girl. Upon arriving in New York City, Slicker and Herbie are taken to the Fort Dix separation center, while Evey is turned over to the U.S. Immigration authorities. Later, Evey learns that she is to be returned to France and after escaping the immigration officials, heads for Times Square, where Slicker and Herbie have gone back to their pre-war trade of selling neckties on the street corner. Evey finds her two foster-uncles just as they are about to be arrested by Collins, who has also returned to his pre-war profession as a police sergeant. With Evey disguised as a boy, Slicker and Herbie then go to the French consul, where they are told that Herbie must be married and employed before he can legally adopt the young girl. Evey suggests Sylvia as a possible mate for Herbie, but the

nurse is already involved with Bill Gregory, a race car driver and designer. Instead, Slicker and Herbie become partners with Bill, even though his race car is being held in hock at Mulroney's Garage. After spending the night in a home-made hammock, pinned to a clothesline outside Sylvia's apartment, Herbie is nearly killed by a jealous husband, who accuses him of being his wife's lover. Acting on Slicker's challenge, the husband cuts the clothesline, sending Herbie crashing into Collins' apartment. The next day, Slicker and Herbie are duped by a crooked real estate salesman into buying a broken-down bus, in which they nevertheless set up housekeeping. Later, the two go to a local bank to apply for G.I. loans in order to finance Bill's car, but, thanks to their lack of automotive knowledge and Herbie's bungling, they are quickly turned down. Herbie suggests that they borrow the money from their old army buddies, and after some of the veterans meet with Bill, the necessary funds are raised. Collins then arrives to take custody of Evey, having traced the orphan through the real estate agent, but when he is accidentally knocked unconscious, Evey and the boys make their escape. Collins is suspended from the police force and, hoping to get his job back, privately stakes out the garage at which Bill's car is being held. After Collins falls asleep, Slicker, Herbie and Bill sneak into the garage and, after a brief fight with the disgraced policeman, tow the car away. Just before the big Gold Cup race, however, Bill, Slicker, Sylvia and Evey are arrested by the reinstated Collins. Herbie then takes the wheel of the midget racer and quickly looses control of it, leaving the racetrack. The police commandeer the limousine of Walter Appleby, an automobile magnate, to chase after Herbie, and Appleby is so impressed by the race car's performance that he orders twenty identical cars and two hundred engines. Bill and Sylvia are then given permission to adopt Evey, and Slicker and Herbie are offered positions with the police force, much to the dismay of Collins. *Adoption. Aliens, Illegal. Nurses. Orphans. Race car drivers. Salesmen. Veterans. Airports. Automobile racing. Banks. Bombs. Chases. Consuls. Disguise. Escapes. Falls from heights. False arrests. Fights. French. Garages. Hypnotism. Jealousy. K.P. duty. Male impersonation. Motion picture theaters. New York City. Officers (Military). Partnership. Police. Ships. United States. Army. United States. Dept. of Immigration. United States. Women's Army Corps.*

Note: This film was a sequel to the highly successful 1941 Universal film *Buck Privates. Buck Privates Come Home* opens with a sequence made up of clips from the 1941 film, including scenes of "Slicker" and "Herbie" selling ties in front of an Army recruitment post and "Slicker" going through basic training. *HR* production charts include Renee Carson in the cast, but her appearance in the released film has not been confirmed.

Box 15 Mar 1947. *DV* 10 Mar 1947. *HR* 5 Nov 1946, p. 2. *HR* 15 Nov 1946, p. 15. *HR* 17 Jan 1947, p. 19. *HR* 24 Jan 1947, p. 6. *HR* 10 Mar 1947, p. 3. *IFJ* 4 Jan 1947, p. 35. *MPHPD* 15 Mar 1947. *NYT* 12 Apr 1947, p. 11. *Var* 12 Mar 1947, p. 12.

LA BUENAVENTURA (Spanish language)

Warner Bros. Pictures, Inc. *Dist* Warner Bros. Pictures, Inc. **1934**; Los Angeles opening: 18 May 1934; Prod: Jan 1934. Sd; b&w. 8 reels, 6,907 ft. 77 min. Spanish language.

Bajo la supervisión de [*Supv*] Manuel Reachi. *Dirigida por* [*Dir*] William McGann. *Argumento cinematográfico de* [*Scr*] Armán Chelieu and John K. Butler. *Continuidad de* [*Continuity*] Betty Reinhardt. *Diálogo de* [*Dial*] Miguel de Zárraga. *Fotografía de* [*Photog*] William Rees. *Escenarista* [*Art dir*] Robert M. Haas. *Cortador* [*Ed*] Frank Magee. *Orquesta Vitafónica dirigida por* [*Vitaphone Orchestra conducted by*] Leo F. Forbstein. *Singing voice of Anita Campillo* Consuelo Melendez.

Song(s): "Serenade" from the opera *Don Pasquale*, music by Gaetano Donizetti, libretto by Donizetti and Giacomo Ruffini; "Una furtiva lagrima" from the opera *Elisir d'amore*, music by Gaetano Donizetti, libretto by Felice Romani; "O Paradiso" from the opera *L'Africaine*, music by Giacomo Meyerbeer, libretto by Eugène Scribe; "Czardis," "Gypsy Love Song," "Always Do as People Say You Should," "Champagne Song," "Ho! Ye Townsmen," "Lily and the Nightingale," "Only in the Play," "Power of the Human Eye" and "Serenade of All Nations," music by Victor Herbert, new lyrics by Warner Bros. staff; and other songs.

Source: Based on the operetta *The Fortune Teller*, music by Victor Herbert, libretto by Harry B. Smith (New York, 4 Nov 1929).

Cast: Enrico Caruso, Jr. (*Enrico Baroni*), Anita Campillo (*Irma [also known as Elvira]*), Luis Alberni (*Fresco*), Alfonso Pedroza (*Sandor*), Antonio Vidal (*Conde de Molnar*), Emilia Leovalli (*Lucía*), Paul Ellis (*Príncipe Nikki*), Germaine de Néel (*Mademoiselle Pompom*), Rosa Rey (*Sofía*), Emilio Fernández

(*Boris*), Francisco Marán (*Muldoni*), Marcela Nivón (*Duquesa*), [Lita Santos (*Gitana*)], [Rafael Navarro], [Raquel Ríos], [Consuelo Melendez].

Romance, with songs. [*Not viewed*]. In France, opera star Enrico Baroni has tired of his mistress Pompom. After a performance, Enrico goes to a cabaret with his manager, Muldoni, and some friends. When Pompom arrives, Enrico leaves the cabaret with his servant, Fresco. Hearing music nearby, Enrico and Fresco discover a band of gypsies. Enrico is fascinated by what seems to be a carefree life and by Irma, a gypsy, who returns his interest. Sofía, Irma's mother, warns her to be careful of Enrico, but when Boris, to whom Irma has been promised since she was young, becomes jealous of Enrico's attentions, Irma insists that she will never marry Boris because she does not love him. Enrico decides to remain with the gypsies, but Fresco summons the police, claiming that Enrico has been kidnapped. Enrico returns to his old life, breaking Irma's heart. Then Sofía tells Irma that she is really the granddaughter of Count Molnar and was kidnapped by Sandor, Sofía's husband, when she was a child. With Sofía's help, Irma is reunited with the count and once again is called by her real name, Elvira. At first Irma rebels against the count's efforts to make her into a lady, but when she sees a picture of Enrico, she decides to make herself worthy of him. A few years later, some friends take Irma to hear Enrico sing. When they visit his dressing room, Enrico finds Irma familiar, but does not really recognize her. He is smitten, however, and visits the count's castle the next day. When Enrico flirts with Irma, telling her she is the only woman he has ever loved, Irma feels betrayed. Unexpectedly the gypsies camp near the castle and, at the same time, Pompom appears, begging Enrico to return to her. Wishing for revenge, Irma dresses as a gypsy again and tells Enrico's fortune. She tells him that once he abandoned a poor girl because he did not love her. Finally, Enrico realizes that Irma and Elvira are the same woman and announces that she will be at his side forever. *Abduction. Class distinction. Gypsies. Romance. Singers. Cabarets. Engagements. Fortune-tellers. Foster parents. France. Grandfathers. Jealousy. Mistresses. Opera. Police. Servants.*

Note: The onscreen credits were taken from a cutting continuity in the Warner Bros. files at USC. The credits include a copyright statement, but no entry for the film was found in the Catalog of Copyright Entries. Some sources credit supervisor Manuel Reachi as a contributor to the screen story and an adaptor. In a memo dated 15 Jan 1934 from the Warner Bros. legal department, which is included in the files at USC, it is noted that the songs in the film used music by Victor Herbert, but the lyrics were by the studio's own writers, not by Harry B. Smith, the operetta's librettist. However, Smith was credited on screen for legal reasons. Memos in the Warner Bros. files list numerous songs that the producers intended to include in the film, but their presence in the final film has not been confirmed.

CM Jun 1934, p. 304. *FD* 18 Sep 1934, p. 7. *NYT* 15 Sep 1934, p. 20.

BUFFALO BILL (Native Americans, Cheyenne)

Twentieth Century-Fox Film Corp. *Dist* Twentieth Century-Fox Film Corp. Apr **1944**; Los Angeles opening: 13 Apr 1944; New York opening: week of 19 Apr 1944; Prod: 26 Jul—early Oct 1943 [©Twentieth Century-Fox Film Corp.; 11 Apr 1944; LP12908]. Sd (Western Electric Recording); col (Technicolor). 10 reels, 8,126 ft. 90 min. PCA cert no. 9533.

[*Exec prod* Darryl F. Zanuck]. *Prod* Harry A. Sherman. *Dir* William A. Wellman. *2d unit dir* Otto Brower. [*Asst dir* Joseph Behm and William Eckhardt]. *Scr* Aeneas MacKenzie, Clements Ripley and Cecile Kramer. *Based on a story by* Frank Winch. [*Contr wrt* John Larkin]. *Dir of photog* Leon Shamroy. *Special photog eff* Fred Sersen. *Technicolor dir* Natalie Kalmus. *Assoc* Richard Mueller. *Art dir* James Basevi and Lewis Creber. *Film ed* James B. Clark. *Set dec* Thomas Little. *Assoc* Fred J. Rode. *Cost* Rene Hubert. *Mus* David Buttolph. *Mus dir* Emil Newman. *Sd* Alfred Bruzlin and Roger Heman. *Makeup artist* Guy Pearce. [*Tech adv* Col. J. G. Taylor, Chief Thundercloud and Joe De Yong]. [*Prod mgr* R. L. Hough and Charles Stallings]. [*Loc mgr* R. C. Moore]. [*Unit mgr* Sidney Bowen]. [*Asst to Harry Sherman* Dick Dickson]. [*Constr supv* Ben Wurtzel]. [*Archery expert* Howard Hill].

Cast: JOEL McCREA [(*William Frederick Cody, also known as Buffalo Bill*)], MAUREEN O'HARA [(*Louisa Frederici Cody*)], LINDA DARNELL [(*Dawn Starlight*)], Thomas Mitchell [(*Ned Buntline*)], Edgar Buchanan [(*Sergeant Chips McGraw*)], Anthony Quinn [(*Yellow Hand*)], Moroni Olsen [(*Senator Frederici*)], Frank Fenton [(*Murdo Carvell*)], Matt Briggs [(*General Blazier*)], George Lessey [(*Schyler Vandevere*)], Frank Orth [(*Sherman*)], [George Chandler

(*Trooper Clancy*)], [Chief Many Treaties (*Tall Bull*)], [Nick Thompson (*Medicine man*)], [Chief Thundercloud (*Crazy Horse*)], [Sidney Blackmer (*Theodore Roosevelt*)], [Edwin Stanley (*Doctor*)], [John Dilson (*President Hayes*)], [Evelyn Beresford (*Queen Victoria*)], [Merrill Rodin (*Bellboy*)], [Talzumbie Dupea (*Old Indian woman*)], [Larry Lawson (*Adjutant*)], [Margaret Martin (*Indian servant*)], [George Sherwood (*Reporter*)], [George Bronson (*Strong man*)], [Harry Tyler, Arthur Loft, Syd Saylor (*Barkers*)], [Robert Homans (*Muldoon, policeman*)], [Billy Bletcher (*Short man*)], [Cordell Hickman (*Black boy*)], [Gerald Mackey, Eddie Nichols, Fred Chapman, George Nokes (*Boys*)], [Cecil Weston (*Maid*)], [John Reese (*Tough guy*)], [Vincent Graeff (*Crippled boy*)], [Fred Graham (*Editor*)], [Thomas Alan Yazloff (*Kit Carson Cody*)], [Clint Sharp], [Cliff Parkinson], [Ben Corbett], [Frank McCarroll], [Frank Cordell], [Phil Schumacher], [John Epper], [George Fiske], [Joe P. Smith], [Jack Carry], [Fred Kennedy], [Henry Wills], [H. Ellingwood], [Buster Wiles], [Lyle Brown], [Jack House], [Larry Dodds], [Don House], [Edward Jauregui], [Jack Shannon], [James Magill], [Kermit Maynard], [Bob Perry], [John Konorez], [Carl Andre], [Merlyn Nelson], [Audrey Scott], [Gordon Jones], [Walter Robbins].

Biography, Western. [*Print viewed*]. In 1877, William Frederick Cody, an army scout at a remote frontier post, and a longtime friend of the Cheyenne Indians, is riding one day when he sees a wagon being attacked by a group of Indians. After rescuing the endangered party, which consists of cavalry sergeant Chips McGraw, Senator Frederici and his daughter Louisa and businessman Murdo Carvell, Bill explains to the senator that the drunken Indians meant no real harm. Later, Louisa invites Bill to a dinner party at her home near the fort, much to the despair of Dawn Starlight, a Cheyenne schoolteacher who is in love with Bill. The dinner is interrupted by Chips, who has brought Yellow Hand, the son of Cheyenne chief Tall Bull, to discuss industrialist Schyler Vandevere's plan to build a railroad line through Cheyenne land. Despite Yellow Hand's warning that it will cause war, Vandevere insists he is going through with his project. Journalist Ned Buntline, another guest, is enthusiastic about covering an Indian war, but Bill fears a tragic result. Vandevere begins his construction, and the Cheyenne, led by Yellow Hand, the war chief, begin a campaign of destruction. Dawn Starlight, who is Yellow Hand's sister, sends him word that if he takes Frederici hostage, he can obtain greater peace terms. Frederici is captured, but Bill negotiates for his release, and soon after, a peace treaty is signed. Ned then returns to the East after telling Bill of his intentions to write about him. Louisa, who has fallen in love with Bill, coaxes the shy scout to propose to her, and they are married. Two years pass as Bill and Louisa enjoy a quiet life. One day, the senator brings news that he and Vandevere have started a company dealing in buffalo robes. Bill agrees to direct the operation but is sickened by the slaughter of the buffalo. Bill's anxiety is temporarily forgotten, however, when Louisa announces that she is pregnant. Meanwhile, Yellow Hand meets with Sioux war chief Crazy Horse, and they declare war on the white man for destroying the buffalo, which are their main food source. While the Indians attack in the North, where there are fewer soldiers, Louisa goes into labor as she and Bill are returning to the fort. Soon Bill is presented with a son, whom he names Kit Carson Cody. Upon their arrival at the fort, Bill and Louisa learn that the Sioux have beaten General George Custer's forces, and General Blazier urges Bill to join the Army. Louisa warns Bill that she will take Kit East if he leaves, but Bill feels compelled to accompany the Army. Bill subverts the general's orders, however, so that the leading group of cavalry meets Yellow Hand's forces at War Bonnet Gorge. There, Bill kills Yellow Hand in hand-to-hand combat, and when the Army reinforcements arrive, the Indians are beaten in a bloody battle, during which Dawn Starlight is killed. Despite his despair over the battle, Bill agrees to go to Washington, D.C., where he is to receive the Congressional Medal of Honor for his heroic actions. During the journey, Bill is surprised to learn that Ned's publications about the exploits of "Buffalo Bill" have made him a celebrity. Once in Washington, however, Bill learns that Kit is seriously ill. Bill rushes to Louisa's house, but the child has already died from diphtheria. Grief-stricken, Bill lashes out at Vandevere and other industrialists, accusing them of persecuting the Indians for their own gain. Powerful political forces then align against Bill and ruin his reputation through slander. Penniless, Bill wanders the streets until his sharpshooting at an arcade catches the eye of Sherman, a sideshow owner. Sherman

hires Bill as part of his show, and when Louisa finally decides to locate her husband, she finds Bill in the humiliating job. The couple reconcile, but Bill decides that he cannot go home because of the way he has treated the Indians. One afternoon, Ned overhears Bill telling some children that Indian children are just like them, and he convinces Bill to start a rodeo show during which he and his Indian friends can demonstrate their skills. Soon Buffalo Bill's Wild West Show has become a success, and as the years pass, Bill travels throughout the world, performing for royalty, heads of state and adoring youngsters. Years later, after his final performance, Bill thanks his fans and announces that he is retiring so that he and Louisa can return to the West. Battles. Cheyenne Indians. Buffalo Bill Cody. Disillusionment. Racism. Scouts (Frontier). Treaties. Banquets. Bison, American. Ned Buntline. Business ethics. Businessmen. Childbirth. Congressional Medal of Honor. Chief Crazy Horse. Dakota Indians. Easterners. Fame. Hero worship. Jealousy. Marriage. Reporters. Retirement. Schoolteachers. Senators. Sideshows. United States. Army. Cavalry. Washington (D.C.). Wild west shows. Chief Yellow Hand.

Note: This film was based on the life of William Frederick "Buffalo Bill" Cody (1846-1917). Cody's legendary exploits as a Pony Express rider, Army scout, Indian fighter, buffalo hunter and showman were popularized in the dime novels of writer Ned Buntline. Although some of the incidents in the film, such as Cody's fight with Cheyenne leader Yellow Hand and his being awarded the Medal of Honor are true, others were not. His wife Louisa, for example, was not the daughter of a senator, and the couple had three other children besides Kit Carson Cody, who actually died of scarlet fever. Numerous films have been made featuring Cody as a character, including the 1926 Sunset Productions film *Buffalo Bill on the U.P. Trail*, starring Roy Stewart; the 1936 Paramount film *The Plainsman*, featuring James Ellison as Cody (see entries below); and the 1976 picture *Buffalo Bill and the Indians or Sitting Bull's History Lesson*, starring Paul Newman. Cody himself appeared in a number of films, including the 1901 Biograph release *Buffalo Bill's Wild West Parade* (see *AFI Catalog of Feature Films, 1893-1910*; A.01833) and the 1917 Essanay release *The Adventures of Buffalo Bill* (see above). The Twentieth Century-Fox Records of the Legal Department, located at the UCLA Arts—Special Collections Library, contains several letters from Cody's relatives, some of which protested that the picture was being made without their permission. Others complained after the film was released that the depiction of Cody was grossly inaccurate. No claims were filed, however, and the studio maintained that because Cody was dead, they did not have to obtain the rights to his life story from any of his surviving relatives.

According to information in the legal records and the Twentieth Century-Fox Produced Scripts Collection, also located at UCLA, the studio purchased the rights to Frank Winch's unpublished story, entitled "Pahaska," from producer Harry Sherman, who had originally intended to make the film at Paramount. Sherman assigned Harrison Jacobs to write the screenplay, and planned to shoot it in Wyoming, according to a Feb 1939 *LAT* news item. Fox's purchase of Sherman's rights to "Pahaska" included the rights to other works by Winch, upon some of which the screenplay may have been based. They include: *The Thrilling Lives of Buffalo Bill, Col. William F. Cody, Last of the Great Scouts and Pawnee Bill, Major Gordon W. Lillie, White Chief of the Pawnees* (1911); *Buffalo Bill as I Knew Him* (1928); and "Buffalo Bill—Frontiersman" (*Ace High Magazine*, 3 Jan 1929—18 Sep 1929). According to a studio press release, "Americana expert" George Milburn was to collaborate with credited writer Aeneas McKenzie on the screenplay, but the extent of his contribution to the completed picture has not been confirmed. A 14 Jun 1943 *HR* news item noted that Sherman originally intended for Lesley Selander to act as the second unit director.

A Jun 1943 version of the screenplay, contained in the scripts collection, includes the following foreword: "In recognition of the valor and devotion of those Indian warriors who are now in the armed forces of our nation, Twentieth Century-Fox Studios dedicates to a race that ever fought for freedom, this story of its greatest friend and foeman." In a 14 Jul 1943 story conference, however, studio production chief Darryl F. Zanuck objected to the dedication, saying "in this we are reminded of a situation which we would rather not have brought up: our ignoble treatment of the American Indian." The story conference also reveals that Vincent Price was originally scheduled to play "Murdo Carvell," but was replaced when the part was cut. *HR* production charts list Price in the cast, however, along with E. J. Ballantine, whose participation in the completed film has not been confirmed. According to several contemporary sources, the buffalo hunting sequence was filmed on the Crow Indian Reservation in Montana, and many sequences were shot on location in Zion National Park and Kanab, Utah. The majority of the Indians in the film were played by Navajo Indians from Arizona.

Box 18 Mar 1944. *Collier's* 18 Mar 1944, pp. 18-19. *DV* 15 Mar 1944, pp. 3, 6. *FD* 17 Mar 1944, p. 6. *HR* 8 Jun 1943, p. 7. *HR* 14 Jun 1943, p. 3. *HR* 15 Jun 1943, p. 6. *HR* 25 Jun 1943, p. 7. *HR* 1 Jul 1943, p. 9. *HR* 16 Jul 1943, p. 7. *HR* 27 Jul 1943, p. 3. *HR* 16 Sep 1943, p. 12. *HR* 17 Sep 1943, p. 9. *HR* 30 Sep 1943, p. 3. *HR* 15 Oct 1943, p. 1. *HR* 21 Mar 1944, p. 19. *HR* 24 Apr 1944, p. 12. *LAT* 15 Feb 1939. *Life* 10 Apr 1944, pp. 109-112, 114, 117. *MPD* 24 Mar 1944. *MPHPD* 18 Mar 1944, p. 1801. *NYT* 12 Sep 1943. *NYT* 20 Apr 1944, p. 22. *Var* 15 Mar 1944, p. 32.

BUFFALO BILL IN TOMAHAWK TERRITORY (Native Americans, Dakota)

Jack Schwarz Productions, Inc. *Dist* United Artists Corp. 8 Feb **1952** [©Jack Schwarz Productions, Inc.; 18 Feb 1952; LP1771]. Sd; b&w. 64 or 66 min. PCA cert no. 15452.

Prod Edward Finney and B. B. Ray. *Dir* Bernard B. Ray. *Story and scr* Sam Neuman and Nat Tanchuck. *Commentary* T. Elbert Hubbard. *Dir of photog* Elmer Dyer. *Spec eff* Ray Mercer. *Film ed* Edward Phillips. *Props* Tom Shaw. *Ward* Harold Dunn. *Mus dir and comp* Frank Sanucci. *Specialty numbers by* The Broome Brothers. *Sd eng* T. T. Triplet. *Makeup* Harry Thomas. *Asst to prod* David Luboff. *Prod asst* Bobby Ray.

Song(s): "On the Old Panhandle Trail," music and lyrics by Max Rich and Allan Flynn.

Cast: Clayton Moore (*Buffalo Bill* [*Cody*]), Slim Andrews (*Cactus*), Chas. Harvey (*Lt. Bryan*), Rod Redwing (*Running Deer*), Shooting Star (*Indian brave*), Chief Yowlachie (*White Cloud*), Chief Thundercloud (*Black Hawk*), Charlie Hughes (*Pinfeathers*), Eddie Phillips (*Blake*), Tom Hubbard (*Bill Stokey*), Sharon Dexter (*Janet*), Helena Dare (*Maria*), Ray Broome, Lee Broome, Joe Broome.

Comedy-drama, **Western**. [*Print viewed*]. In the early days of America's westward expansion, famous scout Buffalo Bill Cody and his pal Cactus are traveling through Indian territory to deliver cattle to Chief White Cloud when they witness a Sioux attack on a wagon train. The two come to the aid of the train, which appears to be a "marrying train," composed solely of women, and succeed in scaring off the attackers. However, when the dust settles, Buffalo Bill and Cactus are surprised to discover that the wagon train is headed by Lt. Bryan, and that the "women" are actually U.S. Cavalry soldiers in disguise. Analyzing the attack, Buffalo Bill concludes that the Sioux retreat was uncharacteristic of Indian ambushes and begins to suspect that the attackers may not have been real Sioux. Furthermore, Buffalo Bill cannot understand why Chief White Cloud would go back on his word and break a peace agreement. When Buffalo Bill and Cactus return to town, they are surrounded by citizens who are angry about the ambush and demand that Buffalo Bill cancel his cattle delivery. The townspeople are being spurred to action by Bill Stokey and Blake, who are trying to stir up trouble with the Indians in order to sabotage the peace effort, which they see as a threat to their plans to dig up gold buried under Indian land. A bruising fistfight ensues, during which Buffalo Bill knocks Stokey unconscious. Janet, who is engaged to Lt. Bryan but is having doubts about becoming an "army wife," has also been swept into Stokey's gang. After the fight, Buffalo Bill leaves the cattle in town and goes to Chief White Cloud to find out if he was behind the recent ambush. En route, he is attacked by a small group of renegade Indians under the command of Running Deer, who is White Cloud's rebellious son, and who is in league with Stokey and his men. The attack is thwarted by White Cloud, who arrives on the scene in time to save Buffalo Bill. Running Deer is later captured by the Sioux, and, when White Cloud refuses to kill him, the dishonored captive kills himself. Now certain that White Cloud is innocent of the wagon train attack, Buffalo Bill returns to the task of delivering the cattle to the Sioux. His mission is confounded, however, when Stokey and his men stampede the cattle. The failure of Buffalo Bill to deliver the cattle results in White Cloud issuing an ultimatum that carries the threat of war. Buffalo Bill tries to diffuse the situation by securing some buffalo for the Sioux, but Stokey and his men sabotage his efforts again, this time by dressing up as Indians and raiding his train. When Buffalo Bill learns the truth about Stokey and his motives, he approaches White Cloud and persuades him to call off the war party. The fake Indians are eventually exposed by Buffalo Bill, and Stokey and Blake are killed. With the threat to the peace treaty eliminated, White Cloud reaffirms his determination to remain friendly with the United States, and Janet and Lt. Bryan resume their romance. *Ambushes. Dakota Indians. Pioneers. Treaties. Wagon trains. The West. Disguise. Engagements. Fathers and sons. Female impersonation. Fistfights. Gold. Gunfights. Scouts (Frontier). Suicide. United States. Army. Cavalry.*

Note: The working title of this film was *Buffalo Bill's Wagon Train.*

Box 16 Feb 1952. *DV* 28 Jan 1952, p. 4. *FD* 29 Feb 1952, p. 7. *HR* 28 Jan 1952, p. 4. *MPHPD* 2 Feb 1952, p. 1222. *Var* 20 Jan 1952, p. 6.

BUFFALO BILL ON THE U. P. TRAIL (Native Americans)

Dist Sunset Productions. 1 Mar **1926**. Si; b&w. 6 reels, 5,104 ft.

Pres Anthony J. Xydias. *Dir* Frank S. Mattison. *Photog* Bert Longenecker. *Tech dir* Jack Pierce. *Film ed* Al Martin.

Cast: Roy Stewart (*Buffalo Bill*), Kathryn McGuire (*Millie*), Cullen Landis (*Gordon Kent, boyhood sweetheart of Millie*), Sheldon Lewis (*Maj. Mike Connel, commander of Post Ellsworth*), Earl Metcalfe (*Sheriff*), Milburn Morante (*"Hearts" Farrel, gambler*), Hazel Howell (*Katy Hale*), Fred De Silva (*Bill Henry, the "other man"*), Felix Whitefeather (*White Spear, only son of the chief*), Jay Morley (*Jim Hale, parson of the plains*), Eddie Harris (*Mose, a runaway slave*), Dick La Reno (*William Rose, owner of the overland*), Harry Fenwick (*Dr. Roy Webb, town-locating agent*).

Western. Winding its way across western Kansas, a wagon train led by Gordon Kent includes Katy Hale, who is running away from her husband with Bill Henry, and Buffalo Bill, who is seen performing kindnesses for an Indian and for a runaway slave. Six months later, Buffalo Bill learns that the railroad is coming through, and he plans with William Rose to build a new town on its route. However, when they refuse train-town locator Roy Webb's offer to "buy in," the latter threatens to change the route, and the entire town moves to a new site, which crosses Kent's property. Enraged, Kent and Buffalo Bill get into a fight with the railroad surveyors, and White Spear starts a buffalo stampede, which endangers Kent's fiancée, Millie. Kent rescues Millie, Buffalo Bill diverts the stampede, Webb agrees to purchase the property rights, and Katy is reunited with her husband. *Bison, American. Buffalo Bill Cody. Indians of North America. Land claims. Railroads. Slaves–Runaway. Stampedes. Union Pacific Railroad. Wagon trains.*

Note: This film was also known as *With Buffalo Bill on the U. P. Trail.* For biographical information about Buffalo Bill Cody, please see the entry above for *Buffalo Bill.*

BUFFALO BILL, PLAINSMAN *see* **YOUNG BUFFALO BILL**

BUFFALO BILL RIDES AGAIN (Native Americans)

Jack Schwarz Productions. *Dist* Screen Guild Productions, Inc. 15 Feb **1947**; *Prod:* 1 Nov–15 Nov 1946 [©Jack Schwarz Productions; 15 Dec 1946; LP874]. Sd; b&w. 70 min.

Pres JACK SCHWARZ. *Prod* Jack Schwarz. *Dir* Bernard B. Ray. *Asst dir* Wesley Barry. *Orig scr* Fran Gilbert and Barney Sarecky. *Dir of photog* Robert Cline. *Film ed* Robert Crandall. *Set dresser* Harry Reif. *Master of props* George Bahr. *Mus comp, arr and cond by* Modest Altschuller. *Sd* Glen Glenn. *Prod mgr* Bobby Ray.

Cast: Richard Arlen (*Buffalo Bill* [*Cody*]), Jennifer Holt (*Dale Harrington*), Lee Shumway (*Steve Harrington*), John Dexter (*Tom Russell*), Gil Patric (*Simpson*), Many Treaties (*Brave Eagle*), Charles Stevens (*White Mountain*), Shooting Star (*Young Bird*), Edward Cassidy (*Sheriff*), Hollis Bane (*Rankin*), Clarke Stevens (*Jeff*), Carl Mathews (*Pete*), Frank McCarroll (*Hank*), Edmund Cobb (*Morgan*), Richard T. Adams (*Sam*), Tom Leffingwell (*Senator Windblower*), Philip Arnold (*Scratchy*), Paula Hill (*Sue Henderson*), [George Sherwood (*Mr. Smith*)], [Fred Graham (*Frank Dawson*)], [Frank O'Connor (*J. B. Jordon*)], [Fred Fox (*Mr. Howard*)], [Dorothy Curtis (*Mrs. Dawson*)].

Western. [*Print viewed*]. Aware that some seemingly worthless western land is actually rich with unmined oil, the J. B. Jordon investment company wants to acquire the land cheaply, form a corporation and sell its stock for a large profit. When the company's plans are thwarted by settlers who refuse to sell, Jordon arranges for a gang of local outlaws to terrorize them. As part of the plan, three members of the gang, including its secret head, businessman Simpson, shoot down Clear Water, an Indian hunter, and frame landowner Tom Russell for the murder by planting Clear Water's furs in Tom's shack. In nearby Redfield, Simpson then tells the sheriff that he saw Tom shoot Clear Water. Before the sheriff can arrest Tom, Clear Water's tribe, led by Brave Eagle, discover the hidden furs and attack Tom's homestead. During the fight, Tom's sweetheart, Dale Harrington, whose father Steve is Tom's partner, dashes off for help and is found by Buffalo Bill Cody. Buffalo Bill, who has been sent by the Army to help the settlers, then stops the Indian attack and convinces Brave Eagle, an old friend, not to exact justice on Tom for three days, by which time he hopes to have discovered the identity of the real killer. Encouraged by Buffalo Bill, Tom allows the sheriff to arrest him and asks Buffalo Bill to look after Dale and Steve. Acting on

Simpson's orders, the outlaws, meanwhile, plot to kill Buffalo Bill by luring him to their hideout and rigging the door so that when he opens it, a rifle automatically fires at him. Buffalo Bill anticipates the trap, however, and after a fierce fight, captures one of the outlaws. The next day, Buffalo Bill arranges for two Indian scouts, Young Bird and White Mountain, to watch the road near the hideout, then reports to Dale and Steve his suspicions that the outlaws want their land because it contains oil. Later, the tight-lipped outlaw, Jeff, breaks out of jail, just as Buffalo Bill and the sheriff are about to release him. Buffalo Bill pursues Jeff, who runs to Simpson for help. Anxious not to be exposed, Simpson shoots Jeff, then tells Buffalo Bill that he killed in self-defense. On the morning of the third day, Young Bird sees Simpson riding to the hideout and follows him. After Simpson orders his men to kidnap Dale, Young Bird is caught outside the hideout. Before Young Bird is imprisoned, he calls out to his horse, which then alerts White Mountain. Steve, meanwhile, leaves his homestead to collect water, and Dale is kidnapped by the outlaws, who leave behind a ransom note. While Steve rushes off to sell his land to gain Dale's release, White Mountain observes Dale with an outlaw and reports to Buffalo Bill. With White Mountain's help, Buffalo Bill sneaks up on the hideout and overwhelms the outlaws. The freed Dale races to town to stop Steve, while Buffalo Bill coerces the outlaws into revealing their leader's identity. At the same time, the Indians, having kept their promise, ride off to claim Tom at the jail. After Steve unwittingly signs his property over to Simpson, Brave Eagle forces the sheriff to release Tom. With the land title in hand, Simpson finally reveals himself to Steve and announces that he and his men are taking over his property. Buffalo Bill, Steve and the sheriff's posse then head for the Harrington homestead and meet up with the Indians and Tom. Buffalo Bill convinces Brave Eagle to join forces with him to defeat the real murderers, and Simpson and his men are finally routed. Later, a grateful Steve, Dale and Tom, who have discovered that their land is indeed oil-rich, bid Buffalo Bill a fond farewell. *Animal traps. Buffalo Bill Cody. Duplicity. Frame-ups. Indians of North America. Land sales. Outlaws. Settlers. Businessmen. Fathers and daughters. Fights. Hideouts. Horses. Hunters. Jailbreaks. Kidnapping. Murder. Oil. Posses. Rescues. Romance. Sheriffs.*

Note: The working title of this film was *Return of Buffalo Bill.* For more information on the depiction of Buffalo Bill Cody in films, see above entry for *Buffalo Bill.*

Box 5 Apr 1947. *DV* 28 Mar 1947. *HR* 1 Nov 1946, p. 2. *HR* 15 Nov 1946, p. 2. *HR* 28 Mar 1947, p. 7. *MPHPD* 5 Apr 1947. *Var* 2 Apr 1947, p. 16.

THE BUFFALO BILL SHOW (Native Americans)

Dist State Rights; Wild West Film Co. Jan 1917. Si; b&w. 5 reels.

Supv William F. Cody. *Dir* John J. O'Brien.

Cast: William F. Cody.

Biography, Documentary. This documentary contains scenes featuring William F. Cody, Indian fights, including the Battle of Little Big Horn, the capture of "The Notorious Outlaw" Buck McCandells, a stage holdup, and other scenes portraying life in the "Wild West." *Indians of North America. Little Big Horn, Battle of the, 1876. United States–History–Indian Campaigns. The West.*

Note: According to contemporary news items, this film was shot years before its release, but could not be shown theatrically until Cody's death on 10 Jan 1917. Modern sources state that Cody was involved in a number of legal battles regarding his film productions and footage for this film may have been part of some litigation. An advertisement for the film claimed that *The Buffalo Bill Show* was the only "authorized" Cody picture and was "taken under the personal supervision of Buffalo Bill." (After Cody's death, Essanay released its own documentary called *The Adventures of Buffalo Bill,* which, like this film, was shot years before its release, see above.) According to this Jan 1917 advertisement, *The Buffalo Bill Show* played simultaneously at the Rialto and Strand theaters in New York City. However, no reviews, or other production information is available. Contemporary sources do not indicate whether the entire production was a recreation of past events or if some of the footage was "live action." John J. O'Brien (also listed as John D. O'Brien) may be the same as John B. O'Brien, once an Essanay actor and scenarist, who may have been involved in the 1913 Essanay Buffalo Bill production. For more historical information about Cody, please see the entry for *Buffalo Bill.*

ETR 3 Mar 1917, p. 916. *MPW* 27 Jan 1917, p. 537, 579.

BUFFALO BILL'S INDIAN WARS *see* **THE INDIAN WARS**

BUFFALO BILL'S WAGON TRAIN *see* **BUFFALO BILL IN TOMAHAWK TERRITORY**

BUFFALO STAMPEDE *see* **THUNDERING HERD**

BUGLES IN THE AFTERNOON (Irish Americans, Native Americans, Dakota)

Cagney Productions, Inc.; A William Cagney Production. *Dist* Warner Bros. Pictures, Inc. 8 Mar 1952; New York City opening: 4 Mar 1952; Prod: early Jun–mid-Jul 1951 [©Cagney Productions, Inc.; 28 Dec 1951; LP1597]. Sd (RCA Recording System); col (Technicolor). 7,612 ft. 84-85 min. Passed by the National Board of Review. PCA cert no. 15325.

Dir Roy Rowland. *Asst dir* William Kissel. *Scr* Geoffrey Homes and Harry Brown. *Dir of photog* Wilfrid M. Cline. *Spec eff* Ralph Webb. *Technicolor color consultant* Mitchell Kovaleski. *Art dir* Edward Carrere. *Film ed* Thomas Reilly. *Set dec* Lyle B. Reifsnider. *Ward* Leah Rhodes. *Mus* Dimitri Tiomkin. *Mus dir* Ray Heindorf. *Sd* C. A. Riggs. *Makeup* Gordon Bau. *Tech adv* Col. C. B. Benton.

Source: Based on the novel *Bugles in the Afternoon* by Ernest Haycox (Boston, 1944).

Cast: RAY MILLAND [(*Sgt. Kern Shafter*)], HELENA CARTER [(*Josephine Russell*)], HUGH MARLOWE [(*Capt. Edward Garnett*)], FORREST TUCKER [(*Pvt. Donovan*)], Barton MacLane [(*Capt. Myles Moylan*)], George Reeves [(*Lt. Smith*)], James Millican [(*1st Sgt. Hines*)], Gertrude Michael [(*May*)], Stuart Randall [(*Bannack Bill*)], William "Bill" Phillips [(*Pvt. Tinney*)], [Sheb Wooley (*Maj. Gen. George Armstrong Custer*)], [John Pickard (*Pvt. McDermott*)], [Dick Rich (*Bierss*)], [John War Eagle (*Red Owl*)], [Charles Evans (*Gen. Terry*)], [Nelson Leigh (*Maj. Reno*)], [Ray Montgomery (*Osborne*)], [Virginia Brissac (*Mrs. Carson*)], [John Halloran (*Big man*)], [Robert Ward Wood (*Cowpoke*)], [Buck Monroe (*Hostler*)], [Terry Wilson (*Bearded man*)], [John Doucette (*Bill*)], [Richard Kipling (*Mr. Russell*)], [Bud Osborne (*Teamster*)], [Hugh Beaumont (*Lt. Cooke*)], [Harry Lauter (*Cpl. Jackson*)], [Robert Malcolm (*Dr. Porter*)], [George Bill (*Man with gun*)], [Walter Coy (*Benteen*)], [Pepe Hern (*First scout*)], [Robert Steele (*Horseman*)], Mary Adams, Lucille Shamburger, Ray Bennett, Franklin Parker.

Western. [Print viewed]. Capt. Kern Shafter of the U.S. Cavalry is stripped of his rank and humiliated before his men for assaulting Capt. Edward Garnett with a saber. Kern, who had assaulted Garnett to avenge the honor of his fiancée, becomes a card-playing drifter and several years later journeys to the Dakota Territory to begin a new life. On the train, he meets the beautiful Josephine Russell, whom he protects from a roughneck, and although he admires her, the two say goodbye upon reaching Bismarck. Kern joins the Seventh Cavalry at Fort Abraham Lincoln, where he encounters his old comrade, Capt. Myles Moylan, who immediately promotes Kern to the rank of sergeant. Kern is far less pleased to discover that Capt. Garnett is also stationed there. Garnett threatens to break Kern unless he leaves the fort, but he insists on remaining. Kern does make one new friend, Pvt. Donovan, a feisty but amiable Irish-American soldier who respects Kern for defeating him in a fistfight. When several miners are murdered by Indians, Garnett, accompanied by a large detachment of men, confronts Chief Red Owl and his warriors on the Sioux reservation. Despite the chief's protests, Garnett sends Kern to arrest the guilty Indians, and just as the incident is about to erupt into a battle, an additional company from the fort appears on a nearby hilltop, and Red Owl agrees to give the murderers up. The Army scout is visibly relieved. The Sioux, he explains, have been pushed back too far and "won't be pushed any further." One evening Kern accompanies Josephine to her home, where, to his distress, he learns that Garnett has also been courting her. Josephine later admits that while she likes Garnett, she also is intrigued by Kern, whom she assumes is running away from some dark event in his past. Kern and Josephine kiss, but he refuses to explain the cause of his enmity with Garnett. Moylan, who knows the reason, realizes that by continually giving Kern dangerous assignments, Garnett is trying to get his old enemy killed. Without informing Kern, Moylan sends word to Washington that he has additional information regarding Kern's case. Meanwhile, Garnett sends Kern and several of his men into dangerous territory, and only by using his wits is the sergeant able to save his men from being massacred by a party of attacking Sioux. Later, Kern visits the Carson farm, where Josephine and Garnett are, like himself, seeking shelter from a storm. Exasperated by Kern's hostility toward Garnett, she asks the men to settle their differences while she cooks dinner. Garnett reminds Kern of his illicit rendezvous years earlier with Alice, then Kern's fiancée, and asserts that he has no intention

of withdrawing his attentions to Josephine. Kern knocks Garnett to the floor, which so angers Josephine that she sends Kern away. Soon after, however, as the soldiers ride out with General George Armstrong Custer to fight the Sioux, she gives Kern her good luck pin. Garnett sends Kern and Donovan into a trap, and they are surrounded by attacking Indians. Mortally wounded, Donovan orders Kern to escape while he provides cover. Donovan sings an Irish ballad and shoots Indians until he finally succumbs, and Kern returns to camp on foot. Eager for revenge, he insists on joining Garnett in battle, but as he rides toward the captain's position, he witnesses the massacre of Custer and his men at Little Big Horn. After sending out a request for help, Kern rides off to join Garnett's men in battle. As he approaches, Garnett shoots at him and the two men fight. Garnett is about to finish Kern when he is himself killed by a Sioux bullet. Kern joins Moylan in battle and is seriously injured. Later, while recuperating in the hospital, Kern learns that because of Moylan's intervention, his original rank of captain has been restored. Josephine then visits him and the two kiss. *Indians of North America. Revenge. Romantic rivalry. Secrets. United States. Army. Cavalry. Attempted murder. Battles. Bismarck (ND). General George Armstrong Custer. Dakota Indians. Escapes. Fistfights. Forts. Gunfights. Honor. Irish Americans. Little Big Horn, Battle of the, 1876. Massacres. Military life. North Dakota. Officers (Military). United States–History–Indian campaigns.*

Note: Ernest Haycox' novel was serialized in *SEP* between 21 Aug and 9 Oct 1943. According to information in the PCA file on the film in the AMPAS Library, portions of the film were shot on location in Kanab, UT, and the picture was reissued in 1963. The Breen Office suggested that the producers consult with the Association of American Indian Affairs, Inc. of New York City for their portrayal of Native Americans. A memo from the PCA on 22 May 1951 suggested that "the slaughter of Indians throughout this script must be held to minimum footage lest we get the general impression of a blood bath." The *NYT* review stated "this film should be given back to the Indians. And judging by the expression of the contributing Sioux, they want no part of it."
The film depicts some of the events that led to the 1876 Battle of Little Big Horn, in which General George Armstrong Custer and all of his men were killed. Many films have featured events surrounding the battle and the life of General Custer. For additional information, please consult the entry below for the 1941 film *They Died with Their Boots On*.
Box 9 Feb 1952. *DV* 31 Jan 1952, p. 3. *Exb* 13 Feb 1952, pp. 3240-41. *FD* 31 Jan 1952, p. 6. *Har* 2 Feb 1952, p. 19. *HCN* 19 Apr 1952. *HR* 1 Jun 1951, p. 21. *HR* 8 Jun 1951, p. 10. *HR* 13 Jul 1951, p. 13. *HR* 31 Jan 1952, p. 3. *LAT* 19 Apr 1952. *MPHPD* 2 Feb 1952, p. 1221. *NYT* 5 Mar 1952, p. 32. *Time* 11 Feb 1952. *Var* 6 Feb 1952, p. 6.

BUGLE'S WAKE see SEMINOLE UPRISING

THE BULL-DOGGER (African Americans)
Norman Film Mfg. Co. **1922.** Si; b&w. 5 reels.
Cast: Bill Pickett, Bennie Turpin, Steve Reynolds, Anita Bush.
African American, Western. [No information about the precise nature of this plot has been found.]. *African Americans. Cowboys. Rodeos.*

Note: Publicity for this film quoted Theodore Roosevelt on the star of the film: "Bill Pickett's name will go down in Western history as being one of the best trained ropers and riders the West has produced." Picket, according to the publicity, performed before the King and Queen of England. The film was shot in and around Wellington, Okmulgee, Oklahoma City and Boley, OK.

BULLWHIP (Native Americans)
Allied Artists Pictures Corp.; A Romson-Broidy Production. *Dist* Allied Artists Pictures Corp. 25 May **1958;** *Prod:* mid-Nov—late Nov 1957 [©Allied Artists Pictures Corp.; 29 Apr 1958; LP10411]. Sd; col (Deluxe); CinemaScope. 7,199 ft. 80-81 min. PCA cert no. 18902.

Exec prod William F. Broidy. *Prod* Helen Ainsworth. *Dir* Harmon Jones. *Asst dir* Ralph Slosser. *Dial supv* David Bond. *Wrt* Adele Buffington. *Dir of photog* John J. Martin. *Art dir* George Troast. *Film ed* Thor Brooks. *Set cont* Eleanor Donahoe. *Set dec* Herman Shoenbrun. *Prop master* Arthur Wasson. *Ward* Bert Henrikson. *Costumer* Marjorie D. Corso. *Mus* Leith Stevens. *Rec* Al Overton. *Makeup artist* Carie Taylor. *Prod supv* Erwin Yessin.

Song(s): "Bullwhip," music and lyrics by Hal Hopper and James Griffith, sung by Frankie Laine.

Cast: GUY MADISON [(*Steve Daly*)], RHONDA FLEMING [(*Julia "Cheyenne" O'Malley*)], James Griffith [(*Karp, later known as Slim Kramer*)], Don Beddoe [(*Judge*)], Peter Adams [(*John Parnell*)], Dan Sheridan [(*Podo*)], Burt Nelson [(*Pine Hawk*)], Al Terr [(*Lem*)], Tim Graham [(*Sheriff Pete*)], Hank Worden [(*Tex*)], Wayne Mallory [(*Larry*)], Barbara Woodell [(*Sarah Mason*)], Rush Williams [(*Judd*)], Don Shelton [(*Hotel keeper*)], Jack Reynolds [(*Sheriff*)], Frank Griffin [(*Keeler*)], J. W. Cody [(*Indian chief*)], Jack Carr [(*Trimble*)], Rick Vallin [(*Marshal*)], Saul Gorss [(*Deputy Luke*)].

Western. [*Print viewed*]. On the eve of his execution for murder, Steve Daly is visited by the corrupt judge who sentenced him. When Steve protests that he killed in self-defense, the judge offers to reverse the verdict to self-defense if Steve will agree to wed a mystery woman he identifies only as "Julia." Explaining that Julia's husband has just died and that, under the terms of his will, she must immediately marry to inherit his estate, the judge tells Steve that he is to sign a blank marriage certificate, never to know his bride's real name. After a brief wedding ceremony, Steve consummates the marriage with a single kiss, and his bride then climbs into her carriage and disappears. Freed from jail and carrying the judge's affidavit reversing his verdict, Steve steps into the street and is fired upon by Karp, a notorious gunslinger. Steve's friend Podo, who has just come to town, shoots at Karp and then gallops off with Steve. At the sheriff's office, meanwhile, Steve's bride, Julia "Cheyenne" O'Malley, pays the judge for arranging the marriage and then offers a bonus to insure Steve's safety. After collecting his money, the judge panics when he learns that Karp has failed to kill Steve and retrieve the affidavit. On the trail outside of town, Steve and Podo are met by two riders, who escort them to meet John Parnell, the owner of a fur trading company. Parnell informs Steve that his bride, Cheyenne, the strong-willed offspring of an Indian princess and a shrewd Irish fur trader, was forced into marriage to comply with her father's will and inherit the family's fur trading company. Parnell continues that under the law, Steve, as Cheyenne's husband, now legally owns the O'Malley trading company. Offering Steve a bonus if he can persuade Cheyenne to guarantee safe passage through Indian country for the Parnell wagons, Parnell procures Steve and Podo a wagon and supplies and points them in the direction of Cheyenne's trail. After Steve departs, Parnell offers Karp $5,000 to guard Steve on his mission. As Cheyenne leads the wagons to her home in Sheridan, Wyoming, thoughts of Steve dog her, causing her to impatiently snap her bullwhip. Nearing the wagon train, Podo and Steve stop for the night. The next morning, Karp rides into their camp and claims that he is seeking employment with the O'Malley wagon train. Steve invites Karp to join them, and suggests that he use an alias, prompting Karp to adopt the name Slim Kramer. When Sarah Mason, a lone settler with an ailing husband, approaches Cheyenne and begs to join the wagon train, Cheyenne refuses. Steve, however, welcomes Sarah as soon as he joins the train. Furious at Steve's intrusion, Cheyenne strikes him with her bullwhip, but he grabs the whip and pulls her from her horse. Indignant, Cheyenne takes refuge in her wagon, and that night, Steve climbs in with her. The next morning, Cheyenne tries to reclaim her authority, but Steve asserts command as her husband. Cheyenne's empathetic Indian friend, Pine Hawk, tries to defend her, but is defeated by Steve. Cheyenne then turns to her Indian blood brothers for support, but they, too, defer to Steve as her husband. Trying a new tactic, Cheyenne notifies the U.S. Marshal that the fugitive Steve Daly can be found in Sheridan. Donning a frilly dress and feigning submission to Steve, Cheyenne then plans a welcome home party for her husband, which, unknown to Steve, the marshal will attend. As they journey to Sheridan, Cheyenne learns of the affidavit and steals the document from Steve's saddlebags. Having witnessed the theft, Karp sneaks into Cheyenne's wagon and pockets the document. On the night of the party, Cheyenne welcomes Steve to her house and then introduces him to the marshal, who puts him under arrest. Realizing that the affidavit proving his innocence is missing, Steve escapes into the woods with Podo. Later, he decides to return and confront Cheyenne. Storming into his wife's bedroom, Steve demands the document and begins to search for it. When Cheyenne discovers that the document has vanished, she confesses her love for Steve and he sweeps her off her feet. The next morning, Steve meets Karp in the woods and learns that he has sold the document to Parnell, who plans to use it to coerce Cheyenne into making him a partner in her business. Just as Cheyenne is about to sign the partnership agreement, Steve barges into the room and snatches the affidavit from Parnell's hand, As Pine Hawk and Podo hold off Parnell's men, Steve gives Parnell a sound thrashing and then embraces Cheyenne. *Affidavits. Bribery. Business competition. Fur traders. Marriage–Forced by circumstances. Women in business. Attempted murder. False accusations. Gunfighters. Indians of North America. Indians of North America–Mixed blood. Judges. Parties. Wagon trains. Whips and whippings. Wills. Wyoming.*

Note: The working title of this film was *Bullwhipped*. The film opens with voice-over narration explaining how the prejudice that the character of

"Cheyenne" faced as an independent woman forced her into marrying a condemned man.

Box 9 Jun 1958. *DV* 29 May 1958, p. 3. *Exh* 25 Jun 1958, p. 4481. *FD* 3 Jun 1958, p. 6. *Har* 31 May 1958, p. 86. *HR* 15 Nov 1957, p. 12. *HR* 23 Nov 1957, p. 10. *HR* 29 May 1958, p. 3. *MPHPD* 31 May 1958, p. 849. *Var* 4 Jun 1958, p. 6.

BULLWHIPPED *see* **BULLWHIP**

BUNDLES FOR FREEDOM *see* **MR. LUCKY**

THE BURDEN OF RACE (African Americans)

Reol Productions Corp. **1921**; Chicago opening: 3 Jan 1922. Si; b&w. 6 reels.

Story Hadley J. Duncan.

Cast: Percy Verwayen, Edna Morton, Lawrence Chenault, Elizabeth Williams, Mabel Young, Arthur Ray.

Drama, African American. At a great university, a young black man who excels in both academic and athletic pursuits, falls in love with a white girl. After graduation, he becomes extremely successful in the world of business, finding in this girl a constant source of inspiration. *African Americans. Businessmen. College life. Students.*

BURDEN OF TRUTH (African Americans)

Allend'or Productions, Inc. *Dist* United Steelworkers of America. Committee on Civil Rights. **1957** [©Allend'or Productions, Inc.; 25 Sep 1957; LP10529]. Sd; b&w. 8 reels. 67 min.

Pres UNITED STEELWORKERS OF AMERICA. COMMITTEE ON CIVIL RIGHTS, DAVID J. McDONALD, I. W. ABEL, HOWARD R. HAGUE, THOMAS SHANE, JOSEPH GERMANO, JOHN W. GRAJCIAR, GILBERT C. ANAYA, BOYD L. WILSON, BERT HOUGH, THOMAS MURRAY, JOSEPH H. NEAL and FRANCIS C. SHANE. *Prod* Algernon G. Walker. *Assoc prod* W. A. Blanchard. *Dir* J. Reid Rummage. *Asst dir* Robert Agnew. [*2d asst dir* Nat Holt, Jr.]. *Wrt* Merl S. Edelman. *Dir of photog* Ralph Woolsey. [*Photog* Roger Sherman]. [*Cam asst* Bob Hossler]. [*Gaffer* Don Carstensen]. *Art dir* Don Ament. *Film ed* Melvin Shapiro. [*Sets* Harry Rief]. [*Ward mistress* Marjorie Corso]. *Mus* Paul Glass. *Sd* Phil Mitchell. [*Boom op* A. B. Roberts]. *Makeup* Carlie Taylor. *Title des* Siegfried Knop. *Assisting Allend'or Productions for the Union: Asst to the prod* Francis C. Shane. *Tech consultant* Thomas Murray, Cass Alvin, Emery F. Bacon and Boyd L. Wilson. *Public relations* Vincent D. Sweeney. [*Head grip* Paul Whitcomb]. [*Prop master* Karl Brainard]. [*Script girl* Diana Loomis].

Cast: Hari Rhodes (*Joe Hamilton*), Shirley Shawn (*Ella Mae Hamilton*), Tom Selden (*Jerry Pearson*), Robert de Coy (*Lloyd Martin*), [*The Present*: Thayer Roberts (*Hiram Pearson*)], [Jeane Wood (*Dark-haired woman*)], [Carolyn Maier (*Blonde woman*)], [and Roy Darmour (*Police sergeant*)], [*The South*: Jacquelyn Lattimore (*Loura Mae*)], [Joel Greene (*Bobby Joe Chitwood*)], [Coleman Francis (*Harvey*)], [Jack Younger (*Buddy*)], [George Offerman (*Archie*)], [Earldon Scales (*Black father*)], [Christopher Stewart (*Black child*)], [and Bill Hughes (*Otis*)], [*In College*: Karl Schanzer (*Bill*)], [Frank Kinsella (*Charlie*)], [Jack Harris (*Mr. Harrison*)], [John Brandt (*Walt*)], [and William Forrest (*Graduation speaker*)], [*Graduation Party*: Jan Shepard (*Gloria*)], [Louis Pollay (*"The lover"*)], [and Tom Riley (*Piano player*)], [*Voices*: Craig Karr (*Newscaster*)], [Chick Hearn (*Fight broadcaster*)], [Larry Berrill (*Baseball broadcaster*)], [and Hank Simms (*Announcer*)], [Members of USW Local 1414 of District #38].

Social, Drama. [*Print viewed*]. Joe and Ella Mae Hamilton, having just moved into a new neighborhood, are confronted by an angry, jeering mob of whites outside their house. As Ella Mae tries to soothe their baby, Joe thinks back to his life before he got married when he worked in a bar to make ends meet: Despite having to face repeated racial indignities and injustices, Joe dreams of joining the Army, going to college and having a career. Joe is brought back to the present by the arrival of police officers. As the officers try to calm the crowd, Joe recalls his college days: Joe attends college on the G.I. Bill and works in a café, where he meets and becomes good friends with Jerry, a white student. Jerry eventually introduces Joe to his future wife Ella Mae, and is often harassed for hanging out with Joe. Jerry resents his father for expecting him to buckle down and join the family real estate business after graduation, but decides that if he has to go into the business, Joe will be his first customer. Joe is returned to the present once again by Jerry's arrival on the scene. As the three friends watch Jerry's hypocritical father on television, preaching American racial and religious equality to a group of refugees, Jerry recalls his father's outrage at Jerry's decision to sell Joe and Ella Mae a house.

Jerry's musings are interrupted when Ella Mae serves dinner. While they eat, Joe remembers his courtship of and marriage to Ella Mae, whose quiet strength and wise advice helped him make some difficult decisions about his life: Despite the reluctance of Joe's boss at the café to award Joe a promotion, life is good for Joe. He is about to graduate from school and he and Ella Mae are becoming serious. As the courtship progresses, Ella Mae introduces Joe to her brother Lloyd, who reared her. Lloyd's assumption that Joe is going to become a teacher bothers Joe, who dreams of joining a public relations department at a major company. Ella Mae balks at Joe's grand plans and challenges him to name companies that would hire a black man for such a position. After Joe and Ella Mae marry, Lloyd and Joe have a heated argument concerning Joe's future plans. Lloyd scoffs at Joe's ambitions and predicts that he will end up working in the steel mill. Lloyd explains that he had big plans too, but grew tired of rejection and prejudice. Lloyd's predictions prove true as Joe is rejected by every company to which he applies and he is forced to seek work at the mill. Even though the work is tough, the mill affords Joe a certain degree of racial equality. He is chosen for a promotion over white competition and he socializes freely with the other men at work and during the mill picnic. Joe and Ella Mae, expecting a child, decide to move out of Lloyd's house. This angers Lloyd, who accuses Joe of not knowing his place and of wanting too much, too soon. Joe explains that he must try to make a better world for the sake of his child. The argument is left unresolved as Joe is brought back to the present, to face the angry mob outside his house. *African Americans. Employment. Friendship. Marriage. Racism. Real estate agents. Bars. College students. Fathers and sons. Foster parents. Hypocrisy. Mobs. Police. Romance. Steel mills. Television.*

Note: The following statement appears in the film's end credits: "The Union and the Producers wish to acknowledge the cooperation of USA District 38 Director Charles J. Smith, the officers and members of Local Union 1414 and the many other people without whose assistance and help this film could not have been made."

BURLESQUE IN HARLEM *see* **BREVITIES OF 1955**

THE BURNING ARROW *see* **THE CHARGE AT FEATHER RIVER**

THE BURNING CROSS (African Americans, Jewish Americans, Swedish Americans)

Somerset Pictures Corp. *Dist* Screen Guild Productions, Inc. 11 Oct **1947**; World premiere in San Francisco, CA: 28 Aug 1947; Prod: 22 May—late May 1947 at Motion Picture Center [©Somerset Pictures Corp.; 1 Sep 1947; LP1187]. Sd (RCA Sound System); b&w. 7,096 ft. 73 or 77 or 79 min. PCA cert no. 12558.

Prod Walter Colmes. *Assoc prod* Selvyn Levinson. *Dir* Walter Colmes. [*Asst dir* George Moskov]. *Orig scr* Aubrey Wisberg. *Dir of photog* Walter Strenge. *Spec eff* Ray Mercer. *Art dir* Frank Sylos. *Film ed* Jason Bernie. *Set des* Jacque Mapes. *Master of props* George Bahr. *Ward* Jimmy Wade. *Mus score* Ralph Stanley. *Sd* Ferol Redd. *Makeup* Ted Larsen.

Cast: Hank Daniels [(*Johnny Larrimer*)], Virginia Patton [(*Doris Greene*)], Dick Rich [(*Lud Harris*)], Joel Fluellen [(*Charlie West*)], John Fostini [(*Tony Areni*)], Raymond Bond [(*Chester Larrimer*)], Betty Roadman [(*Agatha Larrimer*)], Walden Boyle [(*Walter Strickland*)], Alexander Pope [(*Howard Gibbons*)], Richard Bailey [(*Pelham*)], Matt Willis [(*Mort Dauson*)], Ross Elliott, John Doucette [(*Tobey Mason*)], Tom Kennedy [(*Police sergeant*)], Marjorie Manners, Ted Stanhope [(*Elkins*)], Helen Servis, Clinton Rosemond, Glenn Allen [(*Bubby West*)], Maidie Norman [(*Kitty West*)], Jameson Shade, [Jack Shutta (*Hill*)].

Postwar life, Social, Drama. [*Not viewed*]. When wandering ex-serviceman Johnny Larrimer finally returns to his parents' home in Bridgeton, he is depressed to learn that not only has he lost his gas station job, but his best friend, Tony Areni, has become engaged to Johnny's childhood sweetheart, neighbor Doris Greene, as well. Feeling sorry for himself, Johnny begins drinking with locals Lud Harris and Tobey Mason. Lud tells the angry Johnny about an organization that is dedicated to "helping unemployed veterans," and the next day, after he has discussed Johnny with Mort Dauson and Howard Gibbons, leaders of the organization, Lud sends Johnny for a job interview at a machine shop. Although the unionized shop workers are on strike, Johnny accepts the job from the boss, Jim Todd, an organization member. As he is leaving the shop, however, Johnny is confronted and beaten by a striking worker. Later, at home, Johnny

tells Doris that Tony, who did not serve in the war, is a double-crossing "slacker." Infuriated, Doris slaps Johnny, who then provokes a bar fight with Tony. Seeing their opportunity, Lud and Tobey invite Johnny to attend an organization meeting. During the meeting, Gibbons denounces the influx of foreigners to the town and urges his listeners to join one of the many "America Only" associations. Impressed, Johnny applies for membership and is soon initiated into the Ku Klux Klan. Soon after, a rash of violence against blacks, Jews and foreign-born businessmen begins. Tony then reveals to Johnny that he saw him participating in an attack on a Swedish-born florist and warns him that "next time" he will inform the police. Later, Tony is kidnapped by Klan members and dragged to an outdoor meeting. There, Tony witnesses the tar and feathering of one of the strikers and tries to run away. Unaware that Charlie West, a black farmer, is watching the scene from a tree, Lud shoots and kills Tony. Later, Walter Strickland, a special investigator, questions Johnny about Tony's death, but Johnny reveals nothing. After Strickland tells Hill, the local police chief, his suspicions that "nightriders" killed Tony, Hill, a Klan member, apprises Dauson of the investigation. Strickland then convinces Doris to help him uncover Tony's killer by reingratiating herself with Johnny, whom Strickland suspects is somehow involved. The guilt-ridden Johnny, meanwhile, quits his job and informs Lud that he is leaving the Klan. In response, Lud threatens to harm Johnny's parents, compelling Johnny to participate in the Klan's next undertaking—preventing blacks from registering to vote. Johnny is ordered to stop Charlie, an old family friend, from registering, but is unable to dissuade the proud farmer. That night, Charlie is attacked by cloaked Klansmen, and Charlie goes to Hill for help. After a trusting Charlie reveals to Hill that he witnessed Tony's murder, Hill notifies Dauson about the development. Later, Johnny confesses all to Doris and divulges that the Klan is planning an attack on Charlie. Doris, who has forgiven Johnny, tells Strickland about Charlie, and Strickland, in turn, asks Hill to stop the attack. That night, Lud shoots and kills the defiant Charlie, then orders that his house be set on fire with his wife and father trapped inside. Deducing that Johnny is the "squealer," Dauson instructs Lud to "make an example of him." At Doris' urging, Johnny, meanwhile, has confessed to his family and is going to see Strickland when his wheelchair-bound father is beaten, and he is kidnapped by two Klansmen. Just as Lud and the Klan are about to hang Johnny, the police, having tracked the Klansmen's car, arrive on the scene. Johnny pursues the fleeing Lud and beats him into unconsciousness. Later, Dauson and Hill are arrested, and Johnny signs a confession. After Strickland praises Johnny for his courage, Doris pledges to wait for him. *Bigotry. Disillusionment. Extortion. Ku Klux Klan. Murder. Veterans.* African Americans. Antisemitism. Arson. Bars. Childhood sweethearts. Confession (Law). Drunkenness. Engagements. Family relationships. Farmers. Fights. Gas stations. Guilt. Investigations. Italian Americans. Meetings. Paralysis. Police. Rites and ceremonies. Strikes and lockouts. Tar and feathering. Witnesses. Xenophobia.

Note: Although a print of this film was not viewed, the above credits were taken from a cutting continuity deposited with the Copyright Office. The picture opens with a brief narrated montage depicting the history of the Ku Klux Klan in America. Voice-overs spoken by character "Johnny Larrimer" are heard intermittently throughout the film and are finally revealed to be his confession to the police. An article about the film in the Sep 1947 issue of *Ebony* magazine gives the following information about the production: Producer Selvyn Levinson got his inspiration for the project while he was serving in the military during World War II. At his unit in Chengtu, China, an African American staff sergeant was put in charge of an all-white aircraft battery, and Levinson was impressed with the way in which all of the soldiers worked together to make it the "most proficient...on the field." When Levinson sought financing for *The Burning Cross*, he was turned down by "every national bank in the country," according to the *Ebony* article. The picture, which cost $150,000 to make, was financed by "individuals interested in tolerance." Levinson also noted that while the writers with whom he consulted refused to "touch it," many actors volunteered their services on the film.

HR news items and production charts add the following actors to the cast: Rory Mallinson, Betty McMahon, Peggy Wynne, Herbert Wilms, Tom Daley, Victor Zimmerman, Marion Brown, Bill Murphy and Mollie MacIntosh. Their participation in the completed film has not been confirmed, however. According to a *LAT* news item, *The Burning Cross* was the first film to be shot at the newly renovated Motion Picture Center, formerly the Metro Pictures Corp. studio.

In a 12 May 1947 letter to producer-director Walter Colmes, contained in the MPAA/PCA files at the AMPAS Library, PCA director Joseph I. Breen approved the shooting script, but cautioned that "the Negroes throughout the production will at no time be shown as too subservient, and that their dialogue will be cleaned up so that the English will be grammatical." Although Breen had only minor objections to the story, *HR* announced in late Sep 1947 that the Virginia Board of Censors had banned the film, calling it "inhuman and an incitement to crime." The Board felt that the film might "arouse animosity" between blacks and whites, not "believed existing in Virginia." In Oct 1947, *Var* announced that Screen Guild Productions had filed a lawsuit against the Virginia Board before the state court of appeals. The disposition of that suit is not known.

Box 26 Jul 1947. *DV* 21 Jul 1947. *FD* 1 Aug 1947, p. 6. *Ebony* Sep 1947. *HR* 23 May 1947, p. 11, 17. *HR* 27 May 1947, p. 6. *HR* 22 Sep 1947, p. 1. *HR* 25 Sep 1947, p. 15. *HR* 29 Sep 1947, p. 13. *IFJ* 7 Jun 1947, p. 39. *LAT* 23 May 1947. *MPHPD* 26 Jul 1947. *NYT* 20 Feb 1948, p. 19. *Var* 13 Aug 1947, p. 15. *Var* 9 Oct 1947.

THE BURNING HILLS (Native Americans, Latino, Ute)
Warner Bros. Pictures, Inc.; A Warner Bros.—First National Picture. *Dist* Warner Bros. Pictures, Inc. 1 Sep **1956**; New York opening: 23 Aug 1956; Prod: mid-Feb—late Mar 1956 [©Warner Bros. Pictures, Inc.; 1 Sep 1956; LP9287]. Sd (RCA Sound Recording); col (WarnerColor); CinemaScope. 8,456 or 8,975 ft. 93-94 or 97 min. PCA cert no. 17998.

Prod Richard Whorf. *Dir* Stuart Heisler. *Asst dir* Chuck Hansen. *Scr* Irving Wallace. *Dir of photog* Ted McCord. *Art dir* Charles H. Clarke. *Film ed* Clarence Kolster. *Set dec* Frank Miller. *Cost des* Marjorie Best. *Mus* David Buttolph. *Orch* Gus Levene. *Sd* Francis Stahl. *Makeup supv* Gordon Bau. [*Gun instructor* Arvo Ojala].

Source: Based on the novel *The Burning Hills* by Louis L'Amour (New York, 1956).

Cast: TAB HUNTER [(*Trace Jordan*)], NATALIE WOOD [(*Maria Cristina Colton*)], Skip Homeier [(*Jack Sutton*)], Eduard Franz [(*Jacob Lantz*)], Earl Holliman [(*Mort Bayliss*)], Claude Akins [(*Ben Hindeman*)], Ray Teal [(*Joe Sutton*)], Frank Puglia [(*Tio Perico*)], Hal Baylor [(*Braun*)], Tyler MacDuff [(*Wes Parker*)], Rayford Barnes [(*Veach*)], Tony Terry [(*Vicente Colton*)], [Jack Williams (*Farrell*)], [Robert Herron (*Faber*)], [Ron Hargrave], Wayne Burson, Allen Pinson (*Sutton riders*)], [Dale Van Sickel (*Johnny Jordan*)], [Julian Rivero (*Miguel*)], [John Doucette (*Bartender*)], [David McMahon (*Doctor*)], [Tina Menard (*Mexican housewife*)], [Ernesto Zambrano (*Mexican laborer*)].

Western. [*Print viewed*]. After rancher Johnny Jordan is shot in the back and killed, his brother and partner Trace becomes determined to bring the guilty party to justice. Evidence found near Johnny's body reveal that several men were present during his murder: one with a limp, one with elaborate spurs, and one who smoked a certain type of cigarette. Trace's friend Miguel identifies the men as toughs who work for Joe Sutton, a powerful rancher who wants no other settlers on the range. Trace rides into the town of Esperanza, and before he climbs the wall into Sutton's ranch, he notices that several of the horses on the property bear his brother's brand. Now fully convinced that Sutton's men committed the crime, Trace draws his gun and confronts the rancher. Sutton dismisses the accusation, but when Trace threatens to take his evidence to the U.S. Cavalry at Fort Stockwell, the rancher pulls out his own gun. Trace shoots Sutton in self-defense and then escapes over the wall, whereupon the wounded Sutton angrily orders his son Jack and foreman, Ben Hindeman, to "finish the job." The young cowboy, who also was shot, rides out of town but soon loses consciousness. He is found by Maria Cristina Colton, a spirited young woman who keeps a small herd of sheep with her younger brother Vicente and her lazy uncle Perico. Maria is drawn to Trace because he reminds her of her father, a Yankee rancher who married a Mexican woman and was killed while trying to stand up to Sutton. Maria hides Trace in an abandoned mine, and while he recovers from his wound, she creates a false trail to confuse Jacob Lantz, a tracker of mixed Dutch and Ute blood, who is reluctantly working for Sutton. This temporarily slows the scout down, but when Maria realizes that Lantz and the other men in the tracking party are headed toward the mine, she urges Trace to escape and meet her later at an isolated ranch. Furious that Trace has eluded them, Jack shoots Ben and takes control of the gang. Maria brews some coffee for the men, lacing it liberally with jimson weed, and as Jack tries to force Maria to disclose Trace's whereabouts, most of the other men fall ill. Fearing for his sister's life, young Vicente reveals Trace's location, and the poisoned coffee buys Maria only a little time to ride ahead and meet Trace. At the ranch, Trace fights with and finally kills one of Sutton's men. Still just one step ahead of their pursuers, Trace and Maria cleverly conceal their tracks, and once, when Lantz has led the Sutton gang too close to them, Trace attracts a group of Indians to the area. The Indians attack Sutton's men, but three of the ruffians

escape the battle and continue the chase. Maria and Trace arrive at an unfordable river, and while she takes the horse upstream, Trace hides in the rocks and shoots at his enemies. After killing one of them, Trace fights hand to hand with Jack, finally drowning him in the river. Lantz appears with his gun, but instead of shooting at Trace and Maria, he gives them directions to Fort Stockwell. He was ordered to find the escapees, Lantz explains, not kill them, and says that he looks forward to the Cavalry's visit to Sutton's ranch. *Chases. Family relationships. Greed. Murder. Alcoholics. Ambushes. Drugging. Escapes. Evidence. Fear. Fistfights. Gunfights. Gunshot wounds. Indians of North America–Mixed blood. Justice. Laziness. Mexican Americans. Mines. Ranchers. Rivers. Romance. Scouts (Frontier). Sheepherders. Ute Indians.*

Note: Louis L'Amour's novel was serialized in *The Saturday Evening Post* (26 Nov–24 Dec 1955).

Box 4 Aug 1956. *DV* 27 Jul 1956, p. 3. *FD* 27 Jul 1956, p. 6. *HR* 24 May 1955. *HR* 17 Feb 1956, p. 8. *HR* 23 Mar 1956, p. 51. *HR* 27 Jul 1956, p. 3. *LAEx* 25 Mar 1956. *MPHPD* 28 Jul 1956, p. 2. *NYT* 24 Aug 1956, p. 15. *Var* 8 Aug 1956, p. 6.

THE BURNING JOURNEY *see* **BODY AND SOUL** (1947)

BUSTER SE MARIE (French language)

Metro-Goldwyn-Mayer Corp.; controlled by Loew's, Inc.; A Buster Keaton Production. *Dist* Metro-Goldwyn-Mayer Distributing Corp. **1931**. Sd (Western Electric Sound System); b&w. 8 reels. 80 min. Passed by the National Board of Review. French language.

Réalization de [Dir] Edward Brophy. [*Dir* Claude Autant-Lara]. [*Dial dir* André Luguet]. *Dialogue et scenario de [Dial and scr]* Richard Schayer. *Dialogue additionnel de [Addl dial]* Robert E. Hopkins. *Adaptation française de [French adpt]* Ivan Noe. *Photographie de [Photog]* Leonard Smith. *Décorateur [Art dir]* Cedric Gibbons. *Montage de [Ed]* Conrad A. Nervig. *Costumes de [Ward]* René Hubert. *Ingénieur du son [Sd eng]* Douglas Shearer.

Source: Based on the play *Parlor, Bedroom and Bath* by Charles W. Bell and Mark Swan (New York, 24 Dec 1917).

Cast: BUSTER KEATON (*Reggie Irving*), André Luguet (*Jeff Haywood*), Françoise Rosay (*Polly Hathaway*), Jeanne Helbling (*Angelique Embrey*), André Berley (*Detective*), Rolla Norman (*Fred Leslie*), Mona Goya (*Virginia Embrey*), Lya Lys (*Leila Crofton*), George Davis (*Chasseur*), Georgette Rhodes (*Nita Leslie*), Albert Pollet (*Valet*), Mireille (*La femme blonde*), [Paul Morgan].

Comedy. [*Not viewed*]. [The following plot summary is based on the English-language version of this film, *Parlor, Bedroom and Bath*; character names refer to that version. For further information regarding the English-language version, please see the note below and the entry for *Parlor, Bedroom and Bath* in the *AFI Catalog of Feature Films, 1931-40*.] Jeffrey Hayward is in love with Virginia Embrey, but Virginia refuses to marry him until her sister Angelica, who is four years older than she, finds a husband. Frustrated by Virginia's stipulation, Jeff threatens to marry Angelica himself. Meanwhile, outside the Embrey estate, Reginald Irving, a homely billboard painter, is hit by a car while walking along the road. The injured pedestrian is rushed to the Embreys', where Jeff decides to fix him up with Angelica. In order to make Reginald more appealing to the snobbish Angelica, Jeff tells her that Reggie is famous and pays women admirers to surround Reggie and make him seem important. The hapless sign painter, bewildered by all the activity, tries to escape by climbing out of his window, but he is spotted by Jeff, who tackles him and brings him back. Reggie is soon put in charge of managing Angelica's eight million dollar estate. Jeff orders him to stay and continue the hoax until marriage arrangements between him and Angelica are made firm. Believing that Reggie will appear more desirable to Angelica if he is caught having an affair with another woman, Jeff enlists the help of gossip columnist Polly Hathaway, who agrees to meet Reggie at a hotel. Knowing that the half-witted Reggie is incapable of romancing a woman properly, Jeff gives him step-by-step instructions to seduce his date when he gets to the hotel. Jeff's plan goes awry when Reggie mistakes the dejected Nita, a friend of the Embreys', who has just had a quarrel with her husband Frederick, for his date and takes her to the hotel. On the way to the hotel, Reggie's car stalls on railroad tracks and is destroyed by a passing train, forcing the couple to hitchhike in the pouring rain. Drenched, the two arrive at the hotel, while Angelica and Virginia set out in search of them. Nita is shocked when Reggie tries to force his intentions upon her, and she attempts to flee. When Polly arrives at the hotel, she begins to rehearse Jeff's romancing instructions with Reggie. While Polly teaches Reggie how to kiss, Jeff arrives and,

realizing that Reggie has bungled the scheme, warns him that Nita's jealous husband is on his way to kill him. Again, not knowing that it is Polly with whom he is supposed to be caught, Reggie turns to Leila Crofton, another of Angelica's friends, and begins making love to her. Virginia and Angelica burst into the room in the middle of Reggie's attack, but before they are able to react, Frederick arrives on the scene and pulls a gun on Reggie. Jeff manages to save Reggie, but when a gunshot rings out, Polly falls to the floor and is believed to be dead. Everyone flees from the scene when the police arrive, except for Reggie, who tries to hide the body. When Polly regains consciousness, she urges Reggie to use Jeff's lovemaking method on Angelica, and it appears that he and Angelica will become lovers. *Bumblers. Hoaxes. Jealousy. Mistaken identity. Seduction. Automobile accidents. Bellboys. Elopement. Gossip columnists. Hitchhiking. Hotels. Infidelity. Marriage. Police. Romantic rivalry. Sign painters and sign painting. Sisters. Trains.*

Note: M-G-M made French and German versions of the 1931 film *Parlor, Bedroom and Bath*, which was directed by Edward Sedgwick and starred Buster Keaton and Charlotte Greenwood (please see the *AFI Catalog of Feature Films, 1931-40*; F3.3380). The onscreen credits for the French version were taken from a studio cutting continuity. According to the *Var* review, most of this film was shot on location at Buster Keaton's Beverly Hills home. A biography of Keaton notes that when the actor was first shown the working script for this farce comedy, he took an instant disliking to it and indicated that it was the type of comedy he did not appreciate. An earlier film based on the same play was Metro's 1920 production, also entitled *Parlor, Bedroom and Bath*, which starred Eugene Pallette and Ruth Stonehouse, and was directed by Edward Dillon (see *AFI Catalog of Feature Films, 1911-20*; F1.3361).

Other language version(s):

Casanova wider Willen (German language)

1931; Sd.(Western Electric Sound System); b&w.;. German language.

Dir Edward Brophy. *Scr* Richard Schayer. *Photog* Leonard Smith.

German-language cast: Buster Keaton, Marion Lessing, Paul Morgan, Egon von Jordan, Françoise Rosay, Leni Stengel, Gerda Mann, George Davis, Wolfgang Zilzer. [*German version not viewed*]

BY RIGHT OF BIRTH (African Americans, Latino, Native Americans)

Lincoln Motion Picture Co. *Dist* Lincoln Motion Picture Co. **1921**; World premiere in Los Angeles: 22 Jun 1921; Prod: 2 Apr—25 Apr 1921. Si; b&w. 6 reels, 6,000 ft..

Dir Harry Gant. *Scen* Dora Mitchell. *Story* George P. Johnson. *Cam* Harry Gant. *Cost des* Claudius Booker.

Song(s): "Juanita," music and lyrics by John C. Spikes, written to accompany the film.

Cast: Clarence Brooks (*Philip Jones*), Anita Thompson (*Juanita Cooper/Helen Childers*), Webb King (*"Pinky" Webb*), Beatrice George (*Mary Childer, also known as "Mother" Agnes*), Lester Bates (*Frank Cooper*), Lew Meehan (*Manuel Romero*), Minnie Provost (*Minnie Childers*), Baby Ruth Kimbrough (*Helen Childers, as a baby*), Grace Ellenwood (*Geraldine Cooper*), Big Tree (*John Childers*), Lucille Moulton, Nancy Brown, Thelma Worth, Gladys La Vett, Marjory Wakefield.

African American, Social, Drama. [*Viewed print incomplete*]. Juanita Cooper, a student at a university in California, is the foster-daughter of Frank Cooper, a wealthy retired rancher, and his wife Geraldine, who adopted her, believing that she was of American Indian ancestry. She becomes friends with brilliant African-American law student Philip Jones, who is also a popular athlete. When Geraldine loses heavily at bridge, she backs a nefarious scheme of Mexican-American stockbroker Manuel Romero to acquire valuable Oklahoma oil leases belonging to Freedmen. Many of these Freedmen, former black slaves who had Indian owners, and the descendants of these slaves, are unaware that the land allotted by the government to newly-freed slaves contains oil. Romero learns of land belonging to Helen Childers, the missing granddaughter of an aged Indian woman, Minnie Childers. Minnie's son John married a Freedman, and she has not heard from the family since they left Oklahoma for California long ago. In California, while Romero's chauffeur, "Pinky" Webb, a correspondence school detective, does some snooping with Geraldine, Romero sends a forged lease for the property in Helen's name to the government in Oklahoma. Although Pinky does so much walking that at one point his shoes begin to smoke, Geraldine learns that Juanita is actually Helen Childers: After her father was killed in an accident, Frank rescued the baby Helen from a wagon; the baby's

mother was never found. Juanita, upon learning of her heritage, leaves home. "Mother" Agnes, an African-American matron who devotes her life to helping homeless black girls, befriends Juanita. Philip, now an up-and-coming attorney, meets Juanita again while he is fishing and helps her to retrieve her horse, which threw her. He now actively pursues a friendship with her, as race is no longer a concern that could separate them. After learning that the forgery scheme has not worked, Romero finds Juanita and gets her to sign a lease for the land for a small amount of money. Minnie, meanwhile, arrives in California to look for her son and hires Philip as a legal adviser for a substantial yearly salary. When Philip learns of Romero's scheme, they fight, and Romero is killed in an automobile chase. Philip then discovers that "Mother" Agnes is actually Juanita's real mother. The family has a happy reunion in Philip's office, where Juanita introduces "Mother" Agnes to Frank, and Juanita, "by right of birth," acquires her fortune. *African Americans. Foster parents. Lawyers. Long-lost relatives. Mothers and daughters. Parentage. Amateur detectives. Athletes. California. Chauffeurs. Fishing. Forgers and forgery. Grandmothers. Horses. Impersonation and imposture. Indians of North America. Landlords. Law students. Mexican Americans. Oil. Oklahoma. Riding accidents. Universities.*

Note: Interior scenes were shot at Berwilla Studios. According to information in the George P. Johnson Collection at the UCLA Special Collections Library, track scenes were shot at Occidental College and at Los Angeles High School, and other location work was done in Griffith Park. According to *The Sentinel*, Minnie Prevost was an Osage Indian. *The Sentinel* also noted that African-American scenarist Dora Mitchell who had written for the Morosco studio. The newspaper commended her for making the scenario "strikingly free of so many absurdities so often seen in colored productions."

The *Daily Herald* praised the company for making the film "free from racial propaganda such as has been characteristic in several similar productions attempted by other concerns." The *Examiner* stated, "Every detail of the plot supports the theme partly expressed in the title—the right of the transplanted race to a little pride of its own." Information in the Johnson Collection lists L. C. Shumway as being paid for two weeks of work on the film. Shumway, a white actor, was not mentioned in reviews or listed in a final cast sheet. It is possible that he was originally scheduled to play the role of "Manuel Romero."

Billboard 16 Jul 1921. *California Voice (Oakland, CA)* 2 Jul 1921. *ChiDef* 24 Sep 1921, p. 6. *Daily Herald (Los Angeles)* 18 Jun 1921. *LAEx* 23 Jun 1921. *New Age (Los Angeles)* 26 Jun 1921. *Sentinel (San Antonio, TX)* 9 Jul 1921.

C-MAN (Dutch Americans)

Laurel Films, Inc. *Dist* Film Classics, Inc. May **1949**; Prod: New York opening: 27 May 1949 [©Laurel Films, Inc.; 16 May 1949; LP2286]. Sd; b&w. 8 reels, 6,924 ft. 77 min. PCA cert no. 04774.

Exec prod Rex Carlton. *Prod* Joseph Lerner. *Dial dir* Gene Frankel. *Orig scr* Berne Giler. *Dir of photog* Gerald Hirschfeld. *Spec eff* Hugo A. Casolaro and Milton M. Gottlieb. *Art dir* Sal Scappa, Jr. *Film ed* Geraldine Lerner. *Set des* William Noel Salter. *Mus comp and cond* Gail Kubik. *Sd* Reeves Sound Studios. *Makeup* Ira Senz and Danby. *Prod assoc* Ralph Porter. *Unit mgr* George W. Ackerson, Jr. *Const supv* William Nallan. *Elec supv* Arthur Maher.

Song(s): "Do It Now," words and music by Gail Kubik and Larry Neill.

Cast: DEAN JAGGER [(*Cliff Holden, also known as William Hara*)], John Carradine [(*"Doc" Spencer*)], Lottie Elwen [(*Kathe Van Boren*)], Rene Paul [(*Matthew Royal*)], Walter Vaughn [(*Inspector Brandon*)], Adelaide Klein [(*Minnie Hoffman*)], Edith Atwater [(*Lydia Brundage*)], and introducing Harry Landers (*Owney* [*Shore*]), [Jean Ellyn (*Birdie Alton*)], [Walter Brooke (*Joe*)].

Crime, Drama. [*Print viewed*]. In New York City, customs agent Cliff Holden learns that his colleague, Steve Regan, who had been investigating a ring of jewel thieves, has been murdered. Cliff also learns that around the same time, Lydia Brundage purchased an insurance policy for a $500,000 diamond necklace, then reported it stolen in France two weeks later. Cliff's superior, Inspector Brandon, tells him that one of the suspected thieves of the necklace, Matthew Royal, will be flying from Paris to New York, then gives him an airline ticket for a seat next to Royal's. Cliff takes his phony identification establishing him as "William Hara" and immediately leaves for France. While waiting to board the plane in Paris, Cliff meets a Dutch woman, Kathe Van Boren, who is flying to New York to marry her fiancé Joe. In New York, meanwhile, Joe is shot to death in his apartment by gangsters Birdie Alton and Owney Shore, who have broken in to steal Kathe's immigration papers. Back in Paris, Cliff and Kathe board the plane, then realize that they are sitting across the aisle from one another. When Royal takes the seat next to Cliff's and notices Kathe leaning across to speak with him, he offers to trade seats

with her. Sometime after takeoff, Kathe goes back to use the rest room, and is followed by "Doc" Spencer, a disgraced surgeon who is now working for the gang. Doc knocks her out, injects her with a sedative and returns to his seat. When an unconscious Kathe is discovered by the flight attendant, Doc steps forward, "diagnoses" shock, orders an ambulance to be waiting for her when they land, and then puts Lydia's necklace into a bandage and wraps it around her head. After the plane makes an emergency landing, Kathe is rushed into an ambulance, and because they have her immigration papers, Birdie and Owney are permitted inside with Kathe. On the way to the hospital, Kathe begins to wake up, so Owney knocks her out with the butt of his pistol. Birdie tries to grab the necklace, and after the ambulance crashes, Kathe stumbles away, finds the necklace and arrives at Joe's place in a taxi. There, Cliff tells her what happened to Joe, and Kathe explains that she was attacked on the plane, never seeing her assailant. Cliff then tells Kathe to go to the home of his friend, Minnie Hoffman, who will help her hide from the immigration officials who will likely now pursue her. Later, Owney and Birdie break into Joe's place, and after Owney overhears Joe speaking about Doc, Owney escapes and finds Doc at his hotel. Posing as a fellow guest, Cliff goes to Doc's room, where he admits that Royal murdered Steve. Just then, Owney arrives and knocks Cliff unconscious. When he wakes up, Cliff is at Lydia's home, and she introduces herself. She says that while she was in Paris, Royal offered to sell her the stolen necklace for $250,000, and she agreed, saying that she could pay him in New York. After Lydia then offers Cliff $100,000 for the necklace and is rejected, she leaves. Later, Cliff goes back to Lydia's place and while eavesdropping through a window, sees Owney demanding all the money at gunpoint, as Royal stands by. When Owney reaches for the money, Royal suddenly tosses a knife into his back, killing him. Cliff jumps through the window, subdues Royal and calls the police. Later, Kathe arrives with the officers, and Cliff arranges for his new sweetheart, Kathe, to be placed in Minnie's custody. *Airplanes. Aliens. Illegal. Customs officials. Investigations. Jewel thieves. Physicians. Aliases. Ambulances. Apartments. Confession (Law). Dutch. Engagements. Hotels. Hypodermic needles. Insurance. Murder. New York City. Paris (France). Shootings. Stewardesses. Taxicabs. United States. Customs Service.*

Note: The onscreen credits include the following written prologue: "Dedicated to the Customs Agents of the U.S. Treasury Department, without whose assistance this film could not have been made." The film contains intermittent voice-over narration spoken by Dean Jagger. According to a 16 Jun 1949 *HR* news item, *C-Man* was the first Laurel Films production. According to information in the MPAA/PCA Collection at the AMPAS Library, the script was developed from Berne Giler's and producer/director Joseph Lerner's original idea. The *DV* review notes that the story was "based on facts" from the Customs Dept. files. The film was shot on location in New York City.

Box 30 Apr 1949. *DV* 3 Jun 1949, p. 3. *FD* 26 May 1949, p. 6. *HR* 3 Jun 1949, pp. 3-4. *HR* 16 Jun 1949, p. 2. *MPHPD* 23 Apr 1949, pp. 4581-82. *NYT* 28 May 1949, p. 11. *Var* 20 Apr 1949, p. 18.

UN CABALLERO DE FRAC (Spanish language)

Films Paramount; controlled by Paramount Publix Corp. *Dist* Paramount Publix Corp. **1931**; San Juan, Puerto Rico opening: 3 Oct 1931; San Antonio, Texas opening: 1 Jan 1932; Prod: Apr 1931 at the Paramount studios in Joinville, France. Sd; b&w. 10 reels. *Country of origin* France. Spanish language.

Dir Roger Capellani and Carlos San Martín. *Scr* Saint-Granier. *Adpt and Spanish dial* Honorio Maura. *Photog* Ted Pahle.

Song(s): "Dúo de amor," "Canción cómica," "Tonadilla" and "Romanza," music by Charles Borel-Clerc, Paul Barnaby and Milton Ager, lyrics by José Luis Salado.

Source: Based on the play *L'homme en habit* by Yves Mirande and André Picard (Paris, 1922).

Cast: Roberto Rey (*André de Dussange*), Gloria Guzmán (*Totoche*), Rosita Díaz Gimeno (*Susana de Dussange*), Gabriel Algara (*Pierre D'Allouville*), Luis Llaneza (*Buffetaut*), Antonio Martiánez (*Soyer*), Marita Angeles (*Gaby*), José Medina (*Louis*), Kuindós (*Guildé*), Antoñita Colomé (*Ninette*), Antonio Monjardin (*Firmin*), Carlos Martínez Baena (*Maître*), Pedro Elviro "Pitouto", "Antonet", "Béby".

Musical comedy. [*Not viewed*]. Count André de Dussange, a young aristocrat, appears to all the ladies like a legendary prince, but in fact, he is experiencing severe economic problems and is even about to have his furniture seized. One evening, André takes a woman named Totoche away from another man, and from then on, one misfortune

follows another. The count's wife Susana wants a divorce, and her husband's relationship with Totoche the previous evening provides an opening for her, as secretary of the court, to move ahead with the attachment. André loses everything except for his dress dinner suit, which he continues to wear. Dressed so, he is mistaken for an extra in a movie, then he unwittingly attends a funeral. When he reads an advertisement that the Montmartre Follies is seeking a man in tails, he goes to apply. Waiting for him is his wife, who tells him that his uncle has died and that they will inherit a large fortune if they continue as husband and wife, whereupon they reconcile. *Marriage. Nobility. Paris (France). Poverty. Divorce. Funerals. Infidelity. Inheritance. Mistaken identity. Motion picture actors and actresses.*

Note: The working title of this film was *Un hombre de frac*. A French-language version was also made in 1931 at Joinville, entitled *Un homme en habit*, which was directed by René Guissart and Robert Bossis, and starred Fernand Gravey and Suzy Vernon. No information concerning any showings in the U.S. of the French version has been located. In 1927, Paramount released an English-language film based on the same source, entitled *Evening Clothes*, which was directed by Luther Reed and starred Adolphe Menjou and Virginia Valli (see *AFI Catalog of Feature Films, 1921-30*; F2.1558).

EL CABALLERO DE LA NOCHE (Spanish language)
Fox Film Corp. *Dist* Fox Film Corp. 1932; New York opening: 19 Nov 1932; Prod: Aug—Sep 1932. Sd; b&w. 8 reels. Passed by the National Board of Review. Spanish language.
Dirección de [*Directed by*] James Tinling. [*Adpt* Paul Perez and William Kernell]. [*Spanish version by* José López Rubio]. [*Photog* Sidney Wagner].
Song(s): "El día de la ejecución," "Es un ladrón," "Brindemos siempre," "La miniatura," "Jai-jo, jai-jo (Canto de los cazadores)," "Amame," "Unidos siempre (Siempre unidos)," "El caballero de la noche" and "Canción del bandolero," music and lyrics by William Kernell, José Mojica and Troy Sanders, lyrics in Spanish by José Mojica.
Source: Based on the film *Dick Turpin* by Charles Darnton and Charles Kenyon (Fox Film Corp., 1925).
Cast: JOSE MOJICA (*Dick Turpin*), Mona Maris (*Lady Elena*), Andrés de Segurola (*Conde Churlton*), Romualdo Tirado (*Barón Fenwick*), Manuel París (*Tom King*), Lita Santos (*Mary*), [Blanca Vischer], [Carmen Rodríguez].
Adventure, Musical. [*Not viewed*]. In eighteenth century England, a crowd, including Barón Fenwick and Conde Churlton, has gathered to witness a hanging. Dick Turpin, who is a masked bandit wanted by the monarch, rides in a disguise though the crowd singing a song which mocks the wealthy. When guards chase after him, the crowd comes to his rescue and allows him a safe getaway. On the highway, he robs Fenwick and Churlton of a bag of gold and Churlton's snuffbox, which is carved with the likeness of his fiancée, Fenwick's niece, Lady Elena. Dick gallops away and arrives at a tavern, where he is a well-loved guest. He shows the barmaids the snuffbox and proclaims Lady Elena to be his new love, just as she comes into the inn. She angrily takes the box from him and goes to her room. Churlton and Fenwick arrive to meet Elena, and while Fenwick goes to speak with her, Churlton boasts of having cheated a robber out of a bag of gold, and Dick overhears him. Churlton joins Fenwick and Elena, interrupting her protests against her intended marriage. Dick, in his mask, robs the trio of their last bag of gold, yet pointedly, does not take the snuffbox. He escapes from the room, and the men chase after his companion Tom, believing him to be Dick. He then re-enters Elena's room and asks her permission to take the snuffbox. Without waiting for an answer, Dick grabs the box, as Churlton and Fenwick return, and escapes. That evening, Dick, Tom and a group of their followers overtake a group of soldiers on their way to guard Churlton's castle during the wedding festivities. Disguised as Lieutenant Barclay, Dick is ordered by Churlton to guard Elena. The next morning, Churlton and Elena, guarded by Dick, ride in the countryside. Wishing to be alone with Elena, Churlton sends Dick away, only to be accosted by the masked bandit, whom he soon finds locked in an embrace with Elena. Dick escapes and returns disguised again as the lieutenant to guide them back to the castle. Elena receives a letter from Dick asking her to meet him in the evening on her balcony. At the rendezvous, they kiss and Elena asks him to remove his mask. Meanwhile, the real lieutenant informs Churlton of the ruse, and they rush to Elena's room. Dick is alerted by Tom, and he hurries from the room, telling Elena where his campsite will be, but forgetting to collect his mask, which Churlton secretly finds and

pockets. Later that evening, believing that she has snuck off without being noticed, Elena inadvertently leads Churlton's men to Dick's campsite, where they arrest him. Before Dick is to be hanged, Tom gets the hangman inebriated to the point of unconsciousness. He then takes the hangman's hood and parades to the gallows. Dick is led into the square singing, and when Tom fakes a struggle with the noose, Churlton and Fenwick are tricked, and the men are able to elude the soldiers and escape to Elena's awaiting coach. As they pass the tavern where Elena and Dick first met, the barmaids throw flowers in their wake. *Adventurers. Great Britain–History. Masked bandits. Nobility. Romance. Barmaids. Castles. Chases. Drunkenness. Engagements. Escapes. Gold. Guards. Hanging. Hotels. Impersonation and imposture. Officers (Military). Robbery. Snuff boxes and bottles. Uncles.*

Note: The plot summary was based on a screen continuity in the Twentieth Century-Fox Produced Scripts Collection, and the onscreen credits were taken from a screen credit sheet in the Twentieth Century-Fox Records of the Legal Department, both of which are at the UCLA Theater Arts Library. The working titles of this film were *Dick Turpin* and *Tu amor o la vida*. This film was based on the 1925 English-language film produced by Fox entitled *Dick Turpin*, which was directed by John G. Blystone and starred Tom Mix and Kathleen Myers (see *AFI Catalog of Feature Films, 1921-30*; F2.1350).
CM Jan 1933, p. 4.

CABIN IN THE SKY (African Americans)
Metro-Goldwyn-Mayer Corp.; controlled by Loew's Inc. *Dist* Loew's Inc. 9 Apr **1943**; New York opening: 27 Mar 1943; Prod: 31 Aug—29 Oct 1942 [©Loew's Inc.; 9 Feb 1943; LP11861]. Sd (Western Electric Sound System); b&w. 8,862 ft. 98 min. Passed by the National Board of Review. PCA cert no. 8964.
Prod Arthur Freed. *Assoc prod* Albert Lewis. *Dir* Vincente Minnelli. [*Asst dir* Al Shenberg]. *Scr* Joseph Schrank. [*Contr wrt* Marc Connelly]. *Dir of photog* Sidney Wagner. *Art dir* Cedric Gibbons. *Assoc* Leonid Vasian. *Film ed* Harold F. Kress. *Set dec* Edwin B. Willis. *Assoc* Hugh Hunt. *Cost supv* Irene. *Assoc* Shoup. *Men's cost* Gile Steele. *Mus adpt* Roger Edens. *Mus dir* Georgie Stoll. *Orch* George Bassman. *Choral arr* Hall Johnson. [*Dance dir* Archie Savage]. *Rec dir* Douglas Shearer. [*Unit mgr* Charles Levin]. [*Unit prod mgr* Gil Kurland].
Music: "Going Up" by Duke Ellington.
Song(s): "Happiness Is a Thing Called Joe," "Life's Full O' Consequence" and "Li'l Black Sheep," music by Harold Arlen, lyrics by E. Y. Harburg; "Cabin in the Sky" and "Honey in the Honeycomb," music by Vernon Duke, lyrics by John Latouche; "Taking a Chance on Love," music by Vernon Duke, lyrics by John Latouche and Ted Fetter.
Source: Based on the musical play *Cabin in the Sky* book by Lynn Root, lyrics by John Latouche, music by Vernon Duke, as produced by Albert Lewis in association with Vinton Freedley (New York, 25 Oct 1940).
Cast: Ethel Waters (*Petunia Jackson*), Eddie "Rochester" Anderson (*Little Joe Jackson*), Lena Horne (*Georgia Brown*), Louis Armstrong (*The trumpeter*), Rex Ingram (*Lucius/Lucifer, Jr.*), Kenneth Spencer (*Rev. Green/The General*), John W. "Bubbles" Sublett (*Domino Johnson*), Oscar Polk (*The Deacon/[Sgt.] Fleetfoot*), Mantan Moreland (*First Idea Man*), Willie Best (*Second Idea Man*), Fletcher "Moke" Rivers (*Third Idea Man*), Leon "Poke" James (*Fourth Idea Man*), Bill Bailey (*Bill*), Ford L. "Buck" Washington (*Messenger boy*), Butterfly McQueen (*Lily*), Ruby Dandridge (*Mrs. Kelso*), Nicodemus (*Dude*), Ernest Whitman (*Jim Henry*), Duke Ellington and his Orchestra, The Hall Johnson Choir, [Rita Christiani (*Specialty dancer, Hell seq/Jitterbug number*)], [Kathleen Hartsfield, Lawaune Ingram, Jas. Burch, Byron Ellis, Jieno Moxzer, Artie Brandon, June Decuire, Louise Ritchie, Jules Adger, Bernard Bradley, Curry Lee Calmes, Bobby Johnson, Henry Roberts, John Thomas (*Specialty dancers, Hell seq*)], [William Gillespie, Edward Short, Arthur Walker (*"Little Black Sheep" soloists*)], [Meade Lux Lewis (*"Take a Chance on Love" whistling solo*)].
African American, Fantasy, Musical. [*Print viewed*]. Hopeful that her gambling, ne'er-do-well husband Little Joe Jackson has finally reformed, Petunia suggests that he have Rev. Green burn his dice and release the devil's hold on him. A religious woman and loving wife, Petunia is heartened by Little Joe's promise to repent his sins in church. Little Joe soon resumes his gambling, however, when gambler Domino Johnson entices him to return to the casino at Jim Henry's Paradise Café. Petunia later goes in search of Little Joe, only to discover that he has been shot in a gunfight at the Paradise Café. As Petunia prays over her wounded husband, Lucifer, Jr., the ghost of

Little Joe's friend Lucius, enters the room and orders Little Joe to "report to duty." Little Joe does not believe that he is dying until Lucifer, Jr. and his three aides show him his lifeless body. When the General, responding to Petunia's prayers, suddenly appears in the room, Lucifer, Jr. engages him in a battle for Little Joe's soul. While Sgt. Fleetfoot is sent by the General to get a judgment on Little Joe's case from the Lord, Lucifer, Jr. predicts that Little Joe's involvement with vamp Georgia Brown will result in his banishment to Hell. The Lord determines that Little Joe is not fit for Heaven, but he permits Little Joe to return to Earth for six months and prove his worth. With no recollection of his meeting with the Lord or Lucifer, Jr., Little Joe regains consciousness and begins his six-month reprieve. Petunia believes her husband's recovery to be a miracle, but both she and Little Joe are unaware that Lucifer, Jr. and the General will be talking to his conscience and battling for his soul. No sooner does Little Joe resume his daily life than his gambling pals, Jim Henry and Dude, who have been sent by Lucifer, Jr., try to tempt him into a game of dice. Petunia chases Jim and Dude away, but Lucifer, Jr. devises another scheme to distract Little Joe and make him backslide into Hell. Heeding the advice of those working at the Hotel Hades Idea Department, Lucifer, Jr. decides to corrupt Little Joe with riches, and sends him a winning lottery ticket. Little Joe's chances at getting into Heaven improve when he plans to use the money to buy Petunia a washing machine and a house, but when Georgia intervenes, Little Joe returns to the Paradise Café. Petunia succeeds in winning back her husband by going to the casino and singing better than Georgia, but before they leave, a gun battle ensues and Petunia and Little Joe are shot and killed. Furious at Lucifer, Jr.'s meddling, the General sends down a storm and wrecks the Paradise Café. In Purgatory, Petunia is told that she is eligible to pass through the Pearly Gates into Heaven, while Little Joe is rejected. It is only after Little Joe repents and the Lord vouches for him that the General reverses his decision and allows Little Joe to join his wife in Heaven. Moments after he is told of the decision, Little Joe realizes that his brush with the afterlife was all a dream, and vows to change his ways. *African Americans. Afterlife. Compulsive gamblers. The Devil. Marriage. Moral reformation. Religiosity. Biblical characters. Casinos. Churches. Clergy. Death and dying. Dice. Fistfights. Ghosts. Gunshot wounds. Heaven. Infidelity. Jealousy. Singers. Sweepstakes. Temptresses. Tornadoes.*

Note: Actors Ethel Waters and Rex Ingram appeared in the 1940 Broadway production of *Cabin in the Sky* and reprised their roles for this film. The Broadway production also starred Katherine Dunham, Dooley Wilson and Todd Duncan. An Apr 1942 *HR* news item noted that M-G-M purchased the film rights to the musical play for $40,000, and that the producers of the Broadway show lost $25,000 during its New York run. *Cabin in the Sky* marked Vincente Minnelli's first comprehensive screen directorial assignment. Prior to this film, Minnelli had directed stage shows and individual musical numbers in two Judy Garland films. Although some modern sources refer to *Cabin in the Sky* as Lena Horne's first film, she actually made her motion picture debut in the 1938 Million Dollar Production *The Duke Is Tops* (see below) and had also appeared in the 1942 M-G-M film *Panama Hattie.*

According to a Jul 1942 *HR* news item, writer Marc Connelly contributed to the screenplay by "bending the storyline to make 'Happiness Is a Thing Called Joe' a plot point." Modern sources list Eustace Cocrell as a contributor to the screenplay, and note that Busby Berkeley directed one of the film's musical numbers. An early Aug 1942 *HR* news item noted that Gene Kelly was set to direct dances, but his participation in the final film is unlikely. Although news items in *HR* announced that Paul Robeson was being considered for a starring role, and that Cab Calloway was set for an "important" role opposite Waters, neither Calloway nor Robeson appeared in the film. Various news items in *HR* list actors Raymond Turner, Clinton Rosemond and Napoleon Whiting in the cast, but their appearance in the released film has not been confirmed.

According to an Apr 1942 *HR* news item, this picture was to have been the first of three M-G-M "all-Negro" musicals. M-G-M considered producing a second all-black cast film, a motion picture version of George Gershwin's *Porgy and Bess*, but made no additional all-black cast films. *Cabin in the Sky* featured only two songs from the original stage musical, "Taking a Chance on Love" and "Cabin in the Sky." One musical number written especially for the picture, "I Gotta Song," was removed from the film before its release. According to modern sources, the film cost approximately $680,000, making it one of producer Arthur Freed's least expensive musicals of the 1940s. Modern sources note that prominent caricaturist Al Hirschfeld designed posters for the picture. The song "Happiness Is a Thing Called Joe" was nominated for an Academy Award in the category of Best Song.

AmCin Jun 1943, p. 215. *Box* 13 Feb 1943. *DV* 10 Feb 1943, pp. 3-4. *FD* 15 Feb 1943, p. 5. *HR* 7 Apr 1942. *HR* 14 Apr 1942, p. 2. *HR* 25 May 1942, p. 2. *HR* 23 Jul 1942, p. 2. *HR* 31 Jul 1942, p. 4. *HR* 6 Aug 1942, p. 2. *HR* 20 Aug 1942, p. 8. *HR* 24 Aug 1942, p. 7. *HR* 1 Sep 1942, p. 19. *HR* 22 Sep 1942, p. 2. *HR* 2 Oct 1942, p. 2. *HR* 10 Feb 1943, p. 3. *HR* 1 Jun 1943, p. 4. *MPD* 10 Feb 1943. *MPH* 13 Feb 1943. *MPHPD* 13 Feb 1943, p. 1157. *NYT* 28 Mar 1943, p. 19. *Var* 10 Feb 1943, p. 8.

THE CACTUS KID (Native Americans)

Reliable Pictures Corp. *Dist* State Rights; William Steiner. **1934**. Sd; b&w. 6 reels. Passed by the National Board of Review.

Pres BERNARD B. RAY. *Assoc prod* Harry S. Webb. *Dir* Harry S. Webb. *Asst dir* Gene George. *Story* William Nolte. *Dial* Carl Krusada. *Cont* Rose Gordon. *Photog* J. Henry Kruse. *Ed* Fred Bain. *Sd* Oscar Lagerstrom.

Cast: JACK PERRIN (*Cactus Kid* [*Jack*]), Fred Hume (*Jimmie* [*Kane*]), Philo McCullough (*Duncan*), Charles Whitaker ([*"Killer"*] *Plug* [*Perkins*]), Jo [sic] de la Cruz (*Cheyenne*), Jayne Regan (*Beth*), Tom London (*Sheriff*), Kit Guard (*Smiley*), Tina Menard (*Rosie*), Wally Wales (*Andy*), Starlight (*Himself*).

Western. [*Print viewed*]. After presenting rancher Duncan with a catch of wild horses, cowboys "Cactus Kid" Jack and Jimmie Kane ride to town to collect their $1,000 payment from him. While buying a new outfit for Rosie, his saloon girl sweetheart, "Killer" Plug Perkins overhears Jack tell his girl friend Beth, who runs the clothing store, about his profits, and rushes to tell Cheyenne, his half-Indian cohort, about the money. In the saloon, Jimmie, who has been drinking heavily with Duncan, confronts Jack about how the money should be spent, and Jack angrily insists on taking the bankroll himself. Later, however, Jimmie apologizes to Jack, agreeing to invest their profits as Jack wishes, and Jack happily returns the bankroll to him with instructions to ride back to Duncan's ranch and pay off the ranch hands. On the trail to Duncan's, however, Cheyenne hurls a deadly knife at Jimmie's back and, after stealing the money, overcomes his superstitions long enough to help Plug burn Jimmie's body. Soon after, while returning to Duncan's ranch, Jack sees Cheyenne and Plug riding in the distance and hears Cheyenne playing "Swanee River" on his battered harmonica. When Jimmie fails to show up, Jack organizes an exhaustive search but finds no clues. Broke, Jack begins to collect more wild horses to sell to Duncan and, during the round-up, stumbles across Jimmie's belt buckle and a mysterious piece of metal, which he later discovers is a piece from a harmonica. Unimpressed by Jack's finds, the sheriff warns Jack that the townspeople suspect him of killing Jimmie. Determined now to find out what happened to his partner, Jack tracks Cheyenne and Plug to their guarded hideout and eventually draws Cheyenne to his cabin, where he plies him with alcohol. After inspecting Cheyenne's harmonica, Jack sneaks a note to his horse Starlight, who delivers it to Beth. With Smiley, a former boxing champion, Beth rides to Jack's cabin and, dressed in Jimmie's clothes, poses as the dead man. Terrified, Cheyenne confesses to killing Jimmie on Plug's orders. Jack then fights Plug and his men, who are finally arrested by the sheriff. *Cowboys. Indians of North America–Mixed blood. Murder. Outlaws. Thieves. Boxers. Clothes. Confession (Law). Disguise. Drunkenness. False accusations. Fights. Harmonicas. Horses. Knife wounds. Male impersonation. Money. Partnership. Ranchers. Romance. Saleswomen. Saloons. Sheriffs. Superstition.*

Note: Although onscreen credits include a 1934 copyright statement, the title was not found in the copyright records. No reviews were located for the film, but the title is listed in the 1935 *FDYB* as a 1934 Steiner release. In addition, the picture was submitted to the New York State Censor Board on 3 Oct 1934 and was approved with eliminations at that time. The length of the New York print was given as 5,100 feet. Modern sources, which list the film's running time as 56 minutes, include Lew Meehan, George Chesebro, Gordon DeMain and George Morrell as cast members.

LOS CALAVERAS (Spanish language)

Hal Roach Studios, Inc.; Metro-Goldwyn-Mayer Corp.; controlled by Loew's, Inc. *Dist* Metro-Goldwyn-Mayer Distributing Corp. **1931**; San José, Costa Rica opening: 19 Apr 1931; Buenos Aires opening: 8 Jul 1931; Barcelona opening: 30 Sep 1931. Sd (Sistema Western Electric [Western Electric Sound System]); b&w. 6 reels. 63 min. Passed by the National Board of Review. Spanish language.

Dirección [*Dir*] James W. Horne. *Diálogo por* [*Dial*] H. M. Walker. *Fotografía* [*Photog*] Jack Stevens. *Editor de película* [*Film ed*] Richard Currier. *Fonografía* [*Rec*] Elmer Raguse.

Cast: STAN LAUREL [(*Stan Laurel*)], OLIVER HARDY [(*Oliver Hardy*)], [Linda Loredo (*Mrs. Hardy*)], [Anita Garvin (*Mrs. Laurel*)], [Luis Llaneza (*Friend who telephones*)], [Charlie Hall (*Bellboy/Landlord*)], [Charles Dorety (*Drunk*)].

Comedy. [*Print viewed*]. Stan Laurel and Oliver Hardy are about to leave with their wives on a train trip for a vacation. Before their departure, Ollie receives a telephone call from a friend at their lodge telling him that they are to be honored at a stag party that same

evening. All manner of forbidden delights are promised. The boys want to go, so Ollie feigns a sudden illness and arranges for Stan to stay with him while the wives go on without them. Stan and Ollie attempt to leave for their dinner, but have various problems trying to get into their lodge uniforms. Their wives miss the train, return to discover the boys's deception and chase them out of the building. After their wives have divorced them, Stan and Ollie share a room in a boardinghouse with a dog named "Laughing Gravy," whom they conceal from the landlord. After various disasters, they are saved from eviction by the arrival of a letter and check for Stan informing him that he is the beneficiary of an uncle's will. The will, however, stipulates that in order to inherit the money, Stan must abandon Ollie, whom the uncle felt was responsible for holding Stan back. The boys agree to separate, and Ollie keeps the dog. Stan suddenly decides to tear up the check and stay. Ollie is overjoyed to think that his friend has given up everything for him, but Stan makes it clear that his sacrifice is really because he does not want to live without the dog. *Bumblers. Deception. Dogs. Wives. Boardinghouses. Clothes. Divorce. Friendship. Inheritance. Landlords. Lodges (Fraternal organizations).*

Note: This film was a compilation of two English-language shorts made in 1931 by Stan Laurel and Oliver Hardy. The first part of the picture was taken from *Be Big*, and the second part from an expanded version of *Laughing Gravy*, which had a different ending in the English-language version. Apparently the ending described above was filmed for all of the versions, but was changed for the English production, which did not have the plot elements of Stan receiving the letter from his uncle and temporarily deciding to leave Ollie. Instead, Stan and Ollie are told by the boardinghouse keeper to leave, but before they can, a policeman arrives and orders the building quarantined. Unable to stand being with his bumbling tenants and their barking dog, the boardinghouse keeper shoots himself. According to modern sources, a German version may have been made, but no information to verify this has been located. This was the last foreign-language film made by Laurel and Hardy, who learned their lines phonetically for each version. For more information about Laurel and Hardy's career together and their foreign language films, see entry below for *Pardon Us*.

Other language version(s):

Les carottiers (French language)

1931. Sd (Système Western Electric) [Western Electric Sound System]; b&w. 60 min. Passed by the National Board of Review. French language.

Mise en Scène de [*Dir*] James W. Horne. *Photographie de* [*Photog*] Jack Stevens. *Montage* [*Ed*] Richard Currier. *Ingénieur du Son* [*Sd eng*] Elmer Raguse. *Découpage* [*Scr*] H. M. Walker. *Traduction par* [*Translation*] Pierre Weill.

French-language cast: Stan Laurel [(*Stan Laurel*)], Oliver Hardy [(*Oliver Hardy*)], [Germaine de Néel (*Mrs. Hardy*)], [Anita Garvin (*Mrs. Laurel*)], [Jean De Briac (*Friend who telephones*)], [Charlie Hall (*Bellboy/Landlord*)], [Charles Dorety (*Drunk*)]. [*French version viewed*]

CALENDAR GIRL (Irish Americans, Scandinavian Americans)

Republic Pictures Corp. *Dist* Republic Pictures Corp. 31 Jan 1947; Prod: early Jul–early Aug 1946 [©Republic Pictures Corp.; 22 Jan 1947; LP843]. Sd (RCA Sound System); b&w. 88 min. Passed by the National Board of Review. PCA cert no. 11891.

Assoc prod Allan Dwan. *Dir* Allan Dwan. [*Asst dir* Richard Moder]. *Scr* Mary Loos, Richard Sale and Lee Loeb. *Orig story* Lee Loeb. *Photog* Reggie Lanning. *Spec eff* Howard Lydecker and Theodore Lydecker. *Art dir* Hilyard Brown. *Film ed* Fred Allen. *Set dec* John McCarthy, Jr. and George Milo. *Cost supv* Adele Palmer. *Mus dir* Cy Feuer. *Orch* Leo Arnaud. *Dance dir* Fanchon. *Sd* Victor Appel. *Makeup supv* Bob Mark. *Hair stylist* Peggy Gray. "Calendar Girl" *Artist (courtesy of Brown and Bigelow)* Zoe Mozert.

Song(s): "Calendar Girl," "New York is a Nice Place to Visit," "Have I Told You Lately," "Let's Have Some Pretzels and Beer," "A Bluebird is Singing to Me" and "A Lovely Night to Go Dancing," music and lyrics by James McHugh and Harold Adamson.

Cast: Jane Frazee [(*Patricia O'Neil*)], William Marshall [(*Johnny Bennett*)], Gail Patrick [(*Olivia Radford*)], Kenny Baker [(*Byron Jones*)], Victor McLaglen [(*Matthew O'Neil*)], Irene Rich [(*Lulu Varden*)], James Ellison [(*Steve Adams*)], Janet Martin [(*Tessie*)], Franklin Pangborn [(*Dillingsworth*)], Gus Schilling [(*Ed Gaskin*)], Charles Arnt [(*Captain Olsen*)], Lou Nova [(*Clancy*)], Emory Parnell [(*The mayor*)], [Edward Keane (*Battalion chief*)], [Vic Potel (*Swede*)], [Earle Hodgins (*Official*)], [Keith Richards (*Violinist*)], [Gordon Wynne (*Oboe player*)], [Arvon Dale (*Bass fiddler*)], [Helen McAllister (*Sarah*)], [Wanita Charles (*Juanita*)], [Shelah Shutan (*Harriett*)], [Roberta Stevenson (*Roberta*)], [Ralph Montgomery, John

S. Roberts (*Dandies*)], [Burton Jones (*O'Toole*)], [Jack Shea, William Radovich, Lloyd Ford (*Irish Tug O' War men*)], [Chuck Roberson, Wee Willie Davis, Vic Holbrook, Tex Mooney, Mickey Simpson (*Swedish Tug O' War men*)], [Gino Corrado (*Tony, the cook*)], [Spec O'Donnell, Casey MacGregor (*Toughs*)], [Bob Scott, Robert Cherry, Brad Slaven, James Menzies, Snub Pollard, E. L. Davenport (*Mashers*)], [Tommy Ryan, Ralphy Freeto (*Kids*)], [Charles Morton (*Diamond Jim Brady*)], [Ethelreda Leopold (*Rosie O'Grady*)], [Edgar Caldwell].

Comedy-drama, **with songs.** [*Print viewed*]. In turn-of-the-century Greenwich Village, New York, at a boarding house for artists, owner Lulu Varden needs to have her piano moved and so, sets off the fire alarm. When her sweetheart, Irish-American fire chief Matthew O'Neil, arrives with his men and realizes that there is no fire, he becomes angry, so Lulu placates him by inviting him to a party that evening. Before he leaves, Matt learns that the Fire Department's efficiency trophy, which he covets, may go to another fire company headed by Scandinavian Capt. Olsen. As she leaves the boarding house, Patricia O'Neil, Matt's daughter, meets new boarders Steve Davis and Johnny Bennett, who have just arrived from Boston. When artist Steve's sweetheart, Olivia Radford, phones, she reminds him that after three weeks in the Village, he must return to her. That evening at her party, Lulu introduces fledgling composer Johnny to the influential Mr. Dillingsworth, who promises to read Johnny's score when it is completed. Steve asks Pat to pose for a painting he is planning to enter into a calendar contest, offering the first prize of $500 if they win. As Pat poses for Steve, Johnny and poet Byron Jones finish their score, which Johnny then takes to Dillingsworth. Meanwhile, Steve finishes his painting of Pat and asks her to go with him to the upcoming jamboree at the Swiss Gardens. That night, Steve alters his painting of Pat to reveal naked legs, and the painting wins first place. However, when Matt sees the painting of his daughter, he again loses his temper and Steve must hide to avoid him. Later, as Steve prepares to leave for the jamboree, Olivia arrives in town, so Steve asks Johnny to take Pat to the jamboree. Just as Johnny explains that Steve is unable to make it to the jamboree, Olivia and Steve arrive. Steve tells Pat that Olivia is his cousin, and she believes him and thinks that Johnny has lied. Impressed by Steve's score, Dillingsworth is negotiating to buy it, when the mayor arrives to officiate at the game of Tug O' War which will break a tie to award the efficiency trophy. Matt's fire company is about to lose, when one of Olsen's huge Scandinavians loses his grip on the rope. They all celebrate the victory, while Byron and his sweetheart, Tessie, get engaged. *Boardinghouses. New York City–Greenwich Village. Awards. Bankers. Calendars. Contests. Fathers and daughters. Fire departments. Firemen. Irish Americans. Mayors. Musicians. Painters (Of paintings). Paintings. Pianos. Poets. Romance. Scandinavian Americans. Tug of war (Game). United States–History–Social life and customs.*

Note: According to a 10 Apr 1949 article in *NYT*, writers Horace Jackson and Irene Homer filed a plagiarism suit against Republic Studios alleging that they had not been properly compensated for their material. The disposition of the suit is unknown, however, the writers' attorney stated that they received a "'substantial' out-of-court settlement." *CBCS* records the firemen's ethnicity as Swedish, while in the film, they are called "Scandinavians." According to a 21 Nov 1953 ad in *MPH*, this film was re-edited and re-released in 1951 as *Stardust and Sweet Music*.

Box 15 Feb 1947. *DV* 25 May 1946. *DV* 5 Feb 1947. *FD* 14 Feb 1947, p. 10. *HR* 5 Feb 1947, p. 3. *IFJ* 20 Jul 1946, p. 49. *MPH* 21 Nov 1953. *MPHPD* 30 Nov 1946, p. 3335. *MPHPD* 15 Feb 1947. *NYT* 10 Apr 1948. *Var* 12 Feb 1947, p. 14.

CALGARY STAMPEDE see **RIDING HIGH**

CALIFORNIA (Latino)

Metro-Goldwyn-Mayer Corp.; controlled by Loew's Inc. *Dist* Metro-Goldwyn-Mayer Distributing Corp. 7 May 1927 [©Metro Goldwyn Mayer Dist. Corp.; 23 May 1927; LP24255]. Si; b&w. 5 reels, 4,912 ft.

Dir W. S. Van Dyke. *Story* Peter B. Kyne. *Cont* Frank Davis. *Titles* Marian Ainslee and Ruth Cummings. *Photog* Clyde De Vinna. *Film ed* Basil Wrangell. *Settings* Eddie Imazu. *Ward* André-ani.

Cast: Tim McCoy (*Capt. Archibald Gillespie*), Dorothy Sebastian (*Carlotta del Rey*), Marc MacDermott (*Drachano*), Frank Currier (*Don Carlos del Rey*), Fred Warren (*Kit Carson*), Lillian Leighton (*Duenna*), Edwin Terry (*Brig. Gen. Stephen W. Kearny*).

Western. "The war with Mexico serves to bring together American officer and Mexican señorita, the former all ardent and the latter defiant because of the fact that their countries are at war. Coincident with the American victory is the successful conquest by the 'gringo'

of the girl's heart." (*MPNBG* 13 Oct 1927, p. 23.). *Kit Carson. Courtship. Stephen Watts Kearny. Mexicans. Mexico. United States–History–War with Mexico, 1845-1848.*

Var 29 Jun 1927, p. 33.

CALIFORNIA (Irish Americans, Latino)
Paramount Pictures, Inc.; A John Farrow Production. *Dist* Paramount Pictures, Inc. 21 Feb 1947; New York premiere: 14 Jan 1947; Monterey, CA premiere: 27 Jan 1947; Prod: 23 Nov 1945–1 Feb 1946 [©Paramount Pictures, Inc.; 21 Feb 1947; LP860]. Sd (Western Electric Recording); col (Technicolor). 8,760 ft. 97-98 min. Passed by the National Board of Review. PCA cert no. 11220.

Prod Seton I. Miller. *Dir* John Farrow. *Asst dir* Herbert Coleman, [Joe Keller and Ray Kreuger]. [*2d asst dir* Micky Moore and Jim Rosenberger]. *Scr* Frank Butler and Theodore Strauss. *Story* Boris Ingster. *Dir of photog* Ray Rennahan. [*2d cam* Arch Dalzell]. *Spec photog eff* Gordon Jennings. [*Asst spec photog eff, Miniatures* Devereux Jennings]. [*Asst spec optical eff* Paul Lerpae]. *Technicolor color dir* Natalie Kalmus. *Assoc* Robert Brower. *Art dir* Hans Dreier and Roland Anderson. *Ed supv* Eda Warren. *Set dec* Sam Comer and Ray Moyer. *Women's cost* Edith Head. *Men's cost* Gile Steele. *Mus score* Victor Young. *Vocal arr* Ken Lane. *Mus assoc* Phil Boutelje. *Sd rec* Stanley Cooley and John Cope. [*Sd mixer* Philip G. Wisdom]. *Makeup supv* Wally Westmore. [*Tech adv* Dr. John Walton Caughey]. [*Gardener* Loren Holmes]. [*Loc scout and prod aide to John Farrow* Joseph Youngerman]. [*Research dir* Helen Gladys Percey]. [*Research asst* Elvira Smith].

Song(s): "Lily-I-Lay-De-O," "I Shoulda Stood in Massachusetts," "Said I to My Heart," "Carmela," "Gold Rush" and "California or Bust," music by Earl Robinson, lyrics by E. Y. Harburg.

Cast: Ray Milland [(*Jonathan Trumbo*)], Barbara Stanwyck [(*Lily Bishop*)], Barry Fitzgerald [(*Michael Fabian*)], George Coulouris [(*Pharaoh Coffin*)], Albert Dekker [(*Mr. Pike*)], Anthony Quinn [(*Don Luis Rivera y Hernandez*)], Frank Faylen [(*Whitey*)], Gavin Muir [(*Booth Pennock*)], James Burke [(*Pokey*)], Eduardo Ciannelli [(*Padre*)], Roman Bohnen [(*Colonel Stuart*)], Argentina Brunetti [(*Elvira*)], Howard Freeman [(*Senator Creel*)], Julia Faye [(*Wagon woman*)], [Crane Whitley (*Abe Clinton*)], [Joey Ray (*Pennock's partner/Miner*)], [Tommy Tucker (*Elwyn Smith*)], [Frances Morris (*Elwyn's mother/Stoney-eyed woman*)], [Minerva Urecal (*Emma, town matron*)], [Virginia Farmer (*Town matron*)], [Dock McGill (*Coffin's servant*)], [Stanley Andrews (*Higgins*)], [Sam Flint (*Willoughby*)], [Don Beddoe (*Stark*)], [Harry Hayden (*Barrett*)], [Ian Wolfe (*President Polk*)], [Phil Tead (*Eddie, cashier*)], [Jack Baxley (*Cowhand*)], [Kathryn Sheldon (*Gaunt wagon woman*)], [Ethan Laidlaw (*Reb*)], [Gertrude Hoffman (*Old woman*)], [George McDonald, Billy Andrews, Gary Armstrong, Eddie Ehrhart, Albert Ray (*Boys*)], [Diane Ervin (*Wagon woman/Miner's wife*)], [Janet Thomas (*Wagon woman*)], [Alan Bridge (*Town marshal*)], [Bud Geary, Dick Wessel (*Blacksmiths*)], [Tom Fadden, Guy Wilkerson, Ed Randolph, Rex Lease, Frank Hagney, George Magrill (*Strangers*)], [Pepito Perez (*Piano player*)], [Wesley Hopper (*Faro dealer*)], [Lester Dorr (*Mike, the dealer*)], [Al Ferguson (*Card player*)], [Robert R. Stephenson, Phil Dunham (*Barbers*)], [Philip Van Zandt (*Mr. Gunce*)], [Harry Cording, George Anderson, Joe Bernard, Stanley Blystone, William Hunter, James Davies, George Lloyd, Jack Clifford (*Miners*)], [Joe Whitehead (*Miner/Onlooker/Steamship clerk/Delegate*)], [Perc Launders (*Printer*)], [LeRoy Taylor (*Barber shop customer*)], [Joe Gilbert (*Telegraph operator*)], [Lee Phelps (*Bartender*)], [Jimmie Dundee (*Gambler*)], [Jesse Graves (*Black servant*)], [Kernan Cripps (*Shopkeeper*)], [Hal Brown (*Newsboy*)], [Clancy Cooper (*Cavalry N.C.O.*)], [Frank Ferguson (*Cavalry officer*)], [Francis Ford (*Jessie*)], [Si Jenks (*Settler*)], [Louis Mason (*Slim*)], [George Barton (*Farmer*)], [Darby Jones, LeRoy Edwards (*Black slaves*)], [Will Wright (*Chairman*)], [Tony Paton, Fredric Santley, George Melford (*Delegates*)], [Len Hendry (*Spectator*)], [Tom Chatterton (*Joe, chauffeur*)], [Dave Kashner (*Whipman*)], [Martin Garralaga, Pedro Regas (*Mexican sheepherders*)], [Betty Farrington], [John Sheehan], [Eddy Chandler], [Ralph Dunn], [Lane Chandler], [Russ Clark], [Jeff Corey], [William Hall], [Sheik, a horse].

Historical, Western, with songs. [*Print viewed*]. During the California gold rush, a wagon train guided by ex-Army lieutenant Jonathan Trumbo, a deserter, stops in a small town, where Lily Bishop, a woman traveling alone, is thrown out of the saloon and accused of cheating at poker. Lil asks to join the wagon train, but because

Trumbo refuses to take her, kindly old farmer Michael Fabian invites her to ride with him. Throughout the journey, Trumbo is unkind to Lil and she is snubbed by the women. When Lil beats Trumbo at poker one night, he accuses her of cheating. Later he kisses her, but she swears revenge. When news arrives that gold has been found in California, the pioneers abandon their goods and hurry West, and Lil leaves with a rough man named Booth Pennock, determined to make her own fortune. Trumbo tries to apologize to Lil, but Pennock whips him as they ride out. Fabian nurses Trumbo's shoulder and drives him West. Some time later they arrive in Pharaoh City, run by ex-slave trader Pharaoh Coffin, who is determined to make California an independent nation state so that he can rule. In the Golden Lily Saloon, owned by Lil, a farmer named Whitey tells Trumbo that Coffin has been forcing the farmers off their land by charging exorbitant prices for water and protection. Lil rescues Trumbo from a brawl with Pike, Coffin's henchman, but when Trumbo awakens, Lil warns him never to set foot in her saloon again. Later, Trumbo wins Lil's saloon at poker. After he resists Coffin's orders to join his gang, Trumbo is beaten and put on a horse, and following his rescue by two Mexicans, he vows revenge. Meanwhile, Lil moves into Coffin's hacienda. Hoping to convince the state's politicians to resist statehood, Coffin hosts a fiesta, while secretly planning an armed seizure of government property. When Trumbo warns an army captain about the seizure, he is reminded that, as a deserter, he could be court-martialed if Coffin proves to be innocent. Trumbo is given ninety days to find a spokesman for California statehood to appear at the Monterey Convention, where he will be elected as the state's advocate, and the issue of statehood will be decided. Trumbo picks Fabian, and he is elected spokesman. Although Lil warns Fabian that he will be killed if he contravenes Coffin, he gives a speech indicting Coffin for trying to make California an "independent empire." One of Coffin's men tries to shoot Fabian, but a loyal farmer takes the bullet. After Trumbo shoots the assailant, Coffin's supporters abandon him, and Lil sees his treachery for the first time. The next morning, at his hacienda, Coffin asks a padre to marry him and Lil, but she has fled to warn Fabian. She is too late, however, as Fabian is killed in his vineyard by Coffin's gang before Trumbo and his posse arrive. At the hacienda, Trumbo finds Coffin hallucinating that the slaves on his ship have freed themselves and are about to kill him. Lil shoots Coffin and saves Trumbo. Later, they visit Fabian's grave, where Trumbo tells Lil that he will return to the army, and she promises she will wait for him. *California–History–1846-1850. Gold rushes. Megalomania. Ostracism. Political corruption. Revenge. Settlers. Statehood (American politics). Desertion, Military. False accusations. Farmers. Fights. Gamblers. Hallucinations. Irish Americans. Mexicans. Monterey (CA). Murder. Poker (Game). Romantic rivalry. Saloon keepers. Self-sacrifice. Slave traders. Vineyards. Wagon trains. Whips and whippings.*

Note: According to *HR* pre-production news items, screenwriter Albert Hackett was originally scheduled to direct and write this film, but was later replaced. Hackett remained a screenwriter and never did direct a feature film. In Jun and Jul 1945, Alan Ladd and Betty Hutton were scheduled to star in the film. By Sep 1945, Hutton had declined the role in order to go on her honeymoon. Ladd was suspended by Paramount as of 22 Aug 1945 for refusing to report for preparatory work on the film after studio heads refused him more money. By early Nov 1945, Ladd and the studio settled their dispute, but Ray Milland had already been put into the film. *HR* also reported that Victor McLaglen was slated for a role as a "heavy" in this film.

Portions of *California* were shot in Flagstaff and Cameron, AZ, at the Iverson Ranch near Chatsworth, CA, and in Calabasas, CA. As reported in *HR* on 1 Mar 1946, scenic California locations were shot in early Mar 1946 for scenes illustrating the lyrics of introductory music for montages in the film. Among the montage locations were: the Monterey coastline, the Golden Gate Bridge in San Francisco, highway scenes of California redwood forests, the San Juan Capistrano Mission, orange groves at San Bernardino, wild flowers near Bakersfield, the snow-capped mountains of Mount Whitney, Mount San Jacinto and Mount Baldy, peach and apple orchards at Santa Clara and Santa Rosa, and vegetable fields at Bakersfield and in the Imperial Valley. According to an article in the *NYT* on 13 Jan 1946, Paramount recreated a vineyard at Brant's Crags, near Lake Malibu, CA. According to *NYT*, vintage Conestoga wagons were used in the film. According to *Par News*, at the advice of Dr. John Walton Caughey, UCLA history professor, no white-faced Hereford cattle were used in the film because they were not bred in the United States until after the 1840s. The amethyst tiara and necklace worn by Barbara Stanwyck in the film were heirlooms of director John Farrow.

According to a 22 Mar 1946 *HR* news item, because 1946 marked the centennial of the United States' seizure of California from Mexico, Farrow arranged an advance showing of this film in Sacramento for California Governor Earl Warren, heads of the Native Sons and Daughters of the Golden West, and other state leaders. The date of the actual preview was not found, but on 27 Jan

1947, *DV* reported that California historical societies were angered that Paramount had held the film's premiere in New York (on 14 Jan 1947), particularly because California was preparing to celebrate the 100th anniversary of the discovery of gold in Northern California and its adoption into statehood. Paramount reportedly held a special premiere in Monterey, CA two weeks after the New York premiere in response to the protest. Ray Milland and Lizabeth Scott appeared in a *Lux Radio Theatre* broadcast of *California* on 30 Jan 1950.

Box 21 Dec 1946. *DV* 16 Dec 1946, pp. 3, 14. *DV* 23 Jan 1947. *DV* 27 Jan 1947. *FD* 19 Dec 1946, p. 8. *HR* 19 Jan 1945. *HR* 23 Aug 1945, p. 1. *HR* 25 Aug 1945. *HR* 19 Sep 1945, p. 1. *HR* 5 Oct 1945, p. 18. *HR* 9 Nov 1945, p. 1, 3. *HR* 15 Nov 1945, p. 11. *HR* 23 Nov 1945, p. 8. *HR* 11 Jan 1946, p. 13. *HR* 14 Jan 1946, p. 10. *HR* 1 Feb 1946, p. 13, 24. *HR* 1 Mar 1946, p. 8. *HR* 22 Mar 1946, p. 6. *HR* 16 Dec 1946, p. 6. *HR* 3 Jan 1947, p. 2. *MPHPD* 21 Dec 1946, p. 3373. *NYT* 30 Sep 1945. *NYT* 13 Jan 1946. *NYT* 15 Jan 1947, p. 31. *Var* 18 Dec 1946, p. 14.

CALIFORNIA (1949) *see* **THE FIGHTING KENTUCKIAN**

CALIFORNIA CAVALCADE *see* **FRONTIERS OF '49**

CALIFORNIA CONQUEST (Latino)

Esskay Pictures Co. *Dist* Columbia Pictures Corp. Jul **1952**; New York city opening: week of 7 June 1952; Prod: 11 Jun—30 Jun 1951 [©Columbia Pictures Corp.; 2 Apr 1952; LP1614]. Sd (RCA Sound System); col (Technicolor). 8 reels, 7,133 ft. 79-80 min. Passed by the National Board of Review. PCA cert no. 15501.

Prod Sam Katzman. *Dir* Lew Landers. *Asst dir* Charles S. Gould. *Wrt for the screen by* Robert E. Kent. *Dir of photog* Ellis W. Carter. *Spec eff* Jack Erickson. *Technicolor col consultant* Francis Cugat. *Art dir* Paul Palmentola. *Film ed* Richard Fantl. *Set dec* Sidney Clifford. *Mus dir* Mischa Bakaleinikoff. *Sd eng* Josh Westmoreland. *Unit mgr* Herbert Leonard.

Cast: Cornel Wilde [(*Don Arturo Bordega*)], Teresa Wright [(*Julia Lawrence*)], Alfonso Bedoya [(*José Martinez*)], Lisa Ferraday [(*Princess Helena de Gagarine*)], Eugene Iglesias [(*Don Ernesto Brios*)], John Dehner [(*Don Fredo Brios*)], Ivan Lebedeff [(*Count Alexander Rotcheff*)], Tito Renaldo [(*Don Bernardo Mirana*)], Renzo Cesana [(*Fray Lindos*)], Baynes Barron [(*Ignacio*)], Rico Alaniz [(*Pedro*)], William P. Wilkerson [(*Fernando*)], Edward Colmans [(*Junipero*)], Alex Montoya [(*Juan*)], [Hank Patterson (*Sam Lawrence*)], [George Eldredge (*Capt. John C. Fremont*)].

Historical, Drama. [*Print viewed*]. In the years between 1825 and 1841, California, a province of Mexico, is torn by internal strife. While France and Russia attempt to gain a foothold in the rich land, many of California's people hope to be annexed by the United States, a development which they believe would bring them freedom. One of these Californians is Don Arturo Bordega, who rides toward *la Reina de Los Angeles* with the intent of buying defensive weapons from gunsmith Sam Lawrence. Arturo and his servant José are pursued by bandits, but they manage to elude their attackers and arrive safely in Los Angeles. The don and several other Californians, including the ambitious and greedy brothers, Ernesto and Fredo Brios, plan to discuss U.S. interest in the territory with Capt. John C. Fremont at a ball that evening. As Fremont approaches Los Angeles, however, the same bandits attack his coach, killing everyone but him. At the ball that evening, Don Ernesto Brios, who hopes to be named governor of California, seems surprised when Fremont arrives for the meeting. His head wrapped in bandages, Fremont explains that the U.S. has no intention of becoming involved in Mexico's internal conflicts. Annexation would depend on proof that the majority of Californians would support such a move. Following Fremont's departure, Don Fredo hints that Arturo is a threat to their plans, whereupon Ernesto challenges the don to a duel for having insulted him earlier that day. Their furious sword fight ends in Ernesto's death, but at that moment, the bandits, led by José Martinez, attack the gunsmith's shop, killing Sam and stealing his firearms. Sam's beautiful daughter Julia is devastated by her father's murder, and when she learns that Arturo plans to infiltrate Martinez's gang, she follows the don on horseback. Attracted to Julia and concerned for her safety, Arturo orders her to return home, but she, declaring that she is an excellent shot, is determined to avenge her father's death and joins him in pursuit of Martinez. They arrive in Monterey just in time to learn that the Brios brothers hired Martinez to steal the guns. Dressed as a poor laborer, Arturo robs Martinez of his payment and returns to Julia with the bandit in close pursuit. There he feigns admiration for Martinez, calling him the "friend of the people" for opposing the "gringo" takeover of California. Martinez is flattered and accepts Arturo and his "wife" Julia into his gang. The bandits raid and burn the ranches of

many of the California landowners who favor annexation, but at each attack, Arturo secretly leaves the same note: "Be of courage." At Fort Ross, Don Fredo meets with Alexander Rotcheff and Princess Helena de Gagarine, the niece of the Russian czar. Because Don Fredo has paid Martinez to intimidate the landowners and secure a cache of guns, he predicts that there will be no trouble when the czar's soldiers place California under Russian protection. In return for this assistance, the Russians will make Don Fredo governor of the territory. Julia attempts to flee the Martinez gang in order to warn the local citizens of the takeover plans, but she is caught. Don Arturo is whipped for her transgression, after which she grabs a gun, reveals her true identity, and shoots Martinez. Julia then rides to the governor's office for help, while Don Arturo heads for Don Fredo's hacienda just ahead of the remaining bandits. Julia learns that the Mexican governor has no troops to defend the province from the impending Russian attack, but some of the citizens band together and head for the hacienda. Meanwhile, Arturo sneaks into Don Fredo's house and kills the don in a brutal fight. Julia and her group of citizens capture the Russian princess, but the attacking Russian soldiers outnumber the Californians. During the battle, Arturo and Julia load a powder keg onto a wagon, light the fuse, and push the wagon toward the Russians, where it explodes. With the Russian threat removed, Julia and Arturo plan their future together. *Bandits. California–History–To 1846. Mexicans. Russians. Ambition. Duels. Explosions. Fathers and daughters. Firearms. Fort Ross (CA). John Fremont. Gun powder. Impersonation and imposture. Invasions. Knife fighting. Los Angeles (CA). Mexican Americans. Monterey (CA). Munitions. Murder. Raids. Ranchers. Revenge. Romance. Sword fights. Whips and whippings.*

Note: According to information in the PCA file on the film at the AMPAS Library, an early working title was *The Crimson Mask*. A studio-supplied plot summary for the film that is contained in the file credits Robert Shayne with the role of "Capt. John C. Fremont," but that role was played by George Eldredge. Along with its depiction of the Mexican heritage of California, the film highlights a Russian plan to attack and assume control of the territory. Tying this subplot to contemporary fears of Russian/Communist infiltration of the United States, the *Var* reviewer wrote that the plot "purports to show that Russia had her eye on the rich land [of California] even back in those days...." Founded in 1781 on a Spanish grant, Los Angeles was originally known as *Nuestra Señora Reina de los Angeles*, Our Lady Queen of the Angels. In 1812 the Russians established Fort Ross along the northern coast of California as a trading and fur-trapping center. They maintained Fort Ross until 1841.

Box 14 Jun 1952. *DV* 4 Jun 1952, p. 6. *Exh* 30 Jul 1952, p. 3337. *FD* 27 Jun 1952, p. 7. *Har* 14 Jun 1952, p. 94. *HR* 4 Jun 1952, p. 4. *HR* 8 Jun 1951, p. 10. *MPHPD* 14 Jun 1952, p. 1398. *Newsweek* 30 Jun 1952. *NYT* 7 Jun 1952, p. 22. *Time* 23 Jun 1952. *Var* 11 Jun 1952, p. 6.

CALIFORNIA FRONTIER (Latino)

Coronet Pictures, Inc.; Columbia Pictures Corp. of California, Ltd.; H. M. Lang, President. *Dist* Columbia Pictures Corp. of California, Ltd. 15 Dec **1938**; New York premiere: week of 10 Dec 1938; Prod: 22 Sep—28 Sep 1938 [©Columbia Pictures Corp. of California, Ltd.; 30 Nov 1938; LP8458]. Sd (RCA); b&w. 6 reels. 54-55 min. PCA cert no. 4793.

Prod Monroe Shaff. *Dir* Elmer Clifton. *Asst dir* Gordon S. Griffith. *Orig story and scr* Monroe Shaff and Arthur Hoerl. *Photog* Eddie Linden. *Art dir* Vin Taylor. *Film ed* Charles Hunt. *Mus supv* Screen Music, Inc. *Rec* Corson Jowett.

Cast: BUCK JONES ([*Captain*] *Buck Pearson*), Carmen Bailey (*Dolores* [*Cantova*]), Milburn Stone (*Mal Halstead*), Jose Perez (*Juan Cantova*), Soledad Jimenez (*Mama* [*Cantova*]), Stanley Blystone ([*Ted*] *Graham*), Carlos Villarias (*Don Pedro* [*Cantova*]), Paul Ellis (*[Friar] Miguel* [*Cantova*]), Ernie Adams (*Barclay*), Forrest Taylor (*General Wyatt*), Billy Bletcher (*Bellhop*), Glenn Strange (*Blackie*), [Bob Terry].

Western. [*Print viewed*]. Captain Buck Pearson is sent to San Dimas, California, to investigate claims that gold-mad Americans are forcing Mexican landowners from their property. Meanwhile, Ted Graham and his desperados attack the Cantova homestead. Old Don Pedro is killed during the fight. Upon his arrival in San Dimas, Buck has his first encounter with Graham, who is threatening to kill a young Mexican boy, and Buck saves the boy's life. Later, calling at the Land Office, Buck learns that the local agent has been killed and that his frightened assistant Barclay has taken over. Meanwhile, the Cantovas are again under attack. The two oldest children, Juan and Dolores, try to go for help, but are ambushed by Graham and his men. Buck, the first American to help the family, rescues them and they

gratefully acknowledge their new friend. Mal Halstead, the leader of the landgrabbers, forces Barclay to make false claims in the register book, dispossessing the Mexicans of their ancestral property. While hiding in another room, Halstead listens to Buck and Juan when they visit the Land Office, and deduces that Buck is with the government. The desperados return to the Cantova land to force them out, and the ailing Mama tells Juan and Dolores that they must leave. Walking away, they kneel at a roadside statue of the Virgin Mary, and Mama collapses and dies. Juan blames Halstead and his men for Mama's and Don Pedro's deaths and in retaliation, he captures and hangs one of the gang members. A warrant is put out for Juan's arrest. Buck prevents Juan from murdering Barclay, and demands that Barclay turn over all records so that an accurate accounting of ownership can be made. That evening, Buck and Juan return to the Land Office to find Barclay dead and all the records gone. Juan is captured and when Buck comes to his aid, a fight ensues which leaves Juan dead. Buck, who is followed by Dolores, returns to his superiors to report the awful conditions in California and is assigned to return and restore law and order. Buck and Dolores plan to return to the state as husband and wife. *California–History–1846-1850. Government agents. Land rights. Mexicans. Fistfights. Gunfights. Law and order. Mary, Blessed Virgin, Saint. Murder. Racism. Revenge. Undercover operations.*

Note: A modern source adds the following actors to the cast: Tom London, Carl Mathews, Herman Hack, Frank Ellis, George Morrell, Chick Hannon, James Morton, Tom Smith, Tex Phelps and Ray Jones.

FD 13 Dec 1938, p. 8. *HR* 24 Sep 1938, p. 10. *Var* 14 Dec 1938, p. 14.

CALIFORNIA GOLD RUSH (Native Americans)

Republic Pictures Corp. *Dist* Republic Pictures Corp. 4 Feb **1946**; Prod: mid-Apr—late Apr 1945 [©Republic Pictures Corp.; 5 Feb 1946; LP105]. Sd (RCA Sound System); b&w. 6 reels. 55, 57 or 60 min. Passed by the National Board of Review. PCA cert no. 10912.

Series: Red Ryder.

Assoc prod Sidney Picker. *Dir* R. G. Springsteen. [*Asst dir* Don Verk]. *Orig scr* Bob Williams. *Photog* William Bradford. [*2d cam* Joseph Novak]. [*Transparency projection shots* Gordon C. Schaefer]. [*Re-rec and eff mixer* Thomas A. Carman]. [*Re-rec, eff and mus mixer* Howard Wilson]. *Art dir* Frank Hotaling. *Film ed* Charles Craft. *Mus dir* Richard Cherwin. *Sd* Earl Crain, Sr. *Makeup supv* Bob Mark. [*Stunts* Ben Johnson].

Music: "Oh! Susanna" by Stephen Collins Foster.

Source: Based on the comic strip "Red Ryder" by Fred Harman (1938–1964), by special arrangement with Stephen Slesinger.

Cast: WILD BILL ELLIOTT (*Red Ryder*), Bobby Blake [(*Little Beaver*)], Alice Fleming [(*Martha "The Duchess" Wentworth*)], Peggy Stewart [(*Hazel Parker*)], Russell Simpson [(*Colonel Parker*)], Dick Curtis [(*Chopin*)], Joel Friedkin [(*Ernest Murphy*)], Kenne Duncan [(*Felton*)], Tom London [(*Sheriff Peabody*)], Monte Hale [(*Pete*)], Wen Wright [(*The Idaho Kid*)], Dickie Dillon [(*Broken Arrow*)], Mary Arden [(*Woman passenger*)], Jack Kirk [(*Rancher*)], [Nolan Leary (*Eastern passenger*)], [Bud Osborne (*Frank*)], [Freddie Chapman (*Small boy*)], [Budd Buster (*Bellhop*)].

Western. [*Print viewed*]. Colonel Parker is the proprietor of a stagecoach line that has suffered repeated robberies, and one day, during another attack on one of his coaches, his son Ted is killed. Parker is upset but determined to carry the mail to the next stop, much to the dismay of his daughter Hazel, who abhors his pride. One of the passengers, rancher Martha "The Duchess" Wentworth, however, assures Hazel that her nephew, Red Ryder, can ease the Parkers' problems. The Duchess writes a letter requesting Red's help, but hotel clerk Ernest Murphy, who is the secret leader of the gang, takes it instead to Chopin, his psychopathic henchman. Chopin, who has a habit of playing "Oh! Susanna" on his harmonica, advises Murphy to send the letter, and then ambush Red and his Indian ward, Little Beaver, outside the town limits. Red and Little Beaver are to be replaced by The Idaho Kid, a notorious outlaw who is the brother of gang member Felton, and another Indian boy. Disguised as Red, Idaho is then to go to work for Parker and help the gang steal more shipments. Murphy approves of the plan, but as Red and Little Beaver are riding to town, Red kills The Idaho Kid during his ambush attempt. After Broken Arrow, an Indian boy who was kidnapped by Idaho, explains the situation, Red and Little Beaver continue into town. Meanwhile, Chopin, unaware of Idaho's defeat, tells The Duchess that Red is dead and threatens to murder Little Beaver if she reveals their scheme. Devastated, The Duchess returns to the hotel,

where she is greeted by Red. Red warns her to act as if he is Idaho, and she hides her joy upon learning that Little Beaver is safe. Murphy and Chopin, who do not know what Idaho looks like, believe Red's act and send him a note to stay away from the next day's intended stage robbery so that he will not be suspected. Red, who signs on as a driver for Parker, foils the robbery, and when the irate Chopin complains to Murphy, Felton, who is also in the office, spots Red and states that he is not Idaho. Murphy realizes that Red is trying to infiltrate the gang and orders Felton to tell the sheriff that Red is Idaho. Meanwhile, Red arranges to drive a large shipment of gold and Murphy and Chopin kidnap The Duchess so that she will not be able to tell the sheriff the truth. Felton alerts the sheriff and Parker that Red is his outlaw brother, and Parker declares that he has been double-crossed, for Red is now driving the gold wagon. When Chopin and his men attack the wagon, they steal the gold and knock Red unconscious. The sheriff's posse soon comes upon Red, but Little Beaver helps him escape after he is arrested. Red and Little Beaver then follow Felton to the gang's hideout, where The Duchess is being held captive. While Little Beaver gets the posse, Red engages the gang in a fight. Murphy accidentally shoots Chopin while trying to kill Red, and Red is forced to shoot Murphy in self-defense. The rest of the gang is rounded up, and soon after, Parker thanks Red for his help. *Cowboys. Hotel clerks. Impersonation and imposture. Murder. Outlaws. Stagecoach robberies. Ambushes. Aunts. False accusations. Fathers and daughters. Gold. Harmonicas. Indians of North America. Kidnapping. Sheriffs. Wards and guardians.*

Note: Modern sources include Neal Hart, Frank Ellis, Herman Hack, Jim Mitchell, Jess Cavan, Pascale Perry and Silver Harr in the cast. For more information on the "Red Ryder" series, please consult the Series Index and the entry below for *Tucson Raiders.*

DV 22 Feb 1946, p. 3. *HR* 12 Apr 1945, p. 9. *HR* 13 Apr 1945, p. 18. *HR* 20 Apr 1945, p. 10. *HR* 22 Feb 1946, p. 3. *MPHPD* 26 Jan 1946, p. 2818.

CALIFORNIA IN '49 (German Americans, Latino)

Arrow Film Corp. **1924** [©Arrow Pictures Corp.; 13 Nov 1924; LP20846]. Si; b&w. 6 reels.

Dir Jacques Jaccard. *Story* Karl Coolidge.

Cast: Edmund Cobb (*Cal Coleman*), Neva Gerber (*Sierra Sutter*), Charles Brinley (*John Sutter*), Ruth Royce (*Arabella Ryan*), Wilbur McGaugh (*Marsdon*).

Western. Captain John Sutter owns a large tract of land near Sacramento, granted him by the Mexican governor of California. Sutter, planning to create an Empire of the Pacific, is joined in his grand schemes by Arabella Ryan, a handsome adventuress, and Marsdon, an unscrupulous soldier of fortune. When Sutter's daughter, Sierra, finds out that her father is in love with Arabella, she denounces him for defiling the sacred memory of her mother. Sutter is overcome with remorse and angrily orders Marsdon and Arabella from his home. Cal Coleman, a frontier guide and scout who is leading the Donner party across the mountains, is forced to ride for help when their wagon train becomes snowbound in a high mountain pass. Weak from cold and hunger, Cal manages to ride as far as Sutter's fort, whence assistance is dispatched to Donner Pass. Cal is nursed back to health by Sierra, with whom he falls in love. When the Mexican-American settlers decide to revolt against the Mexican government, Cal is elected their leader, and he organizes a successful attack against Fort Sonoma. California is annexed to the United States, Marsdon is killed in a duel with Judge Coleman, Arabella commits suicide, and Cal and Sierra are married. *Adventuresses. California. Duels. Guides. Mexican Americans. Sacramento (CA). Soldiers of fortune. Suicide. John Sutter. Wagon trains.*

Note: *California in '49* is a feature version of the serial *Days of '49*, which was released on 15 Mar 1924.

Var 30 Mar 1927, p. 19.

CALIFORNIA OUTPOST see **OLD LOS ANGELES**

A CALIFORNIA ROMANCE (Latino)

Fox Film Corp. *Dist* Fox Film Corp. 24 Dec **1922** [©William Fox; 24 Dec 1922; LP18997]. Si; b&w. 5 reels, 3,892 ft.

Pres William Fox. *Dir* Jerome Storm. *Scen* Charles E. Banks. *Story* Jules G. Furthman. *Photog* Joseph August.

Cast: John Gilbert (*Don Patricio Fernando*), Estelle Taylor (*Donna Dolores*), George Siegmann (*Don Juan Diego*), Jack McDonald (*Don Manuel Casca*), Charles Anderson (*Steve*).

Romance, **Comedy-drama**. Patricio Fernando, a handsome son of California, loves Dolores, a loyal daughter of Mexico, but he disagrees with her in his opinion that California should join the United States. Believing Patricio a coward, Dolores pledges herself to Juan Diego, a Mexican Army officer who is really the leader of a band of renegades. Diego proves his falsity, however, and Patricio comes to the gallant defense of Dolores and the band of women who have been imprisoned. *Bandits. California–History–To 1846. Mexicans. Patriotism.*

Note: The working title of this film was *Across the Border.*

ETR 23 Dec 1922, p. 219. *FD* 10 Dec 1923. *Var* 17 May 23, p. 26. *MPW* 23 Dec 1922.

THE CALIFORNIA TRAIL (Latino)

Columbia Pictures Corp. *Dist* Columbia Pictures Corp. 24 Mar **1933**; Prod: 12 Nov—21 Nov 1932 [©Columbia Pictures Corp.; 7 Mar 1933; LP3705]. Sd (Western Electric Noiseless Recording); b&w. 7 reels. 65 or 67 min. PCA cert no. 207-R [29 Aug 1934].

Dir Lambert Hillyer. [*Asst dir* Frank Geraghty]. [*Scr* Lambert Hillyer]. *Story* Jack Natteford. *Photog* Benjamin Kline. *Film ed* Gene Milford. [*Sd eng* Lambert Day].

Cast: CHARLES "BUCK" JONES [(*Santa Fe Stewart, the "Yankee Bandit"*)], Helen Mack [(*Dolores Ramirez*)], Luis Alberni [(*Commandante Emilio*)], George Humbart [sic] [(*Don Alberto, mayor*)], Charles Stevens [(*Juan*)], Carlos Villar [(*Governor of California*)], Chrispin Martin [(*Pancho*)], Carmen La Roux [(*Juan's wife*)], Robert Steele [(*Pedro*)], Allan Garcia [(*Sergeant*)], Emile Chautard [(*Don Marco Ramirez*)], [Evelyn Sherman (*Doña Marco*)], [Augie Gomez (*Governor's driver*)], [John Paul Jones (*Lopez*)], [Juan Duval (*Jose*)].

Western. [*Print viewed*]. In 1838, in the town of La Loma, a province of Spanish California, mayor Don Alberto, and his brother, Commandante Emilio, intend to starve the townspeople into giving up their property. Meanwhile, Don Marco Ramirez, a wealthy aristocrat, buys food in order to thwart Alberto's plan. As Marco and Santa Fe Stewart travel to La Loma with the provisions, they are attacked by Indians sent by Emilio. Marco is wounded in the ensuing fight and, as he lies dying, he instructs Santa Fe to take the food to the poor. When Santa Fe arrives in the village, Emilio arrests him as a smuggler and confiscates the food. Meanwhile, Alberto tells Marco's wife, Doña Marco, and daughter Dolores that Santa Fe is responsible for Marco's death. Santa Fe escapes from jail and prevents Juan, a poor villager whose family is starving, from killing Alberto. He then waylays Alberto's clerk, Pancho, who has been entrusted with a gold shipment, and gives the gold to Juan and the other poor people of La Loma to buy food. Then Santa Fe follows Alberto to the Ramirez household and convinces Dolores that Marco was his friend. When troops arrive, Dolores helps Santa Fe escape. One day Santa Fe holds up the governor, who is in disguise so that he may investigate the charges of oppression against the peasants. In town, the governor is arrested for consorting with Santa Fe but Santa Fe manages to escape. Alberto, Emilio and the soldiers leave the fort overnight, after ordering the governor to be shot at dawn. In their absence, the fort is taken over by the townspeople who are led by Santa Fe, just in time to forestall the governor's execution. When Emilio and Alberto return, the governor shoots Emilio and exiles Alberto. Then, the governor appoints Juan to be the new mayor and Santa Fe the commandante, and Dolores is appointed as Santa Fe's wife. *California–History–To 1846. Governors. Mayors. Starvation. Bandits. Disguise. Executions. Family relationships. Forts. Gold. Robbery. Soldiers. Wagon trains. Wealth.*

Note: The working title for this film was *The Yankee Bandit.* Actor George Humbert's surname is spelled "Humbart" in the onscreen credits.

FD 22 Jul 1933, p. 3. *HR* 21 Nov 1932, p. 14. *MPD* 6 Jul 1933, p. 7. *MPH* 29 Jul 1933, p. 28. *Var* 1 Jul 1933, p. 14.

THE CALIFORNIAN (Latino)

Principal Productions, Inc. *Dist* Twentieth Century-Fox Film Corp. 16 Jul **1937**; Prod: began 3 May 1937 [©Principal Productions, Inc.; 16 Jul 1937; LP7521]. Sd (RCA Victor Sound System); b&w. 7 reels, 5,238 ft. 58-59 min. PCA cert no. 3469.

Pres SOL LESSER. *Prod* Sol Lesser. *Assoc prod* Barney Briskin. *Dir* Gus Meins. *Scr* Gilbert Wright. [*Story* Harold Bell Wright]. *Adpt* Gordon Newell. *Photog* Harry Neuman. *Art dir* Harry Oliver. *Film ed* Arthur Hilton and Carl Pierson. *Gowns* Albert De Anna. *Sd eng* Thomas Carmen and [Edward Ullman].

Cast: Ricardo Cortez (*Ramon Escobar*), Marjorie Weaver (*Rosalia Miller*), Katherine DeMille (*Chata*), Maurice Black (*Pancho*), Morgan Wallace (*Tod Barsto*), Nigel de Brulier (*Don Francisco Escobar*), George Regas (*Ruiz*), [Helen Holmes (*Josephine*)], [James Farley (*Sheriff Stanton*)], [Pierre Watkin (*Marshal Morse*)], [Gene Reynolds (*Ramon, as a child*)], [Ann Gillis (*Rosalia, as a child*)], [Richard Botiller (*Pablo*)], [Tom Forman (*Boylan*)], [Bud Osborne (*Murphy*)], [Monte Montague (*Bradford*)], [William Fletcher (*Tax collector*)], [Francisco Del Campo].

Historical, Western. [*Print viewed*]. In California during the mid-1800's, Don Francisco Escobar, a wealthy rancher, throws a party for his young son Ramon before sending him to Seville, Spain to learn to be a gentleman. Ramon and his sweetheart, Rosalia Miller, say their tender goodbyes. Many years later, after the gold rush is over and California has been made part of the United States, a grown Ramon returns from Spain to find that the land and wealth of his people are being plundered by Americans using outrageous tax assessments. These Americans, led by the ruthless Tod Barsto and Sheriff Stanton, have taken Don Francisco's holdings, leaving him poor and helpless. Ramon, donning a black mask and riding a black stallion, assaults Barsto's henchmen and retakes his father's money. At the Escobar ranch, Barsto and his men confront Ramon, who admits his guilt and flees into the countryside, accompanied by his faithful friend Pancho. Later, Ramon sneaks back to see a fearful Rosalia and comforts her by saying, "It is the way of the Californianos." That night, Ramon breaks into Barsto's office, steals a bundle of papers and puts them into his saddlebags for future use. With Pancho, he then rides to the lair of the bandit Ruiz and his gang. Ramon tries to convince Ruiz to join forces with him against the gold-rich Americans, but Ruiz is reluctant to give up his power. His wife Chata, however, supports Ramon and helps him become the leader. When Ramon and the bandits rob a convoy of Barsto's gold, Ruiz wants to keep the money, but Ramon, now known as the "Californian," distributes it to the poor. Furious at Ramon's escapades, Barsto and Stanton send for a marshal from San Francisco and offer a $5,000 reward for Ramon's capture, dead or alive. During a raid on one of Barsto's ranches, Ruiz shoots a peasant, and Ramon tells him he must leave the gang. Ruiz refuses to go and challenges Ramon to a duel using lassos. After Ramon wins, Ruiz takes many of the bandits and leaves. Although Chata wants to stay with Ramon, he tells her that her place is with Ruiz, so she reluctantly follows her husband. The rebuffed Chata then convinces Ruiz to pursue the reward and negotiates with Barsto and Stanton for a bigger payoff. Claiming that Ramon needs her, Chata tricks Rosalia into riding to Ruiz's remote hideout and then sends word to Ramon to meet them alone and unarmed. Before he goes, Ramon gives the saddlebags containing Barsto's papers to Pancho, instructing him to deliver them to the newly arrived marshal. After Ruiz captures and ties Ramon to a tree, he receives his reward from Barsto's men—a bullet in the belly. Having disobeyed Ramon's orders, Pancho rushes with the remaining bandits to rescue Ramon. After the ensuing fight, Barsto wrests the incriminating papers from Pancho and rides away, but Ramon, freed by Chata, rides after Barsto, lassos him and recovers the papers. Marshal Morse, using the papers as evidence, arrests Barsto. Later, at Ramon and Rosalia's wedding, Morse complains that he failed to capture the Californian, and Don Francisco, looking at the happy newlyweds, replies, "I believe he is in safe hands." *Bandits. California–History–1846-1850. Disguise. Fathers and sons. Land rights. Ranchers. Spanish Americans. Betrayal. Duels. Evidence. Kidnapping. Murder. Raids. Revenge. Rewards. Sheriffs. Taxation. Traps. United States. Marshals. Weddings.*

Note: The title of the viewed print was *The Gentleman from California*. A studio trade paper billing sheet lists the film as "Harold Bell Wright's *The Californian*." SAB states that Bell's story was unpublished. Reviews note that the lead character was based on the historical figure Joaquin Murieta. For information on Murieta and other films about him, please see the entry above for *The Avenger*, a 1931 Columbia production. According to a *HR* news item, Richard Arlen was originally cast in the lead role, but he was replaced by Ricardo Cortez a week before shooting began. A *MPH* news item notes that Charles Art Powell, who wrote under the pen name of Gordon Newell, instituted an injunction for $30,000 damages against Sol Lesser, Principal Productions, Inc., Harold Bell Wright and Twentieth Century-Fox Film Corp., charging that he did not receive sufficient exploitation or screen credit for the film. No further information has been located concerning the injunction.

Box 10 Jul 1937. *DV* 1 Jul 1937, p. 3. *FD* 20 May 1937, p. 9. *FD* 7 Jul 1937. *HR* 27 Apr 1937, p. 3. *HR* 1 Jul 1937, p. 2. *MPD* 6 Jul 1937, p. 8. *MPH* 26 Jun 1937, p. 83. *MPH* 10 Jul 1937, p. 50. *MPH* 21 Aug 1937, p. 52. *Var* 7 Jul 1937, p. 13.

THE CALIFORNIAN (1940) *see* **THE MARK OF ZORRO**

CALL HER SAVAGE (Native Americans)

Fox Film Corp. *Dist* Fox Film Corp. 27 Nov **1932**; New York opening: 24 Nov 1932; Prod: 12 Sep—late Oct 1932 [©Fox Film Corp.; 14 Nov 1932; LP3445]. Sd (Western Electric System); b&w. 9 reels, 7,634 or 7,900 ft. 82, 85 or 87 min.

Assoc prod Sam E. Rork. *Dir* John Francis Dillon. [*Asst dir* Jack Boland]. *Scr* Edwin Burke. *Photog* Lee Garmes. *Art dir* Max Parker. [*Film ed* Harold Schuster]. *Ward* David Cox. *Mus dir* Louis De Francesco. *Sd rec* E. Clayton Ward.

Source: Based on the novel *Call Her Savage* by Tiffany Thayer (New York, 1931).

Cast: CLARA BOW [(*Nasa Springer*)], Gilbert Roland [(*Moonglow*)], Thelma Todd [(*Sunny De Lane*)], Monroe Owsley [(*Lawrence Crosby*)], Estelle Taylor [(*Ruth Springer*)], Weldon Heyburn [(*Ronasa*)], Willard Robertson [(*Pete Springer*)], Anthony Jowitt [(*Jay Randall*)], Fred Kohler [(*Silas Jennings*)], Russell Simpson [(*Old man in wagon train*)], Margaret Livingston [(*Molly*)], Carl Stockdale [(*Mort*)], Dorothy Peterson [(*Silas' wife*)], [Arthur Hoyt (*Mr. Russell*)], [Katherine Perry (*Maid*)], [John Elliott (*Hank*)], [Hale Hamilton (*Cyrus Randall*)], [Walter Long (*Man who tries to pick up Nasa*)], [Bert Roach (*Man who does pick up Nasa*)], [Mischa Auer (*Man in restaurant*)], [Douglas Haig (*Pete as a boy*)], [Marilyn Knowlden (*Ruth as a girl*)], [Mary Gordon (*Woman in tenement*)].

Drama. [*Print viewed*]. After an Indian attack on a wagon train, Mort, one of the dying white men, blames his leader Silas Jennings for bringing down the wrath of God in response to Silas' adultery. When Mort calls Silas' lover a harlot, Silas puts his foot on Mort's throat and pushes him to the ground until he is dead. An old man, quoting the Bible, warns Silas that the sins of the fathers are visited upon their children even unto the third and fourth generation. Eighteen years later, in Rollins, Texas, Silas' daughter Ruth falls in love with Ronasa, an Indian, while her husband, Pete Springer, spends much time away on business. After Ronasa, obeying his father, leaves to marry the daughter of another chief, Ruth has a baby, Nasa. She grows up to be a rambunctious woman, who is troubled by her changing, extreme moods. After seeing Nasa whip her gentle, half-breed friend Moonglow, Pete, now one of the richest men in Texas, sends her to a private academy for girls in Chicago. Nasa quickly acquires a reputation in Chicago for her wild behavior. As her coming-out party approaches, Pete gives a story to the newspaper that Nasa's engagement to a man of her choice, Charlie Moffett, will be announced at the party. Nasa explodes with anger and invites man-about-town Larry Crosby. At the party, Larry's mistress, Sunny De Lane, arrives with another man and gets in a hair-pulling fight with Nasa. Larry then proposes to Nasa, who accepts, thinking that it will be a joke on her father. They marry the next afternoon, and Nasa tries to reconcile with her father, but he tells her that he never wants to see her again. Larry comes in drunk late that night, and after they spend a few hours in bed, he dresses to rejoin a poker game. When Nasa, upset, questions the reason he married her, he confesses he did it to get even with Sunny. Nasa goes on a spree, gambling and buying clothes, furs and jewelry with Larry's credit, until Larry's lawyer tells her that he is dangerously ill in New Orleans and advises her to visit him. During the visit, Larry tries to rape her. She hits him over the head with a stool, knocking him out, and when she learns from a doctor that "his mind is affected," she worries for the child with which she is pregnant. One month later, Nasa gives birth to a "seven-month" baby, but she is relieved when the doctor tells her that the baby is healthy. Nasa moves to a cheap boardinghouse. When she needs money for a prescription for the baby, she asks a neighbor's girl to look after the child and picks up a man on the street. She purchases the prescription, but returns to find that her baby has died of smoke suffocation in a fire that started when a lecherous drunk followed the babysitter and dropped a lighted match. Moonglow, who has come with news that Nasa's grandfather has died and left her $100,000, tries to console her, but she vows to get even with life. Nasa divorces Larry and one month later arrives in New York, where she advertises for a male escort. Attracted to her, Jay Randall, the jaded son of a millionaire mine owner, applies, not telling her his real identity. When a brawl erupts in a Greenwich Village restaurant, after a man identifies Jay as a millionaire's son, Nasa enjoys the excitement and confesses that she knew his identity the second day they met. Jay tells his father that he wants to marry Nasa, but his father warns him of her

almost uncontrollable temper and challenges Jay to bring Nasa to a dinner party. To Jay's and Nasa's surprise, Jay's father has invited Larry and Sunny. The dinner turns into a brawl after Larry speaks disrespectfully about Nasa's dead child. Jay rebukes Nasa and calls her "savage." Alone and drunk, Nasa gets violently angry at the men who have made her life miserable. When she learns that her mother is ill, she returns to Texas. Ruth dies after calling Ronasa's name. After Moonglow tells Nasa that Ronasa was the son of an Indian chief who killed himself because he was in love with a beautiful white woman, Nasa realizes that the woman was her mother. She tells Moonglow that she is glad to be a half-breed and takes his hand. *Battle of the sexes. Family relationships. Hereditary tendencies. Indians of North America–Mixed blood. Reputation.* Attempted rape. Chicago (IL). Drunkenness. Fights. Finishing schools. Fires. Gambling. Illegitimacy. Impersonation and imposture. Indians of North America. Infidelity. Inheritance. Marriage. Medicine. Millionaires. Mistresses. Neglected wives. New Orleans (LA). New York City. Prostitution. Restaurants. Self-sacrifice. Snakes. Tests of character. Texas. Wagon trains. Whips and whippings.

Note: This was Clara Bow's first film since she experienced a nervous breakdown in May 1931, after which rumors abounded that she might retire from the screen. According to various unidentified news items in Bow's biographical file at the AMPAS Library, before the breakdown, Bow had suffered through publicized attacks on her by her former secretary, Daisy De Voe, in a court case, and in a series of vicious, smutty articles written by Frederic H. Girnau, who was sentenced to eight years in prison for defamation of character. In Oct 1931, it was announced that Bow would begin a film with her friend, independent producer Sam Rork on 1 Dec. Rork, who had not made a film since 1928, wanted to make his own comeback together with Bow, but he was unable to raise enough money by the time imposed in his contract with Bow. She agreed, however, to wait as he continued to try to raise money. Rork then purchased the motion picture rights to the novel *Call Her Savage*, which had developed some notoriety because of its salacious subject matter, and convinced Fox president Sidney Kent of the soundness of the project.

According to information in the Twentieth Century-Fox Records of the Legal Department at the UCLA Theater Arts Library, Bow's contract with Rork gave her story approval, a condition Kent did not want to incorporate into her contract with Fox, as the studio had never given story approval to an actress before. It was thought that the novel *Call Her Savage* could be agreed upon before signing, and indeed, by 7 May 1932, Bow agreed to do the film with the provision that she must approve the resultant screenplay in writing before shooting began. (Bow did, in fact, approve Edwin Burke's final screenplay on 14 Sep 1932.) Bow's contract called for ten weeks work for $75,000, with a bonus of $25,000 if the total gross rentals reached or exceeded $800,000. (As of Oct 1935, the film had not grossed $800,000.) Bow agreed to reduce her weight to 118 pounds on or before 1 Jul 1932 and to maintain that weight during the term of the contract, and the studio agreed to furnish a masseuse selected by Bow to help with weight reduction and also a voice culture specialist. (Although Bow's weight was over 118 pounds during a large portion of the time involved, the studio did not cancel the contract.) Bow also exercised an option to have filming of the interior scenes shot at Fox's Western Avenue studio, which had been abandoned for some time. (Subsequently, the Western Avenue studio became Fox's "B" picture lot.)

According to correspondence in the MPAA/PCA Collection at the AMPAS Library, the Hays Office was concerned when they learned that Fox was interested in purchasing the novel as a vehicle for Bow. In a letter dated 19 Apr 1932, after the potential project was reported in *FD*, an MPPDA official stated that Fox executives "realize the book contains a great deal of unsuitable picture material, but feel that the title and some parts of the basic story are admirably suited for this undertaking." Although MPPDA president Will H. Hays was "not keen about the property," the official noted that "under the Resolution [passed in 1924 by the MPPDA Board of Directors] any company can buy anything it wants to, but does so at its peril."

In correspondence included in legal records, the author of the novel, Tiffany Thayer (whom Ben Hecht, in a modern source, once referred to as "a fellow pornographer"), stated concerning the origins of the novel, "the background and local color, and some of the incidents, were all based on the life of my wife, who was a resident of Texas and is one-half Osage Indian." The novel has a subplot of incestual desire and includes scenes of promiscuity, sadism, masturbation and lesbianism. In the first treatment, Fox writers Doris Malloy and Leonard Spigelgass removed the offensive sexual situations and much of the theme of the book. In a letter dated 24 Jun 1932, Colonel Jason S. Joy, director of the AMPP Studio Relations Committee, expressed concern that the studio's writers, in this first treatment, had gone too far in expurgating the book. He wrote to Hays, "The book is about as far wrong as it is possible to be. Afraid of this, the studio took most of the real flavor of the story out of the first treatment, with the result that only another stupid picture was in prospect. Somewhere in between there lies a good picture."

Subsequent to this, Joy and his assistant Lamar Trotti, held a number of meetings with Rork, Fox producer Al Rockett, Fox production chief Winfield R. Sheehan and Edwin Burke, who took over as sole screenwriter. Burke retrieved many of the incidents from the novel, and on 22 Aug, his first draft script was sent to the Hays Office for comments. Joy's major objections to this and subsequent drafts were a scene preceding "Nasa's" conception and a scene in a New Orleans hospital between "Nasa" and her husband in which "Crosby," suffering from a venereal disease, physically attacks her. The first scene, which

was similar to the portrayal in the book, had the Indian "Ronasa" accidentally come across "Nasa's" mother (who, in this draft, as in the novel, is named "Clara") in her home crying naked on her bed following a bath. The situation awakens a sexual desire in both, which leads to the beginning of a love-making scene. Joy pointed out that the entire scene would probably be cut by state and local censors and commented, "the affair between Clara [the mother of Nasa] and the Indian is not the result of his seeing her, so much as it is the result of a love that has been unrequited for a long time." This scene was omitted in the final script, and their rendezvous occurs fully-clothed by a stream. In the latter scene, a doctor's diagnosis of "Crosby" was changed from insanity in the first draft to delirium tremens in a later one. (In the final film, the doctor only vaguely tells "Nasa" that "his mind's affected.")

Both Joy and Trotti left the Hays Office and became employees of Fox before the film was completed. (Joy became a scenario editor in charge of consultation with the Hays Office, and Trotti became a writer.) When the film was submitted to the Hays Office for approval, Joy's replacement, James C. Wingate, who had previously been the head of the New York State censor board, ordered a number of cuts. During the hospital scene, in which "Crosby" attempts to rape "Nasa" when she refuses his attempts to make love, and then tries to choke her, Wingate wanted the scene cut so that the emphasis was on the choking rather than the rape: "Endeavor to trim first (sex) part of struggle as much as possible; eliminating neck kissing, and generally re-editing so as to make distinct transition to choking." In a letter Wingate noted the specific changes that were agreed on by Rockett and Rork: "remove one shot of [Monroe] Owsley backing Miss Bow against the wall and kissing her violently on the neck. Also insert close-up of Owsley which would make it evident that the succeeding action is a murderous attack and not an assault at the sex sense. These changes are aimed at eliminating the suggestion of attempted rape, which we feel certain would bring about serious censorship difficulty." The other deletion involved cutting as much of the streetwalking sequence as possible so that the actual "suggestion of soliciting" would be removed.

To attempt to persuade the various state and local censor boards not to cut the picture, Joy sent a letter to boards in New York, Pennsylvania, Virginia, Ohio, Maryland, Kansas, Manitoba, Halifax, New Brunswick, Edmonton, Vancouver, Montreal and Saskatchewan, in which he emphasized the importance of the film as Clara Bow's return to the screen. He wrote, "I doubt if there is any personality today in pictures whose return to the screen after a year's absence could have aroused such universal interest. Every effort, of course, was exerted to find just the right vehicle for Miss Bow, and I am confident her re-appearance will be a revelation to the country....Because it is a new Clara Bow that the screen is presenting, and because there is such necessity, not only of presenting her as a beautiful woman but as an actress, we are all very hopeful that the picture will be judged as a whole for the character study that it is, all parts of which inter-link importantly." Most of the censor boards, however, cut the film at various places. According to a *HR* news item, the British censors refused to pass the film without stating a reason. When Twentieth Century-Fox attempted to obtain a certificate of approval for a re-issue in 1937, PCA director Joseph Breen stated that the film seemed to be "unacceptable," calling it a "sordid story dealing with illegitimacy, attempted rape, prostitution."

According to information in the legal files, David O. Selznick of RKO charged that Rork offered Joel McCrea, on contract to RKO, a bonus to play a role in the film. Modern sources state that McCrea was tested for the role of "Moonglow." In a memo in the legal records, it is noted that "Mr. Selznick is very much aroused over the situation." Gilbert Roland, who played the role in the final film, had had a romance with Bow seven years earlier when they both played in *The Plastic Age*, according to modern sources. According to information in the legal records, Alexander Kirkland was originally cast for the role of "Jay Randall" and Rita LaRoy for the role of "Molly." As Kirkland is listed in *HR* production charts, it is possible that his scenes were shot and then redone with Anthony Jowitt in the role. Reginald Barlow is listed in Fox trade paper billing sheets as appearing in the prologue, while Carl Stockdale is not listed. As Stockdale does play the role of "Mort" in the prologue, it is possible that he replaced Barlow in the role.

Reviews of the film welcomed Bow back to the screen. *LAT* commented, "her fame seems to have been recaptured with remarkable ease....It is generally conceded that her acting has improved, having become more restrained, but she is still sufficiently exuberant in her technique to qualify as a natural actress rather than a cultivated one. Her vitality and sincerity unite [in a] likable personality that disarms criticism and wins for her the whole-hearted approval of the masses....*Call Her Savage* has been condemned by the more discriminating as a flashy, trashy, tasteless and unpleasant exhibit, but not even the most captious deny its superficial appeal to the larger public." Bow's next film, *Hoop-la* (see *AFI Catalog of Feature Films, 1931-40*; F3.1986) was last.

FD 19 Apr 1932, p. 2. FD 16 Sep 1932, p. 6. FD 26 Nov 1932, p. 4. FD 28 Nov 1932, pp. 2, 4-5. HR 24 Oct 1932, p. 6. HR 14 Nov 1932, p. 3. HR 14 Dec 1932, p. 1. MPH 29 Oct 1932, p. 48. MPH 3 Dec 1932, p. 27. NYT 25 Nov 1932, p. 19. Var 29 Nov 1932, p. 18. VarB 18 Nov 1932.

CALL ME YOURS see THE AMAZING MRS. HOLLIDAY

CALL NORTHSIDE 777 (Polish Americans)

Twentieth Century-Fox Film Corp. *Dist* Twentieth Century-Fox Film Corp. 18 Feb **1948**; Prod: 22 Sep—15 Nov 1947 [©Twentieth Century-Fox Film Corp.; 28 Jan 1948; LP1866]. Sd (Western Electric Recording); b&w. 12 reels, 9,969 ft. 110-111 min. PCA cert no. 12397.

[*Exec prod* Darryl F. Zanuck]. *Prod* Otto Lang. *Dir* Henry Hathaway. [*Asst dir* Abe Steinberg and Joe Rickards]. *Scr* Jerome Cady and Jay Dratler. *Adpt* Leonard Hoffman and Quentin Reynolds. *Dir of photog* Joe MacDonald. [*Cam op* Atillio Gabani]. [*Stills* J. C. Milligan and Paul Russell]. *Spec photog eff* Fred Sersen. *Art dir* Lyle Wheeler and Mark-Lee Kirk. *Film ed* J. Watson Webb, Jr. *Set dec* Thomas Little and Walter M. Scott. *Ward dir* Charles Le Maire. *Cost des* Key Nelson. *Mus* Alfred Newman. *Orch arr* Edward Powell. *Sd* W. D. Flick and Roger Heman. *Makeup artist* Ben Nye. [*Makeup* Dick Smith and Thomas Tuttle]. [*Hair stylist* Myrtle Ford]. *Wirephoto by* The Associated Press. [*Tech adv* James P. McGuire]. [*Prod mgr* Sam Wurtzel and R. A. Klune]. [*Scr supv* Stanley Scheuer]. [*Grip* Frank Cory].

Song(s): "Drinking Song," music by Alfred Newman, lyrics by Irene Dzierzgowska.

Source: Based on articles by James P. McGuire, published in the *Chicago Times*.

Cast: JAMES STEWART [(*P. James McNeal*)], Richard Conte [(*Frank Wiecek*)], Lee J. Cobb [(*Brian Kelly*)], Helen Walker [(*Laura McNeal*)], Betty Garde [(*Wanda Skutnik, later known as Wanda Siskovich*)], Kasia Orzazewski [(*Tillie Wiecek*)], Joanne de Bergh [(*Helen Wiecek, later known as Helen Rayska*)], Howard Smith [(*K. L. Palmer*)], Moroni Olsen [(*Chairman of Parole Board*)], John McIntire [(*Sam Faxon*)], Paul Harvey [(*Martin Burns*)], [J. M. Kerrigan (*Sullivan, bailiff*)], [Samuel S. Hinds (*Judge Charles Moulton*)], [George Tyne (*Tomek Zaleska*)], [Richard Bishop (*Warden*)], [Otto Waldis (*Boris*)], [Michael Chapin (*Frank, Jr.*)], [John Bleifer (*Jan Gruska*)], [Addison Richards (*John Albertson*)], [Richard Rober (*Larson*)], [Eddie Dunn (*Patrolman*)], [Percy Helton (*William Decker, mailman*)], [Charles Lane (*Prosecuting attorney*)], [E. G. Marshall (*Rayska*)], [Norman MacKay, Walter N. Greaza (*Detectives*)], [William Post, Jr. (*Police sergeant*)], [George Melford, Charles Miller, Joe Forte, Dick Ryan, George Spaulding (*Parole Board members*)], [Lionel Stander (*Corrigan*)], [Jonathan Hale (*Robert Winston*)], [Lew Eckels, George Cisar, Philip Lord, Duke Watson, George Pembroke (*Policemen*)], [Freddie Steele, George Turner (*Holdup men*)], [Jane Crowley (*Anna Felczak*)], [Robert Karnes (*Spitzer*)], [Larry Blake, Robert Williams, Perry Ivins, Lester Sharpe (*Technicians*)], [Helen Foster, Dollie Caillet (*Secretaries*)], [Abe Dinovitch, Jack Mannick (*Polish men*)], [Henry Kulky (*Bartender in Drazynski's Place*)], [Cy Kendall (*Bartender in Bill's Place*)], [Wanda Perry, Ann Staunton (*Telephone operators*)], [Rex Downing (*Copy boy*)], [Edward Peil, Jr., Buck Harrington (*Bartenders*)], [Stanley Gordon (*Prison clerk*)], [Carl Kroenke (*Guard*)], [Leonarde Keeler (*Himself*)], [Arthur Peterson (*Keeler's assistant*)], [Bill Vendetta (*Himself—Chicago Times photographer*)], [Truman Bradley (*Narrator*)], [Joe Ploski], [Peter Seal].

Newspaper, Drama. [*Print viewed*]. On 9 Dec 1932, during Chicago's violent Prohibition period, police officer John W. Bundy is murdered while he drinks at a speakeasy operated by Wanda Skutnik. Following a tip from a bootlegger, police question Frank Wiecek, who has a minor police record, about his friend Tomek Zaleska, who asserts that he was home at the time of the murder. Finding some inconsistencies in Frank's statements, police hold him on suspicion of the crime. After six weeks of hiding out, Tomek surrenders to the police, and while he maintains that he is innocent, he and Frank are convicted of the murder, based on Wanda's identification of them as the masked assailants, and are sentenced to ninety-nine years at Stateville Penitentiary. On 11 Oct 1944, Brian Kelly, editor of the *Chicago Times*, spots an ad in the personal notices placed by Tillie Wiecek, Frank's mother, offering a $5,000 reward for the killers of Officer Bundy and instructing those with information to "Call Northside 777." Kelly sends reporter P. James McNeal to investigate, and when Jim locates Tillie, who works as a scrubwoman, she tells him that she has saved the reward money over the past eleven years. Although he believes Frank to be guilty, Jim writes a sympathetic article about Tillie. When Kelly asks for a follow-up interview of Frank, Jim hesitates, but writes a second article implying possible police and political corruption after Frank reveals that the police deliberately kept him from seeing his lawyer while he was being interrogated, and that Wanda did not identify him as the killer the first two times she was questioned. The article provokes much response, and Kelly asks Jim to interview Frank's ex-wife Helen, who divorced him after he was imprisoned. Helen tells Jim that Frank begged her to divorce him for the sake of their son, who, Frank felt, needed a name

untainted by the crime. Jim's story about Helen causes Frank to send for him, and at the penitentiary, Frank angrily tells him to stop writing about his family. When the warden informs Jim that the other prisoners believe Frank and Tomek are innocent, Jim interviews Tomek and offers to help him get paroled if he confesses who was with him when he committed the murder. Tomek's protestation of innocence finally convinces Jim that neither of the men are guilty, and he tells Frank that he will now slant the articles in his favor and will dig into the story. After Frank passes a lie detector test, Jim's next article proclaims Frank's innocence. Despite antagonism from police angry that Jim is trying to help a cop killer, he gets access to Frank's booking record, which is dated 23 Dec 1932. What Jim really needs, however, is Frank's arrest record, which, if it is earlier than the booking date, will support Frank's contentions that Wanda had the opportunity to see him before she identified him, and that a police captain induced her to name Frank as one of the killers. Although Jim learns that the police captain died in 1938, he locates the arrest book, which had been separated from the files, and photographs the page listing Frank's arrest date as 22 Dec 1932. After Jim's next article charges political corruption, he is summoned with Kelly to a meeting with the paper's publisher, K. L. Palmer, Sam Faxon from the state's attorney's office and Robert Winston, an aide to the governor. To resolve the governmental objections to the articles, Winston proposes to conduct a hearing of the pardon board the following week. If Frank is exonerated, he will be pardoned, but if not, the paper must agreed to drop the story. Palmer, with Kelly and Jim's consent, agrees. Winston warns, however, that should Frank lose, the record of his failure could hurt his chances to be paroled in thirty years. Martin Burns, the paper's attorney, is skeptical, as he does not think that they have sufficient evidence in Frank's favor. Jim then reveals that he located a photograph showing Wanda arriving at the police station at the same time as Frank, and states that the photo is evidence that Wanda lied about not seeing Frank before she identified him in the police line. Burns, though, maintains that the burden will be on Jim to prove that the photograph was taken on 22 Dec and advises him to discredit Wanda. Working on a tip that Wanda used to run around with a stockyards worker, and thinking that she may still be in the liquor business, Jim circulates her picture in bars in the Polish section behind the stockyards, but gets no leads. He then writes an article about the search and includes his own photo. Two days before the parole board is to convene, a woman sees him in a bar and sells him Wanda's address. Jim finds Wanda, but despite the $5,000 reward, she angrily throws Jim out after he implies she fears retribution from someone. Without Wanda's change of testimony, Burns advises Jim that Frank will lose the hearing, then goes to Springfield to ask that the case be withdrawn so that it will not go on Frank's record. Kelly has Jim break the news to Tillie in person, and although she cries and says that she has no friends left, she is comforted by her faith in God. In a cab on the way to the newspaper office, Jim reads about a new enlargement process that the police have used in a forgery case. He immediately goes to the police photo lab, where the technician, in sympathy with the case because of Jim's articles, agrees to blow up a section of the photograph showing both Frank and Wanda. After calling Burns, Jim flies to Springfield to stall the hearing until Kelly can send the photo over the Associated Press wire to a nearby newspaper office. He tells the parole board that he hopes the enlargement will show the date of a newspaper being hawked in the photo to be 22 Dec 1932. Despite Faxon's objections, the chairman agrees to go to the newspaper office. The wire photo reveals the date to be 22 Dec, and Frank is released from prison. Jim reminds Frank that not many governments in the world would admit such an error. On the outside Frank greets his son, his mother and Helen, who introduces her present husband, Rayska, who promises Frank that he can be with his son anytime. Content, Frank says it is a good world outside. *Chicago (IL). False arrests. Investigations. Polish Americans. Reporters.* Advertisements. Bars. Catholics. Divorce. Editors. Lawyers. Lie detectors and detection. Mothers and sons. Murder. Parole boards. Photographs. Police corruption. Political corruption. Prison wardens. Prisons. Publishers and publishing. Scrubwomen. Speakeasies. Springfield (IL).

Note: The following statement appears after the opening credits: "This is a true story. This film was photographed in the State of Illinois using wherever possible, the actual locales associated with the story." According to information in the Twentieth Century-Fox Records of the Legal Department and the Produced Scripts Collection, located at the UCLA Arts—Special Collections

Library, studio publicity and various newspaper articles, the actual story occurred in much the same manner as was presented in the film. Joe Majczek and Theodore Marcinkiewicz were convicted of the murder of officer William D. Lundy, who was killed on 9 Dec 1932 in a speakeasy owned by Vera Walush in the Southside of Chicago. It was postulated that because the city was preparing for the 1933 World's Fair, Mayor Anton Cermak issued orders for a cleanup of the city, and pressure may have been put on the police department to arrest someone for the murder of the police officer. Majczek's mother Tillie scrubbed floors in office buildings for years to raise money to buy information to free her son, and in 1944, she placed an ad in the *Chicago Times.* Reporter James P. McGuire of the *Times* investigated the story and after proving to the Illinois parole board that Majczek was innocent, Majczek was pardoned by the Governor of Illinois and freed in Aug 1945. (Marcinkiewicz was not released until 1950.) According to a 20 Jun 1947 *HR* news item, Majczek was awarded $24,000 by the Illinois legislature as compensation for his ordeal. Tillie died in 1964, and Majczek, who remarried and became an insurance agent, died in 1983. The real killer or killers were never found.

Time reported on the case in Aug 1945 when Majczek was released. After *Reader's Digest* published a story entitled "Tillie Scrubbed On" in Dec 1946, Twentieth Century-Fox sent producer Otto Lang and writer Leonard Hoffman to Chicago in Jan 1947 to interview participants and writers connected with the story. In Feb 1947, Fox purchased from McGuire the rights to an unpublished story and other material concerning Majczek. McGuire subsequently was hired as a technical adviser on the film. Fox also paid for releases from a number of persons whom they characterized in the film, including Tillie and Joe Majczek and Majczek's former wife. The company failed, however, to obtain a release from Vera Walush, portrayed as Wanda Skutnik in the film, who owned the speakeasy where the murder was committed and whose testimony identifying Majczek as the murderer led to his conviction. Although McGuire, Lang and Fox's legal counsel judged there to be little chance that Walush, who was ill at the time, would file a suit, she did so on May 1950. In her suit, Walush, who was by then known as Mrs. Vera Walush Kasulis, asked for $500,000 and claimed that the picture caused her to be "subject to dishonor and humiliation." Fox settled the suit in Oct 1954, paying Kasulis $25,000 and agreeing not to reissue the film in any theater or to any local television station within the municipal limits of Chicago.

In 2 Aug 1947 memo to Lang, director Henry Hathaway and writer Jay Dratler, executive producer Darryl F. Zanuck commented, "There is a big Polish population in the United States. You will note that I have calmed down some of the dialogue that tends to indicate that all Poles are not on the side of the law, but I think perhaps Dratler should go even further in toning it down. We should not definitely say that this is a Polish neighborhood. Perhaps we could just refer to it as a very tough neighborhood where the people always stick together and protect one another from outsiders, etc." In a 10 Mar 1947 letter from PCA Director Joseph I. Breen to the studio, included in the MPAA/PCA Collection at the AMPAS Library, Breen wrote, "we suggest that you substitute some other word... for 'Polack.' This derogatory reference is liable to give offense to a great many motion picture patrons." The PCA also deemed an early screenplay to be "not acceptable because of its highly questionable portrayal of the police." Later versions of the screenplay were approved, although after filming was completed, the studio cut the scene of the policeman being killed to comply with a Production Code provision that "officers of the law must not be shown dying at the hands of criminals."

According to *HR* news items, Louis King was originally set to direct the picture, which was to star Henry Fonda and Lloyd Nolan. Leopoldine Konstantine was originally signed to play "Tillie Wiecek." Leonarde Keeler, the inventor of the lie detector, played himself in the film, as did *Chicago Times* photographer Bill Vendetta. *Call Northside 777* marked the production debut of Otto Lang, who had previously directed pictures for Fox; the American film debut of Dutch actress Joanne de Bergh; and the screen debut of radio actress Betty Garde. The picture was shot in Chicago at numerous locations including the C.B. & Q. railroad yards, "Skid Row" and "Bughouse Square" in the South Wabash and South State Street slum districts, the Polish quarter and the Criminal Courts building. Scenes were also shot at the Illinois State Prison in Springfield. The photo lab sequence was filmed at the Douglas Aircraft Co. in Santa Monica, CA, and some shooting was done at the *Los Angeles Times* building.

It was Zanuck's intention for the film to use a "semi-documentary" style of mixed realism and drama, which Fox and other studios had used in a number of films made during the previous few years. In a memo dated 5 Mar 1947, he wrote, "While it is our intention to tell a hard-hitting, factual, semi-documentary story like *The House on 92nd Street, 13 Rue Madeleine* and *Boomerang,* we cannot ignore drama any more than these films ignored drama." *DV,* in their review of the film, stated, "This one sticks more closely to the documentary pattern than its predecessors." *HR* commented, "Few motion picture formulas have proved so continuously effective as the semi-documentary technique which takes a real-life story and presents it as a straight-from-the-shoulder statement of facts. Drama, then, is enhanced by its accuracy and emotional strength is drawn from its realism."

On 7 Oct 1948, *Screen Guild Theatre* presented a radio broadcast of *Call Northside 777* with James Stewart, Richard Conte and Pat O'Brien, and on 8 Dec 1949, *Screen Directors' Playhouse* broadcast a version of the story starring Stewart and Bill Conrad.

Box 24 Jan 1948. *Cue* 21 Feb 1948. *DV* 21 Jan 1948, p. 3. *DV* 31 May 1950, p. 5. *DV* 2 Jun 1983. *FD* 21 Jan 1948, p. 6. *HCN* 27 Feb 1948. *HR* 24 Jan 1947, p. 1. *HR* 3 Feb 1947, p. 1. *HR* 7 Mar 1947, p. 14. *HR* 17 Mar 1947, p. 14. *HR* 4 Apr 1947, p. 13. *HR* 20 Jun 1947, p. 7. *HR* 26 Sep 1947, p. 17. *HR* 7 Nov 1947, p. 15. *HR* 21 Jan 1948, p. 10. *HR* 24 Feb 1948, p. 6. *HR* 24 Mar 1948. *LADN* 20 Jun 1947. *LADN* 27 Feb 1948. *LAHE* 20 Jun 1947. *LAT* 29 Sep 1947. *LAT* 27 Feb 1948. *Life* 1 Mar 1948. *Life* 6 Mar 1950. *MPD* 21 Jan 1948. *MPHPD*

24 Jan 1948, p. 4029. *Newsweek* 23 Feb 1948. *New Yorker* 28 Feb 1948. *NYT* 19 Feb 1948, p. 29. *NYT* 26 Jul 1964. *Reader's Digest* Dec 1946, pp. 81-84.. *Time* 27 Aug 1945, p. 23. *Time* 6 Mar 1950. *Var* 21 Jan 1948, p. 8.

THE CALL OF HER PEOPLE (Gypsies)

Columbia Pictures Corp. *Dist* Metro Pictures Corp. 30 Apr **1917** [©Rolfe Photoplays, Inc.; 23 Apr 1917; LP10630]. Si; b&w. 7 reels.

Dir John W. Noble. *Scen* June Mathis. *Cam* Herbert O. Carleton.

Source: Based on the play *Egypt* by Edward Sheldon (New York, 18 Sep 1912).

Cast: Ethel Barrymore (*Egypt*), Robert Whittier (*Young Faro*), William B. Davidson (*Nicholas Van Kleet*), Frank Montgomery (*Faro Black*), William Mandeville (*Gordon Lindsay*), Mrs. Allan Walker (*Mother Komello*), Helen Arnold (*Mary Van Kleet*), Hugh Jeffrey (*Sheriff*).

Drama. Faro Black, the chief of the Gypsies, returns to camp in the South just after Egypt and his son Faro have completed their marriage vows. Angered, the chief tells them that the wedding means nothing, as Egypt is really the daughter of Gordon Lindsay, a wealthy man who is coming to claim her. Thus the lovers are torn apart, but vow to remain true to each other. In her new home, Egypt is unhappy and her love for Faro turns to bitterness when he does not return for her. In truth, Faro is being held prisoner by his relentless father, who, on his death bed, startles Faro with the information that Egypt is not Lindsay's daughter, but a member of the gypsies. After his father dies, Faro goes to Egypt, only to find her engaged to Nicholas Van Kleet. When the sheriff's brother insults Egypt, Faro kills the offender, and the posse sets out after the gypsy. He finds safety in Egypt's apartment, and on the eve of her marriage, the gypsy girl acknowledges her love for Faro. Van Kleet permits them to escape and they return to the gypsies, where Egypt finds happiness among her people. *Duplicity. Fathers and sons. Gypsies. Marriage–Annulment. Parentage. Murder. Posses.*

Note: Exteriors for this film were shot in Florida, while the interiors were filmed in New York.

ETR 9 Jun 1917, p. 54. *Motog* 30 Jun 1917, p. 1397. *MPN* 16 Jun 1917, p. 3793. *MPW* 16 Jun 1917, p. 1796. *NYDM* 2 Jun 1917, p. 24. *NYDM* 9 Jun 1917, p. 30. *Var* 2 Jun 1917, p. 23. *Wid's* 7 Jun 1917, p. 354.

THE CALL OF HIS PEOPLE (African Americans)

Reol Productions Corp. *Dist* Reol Productions Corp. 15 Jul **1921** [©Reol Productions Corp.; 14 Sep 1921; LU17503]. Si; b&w. 6 reels.

Adpt Aubrey Bowser.

Source: Based on the short story "The Man Who Would Be White" by Aubrey Bowser (publication undetermined).

Cast: George Edward Brown, Edna Morton, Mae Kemp, James Steven, Lawrence Chenault, Mercedes Gilbert, Percy Verwayen.

Social, Drama, African American. Nelson Holmes, an African American who has passed for white for twenty years, has advanced himself from office boy to the position of general manager of the Brazilian-American Coffee Syndicate. Nelson is visited by James Graves, a black boyhood friend from the South looking for a job as a Spanish correspondent. Fearing that his secret will be discovered, Nelson urges Graves to pose as a Spaniard, but Graves refuses. Finally Nelson agrees to make Graves his private secretary if he will remain quiet about Nelson's true race, and Graves accepts, though he feels contempt for Nelson. Deeply affected by seeing Graves again, Nelson pays a visit to Graves' sister Elinor, who was his childhood sweetheart. Elinor receives him coldly, however, angered by his denial of his own people, and remains adamant in her refusal to resume their friendship even after Nelson rescues her from a man annoying her. When a representative of the Santos company, a competitor which the syndicate is trying to put out of business, offers Nelson a bribe to destroy some contracts that could ruin his company, Nelson indignantly refuses, but their conversation is overheard by Beauregard Stuart, manager of foreign sales, who earlier was vexed that Nelson had received the promotion to general manager rather than him. That night, Graves overhears Stuart make a deal to get the contracts for the Santos representative. As Stuart is about to take the contracts from the company safe, Graves attacks him, concealing his identity, and during their struggle, retrieves the contracts. After Graves runs off, Nelson returns to the office, and Stuart mistakes him for his attacker, then accuses him of the theft. Graves, meanwhile, shows the contracts to Elinor, saying he now has power over Nelson. Elinor is tempted to destroy the contracts, hoping that Nelson would then be forced to return to his people. The next morning, as Stuart accuses Nelson to their boss, Lionel Weathering, Elinor arrives with the contracts and a letter from Graves, which proves Stuart's guilt. After she leaves, Nelson, extremely grateful for Elinor and Graves' loyalty, finally informs Weathering that he has been passing for white. Weathering assures Nelson that it is the quality and not the color of a man that counts, and Nelson asks Elinor for her hand in marriage, once again proud to be black. *African Americans. Business managers. Childhood sweethearts. Coffee. Racial impersonation. Secretaries. Bribery. Brothers and sisters. Business competition. Employer-employee relations.*

ChiDef 8 Jul 1921, p. 6. *ChiDef* 30 Jul 1921, p. 7.

THE CALL OF THE BLOOD (Native Americans)

Kinemacolor Co. of America. *Dist* Kinemacolor Co. of America. Mar **1913**?. Si; b&w. Length undetermined.

Western. When a pioneer's wife becomes ill, her husband and son decide to take her across the prairie in search of help. Along the way, their wagon is attacked by Indians, who abduct the woman and kill the husband before the arrival of the United States Cavalry. The son is taken to the soldiers' camp, and the woman dies in captivity after giving birth to a daughter. Years later, the boy, who has become a captain in the cavalry, sees the girl, who has grown into womanhood among the Indians, and falls in love with her. When the two finally meet, the young man notices a locket around her neck, and upon inspecting it, he sees the picture of their mother and realizes that he has found his sister. *Abduction. Frontier and pioneer life. Long-lost relatives. Brothers and sisters. Childbirth. Indians of North America. Photographs. United States. Army. Cavalry.*

Note: The film is described as a feature, but it may have been under four reels in length. Kinemacolor, a two-color additive process, was devised in England by Edward R. Turner and popularized by Charles Urban's 1911 film, *The Durbar at Delhi*. Projected at twice the normal speed through an alternating red-orange and blue-green color wheel, the film required a special projector and was said to cause eye strain. The American branch of the Kinemacolor Co. disbanded after only one year.

Var 7 Mar 1913, p. 14.

CALL OF THE COYOTE (Latino)

Imperial Distributing Corp. *Dist* Imperial Distributing Corp. Feb **1934**. Sd (National Recording Company); b&w. 50 min.

Pres William M. Pizor. *Dir* Patrick Carlyle. *Photog* Irving Akers. *Ed* Marshall B. Pollock. *Sd tech* R. E. Carpenter.

Cast: KEN THOMPSON [(*Don Adios*)], Pat Carlyle, Merrill McCormick, Baby Marie Bracco [(*Dolly Barrett*)], Sally Dolling [(*Jane*)], Charles Stevens, Bartlett Carre, Morgan Galloway, Wallace Shepherd, Jack Pollard, Howard Fossett.

Western. [*Print viewed*]. Although Jim Barrett, his friend, Jay, and Chuck Reynolds, the head of a vicious gang of thieves, have equal interests in an Arizona gold mine, only Jim and Jay know its location. Just after one of Reynolds' men murders Jim, Mexican Don Adios and his band of roving cowboys come across Jim's body, on which they find a tiny map to the gold mine. Red, one of Don Adios' men, eagerly pockets the map and thus raises the suspicions of Don Adios. In the nearby town of Williams, meanwhile, Jay and Jim's little daughter Dolly, who has inherited Jim's share of the mine, overhear Reynolds discussing Jim's murder with his henchmen. A moment later, Jane, Dolly's governess, and "Doc," the town physician, question Reynolds about Jim's whereabouts, but Reynolds responds only with screamed threats. Reynolds orders Pete, one of his men, to kidnap Dolly, who has gone off with Doc and Jane, and then shoots and kills Jay in the street. Just before Pete forcibly takes Dolly from Doc, Don Adios and his sidekick, Pancho, ride up and save the child. While Don Adios promises Jane and Doc his protection, Reynolds orders his men to retrieve the map from Red, who was paid by Reynolds to betray Don Adios. At Don Adios' hideout, Pancho cuts a curl from Dolly's head while she sleeps and gives it to the sentimental Don Adios as a momento. As Don Adios admires the curl, a second map to the gold mine falls out of it. Don Adios then learns that Red has betrayed him and, after swearing revenge on Reynolds, orders his men to go to town and wait for the "call of the coyote," his signal to begin fighting. Using Dolly's map, Don Adios and Pancho locate Jim's mine, which they discover is actually a worthless "dry hole." Reynolds and his gang arrive at the mine and, after exchanging brief gunfire with Don Adios and Pancho, are furious to discover Jim's double-cross. Don Adios, still determined to help Dolly and Jane, who was entrusted by Jim to take Dolly to an Eastern boarding school, then gives his call and

alerts his men, who have been rounding up volunteers in Williams. After a gunfight in town, in which Reynolds' henchmen are soundly defeated by Don Adios, Pancho steals Reynolds' ill-gotten gold from the local saloon. As the empty-handed Reynolds vows revenge, Don Adios rides back to Jane and Dolly and happily gives them the gold. Before saying a final goodbye to Jane, Don Adios begs a kiss from her and cuts a heartshape piece of fabric from her dress as a keepsake. His mission completed, he then tells Pancho that it is time for them to seek a "new place," a "new adventure." *Gold mines. Governesses. Maps. Mexicans. Murder. Outlaws. Arizona. Betrayal. Children. Gunfights. Hair. Inheritance. Kidnapping. Mexican-American border region. Rescues. Revenge. Thieves.*

Note: The title card for this film included the subtitle, "A Legend of the Golden West." No contemporary reviews were found for the film. Although the viewed print included a 1934 copyright statement, the title was not found in the copyright records. According to publicity news items, Jose Arias Spanish Orchestra provided music for the picture. It is not known if this credit is for performing or composing. According to the 1935-36 MPA's "Companies Product" section, the film was first released in Feb 1934. A 1936 MPH release chart listed the title, along with several other Imperial titles, as a 15 Mar 1936 re-issue. Modern sources complete the above cast list with the following character names: Charles Stevens (*Pancho*), Patrick Carlyle (*Jim Barret*), Merrill McCormick (*Chuck Reynolds*), Bartlett Carre (*Pablo*), Wallace Shepherd (*Red*), Morgan Galloway (*Doc*), Jack Pollard (*Harry*) and Howard Fossett (*Pete*).

THE CALL OF THE EAST (Japanese Americans)

Jesse L. Lasky Feature Play Co. *Dist* Paramount Pictures Corp. 15 Oct **1917** [©Jesse L. Lasky Feature Play Co., Inc.; 27 Sep 1917; LP11468]. Si; b&w. 5 reels.

Dir George H. Melford. *Asst dir* Roy Marshall. *Story and scen* Beulah Marie Dix. *Cam* Percy Hilburn. *Art dir* Wilfred Buckland and Max Parker.

Cast: Sessue Hayakawa (*Arai Takada*), Tsuru Aoki (*O'Mitsu, his sister*), Jack Holt (*Alan Hepburn*), Margaret Loomis (*Shelia Hepburn*), James Cruze (*Janzo*), Ernest Joy (*Col. Bassett*), Guy Oliver (*Cadger*), Jane Wolff (*Yuri*).

Drama. Alan Hepburn, the son of an American businessman who made his fortune in Japan, resides in Tokyo with his Japanese mistress O'Mitsu. Alan's romance earns the enmity of O'Mitsu's brother Takada, who vows revenge on the American for dishonoring his sister. When Alan's half sister Shelia finds herself irresistibly drawn to Japan, Takada plans poetic justice by seducing the girl. Pretending to be Alan's friend, Takada invites the American to his island home where he then holds him captive. Shelia, learning of her brother's fate, follows him to the island. Dismayed upon discovering that Shelia is the mysterious woman who stole his heart at the Festival of Lanterns, Takada nevertheless intends to exact his revenge until the girl seeks refuge at the image of Kwannon, a sacred spot to the Japanese. Begging her forgiveness, Takada releases Alan and Shelia, but Shelia finds herself strangely drawn to her captor. When Alan informs her that her mother was Japanese, Shelia realizes that she is answering the call of the East and decides to remain behind to become Takada's wife. *Americans in foreign countries. Brothers and sisters. Japan. Japanese. Japanese Americans. Mistresses. Parentage. Revenge. Seduction. Abduction. Shrines.*

Motog 3 Nov 1917, p. 941. *MPW* 3 Nov 1917, p. 707, 756. *NYDM* 6 Oct 1917, p. 13. *NYDM* 27 Oct 1917, p. 20. *Wid's* 29 Nov 1917, p. 768.

CALL OF THE FLESH (*foreign version*) see SEVILLA DE MIS AMORES

CALL OF THE FOREST (Native Amricans)

Adventure Pictures, Inc. *Dist* Lippert Productions, Inc. 18 Nov **1949**; Prod: began late Sep 1947 [©Lippert Productions, Inc.; 15 Dec 1949; LP2721]. Sd (Glen Glenn Sound Recording); b&w. 6 reels, 5,117 ft. 57 min. PCA cert no. 12871.

Prod Edward Finney. *Assoc prod* Morris Landres. *Dir* John F. Link. *Asst dir* Edward Stein. *Scr* Craig Burns. *Dir of photog* Karl O. Struss. *Op* James Knott. *Still photog* Pop Levi. *Spec eff* Robert Clark and Ray Mercer. *Film ed* Asa Boyd Clark. *Master of props* Robert Murdoch. *Ward* Emanuel Barton. *Mus* Karl Hajos. *Sd mixer* Glen Glenn. *Sd rec* Harry Eckles. *Prod mgr* Donald Verk. *Animal trainer* Curley Twiford, Byron Nelson, Bud Hooker, Hugh Hooker and Johnny Goodwin.

Cast: Robert Lowery (*Sam Harrison*), Ken Curtis (*Bob Brand*), Chief Thundercloud (*Stormcloud*), Black Diamond (*King, the stallion*), and Introducing Charlie Hughes (*Bobby Brand*), Martha Sherrill (*Nancy Sommers*), Tom Hanly (*Dan McKay*), Fred Gildart

(*Pinto Peterson*), Eula Guy (*Mrs. Joe*), Jimmy the Crow, Beady the Racoon, Ripple the Deer, Fuzzy the Bear.

Animal, Western, with songs. [*Print viewed*]. Rancher Bob Brand persuades fellow rancher Sam Harrison to help him capture a wild black stallion to give to his seven-year-old son Bobby when he arrives from the East. Together they isolate the stallion, who is the leader of a large herd, lasso him and lock him inside Bob's corral. Bob then leaves to pick up Bobby at the train station, unaware that his scheming neighbors, one of whom is Harrison, suspect that he has discovered Lost Mine, which is located in the badlands near the home of a seemingly crazy old Indian named Stormcloud. After Bob delivers Bobby to the ranch, he presents him with the stallion and tells him that he named the horse King because he was the king of his herd. Bobby notices that King has a splinter stuck in his foot and removes it, after which King appears relieved. In the badlands, meanwhile, Harrison and Gillman are searching for the mine, when suddenly, Stormcloud begins shooting at them. Bob tells Bobby that he plans to leave for a few days to search for the fabled mine and asks Bobby to look after the ranch while he is gone. Days later, King escapes from the corral and gallops into the wilderness some distance away from the ranch. When Bobby finds King, he realizes that he has injured his leg and is unable to stand. Unwilling to desert King, Bobby lies down on the ground next to him, where he stays throughout the night. The next morning, King and Bobby are awakened by Stormcloud, and King appears to have recovered. When Bobby tells him about his father's plan to find the mine, Stormcloud says that he would like to repay Bob, because he has done much to help his people. Stormcloud then recounts a legend which tells how many generations before, his tribe attacked a group of white gold prospectors. Now, Stormcloud explains, the tribe has come to regret the attack. Stormcloud then gives Bobby a Bible which was stolen from one of the prospectors. Bobby goes to the ranch and gives the bible to Bob, who discovers a map to the mine that Stormcloud drew inside the back cover. When Harrison learns about the map, he goes to the ranch, shoots Bob and steals the Bible. The fatally injured Bob falls to the ground, knocks over a lantern and starts a fire, which soon engulfs the entire house. After Bobby escapes the burning house, the sheriff organizes a search party, which includes Harrison. The following day, King awakens Bobby, who fled into a nearby field. Bobby urges his beloved stallion to rejoin his herd, and the horse reluctantly departs. Harrison then arrives, and after Stormcloud accuses him of killing Bob, he shoots Stormcloud in the arm and begins firing at Bobby. Meanwhile, King leads the herd in a stampede toward Harrison, who is trampled to death. Bobby then sees the Bible lying on the ground next to Harrison's corpse, grabs it and rides away on King. *Claim jumpers. Fathers and sons. Mines. Ranchers. Wild horses. Bible. Escapes. Fires. Gifts. Gunshot wounds. Indians of North America. Lassoes. Maps. Murder. Neighbors. Searches. Stampedes. Train stations.*

Note: The working title of this film was *The Flaming Forest*. Although onscreen credits suggest that this film was Charlie Hughes' screen debut, the actor had previously appeared in the 1948 Monogram film *The Fighting Ranger*. Adventure Pictures was not credited onscreen, but was listed in a 15 Apr 1949 *HR* news item. Although there are several songs in the film, no composers or song titles have been determined. On 27 May 1949, *HR* noted that Lippert had acquired the picture and was planning to release it through Screen Guild after adding several days' worth of shooting.

HR 15 Apr 1949, p. 3. *HR* 27 May 1949, p. 3. *MPHPD* 29 Apr 1950, p. 278.

CALL OF THE NAVAJO (Native Americans, Navajo)

New Life Films. **1952?** [©Stanley Earl Taylor; 10 Dec 1952; MP4173]. Sd; col (Kodachrome). 16 mmmm. 42 min.

Dir Stan Taylor. *Narration written by* Marian Taylor. *Photog* Stan Taylor.

Cast: Harris Arthur (*Ashkee*), Jack Drake (*Missionary*), Karl Ashcroft (*Trader*), John Arthur (*Father*), Eva Arthur (*Mother*), Priscilla Arthur (*Sister*), Johnny Arthur (*Brother*), David Hemstreet (*Blind man*), Donald Natoni (*Medicine man*), Eddie Raymond (*Interpreter*), Willard Bass (*Mission school director*), Thomas Atcitty (*Ashkee grown-up*), Harry Elders (*Narrator*).

Religious, Drama. [*Print viewed*]. During a visit to the Eagle Rock Trading Post with his family, Ashkee, a young Navajo boy, spies a beautiful silver belt behind the counter. As Ashkee gazes longingly at the belt, a missionary enters the store and invites everyone to attend a religious service outside. While left alone in the store with a blind customer, Ashkee takes the belt. At that moment Ashkee hears the missionary tell the congregation that God is looking at them right

now. Ashkee comes to his senses, returns the belt, and goes outside to listen to the rest of the service. The following day Ashkee and his family are forced to move their belongings and herd of sheep to an area near a flowing stream because a drought has dried up all the watering holes around their present campsite. As the family settles in, Ashkee takes the sheep out to graze. After suffering through several misadventures, Ashkee returns home to discover that the trader has accused him of stealing the belt which he had coveted. Ashkee insists he did not steal the belt, but neither his father nor the trader believes him. The trader decides that unless the family returns the belt within three days, he will demand their sheep and all their jewelry as payment for the belt. Later, when Ashkee's sister falls ill, Ashkee is convinced that the missionary's God is punishing him for wanting to steal the belt. Ashkee visits the missionary's house to tell him about all the terrible things that have happened and to ask how he can appease this angry God. The missionary assures him that God loves Ashkee and would not cause all this trouble. Ashkee is puzzled and amazed by such a benevolent God. Meanwhile, the missionary decides to help the young boy by trying to find the belt. Later that day during a fierce storm, Ashkee saves his pet lamb Snowflake from a dangerous canyon just as the animal is about to drown. That night the missionary comes to Ashkee's dwelling with his wife and a nurse who tends to Ashkee's sister. The missionary, inspired by Ashkee's love for his pet lamb, shares the biblical story of the shepherd who risks everything to save just one sheep. Ashkee's sister, improving under the nurse's ministrations, thanks the missionary's God for making her better and asks Him to help her family. By the third day, the belt is nowhere to be found, so Ashkee's father rounds up the sheep and gathers together their jewelry to take to the trader. Just as the payment is being made, the missionary rides up with the belt and reveals that the blind customer in the trading post was only pretending to be sightless and had stolen the belt. Ashkee and his family are ecstatic. Ashkee reveals that he has taken the Christian God into his heart and intends to go to mission school so that he can return to the reservation and spread the word of God's love. After an apprehensive start, Ashkee thrives at mission school. He has many ambitions and dreams of playing sports, winning trophies for the school, singing in the choir, studying, going to college and eventually returning to the reservation as a missionary. *Christianity. Faith. False accusations. Missionaries. Navajo Indians. Religious conversion. Blindness. Droughts. Family relationships. Indians of North America–Reservations. Nurses. Robbery. Sermons. Sheepherders. Storms. Trading posts.*

CALL OF THE ROCKIES (Gypsies, Native Americans)

Dist Road Show Pictures, Inc.; Syndicate Pictures Corp. **1931** [©L. E. Goetz; 9 Jan 1931; LP1876]. Sd; b&w. 8 reels. 71 min. Passed by the National Board of Review.

Pres LEON GOETZ and ALBERT DEZEL. *Gen supv* Leon Goetz and Albert Dezel. *Dir* Raymond K. Johnson. *Photog* King Gray and H. H. Brownell. *Film ed* George McQuire. *Mus arr* Dell Youngmeyer. *Orch dir* James G. Henshel.

Cast: BEN LYON (*Matthew*), MARIE PREVOST (*Arleta*), Gladys Johnson (*Sylvia*), Anders Randolph (*Jim [Vance]*), Russell Simpson (*Gunner Bill*), James Mason (*Tony*), The Four Night Hawks.

Historical, Western. [*Print viewed*]. Thompson, a city man, is on vacation in the foothills of the Rockies. After first mistaking him for a government agent because of his riding habit, four mountaineers become friendlier toward Thompson when they learn that he was merely attracted by their singing. The backwoodsmen talk about a government plan to flood a nearby valley that includes their land. One man explains that his grandfather came through that same valley with the first wagon train in 1849 and tells the following story: A small band of pioneers, under the command of Captain Peck, heads West. Three con artists—ex-poker dealer Jim Vance, his gypsy stepdaughter Arleta, and his partner, Tony—approach the wagon train. Arleta plans to swindle the pioneers by selling the caravan's horses to the Indians. The trio approach Matthew, a young scout, and ask if they might join the train. The flirtatious Arleta is attracted to Matthew, but his heart belongs to sweet and lovely Sylvia. As the expedition progresses, food supplies dwindle and many of the pioneers are homesick. A scouting party discovers buffalo, and Arleta rescues Sylvia from a stampede of the herd. The women cement their friendship as the pioneers celebrate and dine on buffalo meat. Matthew nearly succumbs to Arleta's provocative charms during a passionate fandango dance, but finally leaves to be with Sylvia. Jim

and Tony are displeased with Arleta's behavior and decide to exclude her from their future schemes. Weeks later, the wagon train successfully fords a fast-flowing river and sets up camp on the opposite shore. As Jim and Tony plot a morning raid with the Indians, Matthew falls under Arleta's spell and embraces the woman he has learned to love. At daybreak, Arleta is woken by Matthew's dog and learns of her stepfather's conspiracy against the settlers, whom she has grown to respect. As she confronts Jim, the Indians are rustling the horses. "Gunner Bill," one of the settlers, alerts the camp and the Indians are repulsed. Tony is killed by the Indians after they discover that he has tricked them. During a heated argument with Matthew and Arleta, Jim shoots his stepdaughter. As Jim and Matt exchange blows, the buffalo herd stampedes, terrified by the nearby gun battle. Jim is killed by the animals, but Matthew and Arleta escape. Despite her fatal wound, Arleta is able to warn the settlement of the stampede, while Matthew diverts the herd. Her conscience clear, Arleta dies in the arms of Sylvia and Matthew. *Confidence men. Gypsies. Indians of North America. Outlaws. Settlers. Stepchildren. Stepfathers. United States–History–19th century. Buffalo (NY). City slickers. Covered wagons. Death by animals. Gunfights. Horses. Rocky Mountains. Romance. Rustlers. Scouts (Frontier). Seduction. Stampedes. Wagon trains.*

Note: This film was also reviewed under the title *West of the Rockies*. Except for the opening sequence, this film was shot as a silent with music and sound effects added. The film appears to have been produced during the 1920s, but no additional information was found as to the nature of the original production.

FD 12 Jul 1931, p. 10. *MPH* 10 Jan 1931, p. 44. *Var* 14 Jul 1931.

THE CALLAHANS AND THE MURPHYS (Irish Americans)

Metro-Goldwyn-Mayer Corp.; controlled by Loew's Inc. *Dist* Metro-Goldwyn-Mayer Distributing Corp. 18 Jun **1927** [©Metro-Goldwyn-Mayer Distributing Corp.; 11 Jul 1927; LP24254]. Si; b&w. 7 reels, 6,126 ft.

Dir George Hill. *Scen* Frances Marion. *Titles* Ralph Spence. *Photog* Ira Morgan. *Film ed* Hugh Wynn. *Settings* Cedric Gibbons and David Townsend. *Ward* René Hubert.

Source: Based on the novel *The Callahans and the Murphys* by Kathleen Norris (Garden City, New York, 1924).

Cast: Marie Dressler (*Mrs. Callahan*), Polly Moran (*Mrs. Murphy*), Sally O'Neil (*Ellen Callahan*), Lawrence Gray (*Dan Murphy*), Eddie Gribbon (*Jim Callahan*), Frank Currier (*Grandpa Callahan*), Gertrude Olmsted (*Monica Murphy*), Turner Savage (*Timmy Callahan*), Jackie Coombs (*Terrance Callahan*), Dawn O'Day (*Mary Callahan*), Monty O'Grady (*Michael Callahan*), Tom Lewis (*Mr. Murphy*).

Comedy-drama. Mrs. Callahan and Mrs. Murphy, who live on opposite sides of a narrow alley in the tenement district, are quarrelsome friends, although their children, Ellen and Dan, are in love. Dan becomes involved with a gang of bootleggers and disappears. Ellen, meanwhile, gives birth to a child which her mother contrives to adopt without knowledge of its origin. When Dan returns, the couple confesses to having been secretly married. The Callahans and Murphys once again resume their happy existence, with the mothers arguing over the baby's family resemblance. *Adoption. Bootleggers. Family life. Irish Americans. Tenement-houses.*

MPW 16 Jul 1927. *NYT* 12 Jul 1927, p. 29. *Var* 13 Jul 1927, p. 22.

THE CAMERAMAN (Chinese Americans)

Metro-Goldwyn-Mayer Corp.; controlled by Loew's Inc. *Dist* Metro-Goldwyn-Mayer Distributing Corp. 22 Sep **1928** [©Metro-Goldwyn-Mayer Distributing Corp.; 15 Sep 1928; LP25722]. Si; b&w. 8 reels, 6,995 ft.

Prod Buster Keaton. *Dir* Edward Sedgwick. *Scen* Richard Schayer. *Story* Clyde Bruckman and Lew Lipton. *Titles* Joseph Farnham. *Photog* Elgin Lessley and Reggie Lanning. *Tech dir* Fred Gabourie. *Film ed* Hugh Wynn and Basil Wrangell.

Cast: Buster Keaton (*Luke Shannon [Buster]*), Marceline Day (*Sally*), Harry Gribbon (*Cop*), Harold Goodwin (*Stagg*), Sidney Bracy (*Editor*).

Comedy. Tintype photographer Buster falls in love with Sally, a secretary for the Hearst newsreel, and hocks his still camera in order to buy an ancient movie camera. At Sally's urging, Buster photographs news events that may be of interest to the Hearst organization, but all of his attempts turn out badly. Sally tips Buster off about an impending tong war in Chinatown, and he covers all the dangerous action only to discover that he had no film in his camera. The

following day, Buster is filming a regatta and Sally falls overboard from the boat of Stagg, a cowardly Hearst cameraman who deserts her to save himself. Buster rescues Sally and wins her undying love. *Boatracing. Chinatowns. Chinese Americans. Hearst News Service. Newsreel cameramen. Secretaries. Tongs (Secret societies).*

Note: Sources disagree in crediting film editor.
NYT 17 Sep 1928, p. 27. *Var* 19 Sep 1928, p. 12.

CAMINO DEL INFIERNO see **DEL INFIERNO AL CIELO**

LAS CAMPANAS DE CAPISTRANO (Latino, Spanish language)
Producciones Latinas Ltd. *Dist* J. H. Hoffberg Co. Oct **1930**; Los Angeles opening: 3 Oct 1930; Prod: Aug 1930. Sd; b&w. 5,900 ft. 66 min. Spanish language.

Supv Richard C. Kahn. *Dir* Leon De La Mothe. *Scr* B. Wayne Lamont. *Spanish dial* Gabriel Navarro. *Story* Leon De La Mothe. *Photog* Bert Baldridge. *Art dir* José Ignacio Sotomayor. *Film ed* Leon De La Mothe. *Mus comp* Salvador Nuño. *Choral dir* Los hermanos Camacho Vega. *Sd* C. S. Piper.

Song(s): "Camila," "Amar, Vivir" and "Mi Charro," composers undetermined.

Cast: Luis de Ibargüen, Cora Montes, Ricardo Bell, Jr., Antonio Roux, Carmen La Roux, Carlota Cortés, José Ignacio Sotomayor, Salvador Villaseñor, Manuel Camacho Vega, José Arias, Roberto Saa Silva, Israel García, Ernesto Zambrano, Antonio Carral, Elías Guevara, Adolfo Villavicenio, Rafael Blanco, Pedro Valenzuela, José Arias Orchestra.

Melodrama, with songs. [*Not viewed*]. In the 1830's, when General Anastasio Bustamante is the President of Mexico, Governor Manuel Victoria imposes his own rule in Upper California until a revolt breaks out against him. A frightened young woman attempts to free her father from the governor's wrath by informing against the rebellion's leader. During a bloody raid, when the young woman is about to be killed, a mysterious stranger rescues her. When the danger passes, she realizes that her rescuer is the man against whom she informed. *California–History–to 1846. Corruption. Governors. Informers. Mexico–History. San Juan Capistrano Mission (San Juan Capistrano, CA).* Los Angeles (CA). Raids. Uprisings.

Note: This film's working title was *Amor y sacrificio.* It has not been established whether the José Arias Orchestra appeared onscreen or was only heard on the soundtrack.
FD 29 Nov 1931.

THE CAMPUS FLIRT (Swedish Americans)
Famous Players-Lasky Corp. *Dist* Paramount Pictures. 4 Oct **1926**; New York premiere: 18 Sep 1926 [©Famous Players-Lasky Corp.; 5 Oct 1926; LP23181]. Si; b&w. 7 reels, 6,702 ft.

Pres Adolph Zukor and Jesse L. Lasky. *Dir* Clarence Badger. *Story and scr* Louise Long and Lloyd Corrigan. *Titles* Rube Goldberg and Ralph Spence. *Photog* H. Kinley Martin.

Cast: Bebe Daniels (*Patricia Mansfield*), James Hall (*Denis Adams*), El Brendel (*Knute Knudson*), Charles Paddock (*Himself*), Joan Standing (*Harriet Porter*), Gilbert Roland (*Graham Stearns*), Irma Kornelia (*Mae*), Jocelyn Lee (*Gwen*).

Comedy-drama. Patricia Mansfield, a product of wealth and high society, is sent to Colton College by her father, who hopes to eradicate her snobbish veneer. On the train, Pat meets Denis Adams, a prominent athlete who is working his way through school as coach of the girls' track team; he introduces her to track star Charlie Paddock. Through efforts to keep her associates in place, Pat sinks deeper into the mire of antagonism; her only friends are Harriet Porter and Knute Knudson, the Swedish janitor. Trying to escape from Knute's pet mouse, she passes Paddock like a streak of lightning. Joining the fast set, Pat is soon branded as the campus flirt; realizing her foolishness, she sets out to vindicate herself by joining the track team. Before a meet, Graham Stearns abducts Adams, and Pat, in rescuing him, is herself detained. Knute rescues her in time for the race, and, in a screaming finish with chasing policemen, Paddock saves the event by running the last lap. *Athletic coaches. Chases. College life. Courtship. Flirts. Janitors. Mice. Snobs and snobbishness. Swedish Americans. Track and field athletics. University of Southern California. Upper classes.*

Note: This film was shot in part on location at the University of Southern California. *Var* commented concerning Swedish dialect comedian El Brendel: "For attention the star is given a close run by El Brendel (formerly of Brendel and Burt in vaudeville). Brendel will undoubtedly do much more camera work

if this first effort is a criterion. Here he plays a Swede waiter in a school dormitory, extracting successive laughs throughout. His appearance is not unlike Langdon, but that doesn't mean he is mimicking. Not so, Brendel gives every evidence of taking care of himself."
NYT 22 Sep 1926, p. 31. *Var* 22 Sep 1926.

UNA CANA AL AIRE (Spanish language)
Hal Roach Studios, Inc.; Metro-Goldwyn-Mayer Corp.; controlled by Loew's, Inc. *Dist* Metro-Goldwyn-Mayer Distributing Corp. Nov **1930**; Los Angeles opening: 21 Nov 1930; Prod: Aug–Sep 1930. Sd (Sistema Western Electric [Western Electric System]); b&w. 5 reels. 41 min. Passed by the National Board of Review. Spanish language.

Presenta a [*Pres*] Hal Roach. *Dirección* [*Dir*] James W. Horne. *Diálogo por* [*Dial*] H. M. Walker. *Fotografía* [*Photog*] Art Lloyd. *Editor de película* [*Film ed*] Richard Currier. [*Mus* LeRoy Shield]. *Fonografía* [*Rec*] Elmer Raguse.

Music: "Júrame," by María Grever.

Cast: CHARLEY CHASE [(*Carlos*)], Carmen Guerrero [(*Carmen*)], Carmen Granada [(*Juanita*)], Alfonso Pedroza [(*Sr. Pedroza, the client*)], [Enrique Acosta (*Sr. Gilstrom*)], [Dorothy Granger (*Tango partner*)].

Comedy. [*Print viewed*]. Just after Carlos has presented an engagement ring with a miniscule stone to his fiancée Carmen, he receives a phone call from his boss, Sr. Gilstrom, informing him that he must devote his time to Sr. Pedroza, a visiting client from Chicago who expects to be "entertained." Gilstrom gives Carlos the phone numbers of two young "ladies," one for Pedroza, the other for Carlos. However, when Carmen becomes suspicious, Carlos has to explain everything to her and she decides to accompany him. They go by taxi to a hotel where one of the ladies, Juanita, resides. Carlos has been instructed to simply whistle at the hotel's entrance and Juanita will come down. However, when he does this, he is greeted by a cascade of room keys. When Juanita does appear, Carmen is not impressed by her coarse behavior. After they pick up Sr. Pedroza at his hotel, the foursome adjourns to a nightclub, where Pedroza quickly loses interest in Juanita when she reveals that he is wearing a wig. Unaware that Carmen is not a professional escort girl, Pedroza then proposes to Carlos that they change partners, but Carlos resists. When one of the club's floorshow acts is announced as being unable to appear due to the illness of a dancing partner, Pedroza volunteers Carlos so that he can proposition Carmen in his absence. When Carlos returns from performing as a tango dancer, he finds himself being romanced by Juanita, while across the table, Carmen retaliates by flirting with Pedroza, who ridicules the size of the stone in her engagement ring and presents her with a ring with an enormous diamond. Later, as both couples dance, Pedroza sneaks off to an adjacent, curtained booth with Carmen, but they have to leave when the original occupants return. However, Carlos, thinking that Pedroza and Carmen are still there, eavesdrops and hears a seduction taking place. Carlos then inadvertently causes a large number of balloons to explode, making the customers think that a police raid is taking place. They jettison their illegal bottles of liquor, head for the exit and cause much chaos as they attempt to leave the parking lot. Carlos attacks the man in the booth from behind with a vase, but when he sees Pedroza at another table, realizes that he has hit the wrong man. The young lady with the stunned man accuses Pedroza of the deed, while Carlos and Carmen make a fast escape. *Businessmen. Engagements. Escort services. Flirts. Nightclubs. Balloons (Toy). Business ethics. Diamonds. Eavesdropping. Hotels. Mistaken identity. Prohibition. Rings. Tango (Dance). Wigs.*

Note: Carmen Granada's and Alfonso Pedroza's names are misspelled in the onscreen credits. *Una cana al aire* was an expanded version of the two-reel Hal Roach comedy, *Looser Than Loose*, directed by James W. Horne and starring Charley Chase and Thelma Todd. Although a French-language version was also made, entitled *Gare la bombe!*, and starring Chase, Pauline Garon, André Cheron, Georgette Rhodes and Dorothy Granger, its exhibition in the U.S. has not been confirmed.

CANADIAN CAPERS see **RIDING HIGH**

CANAVAN see **IT HAD TO HAPPEN**

CANAVAN, THE MAN WHO HAD HIS WAY see **THE DANGER SIGNAL**

A CANÇÃO DO BERÇO see **TODA UNA VIDA**

LA CANCIÓN DE LOS ANDES *see* EL CARNAVAL DEL DIABLO

LA CANCIÓN PROHIBIDA *see* LA MELODÍA PROHIBIDA

CANE FIRE *see* WHITE HEAT

EL CANTANTE DE NÁPOLES (Spanish language)

Warner Bros. Productions Corp.; La compañia Vitafónica. *Dist* Warner Bros. Productions Corp. **1935**; New York opening: 22 Feb 1935; Prod: Aug 1934. Sd; b&w. 8 reels, 6,963 ft. 77 min. Spanish language.

Supervisada por [*Supv*] Manuel Reachi. *Película dirigida por* [*Dir*] Howard Bretherton. [*Dial dir* Moreno Cuyar]. [*Asst dir* Carrol Sax and Arthur Lueker]. *Argumento* [*Scr*] Elizabeth Reinhardt. [*Scr* Manuel Reachi]. *Fotografía de* [*Photog*] William Rees. [*2d cam* Frank Kesson]. [*Gaffer* Everett Burkholder]. *Escenarista* [*Art dir*] John Hughes. *Cortador* [*Ed*] Frank Magee. [*Ward man* Charles Mack]. [*Ward woman* Ida Greenfield]. *Orquesta Vitafónica dirigida por* [*Vitaphone Orchestra conducted by*] Leo F. Forbstein. *Arreglos* [*Orch arr*] Alberto Conti and Manuel Reachi. [*Sd mixer* Leslie G. Hewitt]. [*Hair* Martha Acker]. [*Makeup* Ed Zimmer]. [*Prod mgr* William Koenig]. [*Unit mgr* Frank Mattison]. [*Scr clerk* Frank Fox]. [*Grip* Whitey Eastman]. [*Props* Herbert Plews]. [*Asst props* Jack More].

Song(s): "Di quelle pira" from the opera *Il trovatore*, music by Giuseppe Verdi, libretto by Salvatore Cammarano; "The Tarantella" and other selections from *Il barbiere di Siviglia*, music by Gioacchino Antonio Rossini, libretto by Giuseppe Petrosellini; "O paradiso" from the opera *L'Africane*, music by Giacomo Meyerbeer, libretto by Eugène Scribe; "Core n'grato," music and lyrics by Cordello; "Neopolitan Nights," music by J. S. Zamecnik, lyrics by Harry D. Kerr; "Addio mia bella Napoli," music and lyrics by Teodoro Cottrau; "Italienischer Salat," music and lyrics by Richard Genee; other songs by Bernhard Kaun and Alberto Conti.

Source: Based on a novel by Armán Chelieu (publication undetermined).

Cast: ENRICO CARUSO, JR. (*Enrico Daspuro*), Mona Maris (*Teresa*), Carmen Río (*María*), Alfonso Pedroza (*Fortuni*), Antonio Vidal ([*Profesor*] *Rubini*), Emilia Leovalli (*Mamá Daspuro*), Enrique Acosta (*Papá Daspuro*), Francisco Marán (*Eduardo*), Martín Garralaga (*Beppo*), María Calvo (*Mamá Corelli*), Rosa Rey (*Doña Rosa*), Elías Guevara, José María Sánchez García (*Empresarios*), "Don Catarino" (*Mensajero*), Terry LaFranconi (*Cancionero*).

Melodrama, with songs. [*Not viewed*]. Enrico Daspuro, the son of a Neopolitan blacksmith, dreams of one day singing opera at La Scala in Milan. To do so he must leave his father's business against his father's wishes. During the festival of Carnival, Enrico sings in public to great acclaim, but because he left the house without his father's permission, he is expelled from the family. While earning his living as a tourist guide, Enrico loses no chance to sing in any café that will allow it. In one of the cafés, Enrico meets Teresa, a woman connected to the world of opera. Although she has a superior attitude, she enthusiastically recommends him to the famous professor Rubini from Milan and gives him the money to journey there. The road to fame is full of pitfalls, however, and far from his sweetheart Maria and his beloved mother, Enrico often feels tormented. Once again, Teresa helps the Neopolitan singer obtain his desired objective, and after achieving professional triumphs, and with his father's pardon, Enrico happily recovers the affection of those he loves. *Art patronage. Fathers and sons. Italy. Opera. Romance. Singers. Blacksmiths. Cafés. Class distinction. Festivals. Milan (Italy). Mothers and sons. Music teachers. Naples (Italy).*

Note: The onscreen credits were taken from a studio cutting continuity. The running time listed above was calculated from footage given in NYSA records. According to her autobiography, Jinx Falkenberg had a small part in this picture. This may have been her film debut.

CM Feb 1935, p. 142. *FD* 26 Feb 1935, p. 38. *HR* 20 Aug 1934, p. 7. *IP* Jan 1934, p. 17. *NYT* 25 Feb 1935, p. 13.

THE CANTOR'S SON (Jewish Americans, Yiddish language)

Eron Pictures, Inc. *Dist* Eron Pictures, Inc. **1937**; New York opening: 25 Dec 1937 [©Mecca Film Laboratory, Inc.; 24 Dec 1937; LP7773]. Sd (RCA The Magic Voice of the Screen); b&w. 10 reels, 8,211 ft. 90 min. PCA cert no. 01849. Yiddish language with English subtitles.

Prod Arthur Block and Samuel M. Segal. *Dir* Ilya Motyleff and [Sidney M. Goldin]. *Scr* Louis Freiman. *English titles by* Julian Leigh. *Dial* Mark Schweid. *Photog* Frank Zucker. *Art dir* Robert Van Rosen.

Ed Leonard Weiss. *Mus score comp and dir by* Alexander Olshanetsky. *Sd rec* Clarence Wall.

Song(s): "Belz," words by Jacob Jacobs, music by Alexander Olshanetsky; "Ask the Stars," words by Dailey Paskman, music by Alexander Olshanetsky.

Cast: MOISHE OYSHER ([*Shloimele, also known as*] *Saul Reichman*), Florence Weiss (*Helen*), Michael Rosenberg (*Yussel Lufchick*), Judith Abarbanel (*Rivkele*), Isidore Cashier (*W. H. Rossovitch*), Judah Bleich (*Zanvel*), Bertha Guttentag (*Malke*), Irving Honigman (*Ben*), Rose Wallerstein (*Clara*), Dan Makarenko (*Zacharoff*), Vicky Marcus (*Shloimele* [*as a child*]), Lorraine Abarbanel (*Rivkele* [*as a child*]).

Yiddish, Musical, Drama. [*Print viewed*]. In the Eastern European town of Belz, Shloimele, the young son of Cantor Zanvel, runs away from his family and friend Rivkele and joins a traveling company of Jewish actors after his father threatens to beat him for consorting with the group. The troupe, after traveling throughout Europe, goes to America, where Shloimele, in a New York ghetto, wishes he could return home. Fifteen years later, after Helen, a cabaret singer at the Roumanian Garden Café, gives the unemployed Shloimele a job as a floor washer, she hears him sing and then convinces the owner to give him a chance to sing with her on stage. Billed as Saul Reichman, Shloimele sings "My Little Town of Belz" in Yiddish and impresses Yiddish radio impresario W. H. Rossovitch, who signs him to sing on his program. Shloimele's success allows him to send money to his father to buy a new *tallis*, a prayer shawl, which pleases Zanvel greatly. When Shloimele sings the Hebrew prayer "*Av Harachamin*" over the radio, a group of men meeting to select a new cantor are greatly impressed as they listen, and they send their representative, Yussel Lufchick, to sign him. With Yussel as his manager, Shloimele tours the United States as a cantor before deciding to return to Belz for his parents' golden wedding anniversary. Helen, who now loves Shloimele, sings as he leaves. In Belz, Shloimele is reunited with his parents, friends and Rivkele, to whom he confesses that he cannot find his real self in America and that she has always been in his heart. They plan to marry, but the day before the wedding, Helen, to whom Shloimele has not written, arrives. After Shloimele explains that Rivkele was his first love, Helen tearfully hugs her and wishes her happiness. The next day as Shloimele prepares to marry Rivkele, he solemnly watches Helen's carriage depart. *Cantors, Jewish. Childhood sweethearts. City-country contrast. Family relationships. Immigrants. Jews. New York City–Second Avenue. Poland. Cabaret performers. Europe. Impresarios. Radio broadcasting. Runaways. Theatrical managers. Theatrical troupes. Unemployment. Unrequited love. Village life. Weddings.*

Note: The Yiddish title of this film was *Dem Khazns Zundl*. According to a *HR* news item dated 8 Aug 1937, this film was planned as the first of six "Yiddish film operas" to be produced by Eron Pictures under the direction of Sidney M. Goldin. Goldin suffered a heart attack in Easton, PA, during the production period, and died on 19 Sep 1937. Goldin, whose film career began in the early 1910s, had been one of the leading directors and writers of films dealing with Jewish life, although he had not directed a film since his 1932 *Uncle Moses*. Goldin was replaced on *The Cantor's Son* by Russian stage director Ilya Motyleff, who before coming to the U.S. in 1934, had been an assistant to Konstantin Stanislavsky, then an associate director of the Moscow Art Theatre, and later a director in Luigi Pirandello's company in Italy and a Broadway director. According to modern sources, this was the only film that Motyleff directed.

This was singer Moishe Oysher's first film. Oysher, who was born in the Bessarabian town of Lipkon, emigrated to Canada when he was thirteen, and the following year began a singing and acting career. Oysher, who also was a cantor for various New York synagogues, was married to co-star Florence Weiss. All reviews list the actress playing "Malke" as Bertha Guttenberg, while screen credits list her as Bertha Guttentag.

FD 29 Dec 1937, p. 8. *HR* 7 Aug 1937. *HR* 21 Jan 1938, p. 7. *Jewish Independent* 13 May 1938. *Jewish Independent* 20 May 1938. *Kansas City Jewish Chronicle* 25 Mar 1938. *MPD* 14 Jan 1938, p. 8. *NYT* 27 Dec 1937, p. 11. *Var* 29 Dec 1937, p. 19.

THE CANYON OF ADVENTURE (Latino)

Charles R. Rogers Productions, Inc. *Dist* First National Pictures, Inc. 22 Apr **1928** [©First National Pictures, Inc.; 14 Feb 1928; LP24984]. Si; b&w. 6 reels, 5,800 ft.

Supv Harry J. Brown. *Dir* Albert Rogell. *Story and scen* Marion Jackson. *Titles* Ford Beebe. *Photog* Ted McCord. *Film ed* Fred Allen.

Cast: Ken Maynard (*Steven Bancroft*), Virginia Brown Faire (*Dolores Castanares*), Eric Mayne (*Don Miguel*), Theodore Lorch (*Don Alfredo Villegas*), Tyrone Brereton (*Luis Villegas*), Hal Salter (*Jake Leach*), Billy Franey (*Buzzard Koke*), Charles Whitaker (*Slim Burke*), Tarzan (*Himself, a horse*).

Adventure. Don Alfredo, a scheming Spanish nobleman, plans to steal the lands of his neighbor, Don Miguel, and marry his worthless son, Luis, to Don Miguel's daughter, Dolores. The plan is foiled by Steven Bancroft, a United States land agent engaged in encouraging the grandees of the new State of California to register their land holdings with the government. Accompanied by two friends disguised as caballeros, Bancroft, who has fallen in love with Dolores, raids the hacienda where she is about to be forced into marriage. After freeing the captive Don Miguel, they turn Don Alfredo and his son over to authorities and continue the wedding, with Bancroft taking the place of the bridegroom. *California. Government officials. Horses. Land rights. Marriage–Arranged. Nobility. Spanish Americans.*
Var 21 Mar 1928, p. 23.

CANYON PASSAGE (Native Americans)
Walter Wanger Productions, Inc.; Universal Pictures Co., Inc. *Dist* Universal Pictures Co., Inc. 26 Jul **1946**; World premiere in Portland, OR: 15 Jul 1946; Prod: mid-Aug—mid-Dec 1945 [©Universal Pictures Co., Inc.; 18 Jul 1946; LP447]. Sd (Western Electric Recording); col (Technicolor). 90-93 min. PCA cert no. 11547.
Pres WALTER WANGER. *Assoc prod* Alexander Golitzen. *Dir* Jacques Tourneur. *Dial dir* Anthony Jowitt. *Asst dir* Fred Frank and [Mack Wright]. *Scr* Ernest Pascal. *Dir of photog* Edward Cronjager. *Spec photog* D. S. Horsley. *Technicolor col consultant* Natalie Kalmus. *Assoc* William Fritzsche. *Art dir* John B. Goodman and Richard H. Riedel. *Film ed* Milton Carruth. *Set dec* Russell A. Gausman and Leigh Smith. [*Const eng* Chauncy Webb]. *Cost* Travis Banton. *Mus dir* Frank Skinner. *Dir of sd* Bernard B. Brown. [*Sd*] *tech* William Hedgcock. *Hair stylist* Carmen Dirigo. *Dir of makeup* Jack P. Pierce.
Song(s): "Rogue River Valley," "I'm Gettin' Married in the Mornin'" and "Silver Saddle," music and lyrics by Hoagy Carmichael; "Ole Buttermilk Sky," music by Hoagy Carmichael, lyrics by Jack Brooks.
Source: Based on the novel *Canyon Passage* by Ernest Haycox (New York, 1945).
Cast: DANA ANDREWS [(*Logan Stewart*)], BRIAN DONLEVY [(*George Camrose*)], SUSAN HAYWARD [(*Lucy Overmire*)], Introducing Patricia Roc [(*Caroline Marsh*)], Ward Bond [(*Honey Bragg*)], Hoagy Carmichael [(*Hi Linnet*)], Fay Holden [(*Mrs. Overmire*)], Stanley Ridges [(*Jonas Overmire*)], Lloyd Bridges [(*Johnny Steele*)], Andy Devine [(*Ben Dance*)], Victor Cutler [(*Vane Blazier*)], Rose Hobart [(*Marta Lestrade*)], Halliwell Hobbes [(*Clenchfield*)], James Cardwell [(*Gray Bartlett*)], Onslow Stevens [(*Jack Lestrade*)], The Devine Kids Tad Devine [(*Asa Dance*)], Denny Devine [(*Bushrod Dance*)], [Dorothy Peterson (*Mrs. Dance*)], [Ray Teal (*Neil Howison*)], [Virginia Patton (*Liza Stone*)], [Francis McDonald (*Cobb*)], [Erville Alderson (*Judge*)], [Ralph Peters (*Stutchell*)], [Jack Rockwell (*Teamster*)], [Joseph P. Mack, Gene Stutenroth, Karl Hackett, Jack Clifford, Daral Hudson, Dick Alexander (*Miners*)], [Wallace Scott (*MacIvar*)], [Chief Yowlachie (*Indian spokesman*)], [Peter Whitney (*Van Houten*)], [Harry Shannon (*McLane*)], [Chester Clute (*Proprietor*)], [Frank Ferguson (*Minister*)], [Eddie Dunn (*Mormon*)], [Harlan Briggs (*Dr. Balance*)], [Jack Baxley (*Immigrant*)], [Mary Newton (*Mother*)], [Jack Ingram (*Pack train leader*)], [Sherry Hall (*Clerk*)], [Danny Jackson (*Stable boy*)], [Casey MaGregor, Frank Arnold (*Poker players*)], [Ann Burr, Janet Ann Gallow (*Girls*)], [David Bair (*Boy*)], [John Berkes (*Man in hallway*)], [Will Kaufman], [Rex Lease].
Western, with songs. [*Print viewed*]. In 1856, Logan Stewart, the proprietor of an Oregon mule train, is nearly robbed of a gold shipment while he sleeps in his Portland hotel room. He tells Lucy Overmine, the fiancée of his best friend, George Camrose, that he thinks the bandit was Honey Bragg, whom he believes had earlier killed two miners, though their murders were blamed on the local Indians. While traveling to the mining town of Jacksonville, Logan and Lucy stop at the ranch of Ben Dance and his family. Logan gives a locket to Caroline Marsh, an English immigrant staying with the Dances, though Lucy doubts his serious intentions. Upon his arrival in Jacksonville, Logan is forced to break up a bar fight between his young friend, Vane Blazier, and Bragg. Meanwhile, Lucy chastises George for his gambling, unaware that the problem is so severe that the banker is embezzling funds to cover his losses. Though he is secretly in love with Lucy, Logan proposes to Caroline, and she accepts, much to the chagrin of the jealous Vane. Later, Logan is

forced to fight Bragg, and though he defeats the murderous outlaw, he refuses to kill him. After learning of George's excessive gambling, Logan agrees to pay his debts if the banker promises to give up poker. Though he takes the money, George continues his gambling, and even as his debt to professional gambler Jack Lestrade mounts, he tries to romance Lestrade's wife Marta. After killing MacIvar, a miner from whom he has been embezzling, George announces his intention to leave Jacksonville and take Lucy along as his wife. While George wants a quick wedding, Lucy's family insists on an elaborate affair, so she prepares to go to San Francisco with Logan to pick out a wedding dress. Before they leave, Logan orders Lestrade to return his ill-gotten winnings to George, but the gambler instead hires Bragg to kill the entrepreneur. Bragg fails in his attempt to murder Logan, but he does kill Logan and Lucy's horses, leaving them stranded in the woods. The two manage to make it back to Jacksonville, only to learn that George has been arrested for the murder of MacIvar. George is found guilty by a kangaroo court, and knowing that his old friend will be lynched that night, Logan breaks the banker out of jail. While George hides in the woods, the townspeople are informed of an Indian uprising, which has been brought on by Bragg's rape and murder of an Indian woman. Learning that the Indians are bound for the Dance ranch, Logan and the miners head there, and discover that both Ben and his son Asa have been killed during an Indian attack. Caroline is found wandering dazed through the woods, and she later breaks her engagement to Logan, telling him that she would rather live on a farm with a man like Vane than in the city with him. Upon his return to Jacksonville, Logan discovers that his general store has been destroyed by the Indians and George has been captured and killed by the townspeople. Despite the setbacks, the resilient Logan heads for San Francisco to arrange for a line of credit to revive his business, with Lucy at his side. *Bankers. Entrepreneurs. Friendship. Murder. Pioneers. Romantic rivalry.* Embezzlement. Engagements. English in foreign countries. Family relationships. Fights. Gambling. General stores. Immigrants. Indians of North America. Miners. Mormons. Mule trains. Newlyweds. Oregon. Outlaws. Poker (Game). Portland (OR). Rainstorms. Rape. Weddings.
Note: Ernest Haycox's novel was serialized in *The Saturday Evening Post* from 13 Jan 1945 to 3 Mar 1945. According to a Feb 1945 *LAEX* news item, producer Walter Wanger had originally intended to cast John Wayne, Thomas Mitchell and Claire Trevor in the film, having had tremendous success with those actors in his 1939 adaptation of another Haycox novel, *Stagecoach* (see *AFI Catalog of Feature Films, 1931-40;* F3.4284). In addition, a May 1945 *NYT* news item states that Robert Siodmak was being considered to direct the picture. According to *LAT*, portions of the film were shot on location near Diamond Lake, OR.
The *DV* review states that Patricia Roc, a British actress who made her American film debut in the picture, was borrowed by Universal from J. Arthur Rank under a "lend-lease" deal between the two production companies. *HR* production charts include Jimmy Aubrey and Walter Doering in the cast, but their appearance in the released film has not been confirmed. *HR* production charts also include Ray Collins in the cast, but he did not appear in the film. According to an article in *SEP*, Hoagy Carmichael, the noted composer, considered his performance as "Hi Linnet" the finest of his career. Carmichael and Jack Brooks's song "Ole Buttermilk Sky" was nominated for an Academy Award, but lost to the Harry Warren-Johnny Mercer tune "On the Atchison, Topeka and Santa Fe" from the M-G-M film *The Harvey Girls.*
Box 27 Jul 1946. *DV* 15 Jul 1946, pp. 3, 14. *FD* 17 Jul 1946, p. 4. *HR* 17 Aug 1945, p. 13 *HR* 24 Aug 1945, p. 15. *HR* 28 Aug 1945, p. 25. *HR* 15 Jul 1946, p. 3. *HR* 12 Aug 1946, p. 8. *LADN* 15 Jul 1946. *LAEX* 6 Feb 1945. *MPHPD* 9 Mar 1946, p. 2883. *MPHPD* 20 Jul 1946, p. 3101. *NYT* 6 May 1945. *NYT* 11 Nov 1945. *NYT* 8 Aug 1946, p. 18. *SEP* 15 Sep 1951. *Var* 24 Jul 1946, p. 14.

UN CAPITÁN DE COSACOS (Spanish language)
Fox Film Corp. *Dist* Fox Film Corp. **1934**; Buenos Aires opening: 29 Aug 1934; Los Angeles opening: 28 Sep 1934; Prod: Apr 1934 [©Fox Film Corp.; 12 Sep 1934; LP4945]. Sd; b&w. 8 reels. Spanish language.
Dirección de [*Directed by*] John Reinhardt. *Original de* [*Orig story*] Joaquín Artegas. [*Orig story* Stuart Anthony and John Reinhardt]. *Adaptación cinematográfica de* [*Screenplay by*] José López Rubio. [*Photog* Harry Jackson]. [*Ed* Ernest Nims].
Song(s): "El boyardo," "Pregúntaselo a ellas" and "Polinka se casa," music by Troy Sanders, lyrics by José Mojica; "Bésame la última vez," music by John Reinhardt, lyrics by José Mojica; "Moon Dreams (Cierra los ojos)," music by Blanche Seaver, lyrics by José Mojica; "Eili Eili" and "Marche heroique," music by Samuel Kaylin, lyrics by José Mojica.
Cast: JOSÉ MOJICA (*Sergio Danikoff*), Rosita Moreno (*Tanya Trainoff*), Tito Coral (*Nicky Baglieff*), Mona Maris (*Olga Nicolaievna*), Andrés de Segurola (*General [Fedor] Petrovich*), Julio

Peña (*Ivan Trainoff*), Paco Moreno (*Zinn*), Martín Garralaga (*Ordenanza*), [Roberto Guzmán (*Flint*)], [José María Sánchez García (*Cook*)], [Carlos Montalbán], [Juan Duval], [Rodolfo Hoyos].

Adventure, Romance, Musical. [*Not viewed*]. In Russia in 1910, Captain Sergio Danikoff is exiled to Komsk, Siberia because of his affair with a woman. When the train on which he is riding makes a stop, Tanya Trainoff, a young woman, joins a nervous-looking man, Ivan, who is her brother. Ivan and the men traveling with him convince Tanya to help them in their scheme to get a twenty-thousand ruble ransom in exchange for the woman they are about to kidnap. Feigning weakness, Tanya keeps Sergio busy while the men kidnap Olga Nicolaievna, the mistress of General Fedor Petrovich, the governor of Siberia. When the train arrives in Komsk, Ivan reports the kidnapping to Petrovich, who is outraged. Sergio begins to search for Olga, and his search leads him to Tanya's house, where a barking dog gives away Ivan's hideout in the adjacent barn. Olga is recovered, and several days later at Petrovich's mansion, when Olga leaves the festivities early because of a headache, Sergio's old friend, Nicky Baglieff, suspects that Sergio has been flirting with Olga and assumes that the headache is a ruse. In order to keep Sergio and Olga from acting on their flirtations, Nicky challenges Petrovich and Sergio to a game of chess. Petrovich and Nicky both become suspicious when they arrive in Sergio's room to see him preparing for a romantic evening. After calling Olga's room to ensure that she has not sneaked out to rendezvous with Sergio, the two men leave Sergio. He is soon joined by Tanya, who confesses that she helped Ivan with the kidnapping and asks Sergio to help free her brother as well as her ill-treated fellow citizens. The following day, Sergio convinces Petrovich to free Ivan and the other prisoners so that Petrovich's men may follow them and investigate what they are truly up to. Petrovich agrees and he holds a festival to celebrate. At the festival, Tanya is attacked by the drunken Petrovich. Hearing her struggle, Ivan comes to her rescue, and they are chased from the celebration by Petrovich's guards. Sergio joins the search for the fugitives, and spotting Tanya in the woods, he leaves the search party in order to reach her without the others' knowledge. As he comes upon her, Tanya's horse throws her, knocking her unconscious. He takes her to a nearby cabin and, after ensuring that she will be okay, rejoins the searchers. At Petrovich's mansion, Sergio is confronted by the governor, who has plans to hang the captured prisoners. Petrovich has the prisoners brought in, and Sergio is shocked to see Tanya among them. Having found out what Sergio did for Tanya, Petrovich has Sergio arrested as well. After a period of initial suspiciousness, the other prisoners join Sergio in a revolt. Armed with a gun, Sergio tells Petrovich that his men have overpowered the guards, and then Nicky, who is in on the plan as well, reads a fake telegram that instructs Sergio to proceed with Petrovich's arrest and removal to St. Petersburg. Petrovich becomes alarmed and asks Sergio to take pity on him because he has less than one year to live. Sergio agrees, and as Petrovich and Olga leave to the taunts of the crowd, he sings a love song to Tanya. *Brothers and sisters. Cossacks. Exiles. Romance. Russia–History–1904-1914. Siberia. Uprisings. Attempted rape. Chess. Dogs. Drunkenness. Festivals. Friendship. Fugitives. Governors. Hanging. Hideouts. Kidnapping. Mansions. Mistresses. Prisoners. Ransom. Riding accidents. Trains.*

Note: The plot was based on a screen continuity in the Twentieth Century-Fox Produced Scripts Collection, and the onscreen credits were taken from a screen billing sheet in the Twentieth Century-Fox Records of the Legal Department, both of which are at the UCLA Theater Arts Library. The Spanish working titles of this film were *Entre dos fuegos, El centauro* and *Cosacos*, and the English working title was *The Cossacks*, which was the title of the original story. According to the legal records, "Joaquin Artegas," who was credited with the original story, was fictitious, and the real authors were Stuart Anthony and John Reinhardt. According to a letter in the legal records, producer Sol M. Wurtzel decided to give the story credit to a fictitious person in order to avoid the impression in Spanish-speaking countries "that our motion pictures were written by Americans, entirely."
La'Opinión 28 Sep 1934.

EL CAPITÁN TORMENTA (Spanish language)

Metropolitan Pictures Corp. *Dist* Metro-Goldwyn-Mayer Corp. **1937**; Mexico City opening: 2 Jul 1936; Los Angeles opening: 30 Jul 1937; Prod: Feb 1936. Sd; col (Hirlicolor (Magnacolor)). 8 reels, 6,343 ft. 70 min. Spanish language.

Prod George A. Hirliman. *Assoc prod* Louis Rantz. *Spanish supv* José Luis Tortosa. *Dir* John Reinhardt. *Scr* Crane Wilbur. *Story*

Gordon Young. *Photog* Mack Stengler. *Mus supv* Abe Meyer. *Sd* Glen Glenn. *Prod mgr* Sam Diege.

Source: Based on the short story "Captain Calamity" by Gordon Young in *Adventure* (publication date undetermined).

Cast: Lupita Tovar (*Magda*), Fortunio Bonanova (*Capitán Bill*), Juan Torena (*Mike*), Movita (*Añana*), Romualdo Tirado (*Hipo*), José Luis Tortosa (*Doctor Kelly*), Roy D'Arcy (*Samson*), George Lewis (*Pedro*), Barry Norton (*Karl*), Paco Moreno (*Alberto*), Agostino Borgato (*Jim*), José Peña "Pepet" (*Joblin*), Rosa Rey (*Madame*), Alberto Gandero (*Gandero*).

Island, Drama. [*Not viewed*]. [The following plot summary is based on the English-language version of this film, *Captain Calamity*; character names refer to that version. For further information regarding the English-language version, please see the note below and the entry for *Captain Calamity* in the *AFI Catalog of Feature Films, 1931-40*.] Captain Calamity, a skipper on the South Seas, pretends to be holding Spanish pirate treasure and, consequently, is pursued by a host of island thieves. While single-handedly fending them off, he falls in love with a young woman named Madge. Eventually, all the crooks are killed or jailed, and Madge and the captain are united. [No additional information on the plot is available.]. *Pirates. Sea captains. South Sea islands. Treasure. Fistfights.*

Note: Unlike the English-language version, *Captain Calamity*, which was produced by Regal Productions, Inc., this Spanish-language version was produced by Metropolitan Pictures Corp., a company set up by Hirliman to make Spanish versions of some of his films. Both version were shot simultaneously at Talisman Studios. According to the *HR* review, portions of both versions were shot on location on Santa Catalina Island, CA. A news item in *HR* on 25 Jan 1936 states that George Hirliman was negotiating with actress Lupita Tovar to appear in the Spanish and English versions of this film; however, she appeared only in the Spanish version. According to a 5 May 1936 *HR* news item, a pig that appeared in the film was barbequed and served to the cast. For information on the English-language version, which also was directed by John Reinhardt and starred George Houston and Marian Nixon, please see the entry for that film in the *AFI Catalog of Feature Films, 1931-40*; F3.0588.

CAPTAIN BUFFALO *see* **SERGEANT RUTLEDGE**

CAPTAIN CALAMITY (*foreign version*) *see* **EL CAPITÁN TORMENTA**

CAPTAIN COURTESY (Latino)

Bosworth, Inc., in association with the Oliver Morosco Photoplay Co. *Dist* Paramount Pictures Corp. 19 Apr **1915** [©Bosworth, Inc.; 31 Mar 1915; LU4878]. Si; b&w. 5 reels.

Dir Lois Weber and Phillips Smalley. *Asst dir* Nate C. Watt. *Cam* Dal Clawson.

Source: Based on the novel *Captain Courtesy* by Edward Childs Carpenter (Philadelphia, 1906).

Cast: Dustin Farnum (*Leonardo Davis, Captain Courtesy*), Courtenay Foote (*George Granville*), Winifred Kingston (*Eleanor*), Herbert Standing (*Father Reinaldo*), Jack Hoxie (*Martinez*), Carl Von Schiller (*Jocoso*), Winona Brown (*Indian girl servant*).

Historical, Drama. In 1840, while California is ruled by Mexico, American settlers are in constant danger from Mexican marauders. After a band of Mexican soldiers led by American renegade George Granville kill the parents of Leonardo Davis, he vows vengeance and begins a career as a masked highwayman who terrorizes the Mexican offenders. Because Leonardo gives his plunder to those Americans who have been robbed, and he protects the women, children, poor, and helpless from attacks, he becomes known as "Captain Courtesy." At the San Fernando Mission, Leonardo falls in love with Eleanor, the orphaned ward of Father Reinaldo. For Eleanor's sake, Leonard renounces his mission of vengeance and joins the California Riflemen. When Granville learns about a cache of gold hidden at the Mission, he organizes an attack. Leonardo crashes through the stained glass window on his horse and rides to General Stephen Kearny's troops encamped in Los Angeles, who then rout the Mexicans. When Granville boldly admits that he slew the Davises, Leonardo fights him, but Eleanor persuades him to spare Granville's life. *Bandits. California–History–To 1846. Mexicans. Revenge. San Fernando Mission (CA). Criminals–Rehabilitation. Disguise. Fights. Gold. Stephen Watts Kearny. Orphans. Renegades. United States. Army. Wards and guardians.*

Note: According to the copyright entry, the subtitle for this film is "A Story of the Mexican Occupation of California, 1840-46." This film was re-issued on 19 Jan 1919, and presented by Jesse L. Lasky in the Paramount Success Series of Famous Players-Lasky Corp. Although only Lois Weber is credited as directing

this film in reviews, a list of titles taken from the film credits both Weber and Phillips Smalley with the direction.

Motog 17 Apr 1915, p. 611. *Motog* 24 Apr 1915, pp. 661-62, 682. *MPN* 17 Apr 1915, p. 47. *MPN* 24 Apr 1915, p. 71. *MPW* 24 Apr 1915, p. 566. *MPW* 25 Jan 1919, p. 541. *NYDM* 14 Apr 1915, p. 28. *Var* 16 Apr 1915, p. 19.

CAPTAIN F. E. KLEINSCHMIDT'S ARCTIC HUNT (Native Americans, Native Alaskans)

Arctic Film Co. *Dist* State Rights. Feb **1914**. Si; b&w. 6 reels.
Prod Capt. Frank E. Kleinschmidt. *Dir* Capt. Frank E. Kleinschmidt.
Cast: Capt. Frank E. Kleinschmidt (*Himself*).

Documentary. This documentary traces the experiences of Capt. Frank E. Kleinschmidt during an expedition to the Arctic. Scenes of Eskimo life include their trading and bartering practices. *Arctic regions. Expeditions. Frank E. Kleinschmidt. Native Alaskans.*

Note: One source lists the film's length as seven reels. According to *MPW*, the film showed was shown in Washington, D.C. before members of Congress "who were then legislating or trying to legislate upon Alaskan affairs. The captain's information in motion pictures was greatly valued by the legislators, who freely declared that nothing less than a trip to a long residence in the territory could have supplied them with the facts recorded in the captain's pictures." *MPW* noted, "The huts of a few Eskimos hanging to the barren rocks of a little island had never been photographed before and make an interesting spectacle."

MPW 21 Feb 1914, p. 956, 996.

CAPTAIN FLY-BY-NIGHT (Latino)

R-C Pictures Corp. *Dist* Film Booking Offices of America. 24 Dec **1922** [©R-C Pictures Corp.; 24 Dec 1922; LP18625]. Si; b&w. 5 reels, 4,940 ft.
Dir William K. Howard. *Scen* Eve Unsell. *Photog* Lucien Andriot.
Source: Based on the novel *Captain Fly-by-Night* by Johnston McCulley (London, 1925).
Cast: Johnnie Walker (*First Stranger*), Francis McDonald (*Second Stranger*), Shannon Day (*Anita*), Edward Gribbon (*Cassara*), Victory Bateman (*Señora*), James McElhern (*Padre Michael*), Charles Stevens (*Indian*), Bert Wheeler (*Governor*), Fred Kelsey (*Gomez*).

Melodrama. First one stranger, then another, arrive at the presidio, each with a government pass and each claiming to have been robbed by the notorious Captain Fly-by-Night and his highwaymen. The soldiers and Señorita Anita believe the first to be Fly-by-Night and the second to be Señor Rocha, Anita's fiancée and emissary of the governor. But the first stranger, to whom Anita is drawn, proves to be on a government mission and exposes the second stranger as Captain Fly-by-Night. *California. Government agents. Highwaymen. Latino. Strangers.*

ETR 30 Dec 1922, p. 278. *MPW* 30 Dec 1922. *Var* 8 Feb 1923, p. 41.

CAPTAIN JOHN SMITH AND POCAHONTAS (Native Americans)

Reliance Productions. *Dist* United Artists Corp. 20 Nov **1953**; *Prod* early Apr—mid-Apr 1953 at Eagle-Lion Studios [©Eclipse Films, Inc.; 20 Nov 1953; LP3479]. Sd; col (Pathècolor). 6,820 ft. 75 min. PCA cert no. 16535.
Prod Aubrey Wisberg and Jack Pollexfen. [*Pres* Edward Small]. *Dir* Lew Landers. *Asst dir* Wilbur McGaugh. *Dial dir* Bill Cottrell. *Orig scr* Aubrey Wisberg and Jack Pollexfen. *Dir of photog* Ellis Carter. *Art dir* Ted Holsopple. *Film ed* Fred Feitshans. *Set dec* Ben Bone. *Ward* Isadore Berne. *Mus* Albert Glasser. *Sd* Jean Speak. *Tech adv* Princess Wyhnemah.
Cast: Anthony Dexter (*Captain John Smith*), Jody Lawrence (*Pocahontas*), Alan Hale, Jr. (*Fleming*), Robert Clarke ([*John*] *Rolfe*), Stuart Randall (*Opechanco*), James Seay (*Wingfield*), Philip Van Zandt (*Davis*), Shepard Menken (*Nantaquas*), Douglas Dumbrille (*Powhatan*), Anthony Eustral (*King James*), Henry Rowland (*Turnbull*), Eric Colmar (*Kemp*), [Francesca di Scaffa (*Mawhis*)], [Joan Nixon (*Lacuma*)], [William Cottrell (*Macklin*)].

Historical, Biography, Drama. [*Print viewed*]. English explorer Captain John Smith, founder of the English colony at Jamestown, Virginia, is summoned to the chambers of King James I to explain the disturbing reports coming out of the colony. Smith explains the situation by telling the king all about the colony, beginning with his arrival there in 1607: While living among the early settlers of Jamestown, Smith is falsely accused of mutiny, arrested and ordered to return to England by Edward Wingfield. Wingfield believes that Smith's presence in Virginia will spoil his plans to turn the colony into a base for privateers. Davis, one of the many disillusioned colonists at Jamestown, expresses the belief shared by many others that they came from England not to be "grubbers of the soil and make

friends with the Indians," but to seek gold and fortunes. Smith is put on a ship bound for England, but he manages to escape and swim back to shore. As soon as he arrives on land, however, Smith encounters an Indian war party about to attack Jamestown. After killing one of the warriors, Smith races to the colony to warn the others. Although his warning gives the colonists enough time to prepare for the attack, they lose many men and much of their provisions in the battle. Soon after Smith is elected leader of the colonists, a position he must share with Wingfield, he leaves on an expedition into the wilderness with two of his allies, John Rolfe and Fleming, hoping to make peace with Indian chief Powhatan. En route, the men meet three Indian maids swimming in a pond, including Powhatan's daughter Pocahontas. Smith falls instantly in love with Pocahontas, but she runs away when he tries to give her a gift. Smith and his companions later meet Nantaquas, the son of Powhatan, who takes them to his father. Powhatan, however, believes that all white men are untrustworthy and orders their immediate beheading. Pocahontas, unable to bear the sight of Smith's execution, saves his life by throwing herself on him just as Opechanco is about to kill him. Pocahontas then insists that Smith marry her as a way to ensure that the peace will be kept. While Smith, Pocahontas and the others make their way back to Jamestown, Wingfield and his allies, Davis and Turnbull, decide to take over the colony so that they can keep their newly discovered gold. The peace between the colonists and the Indians is jeopardized when Opechanco is caught trying to steal a gun from the colonists' stockade. Opechanco is imprisoned, but Wingfield and Davis release him and, in an attempt to spoil the peace, deliver hundreds of the colonists' guns to the Indians. Davis later kills Macklin, a settler who threatened to tell Smith about the gold, and plants Nantaquas' knife in the man's back. In exchange for the weapons, the newly armed braves then engage the colonists in a battle planned by Wingfield. Soon after the war party is called off, Smith sets a trap for Wingfield by announcing that the gold found nearby is Fool's Gold. Wingfield falls for the trap, and Smith defeats him. Badly hurt in a fight with Wingfield, Smith is put aboard a ship sailing for England. Realizing that Jamestown needs Pocahontas' leadership to survive, Smith tells her that he is about to die and leaves her behind to marry Rolfe. Arriving safely in England, Smith makes a full recovery and finishes telling the story of Jamestown. The king then bestows his gratitude upon Smith, and the adventurer prepares for his next mission. *English. Indians of North America. Jamestown (VA). Miscegenation. Pocahontas. Captain John Smith. United States–History–Colonial period, ca. 1600-1775. Virginia. Adventurers. Arson. Battles. Deportation. Escapes. False accusations. Fathers and daughters. Frame-ups. Gold. Jealousy. Kings. Murder. Peace conferences. Princesses. Privateering. John Rolfe. Romance. Self-sacrifice. Tribal chiefs. Whips and whippings.*

Note: Although the first production chart for the film listed it as "3-D," the viewed print was not in 3-D and that process was not mentioned in reviews or other contemporary sources. Some reviews list actress Jody Lawrence as Jody Lawrance. Although the characters of Captain John Smith, Pocahontas and others were based on real-life figures in history, many liberties were taken in the retelling of the incidents portayed in the film. The historical record of the events at colonial Jamestown first appeared in Smith's book *Generall Historie of Virginia*, which was first published in 1624. Pocahontas, born ca. 1595, married John Rolfe in 1614 and some time later moved with him to England, where she died on 21 May 1917. Other filmed versions of the story include a 1948 short entitled *Captain John Smith, Explorer*, a 1955 short entitled *Captain John Smith—Founder of Virginia* and the 1995 Walt Disney Pictures animated feature *Pocahantas*.

Box 13 Mar 1954. *DV* 16 Nov 1953, p. 3. *FD* 3 Dec 1953, p. 6. *HR* 10 Apr 1953, p. 15. *HR* 17 Apr 1953, p. 13. *HR* 16 Nov 1953, p. 3. *MPHPD* 21 Nov 1953, p. 2077. *Var* 18 Nov 1953, p. 6.

THE CAPTAIN OF THE GRAY HORSE TROOP (Native Americans)

Vitagraph Co. of America. *Dist* Greater Vitagraph (V-L-S-E). 7 May **1917** [©Vitagraph Co. of America; 4 May 1917; LP10711]. Si; b&w. 5 reels.
Dir William Wolbert. *Scen* A. Van Buren Powell. *Cam* Reginald E. Lyons.
Source: Based on the novel *The Captain of the Grey Horse Troop* by Hamlin Garland (New York and London, 1902).
Cast: Antonio Moreno (*Capt. George Curtis*), Edith Storey (*Elsie*), Mrs. Bradbury (*Jennie*), Otto Lederer (*Crawling Elk*), Al Jennings (*Cut Finger*), Neola May (*Cut Finger's wife*), Robert Burns (*Cal Streeter*), H. A. Barrows (*Ex-Senator Brisbane*).

Western. Capt. George Curtis is sent from Washington to reform conditions on an Indian reservation. After ousting the reservation

deputy, Curtis comes under fire from the cattlemen who own land adjacent to the reservation. After an Indian kills a white rancher, inciting a lynch mob, Curtis steps in and diplomatically discovers the individual responsible, insisting that it was an isolated incident that should be dealt with in a civilized, legal fashion. The mob wants blood, however, and they attempt to storm the tribe. Curtis, with the help of the now swayed mayor, manages to correct the situation and reestablish peace. *Cattlemen. Indians of North America. Lynching. Murder. Peace. Racism. Soldiers. Vigilantes. Land rights. Mobs.*

Note: The film's working title was *The Long Fight* according to *MPN*. Some scenes in this film were shot in Griffith Park in Los Angeles.

ETR 12 May 1917, p. 1067. *Motog* 19 May 1917, p. 1608. *MPN* 17 Feb 1917, p. 1071. *MPN* 19 May 1917, p. 3161. *MPW* 19 May 1917, p. 1139, 1181. *NYDM* 12 Feb 1917, p. 32. *NYDM* 12 May 1917, p. 28. *Var* 18 May 1917, p. 23. *Wid's* 24 May 1917, p. 335.

CAPTURED IN CHINATOWN (Chinese Americans)

Consolidated Pictures Corp.; A Weiss Production. *Dist* Stage and Screen Productions, Inc. **1935**; Prod: ended 7 May 1935 at Argosy Studios. Sd; b&w. 50 min. Passed by the National Board of Review.
Series: Tarzan, the Police Dog.
Supv Bert Sternbach. *Dir* Elmer Clifton. *Asst dir* Gordon Griffith. *Story* Arthur Durlam. *Cont and dial by* Elmer Clifton and Arthur Durlam. *Photog* Harry Forbes. *Ed* Ralph Holt. *Sd eng* Cliff Ruberg.
Cast: Marion Shilling (*Ann [Parker, also known as Ann Gilmore]*), Charles Delaney (*Bob [Martin]*), Philo McCullough (*Raymond*), Paul Ellis (*Zamboni*), Robert Walker (*Harry*), Bobby Nelson (*Newsboy*), John Elliott (*City editor [Butler]*), Bo Ling (*Joy Ling*), Jimmy Leon (*Wong*), Wing Foo (*Tom Wong*), Paul C. Fong (*[Lieu] Ling*), Tarzan, The Police Dog (*Himself*).
Mystery. *[Print viewed]*. Joy Ling and Tommy Wong are in love, but their families have been feuding for hundreds of years and their fathers forbid them to marry. The day after four more killings occur in a continuing tong war between the Lings and the Wongs, Tommy risks his life by entering the Ling house in order to ask Joy's father, Lieu Ling, if he may marry Joy. Ling rebuffs him, but later Ling and Wong meet and agree to settle the peace with a valuable jade necklace, which Tommy will give to Joy. When *The Daily Herald* reports that the necklace, worth $50,000, is going to be presented that day, a pair of thieves named Harry and Raymond team up with a crook named Zamboni, who is an acquaintance of Ling. Ling agrees to let Zamboni record the peace ceremony and wedding for the Ling and Wong relatives in China to announce the end of the feud. Meanwhile, Bob Martin, Chinatown reporter for *The Chronicle*, reports to work with his talented dog Tarzan and is upbraided by city editor Butler for not having picked up the Ling-Wong story. Although Butler sends Bob out to cover a polo match with his girl friend, reporter Ann Parker, Ann gets an interview with Joy. While Bob is called away to cover a fire, Ann witnesses the peace talks while Zamboni sets up the recording equipment upstairs at the Ling's home, which is also their antique shop. Harry and Raymond, meanwhile, are parked at the curb outside, waiting for Zamboni to make his getaway with the necklace. When Joy goes into her bedroom and admires the necklace in the mirror, Zamboni, who has knocked out Li Foo Ling and taken his robe, accosts her just as Tommy enters. Zamboni stabs Tommy, then runs upstairs with the necklace. Tommy is sure that a Ling has stabbed him, and the feud is immediately resumed. Ann, meanwhile, goes upstairs and sees that the killer is Zamboni, but he locks her in the room that contains the recording equipment, then discards the Chinese garb and knife and hides the necklace in a decorative box. Raymond and Harry, suspicious of Zamboni, enter the shop and accuse Zamboni of double-crossing them. Bob, meanwhile, writes a note to Ann and orders Tarzan to take it to her in her office. When Tarzan finds her missing at the paper, he goes to the Lings' home, carrying the note in his mouth. At the same time, the Ling men meet and, by process of elimination, decide that it was Li Foo who stabbed Tommy. Fearing for their lives, Joy and her father huddle in the shop as the Wong men enter. One of them hurls an ax at a curtain and inadvertently kills Harry. Tarzan, meanwhile, approaches Ann's room from the roof, and she quickly records a message for Bob, then, breaking the skylight, hurls the record through it. Tarzan then runs back to Bob with the record in his mouth. Bob listens to the message, in which Ann pleads with him to come quickly and tells him that she loves him. Raymond, meanwhile, beats up Zamboni, who tells him that Ann has the necklace. Ann quickly locks herself in the room before Raymond can get to her, while Bob and Tarzan race to the scene. Bob breaks the

skylight and descends just as Raymond breaks in and accosts Ann. While Tarzan fights Raymond, Bob catches Zamboni trying to retrieve the necklace and apprehends him. Ann then hears knocking in a trunk and discovers Li Foo, whom she frees. Tarzan brings Raymond's gun to Bob, then retrieves the necklace and chases Zamboni outside. There Tarzan locks Zamboni in a cellar. The police arrive, having been notified of the renewed Ling-Wong violence, and arrest Zamboni. Ling explains the mistaken accusation of Li Foo to Wong. The feud is again called off and the necklace is restored to Joy. Bob then calls in the story to Butler and is about to insult Gilmore, the paper's owner, whom Bob calls "Old Walrus," when Ann informs him that Old Walrus is her father and that Parker is only her pen name. Bob then asks Butler to ask Gilmore if he can marry his daughter, and Bob and Ann kiss. *Chinatowns. Chinese Americans. Dogs. Feuds. Reporters. Thieves. Tongs (Secret societies). Editors. False accusations. Jade. Murder. Necklaces. Newsboys. Peace conferences. Police. Recordings. Rescues. Weddings.*

Note: Although a copyright statement is listed on the film, the title is not listed in copyright records. The name of the actor who played "Li Foo Ling" was not found. This film was the third and last in the "Tarzan, the Police Dog" series. For more information on the series, see entry for *Inside Information* in *AFI Catalog of Feature Films, 1931-40*; F3.2136.

FD 30 Jul 1935, p. 8. *MPD* 31 Jul 1935, p. 12.

CARA O CRUZ *see* DI QUE ME QUIERES

CARAVANE (French language)

Fox Film Corp.; Erik Charell Production. *Dist* Fox Film Corp. **1934**; Prod: une production Erik Charell [an Erik Charell production]. Sd (Western Electric Noiseless Recording); b&w. 11 reels, 9,173 ft. French language.
Directeur de production [Prod dir] Robert T. Kane. *[Supv* André Daven]. *Mise en scène [Dir]* Erik Charell. *D'après la nouvelle de [Based on the novel by]* Melchior Lengyel. *Adaptée a l'écran par [Adpt]* Robert Liebmann and Samson Raphaelson. *Dialogue et chansons de [Dial and songs by]* Bernard Zimmer. *Photographie [Photog]* Ernest Palmer and Theodor Sparkuhl. *Décors [Sets]* William Darling and Ernst Stern. *Cost* Ernst Stern. *Musique et adaptation de mélodies Hongroises [Mus and adpt of Hungarian melodies]* Werner Richard Heymann. *Supervision musicale [Mus supv]* Werner Richard Heymann. *Direction musicale [Mus dir]* Louis DeFrancesco. *[Dir of folk dances* Sammy Lee]. *Ingénieur du son [Sd eng]* A. L. Von Kirbach.
Song(s): "Gypsy Song," by Werner Richard Heymann; "Mon coeur est en Fête," "Ha Cha Cha" and "La chanson du vin," music by Werner Richard Heymann, lyrics by Bernard Zimmer.
Cast: ANNABELLA [(*La princesse Wilma*)], CHARLES BOYER [(*Lazi*)], Pierre Brasseur [(*Lieutenant*)], Conchita Montenegro [(*Tinka*)], Marcel Vallee [(*L'aubergiste*)], Carrie Daumery [(*Mlle. Thomas*)], George Davis [(*Le majordome*)], Jules Raucourt [(*Le baron de Tokay*)], Luis Alberni [(*Le chef des Bohemiens*)], André Cheron [(*Le notaire*)], Robert Graves [(*Le maréchal-des-logis*)], André Ferrier [(*Le curé*)], André Berley [(*Babos, l'intendant*)], [Armand Kaliz (*Colonel of Hussars*)], [Lou Tellegen].
Drama, with songs. *[Not viewed].* [The following plot summary is based on the English-language version of this film, *Caravan*; character names refer to that version. For further information regarding the English-language version, please see the note below and the entry for *Caravan* in the *AFI Catalog of Feature Films, 1931-40*.] When the wine harvest season arrives in the Tokay region of Hungary, the administrator of the Chateau Tokay contracts with the gypsy chief to employ gypsies for three days. Because the quality of the wine depends on the music played during the harvest, the most important part of the contract instructs Lazi, the blasé gypsy violinist, to compose a new song. Lazi finds the inspiration for his song during an embrace with Tinka, a gypsy girl who loves him but towards whom he has grown somewhat ambivalent. That day marks the return to the chateau of Countess Wilma after fourteen years abroad. Wilma, who expects to become the mistress of the estate when she turns twenty-one the next day, is incensed to learn from the executor of her father's will, her uncle, Baron von Tokay, that she must be married by her twenty-first birthday in order to inherit the estate. The baron desires her to marry his son, Lieutenant von Tokay, who has reluctantly left his friends and consorts in Budapest and is expected to arrive that day. Wilma, however, refuses to comply with the baron's wishes and, hearing Lazi's song, proposes to him. Struck by her beauty, Lazi consents. When the aristocratic guests, disgraced by Lazi's presence,

leave the chateau, Wilma opens the house to the gypsies. Although she resists Lazi's attempts to kiss her, she goes with Lazi to an inn, where, dressed as a gypsy, she declares that the "countess" is dead. Lieutenant von Tokay arrives at the inn and, thinking that Wilma is a gypsy, flirts with her. Seeing their mutual interest, Lazi takes Wilma back to the estate, where the gypsies are still celebrating. The lieutenant follows and, after dancing with Wilma, confesses his love; however, when he explains that he is supposed to marry the countess and suggests that Wilma have a clandestine affair with him, she slaps him. At the baron's request, troops arrive to disperse the gypsies, and the lieutenant rides off with Wilma. She allows him to kiss her, but then steals his horse and leaves him stranded. The lieutenant wanders into the gypsy camp, where he finds Tinka crying over her loss of Lazi. He suggests that they try to forget their suffering together, but their attempt at love fails, and the lieutenant discovers that he only wants Wilma. At the estate, when he learns Wilma's true identity, the lieutenant rails at her for marrying a gypsy in order to keep control of her land. Lazi rescues Wilma from a knife attack by the jealous Tinka and then spends the wedding night alone because of a family tradition. Lazi overhears Wilma tell a priest of her unhappiness, and when the priest suggests that Lazi, being a gypsy, would accept one hundred pengö for an annulment, Lazi indignantly tells Wilma that there is not enough money to pay for his love and gives her her freedom for nothing. However, he orders the gypsies to stop playing his music and urges them to steal from the chateau before they leave. Wilma prepares to depart until an innkeeper tells her that the townspeople, fearing a failure of the wine harvest, feel that only she can keep the gypsies from leaving. She then rides out to Lazi and convinces him to play his song so that the harvest can continue. After she and Lazi amicably say goodbye, she discovers that the lieutenant, who learned from Lazi of his break up with Wilma, has taken the reins of her carriage. He and Wilma sing Lazi's song as they happily ride back to the estate. The gypsies also sing as they work, while Lazi gives Trina a necklace that he stole from Wilma, and they embrace as their wagon as they ride off. *Class distinction. Composers. Gypsies. Hungary. Nobility. Officers (Military). Songs. Violinists. Wine and wine making. Deception. Inns. Jealousy. Marriage–Annulment. Mistaken identity. Pride and vanity. Uncles. Wills.*

Note: The onscreen credits for this French-language version were taken from a screen credit sheet in the Twentieth Century-Fox Records of the Legal Department at the UCLA Theater Arts Library. According to information in the legal records, Melchior Lengyel's story was originally written in Hungarian and then was translated into German. Although the French onscreen credits and early billing sheets for the English-language version calls Lengyel's work a novel, information in the legal records confirms that the work was an original story, which had never been published nor copyrighted. Both Erika Gathmann and Hans Kraly translated Liebmann's continuity into English from its original German, but only Kraly's translation was used for the film. Jeannette Marchal translated the English screenplay into French for the French version of the film. Gus Kahn did not receive screen credit for writing the lyrics to the songs in the French version; however, according to correspondence in the legal records, Bernard Zimmer, who did receive screen credit, only translated Kahn's English lyrics. According to the legal records, Annabella, Pierre Brasseur and André Berley came from Fox Europa in Paris to be in the French version. A *DV* news item noted that Annabella was Europe's top star and that André Daven, who supervised the French-language version, was a Fox producer in France. This was the first American film of European producer-director Erik Charell. Although modern sources state that because of the success of Charell's 1931 film for Ufa, *Der Kongress Tanzt* (*Congress Dances*), he was invited by Fox to make this film. News items note that in addition to Charell, a number of the people involved in the production were European, including Charles Boyer, Robert Liebmann, art director Ernst Stern and composer Werner Richard Heymann. Modern sources note that the film was a failure and that afterward, Charell's film career virtually ended. For information on the English-language version, *Caravan,* which was also directed by Charell, and starred Boyer and Loretta Young, please see the entry for that film in the *AFI Catalog of Feature Films, 1931-40*; F3.0600.

CARDIGAN (Native Americans, Cayuga)
Dist American Releasing Corp. 19 Feb **1922** [©American Releasing Corp.; 17 Mar 1922; LP17655]. Si; b&w. 7 reels, 6,788 ft.
Pres Messmore Kendall. *Dir* John W. Noble. *Adpt* Robert W. Chambers. *Photog* John S. Stumar, Ned Van Buren and Max Schneider.
Source: Based on the novel *Cardigan* by Robert William Chambers (New York, 1901).
Cast: William Collier, Jr. (*Michael Cardigan*), Betty Carpenter (*Silver Heels*), Thomas Cummings (*Sir William Johnson*), William Pike (*Captain Butler*), Charles Graham (*Lord Dunmore*), Madeleine Lubetty (*Marie Hamilton*), Hattie Delaro (*Lady Shelton*), Louis Dean

(*Sir John Johnson*), Colin Campbell (*The Weazel*), Jere Austin (*Jack Mount*), Frank Montgomery (*Chief Logan*), Eleanor Griffith (*Dulcina*), Dick Lee (*Quider*), Jack Johnston (*Colonel Cresap*), Florence Short (*Molly Brandt*), George Loeffler (*Patrick Henry*), William Willis (*John Hancock*), Austin Hume (*Paul Revere*).
Historical, Romance. In Johnstown, New York, two years before the American Revolution, young Michael Cardigan, an unwilling subject of King George III, falls in love with the English governor's ward, who is known as Silver Heels. At the outbreak of hostilities between the Colonists and the Indians, Michael is sent by Sir William to carry a peace message to the Cayugas but is intercepted by Britishers; he is saved from being burned at the stake by an Indian runner. In Lexington, Cardigan is admitted to the secret councils of the Minute Men, where he meets Patrick Henry, John Hancock, and Paul Revere and joins in the cause for liberty. Following the famous ride of Paul Revere, the Battles of Lexington and Concord prefigure the retreat of the Redcoats; Cardigan rescues his sweetheart from the advances of Captain Butler, then promises to return to her at the end of the war. *Cayuga Indians. Concord (MA). John Hancock. Patrick Henry. Sir William Johnson. Johnstown (NY). Lexington, Battle of, 1775. Militia. Paul Revere. United States–History–Revolutionary War, 1776-1783.*
    MPW 4 Mar 1922, p. 85. *MPW* 11 Mar 1922, p. 170. *NYT* 20 Feb 1922, p. 7. *Var* 24 Feb 1922, p. 34.

THE CARIBOO TRAIL (Chinese Americans)
    Twentieth Century-Fox Film Corp.; Nat Holt Productions. *Dist* Twentieth Century-Fox Film Corp. Aug **1950**; Los Angeles opening: 21 Jul 1950; *Prod:* mid-Aug—early Oct 1949 at Motion Picture Center Studios. [©Twentieth Century-Fox Film Corp.; 28 Jun 1950; LP377]. Sd (RCA Sound Recording); col (Cinecolor). 7,239 ft. 80 min. PCA cert no. 14183.
    Prod Nat Holt. *Assoc prod* Harry Howard. *Dir* Edwin L. Marin. *Asst dir* William H. Kissel. *2d unit dir* Arthur H. Rosson. *Scr* Frank Gruber. *Story* John Rhodes Sturdy. *Dir of photog* Fred Jackman, Jr. [*Cam op* Robert Gough]. [*Stills* Bob Palmer]. *Cinecolor consultant* Wilton Holm and Clifford Shank. *Art dir* Arthur Lonergan. *Film ed* Philip Martin. *Set dec* Al Orenbach. *Ward* Maria Donovan. *Mus* Paul Sawtell. *Sd rec* Frank McWhorter. *Re-rec* Mac Dalgleish. *Makeup artist* Lee Greenway. *Hair stylist* Lillian Shore. *In Charge of Production* Joseph H. Nadel. [*Scr supv* Vick Evans]. [*Gaffer* William McClellan]. [*Grip* Henry Mack].
    Cast: RANDOLPH SCOTT (*Jim Redfern*), George "Gabby" Hayes (*Grizzly*), Bill Williams (*Mike Evans*), Karin Booth (*Francie [Harrison]*), Victor Jory (*Frank Walsh*), Douglas Kennedy (*Murphy*), Jim Davis ([*Bill*] *Miller*), Dale Robertson (*Will Gray*), Mary Stuart (*Jane Winters*), James Griffith (*Higgins*), Lee Tung Foo (*Ling*), Tony Hughes (*Dr. Rhodes*), Mary Kent (*Mrs. [Martha] Winters*), Ray Hyke (*Jones*), Jerry Root (*Jenkins*), Cliff Clark (*Assayer*), Tom Monroe (*Bartender*), Fred Libby (*Chief White Buffalo*), "Kansas" Moehring (*Stage driver*), Dorothy Adams (*Nurse*), Michael Barret (*Hotel clerk*).
    Western. [*Print viewed*]. Jim Redfern, Mike Evans and Ling, their Chinese cook, have driven a herd of steers from Montana, up the Cariboo Trail, to an area of British Columbia which previously was the site of a major gold rush. Jim hopes to establish a ranch in the Chilcotin area, but Mike is more interested in the possibility that gold may still exist there. When they come to a toll bridge operated by some of Frank Walsh's men, Jim decides the toll is pure robbery and stampedes the cattle across it. Later, an old prospector, Grizzly, and his burro Hannibal join Jim and Mike on their journey. One night while they are all asleep, Walsh's men stampede the cattle through the camp. Mike's left arm is trampled and Jim has to amputate it. As their horses ran off with the cattle, they are forced to proceed on foot, with Hannibal pulling Mike on a litter. A stagecoach passes and they are able to put Mike inside and take him to a doctor in Carson Creek, a town run by Walsh. At the Gold Palace saloon, Jim meets owner Francie Harrison, who is being courted by Walsh but wants nothing to do with him. Walsh then tells Jim that he wants him to reimburse him for the damage he caused to the toll bridge, but Jim refuses to pay. After Ling gives Jim his life's savings of $300 to finance a gold prospecting venture, he, Jim, Mike and Grizzly become equal partners. However, Mike is very angry at Jim, blaming him for his misfortunes. When Jim sees Bill Miller, one of Walsh's men, selling beef with Jim's and Mike's brand still on it, he accuses Miller of

stealing his herd and, in a fair fight, shoots him. Later, in the mountains, Grizzly shows Jim and Ling how to pan for gold, but days pass with no success and they move into Indian country. Meanwhile, Francie visits the still recuperating Mike and asks him to work for her, but Walsh also wants to hire him. In the mountains, Jim discovers a valley which he is sure could be a cattleman's paradise, but he, Grizzly and Ling are captured by Blackfoot Indians. They manage to escape with Hannibal's help, and outrun the Indians, but become separated. While drinking from a stream, Jim finds gold. Unaware of Jim's movements, Ling returns to Carson Creek and asks Francie for a job as a cook. Jim brings gold samples to an assayer, who tells him that they are worth $900, but that he has to collect the cash from Walsh. Jim then goes to the saloon, where Francie welcomes him with an embrace. When Walsh's man, Murphy, brings the cash, Jim discovers that Walsh has deducted $310, the cost of rebuilding his toll bridge. Murphy then stirs up the townspeople with news of Jim's strike, and they declare that he should share his find. With Ling's help, Jim escapes on horseback to the mountains, where he encounters Grizzly and his brother-in-law's widow, Martha Winters, who has come from Montana with 300 head of cattle. As some of her hands have deserted to look for gold, she asks Jim to lead them into the Chilcotin Valley. He agrees to do so in return for a quarter share of the herd. Walsh is informed that Jim is heading his way again and, realizing that the gold boom is clearly over, considers going into the cattle business. As he is hiring men and still considers Mike a partner, Jim goes to see him, but Mike has been drinking heavily and refuses to work for him. The cattle drive moves on, observed all the way by Indians. Back in town, Francie throws Mike out of the saloon and goes to ask Walsh what he is up to, as he, too, suddenly wants to be rid of Mike. Mike reveals to a crowd at the saloon that Walsh has made a deal with the Indians to massacre all the members of the cattle drive. After defending Jim, he and Francie ride off to warn him. The Indians attack at night, lose many men and refuse to attack again until daylight. Walsh decides to stampede the cattle, and they just miss going through the camp site. Mike then arrives and shoots Walsh, who returns fire. After Mike dies in Jim's arms, Jim, Francie and the others finally reach the lush grazing grounds of the Chilcotin Valley. *British Columbia (Canada). Cattle drives. Chilcotin Valley (Canada). Friendship. Gold. Amputees. Chinese Americans. Cooks. Dissipation. Indians of North America. Partnership. Prospectors. Saloon keepers. Saloons. Stampedes. Widows.*

Note: Exteriors were filmed at Gunnison, Colorado and at Bronson Canyon and Republic Studios in Los Angeles. Modern sources add Kermit Maynard to the cast and credit Smith Ballew as Randolph Scott's double.

Box 15 Jul 1950. *DV* 30 Jun 1950, p. 3. *FD* 3 Jul 1950, p. 7. *HR* 30 Jun 1950, p. 3. *MPHPD* 8 Jul 1950, p. 373. *NYT* 1 Sep 1950, p. 17. *Var* 5 Jul 1950, p. 10.

CARMEN JONES (African Americans)

Carlyle Productions; Twentieth Century-Fox Film Corp.; An Otto Preminger Production. *Dist* Twentieth Century-Fox Film Corp. 28 Oct **1954**; Prod: 30 Jun—late Jul 1954 at RKO Radio Studios [©Carlyle Productions; 29 Oct 1954; LP4592]. Sd (Western Electric Recording); b&w (col). 13 reels, 9,666 ft. 105 or 107 min. PCA cert no. 17140.

Prod Otto Preminger. *Dir* Otto Preminger. *Asst dir* David Silver. *Scr* Harry Kleiner. *Dir of photog* Sam Leavitt. *Cam op* Albert Myers. *Art dir* Edward L. Ilou. *Film ed* Louis R. Loeffler. *Mus ed* Leon Birnbaum and George Brand. *Set dec* Claude E. Carpenter. *Cost des* Mary Ann Nyberg. *Mus dir* Herschel Burke Gilbert. *Assoc* Ted Dale. [*Choral dir and voc coach* Jester Hairston]. [*Dance dir* Herbert Ross]. *Sd* Roger Heman and Arthur L. Kirbach. *Mus rec* Vinton Vernon and Murray Spivak. *Prod mgr* Herman E. Webber. *Prod asst* Maximilian Slater. *Casting consultant* Lina Abarbanell. *Fights staged by* John Indrisano. *Title des* Saul Bass.

Song(s): "Dat's Love," "You Talk Just Like My Maw," "Dere's a Cafe on de Corner," "Dis Flower," "Beat Out dat Rhythm on a Drum," "Stan' Up and Fight," "Lift 'Em Up and Put 'Em Down," "Card Song," "Whizzin' Away Along de' Track," "Send Them Along," and "My Joe," music by Georges Bizet, lyrics by Oscar Hammerstein II.

Source: Based on the musical play *Carmen Jones*, music by Georges Bizet, book and lyrics by Oscar Hammerstein II, as produced on the stage by Billy Rose (New York, 2 Dec 1943), which was based on the opera *Carmen*, music by Georges Bizet, libretto by Henri Meilhac and Ludovic Halvy (Paris, 1875), which was based on the short story "Carmen" by Prosper Mérimée in *La Revue des deux mondes* (Paris, 15 Oct 1845).

Cast: Harry Belafonte [(*Joe*)], Dorothy Dandridge [(*Carmen Jones*)], Pearl Bailey [(*Frankie*)], Olga James [(*Cindy Lou*)], Joe Adams [(*Husky Miller*)], Broc [sic] Peters [(*Sgt. Brown*)], Roy Glenn [(*Rum*)], Nick Stewart [(*Dink*)], Diahann Carroll [(*Myrt*)], and the voices of Le Vern Hutcherson [(*Singing voice of Joe*)], Marilynn [sic] Horne [(*Singing voice of Carmen Jones*)], Marvin Hayes [(*Singing voice of Husky Miller*)], [Bernice Peterson (*Singing voice of Myrt*)], [Joseph E. Crawford (*Singing voice of Dink*)], [Margaret Lancaster Hairston (*Singing voice*)], [Sandy Lewis (*T-Bone*)], [Mauri Lynn (*Sally*)], [DeForrest Covan (*Trainer*)].

African American, Drama, Musical. [*Print viewed*]. Cindy Lou travels to a wartime parachute manufacturing plant to say goodbye to her sweetheart Joe. Scheduled to depart for military flying school the next day, Joe is overjoyed to see Cindy Lou and suggests they use his twenty-four-hour pass to get married. Cindy Lou accepts his proposal, even though her concern is aroused when Carmen Jones, a lively and beautiful factory worker who is desired by practically every man at the plant, asks Joe to pick her up that night for a private farewell party. When Carmen fights with another worker for reporting her late arrival to the foreman, Sgt. Brown, whose attentions Carmen has spurned, cancels Joe's leave and orders him to deliver her to the authorities in Masonville. As Cindy Lou watches Joe and Carmen drive away, Sgt. Brown announces that Joe volunteered for the assignment. Riding in the jeep, Carmen suggests that she and Joe stop off for a meal and a little romance. Joe pushes her away, but this only intensifies her attraction to him. Anxious to return to Cindy Lou, Joe opts to take a shorter but more treacherous road to Masonville. The jeep ends up in the river, and Carmen, highly amused, suggests that they catch the Masonville train when it passes through her home town that evening. In her grandmother's house, Carmen gives Joe a peach and begins to brush the mud off his pants. Finally submitting to her charms, Joe kisses her passionately. The next morning, as he dons his shirt, Joe finds Carmen's farewell note, in which she explains that, although she loves him, she cannot tolerate being locked up in jail. Joe is put in the stockade for allowing his prisoner to escape, and Cindy Lou visits him just as a package from Carmen arrives. When Cindy Lou sees the rose inside, she leaves without a word. For weeks, Joe carries the rose with him, dreaming of Carmen as he works in the hot sun. Meanwhile, Carmen, having found work in a Louisiana night spot, waits impatiently for Joe's release. The club stirs with excitement as Husky Miller, a winning prizefighter, arrives with his entourage in an expensive car. Husky sings for the admiring crowd and then introduces himself to Carmen, who rebuffs him. Flustered, Husky orders his manager Rum to persuade Carmen to accompany him to Chicago. Rum and his cohort Dink, promising her diamonds, furs and an expensive hotel suite in exchange for her company, hand Carmen, along with her friends, Frankie and Myrt, train tickets to Chicago. Carmen is tempted but finally decides to remain at the club and wait for Joe's release. Just then, Joe arrives. Overjoyed, Carmen kisses and embraces him, but when he announces that he must depart immediately for flying school, she becomes enraged. Sgt. Brown appears, insults Joe, and starts to leave with Carmen, whereupon Joe gives him a severe beating. Realizing he will go to prison for striking a superior officer, Joe flees with Carmen to Chicago. Because the military police are after him for desertion, Joe remains hidden in a shabby, rented room, while Carmen secretly visits Husky's gym in the hope of obtaining a loan from Frankie. Dressed in satin and diamonds, Frankie claims she has no money of her own, but her efforts to persuade Carmen to leave Joe are fruitless. Carmen, still penniless, arrives at the boardinghouse with a full bag of groceries, leading Joe to wonder aloud how she could have obtained the necessary cash. Following their argument, Carmen visits Husky's hotel suite, where she joins her friends at cards. Drawing the nine of spades, Carmen assumes the card is an omen of impending death and abandons herself to a few final days of drinking and debauchery. Cindy Lou, still in love with Joe, reads about Husky's new girl friend in the newspaper and arrives at Husky's gym just before Joe appears. Brushing Cindy Lou aside, Joe orders Carmen to leave with him, and when she refuses, he threatens Husky with a knife. Carmen helps Joe to escape the military police, but later, during Husky's big fight, Joe finds Carmen in the crowd and pulls her into a storage room. Joe begs Carmen to return to him, but she maintains that their affair is over. Completely broken

down, Joe strangles Carmen to death just before the police arrive. *Jealousy. Love. Obsession. Premarital sex. Temptresses.* African Americans. Boardinghouses. Boxers. Chicago (IL). Defense plant workers. Desertion, Military. Escapes. Fistfights. Gymnasiums. Imprisonment. Louisiana. Managers (Entertainment). Murder. Nightclubs. Soldiers. United States–South. Unrequited love. World War II.

Note: The film's opening title card reads: Oscar Hammerstein's *Carmen Jones.* According to Otto Preminger's autobiography, he and screenwriter Harry Kleiner, who had been Preminger's student at Yale University, decided not to use the text of Hammerstein's musical, or the libretto of Bizet's opera as a basis for the script, but to go back to Prosper Mérimée's short story. Preminger states that he first took the project to friends at United Artists, but they turned him down because they felt they could not risk backing an all-black film.
According to the Twentieth Century-Fox Records of the Legal Department at the UCLA Arts—Special Collections Library, Fox entered into a distribution deal with Preminger's Carlyle Productions in which Fox agreed to advance the film's negative costs, up to $825,000. Fox production head Darryl F. Zanuck was to have final script and cut approval. Preminger was to be paid $110,000 for his services, while Harry Belafonte and Dorothy Dandridge received $1,800 per week, with a ten-week guarantee. Legal records also state that Hammerstein, at the behest of Zanuck, submitted the script to Walter White, the executive secretary of the N.A.A.C.P., for comment. White praised the screenplay, but added that he was opposed to an "all-Negro" show in principle, because of his organization's on-going fight for integration. Although a 23 Dec 1953 *DV* news item stated that Preminger planned to shoot the film in Hollywood, Chicago and South Carolina, studio records indicate that the picture was shot entirely on the RKO lot.
According to legal records, Katherine Hilgenberg was originally hired as the singing voice of "Carmen." Marilyn Horne, whose first name was misspelled in the onscreen credits, sang the part, however. Brock Peters, whose name was also misspelled in the credits, was first considered for the role of "Husky Miller," according to legal records. Dorothy Dandridge received an Academy Award nomination for Best Actress. According to a 24 Oct 1954 *NYT* article, Preminger was reluctant to cast Dandridge because she seemed "too sweet, too regal." Dandridge convinced Preminger to hire her by dressing in flashy clothing and visiting the director, arguing, "Look, I know I can do it. I understand this type of woman. She's primitive, honest, independent, and real—that's why other women envy her." In the same article, Belafonte, when asked if *Carmen Jones* would lead to a greater utilization of black talent in films, replied, "Not really...but I think it will provide some help symbolically. It proves there's no corner of human drama that Negroes cannot play. However, I don't think Hollywood, as a whole, is geared to pioneering of this sort."
HR production charts include Mme. Sul-te-Wan, Archie Savage, Carmen De Lavallade and June Eckstine in the cast, but their appearance in the final film has not been confirmed. A 1 Dec 1957 *NYT* article commented that the film titles designed by Saul Bass, which featured a sinuous animated flame flickering around a rose, introduced design, color and animation to the display of film credits. Modern sources credit John De Cuir as co-art director and Dmitri Tiomkin as co-music director.
Many films have been based on or inspired by the story and opera of *Carmen*, including two 1913 three-reel versions, one with Marion Leonard made by the Monopol Film Co., the other with Marguerite Snow, made by the Thanhouser Corp.; two 1915 versions, a Fox Film Corp. production, directed by Raoul Walsh and starring Theda Bara, and a Jesse L. Lasky production, directed by Cecil B. DeMille and starring Geraldine Farrar (see *AFI Catalog of Feature Films, 1911-20*; F1.0610 and F3.0611); *Gypsy Blood*, directed in 1918 by Ernst Lubitsch and starring Pola Negri; *Loves of Carmen*, produced by Fox Film Corp. in 1927, directed by Raoul Walsh and starring Dolores del Rio (see *AFI Catalog of Feature Films, 1921-30*; F2.3270); the 1948 Columbia film *The Loves of Carmen*, directed by Charles Vidor and starring Rita Hayworth; a 1983 film produced in Spain entitled *Carmen*, directed by Carlos Saura; a 1983 France/Switzerland production entitled *Prenom Carmen*, directed by Jean-Luc Godard; and *Bizet's Carmen*, a 1984 France/Italy production, directed by Francesco Rosi.
AmCin Dec 1954, pp. 610-11, 625-29. *Box* 16 Oct 1954. *DV* 23 Dec 1953. *DV* 28 Sep 1954, p. 3. *Exh* 20 Oct 1954, p. 3856. *FD* 5 Oct 1954, p. 10. *HR* 16 Jul 1954, p. 11. *HR* 23 Jul 1954, p. 11. *HR* 28 Sep 1954, p. 3. *Har* 9 Oct 1954, p. 163. *MPHPD* 16 Oct 1954, p. 179. *NYT* 24 Oct 1954. *NYT* 29 Oct 1954, p. 27. *NYT* 1 Dec 1957. *Var* 6 Oct 1954, p. 6.

EL CARNAVAL DEL DIABLO (Spanish language)

Metropolitan Pictures Corp. *Dist* Metro-Goldwyn-Mayer Corp. **1937**; Mexico City opening: 3 Dec 1936; Los Angeles opening: 1 Oct 1937; Prod: late Jun—Jul 1936 at Pathé Studios. Sd; col (Hirlicolor (Magnacolor)). Length undetermined. Spanish language.

Prod George A. Hirliman. *Assoc prod* Louis Rantz. *Dir* Crane Wilbur. *Dial dir* Carlos F. Borcosque. *Orig story and scr* Crane Wilbur. *Spanish version by* Carlos F. Borcosque. *Photog* Mack Stengler. *Mus supv* Abe Meyer. *Sd* Fred Stahl.

Cast: Fortunio Bonanova, Blanca de Castejón, Enrique de Rosas, Juan Torena, Romualdo Tirado, George Lewis, Blanca Vischer, Jinx Falkenberg, Carlos Montalbán, Anita Gordiano.

Musical comedy. [*Not viewed*]. [The following plot summary is based on the English-language version of this film, *The Devil on Horseback*; character names refer to that version. For further

information regarding the English-language version, please see the note below and the entry for *The Devil on Horseback* in the *AFI Catalog of Feature Films, 1931-40*.] The movie actress Diane Corday has come to the Republic of Alturas on a personal appearance tour with her fiancé, Gary Owen. Gary's father, head of the Owen Coffee Company, sponsors the tour, which includes a radio engagement for both Gary and Diane. When Gary's old school chum, Pancho Granero, hears them both speak over the air, he decides to contact them. Pancho, who has many political enemies, overtakes the train on which Gary and Diane are travelling and insists that they come to his hacienda as his honored guests. Diane's press agent sees an opportunity for a headline story and sends out a bulletin that Diane has been abducted. The news causes an uproar during which diplomatic relations with the American consul at the Alturian capital become strained. The American diplomats demand that General Valdez, the military governor, send an expedition to rescue Diane from "the devil on horseback." Meanwhile, Pancho stages an elaborate fiesta for his guests, and his attentions to Diane prompt a jealous reaction from his lover, Manuela Torres, as well as Gary. An argument ensues in which Pancho punches Gary. Just then, the troops sent to rescue Diane arrive, with Captain Triana in command. Triana has secretly received orders to kill Pancho and when Diane discovers this, she throws herself in front of Pancho to save his life. She then explains that Pancho has not abducted her and that the entire ordeal was a press agent's fiction. Later, the group rides back to the railroad, where they learn that Pancho's friends are once again in power at the capital and that a state of war exists. After goodbyes are said, Pancho and his men ride off to take their part in the fight to free Alturas. *Americans in foreign countries. Bandits. Kidnapping. Motion picture actors and actresses. Romantic rivalry. South America.* Attempted murder. Coffee. Jealousy. Plantations. Rescues. Soldiers. Uprisings.

Note: The two-color Magnacolor process used in this film was alternately listed as "Hirlicolor" and "Hirlacolor" in contemporary sources. Unlike the English-language version, *The Devil on Horseback*, which was produced by Regal Productions, Inc., this Spanish-language version was produced by Metropolitan Pictures Corp., a company Hirliman set up to make Spanish versions of some of his films, and was shot simultaneously with the English version. The working titles of the Spanish version were *El diablo se divierte* and *La canción de los Andes*, and the film was presented by Metro-Goldwyn-Mayer Corp. Portions of the Spanish version were shot on location in Hemet, CA and some scenes may have been shot at Republic Studios. The participation in the completed film of the last two cast members of the Spanish version has not been confirmed. Ann Miller, in her autobiography, states that she appeared as a dancer in this film; as the Spanish version was shot simultaneously with the English version, she may have appeared in both. For information on the English-language version, which also was directed by Crane Wilbur and starred Lily Damita, please see the entry for that film in the *AFI Catalog of Feature Films, 1931-40*; F3.1032.

CARNE DE CABARET (Spanish language)

Columbia Pictures Corp. *Dist* Columbia Pictures Corp. **1931**; New York opening: 8 May 1931; Prod: Feb 1931. Sd; b&w. 88 min. Spanish language.

Dir Christy Cabanne. *Dial dir* Eduardo Arozamena. *Orig story and scr* Jo Swerling. *Spanish dial* René Borgia. *Photog* Al Ziegler.

Source: Inspired by the song "Ten Cents a Dance" by Lorenz Hart and Richard Rodgers.

Cast: Lupita Tovar (*Dorothy O'Neil*), Ramón Pereda (*Bradley Carlton*), René Cardona (*Eddie Miller*), Carmen Guerrero (*Nancy*), Soledad Jiménez (*Madame Blanchard*), Aurora del Real (*Molly*), María Calvo (*Señora Murphy*), Nancy Torres (*Eunice*), Ralph Navarro, Juan Duval, Felipe Flores, Mary O'Keefe, Rodolfo Hoyos.

Romance, Melodrama. [*Not viewed*]. [The following plot summary is based on the English-language version of this film, *Ten Cents a Dance*; character names refer to that version. For further information regarding the English-language version, please see the note below and the entry for *Ten Cents a Dance* in the *AFI Catalog of Feature Films, 1931-40*.] Barbara O'Neill is the prettiest and most popular woman at the "Palais de Dance," a dance hall in New York City. Bradley Carlton, a wealthy patron, visits Barbara, and for no reason gives her $100. When Barbara then asks Bradley for a favor, he agrees to give her friend and neighbor, Eddie Miller, a job and they have dinner. When Barbara arrives home, she sees Eddie packing because he cannot afford to pay his rent. Barbara gives him the $100 and tells him about the job she has arranged. Later, Eddie and Barbara meet in the park and realize that they are in love. Back at the dance hall, Barbara receives a new dress, but is disappointed to find out that

it is from Bradley. Then Eddie arrives and asks Barbara to marry him. Barbara agrees and quits her job. After five months of marriage, Eddie meets Ralph Sheridan, an old friend, and his sister Nancy, and does not tell them that he is now married. They play a game of cards that leaves Eddie $240 in debt, but, because he and Barbara are poor, he keeps the debt secret from her. Meanwhile, Barbara has returned to work at the dance hall, where she occasionally sees Bradley. While Eddie claims to be at a convention, he meets Nancy. Eddie returns to find the rent and utilities past due because he has spent his pay gambling. Later, Barbara finds Eddie packing and he admits that he stole $5,000 from Bradley's office safe, then lost it playing the stock market. Barbara talks him into staying and goes to Bradley to ask for a $5,000 loan. Bradley gives her the money because he loves her, even after she explains why she needs it. The next morning, Barbara presents the money to Eddie, who greedily accepts it, knowing where it came from. When Eddie comes home from work, he throws a fit of jealousy, and Barbara packs her things and returns to the dance hall. Then Bradley arrives with two tickets for the *Ile de France*, so that Barbara may obtain a divorce and marry him. *Dance hall girls. Debt. Gamblers. Marriage. Thieves. Divorce. Friendship. Infidelity. Jealousy. Loans. New York City. Self-sacrifice. Stock market.*

Note: This Spanish-language version of the 1931 film *Ten Cents a Dance*, which was directed by Lionel Barrymore and starred Barbara Stanwyck and Ricardo Cortez (please see the entry for that film in the *AFI Catalog of Feature Films, 1931-40*; F.3.4488), was released in Buenos Aires under the title *El triunfo de un amor* and in Bilbao, Spain under the title *El torbellino del jazz*. Although publicity material for the Spanish version indicates that the director is William Cabana, modern sources note that Cabana is generally assumed to be William Christy Cabanne.

CM Jul 1931, p. 575.

CARNEGIE HALL (Irish Americans)

Federal Films, Inc. *Dist* United Artists Corp. 8 Aug **1947**; New York premiere: 2 May 1947; *Prod:* early Aug—mid-Oct 1946 [©Federal Films, Inc.; 8 Aug 1947; LP1140]. Sd (Western Electric Recording); b&w. 16 reels, 12,126 ft. 135 min. min. PCA cert no. 12197.

Pres BORIS MORROS and WILLIAM LEBARON. *Prod* William LeBaron and Boris Morros. *Dir* Edgar G. Ulmer. *Asst dir* Sal J. Scoppa, Jr. and [George Ackerson]. *Dial dir* Jules Bricken. *Scr* Karl Kamb. *Orig story* Seena Owen. *Dir of photog* William Miller. *Spec eff* Roy W. Seawright. *Art dir* Max Rée. *Prod tech* Eugen Shuftan. *Film ed* Fred R. Feitshans, Jr. *Cost des* Max Rée. *Mus adv* Sigmund Krumgold. *Cond* Charles Previn. *Orch mgr* Daniel Rybb and Maurice Van Praag. *Piano rec* Nadia Reisenberg, Dorothy Eustis, Walter Gross, David Saperton and Rosa Linda. *Rec* Walter Hicks, Richard J. Vorisek and Reeves Sound Studios. *Makeup* Fred C. Ryle. *Prod supv* Samuel Rheiner. *Unit mgr* Geo. W. Ackerson, Jr.

Music: "57th Street Rhapsody" by Mischa and Wesley Portnoff; "Brown Danube" by Hal Borne; Polonaise in A Flat by Frédéric Chopin; "Ritual Fire Dance" by Manuel de Falla; selections from the first and final movements of Concerto for Piano and Orchestra in B Flat Minor, the Concerto for Violin and Orchestra in D Major and selections from Symphony No. 5 in E Minor by Peter Ilyich Tchaikovsky; Prelude to *Meistersinger von Nürnberg* by Richard Wagner; selections from *Rosamunde von Cypren* by Franz Schubert; Final movement of Symphony No. 5 in C Minor by Ludwig van Beethoven; selections from Quintet in E Flat Major by Robert Schumann; "Swan Song" by Camille Saint-Saëns.

Song(s): "The Bell Song" from the opera *Lakmé*, music by Léo Delibes, libretto by Edmond Gondinet and Philippe Gille; "Vocalise," by Sergey Rakhmaninov; "Sequidilla" from the opera *Carmen*, music by Georges Bizet, libretto by Henri Meilhac and Ludovic Halévy; "My Heart at Thy Sweet Voice" from the opera *Samson and Delilah*, by Camille Saint-Saëns; "O sole mio," music by Edoardo de Capua, lyrics by Giovanni Capurra; drinking song from the opera *Don Giovanni*, music by Wolfgang Amadeus Mozart, libretto by Lorenzo da Ponte; aria from the opera *Simon Boccanegra*, music by Giuseppe Verdi, libretto by Francesco Maria Piave; "Beware My Heart," words and music by Sam Coslow; "Sometime We Will Meet Again," music and lyrics by Frank Reyerson, Wilton Moore and Gregory Stone; "The Pleasure's All Mine," music and lyrics by Frank Reyerson and Wilton Moore.

Cast: Marsha Hunt (*Nora Ryan*), William Prince (*Tony Salerno, Jr.*), Frank McHugh (*John Donovan*), Martha O'Driscoll (*Ruth Haines*), Hans Yaray (*Tony Salerno, Sr.*), Joseph Buloff (*Anton Tribik*), Olin Downes (*Himself*), Emile Boreo (*Henry*), Alfonso

D'Artega (*Tschaikowski*), Harold Dyrenforth (*Walter Damrosch, 1891-1909*), Eola Galli, New York Philharmonic Quintette: John Corigliano, Leonard Rose, Michael Rosenker, Wm. Lincer, and Nadia Reisenberg, *and the world's greatest artists in order of appearance:* Walter Damrosch, Bruno Walter, Philharmonic Symphony Orchestra of New York, Lily Pons, Gregor Piatigorsky, Risë Stevens, Artur Rodzinski, Artur Rubinstein, Jan Peerce, Ezio Pinza, Vaughn Monroe and His Orchestra, Jascha Heifetz, Fritz Reiner, Leopold Stokowski, Harry James.

Historical, Show business, Drama, with songs. [*Print viewed*]. Cleaning woman Nora Ryan, an Irish immigrant who works at New York's Carnegie Hall, loves music and revels in listening to the sounds around her. While other charwomen pay little heed to the great musicians who pass through their music hall, Nora tries to hear as many rehearsals as she can. One day, Nora witnesses an angry dispute between conductors Walter Damrosch and the temperamental Tony Salerno. Though Tony unintentionally vents his anger at Nora as he storms out of the concert hall, he later apologizes to her and listens as she tells the story of how, as a child, she came to America and "found heaven" in the just-built Carnegie Hall. She also reveals how she came to adore Damrosch, who allowed her to watch Peter Tschaikowski conducting one night. Tony falls instantly in love with Nora, and the two make a date for the following evening. Nora and Tony eventually marry and have a young son, whom they name Tony Salerno, Jr. The marriage ends tragically, however, when Nora's husband falls down a flight of stairs and dies. In the years that follow, Nora gets a better-paying job and prepares her son for a career as a great concert pianist. Believing that the best way to acquire an appreciation for music is to spend time in a great concert hall, Nora takes Tony, Jr. to Carnegie Hall to attend as many concerts as possible. Nora's interest in her son's lessons grows with time, and she eventually moves to the residence quarters of Carnegie Hall. There, Nora monitors her son's every move and worries that Tony, Jr. will injure his hands playing with other children. One day, when Nora hears her son playing a jazz tune on the piano, she becomes upset and tries to guide him away from the sounds of "Tin Pan Alley." Tony, Jr., however, falls in love with jazz band singer Ruth Haines, and strikes up a friendship with Vaughn Monroe, the band's leader. Much to the dismay of his mother, Tony, Jr. accepts an invitation to tour with the band, and in an ensuing argument, Tony, Jr. accuses Nora of selfishness. He then leaves his mother, severing all ties with her, and marries Ruth. Years pass, and while Tony, Jr. becomes a jazz success, his marriage to Ruth deteriorates. Hoping to repair their marriage, Ruth visits Nora and asks her for advice about her son. After telling Ruth to swallow her pride and return to Tony, Nora has her friend, John Donovan, buy two airplane tickets to Chicago for them. Instead of buying the tickets, though, John surprises Nora and Ruth by taking them to Carnegie Hall to be present for Tony's concert debut there. Nora watches with pride as her son performs his own composition for an appreciative audience. *Carnegie Hall (New York City). Conductors (Music). Mothers and sons. Pianists. United States–History–Social life and customs. Accidents. Composers. Walter Johannes Damrosch. Drunkenness. Irish Americans. Jazz music. Marriage. Opera singers. Orchestras. Rehearsals. Reunions. Scrubwomen. Singers. Peter Ilyich Tschaikowsky. Weddings. Widows.*

Note: The opening credits note that the film was "Produced and Photographed in Carnegie Hall, New York City." Max Rée's onscreen credit reads: "Art director and costumer designer." Peter Ilyich Tchaikovsky (spelled Tschaikowsky in the onscreen credits) conducted the New York Society Symphony Orchestra for the 1891 opening of Carnegie Hall. As depicted in the film, German-born Walter Damrosch was the musical director and the conductor of the New York Society Symphony between 1903 and 1927, as well as a pianist and composer. Olin Downes, who plays himself in the picture, was the music critic for *NYT*.

Carnegie Hall was the first production of Federal Films, a company formed by producers Boris Morros and William LeBaron. According to an Apr 1944 *HR* news item, *Carnegie Hall* was first planned as a Technicolor feature, with a budget of approximately $1,800,000. The same item announced that Ronald Colman was to star in the picture and Serge Koussevitzky, Arturo Toscanini and the Benny Goodman and Paul Whiteman orchestras were to perform. A Mar 1946 *HR* news item announced that the following additional artists were to perform in the film: Jose Iturbi, Vladimir Horowitz, John Charles Thomas, Lauritz Melchior, Mischa Elman, Victor Borge, Alec Templeton, Duke Ellington, Tommy Dorsey and the Boston Symphony. None of these artists, however, appeared in the completed film. The Mar 1946 item also reported that Morros was going to Rome to photograph the Vatican Choir. The Choir was also listed in *HR* production charts, but their participation in the completed film has not been confirmed. Although *HR* production charts add Felix Bressart to the cast,

he did not appear in the completed film. According to a 1946 *Cue* article, workmen cleaned and redecorated Carnegie Hall before shooting began so that it would look new for the scenes set in 1891. A May 1947 *NYT* item noted that a new screen made of Fiberglass, which was designed to eliminate most of the distortion of side viewing, was used commercially for the first time at the New York premiere of the film. According to *HR*, the New York premiere, which occurred in two theaters, benefited the New York Foundling Hospital and the New York Philharmonic Symphony Pension Fund. According to a Mar 1947 *HR* news item, a partial 16mm print of the picture containing footage of Lily Pons, Risë Stevens, Ezio Pinza and other music stars was presented to the Smithsonian Museum in Washington, D.C.

Box 8 Mar 1947. *Cue* 5 Oct 1946, pp. 13-14. *DV* 27 Feb 1947. *FD* 28 Feb 1947, p. 8. *HR* 3 Apr 1944, pp. 1-2. *HR* 7 Mar 1946. *HR* 2 Aug 1946, p. 19. *HR* 11 Oct 1946, p. 11. *HR* 27 Feb 1947, p. 3. *HR* 20 Mar 1947, p. 7. *HR* 25 Apr 1947, p. 9. *IFJ* 17 Aug 1946, p. 39. *MPHPD* 1 Mar 1947. *NYT* 3 May 1947, p. 10. *NYT* 11 May 1947. *Var* 5 Mar 1947, p. 8.

THE CARNEGIE MUSEUM ALASKA-SIBERIAN EXPEDITION *see* THE ALASKA-SIBERIAN EXPEDITION

LES CAROTTIERS *see* LOS CALAVERAS

LA CARTA (Spanish language)

Films Paramount; controlled by Paramount Publix Corp. *Dist* Paramount Publix Corp. 1931; Bilbao, Spain opening: 21 Jan 1931; Los Angeles opening: 20 Feb 1931.. Sd; b&w. Length undetermined. *Country of origin* France. Spanish language.

Dir Adelqui Millar. *Scr* Garrett Fort.

Source: Based on the play *The Letter* by W. Somerset Maugham (London, 24 Feb 1927).

Cast: Carmen Larrabeiti (*Leslie Bennett*), Carlos Díaz de Mendoza (*George Nelson*), Luis Peña Sánchez (*Mr. Joyce*), Cecilio Rodríguez de la Vega (*Philip Bennett*), Lea Niako (*Li-Ti*), Mercedes Servet (*Mrs. Joyce*), Federico Velasco (*Ong-Chi-Seng*).

Drama. [*Not viewed*]. [The following plot summary is based on the English-language version of this film, *The Letter*; character names refer to that version. For further information regarding the English-language version, please see the note below and the entry for *The Letter* in the *AFI Catalog of Feature Films, 1921-30.* F2.3053.] Marooned on a rubber plantation in the East Indies, Leslie Crosbie turns to Geoffrey Hammond for the love and diversion that she does not find with her husband. Hammond falls in love with a Chinese woman, however, and Leslie shoots him dead. Placed on trial for her life, Leslie convinces both the jury and her husband that she killed Hammond in defense of her honor. The Chinese woman has an incriminating letter written by Leslie to Hammond, however, and Leslie must pay to recover it. Her husband foots the bill, and Leslie is faced with a bankrupt and loveless future. *Blackmail. Chinese. East Indies. Infidelity. Marriage. Murder. Plantations. Rubber. Trials.*

Note: The play *The Letter* was based on a short story by William Somerset Maugham, which was published in 1925. While the 1929 English-language version, *The Letter*, which was directed by Jean De Limur and starred Jeanne Eagels and Herbert Marshall, was made at the Paramount studios in Astoria, New York, all the foreign-language versions were produced at the company's studios in Joinville, France. In addition to the Spanish version, which had a U.S. release, the German, which had a San Francisco showing, and the Italian version, which was approved for exhibition in New York state, a French version, entitled *La lettre*, was produced, but no information regarding its release in the U.S. has been located. That version was directed by Louis Mercanton and starred Marcelle Romée and Gabriel Gabrio.

According to information in NYSA records, the Italian version was released at another time under the title *Tragedia d'amore*. Some sources include Joaquín Carrasco in the cast of the Spanish version, but his participation has not been confirmed. For information on other adaptations of the W. Somerset Maugham play, please see the entry for the 1940 Warner Bros. film *The Letter* in *AFI Catalog of Feature Films, 1931-40*; F3.2470.

Other language version(s):

Weib im Dschungel (German language)

1931; San Francisco opening: 8 Jan 1931; Prod: at Paramount studios in Joinville, France. Sd (Western Electric); b&w. 61 min. German language.

Dir Dimitri Buchowetzki. *Writer* Hermann Kosterlitz. *Prod mgr* Paul Reno.

German-language cast: Charlotte Ander, Ernst Stahl-Nachbaur, Erich Ponto, Robert Thoeren, Grace Chiang, Tschang Youling, Dr. Philipp Manning. [*German version not viewed*]

La donna bianca (Italian. language)

1931; Prod: at Paramount studios in Joinville, France. Sd. b&w. 5, 393 ft. 60 min. Italian. language.

Dir Jack Salvatori. *Writer* Mario Bellotti.

Italian-language cast: Matilde Casagrande, Carlo Lombardi, Lamberto Picasso, Hoang Thi-The. [*Italian. version not viewed*].

CM Apr 1931, p. 327. *Var* 8 Apr 1931, p. 19.

CARUSO SINGS TONIGHT *see* THE GREAT CARUSO

LE CAS DU DOCTEUR BRENNER (French language)

First National Pictures, Inc.; controlled by Warner Bros. Pictures, Inc. *Dist* First National Pictures, Inc.; The Vitaphone Corp. 1932. Sd; b&w. 75 min. French language.

Dir Jean Daumery. *Dial* Paul Vialar.

Source: Based on the play *A Kuruzslo* by Emric Földes (copyrighted 9 Jun 1927).

Cast: Simone Genevois (*Lottie*), Jeanne Brumbach (*La mere*), Helena Manson (*L'infirmière*), Michele Beryl (*Anna*), Jean Marchat (*Le docteur Brenner*), Maurice Rémy (*Stéphan Brenner*), Louis Scott (*Le docteur Niergardt*), Bernhard Goetzke, Rene Montis, Alexandre Dréan.

Medical, Drama. [The following plot summary is based on the English-language version of this film, *Alias the Doctor*; character names refer to that version. For further information regarding the English-language version, please see the note below and the entry for *Alias the Doctor* in the *AFI Catalog of Feature Films, 1931-40.*] Karl Muller and his foster brother, Stephan Brenner, leave their farm in the Austrian countryside, and travel to Vienna to study medicine. Karl is in love with his foster sister, Lottie Brenner, and would rather work as a farmer, but in deference to the wishes of his foster mother, Mrs. Brenner, he studies hard and is named valedictorian of his class. Stephan, on the other hand, enjoys drinking and flirting more than studying. One night, while drunk, he performs an illegal operation on his girl friend Anna. After she becomes very ill, he confesses everything to Karl, who agrees to try to help her, even though he does not yet have his license. While Karl is with Anna, she dies, and he takes full blame for the operation in order to spare Mrs. Brenner's feelings. He is not allowed to graduate and spends time in prison. After he leaves prison, he returns home to find that Stephan has died. Karl is eager to return to farming, but after he successfully operates on a boy injured in an accident in front of the house, Mrs. Brenner convinces him to pose as Stephan and continue his work as a surgeon. Karl travels to Vienna to work with earthquake victims and is extremely successful. However, now that he is supposed to be Lottie's brother, they are forbidden to marry. Mrs. Brenner forces Lottie to announce her engagement to another man but, seeing how unhappy she is, remorsefully writes the truth about Karl to his supervisor. Although the board of directors dismisses him, Karl begs to be allowed to operate on his foster mother, who has collapsed in the street. They relent and the operation is a success. No longer a doctor, Karl finally marries Lottie and they return to the land. *Austria. Foster parents. Impersonation and imposture. Mothers and sons. Self-sacrifice. Surgeons. Automobile accidents. Beer gardens. City-country contrast. Drunkenness. Duplicity. Farmers. Foster children. Graduations. Lure of the country. Medical students. Munich (Germany). Operations, Surgical. Prisons.*

Note: For information on the English-language version, *Alias the Doctor*, which was directed by Michael Curtiz and starred Richard Barthelmess and Marian Marsh, please see the entry for that film in the *AFI Catalog of Feature Films, 1931-40*; F3.0062.

CASCARRABIAS (Spanish language)

Paramount-Publix Corp. *Dist* Paramount-Publix Corp. Sep **1930**; Mexico City opening: 11 Sep 1930; Los Angeles opening: 19 Sep 1930.; Prod: mid-Jun—late Jun 1930. Sd; b&w. 11 reels, 8,713 ft. 97 min. Spanish language.

Supv Geoffrey Shurlock. *Dir* Cyril Gardner. *Asst dir* George Yohalem. *Scr* Doris Anderson. *Spanish version* Josep Carner Ribalta. *Photog* Allen Siegler. *Unit mgr* Dan Keefe. *Props* H. Wheeler. *Scr supv* Lydia D'Agostino.

Source: Based on the play *Grumpy* by Horace Hodges and Thomas Wigney Percyval (New York, 24 Nov 1913).

Cast: Ernesto Vilches (*Bullivant*), Carmen Guerrero (*Virginia*), Barry Norton (*Enrique Loder*), Ramón Pereda (*Jarvis*), Andrés de Segurola (*Kul Berci*), Delia Magaña (*Susan*), Paco Moreno (*Ruddock*), Juan Duval (*Kebble*), Celestino Dufau (*Merridew*), Fernando García (*Dawson*).

Comedy-drama, Crime. [*Not viewed*]. Bullivant, a famous criminologist, whom his close friends call "Cascarrabias" (Grouch), as he is perpetually bad—tempered, lives in retirement on an estate on the outskirts of London with his favorite granddaughter Virginia,

whom he expects will marry a nephew, Enrique Loder. However, Enrique has not been heard from for some time as he is away from England. As a result of this, Virginia is being courted by Mr. Jarvis, an older gentleman, whom she met at a party and invited to spend a few days at her grandfather's house. Enrique returns unexpectedly from South Africa, charged with the difficult assignment of secretly transporting a valuable diamond from the mines of Transvaal to his company's office in London. Shortly after greeting his uncle and Virginia, someone attacks Enrique and steals the diamond. Bullivant suspects Jarvis and follows him to London where he attempts to fence the diamond. When Bullivant accuses him, Jarvis returns the diamond and is arrested. Virginia and Enrique reunite. *Criminologists. Diamonds. Grandfathers. Lawyers. Romance. Temper.* Estates. Fences (Criminal). Investigations. London (England). Robbery.

Note: *Cascarrabias* is a Spanish-language version of the 1930 Paramount film *Grumpy,* which was directed by George Cukor and Cyril Gardner, and starred Cyril Maude and Phillips Holmes. Famous Players-Lasky made an earlier film of *Grumpy* in 1923. That version was directed by William De Mille and starred Theodore Roberts and Conrad Nagel (see *AFI Catalog of Feature Films, 1921-30;* F2.2267 and F2.2268).

Cinl Sep 1930, p. 30. *CM* Oct 1930, p. 975. *FD* 31 Oct 1933. *NYT* 30 Oct 1933. *Var* 22 Oct 1930.

CASEY OF THE COAST GUARD *see* SEA SPOILERS

CASTILLOS EN EL AIRE (Spanish language)

Edward Le Baron Productions. *Dist* Monogram Pictures Corp. **1938**; Los Angeles opening: 6 Apr 1938; Prod: mid-Jan—mid-Feb 1938 at Conn Studios. Sd; b&w. 7,545 ft. 84 min. PCA cert no. 4109. Spanish language.

Prod Edward Le Baron. *Dir* Jaime Salvador. *Orig story* Jaime Salvador. *Dial* Miguel de Zárraga, Jr. *Prod mgr* George Gastine.

Song(s): "Un beso de amor," music by Lee Zahler and Harold Raymond, Spanish lyrics by Jaime Salvador.

Cast: Cristina Téllez, Rafael Alcaide, Pilar Arcos (*Sra. Roncallo*), José Peña "Pepet" (*Feliciano Roncallo*), Andrés de Segurola, Emilia Leovalli.

Comedy-drama. [*Not viewed*]. A shy, day-dreaming typist, working in a European city, realizes her greatest dream when she wins a prize of a visit to Hollywood. A bank clerk, who travels to New York on a business trip, passes himself off as a Russian prince and confuses the typist with a South American millionairess. They eventually meet and fall in love. *Bank clerks. Impersonation and imposture. Romance. Typists.* Europe. Hollywood (CA). Millionaires. Mistaken identity. New York City. Princes. Russians. South Americans.

Note: The running time listed above was calculated from footage listed in NYSA records. According to a *MPD* news item, this was the first of a proposed six Spanish-language features to be made by Edward Le Baron Productions for Monogram release. The *NYT* review, which translated the title as *Castles in the Air,* noted that the films were to be made to compete with films from Mexico and Argentina aimed at Spanish-speaking audiences in North and South America. The review also noted that the film was very favorably received at its New York opening at the Teatro Hispano. According to a news item in *HR* on 18 Jul 1938, the production agreement between Le Baron and Monogram was terminated after the release of *Castillos en el aire* when Le Baron charged that the company failed to advance $15,000 for a second picture.

HR 18 Jul 1938, p. 5. *MPD* 16 Feb 1938, p. 7. *NYT* 21 May 1938, p. 9.

CASTLE IN THE DESERT (Chinese Americans)

Twentieth Century-Fox Film Corp. *Dist* Twentieth Century-Fox Film Corp. 27 Feb **1942**; Prod: 23 Sep—mid-Oct 1941 [©Twentieth Century-Fox Film Corp.; 27 Feb 1942; LP11240]. Sd (Western Electric Mirrophonic Recording); b&w. 6 reels, 5,594 ft. 63 min. PCA cert no. 7821.

Series: Charlie Chan.

Prod Ralph Dietrich. *Dir* Harry Lachman. [*Asst dir* Hal Herman and Saul Wurtzel]. [*Dial dir* George A. Wright]. *Orig scr* John Larkin. *Dir of photog* Virgil Miller. *Art dir* Richard Day and Lewis Creber. *Film ed* John Brady. *Set dec* Thomas Little. *Cost* Herschel. *Mus dir* Emil Newman. *Sd* Bernard Freericks and Harry M. Leonard. [*Prod mgr* William Koenig]. [*Dir of pub* Harry Brand].

Source: Based on characters created by Earl Derr Biggers.

Cast: Sidney Toler (*Charlie Chan*), Arleen Whelan (*Brenda Hartford*), Richard Derr (*Carl Detheridge*), Douglas Dumbrille ([*Paul*] *Manderley*), Henry Daniell (*Watson King* [*also known as Cesare Borgia*]), Edmund MacDonald (*Walter Hartford*), Sen Yung (*Jimmy Chan*), Lenita Lane (*Lucy Manderley* [*formerly known as Princess Lucrezia della Borgia*]), Ethel Griffies (*Madame Saturnia*),

Milton Parsons ([*Arthur*] *Fletcher*), Steve Geray (*Dr. Retling*), Lucien Littlefield (*Gleason*), [Eric Wilton (*Wilson*)], [Paul Kruger (*Bodyguard*)], [George Chandler (*Bus driver*)], [Oliver Prickett (*Wigley*)].

Detective, Drama. [*Print viewed*]. At a secluded California desert castle, owned by eccentric millionaire Paul Manderley, tragedy strikes when Professor Gleason, a guest, is poisoned. Others visiting the castle are Manderley's lawyer, Walter Hartford, Walter's wife Brenda, and Manderley's physician, Dr. Retling. Fearing that his wife Lucy will be implicated in the poisoning, because she is the former Princess Lucrezia della Borgia, Manderley bribes Retling and Hartford to take Gleason's body to a hotel in Mojave Wells, the closest town, and make it look as if he died there of a heart attack. Soon after, Honolulu detective Charlie Chan, who is vacationing in San Francisco with his son Jimmy during Jimmy's leave from the Army, receives a note from Lucy asking him to come to the castle. Chan makes the journey, but upon reaching the castle, finds that Lucy did not send the note. Suspecting that the sender wanted him to be a witness to an upcoming crime, Chan stays. Manderley explains that, because he is a medieval scholar studying Cesare Borgia, he wants to live in an atmosphere approximating the fifteenth century. Chan also learns from Retling that Manderley will lose control of his father's estate if he is involved in any scandal. Arriving at the same time as Chan is Watson King, a sculptor commissioned to do a bust of Lucy. Soon after, Jimmy also comes to the castle to pass along a threatening letter that came to the hotel after Chan left. Another visitor is Arthur Fletcher, a private detective representing Gleason's family. After Fletcher falls victim to poison, Retling tries to convince Manderley that Lucy is responsible and must be committed to an insane asylum, but Manderley states that he will turn over control of the estate to Hartford and leave quietly with his wife. Chan discusses the situation with Lucy, and she tells him about her stepbrother Cesare, who was acquitted on a charge of poisoning and then killed in the Spanish war. Chan then obtains a confession from Hartford, Brenda and Retling that they paid Gleason and Fletcher to pretend to be poisoned so that Manderley would be forced to relinquish the estate. Brenda also reveals that Cesare is not dead, and that he wrote to Hartford a month ago demanding money. Chan still believes that there is a killer lurking about, however, and his suspicions are proven correct when Hartford is stabbed to death. After explaining that the murderer needed to get rid of Hartford and then Manderley so that Lucy would inherit the estate, Chan reveals that Watson is the killer and is actually Cesare, having had a facial scar removed so that he would not be recognized. The mystery solved, Chan and Jimmy prepare to leave the castle. *Borgia family. Castles. Chinese Americans. Detectives. Frame-ups. Poisoning.* Arms and armor. Astrologers. California. Carrier pigeons. Confession (Law). Eccentrics. Fathers and sons. Inheritance. Insanity. Lawyers. Middle Ages. Mojave Desert. Physicians. *Romeo and Juliet* (Play). Scars. Scholars. Stepbrothers.

Note: Although a 15 Aug 1941 *HR* news item stated that John Larkin would write the screenplay for this film based on an original story by producer Ralph Dietrich, no other contemporary source confirms Dietrich's contribution to the picture as a writer. According to a studio press release and a *HR* news item, Janis Carter was originally cast as "Brenda Hartford." The *Var* review erroneously lists the film's running time as 51 minutes. *Castle in the Desert* was the last "Charlie Chan" film produced by Twentieth Century-Fox. After the studio helped actor Sidney Toler obtain the rights to the character from Earl Derr Biggers' widow, Toler made more Chan films at Monogram. For additional information about the "Charlie Chan" series, consult the Series Index and see the entry below for *Charlie Chan Carries On.*

Box 7 Feb 1942. *DV* 3 Feb 1942, p. 3. *FD* 4 Feb 1942, p. 6. *HR* 15 Aug 1941, p. 7. *HR* 17 Sep 1941, p. 4. *HR* 23 Sep 1941, p. 2. *HR* 3 Oct 1941, p. 9. *HR* 10 Oct 1941, p. 11. *HR* 26 Nov 1941, p. 7. *HR* 3 Feb 1942, p. 4. *MPD* 3 Feb 1941. *MPHPD* 7 Feb 1942, p. 494. *Var* 4 Feb 1942, p. 8.

CASTLES FOR TWO (Irish Americans)

Jesse L. Lasky Feature Play Co. *Dist* Paramount Pictures Corp. 5 Mar **1917** [©Jesse L. Lasky Feature Play Co.; 23 Feb 1917; LP10261]. Si; b&w. 5 reels.

Pres Jesse L. Lasky. *Dir* Frank Reicher. *Asst dir* Charles Watt. *Story and scen* Beatrice C. de Mille and Leighton Osmun. *Cam* Dent Gilbert.

Cast: Marie Doro (*Patricia Calhoun*), Elliott Dexter (*Brian O'Neil*), Mayme Kelso (*Patricia's secretary*), Jane Wolff, Harriet Sorenson, Lillian Leighton (*Brian's sisters*), Julia Jackson (*Brian's mother*), Horace B. Carpenter (*Neough*), Billy Elmer (*Callahan*), Marie Mills (*Nanny*).

Drama. Heiress Patricia Calhoun visits the Irish home of her grandmother in the hopes of finding the fairies of whom her grandmother so often spoke. There she meets Brian O'Neil who falls in love with her. When Brian's three sisters nag him into agreeing to marry a wealthy American woman in order to save his family's ancestral estate, however, he must put aside his feelings for Patricia whom he thinks is a poor girl. As a practical joke, Patricia makes Brian think that her old maid secretary is actually the heiress and watches him make a fool of himself proposing to the woman. In the end, Patricia's true identity is revealed and Brian is able to marry the woman he loves as well as save his family home. *Brothers and sisters. Family honor. Fortune hunters. Heiresses. Impersonation and imposture. Ireland. Irish. Irish Americans. Marriage–Forced by circumstances. Mistaken identity. Fairies. Practical jokes. Secretaries. Spinsters.*

Note: The title of the original story was *Rich Girl—Poor Girl. The U.S. Catalog of Copyright Entries for Motion Pictures* mistakenly lists the copyright claimant as the Jesse L. Lasky Feature Co.

ETR 10 Mar 1917, p. 976. *Motog* 17 Mar 1917, p. 590. *MPN* 17 Mar 1917, p. 1717. *MPW* 17 Mar 1917, p. 1757, 1827. *NYDM* 10 Mar 1917, p. 26. *Var* 13 Apr 1917, p. 22. *Wid's* 8 Mar 1917, p. 153.

CASTLES IN THE AIR see **CASTILLOS EN EL AIRE**

THE CAT CREEPS *(foreign version) see* **LA VOLUNTAD DEL MUERTO**

CAT PEOPLE (Serbian Americns)

RKO Radio Pictures, Inc. *Dist* RKO Radio Pictures, Inc. 25 Dec **1942**; New York opening: 6 Dec 1942; Prod: 28 Jul—21 Aug 1942 [©RKO Radio Pictures, Inc.; 1 Jan 1943; LP11814]. Sd (RCA Sound System); b&w. 6,534 ft. 73-74 min. PCA cert no. 8693.

Prod Val Lewton. [*Supv* Lou Ostrow]. *Dir* Jacques Tourneur. *Asst dir* Doran Cox. *Wrt* DeWitt Bodeen. *Dir of photog* Nicholas Musuraca. [*Spec eff* Vernon Walker]. *Art dir* Albert S. D'Agostino and Walter E. Keller. *Ed* Mark Robson. *Set dec* Darrell Silvera and Al Fields. *Gowns* Renie. *Mus* Roy Webb. *Mus dir* C. Bakaleinikoff. *Rec* John L. Cass.

Cast: Simone Simon [(*Irene Dubrovna*)], Tom Conway [(*Dr. Louis Judd*)], Jane Randolph [(*Alice Moore*)], Jack Holt [(*Commodore*)], [Kent Smith (*Oliver Reed*)], [Alan Napier (*Carver*)], [Elizabeth Dunne (*Miss Plunkett*)], [Elizabeth Russell (*The cat woman*)], [Mary Halsey (*Blondie*)], [Alec Craig (*Zoo keeper*)], [George Ford (*Whistling cop*)], [Betty Roadman (*Mrs. Hansen*)], [Dot Farley (*Mrs. Agnew*)], [Charles Jordan (*Bus driver*)], [Lon Kerr (*Taxi driver*)], [Leda Nicova (*Patient*)], [Theresa Harris (*Minnie*)], [John Piffle (*Cafe proprietor*)], [Murdock MacQuarrie (*Sheep caretaker*)], [Bud Geary (*Mounted policeman*)], [Eddie Dew (*Street policeman*)], [Connie Leon], [Henrietta Burnside].

Horror, Psychological, Drama. [*Print viewed*]. While sketching a panther at the zoo one day, fashion illustrator Irene Dubrovna meets Oliver Reed, a maritime engineer, and invites him to her apartment. There, she tells Oliver that she feels strangely calmed by the cries of the lions in the zoo and relates the legend of King John of Serbia, who banished the witches from her home village long ago. Oliver, enchanted by the exotic Irene, buys her a kitten as a gift. When the kitten shrinks in fear from Irene, however, Oliver and Irene return it to the pet shop, where Irene's presence drives the caged animals mad. Later, when Oliver tells Irene that he loves her, she voices her apprehension that feelings of love and passion will unleash a beast within her. Oliver dismisses her fears as fairy tales and convinces her to marry him. When, at their wedding celebration, she is greeted as "sister" by a strange, cat-like woman, Irene begs Oliver for patience in consummating their marriage. One month later, Irene laments her feelings of aberrance and Oliver insists that she seek help from Dr. Louis Judd, a psychiatrist. Under Judd's hypnotic spell, Irene tells of the cat women in her Serbian village, whose passion turns them into bloodthirsty panthers. After her session with Judd, Irene returns home, where she finds Oliver visiting with Alice Moore, a woman who works in his office. When she learns that Oliver has confided her fears to Alice, Irene feels betrayed and later that night, unable to sleep, she paces in front of the panther's cage at the zoo. Upon discovering that Irene has not been keeping her appointments with Judd, Oliver accuses her of not wanting to be helped and warns her that they are drifting apart. After Oliver's accusations arouse jealousy in Irene, he angrily storms out of the house, Irene then calls the office and when Alice answers, Irene decides to go there. At a restaurant

around the corner from the office building, Irene sees Oliver seated with Alice. After Alice leaves the restaurant and begins to walk home alone, she senses that she is being followed. Upon hearing a low growl and a rustling of the trees, Alice boards a bus, and later, at the zoo, several sheep are found slain. Leading away from their dead bodies are the paw marks of a large cat, which gradually change into human footprints. Disheveled and sobbing, Irene returns home and dreams that Judd is King John. The next day, she visits the zoo and steals the key to the panther's cage. Later, Irene, Alice and Oliver attend an exhibit of ship models and Irene becomes separated from the others. After leaving the exhibit and returning to her apartment house, Alice decides go swimming in the basement pool. Irene follows her home, and as Alice enters the shadowy basement, she hears a low growl and sees the shadow of a cat. Jumping into the water, Alice calls for help and Irene turns on the lights, claiming to be looking for Oliver. After Irene leaves, Alice picks up her robe and discovers that it has been ripped to shreds. When Alice tells Judd her suspicions that jealousy has transformed Irene into a cat, he discounts her accusations until she shows him the robe. Soon after the pool incident, Oliver informs Irene that he has fallen in love with Alice and she orders him out of the house. Later that night, Judd, Alice and Oliver confer and decide to commit Irene, but when she fails to show up for their meeting, Alice and Oliver return to their office while Judd slips back into the apartment. At the office, Alice and Oliver are menaced by a prowling panther, but Oliver vanquishes the beast with a T-bar in the shape of a cross. Irene then returns to her apartment, where she is greeted by Judd. To prove that Irene's fears are not founded in reality, Judd kisses her and then watches in horror as she changes into a cat and attacks him. Returning to the apartment, Oliver and Alice hear Judd's screams and run up the stairs, passing Irene, who is hiding in the shadows. Wounded by Judd's walking stick, Irene is drawn to the zoo's panther cage and unlocks it with her key. After the beast lunges at her, it runs into the street and is hit by a car. Alice and Oliver then run to the zoo, where they find Irene's dead body lying next to the open cage. *Jealousy. Legends. Marriage. Panthers. Transmutation. Cats. Death by animals. Illustrators. Murder. Psychiatrists. Serbian Americans. Shipbuilders. Swimming. Zoos.*

Note: The film opens with the following written quotation from *The Anatomy of Atavism* a book created for the film purportedly written by one of the characters, Dr. Louis Judd: "Even as fog continues to lie in the valleys, so does ancient sin cling to the low places, the depression in the world consciousness." It closes with the following sonnet from John Donne: "But black sin hath betrayed to endless night. Holy world, both parts and both parts must die." This was the first production of Val Lewton, a former editorial assistant and West Coast story editor for David O. Selznick. Lewton was hired by RKO to form a unit that would produce low-budget horror films. According to an interview with screenwriter DeWitt Bodeen, reproduced in a modern source, the studio allotted a budget of $150,000 per film and dictated the titles to Lewton. Lewton created a production team that at various times included director Jacques Tourneur (who directed Lewton's first three films), editor Mark Robson (who went on to direct five other Lewton films), screenwriter Bodeen and cinematographer Nicholas Musuraca. Under Lewton's patronage, Robert Wise directed his first film, *Curse of the Cat People*. From 1942-1946 Lewton produced eleven films for RKO, ending with the film *Bedlam*.

Cat People exhibited what would become known as Lewton's distinctive style of horror. Lewton used low key lighting to create shadows that obscured the horrific events and intensified psychological horror. *Var* described Lewton's style as "developments of surprises confined to psychological and mental reactions, rather than the transformation to grotesque and marauding characters" (i.e. the monsters of previous horror genres). According to a modern source, Lou Ostrow, Lewton's supervisor at RKO, was so dissatisfied with Lewton's style on this picture that after watching the rushes from the first four days of shooting, he decided to replace Jacques Tourneur as director. Lewton then appealed to studio head Charles Koerner, who reinstated Tourneur. Later, when Ostrow mandated that the panther must appear in the drafting room sequence, Lewton thwarted Ostrow's attempt to make the horror more explicit by instructing Tourneur to shoot the scene with low key lighting, thus leaving the beast into shadows.

HR news items yield the following information about this production: A Jul 1942 item places Carl Brisson in the cast, but his participation in the released film has not been confirmed. In Aug 1942, two units were shooting around the clock to speed completion of the film. During the night, one unit would film the animals for the Central Park sequence, while during the day, the other unit would be working with the actors. The film was such a hit at the box office that it was held over, thus pushing back the releases of the next two Lewton films, *I Walked With a Zombie* and *Leopard Man*, according to a 18 Mar 1943 news item. The film's success led RKO to reunite Kent Smith, Jane Randolph and Simone Simon with screenwriter Bodeen for the 1944 film *Curse of the Cat People* (see entry below). In 1982, director Paul Schrader made another version of the story, also titled *Cat People*, starring Natassia Kinski and Malcolm McDowell.

Box 14 Nov 1942. *DV* 13 Nov 1942, p. 3. *FD* 16 Nov 1942, p. 5. *HR* 13 Jul 1942, p. 6. *HR* 12 Aug 1942, p. 3. *HR* 13 Nov 1942, p. 3. *HR* 17 Feb 1943, p. 10. *HR* 18 Mar 1943, p. 10. *MPHPD* 14 Nov 1942, p. 1005. *NYT* 7 Dec 1942, p. 22. *Var* 18 Nov 1942, p. 8.

THE CATERED AFFAIR (Irish Americans)

Metro-Goldwyn-Mayer Corp.; controlled by Loew's Inc. *Dist* Loew's Inc. 22 Jun **1956**; New York opening: 14 Jun 1956; Prod: 15 Dec 1955—16 Jan 1956 [©Loew's Inc.; 1 May 1956; LP6508]. Sd (Western Electric Sound System); b&w. 10 reels, 8,411 ft. 92-93 min. Passed by the National Board of Review. PCA cert no. 17915.

Prod Sam Zimbalist. *Dir* Richard Brooks. *Asst dir* William Shanks. *Scr* Gore Vidal. *Dir of photog* John Alton. *Art dir* Cedric Gibbons and Paul Groesse. *Film ed* Gene Ruggiero and Frank Santillo. *Set dec* Edwin B. Willis and Hugh Hunt. *Mus* André Previn. *Rec supv* Dr. Wesley C. Miller. [*Sd* Conrad Kahn]. *Hair styles* Sydney Guilaroff. *Makeup* William Tuttle.

Source: Based on the teleplay *The Catered Affair* by Paddy Chayefsky, on *Goodyear Television Playhouse* (NBC, 22 May 1955).

Cast: Bette Davis (*Mrs. Tom* [*Aggie*] *Hurley*), Ernest Borgnine (*Tom Hurley*), Debbie Reynolds (*Jane Hurley*), Barry Fitzgerald (*Uncle Jack Conlon*), Rod Taylor (*Ralph Halloran*), Robert Simon (*Mr. Halloran*), Madge Kennedy (*Mrs. Halloran*), Dorothy Stickney (*Mrs. Rafferty*), Carol Veazie (*Mrs. Casey*), Joan Camden (*Alice* [*Scanlon*]), Ray Stricklyn (*Eddie Hurley*), Jay Adler (*Sam Leiter*), Dan Tobin (*Hotel caterer*), Paul Denton (*Bill*), Augusta Merighi (*Mrs. Musso*), [Sammy Shack, Jack Kenny, Robert Stephenson, Don Devlin (*Cab drivers*)], [Howard Graham (*Joe, a mechanic*)], [Janice Carroll (*Young woman*)], [Joan Bradshaw (*Girl on the phone*)], [Harry Hines (*Counterman*)], [Mae Clarke (*Saleswoman*)], [Jimmie Fox (*Tailor*)], [John Costello (*Bartender*)], [Thomas Dillon (*Father Murphy*)].

Domestic, Comedy-drama. [*Print viewed*]. As New Yorker Tom Hurley completes his shift, his friend, Sam Leiter, tells him the cab they have been wanting to purchase is available at an affordable price. Thrilled that his dream of owning his own cab is about to come true, Tom returns to his cramped Bronx flat to find his wife, grown children and brother-in-law just beginning their day. Daughter Jane remarks that as her fiancé, Ralph Halloran, has been asked to drive a car to California on the following Tuesday, she and Ralph have decided to get married beforehand and honeymoon on the way. Jane's mother Aggie wants to give her daughter a big wedding, but Jane insists that there be "no wedding reception, no nothin,'" just a simple ceremony with immediate family. When Aggie breaks the news to her Irish-born brother Jack, who has lived in the Hurley apartment for the past twelve years, he is thoroughly delighted. Upon learning that he is not invited to the wedding, however, Uncle Jack indignantly exits the apartment. News of the impending marriage travels quickly, and at the fish market, Aggie is besieged with questions from curious friends and neighbors. Why the rush, they ask, is Jane in trouble? Ralph's parents, who live in a nicer part of town, also want a big wedding, and while having dinner at the Hurley apartment that evening, they reminisce about the grand affairs they staged for Ralph's sisters. Just then, Uncle Jack stumbles in and drunkenly announces that because the couple does not consider him part of the immediate family, he will be moving out in the morning. Embarrassed by Jack's behavior and ashamed of her family's sorry financial situation, Aggie insists that Jane have a large wedding, even though, as Tom reminds her, the expense will deplete their savings. Aggie's regrets about her own unceremonious wedding following her brother's offering money to Tom to marry her, and the disappointing years of marriage that followed it, trouble her so deeply that Jane finally consents to having a catered affair. Jane's best friend Alice, who is to be the matron of honor, meets mother and daughter at a bridal salon, but later, she shamefully confesses that her husband has lost his job and that she has no money for a dress. That afternoon, while interviewing the caterer at the Hotel Concourse Plaza, Tom repeatedly expresses horror at the cost of the food, flowers and limousines, and that night, Jane learns that Ralph's mother has invited twice as many guests as she had originally listed. On Sunday, Sam arrives to discuss the cab partnership, and as Jane listens, her father explains that he will be unable to participate. Uncle Jack announces that he has given a wedding invitation to his good friend, Mrs. Rafferty, and when Tom forbids this, Jack again threatens to move out. Aggie argues with Tom, and as the shouting reaches its peak, Jane exclaims that she is calling off the wedding. Later, Ralph and Jane meet Alice and her husband Bill, who have borrowed money in order

to participate in the wedding. Touched, Jane explains that the wedding will be small, as originally planned. Meanwhile, Jack and Mrs. Rafferty decide that as he is moving out of the Hurley house anyway, they should marry and share an apartment. Realizing that when her son leaves for Fort Dix in the fall, she will be alone with her husband for the first time since they were married, Aggie bursts into tears. Tom protests that Aggie should have offered him sympathy rather than criticism for being unable to provide a better life for his children, and when she refuses to listen, he gets drunk and falls asleep. On the morning of the wedding, Aggie gazes at her sleeping husband, and when he finally awakens, she admits that she was wrong. The important thing, she declares, is that together, they witness their daughter's marriage. Aggie then telephones Sam, who drives the now happy couple to church in the new cab. *Family relationships. Financial crisis. Marriage. New York City—Bronx. Weddings. Apartments. Class distinction. Friendship. Guilt. In-laws. Irish Americans. Neighbors. Partnership. Taxicab drivers. Uncles. Unemployment.*

Note: The original television play starred Thelma Ritter and Pat Henning and was directed by Robert Mulligan.

Box 28 Apr 1956. *DV* 25 Apr 1956, p. 3. *Exb* 16 May 1956, pp. 4157-58. *FD* 25 Apr 1956, p. 6. *Har* 28 Apr 1956, p. 66. *HR* 25 Apr 1956, p. 3. *MPHPD* 28 Apr 1956, p. 873. *NYT* 15 Jun 1956, p. 32. *Var* 25 Apr 1956, p. 6.

THE CAT'S-PAW (Chinese Americans)

Harold Lloyd Corp.; William R. Fraser, General Manager. *Dist* Fox Film Corp. 7 Aug **1934**; Prod: 30 Jan—23 Apr 1934 at General Service Studios [©Harold Lloyd Corp.; 17 Aug 1934; LP4895]. Sd (Western Electric Sound System); b&w. 12 reels, 9,155 ft. 100-101 min. Passed by the National Board of Review. PCA cert no. 55.

[*Exec prod* Harold Lloyd]. *Dir* Sam Taylor. [*Fill-in dir* Harold Lloyd]. [*1st asst dir* Walter Mayo]. [*2nd asst dir* Eddie Bernoudy]. *Scr* Sam Taylor. *Photog* Walter Lundin. [*2d cam* Stuart Thompson]. [*Asst cam* Hal Carney and E. William Carter]. [*Gaffer* William McClellan and Ray Jones]. *Art dir* Harry Oliver. *Film ed* Bernard Burton. [*Ward* Peg O'Neil and Miss Anderson]. *Mus dir* Alfred Newman. [*Dance numbers by* Larry Ceballos]. [*Mixer* Bill Fox]. [*Mike man* Bud Swope]. [*Tech dir* William MacDonald]. *Prod mgr* John L. Murphy. [*Chief elec* Cecil Bardwell]. [*Grip* Ralph Hoege]. [*Props* Irving Sindler and Gil Fones]. [*Casting dir* Rex Bailey]. [*Location mgr* Gaylord Lloyd]. [*Asst tech dir* Liell Vedder]. [*Still photog* Eugene Kornman]. [*Publicity dir* Joe Reddy].

Song(s): "I'm Just That Way," music by Harry Akst, lyrics by Roy Turk.

Source: Based on the novel *The Cat's-Paw* by Clarence Budington Kelland (New York, 1934).

Cast: HAROLD LLOYD [(*Ezekiel Cobb*)], Una Merkel [(*Petunia "Pet" Pratt*)], George Barbier [(*Jake Mayo*)], Nat Pendleton [(*Strozzi*)], Grace Bradley [(*Dolores Dace*)], Alan Dinehart [(*Mayor Ed Morgan*)], Grant Mitchell [("*Silk Hat*" *McGee*)], Fred Warren [(*Tien Wang*)], Warren Hymer [("*Spike*" *Slattery*)], J. Farrell Macdonald [(*Pat Shigley*)], James Donlan [(*Red the reporter*)], Edwin Maxwell [(*District Attorney Neal*)], Frank Sheridan [(*Police Commissioner Dan Moriarity*)], Fuzzy Knight [(*Fuzzy*)], Vincent Barnett [(*Vince*)], [David Jack Holt (*Ezekiel as a boy*)], [Charles Sellon (*Dr. Junius P. Withers*)], [James Burke (*Gargan*)], [Frank La Rue (*Jim*)], [Matt McHugh (*Taxi driver*)], [Frederic Burt (*Keen Lung*)], [Samuel S. Hinds (*Mr. Cobb*)], [Alec B. Francis (*Mr. Thatcher*)], [James B. Leong (*Lee Chang*)], [Ivan Linow (*Chee Foo*)], [Jack Kennedy (*Mulligan*)], [Nell Craig (*Mrs. Cobb*)], [Gertrude W. Hoffman (*Mrs. Noon*)], [Tom Herbert (*Drunk*)], [John Ince (*Politician*)], [Dorothy Bay (*Housekeeper*)], [De Witt Jennings, Rychard Cramer (*Policemen*)], [John M. Sullivan (*Jones*)], [George MacQuarrie (*Assistant district attorney*)], [Sam Adams (*Irish policeman*)], [Ernie Alexander, Tom Dugan, John Wray (*Men on street*)], [Noel Madison, Herman Bing, Michael Visaroff (*Gangsters*)], [Dewey Robinson, Constantine Romanoff, Lalo Encinas, Chief Big Tree, Pete Homer (*Chinese guards*)], [Phil Tead, Ernest Wood, Arthur Hoyt, Charles Williams, Billy Dooley, James Mack, Billy Bletcher (*Reporters*)], [Eddie Fetherston, John Kascier, Bob Chapman, Eddie Boland (*Photographers*)], [Sidney Bracy, Fred Walton, George Davis, Rosa Gore, William C. Irving, Vangie Beilby (*Boarders*)], [Jack Don (*Chinese servant*)], [Noah Young].

Comedy-drama. [*Print viewed*]. After living in China with his missionary parents for twenty years, Ezekiel Cobb returns to the

United States to find a wife. When he arrives at the city of Stockport, Ezekiel is baffled by American slang and rudeness, especially when his father's sponsor, Dr. Junius P. Withers, refuses to see him. Ezekiel confides his plight to political boss Jake Mayo, who is touched by Ezekiel's naïveté and sends him to a boardinghouse. That afternoon, Withers dies, causing much consternation for Jake and Mayor Ed Morgan, because Withers was the perenially losing reform candidate for mayor who split the vote so that crooked Morgan was always elected. Jake and Morgan agree that they need another stooge before the election in two days, and so Jake decides to have Ezekiel replace Withers. Jake tells him to be at the city hall the next day for a banquet, at which they will announce his candidacy, but when the time comes, Ezekiel is having tea with his Chinese friend, Tien Wang. Jake begins the banquet and testimonials to the new candidate anyway, and as Ezekiel rushes to city hall, he hears the proceedings on the radio. He is stunned to discover that he is running for mayor, but Jake tells him that it is a matter of principle, even though there is no chance he will win. After Ezekiel accepts, he dines with Petunia "Pet" Pratt, a cynical cigarette girl, at a swanky nightclub, where Ezekiel is dazzled by Morgan's girl friend, Dolores Dace, a glamorous singer who gets him to dance with the chorus girls. The incident creates public support for Ezekiel, who is now perceived as "a regular guy," and he makes himself even more popular by knocking out Morgan, who has drunkenly hit a newsboy. The next day, Ezekiel wins the election by a landslide, and when he tells Pet he must return to China, she shames him into staying. Two months pass as Ezekiel fires Morgan's cronies and vetoes the bills that will result in graft. Jake warns Ezekiel that he is in danger from the political machine he is dismantling, but Ezekiel responds by making Jake the new police commissioner, thereby restoring Jake's belief in honesty. Later that night, Ezekiel is on a date with Pet when Dolores gives him an envelope that she says contains personal letters. She makes him promise to put them in his safe deposit box, which he does the next morning. Unknown to Ezekiel, however, the envelope contains fake deeds, devised by Morgan's gang, which establish him as the owner of a company to which he has awarded a city contract. District Attorney Neal, after hearing allegations that Ezekiel is crooked, opens the box and finds the damning evidence. Ezekiel realizes that by the next day the governor will remove him, but Pet convinces him that he has one day left with which to do good. Ezekiel goes to his office and tells Jake and Pat Shigley, to whom Jake gave the police commissioner's job, to arrest every crook in town and put them in Tien Wang's cellar. Ezekiel then reads to Jake and Pat a story about an ancient Chinese warrior who rid a town of evil men by beheading them, and tells them that Tien has the sword used by the warrior. Despite their forebodings, Jake and Pat carry out his orders, and even arrest Morgan and his gang. Once they are in Tien's cellar, Ezekiel tells them that he will not allow his city to revert to their control, therefore they have a choice of confessing their crimes or being beheaded. Not all of the crooks are convinced, so Ezekiel takes one into another room, and with the help of a Chinese magician, The Great Chang, makes it appear as if the man has been beheaded when they carry his bleeding head through the main room. No one confesses yet, so Ezekiel perpetrates the same trick upon Morgan, after which the others eagerly write confessions. Ezekiel then rushes off to propose to Pet. She accepts, and some time later, the couple visits Tien Wang. After a bit of playful bickering, the couple agrees to stay in Stockport with Ezekiel as mayor rather than return to China as missionaries. *Frame-ups. Innocents. Mayors. Missionaries. Political corruption. Antique dealers. Antique shops. Boardinghouses. China. Chinese Americans. Cigarette girls. Confession (Law). Criminals. District Attorneys. Drunkenness. Executions. Hoaxes. Newsboys. Nightclubs. Police commissioners. Political bosses. Proposals (Marital). Proverbs. Reporters. Romance. Singers. Swords. Telephone.*

Note: Clarence Budington Kelland's novel first appeared as a serial in *The Saturday Evening Post* (26 Aug–30 Sep 1933). Contemporary sources assert that actor Harold Lloyd had never before worked from a published story, or from a story that was not written expressly for him. An unidentified, contemporary news item in the film's production file at the AMPAS Library noted that Lloyd was going to spend $500,000 on this production. According to modern sources, Lloyd paid $25,000 for the film rights to Kelland's novel, and eventually spent $617,000 on the film. According to *HR* news items, Lloyd signed Vincent Lawrence to write the picture's screenplay, and hired Edward Curtis to "assist on dialogue." Their contribution to the completed film has not been confirmed, however. Production was delayed several times due to director Sam Taylor's illness, and according to a *HR* news item, Lloyd directed during at least one of Taylor's absences. *HR* news items reported that Lloyd borrowed actors Grace Bradley and George Barbier from Paramount, Una Merkel from M-G-M, and musical director Alfred Newman from United Artists.

Modern sources assert that Clyde Bruckman worked on the script, and include the following actors in the cast: Jimmy Dime, Don Brodie, Harry Tenbrook, Kit Guard, George Magrill, Jack Herrick, Paul Panzer, James Mason and Harry Wilson (*Gangsters*); Louis Natheaux (*Headwaiter*); Ray Turner (*Bootblack*); Pat Harmon (*Policeman*); Tom London (*Murpb*); Frances Morris and Edward Hearn (*Radio listeners*); Charles McMurphy (*Policeman at elevator*); Sydney Jarvis (*Photo session extra*); Walter James (*Club doorman*); Larry Steers, Pat Somerset and Brooks Benedict (*Club patron*); and James Wang (*Chinese elder*).

Box 11 Aug 1934. *DV* 22 Jan 1934, p. 4. *DV* 17 Jul 1934, p. 3. *DV* 27 Jul 1934, p. 3. *FD* 22 Sep 1933, p. 8. *FD* 24 Jul 1934, pp. 4-5. *FD* 30 Jul 1934, p. 5. *HR* 15 Jun 1933, p. 8. *HR* 5 Jan 1934, p. 1. *HR* 9 Jan 1934, p. 1. *HR* 13 Jan 1934, p. 2. *HR* 24 Jan 1934, p. 3. *HR* 25 Jan 1934, p. 6. *HR* 31 Jan 1934, p. 4. *HR* 2 Feb 1934, p. 4. *HR* 3 Feb 1934, p. 7. *HR* 7 Feb 1934, p. 2. *HR* 17 Feb 1934, p. 4. *HR* 13 Mar 1934, p. 3. *HR* 24 Apr 1934, p. 1. *HR* 26 Apr 1934, p. 2. *HR* 27 Jul 1934, p. 3. *HR* 31 Jul 1934, pp. 6-11. *HR* 17 Aug 1934, p. 1. *IP* Mar 1934, p. 16. *MPD* 28 May 1934, p. 7. *MPH* 12 May 1934, p. 42. *MPH* 16 Jun 1934, p. 30. *MPH* 4 Aug 1934, p. 30. *MPSI* Feb 1935, p. 34. *NYT* 17 Aug 1934, p. 12. *Var* 21 Aug 1934, p. 17.

CATSKILL HONEYMOON (Jewish Americans, Yiddish language)
Martin Cohen Enterprises. *Dist* Pictorial Ventures. 1950; New York opening: 27 Jan 1950 [©Martin Cohen Enterprises; 10 Jan 1950; LP2858]. Sd (RCA Sound); b&w. 8,406 ft. 93 min. Yiddish and English language.
Prod Martin Cohen and [Jack LaMont]. *Dir* Joe Berne. *Dial* Joel Jacobson. *Photog* Charles Downs. *Ed* Jack Kemp and [Cy Braunstein]. *Words and mus comp, arr and cond by* Hy Jacobson. *Extra arrangements by* Dick Bloch and Philip Laskowsky. *Sd rec* Edward Fenton. *Makeup* Vincent Kehoe.
Song(s): "Scattered Toys," words and music by Nick Kenny and Charles Kenny; "Vesti la giubba," from the opera *I pagliacci*, music and libretto by Ruggiero Leoncavallo; aria from the opera *Carmen*, music by Georges Bizet, libretto by Henri Meilhac and Ludovic Halévy; "Hava Nagilah," traditional; additional numbers, including "Catskill Honeymoon," "My Mistake," "Ich Hab Dich Zu Fill Lieb," "Chiri-Bim, Chiri-Bum," "Me and My Concertina," "I'm Singing a Lovesong," "What the Public Wants," "I'm Going Home" and "Sing, Israel, Sing," by Alexander Olshanetsky, Sholom Secunda, Max Kletter and David Meyerowitz.
Cast: Michal Michalesko, Jan Bart, Bas Sheva, Cookie Bowers, Max Bozhyk, Rose Bozhyk, Bobby Colt, Feder Sisters [Sylvia and Miriam], Mike Hammer, Henrietta Jacobson, Julius Adler, Mary La Roche, Abe Lax, Al Murray, David Page, Dorothy Page, Gita Stein, and Introducing Irving Grossman, and Dina Goldberg.

Yiddish, Musical, Comedy. [*Print viewed*]. At Ma Holder's Young's Gap Hotel in Parksville, New York, Mr. and Mrs. Halpern celebrate their fiftieth anniversary with the guests of the hotel. In honor of the occasion, the resort presents a musical and comedy review, with Al Murray as master of ceremonies. Acts include Mary La Roche singing "My Mistake"; Henrietta Jacobson and Julius Adler performing a comedy sketch with a song; Jewish-American tenor Jan Bart singing "Ich Hab dich Zu fill Lieb"; impressionist Cookie Bowers; Irving Grossman and Dina Goldberg performing a comedy sketch and song; singer Abe Lax; David and Dorothy Page singing an aria from *Carmen*; Dina Goldberg and Henrietta Jacobson in the comedy sketch, "Die Galitziane—Die Litvakes," with a song; Yiddish folksongs done in a swing style by The Feder Sisters, Sylvia and Miriam; Bobby Colt singing "Scattered Toys" and "Me and My Concertina"; female cantor Bas Sheva singing "Hava Nagilah" in Hebrew and the aria "Vesti la giubba" from *I pagliacci*; Max Bozhyk, Henrietta Jacobson and Julius Adler performing the comedy sketch "Ten Cents a Bagel"; Jan Bart singing "I'm Singing a Love Song" and another song; and finally, a tribute to Palestine, including the songs "Ich Fuhr Aheim" and "Sing Israel Sing," performed by the entire ensemble. *Jews. Musical revues. Resorts. Cantors, Jewish. Dancers. Impersonations (Comic). Palestine. Singers. Wedding anniversaries.*

Note: The opening credits read "Martin Cohen Enterprises presents Hy Jacobson's Yiddish-American Musical Revue *Catskill Honeymoon*." The credits also noted that the film was shot at Young's Gap Hotel in Parksville, NY. Censors in Ohio cut out English subtitles for a joke about a stutterer, who came to be that way because he was born with his tongue out and was delivered for a circumcision the wrong way. Censors in Maryland cut out both the English subtitles and the Yiddish dialogue for the joke.

Exb 1 Feb 1950, pp. 2792-93. *FD* 6 Feb 1950, p. 11. *LADN* 1 Jul 1950. *LAT* 1 Jul 1950. *NYT* 28 Jan 1950, p. 10. *Var* 1 Feb 1950, p. 20.

CATTLE QUEEN OF MONTANA (Native Americans, Blackfoot, Siksika)

Benedict Bogeaus Productions. *Dist* RKO Radio Pictures, Inc. 18 Nov **1954**; Prod: mid Jul–late Jul 1954 [©RKO Radio Pictures, Inc.; 17 Nov 1954; LP4412]. Sd (RCA Sound Recording); col (Technicolor). 9 reels, 7,944 ft. 88 min. PCA cert no. 17158.

Prod Benedict Bogeaus. *Dir* Allan Dwan. *Asst dir* Nathan Barragar. *Scr* Howard Estabrook. *Story* Thomas Blackburn. *Dir of photog* John Alton. *Art dir* Van Nest Polglase. *Supv ed* James Leicester. *Film ed* Carlo Lodato. *Set dec* John Sturtevant. *Ward des* Gwen Wakeling. *Mus score* Louis Forbes. *Sd supv* Lee Luthaker.

Cast: BARBARA STANWYCK [(*Sierra Nevada Jones*)], RONALD REAGAN [(*Farrell*)], Gene Evans [(*Tom McCord*)], Lance Fuller [(*Colorados*)], Anthony Caruso [(*Natchakos*)], Jack Elam [(*Yost*)], Yvette Dugay [(*Starfire*)], Morris Ankrum [(*Pop Jones*)], Chubby Johnson [(*Nat*)], Myron Healey [(*Hank*)], Rod Redwing [(*Powhani*)], [Byron Foulger (*Land office clerk*)], [Harry Tyler (*Telegraph operator*)], [Paul Birch (*Colonel Carrington*)], [Tom Steele], [Dorothy Andre].

Western. [*Print viewed*]. Texas cattle ranchers Pop Jones and his daughter, Sierra Nevada, arrive in Montana's Buffalo Valley to take ownership of land that once belonged to Pop's family. While bathing in a pond, Sierra is approached by Farrell, a United States Cavalry agent posing as a gunman looking for work at the nearby McCord ranch. After warning Sierra that the local Indians are partial to the scalps of white women, Farrell rides off to McCord's Bear Claw outfit. Later that night, Indians stampede the Jones's cattle, and, in process, kill Pop. They also injure cowhand Nat and knock Sierra unconscious. Tom McCord, who is in league with Natchakoa, the leader of the raiding Indians, takes the pre-emption papers needed by the Jones family to reclaim its property, which he has found on Pop's body. The next day, Sierra and Nat are found by a friendly, young Blackfoot Indian, Colorados, who is returning to his family's village after attending a "white man's school." Colorados takes them to his village, but while Sierra tends to Nat's wounds, Colorados' father, Chief Red Lance, upbraids his son for bringing whites into the camp. Red Lance eventually agrees to let his son prove his assertion that the whites and Indians can live together in peace, and permits the visitors to stay. Later, Natchakoa rejects McCord's orders to kill Sierra and Nat, insisting that to do so he would have to kill Colorados, their protector. McCord instead commissions Farrell to dispose of the two survivors, offering him $2,000 for the deed. When Sierra goes to the land office to claim her land, she is shocked to discover that McCord has already laid claim to it. Realizing that McCord is behind the rustling and the conspiracy to take her family's land, Sierra vows to find proof of this by getting her hands on cattle hide bearing the "new" Bear Claw brand. After finding Nat dead from an Indian arrow, Sierra tries to get at the hide by pretending to accept McCord's offer to buy her out. Sierra is caught trying to steal the hide by one of McCord's henchmen, but she is saved by the arrival of Farrell. Sierra realizes that Farrell is a true friend when he tells her to take the evidence to Cavalry Colonel Carrington. En route to the Army camp, Sierra overhears Natchakoa and McCord discussing plans to kill Colorados on the following day. While Sierra goes to warn Colorados, Farrell visits Carrington with news that he has compiled nearly all the evidence needed to convict McCord. Following the death of Chief Red Lance, Natchakoa challenges Colorados to a knife fight for the right to lead the Blackfoots, but it ends inconclusively, and Colorados lets Natchakoa leave with men who are loyal to him. Farrell rejoins Sierra, and after telling her that he is working for the Army, takes her with him to go after McCord. Farrell and Sierra explode McCord's wagon filled with rifles for the Indians, and a gun battle ensues. Natchakoa and McCord are killed in the battle, leaving Sierra, McCord and Colorados free to begin a new life. *Fathers and sons. Land claims. Montana. Romance. Rustlers. Siksika Indians. Alcoholism. Explosions. Fathers and daughters. Friendship. Gunrunners. Idealists. Impersonation and imposture. Jealousy. Murder. Racism. Ranchers. Self-sacrifice. Stampedes. Undercover agents. United States. Army. Cavalry.*

Note: According to *HR*, some filming took place on location in Montana. Modern sources add Burt Mustin and Roy Gordon to the cast.

Box 27 Nov 1954. *DV* 17 Nov 1954, p. 3. *FD* 7 Dec 1954, p. 12. *HR* 16 Jul 1954, p. 10. *HR* 29 Jul 1954, p. 8. *HR* 30 Jul 1954. *HR* 17 Nov 1954, p. 4. *MPHPD* 20 Nov 1954, p. 218. *NYT* 26 Jan 1955, p. 22. *Var* 17 Nov 1954, p. 6.

CAUGHT IN THE ACT (Italian Americans)

T. H. Richmond Productions. *Dist* Producers Releasing Corp. 17 Jan **1941**; Prod: late Dec 1940 [©Producers Releasing Corp.; 25 Jan 1941; LP10209]. Sd; b&w. 5,392 ft. 60 or 62 min.

Exec prod George R. Batcheller. *Prod* T. H. Richmond. *Assoc prod* Martin Cohn. *Dir* Jean Yarbrough. *Orig story* Robert Cosgriff. *Scr* Al Martin. *Dir of photog* Mack Stengler. *Art dir* Charles Clague. *Sd eng* Corson Jowett. *Prod mgr* Chris Beute.

Cast: Henry Armetta (*Mike Ripportella*), Iris Meredith (*Lucy Ripportella*), Robert Baldwin (*Jim Keene*), Charles Miller (*Leonard Brandon*), Inez Palange (*Mary Ripportella*), Dick Terry (*Henderson*), Joey Ray (*Davis*), Maxine Leslie (*Fay Kingman*), William Newell (*Sergeant Riley*).

Crime, Comedy. [*Not viewed*]. Gangsters Henderson and Davis, who run a protection racket under the name Fidelity Enterprises, attempt to force Leonard Brandon, president of Brandon Construction Company, to purchase their low-quality construction materials. To avoid buying from the thugs, Brandon promotes his scrupulously honest foreman, Italian American Mike Ripportella, to sales. Mike is delighted by the promotion, and leaves that day in high spirits to buy a new suit for his daughter Lucy's wedding. On the way to the store, Fay Kingman, a beautiful blonde, imposes on Mike for a ride because she is being chased by two men. After Mike loses the thugs, Fay thanks him with a kiss which is witnessed by Mike's neighbors. The busybodies report the kiss to Mike's wife Mary, but her rebuke is interrupted when two policemen arrest Mike. Because of his brief encounter with Fay, who was later arrested, the police believe that Mike is a member of the protection racket. Mike learns that Fay is the girl friend of one of the thugs, and while under intense questioning, a befuddled Mike reveals that Brandon is his "boss." The police then arrest Brandon and thereby prevent him from bending to Henderson and Davis' threats. Henderson and Davis, meanwhile, learn that Fay ran away from their thugs because she was upset to learn that they had vandalized construction companies that failed to comply with their demands. When Lucy calls off her wedding because of her father's arrest, her fiancé, reporter Jim Keene, decides to investigate. Mary comes into the police station furious, and is incarcerated with Fay after she slugs a policeman. Jim and Lucy follow her to the station, and based on his investigation, Jim reports to his paper that Brandon is the chief racketeer. Under instructions from Henderson and Davis, their lawyer bails Brandon, Mike and Fay out of jail, and Mike mistakenly thinks Brandon is the real crime boss. Jim and Lucy return to the station to bail the family out, but arrive too late. Jim learns from a policeman where the lawyer resides, and follows the crooked lawyer. Henderson and Davis, meanwhile, believe that Brandon has been operating a protection racket on his own and question Mike and Fay. Mike realizes that the two men are the real criminals and that his boss is innocent. Jim bursts into the apartment just as Henderson and Davis start to brutalize Mike, and he is followed closely by the police. After the racketeers are arrested and Mike and Brandon are cleared, Brandon offers Mike another promotion, but Mike, fearful of the consequences, turns him down. *Construction foremen. False arrests. Police. Promotions. Protection racket. Reporters. Fathers and daughters. Fights. Gossip. Italian Americans. Jails. Lawyers. Weddings. Wives.*

Note: The working title of this film was *It Happened to Me*. The *Exb* review described this film as an "Italian dialect comedy."

Exb 5 Feb 1941, p. 684. *FD* 13 Feb 1941, p. 7. *HR* 27 Dec 1940, p. 10. *HR* 26 May 1941, p. 3. *MPH* 26 Apr 1941, p. 38. *MPHPD* 3 May 1941, p. 126. *Var* 1 Jan 1941. *Var* 12 Feb 1941, p. 18.

LA CAUTIVADORA (Spanish language)

Iberia Productions, Inc. **1931**; San Juan, Puerto Rico opening: 23 Apr 1931; New York opening: 29 May 1931; Prod: Oct 1930 at the Darmour Studios. Sd; b&w. 5,432 ft. 60 min. Spanish language.

Dir Joseph Levering. *Dial dir* Fernando C. Tamayo. *Orig story* Arturo S. Mom. *Dial* Adalberto Elías González. *Mus* Rafael Gama. *Mus performed by* Rafael Gama, and his orchestra.

Song(s): "Yo con tu amor sueño," by Rafael Gama.

Cast: Nelly Fernández ("*La Serpentina*"), Alfonso de Larios ("*El Pesado*"), Julián Rivero, Carmen Granada, Jacinto Jaramillo, Josefina Ramos, Amber Norman, Ted Stroback.

Drama. [*Not viewed*]. "El Pesado" and "La Serpentina," two nightclubs in the Spanish quarter of New Orleans that are located opposite each other, battle to attract customers. Known by the names of their respective establishments, the owners, a man and a woman,

are each obsessed with trying to bring about the ruin of the other. During a vacation from school, Carlos, the younger brother of "El Pesado," falls in love with "La Serpentina," but receives only a pure, maternal affection from her. "La Serpentina" announces that she will dance nude. On the night of her planned dance, her club is packed with people, including her rival. At the climactic moment of the dance, just as she is about to drop the final veil, the police stop the performance to interrogate her about a stolen necklace she is wearing, which was a present from Carlos. Afraid of going to prison, Carlos attempts suicide. The battle between the two proprietors increases until they risk their lives by drinking from two cups, one of which is poisoned; however, when "El Pesado" pretends to have taken the poisoned drink, "La Serpentina" confesses the secret love she has always felt for him. *Business competition. Dancers. New Orleans (LA). Nightclubs. Nightclubs. Attempted suicide. Brothers. Deception. False accusations. Infatuation. Interrogation. Necklaces. Nudity. Poison. Police raids. Students. Thieves. Vacations.*

Note: The working title of this film was *El triunfo de una mujer vencida.* The film was listed as being available for distribution in Spain in 1935-36 under the title *Corazones de acero*, which was the title of Arturo S. Mom's original story, but no information concerning its exhibition at that time has been located. The song "Yo con tu amor sueño" was sung by Samuel Pedraza, but it is not known if Pedraza actually appeared in the film or if only his voice was heard on the soundtrack.

Arte y Cinematografía Jan 1932.

THE CAVALIER (Latino)
Tiffany-Stahl Productions, Inc. 1 Nov **1928** [©Tiffany-Stahl Productions, Inc.; 15 Jun 1928; LP25389]. Sd eff (Photophone); b&w. 7 reels, 6,775 ft.
Dir Irvin Willat. *Scen* Victor Irvin. *Titles* Walter Anthony. *Photog* Jack Stevens and Harry Cooper. *Film ed* Doane Harrison. *Set des* Eugene McMurtrie. *Mus score* Hugo Riesenfeld.
Song(s): "My Cavalier," music by Hugo Riesenfeld, lyrics by R. Meredith Willson.
Source: Based on the short story "The Black Rider" by Max Brand (publication undetermined).
Cast: Richard Talmadge (*El Caballero/Taki*), Barbara Bedford (*Lucia D'Arquista*), Nora Cecil (*Lucia's aunt*), David Torrence (*Ramon Torreno*), David Mir (*Carlos Torreno*), Stuart Holmes (*Sgt. Juan Dinero*), Christian Frank (*Pierre Gaston*), Oliver Eckhardt (*The padre*).
Adventure. El Caballero, a mysterious knight-errant—beloved by the poor, hated by the rich, and feared by the haughty—disguises himself as Taki, an Aztec servant, and rescues Lucía, a Spanish girl of noble birth, from an unhappy marriage with the son of a wealthy Californian. El Caballero, actually a Spanish don, marries Lucía and returns to Spain with her. *Aztec Indians. California–History–To 1846. Disguise. Marriage-Arranged. Nobility. Spaniards.*
FD 4 Nov 1928. *NYT* 31 Oct 1928, p. 28. *Var* 7 Nov 1928, p. 15.

CAVALIER OF THE WEST (Native Americans)
Supreme Features, Inc.; Alfred T. Mannon, President. *Dist* State Rights; Weiss Bros.; Artclass Pictures Corp. 15 Nov **1931**; Prod: ended late Oct 1931 at Tec-Art Studios. Sd (General Sound Corp.); b&w. 65 min. Passed by the National Board of Review.
Assoc prod Geo. M. Merrick. *Dir* John P. McCarthy. *Dial dir* Harry P. Christ. *Story* John P. McCarthy. [*Wrt*] by John P. McCarthy. *Photog* Frank Keeson and Harry Neuman. *Settings* Tec Art Studios, Inc. *Ed* James Morley. [*Rec eng* B. J. Croger]. *Prod mgr* Geo. M Merrick.
Cast: HARRY CAREY (*Captain John Allister*), Carmen La Roux (*Dolores Fernandez*), Kane Richmond (*Lieutenant Wilbur Allister*), Christina Montt (*Chiquita*), Geo. F. Hayes (*Sheriff Bill Ryan*), Theodore Adams (*Lee Burgess*), Maston Williams (*Deputy "Red" Greeley*), Paul Panzer (*Don Fernandez*), P. Narcha (*White Feather*), Ben Corbett (*Sergeant Regan*), Lew Meehan (*Tim Slade*).
Western. [*Print viewed*]. Captain John Allister of the United States Cavalry discovers Deputy Sheriff "Red" Greeley and four companions in the act of attacking a group of Indians. Through a ruse, John proves that their accusation that the Indians were rustling horses was merely an excuse to steal the gold that the Indians were transporting to El Rio. He arrests the men and turns them over to Sheriff Bill Ryan. Lee Burgess, foreman of the ranch owned by Don Fernandez, is secretly allied with Greeley. John and Sheriff Ryan travel to the Fernandez ranch to purchase some horses for the army. Burgess tries to sell them inferior horses for a high price, but John discovers the trick. At the

ranch, they meet Fernandez' daughter Dolores, who much prefers John to Burgess, despite the latter's attempt to pressure her to marry him. The prisoners escape from jail and Greeley is suspected of helping them. Fearing an Indian uprising, John declares martial law. He joins the Indians on their next gold transporting trip, disguised as a cowboy, and prevents any theft. On the evening of Dolores' birthday fiesta, Burgess plans to rob the stagecoach bringing the army payroll into town. Lieutenant Wilbur Allister, John's brother, is guarding the payroll. He has been transferred West to reform his drinking habit under John's supervision. Wilbur is wounded in the holdup and taken to Don Fernandez' ranch to recuperate. During his convalescence, he falls in love with Dolores, not realizing that she is the woman his brother loves. Always the gentleman, John steps aside, but makes Wilbur promise that he will be worthy of Dolores. Under Burgess' influence, however, Wilbur starts drinking and gambling again and then is himself accused of robbing the stage and murdering a man. Using evidence provided by the Indians, John proves that Greeley and Burgess are guilty of the crime and rides off with the army to capture them, leaving Wilbur behind with Dolores. *Brothers. Indians of North America. Outlaws. Romantic rivalry. United States. Army. Cavalry. Birthdays. Convalescence. Cowboys. Deputies. Frame-ups. Gambling. Gold. Gunfights. Gunshot wounds. Impersonation and imposture. Jailbreaks. Jealousy. Martial law. Murder. Proposals (Marital). Ranch foremen. Ranches. Regeneration. Self-sacrifice. Sheriffs. Stagecoach robberies. Trials. The West.*
FD 5 Nov 1931, p. 8. *FD* 22 Nov 1931, 10. *Var* 9 Feb 1932, p. 19.

CAVALRY SCOUT (Native Americans, Cheyenne, Dakota)
Monogram Pictures Corp. *Dist* Monogram Pictures Corp. 13 May **1951**; Prod: mid-Sep—early Oct 1950 [©Monogram Pictures Corp.; 13 May 1951; LP808]. Sd (Western Electric Recording); col (Cinecolor). 8 reels, 7,004 ft. 78 min. PCA cert no. 14954.
Prod Walter Mirisch. *Dir* Leslie Selander. [*Asst dir* William Calihan]. *Story and scr* Dan Ullman. *Addl dial* Thomas Blackburn. *Photog* Harry Neumann. *Col consultant* Wilton R. Holm and Clifford D. Shank. *Art dir* David Milton. *Film ed* Richard Heermance. [*Set dec* Raymond Boltz, Jr.]. *Mus* Marlin Skiles. *Rec by* John Kean. [*Makeup* Leonard Engelman]. [*Hair stylist* Fritzi La Bar]. *Prod mgr* Allen K. Wood. *Set cont* Dorothy Yutzi.
Cast: ROD CAMERON (*Kirby Frye*), Audrey Long (*Claire [Coville]*), Jim Davis (*Lt. [Boyd] Spaulding*), James Millican (*Martin Gavin*), James Arness (*Barth*), John Doucette (*Varney*), William Phillips (*Sgt. Wilkins*), Stephen Chase (*Col. Drumm*), Rory Mallinson (*Corporal*), Eddy Waller (*General Sherman*), Frank Wilcox (*Matson*), Cliff Clark (*Col. Deering*), [Paul Bryar (*Bartender*)].
Western. [*Print viewed*]. In 1876, in the Dakota Territory, pioneers settling in the region find themselves under attack by Indians who fear that they are losing their land. Charged with protecting these settlers are Union Army veterans and former Confederate soldiers, who are stationed at forts along heavily travelled routes. The Indian war parties, composed of Sioux and Cheyenne tribes under the command of Chiefs Sitting Bull and Crazy Horse, become a growing threat as the rapid-fire Gatling gun makes its way into the hands of the Indians. Into this volatile situation arrives Kirby Frye, a former Union Army captain, now a Cavalry scout, who takes up his new post at Red Bluff. Posing as a civilian, Frye makes his new home at an inn operated by Claire Coville, who is the sweetheart of Lt. Boyd Spaulding. During his investigation of the smuggling of ammunition into the territory, Frye suspects that the operation is taking place within the post. This assumption angers Spaulding and his fellow officer, Col. Drumm, who have been overseeing things at Red Bluff until Frye arrived. In order to gain a better knowledge of the shipping activities in the area, Frye seeks employment with the Red Bluff Freight Co., which is run by the crooked Martin Gavin, who is behind the secret selling of Gatling guns to the Indians, but he manages to elude Frye and foil his first attempt to stop the smuggling at a new check point. After a failed attempt by one of Gavin's men, Barth, to kill Frye, Frye and Spaulding join forces to find the would-be killer. They eventually find Barth in the woods and kill him in a bristling gun battle. Later, checkpoint inspectors discover the smuggled arms hidden in bolt of cloth when they fall off the back of a passing coach. After the outlaws scalp the guards at the next checkpoint, they take refuge on an Indian reservation. Claire, who is now Frye's sweetheart, is abducted by Gavin and his men, who suspect that she is spying for Frye. As an

Indian uprising begins, Frye sets a trap for Gavin, and with Claire's help, manages to fight off the Indians and put an end to Gavin's operation. Although Spaulding dies in the battle, Frye and Claire are satisfied with their effort to put an end to the gun-smuggling gang. *Cheyenne Indians. Dakota Indians. Gatling guns. Pioneers. Smuggling. The West. Abduction. Ambushes. Attempted murder. Gunfights. Romance. Scalping. United States. Army. Cavalry. Veterans.*

Note: A *HR* production chart lists Jane Darwell in the cast, but she did not appear in the released film.

Box 21 Apr 1951. *FD* 16 Apr 1951, p. 3. *HR* 16 Apr 1951, p. 3. *HR* 22 Sep 1951, p. 8. *HR* 27 Sep 1951, p. 12. *MPHPD* 21 Apr 1951, p. 809. *NYT* 8 Jun 1951, p. 32. *Var* 18 Apr 1951, p. 24.

THE CAVE GIRL (Native Americans, Aztec)
Inspiration Pictures, Inc. *Dist* Associated First National Pictures. 26 Dec **1921** [©Inspiration Pictures, Inc.; 18 Nov 1921; LP17058]. Si; b&w. 5 reels, 4,405 ft.

Dir Joseph J. Franz. *Scen* William Parker. *Titles* Katherine Hilliker. *Photog* Victor Milner.

Source: Based on the play *The Cave Girl* by Guy Bolton and George Middleton (New York, 18 Aug 1920).

Cast: Teddie Gerard (*Margot*), Charles Meredith (*Divvy Bates*), Wilton Taylor (*J. T. Bates*), Eleanor Hancock (*Mrs. Georgia Case*), Lillian Tucker (*Elsie Case*), Frank Coleman (*Rufus Patterson*), Boris Karloff (*Baptiste*), Jake Abraham (*Prof. Orlando Sperry*), John Beck (*Rogers*).

Melodrama. Margot Sperry, who keeps house for her guardian, a professor who wants to revert to primitive modes of living, finds it difficult to find food in the winter wilderness and resorts to pilfering from the Bates's winter camp. Divvy, engaged to a girl he does not love, meets Margot on one of her raids and falls in love with her. Baptiste, a half-breed employed by the Bates family, is discharged for stealing and burns the camp, driving the family to refuge with Margot. Elsie, hoping to regain Divvy's affections, dresses in boyish clothes similar to Margot's. Joining forces with Baptiste, they capture Margot, and Baptiste takes her in a canoe downstream. Realizing her mistake, Elsie warns Divvy, who bests the half-breed and then rescues Margot from the falls. *Hunger. Indians of North America–Mixed blood. Lure of the primitive. Professors. Waterfalls.*

ETR 18 Mar 1922, p. 1143.

CECIL B. DEMILLE'S UNCONQUERED *see* **UNCONQUERED**

EL CENTAURO *see* **UN CAPITáN DE COSACOS**

THE CHAIR FOR MARTIN ROME *see* **CRY OF THE CITY**

THE CHALLENGE *see* **WHITE FEATHER**

CHAN'S MURDER CRUISE *see* **CHARLIE CHAN'S MURDER CRUISE**

THE CHARGE AT FEATHER RIVER (Native Americans, Cheyenne)
Warner Bros. Pictures, Inc.; A Warner Bros.—First National Picture. *Dist* Warner Bros. Pictures, Inc. 11 Jul **1953**; Vernon, TX premiere: 30 Jun 1953; Prod: late Feb—early Apr 1953 [©Warner Bros. Pictures, Inc.; 4 Aug 1953; LP2780]. Sd (RCA Sound System); col (WarnerColor); Natural Vision 3-Dimension. 8,707 ft. 99 min. PCA cert no. 16407.

Prod David Weisbart. *Dir* Gordon Douglas. *Asst dir* Russell Llewellyn. [*2nd asst dir* James Petsch]. *Wrt* James R. Webb. *Dir of photog* Peverell Marley. [*Cam op* Neal Beckner]. [*Asst cam* Walter Bluemel]. [*Photog tech* Harold Griggs]. [*Stills* Pat Clark]. *Art dir* Stanley Fleischer. *Film ed* Folmar Blangstead. *Set dec* Lyle B. Reifsnider. [*Props* William Robey Cooper]. [*Asst props* L. C. Williams]. *Ward* Marjorie Best. [*Women's ward* Mina Willowbird]. [*Men's ward* Roy Dumont and Charles Mack]. *Orch* Murray Cutter. *Mus* Max Steiner. *Sd* Charles B. Lang. *Makeup artist* Gordon Bau. [*Makeup* Emile LaVigne]. *Natural Vision supv* M. L. Gunzburg. *Visual consultant* Julian Gunzburg, M.D. *Natural Vision consultant* Howard Schwartz. [*Scr supv* Meta Rebner]. [*Grip* Charles Harris]. [*Gaffer* Charles O'Bannon]. [*Best boy* Norman C. McClay].

Cast: Guy Madison [(*Miles Archer*)], Frank Lovejoy [(*Sgt. Baker*)], Helen Westcott [(*Anne McKeever*)], Vera Miles [(*Jennie McKeever*)], Dick Wesson [(*Cullen*)], Onslow Stevens [(*Grover Johnson*)], Steve Brodie [(*Ryan*)], Ron Hagerthy [(*Johnny McKeever*)], Fay Roope [(*Lt. Col. Kilrain*)], Neville Brand [(*Morgan*)], Henry Kulky [(*Smiley*)], Lane Chandler [(*Poinsett*)], [James Brown (*Conner*)], [Rand Brooks (*Adams*)], [Ben Corbett (*Carver*)], [John Damler (*Dabney*)], [Louis Tomei (*Curry*)], [Carl Andre (*Hudkins*)], [Fred Kennedy (*Leech*)], [Dub Taylor (*Danowicz*)], [Ralph Brooke (*Wilhelm*)], [David Alpert (*Griffin*)], [Fred Carson (*Chief Thunder Hawk*)], [Steve Wayne, Bob Roark (*Soldiers*)], [Wayne Taylor (*Signal private*)], [Richard Bartlett (*Sentry*)], [Joe Bassett (*Quartermaster sergeant*)], [Dennis Dengate (*Ordnance sergeant*)], [Vivian Mason (*Mamie*)], [John Pickard (*Officer*)], [Ray Beltram (*Old Indian*)].

Western. [*Print viewed*]. When Cheyenne Indians threaten to disrupt construction of a railroad through Colorado territory they believe is theirs, Lt. Col. Kilrain of the U.S. Cavalry summons Miles Archer, a Civil War veteran and an expert on the region, to Ft. Bellows to organize a special protective guard troop. Archer arrives at the fort only to discover that in addition to the troop, he is also expected to join Sgt. Baker in the rescue of two white women abducted by the Cheyenne five years earlier. Archer initially rejects Kilrain's request, but when he learns that the women, Anne and Jennie McKeever, are the sisters of Johnny McKeever, an old pal of his, he changes his mind. A fighting regiment is then assembled from a group of men who have committed minor offenses at the fort. Among the recruits are Cullen, an inventor; Poinsett, a Southern aristocrat; Ryan, a philanderer; and Grover Johnson, an artist from the East. Before the regiment leaves the fort, a fistfight erupts between Ryan and Baker, who becomes enraged when he finds his wife kissing Ryan. Heading into Cheyenne territory, Archer and his men come across an ailing old Arapaho man, who, before dying, throws his ax at one of the soldiers, hitting him squarely in the back. The men continue on, undaunted, and eventually find the Indian village at which Anne and Jennie are located. It is only after the two sisters are safely brought out of the Indian village that Archer and the others discover that Jennie has become a Cheyenne, and that she is engaged to marry Chief Thunder Hawk. While Anne willingly agrees to return to Fort Bellows, Jennie must be gagged and taken by force. En route to the fort, Archer loses nearly half of his party to Cheyenne attacks and, at one point, discovers that Jennie is secretly signaling the Indians, giving them their exact location. The party finally reaches Fort Bellows only to discover that the fort has been ransacked and that all but one of the men there, a man named Griffin, have been massacred. Griffin tells Archer that the women, including Archer's wife, were sent to Fort Darby. When Archer learns that Fort Darby is the nearest place to get food and water, he decides to lead his party on a four-day journey there. Once again, Archer's party comes under Cheyenne attack and is forced to take shelter on a river island, where a romance between Archer and Anne flourishes. Realizing the danger they are in, Archer sends Baker and Ryan ahead to Fort Darby to get reinforcements. Although Ryan is killed in an Indian ambush, Baker manages to get through to the fort. Back at the river island, the Indian attacks grow in ferocity and result in a full-scale battle. Shortly after Chief Thunder Hawk is killed, reinforcements from Fort Darby arrive, and with their help, the Indians are driven off. Jennie's body, shot up with arrows, is later found next to Chief Thunder Hawk's. With his mission accomplished, Archer professes his love for Anne and asks her to marry him. *Cheyenne Indians. Colorado. Rescues. Romance. United States–History–Indian campaigns. United States. Army. Cavalry. Abduction. Artists. Battles. Civil War veterans. Engagements. Fistfights. Forts. Inventors. Islands. Land claims. Massacres. Officers (Military). Philanderers. Railroads. Sisters. Southerners. Tribal chiefs.*

Note: The working title of this film was *The Burning Arrow*. According to *Var*, *Charge at Feather River* had its premiere at the Plaza Theatre in Vernon, TX, and was the first picture to be shown there. The newly constructed theater was the first in the country built especially for 3-D, widescreen and stereophonic sound films. According to the file for the film in the MPAA/PCA Collection at the AMPAS Library, the river island battle depicted in the film was based on the historic Battle of Beeckers Island, which took place in 1869. Although Larry Chance is credited in the role of "Chief Thunder Hawk" in Feb 1953 studio cast lists, Fred Carson is credited in the part in an Aug 1953 CBCS list. In 1972, according to a *DV* news item, Milton L. Gunzburg filed suit against Warner Bros. and others seeking profits from this and another film, *House of Wax*, which he claimed were contractually due to him and the Natural Vision Corp. Gunzburg also sought $150,000 in damages and an injunction against further showings of the films. The outcome of the suit is not known. Modern sources note that *The Charge of Feather River* was the highest grossing western of 1953.

Box 4 Jul 1953. *Box* 11 Jul 1953. *DV* 30 Jun 1953, p. 3. *FD* 8 Jul 1953, p. 10. *HR* 27 Feb 1953, p. 13. *HR* 3 Apr 1953, p. 9. *HR* 30 Jun 1953, p. 3. *MPHPD* 4 Jul 1953, p. 1901. *NYDM* 6 Apr 1953. *NYT* 16 Jul 1953, p. 17. *Var* 1 Jul 1953, p. 6.

CHARLIE CHAN AND THE CHINESE RING see **THE CHINESE RING**

CHARLIE CHAN AT MONTE CARLO (Chinese Americans)

Twentieth Century-Fox Film Corp. *Dist* Twentieth Century-Fox Film Corp. 21 Jan **1938**; New York opening: week of 17 Dec 1937; Prod: 20 Sep—mid-Oct 1937 [©Twentieth Century-Fox Film Corp.; 21 Jan 1938; LP8366]. Sd (Western Electric Mirrophonic Recording); b&w. 8 reels, 6,465 ft. 71 min. PCA cert no. 3797.

Series: Charlie Chan.

Assoc prod John Stone. *Dir* Eugene Forde. *Asst dir* Saul Wurtzel. *Scr* Charles Belden and Jerry Cady. *Orig story* Robert Ellis and Helen Logan. *Photog* Daniel B. Clark. *Art dir* Bernard Herzbrun. *Art dir assoc* Haldane Douglas. *Film ed* Nick DeMaggio. *Cost* Herschel. *Mus dir* Samuel Kaylin. *Sd* Bernard Freericks and Harry M. Leonard.

Source: Based on the character "Charlie Chan" created by Earl Derr Biggers.

Cast: WARNER OLAND (*Charlie Chan*), Keye Luke (*Lee Chan*), Virginia Field (*Evelyn Grey*), Sidney Blackmer (*Victor Karnoff*), Harold Huber (*Jules Joubert*), Kay Linaker (*Joan Karnoff*), Robert Kent (*Gordon Chase*), Edward Raquello (*Paul Savarin*), George Lynn (*Al Rogers*), Louis Mercier (*Taxi driver*), George Davis (*Pepite*), John Bleifer (*Ludwig*), Georges Renavent (*Renault*), [Constant Franke, André Cheron (*Croupiers*)], [Joseph Romantini, Albert Pollet (*Attachés*)], [Victor Delinsky, Alphonse Martell, Louis Lubitch, Robert Graves, George Sorel, Jean Perry (*Gendarmes*)], [Jean De Briac, Manuel Paris (*Doormen*)], [Eugene Borden (*Hotel clerk*)], [Gennaro Curci, Antonio Filauri, John Picorri (*Waiters*)], [Sherry Hall (*Bartender*)], [Marcelle Corday (*Concierge*)], [Leo White (*French butler*)], [Emile Bistagne], [Art Dupuis].

Detective, Drama. [*Print viewed*]. Charlie Chan and his son Lee attempt to leave Monte Carlo, where Chan is a shareholder in a casino, to go to Paris, where a painting by Lee will be exhibited, but on the road to the Nice airport, their taxi breaks down. Chan and Lee continue on foot until they see an expensive roadster leave another car and find a dead man in the other car. Upon investigating, they learn that the dead man was Renault, a bank messenger on his way to Paris with $1,000,000 in metallurgical bonds, now missing, which belonged to Victor Karnoff, who is staying at the Hotel Imperial. They also discover that three metallurical bonds were that day offered for sale at a Monte Carlo bank by Al Rogers, a bartender at the hotel. Chan recognizes the roadster in front of the hotel and learns that it belongs to Evelyn Grey, who is a resident there. Police inspector Joubert and Chan find her with Paul Savarin, a stock broker and Karnoff's bitter rival. Although she admits stopping by the car, Evelyn says that she fled in fright when she saw Chan and Lee approach. Joubert learns from a messenger that Karnoff's chauffeur Ludwig, who drove Renault and was in league with Savarin, was found dead. Later that day, Karnoff's wife Joan, who earlier begged Rogers to give her back the three bonds, admits to him that she stole them from his room, and he gives her until noon the next day to repay him. The next morning, Evelyn promises Gordon Chase, Karnoff's secretary, that she will not see Savarin again. After Chan learns that Evelyn has been living in luxury with no visible means of income and that Joan pawned jewelry that morning for $25,000, the price of the three bonds, he and Joubert go to interrogate Rogers, but find him dead in his room with an open valise full of Karnoff's bonds. Joubert believes that Rogers committed suicide and that the case is closed, but Chan suggests they go to Karnoff's suite, where they also find Joan, Savarin, Gordon and Evelyn. Joan confesses that Rogers, whom she married seven years earlier and whom she thought had obtained a divorce, was blackmailing her. She had given him the three bonds, but stole them back when she learned of her husband's deal, and had her brother, Gordon, replace them in Karnoff's safe. Chan surmises that Gordon must be the murderer because only he had a key to the valise, and that the valise was found open in Rogers' room, with no damage to its lock. Gordon confesses and berates Evelyn, for whom he says he stole from Karnoff months ago. When he was in danger of being exposed, he murdered Rogers to place the blame on him. Gordon then escapes through a window, but he is run over by a car. Joubert insists that Evelyn and Savarin leave Monte Carlo and gives his friends, Chan and Lee, another send-off in the same, backfiring taxi. *Bonds. Chinese Americans. Deception. Detectives. Monte Carlo (Monaco). Murder. Police inspectors.* Automobile accidents. Bartenders. Bigamy. Blackmail. Business competition. Escapes. Fathers and sons. French. Marriage. Safes. Stockbrokers. Taxicab drivers.

Note: This was Warner Oland's last film. Oland began *Charlie Chan at the Ringside* in Jan 1938, but production was halted due to a dispute between Oland and the studio, according to news items. That film was subsequently produced in the "Mr. Moto" series as *Mr. Moto's Gamble* (see below). Oland died 6 Aug 1938 in Stockholm as he was preparing to sail to the U.S. to work on a new "Charlie Chan" film, after having been in ill since the Spring. This film was his sixteenth role as "Charlie Chan." For information concerning other films in the series, please consult the Series Index and see the entry below for *Charlie Chan Carries On.*

Box 13 Nov 1937. *DV* 1 Nov 1937, p. 3. *FD* 5 Nov 1937, p. 8. *HR* 20 Sep 1937, p. 11. *HR* 18 Oct 1937, p. 11. *HR* 1 Nov 1937, p. 3. *MPH* 20 Oct 1937, p. 43. *MPH* 6 Nov 1937, p. 33. *NYT* 18 Dec 1937, p. 18. *Var* 22 Dec 1937, p. 17.

CHARLIE CHAN AT THE CIRCUS (Chinese Americans)

Twentieth Century-Fox Film Corp. *Dist* Twentieth Century-Fox Film Corp. 27 Mar **1936**; New York opening: week of 18 Mar 1936; Prod: began 6 Jan 1936; retakes early Feb 1936 [©Twentieth Century-Fox Film Corp.; 27 Mar 1936; LP6492]. Sd (Western Electric Noiseless Recording); b&w. 7 reels, 6,500 ft. 71-72 min. PCA cert no. 1978.

Series: Charlie Chan.

Assoc prod John Stone. *Dir* Harry Lachman. *Asst dir* William Eckhardt. *Orig scr* Robert Ellis and Helen Logan. *Photog* Daniel B. Clark. *Art dir* Duncan Cramer. *Film ed* Alex Troffey. *Cost* William Lambert. *Mus dir* Samuel Kaylin. *Sd* Arthur von Kirbach.

Source: Based on the character "Charlie Chan" created by Earl Derr Biggers.

Cast: WARNER OLAND (*Charlie Chan*), Keye Luke (*Lee Chan*), George Brasno (*Tim*), Olive Brasno (*Tiny*), Francis Ford (*John Gaines*), Maxine Reiner (*Marie Norman*), John McGuire (*Hal Blake*), Shirley Deane (*Louise Norman*), Paul Stanton (*Joe Kinney*), J. Carrol Naish (*Tom Holt*), Boothe Howard (*Dan Farrell*), Drue Leyton (*Nellie Farrell*), Wade Boteler (*Lieutenant Macy*), Shia Jung (*Su Toy*).

Detective. [*Print viewed*]. Charlie Chan takes his wife and twelve children to the circus owned by kindly John Gaines and his unscrupulous partner, Joe Kinney. Kinney tells Chan that he has been receiving death threats, after which Kinney and Gaines quarrel over money. Kinney then tries to discipline Caesar, the circus's ape, but the handler, Hal Blake, warns Kinney that he treats Caesar too roughly. Hal seeks solace from his girl friend, Louise Norman, whose sister, aerialist Marie, is Kinney's fiancée. As the show goes on, Chan leaves his family to meet Kinney and discuss his problems. When he arrives at Kinney's wagon, however, Chan, Gaines, and dancing midgets Tim and Tiny discover that Kinney has been murdered. Because the wagon was locked from the inside, and because of the hairs found on the window sill, the others suspect that Caesar climbed through the window and killed Kinney. Chan, however, withholds judgement and turns the case over to Lieutenant Macy, then leaves with his family to continue their vacation. Later that night, however, Tiny appears at their hotel and pleads with Chan to continue the investigation to clear Tim and Gaines, who are being held for questioning. Chan convinces Macy to release Tim and Gaines and to allow the circus to travel on, in hopes that the killer will reveal himself as time passes. Chan, his son Lee and Macy travel with the circus and, despite an attempt on Chan's life that night, reach their destination the next day. They discover that the business wagon's safe has been broken into, and in the safe they find Kinney's insurance policy, naming Marie as the beneficiary, and a marriage certificate stating that Kinney and wardrobe mistress Nellie Farrell were married in Juarez, Mexico on 30 May. The trio later confronts Nellie and her brother Dan, and Nellie asserts that, as Kinney's widow, she is entitled to his half of the circus. Marie retorts that Nellie's claim is false, as Kinney could not have been in Juarez on that date, but before she can offer proof, she has to perform her act. While Marie is in the air, someone shoots her rigging and she falls to the ground. She is seriously injured and the doctor Chan summons states that she must be operated on immediately. While the doctor is tending to Marie, Chan looks through her scrapbook and discovers that on 30 May, Kinney was being held as a witness to a murder in El Paso. While Lee telephones the El Paso police for more information, Caesar is released from his cage. Caesar attempts to kill Marie during the operation but is caught, after which Chan reveals that it is not the true Caeser who was apprehended, but snake handler Tom Holt, disguised as the ape. The police confirm that Holt was the killer in El Paso, and Chan deduces that Kinney covered up for Holt but was later murdered by Holt when they quarreled over money. Holt then attempted to murder Marie,

who is safely recovering at a hospital, because she could reveal the El Paso incident. Holt is arrested, along with Nellie and Dan, who forged the marriage certificate after Kinney's death. Gaines promises Chan lifetime passes to the circus as a reward for his help, and Lee romances Su Toy, a pretty Asian contortionist whom he had been pursuing throughout the investigation. *Chinese Americans. Circus owners. Circus performers. Detectives. Fraud. Murder. Animal trainers. Apes. Brothers. Children. Contortionists. Debt. Disguise. Doughnuts. Dwarfs. Falls from heights. Partnership. Physicians. Police. Sisters. Snakes. Trains. Vacations.*

Note: According to *HR* news items and production charts, June Lang and John Dilson were to be in the cast, but their participation in the final film has not been confirmed. According to a *HR* news item, the film was shot "on location at the Al G. Barnes winter quarters," and a *MPH* pre-release article states that "the Barnes Circus [was] used as a background for production settings." For additional information about the series, please consult the Series Index and see the entry below for *Charlie Chan Carries On*.
    Box 21 Mar 1936. *DV* 12 Mar 1936, p. 3. *FD* 17 Mar 1936, p. 9. *HR* 6 Jan 1936, p. 11. *HR* 7 Jan 1936, p. 4. *HR* 27 Jan 1936, p. 11. *HR* 8 Feb 1936, p. 2. *HR* 12 Mar 1936, p. 3. *MPD* 6 Mar 1936, p. 10. *MPH* 15 Feb 1936, p. 29. *MPH* 28 Mar 1936, p. 41. *NYT* 19 Mar 1936, p. 22. *Var* 25 Mar 1936, p. 15.

CHARLIE CHAN AT THE OLYMPICS (Chinese Americans)

Twentieth Century-Fox Film Corp. *Dist* Twentieth Century-Fox Film Corp. 21 May **1937**; Prod: late Jan—mid-Feb 1937 [©Twentieth Century-Fox Film Corp.; 21 May 1937; LP7170]. Sd (Western Electric Mirrophonic Recording); b&w. 7 reels, 6,400 ft. 71 min. PCA cert no. 3090.

Series: Charlie Chan.

Assoc prod John Stone. *Dir* H. Bruce Humberstone. *Asst dir* Jasper Blystone. *Scr* Robert Ellis and Helen Logan. *Orig story* Paul Burger. *Photog* Daniel B. Clark. *Art dir* Albert Hogsett. *Art dir assoc* Chester Gore. *Film ed* Fred Allen. *Cost* Herschel. *Mus dir* Samuel Kaylin. *Sd* E. Clayton Ward and Harry M. Leonard.

Source: Based on the character "Charlie Chan" created by Earl Derr Biggers.

Cast: WARNER OLAND (*Charlie Chan*), Katherine De Mille (*Yvonne Roland*), Pauline Moore (*Betty Adams*), Allan Lane (*Richard Masters*), Keye Luke (*Lee Chan*), C. Henry Gordon (*Arthur Hughes*), John Eldredge (*Cartwright*), Layne Tom, Jr. (*Charlie Chan, Jr.*), Jonathan Hale (*Hopkins*), Morgan Wallace (*Honorable Charles Zaraka*), Fredrik Vogeding (*Captain Strasser*), Andrew Tombes (*Police Chief Scott*), Howard Hickman (*Dr. Burton*), [Selmer Jackson (*Wright*)], [Edward Keane (*Webster*)], [Arno Frey (*Carlos*)], [Caroline "Spike" Rankin (*Landlady*)], [O. G. "Dutch" Hendrian (*Miller*)], [Billy Wayne (*Steward*)], [Emmett Vogan (*Ship's officer*)], [George Chandler, Al Kikume (*Radio operators*)], [William von Brincken (*Guard*)], [Brooks Benedict (*Henchman*)], [Ferdinand Schumann-Heink (*Officer on Hindenburg*)], [Hans Fuerberg, John Peters (*Radio cops*)], [Minerva Urecal (*Maid*)], [Constant Franke (*Attendant*)], [Paul W. Panzer (*Vendor*)], [Virgil B. Nover, Perry E. Seeley (*Sign language experts*)], [Tom Klune (*Page boy*)], [Ben Hendricks (*Coast Guard officer*)], [Don Brody (*News commentator*)], [Philip Morris, Lee Shumway, Stanley Blystone (*Cops*)], [Glen Cavender, Walter Bonn (*German policemen*)], [David Horsley (*Edwards*)], [Frank Bruno (*Footman*)], [Theresa Harris (*Olympic athlete*)], [Tony Merlo], [Louis Natheaux], [Bill Beggs].

Detective, Drama. [*Print viewed*]. After a pilot testing a device by which his plane is guided by remote control is hijacked, Charlie Chan of the Honolulu police comes on the case. Chan finds the plane with the device, which could be sold for millions to a foreign power, gone and the pilot dead. Later, he also locates the body of the murderer, Miller. Chan, Hopkins, the airplane owner, and Cartwright, the inventor of the device, take the dirigible *Hindenburg* to Berlin to investigate three people traveling there by ocean liner: Dick Masters, an Olympic pole-vaulter and aviator, who did not pilot the plane the day of its disappearance because of an injured shoulder; Yvonne Roland, who visited Miller's room; and Arthur Hughes, an arms dealer, who wanted to buy the device. In Berlin, Chan finds the device hidden in a box in the luggage of Masters' girl friend Betty Adams. He substitutes a book and returns the box to Hopkins. Cartwright tells Chan that Hughes accused Hopkins of double-crossing him and threatened to expose Hopkins' plan to sell the device to a foreign government, and that Hopkins escaped with the box. Masters is now suspected because the box was found in Betty's room and the fact that he was on the boat with Roland. Roland,

however, takes the box to a foreign diplomat, the Honorable Charles Zaraka, who discovers the book instead of the device. After Hughes learns of this, Chan's son Lee, an Olympic swimmer, is kidnapped. Following instructions sent from the kidnapper, Chan brings the device, which he has had removed and replaced with a transmitter, to an agreed upon location. He is then taken to Zaraka's estate, where Hopkins identifies the device. Hughes arrives with his thugs and fights Zaraka's henchmen for the device before he discovers that it is a phony. After the police arrive and Hopkins is shot, Chan reveals that Cartwright shot him, and that earlier Cartwright murdered Miller and made it appear that Hopkins stole the device. Hopkins recovers and Lee wins the hundred meter race. *Chinese Americans. Deception. Detectives. False accusations. Fathers and sons. Inventions. Olympic games. Airplanes. Berlin (Germany). Diplomats. Fights. Hawaii. Hijackers. Hindenburg (Airship). Inventors. Munitions dealers. Murder. Ocean liners. Police. Swimmers.*

Note: This film contained newsreel footage of the dirigible *Hindenburg*, which exploded before the release of the film, and events in the Olympic Games of 1936, including a relay race showing American runner Jesse Owens. This film introduced Layne Tom, Jr. as Charlie Chan's youngest son. John Carradine is listed as a cast member in *HR* production charts, but his participation in the final film has not been confirmed. For information concerning the series, please consult the Series Index and see the entry below for *Charlie Chan Carries On*.
    Box 10 Apr 1937. *DV* 24 Mar 1937, p. 3. *FD* 29 Mar 1937, p. 5. *HR* 25 Jan 1937, p. 11. *HR* 15 Feb 1937, p. 11. *HR* 24 Mar 1937, p. 4. *MPD* 25 Mar 1937, p. 4. *MPH* 6 Mar 1937, p. 49. *NYT* 24 Mar 1937, p. 23. *Var* 26 May 1937, p. 14.

CHARLIE CHAN AT THE OPERA (Chinese Americans)

Twentieth Century-Fox Film Corp. *Dist* Twentieth Century-Fox Film Corp. 8 Jan **1937** Sd (Western Electric Noiseless Recording); b&w. 7 reels, 6,175 ft. 66 or 68 min. PCA cert no. 2796.

Series: Charlie Chan.

Assoc prod John Stone. *Dir* H. Bruce Humberstone. *Asst dir* Sol Michaels. *Scr* Scott Darling and Charles S. Belden. *Story* Bess Meredyth. *Photog* Lucien Andriot. *Art dir* Duncan Cramer and Lewis Creber. *Film ed* Alex Troffey. *Cost* Herschel. *Mus dir* Samuel Kaylin. *Orch* Charles Maxwell. *Sd* George Leverett and Harry M. Leonard.

Song(s): "March Funebre," "Ah, Romantic Love Dream," "King and Country Call," "Carnival Marche" and "Then Farewell" from the opera *Carnival*, music by Oscar Levant, libretto by William Kernell.

Source: Based on the character "Charlie Chan" created by Earl Derr Biggers.

Cast: WARNER OLAND (*Charlie Chan*), BORIS KARLOFF (*Gravelle*), Keye Luke (*Lee Chan*), Charlotte Henry (*Mlle. Kitty*), Thomas Beck (*Phil Childers*), Margaret Irving (*Mme. Lilli Rochelle*), Gregory Gaye (*Enrico Barelli*), Nedda Harrington (*Mme. Anita Barelli*), Frank Conroy (*Mr. Whitely*), Guy Usher (*Inspector Regan*), William Demarest (*Sergeant Kelly*), Maurice Cass (*Mr. Arnold*), Tom McGuire (*Morris*).

Detective, with songs. [*Print viewed*]. At the Rockland State Sanitorium, Gravelle, an opera singing amnesiac, regains his memory when he sees a newspaper article about prima donna Lilli Rochelle, then kills a guard to escape. Inspector Regan calls Charlie Chan in on the case, and as they are in his office discussing it, Lilli comes in, accompanied by her lover and fellow singer, Enrico Barelli, to complain about a threat stating she will die that night. Chan agrees to go to the opera that night, along with Sergeant Kelly, to investigate. Later at the theater, Phil Childers and his girl friend Kitty try to see Lilli but are turned away by Kelly just as Regan and Chan arrive and hear Lilli's husband Whitely and Enrico fighting over Lilli. Meanwhile, in the dressing room of Enrico's wife Anita, Gravelle appears, and although Anita is terrified because he was presumed dead in a theater fire five years ago, she agrees to keep his presence a secret while he carries out his plan of singing Enrico's role on stage. Gravelle then menaces Enrico, who, along with Lilli, locked Gravelle in the burning theater, and soon it is Gravelle rather than Enrico who joins Lilli on stage for their duet. Lilli recognizes Gravelle's voice and faints after she leaves the stage. After Whitely carries Lilli off, the others rush to Enrico's room, only to find that he has been stabbed. While the others search for Gravelle, Phil enters Lilli's room and discovers that she is also dead. Whitely comes in and has Phil arrested, but when Chan questions Phil and Kitty, they tell him that Kitty is Lilli's daughter from her previous marriage to Gravelle and that Lilli refused to acknowledge Kitty in order to keep her past a secret. The young lovers were there to ask Lilli for her permission to marry, as

Kitty is underage. Gravelle, who did not recognize Kitty, is stunned as he overhears. Later, Phil goes to see Regan, leaving Kitty alone, and Gravelle comes in. He gently questions her and plays the piano for her, but she does not remember him and faints from fright. Chan enters, and after Gravelle tells him about Lilli and Enrico's attempt to kill him, Chan flatters him into singing again. Chan arranges to have Anita sing Lilli's role, and during the duet, which involves Gravelle's character stabbing Anita's character, Anita becomes so scared that a police officer shoots Gravelle. Chan then demonstrates that Gravelle's knife is a prop and could not have been used in the murders. He explains that Anita was the only one who had access to Enrico and Lilli when they were alone and unconscious, and that she was also the only one who knew Gravelle was there and could therefore frame him. Anita confesses that jealousy drove her to kill her husband and his lover, and after she is taken away, Chan convinces Kitty to comfort injured Gravelle, thereby saving his life. *Chinese Americans. Detectives. Infidelity. Jealousy. Murder. Opera singers. Amnesia. Disguise. Fathers and daughters. Fathers and sons. Insanity. Long-lost relatives. Mothers and daughters. Police inspectors. Racism. Sanitariums. Stabbings. Threats.*

Note: The film's title card reads: "Twentieth Century-Fox presents Warner Oland vs. Boris Karloff in *Charlie Chan at the Opera.*" Although contemporary reviews call Margaret Irving's character "Lucretia Barrelli," she is called "Anita Barelli" in the film. A *MPD* news item noted that the picture was banned in Germany for having "too many murders." A *HR* news item stated that public response to the film's preview was so positive that Twentieth Century-Fox planned to up the production and advertising budgets for the Charlie Chan series, and that future films would see "Warner Oland co-starred with a top name opposite." The first actor the studio was said to be approaching to star with Oland was Peter Lorre. According to another *HR* news item, this film marked the first time that a DeBrie camera, which was lighter and more quiet than other models, was used in the United States. According to modern sources, H. Bruce Humberstone borrowed some of the sets from *Café Metropole* (see *AFI Catalog of Feature Films, 1931-40*; F3.0551) for this film. Oscar Levant, in his autobiographical writings, states that he was assigned to write an operatic sequence that could take advantage of a Mephistophelian costume that had been created for Lawrence Tibbett in a previous Twentieth Century-Fox film (presumably *Under Your Spell*, see *AFI Catalog of Feature Films, 1931-40*; F3.4856). Levant also relates that the words for the opera were written originally in English by William Kernell and then translated into Italian by "studio linguists." For additional information on the series, please consult the Series Index and see the entry below for *Charlie Chan Carries On.*

Box 5 Dec 1936. *DV* 12 Nov 1936, p. 3. *FD* 16 Nov 1936, p. 7. *HR* 11 Aug 1936, p. 4. *HR* 8 Sep 1936, p. 3. *HR* 14 Sep 1936, p. 23. *HR* 12 Oct 1936, p. 7. *HR* 12 Nov 1936, p. 3. *HR* 13 Nov 1936, p. 3. *MPD* 13 Nov 1936, p. 10. *MPD* 27 May 1937, p. 2. *MPH* 17 Oct 1936, p. 37. *MPH* 28 Nov 1936, p. 68. *NYT* 5 Dec 1936, p. 16. *Var* 16 Dec 1936, p. 21.

CHARLIE CHAN AT THE RACE TRACK (Chinese Americans)

Twentieth Century-Fox Film Corp. *Dist* Twentieth Century-Fox Film Corp. 7 Aug **1936**; Prod: 18 May—mid-Jun 1936 [©Twentieth Century-Fox Film Corp.; 7 Aug 1936; LP6667]. Sd (Western Electric Noiseless Recording); b&w. 7 reels, 6,300 ft. 70 min. PCA cert no. 2353.

Series: Charlie Chan.

Assoc prod John Stone. *Dir* H. Bruce Humberstone. *Asst dir* Aaron Rosenberg. *Scr* Robert Ellis, Helen Logan and Edward T. Lowe. *Story* Lou Breslow and Saul Elkins. [*Contr wrt* Joseph Hoffman]. *Photog* Harry Jackson. *Art dir* Duncan Cramer. *Film ed* Nick De Maggio. *Cost* Herschel. *Mus dir* Samuel Kaylin. *Sd* Alfred Bruzlin and Harry M. Leonard. [*Tech dir* Monroe Liebgold].

Source: Based on the character "Charlie Chan" created by Earl Derr Biggers.

Cast: WARNER OLAND (*Charlie Chan*), Keye Luke (*Lee Chan*), Helen Wood (*Alice Fenton*), Thomas Beck (*Bruce Rogers*), Alan Dinehart (*George Chester*), Gavin Muir (*Bagley*), Gloria Roy (*Catherine Chester*), Jonathan Hale (*Warren Fenton*), G. P. Huntley, Jr. (*Denny Barton*), George Irving (*Major [Gordon] Kent*), Frank Coghlan, Jr. (*Eddie Brill*), Frankie Darro ("*Tip*" *Collins*), John Rogers (*Mooney*), John H. Allen ("*Streamline*" *Jones*), Harry Jans (*Al Meers*), [Robert Warwick (*Chan's chief*)], [Sam Flint (*Ship's captain*)], [Selmer Jackson (*Lansing*)], [Ivan "Dusty" Miller (*Wade*)], [Ed Hart, George Magrill, David Worth, James Flavin (*Detectives*)], [Al Kikume (*Hawaiian detective*)], [Boothe Howard (*Ship's doctor*)], [Sidney Bracy (*Waiter*)], [Jack Mulhall (*Second purser*)], [William Wayne, Les Sketchley, Billie Oakley (*Seamen*)], [Eddie Fetherston, Charles Williams (*Reporters*)], [Max Wagner (*Joe*)], [Harlan Tucker, Sammy Finn, Wilbur Mack, Paul Fix, Norman Willis, Jerry Jerome (*Gangsters*)], [Holmes Herbert, Colin Kenny, Robert E. Homans (*Judges*)], [Lew Hicks, Bob Ellsworth (*Policemen*)], [Lucille Miller

(*Secretary*)], [James Eagles (*Chick Patten*)], [Bobby Tanzel (*Gilroy*)], [Bruce Mitchell (*Gateman*)], [Clyde McAtee, Jack Green (*Pinkerton men*)], [Pat O'Malley (*Track official*)], [David Thursby (*Steward*)], [Ray Hanson (*Third officer*)], [Sam Hayes (*Announcer*)].

Horse race, Detective, Drama. [*Print viewed*]. After jockey "Tip" Collins, riding Avalanche, the horse in the lead in the Melbourne Sweepstakes, fouls another rider, Avalanche is disqualified. Major Gordon Kent, who gave Avalanche as a wedding present to the internationally known American sportsman George Chester when Chester married his daughter Catherine, believes that a big gambling ring is behind the foul. The major has a wire sent to his old friend, the renowned detective Charlie Chan, instructing him to meet their boat in Honolulu on their way to compete in America. However, on the voyage, the major dies seemingly from being kicked by Avalanche in his stall. Chan determines from the position and the shape of the bloodstains that the horse could not have kicked the major. After Chan reveals to his chief and the ship's captain a piece of the ship's winch, the twin of which is missing, which could make a shape identical to that of a horseshoe, the chief suggests that Chan travel with the boat to investigate what they now suspect is a murder. When Chester receives a typed note warning him not to enter Avalanche in the Santa Juanita Handicap, Chan's son Lee, who, against his father's wishes, got on the boat as a cabin boy, determines that the note came from the typewriter of the major's competitor, Warren Fenton. A number of other passengers next receive notes: Fenton, who offered Chester $20,000 for the horse; Bruce Rogers, the major's assistant, who is in love with Fenton's daughter Alice; Denny Barton, who also loves Alice, but whom she has rebuked; and Chester again. After a fire breaks out in the forward hold where Avalanche is kept, Chan is hit in the leg by a bullet fired accidentally by Chester. In Los Angeles harbor, Chan notices that a monkey, who earlier caused Avalanche to bolt, now causes Fenton's horse Gladstone to go wild, while Avalanche does not mind the monkey. Chan suspects that the fire was used as a cover so that the horses could be switched and Fenton's horse could then win the upcoming race with good odds. The switch, involving the application of black dye to Gladstone, was engineered by Avalanche's trainer Bagley working with a gang of gamblers. On the day of the race, Lee creates a diversion so that Chan can enter the stables and switch the horses. Bagley, after noticing the switch, is arrested as he calls a gambler. As the race begins, Al Meers, a track employee in league with the gamblers, switches a device at the three-quarter pole, which is used to time the race, with one fitted with a dart. As Avalanche, in the lead, passes the pole, the dart hits the horse. Avalanche wins anyway, but then falls. As a crowd surrounds Avalanche, someone removes the dart. Chan then gathers Denny, Bagley, Meers, Chester and Fenton in the racing association office. When the dart is found in Fenton's pocket, Fenton accuses Denny of putting it there, but Chester accuses Fenton of wanting to buy Avalanche all along and of murdering Major Kent with the winch shoe because the major would have noticed that the horses had been switched. Chan then points out that no one other than himself, his chief, the captain of the ship and the murderer knew about the winch shoe. He says that he suspected Chester all along because Chester, who admits to gambling losses, did not use his glasses to read the first threatening note he received, which Chester himself sent to throw off suspicion, but that he did use his glasses to read the second note, which Chan, with Lee's help, sent. Chan then reveals blood stains from the dart in the lining of Chester's pocket. Fenton confesses that he knew of the plot to switch horses and tells the commissioner that he will remove his horses from the track. Bruce wins enough money from the race to furnish a flat for himself and Alice. When the ever-enthusiastic Lee pops in with what he thinks is a hot clue, Chan requests that he save it for their next case. *Chinese. Deception. Detectives. Fixed horse races. Gamblers. Horses. Murder. African Americans. Darts (Game). Fires. Gunshot wounds. Honolulu (HI). Horse owners. Jockeys. Los Angeles (CA). Melbourne (Australia). Ocean liners. Stableboys. Threats.*

Note: The Roxy Theatre in New York billed this film as *At the Race Track with Charlie Chan*. *Var* reviewed the film as *Chan at Race Track*. According to *MPH* and *Liberty*, some scenes in the film were shot at the Santa Anita Racetrack in Arcadia, CA, and the film contained footage of "some of the most spectacular events of the recent racing season." *MPH* also notes that the film "has a semi-topical significance in as much as a great Antipodean horse, Pharlap, brought to this country a few years ago [from Australia], died under circumstances that have never been fully explained." *Liberty* notes that

technical director Monroe Liebgold had been a jockey for the well-known horse breeder H. P. Whitney. *HR* production charts lists Neil Fitzgerald and John Mooney as additional actors; their participation in the final film has not been confirmed. For additional information on the series, please consult the Series Index and see the entry below for *Charlie Chan Carries On.*

Box 18 Jul 1936. *DV* 8 Jul 1936, p. 2. *FD* 14 Jul 1936, p. 11. *HR* 18 May 1936, p. 9. *HR* 8 Jun 1936, p. 9. *HR* 8 Jul 1936, p. 4. *Liberty* 26 Aug 1936. *MPD* 9 Jul 1936, p. 4. *MPH* 27 Jun 1936, p. 52. *MPH* 18 Jul 1936, p. 54. *NYT* 15 Aug 1936, p. 6. *Var* 19 Aug 1936, p. 16.

CHARLIE CHAN AT THE RINGSIDE *see* MR. MOTO'S GAMBLE

CHARLIE CHAN AT THE WAX MUSEUM (Chinese Americans)

Twentieth Century-Fox Film Corp. *Dist* Twentieth Century-Fox Film Corp. 6 Sep **1940**; Prod: began mid-May 1940 [©Twentieth Century-Fox Film Corp.; 6 Sep 1940; LP9228]. Sd (RCA "High Fidelity" Recording); b&w. 5,718 ft. 63 min. PCA cert no. 6383.

Series: Charlie Chan.

Assoc prod Walter Morosco and Ralph Dietrich. *Dir* Lynn Shores. [*Asst dir* Jasper Blystone]. *Orig scr* John Larkin. *Dir of photog* Virgil Miller. *Art dir* Richard Day and Lewis Creber. *Film ed* James B. Clark. *Set dec* Thomas Little. *Cost* Herschel. *Mus dir* Emil Newman. *Sd* Bernard Freericks and Harry M. Leonard.

Source: Based on the character "Charlie Chan" created by Earl Derr Biggers.

Cast: Sidney Toler (*Charlie Chan*), Sen Yung (*Jimmy Chan*), C. Henry Gordon (*Dr. Cream*), Marc Lawrence (*Steve McBirney*), Joan Valerie (*Lily Latimer*), Marguerite Chapman (*Mary Bolton*), Ted Osborn (*Tom Agnew [also known as Dagan]*), Michael Visaroff (*Dr. Otto von Brom*), Hilda Vaughn (*Mrs. Rocke*), Charles Wagenheim (*Willie Fern*), Archie Twitchell (*Carter Lane*), Edward Marr (*Grenock*), Joe King (*Inspector O'Mathews*), Harold Goodwin (*Edwards*).

Detective. [*Print viewed*]. Dr. Cream, a plastic surgeon, operates a wax museum featuring figures of infamous criminals as a front for his real business of altering the faces of fugitive criminals. One of these men, Steve McBirney, was convicted by the illustrious detective Charlie Chan and is bent on revenge. After undergoing surgery, McBirney coerces the doctor to lure Chan to the museum on the pretense of participating in a crime solving radio broadcast. Although suspicious of Cream's motives, Chan accepts the invitation, unaware that he is to be electrocuted as he sits in one of Cream's chairs. However, at the last moment, Chan changes seats with Dr. Otto von Brom, another crime expert, and von Brom is murdered. The weapon is not electricity, however, but a poison dart that is blown at him by someone lurking within the museum. The occupants of the museum are unable to call the police because the phone is out of order, and they know that the person who leaves to make the call may be the murderer. As they are sequestered in the museum, terror electrifies the air as the ominous wax dummies appear to come alive. Later, Chan discovers a trap door leading to a secret chamber, where he traces von Brom's murder to Dagan, McBirney's supposedly dead partner who has had his face altered by Cream. After Dagan kills McBirney and attempts to murder Chan, Inspector O'Mathews of the police arrives with his men. Chan then unmasks Dagan as radio broadcaster, Tom Agnew, who killed in order to keep his criminal identity a secret. *Chinese Americans. Criminologists. Detectives. Murder. Plastic surgery. Revenge. Waxworks.* Criminals. Electrocution. Impersonation and imposture. Poison. Police. Radio broadcasting. Surgeons.

Note: For additional information on the series, consult the Series Index and see entry below for *Charlie Chan Carries On.*

FD 1 Aug 1940, p. 6. *HR* 18 May 1940, pp. 6-7. *HR* 26 Jul 1940, p. 4. *MPD* 30 Jul 1940, p. 5. *MPH* 3 Aug 1940, p. 39. *NYT* 28 Sep 1940, p. 9. *Var* 2 Oct 1940, p. 12.

CHARLIE CHAN AT THE WORLD'S FAIR *see* CHARLIE CHAN AT TREASURE ISLAND

CHARLIE CHAN AT TREASURE ISLAND (Chinese Americans)

Twentieth Century-Fox Film Corp. *Dist* Twentieth Century-Fox Film Corp. 8 Sep **1939**; Prod: 17 Apr—13 May 1939 [©Twentieth Century-Fox Film Corp.; 8 Sep 1939; LP9300]. Sd (RCA High Fidelity Recording); b&w. 8 reels, 6,633 ft. 72 or 74 min. PCA cert no. 5321.

Series: Charlie Chan.

[*Exec prod* Sol M. Wurtzel]. *Assoc prod* Edward Kaufman. *Dir* Norman Foster. [*Asst dir* Charles Hall]. *Orig story and scr* John Larkin. *Photog* Virgil Miller. *Art dir* Richard Day and Lewis Creber. *Film ed* Norman Colbert. *Set dec* Thomas Little. *Cost* Herschel. *Mus dir* Samuel Kaylin. *Sd* E. Clayton Ward and William H. Anderson.

Source: Based on the character "Charlie Chan" created by Earl Derr Biggers.

Cast: Sidney Toler (*Charlie Chan*), Cesar Romero (*Rhadini*), Pauline Moore (*Eve [Cairo]*), Sen Yung (*Jimmy Chan*), Douglas Fowley (*Pete Lewis*), June Gale (*Myra Rhadini*), Douglas Dumbrille ([*Stewart Salzbury, alias*] *Thomas Gregory*), Sally Blane (*Stella Essex*), Billie Seward (*Bessie Sibley*), Wally Vernon (*Elmer Kelner*), Donald MacBride (*Chief J. J. Kilvaine*), Charles Halton (*Redley*), Trevor Bardette (*Abdul*), Louis Jean Heydt (*Paul Essex*).

Detective, Drama. [*Print viewed*]. Detective Charlie Chan is accompanying his son Jimmy on the China Clipper from Hawaii to San Francisco, where Jimmy attends college. Also on the plane is Chan's friend, writer Paul Essex, who has just finished a mystery novel about a fake mystic. Paul is pestered by Thomas Gregory, an insurance actuary, who slyly reads a disturbing radiogram that Paul receives. When the plane lands, the passengers discover that Paul has committed suicide. Chan reads the radiogram, which warns of disaster if Zodiac obligations are ignored, then tells Paul's wife Stella about the tragedy. Gregory steals Paul's briefcase, which contains the manuscript, and while Jimmy follows Gregory, Chan goes to police headquarters. There he is greeted by Chief J. J. Kilvaine and introduced to reporter Pete Lewis and magician Rhadini. Rhadini, who operates a magic theater on Treasure Island, and Pete explain that they are on a crusade to expose fake mediums. Their primary target is Dr. Zodiac, whom they suspect is behind the suicides of three of his clients. Chan believes that Paul is the fourth such suicide and states that a suicide induced by blackmail is really murder. Chan, Pete and Rhadini go to Zodiac's mansion and ask to consult with the heavily-masked spiritualist. While Pete and Rhadini proclaim that Zodiac is a fake, Chan cautions that they must be careful because of Zodiac's obvious mental delusions. Later, Chan attends a party Rhadini hosts in honor of San Francisco's Golden Gate International Exposition, where he is fascinated by the mindreading abilities of Eve Cairo, who is Rhadini's assistant and Pete's girl friend. After the party, Chan, Jimmy, Rhadini and Pete return to Zodiac's mansion and find the information with which he has been blackmailing his clients. Chan burns the files, and the next day decides to use Zodiac's vanity to trap him. Rhadini issues a public challenge to Zodiac to subject himself to examination at his theater. Zodiac comes to the theater, but while Rhadini is levitating Eve, the man in the Zodiac mask is murdered and revealed to be Abdul, the medium's servant. Kilvaine then states that Gregory is actually Stewart Salzbury, an insurance detective investigating the suicides, and they offer to help recreate the levitating trick to determine who killed Abdul. When Rhadini performs the act again, he is stabbed in the shoulder. Chan then employs Eve's mindreading ability to help identify the culprit, and while he is questioning her, a hand with a gun appears. The gunman is revealed to be Rhadini, who, as the real Zodiac, had Abdul pose as Zodiac to fool the police into believing that he was dead. Chan demonstrates how Rhadini used his magic wand as a blowgun to kill Abdul and then wounded himself to deflect suspicion. After Rhadini is arrested, Chan smiles as Jimmy falls through a secret trapdoor and releases a pigeon. *Blackmail. Charlatans. Chinese Americans. Detectives. Magicians. Mediums. Murder. Suicide.* Airports. China clipper (Airplane). Clairvoyants. Disguise. Exhibitions. Fathers and sons. Insurance. Jealousy. Levitation. Mansions. Manuscripts. Novelists. Parties. Poison. Police. Reporters. San Francisco (CA). Servants. Treasure Island (CA). Turks. Wives.

Note: According to *HR* news items and production charts, John Carradine and Joyce Compton were to be included in the cast of this film, but their participation in the completed picture is doubtful. A 19 Apr 1939 *HR* news item refers to the film as *Charlie Chan at the World's Fair*. The Golden Gate International Exposition, held on Treasure Island in San Francisco Bay Feb 1939—Oct 1940, provided the backdrop for some of the picture's action. For more information on the series, please consult the Series Index and see the entry below for *Charlie Chan Carries On.*

Box 12 Aug 1939. *DV* 17 Aug 1939, p. 3. *FD* 11 Sep 1939, p. 5. *HR* 14 Apr 1939, p. 2. *HR* 15 Apr 1939, p. 6. *HR* 19 Apr 1939, p. 6. *HR* 20 Apr 1939, p. 6. *HR* 13 May 1939, p. 3. *HR* 17 Aug 1939, p. 3. *MPD* 17 Aug 1939, p. 7. *MPH* 5 Aug 1939, p. 86. *MPH* 26 Aug 1939, p. 55. *NYT* 1 Sep 1939, p. 15. *Var* 23 Aug 1939, p. 20.

CHARLIE CHAN CARRIES ON (Chinese Americans)

Fox Film Corp. *Dist* Fox Film Corp. 12 Apr **1931**; New York opening: week of 20 Mar 1931; Prod: 3 Jan—late Jan 1931 [©Fox Film Corp.; 11 Feb 1931; LP2031]. Sd; b&w. 8 reels, 6,200 ft. 69 min. Passed by the National Board of Review.

Series: Charlie Chan.

Dir Hamilton MacFadden. *Asst dir* Sam Wurtzel. *Scr and dial* Philip Klein and Barry Conners. *Photog* George Schneiderman. *Settings* Joseph Wright. *Film ed* Al De Gaetano. *Cost* Sophie Wachner. *Sd eng* George P. Costello.

Source: Based on the novel *Charlie Chan Carries On* by Earl Derr Biggers (Indianapolis, 1930).

Cast: Marguerite Churchill (*Pamela Potter*), John Carrick (*Mark Kennaway*), Warner Oland (*Charlie Chan*), Warren Hymer (*Max Minchin*), Marjorie White (*Sadie Minchin*), C. Henry Gordon (*John Ross, an alias for Jim Everhard*), William Holden (*Patrick Tait*), George Brent (*Capt. Ronald Keane*), Peter Gawthorne (*Inspector Duff*), John T. Murray (*Dr. Lofton*), John Swor (*Elmer Benbow*), Goodee Montgomery (*Mrs. Benbow*), Jason Robards (*Walter Honeywood*), Lumsden Hare (*Inspector Hanley*), Zeffie Tilbury (*Mrs. Luce*), Betty Francisco (*Sybil Conway*), Harry Beresford (*Kent*), John Rogers (*Martin*), J. Gunnis Davis (*Eben*), James Farley.

Detective, Drama. [*Not viewed*]. Inspector Duff of Scotland Yard gets a call about the murder of wealthy Hugo Morris Drake, who was strangled with a suitcase strap while on an around-the-world tour with a party of other Americans. Dr. Lofton, the tour conductor, discovers that the strap came from his bag. Duff interrogates Walter Honeywood, a theatrical manager occupying the room next to Drake's, who hopes to meet his estranged wife, actress Sybil Conway, at San Remo and persuade her to join him on the trip. Duff then realizes that he cannot hold the twelve remaining tourists because he has no evidence or motive, and after they leave for Paris, Duff learns that Honeywood paid a hotel servant not to reveal that he and Drake exchanged rooms the night Drake was killed. That night, as the party stops over in Nice, a gloved hand fires a shot from some bushes and puts the gun in the hand of the deceased, Honeywood. When Duff arrives the next day, he learns that Honeywood is dead, apparently a suicide. Duff calls Sybil, who meets him at San Remo and says that the murderer is Jim Everhard, a jewel thief to whom she had been unhappily married. Years earlier, when Honeywood and Sybil ran away together, taking two bags of diamonds, Everhard vowed to kill them both. Sybil agrees to point out the killer, but the figure with the gloved hand shoots and kills her. During the next part of the trip, Mark Kennaway, the traveling companion to Patrick Tait, an elderly criminal lawyer, becomes fond of Drake's granddaughter, Pamela Potter, who is continuing the trip to help track down the killer. In Hong Kong, Pam and Mark pass a street merchant who calls out Everhard's name as he passes. When Pam tells the tourist party that Everhard has been spotted, Mark realizes that she has placed herself in danger. As she sends a telegram to Duff, the gloved hand fires a gun at her, but Mark pulls her aside in time. Duff travels to Honolulu, the party's next destination, and after visiting his friend, Inspector Charlie Chan of the Honolulu police, he is shot in the back. Chan prepares to join the party on their voyage to San Francisco, and asks his chief to tell Duff "Charlie Chan carries on." In his cabin on the ship, Chan hears movement by his window and, grabbing a gloved hand holding a gun, pulls the glove off. After clues implicate various male members of the party, the ship approaches San Francisco, and Chan writes identical letters to the suspects. At a party, Chan explains to the guests that Drake was murdered by mistake, for Everhard intended to kill Honeywood. Chan says that in order to save Everhard embarrassment, he has informed him in a note that he will not arrest him until they dock at San Francisco. The tourists then find the letters Chan left for them, while Chan fixes a dummy in front of the window of his own room. As he and Mark wait in the lifeboat, he turns on a switch rigged to light his room. The murderer enters the room and, after shooting at the dummy, is apprehended by Chan and Mark. As the others enter, the murderer is revealed to be John Ross, a limping lumberman who expresses regret over killing Drake, but not Honeywood or Sybil. He then asks Chan how he knew it was him, and Chan reveals that he did not know, but that he wrote the letters to draw the murderer out. Chan then dictates a cable to Duff and, seeing Mark and Pam together, says that they have decided "two shall be one—more later." *Chinese Americans. Detectives. Murder. Ruses. Scotland Yard (London, England). Tourists. China. Egypt. Gunshot wounds. Hong Kong. Honolulu (HI). Hotels. Lawyers. Letters. London (England). Nice (France). Ocean liners. Parties. Photographers. Racketeers. Revenge. Romance. San Remo (Italy). Statues. Thieves. Traveling companions.*

Note: The above plot was based on a screen continuity in the Twentieth Century-Fox Produced Scripts Collection at the UCLA Theater Arts Library. Earl Derr Biggers' novel was serialized in *The Saturday Evening Post* (9 Aug—13 Sep 1930). Some sources erroneously include Luana Alcañiz in the cast of the Spanish version, *Eran trece*. In his autobiography, L. B. Abbott notes that he assisted photographer Sidney Wagner on *Eran trece*. *Eran trece* was the only Spanish version in the Charlie Chan series. In 1940, Twentieth Century-Fox again filmed Biggers' novel as *Charlie Chan's Murder Cruise* (see below).

"Charlie Chan" first appeared on the screen in a 1926 Pathé serial entitled *The House Without a Key*, which starred George Kuwa. Universal produced the next Chan film in 1928, entitled *The Chinese Parrot*, starring Kamiyama Sojin (see below), and in 1929, Fox produced *Behind That Curtain*, directed by Irving Cummings and starring E. L. Park (see *AFI Catalog of Feature Films, 1921-30*; F2.0330). Five of Biggers' six Chan novels were adapted for the screen, while the rest of the Chan films were made from original screenplays. This was the first Chan film to star Warner Oland, who portrayed the detective in sixteen films. After Oland's death in 1938, Sidney Toler took over the lead role in *Charlie Chan in Honolulu*, released in Jan 1939. The last Twentieth Century-Fox entry in the series, *Castle in the Desert*, was released in 1942. Toler, who had bought the screen rights to the Chan character from Biggers' widow, then went to Monogram, which, in 1944, released its first Chan film, *Charlie Chan in the Secret Service*. Toler continued in the role until his death in 1947, after which Roland Winters played Chan in seven films, beginning with *The Chinese Ring* in 1947. Monogram ended the series in 1949 with *The Sky Dragon*.

Keye Luke was featured in several of the Fox and Monogram offerings in the series as "Lee," Chan's "Number One Son," beginning with the 1935 film *Charlie Chan in Paris*. Sen Yung portrayed "James 'Jimmy' Chan," the detective's "Number Two Son," beginning in 1939's *Charlie Chan in Honolulu*. (In the Monogram series, Yung was called "Tommy Chan.") Sol Wurtzel produced most of the Fox Chan series, and frequent directors included H. Bruce Humberstone, Eugene Forde, Hamilton MacFadden and Harry Lachman. The Chan character was also portrayed on the radio by Walter Connolly, Santos Ortega and Ed Begley, and on television by J. Carrol Naish and Ross Martin. Keye Luke provided the voice of Chan in *The Amazing Chan and the Chan Clan*, a Hanna-Barbera cartoon series that ran on CBS from 9 Sep 1972 to 22 Sep 1974. In 1976, the Chan character was parodied along with other famous detectives in the Columbia film *Murder by Death*. The picture, directed by Robert Moore, starred Peter Sellers as "Sidney Wang" and Richard Narita as his son "Willie Wang." With the exceptions of Japanese actors Kuwa and Sojin, who each played Chan once in the 1920s, the detective has been played only by Caucasian actors in American films. Modern sources note that two unauthorized Chan films, featuring Hsu Hsin-yuan, were made by a Chinese company in Shanghai, apparently in the 1930s. Chan's aphorisms were a well-loved component of the films, and a collection of Chan's sayings from the Fox films was published in 1968 under the title *Quotations from Charlie Chan*. In May 1992, Imagine Entertainment announced that it was preparing a new Charlie Chan film for a 1993 release.

Other language version(s):

Eran trece (Spanish language)

1931; New York opening: 4 Dec 1931. Sd; b&w. 9 reels. 79 min. Passed by the National Board of Review. Spanish language.

[*Dir* David Howard]. [*Scr* Philip Klein and Barry Conners]. [*Spanish dial* José López Rubio]. [*Photog* Sidney Wagner].

Song(s): "Mala yerba" by Raúl Roulien; "Crispin" by Mark Hermanns and "L'Amour de l'apache" by Jacques Offenbach.

Spanish-language cast: Juan Torena (*Dick Kennaway*), Ana María Custodio (*Elen Potter*), Rafael Calvo (*Inspector Duff*), Raúl Roulien (*Max Minchin*), Blanca Castejón (*Peggy Minchin*), Miguel Ligero (*Frank Benbow*), Amalia Santee (*Señora Benbow*), Carmen Rodríguez (*Señora Rockwel*), Julio Villarreal (*Doctor Lofton*), José Nieto (*Capitán Kin*), Carlos Díaz de Mendoza (*Walter Decker*), Lia Torá (*Sybil Conway*), Martín Garralaga (*John Ross*), Antonio Vidal (*Paul Nielson*), Ralph Navarro (*Inspector Gardner*), Manuel Arbó (*Charlie Chan*), [Raymond Lopez (*Manservant*)]. [*Spanish version viewed*].

FD 22 Mar 1931, p. 10. *HF* 10 Jan 1931, p. 24. *HF* 17 Jan 1931, p. 24. *HR* 3 Dec 1930, p. 2. *MPH* 24 Jan 1931, p. 47 *MPH* 28 Mar 1931, p. 37. *NYT* 21 Mar 1931, p. 15. *Var* 21 Jan 1931, p. 8. *Var* 25 Mar 1931, p. 24.

CHARLIE CHAN IN ALCATRAZ *see* **DARK ALIBI**

CHARLIE CHAN IN BLACK MAGIC *see* **BLACK MAGIC**

CHARLIE CHAN IN CITY IN DARKNESS *see* **CITY IN DARKNESS**

CHARLIE CHAN IN EGYPT (Chinese Americans)

Fox Film Corp. *Dist* Fox Film Corp. 21 Jun **1935**; Prod: Apr 1935 [©Fox Film Corp.; 21 Jun 1935; LP5882]. Sd (Western Electric Noiseless Recording); b&w. 8 reels, 6,600 ft. 72 min. PCA cert no. 905.

Series: Charlie Chan.

Prod Edward T. Lowe. *Dir* Luis King [sic]. *Orig scr* Robert Ellis and Helen Logan. *Photog* Daniel B. Clark. *Art dir* Duncan Cramer and

Walter Koessler. [*Ed* Al De Gaetano]. *Gowns* Helen Myron. *Mus dir* Samuel Kaylin. *Sd* Albert Protzman.

Source: Based on the character "Charlie Chan" created by Earl Derr Biggers.

Cast: WARNER OLAND [(*Charlie Chan*)], Pat Paterson [(*Carol Arnold*)], Thomas Beck [(*Tom Evans*)], Rita Cansino [(*Nayda*)], Stepin Fetchit [(*Snowshoes*)], [Jameson Thomas (*Dr. Anton Racine*)], [Frank Conroy (*Professor Thurston*)], [Nigel de Brulier (*Edfu Ahmad*)], [James Eagles (*Barry Arnold*)], [Paul Porcasi (*Fouad Soueida*)], [Arthur Stone (*Dragoman*)], [George Irving (*Professor Arnold*)], [Anita Brown (*Snowshoes' friend*)], [John Davidson (*Daoud Atrash, chemist*)], [Gloria Roy].

Detective, Drama. [*Print viewed*]. Charlie Chan goes to Egypt on behalf of the French Archaeological Society to investigate Professor Arnold's excavation of Ameti's tomb, because the artifacts discovered in the tomb have been found in other museums. Once there, however, Chan finds out from the professor's daughter Carol, his son Barry, his brother-in-law, Professor Thurston, and Tom Evans, who is Arnold's young assistant and Carol's boyfriend, that Arnold has been missing for a month. When Carol is overcome by worry over her father, Tom sends for Dr. Anton Racine, who arrives shortly after Carol hallucinates that she is being menaced by Sekhmet, the goddess of vengeance whose statue was guarding Ameti's tomb. Meanwhile, in the basement laboratory, Chan, Thurston and Tom examine Ameti's mummy using an X ray. When Chan notices a bullet in the mummy's chest, they unwrap it and discover not Ameti but Professor Arnold. Thurston then tells Chan that he sold the artifacts to pay off money he had borrowed from Racine. Barry overhears them discussing his father's death and collapses in hysterics, certain that the tomb's curse will kill the entire family. Chan decides to investigate the tomb that night, so with Tom and his helper Snowshoes, he sets off, but once inside the tomb, they are frightened off by a vision of Sekhmet. The next day, Chan goes to Luxor to question Daoud Atrash, the chemist who fills Racine's prescriptions for Carol. That night, when Chan returns to the Arnold house, an autopsy of the professor is underway, and after the others leave, Chan extracts the bullet from near Arnold's heart. Chan then rejoins the others upstairs and questions Racine about Mapouchari, a drug which causes hallucinations and death, and which Chan suspects is placed on Carol's cigarettes to trigger her attacks. They are just about to talk to Barry about the secret treasure his father was trying to find when Barry dies while playing his violin. Later, Chan, Tom and Snowshoes return to the tomb, where they find a secret water passageway. Tom swims to the next room, which is a storage room for Ameti's treasures, but he is shot by someone he recognizes. As he falls, he hits a lever that opens a door between the rooms, and Chan and Snowshoes take him back to the house. After the bullet is removed, Chan takes it for evidence, then goes to search Barry's room. Chan deduces that Barry was killed by a tiny vial of the deadly drug. He demonstrates to Thurston and Racine how the violin's vibrations shattered the glass, releasing the drug in gaseous form. He then tells them it was the hidden treasure room which was the motive for the two murders and the attempt on Tom's life. Upstairs, Racine examines Tom, after which Thurston sends Carol to rest. Alone with Tom, Thurston prepares to stab him in his wounds with Racine's lancet, but Chan arrives just in time. Chan explains that the bullets recovered from Arnold and Tom came from Thurston's gun, and the police then take Thurston away. Tom regains consciousness and is enfolded in Carol's loving embrace. *Archaeologists. Attempted murder. Chinese Americans. Curses. Detectives. Egypt. Murder. Treachery. African Americans. Autopsy. Chemists. Drugging. Family relationships. Gods. Mummies. Physicians. Secret passageways. Servants. Tombs. Treasure. Violins. Visions.*

Note: Director Louis King's name appears as Luis King in the onscreen credits of the print viewed, from which the end credits were missing. According to a *HR* news item, Charles Locher was originally signed for the juvenile lead. For more information on the series, please consult the Series Index and see the entry above for *Charlie Chan Carries On*.

Box 27 Jul 1935. *DV* 31 May 1935, p. 3. *FD* 4 Jun 1935, p. 6. *HR* 1 Apr 1935, p. 6. *HR* 8 Apr 1935, p. 10. *HR* 29 Apr 1935, p. 6. *HR* 31 May 1935, p. 2. *MPD* 1 Jun 1935, p. 4. *MPH* 25 May 1935, p. 51. *MPH* 8 Jun 1935, p. 73, 76. *NYT* 24 Jun 1935, p. 12. *Var* 26 Jun 1935, p. 23.

CHARLIE CHAN IN HONOLULU (Chinese Americans)

Twentieth Century-Fox Film Corp. *Dist* Twentieth Century-Fox Film Corp. 13 Jan 1939; Prod: 31 Oct—late Nov 1938 [©Twentieth Century-Fox Film Corp.; 13 Jan 1939; LP8722]. Sd (Western Electric

Mirrophonic Recording); b&w. 7 reels, 6,074 ft. 67-68 min. PCA cert no. 4861.

Series: Charlie Chan.

[*Prod* Sol M. Wurtzel]. *Assoc prod* John Stone. *Dir* H. Bruce Humberstone. [*Asst dir* Saul Wurtzel]. *Orig scr* Charles Belden. [*Contr wrt* Chandler Sprague]. *Photog* Charles Clarke. *Art dir* Richard Day and Haldane Douglas. *Film ed* Nick DeMaggio. *Set dec* Thomas Little. *Cost* Helen A. Myron. *Mus dir* Samuel Kaylin. *Sd* Joseph E. Aiken and William H. Anderson. [*Casting dir* James Ryan].

Source: Based on the character "Charlie Chan" created by Earl Derr Biggers.

Cast: Sidney Toler (*Charlie Chan*), Phyllis Brooks (*Judy Hayes*), Sen Yung (*James Chan*), Eddie Collins (*Al Hogan*), John King ([*George*] *Randolph*), Claire Dodd ([*Mrs. Elsie Hillman, alias*] *Mrs. Carol Wayne*), George Zucco (*Dr. Cardigan*), Robert Barrat (*Captain Johnson*), Marc Lawrence (*Johnny McCoy*), Richard Lane ([*Mike Hannigan, alias*] *Joe Arnold*), Layne Tom, Jr. (*Tommy Chan*), Philip Ahn (*Wing Foo*), Paul Harvey (*Inspector Rawlins*).

Detective. [*Print viewed*]. Honolulu police detective Charlie Chan is awaiting the arrival of his first grandchild, and after he, his wife and their son-in-law, Wing Foo, rush to the hospital, a call comes in for him to investigate a murder on the freighter *Susan B. Jennings*. Chan's "number two" son James, who wants to become his father's assistant, is persuaded by his little brother Tommy to answer the call himself, and prove to their father that he is a good investigator. Tommy tags along as Jimmy goes to the freighter which has just arrived from Shanghai. There Captain Johnson assumes that Jimmy is Chan and explains that the murdered man's identity is a mystery, and that secretary Judy Hayes was the only eyewitness to the fatal shooting. Jimmy decides to question the rest of the freighter's passengers, who include animal keeper Al Hogan, Mrs. Carol Wayne, psychiatrist Dr. Cardigan, criminal Johnny McCoy, and policeman Joe Arnold, who is taking McCoy back to Shanghai. Judy reveals that her lawyer employer in Shanghai told her to deliver a package containing $300,000 to a man who would meet her in Honolulu. The man identified himself by a pre-arranged signal, but he was shot by an unknown assailant before she gave him the money. First mate George Randolph, who has fallen in love with Judy, takes Jimmy to question the surly crew members, and Jimmy is saved from their ire by Chan, who arrives after having found out about the case from Inspector Rawlins, his boss. Chan questions Carol, who states that she was on the freighter to rest while her suit for divorce was being heard, and that she recently became a widow anyway. Chan finds a wrapper for part of the missing money in the doctor's compartment, and becomes more suspicious of Judy when she slips off the ship to call her employer about the stolen funds. Carol reveals that Randolph gave Judy a gun with which to protect herself, and upon examination of it, Chan finds that it is the same caliber as the murder weapon. Judy then protests to Randolph that she is being framed when he questions her about the missing money that he found hidden in her cabin. Chan and Jimmy find Carol after she has been strangled with a scarf, and Chan reveals that Arnold is actually Mike Harrigan, who, while in league with McCoy, murdered the real Arnold after escaping from prison. While Chan and Cardigan rig a trap for the killer, Chan reveals to the passengers that Carol was really Mrs. Elsie Hillman, the dead man's wife, and Judy states that although she did not know about Carol, she was delivering the money to the man so that he did not have to declare it in a divorce settlement. Chan's trap works when the killer attempts to grab the murder weapon and triggers a camera, and after Cardigan develops the photograph, Johnson is revealed as the murderer. Chan explains that Johnson was after the money, and later killed Carol when she became suspicious. After the case is wrapped up, Chan receives a call from Wing Foo and happily listens as his grandson cries into the phone. *Chinese Americans. Detectives. Fathers and sons. Freighters. Impersonation and imposture. Murder. Brothers. Divorce. Firearms. Grandfathers. Honolulu (HI). Hospitals. Lions. Money. Monkeys. Photographs. Prison escapees. Psychiatrists. Secretaries. Ship crews.*

Note: According to a *HR* news item, Richard Lane was originally signed to play the "romantic lead" opposite Phyllis Brooks. Lane plays criminal "Joe Arnold" in the film, however, while John King plays romantic lead "George Randolph." This was the first film in which Sidney Toler appeared as "Charlie Chan." According to a *HR* news item, associate producer John Stone chose Toler to be the successor of Warner Oland, who played Chan from 1931 until his death in 1938, after seeing him play a Chinese character in the Paramount film

King of Chinatown (see below). Toler was the thirty-fifth actor tested for the role, and *HR* noted that others considered for the part included Leo Carrillo and Cy Kendall, who played Chan in a radio series. Toler portrayed Chan until his death in 1947. This was also the first film in which Sen Yung played "James Chan." Yung replaced Keye Luke, who had portrayed "Lee Chan" in earlier entries in the series. Luke left the series after Oland's death, when he and Twentieth Century-Fox disagreed on his new contract. According to *HR* news items, the search for Luke's replacement was "frantic," and led to casting director James Ryan seeking applicants among Los Angeles Chinese university students and Chinatown residents. *NYT* speculated that *Charlie Chan in Honolulu* would cost $300,000 to produce, and that Toler would receive $15,000 per Chan film. Many reviewers applauded Toler's and Yung's performances and noted that followers of the series would be satisfied with the new actors. The *MPH* review remarked on the novelty of a Chan film being previewed at Grauman's Chinese Theatre, and stated that the 18 Dec 1939 showing was very well received by the "top ranking executives, the most sought after reviewers and commentators and invited guests" who attended. For more information on the series, please consult the Series Index and see the entry above for *Charlie Chan Carries On.*

Box 24 Dec 1938. *DV* 17 Dec 1938, p. 3. *FD* 20 Dec 1938, p. 8. *HR* 9 Aug 1938, p. 2. *HR* 7 Oct 1938, p. 1. *HR* 15 Oct 1938, p. 3. *HR* 19 Oct 1938, p. 4. *HR* 27 Oct 1938, p. 3. *HR* 28 Oct 1938, p. 2. *HR* 31 Oct 1938, p. 2. *HR* 8 Nov 1938, p. 3. *HR* 26 Nov 1938, p. 7. *HR* 12 Dec 1938, p. 3. *HR* 17 Dec 1938, p. 3. *MPD* 21 Dec 1938, p. 8. *MPH* 10 Dec 1938, p. 41. *MPH* 24 Dec 1938, p. 41. *NYT* 18 Dec 1938. *NYT* 31 Dec 1938, p. 7. *Var* 21 Dec 1938, p. 15.

CHARLIE CHAN IN LONDON (Chinese Americans)

Fox Film Corp. *Dist* Fox Film Corp. 12 Sep **1934**; Prod: 9 Jul—early Aug 1934 [©Fox Film Corp.; 14 Sep 1934; LP4951]. Sd (Western Electric Noiseless Recording); b&w. 8 reels, 7,026 ft. 77-79 min. PCA cert no. 171.

Series: Charlie Chan.

Prod John Stone. *Dir* Eugene Forde. [*Asst dir* Ed O'Fearna]. *Orig scr* Philip MacDonald. [*Contr to scr const and dial* Stuart Anthony and Lester Cole]. *Photog* L. W. O'Connell. [*Asst cam* John Schmitz and Robert Surtees]. *Settings* Duncan Cramer. *Gowns* Royer. *Mus dir* Samuel Kaylin. *Sd* E. Clayton Ward. [*Stunts* Joe Flores, Clint Sharp, Walter Nobles and Opal Ernie]. *Stand in* Ann Doran and Alex Chivra.

Source: Based on the character "Charlie Chan" created by Earl Derr Biggers.

Cast: WARNER OLAND (*Inspector Charlie Chan*), Drue Leyton (*Pamela Gray*), Raymond Milland (*Neil Howard*), Mona Barrie (*Lady Mary Bristol*), Alan Mowbray (*Geoffrey Richmond*), Murray Kinnell (*Phillips*), Douglas Walton (*Hugh Gray*), Walter Johnson (*Jerry Garton*), E. E. Clive (*Detective Sergeant Thacker*), George Barraud (*Major Jardine*), Madge Bellamy (*Mrs. Fothergill*), David Torrence (*Home Secretary*), John Rogers (*Lake*), Paul England (*Bunny Fothergill*), Elsa Buchanan (*Alice Rooney*), Perry Ivins (*Kemp*), [Claude King (*Commandant*)], [Reginald Sheffield (*Commander*)], [Helena Grant (*Secretary*)], [Montague Shaw (*Doctor*)], [Phillis Coghlan (*Nurse*)], [Margaret Mann (*Housemaid*)], [Carlie Taylor, Doris Stone (*Guests*)], [Arthur Clayton (*Warden*)].

Detective, Drama. [*Print viewed*]. Pamela Gray goes with Geoffrey Richmond to appeal to the Home Secretary to intervene and stop the planned hanging of her brother Paul, Richmond's former hunt secretary, in three days for the murder of Captain Hamilton of the Royal Air Force, who had been a guest at Richmond's country home at Retfordshire. After the Home Secretary refuses to help, Kemp, his private secretary, instructs Pamela and her fiancé, Neil Howard, to seek the help of Inspector Charlie Chan of the Honolulu police department, who has captured in Honolulu and brought back to London a wanted British criminal. When Neil, who is Paul's barrister, tells Chan that he believes that Paul is guilty, Pamela overhears the conversation and breaks their engagement. Chan, who wants to help, follows her to Retfordshire, where guests are gathered for a hunt. After Lake, the stud groom who Chan suspects, knows more than he admits, is found dead with a suicide note, Chan, while investigating in the study, is almost killed by a missile from an air-blown pistol. The next day, during the hunt, Chan goes to the Farmwell Aerodrome, where he learns that Hamilton, an inventor, had developed a scheme for silencing war planes just before he died. Returning to the hunt, Chan learns that Richmond's fiancée, Lady Mary Bristol, who had important evidence to tell Chan, had a near-fatal riding accident because pepper was put on her horse's eyes. After Chan tells the suspected guests that the murderer's fingerprints will be on the missing plans, he tricks Richmond into firing at him with a gun filled with blanks as Chan seemingly finds the papers. Richmond is revealed to be a spy whom military intelligence has been following for years. Sometime later, Paul, released, has dinner with Pamela and Neil, who

now have been reunited, and Chan. *Americans in foreign countries. Chinese Americans. Detectives. England. False arrests. Murder. Spies. Brothers and sisters. Cruelty to animals. Engagements. Horses. Hunting. Inventions. Lawyers. Riding accidents. Ruses. Sabotage. Secretaries.*

Note: This was the first film of the "Charlie Chan" series that was not based on a particular novel by Chan's creator, Earl Derr Biggers. *NYT* commented that this film, written by Philip MacDonald, a noted detective novelist himself, "maintains the Chan tradition." For information concerning the series, please consult the Series Index and see the entry above for *Charlie Chan Carries On.*

DV 9 Jul 1934, p. 5. *FD* 13 Sep 1934, p. 6. *Har* 15 Sep 1934, p. 146. *HF* 4 Aug 1934, p. 8. *IP* Aug 1934, p. 17. *MPD* 6 Sep 1934, p. 11. *MPH* 22 Sep 1934, p. 42. *NYT* 13 Sep 1934, p. 26. *Var* 18 Sep 1934, p. 11.

CHARLIE CHAN IN MEXICO *see* **THE RED DRAGON**

CHARLIE CHAN IN NEW ORLEANS *see* **DOCKS OF NEW ORLEANS**

CHARLIE CHAN IN NEW YORK *see* **MURDER OVER NEW YORK**

CHARLIE CHAN IN PANAMA (Chinese Americans)

Twentieth Century-Fox Film Corp. *Dist* Twentieth Century-Fox Film Corp. 1 Mar **1940**; New York opening: week of 23 Feb 1940; Prod: began early Oct 1939 [©Twentieth Century-Fox Film Corp.; 8 Mar 1940; LP9651]. Sd (RCA High Fidelity Recording); b&w. 6,061 reels. 67 min. PCA cert no. 5892.

Series: Charlie Chan.

Exec prod Sol M. Wurtzel. *Dir* Norman Foster. *Asst dir* Saul Wurtzel. *Orig scr* John Larkin and Lester Ziffren. *Photog* Virgil Miller. *Art dir* Richard Day and Chester Gore. *Film ed* Fred Allen. *Set dec* Thomas Little. *Cost* Helen A. Myron. *Mus dir* Samuel Kaylin. *Sd* Joseph E. Aiken and William H. Anderson.

Source: Based on the character "Charlie Chan" created by Earl Derr Biggers.

Cast: Sidney Toler (*Charlie Chan [also knwon as Fu Yuen]*), Jean Rogers (*Kathi Lenesch*), Lionel Atwill (*Clivedon Compton*), Mary Nash (*Miss Jennie Finch*), Sen Yung (*Jimmy Chan*), Kane Richmond (*Richard Cabot*), Chris-Pin Martin (*Sergeant Montero*), Lionel Royce (*Dr. Rudolph Grosser*), Helen Ericson (*Stewardess*), Jack La Rue (*Manolo*), Edwin Stanley (*Governor Webster*), Don Douglas (*Captain Lewis*), Frank Puglia (*Achmed Halide*), Addison Richards (*Godley*), Edward Keane (*Dr. Fredericks*), [Charles Stevens (*Native fisherman*)], [Max Wagner, Alan Davis (*Soldiers*)], [Charles Sherlock (*Enlisted man*)], [Eddie Acuff (*Sailor*)], [Harold Goodwin (*Military police*)], [Gloria Roy (*Hostess*)], [Lane Chandler (*Officer*)], [Edward Gargan (*Attendant*)], [Philip Morris (*Plainclothesman*)], [Albert Morin (*Hotel clerk*)], [Jimmy Aubrey].

Detective. [*Viewed print incomplete*]. As the U.S. fleet prepares to navigate the waters of the Panama Canal, Panama City becomes rife with spies. A new group of suspects appears with the arrival of a sea plane bound for Balboa. Among the suspects are novelist Clivedon Compton, matronly school teacher Miss Jennie Finch, sinister scientist Dr. Rudolph Grosser, café proprietor Manolo, singer Kathi Lenesch, cigarette salesman Achmed Halide, government engineer Richard Cabot and government agent Godley. Upon landing, Godley goes to a hat shop owned by Fu Yuen, alias Charlie Chan, to enlist the sleuth's help in unmasking the deadly spy known only as Reiner. Just as Godley is about to divulge Reiner's real identity, he falls to the ground, dead, leaving Chan to expose Reiner before the spy can sabotage the canal. As the other suspects are murdered, one by one, first Compton, then Manolo, Chan learns that the canal's Miraflores locks are to be blown up at ten that night. Chan then sequesters the suspects at the plant, forcing Miss Finch to expose herself as Reiner in order to escape death. With Reiner under arrest, the fleet sails safely through the locks to protect democracy. *Chinese Americans. Detectives. Impersonation and imposture. Sabotage. Spies. Cabaret performers. Cabarets. Fathers and sons. Millinery shops. Murder. Panama Canal (Panama). Scientists. Teachers.*

Note: The viewed print was missing the film's opening credits. For additional information on the series, consult the Series Index and see above entry for *Charlie Chan Carries On.*

DV 1 Feb 1940, p. 3. *FD* 27 Feb 1940, p. 7. *HR* 28 Oct 1938, pp. 5-6. *HR* 3 Feb 1940, p. 3. *MPD* 7 Feb 1940, p. 8. *MPH* 25 Nov 1939, p. 35. *MPH* 10 Feb 1940, p. 38. *NYT* 23 Feb 1940, p. 19. *Var* 21 Feb 1940, p. 12.

CHARLIE CHAN IN PARIS (Chinese Americans)

Fox Film Corp. *Dist* Fox Film Corp. 25 Jan **1935**; New York opening: 21 Jan 1935; Prod: 12 Nov—mid-Dec 1934 [©Fox Film Corp.; 25 Jan 1935; LP5275]. Sd (Western Electric Noiseless Recording); b&w. 7 reels, 6,413 ft. 70 min. PCA cert no. 507.

Series: Charlie Chan.

Prod John Stone. [*Exec prod* Sol M. Wurtzel]. *Dir* Lewis Seiler. [*Orig dir* Hamilton MacFadden]. [*Asst dir* Eli Dunn]. *Scr* Edward T. Lowe and Stuart Anthony. *Story* Philip MacDonald. [*Contr on spec seq* William Allen Johnston]. *Photog* Ernest Palmer. [*Orig photog* Dan Clark]. *Settings* Duncan Cramer and Albert Hogsett. *Gowns* Lillian. *Mus dir* Samuel Kaylin. *Sd* Eugene Grossman. [*Dance double* Betty Bryson and Fred Wallace]. [*Stand in* Alex Chivra and Gladys Howe].

Source: Based on the character "Charlie Chan" created by Earl Derr Biggers.

Cast: WARNER OLAND (*Charlie Chan*), Mary Brian (*Yvette Lamartine*), Thomas Beck (*Victor Descartes*), Erik Rhodes (*Max Corday*), John Miljan (*Albert Dufresne*), Murray Kinnell (*Henri Latouche*), Minor Watson (*Renard*), John Qualen (*Concierge*), Keye Luke (*Lee Chan*), Henry Kolker (*M. Lamartine*), Dorothy Appleby (*Nardi*), Ruth Peterson (*Renee Jacquard*), Perry Ivins (*Bedell*), [George Davis (*Roberts, butler*)], [Auguste Tollaire (*Concierge*)], [Louis Natheaux (*Reporter*)], [Ed Cecil (*Customs officer*)], [Robert Graves, Harry Cording (*Gendarmes*)], [Marty Faust (*Cab driver*)], [Landers Stevens (*Bank attendant*)], [John Dilson (*Information clerk*)], [Samuel T. Godfrey, Rolfe Sedan (*Cashiers*)], [Moore & Allen (*Apache dancers*)], [Gino Corrado (*Head waiter*)], [Wilfred Lucas (*Doorman*)], [Richard Kipling (*Master of ceremonies—Cafe Embassy*)], [Eddie Vitch (*Sketch artist*)], [Paul McVey (*Detective*)], [Gloria Roy].

Detective, Drama. [*Print viewed*]. Honolulu detective Charlie Chan arrives in Paris ostensibly on vacation after solving a noteworthy case in London. He makes an appointment to meet Nardi, a dancer at the Café du Singe Bleu, after her performance that night. Chan first visits Victor Descartes, whose father, Chan's friend, is a director of the Lamartine Bank where Victor works as a clerk. After Victor's fiancée, Yvette Lamartine, the bank president's daughter, arrives with two friends, Max Corday, an intoxicated sketch artist, and Renee Jacquard, the group accompanies Chan to the café. As Max gets out of his car, he bumps into a disgruntled man on crutches in dark glasses, who berates him. After her Apache dance, Nardi is murdered in a back room by a knife thrown by the man on crutches. In Nardi's room, Chan finds a diary containing information about Albert Dufresne. As Chan is leaving the building, the man on crutches drops a cement block from the roof, which nearly hits him. Chan is pleasantly surprised to find in his hotel room his son Lee, who has come to vacation with his father. Chan reveals to Lee that he is really investigating a case for a London banking house and that his accomplice, Nardi, has been murdered. The next day, when Yvette visits her father at the bank, Dufresne, her father's assistant, threatens to show love letters she once wrote him to Victor unless she visits his apartment. While Lee waits at the door, Chan enters the bank and witnesses the office manager, Henri Latouche, have the man on crutches, whom he identifies as Marcel Xavier, a shell-shocked, crippled soldier, escorted out for causing a disturbance. Chan meets with Lamartine and Dufresne and after showing them that bonds issued by the bank are, in fact, forgeries, he instructs Lee to follow Dufresne. That night, as Lee watches from the street, Yvette visits Dufresne, who is packing and is secretly being watched by Xavier. Just as Dufresne is handing Yvette the letters, he is shot from the room that Xavier entered. Xavier escapes with the bonds Dufresne packed, but Lee follows his taxi. Yvette, who grabs the gun when the room is invaded by people, is arrested for murder. When Max and Renee are interrogated by the police, Yvette slips the letters to Chan, who promises to destroy them. Lee returns to the hotel, and when Chan joins him, Lee reports that Xavier got into a limousine after the taxi ride and that it was the same limousine in which Max and Renee drove away from the hotel. Chan visits Max and tells him that he suspects Xavier used his limousine to get rid of his disguise. Max, thinking that Chan may suspect him, reminds him that Xavier bumped into him outside the café. Chan then leaves and Max packs the bonds that were in Dufresne's room, but Chan and Lee stop him from leaving. Chan surmises that Max killed Dufresne, but he still has not found Nardi's murderer. While Lee holds Max at gunpoint, Chan goes to the bank

where Latouche gives him Xavier's address. Victor, appealing to Chan to help Yvette, drives him to find Xavier. At the address, Chan finds a secret panel leading to the Paris sewers, where they find a room with printing and engraving equipment and more forged bonds. Xavier arrives and fires at Chan, but they apprehend him and Chan removes his wig, glasses and mask to reveal Latouche. When the police arrive with Lee, Chan explains that Max and Latouche both used the disguise so that they each could have alibis. Dufresne, their accomplice in the bond forgeries, tried to leave town with their money and was murdered by Max. Chan then tells police inspector Renard that Yvette is his assistant and was sent by him to get important letters from Dufresne. Renard understands and agrees to release her. *Americans in foreign countries. Bonds. Chinese Americans. Detectives. Disguise. Forgers and forgery. Murder. Paris (France). Apache dancers. Artists. Bank clerks. Bank presidents. Cafés. Diaries. Engagements. False arrests. Fathers and sons. Letters. Sewers. Threats.*

Note: According to *DV*, Hamilton MacFadden, the original director, was relieved of his assignment after the film was in production one week. Dan Clark, who did not received screen credit, was the original cameraman. This was the first film in which Keye Luke played the role of Lee Chan. For information regarding the series, please consult the Series Index and see the entry above for *Charlie Chan Carries On*.

Box 2 Feb 1935. *DV* 22 Nov 1934, p. 14. *DV* 22 Dec 1934, p. 3. *FD* 22 Jan 1935, p. 4. *HF* 15 Dec 1934, p. 8. *HR* 9 Nov 1934, p. 8. *HR* 12 Nov 1934, p. 6. *HR* 19 Nov 1934, p. 10, 12. *HR* 22 Dec 1934, p. 3. *HR* 29 Jan 1935, p. 2. *MPH* 5 Jan 1935, p. 35. *NYT* 22 Jan 1935, p. 23. *Var* 29 Jan 1935, p. 14.

CHARLIE CHAN IN RENO (Chinese Americans)

Twentieth Century-Fox Film Corp. *Dist* Twentieth Century-Fox Film Corp. 16 Jun **1939**; New York opening: week of 31 May 1939; Prod: 23 Jan—24 Feb 1939 [©Twentieth Century-Fox Film Corp.; 16 Jun 1939; LP9000]. Sd (RCA High Fidelity Recording); b&w. 7 reels, 6,379 ft. 70 min. PCA cert no. 5160.

Series: Charlie Chan.

Assoc prod John Stone. *Dir* Norman Foster. [*Asst dir* Jasper Blystone]. *Scr* Frances Hyland, Albert Ray and Robert E. Kent. *Story* Philip Wylie. *Photog* Virgil Miller. *Art dir* Richard Day and David Hall. *Film ed* Fred Allen. *Set dec* Thomas Little. *Cost* Herschel. *Mus dir* Samuel Kaylin. *Sd* Bernard Freericks and William H. Anderson.

Source: Based on the character "Charlie Chan" created by Earl Derr Biggers.

Cast: Sidney Toler (*Charlie Chan*), Ricardo Cortez (*Dr. Ainsley*), Phyllis Brooks (*Vivian Wells*), Slim Summerville (*Sheriff Fletcher*), Kane Richmond (*Curtis Whitman*), Sen Yung (*James Chan*), Pauline Moore (*Mary Whitman*), Eddie Collins (*Cab driver*), Kay Linaker (*Mrs. Russell*), Louise Henry (*Jeanne Bently*), Robert Lowery (*Wally Burke*), Charles D. Brown (*Chief of Police King*), Iris Wong (*Choy Wong*), Morgan Conway (*George Bently*), Hamilton MacFadden (*Night clerk*), [Arthur Rankin (*Bellboy*)], [Fred Kelsey (*Sergeant*)], [Virginia Sale (*Maid*)], [Harry Hayden (*Professor*)], [Dick Hogan (*College boy*)], [Barbara MacLain (*College girl*)], [Al Kikume (*Policeman*)], [Ed Stanley (*Chemist*)], [Stanley Blystone (*Policeman*)], [Jack Perry (*Rough drunk*)], [Bob Hale], [Jimmy Aubrey], [Imboden Parrish], [Hank Mann].

Detective. [*Print viewed*]. Sparks fly at the Hotel Eldorado in Reno when Mary Whitman arrives to file for divorce from her husband Curtis and meets Curtis' intended, Jeanne Bently. When Jeanne taunts the defenseless Mary and insults Wally Burke, her former suitor, Mrs. Russell, the owner of the hotel, orders her to leave. Before she can finish packing her bags, however, Jeanne is murdered and Mary, arrested for the crime. Mary's arrest prompts her husband Curtis, a resident of Honolulu, to ask his old friend, Charlie Chan, for help. Charlie accompanies Curtis to Reno, where he meets Sheriff Fletcher, the bumbling law man investigating the case. After winning Mary's release on the grounds of lack of evidence, Charlie visits the murder room, where he finds Dr. Ainsley. Ainsley claims that he is looking for the money that Jeanne won on the night of her murder, suggesting that Burke killed her for her winnings. A search of the room by Charlie and his son Jimmy reveals Jeanne's scrapbook with the pages from the years 1935 and 1936 cut out, and Charlie to surmises that a pair of scissors was the murder weapon. Next, Charlie finds dirt particles on the dead woman's boots, which leads him to an abandoned mine shaft in a nearby ghost town. There, he finds an engineering kit and bank book belonging to George Bently, the dead woman's husband. Bently escapes, but is captured and accused of murder by Sheriff Fletcher, although Charlie is unconvinced of his guilt. Becoming intrigued by

an acid burn on Mary's sleeve that matches a burn found in the rug in Jeanne's room, Charlie traces the acid to Ainsley. The case against the doctor intensifies when Police Chief King discovers that Jeanne had written checks to Ainsley and reveals that the missing pages in the scrapbook related to Jeanne's previous marriage to Mrs. Russell's late husband, whose death had been attended by Dr. Ainsley. Before the detectives can question Mrs. Russell, however, they find her strangled and Ainsley about to administer a hypodermic needle to her. Charlie pulls the needle from his hand and discovers poison in the syringe. Charlie then assembles all the murder suspects and announces that Jeanne had been paying Ainsley to keep silent about the fact that she murdered Russell. Charlie continues that he found the missing money in Ainsley's room, but before he finishes his explanation, Vivian Wells, the hotel's social director who is in love with Ainsley, protests his innocence. Charlie then traps Vivian into exposing a burn on her arm, proving that she murdered Jeanne during a struggle for the acid bottle. *Chinese Americans. Detectives. Divorce. False accusations. Murder. Reno (NV).* Blackmail. Cities and towns, Ruined, extinct, etc.. Evidence. Fathers and sons. Hotels. Mines. Physicians. Poisoning. Police chiefs. Sheriffs. Strangling.

Note: The working title of this picture was *Death Makes a Decree.* It was based on the original screen story "Death Makes a Decree" by Philip Wylie and the character Charlie Chan created by Earl Derr Biggers and Robert E. Kent. According to materials contained in the Twentieth Century-Fox Produced Scripts Collection at the UCLA Theater Arts Library, Paul Perez wrote a version of the screenplay in Dec 1938, but his name does not appear in the final credits. In the Call Bureau Cast Service lists, Sheriff Fletcher's name was originally Foster, Mrs. Russell was named Alice Williamson and Choy Wong was named Sung Li. According to reviews in *HR* and *MPH,* at the time that this picture was produced, this was the most expensive production in the Chan series. For additional information on the series, consult the Series Index and see above entry for *Charlie Chan Carries On.*

DV 27 May 1939, p. 3. *FD* 5 Jun 1939, p. 12. *HR* 11 Jan 1939, p. 5. *HR* 24 Feb 1939, p. 21. *HR* 27 May 1939, p. 3. *MPD* 2 Jun 1939, p. 11. *MPH* 29 Apr 1939, p. 40. *MPH* 3 Jun 1939, p. 38. *NYT* 31 May 1939, p. 27. *Var* 7 Jun 1939, p. 12.

CHARLIE CHAN IN RIO (Chinese Americans)

Twentieth Century-Fox Film Corp. *Dist* Twentieth Century-Fox Film Corp. 5 Sep **1941**; Prod: 8 May—late May 1941 [©Twentieth Century-Fox Film Corp.; 5 Sep 1941; LP10734]. Sd (RCA Sound System); b&w. 6 reels, 5,540 ft. 60 or 62 min. PCA cert no. 7370.

Series: Charlie Chan.

Exec prod Sol M. Wurtzel. *Dir* Harry Lachman. [*Asst dir* William Eckhardt]. *Scr* Samuel G. Engel and Lester Ziffren. *Dir of photog* Joseph P. MacDonald. *Art dir* Richard Day and Lewis Creber. *Film ed* Alexander Troffey. *Set dec* Thomas Little. *Cost* Herschel. *Mus dir* Emil Newman. *Sd* Alfred Bruzlin and Harry M. Leonard. [*Pub dir* Harry Brand].

Song(s): "They Met in Rio" and "I, Yi, Yi, Yi (I Like You Very Much)" music and lyrics by Mack Gordon and Harry Warren.

Source: Based on characters created by Earl Derr Biggers.

Cast: Sidney Toler (*Charlie Chan*), Mary Beth Hughes (*Joan Reynolds*), Cobina Wright, Jr. (*Grace Ellis*), Ted North (*Carlos Dantas [Clarke Denton]*), Victor Jory (*Alfredo Marana [alias of Alfredo Cardozo]*), Harold Huber (*Chief Souto*), Sen Yung (*Jimmy Chan*), Richard Derr (*Ken Reynolds*), Jacqueline Dalya (*Lola Dean*), Kay Linaker (*Helen Ashby [alias of Barbara Cardozo]*), Truman Bradley (*Paul Wagner*), Hamilton MacFadden (*Bill Kellogg*), Leslie Denison (*Rice*), Iris Wong (*Lili [Wong]*), Eugene Borden (*Armando*), Ann Codee (*Margo*).

Detective, Drama, with songs. [*Print viewed*]. In Rio de Janeiro, nightclub singer Lola Dean accepts the proposal of Clarke Denton, then insists on hosting a celebratory dinner for their acquaintances, Ken and Joan Reynolds, Grace Ellis and Bill Kellogg. Clarke agrees and Lola then performs her act, which is watched by Honolulu detective Charlie Chan, his son Jimmy and Rio de Janeiro police chief Souto, who are there to arrest Lola for the murder of Manuel Cardozo in Honolulu a year and a half previously. Chan decides to arrest Lola quietly at her home. After she leaves the club with Clarke, she follows the advice of her secretary, Helen Ashby, and visits Alfredo Marana, a noted psychic. Marana drugs his patients with an herbal ingredient placed on a cigarette that is stimulated by coffee, and after Lola is drugged, Marana records her confessing to killing Manuel because she was in love with him and he would not leave his wife for her. On the way home, Lola persuades Clarke to elope that evening with her to the United States, and she begins to pack immediately. While Helen is telling Lola's guests about the impending elopement, Chan, Jimmy

and Souto arrive, and soon after, Lola is found in her bedroom, stabbed to death, with a broken brooch lying next to her. Helen tells Chan about Lola's visit to Marana and about the persistent attentions of a mysterious man named Paul Wagner. Souto has the two men brought to the house, where Wagner admits that Lola was his ex-wife and that he came to see her earlier in an attempt to win her back. Upon hearing of her engagement to Clarke, however, Wagner left the house. Marana then plays the record of Lola's session and demonstrates his trance-inducing methods on Jimmy. Chan discovers that the pin of the brooch in Lola's room is broken off and deduces that it is imbedded in the killer's shoe. While Chan and Souto investigate, Jimmy finds jewelry taken from Lola's room in the room of Rice the butler. Rice admits to stealing the items but denies killing Lola, and before he can name the murderer, the lights go out and he is shot. Chan then finds the brooch pin in Helen's shoe and suggests that Marana put her in a trance to make her confess. She smokes one of the cigarettes but maintains that she is innocent. After smoking the rest of Helen's cigarette, Chan determines that Marana gave her one that was not drugged in order to protect her. Although Marana, whose real name is Alfredo Cardozo, protests that he killed Lola and Rice to avenge his brother, Helen confesses that she committed the murders because she is actually Barbara Cardozo, Manuel's widow. Helen had wanted to take Lola and the recording to the police the next day, but her elopement with Clarke would have enabled Lola to escape. Rice saw her with Lola's body, and Helen killed him to keep him quiet. Souto arrests Helen, after which Chan informs Jimmy that he has been drafted into the army, and Jimmy replies that the war will be a cinch with him in it. *Chinese Americans. Detectives. Murder. Revenge.* Butlers. Cigarettes. Coffee. Confession (Law). Drugging. Drunkenness. Engagements. Evidence. Fathers and sons. Jewelry. Maids. Mediums. Military service, Compulsory. Nightclubs. Recordings. Rio de Janeiro (Brazil). Secretaries. Singers.

Note: Although Ted North's character is called "Carlos Dantas" in the film's onscreen credits and in reviews, in the picture he is called "Clarke Denton." According to *HR* news items, Virgil Miller was originally assigned as the photographer on this picture, but was replaced by Joseph P. MacDonald, who was promoted after serving as an operative cameraman with Twentieth Century-Fox for eight years. A 30 Apr 1941 *HR* news item noted that Jeanne Kelly had been loaned by Universal to appear in the next Charlie Chan film, and while it was presumably this picture, her participation in the completed film has not been confirmed. *Charlie Chan in Rio* bears a striking resemblance to *The Black Camel,* a 1931 "Charlie Chan" film directed by Hamilton MacFadden, who appears as an actor in the 1941 picture (see entry above). For additional information about the "Charlie Chan" series, consult the Series Index and see the above entry for *Charlie Chan Carries On.*

Box 30 Aug 1941. *DV* 22 Aug 1941. *FD* 22 Aug 1941, p. 5. *HR* 30 Apr 1941, p. 3 *HR* 5 May 1941, p. 3. *HR* 8 May 1941, p. 5. *HR* 9 May 1941, p. 1, 25. *HR* 23 May 1941, p. 9. *HR* 22 Aug 1941, p. 4. *MPH* 23 Aug 1941. *MPHPD* 28 Jun 1941, p. 172. *MPHPD* 13 Sep 1941, p. 262. *Var* 27 Aug 1941, p. 8.

CHARLIE CHAN IN SAN FRANCISCO see **CHARLIE CHAN'S SECRET**

CHARLIE CHAN IN SHANGHAI (Chinese Americans)

Fox Film Corp.; Twentieth Century-Fox Film Corp. *Dist* Twentieth Century-Fox Film Corp. 11 Oct **1935**; Prod: 11 Jul—3 Aug 1935 [©Twentieth Century-Fox Film Corp.; 11 Oct 1935; LP6053]. Sd (Western Electric Noiseless Recording); b&w. 7 reels, 6,300 ft. 70 min. PCA cert no. 1255.

Series: Charlie Chan.

Assoc prod John Stone. *Dir* James Tinling. [*Asst dir* Aaron Rosenberg]. *Orig story and scr* Edward T. Lowe and Gerard Fairlie. *Photog* Barney McGill. *Art dir* Duncan Cramer and Lewis Creber. *Film ed* Nick De Maggio. *Gowns* Alberto Luza. *Mus dir* Samuel Kaylin. *Sd* Albert Protzman. [*Stunts* Chic Collins, Robert Rose and Jack Stoney].

Source: Based on the character "Charlie Chan" created by Earl Derr Biggers.

Cast: WARNER OLAND (*Charlie Chan*), Irene Hervey (*Diana Woodland*), Charles Locher (*Philip Nash*), Russell Hicks (*James Andrews*), Keye Luke (*Lee Chan*), Halliwell Hobbes (*Chief of police [Colonel Watkins]*), Frederik Vogeding (*Burke [Ivan Marloff]*), Neil Fitzgerald (*Dakin*), Max Wagner (*Taxi driver*), [Harry Strang (*Chauffeur*)], [Pat O'Malley (*Belden*)], [James B. Leong (*Telephone operator*)], [Jockey Haefeli (*Crook on boat*)], [David Torrence (*Sir Stanley Woodland*)], [Torben Meyer (*French diplomat*)], [Guy Usher (*President, Chamber of Commerce*)], [Moy Ming (*Diplomat*)], [Willie Wong, Pat Somerset, Phil Tead, Jimmy Phillips, Luke Chan,

Jack Chefe, Colin Kenny (*Reporters*)], [Eddie Lee (*Servant*)], [Jehim Wong (*Ricksha boy*)], [Gladden James (*Forrest, Marloff's valet*)], [William Kum (*Porter*)], [Sam Tong, Walter Wong (*Waiters*)], [Ed Hart, Russell Hopton (*"G" men*)], [Frank Darien, Harrison Greene (*Tourists*)], [Regina Rambeau].

Detective, Drama. [*Print viewed*]. Before Honolulu detective Charlie Chan leaves his boat upon arriving in Shanghai for his first visit in years, supposedly a vacation, a man stuffs a note in his pocket warning him not to leave the ship. At the docks, Chan is greeted by Sir Stanley Woodland's secretary, Philip Nash, and Sir Stanley's niece Diana, before he is surprised by his son Lee, who was sent by his firm to look into the trade situation there. At a banquet that evening in Chan's honor, as Sir Stanley opens a jade box supposedly containing a scroll for Chan, he is shot by a gun set to go off from inside the box. The box had been in Nash's possession all day. Later that night, a man sneaks into Chan's room and, with a silencer on his gun, shoots the figure in Chan's bed and escapes. Chan, fortunately, had slept on a sofa in his son's room and propped pillows to resemble his figure in the bed. The next day, when Chan calls for room service, the switchboard operator telephones Ivan Marloff to inform him that Chan is still alive. Chan next visits Diana and learns that during the previous evening, someone broke into her father's library and searched through his papers. Chan returns to his room where a man identifying himself as the chauffeur of Colonel Watkins, the chief of police, gives him a note instructing Chan to accompany the chauffeur. After Chan leaves, Lee, realizing the ruse, tries to follow his father, but he is subdued by a taxi driver and taken to the house where Chan is being interrogated by Marloff, who is hidden in darkness. Chan and Lee trick the gang into believing that the police have followed Lee, and through Lee's vigorous fisticuffs, manage to escape. Chan then visits James Andrews, a secret agent from Washington, and they discuss Sir Stanley, a secret agent of the British government who was cooperating with the opium committee of the League of Nations and officials in the Chinese government to round up a gang of smugglers who use Shanghai as a clearinghouse. While they talk, Nash, now Andrews' secretary, searches through his belongings. Noticing in a mirror a gun at the door, Chan ducks and avoids being shot. When Nash's fingerprints are found on the gun, he is arrested. In his room, Chan heats the back of a seemingly innocuous letter marked "important" from Sir Stanley to Andrews and discovers a message, which states that Sir Stanley has made an important discovery concerning Ivan Marloff. Chan suspects Andrews because Andrews earlier did not seem interested in the letter, but Andrews then arrives and shows Chan that he knows the secret method of communication. Chan and Andrews search the house where Chan was held, and Chan finds a stamp pad in the fireplace. They then go to police headquarters, where Diana arrives to see Nash, and after she slips him a gun, they escape. Chan returns to his room to find that Lee has trailed the taxi driver who earlier abducted him to a waterfront joint called the Versailles Café. Andrews calls Chan and says that he has cracked the case. When Chan arrives at Andrews' room, he sees Andrews beat a confession out of the chauffeur that Marloff is at the Versailles Café. Andrews leaves with Chan for the café, where, meanwhile, Nash asks Marloff to put him on a boat for America. Calling Nash's escape from jail a trick arranged by Chan, Marloff hits Nash and tells his men to drop him overboard once the boat sails. Upstairs, Chan and Andrews follow the taxi driver into a room where the gang waits hidden. After Chan discovers opium packets in a wine bottle, Andrews suggests that Chan go and signal the police to run the boat to the government dock. Chan delays leaving until the police, whom Lee has called, arrive and capture the gang after a shootout. Chan reveals that it was Andrews' valet who attempted to shoot Chan earlier and that Nash's fingerprints were put on the gun with the stamp pad because the gang felt Nash knew too much about Sir Stanley's investigation. Andrews offers to remove the crooks to his government's boats, but Chan pulls a gun on him and accuses him of being the real head of the gang. Nash had discovered through Sir Stanley's correspondence that the real Andrews neither smoked nor drank, yet the man posing as Andrews earlier accepted Chan's offer of scotch and cigarettes. Lee arrives with a wire photo of Andrews, who was killed three weeks earlier in San Francisco. Chan then sends Nash to comfort Diana. Although he was earlier annoyed that his son was always tying up the phone talking to a girl, Chan allows Lee one phone call to a female friend. *Chinese Americans. Detectives. False*

arrests. Impersonation and imposture. Opium. Shanghai (China). Smuggling. Abduction. Banquets. Chauffeurs. Escapes. Fathers and sons. Fistfights. Interrogation. Nieces. Secret agents. Secretaries. Shootouts. Taxicab drivers. Telephone operators. Waterfronts.

Note: Although the character played by Frederik Vogeding is listed as "Burke" in the onscreen credits, he is called "Ivan Marloff" throughout the dialogue of the film. For more information on the series, please consult the Series Index and see the entry above for *Charlie Chan Carries On*.

Box 14 Sep 1935. *DV* 11 Jul 1935, p. 3. *DV* 3 Aug 1935, p. 3. *DV* 30 Aug 1935, p. 3. *FD* 14 Oct 1935, p. 7. *HR* 30 Aug 1935, p. 3. *MPH* 31 Aug 1935, p. 54. *MPH* 14 Sep 1935, p. 35. *NYT* 14 Oct 1935, p. 21. *Var* 16 Oct 1935, p. 23.

CHARLIE CHAN IN THE JADE MASK *see* **THE JADE MASK**

CHARLIE CHAN IN THE MURDER CHAMBER *see* **BLACK MAGIC**

CHARLIE CHAN IN THE SCARLET CLUE *see* **THE SCARLET CLUE**

CHARLIE CHAN IN THE SECRET SERVICE (Chinese Americans)
Monogram Pictures Corp. *Dist* Monogram Pictures Corp. 14 Feb **1944**; Brooklyn, NY opening: 6 Jan 1944; Prod: early Sep—mid-Sep 1943 [©Monogram Pictures Corp.; 8 Jan 1944; LP12543]. Sd; b&w. 65 min.
Series: Charlie Chan.
Prod Philip N. Krasne and James S. Burkett. *Dir* Phil Rosen. [*Asst dir* George Moskov]. *Orig scr* George Callahan. *Dir of photog* Ira Morgan. *Film ed* Martin G. Cohn. *Set designing* Dave Milton. *Set dec* Al Greenwood. *Mus dir* Karl Hajos. *Sd rec* Glen Glenn. *Prod mgr* George Moskov.
Source: Based on characters created by Earl Derr Biggers.
Cast: Sidney Toler [(*Charlie Chan*)], Mantan Moreland [(*Birmingham Brown*)], Arthur Loft [(*Jones*)], Gwen Kenyon [(*Inez Aranto*)], Sarah Edwards [(*Mrs. Hobbs*)], George Lewis [(*Paul Aranto*)], Marianne Quon [(*Iris Chan*)], Benson Fong [(*Tommy Chan*)], Muni Seroff [(*Peter Lasker*)], Barry Bernard [(*David Blake*)], Gene Stutenroth [(*Louis Vega, also known as Von Vegan*)], Eddie Chandler [(*Lewis*)], Lelah Tyler [(*Mrs. Winters*)], [George Lessey (*Slade*)], [Gene Oliver], [Davison Clark].

Detective, Mystery. [*Print viewed*]. When George Melton, an inventor developing a secret torpedo to demolish German U-Boats, mysteriously dies while opening his closet door and his secret plans disappear, the U.S. Secret Service summons detective Charlie Chan to investigate. Chan, who is visiting Washington, D.C. with his daughter Iris and son Tommy, instructs his offspring to wait for him at the hotel while he proceeds to the Melton house, but the two amateur sleuths decide to conduct their own investigation and follow him there. At the house, Chan is greeted by Secret Service agents Jones and Lewis and a roomful of people whom Melton had invited to a cocktail party prior to his death. Chan begins to question the assembled group: Mrs. Winters, a frivolous socialite; her chauffeur, Birmingham Brown; Louis Vega, a war refugee now involved in the importation of precious metals; Inez Aranto and her wheelchair-bound brother Paul; David Blake, a pompous politician; Mrs. Hobbs, Melton's housekeeper; and Peter Lasker, Vega's valet. When Vega discovers a set of forged plans hidden in the right side of the bookcase, Chan deduces that it was unlikely that Melton secreted them there because he was left-handed. Afterward, Chan sends Lewis back to headquarters to retrieve the completed coroner's report. As Chan and Mrs. Hobbs talk in a room upstairs, a mysterious figure enters the darkened hallway below and removes a painting, revealing a safe hidden behind it. Unable to open the safe, the figure disappears into the darkness. Later, Chan notices that the painting has been moved and discovers the safe. After Chan retires outside to speak to Jones in confidence, Birmingham steps up to the bar to pour himself a drink and notices the reflection of a gun trained at Chan. Birgmingham screams, causing the assailant to miss his target and flee. Chan then requests the key to the safe from Mrs. Hobbs, but soon discovers that the lock has been stripped and won't open. Proceeding to search Melton's lab, Chan, Tommy and Birmingham discover a book about electromagnetic fields written by a scientist named Von Vegan. When a shadowy assailant switches off the lights in the lab and begins to shoot at Chan and the others, Tommy hurls an explosive charge at their attacker, sending him scurrying. As Chan re-adjourns everyone in the living room, Lewis returns with the cororner's report. After scrutinizing the report, Chan calls the group into the hallway to demonstrate how Melton was murdered. Stepping into the closet, Chan pulls the light cord and explains that when Melton pulled the cord, the killer sent

a lethal dose of electricity through the light switch in the living room, causing Melton to be electrocuted. Reconvening the group in the living room, Chan accuses Vega of being the celebrated electrical engineer and author Von Vegan, whose book he found in the laboratory. Chan continues that Vega, a foreign agent, killed Melton in order to steal the scientist's plans. As Vega begins to reply, he collapses, shot in the back. After whispering something to Lewis, Chan begins to question everybody about their acquaintance with Vega. When Lewis, following Chan's instructions, accuses Inez of Vega's murder and begins to manhandle her, Paul springs from his wheelchair to defend his sister. Paul then admits that after recovering from injuries he suffered in an accident, he remained in his wheelchair to test the intentions of his political enemies. Hoping to find the secret plans, Chan reassembles the group at the wall safe, and after fiddling with the lock, he opens the safe, causing a gun secured inside to fire. Chan then deduces that because Vega was shot in the back while everyone else was standing around the piano to his front, the murder weapon must be attached to the gun display on the wall behind the couch. Chan continues that the gun was fired by an electromagnetic field triggered by a switch hidden underneath the piano and accuses Peter of pulling the switch because he was afraid that Vega would implicate him in Melton's murder. After Chan dismisses everyone, Mrs. Winters hurries to leave the room but finds the door blocked by Lewis. Explaining that because she was seated at the piano, she was the only person who could reach the switch, Chan accuses her of Vega's murder and extracts the plans which she had concealed in her fur coat. After thanking Peter for acting as a decoy, Chan concludes that Mrs. Winters killed Vega because she was his accomplice in Melton's murder and feared he would confess and incriminate her. *Chinese Americans. Detectives. Inventors. Murder. Secret plans.* Amateur detectives. Brothers and sisters. Chauffeurs. Electrocution. Fathers and daughters. Fathers and sons. Foreign agents. Handicapped. Housekeepers. Impersonation and imposture. Laboratories. Politicians. Refugees, Political. Safes. Scientists. Secret Service. Washington (D.C.).

Note: This was the first "Charlie Chan" film that Sidney Toler made at Monogram after leaving Twentieth Century-Fox. Toler, who had starred as "Chan" in many of the Fox films, bought the screen rights to the character from the widow of writer Earl Derr Bigger and continued to star as Chan for Monogram until his death in 1947, after which time Roland Winters assumed the role. For additional information on the series, please consult the Series Index and see the entry *Charlie Chan Carries On* in *AFI Catalog of Feature Films, 1931-40*; F3.0663. A modern source adds John Elliott to the cast.

Box 22 Jan 1944. *DV* 11 Jan 1944, p. 3. *FD* 19 Jan 1944, p. 10. *HR* 10 Sep 1943, p. 10. *HR* 17 Sep 1943, p. 9. *MPHPD* 15 Jan 1944, p. 1714. *Var* 12 Jan 1944, p. 24.

CHARLIE CHAN IN THE SHANGHAI COBRA *see* **THE SHANGHAI COBRA**

CHARLIE CHAN ON BROADWAY (Chinese Americans)

Twentieth Century-Fox Film Corp. *Dist* Twentieth Century-Fox Film Corp. 8 Oct **1937**; New York opening: 18 Sep 1937; Prod: 10 Jun—mid-Jul 1937 [©Twentieth Century-Fox Film Corp.; 22 Oct 1937; LP7817]. Sd (Western Electric Mirrophonic Recording); b&w. 7 reels, 6,215 ft. 68 min. PCA cert no. 3570.

Series: Charlie Chan.

Assoc prod John Stone. *Dir* Eugene Forde. *Asst dir* Samuel Schneider. *Scr* Charles Belden and Jerry Cady. *Orig story* Art Arthur, Robert Ellis and Helen Logan. *Photog* Harry Jackson. *Art dir* Lewis Creber. *Film ed* Al De Gaetano. *Cost* Herschel. *Mus dir* Samuel Kaylin. *Sd* George P. Costello and Harry M. Leonard.

Source: Based on the character "Charlie Chan" created by Earl Derr Biggers.

Cast: WARNER OLAND (*Charlie Chan*), Keye Luke (*Lee Chan*), Joan Marsh (*Joan Wendall*), J. Edward Bromberg (*Murdock*), Douglas Fowley (*Johnny Burke*), Harold Huber (*Inspector Nelson*), Donald Wood (*Speed Patten*), Louise Henry (*Billie Bronson*), Joan Woodbury (*Marie Collins*), Leon Ames (*Buzz Moran*), Marc Lawrence (*Thomas Mitchell*), Tashia [sic] Mori (*Ling Tse*), Charles Williams (*Meeker*), Eugene Borden (*Louie*), [William Jeffrey (*Coroner*)], [Sidney Fields (*Porter*)], [Norman Ainsley (*Steward*)], [Philip Morris (*Customs officer*)], [George Regas (*Hindu*)], [Sherry Hall, Creighton Hale, Allen Fox, Franklin Parker, Don Brodie, Billy Wayne (*Reporters*)], [Allen Wood (*Bellhop*)], [George Guhl (*Smitty*)], [Jack Dougherty, Harry Strang, Don Rowan, Eddie Dunn, Carl Faulkner, Lee Shumway, Harry Burns (*Policemen*)], [Billy

O'Brien (*Copyboy*)], [James Blaine (*Detective*)], [Beulah Hutton (*Telephone operator*)], [Harry Depp (*Snapper*)], [Gloria Roy (*Hat check girl*)], [Sam Ash (*Waiter*)], [Blue Washington, Allan Cavan (*Doormen*)], [Art Miles (*Porter*)], [Henry Otho, Monte Vandergrift, Jack Clifford, James Flavin (*Detectives*)], [Charles Haefeli (*Pickpocket*)], [Victor Adams (*Gangster*)], [Paddy O'Flynn, Lester Dorr (*Photographers*)], [Edwin Stanley (*Laboratory expert*)], [Robert Middlemass (*Police official*)].

Detective, Drama. [*Print viewed*]. On an ocean liner approaching New York, a man unsuccessfully tries to steal a small package hidden in a woman's stateroom. The woman then hides the package in the room next to hers, which belongs to the celebrated Honolulu detective Charlie Chan and his son Lee. In New York, newspaper reporter Speed Patten slips into a cab with the woman, whom he knows as Billie Bronson, and she promises to meet him at her hotel at midnight if he will keep quiet. As Speed reports the potential story to his editor Murdock, Murdock gets a call from Billie, who demands twice the amount he was willing to pay one year ago, and he sets up a meeting with her that night. Billie then bribes a bellhop for a key to Chan's room. As she tries to enter, Billie is spotted by Lee, and he follows her to the Hottentot Club, owned by racketeer Johnny Burke. There, mobster Buzz Moran warns Billie to get out of town before morning, after which she goes to Burke's office. Meanwhile, Speed, who has come to the club with photographer Joan Wendall, follows Burke to meet Billie. Billie accuses Burke, her former lover, of giving her the "runaround" because of his involvement with Marie Collins, a dancer in the club, and pulls a gun on Burke as Marie opens the door. Later that day, Inspector Nelson gets word that Billie has been killed and that Lee is being held as a suspect. Nelson orders Lee's release and questions Speed, Burke, Marie and Joan. At the crime scene, Chan notices that a napkin placed over a tray is not in a photograph which Joan took at the time of the murder. Just then, Louie, Burke's man, turns out the lights, and during a scuffle, Burke escapes. When the lights go on, Chan reveals that the key to his hotel room, which is present in the photograph, is now missing along with the napkin. Chan, Lee and Nelson return to Chan's room, where they find that the man on the boat who tried to rob Billie has just been killed. Marie then enters and recognizes him as her husband, Tom Mitchell. On the floor, Chan finds a crumpled page of a diary, which, he realizes, Mitchell was after. Chan finds Murdock in Billie's room, and Murdock explains that he was waiting to buy Billie's diary, which has information on racketeers and politicians in the city. The next day, after reading Speed's newspaper account of the murder, Moran confronts Burke. After Burke knocks down Moran, Moran shoots at him and misses. With his lawyer, Burke goes to police headquarters, where a parafin test to determine whether there are traces of gun powder on his hands proves to be negative. Chan reminds Nelson that the napkin may have been used to cover the gun and warns Burke that he is still investigating him. When Burke finds Lee in his room trying to reconstruct the murder, he gives a black eye to Lee, who hits him back before being thrown out. Burke tries to leave town, but he is apprehended at the airport, along with Marie, and taken back to his office, where Murdock and Moran are also brought. Chan, Lee, Speed, Joan and Nelson also arrive at Burke's office, where Chan reveals that Mitchell was trying to get Billie's diary to ruin Burke, who stole his wife. Murdock then shows a page from the diary, which says that Speed used his newspaper job as a cover for blackmailing. Speed calls the page phony, and Chan accuses him of murder. Chan explains that he first suspected Speed when his newspaper account mentioned that Billie was shot in the back, a fact known only to the police and the murderer. Chan also reveals that he and Nelson planted the phony diary page to draw Speed out. Speed pulls a gun and confesses that he killed Billie because she was going to the district attorney with the diary, which implicated him. He then found Mitchell with the diary and killed him. He is about to shoot Chan when Lee jumps him. In the struggle, Speed is disarmed, while Lee gets a second black eye. *Chinese Americans. Detectives. Diaries. Murder. Reporters.* Bellboys. Blackmail. Bribery. Dancers. Editors. Fathers and sons. Gangsters. Hotels. Keys. New York City. Nightclubs. Ocean liners. Photographs. Police inspectors. Racketeers.

Note: Thomas Beck is listed as a cast member in early *HR* production charts, but his participation in the final film is doubtful. For more information on the series, please consult the Series Index and see the entry above for *Charlie Chan Carries On.*

Box 7 Aug 1937. *DV* 28 Jul 1937, p. 3. *FD* 18 Oct 1937, p. 14. *HR* 5 Jun 1937, p. 2. *HR* 14 Jun 1937, p. 17. *HR* 6 Jul 1937, p. 7. *HR* 9 Jul 1937, p. 6. *HR* 28 Jul 1937, p. 2. *MPD* 31 Jul 1937, p. 3. *MPH* 7 Aug 1937, p. 54. *NYT* 20 Sep 1937, p. 19. *Var* 22 Sep 1937, p. 18.

CHARLIE CHAN'S CHANCE (Chinese Americans)

Fox Film Corp. *Dist* Fox Film Corp. 24 Jan **1932**; New York opening: 22 Jan 1932; Prod: 16 Nov—early Dec 1931 [©Fox Film Corp.; 29 Dec 1931; LP2752]. Sd; b&w. 7 reels, 6,400 or 6,749 ft. 71 or 73 min.

Series: Charlie Chan.

Dir John Blystone. *Asst dir* Jasper Blystone. *Scr* Barry Conners and Philip Klein. *Photog* Joseph August. *2d cam* Charles Fetters. *Asst cam* Harry Webb and Lou Kunkel. *Art dir* Gordon Wiles. *Film ed* Alex Troffey. *Cost* David Cox. *Sd rec* Albert Protzman. *Still photog* Alexander Kahle.

Source: Based on the novel *Behind That Curtain* by Earl Derr Biggers (Indianapolis, 1928).

Cast: Warner Oland (*Charlie Chan*), Alexander Kirkland (*John [R.] Douglas*), H. B. Warner (*Inspector Fife*), Marian Nixon (*Shirley Marlowe*), Linda Watkins (*Gloria Garland*), James Kirkwood (*Inspector Flannery*), Ralph Morgan (*Barry Kirk*), James Todd (*Kenneth Dunwood*), Herbert Bunston (*Garrick Enderly*), James Wang (*Kee Lin*), Joe Brown (*Doctor*), Charles McNaughton (*Paradise*), Edward Peil, Sr. (*Li Gung*).

Detective, Drama. [*Not viewed*]. Charlie Chan, of the Honolulu police, and Inspector Fife of Scotland Yard tour the offices of the New York Police Department with Inspector Flannery, in order to study New York police methods. While dining at a Chinese restaurant, Fife receives a phone call informing him that Sir Lionel Grey, former chief of Scotland Yard, has dropped dead in the offices of Barry Kirk in Wall Street, which was his base of operations. Fife, Flannery and Chan go to the crime scene, and Kirk informs the group that, before his death, Grey was about to solve a big murder case and had invited several guests to a party; he had left the party to take a phone call in Kirk's office and then died mysteriously. The doctor assures the group that Grey died of a heart attack, but Chan notices a dead cat in the room and surmises that the same substance killed them both and that Grey was indeed murdered. The assembled guests are queried, and all seem to be hiding something. In the office, the police discover that the safe has been robbed—a possible motive for the crime—and learn that John R. Douglas, a chemical manufacturer, had made the last phone call to Grey. Chan decides to stay on for the investigation. At a café, Shirley Marlowe meets with John, and he tells her that Grey demanded to know the whereabouts of an Alan Raleigh and threatened to take Shirley, Raleigh's former lover, back to England as an accessory to murder if John would not give the information. John then asks Shirley to marry him. After an interview with one of the assembled guests, Chan is led to Shirley, who confesses to Chan that she fell in love with Raleigh before she discovered the crime that he had committed, which Grey was investigating. When informed, Shirley fled, and she has been pursued by Scotland Yard ever since. Chan promises to keep Shirley's secret and goes to find Li Gung, Raleigh's houseboy. Back at Kirk's office, it is revealed to Kenneth Dunwood, another guest on the night of the murder, and Kirk that gas masks were found at John's chemical factory, which implicates John. Shirley sends a letter to Chan, indicating her plan to tell the police everything. As Shirley prepares to go to the station, an unidentified man drops a gas bomb in her car in an attempt to poison her, but the bomb kills her chauffeur instead. At the station, John is brought in, and he denies his acquaintance with Shirley until she tells him that she's confessed everything. He informs the group that he saw a "Chinaman" enter the building with a basket the day he met with Grey. Chan goes again to Li Gung's home, and the former houseboy tries to kill him with a cleverly designed hidden gun, but a black cat upsets the setup, and the gun shoots Li Gung instead. At the check-in room of the Cosmopolitan Club, Chan discovers Grey's briefcase, which he ascertains from the register was checked in after the murder. He calls Fife and Flannery to watch with him who retrieves it, and the trio are surprised to see Kirk claim the important item. At Kirk's office, the crime solving trio wait with the members of the original party, plus Shirley. When Kirk arrives, Flannery instructs him to answer the door and pretend to be alone. Dunwood enters and thanks Kirk for getting his briefcase. Kirk asks Dunwood when he got his membership card to the club, and it is revealed that Dunwood had not been to the club that day as he had said, but had dropped the case

off just after the murder. Shirley identifies Dunwood as Alan Raleigh, and Dunwood grabs Chan's unloaded gun and covers the group, but Chan quickly subdues him. The lovers, John and Shirley, embrace as Fife announces that Scotland Yard will close the case. The men shake hands and Flannery commends Chan on his crime-solving brilliance. *Chinese Americans. Detectives. Murder. Attempted murder. Capitalists and financiers. Cats. Chemists. Clubs. Gases, Asphyxiating and poisonous. Houseboys. Impersonation and imposture. New York City. Parties. Proposals (Marital). Safes. Scotland Yard (London, England).*

Note: The novel was published serially in *The Saturday Evening Post*, 31 Mar-5 May 1928. The plot summary was based on a screen continuity in the Twentieth Century-Fox Produced Scripts Collection at the UCLA Theater Arts Library. Fox produced a film based on the same source entitled *Behind That Curtain* in 1929, which starred Warner Baxter and E. L. Park and was directed by Irving Cummings (see *AFI Catalog of Feature Films, 1921-30*; F2.0330). For information concerning the Charlie Chan series, please consult the Series Index and the note to *Charlie Chan Carries On* (see above).

FD 24 Jan 1932, p. 11. *HF* 5 Dec 1931, p. 12. *HR* 24 Dec 1931, p. 2. *IP* Feb 1932, p. 33. *MPH* 9 Jan 1932, p. 36. *NYT* 23 Jan 1932, p. 18. *Var* 26 Jan 1932, p. 23.

CHARLIE CHAN'S COURAGE (Chinese Americans)

Fox Film Corp. *Dist* Fox Film Corp. 6 Jul **1934**; Prod: 23 Apr—late May 1934 [©Fox Film Corp.; 6 Jul 1934; LP4813]. Sd; b&w. 7 reels, 6,589 ft. 70-72 or 74 min.

Series: Charlie Chan.

Prod John Stone. *Exec prod* Winfield R. Sheehan. *Dir* George Hadden and Eugene Forde. *Asst dir* Sid Bowen. *Scr* Seton I. Miller. *Photog* Hal Mohr and Arthur Miller. *Cam op* Joseph La Shelle. *Asst cam* W. Abbott and S. McDonald. *Settings* Duncan Cramer. *Film ed* Alex Troffey. *Gowns* Royer. *Mus dir* Samuel Kaylin. *Sd* Alfred Bruzlin. *Still photog* Bill Thomas.

Source: Based on the novel *The Chinese Parrot* by Earl Derr Biggers (Indianapolis, 1926).

Cast: Warner Oland (*Charlie Chan*), Drue Leyton (*Paula Graham*), Donald Woods (*Bob Crawford*), Paul Harvey (*J. P. Madden/Jerry Delaney*), Murray Kinnell (*Martin Thorne*), Reginald Mason (*Alexander Crawford*), Virginia Hammond (*Sally Jordan*), Si Jenks (*Will Holley*), Harvey Clark (*Professor Gamble*), Jerry Jerome (*Maydorf*), Jack Carter (*Victor Jordan*), James Wang (*Wong*), De Witt C. Jennings (*Sergeant Brackett*), Francis Ford (*Hewitt*), Lucille Miller (*Stenographer*), Mary McLaren (*Mother*), Gail Kaye (*Child*), Larry Fisher (*Taxi driver*), Sam McDaniels (*Porter*), Carl Stockdale (*Station lounger*), Lita Chevret, Susan Fleming (*Chorus girls*), Caryl Lincoln (*Leading lady*), John David Horsley (*Leading man*), George Magrill (*Heavy*), Frank Mills (*Prop man*), Sherry Hall (*Assistant director*), James P. Burtis (*Eddie Boston*), Paul McVey (*Director*), Wade Boteler (*Bliss*), Teru Shimada (*Jiu jitsu man*), Paul Hurst, Frank Rice.

Detective, Drama. [*Not viewed*]. Mrs. Sally Jordan asks her faithful, former houseboy, Charlie Chan, now a detective with the Honolulu police force, to personally transport to El Dorado a pearl necklace that she has sold to millionaire J. P. Madden, as something seems suspicious in the transaction. Bob Crawford, son of the jewelry store owner who has set up the deal, precedes Chan to Madden's house to insure that the place is safe and, on the train, meets Paula Graham, a film director's assistant traveling to El Dorado to arrange a film shoot on Madden's property. As they approach the ranch by cab, they hear gunshots. Inside the house, Martin Thorne, Madden's secretary, bends over a body in the bedroom and, when he answers Paula and Bob's knock, tells them that Madden is away and urges Bob to stay, though Bob has revealed that the pearls will arrive the next day by messenger. Chan arrives the next day dressed as a menial, calling himself "Ah Kim," and Thorne hires him as the new cook, as the regular cook is away. While snooping around, Chan notices that a revolver from Madden's collection has been removed and used recently. In Madden's bedroom, he finds bullet holes in the wall and blood stains on the carpet, which someone had attempted to conceal. Believing Madden to have been murdered by Thorne, Bob is amazed when Jerry Delaney, whom he believes to be Madden, shows up. As Bob and Chan drive into the garage one night, they find the dead body of the former cook. The cook's talking Chinese parrot, who made comments suggestive of a murder, is then discovered poisoned, which reveals to Chan that both the cook and the bird witnessed something amiss. Delaney demands that the necklace be handed over, and privately Bob asks Chan for the goods, but Chan is not yet convinced that everything is as it should be and holds on to Mrs. Jordan's property. Chan and Bob

discover a suitcase in the attic that belongs to Delaney and ascertain that he arrived by train the night before Bob's arrival. The movie crew finally arrives, and when the director asks Paula to investigate an old mine where he wants to shoot a scene, a crook jumps out and attacks her. Bob goes looking for Paula, discovers her at the mine and struggles with the crook before finally overpowering him. Paula tells Bob that there is another captive in the mine, Madden. Soon after, Victor Jordan, Sally Jordan's son, arrives at the Madden ranch and blows the whole investigation by telling Delaney that Bob should have handed over the pearls days earlier and demanding that Chan, or "Ah Kim," deliver the pearls as his mother instructed. Delaney uses his left hand to sign a receipt, and Chan, knowing Madden to be right-handed, grabs the pearls and pulls a gun on him. Sergeant Brackett arrives and doesn't believe that "Ah Kim" is really Chan; he gives the pearls back to Delaney, just as Madden enters with a bandaged shoulder. Madden reveals that Delaney, his look alike, has a history of impersonating him and accuses Thorne, rightly, of double-crossing him. The case solved and the pearls safely delivered, Paula, Bob and Chan travel back to San Francisco, and on the rear train platform, Paula and Bob embrace happily. *Chinese Americans. Detectives. Doubles. Impersonation and imposture. Murder. Necklaces. Abduction. Cooks. Fights. Millionaires. Mines. Motion picture crews. Parrots. Ranches. Rescues. Secretaries.*

Note: The plot summary was based on a screen continuity in the Twentieth Century-Fox Produced Scripts Collection at the UCLA Theater Arts Library. Sources conflict concerning the credits for director and cameraman. While production charts list both George Hadden and Eugene Forde as directors and Arthur Miller as the cameraman, reviews and the Fox trade paper advertising billing sheet credits only Hadden as director and lists Hal Mohr as the cameraman. According to a pressbook for the film, this was Hadden's first directorial assignment; he had been theatrical producer David Belasco's "right-hand man" during the last six years of Belasco's life, and had also worked as a dialogue director in films. According to *MPH*, some scenes in this film were shot in the Mojave Desert. Universal Pictures produced a film based on the same source in 1927 entitled *The Chinese Parrot*, directed by Paul Leni and starring Marian Nixon and K. Sojin (see above). For more information on the series, please consult the Series Index and see the entry above for *Charlie Chan Carries On*.

Box 14 Jul 1934. *DV* 23 Apr 1934, p. 2. *DV* 29 Jun 1934, p. 3. *FD* 25 Aug 1934, p. 3. *Har* 21 Jul 1934, p. 114. *HF* 28 Apr 1934, p. 8. *HR* 30 Apr 1934, p. 6. *HR* 21 May 1934, p. 10. *IP* Jun 1934, p. 21. *MPD* 3 Jul 1934, p. 7. *MPH* 26 May 1934, p. 32. *MPH* 1 Sep 1934, p. 33. *NYT* 25 Aug 1934, p. 16. *Var* 28 Aug 1934, p. 15.

CHARLIE CHAN'S GREATEST CASE (Chinese Americans)

Fox Film Corp. *Dist* Fox Film Corp. 15 Sep **1933**; Prod: began mid-Jul 1933 [©Fox Film Corp.; 29 Aug 1933; LP4105]. Sd; b&w. 8 reels, 6,200 ft. 70-71 min. PCA cert no. 1232-R [17 Aug 1935].

Series: Charlie Chan.
Prod Sol M. Wurtzel. *Dir* Hamilton MacFadden. *Asst dir* Percy Ikerd. *Scr* Lester Cole and Marion Orth. *Photog* Ernest Palmer. [*Cam op* Don Anderson]. [*Asst cam* Stanley Little and Robert Mack]. *Settings* Duncan Cramer. *Ed* Alex Troffey. *Gowns* Royer. *Mus dir* Samuel Kaylin. *Sd* George Leverett. [*Asst sd* W. T. Brent]. [*Still photog* Cliff Maupin].
Source: Based on the novel *The House Without a Key* by Earl Derr Biggers (Indianapolis, 1925).
Cast: Warner Oland (*Chalie Chan*), Heather Angel (*Carlotta Eagan*), Roger Imhof (*The beachcomber*), John Warburton (*John Quincy Winterslip*), Walter Byron (*Harry Jennison*), Ivan Simpson (*T. M. Brade*), Virginia Cherrill (*Barbara Winterslip*), Francis Ford (*Captain Hallett*), Robert Warwick (*Dan Winterslip*), Frank McGlynn (*Amos Winterslip*), Clara Blandick (*Minerva Winterslip*), Claude King (*Captain Arthur Temple Cope*), William Stack (*James Eagan*), Gloria Roy (*Arlene Compton*), Cornelius Keefe (*Steve Leatherbee*).

Detective, Drama. [*Not viewed*]. Brothers Amos and Dan Winterslip discuss Dan's latest amour, a shady lady named Arlene Compton of whom the moralistic Amos does not approve. Dan, the family ingrate, throws his brother out of his Honolulu house, and his sister Minerva arrives with the news that another family member, cousin John Quincy Winterslip, is being sent to Honolulu to bring her back to Boston as, in the family's opinion, she's having too much fun. Dan sobers when he sees a newspaper item about the arrival to the islands of a T. M. Brade. During a stopover in San Francisco, John's uncle Roger gives him a strongbox marked "T. M. B." and instructs him to throw it into the Pacific the next day, per Dan's orders. As John is about to toss the box into the sea, he is tackled by an unidentified man who steals the box. On deck, Harry Jennison, Dan's lawyer, and

Barbara, Dan's daughter, also traveling back to Honolulu, decide to marry and telegram Dan with the news. When Dan goes to see Arlene to ask that she return an emerald brooch he had given her as a gift, she lies and says that the brooch is at the jeweler's being repaired and promises to bring it to him later. That evening, the captain on the passenger ship announces a smallpox quarantine that requires the passengers to stay on board until morning. At Dan's home, Minerva finds a prowler and then discovers Dan dead in his den. Captain Hallett at the police station receives the report of the murder, and police detective Charlie Chan is woken up along with his household of several children. At the crime scene, the doctor reports that Dan has been stabbed in the heart and that his arm has been broken. Chan questions Minerva, who remembers only one identifying characteristic of the prowler: a glow-in-the-dark wristwatch with a blurred numeral two. She also tells Chan that she remembers a James Eagan of the Reef & Palm Hotel calling repeatedly the day before the murder. At the hotel, Eagan tries to leave, but Chan reminds him that he had an engagement with Dan, which he had canceled. Eagan admits that Dan insisted on seeing him the night of the murder and that the two met after 11:00 in Dan's garden. Eagan, who hadn't spoken to Dan in twenty-three years, refuses to reveal to Chan the nature of their business transaction. Carlotta, Eagan's daughter, whom John had met on the boat to Honolulu, rebukes John, who has accompanied Chan to the hotel, for questioning her father. Meanwhile, as Carlotta watches the desk of the hotel, Brade, a guest, informs her that he'll be going away for a few days. Koahla, Dan's houseboy, enters with a strongbox for Brade, but leaves when he discovers the latter's absence. Seeing Koahla hiding in some bushes on the hotel grounds, John attacks him and retrieves the box. John now gives the strongbox, which he had earlier tossed into the ocean, to Chan, but they find it empty. Chan finds Amos' dead body on the grounds of the hotel and captures a beachcomber who wears the glowing wristwatch. Later, Chan assembles all the possible suspects at Dan's house for a final meeting at which he plans to reveal the identity of the murderer. When Chan asks Brade about the box, Brade says that Dan stole jewels from his father thirty-five years earlier when Dan was a mate on his father's ship, and that he has scrimped and saved for many years for the chance to reclaim his due. When the emerald brooch, which was found at the crime scene, is produced, both Arlene and Brade claim it. Chan then produces a check for $5,000 which Dan had made out to Eagan, and when Eagan still refuses to explain his relationship with Dan, Chan tells Hallett to arrest him. Carlotta cries out at the injustice and admits that she read her father's diary, which told of an incident thirty-five years earlier in which Eagan, a young bank teller, changed Dan's South American gold into Australian currency. Eagan, being the only man alive who could identify Dan as the thief of Brade's gold, tried to blackmail him. Koahla then admits that he knew of Dan's fear of Brade and stole the box in San Francisco in order to blackmail Dan. Chan then has his son bring in Berkeley, another passenger on the boat, and claims that he is the murderer, as water and seaweed found at the scene of the crime prove that someone swam from the ship on the evening in question. Berkeley tries to make a run for it, but he is caught by Jennison, who breaks his arm in the same fashion that Dan's arm was fractured. Chan then dramatically accuses the real murderer, Jennison, and admits that Berkeley was playing an assigned role. Chan also reveals that Dan's reply to Barbara and Jennison's wedding announcement never reached Barbara and contained a warning to Jennison that unless he broke the engagement, Barbara would be disinherited and the robbery exposed despite injury to both Jennison and himself. Tan lines on Jennison's wrist reveal that he is indeed the owner of the watch, which he lost in the surf, where the beachcomber picked it up following the murder. Jennison pulls an unloaded gun from Chan's pocket, and Chan has no difficulty subduing him. The caper solved, John and Carlotta embrace contentedly in front of the Reef & Surf Hotel, as Chan and family drive by in a new car, a gift from Minerva. *Chinese Americans. Detectives. Honolulu (HI). Murder. Bank tellers. Beachcombing. Blackmail. Brothers. Cousins. Diaries. Fathers and daughters. Hotels. Houseboys. Jewelry. Lawyers. Mistresses. Ocean liners. Revenge. Robbery. San Francisco (CA). Watches.*

Note: The plot summary was based on a screen continuity in the Twentieth Century-Fox Produced Scripts Collection at the UCLA Theater Arts Library. The novel was also published in serial form in *The Saturday Evening Post* (24 Jan-7 Mar 1925). *The House Without a Key* was the first novel in which the character "Charlie Chan" appeared. In 1926, Pathé produced a serial based on

the same source entitled *The House Without a Key*, directed by Spencer Bennett and starring Allene Ray and Walter Miller. For information concerning other films featuring the character of Charlie Chan, please consult the Series Index and see the entry above for *Charlie Chan Carries On*.

FD 7 Oct 1933, p. 4. *HF* 15 Jul 1933, p. 8. *IP* Aug 1933, p. 34. *MPD* 7 Oct 1933, p. 2. *MPH* 5 Aug 1933, p. 36. *MPH* 14 Oct 1933, p. 34, 36. *NYT* 7 Oct 1933, p. 18. *Var* 10 Oct 1933, p. 23.

CHARLIE CHAN'S MURDER CRUISE (Chinese Americans)

Twentieth Century-Fox Film Corp. *Dist* Twentieth Century-Fox Film Corp. 21 Jun **1940**; New York opening: week of 2 May 1940; Prod: began late Jan 1940 [©Twentieth Century-Fox Film Corp.; 21 Jun 1940; LP9750]. Sd (Western Electric Sound System); b&w. 6,315 ft. 70 or 75 min. PCA cert no. 6084.

Series: Charlie Chan.

Exec prod Sol M. Wurtzel. *Assoc prod* John Stone. *Dir* Eugene Forde. [*Asst dir* Saul Wurtzel]. *Scr* Robertson White and Lester Ziffren. *Dir of photog* Virgil Miller. *Art dir* Richard Day and Chester Gore. *Film ed* Harry Reynolds. *Set dec* Thomas Little. *Cost* Helen A. Myron. *Mus dir* Samuel Kaylin. *Sd* Joseph E. Aiken and William H. Anderson.

Source: Based on the novel *Charlie Chan Carries On* by Earl Derr Biggers (Indianapolis, 1930).

Cast: Sidney Toler (*Charlie Chan*), Marjorie Weaver (*Paula Drake*), Lionel Atwill (*Dr. Suderman*), Sen Yung (*Jimmy Chan*), Robert Lowery (*Dick Kenyon*), Don Beddoe (*James Ross*), Leo G. Carroll (*Professor Gordon*), Cora Witherspoon (*Susie Watson*), Kay Linaker (*Mrs. Pendleton*), Harlan Briggs (*Coroner*), Charles Middleton (*Mr. [Jeremiah] Walters*), Claire Du Brey (*Mrs. Walters*), Leonard Mudie (*Gerald Pendleton*), James Burke (*Wilkie*), Richard Keene (*Buttons*), Layne Tom, Jr. (*Willie Chan*), Montague Shaw (*Inspector Duff*).

Detective. [*Print viewed*]. Inspector Duff of Scotland Yard visits Charlie Chan in Honolulu to enlist his aid in trapping a strangler who is lurking among ten members of a world cruise being conducted by Dr. Suderman. Before the inspector can divulge his plan, however, he falls victim to the strangler, and Chan begins his own investigation into the murders. His first stop is a visit to the members of Suderman's party, but when he arrives at the hotel, he finds that another murder has just been committed. The victim, Kenyon, is discovered with a bag containing thirty pieces of silver, and Chan deduces that the man was killed in the room of fellow passenger Gerald Pendleton and his body dragged into Kenyon's room. Chan meets the remaining members of the party when Susie Watson screams upon sighting a man on her balcony, and the group assembles in her room to discover that there is a killer in their midst. In addition to Suderman, the party consists of Kenyon's nephew Dick, Susie's secretary Paula Drake, playboy James Ross, Professor Gordon, an archaeologist, the jumpy Gerald Pendleton and the puritanical Mr. and Mrs. Jeremiah Walters. In a panic, they resume their voyage to San Francisco, and amid a sea of false clues, they share a rather uneventful cruise until Pendleton is murdered on the night that the ship is to dock. Chan finds the traces of a warning that Pendleton had wired to his wife, and deducing that the murderer was absent from the farewell party held at the time of Pendleton's demise, Chan begins to develop negatives from the pictures taken during the party, but the killer steals the evidence. As he flees, the murderer is shot and unmasked as Ross. However, Chan remains skeptical, and at the coroner's inquest, he produces Mrs. Pendleton, who explains that the killer is her demented, vengeful ex-husband and that Ross was only his accomplice. Chan then tricks Gordon into trying to kill his ex-wife, thus exposing him as the true murderer. *Chinese Americans. Cruises. Detectives. Impersonation and imposture. Murder. Revenge. Strangling. Coroners. Fathers and sons. Honolulu (HI). Hotels. Nephews. Parties. Photographs. Playboys. Police inspectors. Professors. San Francisco (CA). Secretaries. Ships.*

Note: The working titles of this film were *Charlie Chan's Cruise, Charlie Chan's Oriental Cruise, Chan's Cruise* and *Chan's Murder Cruise*. According to materials contained in the Twentieth Century-Fox Produced Scripts Collection at the UCLA Theater Arts Library, Robert Ellis and Helen Logan wrote the first treatment for this film, which was followed by a treatment and screenplay written by John Larkin. Their contribution to the final film has not been determined, however. In 1931, Fox filmed another version of Earl Derr Biggers' novel titled *Charlie Chan Carries On* (see above). For additional information on the series, consult the Series Index and see entry above for *Charlie Chan Carries On*.

DV 4 May 1940, p. 3. *FD* 7 May 1940, p. 16. *HR* 3 Feb 1940, pp. 8-9. *HR* 4 May 1940, p. 4. *MPD* 7 May 1940, p. 6. *MPH* 9 Mar 1940, p. 63. *MPH* 11 May 1940, p. 53. *NYT* 3 May 1940, p. 17. *Var* 8 May 1940, p. 12.

CHARLIE CHAN'S SECRET (Chinese Americans)

Twentieth Century-Fox Film Corp. *Dist* Twentieth Century-Fox Film Corp. 10 Jan **1936**; Prod: 26 Aug—21 Sep 1935 [©Twentieth Century-Fox Film Corp.; 10 Jan 1936; LP6049]. Sd (Western Electric Noiseless Recording); b&w. 8 reels, 6,500 ft. 71 min. PCA cert no. 1587.

Series: Charlie Chan.

Assoc prod John Stone. *Dir* Gordon Wiles. *Orig story and scr* Robert Ellis and Helen Logan. [*Scr*] *in collaboration with* Joseph Hoffman. *Photog* Rudolph Maté. *Art dir* Duncan Cramer and Albert Hogsett. *Film ed* Nick De Maggio. *Gowns* Helen Myron. *Mus dir* Samuel Kaylin. *Sd* Al Protzman.

Source: Based on the character "Charlie Chan" created by Earl Derr Biggers.

Cast: WARNER OLAND (*Charlie Chan*), Rosina Lawrence (*Alice Lowell*), Charles Quigley (*Dick Williams*), Henrietta Crosman (*Henrietta Lowell*), Edward Trevor (*Fred Gage*), Astrid Allwyn (*Janice Gage*), Herbert Mundin (*Baxter*), Jonathan Hale (*Warren T. Phelps*), Egon Brecher (*Ulrich*), Gloria Roy (*Carlotta*), Ivan Miller (*Morton*), Arthur Edmund Carew (*Professor Bowan*), [Jerry Miley (*Allen Coleby*)], [William Norton Bailey (*Harris*)], [James T. Mack (*Fingerprint man*)], [Landers Stevens (*Coroner*)], [Francis Ford (*Boat captain*)], [Sid Jordan (*Expert marksman*)], [Charles Earnest (*Diver*)].

Detective, Drama. [*Print viewed*]. During the search for bodies among the wreckage of a boat lost in a storm near Hawaii, detective Charlie Chan finds a diary of Alan Coleby, heir to his father's fortune, which indicates that he was on board and that attempts had recently been made on his life. Chan cables Henrietta Lowell, matriarch of the family and the sister of Alan's deceased father, that Alan's fate is uncertain and flies to San Francisco where Mrs. Lowell, a devoted believer in "psychic research," schedules a séance. Alan returns to the Coleby estate, but upon entering, he is hit by a thrown dagger. The séance is conducted by Carlotta, a medium, and attended by her husband, Professor Bowan, whom Mrs. Lowell supports financially; Mrs. Lowell's two daughters, Alice and Janice; Alice's boyfriend, newspaper reporter Dick Williams; Janice's husband, Fred Gage; Ulrich, a disgruntled servant, who blames his daughter's suicide seven years earlier on Alan for breaking his engagement with her; and Chan. Alan's face appears in the darkened room, and when the lights are turned on, Chan discovers that Alan has been murdered. Chan arranges with Mrs. Lowell to spend the night in the house, which has many secret panels and passages, to investigate. Curious, Mrs. Lowell sneaks away from her home to join Chan in his search for clues. They find a radio receiver, which, Chan surmises, may account for the music they heard during the séance. They also discover that Alan's image appeared when a hidden ultraviolet light was directed toward his face, which was covered with quinine sulfite, a solution that glows when hit by ultraviolet light. Greatly upset, Mrs. Lowell reveals that Professor Bowan knew that if Alan were to return, her patronage would cease. As she agrees with Chan's suggestion that she revise her will, now that she is the legal heir, a shot is fired at her from a hidden doorway, but Chan pushes her out of the way. Just then, Gage enters the house and says that he came because he feared for his mother-in-law's safety. The next day, after seeing a radio transmitter in Ulrich's room, Chan visits Carlotta, who admits the use of the transmitter. She is shocked, however, to learn about the ultraviolet ray. When Chan touches her shortwave coil, Bowan switches on the current, which causes Chan to fall unconscious. Just then, the police arrive, but Bowan escapes. Inspector Morton arrests Carlotta as Chan is revived. Later that day, Mrs. Lowell announces to her family that she plans to sign a new will, which her executor Warren T. Phelps will bring at 8:30 that evening. As the church bells ring at 8:30 and Phelps drives up, Mrs. Lowell is shot through the window. Chan investigates the bell tower and finds a high powered rifle, which had been set to fire at the window when the bell was rung. After Bowan is caught, and he does not confess, Chan calls all the attendees at the first séance back and has Carlotta conduct a new one. When Mrs. Lowell's animated image appears, and it starts to speak, a dagger is thrown at the image, which cracks as the mirror on which it is reflected breaks. When the lights are turned on, Chan reveals that Mrs. Lowell is alive and that a dummy was earlier shot. Gage accuses Ulrich and they struggle, but Chan, who had put graphite on the knife, reveals graphite on Gage's hands and accuses Gage of murdering Alan Coleby to cover evidence

of forgery in the Lowell accounts. After Gage is led away, charges are dropped against Carlotta and Bowan, who agree to leave town, and Chan plans to return to his large family in Honolulu. *Chinese Americans. Detectives. Heirs. Murder. Séances. Bell towers. Charlatans. Diaries. Mediums. Mothers and daughters. Police inspectors. Professors. Radio broadcasting. Revenge. Ruses. Secret passageways. Servants. Shipwrecks. Ultraviolet radiation. Visions. Wills.*

Note: The working title of this film was *Charlie Chan in San Francisco*. In *HR* production charts, George Schneiderman is listed as photographer and Charles McNaughton as a cast member, but their participation in the final film has not been verified. For more information on the series, please consult the Series Index and see the entry above for *Charlie Chan Carries On*.

Box 9 Nov 1935. *DV* 12 Oct 1935, p. 3. *FD* 18 Jan 1936, p. 7. *HR* 26 Aug 1935, p. 7. *HR* 21 Sep 1935, p. 5. *HR* 12 Oct 1935, p. 3. *MPD* 15 Oct 1935, p. 8. *MPH* 26 Oct 1935, p. 76. *NYT* 18 Jan 1936, p. 19. *Var* 22 Jan 1936, p. 15.

CHARLIE CHAN'S ORIENTAL CRUISE *see* **CHARLIE CHAN'S MURDER CRUISE**

EL CHARRO CANTOR *see* **CUANDO CANTA LA LEY**

CHARROS, GAUCHOS Y MANOLAS (Spanish language)
Hollywood Spanish Pictures Co. Mar **1930**; World premiere in Los Angeles: 15 Mar 1930; Prod: late 1929. Sd; b&w. 9 reels. 91 min. Spanish language.

Prod Rodolfo Montes and Xavier Cugat. *Dir* Xavier Cugat. *Scr* Xavier Cugat. *Mus dir* Xavier Cugat.

Music: "Rumba de la escoba" and "Baile del patio," composers undetermined.

Song(s): "Estrellita" by Manuel M. Ponce; "Amapola" by Joseph M. Lacalle; "Mañanitas de Tepic," "Yo con tu amor sueño," "En la playa," "El negro engrupido" and "La princesita," composers undetermined.

Cast: Carmen Castillo, Delia Magaña, Samuel Pedraza, Carlos Gómez "Don Chema" (*Mexican artists*), Paul Ellis, Carmen Granada, Vicente Padula, Carlos Lucanti (*Argentinian artists*), María Alba, Martín Garralaga, Marina Ortiz, José Peña "Pepet" (*Spanish artists*), Romualdo Tirado (*Master of ceremonies*), Luis Alvarez, María Calvo, Luis Elorriaga, Manuel Conesa.

Fantasy, Musical. [*Not viewed*]. The magazine, *Paintings of the People*, initiates a contest to select the best watercolor painting of ethnic peoples and customs. A hungry, bohemian painter invokes his muse to help him to produce the winning painting, and when he experiments with scenes set in Mexico, Argentina and Spain, his paintings come to life. In Xochimilco, Mexico, a young bachelor has a drunken dream that his girl friend is performing Josephine Baker's famous banana dance in a Parisian nightclub. In Buenos Aires, an Italian and a Galician are rivals for the affections of a Creole girl. At the other side of the Hispanic world, a Sevillian girl tells of her tragic romance with a matador, who obstinately continues to appear in the ring despite having been injured. *Argentina. Artists. Bohemians and bohemianism. Contests. Mexico. Paintings. Spain. Bachelors. Josephine Baker. Bullfighters and bullfighting. Creoles. Dancers. Dreams. Drunkenness. Impersonation and imposture. Italians. Magazines. Nightclubs. Paris (France). Romance. Romantic rivalry. Spaniards.*

Note: This film's working title was *Revista musical Cugat*. Some sources indicate that the film was shot at the Tiffany Studios, while others state that it was shot at Universal Studios. These sources also include Don Alvarado and Carmen Guerrero in the cast, but their participation in the released film has not been confirmed. A contemporary news item announced that the producers would also prepare an English-language version, *Hollywood Spanish Follies*, but no evidence has been located to confirm that that film was ever made.

CM Jun 1930, p. 576. *La Opinión* 17 Mar 1930.

THE CHEAT (Japanese Americans)
Jesse L. Lasky Feature Play Co. *Dist* Paramount Pictures Corp. 13 Dec **1915** [©Jesse L. Lasky Feature Play Co., Inc.; 8 Dec 1915; LU7164]. Si; b&w. 5 reels.

Pres Jesse L. Lasky. *Dir* Cecil B. DeMille. *Scen* Hector Turnbull and Jeanie McPherson. *Cam* Alvin Wyckoff. *Art dir* Wilfred Buckland.

Cast: Fannie Ward (*Edith Hardy*), Sessue Hayakawa (*Hishuru Tori*), Jack Dean (*Dick Hardy*), James Neill (*Jones*), Utaka Abe (*Tori's valet*), Dana Ong (*District attorney*), Hazel Childers (*Mrs. Reynolds*), Judge Arthur H. Williams (*Courtroom judge*).

Society, Drama. Edith Hardy, whose obsession with expensive clothes irritates her husband Dick, a stockbroker, complains of Dick's frugality to her admirer, Hishuru Tori, a wealthy Japanese curio dealer who, like Edith, is a member of Long Island's "smart set." After

a friend gives her a stock tip on a copper company, Edith invests the $10,000 raised for the Red Cross Belgian relief fund, with which she, as treasurer, is entrusted. When the company fails, Edith frantically appeals to Tori for help, and agrees that in exchange for the money, she will come to him the next night. When Hardy tells Edith that his investments have capitalized, Edith persuades him to part with $10,000, but Tori, refusing to accept it, becomes enraged, and with his curio iron, brands his seal on her flesh. Writhing with pain, Edith shoots Tori and escapes. To protect Edith, Hardy assumes the blame, but at the trial, Edith climaxes her story by baring her branded shoulder. The enraged crowd nearly lynches Tori, as Hardy's charges are dismissed. *Branding. Embezzlement. Extravagance. Japanese Americans. Marriage. Mobs. Clothes. Curio dealers. Gunshot wounds. Long Island (NY). Racism. Red Cross. Self-sacrifice. Socialites. Speculation. Trials.*

Note: According to a news item, some of the settings in the character Hishura Tori's home contained imported Chinese carved wood furniture. The courtroom judge was former New York Appellate Court Judge Arthur H. Williams. In Feb 1916, members of the Japanese Association of Southern California filed a protest against the showing of this film with the Los Angeles City Council. This film was re-issued by Paramount on 24 Nov 1918, at which time the character played by Sessue Hayakawa was called Burmese and renamed Haka Arakau. *The Cheat* was remade in America in 1923 starring Pola Negri (see *AFI Catalog of Feature Films, 1921-30*; F2.0838); and in 1931 starring Tallulah Bankhead. Marcel L'Herbier directed a French remake in 1937 entitled *Forfaiture*, in which Hayakawa recreated his role. Camille Erlanger wrote an opera based on *The Cheat* entitled *La Forfaiture*, which was the first opera to be based on a motion picture scenario.

MPN 25 Dec 1915, p. 127. *MPW* 20 Nov 1915, p. 1479. *MPW* 18 Dec 1915, p. 2206, 2260. *MPW* 25 Dec 1915, p. 2384. *MPW* 9 Nov 1918, p. 691. *MPW* 30 Nov 1918, pp. 990-91. *NYDM* 25 Dec 1915, p. 40. *NYT* 13 Dec 1915, p. 13. *Var* 17 Dec 1915, p. 18.

CHEATED LOVE (Jewish Americans)
Universal Film Mfg. Co. 16 May **1921** [©Universal Film Mfg. Co.; 7 May 1921; LP16494]. Si; b&w. 5 reels, 4,820 ft.

Dir King Baggot. *Scen* Lucien Hubbard and Doris Schroeder. *Scen and addl story* Sonya Levien. *Photog* Bert Glennon.

Cast: Carmel Myers (*Sonya Schonema*), George B. Williams (*Abraham Schonema*), Allan Forrest (*David Dahlman*), John Davidson (*Mischa Grossman*), Ed Brady (*Scholom Maruch*), Snitz Edwards (*Bernie*), Smoke Turner (*Toscha*), Virginia Harris (*Sophia Kettel*), Inez Gomez (*Rose Jacobs*), Clara Greenwood (*Mrs. Breine*), Meyer Ouhayou (*Sam Lupsey*), Laura Pollard (*Mrs. Flaherty*), Rose Dione (*Madame Yazurka*), Theresa Gray (*Mrs. Leshinsky*), Fred G. Becker (*Charles Hensley*).

Romance. Sonya, a Jewish girl, comes to the United States as an immigrant and works in her father's ghetto grocery store, where she gains the affections of a young settlement worker, David Dahlman. But she loves Mischa, a young doctor who soon arrives from Odessa, and to aid him financially, she distinguishes herself in the local Yiddish theater. Mischa turns her down for a wealthy heiress, however, and owing to the jealousy of Yazurka, a prominent Polish actress, Sonya is refused an important role. During a performance, attended by David, there is a boiler explosion that causes panic in the theater, and Sonya comes from backstage and calms the crowd. Later, rescued by David, she accepts his admiration and love. *Actors and actresses. Explosions. Grocers. Immigrants. Jews. Physicians. Settlement workers. Theater.*

Note: This film was a remake of *The Heart of a Jewess* (United States, 1913), story by Lucien Hubbard and Doris Schroeder, from an idea by John Colton.

FD 29 May 1921.

CHECK AND DOUBLE CHECK (African Americans)
RKO Radio Productions, Inc. 25 Oct **1930**; New York premiere: 31 Oct 1930; Prod: 31 Jul–5 Sep 1930; retakes 9, 11, 16 and 22 Sep 1930. [©RKO Radio Pictures, Inc.; 8 Oct 1930; LP1616]. Sd (RCA Photophone System); b&w. 9 reels, 6,923 ft. 70-71 min. Passed by the National Board of Review.

Prod William LeBaron. *Assoc prod* Bertram Millhauser. *Dir* Melville Brown. [*Asst dir* Fred Tyler]. *Adpt and cont* J. Walter Ruben. *Story and dial* Bert Kalmar and Harry Ruby. *Photog* William Marshall. *Scenery* Max Reé. *Film ed* Claude Berkeley. *Cost* Max Reé. *Rec* George D. Ellis.

Music: "The Perfect Song," by Joseph Carl Breil; "East St. Louis Toodle-O," by James "Bubber" Miley and Duke Ellington; "Old Man Blues," by Duke Ellington and Irving Mills.

Song(s): "Three Little Words" and "Nobody Knows But the Lord," music by Harry Ruby, lyrics by Bert Kalmar.

Cast: Freeman F. Gosden (*Amos*), Charles J. Correll (*Andy*), Sue Carol [(*Jean Blair*)], Irene Rich [(*Mrs. Blair*)], Ralf Harold [(*Ralph Crawford*)], Charles S. Morton [(*Richard Williams*)], Edward Martindel [(*John Blair*)], Rita La Roy [(*Elinor Crawford*)], Russ Powell [(*Kingfish*)], Rosco Ates [(*Brother Arthur*)], Duke Ellington And His Cotton Club Orchestra, [Robert Homans (*Butler*)].

Comedy, with songs. [*Print viewed*]. Wealthy John Blair and his wife are going to the train station to meet Richard Williams, an old family friend, when a traffic jam causes them to be late. The snarl of cars is caused by Amos and Andy, two black men from Harlem who run the Freshair Taxicab Co., whose one vehicle, an old clunker without a top, refuses to start. A policeman helps the baffled Amos and Andy on their way, but the Blairs are too late to meet Richard's train. Richard takes a cab to the Blairs's country home, and on the way he meets their daughter Jean, who was his childhood sweetheart. Richard, whose family moved to the South and fell on hard times after his father's death, is instantly attracted to Jean. She reciprocates his feelings, much to the annoyance of her would-be suitor, Ralph Crawford. Meanwhile, Amos and Andy have returned to their garage office in Harlem, where they receive a phone call from their lady friends, Madame Queen and Ruby Taylor, who want them to go to a dance that evening. Amos and Andy happily agree, although they must wait to join the girls until after their meeting at their lodge, the Mystic Knights of the Sea. Kingfish, who is one of their lodge brothers, arrives and informs them that he has arranged for them to transport Duke Ellington and his Cotton Club Orchestra to the Blairs's home for Jean's birthday party. That night, Amos and Andy then drive the band to the country estate, where Ralph is becoming increasingly jealous of Richard, who has rapidly gained the approval of Mr. and Mrs. Blair. Ralph eavesdrops as Richard confides in Blair that he hopes to find the deed to a large house in Harlem, which was owned by his grandfather. Richard believes that the deed is hidden somewhere on the property and that if he can find it, he can sell the house for a large enough profit to set himself up in business and marry Jean. After his discussion with Blair, Richard runs into Amos and Andy, who used to work for his father in Georgia. Amos and Andy are thrilled to see Richard, and after they reminisce with him, they return to town and attend their lodge meeting. To honor the lodge's founder, who was lost at sea on the same day years previously, two members must go to the old Williams house, which is reputed to be haunted and find a paper marked "Check and Double Check." They then must hide a similarly marked paper to be found the following year and return the note they found to the lodge to prove their completion of the task. Andy draws the unlucky number and chooses Amos to accompany him, after which they are taken to the house and locked in. Ralph and his henchman are already at the house searching for the deed, which is instead found by Amos and Andy. When Ralph discovers Amos and Andy there, he and his henchman terrorize the pair into handing over the paper, which, much to their chagrin, turns out to be the "Check and Double Check" note. Amos and Andy are in turn very disappointed the next day when they discover that they have the deed and not the note, but Amos reasons that the deed, which bears Richard's grandfather's name, must be important and should be given to Richard. Meanwhile, at the Blair estate, Richard bids a sad farewell to Jean, for although he loves her, he feels that he cannot marry her because he did not find the deed. After Richard leaves for the train station, Amos and Andy call the Blairs to find him. They then rush to the station and find Richard just as he is boarding his train. With the deed in hand, Richard thanks Amos and Andy for insuring his future happiness. Several days later, while Amos and Andy are in their garage bemoaning the fact that Madame Queen and Ruby still have not forgiven them for breaking their date to go dancing, they receive part of Jean and Richard's wedding cake as a present. Just then, Ruby calls and tells Andy that she and Madame Queen are no longer angry with them. Amos and Andy then rush out to take the cake to their girl friends, but drop the cake in the street and it is run over by a truck. *African Americans. Deeds. Lodges (Fraternal organizations). Romance. Taxicab drivers. Tests of character. Automobiles. Birthdays. Cake. Financial crisis. Horses. Jealousy. Musicians. New York City–Harlem. Parties. Rainstorms.*

Note: The opening title card of this film reads: "Radio Pictures Presents Amos 'n' Andy (By Arrangement With National Broadcasting Company) in *Check and Double Check.*" Bert Kalmar and Harry Ruby's onscreen credit is for "Story, Dialogue and Music" and Max Rée's credit is for "Scenery and Costumes." *Check and Double Check* was the only film to feature the African-American

characters "Amos" and "Andy," the enormously popular radio personnas of white actors Freeman F. Gosden and Charles J. Correll. In the film, Gosden and Correll were made up to appear black, while on their radio show, they assumed their characters through speech mannerisms. In 1926, Gosden and Correll began their radio show in Chicago with the characters "Sam" and "Henry," who evolved into "Amos" and "Andy" two years later when the actors switched stations. In 1929, the show began broadcasting on NBC, where it stayed until 1948, when Gosden and Correll moved to CBS. Although *Amos 'n' Andy* ended in 1954, Gosden and Correll continued the characters in *The Amos and Andy Music Hall*, which was canceled in 1960, as well as supervising the *Amos 'n' Andy* television show. The television program, which was broadcast on the CBS network from Jun 1951 to Jun 1953, starred African-American actors Spencer Williams as "Andy," Alvin Childress as "Amos" and Tim Moore as "Kingfish." Only African-American actors were featured in the black roles on the television show, which was eventually canceled due to pressure from the NAACP and other groups. Despite the occasional controversy surrounding them, Gosden and Correll's characters are remembered for their astonishing popularity during the 1930s, when approximately forty million Americans tuned into their radios six nights a week to follow their adventures.

Check and Double Check received mostly positive reviews, with *Var* terming it "the best picture for children ever put on the screen." The *MPN* reviewer commented: "RKO, in making this picture, has closely watched the racial situation and is well protected against injuring the feelings of either blacks or whites. In only one scene are the two classes shown together, and then with no familiarity. Southern cities, where racial feelings may be pronounced, will find nothing in the picture to cause objection." The film did not perform well as the box office, however, and no further pictures featuring the team were produced.

"The Perfect Song," which appears over the credits, was the theme song for the "Amos 'n' Andy" radio and televison shows. Some modern sources state that "Ring Dem Bells," written by Duke Ellington and Irving Mills, was performed by Ellington and his orchestra in the film. According to a modern source interview with Ellington, Kalmar and Ruby wrote "Three Little Words" for Ellington's drummer Sonny Greer, but when Greer arrived in Hollywood, he was overcome by stage fright and did not want to sing the song in the film. The song was instead recorded by The Rhythm Boys (Bing Crosby, Harry Barris and Al Rinker) and Ellington's three trumpet players performed to a playback of the song during filming. "Three Little Words" became one of Kalmar and Ruby's most popular songs, and was the title of the 1950 M-G-M film biography of the songwriting team.

FD 12 Oct 1930. *MPN* 4 Oct 1930. *NYT* 1 Nov 1930, p. 23. *Var* 8 Oct 1930, p. 22.

CHEE-AK *see* **IGLOO**

LES CHERCHEUSES D'OR *see* **EL PRÍNCIPE DEL DÓLAR**

CHERI-BIBI (Spanish language)
Metro-Goldwyn-Mayer Corp.; controlled by Loew's, Inc. *Dist* Metro-Goldwyn-Mayer Distributing Corp. **1931**; San José, Costa Rica opening: 17 May 1931; San Juan, Puerto Rico opening: 30 May 1931; Los Angeles opening: 2 Oct 1931; Prod: 7 Jan—2 Feb 1931. Sd (Western Electric Sound System); b&w. 8 reels, 6,634 ft. 74 min. Passed by the National Board of Review. Spanish language.

Dirigida por [*Dir*] Carlos Borcosque. [*Asst dir* Bob Barnes]. *Escenificación de* [*Scr*] Bess Meredyth. *Diálogo por* [*Dial*] Edwin Justus Mayer. *Versión española de* [*Spanish version*] Miguel de Zárraga. *Fotografiada por* [*Photog*] Leonard Smith. *Director artístico* [*Art dir*] Cedric Gibbons. *Editada por* [*Ed*] Peggy O'Day. *Acústica* [*Sd*] Douglas Shearer. [*Double* Jack Chefe].

Source: Based on the novel *Chéri-Bibi et Cécily* by Gaston Leroux (Paris, 1916).

Cast: ERNESTO VILCHES (*Cheri-Bibi/Barón Max von Dyke*), María Ladrón de Guevara (*Cecilia*), María Tubau (*Vera*), Juan Martínez Plá (*Costaud*), José Soriano Viosca (*Duval*), Eduardo Arozamena (*Bourrelier*), Tito Davison (*Juan*), Manuel Arbó (*Raúl*), María Luz Callejo (*María*), Manuel París (*Lacayo*), Max Coll (*Jaimito*), Monina Lamar.

Drama. [*Not viewed*]. [The following plot summary is based on the English-language version of this film, *The Phantom of Paris*; character names refer to that version. For further information regarding the English-language version, please see the note below and the entry for *The Phantom of Paris* in the *AFI Catalog of Feature Films, 1931-40*.] At the Cirque de Paris, society magician and famous disappearing artist Chéri-Bibi performs his act before a well-heeled Parisian audience. While Cecile, his friend and admirer, waits in his dressing room, unable to watch the daring feat, Chéri, with his hands and legs bound, is lowered into a tank of water. The audience grows silent as the clock ticks away, and firemen wait on the sidelines, prepared to rescue the magician should he fail to emerge from the tank in time. To the audience's astonishment, Chéri makes his escape with little time to spare. Cecile lives with her wealthy but ailing father, Bourrelier, who recently added a codicil to his will specifying that if she were to marry the Marquis du Touchais, she would receive

a liberal allowance from his estate. However, when Bourrelier is informed that the marquis is a nobleman, he removes the allowance clause from the will so as not to spoil the young man and allow him to live an idle life. Bourrelier informs the marquis of the change at a party at his residence, and he reacts angrily, accusing Cecile's father of favoring her upstart suitor, Chéri. Bourrelier denies the accusation and later tells Chéri personally that he will not allow him to marry his daughter. Soon after the confrontation between Chéri and Bourrelier, the aged millionaire is murdered. Police Chief Costaud immediately begins an investigation into the murder and questions the guests attending the party. When the marquis is questioned, he lies to Costaud, telling him that Bourrelier privately expressed his fears about Chéri. The magician is promptly arrested and jailed. Though extra security precautions are taken to insure that Chéri does not escape, he manages to free himself from his cell. The magician then attacks a guard, takes his clothes and walks out of the prison unnoticed. Meanwhile, Dr. Gorin, a friend of Chéri's, tells the police that Chéri could not have committed the murder. Another friend of Chéri's, Herman, hides him in the basement of his shop. When Costaud pays Herman a visit, he informs him that the marquis is dying and then searches the shop. Before the police chief can find him, Chéri flees. Having overheard the news of the marquis' impending death, Chéri sneaks into his home and persuades him to admit that he killed Bourrelier. However, the marquis dies before he is able to make the confession. Chéri quickly devises a plan to save himself by bringing the body of the marquis to Dr. Gorin and asking him to perform an operation that would make him resemble the marquis. Chéri then arranges to have his own death announced publicly. The newspapers soon tell stories of the Chéri holding the marquis prisoner before his death. Six months later, Chéri, disguised as the marquis, returns to the marquis' mansion and realizes that Cecile, now married to the marquis, has been unhappy. After Cecile tells Chéri that her love for the magician has never faltered, he reveals himself to her. No sooner does Chéri tell Cecile that he loves her than Costaud and his officers arrive to question the marquis. After fingerprinting the magician, Costaud accuses Chéri of impersonating the marquis and arrests him. Again, Chéri manages to escape, and when he returns to Cecile's house, he forces Vera, the marquis' accomplice in Bourrelier's murder, to confess his guilt. Costaud overhears Vera's confession, and Chéri is vindicated of the crime. *Escapes. Impersonation and imposture. Magicians. Murder.* Confession (Law). False arrests. Fathers and daughters. Fugitives. Marriage–Arranged. Millionaires. Missing persons, Assumed dead. Nobility. Paris (France). Parties. Physicians. Plastic surgery. Police chiefs. Romantic rivalry. Wills.

Note: A *MPH* pre-production news item noted that M-G-M, in a reversal of its usual production procedure, began work on *Cheri-Bibi*, the Spanish version of the film *The Phantom of Paris* before starting on the English version. According to a 21 Jan 1931 *Var* news item, John Robertson was originally set to direct the Spanish version of the film. The onscreen credits for the Spanish version were taken from a studio cutting continuity. Alida Vischer, Luis Llaneza and Juan Duval may have been in the Spanish version, but their participation has not been confirmed. Other films based on Gaston Leroux's story include the 1937 French film *Chéri-Bibi*, directed by Léon Mathot and starring Pierre Fresnay and Jean-Pierre Aumont; and a 1955 French-Italian production, also entitled *Chéri-Bibi*, directed by Marcello Pagliero and starring Jean Richard and Lea Padovani. For information on the English-language version, *The Phantom of Paris*, which was directed by John S. Robertson and starred John Gilbert, please see the entry for that film in the *AFI Catalog of Feature Films, 1931-40*; F3.3443.

CHÉRIE (French language)
Films Paramount; controlled by Paramount Publix Corp. *Dist* Paramount Publix Corp. Dec **1931**; Paris opening: 30 Dec 1930; U.S. premiere in New York: 9 Jun 1931; *Prod*: 1930, at Paramount studios in Joinville, France. Sd (Western Electric); b&w. 7,220 ft. 80 min. *Country of origin* France. French language.
Dir Louis Mercanton. *Scr* Saint-Granier. *Photog* René Guissart.
Song(s): Music by W. Franke Harling and Sam Coslow, lyrics by Saint-Granier.
Source: Based on the novel *Come Out of the Kitchen!* by Alice Duer Miller (New York, 1916) and the play of the same name by A. E. Thomas (New York, 23 Oct 1916).
Cast: Saint-Granier (*Charles Dangerfield*), Marguerite Moreno (*Mrs. Falkner*), Mona Goya (*Olivia Dangerfield*), Janine Guise (*Cora Falkner*), Sunshine Woodward (*Doris*), Jeanne Fusier-Gir (*Mayme*), George Bever (*Weeks*), Marc-Hély (*Mr. Burnstein*), Fernand Gravey (*Burton*), Jacqueline Delubac, Charlotte Martens, Lucien Dayle.

Musical comedy. [*Not viewed*]. [The following plot summary is based on the English-language version of this film, *Honey*; character names refer to that version. For further information regarding the English-language version, please see the note below and the entry for *Honey* in the *AFI Catalog of Feature Films, 1921-30*.] Olivia Dangerfield, daughter of a proud but impoverished Virginia family, is forced to lease the family mansion to a wealthy New York widow to pay off the mortgage. When the servants fail to arrive, with the exception of Doris, a maid, she has her brother Charles impersonate the butler while she herself assumes the position of cook. Mrs. Falkner arrives with her daughter, Cora, and Burton Crane, a prospective match, but Cora falls in love with Charles, the "butler"; through little Doris, Mrs. Falkner learns of the affair, which is confirmed when she sees Charles and Cora together at a Negro jubilee. Then Doris informs Mrs. Falkner that Olivia is the owner of the house, and the incensed widow prepares to leave; but Cora and Charles announce their engagement, leaving clear the path to romance for Olivia and Burton. *Aristocrats. Courtship. Impersonation and imposture. Poverty. Servants. Virginia. Widows. African Americans.*
Note: While the 1930 English-language original, *Honey*, which was directed by Wesley Ruggles and starred Nancy Carroll and Stanley Smith, was made by Paramount in the U.S., all the foreign language versions were produced at the Paramount studios in Joinville, France. In addition to the French, Spanish and German versions, which were exhibited in the U.S., a Swedish language version, entitled *Kärlek måste vi ha*, was produced, but no information has been located concerning a U.S. release. The Swedish version, which opened in Stockholm on 16 Jan 1931, was directed by Gustaf Bergman and starred Margit Rosengren and Nils Ericsson. The working title of the Spanish version was *Dulce como la miel*. The Spanish version played in Santiago, Chile in Jul 1931 under the title *Suegra para dos*.
Alice Duer Miller's novel was filmed twice in Britain by producer Herbert Wilcox. *Come Out of the Pantry* (1935) starred Jack Buchanan and Fay Wray while *Spring in Park Lane* (1948) starred Anna Neagle and Michael Wilding.
Other language version(s):
¡Salga de la cocina! (Spanish language)
1931; Bilbao, Spain opening: 25 Feb 1931; San Juan, Puerto Rico opening: 23 May 1931; New York opening: 24 Jul 1931; *Prod*: Oct 1930 at the Paramount studios in Joinville, France. Sd; b&w. 9 reels, 7,003 ft. 78 min. Spanish language.
Dir Jorge Infante. *Scr* Herman J. Mankiewicz. *Adpt and Spanish dial* Luis Fernández Ardavín. *Photog* René Guissart.
Song(s): by W. Franke Harling and Sam Coslow.
Spanish-language cast: Roberto Rey (*Carlos*), Amparo Miguel Angel (*Alicia*), Miguel Ligero (*Burnstein*), Carmen Jiménez (*Señora Falkner*), Enriqueta Soler (*Rosario*), José Goula (*Fernando*), Paloma Luján (*Mayme*), María Luisa Fernández (*Doris*), Luis Llorens Vidal (*Weeks*). [*Spanish version not viewed*]
Jede Frau hat etwas (German language)
1931; New York opening: 15 May 1931; *Prod*: at Paramount studios at Joinville, France. Sd; b&w. 67 or 85 min. German language.
Dir Leo Mittler. *Dial* Charles Roellinghoff. *Photog* René Guissart. *Mus* W. Franke Harling.
German-language cast: Trude Berliner, Kurt Vespermann, Anny Ann, Willy Clever, Kurt Lilien, Ida Perry, Karl Harbacher. [*German version not viewed*].

CM May 1931, p. 358. FD 24 May 1931, p. 11. FD 14 Jun 1931, p. 16. Var 14 Jan 1931, p. 34. Var 20 May 1931. Var 16 Jun 1931, p. 62.

CHEROKEE UPRISING (Native Americans, Cherokee)
Monogram Pictures Corp.; A Transwestern Picture. *Dist* Monogram Pictures Corp. 8 Oct **1950**; *Prod*: began mid-Aug 1950 [©Monogram Pictures Corp.; 8 Oct 1950; LP455]. Sd (Western Electric Recording); b&w. 6 reels, 5,159 ft. 57 min. PCA cert no. 14818.
Prod Vincent M. Fennelly. *Dir* Lewis Collins. *Asst dir* Melville Shyer. *Orig scr* Dan Ullman. *Dir of photog* Gilbert Warrenton. *Art dir* Dave Milton. *Film ed* Richard Heermance. *Settings* Ray Boltz. *Set cont* Illona [sic] Vas. *Mus dir* Edward Kay. *Rec eng* Tom Lambert.
Cast: WHIP WILSON [(*Bob Foster*)], Andy Clyde [(*Jake Jones*)], Lois Hall [(*Mary Lou Harrison*)], Sam Flint [(*Judge Harrison*)], Forrest Taylor [(*William Welch*)], Marshall Reed [(*Sheriff Joe Conger*)], Iron Eyes Cody [(*Longknife*)], Chief Yowlachie [(*Gray Eagle*)], Lee Roberts [(*Kansas*)], Stanley Price [(*Smokey*)], Lyle Talbot [(*Deputy Marshal Jones*)], [Edith Mills (*Mrs. Strongbow*)].
Western. [*Print viewed*]. U.S. marshal Bob Foster and his partner, Jake Jones, are assigned to investigate a gang of white outlaws operating near Canyon City, who pay their Indian henchmen with whiskey. When Canyon City's Judge Harrison returns to his ranch, his

daughter Mary Lou and their Indian ranch hand, Gray Eagle, greet him. Nearby, Bob and Jake see one of the gang's braves, Longknife, spying on Mary Lou and Gray Eagle from the bushes. After a struggle, Longknife pretends to be knocked unconscious, and Bob and Jake decide to return for him later. As soon as they leave, however, Longknife escapes and goes into town. After telling crooked sheriff Joe Conger that he was attacked by two men, Longknife agrees to go to the gang's hideout with one of his braves, in exchange for some whiskey. At the Harrison ranch, Bob, Jake and Mary Lou listen as Gray Eagle tells them that he would like to help them fight the "bad" Indians. Later, Gray Eagle declares that Longknife is spying on his own people, so they decide to trap him. That evening, while Bob and Jake are pretending to be asleep in their bunkhouse, Longknife and an outlaw named Smokey sneak inside. Bob and Jake suddenly begin fighting with them, and Longknife escapes, but Smokey is shot in the arm while fleeing. After Harrison and Mary Lou come downstairs to see what has happened, Sheriff Conger and Deputy Marshal Jones arrive, and Harrison introduces them to Bob and Jake. At the hideout, the sheriff sends Longknife and another outlaw named Kansas to kill Gray Eagle and kidnap Mary Lou. When Bob, Jake and Harrison return to the ranch and realize what has happened, Harrison fetches the sheriff, and Bob and Jake find Mary Lou. After they return to the ranch, Mary Lou, Jake and Harrison tell the sheriff that Bob has been killed. After Jake insists on accompanying the sheriff to search for Bob's shooter, they go to the outlaws' shack. From his hiding place just outside, Bob sees Longknife sneak up on Jake and take aim at him with his bow and arrow. Bob shoots Longknife, after which he and Jake go to the hideout. Jake finds the sheriff, who draws his gun when Jake tells him that he shot Longknife in self-defense. Bob uses his whip to knock the pistol out of the sheriff's hand, then begins punching him. The sheriff finally confesses to Bob and Jake his part in the gang and warns them that the next wagon train raid will begin in a few hours. While they wait for the braves to gather at the hideout, the sheriff is about to name the gang's leader, when he is killed by an unseen assailant. Meanwhile, Indians have gathered outside the shack and begin shooting flaming arrows to set the roof on fire. Bob sneaks out through the back door, comes around behind the shooter and, after exposing him as the gang's boss, William Welch, the Indian agent, arrests him. In town, Harrison praises Bob and Jake for busting up the gang, after which Bob and Jake say farewell. *Cherokee Indians. Investigations. Outlaws. United States. Marshals. Alcoholism. Bow and arrow. Deputies. Escapes. Espionage. Gunshot wounds. Hideouts. Impersonation and imposture. Indian agents. Judges. Kidnapping. Marshals. Ranchers. Ranchhands. Searches. Self-defense. Traps. Wagon trains. Whips and whippings.*

HR 18 Aug 1950, p. 12. *MPHPD* 11 Nov 1950, p. 563. *Var* 22 Nov 1950, p. 18.

CHERRY BLOSSOM *see* **YIN HUA CHU CHU KAI**

CHEYENNE SUN DANCE (Native Americans, Cheyenne)
1934. Si; b&w. 16mm. 50 min.
Prod Forrest E. Clements.
Educational/Cultural. [*Not viewed*]. This is a field recording of the Cheyenne sun dance of 1933. The complete four-day ceremony is shown, including details of the erection of Medicine Lodge, the painting and decoration of the dancers, building of the altar, all five dances, the consecration of ceremonial food and the chief priest's dance at the end of the ritual. *Cheyenne Indians. Dances. Priests. Rites and ceremonies.*

Note: This educational film was produced by Forrest E. Clements of the University of Oklahoma.
EFC 1943, p. 385.

CHICAGO *see* **IN OLD CHICAGO**

THE CHICAGO FIRE *see* **IN OLD CHICAGO**

CHICKENS COME HOME *(foreign version) see* **POLITIQUERÍAS**

CHIEF CRAZY HORSE (Native Amercans, Dakota, Shoshoni)
Universal-International Pictures Co., Inc. *Dist* Universal Pictures Co., Inc. Apr **1955**; Prod: ended 16 Jul 1954 [©Universal Pictures Co.; 10 Jan 1955; LP4371]. Sd (Western Electric Recording); col (Print by Technicolor); CinemaScope. 10 reels, 7,664 ft. 86 min. PCA cert no. 17183.
Prod William Alland. *Co-Producer* Leonard Goldstein. *Dir* George Sherman. *Asst dir* Marshall Green, [Phil Bowles and Dick Evans]. [*Dial*

dir Jack Daniels]. *Scr* Franklin Coen and Gerald Drayson Adams. *Story* Gerald Drayson Adams. *Dir of photog* Harold Lipstein. *Technicolor color consultant* William Fritzsche. *Art dir* Alexander Golitzen and Robert Boyle. *Film ed* Al Clark. *Set dec* Russell A. Gausman and Ray Jeffers. *Cost* Rosemary Odell. *Mus* Frank Skinner. *Mus supv* Joseph Gershenson. *Sd* Leslie I. Carey and Corson Jowett. *Makeup* Bud Westmore. *Hair stylist* Joan St. Oegger. *Tech adv* David Miller. [*Unit prod mgr* Tom Andre].

Cast: Victor Mature (*Crazy Horse*), Suzan Ball (*Black Shawl*), John Lund (*Major Twist*), Ray Danton (*Little Big Man*), Keith Larsen (*Flying Hawk*), Paul Guilfoyle (*Worm*), David Janssen (*Lt. Colin Cartwright*), Robert Warwick (*Spotted Tail*), James Millican (*General George Crook*), Morris Ankrum (*Red Cloud* [*/Conquering Bear*]), Donald Randolph (*Aaron Cartwright*), Robert F. Simon (*Jeff Mantz*), James Westerfield (*Caleb Mantz*), Stuart Randall (*Old Man Afraid*), Pat Hogan (*Dull Knife*), Dennis Weaver (*Maj. Carlisle*), John Peters (*Sgt. Guthrie*), Henry Wills (*He Dog*), Willie Hunter, Jr. (*Cavalryman*), [Charles Horvath (*Hardy*)], [Bill Williams, Robert St. Angelo (*Sergeants*)], [Reg Parton (*Doctor*)], [Emile Avery (*Captain William Fetterman*)], [David Miller (*Lieutenant*)].

Western. [*Print viewed*]. Major Twist, formerly of the U.S. Cavalry, returns to the Big Horn, once the home of the Lakota Sioux and their most important leader, Chief Crazy Horse. The land, now barren, calls forth a flood of memories for Twist. He tells a story that Crazy Horse related to him of a summer day in 1854, when Conquering Bear, chief of the Great Sioux Nation, returns wounded from a battle with the white man. Before dying, Conquering Bear prophesies that a great warrior will rise up and unite all the tribes of the Lakota to victory against the whites, but that he will die at the hand of a Lakota. Crazy Horse, so named because a wild horse ran through his village on the day of his birth, envisions a warrior wearing a warbonnet of red hawk feathers and riding a golden stallion out of a thunderbolt. In the years that follow, the white man breaks treaties and pushes the Sioux tribes further back. At Laramie, the Sioux Nation is promised that no more forts or roads cutting through the Dakotas will be built and that the sacred Black Hills will be left alone. Many of the Sioux tribes agree to move to reservations in exchange for food and goods, but the proud Lakotas are among those who cling to ancient ways. Crazy Horse, attacked by three Shoshone, who have long been enemies of the Lakota, kills them and recovers feathers of the red-beaked hawk from one. Little Big Man, his cousin, taunts Crazy Horse saying that he will use the three captured Shoshone horses as presents for the hand in marriage of Little Faun, whom Little Big Man also wants for a wife. Meanwhile, Twist, wounded by the Shoshone, falls off his horse into a creek and Little Faun rescues him. As Little Faun has become a woman, her father, Spotted Tail, says she will be known by a woman's name, Black Shawl. Spotted Tail rejects the presents offered by a number of warriors, including Crazy Horse, but Twist, in gratitude to Little Faun, who, he knows, loves Crazy Horse, gives Crazy Horse trade goods to add to his offerings. After Spotted Tail gives his daughter to Crazy Horse, Little Big Man insults Crazy Horse and they battle. Crazy Horse is victorious and Spotted Tail then sends Little Big Man away. Little Big Man follows Twist to Fort Laramie. He gets into a scuffle with a bigoted salesman at the Mantz Brothers Trading Company, and after Jeff Mantz discovers that Little Big Man carries gold, he and his brother Caleb offer him a job. The Mantz brothers ask Commissioner Aaron Cartwright permission to have the Black Hills surveyed with the aim to create a new source of wealth for the American people. When Cartwright refuses, saying such an action would lead to war, Jeff Mantz says disdainfully that Cartwright is part Indian himself. The commissioner's son, Lieutenant Colin Cartwright, acknowledges that his grandmother was an Indian and that they are proud of their heritage. In secret, the Mantz brothers pan for gold in the Black Hills with Little Big Man as a guide and lookout. After they find gold and decide to stake claims, the Mantz brothers kill a neighboring Indian family. When Little Big Man turns away in horror, Jeff Mantz says he will see more bloodshed until the country is "civilized." News of the Mantz's mining claim leads to a rush of prospectors into the Black Hills. When the Sioux Nation takes up arms in a new war, the government has no alternative but to protect the miners and build Fort Phil Kearny deeper into Sioux land. The Sioux leaders argue about how to respond, and Crazy Horse says that they should conduct their campaigns in a military fashion like the cavalry. With Crazy Horse as leader, the Sioux trick troops led by the pompous

Captain William Fetterman into a trap. Now respected in war, the Sioux can go to the fort to talk of peace. Commissioner Cartwright promises that the fort will be destroyed if the Sioux agree to move into a reservation. When some of the Indians are about to consent, Crazy Horse berates them for their short memory of the white man's betrayal. Calling the land sacred, Crazy Horse promises to fight and die for it. The commissioner sadly gives General George Crook permission to bring the Sioux back. Twist rides to warn the Sioux and is wounded and brought to the lodges along with his golden horse, which Crazy Horse believes is the horse from his vision. Warning that Crook has twice the number of men that Crazy Horse has, Twist tries to get Crazy Horse to surrender, but the Lakota warrior argues that Indians have gotten weak from eating the white man's food and from his "coughing sickness," and declares he would rather that his newborn daughter and her sons be dead if they can't live the life of their forefathers. Twist says he has no choice but to fight against him. While trying to leave, Twist falls off his horse because of his injury, and the golden horse walks to Crazy Horse. Black Shawl tells Twist she will care for him. At a ceremony, Crazy Horse is made leader of his people, and he wears the red hawk feathers. When troops cross the river marking Lakota territory, the Lakota attack and kill the Shoshone scouts first, then take the supply wagons and draw the soldiers into a battle so that they will use up their ammunition. During the battle, Lieutenant Cartwright is killed. Crazy Horse sends a captured soldier back with a message to the general warning that any white man who comes into their land will be killed. When Commissioner Cartwright is informed about his son's death, he goes to the Mantz brothers' office and shoots them before killing himself. Upon his return to the village, Crazy Horse finds that his daughter has died from the coughing sickness. At her grave, Black Shawl tells him that General George Armstrong Custer is coming to Big Horn with many soldiers. Crazy Horse devises a plan to defeat Custer by having the Sioux attack from the forest and the Cheyenne from the river, and Custer is routed. After the battle, the Indians separate and one-by-one are defeated and put into reservations. Crazy Horse and some of his young followers hold out deep in the Badlands, but when Black Shawl becomes deathly ill from the coughing sickness, Crazy Horse brings her to the fort, and with the white man's medicine, she almost completely revives by the spring. In the summer, Crazy Horse asks General Crook, who respects him, if they could return to hunt buffalo, saying buffalo provides food, skins for clothing, bone for arrows, hair for ropes, and shoes, and that they are no longer Lakota without the buffalo, but instead are nameless and dead. General Crook agrees to let them go if they will hunt without guns, using traditional weapons, and if they will return before the next snow. Little Big Man, however, taunts Crazy Horse, then stabs him in the back with his bayonet. Seeing the bloodied blade, Little Big Man throws it down and runs out of the fort. Black Shawl and Twist find that Crazy Horse has died, and Twist relates that the prophesy has been fulfilled. *Betrayal. Chief Crazy Horse. Dakota Indians. Officers (Military). United States–History–Indian campaigns.* Black Hills (SD and WY). Conquering Bear (Sioux chieftain). George Crook. General George Armstrong Custer. William Fetterman. Fort Laramie (WY). Fort Phil Kearny (WY). Gold miners. Indians of North America–Reservations. Infant death. Marriage. Murder. Racism. Rescues. Revelation (Theology, inspiration). Shoshoni Indians. Suicide. Trading posts. Treaties. Tuberculosis. United States. Army. Cavalry. Visions.

Note: After the opening credits, the following statement appears: "This is a true story, photographed in the Black Hills of the Dakotas, where it actually happened. It is the story of an American, a leader of his people, one of the great generals of all time—Chief Crazy Horse of the Lakota Sioux." The end credits state the following acknowledgment: "We wish to express our appreciation to the Department of the Interior National Park Service for permission to photograph in the Badlands National Monument, South Dakota. This picture was made with the cooperation of the Oglala Sioux tribe of South Dakota." In a pressbook, director George Sherman claimed that the film was "a faithful depiction of Crazy Horse's life." He commented, "All the kids and a good majority of the grown-ups like to see the Red Men emerge victorious. Kids have always made heroes out of their favorite Indian chiefs of history." *Har* noted that the film was "somewhat different from most stories that deal with a conflict between Indians and whites. This time the Indians are given sympathetic treatment and are depicted as being persecuted by the whites." *MPHPD* predicted that the film would do well at the box office, "if the mistreated-Indian theme hasn't reached the point of diminishing returns."

About the subject of the film, *HR* commented, "Few Indians in American history command such admiration and respect as Crazy Horse....Unfortunately, neither the performance of Victor Mature, in the title role, nor the screenplay

by Franklin Coen and Gerald Drayson Adams, succeeds in getting anything more than a pedestrian concept of the great man on the screen....A forew" says that this is a true story and it is, after a fashion, but it is not a complete or well-rounded presentation of the truth." Other reviews agreed that Mature was miscast in the role.

DV commented that CinemaScope "makes the stock footage scenes inserted here and there seem poor, particularly as the library scenes do not blow up to CinemaScope size with any clarity." *Time* surmised that "there were apparently not enough extras left to stage Custer's last stand at Little Big Horn. So, curiously, the picture dispenses with most of it." *Chief Crazy Horse* was Suzan Ball's first film since early 1954, when her right leg was amputated. *DV* noted, "The doubling-in scenes requiring movement are very good." The film also marked Ray Danton's screen debut and was one of the last of co-producer Leonard Goldstein, who died before the picture's release.

Box 26 Feb 1955. *DV* 22 Feb 1955, p.3. *Exh* 23 Feb, 1955, p.3923 *FD* 22 Feb 1955, p.7. *Har* 26 Feb 1955, pp.35. *HCN* 17 Mar 1955. *HR* 24 Mar 1954. *HR* 16 Jul 1954. *HR* 22 Feb 1955, P.3. *LAEx* 17 Mar 1955. *LAT* 17 Mar 1955. *MPHPD* 26 Feb 1955, p. 337. *NYT* 28 Apr 1955, p.25. *Time* 30 May 1955. *Var* 23 Feb 1955, p.8.

CHIEF RED SLEEVES *see* **WAR DRUMS**

CHIJLKU WO MAWASURU CHIKARA (Japanese language)

Hollywood Nippon Talkie Co.; Japanese Talking Picture Co. **1930**; Los Angeles opening: 26 Jun 1930; Prod: early 1930 at The Monrovia Studio. Sd; b&w. Length undetermined. Japanese language.

Prod Teruo Mayeda. *Supv* James Warwick. *Dir* James Wong Howe and Thomas Hayashi. *Wrt* Wakaba Matsumoto. *Scen* Helen Warwick. *Photog* James Wong Howe. *Prod mgr* George Teraoka. *Dir gen* Tom White.

Cast: Ruth Washizu, Henry Okawa, Taruyo "Jack" Matsumoto (*Father*), Hitoshi Yonemura, Josephine Yamaoka, George Kodama, Gosuke Kawai, Teruo Mayeda, Yuriko Tsuchiya, Kawaye.

Drama. [*Not viewed*]. [The only specific information located concerning the plot indicates that the three main characters are a father and two romantic leads. *Fathers and sons. Japanese.*

Note: Working English-language titles for the film were, *Turning the Earth's Axis, Eternal Passion* and *The Inevitable Urge*. According to articles in *Rafu Shimpo*, this film was the first Japanese talking film made in Los Angeles. A 1 Jan 1930 article referred to the production of Japanese-language films in Hollywood as "the outgrowth of the dream of Teruo Mayeda, noted critic and scenario writer, who has begun producing with a corporation capitalized at $20,000." The film was made in The Monrovia Studio in Monrovia, CA, a facility owned by Tom White. White, according to a 5 Feb 1930 news item, stopped making English-language films to concentrate on foreign-language productions. He "directed the general procedure" of this film, according to a news story. In a modern article on James Wong Howe, who directed and shot the film, White's studio was described as an empty orange-packing shed. Howe previously photographed the film version of the 1925 George Warwick play *Sorrell and Son*, produced in 1927 by Feature Productions (see *AFI Catalog of Feature Films, 1921-30*; F2.5261), Two articles about *Chijlku wo mawasuru chikara* noted that it had a plot similar to *Sorrell and Son. Rafu Shimpo* warned that because of the likeness, "it is expected that the producer will find himself in somewhat of a jam, if he undertakes to produce this story 'as is.'" An article noted that the cast consisted of many second-generation Japanese Americans. Helen Warwick, the scenarist, had worked for the Lasky company.

The 1 Jan 1930 *Rafu Shimpo* article stated that this film was to be the second of Mayeda's productions. The first planned production, which was never realized, was a comedy, also written by Wakaba Matsumoto, entitled *Annoying Age*, about "an old 'hick', who comes to America to see his occidentalized nephew, George, after the latter's absence of ten years. Situations develop 'through the different environments.'" A news article dated 28 Apr 1930 stated that *Chijlku wo mawasuru chikara*, then entitled *Eternal Passion*, was in the process of final cutting, after three months of production, and was then eleven reels in length. The article noted, "The members of the cast were often discouraged on account of many obstacles that they had to face while the picture was being taken at the Monrovia Studio.... More than 100 people assisted in the materialization of this long-cherished dream." The film was previewed in mid-Jun under the title *The Inevitable Urge*. While the photography was praised, the acting was "said to be somewhat uneven" at times, and the dialogue "left much to be desired," according to *Rafu Shimpo*. The film was shown to the public under its Japanese title on 26 and 27 Jun 1930 at the Fox Brooklyn Theatre in Los Angeles for five performance on 26 and 27 Jun 1930. The next public screenings were on 4 and 5 Oct 1930 at the Nishi Hongwanji hall, also in Los Angeles. A sound projector was sent from New York for the latter screenings. According to the article on Howe, the film was shown in Japan, where the accents of the Japanese Americans were thought to be "funny." The article also states that Howe put up $4,500 of the $12,000 production costs.

FIR Apr 1961, p. 219. *Rafu Shimpo* 1 Jan 1930. *Rafu Shimpo* 28 Apr 1930. *Rafu Shimpo* 16 Jun 1930. *Rafu Shimpo* 23 Jun 1930. *Rafu Shimpo* 22 Sep 1930, p. 1, 3. *Var* 5 Feb 1930, p. 4.

A CHILD IN PAWN (African Americans)

D. W. D. Film Corp. **1921**. Si; b&w. 5 reels.

Melodrama (?), African American. No information about the precise nature of this film has been found. *African Americans.*

Note: The D. W. D. Film Corp. was located in Raleigh, NC.

A CHILD OF MYSTERY (Italian Americans)

Universal Film Mfg. Co.; Red Feather Photoplays. *Dist* Universal Film Mfg. Co. 25 Dec **1916** [©Universal Film Mfg. Co.; 15 Dec 1916; LP9741]. Si; b&w. 5 reels.

Dir Hobart Henley. *Scen* Willard Mack. *Cam* George Scoll.

Cast: Gertrude Selby (*Carlotta*), Thomas Jefferson (*Giuseppe*), Paul Byron (*Tom*), Alfred Allen (*Michael Gavotti*), Mark Fenton (*Judge Andrews*), Nanine Wright (*His wife*), Hobart Henley (*Tony*).

Crime, Drama. In New York's Little Italy, Carlotta's life is run by Black Hand leaders who will not let her see her sweetheart Tom. The Black Handers also control the life of prominent Judge Andrews, because years before, after the death of Andrews' daughter, they kidnapped his granddaughter. Only now have they agreed to return her, at a charity ball, for a large ransom. Carlotta momentarily gets away from the Black Hand and goes to the ball alone, where Judge and Mrs. Andrews, startled at her resemblance to their daughter, realize that she is their grandchild. The Black Hand catches up to Carlotta, however, and abducts her again, but Andrews and Tom pursue them, kill the leaders, and take Carlotta back to her rightful home, where she and Tom plan their marriage. *Black Hand (United States). Granddaughters. Italian Americans. Judges. Kidnapping. New York City–Little Italy. Balls (parties). Ransom. Recognition. Rescues.*

ETR 30 Dec 1916, p. 272. *MPW* 30 Dec 1916, p. 1974, 2006.

CHILDREN OF FATE (African Americans)

Colored Players Film Corp. **1927**; Philadelphia showing: Apr 1927; Prod: Nov—Dec 1926. Si; b&w. 8 reels, 7,500 ft.

Dir Roy Calnek.

Cast: Harry Henderson, Shingzie Howard, Lawrence Chenault, Arline Mickey, William A. Clayton, Jr., Howard Augusta, Alonzo Jackson.

African American, Drama. Ross Hampton, a successful gambler, falls victim to the "white plague." Leaving home to reside in a more healthful environment, he reunites with his childhood sweetheart, Virginia Lee, and with her finds health and happiness. *African Americans. Childhood sweethearts. Gamblers. Health. Plague.*

Note: According to a *ChiDef* news story, the planned production cost of this film was to be $25,000.

ChiDef 27 Nov 1926, p. 7. *PittsC* 6 Aug 1927.

CHILDREN OF THE COVERED WAGON *see* **WESTWARD HO THE WAGONS!**

CHILDREN OF THE GHETTO (Jewish Americans)

Box Office Attraction Co. *Dist* Box Office Attraction Co.; Fox Film Corp. 20 Feb **1915** [©William Fox; 8 Feb 1915; LP5180]. Si; b&w. 5 reels.

Pres William Fox. *Dir* Frank Powell. *Scen* Edward José.

Source: Based on the novel *The Children of the Ghetto: A Study of a Peculiar People* by Israel Zangwill (London, 1892) and his play *Children of the Ghetto* (New York, 16 Oct 1899).

Cast: Wilton Lackaye (*Reb Shemuel*), Ruby Hoffman (*Hannah*), Ethel Kaufman (*Esther Ansell*), Frank Andrews (*Moses Ansell*), Louis Alberni (*Pincus, the poet*), Irene Boyle (*Leah*), Victor Benoit (*Reb Shemuel's son*), David Bruce, William R. Hatch, J. Albert Hall.

Drama. In a prologue, actor Wilton Lackaye reads the story *Children of the Ghetto*. Seated opposite him is the character whom Lackaye portrays, Reb Shemuel, a benevolent religious leader. In the main story, Reb Shemuel's son arrives drunk at a Passover feast, insults his father and blasphemes God. When he is injured in a cabaret brawl, Shemuel refuses to see him. Remembering his religious obligation, Shemuel rushes to the hospital and hears his son beg forgiveness before he dies. After the fiancé of a friend of Shemuel's beloved daughter Hannah puts a wedding ring on Hannah's finger in jest and says the marriage vows, Shemuel performs a divorce. Later, Hannah is about to marry David Brandon, when an unsuccessful suitor, Pincus the poet, reminds the congregation that David is a descendant of the priestly tribe of Cohen, who are forbidden to marry divorced women. After David and Hannah marry in a civil ceremony, she becomes estranged from her father, whose sorrow is compounded by the death of his devoted wife. Several years later, Shemuel conducts a lonely Passover seder at a table of empty chairs. Hannah, now widowed, and her two children occupy the chairs, and the old man accepts them lovingly. *Fathers and daughters. Fathers and sons. Jews. Passover.*

Rabbis. Divorce. Drunkenness. Fights. Loneliness. Marriage–Fake. Poets. Reunions.

Note: Wilton Lackaye starred in the original stage production. The Fox Film Corp. became the new name of the Box Office Attraction Co. in Feb 1915, around the time of this film's release.

Motog 6 Mar 1915, pp. 382-83. *MPN* 30 Jan 1915, p. 28. *MPN* 13 Feb 1915, p. 74. *MPN* 20 Feb 1915, p. 53. *MPW* 27 Feb 1915, p. 1290. *Var* 12 Feb 1915, p. 23.

CHIMMIE FADDEN (Irish Americans)

Jesse L. Lasky Feature Play Co. *Dist* Paramount Pictures Corp. 28 Jun **1915** [©Jesse L. Lasky Feature Play Co., Inc.; 9 Jun 1915; LU5501]. Si; b&w. 4-5 reels.

Pres Jesse L. Lasky. *Dir* Cecil B. DeMille. *Tech dir* Wilfred Buckland.

Source: Based on the short story "Chimmie Fadden" by Edward Waterman Townsend in his *Chimmie Fadden; Major Max; and other stories* (New York, ca 1895) and his play of the same name (New York, 13 Jan 1896).

Cast: Victor Moore (*Chimmie Fadden*), Camille Astor (*Hortense, "The Duchess"*), Raymond Hatton (*Larry Fadden*), Mrs. Lewis McCord (*Mrs. Fadden*), Ernest Joy (*Mr. Van Cortlandt*), Anita King (*Fanny Van Cortlandt*), Tom Forman (*Antoine*), Harry De Roy (*Perkins*).

Comedy. Chimmie Fadden, a poor but amiable Irish lad, lives with his mother and brother Larry in New York's Bowery. When Chimmie is arrested for fighting to defend a newsboy from a bully, Fanny Van Cortlandt, a millionaire's daughter on a charity mission, who witnesses the fight, arranges for his release. After Chimmie rescues Fanny from a masher, he becomes a bumbling servant at the Van Cortlandt Long Island mansion, where he falls in love with Hortense, the French maid. One night Chimmie discovers his brother Larry and the valet Antoine stealing the silver. Chimmie knocks Antoine unconscious and hides Larry in a fireplace when Van Cortlandt enters to investigate. Feigning intoxication, Chimmie takes the blame for the noise, and Larry escapes with the silver. The next day Chimmie, now discharged, finds Larry and takes the satchel of silver to return it, but the police arrest him for the crime. After Larry confesses, at the insistence of Mrs. Fadden, Chimmie, now released, finally steals a kiss from Hortense. *Brothers. False arrests. Irish Americans. Self-sacrifice. Servants. Bullies. Charity workers. Confession (Law). Dismissal (Employment). Fights. French Americans. Long Island (NY). Maids. Mansions. New York City–Bowery. Newsboys. Rescues. Robbery.*

Note: The "Chimmie Fadden" stories originally appeared in the *New York Sun*. For the film, Wilfred Buckland designed and oversaw the construction of two New York City street corners, three stories high, based on photographs. Victor Moore played the role of Chimmie Fadden on stage. According to modern sources, DeMille, besides directing the film, produced, wrote and edited it, and Alvin Wyckoff was the cameraman. *Chimmie Fadden Out West*, (see below) released by Lasky in late 1915, was also based on Townsend's short stories.

Motog 17 Jul 1915, p. 139. *MPN* 29 May 1915, p. 46. *MPN* 10 Jul 1915, p. 70. *MPW* 10 Jul 1915, p. 322, 398, 400. *NYDM* 7 Jul 1915, p. 28. *Var* 2 Jul 1915, p. 16.

CHIMMIE FADDEN OUT WEST (Irish Americans)

Jesse L. Lasky Feature Play Co. *Dist* Paramount Pictures Corp. 21 Nov **1915** [©Jesse L. Lasky Feature Play Co., Inc.; 5 Nov 1915; LU6855]. Si; b&w. 4-5 reels.

Pres Jesse L. Lasky. *Dir* Cecil B. DeMille. *Scen* Cecil B. DeMille and Jeanie MacPherson.

Source: Based on the short story "Chimmie Fadden" by Edward Waterman Townsend in his *Chimmie Fadden; Major Max; and other stories* (New York, ca. 1895) and his play of the same name (New York, 13 Jan 1896).

Cast: Victor Moore (*Chimmie Fadden*), Camille Astor (*"The Duchess"*), Raymond Hatton (*Larry Fadden*), Mrs. Lewis McCord (*Mother Fadden*), Ernest Joy (*Mr. Van Cortlandt*), Tom Forman (*Antoine*), Florence Dagmar (*Betty Van Cortlandt*), Harry Hadfield (*Preston*), Ramona the mule (*Herself*).

Comedy. Chimmie Fadden, an Irish Bowery lad, is engaged to Hortense, whom he calls "The Duchess," the lovely French maid of his former employer, millionaire Van Cortlandt. When offered $10,000 to carry out an advertising campaign for Van Cortlandt's Western railroad, Chimmie agrees. As instructed, Chimmie travels to Death Valley, scatters gold nuggets around a deserted mine and reports a gold strike, which creates a sensation. When a government agent investigates, Chimmie arranges to be held-up, but Hortense and Miss Van Cortlandt, in San Francisco to see the Exposition, arrive and have the holdup men arrested. After bluffing the investigator, Chimmie, now famous, makes a record-breaking railway trip to New

York to publicize the railroad. Exploiting the excitement, Van Cortlandt sells stock in the bogus Chimmie Fadden Mining Company. When Chimmie's brother Larry tells Hortense of the swindle, she refuses to marry "a thief." Previously unaware of the company, Chimmie now returns the $10,000 to Van Cortlandt and tells the press about the scheme. Van Cortlandt returns the investments, and Hortense and Chimmie marry. *Advertising. Hoaxes. Irish Americans. Railroads. Death Valley (CA). Fraud. Gold mines. Government agents. Maids. Panama-Pacific International Exposition. San Francisco (CA). Stock market.*

Note: The "Chimmie Fadden" stories, which were also the basis for *Chimmie Fadden,* another 1915 Lasky film (see above listing), were originally published in the *New York Sun.* Some scenes in this film were shot in Death Valley, CA. According to modern sources, DeMille also produced and edited the film. Alvin Wyckoff was the cameraman and Wilfred Buckland was the art director.

Motog 11 Dec 1915, p. 1262. *MPN* 23 Oct 1915, p. 61. *MPN* 27 Nov 1915, p. 87. *MPN* 4 Dec 1915, p. 87. *MPW* 20 Nov 1915, p. 1514. *MPW* 27 Nov 1915, p. 1680, 1732. *NYDM* 4 Dec 1915, p. 28. *NYT* 22 Nov 1915, p. 12. *Var* 26 Nov 1915, p. 23.

CHIN HAI IN SIONG (Chinese language)
Grandview Film Co. **1944.** Sd; b&w. Length undetermined. Chinese language.

Dir Joseph Sunn.

Cast: Wong Hok-sing. [*Not viewed*]. [No information concerning the plot of this film has been located.].

Note: The Cantonese transliterated title is *Qing Hoi Yin Hone.* The English language translation of the title is "Hero in the Sea of Love." This film was probably made in the U.S.

Chinese Times (San Francisco) 24 Jan 1944, p. 7.

CHINATOWN AFTER DARK (Chinese Americans)
Action Pictures, Inc.; Ralph M. Like, Ltd. *Dist* Action Pictures, Inc. 15 Oct **1931**; *Prod:* at International Film Studios. Sd; b&w. 58 min.

Supv Cliff Broughton. *Dir* Stuart Paton. *Author* Betty Burbridge. *Cam* Jules Cronjager. *Film ed* Viola Roehl. *Rec eng* James Stanley.

Cast: Carmel Myers (*Madame Ying Su*), Rex Lease (*Jim Bonner*), Barbara Kent (*Lotus*), Edmund Breese (*Lee Fong*), Frank Mayo (*Ralph Bonner*), Billy Gilbert (*Horatio Dooley*), Lloyd Whitlock (*Detective Captain*), Laska Winter (*Ming Fu*), Michael Visaroff (*Varanoff*).

Mystery. [*Print viewed*]. In Shanghai, Ralph Bonner agrees to deliver a dagger to Lee Fong in San Francisco. Afterward, several attempts are made to steal it from him, but he reaches the United States with the dagger intact. While Ralph and his brother Jim set off into the rainy night to deliver the dagger to Lee Fong, Mr. Varanoff, a crook, conspires with Madame Ying Su to steal the dagger for themselves. Lee Fong is delighted to see the dagger, but just as he reveals a secret jewel in the dagger's hilt, the lights suddenly go out. When they come back on, Lee Fong is dead, and Ralph and the dagger have disappeared. The police suspect Jim, but Lee Fong's white ward, Lotus, has fallen in love with him and defends him. Dissatisfied with the progress of the police, Jim decides to solve the murder himself. He contacts Madame Ying Su and discovers his brother is being held on the premises of her café. Lotus follows Jim to the café. To allay Ying Su's suspicions, Jim offers to question Lotus about the dagger. Instead, he secretly warns her that they are being watched and the two of them try to escape. Lotus manages to get away and arrives with the police just in time to save Jim from death at the hands of Ying Su. They rescue Ralph, who explains the mystery. At last, they discover the dagger where Lee Fong hid it before he died. *Chinese Americans. Daggers. Murder. Gangsters. Jewelry. Kidnapping. San Francisco (CA)–Chinatown. Shanghai (China). Wards and guardians.*

Note: No credits were present on the viewed print.

FD 25 Oct 1931, p. 10. *HR* 11 Nov 1931, p. 3. *MPH* 31 Oct 1931, p. 36. *Var* 24 Nov 1931, p. 21.

CHINATOWN AT MIDNIGHT (Chinese Americans)
Columbia Pictures Corp. *Dist* Columbia Pictures Corp. 19 Jan **1950**; New York opening: 17 Nov 1949; Prod: 19 May—26 May 1949 [©Columbia Pictures Corp.; 18 Jan 1950; LP2761]. Sd (RCA Sound System); b&w. 6,038 ft. 66-67 min. PCA cert no. 14061.

Prod Sam Katzman. *Dir* Seymour Friedman. *Asst dir* Carter DeHaven, Jr. *Wrt for the scr* Robert Libott and Frank Burt. *Dir of photog* Henry Freulich. *Art dir* Paul Palmentola. *Film ed* Edwin Bryant. *Set dec* Frank Tuttle. *Mus dir* Mischa Bakaleinikoff. *Sd eng* Josh Westmoreland. *Unit mgr* Herbert Leonard.

Cast: Hurd Hatfield [(*Clifford Ward*)], Jean Willes [(*Alice*)], Tom Powers [(*Capt. Howard Brown*)], Ray Walker [(*Sam Costa*)], Charles

Russell [(*Fred Morgan*)], Jacqueline de Wit [(*Lisa Marcel*)], Maylia [(*Hazel Fong*)], Ross Elliott [(*Eddie Marsh*)], [Benson Fong (*Joe Wing*)], [Barbara Jean Wong (*Betty Chang*)], [Victor Sen Yung (*Proprietor*)], [Josephine Whitell (*Mrs. Dryden*)].

Crime, Drama. [*Print viewed*]. Interior decorator Lisa Marcel asks Clifford Ward, who is infatuated with her, to steal a white jade vase from G. L. Wing's shop in Chinatown. Ward steals the vase, but when Wing's son Joe attempts to trigger an alarm, Ward kills him and his fiancée, Betty Chang, who was telephoning for help. Removing the receiver from the wounded woman's hand, Ward, speaking in Chinese, reports the robbery and escapes, using a tourist group for cover. The next morning, the police visit the Chinatown telephone exchange and question telephone operator Hazel Fong, who received the call. After Betty dies from her injuries, Hazel becomes the only one who can identify the killer. The police publish a picture of the stolen vase, and one of Lisa's clients discloses that it is in her newly decorated home. To prevent Lisa from implicating him, Ward kills her. The police arrive at Lisa's shop and spot Ward making his escape. During the ensuing chase, Ward sheds his jacket and tie and hides in a soup kitchen line. The next morning, a rubbish collector finds the discarded jacket and gun. An examination of the gun proves that the same person killed Lisa, Betty and Joe. The gun, which was stolen from a pawn shop, provides no further clues, but the police are able to discover Ward's address using the laundry mark in his jacket. The police find stolen articles in Ward's apartment, along with the tape he used to practice Chinese. When they discover a variety of language recordings, they realize that Ward spoke different languages during robberies to mislead witnesses. When Ward spots the police at his apartment, he registers at a cheap hotel. Meanwhile, the police play the recording of Ward's voice for Hazel, who confirms that it is the same man who reported the robbery in Wing's store. At his hotel, Ward suffers a bout of malaria and discovers that he does not have his medication. A drug store clerk refuses to sell him the necessary medicine without a prescription but agrees to give him the medicine if his doctor telephones with an order. Ward, pretending to be a doctor, phones the clerk, and once again, Helen places the call. When she recognizes Ward's voice, she traces the call and informs the police. Ward hears the sirens and runs out of the drugstore, and after a chase over the rooftops of Chinatown, he is fatally wounded. *Chinese Americans. Criminals. Murder. Police. Telephone operators. Antiques. Chases. Dry cleaning. Hotels. Interior decorators. Language and languages. Malaria. Pharmacists. Recognition. Rooftops. San Francisco (CA)–Chinatown. Shootouts. Tourists.*

Note: The film's working title was *Chinatown After Midnight.* The film uses a narrator to create a documentary-like style. Some sources incorrectly identify actor Victor Sen Yung as Victor Sen Yen.

Box 17 Dec 1949. *DV* 18 Nov 1949, p. 4. *HR* 18 Nov 1949, p. 4. *MPHPD* 26 Nov 1949, p. 98. *NYT* 18 Nov 1949, p. 35. *Var* 23 Nov 1949, p. 25.

CHINATOWN CHARLIE (Chinese Americans)
First National Pictures, Inc. *Dist* First National Pictures, Inc. 15 Apr **1928** [©First National Pictures, Inc.; 23 Mar 1928; LP25091]. Si; b&w. 7 reels, 6,365 ft.

Prod C. C. Burr. *Dir* Charles Hines. *Scen* Roland Asher and John Grey. *Story* Owen Davis. *Titles* Paul Perez. *Photog* William J. Miller and Al Wilson. *Film ed* George Amy.

Cast: Johnny Hines (*Charlie*), Louise Lorraine (*Annie Gordon*), Harry Gribbon (*Red Mike*), Fred Kohler (*Monk*), Sojin (*The Mandarin*), Scooter Lowry (*Oswald*), Anna May Wong (*The Mandarin's sweetheart*), George Kuwa (*Hip Sing Toy*), John Burdette (*Gyp*).

Comedy. Charlie, a Chinatown tour guide, attempts to protect one of his female passengers from a gang wanting to steal her ring, reputed to have supernatural powers. He rescues the girl after an escapade at a mandarin's palace in which some acrobats form a human chain across the street two floors aboveground. *Acrobats. Chinese Americans. Clairvoyants. Guides. Tourists.*

FD 17 Jun 1928. *Var* 13 Jun 1928, p. 13.

CHINATOWN NIGHTS (Chinese Americans)
Paramount Famous Lasky Corp. 23 Mar **1929** [©Paramount Famous Lasky Corp.; 23 Mar 1929; LP274]. Talking sequences, sd eff, and mus score (Movietone); b&w. 8 reels, 7,481 ft. [Also si; 7,145 ft.].

Assoc prod David Selznick. *Dir* William A. Wellman. *Scr* Ben Grauman Kohn. *Adpt* Oliver H. P. Garrett. *Dial* William B. Jutte. *Titles* Julian Johnson. *Photog* Henry Gerrard. *Tech dir* Tom Gubbins. *Film ed* Allyson Shaffer.

Source: Based on the short story "Tong War" by Samuel Ornitz (publication undetermined).

Cast: Wallace Beery (*Chuck Riley*), Florence Vidor (*Joan Fry*), Warner Oland (*Boston Charley*), Jack McHugh (*The shadow*), Jack Oakie (*The reporter*), Tetsu Komai (*Woo Chung*), Frank Chew (*The gambler*), Mrs. Wong Wing (*The maid*), Pete Morrison (*The bartender*), Freeman Wood (*Gerald*).

Melodrama. A Chinatown tourist bus is caught in the middle of a tong war, and in the resulting confusion, society woman Joan Fry is left behind. Chuck Riley, the white leader of a tong faction, pulls her from the dangerous streets and keeps her overnight in his apartment. The following morning, Joan leaves, returning later with friends; Chuck again saves her life. Joan falls in love with Chuck and moves in with him, renouncing her former life. She tries to get Chuck to reform, and he throws her out. Joan wanders the streets, and Boston Charley, Chuck's rival, gets her drunk and sends her back to Chuck with a humiliating letter pinned to her frowsy sweater. Chuck, moved by Joan's condition, wrecks his dance hall and leaves Chinatown with her, looking for a new beginning and a brighter tomorrow. *Chinatowns. Chinese Americans. Drunkenness. Socialites. Tongs (Secret societies). Tourists.*

FD 7 Apr 1929. NYT 1 Apr 1929, p. 22. Var 3 Apr 1929, p. 20.

CHINATOWN PICTURES (Chinese Americans)
Dist Capt Lewis. 1915?. Si; b&w. 5 reels.
Drama. [No specific information about the plot of this film has been determined.]. *Chinatowns. Chinese Americans.*

Note: The records of the Kansas State Censors list this film as having been approved for exhibition on on 27 Sep 1915. No reviews or other information about the film has been located.

CHINATOWN SQUAD (Chinese Americans)
Universal Pictures Corp.; Carl Laemmle, President. *Dist* Universal Pictures Corp. 20 May 1935; Prod: 18 Mar—6 Apr 1935 [©Universal Pictures Corp.; 14 May 1935; LP5540]. Sd (Western Electric Noiseless Recording); b&w. 7 reels. 65 or 70 min. PCA cert no. 791.
Pres CARL LAEMMLE. *Exec prod* Stanley Bergerman. *Assoc prod* Maurice Pivar. *Dir* Murray Roth. [*Asst dir* Archie Buchanan and Joe Torillo]. *Scr* Dore Schary. *Orig story* Lawrence G. Blochman. *Addl dial* Ben Ryan. [*Contr wrt* Lawrence G. Blochman and Eliot Gibbons]. *Photog* George Robinson. [*Cam* Harold Smith. *Asst cam* Arthur Gerstle]. [*Process photog* John P. Fulton]. *Art dir* Harrison Wiley. *Film ed* Maurice E. Wright. [*Sd rec* Tommy Ashton]. [*Mixer* Charles Carroll]. [*Boom man* Frank Gorback]. [*Hair* Hazel Rogers]. [*Makeup* William Ely]. [*Tech dir* Archie Hall]. [*Grip* E. Brown, Fred Stoll and Bob Evans]. [*Props* Ernest M. Smith]. [*Script* Connie Earl]. [*Set lighting foreman* Roy Fullerton].
Cast: LYLE TALBOT (*Ted Lacey*), Valerie Hobson (*Janet Baker*), Hugh O'Connell (*Sergeant McLeash*), Andy Devine (*George Mason*), Leslie Fenton ([*Su*] *Quong*), Bradley Page ([*D. D.*] *Palmer*), E. Alyn "Fred" Warren (*John Yee*), Clay Clement ([*Albert*] *Raybold*), Arthur Hoyt ([*William*] *Ward*), Wallis Clarke (*Chief of Detectives Norris*), [Toshia Mori (*Wanda*)], [Henry Armetta (*Italian*)], [Tom Dugan], [Jack Mulhall], [James Flavin], [King Baggott], [Otis Harlan], [Ed LeSaint], [Edward Earle].
Mystery. [*Print viewed*]. On the night of Chinese New Year celebrations in San Francisco, Albert Raybold, a confidence man and agent for Chinese Communist revolutionaries, is knifed to death in the Peking Café, owned by John Yee. Before Sergeant McLeash of the Chinatown police squad arrives on the scene, Yee steals a mystical jade ring from Raybold's corpse and goes into hiding. The ring gives its wearer the power to do irreparable harm to his enemies. Also in the restaurant is ex-cop Ted Lacey, who, tired of the dimwitted McLeash meddling in his cases, quit the force and now drives a sightseeing bus. Lacey helps a mysterious lady dressed in black elude McLeash by including her in his group of tourists. He later discovers she is Janet Baker, a woman who became Raybold's business partner and nearly married him until she found out he was crooked; Raybold lured Janet to Chinatown by sending her a telegram that he had been murdered. Ted agrees to help Janet retrieve incriminating letters that were in Raybold's possession and also hopes to find the killer before McLeash does. McLeash suspects Janet and Yee, as well as D. D. Palmer and William Ward, both of whom Raybold called before he was murdered. Ward was hoping Raybold could get him a monopoly on tea exports to Fuchau, a seaport in China. The night of his death, Raybold

received $70,000 from Yee that he had collected from Chinese-American sympathizers to pay for airplanes which Raybold was going to transport to China that night. Palmer was after a $10,000 commission that Raybold owed him and was meeting Raybold for dinner to collect. Janet disguises herself as a Chinese woman and visits Yee, believing he has her letters, but he locks her up in his restaurant, bound and gagged, and leaves for the Sausalito ferry. Ted follows and is in turn followed by Palmer. Ted is distracted when McLeash goes overboard in an attempt to catch the ferry, and Palmer knifes Yee and throws him overboard. Ted fishes him out and before he dies, Yee gestures that his ring has been stolen. McLeash brings Ted to Chief of Detectives Norris believing he was in cahoots with Yee, but Norris releases him, and he goes to the Peking Café, where he finds Janet and rescues her. Meanwhile, Raybold's secretary, George Mason, who was arrested as a possible suspect, is released by Palmer's lawyer. Palmer agrees to give George a cut if he helps him find the money. Palmer believes Yee's partner, Su Quong, has the letters and the money. Janet contacts George and he tells her to tell Quong that Palmer will give him the ring if Quong gives Palmer the money. All converge at the restaurant, where they discover the money and letters hidden in Raybold's private booth. McLeash then hauls Palmer, George, Janet and Ted to headquarters and, en route, Ted scares George into implicating Palmer as the murderer and gets Palmer to confess. At headquarters, Norris commends Ted for bringing in the murderer and rehires him as a sergeant. Janet looks forward to a life as a policeman's wife. *Chinese Americans. Murder. Police. San Francisco (CA)–Chinatown. Swindlers and swindling. Cafés. Chinese New Year. Communists. Disguise. Ferryboats. Jewelry. Letters. Rescues. Rivalry. Secretaries.*

Note: This film's working titles were *Frisco Lady* and *Frisco Nights*. This film was shot on location in San Francisco, CA.

DV 13 May 1935, p. 3. FD 31 May 1935, p. 7. HR 13 May 1935, p. 3. MPD 7 May 1935, p. 12. MPH 13 Apr 1935, p. 68. MPH 8 Jun 1935, p. 73. MPSI May 1935, p. 22. NYT 30 May 1935, p. 21. Var 5 Jun 1935, p. 54.

THE CHINESE CAT (Chinese Americans)
Krasne-Burkett Productions. *Dist* Monogram Pictures Corp. 20 May 1944; Prod: 11 Jan—19 Jan 1944 [©Monogram Pictures Corp.; 15 Apr 1944; LP12667]. Sd (Western Electric Mirrophonic Recording); b&w. 5,824 ft. 65 min.
Series: Charlie Chan.
Prod Philip N. Krasne and James S. Burkett. *Dir* Phil Rosen. [*Asst dir* Bobby Ray]. *Orig scr* George Callahan. *Dir of photog* Ira Morgan. *Art dir* Dave Milton. *Film ed* Fred Allen and [Martin Cohn]. *Set dec* Tommy Thompson. *Mus supv* David Chudnow. *Mus score* Alexander Laszlo. *Sd rec* Tom Lambert. *Prod mgr* Dick L'Estrange.
Source: Based on characters created by Earl Derr Biggers.
Cast: Sidney Toler [(*Charlie Chan*)], Joan Woodbury [(*Leah Manning*)], Mantan Moreland [(*Birmingham Brown*)], Benson Fong [(*Tommy Chan*)], Ian Keith, Cy Kendall [(*Webster Deacon*)], Weldon Heyburn [(*Harvey Dennis*)], Anthony Ward [(*Catlen*)], John Davidson [(*Carl Kazdas/Kurt Kazdas*)], Dewey Robinson [(*Salos*)], Stan Jolley, Betty Blythe [(*Mrs. Manning*)], Jack Norton, Luke Chan, [Sam Flint].
Detective, Drama. [*Print viewed*]. When Thomas Manning, the second husband of a wealthy socialite, is murdered in his locked study, the police are baffled and the district attorney quickly decides to drop the case. Months later, detective Charlie Chan is passing through town when he is approached by Manning's step-daughter Leah, who asks for help in solving the crime. Chan agrees to review the case, and despite his protests, his college-student son Tommy ignores his studies to help his father. Chan is also aided by cab driver Birmingham Brown who, while terrified of danger, ends up chauffeuring the detective around town. As Leah talks with Chan in his hotel lobby, a man eavesdrops on their conversation. Leah tells Chan that criminologist Dr. Paul Recknik has recently published a book which names her mother as the murderer and accuses police detective Harvey Dennis of covering up the crime because he is in love with Leah. Intrigued, Chan proceeds to a shop to purchase a copy of Recknik's book. Meanwhile, the man in the hotel lobby hurries to a carnival fun house at the end of the pier, where a gang of jewel thieves is headquartered. The man, Kaplan, a member of the gang, reports Chan's activities to twins Carl and Kurt Kazdas. Later, Kurt sneaks out of the hideout to arrange a meeting with Chan. By the time Chan arrives at the fun house, however, he finds Kurt dead, a victim of strangulation. Soon after, Dennis, alerted by Leah, appears at the

fun house and identifies Kurt as a fence specializing in stolen gems. After Chan invites Dennis to join the investigation, they search the headquarters and discover several stale loaves of bread with small statues hidden inside. Next, Chan visits Recknik to discuss his book. Noticing that the criminologist wears gloves, Chan comments that Kurt was killed by a pair of gloved hands, prompting Recknik to explain that he must protect his hands because they were severely burned in a fire. From Recknik's, Chan proceeds to the Manning house to examine the scene of the murder and there finds a statue identical to the ones hidden in the loaves of bread. At the house, Chan is confronted by Manning's partner, Webster Deacon, who vehemently objects to the reopening of Manning's murder. After noting that Deacon sports a large diamond on his ring finger, Chan visits the artist who created the statues. When the artist exposes a concealed compartment at the base of the statue, Chan discovers a diamond hidden inside and surmises that it is part of a stolen collection. At the studio, Chan notices the statue of a large cat identical to one found in Manning's study, and asks to see a copy of the sales receipt. The receipt reveals that the statue was sold to the Sea Tide Art Company, which is located at the pier, adjacent to the Fun House. Next, Chan visits Deacon at his office, and when he begins to question him about the Sea Tide Company, Deacon flees out a back door. Jumping into Birmingham's cab, Chan and Tommy pursue Deacon to the pier, but by the time they arrive, they find Deacon, strangled. Chan, Tommy and Birmingham then return to their hotel room, and when Tommy passes out, Chan opens the door and discovers that someone has been pumping deadly gas into the room through the keyhole. Deciding to examine the cat statue, Chan returns to the Manning house and finds another diamond hidden in a secret compartment. At the Fun House, Chan is captured by Carl, Kaplan and Gannet, another gang member, who demand that he produce the diamond. When Tommy and Birgmingham arrive at the Fun House, the thieves begin to pummel Tommy, intending to coerce Chan into revealing the location of the diamond. After Chan convinces the thieves that Birmingham has the jewel, they begin to chase him, and when Tommy collapses to safety under a table, Chan escapes. Dennis then learns that Chan has gone to the Fun House, he follows him there. Meanwhile, Chan and Birmingham lead the thieves into the Fun House maze. After Chan subdues the crooks with a well-aimed spray of the fire extinguisher, Dennis and Leah arrive and Chan elaborates that Manning and Deacon were partners in the diamond theft. When Manning double-crossed the gang and took the diamonds for himself, Deacon killed him. To prove his supposition, Chan produces the murder weapon with the initials "WD" inscribed on the handle. Chan continues that Deacon killed Kurt after discovering that he was about to betray him. Chan then pulls the murder gloves from Kaplan's pocket and concludes that Kaplan killed Deacon to prevent him from leading Chan to the hideout. *Detectives. Fathers and sons. Jewel thieves. Murder. Taxicab drivers. African Americans. Books. Brothers. Chinese Americans. College students. Criminologists. Diamonds. False accusations. Fun houses. Hideouts. Mazes. Partnership. Piers. Police detectives. Socialites. Statues. Stepchildren. Stepfathers. Twins.*

Note: The onscreen title is listed as "Charlie Chan in *The Chinese Cat.*" The working title of this film was *Murder in the Funhouse.* Although a *HR* production chart places Danny Desmond in the cast, his participation in the released film has not been confirmed. This was the second Monogram entry in the "Charlie Chan" series. For additional information on the series, please consult the Series Index and see the entry for *Charlie Chan Carries On* in *AFI Catalog of Feature Films, 1931-40;* F3.0663.

Box 15 Apr 1944. DV 24 Mar 1944, p. 3. FD 3 Apr 1944, p. 10. HR 7 Jan 1944, p. 6. HR 11 Jan 1944, p. 8. HR 14 Jan 1944, p. 10. HR 24 Mar 1944, p. 3. MPHPD 1 Apr 1944, p. 1826.

A CHINESE GAINS A FORTUNE IN AMERICA (Chinese language, Chinese Americans)

Grandview Film Co. *Dist* State Rights. **1939?.** Sd; b&w. 9 reels, 8,620 ft. Chinese language.

Cast: Yip Foot Yuk (*Chu Wah*), Wai Gim Fong (*His wife*), Fuk Bok (*Father*), Lang Fong (*Mother*), Gong Quon (*Boss of store, Mr. Quon*), Tong Yuck (*Son of boss*), Lee Moh (*Cook*), Ging Hong (*1st son*), Ging Wan (*2nd son*), Su Yu Sing (*2nd son's girl friend*), Su Ping (*Wah's mother*), Lok Suk (*Wah's uncle*).

Drama. [*Not viewed*]. Young Chu Wah leaves his mother and uncle in China and heads for America, where he hopes to make his fortune. A letter of introduction from Wah's uncle secures him a position in

Mr. Quon's store in San Francisco, where Wah works hard and sends money home. He meets a nice young woman to whom he can confide his ambitions. Unfortunately, Mr. Quon's son has ill feelings toward Wah and provokes a fight that results in Wah's dismissal from the store. Wah then discovers that his savings have been stolen, but his girl friend's kindly father lends Wah the money to buy a laundry. The new business gets off to a good start, but the laundry burns down, and Wah gets a job on a farm. Life on the farm suits Wah, and his new employer treats him well, leaving Wah the farm when he dies. Wah is then able to marry his girl friend, and they have two sons. Eighteen years later, Wah, who has become a prosperous farmer and a respected member of the community, is asked to serve as mediator in a local dispute. Wah's eldest son graduates from college and decides to work on the farm with his father. The younger son, however, does not yet share his father's work ethic, and is continually asking for money to spend on his girl friend. When he irresponsibly misplaces an envelope containing Wah's $1,000 contribution to a charity, the young man is remorseful. After declaring his love for his girl friend, he tells his parents that he now knows they are right. Forswearing his extravagent ways, the younger son resolves to join his brother on the farm, promising to work hard and repay his parents. *Chinese Americans. Fathers and sons. Finance–Personal. China. Dismissal (Employment). Farmers. Fights. Immigrants. Laundries. Money. Mothers and sons. Romance. San Francisco (CA). Uncles.*

Note: The summary and cast credits were taken from a translated dialogue continuity contained in the NYSA. The continuity was filed in Nassau County on 16 Oct 1939. Tai Quon Motion Picture Company was also known as Grandview (the English translation of "Tai Quon"), a production company that made Chinese-language films in the United States. The company had offices in San Francisco and Hong Kong, and this film appears to have been shot in both places.

THE CHINESE LILY (Chinese Americans)

Rice and Einstein. **1914?.** Si; b&w. 4 reels.

Dir Arthur W. Rice.

Drama. [No information concerning the plot of this film has been located.]. *Chinese Americans.*

Note: The only information located concerning this film comes from a news item in *MPW* 27 Jun 1914, which announced that the film was being produced in Berkeley, CA. The news item stated, "The sets, costumes and action portray the everyday life and characteristics of the present-day Chinese on the Pacific Coast. The cast is all Chinese, carefully selected to fit each part without make-up. An entirely new phase of Chinese life is presented, without the usual odiferous opium and obnoxious white slave scenes."

MPW 27 Jun 1914, p. 1842.

THE CHINESE PARROT (Chinese Americans)

Universal Pictures Corp.; Universal-Jewel. 23 Oct **1927** [©Universal Pictures Corp.; 24 Aug 1927; LP24331]. Si; b&w. 7 reels, 7,304 ft.

Series: Charlie Chan.

Pres Carl Laemmle. *Dir* Paul Leni. *Scen and adpt* J. Grubb Alexander. *Titles* Walter Anthony. *Photog* Ben Kline.

Source: Based on the novel *The Chinese Parrot* by Earl Derr Biggers (Indianapolis, 1926).

Cast: Marian Nixon (*Sally Phillimore*), Florence Turner (*Sally Phillimore, older*), Hobart Bosworth (*Philip Madden/Jerry Delaney*), Edward Burns (*Robert Eden*), Albert Conti (*Martin Thorne*), K. Sojin (*Charlie Chan*), Fred Esmelton (*Alexander Eden*), Ed Kennedy (*Maydorf*), George Kuwa (*Louie Wong*), Slim Summerville, Dan Mason (*Prospectors*), Anna May Wong (*Nautch dancer*), Etta Lee (*Gambling den habitué*), Jack Trent (*Jordan*).

Mystery. Sally Randall, daughter of a wealthy Hawaiian planter, marries Phillimore, the man of her father's choice, even though she has sworn her love to Philip Madden; tearing from her throat the expensive pearls given her by her father, Madden declares that one day he will buy her at the same price. Twenty years later, now a widow in financial straits, Sally offers the pearls for sale in San Francisco. Accompanied by her daughter, Sally, she is astonished to discover Madden bargaining for the pearls, which she has entrusted to Chan, a Chinese detective, with the sale contingent on her delivery of the jewels to his desert home. Madden is taken prisoner by yeggs and is impersonated by Jerry Delaney, who welcomes Sally and Robert Eden, the jeweler's son. While Chan is secretly conducting an investigation, the jewels are stolen by various parties, but it develops that a Chinese parrot has witnessed the kidnapping and told him about it. *Chinese Americans. Detectives. Hawaii. Jewelry. Kidnapping. Parrots. Plantation owners. San Francisco (CA).*

FD 8 Jan 1928. *NYT* 2 Jan 1928, p. 28. *Var* 11 Jan 1928, p. 27.

THE CHINESE RING (Chinese Americans)
Monogram Pictures Corp. *Dist* Monogram Pictures Corp. 6 Dec 1947; Prod: 21 Aug—early Sep 1947 [©Monogram Pictures Corp.; 20 Nov 1947; LP1381]. Sd (Western Electric Recording); b&w. 67-68 min.
Series: Charlie Chan.
Prod James S. Burkett. *Dir* William Beaudine. *Asst dir* William Calihan, Jr. *Orig scr* W. Scott Darling. *Photog* William Sickner. *Ed* Richard Heermance. [*Set dresser* Ray Boltz, Jr.]. *Mus dir* Edward J. Kay. *Rec* W. C. Smith. *Prod supv* Glenn Cook. *Tech dir* Dave Milton.
Source: Based on characters created by Earl Derr Biggers.
Cast: ROLAND WINTERS [(*Charlie Chan*)], Warren Douglas [(*Sergeant Bill Davidson*)], Mantan Moreland [(*Birmingham*)], Louise Currie [(*Peggy Cartwright*)], Victor Sen Young [(*Tommy Chan*)], Philip Ahn [(*Captain Kong*)], Byron Foulger [(*Armstrong*)], Thayer Roberts [(*Captain Kelso*)], Jean Wong [(*Princess Mei Ling*)], Chabing [(*Lilly Mae*)], George L. Spaulding [(*Dr. Hickey*)], [Paul Bryar (*Sergeant*)], [Thornton Edwards (*Hotel clerk*)], [Lee Tung Foo (*Butler*)], [Richard Wang (*Hamishin*)], [Spencer Chan (*Chinese officer*)], [Kenneth Chuck (*Chinese boy*)], [Jack Mower (*Ballard*)], [Charmienne Harker (*Stenographer*)].
Detective, Drama. [*Print viewed*]. A Chinese princess arrives in San Francisco by boat and visits Detective Charlie Chan at his home. Before an assailant kills the princess by shooting a poison dart through a window, she gives Chan's butler, Birmingham, an ancient Chinese ring. As she dies, the princess writes "Captain K" on a piece of paper, but is unable to finish the captain's name. Chan calls police sergeant Bill Davidson to help him investigate the murder. Bill's friend, reporter Peggy Cartwright, arrives uninvited and identifies the princess as Mei Ling, who came from Asia a few weeks before on a ship captained by two men, Kong and Kelso. Chan soon learns that the princess came to the United States to purchase warplanes for her brother's army in the Orient and brought one million dollars with her. Kelso has received only half his payment, however, and Kong is anxious to receive his share of the arms sales. Peggy searches the princess' apartment, but hides when a masked man enters and ransacks the dresser. Peggy then meets Mei Ling's maid, Lilly Mae, and a boy who lives in the apartment basement. Later, Chan arrives and finds the maid dead. The boy, who is a deaf-mute, tells Chan with gestures that he saw a man enter Mei Ling's apartment. Chan then visits Armstrong, the banker who handled Mei Ling's traveler's checks, and Armstrong tells him that he had to put down one of his vicious guard dogs. Kong and Kelso, anxious to get the rest of their money before their boat sails at midnight, kidnap Chan and Armstrong, bind and gag them, and drive them onto the ship. Birmingham follows and calls Chan's son Tommy, and together they free Armstrong and Chan. Meanwhile, Peggy and Bill arrive, and when Kelso sees Peggy, he abducts her. Bill and the police come to her rescue, and Kong and Kelso are arrested. Chan then explains that it was Armstrong, not Kong and Kelso, who committed the murders. Armstrong stole Mei Ling's money, then swindled Kelso and Kong out of receiving the balance of their payment. He then killed the maid, as well as the boy, whom he buried instead of his dog. Pointing out that Peggy had phoned in her "scoop" implicating Kong and Kelso before he had exposed Armstrong, Chan insists that women are not meant for heavy thinking. *Chinese. Chinese Americans. Detectives. Murder. Sea captains. Swindlers and swindling. Airplanes. Bankers. Butlers. China–History–Civil War, 1945-1949. Deaf-mutes. Fathers and sons. Kidnapping. Maids. Munitions. Princesses. Profiteering. San Francisco (CA). Women reporters.*
Note: The title card on the film reads: "Charlie Chan in *The Chinese Ring*." The film's working titles were *The Red Hornet* and *Charlie Chan and the Chinese Ring*. *IFJ* reviewed the picture as *The Red Hornet*. This film marked the first "Charlie Chan" film to star Roland Winters. Winters was the third actor to portray "Chan" in the series, replacing Sidney Toler after his death earlier in 1947. Toler had replaced Warner Oland in the series, which began with the 1931 Fox film *Charlie Chan Carries On*. Although the CBCS lists Valerie Ardis as "Stenographer," the *Var* review and studio production files list Charmienne Harker in the role. For more information on the series, consult the Series Index and see the above entry for *Charlie Chan Carries On*.
Box 20 Dec 1947. *DV* 9 Dec 1947. *FD* 16 Dec 1947, p. 8. *HR* 20 Aug 1947, p. 6. *HR* 22 Aug 1947, p. 12. *HR* 29 Aug 1947, p. 22. *HR* 9 Dec 1947, p. 3. *IFJ* 2 Aug 1947, p. 34. *MPHPD* 20 Dec 1947. *Var* 17 Dec 1947, p. 20.

CHIP OFF THE OLD BLOCK (German Americans)
Universal Pictures Co., Inc. *Dist* Universal Pictures Co., Inc. 25 Feb **1944**; Prod: 30 Aug—early Oct 1943 [©Universal Pictures Co., Inc.; 10 Mar 1944; LP12600]. Sd (Western Electric Recording); b&w. 7,144 ft. 76-77 min. PCA cert no. 9803.
[*Exec prod* Milton Schwarzwald]. *Assoc prod* Bernard W. Burton. *Dir* Charles Lamont. *Asst dir* Mack Wright. [*Dial dir* Ernest Truex]. *Scr* Eugene Conrad and Leo Townsend. *Orig story* Robert Arthur. *Dir of photog* Charles Van Enger. *Art dir* John B. Goodman and Ralph M. DeLacy. *Film ed* Charles Maynard. *Set dec* R. A. Gausman and E. R. Robinson. *Gowns* Vera West. *Mus dir* Charles Previn. *Orch* Larry Russell and Frank Skinner. *Dance dir* Louis Da Pron. *Dir of sd* Bernard B. Brown. [*Sd*] *tech* Charles Carroll.
Song(s): "My Song," words and music by Lew Brown and Ray Henderson; "Love Is Like Music," music by Milton Schwarzwald, lyrics by Sidney Miller and Inez James; "Is It Good or Is It Bad?" words and music by Charles Tobias; "It's Mighty Nice to Have Met You" and "Spelling Prep," words by William Crago, music by Grace Shannon; "Gotta Give My Feet a Break" and "The Captain's Kids," words and music by Sidney Miller and Inez James; "Sailor Song," music by Sidney Miller and Inez James, lyrics by Eugene Conrad.
Cast: DONALD O'CONNOR (*Donald Corrigan*), PEGGY RYAN (*Peggy* [*Flaherty*]), ANN BLYTH (*Glory Marlow, 3rd*), Helen Vinson (*Glory Marlow, Jr.*), Helen Broderick (*Glory Marlow, Sr.*), Arthur Treacher (*Quentin*), Patric Knowles ([*Commander*] *Judd Corrigan*), J. Edward Bromberg (*Blaney Wright*), Ernest Truex (*Henry McHugh*), Minna Gombell (*Milly*), Samuel S. Hinds (*Dean Manning*), Irving Bacon (*Prof. Frost*), Joel Kupperman (*The Quiz Kid*), [Frank Wilcox (*Edward Storey*)], [The Jivin' Jacks and Jills: Bobby Scheerer, Jerry Antes, Harold Bell, Jack Coffey, Dante DiPaolo, Lowell McPeek, Lou Payetta, Pat Phelan, Cal Rothenberg, George Rowland, Jerry Singer, Ronald Stanton, Jean Davis, Dorothy Webb, Shirley Mills, Peggy Brant, Elaine Campbell, Arlyne Gladden, Verda Jenkins, Irma Jeter, Lu Ann Jones, Iris Kirksey, Connie Roberts, and Barbara Strong], [Leon Belasco (*Piano player*)], [Mantan Moreland (*Porter*)], [Arthur Loft (*Conductor*)], [Gladys Blake (*Receptionist*)], [Eddie Bruce (*Kliegelmeyer*)], [Dorothy Granger (*Cab driver*)], [Vernon Dent (*Scheffer*)], [Sidney Miller (*Soda clerk*)], [George Reed (*Theodore*)], [Jessie Tai Sing (*Sue Chang*)], [Dorothy Babb (*Phyllis*)], [Joe McGuinness, Harry Harvey, Jr., Bill Henderson, Jack Bell, Billy Bestor, John Truel, Robert Coleman, Wally Carter (*Dancers*)], [Jack Gardner (*Elevator operator*)], [Pat Dillon (*Tubb*)], [Jack Lindquist (*Wally*)], [Bruce Bilson (*Red*)].
Youth, Musical comedy. [*Print viewed*]. After writing, directing and starring in the annual musical show at the Sperling Naval Academy, cadet Donald Corrigan is brought before Dean Manning for his many shenanigans. Rather than expelling the teenager, Manning sends Donald home on an extended leave, stating that he may return once he corrects his behavior. Donald meets Glory Marlow III on the train to New York City and becomes immediately smitten. Glory III, who was reared in Hawaii by her aunt and uncle, tells Donald that she is going to New York to live with her mother and grandmother, two famous actresses of the musical theater. Unknown to Glory III, however, is the fact that her mother has just announced her retirement. When her producers, Blaney Wright and Henry McHugh, suggest that Glory III take her place in their new production, Glory, Jr. refuses, as she is intent on keeping her daughter out of the theater. Upon arriving in New York, Donald is met at the train station by love-struck Peggy Flaherty, who causes the jealous Glory III to break her date with Donald. When Glory III tells her mother and grandmother what happened, they tell her about the "Corrigan curse," as they too had fallen in love, then lost, both Donald's father and grandfather. Donald still calls on Glory III that night, but she, bowing to two generations of advice, refuses to see him. The next day, Donald meets with Peggy, and she agrees to square things with Glory III if he agrees to help her audition for some Broadway plays. Glory, however, having ordered Quentin, her butler, to tell Glory III that Donald has left town, impersonates her granddaughter on the phone and tells Donald that Glory III is engaged. The two teenagers, though, run into each other on the streets of New York, and learn about her grandmother's deception. Glory III then invites Donald and Peggy to her recital that night, much to her mother and grandmother's chagrin. Peggy uses the recital as an opportunity to audition for the theatrical producers in attendance, but Blaney and Henry leave before she and Donald

perform their number. Glory III is later offered the lead in the producers' new play, but she refuses, stating that she plans to spend her time working for Chinese war relief and other charities. Donald convinces her to do the play, however, on the condition that all profits be donated to those same charities. Later, Donald's father, Commander Judd Corrigan, returns home, and while eavesdropping on him, Donald and Peggy mistakenly assume that he is a German spy when they hear him discussing plans for Donald's birthday present. After learning that Donald is dating Glory III, Judd goes with his son to Glory III's rehearsal, where he tells Glory, Jr. that he is still in love with her. That night, Donald and Peggy unsuccessfully attempt to steal Judd's blueprints from Scheffer, a German-American sailboat builder. Judd then orders Donald to return to Sperling. Just as her show, *The Third Glory*, is about to open on Broadway, Glory III insists that they perform their final rehearsal at the Academy. Aware that his father is meeting with Scheffer at a nearby boat house, Donald and his cadet friends abduct the boat builder, only to discover that the "spy plans" are the blueprints to Donald's birthday present. Peggy then connives to get Donald to appear with her in the final rehearsal, but he still ends up in the arms of Glory III when they walk offstage together. *Actors and actresses. Cadets. Fathers and sons. Mothers and daughters. Romantic rivalry. Singers. Amateur shows. Blueprints. Brothers and sisters. Butlers. Choirs (Music). Dancers. Drugstores. Eavesdropping. German Americans. Grandmothers. Impersonation and imposture. Maids. Military schools. Musical revues. New York City. Officers (Military). Porters. Recitals. Rehearsals. Theatrical producers. Train conductors. Trains. United States. Navy. Widowers. Widows.*

Note: The working title of this film was *The Third Glory*. *HR* news items and production charts include Walter Catlett in the cast, but he did not appear in the film. According to the *Var* review, actor Donald O'Connor was inducted into the U.S. Army the same week this film was released. This marked the film debut of sixteen-year-old actress Ann Blyth, who had previously appeared on Broadway in the play *Watch on the Rhine*.

Box 19 Feb 1944. *DV* 11 Feb 1944, p. 3. *FD* 14 Feb 1944, p. 7. *HR* 27 Aug 1943, p. 23. *HR* 30 Aug 1943, p. 4. *HR* 31 Aug 1943, p. 3. *HR* 11 Feb 1944, p. 3. *MPHPD* 15 Jan 1944, p. 1715. *MPHPD* 19 Feb 1944, p. 1761. *NYT* 17 Mar 1944, p. 14. *Var* 16 Feb 1944, p. 10.

CHISERA *see* **GUNMEN FROM LAREDO**

CHLOE: LOVE IS CALLING YOU (African Americans)
Pinnacle Productions, Inc. *Dist* State Rights; Pinnacle Productions, Inc. 1 Apr **1934**; *Prod:* at Sun Haven Studios (St. Petersburg, FL). Sd; b&w. 7 reels, 5,802 ft. 64 min.
Pres J. D. TROP. *Dir* Marshall Neilan. *Asst dir* Jack Chapin. *Photog* Max Stengler. *Art dir* Robert Stevens. *Film ed* Helene Turner and Joseph Josephson. *Mus arr* Erno Rapee. *Orig mus* George Henninger.
Cast: Olive Borden (*Chloe, previously known as Betty Ann Gordon*), Reed Howes (*Wade Carson*), Molly O'Day (*Joyce Gordon*), Frank Joyner (*Colonel Gordeon*), Georgette Harvey (*Mandy*), Jess Caven (*Hill*), Gus Smith (*Moses*), Richard Huey (*Ben*), Philip Ober (*Jim Strong*).
Drama. [*Not viewed*]. Mandy, a voodoo practicing nursemaid, leaves the swamps of the Everglades with her half-white daughter Chloe and helper, Jim Strong, to exact revenge on Colonel Gordon, the man she believes is responsible for the lynching of her husband Sam fifteen years earlier. The widowed colonel, whose daughter Betty Ann drowned in the swamps at the same time that Sam was killed, lives with his niece Joyce and oversees the family turpentine factory. As Chloe, Mandy and Jim near the colonel's home, Chloe expresses doubts about her black heritage and rejects the proposal of the devoted Jim. Wade Carson, the new "Yankee" foreman of the turpentine factory, meanwhile, impresses the colonel when he discovers shortages at the factory and establishes that Moses, one of his employees, has been stealing from the company. After Wade fires Moses, Moses swears revenge and then tries to force his attentions on Chloe. Wade comes to Chloe's rescue, however, further aggravating Moses and confusing Chloe with his obvious romantic interest. Later, while Mandy and Moses join forces and plan their voodoo revenge, Chloe and Jim argue about Chloe's attraction to the "white northerner." Then, on the anniversary of Betty Ann's disappearance, Mandy leaves voodoo switches on the colonel's doorstep and initiates a drum-beating ceremony. During the ceremony, Mandy, who is also concerned about Chloe's interest in Wade, drugs her tea and orders Jim to take advantage of her subsequent stupor to assure their marriage. Jim refuses to seduce Chloe, but confronts Wade and tells him that she is half-black and therefore "off-limits." Although Wade

is reluctant to believe Jim about Chloe, he takes seriously his warning that Mandy and Moses are plotting against him and the colonel. Mandy, meanwhile, has been hired by the colonel to wash clothes and, while in his house, steals a photograph of the young Betty Ann. The colonel and Wade then break into Mandy's cabin and there discover clothes that the colonel is sure belonged to Betty Ann. When Chloe identifies the clothes as ones she wore as a child, the colonel becomes convinced she is his daughter. Mandy, however, denies that she kidnapped Chloe to replace her own dead child, and Joyce, who is attracted to Wade, also expresses doubts about Chloe's white parentage. Confused and distraught, Chloe flees into the swamps, while the colonel and Wade, determined to prove their hunch, dig up a grave that the colonel believes contains Mandy's black baby. After they discover "kinky" hair in the gravesite, Wade and the colonel arrest Mandy and rush to save Chloe from the jaws of an alligator. At last assured of her "whiteness," Chloe is free to pursue her romance with Wade. *African Americans. Florida. Long-lost relatives. Miscegenation. Parentage. Revenge. Voodoo. Alligators. Corpses. Dismissal (Employment). Drugging. Employer-employee relations. Everglades (FL). Factories. Fathers and daughters. Foremen. Graves. Lechery. Nieces. Northerners. Proposals (Marital). Rescues. Rites and ceremonies. Romantic rivalry. Swamps.*

Note: No reviews for this film were found. The above plot summary and credits were taken from a dialogue continuity that was submitted on 13 Feb 1934 to the New York State Censor Board. A 26 Jul 1933 *FD* news item refers to this film as a "Kennedy Sunshine Special," an apparent reference to Aubrey Kennedy, the then owner of the picture's production studio. Modern sources add the following additional information: *Chloe* began production on 22 May 1933 in St. Petersburg and featured local people in the cast. At the time of filming, the studio was not called Sun Haven but was renamed Sun Haven in Aug 1933 when T. C. Parker, Jr., a local investor in the project, purchased the facility from Kennedy. Sun Haven then merged with a Tampa studio, Beecroft-Florida Studios, in Dec 1933.

FD 26 Jul 1933, p. 2. *HR* 18 May 1933, p. 4. *MPH* 28 Apr 1934, p. 66.

THE CHOSEN PATH (Italian Americans)
Emory Film Corp. *Dist* Exclusive Features, Inc.; State Rights. Nov **1919**?. Si; b&w. 5 reels.
Story George P. Frazer. *Cam* Edward Wynard.
Cast: Marguerite Leslie (*Mary Willis*), William Betchel (*Fred Willis*), Ray Emory (*Dolly Willis*), Donald Hall (*Donald Turner*), Fred C. Jones (*Tony Leonardo*).
Drama. When Mary Willis leaves her husband Fred for life in the city, Fred puts their daughter Dolly in a convent. Several years pass and Mary is now working in an underworld roadhouse which is financially backed by a suspicious Italian named Tony Leonardo. Mary seeks Dolly out at the convent and induces her to come and work at the roadhouse. When Leonardo falls in love with Dolly, Mary coerces Dolly into marriage with him. Dolly's life is wretched until one night during a raid, Leonardo is killed and Dolly is freed to return to her father. She pleads with him to forgive Mary, and the three are reunited. *Marriage-Forced. Mothers and daughters. Roadhouses. Separation (Marital). Convents. Italian Americans. Lure of the city. Police raids.*

Note: The release date of this film is difficult to determine; while it appears in release charts beginning in Aug 1919, it was not advertised until Nov 1919, and was not reviewed until Feb 1920.

ETR 29 Nov 1919, p. 2198-99. *ETR* 7 Feb 1920, p. 1005.

CHRIST IN CONCRETE *see* **GIVE US THIS DAY**

CIMARRON (Native Americans, Cherokee, Osage)
RKO Radio Pictures, Inc.; A Wesley Ruggles Production. *Dist* RKO Radio Pictures, Inc. 9 Feb **1931**; New York premiere: 26 Jan 1931; *Prod:* 27 Aug—22 Nov 1930; retakes 18 Nov—3 Dec 1930 [©RKO Radio Pictures, Inc.; 31 Dec 1930; LP1930]. Sd (RCA Photophone System); b&w. 13 reels, 11,182 ft. 124 min. Passed by the National Board of Review. PCA cert no. 1029 [2 Jul 1935].
Prod William LeBaron. *Assoc prod* Louis Sarecky. *Dir* Wesley Ruggles. [*2d unit dir* Breezy Eason]. [*Asst dir* Doran Cox, F. D. Langton and Dewey Starkey]. *Scr version and dial* Howard Estabrook. [*Contr wrt* Louis Sarecky]. *Photog* Edward Cronjager. [*Asst cam* Joseph Biroc and Harry Wild]. [*Cam crew—Land rush scenes* Nick Musuraca, Fred Bentley, Joe Novak, Edward Pyle, Pliny Goodfriend, H. Lyman Broening, Ben White, John Thompson, Ed Ullman, Fred Mayer, Rex Wimpy, Frank Redman, Jack Landrigan, Robert Pittack, Harry Jackson, Joe Walters, Edward Henderson, O. H. Borradaile, Guy Bennett, Joe LaShelle, Roy Clark, Elmer Dyer, Ed Kull, Linwood Dunn,

Bob DeGrasse, Fred Hendrickson, Otto Benninger, Rex Curtis, Mack Elliott, Newton Hopcraft, Neal Harbarger, James Daly, Rod Tolmie, E. F. Adams, Ed Kearns, Les Shorr, George Diskant, Emilio Calori, Ted Hayes, Jack Grout, Frank Burgess, Earl Metz, Louis DeAngelis, Harry Underwood, James King, Lothrop Worth, Ed Garvin, Harry Kauffman, Neal Beckner, Al Smalley, Paul Cable, Bill Heckler, Dean Dailey, Maurice Kains, William J. Schuck, Harold Wellman, Willard Barth and Russell Hoover]. *Spec eff* Lloyd Knechtel. [*Asst art dir* Sidney Ullman]. *Film ed* William Hamilton. *Scenery* Max Rée. *Cost* Max Rée. *Rec* Clem Portman. [*Asst rec* Ralph Spotts]. [*Makeup* Ern Westmore]. [*Chief elec* William Johnson]. [*Loc meals served by* Judd Steven]. [*Research* Harold Hendee]. [*Trick rider* Gordon Jones, Bob Erickson, Ken Cooper, Hank Potts, Colonel Whitehorse, Bob Burns, Walt Robbins, "Shorty" Hall, Buff Jones, Charles Johnson, Whitey Sovern, Bud Pope, Rex Cole, Lee Cooper and Pete Janet]. [*Still photog* Fred Hendrickson]. [*Gen press rep* Hyatt Daab].

Source: Based on the novel *Cimarron* by Edna Ferber (New York, 1930).

Cast: Richard Dix (*Yancey Cravat*), Irene Dunne (*Sabra Cravat*), Estelle Taylor (*Dixie Lee*), Nance O'Neil (*Felice Venable*), William Collier, Jr. (*The Kid*), Rosco Ates (*Jesse Rickey*), George E. Stone (*Sol Levy*), Stanley Fields (*Lon Yountis*), Robert McWade (*Louis Hefner*), Edna May Oliver (*Mrs. Tracy Wyatt*), Nancy Dover (*Donna Cravat [as an adult]*), Eugene Jackson (*Isaiah*), [Frank Darien (*Mr. Bixby*)], [Dolores Brown (*Ruby Big Elk, as an adult*)], [Gloria Vonic (*Ruby Big Elk, as a child*)], [Otto Hoffman (*Murch Rankin*)], [William Orlamond (*Grat Gulch*)], [Frank Beal (*Louis Venable*)], [Helen Parrish (*Donna Cravat, as a child*)], [Donald Dilloway (*"Cim," as an adult*)], [Junior Johnson (*"Cim," as a child*)], [Douglas Scott (*"Cim," as a toddler*)], [Reginald Scott (*Yancey, Jr.*)], [Lois Jane Campbell (*Felice, Jr.*)], [Ann Lee (*Aunt Cassandra*)], [Tyrone Brereton (*Dabney Venable*)], [Lillian Lane (*Cousin Bella*)], [Henry Roquemore (*Jouett Goforth*)], [Nell Craig (*Arminta Greenwood*)], [Robert McKenzie (*Pat Leary*)], [William Janney], [George Lollier], [Billy Elmer], [Ethan Laidlaw], [Frank Lackteen], [Mildred Frizelle], [Jack Leonard], [Walter Lewis], [Marion Mirsch], [Lillian West], [Max Barwyn], [Carl Stockdale], [Heinie Conklin], [Barney Furey], [Tim Lonergan], [Helen Trask], [Leo Willis], [Ford West], [Harry Holden], [Alice Adair], [Kay Deslys], [Dorothy Simms], [Dorothy Ray].

Historical, **Drama**. [*Print viewed*]. Inspired by his adventures during the 1889 Oklahoma land rush, Yancey Cravat, a freewheeling lawyer and newspaper editor, convinces his Eastern-bred wife Sabra to leave her stuffy Wichita family and join him in the West. Although Sabra finds Osage, the Oklahoma "boomer town" that Yancey has chosen to start his newspaper, rough and squalid, she settles there with him and, with help from their young black servant Isaiah, undertakes to bring up her son "Cim." Soon after his arrival, Yancey confronts local outlaw and bully Lon Yountis with the murder of the newspaper's previous editor. During an "all-faiths church meeting," which Yancey has been asked to conduct at the town gambling hall, Yancey threatens to identify the editor's killer and is shot at by Lon. In self-defense, Yancey kills Lon, then dismisses his "flock," which includes Dixie Lee, a maligned prostitute whom Yancey had befriended during the land rush. A year later, after the birth of the Cravats' daughter Donna, Osage is besieged by an outlaw gang led by The Kid, an old cowboy friend of Yancey's. Although Yancey kills The Kid during a fierce gun battle, which also claims the life of the loyal Isaiah, he refuses to collect any reward for his deed and bemoans The Kid's downfall. In 1893, a new "Cherokee Strip" land rush is announced, and Yancey, who has never stayed in one place for more than five years, deserts the much-settled Sabra to participate in it. Helped and supported by expert printer Jesse Rickey and department store owner Sol Levy, Sabra, who knows nothing of Yancey's whereabouts, takes over the newspaper. Five years later, dressed in a "Rough Riders" uniform, Yancey returns to Osage just as Sabra and a group of "decent women" are about to try Dixie Lee as a "public nuisance." Yancey successfully defends the misunderstood Dixie in court, then convinces his less tolerant wife of Dixie's essential goodness. After Oklahoma obtains statehood in 1907 and the oil boom has brought prosperity to some of the Osage Indians, Yancey, who has been approached to participate in a political scheme to trick the Indians out of their wealth, writes a provocative editorial favoring citizenship for all American Indians. Despite the heated objections of Sabra, who has always loathed the Indians and who is repulsed by her

son's romantic involvement with an Indian chief's daughter, Yancey publishes the editorial and then disappears. Many years later, after the fortieth anniversary of the newspaper's founding, Sabra is elected as Oklahoma's first Congresswoman. During a luncheon in her honor, a more tolerant Sabra speaks fondly of her Indian daughter-in-law and her long-lost husband. Just before she is to dedicate a statue honoring the Oklahoma pioneers, Sabra hears that a tramp called "Old Yance" has risked his own life to save many oil drillers from a deadly explosion. Sabra rushes to the accident site in time to embrace Yancey before his death, then discovers that the statue has been sculpted in his image. *Marriage. Newspapers. Oklahoma. Settlers. United States–History–Reconstruction, 1865-1898. African Americans. Cherokee Indians. Citizenship. Department store owners. Editors. Family relationships. Gambling houses. Gunfights. Industrial accidents. Intolerance. Jews. Land rushes. Lawyers. Murder. Oil. Osage Indians. Outlaws. Political corruption. Printers. Prostitution. Rough Riders. Self-sacrifice. Servants. Statues. Tramps. Trials. United States–History–War of 1898. United States. Congress. House of Representatives. Wichita (KS). Women in politics. Women reporters.*

Note: The following statement is included in the film's opening credits: "For certain descriptive passages in *Cimarron* Miss Ferber makes acknowledgement to *Hands Up* by Fred E. Sutton and A. B. MacDonald." Sutton and MacDonald's novel was published in New York in 1927. According to an Oct 1932 *LAEx* news item, the studio bid $125,000 for the rights to Ferber's novel. That amount, which was also paid by Universal for the rights to *Strictly Dishonorable*, also produced in 1931 (see *AFI Catalog of Feature Films, 1931-40*; F3.4369), was the highest ever paid by motion picture companies for rights to literary properties, according to the news item. The picture's famous land rush scene, which required a week to film, was shot at Jasmin Quinn Ranch near Bakersfield, CA, according to studio production files. Publicity for the picture notes that 5,000 extras participated in that scene and forty-seven cameras were used to shoot it. An *IP* articles states that the land rush scene was shot by twenty-eight cameramen, six stillmen and twenty-seven assistants, to make a total camera crew of sixty-one, one of the largest group of cameramen ever assembled for one sequence. According to publicity, the Native Americans who appeared in the film were "made up white to appear coppery on the screen." Production files indicate that the film cost $1,434,800 to produce and went over budget by $354,114. Modern sources state that the picture lost $565,000 at the box office in its initial release. Some of this loss was recouped in a 1935 re-issue. The film had its premiere at the Globe Theater in New York, where the top ticket price was $2.00. *Cimarron* won Academy Awards for Best Picture, Best Adaptation and Best Art Direction. It was nominated for Best Direction, Best Actor (Richard Dix), Best Actress (Irene Dunne) and Best Cinematography. *FDYB* included the film in its "one of the year's ten best pictures" list.

Modern sources add the following cast credits: Clara Hunt (*Indian girl*), Bob Kortman (*Killer*) and Dennis O'Keefe (who at that time was known as Bud Flanagan). William Janney is identified in the role of a "worker" by modern sources. In 1960 Anthony Mann directed Glenn Ford and Maria Schell in an M-G-M version of Ferber's novel (see below).

EHW 27 Dec 1930, p. 20. *FD* 18 Jan 1931, p. 10. *IP* Dec 1930, p. 28. *HR* 20 Dec 1930, p. 1, 3. *MPH* 3 Jan 1931, p. 71. *MPH* 17 Jan 1931, p. 58. *MPH* 31 Jan 1931, pp. 27-30. *NYT* 27 Jan 1931, p. 14. *Var* 28 Jan 1931, p. 14.

CIMARRON (Native Americans)

Metro-Goldwyn-Mayer Corp.; controlled by Loew's Inc. *Dist* Loew's Inc. Dec **1960**; World premiere in Oklahoma City, OK: 1 Dec 1960; Prod: late Nov 1959—mid-Feb 1960; addl scenes began mid-Apr 1960 [©Metro-Goldwyn-Mayer Corp.; 7 Dec 1960; LP18009]. Sd (Westrex Recording System); col (Metrocolor); Photographic lenses by Panavision. 8 reels, 12,143 or 13,253 ft. 140 or 147 min. PCA cert no. 19510.

Prod Edmund Grainger. *Dir* Anthony Mann. *Asst dir* Ridgeway Callow. *Scr* Arnold Schulman. *Dir of photog* Robert L. Surtees. *Spec eff* A. Arnold Gillespie, Lee LeBlanc and Robert R. Hoag. *Col consultant* Charles K. Hagedon. *Art dir* George W. Davis and Addison Hehr. *Film ed* John Dunning. *Set dec* Henry Grace, Hugh Hunt and Otto Siegel. *Cost dec* Walter Plunkett. *Mus* Franz Waxman. *Rec supv* Franklin Milton. [*Sd* Wally Wallace]. *Hair styles* Sydney Guilaroff. *Makeup created by* William Tuttle. [*Head wrangler* Dick Webb].

Song(s): "Cimarron," lyrics by Paul Francis Webster, music by Franz Waxman, sung by The Roger Wagner Chorale.

Source: Based on the novel *Cimarron* by Edna Ferber (New York, 1930).

Cast: Glenn Ford [(*Yancey Cravat*)], Maria Schell [(*Sabra Cravat*)], Anne Baxter [(*Dixie Lee*)], Arthur O'Connell [(*Tom Wyatt*)], Russ Tamblyn [(*William "The Kid" Hardy*)], Mercedes McCambridge [(*Sarah Wyatt*)], Vic Morrow [(*Wes Jennings*)], Robert Keith [(*Sam Pegler*)], Charles McGraw [(*Bob Yountis*)], Henry "Harry" Morgan [(*Jesse Rickey*)], David Opatoshu [(*Sol Levy*)], Aline

MacMahon [(*Mavis Pegler*)], Lili Darvas [(*Felicia Venable*)], Edgar Buchanan [(*Neal Hefner*)], Mary Wickes [(*Mrs. Hefner*)], Royal Dano [(*Ike Howes*)], L. Q. Jones [(*Millis*)], George Brenlin [(*Hoss Barry*)], Vladimir Sokoloff [(*Jacob Krubeckoff*)], [Ivan Triesault (*Lewis*)], [Buzz Martin (*Cimarron Cravat, "Cim" as a young man*)], [John Cason (*Suggs*)], [Dawn Little Sky (*Arita Red Feather*)], [Eddie Little Sky (*Ben Red Feather*)], [Clegg Hoyt (*Grat Gotcb*)], [William Challee (*Barber*)], [Helen Westcott (*Miss Kuye*)], [Mickie Chouteau (*Ruby Red Feather*)], [Andy Albin (*Water man*)], [Janet Brandt (*Madam Rhoda*)], [John Pickard (*Cavalry captain*)], [Ted Eccles (*Cim Cravat, age two*)], [Irene James (*Townswoman*)], [James Halferty (*Cim Cravat, age ten*)], [J. Edward McKinley (*Beck*)], [Robert Carson (*Senator Rollins*)], [Barry Bernard (*Butler*)], [Jorie Wyler (*Theresa Jump*)], [Ralph Reed (*Bellboy*)], [Jimmy Lewis (*Hefner boy*)], [Charles Watts (*Mr. Brothers*)], [Rayford Barnes (*Sergeant*)], [Paul Bryar (*Mr. Self*)], [Jack Daly (*Wyatt's man*)], [Coleman Francis (*Mr. Geer*)], [Jack Scroggy (*Mr. Walter*)], [Richard Davies (*Mr. Hodges*)], [Charles F. Seel (*Charles*)], [Mary Benoit (*Mrs. Lancey*)], [Tony Merrill, Bill Remick, Ben Gary, Wilson Wood (*Reporters*)], [Phyllis Douglas (*Sadie*)], [Jeane Wood (*Clubwoman*)], [La Rue Farlow (*Dancer*)], [John Damler (*Foreman*)], [Fred Coby, Robert B. Williams (*Oil workers*)].

Western. [*Print viewed*]. Sabra Cravat's wealthy Kansas City parents try to dissuade her from participating in a land run in the Oklahoma territory with her new husband Yancey, but she is adamant. During the journey, Sabra's knowledge of her husband's character deepens, and when he lends one of his covered wagons to Tom and Sarah Wyatt and their large, destitute family, she experiences his generosity. Upon arriving in Oklahoma and meeting many of Yancey's friends, including a lady of the evening named Dixie Lee, she discovers that he is something of an adventurer. Sabra has her first disagreement with Yancey, however, when he staunchly defends an American Indian family whose wagon has been overturned by a group of angry men. Even though a Cavalry officer states that Ben and Arita Red Feather have the right to participate in the land run, Sabra, a French American, wonders aloud whether Yancey should have risked injury just to help some Indians. At high noon on 22 April 1889, thousands of settlers, who hope to claim one hundred and sixty acres of free land, race wildly on horseback, wagon, bicycle and stagecoach across the prairie. Tom is pushed off the stagecoach, whereupon a frantic Sarah plants a stake into the arid dirt near the starting line. Sam Pegler, an idealistic newspaper owner from Osage, is killed during the run, and Ben Red Feather is lassoed to the ground by a bigoted roughneck named Bob Yountis. After Dixie, angry at Yancey for having married another woman, vengefully claims the land that Yancey had wanted, he decides to forget about ranching and take over Sam's newspaper. The printer, Jesse Rickey, remains in Osage with the paper, the *Oklahoma Wigwam*, while Sam's widow Mavis sadly returns home. Some time later, Bob Yountis and William Hardy, a young troublemaker known as "The Kid," terrorize a Jewish peddler named Sol Levy. Yancey rescues Sol, but The Kid, whose father had been Yancey's friend, refuses to listen to the older man's advice and rides away with his rowdy companions. One night Yountis, leading a band of Indian-hating townspeople, lynches Ben Red Feather and destroys his home. Outraged, Yancey shoots Yountis and then brings Arita and her baby to the Cravat house. When the three arrive home, they discover that Sabra has given birth to a baby boy, whom they name Cimarron. Several years pass, and The Kid, now a feared outlaw, reluctantly joins his cohorts in robbing the Osage bank. Cornered, the robbers take refuge in the schoolhouse, but when his buddy Wes tries to make a child their hostage, The Kid intervenes and is shot. Yancey shoots Wes, thereby earning a large reward, but when he remorsefully tears up the checks, Sabra accuses him of cheating Cim out of his future. Dixie confesses that she still loves Yancey, and when he gently rejects her, she sells her farm and opens a "social club." Meanwhile, Arita's little daughter Ruby is ejected from the schoolhouse. Yancey files a protest, but the townspeople refuse to allow an Indian to attend school. Yancey charges that they are keeping their children's blood pure, but their heads empty. Soon afterward, Yancey leaves town to participate in another land rush, to the bitter disappointment of his wife. During his five-year absence, Sabra obtains a loan from Sol, who has fallen in love with her. Sabra learns from Dixie that Yancey, who spent several years in Alaska, is now a Rough Rider in Cuba. Dixie also confesses that it is Sabra, not her, whom Yancey loves. That year,

Yancey returns, promising to make amends for his absence. Sabra and Cim accept him, and the years pass. One day Yancey excitedly reports that oil has been discovered on the Indian reservation. Tom Wyatt, whose own oil-rich land has made him wealthy, laughs and says that it is he, not the Indians, who owns the oil rights. Yancey writes in his paper that Wyatt swindled the Indians, and the story is reported all over the country. Sabra, meanwhile, worries that Cim is becoming serious about Ruby, whom she considers unfit for her son, but when Yancey tells her that he has been nominated for governor of the territory, she beams. In Washington, Sabra ecstatically dresses for a party, but Yancey learns that Wyatt and his powerful friends will name him governor only if he agrees to cooperate with them. Yancey rejects the post, whereupon Sabra orders him to leave her. Later, Sol, now a successful merchant, lends Sabra a large sum, and she builds the paper into a major enterprise. When Cim informs her that he has married Ruby and is on his way to Oregon, Sabra bitterly complains that he is throwing his life away and then dismisses him from the house. Ten years later, in 1914, Sabra sits at a desk composing an editorial for the newspaper's twenty-fifth anniversary. Sol and Tom want her to be the model for a sculpture exemplifying the pioneer spirit, but Sabra protests that the man who ran away from her was the true pioneer. At a surprise anniversary party, Sabra is reunited with her son and his family. She pays tribute to her husband, claiming that she still hopes for his return, but that day, war is declared. In December, Sabra rereads the letter she has received from Yancey, in which he again apologizes for being a disappointment to her. On the table is an open telegram which states that her husband has been killed in action. *Family relationships. Homesteaders. Idealists. Land rushes. Marriage. Oklahoma.* Adventurers. Bank robberies. Brothels. Childbirth. Desertion (Marital). Editors. French Americans. Friendship. Indians of North America. Jealousy. Jews. Loans. Lynching. Marriage–Mixed. Merchants. Newspapers. Oil magnates. Outlaws. Political corruption. Racism. Reconciliation. Rescues. Shootings. Small town life. Social climbers. Swindlers and swindling.

Note: The film's opening title cards reads: "Metro-Goldwyn-Mayer presents Edna Ferber's *Cimarron*." According to a Sep 1940 *IHR* news item, Wesley Ruggles, who directed the first screen version of Ferber's novel, the 1931 RKO film *Cimarron* (see above), was interested in re-doing the story as a musical for Columbia. In Jul 1941, *HR* then reported that M-G-M planned to team Clark Gable and Norma Shearer in a remake of the 1931 film. Neither project was realized, however. According to a Mar 1958 *DV* news item, producer Edmund Grainger wanted Rock Hudson to play the male lead in this picture, which at that time was to be scripted by Halstead Welles. Welles's contribution to the completed picture has not been determined. *NYT* news item noted that many scenes in the film were shot on location around Tucson and Mescal, AZ.

The land rush scene employed a crowd of 1,000 extras, 700 horses and 500 wagons and buggies. Additional location shooting was completed on ranches in the San Fernando Valley. A Feb 1960 *LAMirror-News* item added that the fictional town of Osage was built on three sound stages comprising over eleven acres at the M-G-M lot, making it the biggest western community in the studio's history. In a 5 Mar 1961 letter printed in *NYT*, Ferber wrote: "I received from this second picture of my novel not one single penny in payment. I can't even do anything to stop the motion-picture company from using my name in advertising so slanted that it gives the effect of my having written the picture....I shan't go into the anachronisms in dialogue; the selection of a foreign-born actress...to play the part of an American-born bride; the repetition; the bewildering lack of sequence....I did see *Cimarron*...four weeks ago. This old gray head turned almost black during those two (or was it three?) hours."

Box 12 Dec 1960, p. 13. *Box* 19 Dec 1960. *DV* 7 Mar 1958. *DV* 6 Dec 1960, p. 3. *Exb* Dec 1960, p. *FD* 6 Dec 1960, p. 6. *Har* 28 Apr 1960, p. 66. *HR* 25 Sep 1940. *HR* 3 Jul 1941. *HR* 26 Oct 1959. *HR* 27 Nov 1959, p. 8. *HR* 6 Jan 1960. *HR* 19 Feb 1960, p. 16. *HR* 15 Apr 1960. *HR* 6 Dec 1960, p. 3. *LAMirror-News* 15 Feb 1960. *MPHPD* 10 Dec 1960, p. 947. *NYT* 10 Jan 1960. *NYT* 17 Feb 1961, p. 12. *NYT* 5 Mar 1961. *Var* 7 Dec 1960, p. 6.

CIRCLE CANYON (Native Americans)

Superior Talking Pictures, Inc. *Dist* State Rights; Superior Talking Pictures, Inc. **1933**; *Prod*: rec at International Film Studios. Sd; b&w. Length undetermined.

Dir Victor Adamson. *Adpt, cont and dial* B. R. Tuttle. *Photog* Bert Longnecker.

Cast: BUDDY ROOSEVELT [(*Chris Morell*)], June Mathews, Clarise Woods, Bob Williamson, Allen Holbrook, Harry Leland, George Hazel, Clyde McClary, Mark Harrison, Ernest Scott.

Western. [*Print viewed*]. Pursued by Sam Black and his gang, Chris Morell orders his adopted daughter Lucy to take their horse and seek shelter at a friend's ranch, while he confronts the outlaws on foot. Chris scares off all but one of Black's horses, thereby stranding the outlaws, but as he makes his escape, he is shot and wounded. Eventually Chris's unconscious body is found by Jim Moore, the

adopted son of Chris's rancher friend, who has just robbed an express office. To divert suspicion from himself, Jim puts his shirt and bandana on Chris and leaves him to be discovered by his aunt, Clara Moore. After Clara questions Chris about his identity, she takes him to her homestead and explains that Jim's father was killed in a range war and lost his ranch to Vic Byrd. At the same time, Lucy arrives at Byrd's ranch and learns that her father Tom, who had abandoned her Indian mother just before she was born, works there. Byrd then meets Jim, who has been recognized as the bandit by Chris, and tells him to "take care of" Chris, while he finds Black. Alerted by his old friend Mat that Lucy is at the Byrd ranch, Chris leaves Clara's to find the child. After murdering Jim for the express money, Byrd locates the still stranded Black and offers to exchange Lucy, whom Black wants, for $5,000 and Chris's scalp. Black agrees to the bargain and heads for Clara's, while Byrd returns to his ranch to secure Lucy. When Chris arrives at Byrd's ranch, he shoots and kills Byrd and, with Mat, prepares to confront Black, who shows up with Clara. Following a stalemated shootout, Black agrees to exchange Clara for Chris, but is tricked by Chris and Mat, who eventually overwhelm the outlaws. As the sheriff arrives to arrest Black, Tom, who has asked Chris not to tell Lucy that he is her father, says goodbye, entrusting his daughter to Chris and Clara's loving care. *Cowboys. Foster children. Homesteaders. Outlaws. Disguise. Gunfights. Gunshot wounds. Horses. Hostages. Indians of North America–Mixed blood. Murder. Nephews. Parentage. Ranchers. Romance. Sheriffs. Thieves.*

Note: Although onscreen credits describe B. R. Tuttle's story as a "magazine" story, no confirmation that it was ever published has been found. The opening frame of the viewed print includes a copyright statement, but the title was not found in the copyright records. The date on the onscreen copyright statement was not readable, and no reviews for the production were located. However, the 1934 *FDYB* lists this title as a 1933 Superior Pictures' release, and the film was submitted to the New York State censor board in 1933. A 1934 John Wayne Lone Star film, *'Neath the Arizona Skies*, was based on the same Tuttle story and screenplay (see entry below). Modern sources complete the above cast list with the following character names: June Mathews (*Clara Moore*), Clarise Woods (*Lucy Morrell*), Bob Williamson (*Jim Moore*), Allen Holbrook (*Vic Byrd*), Harry Leland (*Mat*), George Hazel (*Tom*) and Clyde McClary (*Jim Black*). In addition, modern sources add Johnny Syke and Bud Osborne (*Sheriff*) to the cast.

CIRCLE OF DEATH (Native Americans)

Willis Kent Productions. *Dist* State Rights. **1935**; New York opening: 8 Jun 1935. Sd (International Sound Studios); b&w. 55 min. Passed by the National Board of Review. PCA cert no. 876.

Pres WILLIS KENT. *Dir* J. Frank Glendon. *Asst dir* Bartlett Carré. [*Story* Roy Claire]. *Photog* James Diamond. *Film ed* S. Roy Luby and [Roy Claire]. *Rec eng* J. S. Westmoreland.

Cast: MONTE MONTANA [(*Little Buffalo*)], Tove Lindan [(*Mary Carr*)], Yakima Canutt [(*Yak*)], J. Frank Glendon [(*Sheriff*)], Princess Ahteenah [(*White Fawn*)], Henry Hall [(*J. F. Henry*)], Chas. Whittaker [(*Lane Merrill*)], Benny Corbett [(*Dan Quinn*)], Chief Standing Bear [(*Indian chief*)], Jack Carson [(*Jerry Carr*)], John Ince [(*Bill Carr*)], Dick Botiller [(*Mexican Joe*)], [Marin Sais (*Mary Gordon*)], [Robert Burns (*Storekeeper*)], [Olin Francis (*Deputy sheriff*)], [George Morrell (*Drunk*)].

Western. [*Print viewed*]. In 1878, a group of settlers in a wagon train heading West camp near where Custer and his men were massacred two years previously, and the next day are attacked by the Indians. All the settlers are killed except for an infant boy, who is subsequently adopted by the Indian chief and given the name of Little Buffalo. Twenty-four years later, Little Buffalo enters a town to buy provisions with gold given to him by the Chief, and is met by the hateful jeers of the white customers, one of whom is beaten after trying to molest Little Buffalo's sister, White Fawn. In revenge, the white man reports his sighting of the Indians' gold to his crooked boss, saloon keeper J. F. Henry. Believing that the Indians are getting the gold from the ranch of Bill Carr, who has been kind to them, Henry lures Bill's son Jerry into the saloon to gamble away money borrowed from a cardsharp. In order to pay his gambling debts, Jerry sells his father's cattle to Henry, who then tries to convince Bill to sell him the entire ranch. However, Little Buffalo, after seeing Jerry's sister Mary trying to stop Henry from taking possession of the cattle, brings additional Indians to drive him away and to hide the cattle in a remote valley until Bill can raise more funds. Mary, Little Buffalo and two Indians watch the cattle, and Mary learns that Little Buffalo once attended a white man's school, where he was known as Jim Little. While Little Buffalo is guarding the Carrs' cattle, Henry and his

men attack the Indian camp and kidnap the Chief, but the smoke signals of White Fawn summon Little Buffalo to the rescue. Henry leaves the Chief in the hands of his cruelest henchman, Joe, telling him to extract the location of the gold from the Chief. Joe's torture goes too far, however, bringing the Chief to the point of death, and in revenge, the Indians strangle Joe. With the aid of local deputies, the Indians capture Henry's men, and Little Buffalo brings in Henry. The dying Chief explains that there was never any gold on the Carr ranch and that it was only his old hunting ground. He admits also that Little Buffalo is not his own son, but the white child he saved from the massacre. White Fawn tells Little Buffalo he must leave, as he is not an Indian, and after the Chief's burial, he goes to Mary. *Brothers and sisters. Cattle. Indians of North America. Racism. Ranchers. Cardsharping. Debt. Gambling. Gold. Massacres. Revenge. Saloon keepers. Sexual harassment. Sheriffs. Torture. United States–History–Reconstruction, 1865-1898. Wagon trains.*

Note: Although the viewed print of this film included a copyright statement, the title was not found in copyright records. *FD* lists Roy Claire, not S. Roy Luby, as film editor. Modern sources note that Gaylord Pendleton was billed as Jack Carson and add the following names to the cast: Jack Kirk, Ray Henderson, Artie Ortego, Hank Bell, Budd Buster and Bart Carré. In addition, according to modern sources, *Circle of Death* was Monte Montana's only starring feature.

FD 11 Apr 1935, p. 9. *MPD* 11 Apr 1935, p. 6. *Var* 12 Jun 1935, p. 41.

CISCO AND THE ANGEL see RIDING THE CALIFORNIA TRAIL

THE CISCO KID (Latino)

Fox Film Corp.; Irving Cummings Production. *Dist* Fox Film Corp. 1 Nov **1931**; World premiere in Los Angeles: 6 Oct 1931; New York opening: week of 23 Oct 1931; Prod: began late Jul or early Aug 1931 [©Fox Film Corp.; 18 Sep 1931; LP2524]. Sd (Western Electric System); b&w. 6 reels, 5,533 ft. 60-61 min. Passed by the National Board of Review. PCA cert no. 1742-R [31 Oct 1935].

Series: The Cisco Kid.

Assoc prod William Goetz. *Dir* Irving Cummings. [*Asst dir* Charles Woolstenhulme and Earl Rettig]. *Scr and dial* Al Cohn. *Photog* Barney McGill. [*2d cam* Jack Marta]. [*Asst cam* William Whitley and J. P. Van Wormer]. *Art dir* Joseph Wright. [*Film ed* Alex Troffey]. *Mus score* George Lipschultz. *Sd rec* George P. Costello. [*Dialectician and tech adv* Allan Garcia]. [*Care of horses* Del Maggert]. [*Still photog* Joe List]. [*Bus mgr* William Crawford]. [*Riding double for Conchita Montenegro* Cherié May]. [*Riding double for Warner Baxter* Frank McGrath]. [*Double for Edmund Lowe* Albert Dresden].

Song(s): "My Tonia," words and music by Lew Brown, B. G. DeSylva and Ray Henderson; "Song of the Cisco Kid," words and music by Warner Baxter; "La Cucaracha," Mexican folk song.

Source: Based on the character "The Cisco Kid" created by O. Henry in his short story "Caballero's Way" in *Everybody's Magazine* (Jul 1907).

Cast: Warner Baxter [(*The Cisco Kid*)], Edmund Lowe [(*Sergt. Michael Patrick "Mickey" Dunn*)], Conchita Montenegro [(*Carmencita*)], Nora Lane [(*Sally Benton*)], Frederick Burt [(*Sheriff Tex Ransom*)], Willard Robertson [(*Enos Hankins*)], James Bradbury, Jr. [(*Dixon, U.S.A.*)], Jack Dillon [(*Bouse, U.S.A.*)], Charles Stevens [(*Lopez*)], Chris Martin [(*Gordito*)], Douglas Haig [(*Billy*)], Marilyn Knowlden [(*Annie*)], [Rita Flynn (*Dance hall girl*)], [Consuelo Castillo de Bonzo (*Maria*)], [Allan Garcia], [Del Maggert].

Western. [*Print viewed*]. During President William McKinley's administration, Sergeant Mickey Dunn, a New Yorker stationed near the Mexican border, is excited to hear that his nemesis, The Cisco Kid, for whom there is a $5,000 reward, has been seen in the vicinity. When The Kid, rustling cattle with his cohorts, Gordito and Lopez, sees Dunn and his two men, Dixon and Bouse, on his trail, he instructs Gordito to fire at him so that it will look like he is trying to steal Gordito and Lopez's cattle. The ruse works, The Kid escapes, and Dunn allows Gordito to keep the cattle. At a café in Carrizo, when Sheriff Tex Ransom sees singer Carmencito, whom the sheriff favors, eye The Kid, he shoots the heel off The Kid's boot. The Kid then shoots a glass from the sheriff's hand. After Carmencita helps The Kid escape, he tells her that he trusts no woman and will give his love to none, but nevertheless kisses her passionately. Dunn interrupts them and wounds The Kid as he rides off. The Kid is cared for by widow Sally Benton, whose ranch is in danger of being taken over by Ransom and banker Enos Hankins. Sally's two young children, Billy and Anita, grow to love the visitor. When Dunn romances Carmencita and tries to get information about The Kid's whereabouts, she gives him a false

lead. The Kid recovers, after learning that Hankins plans to take Sally's ranch unless she pays $5,000, he robs Hankins' bank. When Dunn arrives, Carmencita, who earlier was pleased that The Kid risked his life to visit her, runs in front of the departing Kid and feigns being shot. She thus allows The Kid to escape as Dunn goes to comfort her. After The Kid gives Sally the $5,000 from the bank robbery, he starts to ride off as Dunn arrives. Anita, upset that The Kid did not say goodbye, closes the gate in front of his horse and falls as The Kid and his horse jump it. The Kid is captured by Dunn when he rides back to check on Anita, who is not hurt; however, when Dunn learns that The Kid robbed the bank to help Sally, he shakes The Kid's hand and lets him ride to the border. *Deception. Mexican Americans. Mexican-American border region. Officers (Military). Outlaws. Rivalry. Singers. Bank robberies. Bankers. Cafés. Children. Escapes. Flirtation. Nursing back to health. Ranches. Rewards. Rustlers. Sheriffs. Widows.*

Note: The title card for this film in the opening credits reads, "O'Henry's [sic] Romantic Bad Man *The Cisco Kid.*" Al Cohn's unpublished story was originally entitled "The Silver City." According to information in the Twentieth Century-Fox Records of the Legal Department at the UCLA Theater Arts Library, much of the film was shot on property on Ventura Boulevard, thirty miles west of Hollywood. The film was a sequel to the 1929 Fox film *In Old Arizona*, directed by Raoul Walsh, which also starred Warner Baxter and Edmund Lowe and for which Baxter won an Academy Award (see above). The theme song "My Tonia" from the 1929 film was used again in this film. In 1930, Fox produced *The Arizona Kid*, also starring Warner Baxter, which used the character, "The Cisco Kid," without using the name (see above).

After the 1930 film, a number of writers produced work for a new "Cisco Kid" film, including Harvey Fergusson, Herbert Asbury, Clarke Silvernail and Tom Barry, but it is not known if any of this material was used in the final film. Other films based on O. Henry's character include the 1914 three-reel Eclair film entitled *The Caballero's Way*; the 1919 two-reel Universal film entitled *The Border Terror*; the 1939 Twentieth Century-Fox film entitled *The Return of the Cisco Kid*, also starring Warner Baxter (see below); six films starring Cesar Romero, beginning with the 1939 *The Cisco Kid and the Lady*, made by Twentieth Century-Fox (see below).

Gilbert Roland made six films for Monogram in the mid-1940s, beginning with *The Gay Cavalier* in 1946, and Duncan Renaldo, made many films for the same studio, first in 1945, beginning with *The Cisco Kid Returns*, then additional films after Roland left the series. Renaldo also starred with Leo Carrillo in *The Cisco Kid* television series, produced from 1951 to 1955. A 1994 television movie entitled *The Cisco Kid* was broadcast on the TNT cable network. That film was directed by Luis Valdez and starred Jimmy Smits and Cheech Marin. For additional information on "The Cisco Kid," consult the Series Index.

FD 25 Oct 1931, p. 10. *HF* 1 Aug 1931, p. 20. *HF* 22 Aug 1931, p. 20. *IP* Nov 1931, p. 30. *LAHE* 6 Oct 1931. *MPH* 10 Oct 1931, p. 46. *NYT* 24 Oct 1931, p. 20. *Var* 27 Oct 1931, p. 19.

THE CISCO KID AND THE LADY (Latino)

Twentieth Century-Fox Film Corp. *Dist* Twentieth Century-Fox Film Corp. 29 Dec **1939**; Prod: began 11 Sep 1939 [©Twentieth Century-Fox Film Corp.; 29 Dec 1939; LP9616]. Sd (Western Electric Mirrophonic Recording); b&w. 8 reels, 6,600 ft. 73 min. PCA cert no. 5735.

Series: The Cisco Kid.

[*Exec prod* Sol M. Wurtzel]. *Assoc prod* John Stone. *Dir* Herbert I. Leeds. [*Asst dir* Jasper Blystone]. *Scr* Frances Hyland. *Orig story* Stanley Rauh. *Dir of photog* Barney McGill. *Art dir* Richard Day and Chester Gore. *Film ed* Nick De Maggio. *Set dec* Thomas Little. *Cost* Herschel. *Mus dir* Samuel Kaylin. *Sd* George Leverett and William H. Anderson.

Source: Based on the character created by O. Henry.

Cast: Cesar Romero ([*The*] *Cisco Kid*), Marjorie Weaver (*Julie Lawson*), Chris-Pin Martin (*Gordito*), George Montgomery (*Tommy Bates*), Robert Barrat (*Jim Harbison*), Virginia Field (*Billie Graham*), Harry Green (*Teasdale*), Gloria Ann White (*Baby*), John Beach (*Stevens*), Ward Bond (*Walton*), J. Anthony Hughes (*Drake*), James Burke (*Pop Saunders*), Harry Hayden (*Sheriff*), James Flavin (*Sergeant*), Ruth Warren (*Ma Saunders*), [Paul Burns (*Jake*)], [Virginia Brissac (*Seamstress*)], [Adrian Morris (*Drunk*)], [Eddie Dunn (*Jailer*)], [Eddy Waller (*Stage driver*)], [Ivan Miller (*Post commander*)], [Lester Dorr, Harry Strang, Arthur Rankin (*Telegraph operators*)], [Paul Sutton], [Harold Goodwin], [Gladys Blake], [William H. Royle].

Western. [*Print viewed*]. The Cisco Kid, a good-natured, womanizing bandit, is traveling in Arizona when he and his sidekick Gordito see a gang attack a lone man driving a wagon. They chase away the gang, then stop the wagon's runaway horses. The gang's leader, Jim Harbison, doubles back and pretends to be a passerby, although Cisco is not fooled by his pretense of innocence. The men

discover that the driver was traveling with his infant son, and the injured man begs Cisco and Harbison to care for the child in exchange for shares in his gold mine. After dividing the map to the mine in three equal pieces between Cisco, Gordito and Harbison, the man dies. Harbison's men then attempt to kill Gordito and Cisco. Much to Harbison's chagrin, the two bandits have already memorized and destroyed their pieces of the map, and so the group leaves for town to discuss their partnership. On the way, Cisco realizes that they have forgotten the baby, whom he calls Junior, but Junior has been found by schoolteacher Julie Lawson as her stagecoach passes by on the way to town. Cisco is charmed by Julie's beauty, but she is cold to him because of his careless treatment of Junior. When the men reach town, they go to a saloon run by Harbison's partner Teasdale. While Gordito tends to Junior, Cisco becomes enamoured of Harbison's girl friend, dancer Billie Graham. Cisco suspects a trap when Harbison arranges to meet him later to search for the mine, and Cisco therefore asks Julie to look after Junior. While Julie is arguing with her newly arrived fiancé, Tommy Bates, who mistakenly thinks that Junior is her baby, Cisco and Gordito trick Harbison into revealing that he has indeed tried to ambush them. The two bandits return to the saloon, where Cisco gets into an altercation with a drunken Tommy over Julie. Realizing that Julie belongs with Tommy, Cisco turns his romantic attentions to Billie, who reveals that she knows his true identity but will not turn him in. The couple have a falling out when Billie suspects Cisco of stealing Harbison's piece of the map, which she stole from Harbison, and Cisco, Gordito and Tommy wind up in jail after Billie reveals their identities. Later that night, Cisco instructs Harbison to rob a stagecoach while dressed as the Cisco Kid so that Cisco himself will be cleared of suspicion and freed. After Harbison leaves, Cisco and Gordito break out of jail and kidnap the local justice of the peace, Pop Saunders. They take him to Julie's house, where they force him to perform a wedding ceremony for Julie and Tommy. While soldiers search for Harbison, whom they now think is the Cisco Kid, Cisco and Gordito show Tommy the gold mine, which they bequeath to him, Julie and Junior. The soldiers shoot and kill Harbison, thereby freeing Cisco to go on his way. Billie, who has cleared up her misunderstandings with Cisco, accompanies him and Gordito as they leave town, and Cisco promises to find her a fine husband. *Bandits. Duplicity. Gold mines. Infants. Mexicans. Mistaken identity. Partnership. Romance. Abduction. Arizona. Dance hall girls. Drunkenness. Frame-ups. Jailbreaks. Jealousy. Justices of the peace. Maps. Marriage—Forced. Murder. Photographs. Saloons. Schoolteachers. Soldiers. Weddings.*

Note: The working title of this film was *The Adventurer*, and it was the first of six "Cisco Kid" films in which Cesar Romero played the title role. According to *HR* news items, Warner Baxter, who had played the role in three previous films, was originally cast as "Cisco" in this film. Many reviewers praised Romero's performance and noted that he was a worthy successor to Baxter. *HR* news items noted that the film was shot on location at Lone Pine, CA for a week and that associate producer John Stone had taken over production chores from David Hempstead, who had resigned from Twentieth Century-Fox the week before production began. For additional information on the series, consult the Series Index and see entry above for *The Cisco Kid.*

Box 2 Dec 1939. *DV* 25 Nov 1939, p. 3. *FD* 2 Jan 1940, p. 10. *HR* 7 Sep 1939, p. 2, 6. *HR* 8 Sep 1939, p. 4. *HR* 9 Sep 1939, pp. 5-6. *HR* 11 Sep 1939, p. 3. *HR* 14 Sep 1939, p. 7. *HR* 19 Sep 1939, p. 11. *HR* 30 Sep 1939, p. 7. *HR* 7 Oct 1939, p. 6. *HR* 25 Nov 1939, p. 3. *HR* 27 Nov 1939, p. 7. *MPD* 29 Nov 1939, p. 5. *MPH* 2 Dec 1939, p. 41, 44. *NYT* 25 Dec 1939, p. 20. *Var* 29 Nov 1939, p. 14.

THE CISCO KID COMES THROUGH see THE CISCO KID RETURNS

THE CISCO KID IN CHICAGO see VIVA CISCO KID

THE CISCO KID IN NEW YORK see VIVA CISCO KID

THE CISCO KID IN OLD NEW MEXICO see IN OLD NEW MEXICO

THE CISCO KID IN SOUTH OF THE RIO GRANDE see SOUTH OF THE RIO GRANDE

THE CISCO KID RETURNS (Latino)

Monogram Pictures Corp. *Dist* Monogram Pictures Corp. 3 Apr **1945**; Prod: late Oct—early Nov 1944 [©Monogram Pictures Corp.; 19 Mar 1945; LP13251]. Sd; b&w. 64 min. PCA cert no. 10614.

Series: The Cisco Kid.

Prod Philip N. Krasne. *Assoc prod* Dick Lestrange. *Dir* John P. McCarthy. *Asst dir* Eddie Davis. *Orig scr* Betty Burbridge. *Dir of photog* Harry Neumann. *Film ed* Martin Cohen. *Set dec* Ted Driscoll.

Mus dir David Chudnow. *Mus score* Albert Glasser. *Sd rec* Glen Glenn.

Song(s): "Cielito lindo," traditional.

Source: Based on the character created by O. Henry.

Cast: DUNCAN RENALDO [(*The Cisco Kid, also known as Juan Francisco Hernandez*)], Martin Garralaga [(*Pancho*)], Roger Pryor [(*John Harris*)], Cecilia Callejo [(*Rosita Gonzales*)], Fritz Leiber [(*Padre*)], Jan Wiley [(*Jeanette*)], Sharon Smith [(*Nancy Page*)], Vicky Lane [(*Julia, also known as Mrs. Elizabeth Page*)], Anthony Warde [(*Paul Conway*)], Bud Osborne, Eva Puig [(*Tia*)], Cy Kendall [(*Jennings*)], [Emmett Lynn (*Sheriff*)], [Bob Duncan], [Elmer Napier], [Carl Mathews], [Jerry Fields], [Neyle Marx], [Cedric Stevens].

Western. [*Print viewed*]. Outlaw Juan Francisco Hernandez, better known as The Cisco Kid, and Pancho, his companion, stop the wedding of Cisco's girl friend, Rosita Gonzales, to John Harris, a cantina owner, by falsely stating that she is already married to Cisco and that they have a small child. Afterward, Rosita explains to Cisco that she left him because he was unfaithful to her, though he vehemently denies it. Later, Cisco finds his friend Antonio murdered and Stephen Page, Antonio's employer, mortally wounded. With his dying breath, Page asks Cisco to hide his young daughter Nancy, and the outlaw agrees. Cisco is soon accused of committing the murders and kidnapping Nancy. Page's murderer is actually Jennings, a hired gun working for Harris, who in turn, is working for Paul Conway, Page's business adviser, who hopes to take over the businessman's vast estate. Cisco and Pancho go to the local mission to ask the padre's advice, and he tells Cisco that he must keep his promise to the dying Page and care for Nancy. At the same time, a woman claiming to be Mrs. Elizabeth Page arrives at the mission, so Cisco offers to take her and Jeanette, her maid, to the Page hacienda. In actuality, Mrs. Page is an actress named Julia who has been hired by Conway to impersonate Nancy's missing mother. That night, Rosita flies into a jealous fit when she believes she has caught Cisco at the Page estate trying to romance Jeanette. She then goes to Harris and tells him that the outlaw is hiding Nancy. Harris then demands that Conway make him a full partner before he delivers Nancy. The crooked businessman agrees, and together they set a trap for Cisco. That evening, while Cisco calls upon Jeanette, the sheriff and his posse slowly surround the Page hacienda. Pancho, however, warns his friend just in time, and the bandit escapes the trap. After taking Nancy to a new hiding spot, Cisco arranges his own trap for Conway and his gang. He has Pancho bring Conway, "Mrs. Page," Jeanette and the sheriff to the mission to pick up Nancy. The padre, however, insists that "Mrs. Page" sign for the child, as well as pick Nancy out of a group of eight young girls. Cisco then arrives and gives the sheriff a copy of a letter written by Page, in which Page fires Conway, as well as a letter written by the real Mrs. Page. When an examination of the two handwritings exposes Julia, Jeanette confesses all, and Cisco and the sheriff ride off to arrest Harris. As Rosita watches, they capture Jennings as well, and Cisco and Rosita are reunited. *Bandits. Embezzlement. False accusations. Mexican Americans. Murder. Romance. Abduction. Actors and actresses. Business managers. Café owners. Cantinas. Chases. Children. Escapes. Fathers and daughters. Impersonation and imposture. Jealousy. Letters. Maids. Missions. Priests. Sheriffs. Traps. Weddings.*

Note: The working title of this film was *The Cisco Kid Comes Through*. An Oct 1944 *HR* news item lists Pedro de Cordoba in the cast, but his appearance in the released film has not been confirmed. Modern sources include Walter Clinton in the cast. For additional information about the "Cisco Kid" series, consult the Series Index and see the entry above for *The Cisco Kid*.

DV 18 Apr 1945, p. 3. *FD* 3 Apr 1945, p. 6. *HR* 27 Oct 1944, p. 10. *HR* 31 Oct 1944, p. 10. *HR* 18 Apr 1945, p. 3. *MPHPD* 9 Sep 1944, p. 2092. *MPHPD* 7 Jul 1945, p. 2533. *MPHPD* 23 Dec 1945, p. 2242. *Var* 4 Apr 1945, p. 10.

CITIZEN SAINT (Italian Americans)

Clyde Elliott Attractions. *Dist* State Rights. 1947; New York opening: 27 May 1947; Prod: began 16 Dec 1946 at RKO Pathe Studios (Harlem, NYC) [©Clyde Elliott; 12 Apr 1947; LP950]. Sd; b&w. 7 reels. 73 or 78 min.

Pres Clyde Elliott. *Prod* Clyde Elliott. *Dir* Harold Young. *Asst dir* Richard Klopfer. *Scr story* Harold Orlob. *Dir of photog* Don Malkames. *Art dir* Richard Kleepfer. *Film ed* Leonard Anderson. *Mus arr written and cond by* Arthur A. Norris. *Sd rec* Kenneth Upton. *Makeup artist* Fred Ryle. *Casting dir* Max Richard. *Tech adv* Rev. E. V. Dailey. *Prod mgr* Harold Lewis. *Documentary narr* Rev. Cletus McCarthy.

Song(s): "Star That Lights the Midnight Sea," words and music by Arthur A. Norris; "Saint Frances Cabrini," words and music by Harold Orlob.

Cast: Rev. E. V. Dailey, Carla Dare (*Francesca "Cecchina" Cabrini, later known as Mother Cabrini*), Jed Prouty (*Neil Hartley*), Loraine Mae Martin (*Rhea*), Walter Butterworth (*Junior*), Robin Morgan (*Cecchina Cabrini*), Maurice Cavell (*Anton*), William Harrigan (*Father Vail*), June Harrison (*Dorine*), Lucille Fenton (*Antonia Tondini*), Lauretta Campeau (*Salesia*), June DuFrayne (*Veronica*), Julie Haydon (*Sister Delfini*), Clifford Sales (*Billy*), Mary Lee Dearring (*Shirley*), Patty Foster (*Rosemary*), Ralph Simone (*The peddler*), William Sharon (*Prison guard*), Clark Williams (*The prisoner*), Del Casino (*Perry*), Diana Kemble (*Agostini*), Eole Gambarelli (*Euphemia*), Marie Caruso (*Anna*), Donna Moore (*Mother Antonietta*), John Graham (*Doctor Stokes*), Douglas Rutherford (*Father Ryan*), Ann Irish (*The nurse*), Loring Smith (*Doctor Emerson*), Boris Aplon (*Landlord*), George Kluge (*Bishop*), Joy Bannister (*Sister Grace*), Ruth Moore (*Sister Chiera*), Kurt Kupfer (*The baker*), Alma Du Bus (*Committee chairwoman*), Richard Good (*Dr. Riley*).

Biography, **Documentary**. [*Not viewed*]. During the late 1850s, in Italy, the devout young Francesca "Cecchina" Cabrini, dreams of becoming a missionary. Cecchina eventually joins a Catholic religious order and is initiated as a novice. When she reaches adulthood, the young nun demonstrates her organizing abilities and forms the Order of the Missionary Sisters of the Sacred Heart. She is then assigned to duties in America. There, Mother Cabrini, as she is now called, is made the head of the New York State orphanage in New York City. Her devotion to the oppressed and the sick leads her to found sixty-seven hospitals, as well as numerous orphanages, clinics and schools around the United States and Latin America. During her life, Mother Cabrini performs three miracles: she brings Sister Delfini back from the dead, restores the sight of a blind infant, and helps singer Dorine to regain her lost voice. She also intercedes on behalf of a condemned murderer at Sing Sing Prison, saving him from execution. In 1917, at the age of 67, Mother Cabrini dies of malaria in a Chicago hospital. In 1946, she is canonized in Vatican City, and is heralded as the first American to attain sainthood. *Frances Xavier Cabrini, Saint. Catholic Church. Miracles. Nuns. Sainthood.* Blindness. Chicago (IL). Executions. Hospitals. Italian Americans. Italy. New York City. Orphanages. Revivification. Schools. Sing Sing Prison (NY). Singers. Vatican City.

Note: The film's billing sheet, contained in copyright records, includes the following acknowledgement: "With appreciation to Theodore Maynard for use of quotations from his book 'Too Small a World; A Biography of Mother Cabrini.' " Maynard's book was published in Milwaukee in 1945. According to reviews, the film, described as a "semi-documentary," opens and closes with newsreel footage showing Cabrini's canonization by Pope Pius XII in Vatican City. Available descriptions of the picture's narrative are sketchy. A synopsis contained in copyright records states that the story is "told largely by way of artful flashback method, posed against the background of a typical, present-day American family." According to modern biographical sources, Cabrini, who was born in the Lombardy region of Italy in 1850, became a nun in 1877. During the 1880s, she opened seven orphanages in northern Italy as part of her Missionary Sisters of the Sacred Heart order. In 1889, Cabrini and a small group of sisters went to New York City and began working among poor Italian immigrants there. As noted above, she then expanded her efforts around the country and established bases in Chile and Argentina, founding more than sixty convents under her Sacred Heart order. In 1909, Cabrini became a naturalized American citizen. She was beatified in 1938 and canonized in 1946; her feast day is celebrated on 13 November. Many of the institutions she established are still in existence today. As noted in a *HR* news item, two of the beneficiaries of Mother Cabrini's miracles, including a private in the U.S. Army, were still alive at the time this film was made.

According to *HR* news items, in 1944, both PRC Productions and Bing Crosby Productions had "Mother Cabrini" projects in the works. PRC's film, titled *Mother Cabrini*, was to be produced by Leon Fromkess and Martin Mooney and directed by Edgar Ulmer. In Sep 1944, Bing Crosby Productions announced that it was dropping its Mother Cabrini project. PRC's version was apparently also dropped before shooting began. The *NYT* review of *Citizen Saint* notes that William Harrigan, who plays "Father Vail" in the picture, narrates part of the story. It is not known if Rev. E. V. Dailey's and Rev. Cletus McCarthy's narration credit is for writing and/or speaking. According to the *NYT* review, the cast of the film, which was shot at RKO's Harlem studios, was comprised primarily of New York-based actors. The *NYT* review also noted that producer Clyde Elliott also distributed the Italian-made film *The Life and Miracles of Blessed Mother Cabrini*. The 28 Jan 1948 Los Angeles premiere of *Citizen Saint* benefited the Villa Cabrini Blood Bank of Burbank, according to *LAEx*. The film was reviewed twice by *Exb*, once in May 1947 and again in Jun 1948. According to the Jun 1948 review, three minutes were added to the running time after some "changes and editing" were made to the film.

DV 30 Oct 1947. *Exb* 14 May 1947. *Exb* 23 Jun 1948. *HR* 1 Feb 1944, p. 12. *HR* 20 Sep 1944, p. 2. *HR* 25 Sep 1944, p. 3. *HR* 10 Dec 1946. *HR* 30 Oct 1947, p. 3. *LAEx* 20 Jan 1948. *NYT* 28 May 1948, p. 28. *Var* 5 Nov 1947, p. 20.

CITY IN DARKNESS (Chinese Americans)

Twentieth Century-Fox Film Corp. *Dist* Twentieth Century-Fox Film Corp. 1 Dec **1939**; Prod: Began 6 Jul 1939 [©Twentieth Century-Fox Film Corp.; 1 Dec 1939; LP9341]. Sd (RCA "High Fidelity" Recording); b&w. 8 reels, 6,686 ft. 69 min. PCA cert no. 5531.

Series: Charlie Chan.

[*Exec prod* Sol M. Wurtzel]. *Assoc prod* John Stone. *Dir* Herbert I. Leeds. [*Asst dir* Charles Hall]. *Scr* Robert Ellis and Helen Logan. *Photog* Virgil Miller. *Art dir* Richard Day and Lewis Creber. *Film ed* Harry Reynolds. *Set dec* Thomas Little. *Cost* Herschel. *Mus dir* Samuel Kaylin. *Sd* Joseph E. Aiken and William H. Anderson.

Source: Based on the character created by Earl Derr Biggers and a play by Gina Kaus and Ladislaus Fodor (production undetermined).

Cast: Sidney Toler (*Charlie Chan*), Lynn Bari (*Marie Dubon*), Richard Clark (*Tony Madero*), Harold Huber (*Marcel*), Pedro de Cordoba (*Antoine*), Dorothy Tree (*Charlotte Ronnell*), C. Henry Gordon (*Prefect of police*), Douglas Dumbrille (*Petroff*), Noel Madison (*Belescu*), Leo Carroll (*Louis Santelle*), Lon Chaney, Jr. (*Pierre*), Louis Mercier (*Max*), George Davis (*Alex*), Barbara Leonard (*Lola*), Adrienne d'Ambricourt (*Landlady*), Frederik Vogeding (*Captain*).

Detective. [*Print viewed*]. In the fall of 1938, the great powers of Europe struggle to halt the encroaching war by convening at a conference in Munich. As the peace of Europe hangs in the balance, American detective Charlie Chan is drawn into the conflict when Petroff, a foreign agent, is murdered during a Paris blackout. As Chan's investigation progresses, he narrows the suspect list to Tony Madero, a man whom Petroff had framed for forgery because he had objected to Petroff's unwelcome attentions to his wife, Marie Dubon; Alex, Max and Lola, three burglars who had broken into Petroff's house on the night of the murder; Belescu, Petroff's business partner; Louis Santelle, a locksmith in the business of forging passports; and Antoine, Petroff's French butler. When Chan discovers that Petroff died while dictating a telegram about obtaining clearance papers for a special cargo, he begins to suspect that Petroff was a foreign agent dealing in munitions. Chan then traces Petroff and Belescu to Charlotte Ronnell, the head of a spy ring that was shipping munitions to the enemy. After a high speed chase, Charlotte dies in a fiery plane crash, and Antoine admits that he killed Petroff to protect France. *Chinese Americans. Detectives. Foreign agents. Murder. Paris (France). Spies. Americans in foreign countries. Automobile chases. Butlers. Forgers and forgery. France. Locksmiths. Munich agreement, 1938. Munitions. Passports. Thieves.*

Note: The working title of this film was *Charlie Chan in City of Darkness*. For additional information about the Charlie Chan series, consult the Series Index and see the entry above for *Charlie Chan Carries On*.

DV 14 Nov 1939, p. 3. *FD* 20 Dec 1939, p. 7. *HR* 3 Jul 1939, p. 3. *HR* 8 Jul 1939, pp. 5-6. *HR* 15 Nov 1939, p. 3. *MPD* 17 Nov 1939, p. 6. *MPH* 28 Oct 1939, p. 62. *MPH* 18 Nov 1939, p. 44. *NYT* 18 Nov 1939, p. 29. *Var* 22 Nov 1939, p. 14.

THE CITY OF DIM FACES (Chinese Americans)

Famous Players-Lasky Corp. *Dist* Famous Players-Lasky Corp.; Paramount Pictures. 15 Jul **1918** [©Famous Players-Lasky Corp.; 6 Jul 1918; LP12639]. Si; b&w. 5 reels, 4,219 ft.

Pres Jesse L. Lasky. *Dir* George Melford. *Asst dir* Claude Mitchell. *Story and scen* Frances Marion. *Cam* Paul Perry. *Art dir* Wilfred Buckland and Max Parker.

Cast: Sessue Hayakawa (*Jang Lung*), Doris Pawn (*Marcell Matthews*), Marin Sais (*Elizabeth Mendall*), James Cruze (*Wing Lung*), Winter Hall (*Brand Matthews*), Togo Yama (*Foo Sing*), James Wang (*Luk Tim Eli*), George King (*Lee Willie*), Larry Steers (*Ben Walton*).

Drama. Wing Lung, a Chinese merchant, and Elizabeth Mendall, an American, marry and have a son named Jang Lung. Because Elizabeth wants Jang Lung to be raised as a Christian, Wing Lung locks her in the cellar and she becomes demented. Jang meets Marcell Matthews at an Eastern university, and she returns with him to San Francisco to be married. After visiting Chinatown, however, she is disillusioned and breaks off the engagement. The enraged Jang sells Marcell to a marriage broker but tries to rescue her when he learns the true identity of his mother. In the attempt, Jang is mortally wounded, but becomes reconciled to Marcell and his mother before his death. *Chinese. Chinese Americans. Half-castes. San Francisco (CA)-*

Chinatown. Christianity. College students. Insanity. Marriage. Matchmakers. Mothers and sons. Prostitution.

ETR 27 Jul 1918, p. 672. *MPN* 27 Jul 1918, p. 573, 641. *MPW* 20 Jul 1918, p. 459. *MPW* 27 Jul 1918, p. 587. *NYDM* 27 Jul 1918, p. 127. *Var* 9 Aug 1918, p. 33. *Wid's* 14 Jul 1918, pp. 29-30.

THE CITY OF TEARS (Italian Americans)

Bluebird Photoplays, Inc. *Dist* Bluebird Photoplays, Inc. 29 Jun **1918** [©Bluebird Photoplays, Inc.; 13 Jun 1918; LP12552]. Si; b&w. 5 reels.

Dir Elsie Jane Wilson. *Story and scen* Olga Printzlau. *Cam* Alfred Gosden.

Cast: Carmel Myers (*Rosa Carillo*), Edwin August (*Tony Bonchi*), Earl Rodney (*Billy Leeds*), Leatrice Joy (*Maria*), Lottie Kruse (*Katrina*).

Comedy-drama. Rosa Carillo loses her singing job with a bankrupt Italian opera company and goes to work in Tony Bonchi's delicatessen rather than comply with the wishes of artist Billy Leeds, who has offered to "take care" of her. Billy has quarreled with his model and sweetheart Maria, with whom Rosa believes Tony to be in love. When Tony is arrested on a false charge, Rosa tells Billy that she will accept his proposition if he will get Tony out of jail, but she brings Maria to the appointed meeting place to be safe. Tony rushes to the house, and after learning that Maria is his long-lost sister, he proposes to Rosa, while lovers Billy and Maria are reunited. *Artists. Italian Americans. Long-lost relatives. Models. Delicatessens. Dismissal (Employment). False arrests. Opera singers.*

Note: The film's working title was *A Penny's Worth of Love*. Some sources state that the film was distributed by Universal, rather than Bluebird, and that it was released on 8 Jul 1918.

ETR 6 Jul 1918, p. 399. *MPN* 22 Jun 1918, p. 3688. *MPN* 29 Jun 1918, p. 1. *MPN* 6 Jul 1918, p. 117. *MPW* 13 Jul 1918, p. 246. *MPW* 20 Jul 1918, p. 459. *NYDM* 13 Jul 1918, p. 52. *Wid's* 30 Jun 1918, pp. 7-8.

CITY OF THE ANGELS *see* **THE MAN BEHIND THE GUN**

CITY SHADOWS *see* **CITY STREETS**

CITY STREETS (Irish Americans, Italian Americans)

Columbia Pictures Corp. of California, Ltd. *Dist* Columbia Pictures Corp. of California, Ltd. 1 Jul **1938**; Prod: 7 Apr—27 Apr 1938 [©Columbia Pictures Corp. of California, Ltd.; 27 Jun 1938; LP8107]. Sd (Western Electric Mirrophonic Recording); b&w. 7 reels. 62 or 68 min. PCA cert no. 4268.

[*Prod* Wallace MacDonald]. [*Exec prod* Irving Briskin]. *Dir* Albert S. Rogell. [*Asst dir* William Mull]. *Scr* Fred Niblo, Jr. and Lou Breslow. *Orig story* I. Bernstein. [*Contr wrt* Harry Sauber]. *Photog* Allen G. Siegler. *Film ed* Viola Lawrence. *Mus dir* Morris Stoloff. [*Sd eng* George Cooper].

Cast: Edith Fellows (*Winnie Brady*), Leo Carrillo (*Joe Carmine*), Tommy Bond (*Tommy [Francis] Devlin*), Mary Gordon (*Mrs. Devlin*), Helen Jerome Eddy (*Miss North*), Joseph King (*Mike Shanahan*), Frank Sheridan (*Father Ryan*), Arthur Loft (*Dr. Goodman*), George Humbert (*Lupo*), Frank Reicher (*Dr. Ferenc Waller*), Grace Goodall (*Miss Graham*), [Guy Usher (*Judge Wiley*)], [Boyd Irwin (*Dr. Thompson*)], [Margaret Fielding (*Mrs. Chandler*)], [Dick Curtis (*Madden*)], [Minerva Urecal (*Mrs. Grimley*)], [Bess Flowers (*Miss Phillips*)], [Edward Earle (*Mr. Chandler*)], [Eddie Laughton (*Maitre d'hotel*)], [Roger Gray (*Truck driver*)], [George Ovey, Eugene Burr, Alex Palasthy (*Peddlers*)], [Gene Stone, Al Stewart, Harry Bailey, Sam Rice, Joe Palma, E. L. Dale, John Rand, Victor De Linsky, Clarence L. Sherwood (*Vendors*)], [Nick Copeland, James C. Morton, Lew King, Bill Lally (*Drunks*)], [Beatrice Curtis (*Burns*)], [Ann Doran (*Nurse*)], [Lee Shumway (*Doorman*)], [Lew Davis, Ed Cecil (*Waiters*)].

Domestic, Youth, Drama. [*Print viewed*]. Little Tommy Francis Devlin accidentally hits a baseball through the shop window of "Uncle" Joe Carmine, a well-loved shopkeeper in a lower-class New York City neighborhood. When the mother of neighborhood girl Winnie Brady dies, Joe convinces Father Ryan to let him informally adopt her. Joe and Winnie live together with Tommy and his grandmother, Mrs. Devlin, and a dog Winnie names Muriel. Winnie is confined to a wheelchair, so Joe takes her to Dr. Thompson, who says that only Dr. Ferenc Waller, a recent European emigre, can help her. Waller, however, will operate only for a $3,000 fee, so Joe sells his store to make the surgery possible. Dr. Waller only effects a small change in her condition, and Winnie is not able to stand for more than

a few moments. Meanwhile, Joe is trying to sell fruit on a street corner, and one night during a storm, he leaves to buy Winnie a birthday cake. During his absence, a community welfare investigator takes Winnie and places her in an orphanage. Joe becomes a popular visitor at the orphanage, but the superintendent tells him it is in Winnie's best interest that he end his visits, so that she can be adopted by another family. Hoping Winnie will be taken in by a family that can afford proper treatment, Joe tells her he has tired of her, but is so haunted by her cries that he collapses in the street. Joe's illness can be overcome only if he regains his will to live, so Father Ryan takes Winnie from the orphanage by force. She is so afraid that Joe might die that she walks across the room to his bedside and sings his favorite song, "Santa Maria." Later, after Winnie has acquired full use of her legs, Joe buys a catering truck and takes the children on a picnic. *Adoption. Handicapped. Italian Americans. Orphanages. Poverty. Self-sacrifice. Dogs. Grandmothers. Irish Americans. New York City. Operations, Surgical. Physicians. Police. Priests. Social workers. Storekeepers.*

Note: Working titles for this film were *City Shadows* and *No Greater Love.* Copyright records erroneously list assistant director William Mull as William Moe. Author Isadore Bernstein's original story was first filmed by Columbia in 1932 as *No Greater Love* (see below).
DV 17 Jun 1938, p. 3. *FD* 29 Jul 1938, p. 11. *HR* 11 Apr 1938, p. 6. *HR* 17 Jun 1938, p. 3. *HR* 25 Jun 1938, p. 9. *NYT* 25 Jul 1938, p. 18. *Var* 27 Jul 1938, p. 17.

LA CIUDAD DE CARTÓN (Spanish language)
Fox Film Corp. *Dist* Fox Film Corp. **1934**; New York opening: 22 Feb 1934; Prod: Oct–Nov 1933. Sd (Western Electric Noiseless Recording); b&w. 7 reels, 6,799 ft. Passed by the National Board of Review. Spanish language.
[*Prod* John Stone]. *Supervisión de* [*Supv*] Gregorio Martínez Sierra. *Dirección de* [*Dir*] Louis King. *La obra de* [*Orig story*] Gregorio Martínez Sierra. *Adaptación cinematográfica de* [*Scr*] José López Rubio and John Reinhardt. [*Dial* Gregorio Martínez Sierra and José López Rubio]. *Dirección musical de* [*Mus dir*] Samuel Kaylin.
Cast: CATALINA BÁRCENA (*Teresa Collins/Diana Dane*), Antonio Moreno (*Fred Collins*), José Crespo (*Clarence Williams*), Andrés de Segurola (*Morrison*), Luis Alberni (*Craig*), José Rubio (*Gibbons*), Rudolf Amendt (*Primer director*), Carlos Villarías (*Director segundo*), Julio Peña (*Asistente*), Ralph Navarro (*Doctor*), [Francisco Marán (*Mr. Green*)], [Luz Alba (*Hairdresser*)], [Jose Peña "Pepet" (*Make-up man*)], [Sumi Sumida (*Maid*)], [Alfredo Sabato (*Mr. White*)], [Blanca Vischer], [Janet Gaynor, Lionel Barrymore, Robert Young (*Themselves*)].
Show business, Comedy. [*Not viewed*]. Teresa and Fred Collins, happily wed, are having hard times on their ranch in Fresno. Teresa suggests going to San Francisco to borrow money, and because Fred is too timid to go himself, she offers to make the journey. After she acquires the loan, Teresa's train is involved in a wreck. Craig, a publicity agent for Titan Studios, arrives at the disaster scene to look for the famous European star Diana Dane, who was travelling to Hollywood for her first big film. Craig sees Teresa and decides that she is the famous actress, and Teresa, suffering from amnesia, believes him. Teresa is listed as missing, and Fred mourns his wife's death. In Hollywood, Craig gives Teresa the star treatment, and she meets Janet Gaynor, Robert Young and Lionel Barrymore, in addition to having her hair coiffed and her body pampered. Craig tries to arrange a marriage between her and Clarence Williams, another new star, for publicity. When Clarence takes Teresa to a premiere that evening and a dance at the Coconut Grove later, he discovers that she's not a typical Hollywood starlet and begins to fall in love with her. Fred, meanwhile, sees a picture of Teresa as Diana Dane and recognizes her as his wife. He travels to Titan Studios and manages to sneak inside. As Teresa rehearses, Fred calls out desperately to her, and confused to hear the sound of her husband's voice, she falls and is knocked unconscious. Upon waking up, Teresa remembers her identity and cannot remember her life as "Diana Dane." She tries, however, to pretend that she is the European actress, so that she and Fred can continue to make Diana's huge salary, but, in her identity as a farmer's wife, she can no longer act. Fred begs her to go away with him, as the dashed dreams and hopelessness of the "cardboard city" has worn them both down. But Teresa insists that they stay and admits that she has Hollywood "poison." Gibbons, another publicist, finds the couple and offers to promote their film careers, now that their story has been publicized. Gibbons only manages to get Fred a bit part in

a Western, but when he offers to do a dangerous stunt that the other men shy away from, he is so good that Craig gives him a contract. Now a famous Western star, Fred poses on his front lawn for a bus load of tourists. *Amnesia. Hollywood (CA). Mistaken identity. Motion picture actors and actresses. Ranchers. Fresno (CA). Loans. Marriage. Motion picture studios. Motion picture stuntmen and stand-ins. San Francisco (CA). Talent agents. Train wrecks.*

Note: The plot summary was based on a dialogue continuity in the Twentieth Century-Fox Produced Scripts Collection, and the onscreen credits were taken from a screen credits sheet in the Twentieth Century-Fox Records of the Legal Department, both of which are at the UCLA Theater Arts Library. This film was released in Santiago, Chile, and possibly other places, under the title *Hollywood, la ciudad de cartón.* The title was translated in reviews as as "Cardboard City." *NYT* mistakenly lists Roland Young, rather than Robert Young, as one of the stars who welcome "Teresa" to Hollywood.
CM Mar 1934, p. 124. *FD* 28 Feb 1934, p. 8. *NYT* 28 Feb 1934, p. 23.

CIVILIZATION'S CHILD (Jewish Americans)
New York Motion Picture Corp.; Kay-Bee. *Dist* Triangle Film Corp. 23 Apr **1916** Si; b&w. 5 reels.
Supv Thomas Ince. *Dir* Charles Giblyn. *Scen* C. Gardner Sullivan. *Cam* Charles Kaufman.
Cast: William H. Thompson (*Boss Jim McManus*), Anna Lehr (*Berna*), Jack Standing (*Nicolay Turgenev*), Dorothy Dalton (*Ellen McManus*), Clyde Benson (*Jacob Weil*), J. P. Lockney (*Peter Saranoff*), J. Barney Sherry (*Judge Sims*).
Drama. After an idyllic mountain life in Russia, Berna goes to live with her uncle in the Jewish section of Kiev, arriving just as Cossacks massacre most of the Jews in the city. Berna escapes to New York and works at a sweatshop controlled by Boss Jim McManus, but he seduces her, then throws her out on the street, and she becomes a prostitute. Berna later marries Nicolay Turgenev, a young musician, and they soon have a child, but McManus' daughter Ellen falls in love with Nicolay after seeing him perform and convinces him to leave Berna. To make the separation legal, McManus, now a judge, grants Nicolay a divorce and also gives him custody of the child. Almost insane, Berna goes to McManus, denounces him at gunpoint and then kills him. *Immigrants. Infidelity. Jews. Judges. Musicians. Revenge. Russians. Child custody. Cossacks. Divorce. Jews. Kiev (Ukraine). Massacres. Murder. Prostitution. Religious persecution. Sexual harassment. Sweatshops. Uncles.*
Motog 29 Apr 1916, p. 995. *MPN* 29 Apr 1916, p. 2550. *MPW* 29 Apr 1916, p. 820. *MPW* 13 May 1916, p. 1226. *NYDM* 22 Apr 1916, p. 42. *Var* 21 Apr 1916, p. 31. *Wid's* 20 Apr 1916, p. 519.

CLAIR BOOTHE'S MARGIN FOR ERROR *see* **MARGIN FOR ERROR**

CLANCY'S KOSHER WEDDING (Jewish Americans)
R-C Pictures Corp. *Dist* Film Booking Offices of America. 17 Sep **1927** [©R-C Pictures Corp.; 19 Aug 1927; LP24310]. Si; b&w. 6 reels, 5,700 ft.
Pres Joseph P. Kennedy. *Dir* Arvid E. Gillstrom. *Asst dir* Ken Marr. *Scr* J. G. Hawks. *Adpt* Curtis Benton and Gilbert Pratt. *Story* Al Boasberg. *Cam* Charles Boyle.
Cast: George Sidney (*Hyman Cohen*), Will Armstrong (*Timothy Clancy*), Ann Brody (*Mamma Cohen*), Mary Gordon (*Molly Clancy*), Sharon Lynn (*Leah Cohen*), Rex Lease (*Tom Clancy*), Ed Brady (*Izzy Murphy*).
Comedy. Hyman Cohen and Tim Clancy, proprietors of adjacent clothing stores, both resent the fact that their children, Leah and Tom, are exceedingly fond of each other; the Cohens would rather see Leah with Izzy Murphy, a Jewish prizefighter. At a picnic, Izzy and Tom engage in combat for Leah's hand, and Tim and Hyman wager their savings on the fight. Leah, told that Tom's probable victory will cause her father to lose everything, tries to persuade Tom to desist; instead, learning of his father's wager, he topples Izzy. The Cohens are dispossessed, and Hyman is forced to become a peddler; missing their old friends, the Clancys take them in as equal partners in business. *Boxers. Clothing industry. Irish. Jews. Partnership. Peddlers and peddling. Wagers.*
FD 21 Aug 1927. *MPW* 10 Sep 1927. *NYT* 7 Sep 1927, p. 35. *Var* 7 Sep 1927, p. 21.

THE CLANSMAN *see* **THE BIRTH OF A NATION**

CLARENCE E. MULFORD'S HILLS OF OLD WYOMING *see* **HILLS OF OLD WYOMING**

THE CLAY PIGEON (Japanese Americans)

RKO Radio Pictures, Inc. *Dist* RKO Radio Pictures, Inc. Mar **1949**; Prod: late Sep—mid-Oct 1948 [©RKO Radio Pictures, Inc.; 22 Feb 1949; LP2169]. Sd (RCA Sound System); b&w. 5,655 ft. 62-63 min. PCA cert no. 13460.

Prod Herman Schlom. *Dir* Richard Fleischer. [*Asst dir* James Casey and Maxwell Henry]. *Story and scr* Carl Foreman. *Dir of photog* Robert de Grasse. [*Cam op* Charles Burke]. [*Gaffer* Frank Uecker]. [*Stills* Ernie Bachrach]. *Spec eff* Clifford Stine. *Art dir* Albert S. D'Agostino and Walter E. Keller. *Film ed* Samuel E. Beetley. *Set dec* Darrell Silvera and Harley Miller. *Mus dir* C. Bakaleinikoff. *Mus* Paul Sawtell. *Sd* Phil Brigandi and Clem Portman. [*Makeup* Bill Phillips]. [*Hair stylist* Hazel Rogers]. [*Prod mgr* Walter Daniels]. [*Scr supv* Dick Kinon]. [*Grip* Jim Curley].

Cast: BILL WILLIAMS [(*Jim Fletcher*)], BARBARA HALE [(*Martha Gregory*)], Richard Quine [(*Ted Niles*)], Richard Loo [(*Ken Tokoyama, also known as The Weasel*)], Frank Fenton [(*Lt. Comdr. Prentice*)], Frank Wilcox [(*Hospital doctor*)], Marya Marco [(*Helen Minoto*)], Robert Bray [(*Blake*)], Martha Hyer [(*Receptionist*)], Harold Landon [(*Blind veteran*)], James Craven [(*John Wheeler*)], Grandon Rhodes [(*Clark*)], Kenneth Terrell (*Davis*), [Dan Foster (*Bellboy*)], [Ann Doran (*Nurse*)], [Eddie Lee (*Cashier*)], [Harry Cheshire (*Doctor*)], [Jim Nolan (*Faber*)], [Howard Negley (*Sergeant*)], [Joel Friedkin (*Motorist*)], [G. Pat Collins (*Abbott*)], [Joe Bernard (*Hotel manager*)], [Kernan Cripps (*Chief Jones*)].

Crime, Drama. [*Print viewed*]. At the Long Beach Naval Hospital, Seaman First Class Jim Fletcher finally wakes from a coma, two years after he was injured in a Japanese prisoner of war camp. Jim remembers only his name and is disturbed to hear that he has been accused of murderous treason and is scheduled to face a court-martial. That night, the still groggy Jim sneaks out of the hospital and heads for San Diego. News of Jim's escape reaches the U.S. Navy Zone Intelligence Office in Los Angeles, which issues an all-points bulletin for his capture. In San Diego, Jim contacts Martha Gregory, the wife of his best friend Mark, with whom he was imprisoned in the Philippines. Unaware that he has been identified in the newspaper as Mark's killer, Jim introduces himself to Martha, and she feigns friendliness toward him. As Martha is about to call the police, however, Jim realizes his mistake and knocks her out. Later, Jim tries to convince the bound and gagged Martha that he did not inform on her husband for stealing rations from the Japanese guards, a revelation that led to his death, but she continues to fight him. Desperate, Jim calls Ted Niles, a trusted seaman with whom he and Mark were imprisoned, and makes plans to meet him in Los Angeles. Using Mark's gun, Jim forces Martha to drive him to Los Angeles, but along the way, her car is almost run off the road by two men in another vehicle. After Jim passes out at the wheel, Martha notices scars from a severe whipping on his chest and finally believes his story. Stopping at an Oceanside trailer camp, Martha nurses Jim back to health, then insists on accompanying him to Los Angeles. There, while dining at a Chinatown restaurant with Martha, Jim sees Ken Tokoyama, a vicious guard known as "The Weasel" at the prison camp where he was held. Sure that Tokoyama is somehow involved in his troubles, Jim tries to confront him, but loses him in a Chinatown crowd. Later, after the two men from the highway suddenly appear at the restaurant, Jim tells Ted about Tokoyama. Concerned, Ted advises Jim not to leave his hotel and agrees to meet with Martha at his apartment. Ted tells Martha that he has hired a private detective to find Tokoyama and insists that Jim stay low. Jim, however, returns to the restaurant and, seeing a real estate sign on the outside wall, makes inquiries about Tokoyama at the posting agency. Unknown to Jim, the agency is a front for Tokoyama, and he is almost caught by the ex-guard and his two henchmen. Later at their hotel, Jim and Martha receive word from Ted that Tokoyama has booked a train for that night. When Jim arrives at the specified train car, however, he is surprised to find not only Tokoyama there, but Ted as well. Ted implicates himself in Mark's death and admits that, since the end of the war, he and Tokoyama have been involved in a lucrative, illegal business. As Ted and Tokoyama then plan Jim's impending "fall" from the train, Martha uncovers Ted's duplicity and alerts the Navy Zone Intelligence Office, which has been trailing her and Jim, to his predicament. Back on the train, Jim is about to be pushed to his death when the police order an

emergency stop and arrest Ted and Tokoyama. Later, after they learn that Ted and Tokoyama were involved in a multi-million dollar counterfeiting scheme, Jim and Martha announce their marriage plans. *Attempted murder. Betrayal. Counterfeiters and counterfeiting. False accusations. Japanese. Traitors. Veterans. Amnesia. Coma. Hospitals. Long Beach (CA). Los Angeles (CA)–Chinatown. Nursing back to health. Oceanside (CA). Police. Real estate agents. Romance. San Diego (CA). Trains. Widows.*

Note: *The Clay Pigeon* was the first film to be produced at RKO under millionaire aviator Howard Hughes's new directorship. According to *HR*, Lawrence Tierney was first slated to star in this picture, and Sid Rogell was to produce it. Modern sources note that Carl Foreman's story was inspired by an actual incident in which a former serviceman recognized his Japanese prison guard in Los Angeles.
Box 19 Feb 1949. *DV* 9 Feb 1949, p. 3. *FD* 14 Feb 1949, p. 6. *HR* 1 Oct 1948, p. 13. *HR* 15 Oct 1948, p. 17. *HR* 9 Feb 1949, p. 3. *MPHPD* 12 Feb 1949, p. 4493. *Var* 9 Feb 1949, p. 13.

THE CLEMENCEAU CASE (French Americans, Russian Americans)

Fox Film Corp. *Dist* Fox Film Corp. Apr **1915** Si; b&w. 5-6 reels.

Dir Herbert Brenon. *Scen* Herbert Brenon. *Cam* Philip E. Rosen.

Source: Based on the novel *L'affaire Clemenceau* by Alexandre Dumas, *fils* (Paris, 1866).

Cast: Theda Bara (*Iza Dobronowska*), William E. Shay (*Pierre Clemenceau*), Stuart Holmes (*Constantin Ritz*), Frank Goldsmith (*Duke Sergius*), Mrs. Allan Walker (*Marie Clemenceau*), Little Jane Lee (*Janet*), Mrs. Cecil Raleigh (*Countess Dobronowska*), Sidney Shields (*Madame Ritz*).

Drama. Artist Pierre Clemenceau visits the Parisian studio of his friend Constantin Ritz and falls in love with model Iza Dobronowska. Iza ignores the artist, however, until she discovers that her mother Countess Dobronowska is making financial arrangements for her to marry wealthy Russian Duke Sergius. Iza accepts Pierre's proposal, and the two are wed. Scorning her husband, Iza alienates Pierre's family and forms a romantic liaison with Sergius. Pierre learns of her betrayal and kills Sergius in a duel. Disillusioned, Pierre travels to America with Constantin and his new bride. Iza inherits a fortune from Sergius and also sails to America, where she entices Constantin into an adulterous affair. To save his friend's marriage, Pierre lures Iza to his apartment, stabs her to death and then reports his crime to the police. *Artists. French. French Americans. Friendship. Infidelity. Models. Paris (France). Vamps. Confession (Law). Duels. Inheritance. Murder. Nobility. Russian Americans. Russians.*

Note: This film was re-issued by Fox in Jul 1918.
ETR 13 Jul 1918, p. 475. *ETR* 10 Aug 1918, p. 835. *Motog* 17 Apr 1915, p. 633. *MPN* 17 Apr 1915, p. 5. *MPN* 24 Apr 1915, p. 69. *MPN* 13 Jul 1918, p. 256. *MPW* 20 Jul 1918, p. 452. *NYDM* 21 Apr 1915, p. 27. *NYDM* 27 Jul 1918, p. 129. *Var* 23 Apr 1915, p. 18.

CLUB HAVANA (Latino)

Producers Releasing Corp. *Dist* Producers Releasing Corp. 23 Nov **1945**; Prod: mid-May—early Jun 1945 [©Producers Releasing Corp.; 5 Nov 1945; LP13581]. Sd (Western Electric Sound System); b&w. 5,615 ft. 58.5 or 61-62 min. Passed by the National Board of Review. PCA cert no. 10982.

Prod Leon Fromkess. *Assoc prod* Martin Mooney. *Dir* Edgar G. Ulmer. *Asst dir* Eugene R. Anderson. *Scr* Raymond L. Schrock. *Orig story* Fred Jackson. *Dir of photog* Benjamin H. Kline. [*Transparency projection shots* Ray Smallwood]. *Art dir* Edward C. Jewell. *Supv film ed* Carl Pierson. *Set dec* Glenn P. Thompson. *Ward des* Mona Berry. *Mus dir* Howard Jackson. *Sd eng* John Carter. [*Re-rec and eff mixer* Joseph I. Kane]. [*Mus mixer* William H. Wilmarth]. *Dir of makeup* Bud Westmore. *Prod mgr* Raoul Pagel.

Song(s): "Besame Mucho," music and lyrics by Consuela Velazquez; "Tico-Tico no fuba," music and lyrics by Zequinha de Abreu.

Cast: Tom Neal (*Dr. Bill Porter*), Margaret Lindsay (*Rosalind*), Don Douglas (*Johnny [Norton]*), Isabelita (*Isabelita*), Dorothy Morris (*Lucy*), Ernest Truex (*Willy Kingston*), Renie Riano (*Mrs. Cavendish*), Gertrude Michael (*Hetty*), Paul Cavanagh (*Willard [Clifton] Rogers*), Marc Lawrence (*Joe Reed*), Pedro de Cordoba (*Charles*), and introducing Carlos Molina and his Music of the Americas, Eric Sinclair [(*Jimmy Medford*)], Sonia Sorel [(*Myrtle*)], Iris and Pierre, [Susan Kingston].

Drama, with songs. [*Print viewed*]. Following a Reno divorce from her abusive, alcoholic husband, Rosalind rushes home to Miami to meet her boyfriend, Johnny Norton, at the Club Havana, a Latin-flavored nightclub. At the same locale, Lucy, a struggling young

model, is dining with her date, Dr. Bill Porter, an intern, while Clifton Rogers, a noted but penniless promoter, has a business dinner with the wealthy Mrs. Cavendish and her family. Jimmy Medford, the pianist boyfriend of Club Havana singer Isabelita, becomes conscience-stricken when he learns that Joe Reed, a local gambler, has been released from police custody for lack of evience in the murder of Julia Dumont, a performer at the club. Though Jimmy saw the gambler leaving Julia's apartment at the time of the murder, he is reluctant to go to the police, as both he and Isabelita fear Joe's retribution. Later, Mrs. Cavendish agrees to finance Rogers' projects once he consents to marry her, while Johnny breaks Rosalind's heart by telling her that he is in love with another woman. Rosalind then attempts suicide by swallowing a handful of pills, but is saved by Bill. Meanwhile, the newly reconciled Kingstons, an older married couple, plan a romantic dinner at the club, but the two end up doing more arguing than romancing. Jimmy finally decides to call the police, but his phone call is listened in on by Myrtle, the club's telephone operator, who tells Joe of the pianist's actions. Joe then retains a hired killer to murder Jimmy, but the gunman shoots Myrtle instead after she yells a warning to Jimmy while driving away in her car. The gunman is then run over by the mortally wounded telephone operator. While Jimmy is taken to the police station to testify against Joe, Rosalind and Johnny reconcile and leave the nightclub together. *Murder. Nightclubs. Romance. Unrequited love. Attempted suicide. Bands (Music). Conscience. Dancers. Divorce. Gamblers. Hired killers. Latin Americans. Maids. Miami (FL). Models. Physicians. Pianists. Police. Promoters. Proposals (Marital). Singers. Telephone operators.*

Note: While Paul Cavanagh's character is listed as "Willard Rogers" in the film's end credits, he is called "Clifton Rogers" in the film. *HR* production charts include Pamela Blake in the cast, but her appearance in the released film has not been confirmed. According to modern interviews with director Edgar G. Ulmer, German cameraman Eugene Schuftan was the uncredited director of photography on this film, and most of the film's story was made up on the set by the director and his actors.
Box 27 Oct 1945. *FD* 28 Jan 1946, p. 8. *DV* 22 Oct 1945, p. 3. *HR* 11 May 1945, p. 10 *HR* 22 Oct 1945, p. 3. *MPHPD* 21 Jul 1945, p. 2555. *MPHPD* 20 Oct 1945, p. 2686. *Var* 23 Jan 1946, p. 12.

COBRA (Italian Americans)

Ritz-Carlton Pictures. *Dist* Paramount Pictures. 30 Nov **1925** [©Rudolph Valentino; 3 Dec 1925; LP22071]. Si; b&w. 7 reels, 6,895 ft.
Dir Joseph Henabery. *Scr* Anthony Coldewey. *Photog* J. D. Jennings and Harry Fischbeck. *Set des* William Cameron Menzies. *Gowns* Gilbert Adrian.
Source: Based on the play *Cobra* by Martin Brown (New York, 22 Apr 1924).
Cast: Rudolph Valentino (*Count Rodrigo Torriani*), Nita Naldi (*Elise Van Zile*), Casson Ferguson (*Jack Dorning*), Gertrude Olmstead (*Mary Drake*), Hector V. Sarno (*Victor Minardi*), Claire De Lorez (*Rosa Minardi*), Eileen Percy (*Sophie Binner*), Lillian Langdon (*Mrs. Porter Palmer*), Henry Barrows (*Store manager*), Rosa Rosanova (*Marie*).
Society, Drama. Count Rodrigo Torriani, a young Italian, has inherited a debt-ridden palace on the Bay of Naples and a fondness for women. He accepts the offer of New York antique dealer Jack Dorning to work in his shop, and there he falls genuinely in love with Jack's secretary, Mary Drake. Rodrigo is pursued by Elise Van Zile, a worldly-wise woman ambitious to marry him for his money—until she learns that Rodrigo is penniless. Elise turns her attentions, successfully, to Jack, and they get married. She tries to have an affair with Rodrigo on the side, but he at first rejects her. Later, Elise meets Rodrigo at a hotel, but he becomes conscience-stricken and leaves. The hotel burns down, killing Elise. Jack becomes frantic about his wife's disappearance, but Rodrigo leaves town, saying nothing. He returns a year later, learns that Jack knows the truth about Elise, and notes that Jack has regained his equanimity under Mary's care. Although he realizes that Mary's love is his for the asking, he treats their relationship casually and sails away, leaving Jack and Mary to their happiness. *Antique dealers. Friendship. Infidelity. Italian Americans. Naples (Italy). Nobility.*
FD 13 Dec 1925. *NYT* 7 Dec 1925, p. 19.

THE COCK-EYED CRUISE *see* MAD HOLIDAY

CODE OF THE UNDERWORLD *see* MURDER IN VILLA CAPRI

EL CÓDIGO PENAL (Spanish language)

Columbia Pictures Corp.; A Howard Hawks Production. *Dist* Columbia Pictures Corp. **1931**; Mexico City opening: 19 Feb 1931; San Juan, Puerto Rico opening: 14 Mar 1931; New York opening: 10 Apr 1931; Prod: 9 Dec—22 Dec 1930. Sd; b&w. 10 reels, 9,701 ft. 108 min. Spanish language.
Prod supv Ben Pivar. *Dir* Phil Rosen. *Dial dir* Julio Villarreal. *Asst dir* David Selman. *Scr* Fred Niblo, Jr. and Seton I. Miller. *Spanish version* Matías Cirici-Ventalló. *Photog* Joseph Walker.
Source: Based on the play *The Criminal Code* by Martin Flavin (New York, 2 Oct 1929).
Cast: Barry Norton (*Bob Bennet*), María Alba (*Mary Brady*), Carlos Villarías (*Mart Brady*), Manuel Arbó (*Capitán Gleason*), María Calvo (*Katie Ryan*), Julio Villarreal (*Doctor Rinewulf*), Alfredo del Diestro (*MacManus*), Ramón Peón, José Soriano Viosca.
Prison, Drama. [*Not viewed*]. [The following plot summary is based on the English-language version of this film, *The Criminal Code*; character names refer to that version. For further information regarding the English-language version, please see the note below and the entry for *The Criminal Code* in the *AFI Catalog of Feature Films, 1931-40*.] Young Robert Graham, under the influence of alcohol, accidentally kills the son of Thaddeus Parker, who is running for governor, when the man insults Robert's date. Though sympathetic to the boy, district attorney Mark Brady, who wants to run for governor in the upcoming election, decides to go ahead and prosecute Robert. Robert is sent to prison for ten years. After six years of incarceration, Robert's mother dies, and the boy, on the verge of a nervous breakdown, is given a special assignment by Brady, who after losing the election was appointed as the prison's warden. Appalled at what prison life has done to the young man, Brady makes Robert his chauffeur. Robert and Brady's daughter Mary fall in love. Robert is about to be pardoned when Runch, a stool pigeon, is murdered by Robert's cellmate Galloway, and Brady puts Robert in solitary confinement for refusing to inform on his fellow prisoner. After enduring torture in solitary by the brutal head guard Gleason, Robert is slipped a knife with which to kill Gleason, or himself. That evening, as Robert is on the verge of going through with his plan to kill Gleason, Galloway escapes from his cell and kills Gleason himself, in retaliation for the guard's returning him to prison for a minor parole infraction. Then Galloway confesses to the murder of Runch and is subsequently gunned down by guards who have noticed his attempted escape. Robert is reunited with Mary and they receive Brady's blessings. *Murder. Prison wardens. Prisons. Chauffeurs. Confession (Law). Drunkenness. Elections. Fathers and daughters. Governors. Prison escapes. Revenge. Romance.*
Note: This was the Spanish-language version of the 1931 film *The Criminal Code*, which was directed by Howard Hawks and starred Walter Houston and Phillips Holmes. Please see the entry for that film in the *AFI Catalog of Feature Films, 1931-40*; F3.0876. The following actors were listed in publicity in different countries as having appeared in the Spanish-language version: Max Barón, Juan Duval, José Peña "Pepet," Paco Moreno, Hipólito Mora, Manuel Sánchez Navarro, Manuel París, Amelia Suso, Pat Hartigan and Luis Hickus. According to a news item in *CM*, Tito Davison was originally cast for a role in the Spanish version, but was replaced by Ramón Peón. Harry Ham may have been the co-director or dialogue director of the Spanish version. A French version, produced in France in 1932 by Forrester-Parant Productions, was entitled *Criminel*. It was directed by Jack Forrester and starred Harry Baur and Jean Servais, and used some scenes from the American version. The film was remade by Columbia in 1938 as *Penitentiary*. That version was directed by John Brahm and starred Walter Connolly and John Howard (see *AFI Catalog of Feature Films, 1931-40*; F3.3412). In 1950, the film was again remade as *Convicted*, directed by Henry Levin, and starring Glenn Ford and Broderick Crawford.
CM Apr 1931.

THE COHENS AND KELLYS (Irish Americans, Jewish Americans)

Universal Pictures Corp.; Universal-Jewel. 28 Feb **1926** [©Universal Pictures Corp.; 13 Feb 1926; LP22400]. Si; b&w. 8 reels, 7,774 ft.
Series: The Cohens and Kellys
Prod E. M. Asher. *Dir* Harry Pollard. *Scen* Alfred A. Cohn. *Adpt* Harry Pollard. *Photog* Charles Stumar. *Art dir* Charles D. Hall.
Source: Based on the play *Two Blocks Away* by Aaron Hoffman (New York, 30 Aug 1921).
Cast: Charlie Murray (*Patrick Kelly*), George Sidney (*Jacob Cohen*), Vera Gordon (*Mrs. Cohen*), Kate Price (*Mrs. Kelly*), Olive Hasbrouck (*Nannie Cohen*), Nat Carr (*Milton Katz*), Mickey Bennett (*Milton J. Katz*).

Comedy. Jacob Cohen, who owns a dry goods store, and Patrick Kelly, an Irish cop, are constantly at loggerheads, feuding over anything and everything. Kelly's son, Tim, and Cohen's daughter, Nannie, fall in love despite the bickering of their parents; when they cannot get parental consent for their marriage, they secretly wed. Cohen inherits a fortune and moves to the upper East Side, taking Nannie with him. Sometime later, Nannie gives birth to a child; when her parents will not let any of the Kelly clan see the child, Nannie leaves home and goes to live with the Kellys, where Mrs. Cohen soon joins her. Cohen then discovers that Kelly is the rightful heir to the fortune that he himself has inherited, and moved by honesty, he goes to the burly cop and tells him so. The men are reconciled and decide to go into partnership together. *General stores. Inheritance. Irish Americans. Jews. Marriage. Merchants. New York City–East Side. Partnership. Police.*

Note: This was the first of seven pictures made by Universal feature the Cohen and Kelly families. For additional information on the series, consult the Series Index and see entry below for *The Cohens and Kelleys in Africa*.
FD 7 Mar 1926. MPW 6 Mar 1926. NYT 23 Feb 1926, p. 26. Var 24 Feb 1926, p. 42.

THE COHENS AND KELLYS IN AFRICA (Irish Americans, Jewish Americans)
Universal Pictures Corp.; Carl Laemmle, President. *Dist* Universal Pictures Corp. 19 Jan **1931**; New York opening: week of 19 Dec 1930 [©Universal Pictures Corp.; 24 Dec 1930; LP1837]. Sd (Western Electric Sound System); b&w. 8 reels, 7,225 ft. 68 or 70 min.
Series: The Cohens and Kellys.
Pres CARL LAEMMLE. *Prod* Carl Laemmle, Jr. *Assoc prod* Albert DeMond. *Dir* Vin Moore. *Story* Edward Luddy, Lew Lipton and [Vin Moore]. *Scr and dial* William K. Wells. *Cine* Hal Mohr. *Art dir* Charles D. Hall. *Film ed* James Morley. *Supv film ed* Maurice Pivar. *Rec supv* C. Roy Hunter.
Cast: GEORGE SIDNEY (*Mr. [Nathan] Cohen*), CHARLIE MURRAY (*Mr. [Patrick] Kelly*), Vera Gordon (*Mrs. Cohen*), Kate Price (*Mrs. Kelly*), Frank Davis (*Windjammer Thorne*), Lloyd Whitlock (*Sheik [Abdul Hassan Cafa]*), Eddie Kane (*Chief Zulu*), Nick Cogley (*Guide*), Demetrios Alexis (*Sheik's aide*), [Georgette Rhodes, Rene Marvelle (*Dancers*)], [Louis John Bartels].
Comedy, Jungle. [*Viewed print incomplete*]. Patrick Kelly and Nathan Cohen operate a piano business that is faltering due to the lack of ivory for keys. Outside their office they discover Windjammer Thorne, a fast-talking patent medicine salesman who claims to know about ivory conditions in Africa. Under the guidance of Thorne, Cohen and Kelly, accompanied by their wives, depart for Mombasa, which is on the African coast. Before travelling inland to the Zulu village of Gumbo Gumbo, Mrs. Cohen and Mrs. Kelly catch their husbands flirting with two French floozies in a speakeasy. They arrive eventually at the village, where the women stay while Cohen, Kelly, Thorne and their guide trek through the jungle in search of ivory. The wives are kidnapped by a group of gorillas, and the female apes appropriate the women's outer garments. Meanwhile the men, captured by cannibals, dress up in lion skins and effect an escape. Cohen and Kelly, again lost in the brush, wander into another native village where they find an old friend, Sam Ginsberg of Brooklyn, who three years earlier made a deal with the natives and stayed on as their elected chief. Cohen and Kelly make a deal with the chief, betting his huge supply of ivory on the winner of a miniature golf competition, which Ginsberg has introduced to the natives. Cohen defeats Ginsberg's pro in a match with a miraculous stroke on the last hole. Learning from the jungle drums that their wives have been abducted, the husbands fear the worst when they find the female gorillas dressed in their wives' clothing. After they are reunited with Thorne and his men, Thorne tells them their spouses are being held in the harem of Sheik Abdul Hassan Cafa. At the sheik's palace, he agrees to exchange their ivory for their wives. Cohen refuses to sign away the ivory, and a series of chases follow, which result in the release of their wives and the capture of the sheik and his guards. Cohen and Kelly inform their wives of their newly found wealth, for not only have they secured a large shipment of ivory, but they have also sold off their old piano inventory to the natives, who quickly master the instrument. Many of the jungle animals also learn to play, including the gorillas who mimic "Mammy." *Africa. Americans in foreign countries. Irish Americans. Ivory. Jews. Jungles. Wild animals. Abduction. Cannibalism. Chases. Flirtation. Friendship. Golf, miniature. Harems. Marriage. Partnership. Piano makers. Salesmen. Sheiks.*

Note: Although there was an entry for this film in the *AFI Catalog of Feature Films, 1921-30* (F2.0954), its actual release date was 19 Jan 1931. In 1926, Universal released the *The Cohens and Kellys*, the first of a series of eight films featuring the "Cohen and Kelly" characters. *The Cohens and Kellys* was based on Aaron Hoffman's play, *Two Blocks Away* (New York, 1925), and starred Charlie Murray, George Sidney, Vera Gordon and Kate Price (see *AFI Catalog of Feature Films, 1921-30*; F2.0953). *The Cohens and Kellys in Africa* was the sixth entry in the series and the first to be released in the thirties. George Sidney starred in all eight films as "Mr. Cohen," while Vera Gordon and Kate Price left the series in 1931. Other cast members playing continuous featured roles include Mack Swain, J. Farrell MacDonald, Emma Dunn and Esther Howard. For more information consult the Series Index.
FD 21 Dec 1930, p. 10. MPH 8 Nov 1930, p. 41. NYT 20 Dec 1930, p. 20. Var 24 Dec 1930, p. 21.

THE COHENS AND KELLYS IN ATLANTIC CITY (Irish Americans, Jewish Americans)
Universal Pictures Corp. 17 Mar **1929** [©Universal Pictures Corp.; 4 Mar 1929; LP189]. Talking sequences and mus score (Movietone); b&w. 8 reels, 7,401 ft. [Also si; 7,752 ft.].
Series: The Cohens and Kellys.
Dir William James Craft. *Adpt and cont* Earl Snell. *Story* Jack Townley. *Dial and titles* Albert De Mond. *Photog* Al Jones. *Film ed* Charles Craft and Richard Cahoon.
Cast: George Sidney (*Mr. Cohen*), Vera Gordon (*Mrs. Cohen*), Mack Swain (*Mr. Kelly*), Kate Price (*Mrs. Kelly*), Cornelius Keefe (*Pat Kelly*), Nora Lane (*Rose Cohen*), Virginia Sale (*Miss Rosenberg*), Tom Kennedy (*Crook*).
Comedy. After thirty years in the bathing suit business, Cohen and Kelly have fallen on hard times; their merchandise and their business methods are both out of date. While they are away on a selling trip, Cohen's daughter, Rosie, and Kelly's son, Pat, introduce a new line of merchandise into the family business. To promote it, they plan a beauty contest to be held in Atlantic City. Cohen and Kelly return in a rage, and the children sneak off to Atlantic City to avoid involving their parents in the contest. After numerous complications, Rosie wins the contest, the business is saved, and the two families share a happy reunion. *Atlantic City (NJ). Bathing suits. Beauty contests. Businessmen. Irish Americans. Jews. Publicity.*

Note: Some scenes were filmed on location in Atlantic City. For additional information on the Cohens and Kellys series, see entry above for *The Cohens and Kellys in Africa* and consult the Series Index.
FD 24 Mar 1929. NYT 18 Mar 1929, p. 30. Var 20 Mar 1929, p. 12.

THE COHENS AND KELLYS IN HOLLYWOOD (Irish Americans, Jewish Americans)
Universal Pictures Corp.; Carl Laemmle, President. *Dist* Universal Pictures Corp. 28 Mar **1932** [©Universal Pictures Corp.; 17 Mar 1932; LP2926]. Sd (Western Electric Noiseless Recording); b&w. 8 reels. 75 min. PCA cert no. 2922-R [28 Nov 1936].
Series: The Cohens and Kellys.
Pres CARL LAEMMLE. *Prod* Carl Laemmle, Jr. *Assoc prod* Stanley Bergerman. *Dir* John Francis Dillon. *Orig scr* Howard J. Green. *Addl dial* James Mulhauser. *Scen ed* Richard Schayer. *Cine* Jerome Ash. *Art dir* John J. Hughes. *Film ed* Harry W. Lieb. *Supv film ed* Maurice Pivar. *Rec supv* C. Roy Hunter.
Cast: GEORGE SIDNEY (*Mr. [Moe] Cohen*), CHARLES MURRAY (*Mr. [Michael] Kelly*), Norman Foster (*Melville [Cohen]*), June Clyde (*Kitty Kelly*), Emma Dunn (*Mrs. [Sarah] Cohen*), Esther Howard (*Mrs. [Maggie] Kelly*), Luis Alberni (*Mr. [Bladimir Petrosky] Solarsky*), Robert Greig (*Chesterfield*), Edwin Maxwell (*Mr. [Chauncey] Chadwick*), Dorothy Christy (*Mrs. Chadwick*), John Roche (*Gregory Gordon*), [Eileen Percy (*Magazine writer*)], [Genevieve Tobin], [Paul Power], [Boris Karloff], [Vivien Dale], [Anglo Stevenson], [Sidney Fox], [Tom Mix], [Lew Ayres], [Gloria Stuart].
Comedy. [*Not viewed*]. The Cohen and Kelly families have been the best of friends in the small town of Hillsboro for years. Moe and Sarah Cohen's son Melville, who is in love with Michael and Maggie Kelly's daughter Kitty, sends her picture to Continental Productions in Hollywood after they advertise for new actresses. Kitty wins a contract with the company, and her family moves to Hollywood, where they meet with success and buy a mansion. After receiving a postcard from the Kellys saying "wish you were here," the Cohens sell their theatre in Hillsboro and move to Hollywood, but are snubbed on arrival by the now snobbish Kellys. Kelly loses all his money on Kitty's next picture, which is a flop because Kitty's voice does not register well for the new sound films. Now the tables turn, and it is the Cohens who experience success, but relations are no

longer friendly between the two families. Melville sells his songs to motion pictures until songs are no longer a fad in films, and the Cohens once again go broke. Chesterfield, who was a butler for both families at different times, opens an elocution school and now it is his turn for wealth. The Cohens buy back their old jalopy and return to Hillsboro. On the way, they rescue the Kellys, whose car broke down, and upon renewing their friendship, they return to the happy life in Hillsboro they once knew. *Family life. Finance–Personal. Friendship. Irish Americans. Jews. Motion picture producers. Snobs and snobbishness.* Butlers. The Cocoanut Grove (Los Angeles, CA). Contracts. Motion picture actors and actresses. Songwriters.

Note: The plot synopsis is based on the studio cutting continuity. Although the continuity included the song, "Where Are You?" the authors of the song have not been identified. Although the cutting continuity credits call Norman Foster's character "Melville," within the text he is called "Maurice." One scene was filmed on location at the Cocoanut Grove nightclub in the Ambassador Hotel in Los Angeles, CA. Various renowned actors have cameos in this scene, including Genevieve Tobin, Paul Power, Boris Karloff, Vivien Dale, Anglo Stevenson, Sidney Fox, Tom Mix, Lew Ayres and Gloria Stewart. For further information on the series, see *The Cohens and Kellys in Africa* above and consult the Series Index.

FD 24 Apr 1932, p. 10. *IP* Mar 1933, p. 34. *MPH* 19 Mar 1932, p. 39, 42. *NYT* 22 Apr 1932, p. 23. *Var* 26 Apr 1932, p. 54.

THE COHENS AND KELLYS IN TROUBLE (Irish Americans, Jewish Americans)

Universal Pictures Corp.; Carl Laemmle, President. *Dist* Universal Pictures Corp. 23 Mar **1933** [©Universal Pictures Corp.; 16 Mar 1933; LP3730]. Sd (Western Electric Noiseless Recording Sound System); b&w. 7 reels. 69 min. PCA cert no. 2763-R [6 Oct 1936].

Series: The Cohens and Kellys.

Pres CARL LAEMMLE. *Prod* Carl Laemmle, Jr. *Dir* George Stevens. *Scr* Albert Austin and Fred Guiol. *Story* Homer Croy and Vernon Smith. [*Cont* Jack Jungmyeer]. *Cam* Len Powers. [*Cam op* Dick Fryer]. [*Asst cam* Walter Williams and Martin Glouner]. *Art dir* Stanley Fleischer. *Film ed* Robert Carlisle. [*Sd* Jess Moulin]. [*Still photog* Shirley Martin].

Cast: GEORGE SIDNEY (*Nathan Cohen*), CHARLES MURRAY (*Captain Patrick Kelly*), Maureen O'Sullivan (*Molly Kelly*), Frank Albertson (*Bob Graham*), Andy Devine (*Andy Anderson*), Jobyna Howland (*Queenie Truelove*), Maude Fulton (*Fern*), Henry Armetta (*Captain Silva*), [Maurice Black (*Nick*)], [Arthur Hoyt (*Boswell*)], [Max Davidson (*Larsen*)], [Herbert Corthell (*Panhandler*)], [Olive Cooper (*Swedish stewardess*)], [Willie Fong (*Ah Chung*)], [Don Brody (*Chauffeur*)], [Ed Le Saint (*Freighter captain*)], [Jack Raymond].

Sea, Comedy. [*Not viewed*]. Businessman Nate Cohen joins his bootlegger friend, Captain Pat Kelly, on his boat after sixteen years on land. When Kelly's daughter Molly falls in love with Coast Guard officer Bob Graham, who has been hassling Kelly, he refuses to let them marry. In a bar, Kelly meets Queenie Truelove, to whom he was married for eight hours, and she demands $1,200 in alimony. To rid himself of Queenie and her gold-digging friend, Fern, Kelly convinces them his deck hand, Andy Anderson, is millionaire Commodore Van Deusen. When Fern grabs Cohen for a spontaneous double wedding, and Andy passes out from liquor, Kelly moves all to Captain Silva's rum boat, the "Esmeralda," saying it is a hospital boat for Andy. Kelly and Cohen then escape in Kelly's boat, and Kelly goes overboard and is forced to jump into a rowboat. A sea chase ensues in which they nearly crash numerous times, and Cohen ends up towing the rowboat before running out of gas. Meanwhile, Bob and Molly search for Kelly's boat, fearing he is adrift and in danger. Kelly and Cohen spy the "Esmeralda" and come aboard as Silva performs a wedding ceremony for Andy and Queenie, whom Andy thinks is wealthy. When Queenie discovers that Andy is really Kelly's deck hand, she chases Cohen and Kelly off Silva's boat and onto a frigate just as Bob approaches and fires at the rum boat. As the boat sinks, Cohen and Kelly surrender and come aboard Bob's boat. Bob then threatens to arrest Kelly for bootlegging until he agrees to let Bob marry Molly. Kelly accidentally fires a gun round, and the "Esmeralda" explodes, leaving Silva, Andy and Queenie swimming for their lives. *Boats. Bootleggers. Friendship. Gold diggers. Irish Americans. Jews.* Alimony. Bars. Boating accidents. Businessmen. Chases. Drunkenness. Ex-spouses. Explosions. Fathers and daughters. Impersonation and imposture. Marriage–Arranged. Mistaken identity. Prohibition. Proposals (Marital). Sea rescues. Smuggling. United States. Coast Guard. Weddings. Widowers.

Note: Although this film was not viewed, the above credits and plot summary were taken from a studio cutting continuity and dialogue script. This film marks George Stevens' first time as a feature director. Stevens had previously directed only short films. Jack Jungmyeer is credited as the third scenarist (after Austin and Guiol) in *MPH* and copyright records, and is credited with continuity in *DV*. Program notes for a modern screening of the film state that printed on the film's leader are the words: "This print may be used on both Movietone and Disc equipment." In the early thirties, exhibitors had a dual choice of sound systems: the older Vitaphone sound-on-disc system and RCA's Movietone sound-on-film system, which eventually replaced the disc system. This film was the last in a series of seven Cohens and Kellys films. For more information on the series, consult the Series Index and see the entry for *The Cohens and Kellys in Africa* (above).

DV 10 Mar 1933. *FD* 15 Apr 1933, p. 3. *HR* 8 Mar 1933, p. 3. *IP* Mar 1933, p. 34. *MPD* 7 Apr 1933, p. 4. *MPH* 22 Apr 1933, pp. 36-37. *NYT* 17 Apr 1933, p. 16. *Var* 18 Apr 1933, p. 4.

THE COHENS AND THE KELLYS IN PARIS (Irish Americans, Jewish Americans)

Universal Pictures Corp.; Universal Super-Jewel. 15 Jan **1928** [©Universal Pictures Corp.; 3 Jan 1928; LP24820]. Si; b&w. 8 reels, 7,481 ft.

Series: The Cohens and Kellys.

Pres Carl Laemmle. *Dir* William Beaudine. *Story and cont* Alfred A. Cohn. *Scr supv* Joseph Poland. *Titles* Albert De Mond. *Photog* Charles Stumar. *Film ed* Frank Atkinson and Robert Carlisle.

Cast: George Sidney (*Nathan Cohen*), J. Farrell MacDonald (*Patrick Kelly*), Vera Gordon (*Mrs. Cohen*), Kate Price (*Mrs. Kelly*), Charles Delaney (*Patrick Kelly*), Sue Carol (*Sadye Cohen*), Gertrude Astor (*Paulette*), Gino Corrado (*Pierre, Paulette's husband*), Charlie Murray.

Comedy. Nathan Cohen, a Jew, and Patrick Kelly, an Irishman, are quarreling business partners. Accompanied by their wives, they board a liner for France to forestall a marriage between their offspring, Sadye Cohen and Patrick Kelly. Upon arrival in Paris, they find their children already married and nearly divorced. Paulette, an artist's model whom Pat is painting in the nude, is the bone of contention between the newlyweds. Visiting Paulette, Cohen and Kelly quarrel with her husband, Pierre, an apache, and nearly wreck the Café Diable. Pierre challenges Cohen and Kelly to a duel, but the wives rescue their husbands in an airplane; once in the air, the two families make up their differences. *Apaches–Paris. Artists. Businessmen. Irish Americans. Jews. Models. Paris (France). Partnership.*

Note: For additional information on the Cohens and Kellys series, see entry above for *The Cohens and Kellys in Africa* and consult the Series Index.

FD 12 Feb 1928. *NYT* 6 Feb 1928, p. 12. *Var* 8 Feb 1928, p. 16.

THE COHENS AND THE KELLYS IN SCOTLAND (Irish Americans, Jewish Americans)

Universal Pictures Corp. 17 Mar **1930** [©Universal Pictures Corp.; 6 Mar 1930; LP1129]. Sd (Movietone); b&w. 8 reels, 7,600 ft. [Also si; 6,584 ft.].

Series: The Cohens and Kellys.

Pres Carl Laemmle. *Dir* William James Craft. *Scen and dial* Albert De Mond. *Story* John McDermott. *Photog* C. Allen Jones. *Film ed* Harry Lieb. *Rec eng* Joseph R. Lapis and C. Roy Hunter.

Cast: George Sidney (*Cohen*), Charles Murray (*Kelly*), Vera Gordon (*Mrs. Cohen*), Kate Price (*Mrs. Kelly*), E. J. Radcliffe (*McPherson*), William Colvin (*McDonald*), Lloyd Whitlock (*Prince*).

Comedy. Accompanied by their respective spouses, Cohen and Kelly go to Scotland to buy plaids, each having received a tip that the Prince of Morania, a style dictator, is to have a plaid motif in his spring collection. Cohen buys all the plaids of McPherson, while Kelly purchases those of McDonald. Cohen gets into trouble with a stranger on the golf course and is horrified to find that he has insulted the prince; they attend the races where the prince is expected to show himself in plaids, but his clothes are covered by his raincoat. Thinking themselves ruined, each decides to commit suicide; however, when Cohen tries to drown himself, Kelly rescues him. They astound McPherson and McDonald by asking them to buy back the plaids, but when the prince is seen wearing them in a parade, the Scotsmen gladly pay them a fortune. *Clothing industry. Couturiers. Golf. Irish Americans. Jews. Scotland.*

Note: For additional information on the Cohens and Kellys series, see entry above for *The Cohens and Kellys in Africa* and consult the Series Index.

FD 2 Mar 1930. *NYT* 10 Mar 1930, p. 24. *Var* 12 Mar 1930, p. 33.

COHEN'S LUCK (Jewish Americans)

Thomas A Edison, Inc. *Dist* General Film Co. 11 Jun **1915** [©Thomas A. Edison, Inc.; 28 May 1915; LP5437]. Si; b&w. 4 reels.

Pres Thomas A. Edison. *Dir* John H. Collins. *Scen* Lee Arthur.

Source: Based on the play *Cohen's Luck* by Lee Arthur (Chicago, production date undetermined).

Cast: William Wadsworth (*Abe Cohen*), Lillian Devere (*His wife*), Viola Dana (*Minnie Cohen*), Harry Scherr (*Abe Cohen, Jr.*), Duncan McRae (*Sam Blumenthal*), John Walker (*David Moss*), Jessie Stevens (*Mrs. Kitty McGee*), Edward Lawrence (*Timothy Murphy*), Frank A. Lyon (*Steve O'Roque*), Henry Leone (*Laskey*), Robert Brower.

Comedy-drama. Abe Cohen, president of the Buttonhole Makers' Union, loses his job in Sam Blumenthal's East Side sweatshop when he endorses Timothy Murphy for alderman over Steve O'Roque, to whom Blumenthal is indebted. After Murphy helps Cohen start a kosher restaurant, Cohen learns that he and his former co-worker, Kitty McGee, won $10,000 in the lottery. He gives free meals to his customers, but when Kitty discovers that her purse containing half of the ticket was stolen, Cohen clears the "loafers" out. Cohen's daughter Minnie, in love with Blumenthal, secretly marries him, but Blumenthal, already married although separated from his wife, keeps Minnie's ring and their marriage certificate. Doubting the marriage, Cohen turns Minnie out, but when Blumenthal's wife appears, and Minnie's suitor, David Moss, whom Cohen likes, finds her, the marriage is invalidated and Cohen reconciles with his daughter. Mixing with the underworld, Cohen outwits the thief who stole Kitty's ticket. Despite a flood coming down from the apartment above, the ensuing celebration marks Minnie and David's engagement. *Bigamy. Fathers and daughters. Jews. Lotteries. Marriage–Annulment. New York City–Lower East Side. Restaurants.* Clothing industry. Elections. Robbery. Sweatshops. Trade unions.

Note: This film was the first made under Edison's new policy of releasing four reel pictures at regular intervals on the General Film program. William Wadsworth played his role on stage with Annie Russell. Some exteriors for the film were shot in the "ghetto" sections of New York's City's Lower East Side.

EK 1 Jun 1915. *Motog* 12 Jun 1915, p. 975, 985. *MPN* 22 May 1915, p. 47. *MPN* 5 Jun 1915, p. 91. *MPN* 12 Jun 1915, p. 73. *MPW* 5 Jun 1915, p. 1659. *MPW* 26 Jun 1915, p. 2096. *NYDM* 2 Jun 1915, p. 32.

COLLISION see THIEVES' HIGHWAY

COLONEL SPANKY see GENERAL SPANKY

THE COLOR OF HER SKIN see NIGHT OF THE QUARTER MOON

COLORADO PIONEERS (Native Americans)

Republic Pictures Corp. *Dist* Republic Pictures Corp. 14 Nov **1945**; Prod: 12 Mar–23 Mar 1945 [©Republic Pictures Corp.; 29 Oct 1945; LP13627]. Sd (RCA Sound System); b&w. 6 reels. 55-56 or 58 min. Passed by the National Board of Review. PCA cert no. 10855.

Series: Red Ryder.

Assoc prod Sidney Picker. *Dir* R. G. Springsteen. [*Asst dir* Lee Lukather and Al Wood]. *Scr* Earle Snell. *Orig story* Peter Whitehead. *Photog* Bud Thackery. [*2d cam* Enzo Martinelli]. *Spec eff* Howard Lydecker and Theodore Lydecker. [*Transparency projection shots* Gordon C. Schaefer]. *Art dir* Frank Hotaling. *Film ed* Charles Craft. *Set dec* Otto Siegel. *Mus dir* Richard Cherwin. *Sd* Earl Crain, Jr. [*Re-rec and eff mixer* Thomas A. Carman]. [*Re-rec, eff and mus mixer* Howard Wilson]. *Makeup supv* Bob Mark.

Source: Based on the comic strip "Red Ryder" by Fred Harmon (1938–1964), by special arrangement with Stephen Slesinger.

Cast: WILD BILL ELLIOTT (*Red Ryder*), Bobby Blake [(*Little Beaver*)], Alice Fleming [(*Martha "The Duchess" Wentworth*)], Roy Barcroft [(*Bull Reagan*)], Bud Geary [(*Bill Slade*)], Billy Cummings [(*Joe*)], Freddie Chapman [(*Skinny*)], Frank Jaquet [(*Dave Wyatt*)], Tom London [(*Sand Snipe*)], Monte Hale [(*Chuck*)], Buckwheat Thomas [(*Smokey*)], George Chesebro [(*Hank Disher*)], Emmett Vogan [(*Judge*)], Tom Chatterton [(*Father Marion*)], [Edward Cassidy (*Ramsey*)], [Jack Rockwell (*Sheriff*)], [Fred Graham (*Dozier*)], [Howard Mitchell (*Policeman*)], [Gary Armstrong, Bobby Anderson, Roger Williams, Richard Lydon, Robert Goldschmidt, Romey Foley (*Boys*)], [Jack Kirk (*Buggy owner*)].

Western. [*Print viewed*]. In 1899, ranch foreman Red Ryder and his Indian ward, Little Beaver, travel from their home in Blue Springs, Colorado, to Chicago to speak to Ramsey, the representative of a meat packing company. While they are negotiating the price for Red's cattle, two young boys, Joe and Skinny, create a distraction with a stolen wagon, and their adult cohort, Bull Reagan, robs Ramsey. Red follows the boys, who were tricked by Bull into participating, and after a fistfight, turns Bull over to the police. Later, a juvenile court judge listens as Father Marion pleads that the boys, who live in the parish home, are not really bad, just in need of better facilities to keep them off the streets. Red, who has attended the hearing, states that his aunt, Martha "The Duchess" Wentworth, has a large ranch on which the boys could receive fresh air, hard work, discipline and affection if they were sent there for the summer. The judge agrees and Little Beaver waits with the boys while the paperwork is processed. Red returns home, where he learns that a fire has destroyed much of the Duchess' grazing land. One of her neighbors, rancher Dave Wyatt, offers to cover the Duchess' credit at the general store, but she asserts that all will be well once her cattle are shipped. A few days later, Little Beaver arrives, and much to Red's surprise, he brings with him all of the parish boys, not just Joe and Skinny. The Duchess is delighted, and the boys quickly settle into life at the ranch. Only Joe hates the ranch, believing that Red wants to turn him into a "softy." Joe refuses to participate in any activities until one afternoon, Red finds an orphaned colt, and the little animal wins Joe's heart. Red also has found evidence that the fire was arson, although he is baffled about who set it and why. He becomes suspicious of Wyatt when the rancher hires away all of the Duchess' ranch hands, leaving her in jeopardy of not being able to ship her cattle. Red scours the countryside for more hands, but can find only old cowpoke Sand Snipe. While Red is gone, however, Little Beaver teaches the boys how to round up the cattle, and when Red returns, all the cattle are in the canyon waiting for the drive. Still resistant, Joe is about to run away when the colt becomes sick. The illness is not serious, but Joe is persuaded to go with the other boys on the cattle drive and nurse the colt back to health. When the boys are assembled at the campsite soon after, Wyatt and his foreman, Bill Slade, set off an explosion in the cliff face above the camp. Fortunately, only one boy is injured, but the townspeople speak out against Red hiring children to do a man's job. The dissension is temporarily quelled by the excitement over the town's annual buckboard race, but Joe cannot enjoy the proceedings, for Bull, who escaped from custody, has found him and orders him to steal Red's prize money if he is the winner. When Joe attempts to tell Red, he sees Red apparently tampering with Slade's wagon, and after Red wins, Joe assumes that he cheated and, disillusioned, agrees to leave with Bull. That night, Red catches Slade at the ranch house, and Slade confesses that Wyatt instigated the fire and landslide in the hope that the Duchess would be forced to sell her valuable ranch to him. Just then, the sheriff brings in Joe and Bull, who had stolen Red's prize money without Joe's knowledge. Joe learns that Red won the race honestly and Bull is taken away. Later, the boys are about to return to Chicago when Red promises that they can come back during their next summer vacation. As Joe bids farewell to the colt, Red assures him that a horse never forgets its owner, and Joe confesses that he has become a "softy." *Children. Duplicity. Horses. Maturation. Ranch foremen. Ranches.* African Americans. Arson. Aunts. Cattle drives. Chicago (IL). Child custody. Colorado. Criminals. Explosions. Hero worship. Indians of North America. Judges. Landslides. Priests. Prizes and trophies. Racing. Robbery. Wards and guardians.

Note: Modern sources include Horace B. Carpenter, Bill Wolfe, George Morrell, Cliff Parkinson and Jess Cavan in the cast. For more information on the "Red Ryder" series, please consult the Series Index and see the entry below for *Tucson Raiders*.

Box 12 Jan 1946. *DV* 14 Dec 1945, p. 3. *HR* 9 Mar 1945, pp. 13-14. *HR* 16 Mar 1945, p. 48. *HR* 26 Mar 1945, p. 6. *HR* 14 Dec 1945, p. 6. *MPHPD* 21 Jul 1945, p. 2555. *MPHPD* 22 Dec 1945, p. 2768.

COLORADO TERRITORY (Native Americans)

Warner Bros. Pictures, Inc.; A Warner Bros.—First National Picture. *Dist* Warner Bros. Pictures, Inc. 11 Jun **1949**; Prod: late Aug—mid-Nov 1948 [©Warner Bros. Pictures, Inc.; 11 Jun 1949; LP2331]. Sd (RCA Sound System); b&w. 94 min.

Prod Anthony Veiller. *Dir* Raoul Walsh. *Dial dir* Eugene Busch. [*Asst dir* Russell Saunders]. *Wrt* John Twist and Edmund H. North. *Dir of photog* Sid Hickox. *Spec eff* William McGann. *Spec eff* H. F. Koenekamp. *Art dir* Ted Smith. *Film ed* Owen Marks. *Set dec* Fred M. MacLean. *Ward* Leah Rhodes. *Orch* Maurice de Packh. *Mus* David Buttolph. *Sd* Leslie G. Hewitt. *Makeup artist* Perc Westmore.

Cast: JOEL McCREA [(*Wes McQueen*)], VIRGINIA MAYO [(*Colorado Carson*)], DOROTHY MALONE [(*Julie Ann Winslow*)],

Henry Hull [(*Fred Winslow*)], John Archer [(*Reno Blake*)], James Mitchell [(*Duke Harris*)], Morris Ankrum [(*U.S. marshal*)], Basil Ruysdael [(*Dave Rickard*)], Frank Puglia [(*Brother Tomas*)], Ian Wolfe [(*Homer Wallace*)], Harry Woods [(*Pluthner*)], Houseley Stevenson [(*Prospector*)], [Victor Kilian (*The sheriff*)], [Oliver Blake (*Station agent*)], [Jack Montgomery, Artie Ortego (*Deputy marshals*)], [Glenn Thompson, Charles Horvath (*Train guards*)], [Ben Corbett, Bert Dillard, Steve Stephens, Merlyn Nelson, Frosty Royce, Charles Miller (*Posse members*)], [Carl Harbough (*Brakeman*)], [Hallene Hill (*Aunt Georgina*)], [Paul Kruger, George Bell, Robert Filmer (*Deputies*)], [Monte Blue (*U.S. marshal*)], [Carl Andre (*Stage driver*)], [Harry Strang (*Stage guard*)], [Maude Prickett (*Mrs. Wallace*)], [Jack Daley (*Fireman*)], [Fred Kelsey (*Engineer*)], [Gray Eyes (*Old Indian*)].

Western. [*Print viewed*]. Outlaw Wes McQueen escapes from jail and heads for the Colorado Territory, where he is to meet with his boss, Dave Rickard. Before he catches the stagecoach, he stops by his former family farm and learns that everyone he cared about is gone or dead. On the stage, he meets Fred Winslow and his daughter Julie Ann, who have purchased a ranch, sight unseen. When outlaws attack the stage, killing both of the drivers, Wes fights them off and successfully brings the stage into town. Wes's destination is Todos Santos, a ghost town, where Duke Harris and Reno Blake are waiting for him to organize a train robbery. Wes is troubled by the unexpected presence of half-Indian Colorado Carson, as he believes a woman will cause trouble between the two men. After he orders her to leave, however, she warns him about the unreliability of Homer Wallace, the inside man on his team. Impressed by her acumen, Wes allows Colorado to remain with the gang, despite his misgivings. Then, acting on Colorado's warning, Wes tries to scare Wallace into remaining silent. Later, he rides into town to visit the Winslows and learns that the land that they bought is poor and waterless. Wes's attraction to Julie Ann prompts him to visit Dave, who is ill, and disclose that he wants to settle down and live a respectable life. Dave reveals that he has no money and asks his old friend to pull this last job before he quits. On his way back to the hideout, Wes stops again at the Winslows with a new dress for Julie Ann and money to enable them to dig a well. Winslow tries to return the money, explaining that Wes has no chance with Julie Ann, who is in love with Randolph, a man who refuses to marry her. Winslow explains that it was to stop his daughter's involvement with Randolph that they moved West. Back at Todos Santos, Wes learns that his fears that Colorado would cause trouble between the men have been realized. After warning Duke and Reno not to fight until after the robbery, he asks Colorado to move into his room. When she reveals that she is in love with him, he brusquely explains that his plans do not include her. Still wary of Wallace, Wes questions his wife and learns that Wallace has betrayed them. Wes tries to salvage the robbery, but Duke and Reno are captured by the sheriff's men. When Wes and Colorado arrive at Dave's with the money, they discover that he has died. Later, Wes finds Pluthner, another member of Dave's gang, trying to steal the money and kills him, but Wes is himself wounded in the fight. Together with Colorado, Wes asks the Winslows for help, after revealing his real identity. Winslow agrees to help, but Julie Ann, who intends to return to Randolph, tries to turn him in for the reward. A disappointed Wes then leaves with Colorado. After Duke and Reno are hanged, Wes and Colorado return to Todos Santos, where Wes asks Colorado to marry him. There, an Indian riding with the posse spots them and forces them to leave their hideout. Believing they will have a better chance to escape if they separate, Wes rides toward Mexico, leaving Colorado at Todos Santos. There, she overhears the posse plan to surround Wes in the Canyon of the Dead. She begs them not to kill Wes, but the marshal devises a trap, and both Wes and Colorado are killed. Later, Brother Tomas, a traveling monk, discovers the stolen money that Colorado has hidden at Todos Santos and uses it to give new life to the abandoned city. *Betrayal. Colorado. Criminals–Rehabilitation. Outlaws. Fathers and daughters. Friendship. Ghost towns. Hideouts. Indians of North America. Indians of North America–Mixed blood. Jailbreaks. Money. Monks. Murder. Posses. Ranches. Rewards. Romance. Train robberies. Unrequited love.*

Note: The film's working title was *North of the Rio Grande*. According to a 26 May 1950 *LAHE* news item, this was the first U.S. movie to be banned in West Germany, which deemed it "an example of gangster films which glorify anti-social elements." The film is a remake of the 1941 Warner Bros. film, *High Sierra*, written by John Huston and W. R. Burnett.

Box 21 May 1949. *DV* 17 May 1949, p. 3, 6. *FD* 18 May 1949, p. 6. *HR* 27 Aug 1948, p. 13. *HR* 12 Nov 1948, p. 13. *HR* 17 May 1949, p. 3. *LAHE* 26 May 1950. *MPHPD* 21 May 1949, p. 4617. *NYT* 25 Jun 1949, p. 8. *Var* 18 May 1949, p. 8.

THE COLORED AMERICAN WINNING HIS SUIT (African Americans)

Frederick Douglass Film Co. 14 Jul **1916**. Si; b&w. 5 reels.
Prod Rev. W. S. Smith. *Scen* Rev. W. S. Smith.

Cast: Thomas M. Mosley (*Bob Winall*), Ida Askins (*Alma Elton*), Florence Snead (*Bessie Winall*), Marshall Davies (*Jim Sample*), F. King (*Mr. Hinderus*), Fred Leighton (*Col. Goodwill*), Edgar Snead (*Bob's father*), Mrs. E. Snead (*Bob's mother*), Thomas Wheeler (*Alma's father*), Minnie Smith (*Alma's mother*), Fred Quinn (*Detective*).

African American, Drama. Freed from slavery after the Civil War, the Winalls, a poor couple, rent a farm from their former master. The Winalls prosper, eventually buy the farm, and have two children, Bob and Bessie, whom they send to college. Returning to his Virginia home as a lawyer, Bob falls in love with Bessie's roommate Alma Eaton, who becomes a principal at the high school in her North Carolina town. Alma's mother, however, wants her to marry wealthy James Sample instead of Bob, and the couple break up under this familial pressure. When Alma's father, a banker, loses a box of jewels, his white rival Hinderus gives information to the police that results in Eaton's arrest. Hinderus uses his influence to prevent any lawyer from taking Eaton's case. In despair, Mrs. Eaton asks Bob to represent her husband. Bob hires a detective and finds the jewels in the possession of some street children, acquitting Eaton and clearing the way for his marriage to Alma. *African Americans. Bankers. Frame-ups. Lawyers. North Carolina. School superintendents and principals. Detectives. Farmers. Jewelry. Robbery. Slavery–Emancipation. Virginia.*

Note: This film was the first feature made by a black production company. The cast was made up of nonactors from the Jersey City, NJ area. Scenes were shot in Virginia, in Jersey City, and at Howard University in Washington, D.C. The film was cut to four reels sometime after its premiere. One modern source states that the film was originally six, not five, reels. Another modern source credits Dr. G. E. Cannon, the Douglass Film Company's financial backer, as the film's co-producer.

New York Age 20 Jul 1916, p. 6. *New York Age* 14 Jun 1917, p. 6. *New York Age* 9 Aug 1917, p. 6.

COLT .45 (Native Americans)

Warner Bros. Pictures, Inc.; A Warner Bros.—First National Picture. *Dist* Warner Bros. Pictures, Inc. 27 May **1950**; New York opening: 5 May 1950; Prod: mid-Nov—mid-Dec 1949 [©Warner Bros. Pictures, Inc.; 22 May 1950; LP123]. Sd (RCA Sound System); col (Technicolor). 6,653 ft. 74 or 76 min. PCA cert no. 14347.
Prod Saul Elkins. *Dir* Edwin L. Marin. [*Asst dir* Oren Haglund]. *Wrt* Thomas Blackburn. *Dir of photog* Wilfrid M. Cline. *Spec eff* Harry Barndollar. *Technicolor col consultant* Mitchell Kovaleski. *Art dir* Douglas Bacon. *Film ed* Frank Magee. *Set dec* William Wallace. *Orch* Charles Maxell. *Mus* William Lava. *Sd* Dolph Thomas. *Makeup artist* Perc Westmore.

Cast: RANDOLPH SCOTT [(*Steve Farrell*)], RUTH ROMAN [(*Beth Donovan*)], Zachary Scott [(*Jason Brett*)], Lloyd Bridges [(*Paul Donovan*)], Alan Hale [(*Sheriff Harris*)], Ian MacDonald [(*Miller*)], Chief Thundercloud [(*Walking Bear*)], [Lute Crockett (*Judge Tucker*)], [Walter Coy (*Carl*)], [Charles Evans (*Redrock sheriff*)], [Stanley Andrews, Hal Taliaferro (*Drivers*)], [Buddy Roosevelt (*Guard*)], [Art Miles, Barry Regan (*Bystanders*)], [Howard Negley, Charles Sherlock, Nolan Leary, Paul Newland, Franklyn Farnum, Ed Peil, Sr. (*Townsmen*)], [Aurora Navarro (*Indian woman*)], [Jack Watt (*Posseman*)], [Carl Andre, Royden Clark, Clyde Hudkins, Jr., Leroy Johnson (*Indians*)], [Ben Corbett, Kansas Moehring, Warren Fisk, Forrest R. Colee, Artie Ortego, Richard Brehm, Dick Hudkins, Leo McMahon, Bob Burrows, William Steele (*Henchmen*)].

Western. [*Viewed print incomplete*]. While gun salesman Steve Farrell is demonstrating the new Colt .45 repeating pistols to a sheriff, prisoner Jason Brett, who is being transferred to another jail, manages to take the pistols and make his escape. The townspeople are convinced that Steve was Brett's partner and jail him. During the four months that Steve is jailed, Brett begins a long siege of theft and murder. Regular rifles and pistols are no match for his Colt .45 pistols. When Steve is finally released, the sheriff offers him a letter clearing him of the charges against him, providing he reveals Brett's hiding place. Steve, however, proclaims his innocence, and vows to get his guns back from Brett. Steve finds Brett's trail when he happens

on a group of Indians whom Brett has killed to provide a cover for a stagecoach robbery. After Walking Bear, the sole survivor of the slaughter, tells Steve about Brett's plan, Steve boards the stage and fights off the attack with his own set of Colt .45s, despite the attempts of Beth Donovan, the only passenger on the stage, to prevent him. Unknown to Steve, Beth is the wife of Paul Donovan, one of Brett's associates. Later, Steve notices that a white scarf hung outside the stagecoach is being used as a signal and, sure that Beth is part of the gang, tries to bring her to the sheriff. Beth escapes and returns to camp. Although Beth believes that Paul has been forced to work with Brett, he is actually plotting with the bandit to take over the nearby town of Bonanza Creek. Sheriff Harris, who unknown to the town is allied with Brett, agrees to make Steve his deputy, but immediately reveals the fact to Brett, who then plans an ambush for Steve. Steve evades the ambush with the help of Walking Bear's fellow Indians. He captures two members of the gang and brings them back to town. At the hideout, Beth overhears Paul plotting with Brett and realizes her husband is actively working with the gang. After Beth denounces Paul, he locks her in a store room. Later, she manages to escape and hurries into town, planning to reveal everything to the authorities. Donovan stops Beth outside the town, and when she tries to ride past him, shoots her. Steve, hearing the shots, finds Beth lying on the ground and takes her with him to seek refuge with Walking Bear. Beth warns Steve about Paul and Brett's plan to take over Bonanza Creek. Then the Indians discover Donovan's body, shot in the back by a .45. After Steve learns that the Indians intend to go on the warpath, he tries to warn the town, but Brett's men trap and capture him. The Indians kill his captors, but Harris survives. While Steve and the Indians quietly kill many of Brett's men in town, Harris crawls back to warn Brett. Using Beth as a shield, Brett tries to escape, but Beth breaks away and the Indians taunt Brett into using all his powder. Steve then overcomes Brett and is rewarded with Beth's embrace. *Bandits. Firearms. Revenge. Ambushes. False arrests. Gunfights. Gunshot wounds. Indians of North America. Marriage. Murder. Sheriffs. Stagecoach robberies. Uprisings.*

Note: The film begins with the following written foreword: "A gun like any other source of power, is a force for either good or evil, being neither in itself, but dependent upon those who possess it." This was the last film actor Alan Hale made before his death, although the 1950 Columbia film *Rogues of Sherwood Forest*, which was filmed prior to *Colt .45*, was released later.
Box 6 May 1950. DV 3 May 1950, p. 3. FD 3 May 1950, p. 8. HR 3 May 1950, p. 3. MPHPD 6 May 1950, p. 285. NYT 6 May 1950, p. 8. Var 3 May 1950, p. 6.

COLUMN SOUTH (Native Americans, Navajo)
Universal-International Pictures Co., Inc. *Dist* Universal Pictures Co., Inc. Jun **1953**; Prod: 29 Jul—late 1952 [©Universal Pictures Co.; 10 Mar 1953; LP2431]. Sd (Western Electric Recording); col (Technicolor). 7,582 ft. 84-85 min. PCA cert no. 16161.

Prod Ted Richmond. *Dir* Frederick de Cordova. *Asst dir* Fred Frank and [George Lollier]. [*Dial dir* Jack Daniels]. *Story and scr* William Sackheim. *Dir of photog* Charles P. Boyle. *Technicolor col consultant* William Fritzsche. *Art dir* Alexander Golitzen and Hilyard Brown. *Film ed* Milton Carruth. *Set dec* Russell A. Gausman and Ruby Levitt. *Cost* Rosemary Odell. *Mus dir* Joseph Gershenson. *Sd* Leslie I. Carey and Glen E. Anderson. *Hair stylist* Joan St. Oegger. *Makeup* Bud Westmore. *Tech dir* Col. Paul R. Davison, U.S.A., Rtd. [*Unit prod mgr* Percy Ikerd].

Cast: Audie Murphy (*Lt. Jed Sayre*), Joan Evans (*Marcy Whitlock*), Robert Sterling (*Capt. Lee Whitlock*), Ray Collins (*Brig. Gen. [B. N.] Storey [Stone]*), Dennis Weaver (*Menguito*), Palmer Lee (*Chalmers*), Russell Johnson (*Corp. Biddle*), Jack Kelly (*Trooper Vaness*), Johnny Downs (*Lt. Posick*), Bob Steele (*Sgt. McAfee*), James Best (*Primrose*), Ralph Moody (*Joe Copper Face*), Rico Alaniz (*Trooper Chavez*), [Ray Montgomery (*Trooper Keit*)], [Richard Garland (*Lt. Fry*)], [Ed Rand], [Alan Dexter (*Tom Kehler*)], [Sydney Mason (*Garsey*)], [Tyler McVey, Britt Wood (*Millers*)], [Steve Darrell (*Danforth*)], [Jack Ingram (*Veterinarian*)], [Joe Bailey (*Ammunition sentry*)], [Jack George, Ed Colebrook, Jimmy Gray (*Poker players*)], [Boyd Morgan (*Sentry*)], [Kermit Maynard, Monte Montague (*Drivers*)], [Denver Pyle (*Lieutenant*)].

Western. [*Print viewed*]. In Jan 1861, Jed Sayre, a lieutenant in the U.S. Cavalry and commander of New Mexico's Fort Union, is ordered to turn over command of the post to the ruthless Captain Lee Whitlock, who has just arrived from Mississippi with his sister Marcy. Whitlock orders Jed to bring order to the post and tells him that his friendly association with the nearby Navajo Indians must come to an end. During Whitlock and Marcy's first night at the fort, Marcy screams in horror when she sees an Indian peering into her room. Jed and Lt. Chalmers try to quell Marcy's fears by formally introducing her to the Indian, Joe Copper Face, but she runs away in fright and loathing. One day, Whitlock is presented with the body of a dead prospector who was scalped near the fort, and, assuming it to be the act of Navajos, orders to Chief Menguito to turn over the murderers. Jed tries to convince Whitlock that scalping is not a Navajo practice, but his argument is rejected. At a nearby saloon, Jed and Chalmers uncover evidence that the murdered man was killed for his gold pouch by fellow prospector Tom Kehler. After Kehler confesses to the murder, Jed and Chalmers ride into the hills in search of Whitlock, who is about to lead his soldiers in an assault on the Indians to avenge the death of the prospector. Jed and Chalmers arrive at the battle site in time to inform Whitlock that Kehler confessed, and a bloody battle is averted. Later, Jed takes Whitlock to meet Menguito, but the peaceful introduction turns violent when a renegade Navajo engages Whitlock in a fistfight. Menguito apologizes for the incident, but warns Whitlock that his short temper may result in war between the Indians and the whites. Later, at the fort, Marcy insults the visiting Menguito and tells Jed that she still hates the "red-skinned savages." However, Marcy eventually realizes that Jed is right in respecting the Indians, and that he probably saved her brother's life by preventing the battle from taking place. She apologizes to Jed for her behavior, and then indicates that she is in love with him. Meanwhile, at the headquarters of the Ninth Military District in Santa Fe, Union General B. N. Stone, a traitor to the Army, tells local politicians that a civil war is imminent. While visiting Fort Union, Stone persuades Whitlock, a fellow Southerner, to turn traitor with him and join the Confederate army. Leaving the fort with only a few soldiers to defend it, Whitlock leads his regiment into the wilderness to meet up with other Confederate outfits. When Jed finds evidence that Whitlock is conspiring with Stone to desert the Union and join the South, he exposes Whitlock and returns to the fort with soldiers loyal to the Union. Jed and his soldiers arrive back at the fort just as Menguito and the Navajos are about to capture it, and they soon find themselves engaged in a desperate battle to defend it. Things look bad for Jed and the defenders of the fort, until Whitlock, who has had a change of heart, returns to fight on the side of the Cavalry. A single act of bravery by Whitlock saves the fort, and the Indians are surrounded. Whitlock resigns as commander of Fort Union, leaving it under the control of Jed, who will marry Marcy. *Forts. Navajo Indians. New Mexico. Traitors. Tribal chiefs. United States—History—Civil War, 1861-1865. United States. Army. Cavalry. Battles. Bigotry. Brothers and sisters. Confederate States of America. Army. False accusations. Fistfights. Murder. Officers (Military). Poker (Game). Prospectors. Romance. Santa Fe (NM). Scalping. Scouts (Frontier). Soldiers. Southerners.*

Note: Although Ray Collins' character is listed onscreen as "Storey," he is called "Stone" in the film.
Box 16 May 1953. DV 8 May 1953, p. 3 FD 25 May 1953, p. 6. HR 1 Aug 1952, p. 11. HR 22 Aug 1952, p. 10. HR 8 May 1953, p. 3. MPHPD 16 May 1953, p. 1839. Var 13 May 1953, p. 18.

COMANCHE (1958) *see* **TONKA**

COMANCHE (Latino, Native Americans, Comanche)
Carl Krueger Co., Inc. *Dist* United Artists Corp. Mar **1956**; Prod: 24 Aug—5 Oct 1955 [©Carl Krueger Co., Inc.; 3 Mar 1956; LP6409]. Sd (RCA Sound System); col; CinemaScope. 7,848 ft. 87-88 min. PCA cert no. 17714.

Pres CARL KRUEGER. *Prod* Carl Krueger. *Assoc prod* Henry L. Spitz. *Dir* George Sherman. *Asst dir* Henry Spitz and Ignacio Villareal. *Wrt for the scr* Carl Krueger. *Photog* Jorge Stahl, Jr. *Spec eff* David Koehler. *Photog eff* Jack Rabin and Louis De Witt. *Art dir* Ramon Rodriguez. *Film ed* Charles L. Kimball. *Cost* David Berman. *Ward* Georgette Somohano and Adolfo Ramirez. *Mus comp and dir* Herschel Burke Gilbert. *Orch* Walter Sheets and Joe Mullendore. *Sd supv* James L. Fields. *Sd rec* Manuel Topets and Galdino Samperio. *Makeup* Rosa Guerrero. *Hair styles* Pena Lozada. *Prod mgr* Alphonso Sanchez Tello. *Script supv* Bobbie Sierks. [*Stunts* Boyd Stockman].

Song(s): "A Man Is As Good As His Word," music by Herschel Burke Gilbert, lyrics by Alfred Perry, sung by The Lancers, Coral Recording Artists.

Cast: Dana Andrews (*Jim Read*), Kent Smith (*Quanah Parker*), Nestor Paiva (*Puffer*), Henry Brandon (*Black Cloud*), Stacey [sic]

Harris ([*Art*] *Downey*), John Litel (*General Nelson A. Miles*), Lowell Gilmore (*Commissioner Ward*), Mike Mazurki (*Flat Mouth*), Tony Carbajal (*Little Snake*), Introducing Miss Linda Cristal (*Margarita* [*Alvarez*]), Reed Sherman (*Lieutenant* [*John*] *French*), David Moreno, [Carlos Múzquiz], [George Mari], [Fanny Schiller], [José Chavez], [Felipe de Flores], [Lisbeth Tello].

Western. [*Print viewed*]. In 1875, a group of renegade Comanches led by the warlike Black Cloud attacks and burns a Mexican village, kidnaps a number of women, including beautiful young Margarita, and escapes Mexican troops by crossing the border into U.S. territory. Later that day, Quanah Parker, chief of the Comanche Antelope tribe, stops the renegades from massacring of a gang of scalp traders, led by former Cavalry scout Art Downey. Scout Jim Read orders Downey to stay out of the territory, accusing him of having made "a career of Indian hating," which prompts Downey to call Jim an Indian lover. At the Cavalry encampment, Jim meets Commissioner Ward, a government official who has been ordered to end the latest round of Comanche raids into Mexican territory. Gen. Nelson Miles and Jim explain to Ward the roots of the mutual animosity between the Mexicans and the Comanches: When in the early eighteenth century the conquering Spaniards discovered that the land was rich in silver, they forced Comanches to work the mines as slaves. The Comanches rebelled and massacred the Spaniards, who began offering rewards for Indian scalps, even those taken from women and small children. After winning independence from Spain, Mexico officially ended the practice, but by that time, scalp hunting had become big business. Now, Jim concludes, hatred and killing is "a way of life." If the U.S. and Mexico promise to end scalp hunting, Jim maintains, and can persuade respected chief Quanah to approve an "honorable" peace agreement, the raids will cease. Commissioner Ward and Gen. Miles send Jim and his cohort Puffer to negotiate with Quanah, but when Downey informs the distrustful Ward that Jim's mother was the sister of Quanah's mother, an American who had been captured by Indians as a child, he orders the peace talks cut short. While seeking Quanah, Jim and Puffer find Margarita wandering the countryside in a daze and offer her food. They then watch as Downey's gang, anxious for more scalps, shoots at two Comanches. Jim and Puffer rescue one of the wounded Indians and return him to Quanah's stronghold, but Black Cloud accuses Jim of the shooting. The injured Comanche, Quanah's brother, regains his strength and clears Jim and Puffer, after which Jim persuades Quanah to make peace with the U.S. and Mexican governments. Jim tells Quanah they are cousins, and Quanah vows loyalty to his white friend. This infuriates Black Cloud, who gathers his own followers and leaves the village. Jim and Puffer ride off to fetch Ward and Miles for a peace council, but before they leave, Jim promises Margarita that he will return and marry her. On the journey to the army encampment, Jim and Puffer come across a Cavalry unit that has just been massacred by Black Cloud. Gen. Miles soon arrives with Ward, Downey, and a large regiment of soldiers, but Ward, who calls Jim the cousin of a savage, has ordered Miles to subdue Quanah by force, and Jim is unable to prevent their march to Quanah's stronghold. Seeing the soldiers, Black Cloud sends word to Quanah and then traps and destroys a column of troopers led by Ward and Downey. Black Cloud captures Ward and threatens to kill him if Miles and his approaching column refuse the renegade Comanches safe passage from the area. Just then Quanah, leading a huge force of loyal Comanches, threatens to attack Black Cloud. Trapped, the vengeful Black Cloud kills Ward and begins battling Gen. Miles' men. During the battle, Downey's shot misses Jim's back, but Jim's return bullet finds its mark. Next, Jim fights with and finally strangles Black Cloud, and soon the battle ends and Quanah and Gen. Miles shake hands. The Comanches will uphold the peace, Quanah promises, in exchange for the freedom to choose their own teachers, practice their own religion, and think their own thoughts. "From where the sun now stands," he declares, "we will fight no more forever." The agreement made, the troopers start toward home, with Jim and Margarita in the lead. *Battles. Comanche Indians. Massacres. Quanah Parker. Scalping. Scouts (Frontier).* Bounty hunters. Cousins. Government officials. Hate. Indians of North America–Mixed blood. Mexican-American border region. Mexicans. Mexico–History–1867-1910. General Nelson Miles. Officers (Military). Racism. Raids. Renegades. Revenge. Tribal chiefs. United States. Army. Cavalry.

Note: The film was, according to an onscreen acknowledgment, "filmed in its entirety in Durango in Old Mexico for historical authenticity....Most of the characters, places, dates and events in this story are factual." The real Quanah Parker, a chief of the powerful Kwahadie band, grew up fighting whites, even though his mother, Cynthia Parker, was white. In 1874, Quanah led a combined force of over seven hundred Comanche, Kiowa, Arapaho and Cheyenne warriors in an unsuccessful attack on Adobe Walls, an old trading post in the Staked Plain of Texas. That summer, generals Miles and Mackenzie pursued and fought the Indians until, hungry and demoralized, they began to surrender. Quanah Parker, the last of the Comanches to surrender, came in under a flag of truce in Jun 1875. As a reservation Indian, he learned the ways of whites while continuing to lead his people and maintain his customs and heritage as an Indian. The dialogue spoken by Quanah Parker near the film's close was actually uttered by the real-life Chief Joseph, a Nez Perce chief who, upon losing his lands and many of his people during a prolonged flight from the U.S. Cavalry, finally surrendered with the words, "From where the sun now stands, I will fight no more forever."

A pre-release news item in *HR* included Iron Eyes Cody in the cast, but his appearance in the released film has not been confirmed. A *DV* news item noted that Arthur Space, originally cast as "General Eckert" (later listed as "General Miles"), withdrew from the film due to illness, and was replaced by John Litel. Litel, who had already been cast as "Commissioner Ward," was then replaced by Lowell Gilmore.

Box 10 Mar 1956. *DV* 26 Aug 1955. *DV* 5 Mar 1956, p. 3. *Exh* 21 Mar 1956, p. 4122. *FD* 19 Mar 1956, p. 6. *Har* 10 Mar 1956, p. 38. *HR* 5 Mar 1956, p. 3. *MPHPD* 10 Mar 1956, p. 809. *Var* 7 Mar 1956, p. 6.

COMANCHE STATION (Comanche, Native Americans)
Ranown Pictures Corp. *Dist* Columbia Pictures Corp. Mar **1960**; Prod: 10 Jun–26 Jun 1959 [©Ranown Pictures Corp.; ; LP16505]. Sd; col (Eastman Color by Path). 6,570 ft. 74 min. Passed by the National Board of Review.

Dir Budd Boetticher.

Cast: Randolph Scott, Nancy Gates.

Western. [*Print viewed*]. A loner named Jefferson Cody rides into Comanche territory to trade a parcel of goods for a white woman, Nancy Lowe, who had been taken by the Comanches in an attack. After gaining her freedom, Mrs. Lowe asks Cody if a man would still want a woman who had been abused by the Comanches. He would take her back if her loved her enough, Cody replies. Although Cody claims he rescued her because it "seemed like a good idea," she learns when they arrive at Comanche Station that her husband has offered a $5,000 reward for her safe return. At the station, Cody and Mrs. Lowe encounter Frank, Dobie, and Ben Lane, the latter an unscrupulous bounty hunter whom Cody had court-martialed when both were in the army years before. Cody suspects Lane is carrying Comanche scalps, even though Lane claims he was in the area to search for Mrs. Lowe. That night, while the group awaits the stage that will carry Mrs. Lowe back home to Lordsburg, Lane tells Frank and Dobie that because the woman's husband has offered to pay the reward whether she is returned dead or alive, he plans to kill both her and Cody and then claim the money. The next morning, the station master rides up with an arrow in his chest, declaring that because some white bounty hunters brutally raided a Comanche village, the Indians attacked the stage coach, along with every other white in the area. Fearing for their safety, the the group decides to leave Comanche Station and ride to Lordsburg on horseback. When they stop for a rest, Mrs. Lowe washes her clothes in the river, and when she hears some Comanche whoops, she looks up and sees that Frank has been shot with an arrow. The party continues towards Lordsburg, and while Lane hints that he might like to have Mrs. Lowe for himself, Dobie begins to have second thoughts about killing her for the reward. That night, Cody, suspecting that Lane plans foul play, disarms Lane and Dobie and orders them to ride away. In the morning, Lane and Dobie position themselves in the rocks above the trail, and Lane produces a rifle he'd hidden away. When Dobie refuses to help Lane shoot Cody and Mrs. Lowe, who are about to ride by, Lane shoots him, thereby alerting Cody and Mrs. Lowe to trouble. Cody takes Mrs. Lowe to the safety of the rocks and then looks for Lane. The latter is about to shoot Mrs. Lowe when Cody appears. Lane spins around to kill Cody, but Cody is too fast and Lane dies. Cody then safely delivers Mrs. Lowe to her son and her husband, who, it is now revealed, was unable to retrieve his wife himself because of blindness. Mrs. Lowe thanks Cody, who, before receiving his reward money, turns his horse around and rides away. *Bounty hunters. Comanche Indians. Rescues. Traders.* Abduction. Ambushes. Raids. Rape.

Box 29 Feb 1960. *DV* 24 Feb 1960, p. 3. *FD* 29 Feb 1960, p. 6. *HR* 24 Feb 1960, p. 3. *MPHPD* 12 Mar 1960, p. 620. *Var* 24 Feb 1960.

COMANCHE TERRITORY (Native Americans, Comanche)

Universal-International Pictures Co., Inc. *Dist* Universal Pictures Co., Inc. May **1950**; New York opening: week of 7 Apr 1950; Prod: early Aug–mid-Sep 1949 [©Universal Pictures Co., Inc.; 17 Mar 1950; LP20]. Sd (Western Electric Recording); col (Technicolor). 6,827 ft. 76 or 78 min. PCA cert no. 14175.

Prod Leonard Goldstein. *Dir* George Sherman. [*Asst dir* John F. Sherwood]. *Scr* Oscar Brodney and Lewis Meltzer. *Story* Lewis Meltzer. *Dir of photog* Maury Gertsman. *Spec photog* David S. Horsley. *Technicolor color dir* William Fritzsche. *Art dir* Bernard Herzbrun and Richard H. Riedel. *Film ed* Frank Gross. *Set dec* Russell A. Gausman and Joseph Kish. *Cost* Yvonne Wood. *Mus* Frank Skinner. *Choreography* Harold Belter. *Sd* Leslie I. Carey and Richard DeWeese. *Hair stylist* Joan St. Oegger. *Makeup* Bud Westmore.

Cast: MAUREEN O'HARA (*Katie [Howard]*), MACDONALD CAREY (*James Bowie*), Will Geer (*Dan'l Seeger*), Charles Drake (*Stacey Howard*), Pedro De Cordoba (*Quisima*), Ian MacDonald (*Walsh*), Rick Vallin (*Pakaneh*), Parley Baer (*Boozer*), James Best (*Sam*), Edmund Cobb (*Ed*), Glenn Strange (*Big Joe*), [Iron Eyes Cody (*Indian*)].

Historical, Western. [*Print viewed*]. Frontiersman James Bowie arrives in the Mexican-controlled territory of Texas in the 1820s, where he is saved by Dan'l Seeger, an ex-Congressman, from a group of attacking Comanche Indians. Dan is shot during the rescue, and after Jim removes the bullet from his shoulder, the two are captured by the Comanches and taken back to their village. They are saved from execution by the arrival of Quisima, the elderly chief of the tribe, who is impressed by both Jim's manner of speech and his knife. Jim teaches the Comanches how to make the famous Bowie knife and, in return Quisima agrees to allow the United States to mine for silver on Comanche land after the tribe renews its treaty with the government. Upon leaving the Indian village, however, Dan confesses that he was sent from Washington, D.C. to ratify the treaty in question, but it was stolen from him. The two then travel to Crooked Tongue, where Jim hopes to discover the culprits by pretending to be a silver buyer. Upon arriving in town, Jim immediately runs afoul of Katie Howard, owner of both the local bank and saloon. Dan recognizes Katie's perfume as the scent of the person who shot him and openly demands that she return the stolen treaty, which leads to a barroom brawl. Katie is then ordered by her brother Stacey to romance Jim, as he hopes the wealthy frontiersman will buy their silver in the future. Later, Jim and Katie are forced to go to the Comanche village and meet with Quisima. The chief's son Pakaneh accuses "the white man" of breaking his treaty. When Jim pledges his word that the new treaty is on its way, he is forced to fight Pakaneh to prove his sincerity. Katie then confesses to stealing the treaty to help the settlers, but Jim convinces her that the treaty will bring both peace and prosperity to the area, so she agrees to return it. Although Stacey lies to her that he has destroyed the treaty, Katie throws a big party to convince the settlers to accept the treaty's terms. Later, Stacey takes the treaty to Quisima, having augmented it with a provision that insists that the Indians turn over their guns. The old chief agrees, not knowing that Stacey and his men plan to kill the disarmed Comanches, then begin silver mining on their land. Learning of Stacey's deception, Jim and Dan ride to the Comanche village to warn them of the planned attack, but the Indians have little with which to defend themselves, having already given up their rifles. Katie, previously unaware of her brother's plans, steals the wagon filled with the Comanches' guns and rides to the Indian village. She arrives there just in time to arm Quisima's warriors in their battle against Stacey's men. Seeing that defeat is imminent, Stacey tries to escape, only to be ridden down and captured by Jim. With peace restored, Jim heads back for Washington to meet with President Andrew Jackson, but promises Katie to return soon. *James Bowie. Brothers and sisters. Comanche Indians. Government agents. Land rights. Saloon keepers. Texas. Treaties. Bankers. Bartenders. Chases. Deception. Escapes. Fathers and sons. Fights. Gambling. Gunshot wounds. Knives. Parties. Peace pipes. Perfume. Rescues. Rifles. Silver mines. Smuggling. Women in business.*

Note: The working title of this film was *The Bowie Knife*. The film included one song, but its title and composer have not been determined. This film is a fictionalized account of elements in the life of American pioneer James Bowie. Born in Logan County, KY, in 1796, Bowie moved to San Antonio, TX in 1828, becoming a Mexican citizen in 1830. Bowie joined the Texas battle for independence in 1832, and while serving as a colonel in the Texas revolutionary army, died in 1836 at the battle of the Alamo. He is noted for inventing the knife that carries his name.

Box 15 Apr 1950. *DV* 5 Apr 1950, p. 3. *FD* 10 Apr 1950, p. 6. *HR* 5 Aug 1949, p. 13. *HR* 5 Apr 1950, p. 3. *MPHPD* 8 Apr 1950, p. 253. *NYT* 8 Apr 1950, p. 9. *Var* 5 Apr 1950, p. 6.

COME LIVE WITH ME (Austrian Americans)

Metro-Goldwyn-Mayer Corp.; controlled by Loew's Inc. *Dist* Loew's Inc. 31 Jan **1941**; Los Angeles opening: 29 Jan 1941; Prod: 7 Oct–30 Nov 1940 [©Loew's Inc.; 23 Jan 1941; LP10217]. Sd (Western Electric Sound System); b&w. 9 reels, 7,761 ft. 85 min. Passed by the National Board of Review.

Prod Clarence Brown. *Dir* Clarence Brown. [*Asst dir* Walter Strohm]. *Scr* Patterson McNutt. *Orig story* Virginia Van Upp. *Dir of photog* George Folsey. *Art dir* Cedric Gibbons. *Assoc* Randall Duell. *Film ed* Frank E. Hull. *Set dec* Edwin B. Willis. *Gowns* Adrian. *Mus score* Herbert Stothart. *Rec dir* Douglas Shearer.

Cast: JAMES STEWART (*Bill Smith*), HEDY LAMARR (*Johnny Jones*), Ian Hunter (*Barton Kendrick*), Verree Teasdale (*Diana Kendrick*), Donald Meek (*Joe Darsie*), Barton MacLane (*Barney Grogan*), Edward Ashley (*Arnold Stafford*), Ann Codee (*Yvonne*), King Baggott (*Doorman*), Adeline de Walt Reynolds (*Grandma*), Frank Orth (*Jerry*), Frank Faylen (*Waiter*), Horace MacMahon (*Taxi driver*), Greta Meyer (*Frieda*).

Romance. [*Print viewed*]. Middle-aged New York publisher Barton Kendrick and his wife Diana have a "modern" marriage in which each allows the other romantic freedom. Diana secretly wishes the situation were different, but Bart revels in his relationship with the beautiful Johnny Jones. Johnny, a Viennese refugee who has been staying illegally in New York since her temporary visa expired, is in love with Bart but won't accept his marriage proposal because she is worried that Diana will be hurt. When immigration official Barney Grogan comes to Johnny's apartment to tell her to report for deportation, he informs her, off the record, that if she marries an American citizen she will not be deported, then gives her a week to find a husband. While Johnny is thinking things over in a diner, she encounters Bill Smith, an aspiring writer who is completely broke. She gets the idea to marry him and invites herself back to his apartment. When she proposes, he is reluctant, but eventually agrees and convinces her to draw up a contract whereby she will pay him $17.80 each week. Two months later, Bill has fallen in love with Johnny. Meanwhile, Bart knows that Johnny has been granted residency, but she won't tell him how. One night, when Bart proposes and says that his divorce can be arranged in six weeks, she confesses that she is married. She then goes to see Bill a day early, and she shows her his novel based on their marriage, *Without Love*. She is touched, but wants him to give her a divorce right away, and tells him that she loves someone else. Though heartbroken, he agrees to the divorce. After some revisions, Bill sends his unfinished novel to some publishers, one of whom is Bart. Diana, who reads all of Bart's submissions, calls Bart to tell him about the wonderful new writer she has discovered, and when he reads the unlikely plot, Bart finds it too familiar. He then invites Bill to his office, and as he staunchly defends the "older man" in Bill's story, Diana realizes that Bart is the real older man. She convinces Bart to give Bill a $500 advance, and Bill thinks that he now has a chance with Johnny. Diana then tells Bart that she will give him a divorce as soon as Bart is convinced that Johnny really loves him and not Bill. Bill goes to see Johnny to repay her and tells her that before he agrees to a divorce, they must take a trip together. After leaving New York, they stop at a roadside restaurant, where she secretly calls Bart, who promises to come for her right away. They then drive to a farm owned by Bill's kindly grandmother. Later that night, while staying in rooms divided by a three-quarter wall, neither Bill or Johnny can get to sleep. After Bill tells Johnny how fireflies show their love and recites a romantic poem, she falls in love and turns her flashlight on and off like a firefly. Just then Bart arrives, and Bill soon realizes that Bart is his romantic rival. The men argue, but after Bill goes to his room, Johnny sends away Bart, who finally realizes that he still loves Diana. When Johnny goes upstairs, she flashes the light again and they kiss over the wall that bears one of Grandma's Shakespeare-quoting samplers, "All's well that ends well." *Immigrants. Marriage of convenience. Novelists. Open marriage. Publishers and publishing. Romance. Romantic rivalry. Austrians. Contracts. Deportation. Diners (Restaurants). Divorce. Farms. Financial crisis. Fireflies. Grandmothers. Needlework. New York City. Poetry. Restaurants. United States. Dept. of Immigration. War refugees.*

Note: The romantic poem recited by "Bill" in the film, was Christopher Marlowe's "Come Live with Me," first published in *The Passionate Pilgrim* in

1599. This film marked the motion picture debut of actress Adeline de Walt Reynolds. According to M-G-M publicity materials contained in the AMPAS Library file on the film, Reynolds was an Iowa farmer's wife who entered college in her sixties and graduated from the University of California at Berkeley at age seventy. She was discovered by director Clarence Brown in a local theatrical production and continued to act in films and on the stage until her death in 1961.

Box 1 Feb 1941. *DV* 23 Jan 1941. *FD* 30 Jan 1941, p. 11. *HR* 4 Oct 1940, p. 8. *HR* 7 Oct 1940, p. 1. *HR* 22 Nov 1940, p. 8. *HR* 22 Jan 1941, p. 1. *HR* 23 Jan 1941, p. 3. *MPH* 25 Jan 1941. *MPHPD* 11 Jan 1941, p. 39. *NYT* 28 Feb 1941, p. 17. *Var* 22 Jan 1941, p. 16.

COME ON, COWBOY! (African Americans)

Goldmax Productions; Toddy Pictures Co. **1949?**. Sd; b&w. 7 reels, 6,453 ft. 72 min.

Exec prod Ted Toddy.

Song(s): "I Can't Get Him Off My Mind," "Do That Thing," composers undetermined; "Boll Weevil," traditional.

Cast: Mantan Moreland (*Mantan Moreland*), Mauryne Brent, Johnny Lee, F. E. Miller.

African American. [*Not viewed*]. New Yorker Mantan Moreland is sent out West by his boss, Fred Wilson, to prepare Wilson's ranch for his arrival with his new bride. The ranch has not been occupied for five years and has become something of a ghost ranch. Mantan takes his pal Steve with him and in the town of Dry Gulch they become involved with a girl called Flo. The ranch is being used as a hideout by the outlaw Dice and his gang. Mantan and Steve meet Lee, a former bartender, and they all head off to clean up the ranch. The outlaws make them believe that the place is haunted, however, and scare them off. Later, when the outlaws leave to rob a bank, Mantan and his pals return to resume the clean-up. Later, the sheriff trails the bank robbers to the ranch and Mantan and his friends assist in their capture. Finally, at a luncheon for Fred Wilson and his wife, Mantan makes a speech thanking them for sending him West, but indicates that he prefers to return to New York. *African Americans. Cowboys. Horses. Outlaws. Bartenders. City-country contrast. Horses. New York City. Sheriffs. Singers. The West.*

Note: The summary for this film was derived from a 1949 dialogue continuity deposited with the NYSA. The film was not registered for copyright and no reviews have been located.

COME ON OVER (Irish Americans)

Goldwyn Pictures Corp. **1922**; Los Angeles, Chicago, and Clevland premieres: 11 Mar 1922 [©Goldwyn Pictures Corp.; 25 Feb 1922; LP17582]. Si; b&w. 6 reels, 5,556 ft.

Dir Alfred E. Green. *Story and scen* Rupert Hughes. *Photog* L. William O'Connell. *Art dir* Cedric Gibbons.

Cast: Colleen Moore (*Moyna Killiea*), Ralph Graves (*Shane O'Mealia*), J. Farrell MacDonald (*Michael Moraban*), Kate Price (*Delia Moraban*), James Marcus (*Carmody*), Kathleen O'Connor (*Judy Dugan*), Florence Drew (*Bridget Moraban*), Harold Holland (*Myle Moraban*), Mary Warren (*Kate Moraban*), Elinor Hancock (*Mrs. Van Dusen*), Monte Collins (*Dugan*), C. E. Mason (*Barney*), C. B. Leasure (*Priest*).

Comedy. Shane O'Mealia emigrates from Ireland to the United States, having promised to send for his sweetheart, Moyna Killiea, when he has earned money for her passage. He lives with the Morahans in New York, where he is unlucky in finding jobs and is constantly seen with Judy Dugan, for whose father he finds a job and whom he induces to take the temperance pledge. Secretly, Morahan goes to Ireland and brings back Moyna and her mother. As a result of a misunderstanding, Moyna believes that Shane and Judy are engaged to be married, and she vanishes. When found, she refuses to see Shane until his employer's sister, Mrs. Van Dusen, gives her a frock to wear to a party. At first Shane does not recognize her in her finery, but when he dances into her arms they are happily reunited. *Immigrants. Irish Americans. New York City. Temperance.*

Note: The working title of this film was *Darling*.

ETR 25 Mar 1922, p. 1217. *FD* 19 Mar 1922. *MPW* 25 Mar 1922, p. 401. *MPW* 1 Apr 1922, p. 544. *Var* 17 Mar 1922, p. 41.

COME OUT OF THE KITCHEN (African Americans)

Famous Players-Lasky Corp. *Dist* Famous Players-Lasky Corp.; Paramount Pictures. 11 May **1919** [©Famous Players-Lasky Corp.; 7 May 1919; LP13684]. Si; b&w. 5 reels.

Pres Adolph Zukor. *Dir* John S. Robertson. *Asst dir* Frank Walton. *Scen* Clara Beranger. *Cam* Jacques Monteran and Hal Young.

Source: Based on the novel *Come Out of the Kitchen!* by Alice Duer Miller (New York, 1916).

Cast: Marguerite Clark (*Claudia Daingerfield*), Frances Kaye (*Elizabeth Daingerfield*), Bradley Barker (*Paul Daingerfield*), Albert M. Hackett (*Charles Daingerfield*), George Stevens (*Mr. Daingerfield*), May Kitson (*Mrs. Daingerfield*), Eugene O'Brien (*Burton Crane*), Frederick Esmelton (*Solon Tucker*), Craufurd Kent (*Randolf Weeks*), Augusta Anderson (*Mrs. Faulkner*), Rita Spear (*Cora Faulkner*), Frances Grant (*Mammy Jackson*), George Washington (*"Snowball"*).

Comedy. When the head of an aristocratic, but impoverished, Virginia family must be treated for his illness by a New York specialist, his daughter, Claudia Daingerfield, raises money by leasing their old Southern mansion to Burton Crane. The only condition Crane makes is that the black servants be replaced by white servants. Claudia and her brothers and sister take on the roles of servants, with calamitous results. When Claudia is introduced to Burton as his cook, he immediately falls in love with her. Claudia overcomes her lack of culinary skills by smuggling Mammy Jackson into the house to do the cooking. The other "servants" are all let go, and the father survives the dangerous operation. When Claudia's true identity is revealed, Burton recognizes her pluck, and she accepts his offer of marriage. *Aristocrats. Cooks. Family life. Impersonation and imposture. Mansions. Servants. Southerners. Virginia. African Americans. Operations, Surgical. Poverty.*

Note: A. E. Thomas wrote a stage play based on the Duer novel, also titled *Come Out of the Kitchen*, which had its premiere in New York on 23 Oct 1916. Some scenes for this film were shot in Pass Christian, MS. One source lists the actor who plays Mrs. Faulkner as Mrs. August Anderson. Among the remakes of this film are a 1930 Paramount film called *Honey*, and two British films called *Come Out of the Pantry* (1935) and *Spring in Park Lane* (1948). The 1935 film was directed by Jack Raymond and starred Jack Buchanan and Fay Wray, the 1948 was directed by Herbert Wilcox and starred Anna Neagle and Michael Wilding.

ETR 17 May 1919, p. 1821. *ETR* 24 May 1919, p. 1939. *MPW* 5 Apr 1919, p. 108. *MPW* 24 May 1919, p. 1225. *NYT* 12 May 1919, p. 11. *Var* 16 May 1919, p. 54. *Wid's* 25 May 1919, p. 15.

EL COMEDIANTE (Spanish language)

John H. Auer Productions, Ltd. *Dist* Paramount Publix Corp. **1931**; Panama City, Panama opening: 10 Jul 1931; New York opening: 31 Jul 1931; Prod: Mar—Apr 1931 at Metropolitan Studios. Sd; b&w. 7 reels, 6,493 ft. 72 min. Spanish language.

Supv John H. Auer. *Dir* Ernesto Vilches and Leonard H. Fields. *Scr* Ernesto Vilches and Leonard H. Fields. *Photog* Gilbert Warrenton. *Film ed* Lou Sackin. *Mus comp* Giuseppe Miceli. *Sd* R. S. Clayton and William R. Fox.

Source: Based on the play *Sullivan* by Mélesville (production date undetermined).

Cast: Ernesto Vilches (*Jorge Sullivan*), Angelita Benítez (*Leila Jenkins*), José Soriano Viosca (*Mr. Jenkins*), Barry Norton (*Federico*), María Calvo (*Arabela*), Manuel Arbó (*Peacock*), Antonio Vidal (*Dixon*), José Peña "Pepet" (*John*), Gabry Rivas.

Drama. [*Not viewed*]. The daughter of an English millionaire falls in love with Jorge Sullivan, a famous comedic actor. He also loves her, but does not realize that she is the millionaire's daughter. The comedian allows himself to be persuaded by the millionaire to disenchant one of his daughters and gives his word to discredit himself verbally in her presence at dinner. Although stricken by grief at finding out the target of deception is his loved one, Sullivan does keep his promise. *Actors and actresses. Class distinction. Pledges. Romance. Self-sacrifice. Deception. Fathers and daughters. Millionaires.*

Note: The play appears to have been written in the nineteenth century. It was adapted by T. W. Robertson into the play *David Garrick*, which was produced in 1864 in London. The running time listed above was calculated from footage given in NYSA records. Some sources include in the cast Eduardo Arozamena, Paco Madrid and Romualdo Tirado, but their participation in the film has not been confirmed.

CM Aug 1931, p. 601.

COMING OUT PARTY (Swedish Americans)

Fox Film Corp.; Jesse L. Lasky Productions. *Dist* Fox Film Corp. 9 Mar **1934**; Prod: 6 Nov—mid-Dec 1933 [©Fox Film Corp.; 26 Feb 1934; LP4512]. Sd (Western Electric Noiseless Recording); b&w. 8 reels, 7,224 ft. 77 or 79-80 min. Passed by the National Board of Review.

Prod JESSE L. LASKY. [*Exec prod* Winfield R. Sheehan]. *Dir* John Blystone. [*Asst dir* Jasper Blystone]. *Scr* Gladys Unger and Jesse Lasky, Jr. *Orig story* Becky Gardiner and Gladys Unger. [*Contr wrt* Alice-Leone Moats and Barry Trivers]. *Photog* John Seitz. *Settings* William

Darling. [*Ed* Dorothy Spencer]. *Cost* Rita Kaufman. *Mus dir* Louis De Francesco. *Sd* George Leverett.

Song(s): "I Think You're Wonderful," music by Burton Lane, lyrics by Harold Adamson.

Cast: Frances Dee (*Joy [Joyce] Stanhope*), Gene Raymond (*Chris Hansen*), Alison Skipworth (*Miss Vanderoe*), Nigel Bruce (*Troon*), Harry Green (*Harry Gold*), Gilbert Emery (*Mr. Stanhope*), Marjorie Gateson (*Mrs. Stanhope*), Clifford Jones (*Jimmy Wolverton*), [Jessie Ralph (*Nora*)], [Germaine de Neel (*Louise*)], [Paul Porcasi (*Manager*)], [Gwen Phillips (*Debutante, Ann Waring*)], [Harold Minjir (*Mr. Greenvalley*)], [Eugene Borden (*French clerk*)], [Paul McVey (*Clerk in Tiffany's*)], [Claire Du Brey (*Mrs. Winfield*)], [Gladys Blake (*Secretary*)], [Vesey O'Davoren (*Second butler*)], [Jimmy Grant (*Singer*)], [Lyman Williams (*Charlie*)], [Belle Daube (*Dowager*)], [Carlyle Moore, John Arledge (*Drunk party crashers*)], [Arthur Belasco (*Captain of detectives*)], [William Augustin (*Irish detective*)], [Jack Trainor (*Jewish detective*)], [Claude King (*Attorney*)], [Tony Merlo (*Waiter*)], [George Humbert (*Head waiter*)], [Jerry Jerome (*Chauffeur*)], [Harry Hollingsworth (*Doorman*)], [Pat Hartigan (*Cop*)], [Sherry Hall (*Cameraman*)], [Frederic Howard (*Reporter*)], [Jean De Briac], [Finis Barton], [Consuelo Baker], [William Lawrence], [Edward Norris], [Mae Madison], [Jennie Gray], [Mary Blackwood], [Anne Nagel], [Frank Moran], [Sumner Getchell], [Betty Flournoy], [Patricia Scott], [Helen Peterson], [Jeanne Ruwe], [Maury Ginn, Jr.], [John Ruwe].

Society, Romance, Drama. [*Print viewed*]. Joy Stanhope, a Park Avenue debutante whose coming out party promises to be the winter's biggest event, has been carrying on a secret romance with Chris Hansen, a violinist in a jazz band living in a one-room apartment whose parents were Swedish immigrants. Although Chris sees Jimmy Wolverton, deemed the most sought after bachelor in New York, flirt with Joy, his jealousy is not aroused when Joy breaks their date because her mother insists that she accompany Jimmy to a Long Island party. As Jimmy grows very intoxicated while driving to the party, Joy suggests that they stop at a roadhouse. In a private room, Jimmy tries to grab Joy, but after she rebuffs his advances, he falls asleep. Later, Joy revives Jimmy with coffee, and they start to leave, but Chris, performing with his band at the roadhouse, sees them together and insults Joy, who then slaps him. Later that night, Joy goes to Chris's room to explain, and although he dishearteningly tries to tell her that her social standing will keep them apart, they end the argument in an embrace. When the night of her party arrives, Joy anxiously queries Chris's Jewish boss, bandleader Harry Gold, whether Chris has returned from Chicago, where he was playing. When Harry wonders whether Chris may have been detained, Joy breaks down and cries. Figuring out that she is pregnant, Harry urges her to marry Chris despite her parents' objections and vows to get him back in time for the party. When Chris does arrive, he excitedly tells Joy that he has been chosen to accompany a great operatic star on a one-year European concert tour and must sail immediately. She agrees to wait for him and, unwilling to spoil his "chance in a lifetime," does not reveal her condition. During the party, Joy, dazed and distressed, does nothing to stop Jimmy when, on a whim, he takes her to elope. Meanwhile, Troon, the Stanhope's Scottish family butler, who has helped Joy communicate secretly with Chris in the past, learns from Harry about Joy's predicament. Troon goes to the boat to tell Chris, but they return to learn that Joy and Jimmy have already married. After Harry encourages Chris to fight for Joy, he tries to visit Joy, who has since undergone a nervous breakdown, but her father will not allow him to see her. However, Jimmy, realizing that Joy loves Chris, agrees to let her decide if she wants an annulment. When Joy sees Chris, they kiss, and as the film ends, the 1934 Social Register book is thrown into a trash can. *Class distinction. Debutantes. Family relationships. Musicians. Pregnancy. Romance. Upper classes. Band leaders. Butlers. Cads. Drunkenness. Elopement. Jews. Marriage–Annulment. Nervous breakdown. Roadhouses. Scottish Americans. Swedish Americans.*

Note: The opening credits of the film appear in the form of invitation cards, the first reading "Fox Film invites you to Jesse L. Lasky's *Coming Out Party* R.s.v.p. 715 Park Avenue." *NYT* called the film *Coming-Out Party*. The working title was *Society Debut*. This was British actor Nigel Bruce's first American film. According to a *DV* news item, a number of "debs and sub-debs" from all parts of the United States were cast in the film. Although "Joy's" pregnancy is not overtly mentioned in the film, reviews state that during the night of her argument with "Chris" at the roadhouse, their "love is consummated" in his room, and she discovers that she is pregnant just before he is called off to Europe. *FD* commented, "It looks like considerable cutting

and editing eliminated some scenes that would have served to make the film more coherent."

DV 15 Jan 1934, p. 3. *FD* 17 Mar 1934, p. 4. *Har* 24 Mar 1934, p. 47. *HF* 25 Nov 1933, p. 12. *HF* 9 Dec 1933, p. 12. *HR* 6 Nov 1933, p. 1. *MPD* 22 Jan 1934, p. 4. *MPH* 27 Jan 1934, p. 41. *NYT* 17 Mar 1934, p. 11. *Var* 20 Mar 1934, p. 16.

COMMON CLAY (*foreign version*) see **DEL MISMO BARRO**

CONDUCTOR 1492 (Irish Aericans)
Warner Bros. Pictures, Inc. *Dist* Warner Bros. Pictures, Inc. 12 Jan **1924** [©Warner Bros. Pictures, Inc.; 25 Dec 1923; LP20761]. Si; b&w. 7 reels, 6,500 ft.

Dir Charles Hines and Frank Griffin. *Story* Johnny Hines. *Photog* Charles E. Gilson. *Film ed* Clarence Kolster.

Cast: Johnny Hines (*Terry O'Toole, "Conductor 1492"*), Doris May (*Noretta Connelly*), Dan Mason (*Mike O'Toole*), Ruth Renick (*Edna Brown*), Robert Cain (*Richard Langford*), Fred Esmelton (*Denman Connelly*), Byron Sage (*Bobby Connelly*), Michael Dark (*James Stoddard*), Dorothy Burns (*Mrs. Brown*).

Comedy-drama. Terry O'Toole, a young Irishman, arrives in America and gets a job as a streetcar conductor. He rescues the son of company president Denman Connelly; foils the attempts of crooks to gain control of the company; and marries Connelly's daughter, Noretta. *Immigrants. Irish Americans. Streetcar conductors. Streetcars.*
FD 23 Mar 1924. *MPW* 23 Feb 1924. *Var* 19 Mar 1924, p. 27.

CONFESSIONS OF A NAZI SPY (German Americans)
Warner Bros. Pictures, Inc.; A First National Picture. *Dist* Warner Bros. Pictures, Inc. 6 May 1939; World premiere in Beverly Hills: 27 Apr 1939; Prod: 1 Feb—18 Mar 1939 [©Warner Bros. Pictures, Inc.; 6 May 1939; LP8823]. Sd; b&w. 11 reels. 102 or 110 min. PCA cert no. 5084.

[*Exec prod* Jack L. Warner and Hal B. Wallis]. [*Assoc prod* Robert Lord]. *Dir* Anatole Litvak. [*2d unit dir* Claude E. Archer]. *Dial dir* Ted Thomas. [*Asst dir* Chuck Hansen]. *Scr* Milton Krims and John Wexley. *Photog* Sol Polito and [Ernest Haller]. [*2d cam* John Polito]. [*Asst cam* Frank Evans]. [*Gaffer* Frank Flanagan]. *Art dir* Carl Jules Weyl. *Film ed* Owen Marks. *Gowns* Milo Anderson. [*Ward* Dick Moder and Cora Lobb]. *Mus dir* Leo F. Forbstein. *Sd* Robert B. Lee. [*Hair* Ruby Felker]. [*Makeup* Joe Stinton and Bob Cowan]. *Tech adv* Leon G. Turrou. *Narr* John Deering. [*Unit mgr* Louis Baum]. [*Scr clerk* Jean McNaughton]. [*Grip* Harold Noyes]. [*Props* M. Goldman]. [*Asst prop man* H. Goldman]. [*Best boy* Bill Conger]. [*Still photog* Mack Elliott]. [*Pub* Frank Heacock].

Source: Based on articles by Leon G. Turrou, as told to David G. Wittels in *The New York Post* (5 Dec 1938—4 Jan 1939).

Cast: Edward G. Robinson (*Edward Renard*), Francis Lederer ([*Kurt*] *Schneider*), George Sanders ([*Franz*] *Schlager*), Paul Lukas (*Dr. [Karl F.] Kassell*), Henry O'Neill (*Attorney Kellogg*), Dorothy Tree (*Hilda Keinhauer*), Lya Lys (*Erika Wolff*), Grace Stafford (*Mrs. Schneider*), James Stephenson (*British military intelligence agent*), Celia Sibelius (*Mrs. [Liza] Kassell*), Joe Sawyer (*Werner Renz*), Sig Rumann ([*Dr. Julius Gustav*] *Krogman*), Lionel Royce (*Hintze*), Henry Victor (*Wildebrandt*), Hans von Twardowsky ([*Max*] *Helldorf*), John Voigt ([*Johann*] *Westphal*), Frederick Vogeding (*Captain Richter*), Willy Kaufman (*Greutzwald*), Robert Davis (*Captain Straubel*), William Vaughn (*Captain von Eichen*), George Rosener (*Klauber*), Frederick Burton (*U.S. District Court Judge*), Ely [sic] Malyon (*Mrs. [Mary] MacLaughlin*), Bodil Rosing (*Passenger on boat [Anna Keller]*), [Fred Tozere (*Phillips*)], [Frank Mayo (*Staunton*)], [Lucien Prival (*Kranz*)], [Martin Kosleck (*Goebbels*)], [Ward Bond (*American Legionnaire*)], [Alec Craig (*Postman*)], [Jack Mower (*McDonald*)], [Jean Brooks (*Kassell's nurse*)], [Robert Emmett Keane (*Harrison*)], [Charles Sherlock (*Young*)], [Edward Keane, William Gould, John Hamilton (*F.B.I. men*)], [Selmer Jackson (*Custom official*)], [Emmett Vogan (*Hotel clerk*)], [John Ridgely (*Army hospital clerk*)], [Egon Brecher (*Nazi agent*)], [Edwin Stanley (*U. S. official*)], [Niccolai Yoshkin (*The Man*)], [John Conte (*Announcer's voice*)], [Charles Trowbridge (*Major Williams*)], [Tommy Bupp (*Shoeshine boy*)], [Ferdinand Schumann-Heink].

Espionage, Drama. [*Print viewed*]. In a small Scottish town in the late 1930's, Mrs. Mary MacLaughlin operates a secret international Nazi postal office out of her home. Her services are provided to agents working all over the world, including Kurt Schneider, an American soldier living in New York. Dr. Karl F. Kassell, a U.S. Navy Reserve officer, also works for the Nazis—he heads the New York German

Bund and is devoted to the "purification" of the German race. Schneider's career as a spy begins with orders to report to the Nazis on the number of American troops stationed in the New York area. He carries this task out successfully, but complains when he is paid by the Nazis a meager monthly wage of fifty dollars. Meanwhile, at a New York Bund rally, Gestapo agents forcibly remove a dissenting voice from the meeting. Subversive Nazi activities are also taking place on board the German ocean liner *Europa*, where Franz Schlager is the ship's Nazi leader. Schlager works closely with the ship's beauty salon operator, Hilda Keinhauer, who reports passenger Anna Keller when she learns that Keller does not sympathize with the Nazi regime. Upon his arrival in New York, Schlager is instructed to make contact with Schneider and give him a new assignment. Impatient for better work, Schneider sends a letter to Nazi officials in Germany, but when the letter is intercepted in Scotland, Mrs. MacLaughlin is arrested. The evidence found in MacLaughlin's home prompts an F.B.I. investigation, led by Edward Renard, into Nazi espionage activities in the United States. Federal agents are soon tipped off to one of Schneider's assignments and arrest the Nazi operative. Schneider is brought to Renard for questioning, and Renard cleverly extracts a full confession from him. When Hilda Keinhauer, whom Schneider implicates, is arrested, she unintentionally implicates Kassell. Renard surprises Kassell at his office, and he, too, eventually cracks under pressure, naming others involved in the spy ring. A nationwide dragnet is ordered, and many more agents are arrested, including Hintze and Wildebrandt, who are later released. Although Renard tries to protect Kassell from Hintze and Wildebrandt, he is too late to prevent them from abducting him and forcing him to board the German liner S. S. *Bismarck* for Germany. Renard sends orders for the ship to stop and surrender Kassell, but the captain refuses to obey them. When the ship docks in Germany, the Gestapo orders Kassell to file formal charges of harassment and intimidation against the F.B.I. Meanwhile, Dr. Julius Gustav Krogman, a German government official, appears at Renard's office to advise Keinhauer to lie and say that she was forced to sign a false confession. Renard dismisses Krogman from his office, and realizes that the official's attempt to intercede on Keinhauer's behalf proves the German government's complicity in the espionage crimes. The spy case goes before a grand jury, and four of the major participants in the spy ring are convicted and sentenced. *Espionage. German Americans. Germany. Navy. Investigations. Nazism. United States. Federal Bureau of Investigation.* Abduction. Berlin (Germany). Joseph Paul Goebbels. Hermann Göring. Hairdressers. Adolf Hitler. Hotels. Infidelity. Informers. Interrogation. Lawyers. Military bases. New York (State). Nurses. Patriotism. Physicians. Postal service. Propaganda. Sea captains. Ships. Trials. United States. Navy.

Note: Actress Eily Malyon's name is spelled "Ely Malyon" in the opening credits. The working title of this film was *Storm over America.* Contemporary sources indicate that this film, presented in a semi-documentary form, was the first of the anti-Hitler films made in Hollywood before the start of World War II. Much of the film was based on a highly publicized German spy trial that took place in New York in 1938. In late Oct 1938, according to a *HR* news item, Warner Bros. sent contract writer Milton Krims to New York to cover the trial of eighteen individuals charged with spying for the German government. The trial took place between 29 Nov and 2 Dec 1938 and resulted in the conviction of four individuals (fourteen of the accused spies were still at large). Producer Harry Warner's involvement in anti-Nazi activities was widely known in Hollywood in the late 1930s, as was that of star Edward G. Robinson, who, according to a late 1938 *HR* news item, was affiliated with a group called the "Hollywood Anti-Nazi League for the Defense of American Democracy."

According to the file for the film in the MPAA/PCA Collection at the AMPAS Library, soon after Warner Bros. expressed interest in the spy trial, the Charge d'Affairs of the German Counsel in Los Angeles sent a letter to the PCA requesting that it prevent the studio from producing the picture. The PCA also received a letter of protest from an official at the Paramount Foreign Department in New York, who voiced his opposition to Warners' plan to make an anti-Nazi film, calling it a "big mistake." The Paramount official accused Warners of ignoring the example set by Charlie Chaplin, who had, he claimed, decided that a picture burlesquing Adolf Hitler would be too dangerous to film. He also warned that if the picture were made, Warners would have "on their hands the blood of a great many Jews in Germany."

Ignoring the opposition to the script, Warner Bros. went ahead with the picture, and on 6 Dec 1938, a *HR* article announced that the studio was rushing production on the film to meet a targeted 15 Jan 1939 release date. Although the casting was not yet completed, the production on the Krims script was set to begin (on a twenty-four hour basis) the following day. The article also stated that the cast would be made up entirely of unknown actors—all non-Aryans. Krims's script was reportedly polished aboard a Hollywood-bound train by Krims and producers Jack Warner and Hal Wallis. The first draft of the script was submitted to the PCA by late Dec 1938, at which time the PCA informed Warner Bros. that although the screenplay appeared to be "technically" within the provisions of the Production Code, because of its controversial nature it could be rejected by censor boards fearing that the exhibition of the film would result in public disorder or incite a riot.

The PCA file also contains a series of "notes and observations" on the story by PCA official Karl Lischka, who wrote on 22 Jan 1939 that the story was in violation of the Code because "Hitler and his government are unfairly represented." Lischka took issue with the story's portrayal of Hitler as a "screaming madman and a bloodthirsty persecutor," and instead praised the German leader's "phenomenal public career and his unchallenged political and social achievements." Lischka said that the story's inference that the German government was a direct sponsor of agitation in the United States constituted a "grave accusation which lacks proof." He also criticized "extraneous" elements of the story, including the abolition of Christian schools and the dismemberment of Czechoslovakia. Lischka concluded that if the film were made it would be "one of the most lamentable mistakes ever made by the industry."

Although Warner Bros. planned to start production on the picture in early Dec 1938, filming did not begin until 1 Feb 1939. In early Jan 1939, Leon G. Turrou, the U. S. government agent who broke the spy ring, was hired by Warner Bros. as a technical adviser. According to modern sources, the publication of Turrou's articles on the Nazi spy trials in New York were delayed for five months, following the issuance of a Jun 1938 restraining order blocking their publication. A contemporary news item notes that Turrou quit his job at the F.B.I. just prior to selling his article on the spy trial to the *New York Post.* Turrou also wrote a book on the case, entitled *Nazi Spies in America*, which was published in New York in 1939, and which he sold to Warner Bros. for $25,000.

A *HR* pre-production article notes that because the studio encountered casting difficulties in Hollywood, director Anatole Litvak traveled to the East Coast to cast many of the parts. A number of Hollywood actors reportedly refused parts in the picture because they feared that their participation in the film would result in reprisals by the Nazis against their relatives in Germany. Anna Sten and Marlene Dietrich were among those originally announced for leading feminine roles.

Warner Bros. publicity material on the film notes that because the subject matter of the picture was considered to be highly controversial, extreme precautions were taken to insure the safety of those working on the production. Four uniformed studio policemen were posted near the sound stage to bar the press and anyone else not directly involved in the film, including Warner Bros. executives, from the set. To insure the secrecy of the script, only ten copies of it were mimeographed (as opposed to the usual 150 copies made for a production of this size), and most of the actors got their lines one day at a time. More than a dozen people associated with the film took up residence on the Warner Bros. lot and lived there throughout the production. Despite the heavy security, sabotage was suspected on the set when a boom holding one of the cameras collapsed and narrowly missed hitting director Anatole Litvak. The publicity material also notes that after the first ten principal players were chosen for the picture, Warner Bros. decided to remain silent about further casting news and announced that subsequent cast additions would be referred to by numbers instead of names.

Warner Bros., in fact, went to great lengths to conceal the identity of those actors who wished to remain anonymous. Not only did the actors receive fictitious names, such as Celia Sibelius, Robert Davis and John Voigt, but makeup artists had the actors so heavily made up that, according to Warner Bros. publicists, "even their best friends won't recognize them on the screen." However, employment contracts in the Warner Bros. production file reveal the true identities of the actors: "Robert Davis" was actually Rudolf Amendt; "John Voigt" was Wolfgang Zilzer and "Celia Sibelius" was Hedwiga Reicher. "Jean Brooks," who was credited as "Kassell's nurse," may have been actress Lotte Palfi, who tested for the role on 8 Feb 1939, or Louise Golm. The production file also indicates that Hans von Morhart was originally contracted for the part of "Kranz." Although their appearance in the released film has not been confirmed, studio records of the daily production activity on the film indicate that following actors were scheduled to appear in the film: Tempe Pigott, Ray Miller, Ed Meski, John Harron, Walter Bonn, Dave Wengren, Lester Scharff, George Offerman, Fred Graham, Stan Pomeroy, Jack Storey, Frederick Jehrman, Rudolph Steinbeck, Sherwood Bailey and Walter Moore.

Pre-release news items in *HR* and *NYT* note that set designer Carl Jules Weyl designed eighty-three sets for the film (breaking all previous records for the number of sets on a Warner Bros.' film), that cameraman Ernest Haller took over the photography of the film when Sol Polito fell ill, and that the film was budgeted at $1,500,000. Studio publicity records indicate that Warner Bros. dance director Bill O'Donnell was put in charge of preparing 350 bit players for the Bund camp military sequence.

In May 1939, according to news items in *HR*, German-American Bund leader Fritz J. Kuhn tried to block the release of the film by filing a $5,000,000 libel suit against Warner Bros., and requested a temporary injunction against the film's exhibitors. A federal judge denied Kuhn's request for an injunction, and after failing to win an appeal, Kuhn was instructed by the judge (at Warner Bros.' request) to answer specific questions in reference to the history and constitution of the Bund, in addition to naming the characters in the film who he claimed represent himself and other Bund members. In Sep 1939, *HR* noted that Warner Bros. filed a legal answer to Kuhn's suit, in which the studio requested a jury trial to hear its proof that the Bund was an "active militant propaganda agency" of the German government, and that its members were "abusing the rights and privileges of American citizens." Modern sources note that Kuhn's suit was dropped following charges that he embezzled Bund funds. Kuhn's suit coincided with a similar one filed by one of the convicted spies,

Katherine Moog (who was portrayed by Lya Lys in the film), in Jul 1939. Moog, also known as Katherine Moog Busch, eventually lost her $75,000 suit, in which she claimed that the portrayal of herself as the character of "Erika Wolf" constituted libel. Modern sources note that although an early draft of the screenplay used the actual names of the defendants in the New York spy case, the name of the character portraying Moog was always referred to as "Erika Wolf." Moog's identity was allegedly concealed from the outset because of her ties to high-ranking U. S. government officials.

The film did record-breaking box office business around the world and was re-released in 1940 with a new ending that included footage showing the effects of the Nazi occupation of Norway, Holland and Belgium. *Confessions of a Nazi Spy* was banned in Japan and eighteen Latin American and European nations, including Ireland, Italy, Denmark, Norway, Argentina, Costa Rica, Sweden, Belgium and Brazil. *HR* notes that in an attempt to reverse Brazil's decision to ban the film, Harry Warner personally cabled the Brazilian government and offered to turn over all of the film's Brazilian receipts to the Red Cross. Germany reacted with expected outrage at the film, and issued an official warning to the Hollywood film community that it would ban all future films that used cast or crew members employed in the film. According to an *LAEx* article, the U.S. State Department was notified that German Propaganda Minister Joseph Goebbels had ordered the Nazi-run German film industry to produce a series of "documentary" films bearing upon American unemployment, gangsterism and judicial corruption in retaliation for Warner Bros.' release of *Confessions of a Nazi Spy.*

Following the release of the film, many instances of vandalism and threats were reported by theater owners, and one news item told of seven theater operators who screened the film in Warsaw and reportedly were hanged following the German occupation. In addition, an Aug 1939 *HR* news item noted that five Danzig citizens were arrested by Nazi authorities for having traveled to Gdynia, Poland, to see the film. Reported incidents of lesser seriousness ranged from the mysterious disappearance of three prints of the film from a Swiss War Department truck in Berne, Switzerland, as reported in *HR*, to the vandalism done to a print of a Warner Bros. western that was mistaken for *Confessions of a Nazi Spy* during a break-in at a Hobbs, New Mexico, theater. In his autobiography, Jack Warner wrote that the film probably put him on Adolf Hitler's personal death list.

In Sep 1941, the *NYT* reported that Harry Warner was called to testify before the Senate subcommittee hearings into alleged war propaganda in Hollywood films. Four Warner Bros. films, including *Confessions of a Nazi Spy*, were named as "propaganda films" in a resolution co-authored by Senator Gerald P. Nye. Harry Warner testified that the picture was "factual," and that Senator Nye had personally endorsed the film after attending a private screening of it in May 1939. Director Anatole Litvak was also subpoenaed to appear before the investigating committee.

Confessions of a Nazi Spy was selected as one of the best films of 1939 by the National Board of Review.

DV 28 Apr 1939, p. 3. *FD* 28 Apr 1939, p. 8. *HR* 6 Dec 1938, p. 1, 6. *HR* 8 Dec 1938, p. 7. *HR* 30 Dec 1938, p. 1. *HR* 4 Jan 1939, p. 3. *HR* 13 Jan 1939, p. 1. *HR* 17 Jan 1939, p. 3. *HR* 7 Mar 1939, p. 3. *HR* 18 Mar 1939, pp. 6-8. *HR* 28 Apr 1939, p. 3. *HR* 13 May 1939, p. 1. *HR* 6 Jun 1939, p. 1. *HR* 1 Jul 1939, p. 2. *HR* 10 Jul 1939, p. 4. *HR* 14 Jul 1939, p. 1. *HR* 15 Jul 1939, p. 1. *HR* 20 Jul 1939, p. 1. *HR* 10 Aug 1939, p. 5. *HR* 22 Aug 1939, p. 1. *HR* 30 Aug 1939, p. 4. *HR* 6 Sep 1939, p. 1. *HR* 5 Oct 1939, p. 4. *HR* 11 Jun 1940, p. 3. *HR* 19 Jul 1940, p. 3. *LAEx* 6 Jun 1939. *MPD* 28 Apr 1939, p. 3. *MPH* 29 Apr 1939, pp. 50-51. *NYT* 5 Feb 1939. *NYT* 29 Apr 1939, p. 13. *NYT* 2 Jun 1940. *NYT* 3 Jun 1940, p. 11. *NYT* 26 Sep 1941. *Var* 3 May 1939, p. 16.

THE CONFLICT see **HER OWN PEOPLE**

THE CONJURE WOMAN (African Americans)
Micheaux Film Corp. **1926.** Si; b&w. Length undetermined. [Feature length assumed.].
Cast: Evelyn Preer, Percy Verwayen.
Melodrama (?), African American. No information about the precise nature of this film has been found. *African Americans. Magicians.*

¿CONOCES A TU MUJER? (Spanish language)
Fox Film Corp. *Dist* Fox Film Corp. **1931**; Panama City, Panama opening: 11 Sep 1931; San Juan, Puerto Rico opening: 13 Sep 1931; New York opening: 25 Sep 1931; Prod: Jun 1931. Sd; b&w. 8 reels, 6,867 ft. 76 min. Spanish language.
Dir David Howard. *Asst dir* Sid Bowen. *Dial dir* Francisco Moré de la Torre. *Scr* Leon Gordon and Lynn Starling. *Spanish version by* Matías Cirici-Ventalló. *Photog* Sidney Wagner.
Cast: Carmen Larrabeiti (*Laura Drake*), Rafael Rivelles (*Robert Felton*), Ana María Custodio (*Tulula*), Manuel Arbó (*Heriberto Drake*), Miguel Ligero (*Tim*), Enriqueta Soler (*Lita*), Rafael Calvo (*Seco*), Raúl Lechuga (*Capitán*), Hipólito Mora (*Simón*), Emma Roldán.
Society, Comedy. [*Not viewed*]. [The following plot summary is based on the English-language version of this film, *Don't Bet on Women*; character names refer to that version. For further information regarding the English-language version, please see the note below and the entry for *Don't Bet on Women* in the *AFI Catalog of Feature Films, 1931-40*.] Roger Fallon, a confirmed bachelor who

believes that all women are bad but fascinating, fends off women five years after his divorce. When his former wife Doris asks him to draw up a trust fund because she plans to marry a man who cannot support her, Roger consents and consults smug, self-satisfied attorney Herbert Drake. According to Drake, women are bad because men allow them to be bad, and he argues that it is an art to control women without letting them know that they are being controlled. Drake further states that he has absolute trust in his wife Jeanne. To get away from women, Roger and his friend Chipley Duff plan a yachting trip, but before they leave, Roger rescues a girl, Tallulah Hope, who calls for help in the water. Tallulah, it turns out, is a guest of the Drakes. Jeanne arrives on the boat and invites Roger and Chip to a party, where Drake, further perturbed by Roger's views, wagers $10,000 that Roger cannot kiss the first woman who enters the veranda within forty-eight hours. When Jeanne enters, Roger offers to call the bet off to avoid embarrassing Drake, but Drake, insulted, insists the bet is on. Jeanne, learning of the bet from Tallulah, coyly tells her anxious husband that it will allow her to learn whether she is a good woman or not. After Jeanne goes horseback riding with Roger, allows him to kiss her hand and encourages his flirtations, Drake refuses to go with her to Roger's apartment for dinner. Roger, who is falling in love, worries that if he kisses Jeanne, he will be left with a broken heart. That night, Jeanne, drunk with champagne and falling for Roger, entices him, but Roger, sincerely in love, refuses to love her under the existing taudry situation. Upset, Jeanne responds by saying that he couldn't be true to any woman because he is not even true to himself. Drake, who followed and overheard the conversation, happily tears up Roger's check to pay the wager. Before she leaves, Jeanne, curious to see if she missed anything, kisses Roger goodbye, to her husband's distress. *Bachelors. Battle of the sexes. Flirtation. Kisses. Marriage. Misogyny. Tests of character. Wagers. Ex-spouses. Lawyers. Rescues. Riding. Yachts and yachting.*

Note: For information on the English-language version, *Don't Bet on Women*, which was directed by William K. Howard and starred Edmund Lowe and Jeanette MacDonald, please see the entry for that film in the *AFI Catalog of Feature Films, 1931-40*; F3.1095. The running time listed for the Spanish language version was calculated from footage given in NYSA records. Some sources state that Nicolás Jordán de Urríes contributed dialogue to the Spanish version.

CM Oct 1931, p. 750.

THE CONQUEROR (Native Americans, Cherokee)
Fox Film Corp.; A Standard Picture. *Dist* Fox Film Corp. 16 Sep **1917** [©William Fox; 9 Sep 1917; LP11362]. Si; b&w. 8 reels.
Dir R. A. Walsh. *Scen* R. A. Walsh. *Story* Henry Christeen Warnack. *Cam* Dal Clawson. *Set des* George G. Grenier.
Cast: William Farnum (*Sam Houston*), Jewel Carmen (*Eliza Allen*), Charles Clary (*Sidney Stokes*), J. A. Marcus (*Jumbo*), Carrie Clarke Ward (*Mammy*), William Chisholm (*Dr. Spencer*), Robert Dunbar (*Judge Allen*), Owen Jones (*James Houston*), William Eagle Shirt, Chief Birdhead, Little Bear (*Indian chiefs*).
Historical, Drama. The young Sam Houston leads a contented life among the Cherokee Indians until he meets proud Eliza Allen, the blue blooded "rose of Tennessee." In order to win Eliza's favor, Sam enters politics and climbs his way to the office of governor of Tennessee. In his second term, Eliza consents to marry him. His happiness is short lived however, when he discovers that her reason for marriage was to attain the status of first lady. Heartbroken, Houston leaves her and goes to Texas, where he is followed by the repentant Eliza. But before she can reach him, Eliza is forced by a marauding band of Mexicans to take refuge in a convent. Houston, with the aid of his faithful Cherokees, drives the Mexicans to the convent where he arrives just in time to save Eliza from an assault at the hands of the Mexican leader. It is there that he discovers his wife's love, and together they start over to seek happiness and fame. *Cherokee Indians. Governors. Sam Houston. Marriage of convenience. Politics. Texas. United States–History–War with Mexico, 1845-1848. Convents. Mexicans. Rescues. Tennessee.*

Note: The story included in the copyright descriptions was entitled "A Man's Revenge." The film opened in New York on 10 Sep 1917 and was released on the open market as an individual attraction. *Wid's* credits Chester B. Clapp with the scenario, while other sources credit director Walsh. *Wid's* also gives the length as 10 parts. Walsh, in his autobiography, related that 30 Sioux Indians from the Pine Ridge agency in South Dakota appeared in the film, and some injuries were suffered when a chief used a real tomahawk in a battle scene rather than a rubber-tipped one.

Motog 13 Oct 1917, p. 783. *MPN* 29 Sep 1917, p. 2205. *MPW* 11 Aug 1917, pp. 904-05. *MPW* 29 Sep 1917, p. 2006. *MPW* 13 Oct 1917, p. 297. *NYDM* 22 Sep 1917, p. 25. *NYT* 11 Sep 1917, p. 11. *Var* 21 Sep 1917, p. 44. *Wid's* 25 Oct 1917, pp. 678-79.

CONQUEST OF COCHISE (Native Americans, Apache, Comanche)
Columbia Pictures Corp. *Dist* Columbia Pictures Corp. Sep **1953**; Los Angeles opening: 2 Sep 1953; Prod: 11 Dec—22 Dec 1952 [©Columbia Pictures Corp.; 3 Sep 1953; LP2887]. Sd (Western Electric Recording); col (Technicolor). 8 reels, 6,359 ft. 70 min. PCA cert no. 16328.

Prod Sam Katzman. *Assoc prod* Herbert Leonard. *Dir* William Castle. *Asst dir* Sam Nelson. *Scr* Arthur Lewis and De Vallon Scott. *Story* De Vallon Scott. *Dir of photog* Henry Freulich. *Technicolor col consultant* Francis Cugat. *Art dir* Paul Palmentola. *Film ed* Al Clark. *Set dec* Sidney Clifford. *Mus dir* Mischa Bakaleinikoff. *Sd eng* Josh Westmoreland.

Cast: John Hodiak [(*Cochise*)], Robert Stack [(*Major Burke*)], Joy Page [(*Consuelo de Cordova*)], Rico Alaniz [(*Felipe*)], Fortunio Bonanova [(*Mexican minister*)], Edward Colmans [(*Don Francisco de Cordova*)], Alex Montoya [(*Garcia*)], Steve Ritch [(*Tukiwah*)], Carol Thurston [(*Terua*)], Rodd Redwing [(*Red Knife*)], Robert E. Griffin [(*Sam Maddock*)], Poppy del Vando [(*Señora de Cordova*)], [John Crawford (*Bill Lawson*)], [Joseph Waring (*Running Cougar*)], [Guy Edward Hearn (*General Gadsden*)].

Western. [*Print viewed*]. In 1853, shortly after the end of the war between Mexico and the United States, Apache and Comanche Indians are stepping up their attacks on Mexican ranchers living in the Tucson area. In the hope of putting an end to the Indian raids, Cavalry General Gadsden sends Major Burke to the territory to make peace. Before Burke leaves, Gadsden warns him that the Apache warriors, under the leadership of Cochise, are ferocious fighters. In Tucson, Burke meets town leader Sam Maddock, but is unaware that Maddock is the instigator of trouble between the Indians and the settlers, and that he is forcing the Mexicans out of their homes and taking their land. One Mexican, Felipe, the son-in-law of landowner Don Francisco De Cordova, is especially embittered by the Indian raids, having lost his wife to an Apache arrow. Felipe is equally suspicious of the Americans, who he believes are also interested in taking the Mexicans' land. When Burke is invited to dine at Don Francisco's hacienda, he meets the beautiful Consuelo, Don Francisco's daughter. The visit is interrupted, however, by the unexpected arrival of Cochise. After Cochise and Burke discuss the Cavalry's presence, Cochise leaves vowing to remain at peace with the Americans. Running Cougar, the renegade Comanche leader, rejects the peace agreement, and leads a bloody raid on Don Francisco's hacienda. Cochise and his men arrive in time to save the hacienda, and Running Cougar is killed. Angered by the killing of his brother, the once-peaceful Red Knife announces that he will no longer abide by the peace treaty, even if it means war with the Apaches. Fearing a war with the Comanches, the other Apaches side with Running Cougar, and decide to join the fight against the whites. Realizing that his people are no longer interested in the treaty, Cochise and his wife Terua go to Tucson to meet with Burke. Maddock, meanwhile, conspires with Felipe to kill Cochise, but Felipe accidentally kills Terua instead. Cochise finds the rifle that was used to kill his wife, but before assuming that it was an American who killed her, he decides to give Burke a chance to prove otherwise. Cochise sends a raiding party to Tucson to find a hostage who will be used to force Burke to visit them. In Tucson, the raiding party kills Maddock before abducting Consuelo. Soon after Burke arrives at the camp, he is given four days to prove that the Americans were not responsible for the death of Terua, or face war. While in captivity, Consuelo falls in love with Cochise, who takes her to a romantic place in the wilderness. Back in Tucson, Burke discovers that the rifle used to murder Terua belonged to Corporal Carter, who admits that he got drunk one night and left it at Maddock's saloon. Tracing the rifle to Felipe, Burke wrings a confession from him and takes him to Cochise. The war dance is called off; however, Felipe, who remains unrepentant, makes another unsuccessful attempt to kill Cochise. Felipe is then killed by one of the Apaches. Cochise goes to Red Knife to persuade him to call off the war, but Red Knife refuses to accept Cochise's story and orders his death. Burke and his men arrive in time to save Cochise, and with the help of Apaches who are loyal to Cochise, the Comanches are defeated. Consuelo wishes to remain with Cochise as his wife, but the Apache leader refuses to let her "live the life of a renegade" and

insists that she leave with Burke. Consuelo accepts Cochise's wishes and leaves with the hope that the bloodshed has ended. Apache Indians. Arizona. Cochise. Comanche Indians. Mexican Americans. United States–History–Indian campaigns. United States. Army. Cavalry. Abduction. Ambushes. Attempted murder. Brothers. Brothers-in-law. Haciendas. Land claims. Lynching. Marriage. Murder. Oaths. Rescues. Revenge. Romance. Torture. Treaties. Tribal chiefs. Tucson (AZ).

Note: The MPAA/PCA Collection at the AMPAS Library contains a letter, dated 28 Nov 1952, from the PCA to Columbia production head Harry Cohn, in which PCA official Joseph I. Breen urged the studio to avoid excessive violence in the film, and to use caution in the characterization of Mexicans. In particular, Breen expressed concern about one scene in which "Felipe" was to have committed suicide in order to avoid punishment under the law, and another scene showing the lynching of a Mexican farmer. Although the lynching scene remained in the final film, the suicide was eliminated. For more information about the real-life Cochise, see entry below for *Fort Apache*.

Box 29 Aug 1953. *DV* 21 Aug 1953, p. 3. *FD* 21 Aug 1953, p. 7. *HR* 21 Aug 1953, p. 3. *Var* 26 Aug 1953, p. 6.

CONTRA LA CORRIENTE (Spanish language)
R. N. S. Productions, Ltd. **1936**; New York opening: 6 Mar 1936; Prod: 14 Mar—early Apr 1935 at Talisman Studios; filming of additional scenes ended early Jul 1935 [©Ramón Novarro Samaniegos; 13 Aug 1935; LP5711]. Sd (Balsley y Phillips); b&w. 10 or 11 reels, 7,987 ft. 89 min. Passed by the National Board of Review. PCA cert no. 1158. Spanish language.

[*Prod* Ramón Novarro]. *Escrita y dirigida* [*Written and directed by*] Ramón Novarro. *Director ayudante* [*Asst dir*] Antonio Samaniego. *Libreto y continuidad* [*Scr*] Ramón Novarro. [*Orig story* Ramón Novarro]. *Fotografía por* [*Photog*] Edward Snyder. [*Photog*] Jerry Ash]. *Arquitecto escenógrafo* [*Art dir*] Eduardo Samaniego. *Ayudante* [*Asst art dir*] Stephen Stepanian. *Corte de película por* [*Ed*] Ethel Davey. *Partitura compuesta y dirigida por el* [*Score comp and dir*] Profesor Juan Aguilar. *Tango por* [*Tango by*] Ernesto Piedra. *Sonido por* [*Sd*] Karl Zint.

Cast: José Caraballo (*Alberto Dortel*), Luana Alcañiz (*Rosalía Martin*), Alma Real (*Mrs. [Dolores Palacios de] Martin*), Ramón Guerrero (*Mr. [Frank] Martin*), Marina Ortiz (*Tía Pascuas*), Luis Díaz Flores (*Carlos Marco*), Nena Sandoval (*Juana*), Carmen Samaniego (*Maruca*), Luz F. Morán (*Sra. Torres*), John Pérez (*Ricardo Gavilán*), [Corazón Montes], [José Peña "Pepet"].

Domestic, Comedy-drama. [*Viewed print incomplete*]. At the 1932 Olympic games in Los Angeles, Rosalía Martin, a wealthy, local society girl, is attracted to Argentina's swimming champion, Alberto Dortel, who wins the world championship. Rosalía's suitor, Carlos Marco, introduces the two, and when Rosalía invites Alberto to a cocktail party at her home, he shyly refuses. The next day, his friend, through a prank, gets Alberto to enter the house, and Rosalía brings him into the party. He comes the following day to give her a swimming lesson, and they engage in a serious conversation about life. Later, Rosalía suggests that they go to a nightclub, but Alberto says he does not have enough money to take her there and will not allow her to treat him. Instead, they dance to music from the club over the radio and embrace. She kisses him and he tries to tell her that he loves her, but she asks him not to talk about it until the next day. Alberto returns to the Olympic Village and finds out that his team is to leave the next evening. The next day, Alberto tells Rosalía that he must leave and confesses that he also loves her. He worries that his poverty will stand in the way of their love, and before he boards his train, Rosalía gives him a book of love poems. Alberto, however, decides to remain in Los Angeles and surprises Rosalía as she returns to her limousine. Rosalía's father, realizing the two are in love, gives Alberto a job as a chauffeur without her knowledge. He and Rosalía almost have a collision one day, and when she realizes his position, she angrily says he should get another one. Her father then sees that Alberto is the type of man he wants for Rosalía and suggests that they marry. After the wedding, they honeymoon in Paris and London, then return to Los Angeles. Following the birth of their child, Alberto and Rosalía drift apart, as he does not care for her social life and spends much time working. At a party in their home, after an argument between Rosalía and Alberto, Carlos tries to flirt with her. Alberto then tells his father-in-law that he wants to give Rosalía her freedom. Greatly upset, Mr. Martin tells his daughter, who cries on his shoulder when she realizes Alberto's feelings. Rosalía complains that Alberto never forbids her to do anything or go anywhere and wonders why her husband does not slap her once in awhile. Meanwhile, in a nightclub,

Alberto overhears Carlos brag to two of his pals that he will be able to win Rosalía in a week. Alberto punches Carlos, and soon the police break up their fight. Rosalía wants to ask her husband's forgiveness, but he does not come home because he is jailed. The next day, they argue and he slaps her. Rosalía then cries, and when he threatens divorce, she begs him on her knees to stay. They embrace, and she puts a note on the door saying that the house is quarantined for smallpox, so that they can be alone together. *Argentines. Class distinction. Los Angeles (CA). Manhood. Marriage. Olympic Games, Los Angeles, 1932. Socialites. Swimmers. Temper. Tests of character. Athletes. Chauffeurs. Dancing. Divorce. Employment. Fathers and daughters. Fistfights. High society. Honeymoons. Jails. Nightclubs. Parties. Poetry. Police. Romantic rivalry. Shyness. Trains. Weddings.*

Note: One reel was missing from the print viewed. Some plot information was taken from a synopsis in the copyright descriptions. News items refer to this film under its English-language title *Against the Current*. This was actor Ramón Novarro's first film as a producer, director and writer. According to a *FD* news item, this was to be the first of six of Novarro's productions, and he originally planned to shoot it at the old Tiffany studios. Eventually the film was shot at the Talisman studios over a sixteen-day shooting period. Additional photography took place in and around Los Angeles. Final dubbing occurred in mid-Jul under Novarro's supervision. Sources disagree concerning the cost. A *NYT* article states that Novarro spent $200,000, while the *HR* review says the film had a "reputed cost of $60,000." According to *FD*, José Caraballo was the champion swimmer of Argentina and Spain, and Luana Alcañiz was a premier Spanish dancer. The *HR* review noted that preceding the picture, Novarro appeared on screen to give a tribute to Rex Ingram, the director who discovered him, and to ask his audience to support *Contra la corriente*. According to *NYT*, Novarro planned for the premiere to take place in the small Mexican town in which he spent his boyhood. No information has been located, however, concerning any showing of the film before its opening in New York in Mar 1936, other than a private preview in Aug 1935. The film had its Los Angeles premiere on 24 Jul 1936, with Novarro making a personal appearance. According to an ad, the film was distributed in South America by Radio Films, S.A.E. It is not known if RKO was involved in the distribution of the film in the U.S. Although the copyright register states that the film is eleven reels in length, the print at the Library of Congress is ten reels and does not contain Novarro's introductory dedication. In a Jul 1935 *NYT* article, Novarro indicated that he was happy to be free from studio obligations and that he had just written a play critical of Hollywood.

FD 21 Mar 1935, p. 6. *FD* 12 Mar 1936, p. 18. *HR* 11 Mar 1935, p. 3. *HR* 1 Apr 1935, p. 15. *HR* 9 Jul 1935, p. 2. *HR* 3 Aug 1935, p. 6. *HR* 25 Jul 1936, p. 4. *NYT* 7 Jul 1935. *NYT* 10 Mar 1936, p. 27.

COPACABANA (Latino)

Beacon Productions, Inc.; A Sam Coslow Production. *Dist* United Artists Corp. 30 May **1947**; Prod: 22 Nov 1946–22 Jan 1947 at Samuel Goldwyn Studios [©Beacon Productions, Inc.; 30 May 1947; LP1323]. Sd (Western Electric Recording); b&w. 10 reels, 8,248 ft. 92 min. PCA cert no. 12290.

Prod Sam Coslow. *Assoc prod* Walter Batchelor. *Pres by* David L. Hersh. *Dir* Alfred E. Green. *Dial dir* Irvin Berwick. *Asst dir* Harold Godsoe. *Orig story* Laslo Vadnay. *Scr* Laslo Vadnay, Alan Boretz and Howard Harris. *Addl dial* Sydney P. Zelinka. *Dir of photog* Bert Glennon. *Spec photog eff* John Fulton. *Prod des* Duncan Cramer. *Film ed* Philip Cahn. *Set dec* Julia Heron. *Cost des* Barjansky. *Mus dir and incidental mus* Edward Ward. *Mus arr* Jack Mason, Harold Zweifel and Bob Gordon. *Mus adv* Eddie Durant. *Mus ed* Weldon Hancock. *Mus numbers staged by* Larry Ceballos. *Sd* Fred Lau. *Makeup supv* Bob Stephanoff. *Hair stylist* Marie Clark. *Prod asst* Sid Ross. *Asst to prod* Dave Sebastian. *Prod mgr* Raoul Pagel.

Song(s): "Tico-Tico no fuba," music by Zequinha de Abreu, English lyrics by Ervin Drake; "Go West, Young Man," music and lyrics by Bert Kalmar and Harry Ruby; "Stranger Things Have Happened," "Je Vous Aime," "My Heart Was Doing a Bolero," "Let's Do the Copacabana" and "I Haven't Got a Thing to Sell," music and lyrics by Sam Coslow.

Cast: GROUCHO MARX [(*Lionel Q. Devereaux*)], CARMEN MIRANDA [(*Carmen Novarro/Fifi*)], STEVE COCHRAN BY ARR WITH SAMUEL GOLDWYN [(*Steve Hunt*)], ANDY RUSSELL [(*Himself*)], GLORIA JEAN [(*Anne*)], Abel Green, Louie Sobol, Earl Wilson (*Themselves*), De Castro Sisters, Paul & Eva Reyes, Ralph Sanford [(*Liggett*)], Igor Dega, Kay Gorcey, Merle McHugh, Dee Turnell, Maxine Fife, Toni Kelly, Chili Williams, Abigail Adams, Jill Meredith, and The Famous "Copa Girls."

Show business, Musical comedy. [*Print viewed*]. In New York City, Lionel Q. Devereaux and his girl friend, Brazilian singer Carmen Novarro, are given twenty-four hours to pay their hotel bill. With the help of gullible singer Andy Russell, Lionel, posing as an agent, convinces producer Steve Hunt to let Carmen audition for the Club

Copacabana. When Hunt asks whom else Lionel represents, he invents a veiled beauty from Paris named Fifi and convinces Carmen to personify her. Steve hires both Carmen and Fifi, who is a sensation in the press. Lionel tells Steve that he and Carmen are engaged to keep him away from her, but Steve asks out Fifi instead. Lionel then asks Andy to play cupid with Steve and his secretary, Anne, who is in love with him. Andy urges Anne to sing her feelings to Steve, but he is indifferent to her lovemaking. After Anatole Murphy, a Hollywood producer, makes an offer to Steve to take over Lionel's contract on Fifi, a slick agent named Liggett convinces Lionel to sell Fifi's contract to him for $5,000. Liggett in turn receives $100,000 from Murphy. Liggett becomes suspicious when he sees Fifi get into a cab and Carmen get out of it. After Anne confides in Carmen that Fifi is ruining her chances at love with Steve, Lionel and Carmen stage a fight in her dressing room between Carmen and Fifi, which is followed by Fifi's disappearance. Lionel later reports that she was found dead in the river and that he is glad he killed her. He is overheard, however, and blamed for Fifi's murder. During his interrogation, Lionel explains that he made up Fifi. Steve confesses that he courted Fifi only for business and that he loves Ann. Carmen then enters dressed as Fifi, and when Steve removes her veil, Carmen and Fifi are proven to be one and the same. Lionel kisses Carmen, and Murphy offers to buy the girl and the story for a Hollywood picture. Lionel subsequently receives credit for everything on the production, which opens with a song about the Club Copacabana. *Copacabana Nightclub (New York City). Deception. Impersonation and imposture. Latin Americans. Nightclub entertainers. Romantic rivalry. Theatrical agents. French. Hotels. Motion picture producers. New York City–Times Square. Nightclub owners. Secretaries. Singers. Theatrical producers.*

Note: The film's title was taken from Monte Proser's famous New York nightclub, the Copacabana, which was located at 10 East 60th St. According to a Jun 1944 *HR* news item, independent producer Jack Skirball was originally set to make the picture, with assistance from Proser. At that same time, George Raft was announced as the film's possible lead. This was the first film in which Groucho Marx appeared without his brothers. It is also the first film in which Groucho appeared in his own mustache, rather than a greasepaint one. This was Carmen Miranda's first film after leaving Twentieth Century-Fox, the studio to which she had been under contract since 1940. The film included cameo appearances by Broadway writers Abel Green (the editor of *Variety*), Louie Sobol (*New York Journal-American*), and Earl Wilson (*New York Post*). At the time of the production, Groucho Marx was married to Kay Gorcey, who had a small role in this film.

HR news items add Chester Clute, Richard Elliott, Frank Scannel, Pierre Andre and Andrew Tombes to the cast, but their participation in the completed film has not been confirmed. Pierre Andre was signed to perform a specialty dance number with Dee Turnell, according to *HR*. In mid-Feb 1947, *HR* reported that producer Sam Coslow was considering reshooting scenes in which Miranda appears in a blonde wig, because of mail from Brazilian fans stating that they prefer her as a brunette. The reshot scenes were to be inserted in South American release prints only, according to the item. As reported in *LAT* on 14 Jul 1953, Murray P. Koch sued Coslow and George Frank for $80,000, money he claimed to have advanced Beacon to aid in the making of this film. Along with Walter Batchelor and David Hersh, both of whom were dead by the time the suit was filed, Frank and Coslow held a controlling interest in Beacon, which was deemed insolvent. The disposition of this lawsuit is not known. According to *HR*, the film was obtained for re-release by Hal R. Makelim's Atlas Pictures Co. in Jan 1954. The film was also re-issued in Jul 1972.

Box 21 Jun 1947. *DV* 23 Apr 1947. *FD* 21 May 1947, p. 7. *HR* 16 Jun 1944, p. 1. *HR* 22 Jun 1944, p. 3. *HR* 22 Nov 1946, p. 21, 27. *HR* 3 Dec 1946, p. 11. *HR* 6 Dec 1946, p. 8. *HR* 9 Dec 1946, p. 12. *HR* 20 Dec 1946, p. 25. *HR* 22 Jan 1947, p. 4. *HR* 19 Feb 1947, p. 19. *HR* 21 May 1947, p. 3. *HR* 15 Jul 1947, p. 6. *HR* 6 Jan 1954. *IFJ* 4 Jan 1947, p. 35. *LAT* 14 Jul 1953. *MPHPD* 24 May 1947. *NYT* 12 Jul 1947, p. 7. *Var* 21 May 1947, p. 15. *Var* 12 Jul 1972.

CORAZONES DE ACERO see LA CAUTIVADORA

CORAZONES DE PLOMO see TODA UNA VIDA

CORPUS DELICTI see SHADOWS OVER CHINATOWN

COSACOS see UN CAPITáN DE COSACOS

COSAS DE LA VIDA see ASí ES LA VIDA

COSÌ È LA VITA (Italian language)

Thalia Amusement Corp. *Dist* Thalia Amusement Corp. **1931**; New York opening: 21 Nov 1931; Prod: completed mid-Oct 1931 at Metropolitan Studios in Fort Lee, N.J.. Sd; b&w. 8 reels. 70 or 75 min. Italian language.

Pres William Reutemann. *Dir* Eugene Roder. *Scr* Eugene Roder. *Orig story* Armando Cennerazzo. *Photog* Frank Zucker. *Mus dir* Pio Fantoni.

Cast: Miriam Battista (*Immacolata*), Ascanio DeRosa, Adriana Dori, Eduardo Cianelli, Pierre Nigi, Augusta Merighi, Vannette Van, Frank Allara, Allesandro Immella.

Melodrama. [*Not viewed*]. In Naples, wealthy Isabella and Don Fortunado Albano are the proud parents of a new baby girl, Immacolata. When Count Armando, Fortunado's best friend, whom Isabella mistrusts, arranges to send Fortunado away to America on business, much to Isabella's chagrin, he promises to care for Fortunado's wife and young daughter. True to his word, he visits regularly and insists that Isabella join him for an evening of dancing and music. Isabella languishes at the news that her husband will be gone for another year, and she agrees to go out on the town. Armando convinces her to drink champagne and then kisses her. Later, Isabella confesses to Carmela Parisi, the gardener Nicola's wife, how distressed she feels at her husband's absence, and she convinces Carmela to come away with her to the family's country villa. Fortunado returns home unexpectedly and demands that Nicola take him to his wife. When he arrives, Isabella is ill, no longer wanting to live, and she eventually dies. Years later, Immacolata, now a beautiful young girl, receives her education in a convent. Fortunado arrives one day to take her home, and Immacolata and Salvatore, the son of Nicola and Carmela, enjoy a happy reunion, pledging never to be separated again. On Immacolata's twentieth birthday, her father plans a party and invites Count Alfredo Spadaro, a gentleman interested in marrying the girl. Fortunado and the count interrupt Immacolata and Salvatore, but Fortunado believes that she is only ordering flowers from the gardener's son. At the feast, Carmela and Nicola dance the Tarantella. Spadaro proposes to Immacolata, and the next day, Salvatore tells his mother that he hates Spadaro because the man loves Immacolata. Carmela scolds her son, reminding him of his poverty and the impossibility of a union with Fortunado's daughter. Meanwhile, Fortunado urges his daughter to accept the count's proposal. She tells him about her love for Salvatore, and Fortunado sends the boy away, reminding him of the importance of knowing one's place in the world. Angered and jealous, Salvatore approaches Immacolata and Spadaro sitting in his car with a gun in his hand. A short time later, the count stands trial for the murder of Salvatore. The count claims to have killed Salvatore in self-defense, but Immacolata contradicts him and says she hopes to be reunited with Salvatore in heaven. When Carmela testifies, she asks to speak privately with the judge and Immacolata, and confesses that Salvatore was not her son but was Isabella's illegitimate baby, to whom she gave birth at the villa before she died. Carmela raised the baby as her own, after promising to keep Isabella's secret forever. Immacolata returns to her father and tells him nothing of Carmela's story. The charges are dropped against the count for lack of evidence, and Immacolata resigns herself to be an obedient and dutiful wife. A Catholic marriage ceremony ensues. *Brothers and sisters. Class distinction. Gardeners. Illegitimacy. Naples (Italy). Nobility. Parentage. Romantic rivalry. Secrets. Unrequited love. Birthdays. Confession. Engagements. Infidelity. Jealousy. Seduction. Trials. Weddings.*

Note: The film's English title was given in NYSA as *Such Is Life* and in *Var* as *Life Is Like That*. According to correspondence at NYSA, the film's title was changed in Nov 1932 to *Il segreto di una morta (The Secret of the Death)* and changed again in May 1933 to *Brother and Sister (Frate e suora)*. The above plot summary was based on a dialogue continuity deposited at NYSA. A news item in *FD* notes that Miriam Battista, a former child actress, made her return to the screen in this film. Sources disagree concerning the spelling of some of the actors' names. While *FD* lists Ascanio DeRosa, Pierre Nigi and Vannette Van, *Var* lists Ascanio de Rose, Pierce Nigi and Wannette Vanni. *Var* commented concerning the film, "Poorly acted and photographed the same way. Direction is way off. The sound is terrible."

FD 19 Oct 1931, p. 6. *FD* 8 Nov 1931, p. 5, 11. *Var* 1 Dec 1931, p. 21.

COSMO JONES THE CRIME SMASHER *see* **CRIME SMASHER**

THE COSSACKS *see* **UN CAPITáN DE COSACOS**

COSSACKS BEYOND THE DANUBE *see* **COSSACKS IN EXILE**

COSSACKS IN EXILE (Ukrainian language)
Avramenko Film Co. 1939; New York opening: 28 Jan 1939; Prod: began mid-Jul 1938 in Newton, NJ. Sd (Variray Blue Seal Recording); b&w. 82 min. Ukrainian language.
Assoc prod Michael J. Gann. *Entire prod conceived and prod* Vasile Avramenko. *Dir* Edgar G. Ulmer. *Scr* V. Avramenko. *Cam* W. Miller and Leo Lipp. *Film ed* Jack Kemp. *Comp, mus arr and supv* Anthony Riudnicky. *Ukrainian* [*adv*] L. Biberowich. [*Scr supv* Shirley Ulmer].

Source: Based on the operetta *Zaporozheta za Dunayem* by Semen Artemowsky (St. Petersburg, 1863).
Cast: MARIA SOKIL (*Odarka*), Michael Shvetz (*Ivan Karas*), Nicholas Harlash (*Sultan*), Alexis Tcherkasshy (*Andrey*), Helen Orlenco (*Pxana*), D. Creona (*Kobzar*), Vladimir Zelitsky (*Selih-Agha*), General V. Kikevitch (*Kalnyshewky*), S. Mostowy (*Prokip*), L. Biberowich (*Catherine II*), N. Mandryka (*General Tekely*), Jean Harasymyk (*Hassan*), Anna Mushinsky (*Neboha*), F. Braznick (*Old Cossack*), E. Bodnar, h. Vepruk (*Oxana's friends*), N. Trach, E. Wolk, J. Finchuk, W. Bilous, O. Guzda, A. Hukalo, M. Vynnychok, S. Hancharyk, N. Bulawka (*Cossacks, Turks, Russians*), William Yacyna (*Solo dance*).

Musical, Historical. [*Print viewed*]. The Zaporogian Cossacks are the pride of the Ukraine, but the Imperial government in Moscow opposes them. When the men at a Zaporogian fort learn that Moscow is sending soldiers to destroy their unit, they decide to appeal directly to Czarina Catherine. Meanwhile, Oxana, a Ukranian village girl, is in love with fellow villager Andrew and rejects the overtures of her older suitor, Prokip. When news comes that Catherine has refused Ukranian pleas and that the soldiers will now be required to join the ranks of the Russian army, the Cossacks decide to destroy their fort and leave the Ukraine, accompanied by their families. The commander of the fort is captured and exiled to a Siberian monastery, where he prays for the freedom of his people. The other Cossacks flee on the Danube River to Turkey, where they live in peace, but still yearn for their homeland. Ivan Karas and his wife Odarka, Oxana's parents, worry about her because Andrew did not arrive in Turkey with the rest of the villagers and Prokip continues to pursue her. One day, after the Cossacks have helped the Turks in their battle against the Arnauts, the Sultan of Turkey arrives at Ivan's village to see for himself what the Cossacks are really like. Although the sultan does not reveal his true identity, Ivan treats him very warmly. The sultan is so impressed with Ivan that he invites him to "the sultan's palace," pretending to be the sultan's emissary. At the palace, Ivan is dressed in royal finery and shown to the harem, still unaware that his escort is the sultan. While they talk, Ivan reveals that he would like to meet the sultan to ask if the homesick Cossacks could now return to their own country. As Ivan is being entertained by the sultan, Oxana looks toward the Danube, waiting for Andrew. When Andrew finally arrives, Prokip sees the lovers embrace and becomes so jealous that he arranges for the couple to be arrested by the Turks as spies. Soon Ivan returns home, dressed in new Turkish finery, and impresses Odarka. When they learn what has happened to Oxana and Andrew, she insists that he go to the Pasha, the local Turkish official. Thinking that Ivan's Turkish clothing is the disguise of a spy, the Pasha plans to hang him as well as Oxana and Andrew. They are all saved just in time, however, when the sultan arrives and sets them free, then orders Prokip arrested. Finally revealing his true identity, the sultan then orders that the Cossacks be allowed to return home. Following a joyous celebration, the Cossacks set sail for their homeland. *Cossacks. Marriage. Romance. Russia–History. Sultans. Turkey–History. Ukrainians. Battles. Catherine I, Empress of Russia, 1684-1727. Danube River. Harems. Impersonation and imposture. Jealousy. Officers (Military). Spies.*

Note: This film was also known as *Cossacks Beyond the Danube*. It was shot in the Ukrainian langauge in Newton, NJ, partially at the Little Flower Monastery. The viewing print had English subtitles. According to reviews, the film was also shown with English subtitles at its New York opening in late Jan 1939. The *Var* review pointed out that the operetta on which the film was based had remained very popular since its first production. Another film, based on the same operetta, was released in New York in Sep 1938, under the title *Zaporozets za Dunayem* [*Cossacks Beyond the Danube*]. Some sources confuse that film, made in Russia in the Ukrainian language, and directed by Y. P. Kavaledge, with the American-made, Edgar Ulmer-directed film. According to modern sources, the success of Ulmer's previous Ukrainian musical made for Vasile Avramenko's company, *Natalka Poltavka*, made *Cossacks in Exile* possible. In a modern interview, Ulmer indicated that he shot the film in the same area that he shot *The Singing Blacksmith*. Modern sources have commented on Ulmer's very stylized use of silhouettes and shadows in *Cossacks in Exile*.

FD 2 Feb 1939, p. 7. *MPD* 8 Jul 1938, p. 8. *NYT* 28 Jan 1939, p. 19. *Var* 15 Feb 1939, p. 13.

COTTON AND CATTLE (African Americans)
Westart Pictures. 1921; Brooklyn showing: 30 Jun 1921. Si; b&w. 5 reels.

Dir Leonard Franchon. *Wrt* W. M. Smith. *Photog* A. H. Vallet.

Cast: Al Hart (*Bill Carson*), Jack Mower (*Jack Harding*), Robert Conville (*Buck Garrett*), Edna Davies (*Edna Harding*), Ethel Dwyer (*Ethel Carson*).

Western. Because Buck Garrett threatens to foreclose the mortgage on her father's cotton plantation, Ethel Carson enlists the aid of her sweetheart, rancher Jack Harding, and his cowboys in quickly picking the crop for market. Garrett gets an idea from a newspaper, and the next day Carson receives a note from "the night rider" warning him to cease harvesting. Carson stubbornly refuses, and his harassment begins: the black pickers are frightened away by hooded men, their huts are burned, Carson is kidnapped. Donning the cloak of a felled "night rider," Jack finds Carson, subdues the band's leader, and unmasks Garrett. (Locale: Oklahoma.). *African Americans. Cotton. Cowboys. Farmers. Mortgages. Oklahoma. Plantations. Ranchers. Terrorism.*

ETR 26 Mar 1921, p. 1559.

COUNSELLOR AT LAW (Jewish Americans)

Universal Pictures Corp. *Dist* Universal Pictures Corp. 25 Dec **1933**; Prod: ended 21 Oct 1933 [©Universal Pictures Corp.; 5 Dec 1933; LP4314]. Sd; b&w. 78 or 80 min. PCA cert no. 4104-R [5 Feb 1938].

Pres CARL LAEMMLE. *Prod* Carl Laemmle, Jr. *Dir* William Wyler. *Scr* Elmer Rice. *Cam* Norbert Brodine. *Art dir* Charles D. Hall. *Film ed* Daniel Mandell. [*Supv film ed* Maurice Pivar]. *Sd supv* Gilbert Kurland.

Source: Based on the play *Counsellor-at-Law* by Elmer Rice (New York, 6 Nov 1931).

Cast: John Barrymore (*George Simon*), Bebe Daniels (*Regina "Rexy" Gordon*), Doris Kenyon (*Cora Simon*), Isabel Jewell (*Bessie Green*), Melvyn Douglas (*Roy Darwin*), Onslow Stevens (*John P. Tedesco*), Thelma Todd (*Lillian La Rue*), Clara Langsner (*Lena Simon*), J. Hammond Dailey (*Charlie MacFadden*), Mayo Methot (*Mrs. Zadorah Chapman*), Bobby Gordon (*Henry Susskind*), Malka Kornstein (*Sarah Becker*), Vincent Sherman (*Harry Becker*), Marvin Kline (*Herbert Howard Weinberg*), T. H. Manning (*Peter J. Malone*), John Qualen (*Johan Breitstein*), Angela Jacobs (*Goldie Rindskopf*), Richard Quine (*Richard Dwight*), Barbara Perry (*Dorothy Dwight*), Elmer H. Brown (*Francis Clark Baird*), Conway Washburn (*Arthur Sandler*), Frederick Burton (*Crayfield*), [Victor Adams (*David Simon*)].

Drama. [*Print viewed*]. At the bustling Manhattan law offices of Simon and Tedesco, highly successful Jewish attorney George Simon, who has risen from the slums of New York, returns to his roots when he bails out Sarah Becker's son Harry, a young Communist who has been brutalized by the police, but grows rich on sensational cases like the murder trial of Mrs. Zadorah Chapman and the breach of promise suit of the seductive Lillian La Rue. Simon's devoted secretary, Regina "Rexy" Gordon, is always at his side, and secretly loves him. Simon's socialite wife Cora is embarrassed by his notoriety and uncomfortable with his heritage. She begs him to decline a $100,000 case against one of her society friends. He reluctantly agrees but is soon threatened with disbarment when upper-class attorney Francis Clark Baird discovers that years before he created a false alibi for Johan Breitstein, another friend from his old neighborhood. Desperate to save his career, Simon cancels his plans to go to Europe with Cora, while his investigator, Charlie MacFadden, searches for information to use against Baird. Simon, meanwhile, grows morose because he is convinced that his career is finished. His depression deepens after he hears that Harry Becker, who railed at him for forsaking his roots and buying into the capitalist system, has died of his injuries. Charlie discovers that Baird is leading a double life, keeping a girl friend and illegitimate child in Pennsylvania, and Simon uses the information to silence Baird. Triumphant, he sends a telegram to Cora asking her to disembark the ship and postpone the trip until he can join her, but she refuses. Simon, suspicious that she is having an affair, calls her socialite friend, Roy Darwin, and discovers that he has left on the same boat. Depressed and alone in the office, Simon decides to commit suicide, but just as he is about to jump from the skyscraper's window, Rexy returns unexpectedly. After her scream stops him, a phone call, begging him to take another sensational case, revives his spirits. He gleefully kisses Rexy and they depart together to investigate the case. *Class distinction. Ethics. Jews. Lawyers. Attempted suicide. Blackmail. Breach of promise. Communists.*

Depression, Mental. Detectives. Infidelity. Marriage–Mixed. Mothers and sons. New York City. Secretaries. Skyscrapers. Socialites. Telephone operators. Unrequited love.

Note: According to a *HR* news item, Paul Muni, who played "George Simon" in the New York stage production, declined the lead role in the film. The following actors reenacted their Broadway roles for the film: Clara Langsner, J. Hammond Dailey, Malka Kornstein, Marvin Kline, T. H. Manning, John Qualen, Angela Jacobs, Elmer H. Brown and Conway Washburn. According to modern sources, Vincent Sherman had appeared in the Chicago production of the play. Modern sources note that Barrymore was paid $25,000 a week for his performance, and add George Humbert and Jack Mower to the cast.

FD 28 Nov 1933, p. 4. *HR* 17 May 1933, p. 3. *HR* 23 Oct 1933, p. 2. *HR* 18 Nov 1933, p. 3. *MPH* 25 Nov 1933, p. 35. *NYT* 8 Dec 1933, p. 31. *Var* 12 Dec 1933, p. 19.

COUNSELOR AT GUN-LAW *see* **ROLL THUNDER ROLL!**

COUNT OF ARIZONA *see* **MY AMERICAN WIFE**

A COUNTRY WEDDING *see* **WIEJSKIE WESELE**

THE COURAGE OF TEN *see* **THE MEN**

THE COURAGEOUS COWARD (Japanese Americans)

Haworth Pictures Corp. *Dist* Robertson-Cole Co. through Exhibitors Mutual Distributing Corp. 14 Apr **1919** [©The Haworth Pictures Corp.; 27 Feb 1919; LU13446]. Si; b&w. 5 reels.

Dir William Worthington. *Scen* Frances Guihan. *Story* Thomas J. Geraghty. *Cam* Dal Clawson. *Art dir* Milton Menasco.

Cast: Sessue Hayakawa (*Suki Iota*), Tsuru Aoki (*Rei Oaki*), Toyo Fujita (*Tangi*), George Hernandez (*Big Bill Kirby*), Francis J. McDonald (*Tom Kirby*), Buddy Post (*Cupid*).

Drama. Suki Iota, a Japanese-American law student, falls in love with his guardian's niece Rei Oaki, who has just arrived from Japan to cultivate her singing voice. After Suki goes East to law school, Rei, thinking Suki wants an American girl, gets Tom Kirby, the son of the Chinatown boss, to teach her American ways of dress and behavior. On his return, Suki is displeased with Rei's change and believes her to be Tom's girl when he sees them celebrating the Chinese New Year. Suki is appointed assistant district attorney and, with the whole city watching because of anonymous death threats sent to him, he steadfastly prosecutes a murder case until Tom confesses to him. To protect Rei, Suki removes himself from the case. Branded a coward and a traitor to justice, Suki remains silent until Tom publicly confesses. Now regarded as a hero, Suki defends Tom. Rei confesses she never loved Tom, and her romance with Suki begins anew. *Chinatowns. Cultural conflict. District attorneys. Japanese. Japanese Americans. Ostracism. Social customs. Chinese New Year. Confession (Law). Law students. Singers.*

ETR 26 Apr 1919, p. 1597. *MPN* 26 Apr 1919, p. 2711. *MPW* 26 Apr 1919, p. 579. *Var* 25 Apr 1919, p. 80.

COVERED WAGON DAYS (Latino)

Republic Pictures Corp. *Dist* Republic Pictures Corp. 22 Apr **1940**; Prod: mid Mar–late Mar 1940 [©Republic Pictures Corp.; 22 Apr 1940; LP9626]. Sd (RCA High Fidelity Recording); b&w. 6 reels. 56 min.

Series: The Three Mesquiteers.

Assoc prod Harry Grey. *Dir* George Sherman. [*Asst dir* William O'Connor and Mike Eason]. *Orig scr* Earle Snell. *Photog* William Nobles. *Film ed* Bernard Loftus. *Mus score* Cy Feuer. *Prod mgr* Al Wilson.

Source: Based on characters created by William Colt MacDonald.

Cast: Robert Livingstone (*Stony Brooke*), Raymond Hatton (*Rusty Joslin*), Duncan Renaldo (*Rico*), Kay Griffith [(*Maria*)], George Douglas [(*Ransome*)], Ruth Robinson [(*Mama Rinaldo*)], Paul Marion [(*Carlos*)], John Merton [(*Gregg*)], Tom Chatterton [(*Major Norton*)], Guy D'Ennery [(*Diego*)], Tom London [(*Martin*)], Reed Howes [(*Stevens*)].

Western. [*Print viewed*]. Stony Brooke, Rusty Joslin and Rico, the Three Mesquiteers, are riding to Mexico to celebrate the marriage of Rico's brother Carlos when they are stopped at the border by officials who are investigating a ring smuggling silver into the United States. Unknown to the trio, the smugglers are operating by means of a tunnel that links a silver mine on each side of the border, and the Juanita mine on the Mexican side is owned by Rico's uncle, but has been closed for years. The smugglers, led by Ransome, the owner of the mining supply depot, attempt to buy the mine, but when the old man refuses to sell, Ransome orders him slain and frames Carlos for

the murder. After Carlos is arrested, Ransome's men organize a lynch mob, but the Mesquiteers save Carlos from the hangman's noose and hide him in the hills. Feigning friendship for Carlos, Ransome sends Maria, Carlos' bride with a message for the fugitive, and then arranges for his men to follow her to the hideout. The Mesquiteers hold off the bushwackers while Carlos and Maria flee in her carriage, but when Carlos is wounded during the escape, Maria takes him to the army post, where he is arrested for murder. During Carlos' trial the next day, Stony sneaks into Ransome's store and discovers the entrance to a hidden mine shaft in the cellar. Meanwhile, Rico and Rusty visit the Juanita mine, where they also discover the hidden shaft housing the smuggled silver. As the Mesquiteers struggle with Ransome and his men, a keg of dynamite explodes, and in the chaos, Ransome escapes. Stony pursues him and forces a confession, thus exonerating Carlos of all guilt. Confession (Law). Cowboys. Explosions. Frame-ups. Mexican Americans. Mexican-American border region. Murder. Silver mines. Smuggling. Brothers. Lynching. Mobs. Uncles. Weddings.

Note: A HR production chart places Al Taylor, Lee Shumway, Barry Hays and Elias Gomboa in the cast, but their participation in the final film has not been confirmed. Modern sources add Dick Alexander, Art Mix, Jack Montgomery, Edward Hearn, Frank McCarroll, Jack Kirk, Herman Hack, Ken Terrell and Tex Palmer to the cast. For additional information on the series, consult the Series Index and see entry for The Three Mesquiteers in (see AFI Catalog of Feature Films, 1931-40; F3.4617).

FD 9 May 1940, p. 8. HR 16 Mar 1940, pp. 6-7. MPH 6 Apr 1940, p. 27. MPH 11 May 1940, p. 52. Var 8 May 1940, p. 12.

THE COWBOY AND THE INDIANS (Native Americans)

Gene Autry Productions. *Dist* Columbia Pictures Corp. Sep **1949**; Prod: 14 Mar—28 Mar 1949 [©Gene Autry Productions; 30 Sep 1949; LP2668]. Sd (RCA Sound System); b&w. 68 or 70 min. PCA cert no. 13748.

Prod Armand Schaefer. *Dir* John English. [*Asst dir* Jack Corrick]. *Wrt* Dwight Cummins and Dorothy Yost. *Dir of photog* William Bradford. *Art dir* Harold MacArthur. *Film ed* Henry Batista. *Set dec* Louis Diage. *Mus supv* Paul Mertz. *Mus dir* Mischa Bakaleinikoff. [*Sd* Frank Goodwin].

Song(s): "One Little Indian Boy," words and music by Robert Bilder; "America," words Samuel Francis Smith, music by Henry Carey; "Silent Night," German words by Joseph Mohr, music by Franz Gruber. "Here Comes Santa Claus," words and music by Gene Autry and Oakley Haldeman.

Cast: Gene Autry [(*Gene Autry*)], and Champion World's Wonder Horse, Sheila Ryan [(*Dr. Nan Palmer*)], Frank Richards [(*"Smiley" Martin*)], Hank Patterson [(*Tom Garber*)], Jay Silverheels [(*Lakobna*)], Claudia Drake [(*Lucy Broken Arm*)], George Nokes [(*Rona*)], Charles Stevens [(*Broken Arm*)], Alex Frazer [(*Fred Bradley*)], Clayton Moore [(*Luke*)], [Frank Lackteen (*Blue Eagle*)], [Chief Yowlachie (*Chief Long Arrow*)], [Lee Roberts (*Joe*)], [Nolan Leary (*Sheriff Don Payne*)], [Maudie Prickett (*Miss Summers*)], [Harry Mackin (*Bob Collins*)], [Charles Quigley (*Henderson*)], [Gilbert Alonzo (*Lucy's son*)], [Roy Gordon (*Congressman Lawrence*)], [Jose Alvarado (*Indian boy*)], [Ray Beltram (*Old Indian*)], [Felipe Gomez (*One Mary*)], [Ro Mere Darling (*Two Mary*)], [Shooting Star, Iron Eyes Cody (*Indians*)].

Western, with songs. [*Print viewed*]. At the Bar B Ranch, new owner Gene Autry is angry when he discovers that nearby Indians are grazing sheep on his land. He sets out to complain to Chief Long Arrow, but when he arrives on the reservation, he learns that One Mary, the chief's aging relative, is very ill. Concerned, Gene brings her to the trading post and summons a doctor. At the trading post, Gene stops the proprietor, "Smiley" Martin, from cheating Lakohna, an Indian. Then, over Martin's objections, Gene brings One Mary into the post to wait for the doctor. When Nan Palmer, the doctor, arrives, she determines that One Mary is suffering from malnutrition. Gene is shocked by the news and decides to allow the Indians to continue grazing their herds on his land. From Long Arrow's grandson Rona, Gene learns that the Indians do not get enough to eat. Later, Gene encounters Nan at the schoolhouse and helps her inoculate the children. As a favor to Nan, Gene brings medicine to Broken Arm at the reservation. There, he tries to stop some men claiming to be government agents from taking Broken Arm's sheep away from him, but they manage to drive the sheep over a cliff to their deaths. Later, the men are revealed to be cohorts of Martin, who are trying to force Broken Arm's wife Lucy to sell a priceless blanket, but Henderson, the head of the Indian Bureau, refuses to jail them unless he has solid

proof that they are harming the Indians. Gene asks Bob Collins, a reporter, to write an expose for the paper, but Bob is not interested in the story. Then Gene telephones Congressman Lawrence, who asks Gene to write a full report. Gene learns that the Indians have lost many sheep, and that they have no water on the reservation with which to irrigate their corn. Without sheep for wool, the Indians are unable to weave the blankets that they sell for money to buy supplies. Thus, Martin is able to cheat them out of their possessions and sell them to curio dealer Fred Bradley. One of his partners covets the necklace that belongs to Long Arrow. Because he knows that the necklace is the property of the tribe, and that Long Arrow would never sell it, Martin decides to kill him, steal the necklace and pin the murder on Lakohna. After Long Arrow is discovered fatally wounded, Gene advises Lakohna to hide until he can discover the identity of the real murderer. That night, Gene and Lakohna sneak into the trading post looking for proof that Martin was behind the attack on Long Arrow. They are discovered and chased by Martin and his confederates. In the morning, Gene and Lakohna are trapped in the rocks, but are saved by the arrival of more Indians. Shortly after, the sheriff arrives with a posse, and Martin is arrested, after which the necklace is returned to Lakohna, who is now the tribe's chief. Bob writes the story, and the resulting publicity causes many people to send gifts to the Indians, and Congress grants the tribe an appropriation. Later, Nan, whose real name is Nanusha, reveals that she is half-Indian and will marry Lakohna. Indians of North America. Ranchers. Starvation. Trading posts. Women physicians. Children. Congressmen. Frame-ups. Grandfathers. Gunfights. Indians of North America–Mixed blood. Indians of North America–Reservations. Murder. Necklaces. Reporters. Sheep. Sheriffs. Swindlers and swindling. Tribal chiefs. Tribal life. Vaccination.

Note: The song "Here Comes Santa Claus" became a Christmas "perennial." This film marked the first time that Jay Silverheels and Clayton Moore appeared together. They later starred in the television program The Lone Ranger.

Box 17 Dec 1949. MPHPD 5 Nov 1950, p. Var 2 Nov 1949, p. 22.

THE COWBOY AND THE PRIZEFIGHTER (Native Americans)

Equity Pictures, Inc. *Dist* Eagle Lion Films, Inc.; controlled by Pathe Industries, Inc. Dec **1949**; Prod: began mid-Aug 1949 [©Pathe Industries, Inc.; 5 Dec 1949; LP2710]. Sd (Glen Glenn Sound System); col (Cinecolor). 7 reels, 5,338 ft. 59-60 min. PCA cert no. 14147.

Series: Red Ryder.

Prod Jerry Thomas. *Assoc prod* Bartlett Carre. *Dir* Lewis D. Collins. *Asst dir* Joseph Wonder. *Dial dir* Gloria Welsch. *Scr* Jerry Thomas. *Dir of photog* Gilbert Warrenton. *Film ed* Joseph P. Gluck. *Set dec* Vin Taylor. *Dir of ward* Bert Offord. *Mus comp and dir by* Ralph Kraushaar. *Mus supv* David Chudnow. *Sd supv* Glen Glenn. *Dir of makeup* Jack Casey. *Asst to the prod* Fred W. Kline.

Source: Based on the comic strip "Red Ryder" by Fred Harman (1938–1964), by special arrangement with Stephen Slesinger.

Cast: Jim Bannon (*Red Ryder*), Little Brown Jug (*Little Beaver*), Emmett Lynn (*Buckskin Blodgett*), Marin Sais (*Duchess*), Don Haggerty [(*Steve Stevenson*)], Karen Randle (*Sue Evans*)], John Hart [(*Mark Palmer*)], Lane Bradford, Marshall Reed [(*Bart Osborne*)], Forrest Taylor [(*Stevenson*)], Frank Ellis, Bud Osborne, Lou Nova [(*Bull, the prizefighter*)].

Western. [*Print viewed*]. Outside a western town, newcomer Steve Stevenson shoots a ranch hand to prevent him from killing rancher Red Ryder, who had just fired the hand from his Painted Valley ranch. As thanks, Red offers Steve the dead man's job on the ranch, which Red owns with his aunt, Duchess. At the ranch house, Steve explains that he is from the town of Indian Gap, where his gambling father, Miles, was murdered a few months earlier. Official reports called the death a suicide prompted by Miles' financial trouble, but Steve believes that crooked prizefight promoter Mark Palmer had a hand in Miles' death. Earlier, Palmer set up a fixed fight between the Stevenson ranch foreman and his man, Bull. The bets were covered by Charlie, the local gambling house proprietor. When Miles' man lost the fight, the townspeople, who lost considerable money, turned against him, and he was given thirty days to get off his ranch. Now Steve rides out with Red, his friend Buckskin Blodgett, and Little Beaver, an Indian boy, and come upon a stagecoach being robbed by a group of bandits. Buckskin and Red fight off the thieves, and the $5,000 gold payroll is saved. In town, Steve discovers that Palmer was on the stagecoach, and confronts him. Also on board was Sue Evans,

who, through Charlie, has come to work at the Silver Dollar Saloon for owner Bart Osborne. Osborne and Palmer plan to force Red to fight Bull, then discredit him after Bull wins and the townspeople lose their bets. Steve decides to fight in Red's place. Buckskin, meanwhile, has eavesdropped on Osborne and Palmer plotting with Duke Samson, the leader of the bandits, to steal the payroll during the fight. Buckskin is caught and knocked out, however, and suffers a temporary case of amnesia. At the fight, Steve is knocked out after Bull punches him with a lead pipe in his hand. After the heist, a bank employee races to get the sheriff, and a posse brings in the bandits after a gunfight and chase in which Samson is killed. Later, in town, a man tells Red that Osborne has started a rumor that Red is a coward. In the saloon, after Palmer, Osborne and Bull split their profits, Red fights Bull and accuses him of being armed with a lead pipe when it flies out of Bull's hand and hits Buckskin in the head. With Buckskin, whose amnesia is cured by the blow, as a witness, Osborne and Palmer are arrested. Later, at Red's ranch house, Steve reports that Palmer admitted to killing Steve's father. It turns out that Sue was working for Osborne in order to repay a gambling debt owed by her brother, who is Charlie. Steve suggests that Sue quit her job and marry him, and Duchess threatens to hit Buckskin again so that he is not so ornery. *Amnesia. Fixed fights. Promoters. Ranchers. Bandits. Bank robberies. Brothers and sisters. Debt. Fathers and sons. Murder. Payrolls. Rescues. Saloon keepers. Stagecoach robberies. Wagers.*

Note: Actor Don Kay Reynolds, who played "Red Ryder's" Indian ward "Little Beaver," was listed as "Little Brown Jug" in his onscreen credit. Modern sources add Steve Clark and Ray Jones to the cast. *The Cowboy and the Prizefighter* was the fourth and final entry in Equity Picture's "Red Ryder" series. For additional information on the "Red Ryder" series, please consult the Series Index and see the entry below for *Tucson Raiders*.

Box 21 Jan 1950. *DV* 9 Mar 1950, p. 3. *FD* 19 Jan 1950, p. 12. *HR* 26 Aug 1949, p. 12. *HR* 10 Mar 1950, p. 3, 6. *MPHPD* 14 Jan 1950, p. 154. *Var* 22 Feb 1950, p. 6.

COWBOY HOLIDAY (Latino)
Beacon Productions, Inc. *Dist* State Rights. 1 Jan **1935**; Prod: late Nov 1934 at Alexander Brothers Studios. Sd; b&w. 56-57 min. Passed by the National Board of Review.
Prod Arthur Alexander. [*Supv* Max Alexander]. *Dir* Bob Hill. *Asst dir* Myron Marsh. *Story* "Roc" Hawke [sic]. *Photog* Gil Warrenton. *Ed* Holbrook Todd. *Tech dir* Fred Preble.
Cast: BIG BOY WILLIAMS [(*Buck Sawyer*)], Janet Chandler [(*Ruth Hopkins*)], Julian Revaro [sic] [(*Pablo Escobar, The Juarez Kid*)], Dick Alexander, John Elliott, Julia Bejarano, Alma Chester.
Western. [*Print viewed*]. Cowboy Buck Sawyer is on his way to a vacation in Waco, Texas, and stops at the house of an old friend, Hank. Hank is in distress because there have been a series of robberies in his county that the residents are blaming on the Juarez Kid, who is really Pablo Escobar. Rumors abound that Hank will be recalled as sheriff in favor of his deputy, Walt Gregor. Hank's mother believes that Walt is framing Hank. Meanwhile, a large man escapes capture and while hiding in a cave, changes out of a Mexican costume. Buck decides to leave for Waco, but on his way out, he is stopped by some men who accuse him of being the Juarez Kid because of his size. Buck knows that Escobar is a small man and after being released, heads into the hills where he hears the disguised man's horse whinny and discovers the costume in the cave. That evening, the Juarez Kid kills a rancher named Hopkins to get the money he paid him for some cattle. Buck rides to the scene, but Ruth, Hopkins' daughter, believes he is the killer and calls her ranch hands for help. Buck escapes but one of the ranch hands shoots him in the arm. Seeing a cabin, Buck enters and makes himself at home, unaware that the two inhabitants are spying on him from a trapdoor in the floor that connects to a small mine. The man, seeing no gun on Buck, advances and Buck recognizes him as Escobar, then faints from the bullet wound. Some time later, Escobar finds gold in the mine while Buck visits Ruth. Walt then arrives and questions Escobar's mother about seeing any strangers. She claims to have seen no one, but Walt sees the hunk of gold ore. Meanwhile, Ruth's ranch hands have gotten rid of Buck, but Hank arrives to tell her that she has misconstrued Buck's actions. At Escobar's cabin, Buck, Escobar and Mama come up with a plan to get Walt. They call him out to the cabin and Mama agrees to sell him the property. That evening, as Mama, Escobar, Hank, Ruth and Buck watch, Walt, disguised as the Juarez Kid, comes to get his money back. They trick Walt into shooting at Mama's bed and after he takes off, with Buck following, Hank and Escobar remove his bullets from the empty bed. His bullets match those that killed Mr. Hopkins, and after Buck

subdues him, Walt confesses to the crimes and apologizes. Ruth apologizes to Buck and hires him as her ranch foreman. *Disguise. Impersonation and imposture. Mexican Americans. Robbery. Sheriffs. Bandits. Confession (Law). Deputies. False accusations. Gold mines. Mothers and sons. Murder. Ranchers. Texas.*

Note: According to modern sources, "Rock" Hawkey, which is spelled "Roc" Hawke in the onscreen credits, is a pseudonym for director Bob Hill. Modern sources include Frank Ellis and William Gould in the cast.

FD 26 Dec 1934, p. 6. *HR* 26 Nov 1934, p. 15. *MPD* 16 Jan 1935, p. 26, 28. *MPH* 26 Jan 1935, p. 46.

COWBOY JOE *see* **SHUT MY BIG MOUTH**

CRADLE OF FEAR *see* **CROSSFIRE**

THE CRADLE OF SOULS *see* **THE GREATEST THING IN LIFE**

THE CRASH (Irish Americans)
First National Pictures, Inc. *Dist* First National Pictures, Inc. 7 Oct **1928** [©First National Pictures, Inc.; 12 Jun 1929; LP457]. Si; b&w. 8 reels, 6,225 ft.
Pres Richard A. Rowland. *Dir* Eddie Cline. *Cont* Charles Kenyon. *Titles* Dwinelle Benthall and Rufus McCosh. *Photog* Ted McCord. *Film ed* Al Hall.
Source: Based on the short story "The Wrecking Boss" by Frank L. Packard in *The Night Operator* (New York, 1919).
Cast: Milton Sills (*Jim Flannagan*), Thelma Todd (*Daisy McQueen*), Wade Boteler (*Pat Regan*), William Demarest (*Louie*), Fred Warren (*Corbett*), Sylvia Ashton (*Mrs. Carleton*), De Witt Jennings (*Superintendent Carleton*).
Melodrama. Jim Flannagan, a two-fisted, hard-fighting Irishman, returns from the war to White Cloud, a railroad junction high in the Sierras, and is put in charge of a wrecking crew. He becomes fascinated with Daisy, soubrette of a traveling theatrical troupe, and she accepts his offer of marriage. Although she is a good cook and housekeeper, her free and easy ways arouse Jim's suspicious jealousy; when he fights with Louie, manager of the show troupe, Daisy leaves him. Jim takes to drinking and misses a call to clear a wreck, and he is discharged. Then Regan, a friend, sends for Daisy, and she returns with their child, a baby girl; although overjoyed, Jim's old jealous doubt returns, and, her pride offended, Daisy returns to the city. Her train collides with a fast freight, and against orders Jim joins the crew and retrieves the miraculously unharmed Daisy from the wreck. They are thus reunited. *Drunkenness. Irish Americans. Jealousy. Marriage. Sierra Nevada Mountains (CA and NV). Theatrical troupes. Train wrecks. Veterans. Wreckers.*

FD 11 Nov 1928. *Var* 7 Nov 1928, p. 26.

CRASH DIVE (African Americans)
Twentieth Century-Fox Film Corp. *Dist* Twentieth Century-Fox Film Corp. 14 May **1943**; World premiere in New York: 28 Apr 1943; Prod: late Jul—mid-Nov 1942; addl scenes began on 18 Dec 1942 [©Twentieth Century-Fox Film Corp.; 14 May 1943; LP12147]. Sd (Western Electric Recording); col (Technicolor). 12 reels, 9,552 ft. 105 min. PCA cert no. 8731.
[*Exec prod* Darryl F. Zanuck and William Goetz]. *Prod* Milton Sperling and Lee Marcus]. *Dir* Archie Mayo. [*Asst dir* Art Jacobson and Johnnie Johnson]. [*2d unit dir* Otto Brower]. [*Fill-in dir* Edward Ludwig]. *Scr* Jo Swerling. *Orig story* W. R. Burnett. *Dir of photog* Leon Shamroy. *Spec photog eff* Fred Sersen. *Technicolor dir* Natalie Kalmus. *Assoc* Henri Jaffa. *Art dir* Richard Day and Wiard B. Ihnen. [*Loc art dir* James Havens]. *Film ed* Walter Thompson and Ray Curtiss. *Set dec* Thomas Little. *Set des* Paul S. Fox. *Cost* Earl Luick. *Mus* David Buttolph. *Mus dir* Emil Newman. *Sd* Bernard Freericks and Roger Heman. *Makeup artist* Guy Pearce. *Tech adv* M. K. Kirkpatrick, Commander, U.S.N. and [William Calkins].
Cast: TYRONE POWER, U.S.M.C.R. [(*Lt. Ward Stewart*)], ANNE BAXTER [(*Jean Hewlitt*)], DANA ANDREWS [(*Lt. Comm. Dewey Connors*)], James Gleason [(*McDonnell*)], Dame May Whitty [(*Grandmother*)], Henry Morgan [(*Brownie*)], Ben Carter [(*Oliver Cromwell Jones*)], Charles Tannen [(*Hammond*)], [Frank Conroy (*Capt. Bryson*)], [Florence Lake (*Doris*)], [John Archer (*Curly*)], [George Holmes (*Crew member*)], [Minor Watson (*Admiral Bob Stewart*)], [Kathleen Howard (*Miss Bromley*)], [David Bacon (*Lieutenant*)], [Stanley Andrews (*Captain*)], [Paul Burns (*Clerk*)], [Gene Rizzi, Malcolm McTaggart, Harry Carter (*Sailors*)], [Frank Dawson (*Butler*)], [Edward McWade (*Crony*)], [Paul Stanton, James

Eagles (*Officers*)], [Betty McKinney, Ruth Jordan, Dorothy Brent, Sally Harper, Ruth Thomas, Sue Jolley (*Schoolgirls*)], [Floyd Shackelford (*Porter*)], [Trudy Marshall (*Telephone operator*)], [Chester Gan, Bruce Wong (*Waiters*)], [Peter Leeds (*Shore police*)], [Gene Collins (*Boy*)], [Netta Packer (*Mother*)], [Nick Vehr (*Russian officer*)], [William Yetter (*Lieutenant of tanker*)], [John Mylong (*Captain of submarine*)], [Lionel Royce (*Captain of Q-boat*)], [Frederick Brunn], [Hans von Morhart (*Y-gun operator*)], [Sigurd Tor (*German soldier*)], [Otto Reichow (*German*)], [Hans Moebus (*German officer*)], [Thurston Hall (*Texan*)], [Leila McIntyre], [Cecil Weston], [Edward Earle], [James Metcalf].

Sea, **World War II**, **Drama**. [*Print viewed*]. Lt. Ward Stewart delights in the maneuverability and speed of his PT boat, and is disappointed when his uncle, Admiral Bob Stewart, asks him to join the submarine branch of the Navy. Stewart agrees that it is his duty to serve where he is most needed, but requests a weekend leave before assuming his new post as executive officer aboard the *Corsair*, which is captained by Dewey Connors. During his train trip to Washington, D.C., Stewart meets teacher Jean Hewlitt. Stewart is instantly attracted to Jean, but his rakish behavior irritates her. He persuades her to go to a party with him, but she does not keep their dinner date for the following evening. Undeterred, Stewart is pleased to discover that she teaches at the Bromley School for Girls, located in New London, Connecticut, which is also the site of the Naval submarine base. Unknown to Stewart, Jean is Connors' girl friend, and after her return to New London, Jean, who wants to believe that she prefers the stable Connors to the devil-may-care Stewart, asks Connors if they can marry before he leaves on his next mission. Connors wants to wait until after he receives a promotion, however, so he tells Jean that they can marry when he returns. The *Corsair* sails that night, and during the journey, black messman Oliver Cromwell Jones discovers that his friend McDonnell is secretly taking nitroglycerin pills for a heart condition. One afternoon, the sub is fired upon by a German Q-boat disguised as a Swedish scow, and Connors decides to play "possum" and allow the Germans to think that they have been sunk. The strategy pays off and the *Corsair* sinks the Q-boat, then returns to New London. After their arrival, Connors goes to Washington, where he receives a promotion, while Stewart continues his pursuit of Jean, who does not know that he serves under Connors. Meanwhile, McDonnell explains to Oliver that he needs to go on one more mission to atone for his cowardice during World War I, and Oliver promises to keep McDonnell's condition a secret. One evening, Stewart takes Jean to meet his feisty grandmother, then proposes to her the next morning on their way back to the school. Deeply in love with Stewart, Jean accepts, but when Stewart learns soon after that Connors intends to propose to her as well, he informs Jean that they can no longer see each other. As Jean is telling Stewart that he is the one she loves, they realize that Connors has overheard their conversation. Before the situation can be resolved, the men are sent on a mission to find a secret German naval base. Stewart tries to explain matters to Connors and maintain their friendship, but Connors coldly repulses him and attends only to business. Just as the *Corsair* is getting low on fuel, they find the base and follow a tanker into the mine-strewn harbor. Stewart leads the landing party, which blows up the ammunition dumps as the *Corsair* fires on the anchored ships. McDonnell is killed in the raid while saving Oliver and Stewart, who swim through the oil-covered, flaming water back to the sub. Because the periscope has been damaged, the fleeing sub cannot resubmerge, and Connor is forced to stay on deck and guide her through the mines and bombardments from land and sea. He is wounded but not fatally, and Stewart gets him below just before the *Corsair* submerges. The men make peace, and soon after the *Corsair*'s return to New London, Stewart and Jean are married. *Friendship. New London (CT). Officers (Military). Romantic rivalry. Submarine warfare. United States. Navy. African Americans. Battles. Cigarettes. Engagements. Fires. Germany. Navy. Girls' schools. Grandmothers. Heart disease. Sailors. Schoolteachers. Self-sacrifice. Trains. Uncles. Washington (D.C.). Womanizers.*

Note: The working titles of this film were *SS 111* and *Submarine School*. On 25 Aug 1942, after *Crash Dive* had been selected as the film's title, Twentieth Century-Fox announced that it was considering renaming the picture again, because of fears that "the ticket buyers might connect the title with an airplane story." After the opening credits, a written prologue reads: "The cooperation and assistance of the officers and men of the U.S. Navy submarine base, New London, Connecticut, is gratefully acknowledged." On 12 Sep 1942, *PittsC*

stated that the film would "touch lightly on the seaman life of Dorie Miller," an African American messman who was awarded the Navy Cross for his heroic actions aboard the U.S.S. *Arizona* during the attack on Pearl Harbor. Although Miller is not directly portrayed in the picture, *PittsC* noted that Ben Carter's character, "Oliver Cromwell Jones," would be depicted as "a heroic mess attendant, very much a part of the plot, and a fighting man among fighting men." According to a *HR* news item, John Payne and Randolph Scott were originally set to star in the picture. Another *HR* news item noted that William Perlberg was scheduled to produce the film. He was replaced by Milton Sperling, who, on 10 Sep 1942, left the studio to join the Marine Corps. Lee Marcus then stepped in to act as producer while the film was still shooting. The picture was also Tyrone Power's last before enlisting in the Marine Corps as a private. Although Power was originally set to report for duty on 1 Oct 1942, he was granted a deferment to finish the picture. He did not make another film until 1946, when he starred in *The Razor's Edge*. Much background footage was shot on location at the U.S. Naval submarine base in New London, CT, and the Navy supplied equipment and granted access to submarines and servicemen. Although *HR* production charts include Charley Grapewin in the cast, he is not in the completed picture. Information in the MPAA/PCA Collection at the AMPAS Library indicates that prints of the picture were made with an incorrect certificate number—8371—instead of the correct one—8731. A *HR* news item noted that Norman Nesbett was to be the narrator of a "special trailer" for the picture. *HR* also reported that in conjunction with the film's opening at Grauman's Chinese Theatre on 27 May 1942, the Navy would be "setting up a recruiting station in the lobby" and would "keep it there all through the run of the film." The picture received an Academy Award for special effects (Fred Sersen, photography, and Roger Heman, sound).

AmCin Jul 1943, p. 257. *Box* 24 Apr 1943. *DV* 22 Apr 1943, p. 3. *FD* 22 Apr 1943, p. 7. *HR* 29 Jan 1942. *HR* 6 Apr 1942, p. 2. *HR* 30 Jun 1942, p. 2. *HR* 17 Jul 1942, p. 1. *HR* 7 Aug 1942, p. 9. *HR* 25 Aug 1942, p. 2. *HR* 26 Aug 1942, p. 4. *HR* 27 Aug 1942, p. 1. *HR* 31 Aug 1942, p. 1. *HR* 1 Sep 1942, p. 3. *HR* 11 Sep 1942, p. 1. *HR* 7 Oct 1942, p. 1. *HR* 16 Oct 1942, p. 11. *HR* 3 Nov 1942, p. 6. *HR* 18 Dec 1942, p. 4. *HR* 1 Mar 1943, p. 3. *HR* 19 Apr 1943, p. 1. *HR* 22 Apr 1943, p. 3. *HR* 3 May 1943, p. 1, 6, 8. *HR* 14 May 1943, p. 8. *MPD* 22 Apr 1943, p. 1, 6. *MPH* 24 Apr 1943. *MPHPD* 24 Apr 1943, p. 1273. *NYT* 29 Apr 1943, p. 25. *NYT* 6 Jun 1943. *PittsC* 12 Sep 1942, p. 20. *Var* 21 Apr 1943, p. 8.

CRASHIN' THRU (Native Americans)

R-C Pictures Corp. *Dist* Film Booking Offices of America. 1 Apr 1923 [©R-C Pictures Corp.; 16 Mar 1923; LP18773]. Si; b&w. 6 reels, 6,500 ft.

Dir Val Paul. *Adpt* Beatrice Van. *Photog* William Thornley and Robert De Grasse.

Source: Based on the short story "If a Woman Will" by Elizabeth Dejeans in *Blue Book Magazine* (Feb–Apr 1919).

Cast: Harry Carey (*Blake*), Cullen Landis (*Cons Saunders*), Myrtle Stedman (*Celia*), Vola Vale (*Diane*), Charles Le Moyne (*Saunders*), Winifred Bryson (*Gracia*), Joseph Harris (*Holmes*), Donald MacDonald (*Allison*), Charles Hill Mailes (*Benedict*).

Western. Gracia, a half-breed Indian girl, plots with Cons Saunders to steal cattle from Blake because he is oblivious to her charms. With his stock gone, he cannot repay the money he owes his Uncle Benedict, and when Benedict is murdered, Blake is suspected. Because Blake has taken care of Saunders (Cons's father) for the many years he has been without the use of his legs, the latter is finally conscience-stricken and confesses to the crime, thus freeing Blake to marry Diana. *Debt. Indians of North America–Mixed blood. Invalids. Murder. Rustlers.*

Note: The working title of this film was *The One Man*.

FD 1 Apr 1923. *MPW* 7 Apr 1923. *Var* 19 Apr 1923, p. 36.

CRIME AND PUNISHMENT (Russian Americans)

Arrow Film Corp.; Gold Rooster Plays. *Dist* Pathé Exchange, Inc. 25 Feb **1917**. Si; b&w. 5 reels.

Dir Lawrence B. McGill. *Scen* Charles Taylor. *Cam* Henry Cronjager.

Source: Based on the novel *Crime and Punishment* by Fyodor Dostoevsky (Russia, 1866).

Cast: Derwent Hall Caine (*Rodion Raskolnikoff*), Cherrie Coleman (*Dounia, his sister*), Lydia Knott (*His mother*), Carl Gerard (*Razamouhin Porkovitch*), Sidney Bracey (*Andreas Valeskoff*), Marguerite Courtot (*Sonia Marmeladoff*), Robert Cummings (*Porphyus*).

Drama. University student Rodion Raskolnikoff is forced to flee Russia for publishing a radical treatise advocating lawlessness for the good of society. He arrives on the shores of America, still preaching the same doctrine. Touched by the poverty on the East Side of New York, Rodion kills a pawnbroker who oppresses the people in his neighborhood, robs his safe, and uses the money for charitable purposes, managing to keep the guilt from himself. When the crime is fastened upon Porphyus, an innocent man, however, Rodion is caught in the struggle between conscience and his creed, until Sonia,

a poor young Russian girl, instills in him a sense of the wrong of his act by converting him to a belief in God. Conscience stricken, Rodion rejects his credo and acknowledges his guilt. *Conscience. False accusations. Guilt. Murder. Poverty. Religious conversion. Revolutionaries. Robbery. Russian Americans. College students. Exiles. New York City–East Side. Pawnbrokers.*

Note: Dostoevsky's novel was first published in *Russky Vestnik Magazine* in 1866. Among the many other film adaptations of Dostoevsky's novel are: the 1923 German film *Raskolnikow*, directed by Robert Wiene; the 1935 French film *Crime et Chatiment*, starring Harry Baur and directed by Pierre Chenal; the 1935 Columbia production, starring Peter Lorre and directed by Josef von Sternberg; the 1956 French film *Crime et Chatiment*, starring Jean Gabin and Robert Hossein and directed by Georges Lampin; the 1959 Allied Artists release *Crime and Punishment USA*, starring George Hamilton and directed by Denis Sanders; and the 1969 Russian production, directed by Lev Kulijanov.

ETR 17 Feb 1917, p. 773. *MPN* 24 Feb 1917, p. 1255. *MPW* 24 Feb 1917, p. 1211. *MPW* 3 Mar 1917, p. 1408. *NYDM* 17 Feb 1917, p. 26. *Wid's* 15 Feb 1917, p. 111.

CRIME BUSTER *see* **CRIME SMASHER**

CRIME SMASHER (African Americans)

Monogram Pictures Corp. *Dist* Monogram Pictures Corp. 29 Jan 1943; Prod: 14 Nov—late Nov 1942 [©Monogram Pictures Corp.; 1 Jan 1943; LP11783]. Sd; b&w. 5,525 ft. 62 min.

[*Exec prod* Trem Carr]. *Prod* Lindsley Parsons. *Dir* James Tinling. [*Asst dir* William Strohbach]. *Scr* Michael L. Simmons and Walter Gering. *Orig story* Walter Gering. *Dir of photog* Mack Stengler. *Tech dir* Dave Milton. *Film ed* Carl Pierson. *Mus dir* Edward Kay. *Sd dir* Glen Glenn. *Prod mgr* William Strohbach.

Source: Based on the radio series *Cosmo Jones* created by Walter Gering (broadcast undetermined).

Cast: Edgar Kennedy [(*Murphy*)], Richard Cromwell [(*Pat Flanagan*)], Gale Storm [(*Susan*)], and Mantan Moreland [(*Eustace Smith*)], Frank Graham [(*Cosmo Jones*)], Gwen Kenyon [(*Phyllis Blake*)], Herbert Rawlinson [(*James J. Blake*)], Tristram Coffin [(*Jake*)], Charles Jordan [(*Biff*)], Vince Barnett, Emmett Vogan, Maxine Leslie, Mauritz Hugo, Sam Bernard, [Gil Stanley (*Tommy Hayes*)].

Detective, Comedy-drama. [*Print viewed*]. The police are unable to abate a crime wave that has hit their big city. Nightclub owner Jake Pelotti, meanwhile, wins $20,000 at the racetrack, but his wife is forced to use the winnings to pay ransom to Pelotti's competitor, Biff, when he kidnaps him. After he is released, Pelotti is angry that Biff has taken his money, and kills Biff's thug, Tony. Professor Cosmo Jones, a correspondence course detective, is walking in front of the police station when Tony's body is thrown from a car. Cosmo reports the finding to police chief Murphy, who is under pressure from the police commissioner to clean up the city. Cosmo wants to be hired as a special investigator, but Murphy refuses. After Cosmo accepts a ride from Sergeant Pat Flanagan, Pat averts the kidnapping of Phyllis Blake, the daughter of wealthy oil tycoon, James J. Blake. Cosmo stays behind to investigate and encounters a janitor named Eustace Smith, who has found the body of Mike Andrews, a bystander who was injured during the attempted kidnapping. To avoid her father's wrath, Phyllis and her boyfriend, Tommy Hayes, deny that she was almost kidnapped, and Pat is demoted for shooting Mike. As Pat refuses to marry his fiancée Susan, the commissioner's secretary, until he is promoted, she helps Cosmo with his investigation, and Cosmo makes Eustace his assistant. Tommy, who secretly works for Biff, later succeeds in kidnapping Phyllis, and her outraged father demands a shakeup of the police department after three days of apparent inaction. Pat and Cosmo join forces and obtain Blake's cooperation to bring the kidnappers out into the open by publishing a false report of a ransom note. Biff murders Pelotti, believing that he was trying to cut in on his action, and then sends an actual ransom demand. Hoping to protect Blake, Cosmo gives him a satchel containing counterfeit money, but Blake abandons Cosmo when Biff makes a new arrangement. Cosmo then accidentally switches satchels with a doctor at a drugstore, and leaves a note there for Murphy and Pat with the address of the new meeting place. Cosmo and Eustace are abducted by the gangsters and interrogated along with Blake. Biff, angry that there is no money in either satchel, threatens to deface Eustace with a scalpel, until Pat and Murphy arrive and fire at him. While Biff and his thugs return the fire, Cosmo and Blake rescue Phyllis. Eustace knocks one thug out while Pat shoots Biff in self-defense, and the gangsters are arrested. The commissioner thanks Cosmo for his diligence, and with the promise of a promotion, Pat can

now marry Susan. *Amateur detectives. Kidnapping. Murder. Police. African Americans. Engagements. Gangsters. Gunfights. Impersonation and imposture. Nightclubs. Police commissioners. Professors. Socialites. Tycoons.*

Note: The working title of this film was *Adventures of Cosmo Jones*. The title card of the film reads: "Cosmo Jones in *Crime Smasher*." Contemporary sources also referred to the film as *Crime Buster* and *Cosmo Jones the Crime Smasher*. According to Monogram publicity information, Frank Graham was known as the "man of many voices," who for three years portrayed "Jones" and other characters on the CBS radio series *Cosmo Jones*.

Box 20 Feb 1943. *DV* 13 Nov 1942. *DV* 12 Feb 1943. *FD* 18 Feb 1943, p. 4. *HR* 13 Nov 1942, p. 8. *HR* 20 Nov 1942, p. 6. *HR* 12 Feb 1943. *MPH* 20 Feb 1943. *MPHPD* 12 Dec 1942, p. 1055. *MPHPD* 20 Feb 1943, p. 1170.

EL CRIMEN DE MEDIA NOCHE (Spanish language)

Reliable Pictures Corp. *Dist* Reliable Pictures Corp. **1936**; New York opening: 21 Feb 1936; Prod: Oct 1935. Sd; b&w. 5,657 ft. 63 min. Spanish language.

Prod Bernard B. Ray and Harry S. Webb. *Assoc prod* Moe Sackin. *Dir* Bernard B. Ray. *Dial dir* Jesús Topete. *Orig story and scr* John Thomas Neville. *Asst* Ira S. Webb. *Spanish dial* René Borgia. *Photog* Pliny Goodfriend. *Ed* William Austin.

Cast: Ramón Pereda (*David Graham*), Adriana Lamar (*Diana Sullivan*), Juan Torena (*Alberto Burke*), José Luis Tortosa (*James A. Sullivan*), Aura de Silva (*Kate*), Jaime Devesa (*Withers*), Rosa Rey (*Señora Ryan*), José Peña "Pepet" (*Doctor McNeill*), Lucio Villegas (*Doctor Kelly*), Carlos Montalbán (*Johnny*), Jesús Topete (*Louvain*), Ramón Muñoz (*Silverstein*), Gerardo Gómez (*Bonelli*), Raúl Lechuga (*Morgan*), Israel García (*Perkins*), Agustín Guzmán (*Oficial de la radio*), Carlos de la Paz (*McCoy*), Antonio Manfredi (*Finnegan*).

Police, Mystery. [*Not viewed*]. [The following plot summary is based on the English-language version of this film, *Midnight Phantom*; character names refer to that version. For further information regarding the English-language version, please see the note below and the entry for *Midnight Phantom* in the *AFI Catalog of Feature Films, 1931-40.*] Lieutenant Dan Burke bursts into the office of Police Chief James Sullivan to ask for the hand of his daughter, Diane, and Sullivan acquiesces, although he would have preferred that she marry the eminent criminologist Professor David Graham. Dan is later dispatched to pursue a gang of bank robbers, and when their car crashes, he discovers that his half-brother Johnny was in on the job. Before dying in Dan's arms, Johnny explains that he was broke and didn't know what he was getting into when he joined the gang. Dan makes an attempt to cover up Johnny's identity; however, he is found out and Sullivan demands that Diane break off the engagement. Sullivan later invites Professor Graham to police headquarters to lecture on the science of criminology, and Captain Bill Withers, who has been ordered by Sullivan to prevent Dan from obtaining a marriage license, introduces Graham to the police force. At the midnight lecture in a darkened room, various convicts are brought before Graham, who diagnoses their criminal tendencies with surprising accuracy just from their appearance. When the lights go back on, it appears that Sullivan has had a heart attack and Police Surgeon Kelly, who had recently given Sullivan a clean bill of health, is called in. Graham asserts that Sullivan was murdered with a rare jungle poison affixed to a dart, and suspicion falls on a number of people present at the lecture. Sullivan had recently reorganized the department, eliminating graft and corruption, and a number of police officers had been disgruntled. Mary Ryan, a tough policewoman, had been angry at Sullivan because she believed that he had allowed her daughter Kathleen, who worked as Sullivan's secretary, to become too attached to him, and she subsequently threatened him with a scandal. Dan has a clear-cut motive because Sullivan had forbidden his daughter to marry him, and, in addition, Sullivan had been receiving strange and threatening anonymous phone calls. A needle is eventually found in the room, but as Kelly is about to explain why it could not have been the instrument that killed Sullivan, he collapses to the floor, dead. Graham declares that Dan killed the two men by blowing the poisoned darts out of his cigar, and he explains that Dan's tendency to crime is a hereditary trait which he shared with his half-brother. However, Dan cleverly traces the murder weapon to Graham, and Graham is arrested for the murders. Six months later, while Dan and Diane share a picnic, they read of Graham's execution in the newspaper. Graham confessed in prison that he had diagnosed himself as a criminal, and when he realized that he could not win Diane, he became obsessed with committing the perfect crime.

Criminologists. Detectives. Murder. Police chiefs. Romantic rivalry. Darts (Game). Engagements. Executions. Fathers and daughters. Graft. Half brothers. Hereditary tendencies. Lectures. Mothers and daughters. Poison. Police. Secretaries. Surgeons. Thieves.

Note: The Spanish and English language versions of this film were shot simultaneously. The title of the Spanish-language version was translated in reviews as "The Crime at Midnight." The Spanish version was advertized in New York under the title *El fantasma de media noche*. The running time listed for the Spanish version was calculated from footage in NYSA records. For information on the English-language version, *Midnight Phantom*, which was directed by Bernard B. Ray and starred Reginald Denny, please see the entry for that film in the *AFI Catalog of Feature Films, 1931-40*, F3.2864.

CM Dec 1935, p. 748.

EL CRIMEN DE WALL STREET *see* EL CUERPO DEL DELITO

THE CRIMINAL (Italian Americans)
New York Motion Picture Corp.; Kay-Bee. *Dist* Triangle Film Corp. 2 Dec **1916**. Si; b&w. 5 reels.

Pres Thomas H. Ince. *Supv* Thomas H. Ince. *Prod* Thomas H. Ince. *Dir* Reginald Barker. *Scen* C. Gardner Sullivan. *Cam* Charles Kaufman. *Art dir* Robert Brunton.

Cast: Clara Williams (*Naneta*), William Desmond (*Donald White*), Enid Willis (*The baby*), Joseph J. Dowling (*Carlos Lupoli*), Gertrude Claire (*Mother Marie*), Charles K. French (*Pietro*), Walt Whitman (*Police magistrate*).

Drama. Italian immigrant Naneta finds a baby at her tenement and takes care of it, then asks writer Donald White, who frequents the restaurant where she works, to read the note pinned to the child. The note explains that the baby is illegitimate. The police arrest Naneta for kidnapping, but she refuses to clear herself by detailing the baby's origins because she herself had been illegitimate, and does not want the baby so labeled. Finally, Donald comes to the authorities and explains everything, and then, to Naneta's delight, he proposes to her, and the couple decides to adopt the baby. *Authors. Foundlings. Illegitimacy. Immigrants. Italian Americans. Self-sacrifice. Adoption. False arrests. Police. Tenement-houses.*

Motog 11 Nov 1916, p. 1094. *MPN* 4 Nov 1916, p. 2866. *MPW* 4 Nov 1916, p. 691. *MPW* 2 Dec 1916, pp. 1286-87. *MPW* 9 Dec 1916, p. 1549. *NYDM* 28 Oct 1916, p. 26. *Var* 27 Oct 1916, p. 27. *Wid's* 26 Oct 1916, p. 1059.

THE CRIMINAL CODE (*foreign version*) *see* EL CÓDIGO PENAL

THE CRIMSON FOG *see* OUT OF HE CRIMSON FOG

THE CRIMSON KIMONO (Japanese Americans)
Globe Enterprises, Inc. *Dist* Columbia Pictures Corp. 14 Sep **1959**; Prod: 16 Feb—10 Mar 1959 [©Columbia Pictures Corp.; 1 Oct 1959; LP14532]. Sd (RCA Sound System); b&w. 10 reels, 7,317 ft. 80-82 min. PCA cert no. 19349.

Prod Samuel Fuller. *Dir* Samuel Fuller. *Asst dir* Floyd Joyer. *Wrt* Samuel Fuller. *Dir of photog* Sam Leavitt. *Art dir* William E. Flannery and Robert Boyle. *Film ed* Jerome Thoms. *Set dec* James A. Crowe. *Cost* Bernice Pontrelli. *Mus comp and cond* Harry Sukman. *Orch* Leo Shuken and Jack Hayes. *Rec supv* John Livadary. *Sd* Josh Westmoreland. *Makeup supv* Clay Campbell. *Hair styles supplied by* Helen Hunt. [*Stand-in* Allen Pinson and Stacey Morgan].

Cast: Victoria Shaw [(*Christine Downes*)], Glenn Corbett [(*Detective Sgt. Charlie Bancroft*)], James Shigeta [(*Detective Joe Kojaku*)], Anna Lee [(*Mac*)], Paul Dubov [(*Casale*)], Jaclynne Greene [(*Roma*)], Neyle Morrow [(*Hansel, also known as Paul Sand*)], Gloria Pall [(*Sugar Torch*)], Barbara Hayden [(*Mother*)], George Yoshinaga [(*Willy Hidaka*)], Kaye Elhardt [(*Nun*)], Aya Oyama [(*Sister Gertrude*)], George Okamura [(*Karate*)], Reverend Ryosho S. Sogabe [(*Priest*)], Robert Okazaki [(*Yoshinaga*)], Fuji [(*Shuto*)], [Robert Kino (*Announcer*)], [Jack Carol (*Specialist*)], [Brian O'Hara (*Police captain*)], [David McMahon (*Uniformed policeman*)], [Harrison Lewis (*Waiter*)], [Walter Burke (*Ziggy*)], [Torau Mori (*Kendo referee*)], [Edo Mita (*Japanese gardener*)], [Chiyo Toto (*Japanese woman*)], [Katie Sweet (*Little girl*)], [Stafford Repp (*City librarian*)], [Nina Roman (*College girl*)], [Rollin Moriyama], [Carol Nugent].

Police, Drama. [*Print viewed*]. In Los Angeles' Little Tokyo neighborhood, a stripper named Sugar Torch is shot and killed one night. Homicide detectives Charlie Bancroft and Joe Kojaku learn while examining the Japanese art that adorns the dancer's dressing room that she had been developing a new act. In the narative paintings, Sugar is dressed as a geisha, and she and her Japanese lover

are killed onstage by a jealous karate expert. Joe, who knows everyone in Little Tokyo, questions local kendo and karate practitioners about the identity of the male characters in the new act, while Charlie seeks out Christine Downes, the artist who painted the portrait of Sugar in her kimono. Back at the apartment they share, Joe confesses to Charlie that because his girl friend was reared in Japan and he in the United States, they argue about the "old country" constantly. Later Charlie questions Chris, an art student at the University of Southern California, about the man who commissioned Sugar's portrait, Mr. Hansel. As she sketches Hansel's portrait, Charlie flirts with Chris and she smiles. Joe discovers from two nuns that a formidable Korean man named Shuto, who was to be the karate expert in the strip tease act, knows his old friend, Mr. Yoshinaga. Joe finds the kindly Yoshinaga in the local Buddhist temple, where he has come to observe the anniversary of his son's death. After the private ceremony, he leads Joe through Little Tokyo to the Koga Rice Cake Co. Shuto, who works at the factory, panics when he sees the detective, and Joe loses sight of him during the ensuing chase. Charlie's friend Mac, an eccentric but endearing artist who lives on Skid Road, worries that because Chris's sketch of Hansel has now been broadcast on television, the criminal might try to kill her. As feared, someone takes a shot at Chris that night. For her protection, she moves in with Charlie and Joe, and when fear causes her to burst into tears, Charlie kisses her. Later, Charlie and Joe visit Roma, a wigmaker, who knows Hansel, but she provides little information. They then learn that Hansel has just left his position as an Asian specialist at the public library, where he was known by his actual name, Paul Sand. That evening, Joe and Chris realize while talking together that they are deeply in love. Afraid of hurting Charlie, Joe resolves to hide his feelings from his friend, but becomes sullen and uncommunicative. Worried by Joe's moodiness, Charlie fears that Chris may have inadvertently expressed prejudice toward Joe, and this concern causes Chris to realize the depth of the men's friendship. Joe and Charlie face off in the Nisei Week kendo demonstration, and Joe surprises everyone by attacking his friend mercilessly. Later, Joe confesses his love for Chris. When Charlie looks up and gravely asks Joe if he intends to marry Chris, Joe assumes that his friend's anger is based on racism and is devasted. After expressing his confusion to Chris, Joe packs his bags, resigns from the force, and prepares to leave town. Chris and Charlie try to persuade him that neither of them feels anything but love for him, but Joe cannot believe this. As Chris is speaking, she suddenly sees Hansel. When Charlie and Joe corner him, Hansel claims that as an Asian specialist, he only meant to advise Sugar Torch on her act. When they ask Hansel why he shot the stripper, Roma appears and takes a shot at Charlie. Joe pursues her through the Nisei Week parade and is finally forced to shoot her. As they await the ambulance, the distressed woman admits it was she who killed Sugar. Having assumed that Hansel preferred the stripper to her, the wigmaker killed her rival, but later realized there was nothing between the two. Joe takes this in and immediately turns and apologizes to Charlie. As the friends reconcile, Chris runs into Joe's arms and they kiss. *Friendship. Japanese Americans. Los Angeles (CA)–Little Tokyo. Murder. Asian Americans. Romantic rivalry. Alcoholics. Artists. Attempted murder. Buddhism. Chases. Detectives. False accusations. Jealousy. Karate. Kendo. Korean Americans. Libraries and librarians. Murder. Parades. Racism. Rites and ceremonies. Strip-tease. Wigs.*

Note: The film's working title was *The White Kimono*. The *MPHPD* reviewer remarked about the film, "For the first time, an American film tells a story in which a Japanese boy wins the white girl....Shigeta's clean cut appearance will temper the shock of the fadeout kiss and the ultimate Japanese boy-American girl relationship." The *Var* reviewer was not pleased with the picture. "Although Fuller's attempts to probe racial prejudice were undoubtedly motivated by a worthy desire, it doesn't work out very well....the racial tolerance plea gets cheapened by its inclusion in a film of otherwise straight action." The *MPHPD* reviewer noted that this picture marked the film debuts of both James Shigeta and Glenn Corbett. Much of the picture was filmed in the Little Tokyo section of Los Angeles.

Box 14 Sep 1959. *DV* 9 Sep 1959, p. 3. *Exh* 23 Sep 1959, p. 4637. *FD* 14 Sep 1959, p. 7. *Har* 12 Sep 1959, p. 147. *HR* 9 Sep 1959, p. 3. *LAEx* 29 Mar 1959. *MPHPD* 12 Sep 1959, p. 403. *Var* 9 Sep 1959, p. 6.

THE CRIMSON MASK *see* CALIFORNIA CONQUEST

THE CRIMSON SKULL (African Americans)
Norman Film Mfg. Co. **1922**; New York State opening: 20 Apr 1922; Prod: Oct 1921. Si; b&w. 6 reels, 5,934 ft.

Cast: Anita Bush (*Anita Nelson*), Lawrence Chenault (*Bob Calem*), Bill Pickett, Steve Reynolds.

African American, Mystery, Western. [*Not viewed*]. When the peaceful black city of Boley, Oklahoma falls under the control of an outlaw known as "The Skull" and his band of henchman, "The Terrors," the Boley Law and Order League offers a one-thousand dollar reward for the Skull's capture, dead or alive. The League also forces the resignation of the sheriff, a Skull puppet, and gives the job to the respected Lem Nelson, a cattleman and owner of the Crown C ranch. Bob Calem, the Crown C foreman, volunteers to infiltrate the Skull's gang in order to hasten the criminals' capture. When Steve Reynolds, a one-legged cowboy, and Anita Nelson, Lem's daughter, as well as Bob's sweetheart, are kidnapped by the gang, Bob helps them to escape. He is accused of being a traitor, but the gang cannot decide whether Bob is guilty or innocent, so they leave his fate to the test of "The Crimson Skull," in which one drop of blood will determine whether he lives or dies. [No further information regarding the plot has been located.]. *African Americans. Cowboys. Oklahoma. Outlaws. Ranch foremen. Trials. Fathers and daughters. Handicapped. Kidnapping. Ranchers. Romance. Sheriffs.*

Note: Norman Film Manufacturing Co. was located in Jacksonville, FL. According to its pressbook, the film was produced in "the All-Colored City of Boley, Okla." Lawrence Chenault, who played three roles, including the film's hero and villain, had earlier been a member of the Anita Bush Dramatic Stock Company. Bush, who made her motion picture debut in *The Crimson Skull*, started acting in New York theater in 1903, and following her success at the Lincoln Theater in Harlem, became known as "The Little Mother of Colored Drama." The pressbook stated that the film's "action and story [are] on a par with white productions with the drawing feature of a cast composed entirely of colored artists. (There is not a white character in it.) And a story free from the usual mimicry of the colored man; free from 'race problems' that engender friction." Publicity material stated that the cast included "30 colored cowboys." According to *ChiDef*, actor Steve Reynolds appeared in person when the film showed in Nashville in Nov 1922.

ChiDef 18 Nov 1922, p. 7.

CROOKED MONEY *see* **WHILE THOUSANDS CHEER**

CROSS ROADS (Latino, Native Americans, Yaqui)
William M. Smith Productions. *Dist* Merit Film Corp. Dec **1922**. Si; b&w. 5 reels, 4,500 ft.

Dir? Francis Ford.

Cast: Franklyn Farnum (*The Hero*), Shorty Hamilton (*Onate*), Al Hart (*The Yaqui*), Genevieve Bert (*Jackie*).

Western. "A young Westerner on the Mexican border is prevented from being made sheriff by a cunning Mexican, Onate, who forges the papers and makes himself sheriff. He immediately starts proceedings against the real sheriff and forces him to kill a man in own defense. The Westerner escapes and is befriended by a lonely girl, Jackie, whom everyone shuns because of a belief that she brings bad luck. He is pursued and imprisoned by Onate's men, but Jackie obtains a pardon from the governor and Onate's faithful servant, the Indian, turns traitor for the sake of her American friend. Onate is punished, the sheriff's commission is restored to the right man, and Jackie finds that her curse has finally been removed." (*MPW* 6 Jan 1923, p. 61.). *Mexicans. Sheriffs. Superstition. Yaqui Indians.*

Note: This film was probably directed by Francis Ford, who directed several other Farnum features for Smith in this period. *The Lariat Thrower* (licensed in New York State 2 Dec 1922, produced by William M. Smith Productions in 5 reels, and starring Franklyn Farnum) may be the same film.

CROSSFIRE (Jewish Americans, Irish Americans)
RKO Radio Pictures, Inc. *Dist* RKO Radio Pictures, Inc. 15 Aug **1947**; New York opening: 22 Jul 1947; *Prod:* 4 Mar—28 Mar 1947; retakes 31 Mar and 22 Apr 1947 [©RKO Radio Pictures, Inc.; 22 Jul 1947; LP1194]. Sd (RCA Sound System); b&w. 7,696 ft. 86 min. PCA cert no. 12325.

Pres DORE SCHARY. *Prod* Adrian Scott. *Dir* Edward Dmytryk. *Asst dir* Nate Levinson and [Cliff Reid]. *Dial dir* William E. Watts. *Scr* John Paxton. *Dir of photog* J. Roy Hunt. *Spec eff* Russell A. Cully. *Art dir* Albert S. D'Agostino and Alfred Herman. *Film ed* Harry Gerstad. *Set dec* Darrell Silvera and John Sturtevant. *Mus dir* C. Bakaleinikoff. *Mus* Roy Webb. [*Mus performed by* Kid Ory's Creole Jazz Band]. *Sd* John E. Tribby and Clem Portman. *Makeup supv* Gordon Bau. [*Stand-in* B. Scott, C. Bidwell, Sam Lufkin and Charles Cirillo].

Source: Based on the novel *The Brick Foxhole* by Richard Brooks (New York, 1945).

Cast: ROBERT YOUNG ([*Captain*] *Finlay*), ROBERT MITCHUM ([*Sgt. Felix*] *Keeley*), ROBERT RYAN ([*Sgt.*] *Montgomery*), Gloria Grahame (*Ginny* [*Tremaine*]), Paul Kelly (*The man*), Sam Levene ([*Joseph*] *Samuels*), Jacqueline White (*Mary Mitchell*), Steve Brodie (*Floyd* [*Bowers*]), George Cooper ([*Corp. Arthur*] *Mitchell*), Richard Benedict (*Bill* [*Williams*]), Richard Powers (*Detective* [*Dick*]), William Phipps (*Leroy*), Lex Barker (*Harry*), Marlo Dwyer (*Miss Lewis*), [Harry Harvey (*Man in hallway*)], [Carl Faulkner (*Deputy*)], [Jay Norris, Robert Bray, George Turner, Don Cadell (*M.P.s*)], [Philip Morris (*Police sergeant*)], [Kenneth McDonald (*Major*)], [Allen Ray (*Soldier*)], [Bill Nind (*Waiter*)], [George Meader (*Police surgeon*)].

Postwar life, Drama. [*Print viewed*]. In a dark Washington, D.C. apartment, two men beat up another man and leave him for dead. A short time later, police captain Finlay, who has been called to the murder scene, questions Miss Lewis, the woman who discovered the body. Miss Lewis tells Finlay that, earlier in the evening, she and the victim, Joseph Samuels, were drinking in a bar with a trio of recently discharged soldiers, one of whom Samuels then invited to his apartment. After Miss Lewis states that she left Samuels alone with the soldier, returning only after Samuels failed to answer his phone, army sergeant Montgomery appears at the door, looking for Corp. Arthur "Mitch" Mitchell. Montgomery claims that he and another friend, Floyd Bowers, were with Mitch in Samuels' apartment, but that Mitch left abruptly, promising to return soon. As he has found the corporal's wallet in the apartment, Finlay determines to locate Mitch and brings his best friend, Sgt. Felix Keeley, in for questioning. While maintaining his friend's innocence, Keeley tells Finlay that Mitch, a painter, is suffering from post-war depression and is estranged from his wife Mary. Finlay then re-questions Montgomery, a former policeman, who describes Samuels as a draft-dodging "Jewboy." Montgomery repeats that, after following Mitch to Samuels' apartment, he and Bowers left shortly after Mitch. Concerned for Mitch, Keeley sends all of the servicemen in their hotel to search for him. With his friends's help, the corporal manages to elude some M.P.'s, and flees to a movie theater with Keeley. Mitch then tells Keeley his version of that night's events: After Samuels takes Mitch to his apartment, Montgomery bursts in with Floyd and picks a fight with Samuels. Suddenly ill, Mitch leaves Samuels' and meets a sympathetic taxi dancer named Ginny Tremaine, who invites him to wait for her at her place. There Mitch runs into an odd man, who claims at first to be Ginny's husband, then insists he is not. Unnerved by the man, Mitch leaves and staggers back to the hotel. Back in the theater, Keeley informs Mitch that Mary is in town, anxious to see him, then hears that Floyd has been found hiding out in Maryland. Before the police can question Floyd, Montgomery appears at his door, demanding that they "get their story straight." A nervous Floyd agrees to corroborate Montgomery's story to the police and promises not to speak to anyone about the incident. When Keeley and another soldier, Bill Williams, come knocking, Montgomery hides and eavesdrops as Floyd reveals that he called his friend Leroy, who was in the bar briefly with Mitch and Samuels. After Keeley and Bill leave, an enraged Montgomery beats and strangles Floyd, leaving him for dead. Later, Finlay questions Keeley about Floyd's murder and learns about Ginny. Keeley then meets with Mary and directs her to the movie theater where Mitch is still hiding. After reuniting with her confused husband, Mary offers to question the taxi dancer on his behalf and goes with Finlay to Ginny's apartment. Neither Ginny nor the strange man, however, can provide a convincing alibi for Mitch. Frustrated, Finlay re-interrogates Montgomery, who unwittingly exposes himself as the killer when he displays his hatred of Jews and thereby supplies a motive for the crime. Delivering a passionate speech on the evils of antisemitism, Finlay then convinces a frightened Leroy, who has been found by Keeley, to participate in a plot to trap Montgomery. In a men's room, Leroy tells Montgomery that he has just spoken with Floyd and that Floyd is demanding blackmail money from him. After Leroy gives him an address for Floyd, which lists the correct building but the wrong apartment number, Montgomery sneaks into Floyd's apartment. There he is startled to run into Finlay, who calmly points out that the only way that Montgomery could have known which apartment belonged to Floyd was if he had been there earlier. In a panic, Montgomery runs out of the building, but is shot dead in the street by Finlay. *Antisemitism. Investigations. Murder. Police detectives. Veterans. Apartments. Bathrooms. Hotels. Motion picture theaters. Post-traumatic stress disorder. Separation (Marital). Taxi dancers. Traps. United States. Army. Washington (D.C.).*

Note: The working titles of this film were *The Brick Foxhole* and *Cradle of Fear*. In Richard Brooks's novel, the character "Montgomery" kills "Samuels" not because he is a Jew, but because he is a homosexual. PCA director Joseph I. Breen described the novel in a 17 Jul 1945 letter to RKO executive William Gordon, contained in the MPAA/PCA files at the AMPAS Library, as "thoroughly and completely unacceptable, on a dozen or more counts." In Feb 1947, however, after screenwriter John Paxton had completely eliminated the homosexual plot line from the story, Breen endorsed the project, but cautioned that the final film should contain "no suggestion of a 'pansy' characterization about Samuels or his relationship with the soldiers."

Contemporary news items add the following information about the production: In Mar 1946, Dick Powell, who had previously starred in two successful Edward Dmytryk/Adrian Scott/John Paxton pictures, *Murder My Sweet* and *Cornered*, was announced as the film's probable star. Robert Young eventually agreed to do the picture on condition that it be shot on a twenty-four day schedule, which it eventually was. RKO borrowed Gloria Grahame from M-G-M for the production.

A Mar 1947 *NYT* article described *Crossfire* as one of the first Hollywood films of the 1940s to "face questions of racial and religious prejudice with more forthright courage than audiences have been accustomed to expect." While RKO was producing *Crossfire*, Twentieth Century-Fox was making *Gentleman's Agreement*, another story about antisemitism. RKO raced to beat the much "ballyhooed" Fox picture to the theaters, releasing *Crossfire* several months before *Gentleman's Agreement*. In Jul 1947, RKO screened *Crossfire* for representatives of various Los Angeles religious groups. In addition, several surveys, which were designed to gauge the audience's prejudices, were conducted before and after screenings of the film. *Crossfire* received both praise and criticism for its depiction of antisemitism in America and was the subject of many editorials. Some Jewish leaders protested Montgomery's extreme brand of antisemitism, which they felt could be too easily dismissed by the audience.

Crossfire was Dmytryk's and Scott's last film for RKO. In Oct 1947, the House Committee on Un-American Activities (HUAC) called the filmmakers as "unfriendly" witnesses before their Congressional hearings. HUAC, which was formed by Congress in 1938 to investigate a variety of political extremists, had dedicated itself solely to exposing communist and left-wing activities after World War II, and, in late 1947, turned its attention specifically to the film industry. Scott and Dmytryk became the first two members of the infamous "Hollywood Ten," a group of producers, writers and directors who were indicted for contempt of Congress when they refused to state whether they were or had been communists. Other members of the Hollywood Ten included screenwriters Alvah Bessie, Lester Cole, John Howard Lawson, Dalton Trumbo, Ring Larnder, Jr., Samuel Ornitz and Albert Maltz and producer-director Herbert Biberman. In Apr 1948, the Hollywood Ten were tried at the Federal Court in Washington, D.C., and were convicted of contempt of Congress. All ten served prison terms and, for many years, were blacklisted from the film industry. Some, including others who were implicated in later years, continued to write using pseudonyms. In Jan 1948, Dmytryk, whose contract at RKO was dropped after the indictment, sued the studio for $1,783,425, claiming anguish, loss of salary, screen fame and artistic reputation as well as personal humiliation due to his firing. The disposition of that lawsuit has not been discovered. In Sep 1950, however, the imprisoned Dmytryk broke his silence, stating that he was once a member of the Communist Party, and was released early from jail. When Dmytryk testified a second time for HUAC in 1951, he implicated others, including Scott, as communists, and thereby removed himself from Hollywood's blacklist. His next American-made film was the 1952 picture *Mutiny*. Scott, however, continued to be blacklisted and never produced another picture.

Because of its modest $589,000 budget, *Crossfire* was touted as a model "sleeper" hit. According to modern sources, it grossed $1,270,000 and was RKO's biggest hit of 1947. *Crossfire* received an Academy Award nomination for Best Picture, but lost to *Gentleman's Agreement*. It was also nominated for Best Supporting Actor (Ryan), Best Supporting Actress (Grahame), Best Director and Best Screenplay (Adaptation). In Sep 1947, *Crossfire* was named Best Social Film at Cannes. In Dec 1947, *Ebony* magazine, an African-American publication, gave the film its annual award for "improving interracial understanding."

Box 28 Jun 1947. *DN* 4 Dec 1947. *DN* 9 Mar 1948, p. 23, 26. *DV* 25 Jun 1947. *FD* 27 Jun 1947, p. 8. *HR* 15 Mar 1946, p. 1. *HR* 4 Dec 1946, p. 11. *HR* 6 Mar 1947, p. 4. *HR* 11 Mar 1947, p. 11. *HR* 25 Jun 1947, p. 3. *HR* 6 Aug 1947, p. 8. *HR* 30 Sep 1947, p. 3. *HR* 8 Jan 1948, p. 1. *HR* 11 Sep 1950, p. 8. *IFJ* 15 Mar 1947, p. 41. *Life* 30 Jun 1947, pp. 71-73. *MPHPD* 28 Jun 1947, p. 3701. *NYT* 16 Mar 1947. *NYT* 6 Jul 1947. *NYT* 23 Jul 1947, p. 19. *NYT* 25 Jan 1948. *Var* 25 Jun 1947, p. 8.

CROSSOVER see **PINKY**

THE CROWD ROARS (*foreign version*) *see* **LA FOULE HURLE**

CROWDED PARADISE (Latino)

IMPS, Inc. *Dist* Tudor Pictures, Inc. Jun 1956; Prod: began 12 May 1954. Sd; b&w. 10 reels, 8,543 ft. 93-94 min. PCA cert no. 18105. English language with Spanish-language sequences.

Pres BEN GRADUS. *Prod* Ben Gradus. *Assoc prod* Walter Sachs. *Dir* Fred Pressburger. *Loc seq in New York and Puerto Rico dir* by Ben Gradus. *Asst dir* C. James Di Gangi. *Wrt* Arthur Forrest. *Addl scenes by* Marc Connelly. *Dir of photog* Boris Kaufman. *Op cam* Morris Hartzband. *Optical eff* Cineffects, Inc. of N.Y. *Prod des* Richard Sylbert. *Art dir* Carl Kent. *Film ed* Rita Roland. *Ed asst* Irving Sachs,

Lucy Sabsay and Neil Matz. *Ward* Florence Transfield and Beatrice Leon. *Mus comp and dir* David Broekman. *Sd rec* James Gleason and William Schwartz. *Makeup* Eddie Senz. *Hairdresser* Helen Grizuk and Maria Stevens. *Scr clerk* Faith Elliott and Patricia Jaffe. *Prod asst* Barbara Wiegand and Fabio Coen. *Tech adv* Miriam Colon. *Tech consultant* Clarence O. Senior and Joseph Monserrat.

Song(s): "Moon Magic," based on a Puerto Rican folk theme, music by Terry Stern and David Broekman, lyrics by Sammy Gallop; "Mi Rumbon" and "Pastilellero," written by William Gonzalez; "Violetta," by Rafael Alers.

Cast: HUME CRONYN [(*George Heath*)], NANCY KELLY [(*Louise Heath*)], And Introducing Mario Alcalde [(*Juan Negron Figueroa*)], Starring Frank Silvera [(*Papa Diaz*)], and Enid Rudd [(*Felicia Diaz*)], With David Opatoshu [(*Jack Kaufer*)], Ralph Dunn [(*Detective Green*)], Carlos Montalban [(*Uncle Felipe*)], Santos Ortega, Miriam Colon [(*Cousin Maria Rodriquez*)], Marita Reid [(*Mrs. Diaz*)], Stefan Schnabel [(*Fat drunk*)], Charles Welch, Miguel A. Rodriguez, Elliott Sullivan, Henry Silva, Mary Bell, Bert Freed, Nita De Soto, Rock Rogers, Jack Davis, Mike Keane, John Graham, Carolyn Sullivan, William E. Gonzalez, Angel Luis Diaz Lebron, Gilberto Diaz Lebron.

Social, Drama. [*Print viewed*]. Juan Negron Figueroa, a young auto mechanic, plans to leave his home in Puerto Rico to go to New York City and marry Felicia Diaz, a Puerto Rican American who lives in New York, whom he met when she vacationed in Puerto Rico. On New York's upper West Side, Felicia's father objects to the couple's plans. Proud of his own rise from an impoverished immigrant to a skilled union worker, he does not want Felicia to marry a newcomer like he once was, feeling he will then have slaved twenty years for nothing. With a jar containing eighty-five dollars in coins that his mother saved for him to pay for music at the wedding, Juan arrives in New York and lives with a cousin and her family. When Juan visits Felicia, he meets the bigoted superintendent of her building, George Heath, a recovering alcoholic and ex-convict who lives in the basement with his blind wife Louise. George spent two years in prison after slashing Louise with a broken bottle while intoxicated, which blinded her. She now keeps money under lock and key, and makes him promise not to drink whenever she doles him out some money. Louise thinks of Felicia as her best friend, but George, although he lusts after the young girl, hates Puerto Ricans. He tries to taunt Juan, asking why, if his country is the "paradise" that he describes, do so many of "you people" leave, and Juan replies that it is too crowded. Juan and Papa Diaz argue about his ability to get a job, and Juan brags that he can find work as a mechanic that will pay seventy to eighty dollars a week; however, because of discrimination against Puerto Ricans and the fact that he is unfamiliar with the equipment used in New York garages, Juan settles for a job as a dishwasher in a cafeteria. When a boxing promoter cannot get his South American heavyweight fighter into the U.S. because the fighter had once been in jail, he calls an underworld colleague, Jack Kaufer, for help. Jack, who had been in prison with George, contacts him, knowing that his apartment house is filled with Puerto Ricans, one of whom, he hopes, will sell his birth certificate that could then be used to show the fighter is an American citizen. Jealous of Felicia's love for Juan, George arranges for the police to film Juan selling his birth certificate to Kaufer. Juan, feeling that he can't ask Felicia to marry him on the wages he receives as a dishwasher, argues with her when she says she will get a job also. They decide to marry first and argue later, and go to look at apartments. After a landlady who promised Felicia a nice apartment, reneges on their agreement after meeting Juan, the couple is misled concerning a noisy, dark apartment run by a Puerto Rican landlord and his wife. Juan then decides to sell his birth certificate for $800; however, before the deal is consummated, he changes his mind, saying that it is not for sale because his mother's name is on it. At his cousin's crowded apartment, Juan tells Felicia that he will go to trade school for six months to learn all about the new gadgets so that he can make a decent salary. When he kills an animal crawling under the bed with repeated whacks of a broom, Felicia runs home in disgust. Because George has locked the inside door, she knocks on his window, and in the vestibule, George, intoxicated, makes indecent proposals to her, then grabs her when she refuses his entreaties. She bites his hand and escapes. Not wanting to hurt Louise, Felicia refuses to let her father call the police. Meanwhile, Detective Green asks for Juan's help in capturing Kaufer. Juan refuses, saying he plans to return to Puerto Rico. Green talks to him about being a patrolman in his

neighborhood, which, over the years, housed Irish, Jews and Italians. He relates the rough time that members of those groups had and predicts that Juan also will do all right if he gives himself time. Green says that it may take up to two months to get evidence against Kaufer, but Juan only agrees to help until he leaves in a few days. When Papa Diaz sees how unhappy his daughter is, he agrees to let her marry Juan. She decides she can suffer for six months, living in Juan's cousin's crowded apartment while Juan is in trade school, and she and Juan reconcile. While Louise waits in the Diaz apartment for the wedding party to return from the church, George breaks into the locked drawer where she hides her coins. He gets drunk in a bar and insults a Spanish-speaking man, who walks away rather than get into a fight with him. George then launches into a harangue against Puerto Ricans to a couple of drunken men, one of whom takes George to his apartment and shows him a souvenir German hand grenade that he bought at an army base. Meanwhile, Louise, finding her apartment broken into, calls the police. George comes to the wedding party at the Diaz apartment, and when he sees Juan and Felicia dancing, he destroys the wedding cake. Juan protects George from Papa Diaz, who is furious, and George threatens the group with the grenade. Louise then enters with the police, and when George sees them, he throws the grenade. Juan retrieves it and throws it out the window, but it does not explode, as it is empty. The police allow George to dress before arresting him, and as Louise ties his tie, he violently kisses her. She breaks away and slaps him, then berates him for intending to murder the group at the wedding. Detective Green comes by and tells Juan that he won't be able to use him to capture Kaufer, now that George has been arrested, but that Kaufer is bound to slip up sometime. Juan invites Green to join the celebration, and the couple vow that they both can learn from each other. *Bigotry. Class distinction. Discrimination in employment. Discrimination in housing. Engagements. Immigrants. New York City. Puerto Ricans. Superintendents. Alcoholics. Apartments. Attempted rape. Bars. Blindness. Cousins. Dishwashing. Employment agencies. Ex-convicts. Fathers and daughters. Fraud. Grenades. Jealousy. Landladies. Lechery. Mechanics. Police detectives. Puerto Rico. Thieves. Traps. Undercover operations. Weddings.*

Note: This film was shot in New York City and in Puerto Rico. Location shooting was done in East Harlem and Manhattan, while interiors were shot at the Fox Movietone Studios in New York. *MPH* praised Boris Kaufman's cinematography, saying he "has caught with a documentarian's eye the essence of his authentic locations, New York's West Side and Puerto Rico." *Var* commented that the film was "produced in almost documentary style" and called it "an arty theatre entry." Many of the actors were from the New York stage. Reviews were generally positive concerning the film's subject matter and the acting. *Cue* praised the film for its depiction of "racial bigotry and economic ostracism, residential restrictions imposed in Harlem's 'yellow ghetto,' and the prejudices of long-time Puerto Rican residents who look upon their newly arrived compatriots as 'foreigners.'" *NYT* wrote, "Although it fails to solve the many problems besetting Manhattan's burgeoning Puerto Rican population, *Crowded Paradise*... dramatizes a few of these ills with restraint and compassion." They criticized, however, the film's "sleazy facade." *MPH* called Mario Alcalde "a sort of Latin Brando type with a casual, natural acting style." Reviews predicted that the film would be appreciated by Puerto Rican-American audiences, and *Var* commented, "N.Y. City officials perhaps will be far from happy over some of the scenes or the closeups of ramshackle apartment structures." According to information in the MPAA/PCA Collection at the AMPAS Library, PCA director Joseph I. Breen complained to the production company about a scene in which "George" uses a broken bottle as a weapon, and one in which he pleads to be allowed to keep Felicia's shoe as a momento. He wrote the action "could be indicative of the fact that he is a sex pervert. This well-known token of fetishism—the shoe—we feel too plainly indicates that he is possibly a pervert."

Box 30 Jun 1956. *Cue* 23 Jun 1956. *DV* 8 May 1956, p. 3. *Exh* 25 Jul 1956, pp. 4193-94. *FD* 14 May 1956, p. 8. *HR* 27 Feb 1956. *MPD* 10 May 1956. *MPHPD* 12 May 1956, p. 889. *NYT* 9 May 1954. *NYT* 22 Jun 1956, p. 15. *Var* 5 May 1954. *Var* 9 May 1956, p. 6.

THE CROWNING EXPERIENCE (African Americans)

Moral Re-Armament. *Dist* Moral Re-Armament. **1960**; World premiere in New York City: 21 Oct 1960. Sd (Westrex Recording System); col (Technicolor). 11 reels, 8,987 ft. 102 min. PCA cert no. 19509.

[*Prod* Donald Birdsell]. [*Dir* Rickard Tegström, Marion Clayton Anderson and Harold Schuster]. [*Scr* Alan Thornhill and Cecil Broadhurst]. *Photog* Rickard Tegström. *Mus dir* Paul Dunlap. [*Mus comp and cond* George Fraser]. [*Asst to mus comp and cond* Richard Hadden, Frances Hadden, John Hopcraft, Herbie Allen, Waldemar Smith and Cecil Broadhurst]. *Mus rec* David Forrest. [*Sd* Jack Dickson].

Song(s): "Sweet Potato Pie," "The World Walked into My Heart Today," "I've Gotta Scoop," "There's Always Room for One More," and other original songs by Will Reed and George Fraser.

Source: Based on the play *The Crowning Experience* by Alan Thornhill and Cecil Broadhurst (Detroit, 25 Dec 1958).

Cast: Muriel Smith [(*Emma C. Tremaine*)], Ann Buckles [(*Sarah Miller Spriggs*)], Louis Byles [(*Charlie Winter, as a man*)], [Vernon Slaughter (*Emma's faithful retainer*)], [George McCurdy (*Charlie Winter, as a boy*)], [William Pawley, Jr. (*Mr. Spriggs*)], [Phyllis Konstam Austin (*Mrs. Spriggs*)], [Anna Marie McCurdy (*Julie*)], [Robert Anderson (*Blaney*)], [Cecil Broadhurst (*Editor*)], [Angelo Pasetto].

Religious, Social, Drama, with songs. [*Print viewed*]. In Washington, D.C., Emma C. Tremaine remembers her past: An African American, Emma teaches small children of her race at an open-air school and hopes one day to have a real college there. Charlie Winter, who can't read, is brought to the school by police who caught him stealing a pair of shoes. The police are deferential to Sarah Miller Spriggs, a white woman who is editor of the school paper, and leave Charlie in her care. Charlie is critical of Sarah because her parents have money, and when Emma tries to talk to him, he lashes out that he does not want people to be nice to him and desires revenge because his mother died from not getting enough to eat. Charlie is attracted, though, to Emma's daughter Julie. With the financial backing of Sarah's parents, Emma's dream of a college becomes a reality in ten years, and Charlie and Julie graduate. After the ceremony, Blaney, a white Communist, explains to Charlie and Julie he is working to bring an end to exploitation. As Emma becomes a voice for education throughout the country, Julie, who has to take care of the college, berates her mother for her seemingly endless rounds of banquets and speeches. When Charlie tells Emma that he and Julie are getting married, and that Blaney, who has been recruiting other students, will set them up in Washington, Emma is angered, but she gives them her blessing. A number of years later, Emma is chosen as a guest speaker at the Washington Ladies' Literary Club, the first of her race to be invited, Sarah, now a top reporter, brags she can get a scoop. Some of the club members, including Sarah's mother, argue that inviting Emma is a mistake. When she arrives, there is some uneasiness and snubbing, until Emma relates a lesson she learned from her mother: there's always room for one more. Even though she grew up in a three-room shack in a family of sixteen, her mother always made room for friends and neighbors. She then reveals she has received a letter from the President of the United States, who requests that she serve on the National Advisory Board. Back at the college, Emma overhears Charlie criticize her philosophy to a group of students, whom he encourages to join him in a mass rally. Emma refuses to allow it, reminding them of Lincoln's ideal of malice toward none and charity toward all. When the students agree with Charlie, Emma, distraught, prays for God to show her the answer. She then admonishes Julie and Charlie, telling them not to come back until they feel differently. During the next eight years, life is difficult for Julie, who learns that Charlie has become a trained revolutionary. When Sarah's chief sends her to cover a Moral Re-Armament conference on Mackinac Island, Michigan, she invites Emma to join her. At the conference, top-level people from all over the world, representing government, labor and business, try to solve world issues by understanding the roots of human nature. Julie, to whom Emma has not spoken for years, is at the conference also. She tells her mother that when Blaney moved in with her and Charlie, she moved out. Sarah explains to Emma that she felt the need for wisdom greater than her own when she realized that a breakdown in civilization was occurring. Emma agrees that, despite her faith in education, there has been a breakdown in the morals of youth, of which Blaney and thousands like him take advantage. Sarah believes that only an ideology superior to Blaney's can work. Moral Re-Armament, she tells Emma, advises that one should begin with one's self to correct problems in the world. Sarah encourages Emma to write her thoughts about herself, and Emma complies, then reads them to Sarah: that she is full of self-importance and too busy; that she failed Julie; and that she never gave Charlie a purpose big enough for which to live and thus let Blaney take over his life. Meanwhile, although Blaney warns Charlie to forget Julie, Charlie goes to see her at the conference, where he sees participants of all races and peoples. Sarah's mother, who earlier snubbed Emma because of racism, rises

out of her wheelchair and confesses that generations have been kept in bondage because of her type of pride—she used tolerance and patronage as a balm, and confesses to Emma that in her heart, she refused to meet her as a woman. She asks Emma's forgiveness and they cry together. Emma confesses having an ache still in her heart for a boy she once loved like a son, whom she failed. Charlie listens to voices from his past and realizes that he has never really believed that man is shaped by his economic environment. He feels that if human nature can be changed, as Moral Re-Armament affirms, it is the most revolutionary fact in history and makes Blaney's ideas seem small and out-of-date. He takes the arms of Emma and Julie and tells them of his decision to stay. People from the conference walk together, and Emma explains that remaking the world by being a part of the great unifying force is the crowning experience of her life. *African Americans. African-American leadership. Mary McLeod Bethune. Colleges. Communism. Moral rearmament. Mothers and daughters. Religion. Religious conversion. Schoolteachers. Social reform. Women in politics. Clubs. College sports. Confession (Religion). Mackinac Island (MI). Marriage. Meetings. Prayer. Racism. Reporters. Revenge. Revolutionaries. Separation (Marital). Snobs and snobbishness. Speeches. Washington (D.C.). Wheelchairs.*

Note: After the opening credits, the film begins with the following statement: "This story is inspired by the life of Mary McLeod Bethune, who was born of slave parents and rose to become adviser to the President." According to information in the Moral Re-Armament, Inc. Collection at the Library of Congress Manuscripts Division, Moral Re-Armament (MRA) was organized in 1938 in London. A precursor organization, the Oxford Group, began in the early 1920s. MRA's leader was Frank Buchman, originally a Lutheran minister from Pennsylvania, who also has been said to have inspired Alcoholics Anonymous. The group did not align itself with any specific religious denomination, preferring an ecumenical approach and including among its adherents Buddhists and Hindus, in addition to Protestants and Catholics. Buchman achieved success in converting people to the group's ideas and goals through emotional group confessional techniques. MRA's four core teachings were absolute honesty, purity, love and unselfishness. In 1939, the group advocated efforts to prevent war, and following World War II, it initiated a campaign to offer an alternative to international communism, concentrating its work in Europe, Japan, Africa, Asia and South America. Critics of the organization have associated it with appeasement in regard to its attitude towards Nazi Germany, and pro-fascism. MRA attracted a number of world leaders, such as Mahatma Gandhi and West German Chancellor Konrad Adenauer. In a souvenir booklet published by Random House for the film's premiere, Gandhi is quoted as saying, "Moral Re-Armament is the best thing that ever came from the West to the East." According to the *MPD* review of the film, the goal of MRA was to "put right what is wrong in the world" by starting with the individual. Rajmohan Gandhi, grandson of the Mahatma, stated MRA's philosophy: "Human nature can be changed—that is the root of the answer. National economies can be changed—that is the fruit of the answer. World history can be changed—that is the destiny of our age." MRA was responsible for the "Up with People" musical programs of the 1960s. Buchman died in 1961, and by 1975, MRA was being phased out as an active organization.

The character of "Emma Tremaine" in *The Crowning Experience* was based on the African-American educator and presidential adviser Mary McLeod Bethune. According to the souvenir booklet produced for the film's premiere, Bethune was born in Jul 1875 in Mayesville, SC, the youngest of seventeen children, to former slaves. She was the founder and president of Bethune-Cookman College in Daytona, Florida; advised Presidents Hoover and Roosevelt; founded the National Council of Negro Women; and was the vice-president of the National Association for the Advancement of Colored People. According to an unpublished biography of Buchman by MRA's director Ray Foote Purdy, in the Moral Re-Armament, Inc. Collection, after Bethune visited an MRA Assembly, she "lost her passionate protagonism of race and felt she must carry in her heart as a forgiven sinner the compassion for all men everywhere that God imposed upon her." Before she died in 1955, Bethune requested that the following inscription, from a statement she made at an Assembly in Caux, Switzerland, be placed on her tombstone at Bethune-Cookman College: "Moral Re-Armament. To be a part of this great uniting force of our age is the crowning experience of my life."

According to the Purdy biography, African-American actress and singer Muriel Smith (who previously had been in *Carmen Jones* and *The King and I* on Broadway) visited MRA's Assembly at Mackinac Island, MI in 1958 and became involved with the group. (Assemblies had been held at Mackinac since 1942.) In the souvenir booklet for the film, Smith writes, "The historical past of my people and their emergence from the bonds of slavery are in the records of history as one of the great miracles of this age. We are equipped to understand the meaning of slavery. We know what is the real meaning of victory through peace. We have been prepared by history for the supreme part in this our nation's task in setting the whole world free." Smith urged that a play based on Bethune's life be written. The play, starring Smith and Ann Buckles, who also had become involved with MRA and who acts in the film, was presented at Christmas, 1958 in Detroit, and then for four months in Atlanta and seven weeks at the National Theatre in Washington, D.C. During the Atlanta run, according to the Purdy biography, Smith received a number of offers from Samuel Goldwyn to star in the film version of *Porgy and Bess*. Although she acted in *The Crowning Experience* for no salary, she refused the Goldwyn offer and

challenged him instead to make a film version of the play.

According to the Purdy biography, most of this film, the first produced by MRA, was shot at Mackinac Island, MI, with some scenes filmed at the home of Mrs. Francis Crosby on the California coast, south of San Francisco. *FD* stated that the film was produced with Screen Gems facilities. Joel McCrea narrated a special prologue to the film, which was recorded at Mackinac Island. Sources disagree concerning the film's director. While no director is listed in the onscreen credits, a number of sources, including ads for the film, the Purdy biography and the souvenir booklet state that Rickard Tegström (who received an onscreen "Photographed by" credit) "directed and filmed" the picture; Marion Clayton Anderson is credited as director in some reviews; and Harold Schuster is listed as director in the *Los Angeles Mirror* review. Publicity for the film noted that Tegström, a Swedish documentarist, had made films for Walt Disney. Most of the film's cast were non-professionals. Louis Byles, who played "Charlie Winter," was a Jamaican attorney who helped draft the constitution of the West Indies Federation, according to the souvenir booklet. Internationally known MRA adherents appearing in the film included Rajmohan Gandhi, South African revolutionary leader William Nkomo, Chancellor Adenauer, Chief Walking Buffalo of the Stoney (Sioux) Indians, and missile expert Dr. S. Douglas Connell. The film was exhibited for the press and the film industry in Hollywood in Feb 1960 and had its world premiere in New York on 21 Oct 1960; delegates from over sixty United Nations countries attended, according to *HR*. After New York, the film played in Los Angeles, South Africa, the Congo, Finland, Norway, Denmark, Switzerland and other European countries, according to *HR*. Twentieth Century-Fox began negotiations with MRA prior to the New York premiere to handle the worldwide distribution, but the deal did not materialize because Fox insisted that its DeLuxe Laboratories get the contract for making prints, and MRA previously had contracted with Technicolor. According to *DV*, an MRA executive commented, "After all, how would it look if we broke a contract."

The film was banned from the San Francisco Film Festival because it "embarrasses the Russians," according to *Limelight*. The Legion of Decency issued a statement that the film should be viewed by Catholics with certain reservations, as it "relies too heavily upon emotional argument and because the religious expression which it gives to personal reform is theologically ambiguous," according to *Var*. In its review, *Var* commented, "As well-meaning as it is, [this] film is a tepid drama-with-songs, episodic in structure and lacking in the kind of sock emotional impact that should grow naturally out of the narrative itself. Without meaning to be flip, it's like an extended tv commercial, full of endorsements for the product (MRA), and of the need for it, but which never defines the product except in the most general terms.... Except in its opening sequences showing the educator (played by Muriel Smith) teaching in a little open-air school, [the] film never quite touches the heart as it should, perhaps because the screenplay tries to cover too much ground in too great a hurry and hasn't time to develop interesting characterization." *Var* did praise Smith, however, noting, "What vitality the film has comes almost entirely from Miss Smith's warm and dignified performance and in her delivery of about six of the picture's 11 original songs." *Var* concluded that the film "does provide a pretty (if not profound) picture of the U.S., especially its race relations. Thus it could prove to be of value overseas in the west-east information war." Although *FD* called the film a "happy picture," it commented, "its acting and dialogue are for the most part amateurish, its tempo, excepting when it takes to music, slow, and its dramatic scenes weak."

BHCN 4 Feb 1960. *Cue* 29 Oct 1960. *DV* 12 Oct 1960. *DV* 24 Oct 1960, p. 4. *Exh* 7 Dec 1960, p. 4775. *FD* 2 Sep 1960, p. 1, 4. *FD* 28 Oct 1960, p. 6. *HCN* 1 Dec 1960. *HCN* 27 Apr 1961. *HR* 3 Feb 1960. *HR* 8 Feb 1960, p. 3. *HR* 2 Sep 1960. *HR* 18 Oct 1960. *HR* 21 Oct 1960. *HR* 28 Nov 1960. *HR* 29 Nov 1960. *HR* 13 Dec 1960. *HR* 2 Feb 1961. *LAEx* 1 Dec 1960, sec. 3, p. 18. *LAMirror* 21 Oct 1960, pt. II, p. 5. *LAMirror* 1 Dec 1960. *LAT* 1 Dec 1960. *Limelight* 27 Oct 1960. *MPD* 24 Oct 1960. *MPHPD* 29 Oct 1960, p. 901. *NYT* 24 Oct 1960, p. 25. *Var* 26 Oct 1960, p. 6. *Var* 16 Nov 1960.

THE CROW'S NEST (Native Americans)

Sunset Productions. *Dist* Aywon Film Corp. 15 Sep **1922**. Si; b&w. 5 reels, 4,403-4,700 ft.

Pres Anthony J. Xydias. *Dir* Paul Hurst. *Story* William Lester. *Photog* William Nobles.

Cast: Jack Hoxie (*Esteban*), Ruddel Weatherwax (*Esteban, as a boy*), Evelyn Nelson (*Patricia Benton*), Tom Lingham (*Beaugard*), William Lester (*Pecos*), William Dyer (*Timberline*), Mary Bruce (*Margarita*), Bert Lindley (*John Benton*), Augustina Lopez (*The Squaw*).

Western. Esteban, a white boy, is reared by an Indian squaw, whom he believes to be his mother and from whom Beaugard steals the papers documenting Esteban's birth and his right to inherit a ranch. When he is grown, Esteban falls in love with Patricia Benton, Beaugard "exposes" Esteban to Patricia, and the villain taunts the lad that he has no right to a white woman. After a series of adventures in which Esteban recovers Patricia from Beaugard's grasp, the couple happily learn the truth from Esteban's "mother." *Indians of North America. Inheritance. Parentage. Racism.*

MPN 2 Dec 1922, p. 2798. *MPW* 25 Nov 1922. *Var* 17 Nov 1922, p. 41.

LA CRUZ Y LA ESPADA (Spanish language)

Fox Film Corp. *Dist* Fox Film Corp. **1934**; New York opening: 1 Feb 1934; *Prod:* Oct 1933. Sd (Western Electric Noiseless Recording); b&w. 8 reels. 73 min. Passed by the National Board of Review. Spanish language.

[*Prod* John Stone]. *Dirección de* [*Dir*] Frank Strayer. [*Dial dir* Miguel de Zárraga]. *Obra original de* [*Orig story by*] Miguel de Zárraga. *Adaptación cinematográfica de* [*Scr*] Paul Schofield and William DuBois. [*Dial* Miguel de Zárraga]. *Dirección musical de* [*Mus dir*] Samuel Kaylin.

Song(s): "Singsong of the Children," "Song of the Grapes," "Song of the Miller," "Song of the Muleteers," "Song of the Miners" and "Jota No. 3," music by Troy Sanders, lyrics by José Mojica; "Gracia plena," words and music by Mario Talavera; "Funeral," words and music by Ernesto Lecuona; "Alleluia," words and music by Frederick Hummel; "Carmela," Spanish California folksong.

Cast: JOSÉ MOJICA (*Hermano Francisco*), Juan Torena (*José Antonio [Romero]*), Anita Campillo (*Carmela*), Lucio Villegas (*Padre Superior*), Carmen Rodríguez (*Tía Mónica*), Paco Moreno ([*Hermano*] *Pedro*), Carlos Montalbán (*Esteban*), Martín Garralaga (*Jaime*), Julián Rivero (*El Mestizo*), [F. A. Armenta (*The Indian*)], [Rudolph Galante (*Vaquero*)], [Soledad Jiménez (*Sra. Moreno*)], Enrico Ames, Jesús Mena.

Historical, Musical, Drama. [*Print viewed*]. In California, in the late eighteenth century, José Antonio Romero lives in a village near one of Junípero Serra's Franciscan missions. When gold is discovered, José gets a group of men together to form a prospecting expedition. José goes to talk to his good friend, Brother Francisco, and tells him that he wants to find gold so that he can give a good life to his beloved, Carmela. Meanwhile, Carmela tells her aunt that she is not sure if she loves José. Bandits, led by El Mestizo, arrive at the mission and kidnap Carmela. Brother Francisco pursues then rescues her, and realizes that she is his friend José's beloved. At the chapel, Carmela is surprised to learn that her rescuer is Brother Francisco, and she asks why he gave up the world for a religious vocation. He tells her that it was because of his sorrow over a woman. Jaime arrives from the mining camp and tells Francisco that Esteban has been stabbed. Francisco volunteers to go to render medical aid and, on his way back from the camp, shelters from a storm in a cave where he discovers gold. Francisco then battles with temptation. His evil conscience tells him to take the beautiful Carmela and the gold. Francisco imagines that he goes to Carmela and tells her that he has burned his novitiate's clothing. However, Francisco overcomes these temptations and later writes to José telling him of the gold's location. In a cantina back at the village, a drunken local tells José that Carmela and Francisco have been seen flirting. José madly confronts Francisco, who denies all charges of infamy. After José attacks his old friend with a knife, Francisco tells him that Carmela is completely pure and José begs for the brother's forgiveness. Carmela arrives and Francisco says that José has asked him to sing at their wedding. At the ceremony, Francisco joyously sings their wedding song. *California–History–To 1846. Franciscans. Gold mines. Missions. Religiosity. Aunts. Bandits. Caves. Cock-fighting. False accusations. Fiestas. Fights. Folk dancing. Jealousy. Kidnapping. Rescues. Stabbings. Visions. Weddings.*

Note: The working titles of this film were *Romance de California* and *Oro de California*. Although the screen credits list Amado Nervo among the film's songwriters, no song written by him was located in the cue sheets for the film in the Twentieth Century-Fox Records of the Legal Department in the UCLA Arts—Special Collections Library. During the film's pre-production period, Carmen Samaniego, Carlos Villarías and María Calvo were announced as cast members, but their participation in the completed film has not been confirmed. According to *DV*, the film "has been one of Fox's biggest grossers among Spanish versions." *DV* also stated that Fox at one time thought about producing an English version, and that the version which opened in Los Angeles had English titles.

DV 19 Jul 1934, p. 1. *NYT* 5 Feb 1934, p. 19.

CRY OF THE CITY (Italian Americans)

Twentieth Century-Fox Film Corp. *Dist* Twentieth Century-Fox Film Corp. Oct **1948**; New York opening: 29 Sep 1948; *Prod:* 26 Dec 1947—24 Feb 1948; mid-Mar 1948 [©Twentieth Century-Fox Film Corp.; 29 Sep 1948; LP2075]. Sd (Western Electric Recording); b&w. 10 reels, 8,554 ft. 95 min. PCA cert no. 12957.

[*Exec prod* Darryl F. Zanuck]. *Prod* Sol C. Siegel. *Dir* Robert Siodmak. [*Asst dir* Jasper Blystone]. [*Dial dir* Michael Audley]. *Scr* Richard Murphy. *Dir of photog* Lloyd Ahern. [*Cam op* Paul Lockwood]. [*Stills* Cliff Maupin]. *Spec photog eff* Fred Sersen. *Art dir* Lyle Wheeler and Albert Hogsett. *Film ed* Harmon Jones. *Set dec* Thomas Little and Ernest Lansing. *Ward dir* Charles LeMaire. *Cost des* Bonnie Cashin. *Mus* Alfred Newman. *Mus dir* Lionel Newman. *Orch arr* Herbert Spencer, Earle Hagen, [Edward Powell and Louis Bacigalupi]. *Sd* Eugene Grossman and Roger Heman. *Makeup artist* Ben Nye. [*Makeup* Harry Maret and Pat McNally]. [*Hair stylist* Linda Cross]. [*Prod mgr* Sid Bowen]. [*Unit mgr in New York* Robert Snody]. [*Scr supv* Rose Steinberg]. [*Grip* Eddie Ledgerwood].

Source: Based on the novel *The Chair for Martin Rome* by Henry Edward Helseth (New York, 1947).

Cast: Victor Mature [(*Lt. Vittorio Candella*)], Richard Conte [(*Martin Rome*)], Fred Clark [(*Lt. Jim Collins*)], Shelley Winters [(*Brenda*)], Betty Garde [(*Miss Frances Pruett*)], Berry Kroeger [(*Niles*)], Tommy Cook [(*Tony Rome*)], Debra Paget [(*Teena Riconti*)], Hope Emerson [(*Rose Given*)], Roland Winters [(*Ledbetter*)], Walter Baldwin [(*Orvy*)], [June Storey (*Miss Boone*)], [Tito Vuolo (*Papa Rome*)], [Mimi Aguglia (*Mama Rome*)], [Konstantin Shayne (*Dr. Veroff*)], [Howard Freeman (*Sullivan*)], [Dolores Castle (*Rosa*)], [Claudette Ross (*Rosa's daughter*)], [Tiny Francone (*Perdita*)], [Elena Savonarola (*Francesca*)], [Vito Scotti (*Julio*)], [Thomas Ingersoll (*Priest*)], [Robert Karnes, Charles Tannen (*Interns*)], [Oliver Blake (*Caputo*)], [Antonio Filauri (*Vaselli*)], [Joan Miller (*Vera*)], [Ken Christy (*Loomis*)], [Emil Rameau (*Dr. Niklos*)], [Eddie Parks (*Mike*)], [Charles Wagenheim (*Counterman*)], [Kathleen Howard (*Miss Pruett's mother*)], [John Cortay (*Policeman*)], [George Beranger (*Barber*)], [Harry Carter (*Policeman in elevator*)], [Jane Nigh, Ruth Clifford (*Nurses*)], [Davison Clark (*Mounted policeman*)], [Tom Moore (*Doctor*)], [Michael Stark (*Policeman*)], [Martin Begley (*Bartender*)], [Michael Sheridan (*Detective*)], [Tommy Nello (*Newspaper vendor*)], [George Melford], [Helen Troy], [Robert Adler], [Harry Seymour].

Film noir, Police, Gangster. [*Viewed print incomplete*]. Hoodlum Martin Rome, who has killed a policeman during a robbery, is in a hospital prison ward about to be operated on, and is being prayed over by his parents, brothers and sisters and a priest. New York City police lieutenants Vittorio Candella, who grew up in the same Italian neighborhood as Rome, and Jim Collins wait outside to question him. Niles, a lawyer, also wants to see Rome to ask him to confess to his involvement in the killing of a Mrs. de Grazia and thereby save an innocent man who has been arrested for the crime. Rome refuses to cooperate, but later, as he recovers from the surgery, Candella interrogates him about a ring found in his possession, a ring stolen from Mrs. de Grazia, who was tortured until she revealed the whereabouts of her jewels and was then strangled. Although Rome is headed for the electric chair for killing the police officer, he denies involvement in the de Grazia murder and says he won the ring in a crap game. After Candella leaves, Rome asks his middle-aged nurse, Miss Francis Pruett, to take a note to his girl friend, Teena Riconti, telling her to go into hiding as she may be arrested as an accomplice. When Niles offers to defend Rome in exchange for his confession to the de Grazia killing, Rome again refuses. Candella then visits Rome's parents, whom he knows, looking for information about Rome's girl friends. Meanwhile, Rome has been moved to a prison, where a trusty offers to help him escape. After Rome escapes from his cell by means of a duplicate key, Candella and Collins are tipped off that Rome is at Teena's place, but find only his younger brother Tony there. Rome goes to Niles' office, threatens him with a knife and, while looking for cash in his safe, discovers the de Grazia jewels in a hidden compartment. Niles tries to shoot Rome but accidentally shoots his secretary and is stabbed to death by Rome, who takes the jewels and a gun and heads to his parents' place. Although his father disowns him, his mother tries to help but cannot understand why he kills. Another of Rome's girl friends, Brenda, drives Rome to meet a Madam Rose, but as he is still suffering from the after-effects of the surgery, he passes out en route. Brenda locates an unlicensed doctor, Dr. Veroff, who treats him as they drive around. Rome tells Rose he knows she was in on the de Grazia job and that Niles gave him the jewels, which he now wants to trade for a car, $5,000 and a way out of the country. Rose agrees to meet him the next day to make the exchange. Meanwhile, Candella questions several unlicensed doctors, including Veroff, who admits he treated Rome. Rome phones Candella at police headquarters in an attempt to double-cross Rose, but when Rose and Rome meet, she draws a gun on him and together they go to a locker

in a subway station where Rose is arrested by two plainclothesmen. During the ensuing fracas, Rose accidentally shoots Candella and Rome escapes. Later, Lt. Collins discovers that Candella has walked out of the hospital where he was being treated and has gone to Miss Pruett's house, looking for Teena. She, however, has left to meet Rome at a church. Rome, meanwhile, asks Tony to take their mother's savings money and bring it to him. When Rome tells Teena that they are going to leave the country, she responds that she no longer loves him and will not go with him. Candella then finds them, and after telling Teena to go home, prepares to take Rome in. As they leave the church, Rome hands his gun to Candella but then slugs the ailing cop and limps away. Candella shoots him, and Tony returns to find his brother dead. As the police arrive, Tony confesses that he could not steal from his mother, and after he helps Candella into a police car, he cries. *Criminals. Family relationships. Italian Americans. Murder. New York City. Police detectives.* Aged women. Brothers. Churches. Confession (Law). Fathers and sons. Gunshot wounds. Hospitals. Investigations. Jewel thieves. Lawyers. Masseurs. Mothers and sons. Murder. Nurses. Operations, Surgical. Physicians. Priests. Prison escapes. Prisons. Stabbings. Subways. Wounds and injuries.

Note: This film's working titles were *The Chair for Martin Rome* and *The Law and Martin Rome*. According to documents in the Twentieth Century-Fox Records of the Legal Department and the Twentieth Century-Fox Produced Scripts Collection at the UCLA Arts—Special Collections Library, the studio purchased rights to Henry Helseth's novel *The Chair for Martin Rome* in Mar 1947 for $22,500. A first draft screenplay by Ben Hecht and Charles Lederer was ready by early Jun 1947. John Monks, Jr. contributed additional drafts, but the final draft was the same as that turned in by Richard Murphy in early Dec 1947. The extent of the contribution of the earlier writers to the released film has not been determined. In the novel, neither of the principal male characters was of Italian ancestry. The police lieutenant was named "Saul Mendel," while "Martin Rome's" ethnicity was unspecified although he was described as a tall, blonde guy with blue eyes.
An undated studio press release in the *AMPAS* Library, probably from mid-1947, announced Lon McCallister in the role of the "baby-faced killer." At that time, the production was to be shot in San Francisco. According to another press release, Victor Mature and Richard Conte were originally cast in the other's role, but when it was deemed unwise for Mature to play another criminal, Conte, whose two previous roles had been highly sympathetic, assumed the hoodlum's role. Randy Stuart and Lisa Howard were originally cast as "Teena." Hope Emerson made her screen debut in the picture. Although set in New York, most of the film was shot in Los Angeles. The hospital scenes, for example, were shot at Los Angeles County Hospital. However, in mid-Mar 1948, the production moved to New York for a few days of shooting on Sixth Avenue, Hester, Mott and Grand Streets. Additional New York filming took place near King and Houston Streets and in a subway station at Fourth Avenue and Eighteenth Street.
The *CBCS* and the studio's cutting continuity list characters played by Eddie Parks, Martin Begley and George Melford but they were not seen in the viewed, incomplete print. Various reviews incorrectly list the character portrayed by Betty Garde as "Mrs. Pruett." Two sequences included in the film's cutting continuity, but missing from the print viewed, feature Shelley Winters: In her first appearance in the film, she visits a photographic studio in an attempt to locate Madam Rose, who had been in show business, for Rome. Later, when Dr. Veroff treats Rome, he asks "Brenda" to get him some alcohol and she goes into a bar where a salesman tries to pick her up.
Early in Jun 1947, as the studio was about to release the film under the title *The Law and Martin Rome*, a Baltimore, Maryland attorney Morton E. Rome wrote to the studio, "It is my opinion that the showing of such a picture...would damage my own personal career and hold me up to ridicule....I have no desire to engage in litigation over this matter, unless I am forced to. If you are willing to change the name of the picture, I shall be happy to forget the whole affair." Studio inter-office correspondence reveals that, as exhibitors were reacting unfavorably to the current title, a decision was made to change the title to *Cry of the City*. Alfred Newman's score includes another re-use of his *Street Scene* theme.
Box 25 Sep 1948. *DV* 10 Sep 1948, p. 3. *FD* 10 Sep 1948, p. 5. *HR* 10 Sep 1948, p. 3, 9. *HR* 4 Oct 1948, p. 5. *MPHPD* 4 Sep 1948, p. 4303. *MPHPD* 18 Sep 1948, p. 4317. *NYT* 30 Sep 1948, p. 32. *Var* 15 Sep 1948, p. 15.

CRY OF THE HUNTED (Cajuns)
Metro-Goldwyn-Mayer Corp.; controlled by Loew's Inc. *Dist* Loew's Inc. Aug 1953; *Prod:* mid-Sep—late Sep 1952 [©Loew's Inc.; 3 Mar 1953; LP2483]. Sd (Western Electric Sound System); b&w. 7,128 ft. 78 min.
Prod William Grady, Jr. *Dir* Joseph H. Lewis. *Asst dir* Joel Freeman. *Scr* Jack Leonard. *Story* Jack Leonard and Marion Wolfe. *Dir of photog* Harold Lipstein. *Spec eff* A. Arnold Gillespie and Warren Newcombe. *Art dir* Cedric Gibbons and Malcolm Brown. *Film ed* Conard A. Nervig. *Set dec* Edwin B. Willis and Ralph Hurst. *Mus dir* Rudolph G. Kopp. *Rec supv* Douglas Shearer. *Makeup created by* William Tuttle.
Cast: Vittorio Gassman (*Jory*), Barry Sullivan (*Lt. Tunner*), Polly Bergen (*Janet Tunner*), William Conrad (*Goodwin*), Mary Zavian

(*Ella*), Robert Burton (*Warden Keeley*), Harry Shannon (*Sheriff Brown*), Jonathan Cott (*Deputy Davis*), [Nolan Leary (*Medic*)], [Jay Lawrence (*Deputy*)], [Eugene Mazzola (*Albert Jory*)], [Harry Cheshire (*Doctor*)], [Helen Winston (*Nurse*)], [Frank Arnold (*Fisherman*)], [Sonia Charsky (*Swamp woman*)], [George Selk (*Josh*)], [Inez Palange (*Old woman*)], [Fred Santley (*Ticket clerk*)].
Crime, Prison, Drama. [*Print viewed*]. At the Branville State Penitentiary, Warden Keeley conveys to Lt. Tunner, the head of maximum security, the district attorney's dissatisfaction with the way that Tunner is handling the Jory case. Jory, a Cajun convicted of robbery, has steadfastly refused to divulge the names of his partners in crime. Frustrated by Jory's silence, Tunner attempts to beat the information from him. After Jory finally agrees to identify his accomplices, he is escorted to the district attorney's office by Goodwin, the police officer who hungers for Tunner's job. On the drive downtown, their car collides with another vehicle and Jory escapes. Certain that Jory will go home to Louisiana, the warden dispatches Tunner to bring him back. In Louisiana, Tunner is met by Sheriff Brown, who disdains Tunner's humane methods and suggests that a shotgun would prove more efficacious. Informed that Jory has hopped a freight train headed toward Louisiana, the sheriff and Tunner stop the train to search it. Jory jumps from the boxcar, dives into the river and swims to freedom. The sheriff fires at the fugitive, infuriating Tunner. Hunted by dogs, Jory plunges into the bayou and heads for home. Upon reaching his shack, Jory finds Tunner waiting for him. After making a deal with Jory to return peacefully, the compassionate Tunner reunites Jory with his wife Ella and then steps out of the shack so that they can share a moment in private. When Jory refuses to flee, Ella taunts him about being a coward and then calls to Albert, the son he has never seen. Upon meeting the boy, Jory vows never to return to prison, and Ella knocks Tunner unconscious. Overwhelmed with thirst upon awakening, Tunner drinks some swamp water and becomes delirious with swamp fever. After being tortured by hallucinations of chasing Jory, Tunner finally regains consciousness to find his wife Janet and Goodwin at his bedside. Although Goodwin informs Tunner that he is taking over the case, Tunner refuses to relinquish control. The next day, Janet flies home, and Goodwin and Tunner propel a boat into the bayous in search of Jory. As night falls, the two set up camp in a graveyard. Spooked by a series of haunting cries, the two trace the sounds to a crazed old woman, who claims that Jory stole some food from her. The next day, Goodwin bullies one of the swamp dwellers into revealing the direction in which Jory was headed. Alerted to the approaching intruders by gunshots, Jory is goaded by Ella into taking up firearms. Tunner, meanwhile, decides to split up with Goodwin and search the swamp on foot. Declaring that he is giving up the hunt, Goodwin then returns to town. While trudging through the dank swamplands, Tunner finds an abandoned canoe and commandeers it. Slipping unseen into the water, Jory overturns the canoe. On shore, the two men battle, and Tunner hurls Jory into a protruding broken tree limb, wounding him. Jory then flings Tunner into a pit of quicksand. As Tunner sinks into the pit, Jory's conscience wins out, and he rescues Tunner from certain death. That night, Jory confesses that Logan, the man who planned the robbery, offered him $5,000 for his silence. When Jory becomes delirious from his infected wound, Tunner loads him into the canoe and paddles into the swamp, their water supply depleted. As night falls, Tunner rows to shore. Raving, Jory mistakes him for Logan and runs into the swamp, but Tunner loads him back into the canoe and begins to paddle again. As alligators trail in their wake, the boat overturns, and Tunner snatches Jory from the creatures' jaws and lugs him to shore. Later, Tunner hears the sound of a boat motor and Goodwin's voice calling to him. Parched, Tunner struggles to respond. Unable to speak, Tunner ignites the brush with his cigarette lighter. Spotting the smoke, Goodwin comes to the rescue and pulls Jory and Tunner to safety. Some time later, Jory has completed his prison sentence and is released, a free man. As he purchases a train ticket to Louisiana, Tunner wishes him luck. *Bayous (LA). Cajuns. Chases. Fugitives. Police. Prison escapees. Swamps.* Aged women. Alligators. Cemeteries. Fathers and sons. Fever. Fights. Hallucinations. Prison wardens. Prisons. Quicksand. Sheriffs. Trains. Wives. Wounds and injuries.
Note: Although "Jory" is shown escaping on the Angels Flight funicular in Los Angeles, the context of the story makes it clear that the prison is not located in California.

Box 28 Mar 1953. *DV* 9 Mar 1953, p. 3. *Exb* 25 Mar 1953, p. 3486. *FD* 6 Apr 1953, p. 10. *Har* 14 Mar 1953, p. 43. *HR* 12 Sep 1952, p. 8. *HR* 19 Sep 1952, p. 14. *HR* 10 Mar 1953, p. 3. *MPHPD* 14 Mar 1953, p. 1758. *Var* 11 Mar 1953, p. 6.

CRY OF THE WEREWOLF (Gypsies)

Columbia Pictures Corp. *Dist* Columbia Pictures Corp. 17 Aug 1944; New York opening: 11 Aug 1944; Prod: 8 May—27 May 1944 [©Columbia Pictures Corp.; 11 Aug 1944; LP12815]. Sd (Western Electric Mirrophonic Recording); b&w. 5,668 ft. 62-63 min.

Prod Wallace MacDonald. *Dir* Henry Levin. [*Asst dir* Milton Feldman]. [*Dial dir* Herman Rotsten]. *Scr* Griffin Jay and Charles O'Neal. *Story* Griffin Jay. *Dir of photog* L. W. O'Connell. *Art dir* Lionel Banks and George Brooks. *Film ed* Reg Browne. *Set dec* Robert Priestley. *Mus dir* Mischa Bakaleinikoff. [*Tech adv* Dr. Fraime Sertorodos].

Cast: Nina Foch [(*Celeste*)], Stephen Crane [(*Bob Morris*)], Osa Massen [(*Elsa Chauvet*)], Blanche Yurka [(*Bianca*)], Barton MacLane [(*Lt. Barry Lane*)], [Ivan Triesault (*Yan Spavero*)], [John Abbott (*Peter Althius*)], [Fred Graff (*Pinkie*)], [John Tyrrell (*Mac*)], [Robert Williams (*Max*)], [Fritz Leiber (*Dr. Charles Morris*)], [Milton Parsons (*Adamson*)].

Horror. [*Print viewed*]. At the Latour Museum in New Orleans, Louisiana, tour guide Peter Althius relates the legend of Marie Latour, the former mistress of the building, who was rumored to be a werewolf. Later that night, Yan Spavero, the janitor at the museum, visits Celeste, a gypsy princess and Marie's daughter, to warn her that Dr. Charles Morris, the museum's director, has discovered the secret behind her mother's grave and plans to publish it in a manuscript. The following day, Celeste enters the museum and disappears behind a secret panel that is embedded in the mantlepiece of a fireplace. That night, Elsa Chauvet, the doctor's Transylvanian assistant, becomes concerned when she finds a devil doll on the doctor's desk. Scoffing at the doll, which portends death, Morris asks Elsa to meet his son Bob at the airport. After Elsa departs, Peter hears unearthly screams and howls emanating from behind the mantlepiece and enters the secret passage to investigate. Upon returning to the museum with Bob, Elsa notices pages from the doctor's manuscript blazing in the fireplace, and soon after, Peter appears, lumbering in a trance. After they discover the doctor's slain body, the police are summoned and Lt. Barry Lane comes to investigate. Bob discloses that his father was researching the legend of Marie Latour, but Lane dismisses his fears about werewolves until the lab report reveals that wolf fur was found under the doctor's fingernails. Informed by the lab that a woman's hand print was also discovered on the panel door, Lane begins to suspect Elsa, but when her fingerprints fail to match those found at the murder scene, he comes to think that Yan may have been her accomplice. As Bob and Elsa piece together the charred fragments of his father's notes, Elsa voices her belief that the doctor was killed by supernatural causes. Later, as they leave the museum, Bob proposes to Elsa and she accepts. Their departure is watched by Yan, who then sneaks into the lab and destroys the remnants of the manuscript. The next day, the police discover Yan's fingerprints on the lab door and, suspecting that he is the killer, launch a manhunt to find him. Yan seeks refuge at the gypsy camp, but Celeste, fearing that his presence will jeopardize her status as a gypsy princess, declares that he must die. When Yan's mutilated body is found, Celeste is summoned to testify at an inquiry into his death. At the hearing, Bob learns that the gypsies return to New Orleans once a year to bury their dead, who are stored at the Adamson funeral parlor. Bob then ventures to the funeral parlor, but Adamson refuses him access to the gypsies' records which are stored in the basement. Their conversation is interrupted by the arrival of the gypsies, and after Adamson excuses himself to greet his clients, Bob sneaks into the basement to examine the records. As he reaches for the files, he hears the sound of a woman's footsteps, and when the footsteps turn into the padding of a wolf, Bob escapes into the elevator. Upstairs, Bob meets Celeste, who offers to explain the customs of her people if he will escort her back to the camp. After his visit with Celeste, Bob returns to the museum, bewitched, and informs Elsa that he no longer suspects the gypsies of being involved in his father's death. Realizing that Celeste has put a spell on Bob, Elsa determines to uncover the secret of Marie Latour. Returning to the museum later that night, Elsa is confronted by Celeste, who, out of jealousy, decides to transform her rival into a sister werewolf. Later, Bob hears a cat meowing in the secret passage, and when he opens the door, a dazed Elsa appears and confesses that she killed his father.

Suspecting that Celeste has cast a spell on Elsa, Bob summons the police. When Bob suggests that the basement chamber holds the secret of his father's death, Lane and several of his men descend into the passage to investigate. After locating the crypt of the gypsy queen, they hear a wolf growl and begin to fire their guns. Upstairs, Elsa awakens from her trance, and a wounded Celeste appears and incites her to kill Bob. When Bob exhorts Elsa to exercise her own will, Celeste, weakened by her wounds, turns into a wolf and attacks Bob. At that moment, the police burst into the room and slay the wolf. With the death of Celeste, the spell on Elsa is broken, and as Lane examines the body of the wolf, he begins to believe in the supernatural. *Gypsies. Murder. Museums. Werewolves. Cats. Curators. Fathers and sons. Fingerprints. Gunshot wounds. Investigations. Janitors. Jealousy. Legends. Manuscripts. New Orleans (LA). Police. Scientists. Secret passageways. Spells. Tombs.*

Note: The working title of this film was *Bride of the Vampire*. The picture begins with the following written prologue: "The ancient belief is still held by many that anything that happens in the world is never lost. No sparrow falls unnoted—no tree crashes in the forest unheard. The sorrows, the joys, the love and the hates of past generations live on in people's memories, in their legends and their stories. Perhaps our story is something that has lived on in a person's memory or perhaps it is just a legend—" According to a *HR* news item, Dr. Fraime Sertorodos, a Transylvanian psychiatrist, provided technical advice for the film. This picture marked the acting debut of Stephen Crane and the directorial debut of former dialogue director Henry Levin.

Box 26 Aug 1944. *DV* 5 Sep 1944, p. 6. *FD* 23 Aug 1944, p. 8. *HR* 28 Apr 1944, p. 1. *HR* 2 May 1944, p. 9. *HR* 10 May 1944, p. 9. *HR* 12 May 1944, p. 22. *HR* 5 Sep 1944, p. 8. *MPHPD* 24 Jun 1944, p. 1958. *MPHPD* 19 Aug 1944, p. 2053. *NYT* 12 Aug 1944, p. 16. *Var* 16 Aug 1944, p. 16.

CRY TOUGH (Latino)

Canon Productions. *Dist* United Artists Corp. Aug 1959; Prod: early Sep—late Sep 1958 at Universal-International studios and M-G-M studios [©Anne Productions, Inc.; 7 Aug 1959; LP15205]. Sd (Westrex Recording System); b&w. 7,500 ft. 83-84 min. PCA cert no. 19169.

Prod Harry Kleiner. *Dir* Paul Stanley. *Asst dir* Philip Bowles. *Scr* Harry Kleiner. *Photog* Philip Lathrop and Irving Glassberg. *Art dir* Edward Carrere. *Film ed* Frederic Knudtson. *Set dec* Russell Gausman and William Tapp. *Mus* Laurindo Almeida. *Sd* Leslie I. Carey and Don McKay. *Prod mgr* Thomas P. Shaw.

Source: Based on the novel *Cry Tough!* by Irving Shulman (New York, 1949).

Cast: JOHN SAXON [(*Miguel Estrada*)], LINDA CRISTAL [(*Sarita*)], Joseph Calleia [("*Papa*" *Estrada*)], Harry Townes [(*Carlos Mendoza*)], Don Gordon [(*Incho*)], Perry Lopez [(*Toro*)], Frank Puglia [(*Lavandero*)], Penny Santon [(*Senora Estrada*)], Joe De Santis [("*Boss*" *Juan Cortez*)], Barbara Luna [(*Tina Estrada*)], Arthur Batanides [(*Alvears*)], Paul Clarke [(*Emilio*)], [John Sebastian (*Alberto Estrada*)], [Nira Monsour (*Dolores*)].

Gangster, Social, Drama. [*Print viewed*]. Miguel Estrada returns home to his Spanish Harlem tenement after serving a one-year prison sentence for assisting some racketeers in the commission of a crime. On the way to his family's apartment, Miguel visits his friends in the Carlos Mendoza mob, not to take up his old position in the gang, but rather, as he tells them, to celebrate old times. Refusing to believe that Miguel really wants to go straight, Mendoza argues that the first generation of Puerto Ricans born in the "land of the big dollar" can either make it "the slow, hard way," or "break out fast at the point of a gun." With Miguel's intelligence and loyalty, Mendoza argues, the gang could crush the rival mob of "Boss" Juan Cortez, a crooked politician, and take control of the *barrio*. Miguel adamantly rejects Mendoza's offer and then, somewhat apprehensively, goes home, where his family is celebrating the birth of his uncle Alberto Estrada's seventh child. Just before Miguel appears at the door, his father, whom everyone calls "Papa," tells the young man's mother and sister Tina that Miguel has disgraced the family name. Everyone except Papa is happy to see him, but the old man grudgingly allows him to enter. Although he is glad to be with his family, Miguel wants desperately to get them out of the "rat trap" they share. His father assures him that his children will escape the *barrio*, but Miguel, who notes that the Irish, Jews and Italians "busted out before us," is impatient for a better life for both his own and his father's generation. The next morning, Miguel returns to his old job at a laundry establishment owned by Cortez, who secretly uses the business as a front for his illegal activities. At work, Tina's young sweetheart Emilio asks for Miguel's *benedición*, or blessing, on their planned marriage, hinting

that he has amassed money illegally. When the laundry boilers suddenly explode, Miguel realizes that Mendoza has paid Emilio to jam the valves and boldly orders the gangster to "lay off Emilio." Later, as he is leaving Mendoza's nightclub, he is mesmerized by one of its "hostesses," the beautiful Sarita, and agrees to meet her after work. That night, Mendoza's men trick Miguel into committing a robbery, but he escapes the scene and ruins their plans. In retaliation, they beat him. Miguel staggers up to Sarita's room, where he remains for the next ten days. Having fallen in love with Sarita, he proposes to her, but she insists that marriage would tie her down. When an immigration officer appears downstairs, Sarita admits that she is an illegal immigrant from Cuba. Following her arrest, Miguel asks Mendoza to arrange for her release. Sarita then marries Miguel and moves in with his family, while Miguel, eager to give his new wife everything she desires, asks Cortez for a raise. Cortez refuses this request but offers the young man twice his current salary to maintain the laundry's dangerous machinery. Miguel accepts and returns home, only to find that Sarita has left him. Furious, Miguel offers to work for Mendoza if the crook finds Sarita for him. Mendoza orders Miguel to lead his men, including Emilio, in a robbery, and during the heist, the police arrive, forcing the robbers to hide in the cellar. Toro, a Mendoza thug who has always been jealous of Miguel, threatens his rival with a knife, and during the fight, Miguel kills him. Later, in the penthouse apartment Miguel has rented with the stolen money, Mendoza arrives with Sarita, and when she angrily declares that she has to be free, he locks her in the bedroom. The police question Miguel about Toro's death, but he remains silent, even when they threaten to question Emilio, who at that moment is buying a wedding dress with Tina. Seeing the police, Emilio panics and races in front of a car to his death. At the boy's funeral, Tina blames Miguel for the loss of her fiancé, and Papa publicly disowns his wayward son. Half crazy with guilt and frustration, Miguel decides to rob the Cortez laundry, a plan Mendoza labels as suicidal. Before the robbery, Sarita tearfully apologizes to her husband, but he declares that he no longer has feelings. The daring robbery proceeds as planned until Papa arrives for work and pulls the burglar alarm. Miguel escapes the subsequent shootout, but because he has botched the job, Mendoza's men decide to kill him. Two of the thugs chase him across a rooftop, and when he tries to leap to another building, he falls. Papa and Sarita, kneeling over Miguel's broken body, blame themselves for his misfortune, but just before he dies, he absolves them of guilt and receives his father's cherished blessing. *Criminals–Rehabilitation. Family honor. Fathers and sons. Gangsters. Immigrants. New York City–Spanish Harlem. Puerto Ricans. Accidental death. Aliens, Illegal. Brothers and sisters. Chases. Cuban Americans. Engagements. Ex-convicts. Falls from heights. Funerals. Latino. Knife fighting. Laundries. Marriage–Forced by circumstances. Moral corruption. Nightclubs. Political bosses. Rivalry. Robbery. Superstition. Tenement-houses.*

Note: An onscreen narrative reads: "In the heart of New York City, there is a steaming jungle of tenements inhabited by America's newest wave of immigrants, the Puerto Ricans. Surrounded by the great city, they are isolated within it. They call their little world the *Barrio*, the Spanish word for 'district.'" According to information in the MPAA/PCA file on the film, Irving Shulman's novel was originally to have been produced by Mort Briskin for Morjay Productions, Inc., and released by RKO Radio Pictures, Inc. Hecht-Hill-Lancaster bought the story from Irving Shulman in 1955. Canon Productions and Anne Productions, Inc., the film's copyright claimant, appear to be companies set up by Hecht-Hill-Lancaster specifically for this production. A 1958 item in *DV* stated that producer/writer Harry Kleiner completely revamped Shulman's "mid-depression novel about a Jewish family in Brooklyn." According to a 12 Oct 1958 article in *LAEx*, Kleiner spent two weeks in Spanish Harlem interviewing hundreds of locals on all aspects of life there. Although the *Var* review noted that *Cry Tough* marked the screen's first attempt at depicitng "second generation Puerto Ricans in Manhattan," most reviewers complained about the film's lack of realism. *Cry Tough* was television director Paul Stanley's first effort at theatrical filmmaking.

Box 10 Aug 1959. *DV* 28 Jul 1959, p. 3. *Exb* 29 Jul 1959, p. 4611. *FD* 31 Jul 1959, p. 6. *Har* 1 Aug 1959, pp. 122-23. *HR* 5 Sep 1958, p. 8. *HR* 26 Sep 1958, p. 10. *HR* 28 Jul 1959, p. 3. *LAEx* 12 Oct 1958, p. 1, 4. *MPHPD* 1 Aug 1959, p. 356. *NYT* 17 Sep 1959, p. 48. *Var* 29 Jul 1959, p. 6.

CUANDO CANTA LA LEY (Spanish language)

Darío Productions, Inc. *Dist* Paramount Pictures, Inc. **1940**; Santiago, Chile premiere: 19 Dec 1939; Los Angeles opening: 7 Feb 1940; Prod: Apr 1939. Sd; b&w. 9 reels. 67 or 77 min. PCA cert no. 5379. Spanish language.

Prod Darío Faralla. *Dir* Richard Harlan. *2d unit dir* Irving Applebaum. *Dial dir* Gabriel Navarro. *Asst dir* William Faralla. *Orig* *scr* Jack Natteford, Enrique Uhthoff and Richard Harlan. *Spanish version wrt* Enrique Uhthoff. *Photog* Jerry Ash and William Sickner. *Art dir* Ralph Berger. *Set dec* Glenn P. Thompson. *Mus dir* Lud Gluskin. *Mus arr* Lucien Moraweck. *Chorus dir* Harry Simeone. *Sd* Hal Baumbaugh. *Makeup* Max Factor.

Song(s): "El loco," "Río Grande," "Por tus ojos," "Huapango" and "March," music and lyrics by Tito Guízar and Nenette Noriega.

Cast: Tito Guízar (*Alberto Galindo*), Tana (*María Luisa Pineda*), Martín Garralaga (*Adobe*), Paul Ellis (*Eduardo Pineda*), Pilar Arcos (*Rosa Pineda*), José Luis Tortosa (*Señor Vázquez*), Carlos Ruffino (*Montoya*), Carlos Montalbán (*José*), Raúl Lechuga (*Pedro*), José Peña "Pepet" (*Miguel*), "Arroyito" (*Chico*).

Western, with songs. [*Not viewed*]. On the trail of a murderer and bond thief, Eduardo Pineda, Alberto Galindo, a Mexican secret service agent, joins forces with Adobe, an insurance company detective. Tracing Pineda to a ranch owned by his relative, María Luisa, the pair go undercover and obtain jobs as ranch hands. Their deception pays off when Pineda comes to visit María Luisa. After Montoya, the ranch foreman, tries to kill Alberto, the secret service operative follows Pineda and discovers the cache of stolen bonds. When Montoya and his men come to Pineda's defense, a gun battle ensues in which Alberto and Adobe vanquish the criminals. *Government agents. Impersonation and imposture. Thieves. Bonds. Mexicans. Ranch foremen. Ranches.*

Note: The working title of this film was *El charro cantor*. It was shown in Santiago, Chile under the title *El rancho del pinar*. The picture was filmed on location at the Morrison and Major French ranches in CA. According to the *Var* review, this was the fourth and final of Paramount's series of Spanish-language films produced for the Latin American market.

DV 25 May 1939, p. 3. *FD* 5 Jun 1939, p. 13. *HR* 26 May 1939, p. 3. *MPH* 3 Jun 1939, p. 38. *Var* 31 May 1939, p. 14.

CUANDO EL AMOR RÍE (Latino, Spanish language)

Fox Film Corp. *Dist* Fox Film Corp. Dec **1930**; New York opening: 26 Dec 1930; Prod: mid-Aug–early Sep 1930. Sd; b&w. 6 reels, 5,111 ft. 57 min. Passed by the National Board of Review.

Presenta [*Pres*] William Fox. *Supervisión de* [*Supv*] John Stone. *Dirección de* [*Dir*] David Howard. [*Dir* William J. Scully]. [*Scr* Lynn Starling]. [*Contr to scr* John Stone]. [*Story* Lynn Starling]. [*Spanish version* Francisco Moré de la Torre]. [*Photog* Lucien Andriot]. [*Film ed* Ralph Dixon]. [*Sd* Frank MacKenzie]. [*Riding double for José Mojica* Morris Weidman].

Song(s): "Mi serenata," music and lyrics by María Grever; "Sonried," music and lyrics by William Kernell, Spanish lyrics by José Mojica; "Horses and Women" and "Recuerda," music and Spanish lyrics by José Mojica and Troy Sanders; "Nena," music by William Kernell, Spanish lyrics by José Mojica.

Cast: José Mojica [(*Emilio Rodríguez de Viana*)], Mona Maris [(*Elvira Alvarado*)], Carlos Villarías [(*Don José Alvarado*)], Carmen Rodríguez [(*Sra. de Alvarado*)], René Cardona [(*Manuel*)], Rosita Granada [(*Anita*)], Rafael Valverde [(*Alonso*)].

Melodrama, with songs. [*Not viewed*]. Emilio Rodríguez de Viana, a congenial but mysterious trainer of wild horses, works on Don José Alvarado's ranch in California, but is warned to stay away from his daughter, Elvira, who is betrothed to Manuel, son of a neighboring rancher. Emilio discovers that his friend Anita has been involved with Manuel and that they have had a daughter together. Emilio professes his love for Elvira, but social barriers keep them apart. On the eve of Elvira's wedding to Manuel, Anita visits her and reveals all. Eventually, Don José approves of a marriage between Emilio and his daughter, while Manuel is obliged to marry Anita. *Class distinction. Engagements. Fathers and daughters. Latino. Horse trainers. Ranches. Wild horses. California. Cantinas. Children. Marriage. Mothers and daughters. Romantic rivalry. Seduction.*

Note: According to documents in the Twentieth Century-Fox Records of the Legal Department and the Twentieth Century-Fox Produced Scripts Collection at the UCLA Arts—Special Collections Library, William J. Scully participated in the direction of this film, but David Howard was accorded the official credit. Some sources include Juan Torena and Luana Alcañiz in the cast, but their participation in the released film has not been confirmed and is doubtful.

This film played in Barcelona, Spain under the title *Ladrón de amor* and in Havana, Cuba as *El domador de mujeres*.

FD 18 Oct 1933. *CM* Mar 1931, p. 216. *NYT* 17 Oct 1933. *Var* 22 Apr 1931.

¿CUÁNDO TE SUICIDAS? (Spanish language)

Films Paramount; controlled by Paramount Publix Corp. *Dist* Paramount Publix Corp. **1932**; Bilbao, Spain opening: 27 Jan 1932; San Juan, Puerto Rico opening: 3 Apr 1932; Los Angeles opening: 10 Mar 1933; Prod: Aug 1931 at Paramount studios in Joinville, France. Sd; b&w. 9 reels, 7,250 ft. 81 min. *Country of origin* France. Spanish language.

Dir Manuel Romero. *Scr* Saint-Granier. *Adpt and Spanish dial* Claudio de la Torre.

Source: Based on the novel *Quand te tues-tu? (Histoire d'un suicide)* by André Dahl (Paris, 1930).

Cast: Fernando Soler (*Xavier du Venoux*), Imperio Argentina (*Gaby*), Manuel Russell (*León Mirol*), Carmen Navascués (*Viuda Dumonthal*), José Isbert (*Petavey*), María Anaya (*Virginia*), Enrique de Rosas (*Moisés*), Manuel Vico (*Grillard*), Carlos Martínez Baena (*Abraham*).

Comedy. [*Not viewed*]. Viscount Xavier du Venoux has decided to kill himself as he can no longer live without the love of a woman. León Mirol, a happy, carefree friend, who has never worked and has no profession, has the opportunity to inherit a large sum from his uncle if he agrees to marry a widow within a year after the millionaire's death. Seeing that Leon is in serious difficulty and that he faces a bleak future without the inheritance, Gaby, his girl friend, looks for a suitable candidate, but, being very jealous and fearing that she may lose her boyfriend, she cannot find anyone trustworthy. When all is almost lost, León finds out about Xavier's intention and immediately suggests that he marry Gaby, as she will then instantly become a widow. Xavier sees no reason not to help his friend, until after the ceremony, he feels that fortune has smiled upon him and, thenceforth, forgets all about killing himself. *Friendship. Inheritance. Suicide. Nobility. Uncles. Widows.*

Note: The running time was calculated from footage given in NYSA records. The working title of this film was *¿Cuándo te matas?* No reviews were located for this film. The French-language version of this film, entitled *Quand te tues-tu?*, was shot before the Spanish-language version, but no information has been located concerning any showings of the French version in the U.S. The French version was directed by Roger Capellani and starred Robert Burnier, Simone Vaudry, Noël-Noël and Madeleine Guitty.

THE CUB REPORTER (Chinese Americans)

Phil Goldstone Productions. Aug **1922**. Si; b&w. 5 reels.

Dir Jack Dillon. *Scen* George Elwood Jenks. *Photog* Harry Fowler.

Cast: Richard Talmadge (*Dick Harvey*), Jean Calhoun (*Marion Rhodes*), Edwin B. Tilton (*Harrison Rhodes*), Wilson Hummel (*Mandarin*), Lewis Mason, Ethel Hallor (*Crooks*).

Newspaper, Adventure. "Harvey, of the Morning Times, is called upon to do one daredevil stunt after another in his efforts to recover the Sacred Jewel of Buddha.... He dives head first through a skylight into the den of the Tong and gets away with the Jewel. Then he braves the underground passages of the Chinese underworld to rescue the girl stolen by the Tong and held as hostage for the return of the jewel. He proves too much for a whole squad of Chinamen and escapes with the beautiful girl." (*MPW* 30 Sep 1922, p. 396.). *Chinese Americans. Daredevils. Hostages. Reporters. Tongs (Secret societies).*

FD 4 Sep 1922. *Var* 22 Sep 1922, p. 42.

CUBAN FIREBALL (Latino)

Republic Pictures Corp. *Dist* Republic Pictures Corp. May **1951**; Prod: mid-Sep—late Sep 1950 [©Republic Pictures Corp.; 15 Feb 1951; LP757]. Sd (RCA Sound System); b&w. 7,016 ft. 78 min. Passed by the National Board of Review. PCA cert no. 15019.

Pres HERBERT J. YATES. *Assoc prod* Sidney Picker. *Dir* William Beaudine. [*Asst dir* Lee Lukather]. *Scr* Charles E. Roberts and Jack Townley. *Story* Charles E. Roberts. *Dir of photog* Reggie Lanning. *Spec eff* Howard Lydecker and Theodore Lydecker. *Optical eff* Consolidated Film Industries. *Art dir* Frank Hotaling. *Film ed* Tony Martinelli and [Arthur Roberts]. *Set dec* John McCarthy, Jr. and Charles Thompson. *Cost des* Adele Palmer. *Mus* Stanley Wilson. *Sd* Earl Crain, Sr. *Makeup supv* Bob Mark. *Hair stylist* Peggy Gray.

Song(s): "A Slave" and "Lost and Found," music and lyrics by Jack Elliott and Aaron Gonzales; "Un poquito de tu amor," English lyrics by Julio Gutierras.

Cast: Estelita Rodriguez [(*Estelita Rodriguez*)], Warren Douglas [(*Tommy Pomeroy*)], Mimi Aguglia [(*Señora Martinez*)], Leon Belasco [(*Hunyabi*)], Donald MacBride [(*Captain Brown*)], Rosa Turich [(*Maria*)], John Litel [(*Pomeroy, Sr.*)], Tim Ryan (*Detective Bacon*), Russ Vincent [(*Ramon*)], Edward Gargan [(*Ritter*)], Victoria Horne [(*Maid*)], Jack Kruschen [(*Lefty*)], Pedro de Cordoba [(*Don Perez*)], [Olan Soule (*Jimmy*)], [Tony Barr (*Estaban Martinez*)], [Luther Crockett (*Rafferty*)], [Julian Rivero], [Nacho Galindo], [Eumenio Blanco], [Harry Vejar (*Janitor*)], [Eddie Parks, Harry Tyler (*Drunks*)], [Pat Shade (*Bellboy*)], [Manuel Paris (*Headwaiter*)], [Douglas Evans (*Atkins*)], [Pat Gleason (*Murphy*)], [Lois Hall (*Stewardess*)], [John Crawford (*Photographer*)].

Comedy, with songs. [*Print viewed*]. In Havana, Cuba, Estelita Rodriguez, a singer hired to entertain for employees at a cigar factory, faces dismissal when she is caught performing an unflattering impersonation of her boss, Señora Martinez. Estelita finds an unexpected escape from her troubles at work when Don Perez, an attorney, tells her that she has inherited the estate of her oil tycoon grandfather, Patrick Renaldo O'Hara. Perez explains that to claim the $20,000,000 inheritance, Estelita must travel to Los Angeles to be present at the estate settlement. Before leaving for Los Angeles with her cousin Maria, Estelita attends a going away party held in her honor, and turns down a marriage proposal from Señora Martinez' fortune-hunting son Estaban. On her flight to Los Angeles, a stewardess advises Estelita to disguise herself to avoid "wolves" who might be after her money. Estelita takes the advice seriously and dresses herself in the disguise she used to impersonate Señora Martinez. When Mr. Pomeroy, the general manager of the O'Hara Oil Co. and his son Tommy greet Estelita at the airport, she tells them that her name is Maria and that she is Estelita's aunt. After making certain that Tommy is not a fortune-hunter, Estelita falls in love with him. Chaos ensues, however, when Estelita tries, with great effort, to impersonate her cousin for the public while at the same time trying to show Tommy her true self. The situation is further complicated when a maid, after overhearing a plan do "get rid" of Estelita, believes that the heiress will be murdered. The maid tells the police about the plan, and Detective Bacon begins an investigation. Later, when Ramon, an old friend of Estelita, makes an unexpected visit, he blackmails her, and demands $5,000 in exchange for his silence. When Bacon learns that Maria is Estelita's legal heir, he sees a possible motive for Maria to kill Estelita and places a twenty-four-hour watch on her. Things become even more complicated for Estelita when two immigration officers arrive at her hotel room demanding to see Maria. Estelita's hopes of fooling the officers are nearly dashed when her dog Pepito jumps out of the hotel room window with the fake nose and glasses she was using for her disguise. While Estelita tries to retrieve her disguise by climbing onto the ledge outside her window, Señora Martinez arrives, determined to prevent Estelita from marrying anyone but her son. Realizing that Señora Martinez might easily be mistaken for "Maria," Estelita tries to keep her out of view by forcing her into a closet. A struggle between the two women ensues, and the maid, witnessing the struggle, believes that the suitcase the two women are fighting over contains the dead body of the heiress. The maid alerts the police, and the following day, assuming that Señora Martinez is Maria, they arrest her for Estelita's murder. As newspaper headlines report the apparent murder of the heir to the O'Hara fortunes, Estelita goes to Ramon for help. Ramon, who is only interested in Estelita's fortunes, refuses to help and demands his blackmail money. Estelita is eventually saved when Tommy arrives and trounces Ramon in a fistfight. Though Estelita's ruse is exposed, Tommy forgives her, and they marry. *Blackmail. Cubans. Disguise. Impersonation and imposture. Inheritance. Singers. Cigar and cigarette manufacturers. Cousins. Employer-employee relations. Fathers and sons. Fortune hunters. Hotels. Los Angeles (CA). Maids. Police detectives. Romance.*

Note: *HR* production charts list Arthur Roberts as the film's editor, but only Tony Martinelli is credited onscreen. According to memos in the file on the film in the MPPDA/PCA Collection at the AMPAS Library, the Breen Office negotiated the elimination of some situations and dialgoue from the film that might "prove highly offensive to the sensibilities of Cuban nationals." Among the changes noted was the elimination of a questionable reading of "Little Red Riding Hood" in dialect.

Box 7 Apr 1951. *DV* 7 Mar 1951, p. 6. *FD* 9 Mar 1951, p. 8. *HR* 15 Sep 1950, p. 11. *HR* 22 Sep 1950, p. 8. *HR* 7 Mar 1951, p. 4. *MPHPD* 31 Mar 1951, p. 786. *Var* 14 Mar 1951, p. 7.

CUBAN PETE (Latino)

Universal Pictures Co., Inc. *Dist* Universal Pictures Co., Inc. 26 Jul **1946**; Prod: mid-Apr—early May 1946 [©Universal Pictures Co., Inc.; 18 Jul 1946; LP446]. Sd (Western Electric Recording); b&w. 61 min. PCA cert no. 11734.

Exec prod Howard Welsch. *Assoc prod* Will Cowan. *Dir* Jean Yarbrough. *Dial dir* Bob O'Connor. [*Asst dir* Fred Frank]. *Scr* Robert Presnell, Sr. and M. Coates Webster. *Orig story* Bernard Feins. *Dir of photog* Maury Gertsman. *Art dir* Jack Otterson and Abraham Grossman. *Film ed* Otto Ludwig. *Set dec* Russell A. Gausman and T. F. Offenbecker. *Gowns* Vera West. *Mus dir* Milton Rosen. *Dir of sd* Bernard B. Brown. [*Sd*] *tech* Jess Moulin. *Hair stylist* Carmen Dirigo. *Dir of makeup* Jack P. Pierce.

Music: "The Breeze and I" by Ernesto Lecuona.

Song(s): "Cuban Pete," music and lyrics by José Norman; "El Cumbanchero," music and lyrics by Rafael Hernandez; "Lullaby," music and lyrics by Bill Driggs, based on the traditional Mexican folk song "Cielito lindo;" "After Tonight," music by Jack Brooks, lyrics by Milton Schwarzwald; "Rhumba Matumba," music and lyrics by Bobby Collazo.

Cast: DESI ARNAZ AND HIS ORCHESTRA, Joan Fulton [(*Ann Willliams*)], Beverly Simmons [(*Brownie*)], Don Porter [(*George Roberts*)], Jacqueline de Wit [(*Theresa Lindsay*)], Pedro DeCordoba [(*Manuel Perez*)], Igor and Yvette, Ethel Smith, The King Sisters, [Del Sharbutt (*Radio announcer*)], [Eddie Parks (*Alvin*)], [Charles Jordan (*Police sergeant*)], [Roseanne Murray (*Receptionist*)], [Shirley O'Hara (*Girl*)], [Rico De Montez (*Cuban driver*)], [Ellen Corby, Ann Lawrence, Peggy Leon, Diane Carroll (*Screaming patients*)], [Robert O'Connor (*Cuban servant*)], [Chuck Bedell (*Barker*)], [Cleo Morgan (*Nurse*)], [Samuel Schultz (*Boy*)], [Peter Seal (*Cossack*)], [Ruth Lee (*Woman on the table*)].

Musical, Romantic comedy. [*Print viewed*]. Screwball perfume manufacturer Theresa Lindsay informs George Roberts of the Roberts Advertising Agency that she has decided to change the musical programming of her radio show from Russian to Cuban. Furthermore, Theresa insists that the unknown Desi Arnaz and His Cuban Rhythm Band be imported from Cuba to New York City to star on her show. When the bandleader refuses George's phone and telegram offers, the desperate advertising executive sends Ann Williams, his assistant, to Cuba to personally pursue Desi. She finds Desi and his group working on a plantation on the outskirts of Havana. Desi tells Ann that he refused the radio offer because his sister and brother-in-law were killed in New York City, and that he has been taking care of his orphaned niece Brownie ever since. With Brownie's help and a bit of romance, Ann convinces Desi to go to New York, but he soon becomes disenchanted when he learns that George paid Ann a $5,000 bonus to get him to appear on Theresa's show. Matters are further complicated when Theresa announces that she plans to perform on the radio program with Desi and his band. When Desi refuses to sing with her, Theresa attempts to enlist Brownie's aid by taking the little girl's sick parrot, José, to Alvin, her physician. Instead, Theresa is arrested when the parrot disrupts the doctor's office. Ann then agrees to arrange for Theresa's release from police custody only if the radio sponsor agrees never to sing with Desi. With Theresa at a safe distance, the radio show is a great success, and Desi and Ann are happily united. *Advertising agencies. Band leaders. Cubans. Radio sponsors. Romance. Americans in foreign countries. Bands (Music). Children. Cuba. Eccentrics. New York City. New York City–Coney Island. Nieces. Nightclubs. Organists. Orphans. Parrots. Perfume. Plantations. Police. Radio programs. Rehearsals. Singers. Sisters.*

Note: The José Norman song "Cuban Pete" became one of the signature songs for actor-singer Desi Arnaz and gained new popularity in 1994, when it was performed by comedic actor Jim Carrey in the New Line film *The Mask*.
Box 27 Jul 1946. *DV* 19 Jul 1946, p. 3. *HR* 19 Apr 1946, p. 21. *HR* 19 Jul 1946, p. 3. *MPHPD* 29 Jun 1946, p. 3066. *MPHPD* 14 Sep 1946, p. 3198. *Var* 24 Jul 1946, p. 26.

EL CUERPO DEL DELITO (Spanish language)

Paramount Publix Corp. *Dist* Paramount Publix Corp. May **1930**; Madrid, Spain opening: 21 May 1930; San Juan, Puerto Rico opening: 30 May 1930; San Antonio, Texas opening: 7 Jun 1930; Prod: mid-Mar 1930. Sd; b&w. 9 reels. Spanish language.

Series: Philo Vance.

Presentan [*Pres*] Adolph Zukor and Jesse Lasky. *Gerente General de los Estudios de California* [*General mgr of the California Studios*] B. P. Schulberg. [*Supv* Geoffrey Shurlock]. *Dirección de* [*Dir*] Cyril

Gardner and A. W. Pezet. [*Dial dir* A. W. Pezet]. [*Asst dir* Jack Wagner, Lou Asher and Geo. Hippard]. *Adaptación cinematográfica* [*Scr*] Bartlett Cormack. *Versión española* [*Spanish version*] J. Carner-Ribalta. *Fotografía* [*Photog*] Henry Gerrard. [*Sd* Harry M. Lindgren]. [*Unit mgr* Dan Keefe].

Source: Based on the novel *The Benson Murder Case* by S. S. Van Dine (New York, 1926).

Cast: Antonio Moreno (*Harry Gray*), Ramón Pereda (*Philo Vance*), Andrés de Segurola (*Andrew* [*Antonio*] *Benson*), Barry Norton (*Adolph Mahler*), María Alba (*Miss Delroy*), María Calvo (*Mrs.* [*Paula*] *Banning*), Carlos Villarías (*Fiscal* [*District Attorney*] *Markham*), Vicente Padula (*Sargento Heath*), Manuel Conesa (*Albert Brecher*), [Ralph Navarro], [María Teresa Renner], [Eumenio Blanco].

Detective. [*Not viewed*]. The Wall Street crash of 1929 brings tragedy to thousands, and only a small group of astute investors are able to retrieve their funds. Financial adviser Antonio Benson is one of the few to survive the disaster. He escapes from his ruined clients, whose funds he has mismanaged, by hiding out at his country home; however, someone finds him and kills him. The principal suspects are: Miss Delroy, a Broadway actress, who was robbed of her valuable pearls after she endorsed a worthless check; Adolph Mahler, the originator of the check; widow Paula Banning, who has lost a great deal of money and is pursuing Mahler, her lover, as he attempts to recover the check; gambler Harry Gray and Albert Brecher, Benson's manservant. After abandoning several false leads, the district attorney in charge of the murder investigation turns to amateur detective Philo Vance for help. Vance, while following an apparently harebrained theory, discovers the murderer. *Amateur detectives. Murder. Stockbrokers. Actors and actresses. Butlers. District attorneys. Gamblers. Investors. Jewelry. New York Stock Exchange. Stock market crash of 1929. Widows.*

Note: The onscreen credits were taken from a cutting continuity. The film is a Spanish-language version of the 1930 film *The Benson Murder Case* (see *AFI Catalog of Feature Films, 1921-30*; F2.0352), which was directed by Frank Tuttle and starred William Powell and Natalie Moorhead. The Spanish version had two working titles; *Juego, amor y sangre* and *El crimen de Wall Street*. For additional information on other Philo Vance films, see entry for *The Kennel Murder Case* in *AFI Catalog of Feature Films, 1931-40*; F3.2259.
CM Jul 1930, p. 676.

CUERPO Y ALMA (Spanish language)

Fox Film Corp.; Alfred Santell Production. *Dist* Fox Film Corp. **1931**; New York opening: 5 Jun 1931; Prod: Apr 1931. Sd; b&w. 10 reels, 8,665 ft. 96 min. Passed by the National Board of Review. Spanish language.

Prod WILLIAM FOX, PRESENTA [PRES]. [*Dir* David Howard]. [*Scr* Jules Furthman]. [*Spanish version by* Matías Cirici-Ventalló].

Song(s): "Ride On Vaquero," by L. Wolfe Gilbert and Abel Baer, Spanish lyrics by César Barja; "I May Be Gone for a Long, Long Time," music by Albert Von Tilzer, lyrics by Lew Brown, Spanish lyrics by Matías Cirici-Ventalló; "Dark Town Strutters Ball," words and music by Shelton Brooks.

Source: Based on the unproduced and unpublished play *Squadrons* by Elliott White Springs and A. E. Thomas, which was based on the short story "Big Eyes and Little Mouth" by Elliott White Springs in *Nocturne Militaire* (1927).

Cast: Jorge Lewis (*Ted*), Ana María Custodio (*Carla*), José Alcántara (*Philip*), José Nieto (*Tap*), Enriqueta Soler (*Alice* [*Lester*]), Rafael Calvo (*General de Brigada*), Carlos Villarías (*Comandante Burke*), Félix de Pomés (*Comandante Knowles*), [Martín Garralaga (*Young*)], Max Barón.

Aviation, War, Espionage, Drama. [*Not viewed*]. [The following plot summary is based on the English-language version of this film, *Body and Soul*; character names refer to that version. For further information regarding the English-language version, please see the note below and the entry for *Body and Soul* in the *AFI Catalog of Feature Films, 1931-40*.] During World War I, Mal Andrews and Tap Johnson, American flyers attached to the Royal Air Force Squadron, scold their rakish buddy Jim Watson, who is having an affair after only being married for a year. General Trafford Jones arrives at Air Force headquarters to announce that the squadron is a disgrace to the flying corps. He orders Jim to go alone to shoot down an enemy balloon, a mission from which Jim knows he will not return. At the last moment, Mal surreptitiously joins Jim in his plane. The fliers battle with the enemy balloon, and Jim is shot, but Mal manages to fly the plane and

destroy the German balloon before landing. He then sends the plane back up so it will appear as if Jim has died like a hero. Back at headquarters, Carla, Jim's widow, arrives in search of him, but the men believe that she is "Pom Pom," Jim's mistress. The fliers tell Carla of Jim's death and of the wife who must never know about Pom Pom's existence, and Mal gives Carla a watch and the letters that Pom Pom had sent to Jim. Mal, who knows nothing about women nor liquor, and a distraught Carla spend the evening together. When they end up at Carla's apartment, she scolds him for pretending to be a tough guy when he actually has been dumping his liquor in flower pots, and she admits to having done the same. Mal, by revealing his true identity as a romantic novice rather than a ladies' man, wins Carla's heart. Back at the aviators' headquarters, Tap scolds Mal for spending time with Jim's former girl friend, and Mal promises to stop seeing Pom Pom. Carla later arrives to visit Mal, who receives her coldly and accuses her of sullying him before his next mission. Major Burke of Army Intelligence calls on Jim and asks him questions about Pom Pom, who is about to be accused of espionage. Mal denies her guilt until Burke brings in the real Pom Pom, Alice Lester. The men believe that Carla is an impostor, and when Tap is announced dead, Mal realizes that Carla had overheard the details of his mission. Mal goes to Carla's apartment intending to shoot her, but he realizes that he loves her more than ever, and they are caught trying to escape. Back at headquarters, Carla reveals her true identity as Jim's wife and produces "Pom Pom's" letters, which prove Lester's guilt. On the flying field, as Mal prepares for his next mission, the lovers bid farewell and promise that they will wait for each other either in this world or the next. *Air pilots. Americans in foreign countries. Espionage. Great Britain. Air Force. Innocents. Mistaken identity. Mistresses. Widows. World War I.* Aerial combat. Balloons (Hot air). Heroism. Letters. Poisoning. Romance. Suicide.

Note: The plot summary was based on a screen continuity in the Twentieth Century-Fox Produced Scripts Collection, and the onscreen credits were taken from a screen billing sheet in the Twentieth Century-Fox Records of the Legal Department, both of which are at the UCLA Theater Arts Library. For information on the English-language version, *Body and Soul*, which was directed by Alfred Santell and starred Charles Farrell and Elissa Landi, please see the entry for that film in the *AFI Catalog of Feature Films, 1931-40*; F3.0406. The working title of the Spanish-language version was *Escuadrones*. An article appearing in *Fortune* magazine in Aug 1931 states that the Spanish-language version of this film was made with a Spanish troop imported from Barcelona and Madrid with a Spanish co-director for distribution in Spain, Central and South America. (No information concerning the name of the Spanish co-director has been located; as the director of the Spanish-language version was David Howard, the co-director referred to in the article may have been a dialogue director. The "Spanish troop" was not imported specifically for this film, but for a number of Fox Spanish-language films). The film was dubbed into six other languages for distribution abroad. Some sources state that Francisco Moré de la Torre collaborated on the Spanish-language version of the script, but this has not been confirmed.

CM Sep 1931, p. 670. *Fortune* Aug 1931, pp. 27-34, 114-19.

CUESTA ABAJO (Spanish language)

Exito Corp. *Dist* Paramount Pictures, Inc. **1934**; New York opening: 10 Aug 1934; Prod: May 1934 at Eastern Service Studios, Inc. [©Exito Corp., Inc.; 10 Aug 1934; LP4893]. Sd; b&w. 8 reels. 74-75 min. Spanish language.

[*Supv* Robert Snody]. *Dirección de* [*Dir*] Louis Gasnier. [*Asst dir* Fred Scheld and Warren Murray]. *Argumento y adaptación cinematográfica* [*Story and scr*] Alfredo Le Pera. *Fotografía* [*Photog*] George Webber. *Dirección musical de* [*Mus dir*] Alberto Castellanos. [*Sd* C. A. Tuthill]. *Supervisión tecnico de* [*Tech supv*] Samuel E. Piza.

Song(s): "Por tu boca roja," "Criollita, decí que sí," "Cuesta abajo," "Mi Buenos Aires querido," "Viejos tiempos," "En los campos en flor," and "Olvido," music by Carlos Gardel, lyrics by Alfredo Le Pera; "Amores de estudiante," music by Carlos Gardel, lyrics by Alfredo Le Pera and Mario Battistella.

Cast: CARLOS GARDEL (*Carlos Acosta*), Mona Maris (*Raquel*), Vicente Padula (*Jorge Linares*), Anita Campillo (*Rosa*), Jaime Devesa (*Bastida*), Guillermo Arcos (*Don Pedro*), Suzanne Dulier (*Aida*), Manuel Peluffo (*Gutiérrez*), Carlos Spaventa (*Corrales*), Cornejo, Ingrata (*Bailarines criollos*), [Alfredo Le Pera (*Man in club*)].

Romance, Drama, with songs. [*Viewed print incomplete*]. In Buenos Aires, university students frequent a café run by the father of Rosa, a wholesome, lively girl. Carlos Acosta, whose wife Raquel continually flirts with other men, is in love with Rosa. After leaving Raquel and traveling to Paris and New York, Carlos returns to Buenos

Aires, where he is reunited with Rosa. *Romantic rivalry. Separation (Marital). Vamps.* Buenos Aires (Argentina). Cafés. College life. New York City. Paris (France). Restaurateurs.

Note: The print viewed was incomplete, lacking several narrative sections. This film was the first of four Spanish-language musicals, produced in New York, starring the famous singer Carlos Gardel.

CM Sep 1934, p. 492. *FD* 18 Jul 1934, p. 7. *NYT* 15 Aug 1934, p. 13.

CUORE D'EMIGRANTE (Italian Americans, Italian language)

S. Luisi & Co. **1932**; Prod: completed early Nov 1931 at the Metropolitan Studios in Fort Lee, NJ. Sd; b&w. 6 reels, 5,326 ft. 59 min. Italian language.

Prod Angelo De Vito. *Dir* Harold Godsoe. *Photog* Frank Zucker.

Song(s): "Far Away from You" and "Sky Blue Sea," songwriter unknown.

Cast: Carlo Renard, Yolanda Carluccio, Rafaelo Bougini.

Drama, with songs. [*Not viewed*]. At the lower Manhattan home of Francesco "Don Ciccio" Mauri, a Neapolitan who has lived in America for most of his life, a birthday party for his Americanized daughter Elsie is in full swing. Elsie's American boyfriend, Mr. Gravesend, arrives with a bracelet for the girl, and she hugs him in gratitude, upsetting her father, who disapproves of such free "American style" behavior. At Don Ciccio's request, Mario, the friend of Don Ciccio's other, more traditional daughter Elena, sings a sentimental Neapolitan song, a tune which the older guests enthusiastically enjoy. Elsie puts an end to their merriment, however, by turning on the radio to a jazz station and by asking her friend Susie to dance for them. Don Ciccio is disgusted, as are his friends. The dance is interrupted by the sound of a shot from the street, and Don Ciccio's son Mickey arrives, followed by a policeman who inquires about the shooting. Mickey responds to his father's questions by telling him to shut up. The revelers then leave, to Elsie's chagrin, and as Elena walks with Mario, he relates that in Naples parents are properly treated with respect. As they embrace, a policeman, who is a family friend, separates them, and the boy, not understanding English, is confused. Shortly thereafter, the couple declare their love for one another. When Don Ciccio offers to find his son a good, clean job, Mickey ignores the paternal suggestion. Elena arrives home one day to find Elsie maligning her father. They argue, and Elena calls her sister a "flapper," then tells her father that she has been laid off. When Mario arrives, she reveals that the previous night, her lecherous boss asked her to work overtime and kissed her by force, which disgusted her. Because she did not respond, she was fired. Mario suggests that they go to Naples, but she fears that her father would die if she left; however, Mario convinces her to go the next day by ship. Due to his sadness, Don Ciccio stays home from work for the first time in twenty years. Mickey, who had overheard his father offering Elena his life savings of five hundred dollars, comes to the bank to try to withdraw the money. The cashier calls Don Ciccio, who goes to the bank and seeing his son, understands what Mickey has tried to do. He tells the manager to give his son the cash, then goes home and finds out that Elena is leaving. He cries out that he has slaved for twenty years and deprived himself for his children, but tells her to go. He angrily decides to turn Mickey in, but Elena stops him from calling the police, and he admits he can't turn his son in. After assuring himself that Mario loves Elena, Don Ciccio decides to accompany the couple to Naples. Elsie and Mr. Gravesend arrive and announce that they've been married, and Don Ciccio is very relieved. He kisses his dead wife's picture and tells Elsie to leave a key for Mickey, with the hope that his mother's picture will encourage the boy to reform. Mickey returns home to find the house empty. He receives his father's message from a neighbor, embraces his mother's photo, and then sobs, dropping the stolen money on the ground. Sometime later in Naples, Don Ciccio, Elena, Mario and their baby receive a letter informing them that Mickey has indeed reformed himself and become a great contractor. *Assimilation (Sociology). Cultural conflict. Family life. Immigrants. Italian Americans. Widowers. Banks.* Birthdays. Dismissal (Employment). Marriage. Moral reformation. Naples (Italy). New York City. Photographs. Romance. Slavery–Emancipation. Songs.

Note: The plot summary was taken from a dialogue continuity deposited at the NYSA. The working title of this film was *The Immigrant*. The film was also known by its English title of *The Immigrant*, under which it is listed in the *AFI Catalog of Feature Films, 1931-40*; F3.2106. In Apr 1932, the film's title was changed to *Santa Lucia Luntana*, and in Mar 1934, it was changed again to *My Son (Mio figlio)*, according to NYSA records.

FD 4 Nov 1931, p. 4. FD 8 Nov 1931, p. 5.

THE CUP OF FURY (German Americans)
Eminent Authors Pictures, Inc. *Dist* Goldwyn Distributing Corp. Jan **1920** [©Rupert Hughes; 31 Dec 1919; LP14707]. Si; b&w. 6-7 reels.
Pres Samuel Goldwyn and Rex Beach. *Dir* T. Hayes Hunter. *Asst dir* Claude Camp. *Scen* E. Richard Schayer. *Cam* Abe Scholtz.
Source: Based on the novel *The Cup of Fury* by Rupert Hughes (New York, 1919).
Cast: Helene Chadwick (*Marie Louise, "Mamise"*), Rockcliffe Fellowes (*Davidge*), Frank Leigh (*Nicky*), Clarissa Selwyn (*Lady Clifton-Wyatt*), Kate Lester (*Lady Webling*), Herbert Standing (*Sir Joseph Webling*), Florence Deshon (*Polly Widdicombe*), Dwight Crittenden (*Major Widdicombe*), Sydney Ainsworth (*Verrinder*), H. A. Morgan (*Jake*), Marion Colvin (*Abbie*), Wade Boteler (*Larry*), Elinor Hancock (*Mrs. Prothero*).
Espionage, Drama. When Marie Louise's foster parents commit suicide in order to avoid charges of treason, she emigrates from Germany to America. Once there, she is met with suspicion wherever she goes. One day she meets Davidge, an American shipbuilder, and induces him to give her a job in the shipyards as her contribution ot the war effort. While at work in the plant, Marie is approached by Verrinder, a German spy, who attempts to enlist her in his plot to sabotage the operations. Marie, with Davidge's help, foils Verrinder's scheme and is vindicated of all suspicion when the next vessel launched is named for her. At dockside, Davidge announces their engagement. *Espionage. German Americans. Germans. Immigrants. Patriotism. Sabotage. Shipyards. World War I.* Foster parents. Germany. Shipbuilders. Spies. Suicide. Treason.
Note: Rupert Hughes' novel was serialized in *The Red Book Magazine* from Sep 1918 to Jun 1919. This was the first production of Eminent Authors' Pictures, Inc., a company formed to produce films from the works of a select number of famous authors. The individual author would, according to a news item, "have the final power of direction and supervision of his work." According to news items, Rupert Hughes worked with Anthony Paul Kelly on the adaptation of the film. One news item credits Eve Unsell with work on the adaptation. Rex Beach was the president and Samuel Goldwyn was the chairman of the board of directors of the company. The film was made at the Goldwyn studios in Culver City, CA. It had its premiere in Los Angeles in Jan 1920.
ETR 24 Jan 1920, p. 807. MPN 7 Feb 1920, p. 1391. MPN 24 Apr 1920, p. 3737. MPW 7 Jun 1919, p. 1469. MPW 21 Feb 1920, p. 1291. NYMT 11 Apr 1920. Wid's 11 Apr 1920, p. 7.

THE CURSE OF CAPISTRANO *see* **THE MARK OF ZORRO** (1920)

CUSTER'S LAST FIGHT (Native Americans, Cheyenne, Dakota)
Dist Quality Amusement Corp. **1925.** Sd; b&w. 4,250 ft.
Prod under the personal supv of Thomas H. Ince. *Story* Richard V. Spencer. *Ed and titled by* Inez A. Ridgway.
Western. [*Print viewed*]. The Cheyenne and Sioux nations, both bitterly opposed to the advance of white civilization, join forces in attempting to stem the flow of westward-moving immigrants in Wyoming and Montana by attacking immigrants and forts on the Bozeman wagon trail in Montana. In 1868, Congress orders several forts closed and grants the Sioux exclusive use of a vast territory, filling the Indians with pride and insolence. Soon, however, the Northern Pacific Railroad sends a survey team to the area in 1873. When two of the surveyors wander away from the main group, a warrior named Rain-in-the-Face kills them both. During the following year, agent James McLaughlin overhears the warrior boasting of his kill at a government Indian post and wires Fort Abraham Lincoln for help. Capt. Tom Custer, the brother of Gen. George Armstrong Custer, arrests Rain-in-the-Face, but the Indian later escapes. Lured by gold discovered in the Black Hills, white settlers and adventurers ignore the government ban and flood into Sioux territory. In 1875, the Sioux are notified that by the following year, they must reside only on designated reservations, but Sitting Bull, the medicine man of the Sioux, defies the order. In early 1876, Gen. Terry, Col. Gibbon, and Gen. Crook join Custer in attempting to force the Indians onto the reservations. Terry's force of twelve-hundred men moves into Montana to join Gibbon's column. They set up camp near the Big Horn Mountains, in whose valleys the Indians are preparing to fight. Meanwhile, Custer and his Seventh Cavalry are sent into the area. Their scouts, Crow Indians who are enemies of the Sioux, report a large encampment of the enemy on the Little Big Horn River. Custer orders Maj. Reno to storm the Indian village, planning to join the attack from higher ground. The Indians at the camp, who comprise a far larger group than Custer expects, are celebrating a Sun Dance, but

when Reno attacks, they force him to retreat. As Custer approaches the village, Reno finds himself engaged in battle on the opposite side of the river and decides that it is too dangerous to leave this position. Greatly outnumbered, Custer and the Seventh Cavalry fight bravely, while Tom fights Rain-in-the-Face, who cuts out his heart. As Sitting Bull "makes medicine" for victory at a safe distance, Rain-in-the-Face and his brother Gall then charge their enemies, and Custer, along with every soldier in his detachment, is killed. Following the battle, Indian squaws and youths swarm onto the field to strip and mutilate the bodies. The body of Custer is left untouched, however, as he is recognized as a "great chief." The Indians sing in celebration all through the night, but when Terry and Gibbon approach with the infantry, they flee. Terry weeps over Custer's body, and the 212 men who died in the battle are buried on the field. Upon hearing this news, Mrs. Custer and the other women of Fort Abraham Lincoln are stricken with grief. The pursuit of Sitting Bull lasts for several years. Deserted by Rain-in-the-Face, Sitting Bull and the starving remnants of his band surrender at Fort Buford in 1881. At an Indian agency in 1890, Sitting Bull initiates the Ghost Dance, a religious ceremony intended to hasten the day when the ghosts of dead Indians will return and drive great herds of ponies and buffalo. On this day, the belief goes, the "paleface" will be smothered in the earth, and the Indian will again reign supreme. During the Ghost Dance, many Indians go into a trance, and Sitting Bull states that one of the celebrants is in communication with spirits. So powerful is the Ghost Dance that Sitting Bull is arrested, but because he resists, he is killed by an Indian policeman. At Custer's funeral, a large monument is erected and the U.S. flag flies. *Battles. General George Armstrong Custer. Dakota Indians. Heroism. Indians of North America. Little Big Horn, Battle of the, 1876. Sitting Bull.* Black Hills (SD and WY). Braggarts. Cheyenne Indians. Cowardice. Dancing. Massacres. Medicine men. Montana. Murder. Officers (Military). Rites and ceremonies. Trance. United States–History–Indian campaigns. United States. Army. Cavalry. Wyoming.
Note: This film is an expanded version of a 1912 Bison three-reel film, *Custer's Last Raid*, originally produced by the New York Motion Picture Co. and distributed by the Tower Film Corp. In the 1925 version, there are more intertitles, which differ in appearance from those used in the 1912 film. The battle scenes were lengthened, and some of the actions that do not occur or that are merely described by intertitles in the 1912 release were fully dramatized in the later version. Modern sources list the 1912 cast members as Francis Ford, Anna Little, Grace Cunard, William Eagleshirt, J. Barney Sherry, Charles K. French, Lillian Christie, Snowball and Art Acord, and credit Ray Smallwood as the photographer. The Ghost Dance religion was founded in 1888 by a Paiute Indian named Wovoka, son of the mystic Tavibo. In Nov 1890, after the Ghost Dance had been banned from Sioux reservations, Kicking Bear and Short Bull, both Miniconjou Tetons, invited Sitting Bull to join them in defying the ban. Before he could leave the Standing Rock Reservation in North Dakota, however, Indian police attempted to arrest him. In the scuffle, he and seven of his warriors were killed. For more information about Custer and the Battle of Little Big Horn, please see the entry below for *They Died With Their Boots On.*

CUSTER'S LAST STAND (Native Americans, Cheyenne, Dakota)
Exploitation Pictures, Inc.; Weiss Productions, Inc.; A Weiss-Mintz Exploitation Serial. *Dist* State Rights; Stage and Screen Productions, Inc. 2 Apr **1936**; Prod: recorded at International Film Studios. Sd; b&w. 9 reels. 94 min. Passed by the National Board of Review.
Pres GEORGE M. MERRICK. *Supv* Louis Weiss. *Dir* Elmer Clifton. *Asst dir* Adrian Weiss. *Orig scr* George Arthur Durlam, Eddy Graneman and Bob Lively. *Photog* Bert Longenecker. *Film ed* Holbrook Todd and George M. Merrick. *Mus dir* Hal Chasnoff. *Sd eng* T. T. Triplett. *Prod mgr* George M. Merrick. [*Prod*] *Assistant* Bill Salzman.
Cast: Rex Lease (*Kit Cardigan*), Lona Andre (*Belle Meade*), William Farnum (*Fitzpatrick, Indian agent*), Ruth Mix (*Mrs. Elizabeth Custer*), Jack Mulhall (*Lieutenant Cook*), Nancy Caswell (*Barbara Trent*), George Chesboro (*Lieutenant Roberts*), Dorothy Gulliver (*Red Fawn*), Frank McGlynn, Jr. (*Gen. George A. Custer*), Helen Gibson (*Calamity Jane*), Josef Swickard (*Major [Henry] Trent*), Chief Thundercloud (*Young Wolf*), Reed Howes (*Tom "Keen" Blade*), Bobbie Nelson (*Bobby [Nelson]*), Robert Walker (*Henchman Pete*), Marty Joyce (*Buzz*), Milburn Moranti (*Buckskin*), George Morrell (*Sergeant Flannigan*), Creighton Hale (*Hank*), Ted Adams (*Buffalo Bill [/Barney]*), Carl Mathews (*Curley [/True Eagle]*), Allan Greer (*Wild Bill Hickok*), High Eagle (*Crazy Horse*), Howling Wolf (*Sitting Bull*), Big Tree (*Medicine Man*), Iron Eyes (*Brown Fox*), Chick Davis (*Rain-in-the-face*), Bill Desmond (*Wagon*

master), Walter James (*Judge Hooker*), James Sheridan (*Jim*), Ken Cooper (*Spike*), Budd Buster (*Major Ware*), Carter Wayne (*Striker Martin*), Cactus Mack (*Lieut. Weir*), Barney Fury (*Sergeant Peters*), Lafe McKee (*Captain Benteen*), Franklyn Farnum (*Major Reno*), Ed Withrow (*Blue Crow*), Artie Ortego (*Quirk*), [Patter Poe (*Crow Scout*)], [Mabel Strickland (*Mabel*)], [''Sunday'' (*Sunday*)], [Lone Star, Humming Bird, I. R. Swift Eagle, Tall Tree, Little Eagle, Lone Pine, Herb Jackson, J. Spencer (*Renegades*)].

Historical, Western. [*Print viewed*]. When Indians raid a group of white settlers, the Indians' medicine man is killed, and Major Henry Trent collects the man's arrow, which bears directions to a cave in the Black Hills filled with gold. In Black Pool, casino owner Tom ''Keen'' Blade, who secretly sells liquor to the Indians, befriends Young Wolf, who needs the magic arrow for its healing powers. Blade then kills three of the four white survivors of the skirmish, including John Cardigan, who was in search of the arrow. A year later, Trent, his daughter Barbara, and grandson Bobby come to Fort Henry just as General George A. Custer arrives and restores sobriety to the 7th U.S. Cavalry headquarters. Meanwhile, Sioux and Cheyenne Indian chiefs plan their attack on the white man to stop the gold prospectors and settlers who are encroaching on their sacred grounds. At the powwow, Crazy Horse, leader of the Cheyenne, marks Little Big Horn as the communal village which will serve as their fortress. The Trents are then ambushed by Young Wolf's men, but they survive, and the arrow remains intact. While Custer and Chief Brown Fox have a powwow concerning three braves captured at Black Pool for trading ''fire-water'' for pelts, Blade kills the Indian who is about to reveal Blade's guilt, and Indians raid the fort. The Indians eventually retreat, but the incident propels the Sioux and Cheyenne to Little Big Horn. Next, Blade schemes with the crooked Judge Hooker to arrest the Trents for inciting a riot with the Indians, and a jury sentences them to die in an hour. Ex-lieutenant Roberts, who testified against the Trents, has a change of heart, however, and rescues them. Custer's head scout, Kit Cardigan, then kills Hooker in a duel, and Roberts acknowledges Blade's guilt in Kit's father's murder. After Bobby finds the arrow, Young Wolf attacks him, but Kit saves him and gives the arrow to his Indian friend, Red Fawn. He then proposes to Barbara as the war begins. At Little Big Horn, the Indians massacre Custer and his men, including Roberts, and the American flag falls. After finally killing Blade in a duel, Kit gets his discharge from the army and unites with Barbara. *Black Hills (SD and WY). Cheyenne Indians. Chief Crazy Horse. General George Armstrong Custer. Dakota Indians. Duplicity. Indians of North America. Little Big Horn, Battle of the, 1876. Moral reformation. Murder. Prospectors. Religious articles. Scouts (Frontier). Settlers. Sitting Bull. United States. Army. Cavalry. Casino owners. Drunkenness. Duels. False arrests. Fathers and daughters. Grandsons. Liquor. Magic. Medicine men. Proposals (Marital). Raids. Rescues. Saloons.*

Note: Prior to the feature release, Stage and Screen Productions released a serial version of *Custer's Last Stand* through state rights exchanges starting 2 Jan 1936; the first episode was five reels and was followed by fourteen two-reel episodes. *HR* announced on 23 Jan 1936 that the serial was to be distributed by RKO in India, and was set for release in fourteen foreign countries. This film was compiled from the first of three Weiss-Mintz serials. The second serial, *The Clutching Hand*, was also released as a feature, but the third, *The Black Coin* was released only as a serial. In Mar 1936, *HR* stated that Lloyds of London was involved in a lawsuit filed by Western Costume Company over props and scenery that were stolen while the production was on location at Vasquez Rocks in the Angeles National Forest. No reviews were found for the feature, although *MPH* reviewed the first three chapters of the serial on 30 Nov 1935. Modern sources list the following additional cast members for the serial, although some of the actors may not have appeared in the feature: Whitey Sovern, Buddy Fisher, Charles Hunter, William Hunt, White Feather, Walter Gable, Bill Thompson, William Bartlett and Red Star Cody.

Other films based on General Custer include the 1909 Selig Polyscope film *On the Little Big Horn or Custer's Last Fight*, starring Paul McCormick, Jr.; the 1916 Vitagraph film *Britton of the Seventh* directed by Lionel Belmore and starring Darwin Karr and Charles Kent (see above); *Custer's Last Fight*, a 1925 re-issue of a Thomas Ince film, and the 1926 Universal film *The Flaming Frontier*, directed by Edward Sedgwick and starring Hoot Gibson and Anne Cornwall (see below) and the 1941 Warner Bros. film *They Died with Their Boots On*, directed by Raoul Walsh and starring Errol Flynn and Olivia de Havilland (see below). There was also a the 1968 U.S.—Spanish co-production *Custer of the West*, directed by Robert Siodmak and starring Robert Shaw, Mary Ure and Robert Ryan; and the 1991 ABC Television film *Son of the Morning Star*, directed by Mike Robe and starring Gary Cole, Rosanna Arquette and Dean Stockwell.

HR 23 Jan 1936, p. 2. *HR* 7 Mar 1936, p. 4. *MPH* 30 Nov 1935, p. 66.

THE CYCLONE (Chinese Americans)

Fox Film Corp. *Dist* Fox Film Corp. Jan—Feb **1920** [©William Fox; 25 Jan 1920; LP14672]. Si; b&w. 5 reels.

Dir Cliff Smith. *Scen* J. Anthony Roach. *Story* Col. Todhunter Marigold. *Cam* Frank Good.

Cast: Tom Mix (*Sergeant Tim Ryerson*), Colleen Moore (*Sylvia Sturgis*), Henry Hebert (*Ferdinand Baird*), William Ellingford (*Silas Sturgis*).

Northwest, Drama. Sergeant Tim Ryerson of the North West Mounted Police is commissioned to round up a gang that smuggles Chinese laborers across the border. While visiting his fiancée, Sylvia Sturgis, at her father's ranch, Tim becomes suspicious of ranch foreman Ferdinand Baird, who is the leader of the smugglers. One night, Tim catches Baird smuggling Chinese across the border to the United States, but Baird escapes and flees to the Sturgis house where he abducts Sylvia. Tim pursues Baird to Vancouver's Chinatown where he raids the smuggler's headquarters and rescues Sylvia. *Canadian-American border region. Chinese. North West Mounted Police. Ranch foremen. Smuggling. Abduction. Chinatowns. Ranches. Vancouver (Canada).*

Note: The Canadian Royal North West Mounted Police cooperated in the making of this film.

ETR 24 Jan 1920, p. 815. *MPN* 31 Jan 1920, p. 1321. *MPW* 31 Jan 1920, p. 776. *Var* 27 Feb 1920, p. 46. *Wid's* 18 Jan 1920, p. 15.

CYCLONE FURY (Native Americans)

Columbia Pictures Corp. *Dist* Columbia Pictures Corp. Sep **1951**; Prod: 8 Jan—11 Jan 1951 [©Columbia Pictures Corp.; 15 Aug 1951; LP1227]. Sd (Western Electric Recording); b&w. 6 reels, 4,777 ft. 54 min. PCA cert no. 15207.

Series: The Durango Kid.

Prod Colbert Clark. *Dir* Ray Nazarro. [*Asst dir* Gilbert Kay]. *Wrt* Barry Shipman and Ed. Earl Repp. *Dir of photog* Henry Freulich. *Art dir* Charles Clague. *Film ed* Paul Borofsky. *Set dec* George Montgomery. *Mus supv* Paul Mertz. *Mus dir* Mischa Bakaleinikoff. [*Sd eng* Russell Malmgren].

Song(s): ''Trumpet Polka,'' by Smiley Burnette; ''I'll Be Gettin' Some Sleep'' and ''That's the Wind Singin' a Cowboy Song,'' composers undetermined.

Cast: CHARLES STARRETT [(*Steve Reynolds/The Durango Kid*)], Fred F. Sears [(*Capt. Barbam*)], Clayton Moore [(*Grat Hanlon*)], Bob Wilke [(*Bunco*)], Merle Travis and his Bronco Busters, Smiley Burnette [(*Smiley Burnette*)], [Louis Lettieri (*Johnny*)], [George Chesebro (*Bret Fuller*)], [Frank O'Connor (*Doc*)], [Jay Silverheels].

Western, with songs. [*Print viewed*]. In the 1880s, Steve Reynolds is employed as a government agent to help tame the remnants of the once-vast herds of wild mustangs in the West for use by the Army. In Arizona, Steve leases 15,000 acres of the finest grazing land to Bronc Masters to raise horses for the Army, but later learns that Bronc has died from being thrown by a horse. Suspecting foul play, Steve begins to investigate. Grat Hanlon, who has tried to get Bronc off the land, sends his colleague Bunco to follow Steve so that he won't interfere with their men who are running off the horses. At Bronc's ranch, the Durango Kid, a masked man on a white horse, sees four men, including Grat and Bunco, firing guns to herd horses. He climbs a tree and jumps the rear two. After a gun battle, Grat and Bunco ride off. At a town meeting to award the contract for delivering horses to the Army, Grat claims he can supply 300 head a month, an amount no other rancher can match. He admits he plans to use Bronc's herd, contending they will become the property of the first man who can round them up, but Steve introduces the herd's new owner, an Indian boy named Johnny, whose father saved Bronc's life. After Johnny's parents died in a smallpox epidemic that killed many Indians, Bronc legally adopted Johnny. Steve vows to deliver the 300 head per month with Johnny. Grat, who hates Indians, sends a henchman to Johnny's hotel room, but the boy escapes, falling out the window. Laid up with a broken leg, Johnny gives Steve's sidekick, Smiley Burnette, a message to take to Chief Running Wolf to have him start rounding up the horses. Grat overhears the message and sends his henchmen to stop Smiley from reaching Indian country. After one of the henchmen shoots at Smiley, the Durango Kid shoots one of the pursuers, then sends the other off to hobble home without his boots. Although Smiley inadvertently burns up the message while sending

smoke signals, he is able to relay it verbally to the Indians. Grat next comes up with a plan to delay the transaction between the Army and Johnny by having his men rob the bank where Captain Barham keeps $15,000 of government money, which he plans to use for the deal. When the bank is robbed by four masked men, the Durango Kid follows them, and when they split in pairs, he pursues the two with the money bags and recovers them. Grat, meanwhile, threatens to arrange a new deal with an officer who outranks the captain, Colonel W. S. Fawcett at nearby Fort Starr. When the Durango Kid returns the money, Grat calls for Bunco, and the Kid hits him. As the Kid rides off, Grat begins a gunfight, but the Kid shoots the gun from his hand. Grat then receives a telegram from Colonel Fawcett, who says he'll listen to his proposition the next day. As Grat prepares to leave for the fort, he instructs Bunco to get a henchman to finish Steve off. Steve knocks out the henchman, then sends Smiley to find wranglers to help get the horses to town. The Durango Kid then meets with Chief Red Wing and his Indians, and explains that bad white men will steal from Johnny if the horses are not at Cyclone Canyon soon. The Indians send a smoke signal to another tribe for help. The next day, Grat returns with the colonel's signature on a new contract that will take effect at six if the horses are not delivered. When Bunco tells Grat that the Indians have rounded up more than 300 horses and delivered them to wranglers working for Steve and Johnny, Grat orders him to get his men together to stop them. They plan to capture the horses at Little Neck Canyon, which the horses have to pass through. As six o'clock approaches, the Kid and his followers chase off Grat's gang in a gun battle. In town, the Kid finds Grat at his safe and shoots a gun from his hand, then bests him in a fistfight. At five minutes before six, the horses, led by Smiley, run through the town's main street and are put into corrals. Later, Steve tells the captain, Johnny and Smiley that Grat has confessed to Bronc's murder. Johnny tells Steve to thank his friend, the Durango Kid. *Children. Government agents. Horse thieves. Horses. Indians of North America. Masked bandits. Orphans. Ranchers. Arizona. Bank robberies. Coffins. Hotels. Messengers. Officers (Military). Racism. United States–History–19th century. United States. Army. Wounds and injuries.*

Note: The working title of this film was *Cyclone Canyon.* For information about the "Durango Kid" series, please see the entry below for *Laramie.* *Box* 1 Sep 1951. *DV* 10 Aug 1951, p. 3. *Exb* 15 Aug 1951, p. 3125. *FD* 14 Aug 1951, p. 6. *HR* 5 Jan 1951, p. 10. *HR* 10 Aug 1951, p. 3. *MPD* 14 Aug 1951. *MPHPD* 18 Aug 1951, p. 982. *Var* 15 Aug 1951, p. 6.

CYCLONE OF THE SADDLE (Native Americans)
Weiss Productions, Inc.; A Range Rider Western. *Dist* State Rights; Superior Talking Pictures, Inc. Dec **1935**; Prod: began 7 Mar 1935 at Argosy Studios. Sd (International Recording); b&w. 6 reels, 4,804 ft. 55 min. Passed by the National Board of Review.
Pres GEO. M. MERRICK. *Supv* Louis Weiss. *Dir* Elmer Clifton. *Story and dial* Elmer Clifton and Geo. M. Merrick. *Photog* Eddie Linden. *Sd eng* Cliff Ruberg.
Song(s): "The Old Wagon Train," "Goin' Home" and "There's No Place Like Home," composer unknown.
Cast: Rex Lease (*Andy [Thomas]*), Janet Chandler (*Sue*), Bobby Nelson (*Dick*), Yakima Canutt (*Snake*), Helen Gibson (*Ma*), Milburn Moranti (*Pa*), Chick Davis (*High Hawk*), Chief Standing Bear (*Porcupine*), Chief Thunder Cloud (*Yellow Wolf*), George Chesebro (*Cherokee [Carter]*), Art Mix (*Pioneer*), Bill Desmond (*Wagon master*), Black Fox, the Scholar Horse [(*Black Fox*)], [Range Ranglers Band], [George Morrell].
Western, with songs. [*Print viewed*]. Andy Thomas, a member of the United States Cavalry, goes undercover in order to stop a gang of outlaws who are selling guns and whiskey to the Indians and are conspiring with them to rob passing wagon trains. Introducing himself as "Johnson," Andy hooks up with a wagon train, whose members include a young boy named Dick, his pretty older sister Sue, and their parents. The next day, while Dickie is out riding, his horse, Black Fox, sees a group of menacing Indians and whinnies in order to warn Dickie, who races back to the wagon train to sound the alarm. A gun and arrow battle ensues in which Dickie and Sue's father is killed. After Pa's funeral, two outlaws, Cherokee Carter and his partner, Snake, infiltrate the wagon train by posing as victims of the Indian attack in need of protection. Cherokee harasses Sue and challenges Andy's riding skill by betting that he cannot stay on top of one of Cherokee's wild ponies. Andy succeeds in riding the pony, earning the nickname "Cyclone of the Saddle," and Cherokee vows

revenge. Dickie, Sue and Ma return safely to their homestead, but Cherokee shows up to menace Sue, and Dickie shoots him in the hand. A furious Cherokee kills two Indian braves, steals their ponies, and then plants them on Dickie and Sue's homestead. When the Indians arrive to reclaim their property, they kidnap Dickie and Black Fox. Black Fox manages to escape, however, and, carrying an Indian charm in his mouth, he goes straight to Andy. Cherokee lies to the Indian chief Yellow Wolf, telling him that other white men killed the braves. The Indians prepare to attack, while Andy, disguised in Indian garb, rescues Dickie and sends him to the fort to alert the soldiers to the impending battle. After a brief fight, the Indians surrender and express their willingness to sign a new peace treaty. Realizing that they had been duped by Cherokee, they request that he be delivered to them to face judgment by the "Great Spirit in the Sky." Andy and Sue embrace in a meadow, and he promises to build her a house by the river as soon as his enlistment is over. *Homesteaders. Horses. Impersonation and imposture. Indians of North America. Outlaws. Robbery. Brothers and sisters. Disguise. Forts. Gunrunners. Horse thieves. Kidnapping. Rescues. Revenge. Romance. Treaties. United States. Army. Cavalry. Wagon trains.*
Note: Although the opening credits of the viewed print included a 1935 copyright statement, the title was not listed in the copyright catalog. According to modern sources, the cast also included Glenn Strange (*Band singer/townsman*).
Exb 1 Aug 1935. *FD* 3 Apr 1935, p. 11. *HR* 7 Mar 1935, p. 3.

THE CYCLONE RANGER (Latino)
Spectrum Pictures Corp.; Ray Kirkwood's Production. *Dist* State Rights; Spectrum Pictures Corp. 15 Mar **1935**. Sd; b&w. 5,382 ft. 60 or 65 min. Passed by the National Board of Review. PCA cert no. 952.
Supv Ray Kirkwood. *Dir* Bob Hill. [*Wrt*] *by* Oliver Drake. *Photog* Don Keyes.
Cast: BILL CODY [(*The Pecos Kid*)], Nena Quartaro [(*Nita Garcia*)], Eddie Gribbon [(*Duke*)], Solidad Jimines [sic] [(*Doña Castelar*)], Earl Hodgins [(*Pancho Gonzales*)], Zara Tazil [(*Martha*)], Donald Reed [(*Juan Castelar*)], Colin Chase [(*Sheriff Luke Saunders*)], [Bud Buster (*Clem Rankin*)], [Jerry Ellis (*Pete*)], [Anthony Natale (*Felipe*)], [Bill Moore, Buck Morgan, Bud Pope, Frank Gates, Barney Beasley, Ace Cain (*Outlaws*)].
Western. [*Viewed print incomplete*]. The Pecos Kid, who is the leader of a band of cattle rustlers, shows his friend, Juan Castelar, a newspaper ad requesting information regarding Juan's whereabouts because his mother, Doña Castelar, is seriously ill. The ad was placed by Nita Garcia, whom Juan explains is his mother's ward. Juan tells Pecos that he ran away from home fifteen years before seeking adventure, but now it is time to return. Juan, Pecos and their friend, Pancho Gonzales, the Doña's servant who cares for Juan, agree to quit the gang and go to Juan's ranch in Mexico, where they will have a fresh start. Just then, Duke and other gang members arrive with Clem Rankin, a local loan shark whom they have kidnapped. Pecos is furious with Duke, telling him that the gang only rustles cattle and does not perpetrate violent crimes such as kidnapping or murder. Pecos orders Duke to free Rankin, after which he tells Duke that he is now the head of the gang. The three friends leave, but they are soon pursued by Sheriff Luke Saunders and his posse, who have been told about the kidnapping by Rankin. Juan is shot in the chase, and while Pecos and Pancho try to help him, Juan knows that they will not be able to elude capture with him holding them back. Juan commits suicide, and Pancho and Pecos sadly continue to the ranch to tell Doña Castelar the news. Once they arrive, however, they discover that the Doña is blind, and she mistakes Pecos for Juan as Juan had given him his ring. Nita also thinks Pecos is Juan, and the two former bandits do not have the heart to tell the truth to her or the kindly blind woman, who is overjoyed by her "son's" return. They settle into life on the ranch until one day Duke and his men appear. Duke tells the Doña and Nita that he is the Pecos Kid, and Pecos and Pancho are forced to go along with the charade. Duke wants to steal the ranch's cattle, but Pecos stalls him for a week, and when Duke complains about waiting, Pecos promises to give him the deposit for the cattle's sale after the roundup. That night, Duke steals the deposit money, and before Pecos and Pancho can apprehend him, they are captured by Duke's men. At their hideout, Duke orders his men to raid the herd anyway. Pecos manages to escape, then returns to free Pancho. Meanwhile, Saunders arrives at the ranch house and shows Nita a wanted poster of Pecos, and tells her that the real Juan is dead. Pancho arrives and

after telling him of Pecos' good intentions, asks for his help in catching Duke. Pancho promises that he and Pecos will return with Saunders to jail in exchange for his assistance, and the men and Nita ride to the rescue. They reach the herd, where Pecos is fighting with Duke. The gang is rounded up, and Duke is stabbed in the fight with Pecos. Saunders tears up the wanted poster and wishes Pecos good luck in his new life. Pecos promises to go straight, and he and Nita happily embrace. *Impersonation and imposture. Mexican Americans. Mexicans. Mistaken identity. Moral reformation. Mothers and sons. Rustlers. Bandits. Blindness. Kidnapping. Knife wounds. Mexican-American border region. Posses. Ranches. Self-sacrifice. Servants. Sheriffs. Suicide. Wards and guardians.*

Note: Although there is a copyright statement on the opening title card of this film, the title is not listed in the copyright catalog. The onscreen credits of the print viewed include those for producer Ray Kirkwood, writer Oliver Drake and the cast; other credits were obtained from contemporary sources. According to a *FD* news item, this was the second in a proposed series of eight westerns featuring Cody and his Arabian horse, "Chico." The plots of *The Cyclone Ranger* (see below) and the 1933 Western Star Productions picture *Gun Law* (see *AFI Catalog of Feature Films, 1931-40*; F3.1749), both of which were written by Oliver Drake, bear a striking resemblance to each other, although no information has been located to verify that the later picture was a remake of the earlier one. Modern sources include Herman Hack in the cast.

Box 30 Mar 1935. *FD* 7 Feb 1935, p. 15. *FD* 20 Mar 1935, p. 11. *MPD* 23 Mar 1935, p. 3. *MPH* 6 Apr 1935, p. 54. *Var* 22 May 1935, p. 17.

CYNTHIA'S SECRET see DARK DELUSION

DADDY'S GONE A-HUNTING see WOMEN LOVE ONCE

DÄMON DES MEERES (German language)

Warner Bros. Pictures, Inc. *Dist* Warner Bros. Pictures, Inc. **1931**; Berlin opening: 2 Mar 1931. Sd; b&w. Length undetermined. German language.

Supv Heinz Blanke. *Dir* Michael Curtiz. *Scr* Ulrich Steindorff. *Photog* Sid Hickox.

Source: Based on the novel *Moby Dick, or The Whale* by Herman Melville (New York, 1851).

Cast: Wilhelm Dieterle, Lissy Arna, Anton Pointner, Karl Etlinger, Carla Bartheel, Lothar Mayring, Bert Sprotte, Otto Kottke, Reginald Pasch, John Eskridge, Adolph Milar.

Sea, Adventure. *[Not viewed].* [This is the German-language version of the 1930 English-language film, *Moby Dick*. The plot of that film is similar to that of the 1926 film *The Sea Beast*, which is given below; character names refer to that film. For further information regarding the English-language version, please see the note below and the entry for *Moby Dick* in the *AFI Catalog of Feature Films, 1921-30*.] Ahab Ceeley and his half brother, Derek, are rivals for the hand of Esther Harper, a minister's beautiful daughter. Because Esther favors his brother, Derek pushes Ahab overboard on a whaling trip; Ahab's leg is chewed off by Moby Dick, a white whale; and he returns to Esther a broken and embittered man. Ahab, believing that Esther no longer loves him, becomes captain of a whaler and obsessively sets out to kill Moby Dick. Ahab learns of Derek's treachery and, after killing the whale, kills Derek. Ahab return to New Bedford and, his obsession gone, settles down with Esther. *Clergy. Courtship. New Bedford (MA). Sea captains. Whales and whaling.*

Note: The 1930 English-language version, entitled *Moby Dick*, was directed by Lloyd Bacon and starred John Barrymore and Joan Bennett. Other films based on the same source include the 1926 Warner Bros. film entitled *The Sea Beast*, which was directed by Millard Webb and starred John Barrymore and Dolores Costello (see *AFI Catalog of Feature Films, 1921-30*; F2.4858) and the 1956 Warner Bros. release *Moby Dick*, which was produced and directed by John Huston and starred Gregory Peck and Richard Basehart. In 1954, NBC-TV broadcast a *Hallmark Hall of Fame* production, *Moby Dick*, which was produced and directed by Albert McCleery and starred Victor Jory and Hugh O'Brian.

THE DAGO see THE ITALIAN

DAKOTA INCIDENT (Native Americans, Cheyenne)

Republic Pictures Corp. *Dist* Republic Pictures Corp. 23 Jul **1956**; Prod: mid-Dec 1955—early Jan 1956 [©Republic Pictures Corp.; 14 Jun 1956; LP6813]. Sd (RCA); col (Trucolor). 88 min. PCA cert no. 17945.

Prod HERBERT J. YATES. *Assoc prod* Michael Baird. *Dir* Lewis R. Foster. *Asst dir* Leonard Kunody. *Wrt* Frederic Louis Fox. *Dir of photog* Ernest Haller. *Spec eff* Howard Lydecker and Theodore Lydecker. *Optical eff* Consolidated Film Industries. *Art dir* Walter Keller. *Film ed* Howard Smith. *Set dec* John McCarthy. *Set des* George Milo. *Cost des* Adele Palmer. *Mus* R. Dale Butts. *Sd* Melvin M. Metcalfe and Howard Wilson. *Makeup supv* Bob Mark.

Cast: Linda Darnell [(*Amy Clarke*)], Dale Robertson [(*John Banner*)], John Lund [(*Carter Hamilton*)], Ward Bond [(*Senator Blakeley*)], Regis Toomey [(*Minstrel*)], Skip Homeier [(*Frank Banner*)], Irving Bacon [(*Tully Morgan*)], John Doucette [(*Rick Largo*)], Whit Bissell [(*Mark Chester*)], William Fawcett [(*Matthew Barnes*)], Malcolm Atterbury [(*Bartender-desk clerk*)], Diane DuBois [(*Giselle*)], Charles Horvath [(*Indian leader*)], Rankin Mansfield (*Mr. Cooper*), Eva Novak (*Mrs. Cooper*), [Fred Coby, Bob Hinkle (*Bystanders*)], Eddie Baker (*Townsman*).

Western. [*Print viewed*]. On the run after a bank robbery, Rick Largo convinces his cohort, Frank Banner, to shoot Frank's brother John, then split the booty two ways. Johnny, however, only pretended to be dead after being shot, and when he shows up in town challenges his brother to a shoot-out, even though Frank swears that Largo fired the bullet. Frank misses and Johnny spares his life, then tells him to get out of town. Johnny next has a shootout with Largo, during which Largo is killed. With his vengeance completed, Johnny decides to find a horse so that he can get to Laramie, Wyoming, where he plans to buy a ranch. Meanwhile, saloon singer Amy Clarke also determines to get to Laramie so that she can retrieve money stolen from her by her crooked agent and former sweetheart. The stagecoach to Laramie is full, but Amy bribes the clerk with one of her scented garters and gets a place. When the stage arrives, the driver and horses are full of Cheyenne Indian arrows, and all the passengers are dead. Undaunted, Amy insists on taking the stage anyway and convinces Johnny to drive the coach and harness his newly-purchased horse to the rig. Although Amy's French maid Giselle refuses to accompany her mistress, four other passengers do: the bombastic Senator Blakeley, who continually espouses the Indian cause despite only knowing them in "the literary sense"; Carter Hamilton, a bank clerk sought for the robbery committed by Johnny and his gang, who is determined to follow the outlaw until he can turn him in; Mark Chester, a gold speculator from Pennsylvania; and Minstrel, Amy's accompanist, companion and protector. En route, the group stops to rest and finds Frank's corpse pierced with Cheyenne arrows. A short time later, they break a wheel and crash, and move the stage to the safety of a dry gully while they make repairs. Their precautions do not protect them from a Cheyenne attack, during which Chester is killed. A full-scale rifle battle ensues and, with each Indian attack, Amy ridicules Blakeley for his support of the "savages," but he continues to find excuses for the brutality. The Indians wait in the rocks above while the stranded travelers begin to feel the effects of thirst. When Hamilton and Johnny decide to try to steal one of the Indians' horses and get help, Hamilton is injured and Johnny shoots the Indian, saving Hamilton's life. When the two arrive back in the gully, they find Blakely flirting with Amy, who insults him by calling him "father" and incurs Johnny's jealousy. As the group continues to suffer from heat and thirst, Minstrel sees a mirage and insists on going to it, with Hamilton, in his own state of delirium, believing that Johnny lied about the lack of water. Minstrel is shot by the Indians, and Amy once again chides Blakeley, telling him to go and prove his pacifist methods by talking peace to the Indians. Blakeley goes out with open arms and words of brotherhood, but the Indians shoot him. As he dies, Blakeley concedes to Amy, who feels responsible for his death, that indeed words may not be enough, but that, perhaps, the Indians just did not understand. Soon Hamilton, too, is near death and Johnny decides to risk his own life for Hamilton by retrieving a canteen that the Indians planted as a lure. He takes the canteen but finds it dry, and then begins to taunt the Indians. Just then the gully begins to fill up with water, and Amy, bringing a drink to Hamilton, discovers him dead. An Indian attacks Johnny, and Johnny almost drowns him, but decides to spare his life, telling him to return to his people and report that a white man gave him back his life. Johnny tells Amy that he will keep his promise to the dying Hamilton to clear his name and return the money to the bank. She says that she no longer cares about her former sweetheart, and the two embrace just as the Indians return. The Indian whose life was spared brings two horses as a gift, and the couple regret that Blakeley could not have lived to see this act of friendship. *Cheyenne Indians. Friendship. Gunfights. Moral reformation. Romance. Stagecoaches. Bank clerks. Bank robberies. False accusations. Fratricide. Laramie (WY). Mirages. Reputation. Senators. Singers. Thirst.*

Note: A 17 Jan 1956 letter to the MPAA found in the file on this film in the MPAA/PCA Collection at the AMPAS Library states that the film was being produced by Landmark Productions, but no other source mentions that corporate name.
Exb 25 Jul 1956, p. 4197. *Har* 28 Jul 1956, p. 120. *HR* 16 Dec 1955, p. 16. *HR* 30 Dec 1955, p. 12. *HR* 25 Jul 1956. *MPD* 8 Aug 1956. *Var* 25 Jul 1956.

THE DALTON GANG (Native Americans, Navajo)

Lippert Productions, Inc. *Dist* Screen Guild Productions, Inc. 21 Oct **1949**; Prod: late Jun—early Jul 1949 at Nassour Studios [©Lippert Productions, Inc.; 22 Oct 1949; LP2590]. Sd (Glen Glenn Sound Co.); b&w. 6 reels, 5,297 ft. 58-59 min. PCA cert no. 16076.

Pres ROBERT L. LIPPERT. *Prod* Ron Ormond. *Assoc prod* Ira Webb and June Carr. *Dir* Ford Beebe. *Asst dir* Austin Jewell. *Dial [dir]* Gloria Welsch. *Wrt* Ford Beebe. *Dir of photog* Ernest Miller. *Cam op* Archie Dalzell. *Spec eff* Ray Mercer. [*Stills* James Doolittle]. *Art dir* Fred Preble. *Film ed* Huck Winn. *Set dec* Theodore Offenbecker. *Ward* Alfred Berke. *Mus dir* Walter Greene. *Sd eng* Glen Glenn and Earl Snyder. *Makeup artist* Paul Stanhope. *Scr supv* Moree Herring.

Cast: Don Barry [(*Larry West, also known as Rusty Stevens*)], Robert Lowery [(*Blackie Mullet*)], James Millican [(*Sheriff Jeb Marvin*)], Greg McClure [(*Missouri Ganz*)], Betty Adams [(*Polly Medford*)], Byron Foulger [(*Amos Boling*)], J. Farrell MacDonald [(*Judge Price*)], George Lewis [(*Chief Irahu*)], Ray Bennett [(*J. J. Gorman*)], Marshall Reed [(*Joe*)], Cliff Taylor [(*Dr. Water*)], Cactus Mack [(*Ed, stagedriver*)], [Lee Roberts (*Mac*)].

Western. [*Print viewed*]. In the western town of Rincon, Blackie Mullet, Missouri Ganz and Mac, outlaw brothers formerly known as the Dalton Gang, rob a bank, then kill a U.S. marshal while escaping. On his way to town to investigate the murder, Santa Fe marshal Larry West rescues a man named Joe after he is shot by the gang. Larry accompanies the wounded Joe into town, where he sees a wanted poster calling for the arrest of Navajo chief Irahu, whose braves have been blamed for the gang's crimes. Blackie tells newspaper editor Amos Boling that a marshal has been shot, and Joe agrees to pose as the marshal, while Larry takes the name Rusty Stevens and begins working undercover. Inside his print shop, Amos informs Larry that Blackie, who has taken a job with the Rincon Land and Water Company, has been living in town with his brothers. Then, Amos' assistant, Polly Medford, whose father, a land agent, was murdered by the gang, tells Larry that Irahu is innocent. At the Navajo village, Irahu tells Larry that the gang shot Medford before he could sign the lease for their reservation and framed Irahu for the crime. Convinced of Irahu's innocence, Larry refuses to serve the warrant, then resigns his post. Later, Larry goes to see Rincon Land and Water representative J. J. Gorman, hoping to infiltrate the gang. Mac, who has just returned from Santa Fe, recognizes Larry as the marshal sent to investigate the gang's crimes and dissuades Gorman from hiring him. After Larry leaves, Mac explains that Larry is actually the marshal, so Gorman instructs Missouri to provoke a fight so that he can shoot him in "self-defense." Later, Sheriff Jeb Marvin rides out to serve the warrant on Irahu, and when he returns, Blackie reports that Larry has been arrested for killing Missouri. Larry reveals that he is the real marshal, but when he asks Joe to verify this for the sheriff, he inexplicably refuses. Polly tells Irahu about Larry's imprisonment, and Irahu sends his braves to break him out of jail. After they use their horses to pull the bars out of his cell window, Larry escapes, then tells Amos to find Judge Price, while he sneaks in through Blackie's window at the hotel. At gunpoint, Blackie confesses that the land company wants to steal the reservation because of the watering hole there. Larry then attempts to arrest Blackie and is forced to shoot him when he resists. They go to the judge, where Blackie admits that the company's lease on the reservation is a forgery. The judge writes out warrants for the rest of the gang, and after Larry leaves to get Jeb, Blackie shoots the judge, then goes to the hotel. When Amos and Jeb arrive at the judge's home to get the warrants, they find his corpse. Then, Larry and Jeb enlist the help of Irahu's braves in arresting the gang, who are holed up at the hotel. A shootout begins, the gang surrenders, and everyone except Jeb, Blackie and Larry is shot. After Larry arrests Blackie, he learns that his superior refused to accept his resignation. Larry then proposes to Polly, and she happily accepts. *Arrests. Brothers. Confession (Law). Editors. Frame-ups. Land rights. Navajo Indians. Undercover operations. United States. Marshals. Escapes. Gunfights. Gunshot wounds. Hotels. Indians of North America–Reservations. Jailbreaks. Judges. Murder. Outlaws. Proposals (Marital). Sheriffs. Stagecoaches. Warrants.*

Note: The title on the viewed print was *The Outlaw Gang*, the film's television release title. Ford Beebe's onscreen credit reads: "Written and directed by Ford Beebe." Although he is not credited onscreen as producer, some reviews call this picture a Donald Barry Production. *HR* production charts include Tom Neal and Margia Dean in the cast, but their participation in the released film has not been confirmed. Modern sources include the following actors in the cast: Dick Curtis and Stanley Price.
DV 2 Nov 1949, p. 3. *HR* 24 Jun 1949, p. 12. *HR* 1 Jul 1949, p. 10. *HR* 2 Nov 1949, p. 3. *MPHPD* 28 Jan 1950. *NYT* 25 Nov 1949, p. 27. *Var* 30 Nov 1949, p. 6.

LA DAMA ATREVIDA (Spanish language)

First National Pictures, Inc.; controlled by Warner Bros. Pictures, Inc. *Dist* First National Pictures, Inc.; The Vitaphone Corp. **1931**; New York opening: 20 Mar 1931. Sd; b&w. 8 reels, 7,094 ft. 79 min. Spanish language.

[*Supv* Henry Blanke]. *Director [Dir]* William McGann. [*Dial dir* Guillermo Prieto Yeme]. [*Asst dir* Louis Marlowe]. [*Scr* Forrest Halsey and Kathryn Scola]. *Adaptada al español por [Spanish adpt]* Alvaro Gimeno. *Fotografía por [Photog]* Frank Kesson. *Editada por [Ed]* George Amy. *Dirección musical de [Mus dir]* Leo Forbstein.

Song(s): "Ojos tristes," words by Alfredo Aguilar Alfaro, music by Guty Cárdenas; "Piña madura," words and music by Guty Cárdenas.

Cast: Ramón Pereda [(*Jack Norton*)], Luana Alcañiz [(*Margarita Townsend*)], Martín Garralaga [(*Carlos Townsend*)], Lygia de Golconda [(*Juliana Fleming*)], Alfredo del Diestro [(*Mr. Fleming*)], Delia Magaña [(*Chinese woman*)], Antonio Vidal [(*Farrell*)], Guty Cárdenas [(*Singer*)], [Paco Moreno (*Mayordomo*)].

Melodrama. [*Viewed print incomplete*]. [The following plot summary is based on the English-language version of this film, *The Lady Who Dared*; character names were taken from that version.] Margaret Townsend, the wife of American Vice-Consul Charles Townsend, feels neglected because her husband spends most of his time working. To amuse herself, she accepts a dinner invitation from Julianne Boone-Fleming and her husband Seton. Jack Norton, a big-game hunter, has also been invited. Seton pretends to be drunk, and when Julianne leaves with him, Norton begins to warn Margaret that she should not have come. When he realizes he is being watched by the butler, Norton plays his part, kissing Margaret as the butler takes a picture to use for blackmail. Knowing that Norton is suspected of smuggling, Margaret returns and warns the Boone-Flemings that the Treasury agent, Farrell, suspects them of smuggling and that she is worried about the discovery of the photos. Julianne then calls Norton, one of her partners in the smuggling operation, to tell him to take the evidence with him to New York. Meanwhile, Margaret, who has been hiding in the house, snatches an envelope that she thinks contains the photos and escapes. Norton sees another envelope and pockets it. When Margaret discovers that she has the wrong envelope, she searches Norton's hotel room for the other, but Norton discovers her there and gives her the photos. He explains that he and Julianne have a child, and she has threatened to expose him to their daughter unless he goes along with her plans. Margaret tells Norton of Farrell's suspicions just as the agents, including Charles, arrive to search his luggage. Margaret hides, and to protect her identity, Norton confesses to the smuggling. Margaret gets safely away and plants evidence in the Boone-Flemings' luggage before tipping off the authorities. They are arrested and face a lengthy prison sentence. At the same time that Norton is being deported, Charles tells the story to his very interested wife. *Blackmail. Smuggling. Butlers. Diplomats. Fatherhood. Illegitimacy. Neglected wives. Self-sacrifice. United States. Treasury Department.*

Note: *La dama atrevida* is a Spanish-language version of the 1931 film *The Lady Who Dared*, directed by William Beaudine and starring Billie Dove, Sidney Blackmer and Conway Tearle (see *AFI Catalog of Feature Films, 1931-40*; F3.2359). Although the English-language version credits Kenneth J. Saunders with the story, and the Spanish-language version states that the film was based on Saunders' novel *The Devil's Playground*, according to notes in the file on the film in the Warner Bros. collection at the USC Cinema-Television Library, the film was actually based on W. E. Scutt's short story "The Whisper Market" in *Snappy Stories* (18 Jan 1918). For the Spanish-language version, the setting was changed from South America to China. According to modern sources, Alvaro Gimeno, the Spanish adaptor, also known as Alvaro Jimeno and Guillermo Prieto Yeme, the dialogue director, are the same person.
CM Jun 1931, p. 469. *FD* 7 Jun 1931, p. 11. *MPH* 1 Nov 1930. *NYT* 6 Jun 1931, p. 16. *Var* 9 Jun 1931, p. 18.

DAMIEN (Hawaiians)

Hawaiian Productions, Ltd. *Dist* Theatre Hawaii Ltd. **1950** Sd (Western Electric Mirrophonic Recording); b&w. 8 reels.

Prod Gene Fowler, Jr. and Tambi Larsen. *Dir* John Kneubuhl. *Wrt* John Kneubuhl. *Photog* George Tahara. *Prod des* Tambi Larsen. *Supv ed* Gene Fowler, Jr. *Film ed* Marjorie Fowler. *Mus* James Wolfe. *Sd* Yung Kang.

Cast: Russell Collins (*Joseph Damien de Veuster*), Stephan Desha (*Keaka*), Arlene Kim (*Milo*), Glenn Alana (*Kamuela*), Herman Luis (*Bishop*), Norman Wright (*Father Boniface*), Lydia Wright (*Princess Liliuokalani*), Martha Hohu (*Keakina*), David Kahamkahi (*Amalu*), Emily Taylor (*Pua*), Sargeant Kahanamoku (*Nueka*), Roger Kanealii (*The Kahuna*), Barry Yap (*Petero*), Tom Mullahey (*Trooper*), Phil Bolton (*Board of Health Chairman*), Arnold Spencer, Pat Hallaran, Henry Thompson, Russell Cades (*Board of Health members*), Gene Fowler (*Narrator*).

Biography, Historical, Drama. [*Not viewed*]. In 1866, on the island of Hawaii, the United States government decrees that all lepers must report for deportation to a settlement on the island of Molokai. When one of the notices is posted on the door of Father Joseph Damien de Veuster's rectory, the priest tears down the sign, distressed because several of his ailing parishioners are to be exiled to Molokai. As Damien attempts to comfort the exiles, a trooper interrupts him with news that one of his parishioners, Keaka, has attacked a guard and taken refuge in the hills with his leper wife. Following Keaka into the hills, Damien assures him that he may accompany his wife to Molokai, and Keaka chooses to join his wife in her journey to the "island of the dead." Seven years later, Damien is summoned by the bishop to assist in the dedication of a new church on the island of Maui. After the ceremony, the bishop appeals for a volunteer to go to the leper settlement, and Damien pleads to be the one chosen. Soon after, Damien arrives on Molokai and is met by three men carrying a corpse and a furious old man pelting him with stones. In terror, Damien runs to the little chapel standing alone by the sea under the cliffs. Bursting through the door, Damien collapses at the alter when the figure of a man turns to embrace him. Fearful at first, Damien recognizes the man as Keaka, welcoming him to the island. Behind them, three people shyly come forward to meet the priest: Milo, a young girl whose mother is dying of leprosy, and Amalu and Pua, who have accompanied their ailing relatives to the island. In Honolulu, meanwhile, the Board of Health convenes to allot funds for the leper colony. Although the Board is supportive, budget constraints dictate that only thirty-five dollars for lumber may be apportioned. On Molokai, the lumber is shaped into coffins for victims of the disease. When a Hawaiian family refuses a Christian burial for their child, Damien, despairing that he will not be able to establish a Christian congregation, returns defeated to the chapel and tells his four healthy friends that they must leave the island. In unison, they insist on staying with their beloved priest. Soon after, Kamuela, a recent arrival, storms into the chapel and spits on Damien's extended hand of greeting. Kamuela, a young leper from the city, charges that he has been refused shelter because he is a Protestant. In a heated exchange, Kamuela takes a pipe from the priest's pocket, places it in his mouth and then dares the priest to smoke it. When Damien lights up the pipe and invites Kamuela to spend the night in the chapel, he and the young leper become friends. Desperate for supplies, Damien travels to Honolulu, violating a law that forbids the inhabitants of the colony to leave the island. Damien's pleas to the Board of Heath move the members to empty their own pockets to provide supplies for the leper colony. With these funds, Damien buys lumber, tools and pipe to build a system to supply water to the waterless settlement. On Molokai, the lepers who have been won over by Damien's dedication, load the supplies into wagons and begin to build the pipeline and new housing. On Damien's birthday, the pipeline is finally completed. As the visiting members from the Board of Health turn the spigot, water splashes and gushes out, and Keaka fills several pitchers with water to take to the priest's new house. On the porch, Keaka notices that Milo is in tears, but when he approaches her, she runs away. After the visitors depart, Damien searches for Milo and finds her in a crumbling old shack. There she confides that she has fallen victim to the dreaded disease. Some time later, Princess Liliuokalani, the Regent of Hawaii, visits the settlement. Milo, ravaged by the disease, is now unable to walk or stand, and Kamuela is bandaged to his neck. Side by side, the princess and the priest walk to meet the inhabitants of the colony. Twelve years after Damien's arrival on the island, Kamuela rumages through the priest's desk to find the Princess' letter bestowing the order of Kalakawa on Father Damien. When Damien snaps at Kamuela, Kamuela hobbles on his crutches out of the house, weeping. Bitter and angry that his appeals for aid have fallen on deaf ears, Damien himself now has fallen victim to the disease. When Keaka implores him to seek treatment in Honolulu, Damien refuses, claiming that his work is his life. Damien then extends his hand to Keaka, and together, they return to their labors. *Hawaiians. Leprosy. Molokai (HI). Priests. Joseph Damien de Veuster. Coffins. Corpses. Exile. Health officials. Self-sacrifice.*

Note: The credits for this film were taken from a continuity transcribed from a print at the Bishop Museum Archives in Honolulu, Hawaii. The cast end credits are presented in a different order than the opening cast credits in the film. The picture opens with the following written acknowledgement: "People of all races and creeds in Hawaii had a part in telling this story. To them the Producers express their gratitude, and especially to the patients and staffs of Hale Mohalu and Kalaupapa on the island of Molokai." Leprosy, or Hansen's disease, is a chronic infectious disease caused by Mycobacterium leprae that affects the skin and superficial nerves. It is found mainly, but not exclusively, in tropical regions. The disease produces numerous skin and nerve lesions, which, if left untreated, enlarge and may result in severe disfigurement.

Belgian-born Father Damien (Joseph Damien de Veuster 1840—1888), was a Roman Catholic priest who served as a missionary at the Kalaupapa Leper Colony on Molokai, HI. Suffering from leprosy himself, Father Damien succumbed to the disease after spending sixteen years among the outcasts. According to materials contained in the Bishop Museum Archives, the film was copyrighted and released in 1950, but additional footage was shot and added in 1952. According to materials contained in the copyright files, the story was adapted from a play by John Kneubuhl produced by Theatre Hawaii Ltd. Modern sources note that the film was shot on location on Oahu and at the Kalaupapa settlement on Molokai. The picture was originally filmed on 16mm stock and later blown up to 35 mm. In Feb 1978, Hawaiian Public Television broadcast a television program about the missionary, titled *Damien* and starring Terence Knapp and produced and directed by Nino Martin. The original chapel and the house in which Father Damien lived was restored in the early 1990's.

DAN (African Americans)

All-Star Feature Corp. Aug **1914**. Si; b&w. 5 reels.

Dir John H. Pratt and George Irving. *Scen* Hal Reid. *Mus accompaniment comp* Manuel Klein.

Cast: Lew Dockstader (*Dan*), Hal Reid (*Colonel Dabney*), Gail Kane (*Grace Dabney*), Lois Meredith (*Lila Dabney*), Beatrice Clevenger (*Elsie Hammond*), George Cowl (*Raoul Dabney*), W. D. Fischter (*John Hammond*), Jonas Watts (*William Conklin*), John H. Pratt (*Stonewall Jackson*).

Historical, War, Drama. Dan, the loyal slave of the aristocratic Dabney family, is overjoyed when Raoul becomes engaged to Northerner Elsie Hammond and his sister Grace becomes engaged to Elsie's brother John. When the Civil War breaks out, the heartbroken Hammonds return North and John joins the Union army. Raoul joins the Confederacy, but his vindictive overseer, Jonas Watts, becomes a Union officer. Watts takes Grace prisoner, but before he can act on his desires, John rescues her. He then encounters Raoul and is obliged to arrest him, but Dan comes to his aid by throwing red peppers into his captors' eyes. When John is arrested by Confederates, Raoul frees him for Grace's sake, but when his superiors discover his treason, he is sentenced to death. Stonewall Jackson, a family friend, tries to obtain a stay of execution for Raoul, but in the meantime, Dan visits him and convinces his master to blacken his face and take the slave's place. He does, and Dan is executed. After the war, Raoul and Elsie, and John and Grace marry and settle on the Dabney estate. *Disguise. Loyalty. Self-sacrifice. Slaves. Southerners. Treason. United States–History–Civil War, 1861-1865. Attempted rape. Brothers and sisters. Executions. General Thomas Jonathan Jackson. Marriage. Rescues.*

Note: Lew Dockstader, founder of the Dockstader's Minstrals, played the role of Dan in black face.

Motog 15 Aug 1914, pp. 239-40. *MPN* 8 Aug 1914, p. 55. *MPW* 8 Aug 1914, p. 813. *NYDM* 5 Aug 1914, p. 26. *Var* 4 Sep 1914, p. 13.

DANCE HALL DAISY *see* LAZY RIVER

DANCE HALL HOSTESS (Irish Americans)

Golden Arrow Productions, Inc. *Dist* Mayfair Pictures Corp. 1 Jul **1933**; Prod: began late Apr 1933 at Darmour Studios [©Mayfair Pictures Corp.; 7 Jun 1933; LP3949]. Sd; b&w. 8 reels. 66, 71 or 73 min.

Pres George W. Weeks. *Supv* Lester F. Scott, Jr. *Dir* Breezy Eason. *Asst dir* Leigh Smith. *Story* Tom Gibson. *Cont and adpt* Betty Burbridge. *Photog* Jules Cronjager. *Ed* Byron Robinson. *Rec eng* Homer Ackerman.

Cast: Helen Chandler (*Nora Marsh*), Jason Robards (*Jerry Raymond*), Edward J. Nugent (*Patrick Gibbs, Jr.*), Natalie Moorhead

(*Clare*), Alberta Vaughn (*Myra*), Jane Keckley (*Mrs. Gibbs*), Ronnie Cosbey (*Donnie*), Clarence Geldert (*Sheriff*).

Society, Comedy-drama. [*Not viewed*]. Patrick Gibbs, Jr., a wealthy, jaded alcoholic, goes one evening to a cheap dance hall, where he is attracted to Nora Marsh, a taxi dancer who plans to marry taxicab driver Jerry Raymond as soon as his cab is paid for. When Pat complains that his life has been wrecked by always having had too much money, Nora wistfully tells him that her dream of a luxurious life would be to have a new pair of stockings every day of the year. She soon receives a package containing 365 pairs of stockings, and Jerry, hot-tempered, jealous and Irish, explodes. The next night at the dance hall, Pat seeks consolation from Nora because of his sister Clare's announced marriage to a "second-rate" prince. Pat offers to see Nora home, and they get into Jerry's cab. He silently seethes as he takes Nora to her rooming house and afterward, unable to control himself, drives recklessly and crashes the cab into a tree to avoid a collision. Although he and Pat are unhurt, the cab is wrecked. He then loses his job and has a furious argument with Nora. To afford luxuries for Nora, Jerry gets work with a beer-runner, but he is caught by a prohibition squad and sent to prison. Unaware of his fate, Nora thinks that he has deserted her, and she accepts Pat's proposal, but warns him that she will always love Jerry. Pat believes they will have a successful marriage, but Nora is snubbed by his family, particularly Clare, who has since married Prince Bodelski. Pat soon neglects Nora and begins to frequent his old drinking haunts, unmindful of warnings from Dr. Cromwell, the family physician. In a year, a son, Donnie, is born to Nora. Three years later, Pat, Nora and Donnie join Clare and the prince at the elder Mrs. Gibbs's estate. Clare calls an agency for a chauffeur and Jerry, now out of prison, is sent. Attracted to him, Clare hires Jerry, but later jealously spies on him and Nora talking. After Clare hints to Pat about an affair between Nora and Jerry, Nora, very uncomfortable, asks Jerry to leave. He agrees, but as they say goodbye late one night, Pat drives up and sees them. A few hours later, Pat is found dead in the garage from carbon monoxide poisoning. Clare attempts to place the blame on Nora and Jerry, and when it is discovered that they had once been sweethearts and that Jerry has left, he is found and arrested. However, Dr. Cromwell tells the sheriff that earlier that day he told Pat he would soon die because of his heavy drinking. The doctor's conviction that Pat was a suicide results in Jerry's release. A few months later, he and Nora are married and living happily, their only possessions being a country cottage, a paid-for taxicab and Donnie. *Alcoholics. Dance hall girls. Jealousy. Taxicab drivers. Wealth. Automobile accidents. Bootleggers. Brothers and sisters. Children. Class distinction. False arrests. Gossip. Hosiery. Irish Americans. Marriage. Physicians. Princes. Prohibition. Sheriffs. Snobs and snobbishness. Suicide.*

FD 26 Aug 1933, p. 4. *Har* 26 Aug 1933, p. 135. *HF* 29 Apr 1933, p. 8. *MPD* 25 Aug 1933, p. 14. *MPH* 2 Sep 1933, p. 37.

DANCING PIRATE (Latino)
Pioneer Pictures, Inc. *Dist* RKO Radio Pictures, Inc. 22 May **1936**; Prod: 15 Jan—mid-Mar 1936 at United Artists Studios [©Pioneer Pictures, Inc.; 22 May 1936; LP6422]. Sd (Western Electric Wide Range Noiseless Recording); col (Technicolor). 85 min. PCA cert no. 2162.
Prod John Speaks. *Exec prod* Merian C. Cooper. *Dir* Lloyd Corrigan. *Scr* Ray Harris and Francis Edwards Faragoh. *Adpt* Jack Wagner and Boris Ingster. *Photog* William V. Skall. *Photog eff* Willis H. O'Brien. *Technicolor color dir* Natalie Kalmus. *Art dir* W. B. Ihnen. *Designed in color by* Robert Edmond Jones. *Ed* Archie F. Marshek. *Mus dir* Alfred Newman. *Dance dir* Russell Lewis. [*Sd* Fred Lau]. *Rec* Oscar Lagerstrom. [*Makeup* Max Factor].
Song(s): "When You're Dancing the Waltz" and "Are You My Love?" words and music by Richard Rodgers and Lorenz Hart.
Source: Based on the short story "Glorious Buccaneer" by Emma Lindsay Squier in *Collier's* (27 Dec 1930).
Cast: Charles Collins (*Jonathan Pride*), Frank Morgan (*Alcalde* [*Don Emilio*]), Steffi Duna (*Serafina*), Luis Alberni (*Pamfilo*), Victor Varconi (*Don Baltazar*), Jack La Rue (*Chago*), Alma Real (*Blanca*), William V. Mong (*Tecolote*), Mitchell Lewis (*Pirate chief*), Julian Rivero (*Shepherd*), John Eberts (*Mozo*), Cansino Family (*Royal Cansinos*), [Harold Waldridge (*Orville*)], [Vera Lewis (*Orville's mother*)], [Nora Cecil (*Landlady*)], [Ellen Lowe (*Miss Ponsonby*)], [Max Wagner (*Pirate mate*)], [James Farley (*Sailor*)].

Historical, Comedy, with songs. [*Print viewed*]. One evening in 1820, dancing master Jonathan Pride, who specializes in teaching the waltz, is ambushed by pirates on the streets of Boston. Forced into hard labor, Jonathan sails around South America with the pirates and ends up on the coast of California, where he eventually tricks his way to freedom. Possessing only his aunt's umbrella and music box, Jonathan wanders into a Spanish village, whose alerted inhabitants greet him with cannon fire and gunshots. Caught hiding in the bedroom of Serafina, the alcalde's beautiful daughter, Jonathan is arrested and sentenced to hang without a trial. Despite Jonathan's protestations of innocence, the buffoonish alcalde, Don Emilio, and the jailer, Pamfilo, insist on the execution until Serafina hears that Jonathan is a dancing teacher who knows the waltz. With the other women behind her, Serafina forces a stay of execution for Jonathan, who gratefully offers to teach her the waltz. After overcoming an initial misunderstanding concerning the placement of hands, Jonathan mesmerizes Serafina, herself an accomplished dancer, with his waltz lessons. Before Jonathan can win permanent freedom, however, Don Baltazar and his men, renegade soldiers from Monterey, arrive and make him their prisoner. Don Emilio, who believes that Baltazar is still a respected military leader, treats him as an honored guest, and Serafina encourages his amorous affections in order to delay Jonathan's departure. Eventually, Baltazar strikes a lucrative marriage deal with Don Emilio and is about to wed Serafina when Jonathan, who has escaped his captors, shows up with a band of rope-wielding Indians. Once Baltazar and his men are tied up and revealed, Serafina continues her wedding, with Jonathan as her groom. *California–History–To 1846. Dance teachers. Dancers. Latino. Mistaken identity. Pirates.* Boston (MA). *Escapes. Executions. Imprisonment. Indians of North America. Kidnapping. Marriage–Arranged. Mayors. Renegades. Ships. Soldiers. Village life. Weddings.*

Note: Onscreen credits state that this film was the first color "dancing musical," and was "filmed 100% in new Technicolor." It was Pioneer Pictures' second and last three-strip Technicolor feature to be distributed by RKO. According to *HR*, Robert Benchley, on loan from M-G-M, teletyped dialogue for the film from New York, but was later replaced by credited writers Francis Edwards Faragoh and Ray Harris. The extent of Benchley's contribution to the final film, if any, has not been determined. A *HR* news item described color director Robert Edmond Jones's aesthetic approach as "imaginative" rather than "realistic," as he was attempting to "synchronize color, music and dancing" throughout the picture. Charles Collins, a veteran New York and London stage performer, made his screen debut in this production. *HR* production charts add Sherman Sanders and Cy Kendall to the cast, but their participation in the final film has not been confirmed.

DV 6 May 1936, p. 3. *FD* 8 May 1936, p. 7. *HR* 16 Jan 1936, p. 4. *HR* 21 Jan 1936, p. 4. *HR* 28 Jan 1936, p. 14. *HR* 16 Mar 1936, p. 10. *HR* 6 May 1936, p. 3. *MPD* 7 May 1936, p. 6. *MPH* 9 May 1936, p. 38. *MPH* 16 May 1936, p. 33, 47-50. *MPSI* May 1936, p. 26. *NYT* 18 Jun 1936, p. 19. *Var* 24 Jun 1936, p. 29.

DANGER ISLAND *see* **MR. MOTO IN DANGER ISLAND**

THE DANGER SIGNAL (Irish Americans)
George Kleine. *Dist* Kleine-Edison Feature Service. 1 Dec **1915** Si; b&w. 5 reels.
Dir Walter Edwin.
Source: Based on the short story "Canavan, the Man Who Had His Way" by Rupert Hughes in *The Saturday Evening Post* (11 Sep 1909).
Cast: Arthur Hoops (*Danny Canavan/Dennis Canavan*), Ruby Hoffman (*Beatrice Newnes*), John Davidson (*Rodman Cadbury*), Frank Belcher (*Boss Havens*), Tom Walsh (*Roscoe Newnes*), Billy Sherwood (*Henry Cadbury*), Della Connor (*Amy Carroll*), Florence Coventry (*Mrs. Canavan*).
Drama. Danny Canavan, the large, yet cowardly son of a stern Irish-American blacksmith, is scorned and abused by his wife, father, and his father's helpers. After insurance company president Rodman Cadbury's carriage runs over Danny, his wife gives him more brow-beatings, and when he recovers, she gets him a job working on the subway. One day Danny is given a red flag as a danger signal to warn traffic of dynamite blasts. Amazed by his power to have commands obeyed, Danny develops self-confidence. After asserting his independence and thrashing one of his father's employees, Danny wins the favor of a political boss, and soon assumes leadership of a political party. Soon Danny revokes an indictment against Cadbury, and forces Cadbury and his wife to sponsor him socially. In England, he purchases a horse which wins the English Derby. After Cadbury dies in an accident during an international polo match, Danny, now a widower, marries Cadbury's widow, Beatrice. Although she

complains about his lack of polish, after Danny relates his rise to the top, she acknowledges her love for him. *Ambition. Cowardice. Personality change. Political bosses. Self-confidence. Social climbers. Timidity. Accidents. Blacksmiths. Dynamite. English Derby. Etiquette. Fights. Horses. Irish Americans. Polo. Subways.*

Note: The film's pre-release title was *Canavan, the Man Who Had His Way.* There was a trade showing of the film on 14 Nov 1915. According to reviews, at the beginning of the film, a shot introducing Arthur Hoops was hand colored to show him carrying a red flag. According to the *Var* review, the original story was inspired by the life of former Tammany Hall boss Richard Croker. Goldwyn Pictures released a film based on the same source, entitled *Hold Your Horses,* on 28 Jan 1921. This version was directed by E. Mason Hopper, and starred Tom Moore (see below). The 1936 Twentieth Century-Fox production *It Had to Happen* was also based on the same source; it was directed by Roy Del Ruth and starred George Raft and Rosalind Russell (see below).

MPN 27 Nov 1915, p. 57, 98. *MPN* 11 Dec 1915, p. 29. *MPW* 20 Nov 1915, p. 1510. *MPW* 27 Nov 1915, p. 1732. *NYDM* 4 Dec 1915, p. 31. *Var* 19 Nov 1915, p. 23. *Wid's* 2 Dec 1915.

DANGEROUS DAYS (German Americans)

Eminent Authors Pictures, Inc.; A Reginald Barker Production. *Dist* Goldwyn Distributing Corp. 14 Mar **1920** [©Mary Roberts Rinehart; 23 Mar 1920; LP14917]. Si; b&w. 7 reels, 6,662 ft.

Pres Samuel Goldwyn and Rex Beach. *Dir* Reginald Barker. *Scen and titles* Mary Roberts Rinehart. *Scen* Charles Kenyon, J. G. Hawks and Thompson Buchanan. *Cam* Percy Hilburn.

Source: Based on the novel *Dangerous Days* by Mary Roberts Rinehart (New York, 1919).

Cast: Lawson Butt (*Clayton Spencer*), Clarissa Selwynne (*Natalie Spencer*), Rowland Lee (*Graham Spencer*), Ann Forrest (*Anna Klein*), Stanton Heck (*Herman Klein*), H. Milton Ross (*Dunbar*), Pauline Starke (*Delight Haverford*), Bertram Grassby (*Rodney Page*), Frank Leigh (*Rudolph Klein*), Eddie McWade (*Dr. Haverford*), Barbara Castleton (*Audrey Valentine*), Florence Deshon (*Marion Hayden*).

Espionage, Drama. Rudolph Klein, a German spy, tries to persuade his brother Herman, a trusted employee of the Spencer Steel Works, to blow up the munitions factory. When World War I breaks out, Spencer's son Graham decides to enlist in the army, but when his mother Natalie, a cold-hearted social butterfly, objects, he wavers in his decision. Rudolph persuades Herman that Graham is trying to seduce his daughter Anna, and, for revenge, Herman finally agrees to blow up the plant. Anna overhears the conspiracy and rushes to warn the Spencers, but gets caught in the explosion instead. Her death cements Graham's resolution to enlist and he goes off to war. Natalie then decides to leave Spencer, freeing him for Audrey Valentine, a widow who has lost her son at the front. *Espionage. German Americans. Germans. Ordnance. Sabotage. Spies. World War I. Brothers. Explosions. Mothers and sons. Revenge. Socialites. Steel industry.*

Note: The novel was serialized in *Pictorial Review,* Winter-Spring 1919. In Apr 1920, Eminent Authors Pictures, Inc. commenced suit for an injunction to prevent further exhibition of *Dangerous Hours,* produced by Thomas H. Ince and released in Feb 1920, because Eminent Authors claimed to have exclusive and prior right to the title *Dangerous Days,* and that the similarity in titles would mislead the public and benefit the Ince organization, as the novel *Dangerous Days* was widely known. No further information concerning the suit has been located.

ETR 27 Mar 1920, p. 1884. *MPN* 31 Jan 1920, p. 1258. *MPW* 27 Mar 1920, p. 2175. *NYT* 15 Mar 1920, p. 53. *Wid's* 21 Mar 1920, p. 21.

DANGEROUS HOURS (Russian Americans)

Thomas H Ince Productions; A Paramount-Artcraft Special. *Dist* Famous Players-Lasky Corp. 29 Feb **1920** [©Thomas H. Ince; 24 Nov 1919; LP14488]. Si; b&w. 7 reels.

Pres Thomas H. Ince. *Dir* Fred Niblo. *Scen* C. Gardner Sullivan. *Cam* George Barnes.

Source: Based on the short story "A Prodigal in Utopia" by Donn Byrne in *The Saturday Evening Post* (production date undetermined).

Cast: Lloyd Hughes (*John King*), Barbara Castleton (*May Weston*), Claire DuBrey (*Sophia Guerni*), Jack Richardson (*Boris Blotchi*), Walt Whitman (*Doctor King*), Lew Morrison (*Michael Regan*), Gordon Mullen (*Andrew Felton*).

Drama. During a strike at the Paterson, New Jersey, silk mills, young John King falls under the spell of Bolshevist agitator Sophia Guerni. When Guerni and her confederate Boris Blotchi decide that their next target will be the peaceful strike at the Weston shipyards, John assents, although his childhood sweetheart May Weston runs the plant and also supports John's poverty-stricken father, Dr. King.

However, when John overhears his cohorts extorting money from May, he intervenes and is seriously wounded. After subduing John, the agitators bomb the plant where May and Dr. King have taken refuge. Shaken by the violence, John drives back the mob and renounces his revolutionary doctrine. May then forgives him and the two are reunited. *Bolshevists and Bolshevism. Labor agitators. Mobs. Strikes and lockouts. Explosions. Extortion. Paterson (NJ). Shipyards. Textile mills.*

Note: The working title of this film was *Americanism (Versus Bolshevism).* This film was shown privately in New York in Dec 1919. Sources vary in listing release dates; the film may have been released 25 Jan 1919. In Apr 1920, Eminent Authors Pictures, Inc. commenced suit for an injunction to prevent further exhibition of *Dangerous Hours* under that title, because Eminent Authors claimed to have exclusive and prior right to the use of the title *Dangerous Days.* Eminent Authors produced *Dangerous Days,* which was released in Mar 1920, and claimed that the similarity in titles would mislead the public and benefit the Ince organization, as the novel *Dangerous Days* was widely known. No further information concerning the suit has been located. Also in Apr 1920, *Dangerous Hours* was canceled from showing at Keith's 81st Street Theatre in New York because the Keith management thought that the Bolshevism outlined in the film, while renounced by the main character, was potentially antagonistic. *Var* commented that the film "brings home to an audience the moral that there are insidious forces ostensibly transported to America to sow the seed of discontent among the peaceful, toiling class whose wont it is to follow their occupations without complaining, and do until aroused to a frenzied state of hysteria by 'the blind not leading the blind, but in advance of the vultures'.... The film is grossly exaggerated in spots and could not in many instances be held up to actual incident for comparison, and, therefore, it often sounds unconvincing."

ETR 14 Feb 1920, p. 1109. *MPN* 17 May 1919, p. 3235. *MPN* 14 Feb 1920, p. 1687. *MPW* 14 Feb 1920, p. 971, 1116. *NYMT* 14 Feb 1920. *Var* 6 Feb 1920, p. 53. *Var* 16 Apr 1920, p. 39. *Wid's* 8 Feb 1920, p. 22.

DANGEROUS INTRIGUE (Slavic Americans)

Columbia Pictures Corp.; Harry Cohn, President. *Dist* Columbia Pictures Corp. 4 Jan **1936**; Prod: 29 Oct—12 Nov 1935 [©Columbia Pictures Corp.; 20 Dec 1935; LP6012]. Sd (Western Electric Noiseless Recording); b&w. 6 reels. 57 or 59 min. PCA cert no. 1787.

[*Prod* Robert North]. *Assoc prod* Harry L. Decker. *Dir* David Selman. [*Asst dir* Cliff Broughton]. *Scr* Grace Neville. *Story* Harold Shumate. *Photog* George Meehan. *Film ed* Al Clark. [*Sd eng* Edward Bernds].

Cast: Ralph Bellamy ([*Dr.*] *Tony* [*Halliday, also known as John Davis*]), Gloria Shea (*Greta* [*Kosovic*]), Joan Perry (*Carol* [*Elder*]), Fred Kohler, Sr. (*Brant*), Fredrik Vogeding (*Joe Kosovic*), Edward Le Saint (*Dr. Miller*), Georgie Billings (*Danny* [*Brant*]), Boyd Irwin, Sr. (*Dr. Wagner*), Gene Morgan (*Taxi Driver*), Stanley Andrews (*Mr. [John] Mitchell*), [Robert Middlemass (*Koenig*)], [Arthur Rankin (*Orderly*)], [Nick Baskovitch (*Zivok*)], [John Northpole (*Sleveki*)], [Fred Walton (*Scottish man*)], [George Lloyd (*Foreman*)], [Nellie V. Nichols (*Italian woman*)], [Sarah Edwards (*Superintendent of nurses*)], Brandon Evans (*Superintendent of hospital*), [John Picorri (*Doctor with pince nez*)], [Tina Marshall (*Farmer*)], [Beatrice Blinn (*Teacher*)], [Jack Carlyle (*Cop*)], [Broderick O'Farrell (*Druggist*)], [Ann Doran (*Floor nurse*)], [Walden Boyle (*Intern*)], [Eva Novak (*Nurse*)], [Francis Morris, Betty May (*Student nurses*)], [Lillian Rich (*Wagner's nurse*)], [Cecil Weston (*Tony's nurse*)], [Edward Mortimer, Carlton E. Griffin (*Doctors*)], [Phillips Smalley (*Business man*)], [Edward Peil, Sr. (*Detective*)], [Pat Somerset, Arthur Stuart Hull (*Club members*)], [William Worthington, Brandon Beach, Charles Meakin (*Executives*)], [George Ducount (*Yeneff*)], [Earl Bunn, Richard Botiller (*Tramps*)], [John Tyrrell (*Clerk*)], [Harry Vahar (*Inspector*)], [Charles DeLamont (*Fruit peddler*)].

Medical, Drama. [*Print viewed*]. At New York's Mitchell Memorial Hospital, Dr. Tony Halliday is near collapse from nervous exhaustion. While he is treating a poor Italian child, the hospital's patron, John Mitchell, brings in his daughter. Tony angers Mitchell by operating on his daughter after the Italian, and when the girl later dies of thrombosis, Mitchell accuses Tony of negligence, which causes him to quit. Then Tony's fiancée Carol Elder tells him that she does not want to be engaged to a doctor who works at a clinic. Tony leaves in shock and contracts amnesia. After wandering aimlessly, Tony, using the name John Davis, finds employment at the Crocker Steel Works in Scranton, PA. One day an accident occurs at the steel works and Tony enters the company's hospital and instinctively takes over. Later, Tony meets mill school teacher Greta, who is daughter of Joe Kosovic, a steel worker. When Greta sees some children playing the "steel game," dropping bricks on people, Joe guesses that the recent spate of accidents were caused by a rival who wants to take over the plant.

Brant, who has been paid by a rival mill for sabotage, blames the accidents on Tony. Brant's son, Danny, is injured when he follows his father to the mill and must be immediately operated on by Tony. When Brant learns this, he sacrifices his life to prevent the detonation of the works. Tony's old friends see his picture in the newspaper and recognize him, but he refuses to return to New York, preferring to remain with Greta. *Amnesia. Hospitals. Operations, Surgical. Physicians. Dances. Engagements. Industrial accidents. New York City. Nurses. Scranton (PA). Slavic Americans. Steel mills.*

Note: The working title of this film was *Doctor Steele*.

DV 30 Oct 1935, p. 2. *DV* 26 Nov 1935, p. 4. *FD* 18 Jan 1936, p. 7. *MPD* 17 Feb 1936, p. 8, 10. *Var* 22 Jan 1936, p. 15.

DANGEROUS MISSION (Native Americans)

RKO Radio Pictures, Inc. *Dist* RKO Radio Pictures, Inc. Jun **1954**; Prod: late Jul 1953 [©RKO Radio Pictures, Inc.; 25 Feb 1954; LP3544]. Sd (RCA Sound System); col (Technicolor); 3-D. 6,740 ft. 75 min. PCA cert no. 16641.

Prod Irwin Allen. *Dir* Louis King. *Asst dir* James W. Lane. *Scr* Horace McCoy, W. R. Burnett and Charles Bennett. *Story* Horace McCoy and James Edmiston. *Dir of photog* William Snyder. *Photog eff* Harold Wellman. *Technicolor col consultant* Monroe W. Burbank. *Art dir* Albert S. D'Agostino and Walter Keller. *Ed supv* Frederic Knudtson. *Film ed* Gene Palmer. *Set dec* Darrell Silvera and John Sturtevant. *Cost* Michael Woulfe. *Mus* Roy Webb. [*Mus dir* C. Bakaleinikoff]. *Sd* Frank McWhorter and Clem Portman. *Makeup artist* Mel Berns. *Hair stylist* Larry Germain.

Music: "One for My Baby and One More for the Road," music by Harold Arlen.

Cast: VICTOR MATURE [(*Matt Hallett*)], PIPER LAURIE [(*Louise Graham*)], WILLIAM BENDIX [(*Joe Parker*)], VINCENT PRICE [(*Paul Adams*)], Betta St. John [(*Mary*)], Steve Darrell [(*Katoonai*)], Marlo Dwyer [(*Mrs. Elster*)], Walter Reed [(*Dobson*)], Dennis Weaver [(*Pruitt*)], Harry Cheshire [(*Elster*)], [George Sherwood (*Mr. Jones*)], [Maureen Stephenson (*Mrs. Jones*)], [Fritz Apking (*Hawthorne*)], [Ken Dibbs (*Johnny Yonkers*)], [Bert Moorehouse (*Piano player*)], [John Carlyle, Chet Marshall (*Bellhops*)], [Frank Griffin (*Tedd*)], [Virginia Linden (*Mrs. Brown*)], [Trevor Bardette (*Kicking Bear*)], [Helen Brown (*Miss Thorndyke*)], [Frank Wilcox (*Jeremiah Kern*)], [Roy Engel (*Hume*)], [Chester Jones (*Porter*)], [Richard Newton (*Young Man Boone*)], [Bill White, Jr. (*Hotel clerk*)], [Charles Cane (*Barrett*)], [Grace Hayle (*Mrs. Alvord*)], [Jack Chefe (*Headwaiter*)], [Steve Rowland (*Parking lot attendant*)], [Russ Thorson (*Radio man*)], [Don Dillaway (*Praskins*)], [Robert Carraher (*Ranger*)], [Jim Potter (*Cobb*)], [Wymer Gard (*Fletcher*)], [Mike Lally, Ralph Volkie, Sam Shack, Craig Moreland (*Firefighters*)], [Ann Dore].

Crime, Northwest, Drama. [*Print viewed*]. At a New York nightclub after hours, while a man plays "One for My Baby" on the piano, cashier Louise Graham inadvertently witnesses a murder. Fearing for her life, Louise flees the state. Gangster Johnny Yonkers is charged with the crime, but to prove his case, the district attorney needs an eyewitness and so sends New York police officer Matt Hallett to find Louise. After tracing her to Glacier National Park in Montana, Matt poses as a guest at the resort hotel in which Louise is employed. There Matt also meets Mary, an Indian girl who works with Louise; ranger Joe Parker and Paul Adams, a commercial photographer on assignment at the hotel. That evening, Matt escorts Mary to a dance at a luxurious house built into the side of a mountain. As Paul dances with Mary, Parker shows Matt a wanted poster for Mary's father, Katoonai, who is accused of murder. Later, Matt asks Louise to dance, but when the song "One for My Baby" is played on the jukebox, she becomes agitated. Soon after, an avalanche sends rocks cascading into the house, causing the power lines to explode. Parker is impressed when Matt scales the electrical pole outside the house and disables the power. The next day, Matt invites Louise to go walking and asks her why she was upset by the song the previous evening. The strains of the tune bring back terrifying memories to Louise, and she screams. Later that afternoon, Mary gives a special presentation at the school she once attended, but when she sees her father peering proudly from a trap door in the ceiling, she faints. That evening, at the hotel bar, Elster, an emissary from Yonkers posing as a jovial guest, approaches Paul and warns him that Yonkers is impatiently waiting for him to eliminate Louise. Nervously, Paul seeks out Louise and asks her to go for a ride, but before they can leave, Parker commandeers him and Matt to help fight a forest fire. As they battle the fire, the three are

trapped in the flames and Matt saves Paul's life. Upon returning to the lodge, Paul, who is involved in a clandestine affair with Mary, uses his concern for the girl as a pretense to talk to Louise alone. After they drive away in Paul's car, Matt is called to the phone, and after he hangs up, he shows Parker his police badge and asks the ranger's help in arresting Paul. As Paul and Louise drive along a mountain road, a bulletin from ranger headquarters comes over their car radio, warning that Paul is a dangerous gunman dispatched to kill Louise. Screaming in fear, Louise jumps out of the car and Paul swerves around, trying to run her over. Pushed over the roadside embankment, Louise lands safely in the brush and pulls herself back onto the road, where she is picked up by a motorist and taken to the ranger station. Paul, meanwhile, speeds to Mary's room and informs her that the rangers want to arrest him. Lying that his car was stolen and used in a robbery, Paul enlists Mary's help in fleeing the park. Matt, meanwhile, picks Louise up at the ranger's station, and after confessing that he has fallen in love with her, presses her to return to New York and testify against Yonkers. Upon reaching the lodge, they find a note from Mary, and when a fisherman directs them to Paul's abandoned car, Louise leads Matt to an Indian cave in which she thinks Paul may be hiding. At the cave, they encounter Katoonai, who fears that Mary and Paul will cut across the glacier to exit the park. As Mary and Paul approach the glacier, Katoonai sees them and instructs Matt to pin down Paul with gunfire while he climbs onto the ledge above. Paul spots Katoonai, however, and shoots him from his perch, sending him careening to his death. Horrified, Mary struggles with Paul, who throws her against the rocks and takes her hostage, forcing her to continue. Matt and Louise follow, and Mary grapples with Paul again, sending his gun flying into the snow. Matt then jumps Paul, and as the two men fight, Louise reaches for the discarded gun. The added weight causes the glacier to crumble, plummeting Louise to an ice shelf below. After throwing Paul into a snowbank, Matt, with Mary's help, lowers himself by rope to rescue Louise. Regaining his balance, Paul grabs for the gun and fires at Matt. The sound of the gunshots triggers the collapse of the glacier, causing it to topple over and crush Paul. After tying the rope around Louise's waist, Matt pulls her to safety. Drawn by the sound of gunfire, the rangers then appear, and in relief, Matt and Louise kiss. *Assassins. Glacier National Park (MT). Impersonation and imposture. Murder. Rangers. Resorts. Undercover agents. Witnesses. Accidental death. Avalanches. Explosions. Fathers and daughters. Forest fires. Fugitives. Glaciers. Indians of North America. New York City. Photographers. Songs. Speeches.*

Note: The working titles of this picture were *Rangers of the North* and *The Glacier Story*. The film opens with the following written acknowlegement: "The cooperation of the U.S. Department of the Interior, National Park Service, and Glacier National Park is gratefully acknowledged." Location scenes were shot at Glacier National Park in Montana, according to the *Var* review.

Box 27 Feb 1954. *DV* 24 Feb 1954, p. 3. *FD* 25 Feb 1954, p. 10. *Har* 27 Feb 1954, p. 35. *HR* 24 Jul 1953, p. 9. *HR* 24 Feb 1954, p. 3. *MPHPD* 27 Feb 1954, p. 2197. *NYT* 6 Mar 1954, p. 13. *Var* 24 Feb 1954, p. 6.

DANGEROUS MONEY (Chinese Americans)

Monogram Pictures Corp. *Dist* Monogram Pictures Corp. 12 Oct **1946**; Prod: mid–late Jun 1946 [©Monogram Pictures Corp.; 29 Sep 1946; LP656]. Sd (Western Electric Mirrophonic Recording); b&w. 66 min. PCA cert no. 11824.

Series: Charlie Chan.

Prod James S. Burkett. *Dir* Terry Morse. *Asst dir* Wesley Barry. *Scr* Miriam Kissinger. *Dir of photog* William Sickner. *Tech dir* Dave Milton. *Supv film ed* Richard Currier. *Ed* William Austin. *Mus dir* Edward J. Kay. *Rec* Tom Lambert. *Makeup* Harry Ross. Glenn Cook.

Source: Based on characters created by Earl Derr Biggers.

Cast: Sidney Toler [(*Charlie Chan*)], Gloria Warren [(*Rona Simmonds*)], Victor Sen Young [(*Jimmy Chan*)], Rick Vallin [(*Tao Erickson*)], Joseph Crehan [(*Captain Black*)], Willie Best [(*Chattanooga Brown*)], John Harmon [(*Freddie Kirk*)], Bruce Edwards [(*Harold Mayfair*)], Dick Elliott [(*P. T. Burke*)], Joe Allen, Jr. [(*George Brace*)], Amira Moustafa [(*Laura Erickson*)], Tristram Coffin [(*Scott Pearson*)], Alan Douglas [(*Mrs. Whipple, also known as Joseph Murdock*)], Selmer Jackson [(*Ship's doctor*)], Dudley Dickerson [(*Big Ben*)], Rito Punay [(*Pete*)], Elaine Lange [(*Cynthia Martin*)], Emmett Vogan [(*Professor Henry Martin*)], Leslie Dennison [(*Reverend Whipple, also known as Lane*)], [Jerry Groves (*Polynesian*)], [Kit Carson (*Seaman*)], [Mavis Russell (*Kirk's assistant*)], [Don McCracken (*Junior officer*)].

Detective, Comedy-drama. [*Print viewed*]. On a foggy night on board a ship bound for Samoa and Australia, undercover agent Scott Pearson tells detective Charlie Chan that he is being sent to Samoa to investigate the sudden appearance of money and artworks stolen from Philippine banks during the Japanese invasion. Later, while the passengers gather in the salon for a ceremony to celebrate the crossing of the equator, Pearson is stabbed in the back and killed. After warning the other passengers to stay where they are, Chan and the captain examine Pearson's room and discover that it has been searched. The captain reassures Chan that Pearson's portfolio is in his office safe, and Chan notices that Pearson's papers mention a man named Lane, but do not identify him. Later, Chan questions the ship's passengers, who include Freddie Kirk, an exhibition knife-thrower; P. T. Burke, a trader in cotton; Professor Henry Martin, an ichthyologist, and Henry's wife Cynthia; Tao Erickson, a half-Polynesian who owns a restaurant on Samoa, and Tao's Polynesian wife Laura; missionaries Rev. and Mrs. Whipple; and Rona Simmonds, an English tourist in love with the ship's purser, George Brace. After he dismisses most of the passengers, Chan speaks privately to Rona and George and, while advising them to speak the truth, asks them to identify Lane. George, however, insists that they have nothing to reveal. Later, Chan sets a trap to catch the killer, but, although an attempt is made on the detective's life, the killer avoids discovery. Chan's son Jimmy checks the knife used in the attack against Pearson for fingerprints, but finds none. Chan then learns that Burke and Kirk are blackmailing Rona. The ship docks in Samoa, giving Chan twenty-four hours to solve the murder before he must leave for Australia. His oldest son sends him a telegram, which explains that Rona's father was an Australian, who was stranded during the war in Manila with valuable art objects, and Rona is now trying to discover their whereabouts. Chan discovers that Rona is traveling under papers that were falsified by Brace and that is why Burke is blackmailing her. Chan questions Burke, but Burke is killed by a thrown knife before he can reveal anything. Meanwhile, Jimmy and Chan's assistant, Chattanooga Brown, stumble upon money hidden in a fish museum near the Ericksons' restaurant. After Kirk is killed, the rest of the suspects converge on the fish museum. Chan learns that Whipple is the head of a gang, which includes the Ericksons, Burke and Kirk, and which planned to sell the stolen art works. The Whipples are then revealed to be Lane and his valet, Joseph Murdock, who was dressed as a woman. Murdock, the murderer, shot the blades through a gun and thus was able to escape detection. *Chinese Americans. Detectives. Murder. Samoan Islands. Ships. Treasure.* African Americans. Blackmail. Fathers and sons. Female impersonation. Forgers and forgery. Ichthyologists. Knife throwing. Money. Museums. Polynesians. Restaurants. Traders.

Note: The film's working title was *Hot Money*. The title card reads "Charlie Chan in *Dangerous Money*". *HR* news items add the following information about the production: Prior to his appearance in this film, Rick Vallin served a term in the U.S. Coast Guard. Restaurateur "Don the Beachcomber" gave technical advice on the South Sea Islands. For additional information about the "Charlie Chan" series, consult the Series Index and see the entry above for *Charlie Chan Carries On*.

Box 12 Oct 1946. *DV* 16 Oct 1946, p. 3. *HR* 16 May 1946, p. 13. *HR* 12 Jun 1946, p. 2. *HR* 13 Jun 1946, p. 12. *HR* 14 Jun 1946, p. 38. *HR* 7 Oct 1946, p. 3. *MPHPD* 7 Sep 1946, p. 3186. *MPHPD* 12 Oct 1946, p. 3250.

DANGEROUS PARADISE (foreign version) see TROPENNÄCHTE

DANGEROUS TO KNOW (Chinese Ameicans)

Paramount Pictures, Inc. *Dist* Paramount Pictures, Inc. 11 Mar **1938**; Prod: late Nov—late Dec 1937 [©Paramount Pictures, Inc.; 11 Mar 1938; LP7875]. Sd (Western Electric Mirrophonic Recording); b&w. 7 reels. 70 min. Passed by the National Board of Review. PCA cert no. 3989.

Pres ADOLPH ZUKOR. [*Prod* Edward T. Lowe]. [*Exec prod* William LeBaron]. *Dir* Robert Florey. [*Asst dir* Stanley Goldsmith]. *Scr* William R. Lipman and Horace McCoy. *Photog* Theodor Sparkuhl, [Karl Struss and Charles Schoenbaum]. *Art dir* Hans Dreier and John Goodman. *Ed* Arthur Schmidt. *Int dec* A. E. Freudeman. *Cost* Edith Head. *Mus dir* Boris Morros. *Sd rec* Harry Lindgren and Richard Olson.

Music: Selections from the music of Peter Ilyich Tchaikovsky.

Source: Based on the play *On the Spot* by Edgar Wallace (London, 2 Apr 1930).

Cast: Anna May Wong (*Madame Lan Ying*), Akim Tamiroff (*Stephen Recka*), Gail Patrick (*Margaret Van Kase*), Lloyd Nolan (*Inspector Brandon*), Harvey Stephens (*Philip Easton*), Anthony Quinn (*Nicolai [Nicky] Kusnoff*), Roscoe Karns (*Duncan*), Porter

Hall (*Mayor Bradley*), Barlowe Borland (*Butler*), Hedda Hopper (*Mrs. Carson*), Hugh Sothern (*Harvey Greggson*), Edward Pawley (*John Rance*), Eddie Marr (*Crouch*), Harry Worth (*Hanley*), Robert Brister (*Councilman Murkil*), Pierre Watkin (*Senator Carson*), [Garry Owen (*Mike Tookey*)], [Donald Brian (*Judge Parker*)], [Stanley Blystone (*Motorcycle cop*)], [Terry Ray (*Secretary*)], [Rita La Roy (*Mrs. Barnett*)], [Harvey Clark (*Mr. Barnett*)], [Jack Knoche (*Messenger*)], [Gino Corrado (*Headwaiter*)], [George Melford (*Councilman at party*)], [Rudolph Myzet (*Musician at party*)], [Andre P. Marsaudon (*Second butler*)], [Perry Ivins (*Pompous man*)], [Margaret Randall (*Phone girl*)], [Wade Boteler (*Old time uniformed policeman*)], [Ivan Miller (*Policeman*)], [Frank Melton (*Man at racetrack*)], [Grace Benham, Lynn Bailey, Larry Steers, Estelle Etterre, Harry Myers, David Newell, Cyril Ring, Sheila Darcy, Blanca Vischer (*Guests at party*)], [John Hart], [Joyce Mathews], [Carol Parker], [Ruth Rogers], [Suzanne Ridgway].

Gangster, Melodrama. [*Print viewed*]. At City Hall, Nicolai "Nicky" Kusnoff, gangster Stephen Recka's henchman, overhears city councilman Murkil plotting with John Rance to take over the mayor's office. Madame Lan Ying, Recka's mistress, hosts a birthday party for him, which is attended by those who want a share in his city-wide power. Recka becomes interested in socialite Margaret Van Kase when she attends the party without an invitation. That evening, Recka coldly murders Rance after forcing him to write a suicide note. City inspector Brandon believes Recka is responsible for eight deaths, but has no evidence to convict him. Brandon and Recka share the same birthday, and for the seventh year in a row, Brandon refuses Recka's birthday "gift," a bribe. At the racetrack, Nicky reports to Recka on Margaret's fiancé, a handsome bond salesman named Philip Easton. Recka, who models himself after Napoleon Bonaparte, buys a large amount of bonds from Phil, then attends a society dinner with Margaret. Nicky impetuously reveals to Lan Ying that Recka plans to wed Margaret, after which Lan Ying warns Recka that trying to enter society is reaching beyond his grasp. Recka arranges with Crouch and Hanley to rob Phil's bonds in a manner that makes Phil appear an accessory to the crime. When Margaret calls on Recka, he promises to have Phil freed if she will marry him. Crouch and Hanley double-cross Recka, however, and keep the bonds, then are caught speeding by the police. After Lan Ying gives Phil airplane tickets that Recka had bought for a flight with Margaret, Brandon arrests Nicky to keep him from murdering Phil. Lan Ying refuses a large check offered by Recka and warns him that she will not be waiting if he returns, playing a record of "Thanks for the Memory" as a farewell. Although still determined to marry Margaret, Recka is nonetheless confused and lonely and plays a Tchaikovsky piece on his pipe organ. Behind him Lan Ying commits suicide with a knife, and just as Recka realizes something unexpected has happened, Brandon enters and arrests him. Brandon intends that Recka be convicted as the murderer of Lan Ying and thus pay for any other crimes for which he was never tried. Nicky foolishly imagines himself as Recka's successor, while Phil and Margaret fly to their honeymoon. *Ambition. Chinese Americans. Class distinction. Gangsters. Mistresses. Socialites. Suicide.* Abduction. Bonds. Loneliness. Marriage—Forced. Mayors. Music. Napoleon I, Emperor of the French, 1769-1821. Organs. Parties. Police. Romantic rivalry.

Note: Edgar Wallace's play opened in New York on 29 Oct 1930 and was published as a novel in 1932. According to Wallace biographers, the play was written in four days and was based on the career of Al Capone. Anna May Wong reprised her stage role from the New York production in the movie. Passages from symphonies by Peter Ilyich Tchaikovsky, played by "Recka" during numerous scenes, were blended into the musical score. Early *HR* production charts list Charles Schoenbaum as photographer. According to contemporary sources, Wong capitalized on the success of the film when she toured on behalf of Chinese war relief.

DV 24 Feb 1938, p. 3. *FD* 14 Mar 1938. *HR* 29 Nov 1937, p. 10. *HR* 20 Dec 1937, p. 14. *HR* 24 Feb 1938, p. 2. *MPD* 2 Mar 1938, p. 4. *MPH* 29 Jan 1938, p. 39. *MPH* 5 Mar 1938, p. 40. *Motion Picture Review* 26 Feb 1938. *NYT* 11 Mar 1938, p. 15. *Var* 16 Mar 1938, p. 15.

DANGEROUS VENTURE (Native Americans)

Hopalong Cassidy Productions, Inc. *Dist* United Artists Corp. 23 May **1947**; Prod: began late Jul 1946 [©Hopalong Cassidy Productions, Inc.; 23 May 1947; LP1013]. Sd (Western Electric Wide Range System); b&w. 6 reels, 5,335 ft. 59 min. Passed by the National Board of Review. PCA cert no. 12177.

Series: Hopalong Cassidy.

Prod Lewis J. Rachmil. [*Exec prod* William Boyd]. *Dir* George Archainbaud. *Asst dir* George Tobin. *Scr* Doris Schroeder. *Dir of photog* Mack Stengler. *Art dir* Harney T. Gillett. *Film ed* Fred W. Berger. *Set dec* George Mitchell. *Ward* Earl Moser. *Mus* David Chudnow. *Sd rec* Sound Services, Inc. *Sd* Frank Hansen.

Source: Based on characters created by Clarence E. Mulford.

Cast: WILLIAM BOYD (*Hopalong Cassidy*), Andy Clyde (*California Carlson*), Rand Brooks (*Lucky Jenkins*), Fritz Leiber (*Xeoli*), Douglas Evans (*Dr. [Grimes] Atwood*), Harry Cording ([*Dan*] *Morgan*), Betty Alexander (*Sue [Harmon]*), Francis McDonald ([*Bill*] *Kane*), Neyle Morrow (*José*), Patricia Tate (*Talu*), Bob Faust (*Stark*), Ken Tobey (*Red*), Jack Quinn (*Marshal*), Bill Nestell (*Pete*).

Western. [*Print viewed*]. José, a young Talnec Indian, is accused of rustling by ranchers Dan Morgan and Bill Kane, and is rescued by rancher Hopalong Cassidy and his partners, California Carlson and Lucky Jenkins. In reality, Morgan's men have been rustling local cattle while dressed as Indians, and Morgan has been blaming the crimes on an elusive band of Indians, called "ghost" Indians, who live a secluded life on a mesa. In town, Hoppy meets young Dr. Sue Harmon, an archaeologist who has come to study artifacts of the Talnecs to prove her father's theory that they are direct descendents of the Aztecs. With Sue is Dr. Grimes Atwood, who is leading the exhibition into the Talnec territory. Because Hoppy gives his word that white men will not touch the sacred Talnec burial grounds, which are filled with invaluable treasures, Xeoli, the tribal chief and José's grandfather, agrees to let the expedition take place. Morgan refuses to let the archaeologists pass through his ranch, until Atwood learns from Hoppy that he is behind the rustling and makes a pact with Morgan to protect him if he will help him ravage the burial grounds. In order to distract Hoppy, Sue and the others while he rustles a herd through the hills, Morgan stages an Indian raid in which the expedition's camp is set on fire. Hoppy sees Atwood flee before the raid, and becomes suspicious of him. While searching for the burial grounds, Morgan and Atwood see José, who realizes what they are doing, and Morgan shoots him to prevent him from warning the other Indians. Xeoli mistakenly believes that Hoppy is responsible for wounding his grandson and betraying the tribe, but José makes an oath on his life that Hoppy is their friend. The oath requires a human sacrifice by fire if José is wrong, and Xeoli decides to make Hoppy take José's place as the sacrificial victim. Hoppy peacefully disarms Xeoli, however, and refuses to accompany him back to the ritual site, and so Xeoli decides to take José's place himself. Although José maintains that Morgan is the one who shot him, his sister Talu lures California, whom she believes to be Hoppy, back to the Indian camp for the sacrifice. Meanwhile, as Hoppy attempts to stop Morgan and Atwood from robbing the graves, the Indians prepare to burn California. Hoppy comes to the rescue in time, and engages in a gunfight with Morgan and his men. Atwood is killed while trying to steal from the Indians' altar and falls into the fire pit. Hoppy and Lucky bring down the gang, and Lucky, who has been made a deputy, arrests Morgan. On Hoppy's advice, the Talnecs then move off the mesa to live in the valley with the white man. *Archaeologists. Expeditions. Indians of North America. Ranchers. Rustlers. Thieves. Brothers and sisters. Burial grounds. Fires. Grandfathers. Gunfights. Human sacrifice. Oaths. Relics and reliquaries. Rescues. Rites and ceremonies.*

Note: For additional information on the series, consult the Series Index and see the entry for *Hop-Along Cassidy* in the *American Film Institute Catalog of Feature Films, 1931-40*; F3.1990.

Box 1 Mar 1947. *DV* 17 Feb 1947. *FD* 25 Feb 1947, p. 8. *HR* 26 Jul 1946, p. 15. *HR* 17 Feb 1947, p. 3.

DANGERS OF THE ARCTIC (Native Americans, Native Alaskans)
Explorers Film Co. *Dist* Principal Distributing Corp. **1932**; New York opening: 29 Jun 1932. Sd; b&w. 58 or 60 min.

Dir Earl Rossman. *Photog* Earl Rossman. *Mus* Michael Hoffman. *Narr* Earl Rossman.

Documentary. [*Not viewed*]. Explorer Earl Rossman travels to the Arctic. According to the film, the Alaskan salmon canning business annually provides over \$7,000,000 in profits, which is over twice the sum paid to Russia for the area. Footage includes scenes of salmon fishing, glaciers breaking up and harpooning of whales and Walrus Island, which is said to be the home of the widest variety of birds in the North. A single Eskimo builds an igloo as protection from a snowstorm, which hides his sled with snow. The Eskimo is only able

to locate two of his reindeer, and he uses one as food, eating the flesh raw. In order to travel home, he skins the reindeer and freezes its hide, using it as a sled which he attaches to the surviving reindeer with strips of skin. The Eskimo later participates in a reindeer roundup, in which the animals are herded into an area bounded by fences made of ice. After selection of the best reindeer, the rest are released. In addition, Rossman charters a plane in Fairbanks, Alaska, and flies over Mt. McKinley. *Alaska. Arctic regions. Explorers. Fishing. McKinley, Mount (AK). Native Alaskans. Wild animals.*

FD 2 Jul 1932, p. 6. *HR* 29 Jun 1932, p. 7. *MPH* 9 Jul 1932, p. 36. *NYT* 30 Jun 1932, p. 26. *Var* 12 Jul 1932, p. 25.

DANIEL BOONE (Native Americans)
George A. Hirliman Productions, Inc. *Dist* RKO Radio Pictures, Inc. 17 Oct **1936**; Prod: 22 Jul—mid-Sep 1936 [©RKO Radio Pictures, Inc.; 12 Oct 1936; LP6632]. Sd (RCA "High Fidelity" Sound System); b&w. 75 or 77 min. PCA cert no. 2500.

Prod George A. Hirliman. *Assoc prod* Leonard Goldstein. *Dir* David Howard. *Asst dir* George Sherman and William O'Connor. *Scr* Daniel Jarrett. *Orig story* Edgecumb [sic] Pinchon. *Photog* Frank Good. *Art dir* Frank Sylos. *Film ed* Ralph Dixon. *Supv film ed* Joseph H. Lewis. *Mus dir* Hugo Riesenfeld and Arthur Kaye. *Mus supv* Abe Meyer. *Sd rec* Hal Bumbaugh. *Makeup* Max Factor. *Prod mgr* Charles Hunt.

Song(s): "Make Way," words and music by Jack Stern and Harry Tobias; "In My Garden," words by Grace Hamilton, music by Jack Stern.

Cast: GEORGE O'BRIEN [(*Daniel Boone*)], Heather Angel [(*Virginia Randolph*)], John Carradine [(*Simon Girty*)], Ralph Forbes [(*Stephen Marlowe*)], George Regas [(*Black "Blackie" Eagle*)], Dickie Jones [(*Master Jerry*)], Clarence Muse [(*Pompey*)], Huntley Gordon [(*Sir John Randolph*)], Harry Cording [(*Joe Burch*)], Aggie Herring [(*Mrs. Burch*)], Crawford Kent [(*Attorney General*)], Keith Kenneth [(*Commissioner*)], Tom Ricketts, Baron Lichter.

Biography, with songs. [*Print viewed*]. In 1775, frontiersman Daniel Boone prepares to lead a group of Colonial settlers from their home in Yadkin, North Carolina, across the Cumberland Mountains to a region known as Kain-tu-kee. Before leaving, Daniel sets out on a "hunting" trip with his Indian friend, Black "Blackie" Eagle, and finds his prey, the dreaded white renegade Simon Girty, who, with his small band of outlaw Indians, have murdered numerous settlers. Daniel and Black Eagle capture Girty but learn that, because of a recently signed treaty with the Indians, Girty cannot be tried for his crimes. Although he and the revenge-hungry settlers are frustrated by the law, they agree to free Girty to avoid trouble with the Indians. On the way to Kain-tu-kee, Daniel asks dandy Stephen Marlowe, who is in love with the pretty aristocratic settler Virginia Randolph, to ride ahead and tell the men who are driving the cattle herd to return to the main group. Marlowe, however, ignores Daniel's order, and the cattle herders are murdered that night by Girty. Furious, Daniel tells Marlowe to leave the group, but changes his mind when Virginia intercedes on Marlowe's behalf. Unknown to Virginia and Daniel, Marlowe and his rich political cohorts from Richmond are plotting to seize the land settled by Daniel by enforcing a law that requires squatters to acquire a legal title to their land claims by a certain date. Consequently, as soon as the new fortified settlement of Boonesborough is developed, Daniel is forced to ride to Richmond to save it from the Virginian politicians. In spite of Daniel's pleas, Marlowe refuses to bend the law, and Daniel rides sadly back to Boonesborough. Before reaching the settlement, Daniel is captured by Girty but is saved from a flaming death by Black Eagle. The settlers do battle with Girty and the Indians for nine exhausting days and, with the help of a well-timed rain storm, finally defeat the Indians. Girty, however, refuses to surrender and murders Daniel's special friend, little Master Jerry. Filled with vengeance, Daniel kills Girty after a long fight. With Virginia at his side, Daniel then leads the surviving settlers west to pioneer more virgin territory. *Daniel Boone. Simon Girty. Indians of North America. Kentucky. Politicians. Settlers. United States—History—Colonial period, ca. 1600-1775. Aristocrats. Boonesboro (KY). Children. Cumberland Mountains. Escapes. Fights. Land claims. Massacres. Murder. Rainstorms. Renegades. Richmond (VA). Treaties. Yadkin Riverh (NC).*

Note: The film's foreword states that while the story is "imaginative in some aspects," it is "faithful to the character and times." According to historical records as noted in modern sources, in 1775, as part of an agreement with Richard Henderson's Transylvania company, Daniel Boone led a group of

settlers, which included his wife and daughter, from Yadkin, North Carolina to the Indian territory known as Kain-tu-kee. In the process of establishing Boonesborough (later spelled Boonesboro), he and his followers fought with and were captured by Indians. Instead of being named the fourteenth colony, the newly settled land was incorporated by Virginia as a county. Richard Henderson never succeeded in procuring legal title to the land. Simon Girty, called "The Great Renegade," led raids against settlers and soldiers, but not until 1778, after his participation in the American Revolution.

Although a *HR* news item announced that the film was to have its premiere in Louisville, KY, release charts indicate that the national release date preceded the proposed premiere date. Many films and television shows based on the life of Daniel Boone have been made, including the 1923 short film *Daniel Boone*, which was part of the Yale University Press's *Chronicles of America* series; *Daniel Boone Thru the Wilderness*, a 1926 Sunset Productions film starring Roy Stewart and directed by either Frank S. Mattison or Robert N. Bradbury (see *AFI Catalog of Feature Films, 1921-30*; F2.1197); *Young Daniel Boone*, a 1950 Monogram production starring David Bruce and directed by Reginald LeBorg; *Daniel Boone, Trail Blazer*, a 1956 Republic picture starring Bruce Bennett and directed by Albert C. Gannaway and Ismael Rodriguez (see below), and the NBC television series *Daniel Boone*, which starred Fess Parker and ran from 1964 to 1969.

DV 18 Sep 1936, p. 3. *FD* 22 Sep 1936, p. 8. *FD* 30 Sep 1936, pp. 16-17. *HR* 14 Jul 1936, p. 4. *HR* 8 Sep 1936, p. 7. *HR* 18 Sep 1936, p. 4. *HR* 16 Oct 1936, p. 3. *MPD* 19 Sep 1936, p. 2. *MPH* 31 Oct 1936, p. 41. *NYT* 24 Oct 1936, p. 23. *Var* 28 Oct 1936, p. 14.

DANIEL BOONE, TRAIL BLAZER (Native Americans, Cherokee, Shawnee)

Gannaway-Ver Halen Productions; An Albert C. Gannaway Production. *Dist* Republic Pictures Corp. 14 Sep **1956**; *Prod*: mid-Aug—mid-Sep 1955 [©Republic Pictures Corp.; 14 Jun 1956; LP7359]. Sd (RCA Sound System); col (Trucolor by Consolidated Film Industries). 6,809 or 7,685 ft. 76 min. Passed by the National Board of Review. PCA cert no. 17933.

Exec prod Ben Costanten and C. J. Ver Halen. *Prod* Albert C. Gannaway. *Dir* Albert C. Gannaway and Ismael Rodriguez. *Asst dir* Jaime L. Contreras and Robert G. Vreeland. *Scr* Tom Hubbard and Jack Patrick. *Photog* Jack Draper. *Supv ed* Leon Barsha. *Ed* Fernando A. Martinez. *Mus comp and cond* Raul Lavista. *Sd* James L. Fields and Nicolas de la Rosa. *Tech adv* Charles Heard, Billy Coontz and Tex Lambert. *International coordination* William O'Dwyer.

Song(s): "Dan'l Boone," "Stand Firm in the Faith" and "Long Green Valley," music by Albert C. Gannaway, lyrics by Hal Levy.

Cast: Bruce Bennett (*Daniel Boone*), Lon Chaney (*Blackfish*), Faron Young (*Faron Callaway*), Kem [sic] Dibbs (*Simon Girty*), Damian O'Flynn (*Andy Callaway*), Jacqueline Evans (*Rebecca Boone*), Nancy Rodman (*Susannah Boone*), Freddy Fernandez (*Israel Boone*), Carol Kelly (*Jemima Boone*), Eduardo Noriega (*Squire Boone*), Fred Kohler, Jr. ([*Otis*] *Kenton*), Gordon Mills (*John Holder*), Claude Brook (*James Boone*), Joe Ainley (*General Hamilton*), Lee Morgan (*Smitty*).

Western, with songs. [*Print viewed*]. In 1775, Daniel Boone leads his family and a small group of settlers into the Kentucky wilderness to establish a fort and trading post for the Transylvania Company. His son James and several other scouts follow the main party, but when the smaller party camps for the night, they are attacked by a group of Shawnee Indians, and young James is killed and scalped. A British general named Hamilton has been offering the Shawnees rifles in exchange for the scalps of American rebels. Most of these deals are brokered by Simon Girty, a Cherokee who speaks with a French accent and wears a British uniform. When Boone finds his son's body and carries it back to the small fort, Andy Callaway, another settler, argues that they should return to civilization. Boone, however, believes that their settlement of Boonesboro will be the gateway to the West and insists on remaining. Andy's son Faron, who is loved by Boone's daughter Susannah, shares Boone's enthusiasm. Soon afterward, Blackfish, chief of the Shawnee Indians, visits the fort in the company of Girty to warn Boone against settling the area. Boone and Blackfish are blood brothers, but when Boone calls Girty a "serpent," the chief sternly replies, "He's Shawnee now." Worried about the safety of his brother Squire, who is bringing a group of children to the fort, Boone and several other settlers head out to meet the wagons. The children, several of them Boones, sing about "Dan'l Boone," but just before the famed pioneer arrives, the wagons are captured by Shawnees. That night, Boone uses cunning to free the wagon from the Indians, but two of the men become Shawnee prisoners. Boone later walks into the Shawnee village, but before Blackfish talks peace with him, he is forced to endure the blows of many of the warriors' tomahawks. At a council meeting, Boone argues that the settlers want only to live in peace and share the wealth of the

land with the Indians. Blackfish agrees to send his two sons to meet at a waterfall to discuss peace, but when the young warriors arrive, Girty secretly has them shot. Holding the body of one of his sons aloft, Blackfish later cries, "The earth will run red with the blood of white men!" and Boone barely escapes with his life. Later, Boone finds White Fox, Blackfish's other son, by the waterfall, mumbling "Girty!" Boone carries the feverish White Fox back to the fort, where he fervently hopes the Indian will regain his health. At night, several warriors quietly enter the fort, and although Boone orders the settlers to hold their fire, Callaway shoots, shouting, "Well, they're savages, aren't they?" One of the white prisoners escapes from the Shawnee village, but as he approaches the fort, the full contingent of attacking Indians begins shooting. The settlers fight hard but are soon overwhelmed, and things look hopeless when White Fox dies. Callaway is killed while approaching Blackfish and Girty with a white flag, and afterward, Blackfish enters the fort. He is shocked to see Boone supporting the upright body of White Fox, who, although dead, stares ahead with open eyes. Boone quietly asks Blackfish to act as though he is speaking with his son, and when Boone points the dead man's hand toward Girty, the villain assumes that his treachery has been revealed. As Girty turns to run away, Blackfish flings an axe at him. The bereaved chief then carries his son's body away from the fort, leaving it open to future westward travelers. *Daniel Boone. Boonesboro (KY). Settlers. Shawnee Indians. Treachery. Battles. Bounty hunters. Chases. Cherokee Indians. Children. Cowardice. English in foreign countries. Escapes. Family relationships. Forts. Simon Girty. Henry Hamilton. Infatuation. Murder. Raids. Revenge. Ruses. Tests of character. United States–History–Revolutionary War, 1776-1783.*

Note: The working titles of this film were *Adventures of Daniel Boone* and *Dan'l Boone*. An onscreen copyright notice states: "Copyright MCMLV by Daniel Boone Inc." This statement conflicts with information contained in the copyright registration, in which the picture is listed as Republic Pictures Corp. and the year of registration given as 1956. Actor Faron Young, who sings "Long Green Valley" in the film, was a country singer. As depicted in the film, Daniel Boone and his family guided settlers into Kentucky in 1775, erecting a fort on the site of what is now Boonesboro. From that year on, settlers endured frequent Shawnee and Tory attacks, and in 1778, Boone was briefly held at the Shawnee village of Chillicothe. Simon Girty was an American soldier who in 1878 began to lead Indian and British attacks on Americans along the northern and western frontier. In 1796, he escaped into Canada, and in 1818, he died. Henry Hamilton, who commanded the frontier post of Detroit, was known among the region's Indians as the "Hair Buyer" because he paid bounties for rebel scalps during the Revolution.

Because the picture was filmed in Mexico rather than Kentucky, Congressman Eugene Siler attempted to organize a Kentucky boycott of the film. A 29 Mar 1956 *DV* news item noted that the AFL-CIO had also planned a boycott of the film, in order to "teach a lesson to an American employer who ran away to a foreign country whereby he escaped paying American union wage rates to American workmen." Gannaway-Ver Halen Productions asserted that inclement weather prevented shooting in Kentucky, the story's locale. Gannaway also claimed that some of the film's financing originated in Mexico. A 26 Apr 1956 *LAT* news item reported that the boycott had been lifted following "an agreement on the part of the producer not to engage in 'runaway' foreign production in the future." For additional information on other films featuring Daniel Boone, see entry above for *Daniel Boone*.

Box 16 Mar 1957. *DV* 29 Mar 1956, pp. 1-2. *DV* 26 Apr 1956, p. 1, 4. *DV* 7 Feb 1957, p. 3. *Exh* 31 Oct 1956, p. 4243. *HR* 19 Aug 1955, p. 15. *HR* 16 Sep 1955, p. 11. *LAT* 26 Apr 1956. *MPHPD* 17 Nov 1956, p. 146. *Var* 13 Feb 1957, p. 6.

THE DARING CABALLERO (Latino)

Inter-American Productions, Inc. *Dist* United Artists Corp. 14 Jun **1949**; *Prod*: began mid-Dec 1949 [©Inter-American Productions, Inc.; 24 Jun 1949; LP2480]. Sd (RCA Sound System); b&w. 6 reels, 5,418 ft. 60-61 min. PCA cert no. 13653.

Series: The Cisco Kid.

Prod Philip N. Krasne and Duncan Renaldo. *Dir* Wallace Fox. *Asst dir* Louis Germonprez. *Scr* Betty Burbridge. *Orig story* Frances Kavanaugh. *Dir of photog* Lester White. [*Gaffer* James Punter]. [*Stills* Al St. Hilaire]. *Art dir* Edward Jewell. *Film ed* Marty Cohn. *Set dec* Helen Hansard. *Property masters* Gene Stone. *Ward* Robert Richards. *Mus comp and cond* Albert Glasser. *Sd* Garry Harris. *Makeup artist* Arthur Dupuis. *Property master* Gene Stone. [*Scr supv* Arnold Leven]. [*Grip* Charles Turner].

Source: Based on the character created by O. Henry.

Cast: Duncan Renaldo [(*The Cisco Kid*)], Leo Carillo [(*Pancho*)], Kippee Valez [(*Kippee Valez*)], Charles Halton [(*Hodges*)], Pedro de Cordoba [(*Padre*)], Stephan Chase [(*Mayor Brady*)], David Leonard [(*Patrick Del Rio*)], Edmund Cobb [(*Marshal Scott*)], Frank Jaquet [(*Judge Perkins*)], Mickey Little [(*Bobby Del Rio*)].

Western. [*Print viewed*]. In Del Rio, Texas, cowboy The Cisco Kid and his sidekick Pancho arrive at a mission, which is the home of young Bobby Del Rio. The padre tells Cisco that Bobby's father, Patrick Del Rio, who founded the town's bank, has been sentenced to die for a murder he did not commit. Cisco poses as a waiter delivering food to Del Rio's cell and breaks him out of jail. Cisco, Pancho and Del Rio then go to the mission's cellar to hide. Del Rio tells them that one day at the bank, he discovered that $90,000 in sequential bills were missing. When he asked his clerk to bring him the serial numbers of the missing bills, the clerk was shot by an unseen assailant. Shortly thereafter, Del Rio was arrested, and at his trial, a bank employee named Hodges testified that he had seen Del Rio shoot the man. Unknown to Del Rio, the real culprits, Hodges and Mayor Brady, are keeping the money inside a safe-deposit box at the bank until they can find the serial numbers list. Suspicious of Hodges, Cisco takes a bag of coins to the bank and asks him to exchange them for a $1,000 bill. Hodges offers Cisco two $500 bills, which he accepts. On the street outside, meanwhile, Marshal Scott mistakes Pancho for Cisco and arrests him on a trumped-up charge. Cisco then goes to Brady's office and forces him at gunpoint to phone Scott and order Pancho released. Later, Cisco shows Del Rio the bills that Hodges gave him and asks for the list, which was given to bank employee Kippee Valez. Meanwhile, Hodges and Brady learn that Bobby is being kept at the mission and go there with a search warrant. The padre complies with the warrant and begins to show them around, while Cisco and Pancho rush to the cellar to hide Del Rio. Cisco then goes to the bank to look for the list and finds a safe-deposit box key. He is about to open the box, when Brady emerges from the shadows, and they begin to fight. After Cisco knocks out Brady, he and Pancho escape, then fetch Kippee, who shows them where the list is. As expected, the numbers on the list do not match the bills, but Cisco and Pancho find the stolen bills inside the safe-deposit box. At that moment, Cisco, Pancho and Kippee hear Brady and Hodges sneaking into the bank and quickly hide. After Brady finds his spare key, he and Hodges enter the vault. Cisco then locks them inside and sends Pancho to fetch Judge Perkins. A short time later, inside the vault, Hodges falls asleep, so Brady places the bills into his own box. After Pancho and the judge arrive at the bank, Cisco reassembles the jury from Del Rio's first trial, then orders Kippee to open the vault. When Brady and Hodges step out with the empty box, Cisco asks for Brady's key and finds the money inside his box. In retaliation for his betrayal, Hodges shoots Brady, and is promptly arrested. After they learn that Del Rio has been freed, Cisco and Pancho say farewell. *Bank robberies. Betrayal. Cowboys. Frame-ups. Mexican Americans. Cellars. Conspiracy. False arrests. Hideouts. Impersonation and imposture. Jailbreaks. Judges. Juries. Mayors. Missions. Priests. Revenge. Safe-deposit boxes. Shootings. Trials. Vaults. Waiters. Warrants.*

Note: The title on the viewed print was *Guns of Fury*. This was the first Cisco Kid picture to be produced by United Artists. For additional information on the series, please consult the Series Index and see the above entry for *The Cisco Kid*.

Box 6 Aug 1949. DV 27 Jun 1949, p. 3. FD 2 Aug 1949, p. 5. HR 2 Dec 1948, p. 3. HR 17 Dec 1948, p. 13. HR 27 Jun 1949, p. 3. MPHPD 20 Aug 1949, p. 4722. Var 29 Jun 1949, p. 20. Var 27 Jul 1949, p. 12.

DARK ALIBI (Chinese Americans)

Monogram Pictures Corp. *Dist* Monogram Pictures Corp. 25 May 1946; Prod: began mid-Dec 1945 [©Monogram Pictures Corp.; 26 Mar 1946; LP184]. Sd (Western Electric Mirrophonic Recording); b&w. 60-61 min. PCA cert no. 11408.

Series: Charlie Chan.

Prod James S. Burkett. *Dir* Phil Karlson. *Asst dir* Theodore Joos. *Orig scr* George Callahan. *Photog* William Sickner. [*2d cam* Al Niclin]. [*Spec eff* Larry Glickman and Mario Castegnaro]. *Tech dir* Dave Milton. *Supv film ed* Richard Currier. *Ed* Ace Herman. [*Set dresser* Max Pittman]. *Mus dir* Edward J. Kay. *Rec* Tom Lambert. [*Re-rec and eff mix* Joseph I. Kane]. [*Mus mix* William H. Wilmarth]. *Prod mgr* Glenn Cook.

Source: Based on characters created by Earl Derr Biggers.

Cast: Sidney Toler [(*Charlie Chan*)], Mantan Moreland [(*Birmingham Brown*)], Ben Carter [(*Carter*)], Benson Fong [(*Tommy Chan*)], Teala Loring [(*June Harley*)], George Holmes [(*Hugh Kensey*)], Joyce Compton [(*Emily Evans*)], John Eldredge [(*Morgan*)], Russell Hicks [(*Warden*)], Tim Ryan [(*Foggy*)], Janet Shaw [(*Miss Petrie*)], Edward Earle [(*Thomas Harley*)], Ray Walker [(*Danvers*)], Milton Parsons [(*Johnson*)], Edna Holland [(*Mrs. Foss*)],

Anthony Warde [(*Jimmy Slade*)], George Eldredge [(*Brand*)], Meyer Grace [(*Doorman*)], [William Ruhl (*Thompson*)], [Minerva Urecal (*Mrs. Foss*)], [Frank Marlowe (*Barker*)].

Detective, Drama. [*Print viewed*]. When ex-convict Thomas Harley arrives at the boarding house where he lives with his daughter June, he is arrested for robbing a bank and killing a bank guard. Although he claims that he was summoned to the Carey Theatrical Warehouse by a note from his former cell mate, Dave Wyatt, and subsequently locked inside, the police do not believe his alibi because Wyatt has been dead for eight years. After fingerprints found at the scene are identified as belonging to Harley, he is condemned to death. Determined to prove her father innocent, June contacts detective Charlie Chan, who agrees that the case against her father is suspect. Together with June's boyfriend, prison guard Hugh Kensey, Chan questions Mrs. Foss, the boardinghouse landlady, who often rents to ex-convicts. They discover that the note purporting to be from Wyatt was written on Foss's typewriter. Chan then questions the other boarders: Miss Petrie, who works for a small salary at a social foundation; Mr. Johnson, a bookkeeper for the Carey Theatrical company; Mr. Danvers, a salesman of bank alarm systems; and Emily Evans, a showgirl whose costume was found in the warehouse. Both Danvers and Evans had traveled to other cities immediately before banks in those locations were robbed. The next day, Chan, his son Tommy, and his chauffeur, Birmingham Brown, drive to the prison, where an unknown assailant shoots at them. Chan becomes convinced that the fingerprints found at the scene were forged. After studying the police reports, Chan discovers that although a different man was convicted for each of the previous robberies, each man had been jailed in the same prison and the *modus operandi* used was identical in each case. Miss Petrie is revealed to be the wife of Jimmy Slade, a convict trustee, who is employed in the fingerprint bureau of the prison. When Petrie disappears, Chan, Birmingham and Tommy hurry to the warehouse. There, they locate Johnson, and later, Petrie is killed by a truck outside the warehouse. When Chan returns to the prison and discovers that the fingerprint cards have been tampered with, Slade overhears Chan and is wounded while trying to escape. After stating that he will not take the rap, Slade dies. Chan then takes prints of all the boarders at the boarding house and finds Johnson's on one of the prison cards. Chan then returns to the warehouse and uncovers the equipment necessary for forging fingerprints in the truck that killed Petrie. Danvers then tries to kill Chan, as he did Johnson, to stop him from talking. After Harley is freed, Chan explains that Slade sent the prints to Johnson, who copied them for Danvers, who carried out the robberies. He adds that Kensey was the leader of the gang, and when Harley opposed his marriage to June, the guard framed him. *Chinese Americans. Ex-convicts. Fathers and daughters. Fingerprints. Frame-ups. Murder. Private detectives. Alibi. Bank robberies. Boardinghouses. Chauffeurs. Fathers and sons. Forgers and forgery. Landladies. Prisons. Warehouses.*

Note: The film's working titles were *Fatal Fingerprints*, *Fatal Fingertips* and *Charlie Chan in Alcatraz*. The opening title card reads: Charlie Chan in *Dark Alibi*. The CBCS lists Minerva Urecal as "Mrs. Foss" but production information included in the file on the film at the AMPAS Library states that she was replaced by Edna Holland, who is listed in the onscreen credits. For more information on the Charlie Chan series consult the Series Index and see the entry above for *Charlie Chan Carries On.*

Box 30 Mar 1946. DV 10 Jul 1946, p. 3. FD 24 Apr 1946, p. 11. HR 19 Apr 1946, p. 3. MPHPD 19 Jan 1946, p. 2809. MPHPD 27 Apr 1946, p. 2962.

THE DARK AT THE TOP OF THE STAIRS (Jewish Americans)

Warner Bros. Pictures, Inc. *Dist* Warner Bros. Pictures, Inc. 8 Oct 1960; World premiere in New York: 22 Sep 1960 [©Warner Bros. Pictures, Inc.; 8 Oct 1960; LP21318]. Sd (RCA Sound Recording); col (Technicolor). 123 min. PCA cert no. 19612.

Prod Michael Garrison. *Dir* Delbert Mann. *Asst dir* Russell Llewellyn. *Dial supv* Norman Stuart. *Scr* Harriet Frank, Jr. and Irving Ravetch. *Dir of photog* Harry Stradling, Sr. *Art dir* Leo K. Kuter. *Film ed* Folmar Blangsted. *Set dec* George James Hopkins. *Cost des* Marjorie Best. *Mus* Max Steiner. *Orch* Murray Cutter. *Sd* Stanley Jones. *Makeup supv* Gordon Bau.

Source: Based on the play *The Dark at the Top of the Stairs* by William Inge (New York, 5 Dec 1957), as produced by Saint-Subber and Elia Kazan (New York, 5 Dec 1957).

Cast: ROBERT PRESTON [(*Rubin Flood*)], DOROTHY McGUIRE [(*Cora Flood*)], Eve Arden [(*Lottie*)], Angela Lansbury [(*Mavis Pruitt*)], Shirley Knight [(*Reenie Flood*)], Lee Kinsolving [(*Sammy Golden*)], Frank Overton [(*Morris*)], Robert Eyer [(*Sonny Flood*)],

Penny Parker [(*Flirt Conroy*)], Ken Lynch [(*Harry Ralston*)], [Nelson Leigh (*Ed Peabody*)], [Dennis Whitcomb (*Punky Givens*)], [Emerson Treacy (*George Williams*)], [Ben Erway (*Joseph Moody*)], [Helen Brown (*Mrs. Haycox*)], [Jean Paul King (*Mr. Delman*)], [John Eiman, Mike Chain, Bobby Beekman, Butch Hengen (*Boys*)], [Helen Wallace (*Lydia Harper*)], [Peg LaCentra (*Edna Harper*)], [Paul Birch (*Jonah Mills*)], [Mary Patton (*Mrs. Ralston*)], [Paul Comi (*Jenkins*)], [Addison Richards (*Harris*)], [Robin Warga (*Harold*)], [Charles Seel (*Percy Weems*)], [Stoddard Kirby (*Cadet*)].

Domestic, Historical, Drama. [*Print viewed*]. In the 1920s, Rubin Flood, a traveling harness and saddle salesman, lives in a small Oklahoma town with Cora, his wife of seventeen years, their teenage daughter Reenie, and younger son Sonny. When Rubin is about to leave on a road trip, his company's owner tells him that he is facing bankruptcy due to the increasing popularity of motorized vehicles, and has to lay him off. To bolster his confidence, Rubin stops at the local pharmacy and, in a back room, drinks some "prescription" alcohol. While there, he meets Harry Ralston, whose daughter is good friends with Reenie. Rubin does not like the nouveau riche Ralston, who shot himself in the foot in order to collect insurance money with which to indulge his nagging wife, and then invested some of the cash in oil wells and became rich. Meanwhile, Cora is helping Reenie buy a dress for Ralston's daughter's birthday party to be held at the country club. Reenie, however, has low self-esteem and regards herself as a wallflower. Later, after Rubin and Cora have an argument about the cost of Reenie's dress, Cora complains that she always has to scrimp to make ends meet. Sonny, friendless, insecure and scared of the dark, returns home having been teased by some local boys, and Rubin attempts to teach him how to box, but accidentally hits him hard, further angering the over-protective Cora. When Cora accuses Rubin of having a relationship with Mavis Pruitt, a young widow who runs a beauty parlor, he slaps her, then drives off. Upset by her parents' dispute, Reenie runs off distractedly into the street, causing a young man, Sammy Golden, to crash his car into a tree. Unhurt, Sammy, a student at a nearby military school, takes Reenie to a soda fountain and tells her that his mother, a movie actress, has virtually abandoned him. Rubin, meanwhile, shows up, slightly intoxicated, at Mavis's house, which also serves as her place of business, and scandalizes her customers, Lydia and Edna Harper, two gossiping sisters. Rubin tells Mavis that he needs her but that, at the same time, he is a family man and has never been unfaithful to Cora. Unable to seduce Mavis, Rubin falls asleep on her sofa. Four days later, on the night of the country club party, Lottie, Cora's older sister, and her husband Morris, whom Cora has phoned after her fight with Rubin, come from Oklahoma City for dinner. Cora breaks down and tells Lottie that she does not know where Rubin is and asks if she and the children can move in with her. Rubin returns during dinner and apologizes to Cora for hitting her. However, Cora receives a phone call from one of the Harper sisters detailing Rubin's recent activities. The sister's gossip provokes Rubin into bringing the crux of their recent problems into the open and he accuses Cora of rejecting him sexually. Cora responds that she can not make love at night after days filled with bitter feuding over money. Rubin also tries to give advice to Morris, who is dominated by Lottie. When Reenie's friend, Flirt Conroy, and her date arrive with Reenie's blind date for the party, Reenie is delighted to discover that he is Sammy Golden. Lottie, a bigot who has previously voiced anti-Catholic sentiments, realizes that Sammy is Jewish. When Sammy suggests to Rubin that he may not want his daughter to go out with him and offers to leave, Rubin refuses to consider that. After the young people leave for the party, Lottie, who is childless, confesses to Cora that Morris no longer makes love to her and that she has never enjoyed sex and states that she wishes someone loved her enough to hit her. At the party, Reenie and Sammy get along very well but, during an innocent kiss, are discovered by hosts Ralston and his wife. Mrs. Ralston accuses Reenie of turning her daughter's party into a petting party and, when she learns that Sammy is Jewish, tells Reenie that she has put them in a very embarrassing situation, as the country club is restricted and does not allow Jews as members. Although Ralston insists that his wife does not know what she is saying, Sammy feels that she does and is "the voice of the world." Sammy and Reenie leave, and while he is driving her home, Sammy tells Reenie that they can never be friends, that he will always have to be on the outside looking in. Reenie begs to stay with him, but Sammy tells her that he wants to drive around by

himself for a while. When Reenie finds her father trying to sleep on the sofa, he tells her that her mother does not know that he has lost his job. The next morning, Flirt brings the news that Sammy has tried to commit suicide and is in the hospital. While Reenie tells Sammy, whose mother has ignored his plea for help, that she wants to counteract all the people who have rejected him and have him become part of her family, Cora tries to make Sonny understand that she has kept him too close to her and that he must learn to stand on his own two feet. When Reenie returns home, her mother tells her that she has just phoned the hospital and learned that Sammy died after Reenie left. Later that day, Cora, posing as a customer, goes to visit Mavis. When she reveals that she is Rubin's wife, Mavis tells her that she has been in love with Rubin for years but that their relationship has never been consummated. After Mavis tells her about Rubin losing his job, she also advises Cora not to resist her husband's conjugal demands. Meanwhile, Rubin has a successful interview for a job selling oil drilling equipment, with a company whose president respects his native selling ability and knowledge of the territory. After the interview, Rubin finds Cora waiting for him, and she apologizes to him, tells him about Sammy's death and that she has sent the broken-hearted Reenie to stay with Lottie for a few days. Cora also admits that she has been to see Mavis and confesses that she has been mistaken about her. Rubin tells her that he is doing the best he can, that he loves and needs her. They return home to find that Sonny has made friends with one of his former tormentors and, as Cora awaits her husband in their upstairs bedroom, Rubin persuades the boys to go off to an afternoon movie. Adolescents. Antisemitism. Family life. Jews. Marriage. Salesmen. Sex. Unemployment. Automobile accidents. Beauty shops. Bigotry. Blind dates. Catholic Church. Children. Country clubs. Drugstores. Drunkenness. Fathers and daughters. Financial crisis. Gossip. Henpecked husbands. Military schools. Mothers and sons. Oklahoma. Parenthood. Parties. Phobias. Saddlery. Self-confidence. Sisters. Small town life. Suicide. Widows.

Note: William Inge's play had a thirteen month run on Broadway with Pat Hingle as "Rubin" and Teresa Wright as "Cora." Frank Overton, as Cora's brother-in-law, was the only person from the Broadway production to be cast in the film. Shirley Knight received an Academy Award nomination as Best Supporting Actress for her work on the film.

FD 15 Sep 1960. *Har* 17 Sep 1960. *HR* 12 Sep 1960. *LAT* 29 Sep 1960. *MPD* 14 Sep 1960. *MPH* 17 Sep 1960. *NYT* 23 Sep 1960, p. 33. *Var* 14 Sep 1960.

DARK DELUSION (Chinese Americans)
Metro-Goldwyn-Mayer Corp.; controlled by Loew's Inc. *Dist* Loew's Inc. Jun **1947**; New York opening: 25 Jun 1947; Prod: mid-Oct—early Dec 1946 [©Loew's Inc.; 14 May 1947; LP1012]. Sd (Western Electric Sound System); b&w. 8,069 ft. 90 min. Passed by the National Board of Review. PCA cert no. 12166.
Series: Dr. Gillespie.
Prod Carey Wilson. *Dir* Willis Goldbeck. [*Asst dir* Bill Lewis]. *Orig scr* Jack Andrews and Harry Ruskin. *Dir of photog* Charles Rosher. *Art dir* Cedric Gibbons and Stan Rogers. *Film ed* Gene Ruggiero. *Set dec* Edwin B. Willis. *Cost supv* Irene. *Mus score* David Snell. *Rec dir* Douglas Shearer. *Makeup created by* Jack Dawn.
Source: Based on characters created by Max Brand.
Cast: Lionel Barrymore (*Dr. Leonard Gillespie*), James Craig (*Dr. Tommy Coalt*), Lucille Bremer (*Cynthia Grace*), Jayne Meadows (*Mrs. Selkirk*), Warner Anderson (*Teddy Selkirk*), Henry Stephenson (*Dr. Evans Biddle*), Alma Kruger (*Molly Byrd*), Keye Luke (*Dr. Lee*), Art Baker (*Dr. Sanford Burson*), Lester Matthews (*Wyndham Grace*), Marie Blake (*Sally*), Ben Lessy (*Gin Rummy player [Napoleon]*), Geraldine Wall (*Miss Rowland*), Nell Craig (*Nurse Parker*), George Reed (*Conover*), Mary Currier (*Nurse Workman*), [Clarke Hardwicke (*Intern*)], [Eddie Parke (*Mild little man*)], [Bruce Cowling (*Dr. Williams*)], [William Tannen (*Chauffeur Walters*)], [Russell Hicks (*Mr. Logan*)], [John Burton (*Minister*)], [Mary Stuart (*Bride*)], [Michael Kirby (*Groom*)], [Vesey O'Davoren (*Butler*)], [Margaret Bert (*Mrs. Harris*)], [Jim Nolan (*Orderly*)], [Ransom Sherman (*Tomlin*)], [William Forrest (*Detective Jordan*)], [Ruth Lee (*Nurse*)], [Frances Chung (*Toots*)], [Harold Miller (*Patient*)], [Pietro Sosso (*Servant*)], [Polly Bailey (*Scrub woman*)], [Jack Rice (*Floorwalker*)], [Dick Paxton (*Western Union messenger*)], [Gary Gray (*Boy*)], [Hal Hackett], [Sammy McKim].
Medical, Drama. [*Print viewed*]. At Blair General Hospital in New York City, Dr. Tommy Coalt, an accomplished surgeon with a brusque bedside manner, is temporarily reassigned to a doctor's office in the small town of Bayhurst by head surgeon Dr. Leonard Gillespie.

Tommy is asked to take over Dr. Sanford Burson's private practice for six weeks while Burson is out of town. En route to Bayhurst, Tommy gets lost and stops to ask a young woman for directions. He notices that the woman is behaving in a strange manner, but when he asks her about her problem, she runs away. Tommy's first house call in Bayhurst is to Wyndham Grace, the town's wealthiest and most prominent citizen, who wants Tommy to put his signature on a document that will authorize the commitment of his daughter Cynthia to an insane asylum. Tommy immediately recognizes Cynthia as the woman he met by the road, and flatly rejects Wyndham's assertion that she is a schizophrenic. Dr. Evans Biddle, the only other doctor in Bayhurst, has signed the asylum admission papers, but Tommy is certain that Cynthia is not seriously ill. After leaving the Graces, Tommy visits the Selkirks, a young couple in the process of adopting a baby boy. Tommy tells Mrs. Selkirk that her husband Teddy must stop avoiding the physical examination required by law before they can finalize the adoption of their baby. While at the Selkirks', Tommy receives an urgent telephone call from Walters, the Grace family chauffeur, who has found Cynthia behaving oddly at a department store. Tommy races to the store, and arrives in time to witness Cynthia shoplifting merchandise. When Tommy asks Cynthia what she has just done, her thoughts become clouded, and she is slow to realize what has happened. Tommy tells Cynthia that she suffers from kleptomania, but insists that he must perform more studies to determine the cause of her behavior. Later, after accidentally starting a fire at her birthday party, Cynthia flees from her father's house, and takes refuge in Tommy's office. The following day, Wyndham telephones Dr. Gillespie to tell him about his daughter's disappearance. Later, when Teddy presents Tommy with a medical examination report, Tommy realizes that the report is a fake and demands that Teddy submit to a real examination. Dr. Gillespie then makes an unannounced visit to Bayhurst and tells Tommy that he may be facing a number of criminal charges, including kidnapping and malpractice. After convincing Dr. Gillespie that Cynthia does not require institutionalization, Tommy tries to diagnose her problem using "narcosynthesis," a procedure involving truth serum. During the procedure, Cynthia tells Tommy that she did not see a doctor after a fall from a horse months earlier. Tommy takes Cynthia to Brookline Hospital, where he soon discovers a blood clot in her brain. Meanwhile, in Bayhurst, Dr. Lee, a Chinese-American doctor from New York, takes over for Tommy during his absence and learns that Teddy has been hiding a heart condition from doctors. However, an impromptu physical examination shows that Teddy's concerns are unfounded and that he is healthy enough to adopt. Weeks pass, and Tommy returns to Bayhurst with Cynthia, who has fully recovered from her brain surgery. When Dr. Burson returns, he asks Tommy to stay in Bayhurst and hires him to help him in his practice. *Hospitals. Mental illness. Physicians. Small town life. Surgeons.* Adoption. Brain surgery. Chases. Chauffeurs. Chinese Americans. Deception. Dismissal (Employment). Fathers and daughters. Fires. Heart disease. Hypnotism. Kleptomania. New York City. Poliomyelitis. Riding accidents. Truth serums. Weddings.

Note: Working titles for this film were *Cynthia's Secret* and *The Personal Touch. HR* production charts list Edward Arnold in the cast, but he did not appear in the final film. *Dark Delusion* was the last in M-G-M's "Dr. Gillespie" series. For more information on the series, consult the Series Index and see the entry above for *Calling Dr. Gillespie* and *Young Dr. Kildare* in *AFI Catalog of Feature Films, 1931-40*; F3.5251.

Box 12 Mar 1947. *DV* 8 Apr 1947. *FD* 9 Apr 1947, p. 7. *HR* 18 Oct 1946, p. 10. *HR* 29 Nov 1946, p. 14. *HR* 8 Apr 1947, p. 3. *MPHPD* 12 Apr 1947. *NYT* 26 Jun 1947, p. 19. *Var* 9 Apr 1947, p. 16.

DARK MANHATTAN (African Americans)
Randol-Cooper Productions, Inc. *Dist* Rinaldo Films. **1937**; World premiere in Los Angeles: 13 Feb 1937; New York opening: week of 12 Mar 1937; *Prod*: late Dec 1936—5 Jan 1937. Sd; b&w. 77 min. PCA cert no. 3033.

Exec prod George Randol. *Assoc prod* Ben Rinaldo. *Dir* Harry Fraser. *Asst dir* William Nolte. *Orig story and scr* George Randol. *Photog* Arthur Reed. *Film ed* Arthur Brooks. *Mus* Ben Ellison and Harvey Brooks. *Sd* Corson Jowett. *Tech supv* Roland Price.

Cast: RALPH COOPER (*[James A.] Curly Thorpe*), Cleo Herndon (*Flo Gray*), Clarence Brooks (*Larry [B.] Lee*), Jess Lee Brooks (*Lieut. Ballot*), Sam McDaniels (*Jack Jackson*), Corny Anderson (*Atty. Brown*), Rubeline Glover (*Miss Hall*), James Adamson (*Lem*), [Nicodemus (*Pete*)], [Jack Liney (*Butch Williams*)], [Jack Clisby], [Charles Battersby].

African American, Gangster, Drama. [*Print viewed*]. When Larry B. "L. B." Lee, the top numbers banker in Harlem, visits the poolroom of one of his accounts, Jack Jackson, he witnesses James A. "Curly" Thorpe break up a knife fight and, impressed with his performance, asks Curly to join his organization, which he emphasizes does not use underhanded methods. Curly quickly distinguishes himself as tough on district operators, whose business is declining, and grows ambitious in his desire to be the most talked about man in Harlem. He also wants to steal the affections of L. B.'s girl friend, Flo Gray, a radio singer who appears at the Club Congo. After L. B., who has been warned by his doctor to take a rest, has a heart attack while dining with Flo, Curly runs the operation while L. B. recuperates. Curly institutes gangster methods to force smaller operations to pay for protection, and doubles the bank's income, which causes ten days of gang warfare and police raids, culminating in a district attorney's effort to smash the numbers racket. Although Curly and Flo keep newspaper reports away from L. B., the heads of the other numbers banks reveal the situation to him, after which he promises to redistribute the money his bank made. Curly, however, refuses to part with the money made since he took over and prevails upon L. B. to take a trip for his health. After Curly tells the bankers' association that he wants twenty percent from every banker for protection, Butch Williams, a rival who operates at the Club Congo, offers protection for five percent. During a shoot out at the club, Curly is mortally wounded, and he dies in the arms of Flo, who has grown to love him. *African Americans. Ambition. Gangsters. New York City--Harlem. Numbers racket.* Billiards and billiard parlors. Clubs. District Attorneys. Gang wars. Gunshot wounds. Heart disease. Knife fighting. Physicians. Police raids. Radio broadcasting. Singers.

Note: Before the opening credits of this film, a title card reads: "We dedicate this picture to the memories of R. B. Harrison, Bert Williams, Florence Mills and all of the pioneer Negro actors who by their many sacrifices made this presentation possible." According to an 11 Dec 1936 *HR* news item, Randol-Cooper Productions was "formed to produce pictures for theaters catering largely to Negro trade," and this was to be the first of six features planned for the year. The news item also states that Leslie Goodwins was going to direct, Ralph Like was to be the associate producer, Nina Mae McKinney would play opposite Ralph Cooper, and that shooting would begin on 18 Dec at Talisman studios. No information has been located to confirm that Goodwins, Like or McKinney were actually involved with the film, or that the Talisman studios were used. A 6 Jan 1937 *HR* news item states that filming wound up the previous day at International studios, however, modern sources state that the film was shot at the old Grand National studio in Hollywood.

According to a 6 Feb 1937 news item in *PittsC*, on 4 Feb "pandemonium broke out at the Tivoli theater [in Los Angeles when the film] failed to have the gala world premiere as advertised several weeks in advance." The event reportedly turned into a riot when, instead of the premiere showing of the film, the audience was shown other films. The article also notes that in the foyer of the theater, "many actors who worked on the film told of not being paid for their work," and that the AMPAS, in a statement to the press about the "unhappy incident," called the producers of the film "fly by night wild cats that spring up over night."

A 22 Dec 1936 *HR* news item states that because of a possible ban on films in which white men speak lines in films exhibited in theaters catering to the black trade in New York, Illinois and Pennsylvania, the producers lined up two sets of extras and supporting players, one containing white actors and the other all black, pending word from the Hays Office. In Jan 1937, according to a *HR* news item, it was decided that the film would have an all-black cast.

According to the file for the film in the MPAA/PCA Collection at the AMPAS Library, the PCA, on 23 Dec 1936, informed Randall [sic] Cooper Productions that the film was "in violation of the Code" because it failed to present the "numbers" racket as a "definite illegal activity," and because it failed to "show the police as being active in suppressing the racket." The PCA also noted in the letter that it was their understanding that omitted from the film would be the "indication that the gangsters who muscle in on the racket are white gangsters, [which would] eliminate any suggestion of conflict between whites and negroes." In addition to this, the PCA insisted on the elimination of the showing of machine guns in the hands of gangsters, illicit sex between "Flo" and "Curly," and any suggestion that "Flo" is a loose woman.

Although *Var* calls the film a "Renaldo Films release," the distributor was probably Rinaldo Films, as Ben Rinaldo was listed as associate producer in the credits. *Var* called the film the "best technically ever made with complete colored cast." Modern sources state that the film was produced by Million Dollar Pictures, Renaldo Films and Cooper-Randol Productions; that it was the first black film produced in Hollywood; that Arthur Brooks wrote the screenplay; that Nicodemus' last name was Stewart; that Roy Glenn was in the cast; and that actor Ralph Cooper, sometimes billed as "the Bronze Bogart," co-directed with Harry Fraser.

HR 11 Dec 1936, p. 4. *HR* 22 Dec 1936, p. 11. *HR* 6 Jan 1937, p. 9. *HR* 13 Feb 1937, p. 4. *PittsC* 6 Feb 1937, sec. II, p. 6. *PittsC* 20 Feb 1937, p. 19. *Var* 17 Mar 1937, p. 15.

THE DARK MIRROR (Gypsies)

Famous Players-Lasky Corp. *Dist* Famous Players-Lasky Corp.; Paramount-Artcraft Pictures. 16 May **1920** [©Thomas H. Ince; 27 Mar 1920; LP14935]. Si; b&w. 5 reels, 5,084 ft.

Supv Thomas H. Ince. *Dir* Charles Giblyn. *Scen* E. Magnus Ingleton. *Cam* John S. Stumar.

Source: Based on the novel *The Dark Mirror* by Louis Joseph Vance (Garden City, NY, 1920).

Cast: Dorothy Dalton (*Priscilla Maine/Nora O'Moore*), Huntley Gordon (*Dr. Philip Fosdick*), Walter Neeland (*Red Carnahan*), Jessie Arnold (*Inez*), Lucile Carney (*Addy*), Pedro de Cordoba (*Mario*), Donald MacPherson (*The nut*), Bert Starkey (*Charlie the Coke*).

Drama. Priscilla Maine, a wealthy young woman, is plagued by visions filled with menacing people and strange adventures. She confides these to Dr. Philip Fosdick, a young physician. Later, while reading a newspaper account of a crime, Philip recognizes the people from Priscilla's dreams and investigates. He discovers that Priscilla has a twin sister living in the slums named Nora O'Moore who has just escaped from the clutches of gang leader Red Carnahan. Carnahan discovers Nora's hiding place and, dragging her to a lake, drowns her. Priscilla envisions the lake and is drawn to it; there she finds Carnahan who becomes so terrified at Priscilla's resemblance to his victim that he drowns himself in fear. Priscilla faints and is nursed back to health by Philip. They then discover that Priscilla's father had married a gypsy who gave birth to twin daughters: her mother ran off with Nora while Priscilla remained with her father. With the mystery solved, Philip and Priscilla marry. *Dreams. Extrasensory perception. Gangsters. Parentage. Physicians. Sisters. Twins. Visions.* Drowning. Gypsies. Lakes. Murder. Newspapers. Nursing back to health. Slums. Suicide.

Note: This was the first film of Donald MacPherson.

ETR 15 May 1920, p. 2740. *MPN* 22 May 1920, p. 4400. *MPW* 15 May 1920, p. 983. *NYMT* 16 May 1920. *NYR* 15 May 1920. *Var* 14 May 1920, p. 34. *Wid's* 23 May 1920, p. 9.

DARK VIOLENCE *see* ANGEL IN EXILE

DARK WATERS (Cajuns, Creoles, African Americans)

Benedict Bogeaus Productions, Inc. *Dist* United Artists Corp. 10 Nov **1944**; Prod: 15 May—20 Jul 1944 at General Service Studios [©Dark Waters Productions, Inc.; 15 Sep 1944; LP13028]. Sd (Western Electric Mirrophonic Recording); b&w. 8,055 ft. 90 min.

Exec prod James Nasser. *Prod* Benedict Bogeaus. *Prod assoc* Arthur M. Landau. *Asst to prod* Carley Harriman. *Dir* Andre De Toth. *Asst dir* Joseph Depew. *Scr* Joan Harrison and Marian Cockrell. *Addl dial* Arthur Horman. *Cine* Archie Stout and John Mescall. *Spec eff* Harry Redmond, Jr. *Art dir* Charles Odds. *Film ed* James Smith. *Set dec* Maurice Yates. *Cost for Miss Oberon* Rene Hubert. *Ward* Greta. *Mus score and dir* Miklos Rozsa. [*Dance dir* Jack Crosby]. *Sd tech* Frank Webster. *Makeup artist* Edward Larsen. *Hair stylist* Scotty Rackin. [*Unit mgr* Len Boyd].

Source: Based on the novel *Dark Waters* by Frank and Marian Cockrell (New York, 1944).

Cast: MERLE OBERON [(*Leslie Calvin*)], FRANCHOT TONE [(*Dr. George Grover*)], THOMAS MITCHELL [(*Mr. Sydney*)], FAY BAINTER [(*Aunt Emily Lamont/May*)], Elisha Cook, Jr. [(*Cleeve*)], John Qualen [(*Uncle Norbert Lamont/Pinky*)], Rex Ingram [(*Pearson Jackson*)], Nina May [sic] McKinney [(*Florella*)], Odette Myrtle [(*Mama Boudreaux*)], Eugene Borden [(*Papa Boudreaux*)], [Eileen Coghlan (*Jeanette*)], [Alan Napier (*The doctor*)], [Rita Beery (*The nurse*)], [Gillian Perreau (*Yvette Boudreaux*)].

Psychological, Drama. [*Print viewed*]. When the ship that is carrying Leslie Calvin and her wealthy parents from Batavia to America sinks, Leslie, one of only four survivors, is haunted by the death of her parents. Just before she is to be released from the New Orleans hospital in which she is recuperating, Leslie writes a letter to her only living relative, her mother's sister, Emily Lamont, whom she has never met. Emily writes back from Belleville, Louisiana, explaining that she and her husband Norbert are residing at the ancestral plantation there and inviting Leslie to stay with them. Leslie travels to Belleville, but when no one appears to meet her at the train station, the neurotic Leslie faints from the heat. The town physician, George Grover, is summoned to treat Leslie and convinces her to accompany him to his office. There, Leslie confides her fears about being alone and her recurring nightmares about her rescue. Feeling compassion for the distraught Leslie, George offers to drive her to the plantation. There, they are met by the overbearing Mr. Sydney, who introduces himself as a guest of the Lamonts, and Leslie's eccentric aunt Emily, who claims that she never received Leslie's telegram notifying them of her arrival. Before departing, George cautions Sydney that Leslie is emotionally unstable and needs to forget her traumatic ordeal. After Emily escorts Leslie to her room, Sydney extracts her telegram from his coat pocket and tosses it in the wastebasket. At dinner that night, Sydney urges Leslie to relate the tale of her tragic voyage, sending her running from the table, hysterical. The next morning, Sydney and Cleeve, the overseer, take Leslie on a tour of the plantation and force her to tread perilously on a ledge along the bayou. As Cleeve is about to coerce the terrified Leslie into joining him for a boat ride, George appears and invites her to join him on his rounds. At a bayou shack, George introduces Leslie to the Boudreaux family, who ask them to lunch. Leslie's spirits are uplifted, until she attends a movie with the Lamonts and Sydney that night and views a newsreel depicting the sinking of a ship by a German submarine. The next day, as Leslie suns herself in the garden, Pearson Jackson appears to ask for her help. Pearson explains that he worked on the plantation for twelve years until the Lamonts arrived and Cleeve fired him. That night, George takes Leslie to a dance, and Leslie recalls that as a girl she would dance for her mother, who was unable to walk. When George kisses her and proposes, Leslie runs into the house, asserting that she can never see him again. Agitated, Leslie then confides to her aunt that she can never marry because she suffers hallucinations and belongs under the water with her mother and father. After going to bed, Leslie hears a voice calling her name and wanders outside, seeking its source. She is startled by Pearson, who has also heard the voice and warns her that spirits are pursuing her. Terrified, Leslie takes refuge in the house and phones George, who is out on a housecall. After leaving a message for George, Leslie questions Emily about Cleeve and Sydney and charges that one of them is trying to drive her insane. When Emily begins to reminisce about Leslie's mother's love of dancing, Leslie realizes that she is an impostor. The next day, Pearson warns Leslie that her aunt and uncle are impostors and arranges to meet her in the bayou that evening. When Leslie goes to the appointed meeting place, however, she finds Pearson's dead body. Leslie decides to catch the next train leaving Belleville, but is prevented from doing so by Emily, who summons her to her room. The next morning, George returns Leslie's phone call, and Leslie insists that he immediately come to the plantation. When he arrives, Leslie apprises him of Pearson's murder and claims that her aunt and uncle are impostors. Incredulous, George writes out a prescription for a tranquilizer. After sending Leslie to her room for a rest, George informs Sydney that he is certain that Leslie is suffering from delusions and will arrange for her to see a psychiatrist. In her room, Leslie, desolate, looks at the prescription and realizes that George has actually written a note, warning her of danger and promising to return with help. After George departs, Sydney addresses Norbert as Pinky and Emily as May. When May, who has been hired by Sydney to pose as Emily, objects to harming Leslie, Sydney reminds her that she and Pinky are already implicated in the Lamonts' murder. At the boathouse, meanwhile, Cleeve has taken George prisoner. After George tricks Cleeve into admitting that he murdered the Lamonts, he begins to taunt Cleeve about performing Sydney's dirty work. Soon after, Sydney appears with Leslie. After demonstrating how he used a phonograph to call out Leslie's name, Sydney explains that he engineered the diabolical plot to drive Leslie mad and acquire her inheritance. Sydney then orders Cleeve, George and Leslie into a motorboat, but when he commands Cleeve to kill George and Leslie while motoring into the bayou, Cleeve balks and the two men begin to argue. In the confusion, Leslie and George jump overboard and hide in the water lilies. When Leslie collapses with terror, George helps her ashore and Cleeve and Sydney follow. Cleeve charges into the swamp, but sinks into a bog of quicksand and drowns. George then calls to Sydney and offers to lead him out of the swamp in exchange for his gun. After Sydney discards his weapon, George picks it up and orders him back into the boat. When Leslie climbs in and follows George's instruction to start the engine, she realizes that she is recovered at last. *Drowning. Impersonation and imposture. Inheritance. Louisiana. Mental illness. Physicians. Psychological torment.* Aunts. Boating accidents. Hospitals. Murder. Overseers. Plantations. Proposals (Marital). Quicksand. Swamps. Uncles.

Note: Frank and Marian Cockrell's novel was serialized in *The Saturday Evening Post* from 19 Feb 1944 to 11 Mar 1944. The viewed print was considerably shorter than the original release length. Nina Mae McKinney's name was misspelled "Nina May" in the onscreen credits. News items in *HR* yield the following information about this production: In Apr 1944, producer Benedict Bogeaus announced that he was seeking Jennifer Jones and George Murphy to play the leads. Barton Hepburn was tested for a feature role, but did not appear in the film. Cecil Cunningham was to portray Merle Oberon's mother in the picture, but that character did not appear in the completed film. According to a Jun 1944 news item, Franklyn Farnum, Wilbur Mack, Maude Fealy and Ray Cordell appeared as extras in the movie theater scene. *HR* news items add Frank Dawson, Paul Burns, William Randolph, Ian Wolfe, Gino Corrado, Louise and Alice Kerbrat, Gerald Perreau, Fleurette Zama, Diana Martin, Diana Du Bois, Rose Plummer, Margaret Tealy, Dorothy Vernon, Donald Kerr, Art La Forrest, Rex Moore and Bud Rae to the cast, but their participation in the released film has not been confirmed. On 27 Nov 1944, *Lux Radio Theatre* broadcast a radio version of the story starring Merle Oberon.

Box 18 Nov 1944. *DV* 31 Oct 1944, p. 3, 8. *FD* 31 Oct 1944, p. 6. *HR* 10 Apr 1944, p. 8. *HR* 10 May 1944, p. 7. *HR* 15 May 1944, p. 4. *HR* 5 Jun 1944, p. 11. *HR* 14 Jul 1944, p. 14. *HR* 23 Jun 1944, p. 8. *HR* 27 Jun 1944, p. 2. *HR* 13 Jul 1944, p. 7. *HR* 20 Jul 1944, p. 2, 6. *HR* 31 Oct 1944, p. 4. *HR* 27 Nov 1944, p. 6. *MPHPD* 8 Jul 1944, p. 1983. *MPHPD* 4 Nov 1944, p. 2165. *NYT* 22 Nov 1944, p. 25. *Var* 1 Nov 1944, p. 10.

DARLING *see* COME ON OVER

DARLING MINE (Irish Americans)
Selznick Pictures Corp. *Dist* Select Pictures Corp. 16 Aug 1920 [©Select Pictures Corp.; 8 Aug 1920; LP15545]. Si; b&w. 5 reels.

Pres Lewis J. Selznick. *Dir* Laurence Trimble. *Scen* John Lynch and Laurence Trimble.

Cast: Olive Thomas (*Kitty McCarthy*), Walter McGrail (*Roger Davis*), Walt Whitman (*James McCarthy*), Barney Sherry (*Gordon Davis*), Margaret McWade (*Agnes McCarthy*), Betty Schade (*Vera Maxwell*), Richard Tucker (*Jay Savoy*), Colin Kenny, Andrew Arbuckle, Mrs. George Hernandez.

Drama. Impelled by a note from her Aunt Agnes in America, Kitty McCarthy travels from Ireland to New York City, where she meets Gordon Davis, a successful playwright, who directs her to her aunt's address on the East Side. There Kitty discovers her aunt living in a tenement, a confirmed alcoholic. Through her niece's care, Agnes is cured, and one day Davis appears and offers Kitty a part in a comedy that he has written. She accepts, and once backstage meets Vera Maxwell, the victim of an unhappy affair with Oscar Savoy. Kitty brings the lovelorn couple back together but is unsuccessful in arranging her own romance with Davis' nephew Roger until Davis finally intervenes, and all ends happily. *Alcoholism. Aunts. Immigrants. Irish. New York City–East Side. Playwrights. Actors and actresses. Tenement-houses.*

ETR 4 Sep 1920, p. 1512. *MPN* 18 Sep 1920, p. 2311. *MPW* 28 Aug 1920, p. 1213.

THE DAUGHTER OF DAWN (Native Americans, Comanche, Kiowa)
Texas Film Co. Oct 1920 [©Richard E. Banks; 20 Oct 1920; LP16293]. Si; b&w. 6 reels.

Dir Norbert Myles. *Scen* Norbert Myles.

Western. Rivalry develops between Comanche Indians White and Wolf for the hand of Dawn, the daughter of the chief, but Dawn loves White. When the chief sets up a test of bravery for the men, noble White passes, but cowardly Wolf fails and is banished from the camp. Wolf becomes a traitor and goes to the Kiowas (who have stolen the Comanche ponies, and are occupying their territory), to offer to lead them to the Comanche camp in order to steal away their women. The Kiowas kidnap the women while the Comanches are away on a hunt and Wolf takes Dawn. The Comanches go on the warpath against the Kiowas, overpowering them. White fights with Wolf and leaves him for dead. Wolf dies in the arms of Wanada, who had loved him, and in despair she kills herself. Back in the Comanche camp, White and Dawn are happy, together at last. *Abduction. Comanche Indians. Kiowa Indians. Rivalry. Traitors. Tribal chiefs. Courage. Suicide.*

Note: This film was produced in Oklahoma. According to a news item, only Native American Indians appeared in the film. It had its premiere in Los Angeles in Oct 1920. It was licensed for reissue in New York on 2 Apr 1924; at that time, the names of Chief Buffalo Bear and Princess Buffalo Bear were associated with the film, but the nature of their specific involvement is not known.

MPN 16 Oct 1920, p. 2972.

A DAUGHTER OF HER PEOPLE (Yiddish language)
Standard Film Co. *Dist* Quality Film Corp. 1932; Pittsburgh showing: Mar 1933; Prod: recorded by Atlas Soundfilm Recording Studios; ended late May 1932. Sd (Cineglow Sound System); b&w. 7,271 ft. 75 min. Yiddish language.

Pres HARRY S. BROWN. [*Prod* Harry S. Brown]. *Dir* George Roland. *Scr adpt* Jeanette Schiller Brown. *Dial* Jacob Mestel. *Photog* "Buddy" Harris and Carl Berger. *Film ed* Jean Roland. *Mus score* I. J. Hochman. *Rec eng* Lyman J. Wiggin.

Source: Based on the novel *Judith Trachtenberg* by Karl Emil Franzos (New York, 1891).

Cast: Joseph Greenberg [(*The narrator*)], Chaim Shneyer, Morris Dorf, Jacob Mestel, Michael Rosenberg, Ben Basenko, Helen Blay.

Historical, Yiddish, Drama. [*Print viewed*]. On the anniversary of the death of Judith Trachtenberg, a man, at night, searches for her grave and then tells her story to three comrades: In the nineteenth century, Judith, who is reared in a Jewish ghetto in a part of Poland that belongs to Austria, meets Count Agenor Baranowski during a ball at the home of her father's business associate, Prefect von Wroblewski. After the count saves her from the unwanted attentions of an intoxicated Polish officer, Judith and the count become lovers. Because of the liaison, she is rejected by her father and brother, so she begins to live with the count. After she becomes pregnant, the count fakes a marriage with her, to assuage her guilt. The Jews then, according to their custom, conduct a burial service for Judith and bury a rosebush in her place, as her father is heartbroken. When the count learns that the state of Sachsen-Weimer countenances mixed marriages, he and Judith go there to legalize their union. Their marriage is also validated in Austria by Count Metternich, but when they return and Judith is still not accepted by her people, she drowns herself in a lake. After the story is concluded, as the sun rises, Judith appears to the group in tears before disappearing. *Jews–History. Legends. Marriage–Mixed. Ostracism. Suicide. Austria–History. Balls (Parties). Drowning. Graves. Marriage–Fake. Nobility. Poland–History. Rabbis. Rites and ceremonies.*

Note: The Yiddish title of this film is *Yidishe Tochter*. The film was a re-release of a silent film with a talking framing sequence and dubbed Yiddish narration added to the original film. The additional material was shot in New York in 1932. An opening title states that the story is based on an old Jewish legend discovered by a student who carefully researched the romance. The *Var* review of a 1933 New York showing states that the Vilna Troupe appeared in the original silent film; however, a *FD* news item states that the Vilna Troupe appeared in the sequences filmed in 1932. Modern sources state that the original film was the 1920 German film *Judith Trachtenberg*. That film was produced by Neos-Film and distributed by Doktram-Film, and had its premiere in Berlin in Dec 1920. It was 7 reels and 2,373 meters in length before censorship cuts. The following credits for that film come from modern sources: *Dir* Henrik Galéen; *Script* Franz Schulz; *Cam* Gotthardt Wolf; *Art dir* Eduard Peter; *Art adviser* Karl Jacob Hirsch; *Jewish adviser* Jacob Steinbach; *Cast* Leontine Kühnberg (*Judith Trachtenberg*), Ernst Deutch (*Her brother*), Leonhard Haskel (*Her father*), Paul Otto (*Count Agenor Baranowski*), Hermann Vallentin (*Prefect von Wroblewski*), Max Adalbert, Friedrich Kühne, Ernst Pröckl, Margarete Kupfer, Frieda Richard.

The above plot summary of the original silent film was based on a review of *Judith Trachtenberg*. However, speculation exists that the silent film may have been a Polish film, which, under the English title of *Rachael the Outcast*, was submitted to the New York State censors in Apr 1922. The silent film within *A Daughter of Her People* has a shot of a signpost in Polish, and modern sources state that the plot of *Rachael the Outcast* "suggests *Judith Trachtenberg*." No further information regarding the original silent film has been located.

The added scenes in the 1932 version features actors from the Yiddish Art Players. This version includes scenes that appear at the beginning and end to introduce and conclude the story, in addition to two scenes in the middle of Judith's father coming to see the rabbi, and the rabbi telling another man after Judith's death that it will be alright to say the *Kaddish*, or the prayer for the dead, and to "sit *shiva*," or mourn, for Judith.

According to a *Var* news item, management for the Avenue Cinema in Pittsburgh, a foreign film theater, bought the film sight unseen as an "all-talker," and they were ready to junk it when they saw what arrived. However, as they had no other booking available, they played the film, and it did the best business there in months.

FD 12 May 1932, p. 8. *FD* 5 Jun 1932, p. 4. *Der Kinematograph* 3 Apr 1921. *Var* 28 Mar 1933. *Var* 23 May 1933, p. 19.

DAUGHTER OF MINE (Jewish Americans)
Goldwyn Pictures Corp. *Dist* Goldwyn Distributing Corp. 30 Mar 1919 [©Goldwyn Pictures Corp.; 21 Mar 1919; LP13523]. Si; b&w. 5 reels, 4,680 ft.

Pres Samuel Goldwyn. *Dir* Clarence G. Badger. *Story and scen* Hugo Ballin. *Cam* Marcel Le Picard. *Art dir* Hugo Ballin.

Cast: Madge Kennedy (*Rosie Mendelsohn/Lady Diantha*), John Bowers (*George Howard/Byron Mulvaney*), Tully Marshall (*Papa Mendelsohn/Lord Noblebrow*), Arthur Carew (*Joseph Rayberg/Baron Landsandhome*), Abraham Schwartz (*Rabinowitch/The major domo*).

Drama. Rosie Mendelsohn, the daughter of a kindly Jewish tailor in New York's East Side ghetto, ends her romance with struggling author George Howard because of her father's objections to her marriage to a gentile. After George leaves, Rosie attempts to find him by becoming a private secretary to publisher Joseph Rayberg, whom she persuades to publish a contest in which authors would send in endings to part of a manuscript she claims to have found. Rayberg, intent on seducing Rosie, agrees to publish the manuscript (which is a version of George's novel that she had typed earlier, and actually is a humorously idealized story of her own life) only after Rosie agrees to have sex with him when the contest is over. When George, down-and-out, submits the rest of his story, Rayberg locks Rosie in his office, but she escapes into George's arms and they go to her father who relents and blesses their union. *Contests. Fathers and daughters. Jews. Marriage–Mixed. New York City–Lower East Side. Novelists. Escapes. Publishers and publishing. Secretaries. Self-sacrifice.*

Note: This film was partially shot on Ludlow Street in New York City. Reviews list the leading male character as both "George Howard" and "Charles Howard." Hugo Ballin, who wrote the story, was Goldwyn's art director since the company's formation.

ETR 3 May 1919, p. 1683. *MPN* 17 May 1919, p. 3278. *MPW* 10 May 1919, p. 935. *Var* 2 May 1919, p. 59. *Wid's* 27 Apr 1919, p. 23.

DAUGHTER OF RAMONA *see* DAUGHTER OF THE WEST

THE DAUGHTER OF ROSIE O'GRADY (Irish Americans)

Warner Bros. Pictures, Inc.; A Warner Bros.—First National Picture. *Dist* Warner Bros. Pictures, Inc. 29 Apr **1950**; New York opening: week of 30 Mar 1950; Prod: early Aug—early Oct 1949 [©Warner Bros. Pictures, Inc.; 29 Apr 1950; LP84]. Sd (RCA Sound System); col (Technicolor). 9,408 ft. 104 min.

Prod William Jacobs. *Dir* David Butler. [*Asst dir* Phil Quinn]. [*2d asst dir* Lee White]. *Scr* Jack Rose, Melville Shavelson and Peter Milne. *Story* Jack Rose and Melville Shavelson. *Dir of photog* Wifrid M. Cline. [*Cam op* George Nogle]. [*Asst cam* Harry Marsh and Bob Burkitt]. [*Stills* D. B. Graybill]. [*Gaffer* Frank Flanagan]. [*Cam tech* Paul Hill]. *Spec eff dir* William McGann. *Spec eff* H. F. Koenekamp. *Technicolor color dir* Mitchell Kovalelski. *Art dir* Douglas Bacon. *Film ed* Irene Morra. [*Asst ed* Bob Swanson]. *Set dec* Ben Bone. [*Props* L. B. Reifsnider]. [*Asst props* Ben L. Goldman]. [*Props for Prinz unit* Harry Goldman]. *Miss Haver's ward* Travilla. *Ward* Marjorie Best. [*Men's ward* Ted Schultz and Roe Ramsey]. [*Women's ward* Patricia Davidson]. [*Ward for Prinz unit* Bob O'Dell]. *Orch* Frank Perkins. *Mus adpt* David Buttolph. *Mus dir* Ray Heindorf. *Mus numbers staged and dir by* LeRoy Prinz. [*Asst dance dir* Eddie Prinz and Eddie Graham]. *Sd* Dolph Thomas. *Makeup artist* Perc Westmore. [*Makeup* Eddie Allen and Monty Westmore]. [*Hair stylist* Tillie Starriett]. [*Scr supv* Fred Applegate]. [*Best boy* Gilbert Germaine]. [Charles Harris]. [*Pub* Ralph Huston]. [*Stand-in for June Haver* Shirley Clark]. [*Stand-in for Marsha Mae Jones* Ann Urcan]. [*Stand-in for Debbie Reynolds* Alma Maison]. [*Stand-in for Sean McClory* Fred Stromsoe, Jr.].

Music: "Semper Fidelis March" and "The Thunderer" by John Philip Sousa; "Chatterbox Rag," composers undetermined.

Song(s): "The Daughter of Rosie O'Grady," music by Walter Donaldson, lyrics by Monty C. Brice; "As We Are Today," music by Ernest Lecuona, lyrics by Charles Tobias; "A Farm on Old Broadway," "What Am I Going to Tell Them At the Yacht Club?" "My Own True Love and I" and "Winter Serenade," music and lyrics by M. K. Jerome and Jack Scholl; "The Rose of Tralee," music by Charles Glover, lyrics by Mordaunt Spencer; "Moonlight Bay," music by Percy Wenrich, lyrics by Edward Madden; "Just One Girl," music by Lyn Udall, lyrics by Karl Kennett; "O Little Town of Bethlehem," music by Lewis H. Redner, lyrics by Phillips Brooks; "The Picture That's Turned to the Wall," music and lyrics by Charles Graham; "Ma Blushin' Rosie," music by John Stromberg, lyrics by Edgar Smith.

Cast: JUNE HAVER [(*Patricia O'Grady*)], GORDON MACRAE [(*Tony Pastor*)], James Barton [(*Dennis O'Grady*)], Cuddles Sakall [(*Miklos Teretzky*)], Gene Nelson [(*Doug Martin*)], Sean McClory [(*James Moore*)], Debbie Reynolds [(*Maureen O'Grady*)], Marsha Jones [(*Katie O'Grady*)], Jane Darwell [(*Mrs. Murphy*)], Virginia Lee [(*Virginia Lee*)], [Irene Seidner (*Mrs. Teretzky*)], [Jack Lomas (*Sergeant*)], [Carl Harbough (*Doorman*)], [Kendall Kapps (*Actor*)], [Bert Hanlon (*Assistant stage manager*)], [Karl Davis (*Roughneck*)], [Charles Sherlock (*Stagehand*)], [Joel Friedkin (*Doctor*)], [Pat Flaherty (*Bartender*)], [Baron Lichter (*Piano player*)], [Oscar O'Shea (*Mr. Flannigan*)], [Jack Daley, Fred Kelsey (*Policemen*)], [Sue Casey

(*Pretty girl*)], [Spec O'Donnell (*Small boy*)], [Glen Turnbull (*Hoffer*)], [Michael Ross].

Historical, Show business, Musical. [*Print viewed*]. After attending a parade honoring soldiers returning from the Spanish-American War, sisters Patricia and Maureen O'Grady pass in front of Tony Pastor's vaudeville theater on the way to bring lunch to their father Dennis, a streetcar conductor. Tony, who is standing outside dressed as a bum, begs them for some food, and they give the lunch to him. Meanwhile, Dennis' friend, Miklos Teretzky, advises the overprotective father to tell his motherless daughters about men before it is too late. Unknown to Dennis, his oldest daughter Katie is secretly married to James Moore, a returning soldier, and is pregnant. They have not revealed their marriage because the wartime housing shortage has left them unable to find an apartment of their own. Later, Pat learns that the man who ate their father's lunch was not a bum as he appeared, but an actor, and marches straight to the theater to scold him. Tony apologizes, and after learning that Pat's mother was a well-known vaudeville performer, immediately writes a song about the "Daughter of Rosie O'Grady." He then drops in on the sisters to play the song for Pat and is still there when Dennis comes home. Dennis blames the death of his wife Rosie on the hard life of vaudeville and consequently is violently opposed to anything to do with the theater. For this reason, Pat tells her father that Tony is a college student, and impressed, Dennis decides that he should date Katie. During a dinner party with Tony and some of the other actors from his theater, who are posing as students, Pat secretly tells Tony that she wants to go on the stage. Tony insists that they first tell her father the truth about his profession, after which the furious Dennis bans Tony from his house until he gives up the theater, then locks Pat in her room. Pat sneaks out and, while staying with Miklos and his wife, becomes a hit at Tony's theater. When Dennis learns that one of his daughters is expecting twins, he decides it must be Pat and, although he is not a drinking man, immediately gets drunk. The bartender calls a policeman, and Jim, who is now working as a policeman, comes to take him home. Later, Tony helps Jim and Katie find an apartment. When Dennis learns about it, he disowns all his daughters. At Tony's Christmas party, Miklos tells Pat that her father is very ill. Hearing this Tony sends Pat home, telling Miklos that he loves her too much to let anything come between her and her father. Pat and Maureen arrive at Dennis', each carrying a Christmas tree and presents. Then Jim, also carrying a tree, arrives to tell the family that Katie is home awaiting the birth of twins. The family is reconciled, and for the first time, Dennis sees Pat on stage. She introduces her father, who does one of his old routines. Just then, Jim arrives to announce the birth of triplets, and a contented Tony presents Pat with an engagement ring. *Fathers and daughters. Tony Pastor. Romance. Sisters. Vaudevillians. Acrobats. Christmas. Drunkenness. Friendship. Impersonation and imposture. Irish Americans. Marriage–Secret. New York City. Parades. Police. Pregnancy. Streetcars. United States–History–Social life and customs. United States–History–War of 1898. Veterans. Widowers.*

Note: The film's working title was *A Night At Tony Pastor's*. Antonio Pastor was born in 1837 and, as a child, made his first theatrical appearance with impressario P. T. Barnum. Displeased with the vulgarity of variety theater, Pastor opened his own theater, which he named Tony Pastor's Opera House, and banned drinking and smoking. He always appeared in his own shows as a singer of popular ballads. In 1881, he presented the first performance of what later became known as vaudeville at the Fourteenth Street Theater and operated it for twenty-seven years. Stars such as Weber and Fields and Lillian Russell appeared at the theater. Pastor died in 1908. A 17 Nov 1942 *HR* news item notes that the film was to have starred George Raft.

Box 1 Apr 1950. *DV* 29 Mar 1950, p. 3, 8. *FD* 3 Apr 1950, p. 6. *HR* 17 Nov 1942, p. 1. *HR* 5 Aug 1949, p. 13. *HR* 7 Oct 1949, p. 11. *HR* 29 Mar 1950, p. 3. *MPHPD* 1 Apr 1950, p. 245. *NYT* 31 Mar 1950, p. 36. *Var* 29 Mar 1950, p. 11.

DAUGHTER OF SHANGHAI (Chinese Americans)

Paramount Pictures, Inc. *Dist* Paramount Pictures, Inc. 21 Jan **1938** [©Paramount Pictures, Inc.; 17 Dec 1937; LP7674]. Sd (Western Electric Mirrophonic Recording); b&w. 7 reels, 5,607 ft. 60 or 67 min. Passed by the National Board of Review. PCA cert no. 3775.

Pres ADOLPH ZUKOR. [*Prod* Edward T. Lowe]. [*Exec prod* William LeBaron]. *Dir* Robert Florey. [*Asst dir* Stanley Goldsmith]. *Scr* Gladys Unger and Garnett Weston. [*Addl dial* William Hurlbut]. *Photog* Charles Schoenbaum. *Art dir* Hans Dreier and Robert Odell. *Ed* Ellsworth Hoagland. *Int dec* A. E. Freudeman. *Mus dir* Boris Morros. *Sd rec* Charles Hisserich and Richard Olson.

Cast: Anna May Wong (*Lan Ying Lin*), Charles Bickford (*Otto Hartman*), Larry Crabbe (*Andrew Sleete*), Cecil Cunningham (*Mrs.*

Mary Hunt), J. Carrol Naish (*Frank Barden*), Anthony Quinn (*Harry Morgan*), John Patterson (*James Lang*), Evelyn Brent (*Olga Derey*), Philip Ahn (*Kim Lee*), Fred Kohler (*Captain Gulner*), Guy Bates Post (*Lloyd Burkett*), Virginia Dabney (*Rita, a dancer*), [Ching Wah Lee (*Quan Lin*)], [Frank Sully (*Jake Kelly*)], [Ernest Whitman (*Sam Blike*)], [Maurice Liu (*Ah Fong*)], [Mrs. Wong Wing (*Amah*)], [Paul Fix (*Miles*)], [Gwen Kenyon (*Phone girl*)], [Charles Wilson (*Schwartz*)], [John Hart (*Sailor*)], [Layne Tom, Jr. (*Chinese candy vendor*)], [Michael Wu (*Yung Woo*)], [Mae Busch (*Lil*)], [William Powell (*Carib waiter*)], [Carmen Bailey, Paulita Arvizu, Carmen La Roux, Tina Menard (*Dancers*)], [Gino Corrado (*Interpreter*)], [Alex Woloshin, Agostino Borgato (*Gypsies*)], [Bruce Wong (*Chinese*)], [Andre P. Marsaudon (*South American*)], [Billy Jones, Jimmie Dundee, Chick Collins (*Seamen who fight*)], [Harry Strang (*Sailor*)], [Lee Shumway (*Ship's officer*)], [Pierre Watkin (*Mr. Yorkland*)], [Rebecca Wassem], [Marie Burton], [Paula de Cardo], [Alma Ross], [Blanca Vischer], [Norah Gale], [Harriette Haddon], [Joyce Mathews], [Helaine Moler].

Detective. [*Print viewed*]. Lan Ying Lin's father, an importer of Oriental antiques, is murdered by smugglers after he refuses to help them smuggle illegal aliens into San Francisco. Detective Kim Lee is assigned to the case and meets with Lan Ying and family friend Mrs. Mary Hunt the night of the murder. Lan Ying is distrustful of the policeman's ability to solve the case and decides to crack the smuggling ring herself. Because her father thought that a man named Otto Hartman living in the Central American town of Port O'Juan, is the head of the smugglers, Lan Ying travels there. After some investigation, Lan Ying locates Hartman and hires on at his nightclub as a dancer. She finds his business ledger and discovers that he is not the chief of the smugglers after all. Kim Lee also comes to Port O'Juan after working undercover for the captain of the smugglers' ship *Jenny Hawk*. He meets Hartman through the captain and recognizes Lan Ying in the club, where they manage to speak privately. She reveals the location of Hartman's ledger and agrees to sneak aboard the ship dressed as a man. Hartman finds Kim Lee with the book and they struggle, until one of the refugees shoots Hartman, which allows Kim Lee to board the ship with no problems. After they set sail, one of the immigrants discovers Lan Ying is a woman, and they all attack her. Kim Lee comes to her aid, but he is knocked unconscious and drops the ledger. The captain finds it and suspects Kim Lee and Lan Ying of being spies. When the smugglers' seaplane meets the ship, they tie up the couple and put them over the plane's bomb doors. The smugglers open the doors as they are flying over the ocean, but Kim Lee and Lan Ying cling to the inside, and they swim ashore when the plane eventually lands. Kim Lee and Lan Ying stumble upon Mrs. Hunt's estate and discover that she is the head of the smuggling ring. She holds them captive, but Kim Lee is able to phone the Federal police, and he escapes with the help of Kelly, Mrs. Hunt's honest chauffeur. After a gunfight between the smugglers and the police, Mrs. Hunt and her cohorts are arrested. Kim Lee proposes marriage to Lan Ying, and she accepts. *Chinese Americans. Detectives. Immigrants. Smuggling. Undercover operations. Aliens, Illegal. Attempted rape. Central America. Chauffeurs. Gunfights. Male impersonation. Murder. Nightclubs. Proposals (Marital). San Francisco (CA). Seaplanes. Ship crews. Socialites.*

Note: The Release Dialogue Script in the Paramount story files at the AMPAS Library provided some opening credits which were missing from the viewed print. A pre-release title of the film was *Across the River*. Included in the Paramount story files is the story "Honor Bright" by Garnett Weston, and a script by William Hurlbut, however, the authors' contribution to the final film has not been determined.

DV 11 Dec 1938, p. 3. FD 21 Dec 1937, p. 4. HR 11 Dec 1937, p. 2. MPD 15 Dec 1937, p. 4. MPH 18 Dec 1937, p. 51. NYT 24 Dec 1937, p. 21. Var 29 Dec 1937, p. 17.

A DAUGHTER OF THE CONGO (African Americans)
Micheaux Pictures. 1930; New York opening: 5 Apr 1930. Talking sequences and mus score; b&w. 9 reels, 7,934 ft. [Also si.].

Dir Oscar Micheaux.
Song(s): "That Gets It," music and lyrics by Roland Irving and Earl B. Westfield.
Source: Based on a story by Henry Downing.
Cast: Kathleen Noisette (*Lupelta*), Loretta Tucker, Clarence Reed, Willor Lee Guilford, Daisy Harding, Roland Irving.

African American, Adventure. [*Not viewed*]. Lupelta, a mulatto girl who was stolen as a baby and brought up by an African tribe, is betrothed to the powerful chief Lodango. As she travels with her maid

to Lodango's village, she stops to bathe and is captured by Arab slave hunters. Meanwhile, Captain Paul Dale of the African-American 10th United States Cavalry, assisted by First Lieutenant Ronald Brown, operates a constabulary in the small republic of Liberia, where Lupelta's tribe lives. During a reconnaissance mission, they encounter the slave hunters, rescue Lupelta and imprison the men responsible for her capture. Dale and Brown then take Lupelta to a mission school, where she excels remarkably, despite her tendency to return to some of her wild native ways. Through her industry, beauty, and intelligence, Lupelta soon becomes one of the most popular girls in Monrovia. *African Americans. African Americans–Mixed blood. Africans. Arabs. Liberia. Missions. Slave traders. Tribal chiefs. United States. Army. Cavalry. Rescues.*

Note: Some of the above plot summary was taken from modern sources. *New York Age* stated that this was the first talking picture produced by an African-American company.

New York Age 5 Apr 1930, p. 6. New York Age 12 Apr 1930, p. 6. PittsC 12 Apr 1930, pt. II, p. 7. PittsC 30 Apr 1930, pt. II, p. 7.

THE DAUGHTER OF THE DON (Latino)
Monrovia Feature Film Company; Moe Streimer Feature Films. *Dist* State Rights. 13 Aug **1916** [©Winfield Hogaboom; 7 Aug 1916; LU9045]. Si; b&w. 10 reels.

Dir Henry Kabierske. *Asst dir* Costello (full name unknown). *Story and scen* Winfield Hogaboom.
Cast: Hal Cooley (*Lieutenant Nelson*), Marie McKeen (*Ysabel Hernandez*), V. O. Whitehead (*Don Hernandez*), William Ehfe, Grant Churchill.

Historical, Drama. In 1846 California, Lieutenant Nelson of the American army and Ysabel Hernandez, the daughter of a California don, fall in love. Warfare between the Americans and the Californians soon breaks out, however, and Ysabel puts on man's dress and joins Pico's Californian army, distinguishing herself by her horsemanship. After many shifts of fortune, the Americans are victorious in the final battle in Los Angeles, in which Nelson narrowly escapes killing Ysabel. Holliday, the treacherous Englishman whose deceptions helped to start the hostilities, kidnaps Ysabel and her brother's fiancée, but Nelson and several others come to the rescue and the lovers are united. *California–History–1846-1850. Loyalty. Male impersonation. Officers (Military). Soldiers. Combat. Duplicity. English. Kidnapping. Los Angeles (CA). Nobility. Pio Pico. Rescues. Spaniards. United States. Army.*

Note: The film had its premiere in Los Angeles on 13 Aug 1916, but it does not appear to have received wider distribution during 1916. Streimer put the film on the state rights market in Jun 1917. In the spring of 1920, Arrow Film Corp. acquired the film, now a six-reeler, and announced that it had been sold to several state rights markets, though the film may not have played theaters in this form until late 1921 or 1922. Scenes from the film were shot in the San Pedro, CA harbor. Some reviews of the film's 1921-22 release claim that it is based on a novel by Hogaboom, but this is probably an error.

MPW 8 Jul 1916, p. 237. MPW 29 Jul 1916, p. 776. MPW 5 Aug 1916, p. 931. MPW 18 Nov 1916, pp. 1021-22. MPW 16 Jun 1917, p. 1797. MPW 15 Apr 1922, p. 764. Var 1 Sep 1916, p. 21.

A DAUGHTER OF THE OLD SOUTH (Creoles)
Famous Players-Lasky Corp. *Dist* Famous Players-Lasky Corp.; Paramount Pictures. 24 Nov **1918** [©Famous Players-Lasky Corp.; 3 Oct 1918; LP12942]. Si; b&w. 5 reels, 4,362 ft.

Pres Adolph Zukor. *Dir* Emile Chautard. *Scen* Margaret Turnbull. *Story* Alicia Ramsay and Rudolph de Cordova. *Cam* Jacques Bizeul.
Cast: Pauline Frederick (*Dolores Jardine*), Pedro De Cordoba (*Pedro de Alvarez*), Vera Beresford (*Lillian Hetherington*), Rex MacDougall (*Richard Ferris*), Mrs. T. Randolph (*Dolores' grandmother*), Myra Brooks (*The housekeeper*), J. P. Laffey (*Mr. Hetherington*).

Drama. Although Dolores Jardine's grandmother has betrothed her to the wealthy young Spaniard, Pedro de Alvarez, she is determined to marry a man of her own choosing. She falls in love with novelist Richard Ferris who, although initially attracted by her beauty and Creole charm, abandons the girl when his old flame Lillian Hetherington suddenly appears. Seeking revenge, Dolores invites Richard to dinner and conceals Lillian behind a curtain. After overhearing Richard promise to marry Dolores, Lillian leaves in disgust and Dolores wanders into the woods distraught. Pedro prevents her from drowning herself and takes her to his heart. *Creoles. Novelists. Revenge. Attempted suicide. Drowning. Grandmothers. Marriage-Arranged. Spaniards.*

ETR 7 Dec 1918, pp. 67-68. *MPN* 26 Oct 1918, p. 2714. *MPW* 26 Oct 1918, p. 546. *MPW* 30 Nov 1918, pp. 991-92. *NYDM* 30 Nov 1918, p. 811. *Var* 18 Oct 1918, p. 38. *Wid's* 25 Oct 1918, p. 4.

A DAUGHTER OF THE SIOUX (Native Americans, Dakota)

Davis Distributing Division, Inc. **1925** [©Davis Distributing Division, Inc.; 28 Dec 1925; LP22182]. Si; b&w. 5 reels, 4,700 ft.

Dir Ben Wilson. *Asst dir* Archie Ricks. *Adpt* George W. Pyper. *Photog* William Fildew.

Source: Based on the novel *A Daughter of the Sioux, a Tale of the Indian Frontier* by Gen. Charles King (New York, 1903).

Cast: Ben Wilson (*John Field*), Neva Gerber (*Nanette*), Robert Walker (*Eagle Wing*), Fay Adams (*Trooper Kennedy*), William Lowery (*Big Bill Hay*), Rhody Hathaway (*Maj. John Webb*).

Western. John Field, a government surveyor, suspects that Nanette, known at Fort Frayne as the "daughter of the Sioux," is giving information about the fort's defenses to the Indians. Eagle Wing, a renegade, incites the Sioux to attack a number of isolated settlers, and John rides after him, bringing him back to the fort. An old scout recognizes Nanette, apparently an Indian squaw, as a white child stolen long ago by the Sioux. Nanette admits this truth and further reveals that Eagle Wing is, in actuality, the son of Big Bill Hay. John, who has fallen in love with the dark-browed Nanette, declares his love for her. *Dakota Indians. Forts. Parentage. Scouts (Frontier). Spies. Surveyors.*

FD 11 Oct 1925.

DAUGHTER OF THE TONG (Chinese Americans)

Metropolitan Pictures Corp. *Dist* State Rights. Aug **1939**. Sd; b&w. 56 min. PCA cert no. 5358.

Pres HENRY S. WEBB. *Prod* Lester F. Scott, Jr. *Dir* Raymond K. Johnson. *Asst dir* Ray Nazarro. *Story* George H. Plympton. *Cont* Alan Merritt. *Photog* Elmer Dyer. *Film ed* Charles Diltz. *Mus dir* Lee Zahler. *Sd tech* Clifford Ruberg.

Cast: Evelyn Brent [(*The Illustrious One also known as Carney and The Daughter of the Tong*)], Grant Withers [(*Ralph Dickson*)], Dorothy Short [(*Marion Morgan*)], Dave O'Brien [(*Jerry Morgan*)], Richard Loo [(*Wong*)], Dirk Thane [(*Slade*)], Harry Harvey [(*Mugsy*)], Budd Buster [(*Lefty*)], Robert Frazer [(*Williams*)], Hal Taliaferro [(*Lawson*)], [James Coleman (*Hardy*)].

Crime, Drama. [*Print viewed*]. A reign of terror, blackmail and murder pervades the Chinatown district of Pacific City, which is ruled by the Carney gang, a band so strong politically that the local authorities are powerless against its activities. The leader is known by rumor as "Carney", but that name is merely the alias of a beautiful Chinese girl called "The Illustrious One" who is hailed by her gangsters as "Daughter of the Tong." When Wilson, the federal agent who had been investigating the case, is murdered, the F.B.I. sends agent Ralph Dickson to impersonate Gallagher, a notorious Eastern gun man who Carney has hired to do her dirty work. Posing as Gallagher, Dickson is met at the bus station by one of Carney's men who takes him to the hotel. There Dickson is suprised to find Marion Morgan, a woman he met at the bus station, and discovers that she is being held hostage by Carney's gang. Dickson frees Marion and takes her to F.B.I. headquarters where she tells the agents that her brother Jerry is held captive by Carney's gang. Marion continues that Jerry had been Carney's partner in an importing business until he discovered that it was really a front for Carney's smuggling ring. Marion's story gives Dickson an idea about how to expose Carney, and he returns to the hotel, still posing as Gallagher. Carney then introduces herself to him and orders him to kill Jerry. Instead, Dickson pulls a gun and is aided in his escape by Lefty, also an F.B.I. agent who has infiltrated the gang. Jerry and Dickson speed away with the gang in hot pursuit, but are overtaken and returned to Carney's headquarters. Before Carney can order their elimination, however, government agents, led by Marion and Lefty, burst in and arrest the gang. *Chinese Americans. Government agents. Hired killers. Impersonation and imposture. Murder. Smuggling. United States. Federal Bureau of Investigation.* Brothers and sisters. Chases. Escapes. Gangsters. Hostages.

FD 28 Aug 1939, p. 7. *Var* 16 Aug 1939, p. 16.

DAUGHTER OF THE WEST (Native Americans, Navajo)

Martin Mooney Productions, Inc. *Dist* Film Classics, Inc. 15 Feb **1949** [©Martin Mooney Productions, Inc.; 25 Mar 1949; LP2283]. Sd (RCA Sound System); col (Cinecolor). 9 reels, 6,930 ft. 73 or 76-77 min. PCA cert no. 13475.

Prod Martin Mooney. *Assoc prod* Robert E. Callahan. *Dir* Harold Daniels. *Asst dir* Frank Fox. *Dial dir* Jack Daly. *Adpt* Irwin R. Franklin. *Scr* Raymond L. Schrock. *Photog* Henry Sharp. *Cinecolor consultant* Henry J. Staudigal. *Art dir* George Van Marter. *Ed* Douglas W. Bagier. *Ward* Bob Martin. *Mus score* Irving Gertz. *Based on orig mus by* Victor Granados and Juan Duval. *Sd eng* Ferol Redd. *Makeup artist* Harry Rose. *Hair stylist* Gail McGarry. *Prod mgr* George Moskov. *Prod asst* Leon Chooluck. *Tech dir* Robert E. Callahan.

Song(s): "Autumn Harvest," words and music by Victor Granadas and Juan Duval.

Source: Based on the novel *Daughter of Ramona* by Robert E. Callahan (New York, 1930).

Cast: Martha Vickers [(*Lolita Moreno*)], Philip Reed [(*Navo White Eagle*)], Donald Woods [(*Ralph Connors*)], Marion Carney [(*Okeema*)], Pedro de Cordoba [(*Indian chief*)], James J. Griffith [(*Jed Morgan*)], William Farnum [(*Father Vallejo*)], Luz Alba [(*Wateeka*)], Tommy Cook [(*Ponca*)], Anthony Barr [(*Yuba*)], Helen Servis, Milton Kibbee, [Willow Bird (*Medicine man*)].

Western. [*Print viewed*]. At her home at California's Mission San Juan Capistrano, Lolita Moreno, who unknown to her is the daughter of the slain Indian heroine Ramona, prepares to leave for a new teaching job at a Navajo reservation in Arizona. Before she boards the stagecoach, Lolita says farewell to her guardian, Father Vallejo, who gives her a cross pendant which belonged to her mother, but does not reveal her mother's identity. When the stage is still several miles from the reservation, the driver stops and explains that his route ends there. Dismayed, Lolita gets out, then agrees to deliver a package to a reservation resident named Navo White Eagle. Sometime later, Navo arrives in a horse-driven cart, collects the package from Lolita and offers her a lift to the reservation. When they arrive, Navo takes Lolita to her hosts, Mr. and Mrs. Beggs, who operate the reservation's trading post. There, Lolita meets the man who hired her, Indian agent Ralph Connors, who is secretly planning to steal some of the reservation's land because of a rich copper vein located there. Later, the chief's daughter Okeema quarrels with her lover Yuba, who has sensed her feelings for Navo. Yuba tells Connors that Navo has been selected as the tribe's new spokesman, and after he overhears Navo rejecting Okeema's romantic advances, Connors persuades her to come to his office that evening. There, Connors gives Okeema an ink pad, tells her to put her fingerprints onto a stack of documents bearing his agency's letterhead, then tries to seduce her. Later, Navo's mother Wateeka invites Lolita to dinner, and comments on Lolita's crucifix, saying she recalls seeing it on a young bride at the Mission San Diego. At a harvest festival hosted by Connors, Navo finds the drunken chiefs sleeping in the back of Yuba's wagon. After Yuba is arrested, he is shot in the back by Connors' henchman, Jed Morgan. Later, Jed and a vengeful Okeema implicate Navo in the shooting, and he is arrested. When the chief learns of the charge, he obtains permission from Connors to administer tribal justice to Navo. The tribe decides to banish Navo from the reservation, but he refuses to leave, and instead, demands a trial by fire. Navo then walks several feet over burning hot embers to prove his innocence. After she overhears Connors saying that he plans to kidnap and marry Lolita, Okeema guiltily confesses her misdeed to Wateeka, while Navo eavesdrops. Later, Lolita reports to a fort, where warrants are issued for the arrest of Connors and Jed. When Okeema kills herself by jumping from a bridge, the chief, who knows that his daughter died for Connors' love, buries her on the land adjoining Connors' office in protest of his actions. After Connors and Jed try to escape with the illegally obtained land transfers, they are captured and sentenced to death. Later, Navo is appointed Indian agent for the reservation, and he and Lolita kiss. *Conspiracy. Indians of North America–Reservations. Land rights. Navajo Indians. Alcoholism. Arizona. Arrests. Bridges. Confession (Law). Crucifixes. Eavesdropping. Family relationships. Festivals. Forts. Fraud. Funerals. Indian agents. Jumps from heights. Kisses. Missions. Postal workers. Romantic rivalry. San Juan Capistrano Mission (San Juan Capistrano, CA). Seduction. Shootings. Stagecoaches. Suicide. Teachers. Wards and guardians. Warrants.*

Note: The working title of this film was *Daughter of Ramona*. The *Var* review noted that the story deals with "the daughter of Ramona, heroine of an earlier book-film classic." In 1936, Fox released *Ramona*, which starred Loretta Young and Don Ameche and was directed by Henry King.

Box 2 Apr 1949. *DV* 28 Mar 1949, p. 3. *FD* 19 Apr 1949, p. 8. *HR* 10 Sep 1948, p. 12. *HR* 17 Sep 1948, p. 12. *HR* 28 Mar 1949, p. 3. *MPHPD* 2 Apr 1949, p. 4558. *Var* 30 Mar 1949, p. 13.

DAUGHTERS COURAGEOUS (Portuguese Americans)

Warner Bros. Pictures, Inc.; A First National Picture; Jack L. Warner in charge of production. *Dist* Warner Bros. Pictures, Inc. 22 Jul 1939; Prod: 10 Feb—late Mar 1939 [©Warner Bros. Pictures, Inc.; 22 Jul 1939; LP8979]. Sd; b&w. 12 reels. 100 or 107 min. PCA cert no. 5223.

Exec prod Hal B. Wallis. *Assoc prod* Henry Blanke. *Dir* Michael Curtiz. *Dial dir* Irving Rapper. [*Asst dir* Sherry Shourds]. *Scr* Julius Epstein and Philip G. Epstein. *Photog* James Wong Howe and [Ernest Haller]. *Art dir* John Hughes. *Film ed* Ralph Dawson. *Gowns* Howard Shoup. *Mus dir* Leo F. Forbstein. *Mus* Max Steiner. *Orchestral arr* Ray Heindorf. *Sd* C. A. Riggs and Oliver S. Garretson. *Makeup* Perc Westmore. [*Unit mgr* Frank Mattison].

Source: Suggested by the play *Fly Away Home* by Dorothy Bennett and Irving White (New York, 15 Jan 1935).

Cast: John Garfield (*Gabriel Lopez*), Claude Rains (*Jim Masters*), Jeffrey Lynn (*Johnny Heming*), Fay Bainter (*Nan Masters*), Donald Crisp (*Sam Sloane*), May Robson (*Penny*), Frank McHugh (*George*), Dick Foran (*Eddie Moore*), George Humbert (*Manuel Lopez*), Berton Churchill (*Judge Hornsby*), Priscilla Lane (*Buff Masters*), Rosemary Lane (*Tinka Masters*), Lola Lane (*Linda Masters*), Gale Page (*Cora Masters*), [Wilfred Lucas, Jack Mower (*Conductors*)], [Nat Carr (*Court clerk*)], [George Chesebro (*Proprietor*)], [Tom Dugan (*Joe, waiter*)], [Jack Gardner (*Tim*)], [Ray Cooke (*Bill*)], [Leyland Hodgson (*Actor*)], [John Harron (*Stage manager*)], [George Ovey (*Ticket agent*)], [Hobart Cavanaugh (*Tourist*)], [Alice Connor], [Maris Wrixon], [Creighton Hale], [William Hopper].

Domestic, Drama. [*Print viewed*]. After wandering the globe for twenty years, Jim Masters returns home to Carmel, California, where his wife Nan and daughters Buff, Tinka, Linda and Cora still live. Just before Jim's unexpected return, Nan had won the approval of her daughters to marry Sam Sloane, a prosperous pillar of the community. At first the girls resent the intrusion of this stranger who calls himself their father, and make a pact to ignore him so that he will leave. However, Jim gradually wins them over with his worldly understanding of life. Buff is fascinated by Gabriel Lopez, the son of a Portuguese fisherman, but her mother, who knows Gabriel's troubled history well because she is often called upon to intervene between him and Judge Hornsby, disapproves of the match. Despite her mother's warnings, Buff begins dating Gabriel. When Jim lies to Nan about Buff's whereabouts after a missed curfew, Buff thanks him for helping her out. Jim gains even more respect when he secretly brings Nan flowers and a cake for her birthday, which everyone else had forgotten, and allows Sam to take the credit. Regardless, Sam tells Jim that he is concerned that his presence is disrupting the family and persuades him to leave. Before he goes, Nan begs Jim to take back his advice to Buff that she elope with Gabriel, sensing that Gabriel will do to Buff what Jim had done to her. In Gabriel, Jim sees his own nonconformist attitudes and wanderlust, and through Jim's persuasion, Gabriel comes to realize that he is not cut out for a conventional family life. In the end, Gabriel and Jim, two kindred spirits, go off to travel the world together, leaving Nan behind to marry homebody Sam, and preventing Buff from repeating her mother's mistake. *Desertion (Marital). Family life. Fathers and daughters. Mothers and daughters. Nonconformists. Billiards and billiard parlors. Birthdays. Drowning. Elopement. Engagements. Fishing boats. Fishing villages. Judges. Juvenile delinquents. Missing persons, Assumed dead. Portuguese Americans. Weddings.*

Note: Working titles for this film were *American Family, A Family Affair, Family Affair, Fly Away Home* and *Family Reunion.* Contemporary sources note that cameraman Ernest Haller took over filming when James Wong Howe fell ill with the flu. A Feb 1939 *HR* news item noted that Irving Rapper was set as dialogue director, but his participation in the film has not been confirmed. Although not a sequel, this film was a follow-up to the 1938 Warner Bros. film *Four Daughters* (see *AFI Catalog of Feature Films, 1931-40*; F3.1452), which had the same cast. According to a *HR* pre-release news item, Jack Warner personally wrote to 14,000 exhibitors to draw their attention to the film, much in the same way he did with *Four Daughters.* In addition, Warner Bros. plugged the film with a contest called the "Typical Daughters Contest," the winners of which were awarded with a Hollywood screen test. *HR* also notes that Warner Bros. held up the release of the picture to coincide with National Daughters Day (23 July). *Daughters Courageous* was remade in 1942 by Warner Bros. as *Always in My Heart,* directed by Jo Graham and starring Kay Francis and Walter Huston; and again in 1954 as *Young at Heart,* directed by Gordon Douglas and starring Kay Francis and Frank Sinatra.

DV 15 Jun 1939, p. 3. *FD* 16 Jun 1939, p. 6. *HR* 10 Feb 1939, p. 6. *HR* 11 Feb 1939, p. 7. *HR* 18 Feb 1939, p. 3. *HR* 25 Mar 1939, p. 7. *HR* 13 May 1939, p. 3. *HR* 15 Jun 1939,

p. 3. *HR* 30 Jun 1939, p. 4. *HR* 21 Aug 1939, p. 13. *MPD* 15 Jun 1939, p. 6. *MPH* 8 Apr 1939, p. 50. *MPH* 24 Jun 1939, p. 39. *NYT* 24 Jun 1939, p. 14. *Photo* Aug 1939, p. 45. *Var* 21 Jun 1939, p. 16.

DAVY CROCKETT AND THE RIVER PIRATES (Native Americans, Chickasaw)

Walt Disney Productions. *Dist* Buena Vista Film Distribution Co., Inc. 17 Jul **1956** [©Walt Disney Productions; 10 Apr 1956; LP8892]. Sd (RCA Sound Recording); col (Technicolor). 7,290 ft. 81 min. PCA cert no. 17944.

Pres WALT DISNEY. *Prod* Bill Walsh. *Dir* Norman Foster. *Asst dir* Ivan Volkman. *Wrt* Tom Blackburn and Norman Foster. *Photog* Bert Glennon. *Spec processes* Ub Iwerks. *Matte artist* Peter Ellenshaw. *Art dir* Feild Gray. *Ed* Stanley Johnson. *Set dec* Emile Kuri and Bertram Granger. *Cost* Carl Walker. *Mus* George Bruns. *Orch* Edward Plumb. *Sd* Robert O. Cook. *Makeup artist* David Newell and Phil Sheer. *Unit mgr* John Grubbs.

Song(s): "Ballad of Davy Crockett, "King of the River" and "Yaller, Yaller Gold," words by Tom Blackburn, music by George Bruns.

Cast: Fess Parker (*Davy Crockett*), Buddy Ebsen (*George Russel*), Jeff York (*Mike Fink*), Kenneth Tobey (*Jocko*), Clem Bevans [(*Cap'n Cobb*)], Irvin Ashkenazy [(*Moose*)], Mort Mills [(*Sam Mason*)], Paul Newlan [(*Big Harpe*)], Frank Richards [(*Little Harpe*)], Troy Melton, Hank Worden, Dick Crockett, Walter Catlett [(*Colonel Plug*)].

Adventure, Historical, with songs. [*Print viewed*]. In 1810 in the wilderness of Ohio, frontiersman Davy Crockett and his friend, George Russel, head toward the Ohio River after a successful fur trapping expedition. Davy and George reach the small port of Maysville, Kentucky, where they meet the legendary boatman, Mike Fink, who brags about his status as the "King of the River." Mike advises Davy and George to go downriver to New Orleans to get the best price for their furs, offering them a ride on his keelboat, the "Gullywhumper," for the outrageous sum of $1,000. Davy and George then meet Cap'n Cobb, the elderly owner of the "Bertha Mae," who is stuck in Maysville because his crew, fearful of reported Indian attacks on the river, has abandoned him. Cobb offers Davy and George the use of his boat, hoping that Davy, whose bravery is legendary, will be able to attract a new crew. Davy and George set off to recruit boatmen, and George happens into the nearest tavern, where he is tricked into drinking too much by Mike and his men. After rounding up his crew, Davy enters the tavern to find a drunk George swinging from the chandelier and learns to his dismay that George has foolishly challenged the "Gullywhumper" to a race to New Orleans, the stakes being the title of "King of the River" and Davy's fur cargo. The following day, the race begins with a cannon blast as the onlookers laugh at the ineptitude of Davy's crew. Out on the river, Mike's crew cheats by removing a buoy warning of a dangerous channel ahead, but the "Bertha Mae" makes it safely through the rapids. The next day, Mike passes the landmark "Cave-in-Rock" and is flagged down by a group of men claiming that the cave now houses a saloon. Mike, well ahead of Davy, prepares to put ashore, unaware that the tavern is a ruse devised by the bandit Sam Mason, whose henchmen, disguised as Indians, are hiding in the brush. Mason's "Indians" attack the "Gullywhumper," but Davy and his crew come up from behind, causing the attackers to flee. Later, as a result of an act of sabotage by Mike, the "Bertha Mae's" rudder breaks, but Davy and George gain a lead in the race when they succeed in keeping Mike distracted in a riverfront tavern. The "Bertha Mae's" lead turns out to be short-lived, however, when Davy stops to pick up an old man stranded on an island with a large menagerie. The "Gullywhumper" passes by, but just when all seems lost, the old man returns Davy's kindness by telling him of a secret river shortcut. Davy and his men catch up and narrowly win the race, and Mike, now greatly humbled, hands over his red feather, the symbol of his status as "King of the River." Davy refuses the feather, wanting only his fur cargo, and he and Mike end up becoming friends. Davy and George subsequently return north on Mike's boat, but soon tire of life on the river and bid Mike farewell. Once ashore, the two are captured by Chickasaw Indians and brought before Chief Red Horn, who informs Davy that all of the local tribes are preparing for war against the white man in retaliation for attacks on an allied tribe living on the Ohio River. Davy explains to the chief that the Indians began the conflict by attacking riverboats, but the chief soon convinces him of the Indians' innocence, leading Davy to surmise that the attacks were carried out

by bandits posing as Indians. Davy and George vow to bring the killers to justice, so Red Horn gives them until the next full moon to make good on their promise. Returning to the river, Davy and George locate Mike, who agrees to help pursue the bandits. Davy devises a plan in which Mike will pose as a banker traveling upriver with a cargo of gold. Calling himself J. J. McGillicuddy, Mike enters a riverfront tavern and loudly brags about his wealth in the hope of flushing out someone connected to the bandits. Soon a well-dressed man carrying a banjo introduces himself as Colonel Plug and asks for a ride upriver. Once on Mike's boat, Plug, who works for Mason, loudly sings a ditty entitled "Yaller, Yaller Gold" as a means of signaling to his boss that a profitable target is approaching. Suspicious of Plug, Davy quickly gags him and sends him down into the hold while his crew prepares to do battle with Mason's men. During the protracted battle, Davy's crew prevails over Mason's phony Indians, and Davy and Mike eventually succeed in capturing Mason. Davy and Mike once again say goodbye, satisfied that an Indian war has been averted and that the river is now safe. *Adventurers. Boatracing. Davy Crockett. River boats. Rivers. Bandits. Braggarts. Caves. Cheating. Chickasaw Indians. Drunkenness. Fistfights. Friendship. Fur trappers. Impersonation and imposture. Indians of North America. Mississippi River. New Orleans (La). Ohio River. Ruses. Sailors. Saloons. Tribal chiefs. Wilderness areas.*

Note: Like its predecessor, *Davy Crockett, King of the Wild Frontier* (see below), this film is comprised of two episodes that originally aired on ABC's "Disneyland" television show. "Davy Crockett's Keelboat Race," shown in two parts, premiered on 18 Nov 1955, followed by "Davy Crockett and the River Pirates," which aired in early 1956. Although Crockett and the famed riverboat captain Mike Fink were contemporaries and were most likely acquainted, the events depicted in the film are based entirely on frontier legend. According to publicity material contained in the AMPAS Library file on this film, outdoor scenes were shot on location on the Ohio River, in the port of Shawneetown, IL and in Uniontown, PA.

In an article dated Nov 1955, *Fortnight* magazine reported that because of the immense popularity of the song "Ballad of Davy Crockett," which was written for *Davy Crockett, King of the Wild Frontier*, Disney executives had high hopes for "King of the River" and "Yaller, Yaller Gold." However, by the time of the theatrical release of *Davy Crockett and the River Pirates*, the "Crockett craze" was long over, leading the *Newsweek* reviewer to conclude that "children may be moved to attend this movie only by the sort of sentimental curiosity that sends adults to revivals of the old silent pictures." In fact, according to the *NYT* magazine, sales of Crockett merchandise had already plummeted by Dec 1955, approximately seven months after the fad began. For information on other film versions of the Crockett legend, see entry below for *Davy Crockett, Indian Scout*. For biographical information on Crockett, see entry below for *Davy Crockett, King of the Wild Frontier*.

DV 16 Jul 1956, p. 3. *Exb* 25 Jul 1956, p. 6. *Fortnight* Nov 1955. *Har* 21 Jul 1956, p. 114. *HR* 16 Jul 1956, p. 3. *Newsweek* 20 Aug 1956. *NYT* 11 Dec 1956, p. 21. *MPHPD* 28 Jul 1956, p. 2. *Var* 18 Jul 1956.

DAVY CROCKETT, INDIAN SCOUT (Native Americans)

Edward Small Productions, Inc.; Reliance Pictures, Inc. *Dist* United Artists Corp. 6 Jan **1950** [©Reliance Pictures, Inc.; 7 Jan 1950; LP2745]. Sd (Western Electric Recording); b&w, 6,399 ft. 71 min. PCA cert no. 13354.

Pres EDWARD SMALL. *Assoc prod* Grant Whytock and Bernard Small. *Dir* Lew Landers. *Asst dir* Harold Knox. *Scr* Richard Schayer. *From a story by* Ford Beebe. *Dir of photog* George Diskant and John Mescall. *Art dir* Rudolph Sternad and Martin Obzina. *Film ed* Stuart Frye and Kenneth Crane. *Set dec* C. I. Steenson and Howard Bristol. *Ward* Edward Lambert and Elmer Ellsworth. *Mus* Paul Sawtell. *Sd* L. J. Meyers. *Makeup* Don Cash.

· **Cast:** George Montgomery (*Davy Crockett*), Ellen Drew (*Frances [Oatman]*), Philip Reed (*Red Hawk*), Noah Beery, Jr. (*Tex*), Paul Guilfoyle (*Ben*), Addison Richards (*Captain Weightman*), Robert Barrat (*Lone Eagle*), Erik Rolf (*Mr. Simms*), William Wilkerson (*High Tree*), John Hamilton (*Colonel Pollard*), Vera Marshe (*Mrs. Simms*), Jimmy Moss (*Jimmy Simms*), Chief Thundercloud (*Sleeping Fox*), Kenneth Duncan (*Sergeant Gordon*), Ray Teal (*Captain McHale*).

Western. [*Print viewed*]. In 1848, after an Army platoon escorting a wagon train of homesteaders to a fort is attacked, Col. Pollard holds an informal hearing in his office. When Pollard reveals his suspicion that a spy has been operating in their midst, an angry homesteader named Mr. Simms accuses Red Hawk, an Indian guide, of being the spy. This prompts Red Hawk's partner, an Army scout named Davy Crockett, who shares his famous uncle's name, to give the following testimony: During the long journey to the fort, Davy and Red Hawk learn about the threat of a local Indian uprising. After they rescue a lone wagon from some braves, Davy and Red Hawk meet passenger

Frances Oatman, who is part Kiowa Indian. Frances says that she hired her supposedly deaf-mute driver, Ben, for the journey west in search of a teaching job, and Davy encourages her to join the wagon train. One night, at the homesteaders' camp, Red Hawk learns that an attack is imminent, so he and Davy inform Capt. Weightman. Just then, a messenger arrives with news that braves from other tribes are gathering in preparation for battle. Inside his tent at the camp, Weightman is assured by the spy, an Indian chief named Lone Eagle who is posing as Weightman's trusted Indian agent, that a general uprising is unlikely. Suspicious of Frances, Red Hawk sneaks into her wagon and learns that she attended a missionary school for Indians. Later, Davy overhears Ben speaking to an Indian stable hand and realizes that Frances lied about him. The next morning, Davy, Red Hawk and the cavalry ride out with the wagon train, followed by Lone Eagle and the Indian stable hand. Davy, who has purposely left their route undecided, refuses to say which of two mountain passes they will take. When the road forks, Davy picks the dry South Pass, knowing that the camp will be warned that there will be no water for the next leg of the journey. Davy then instructs Red Hawk to follow anyone who leaves the camp. Once everyone is asleep, Davy captures Ben trying to sneak away and learns that he is spying for Lone Eagle. Meanwhile, Red Hawk follows Frances when she tries to slip away from the camp to warn her father, Lone Eagle. The next morning, Lone Eagle sends braves from several tribes to ambush the wagon train at South Pass. When Frances overhears her father vowing to kill women and children, she decides to return to warn Davy and Red Hawk of the attack, but they refuse to believe her until a messenger arrives with the same warning. Later, while returning with news of the altered route, a messenger is shot, and the message intercepted. Lone Eagle then quickly moves his braves to the new location. Marching well ahead of the homesteaders, the cavalry enters the pass, and the Indians use explosives to cause an avalanche, which cuts off the cavalry from the homesteaders. In order to get back to where the homesteaders are being attacked by braves, Davy uses a wagon full of explosives to blast a hole through the side of the avalanche. After they are rescued, the homesteaders are escorted safely to the fort, where Pollard decides to dismiss the charges against Frances and hire her as the fort's teacher. *False accusations. Indians of North America. United States. Army. Cavalry. Wagon trains. Ambushes. Avalanches. Camps. Explosives. Family relationships. Forts. Guides. Homesteaders. Indian agents. Kiowa Indians. Messengers. Mountains. Officers (Military). Rescues. Shootings. Stableboys. Tents.*

Note: The television release title of this film was *Indian Scout*. A modern source identifies that the film contains footage from United Artists' 1940 release *Kit Carson* (see below). Born in 1786 in Tennessee, American frontiersman and politician Davy Crockett distinguished himself in Andrew Jackson's campaign against the Creek Indians. In 1821, Crockett was elected to the Tennessee state legislature, and in 1827, to Congress. He died in 1836 fighting for Texas at the Alamo. His character was featured in several films, beginning in 1908 with *Davy Crockett in Hearts Divided*. Subsequent pictures include Paramount's *Davy Crockett*, released in 1916, and Sunset's *Davy Crockett at the Fall of the Alamo*, released in 1926. Disney produced two pictures dealing with Crockett's character, *Davy Crockett, King of the Wild Frontier*, released in 1955, and *Davy Crockett and the River Pirates*, released in 1956. Several television productions featuring the character were broadcast during the 1950s.

Box 14 Jan 1950. *DV* 9 Jan 1950, p. 3. *FD* 12 Jan 1950, p. 5. *HR* 9 Jan 1950, p. 4. *MPHPD* 14 Jan 1950, p. 153. *NYT* 17 Mar 1950, p. 28. *Var* 11 Jan 1950, p. 6.

DAVY CROCKETT, KING OF THE WILD FRONTIER (Native Americans, Creek)

Walt Disney Productions. *Dist* Buena Vista Film Distribution Co., Inc. Jun **1955**; New York opening: 25 May 1955 [©Walt Disney Productions; 18 Mar 1955; LP5195]. Sd (RCA Sound Recording); col (Technicolor). 8,340 ft. 90 or 93-95 min. PCA cert no. 17448.

Pres WALT DISNEY. *Prod* Bill Walsh. *Dir* Norman Foster. *Asst dir* James Judson Cox. *Wrt* Tom Blackburn. *Photog* Charles Boyle. *Spec processes* Ub Iwerks. *Matte eff* Peter Ellenshaw. *Art dir* Marvin Aubrey Davis. *Spec artwork* Joshua Meador, Art Riley and Ken Anderson. *Ed* Chester Schaeffer. *Set dec* Emile Kuri and Pat Delaney. *Cost* Norman Martien. *Mus* George Bruns. *Orch* Edward Plumb. *Sd* C. O. Slyfield and Robert Cook. *Makeup artist* Lou Phillippi. *Unit prod mgr* Hank Spitz.

Song(s): "Ballad of Davy Crockett," words by Tom Blackburn, music by George Bruns; "Farewell," words by Davy Crockett, music by George Bruns.

Cast: Fess Parker (*Davy Crockett*), Buddy Ebsen (*George Russel*), Basil Ruysdael [(*Andrew Jackson*)], Hans Conried [(*Thimblerig*)], Ken Tobey [(*Col. Jim Bowie*)], Helene Stanley [(*Polly Crockett*)], Don Megowan [(*Col. Billy Travis*)], William Bakewell [(*Tobias Norton*)], Pat Hogan [(*Chief Red Stick*)], Nick Cravat [(*Bustedluck*)], Mike Mazurki [(*Bigfoot Mason*)], Jeff Thompson (*Charlie Two Shirts*)], Henry Joyner [(*Swaney*)], Colonel Campbell Brown [(*Bruno*)], [Benjamin Hornbuckle (*Henderson*)], [Hal Youngblood (*Opponent political speaker*)], [Jim Maddux, Robert Booth (*Congressmen*)], [Eugene Brindel (*Billy*)], [Ray Whitetree (*Johnny*)].

Biography, Western, with songs. [*Print viewed*]. In 1813 in the Mississippi Territory, General Andrew Jackson demands that his aide, Major Tobias Norton, locate his missing scout, Davy Crockett, who is soon found in the woods attempting to "grin down" a bear. Although Jackson finds Davy's behavior odd, Davy is his most trusted and intuitive scout, so he assigns him to lead Norton and his squad on a reconnaissance mission into dangerous Indian territory. Dismissing the scout as a simpleton, Norton ditches Davy and his sidekick, George Russel, at the first opportunity. Once alone, Davy and George spy an Indian war party and Davy recognizes Red Stick, the fearsome Creek chief, who is clearly inciting his warriors to battle. Davy and George rush back to Norton, but his men are already under siege by the Creek warriors. Greatly outnumbered, Davy and George succeed in routing the Indians by yelling "charge!" and imitating the sounds of a large brigade. When Davy reports back to Jackson that the Creek are preparing for war, Jackson plans an offensive. Davy kills the Creek's lookout, enabling Jackson's troops to launch a surprise attack and easily win the battle; however, much to Jackson's frustration, Red Stick eludes capture. Davy and George head off in search of Red Stick, but George is soon captured by Red Stick's braves. Just as the Indians are about to set George afire, Davy appears and suggests that he and Red Stick engage in hand-to-hand combat in order to settle the Creek War once and for all. Although Red Stick attempts to cheat, Davy gains the upper hand and spares Red Stick's life in exchange for peace. After spending the winter with his wife Polly and their two sons, Davy leaves with George come springtime, promising Polly he will soon be ready to settle down. While traveling west of the Tennessee River in search of land on which to file a claim, Davy and George encounter a group of men in the midst of a shooting contest. Davy goes up against Bigfoot Mason, the scourge of the community, and easily beats him. Later, Davy learns that Bigfoot and his underlings have been running Indians off their rightful land, then selling the stolen plots to unsuspecting settlers. Davy accepts the position of magistrate offered by the desperate settlers and engages in a fistfight with Bigfoot as a means of resolving the conflict, eventually beating Bigfoot to a pulp. Bigfoot and his cohorts are hauled off to jail, after which the grateful locals ask Davy to run as their representative for the Tennessee State Legislature. As Davy throws himself into his campaign, he receives word that Polly has taken ill and died. Davy beats his opponent, the corrupt lawyer Amos Thorpe, in a landslide victory. In Nashville, Davy is reunited with Gen. Jackson and Jackson suggests that Davy run for U.S. Congress. In the next election, Jackson is elected President and Davy wins a seat in the House of Representatives. Later, President Jackson sends Davy on a speaking tour, ostensibly in order to groom him for a future presidential run. However, George shows up to inform Davy that Jackson has sent him away because he wants to get a bill detrimental to the Indians passed and knows that Davy will try to block it. Davy rushes back to Washington just in time and, coonskin cap in hand, makes an impassioned speech on behalf of the Indians, after which Jackson's bill is voted down. Nevertheless, Jackson's betrayal destroys Davy's enthusiasm for politics, and he leaves the Capitol to return to the frontier with George. The pair soon decides to head to Texas in order to help defend the besieged Alamo against the Mexican army. On the way, Davy and George are joined by a gambler named Thimblerig and a Comanche Indian dubbed Bustedluck, who serves as their guide. The group manages to break into the Alamo, where Davy finds Col. Jim Bowie seriously ill. After the Mexican army begins shelling the fort, George volunteers to carry a message requesting more U.S. troops. Davy's excellent shooting helps Bowie's men keep the Mexicans at bay, but George returns with the bad news that the army cannot spare any more soldiers. As the situation appears hopeless, Bowie gives his men the chance to escape the fort under cover of darkness, but everyone present, including the cowardly Thimblerig, decides to stay and fight. The men defend the

fort valiantly, but after a protracted battle, the Mexican troops succeed in entering the fort. In a final display of heroism, Bowie fights from his sickbed, while Davy's journal closes with the motto: "1836: Liberty and Independence Forever." *Adventurers. Davy Crockett. Scouts (Frontier). United States–History–19th century. Wilderness areas. Alamo (San Antonio, TX). Battles. Bears. James Bowie. Cheating. Creek War, 1813–1814. Fistfights. Friendship. Gamblers. Heroism. Homesteaders. Indians of North America. Andrew Jackson. Land rights. Mississippi–History. Political alliances. Political campaigns. Rescues. Speeches. State governments. Tennessee. Texas–History. United States. Army. Cavalry. United States. Congress. House of Representatives. Widowers.*

Note: Onscreen credits include the following acknowledgement: "We extend our thanks and gratitude to the members of the Cherokee Indian Nation of North Carolina, to the Forest Rangers of the Great Smokey Mountains National Park, and to the people of Tennessee and Texas for their generous cooperation in the filming of this story." This film is comprised of the three episodes originally produced for the *Disneyland* television show, collectively titled "Davy Crockett." The episodes, titled "Davy Crockett, Indian Fighter," "Davy Crockett Goes to Congress" and "Davy Crockett at the Alamo," aired on the ABC network on 15 Dec 1954, 26 Jan 1955 and 23 Feb 1955, respectively. The episodes are introduced and linked together in the film with lyrics from the show's theme song, "Ballad of Davy Crockett," and with animation and graphics depicting maps, frontier scenes and pages from Davy's diary.

Although Davy's onscreen exploits and frontier adventures are fictitious, the film's major events and settings are based on the life of the real Davy Crockett (1786-1836). Born in eastern Tennessee, Crockett first attracted attention for his heroism during the Creek Indian War (1813-1815). He subsequently served two terms in the Tennessee State Legislature and three terms as a U.S. Congressman. In contrast to the film's depiction of him, there is no historical evidence suggesting that Crockett was particularly sympathetic to Native Americans. Rather, his eventual falling out with President Andrew Jackson, a former mentor, was the result of a heated dispute pertaining to settlers' rights. After losing his last Congressional run in 1835 because of well-organized opposition from Jackson's Democratic Party, Crockett went to Texas to help in the fight against the Mexican army. Along with James Bowie and approximately one hundred eighty-seven others, Crockett was killed at the Alamo on 6 Mar 1836.

According to publicity material contained in the AMPAS Library file on the film, Walt Disney saw Fess Parker in a small part in the thriller *Them!* and suggested he be called in to read for the part of Davy. Parker was selected for the role from a field of several candidates, becoming the first adult player to be put under long-term contract by Disney. Many of *Davy Crockett's* exteriors were shot in Tennessee's Great Smokey Mountains, with the chambers of the Tennessee State Legislature in Nashville doubling for those of U.S. Congress circa 1827. Two hundred Cherokees still living in the Great Smokey Mountains appeared in the film as Creek Indians. A replica of the Alamo was built on a soundstage, although the onscreen acknowledgement indicates that some exteriors were shot on location in Texas.

By the time *Davy Crockett, King of the Wild Frontier* was released in early Jun 1955, "Ballad of Davy Crockett" was being played regularly on TV and radio's "Your Hit Parade," and the "Crockett craze" was in full swing. According to an article in the Nov 1955 edition of *Fortnight* magazine, writer Tom Blackburn first came up with the idea of using a ballad, rather than oral narration, to connect dramatic episodes in a screenplay while working on Warner Bros.' *Daniel Boone.* Producer Milton Sperling reportedly hated both the idea and the resulting ballad, and promptly fired Blackburn, after which Blackburn was hired by Walt Disney, who enthusiastically endorsed "Ballad of Davy Crockett." The song began attracting attention immediately after the premiere of the "Davy Crockett" television show and by Nov 1955, *Fortnight* reported that forty-one versions had been recorded and 10 million copies sold, including 1.5 million copies of the version sung by Fess Parker. According to a modern source, "Ballad of Davy Crockett" was the number one song in terms of airplay in 1955. *Fortnight* also reported the sale of 5.5 million Davy Crockett books and 6 million coonskin caps, as well as large numbers of Crockett toys, costumes, lunchboxes, guitars and even curtains. At the high end of the Crockett merchandising phenomenon was Steuben's glass bowl etched with scenes from Davy's adventures, which carried a price tag of $1,500.

Disney followed up this film with *Davy Crockett and the River Pirates,* released in 1956 (see entry above). Jul 1963 news items in *DV* and the *LAEx* reported that Walt Disney and Fess Parker were planning to shoot a Davy Crockett feature film in the Florida Everglades; however, there is no indication that the film was ever produced. Walt Disney Productions revived the Crockett television show in 1988 with five new episodes, collectively entitled *Davy Crockett: Rainbow in the Thunder,* which premiered on 20 Nov on NBC's "The Magical World of Disney." For information on earlier films based on the life of Crockett, see above entry for *Davy Crockett, Indian Scout.*

Box 21 May 1955. *DV* 17 May 1955, p. 3. *DV* 29 Jul 1963. *Exb* 1 Jun 1955, p. 3969. *FD* 19 May 1955, P. 6. *Fortnight* Nov 1955, p. 38. *Har* 21 May 1955, p. 84. *HR* 17 May 1955, p. 3 *LAEx* 23 Jul 1955. *MPHPD* 21 May 1955, p. 441. *NYT* 26 May 1955, p. 36. *Var* 18 May 1955, p. 8.

DAY OF DECISION (Native Americans, Navajo, Pima)
Dist Presbyterian Church. **1955.** Sd; col. 44 min.

Educational/Cultural. [*Not viewed*]. The wedding of a Navajo bride and a Pima groom provides the basis for flashbacks into the

history and life of both tribes. Conflicts, customs, joys and sorrows are shown, followed by progress to new living standards, new sociological concepts and a new faith in God. *Navajo Indians. Pima Indians. Religiosity. Weddings.*

Note: This film was listed in an educational film catalog.

THE DAY THEY GAVE BABIES AWAY *see* **ALL MINE TO GIVE**

THE DAY THEY ROBBED THE BANK OF ENGLAND (Irish Americans)

Summit Film Productions, Ltd.; Metro-Goldwyn-Mayer presents. *Dist* Loew's Inc. Jul **1960**; Prod: early Sep—early Oct 1959 at M.G.M. British Studios, Boreham Wood, England [©Summit Film Productions Ltd.; 31 Dec 1959; LP19148]. Sd (Westrex Recording System); b&w; Metroscope. 9 reels, 7,645 ft. 85 min. PCA cert no. 19475.

Prod Jules Buck. *Assoc prod* Dora Wright. *Dir* John Guillermin. *Asst dir* David Orton. *Scr* Howard Clewes. *Film adpt* Howard Clewes and Richard Maibaum. *Dir of photog* Georges Perinal. *Cam op* Chic Waterson. *Stills cam* David Boulton. *Spec eff* Tom Howard. *Art dir* Peggy Gick and Scott MacGregor. *Film ed* Frank Clarke. *Cost des* Ivy Baker. *Mus comp and cond by* Edwin Astley. *Rec supv* A. W. Watkins. *Sd rec* Cyril Swern and J. B. Smith. *Makeup* Freddie Williamson. *Hairdressing* Joan Johnstone. *Prod mgr* David Middlemas. *Administration* Roy Simpson. *Cont* Angela Martelli. *Tech adv* Brig (Rtd.) A. H. Swinton, M.C.

Source: Based on the novel *The Day They Robbed the Bank of England* by John Brophy.

Cast: ALDO RAY [(*Charles Norgate*)], Elizabeth Sellars [(*Iris Muldoon*)], Peter O'Toole [(*Lt. Monte Fitch*)], Kieron Moore [(*Walsh*)], Albert Sharpe [(*Tosher*)], Joseph Tomelty [(*Cohoun*)], Wolf Frees [(*Dr. Hagen*)], John Le Mesurier [(*Greene*)], Miles Malleson [(*Assistant curator*)], Colin Gordon [(*Benge*)], Andrew Keir [(*Sergeant of the Guard*)], Hugh Griffith [(*O'Shea*)], [Michael Golden (*Gamekeeper*)], [Peter Myers (*Piers*)], [Michael Brennan (*Walters*)], [Erik Chitty (*Gudgeon*)], [Frederick Piper], [Charles Lloyd-Pack], [The Scots Guards].

Crime, Drama. [*Print viewed*]. Early in the twentieth century, as Ireland struggles for independence, Charles Norgate, an Irish American, arrives in London to undertake the robbery of the inviolate Bank of England, which has never been robbed in its 200-year existence. Mrs. Michael Muldoon, a widow whose husband died years earlier in the attempt by Irish revolutionaries to take over the Armory, previously had been sent to New York by the movement to hire Norgate. The movement desires to rob the bank of a million pounds as part of their political offensive. Norgate, a professional who had once been a mining engineer, gains their confidence by saying that he still has his roots in Ireland. Told that the bank is considered impregnable, he decides to find a weakness in the "Bank Picket," Her Majesty's Brigade of Guards, which keeps watch on the gold. Norgate becomes friends with Lt. Monte Fitch of the Guard, and after he expresses an interest in architecture, Fitch tells him about the museum that houses the designs of the bank's architect, Sir John Soane. At the museum, Norgate breaks into the case containing the plans and traces them. Walsh, one of the revolutionaries who dislikes Norgate, believes there is no way they can get into the vault and tries to talk Mrs. Muldoon, of whom he is enamored, into leaving the movement with him, but she refuses. Although she had an affair with Norgate in New York, she now wants no longer to be involved with him either. Since the plans have no scale, Norgate gets Fitch to show him the vault and learns that the guards walk at exactly the same pace. By counting the paces, he figures out the corridor's length. When he learns that the guards are plagued by rats and that the floor has been reinforced, he goes to the Sewage Commission Records Department and discovers that an underground river, which has been sealed up for forty years, runs under the bank. Norgate finds an old "Tosher," a scavenger of the Thames, and after identifying himself as an archaeologist trying to examine ruins of a Roman temple, persuades the Tosher to show him where the river had been walled up. The group purchases a warehouse around it and digs through until they come through to the river. They plan to dig a thirty-foot tunnel during the first weekend in August, in which the Monday is a bank holiday. Before they start, Norgate taunts Mrs. Muldoon, saying she is afraid of herself and what her dead husband might think, and she responds to his kisses. As they begin to dig, the Tosher, running from the police, enters the area, and Norgate decides he should stay with them. Lt.

Fitch, on duty over the vault, begins to get suspicious of Norgate and learns that he has checked out of his hotel. Walsh, with whom Norgate has fought, hits a gas pipe with his pick and the lights go low until Norgate plugs the hole with a piece of wood and mud. Fitch then commands the keeper, Mr. Greene, to open the vault door, but it can only be opened if the three officials who have keys use them together, and one, Mr. Peabody, is away on holiday. To the displeasure of Greene, Fitch orders that Peabody be found and brought to the vault. Meanwhile, O'Shea, one of the revolutionaries, announces that the Irish Home Rule bill is to be reintroduced, and the theft must be stopped, as nothing can be allowed to jeopardize passage of the bill. After an argument with O'Shea, who says that the movement will disassociate itself from the thieves as they did when Mrs. Muldoon's husband died, she convinces Walsh to go with her to inform Norgate. Walsh arrives as Norgate is about to get through the floor of the vault, and astounded by the gold bars there, Walsh says nothing. They get a million pounds worth of bullion and are about to dynamite through a sealed entrance, where Cohoun, another of the group, is to be waiting with a tug, when Mrs. Muldoon appears and says she sent Cohoun away. Despite her pleas, Walsh and Norgate decide to take the gold through the warehouse. When Norgate realizes that Tosher, whom Walsh had knocked cold as he rushed past, has not come out, he goes in search of him. Tosher, meanwhile, has revived, and carrying a bust from a Roman ruin, he looks for Norgate and arrives in the vault. Norgate finds him there, and Tosher, when he sees "the Queen's yellow," realizes that Norgate is not the gentleman he thought he was. Just then, Flynn and the guard open the vault door, as Peabody has been located and brought back to London. On the street, as a bobby passes by, the gold breaks through a cart that Walsh, in his greed, has overloaded. When Norgate is led to a police wagon in handcuffs, Mrs. Muldoon looks in his eyes with tears in hers. She walks off, and the Tosher wanders away carrying the bust. *Bank of England. Bank robberies. Guards. Irish. Irish Americans. Revolutionaries. Gold. Impersonation and imposture. London (England). Museums. Sewers. John Soane. Thames River (England). Tunnels. Vaults. Widows.*

Note: The opening credits contain the following statement: "The producers gratefully acknowledge the assistance given them by the War Office and Her Majesty's Brigade of Guards in providing officers and men for this production. Thanks are especially due to the Scots Guards." According to the pressbook for the film, it was inspired by a number of actual incidents in the history of the Bank of England. In the 1840s, an employee of a sewer maintenance company, while repairing some brick work, discovered a ventilation shaft that went under the Bank floor from a dried-up stream. He wrote letters to a director of the Bank of England boasting he could break into the vaults, and after he stated a specific time in which he would do this, armed guards were instructed to wait inside the vault. When the man broke through the floor, he was given a bonus of 1,000 pounds for his honesty. In 1872, the Bank was robbed of five million dollars, the only time such a robbery was successful. Three Americans involved were sentenced to life imprisonment, but were pardoned after twenty years by Queen Victoria. According to *NYMirror*, the story of Irish revolutionaries robbing the Bank had become an Irish legend. The pressbook relates that the Bank declined to give permission to film its vaults for security reasons, but that the sets were based on sketches and old prints from the British Museum of the vaults as they looked in 1900. The London County Council refused to give permission for the company to film in the sewers, so these were reconstructed on the studio lot. Her Majesty's Scots Guards, including the Regimental Pipers, were filmed on their nightly parade from Wellington Barracks opposite Buckingham Palace to the bank. The nightly walk had routinely taken place since the Gordon Riots of 1780. This was the first time permission was granted to a film company to have the road and footpaths fronting the Palace cleared. Other scenes were shot at Hertfordshire and Buckinghamshire, and at dockyard locations in London. The London newspaper the *Evening News* commented concerning Peter O'Toole's performance: "It happened again this week—that magical moment in the critic's routine when a magnetic spark seems to come out of the screen and he knows that he is seeing the birth of a great star.... I have an idea that Peter O'Toole is going to blaze a fiery trail over our screens that will make some other reigning satellites look stale." According to *NYT*, after David Lean saw the film at its London premiere, he called O'Toole and asked him to test for the title role in *Lawrence of Arabia*.

Box 1 Aug 1960. *Exh* 20 Jul 1960, pp. 4721-22. *FD* 19 Jul 1960, p. 10 *Green Sheet* Aug 1960. *Har* 23 Jul 1960, p. 118. *HR* 4 Sep 1959, p. 10. *HR* 2 Oct 1959, p. 12. *HR* 18 Jul 1960, p. 3. *LAT* 4 Aug 1960. *MPD* 18 Jul 1960. *MPHPD* 23 Jul 1960, p. 781. *Newsweek* 1 Aug 1960. *NYMirror* 13 Jul 1960. *NYP* 14 Aug 1960. *NYT* 5 Sep 1960, p. 11. *NYT* 5 Feb 1961. *Var* 25 May 1960, p. 6.

DE BOTE EN BOTE *see* **PARDON US**

¡DE FRENTE, MARCHEN! (Spanish language)

Metro-Goldwyn-Mayer Corp.; controlled by Loew's, Inc.; Una Producción de Buster Keaton. *Dist* Metro-Goldwyn-Mayer Distributing Corp. Dec **1930**; San Juan, Puerto Rico opening: 11 Dec

1930; Madrid, Spain opening: 18 Dec 1930; Los Angeles opening: 23 Jan 1931.; Prod: Jun—Jul 1930. Sd (Western Electric Sound System); b&w. 11 reels, 8,658 ft. 96 min. Spanish language.

[*Supv* George Kann]. *Dirigida por* [*Dir*] Edward Sedgwick. [*Dial dir* Salvador de Alberich]. *Arreglo* [*Scr*] Richard Schayer. *Argumento* [*Story*] Al Boasberg and Sidney Lazarus. *Adaptación española* [*Spanish adpt*] Salvador de Alberich. *Fotografiada por* [*Photog*] Leonard Smith. *Director artístico* [*Art dir*] Cedric Gibbons. *Editada por* [*Ed*] George Boemler. *Bailes por* [*Dances staged by*] Sammy Lee. *Acústica por* [*Sd*] Douglas Shearer. [*Sd*] Karl E. Zint].

Cast: BUSTER KEATON (*Canuto de la Montera*), Conchita Monteño (*Mary*), Juan de Landa (*El sargento Gruñón*), Romualdo Tirado (*Pepe Alegría, "El tranquilo"*), Martín Garralaga (*El capitán Scott*), Victor Potel (*Adormidera*), Francisco Madrid (*Sánchez*), Herbert Von Morhart (*Fritz*), Gabry Rivas (*El comandante*), Rosita Granada (*Rosita*), [Lolita Méndez].

War, Comedy. [*Not viewed*]. The fabulously wealthy Canuto de la Montera is seeking a new chauffeur as his previous driver decided to enlist in the army. However, due to a misunderstanding, Canuto finds himself enlisted and shipped to France. Canuto's aristocratic behavior and demands are constantly deflated by his tough sergeant, and he finds peace only with Mary, a canteen girl. When sent to the front, Canuto unwittingly becomes a hero. *France. Officers (Military). Soldiers. United States. Army. World War I. Canteens (War-time, emergency, etc.). Chauffeurs. Germans. Heroes. Military service, Compulsory. Wealth.*

Note: This was a Spanish-language version of the 1930 film *Doughboys*, which was directed by Edward Sedgwick and starred Buster Keaton and Sally Eilers (see *AFI Catalog of Feature Films, 1921-30*; F2.1425). The cast and crew credits for the Spanish version were annotated from a studio cutting continuity.
CM Dec 1930. *Var* 22 Apr 1931.

DE LA SARTÉN AL FUEGO (Spanish language)

Metropolitan Pictures Corp. *Dist* Twentieth Century-Fox Film Corp. **1935**; New York opening: 11 Dec 1935; Prod: Oct 1935. Sd; col (Hirlicolor (Magnacolor)). 7,400 ft. 82 min. Spanish language.

Prod George A. Hirliman. *Assoc prod* Louis Rantz. *Dir* John Reinhardt. *Scr* Roger Whately. *Orig story* J. D. Newsom. *Spanish version* José Luis Tortosa. *Photog* Mack Stengler. *Art dir* Lewis J. Rachmil. *Ed* Tony Martinelli. *Sd* David Stoner. *Prod mgr* Sam Diege.

Cast: Rosita Moreno (*Ivonne Cartier*), Juan Torena (*Gary Linton*), Romualdo Tirado (*Alfred Gibbons*), José Luis Tortosa (*Henri Rilet*), Corazón Montes (*Luisa Rilet*), Rudolph Amendt (*Sargento Groebner*), Martín Garralaga (*Subteniente Cartellini*), Lou Hicks (*Inspector Donnegan*), Elisa Muriel.

Comedy. [*Not viewed*]. [The following plot summary is based on the English-language version of this film, *The Rest Cure*; character names refer to that version. For further information regarding the English-language version, please see the note below and the entry for *The Rest Cure* in the *AFI Catalog of Feature Films, 1931-40*.] Ex-racketeer Americans Dan Linton and Spike Connover hide out in Paris from their enemies. At a café, they charm Mrs. Louise Rillette and Naomi until interrupted by Perrelli, a rival gangster who appears to be carrying a machine gun. Louise then suggests that Dan and Spike volunteer for the Foreign Legion for a rest cure and go to Morocco. While on their way, Dan and Spike get involved with the misconduct of Captain Henri Rillette. In the legion, Dan and Spike generally misbehave, and Dan interrupts Spike's date with Honey Evans, an exotic cabaret performer, causing a fight between them which results in a sentence of six months hard labor in a prison camp for them. Later, Dan and Spike are reunited and save Louise, Naomi, and the general's wife from being kidnapped by Arab brigands led by Abdul Ben Abou and Ali. When their secure camp is besieged, Dan and Spike lead the legionnaires to victory and are pardoned. Dan and Naomi then swear their love. *Americans in foreign countries. Arabs. France. Army. Foreign Legion. Gangsters. Morocco. Paris (France). Bombs. Cabaret performers. Kidnapping. Rescues.*

Note: Unlike the English-language version, *The Rest Cure*, which was produced by Regal Productions, Inc., the Spanish-language version, which was shot simultaneously with the English version, was produced by Metropolitan Pictures Corp., a company set up by Hirliman to produce Spanish versions of some of his films. The Spanish version was released in Mexico on 2 Jul 1936 under the title *La legión extranjera*. The running time listed for the Spanish version was calculated from footage given in NYSA records. For information on the English-language version, which was directed by Crane Wilbur and starred

Reginald Denny, please see the entry for that film in the *AFI Catalog of Feature Films, 1931-40*; F3.3698.
CM Feb 1936, p. 76.

DEAD MEN TELL (Chinese Americans)

Twentieth Century-Fox Film Corp. *Dist* Twentieth Century-Fox Film Corp. 28 Mar **1941**; Prod: mid-Dec 1940—mid-Jan 1941 [©Twentieth Century-Fox Film Corp.; 28 Mar 1941; LP10394]. Sd; b&w. 6 reels, 5,383 or 5,441 ft. 60-61 min. PCA cert no. 6981.

Series: Charlie Chan.

Assoc prod Walter Morosco and Ralph Dietrich. *Dir* Harry Lachman. [*Asst dir* Saul Wurtzel]. *Orig scr* John Larkin. *Dir of photog* Charles Clarke. *Art dir* Richard Day and Lewis Creber. *Film ed* Harry Reynolds. *Set dec* Thomas Little. *Cost* Herschel. [*Mus dir* Emil Newman]. *Sd* Alfred Bruzlin and Harry M. Leonard. [*Pub dir* Harry Brand].

Source: Based on characters created by Earl Derr Biggers.

Cast: Sidney Toler (*Charlie Chan*), Sheila Ryan (*Kate Ransome*), Robert Weldon (*Steve Daniels*), Sen Yung (*Jimmy Chan*), Don Douglas (*Jed Thomasson*), Katharine Aldridge (*Laura Thursday*), Paul McGrath (*Charles Thursday*), George Reeves (*Bill Lydig*), Truman Bradley (*Captain Kane*), Ethel Griffies (*Miss [Patience] Nodbury*), Lenita Lane (*Dr. Anne Bonney*), Milton Parsons (*Gene La Farge*), [Lee Tung-Foo (*Wu Mei*)], [Ralph Dunn, Lee Phelps (*Detectives*)], [Stanley Andrews (*Inspector Vesey*)], [Pat Flaherty (*Policeman*)], [Tim Ryan (*Red Eye*)], [Jimmy Aubrey (*English sailor*)], [John Wallace (*Peg Leg*)], [Charles Tannen (*Sailor*)].

Detective, Drama. [*Print viewed*]. On the night before his ship, the *Suva Star*, is to leave for Cocos Island on a treasure hunt, Captain Kane discusses the journey's sponsor, Miss Patience Nodbury, with Steve Daniels, who helped arrange the trip. Just then Charlie Chan, a lieutenant in the Honolulu police, arrives to look for his son Jimmy, who has stowed away in search of adventure. Miss Nodbury explains to Chan that she tore the treasure map, drawn by her pirate ancestor, Black Hook Nodbury, into four pieces and mailed three of them to other passengers. She also tells Chan that Black Hook, who had a peg leg and a hook, appears to each of the Nodburys as they are about to die. After Miss Nodbury retires to her stateroom, she hears the tap of Black Hook's peg leg and the scratching of his hook on her door. The elderly woman opens the door, sees her ancestor and dies of a heart attack, after which the pirate gets her piece of the map. Meanwhile, the ship's passengers, claiming that they received a mysterious message from Steve, arrive and are introduced to Chan. They include Bill Lydig, a journalist about whom Chan is curious because he thought Lydig was dead, mortician Jed Thomasson, typist Kate Ransome and newlyweds Charles and Laura Thursday. Kate discovers Miss Nodbury's body, after which Chan finds part of the Black Hook disguise that someone wore to frighten the elderly woman to death. When Chan sends Jimmy ashore to telephone the police, the youngster overhears a suspicious conversation between Dr. Anne Bonney, a psychoanalyst, and her patient, Gene La Farge, who are both passengers on the *Suva Star*. Back on the ship, Gene admits that he saw Miss Nodbury's corpse but denies that he killed her. Laura and Thomasson give their pieces of the map to Chan for safekeeping, after which Jimmy finds the rest of the disguise and a map piece in Steve's room. Steve protests that he is being framed, after which it is discovered that the two map pieces Chan had were stolen. The group then finds Kate, who had fainted after reading in a magazine that Lydig is really an escaped murderer. Before Lydig can be questioned, however, he is found dead of suffocation in the diving bell below deck. Chan then goes ashore and finds Kane, who reveals that he has not met any of his passengers yet. When Chan questions the captain about his strange behavior, Kane explains that many years ago, he went on a treasure hunt to Cocos Island with his partner, but that the man left him there to die. Believing that his former partner would not be able to resist returning to the island, Kane arranged the journey so that he could find and kill the man. After Chan calls the police, Inspector Vesey arrives and arrests Steve because of the circumstantial evidence against him. Chan, who has the map piece found in Steve's room, uses himself as bait to trap the real killer. While Chan waits, Black Hook stalks him. Jimmy's signal alerts his father, and Chan captures the pirate, who is Thomasson in disguise. Kane reveals that Thomasson is his former partner, and Thomasson admits to killing Miss Nodbury and Lydig, who had stolen the map pieces from Chan's pocket. Vesey arrests Thomasson, and Chan watches in amusement

when Jimmy falls into the water again, as he has been doing throughout the evening. *Chinese Americans. Detectives. Murder. Superstition. Treasure hunts. Waterfronts. Aged women. Circumstantial evidence. Disguise. Fathers and sons. Maps. Newlyweds. Parrots. Pirates. Psychoanalysts. Sea captains. Ships. Stowaways.*

Note: According to *HR* news items, Jean Rogers was to appear in this film as "Laura Thursday," but was replaced after shooting began by Katharine Aldridge when she became ill with the flu. *HR* production charts include Fay Helm in the cast, but her participation in the completed film has not been confirmed. For additional information about the series, consult the Series Index and the above entry for *Charlie Chan Carries On.*

Box 29 Mar 1941. *DV* 21 Mar 1941. *FD* 18 Apr 1941, p. 10. *HR* 17 Dec 1940, p. 4. *HR* 18 Dec 1940, p. 2. *HR* 20 Dec 1940, p. 11. *HR* 24 Dec 1940, p. 3. *HR* 10 Jan 1941, p. 8. *HR* 21 Mar 1941, p. 3. *MPH* 29 Mar 1941, p. 41. *MPHPD* 22 Feb 1941, p. 63. *NYT* 17 Apr 1941, p. 29. *Var* 26 Mar 1941, p. 18.

DEADLINE ALLEY *see* **HEADLINE HUNTERS**

DEATH MAKES A DECREE *see* **CHARLIE CHAN IN RENO**

DEATH OF A SCOUNDREL (Czech Americans)
Charles Martin Productions, Inc. *Dist* RKO Radio Pictures, Inc. Nov **1956**; New York opening: 5 Nov 1956.; Prod: early Jan—early Feb 1956 at Samuel Goldwyn Studios [©Charles Martin Productions, Inc.; 31 Oct 1956; LP7263]. Sd (Western Electric Recording); b&w. 10,748 ft. 119 min. PCA cert no. 17862.

Prod Charles Martin. *Assoc prod* J. Herbert Klein. [*Exec prod* Jack Wilens]. *Dir* Charles Martin. *Asst dir* Frank Fox. *Wrt by* Charles Martin. *Dir of photog* James Wong Howe. *Art dir* Rudi Feld. *Supv ed* Conrad Nervig. [*Film ed* John Hoyt and George Gittens]. *Set dec* Ross Dowd. *Gowns* Waldo. *Ward woman* Rosamonde Price. *Ward man* Charles Arrico. *Orch* Murray Cutter. *Sd* John Kean. *Hair stylist* Olga Collings. *Makeup artist* Karlie Taylor. *Scr supv* Pat Miller. *Tech adv* Irwin Berger.

Cast: George Sanders [(*Clementi Sabourin*)], Yvonne De Carlo [(*Bridget Kelly*)], Zsa Zsa Gabor [(*Mrs. Ryan*)], Victor Jory [(*Leonard Wilson*)], Nancy Gates [(*Stephanie North*)], Coleen Gray [(*Mrs. Edith Van Renassalear*)], John Hoyt [(*Mr. O'Hara*)], Lisa Ferraday [(*Zina Monte*)], Tom Conway [(*Gerry Monte*)], Celia Lovsky [(*Mrs. Sabourin, mother*)], Werner Klemperer [(*Herbert, lawyer*)], Justice Watson [(*Butler*)], John Sutton [(*The actor*)], Curtis Cooksey [(*Oswald Van Renassalear*)], Gabriel Curtiz [(*Max Freundlich*)], Morris Ankrum [(*Captain Lafarge*)].

Drama. [*Print viewed*]. After Bridget Kelly, assistant to the corrupt New York financier Clementi Sabourin, finds her boss dead in the bedroom of his New York mansion, she tells the police that Clementi was an evil genius, and recounts his history: Freed from a Nazi prison camp in Czechoslovakia, Clementi travels to Italy to see his brother, Gerry Monte, and learns that Gerry has opened an antique shop with Clementi's money and married his girl friend Zina. Clementi vengefully turns Gerry in as an illegal immigrant in exchange for a U.S. visa, and his brother is killed during his subsequent arrest. Just before he disembarks in New York, Clementi meets oilman Leonard Wilson, to whom he describes his theory on how to obtain wealth dishonestly. Wilson later drops his wallet while exchanging money, and Clementi follows Bridget Kelly to a bar after she picks it up. Although Wilson suspects Clementi, police do not find the wallet on him. However, Clementi later steals the wallet from Bridget when he goes home with her, and is chased into the street by her friend Jack. Jack shoots Clementi in the shoulder, and is then killed by a truck. When a doctor treats his wound with a revolutionary new medicine called penicillin, Clementi falsely endorses Wilson's $20,000 check to buy stock in the pharmaceutical company that makes the antibiotic. Clementi's investment precedes public announcement about the medical breakthrough, and he immediately earns over one hundred thousand dollars. Soon after, Clementi meets wealthy widow Ryan at the brokerage firm, and encourages her to follow his investment advice. After Mrs. Ryan also turns a profit, Clementi convinces her to pay him $20,000 for his shares, and then exchanges her check for Wilson's check. Clementi's broker, O'Hara, learns that Clementi's original check was bad and blackmails him into paying $5,000 and starting an investment business in which he is the junior partner. Clementi then buys a mansion and hires Bridget as his assistant. When Wilson's Canadian oil company starts to fail, Clementi and Bridget travel to Canada, where Clementi returns the check and offers to buy the company, after revealing that he has published Wilson's confidential financial statement and caused his stock to

plummet. Clementi returns to New York while Bridget convinces Wilson to sell. Bridget later arranges to bring a newspaperman to the oil fields, just as an engineer reports that they have struck oil. Clementi sells the Wilson stock after having made a handsome profit, but the company actually strikes oil and the stock skyrockets. Mrs. Ryan is thrilled that Clementi's advice has worked to her advantage and throws him a lavish party. Clementi invites Mrs. Ryan's attractive secretary, Stephanie North, to the party, but spends most of his time flirting with Edith, the wife of wealthy department store owner Oswald Van Renassalear. Mrs. Ryan humiliates Stephanie when she discovers her at the party, and while comforting Stephanie, Clementi learns of her ambition to be an actress. The next day, he arranges to back a Broadway play on the condition that Stephanie gets the lead role, but she is unaware that he did more than just put in a good word for her. In the meantime, Clementi uses a two million dollar investment from Mrs. Ryan to create a false company called "Sabouranium," with which he plans to accept investments and then go into receivership. To everyone's surprise, Stephanie's performance is a huge success, and on the night of the opening, Clementi tries to seduce her. Stephanie mocks him and leaves, however, so he has her fired the next day. Clementi is later moved by her genuine distress and confides to Bridget that he wanted Stephanie because she is "good." After Bridget admits that she has fallen in love with him, Clementi advises her that his only interest is money, then tells the producer to reinstate Stephanie in the show. Clementi pursues a romance with Edith, and arranges for her to catch her husband and Bridget at a restaurant together. Edith later files for divorce, and Clementi makes plans to take over Oswald's company, in which she holds the controlling shares. Before he flies to Chicago to see her, however, he is confronted by Zina, who has come to avenge Gerry's death. Clementi plays on Zina's emotions and convinces her not to kill him but to join him in Chicago. Zina poisons herself after she sees Clementi with Edith, but leaves a statement accusing Clementi of her murder. Clementi is arrested for manslaughter and released on bail, but panics when his lawyer, Herbert, tells him that the district attorney intends to deport him to Czechoslovakia. Newspapers soon report that Clementi is also suspected of embezzlement, and a desperate Clementi sends for his elderly mother in Europe. Clementi's mother is thrilled that her son has finally sent for her, but her joy turns to horror when Clementi asks her to claim that he is the illegitimate son of a Swiss man, so that he will be deported to Switzerland, where he can keep his money in a private account. Clementi is rejected by his mother, and newspapers decry him as a "barbarian" who represents the moral corruption of society. Bridget leaves Clementi, and suggests that he return the money he stole from investors. At his office, Clementi signs over the stock certificates to the original buyers. O'Hara finds him in the office, and, desperate to save himself, shoots Clementi. The wounded Clementi then fatally shoots O'Hara during a struggle over the gun. Clementi stumbles home, and when his mother refuses to forgive him, he calls Bridget, begs for her forgiveness, and dies. Bridget now turns the stock certificates over to the police, and sadly leaves the mansion. *Czechoslovakian Americans. Duplicity. Embezzlement. Fraud. Greed. Immigrants. Moral corruption. Revenge. Stocks. Accidental death. Actors and actresses. Brothers. Canada. Class distinction. Gunshot wounds. Informers. Lawyers. Love affairs. Mothers and sons. New York City. Oil companies. Parties. Passports. Penicillin. Plays. Proposals (Marital). Socialites. Stockbrokers. Theatrical backers. Unrequited love.*

Note: Charles Martin's onscreen credit reads: "Produced, Written and Directed by Charles Martin." According to a modern source, this film was retitled *The Loves and Death of a Scoundrel* for marketing purposes. Although a Jan 1956 *HR* production chart places George Brent in the cast, he does not appear in the released film Reviews noted the resemblance between "Clementi Sabourin" and real-life New York financier Serge Rubinstein, an amoral Russian-born immigrant who had a genius for manipulating money. Rubinstein, a renowned playboy and swindler, was convicted of evading the draft in 1947. He was murdered in Jan 1955, and although an intensive investigation followed, the killer was never identified.

Box 1 Nov 1956. *DV* 31 Oct 1956, p. 3. *Exh* 14 Nov 1956, pp. 4250-51. *FD* 31 Oct 1956, p. 6. *Har* 3 Nov 1956, p. 175. *HR* 13 Jan 1956, p. 15. *HR* 3 Feb 1956, p. 12. *HR* 31 Oct 1956, p. 3. *MPHPD* 3 Nov 1956, p. 129. *NYT* 6 Nov 1956, p. 30. *Var* 24 Oct 1952. *Var* 31 Oct 1956, p. 6.

DEATH VALLEY *see* **MYSTERY RANCH**

DEBBIE'S ESCAPE *see* **BUCCANEER'S GIRL**

THE DEBT *see* **HIS DEBT**

THE DEBT OF HONOR *see* **HER DEBT OF HONOR**

A DEBTOR TO THE LAW (African Americans)
Norman Film Mfg. Co. **1924**. Si; b&w. 6 reels.
Cast: Henry Starr.
Western, African American. No information about the precise nature of this film has been found. *African Americans.*

DECEIT (African Americans)
Micheaux Film Corp. 1 Mar **1923**. Si; b&w. 6 reels.
Pres Oscar Micheaux. *Dir* Oscar Micheaux.
Cast: Evelyn Preer (*Doris Rutledge/Evelyn Bently*), William E. Fontaine, George Lucas, Norman Johnston (*Alfred DuBois/Gregory Wainwright*), A. B. De Comathiere (*Reverend Bently*), Cleo Desmond (*Charlotte Chesbro*), Louis De Bulger (*Mr. Chesbro*), Mabel Young (*Mrs. Levine*), Cornelius Watkins (*Gregory Wainwright, as a boy*), Mrs. Irvin C. Miller (*Mrs. Wainwright*), Ira O. McGowan (*Mr. Wainwright*), Lewis Schooler (*Actor*), Jerry Brown (*Actress*), James Carey (*Banker*), Viola Miles, Mary Watkins (*Teachers*), J. Coldwell, F. Sandfier, Jesse Billings, Allen Dixon (*Preachers*), Leonard Galezio, William Petterson, Sadie Grey (*Censors*), William Petterson, Melton Henry (*Rescue party*), N. Brown.
African American, Melodrama. Alfred Dubois and his charming secretary organize a film production company. Their first film is entitled *The Hypocrite.* All goes well with the production until Dubois must show his film to the censor board, which includes a delegation of preachers headed by the recalcitrant and conservative Christian P. Bently. Upon viewing the film, Bently expresses violent disapproval and persuades the censors to reject it. Dubois is persistent, though, and appeals to the board to screen the film for a less biased audience to decide if the sequence in question warrants the film's rejection. The film is projected as the new committee members look on. *Actors and actresses. African Americans. Bankers. Censorship. Clergy. Motion picture producers. Schoolteachers. Secretaries.*

DEEP IS THE WELL *see* **THE WELL**

DEERSLAYER (Native Americans, Mohegan, Huron)
Cardinal Pictures Corp. *Dist* Republic Pictures Corp. 22 Nov **1943**; Prod: began 8 Jun 1943 [©Republic Pictures Corp.; 28 Oct 1943; LP12371]. Sd (RCA Sound System); b&w. 7 reels, 6,051 ft. 65 or 67 min. Passed by the National Board of Review. PCA cert no. 9532.
Prod P. S. Harrison and E. B. Derr. *Dir* Lew Landers. *Asst dir* Eddie Stein. *Story trmt and scr* P. S. Harrison and E. B. Derr. *Adpt of trmt* John W. Krafft. *Dir of photog* Arthur Martinelli. *Film ed* George McGuire. *Set dec* William Kiernan. *Sd* Fred Stahl. *Dir of makeup* William Knight.
Source: Based on the novel *The Deerslayer: Or, the First War-Path, A Tale* by James Fenimore Cooper (Philadelphia, 1841).
Cast: Bruce Kellogg (*Deerslayer*), Jean Parker (*Judith Hutter*), Larry Parks (*Jingo-Good*), Warren Ashe (*Harry March*), Wanda McKay (*Hetty Hutter*), Yvonne de Carlo (*Wah-Tah*), Addison Richards (*Hutter*), Johnny Michaels (*Bobby Hutter*), Phil Van Zandt (*Briarthorn*), Trevor Bardette (*Chief Rivenoak*), Robert Warwick (*Chief Uncas*), Many Treaties (*Chief Brave Eagle*), Clancy Cooper (*Barlow*), Princess Whynemah (*Duenna*), William Edmunds (*Huron sub-chief*), Charles Brunner (*Messenger*), Steve Clark (*Doctor*).
Historical, Drama. [*Not viewed*]. In the late 1700s, Huron chief Rivenoak leads his warriors in raids against white settlers and their allies, the Mohican and Delaware tribes, after many years of peace. Among those on the defense are Deerslayer, a white man reared by the Mohican chief Uncas, and Uncas' own son, Jingo-Good. The Hurons are aided by Briarthorn, a traitorous Mohican who is in love with the Delaware princess Wah-Tah, the betrothed of Jingo-Good. After Briarthorn kills Chief Brave Eagle, Wah-Tah's father, and kidnaps Wah-Tah, Jingo-Good vows revenge. Meanwhile, Deerslayer comes to the rescue of Hetty Hutter and her little brother Bobby, who are being attacked by Huron warriors. Deerslayer helps them reach the "Arc," a houseboat used as a ferry by their father. Bobby is in desperate need of a doctor, however, so Deerslayer goes to the stockade, where the settlers agree to provide a doctor and an escort if Deerslayer does

them a service in return. Deerslayer acquiesces and is sent in search of his old friend, Harry March, who is escorting sixty-five eastern women to the stockade, where they are to be wed to the frontiersmen. Deerslayer finds Harry as he is crossing the rapids of a dangerous river in an attempt to avoid going the long way around. After signaling to the women to wait on the other side, where they will be safe from the Hurons, Deerslayer and Harry go to the Arc to help defend the Hutters. They also vie for the affections of Hetty's older sister Judith, but she maintains a friendly distance from the men. Jingo-Good's thirst for revenge is increased when Chief Uncas is killed, and the Hurons further anger Deerslayer when they capture Hutter and Harry. Hetty, who knows that the Hurons will not harm a mentally unbalanced person, pretends to be insane and gains access to the Huron camp, where she obtains Hutter and Harry's release by offering a valuable ransom. Deerslayer and Jingo-Good then attempt to rescue Wah-Tah, and although the two Indians escape, Deerslayer is captured. He is not held prisoner for long, however, as Jingo-Good soon rescues him. The Hurons, enraged over their interference, attack the Hutters' lake home, and Hutter and Hetty are killed in the battle. A contingent of settlers from the stockade arrive in time to subdue the uprising and save Deerslayer, Jingo-Good and the others. Later, after Judith admits that she loves Harry, Deerslayer returns to the river to escort the women to their waiting grooms. *Huron Indians. Kidnapping. Mohegan Indians. Raids. Scouts (Frontier). Settlers. United States–History–Colonial period, ca. 1600-1775. Family relationships. Houseboats. Marriage–Arranged. Murder. Ransom. Rescues. Rivers. Romantic rivalry. Sisters. Traitors.*

Note: According to *HR* news items, this film was shot on location at Lake Elsinore, CA, and actor Johnny Michaels was borrowed from Paramount for the production. *Deerslayer* was the only picture written and produced by P. S. Harrison, a longtime film critic and the publisher of *Harrison's Reports* [*Har*]. The *Har* review, which was written by Harrison's friend Abram F. Myers, noted that the producers were considering a "series of pictures based on the writings of James Fenimore Cooper." *HR* news items also noted that Harrison and Derr were working on a screenplay for *The Last of the Mohicans*, in which they intended to star Bruce Kellogg and Warren Ashe. *Deerslayer* was not well received, however, and the *DV* reviewer termed it "a museum piece that should be kept handy to show to any film critics who might hanker to turn producers in the future." Derr and Harrison did not produce any more pictures together. Other films based on Cooper's novel include Twentieth Century-Fox's 1957 release, *The Deerslayer*, which was directed by Kurt Neumann and starred Lex Barker, Rita Moreno and Forrest Tucker (see below), and a 1978 television movie directed by Dick Friedenberg and starring Steve Forrest and Ned Romero.

Box 13 Nov 1943. *DV* 3 Nov 1943, pp. 3-4. *FD* 9 Nov 1943, p. 7. *Har* 13 Nov 1943. *HR* 8 Jun 1943, p. 9. *HR* 23 Sep 1943, p. 1. *HR* 1 Oct 1943, p. 6. *HR* 3 Nov 1943, p. 3. *HR* 23 Nov 1943, p. 8. *HR* 20 Dec 1943, p. 3. *MPD* 4 Nov 1943. *MPH* 6 Nov 1943. *MPHPD* 23 Oct 1943, p. 1599. *MPHPD* 6 Nov 1943, p. 1615. *Var* 10 Nov 1943, p. 35.

THE DEERSLAYER (Native Americans, Mohegan, Huron)
Twentieth Century-Fox Film Corp. *Dist* Twentieth Century-Fox Film Corp. 3 Oct **1957**; Prod: late Apr—late May 1957 [©Twentieth Century-Fox Film Corp.; 11 Sep 1957; LP9261]. Sd; col (DeLuxe). Cinemascope. 6,992 ft. 76 min.
Exec prod E. J. Baumgarten. *Prod* Kurt Neumann. *Dir* Kurt Neumann. *Asst dir* Herbert Mendelson. *Scr* Carroll Young and Kurt Neumann. *Dir of photog* Karl Struss. *Art dir* Theodore Holsopple. *Film ed* Jodie Copelan. *Mus* Paul Sawtell and Bert Shefter. *Sd* Steve Bass.
Source: Based on the novel *The Deerslayer: Or, the First War-Path, A Tale* by James Fenimore Cooper (Philadelphia, 1841).
Cast: Lex Barker (*The Deerslayer*), Rita Moreno (*Hetty Hutter*), Forrest Tucker (*Harry Marsh*), Cathy O'Donnell (*Judith Hutter*), Jay C. Flippen (*Old Tom Hutter*), Carlos Rivas (*Chingachgook*), John Halloran (*Old warrior*), Joseph Vitale (*Huron chief*), Rocky Shahan, Phil Schumacher, George Robotham, Carol Henry.
Historical, Drama. [*Not viewed*]. After The Deerslayer, a white man reared by the Mohicans, and his blood brother Chingachgook, a Mohican chief, save trader Harry Marsh from the hostile Huron Indians, they learn that the Hurons will attack bounty hunter Old Tom Hutter and his two daughters, Hetty and Judith, who live on a floating raft fort on the river. The Deerslayer and Chingachgook decide to help the beleaguered family, but soon learn that Hutter hates the Indians because they scalped his wife years before and has since devoted his life to collecting Indian scalps. The Hurons are determined to retrieve the scalps of their dead so that their souls may rest in peace. On a scouting mission, The Deerslayer and Chingachgook discover the Hurons building a raft to attack the fort. They are trapped when they attempt to set fire to the raft, but are

rescued by Marsh and Hutter, who kill and scalp two of the Hurons. Later, the Hurons attack, and Hutter is captured by the Indians. Marsh wants to take Hutter's gold and scalps, but The Deerslayer decides to use the scalps to bargain for Hutter's release. Meanwhile, from a notation in Hutter's Bible, The Deerslayer learns that Hetty is an Indian whom Hutter stole and reared as his own daughter. Unaware that Marsh has stolen the scalps from his pouch, The Deerslayer meets with the Hurons, who agree to the trade. When they discover that the scalps are missing, however, the Hurons capture The Deerslayer, Chingachgook, Hetty and Judith. As the Hurons prepare to kill their prisoners, Marsh comes to their rescue, using a cannon that he stole from Hutter's fort. Hutter is killed during the ensuing battle. Judith then accompanies Marsh back to Albany, while The Deerslayer, Chingachgook and Hetty return to the Mohicans. *Fathers and daughters. Huron Indians. Mohegan Indians.* Blood brotherhood. Bounty hunters. Forts. Kidnapping. Parentage. Rafts. Raids. Rescues. Rivers. Robbery. Scalping. Scouts (Frontier). Trappers. United States–History–Colonial period, ca. 1600-1775.

Note: Portions of the film were shot on location in Northern California. For information on other film versions of James Fenimore Cooper's novel, see the entry above for the 1943 Republic film *Deerslayer*.

Box 21 Sep 1957. *DV* 12 Sep 1957, p. 3. *Exb* 16 Oct 1957, p. 4391. *FD* 3 Oct 1957, p. 10. *Har* 21 Sep 1957, p. 150. *HR* 3 May 1957, p. 13. *HR* 17 May 1957, p. 17. *HR* 12 Sep 1957, p. 3. *MPHPD* 28 Sep 1957, p. 545. *Var* 18 Sep 1957, p. 6.

THE DEFENDERS *see* **A SISTER OF SIX**

THE DEFIANT ONES (African Americans)
Lomitas Productions, Inc.; Curtleigh Productions, Inc. *Dist* United Artists Corp. 20 Oct **1958**; New York opening: 24 Sep 1958; Prod: late Feb—early Apr 1958 [©Lomitas Productions, Inc. & Curtleigh Productions, Inc.; 13 Aug 1958; LP13779]. Sd (Westrex Recording System); b&w. 8,673 ft. 97-98 min. PCA cert no. 18985.
Pres STANLEY KRAMER. *Prod* Stanley Kramer. *Dir* Stanley Kramer. *Asst dir* Paul Helmick. *Wrt by* Nathan E. Douglas and Harold Jacob Smith. *Dir of photog* Sam Leavitt. *Cam op* Al Myers. *Spec eff* Alex Weldon. *Prod des* Rudolph Sternad. *Art dir* Fernando Carrere. *Film ed* Frederic Knudtson. *Set dec* Joe Kish. *Prop master* Art Cole. *Cost supv* Joe King. *Mus* Ernest Gold. *Sd eng* James Speak. *Sd eff* Walter Elliott. [*Sd ed* John Mick and Wayne B. Fury]. *Makeup* Don Cash. *Prod mgr* Clem Beauchamp. *Company grip* Morris Rosen. *Scr supv* John Franco. *Chief gaffer* James Almond. [*Dog trainer* Cindy James].
Song(s): "Long Gone," adapted from "Long Gone (From Bowlin' Green)," music by William C. Handy, lyrics by Chris Smith.
Cast: TONY CURTIS [(*John "Joker" Jackson*)], SIDNEY POITIER [(*Noah Cullen*)], Theodore Bikel [(*Sheriff Max Muller*)], Charles McGraw [(*Capt. Frank Gibbons*)], Lon Chaney [(*Big Sam*)], King Donovan [(*Solly*)], Claude Akins [(*Mac*)], Lawrence Dobkin [(*Editor*)], Whit Bissell [(*Lou Gans*)], Carl Switzer [(*Angus*)], Kevin Coughlin [(*Billy*)], Cara Williams [(*Billy's mother*)].
Social, Drama. [*Print viewed*]. When a truck transporting chain gang convicts back to prison crashes on a rainswept Southern road, two of the prisoners escape: Noah Cullen, a black man who reacts violently to racial insults, and John "Joker" Jackson, a Southern white bigot. While the two try unsuccessfully to break the three-foot chain that binds them together, Sheriff Max Muller, under pressure from the governor, organizes a posse of state troopers and civilian volunteers. Muller reminds the well-armed troopers and local hunters that the convicts are men, "not rabbits," and his refusal to allow one volunteer's brutal Dobermans off the leash angers police captain Frank Gibbons, who would just as willingly capture the men dead as alive. Meanwhile, Joker and Cullen argue about which direction they should take. Noah, who realizes he has little chance of attaining freedom in the South, finally convinces his reluctant partner to proceed around the swamp and then try to jump a train to Ohio. While attempting to cross a rushing river, Cullen loses his footing, and the two are carried away by the rapids. Joker eventually grabs onto a branch, but when Cullen thanks him for pulling him out of the river, the white man snarls a cutting response. The convicts manage to kill a frog, and as they devour it, Joker advises Cullen to be less sensitive about racial epithets. Countering the white man's claim that "I didn't make the rules," Cullen answers that Joker breathed in his racism at birth and has been spitting it out ever since. In order to avoid the detection of a passing farmer, Cullen and Joker leap into a clay pit, and only by coordinating their efforts are they able to climb back out. That evening, as the men wait for the cover of darkness

before sneaking into a small settlement, they begin to discuss their past experiences and future hopes. Their attempt to break into the general store for food, however, produces disastrous results: Joker seriously injures his wrist, and the townspeople capture them. The locals are about to lynch the escaped convicts, when Big Sam, who had been a convict himself, rescues and later frees the men. At the same time, Gibbons, exasperated with what he considers the slow pace of the pursuit, threatens that Muller will lose his job if the posse fails to recapture the prisoners. A portable radio carried by one of the civilians endlessly blares rock and roll, which further erodes the tempers of the pursuers. The next day, Cullen and Joker are surprised when a young boy named Billy aims a shotgun at them, but they easily overcome the youngster, who leads them to his farm. There they hungrily devour a meal and hammer the chain from their wrists. Billy's mother, whose husband had abandoned her eight months before, is attracted to Joker, and as she tends to his injury, she confesses that she is deeply lonely. While Cullen sleeps, the couple makes love, and in the morning, the woman announces that she wants to escape in her car with Joker. Reluctant to abandon Cullen at first, Joker finally agrees to the plan just as Cullen appears. The woman advises Cullen to take the shortcut through the swamp to the railroad tracks, but after he leaves, she admits that the swamp is impenetrable bog and quicksand. Furious at his own inadvertent betrayal of Cullen, Joker pushes the woman away and starts to go after his cohort. The boy shoots Joker in the shoulder, and when the injured man finally locates Cullen in the swamp, he protests that he is too weak to go on. The posse has now reached the woman's farm. Proceeding through the swamp, Muller threatens to shoot the Dobermans if Gibbons removes their muzzles. Cullen and Joker, hearing the train whistle, stumble up the hill as the train crosses a trestle. Cullen leaps on, but he cannot hold onto Joker, and both men tumble to the ground. Cradling Joker's head against his chest, Cullen muses, "We gave 'em a hell of a run for it, didn't we?" As Muller, who wants to confront the prisoners alone, approaches the men, Cullen sings his blues anthem, "Long Gone," and then laughs. *African Americans. Prison escapees. Racism. Transformation. United States–South.* Attempted murder. Betrayal. Blues music. Chain gangs. Children. Dogs. Ex-convicts. Humanitarianism. Loneliness. Love affairs. Lynching. Neglected wives. Police. Posses. Radios. Rapids. Self-sacrifice. Sheriffs. Swamps. Trains. Truck accidents.

Note: According to a Jul 1958 *NYT* news item, the film's river-crossing sequence was photographed on the Kern River, near Kernville, CA. To film the scene, Tony Curtis and Sidney Poitier were shackled together wearing rubber diving suits under their prison clothing. While wading though the swiftly running, thirty-eight degree river, they were carried away by the rapids and finally caught by stunt men at a designated position one hundred yards downstream. United Artists production notes on the film contained in the AMPAS Library add that the production was filmed on a closed set because of the provocative nature of the topic. A 1 Jan 1959 *NYT* news item revealed that Nathan E. Douglas, credited onscreen as co-author of the screenplay, was a pseudonym for Nedrick Young, who had been blacklisted in 1953 for invoking the Fifth Amendment as an "unfriendly witness" before the House Un-American Activities Committee.

Two weeks later, the Academy of Motion Picture Arts and Sciences repealed an amendment that prohibited Academy Award recognition to anyone admitting or refusing to deny membership in the Communist Party. Douglas and his co-author Harold Jacob Smith were then nominated and later won the Academy Award for Best Screenplay. The controversy surrounding the issue continued, however, and in a Sep 1959 *NYT* news item, it was charged that the American Legion singled out independent producers for employing blacklisted talent while ignoring the major studios. Stanley Kramer and United Artists were among those criticized for producing a picture using a blacklisted writer. According to a 30 Jul 1996 *HR* article, The Writers Guild of America had officially restored Young's credit, along with credits for the writers of nine other films written by blacklisted writers.

This picture was also nominated for an Academy Award for Best Picture, Best Director, Best Actor (both Tony Curtis and Sidney Poitier), Best Supporting Actor (Theodore Bikel), and Best Supporting Actress. It received an Academy Award for Best Cinematography, as well as garnering three New York Film Critics awards: Best Motion Picture, Best Direction and Best Writing. It also won a Golden Globe award for Best Motion Picture (Drama), and Sidney Poitier won the award for Best Foreign Actor at the Berlin Film Festival. The film was acclaimed for its promotion of race relations, winning the 1959 annual Brotherhood Media Award presented by the National Conference of Christians and Jews and the Prague Film Festival Award for films designed to promote "better relations between people."

Special screenings for integrated audiences in several Southern cities were arranged by the Protestant Film Council to promote an "understanding between the races," according to a 7 Feb 1961 *HR* news item. An 11 Apr 1959 *LAT* news item added, however, that a screening at a theater in Montgomery, Alabama, was canceled when the White Citizen's Committee Council protested that the film

would give "moral support and financial gain to subversive propagandists." According to a modern source, Curtis insisted that he and Poitier share top billing; in the final credits, Poitier was billed under Curtis. *The Defiant Ones* was remade for television in 1986. The remake was directed by David Lowell and starred Robert Urich and Carl Weathers.

AmCin Jul 1958, pp. 484-85, 500, 502. *Box* 11 Aug 1958. *DV* 5 Aug 1958, p. 3. *FD* 5 Aug 1958, p. 8. *Har* 9 Aug 1958, p. 127. *HR* 28 Feb 1958, p. 29. *HR* 4 Apr 1958, p. 8. *HR* 5 Aug 1958, p. 3. *HR* 7 Feb 1961. *HR* 2 Jul 1961. *HR* 30 Jul 1996, p. 1, 11. *LAEx* 2 Oct 1958. *LAT* 11 Apr 1959. *MPH* 26 Jul 1958. *MPHPD* 9 Aug 1958, p. 937. *NYT* 16 Jul 1958. *NYT* 25 Sep 1958, p. 29. *NYT* 1 Jan 1959. *NYT* 14 Jan 1959. *NYT* 3 Sep 1959. *Var* 6 Aug 1958, p. 6.

DEFYING THE LAW (Chinese Americans, Italian Americans)
William B. Brush Productions. *Dist* Gotham Productions. **1924**; New York premiere: 3 Jun 1924 [©Gotham Productions; 15 Apr 1924; LP20115]. Si; b&w. 5 reels.

Dir Bertram Bracken. *Story* Bertram Bracken and John T. Prince. *Titles* Andrew Bennison. *Photog* Gordon Pollock. *Film ed* Leonard Wheeler.

Cast: Lew Cody (*Pietro Savori*), Renée Adorée (*Lucia Brescia*), Josef Swickard (*Michelo Brescia*), Charles "Buddy" Post (*Francisco*), Naldo Morelli (*Guido Savori*), Dick Sutherland (*Luigi Bevani*), James B. Leong (*Dr. Chong Foo*), Evelyn Adamson (*Maria Baretto*), Kathleen Chambers (*Sylvia Baretto*), Marguerite Kosik (*Alicia Bevani*).

Melodrama. Discouraged with life, Michelo throws his daughter Lucia into the sea, but she falls into a fisherman's boat and is taken to a fishing village. Francisco kidnaps her and takes her to the headquarters of smuggler Dr. Chong Foo, located in a studio occupied by Pietro Savori, an unwilling partner. Chong Foo kills Savori to gain the girl for himself, but Bevani comes to the rescue and saves Lucia for her sweetheart, Guido. *Chinese Americans. Fatherhood. Fishermen. Italian Americans. Kidnapping. Smuggling.*

Var 11 Jun 1924, p. 31.

DEL INFIERNO AL CIELO (Spanish language)
Fox Film Corp. *Dist* Fox Film Corp. **1931**; New York premiere: 27 Feb 1931; Prod: Jan 1931. Sd; b&w. Length undetermined. Spanish language.

Presenta [*Pres*] William Fox. [*Prod* Raoul Walsh]. [*Dir* Richard Harlan]. [*Asst dir* Sid Bowen]. [*Scr* Edwin Burke]. [*Addl dial* Paul Perez]. [*Spanish version written by* Francisco Moré de la Torre].

Song(s): "I Have a Thought in My Heart for You," by Sol Hoopii, Jr.

Source: Based on the novel *The Man Who Came Back* by John Fleming Wilson (New York, 1912) and the play of the same title by Jules Eckert Goodman (New York, 2 Sep 1916).

Cast: Juan Torena (*Esteban Randolf*), María Alba (*Angela*), Carlos Villarías (*Tomás Randolf*), Ralph Navarro (*Traves* [/*Detective Harrison*]), Carmen Rodríguez (*Tía Isabel*), Lucio Villegas ([*Carlos*] *Resling*), [Juan Aristi Eulate (*Capitán Garlon*)], [Ramón Peón], [Virginia Ruiz].

Social, Drama. [*Not viewed*]. [The following plot summary is based on the English-language version of this film, *The Man Who Came Back*; character names refer to that version. For further information regarding the English-language version, please see the note below and the entry for *The Man Who Came Back* in the *AFI Catalog of Feature Films, 1931-40*.] New York millionaire Thomas Randolph becomes furious when he learns that his spoiled, wastrel son Stephen has been involved in yet another highly publicized scandal. This incident, coupled with Stephen's reckless financial handlings, prompts Thomas to cut off his support and force him to work for a living. Stephen rejects his father's decision that he work at his San Francisco shipping company, and instead falls in love with Angie, a San Francisco cabaret singer who promises to follow him wherever he goes. When Stephen threatens to soil the Randolph name and never return if his father cuts him off, Thomas decides to teach his son a lesson by having him shanghaied and taken to China. Four months later, Stephen runs into Angie in a Chinese drug den, known in Shanghai as "Slackjaw Palace," where Angie pretends to be high on dope, unable to recognize him. Stephen tries to strangle Angie in order to get her to stop her drug habit, and they soon resume their romance. One year later, Stephen and Angie, living in Hawaii, are visited by Captain Trevelyan, a mutual acquaintance who appears to have developed a fondness for Angie. In the hope that Angie will leave Stephen when she learns that her sweetheart has returned to his alcoholic ways, Trevelyan tells her that he has seen Stephen on a drinking jag. While Angie feigns drug addiction to test Stephen's resolve to love her, Stephen's aunt arrives

with news that his father is ill, forcing him to choose between staying by Angie's side, and going to his father's sickbed. After some deliberation, Stephen decides to stay with Angie. When Thomas decides that Stephen has learned his lesson, he summons him back to New York with a promise that he will take him into his firm, but only on the condition that he and Angie remain apart. Later, Thomas informs his son that he has had Angie watched while he was away, and tells him that she has left Honolulu with Captain Trevelyan. At that moment, Trevelyan and Angie enter and Thomas explains that he was satisfied with Angie's conduct under Trevelyan's surveillence, so he brought her over to be with Stephen. *Abduction. Alcoholism. Dissipation. Drug addicts. Fathers and sons. Irresponsibility. Moral reformation. Scandal. China. Drugs. Family relationships. Honolulu (HI). Impersonation and imposture. Millionaires. Morphine. Opium dens. San Francisco (CA). Shanghaiing. Singers. Spies.*

Note: The novel on which the film is based was first published as a short story in *American Mercury* in Nov 1912. The onscreen credits listed for this Spanish-language version were taken from a screen credit sheet in the legal records. The Spanish version was shown in Barcelona, Spain under the title *Camino del infierno* and in Santiago, Chile under the title *Regeneración*. Another film based on the same source was the 1924 Fox film *The Man Who Came Back*, directed by Emmett Flynn and starring George O'Brien and Dorothy MacKaill (see *AFI Catalog of Feature Films, 1921-30*; F2.3429). This film was also dubbed in German, Italian, French and Japanese. For information on the English-language version, *The Man Who Came Back*, which was directed by Raoul Walsh and starred Janet Gaynor and Charles Farrell, please see the entry for that film in the *AFI Catalog of Feature Films, 1931-40*; F3.2718.

DEL MISMO BARRO (Spanish language)
Fox Film Corp. *Dist* Fox Film Corp. Sep **1930**; New York opening: 19 Sep 1930; Prod: Jun—Jul 1930. Sd; b&w. 10 reels. 93 min. Spanish language.

Supv John Stone. *Dir* David Howard. *Scr* Jules Furthman. *Spanish version* Francisco Moré de la Torre. *Photog* Ross Fisher. *Film ed* Louis Loeffler.

Source: Based on the play *Common Clay* by Cleves Kinkead (New York, 26 Aug 1915).

Cast: Mona Maris (*Elena Neal*), Juan Torena (*Jorge Fullerton*), Vicente Padula (*Sr. Fullerton*), Carlos Villarías (*Filson*), Roberto Guzmán (*Yute*), María Calvo (*Sra. Neal*), Rafael Valverde (*Edwards, el mayordomo*), René Cardona (*Bobby*), Consuelo de los Angeles (*Ana Fullerton*), Marcela Nivón (*Sra. Fullerton*), [Luana Alcañiz], [Julio Villarreal], [Agnes Aranis], [Marina Alcañiz], [Nelly Fernández].

Social, Drama. [*Not viewed*]. After the police arrest Elena Neal during a routine raid on a nightclub, the judge at her trial realizes that she is a naïve, inexperienced young woman and frees her on the condition that she does not become a repeat offender. Ellen takes a job as a maid with the Fullerton family, but finds herself pursued not only by the majordomo, but by the handsome young master, Jorge, and his brazen friends. Elena winds up pregnant and gives birth to a baby boy, but rejects Sr. Fullerton's desire to buy her silence, confident that Jorge will not forget his promises to her despite the fact his family name will be involved in a scandal. While investigating Elena's past, the Fullerton's lawyer discovers that she is actually his own daughter. Elena's mother had been from humble circumstances and had left the lawyer to avoid impeding his chances for a brilliant career. Upon learning of these revelations, Sr. Fullerton refuses to become further involved in the sordid, sentimental events. Tired of being compromised by all the hypocrisy, Elena withdraws the lawsuit by which she hoped to have her child's paternity established and thus wins from Jorge the response she wanted. *Fathers and sons. Hypocrisy. Illegitimacy. Lawyers. Scandal. Seduction. Class distinction. Judges. Maids. Nightclubs. Parties. Police raids.*

Note: This film's working titles were *Arcilla* and *Barreras sociales*. The film is a Spanish-language version of the 1930 film *Common Clay*, which was directed by Victor Fleming and starred Constance Bennett and Lew Ayres (see *AFI Catalog of Feature Films, 1921-30*; F2.0986).

CM Oct 1930, p. 977.

DELICIOUS (Scottish Americans, Russian Americans)
Fox Film Corp. *Dist* Fox Film Corp. 26 Dec **1931**; New York opening: 25 Dec 1931; Prod: 29 Aug–10 Nov 1931 [©Fox Film Corp.; 3 Dec 1931; LP2697]. Sd (Western Electric System); b&w. 11 reels, 9,564 ft. 106 min. Passed by the National Board of Review.

Dir David Butler. [*Asst dir* Ad Schaumer]. *Story* Guy Bolton. *Adpt* Guy Bolton and Sonya Levien. *Photog* Ernest Palmer. [*2d cam* Don Anderson]. [*Asst cam* Stanley Little and John Miehle]. *Art dir* Joseph

Wright. [*Film ed* Irene Morra]. [*Cost* Guy Duty]. *Sd rec* Joseph Aiken. [*Still photog* Anthony Ugrin].

Music: "You Started It" and "New York Rhapsody" by George Gershwin.

Song(s): "Delishious," "Dream Sequence," "Somebody from Somewhere," "Katinkitschka" and "Blah-Blah-Blah-Blah with You," music by George Gershwin, lyrics by Ira Gershwin.

Cast: JANET GAYNOR [(*Heather Gordon*)], CHARLES FARRELL [(*Larry Beaumont*)], El Brendel [(*Jansen*)], Raul Roulien [(*Sascha*)], Lawrence O'Sullivan [(*Inspector O'Flynn*)], Manya Roberti [(*Olga*)], Virginia Cherrill [(*Diana Van Bergh*)], Olive Tell [(*Mrs. Van Bergh*)], Mischa Auer [(*Mischa*)], Marvine Maazel [(*Toscha*)], [Jeanette Gegna (*Momotschka*)], [*Dream sequence*: Frankie Adams, Norman Pringle, R. Saeger, W. Phelps, Walter O'Malley, Arthur Bronson, Dick Stevens, Al Smith, Paul Sautter, Roy Rockwood, J. Harold Reeves, Randall Reynolds, Frank Kneeland, Bob Knickerbocker, J. Kessler, A. J. Cristy, Rudy Caffero, F. Doland, J. Malone, Jack Thireaux, Charles Owens, Bert Le Baron, Harry Lauder, Austin Grout, Will Gordon, B. Gordon, Al Gordon, Carter Gibson, Harry Weil, F. Moorten, Fred Herbert (*Cameramen-singers*)], [Ed Parker, John Dennis, Pete Rasch, Tony Stabenau, Ed Schaefer, Bob Reeves, Kelly Knutsen, Ed O'Neill, Fred Lindstrand, Jack Norbeck, Jack Grant, Charles Hall (*Policemen*)], [Mark Cook, Enrico Cucinelli, Jack Egan (*Reporters*)], [Kenneth Rowley, Durwood von Zeuthen, R. H. Bloem, George Scheller, Harold Erickson, John Westervelt, Allan Watson, William Hargreaves (*Uncle Sams*)].

Musical comedy. [*Not viewed*]. On a ship headed from Europe to America, immigrants sing and have fun in steerage. Heather Gordon, a Scottish woman whose parents have died, is going to live with an uncle in Idaho. Her Russian friend Sascha, who wants to make it as a composer in New York City, is traveling with relatives. Wealthy Americans Larry Beaumont and Diana Van Bergh travel in first-class. Diana's mother wants the two married and Larry has proposed, but Diana has merely stated that she will think about it. Heather and Sascha sneak into the first-class section for some fun, but they are spotted and chased. In the ship's stable, Heather meets Larry and mistakes him for a groom. Sascha and Heather meet up again in the ship's music room, where they are caught by the crew and accused of shipboard thefts. Larry, however, along with his Swedish valet Jansen, vouches for the pair. After Heather has a dream about her arrival in America, in which she is greeted by "Mr. Ellis" and a welcoming committee, who give her the key to the city, the ship arrives at Ellis Island, where Heather discovers that her uncle now refuses to take her in. According to the law, she must be sent back to Europe. Sascha offers to marry her so that she can stay, but she refuses, saying that she doesn't love him that way. Larry cannot see Heather before she departs, but he leaves a letter for her with Diana, whose mother tears it up. While Inspector O'Flynn, who is sent to make sure that Heather stays on the boat, is distracted by Jansen, Heather hides in a horse van, which is lowered directly onto a train. The horse turns out to belong to Larry, and Heather arrives at his mansion just as O'Flynn drives up to question him. Jansen hides Heather, but she is eventually discovered by Larry, who finds out that she never got his letter. Larry offers to help the girl, but she goes away during the night, leaving a note explaining that she cannot accept anything from him. Heather goes to Sascha and his family, who put her to work in a café show disguised as a Russian. Olga, one of Sascha's relatives, sends Larry a telegram explaining where Heather is. O'Flynn almost catches Heather, but he is fooled with the help of Larry, Jansen, and Olga. Diana and her mother show up to invite Heather and the Russians to play at the engagement party for Diana and Larry the following week. Heather, who has fallen in love with Larry, is crushed, and when Sascha proposes to her again, she accepts. The Russians buy them a radio as a wedding present, and they are all listening to Larry's polo game when they hear that he has been injured. Heather rushes to Larry's, where Diana lets her in, but then calls the police. Sascha realizes who Heather really loves and calls off the marriage. Meanwhile, Jansen proposes to Olga and she accepts. Heather escapes with O'Flynn hot on her tail and, after a mad chase around the city, gives herself up. A judge orders her deported, and she is sent to a ship bound for Europe. Larry, however, finally realizes Diana's true nature and rushes to board Heather's ship. On the ship he proposes to Heather, who accepts, and they plan to be married by the captain on the high seas. *Class distinction. Deportation. Immigrants. New York City.*

Romance. Scots. Ships. Wealth. Cafés. Chases. Dreams. Engagements. False accusations. Horses. Judges. Mistaken identity. Mothers and daughters. Parties. Polo. Proposals (Marital). Radio broadcasting. Russians. Swedish Americans. Uncles. Valets.

Note: The plot summary was based on a screen continuity in the Twentieth Century-Fox Produced Scripts Collection, and the onscreen credits were taken from a screen credit sheet in the Twentieth Century-Fox Records of the Legal Department, both of which are at the UCLA Theater Arts Library. This film's working titles were *Sky Line* and *Skyline*. According to information in the legal records, the story was based on a play by Guy Bolton, which had been produced in London, but no other information concerning the play has been located. Also, according to the legal records, Buddy DeSylva was connected with the film's production in some unspecified manner.

The opening credits read, "Janet Gaynor and Charles Farrell in *Delicious* with George Gershwin Music." This was the first film for which George and Ira Gershwin wrote the full score. According to the legal records, the Gershwins were signed to compose eight songs for the film, in addition to the score, including theme and incidental music. The records include an assignment for the song "Mischa-Jascha-Toscha-Sascha," which was not included in the final film. Gershwin's "New York Rhapsody," which was entitled "Rhapsody in Rivets" during production, was highly praised by the critics. *MPH* commented, "Gershwin's 'New York Rhapsody,' which is presented against a striking background of New York life, is an outstanding feature of the production and probably constitutes one of the finest, if not the finest, musical composition originally conceived for motion pictures." *Var* remarked that this composition, "which the composer is booked to play in concert shortly, is mutilated as spotted in sections in this script....Gershwin's new rhapsody is cut in pieces when first used as the musical background in a studio scene, but later gets into full play in a symbolic manner as Janet [Gaynor] wanders through the city in a daze." *NYT* notes that Marvine Maazel played the composition in the film. The work was also entitled "Second Rhapsody." *FD* reported on 5 Jul 1931 that a rehearsal of "Second Rhapsody" had been given under the auspices of NBC. The premiere of the work on New York on Christmas Day, 1931 occurred one day before the opening on Broadway of the Gershwins' musical *Of Thee I Sing*. According to modern sources, the song "Blah-Blah-Blah-Blah with You" was originally entitled "Lady of the Moon" and written for the never produced Florenz Ziegfeld musical *East Is West*, then revised and retitled as "I Just Looked at You" for the musical *Show Girl*, but discarded from that. Modern sources also state that the song "Thanks to You" was written for this film but dropped and that George Gershwin may have played the piano for some of the songs in the film.

According to the legal records, Alfred Cordova was originally cast in the role of "Sascha." The legal records also contain information about a $1,500,000 suit by Corinne Swenson, also known as Marie Manix, for the alleged unauthorized use of her story "Lucky Molly Bawn." The suit was settled in May 1933 when the studio bought the story for $3,000. A *Var* news item, dated 31 Jun 1935, stated that Twentieth Century-Fox was remaking *Delicious* under the title of *The Immigrant*. That title was the working title for the 1936 film *Paddy O'Day*, which starred Jane Withers (see below). While the plot of the later film has similarities to *Delicious*, neither of the writers of the earlier film are credited in connection with *Paddy O'Day*.

FD 5 Jul 1931, p. 5. *FD* 27 Dec 1931, p. 10. *HF* 5 Sep 1931, p. 20. *HR* 1 Dec 1931, p. 3. *HR* 31 May 1933, p. 4. *IP* Jan 1932, p. 32. *MPH* 12 Dec 1931, pp. 35-36. *NYT* 26 Dec 1931, p. 15. *Var* 29 Dec 1931, p. 166. *Var* 31 Jun 1935.

THE DELICIOUS LITTLE DEVIL (Irish Americans)
Universal Film Mfg. Co. *Dist* Universal Film Mfg. Co. May **1919** [©Universal Film Mfg. Co.; 18 Apr 1919; LP13628]. Si; b&w. 6 reels, 5,650 ft.

Pres Carl Laemmle. *Dir* Robert Z. Leonard. *Scen* Harvey F. Thew. *Cam* Allan Zeigler.

Source: Based on the short story "Kitty, Mind Your Feet" by Harvey F. Thew and John B. Clymer (publication undetermined).

Cast: Mae Murray (*Mary McGuire*), Harry Rattenbury (*Patrick McGuire*), Richard Cummings (*Uncle Barnley*), Rudolpho De Valintine (*Jimmie Calhoun*), Ivor McFadden (*Percy*), Bertram Grasby (*Duke de Sauterne*), Edward Jobson (*Michael Calhoun*), William Mong (*Larry*).

Comedy. When Mary McGuire loses her job as a hat check girl, she decides to help her mother, a washerwoman, support her father and uncle, two drinking layabouts, by becoming a dancer. She applies for the job of lead dancer and hostess at a roadhouse cabaret and gets it by pretending to be Gloria De Moin, the notorious Spanish dancer and mistress of the Duke de Sauterne, who, according to the newspapers, recently disappeared. While at the cabaret, Mary constantly has to hide her virtuous past to keep her job. She falls in love with Jackie Calhoun, the son of a millionaire contractor, who is afraid to propose because of her supposed past. Jackie's father tries to end the romance by throwing a party and inviting the duke. When Mary's father and uncle also show up, Jackie's father discovers that he and Mary's father, both Irish, had been bricklayers together, so he agrees to the marriage. *Cabarets. Dancers. Family relationships. Impersonation and imposture. Dismissal (Employment). Hat check girls. Irish Americans. Nobility. Parties. Washerwomen.*

Note: The actor listed as Rudolpho De Valintine later became known as Rudolph Valentino.

ETR 10 May 1919, p. 1771. *MPN* 3 May 1919, p. 2894. *MPW* 26 Apr 1919, p. 577. *Var* 18 Apr 1919, p. 53. *Wid's* 20 Apr 1919, p. 23.

DELIVERANCE (Immigrants)

Helen Keller Film Corp. *Dist* George Kleine. 18 Aug **1919** [©Edwin Leibfreed; 26 Mar 1919; LU13725]. Si; b&w. 9 reels.

Pres Edwin Leibfreed. *Prod* George Foster Platt. *Dir* George Foster Platt. *Story and scen* Dr. Francis Trevelyan Miller. *Titles* Joseph White Farnham. *Cam* Arthur Todd and Lawrence Fowler. *Ed* Joseph White Farnham. *Mus accompaniment arr* Dr. Anselm Goetzl.

Cast: First episode: Little Etna Ross (*Helen Keller*), Edythe Lyle (*Anne Sullivan*), Roy Stewart (*Captain Keller*), Betty Schade (*Mrs. Kate Keller*), Tula Belle (*Nadja*), John Cosgrove (*Nadja's father*), Mary Tolenski (*Nadja's mother*), Joy Montana (*Joy*), Edythe Chapman (*Sarah Fuller*), Jenny Lind (*Pickaninny Martha Washington*), Sarah Lind (*Old Black Mammy*), James Dunn (*Life saver*), James Warfield (*Dr. Alexander Graham Bell*), Davies Thompson (*Rev. Phillips Brooks*), Elmo Lincoln (*Ignorance*), Charlotte Mesreau (*Knowledge*), Harold Judson (*George Washington*).

Second episode: Ann Mason (*Helen Keller*), Edythe Lyle (*Anne Sullivan*), Flora Braidwood (*Nadja*), Josef de Serino (*Josef*), Ivan Tchkowski (*The "old music master"*), Herbert Hayes (*Ulysses*), Thomas Jefferson (*Joseph Jefferson*), James Howarth (*Mark Twain*), Henry Russell (*A Radcliffe professor*),

Third episode: Helen Keller (*Herself*), Mrs. Anne Sullivan Macy (*Herself*), Mrs. Kate Adams Keller (*Herself*), Phillips Brooks Keller (*Helen's brother, himself*), Polly Thomson (*Helen's secretary, herself*), Ardita Mellinino (*The regenerated Nadja*), Parke Jones (*Nadja's son*).

Documentary, Drama. In her infancy, Helen Keller loses her sight and hearing. When Helen is seven, her parents hire Anne Sullivan, who herself was blind for seventeen years, to educate her. Ignorance, depicted as an allegorical figure, seeks Helen as his victim, while Knowledge, a woman robed in white, struggles to raise Helen to the realm of spiritual freedom. Despite Helen's often unmanageable willfulness, the tender care of her parents and Anne's patient instruction enable Helen to learn the names of objects and places through a system of signs. Later, through the efforts of noted educator Sarah Fuller, Helen learns oral speech. Meanwhile, Nadja, the daughter of an immigrant agricultural laborer, is unwilling to take advantage of educational opportunities in her school, and although she has all her faculties, is handicapped by Ignorance. After college, Helen meets some of the distinguished men of her time. Nadja, who works in a sweatshop, is rescued from an unpleasant incident by Josef, an immigrant violinist. They marry, but Josef, worn out by his failure to get work, dies before their child is born. Later, Nadja's child returns from World War I blind, and Nadja takes him to Helen, her childhood friend, for advice. Helen begins hospital work with Nadja to help with the rehabilitation of blind and crippled soldiers. Helen inspires councils dealing with the great world problems, and is seen horseback riding, in an airplane, and christening a ship. She sends words of cheer to farmers, laborers and immigrants. Finally, Helen, Nadja and Josef as a boy appear on horseback leading a great concourse of people in a demonstration of the ideals of the world's new era. *Blindness. Deaf-mutes. Education. Good Samaritans. Helen Keller. Anne Sullivan. Teachers. Sarah Fuller. Hospitals. Immigrants. Moral reformation. Sweatshops. Unemployment. Violinists. War victims.*

Note: Dr. Francis Trevelyan Miller, who wrote the story and scenario, was an historian, editor emeritus of *The Journal of American History* and a friend of Helen Keller. Edwin Leibfreed, the copyright claimant, who presented the version shown in New York, also wrote some insert titles in verse. The film had its premiere in nine reels at the Lyric Theatre in New York on 18 Aug 1919. Dr. Anselm Goetzl of the Metropolitan orchestra, who arranged the accompanying music, conducted the augmented orchestra at the opening. The film was divided into three acts, the first entitled "Childhood," the second "Maidenhood," and the third "Womanhood." According to a news item, director George Foster Platt shot the film in a style that emphasized the playing of scenes as they would be played on stage, and used very few close-ups or "cutaways." After the New York run, George Kleine acquired the distribution rights.

He had the negative of over 40,000 feet recut to various lengths between six and seven reels for the standard version, and ten reels for road shows. He also had new titles written. After test showings in Atlanta, Madison, WI and possibly a few other cities, he planned in Feb 1920 to open the film in Cleveland, Cincinnati and Columbus, OH before releasing it elsewhere, but it is unclear when the film was actually exhibited. George Kleine presented his version which had the subtitle "My Message to the World."

ETR 30 Aug 1919, p. 1089. *MPN* 30 Aug 1919, p. 1843, 1873. *MPN* 14 Feb 1920, p. 1677. *MPW* 23 Aug 1919, p. 1122. *MPW* 30 Aug 1919, p. 1369. *MPW* 21 Feb 1920, p. 1150. *NYT* 19 Aug 1919, p. 10. *Var* 22 Aug 1919, p. 76. *Wid's* 24 Aug 1919, p. 22.

DEM REBNS KOYEKH *see* THE RABBI'S POWER

DEMOCRACY; OR A FIGHT FOR RIGHT *see* INJUSTICE

DENNY FROM IRELAND (Irish Americans)

W. H. Clifford Photoplay Co.; Shorty Hamilton Series. *Dist* State Rights; Ernest Shipman. May **1918**. Si; b&w. 5 reels.

Dir W. H. Clifford. *Scen* W. H. Clifford.

Cast: Shorty Hamilton (*Denny O'Hara*), Ellen Terry (*Eileen O'Connor*), Florence Drew (*Mrs. O'Hara*), Andrew Arbuckle (*Priest*), Pomeroy Cannon (*Sheriff*), Ralph Bell (*Express agent*), Louis Morrison (*Landlord*), U. G. Calvin (*Detective*).

Western, Comedy-drama. As Irishman Denny O'Hara celebrates his marriage to Eileen O'Connor, the landlord evicts his sick mother. After finding her dead, Denny goes after the landlord but discovers that he already has been shot by a poacher. The priest suspects that Denny will be blamed for murder and convinces him to board the next ship for America. Denny settles in Arizona, where he plans to make his fortune and then send for Eileen, but earning it proves so difficult that he decides to rob a shipment of money. Although another robber has preceded him, Denny locates the hidden money and buries it on his ranch, and soon Eileen joins him in Arizona. Before long a detective traces the crime to Denny, but the sheriff, who has made Denny a deputy, declares that the Irishman has found the money and the thieves. Repentant, Denny captures the robbers and turns over the money, thereby clearing his name and his conscience. *Arizona. Immigrants. Ireland. Irish. Murder. Robbery. Sheriffs. Detectives. Eviction. Landlords. Moral reformation. Mothers and sons. Poachers. Priests. Ranches. Thieves.*

Note: Clifford Photoplay Co. first announced the film was available for the state rights market in Dec 1917, but it is unclear whether the film was released at that time. Ernest Shipman, formerly the sales manager of Clifford Photoplay, took over the distribution of the Shorty Hamilton series in mid-1918 and released *Denny from Ireland* in May 1918, when it was reviewed in trade journals. Victor Kremer, general manager of Clifford Photoplay when the film was first announced, bought the distribution rights to the Hamilton series in early 1919 and placed the film on the state rights market again later that year.

MPW 11 May 1918, p. 2860. *MPW* 11 May 1918, p. 896. *MPW* 18 May 1918, p. 1042. *NYDM* 15 Dec 1917, back cover.

DEPORTED (Italian Americans)

Universal-International Pictures Co., Inc. *Dist* Universal Pictures Co., Inc. Oct **1950**; Prod: late Sep—late Nov 1949 [©Universal Pictures Co., Inc.; 16 Nov 1950; LP533]. Sd (Western Electric Recording); b&w. 10 reels, 7,966 ft. 88-89 min. PCA cert no. 14339.

Prod Robert Buckner. *Dir* Robert Siodmak. *Asst dir* Ronnie Rondell. *Scr* Robert Buckner. *Story* Lionel Shapiro. *Dir of photog* William Daniels. *Spec photog* David S. Horsley. *Art dir* Bernard Herzbrun and Nathan Juran. *Film ed* Ralph Dawson and Russell Schoengarth. *Set dec* Russell A. Gausman and John Austin. *Miss Toren's gowns* Orry-Kelly. *Mus dir* Walter KoZcharf. *Sd* Leslie I. Carey and Joe Lapis. *Hair stylist* Joan St. Oegger. *Makeup* Bud Westmore.

Cast: Marta Toren (*Countess Christine di Lorenzi*), Jeff Chandler (*Vic Smith, also known as Vittorio Mario Sparducci*), Claude Dauphin (*Vito Bucelli*), Marina Barti (*Gina Carapia*), Richard Rober (*Bernardo Gervaso*), Silvio Minciotti (*Armando Sparducci*), Carlo Rizzo (*Guido Caruso*), Mimi Aguglia (*Teresa Sparducci*), Adriano Ambrod (*Father Genaro*), Michael Tor (*Ernesto Pampiglione*), Ermino Spalla (*Beniamino Barda*), Dino Nardi (*Donati*), Guido Celano (*Aldo Brescia*), Tito Vuolo (*Postal clerk*).

Gangster, Drama. [*Not viewed*] Gangster Vic Smith is deported from the United States to Italy, where he was born under the name Vittorio Mario Sparducci. After arriving by ship in Naples, Vic is met by Vito Bucelli, an Italian policeman, who informs the gangster that he must leave that afternoon for his home town of Marbella, where he is required to remain for the next thirty days. As he enters a taxicab, Vic meets Gina Carapia, a beautiful young woman who lures him into a trap set by his old henchman, Bernardo Gervaso. Gervaso demands

his "cut" of the $100,000 Vic was convicted of stealing, but Vic insists that he left the money behind in America, and, having served five years in prison as well as being deported for the theft, feels he is entitled to the entire sum. Vic then beats up Gervaso and orders him to stay away. In Marbella, Vic is treated to a hero's welcome, as the townspeople are under the impression that he is a "local boy who made good," and is returning to Italy after completing a mysterious government mission. His uncle, Armando, goes so far as to insist that Vic come to live with him and his family. Soon thereafter, Vic becomes involved with Countess Christine di Lorenzi, a wealthy widow who is responsible for the distribution of American relief supplies to the town's poor. Vic then hatches a plan with Guido Caruso, the head of the local black market, to use his hidden money in America to buy massive amounts of relief supplies, then hijack the shipment and sell the much-needed food and medicine on the black market. When the relief supplies arrive, a great festival is held, and Christine tells the townspeople that Vic is their benefactor. Despite feeling pangs of guilt, Vic still plans to steal the relief supplies until the unexpected appearance of Bucelli, who has come to Marbella to check up on Vic. Afraid that the policeman will rightfully blame him for the hijacking, Vic insists that Caruso call off the heist, but the black marketeer insists on going ahead with the plan. As Caruso and his men enter the warehouse holding the relief materials, Vic is waiting for them and quickly captures Caruso, only to be captured himself by Gervaso, who has recently joined Caruso's gang. Vic is saved, however, by the arrival of Bucelli and the police, who capture Caruso and his gang after a fierce battle. Gervaso is then killed while fighting with Vic after he accidentally overturns a pile of packing cases on top of himself. The next morning, Vic and Bucelli head for the railroad station, as Vic has been summoned to Rome to explain his involvement with Caruso. Christine joins them on board the train, announcing that she is in love with Vic, and despite knowing all about his past, is willing to stand by him in court. *Americans in foreign countries. Deportation. Gangsters. Italian Americans. Italy. Black market. Deception. Hijackers. Love. Naples (Italy). New York City. Royalty. Uncles. Warehouses. Widows.*

Note: According to a *NYT* news item, this film was shot on location in Italy, in the cities of Rome, Naples and Siena. Portions of the film were shot at the seventeenth century villa belonging to Count Ranuccio Bianchi-Bandinelli, a prominent Italian political figure, who reportedly met the filmmakers and offered them the use of his home just outside Siena. The *NYT* article also states that only two Universal contract players—Jeff Chandler and Marta Toren—were used in the film, as producer-writer Robert Buckner cast the remaining roles in Rome. Contemporary sources vary greatly on the spelling of the Italian actors' names. According to the *NYT*, the film's budget was drastically cut by the use of Italian cast and crew members, whose salaries were a fraction of their American counterparts. The *DV* review pointed out the similarity between Jeff Chandler's character "Vic Smith" and Charles "Lucky" Luciano, the noted Italian-American Mafia chief who was deported from the United States to his native Italy in 1946.
AmCin Jan 1950, pp. 10-11, 20. *Box* 28 Oct 1950. *DV* 18 Oct 1950, p. 3. *FD* 19 Oct 1950, p. 6. *HR* 23 Sep 1950, p. 15. *HR* 18 Oct 1950, p. 3. *MPHPD* 21 Oct 1951, p. 537. *NYT* 6 Nov 1949. *NYT* 2 Nov 1950, p. 39. *Var* 18 Oct 1950, p. 6.

THE DEPTHS BELOW see **THE DEVIL'S PLAYGROUND**

DER SPUK UM MITTERNACHT see **NOCHE DE DUENDES**

DER VILNER SHTOT KHAZN see **OVERTURE TO GLORY**

DESERT GOLD (Latino, Native Americans, Yaqui)
Zane Grey Pictures, Inc. *Dist* W. W. Hodkinson Corp. through Pathé Exchange, Inc. 22 Nov **1919** [©Benj. B. Hampton; 20 Sep 1919; LP15775]. Si; b&w. 5-7 reels.
Pres Benjamin B. Hampton and Eltinge F. Warner. *Dir* T. Hayes Hunter. *Asst dir* Claude Camp. *Scen* Fred Myton. *Cam* Abraham Scholtz and A. L. Todd.
Source: Based on the novel *Desert Gold* by Zane Grey (New York, 1913).
Cast: E. K. Lincoln (*Dick Gale*), Margery Wilson (*Mercedes Castanada*), Eileen Percy (*Nell*), W. Lawson Butt (*The Yaqui*), Russell Simpson (*Ladd*), Walter Long (*Rojas*), Arthur Morrison (*Lash*), Edward Coxen (*Captain George Thorne*), Frank Lanning (*Papago Indian son*), Frank Brownlee (*Jonas Warren*), William H. Bainbridge (*Jim Belding*), Laura Winston (*Mrs. Belding*), Mrs. Dark Cloud (*Papago Indian mother*), Mary Jane Irving (*The child*).
Western. Jonas Warren, searching the desert for his daughter, finds the man who took her away, who then produces a marriage certificate to pacify Warren's anger. After the husband finds a gold mine and uses

the certificate to mark it, they die in a sand storm. Later, Dick Gale, an Easterner in search of adventure, rescues his friend Captain George Thorne and the captain's sweetheart, Mercedes Castanada, from the Mexican bandit Rojas. Dick takes Mercedes to the ranch of Jim Belding, where Dick falls in love with Belding's adopted daughter Nell. When Rojas arrives with a band of outlaws, Dick, with the ranch cowboys, escorts Mercedes to the mountains, led by Dick's friend, a Yaqui Indian. After the Yaqui throws Rojas off a cliff and locates a water source for the ranch, he shows Nell the gold mine. The marriage certificate of her parents proves that the mine is hers. Since she now knows she is not illegitimate, she can marry Dick. *Deserts. Gold mines. Marriage licenses. Parentage. Sandstorms. Yaqui Indians. Bandits. Falls from heights. Mexicans. Ranches. Rescues.*

Note: While sources call this both a six and seven reel film, *Wid's* lists its length as 4,785 feet. Zane Grey's novel was serialized in *Popular* magazine, beginning on 1 Mar 1913. The novel was filmed twice again: by Famous Players-Lasky in 1926, with Neil Hamilton starring and George B. Seitz directing, and by Paramount in 1936, with Buster Crabbe starring and James Hogan directing (see below).
ETR 8 Nov 1919, p. 1982. *MPN* 13 Sep 1919, pp. 2247-48. *MPW* 15 Nov 1919, p. 363. *Var* 7 Nov 1919, p. 104. *Wid's* 16 Nov 1919, p. 21.

DESERT GOLD (Latino, Native Americans, Yaqui)
Famous Players-Lasky Corp. *Dist* Paramount Pictures. 19 Apr **1926**; New York premiere: ca21 Mar 1926 [©Famous Players-Lasky Corp.; 20 Apr 1926; LP22626]. Si; b&w. 7 reels, 6,900 ft.
Pres Adolph Zukor and Jesse L. Lasky. *Supv* Hector Turnbull and B. P. Schulberg. *Dir* George B. Seitz. *Scen* Lucien Hubbard. *Photog* Charles Edgar Schoenbaum.
Source: Based on the novel *Desert Gold, a Romance of the Border* by Zane Grey (New York, 1913).
Cast: Neil Hamilton (*Lt. George Thorne*), Shirley Mason (*Mercedes Castanada*), Robert Frazer (*Dick Gale*), William Powell (*Landree*), Josef Swickard (*Sebastian Castanada*), George Irving (*Richard Stanton Gale*), Eddie Gribbon (*One Round Kelley*), Frank Lackteen (*Yaqui*), Richard Howard (*Sergeant*), Bernard Siegel (*Goat herder*), George Rigas (*Verd*), Ralph Yearsley (*Halfwit*), Aline Goodwin (*Alarcon's wife*).
Western. Dick Gale, the fun-loving son of a respectable New York lawyer, is given an ultimatum by his father to either get a job or get out. He goes west, and at the border town of Casita, finds Lieutenant George Thorne, a U.S. Cavalry commander, trapped by Landree, an unscrupulous outlaw and killer, who has plundered the villa of Don Sebastian Castanada, one of the old Spanish land-holders, in an attempt to capture his daughter, Mercedes, whom Thorne loves. She has escaped disguised as a peon boy with the help of an Indian, Yaqui, whom she earlier nursed to health. After Thorne is injured as he and Dick rescue Mercedes, Dick and Mercedes, with Yaqui as their guide, flee into the desert. A sandstorm turns back the villains, their horses are lost, and the Indian guide is injured. Thorne returns to the fort unaware of their plight. They are tracked down by Landree's men; the Yaqui precipitates a landslide, which blocks their path but costs him his life. Thorne rescues the party, and, realizing the love of Dick and Mercedes, relinquishes his own claim on her. *Deserts. Latino. Mexican-American border region. Outlaws. Sandstorms. Yaqui Indians.*

Note: See entries above and below for information on other film adaptations of Zane Gray's novel.
FD 4 Apr 1926. *MPW* 10 Apr 1926. *NYT* 23 Mar 1926, p. 24. *Var* 24 Mar 1926, p. 39.

DESERT GOLD (Native Americans)
Paramount Productions, Inc. *Dist* Paramount Productions, Inc. 27 Mar **1936**; Prod: began 19 Dec 1935; addl shooting: 22 Jan—23 Jan 1936 [©Paramount Productions, Inc.; 27 Mar 1936; LP6250]. Sd (Western Electric); b&w. 6 reels. 58-59 min. Passed by the National Board of Review. PCA cert no. 1931.
Pres ADOLPH ZUKOR. [*Prod* Harold Hurley]. *Assoc prod* William T. Lackey. *Dir* James Hogan. *Scr* Stuart Anthony and Robert Yost. *Photog* George Clemens. *Art dir* Hans Dreier and David Garber. *Ed* Chandler House. *Int dec* A. E. Freudeman. *Sd rec* Walter Oberst.
Source: Based on the novel *Desert Gold, A Romance of the Border* by Zane Grey (New York, 1913).
Cast: Larry "Buster" Crabbe (*Moya, chief of an Indian tribe*), Monte Blue (*Chetley Kasedon*), Glenn Erikson (*Glenn Kasedon*), Frank Mayo (*Bert Lash*), Walter Miller (*Hank Lade*), Raymond Hatton (*Doc Belding*), Marsha Hunt (*Judith Belding*), Robert Cummings (*Fordyce [Ford] Mortimer*), Tom Keene (*Randolph Gale*), [John

Merkyl, Anders Van Haden (*Elders*)], [Si Jenks (*Driver*)], [James P. Burtis (*Sleeping passenger*)], [Ed Thorpe (*Indian*)], [Philip Morris (*Sentry*)], [Willis Marks (*J. T. Winters, assayer*)], [Gertrude Simpson (*Guest*)], [Billy Bletcher], [Robert McKenzie].

Western. [*Print viewed*]. In Arizona, Moya, an Indian schooled in the white man's ways, becomes chief of his small tribe upon his father's death. In town, Moya is approached by Chetley Kasedon, who wants to be made a partner in mining the tribe's hidden gold mine. When Moya refuses, Chet's henchmen trail and kidnap him in order to force him to lead them to the mine, which is located in the Superstition Mountains. Meanwhile, in a stagecoach, Eastern mining engineer Randolph Gale, traveling with his young tenderfoot friend, Fordyce Mortimer, called "Ford," meets Doctor Belding and his daughter Judith, who are returning from Tuscon for Judith's wedding. In town, Randolph then meets Chet, who tells him he is searching for the richest gold mine in that part of the country and advises him that the mine will belong to the first white man who finds it. Chet's brother Glenn, who is familiar with the Superstition Mountains, leads Randolph and Ford into the hills, then leaves them to search for the mine. Upon entering the mountains, Randolph and Ford find Chet whipping Moya. Despite Randolph's protestations, Chet continues the beating, and Moya refuses to reveal the whereabouts of the mine. Under cover of night, Randolph creeps into Chet's mountain camp and takes Moya's bleeding body to Doc. There, Randolph learns that Judith, with whom he has fallen in love, is engaged to Chet, but has stopped wearing her engagement ring. Out of gratitude for saving his life, Moya makes Randolph a member of his tribal family and gives him a thoroughbred horse named "Drako," who was bred by the tribe. Moya also hires Randolph, saying he needs a white man to help make the mine profitable. After Moya shows him the mine, Randolph has Moya's gold specimens analyzed by assayer J. T. Winters, who reports to Chet that Randolph has located the mine. While Chet prepares to marry Judith, his henchman attempts to abduct Randolph and Ford, but Randolph knocks him out and rushes to stop the wedding. With her father's help, Randolph kidnaps Judith in her wedding dress and hides her at Moya's mining camp, where he realizes she loves him. Chet follows with his armed henchmen and opens fire on the camp from behind some rocks, killing an Indian guide who was on his way to retrieve Moya from the village. Judith bravely mounts Drako, who leads her to the Indian village, while Randolph uses dynamite to expose Chet's men. As Randolph fights Chet on a cliff, Moya arrives and shoots him, and he falls to his death, leaving Judith free to marry Randolph. *Claim jumpers. Gold mines. Indians of North America. Romantic rivalry. Thieves. Abduction. Arizona. Assayers. Brothers. Dentists. Dynamite. Engineers. Falls from heights. Gunfights. Horses. Mining towns. Mountains. Physicians. Rescues. Tenderfoots. Toothache. Torture. Tribal chiefs. Weddings. Whips and whippings.*

Note: The title card on viewed print reads: "Zane Grey's *Desert Gold.*" Grey's novel was serialized in *Popular* magazine, beginning 1 Mar 1913. Other versions of Grey's novel include the 1919 film of the same title produced by Zane Grey Pictures, Inc., directed by T. Hayes Hunter and starring E. K. Lincoln and Margery Wilson and the 1926 Paramount film of the same title directed by George B. Seitz and starring Neil Hamilton and Shirley Mason (see above).

DV 19 Dec 1935, p. 7. *DV* 22 Jan 1936, p. 2. *DV* 17 Feb 1936, p. 3. *FD* 8 May 1936, p. 7. *HR* 17 Feb 1936, p. 3. *MPD* 18 Feb 1936, p. 5. *MPH* 8 Aug 1936, p. 42. *Var* 13 May 1936, p. 14.

DESERT PURSUIT (Arab Americans, Native Americans)
Monogram Pictures Corp. *Dist* Monogram Pictures Corp. 11 May 1952; Prod: late Oct—mid-Nov 1951 [©Monogram Pictures Corp.; 21 Apr 1952; LP1659]. Sd; b&w. 6,404 ft. 71 min. PCA cert no. 15668.
Prod Lindsley Parsons. *Assoc prod* Wayne Morris and Ace Herman. *Dir* George Blair. *Asst dir* Rex Bailey. *Scr* W. Scott Darling. *Photog* William Sickner. *Film ed* Leonard Herman. *Ward* Jack Dowsing. *Mus dir* Edward J. Kay. *Sd* Frank Webster and Tom Lambert. *Makeup* Lou Phillipi. *Hair stylist* Hazel Keithley. *Scr supv* Ilona Vas.
Source: Based on the short story "Horse Thieves' Hosana" by Kenneth Perkins in *Blue Book Magazine* (publication date undetermined).
Cast: Wayne Morris (*Ford Smith*), Virginia Grey (*Mary Smith*), Anthony Caruso (*Hassan*), George Tobias (*Ghazili*), John Doucette (*Kafan*), Emmett Lynn (*Leatherface*), Bill Wilkerson (*Young brave*), Robert Bice (*Tomaso*), Gloria Talbot (*Young squaw*), Frank Lackteen (*Priest*).

Western. [*Not viewed*]. Ford Smith has made a valuable gold strike in Nevada and is about to set off for California via Death Valley when his pal, Leatherface, warns him that three Arabs, Hassan, Ghazili and Kafan, intend to attack him and steal his gold. On the eve of his departure, Mary Smith, who has been fired from her job as a blackjack dealer in Carson City because she would not "accomodate" a gambler friend of her employer, rides into Ford's camp. Ford and Mary make plans to cross Death Valley to San Bernardino together but their journey turns into an ordeal and they are overtaken by the three Arabs mounted on camels. Ford and Mary manage to escape but continue to be pursued and are about to lose hope of reaching civilization when they come upon a settlement of Mission Indians holding a Christmas Eve ceremony. The Indians feed and shelter Ford and Mary, but when the Arabs arrive, the Indians are awestruck and receive them as the "Three Wise Men" of the Bible. The Arabs take advantage of the situation and try to force Ford to give them his gold to use as one their "gifts." Instead, Ford gives a handful of gold to the tribal chief conducting the ceremonies. In return for this generosity, the chief provides Ford and Mary with a bodyguard for the rest of their journey. The next day, when the Arabs attack again, Ford, Mary and their Indian friend defeat them, killing two, while the third escapes on his camel. When they reach San Bernardino, Ford and Mary realize that they are in love and decide to marry. *Arabs. California–History. Camels. Christmas. Death Valley (CA). Deserts. Gold. Indians of North America. Missions. Bodyguards. Camps. Chases. Gifts. Gunfights. Religion. Romance. San Bernardino (CA). Tribal chiefs.*

Note: This film's working title was *Starlight Canyon*. According to the *HR* review, the picture includes a foreword which explains that a camel corps, manned by Arabs, was used during the Civil War by Confederate forces attempting to capture California.

Box 26 Jul 1952. *DV* 3 Jul 1952. *HR* 26 Oct 1951, p. 16. *HR* 3 Jul 1952. *MPH* 12 Jul 1956. *Var* 9 Jul 1952.

THE DESERT RIDER (Latino)
Metro-Goldwyn-Mayer Corp.; controlled by Loew's Inc. *Dist* Metro-Goldwyn-Mayer Distributing Corp. 11 May **1929** [©Metro-Goldwyn-Mayer Distributing Corp.; 8 Aug 1929; LP286]. Si; b&w. 6 reels, 4,943 ft.
Dir Nick Grinde. *Scr* Oliver Drake. *Story* Ted Shane and Milton Bren. *Titles* Harry Sinclair Drago. *Photog* Arthur Reed. *Film ed* William Le Vanway. *Ward* Lucia Coulter.
Cast: Tim McCoy (*Jed Tyler*), Raquel Torres (*Dolores*), Bert Roach (*Friar Bernardo*), Edward Connelly (*Padre Quintada*), Harry Woods (*Williams*), Jess Cavin (*Black Bailey*).
Western. "Bandit gang robs rider of pony express of government land grant belonging to Mexican girl. Jed Tyler tracks down the bandits and saves the ranch for the girl." (*MPNBG* 15 Mar 1930, p. 77.). *Bandits. Land rights. Mexicans. Pony Express.*
FD 7 Jul 1929. *Var* 10 Jul 1929, p. 24.

DESERT STATION *see* **APACHE TRAIL**

THE DESERTER *see* **ARROW IN THE DUST**

DESHABILLÉ *see* **DOS MÁS UNO, DOS**

DESPERADOES OF DAKOTA *see* **PHANTOM OF THE PLAINS**

DESPERATE (Czech Americans)
RKO Radio Pictures, Inc. *Dist* RKO Radio Pictures, Inc. Jun **1947**; Prod: late Nov—late Dec 1946 [©RKO Radio Pictures,Inc.; 31 May 1947; LP1069]. Sd (RCA Sound System); b&w. 6,584 ft. 73 min. PCA cert no. 12132.
Prod Michel Kraike. *Dir* Anthony Mann. [*Asst dir* Nate Levinson]. *Scr* Harry Essex. *Addl dial* Martin Rackin. *Story* Dorothy Atlas and Anthony Mann. *Dir of photog* George E. Diskant. *Spec eff* Russell A. Cully. *Art dir* Albert S. D'Agostino and Walter E. Keller. *Film ed* Marston Fay. *Set dec* Darrell Silvera. *Mus dir* C. Bakaleinikoff. *Mus* Paul Sawtell. *Sd* Earl A. Wolcott and Roy Granville.
Cast: Steve Brodie (*Steve Randall*), Audrey Long (*Ann Randall*), Raymond Burr (*Walt Radak*), Douglas Fowley (*Pete*), William Challee (*Reynolds*), Jason Robards ([*Lieutenant Louie*] *Ferrari*), Freddie Steele (*Shorty* [*Abbott*]), Lee Frederick (*Joe* [*Daily*]), Paul E. Burns (*Uncle Jan*), Ilka Gruning (*Aunt Klara*), [Larry Nunn (*Al Radak*)], [Robert Bray, Bill Wallace, Carl Saxe (*Policemen*)], [Carl Kent (*Detective*)], [Carol Forman (*Mrs. Roberts*)], [Erville Alderson (*Simon Pringle*)], [Teddy Infuhr (*Richard*)], [Perc Launders (*Manny*)], [Ralfe Harolde (*Doctor with Walt*)], [Kay Christopher,

Leza Holland (*Nurses*)], [Jay Norris, Michael Visaroff, Ernie Adams (*Villagers*)], [Milt Kibbee (*Mac*)], [Dick Elliott (*Sheriff Hat Lewis*)], [Charles Flynn (*State trooper*)], [Art Miles (*First truck driver*)], [Glen Knight (*Second truck driver*)], [Hans Herbert (*Reverend Alex*)], [Elena Warren (*Mrs. Oliver*)], [Robert Clarke (*Bus driver*)], [Netta Packer, George Anderson (*Train passengers*)], [Don Kerr (*Vendor on train*)], [Frank O'Connor (*Conductor*)], [William Bailey, Marshall Ruth (*Traveling salesmen*)], [Jack Baxley (*Dr. Wilson*)], [Joe Recht (*Bellhop*)], [Eddie Parks (*Mr. Frank*)], [Graham Covert].

Road, Film noir. [*Print viewed*]. On the night of his four-month wedding anniversary, trucker Steve Randall, who has just gotten out of the army, is offered a high-paying job and reluctantly accepts it. When Steve arrives at his pick-up point, however, he discovers that the job involves shipping stolen furs for a gang of thieves, who are led by Walt Radak, an acquaintance of Steve's. After Steve refuses to load the furs, Walt threatens him with a gun, then is surprised by the arrival of a policeman. Steve alerts the officer by flashing his headlights, and the officer begins firing at the gang. In the ensuing chaos, the policeman is shot, and Steve pulls away from the loading platform, causing Al, Walt's younger brother, to fall to the ground. Although Walt and his men, Shorty Abbott, Reynolds and Joe Daily, escape capture, Al is apprehended by the police, and Steve is nabbed by Walt. Furious at Steve for exposing Al, Walt tries to force him to tell the authorities that he made Al participate in the robbery, but Steve refuses and is beaten. After he gives the police Steve's license plate number, Walt threatens to cut Ann, Steve's wife, with a broken bottle. To protect Ann, Steve agrees to go to the police, but as he and Reynolds are pulling up to the station, he knocks Reynolds out and escapes. Steve and Ann are reunited on a west-bound train, but when they discover that Steve's photograph has been published in the newspaper, they get off at the first stop. Walt, meanwhile, becomes determined to find Steve after he learns that Al will probably be executed for the policeman's murder, and hires Pete, a private detective, to track him. After Steve and Ann catch a bus, they spend the night in a hotel, where Ann begs Steve to give himself up. Although Steve refuses to reveal the reason behind his flight, he does agree to go to Ann's aunt Klara and uncle Jan's farm. With his last ninety dollars, Steve buys a dilapidated car from a crooked car salesman and repairs it in his yard. Upon seeing how well the car runs, the salesman refuses to give it to Steve, and Steve is forced to steal it. When the jalopy breaks down on the highway, Steve and Ann, who has just confessed to Steve that she is pregnant, are picked up by a sympathetic man, who turns out to be a sheriff. The sheriff hears about the car theft and is about to return Steve and Ann when he crashes into a tree. Leaving the unconscious sheriff behind, Steve and Ann sneak a ride on a truck and eventually arrive at their relatives' farm. The money-grubbing Pete, meanwhile, shows Walt a recently mailed letter from Klara and Jan inviting Steve and Ann to visit, and Walt pays Pete to go to their farm. At the farm, Steve is finally convinced of Ann's safety and goes to the police. Although Lieutenant Louie Ferrari doubts Steve's story, he allows him to leave in the hope that he will lead the police to the gang. Aunt Klara then insists that Ann and Steve be married in a traditional Czech ceremony, and during the reception, Pete wanders in and spots Steve. When Pete reports back to Walt, he is followed by the police, who begin shooting at the gang. Once again, Walt escapes capture, but is seriously wounded and is bedridden for two months. Just before Ann's baby is due, the revenge-hungry Walt shows up at the farm with Reynolds. Steve and Ann flee in time, but must head for a hospital when Ann goes into labor. Weeks later, Steve, who has resumed work as a truck driver, reads about Al's impending execution and then is shot at by Walt and Reynolds. After Steve sends Ann and his baby to California, where they hope to buy a gas station, he prepares to face Walt. Steve then encounters Ferrari, who informs him that Shorty confessed and attested to Steve's innocence. When Steve returns to his apartment, he is met by a gun-wielding Walt, who tells him he will shoot him in fifteen minutes—midnight—the same time that Al is to die. Minutes before the deadline, however, Ferrari and the police show up, and after pursuing his nemesis to the top floor, Steve shoots and kills Walt. Exonerated by Ferrari, Steve leaves for California. *False accusations. Fugitives. Murder. Newlyweds. Revenge. Robbery. Aunts. Automobile accidents. Brothers. Buses. Czechoslovakian Americans. Farmers. Gunfights. Gunshot wounds. Hospitals. Infants. Police. Pregnancy. Private detectives. Salesmen. Sheriffs. Trains. Truck drivers. Uncles. Veterans. Wedding anniversaries. Weddings.*

Note: The working titles of this film were *Flight* and *Desperate Flight*. According to a Jun 1946 *HR* news item, producer Michel Kraike worked on the picture's script.

Box 17 May 1947. *DV* 15 May 1947. *FD* 20 May 1947, p. 5. *HR* 26 Jun 1946, p. 3. *HR* 22 Nov 1946, p. 27. *HR* 20 Dec 1946, p. 35. *HR* 15 May 1947, p. 3. *MPHPD* 17 May 1947. *Var* 14 May 1947, p. 15.

DESPERATE FLIGHT *see* **DESPERATE**

DEUDOS Y DUENDES *see* **NOCHE DE DUENDES**

THE DEVIL *see* **DRUMS O' VOODOO**

THE DEVIL HORSE (Native Americans)

Hal E. Roach Studios, Inc. *Dist* Pathé Exchange, Inc. 12 Sep 1926 [©Pathé Exchange, Inc.; 6 Mar 1926; LU22462]. Si; b&w. 6 reels, 5,853 ft.

Dir Fred Jackman. *Story* Hal Roach. *Photog* Floyd Jackman and George Stevens.

Cast: Rex (*The Devil Horse*), The Killer (*A Black and White* [*horse*]), Lady (*Herself, a horse*), Yakima Canutt (*Dave Garson*), Gladys Morrow (*Marion Marrow*), Robert Kortman (*Prowling Wolf*), Roy Clements (*Major Morrow*), Master Fred Jackson (*Young Dave*).

Western. A wagon train of Montana settlers is attacked by Indians, and all but young Dave Garson are slaughtered. Years pass, and Dave grows to manhood hating the Indians and shouting for the cavalry. Prowling Wolf, a renegade Indian, kidnaps the major's daughter, and Dave, riding the much-feared Devil Horse, rescues her. The following day, the Indians attack the fort and destroy the ammunition stores. Dave rides for help and, reaching a wagon train, sends shells and powder back to the fort. *Forts. Horses. Indians of North America. Montana. Settlers. United States. Army. Cavalry. Wagon trains.*

MPW 12 Jun 1926.

DEVIL MONSTER (*foreign version*) *see* **EL DIABLO DEL MAR**

THE DEVIL ON HORSEBACK (foreign version) *see* **EL CARNAVAL DEL DIABLO**

DEVIL'S CANYON *see* **FLAMING FEATHR**

THE DEVIL'S CLAIM (Persian Americans)

Haworth Pictures Corp. *Dist* Robertson-Cole Distributing Corp. 2 May 1920 [©Haworth Pictures Corp.; 8 Jun 1920; LU15399]. Si; b&w. 5 reels.

Dir Charles Swickard. *Story and scen* J. Grubb Alexander. *Cam* Frank D. Williams.

Cast: Sessue Hayakawa (*Akbar Khan/Hassan*), Rhea Mitchell (*Virginia Crosby*), Colleen Moore (*Indora*), William Buckley (*Spencer Wellington*), Sidney Payne (*Kemal*), Joe Wray (*Salim*).

Drama. Akbar Khan, a Hindu novelist living in Greenwich Village, uses his love affairs as inspiration for his books. When he exhausts all the story material from his affair with Indora, a young Persian girl, he deserts her. Virginia Crosby, a social worker, takes pity on Indora, who has failed in an attempt to kill Khan, and offers to win him back for her. Virginia pretends to fall in love with Khan and inspires him with tales of the devil's trademark, the emblem of a band of devil worshipers whose hero is named Hassa. In these tales, Hassa and a beautiful Hindu woman lead a series of adventures based upon the motif of devil worship. When Virginia jilts Khan before the last installment of the serial is written, she sends Indora to take her place, and Khan finally discovers his love for her. *Desertion (Marital). The Devil. Hindus. New York City–Greenwich Village. Novelists. Persians. Storytellers. Social workers.*

Note: The working title of this film was *The Devil's Trade-Mark*.

ETR 15 May 1920, p. 2738. *MPN* 22 May 1920, p. 4404. *MPW* 15 May 1920, p. 984. *NYMT* 9 May 1920. *Var* 14 May 1920, p. 35. *Wid's* 16 May 1920, p. 17.

THE DEVIL'S DAUGHTER (African Americans)

Lenwal Productions. *Dist* Sack Amusement Enterprises, Inc. Dec? 1939. Sd (Variray Blue Seal Recording); b&w. 65 min.

Prod Arthur Leonard. *Dir* Arthur Leonard. *Story* George W. Terwilliger. *Photog* Jay Rescher. *Asst cam* Tom Priestley. *Ed* Samuel A. Datlowe. *Ward* Renie. *Mus score* John Killam. *Sd* Dean Cole. *Makeup* Richard Willis. *Narr* Leon Lee. *Loc mgr* Syl Priestley.

Cast: Nina Mae McKinney (*Isabelle Walton*), Jack Carter (*Philip Ramsay*), Ida James (*Sylvia Walton*), Hamtree Harrington (*Percy Jackson*), Willa MacLane (*Elvira*), Emmett Wallace (*John Lowden*).

African American, Jungle, Comedy-drama. [*Print viewed*]. In Jamaica, after a song and a cockfight, Percy Jackson, a Harlem confidence man with dice, tries to win the fighter roosters. However, the Jamaicans catch on to Percy, even though Elvira, Sylvia Walton's servant, likes him. Sylvia also is recently arrived from New York and is the educated younger half sister of Isabelle Walton, who has been running their late father's banana plantation, although he willed it to Sylvia. While she has long been loved by John Lowden, Sylvia now favors her overseer, Philip Ramsay, irritating John. Elvira takes Percy to Isabelle, who is now hiding out in the jungle, and Isabelle tells Percy that his soul has been transferred into a particular pig, which must be protected. Sylvia is unnerved by Jamaican superstitions, and anxious to maintain control of the plantation, Isabelle hopes to scare her into returning to New York. Philip proposes marriage to Sylvia, but she waits to give him her answer, agreeing to meet Isabelle and proposing to split the estate with her. Isabelle wants all or nothing, however, and also wants John's love for herself. Subsequently, Isabelle has Sylvia's drink drugged, so that Isabelle, whose mother was Haitian, can subject her to the obeah blood dance ritual. John overhears Philip planning to leave with Sylvia's money, and after a fight, Philip confesses Isabelle's plans. As Isabelle recites the death incantation, John interrupts the ceremony. Elvira and Percy also arrive on the scene, having spent the evening searching for Percy's "soul" pig, unaware that the cook has already slaughtered it. John reunites the two sisters, and after Isabelle explains to Percy that the pig story was a joke, they all sit down for a meal of roast pork. *African Americans. Half sisters. Jamaica. Rivalry. Superstition. Cock-fighting. Confession. Confidence men. Jungles. Pigs. Plantations. Proposals (Marital). Rites and ceremonies. Romance. Singers. Witchcraft.*

Note: *The Devil's Daughter* was also reviewed under the title *Pocomania*, a word used by "Isabelle" to describe the "obeah." According to *FD*, the picture was filmed in Jamaica. Modern sources specify the location as Kingston, Jamaica, and note that it marked the only time a black American film was made there. Modern sources also, indicate that the production company was Domino Film Corp. Although reviews and modern sources commonly identify "Isabelle" as a practitioner of voodoo, this word is never used in the film. Instead, her supposed magical power is called "obeah."

Exb 13 Dec 1939. *FD* 14 Dec 1939, p. 6. *MPD* 12 Dec 1939, p. 6. *MPH* 9 Dec 1939, p. 74.

THE DEVIL'S DISCIPLE (African Americans)

Micheaux Film Corp. **1925**; Harlem opening: 18 Oct 1925. Si; b&w. Length undetermined.

Prod Oscar Micheaux. *Dir* Oscar Micheaux.

Cast: Evelyn Preer, Lawrence Chenault, Percy Verwayen.

Drama, African American. In Harlem, a beautiful, vain African-American girl falls in love with a degenerate man. She is not able to reform him and is herself dragged down because of him. *African Americans. Love affairs. Moral corruption. New York City–Harlem.*

Note: Scenes of this film were shot in Harlem. In an Mar 1925 interview in *ChiDef*, Oscar Micheaux stated that Paul Robeson, star of Micheaux's earlier film *Body and Soul* (see above) was going to star in this film.

ChiDef 28 Mar 1925, p. 6. *New York Age* 17 Oct 1925, p. 6.

DEVIL'S DOORWAY (Native Americans, Shoshoni)

Metro-Goldwyn-Mayer Corp.; controlled by Loew's Inc. *Dist* Loew's Inc. Sep **1950**; Prod: 15 Aug—mid-Oct 1949 [©Loew's Inc.; 12 May 1950; LP115]. Sd (Western Electric Sound System); b&w. 9 reels, 7,590 ft. 84 min. Passed by the National Board of Review. PCA cert no. 14216.

Prod Nicholas Nayfack. *Dir* Anthony Mann. [*Asst dir* Reg Callow]. *Wrt* Guy Trosper. *Dir of photog* John Alton. *Spec eff* A. Arnold Gillespie. *Art dir* Cedric Gibbons and Leonid Vasian. *Film ed* Conrad A. Nervig. *Set dec* Edwin B. Willis. *Assoc* Alfred E. Spencer. *Cost* Walter Plunkett. *Mus* Daniele Amfitheatrof. *Rec supv* Douglas Shearer. *Hairstyles des by* Sydney Guilaroff. *Makeup created by* Jack Dawn.

Cast: Robert Taylor (*Lance Poole*), Louis Calhern (*Verne Coolan*), Paula Raymond (*Orrie Masters*), Marshall Thompson (*Rod MacDougall*), James Mitchell (*Red Rock*), Edgar Buchanan (*Zeke Carmody*), Rhys Williams (*Scotty MacDougall*), Spring Byington (*Mrs. Masters*), James Millican (*Ike Stapleton*), Bruce Cowling (*Lt. Grimes*), Fritz Leiber (*Mr. Poole*), Harry Antrim (*Dr. C. O. MacQuillan*), Chief John Big Tree (*Thundercloud*), [Tom Fadden (*Bob Trammel*)], [Titus Spencer (*Painter*)], [Vivian Brown (*Mrs. Campbell*)], [Bertha Cody (*Mary*)], [George Sky Eagle (*Lone Bear*)], [Henry Marco (*Jimmy*)], [Dan Foster (*Rancher*)], [Dabbs Greer (*Spud*

Keith)], [Harold A. Deane (*Surveyor*)], [Cecil Smith (*Indian*)], [Frank Conlan (*Telegrapher*)], [William "Bill" Phillips, John Maxwell, Lee Phelps, Roy Butler, Philo McCullough, William Norton Bailey (*Posse*)], [Buddy Messenger].

Western. [*Print viewed*]. Lance Poole, a Shoshone Indian, returns to his home in Medicine Bow, Wyoming, having won the Congressional Medal of Honor for his service in the Civil War. Despite his honorable war record, Lance is shunned by the white townspeople, who bear a grudge against him and his father because of their hold on the richest land in the region. Lance becomes embittered against the white men in Medicine Bow after his father dies because a white doctor refused him prompt medical attention after Lance himself is refused service at a local saloon. When Verne Coolan, a prejudiced lawyer, threatens to take Lance's land away under a new homesteading law, Lance hires Orrie Masters, a female attorney who has recently settled in Medicine Bow, to take his case. Complications soon arise when Lance discovers that, as a ward of the government, he is not entitled to file a claim to keep his land. Orrie tries to circumvent the homesteading law by circulating a petition to allow Lance to keep at least a portion of his land, but Coolan thwarts her attempt by spreading word through town that Lance has killed one of his men. Coolan then assembles an army composed of sheepherders to take the land by force, and a bloody battle ensues. Having suffered great losses in the battle, Lance and his Shoshone Indian fighters take refuge in Lance's cabin, and quickly turn it into a makeshift fortress. After calling in U.S. Cavalry troops and negotiating a truce with the sheepherders, Orrie makes an unsuccessful attempt to persuade Lance to give up his losing fight. Lance refuses to heed Orrie's advice, insisting that it would be shameful to give up his land to the sheepherders, and continues the fight. Lance kills Coolan, but when the Cavalry fighters join the sheepherders, Lance's men are overwhelmed and forced to surrender. Lance is shot during one last skirmish and, in the final moments of his life, gives the Cavalry commander a farewell salute. *Bigotry. Gunfights. Land claims. Shoshoni Indians. Civil War veterans. Congressional Medal of Honor. Death and dying. Fathers and sons. Fortresses. Funerals. Gunshot wounds. Homesteaders. Indians of North America–Reservations. Lawyers. Medicine Bow (WY). Posses. Sheepherders. United States. Army. Cavalry. Women lawyers.*

Note: Two *HR* production charts in mid-Sep 1949 referred to this film as *Devil's Holiday*. Although a Sep 1949 *DV* news item states that Frank McGrath was cast in this film, his participation in the released film has not been confirmed. That same news item adds that location shooting was done around Grand Junction, Colorado.

Box 13 May 1950. *DV* 14 Sep 1949, p. 2. *DV* 15 May 1950, p. 3. *FD* 18 May 1950, p. 6. *HR* 12 Aug 1949, p. 11, 12 *HR* 9 Sep 1949, p. 12. *HR* 7 Oct 1949, p. 10. *MPHPD* 6 May 1950, p. 287. *NYT* 10 Nov 1950, p. 35. *Var* 17 May 1950, p. 6.

THE DEVIL'S HOLIDAY (*foreign version*, 1931) *see* **LA FIESTA DEL DIABLO**

DEVIL'S HOLIDAY (1950) *see* **EVIL'S DOORWAY**

THE DEVIL'S MATCH (African Americans)

Ben Strasser Co. *Dist* American Colored Film Exchange. **1923**; New York showing: 15 Mar 1923. Si; b&w. 5 reels.

Dir Ben Strasser.

Cast: Walter Long (*The minister*), Bobby Smart.

Comedy-drama, African American. A minister attempts to clean up a small town. *African Americans. Ministers. Small town life.*

Billboard 31 Mar 1923.

THE DEVIL'S PLAYGROUND (Latino)

Columbia Pictures Corp. of California, Ltd. *Dist* Columbia Pictures Corp. of California, Ltd. 24 Jan **1937**; Prod: 8 Sep—19 Oct 1936 [©Columbia Pictures Corp. of California, Ltd.; 18 Jan 1937; LP6865]. Sd (Western Electric Noiseless Recording); b&w. 8 reels. 74 min. PCA cert no. 2833.

Assoc prod Edward Chodorov. *Dir* Erle C. Kenton. [*Asst dir* Cliff Broughton]. *Scr* Liam O'Flaherty, Jerome Chodorov and Dalton Trumbo. [*Story* Norman Springer]. *Photog* Lucien Ballard. *Spec camera eff* Ganahl Carson. *Art dir* Stephen Goossón. *Film ed* Viola Lawrence. *Cost* Ernst Dryden. *Mus dir* Morris Stoloff. [*Sd eng* Edward Bernds].

Cast: RICHARD DIX (*Jack Dorgan*), DOLORES DEL RIO (*Carmen*), CHESTER MORRIS (*Robert Mason*), George McKay (*Red Anderson*), John Gallaudet (*Jones*), Pierre Watkins (*Submarine commander*), Ward Bond (*Sidecar Wilson*), Don Rowan (*Reilly*),

Francis McDonald (*Romano*), Stanley Andrews (*Salvage boat commander*), Jimmy Smith, and his orchestra, [Gene Morgan (*Orderly*)], [Arthur Loft (*Damage control officer*)], [Garry Owen (*Radio man*)], [Harvey Clark (*Real estate man*)], [Lucille Ward (*Neighbor lady*)], [James T. Mack (*Minister*)], [Si Jenks (*Telephone man*)], [Miki Morita (*Houseboy*)], [Herbert Ashley (*Bartender*)], [Corbet Morris (*Furniture salesman*)], [Jack Pennick (*Gob*)], [Arthur Stuart Hull (*Rear admiral*)], [Harry Bernard (*Husband*)], [Tina Menard, Blanca Vischer (*Spanish girls*)], [William J. Worthington (*Vice admiral*)], [Art Dupuis (*Dance hall attendant*)], [Nick Copeland (*Ticket taker*)], [Eddie Fetherston, Reginald Simpson (*Sailors*)], [Sammy Blum (*Bartender*)], [Dorothy Dehn (*Girl*)], [Ernest Shield (*Waiter*)], [Frank Marlowe (*Civilian*)], [Wesley Hopper (*Diver*)], [William Arnold, Robert Fiske, Bud Geary (*Officers*)], [Bruce Wong (*Chinese waiter*)], [Edward Hearn (*Surgeon*)], [Lutra Winslow (*Marcia*)], [Buddy Roosevelt (*Deck officer*)], [Ann Doran], [Alma Chester], [Beatrice Curtis], [Ed Hart].

Military, Sea, Drama. [*Print viewed*]. Ace Navy diver, Jack Dorgan and his aide for many years, Robert Mason, are separated when Jack receives orders to relocate to San Diego as a diving instructor and Bob is named chief petty officer of a submarine. In San Diego, Jack is consoled when he realizes his dream of owning a house but soon becomes bored with his new lifestyle and decides to go out for a night on the town. At a dance hall, Jack meets Carmen, a beautiful taxi dancer. Jack is immediately infatuated with Carmen, who tells him a misleading hard-luck story. Jack believes Carmen's story and asks her to marry him. Before they can go on a honeymoon, however, Jack is sent away on a salvage job. Carmen becomes bored and soon returns to her job at the dance hall. One night, Bob, who is on shore leave, visits the dance hall and falls in love with Carmen. Carmen does not reveal her marriage, and she and Bob enjoy one another's company for the remainder of the time that Jack is away. When Jack returns home, he is incensed to find Bob in Carmen's arms and throws Bob out of his house. Back at sea, Bob's submarine collides with an old shipwreck and sinks. Several crew members manage to escape and they alert the Navy. When Jack is called in to rescue the stranded crew, he refuses to help because Bob is on board. Carmen is outraged at Jack's behavior and confronts him, explaining that Bob is not guilty of any wrongdoing. Jack realizes how foolish he has been and rushes to the submarine site, where the trapped men are close to asphyxiation. Attaching an air hose to the submarine, Jack saves Bob and the rest of the crew. After recuperating, Bob and Jack are sent to China, and Carmen returns to the dance hall. *Divers and diving. Marriage. Submarine boats. United States. Navy. Vamps. Dancers. Friendship. Houses. Infidelity. Jealousy. Mexican Americans. Salvage operations. San Diego (CA). Shipwrecks.*

Note: The film's working title was *The Depths Below*. Re-release prints were retitled *Submarine. The Devil's Playground* was a remake of the 1928 Columbia film *Submarine*, directed by Frank Capra and starring Jack Holt (see *AFI Catalog of Feature Films, 1921-30;* F2.5454). The 1931 Columbia film *Fifty Fathoms Deep* was also based on the same story (see below).

DV 6 Dec 1936, p. 3. FD 16 Feb 1937, p. 7. HR 24 Aug 1936, p. 10. HR 19 Oct 1936, p. 34. HR 11 Feb 1937, p. 3. MPD 18 Jan 1937, p. 5. MPH 10 Oct 1936, p. 42. MPH 27 Feb 1937, p. 60. NYT 15 Feb 1937, p. 12. Var 27 Feb 1937, p. 14.

THE DEVIL'S SADDLE (Native Americans, Hopi)
Charles R. Rogers Productions, Inc. *Dist* First National Pictures, Inc. 10 Jul **1927** [©First National Pictures, Inc.; 11 Jul 1927; LP24160]. Si; b&w. 6 reels, 5,488 ft.
Pres Charles R. Rogers. *Dir* Albert Rogell. *Adpt* Marion Jackson and Charles R. Rogers. *Photog* Ross Fisher.
Source: Based on the short story "The Devil's Saddle" by Kenneth Perkins in *Argosy All-Story Weekly* (30 Oct—4 Dec 1926).
Cast: Ken Maynard (*Harry Morrel*), Kathleen Collins (*Jane Grey*), Francis Ford (*Pete Hepburn*), Will Walling (*Sheriff Morrel*), Earl Metcalfe ("*Gentle*" *Ladley*), Tarzan (*A horse*), Paul Hurst ("*Swig*" *Moran*).
Western. "Concerns the early lives of Hopi Indians. Evolves around the invasion of their lands by prospectors. Hero is center of plot of gang of lawless whites to convice Indians he killed one of their number. Finally clears himself." (*MPNBG* 13 Oct 1927, p. 27.) "The strongest situations are those near the end where the hero corners the villain, hog-ties him and delivers him to the Indians... the Indians are seen setting fire to the hero's father's home in revenge for the father's failure to punish the son whom they had thought guilty of the murder; they had demanded the same law for the whites as for the

Indians." (*Har* 13 Aug 1927, p. 130.). *Family relationships. Hopi Indians. Law (Concept). Murder. Prospectors.*

FD 14 Aug 1927. Har 13 Aug 1927, p. 130. MPNBG 13 Oct 1927, p. 27.

THE DEVIL'S TRADE-MARK *see* **THE DEVIL'S CLAIM**

DI QUE ME QUIERES (Spanish language)
William Rowland Productions. *Dist* RKO Radio Pictures, Inc. Nov **1938**; Mexico City opening: 2 Feb 1939; San Juan, Puerto Rico opening: 21 Mar 1939; New York opening: mid-Apr 1939; *Prod:* began 22 Aug 1938 at the Eastern Service Studios, Inc., Astoria, NY. Sd; b&w. 7,591 ft. 84 min. Spanish language.
Prod William Rowland. *Assoc prod* Thomas Allen Moore. *Dir* Robert Snody. *Asst dir* Saul Harrison. *Scr* Francisco J. Ariza. *Orig story* William Rowland and Robert Snody. *Photog* William Miller and Bill Kelly. *Mus dir* Nathaniel Shilkret.
Song(s): "Lejos de mi tierra," "No sé por qué te quiero," "Calientito," "El mariachi," "Duerme" and "Di que me quieres," words and music by Nilo Menéndez, Terig Tucci and Rubén F. de Olivera.
Cast: Jorge Lewis (*Carlos Madero*), Eva Ortega (*Mercedes García*), Paul Ellis (*Rafael*), Martín Garralaga (*M. Desparrat*), Azucena Maizani (*Actuante*), Rosita Ríos (*Nina*), Ramiro Gómez (*Manuel López*), Manuel de Moya (*Rullan*), "Don Mario" (*Maestro de ceremonias*), "Don Alberto", Julián Benedet, Lita Santos, Alfonso Pedroza, Alberto Camacho, Francisco Carmona, Leopoldo Gutiérrez, José Hernández, Hernán Belmonte, Francisco Madrid, Benjamin Rico, *Song and dance numbers featuring:* Don Julio, Monna Montes, Gloria Belmonte, Joyita y Maravilla, Dan Carthay, Dorita y Varela, Hermanos Duval, Mildred y Maurice.
Musical. [*Not viewed*]. Carlos Madero, a composer of popular songs, puts to good use a twenty-five dollar tip given anonymously to him by his secret admirer, Mercedes Garcia. Soon Carlos' fortune increases, enabling him to travel to New York. Eventually, Carlos is able to open a luxurious nightclub. The owner of five similar establishments plans to take advantage of the fact that Carlos doesn't have much money and tries to appropriate the nightclub to add it to his own chain. A soft-hearted gambler comes to Carlos' aid, however, and gets the money necesssary to stop Carlos' ambitious rival. Mercedes drives to New York in search of her fortune and goes to Carlos' nightclub when she gets a job as a singer with a band. Finally, she and Carlos fall in love. *Lure of the city. New York City. Nightclubs. Singers. Songwriters. Business competition. Gamblers. Good Samaritans. Romance.*
Note: Working titles of this film were *Cara o cruz* and *La fascinadora*. The *NYT* review translated the film's title as *Say That You Love Me.*

CM Nov 1938, p. 564. HR 3 Sep 1938, p. 9. Imparcial Films 25 Sep 1939. MPD 17 Aug 1938, p. 15. MPD 31 Aug 1938, p. 4. NYT 24 Apr 1939, p. 13.

EL DÍA QUE ME QUIERAS (Spanish language)
Exito Productions, Inc. *Dist* Paramount Pictures, Inc. **1935**; Havana, Cuba opening: 5 Jul 1935; San Juan, Puerto Rico opening: 11 Jul 1935; New York opening: 23 Aug 1935; *Prod:* Jan 1935 at the Eastern Service Studios, Inc. in Astoria, Long Island [©Exito Productions, Inc.; 16 Apr 1935; LP5473]. Sd (Sistema Sonoro "Western Electric" a prueba de ruidos [Western Electric Sound System]); b&w. 9 reels. 82 min. PCA cert no. 765. Spanish language.
[*Supv* Robert Snody]. *Dirección de* [*Dir*] John Reinhardt. [*Asst dir* Fred Scheld]. [*Guión y argumento original*] [*Scr and orig story*] Alfredo Le Pera. *Fotógrafo* [*Photog*] William Miller. *Dirección musical de* [*Mus dir*] Terig Tucci. *Supervisor técnico* [*Tech supv*] Samuel E. Piza.
Song(s): "El día que me quieras," "El tango dramático," "Guitarra mía," "Jurar en vano," "Volver," "Mi suerte es negra" and "Sus ojos se cerraron," music by Carlos Gardel, lyrics by Alfredo Le Pera; "Bajo el cielo tropical (Sol tropical)," music by Terig Tucci, lyrics by Alfredo Le Pera.
Cast: CARLOS GARDEL (*Julio Argüelles* [*/Julio Quiroga*]), ROSITA MORENO (*Margarita/Marga*), Tito Lusiardo (*Rocamora*), Manuel Peluffo (*Saturnino*), Del Campo (*Daniel Dávila*), José Luis Tortosa (*Sr.* [*Pedro*] *Dávila*), Fernando Adelantado (*Carlos "Argüelles"*), Susanne Dulier (*Pepita*), Celia Villa (*Juanita*), [Giulio de Capua (*Opera enthusiast*)].
Melodrama, with songs. [*Print viewed*]. Julio Argüelles, the son of a very rich Buenos Aires businessman, prefers to devote his career to Creole music and song and, with a couple of friends, forms the trio

"Los Gorjeadores." Determined to live his own life, Julio opposes his father's plans and, instead of marrying an heiress, decides to take his chances with Margarita, a dancer, and breaks all contact with his family. Living in poverty and with his young daughter Marga to support, Julio, in desperation, goes to his father's house to ask for the money necessary to save his wife who is deathly ill. Pedro Dávila, in charge of business affairs for his father, surprises Julio stealing, and although he escapes, Julio returns too late to save his wife. Years later, Marga has become a pretty young woman, a dancer like her late mother. Julio has become successful in a large part of the world under the surname Quiroga. En route to Buenos Aires, the Dávila family find themselves on the same boat as Marga and Julio. Daniel, the manager's son, falls in love with Marga during the voyage, and although he discovers the singer's past, this cannot obstruct the happiness of the two young people. *Dancers. Family relationships. Musicians. Poverty. Buenos Aires (Argentina). Businessmen. Creoles. Disease. Heiresses. Marriage. Motion picture studios. Romance. Thieves.*

Note: *NYT* gave the English translation of the title as "The Day You Love Me." Actor and singer Carlos Gardel died in an airplane accident in Colombia on 24 Jun 1935, according to *Var*, which noted that he had planned to make two further films for Paramount. According to some sources, Agustín Cornejo and Alberto Infanta were also in the cast, but their participation in the film has not been confirmed.

CM Jun 1935, p. 340. *NYT* 27 Aug 1935, p. 23.

EL DIABLO DEL MAR (Spanish language)
Theater Classic Pictures. **1936**; Mexico City opening: 12 Dec 1935; New York opening: 27 Mar 1936; Prod: Feb 1935 at the Argosy and Mascot studios. Sd; b&w. 6,180 ft. 65 min. Spanish language.
Prod S. Edwin Graham. *Dir* Juan Duval. *Orig story* Thelma Brooks and Terry Grey. *Scr* Juan Duval and Terry Grey. *Spanish dial* Manuel París. *Photog* H. O. Carleton. *Mus* Emilio Osta.
Cast: Ramón Pereda (*José*), Movita Castañeda (*Maya*), Carlos Villarías (*El capitán*), Barry Norton (*Roberto*), Carmen Bailey, Julia Bejarano, Ramón Muñoz, Daniel F. Rea, Antonio Cabrera.
Sea, Adventure. [*Not viewed*]. [The following plot summary is based on the English-language version of this film, *Devil Monster*; character names refer to that version. For further information regarding the English-language version, please see the note below and the entry for *Devil Monster* in the *AFI Catalog of Feature Films, 1931-40*.] José Francisco has been missing at sea for six years. His mother sees a newspaper story that suggests there may be survivors of the wreck on a distant island. She asks Robert, who has fallen in love with José's girl friend Louise, to check the islands when he is on a tuna fishing expedition with his father. Louise holds out hope that José is still alive. Robert and his father find José on one of the islands, where he has gained the natives' respect as a skilled fisherman. He is in love with the local chief's daughter and unwilling to return to civilization, so Robert, his father and the crew members abduct José. He is assigned to help look for tuna, and he eventually takes them to a productive area, where they encounter the "devil monster," a giant manta ray. Robert is knocked overboard, but José goes to his rescue even though he suspects that Robert wishes to marry Louise. In the rescue, José loses an arm. The boat returns to harbor, and José is reunited with his mother and girl friend. *Fishermen. Islands. Missing persons. Mobulidae. Mothers and sons. Romantic rivalry. Abduction. Rescues. Shipwrecks. Tribal chiefs. Tribal life.*

Note: The title of this Spanish-language version was translated in reviews as "The Sea Devil." The actor listed in the Spanish version as Antonio Cabrera may have been the same as Donato Cabrera, who was in the English language version. For information on the English-language version, *Devil Monster*, which was directed by S. Edwin Graham and starred Barry Norton and Blanche Mehaffey, please see the entry for that film in the *AFI Catalog of Feature Films, 1931-40*, F3.1029.

FD 2 Apr 1936, p. 12. *NYT* 1 Apr 1936, p. 29.

EL DIABLO SE DIVIERTE *see* **EL CARNAVAL DEL DIABLO**

DIAMOND HANDCUFFS (African Americans)
Cosmopolitan Productions. *Dist* Metro-Goldwyn-Mayer Distributing Corp. **5 May 1928** [©Metro-Goldwyn-Mayer Distributing Corp.; 5 May 1928; LP25253]. Si; b&w. 7 reels, 6,057 or 6,070 ft.
Dir John P. McCarthy. *Adpt* Willis Goldbeck. *Story* Carey Wilson. *Cont* Bradley King. *Titles* Joe Farnham. *Photog* Henry Sharp. *Film ed* Sam S. Zimbalist. *Set des* Alexander Toluboff. *Ward* David Cox.
Source: Based on the short story "Pin Money" by Henry C. Vance in *Snappy Stories* (2 Dec 1921).

Cast: Act I: Lena Malena (*Musa*), Charles Stevens (*Niambo*), **Cast—Act II:** Lena Malena (*Musa [as a maid]*), Conrad Nagel (*The Husband, John*), Gwen Lee (*The Wife, Cecile*), John Roche (*The Friend, Jerry Fontaine*), **Cast—Act III:** Lena Malena (*Musa [as a cafe dancer]*), Eleanor Boardman (*Tillie*), Lawrence Gray (*Larry*), Sam Hardy (*Spike*).
Drama. Three stories dealing with the pursuit of a diamond that brings only misfortune to its owner: I. In South Africa, a mine worker loses his life for stealing a diamond he has found. Before he dies, he gives the stone to Musa, a local girl. II. The gem becomes known as the Shah diamond and ends up in a New York City jewelry store window, where Cecile, an upper-class matron, admires it. Her husband leaves her when he discovers that Jerry, a family friend, has given Cecile the diamond, under the pretense that it is a glass trinket. Musa, now Cecile's maid, is again the recipient of the gem. III. The diamond is stolen by a gang of thieves. Tillie, the roughly-treated "woman" of Spike, café owner and gangster, admires the diamond. Larry, who really loves her, secretly gives her money to go to a sanitarium in order to cure her lung disease. Instead, Tillie uses the money to buy the diamond. That night, Spike is killed when police raid his café, and a black dancer named Musa dies from a bullet wound she receives while trying to retrieve the diamond. Tillie accepts a modest diamond from Larry and becomes his wife. *African Americans. Dancers. Diamonds. Gangsters. Maids. New York City. South Africa. Tuberculosis.*

MPW 2 Jun 1928. *Var* 11 Jul 1928, p. 25.

DIAMOND IN THE HAYSTACK *see* **TOP O' THE MORNING**

DIANE OF STAR HOLLOW (Italian Americans)
C. R. Macauley Photo Plays. *Dist* Producers Security Corp. Mar **1921**. Si; b&w. 6 reels.
Dir Oliver L. Sellers. *Scen* Joseph Farnham. *Photog* Lucien Tainguy.
Source: Based on the short story "Diane of Star Hollow" by David Potter (publication undetermined).
Cast: Bernard Durning (*Sgt. Pat Scott*), Evelyn Greeley (*Diane Orsini*), George Majeroni (*Alessandro Orsini*), Fuller Mellish (*Father Lorenzo*), George E. Romain (*D. Crispi*), Freeman Wood (*Dick Harrison*), Al Hart (*Hanscom*), Louis J. O'Connor (*Sheriff*), Joseph Gramby (*Pietro*), Sonia Marcelle (*Carlotta Orsini*), Charles Mackay (*Dr. Ogden*), May Hopkins (*Jessie*), Julia Neville (*Jessie's mother*).
Crime, Melodrama. Patrick Scott, local chief of state constabulary, loves Diane Orsini, whose father, a rich Italian, is suspected of being head of the Black Hand. Scott is detailed to obtain evidence and capture the gang and its leader. This investigation results in several tense situations—the last one an all-out gun fight in which Pat is injured and Orsini's henchmen are killed. Pat later recovers both his health and Diane, and Orsini, having incurred his daughter's animosity and seen his empire destroyed, commits suicide. *Black Hand (United States). Gunfights. Italian Americans. Secret societies. Suicide.*

FD 10 Apr 1921. *Var* 29 Apr 1921, p. 41.

DIANE OF THE GREEN VAN (Native Americans, Seminole)
Winsome Stars Corp. *Dist* Robertson-Cole Co. through Exhibitors Mutual Distributing Corp. 6 Apr **1919**. Si; b&w. 5 reels, 4,800 ft.
Pres F. Laws Hutton. *Dir* Wallace Worsley. *Scen* Thomas J. Geraghty. *Cam* Robert Newhard.
Source: Based on the novel *Diane of the Green Van* by Leona Dalrymple (Chicago, 1914).
Cast: Alma Rubens (*Diane Westfall*), Nigel Barrie (*Philip Poynter*), Lamar Johnstone (*Carl Granberry*), Josephine Crowell (*Aunt Agatha*), Harry von Meter (*Baron Tregar*), Wedgwood Nowell (*Prince Ronador*), Ed Brady (*Themar*), Alfred Hollingsworth (*Micco*), Irene Rich (*Keela*), Sydney Hayes.
Drama. Diane Westfall, the heiress to the Westfall millions, seeks adventure in a green van to escape her boredom. Unknown to her, however, four men pursue her: her cousin Carl, who wants her inheritance; Baron Tregar of the Balkan country of Houdania, who is looking for the rightful heir to his country's throne and thinks that it may be Diane because of a document Carl found; Prince Ronador, who was foiled in his attempt to kill Diane to get control of the throne, and thus is trying to marry her; and Philip Poynter, an American friend of the Baron's, who falls in love with Diane and tries to protect her. Diane discourages Philip's attentions after the Prince

denounces him, but when she gets to the Everglades, she learns from the Seminole medicine man Mic-co that Philip is the only one who loves her for herself. She marries Philip after Mic-co reveals that he is her father and the heir to the Houdania throne but he wanted to escape the position. *Adventurers. Balkan Peninsula. Everglades (FL). Heiresses. Imaginary lands. Long-lost relatives. Seminole Indians. Cousins. Medicine men. Nobility. Usurpers.*

Note: This was the first film produced by Alma Rubens' company, Winsome Stars Corporation. The film was shot in Brunton studios in Los Angeles and in the Florida Everglades using Seminole Indians in minor roles.

ETR 19 Apr 1919, p. 1525. *MPN* 5 Apr 1919, p. 2140. *MPW* 19 Apr 1919, p. 429. *Var* 11 Apr 1919, p. 55. *Wid's* 16 Mar 1919, p. 9.

DIARY OF THE SANTA FE *see* SANTA FE TRAIL

DICK TURPIN *see* EL CABALLERO DE LA NOCHE

DIMPLES (Racial impersonation)

Twentieth Century-Fox Film Corp.; Darryl F. Zanuck in charge of production. *Dist* Twentieth Century-Fox Film Corp. 16 Oct **1936**; New York opening: week of 9 Oct 1936; Prod: early May—mid-Jun 1936 [©Twentieth Century-Fox Film Corp.; 16 Oct 1936; LP6956]. Sd (Western Electric Noiseless Recording); b&w. 8 reels, 7,108 ft. 78 min. PCA cert no. 2352.

Assoc prod Nunnally Johnson. *Dir* William A. Seiter. *Asst dir* Booth McCracken. *Scr* Arthur Sheekman and Nat Perrin. [*Orig idea* Nunnally Johnson]. *Photog* Bert Glennon. *Art dir* William Darling. *Film ed* Herbert Levy. *Set dec* Thomas Little. *Cost* Gwen Wakeling. *Mus dir* Louis Silvers. *Dance dir* Bill Robinson. *Sd* Eugene Grossman and Roger Heman.

Song(s): "Hey, What Did the Blue Jay Say," "He Was a Dandy," "Picture Me Without You" and "Dixie-anna," music and lyrics by Jimmy McHugh and Ted Koehler; "Wings of the Morning," spiritual, music by Jimmy McHugh.

Cast: SHIRLEY TEMPLE (*Dimples Appleby*), Frank Morgan (*Prof. Eustace Appleby*), Robert Kent (*Allen Drew*), Helen Westley (*Mrs. Caroline Drew*), Stepin Fetchit (*Cicero*), Astrid Allwyn (*Cleo Marsh*), Delma Byron (*Betty Loring*), The Hall Johnson Choir (*Choir*), Berton Churchill (*Colonel Loring*), Paul Stanton (*Mr. St. Clair*), Julius Tannen (*Hawkins*), John Carradine (*Richards*), Billy McClain (*Rufus*), Jack Clifford (*Uncle Tom*), Betty Jean Hainey (*Topsy*), Arthur Aylesworth (*Pawnbroker*), Leonard Kibrick, Warner Weidler, Walter Weidler, George Weidler (*Children's band*), Jesse Scott, Thurman Black (*The Two Black Dots*), [Herman Bing (*Proprietor*)], [Greta Meyer (*Proprietor's wife*)], [Robert Murphy, Fred Kelsey, A. S. "Pop" Byron, Herbert Ashley (*Policemen*)], [Harry McCrillis, Ed Cook, Walter Dennis, Alex Hirshfeld (*Additional members of children's band*)], [Margaret Bloodgood (*Mrs. O'Casey*)], [Francis McDonald, Douglas Fowley (*Strangers*)], [Fred Silva (*Call boy*)], [Fred Wallace (*Usher*)], [Edward LeSaint, Homer Dickinson, Wilfred Lucas (*Creditors*)], [Martin Turner (*Coachman*)], [David Thursby (*Customer*)], [William H. Turner (*Doorman*)], [Charles Tannen (*Box office man*)], [Maybelle Palmer].

Historical, Show business, Musical, Comedy-drama. [*Print viewed*]. In the New York of 1850, "decent folk' are beginning to tolerate the theater, while "young radicals" argue against slavery. Dimples Appleby, who leads a band of children street singers, lives with her grandfather, Professor Eustace Appleby, an old actor down on his luck who now teaches acting, singing and birdcalls, and who has resorted to petty theft, rumors of which Dimples refuses to believe. The children perform at the Drew estate uptown, and Dimples is apprehended trying to escape after furs are discovered to be missing. Informed of this, the professor returns with the furs and reports that he valiantly fought a thief to get the furs back. Before leaving, Dimples sees the professor snatch a cuckoo clock. The next day, she returns it to Mrs. Caroline Drew and says that she stole it herself. The kindly Mrs. Drew is interrupted in her talk with Dimples when she learns that her beloved nephew Allen is breaking his engagement with Betty Loring, the daughter of Mrs. Drew's friend, Colonel Loring, because of his infatuation with actress Cleo Marsh. Shocked, Mrs. Drew, who hates the theater, orders Allen to break with the actress, and Allen sadly says he will leave his aunt's home. After he goes, Dimples sees Mrs. Drew crying. Mrs. Drew takes Dimples back to the professor's shabby quarters and asks him to let Dimples live with her for the girl's sake. Dimples overhears her offer the professor $5,000, and after Mrs. Drew leaves, Dimples tearfully asks

the professor not to sell her, whereupon he vows he would not do that for all the money in the world. Although cut off financially from his aunt, Allen has enough savings to produce the first performance of *Uncle Tom's Cabin*. He auditions Dimples for the role of "Eva," and hires the professor as his assistant. After the professor loses Allen's last $800 to a gang of con-artists, Allen's creditors threaten to have someone put in jail if the company does not pay its bills. To save her grandfather, Dimples agrees to live with Mrs. Drew for the $5,000. When the professor calls on Mrs. Drew for the money, he finds Dimples crying because she is lonesome without him, and he returns Mrs. Drew's check. Before he leaves with Dimples, however, he convinces Mrs. Drew, who is attentive to his flirtations, that a worthless watch which he got from the conmen was given to Napoleon by Josephine and accepts $1,000 from Mrs. Drew for the watch. As the play is about to begin without Cleo, who left Allen when his money was gone, Dimples brings Betty, whose father forbade her to attend, to see Allen backstage. Meanwhile, Colonel Loring declares the watch to be a fake, and with police in tow, Mrs. Drew and the colonel arrive at the theater to have the professor arrested. To avoid them, the professor dons an "Uncle Tom" costume and in blackface, performs the role until the actor cast as "Uncle Tom" also appears onstage in blackface. The professor is arrested upon exiting the stage, but the police, Mrs. Drew and Colonel Loring agree to remain until the end of the play rather than disrupt it. Moved to tears by Eva's deathbed scene, as played by Dimples, Mrs. Drew calls the play beautiful and tells the police to let the professor go. A year later, after a performance, Allen, now with Betty, announces to an audience which includes the professor, who kisses Mrs. Drew's shoulder, the first presentation in New York of a minstrel show, in which Dimples is starred. *Actors and actresses. Grandfathers. New York City–History. Uncle Tom's Cabin (Novel). Wards and guardians. Aunts. Confidence men. Engagements. Minstrel shows. Self-sacrifice. Thieves.*

Note: The first treatment of this film was entitled "Under the Gaslight." During production, the title of the film was changed from *Dimples* to *The Bowery Princess*, but it was changed back before the film's release. The following cast suggestions were listed in material in the Twentieth Century-Fox Produced Scripts Collection at the UCLA Theater Arts Library: W. C. Fields as "Professor Eustace Appleby"; Edna May Oliver as "Mrs. Caroline Drew"; Michael Whalen as "Allen Drew"; Claude Gillingwater as "Colonel Loring"; Warren Hymer as "Patrolman"; and Borrah Minevitch and His Gang. A *HR* news item from Dec 1935 states that Twentieth Century-Fox was negotiating with Paramount to borrow Fields for the film. Joseph Cawthorn is listed as a cast member in a *HR* production chart; his participation in the final film has not been confirmed. The copyright music register lists the song "Oh, Mister Man Up in the Moon," by Ted Koehler and Jimmy McHugh as having been written for this film, but it was not included in the final film. Stepin Fetchit's name is not in the opening or closing credits of the video release of the film, but his name was included in the opening and closing credits of the 1936 release. In a *NYT* article, Bill Robinson was quoted saying about Shirley Temple, "The kid might not be a perfect tap dancer, but I want 'em to find me another her age who could learn five of my routines in a week." In a modern source, Frank Morgan was quoted saying about Temple that "she is the greatest actress I ever played with."

Box 3 Oct 1936. *DV* 23 Sep 1936, p. 3. *FD* 26 Sep 1936, p. 7. *HR* 21 Dec 1935, p. 3. *HR* 11 May 1936, p. 13. *HR* 8 Jun 1936, p. 8. *HR* 23 Sep 1936, p. 3. *MPD* 24 Sep 1936, p. 12. *MPH* 27 Jun 1936, p. 52. *MPH* 17 Oct 1936, p. 47. *NYT* 10 Oct 1936, p. 21. *Var* 14 Oct 1936, p. 15.

DINTY (Chinese Americans, Irish Americans)

Marshall Neilan Productions. *Dist* Associated First National Pictures, Inc. 29 Nov **1920** [©Marshall Neilan Productions; 3 Jan 1921; LP16312]. Si; b&w. 6-7 reels, 6,587 ft.

Prod Marshall Neilan. *Dir* Marshall Neilan and John McDermott. *Asst dir* Tom Held and George Dromgold. *Scen* Marion Fairfax. *Story* Marshall Neilan. *Cam* David Kesson, Charles Rosher and Foster Leonard. *Art dir* Ben Carré. *Film ed* Daniel Gray. *Cutter* Bessie Mason. *Cont man* Charles Smith.

Cast: Wesley Barry (*"Dinty" O'Sullivan*), Colleen Moore (*Doreen O'Sullivan*), Tom Gallery (*Danny O'Sullivan*), J. Barney Sherry (*Judge Whitely*), Marjorie Daw (*Ruth Whitely*), Pat O'Malley (*Jack North*), Noah Beery (*Wong Tai*), Walter Chung (*Sui Lung*), Kate Price (*Mrs. O'Toole*), Tom Wilson (*Barry Flynn*), Aaron Mitchell (*Alexander Horatius Jones*), Newton Hall (*The tough one*), Young Hipp (*Wong Tai's son*), Hal Wilson.

Drama. Upon arriving in San Francisco from Ireland, Doreen O'Sullivan discovers that her husband has been killed in an accident. To support herself and her infant son Dinty, Doreen labors as a scrub woman until, at the age of twelve, Dinty becomes the family's breadwinner by selling newspapers. Meanwhile, in Chinatown,

wealthy opium smuggler Wong Tai kidnaps Judge Whitely's daughter in retribution for the judge's sentencing of Wong Tai's son to prison. Dinty, whose work as a newsboy has familiarized him with the Chinese underworld, leads the police to Wong Tai's hideout and saves the judge's daughter from a torturous death. To show his gratitude, Judge Whitely adopts Dinty, whose mother recently had succumbed to tuberculosis, and Dinty begins life anew. *Abduction. Adoption. Chinese Americans. Immigrants. Irish Americans. Newsboys. Rescues. San Francisco (CA). San Francisco (CA)–Chinatown. Charwomen and cleaners. Judges. Mothers and sons. Opium. Revenge. Smuggling. Tuberculosis.*

Note: Some scenes in this film were shot in San Francisco. The estate of A. B. Spreckles, located in San Francisco, was used as a background in the film. According to a news item, Marshall Neilan directed the Chinatown scenes, while John McDermott directed the Irish scenes.

ETR 4 Dec 1920, p. 18. *MPN* 5 Jun 1920, p. 4658. *MPN* 13 Nov 1920, p. 3699. *MPN* 4 Dec 1920, p. 4345. *MPN* 11 Dec 1920, pp. 4398-99. *MPW* 11 Sep 1920, p. 196. *MPW* 4 Dec 1920, p. 640. *MPW* 18 Dec 1920, p. 901. *MPW* 25 Dec 1920, p. 1072. *NYMT* 28 Nov 1920. *NYR* 27 Nov 1920. *NYT* 22 Nov 1920, p. 13. *NYTr* 22 Nov 1920. *Var* 26 Nov 1920, p. 34. *Wid's* 28 Nov 1920, p. 9.

EL DIOS DEL MAR (Spanish language)

Paramount Publix Corp. *Dist* Paramount Publix Corp. Oct **1930**; Los Angeles opening: 17 Oct 1930; Prod: mid—late Aug 1930. Sd (Sistema Western Electric); b&w. 8 reels, 6,444 ft. 72 min. Spanish language.

[*Supv* Geoffrey Shurlock]. [*Dir* Eduardo Venturini]. [*Asst dir* William Kaplan and H. Hamm]. *Dirección de diálogo* [*Dial dir*] Paco Moreno. *Versión española* [*Spanish version*] J. Carner-Ribalta. *Argumento* [*Story*] John Russell. *Fotografía* [*Photog*] David Abel. [*2d cam* George Clemmons and Dan Fapp]. [*Unit mgr* Jack Voshell]. [*Props* Joe Youngerman].

Source: Based on the short story "The Lost God" by John Russell in *Where the Pavement Ends* (New York, 1919).

Cast: Ramón Pereda (*Leandro Dupré*), Rosita Moreno (*Mariana*), Julio Villarreal (*Korff*), Manuel Arbó (*Pancho*), Paco Moreno (*Gil*), José Peña "Pepet" (*Nick, el perlero*).

Adventure, Sea. [*Not viewed*]. Captain Leandro Dupré, skipper of the schooner "Niña bonita," is having the worst streak of bad luck since he arrived in the Melanesian Islands seeking his fortune. After losing all of his savings gambling, and breaking up with his girl friend, Mariana, he has also lost the schooner in a race against rival captain Korff when he stopped to rescue a castaway. While Korff celebrates his victory, the castaway insists upon rewarding Leandro with a handful of pearls and tells him where he can find more. Later, as soon as Leandro has recovered his boat by selling the pearls, he sets sail secretly and heads for a group of islands inhabited by cannibals. Mariana stows away on board. From inside a diving suit, Leandro marvels at the amazing pearl bed he discovers, without realizing that, above, Korff has followed him and is preparing to take over his boat. However, the cannibals counterattack, rout Korff's men and prepare to sacrifice Mariana and Leandro's crew. When Leandro emerges from the depths, however, encased in the diving suit, the cannibals think that this strange monster must be the sea god and obey Leandro's orders to release the crew. *Adventurers. Cannibalism. Divers and diving. Pearl diving. Schooners. Sea captains. Castaways. Gods. Human sacrifice. Melanesia. Pearls. Racing. Rescues. Romance. Stowaways. Traders. Wagers.*

Note: This film is a Spanish-language version of the 1930 Paramount film, *The Sea God*, which was directed by George Abbott and starred Richard Arlen and Fay Wray (see *AFI Catalog of Feature Films, 1921-30*; F2.4861). The onscreen credits were derived from a studio cutting continuity. According to contemporary sources, cinematographer Lionel Lindon may have shot the underwater sequences.

Cinl Dec 1930, p. 30. *CM* Jan 1931, p. 22.

DIPLOMANIACS (Native Americans)

RKO Radio Pictures, Inc. *Dist* RKO Radio Pictures, Inc. 12 May **1933**; New York opening: week of 28 Apr 1933; Prod: late Feb—late Mar 1933 [©RKO Radio Pictures, Inc.; 28 Apr 1933; LP3868]. Sd (RCA Photophone System); b&w. 7 reels. 59 or 63 min.

Exec prod Merian C. Cooper. *Assoc prod* Sam Jaffe. *Dir* William A. Seiter. [*Asst dir* Ed Killy]. *Scr* Joseph L. Mankiewicz and Henry Myers. *Orig story* Joseph L. Mankiewicz. *Photog* Edward Cronjager. [*2d cam* Harry Wild and Robert De Grasse]. [*Asst cam* Charley Burke and George Diskant]. *Settings* Van Nest Polglase and Al Herman. *Film ed* William Hamilton. *Mus dir* Max Steiner. *Dance numbers staged by* Larry Ceballos. *Rec* John E. Tribby.

Song(s): "Sing to Me," words and music by Harry Akst and Edward Eliscu; "Annie Laurie," traditional.

Cast: BERT WHEELER [(*Willy Nilly*)], ROBERT WOOLSEY [(*Hercules Glub*)], Marjorie White [(*Dolores*)], Louis Calhern [(*Winklereid*)], Phyllis Barry [(*Fifi*)], Hugh Herbert [(*Chow-Chow*)], Edgar Kennedy [(*Presiding delegate*)], Richard Carle [(*The captain*)], William Irving [(*Schmerzenpuppen*)], Neely Edwards [(*Puppenschmerzen*)], Billy Bletcher [(*Schmerzenschmerzen*)], Teddy Hart [(*Puppenpuppen*)], Charles Coleman [(*The butler*)], Edward Cooper [(*Chief Adoop*)], Dewey Robinson [(*Luke the Hermit*)].

Comedy. [*Print viewed*]. Dimwitted barber Willy Nilly confuses the instructions of his partner, Hercules Glub, and instead of finding a spot for their barbershop where they would have no competition, he locates the business on an Oklahoma Indian reservation, where they are guaranteed no customers. After shaving Luke the Hermit, the only local resident with facial hair, Willy and Hercules are whisked away by a group of oil-rich Adoop Indians, whose Oxford-educated chief offers them a million dollars to represent the tribe at the Geneva peace talks. If they succeed in promoting peace, the Chief tells them, they will receive another million dollars; if they fail, however, they will be killed. Forcefully persuaded, Willy and Hercules sail for Geneva with the Chief's secret papers. Also on board the steamship are Winklereid, an evil "conspirator," who plots with the equally evil Chow-Chow and the cellophane-wrapped, virgin-vamp Dolores, to steal the diplomats' money and the Chief's papers. While Dolores plies her vampish wares on Willy, Hercules gets drunk with Winklereid and the ship's tippling captain, who drunkenly steers the boat in endless circles. After a record-breaking eight-month voyage, Willy and Hercules arrive in Paris, where Hercules becomes the target of Fifi, another vamp. At last in Geneva, Hercules and Willy are spied upon by Winklereid and his cohorts, Schmerzenpuppen, Puppenschmerzen, Schmerzenschmerzen and Puppenpuppen. Protected by the omniscient Adoops, Willy and Hercules, who have prepared an impromptu peace treaty, survive the conspirators' assassination attempts and arrive safely at the conference. During their unique "harmony-among-nations" speech, Winklereid tosses a bomb into the room, which explodes and blackens the faces of all present. After the war-loving delegation sings a song of peace, Winklereid, determined to ensure a continuing market for his employer's explosive bullets, steals Willy's treaty and forges the names of the delegates on it. Willy and Hercules, believing that they have succeeded, return to America, only to discover that war has been declared and that they have been drafted. *Barbers and barbershops. Conspiracy. Diplomats. Indians of North America. Peace. War. Ammunition. Bombs. Drunkenness. Forgers and forgery. Geneva (Switzerland). Hermits. Indians of North America–Reservations. Military service. Compulsory. Money. Oklahoma. Paris (France). Peace conferences. Sea captains. Steamboats. Thieves. Treaties. Vamps.*

Note: The working title of this film was *In the Red*.

FD 27 Mar 1933, p. 4. *FD* 29 Apr 1933, p. 3. *HF* 25 Feb 1933, p. 12. *HR* 8 Apr 1933, p. 2. *IP* Mar 1933, p. 20. *MPD* 29 Apr 1933, p. 4. *MPH* 15 Apr 1933, pp. 29-30. *NYT* 29 Apr 1933, p. 14. *Var* 4 May 1933, p. 12.

DIPLOMÁTICO DE SALÓN see DON JUAN DIPLOMÁTICO

DIRTY GERTIE FROM HARLEM, U.S.A. (African Americans)

Sack Amusement Enterprises. *Dist* State Rights. **1946**. Sd; b&w. 5,374 ft. 60 min.

Pres ALFRED N. SACK. *Prod* Bert Goldberg. *Dir* Spencer Williams. *Orig story and scr adapt* True T. Thompson. *Dir of photog* John L. Herman. *Asst cam* Gordon Yoder. *Art dir* Ted Solomon. *Props* J. L. Block. *Sd eng* Dick Byers. *Makeup* Frillia.

Cast: Francine Everette (*Gertie LaRue*), Don Wilson (*Diamond Joe*), Kathrine Moore (*Stella Van Johnson*), Alfred Hawkins (*Jonathan Christian*), Boykin (*Ezra Crumm*), L. E. Lewis (*Papa Bridges*), Inez Newell (*Mama Bridges*), Piano Frank (*Larry*), John King (*Al*), Shelly Ross (*Big Boy*), Hugh Watson (*Tight Pants*), Don Gilbert (*Manager*), Spencer Williams (*Old Hager*), July Jones, and Howard Gallaway, 6-Harlem Beauties-6 (*Specialties*).

African American, Island, Drama. [*Print viewed*]. When famous Harlem stripper Gertie LaRue arrives on the island of Rinidad, she is given celebrity treatment and taken to the Paradise Hotel, where she and her assistant, Stella Van Johnson, are placed in the posh bridal suite. The hotel's proprietor, Diamond Joe, is smitten with Gertie, but Gertie ignores Stella's suggestion that she take an interest in him.

Meanwhile, in their private dormitory room, members of Gertie's troupe discuss Gertie's past relationship with a generous Harlem man named Al, whom Gertie treated poorly and deserted. Also staying at the hotel is the pious Mr. Jonathan Christian and his assistant Ezra Crumm, two missionaries who have come to the island to teach about sin. Having witnessed Gertie's flirtatious behavior on the boat, Mr. Christian tells Ezra that she is a "painted trollop." Gertie remains true to her reputation as a gregarious flirt when she joins a sailor named Tight Pants and a soldier named Big Boy for a drink at the Diamond Palace lounge. There, Larry, the bar's piano player, recognizes Gertie and plays a tune intended to stir memories of her troubled past in Harlem and her relationship with his friend Al. When Gertie returns to the hotel drunk and in the company of the two military men, Mr. Christian watches in horror as she kisses both of them. He also sees Gertie throw a liquor bottle at a hallucination of Al that has suddenly haunted her. Gertie faints when Mr. Christian emerges from the shadows, and when she regains consciousness, she misinterprets his actions and accuses him of trying to take advantage of her. Later that day, Gertie, having been spooked by bad omens since her arrival on the island, goes to a fortune teller, an old woman named Old Hager, who looks into her crystal ball and sees Gertie's misdeeds and has a vision of a man coming after her. However, neither the medium's portents nor Mr. Christian's best efforts to have the Diamond Palace shut down prevent Gertie from taking the stage and performing her striptease. During her act, Mr. Christian, who has been watching the show with interest, takes to the stage and orders an end to the show. A brawl ensues when he grabs Gertie, but Diamond Joe whisks her out of the club and takes her back to the hotel. Alone in her room, Gertie is unhappy with the image she has caught of herself in the mirror, and while she is thinking, Al bursts into the room from the balcony and shoots her. When Stella and the police rush into the room, Al tells them that he killed her because he loved her. *African Americans. Burlesque dancers. Femmes fatales. Islands. Missionaries. Romantic obsession. Drunkenness. Entertainers. Fortune-tellers. Hallucinations. Hotels. Musicians. New York City–Harlem. Shootings. Strip-tease.*

Note: Although the viewed print contained a copyright statement by True Thompson, the film was not listed in the *Catalog of Copyright Entries* for motion pictures. As noted in modern sources, the storyline of the film is loosely based on W. Somerset Maugham's short story "Miss Thompson," in *The Smart Set* (Apr 1921). The short story was adapted for the stage by John Colton and Clemence Randolph as *Rain* (New York, 7 Nov 1922), and adapted for motion pictures several times. For information on other film adaptations of the story, consult the entry for the 1932 Lewis Milestone-directed United Artists release of *Rain*, starring Joan Crawford (see *AFI Catalog of Feature Films, 1931-40*; F3.3606). Although contemporary reviews or an exact release date for the film have not been located, a completed script of the film was submitted to NYSA in 1947. A modern source states that this film was made in Fort Worth, San Antonio and Dallas, TX. A phonograph recording of "Blues in the Night" by Harold Arlen and Johnny Mercer is heard in the film.

DISTANT DRUMS (Native Americans, Seminole)

United States Pictures, Inc. *Dist* Warner Bros. Pictures, Inc. 29 Dec **1951**; Prod: late Mar—late May 1951 [©United States Pictures, Inc.; 17 Dec 1951; LP1380]. Sd (RCA Sound System); col (Technicolor). 9,052 ft. 100-101 or 103 min. PCA cert no. 15280.

Prod Milton Sperling. *Dir* Raoul Walsh. [*Asst dir* Russ Saunders]. *Scr* Niven Busch and Martin Rackin. *From a story by* Niven Busch. *Dir of photog* Sid Hickox. *Technicolor col consultant* Mitchell Kovaleski. *Art dir* Douglas Bacon. *Film ed* Folmar Blangsted. *Set dec* William Wallace. *Ward* Marjorie Best. *Orch* Murray Cutter. *Mus* Max Steiner. [*Comp of percussion composition* Ray Heindorf]. *Sd* Oliver S. Garretson. *Makeup artist* Gordon Bau. [*Double for Gary Cooper* Slim Talbot].

Cast: GARY COOPER [(*Capt. Quincy Wyatt*)], Mari Aldon [(*Judy Beckett*)], Richard Webb [(*Lt. Richard Tufts*)], Ray Teal [(*Private Mohair*)], Arthur Hunnicutt [(*Monk*)], Robert Barrat [(*General Zachary Taylor*)], [Clancy Cooper (*Sgt. Shane*)], [Larry Carper (*Chief Ocala*)], [Dan White (*Cpt. Peachtree*)], [Mel Archer (*Pvt. Jeremiah Hiff*)], [Angelita McCall (*Amelia*)], [Lee Roberts (*Pvt. Tibbett*)], [Gregg Barton (*Pvt. James Tasher*)], [Sheb Wooley (*Pvt. Jessup*)], [Warren MacGregor (*Pvt. Sullivan*)], [George Scanlan (*Bosun*)], [Carl Harbaugh (*Duprez*)], [Beverly Brandon (*Mme. Duprez*)], [Sidney Capo (*Indian boy*)].

Historical, War, Drama. [*Print viewed*]. In 1840, seven years after the beginning of the Seminole Indian war in Florida, U.S. Army General Zachary Taylor sends for naval officer Lieutenant Richard Tufts from the North to undertake a special mission to defeat the Indians. Upon his arrival in Florida, Tufts meets his scout, Monk, who guides him through the alligator-ridden swamp to the island home of the mission's commander, Capt. Quincy Wyatt, a reclusive widower and an expert swamp fighter. After bidding farewell to his five-year-old son, whose mother was a Creek princess, Wyatt goes with Tufts and Monk to Army headquarters, where they receive their official instructions from General Taylor and inspect their troops. Wyatt and his company then pursue the first objectives of their mission—to recapture a western fortress taken by the Seminoles and free the white prisoners being held captive there. No sooner do Wyatt and his men free the prisoners, among whom is the beautiful Judy Beckett, than they are pursued by the Seminoles and forced to abandon their plans to board a rescue boat on Lake Okeechobee. Wyatt commands his forces to beat a hasty retreat deep into the Everglades, where a brush fire is set to hold back the approaching Indians. The fire keeps the Indians temporarily at bay, but things look bad for Wyatt when the drumbeat of the Indian battle cry is sounded and the platoon is faced with little room for escape. Thinking quickly, Wyatt decides to send his platoon with Sgt. Shane, while he and Tufts stay behind to build canoes, which will be used to rendezvous with the platoon at the Indian burial grounds. During this time, a romance is sparked between Wyatt and Judy, who tells Wyatt that she is intent on returning to Savannah to take revenge upon the man who killed her father. When the canoes are completed, Wyatt, Tufts and Judy journey to the burial grounds, but Shane and the platoon are not there when they arrive. They decide to wait, but the only person who emerges from the darkness is Monk, who arrives with news that the platoon has been ambushed and massacred by the Seminoles. Meanwhile, General Taylor, fearing that Wyatt's platoon has met its demise in the Florida swamps, calls off his search for the fighters and orders his men to rescue Wyatt's son. When Wyatt and the others finally make it to Wyatt's island, they find it burned out and the boy missing. Fearing that his son is dead, Wyatt decides to end his retreat and fight his attackers. After he defeats Chief Ocala, the Seminole chief, in a daring underwater fight, the rest of the Seminole warriors capitulate and flee in fear. Wyatt's success is made sweeter when General Taylor safely delivers his son and Judy decides to stay with him on the island. *Everglades (FL). Indians of North America. Romance. Seminole Indians. Seminole War, 2d, 1835-1842. United States. Army. Alligators. Explosions. Fathers and sons. Fires. Forts. Graves. Indians of North America–Mixed blood. Islands. Lakes. Officers (Military). Prisoners. Recluses. Rescues. Snakes. Soldiers. Swamps. Zachary Taylor. Widowers.*

Note: *Distant Drums* includes the following written epilogue: "This picture was photographed in the heart of the Florida Everglades, at Silver Springs and at Castillo de San Marcos in the Southeastern National Monuments through the courtesy of the United States Department of the Interior, National Park Service." According to contemporary news items, United States Pictures used the title of Dan Totheroh's play *Distant Drums*, which it had purchased in 1946, for this film, even though the play, which was filmed in 1946 as *South of St. Louis*, bears no resemblance to the film.

The character of "Chief Ocala" may have been based on the real-life Seminole chief, Chief Osceola, who led the battle against the United States during the second Seminole war and was captured by the Americans while surrendering. The second war between the Seminoles and the United States was sparked when a majority of the Seminole Indian chiefs in Florida refused to honor the treaty of removal signed by a small number of Seminole chiefs. For more information about Osceola, see entry below for *Naked in the Sun*. Studio publicity material in the *AMPAS* production file indicates that Mel Archer, a long distance swimming champion, and David Rochlen, a Santa Monica, CA, lifeguard, were given roles in the film because of their underwater expertise. Although Archer is credited in the picture, Rochlen's appearance in the released film has not been confirmed.

The file for the film in the MPAA/PCA Collection at the *AMPAS* Library contains a letter dated 20 Mar 1951 from PCA director Joseph I. Breen to producer Milton Sperling in which Breen urged Sperling to change the opening narration of film. The narration apparently referred to the Seminole Indians as "more vile than the rattlesnakes" and "sadistic and bloodthirsty." Breen suggested that "something far less derogatory should be substituted, in order to avoid justified complaint." According to a May 1951 article in *AmCin*, a camera vehicle called the "swampmobile" was used to shoot scenes in inaccessible areas of the Florida Everglades. Modern sources add Kenneth MacDonald to the cast. Modern sources note the similarities between *Distant Drums* and Raoul Walsh's 1945 World War II picture *Objective, Burma!*.

AmCin May 1951, p. 206. *Box* 8 Dec 1951. *DV* 29 Nov 1951, p. 3. *FD* 29 Nov 1951, p. 6. *HR* 23 Mar 1951, p. 11. *HR* 25 May 1951, p. 11. *HR* 29 Nov 1951, p. 3. *LADN* 29 May 1951. *MPHPD* 1 Dec 1951, p. 1126. *NYT* 26 Dec 1951, p. 19. *Var* 5 Dec 1951, p. 6.

THE DIVIDING LINE *see* **THE LAWLESS**

THE DIVINE YOUNG LADY *see* **THE AMAZING MRS. HOLLIDAY**

A DIVORCE OF CONVENIENCE (Latino)
Selznick Pictures Corp. *Dist* Select Pictures. May **1921** [©Selznick Pictures Corp.; 8 May 1921; LP16545]. Si; b&w. 5 reels, 4,995 ft.
Dir Robert Ellis. *Scen* Sarah Y. Mason. *Story* Victor Heerman. *Photog* Alfred Gondolfi.
Cast: Owen Moore (*Jim Blake*), Katherine Perry (*Helen Wakefield*), George Lessey (*Senator Wakefield*), Nita Naldi (*Tula Moliana*), Frank Wunderley (*Blinkwell Jones*), Dan Duffy (*Mr. Hart*), Charles Craig (*Mr. Holmes*).
Domestic, Comedy. Spanish coquette Tula Moliana finds herself encumbered with two husbands, and in order to get a divorce from the first, Senator Wakefield, she engages Jim Blake, the fiancé of Helen, the senator's daughter, to be her corespondent. Jim agrees to help her but finds himself entangled in a web of deceit and has difficulty in making excuses to Helen for the numerous adventures in which he becomes involved, especially when his life is threatened by a jealous rival pursuing Tula. Matters are cleared up when Helen discovers he has been victimized, and Tula accepts her first husband.
Bigamy. Divorce. Spaniards. United States. Congress.

DIXIE (African Americans)
Paramount Pictures, Inc. *Dist* Paramount Pictures, Inc. **1943**; New York opening: 23 Jun 1943; Prod: 26 Oct 1942—5 Jan 1943 [©Paramount Pictures, Inc.; 24 Jun 1943; LP12571]. Sd (Western Electric Mirrophonic Recording); col (Technicolor). 9 reels, 8,065 ft. 88-89 min. Passed by the National Board of Review. PCA cert no. 8953.
[*Exec prod* B. G. DeSylva]. *Assoc prod* Paul Jones. *Dir* A. Edward Sutherland. [*Asst dir* Alvin Ganzer]. [*2d asst dir* H. Kaplan]. [*2d unit asst dir* Henry Kessler]. [*Dial dir* L. Allen]. *Scr* Karl Tunberg and Darrell Ware. *Adpt* Claude Binyon. *Story* William Rankin. [*Contr wrt* Barney Dean and Arthur Phillips]. [*Contr wrt for "Blind man gag"* Leo Sherin]. *Dir of photog* William C. Mellor. [*2d unit cam* Loyal Griggs]. [*2d unit asst cam* Frank Dugas]. *Spec eff* Gordon Jennings. *Process photog* Farciot Edouart. *Technicolor color dir* Natalie Kalmus. *Assoc* Morgan Padelford. *Art supv* Hans Dreier. *Art dir* William Flannery. *Ed* William Shea. *Settings* Raoul Pène duBois. *Set dec* Ray Moyer. *Cost* Raoul Pène duBois. [*2d unit men's ward* Fred Starnes]. [*2d unit women's ward* Irmgard Batchler]. *Mus dir* Robert Emmett Dolan. *Vocal arr* Joseph J. Lilley. *Mus asst* Arthur Franklin. *Dances staged by* Seymour Felix. [*Asst dance dir* A. Mann]. [*Asst to Seymour Felix* B. Goodstein]. [*Dance coach and asst to Seymour Felix* George Dobbs]. [*Dance coach to Bing Crosby* S. Ledner]. [*Dance rehearsal pianist* E. Frazier]. *Sd rec* Earl Hayman and John Cope. *Makeup artist* Wally Westmore. [*2d unit makeup* Max Asher]. [*Hair supv* Leonora Sabine]. [*2d unit hair* Maudlee McDougal]. [*Dial coach* Frances Dawson]. [*Scr clerk* Grace Dubray]. [*Unit mgr* H. Schwartz]. [*Loc mgr* N. Lacey]. [*2d unit grip* Jack Frances, H. Murray, W. Collins, Ed Manriquez and Paul Way].
Song(s): "If You Please," "Kind'a Peculiar Brown," "She's from Missouri," "A Horse That Knows the Way (Back Home)" "Laughing Tony," "Sunday, Monday or Always" and "Miss Jemima Walks By," music by James Van Heusen, lyrics by Johnny Burke; "Buffalo Gal (Won't You Come Out Tonight?)" music and lyrics by William Cool White; "Oh! Dem Golden Slippers," music and lyrics by James Bland; "Turkey in the Straw," traditional; "Swing Low, Sweet Chariot," music and lyrics by Henry Thacker Burleigh; "Roll Out! Heave Dat Cotton," music and lyrics by W. M. Hays; "Shew! Fly, Don't Bother Me," music by Frank Campbell, lyrics by Billy Reeves; "Jimmy Crack Corn (The Blue Tail Fly)," music and lyrics attributed to Daniel Decatur Emmett.
Cast: Bing Crosby [(*Daniel Decatur Emmett*)], Dorothy Lamour [(*Millie Cook*)], Marjorie Reynolds [(*Jean Mason*)], Billy De Wolfe [(*Mr. Bones*)], Lynne Overman [(*Mr. Whitlock*)], Raymond Walburn [(*Mr. Cook*)], Eddie Foy, Jr. [(*Mr. Pelham*)], Grant Mitchell [(*Mr. Mason*)], [Clara Blandick (*Mrs. Mason*)], [Tom Herbert (*Homer*)], [Olin Howlin (*Mr. Devereaux*)], [Robert Warwick (*Mr. La Plant*)], [Stanley Andrews (*Mr. Masters*)], [Norma Varden (*Mrs. La Plant*)], [Hope Landin (*Mrs. Masters*)], [James Burke (*River boat captain*)], [George H. Reed (*Lucius*)], [Jimmy Conlin, George Anderson, Harry C. Bradley, William Halligan (*Publishers*)], [Wilbur Mack (*Asst. in publisher's office*)], [Henry Roquemore (*Man in audience*)],

[Brandon Hurst (*Dignified man in audience*)], [Sam Flint (*Southern colonel*)], [Dell Henderson (*Stage manager*)], [Harry Barris (*Drummer*)], [Isabel Randolph (*Woman in Maxwell Theatre*)], [Joe Cunningham (*Man in Maxwell Theatre*)], [Fortunio Bonanova (*Waiter in restaurant*)], [Brandon Hurst (*Man in restaurant*)], [Josephine Whittell (*Woman in restaurant*)], [Willie Best (*Steward*)], [Paul McVey (*Headwaiter, 1st restaurant*)], [Charles La Torre (*Captain of waiters*)], [Charles R. Moore (*News vendor*)], [Tom Kennedy (*Barkeeper*)], [Charles Cane, Edward Emerson, Cyril Ring (*Firemen*)], [Dudley Dickerson (*Black boiler room attendant*)], [Harry Tyler (*Blind man*)], [Carl Switzer (*Boy*)], [John "Skins" Miller, Donald Kerr, Fred Santley, Warren Jackson, Jimmy Ray, Hal Rand, Charles Mayon, Allen Ray, Jerry James, James Clemons (*Specialty members of minstrel show*)], [Ethel Clayton].
Biography, Musical. [*Print viewed*]. In the mid-1800s in Ohio, Daniel Decatur Emmett, who works at a feed store but yearns to be a performer, is romancing his fiancée, Jean Mason, when they hear the fire alarm ringing. They discover that Jean's house has burned down because of Dan's careless placement of his 3orncob pipe. Jean's father refuses to allow Dan to marry Jean unless he earns $1,000 within the next six months. To this end, Dan takes a ferry headed for New Orleans, and during the ride he meets Mr. Bones, an accordion-playing opportunist. Bones cheats Dan of his $500 inheritance in a rigged card game and then disappears. Not to be outsmarted, Dan places an advertisement in a New Orleans newspaper for an accordion player, and when Bones responds to the ad, Dan attempts to force him into returning his money. The money has already been spent, however, so Bones promises to make Dan a partner in his next venture. Bones takes Dan to a boardinghouse run by Mr. Cook, who is sympathetic to actors, and his daughter Millie, who resents her father's leniency. Cook gets Bones a paying audition at the Maxwell Theatre, and Millie insists that Bones's friends and fellow boarders, Dan, Whitlock and Pelham, perform with him so that they can all pay their rent. Unfortunately, both Dan and Bones got black eyes during an altercation at a restaurant where they were unable to pay their bill. Millie suggests that they paint their faces to cover up their black eyes and go as black men. The audition is a rousing success, and Millie and Dan fall in love. Two weeks later, Bones sells the Maxwell Theatre his idea for a new show featuring twenty-four performers. Dan writes all the music for the minstrel show, but his conscience troubles him because of his engagement to Jean, and he snubs Millie. Bones takes advantage of Millie's situation and proposes to her, and she accepts. On opening night, the theater burns down because Dan is again careless with his pipe, and they thereby lose their jobs. Dan recognizes that Millie is his true love and reunites with her, but as he is out of work, he decides to return home and break off his engagement with Jean. When he discovers that Jean has been permanently paralyzed by a debilitating illness, however, he writes to Millie, breaking off their engagement, and marries Jean. The newlyweds move to New York with the hope that Dan can sell his music there. One day, Mr. Cook visits their apartment and tells Jean about Dan's previous engagement to Millie. When Dan returns that day having sold ten of his songs for only $100, Jean insists that they move to New Orleans so that he can rejoin his friends in a show there. Millie is furious that her father has brought Dan back to the boardinghouse until she sees that Jean is disabled, and gains new respect for him. When Dan and Bones learn that Devereaux, the owner of the opera house where they want to book their show, likes to gamble, they arrange a game with him. Bones wins the card game, and they intimidate Devereaux, a snob who does not think their show is worthy of his establishment, into giving them a booking. Devereaux later insists that he will cancel the show if the opening night is not successful. Jean meanwhile watches Dan and Millie carefully, and, heartbroken when she detects intimacy between them, decides to leave Dan. On opening night, Jean sends a letter to Dan backstage, which she hopes he will find after the show, informing him that she is leaving him so that he and Millie can be together. Millie notices Jean crying during one of Dan's love songs, and discovers Jean's note backstage. Millie burns the note and tells Jean that she has just become engaged to Bones. Unknown to Millie, the burning letter was not completely extinguished and has started a fire backstage. As Dan performs his slow ballad, "Dixie," he sees stageworkers offstage trying to extinguish the fire. Dan starts singing faster and faster and draws the entire chorus into the song. The audience, previously

unaffected by the show, becomes roused by the moving tribute to the South, and sings along. The fire is extinguished, the show is a huge success, and Jean and Dan remain happily married. *Composers. Daniel Decatur Emmett. Marriage. Minstrel shows. Musicians. Southerners. Actors and actresses. Boardinghouses. Engagements. Fathers and daughters. Fires. Gambling. Infidelity. Music publishers and publishing. New Orleans (LA). Ohio. Paralysis. Proposals (Marital). Racial impersonation. Self-sacrifice.*

Note: Southerner Daniel Decatur Emmett, who was born in Ohio in 1815, was best known as the composer of the song "Dixie." Modern historians indicate that Emmett was an abolitionist, however, the song became an unofficial anthem for the Confederacy during the Civil War. As depicted in the film, Emmett was one of the originators of blackface entertainment in the theatre. In New York in 1843, Emmett, Billy Whitlock, Frank Pelham and Frank Brower performed in blackface, billing themselves as the Virginia Minstrels. This is the first known performance in which blackface performers were called minstrels, although blackface performances were common in circuses. Although dancer Louis Da Pron is listed in the CBCS as a "Minstrel dancer," a memo contained in the Paramount Collection at the AMPAS Library states that Da Pron "is no longer in the picture and his name should be removed from the cast sheet thereof." According to an article in *Down Beat*, Lou Bonnie provided the banjo music on the score. An early *HR* news items reported that Paramount considered adding Fred Astaire to the cast. *Dixie* marked Billy De Wolfe's feature film debut.

AmCin Jul 1943, p. 257, 268. *Box* 3 Jul 1943. *DV* 24 Jun 1943, p. 3, 7. *Down Beat* 15 Jul 1943, p. 9. *FD* 24 Jun 1943, p. 6. *HR* 24 Jun 1943, p. 3. *HR* 29 Jun 1943, p. 4, 5. *MPH* 26 Jun 1943. *MPHPD* 26 Jun 1943, p. 1385. *NYT* 24 Jun 1943, p. 26. *Var* 30 Jun 1943, p. 8.

DOCKS OF NEW ORLEANS (Chinese Americans)

Monogram Pictures Corp. *Dist* Monogram Pictures Corp. 21 Mar 1948; Prod: 17 Nov—25 Nov 1947 [©Monogram Pictures Corp.; 21 Mar 1948; LP1610]. Sd (Western Electric Recording); b&w. 7 reels, 5,802 ft. 64 min. PCA cert no. 12895.

Series: Charlie Chan.

Prod James S. Burkett. *Dir* Derwin Abrahams. *Asst dir* Theodore Joos. *Orig scr* W. Scott Darling. *Photog* William Sickner. [*Cam op* John Martin]. [*Stills* Jim Fullerton]. *Supv film ed* Otho Lovering. *Ed* Ace Herman. [*Set dec* Ken Schwartz]. *Mus dir* Edward J. Kay. *Rec* Tom Lambert. [*Hair stylist* Lela Chambers]. *Prod supv* Glenn Cook. *Tech dir* Dave Milton. [*Scr supv* Mary Chaffee]. [*Grip* George Booker].

Source: Based on characters created by Earl Derr Biggers.

Cast: Roland Winters [(*Charlie Chan*)], Virginia Dale [(*René*)], Mantan Moreland [(*Birmingham Brown*)], John Gallaudet [(*Capt. Pete McNally*)], Victor Sen Young [(*Tommy Chan*)], Carol Forman [(*Nita Aguirre*)], Douglas Fowley [(*Grock*)], Harry Hayden [(*Oscar Swendstrom*)], Howard Negley [(*André Pareaux*)], Stanley Andrews [(*Theodore Von Scherbe*)], Emmett Vogan [(*Henri Castanero*)], Boyd Irwin [(*Simon Lafontanne*)], Rory Mallinson [(*Thompson*)], George J. Lewis [(*Sgt. Dansiger*)], [Diane Fauntelle (*Mrs. Swendstrom*)], [Ferris Taylor (*Dr. Dooble, coroner*)], [Haywood Jones (*Mobile*)], [Eric Wilton (*Butler*)], [Forrest Matthews (*Detective*)], [Wally Walker (*Chauffeur*)], [Larry Steers (*Doctor*)], [Paul Conrad (*Man from D.A.'s office*)], [Frank Stephens (*Sergeant*)], [Fred Miller (*Armed guard*)], [Charlie Jordan (*Fingerprint expert*)].

Detective, Drama. [*Print viewed*]. Simon Lafontanne, head of the Lafontanne Chemical Co., goes to consult with Chinese-American private detective Charlie Chan, as he thinks that he has an enemy who is having him followed everywhere he goes. The trouble started when he entered into a partnership with two foreigners, Henri Castanero and Theodore Von Scherbe, to ship a chemical to South America. After Chan agrees to investigate further at Lafontanne's office, Lafontanne discovers that his chauffeur has been beaten up and his car stolen. The next morning, at his office, Lafontanne's secretary René, who is also his niece, tells him that his new partners are waiting to speak with him. Castanero and Von Scherbe are concerned about the possibility of one of them dying suddenly and have added a clause to their agreement, whereby in the event of the death of any of the principals, his share will revert to the survivors. After Lafontanne signs the clause reluctantly, Oscar Swendstrom shows up at the office, brandishing a gun and claiming that Lafontanne stole his formula for the chemical. René phones police captain Pete McNally to have Swendstrom arrested, but when McNally and his assistant, Dansiger, arrive, they find Lafontanne dead in his office. Chan then shows up to keep his appointment, and the police tell him that they think Lafontanne may have died from a heart attack. Although Chan investigates and finds a shattered tube in the office radio, the police take Swendstrom in for questioning. Meanwhile, Tommy, Chan's

"number two" son, and chauffeur Birmingham Brown locate Lafontanne's car. Chan looks it over and finds some cigarette ash containing traces of a Mexican bark. Later, Chan discovers that a certain sound frequency will cause the glass in radio tubes to shatter. Chan then visits Castanero, and while he is there, André Pareaux and Nita Aguirre, who have an interest in diverting the chemical shipment for their own use, arrive. Pareaux offers Chan one of his specially made cigarettes, in which Chan detects the same material he found in Lafontanne's car. Later, a letter is delivered to Castanero, which prompts him to phone McNally to report that he is in great danger. However, by the time the police arrive, Castanero is dead under circumstances similar to Lafontanne's demise. Chan investigates Pareaux and finds that he has had various aliases and is apparently after the formula. Swendstrom finally tells McNally that Von Scherbe is the murderer, then he, too, is murdered. All of the suspects in the case are invited to Chan's house. Pareaux and Aguirre, along with henchman Grock, arrive early and knock out Birmingham and Tommy, then demand information from Chan about the Lafontanne deal and the formula. In response, Chan tells them that a radio tube he is holding contains a deadly poison gas. He then plays a recording of a soprano singing a note which is of a pitch high enough to shatter the glass. Chan tells Pareaux and his associates that the gas is in the room and they panic. Tommy and Birmingham break in, but discover that there was no poison gas in the tube. McNally and his men arrive and arrest Pareaux and company, but Chan explains that it was Swendstrom who had used the gas in the tubes to kill his former business partner and who had also carried out the subsequent murders. Swendstrom's wife was in on the crimes as it was her singing voice on the radio programs that triggered the shattering of the tubes. *Chemical formulas. Chinese Americans. Foreign agents. Gases, Asphyxiating and poisonous. Murder. Private detectives. Radios. African Americans. Aliases. Boogie-woogie music. Cigarettes. Docks. Fathers and sons. Glass. Nieces. Partnership. Police. Radio programs. Recordings. Singers.*

Note: The film's main title card reads: Charlie Chan in *Docks of New Orleans*. The film's working title was *Charlie Chan in New Orleans*. Despite the title, the docks are seen only very briefly during the credit titles. Although not acknowledged in the onscreen credits, the film's story was derived from Monogram's 1938 picture, *Mr. Wong, Detective* (see entry below). For additional information on the "Charlie Chan" series, please see the above entry for *Charlie Chan Carries On* and consult the Series Index.

Box 21 Aug 1948. *DV* 29 Apr 1948, p. 3. *FD* 5 May 1948, p. 8. *HR* 14 Nov 1947 p. 14. *HR* 29 Apr 1948, p. 3. *MPHPD* 6 Mar 1948, p. 4086. *MPHPD* 20 Mar 1948, p. 4101, 4103. *Var* 17 Mar 1948, p. 8.

DR. GILLESPIE'S CRIMINAL CASE (Chinese Americans)

Metro-Goldwyn-Mayer Corp.; controlled by Loew's Inc. *Dist* Loew's Inc. **1943**; Prod: 23 Nov 1942—mid-Jan 1943 [©Loew's Inc.; 6 May 1943; LP12074]. Sd (Western Electric Sound System); b&w. 9 reels, 8,000 ft. 89 min. Passed by the National Board of Review. PCA cert no. 9140.

Series: Dr. Gillespie.

Dir Willis Goldbeck. [*Asst dir* Al Raboch]. *Orig scr* Martin Berkeley, Harry Ruskin and Lawrence P. Bachman. *Dir of photog* Norbert Brodine and [Charles Lawton]. *Art dir* Cedric Gibbons. *Assoc* William Ferrari. *Film ed* Frank Hull. *Set dec* Edwin B. Willis. *Assoc* Edward G. Boyle. *Gowns* Irene. *Mus score* Daniele Amfitheatrof. *Rec dir* Douglas Shearer.

Cast: Lionel Barrymore [(*Dr. Leonard Gillespie*)], Van Johnson [(*Dr. Randall ["Red"] Adams*)], Keye Luke [(*Dr. Lee Wong How*)], Alma Kruger [(*Molly Byrd*)], Nat Pendleton [(*Joe Weyman*)], Margaret O'Brien [(*Margaret*)], Donna Reed (*Marcia Bradburn*), John Craven (*Roy Todwell*), Michael Duane (*Sergeant Patrick J. Orisin*), William Lundigan (*Alvin F. Peterson*), Walter Kingsford (*Dr. Walter Carew*), Marilyn Maxwell (*Ruth Edly*), Henry O'Neill (*Warden Kenneson*), Marie Blake (*Sally*), Frances Rafferty (*Irene*), [Nell Craig (*Nurse Parker*)], [Arthur Loft (*Dr. Post*)], [Milton Kibbee (*Briggs*)], [Robert Emmet O'Connor (*Samson*)], [Boyd Davis (*Mr. Coleman*)], [Richard Crane (*Sailor*)], [Aileen Pringle (*Chaperon*)], [Edna Holland (*Nurse Morgan*)], [Lorin Raker (*Price*)], [Richard Bartell (*Botsford*)], [Katharine Booth (*Cashier*)], [William Haade (*Driver*)], [Ralph Dunn, Roy Barcroft, Lee Phelps, Captain Somers (*Guards*)], [Douglas Fowley (*Wallace*)], [Barbara Bedford (*Secretary*)], [Patricia Barker (*Edith*)], [Janet Chapman (*Mary*)], [Yvette Duguay (*Aggie*)], [Irene Tedrow (*Nurse Dodd*)], [Herbert Vigran (*Orderly*)], [Gertrude W. Hoffman (*Grandmother*)], [Byron

Foulger (*Father*)], [George Irving (*Rear Admiral*)], [John Dilson (*Green*)], [Matt Moore (*Harper*)], [Edward Keane (*Stiles*)], [Edward Earle (*Morris*)], [Grant Withers (*Waddy*)], [George Lynn (*Mack*)], [Ted Adams (*Stapleton, guard*)], [Jerry Jerome, Chick Collins (*Convicts*)], [Don Cadell (*Big Marine*)], [Helen Dickson (*Dowager hostess*)], [Marianne Quon (*Lee Ti Fang*)], [Almeda Fowler (*Nurse Trippett*)], [Margaret Adden (*Nurse*)].

Medical, Drama. [*Print viewed*]. One year after her former fiancé, Roy Todwell, was sentenced to life in prison for murder, socialite Marcia Bradburn goes to visit Dr. Leonard Gillespie. The wheelchair-bound Gillespie, who lives and works at New York City's Blair General Hospital, testified unsuccessfully at Roy's trial, hoping to convince the jury that Roy was insane and should be put in a sanitarium. Marcia wants to accept the proposal of Sergeant Patrick J. Orisin, but is afraid that if Roy reads about it in the newspaper, he will react violently. Gillespie tells her not to worry, but after she leaves, he telephones Warden Kenneson at the penitentiary where Roy is incarcerated and says that he will be flying in for a visit. Gillespie is currently searching for a new chief assistant and encourages an intense rivalry between the two candidates, Randall "Red" Adams who wants to join the Army medical corps, and Brooklyn-born Chinese American Lee Wong How, who is learning Chinese in the hope of going to China. One of Lee's patients is Alvin F. Peterson, a young man who lost both legs in the attack on Pearl Harbor. Lee tells Peterson that a special operation to put on artificial limbs is going to be performed on him. The uninterested and embittered Peterson has been burning unread letters from his girl friend, and Gillespie advises Lee and head nurse Molly Byrd never to leave the extremely depressed Peterson alone. On Friday evening, after interrupting Red's romantic date with wealthy social services worker Ruth Edly, Gillespie takes Red with him to the penitentiary, in the hope of convincing the warden to transfer Roy to a sanitarium. The warden lets Gillespie go to the prison hospital, where Roy works, and Roy cheerfully tells him that he remembers nothing of his earlier violent episodes. Despite Roy's demeanor, Gillespie is convinced that the young man is still dangerously insane. Back at the hospital, Gillespie and Lee try to get Peterson to walk on his new limbs, but he refuses to cooperate. Gillespie, who has gotten hold of a letter from Peterson's girl friend, gives him the letter, which confirms that she still loves him. Just then, chief administrator Dr. Walter Carew announces that there is a terrible infection in the children's post-surgical ward, and Gillespie assigns Red and Lee to the case. The doctors use every means at their disposal to reduce the girls' fevers, and Lee and Red even resort to hours of flapping ice-cold sheets on one child, Margaret, who is near death. Their joint effort makes them realize that they are more friends than rivals. One of the nurses, Miss Dodd, dies from the same fever, but Margaret eventually recovers. A short time later, Marcia brings Gillespie a letter that Roy sent to her, and Gillespie immediately travels to the penitentiary. Meanwhile, Lee brings a visitor to Peterson, Mr. Coleman, a wealthy friend of Gillespie who secretly paid for Peterson's operation. When Coleman reveals that he lost his legs in an accident but has gotten by very well with artificial limbs, Peterson is inspired and determines to learn to walk. At the penitentiary, Gillespie argues Roy's case in front of the prison board, explaining that he is a "timebomb." A board member then points out that Roy, whose violence had supposedly been triggered by shrill noises, has not reacted at all to the daily prison whistles and therefore must be faking. Just at that moment, however, as Roy reads about Marcia's engagement, the noon whistle blows and his mind snaps. With two accomplices, Roy goes to the warden's office with smuggled guns and kills a board member. The three convicts then exchange clothes with some board members, take them hostage and leave through the prison gate. After the convicts escape, the police slowly approach the deserted cabin in which they are hiding and Gillespie calls out to Roy, telling him that he is still insane because he never remembers his crimes. After taking the other prisoners' guns, Roy leaves the shack and shoots wildly, but is killed by the police. Some weeks later, Red goes to Ruth's apartment for their long-awaited date, but finds that Gillespie, Lee and other hospital staff members are there, along with the surviving fever patients, Marcia, her new husband and a now ambulatory Peterson. *Amputees. Chinese Americans. Hospitals. Paraplegics. Physicians. Rivalry. Children. Depression, Mental. Disease. Engagements. Fever. Firearms. Good Samaritans. Hostages. Insanity. Language and languages. Letters.*

Murder. New York City. Nurses. Operations, Surgical. Pearl Harbor (HI), Attack on, 1941. Prison escapes. Prison wardens. Prisons. Romance. Shootouts. Socialites. Soldiers.

Note: Working titles of the film were *Dr. Gillespie's Prison Story* and *Dr. Gillespie's Criminal Story*. The characters of "Marcia Bradburn" and "Roy Todwell" had previously appeared in the film *Calling Dr. Gillespie*, although in the earlier film, actor Phil Brown had portrayed Roy. Actress Katharine Booth made her motion picture debut in the film. *HR* news items include William G. Fisher, Betty Jane Nichols, Jeanette Alice Winkler, Diane Toien, Geraldine Pinker and Marion Salerno in the cast, but their appearance in the released film has not been confirmed. The *Var* review incorrectly identified the film's editor as Laurie Vejar. For additional information on the Dr. Gillespie series, see the entry for *Young Dr. Kildare* in *AFI Catalog of Feature Films, 1931-40*; F3.5251, and consult the Series Index.

Box 8 May 1943. *DV* 5 May 1943, p. 3, 15. *FD* 11 May 1943, p. 6. *HR* 23 Jul 1942, p. 9. *HR* 23 Nov 1942, p. 3. *HR* 27 Nov 1942, p. 8. *HR* 13 Jan 1943, p. 8. *HR* 14 Jan 1943, p. 12. *HR* 22 Jan 1943, p. 10. *HR* 5 May 1943, p. 6. *MPH* 8 May 1943. *MPHPD* 6 Mar 1943, p. 1192. *MPHPD* 8 May 1943, p. 1302. *Var* 5 May 1943, p. 16.

DR. GILLESPIE'S NEW ASSISTANT (Chinese Americans)
Metro-Goldwyn-Mayer Corp.; controlled by Loew's Inc. *Dist* Loew's Inc. Dec 1942—Jan 1943; *Prod:* 13 Aug—19 Sep 1942 [©Loew's Inc.; 13 Nov 1942; LP11698]. Sd (Western Electric Sound System); b&w. 9 reels, 7,882 ft. 86-87 min. Passed by the National Board of Review. PCA cert no. 8889.

Series: Dr. Gillespie.

Dir Willis Goldbeck. [*Asst dir* Albert Kelley]. *Orig scr* Harry Ruskin, Willis Goldbeck and Lawrence P. Bachman. *Dir of photog* George Folsey. *Art dir* Cedric Gibbons. *Assoc* Urie McCleary. *Film ed* Ralph Winters. *Set dec* Edwin B. Willis. *Assoc* Edward G. Boyle. *Mus score* Daniele Amfitheatrof. *Rec dir* Douglas Shearer. [*Unit mgr* Art Smith]. [*Tech adv* Dr. H. H. Conway].

Source: Based on characters created by Max Brand.

Cast: Lionel Barrymore (*Dr. Leonard Gillespie*), Van Johnson (*Dr. Randall ["Red"] Adams*), Susan Peters (*Mrs. Howard Allwinn Young [also known as Claire Merton]*), Richard Quine (*Dr. Dennis Lindsay*), Keye Luke (*Dr. Lee Wong How*), Alma Kruger (*Molly Byrd*), Nat Pendleton (*Joe Weyman*), Horace McNally (*Howard Allwinn Young*), Frank Orth (*Mike Ryan*), Walter Kingsford (*Dr. Walter Carew*), Nell Craig (*Nurse Parker*), Marie Blake (*Sally*), George H. Reed (*Conover*), Ann Richards (*Iris Headley*), Rose Hobart (*Mrs. Black*), Eddie Acuff (*Clifford Genet*), [Shirley Warde (*Nurse Jordan*)], [Harry Strang (*Cop*)], [Leigh Sterling (*Intern*)], [Wally Cassell (*Gangster*)], [Hal K. Dawson (*Shumate*)], [Paul McVey (*Manager*)], [Dorothy Vaughn (*Maid in hotel*)], [Dorothy Adams (*Mrs. Alberts*)], [Arthur Shields (*Mr. Kipp*)], [Georgia Caine (*Mrs. Kipp*)], [Jacqueline White (*Telephone operator*)], [Dick Simmons (*Dr. Fletcher*)], [Edith Evanson (*Hilda*)], [Pamela Blake (*Jimmy James*)], [Sarah Padden (*Neighbor*)], [Paul Fix (*Husband*)], [Dorothy Morris (*Wife*)], [Betty Jaynes, Sylvia Field, Estelle Etterre (*Nurses*)], [Ernie Alexander (*Elevator boy*)].

Medical, Drama. [*Print viewed*]. Blair General Hospital's Dr. Leonard Gillespie has been working so hard that his friends, chief administrator Dr. Walter Carew and head nurse Molly Byrd, are concerned. When the wheelchair-bound Gillespie falls asleep on a hospitalized patient, they demand that he finally select a new assistant. Gillespie agrees to make his choice by asking a very difficult question of all the new interns; the one who answers it correctly will have the position. Three doctors surprise Gillespie by answering the question correctly: Dr. Randall "Red" Adams of Kansas City, Dr. Lee Wong How of Brooklyn and Dr. Dennis Lindsay, an Australian on temporary assignment at Blair to study tropical diseases. Because he cannot decide among them, Gillespie resolves to give all three a chance. Meanwhile, Howard Allwin Young, the son of one of Gillespie's oldest friends, stop for lunch at an inn with his new bride, dress designer Claire Merton. At almost the same moment that Gillespie calls them to offer his congratulations, Claire suddenly loses all memory of who she is. Gillespie suggests that Howard bring Claire to the hospital, where he and Red try to determine what has caused her amnesia. Though she has no apparent signs of physical or emotional trauma, she can give no information about her life and is reluctant to go home with Howard. Instead, she suggests that they annul the marriage. Red takes her to her apartment and has no success in jogging her memory. When Red discusses the case with his mentor, Gillespie guides him to the only logical conclusion—Clair is faking. To find out what Clair is trying to hide, Red decides to see if he can find her personal physician. Red finally locates the doctor, who has

enlisted in the Army. The doctor's receptionist, Mrs. Black, will only let Red see Claire's information card, but Red discovers that Claire had listed herself as a married woman with a two-year-old child. When Gillespie confronts Claire with the information, she collapses, but later confesses that she was married in Texas at age sixteen and was soon widowed by her criminal husband, who left her with a baby. After leaving the baby with her mother, Claire became a successful fashion designer in New York and fell in love with Howard. The reason why she feigned amnesia was that during lunch at the inn, she had tried to tell him about her earlier marriage, but Howard, thinking that she was teasing, made a cruel joke about "second-hand wives." She is convinced that Howard would never understand or accept her child, so she decides to go back to Texas and asks Gillespie and Red not to tell Howard anything. Red and Gillespie are sure that Claire is still hiding something, so Red decides to try to get more information out of Mrs. Black. The next day, after getting Mrs. Black drunk and stealing Claire's file, Red reveals to Gillespie that the file confirmed that Claire was unable to have any more children, but did not know. Gillespie then calls Howard and lectures him about bigotry and prejudice after telling him about Claire's past. After Howard says that he loves Claire and wants both her and her child, Gillespie opens the door to another office and Claire, who has been waiting, is happily reunited with Howard. While Red has been working on Claire's case, Lee and Lindsay have resolved their own and Gillespie says that he cannot fire any of them. Lindsay has been ordered back to Australia, but Lee and Red will both act as Gillespie's assistants. *Amnesia. Deception. Hospitals. Paraplegics. Physicians. Rivalry. Australians. Bigotry. Chinese Americans. Couturiers. New York City. Newlyweds. Nurses. Receptionists. Restaurants.*

Note: This film marked the directorial debut of Willis Goldbeck, who previously had written the "Dr. Kildare" and "Dr. Gillespie" films. According to news items in *HR*, Edna Holland and Edith Evanson were cast in the film, but their appearances have not been confirmed. Although Selmer Jackson is listed in the CBCS as "Dr. Harrison," he was not in the released film. A news item in *HR* on 20 Aug 1942 noted that Dr. H. H. Conway was to be the technical adviser on the film, taking over from the usual series adviser, Dr. Charles Mandell, who had recently entered the Army. The extent of Mandell's participation on this film has not been determined.

This was the first of four films in the Dr. Gillespie series in which Van Johnson portrayed "Dr. Red Adams," and Keye Luke portrayed "Dr. Lee Wong How." Johnson left the series in 1944 and Luke's final picture in the series was the last, *Dark Delusion* in 1947 (see above). Johnson and Luke assumed the role of Gillespie's "assistant," which had previously been occupied by Lew Ayres in films that were part of the Dr. Kildare series. Luke also portrayed Dr. How in the 1944 picture *Andy Hardy's Blonde Trouble*. For additional information on the "Dr. Kildare" and "Dr. Gillespie" series, consult the Series Index and see the entry for *Young Dr. Kildare* in AFI Catalog of Feature Films, 1931-40; F3.5251.

Box 14 Nov 1942. DV 11 Nov 1942, p. 3. FD 12 Nov 1942, p. 5. HR 21 Jun 1942, p. 6. HR 23 Jul 1942, p. 9. HR 31 Jul 1942, p. 4. HR 14 Aug 1942, p. 6. 8. HR 17 Aug 1942, p. 6. HR 20 Aug 1942, p. 3. HR 11 Sep 1942, p. 8. HR 18 Sep 1942, p. 3. HR 11 Nov 1942, p. 3. MPD 12 Nov 1942. MPHPD 15 Nov 1942, p. 1005. STR 14 Nov 1942. Var 11 Nov 1942, p. 8.

DR. GILLESPIE'S PRISON STORY *see* **DR. GILLESPIE'S CRIMINAL CASE**

DR. RED ADAMS *see* **BETWEEN TWO WOMEN**

DOCTOR STEELE *see* **DANGEROUS INTRIGUE**

THE DOCTOR'S HUSBAND *see* **EMERGENCY WEDDING**

THE DOCTOR'S SECRET *(foreign version) see* **EL SECRETO DEL DOCTOR**

DOCTORS DON'T TELL *see* **THREE ACES WEST**

THE DOGY *see* **THE TROUBLE BUSTER**

DOING OUR BIT *see* **DOING THEIR BIT**

DOING THEIR BIT (Irish Americans)
Fox Film Corp. *Dist* Fox Film Corp. 4 Aug 1918 [©William Fox; 4 Aug 1918; LP12735]. Si; b&w. 5 reels.
Dir Kenean Buel. *Story and scen* Kenean Buel. *Cam* Joseph Ruttenberg.
Cast: Jane Lee (*Janie O'Dowd*), Katherine Lee (*Kate O'Dowd*), Franklyn Hanna (*Michael O'Dowd*), Gertrude Le Brandt (*Bridget McCann O'Dowd*), Alex Hall (*Miles O'Dowd*), Beth Ivins (*Patricia O'Dowd*), Kate Lester (*Mrs. Velma Vanderspent*), William Pollard

(*Alfred Caesar Vanderspent*), Jay Strong (*Jerry Flynn*), Aimee Abbott (*Mrs. Mary Flynn*), Edwin Sturgis, R. R. Neill (*German spies*).
Espionage, World War I, Comedy-drama. Little Kate and Janie O'Dowd are sent to their wealthy American uncle, Michael O'Dowd, after their Irish father loses his life on a World War I battlefield. Having been locked accidentally into O'Dowd's munitions plant one evening, the children catch sight of their intoxicated cousin Miles O'Dowd admitting two men into the factory. The girls recognize the two as spies they had seen on the boat to America sending signals to a German submarine. After the spies knock Miles cold, the children trap them in a die-stamping machine until help arrives. Miles and factory worker Jerry Flynn, who loves young Patricia O'Dowd, enlist and are soon joined by Alfred Vanderspent, whose wealthy mother's plot to falsify his birth records is foiled by the children. *Children. Cousins. Germans. Irish. Munitions factories. Sisters. Spies. Drunkenness. Factory workers. Military service, Voluntary. Mothers and sons. Soldiers. Submarine boats. Uncles. World War I.*
Note: An alternate title for this film was *Doing Our Bit*.
ETR 10 Aug 1918, p. 841. MPN 17 Aug 1918, p. 1042, 1122. MPW 10 Aug 1918, p. 892. MPW 17 Aug 1918, p. 1015. NYDM 24 Aug 1918, p. 274. Var 23 Aug 1918, p. 42. Wid's 4 Aug 1918, pp. 11-12.

DOLLAR DIZZY *(foreign version) see* **EL PRÍNCIPE DEL DÓLAR**

THE DOLLY SISTERS (Hungaian Americans)
Twentieth Century-Fox Film Corp. *Dist* Twentieth Century-Fox Film Corp. Nov **1945**; World premiere in Chicago: 5 Oct 1945; Prod: 18 Jan—20 Apr 1945 [©Twentieth Century-Fox Film Corp.; 5 Oct 1945; LP101]. Sd (Western Electric Mirrophonic Recording); col (Technicolor). 13 reels, 10,251 ft. 114 min. PCA cert no. 10827.
[*Exec prod* Darryl F. Zanuck]. *Prod* George Jessel. *Dir* Irving Cummings. [*Asst dir* Henry Weinberger]. *Orig scr* John Larkin and Marian Spitzer. *Dir of photog* Ernest Palmer. [*2d cam* Lou Kunkel]. *Spec photog eff* Fred Sersen. [*Miniatures* Ralph O. Hammeras]. *Technicolor dir* Natalie Kalmus. *Assoc* Richard Mueller. *Art dir* Lyle Wheeler and Leland Fuller. *Mus set des by* Joseph C. Wright. *Film ed* Barbara McLean. *Set dec* Thomas Little. *Assoc* Walter M. Scott. *Cost* Orry Kelly. *Mus dir* Alfred Newman and Charles Henderson. *Orch arr* Gene Rose. *Dances staged by* Seymour Felix. *Sd* Arthur L. Kirbach and Roger Heman. [*Mus mixer* Paul Neal and Murray Spivack]. *Makeup artist* Ben Nye. [*Prod mgr* R. A. Klune]. [*Scr supv* Doris Drought]. [*Research dir* Frances C. Richardson]. [*Research asst* Gertrude Kingston].
Music: "Hungarian Dance No. 5" by Johannes Brahms; "I Never Knew I Could Love Anybody Like I'm Loving You" by Tom Pitts, Ray Egan and Roy K. Marsh.
Song(s): "I'm Always Chasing Rainbows," music by Harry Carroll, lyrics by Joseph McCarthy; "I Can't Begin to Tell You," music by James Monaco, lyrics by Mack Gordon; "The Vamp," music and lyrics by Byron Gay; "Give Me the Moonlight, Give Me the Girl," music by Albert Von Tilzer, lyrics by Lew Brown; "We Have Been Around" and "Don't Be Too Old Fashioned (Old Fashioned Girl)," music by Charles Henderson, lyrics by Mack Gordon; "Carolina in the Morning," music by Walter Donaldson, lyrics by Gus Kahn; "Powder, Lipstick & Rouge," music and lyrics by Mack Gordon and Harry Revel; "The Darktown Strutters' Ball," music and lyrics by Shelton Brooks, special lyrics by Charles Henderson, French lyrics by Georges Kessel; "Arrah Go On, I'm Gonna Go Back to Oregon," music by Bert Grant, lyrics by Sam Lewis and Joe Young; "Smiles," music by Lee G. Roberts, lyrics by J. Will Callahan; "Oh! Frenchy," music by Con Conrad, lyrics by Sam Ehrlich; "Pack Up Your Troubles in Your Old Kit Bag and Smile, Smile, Smile," music by Felix Powell, lyrics by George Asaf; "The Sidewalks of New York," music and lyrics by Charles B. Lawlor and James W. Blake; "Mademoiselle from Armentières," composer undetermined.
Cast: Betty Grable [(*Yansci "Jenny" Dolly*)], John Payne [(*Harry Fox*)], June Haver [(*Roszika "Rosie" Dolly*)], S. Z. Sakall [(*Latsie Dolly*)], Reginald Gardiner [(*Tony, Duke of Breck*)], Frank Latimore [(*Irving Netcher*)], Gene Sheldon [(*Professor Winnup*)], Sig Ruman [(*Ignatz Tsimmis*)], Trudy Marshall [(*Lenora Baldwin*)], [Collette Lyons (*Flo Daly*)], [Evon Thomas (*Jenny, as a child*)], [Donna Jo Gribble (*Rosie, as a child*)], [Robert Middlemass (*Oscar Hammerstein*)], [Paul Hurst (*Tim Dowling*)], [Lester Allen (*Morrie Keno*)], [Frank Orth (*Stage manager*)], [Herbert Ashley (*Fields*)], [William Nye (*Bartender*)], [Peter Cusanelli (*Waiter at Little Hungary*)], [Al Murphy (*Waiter*)], [Walter Soderling, Albert Pollet

(*Conductors*)], [Rudolf Lindau (*Busboy*)], [Audrey Betz (*Cashier*)], [Harry Seymour (*Pianist*)], [George Davis (*French juggler*)], [Trude Berliner (*German actress*)], [Igor Dolgoruki (*Russian actor*)], [Nino Bellini (*French actor*)], [Theresa Harris (*Ellabelle*)], [Roberta Daniel, Nanette Ballon, Carmen Beretta (*French maids*)], [Eugene Borden, Alphonse Martell (*Chauffeurs*)], [Mary Currier (*Hammerstein's secretary*)], [Claire Richards (*Operator*)], [Maria Bibikov (*Waitress*)], [Andre Charlot (*Phillipe*)], [Edward Kane (*Sam Harris*)], [Mae Marsh (*Flower lady*)], [Else Janssen (*Kathi*)], [Tommy Mack (*Baggage man*)], [Frank Penny (*Counterman*)], [Aldo Nadi (*King*)], [Henri De Soto (*Chef*)], [Serge Krizman (*Baltic officer*)], [Ricki Van Dusen (*Madame Polaire*)], [Wedgewood Nowell (*Footman*)], [Gino Corrado, Jean De Briac (*French trainmen*)], [Larry Thompson (*Sergeant*)], [Virginia Brissac (*Nun*)], [Frank Ferguson, Franklin Parker (*Reporters*)], [Howard Negley (*Cameraman*)], [J. C. Fowler (*Al Smith*)], [Betty Farrington (*Mrs. Al Smith*)], [Sam Garrett (*Will Rogers*)], [Albert Petit (*Croupier*)], [George O'Hara (*Frank Tinny*)], [J. Farrell MacDonald (*Doorman*)], [James Burke (*Policeman*)], [Julius Tannen], [James Metcalfe], [Phil Tead], [Craufurd Kent].

Show business, **Biography**, **Comedy-drama**, **Musical**. [*Print viewed*]. In 1904, Hungarian sisters Yansci and Roszika Dolly immigrate to America with their uncle Latsie, and their first stop is a New York City restaurant run by Latsie's friend, Ignatz Tsimmis. To amuse themselves, the girls dance as the restaurant's band plays folksongs, much to the delight of the patrons. In 1912, the girls, now grown, are called Jenny and Rosie, and still love to dance and sing popular songs at Tsimmis'. Needing money to pay Uncle Latsie's debts, Jenny and Rosie persuade Tsimmis to book them elsewhere, and he gets them a job in upstate New York. On the train, the sisters meet singer Harry Fox, who lies about how successful he is, and he is chagrined to discover later that he has been billed below the unknown sisters and Professor Winnup's educated seal. Harry overcomes his embarrassment and over the next several days, romances Jenny. The couple fall in love despite Rosie's dislike of Harry, and on the day the Dollys leave, Jenny promises Harry that she will wait for him. Back in New York City, the sisters try to advance their career but have no luck, until one day, they meet Harry again. Harry and Jenny are delighted to be reunited, and Harry assures the girls that, with his help, they can catch the eye of impressario Oscar Hammerstein, who is looking for exotic acts. Harry installs the girls in an expensive hotel suite and clothes them in lavish outfits, then arranges for Hammerstein to visit. Re-assuming their Hungarian accents, the girls audition for Hammerstein, who is so impressed by them that two weeks later, they are starring in one of his shows. By 1915, Rosie and Jenny are very successful and are about to embark on their first tour of Paris. One day, Harry visits Jenny and admits that he wishes to end their relationship because she has hit the big time while he is still struggling. They resolve their problems though, when song publisher Sam Harris admires one of Harry's compositions, and Jenny retires to marry Harry. On the eve of Harry's first Broadway show, however, he enlists in the Army and is sent overseas. Jenny then accompanies Rosie to Paris, and the Dolly Sisters conquer the Folies Bergere. They then become the toast of London, where Jenny attracts the attention of Tony, the Duke of Breck. A magazine photograph of the couple enrages Harry, who goes to see Jenny while on leave. Harry, who is returning to the United States, demands that Jenny come with him, but she cannot leave Rosie, as they have signed with the Folies Bergere for another season. The heartbroken Jenny files for divorce after Harry leaves her, then immerses herself in a whirlwind of performing, gambling and refusing Tony's marriage proposals. Meanwhile, Rosie has fallen in love with American department store owner Irving Netcher. Back in New York, Harry achieves success and pursues the beautiful Lenora Baldwin. One night, Jenny overhears Rosie tell Irving that they must wait to be married, and in order to free Rosie, Jenny agrees to marry Tony. As they are driving to town for the ceremony, however, Jenny's emotions disorient her and she drives the car off a cliff. Tony is unharmed by the accident, but Jenny is seriously disfigured. On the night that he becomes engaged to Lenora, Harry learns of Jenny's accident, and Jenny is comforted by the telegram he sends. Jenny urges Rosie to marry Irving immediately, and after the couple leave on their honeymoon, Jenny's beauty is saved through plastic surgery. Rosie and Irving soon welcome Jenny to New York, although they are dismayed to discover that she has sold her jewelry to pay her medical bills. Irving agrees to allow Rosie to return to the

stage with Jenny, and the sisters are soon appearing at an all-star benefit. Harry is also on the bill, and when Lenora sees Harry watching Jenny, she realizes that he still loves her. Lenora then tells Rosie that she will not be marrying Harry, and watches as Harry invites Jenny to join him onstage for a song. The couple reconcile as they sing together, and happily gesture for Rosie to join them. *Jenny Dolly. Rosie Dolly. Entertainers. Loyalty. Romance. Sisters.* Ambition. Automobile accidents. Cards. Divorce. Gambling. Oscar Hammerstein. Hungarian Americans. Jealousy. Military service, Voluntary. Photographs. Racial impersonation. Restaurants. Seals (Animals). Songwriters. Trains. Uncles. Wealth. World War I.

Note: *The Dolly Sisters* is based on the lives of Yansci and Roszika Deutch, twin sisters who were born near Budapest, Hungary in 1892 and immigrated to the United States in 1900. [In the film, their Hungarian first names are spelled Jansci and Rozsicka, a less-used alternative spelling. Also, the sisters in the film are not twins.] The dark-haired sisters, who became famous under the names Jenny and Rosie Dolly, were as well known for their beauty, romantic attachments and exploits in European casinos as for their dancing. Although the sisters were indeed world-famous dancers, much of the film's story is fabricated. Rosie's first husband was songwriter Jean Schwartz, and after their divorce in 1921, she married millionaire Mortimer Davis, Jr. in 1927. After divorcing Davis, Rosie married department store owner Irving Netcher in 1932. Jenny was married to Harry Fox from 1914 to 1920, and married lawyer Bernard Vinnisky in 1935. The sisters, who began their career in 1907 in vaudeville, went on to star in musical shows produced by Florenz Ziegfeld, Oscar Hammerstein and Charles Cochran, and perform in plays in New York, London and Paris. In 1915, Jenny starred in the Kalem Co. film *The Call of the Dance*, directed by George L. Sargent, and Rosie appeared in Fine Arts Film Co.'s picture *The Lily and the Rose*, which was produced by D. W. Griffith. In 1918, the twins were directed by Leonce Perret in *The Million Dollar Dollies* (see *AFI Catalog of Feature Films, 1911-1920*; F1.0571, F1.2497 and F1.2943). The sisters retired in 1927, but because of their highly publicized gambling exploits, their fame persisted. Jenny adopted two young Hungarian orphans, Klari and Manzi, in 1929, and was seriously injured in an automobile accident in 1933. After her recovery, Jenny returned to the United States with her daughters and married Vinnisky. Jenny committed suicide in 1941, and Rosie died of a heart attack in 1970. According to information in the Twentieth Century-Fox Records of the Legal Department and the Produced Scripts Collection, both of which are located at the UCLA Arts—Special Collections Library, when Rosie sold the rights to the story of the Dolly Sisters to Fox for $52,500, the studio was forbidden to include in the film any information about Jenny's adoption of Klari and Manzi or her suicide. The studio records also reveal that the film was partly based on a fourteen-page biography of the sisters, written by Rosie, as well as scrapbooks, correspondence, newspaper clippings, etc. that she supplied.

HR news items announced that Fox was producing a film about the Dollys in May 1943, and later news items and studio records reveal that Alice Faye was originally scheduled to play "Jenny." Faye declined to make another musical, however, and instead appeared in the drama *Fallen Angel*. The film's production was delayed due to Betty Grable's pregnancy, and during her temporary retirement from the screen, Fox considering casting other actresses, including Gale Robbins, Janet Blair, Vivian Blaine, Patricia Romero and the Dowling Twins, Constance and Connie. Studio records indicate that Robert Wyler may have worked on the screenplay, although his contribution to the completed film is doubtful. A 15 Sep 1943 *HR* news item stated that Eugene R. O'Neil was to work with producer George Jessel on the film, but the extent of his contribution to the finished film, if any, has not been determined. *HR* news items and a studio press release note that John Stahl was originally scheduled to direct the picture, Milton Berle was set to play "Professor Winnup" and Jessel was set to play himself in the picture. According to studio records, Jessel was to play the master of ceremonies in the benefit show sequence at the end of the picture. Jessel, who knew the Dolly Sisters, also wrote a foreword about them included in early versions of the screenplay, but it was not used in the finished picture. A *HR* news item noted that Jessel would not appear in the picture due to the pressures of his producing schedule.

The film marked Jessel's debut as a motion picture producer, and also marked the return to the screen of actor John Payne, who had served in the military for two years. Studio records indicate that J. Edward Bromberg was originally signed to play "Oscar Hammerstein," but the casting was protested by Hammerstein's grandson, Oscar Hammerstein, II, who feared that Bromberg would "give the public a visual and mental impression that may be totally different" from what he and production chief Darryl F. Zanuck were contemplating in connection with a biographical film about Hammerstein. [That film, which they intended to call *Romance with Music*, was not made.] Zanuck assured Hammerstein that the role would be recast "with a more perfect physical double in an effort to match original photographs." Robert Middlemass appears in the role in the completed film. *HR* news item and a studio press release include the following actors in the cast, although their participation in the finished picture has not been confirmed: Fefe Ferry, Helen Kimball, Lois Barnes, Lucille Barnes, Jan Bryant, Juanita Cole, Ann Corcoran, Virginia De Luce, Marietta Elliott, Donna Hamilton, Marjorie Holliday, Savona King, Elaine Langan, Eve Miller, Martha Montgomery, Mary Jane Shores and Yvonne Vautrot. S. Z. Sakall was borrowed from Warner Bros. for the production. The film received an Academy Award nomination for the song "I Can't Begin to Tell You," written by James Monaco and Mack Gordon. Monaco died on 16 Oct 1945; *The Dolly Sisters* was his last screen assignement.

Several lawsuits concerning the film were filed, including one by songwriter

Jean Schwartz, who was Rosie's first husband. Even though the studio's legal records indicate that Rosie had obtained a release from Schwartz and several other current or former family members, allowing for the use of his "name, likeness, actions and activities, in fact or in fiction," *HR* and *LAEx* news items reported that Schwartz had demanded $100,000 in damages. Schwartz made numerous allegations, including that his career had been damaged by his not being characterized in the film; that there was a breach of oral contract by the studio to employ him as a technical director; that Rosie had misled him to believe his songs would be included in the production; and that the picture presented a gross distortion of history by portraying comedian/actor Harry Fox [Jenny's first husband] as a songwriter, when, in fact, Schwartz was the only songwriter married to either sister. The highly publicized trial, at which Rosie and Jessel testified, was dismissed on 1 Apr 1947 by Judge Campbell E. Beaumont, who stated that Schwartz could not have been injured by a film in which he was not named or characterized. Harry Fox also filed suit against the studio, Jessel and Rosie in Mar 1946, claiming that his reputation had been injured by the film's portrayal of him as a "lowly songwriter," according to a *LAHE* news item. The same news item also reported that Fox asserted that Rosie "induced him to agree to the film portrayal as part of a 'conspiracy' to injure him." The disposition of Fox's suit has not been determined. The legal files indicate that several other complaints or suits were lodged against the studio, one by Jenny's daughter Klari and another by Beatrice Fox White, who was Harry Fox's third wife, but their exact nature and disposition have not been determined.

Box 29 Sep 1945. *DV* 26 Sep 1945, p. 3, 7. *FD* 28 Sep 1945, p. 12. *HR* 28 May 1943, p. 3. *HR* 22 Jun 1943, p. 5. *HR* 4 Aug 1943, p. 6. *HR* 15 Sep 1943, p. 1. *HR* 23 Sep 1943, p. 3. *HR* 21 Oct 1943, p. 11. *HR* 15 Dec 1943, p. 1. *HR* 22 Dec 1943, p. 1. *HR* 13 Jan 1944, p. 31. *HR* 7 Mar 1944, p. 1. *HR* 30 Jun 1944, p. 1. *HR* 12 Jul 1944, p. 6. *HR* 30 Oct 1944, p. 1. *HR* 26 Dec 1944, p. 2. *HR* 12 Jan 1945, p. 2, 17. *HR* 19 Jan 1945, p. 10. *HR* 26 Feb 1945, p. 4. *HR* 27 Feb 1945, p. 2. *HR* 15 Mar 1945, p. 2. *HR* 5 Apr 1945, p. 7. *HR* 27 Apr 1945, p. 11. *HR* 26 Sep 1945, p. 3, 8. *HR* 1 Oct 1945, p. 21. *HR* 17 Oct 1945, p. 1. *HR* 19 Nov 1945, p. 6. *HR* 1 Feb 1946, p. 5. *HR* 20 Mar 1946, p. 1, 14. *LAEx* 7 Mar 1947. *LAEx* 8 Mar 1947. *LAEx* 12 Mar 1947. *LAEx* 14 Mar 1947. *LAEx* 20 Mar 1947. *LAEx* 28 Mar 1947. *LAEx* 29 Mar 1947. *LAEx* 2 Apr 1947. *LAHE* 20 Mar 1946. *MPD* 26 Sep 1945, p. 1, 7. *MPHPD* 29 Sep 1945, p. 2661. *NYT* 15 Nov 1945, p. 24. *Var* 26 Sep 1945, p. 14.

DON JUAN DIPLOMÁTICO (Spanish language)

Universal Pictures Corp.; A Carl Laemmle Jr. Production. *Dist* Universal Pictures Corp. **1931**; Los Angeles opening: 13 Feb 1931; Prod: Nov—Dec 1930. Sd; b&w. 8 reels. Spanish language.

Supv Paul Kohner. *Dir* George Melford. *Dial dir* Enrique Tovar Avalos. *Scr* Benjamin Glazer and Tom Reed. *Spanish vers* Baltasar Fernández Cué. *Photog* George Robinson. *Art dir* Herman Rosse. *Film ed* Arturo Tavares. *Sd supv* C. Roy Hunter.

Source: Based on the play *The Command to Love* by Rudolph Lothar and Fritz Gottwald (New York, 20 Sep 1927).

Cast: Miguel Faust Rocha (*Marqués de Valmi*), Lia Torá (*Elena*), Celia Montalván (*Mona*), Juan Aristi Eulate (*Embajador*), Enrique Acosta (*Ministro de la guerra*), Eduardo Arozamena (*Doctor*), Julio Villarreal (*Ministro de relaciones exteriores*), Rafael Navarro (*Emilio, secretario del marqués*), Manuel Mendoza López (*Martel, consejero de la embajada*).

Romantic comedy. [*Not viewed*]. [The following plot summary is based on the English-language version of this film, *The Boudoir Diplomat*; character names refer to that version. For further information regarding the English-language version, please see the note below and the entry for *The Boudoir Diplomat* in the *AFI Catalog of Feature Films, 1921-30*.] The ambassador of the Kingdom of Luvaria orders Baron Belmar, his attaché, to win the interest of Mona, wife of the war minister, who opposes a treaty the ambassador very much wants signed. However, his mission is complicated by the fact that Helene, the ambassador's wife, is extremely jealous of every woman he meets, for she was responsible for getting him his appointment as attaché. Belmar, nevertheless, is in love with Greta, who will not marry him until he is proven worthy of her trust. After many narrow escapes from exposure of the personal intrigue, he manages to sway the attentions of Mona, who persuades the war minister to sign the treaty, thus gaining Belmar an appointment as ambassador to Peru and Greta as his wife. *Diplomats. Imaginary lands. Nobility. Peru. Treaties.*

Note: Universal remade the 1930 film, *The Boudoir Diplomat*, which was directed by Malcolm St. Clair and starred Betty Compson, Mary Duncan and Ian Keith, in Spanish, French and German versions. The working title of the Spanish-language version was *Diplomático de salón*. Arthur Gregor was initially signed to direct the Spanish version, but he was replaced by George Melford. While the Spanish and German versions were reviewed at the time of their showings in the U.S., no reviews for the French version have been located, and it is not known if that version was exhibited in the U.S. According to NYSA records, the German version had an alternate title of *Beehrt sich Vorzufaebren*. Onscreen credits for the German version were taken from a studio cutting continuity.

Boudoir diplomatique (French language)

1931; Sd. b&w. French language.

Dir Marcel De Sano. *Scr* Benjamin Glazer and Tom Reed.

French-language cast: Arlette Marchal, Tania Fédor, Ivan Petrovich, Marcel de Garcin, André Nicolle, André Cheron. [*French version not viewed*]

Liebe auf Befehl (German language)

1931; Berlin opening: late Feb 1931; Chicago opening: 12 Mar 1931; Sd. b&w. 8 reels, 7,045 ft. 78 or 80 mins. German language.

Produktionleitung [*Prod supv*] Paul Kohner. *Regie* [*Dir*] Ernst L. Frank and Johannes Riemann. *Regie assistent* [*Asst dir*] Alfred Stern. *Drehbuch* [*Scr*] Dr. Ernst E. Redlich and Werner Klingler. *Dialog* Johannes Riemann and Dr. Ernst E. Redlich. *Bauten* [*Art dir*] Hermann Rosse. *Photographie* [*Photog*] Charles Stumar. *Tonschnitt* [*Ed*] Lou Sackin. *Tonschnittleitung* [*Supv ed*] Maurice Pivar. *Musik* Heinz Romheld. *Kostume* André-ani. *Tonaufnahmeleiter* [*Rec supv*] C. Roy Hunter.

German-language cast: Johannes Riemann (*Marquis de Saint Lac*), Olga Tschechova (*Manuela*), Hans Junkermann (*Der Kriegsminister*), Tala Birrell (*Marie-Anne*), Arnold Korff (*Der Gesandte*), Albert Conti (*Emile*), Paul Weigel (*Dr. Munaterra*). [*German version not viewed*].

FD 7 Jun 1931, p. 11. *Var* 18 Mar 1931, p. 34. *Var* 22 Apr 1931, p. 19. *Var* 9 Jun 1931, p. 19.

DON MIKE (Latino)

R-C Pictures Corp. *Dist* Film Booking Offices of America. 25 Jan or 27 Feb **1927** [©R-C Pictures Corp.; 27 Jan 1927; LP23596]. Si; b&w. 6 reels, 5,723 ft.

Pres Joseph P. Kennedy. *Dir* Lloyd Ingraham. *Asst dir* Douglas Dawson. *Story* Frank M. Clifton. *Cont* Lloyd Ingraham. *Photog* Ross Fisher.

Cast: Fred Thomson (*Don Miguel Arguella*), Silver King (*Rey de Plata, a horse*), Ruth Clifford (*Mary Kelsey*), Noah Young (*Reuben Pettingill*), Albert Prisco (*Don Luis Ybara*), William Courtright (*Gómez*), Tom Bates (*Jason Kelsey*), Norma Marie (*Dolores*), Carmen Le Roux (*Carmen*).

Romance. Don Miguel Arguella, owner of a vast California estate, is holding a fiesta when message arrives of a lost party in the desert; he rescues the pioneers, headed by Reuben Pettingill and including Jason Kelsey and his daughter Mary, to whom Don Mike is attracted. The *alcalde*, Don Luis Ybara, is embittered because of Don Miguel's interference in his persecution of Carmen, a girl on the estate. Pettingill, learning that "Don Mike" has neglected to record the boundaries of his land, files claim to the greater part of the estate and persuades Kelsey to promise him Mary. Don Luis is found murdered, and Pettingill offers a reward for the capture of Don Mike. General é Frémont hears of the incident and sends a group of soldiers to the rancho, while Don Mike, dressed as a monk, attends the wedding as the officiating priest. A struggle ensues, and Pettingill is unmasked as the murderer and usurper. *California. Courtship. Frontier and pioneer life. Horses. Land rights. Mayors. Murder. Spaniards.*

FD 20 Feb 1927. *MPW* 5 Mar 1927. *Var* 23 Feb 1927, p. 16.

DON Q, SON OF ZORRO (Latino)

Elton Corp. *Dist* United Artists Corp. 20 Sep **1925** [©Elton Corp.; 8 Jul 1925; LP21637]. Si; b&w. 11 reels, 10,264 ft.

Dir Donald Crisp. *Asst dir* Frank Richardson. *Scenario ed* Lotta Woods. *Photoplay* Jack Cunningham. *Photog* Henry Sharp. *Lighting eff* William S. Johnson. *Addl photog* E. J. Vallejo. *Supv art dir* Edward M. Langley. *Consulting artist* Harry Oliver. *Asst art dir* Francesc Cugat, Anton Grot and Harold Miles. *Film ed* William Nolan. *Ward* Paul Burns. *Mus score* Mortimer Wilson. *Prod mgr* Theodore Reed. *Props* Howard MacChesney. *Research dir* Arthur Woods. *Gen mgr* Robert Fairbanks. *Tech eff* Ned Mann.

Source: Based on the novel *Don Q's Love Story* by Hesketh Prichard and Kate Prichard (New York, 1925).

Cast: Douglas Fairbanks (*Don éCésar de Vega/Zorro*), Mary Astor (*Dolores de Muro*), Jack McDonald (*General de Muro*), Donald Crisp (*Don Sebastian*), Stella De Lanti (*The Queen*), Warner Oland (*The Archduke*), Jean Hersholt (*Don Fabrique*), Albert MacQuarrie (*Colonel Matsado*), Lottie Pickford Forrest (*Lola*), Charles Stevens (*Robledo*), Tote Du Crow (*Bernado*), Martha Franklin (*The Duenna*), Juliette Belanger (*Dancer*), Roy Coulson (*Her admirer*), Enrique Acosta (*Ramón*).

Historical, **Adventure**. Don César de Vega, a dashing young Californian, is sent by his father, Zorro, to Spain in order to broaden himself as is the tradition of the family. There he falls in love with a beauty named Dolores and also, owing to his prowess, gains favor with the Spanish court and the visiting Austrian Archduke. When the archduke is assassinated by one of the queen's guards and Don César is accused, the only witness refuses to clear Don César. So as to gain time to unmask the real criminals, Don César then feigns suicide, and with the help of his father, who has come to Spain, he succeeds in solving the mystery. His reward is the love of Dolores. *Assassination. California. Royalty. Spain. Suicide.*

Note: For information on other "Zorro" films, consult the entry below for the 1920 film *The Mark of Zorro*.

FD 21 Jun 1925. *NYT* 16 Jun 1925, p. 24. *Var* 17 Jun 1925, p. 35.

DON RENEGADE *see* **THE MARK OF THE RENEGADE**

DON RICARDO RETURNS (Latino)

PRC Pictures, Inc.; controlled by Pathe Industries, Inc. *Dist* Producers Releasing Corp. 5 Nov **1946**; Prod: early Aug—mid-Aug 1946 [©Pathe Industries, Inc.; 5 Nov 1946; LP686]. Sd (RCA Sound System); b&w. 6,213 ft. 63 or 67 min. PCA cert no. 11940.

Prod J. S. Burkett. *Assoc prod* Renault Duncan. *Dir* T. O. Morse. *Asst dir* Clarence Eurist. *Orig story* Johnston McCulley. *Scr* Jack DeWitt and Renault Duncan. [*Stills* M. B. Paul]. *Dir of photog* Vincent Farrar and Ben Kline. *Spec eff* Ray Mercer. *Film ed* George McGuire. *Master of props* Joe Montenaro. *Mus dir* Alexander Steinert. *Sd eng* Percy Townsend. *Dir of makeup* Bob Cowan. *Prod mgr* Cy Roth. [*Fencing instructor* Fred Cavens and Joanna De Tuscan].

Cast: Fred Coby [(*Don Ricardo, also known as Manuel*)], Isabelita [(*Dorotea*)], Paul Newlan [(*Lugo the Huge*)], Anthony Warde [(*Don Luera*)], Martin Garralaga [(*Miguel Porcoreno*)], Claire Du Brey [(*Teresa Flores*)], Michal [sic] Vizaroff [(*Capt. Martinez*)], [David Leonard (*Father Carlos*)].

Historical, **Western**. [*Print viewed*]. In 1835, in Monterey, Alta California, the duplicitous Spaniard Luera is concerned because the ship on which he had his cousin, Don Ricardo, the owner of Rancho San Luis Rey, shanghaiied two years before, is finally returning to port. Determined to have Don Ricardo declared dead so that he can inherit his ranch and marry his fiancée, Dorotea, Luera orders his guards to go to the port and kill Don Ricardo on sight. Having jumped ship, Don Ricardo, meanwhile, appears in a cantina and, after becoming involved in a fight with the owner, is aided by Lugo the Huge, a childhood friend. Lugo recognizes the much-changed Don Ricardo by a scar on his face and pledges to help him. Lugo and Don Ricardo are then surprised by Capt. Martinez, the man whom Luera hired to shanghai Don Ricardo, and Luera's guards. Don Ricardo and Lugo quickly overwhelm their attackers, however, and force Martinez to implicate Luera in the kidnapping before letting him go. Later, after Lugo tells Don Ricardo that Luera has been putting his labels on goods produced at Dorotea's ranch, El Camino, Don Ricardo vows to find enough evidence to convict him. Martinez, meanwhile, is confronted by Luera and his vicious overseer, Miguel Porcoreno, and assures him that Don Ricardo drowned while trying to flee the ship. After Luera breaks the "news" to Dorotea, he prepares to leave for San Diego, where he will have Don Ricardo officially declared dead and himself the new proprietor of San Luis Rey. The faithful Dorotea refuses to believe that Don Ricardo is dead, however, and rejects Luera's explanation that he abandoned her in order to have "an adventure." Don Ricardo and Lugo, meanwhile, seek refuge in the local mission, which is run by Father Carlos. After Don Ricardo tells Father Carlos that he is planning to engage Luera in a duel with swords, the priest advises him to go incognito until he is ready to fight. To that end, Lugo and Don Ricardo, using the name Manuel, convince the unsuspecting Porcoreno to hire them as laborers at San Luis Rey. At the first opportunity, Don Ricardo sneaks into his house and retrieves his sword and the deed to the ranch. Soon after, Father Carlos secretly reunites Don Ricardo and Dorotea at the mission, and Dorotea, who has been honing her fencing skills with Luera, practices daily with her fiancé in preparation for the duel. When Luera finally returns from San Diego, having been made a don by the governor, Porcoreno reports to him that Dorotea has been meeting someone in secret. Angry and jealous, Luera rushes to see Dorotea at El Camino, while she sends a servant to fetch "Manuel" and Lugo at San Luis Rey. Before he can go to Dorotea, however, Don Ricardo is summoned by

Porcoreno, who, having sensed that he is not an ordinary "peon," asks him to look over the ranch's account books. When Lugo arrives at El Camino, he tries to eavesdrop on Luera's conversation with Dorotea, but Luera orders him to leave. Lugo challenges Luera's authority, however, and slugs him, after which Luera tries to arrest Lugo and inadvertently provokes the workers to revolt. While the laborers create havoc at El Camino, Don Ricardo, having found the evidence he needs in Luera's account books, escapes from San Luis Rey and, dressed in his formal clothes, challenges his startled cousin to a duel. Luera agrees on condition that no seconds be present and the fight be to-the-death, but then resorts to unfair tactics in order to kill Don Ricardo after wounding him. With the help of Dorotea and Lugo, however, Don Ricardo gets the upper hand and corners Luera, who is then led off by a sergeant sent by Father Carlos. Later, with his land restored, Don Ricardo instructs the priest to announce his impending marriage to Dorotea. *California–History. Duplicity. Impersonation and imposture. Nobility. Spanish Americans. Sword fights. Cantinas. Cousins. Duels. Engagements. Evidence. Fights. Friendship. Missions. Overseers. Peasantry. Priests. Recognition. Scars. Uprisings. Wounds and injuries.*

Note: Michael Vizaroff's name is misspelled "Michal" in the onscreen credits. Although onscreen credits describe Johnston McCulley as the "author of 'Zorro,'" the serialized novel in which McCulley's Zorro character first appeared was titled *The Curse of Capistrano*. It was later published in book form under the title *Mark of Zorro*. According to publicity material deposited with the copyright records, some scenes in this film were shot at the San Fernando Mission in Southern California.

Exb 25 Dec 1946. *Har* 21 Dec 1946. *MPHPD* 7 Dec 1946, p. 3347.

DOÑA MENTIRAS (Spanish language)

Cinéstudio Continental; controlled by Paramount Publix Corp. *Dist* Paramount Publix Corp. Nov **1930**; Valencia (Spain) opening: 5 Nov 1930; Los Angeles opening: 21 Nov 1930.; Prod: May—Jun 1930 at Paramount studios in Joinville, France. Sd; b&w. 7,217 ft. 80 min. *Country of origin* France. Spanish language.

Dir Adelqui Millar. *Scr* John Meehan and Garrett Fort. *Spanish dial* María Luz Morales.

Source: Based on the play *The Lady Lies* by John Meehan (New York, 26 Nov 1928).

Cast: Carmen Larrabeiti (*Luisa Rollan*), Félix de Pomés (*Roberto Deval*), Miguel Ligero (*Carlos Tellier*), Carmen Ruiz Moragas (*Gilda Montel*), Julio Peña (*Bob Deval*), Helena D'Algy (*Ana María Lemontier*), Modesto Rivas (*Antonio Renaud*), Mercedes Servet (*Amelia Renaud*), Carmelita Fernández García (*Adelina Deval*).

Domestic, **Drama**. [*Not viewed*]. Lawyer Roberto Deval, a widower for six years, lives alone in Paris while his two chldren are studying at foreign colleges. Bob, the older child, and his sister Adelina are facing the difficulties of growing up without the support of a complete, stable family situation. As Adelina's birthday approaches, the ever-busy Roberto takes a break from work to buy her a present. At a ladies' fashion store, he has the good fortune to be served by Luisa Rollan, a pleasant salesclerk, who helps him make his selection. A few days later, Roberto bumps into Luisa again and thus begins a friendship which turns into love. When Bob and Adelina return to their father's house on vacation and find out about the romance, they cruelly try to break it up, but Luisa ends up gaining their confidence and approval, and they all work together to prepare her wedding to Roberto. *Brothers and sisters. Fatherhood. Lawyers. Romance. Salesclerks. Widowers. Class distinction. Courtship. Paris (France). Students.*

Note: Paramount's 1929 film *The Lady Lies*, directed by Hobart Henley and starring Walter Huston and Claudette Colbert, (see *AFI Catalog of Feature Films, 1921-30*; F2.2933) was remade in 1930 in five foreign versions. The foreign-language versions were shot at Paramount's Joinville studios, just outside Paris. According to censorship records at the NYSA, the Spanish, Italian, Swedish and German versions were passed for exhibition in New York state, but no evidence has been found to indicate that the French version was released in the U.S. The French-language versions was, however, exhibited in Montreal, Canada, in early Nov 1930. That version was titled *Une femme a menti* and was directed by Charles de Rochefort, adapted by Léopold Marchand and Hermann Kosterlitz, and starred Louise Lagrange and Paul Capellani. Some sources credit Luis Fernández Ardavín as dialogue director of the Spanish version but his participation has not been confirmed.

Running times for the various versions have been calculated from footage contained in NYSA records. The Swedish version, unlike the Spanish, was set in New York City. A Swedish reviewer, who had seen both the French and Swedish versions, commented that the Swedish was better in sound quality, but that its pace was too slow in comparison with the French version.

Other language version(s):
Perché no? (Italian language)
1930; San Francisco opening: 22 Jan 1931. Sd; b&w. 7,084 ft. 79 min.;. Italian language.
Dir Amleto Palermi.
Italian-language cast: Maria Jacobini, Livio Pavanelli, Oreste Bilancia, Sergio Fonsilli, Marcella Sabbatini. [*Italian version not viewed*]
Vi två (Swedish language)
1930; Stockholm opening: 18 Sep 1930; New York opening: mid-Feb 1931. Sd; b&w. 8,833 ft. 98 min.;. Swedish language.
Dir John W. Brunius. *Swedish adpt* Elsa af Trolle and Per Stille.
Swedish-language cast: Edvin Adolphson (*Robert Rossiter*), Anne-Marie Brunius (*Josephine, his daughter*), Ragnar Falck (*Bob, his son*), Margit Manstad (*Joyce Roamer, salesperson*), Erik "Bullen" Berglund (*Charles Tyler*), Märta Ekström (*Miriam Pearson*), Ivan Hedqvist (*Henry Tuttle*), Anna-Lisa Fröberg (*Amelie Tuttle*), Brita Vieweg (*Ann Gardner*), Ragna Broo-Juter (*Bernice*), Elsa de Castro. [*Swedish version not viewed*]
Seine Freundin Annette (German language)
1931; Berlin opening: 21 Apr 1931. Sd; b&w. 6,715 ft. 75 min.;. German language.
Dir Felix Basch. *German adpt* Hermann Kosterlitz.
German-language cast: Lissy Arna, Fritz Delius, Peter Wolff, Eva Brigitte Hartwig, Hadrian Maria Netto, Lotte Lorring, Philipp Manning, Grete Felsing. [*German version not viewed*].
Var 14 Jan, 1931.

¿DÓNDE HAS PASADO LA NOCHE? *see* **NO DEJES LA PUERTA ABIERTA**

DON'T BET ON WOMEN (*foreign version*) *see* **¿CONOCES A TU MUJER?**

DOOMED CARAVAN (Latino)
Harry Sherman Productions. *Dist* Paramount Pictures, Inc. 10 Jan **1941**; *Prod:* began Apr 1940; Sep—mid Oct 1940 [©Paramount Pictures, Inc.; 10 Jan 1941; LP10167]. Sd; b&w. 60 min. Passed by the National Board of Review.
Series: Hopalong Cassidy.
Prod Harry Sherman. *Assoc prod* Jos. W. Engel. *Dir* Lesley Selander. *Asst dir* Derwin Abrahams. *Scr* Johnston McCulley and J. Benton Cheney. *Photog* Russell Harlan. *Art dir* Lewis J. Rachmil. *Supv ed* Sherman A. Rose. *Ed* Carrol Lewis. *Set dec* Emile Kuri. *Props* Henry Donovan. *Ward* Earl Moser. *Mus dir* Irvin Talbot and John Leipold. *Sd* Chas. Althouse. *Sd rec* Cinema Service Studios.
Source: Based on characters created by Clarence E. Mulford.
Cast: William Boyd (*Hopalong Cassidy*), Russell Hayden (*Lucky Jenkins*), Andy Clyde (*California Jack*), Minna Gombell (*Jane Travers*), Morris Ankrum (*Stephen Westcott*), Georgia Hawkins (*Diana Westcott*), Trevor Bardette (*Ed Martin*), Pat J. O'Brien (*Jim Ferber*), Raphael Bennett (*Pete Gregg*), Jose Luis Tortosa (*Don Pedro*).
Western. [*Print viewed*]. In old California, as a favor to a mine owner friend, ranch hand Hopalong Cassidy, his sidekick, Lucky Jenkins, and other ranch hands escort a load of gold bullion safely to Crescent City. When they deliver the gold to Jane Travers, owner of the Crescent City Freight Company, she informs "Hoppy" that unidentified outlaws have burned several of her storehouses and have robbed her wagon train shipments. Although she has called for U.S. troopers to guard her next shipment, Hoppy agrees to ride along as extra insurance. Hoppy becomes suspicious of the troopers when they arrive because of their motley uniforms and behavior, and tells Jane that he and his men will not ride along with her after all. Instead, they locate the area where the outlaws have intercepted and killed the real troopers, and Hoppy then gallops to meet the wagon train, knowing that it must be in trouble. Hoppy and his men trick the outlaws, led by Jim Ferber, into believing that they are the real troopers, and the outlaws flee. Hoppy and his men then accompany a grateful Jane to Eldorado. There, Jane's companion, Diana Westcott, joyfully greets her uncle, Stephen Westcott. Westcott behaves strangely, however, and Hoppy suspects him of involvement with the outlaws. He and Lucky consult with governor Don Pedro, who informs them that he has called for state troopers to help quiet the uprising between local Mexican and American residents. A local monk indicates that the dissent is being fomented by a local rancher,

Ed Martin. Lucky, who is enamored of Diana, leaks the news of the troopers to Westcott, who works with Martin and concocts a plan to take over the town. Westcott urges Don Pedro to throw a fiesta; however, Martin takes everyone hostage at the party and declares his sovereignty. Hoppy escapes with Diana and takes refuge in the home of a friend of Jane's grizzled foreman, California Jack. Disguised as the monk, Hoppy gains entry to visit the hostages and sneaks in guns under his robes. The tables turn on Martin when Hoppy and friends thwart their own execution and Martin is killed. Jane joins Hoppy and their men when they battle the rest of the outlaws being led by Westcott. Hoppy finally captures Westcott, and he and the rest of the outlaws are brought to justice. With peace restored to Eldorado, the wagon train heads home. *Bandits. Freight lines.* Cultural conflict. Governors. Gunfights. Hostages. Impersonation and imposture. Mexican-American border region. Mexicans. Parties. Ranchers. Ranchhands. Rescues. Uncles. Uprisings. Wagon trains. Women in business.

Note: Although a *HR* news item indicates that writer Johnston McCulley sold his novel, *The Guardian Devil*, to Paramount for this film, Paramount Produced Properties listings indicate that the story was an original, and no publication information for the title listed above has been found. According to a Sep 1940 *HR* news item, production was interrupted for four months to allow time for actor William Boyd to heal from a leg injury. A modern source adds Ed Cassidy to the cast. This film was shot on location in Kernville, CA, and surrounding areas. For additional information on the series, consult the Series Index and see the entry for *Hop-Along Cassidy* in the *AFI Catalog of Feature Films, 1931-40*; F3.1990.
Box 18 Jan 1941. *DV* 3 Jan 1941. *FD* 17 Jan 1941, p. 7. *HR* 15 Mar 1940. *HR* 18 Sep 1940. *HR* 12 Aug 1940, p. 3. *HR* 15 Oct 1940, p. 4. *HR* 3 Jan 1941, p. 3. *MPH* 11 Jan 1941. *Var* 8 Jan 1941, p. 24.

DOOMED TO DIE (Chinese Americans)
Monogram Pictures Corp.; Scott R. Dunlap, in charge of production. *Dist* Monogram Pictures Corp. 12 Aug **1940**; *Prod:* began mid-Jun 1940 [©Monogram Pictures Corp.; 19 Jul 1940; LP9855]. Sd; b&w. 67 min. PCA cert no. 6505.
Series: Mr. Wong.
[*Exec prod* Scott R. Dunlap]. *Assoc prod* Paul Malvern. *Dir* William Nigh. [*Asst dir* Glen Cook]. *Scr* Michel Jacoby. *Orig story* Ralph Bettinson. *Photog* Harry Neumann. *Film ed* Robert Golden. [*Mus dir* Edward Kay]. *Sd eng* Karl Zint. *Tech dir* E. R. Hickson. *Prod mgr* Charles J. Bigelow.
Source: Based on characters created by Hugh Wiley in the "James Lee Wong" short stories in *Collier's*.
Cast: BORIS KARLOFF (*James Lee Wong*), Grant Withers (*Capt. Bill Street*), Marjorie Reynolds (*Bobby [Logan]*), Melvin Lang ([*Cyrus*] *Wentworth*), Guy Usher ([*Paul*] *Fleming*), Catherine Craig (*Cynthia Wentworth*), William Stelling (*Dick Fleming*), Harry Brandon (*Victor Martin*), [Wilbur Mack (*Mathews*)], [Kenneth Harlan], [Richard Loo], [Tris Coffin], [William Willmering], [Mike Donovan], [Jack Kennedy], [Maxine Leslie].
Detective. [*Print viewed*]. Despondent because of his increasing business losses and the tragic loss of his ship, the *Wentworth Castle* in a fire at sea, shipping magnate Cyrus Wentworth signs his will, leaving everything to his daughter Cynthia. Soon after, Cyrus' business rival, Paul Fleming, offers to consolidate their shipping lines, but Wentworth throws him out of his office. Fleming is in the outer office speaking to Mathews, a Wentworth employee, when his son Dick comes to inform Cyrus that he is planning to marry Cynthia. As Mathews and Fleming listen to the heated argument coming from Cyrus' office, a shot rings out and Cyrus is found dead. The police are summoned and Captain Bill Street arrests Dick for the murder. When Dick claims that he had already left for the office when the shot was fired, Cynthia's friend, reporter Bobby Logan, sends for special detective James Lee Wong to investigate. Suspecting a revenge motive for the shipowner's death, Wong goes to Chinatown to investigate. There he learns that Kai Ling was smuggling bonds from China aboard the *Wentworth Castle*, and is now missing. Wong also suspects Ludlow, the disgruntled Wentworth chauffeur, and follows him to the shipping office where he watches him burn some documents. After several more shootings, including the murder of Kai Ling, Wong discovers that Ludlow, Kai Ling and attorney Victor Martin were involved in a smuggling ring, and that Ludlow killed Cyrus in order to destroy all evidence of his involvement. Under Wong's scrutiny, the guilty man confesses and Dick is exonerated of all murders. *Chinese Americans. Detectives. False accusations. Murder. Shipping. Smuggling.* Business competition. Chauffeurs. Chinatowns. Confession (Law). Family relationships. Lawyers. Police. Reporters. Wills.

Note: The working title of this film was *Shadows over Chinatown*. For additional information about the series, consult the Series Index and see entry below for *Mr. Wong, Detective*.

DV 5 Aug 1940, p. 3. *FD* 3 Sep 1940, p. 3. *HR* 15 Jun 1940, pp. 6-7. *HR* 6 Aug 1940, p. 3. *MPD* 8 Aug 1940, p. 8. *NYT* 30 Jul 1940, p. 16. *MPH* 3 Aug 1940, p. 42. *Var* 7 Aug 1940, p. 14.

DOS MÁS UNO, DOS (Spanish language)

Fox Film Corp. *Dist* Fox Film Corp. **1934**; New York opening: 26 Oct 1934; Prod: Jun 1934 [©Fox Film Corp.; 29 Sep 1934; LP4980]. Sd (Western Electric); b&w. 8 reels, 6,830 ft. 76 min. PCA cert no. 199. Spanish language.

[*Prod* John Stone]. *Dirección de* [*Dir*] John Reinhardt. [*Asst dir* Sam Schneider]. [*Dial dir* José López Rubio]. *Adaptación cinematográfica de* [*Scr*] Anthony Coldeway and Hilda Hess. *Versión española de* [*Spanish version*] José López Rubio. [*Contr wrt* John Reinhardt]. [*Photog* Harry Jackson]. [*Ed* Fred Allen]. [*Cost* Royer]. [*Mus dir* Samuel Kaylin]. [*Sd* E. Clayton Ward].

Source: Based on the film *Don't Marry*, story by Philip Klein and Sidney Lanfield, screenplay by Randall H. Faye (Fox Film Corp., 1928).

Cast: Rosita Moreno (*Peggy/Elena* [*Carson*]), Valentín Parera (*Carlos* [*Bentley*]), Andrés de Segurola (*Sir Eduardo* [*Bentley*]), Carmen Rodríguez (*Tía Carolina*), Rafael Storm (*Henry*), Carlos Montalbán (*Ronald*), Lucio Villegas (*Jenkins*), Carlos Villarías (*Rodney*).

Romantic comedy. [*Not viewed*]. In England, childhood friends Elena Carson, a modern girl who likes to wear trousers, and Carlos Bentley, a stuffy archaeologist, fail to recognize one another when Elena crashes into Carlos' car on a winding road. Elena returns to the home of her staid aunt Carolina and then visits family friend Don Eduardo, Carlos' uncle. The two realize that Elena is the recklessly driving "flapper" about whom Carlos spoke, and agree to keep her identity a secret. At a tea, which Carlos and Don Eduardo attend, Elena arrives in an old-fashioned dress and conducts herself like a Victorian lady. Carlos, who prefers "pre-war" women, is immediately won over by her traditional charms. Elena tells him that the girl who crashed into him was her wild cousin Peggy, with whom she is often confused. At a costume ball, Carlos proposes to Elena, and before she can accept, he announces the news to Aunt Carrie and the party. Elena admits to Don Eduardo that she loves Carlos, but states that she wants him to love her for the woman whom she truly is. The two contrive a vacation at Don Eduardo's beach house, where Elena does her best to annoy Carlos by forbidding him to smoke his pipe, insisting on playing croquet daily, and showing up for a swimming lesson in an old-fashioned bathing suit, which prompts the laughter of everyone on the beach. As Carlos' patience wears thin, Elena shows up as "Peggy," looking very fetching as she reads a book about archaeology. At "Peggy's" insistence, Carlos breaks his date to take Elena and Aunt Carrie to an abbey near by, and instead assists her in racing Don Eduardo's boat in the regatta. Carlos and Peggy win the race, and at the yachting club, where Elena receives a trophy, the two meet on the terrace and almost kiss, but Carlos pulls away in horror at his supposed infidelity. Back in England, "Peggy" begins to despair as Carlos will not return her letters nor her phone calls. Elena and Carlos wed, and on their honeymoon cruise, she insists that he sleep in the sitting room. Meanwhile, "Peggy" calls and demands that Carlos visit her in her room, where the two embrace passionately. Carlos returns to Elena's room to confess all and finds Elena in the corridor with Henry, an old beau who recognized her as he walked past her room. When the two flee, Carlos finds a steward and searches for them room by room. Finding Elena and Henry, he throws out the latter and demands an explanation from Elena for her wedding night infidelity. As he admits that he loves her cousin Peggy, Elena's old-fashioned nightie slips to reveal Peggy's negligee, and Carlos realizes the ruse. He calls her Peggy and kisses her, and the steward discovers Elena's old-fashioned nightcap and gown that the happy couple have tossed from their porthole. *Impersonation and imposture. Romance. Tests of character. Archaeologists. Aunts. Automobile accidents. Beaches. Boatracing. England. Honeymoons. Masked balls. Proposals (Marital). Uncles. Vacations.*

Note: The onscreen credits were taken from a screen credit billing sheet in the Twentieth Century-Fox Records of the Legal Department at the UCLA Theater Arts Library, and the plot was based on a screen continuity in the Twentieth Century-Fox Produced Scripts Collection at the USC Library. The working titles of this film were *¡No te cases!* and *Deshabillé*. The film was released in Madrid under the title *¡Ojo, solteros!*. This film was based on a 1928 Fox film entitled *Don't Marry*, which was directed by James Tinling and starred Lois Moran and Neil Hamilton (see *AFI Catalog of Feature Films, 1921-30*; F2.1406). According to material in the Produced Scripts Collection, a new ending was added to the final script. In the original ending, the character Henry does not appear, and Carlos does not search with the steward for Elena's whereabouts; after Carlos confesses his love for Peggy to Elena, Elena admits that they are the same woman.

CM Oct 1934, p. 552. *FD* 30 Oct 1934, p. 4. *HR* 18 Jun 1934, p. 16. *NYT* 27 Oct 1934, p. 20.

DOS NOCHES (Spanish language)

Fanchon Royer Pictures, Inc. *Dist* J. H. Hoffberg Co. **1933**; Panama City, Panama opening: 16 Jun 1933; San Juan, Puerto Rico opening: 15 Jul 1933; New York opening: 28 Jul 1933; Prod: Jan—Feb 1933. Sd; b&w. 6 reels. 62 min. Spanish language.

Prod Jack Gallagher. *Dir* Carlos F. Borcosque. *Story* Frank E. Fenton and John Thomas Neville. *Scr* Albert Benham and John Thomas Neville. *Spanish dial* Miguel de Zárraga. *Photog* Ernest Miller.

Cast: José Crespo (*Boris Krinsky*), Conchita Montenegro (*Sandra Milaikov*), Romualdo Tirado (*Paul Denisy*), Antonio Cumellas (*Capitán Alba*), Carlos Villarías (*General Sánchez del Valle*), Juan Martínez Plá (*Méndez*), Paul Ellis (*Pierre Duval*), Enrique Acosta (*Manuel Jiménez Blanco*), Martín Garralaga (*Pedro Hernández*), Lita Santos (*Diana Gordon*), Manuel Noriega, Fernando G. Toledo.

Adventure. [*Viewed print incomplete*]. [The following plot summary is based on the English-language version of this film, *Revenge at Monte Carlo*; character names refer to that version. For further information regarding the English-language version, please see the note below and the entry for *Revenge at Monte Carlo* in the *AFI Catalog of Feature Films, 1931-40*.] Following President Alarcon's ouster from rule in the mythical republic of Luvania, a group of aristocrats plot in Monte Carlo for Alarcon's return and sign a manifesto pledging their fortunes to that cause. After Francisco Hernandez's father and brother are arrested as conspirators, secret intelligence chief Mendez offers Hernandez the chance to save their lives if he secures the manifesto in Monte Carlo. Reluctantly, Hernandez agrees and meets the conspirators at the Hotel Moderne in Monte Carlo, where he is given the manifesto after he explains that his brother is ill. As Hernandez hands it to Mendez outside the hotel, international crook Boris Krinsky grabs it and takes off in his fast car, planning to sell it for ten million dollars. Krinsky becomes smitten with Parisian ballet dancer Landra and goes to her dressing room, where he is turned away by her maid. Alba, Krinsky's former captain in the Luvanian Foreign Legion, whom Krinsky has hated for many years, also courts Landra, but he is also turned away that night. When Krinsky and his pal, Spike Maguire, a New York gang member, return to the hotel, they find Mendez searching for the papers, and Krinsky says he has secreted them in a vault. Landra, who loathes Krinsky, invites him to her room for a midnight supper. She reveals that Alba told her about the manifesto and proposes that they become partners in selling it, as she can set up a meeting at her castle near the Italian border with representatives of the conspirators. Aware that Krinsky has spoiled past deals because of his involvement with women, Spike wires a group of French Apaches, led by Gaston, to protect Krinsky. After seeing Hernandez and his men at a casino, Krinsky and Landra leave in their American roadster which soon outdistances their pursuers. As Krinsky hands Landra the manifesto to protect in her purse, they miss the turnoff to her castle, and when they skid while turning around, Hernandez and his men are able to capture them and the document. Landra's anger is mollified when Krinsky reveals that the papers Hernandez took were forged and that the real manifesto is still hidden. At the castle, Alba and his followers interrupt Krinsky and Landra's pursuance of romance and take Krinsky to the torture chamber in the dungeon. Alba, who was the cause of the scars on Krinsky's back while they were in the Legion, whips him again, until Spike and Gaston arrive and capture Alba and the others. Krinsky, who has learned that Landra's uncle and brother are part of the conspiracy to restore Alarcon to power, auctions the manifesto, which Mendez buys for two-and-one-half million dollars. Mendez discovers, however, when he opens the envelope, that Krinsky, to help Landra, has burned the incriminating signatures. *Aristocrats. Ballerinas. Criminals. Monte Carlo (Monaco). Mythical lands. Romance. Secret documents. Americans in foreign countries. Apaches-Paris. Auctions. Casinos. Castles. Chases. Conspiracy. Coups 'd'état. Family relationships. Forgers and forgery. Gangsters. Hotels. Maids. Romantic rivalry. Torture. Whips and whippings.*

Note: This was a Spanish-language version of *Revenge at Monte Carlo*, which was directed by Breezy Eason and starred June Collyer and José Crespo (see *AFI Catalog of Feature Films, 1931-40*; F3.3713). The working titles of the Spanish version were *Venganza en Monte Carlo* and *La república no peligra*. The incomplete print viewed contained no credits. When shown in Santiago, Chile, this film was entitled *Amante y traidora*.

CM May 1933, p. 260.

DOUBLE CROSSED *see* **SET FREE**

DOUBLE DEAL (African Americans)

Argus Pictures, Inc.; A Dixon R. Harwin Production. *Dist* International Road Shows, Inc. Dec? 1939; Brooklyn (New York) opening: 2 Apr 1939. Sd; b&w. 6 reels, 5,370 ft. 55 or 59-60 min. PCA cert no. 5831.

[*Exec prod* Jack Goldberg]. [*Dir* Arthur Dreifuss]. *Asst dir* Ralph Slosser. [*Scr* Arthur Hoerl]. [*Addl dial* F. E. Miller]. *Photog* Mack Stengler. *Gowns* J. I. Ree. *Miss Le Gon's furs by* H. J. Stearnes. *Mus dir* Ross Di Maggio. *Sd rec* Glen Glenn. *Coiffures* Ruth. *Unit mgr* William C. Kent.

Song(s): "Jitterbugs Cuttin' Rugs" and "Hole in the Wall," music and lyrics by Shelton Brooks; "Gettin' in Right with You," music and lyrics by Peter Tinturin and Harry Tobias.

Cast: Monte Hawley (*Jim McCoy*), Jeni Le Gon (*Nita Walker*), Eddie Thompson (*Dude Markey*), Florence O'Brien (*Sally*), Freddie Jackson (*Tommy McCoy*), Maceo Sheffield ([*Murray*] *Howard*), Buck Woods (*Sharpie*), Tommy Southern (*Eric*), Vernon McCalla (*Inspector*), Jack Clissby (*Xavier*), Arthur Ray (*Harmon*), Charles Gordon (*Lanny*), F. E. Miller (*Slim*), Shelton Brooks (*Himself*), [Charles Hawkins (*Snively*)].

African American, Crime, Drama, with songs. [*Print viewed*]. Murray Howard owns a nightclub where entertainer Nita Walker dances and sings. Although admired by Dude Markey, she is already in love with Jim McCoy. Snively, the club manager, in turn loves Sally, a cigarette girl and aspiring performer. She, however, likes Slim, who is penniless. Dude and Howard offer Jim's little brother Tommy a job, on condition he ask no questions. Tommy had earlier rejected his brother's offer of a Pullman job, despite it being a respectable position. Tommy discovers to his dismay that Dude is a criminal when he accompanies him on a safecracking job that results in the murder of a night watchman. Dude brings the stolen jewels back to Howard, who puts them in his safe as Dude secretly notes the combination. In the nightclub, after Shelton Brooks sings "Hole in the Wall," Dude asks Snively to fix him up with Nita, who then directs her singing of "Gettin' in Right with You" toward Dude. Jim becomes jealous, and when he goes to Nita's dressing room and Dude enters, a fight ensues between the two men. The fracas is broken up by Lanny, a policeman. Howard warns Dude to lay off Jim. When Jim escorts Sally and Nita to the their rooms, he finds Tommy waiting for him, and an inspector arrives to tell them of the recent robbery and murder. Later, Jim joins Dude and some others in a poker game. Dude removes the jewels, then takes advantage of Jim's presence by accusing him of robbing the safe, having dropped a slip of paper with the combination into his pocket. Jim escapes and, noticing the number 271 on the back of the piece of paper, asks Slim to see if it is someone's "lucky" number. Meanwhile, Nita has found Dude's gun in her dressing room with three cartridges missing. Howard is unhappy that Dude has not caught Jim, and Dude suggests they bring in Tommy instead. Dude tries to convince Nita to elope with him. Slim has found out that Dude was playing the number 271, and Nita tells Howard. However, Dude overhears and shoots Howard through the window, and Tommy is blamed. That night, Jim catches Dude picking up the diamonds where he had hid them, and after a pursuit to Nita's, they fight. Lanny arrives and Dude is shot. With the reward money, Jim becomes the new owner of the nightclub, which clears the way for his marriage to Nita. Slim becomes the new club manager, while Sally becomes the new entertainer. *African Americans. Brothers. Entertainers. False accusations. Nightclubs. Thieves. Fights. Friendship. Gambling. Gunshot wounds. Jealousy. Jewelry. Murder. Nightclub owners. Poker (Game). Police. Rewards. Romantic rivalry. Safes. Singers.*

Note: According to the onscreen credits, the film was copyrighted by Argus Pictures, but no record of copyright registration has been found. According to unidentified contemporary clippings from the black press, this was "the first Class A film made solely for colored consumption." One article indicates that Argus, which was located in Hollywood, secured the best in technical resources and crew for the production, including a ten-piece Swing orchestra. The cast of one hundred included a retired Los Angeles police captain. According to

modern sources, the cast also included Blue Washington, and Bert Goldberg was co-executive producer with Jack Goldberg. The file for the film in the MPAA/PCA Collection at the AMPAS Library contains a letter dated 19 Oct 1939, in which the PCA warned producer D. R. Harwin to avoid filming the "bump and kootch movements" in the dance sequence, and to remove any sexual suggestiveness in the dialogue between "Dude" and "Sharpie." In addition, the PCA urged the producer to "minimize the showing of the slot machines... details of the jewelry store break-in...and killing of policemen by criminals."

DV 21 Nov 1939, p. 3. *FD* 14 Dec 1939, p. 6. *MPD* 13 Dec 1939, p. 6. *MPH* 16 Dec 1939, p. 28. *NYT* 31 Aug 1941.

THE DOUBLE O (Latino)

Ben Wilson Productions. *Dist* Arrow Film Corp. 29 Nov 1921 [©Arrow Film Corp.; 3 Dec 1921; LP17272]. Si; b&w. 5 reels.

Dir Roy Clements. *Scen* Roy Clements. *Photog* King Gray.

Cast: Jack Hoxie (*Happy Hanes*), Steve Clemento (*Cholo Pete*), William Lester (*Mat Haley*), Ed La Niece (*Jim*), Evelyn Nelson (*Frances Powell*).

Western. Happy Hanes, foreman of the Double O Ranch (which is near the Mexican border), and his pal, Jim, incur the enmity of the ranch manager and Cholo Pete, who are in league with cattle rustlers. He insults the new ranch owner, Frances Powell, by offering to "sell" Pete for a kiss from her (saying he won Pete in a game), and she dismisses him. Mat Haley, the manager, angered by Frances' refusal to marry him, has Pete kidnap her, but Happy rescues her. Mexican bandits capture Happy and hold him for ransom, but Frances rescues him and the two are happily married. *Kidnapping. Mexican Americans. Mexican-American border region. Mexicans. Ranch foremen. Ranchers. Ransom. Rustlers.*

DOUGHBOYS *(foreign version) see* ¡**DE FRENTE, MARCHEN!**

DOUGHBOYS IN IRELAND (Irish Americans)

Columbia Pictures Corp. *Dist* Columbia Pictures Corp. 7 Oct 1943; Prod: 12 Jul—27 Jul 1943 [©Columbia Pictures Corp.; 7 Oct 1943; LP12307]. Sd; b&w. 5,633 ft. 61 min.

Prod Jack Fier. *Dir* Lew Landers. *Asst dir* William Mull. *Orig scr* Howard J. Green. *Addl dial* Monte Brice. *Dir of photog* L. W. O'Connell. *Art dir* Lionel Banks. *Assoc* Paul Murphy. *Film ed* Mel Thorsen. *Set dec* Frank Tuttle. *Mus dir* M. W. Stoloff. *Sd eng* Tom Lambert.

Song(s): "Mother Machree," words and music by Rida Johnson Young, Ernest R. Ball and Chauncey Olcott; "My Wild Irish Rose," words and music by Chauncey Olcott; "When Irish Eyes Are Smiling," words by Chauncey Olcott and George Graff, Jr., music by Ernest R. Ball; "I Have Faith," "Little American Boy," words and music by Yetta Cohen; "There Must Be an Easier Way," composer undetermined.

Cast: Kenny Baker (*Danny O'Keefe*), Jeff Donnell (*Molly Callahan*), Lynn Merrick (*Gloria Gold*), Guy Bonham (*Chuck Mayers*), Red Latham (*Corny Smith*), Wamp Carlson (*Tiny Johnson*), Bob Mitchum (*Ernie Jones*), Buddy Yarus (*Jimmy Martin*), Harry Shannon (*Michael Callahan*), Dorothy Vaughan (*Mrs. Callahan*), Larry Thompson (*Captain*), Syd Saylor (*Sergeant*), Herbert Rawlinson (*Larry Hunt*), Neil Reagan (*Musical captain*), Constance Wood (*Miss Wood*), Harry Anderson (*Soldier*), James Carpenter (*Sentry*), Craig Woods (*Corporal*), Muni Seroff (*Nick Greco*).

Military, Show business, Comedy-drama, with songs. [*Not viewed*]. As Danny O'Keefe, the band leader and vocalist at the Club Shamrock in New York City, is about to be inducted into the Army along with three members of his orchestra, Chuck Mayers, Corny Smith and Tiny Johnson, he asks Gloria Gold, a singer at the club, to wait for him. The ambitious Gloria insincerely pledges her love to Danny and promises to write him daily, although in reality, Gloria's only interest lies in pursuing a Broadway career. At training camp, Danny spends every spare minute writing lengthy letters to Gloria, who, too busy to reply, instructs her elderly secretary to respond to Danny's letters, signing the singer's name. With basic training completed, Danny and his friends are sent to Ireland. While Danny is on sentry duty one day, Molly Callahan drives her donkey cart to the edge of the Army camp. When Danny demands that she leave, Molly becomes insulted and reports the incident to her father, Michael Callahan. Michael relates the offense to several dozen more Callahans, and as a result, every American soldier who looks at an Irish girl receives a sound trouncing at the hands of the Callahans. To prevent further confrontations, the top sergeant demands that Danny apologize to Molly. At the Callahan home, Danny wins over Molly and

her entire family by singing Irish ballads, and the family then decides to convert a nearby mansion into an entertainment center for the soldiers. Realizing that Molly has fallen in love with him, Danny, fearful of igniting another feud, begins to court her, although he is still in love with Gloria. When Gloria appears at the camp during a tour of Army outposts and greets him casually, however, Danny begins to have doubts about his infatuation with the singer. Molly, meanwhile, has overheard a conversation about Danny's apparent romance with Gloria, and brokenhearted, is ready to give him up without a fight. Encouraged by her mother to fight for her man, Molly returns to the camp to speak to Danny, but she is too late because his unit has just been sent on a commando raid. While his life is in danger, Danny realizes that he truly loves Molly. Danny is severely wounded in the raid and hospitalized. In his delirium, he keeps calling for Gloria, but only Molly is there. Molly is shattered until she learns that Danny only wants to speak to Gloria to inform her that he is in love with Molly. All ends happily as Danny, now recovered, rides back to camp in Molly's donkey cart. *Ambition. Band leaders. Ireland. Irish Americans. Romance. Singers. Soldiers.* Family life. Feuds. Hospitals. Letters. Military posts. Musicians. New York City. Secretaries. Songs. Unrequited love. War injuries.

Note: According to a Jan 1943 news item in *HR*, Columbia originally sought Bonita Granville to appear in this picture.

DV 11 Nov 1943, p. 3. *HR* 27 Jan 1943, p. 3. *HR* 11 Nov 1943, p. 3. *MPH* 9 Oct 1943. *MPHPD* 18 Sep 1943, p. 1545. *MPHPD* 9 Oct 1943, p. 1574. *Var* 15 Dec 1943, p. 8.

THE DOVE (Latino)

Norma Talmadge Productions. *Dist* United Artists Corp. 7 Jan **1927**; New York premiere: 31 Dec 1927 [©Joseph Schenck; 16 Jan 1928; LP24864]. Si; b&w. 9 reels, 9,100 ft.

Pres Joseph M. Schenck. *Dir* Roland West. *Adpt* Roland West and Willard Mack. *Adpt, cont and titles* Wallace Smith. *Cont* Paul Bern. *Photog* Oliver Marsh. *Art dir* William Cameron Menzies. *Film ed* Hal Kern.

Source: Based on the play *The Dove* by Willard Mack and Gerald Beaumont (New York, 11 Feb 1925).

Cast: Norma Talmadge (*Dolores*), Noah Beery (*Don José Maria y Sandoval*), Gilbert Roland (*Johnny Powell*), Eddie Borden (*Billy*), Harry Myers (*Mike*), Michael Vavitch (*Gómez*), Brinsley Shaw (*The Patriot*), Kalla Pasha (*The Comandante*), Charles Darvas (*The Comandante's Captain*), Michael Dark (*Sandoval's Captain*), Walter Daniels (*The Drunk*).

Romance. Dolores, a dance hall girl known as "The Dove," is in love with a gambler named Johnny Powell. Don José, a wealthy caballero smitten by Dolores' beauty, frames Powell on a murder charge. Dolores bargains with Don José to release Powell in exchange for her freedom, but on the eve of her marriage to Don José, Powell returns from exile to claim Dolores. After an unsuccessful escape, Powell and Dolores are about to be shot when a crowd of bystanders forces Don José to release them. He relents, frees the prisoners, and gives them his carriage in which to depart. *Dance hall girls. Frame-ups. Gambling. Mexicans. Murder.*

FD 8 Jan 1928. *NYT* 3 Jan 1928, p. 28. *Var* 11 Jan 1928, p. 20.

DOWN BY THE RIO GRANDE (Latino)

Phil Goldstone Productions. **1924**; New York State license: 20 May 1924. Si; b&w. 5 reels, 4,800 ft.

Dir Alvin J. Neitz. *Scen* Donald Fitch. *Story* Julio Sabello. *Photog* Roland Price.

Cast: William Fairbanks, Dorothy Revier, Andrew Waldron, Olive Trevor, Jack Richardson, Milton Ross.

Melodrama. "The script... [tells] of a Spanish family who own an extensive ranch, with the deed to the property ultimately finding its way to the rightful owner, the unspoken-of relative (Fairbanks), after a villainous cousin has possessed the papers and stated marriage to the daughter as the price of his silence." (*Var* 18 Jun 1924, p. 23.). *Land claims. Ranches. Rio Grande. Spaniards.*

FD 22 Jun 1924. *Var* 18 Jun 1924, p. 23.

DOWN TO THE SEA (Greek Americans)

Republic Pictures Corp. *Dist* Republic Pictures Corp. 25 Aug **1936**; Prod: began 9 May 1936 [©Republic Pictures Corp.; 20 Jul 1936; LP6477]. Sd (RCA Victor "High Fidelity" Sound System); b&w. 7 reels, 6,163 ft. 67 or 69 min. Passed by the National Board of Review. PCA cert no. 2283.

Prod Nat Levine. *Supv* Armand Schaefer. *Dir* Lewis D. Collins. [*Asst dir* Harry Knight]. *Scr* Wellyn Totman and Robert Lee Johnson. *Orig story* Eustace L. Adams, Wellyn Totman and William A. Ulman, Jr. *Photog* Harry Neumann. *Spec eff* Bud Thackeray. *Film ed* Charles Craft. *Supv ed* Murray Seldeen. [*Mus score* Arthur Kaye]. *Mus supv* Harry Grey. [*Sd* Robert Pritchard]. *Sd eng* Terry Kellum.

Cast: Russell Hardie [(*Johnny Kamines*)], Ben Lyon [(*Steve Londos*)], Ann Rutherford [(*Helen Pappas*)], Irving Pichel [(*Alex Grenaris*)], Fritz Leiber [(*Gregory Pappas*)], Vince Barnett [(*Hector*)], Maurice Murphy [(*Luis*)], Nigel de Brulier [(*Demetrius*)], Paul Porcasi [(*Vasilios*)], Vic Potel [(*Andy*)], Karl Hackett [(*Joe*)], Francisco Maran [(*George*)], Frank Yaconelli [(*Pete*)], Mike Tellegan [(*Cimos*)], [John Picorri (*Greek proprietor*)].

Sea, Drama. [*Print viewed*]. Trouble is brewing between rival factions of Tarpon Springs, Florida, a Greek community of sponge gatherers, when Johnny Kamines returns from college to visit his childhood friends, Steve Londos and Helen Pappas. Steve is the chief diver on a boat owned by Helen's gruff father, Captain Gregory Pappas, and captained by Alex Grenarias. Alex and Steve occasionally dive illegally in the shallow waters reserved for "hookers," the sponge gatherers who use long hooks. Although their actions anger the hookers, Pappas' power and prestige prevent them from redressing the situation. Steve and Helen are engaged, despite Helen and Johnny's strong feelings for each other. Johnny therefore strives to protect Helen's feelings the day after she arrives, when he finds Steve drunk at Alex's house, where he was to turn in money he raised in an annual drive to help crippled divers. The girls entertaining Steve and Alex steal the collection money, and after Johnny uses his tuition money to replace it, he must begin working on the Pappas boat. One day, Johnny tries to stop Alex and Steve from poaching sponges but to no avail. While Steve is diving, he grabs the hook of a one sponger and almost drowns him. Johnny saves the man, Luis, who works with his father Demetrius, and then joins the battle on the side of the hookers. The next afternoon, Johnny brings the sheriff to the auction where the sponges from Alex's boat are being sold. After verifying that the catch was poached, the sheriff arrests Alex and his crew. Once they are released on bail, Alex and Steve look for Johnny, but when they do not find him at Luis' boat, the spiteful Alex hits Demitrius, who falls into the water and drowns. Steve then finds Helen and Johnny together and returns Johnny's tuition money to him. Helen prevents the men from fighting and, after Johnny leaves, breaks her engagement to Steve. Pappas enters the argument, telling Steve that he must leave that night on the boat to avoid prosecution, and ordering Helen to marry Steve when he returns in three months. After Pappas collapses, Steve and Helen agree to carry out his wishes. Meanwhile, Luis finds Steve's medallion on the dock by his boat and assumes that he is responsible for Demitrius' disappearance. The hookers chase Pappas' boat, and when Alex sees them coming, he brings Steve up too quickly from his dive in hopes of killing him before he tells the hookers the truth about the murder. Steve gets a severe case of the bends, and when Johnny deduces the reason behind Alex's actions, Alex knocks him out and puts him into Steve's diving suit. When the hookers storm the boat, they mistake Johnny for Steve and try to cut his airline. While everyone is fighting, however, Steve crawls on deck and attempts to raise Johnny himself. In the end, Alex is thrown to the sharks, Johnny is rescued and prevents anyone from being arrested, and the three childhood friends are reconciled before Steve dies. *Class distinction. Divers and diving. Greek Americans. Murder. Poachers. Romantic rivalry.* Charity. Cooks. Drowning. Drunkenness. Fathers and daughters. Fights. Florida. Handicapped. Paralysis. Religion. Rescues. Self-sacrifice. Sharks. Ship crews. Ship owners. Sponges. Thieves.

Note: The working titles of this film were *Beneath the Seas*, and *Twenty Fathoms Below*. It was reviewed by the *NYT* as *Down Under the Seas*, and called *Beneath the Seas* by *MPH*'s "In the Cutting Room." The onscreen credits note that the picture's underwater scenes were filmed at Silver Springs, FL, and dedicate the film to the Greek community of Tarpon Springs, FL, who cooperated in the production. *HR* production charts include Dorothy Ates in the cast; her participation in the completed film has not been confirmed, however. Although Irving Pichel's character is listed as Alex Fotakis in contemporary reviews, he is called Alex Grenaris in the film.

Box 11 Jul 1936. *DV* 27 Jun 1936, p. 3. *FD* 5 Dec 1935, p. 12. *FD* 17 Apr 1936, p. 12. *FD* 30 Jun 1936, p. 14. *HR* 9 May 1936, p. 2. *HR* 18 May 1936, p. 9. *HR* 27 Jun 1936, p. 3. *MPD* 1 Jul 1936, p. 11. *MPH* 30 May 1936, p. 34. *MPH* 11 Jul 1936, p. 105. *NYT* 10 Aug 1936, p. 10. *Var* 12 Aug 1936, p. 19.

DOWN UNDER THE SEAS *see* **DOWN TO THE SEA**

DRáCULA (Spanish language)
Universal Pictures Corp. *Dist* Universal Pictures Corp. **1931**; Havana, Cuba opening: 11 Mar 1931; New York opening: 24 Apr 1931; Prod: 23 Oct–Nov 1930. Sd (Sistema Western Electric [Western Electric Sound System]); b&w. 11 reels. 103 min. Spanish language.
Presenta [*Pres*] Carl Laemmle. *Producida por* [*Prod*] Carl Laemmle, Jr. *Productor asociado* [*Assoc prod*] Paul Kohner. *Dirigida por* [*Dir*] George Melford. [*Dial dir* Enrique Tovar Avalos]. [*Asst dir* Jay Marchant and Charles Gould]. [*Scr* Garrett Fort]. *Versión española de* [*Spanish version*] B. Fernández Cué. *Fotografo* [*Photog*] George Robinson. *Director artistico* [*Art dir*] Charles D. Hall. *Editor del film* [*Film ed*] Arturo Tavares. *Supervisor de la edición del film* [*Supv film ed*] Maurice Pivar. *Supervisor de acústica* [*Sd supv*] C. Roy Hunter. [*Makeup* Jack P. Pierce].
Source: Based on the novel *Dracula* by Bram Stoker (London, 1897).
Cast: Carlos Villar (*Conde Drácula*), Lupita Tovar (*Eva*), Barry Norton (*Juan Harker*), Pablo Alvarez Rubio (*Renfield*), Eduardo Arozamena (*Van Helsing*), José Soriano Viosca (*Doctor Seward*), Carmen Guerrero (*Lucía*), Amelia Senisterra (*Marta*), Manuel Arbó (*Martín*).
Horror. [*Print viewed*]. [The following plot summary is based on the English-language version of this film, *Dracula*; character names refer to that version. For further information regarding the English-language version, please see the note below and the entry for *Dracula* in the *AFI Catalog of Feature Films, 1931-40*.] English businessman Renfield has a harrowing journey to Transylvania, where he is to arrange a lease of the Carfax Abbey in England for Count Dracula. Unknown to Renfield, Dracula is a centuries-old vampire, who lives off the blood of humans and cannot withstand the light of day. Renfield is greeted at Dracula's castle by Dracula himself, but after he passes out from drinking drugged wine, his host descends upon him to feed on his blood. Renfield, weakened by the attack, and Dracula board an England-bound ship which also carries the coffin in which Dracula sleeps during the day and several coffins filled with his native soil, which is required for his survival. When the ship docks at Whitby Harbor, the entire crew is found dead. Only Dracula and Renfield, who appears to have gone insane, survive. Renfield is installed in Dr. Seward's sanitarium, where the physician studies his strange habit of consuming the blood of small animals. Meanwhile, Dracula drains the blood of the female population of London. One night at the opera, Dracula introduces himself to Dr. Seward and meets his daughter Mina, her fiancé, John Harker, and friend Lucy. Lucy is enchanted by Dracula's romantic manner, and later, Dracula attacks and kills her. German scientist Van Helsing arrives in London to assist Dr. Seward, and correctly assesses the situation. As Carfax Abbey is next to Seward's estate, Dracula has easy access to its occupants, and he takes advantage of his ability to transform himself into a bat to attack his next victim, Mina. However, she does not die immediately, but undergoes a change over several nights. Van Helsing confirms for Seward and Harker that Dracula truly is a vampire when Dracula's reflection does not appear in the mirror of a cigarette box. Meanwhile, Renfield constantly escapes from the hospital as ordered by his master, Dracula. Despite the precautions of Van Helsing to prevent Dracula's entry into Mina's room, he hypnotizes her maid to open the windows to admit him. Mina succumbs to a final bonding with Dracula and becomes a vampire. She confesses to Van Helsing that she has seen Lucy since she was buried, which confirms his suspicions that the "woman in white" who has been attacking young children is Lucy. Dracula tries to hypnotize Van Helsing to force him to do his will, but Van Helsing resists and is saved by his crucifix, upon which Dracula cannot look. Dracula, followed by Renfield, takes Mina to Carfax Abbey, where he plans to make her final transition to vampirism. Van Helsing and John follow Renfield there, but when Dracula discovers their presence, he kills Renfield. Dawn approaches, and when Van Helsing finds Dracula in his coffin, he drives a stake through his heart, killing him for eternity. At the same time that Dracula is killed, Mina is released from his spell. With the horror ended, John and Mina reunite. *Death and dying. England. Metamorphosis. Murder. Physicians. Vampires.* Bats. Castles. Coffins. Corpses. Engagements. Germans. Hypnotism. London (England). Maids. Nobility. Opera. Romantic rivalry. Sanitariums. Ships. Storms. Superstition. Transylvania (Romania). Whitby (England).

Note: Universal simultaneously made a Spanish-language version of the 1931 *Dracula*. The English-language version was directed by Tod Browning and starred Bela Lugosi. Please see the entry for that film in the *AFI Catalog of Feature Films, 1931-40*; F3.1121. Both versions utilized the same sets. Most of the Spanish-language version was shot at night, while the English-language version was shot during the day. The actor who plays Dracula in the Spanish version is billed on screen as Carlos Villar, but was more commonly known as Carlos Villarías.
Many films have been based on the Dracula legend. A partial listing includes the following: The 1921 German production *Nosferatu—Eine Symphonie des Grauens*, which was unofficially based on Bram Stoker's novel, directed by Friedrich Wilhelm Murnau and starring Max Schreck; the 1932 German-French film *Vampyr*, directed by Carl Theodor Dreyer and starring Julian West and Henriette Gérard; the 1956 Italian film *I Vampiri*, directed by Riccardo Freda and starring Gianna Maria Canale and Antoine Balpêtré; the 1958 British film *Dracula*, directed by Terence Fisher and starring Peter Cushing and Christopher Lee; the 1973 British television production of *Dracula*, directed by Dan Curtis and starring Jack Palance; the 1979 American *Dracula*, directed by John Badham and starring Frank Langella, Laurence Olivier, Donald Pleasance and Kate Nelligan; the 1979 German film *Nosferatu: Phantom der Nacht*, directed by Werner Herzog and starring Klaus Kinski and Isabelle Adjani; and the 1992 film *Bram Stoker's Dracula*, directed by Francis Ford Coppola and starring Gary Oldman and Winona Ryder.
Cinl Mar 1931, p. 36.

THE DRAGON'S SHADOW *see* **THE MIDNIGHT PATROL**

DRAGOON WELLS MASSACRE (Native Americans, Apache)
Lindsley Parsons Productions, Inc. *Dist* Allied Artists Pictures Corp. 28 Apr **1957**; Prod: early Jul–early Aug 1956 [©Allied Artists Pictures Corp.; 3 Apr 1957; LP8010]. Sd; col (Eastman Color); CinemaScope. 7,910 ft. 87-88 min. PCA cert no. 18220.
Prod Lindsley Parsons. *Assoc prod* John H. Burrows. *Dir* Harold Schuster. *Asst dir* Kenneth Walters and Lindsley Parsons, Jr. *Scr* Warren Douglas. *Orig story* Oliver Drake. *Photog* William H. Clothier. *Film ed* Maurice Wright. *Mus* Paul Dunlap. *Sung by* Roger Wagner Chorale. *Rec* Tom Lambert. *Makeup* Willard Colee. *Hairdresser* Vou Lee Giokaris. *Set continuity* Bobbie Sierks. *Chief set electrician* Lloyd L. Garnell. *Casting* Fred H. Messenger.
Cast: Barry Sullivan (*Link Ferris*), Mona Freeman (*Ann Bradley*), Dennis O'Keefe (*Capt. Matt Riordan*), Katy Jurado (*Mara Fay*), Jack Elam (*Tioga*), Sebastian Cabot (*Jonah McAdam*), Casey Adams (*Phillip Scott*), Trevor Bardette (*Marshal Bill Haney*), Jon Shepodd (*Tom*), Hank Worden (*Hopi Charlie*), Warren Douglas (*Jud*), Judy Stranges (*Susan*), Alma Beltran (*Station agent's wife*), John War Eagle.
Western. [*Not viewed*]. In 1860, a prison wagon transporting two outlaws, Link Ferris and Tioga, is traveling through the Arizona desert country toward Fort Dragoon, accompanied by Marshal Bill Haney and his assistant Tom. On the way, they come across, in turn, Indian trader Jonah McAdam; Capt. Matt Riordan, the only survivor of a cavalry company ambushed by Apaches; and a stagecoach carrying an engaged couple, Phillip Scott and Ann Bradley, and entertainer Mara Fay. Realizing that the Apaches are bound to attack again, they all join forces in an effort to reach Fort Dragoon safely. Jonah, who unbeknown to the others, has been supplying the Apaches with guns and whiskey, murders Jud, the driver of the prison wagon. Link wants to shoot Jonah, but Capt. Riordan insists that he stand trial. Subsequent attacks by the Apaches destroy the wagons and claim the lives of Tom, Tioga and Phillip. The rest reach Fort Dragoon, only to find the stockade surrounded by Apaches. The men cut cards to see who will ride the only remaining horse to Fort Buchanan for help. Link gets the assignment, and he is captured and wounded by the Apaches. Meanwhile, Mara and Ann, who used to be romantically involved with Capt. Riordan, have developed a strong dislike for each other, and their mutual animosity finally erupts in a savage fight. The next morning, the Apaches offer to trade Link for Jonah, and Capt. Riordan, seeing no alternative, agrees to the exchange. Capt. Riordan, Link and Marshal Haney then set off for Fort Buchanan together. At the Indians' encampment, they discover Jonah urging the Apaches to massacre all of the whites, and Link is compelled to shoot him. A band of whites unexpectedly arrives and dispatches the Apaches. After Marshal Haney gives Link his freedom, he and Ann, who have fallen in love, depart together. *Apache Indians. Convicts. Massacres. Officers (Military). Traders. Wagon trains.* Ambushes. Arizona. Duplicity. Engagements. Entertainers. Fights. Forts. Marshals. Romantic rivalry. United States. Army. Cavalry.
Note: This film's working title was *Massacre at Dragoon Wells*. The film was shot in Kanab, UT.

Box 4 May 1957. *DV* 11 May 1953. *DV* 5 Jul 1956. *DV* 3 May 1957, p. 3. *Exb* 12 Jun 1957. *FD* 3 May 1957, p. 6. *Har* 11 May 1957, p. 74. *HR* 6 Jul 1956, p. 8. *HR* 27 Jul 1956, p. 12. *HR* 3 May 1957. *MPHPD* 4 May 1957, p. 361. *NYT* 6 May 1957, p. 25. *Var* 8 May 1957, p. 6.

DRAY TEKHTER *see* **THREE DAUGHTERS**

THE DREAM OF HOME *see* **TILL THE END OF TIME**

DREAM WIFE (Middle Eastern Americans)

Metro-Goldwyn-Mayer Corp.; controlled by Loews Inc. *Dist* Loew's Inc. 19 Jun **1953**; Prod: mid-Sep–late Oct 1952 [©Loew's Inc.; 6 Mar 1953; LP2716]. Sd (Western Electric Sound System); b&w. 9,120 ft. 99 min. Passed by the National Board of Review. PCA cert no. 16307.

Prod Dore Schary. *Dir* Sidney Sheldon. *Asst dir* Arvid Griffen. *Scr* Sidney Sheldon, Herbert Baker and Alfred Lewis Levitt. *Dir of photog* Milton Krasner. *Spec eff* A. Arnold Gillespie and Warren Newcombe. *Art dir* Cedric Gibbons and Daniel B. Cathcart. *Film ed* George White. *Set dec* Edwin B. Willis and Alfred E. Spencer. *Women's cost des* Helen Rose. *Men's cost des* Herschel McCoy. *Mus* Conrad Salinger. *Rec supv* Douglas Shearer. *Hairstyles* Sydney Guilaroff. *Makeup created by* William Tuttle.

Song(s): "Tarji's Song" and "Ghi-li, Ghi-li, Ghi-li," music and lyrics by Charles Wolcott and Jamshid Sheibani.

Cast: CARY GRANT (*Clemson Reade*), DEBORAH KERR (*Effie*), WALTER PIDGEON (*Walter McBride*), and introducing Betta St. John ([*Princess*] *Tarji*), Eduard Franz (*Khan [of Bukistan]*), Buddy Baer (*Vizier*), Les Tremayne (*Ken Landwell*), Donald Randolph (*Ali*), Bruce Bennett (*Charlie Elkwood*), Richard Anderson (*Henry Malvine*), Dan Tobin (*Mr. Brown*), Movita (*Rima*), Gloria Holden (*Mrs. Landwell*), June Clayworth (*Mrs. Elkwood*), Dean Miller (*George*), Steve Forrest (*Louis*), Jonathan Cott (*Marine*), Patricia Tiernan (*Pat*), [Mary Lawrence (*Mrs. Malvine*)], [Faire Binney (*Mrs. Parker*)], [Dan Barton (*Marine*)], [Edward Cassidy (*Customs official*)], [Perry Sheehan (*Evelyn, a receptionist*)], [Virginia Mullen (*Annie*)], [Marie Brown (*Miss Temple*)], [Dick Rich (*Delivery man*)], [Bert Moorhouse (*Attlow*)], [Jimmy Moss (*Small boy*)], [Gail Bonney (*"Mommy"*)], [Lillian Culver (*Woman at airport*)], [Forbes Murray, Donald Dillaway, Gayne Whitman (*Men at airport*)], [John Alvin, Dorothy Kennedy (*Reporters*)], [William Hamel, Allen O'Locklin (*Clerks*)], [Aram Katcher, Andre d'Arcy, William McCormick, Bernie Gozier, Mohamed Ilbagi (*Bukistanians*)], [Jim Cronin, Paul F. Smith (*Bellhops*)], [Alphonse Martel (*Head waiter*)], [Jack Chefe (*Captain*)], [Margie Liszt (*Woman cab driver*)], [Charles Sullivan (*Truck driver*)], [William Vedder (*Old man*)], [Vernon Rich (*McBride's assistant*)], [Robert E. Nichols, Dabbs Greer (*Elevator boys*)], [Kathleen Freeman (*Chambermaid*)], [Aram Katcher (*Messenger*)], [Rudy Rama (*Servant*)], [Bob Lugo (*Guard*)], [Hassan Khyyam (*Bukistanian priest*)], [Gordon Richards (*Sir Cecil*)], [Beryl McCutcheon, Margaret Hedin, Inez Gorman (*Secretaries*)], [Jack George (*Clarence*)], [Kay Riehl], [Jean Andren], [Harry Stanton], [Steve Carruthers], [James Farrar].

Romantic comedy. [*Print viewed*]. While on a business trip to the Middle Eastern country of Bukistan, American salesman Clemson Reade is invited to the home of the Khan of Bukistan. There he meets the Khan's beautiful daughter, the princess Tarji, who performs a seductive dance for him. During the dance, the Khan tells Clemson that Tarji has been "trained" to devote her life to pleasing the man she marries. Clemson is fascinated by prospect of an utterly devoted wife, but he leaves Bukistan the following week to marry his American fiancée, Priscilla "Effie" Effington. Back in New York, Clemson visits Effie at the State Department, where she works, only to be brushed aside by her attention to an oil crisis. Later that night, Effie spoils a romantic evening planned by Clemson when she tells him that the wedding must be postponed until after the oil deal is signed. When Effie's partner, Walter McBride, drops by to discuss the oil contract, Clemson realizes that his desire for a "full-time wife" cannot be reconciled with Effie's demand for a "part-time husband," and he calls off the engagement. The following day, while meeting with his male colleagues and bemoaning the progress made by women seeking their independence, Clemson hits upon the idea of marrying Tarji, the one woman he knows who was "trained from that day she was born to be a dream wife." Clemson cables a marriage proposal to Tarji, and in three weeks the princess' acceptance arrives with a delivery of goats as her dowry. Meanwhile, at the State Department, McBride, worried that a misstep by Clemson in the

courting of Tarji will result in a collapse of the oil deal, assigns Effie to chaperone the two and ensure that their courtship goes smoothly. Soon after Tarji arrives in New York, Clemson becomes frustrated when he learns that Eastern custom forbids any physical contact with his new fiancée until after their marriage. To make matters worse, Clemson is told that the wedding date has been set by the Khan and that it will not be for another three months. Under Effie's tutelage, Tarji soon learns how to speak English, and appreciate the emancipated life that Western women enjoy. One day, while walking in the city, Tarji meets a number of young men, and innocently leads them to believe that she is available for dates. Later that night, confusion abounds when the men that Tarji met on the street arrive at her hotel room expecting to spend time with the princess. A fistfight ensues, and Tarji is jailed as a result. Angered by news of the scandal, the Khan rushes to America and announces the end of his daughter's romance with Clemson. With the oil contract in peril, Effie uses her charm to win the friendship of the Khan, and persuades him to let Tarji marry Clemson. The day before he and Tarji are to marry, however, Clemson rediscovers his love for Effie and decides to break off his engagement. Tarji breaks the engagement first, though, and tells him that she prefers to marry someone that she chooses herself. After extracting a promise from the Khan to sign the oil agreement, Effie turns her attention to Clemson, and the two embrace in a kiss. *Battle of the sexes. Cultural conflict. Muslims. Oil magnates. Princesses. Salesmen. United States. Dept. of State. Women in politics. Women's rights. Americans in foreign countries. Dancers. Diplomats. Dowry. Drunkenness. Earthquakes. Engagements. Fathers and daughters. Goats. Jealousy. Language and languages. Middle East. Mistaken identity. Oil. Proposals (Marital). Weddings.*

Note: The film's opening credits are presented after a speech delivered by the "Kahn of Bukistan," who addresses the audience in gibberish which is "translated" by subtitles. A 1951 *Var* news item noted that M-G-M purchased the story on which this film was based for approximately $50,000. *Dream Wife* marked the screen debut of stage actress Betta St. John, who changed her name from Betta Streigler. The file for the film in the MPAA/PCA Collection at the AMPAS Library contains a letter, dated 27 Nov 1951, written by Joseph Breen of the PCA and sent to Dore Schary, in which Breen warned the producer that the "basic story" of the script or treatment was in violation of the Production Code. Breen wrote that the presentation of the U.S. State Dept. and the fictitious country of Bukistan constituted a violation of the Production Code. While commending the studio for making it clear that Bukistan was a fictitious country, Breen nevertheless asserted that it was a "rather thin veil" through which it was clear to see that the locale of the story was the Near East. [Both the film and studio publicity identified "Bukistan" as a Middle Eastern country.] Breen went on to write that the story "ridicules the way of life, the customs, and habits of people unmistakably identified as present day natives of the explosive Near East territory." Although Breen informed Schary in Sep 1952 that the story, which was probably revised and then resubmitted, seemed to "meet the provisions of the Code," he later appealed to Schary to consider the possiblity that the exhibition of the film might lead to charges that Hollywood was propagandizing. Breen emphasized that the "whole Middle East, predominately Moslem, is in a very touchy state of mind right now." He further noted that the film might "influence public opinion in connection with the troubled question of the State of Israel," and that the charges of propagandizing might result in "serious damage throughout the Moslem world, not only to the company involved, but to our industry in general, and in fact to the whole foreign policy of the United States in that area." *Dream Wife* received an Academy Award nomination in the category of Best Costume Design.

Box 14 Mar 1953. *DV* 9 Mar 1953, p. 3. *FD* 16 Mar 1953, p. 10. *HR* 19 Sep 1952, p. 14. *HR* 31 Oct 1952, p. 12. *HR* 9 Mar 1953, p. 3. *MPHPD* 14 Mar 1953, p. 1758. *NYT* 30 Jul 1953, p. 20. *Var* 19 Mar 1951. *Var* 11 Mar 1953, p. 6.

DIE DREIGROSCHENOPER (German language)

Warner Bros. Pictures, Inc.; Gemeinschaft mit Tobis. *Dist* Warner Bros. Pictures, Inc. **1931**; Berlin opening: 19 Feb 1931; Prod: in Berlin, Germany. Sd; b&w. 97 min. *Country of origin* Germany. German language.

Dir G. W. Pabst. *Scr* Leo Lania, Béla Balázs and Ladislaus Vajda. *Photog* Fritz Arno Wagner. *Settings* Andre Andreiev. *Ed* Hans Oser. *Mus dir* Theo Makeben. *Mus* Kurt Weill. *Sd* A. Jansen.

Source: Based on the opera *Die Dreigroschenoper*, book and libretto by Berthold Brecht, music by Kurt Weill (Berlin, 13 Oct 1928), which was based on the play *The Beggar's Opera* by John Gay (London, 29 Jan 1728).

Cast: Rudolph Förster (*Mackie Messer*), Carola Neher (*Polly Peachum*), Reinhold Schünzel (*Tiger Brown*), Fritz Rasp (*Peachum*), Valeska Gert (*Mrs. Peachum*), Lotte Lenya (*Jenny*), Herman Thimig (*The pastor*), Ernst Busch (*The street singer*), Wladimir Sokoloff (*Jailer*), Paul Kemp, Gustav Püttjer, Oscar Höcker, Kraft Roschig (*Mackie's gang*), Herbert Grünbaum (*Filch*).

Musical, Social, Drama. [*Print viewed*]. As he is leaving Jenny at the doors of a brothel, Mackie Messer, a pimp and gangster, sees Polly Peachum, the daughter of the king of beggars, on the street with her mother and immediately invites them into a local pub for a drink. He has already decided that he will marry Polly and instructs his men to steal a wedding dress and a complete set of home furnishings, including a grandfather clock. He orders them to invite Tiger Brown, the chief of police to the ceremony. While one of Mackie's men dances with Mrs. Peachum, Mackie and Polly come to an understanding. That evening Polly and Mackie are married, and Brown is one of the guests. Every beggar in London owes allegiance to Peachum; no one can beg without a license from the king of beggars. Peachum is furious when he learns of Polly's marriage, and out of revenge, he demands that Brown arrest Mackie. When Brown refuses, Peachum threatens to disrupt the approaching coronation of the English queen, which will cost Brown his job. When Polly learns of her father's actions, she warns Mackie to go into hiding, asking him to stay away from other women, particularly those in the brothel. Mackie turns over his business to Polly, but he has no intention of passing up his regular visit to Jenny. Knowing his habits, Mrs. Peachum brings the police to the brothel to wait for Mackie. She tells Jenny of Mackie's marriage and asks her to betray him. Angered by the news, Jenny signals to the police when Mackie arrives, but has a change of heart and helps him escape over the roofs. He hides with another prostitute, but the police capture him when he leaves her room. Meanwhile, under Polly's leadership, Mackie's gang has taken over a bank; from now on they will rob people legally. Peachum, believing that Brown was responsible for Mackie's escape, organizes the beggars. When Mrs. Peachum tells him that Polly is now married to a bank president, he tries to stop the demonstration, but the poor people have organized and no one can stop them. The demonstration stops the coronation. Feeling remorse for her part in Mackie's imprisonment, Jenny helps him escape. Mackie and Brown take refuge in the bank and reminisce about their service as soldiers in the Indian army. Having lost power over his beggars, Peachum comes to Mackie and asks to to join in his future exploits. *Beggars. Moral corruption. Political corruption. Prostitution. Thieves.* Bankers. Betrayal. Brothels. Coronations. Jailbreaks. Jails. London (England). Police. Poverty. Priests. Riots. Weddings.

Note: According to *Var*, this film, which is known in English as *The Threepenny Opera*, was the first to run in Warner Bros.' new foreign language theater on Broadway in New York City. *NYT* notes that Carola Neher, Lotte Lenya and Rudolph Förster reprised their stage roles for the film and comments that only Förster's face seemed suitable to the screen. *NYT* also mentions lawsuits brought against the production by Kurt Weill and Berthold Brecht, who were hired to adapt their play to the screen. According to modern sources, when *Die Dreigroschenoper* was sold to Warner Bros., Brecht stipulated that nothing in the original stage version could be changed. He intended the movie to be a severe satire of capitalism, but Pabst wanted it to be more entertaining. Claiming that certain important ideological elements were deleted from the original play, Brecht and Weill sued the German production company in Berlin, asking for the production to be stopped on copyright grounds. Brecht, who quit in the midst of production, was accused of breach of contract and his suit was turned down. Weill, who continued working with the producers until fired, won his case. The German film was banned by the Nazis in August 1933 because of its unmistakable relevance to the political and social circumstances in Germany at the time. The German censors destroyed the original negative and every print they could find. Carola Neher was executed by the Nazis in 1940. In 1960, a reconstructed print was released, compiled by Thomas Brandon with the help of the Museum of Modern Art in New York. A French version entitled *L'Opera de quat'sous* was made simultaneously with the German film. According to modern sources, the running time of the original German version was 113 minutes. A shortened version was released in the United States and Great Britain. Among the songs in the movie were "The Ballad of Mackie Messer," "Love Duet," "Barbara," "Is It a Lot I'm Asking?" "The Ballad of the Ship with Fifty Cannons" and "The Song of the Heavy Cannon." Other films based on *The Beggar's Opera* include: a British film, *The Beggar's Opera*, made in 1953; a 1964 German version entitled *The Threepenny Opera*, and television versions made in 1967, 1972 and 1973 all entitled *The Beggar's Opera*.

Other language version(s):

L'opera de quat' sous (French language)

1930. Sd; b&w. 90 min. French language.

Dir G. W. Pabst. *Asst dir* Solange Bussi. *Scr* Leo Larna, Lladislaus Vajda and Béla Balázs. *Adpt* André Mauprey, Solange Bussi and Ninon Steinhoff. *Photog* Fritz Arno Wagner. *Mus* Kurt Weill. *Mus arr* Theo Mackeben. *Lyrics* André Mauprey. *Dec* Andre Andrejew. *Ed* Henri Rust.

Florelle (*Polly Peachum*), Lucy de Matha (*Mrs. Peachum*), Margo Lion (*Jenny*), Albert Préjean (*Mackie*), Gaston Modot (*Peachum*),

Jacques Henley (*Tiger Brown*), Antonin Artaud (*A beggar*), Marie-Antoinette Buzet, Bill-Bocketts, Arthur Duarte, Marcel Merminod, Pierre Léaud, Wladimir Sokoloff, Albert Broquin, Herman Thimig. [*French version not viewed*].

FD 24 May 1931, p. 11. *NYT* 29 Mar 1931, p. 6. *NYT* 18 May 1931, p. 21. *Var* 20 May 1931, p. 16.

DRIFTING WESTWARD (Latino)

Monogram Pictures Corp.; A Scott R. Dunlap Production. *Dist* Monogram Pictures Corp. 25 Jan **1939**; Prod: began early Dec 1938 [©Monogram Pictures Corp.; 18 Jan 1939; LP8562]. Sd; b&w. 6 reels. 58 min.

Supv Robert Tansey. *Dir* Robert Hill. *Asst dir* Edward M. Saeta. *Orig scr* Robert Emmett. *Photog* Bert Longenecker. *Art dir* E. R. Hickson. *Film ed* Howard Dillinger. *Mus dir* Abe Meyer. [*Sd rec* Glen Glenn]. *Prod mgr* Charles J. Bigelow.

Cast: JACK RANDALL [(*Jack Clark*)], Edna Duran [(*Wanda Careta*)], Frank Yaconelli [(*Lopez*)], Julian Rivero [(*Don Careta*)], Stanley Blystone [(*Carga*)], Carmen Bailey [(*Nicki*)], Octavio Giraud [(*Manuel Careta*)], Dave O'Brien [(*Trigger*)], Rosa Turich, Dean Spencer [(*Red*)], Rusty the Wonder Horse, [James Sheridan (*Piute*)].

Western. [*Print viewed*]. In their search for the hidden map to a silver mine, bandits Manuel and Carga break into the house of Don Careta, Manuel's brother. Fearing for the safety of his daughter Wanda, Don Careta sends for Jack Clark, the son of his old friend, to protect the family. Learning of Jack's impending arrival, Manuel, Carga and their accomplice, Nicki hire a gunman to eliminate him. Jack, who is on his way to Santa Fe with his pal Lopez, accidentally runs into the gunman, who is killed in a fight with the sheriff. Finding Carga's letter on the body, Jack decides to take the killer's place and presents himself as the hired gun. Jack's ruse is discovered when Piute, Carga'a Indian spy, overhears Jack conferring with Don Careta, and he then informs Carga. Deciding to eliminate all those who stand in the way of the map, Carga kidnaps Wanda and Careta and imprisons them in a mountain cabin. When Jack rides to their rescue, he is overpowered by Carga's man, Trigger, and Carga threatens to blow them all up unless Careta gives him the map. Careta agrees to hand over the map at the hacienda, but Carga double-crosses him and sets the charge of dynamite to explode anyway. After Carga leaves them to search the Careta house for the map, Jack's faithful horse Rusty appears and saves his master. Jack and Lopez then ride to the ranch, where Lopez kills Piute. Unarmed, Jack enters the house and finds an old gun belonging to Careta's father. In the ensuing fight, Jack overpowers Carga and afterwards finds the map hidden in the gun. After capturing the rest of the gang, Jack proposes to Wanda. *Impersonation and imposture. Maps. Mexican Americans. Outlaws. Treasure. Brothers. Dynamite. Fathers and daughters. Gunfights. Hired killers. Horses. Indians of North America. Kidnapping. Ranches. Silver mines.*

Note: The working title of this picture was *Santa Fe Bound*. In the film, Randall's character is called "Jack Clark," but *Var* identifies him as "Jack Martin."

HR 10 Dec 1938, pp. 6-7. *Var* 15 Feb 1939, p. 13.

DRINK TO ME ONLY *see* **THE BIG HANGOVER**

DRUM BEAT (Native Americans, Modoc)

Ladd Enterprises, Inc.; A Jaguar Production. *Dist* Warner Bros. Pictures, Inc. 13 Nov **1954**; Los Angeles opening: 10 Nov 1954; Prod: early Jun—mid-Jul 1954 [©Ladd Enterprises, Inc.; 13 Nov 1954; LP5775]. Sd (RCA Sound Recording); col (Warnercolor); CinemaScope. 9,660 ft. 107 min. PCA cert no. 17087.

Dir DELMER DAVES. *Asst dir* William Kissel. *2d unit dir* John Waters. *2d unit asst dir* Eli Dunn. *Written by* Delmer Daves. *Dir of photog* J. Peverell Marley. *2nd unit photog* Sid Hickox. *Spec eff* H. F. Koenekamp. *Color consultant* Philip Jefferies. *Art dir* Leo K. Kuter. *Film ed* Clarence Kolster. *Set dec* William L. Kuehl. *Ward* Moss Mabry. *Mus* Victor Young. *Orch* Leo Shuken and Sid Cutner. *Sd* C. A. Riggs. *Makeup artist* Gordon Bau. *Tech adv* Ben Corbett and George Ross.

Song(s): "Drum Beat," music by Victor Young, lyrics by Ned Washington.

Cast: ALAN LADD [(*Johnny Mackay*)], Audrey Dalton [(*Nancy Meek*)], Marisa Pavan [(*Toby*)], Robert Keith [(*Bill Satterwhite*)], Rodolfo Acosta [(*Scarface Charlie*)], Charles Bronson [(*Captain Jack*)], Warner Anderson [(*General Canby*)], Elisha Cook, Jr.

[(*Crackel*)], Anthony Caruso [(*Manok*)], Richard Gaines [(*Dr. Thomas*)], Edgar Stehli [(*Jesse Grant*)], Hayden Rorke [(*President Ulysses S. Grant*)], Frank de Kova [(*Modoc Jim*)], Perry Lopez [(*Bogus Charlie*)], Willis Bouchey [(*General Gilliam*)], Peter Hansen [(*Lt. Goodsall*)], George Lewis [(*Captain Clark*)], Isabel Jewell [(*Lily White*)], Frank Ferguson [(*Mr. Dyar*)], Peggy Converse [(*Mrs. Grant*)], [Pat Lawless (*O'Brien*)], [Paul Wexler (*William Boddy*)], [Richard Cutting (*Colonel Meek*)], [Strother Martin (*Scotty*)], [Rico Alaniz (*Medicine man*)], [John Veitch (*Young soldier*)], [George Ross, Victor Millan (*Sentries*)], [Maurice Jara, Chief Jonas Applegarth, Felix Noriego (*Indians*)], [James Griffith (*Veteran*)], [Frank Gerstle (*Officer*)], [Carol Nugent (*Nellie Grant*)], [Michael Daves (*Young Boddy*)], [Juney Ellis (*Mrs. Boddy*)], [Leonard Penn (*Miller*)], [Oliver Blake (*Minister*)], [George Lloyd (*Settler*)], [Dee Carroll (*Young widow*)], [Richard Hale (*General Sherman*)], [Denver Pyle (*Fairchild*)], [Rayford Barnes (*Captain Summer*)], [Norman Willis (*Guard*)], [Ken Smith], [Ron Hargrave], [Dan Borzage], [Kay Kuter], [Arthur Space].

Western. [*Print viewed*]. In 1872, Indian fighter Johnny Mackay goes to Washington to discuss, with President Ulysses S. Grant, the situation on the California-Oregon border where a renegade Modoc Indian chief, Captain Jack, is causing problems. Grant wants Johnny, whose parents, brothers and sisters were all killed by Indians, to persuade Captain Jack, whom Johnny has known for a long time, to return to the reservation without violence and appoints him Peace Commissioner. Johnny escorts Nancy Meek, the niece of a retired army colonel, back west. On the stagecoach journey between Sacramento and Oregon, they are attacked by Indians led by Modoc Jim, one of Captain Jack's men. After stage driver Bill Satterwhite's lady friend, Lily White, is killed, Bill swears vengeance on all Modocs. When Johnny drives Nancy to her uncle's ranch, they discover that it has been raided and burned, and her aunt and uncle killed. At Fort Klamath, Toby and Manok, the daughter and son of the old Modoc chief, tell Johnny that most of the Modoc want peace but are unable to control Captain Jack. Toby suggests that Johnny kill Captain Jack, but he tells her he intends to talk peace with him. Toby, in love with Johnny, who saved her life years earlier, wants to be his woman so that no Modoc will kill her, but he gently refuses her offer. At Lost River, Captain Jack's territory, Johnny reminds Jack that he signed a treaty agreeing to live on the reservation. Jack, however, wants to take over all of Lost River and drive out the settlers. As Johnny leaves, Bill rides up and starts shooting, killing Modoc Jim and causing the other Indians to go on a rampage of killing. The Modoc occupy a mountain stronghold, which the army, led by General Gilliam, attempt to storm, but they are defeated and have to retreat to the fort. Later, General Canby is instructed by the Secretary of War to cease all operations against the Modoc and make another attempt to achieve peace, but a peace with honor. Manok and Toby arrange a meeting between Captain Jack, Johnny, Canby and other interested parties, and both sides agree not to carry firearms to the meeting. Meantime, as Johnny and Nancy are falling in love, Johnny asks her to promise that she will leave if the peace talks fail. Toby, who fears that Captain Jack will kill all the whites, warns Nancy, and she tries unsuccessfully to persuade Johnny not to go. At the meeting, Captain Jack reiterates his demand that all the settlers leave the Lost River area, then suddenly, draws a gun and starts shooting at the peace party. General Canby is killed and Johnny injured. While attempting to save Johnny from being scalped, Toby is killed. President Grant authorizes Johnny to track down the renegades, but troopers, already on their trail, are ambushed. When Johnny rides out with the rest of the soldiers, Captain Jack and two of his braves, Scarface Charlie and Bogus Charlie, split up, and Johnny pursues Captain Jack while Bill and Manok go after the others. Manok catches and kills Bogus Charlie, but Bill is surprised when Scarface Charlie tells him that, if they are treated well, they will surrender. Meantime, after initially being pinned down by Captain Jack's rifle-fire, Johnny overpowers him in a rapidly flowing stream and takes him back to the fort as a prisoner of war. After Captain Jack's trial, as preparations are made for his hanging, Johnny visits him in his cell. They discuss meeting one day in their respective heavens and part as friends. Peace finally comes to the area, and Johnny and Nancy plan a life together. *Modoc Indians. Oregon. Peace. Renegades. Tribal chiefs. United States. Army. Cavalry. Brothers and sisters. Burial. California. Forts. Ulysses Simpson Grant. Gunrunners. Indians of North America–Reservations. Massacres. Nieces.*

Peace conferences. Romance. Self-sacrifice. Settlers. William Tecumseh Sherman. Stagecoaches. Storekeepers. Telegraph. Treachery. Unrequited love. Washington (D.C.).

Note: This was the first production of Alan Ladd's own company. Although there is no "Producer" credit on the film it is likely that Delmer Daves assumed that role. The main title reads: "Delmer Daves' *Drum Beat*." The film was shot around Sedona and in the Coconino National Forest, Arizona. *Time* reported that the film was made at a low cost of $1,100,000. The opening titles state that the story is based upon historical fact and that fictional incidents and characters have been introduced only where necessary to dramatize the truth. This was the first film in which Charles Buchinsky was billed as Charles Bronson.

Box 6 Nov 1954. *DV* 9 Apr 1954. *DV* 3 Nov 1954. *Exb* 17 Nov 1954, p. 3872. *FD* 10 Nov 1954. *Har* 6 Nov 1954, p. 179. *HCN* 11 Nov 1954. *HR* 3 Nov 1954, p. 4. *LAEx* 11 Nov 1954. *LAT* 11 Nov 1954. *MPD* 8 Nov 1954. *MPHPD* 6 Nov 1954, p. 201. *NYT* 18 Nov 1954, p. 42. *Time* 22 Nov 1954. *Var* 3 Nov 1954, p. 6.

DRUMS ACROSS THE RIVER (Native Americans, Ute)
Universal-International Pictures Co., Inc. *Dist* Universal Pictures Co., Inc. Jun 1954; *Prod*: Oct 1953 [©Universal Pictures Co.; 11 May 1954; LP3684]. Sd (Western Electric Recording); col (Technicolor). 7,033 ft. 77-78 min. PCA cert no. 16863.

Prod Melville Tucker. *Dir* Nathan Juran. *Asst dir* Tom Shaw. *Scr* John K. Butler and Lawrence Roman. *Story* John K. Butler. *Dir of photog* Harold Lipstein. *Technicolor col consultant* Monroe W. Burbank. *Art dir* Bernard Herzbrun and Richard H. Riedel. *Film ed* Virgil Vogel. *Set dec* Russell A. Gausman and Julia Heron. *Cost* Jay Morley, Jr. *Mus dir* Joseph Gershenson. *Sd* Leslie I. Carey and Richard DeWesse. *Hair stylist* Joan St. Oegger. *Makeup* Bud Westmore.

Cast: AUDIE MURPHY (*Gary Brannon*), WALTER BRENNAN (*Sam Brannon*), LYLE BETTGER (*Frank Walker*), Lisa Gaye (*Jennie*), Hugh O'Brian (*Morgan*), Mara Corday (*Sue*), Jay Silverheels (*Taos*), Emile Meyer (*Nathan Marlowe*), Regis Toomey (*Sheriff Jim Beal*), Morris Ankrum (*Chief Ouray*), Bob Steele (*Billy Costa*), James Anderson (*Jed Walker*), George Wallace (*Les Walker*), Lane Bradford (*Ralph Costa*), Howard McNear (*Stilwell*), Gregg Barton (*Fallon*), [Ken Terrell (*Red Knife*)], [Phil Chambers (*Dave Partridge*)], [Chief Yowlachie (*Medicine man*)], [Steve Darrell (*Carmody*)], [Ewing Mitchell (*Colonel*)], [Edmund Cobb (*Second deputy*)], [Cliff Lyons (*Hank*)], [Robert Bray (*Ed Crockett*)], [Andy Brennan (*Jim Decker*)], [Rusty Wescoatt (*Townsman*)], [Larry Williams], [Joseph Morrisey], [Brick Sullivan], [Steve Raines], [Harry Raven], [Lee Morgan].

Western. [*Print viewed*]. Crown City, Colorado, once a busy gold mining town, is now miles away from the nearest gold vein, which lies across the San Juan River, in Ute Indian country. Many of the townspeople have been driven to desperation by hard times, including Gary Brannon, who, with his father Sam, operates a freight company. Gary falls in with a group of men, led by Frank Walker, who are planning to seize gold-rich land located in territory assigned to the Ute Indians as part of a peace treaty. On the night of their planned river crossing, Sam tries unsuccessfully to dissuade Gary from joining the men. While Sam has maintained a delicate friendship with the Ute chief, Ouray, Gary harbors deep resentment for the Utes, who killed his mother. Sam is determined to stop Walker and his men from using Gary and Nathan Marlowe, the first settler of Crown City, to start a war with the Indians, and follows their wagons. Sam catches up with the raiding party just in time to prevent his son from killing the chief's son, Red Knife, and urges him instead to use the Indian as a hostage. During a gun battle between a Ute hunting party and Walker's men, Sam manages to bring about a temporary cease-fire by telling the Utes that they have Red Knife, and that they will turn him over only when the Utes release their hostage, Marlowe. The next day, as Sam prepares the hostage exchange, Walker signals his men to fire at the Indians, and the temporary truce is broken. When Sam is wounded in the gun battle, Gary realizes that his father is right, and decides to sever his ties with Walker. Gary later tells the Ute chief that only a small band of instigators are responsible for the recent fighting. The dying Ouray does not believe the white man's promises of peace, but instructs his son Taos to deliver Gary safely home. Gary arrives in Crown City just in time to prevent Walker and his men from marching on the Ute village. Walker, however, quickly devises a new plan to get his men across the San Juan River again: He takes Sam hostage and coerces Gary into robbing a gold-filled stagecoach, killing its driver and guard, and planting evidence implicating the Utes. After he has been convicted of the crime and preparations are made for his hanging, Gary sends a message to Walker, offering, in exchange for his freedom, to tell him where he hid the gold shipment. The ploy works,

and Sam is sent to break his son out of prison and deliver him to Walker. Instead of leading Walker and his men to the gold shipment, though, Gary takes them to the sacred Ute burial ground, knowing that the Indians will engage the men in a bloody battle there. After the Indians massacre Walker's gang, Gary proudly observes the signing of a new treaty with the Indians, and looks forward to starting a new life with his sweetheart Jennie. *Fathers and sons. Gold miners. Land claims. Ute Indians. Blackmail. Burial. Colorado. Confession. Fistfights. Frame-ups. Freight lines. Gunshot wounds. Hostages. Romance. Stagecoach robberies. Treaties. Tribal chiefs.*

Box 15 May 1954. *DV* 10 May 1954, p. 3. *FD* 2 Jun 1954, p. 6. *HR* 9 Oct 1953, p. 10. *HR* 30 Oct 1953, p. 10. *HR* 10 May 1954, p. 3. *MPHPD* 22 May 1954, pp. 1-2. *Var* 19 May 1954, p. 6.

DRUMS ALONG THE MOHAWK (Native Americans)

Twentieth Century-Fox Film Corp.; Darryl F. Zanuck's production of. *Dist* Twentieth Century-Fox Film Corp. 10 Nov **1939**; New York opening: week of 4 Nov 1939; Prod: 28 Jun—late Aug 1939 [©Twentieth Century-Fox Film Corp.; 10 Nov 1939; LP9429]. Sd (Western Electric Mirrophonic Recording); col (Technicolor). 12 reels, 9,303 ft. 100 or 103 min. PCA cert no. 5530.

Assoc prod Raymond Griffith. *Dir* John Ford. [*Asst dir* Ed O'Fearna, Wingate Smith and F. E. Johnson]. *Scr* Lamar Trotti and Sonya Levien. [*Contr to trmt* William Faulkner and Bess Meredyth]. *Dir of photog* Bert Glennon and Ray Rennahan. [*Cam op* I. Rosenberg]. [*Asst cam* Charles Bohny]. [*Gaffer* Fred Hall]. *Technicolor dir* Natalie Kalmus. *Assoc* Henri Jaffa. [*Technicolor tech* Nelson Cordes and John Gustafson]. [*Technicolor asst cam* John Lees]. [*Technicolor service man* Fritz Borsch]. [*Technicolor film loading* Al Baalas]. [*Technicolor continuity* Henry Staudigl]. *Art dir* Richard Day and Mark-Lee Kirk. *Film ed* Robert Simpson. [*Asst cutter* Jack Wells and Mary Crumley]. *Set dec* Thomas Little. [*Set dresser* Fred Rhodes]. *Cost* Gwen Wakeling. [*Ward* Robert Varnado, Harry Kernell, Norman Martien, Joe Kane, Josephine Perrin, Ollie Hughes and Grace Wilson]. [*Tailor* George Koich]. [*Mus dir* Louis Silvers]. *Mus* Alfred Newman. *Sd* E. Clayton Ward and Roger Heman. [*Asst sound* H. A. Root]. [*Boom man* Harry Roberts]. [*Cableman* Harry Leonard and Mert Strong]. [*Hair* Myrtle Ford, Irene Beshon, Marie Brasselle and A. Barr]. [*Makeup* Norbert Miles, Newton House, Bob Cowan and Steve Drumm]. [*Tech adv* Thorton Edwards]. [*Prod mgr* Ralph Dietrich]. [*Unit mgr* B. F. McEveety, Duke Goux and W. F. Fitzgerald]. [*Scr clerk* Meta C. Sterne]. [*Grip* Phil Mandella]. [*Props* Joe Behm]. [*Best boy* John Grady]. [*Asst prop man* Tom Shaw and Stanley Detlie]. [*Still photog* Frank Powolny].

Source: Based on the novel *Drums Along the Mohawk* by Walter D. Edmonds (Boston and New York, 1936).

Cast: Claudette Colbert (*Lana "Magdalena"* [*Borst*]), Henry Fonda (*Gilbert Martin*), Edna May Oliver (*Mrs. McKlennar*), Eddie Collins (*Christian Reall*), John Carradine (*Caldwell*), Dorris Bowdon (*Mary Reall*), Jessie Ralph (*Mrs. Weaver*), Arthur Shields (*Reverend Rosenkrantz*), Robert Lowery (*John Weaver*), Roger Imhof (*General Nicholas Herkimer*), Francis Ford (*Joe Boleo*), Ward Bond (*Adam Hartman*), Kay Linaker (*Mrs. Demooth*), Russell Simpson (*Dr. Petry*), Spencer Charters (*Innkeeper*), Si Jenks (*Jacob Small*), J. Ronald Pennick (*Amos Hartman*), Arthur Aylesworth (*George Weaver*), Chief Big Tree (*Blue Black*), Charles Tannen (*Dr. Robert Johnson*), Paul McVey (*Capt. Mark Demooth*), Elizabeth Jones (*Mrs. Reall*), Beulah Hall Jones (*Daisy*), Edwin Maxwell (*Reverand Daniel Gros*), Robert Greig (*Mr. Borst*), Clara Blandick (*Mrs. Borst*), Clarence H. Wilson (*Paymaster*), Lionel Pape (*General*), [Mae Marsh].

Adventure. [*Print viewed*]. In 1776, after marrying Gilbert Martin, Lana "Magdalena" Borst leaves her luxurious home in Albany, New York to set out for her husband's farm in Deerfield, in the perilous territory of the Mohawk Valley in upstate New York. Soon after arriving in Deerfield, Lana is startled by the presence of Gilbert's Indian friend, Blue Back, in their small cabin, and becomes hysterical. Gilbert strikes his new wife to bring her back to her senses, and when Lana insists on returning to Albany, he refuses to go and she decides to stay by his side. Unaccustomed to the rugged conditions, Lana has a hard time adjusting, but soon is working the fields of her farm with her husband. At German Flats, the nearest settlement to Deerfield, Gilbert and Lana meet many of the local residents and learn that the revolution that has followed the signing of the Declaration of Independence has now become a full-scale war, requiring the

dispatch of additional troops to Boston. When Indians, led by Tory Caldwell, attack and burn the Martins' farm, Lana faints while fleeing and miscarries her first child. Empty-handed, the Martins turn to the widow McKlennar, who offers them a home and work on her land. Life goes on peacefully until word comes of an impending Indian attack and Gilbert and the other men form a backwoods militia to protect their land. Ill-equipped and ill-trained, the men fight off the attack with their lives and Gilbert returns home, wounded and delirious. Soon after, Lana gives birth to a son and a period of peace ensues until the Indians regroup and attack once more. Seeking refuge in the fort, the men and women fight side-by-side and, in the struggle, Mrs. McKlennar is mortally wounded. When the ammunition runs dangerously low, Joe Boleo goes for reinforcements, but when he is killed, Gilbert takes his place, making a desperate dash through the enemy line and outrunning his pursuers to reach the nearest fort for help. Just as the Indians breech the wall of the fort, Gilbert and the troops arrive to defeat the attackers and restore peace to the valley. With the farm that Mrs. McKlennar gave to them before she died, Gilbert and Lana can now start their lives over. *Farmers. Indians of North America. Land rights. New York (State). Settlers. Soldiers. United States–History–Revolutionary War, 1776-1783. American loyalists. Arson. Clergy. Drunkenness. Forts. Gunfights. Miscarriage. Nursing back to health. Rescues. Rural life. Sieges. Weddings. Widows.*

Note: This film marked director John Ford's first Technicolor film, and followed Twentieth Century-Fox's successful teaming of producer Darryl Zanuck, director John Ford, screenwriter Lamar Trotti and star Henry Fonda in *Young Mr. Lincoln* (see *AFI Catalog of Feature Films, 1931-40*; F3.5256). According to early 1937 *HR* news items, Fox initially set Warner Baxter for the male lead and listed Henry King as the director. A studio press release noted that Nancy Kelly was originally set for the female lead and that Don Ameche was considered for the role that was eventually given to Fonda. The press release reported that Ameche was unable to take the assignment because he was tied up with *Hollywood Cavalcade* (see *AFI Catalog of Feature Films, 1931-40*; F3.1956). An Aug 1939 *HR* news item notes that novice actress Linda Darnell was pulled from the cast of the film because Zanuck had decided that she would be better suited for a role as society girl in *Public Debutante No. 1* (see below), a film in which she did not finally appear. Although the film credits Ward Bond with the role of Adam Hartman, reviews erroneously list his character as "Adam Helmer."

A Mar 1937 *HR* news item announced that William Faulkner was signed to write the screenplay for the film, however material contained at the Twentieth Century-Fox Produced Scripts Collection at the UCLA Theater Arts Library suggests that Faulkner's sole contribution was that of an early treatment of the story. A modern source notes that the final film was almost entirely devoid of Faulkner's contributions. The UCLA files also indicate that Zanuck criticized Sonya Levien's first draft of the continuity, dated 2 Dec 1938, for having too much emphasis on the epic nature of the story rather than the more personal tale of Gilbert and Lana, which he preferred. In Apr 1939, Zanuck, after having read Lamar Trotti's draft of the screenplay, argued against the script's "flag waving patriotism" and reasserted his desire to see the clash of personalities between Lana and Gilbert more fully developed. According to the Twentieth Century-Fox Records of the Legal Department at the UCLA Theater Arts Library, Zanuck purchased the rights to the film for $25,000.

According to *HR*, some scenes were shot at Cedar City, Utah, where 350 local residents were used as extras. A biography of Ford notes that filming began without a completed script, and that rain and unpredictable lighting conditions in Utah's Wasatch Mountains forced many production delays. The biography also indicates that Ford, pressed for time at the Utah location, decided to forgo filming a large-scale battle scene, which had been scheduled for a three-week shoot, and instead used footage taken from an unscripted description of the battle spoken by Fonda. The sequence was taken from an improvised conversation between Ford and Fonda that had been filmed and later edited with Ford's questions removed. The result was a continuous shot of Fonda giving a descriptive narration of the battle scene. Modern sources add actors Tom Tyler (*Morgan*) and Noble Johnson (*Indian*) to the cast, and note that Mae Marsh played a pioneer woman in the film.

Edna May Oliver was nominated for an Academy Award for Best Supporting Actress in her role as Mrs. McKlennar. A radio dramatization of *Drums Along the Mohawk*, featuring Colbert and Fonda, aired on Kate Smith's radio program on 3 Nov 1939.

DV 3 Nov 1939, p. 3. *FD* 6 Nov 1939, p. 5. *HR* 22 Feb 1937, p. 4. *HR* 10 Mar 1937, p. 3. *HR* 17 Mar 1937, p. 3. *HR* 24 Jun 1939, p. 3. *HR* 29 Jun 1939, p. 16. *HR* 10 Aug 1939, p. 1. *HR* 19 Aug 1939, p. 6. *HR* 3 Nov 1939, p. 8. *MPD* 6 Nov 1939, p. 8. *MPH* 30 Sep 1939, p. 47. *MPH* 11 Nov 1939, p. 11. *NYT* 4 Nov 1939, p. 38. *Var* 8 Nov 1939, p. 14.

DRUMS O' VOODOO (African Americans)

International Stageplay Pictures, Inc. *Dist* State Rights. **1934**; New York opening: week of 11 May 1934; Prod: completed late Mar 1933 at Atlas Soundfilm Recording Studios (New York). Sd (Cineglow Sound System); b&w. 7 reels. 70 min.

Pres Robert Mintz. *Prod* Louis Weiss. *Dir* Arthur Hoerl. *Scr* J. Augustus Smith. *Photog* Walter Strenge and J. Burgi Contner. *Film ed* Joe Silverstein. *Sd eff* Lyman J. Wiggin and Verne T. Brayman.

Source: Based on the play *Louisiana* by J. Augustus Smith (New York, 27 Feb 1933).

Cast: Laura Bowman (*Aunt Hagar*), Edna Barr (*Myrtle Simpson*), Lionel Monagas (*Ebenezer*), J. Augustus Smith (*Amos Berry*), Morris McKenny (*Thomas Catt*), A. B. Comathiere (*Deacon Dunson*), Alberta Perkins (*Sister Knight*), Fred Bonny (*Brother Zero*), Paul Johnson (*Deacon August*), Trixie Smith (*Sister Marguerite*), Carrie Huff (*Sister Zuzan*).

African American, Drama. [*Not viewed*]. Thomas Catt, the proprietor of a "jook," a Southern cabaret-brothel, desires young, virginal Myrtle Simpson, the niece of preacher Amos Berry and the fiancée of the grandson of Aunt Hagar, the local voodoo high priestess. Although Catt threatens to expose Amos' past to his congregation if he refuses to "give" Myrtle to him, Amos resists Catt's attempts at blackmail, while Aunt Hagar activates some of her voodoo spells. Later, during one of Amos' spirited revival meetings, Catt bursts in and, after drawing his razor, announces that he has come to claim Myrtle. Defied by both Aunt Hagar's grandson and Amos, Catt starts to reveal to the congregation that Amos had once murdered a man. In the middle of his exposé, however, Catt is struck by a bolt of lightning and is blinded, a fate that had been predicted by Aunt Hagar. Catt is then smothered in a pool of quicksand, and Myrtle and Amos are at last freed from their tormentor. *Blackmail. Nieces. Pimps. Preachers. Voodoo. Women priests. Blindness. Brothels. Cabarets. Churches. Curses. Lightning. Predictions. Quicksand. Revivals. Virginity.*

Note: The working titles of this film were *Louisiana* and *Voodoo*. *HR* reviewed the picture as *Louisiana*. New York State Censor Board records from 1934 indicate that the film was retitled *The Devil*. In 1981, the film was found by historian-producer Alex Gordon. According to a press release for the re-issue, the picture was also known as *She Devil* during its initial run. Modern sources list the title as *Voodoo Devil Drums* and *Voodoo Drums*. Most of the all-black cast, including playwright J. Augustus Smith, also appeared in the stage play, which was produced on Broadway by the Negro Theatre Guild. The play was one act long and was only performed eight times, partly because of the criticism of Brooks Atkinson of *NYT*. *HR* commented that the play was "transferred to screen from stage intact, including the painted scenery, the long speeches and the stage technique." The *Var* review adds the following description: "There are snatches of jungle worship dancing, but all clean. Only spicy shot is a girl's snakehips dance in a brief brothel scene. The voodooists' tom-toms beat a monotone through the picture, a la *Emperor Jones*....Typical antics of his [the preacher's] fananatical congregation add to the effectiveness. White audiences have seen samples of the same thing through the newsreels and travelogs." Sources disagree on the producer credit. One review credits Robert Mintz as producer, while others credit Louis Weiss. New York State Censor Board records indicate that substantial footage was cut from the film before the Board approved it for distribution.

Modern sources note that by using the original cast, costumes, script and authentic spirituals and voodoo music, the budget was kept to a minimum. Modern sources list Ben Berk as production manager and Sam Corso as art director. Additional cast members from modern sources include James Davis (*Brother Zumee*), Ruth Morrison (*Sister Gaghan*), Harriet Daughtry (*Sister Lauter*), Bennie Small (*Bou Bouche*), Pedro Lopez (*Marcon*), Jennie Day, Gladys Booker, Herminie Sullivan, Lillian Exum, Edith Woodby, Mabel Grant, Marion Hughes, Madeline Smith, Theresa Harris, Dorothy St. Claire, Eleanor Hines, Pauline Freeman, Annabelle Smith, Jacqueline Ghant, Annabelle Ross and Harriett Scott (*Members of the Flat Rock Washfoot Baptist Church*), Cherokee Thornton, Arthur McLean, DeWitt Davis, Rudoph Walker, Marvin Everhart, Jimmie Cook, Irene Bagley, Sally Timmons, Beatrice James and Marie Remsen (*Voodoo Dancers*). *Drums O'Voodoo* is unrelated to the short film entitled *Voodoo*. The later film was produced in 1933 by Principal Pictures.

FD 9 Mar 1933, p. 2. *FD* 21 Mar 1933, p. 4. *FD* 12 May 1934, p. 4. *HR* 14 Jun 1934, p. 3. *Var* 15 May 1934, p. 27.

DRUMS OF DESTINY (Crescent Pictures Corp., Mar 1937) *see* **OLD LOUISIANA**

DRUMS OF DESTINY (Native Americans, Cree, Seminole)
Crescent Pictures Corp. *Dist* Crescent Pictures Corp. 12 Jun 1937. Sd; b&w. 6 reels, 5,702 ft. 60 or 62 min. PCA cert no. 3463.

Prod E. B. Derr. *Assoc prod* Bernard A. Moriarty. *Dir* Ray Taylor. *Asst dir* Theodore Joos. *Scr* Roger Whately and John T. Neville. *Orig story* Roger Whately. *Photog* Arthur Martinelli. *Film ed* Finn Ulback. *Mus dir* Abe Meyer. *Rec eng* Karl Zint. *Prod supv* Frank Melford.

Cast: Tom Keene (*Capt. Jerry Crawford*), Edna Lawrence (*Rosa Maria Dominguez*), Budd Buster (*Kentuck*), Robert Fiske (*Holston*), Carlos De Valdez (*Don Salvador Dominguez*), David Sharpe (*Crawford's brother*), Raphael Bennett (*Jenkins*), John Merton (*Fiske's henchman*), Aurora Navarro (*Rosa Maria's duenna*), William Hazlett.

Historical, Drama. [*Not viewed*]. In the early 1800's, Captain Jerry Crawford, the commander of a platoon of U.S. Army militia in Mississippi, is sent to the Florida border to protect Americans endangered by Seminole and Cree Indians, who have been raiding their sparsely populated settlements and then escaping to Florida, which belongs to Spain. After a raid on a farmhouse, Crawford becomes convinced that someone is illegally supplying the Indians with guns. Crawford's younger brother, who is leading an ammunitions train to his brother's outpost, is ambushed by renegade Americans led by Holston, the provost marshal who is the power behind Spanish Governor Don Salvador Dominguez. After learning that his brother has been sentenced to death, Crawford crosses the border, thus disobeying orders, to rescue him. He comes across the governor's daughter, Rosa Maria, whose carriage has broken down, and helps her. In Potaluna, Florida, Crawford speaks with Don Salvador on his brother's behalf and receives a stay of execution, while he gets proof from Washington that Holston is a criminal. He is then allowed to set up camp outside the city. Holston arrests Don Salvador and orders Bill's immediate execution, but Crawford rescues his brother just before he is to be shot by a firing squad. Crawford's troops wipe out Holston's followers, as Crawford fights Halston and saves the governor. Crawford also wins the hand of Rosa Maria, with whom he has fallen in love. *Boundaries. Brothers. Cree Indians. Florida–History. Gunrunners. Mississippi–History. Officers (Military). Seminole Indians. United States. Army. Ammunition. Battles. Fathers and daughters. Firing squads. Military posts. Rescues. Romance. Spaniards. Territorial governors.*

Note: Reviews note that the film was based on fact and was one of a series of American history action films produced by E. B. Derr and starring Tom Keene. According to a *Var* news item, in Aug 1936, E. B. Derr purchased an original story by John T. Neville entitled "Drums of Destiny" which dealt with the Louisiana Purchase; the film made from that story was called *Old Louisiana* and also starred Tom Keene (see below). Apparently Derr kept the title of that story for this later film. According to modern sources, Chief Flying Cloud was also in the cast.

Box 26 Jun 1937. *DV* 8 Jun 1937, p. 3. *FD* 15 Jun 1937, p. 9. *Har* 17 Jul 1937, p. 114. *MPD* 11 Jun 1937, p. 2. *MPH* 19 Jun 1937, p. 60. *Var* 6 Aug 1936. *Var* 10 Nov 1937, p. 19.

DRUMS OF THE DESERT (Native Americans, Navajo)
Paramount Famous Lasky Corp. 4 Jun 1927 [©Paramount Famous Lasky Corp.; 4 Jun 1927; LP24049]. Si; b&w. 6 reels, 5,907 ft.

Pres Adolph Zukor and Jesse L. Lasky. *Dir* John Waters. *Scr* John Stone. *Photog* C. Edgar Schoenbaum.

Source: Based on the short story "Desert Bound" by Zane Grey in *McCall's* (publication date undetermined).

Cast: Warner Baxter (*John Curry*), Marietta Millner (*Mary Manton*), Ford Sterling (*Perkins*), Wallace MacDonald (*Will Newton*), Heinie Conklin (*Hi-Lo*), George Irving (*Prof. Elias Manton*), Bernard Siegel (*Chief Brave Bear*), Guy Oliver (*Indian agent*).

Western. Chief Brave Bear and his people gather at the Navajo reservation to confront a problem: a group of men, headed by Will Newton, seeks to force them off their desert lands. Perkins and Hi-Lo meet the exploring party of Elias Manton and his daughter, Mary; posing as desert rats, they are hired as guides. They encounter John Curry, a friend of the Indians whose cordiality arouses their suspicion; Newton tries, unsuccessfully, to dissuade them from continuing their work in the desert and casts aspersions on Curry. Manton is kidnapped by Newton's men, but Curry rescues him after a search. Newton starts for the oil claims, while the Navajo prepare to defend their sacred altars. Curry tries unsuccessfully to placate the Indians and is shot by Newton, who fails to listen to reason. United States Cavalry arrive and place Newton's men under arrest, and Mary realizes the worth of her protector. *Arizona. Land rights. Navajo Indians. Oil. United States. Army. Cavalry.*

Note: Photographed on location at an Arizona Navajo reservation.
FD 21 Aug 1927. *Var* 10 Aug 1927, p. 26.

THE DUDE GOES WEST (Native Americans, Paiute)
Allied Artists Productions, Inc.; A King Bros. Production. *Dist* Monogram Pictures Corp. 30 May 1948; *Prod:* late Nov—late Dec 1947 [©Allied Artists Productions, Inc.; 30 May 1948; LP1691]. Sd (Western Electric Recording); b&w. 7,826 ft. 87 min. PCA cert no. 12936.

Prod Maurice King and Frank King. *Asst to prod* Arthur Gardner. *Dir* Kurt Neumann. *Asst dir* Frank S. Heath. *Dial dir* Jo Graham. *Orig scr* Mary Loos and Richard Sale. *Dir of photog* Karl Struss. [*Cam op* Bob Martin]. [*Stills* Madison Lacey]. *Spec eff* Ray Mercer. [*Art dir*

Gordon Wiles and Ernest R. Hickson]. *Film ed* Richard Heermance and [William Zeigler]. *Set dec* Sidney Moore. [*Cost* Lorraine MacLean]. *Mus comp and cond* Dimitri Tiomkin. [*Mus dir* Edward Kay]. *Sd eng* Tom Lambert. [*Makeup* Emile LaVigne]. [*Hair stylist* Carla Hadley]. *Prod mgr* Herman E. Webber. *Tech adv* Herman King. [*Scr supv* Jules Levy]. [*Grip* Harry Lewis].

Song(s): "Old Dan Tucker," traditional.

Cast: EDDIE ALBERT (*Daniel Bone*), GALE STORM (*Liza Crockett*), James Gleason (*Sam Briggs*), Gilbert Roland (*Pecos Kid*), Binnie Barnes (*Kiki Kelly*), Barton MacLane (*Texas Jack* [*Barton*]), Harry Hayden (*Horace Hotchkiss*), Catherine Doucet (*Grandma Crockett*), Sarah Padden (*Mrs. Hallahan*), Douglas Fowley (*Beetle*), Olin Howlin (*Finnegan*), Francis Pierlot (*Mr. Brittle*), [Chief Yowlachie (*Running Wolf*)], [Edward Gargan (*Conductor*)], [Tom Fadden (*J. J. Jines*)], [Si Jenks (*Horse trader*)], [George Meeker (*Gambler*)], [Frank Yaconelli (*Train passenger*)], [Charles Williams (*Harris*)], [Tom Tyler (*Spiggoty*)], [Lee "Lasses" White (*Baggage master*)], [Ben Weldon (*Porgy*)], [Iron Eyes Cody], [Dick Elliott].

Comedy, Western. [*Print viewed*]. In 1876, Daniel Bone abandons his father's gunsmith business in Brooklyn and heads West to set up shop in Arsenic City, Nevada, site of a gold rush. On board the train west, Dan, an avid reader, learns western history and teaches himself Indian sign language. After changing trains in Kansas City, Dan meets Liza Crockett, who is also going to Arsenic City, and the Pecos Kid. During the onboard Sunday services, Dan sees Pecos steal Liza's purse and, after a brief scuffle with him on the railroad car platform, pushes him off the train, relieving him of his gun while simultaneously saving the purse. However, Liza thinks Dan has stolen her purse. Meanwhile, Pecos, who had planned to leave the train at that point anyway, is met by his cohort Beetle and swears to him that he will get even with Dan, the "dude." In Carson City, Dan learns that the stagecoach to Arsenic City is fully booked for weeks ahead, and buys an old bakery wagon, a horse, Stetson and boots. At the Red Dog Saloon, Dan observes gold miner Sam Briggs being cheated in a card game and intervenes on his behalf. Later, Dan shows Sam a gun made by his father, which looks like a pipe. Sam joins Dan on the trip to Arsenic City and along the way, Sam tells Dan that he knew Liza's father, a prospector who struck a motherlode but was killed in an ambush without revealing the location of the strike. Meanwhile in Arsenic City, Texas Jack Barton and his gang hold up the bank and, during their getaway, Jack is shot in the leg. Dan finds him in the desert, and Jack claims to have shot himself in the leg. When Dan shows Jack the gun he took from Pecos, he earns Jack's respect. Jack tells him that Pecos is the best shot in Nevada after him, but after Dan proves that he is a far better shot than Jack, Jack asks him to join his gang. When Dan declines, Jack slugs him and takes his horse and wagon, leaving him to walk to Arsenic City. Liza happens along in a buckboard and reluctantly agrees to take him into town. On the way, they are attacked and taken prisoner by Paiute Indians. From his reading, Dan remembers that the Paiutes are superstitious and, by way of some basic magic and his knowledge of sign language, is able to trick the chief, Running Wolf, and becomes his blood brother. After Dan tells the chief that Liza is his squaw, they stay with the tribe for several days. Eventually Dan and Liza reach Arsenic City, where Dan finds his wagon with a note of apology from Jack and learns that Jack has a $5,000 reward on his head. Liza, who did not appreciate the hard labor she had to perform as Dan's "squaw," is anxious to part company with him. She goes to see lawyer Horace Hotchkiss, who claims to have been her father's best friend and is particularly interested to learn that she may have a map to the gold strike. Hotchkiss is in cahoots with Kiki Kelly, a saloonkeeper, and with Pecos, who killed Liza's father. Pecos was supposed to have stolen the map from Liza while on the train. In the saloon, Pecos challenges Dan to a gunfight, which Dan wins by shooting the gun out of his hand. Outside, Dan discovers two of Pecos's henchmen trying to rob Liza. When he shoots them dead, Liza faints and Dan takes her to her hotel room, where he discovers the map, memorizes it, then burns it. Liza now has to trust Dan as he is the only person who knows the location of the mine. Pecos sets a trap for his rival, Jack, and is about to have him lynched when Dan and Sam stop the proceedings. They are able to free Jack, but Kiki shoots and kills Sam. Later, Dan enlists the Indians' help in beginning mining operations and arranges for two Indians to kidnap Liza and bring her to the mine, where he shows her a large quantity of gold. On their way back into Arsenic City, Dan and

Liza, who realize they are in love, are stopped by Pecos and Kiki, who demand to know the location of the mine. Kiki and Pecos, in turn, are held up by Texas Jack, who shoots Kiki. After Pecos shoots Jack, Dan shoots Pecos with his pipe gun. Dan and Liza are then pursued by Pecos' men, but Dan's Indian friends ride to their rescue. Running Wolf escorts them back into town and Liza officially becomes Dan's "squaw." *Bandits. Gold mines. Gunsmiths. Nevada. Paiute Indians. Tenderfoots. Bank robberies. Books. Deserts. Easterners. Firearms. Fistfights. Gunfights. Gunshot wounds. Lawyers. Lynching. Magic. Maps. Murder. New York City—Brooklyn. Rites and ceremonies. Romance. Saloon keepers. Saloons. Sign language. Trains. Wagons.*

Note: This film's working title was *The Tenderfoot*. Although onscreen credits list Richard Heermance as editor, *HR* production charts and copyright records list William Zeigler. According to Aug 1947 *HR* news items, background shots for *The Tenderfoot* were made at the Bowie (Texas) Rodeo and a cattle stampede was staged near Winemucca, NV. None of this footage appears in the released film, however. A 20 Nov 1947 *LAT* news item includes Milburn Stone in the cast, but he was not seen in the viewed print.

Box 1 May 1948. *DV* 22 Apr 1948, p. 3, 11. *FD* 27 Apr 1948, p. 6. *HR* 20 Aug 1947, p. 13. *HR* 22 Aug 1947, p. 9. *HR* 5 Dec 1947, p. 12. *HR* 22 Apr 1948, p. 3. *LAT* 20 Nov 1947. *MPHPD* 31 Jan 1948, p. 4038. *MPHPD* 1 May 1948, p. 4145. *Var* 28 Apr 1948, p. 8.

THE DUDE RANCH *see* **LOOKOUT SISTER**

I DUE GEMELLI (Italian language, Italian Americans)
Victoria Italian Film Company. *Dist* Victoria Italian Film Company. **1938?.** Sd; b&w. 4 reels. Italian language.

Song(s): "Neapolitan Night," "I due gemelli," and other songs, composers undetermined.

Cast: Carlo Buti (*Singer*), Ria Rosa (*Singer*).

Musical comedy. [*Not viewed*]. A young couple gives a party to celebrate the birth of their twins. Among the guests are radio announcer Professor Misery, his wife, Gervasa Cocozza, Donna Angelina Cipuduzza and her husband, Don Paolino Onion. The guests are rude and ungracious and the father is anxious for them all to leave. Eventually they turn on the radio and listen to Carlo Buti and Ria Rosa perform Italian songs. *Italian Americans. Italians. Showers (Parties). Twins. Marriage. Radio broadcasting. Singers.*

Note: The film's title was translated into English as "The Twins." The plot summary and credits were obtained from a translated dialogue continuity deposited with the NYSA. Although no reviews or additional credit information was located, records at the NYSA indicate that the film was made in the U.S. and was approved for exhibition in New York state in 1938. Although the continuity includes lyrics to several songs, only two titles and none of the composers could be verified. Other information at the NYSA suggests that the film was based on "the song of the same name."

DUEL IN THE SUN (Native Americans)
Vanguard Films, Inc. *Dist* Selznick Releasing Organization. **1947;** World premiere in Los Angeles: 31 Dec 1946; New York opening: week of 8 May 1947; Prod: 1 Mar 1945—Sep 1946; addl scenes May 1947 [©Vanguard Films, Inc.; 31 Dec 1946; LP982]. Sd (Western Electric Recording); col (Technicolor). 12,122 ft. 134-136 min. PCA cert no. 11649.

Pres DAVID O. SELZNICK. *Dir* KING VIDOR and [William Dieterle]. *Asst dir* Lowell J. Farrell and [Harvey Dwight]. *2d unit dir* Otto Brower, Reaves Eason, [William Cameron Menzies and Chester Franklin]. [*2d asst dir* Bert Chervin and Arthur Fellows]. *Scr* David O. Selznick. *Adpt* Oliver H. P. Garrett. *Dir of photog* Lee Garmes, Hal Rossen and Ray Rennahan. *Addl photog* Charles P. Boyle and [Allen Davey]. [*Cam op* Edward P. Fitzgerald and Harry Webb]. [*Stills* Alfred St. Hilaire and Madison Lacy]. [*Chief elec* Homer Plannette and Edward Petzoldt]. *Spec eff* Clarence Slifer and Jack Cosgrove. [*Effects ed* Charles Freeman]. *Col dir* Natalie Kalmus. *Assoc* Morgan Padelford. *Prod des* J. McMillan Johnson. *Art dir* James Basevi. *Assoc art dir* John Ewing. *Supv film ed* Hal C. Kern. *Assoc* Wm. Ziegler and John Faure. [*Asst film ed* Wayland M. Hendry and Noel Coppleman]. *Int dec* Emile Kuri. [*Props mgr* Fred Widdowson and John Brent]. [*Props on the set* Arden Cripe]. *Cost* Walter Plunkett. [*Ward superintendent* Frank Beetson, Elmer Ellsworth and Ann Peck]. *Mus wrt and cond* Dimitri Tiomkin. [*Mus coordinator* Audray Granville]. *Solo dances created by* Tilly Losch. *Group dances by* Lloyd Shaw. *Sd dir* James G. Stewart. *Rec* Richard De Weese. [*Mus ed* George Emick]. [*Makeup* Blagoe Stephanoff and Norbert Miles]. [*Hair* Gail McGarry and Margaret Martin]. *Scenario asst* Lydia Schiller. [*General mgr* Charles Glett]. [*Visual consultant* Josef von Sternberg]. [*Prod mgr* Argyle Nelson and Richard Johnston]. [*Asst prod mgr* Fred Ahern]. [*Unit mgr* Glenn Cook and Bill McGarry]. [*Scr clerk* Adele Cannon,

Donna Norridge and Agnes Pottage]. [*Tech adv on ranch life details* Ralph McCutcheon and J. T. Harris]. [*Tech adv on 19th cent dances* Lloyd Shaw]. [*Tech adv for barbeque scene* Captain Charles Ellison]. [*Tech adv on railroad const* Walter Haven]. [*Tech adv on the cavalry charge* Major Phillip J. Kieffer]. [*Tech adv on barroom scenes* Carl Preed]. [*Tech adv on Texas dialect* Lucille Scholsberg and Dan White]. [*Tech adv on guns and gunplay* Fred Andrews]. [*Research* Ann Harris]. [*Casting dir* Ruth Burch]. [*Construction superintendent* Harold Fenton]. [*Head grip* Morris Rosen and Raymond Bahns]. [*Green man* Roy McLaughlin]. [*Drapes* Harry Apperson]. [*Chief eff projectionist* Robert Hansard].

Song(s): "Gotta Get Me Somebody to Love," music and lyrics by Allie Wrubel and "Headin' Home," music by Dimitri Tiomkin, lyrics by Frederick Herbert.

Source: Suggested by the novel *Duel in the Sun* by Niven Busch (New York, 1944).

Cast: Jennifer Jones [(*Pearl Chavez*)], Joseph Cotten [(*Jesse McCanles*)], Gregory Peck [(*Lewt McCanles*)], Lionel Barrymore [(*Senator McCanles*)], Herbert Marshall [(*Scott Chavez*)], Lillian Gish [(*Laura Belle McCanles*)], Walter Huston [(*Jubal Crabbe, the sinkiller*)], Charles Bickford [(*Sam Pierce*)], Harry Carey [(*Lem Smoot*)], Joan Tetzel [(*Helen Langford*)], Tilly Losch [(*Mrs. Chavez*)], Butterfly McQueen [(*Vashti*)], Scott McKay [(*Sid*)], Otto Kruger [(*Mr. Langford*)], Sidney Blackmer [(*The lover*)], Charles Dingle [(*Sheriff Hardy*)], [Francis McDonald, Victor Killian (*Gamblers*)], [Griff Barnett (*The jailer*)], [Frank Cordell (*Ken*)], [Dan White (*Ed*)], [Lane Chandler (*Captain, U.S. Cavalry*)], [Lloyd Shaw (*Caller at barbecue*)], [Thomas Dillon (*Engineer*)], [Robert McKenzie (*Bartender*)], [Steve Dunhill].

Western, Melodrama. [*Print viewed*]. Before Scott Chavez is hanged for the murder of his Indian wife and her lover, he makes his beautiful but unrefined daughter Pearl promise that she will grow up to be a lady like Laura Belle McCanles, his former sweetheart. Laura Belle offers Pearl a home on Spanish Bit, the Texas cattle ranch where she lives with her husband, "Senator" McCanles, and her two sons, Jesse and Lewt. Although McCanles, who is confined to a wheelchair, is hostile toward Pearl, her beauty immediately attracts the attentions of both Jesse and Lewt. One night, when Pearl goes to bed, Lewt forces his way into her room and kisses her. Although Pearl loves the kindhearted Jesse, she is physically drawn to the wild, handsome Lewt and, despite the prayers of preacher Jubal Crabbe, who is known as "the sinkiller," cannot resist him. When a railroad company wins the legal right to build tracks through the million-acre McCanles ranch, McCanles gathers all the ranch hands to defend the border against the railroad crew. In order to prevent bloodshed, Jesse, a lawyer, takes the side of the railroad and is banned from the ranch by his father. When Lewt returns from El Paso, he takes advantage of the deserted house to seduce Pearl. Jesse finds them together and confesses that although he loves her, he will never forget what he has seen. Pearl now pushes Lewt to marry her, but when he makes it clear that he has no intention of being tied down, she quickly becomes engaged to Sam Pierce, a much older cowhand. Lewt is overcome with jealousy and kills Sam. After a reward is posted for Lewt's capture, McCanles sends Lewt, his favorite son, to Mexico. Before Lewt goes into hiding, he derails a train carrying explosives that is headed for Spanish Bit. He then stops at the ranch to say goodbye to Pearl, who begs to come with him. Lewt roughly rejects her, and Pearl is left alone with McCanles and the dying Laura Belle. Faced with losing his wife so soon after losing both his sons, McCanles tells Laura Belle that although he has always blamed her for the injury he received while chasing her when he thought she was running away to join Chavez, he realizes now it was his own jealousy that was responsible. After begging his wife's forgiveness, Laura Belle dies. Unaware that his mother is dead, Jesse returns to the ranch to see her. Pearl has suffered a breakdown since Laura Belle's death, and Jesse, who is now engaged to Helen Langford, the daughter of a railroad man, takes her away from the ranch. Lewt comes after Pearl and, when Jesse refuses to let him near her, shoots his brother. Jesse survives and is reconciled with his father, but Pearl understands that Lewt will eventually kill Jesse. In order to prevent that, she agrees to meet Lewt at Squaw's Head Rock, intending to kill him. Pearl's first shot wounds Lewt, who not quite dead, returns her fire, wounding her. The two dying lovers crawl toward each other and die together under the blazing sun.

Brothers. Fathers and sons. Indians–Mixed blood. Jealousy. Lechery. Engagements. Explosions. Fathers and daughters. Funerals. Handicapped. Horses. Murder. Railroads. Ranchers. Revenge. Seduction. Shootings. Texas. Train wrecks.

Note: Niven Busch's novel was purchased by RKO in 1944. According to a 16 Nov 1944 *HR* news item, the studio intended to star John Wayne and Hedy Lamarr in Busch's adaptation of his novel. A 2 Aug 1944 letter sent from MPAA head Joseph I. Breen to William Gordon at RKO included in the MPAA/PCA files at the AMPAS Library, objected to Busch's script because "it seems to be a story of illicit sex and murder for revenge, without the full compensating moral values required by the Code." Busch wanted to borrow Jennifer Jones from David O. Selznick's company, but according to modern sources, Selznick did not want Jones to appear in a film with a first-time producer. In Nov 1944, Selznick purchased the rights to the novel from RKO and enlarged the concept of the film to provide a suitable showcase for his star. He hired King Vidor to direct, and wrote the script himself from an adaptation by Oliver H. P. Garrett. According to modern sources, Selznick invented the ending in which "Pearl" and "Lewt" kill each other. In the novel, Pearl kills Lewt and then rides away to join "Jesse." Later, Selznick added the opening scenes with Tilly Losch and Herbert Marshall to "explain" Pearl's background, according to modern sources.

Scenes were filmed on location in Tucson, AZ, and Lasky Mesa and Sonora, CA and, according to contemporary sources, inclement weather in Arizona and California interfered with filming. A strike by employees of the International Association of Theatrical Stage Employees, the Screen Actors' Guild, and the Teamsters' Union interrupted the production in Apr 1945. In early Nov 1945, the production was suspended again because of Jones's illness. Then, in Aug 1946, shortly before the end of filming, differences with Selznick forced Vidor to walk off the set. According to a 19 May 1946 *NYT* article, Selznick asked William Dieterle to complete the picture. Although Dieterle is credited in the program for the film's initial release with directing "a substantial number of key sequences and scenes throughout the entire picture," Selznick had decided that Vidor should receive sole screen credit for the film. The *NYT* article reports that Dieterle protested this decision to the Screen Directors Guild, which agreed that only Vidor should receive credit. The program also acknowledges the help of directors Josef von Sternberg, William Cameron Menzies and Chester Franklin, although the exact nature of their respective contributions was not mentioned. A 6 Apr 1945 memo from Selznick to Joseph McMillan Johnson, head of Selznick's Art Department, reprinted in a modern source, indicates that von Sternberg acted as special visual consultant on the film. A 16 Aug 1945 memo from Selznick to Vidor indicates that Franklin and Menzies acted as second unit directors. A 19 Jan 1947 *NYT* article reports that a 1946 strike at the Technicolor plant prevented the processing of enough prints for nationwide release, and that Selznick was barely able to open the film at two theaters in Los Angeles in time to qualify for the 1946 Academy Awards.

After Selznick sold abandoned properties to RKO and 20th Century-Fox, United Artists, which had agreed to release *Duel in the Sun*, objected that he had broken his contract with the company and refused to distribute the film, according to a 2 Dec 1946 *HR* report. On 18 Nov 1946, *HR* reported a rumor that M-G-M would release the film, which was denied by the studio. Selznick then formed his own distribution company, Selznick Releasing Organization, according to a *HR* article on 12 Dec 1946. On 20 Dec 1946, *HR* reported that Selznick intended to file a suit for damages against United Artists and co-owners Mary Pickford and Charles Chaplin for maliciously conspiring to deprive his company of a distribution agreement executed in Oct 1942. The matter was eventually settled out of court.

Information in the MPAA/PCA files reveals that Selznick worked closely with the MPAA to ensure that the film would meet Production Code requirements. Despite the MPAA's approval of the finished picture, the National Legion of Decency condemned the film. They protested that even though the characters of Lewt and Pearl die, there is no sense that what they did was wrong. After Selznick recut the film a month later, the Legion gave it a "B" (objectional in parts for all) rating. In May 1947, a second re-edited version was released with an added prologue and epilogue. The prologue emphasized that the "Sinkiller" was not an ordained minister, in response to protests from Protestant churchmen, who felt the character made ministers appear ludicrous. The epilogue summarized the awards that the film had won and informed audiences that the main characters died because they violated the laws of God. According to a 10 Jun 1947 article in *Look*, a sexy dance in the "sump" scene was cut, and the scene in which Lewt forces himself on Pearl was shortened to eliminate any indication that a rape had occurred.

On 19 Jun 1947, Mississippi Representative John E. Rankin introduced House Resolution 250, which called for the House to demand that the District of Columbia police close a theater which was showing the film because it was "filthy, debasing, and insulting to the moral instincts of decent humanity." New York Representative Emanuel Celler objected that passing the resolution would make Rankin, who had not seen the picture, the "keeper of the nation's morals" and added that the film was no longer playing in the District of Columbia. The House Resolution never emerged from the District of Columbia Committee, where it was sent for study. Eventually, the film was passed by censor boards throughout the country, with the exception of Memphis, TN, where it was not shown until 1959.

A 7 Apr 1946 *NYT* article reported that, to sell the film, which cost between five and six million dollars, according to contemporary sources, Selznick spent another two million dollars on exploitation, and initiated a policy of saturation booking: Wherever the film opened, Selznick blanketed the area with multiple screenings. According to a 10 May 1947 *Cue* article, this was the first film to be marketed in this way. The article continued that in New York, for example,

the film was shown simultaneously in fifty theaters. Lillian Gish was nominated for Best Supporting Actress for her portrayal of ''Laura Belle'' and Jennifer Jones's performance received an Oscar nomination for Best Actress.

AmCin Feb 1946, p. 40. *Cue* 10 May 1947. *DV* 31 Dec 1946, p. 3, 16. *DV* 2 May 1947. *FD* 31 Dec 1946, p. 4. *Har* 25 Jan 1947, p. 13. *HR* 16 Nov 1944, p. 3. *HR* 9 Nov 1945, p. 3. *HR* 4 Dec 1945, p. 9. *HR* 4 Jan 1946, p. 1, 7. *HR* 27 Mar 1946, p. 2. *HR* 18 Nov 1946, pp. 1-2. *HR* 20 Nov 1946, p. 1, 4. *HR* 2 Dec 1946, p. 1, 8. *HR* 12 Dec 1946, p. 1, 4. *HR* 20 Dec 1946, p. 1, 31. *HR* 23 Dec 1946, p. 1, 3. *HR* 31 Dec 1946, p. 3. *HR* 9 Jan 1947, p. 2. *Look* 10 Jun 1947. *LAT* 18 Apr 1945. *MPD* 31 Dec 1946. *MPHPD* 17 Mar 1945, p. 2366. *MPHPD* 6 Apr 1946, p. 2926. *MPHPD* 14 Dec 1946, p. 3363. *NYT* 8 Apr 1945. *NYT* 19 May 1946. *NYT* 7 Apr 1946. *NYT* 19 Jan 1947. *NYT* 8 May 1947, p. 30. *Time* 17 Mar 1947. *Var* 1 Jan 1947, p. 14.

DUEL ON THE MISSISSIPPI (Creoles)

Clover Productions, Inc. *Dist* Columbia Pictures Corp. Oct **1955**; Prod: 7 Dec—17 Dec 1959 [©Columbia Pictures Corp.; 15 Aug 1955; LP5219]. Sd (RCA Sound Recording); col (Technicolor); 1.85. 8 reels, 6,470 ft. 72 min. PCA cert no. 17350.

[*Prod* Sam Katzman]. *Dir* William Castle. *Asst dir* Irving Moore. *Story and scr* Gerald Drayson Adams. *Dir of photog* Henry Freulich. *Spec eff* Jack Erickson. *Technicolor color consultant* Henri Jaffa. *Art dir* Paul Palmentola. *Film ed* Edwin Bryant. *Set dec* Sidney Clifford. *Mus cond* Mischa Bakaleinikoff. *Sd* Josh Westmoreland. *Unit mgr* Leon Chooluck.

Cast: Lex Barker [(*André Tulane*)], Patricia Medina [(*Lili Scarlet*)], Warren Stevens [(*Hugo Marat*)], Craig Stevens [(*René LaFarge*)], John Dehner [(*Jules Tulane*)], Ian Keith [(*Jacques Scarlet*)], Chris Alcaide [(*Anton*)], John Mansfield [(*Louie*)], Celia Lovsky [(*Celeste Tulane*)], Lou Merrill [(*Georges Gabriel*)], Mel Welles [(*Sheriff*)], [Jean Del Val [(*Bidault*)], [Baynes Barron (*Gaspard*)], [Vince M. Townsend, Jr. (*Benedict*)].

Historical, Drama. [*Print viewed*]. In early nineteenth-century Louisiana, a band of raiders led by Hugo Marat attack black workers on the plantation of Jules Tulane and kill one of the overseers. The raiders also steal Tulane's large harvest of cut sugarcane to sell on the black market. This group, along with other raiders and pirates, threaten to destroy the river empire of plantations that the Creole aristocracy has developed since early settlement. Lili Scarlet, who with her father and Hugo runs a gambling boat, admonishes Hugo for the killing, but not the theft. Lili's hatred of the Tulanes began when the aristocracy prevented her father Jacques, a ''delta man'' and former Lafitte pirate, from purchasing the estate of René LaFarge, a friend of Jules Tulane's son André. After being alerted by a wounded worker, André catches Lili and threatens her with ten years in prison unless she shows him the secret location of the raiders' hideout at Bastille Bayou. Lili pretends to agree but manages to trick André and escape. Soon after, Jules is ordered to appear in court for non-payment of a $30,000 note issued by refinery owner Georges Gabriel. The Tulane sugarcane had been promised as security for payment of the note, and now Jules, who suffers from malaria, is threatened with five years in prison. When André protests that his father would die in prison, Lili, who has purchased the note from Gabriel, offers to cancel the debt if André enters into bonded servitude to her for three years. He agrees, despite his father's objection. When André challenges Hugo to a duel following some insulting remarks, Hugo, who is an expert swordsman, agrees to fight with rapiers at daybreak. Lili pleads with André's parents to stop him, but Jules and his wife Celeste inform Lili that family honor is more precious to the Tulanes than life. The next morning, Lili insists on being the referee and stops the duel when first blood is drawn. She commands André never to challenge anyone to a duel again, and André is impressed with her spirit. On the gambling boat that night, Gabriel offers to help the Tulanes, and André, suspecting that he is in cahoots with the raiders, gives him false information bout LaFarge's sugarcane. The next night, Lili succeeds in enticing André, but a brawl downstairs in the gambling area interrupts their embrace. Lili, Jacques and André are then arrested and taken to the parish prison. Lili is angry with Hugo, who was responsible for the fight, but Jacques reminds her that they cannot buy him out, as the banks, owned by the Creole aristocracy, would never loan them money. André, however, tries to convince Lili that Hugo and his raiders are intent on ruining her family as well as the planters. He then proposes marriage, saying that she is the loveliest and most courageous woman he has met, and they kiss. The next day, Hugo bails out Lili and Jacques, and she says she will get money within an hour to release André. Sometime later, Gabriel bails out André, and states that he saw the Scarlets riding south to the river. Acting on Hugo's orders, Gabriel sets André up to be murdered, but

André eludes Hugo's thugs, and Hugo then shoots Gabriel in the back. André's plan to trap the raiders backfires, and, believing that Lili has deceived him, he returns to the gambling boat. After knocking out a guard, however, André finds that Lili and her father are Hugo's prisoners, and that the bags of LaFarge's sugarcane are on the boat, which is to leave for Bastille Bayou. When Hugo finds André, Lili, to stall for time, taunts Hugo, saying she is afraid to fight a duel with André. Hugo takes up the challenge, slaps André's face, and André chooses machetes for their duel at daybreak at Bastille Bayou. Afraid that even if André wins the duel the raiders will kill him, Lili escapes and swims to shore, then goes to the Tulane plantation, where she gives Jules his note back and convinces him and LaFarge to round up the planters. Celeste now says it is high time for the aristocracy to realize that ''it does not matter where you comes from, but what you are'' and says she hopes André has the good fortune to bring her into the family. Lili leads the planters on the ride to Bastille Bayou. The duel is interrupted by the riders, who capture the raiders, and André chases Hugo to the boat, where their fight ends in the gambling hall as André kills Hugo. Later, Lili tells André that he has a ''delta woman,'' and he threatens to send her to parish prison unless she enters into ''bonded servitude'' to him for the rest of her life. He then kisses her and picks her up, telling her that he is taking her home, as her father watches approvingly. *Battle of the sexes. Class distinction. Creoles. Gambling ships. Louisiana. Plantations. Raids. Revenge. Romance. Servants. African Americans. Bayous. Debt. Duels. Duplicity. Escapes. Family honor. Fathers and daughters. Fights. Lechery. Malaria. Mississippi River. Murder. New Orleans (LA). Ostracism. Partnership. Prisons. Proposals (Marital). Sugar. Thieves. Traps. Trials. United States–History–19th century.*

Note: The working title of this film was *Lili Scarlet.* Some scenes were shot at Algiers, Louisiana.

Box 24 Sep 1955. *DV* 9 Dec 1954. *DV* 21 Sep 1955, p. 3. *Exb* 5 Oct 1955, p. 4037. *FD* 21 Sep 1955, p. 10. *Har* 24 Sep 1955, p. 154. *HR* 21 Sep 1955, p. 3. *MPD* 22 Sep 1955. *MPHPD* 24 Sep 1955, p. 602. *Var* 21 Sep 1955, p. 6.

THE DUKE IS TOPS (African Americans)

Million Dollar Productions, Inc. *Dist* Million Dollar Productions, Inc. 1 Jul **1938**; World Premiere in Pittsburgh, PA: 15 Jul 1938; Prod: mid-Feb 1938. Sd; b&w. 8 reels, 6,627 ft. 74 min. PCA cert no. 4215.

Pres HARRY M. POPKIN. *Assoc prod* Leo C. Popkin. *Supv* Halley Harding. *Dir* William Nolte. *Asst dir* Herman Webber. *Scr adpt* Phil Dunham. *Photog* Robert Cline and Henry Kruse. *Film ed* Alice Greenwood. *Supv film ed* Arthur A. Brooks. *Set des* Vin Taylor. *Mus dir* Lou Frohman. *Mus* Ben Ellison and Harvey Brooks. *Mus arr* Phil Moore. *Ensemble numbers* Lew Crawford. *Rec eng* Glen Glen [sic]. *Prod mgr* Walter ''Buck'' Jones.

Song(s): ''I Know You Remember'' and ''Don't Let Our Love Song Turn Into a Blues,'' words and music by Ben Ellison and Harvey Brooks; ''Harlem is Harmony,'' ''When You Smoke'' and ''Thursday Evening Swing,'' composers undetermined.

Cast: RALPH COOPER (*Duke Davis*), Lena Horne (*Ethel Andrews*), Lawrence Criner (*Doc Dorando*), Monte Hawley (*George Marshall*), Neva Peoples (*Ella*), Vernon McCallum (*Mason*), Edward Thompson (*Ferdie Fenton*), Johnny Taylor (*Dippy*), Ray Martin (*Joe*), Guernsey Morrow ([*Ed*] *Lake*), Charlie Hawkins (*Sam*), *Specialties*; Willie Covan, The Basin Street Boys, Rubber Neck Holmes, The Cats and the Fiddle, Marie Bryant Swing Band, and Harlemania Orchestra, [Everett Brown (*Sheriff*)], [Arthur Ray (*Druggist*)].

African American, Show business, Musical. [*Print viewed*]. Duke Davis, singer Ethel Andrew's sweetheart, manager, and producer, finds himself in a dilemma when George Marshall, a New York booking agent, offers Ethel an opportunity to leave the show ''Sepia Scandals,'' which is touring small towns, for New York City. Because Marshall has stipulated that Ethel must go without Duke, Duke anguishes over whether to encourage her departure, but he eventually consents to it when Marshall promises to launch her New York career. Ethel initially rejects Marshall's offer when she realizes that she will be separated from Duke, but when Duke tells her that he has sold their contract for a personal profit, she is heartbroken and changes her mind. Later, Ethel's friend Ella discovers that Duke, knowing that Ethel would never leave him willingly, intentionally angered her in order to force her to do what he thought was best for her. Ella agrees to keep his good motives a secret from Ethel. While Ethel's New York stint gets off to a successful start, Duke finds himself destitute and desperately seeks backing for his vaudeville show from

booking agent Ed Lake. Lake, however, says that vaudeville is dead and rejects Duke's proposal. Although Duke later convinces Mr. Mason, a theater owner who had played his earlier show, to produce his new show, called "The Mobile Merry Makers," the show is a failure and Duke winds up having to support himself by working as a barker for Doc Dorando's traveling medicine show. Duke injects some much-needed showmanship into Dorando's pitch and, along with Dippy, an unemployed property man, they take to the road with their product, "Doc Dorando's Universal Elixir." A year passes and one day, while listening to the radio, Duke hears that a show in which Ethel was appearing has flopped and he rushes to New York to be with her. Ella tells Ethel the truth about Duke, and when Duke arrives in New York, he meets with Ferdie Fenton, producer and club owner, who has been blamed for rushing Ethel's career and causing her failure. Duke soon secures permission from Fenton to create a new show and he and Ethel appear on stage together, reunited at last. *African Americans. Dancers. Self-sacrifice. Show business. Singers. Theatrical managers. Theatrical producers. Barkers (Carnival). Cats. City-country contrast. Confidence men. Contracts. Fires. Fraud. Medicine shows. New York City–Broadway. Nightclubs. Romance. Sheriffs. Show girls. Theatrical agents. Theatrical backers. Unemployment.*

Note: *The Duke Is Tops* was re-released in 1944 as *The Bronze Venus*, with Lena Horne's name appearing above the title. This film marked the motion picture debut of Horne, whom the *Var* reviewer called "a rather inept actress, but something to look at and hear." A modern source claims that Horne replaced Nina Mae McKinney as the female lead in the middle of filming when McKinney became ill. Modern sources also note that the film was shot on a shoestring budget in ten days, and that Horne's husband refused to let her attend the NAACP charity premiere of the film in Pittsburgh, PA because she was never paid for her work in the picture.

Exb 28 Jun 1939, p. 338. *PittsC* 18 Jun 1938, p. 20. *Var* 20 Jul 1938, p. 12.

DULCE COMO LA MIEL *see* CHÉRIE

THE DUNGEON (African Americans)
Micheaux Film Corp. 22 May **1922**. Si; b&w. 7 reels, ca 6,300 ft.
Pres Oscar Micheaux. *Prod* Oscar Micheaux. *Dir* Oscar Micheaux. *Story* Oscar Micheaux.

Cast: William E. Fountaine, Shingzie Howard (*Myrtle Downing*), J. Kenneth Goodman, W. B. F. Crowell (*Gyp Lassiter*), Earle Browne Cook, Blanche Thompson.

African American, Crime, Drama. One night, Myrtle Downing, who is engaged to young lawyer Stephen Cameron, dreams that she has married Gyp Lassiter, a criminal and Cameron's chief enemy. The next morning, Myrtle reads the newspaper announcement of her marriage to Lassiter and realizes that the night before was no dream, but that Lassiter drugged, then married her while she was in a hypnotic condition. Lassiter then takes Myrtle to a lonely house where he locks her in a dungeon. Lassiter then tells her about his many wives, all of whom he killed when they tried to escape, and Myrtle realizes that if she tries to expose him she will face the same fate as the others. Soon the discouraged Cameron goes to Alaska and becomes rich on a claim. When claim jumpers try to swindle him out of his property, he is saved by prizefighter Chick Barton, who informs him that redistribution of the Congressional districts in his hometown, Cartersville, has permitted blacks to run for Congress. When he learns that Lassiter himself is being groomed for office, Cameron returns to Cartersville to run against Lassiter and hopefully prevent his election. Meanwhile, Myrtle learns that her husband has agreed to permit racial segregation and thus force blacks to leave the city's best neighborhoods, in return for money and a seat in Congress. Myrtle tries more than once to escape to warn the community of the danger presented by Lassiter's election, and when she finally succeeds, she has him exposed in a Black newspaper. An enraged Lassiter finds Myrtle, carries her to his dungeon, where he plans to torture and kill her, but Cameron manages to rescue Myrtle and in the ensuing struggle kills his evil rival. *African Americans. Drugging. Dungeons. Elections. Hypnotism. Lawyers. Marriage–Forced. Murder. Political corruption. Segregation. Alaska. Boxers. Claim jumpers. Dreams. Newspapers. Real estate. Rescues.*

ChiDef 8 Apr 1922, p. 6. *ChiDef* 8 Jul 1922. *ChiDef* 24 Mar 1923, p. 6.

THE DUSTY ROAD *see* LET FREEDOM RING

THE EASIEST WAY (*foreign version*) *see* QUAND ON EST BELLE

EAST AND WEST *see* MAZEL TV

EAST END CHANT *see* LIMEHOUSE BLUES

EAST IS EAST *see* JAPANESE WAR BRIDE

EAST IS WEST (Chinese Americans)
Constance Talmadge Productions. *Dist* Associated First National Pictures. Oct **1922**; Cleveland and Des Moines premieres: ca15 Oct 1922 [©Joseph M. Schenck; 7 Nov 1922; LP18405]. Si; b&w. 8 reels, 7,737 ft.
Prod Joseph M. Schenck. *Dir* Sidney Franklin. *Scen and adpt* Frances Marion. *Photog* Antonio Gaudio. *Art dir* Stephen Goosson.

Source: Based on the play *East Is West* by Samuel Shipman and John B. Hymer (New York, 25 Dec 1918).

Cast: Constance Talmadge (*Ming Toy*), Edward Burns (*Billy Benson*), E. A. Warren (*Lo Sang Kee*), Warner Oland (*Charley Yong*), Frank Lanning (*Hop Toy*), Nick De Ruiz (*Chang Lee*), Nigel Barrie (*Jimmy Potter*), Lillian Lawrence (*Mrs. Benson*), Winter Hall (*Mr. Benson*), Jim Wang (*Proprietor of love boat*).

Melodrama. Ming Toy, the eldest of Hop Toy's many children, is rescued from the auction block by Billy Benson and sent to the United States in the care of Lo Sang Kee. There she continues her interest in western ways and attracts the attention of a powerful Chinatown figure, Charley Yong. When Charley Yong demands the hand of Ming Toy, she is again rescued by Benson. There ensues a chase, Billy takes Ming Toy to his home and declares his love, and Charley Yong acquiesces when it is revealed that Ming Toy, as a baby, was kidnapped from American parents. *Chinese Americans. Kidnapping. San Francisco (CA)–Chinatown.*

Note: For information on the 1930 film adaptation of Samuel Shipman's play see entry below.

ETR 9 Sep 1922, p. 1021. *FD* 3 Sep 1922. *MPW* 9 Sep 1922. *MPW* 23 Sep 1922. *Var* 20 Oct 1922, p.40.

EAST IS WEST (Chinese Americans)
Universal Pictures Corp. *Dist* Universal Pictures Corp. 23 Oct **1930**; Prod: Aug-Sep 1930 [©Universal Pictures Corp.; 11 Oct 1930; LP1628]. Sd (Movietone); b&w. 8 reels, 6,683 ft. 74 min.
Pres Carl Laemmle. *Assoc prod* E. M. Asher. *Scr* Tom Reed. *Dir* Monta Bell. *Adpt* Winifred Eaton. *Addl dial* Tom Reed. *Photog* Jerry Ash. *Spec eff photog* Frank H. Booth. *Film ed* Harry Marker. *Rec eng* C. Roy Hunter.

Source: Based on the play *East Is West* by Samuel Shipman and John B. Hymer (New York, 25 Dec 1918).

Cast: Lupe Vélez (*Ming Toy*), Lew Ayres (*Billy Benson*), Edward G. Robinson (*Charlie Yong*), Mary Forbes (*Mrs. Benson*), E. Alyn Warren (*Lo Sang Kee*), Henry Kolker (*Mr. Benson*), Tetsu Komai (*Hop Toy*), Edgar Norton (*Thomas*), Charles Middleton (*Dr. Fredericks*).

Romance, Drama. [The plot is essentially the same as that of the 1922 Constance Talmadge Production of the same title (see above).]. *Chinese Americans. Kidnapping. San Francisco (CA)–Chinatown. Americans in foreign countries. Auctions.*

Note: The Spanish-language version of the film had the working title *El barco del amor* and was filmed simultaneously with the English version. A 1922 silent version of *East Is West* was directed by Sidney Franklin and starred Constance Talmadge and Edward Burns (see above).

Other language version(s):
Oriente y Occidente (Spanish language)
1930; San José de Costa Rica opening: 30 Nov 1930; Los Angeles opening: 26 Dec 1930. Sd; b&w. 10 reels. 93 min. Spanish language.
Supv Paul Kohner. *Dir* George Melford. *Asst dir* Jay Marchant. *Dial dir* Enrique Tovar Avalos. *Spanish version* Baltasar Fernández Cué. *Photog* George Robinson. *Art dir* Herman Rosse. *Film ed* Arturo Tavares. *Sd supv* C. Roy Hunter. *Mus comp* Heinz Romheld.
Song(s): "Júrame," music and lyrics by María Grever.
Spanish-language cast: Lupe Vélez (*Ming Toy*), Barry Norton (*Billy Benson*), Manuel Arbó (*Charlie Yong*), Daniel F. Rea (*Lo Sang Ki*), Tetsu Komai (*Hop Toy*), Marcela Nivón (*Sra. Benson*), José Soriano Viosca (*Sr. Benson*), André Cheron (*Tomás*), Lucio Villegas (*Dr. Fredericks*). [*Spanish version not viewed*].

CM Mar 1931, p. 237. *Cinl* Dec 1930, p. 30.

EAST OF BROADWAY (Irish Americans)

Encore Pictures. *Dist* Associated Exhibitors, Inc. 23 Nov **1924** [©Associated Exhibitors, Inc.; 11 Dec 1924; LU20888]. Si; b&w. 6 reels, 5,785 ft.

Dir William K. Howard. *Scen and adpt* Paul Schofield. *Photog* Lucien Andriot.

Source: Based on the short story "Tropic of Capricorn" by Richard Connell in *The Sins of Monsieur Pettipon, and other Humorous Tales* (New York, 1922).

Cast: Owen Moore (*Peter Mullaney*), Marguerite De La Motte (*Judy McNulty*), Mary Carr (*Mrs. Morrisey*), Eddie Gribbon (*Danny McCabe*), Francis McDonald (*Professor Mario*), Betty Francisco (*Diana Morgan*), George Nichols (*Officer Gaffney*), Ralph Lewis (*Commissioner*).

Comedy. Peter Mullaney, the son of Irish immigrants living on the East Side of Manhattan, has one ambition in life: to become one of New York's Finest. He goes to the Police Training School and is about to be rejected for not meeting the height qualification when he demonstrates his prowess in a fight. The commissioner then decides to give Peter a chance to make the force, if he scores well on the written examination. Peter declares the Tropic of Capricorn to be in the Bronx and fails to pass; the commissioner, however, allows him to wear the uniform for one night in order not to disappoint Peter's girl, Judy McNulty. Walking the beat with Officer Gaffney, he becomes involved in preventing a robbery, during which Gaffney is shot. Peter comes to his aid and captures the robbers, being himself hurt in the process. In the hospital, the commissioner, on account of his bravery, pins a shield on him, and Peter and Judy make plans to be married. *Irish Americans. New York City–East Side. Police. Robbery.*

FD 16 Nov 1924. *MPW* 22 Nov 1924. *NYT* 12 Nov 1924, p. 13. *Var* 12 Nov 1924, p. 25.

EAST OF FIFTH AVENUE *see* **OBEY THE LAW**

EAST OF THE RIVER (Italian Americans)

Warner Bros. Pictures, Inc.; A Warner Bros.—First National Picture; Jack L. Warner, in charge of production. *Dist* Warner Bros. Pictures, Inc. 9 Nov **1940**; New York opening: week of 28 Oct 1940; Prod: began late Jul 1940 [©Warner Bros. Pictures, Inc.; 9 Nov 1940; LP10035]. Sd (RCA Sound System); b&w. 8 reels. 73 min. PCA cert no. 6562.

[*Exec prod* Bryan Foy and Hal B. Wallis]. *Assoc prod* Harlan Thompson. *Dir* Alfred E. Green. *Dial dir* Hugh MacMullan. [*Asst dir* Les Guthrie]. *Scr* Fred Niblo, Jr. *Orig story* John Fante and Ross B. Willis. *Photog* Sid Hickox. *Art dir* Hugh Reticker. *Film ed* Thomas Pratt. *Gowns* Howard Shoup. *Mus dir* Leo F. Forbstein. *Mus* Adolph Deutsch. *Sd* Stanley Jones. *Makeup* Perc Westmore. *Tech adv* Marie Jenardi.

Cast: JOHN GARFIELD (*Joe Lorenzo*), BRENDA MARSHALL (*Laurie Romayne*), MARJORIE RAMBEAU ([*Mama*] *Teresa Lorenzo*), George Tobias (*Tony*), William Lundigan (*Nick Lorenzo*), Moroni Olsen (*Judge Davis*), Douglas Fowley (*Cy Turner*), Jack LaRue (*Scarfi*), Jack Carr (*"No Neck" Griswold*), Paul Guilfoyle (*Balmy*), Russell Hicks (*Warden*), Charley Foy (*Customer*), Ralph Volkie, Jimmy O'Gatty (*Henchmen*), Robert Homans (*Patrolman Shanahan*), Joe Conti (*Jo, as boy*), O'Neill Nolan (*Nick, as boy*), [William Pawley (*Dave Carter*)], [John Kelly (*The dope*)], [George Humbert (*Peddler*)], [Eddy Chandler (*Watchman*)], [Al Herman (*Hotdog vendor*)], [Jack Mower, Frank Mayo, Cliff Saum (*Guards*)], [Al Lloyd, Tom Wilson, Sol Gorss, Jack Wise, Paul Panzer, Don Turner (*Prisoners*)], [Edwin Stanley (*Commencement speaker*)], [William Marshall (*Usher*)], [Edward Fielding (*President*)], [Jerry Mandy (*Mr. Lomardo*)], [Richard Clayton (*Delivery boy*)], [Creighton Hale (*Houseman*)], [Charles Sherlock (*Second houseman*)], [Arch Hendricks (*Captain McNamara*)], [Howard Mitchell (*Detective*)], [Murray Alper (*Dink Rogers*)], [Al Rhein (*Dealer*)], [George Lloyd (*Charlie, bartender*)], [Demetris Emanuel (*Manuel*)], [Hector Sarno (*Pop Fiaschetti*)], [John Sheehan (*Bartender*)], [Ann Edmonds (*Marie Carmine*)], [Armand "Curly" Wright (*Bruno*)], [Fred Graham, Ralph Sanford, Pat O'Malley, Roy Barcroft (*Cops*)].

Gangster, Drama. [*Print viewed*]. On New York's Lower East Side, Mama Teresa Lorenzo labors in her spaghetti restaurant, determined to keep her young son Joe honest. When Joe and his friend Nick get into trouble for slugging a railroad detective, Mama saves the boys from the reformatory by promising to discipline Joe and adopt the homeless Nick. While Nick earns straight A's in school and continues

on to college, Joe turns to gambling and crime. Joe finances Nick's education and leads his family to believe that he is running a ranch in California, but is actually serving a prison term in San Quentin. Upon finishing his sentence, Joe returns to New York to attend Nick's college graduation and brings his girl friend, Laurie Romayne, who is wanted on a forgery charge, with him. In New York, Laurie, touched by Mama's kindness and concern, begins to help with the household chores and discovers that she enjoys the honest life. Meanwhile, Joe plots revenge on Scarfi and Cy Turner, the two gangsters he blames for sending him to Quentin. Joe informs the police of a robbery that the two are planning, but Turner escapes the police trap. When Scarfi is sent to the electric chair for shooting a policeman, Turner vows to take Joe's life in revenge. To avoid Turner's thugs, Joe leaves town, but Laurie decides to stay with Mama. In Joe's absence, Laurie gets a job, and she and Nick fall in love and decide to marry. In Mexico, Joe learns of their plans and returns to stop the wedding. He threatens to expose Laurie's past unless she gives Nick up, but Mama, learning of Joe's treachery, renounces him as her son. Joe relents, and after delivering Laurie to the church, he eludes the clutches of Turner's thugs by slugging a policeman and getting arrested. *Brothers. Criminals–Rehabilitation. Gangsters. Italian Americans. Mothers and sons. New York City–East Side. Adoption. Forgers and forgery. Frame-ups. Gambling. Molls. Police. Restaurants. Revenge. San Quentin Federal Penitentiary (CA). Traps. Weddings.*

Note: The working titles of this film were *Mama Ravioli* and *Bad Boy*. According to news items in the *HR*, Raoul Walsh was originally scheduled to direct and Ida Lupino was slated for Brenda Marshall's role.

DV 3 Dec 1940, p. 3. *FD* 31 Oct 1940, p. 4. *HR* 12 Jul 1940, p. 1. *HR* 19 Jul 1940, p. 5. *HR* 26 Jul 1940, pp. 8-9. *HR* 3 Dec 1940, p. 4. *MPD* 4 Nov 1940, p. 3. *MPH* 2 Nov 1940, p. 35, 58. *NYT* 28 Oct 1940, p. 21. *Var* 30 Oct 1940, p. 14.

EAST SIDE *see* **THE HEART OF NEW YORK**

EAST SIDE SADIE (Jewish Americans)

Dist Worldart Film Co. **1929**; New York showing: 20 May 1929. Mus score and talking sequences; b&w. 6 reels, 5,500-6,100 ft. [Also si.].

Dir Sidney M. Goldin. *Story* Sidney M. Goldin. *Titles* Sam Citen. *Photog* Frank Zucker. *Film ed* Sam Citen.

Cast: Bertina Goldin, Jack Ellis, Boris Rosenthal, Lucia Backus Seger, Abe Sinkoff, John Halliday, Al Stanley, Maechivinko, Mark Schweid.

Drama. A Jewish sweatshop seamstress contributes her meager earnings to her boyfriend's college education, but he falls into the hands of a marriage broker, who matches him with a wealthy girl. Given a beating by the seamstress' brother just before the wedding, the boy awakens to the girl's sacrifices and is reunited with her. (Sources are somewhat confusing about the story line. The boy may be Irish and have a Jewish stepfather. There is also a vague reference to a comedy scene on a tenement roof involving some Italians. Sound sequences include singing children, a cantor singing a wedding prayer, and some shouting during the wedding.). *Brothers and sisters. Education. Irish Americans. Italian Americans. Jews. Matchmakers. New York City–East Side. Seamstresses. Sweatshops. Weddings.*

FD 2 Jun 1929.

EAST SIDE STORY *see* **HOUSE OF STRANGERS**

EAST SIDE WEST SIDE (Fox Film Corp., Oct 1931) *see* **SKYLINE**

EAST SIDE, WEST SIDE (1939) *see* **THE ESCAPE**

EASY COME, EASY GO (Irish Americans)

Paramount Pictures, Inc.; A John Farrow Production. *Dist* Paramount Pictures, Inc. 7 Mar **1947**; New York opening: 5 Feb 1947; Prod: 10 Oct–16 Nov 1945; added scenes 26 Nov 1945 [©Paramount Pictures, Inc.; 31 Jan 1947; LP862]. Sd (Western Electric Recording); b&w. 8 reels. 77 min. Passed by the National Board of Review. PCA cert no. 11255.

Prod Kenneth Macgowan. *Dir* John Farrow. [*Asst dir* Oscar Rudolph]. *Scr* Francis Edwards Faragoh, Anne Froelick and John McNulty. *Dir of photog* Daniel L. Fapp. [*2d cam* Haskell Boggs]. *Process photog* Farciot Edouart. [*Spec photog eff* Gordon Jennings]. [*Spec eff asst* Paul Lerpae and Loyal Griggs]. *Art dir* Hans Dreier and Haldane Douglas. *Ed supv* Eda Warren. *Ed* Thomas Scott. *Set dec* Sam Comer and Maurice Goodman. *Cost* Dorothy O'Hara. *Mus score* Roy Webb. *Sd rec* Stanley Cooley and Don Johnson. [*Mus mixer* Philip G. Wisdom]. *Makeup supv* Wally Westmore.

Source: Based on sketches compiled in the book *3rd Avenue, New York* by John Lawrence McNulty (Boston, 1946).

Cast: BARRY FITZGERALD [(*Martin L. Donovan*)], DIANA LYNN [(*Connie Donovan*)], SONNY TUFTS [(*Kevin O'Connor*)], Dick Foran [(*Dale Whipple*)], Frank McHugh [(*Carey*)], Allen Jenkins [(*Nick*)], John Litel [(*Tom Clancy*)], Arthur Shields [([*Timothy*] *Mike Donovan*)], Frank Faylen [(*Boss*)], James Burke [(*Harry Weston*)], George Cleveland [(*Gilligan*)], Ida Moore [(*Angela Orange*)], Rhys Williams [(*Priest*)], Oscar Rudolph [(*Bookie*)], [Gene Stone (*Bookie*)], [Lou Lubin (*Mr. Weiss, tailor*)], [Frank Puglia (*Italian grocer*)], [Erno Verebes (*Mopsy Marek*)], [Olin Howlin (*Gas man*)], [Howard Freeman (*Magistrate*)], [Hobart Cavanaugh (*Mr. Higgins, repair shop manager*)], [Byron Foulger (*Sporting goods shop proprietor*)], [Houseley Stevenson (*Doctor*)], [Tom Fadden (*Sanitation man/grocery clerk*)], [Tom Dugan (*Sanitation man*)], [Joey Ray (*Mr. X*)], [Howard Mitchell (*Bailiff*)], [Chester Clute (*Waiter*)], [Rex Lease, Ted Rand, Stanley Price, Pat McVeigh (*Gamblers*)], [Phil Monte (*Gambler and bookie*)], [Crane Whitley (*Prosecutor*)], [Matt McHugh (*Worker*)], [Charles Sullivan (*Cabbie*)], [Perc Launders, Jimmie Dundee (*Bartenders*)], [Eddie Fetherston (*Passenger*)], [Antonio Filauri (*Grocer*)], [Stanley Andrews, Jack Shea, John Sheehan, Chuck Hamilton (*Detectives*)], [James Flavin, Eddy Chandler (*Plainclothesmen*)], [G. Pat Collins (*Desk sergeant*)], [Tom P. Dillon (*Cop*)], [Polly Bailey (*Housewife*)], [Robert R. Stephenson (*Alex the delicatessen man/sanitation man*)], [Lorin Raker (*Restaurant manager*)], [Harry Hayden (*Bank teller*)], [Syd Saylor (*Milkman*)], [Philip Van Zandt (*Mailman*)], [Myron Geiger, Tommy Summers, Dario Piazza, David Wold, Dan Borzage, Charles Campbell, John Jennings, James Davies, James Cornell, Patricia West, Betty Hill, Julia Faye, Diane Ervin, Patricia Harmon, Miriam Snitzer, Jean Marshall (*Neighbors*)], [Freddie Chapman, Vincent Graeff, Mickey McGuire, Henry Blair (*Boys*)], [Jack Murphy], [Edwin Chandler].

Gambling, Comedy-drama. [*Print viewed*]. New York Irishman Martin L. Donovan, a charismatic, compulsive gambler affectionately referred to as "Himself," is released after being caught in a raid at a bookie joint, when he finally promises to do legitimate work. Although Martin's daughter Connie tries to take care of the family boardinghouse, Martin's boarders are captivated by his dreams of wealth and place bets with him, and are then unable to pay rent. Fearing that he will lose Connie to marriage, Martin starts a rivalry for her affection between policeman Dale Whipple and returning "seabee" Kevin O'Connor. Kevin, whom Connie has loved since she was a girl, wins Connie's heart, and she shares his dream of opening an automobile repair shop. Hoping to keep Connie with him, Martin lures Kevin into spending all his earnings as a cab driver on bets. Although depressed by his overwhelming losses, Kevin proposes to Connie, but loses the money for an engagement ring, when he follows Martin's gambling advice. Kevin is then arrested with Martin in a police raid, and is accused of participating in a robbery, in which his stolen cab was used. Connie posts bail with the deed to her house, but leaves Kevin for Dale because of his gambling. Without Connie there, everything falls apart at the boardinghouse. The disgusted renters move out and bill collectors pound on Martin's door. Martin's last hope for solvency disappears when his brother Timothy, who has just returned after a twenty-year absence, reveals he is as poor as Martin. Martin then goes to work with Timothy, a diver for the police, and one day while diving into the East River, Martin finds a satchel filled with money. Martin spends the cash profligately, favoring the motto, "easy come, easy go," and the money soon runs out. When Connie learns that Martin has lost his fortune and his friends, she pawns Dale's engagement ring, and, at the urging of former boarder Mrs. Angela Orange, bets the money on a horse named "Easy Come, Easy Go." Before the race is finished, the betting house is raided and both women are arrested. Connie is embarrassed when Dale turns out to be the arresting officer, and he worries that his reputation with the police force will be damaged. After Connie is released, she learns that "Easy Come, Easy Go" won the race, and reunites with Martin and Kevin. Martin is hit by a car shortly after, and although he is not severely injured, he goes into shock. A kindly priest talks Martin out of his coma using racing metaphors, and Martin's faith in life is restored. *Fathers and daughters. Finance–Personal. Gambling. Romantic rivalry. Automobile accidents. Boardinghouses. Bookies. Debt. Divers and diving. Engagements. False arrests. Irish Americans. Money. New York City. Pawnbrokers. Police. Priests. Raids. Taxicab drivers. Veterans. Wagers.*

Note: The working titles of this film were *Third Avenue* and *Too Good to Be True*. John McNulty's book was originally published in the early 1940s as a series of sketches in *The New Yorker* magazine. Paramount released a song, "Easy Come, Easy Go," music and lyrics by Jay Livingston and Ray Evans, in conjunction with the release of this film, but the song was not heard in the viewed print.

Box 1 Feb 1947. *DV* 3 Feb 1947. *FD* 4 Feb 1947, p. 12. *HR* 1 May 1945, p. 5. *HR* 11 Oct 1945, p. 6. *HR* 20 Nov 1945, p. 10. *HR* 26 Nov 1945, p. 14. *HR* 1 Feb 1946, p. 6. *HR* 3 Feb 1947, p. 3. *IFJ* 10 Nov 1947, p. 50. *MPHPD* 8 Feb 1947. *NYT* 6 Feb 1947, p. 29. *Var* 5 Feb 1947, p. 12.

EASY MONEY (African Americans)

Reol Productions Corp. **1922**; License application, New York State: 29 Mar 1922 [©Reol Productions Corp.; 6 Mar 1922; LU17737]. Si; b&w. 6 reels, 5,500 ft.

Story J. Rufus Brown.

Cast: Sherman H. Dudley (*Andy Simpson*), Edna Morton (*Margie Watkins*), H. L. Pryor, Inez Clough, Alex K. Shannon, Percy Verwayen.

African American, Comedy-drama. Andy Simpson, constable, blacksmith and all-round mechanic of Millbrook, a thrifty little southern town, is looked upon as slow, plodding, and lacking in ambition by all save Margie Watkins, his sweetheart and daughter of the bank president. Margie, however, becomes attracted to J. Overton Tighe (a partner of James Bradford, notorious promoter of "wildcat" investments), who is newly arrived in town in an expensive car. Despite Andy's warnings, the townspeople eagerly buy shares in a phony stock promoted by Tighe. Mrs. Watkins even persuades her husband to invest some of the bank's funds in the enterprise. Even after he finds conclusive evidence, Andy hesitates to arrest Tighe, for an arrest would mean the ruin of Margie's father. Margie, apparently disregarding Andy's advice, continues her affair with Tighe, and they become engaged. Tighe finds oil on Andy's land and buys it for a song. Andy finally exposes Tighe's real business in Millbrook (which is more serious than swindling), arrests Tighe, and in the end turns the tables on the shrewd promoter and himself gets the easy money. *African Americans. Bankers. Blacksmiths. Constables. Deception. Mechanics. Small town life. Speculation. United States–South.*

EASY STREET (African Americans)

Micheaux Pictures. **1930**; Pittsburgh, PA opening: 16 Oct 1930. Sd; b&w. 5 reels, 4,974 ft.

Pres Oscar Micheaux. *Dir* Oscar Micheaux.

Cast: Richard B. Harrison, Alice B. Russell, William A. Clayton, Willor Lee Guilford, Lorenzo Tucker.

African American, Crime, Drama. [An ad for the film calls it, "A sensational story of Love, Finance, Gang Life, City Slickers, and their attempt to swindle an old man of honestly earned money. A plot sensational with Surprise, Action, Love, Suspence and Intrigue." No additional information about the plot has been located.]. *African Americans. Aged men. Gangsters. Romance. Swindlers and swindling.*

Note: The film was approved for exhibition in New York state on 16 Oct 1930, according to NYSA records.

PittsC 11 Oct 1930, pt. II, p. 8.

EASY STREET (1938) *see* BREAKING THE ICE

ECHEC AU ROI (French language)

RKO Radio Pictures, Inc. *Dist* RKO Radio Pictures, Inc. **1931**; World premiere in Los Angeles: 27 Dec 1930; Chicago opening: 6 Mar 1931. Sd; b&w. 86 min. French language.

Prod William LeBaron. *Dir* Léon D'Usseau and Henri de la Falaise. *Scenario and dial* Robert Harari. *Scenario* J. Walter Ruben. *Photog* Leo Tover. *Ed* Milner Kichen. *Sd* Paul Saulkner.

Source: Based on the play *The Queen's Husband* by Robert Emmet Sherwood (New York, 25 Jan 1928).

Cast: Françoise Rosay (*La reine*), Pauline Garon (*La princesse Anne*), Emile Chautard (*Le roi Eric VIII*), Jules Raucourt (*Le général Bellum*), George Davis (*Phipps*), Ivan Lebedeff (*Le docteur*), Jacques Jou-Jerville (*Le marquis de Birsen*), Frank O'Neill (*Granton*), Roland Mars (*Le major Blent*), Robert Harari (*Le docteur Felman*), Arthur Hurni (*Carpoff*), Albert Petit.

Comedy-drama. [*Not viewed*]. [The following plot summary is based on the English-language version of this film, *The Royal Bed*; character names refer to that version. For further information regarding the English-language version, please see the note below and the entry for *The Royal Bed* in the *AFI Catalog of Feature Films, 1931-40*.] More interested in playing checkers with the servants than

in governing his people, King Eric VIII is dominated by Martha, his queen, a humorless woman who believes in doing her royal duty above all else. Her daughter, Princess Anne, however, loves commoner Freddie Granton, the king's secretary, and refuses to marry her mother's political choice, the foppish Prince William. After the queen leaves for a promotional tour of America, a long-fomenting revolution erupts on the night of Anne's birthday ball, and the palace is bombed. The king agrees to meet with the revolution's leader and, after hearing his cause, promises him that if the revolutionaries lay down their arms, he will oust General Northrup, the powerful, dictatorial premier. After some manipulation and collaboration, the king rids the country of Northrup, while insuring better living conditions for his subjects. With the uprising squelched and the queen back from America, Anne's wedding to William proceeds as planned, though under protest from the princess. Minutes before the ceremony, however, the rejuvenated king, in final defiance of his wife, secretly marries Anne and Freddie himself and arranges for their passage to common freedom. *Fathers and daughters. Marriage-Arranged. Mythical lands. Royalty. Transformation. Usurpers. Balls (Parties). Checkers (Game). Elopement. Fops. Officers (Military). Revolutionaries. Servants. Uprisings.*

Note: The French version of the film screened in Los Angeles and Chicago under the title *Le roi s'ennuie.* According to modern sources, the working titles of the French version were *Le mari de la reine* and *Le roi s'ennuie.* For information concerning the English-language version, *The Royal Bed,* which was directed by Lowell Sherman and starred Lowell Sherman and Mary Astor, please see the entry for that film in the *AFI Catalog of Feature Films, 1931-40;* F3.3845.

THE EDDIE CANTOR STORY (Jewish Americans)
Warner Bros. Pictures, Inc.; A Warner Bros.-First National Picture. *Dist* Warner Bros. Pictures, Inc. Dec 1953; New York premiere: 23 Dec 1953; Los Angeles premiere: 29 Dec 1953; Prod: 2 Jan–3 Mar 1953; addl scenes Aug—early Sep 1953 [©Warner Bros. Pictures, Inc.; 3 Feb 1954; LP4396]. Sd (RCA Sound System); col (Technicolor). 13 reels, 10,471 ft. 115-116 min. Passed by the National Board of Review. PCA cert no. 16034.
Prod Sidney Skolsky. *Dir* Alfred E. Green, [George Stevens and Gordon Douglas]. *Asst dir* Al Alleborn. [*2d asst dir* Gibson Graham]. *Scr* Jerome Weidman, Ted Sherdeman and Sidney Skolsky. *From a story by* Sidney Skolskyd. *Dir of photog* Edwin DuPar. [*Cam* Ted McCord]. *Technicolor color consultant* Mitchell G. Kovaleski. *Art dir* Charles H. Clarke. *Film ed* William Ziegler. *Set dec* William Wallace. *Ward* Howard Shoup and Marjorie Best. *Mus dir* Ray Heindorf. *Mus numbers staged and dir by* LeRoy Prinz. *Orch* Frank Comstock and Gus Levene. *Vocal arr* Charles Henderson. [*Dance asst* Eddie Prinz]. *Sd* C. A. Riggs and David Forrest. *Makeup artist* Gordon Bau.
Song(s): "Meet Me Tonight in Dreamland," music by Leo Friedman, lyrics by Beth Slater; "Bedelia," music by Jean Schwartz, lyrics by William Jerome; "Will You Love Me in December as You Do in May?" music by Ernest R. Ball, lyrics by James J. Walker; "Be My Little Baby Bumble Bee," music by Henry I. Marshall, lyrics by Stanley Murphy; "If I Was a Millionaire," music by Gus Edwards, lyrics by Will D. Cobb; "Love Me and the World Is Mine," music by Ernest R. Ball, lyrics by Dave Reed, Jr.; "Row, Row, Row," music by James V. Monaco, lyrics by William Jerome; "How Ya' Gonna' Keep 'Em Down on the Farm After They've Seen Paree?" music by Walter Donaldson, lyrics by Sam M. Lewis and Joe Young; "Oh, You Beautiful Doll," music by Nat D. Ayer, lyrics by Seymour Brown; "If You Knew Susie Like I Know Susie," music and lyrics by B. G. De Sylva and Joseph Meyer; "Bye, Bye, Blackbird," music by Ray Henderson, lyrics by Mort Dixon; "Pretty Baby," music and lyrics by Gus Kahn, Tony Jackson and Egbert Van Alstyne; "Yes, Sir, That's My Baby,"music by Walter Donaldson, lyrics by Gus Kahn; "Josephine Please No Lean on the Bell," music and lyrics by Ed G. Nelson, Harry Pease and Duke Leonard; "Yes! We Have No Bananas," music and lyrics by Frank Silver and Irving Cohn; "Tip Toe Through the Tulips with Me," music by Joe Burke, lyrics by Al Dubin; "Ida, Sweet as Apple Cider," music by Eddie Munson, lyrics by Eddie Leonard; "Makin' Whoopee," music by Walter Donaldson, lyrics by Gus Kahn; "Now's the Time to Fall in Love," music and lyrics by Al Sherman and Al Lewis; "(I'd Love to Spend) One Hour with You," music by Richard A. Whiting, lyrics by Leo Robin; "Margie," music by Con Conrad and J. Russel Robinson, lyrics by Benny Davis; "When I'm the President," music and lyrics by Al Lewis and Al Sherman; "Ma, He's Making Eyes at Me," music by Con Conrad, lyrics by Sidney Clare.

Cast: Keefe Brasselle [(*Eddie Cantor*)], Marilyn Erskine [(*Ida [Tobias] Cantor*)], Aline MacMahon [(*Grandma Esther*)], Arthur Franz [(*Harry Harris*)], Alex Gerry [(*David Tobias*)], Greta Granstedt [(*Rachel Tobias*)], Gerald Mohr [(*Rocky Kramer*)], William Forrest [(*Flo Ziegfeld*)], Jackie Barnett [(*Jimmy Durante*)], Richard Monda [(*Eddie Cantor, age 13*)], Marie Windsor [(*Cleo Abbott*)], Douglas Evans [(*Leo Raymond*)], Ann Doran [(*Lillian Edwards*)], Hal March [(*Gus Edwards*)], Will Rogers, Jr. [(*Will Rogers*)], [Eddie Cantor, Ida Cantor (*Themselves*)], [Susan Odin (*Ida Tobias, age 11*)], [Owen Pritchard (*Harry Harris as a boy*)], [James Flavin (*Kelly the policeman*)], [Peter De Bear (*Rocky as a boy*)], [Eddie Sands (*Nails*)], [Michael Kanner (*George Jessel as a child*)], [Julie Newmeyer (*Showgirl*)], [David Alpert (*Mr. Berk*)], [Harry Mendoza (*Magician*)], [Chick Chandler (*Lesser*)], [Ralph Volkie (*Slats*)], [Bill O'Brien (*Proprietor*)], [Diane Dawson (*Secretary*)], [Dave Newell (*Policeman*)], [Mickey Simpson (*Headwaiter*)], [James Craven (*Bert Glenville*)], [Norma Amigo (*Rocky's friend*)], [Robert Jordan (*Customer*)], [Kathleen Case (*Francey*)], [Richard Gordon (*Glenville's friend*)], [Tris Coffin (*Director*)], [Barbara Pepper (*Patron*)], [Don Dillaway (*Coronet player*)], [Michael Pierce (*Western Union boy*)], [Jack Gargan (*Stage manager*)], [Jim Dale (*Caddy*)], [Joel Smith (*Rocky's benchman*)], [Marilee Phelps (*Nurse*)], [Arthur Space (*Phil*)], [Kermit Maynard (*Willie*)], [Barry Brooks (*Alvin*)], [Ned Young (*Jack*)], [Mira McKinney (*Pianist*)], [Gail Ganley (*Natalie Cantor*)], [Steffi Sydney (*Edna Cantor*)], [John Anderson (*Bobby*)], [Albert Walters (*Eddie at 15*)], [Marcoreta Hellman], [Ed Haskett], [Charles Morton], [Paul Birch], [Faire Binney], [Eva Novak], [Cameron Grant], [Bob Stephenson], [George Spaulding], [Howard Brody], [Ralph Gibson], [Pat Mazzoti], [John Gardner], [Billy Perna], [Henry Fladwed], [Le Roy Strand], [Gary Stewart], [Don Bender], [Dickie Leroy], [Jimmy Moss], [Whitey Haupt].

Biography, Musical. [*Print viewed*]. Eddie Cantor and his wife Ida arrive at Warner Bros. studios in Burbank, CA, for a private screening of *The Eddie Cantor Story.* Just before the film rolls, Cantor whispers, "Ida, I've never been so nervous in all my life." The story begins on New York's East Side in 1904. Thirteen-year-old Eddie Cantor, eager to be accepted by the neighborhood hoodlum, Rocky Kramer, entertains a crowd at a political rally by singing, unaware that Rocky and his gang are using the opportunity to pick the listeners' pockets. After a kindly Irish cop escorts Eddie home to his Grandma Esther, Eddie sets off to deliver Sabbath candles to the home of merchant David Tobias, whose daughter, Ida, invites Eddie to stay for dinner. Soon after, Mr. Burke from the Educational Alliance persuades Grandma Esther to send Eddie to the Surprise Lake Camp for boys. Eddie's vocal performances make him an instant hit with the campers and on the way home, he wins a contest at Miners' Bowery Theatre. In the audience is Mr. Lesser, a producer who arranges for Eddie to join the Gus Edwards Kid Kabaret. For the next several years, Eddie travels with the show, sending Grandma Esther souvenir spoons from each of the cities he visits. When Eddie becomes too old for the Kid Kabaret, he returns home. Rocky Kramer, now a crooked politician with Tammany Hall, offers Eddie a job at his nightclub on Coney Island. Although nothing more than a singing waiter, Eddie, who is still fond of his childhood sweetheart Ida, boasts that he is the star of the show to impress her father. One evening, Ida and her family, accompanied by another of Ida's admirers, Harry Harris, visit the club. Horrified, Eddie sets down his tray and provides his audience with an unscheduled solo performance, but Ida's family nevertheless discovers the truth. Ida is angry at Eddie for lying, but when he tells her that a famous producer wants him to perform in London, and that he wants Ida to accompany him as his wife, she happily elopes with him. Upon discovering that the producer is broke, however, the newlyweds return home. Eddie remains unemployed until Jimmy Durante, the piano player at Kramer's club, gets him a spot in a Los Angeles show entitled *Canary Cottage.* The show is a success, but its star, Cleo Abbott, is jealous of Eddie's popularity. To get rid of the scene stealer, Abbott pretends that famous theatrical producer Florenz Ziegfeld wants Eddie to perform in his new *Follies.* The ambitious Eddie joyfully returns to New York, only to discover that Ziegfeld has never heard of him, but Eddie, who now has not only Ida but a new baby daughter to support, persuades Ziegfeld to try him out that evening. His performance of "How Ya' Gonna' Keep 'Em Down on the Farm After They've Seen Paris" is such a hit that Ziegfeld signs him to a traveling show that includes Will Rogers in its cast. As time

passes, Ida has a second daughter while Eddie is on the road, but Eddie later returns to Broadway to star in Ziegfeld's new *Follies*. On opening night, Grandma Esther, bursting with pride and all dressed up for the show, dies peacefully in a chair. Overwhelmed with grief, Eddie is able to perform a rousing version of "If You Knew Susie Like I Know Susie" only by imagining that Grandma Esther is the sole member of the audience. During the next several years, Eddie's popularity grows as he becomes identified with hit songs such as "Bye, Bye Blackbird," "Pretty Baby," and "Yes, Sir, That's My Baby." On the night that Ida gives birth to their third baby girl, Eddie performs for the Prince of Wales and visits the hospital in blackface. Ida later begs her husband to take a vacation with the family, but Eddie, explaining that he must work hard to stay on top, suggests that they build a house on Long Island instead. Eddie's successful new show makes his schedule even more hectic. In 1929, while recovering in the hospital from the birth of yet another daughter, Ida learns from the newspaper that "Cantor Says Vacation Is Out." Weeping, Ida declares that because she and the children are not an important part of Eddie's life, their marriage is over. Eddie is crushed and offers to take Ida and his five daughters to London, but as they are planning the trip, the stock market crashes and he loses everything. With Ida's approval, Eddie returns to work in a new show entitled *Whoopee* and later performs in his own weekly radio show, ending each program with the tune, "(I'd Love To Spend) One Hour with You." Harry, now the family's doctor, advises Eddie to relax and spend time with family, and when Eddie stubbornly refuses, they argue. Harry declares that Eddie has always needed applause to replace the love he never received from a mother and father, while Eddie accuses his old friend of still loving Ida. Not long after, Eddie learns that Rocky has been indicted for murder, and soon after, while working late on a show, he suffers a heart attack. Eddie recovers, but becomes morose and quits working. Ziegfeld thinks that Eddie is scared, and Ida wires Harry for help. When Eddie is invited to speak at the boys camp he attended as a youth, he tells the boys that his experience at camp prevented him from joining up with Rocky, who by this time has been sentenced to death. The boys plead for a song, whereupon Eddie, reluctantly at first, sings a few of his famous tunes. Declaring that he has at last grown up, Eddie launches a string of performances for charity shows. In the projection room, the lights come up and as Eddie and Ida prepare to leave, Eddie exclaims "I never looked better in my life!" *Ambition. Eddie Cantor. Musical revues. Show business. United States–History–Social life and customs. Vaudeville. Burlesque. Camps. Charities. Child actors and actresses. Childbirth. Depression, Mental. Fame. Family life. Gangs. Gangsters. Grandmothers. Heart disease. Jealousy. Jews. Marriage. New York City–Broadway. New York City–East Side. Physicians. Radio programs. Romantic rivalry. Social workers. Theatrical producers. Vocational obsession. Ziegfeld Follies. Florenz Ziegfeld, Jr..*

Note: The working title of this film was *The Story of Eddie Cantor*. Eddie Israel Iskowitz Cantor (1892-1964), was born in New York. Cantor's parents, immigrants from Russia, died when he was a small child and, as the film depicts, he was thereafter raised by his grandmother. According to a *HR* news item, dated Aug 1948, Lou Edelman was set to produce a Cantor biography for Warner Bros. with the working title *The Life of Eddie Cantor*, but the project was dropped when Cantor and studio executives could not agree on the final script. Sidney Skolsky, a syndicated gossip columnist, had previously produced *The Jolson Story* (1946), which was also directed by Alfred E. Green. *HR* noted in Oct 1951 that Eddie and Ida Cantor were "greatly moved" by Skolsky's screen treatment and the film was made with the their approval and active participation. Cantor was said to have been impressed by how much Keefe Brasselle resembled him, especially once Brasselle was in the special make-up created for the role. According to a Jan 1953 article in *LAMirror*, make-up artist Gordon Bau spent eight months developing techniques to transform Brasselle into Eddie Cantor at various ages. Bau's innovations included large life-like plastic ears and an eye lining technique designed to give Brasselle's eyes the popping-out quality for which Cantor's were famous.

DV news items indicate that George Stevens directed several additional scenes for the film in Aug 1953 and that Gordon Douglas shot one exterior scene in early Sep 1953. Eddie Cantor's voice was dubbed onto the soundtrack for all of the featured songs and the original soundtrack album was released by Capitol Records in 1954. *The Eddie Cantor Story* had gala premieres in New York City and Los Angeles, on 23 Dec and 29 Dec 1953. Although the film received some positive notices, most reviews were mixed; the general consensus was that Cantor's life story had been oversentimentalized. The majority of critics felt that Brasselle overplayed Cantor's mannerisms, leading to a performance that *Cue* described as "uncomfortable, exaggerated and ugly." *The New Yorker* termed the portrayal "disconcerting," noting that Brasselle's "efforts to make his eyes pop out in the manner of the master frequently conveys the impression he is being strangled." The *HR*, however,

praised Brasselle's performance and instead criticized the make-up job which gave the actor a "mask-like expression that sometimes is almost grotesque."

Box 19 Dec 1953. *Cue* 26 Dec 1953. *DV* 10 Aug 1953. *DV* 4 Sep 1953. *DV* 17 Dec 1953, p. 3. *Exh* 30 Dec 1953, pp. 3672-73. *FD* 17 Dec 1953, p. 8. *Har* 19 Dec 1953, p. 202. *HR* 4 Aug 1948. *HR* 17 Oct 1951. *HR* 3 Dec 1951. *HR* 9 Dec 1953, p. 3. *LAEx* 30 Dec 1953. *LAMirror* 5 Jan 1953. *MPD* 17 Dec 1953. *MPHPD* 19 Dec 1953, p. 2109. *New Yorker* 26 Dec 1953. *NYT* 26 Dec 1953 p. 10. *Var* 23 Dec 1953, p. 6.

EDGE OF THE CITY (African Americans)

Metro-Goldwyn-Mayer Corp.; controlled by Loew's Inc.; Jonathan Productions, Inc. *Dist* Loew's Inc. 4 Jan 1957; Los Angeles opening: 20 Mar 1957; Prod: late Mar–late May 1956 [©Loew's Inc.; 26 Dec 1956; LP7542]. Sd (Westrex Recording System); b&w. 9 reels, 7,662 ft. 85 min. PCA cert no. 18313.

Prod David Susskind. *Assoc prod* C. J. Di Gangi. *Dir* Martin Ritt. *Asst dir* Don Kranze. *Story and scr* Robert Alan Aurthur. *Dir of photog* Joseph Brun. *Art dir* Richard Sylbert. *Film ed* Sidney Meyers. *Cost* Anna Hill Johnstone. *Mus comp and cond* Leonard Rosenman. *Sd* James Gleason. [*Makeup* Herman Buchman]. *Titles des by* Saul Bass. [*Scr supv* Marie Kenney]. [*Casting* Ethel Winant]. [*Prod coordinator* Renee Valente]. [*Exec asst to the prod* Michael Abbott].

Source: Based on the teleplay *A Man Is Ten Feet Tall* by Robert Alan Aurthur on *Philco Television Playhouse* (NBC, 2 Oct 1955).

Cast: John Cassavetes [(*Axel Nordmann, also known as Axel North*)], Sidney Poitier [(*Tommy Tyler*)], Jack Warden [(*Charles Malik*)], Kathleen Maguire [(*Ellen Wilson*)], Ruby Dee [(*Lucy Tyler*)], Val Avery [(*Brother*)], Robert Simon [(*Mr. Nordmann*)], Ruth White [(*Mrs. Nordmann*)], William A. Lee [(*Davis*)], John Kellogg [(*Detective*)], David Clarke [(*Wallace*)], Estelle Hemsley [(*Lucy's mother*)], [Charles Jordan (*Old Stevedore*)], [Ralph Bell (*Nightboss*)].

Drama. [*Print viewed*]. Axel Nordmann, a troubled young man, arrives one evening at a New York City freight train depot looking for a job. When the night watchman tells him he has to wait until the morning, Axel falls asleep in the yard, and the next morning is woken up by Tommy Tyler, a kindly black stevedore, who befriends him. When Axel asks to speak to Charles Malik, Malik pretends to recognize him and hires him, aware that Ed Favors, a mutual friend with illicit connections, has sent him. Axel joins Malik's crew as a stevedore and quickly learns that he is required to give Malik a portion of his earnings in exchange for having received the job. Malik, a racist, also demands that Axel stay away from Tommy if he wants to continue to work. When Tommy offers to help Axel find an apartment in his neighborhood, Axel at first angrily refuses, but then accepts his kindness. The next day, Tommy gives Axel his very own stevedore's hook and has him transferred to his own gang. Malik begins to taunt Axel, who has been calling himself Axel North, about his dealings with Favors, and Axel decides to be honest with Tommy by telling him his real name and that he is from Gary, Indiana. Later, at a bar, Axel tells Tommy about the tragedy that has ruined his life: After the death of his much-loved brother Andy, who was killed in a car accident while Axel was driving, his father, a strict police officer, blamed Axel for killing his favorite son. One night, Axel has dinner with Tommy, his wife Lucy, and their friend, Ellen Wilson, a white social worker who, like Lucy, is well-educated and motivated by leftist political causes. The four go dancing at a Latin nightclub, and when Axel is recognized by a drunken soldier, he flees in embarrassment. Sometime later as Axel is beginning to benefit from Tommy's philosophy that he must behave like "a man ten feet tall," Malik continues to taunt Axel with oblique references to his past. Axel finally confesses to Tommy the whole story: He enlisted in the Army as a way of dignifying himself in his family's eyes, but then deserted because the sergeant criticized him unrelentingly. Tommy tells Axel that he will always stand by him, and later Ellen, with whom Axle has fallen in love, also pledges her support. At work, Axel decides finally to stand up to Malik and the two begin to fight. Tommy intervenes and when Malik makes a racist comment to him, the two longtime enemies go at it with their stevedore's hooks. Tommy is stabbed in the back and dies in Axel's arms. When the police detective arrives, all the workers deny having seen anything, and Axel, too, keeps quiet. Axel goes home and calls his parents for the first time in years and tells them that he wants to come home. Before Axel leaves for Gary, he goes to see Lucy, who insists on knowing how Tommy was killed. When Axel finally tells her haltingly that Tommy was killed in a fight, she screams at him for not going to the police and then kicks him out. Prompted by Ellen to do what is right, Axel goes back to work, has the detective called, and tells Malik that he is going to turn him in. Malik

grabs his hook and the two engage in a vicious fight, which Axel finally wins. Axel then drags Tommy's murderer to the detective, as the other workers watch and follow. *African Americans. Dock workers. Guilt. Murder. New York City. Racism. Transformation. Aliases. Blackmail. Desertion, Military. Fistfights. Nightclubs. Police detectives. Recognition. Romance. Social workers. Stabbings. Unemployment.*

Note: The working title of this film was *A Man Is Ten Feet Tall.* Author Robert Alan Aurthur and producer David Susskind also made the television drama upon which this film is based, titled *A Man Is Ten Feet Tall.* Aurther is credited onscreen only as the film's writer, however. The teleplay starred Sidney Poitier, and in his autobiography, Poitier noted that in order to be hired for the part, NBC's legal department required that he sign a statement repudiating his relationships with Paul Robeson and Canada Lee, whom the legal department had deemed to be "dangerous people." After Poitier refused, Aurthur and others worked out a compromise which allowed him to take the role. Another modern source states that Poitier's appearance in *A Man Is Ten Feet Tall* marked the first time that a black actor was cast in major role in a television drama, and that when the teleplay was aired, Philco received numerous complaints and threats of cancellation. According to Poitier's autobiography, the complaints were partly directed at Hilda Simms, the actress who played his wife, a very light-skinned black woman who looked white.

The film version of *Edge of the City* was shot on location in Brooklyn and Harlem. The *Var* review commented that the picture was a "milestone" in cinema history because it showed a black man as "a fully-integrated, first-class citizen," rather than as a "problem." The review goes on to suggest, however, that the representation of equality between whites and blacks in the film might raise the issue of how the film should be marketed in the South, "in light of the current tension over integration." In a modern interview, director Martin Ritt recalled that "Tommy Tyler's" death sparked a near riot in one theater where the film was shown. According to correspondence on the file on the film in the MPAA/PCA Collection at the AMPAS Library, the PCA was worried about the possibility that John Cassavetes' character "Axel" might be viewed as homosexual. In a letter dated 16 Mar 1956 to producer Susskind, PCA official Geoffrey Shurlock cited as problematic Axel's "almost psychopathic aversion to women," and requested that a scene be cut in which Axel demonstrates "a rather unusual reaction to the couple he sees necking in the movie." He also asked Susskind to remove a moment of dialogue in which "Malik" teases Axel and Tommy by announcing to the work crew that they are getting married. Neither of these scenes appears in the finished film. *Edge of the City* was the first film venture for Susskind, Aurthur and Ritt who, prior to this project, worked in television and theater.

Box 5 Jan 1957. *DV* 26 Dec 1956, p. 3 *Exb* 9 Jan 1957, pp. 4273-74. *FD* 3 Jan 1957, p. 8. *Har* 29 Dec 1956, p. 206. *HR* 18 May 1956, p. 16. *HR* 27 Apr 1956, p. 8. *HR* 26 Dec 1956, p. 3. *MPD* 27 Dec 1956. *MPHPD* 29 Dec 1956, p. 201. *NYT* 30 Jan 1957, p. 33. *Var* 22 Aug 1956. *Var* 2 Jan 1957, p. 6.

EDNA FERBER'S CIMARRON *see* CIMARRON

EDNA FERBER'S SHOW BOAT *see* SHOW BOAT

EL QUE A HIERRO MATA (Latino)

Cuautla. 1927?; Prod: 1926. Si; b&w. Length undetermined.

Dir Miguel Angel Alvarez. *Story* Ana M. de Ramírez. *Adpt* Antonio M. Ramírez. *Photog* Antonio M. Ramírez.

Drama?. [*Not viewed*]. [No information has been located concerning the plot of this film.].

Note: According to an 8 Nov 1926 article in *La Opinión, El que a hierro mata* (which translates into English as "He Who Kills with the Sword") was made by a group of Mexican Americans working in the Hollywood studios. They formed the company Cuautla, of which Antonio M. Ramírez was the president. Others involved in the company include Juan B. Quiñones, Fernando Parra, David Galván, Amparo Ramos and Julia S. Provencio. Sets for the film were built in a large yard on Figueroa Street in Los Angeles. No information has been located concerning the exhibition of this film.

La Opinión 8 Nov 1926.

ELEVEN P.M. (African Americans)

Maurice Film Co. **1928.** Sd; b&w. 6 reels.

Pres RICHARD D. MAURICE. *Dir* Richard D. Maurice. *Scr* Richard D. Maurice.

Cast: H. Marion Williams (*Roy Stewart*), Sammie Fields (*Frank Perry*), Leo Pope (*Bennie Madison*), Orine Johnson (*June Blackwell/Hope Sundaisy*), Richard D. Maurice (*Sundaisy*), Wanda Maurice (*Little Hope*), Eugene Williams (*Harry Brown*), J. M. Stephens (*Reverend Hacket*).

African American, Crime, Fantasy. [*Print viewed*]. Louis Perry, a young African-American athlete and writer, hands editor Harry Brown, of the religious paper *Search Light*, an incomplete manuscript he is writing. Perry tells Brown he believes that, by thinking, it is possible for human beings to take refuge in a lower form of animal existence. Although skeptical, Brown asks Perry to finish the story that night, as they go to press early in the morning, and arranges to collect the story at 11 p.m. When prizefight promoter Roy

Stewart learns that one of his fighters has broken his thumb, he calls Perry and arranges for him to fight at the midnight bout, as he wants to get even with "that high-hatted Perry" and plans to pick Perry up at 11 p.m. Meanwhile, Perry's sweetheart June telephones to say that she and her mother will call for him at 11 p.m. to attend a midnight affair, then hangs up before Perry can protest. Perry reads a bit of his manuscript with his dog on his lap and, drifting off to sleep, begins to dream: Stewart, mortally wounded by a rival criminal, stumbles into the home of half-breed street fiddler Sundaisy and makes him promise to find his son Clyde and see that he gets the proper education and does not become a criminal. He gives Sundaisy a wallet full of money, but a hand reaches through the window and steals it. Meanwhile, Clyde and a gang of boys steal vegetables from a wagon. As he chases Clyde, the owner runs into Sundaisy, who learns that Clyde works in "Old Maggie's soup joint." There he meets June, Old Maggie's step-daughter, who wishes someone would take her away from the horrible place. As Sundaisy talks with Clyde, who washes dishes at the kitchen, a patron grabs June's hand and she accidentally spills coffee on him. She slaps a man who laughs at her, and after Sundaisy punches him, Maggie tells June to leave. Sundaisy walks with her and Clyde to the YMCA, where he is told that Brown wants him to come to his house. At Brown's home, Brown introduces them to the Reverend Hacket, who runs a school for boys. Hacket agrees to take Clyde and encourages Sundaisy to marry June, so that she will be free of Old Maggie. As June is pleased, Sundaisy agrees. Hacket performs the marriage, then brags to two women companions that Brown has raised $10,000 for him and that he got $2,000 from Sundaisy, both of whom he calls "suckers." Next Hacket sends Clyde to a gang, where he gets his "schooling" in crime. Twelve years later, Clyde visits Sundaisy and June, who now have a daughter named Hope, and says that he wants to repay his debt. Sundaisy refuses and Hope backs away in fear. A few days later, Clyde tempts June to leave her home and reveals that her marriage is not legal, as Hacket was only a cheap crook. June plans to come back for Hope, but Clyde takes her to a madam. When Hope tells Sundaisy that June left with the "Devil Man," he cries. During the next twelve years, Sundaisy travels with Hope and they entertain on street corners. June, ashamed and filled with remorse, lives in the slums of a big city. Clyde, who has been watching Hope perform for two weeks, sends a cohort to get her. The man, though, warns that he will have trouble with Perry if he fools with Hope, as Perry is Hope's boyfriend. By saying that Sundaisy has been hit by an automobile, Clyde's cohort gets Hope to go with him to Clyde's room, where he tries to kiss and embrace her. A friend of Perry's, who has overheard Clyde, tells Perry, who races to Clyde's café and engages in a fight with his gang. Hope hits Clyde in the eye, and Perry knocks Clyde down. Perry's pal then bluffs having a gun in his pocket and they escape with Hope. Meanwhile, Sundaisy sits on a stoop with his dog Mickey and philosophizes that maybe he will return someday to a life like Mickey's, just eating, sleeping and playing, with no worries and sorrows, and no Hell when he dies. Perry then drives up with Hope, and when Sundaisy learns what happened, he asks Perry to take care of Hope if he does not return. Sundaisy enters Clyde's club and pulls a knife, but before he can attack, he collapses from heart trouble. He vows to come back, then falls dead. Sometime later, Perry learns that Hope is to be the featured attraction at Clyde's new cabaret, The Blue Heaven, and is enraged. He witnesses her erotic dance, and when Clyde kisses her afterward, Perry walks away and out the stage door, where he is knocked out and robbed by two thugs. After wandering the streets in a daze, Perry awakens in a hospital, deranged from mental strain and the slight blow to the head. Perry's friend, who drunkenly tried to fight Clyde and was thrown out, is also hospitalized, shaking from an alcoholic fit, and put in a bed next to Perry, then shakes Perry until he recovers. Meanwhile, Clyde, while drinking, sees an apparition of Sundaisy. He lashes out with his bottle, but Sundaisy disappears. As Hope sits with May, another dancer, Clyde comes in. Hope's dog barks, then changes into Sundaisy and attacks Clyde, biting his throat. Perry arrives and embraces Hope, while May sees Sundaisy's head attached to the dog's body. Before dying, Clyde relates Sundaisy's vow to return. Perry comforts and kisses Hope, the suddenly awakens from his dream to find Brown, Stewart, June and her mother waiting. When Brown asks if the story is ready, he says he just dreamed the last chapter. He then goes to type the story, as Brown looks at his watch, which shows that it is 11 p.m. *African Americans. African Americans–*

Mixed blood. Authors. Dreams. Reincarnation. Street entertainers. Alcoholics. Boxing. Cabarets. Dancing. Death by shock. Dishwashing. Dismissal (Employment). Dogs. Fathers and daughters. Fights. Gangs. Hospitals. Impersonation and imposture. Kitchens. Marriage–Fake. Oaths. Promoters. Prostitution. Religion. Robbery. Stepmothers.

Note: Richard D. Maurice's onscreen credit reads "Written and directed under the personal supervision of Richard D. Maurice." According to modern sources, the Detroit-based Maurice Film Co. was organized in 1920 by Richard and Vivian Maurice.

ELI ELI (Yiddish language)

Cinema Service Corp. *Dist* Cinema Service Corp. **1940**; New York opening: 27 Sep 1940; Prod: began Jun 1940 in Fort Lee, NJ. Sd; b&w. 9 reels, 7,244 ft. 88-89 min. Yiddish language with English subtitles.

Dir Josef Seiden. *Asst dir* H. Rosen. *Story* I. Frankel. *Photog* Don Malkames and Charles Levine. *Sets* J. Allstadt. *Mus* Sholom Secunda. *Sd* M. Dichter and P. Jacobs.

Cast: ESTHER FIELD (*Hannah [Shapiro]*), Lazar Freed (*Mendel [Shapiro]*), Muni Serebroff (*Morris [Shapiro]*), Paula Lubelska (*Jennie [Shapiro]*), Rose Greenfield (*Mollie*), David Yanover (*Harold*), Eddie Friedlander (*Danny*), Max Badin (*Michel*), Mae Schoenfeld (*Shlime*), Irving Jacobson (*David*), [Isidor Frankel], [Herman Rosen].

Yiddish, Elderly, Domestic, Melodrama, with songs. [*Print viewed*]. Mendel and Hannah Shapiro, an elderly Jewish couple who run a small farm in New Jersey, must get money to meet their mortgage payment to the bank by the next day to keep their farm. Mendel calls their children, Mollie, in Philadelphia, and Morris, in New York, to come right away. His neighbor Michel believes that most children do not properly care for their parents and insinuates that Mendel's children would not come to visit if they knew that their parents needed money. Mendel, however, assures Michel that children are the best investment one can make. Michel's cynicism proves to be prescient when Morris, a doctor, explains that he has used Mendel's money to fix up his office and to bring two relatives from Europe and suggests that his parents sell their farm and live apart, one with each of their children. Although Mendel and Hannah, having lived together for fifty-five years, are shocked at the suggestion, they sadly agree to comply. After three months with Mollie and her husband Harold in Philadelphia, Mendel, in a letter to Michel, acknowledges that he was right about children, while Hannah, now very lonely living in New York with Morris and his wife Jennie, imagines her husband calling her. Michel visits Mendel and, after assuring him that his house will always be open to him, insists Mendel take a loan of fifty dollars. The next day, when Mollie, who continually nags her father, questions him about the source of the money that he used to buy a lottery ticket from one of his old friends, Mendel angrily tells her to mind her own business. Meanwhile, in New York, Jennie berates Hannah for taking a birthday gift to Morris at his office, and Hannah is disheartened that she is not invited to the birthday celebration for her son given by Jennie's snooty mother. In Philadelphia, when Mollie finds the rent money missing, she accuses her father of being a thief. Mollie sends for Morris, who sadly arranges for Mendel to be admitted to an Old Folks' Home. In New York, Hannah hallucinates that she is a young mother, and she is put into a sanitarium. Meanwhile, when Mollie and Harold's indolent son Danny learns that his grandfather has been sent away for stealing, he confesses that he took the money for a weekend trip to Atlantic City. Worried that Hannah has not written recently, Mendel travels to New York. With Morris, he visits his wife, who babbles about her beautiful baby. When the doctor suggests that the atmosphere of their old home might help Hannah, Mendel returns to New Jersey to ask Michel for help and finds that Michel died six months earlier and made him heir to his farm. Sometime later, Mendel happily feeds his chickens, while Hannah prepares a meal for their visiting children. Danny, who now milks ten cows in half an hour, has reformed due to farm life and stands to inherit the farm. Morris, who has left an important conference to come, arrives with Jennie, Mollie and Harold, and Hannah asserts that children are, in fact, worthwhile. After the meal, when Hannah learns that unless Morris gets $2,000, he will lose his home, she convinces Mendel to go to the bank to get the money for their son. *Aged persons. City-country contrast. Family relationships. Farms. Jews. Neighbors. Separation (Marital). Birthdays. Confession. False accusations. Hallucinations. Inheritance. Moral reformation. Mortgages. New Jersey. New York City. Parties. Philadelphia (PA). Physicians. Retirement homes. Sanitariums.*

Note: The screen credits for the film read "Cinema Service Corp. Presents 'The Yiddishe Mama' (Esther Field) in *Eli Eli*." This film was reissued in Mar 1949. Although the film includes songs, no information concerning their identity has been located.

Exb 16 Oct 1940. *MPD* 11 Jul 1940. *Var* 9 Oct 1940, p. 18.

ELLIS ISLAND (Immigrants)

Invincible Pictures Corp. *Dist* Chesterfield Motion Pictures Corp. 5 Nov **1936** [©Invincible Pictures Corp.; 10 Dec 1936; LP6785]. Sd (RCA Victor "High Fidelity" Sound System); b&w. 7 reels. 65-66 min. Passed by the National Board of Review. PCA cert no. 2800.

Prod Maury M. Cohen. *Supv* Herbert S. Cohen. *Dir* Phil Rosen. *Asst dir* Milton R. Brown. *Orig story and scr* Arthur T. Horman. [*Photog* M. A. Andersen]. *Settings* Edward C. Jewell. *Film ed* Holbrook Todd. *Sd eng* Richard Tyler.

Cast: Donald Cook [(*Gary*)], Peggy Shannon [(*Betty Parker*)], Jack La Rue, Joyce Compton [(*Adele*)], Bradley Page, Johnny Arthur [(*Kit*)], George Rosener, Maurice Black, Matty Fain, Bryant Washburn, Monte Vandergrift, Lew Kelly, [Captain E. H. Calvert].

Crime, Drama. [*Print viewed*]. In 1926, after a New York federal reserve bank is robbed of a million dollars, Ted Kedrick, Jan Imarski and Anton Lonelli are each sentenced to ten years in prison for the theft, but the money is never found. In 1936, they are released. As Kedrick is about to be deported through Ellis Island, a crook posing as Peter James of the Treasury Department offers to spring him if he will split the million fifty-fifty. A gang of thieves intervenes and abducts Kedrick to a warehouse, where they beat him to make him talk, but he resists. Kedrick's niece, Betty Parker, who has come to the island to say good-bye, is suspected of helping Kedrick escape. Gary, an Ellis Island official, believes that Betty is innocent, and he goes with his friend Kit to warn her. She tells them that strange men once approached her about the bank heist, but she told them that the only name she remembered was Dan Kilemo. The man posing as James locates Kedrick and helps him escape. When Kedrick says he will only talk to his niece, "James" gets him drunk and deposits him on Betty's couch, then bugs the room and waits in the room above Betty's apartment. Gary and Kit take Betty home. Gary discovers the bug and "James," but thinks "James" is a real government agent. While Gary and "James" are upstairs, the gang kidnaps both Kedrick and Betty, with the hope that Kedrick, to save Betty, will talk. Gary then researches the name "Kilemo" and discovers that a man named Dan Kilemo was interred at the Rosedale Cemetery in New Jersey shortly after the robbery. The first and second letters of Kedrick, Imarski and Lonelli spell Kilemo. At the cemetery, the gang digs up Kilemo's grave after tying Kedrick and Betty to trees. Kit then remembers that the real James showed up at Ellis Island, and he warns Gary, who tries to hold up the thieves himself, but only gets himself tied to a tree. As daylight comes, the gang unearths the coffin and while they transport the money bags from the coffin to the car, Kit releases the hostages. The James impostor then takes off in the getaway car and Gary, Kit, Kedrick and Betty follow, with the thieves in pursuit. Gary apprehends "James" and hides in a barn with the others, as the thieves arrive. Gary then removes the money from the getaway car and pushes the car out of the barn into the thieves' hands while releasing the farmer's honey bees. The thieves take cover, and the real James arrives with the police and arrests them. Kit's fiancée Adele, who had threatened to marry someone else when she saw him with a blonde, arrives fearing for his life, and Kit drives her to a neighboring justice of the peace with Gary and Betty as witnesses. *Bank robberies. New York City–Ellis Island. Nieces. Thieves. Bees. Cemeteries. Chases. Deportation. Drunkenness. Engagements. Escapes. False accusations. Farms. Federal Reserve bank. Government agents. Graves. Impersonation and imposture. Interrogation. Kidnapping. Marriage. Wiretapping.*

Exb 15 Dec 1936, p. 31. *HR* 25 Nov 1936, p. 3. *MPD* 30 Nov 1936, p. 8.

ELLIS ISLAND (1938) *see* GATEWAY

ELSA MAXWELL'S PUBLIC DEB NO. 1 (Russian Americans)

Twentieth Century-Fox Film Corp. *Dist* Twentieth Century-Fox Film Corp. 13 Sep **1940**; Prod: Began 8 Apr 1940 [©Twentieth Century-Fox Film Corp.; 13 Sep 1940; LP9929]. Sd (Western Electric Mirrophonic Recording); b&w. 7,247 ft. 79 min. PCA cert no. 6234.

Prod Darryl F. Zanuck. *Assoc prod* Gene Markey. *Dir* Gregory Ratoff. [*Asst dir* Fred Spencer]. *Scr* Karl Tunberg and Darrell Ware. *Story* Karl Tunberg and Don Ettlinger. *Dir of photog* Ernest Palmer.

Art dir Richard Day and Rudolph Sternad. *Film ed* Robert Simpson. *Set dresser* Thomas Little. *Cost* Travis Banton. [*Jewels by* Laykin et Cie]. *Mus dir* Alfred Newman. [*Dances staged by* Nicholas Castle and Geneva Sawyer]. *Sd* W. D. Flick and Roger Heman.

Cast: George Murphy (*Alan Blake*), Brenda Joyce (*Penny Cooper*), Elsa Maxwell (*Herself*), Mischa Auer (*Grisha*), Charlie Ruggles (*Milburn [Cooper]*), Ralph Bellamy (*Bruce Fairchild*), Maxie Rosenbloom (*Eric*), Berton Churchill (*Magistrate*), Franklin Pangborn (*Bartender*), Hobart Cavanaugh (*Mr. Schilitz*), Lloyd Corrigan (*Hugh Stackett*), Ivan Lebedeff (*Feodor*), Charles Judels (*Ivan*), Elisha Cook, Jr. (*Communist*), Selmer Jackson (*Lawyer*), Luis Alberni (*Frontenac*), Hal K. Dawson (*Layout man*), Charles Wilson (*Sergeant*), Dick Rich, William Pawley (*Legionnaires*), Mary Gordon (*Landlady*), Addison Richards (*Sanford*), Paul Stanton, Joseph Crehan, Douglas Wood (*Directors*), Ralph Dunn (*Policeman*), John Dilson (*Clerk*), Chester Clute (*Car payment man*), Herman Bing (*Dutchman*), [Joseph Marievsky (*Chauffeur*)], [Ted Arkin (*Sailor*)], [Dorothy Roberts (*Sailor's lady*)], [Charles Tannen, Robert Shaw, Milburn Stone, Stanley Taylor, Arthur Rankin, Alan Davis, Billy Newell (*Reporters*)], [Lillian Porter (*Hat check girl*)], [Lee Shumway (*Legionnaire*)], [Adrian Morris (*Guard*)], [Alexis Tcherkassky (*Dimitri*)], [Don Forbes, John Wald (*Announcers*)], [Orlando A. Martin (*Orchestra leader*)], [Walter Bonn (*Doorman*)], [Louise Lorimer (*Secretary*)], [George Dobbs, Billy Wayne (*Photographers*)], [Ed Cecil (*Waiter*)], [Margaret Armstrong (*President*)], [Harry Depp (*Grocery clerk*)], [Adia Kuznetzoff], [Kathryn Sheldon].

Society, Comedy-drama. [*Print viewed*]. A Communist rally is held at New York City's Union Square. A number of Legionnaires decide to break up the rally, causing a riot. At night court, the magistrate sentences each Communist to "thirty dollars or thirty days." When Penny Cooper, heiress to the Cooper's Soup fortune and café society's number one debutante, faces the gavel, however, the judge immediately drops the charges against her and all the others. Returning home, Penny is greeted by her new butler and political tutor, Grisha, a shady character at best. Waiting for Penny is her boyfriend, Bruce Fairchild. Bruce, a Republican lawyer, tells Penny he has been asked to run for Congress. Penny is thrilled, thinking Bruce will carry the Communist banner. Penny's uncle Milburn arrives in a cab from Palm Beach and tells Penny that, as she represents Cooper's Soup to the masses, she must stay out of the news. Just then, Grisha arrives with headlines proclaiming Penny's new Communist allegiance. Women's groups begin a boycott of Cooper's Soup, causing sales to plummet. Milburn addresses a meeting of the board of directors, telling them society hostess Elsa Maxwell will endorse the soup for $25,000. When Elsa arrives, however, she announces that she can not endorse the soup and that Penny needs to "be taken out to the woodshed." Later, at the Russian restaurant Red Samovar, Penny and Bruce have dinner. Their waiter, Alan Blake, is no Russian and no waiter. After dropping a olive in Penny's cleavage and spilling Bruce's soup, Alan stirs Penny's ire when he responds in the negative to her questions about Communism. Upset at Alan's impertinence, Penny has Alan fired. Alan, in turn, turns Penny over his knee and spanks her, just as the press arrives. Alan is proclaimed an American hero by the newspapers, which he reads from his jail cell. Back at home, Cooper's Soup nears bankruptcy. Penny claims not to care until Grisha reminds her that the revolution needs her money. Penny drops the charges against Alan and leaves the jail with him while reporters eagerly proclaim "Love at First Slap." Alan agrees to their phony romance when he is made vice president of Cooper's Soup. As the headlines of Penny and Alan's romance fill the society pages, the sales of Cooper's Soup skyrocket. Taking a night off from café society, Alan and Penny go to a blue-collar dance where they find mutual attraction. But when Alan starts telling Penny the ways of the world, she angrily storms home. Catching her at the door, Alan kisses her, telling her "the physical approach is the only one you understand." Upset, Penny fires Alan. The next day, Penny works out with her boxing instructor Eric. Alan calls, telling Penny that he has taken a job on a ship to South America. Penny shows authentic concern until she hears Alan's landlady in the background. At her costume birthday party, Alan thinks he has won Penny's heart, but she dances every dance with Bruce. At the bartender's suggestion, Alan decides to slip Bruce a "Mickey." When he discovers that Bruce and Penny are engaged and that Penny plans sell the soup company and

give all the money to the Communist party, Alan instead gives Penny the "Mickey". The next morning, Penny finds herself chained to a bed at the deserted Sugar Ridge Hotel, which Alan had managed at one time. She escapes and is about to sell the soup company to Milburn's drinking buddy, Hugh Stackett, when Eric enters the room, informing them that Russia has just invaded Finland. Penny realizes that Communism isn't what she thought it was and learns that Grisha is no more than a petty thief. She tears up the transfer papers and knocks out Grisha as Alan and Bruce arrive. Penny tells Alan she despises him, but when he kisses her, the "physical approach" works again. Penny throws her Communist manual out the window where a dog then sniffs at it. Communism. Costume parties. Heiresses. Politics. Romance. Waiters. Bartenders. Butlers. Drugging. Benjamin Franklin. Hoaxes. Hotels. Judges. Kidnapping. Abraham Lincoln. Political campaigns. Politicians. Reporters. Restaurants. Riots. Russian Americans. Socialites. Soup industry. Thieves. Trials. Uncle Sam (Fictional character). Uncles.

Note: Working titles for this film include *Public Relations*, *Princess and the Pauper*, and *The Public Be Damned*. The film is also known under the title *Public Deb. No. 1*. Material in the Twentieth Century-Fox Produced Script Collection at the UCLA Theater Arts Library indicate that Elsa Maxwell wrote the first draft of this screenplay, though she received no writing credit nor is there any indication that material from that draft was used. *HR* reported that director Sidney Lanfield severed his relationship with Fox after fifteen years when he refused to direct this film. According to a Twentieth Century-Fox press release, this was the fourth film for which Fox had borrowed George Murphy from M-G-M. Linda Darnell was cast at one time in the lead role in this film, but was later replaced by Brenda Joyce. Press releases note that the Brenda Joyce's wardrobe was worth $275,000, but the actual rental cost was $50,000. A freestanding, wheeled dance floor was built for the film, which, when attached to the camera, allowed the camera to dolly around Murphy and Joyce during the dance sequence. In addition, the make-up for Elsa Maxwell for the costume party sequence reportedly took two hours each day to apply. Mickey Rooney wrote a song entitled "Public Deb. #1" and auditioned it before the Fox music department, in hopes of selling it for this film. It was not used or purchased, however. The film makes reference to the 30 November 1939 invasion of Finland by the Soviet Union which resulted in the Treaty of Moscow of 12 March 1940, and led to the partial annexation of Finland by the Soviet Union.

FD 18 Sep 1940, p. 6. *HR* 30 Mar 1940, p. 5. *HR* 23 Aug 1940, p. 3. *MPD* 27 Aug 1940, p. 9. *MPH* 25 May 1940, p. 40. *MPH* 31 Aug 1940, p. 53. *NYT* 18 Sep 1940, p. 19. *Var* 28 Aug 1940, p. 20.

EMERGENCY WEDDING (Immigrants)
Columbia Pictures Corp. *Dist* Columbia Pictures Corp. Nov **1950**; *Prod:* 31 Mar–3 May 1950 [©Columbia Pictures Corp.; 1 Nov 1950; LP966]. Sd (Western Electric Recording); b&w. 7,026 ft. 78 min. PCA cert no. 14528.

Prod Nat Perrin. *Dir* Edward Buzzell. [*Asst dir* Earl Bellamy]. *Scr* Nat Perrin and Claude Binyon. *Story* Dalton Trumbo. *Dir of photog* Burnett Guffey. *Art dir* Carl Anderson. *Film ed* Al Clark. *Set dec* Earl Bellamy. *Gowns* Jean Louis. *Mus dir* Morris Stoloff. *Mus score* Werner R. Heymann. *Sd eng* Lambert Day. *Makeup* Clay Campbell. *Hair styles* Helen Hunt.

Cast: LARRY PARKS [(*Peter Judson Kirk, Jr.*)], BARBARA HALE [(*Dr. Helen Hunt*)], Willard Parker [(*Vandemer*)], Una Merkel [(*Emma*)], Alan Reed [(*Tony*)], Eduard Franz [(*Dr. Heimer*)], Irving Bacon [(*Filbert*)], Don Beddoe [(*Forbish*)], Jim Backus [(*Ed Hamley*)], [Teru Shimada (*Ito*)], [Myron Welton (*Freddie*)], [Ian Wolfe (*Dr. White*)], [Helen Spring (*Miss Toomey*)], [Greg McClure (*Richard Andrews*)], [Queenie Smith (*Rose*)], [Jerry Mickelsen (*Newsboy*)], [George Meader (*Motel manager*)], [Dorothy Vaughn (*Woman patient*)], [Cosmo Sardo (*Headwaiter*)], [Joe Palma, Frank Arnold (*Waiters*)], Sydney Mason, Boyd Davis, Pierre Watkin (*Doctors*), [Wilson Benge (*Frederick, the butler*)], [Thomas F. Martin (*Bartender*)], [Myron Healey, Mike Lally, Warren Mace, Shirley Ballard, Jean Willes, Mary Emery (*Guests*)], [Stephen Chase (*Kirk*)], [Thomas Patrick McCormick (*Baby*)], [Billy Nelson (*Cab driver*)], [James O'Gatty (*Pedestrian*)], [Ted Jordan (*Orderly*)], [William E. Green (*Chairman*)], [Vince Gironda (*Gym instructor*)], [James Conaty, James Carlisle (*Committee men*)], [Bobby Johnson (*Sammy*)], [Vivian Mason (*Kitty*)], [Kathleen O'Malley (*Mabel*)], [Louise Kane (*Switchboard girl*)], [Beatrice Gray (*Newsboy's mother*)], [Harry Harvey (*Dr. Wilson*)], [William Forrest (*Personnel director*)], [Frank Cady (*Mr. Hoff*)], [Ann Tyrrell (*Miss Nielson*)], [Raymond Largay (*Mr. Hill*)], [Shirley Whitney (*Nurse*)], [Merry McGovern (*Bratty girl*)], [Simon "Stuffy" Singer, Robert Lyden (*Little boys*)], [Paul Bradley, John Kascier, Richard LaMarr (*Barbers*)], [Elizabeth Flournoy (*Saleswoman*)], [Mary Newton (*Governess*)], [Ruth Warren (*Shopper*)], [Henry Sylvester, Ted Stanhope (*Clerks*)], [Muriel

Maddox (*Mrs. Crain*)], [Marjorie Stapp (*Mrs. Young*)], [Beverly Crane (*Mrs. Hayes*)], [Bobby Larson (*Bellboy*)], [Edna Sturgeon (*Dignified woman*)], [Elsa Peterson], [Lucille Shamburger], [Arthur Howard], [Virginia Cruzon], [Eric Wilton], [Emil Sitka], [Grace Burns].

Comedy. [*Print viewed*]. After the death of his father, Peter Judson Kirk, Jr. vows that from now on, he will do as he pleases, which is mainly to chase beautiful women. He meets his match, however, in attractive physician Dr. Helen Hunt, with whom he hitches a ride to Los Angeles after his car is demolished in an accident. Peter is delighted when Helen's car needs a repair that will require them to spend the night at a nearby motel. Even though he has only known Helen a short time, Peter immediately proposes marriage, but Helen turns him down, stating firmly that she wants a career, not marriage. When Peter insists that marriage would not interfere with her profession, Helen succumbs to his entreaties and marries him. In Los Angeles, Peter's resolve is tested immediately when a romantic dinner at home is interrupted by an emergency call. After several such calls, Helen is summoned to a delivery and is gone for the rest of the evening. When she finally returns, she mentions the name of a former suitor and current patient, Vandemer, and Peter instantly becomes jealous. The next morning, Peter's jealousy is again roused when he remembers that Helen accepts male patients. He hurries to her office and there overhears her laughing with a male patient and breaks into the examining room. Once again he must apologize for his jealousy, but that same night, when Peter and Helen go dancing, they encounter Van, and Peter challenges him to a fight. A few days later, Van throws a surprise party for Helen and Peter, but Peter misunderstands and makes a jealous scene. Furious, Helen accuses Peter of laziness and charges that he does nothing because he is afraid of failure. After she leaves him, Peter tries various jobs, but succeeds at none of them. Later, a newsboy is badly injured when he saves Peter from being run over by a car. At the hospital, Dr. Heimer, a highly-qualified foreign surgeon, is unable to operate because he has not completed the required American internship. Peter induces him to operate anyway and later asks for Helen's help in overturning the internship requirements. Helen explains that the internship laws ensure that doctors trained abroad will meet U. S. standards and that what is really needed are more hospitals where foreign doctors can work as interns. Peter then builds a new hospital. Helen, meanwhile, has gone to Reno for a divorce. Convinced that he is now a man that Helen could love, Peter flies after her, but she tells him that she plans to marry Van, who does not have a jealous bone in his body. When Van learns that Peter is in Reno, however, he reveals that he is just as jealous as Peter. Disgusted with both men, Helen is ready to leave, but the hotel maid persuades her that jealousy means the men really love her. Realizing that the maid is right, Helen reconciles with Peter. *Jealousy. Marriage. Physicians. Wealth. Automobile accidents. Barbers and barbershops. Drunkenness. Hospitals. Immigrants. Interns (Medicine). Maids. Nurses. Reno (NV). Romantic rivalry. Self-sacrifice. Trials.*

Note: The film's working titles were *The Doctor's Husband* and *That Bedside Manner*. The 1941 Columbia film *You Belong to Me* was also based on Dalton Trumbo's story. At the time this film was released, Trumbo, one of the Hollywood Ten, was serving a prison term for refusing to testify in front of the U.S. House of Representatives Committee on Un-American Activities (HUAC). For additional information on HUAC, see entry above for *Crossfire*.

Box 11 Nov 1950. *DV* 10 Nov 1950, p. 3. *FD* 15 Nov 1950, p. 6. *HR* 29 Mar 1950, p. 2. *HR* 31 Mar 1950, p. 12. *HR* 10 Nov 1950, p. 3. *MPHPD* 18 Nov 1950, p. 570. *NYT* 12 Nov 1950. *NYT* 22 Dec 1950, p. 19. *Var* 15 Nov 1950, p. 6.

THE EMPEROR JONES (African Americans)
John Krimsky and Gifford Cochran, Inc. *Dist* United Artists Corp. 29 Sep 1933; New York opening: week of 19 Sep 1933; Prod: 25 May–late Jul 1933 at Eastern Service Studios, Inc. [©John Krimsky and Gifford Cochran, Inc.; 29 Sep 1933; LP4347]. Sd (Western Electric Noiseless Recording); b&w. 9 reels. 80 min. Passed by the National Board of Review. PCA cert no. 1316-R [29 Aug 1935].

Pres JOHN KRIMSKY and GIFFORD COCHRAN. *Supv* William C. de Mille. *Dir* Dudley Murphy. *Asst dir* Joseph H. Nadel. *Scr* Du Bose Heyward. *Photog* Ernest Haller. *Art dir* Herman Rosse. *Film ed* Grant Whytock. *Incidental mus comp and dir by* Frank Tours. *Vocal arr* J. Rosamond Johnson. *Synchronization* Max Manne. *Sd eng* Joseph Kane. *Prod mgr* J. Edward Shugrue and [George Knafka].

Song(s): "Emperor Jones," music and lyrics by Allie Wrubel; "Now Let Me Fly," "I'm Travelin'" and "Water Boy," composer undetermined; and other songs.

Source: Based on the play *The Emperor Jones* by Eugene O'Neill (New York, 1 Nov 1920).

Cast: PAUL ROBESON (*Brutus Jones*), Dudley Digges (*Smithers*), Frank Wilson (*Jeff*), Fredi Washington (*Undine*), Ruby Elzy (*Dolly*), George Stamper (*Lem*), [Jackie Mabley (*Marcella*)], [Blueboy O'Connor (*Treasurer*)], [Brandon Evans (*Carrington*)], [Taylor Gordon (*Stick-Man*)].

African American, Drama, with songs. [*Print viewed*]. At the Hezekiah Baptist Church, prayers are offered for Brutus Jones, who is about to leave town for a job as a Pullman porter. Before boarding his train, Jones bids farewell to his sweetheart, Dolly, who fears for his well-being. Her concerns prove valid when Jones's buddy, Jeff, initiates him to the very lifestyle she feared. In Harlem, Jones takes Jeff's girl friend Undine as his mistress. Later, when Jones is transferred to the car of the President of the United States, he overhears illicit monetary dealings and then blackmails a financier into investing his savings of $300. The now fashionable Jones, resolving to "travel light," drops Undine in favor of Belle La Due. When Undine attacks Belle at a nightclub, Jones leaves both women behind and encounters Jeff gambling in a pool hall. There the two men gamble in a high-stakes crap game, but when Jones discovers that Jeff is using loaded dice, he starts a fight and accidentally kills Jeff. Jones is sent to prison for the murder, but escapes after refusing to obey a guard's brutal order to beat a tortured fellow prisoner. He returns to Dolly, and after filing through his chains, discards his prison uniform and obtains work as a ship's stoker on a vessel bound for Kingston, Jamaica. On the way, Jones jumps ship and is taken prisoner by a dictator, General Peters, and sold for five dollars to Smithers, a crooked white trader and gunrunner. After gambling with the other prisoners, Jones obtains their money and, by threatening to become a competitor, bluffs Smithers into making him a partner. When the general and his treasurer complain about receiving a dishonest bill from Smithers and Jones, the general orders Jones's execution. Jones, however, foils the execution by replacing the drunken aide Quacko's bullets with blanks. Awed by Jones's apparently miraculous escape from death, and believing his claim that he can only be killed by silver bullets, the general's troops accept Jones as their new ruler. Proclaiming himself the Emperor Jones, over the next two and a half years he doubles taxes, elaborately furnishes his palace and buys ornate uniforms for his men. Jones continues to loot the country, sending money away so that he can leave a wealthy man, until the people realize his scheme and revolt. One day, when Jones orders floggings and the burning of a village for the attack on a tax collector, Jones's troops abandon him. The next evening, Jones, believing that he can find his way to the forest and escape on a French ship, becomes lost in the swamps and forest and is frightened by the sound of beating drums. After seeing and hearing scenes from his past, Jones prays for forgiveness. The sight of a voodoo figure sends Jones in a hysterical rush to the camp, where his former guards shoot him with a silver bullet. *African Americans. Emperors. Gambling. Jungles. Moral corruption. Traders. Bullets. Chain gangs. Dice. Dictators. Embezzlement. English. Executions. Fear. Islands. Jamaica. Manslaughter. Mistresses. Nightclubs. Palaces. Partnership. Porters. Pride and vanity. Prison escapes. Prostitution. Slavery. Soldiers. Swamps. Trains. Trains–Pullman cars. Uniforms. Uprisings. Visions.*

Note: This film marked the film debut of Paul Robeson. Publicity material for the film, preserved at the AMPAS Library, indicates that Ruby Elzy, who was an assistant to composer Rosamund Johnson, was cast as "Dolly" after helping to lead the spiritual singing in the church scene. Reviews list the role of Lem as having been played by George Haymid Stamper, while the film lists his name as George Stamp. Dudley Digges was the only non-black member of the cast. *Var* noted that the film was not likely to be seen by white theatergoers in the South, and that its business, even in black theaters, was questionable due to objections of black exhibitors to the use of the word "nigger." A 10 Oct 1933 *HR* news item noted that United Artists deleted the word from prints that were "destined to be shown in Negro theatres," but continued to show the original print in regular runs. Although the picture received many favorable reviews at the time of its release, three years later a conference of Marcus Garvey's United Negro Improvement Association, held in Canada, condemned the film.

According to modern sources, playwright Eugene O'Neill, who had long been interested in making a film version of his play, originally worked out a silent treatment. Producers John Krimsky and Gifford Cochran used the money they made by their sponsorship of the German film *Maedchen in Uniform* to finance *The Emperor Jones*, which was their first producing venture, and which cost approximately $250,000. Dudley Murphy reportedly convinced the neophyte producers that *The Emperor Jones* would make a successful film, and wrote a treatment presenting the story in chronological fashion, as opposed to O'Neill's flashback monologue, which Du Bose Heyward then completed in screenplay

form. Modern sources note that although a location shoot in Haiti was originally planned, art director Herman Rosse convinced the producers that a more effective jungle set could be created in the studio. The outdoor chain gang sequence was filmed in a stone quarry near Westchester, New York. Modern sources also note that actor Lorenzo Tucker worked three days as an extra in the Harlem Cabaret scene, and that all of Fredi Washington's scenes were reshot after the producers decided that she looked too white in the early rushes. Fearing that audiences would think that Robeson was embracing a white woman, the producers had Washington made up with a thick layer of dark pancake makeup for the second round of filming. According to a biography of Robeson, he later regretted having made the picture because it deviated too much from O'Neill's play. Black actor Charles Gilpin originally played the title role in the Broadway play, marking the first time that an important black role was not played by a white actor in blackface. Paul Robeson replaced Gilpin for a revival of the play in 1924. In late 1924, Robeson performed and sang portions of the play on a New York radio program, marking the first time an O'Neill play was broadcast over the radio. A Kraft Theatre teleplay of *The Emperor Jones*, produced and directed by Fielder Cook and starring Rex Ingram and Everett Stone, aired on the NBC network on 23 Feb 1955, and a made-for-television version of the play, starring Kenneth Spencer and Harry H. Corbet, aired on the ABC television network on 13 Apr 1958.

FD 16 Sep 1933, p. 4. *HR* 24 May 1933, p. 1. *HR* 15 Sep 1933, p. 3. *HR* 16 Sep 1933, p. 3. *HR* 10 Oct 1933, p. 9. *MPD* 16 Sep 1933, p. 4. *MPH* 23 Sep 1933, p. 33. *NYT* 16 Jul 1933. *NYT* 20 Sep 1933, p. 26. *Newsweek* 23 Sep 1933, p. 32. *Time* 25 Sep 1933, p. 31. *Var* 26 Sep 1933, p. 15.

THE EMPIRE BUILDERS see **IT'S A GREAT LIFE**

EMPIRE, INC. see **THE BLACK KING**

EN ALAS DEL AMOR see **LAS FRONTERAS DEL AMOR**

EN CADA PUERTO UN AMOR (Spanish language)

Metro-Goldwyn-Mayer Corp.; controlled by Loew's, Inc. *Dist* Culver Export, Inc. **1931**; New York opening: 27 Mar 1931; Prod: Nov—Dec 1930. Sd (Western Electric Sound System); b&w. 10 reels, 8,391 ft. 93 min. Passed by the National Board of Review. Spanish language.

[*Supv* Frank Davis]. *Dirigida por* [*Dir*] Marcel Silver. [*Dial dir* Carlos F. Borcosque]. [*Asst dir* Robert Barnes]. *Escenario y diálogo por* [*Scr and dial*] Laurence Stallings and W. L. River. *Diálogo adicional por* [*Addl dial*] Charles MacArthur. *Versión española por* [*Spanish version*] Edgar Neville. *Fotografiada por* [*Photog*] Leonard Smith and Harold Rosson. *Director artístico* [*Art dir*] Cedric Gibbons. *Editada por* [*Ed*] Peggy O'Day. *Acústica por* [*Sd*] Douglas Shearer.

Source: Based on the novel *Way for a Sailor* by Albert Richard Wetjen (New York, 1928).

Cast: José Crespo (*Jack*), Conchita Montenegro (*Elena*), Juan de Landa (*Trípode*), Romualdo Tirado (*Timón*), Elena Landeros (*Margot*), Rosita Granada (*Lulú*).

Drama. [*Not viewed*]. [The following plot summary is based on the English-language version of this film, *Way for a Sailor*; character names refer to that version. For further information regarding the English-language version, please see the note below and the entry for *Way for a Sailor* in the *AFI Catalog of Feature Films, 1921-30*.] Jack, a sailor, along with his buddies Tripod and Ginger, feels himself an indomitable force until he falls for Joan, who repeatedly repels his advances every time he comes into port, and only after a number of years is he able to see her alone. Finally he wins her and they are married, but Joan, learning he plans to return to the sea, leaves him. Later, having become a quartermaster on an ocean liner, he finds her still unforgiving; then a storm wrecks the ship on which all are traveling, and to her grief he is lost with Tripod and Ginger, but the trio is rescued by a whaling vessel and returned to port. After receiving Jack's message, Joan, having realized her true feelings, is reunited with him. *Courtship. Ocean liners. Sailors. Ships. Whales and whaling.*

Note: The onscreen credits were taken from a studio cutting continuity. The working titles of this film were *¡Paso al marino!* and *La ruta del marino*. The English-language version, *Way for a Sailor*, which was released in late 1930, was directed by Sam Wood and starred John Gilbert and Wallace Beery. Some sources include Raquel Davido and Luis Nava in the cast of the Spanish version, but their participation in the released film has not been confirmed. According to modern sources, Marcel Silver was removed as the film's director for budgetary reasons, but presumably was replaced by another director, whose name has not been determined.

Cinl May 1931, p. 31. *CM* Jun 1931, p. 438. *HF* 22 Nov 1930, p. 24.

EN LOS BRAZOS DE ELLA see **LA LEY DEL HAREM**

EN MITAD DEL CAMINO DEL CIELO see **SOMBRAS DEL CIRCO**

ENCHANTED see **SHAMROCK HILL**

ENCHANTED DREAM see **SHAMROCK HILL**

END OF THE RAINBOW see **NORTHWEST OUTPOST**

THE END OF THE TRAIL see **FURY AT FURNACE CREEK**

THE END OF THE WORLD see **THE WORLD, THE FLESH AND THE DEVIL**

THE ENEMY WITHIN see **THE HUN WITHIN**

ENSENADA see **HOLD BACK THE DAWN**

ENTRE DOS FUEGOS see **UN CAPITÁN DE COSACOS**

ERAN TRECE see **CHARLIE CHAN CARRIES ON**

ERSTWHILE SUSAN (German Americans)

Realart Pictures Corp. *Dist* Realart Pictures Corp. 16 Nov **1919** [©Realart Pictures Corp.; 26 Oct 1919; LP14386]. Si; b&w. 6 reels, 5,380 ft.

Dir John S. Robertson. *Asst dir* Shaw Lovett. *Scen* Kathryne Stuart. *Cam* Roy Overbaugh.

Source: Based on the novel *Barnabetta* by Helen R. Martin (New York, 1914) and the play *Erstwhile Susan* by Marian De Forest (New York, 18 Jan 1916).

Cast: Constance Binney (*Barnabetta Dreary*), Jere Austin (*David Jordan*), Alfred Hickman (*Dr. Edgar Barrett*), Mary Alden (*Juliet Miller, known as Erstwhile Susan*), Anders Randolph (*Barnaby Dreary*), Georges Renavent (*Emanuel Dreary*), Bradley Barker (*Jacob Dreary*), Leslie Hunt (*Abel Buchter*).

Rural, Drama. Barnabetta Dreary's grim life of slaving for her Pennsylvania Dutch father Barnaby and her two brothers, is surprisingly changed when Barnaby marries Juliet Miller. Known as Erstwhile Susan, she becomes fond of Barnabetta, and because she retains control of her fortune, induces the other Drearys to relieve Barnabetta of some of her drudgery. After Barnaby has a stroke brought on when Susan proposes sending Barnabetta to school, she goes to a prep school where the president, Doctor Barrett, and a trustee, State Senator Jordan, both fall for her newly acquired charm, to the dismay of Jordan's sister who loves Barrett. When the sister interferes with Barnabetta's plan to work in the school after graduation, Barnabetta helps Jordan win his campaign for governor, and after exposing him to her family's crude table manners, Barnabetta accepts Jordan's marriage proposal, while Susan succeeds in reforming Barnaby and his sons. *Class distinction. Drudges. Family life. High schools. Pennsylvania Dutch. Stepmothers. Elections. Governors. Jealousy. Physicians. Stroke. Trusts and trustees.*

Note: The film marked Constance Binney's first starring role.

ETR 15 Nov 1919, p. 2058. *MPN* 22 Nov 1919, p. 3788. *MPW* 13 Dec 1919, p. 854. *Var* 12 Dec 1919, p. 45. *Wid's* 7 Dec 1919, p. 5.

THE ESCAPE (Italian Americans)

Twentieth Century-Fox Film Corp. *Dist* Twentieth Century-Fox Film Corp. 6 Oct **1939**; Prod: late Mar—21 Apr 1939 [©Twentieth Century-Fox Film Corp.; 6 Oct 1939; LP9212]. Sd (RCA High Fidelity Recording); b&w. 5,223 ft. 58 or 62 min. PCA cert no. 5291.

Exec prod Sol M. Wurtzel. *Dir* Richard Cortez. [*Asst dir* Jasper Blystone]. *Orig scr* Robert Ellis and Helen Logan. *Dir of photog* Edward Cronjager. *Art dir* Richard Day and Haldane Douglas. *Film ed* Fred Allen. *Set dec* Thomas Little. *Cost* Herschel. *Mus dir* Samuel Kaylin. *Sd* Joseph Aiken and William H. Anderson.

Cast: Kane Richmond (*Eddie Farrell*), Amanda Duff (*Juli Peronni*), June Gale (*Annie Qualen*), Edward Norris (*Louie Peronni*), Henry Armetta (*Guiseppi Peronni*), Frank Reicher (*Dr. Shumaker*), Scotty Beckett (*Willie Rogers*), Leona Roberts (*Aunt Mamie Qualen*), Rex Downing (*Tommy Rogers*), Jimmy Butler (*Jim Rogers*), Roger McGee (*Swat*), Richard Lane (*David Clifford*), Jack Carson (*Chet Warren*), Matt McHugh (*Pete*), Helen Ericson (*Helen Gardner*), [Robert Scott (*Mickey*)], [Nick Copeland (*Chummy*)], [Selmer Jackson (*Mr. Henley*)], [Aggie Herring (*Mrs. Nearny*)], [Robert Lowery (*Ambulance driver*)], [Jerry Jerome, Sammy Finn, John Harmon (*Gangsters*)], [Ivan Miller (*Police captain*)], [Al Hill (*Lefty*)], [James Mack, Sr. (*Watchman*)], [Sandra Lee Richards (*Clifford Child*)], [David Newell, Terry Ray, Jack Easton, Garland Weaver

(*Reporters*)], [Thomas E. Jackson (*Police lieutenant*)], [Stanley Blystone (*Policeman*)], [Edward Keane (*Captain of detectives*)], [Agnes Steele (*Matron*)], [Bruce Mitchell (*Sergeant*)], [Freddie Walburn (*Boy*)], [Jessie Arnold], [Mary Gordon], [Milton Kibbee], [Pat O'Malley].

Crime, Drama. [*Print viewed*]. As newspaper headlines announce the death of New York gangster Louie Peronni, reporter Chet Warren gets the inside story from Dr. Shumaker, the Peronni family doctor. After Louie returns home from prison to his East Side neighborhoood, he is shot by a rival gangster and learns that Annie Qualen, his wife by a secret marriage, has born him a child but has put the child up for adoption rather than rear it with a gangster father. He also discovers that his sister, Juli, a schoolteacher, has become engaged to Eddie Farrell, the neighborhood policeman, who was once Louie's childhood friend. Louie, who hates policemen, breaks up the engagement by telling Juli that he was the man who killed Eddie's policeman father in a robbery. Then, following the death of their father, the three Rogers boys, Jim, Tommy and Willie, come to live with Annie, who is their cousin, and her mother Mamie. Jim, the oldest, looks for work while Tommy and Willie go to school. Tommy becomes the chum of Swat, leader of the neighborhood delinquents, while Willie becomes friends with Eddie, who shows him the better side of the neighborhood. When Mamie becomes ill and Annie is arrested while working in a dance hall, a city welfare worker threatens to take the boys away, but Shumaker convinces him to wait. Jim gets a job working nights in a fur warehouse. Tommy and Swat go to Louie and his gang, led by Chummy Miller, telling them that they can steal furs from under Jim's eyes. Louie sends the boys away, realizing that the gang can steal the $50,000 worth of furs themselves. As Tommy and Swat watch, Louie and his gang steal the furs, killing the watchman and running over Willie during their escape. Learning that Jim has been arrested as an accomplice and that Willie is seriously injured, Tommy goes to the police and tells all. After Louie is arrested, his gang kidnaps the district attorney's baby to make an exchange. Annie goes to the police station to tell Louie that the kidnapped child is their baby. Eddie helps Louie escape and the two go to the gang's hideout. Before going inside, Louie tells Eddie that he lied to Juli, that Chummy Miller actually killed his father. Inside the hideout, Louie sees his child for the first and only time as, in the ensuing shoot-out, he is killed by Miller, who is then killed by Eddie. As he dies, Louie asks Eddie not to tell anyone he is the child's father and preys for his family's forgiveness. As Dr. Shumaker finishes the story, Chet decides to tear up his notes and follow the doctor on another story: the birth of a neighborhood baby and the beautiful nurse who assisted. *Adoption. Gangsters. Italian Americans. Marriage–Secret. New York City–East Side. Orphans. Police. Self-sacrifice. Boy Scouts. Brothers. Brothers and sisters. Cousins. Engagements. Gunshot wounds. Juvenile delinquents. Kidnapping. Murder. Physicians. Prostitution. Reporters. Rivalry. Robbery. Social workers. Teachers.*

Note: The working title for this film was *East Side, West Side.* According to a news item in *HR*, added scenes, which began filming on 25 Jul 1939, involved Jack Carson as newspaperman "Chet Warren" learning the story in flashback. These were filmed three months after the initial shoot.

FD 9 Nov 1939, p. 8. *HR* 1 Apr 1939, p. 6. *HR* 21 Apr 1939, p. 7. *HR* 26 Jul 1939, p. 7. *HR* 9 Nov 1939, p. 3. *MPH* 16 Sep 1939, p. 63. *MPH* 11 Nov 1939, p. 17. *NYT* 3 Nov 1939, p. 17. *Var* 8 Nov 1939, p. 14.

ESCAPE (German Americans)

Metro-Goldwyn-Mayer Corp.; controlled by Loew's Inc.; A Mervyn LeRoy Production. *Dist* Loew's Inc. 1 Nov **1940**; Prod: early May—1 Jun 1940; additional scenes early Sep 1940 [©Loew's Inc.; 4 Nov 1940; LP10038]. Sd (Western Electric Sound System); b&w. 11 reels. 102-104 min. Passed by the National Board of Review. PCA cert no. 6501.

[*Prod* Lawrence Weingarten]. *Dir* Mervyn LeRoy. [*Addl scenes dir* George Cukor]. [*Asst dir* Al Shenberg]. *Scr* Arch Oboler and Marguerite Roberts. *Dir of photog* Robert Planck. *Art dir* Cedric Gibbons. *Art dir assoc* Urie McCleary. *Film ed* George Boemler. *Set dec* Edwin B. Willis. *Gowns* Adrian. *Men's cost* Gile Steele. *Rec dir* Douglas Shearer. *Hair styles for Miss Shearer* Sydney Guilaroff. *Makeup created by* Jack Dawn. [*Tech adv* Raul Huldeschinsky]. [*Tech expert* Henry Noerdlinger].

Source: Based on the novel *Escape* by Ethel Vance (Boston, 1939).

Cast: NORMA SHEARER (*Countess [Ruby] Von Treck*), ROBERT TAYLOR (*Mark Preysing*), Conrad Veidt (*General Kurt Von Kolb*), Nazimova (*Emmy Ritter*), Felix Bressart (*Fritz Keller*), Albert

Basserman (*Dr. Arthur Henning*), Philip Dorn (*Dr. Ditten*), Bonita Granville (*Ursula*), Edgar Barrier (*Commissioner*), Elsa Basserman (*Mrs. Henning*), Blanche Yurka (*Nurse*), Lisa Golm (*Anna*), [Marek Windheim (*Hotel clerk*)], [Gretl Sherk (*Hilda Keller*)], [Lotte Palfi (*Julie, the countess' maid*)], [Janet Shaw (*Greta*)], [Florine McKinney, Gerta Rozan, Anya Taranda (*Students*)], [Marianne Mosner (*Maria*)], [Ann Sheldon (*Helene*)], [Christina Montez (*Suzanne*)], [Adolph Milar (*Salesman*)], [Fredrik Vogeding, Hans Joby (*Passport officials*)], [Erwin Kalser (*Bartender*)], [Henry Rowland (*Bellboy*)], [Wolfgang Zilzer (*Pavillion attendant*)], [Frederick Giermann, Helmut Dantine (*Porters*)], [William Yetter (*Heinrich*)], [Fred Wolff (*Waiter*)], [Ernst Deutsch (*Baron von Reiber*)], [Maria Ray (*Baroness*)], [Kay Deslys (*Waitress*)], [Albert d'Arno (*Elevator man*)], [Howard Lang (*Dr. Heinrich*)], [Edit Angold (*Servant*)], [William Edmunds (*Waiter, White Swan*)], [Henry Victor, Hans Schumm (*Policeman*)], [Edouard Faust (*Proprietor, beer garden*)], [Arno Frey (*Commandant*)], [Walter Bonn (*Guard, concentration camp*)], [Winter Hall (*Priest*)], [Thomas Monk (*Priest's assistant*)].

War, Drama. [*Print viewed*]. In 1936, in a concentration camp in the Bavarian Alps, German-born actress Emmy Ritter awaits her death at the hands of the Nazis, only comforted by camp physician Dr. Ditten, who secretly allows her to write a letter to her American-born son, Mark Preysring. Unknown to them, Mark has arrived in Germany searching for Emmy, and after a terrified old friend reveals that she may have been arrested for trying to smuggle money out of the country, Mark goes to the authorities. He learns that Emmy, who had been helping refugees and "enemies" of the German state, has been sent to a concentration camp. Mark then goes to a small Bavarian town in which an old servant of Emmy's, Fritz Keller, lives, but Fritz pretends not to know Mark. One afternoon, a despondent Mark meets Countess Ruby Von Treck, an American-born widow of a German nobleman, who runs a finishing school in her home. Ruby is sympathetic to Mark and asks her lover, Nazi General Kurt Von Kolb, about Emmy and learns where she is confined. Ruby then goes to see Mark at his hotel, but can't bring herself to tell him. Mark begins to fall in love with Ruby, but when he learns that she is friends with a Nazi general, he turns against her. When Kurt reveals that Emmy is about to be executed, though, Ruby invites Mark to meet her at a concert and tells him about Emmy, then advises him to go home. Mark is enraged by her apparent callousness and lashes out at her. After the concert, she introduces him to Ditten, an old friend, who asks Mark to go with him for a drink. Unaware that Mark is Emmy's son, Ditten at first asks him to send some American medical journals to him, but when he realizes who Mark is, he gives him Emmy's letter. When some Gestapo officers come into the café, Ditten leaves, but invites Mark to his apartment the following evening. Back at his hotel, Mark finds Fritz waiting for him, remorseful over his earlier behavior. Fritz admits that he was too afraid to speak to Mark openly, but offers to properly bury Emmy. The next morning, in the concentration camp, Emmy seems to have a heart attack and Ditten pronounces her dead. That night, however, when Mark goes to visit him, Ditten secretly reveals that he administered a drug to Emmy to produce a coma-like state that simulates death. Mark is shocked, but when he realizes that Ditten has given Emmy her only chance, Mark arranges for Fritz to claim the body, then meet him at an inn near the camp. Mark waits, but Fritz does not come, and soon two members of the Gestapo arrive and question him. Suspicious when Mark says that he is waiting for Ditten, they take him to the camp for questioning. Ditten tells the Gestapo that Mark has come for his dead mother's body, and soon Fritz arrives with the proper papers to claim her. Though still suspicious, the Gestapo release the body to Mark and Fritz. After they leave the camp, Mark finally revives Emmy, but because snow and debris on the road blocks their truck, Mark decides to take her to Ruby's house, hoping that she will help. She says she doesn't want to help, but does, even though Kurt has seen Fritz' truck and suspects that something is wrong. The next morning, Ruby obtains a passport for Emmy from one of the girls who is against the Nazis, then sends the rest of the girls off to ski. When Kurt arrives, he is suspicious of Mark, whom Ruby dismisses as someone with a crush on her. She secretly sends Mark away with Emmy and promises to join him later, even though she knows that Kurt will never let her go. After they leave, Ruby prevents Kurt from stopping them by revealing her love for Mark and taunting him, causing him to have a heart attack. As Kurt dies, she promises not to leave him, knowing that Mark and Emmy are

free. *Americans in foreign countries. Courage. Escapes. German Americans. Germany. Mothers and sons. Nazism. Political prisoners. Actors and actresses. Heart disease. Hotels. Ice skaters and ice skating. Physicians. Self-sacrifice. Skiing.*

Note: Opening cast credits for the film identify Norma Shearer's character as "The Countess," Conrad Veidt's character as "The General," Albert Basserman's character as "The Lawyer," Felix Bressart's character as "Fritz" and Philip Dorn's character as "The Doctor." End credits list the character names as indicated in the credits above. Character names for the other leading actors, Robert Taylor, Nazimova and Bonita Granville, are the same in both places. According to the film's pressbook, the name Ethel Vance was a pseudonym used by the real authoress of *Escape* to protect relatives living in Nazi Germany. Modern sources have confirmed that Vance was the pen name of novelist Grace Zaring Stone, who previously had written *The Bitter Tea of General Yen* (see *AFI Catalog of Feature Films, 1931-40*; F3.0353). Stone's daughter, Eleanor Perenyi, was living in occupied Europe at the time, and her husband, Ellis Stone, was the United States Naval attache in Paris. Stone felt that her relatives might be in danger if her real name were attached to the book, thus she used a pseudonym that was not even known to M-G-M when that studio purchased the rights to the novel.

An article in *Pacific Coast Musician* on 2 Nov 1940 noted that no music credits were given for the film for the reason that the composers also had relatives in Germany and feared for their safety. No music credits were given in contemporary reviews or in onscreen credits, nor were any music credits cited within the film's cutting continuity, a departure from most M-G-M films of the time. Additional scenes were shot for the film in early Sep 1940 by director George Cukor. A news item notes that Edgar Barrier, who played "The Commissioner," made his motion picture debut in the film. Elsa Basserman, the wife of actor Albert Basserman, who portrayed his wife in the film, made her motion picture debut in the film. Actor Helmut Dantine, who had a minor role as a partner in the film, also made his debut in *Escape*. Modern sources credit Jack D. Moore with set decoration.

DV 31 Oct 1940, p. 3. *FD* 31 Oct 1940, p. 4. *HR* 23 Apr 1940, p. 8. *HR* 6 May 1940, p. 2. *HR* 9 May 1940, p. 11. *HR* 11 May 1940, p. 6. *HR* 5 Sep 1940, p. 13. *HR* 31 Oct 1940, p. 3. *MPD* 30 Oct 1940, p. 14. *MPH* 2 Nov 1940, p. 35. *NYT* 1 Nov 1940, p. 33. *Var* 30 Oct 1940, p. 14.

ESCAPE FROM RED ROCK (Native Americans, Apache, Latino)

Regal Films, Inc. *Dist* Twentieth Century-Fox Film Corp. Jan **1958**; Prod: late Jul–early Aug 1957 [©Twentieth Century-Fox Film Corp.; 27 Nov 1957; LP10609]. Sd (RCA Sound Recording); b&w; Regalscope. 6,757 ft. 75 min. PCA cert no. 18761.

Prod Bernard Glasser. *Dir* Edward Bernds. *Asst dir* Leonard Shapiro. *Wrt by* Edward Bernds. *Dir of photog* Brydon Baker. *Art dir* Rudi Feld. *Supv ed* John F. Link. *Set dec* Walter M. Scott and Maurice Mulcahy. *Prop master* Neil Wheeler. *Ward* Clark Ross. *Mus comp and cond* Les Baxter. *Sd* Ben Winkler and Harry M. Leonard. *Makeup* Louis Hippe. *Hair stylist* Josephine Sweeney. *Prod mgr* H. E. Mendelson. *Script supv* Joan E. Buck. *Dial coach* Henry Staudigl. [*Double* Roydon Clark and Sailor Vincent].

Cast: Brian Donlevy [(*Bronc Grierson*)], Eilene Janssen [(*Janie Acker*)], Gary Murray [(*Cal Bowman*)], Jay C. Flippen [(*Sheriff John Costaine*)], William Phipps [(*Arky Shanks*)], Michael Healey [(*Joe Skinner*)], Nesdon Booth [(*Peter Acker*)], Daniel White [(*Al Farris*)], Andre Adoree [(*Guard*)], Courtland Shepard [(*Rube Boyce*)], Tina Menard [(*Maria Chavez*)], Natividad Vacio [(*Miguel Chavez*)], Zon Murray [(*Krug*)], Rick Vallin [(*Judd Bowman*)], [Ed Hinton (*Tarrant*)], [Frosty Royce (*Coach driver*)], [Frank Richards (*Price*)], [Linda Dangcil (*Elena Chavez*)], [Eumenio Blanco (*Mayor*)], [Elena Da Vinci (*Antonia Chavez*)], [Hank Patterson (*Grover*)], [Eileene Stevens (*Mrs. Donnely*)], [Frank Marlowe (*Manager*)], [Joe Becker (*Clerk*)], [Dick Crockett (*Krug Henchie*)].

Western. [*Not viewed*]. When young rancher Cal Bowman assaults two men for accusing his brother Judd of robbery and murder, Sheriff John Costaine breaks up the fight. Although Costaine is sympathetic to Cal's loyalty, he warns Cal that he cannot defend Judd, a fugitive from the law, from the whole world. While they are talking, Deputy Al Farris brings in seventeen-year-old Janie Acker, who has run away from her brutal father Peter. When Peter appears to claim his daughter, Costaine reluctantly turns her over to him with a warning to stop beating the girl. Upon returning to his ranch, Cal finds outlaw Bronc Grierson and his henchmen, Rube Boyce, Joe Skinner and Arky Shanks, waiting for him. When Cal sees a wounded Judd with the outlaws, he realizes that the accusations are true. Judd is badly in need of medical attention, but Bronc refuses to let him see a doctor until Cal finds out when the next shipment of gold is due at the Railway Express office. To save his brother, Cal acquiesces to the outlaws' demands, and during the robbery, watches helplessly as an innocent woman bystander is killed, and Boyce shot to death. When Janie warns Cal that a posse has been formed to lynch him, Cal rides

back to the ranch, and finding his brother dead, flees to the Mexican border with Janie. After a dangerous journey through Apache country, they stop at a little town on the Arizona side of the border and are given refuge by Miguel Chavez and his wife Maria, who think that Cal and Janie are eloping. After arranging their marriage, Miguel sends Cal and Janie to the home of Mr. Willis, a friend of the Apache who can give them safe passage to Mexico. When they arrive at the Willis ranch, however, they find that Willis and his wife have been massacred by the Indians. The Willis' infant son has survived, and rather than abandon the child, Cal and Janie remain with him at the ranch. Soon after, Bronc and his gang, also on their way to Mexico, stumble upon the ranch. When Arky and Skinner decide to kidnap Janie and kill Cal, Bronc, softened by the infant, opposes them. At that moment, the posse arrives, and after Janie sends them on a wild goose chase, Bronc disarms Arky and Skinner. As Bronc leads his gang across the border, they are attacked and killed by the Apache. Costaine and his men then appear just in time to save Janie and Cal, and convinced that Cal is innocent of all crimes, the sheriff frees him so that he and Janie can start a new life in California. *Apache Indians. Battered children. Brothers. False accusations. Fugitives. Outlaws. Ranchers. Robbery. Runaways. Sheriffs. Boundaries. Fathers and daughters. Infants. Mexican Americans. Murder. Posses.*

Note: Although the film was not viewed, the above credits were taken from a continuity contained in the Copyright files.

Box 20 Jan 1958. *DV* 13 Jan 1958, p. 3. *Exh* 11 Dec 1957, p. 4414. *FD* 23 Jan 1958, p. 7. *Har* 18 Jan 1958, pp. 10-11. *HR* 26 Jul 1957, p. 13. *HR* 9 Aug 1957, p. 13. *HR* 13 Jan 1958, p. 3. *MPHPD* 18 Jan 1958, p. 683. *Var* 15 Jan 1958, p. 7.

ESCAPE IF YOU CAN *see* SO YOUNG, SO BAD

ESCAPE IN THE FOG (Chinese Americans)

Columbia Pictures Corp. *Dist* Columbia Pictures Corp. 5 Apr **1945**; Prod: 6 Dec–22 Dec 1944 [©Columbia Pictures Corp.; 5 Apr 1945; LP13268]. Sd (Western Electric Mirrophonic Recording); b&w. 5,645 ft. 60 or 63 min. PCA cert no. 10674.

Prod Wallace MacDonald. *Dir* Oscar Boetticher, Jr. [*Asst dir* Milton Feldman]. [*Dial dir* Milton Stiefel]. *Orig scr* Aubrey Wisberg. *Dir of photog* George Meehan. [*2d cam* Gert Andersen]. *Art dir* Jerome Pycha, Jr. *Film ed* Jerome Thoms. *Set dec* Joseph Kish. [*Sd eng* Philip Faulkner]. [*Research dir* Marianne Nussbaum].

Cast: Otto Kruger [(*Paul Devon*)], Nina Foch [(*Eilene Carr*)], William Wright [(*Barry Malcolm*)], Konstantin Shayne [(*Schiller*)], Ivan Triesault [(*Hausmer*)], Ernie Adams [(*George Smith*)], [Mary Newton (*Mrs. Devon*)], [Ralph Dunn (*Police sergeant*)], [John Tyrrell (*Brice*)], [Charles Jordan (*Simmons*)], [Noel Cravat (*Kold*)], [John H. Elliott (*Thomas*)], [Robert Williams (*Officer on bridge*)], [Eddie Parker (*Officer Sullivan*)], [Wing Foo (*Chang Yong*)], [Leslie Denison (*Gale*)], [Dick Jensen, Joseph Palma, Elmo Lincoln (*Officers*)], [Jim Lim, William Yip (*Chinese*)], [Leroy Taylor (*Plainclothesman*)], [Chuck Hamilton (*Doorman*)], [Emmett Vogan (*Port director*)], [Edmund Cobb (*Detective*)], [Shelley Winter (*Taxi driver*)], [Jessie Arnold (*Screaming woman*)], [Harrison Greene (*Mr. Boggs*)], [Tom P. Dillon (*Lt. Commander*)], [Chin Kuang Chow (*Chinese boy*)], [Frank O'Connor (*Police clerk*)], [Frank Mayo (*Bartender*)], [Victor Travers], [Heinie Conklin].

Espionage, Drama. [*Print viewed*]. Eilene Carr has a nightmare in which she is strolling along the Golden Gate Bridge on a foggy San Francisco night when a cab pulls over, three men jump out and two of them poise a knife at the other's throat. Eilene screams, and at the Rustic Dell Inn, outside of San Francisco, her shrieks bring the innkeeper and Barry Malcolm, a guest, rushing into her room to awaken her from her nightmare. Once she is alert, Eilene recognizes Barry as the intended murder victim in her dream. At breakfast the next morning, Eilene tells Barry that she is recuperating from shock suffered when the hospital ship on which she was serving as a nurse was sunk during battle. Barry is mysterious about his work, but when he receives a phone call directing him to a meeting in San Francisco that afternoon, he asks Eilene to accompany him into the city. George Smith, a man in the hotel lobby, overhears Barry's conversation and notifies Schiller, the owner of the Golden Gate watch repair shop in San Francisco about Barry's plans. Upon reaching the city, Barry visits his contact, Paul Devon, the leader of a group of government undercover agents. After informing Barry that he is being sent to Hong Kong to coordinate an underground group there, Devon tells him that an agent will pick him up in a taxi cab at his hotel at 10:30 that night and hands him a top secret pouch containing the names of double

agents operating in Japan. After Barry leaves Devon's house, Schiller rings the doorbell and gains admittance by claiming that he has come to adjust Devon's grandfather clock. When Devon's butler leaves the room, Schiller opens the back of the clock and removes a small recording cyclinder that he had previously placed there. Upon returning to his shop, Schiller and Smith listen to Barry's recorded conversation and learn his misson. Resolving to gain possession of the list of double agents, the spies trace Barry to the Cumberland Hotel. After dining at the Caravan Club that night, Barry tells Eilene that he must leave on a mission and asks her to wait for him in the hotel lobby while he goes to his room to retrieve his suitcase. When Barry disappears into the elevator, Smith calls the hotel doorman and, pretending to be Barry, instructs him to send the man waiting out front in the cab to his room and dismiss the taxi. The vehicle departs, and another taxi driven by one of the spies replaces it in front of the hotel. After Barry drives away in the cab, Eilene is overcome by a strange sensation and stumbles into the street, where she is knocked down by an oncoming car. The blow to her head causes Eilene to recall the nightmare images of Barry's peril, and she hurries to Devon's house. Devon refuses to take Eilene's premonition seriously until the agent calls from the hotel informing him that Barry is missing. Hurrying to the bridge, the site of her nightmare, Eilene watches as a cab pulls over and three men jump out. Eilene screams, and a nearby guard runs to her rescue. When the guard appears, two of the men hop back into the cab and speed away, leaving Barry, who has thrown the pouch into the water, behind. The harbor patrol is unable to locate the pouch, but, Eilene recalls hearing a boat pass beneath the bridge. Thinking that the packet may have landed on the deck of the boat, Barry querries the port director, who denies that a ship was in the vicinity that night. In reality, an experimental Navy ship passed under the bridge, but the director lacks the authority to divulge that information. While Barry calls an agent friend for help in locating the ship, Smith, who has followed him to the office of the Port Authority, deduces that the packet may have fallen onto a passing ship and notifies Schiller. To insure the return of the pouch, Schiller places an advertisement in the classifieds offering a reward for it. Meanwhile, Barry receives a message from his friend, directing him to a boat docked in the Half Moon Bay harbor. After giving Eilene the note for safekeeping, Barry proceeds to the harbor. While waiting Barry's return, Eileen reads the paper and, noticing the ad, telephones the interested party and is directed to Schiller's shop. There she is taken captive, and when Schiller finds the note with the ship's name on it, he calls the Half Moon Bay harbor police. Impersonating the director of the Port Authority, Schiller orders a messenger to deliver the package to the office in San Francisco. Soon after, Barry arrives at the harbor, and when he learns that the pouch is enroute to San Francisco, he orders the messenger intercepted. When Barry returns to his hotel room that night, he finds a note demanding the packet in exchange for Eilene's life and directing him to Chinatown. Meanwhile, at the Devon house, Devon notices that his grandfather clock has stopped and finds the recording device hidden in the back. Devon proceeds to Schiller's repair shop in Chinatown while Smith escorts Barry at gunpoint to the same shop. After procuring the pouch, Schiller and Smith chain Barry to a table, turn on the gas and leave him and the bound Eilene to perish in the impending explosion. Seizing a jeweler's magnifiying glass, Barry cleverly pens "hail Japan" on it, holds it to a window and illuminates it with his lighter. Angered by the slogan, some passing Chinese smash the window just as Devon and the police arrive. To avoid the police dragnet, Smith and Schiller separate and accidentally shoot each other in the fog. Later, Barry and Eilene return to the bridge and embrace. *Nightmares. Secret documents. Spies. Undercover agents.* Chinese Americans. Clocks. Fog. Hotels. Nurses. Police. Post-traumatic stress disorder. Predictions. San Francisco (CA)–Chinatown. San Francisco (CA)–Golden Gate Bridge. Surveillance devices. Taxicabs. World War II.

Note: The working title of this film was *Out of the Fog.* According to a pre-production *HR* news item, William Castle was originally to have directed this picture and Lynn Merrick was to have played the female lead.

Box 3 Mar 1945. *DV* 21 May 1945, p. 3. *HR* 24 Nov 1944, p. 18. *HR* 15 Dec 1944, p. 18. *HR* 21 May 1945, p. 3. *MPHPD* 10 Feb 1945, p. 2310. *MPHPD* 19 May 1945, p. 2453.

ESCAPE TO FREEDOM see **JOURNEY TO FREEDOM**

ESCAPE TO GLORY (German Americans)

Columbia Pictures Corp. *Dist* Columbia Pictures Corp. 28 Nov **1940**; Prod: 19 Aug—23 Sep 1940 [©Columbia Pictures Corp.; 14 Oct 1940; LP10237]. Sd; b&w. 73 min. PCA cert no. 6656.

Prod Samuel Bischoff. *Dir* John Brahm. [*Asst dir* C. C. Coleman]. *Scr* P. J. Wolfson. *Story* Sidney Biddell and Fredric Frank. *Dir of photog* Franz Planer. *Art dir* Lionel Banks. *Film ed* Al Clark. *Miss Bennett's gowns* Irene. *Mus dir* M. W. Stoloff. [*Sd eng* Lodge Cunningham]. *Stand-in for Pat O'Brien* Bert Kennedy. *Stand-in for Constance Bennett* Kay Smith. *Stand-in for Alan Baxter* Thor Liljiucrantz. *Stand-in for Stanley Logan* Casey Whitney. *Stand-in for Melville Cooper* Joe Murphy. *Stand-in for John Halliday* James Flatley. *Stand-in for Jessie Busley* Ida Schumaker. *Stand-in for Marjorie Gateson* Frances Gehraty.

Cast: Pat O'Brien (*Mike Farrough*), Constance Bennett (*Christine Blaine*), John Halliday (*John Morgan*), Melville Cooper (*Penney*), Alan Baxter (*Larry Perrin*), Edgar Buchanan (*Charles Atterbee*), Marjorie Gateson (*Mrs. Winslow*), Francis Pierlot (*Professor Mudge*), Jessie Busley (*Mrs. Mudge*), Stanley Logan (*Captain Hollister*), Frank Sully (*Tommy Malone*), Erwin Kalser (*Dr. Behrens*), Don Beddoe (*Chief engineer*), Leslie Denison (*First mate*), [Bruce Bennett (*Lieutenant*)], [Dick Rich (*Harry*)], [Olaf Hytten (*Agent*)], [Frank Baker, Arthur Mulliner (*Detectives*)], [Frank Benson, Dave Dunbar, James Kilgannon, Bobby Hale (*Sailors*)], [Rex Post (*First mate*)], [Douglas Gordon (*Lookout*)], [Hans Schumm (*Submarine commander*)], [Norbert Schiller (*Submarine first officer*)], [Franz Von Altenberger (*Submarine radio operator*)], [Fred Wolff, Hans Von Morhart, Paul Michael (*German sailors*), [Arno Frey (*Submarine gunner*)], [James Flatley (*Double for "John Morgan"*)], [John Kascier (*Double for "Professor Mudge"*)], [Steve Benton (*Double for "Charles Atterbee"*)], [Kay Smith (*Double for "Christine Blaine"*)], [Crete Sipple (*Double for "Mrs. Mudge"*)], [Ione Reed (*Double for "Mrs. Winslow"*)], [Wyndham Standing].

War, Drama. [*Print viewed*]. Amid rumors of war in Europe, a group of Americans rush homeward aboard a British freighter. On board are Mike Farrough, an American soldier of fortune; John Morgan, a district attorney who has put his office at the service of gangsters; Christine Blaine, Morgan's secretary and sweetheart; Larry Perrin, a fugitive murderer trailing Morgan to avenge a double-cross; Professor and Mrs. Mudge, an elderly couple; and Dr. Behrens, a German doctor. One day out of Liverpool, war is declared, and soon after, the freighter is halted to take on guns. When a German submarine appears, Farrough mans a gun and cripples the U-boat's periscope. Dr. Behrens, torn between ethics and his love for his fatherland, sends signals to the submarine with a shortwave transmitter. As the submarine tracks its prey, Perrin watches for his chance to kill Morgan, while Farrough and Christine fall in love. Discovering that the doctor has been signaling the submarine, Farrough places the transmitter aboard a small boat loaded with depth charges. To decoy the submarine away from the freighter, Perrin volunteers to pilot the boat in a suicide mission, and forces Morgan to accompany him. When the submarine attacks the decoy, the depth charges explode, sinking the sub and saving the freighter at the cost of Morgan's and Perris' lives. *Freighters. Revenge. Soldiers of fortune. Submarine boats. World War II.* Americans in foreign countries. Betrayal. District Attorneys. Explosions. Fugitives. Gangsters. German Americans. Germany. Navy. Liverpool (England). Murder. Patriotism. Physicians. Professors. Romance. Secretaries. Self-sacrifice.

Note: The working titles of this film were *Passage West* and *Submarine Zone.*

DV 19 Nov 1940, p. 3. *HR* 23 Aug 1940, pp. 8-9. *HR* 19 Nov 1940, p. 3. *MPH* 23 Nov 1940, p. 45. *NYT* 7 Apr 1940, p. 3. *Var* 20 Nov 1940, p. 16.

ESCAPE TO RED ROCK see **ESCAPE FROM RED ROCK**

ESCLAVAS DE LA MODA (Spanish language)

Fox Film Corp. *Dist* Fox Film Corp. **1931**; New York opening: 3 Jul 1931; Prod: Apr–May 1931. Sd; b&w. 8 reels, 6,789 ft. 75 min. Passed by the National Board of Review. Spanish language.

Pres WM. FOX. [*Dir* David Howard]. [*Dial dir* Francisco Moré de la Torre]. [*Adpt and dial* Howard J. Green]. [*Spanish version by* Matías Cirici-Ventalló]. [*Photog* Sidney Wagner]. [*Sd* Bernard Freericks].

Source: Based on the short story "On Your Back" by Rita Weiman in *Liberty* (22 Feb 1930).

Cast: Carmen Larrabeiti (*Julia*), Julio Peña (*Mario*), Blanca Castejón (*Dora [Durke]*), Ralph Navarro (*Larry*), Félix de Pomés ([*David*] *Morton*), Enriqueta Soler (*Gaby*), Paco Moreno (*Víctor*), Rafael Calvo (*Tyler*), [Robert Cartier (*Mario, de niño*)], [Nelly Fernández].

Drama. [*Not viewed*]. [The following plot summary is based on the English-language version of this film, *On Your Back*; character names refer to that version. For further information regarding the English-language version, please see the note below and the entry for *On Your Back* in the *AFI Catalog of Feature Films, 1921-30*.] Julianne rises from the rank of a Broadway modiste to owner of a fashionable Fifth Avenue salon, guided by a worn deck of cards and her faith in the future of her only son, Harvey, whom she sends to college. "Lucky" Jim Seymour suggests a plan by which she can benefit financially—extending credit to struggling showgirls under the egis of broker Raymond Pryer. Jeanne Burke, who is having an affair with Pryer, meets Harvey in a college town and becomes engaged to him; following graduation, Harvey takes a job in Pryer's office but leaves when he learns of her affair. Julianne, who disapproves of the girl, presses for payment of her account under threat of exposure, but Jeanne counters with the threat of revealing the particulars of Julianne's sideline activities. Ultimately, the mother relents. *Brokers. Couturiers. Debt. Motherhood. New York City. Show girls. Students.*

Note: The onscreen credits were taken from a screen credit sheet in the Twentieth Century-Fox Records of the Legal Department at the UCLA Theater Arts Library. The working title of this film was *Sobre su espalda*. This was the Spanish language version of Fox's 1930 English language release *On Your Back*, which was directed by Guthrie McClintic and starred Irene Rich and Raymond Hackett. The running time was calculated from footage given in NYSA records.
CM Oct 1931, p. 750.

ESKIMO (Native Americans, Native Alaskans)
Metro-Goldwyn-Mayer Corp.; controlled by Loew's, Inc.; W. S. Van Dyke's Production. *Dist* Metro-Goldwyn-Mayer Corp. 10 Jan **1934**; New York opening: 14 Nov 1933; Prod: late Jul 1932—late May 1933 [©Metro Goldwyn Mayer Corp.; 9 Jan 1934; LP4413]. Sd (Western Electric Sound System); b&w. 12 reels. 117 or 120 min. Passed by the National Board of Review.

Prod Hunt Stromberg. *Dir* W. S. VAN DYKE. *Asst dir* Frank Messenger and Edward Hearn. *Translated to the screen* John Lee Mahin. *Photog* Clyde De Vinna, Josiah Roberts, George Nogle and Leonard Smith. [*Asst cam* Dale Deverman and William James Knott]. *Film ed* Conrad A. Nervig. *Rec* C. S. Pratt and H. D. Watson. [*Location camp chef* Emil Ottinger]. [*Still photog* Roy Clark].

Source: Based on the book *Storfanger* by Peter Freuchen (Copenhagen, 1927) and his book *Die Flucht ins weisse Land* (Berlin, 1929).

Cast: [Mala (*Himself*)], [Lotus (*Iva*)], [Joseph Sauers (*Sergeant Hunt*)], [W. S. Van Dyke (*Inspector White*)], [Peter Freuchen (*Captain*)], [Edgar Dearing (*Constable Balk*)], [Harold Seabrook].

Drama. [*Print viewed*]. When Mala, the best hunter in his remote Eskimo village, hears tales from other tribesmen about the White Man's ship and the guns that the White Man trades for fox skins, he is greatly impressed. Later Mala's wife Aba, who longs for the White Man's goods, suggests that Mala and their family travel to the ship, and Mala, who is concerned about providing food for the long winter, agrees. After a 500 mile journey across the frozen tundra, during which Mala graciously offers Aba's sexual services to a womanless hunter, Mala and his family arrive at Tjaranak, an inlet where the White Man's ship is harbored. Mala barters with the unscrupulous captain of the ship and trades his valuable skins for a rifle. Taken with Aba, the captain then insists she remain with him and seduces her with alcohol and useless gifts. The next day, an angry Mala forces the captain to promise to leave Aba alone while he and a group of men are away whale hunting. Later, the sailors begin to drink, and the captain orders two of his men to bring Aba to the ship. Dragged from her igloo against her will, Aba is forced to drink and is raped by the captain. The next morning, still drunk, she stumbles from the ship and collapses in the snow, where she is mistaken for an animal and is shot by a sailor. When Mala returns from the whale hunt, he is told that his wife "sleeps" and learns about the circumstances of her death. Enraged, he kills the captain with a harpoon and rushes back to his tribe with his children. Back in his village, Mala grieves for Aba but leads his tribesman in a successful caribou hunt. While staring at a slain caribou, however, Mala sees the image of the captain and

consults with a Wise Old One about his vision. The Wise Old One advises him to ask the Spirits for a new name, so that the captain cannot follow him, and Mala goes to a sacred hilltop to pray. Inspired by a bird that flies overhead, Mala takes the name Kripik and begins to dance and chant. He then notices that Iva, the second wife of another hunter, has followed him and reveals to her his new name. With his new identity, Mala warms to Iva, who has always loved him and has been offered to him by her husband, and agrees to "lie down" with her. Out of respect for Mala, the other hunter offers him his first wife as well and announces that he is leaving the village for good. While Mala enjoys his new family, a Royal Canadian Mounted Police post is established in the Tjaranak inlet, and after the two Mounties in charge learn of the captain's killing, they set out to find and arrest Mala. Near his village, Mala comes across the nearly frozen bodies of the Mounties and reluctantly takes them to his igloo. After they recover sufficiently, the Mounties question Mala about his identity and, through their English speaking Eskimo guide, learn that he is the captain's killer. Although grateful to Mala, the Mounties trick him into leaving his family by telling him that they need his help in securing food at the inlet. While Mala is out wolf hunting for the post, Inspector White arrives and demands that Mala be treated like a prisoner. Reluctantly the Mounties tell Mala, who has learned that his family is alone and starving in the village, that he cannot go home and, breaking a promise they made to him, shackle him to his bed. Enduring great pain and injury, Mala wriggles his hand out of the shackle and, with his dog team, escapes before daylight. The Mounties dutifully pursue him, aware that with his injured hand his chances of a successful flight are limited. After a grueling journey, Mala finally is rescued by his eldest son near his deserted village. Determined not to be re-captured by the traitorous white men, Mala announces that he is leaving the family but is followed by the loyal Iva. As they head for an ice floe, Mala and Iva are pursued by the approaching Mounties. Unable to stop Mala without shooting him, the Mounties decide at last to give the brave Eskimo his freedom. *Arctic regions. Cultural conflict. Honor. Murder. Native Alaskans. North West Mounted Police. Accidental death. Aged men. Betrayal. Chases. Dogsledding. Drunkenness. Escapes. Fur traders. Grief. Hunger. Hunting. Ice floes. Imprisonment. Polygamy. Rape. Rites and ceremonies. Sailors. Sea captains. Ships. Village life. Visions. Whales and whaling.*

Note: The onscreen credits contain the following statement: "The Expedition to the Arctic began in April 1932...In November of 1933, the record was complete. Excepting the characters of the Canadian Police, there are no actors in this record...entire story told by primitive Eskimos in Native tongue, in Native custom...The Books by Peter Freuchen were notable for their discussion of the Moral Code of the Eskimos...this record attempts to present that Code...a strong, primeval Creed belonging to the farthest wilderness of the endless North...." Sub-titles were used in the film to translate Eskimo dialogue. In spite of the film's "no actor" claims, the Eskimo performers appear to be well-trained and "made up" for their parts. An unidentified contemporary source in the AMPAS files states that Mala, a genuine Eskimo, came to Los Angeles a year or two before the production began to work as a cameraman. Originally hired as a guide for *Eskimo*, he convinced the filmmakers of his acting talent and was cast in the lead. According to modern sources, producer Hunt Stromberg was so impressed with Mala's performance in the film that he signed him to an M-G-M contract. In his later films, Mala usually portrayed Polynesian characters. Lotus also made her screen debut in this film. She later changed her name to Lotus Long and, like Mala, played Asian characters.

A late Jul 1932 *HR* news item announced that location shooting for the production had begun in the Arctic. According to an informal production newsletter, which was edited by author Peter Freuchen, the film crew had its camp in Teller, AK. An Oct 1932 *HR* news item claimed that the *Eskimo* crew was "iced in" during shooting and had to be rescued by a dog sled team. *FD* news items indicate that Van Dyke completed the direction of the film in May 1933, and that other members of the crew, including still photographer Roy Clark, returned from the Arctic in Apr 1933, after a ten-month stay. The location camp chef, Emil Ottinger, was hired from the kitchen of the Roosevelt Hotel in Hollywood, according to an unidentified contemporary source found in the AMPAS files. The same source also noted that the production cost $1.5 million and employed forty-two cameramen and technicians and six airplane pilots.

The film's preview running time was 160 minutes, indicating that a large amount of footage was cut for the final release prints. According to a *HR* news item, Freuchen spent several weeks lecturing throughout the country in connection with the film's opening. Conrad Nervig won an Academy Award for Best Editing for his work on the production. Modern sources add Edward Hearn as "the Captain's mate" to the cast. Hearn was an assistant director on the production.

DV 16 Sep 1933, p. 3. *FD* 5 Apr 1933, p. 6. *FD* 20 May 1933, p. 4. *FD* 6 Nov 1933, p. 6. *HH* 1 Jun 1933, pp. 5-8. *HR* 25 Jul 1932, p. 1. *HR* 16 Oct 1932, p. 3. *HR* 29 Oct 1932, p. 3. *HR* 12 Dec 1933, p. 2. *IP* Apr 1933, p. 30. *MPD* 15 Nov 1933, p. 2. *MPH* 18 Nov 1933, p. 36. *NYT* 15 Nov 1933, p. 25. *Var* 21 Nov 1933, p. 14.

ESPÉRAME (Spanish language)

Films Paramount; controlled by Paramount Publix Corp. *Dist* Paramount Publix Corp. **1933**; San Juan, Puerto Rico opening: 24 Feb 1933; Madrid opening: 27 Feb 1933; New York opening: 30 Jun 1933; Prod: Oct--Nov 1932 at Paramount studios in Joinville, France. Sd; b&w. 7 reels, 6,279 ft. 70 min. *Country of origin* France. Spanish language.

Supv Florián Rey. *Dir* Louis Gasnier. *Story and scr* Louis Gasnier. *Dial* Alfredo Le Pera. *Photog* Harry Stradling. *Accompaniment* Don Azpiazu, Orchestra.

Song(s): "Estudiante," "Me da pena confesarlo" and "Criollita de mis amores," music by Carlos Gardel, lyrics by Alfredo Le Pera and Mario Battistella; "Por tus ojos negros," music by Don Azpiazu, lyrics by Alfredo Le Pera and Carlos Lenzi; "No es de hombres lamentarse," music and lyrics by Marcel Lattés.

Cast: Carlos Gardel (*Carlos de Acuña*), Goyita Herrero (*Rosario Aguilar*), Lolita Benavente (*Juanita*), Manuel París (*González*), Jaime Devesa (*Esteban Márquez*), Manuel Bernardos (*Sebastián*), Matilde Artero (*Pepita*), José Argüelles (*Mozo*), León Lavalle (*Aguilar*), Luis Arnedillo.

Drama, with songs. [*Not viewed*]. During a masked ball, Rosario Aguilar becomes attracted to a likable young man who sings very well, but just before the time to remove the disguises, the young man suddenly leaves the hall and Rosario is left not knowing his identity. With the sudden death of Señor de Acuña, an old friend of the Aguilars', his son Carlos discovers to his surprise that his inheritance consists only of debts. He decides to take advantage of his singing ability to make a living in nightclubs. Acclaimed by the most distinguished audiences in Buenos Aires, Carlos cannot forget that evening which had such a sad ending, nor the mysterious masked lady with whose eyes he fell in love. When someone in the club tells Carlos that a certain Esteban Marquez is ruining Señor Aguilar by cheating him at gambling and is seeking to marry his daughter, Carlos has a hunch, attends the engagement party and realizes that Rosario is the woman he is seeking. Encouraged by the discovery, Carlos openly challenges Márquez, confronts him with a witness and forces him to return the stolen money. Aguilar recognizes the son of his old friend, and he is happy that Rosario has reunited the two families. *Buenos Aires (Argentina). Masked balls. Romance. Singers. Debt. Engagements. Fraud. Gambling. Inheritance. Nightclubs. Parties.*

Note: The running time listed above was calculated from footage given in NYSA records. *NYT* gives the English translation of the title as "Wait for Me." *NYT* 3 Jul 1933, p. 14.

ESTRELLADOS (Latino, Spanish language)

Metro-Goldwyn-Mayer Corp.; controlled by Loew's, Inc.; Una Producción de Buster Keaton/Una Producción de Eduardo Sedgwick. *Dist* Metro-Goldwyn-Mayer Distributing Corp. Jul **1930**; Havana, Cuba opening: 14 Jul 1930; Barcelona, Spain and New York openings: 17 Oct 1930.; Prod: Mar 1930. Sd (Western Electric Sound System); b&w. 11 reels, 95 min. Passed by the National Board of Review. Spanish language.

[*Supv* George Kann]. *Dirigida por* [*Dir*] Eduardo Sedgwick. [*Dial dir* Salvador de Alberich]. *Arreglo cinemátografico de* [*Scr*] Paul Dickey. *Argumento de* [*Story*] Richard Shayer. *Adaptación y diálogo en español de* [*Spanish adpt and dial*] Salvador de Alberich. *Fotografiada por* [*Photog*] Leonard Smith. *Director artístico* [*Art dir*] Cedric Gibbons. *Editada por* [*Ed*] George Boemler. *Vestuario por* [*Ward*] David Cox. *Música de* [*Mus*] Fred E. Ahlert. *Bailes dirigidos por* [*Dances staged by*] Sammy Lee. *Acústica por* [*Sd*] Douglas Shearer. [*Sd* William W. Hedgecock and Antonio Samaniego].

Song(s): "La reina de mi corazón" and "Estrellados," music by Fred E. Ahlert, Spanish lyrics by Salvador de Alberich.

Cast: BUSTER KEATON (*Canuto Cuadratín*), Raquel Torres (*Elvira [de Rosas]*), María Calvo (*La mamá*), Don Alvarado (*Larry Mitchell*), Juan de Homs (*Un director*), Carlos Villarías (*Jack Colier [Master of ceremonies]*), Lionel Barrymore, William Haines, John Miljan, Gwen Lee, Cecil B. De Mille, Fred Niblo, [Salvador de Alberich (*Un director*)], [Enrique Acosta (*Chamber of Commerce president*)], [Edgar Dearing (*Guard*)], [Lottice Howell (*Singer*)], [Manuel Conesa], [Renée Torres].

Comedy, with songs. [*Print viewed*]. Elvira de Rosas has won a beauty contest in her home town of Rioseco, Kansas. Her prize is a trip to Hollywood, accompanied by her formidable mother and the timid Canuto Cuadratín who is acting as her business manager. On the

train to California, Elvira has the good fortune to meet the famous movie star Larry Mitchell, who offers to introduce her to the management and stars at the Metro-Goldwyn-Mayer studios. Although he is not permitted to enter the studio, Canuto sneaks in, becomes involved in the shooting of a scene and is mistaken for an actor with disastrous results. Larry becomes infatuated with Elvira and invites her to his home. Canuto and Sra. de Rosas arrive in time to interrupt Larry's declaration of love, and Larry receives a severe reprimand from Elvira's mother. The repentant suitor, attempting to further ingratiate himself with Elvira, finds a small part for Canuto in a musical comedy, and he suddenly becomes a hit, but loses his secret love, Elvira, who accepts Larry's proposal of marriage. *Beauty contests. Bumblers. Motion picture actors and actresses. Motion picture crews. Motion picture directors. Motion picture studios. Chambers of commerce. Grauman's Chinese Theatre (Los Angeles, CA). Guards. Latino. Kansas. Managers (Entertainment). Mothers and daughters. Motion picture premieres. Proposals (Marital). Romance. Unrequited love.*

Note: This was a simultaneously shot, Spanish-language version of the 1930 film *Free and Easy* (see *AFI Catalog of Feature Films, 1921-30*; F2.1959), which was also directed by Edward Sedgwick and starred Buster Keaton and Anita Page. Some shots, which featured Anita Page, Robert Montgomery, Trixie Friganza and Jackie Coogan, were reused from the English version but were dubbed. A sequence in the English version featuring Dorothy Sebastian and Karl Dane was not used in *Estrellados*.

CM Jul 1930, p. 676. *Cinl* Jul 1930, p. 29.

ETERNAL FOOLS (EWIGE NARANIM) (Jewish Americans, Yiddish language)

Judea Films. 23 Sep **1930** [©Joseph Seiden; 4 Oct 1930; LU1640]. Sd; b&w. 8 reels, 6,120 ft. Yiddish language.

Dir Sidney M. Goldin. *Scen and dial* H. Kalmonowitz. *Photog* Charles Levine and Sam Schwartz. *Film ed* Louis Schwartz. *Rec eng* Douglas Shearer.

Source: Based on the Yiddish play *Ewige Naranim* by H. Kalmonowitz (production undetermined).

Cast: Yudel Dubinsky (*Grandfather*), Jehuda Bleich (*Morris Rothstein, father*), Bella Gudinsky (*Mother*), Seymour Rechtzeit (*Son*), Isadore Meltzer (*Comedian*), Charlotte Goldstein (*Daughter*), Beatrice Miller (*Son's Wife*), Eddie Friedlander, Gertie Krause (*Babies*).

Domestic, Drama. Morris Rothstein, a factory worker of ordinary means, makes many sacrifices in order that his children may reap the benefit of his labor. In later years, when he has attained wealth and a comfortable position, he finds that his children no longer consider him in their plans, and his daughter-in-law takes over the management of the household. Completely disillusioned, Rothstein decides to destroy the fruit of all his labor, but his father stops him by reminding him that his children's behavior is no different from that of his own and that he too once treated his father in the same manner. He affirms that "we must not destroy what we have built. We must go on." *Children. Family life. Family relationships. Fatherhood. Jews. Self-sacrifice.*

THE ETERNAL JEW (Yiddish language)

Seiden Films, Inc.; Jewish Talking Picture Co. *Dist* Jewish Talking Picture Co. Feb **1933**; Prod: ended late Jan 1933 [©Jewish Talking Picture Co.; 28 Feb 1933; LU3691]. Sd (Seiden Sound System); b&w. 6 reels, 5,710 ft. 63 min. Yiddish language with English subtitles.

Supv Abraham Leff. *Dir* George Roland. *Story* Abraham Armband. *Photog* Sam Rosen. *Ed* Jean Roland. *Mus* Al Kay. *Sd eng* Murray Dichter. *Tech dir* Manuel Peluffo.

Cast: [Leibele Waldman (*The cantor*)], [Celina Breene (*The first child*)], [Rubin Wendorf], [Morris B. Samuylow], [Barney Schechtman], [Bernard Holtzman].

Religious, Yiddish, Drama, with songs. [*Print viewed*]. A rabbi and a *shamis*, the rabbi's assistant in the synagogue, tell the Biblical story of Abraham to a group of children. The rabbi says that with Abraham, the history of the Jewish people commences, and that Abraham's story relates man's progress from idolatry to the conviction that there is only one God. The rabbi narrates the following scenes: After a big star appears over Babylonia and devours four smaller stars, the soothsayers of King Nimrod predict that a man will be born who will overthrow the throne of all kings. Nimrod declares that all newly-born male children shall be killed, and after 70,000 are slaughtered, the wife of Tereh hides in a cave to give birth to a baby, who is named Abram. The child is nourished by angels with milk and honey after his

mother flees, fearful of the spirit of God that appears on the baby's face. As a man, Abram, whose father is an idol maker, rejects idolatry and, after marrying Sarai, leaves with her, his father and his cousin Lot in search of a supreme God. After Abram is captured by soldiers of Amraphel, king of Shinar, his sincerity so impresses the king that he is freed. Abram, upon discovering that Lot has taken an idol with him, destroys it. At the city of Haran, where Abram finds the people sinful and intolerant, Tereh dies. Lot's wife sacrifices the child of Lot's servant to Moloch, the god of Babylonia, as is the custom. Abram and his party barely escape slaughter during an Arab attack. In Canaan, Abram builds an altar to God and soon prospers, but Lot's jealousy leads Abram to give Lot a choice of land, whereupon Lot chooses the plains of Jordan. God promises Abram that all the land within sight will belong to him and his descendants forever. Four Mesopotamian kings invade Canaan and defeat its five kings. Lot sends a servant to Abram for help, and with God's help and 318 armed servants, Abram, who has no knowledge of battle, fights the kings and rescues Lot. As he reaches old age, Abram, who has gained recognition in Canaan as the high priest, fears he will be childless. Because Sarai is childless, Hagar, Sarai's Egyptian handmaiden, bears Abram a son, in accordance with the custom of the time. The son Ishmael inherits his mother's unruly spirit. The *shamis* then tells the story of Sodom and Gomorrah and explains that God refused Abram's plea that he not destroy the sinful cities because Abram could not find even ten righteous people living there. God tells Abram that his name shall in the future be Abraham and that Sarai's shall be Sarah. She bears him a son, Isaac, but the priests of the land demand that the first born son shall be sacrificed to Moloch, a practise to which Abraham earlier refused to object because he didn't want to interfere with the customs of the land. Meanwhile, Sarah realizes that Hagar is trying to usurp her position, and because of this and Ishmael's wild nature, she asks Abraham to cast them out. Painfully, Abraham complies, and the mother and son go off into the wilderness. After Hagar gives Ishmael the last drop of water she has, they fall exhausted, and she puts the boy under a shrub and prays to her idol to do with her son what it wills. In Canaan, Abraham gives a feast the day Isaac is weaned. Later, as Abraham holds Isaac on his lap and envisions the sacrifice that Moloch demands, an angel's hand stays his and Isaac is saved. With the story ended, the children tell the rabbi and the *shamis* the lessons they've learned: that humanity should live in harmony and that their forefathers had a mission to make brothers of humanity. The rabbi says that Abraham did not falter in his mission to humanity and tells the children that they must not despair against the persecution and intolerance of the present day, but carry on the mission for the betterment of the world and the brotherhood of mankind. *Biblical characters. Idolatry. Jews–History. Religion. Religiosity. Revelation (Theology, inspiration). Angels. Babylon. Banquets. Battles. Childbirth. Children. Cousins. Egyptians. Fire. Fortune-tellers. Human sacrifice. Kings. Maids. Marriage. Murder. Ostracism. Rabbis. Soldiers.*

Note: The print viewed was a re-release by Cinema Service Corp. entitled *Avrum Ovenu* or, in English, *Father Abraham*. The film itself was a re-release of a silent film, with narration, an opening section and a few additional sections added. According to *Exh*, this was the first production of Abraham Leff, an operator of motion picture theaters in the Bronx. According to a *FD* news item, Larry Barren handled release of the film for Jewish Talking Picture Co. for metropolitan territories, while Joseph Seiden handled world rights. Modern sources state that the silent film was entitled *Story of the Bible*. Although the film includes songs, no information concerning their identity has been located.

Exh 10 Feb 1933, p. 2. *FD* 23 Jan 1933, p. 2. *FD* 1 Feb 1933, p. 6. *NYT* 2 Feb 1933.

ETERNAL PASSION *see* **CHIJLKU WO MAWASURU CHIKARA**

THE ETERNAL SONG *see* **A BRIVELE DER MAMEN**

EVANGELINE (Cajuns)

Fox Film Corp. *Dist* Fox Film Corp. 21 Sep **1919** [©William Fox; 19 Aug 1919; LP14135]. Si; b&w. 6 reels, 5,200 ft.

Dir R. A. Walsh. *Scen* R. A. Walsh. *Cam* J. D. Jennings. *Asst cam* Benjamin Bail. *Titles and inserts photog* Richard W. Maedler.

Source: Inspired by the poem *Evangeline, A Tale of Acadie* by Henry Wadsworth Longfellow (Boston, 1847).

Cast: Miriam Cooper (*Evangeline*), Albert Roscoe (*Gabriel*), Spottiswoode Aitken (*Benedict Bellefontaine*), James Marcus (*Basil*), Paul Weigel (*Father Felician*).

Historical, Drama. A father reads to his daughter and her fiancé who have been quarreling, Longfellow's poem "Evangeline": In 1775, in the village of Grand-Pre in the valley of Arcadia, a wedding

ceremony attended by all the happy villagers, between Evangeline, the daughter of the wealthiest farmer in the region, and Gabriel, the son of a blacksmith, is stopped by British soldiers who exile the French Arcadians. Gabriel and Evangeline are torn apart and put on separate boats heading south. Gabriel's boat takes him to the lowlands of Louisiana where he and his father prosper, but he refuses other women, longing for Evangeline. For years she searches for Gabriel, also refusing others, and once they almost meet. When they are very old, Gabriel, dying of pestilence, comes to the almshouse where Evangeline is a nurse and dies in her arms. The modern-day lovers, moved by the tale, forgive each other. *Acadia (Nova Scotia). Cajuns. Engagements. Exiles. Fidelity. Louisiana. Poetry. Reunions. United States–History–Revolutionary War, 1776-1783. Village life. Weddings. English. Fathers and daughters. Nurses. Plague. Poorhouses. Soldiers.*

Note: Some scenes were filmed at a ranch near Silver Lake, CA. The film was endorsed by the American Longfellow Society. Publicity indicates that close to 1,000 people were used in the film. The copyright entry and some of the reviews give the film's length as five reels. Among the other screen versions of Henry Wadsworth Longfellow's poem are the 1913 Canadian feature directed by E. P. Sullivan and William Cavanaugh, and the 1929 Fox film starring Dolores Del Rio and directed by Edwin Carewe (see below).

ETR 23 Aug 1919, p. 991. *MPN* 23 Aug 1919, p. 1697. *MPW* 23 Aug 1919, p. 1177. *NYMT* 17 Aug 1919. *NYT* 20 Aug 1919, p. 12. *Var* 15 Aug 1919, p. 71. *Var* 22 Aug 1919, p. 77. *Wid's* 24 Aug 1919, p. 3.

EVANGELINE (Cajuns)

Edwin Carewe Productions; Feature Productions, Inc. *Dist* United Artists Corp. 24 Aug **1929**; New York opening: 27 Jul 1929 [©Edwin Carewe-Feature Productions, Inc.; 1 Jul 1929; LP531]. Mus score and sd eff (Movietone); b&w. 9 reels, 8,268 ft. [Also si; 7,862 ft.].

Dir Edwin Carewe. *Asst dir* Jack Boland. *Scr and titles* Finis Fox. *Photog* Robert B. Kurrle and Al M. Green. *Lighting eng* C. P. Drew. *Film ed* Jeanne Spencer. *Settings* Stephen Goosson. *Master of ward* Charles Huber. *Mus synchronization* Hugo Riesenfeld. *Tech adv* Eugene Hornbostel. *Prod mgr* Louis M. Jerome. *Props* Gene Rossi. *Chief prod aide* Wallace Fox. *Historian* Finis Fox.

Source: Based on the poem *Evangeline, A Tale of Acadie* by Henry Wadsworth Longfellow (Boston, 1847).

Cast: Dolores Del Rio (*Evangeline*), Roland Drew (*Gabriel*), Alec B. Francis (*Father Felician*), Donald Reed (*Baptiste*), Paul McAllister (*Benedict Bellefontaine*), James Marcus (*Basil*), George Marion, Sr. (*René La Blanc*), Bobby Mack (*Michael*), Lou Payne (*Governor-General*), Lee Shumway (*Colonel Winslow*).

Historical, Drama. In the quiet Nova Scotian village of Grand-Pré lives the fair, beloved Evangeline with her father, Benedict Bellefontaine, a prosperous and honored farmer of the Acadian community. Though she admires and is loved by Baptiste, son of the notary, she is pledged to Gabriel, son of Basil, the village smith. Before they can be married, France and England declare war; the Acadians, bound by allegiance to England and by ties of kinship to France, refuse to take up arms against France, and as a result are ordered deported. As the men are herded aboard a British man-o'-war, the governor-general sets fire to the village of Grand-Pré. Suffering from exposure and broken by the sight, Benedict dies in the arms of Evangeline, who then departs for unknown lands with Father Felician. They arrive at Bayou Têche, Louisiana, where former residents of Grand Pré have established a settlement, just missing Gabriel. Through the wilds of the gulf coast, Evangeline suffers many hardships in search of her beloved, refusing the hand of Baptiste, who has meanwhile become a prosperous land owner. Basil offers to aid her in her search for Gabriel, but they are separated by a storm on the rapids. Traveling alone through unexplored country, Evangeline arrives at a settlement of Jesuits; she becomes a Sister of Mercy, though ever hopeful of finding Gabriel. At the end of the war, Evangeline is sent to Philadelphia to care for the maimed and friendless; there, in an almshouse, she is at last reunited with her long-sought beloved. *Acadia (LA). Acadia (Nova Scotia). Cajuns. Colonies. Courtship. Farmers. Philadelphia (PA). Priests. Sisterhoods. United States–History–French and Indian War, 1755-1763. Village life.*

Note: For the 1919 filmed adaptation of Henry Wadsworth Longfellow's poem, see entry above.

FD 14 Aug 1929. *NYT* 29 Jul 1929, p. 23. *Var* 31 Jul 1929, p. 17.

EVER FOR EACH OTHER *see* **ALL THE FINE YOUNG CANNIBALS**

EVER IN MY HEART (German Americans)
Warner Bros. Pictures, Inc. *Dist* Warner Bros. Pictures, Inc. 28 Oct 1933 [©Warner Bros. Pictures, Inc.; 22 Nov 1933; LP4253]. Sd; b&w. 8 reels. 70 min. PCA cert no. 2628-R [3 Sep 1936].
[*Exec prod* Hal B. Wallis]. [*Supv* Robert Presnell]. *Dir* Archie Mayo. *Asst dir* Frank Shaw. *Story* Beulah Marie Dix and Bertram Milhauser. *Adpt* Bertram Milhauser. *Photog* Arthur Todd. [*Asst cam* Carl Guthrie]. [*1st cam* Leon Shamroy]. [*2d cam* Al Green]. *Art dir* Anton Grot. *Ed* Owen Marks. *Gowns* Earl Luick. *Vitaphone Orch cond by* Leo F. Forbstein. [*Sd* Dolph Thomas]. [*Hair* Dot Carlson]. [*Chief elec* Charles Alexander]. [*Grip* Glen Harris]. [*Props* Morris Goldman].
Cast: Barbara Stanwyck (*Mary [Archer]*), Otto Kruger (*Hugo [Wilbrandt]*), Ralph Bellamy (*Jeff*), Ruth Donnelly (*Lizzie*), Laura Hope Crews (*Grandma Archer*), Frank Albertson (*Sam*), Ronnie Crosby (*Teddy*), Clara Blandick [(*Anna*)], Elizabeth Patterson, Willard Robertson, Nella Walker [(*Martha Sewell*)], George Cooper (*Lefty*), Wallis Clark (*Enoch Sewell*), Harry Beresford [(*Eli*)], Virginia Howell [(*Serena*)], Ethel Wales, [Florence Roberts (*Eunice*)], [Frank Reicher (*Dr. Hoffman*)].
Drama. [*Print viewed*]. Mary Archer expects to marry her cousin Jeff when he comes home from studying in Europe in 1909, but when she meets his German friend, Hugo Wilbrandt, she falls hopelessly in love. Despite her family's opposition, the two are married and Hugo takes a position as a college professor. They are extremely happy and grow closer with the birth of a baby boy, after which, Hugo proudly becomes a United States citizen. When the war breaks out, however, Hugo is snubbed by the community and dismissed from his position because of anti-German sentiment. After their child dies, some neighborhood kids stone the boy's dachshund nearly to death, and Hugo, taking pity on his beloved pet, fires a bullet into the dog. When Mary's grandmother offers Hugo a job in the family mill if he will change his Germanic name, he refuses, saying he is not ashamed of it. After Mary becomes ill, Hugo sends her to live with her family and leaves for Germany, saying he will return. However, Mary later gets a letter in which Hugo writes, "They let me be a citizen, but they won't let me be an American," and announces that he is going to fight for *his* people. Mary divorces Hugo and plans to marry Jeff, who joins the army and is sent to France. Mary follows him and goes to work in a canteen. There, she sees Hugo dressed as an American soldier and learns from Jeff that a German spy is in the area. That night, Hugo meets Mary in her room and she realizes that she is still deeply in love with him. Certain that he is the spy, she must choose between her own feelings and her duty to her country. He spends the night with her, and as dawn breaks, she poisons their wine and they die together. *Bigotry. German Americans. Romance. Dogs. Germany. S.S.Lusitania. Marriage. New England. Patriotism. Professors. Spies. Suicide. World War I.*
Note: According to *FD*, George Cooper replaced Frank McHugh who was filming *House on 56th Street*. In other cast changes Frank Albertson replaced Edwin Phillips, Wallis Clark replaced Henry O'Neill and Laura Hope Crews was added. News items in *FD* indicate that Kay Francis and Paul Muni were considered for the leads. Papers contained in the production files at the AMPAS Library report that the film cost $243,000. Modern sources list Donald Meek (*Storekeeper*), Ethel Wales, George Renavent and Claire DuBrey among the players. Modern sources also add the following characters: Elizabeth Patterson (*Clara*).
DV 22 Sep 1933, p. 3. *FD* 19 May 1933, p. 4. *FD* 13 Oct 1933, p. 10. *HR* 22 Sep 1933, p. 3. *MPD* 13 Oct 1933, p. 2. *MPH* 21 Oct 1933, p. 40. *NYT* 13 Oct 1933, p. 25. *Var* 17 Oct 1933, p. 19.

EVER THE BEGINNING *see* **MY GIRL TISA**

THE EVIL HALF *see* **WOLVES OF THE NORTH**

EWIGE NARANIM *see* **ETERNAL FOOLS (EWIGE NARANIM)**

THE EXILE (African Americans)
Micheaux Film Corp. *Dist* Micheaux Film Corp. **1931**; New York opening: 16 May 1931; Prod: completed mid-Mar 1931 at Metropolitan Studios, Fort Lee, NJ [©Oscar Micheaux; 16 May 1931; LP2489]. Sd; b&w. 9 reels. 93 min.
Pres FRANK SCHIFFMAN. *Dir* OSCAR MICHEAUX. *Scr* Oscar Micheaux. *Photog* Lester Lang and Walter Strenge. *Synchronization and score by* Donald Heywood. *Dances and ensembles staged by* Leonard Harper.
Source: Based on the short story "The Conquest" by Oscar Micheaux (publication undetermined).

Cast: Eunice Brooks (*Edith Duval*), Stanley Morrell (*Jean Baptiste*), Celeste Cole (*A singer*), Katherine Noisette (*Madge*), Charles Moore (*Jack Stewart*), Nora Newsome (*Agnes*), George Randol (*Bill Prescott*), A. B. Comathiere (*An outlaw*), Carl Mahon ("*Jango*"), Lou Vernon (*District Attorney*), Louise Cook, Roland Holder, Don Heywood, and his band, Leonard Harper, and his Chorines.
African American, Drama. [*Print viewed*]. Edith Duval, a former maid, occupies a Southside Chicago mansion after it is abandoned by its wealthy meat packer owner. She is part of a wild crowd that likes to gamble, dance and have a good time. One night, when she throws a huge party for her friends, Jean Baptiste, a sincere young black man, draws her away from the crowd and confesses his love for her. Edith is delighted and tells Jean her plans to turn the house into a gambling club. Outraged by the suggestion, Jean declares his desire to take her away to a farm in South Dakota to earn an honest living. Edith, however, scornfully sends him away. Five years later, Jean has become such a successful farmer that he needs a hand with the chores and asks his new neighbors for help. Jean and the head of the family agree that the son will work for him. Meanwhile, Agnes, the daughter, is very attracted to Jean and, although he returns her love, he breaks off the romance because she is white and he is afraid that if they marry, she will face a difficult life. Brokenhearted, Jean returns to Chicago. There, he visits Edith's nightclub, and determined to put Agnes behind him, he proposes to Edith again. This time she happily accepts. Unfortunately, an old lover of Edith shoots her in a jealous rage and Jean is accused of her murder. Upon seeing his name in the paper, Agnes decides to go to his aid. Her father agrees, and before she goes, he tells her that her mother was of Ethiopian descent, so it is all right for her to marry Jean. Just as she arrives in Chicago, she meets Jean, who has been completely cleared of the crime. The two set off for a happy married life in South Dakota. *African Americans. City-country contrast. Farmers. Miscegenation. Nightclubs. African Americans–Mixed blood. Chicago (IL). Dancers. Ethiopians. False accusations. Fathers and daughters. Gambling. Jealousy. Maids. Marriage. Murder. Parties. Proposals (Marital). Romance. South Dakota.*
Note: This film, which was billed as the "first Negro talker," was Micheaux's first sound film. The *Var* review notes that it "runs" only partly in dialogue, the rest of the film using sound synchronization. According to *Var*, Frank Schiffman was the general manager of Leo Brecher Theater Enterprises and personally operated the Lafayette in Harlem. *Var* also notes that the initial estimated cost of the film was approximately $4,500, and that its final cost was $15,000. Roland Holder does a tap dance and Louise "Jota" Cook, a nightclub entertainer, does a "muscle dance" in the film.
Modern sources note that Micheaux filmed the outside of steel magnate Charles Schwab's New York City mansion, without authorization, to represent the Duval mansion in the film. They note further that after a successful premiere in New York, the first showing in Pittsburgh was halted midway by two women members of the Pennsylvania Board of Censors, because, they claimed, it lacked a seal indicating that it had been passed by the state censor board. There was speculation at the time that the real reason was that certain scenes showed a black man making love to a light-skinned woman. Modern sources give the following information about the production: that Micheaux thought that his ending, which ultimately skirted the issue of interracial love, would allow the picture to be shown; that a second version of *The Exile* was made because Micheaux was unhappy with Stanley Morrell's performance; and that many scenes were reportedly reshot with Lorenzo Tucker in the lead role, and advertisements were printed announcing him in the starring role. No extant prints of the Tucker version have been located, and it is possible the film may not have been completed.
FD 15 Mar 1931, p. 5. *Var* 27 May 1931, p. 57.

THE EYES OF FATHER TOMASINO *see* **THE MIDNIGHT STORY**

EYES OF YOUTH (African Americans)
Quality Amusement Co. 25 Jan **1920**. Si; b&w. Length undetermined.
Source: Based on the play *Eyes of Youth* by Charles Guernon, Max Marcin (New York, 22 Aug 1917).
Cast: Abbie Mitchell.
African American, Drama. The play upon which the film is based is about a woman, about to choose among several suitors and careers, who visits a medium and is shown in a crystal ball the future that will result from each of her possible choices. [No other information concerning the film's plot has been located.]. *African Americans. Mediums. Crystal balls.*
Note: This all-black film is probably based on a theatrical production staged by The Lafayette Players, a Harlem company. A contemporary newspaper article describes the film as a feature, but its exact length has not been determined.

Other filmed versions of the play include a 1919 Garson Production, directed by Albert Parker and starring Clara Kimball Young and Gareth Hughes (see *AFI Catalog of Feature Films, 1911-20*; F1.1237) and a 1927 film entitled *The Love of Sunya*, also directed by Parker, starring Gloria Swanson and produced by her own company (see *AFI Catalog of Feature Films, 1921-30*; F2.3241).

F-4 see THE HUN WITHIN

THE FABULOUS SENORITA (Latino)

Republic Pictures Corp. *Dist* Republic Pictures Corp. 1 Apr **1952**; Los Angeles opening: 6 Mar 1952; *Prod:* late Sep—late Oct 1951 [©Republic Pictures Corp.; 29 Feb 1952; LP1641]. Sd (RCA Sound System); b&w. 7,202 ft. 80 min. PCA cert no. 15649.

Pres HERBERT J. YATES. *Assoc prod* Sidney Picker. *Dir* R. G. Springsteen. [*Asst dir* Lee Lukather]. *Scr* Charles E. Roberts and Jack Townley. *Story* Charles R. Marion and Jack Townley. *Dir of photog* Jack Marta. *Spec eff* Howard Lydecker and Theodore Lydecker. *Optical eff* Consolidated Film Industries. *Art dir* Al Ybarra. *Film ed* Tony Martinelli. *Set dec* John McCarthy, Jr. and George Milo. *Cost supv* Adele Palmer. *Mus* Stanley Wilson. *Dance dir* Antonio Triani. *Sd* Earl Crain, Sr. *Makeup supv* Bob Mark. *Hair stylist* Peggy Gray.

Song(s): "La Virgen de la Macarena," words and music by B. B. Monterde and A. O. Calero; "You've Changed," words and music by Edward Heyman, Tony Martin and Victor Young; "A Caridad le da el Santo," words and music by R. Silva.

Cast: Estelita [(*Estelita Rodriguez*)], Robert Clarke [(*Jerry Taylor*)], Nestor Paiva [(*Jose Rodriguez*)], Marvin Kaplan [(*Clifford Van Kunkle*)], Rita Moreno [(*Manuela Rodriguez*)], Leon Belasco [(*Senor Gonzales*)], Tito Renaldo [(*Pedro Sanchez*)], Tom Powers [(*Delaney*)], Emory Powell [(*Dean Bradshaw*)], Olin Howlin [(*Justice of Peace*)], Vito Scotti [(*Estaban*)], Martin Garralaga [(*Police Captain Garcia*)], Nita Del Rey [(*Felice*)], Frank Kreig [(*Cab driver*)], [Clark Howat (*Davis*)], [Dorothy Neumann (*Mrs. Black*)], [Norman Field (*Dr. Campbell*)], [Arthur Walsh (*Pete*)], [Frances Dominguez (*Amelia*)], [Charlie Sullivan (*Taxi driver*)], [Betty Farrington (*Janitress*)], [Elizabeth Slifer (*Wife of Justice of Peace*)], [Joan Blake (*Betty*)].

Romantic comedy, with songs. [*Print viewed*]. In Cuba, businessman Jose Rodriguez finds himself in a dilemma when loan officer Senor Gonzales tells him that he will approve his loan only if Gonzales' son Estaban is permitted to marry his daughter Manuela. Jose reluctantly consents to the arrangement, but soon after, Manuela's boyfriend, Pedro Sanchez, asks him to give his blessing to their marriage. When Manuela learns of her father's arrangement, she and Pedro, with the help of her sister Estelita, try to elope. While hurriedly packing Manuela's belongings, however, Estelita is accidentally knocked unconscious by a flying suitcase. Finding Estelita in distress, Jerry Taylor, an American professor at Whitmore College, takes her in his arms and carries her to safety. Gonzales, angered by the sight of a woman whom he thinks is his future daughter-in-law in another man's arms, calls the police. Estelita, who has fallen in love with Jerry, is disappointed when the professor tells her that he is returning to America soon, and tries to prevent him from leaving by telling the police that he kidnapped her. Meanwhile, newspapers report Manuela's engagement to Estaban, but she has already secretly married Pedro. Soon after Jerry is released from jail, he goes to the Rodriguezes and gives Estelita a spanking. Later, confusion ensues when Estelita, impersonating Manuela, tells Jerry that he spanked her identical sister. Having never met the real Manuela, Jerry believes the lie and apologizes to "Manuela." Continuing her deception, Estelita persuades her father to send Manuela to California to complete her education, and then secures her own passage abroad by convincing her father that Manuela will need her help there. As part of Estelita's plan, Pedro, disguised as a police officer, arrests Estaban for a traffic violation, thus giving Pedro and Manuela the opportunity to elope. Estelita, hoping to find Jerry, and still posing as Manuela, then boards the plane to California without her sister. More complications arise for Estelita at Whitmore College when Jerry shows little interest in her arrival, and when honors student Clifford Van Kunkle falls in love with her. Estelita is eventually expelled from the school when she is caught singing at a nearby nightclub and embroiled in a scandal involving Jerry and the dean of the college, Dean Bradshaw. While awaiting the arrival of her father, who has been summoned by the school, Estelita panics and orders Manuela to come to California immediately. The Rodriguez sisters manage to keep up their charade long enough for Estelita and

Jerry to take their place at the altar, but just as they are about to be married, Jose, under the impression that it is Manuela who is about to marry Jerry, bursts into the chapel with a gun. After learning the truth, though, Jose accepts Manuela's marriage to Pedro and permits Estelita to stay in California and marry Jerry. *Cubans. Elopement. Fathers and daughters. Impersonation and imposture. Professors. Sisters. Americans in foreign countries. Bankers. Blackmail. Dancers. Engagements. False accusations. Fistfights. Loans. Marriage–Arranged. Marriage–Secret. Nightclubs. Pregnancy. Scandal. Singers. Sneezing.*

Note: Working titles for this film were: *Girl From Panama* and *An Old Spanish Custom*. Estelita's onscreen credit reads, "Estelita, the Toast of Pan America." She is credited in some reviews as Estelita Rodriguez.

Box 29 Mar 1952. *DV* 24 Oct 1951. *DV* 7 Mar 1952, p. 3. *Exh* 9 Apr 1952, p. 3271. *FD* 3 Apr 1952, p. 10. *Har* 22 Mar 1952, pp. 46-47. *HR* 28 Sep 1951, p. 23. *HR* 19 Oct 1951, p. 13. *HR* 10 Mar 1952, p. 3. *MPHPD* 29 Mar 1952, p. 1298. *Var* 26 Mar 1952, p. 6.

THE FACE AT YOUR WINDOW (Russian Americans)

Fox Film Corp. *Dist* Fox Film Corp. 31 Oct **1920** [©William Fox; 12 Nov 1920; LP15924]. Si; b&w. 7 reels.

Pres William Fox. *Dir* Richard Stanton. *Scen* Edward Sedgwick. *Story* Max Marcin. *Cam* Horace G. Plimpton, Jr.

Cast: Gina Reilly (*Ruth Kravo*), Earl Metcalfe (*Frank Maxwell*), Edward Roseman (*Comrade Kelvin*), Boris Rosenthal (*Ivan Koyloff*), Walter McEwen (*Hiram Maxwell*), Diana Allen (*"Dot" Maxwell*), Alice Reeves (*Ethel Harding*), Fraser Coulter (*Nicholas Harding*), William Corbett (*Steve Drake*), Robert Cummings (*Kravo*), Henry Armetta (*Danglo*), Frank Farrington (*District attorney*).

Social, Drama. Hiram Maxwell and Nicholas Harding, both factory owners, exhibit two different philosophies of management: Maxwell is sympathetic to his employees while Harding remains blind to the needs of his workers. Maxwell's son Frank is engaged to Harding's daughter Ethel but fancies Ruth Kravo, a Russian immigrant who also works at the factory. While leaving the factory one night, Frank is stabbed in the back, and Ruth is arrested although her jealous labor agitator admirer Ivan Koyloff is the more likely suspect. Released on lack of evidence, Ruth becomes a secret agent, spying on her fellow Russians. One day a stranger, Comrade Kelvin, comes to town and secretly organizes the workers, preparing them to strike. The employers, fearing trouble, meet and decide to cooperate with the men. Harding reneges on his promises, however, and the next morning issues an order for longer hours and no wage increase. This precipitates a revolt among the workers, and the American Legion is called to establish peace. Frank calms the mob with a patriotic speech, and one of the labor leaders steps forth and offers his hand, while Frank extends his other hand to Ruth. *Employer-employee relations. Factories. Factory owners. Immigrants. Labor agitators. Mobs. Russian Americans. Strikes and lockouts. American Legion. Bolshevists and Bolshevism. False arrests. Knife wounds. Labor leaders. Patriotism. Secret agents.*

Note: The copyright catalog states the length of this film is eight reels, *MPW* states six reels and *Wid's* lists 7,000 feet. Although not an obvious element in the final film, a pre-production news item describes the story as a cautionary tale about runaway immigration. Advertisements for the film include pictures of hooded Klansmen, and one review mentions the fact that the American Legion members were dressed inexplicably in traditional Ku Klux Klan robes. One source credits Max Marcin, who was a well-known playwright, with writing the "drama," but it is unclear whether this term refers to a stage play or an original screen story. All other sources credit Marcin with the "story," and no evidence of the existence of a stage play has been found.

ETR 11 Dec 1919, p. 126. *MPN* 7 Aug 1920, pp. 1046-47. *MPW* 11 Dec 1920, p. 768. *Wid's* 14 Nov 1920, p. 19.

THE FACE BEHIND THE MASK (Hungarian Americans)

Columbia Pictures Corp. *Dist* Columbia Pictures Corp. 16 Jan **1941**; *Prod:* 6 Nov—26 Nov 1940 [©Columbia Pictures Corp.; 10 Feb 1941; LP10254]. Sd (Western Electric Mirrophonic Recording); b&w. 6,123 ft. 66 or 69 min. PCA cert no. 6850.

[*Exec prod* Irving Briskin]. [*Prod* Wallace MacDonald]. *Dir* Robert Florey]. [*Asst dir* Milton Carter and William Mull]. *Scr* Allen Vincent and Paul Jarrico. *Story* Arthur Levinson. *Dir of photog* Franz Planer. *Art dir* Lionel Banks. *Film ed* Charles Nelson. *Mus dir* M. W. Stoloff. [*Sd eng* George Cooper].

Source: Based on the radio play *Interim* by Thomas Edward O'Connell (broadcast undetermined).

Cast: PETER LORRE (*Janos Szabo*), Evelyn Keyes (*Helen Williams*), Don Beddoe (*Jim O'Hara*), George E. Stone (*Dinky*), John Tyrrell (*Watts*), Stanley Brown (*Harry*), Al Seymour (*Benson*), James Seay (*Jeff* [*Jeffries*]), Warren Ashe (*Johnson*), Charles Wilson

(*Chris O'Brien*), George McKay (*Terry Finnegan*), [Ben Taggart (*Dr. Jones*)], [Mary Currier (*Nurse Kritzer*)], [Sarah Edwards (*Mrs. Perkins*)], [Frank Reicher (*Dr. Cheever*)], [Ralph Peters (*Cook*)], [Al Hill (*Horton*)], [Walter Soderling (*Harris*)], [Lee Prather (*Immigration officer*)], [David Oliver (*Steward*)], [John Dilson (*Anderson*)], [Joel Friedkin (*Mr. Perkins*)], [Lee Phelps (*Brown*)], [Sam Ash (*Cary*)], [Ed Stanley (*Dr. Beckett*)], [Claire Rochelle (*Nurse Bailey*)], [Walter Merrill (*Joe*)], [Harry Strang (*Clerk Stimson*)], [Al Bridge (*Horgan*)], [Lee Shumway (*Policeman*)], [Eddie Foster (*City slicker*)], [Chuck Hamilton (*Gas station attendant*)], [Bill Lally (*Wilson*)], [Al Rhein], [Ernie Adams], [Victor Travers], [E. L. Dale], [Almeda Fowler], [Bessie Wade], [Jack Gardner].

Crime, Drama. [*Print viewed*]. Hungarian immigrant Janos Szabo docks in New York, brimming with enthusiasm for his new land. On the street he is befriended by police lieutenant Jim O'Hara, who sends him to Terry Finnegan's hotel. There, Janos rents a room and works as a dishwasher in the café, dreaming of the day when he will be able to send for his sweetheart in Hungary. Janos' dreams are shattered, however, when his face is hideously disfigured in a hotel fire. Feeling responsible for directing Janos to the hotel, O'Hara leaves a note for him at the hospital. Janos eagerly awaits the removal of his bandages so that he can look for work as a watchmaker but then sees his grisly reflection in the mirror. Unable to find employment because of his appearance, Janos writes his fiancée a farewell letter and is contemplating suicide when a passerby asks him for a match. Horrified by Janos' face, the man runs away, dropping his wallet in haste. Then, from out of the shadows steps Dinky, a petty thief who suggests they split the money in the man's wallet. Dinky and Janos become friends and roommates, but soon the money is gone and they are reduced to living in a junkyard. When Dinky becomes ill and desperately needs medical attention, Janos uses his mechanical aptitude to rob a safe. Janos' criminal abilities bring him to the attention of Watts and Benson, two former members of Dinky's gang, who propose they go into partnership. Hoping to raise enough money to pay for plastic surgery, Janos accepts their offer and visits Dr. Cheever, a plastic surgeon. Dr. Cheever is on vacation, but his assistant offers to make Janos a temporary mask until the doctor returns. Soon after Janos and his gang rob the opera box office, Jeff Jeffries, the gang's former leader who has just been released from prison, arrives to challenge Janos' authority. Janos appeases Jeff by offering him a cut from the robbery and welcoming him to join the reconstituted gang. Janos' new mask conceals his hideous appearance, but when Dr. Cheever offers no hope for surgery, Janos angrily runs out of the office and into the street, where he collides with Helen Williams, a blind girl. Janos offers to carry Helen's boxes of beads home, and a friendship springs up between the disfigured man and the sightless girl. When Helen tells Janos that she is content to live in a world of sounds, he bitterly spits out the story of his disfigurement and receives sympathy from Helen. Later, when Helen hears a radio broadcast discussing Janos' most recent theft, she denounces the robbers, and Janos decides to go straight. After announcing his intentions to the gang, Janos gives Dinky his new address and confides that has bought a house in the country and plans to marry Helen. Jeff, however, is suspicious of Janos' motives, and when he finds the card that O'Hara gave Janos in the hospital, he is certain he has been double-crossed and beats Janos' address out of Dinky. The next morning, Janos drives Helen to their new house. As they sit down to their first breakfast together, Jeff arrives to interrupt their newfound tranquility. While Jeff occupies Janos in the house, the others plant a bomb in his car. Their task completed, the gang drives off and then shoots Dinky, pushing him out of the car and leaving him for dead. Wounded, Dinky drags himself to a gas station to warn Janos about the bomb. Because Janos does not have a phone, Dinky calls his neighbors and asks them to bring him to the phone. As Janos drives away with his neighbors, Helen decides to unpack the car. When Dinky warns him about the bomb, which is connected to the car radio, Janos rushes home, arriving just as Helen turns on the radio and detonates the bomb. After Helen dies in his arms, Janos visits Dinky and learns of Jeff's plans to fly to Mexico that night. Janos forces Dinky to promise that he will return home to his mother and buy a farm, and then leaves. Soon after, O'Hara receives an anonymous letter, informing him that Jeff's gang can be found in a patch of the Arizona desert one week from Friday and instructing him that the reward is to be paid to Dinky's mother. Meanwhile, Jeff and

the others board the plane for Mexico, unaware that Janos is their pilot. Janos lands the plane in the desert, sentencing them to die. After tying Janos to the plane, the gang, crazed with thirst, strikes out into the desert to look for help. One week later, O'Hara arrives to keep his appointment and finds the bodies scattered throughout the desert and a note on Janos' body thanking him for his kindness. Burns. Disfiguration. Disillusionment. Thieves. Arizona. Blindness. Bombs. Deserts. Despair. Fires. Hotels. Hungarian Americans. Immigrants. Masks. New York City. Physicians. Plastic surgeons. Police. Revenge. Rewards. Self-sacrifice.

Note: The film opens with the following prologue: "Just a few years ago—when a voyage to America meant adventure and not flight...when a quota was a number and not a lottery prize to be captured by a lucky few..." A pre-production news item in *FD* lists Irmgard von Cube as the film's author, but the extent of von Cube's contribution to the released film has not been determined. This was director Robert Florey's first picture under his Columbia contract. According to a modern source, Peter Lorre's "mask" was created by using white powder and two pieces of tape.

Box 15 Feb 1941. *DV* 24 Feb 1941. *FD* 26 Jun 1940. *FD* 15 Feb 1941, p. 10. *HR* 22 Nov 1940, p. 8. *HR* 24 Apr 1941, p. 4. *MPHPD* 5 Apr 1941, p. 100. *NYT* 7 Feb 1941, p. 23. *Var* 12 Feb 1941, p.14.

THE FACE OF MARBLE (Haitian Americans)
Monogram Pictures Corp. *Dist* Monogram Pictures Corp. 19 Jan **1946**; Prod: early—mid Oct 1945 [©Monogram Pictures Corp.; 19 Jan 1946; LP223]. Sd (Western Electric Mirrophonic Recording); b&w. 7 reels. 72 min. PCA cert no. 11286.

[*Prod* Jeffrey Bernerd]. *Dir* William Beaudine. *Asst dir* Theodore Joos. *Scr* Michel Jacoby. *Orig story* William Thiele and Edmund Hartmann. *Dir of photog* Harry Neumann. [*2d cam* Al Nicklin]. *Spec eff* Robert Clark. [*Spec optical eff* Larry Glickman]. [*Transparency projection shots* Mario Castenaro]. *Ed* William Austin. *Set dec* Vin Taylor. *Mus dir* Edward Kay. *Sd rec* Tom Lambert. [*Re-rec and eff mixer* Joseph I. Kane]. [*Mus mixer* William H. Wilmarth]. *Prod mgr* Glenn Cook. *Tech dir* David Milton.

Cast: John Carradine [(*Professor Charles Randolph*)], Claudia Drake [(*Elaine*)], Robert Shayne [(*David Cochran*)], Maris Wrixon [(*Linda Sinclair*)], Willie Best [(*Shadrach*)], Thomas E. Jackson [(*Norton*)], Rosa Rey [(*Maria*)], [Neal Burns (*Detective, Jeff*)], [Donald Kern, Allan Ray (*Photographers*)], [General, a dog (*Brutus*)], [Clark Kuney (*Fisherman, corpse*)], [Carl Wester (*Cop*)].

Horror, Science fiction. [*Print viewed*]. In the basement laboratory of a lone cliffhouse, Professor Charles Randolph, a brain surgeon, is aided by fellow scientist David Cochran in attempting the revivification of a recently drowned sailor, using electric shock. As Charles's young wife Elaine enters the lab, the victim's body stirs, his hair turns white, and his face becomes frozen, like marble, before he again dies. Charles then has the coast guard return the body to the scene of the shipwreck. After Elaine unsuccessfully pleads with David to stop her husband's sinister experiments, Maria, the house maid who is maniacally devoted to Elaine, places a voodoo doll under David's pillow to make him fall in love with Elaine and support her. Her plot fails, however, when David burns the voodoo doll in acid, and Maria places a curse on the house. Meanwhile, after the coroner finds the sailor's death to be caused by electric shock, not drowning, homicide inspector Norton accuses Charles of tampering with the corpse. Charles next kills Elaine's faithful Great Dane, Brutus, and shocks him alive again. Although the dog is now immortal, he becomes extremely dangerous. Then in an effort to keep David at the house, Charles sends for his fiancée, Linda Sinclair. On her first night there, Brutus enters through Linda's closed bedroom window and terrifies her. The next morning, Norton announces that local stock farm animals were found dead with their throats ripped apart and their blood drained. Realizing that Brutus was responsible, Elaine becomes angry at Charles. Linda and David prepare to leave, but that night, still hoping that David will choose Elaine, Maria places a deadly potion in Elaine's room, believing Linda is sleeping there, and Elaine is asphyxiated. David and Charles revivify her, but, in her delirium, she calls only David's name, and Linda is convinced that Elaine is in love with him. When Charles finds an incense burner in Elaine's room, he realizes that Maria killed her with a root used in the voodoo death ritual. Maria then places Elaine in a trance and orders her to stab Charles. Maria accuses David of the murder, and Norton arrests him. David fears Linda will not be safe at the house with Maria and flees the police, while Shadrach, the butler, confesses he saw Elaine stab Charles. At the house, Brutus and Elaine nearly attack

Linda, but David's sudden arrival saves her. Later, Maria is found dead from the death root, and two pairs of footprints, human and canine, are seen walking out to sea. *Experiments, Human. Mad scientists. Revivification. Voodoo. Asphyxia. Brain surgery. Butlers. Cruelty to animals. Death and dying. Dogs. Electrocution. Engagements. Loyalty. Marriage. Murder. Obsession. Police inspectors. Psychological torment. Romantic rivalry. Spells. Suicide.*

Box 26 Jan 1946. *DV* 17 Jan 1946, p. 3. *FD* 19 Feb 1946, p. 10. *HR* 5 Oct 1945, p. 20. *HR* 19 Oct 1945, p. 14. *HR* 17 Jan 1946, p. 3. *MPHPD* 26 Jan 1946, p. 2818. *Var* 13 Feb 1946, p. 10.

FAIR LADY (Italian Americans)
Bennett Pictures Corp. *Dist* United Artists Corp. 19 Mar **1922** [©Bennett Pictures Corp.; 18 Mar 1922; LP17661]. Si; b&w. 7 reels, 6,400 ft.
Prod Whitman Bennett. *Dir* Kenneth Webb. *Scen* Dorothy Farnum. *Photog* Harry Stradling and Edward Paul.
Source: Based on the novel *The Net* by Rex Beach (New York, 1912).
Cast: Betty Blythe (*Countess Margherita*), Thurston Hall (*Caesar Maruffi*), Robert Elliott (*Norvin Blake*), Gladys Hulette (*Myra Nell Drew*), Florence Auer (*Lucrezia*), Walter James (*Gian Norcone*), Macey Harlam (*Count Modena*), Henry Leone (*Riccardo*), Effingham Pinto (*Count Martinello*), Arnold Lucy (*Uncle Bernie Drew*).
Crime, Melodrama. In Sicily, Cardi, a Mafia leader of unknown identity, sends warnings to Countess Margherita that she must not marry Count Martinello. En route to the wedding Martinello is murdered by Cardi's band, and Norvin Blake, a wounded young American, makes his way to the countess and breaks the news, and she swears to avenge the death of her beloved. Several years later, in New Orleans, Margherita, posing as a nurse, meets Blake, and he declares his love for her. Recognizing Norcone, a giant laborer, as the leader of the band that killed Martinello, Blake has him arrested after engaging him in a hand-to-hand fight. Maruffi, a suitor for the hand of Margherita, is discovered to be Cardi. The Italian-Sicilian colony is aroused against him, and during a fight between Blake and Cardi, the latter is stabbed by Margherita's maid; Blake finally wins Margherita. *Italian Americans. Italians. Mafia. New Orleans (LA). Nobility. Nurses. Revenge. Sicily.*

ETR 25 Mar 1922, p. 1221. *FD* 26 Mar 1922. *MPW* 1 Apr 1922, p. 554. *MPW* 22 Apr 1922, p. 875. *Var* 24 1922, p. 41.

THE FALL OF A NATION (Immigrants)
National Drama Corp. *Dist* V-L-S-E, Inc. 18 Sep **1916** [©National Drama Corp.; 6 Jun 1916; LP8495]. Si; b&w. 7-8 reels.
Dir Thomas Dixon. *Scen* Thomas Dixon. *Cam* William C. Thompson, John W. Boyle, Claude H. "Bud" Wales and Jack R. Young. *Art dir* G. H. Percival. *Tech dir* H. L. Jackson. *Mus accompaniment comp* Victor Herbert. *Asst to the dir* Bartley Cushing and George L. Sargent.
Source: Based on the novel *The Fall of a Nation: A Sequel to The Birth of a Nation* by Thomas Dixon (Chicago and New York, 1916).
Cast: Lorraine Huling (*Virginia Holland*), Percy Standing (*Charles Waldron*), Arthur Shirley (*John Vassar*), Flora MacDonald (*Angela Benda*), Paul Willis (*Billy*), Philip Gastrock (*Thomas*), C. H. Geldart (*General Arnold*), Leila Frost, Edna May Wilson, Mildred Bracken, May Geraci, Beulah Burns, A. E. Witting, Ernest Butterworth.
Drama. American millionaire Charles Waldron heads a German-backed conspiracy to overthrow the United States by arming the nation's immigrants. The takeover succeeds, and Charles appoints himself Prince. Virginia Holland, a suffragette and a peace activist, feigns support for the new regime and is given a high government position by Charles, who always has loved her. In secret, however, Virginia rejects her commitment to peace and organizes the "Daughters of Jael," a group of women dedicated to the overthrow of the immigrant government. The women first flirt with the soldiers of the occupying army and then, when the men drop their guard, they kill them. With the help of other vigilante groups, the women finally restore the United States government, and Virginia makes plans to marry Congressman John Vassar who, before the immigrant takeover, had been lobbying hard for increased American military preparedness. *Conspiracy. Coups d'état. Secret societies. Women in politics. Immigrants. Millionaires. Pacifism and pacifists. Soldiers. Suffragettes. United States. Congress.*
Note: Victor Herbert's score for this film was the first original score to be written entirely for a film. The score for *Civilization* by Victor Schertzinger was

written later, although that film was released earlier. According to contemporary news items, *The Fall of a Nation* was shown extensively in the European war zones and in various cities of Russia. This was the first film of the National Drama Corp., whose studio was in Hollywood. The film had its premiere in New York on 6 Jun 1916 and showed in other big cities before its national release on 18 Sep 1916 by V-L-S-E, Inc. Bartley Cushing and George L. Sargent were described in various sources as assistants to the director. Cushing also was described as the principal stage director. Because Sargent was a director in his own right, and Thomas Dixon, who is credited in reviews as the director, was a novelist and playwright, the division of responsibility of the film is unclear. According to the 1918 *MPSD*, Wiley J. Gibson worked on the film in some capacity, and Henry I. MacMahon was the press representative.

Motog 24 Jun 1916, p. 1450. *MPN* 10 Jun 1916, p. 3551. *MPN* 24 Jun 1916, p. 3877. *MPN* 16 Dec 1916, p. 3781. *MPW* 24 Jun 1916, p. 2256. *MPW* 7 Oct 1916, p. 135. *NYDM* 3 Jun 1916, p. 26. *NYDM* 10 Jun 1916, p. 25. *NYDM* 17 Jun 1916, p. 22. *NYDM* 26 Aug 1916, p. 30. *NYT* 7 Jun 1916, p. 11. *Var* 9 Jun 1916, p. 23. *Wid's* 15 Jun 1916, p. 651.

A FALLEN IDOL (Hawaiians)
Fox Film Corp. *Dist* Fox Film Corp. 18 May **1919**. Si; b&w. 5 reels.
Dir Kenean Buel. *Asst dir* John Kellette. *Scen* E. Lloyd Sheldon. *Cam* Joseph Ruttenberg.
Cast: Evelyn Nesbit (*Princess Laone*), Lillian Lawrence (*Mrs. Parrish*), Sidney Mason (*Keith Parrish*), Lyster Chambers (*Stephen Brainard*), Pat J. Hartigan (*Brainard's chief mate*), Harry Semels (*Tushau*), Thelma Parker (*Lato*), Marie Newton (*Elsie Blair*), Fred C. Williams (*Keith's father*).
Drama. Princess Laone, a Hawaiian composer staying in Santa Barbara as the protégée of society matron Mrs. Parrish, falls in love with her nephew, Keith Parrish. Mrs. Parrish convinces Laone that they must not marry because of the difference in their races, so when Keith proposes, Laone refuses and attempts to drown herself. Keith rescues her, but then goes to New York to see his dying father. When he returns, he finds that Laone left for Hawaii with playboy and smuggler Stephen Brainard after Mrs. Parrish told her that Keith had deserted her. Keith goes to Hawaii where Laone repulses him, because, on Brainard's yacht, she was forced to have sex with the playboy rather than be given to the crew. After Keith is arrested for stealing a necklace that Laone knows was smuggled by Brainard, she returns to Brainard's yacht for proof to clear Keith. After a fight, Laone summons the harbor patrol, Brainard is arrested with the incriminating papers, and Laone and Keith become lovers again. *False arrests. Hawaiians. Princesses. Racism. Rape. Yachts and yachting. Attempted suicide. Composers. Fights. Rescues. Robbery. Santa Barbara (CA). Smuggling. Socialites.*
Note: Some scenes were filmed near Miami, FL. The working title of this film was *Love Redeemed.*
ETR 31 May 1919, p. 2015. *MPN* 31 May 1919, p. 3663. *NYMT* 18 May 1919. *Var* 23 May 1919, p. 57. *Wid's* 26 Oct 1919, p. 25.

FALSE EVIDENCE (Scottish Americans)
Metro Pictures Corp. *Dist* Metro Pictures Corp. 21 Apr **1919** [©Metro Pictures Corp.; 24 Apr 1919; LP13650]. Si; b&w. 5 reels.
Dir Edwin Carew. *Asst dir* Webster Cullison. *Scen* Finis Fox. *Cam* John Arnold.
Source: Based on the novel *Madelon* by Mary E. Wilkins Freeman (New York, 1896).
Cast: Viola Dana (*Madelon MacTavish*), Wheeler Oakman (*Burr Gordon*), Joe King (*Lot Gordon*), Edward J. Connelly (*Sandy MacTavish*), Patrick O'Malley (*Richard MacTavish*), Peggy Pearce (*Dorothy Fair*), Virginia Ross (*Samanthy Brown*).
Northwest, Drama. Scotsman Sandy MacTavish, living in the small California village of Redwoods, betrothes his baby Madelon, as is the village custom, to wealthy Lot Gordon. When Madelon grows up and falls in love with Lot's cousin Burr, Sandy's sense of honor will not let him release her. After Madelon learns of Burr's betrothal to Dorothy Fair, the village flirt, she stalks out of a dance into the woods, where Lot tries to kiss her. Not knowing who he is, Madelon stabs Lot, and Burr, without Madelon's approval, takes the blame for the crime. When Madelon's pleas for Burr incite the townspeople, she convinces Lot to write a statement absolving Burr of the crime in return for her hand in marriage when he recovers. After she stops Burr's lynching at the last moment, Madelon is freed from her obligation to Lot when a redwood falls on him just before their wedding night, leaving her and Burr free to marry. *California. Lynching. Marriage–Arranged. Scottish Americans. Social customs. Village life. Cousins. Dances. Fathers and daughters. Flirts. Kisses. Knife wounds. Self-sacrifice. Trees.*
Note: The title of this film was changed from *Madelon of the Redwoods.*

ETR 26 Apr 1919, p. 1609. *MPN* 3 May 1919, p. 2895. *MPW* 3 May 1919, p. 714. *Var* 25 Apr 1919, p. 80.

A FAMILY AFFAIR see **DAUGHTERS COURAGEOUS**

FAMILY REUNION see **DAUGHTERS COURAGEOUS**

THE FAMILY WAY see **FULL OF LIFE**

FANNIE HURST'S SYMPHONY OF SIX MILLION see **SYMPHONY OF SIX MILLION**

EL FANTASMA DE MEDIA NOCHE see **EL CRIMEN DE MEDIA NOCHE**

THE FAR HORIZONS (Native Americans, Hidatsa, Shoshoni)

Paramount Pictures Corp. *Dist* Paramount Pictures Corp. Jun **1955**; New York opening: 20 May 1955; Prod: early Jul—late Aug 1954 [©Paramount Pictures Corp.; 6 Jan 1955; LP4799]. Sd (Western Electric Recording); col (Technicolor); VistaVision. 12 reels, 9,695 ft. 107-108 min. PCA cert no. 17254.

Prod William H. Pine and William C. Thomas. *Dir* Rudolph Maté. *2d unit dir* C. C. Coleman, Jr. *Asst dir* William McGarry. *Wrt for the screen by* Winston Miller and Edmund H. North. *Dir of photog* Daniel L. Fapp. *2d unit photog* William Williams. *Spec photog eff* John P. Fulton. [*Process photog* Farciot Edouart]. *Technicolor color consultant* Richard Mueller. *Art dir* Hal Pereira and Earl Hedrick. *Ed* Frank Bracht. *Set dec* Sam Comer and Otto Siegel. *Cost* Edith Head. *Mus* Hans Salter. *Sd rec* Gene Merritt and Gene Garvin. *Makeup supv* Wally Westmore. *Tech adv* Donald R. O. Hatswell.

Source: Based on the novel *Sacajawea of the Shoshones* by Della Gould Emmons (Portland, OR, 1943).

Cast: FRED MacMURRAY [(*Capt. Meriwether Lewis*)], CHARLTON HESTON [(*Lt. William Clark*)], DONNA REED [(*Sacajawea*)], BARBARA HALE [(*Julia Hancock*)], William Demarest [(*Sgt. Cass*)], Alan Reed [(*Charboneau*)], Eduardo Noriega [(*Cameahwait*)], Larry Pennell [(*Wild Eagle*)], Herbert Heyes [(*President Thomas Jefferson*)], [Lester Matthews (*Mr. Hancock*)], [Ralph Moody (*Le Borgne*)], [Argentina Brunetti (*Old crone*)], [Julia Montoya (*Crow woman*)], [Helen Wallace (*Mrs. Hancock*)], [Walter Reed], [Bill Phipps], [Tom Monroe], [LeRoy Johnson], [Joe Canutt], [Bob Herron], [Herman Scharff], [Al Wyatt], [Voltaire Perkins], [Vernon Rich], [Bill Walker], [Marguerite Martin], [Frank Fowler], [Fran Bennett].

Historical, **Adventure**. [*Print viewed*]. Capt. Meriwether Lewis, secretary to President Thomas Jefferson, is visiting the home of Congressman Hancock, whose lovely daughter Julia has won his heart. He is about to reveal his feelings to her when news arrives that the United States has purchased the Louisiana Territory from France, thereby more than doubling the young nation's size. Lewis greets his old friend, Lt. William Clark, who has just arrived at the Hancock home, but then learns that the President has recalled him to Washington. At the White House, Jefferson places Lewis in charge of a military expedition that is to explore and chart the new territory from the Mississippi to the Continental Divide. Jefferson orders Lewis to continue even beyond the boundary of the purchase, however, proceeding, if possible, to the Pacific Ocean. Lewis wants Clark to share the command of the expedition, but when he returns to the Hancock estate, he learns that his friend and Julia have become engaged. Because Clark was unaware of Lewis' feelings for Julia, the captain forgives him, but his pain at losing Julia is evident. Later, in Wood River, near St. Louis, the two meet the flinty Sgt. Cass, along with most of the men who will accompany them, and Clark is annoyed to learn that a paperwork error has delayed his promotion to the rank of captain. The expedition journeys first up the Missouri in a large keelboat, mapping the river as they go. Upon arriving at a Minitari Indian village, Lewis assures the chief that the United States hopes for peaceful and friendly relations with the tribe. Although the tribal leader publicly acknowledges the sovereignty of the U.S., he secretly plans for his warriors to ambush the expedition when it resumes its course. Assisting him is a French trader named Charboneau, who agrees to lead Lewis and Clark into the trap in exchange for a captured Shoshoni slave named Sacajawea. Seeing a chance to escape slavery and return to her people, Sacajawea asks if she might serve as the expedition's guide, but Clark distrusts Indians and refuses her request. After the white men leave, Sacajawea witnesses a war dance and realizes that the white men are heading into an ambush. She therefore steals a horse and secretly rides ahead

of the departing war party, arriving at the expedition's camp in time to prepare the soldiers for battle. After they defeat the Indians, Clark invites her to remain with the expedition. Continuing up the Missouri, the party splits up, with Lewis' group exploring one fork of the river, and Clark's the fork recommended by Sacajawea. After Sacajawea leaps into the strong current to rescue Clark's book of maps, he begins to call her Janie, a name, he remarks, that means "beautiful." Later, Clark falls ill, and as Sacajawea nurses him back to health, she realizes she is in love with him. Following his recovery, Clark tries to bolster the flagging spirits of the men, but when he dances with Sacajawea, Charboneau attacks him with a knife and claims that she is his. Sacajawea later declares that because he fought for her, Clark now possesses her. Clark gently rebuffs her because of her race, and even though he is unable to explain his reservations, she promises to wait for his marriage proposal. Both parties now reunited, the expedition finally reaches the village led by Sacajawea's brother Cameahwait. The Shoshonis are grateful to the explorers for returning their abducted sister and agree to provide horses for their journey over the mountains. Opposed to this plan is Wild Eagle, the warrior to whom Sacajawea had been promised before her capture. That night, Sacajawea again offers herself to Clark, but he allows her to remain in the tent only to prevent her from being given to Wild Eagle. Cameahwait guides the expedition over the mountains to the river "that leads to the great salt water." A messenger is sent ahead of the party to advise the Nez Perce that the white men are friends. Wild Eagle, however, kills the messenger and paddles into Nez Perce country intending to lay a trap. Meanwhile, Lewis accuses Clark of disregarding the feelings of both Sacajawea and Julia, and demands that the Shoshoni princess be sent home. Seeing that Clark intends to bring Sacajawea along, Lewis uses his superior rank to assume full command of the expedition, and orders Clark to leave her onshore. As the party canoes downriver, Sacajawea keeps pace with them by running along the shore until she collapses from exhaustion. Clark kisses her and places her in his canoe, whereupon Lewis threatens to have him court-martialed, and the two brawl. The party continues down the river until it encounters the Nez Perce ambush devised by Wild Eagle. During the subsequent battle, Clark kills Wild Eagle, and Lewis removes the rope blocking the river. When the expedition finally reaches the Pacific Ocean, the slain are buried, and Lewis claims all of the land between the Rockies and the Pacific for the United States. Back in Washington, D.C. in 1806, Lewis and Clark introduce Sacajawea to President Jefferson. Later, Julia and "Janie" discuss the responsibilities of being a white man's wife, and Julia realizes that Clark loves the Shoshoni woman. "You love him, too, don't you?" Sacajawea asks upon noting Julia's sadness. When Julia realizes that Lewis intends to have Clark court-martialed on her account, she asks Lewis to forego his plan, and to Clark's surprise and gratitude, Lewis desists. At a White House reception later that day, Julia tells Clark that "Janie" has returned to her own people, reading him a letter that Sacajawea dictated. In it, she explains that although the white people were kind to her, they were not her people, the U.S. not her country. "Have happy memories, like ours were, my love," she writes, "all the days of your life." *William Clark. Explorers. Guides. Meriwether Lewis. Lewis and Clark Expedition, 1803–1806. Marriage-Mixed. Romantic rivalry. Sacajawea. Shoshoni Indians. Accidents. Ambushes. Battles. Canoes and canoeing. Toussiaint Charbonneau. Columbia River. Diplomats. Feuds. Fever. Fistfights. French Canadians. Friendship. Hidatsa Indians. Indians of North America. Thomas Jefferson. Letters. Louisiana. Louisiana Purchase. Maps. Missouri River. Rivers. Trappers. Tribal chiefs. Washington (D.C.). The West.*

Note: In the onscreen credits, the film is subtitled "The Story of the Lewis and Clark Expedition. The working titles of this film were *Beyond the Blue Horizon*, *Blue Horizons*, *Two Captains West*, *Lewis and Clark*, and *Sacajawea of the Shoshones*. A *LAT* news item dated 30 Apr 1953 reported that producers Pine and Thomas were negotiating with M-G-M to have Leslie Caron play "Sacajawea". Location filming was done near Jackson Hole, Wyoming, according to the *HR* production charts and reviews. Sacajawea, or "Birdwoman," of the Shoshoni tribe, not only guided the Lewis and Clark Expedition throughout much of its three-year journey, but also acted as a diplomat to some fifty tribes encountered by the explorers. She was sold and married to Canadian trapper Toussaint Charbonneau, who accompanied her on the expedition. The tribe referred to in the film as Minitari is more commonly known as the Hidatsa tribe. This picture was re-released in 1961 as *Untamed West*.

Box 28 May 1955. *DV* 20 May 1955, p. 3. *Exh* 1 Jun 1955, p. 3970. *FD* 24 May 1955, p. 11. *Har* 21 May 1955, p. 83. *HR* 9 Jul 1954, p. 6. *HR* 20 Aug 1954, p. 8. *HR* 20 May 1955, p. 3. *LAT* 30 Apr 1953. *MPHPD* 21 May 1955, p. 441. *NYT* 21 May 1955, p. 11. *Var* 25 May 1955, p. 6.

THE FARMER'S DAUGHTER (Swedish Americans)

RKO Radio Pictures, Inc.; A Dore Schary Production. *Dist* RKO Radio Pictures, Inc. 26 Mar **1947**; World premiere in New York: 25 Mar 1947; Prod: early May—early Sep 1946 [©RKO Radio Pictures, Inc.; 25 Mar 1947; LP995]. Sd (RCA Sound System); b&w. 96 min. PCA cert no. 11735.

Dir H. C. Potter. *Asst dir* James Casey. *Wrt* Allen Rivkin and Laura Kerr. *Dir of photog* Milton Krasner. *Spec eff* Russell A. Cully. *Mont* Harold Palmer. *Art dir* Albert S. D'Agostino and Feild Gray. *Film ed* Harry Marker. *Set dec* Darrell Silvera and Harley Miller. *Miss Loretta Young's cost des by* Edith Head. *Mus dir* C. Bakaleinikoff. *Mus* Leigh Harline. *Orch arr* Gil Grau. *Sd* Francis M. Sarver and Clem Portman. *Asst to the prod* Edgar Peterson.

Source: Suggested by the play *Juurakon Hulda* by Juhni Tervataa (published Helsinki, 1937).

Cast: LORETTA YOUNG (*Katrin Holstrom*), JOSEPH COTTEN (*Glenn Morley*), ETHEL BARRYMORE (*Mrs. [Agatha] Morley*), Charles Bickford ([*Joseph*] *Clancy*), Rose Hobart (*Virginia [Thatcher]*), Rhys Williams (*Adolph*), Harry Davenport (*Dr. Matthew Sutven*), Tom Powers (*Nordick*), William Harrigan (*Ward Hughes*), Keith Andes (*Sven*), Harry Shannon (*Mr. Holstrom*), Lex Barker (*Olaf*), Thurston Hall (*Wilbur Johnson*), Art Baker (*A[nders] J. Finley*), Don Beddoe (*Einar*), James Aurness (*Peter*), Anna Q. Nilsson (*Mrs. Holstrom*), John Gallaudet (*Van*), William B. Davidson (*Eckers*), Cy Kendall (*Sweeney*), Frank Ferguson (*Martinaan*), William Bakewell (*Windor*), Charles Lane (*Jackson*), [Vic Potel (*Farmer*)], [Jessie Arnold (*Motel manager*)], [Drew Miller (*Mechanic*)], [Eleanor Vogel (*Rooming house manager*)], [Sven Hugo Borg (*Dr. Mattson*)], [Bill Caldwell (*Milk truck driver*)], [Mary Newton, John Landon (*Secretaries*)], [Ben Erway, Douglas Evans, Carl Hansen, Harry Denny, Elsa Peterson, Beth Beldon (*Politicians*)], [Lee Kass, Robert Strong, Al Cavens, Mike Lally (*Photographers*)], [Eddie Arden (*Elevator operator*)], [Charles McGraw (*Fisher*)], [Joe Gilbert (*Reporter*)], [Carl Kent, Tony Barrett (*Announcers*)], [Robert Clarke (*Assistant announcer*)], [Jason Robards (*Night editor*)], [Janet Burston (*Girl*)], [Jerome Franks (*Route man*)], [Jim Pierce (*Policeman*)], [Dick Rush (*Polling place owner*)], [Michael Chapin (*Boy*)], [William Bailey (*Father*)], [Hazel Keener (*Mother*)], [Bess Flowers], [Florence Wix], [Dorothy Curtis], [Art Howard], [Larry Steers], [Major Sam Harris], [Jack Gargan], [Mel Wixon], [Brandon Beach], [James Conaty], [Stuart Holmes].

Political, Comedy-drama. [*Print viewed*]. Swedish-American Katrin Holstrom bids farewell to her Midwestern farm family and heads for Capital City, where she plans to pursue a career in nursing. While waiting for the bus, she is picked up by barn painter Adolph, who tries to force her to spend the night in an auto court by pretending his jeep is broken. When Katie shows Adolph just how well the jeep is running, he becomes flustered and backs into a car. The trusting Katie advances Adolph the necessary repair money and is dumbstruck when she discovers the next morning that he has left her nearly penniless at the auto court. Katie eventually makes her way to Capital City, but instead of reporting to nursing school, she takes a temporary job as a maid to rebuild her savings. Although her employers—Glenn Morley, a young Congressman and son of a former U.S. Senator, and his kind but worldly mother Agatha—are impressed by her openness, Katie's supervisor, the crusty Joseph Clancy, warns her not to talk politics while serving. During a political party celebrating the victory of Glenn's fellow Congressman, Wilbur Johnson, however, Katie ignores Clancy's advice and reveals her hostile feelings about Johnson. Later, Glenn, who is attracted to Katie, asks her why she dislikes Johnson, and she tells him that she believes in the right to a minimum wage, legislation that Johnson opposes. Although Glenn is romantically connected to Virginia Thatcher, a political reporter, he and Katie grow close over the next few weeks. Later, when Katie announces that she is leaving for nursing school, Glenn, who is headed for Europe, implores her to stay. She agrees to remain until he returns from Europe, and he suggests that during his absence, she take some night classes. Soon Katie is studying economics and politics and is helped by Clancy and Agatha. Glenn's homecoming coincides with Johnson's sudden death, and Katie finds herself at odds with Glenn's party's choice for his replacement—Anders J. Finley. During a rally for Finley, Katie stands up and begins questioning his dubious voting record. Her protests stir up the partisan crowd, and reports about her behavior attract the attention of the opposition party. To Katie's surprise, the opposition party leader invites her to run against Finley, and even though Agatha swears to fight her, Katie accepts. Although saddened by Katie's disaffection, Glenn helps her to improve her oratorical skills and wishes her well in the race. As the election nears, Finley's lead over Katie grows narrower and narrower. Then, just two days before the election, Adolph approaches Agatha and Finley and infers that, during their trip to Capital City, he and Katie slept together. Although Agatha at first orders Finley not to repeat Adolph's story, she finally agrees with her cronies that using Adolph's lie is the only way to win. Glenn, however, announces he will quit the party if Adolph's story is printed, and when it does appear the next day, he drives to the Holstrom farm, where Katie has gone. Katie accepts Glenn's proposal, but is admonished by her father not to quit the race, but to fight for the truth. Moved by Mr. Holstrom's words, Katie and Glenn return to Capital City and are joined by a repentant Agatha, who gets Finley drunk enough to admit that he is a white supremacist. Finley also tells Agatha that he paid Adolph to lie about Katie and reveals where his fascist cohorts are hiding him. Katie and Glenn track Adolph to a remote lake and, after a fierce fight with Finley's men, are able to force Adolph to issue a public retraction. Katie then wins the election by a landslide and is carried by Glenn over the threshold at the House of Representatives. Congressmen. Elections. Maids. Political corruption. Politics. Romance. Butlers. City-country contrast. Drunkenness. Duplicity. Education. Farmers. Fathers and daughters. Fights. Ice skaters and ice skating. Lakes. Lechery. Mothers and sons. Proposals (Marital). Racism. Rallies. Reporters. Scandal. Speeches. Swedish Americans. United States–Midwest. United States. Congress. House of Representatives.

Note: The working title of this film was *Katie for Congress*. Actors James Arness (who appeared as James Aurness) and Keith Andes made their screen debuts in the picture. Contemporary news items provide the following information about the production: Producer David O. Selznick bought the rights to Juhni Tervataa's play in 1944 and intended it as a vehicle for contract star Ingrid Bergman. When Bergman and Selznick's professional relationship ended in late 1945, however, the title role became open. (Modern sources note that when Bergman dropped out, Selznick struck a deal with RKO that included the rights to the play, the Americanized screenplay, and the services of his contractee, Joseph Cotten, as well as producer Dore Schary, who had not yet been named RKO production chief, in exchange for partial ownership of the property.) Some scenes for the film were shot in Petaluma, north of San Francisco, and other Bay Area locations. Four hundred and fifty extras were called for the political rally scene at the Ebell Theatre in Los Angeles. In addition, some filming was done at the M-G-M studios.

Production was delayed for a week in late Jul 1946 when Loretta Young was hospitalized with the flu. Although RKO wanted the picture to be completed in time for the Nov 1946 Congressional elections, it wasn't released until Mar 1947. Once the "political" deadline had passed, RKO changed the film's title to *The Farmer's Daughter*. HR announced that a Swedish folk song, "High Mountains and Deep Valleys," was to be used in the film, but no song was heard in the viewed print. Loretta Young won an Academy Award for Best Actress for her performance in the picture. Charles Bickford, who returned to the screen after a two-year absence, was nominated as Best Supporting Actor. Joseph Cotten and Loretta Young reprised their roles in a *Lux Radio Theatre* broadcast on 5 Jan 1948. On 14 Jan 1962, a televised version of Tervataa's play, starring Lee Remick and Peter Lawford and directed by Fielder Cook, was broadcast on NBC's *Theater '62*. Bickford revived his role as "Clancy" for that program. Young revived her role for an episode of her NBC anthology program *The Loretta Young Theater*, which was broadcast between Aug 1953 and early Sep 1961. Between 1963 and 1966, ABC broadcast *The Farmer's Daughter*, a television series starring Inger Stevens and William Windom that was also loosely based on Tervataa's play.

Box 22 Feb 1947. *DV* 19 Feb 1947. *FD* 24 Feb 1947, p. 7. *HR* 26 Mar 1946, p. 3. *HR* 24 Apr 1946, p. 12. *HR* 10 May 1946, p. 5. *HR* 22 May 1946, p. 14. *HR* 27 May 1946, p. 31. *HR* 29 Jul 1946, p. 1. *HR* 30 Jul 1946, p. 7. *HR* 23 Aug 1946, p. 3. *HR* 6 Nov 1946, p. *HR* 19 Feb 1947, p. 6. *HR* 27 Feb 1947, p. 3. *HR* 14 Mar 1947, p. 9. *Life* 5 May 1947, pp. 67-69. *Look* 18 Mar 1947, pp. 92-94. *MPHPD* 1 Mar 1947, p. 3502. *NYT* 26 Mar 1947, p. 31. *Var* 29 Feb 1947, p. 6.

LA FASCINADORA *see* **DI QUE ME QUIERES**

FASHION ROW (Russian Americans)

Tiffany Productions, Inc. *Dist* Metro Pictures. 3 Dec **1923** [©Tiffany Productions, Inc.; 5 Dec 1923; LP19732]. Si; b&w. 7 reels, 7,300 ft.

Prod M. Leonard. *Dir* Robert Z. Leonard. *Scen* Sada Cowan and Howard Higgin. *Titles* Alfred A. Cohn. *Photog* Oliver T. Marsh. *Art dir* Horace Jackson.

Cast: Mae Murray (*Olga Farinova/Zita, her younger sister*), Earle Foxe (*James Morton*), Freeman Wood (*Eric Van Corland*), Mathilde Brundage (*Mrs. Van Corland*), Elmo Lincoln (*Kaminoff*), Sidney Franklin (*Papa Levitzky*), Madame Rosa Rosanova (*Mama Levitzky*), Craig Biddle, Jr. (*A press agent*).

Melodrama. Two peasant sisters flee Russia during the revolution and sail to America. One, Olga Farinova, masquerades as a princess, becomes a noted actress, and marries a millionaire's son. Olga repudiates her sister, Zita, who has no illusions about her past life or present poverty. When Olga is shot by Kaminoff, a rejected suitor, Zita is adopted into the husband's family. *Actors and actresses. Impersonation and imposture. Millionaires. Peasantry. Refugees, Political. Russia–History–Revolution, 1917-1921. Russian Americans. Sisters.*

FD 2 Dec 1923. *MPW* 8 Dec 1923. *Var* 31 Jan 1924, p. 23.

FAST WORK (*foreign version*) *see* **LOCURAS DE AMOR**

FATAL FINGERPRINTS *se* **DARK ALIBI**

FATAL FINGERTIPS *see* **DARK ALIBI**

THE FATAL HOUR (Chinese Americans)
Monogram Pictures Corp.; Scott R. Dunlap in charge of production. *Dist* Monogram Pictures Corp. 15 Jan **1940**; Prod: began 28 Nov 1939 [©Monogram Pictures Corp.; 10 Jan 1940; LP9350]. Sd (Western Electric Sound System); b&w. 8 reels. 68 min. PCA cert no. 5984.
   Series: Mr. Wong.
   Assoc prod William Lackey. *Dir* William Nigh. *Asst dir* W. B. Eason. *Scr* Scott Darling. *Adpt* Joseph West. *Dir of photog* Harry Neumann. *Film ed* R. F. Schoengarth. *Ward* Louis Brown. *Mus dir* Edward Kay. *Rec eng* Karl Zint. *Tech dir* E. R. Hickson. *Prod mgr* Chas. J. Bigelow.
   Source: Based on characters created by Hugh Wiley in the "James Lee Wong" short stories in *Collier's*.
   Cast: BORIS KARLOFF [(*James Lee Wong*)], Marjorie Reynolds [(*Bobbie Logan*)], Grant Withers [(*Captain Bill Street*)], Charles Trowbridge [(*Forbes*)], Frank Puglia [(*Hardway Harry Lockett*)], Craig Reynolds [(*Frank Belden, Jr.*)], Lita Chevret [(*Tanya Sarova*)], Harry Strang, Hooper Atchley, Jason Robards [(*Griswold*)], Richard Loo, Jack Kennedy [(*Mike*)], [John Hamilton (*Belden, Sr.*)], [I. Stanford Jolley (*Soapy*)], [Pauline Drake (*Bessie*)].
   Crime, Drama. [*Print viewed*]. When Detective Dan Grady is murdered while on smuggling detail in Chinatown, his friend Bill Street, captain of homicide, investigates with James Lee Wong, "the Chinese copper." Wong finds a rare jade figurine in Dan's desk and visits Chinatown jeweler Belden, who specializes in Oriental imitations. With the help of female reporter Bobbie Logan, Street locates a witness who saw Dan in the Club Neptune the night he was murdered. The club is run by crooked gambler "Hardway Harry" Lockett, who is part of Belden's smuggling ring. Lockett's moll, Tanya Sarova, wants out of the smuggling ring in order to marry Belden's innocent son Frank. When Belden learns of his son's plans to marry, he threatens to talk if Lockett has Frank killed. That night, Belden is killed in his store, which Wong realizes is filled with smuggled jade. Tanya is then found dead, and Frank is arrested on suspicion of murder. The next morning, Street calls all the suspects to his office, and Frank insists that Tanya was dead when he arrived at her apartment and that the radio had been on. During the interrogation, Griswold, the writer of a mystery radio play which Belden sponsored at the request of his financial adviser, Mr. Forbes, is murdered in Street's office. Wong discovers that the play was aired at the exact time Tanya was murdered and contains a gunshot fired at exactly the time a switchboard operator heard one over the phone. A ballistics report then reveals that Tanya, Belden and Dan were all killed with the same gun. Wong goes to Tanya's apartment and finds Forbes, whom he now knows killed Tanya because she was leaving him for Frank. Forbes had rigged a cord to unhook Tanya's phone so the operator could hear the shot on the radio and place the murder during Frank's visit. Forbes now pulls a gun on Wong, who is saved by Bobbie, and Street arrests the killer. *Chinese Americans. Detectives. Murder. San Francisco (CA)–Chinatown. Smuggling. Women reporters. Fathers and sons. Frame-ups. Gems. Jealousy. Jewelers. Molls. Nightclubs. Playwrights. Police. Radio broadcasting. Romantic rivalry.*
   Note: The working title for this film was *Mr. Wong at Headquarters*. For more information on the series, see the entry for *Mr. Wong, Detective* (below) and consult the Series Index.
   FD 24 Jan 1940, p. 4. *HR* 27 Nov 1939, p. 5. *HR* 2 Dec 1939, p. 6. *MPH* 30 Dec 1939, p. 53. *MPH* 20 Jan 1940, p. 46. *NYT* 13 Jan 1940, p. 11. *Var* 17 Jan 1940, p. 24.

FATE DECIDES *see* **TOYS OF FATE**

FATE IN THE BALANCE *see* **THE GRAY TOWERS MYSTERY**

FATE'S CHESSBOARD (Native Americans, Seminole)
Florida Feature Films Co. **1916**?. Si; b&w. 5 reels.
   Supv Thomas J. Peters.
   Drama. [No specific information about the plot of this film has been determined.]. *Seminole Indians.*
   Note: This film, which was completed by Aug 1916, may never have been released. According to a news item, the film's release was to be held up until *The Human Orchid*, an earlier production of the Florida Feature Films Co., sold to most territories on a state rights basis. According to a modern source, *Fate's Chessboard* concerned the Seminole Indians and had a working title of *Fate's Bond*. The modern source also notes that the Florida Feature Films Co. was no longer in operation by the end of 1916. A two-reel Blazed Trail production, released by Arrow Film Corp. in 1920, and also entitled *Fate's Chessboard*, was unrelated to the 1916 film. Florida Feature Films Co. earlier was called Field Feature Films Co. *Fate's Chessboard* may have been made during the time that the company was known by its former name.
   MPW 26 Aug 1916, p. 1416. *MPW* 2 Sep 1916, p. 1564.

FATHER ABRAHAM *see* **THE ETERNAL JEW**

FATHER DUFF OF THE FIGHTING 69TH *see* **THE FIGHTING 69TH**

FATHER DUNNE'S NEWSBOYS HOME *see* **FIGHTING FATHER DUNNE**

FATHOMS DEEP *see* **THE RED MENACE**

THE FBI STORY (Native Americans, Osage)
Warner Bros. Pictures, Inc.; A Mervyn LeRoy Production. *Dist* Warner Bros. Pictures, Inc. Oct **1959**; New York opening: 24 Sep 1959; Prod: mid-Aug—mid-Ded 1958 [©Warner Bros. Pictures, Inc.; 10 Oct 1959; LP17156]. Sd (RCA Sound Recording); col (Technicolor). 13,398 ft. 149 min. PCA cert no. 19140.
   Dir Mervyn LeRoy. *Asst dir* David Silver and Gil Kissel. *Scr* Richard L. Breen and John Twist. *Dir of photog* Joseph Biroc. *Art dir* John Beckman. *Film ed* Philip W. Anderson. *Set dec* Ralph Hurst. *Cost des* Adele Palmer. *Mus* Max Steiner. *Orch* Murray Cutter. *Sd* M. A. Merrick. *Makeup supv* Gordon Bau.
   Source: Based on the book *The FBI Story: A Report to the People* by Don Whitehead (New York, 1956).
   Cast: James Stewart [(*Chip Hardesty*)], Vera Miles [(*Lucy Hardesty*)], Murray Hamilton [(*Sam Crandall*)], Larry Pennell [(*George Crandall*)], Nick Adams [(*Jack Graham*)], Diane Jergens [(*Jennie Hardesty*)], Jean Willes [(*Anna Sage*)], Joyce Taylor [(*Anne Hardesty*)], Victor Millan [(*Mario*)], Parley Baer [(*Harry Dakins*)], Fay Roope [(*Dwight McCutcheon*)], Ed Prentiss [(*U.S. marshal*)], Robert Gist [(*Medicine salesman*)], Buzz Martin [(*Mike Hardesty*)], Kenneth Mayer [(*Casket salesman*)], Paul Genge [(*Suspect*)], [Michael Garrett (*Insurance salesman*)], [Les Hellman (*Kirby*)], [John Truax (*Boyd*)], [Will J. White (*Silvano*)], [Sid Kane (*Metzger*)], [Gil Smith (*Mike Hardesty, age 6*)], [Rickey Kelman (*Mike Hardesty, age 10*)], [Robin Eccles (*Anne Hardesty, age 4*)], [Dawn Menzer (*Anne Hardesty, age 8*)], [Kimberly Beck (*Jennie Hardesty, age 2*)], [Jennie Lynn (*Jennie Hardesty, age 4*)], [Michael Switlick (*Anne's 3-year-old son*)], [Al Paige (*Checker*)], [Richard Boyer (*Ticket agent*)], [Eleanor Audley (*Mrs. King*)], [John Damler (*Denver S.A.C.*)], [George Pembroke (*Chief of C.A.B.*)], [Al Tonkle (*Druggist*)], [Rand Harper (*Assistant Denver S.A.C.*)], [Will White (*J. Edgar Hoover*)], [Luana Anders (*Mrs. Graham*)], [Mary Ann Edwards (*Marge*)], [Elizabeth Harrower (*Clerk*)], [William J. Thomas (*Janitor*)], [Forrest Taylor (*Minister*)], [George Selk (*Organist-janitor*)], [Ann Doran (*Mrs. Ballard*)], [Al McGranary (*Mr. Ballard*)], [Audley Anderson, Elmore Vincent, Britt Nolan (*Farmers*)], [Vera Denham, Fern Barry, Ella Ethridge (*Farmers' wives*)], [David McMahon, John Pickard, Tom Monroe (*Klansmen*)], [Terry Frost (*Craig*)], [Harold McNulty (*Lum Fong*)], [Roy Gordon (*Emmet Reese*)], [Indian sequence: Rocky Ybarra (*Indian killed*)], [Jim Porcupine (*Indian at switchboard*)], [Vince St. Cyr (*Dan Savage Horse*)], [Eddie Little Sky (*Henry Roanborse*)], [Chief Yowlachie (*Harry Willowtree*)], [Charles Bruner (*Bill Smith*)], [Dorothy Sky Eagle (*Rita Smith*)], [Emily All Runner (*Servant girl*)], [Charles Soldani (*Indian on train*)], [and Mary Lou Clifford (*Indian switchboard girl*)], [Guy Teague (*Deputy marshal*)], [Paul Smith (*Albert Shaw*)], [Kay Kuter (*Barber*)], [Trippy Elam (*Shoeshine boy*)], [Sam Flint (*Doctor*)], [Bob Petersen

(*Pretty Boy Floyd*)], [Maurice Wells (*Speaker*)], [Mike Smith (*George Crandall, age 12*)], [Burt Mustin (*Schneider*)], [Guy Wilkerson (*Eberhardt*)], [William Phipps (*Baby Face Nelson*)], [Grandon Rhodes (*Minister*)], [Theona Bryant (*Edith Crandall*)], [Bob Peoples (*Sam Cowley*)], [Scott Peters (*John Dillinger*)], [Herbert Armstrong (*Frank Nash*)], [Jack E. Henderson (*Hardware store owner*)], [Jane Crowley (*Ma Barker*)], [Alan Craig (*Fred Barker*)], [George Khoury (*Alvin Karpis*)], [Angelo DeMeo (*Fred Hunter*)], [Stacy Keach (*Machine Gun Kelly*)], [John Quijada, Gabriel Del Valle, James Porta (*Argentine policemen*)], [Paul Denton, Charles Bateman (*FBI agents*)], [Arthur Gilmour, Patrick Whyte (*Majors*)], [Robert Clarke (*Bartender*)], [Ray Montgomery, Nesdon Booth (*Drivers*)], [Jack Tesler (*Operator*)], [Dorothy Neumann (*Landlady*)], [Ben Erway, Charles Postal (*Justice Dept. lawyers*)], [Jerry Brent (*Western Union boy*)], [William Lovett, Roy Thinnes, Judd Holdren, Morgan Lane, Lowell Brown, Grant Scott, Jeanne Dante, Shirley Bonne, Joan Dupuis, Susan Davis, Barbara Beall (*Guests at party*)], [Herman Rudin (*Hoodlum*)], [Selene Walters (*Polly*)], [Carroll House (*Dover*)], [James Vickery (*Schaeffer*)], [Ed Wagner (*Sawyer*)], [John Varnum (*Breckenridge*)].

Historical, Drama. [*Print viewed*]. Longtime FBI agent Chip Hardesty relates the history of the agency as he has experienced it to an audience of agency recruits: In 1924, before the FBI is actually a government bureau, Chip and his colleague, Sam Crandall, learn that their ineffective and highly politicized organization has a new director, J. Edgar Hoover. That afternoon, Chip proposes to his sweetheart, a pretty Tennessee librarian named Lucy. Before she accepts, she exacts a promise from him that, directly after he meets the new director on their post-honeymoon trip to Washington, D.C., he will resign from the Bureau, which she considers too unrewarding for a brilliant young lawyer like Chip. The newlyweds join Sam on the train to Washington, and are surprised when Sam makes an emotional plea for Chip to remain in the FBI, which he believes could be an effective crime-fighting force under its new leader. So moved is Chip by Hoover's first speech to the agents, an address that demonstrates the director's fire and drive, that he decides to remain in the Bureau for several more years. Disappointed but determined to support her husband, Lucy agrees to the plan, and the next day, the couple is sent south to investigate the terrorist activities of the Ku Klux Klan. On the night Lucy gives birth to their first child, Mike, Chip and Sam finally arrest the Klansmen as they attempt to destroy a newspaper and murder its editor. During the next few years, Chip tackles assignments in various parts of the country while Lucy has two more children, Anne and Jennie. The Hardesty family then settles in Ute City, Oklahoma, as Chip tries to discover who is murdering local Osage Indians, a poor band made suddenly wealthy by the discovery of oil deposits on their land. The Indians fall prey to a veritable circus of salesmen, who peddle everything from patent medicines to casket linings in "official Osage colors." On the night Chip finally arrests white banker Dwight McCutcheon and his nephew for murdering rich Indians and then quietly appropriating their estates, Lucy suffers a miscarriage, and Chip promises to take the family away from "this God-forsaken place." His following assignments take them to the Midwest, where the FBI has begun to track down dangerous gangsters such as Pretty Boy Floyd, Baby Face Nelson, John Dillinger and Ma Barker. After Congress allows the FBI to arm its agents, Sam is killed in a gun battle, leaving a young son named George behind. As the Bureau intensifies its war on the underworld and more agents lose their lives, Lucy's concern for Chip's safety becomes too much for her to bear, and she begs him to resign. When he refuses, she takes the children to live with her parents in Tennessee. Several months and, and finally, Lucy realizes what her husband and family already know: the family must be reunited. On the very day on which she brings the children home, however, Chip is reassigned and the family moves to Washington, D.C. Years later, during World War II, thousands of agents are accepted into the FBI and instructed to round up "enemy aliens." One of the recruits is Sam's son George, who, while struggling through the Bureau's rigorous training program, becomes seriously involved with Chip's daughter Anne, now an attractive young woman. Young Mike Hardesty joins the Marines and is sent to the Pacific, and Chip is dispatched to Argentina to aid in the interception of coded submarine messages. George is stationed in the jungle there, and he, Chip and a heroic agent named Mario are forced to flee approaching *federales*. In 1945, the Hardesty family is grieved

to learn that young Mike has been killed during the landings at Iwo Jima. Following the war, the FBI faces a new threat: international Communism. Using its extensive lab facilities and research capabilities, the FBI tracks down and arrests spies. Chip directs one such case from his desk in Washington. With the help of telephones and radios, the veteran agent coordinates the extended pursuit and ultimate arrest of two New York based Communist spies. The story of his adventurous life with the FBI over, Chip concludes the day's lecture and joins his waiting family, which now includes a grandson named Mike. Their drive takes them past several of Washington's most famous monuments to freedom, including the sculpture commemorating the landing at Iwo Jima. *Arrests. Family relationships. Investigations. Marriage. Patriotism. United States. Federal Bureau of Investigation. Argentina. Bombings. Chases. Communism. Escapes. Espionage. Explosions. Forensics. Gangsters. Grief. Heroism. J. Edgar Hoover. Indians of North America. Interrogation. Jungles. Ku Klux Klan. Lawyers. Libraries and librarians. Miscarriage. Murder. New York City. Oklahoma. Osage Indians. Parricide. Self-sacrifice. Separation (Marital). Shootouts. Spies. Swindlers and swindling. Terrorism. Washington (D.C.). World War II.*

Note: A Dec 1956 *HR* news item reported that Warners had purchased *The FBI Story* from Pulitzer Prize winner Don Whitehead for "a reported sum well over $100,000." The same item stated that Martin Rackin would produce the picture. FBI Director J. Edgar Hoover wrote the foreword to the Don Whitehead book on which the film was based. According to news items, in 1957, Gramercy Pictures bought the rights to a 1950 novel by Mildred and Gordon Gordon, which was also titled *The F.B.I. Story*, and planned to adapt it for the screen using the same title. In Nov 1958, however, the MPAA board announced that it was awarding title rights to Warner Bros., who, according to a *Var* news item, had approval of the FBI to use the title." Later, the Gordons filed a plagiarism suit against Warner Bros., claiming that they submitted a script titled *F.B.I. Story* to the studio before Warners purchased Whitehead's book. Warner Bros. argued that its film was a documentary based on the Whitehead book, while the Gordons argued that the film was work of fiction. The Gordons were awarded $54,000 in damages. According to a 26 Sep 1959 *LAT* article, this was the first film to be made with the full cooperation of the FBI. Portions of the film were shot in Washington, D.C. and New York City, including Yankee Stadium and Central Park.

AmCin May 1959, pp. 286-87, 305-09. *Box* 24 Aug 1959. *Box* 31 Aug 1959. *DV* 18 Aug 1959, p. 3. *DV* 12 Aug 1965. *DV* 20 Aug 1965. *Exh* 26 Aug 1959, p. 4618. *FD* 18 Aug 1959, p. 6. *Har* 22 Aug 1959, p. 134. *HR* 15 Aug 1958, p.8. *HR* 19 Dec 1958, p. 18. *HCN* 24 Sep 1960. *HR* 11 Dec 1956. *HR* 5 Feb 1957. *HR* 18 Aug 1959, p. 3. *LAT* 26 Sep 1959. *MPHPD* 22 Aug 1959, p. 380. *NYT* 25 Sep 1959, p. 23. *Var* 7 Nov 1958. *Var* 19 Aug 1959, p. 6.

THE FEARLESS LOVER (Irish Americans)
Perfection Pictures Corp. 1 Feb **1925** [©Perfection Pictures Corp.; 2 Mar 1925; LP21191]. Si; b&w. 5 reels, 4,656 ft.
Dir Henry MacRae. *Story* Scott Dunlap. *Photog* Allen Thompson.
Cast: William Fairbanks (*Patrick Michael Casey*), Eva Novak (*Enid Sexton*), Tom Kennedy (*Tom Dugan*), Lydia Knott (*Mrs. James Sexton*), Arthur Rankin (*Ted Sexton*), Frankie Darrow (*Frankie*).

Melodrama. Patrick Michael Casey, a young patrolman and the second generation of his family on the force, arrests the brother of Enid Sexton, the girl with whom he is in love. Patrick learns that the boy was forced into a life of crime by Tom Dugan, notorious crook, and determines to bring Dugan to justice. Patrick succeeds in arresting Dugan and thus effects the release of Enid's brother from jail. Enid and Patrick make plans to pound the beat of life together. *Brothers and sisters. Irish Americans. Police.*

Note: *Var* commented, "The policeman is of course Irish, courageous, witty, acrobatic... ".
Var 15 Jul 1925.

THE FEATHERED SERPENT (Chinese Americans)
Monogram Pictures Corp. *Dist* Monogram Pictures Corp. 19 Dec **1948**; Prod: late Sep—early Oct 1948 [©Monogram Pictures Corp.; 9 Jan 1949; LP2171]. Sd (Western Electric Recording); b&w. 60 min.
Series: Charlie Chan.

Prod James S. Burkett. *Dir* William Beaudine. *Asst dir* William Calihan. *Story and scr* Oliver Drake. [*Addl dial* Hal Collins]. *Photog* William Sickner. [*Cam op* John Martin]. [*Stills* Eddie Jones]. [*Gaffer* Lloyd Garnell]. *Spec eff* Ray Mercer. *Tech dir* David Milton. *Supv film ed* Otho Lovering. *Ed* Ace Herman. [*Set dec* Ray Boltz]. *Mus dir* Edward J. Kay. *Rec* Tom Lambert. [*Makeup* Webb Overlander]. *Prod mgr* Allen K. Wood. [*Scr supv* Ilona Vas]. [*Grip* Harry Lewis].
Source: Based on characters created by Earl Derr Bigger.
Cast: ROLAND WINTERS [(*Charlie Chan*)], Keye Luke [(*Lee Chan*)], Mantan Moreland [(*Birmingham*)], Victor Sen Young [(*Tommy Chan*)], Carol Forman [(*Sonia Cabot*)], Robert Livingston

[(*John Stanley*)], Nils Asther [(*Professor Paul Evans*)], Beverly Jons [(*Joan Farnsworth*)], Martin Garralaga [((*Pedro*)], George J. Lewis [(*Captain Juan*)], Leslie Dennison [(*Professor Farnsworth*)], [Jay Silverheels (*Diego*)], [Charles Stevens (*Manuel*)], [Milton Ross (*Pete*)], [Fred Cordova (*Felipe*)], [Erville Alderson (*Professor*)], [Juan Duval (*Dr. Castelar*)], [Frank Leyva (*Jose*)].

Detective, **Drama**. [*Print viewed*]. In San Pablo, Mexico, an expedition prepares to look for two archaeologists, Professors Scott and Farnsworth, who have been searching for the lost Aztec Temple of the Sun, but have been missing for months. Detective Charlie Chan, en route to Mexico City for a vacation with his two sons, Lee and Tommy, and his chauffeur, Birmingham, finds Scott delirious as he collapses on his way into San Pablo. Scott explains that after he and Farnsworth found the temple, they were held hostage and forced to unearth a fortune of jade and gold. Before Scott can name his captor, however, he is knifed to death. The search party includes Farnsworth's sister Joan, who is also his heir; her fiancé, archaeologist John Stanley; Farnsworth's fiancée, Sonia Cabot; and archaeologist Professor Paul Evans. While Chan discusses the case with Captain Gonzales, a poison dart is shot through the window, and Lee sees an Aztec Indian fleeing the scene. Chan and his sons join the expedition, which camps at the foot of the Diablo mountains in search of a stone containing ancient hieroglyphics that Scott said will lead them to the secret opening of the temple. While on night watch, Birmingham catches an Indian named Manuel fleeing the camp, and Chan and Lee follow him. Meanwhile, Stanley sneaks into the secret temple, where he is holding Farnsworth hostage in order to unearth the tomb of an ancient king that contains a fortune in antiques. Stanley orders his henchman, Diego, to kill Chan, but Diego is shot by Pedro, the camp cook, who turns out to be a member of the Mexican secret service. Chan removes Diego's wig and reveals that he was not an Aztec, but an American disguised in order to cast suspicion on the Indians. Stanley, meanwhile, threatens to kill Joan and Sonia if Farnsworth does not cooperate. After Sonia is killed at the camp with Èvans' knife, two search parties go out. Chan's sons find the rock containing directions to the temple, but do not know how to enter it. When Birmingham inadvertently sits on the rock and is pulled inside, Lee and Tommy think he has disappeared. Stanley holds up Joan and a Mexican guide named Jose and brings them into the temple, where Manuel shoots Jose. Chan and his sons finally realize that the rock, which is marked by a symbol of a feathered serpent, is the temple's entrance and enter with Pedro. They knock out Stanley, then Chan explains that Stanley killed Sonia because she had been helping him smuggle Aztec treasures and he wanted to silence her. Chan now prepares for his vacation in Mexico City, but he is assured that the police there also will be needing his help. *Archaeologists. Detectives. Expeditions. Hostages. Mexico. Treasure. Antiques. Aztec Indians. Brothers and sisters. Chinese Americans. Engagements. Fathers and sons. Impersonation and imposture. Mexico–History. Mexico. Secret Service. Murder. Temples. Tombs. Valets.*

Note: The opening title card for this film reads: "Charlie Chan in *The Feathered Serpent*." For additional information on this series, please consult the Series Index and see the entry above for *Charlie Chan Carries On*.

Box 11 Jun 1949. *DV* 20 Jan 1949, p. 3. *HR* 8 Oct 1948, p. 14. *HR* 20 Jan 1949, p. 3. *MPHPD* 12 Feb 1949, p. 4494.

FELIZ ACCIDENTE see **TRES AMORES**

FEU MON ONCLE see **NOCHE DE DUENDES**

FIDDLERS GREEN see **THE RAGING TIDE**

FIDELE see **FOR THE DEFENSE**

FIELDS OF HONOR (French Americans)

Goldwyn Pictures Corp. *Dist* Goldwyn Pictures Corp. 14 Jan **1918** [©Goldwyn Pictures Corp.; 10 Jan 1918; LP11920]. Si; b&w. 5 reels.

Dir Ralph W. Ince. *Cam* George Hill. *Art dir* Hugo Ballin.

Source: Based on the short story "Field of Honor" by Irvin S. Cobb in *The Saturday Evening Post* (13 May 1916).

Cast: Mae Marsh (*Marie Messereau*), Marguerite Marsh (*Helene*), George Cooper (*Paul*), John Wessel (*Hans Grossman*), Vernon Steele (*Robert Vorhis*), Neil Moran (*Judge Vorhis*), Maud Cooling (*Mrs. Vorhis*), Ned Hay (*Lawrence Caltbrop*), Edward Lynch (*Schwartzman*), "Mother" Marsh (*Extra in shipboard scene*).

World War I, **Drama**. Marie Messereau, with her sister Helene and brother Paul, emigrates from France to America, the land of promise,

accompanied by Helene's German fiancé, Hans Grossman. The four find employment, and all goes well until Paul and Hans are called back to Europe to fight in World War I. Robert Vorhis falls in love with Marie, but because a rejected suitor tells him that Marie's reputation is stained, he accompanies his parents to California to forget her. Helene contracts tuberculosis, and when Marie, in seeking the location of a hospital for consumptives, asks several men their address, she is arrested for streetwalking. Robert's father, Judge Vorhis, acquits her, but upon returning home, she discovers that Paul and Hans have been killed in battle and that her sister has committed suicide. Broken, Marie decides to return to France and is about to sail when Robert, who has been unable to forget her, rushes up the gangplank and takes her in his arms. *French Americans. Immigrants. Reputation. World War I. Brothers and sisters. California. France. Germans. Hospitals. Judges. Libel and slander. Prostitution. Ships. Sisters. Suicide. Tuberculosis.*

Note: Several sources imply that Cobb also wrote the scenario. The mother of Mae and Marguerite Marsh made her screen debut in this film as an extra. According to publicity for this film, Mae Marsh initiated an agreement with Goldwyn Pictures that her films would be exhibited without rental cost at any chartered social service or settlement house institution in the United States which requested them.

ETR 19 Jan 1918, p. 555. *ETR* 2 Feb 1918, p. 763. *MPN* 9 Feb 1918, p. 890. *MPW* 19 Jan 1918, p. 411. *MPW* 2 Feb 1918, p. 684. *NYDM* 26 Jan 1918, p. 19. *Var* 18 Jan 1918, p. 42. *Wid's* 24 Jan 1918, pp. 892-93.

LA FIESTA DEL DIABLO (Spanish language)

Films Paramount; controlled by Paramount Publix Corp. *Dist* Paramount Publix Corp. Feb **1931**; Bilbao, Spain opening: 11 Feb 1931; Los Angeles opening: 19 Jun 1931.; Prod: Sep 1930 at Paramount studios in Joinville, France. Sd; b&w. 10 reels, 8,378 ft. 93 min. *Country of origin* France. Spanish language.

Dir Adelqui Millar. *Orig story and scr* Edmund Goulding.

Cast: Carmen Larrabeiti (*Hallie Hobart*), Tony D'Algy (*David Stone*), Félix de Pomés (*Mark Stone*), Miguel Ligero (*Charlie Thorne*), Amelia Muñoz (*Telefonista*), Manuel Vico (*Ezra Stone*), Manuel Russell (*Doctor Reynolds*), Pedro Barreto (*Kent Carr*), Mercedes Servet (*Tía Betty*), José Sierra de Luna (*Hammond*), Carlos Díaz de Mendoza (*Monk McConnell*).

Melodrama. [*Not viewed*]. [The following plot summary is based on the English-language version of this film, *The Devil's Holiday*; character names refer to that version. For further information regarding the English-language version, please see the note below and the entry for *The Devil's Holiday* in the *AFI Catalog of Feature Films, 1921-30*.] Hallie Hobart, a man-hating manicurist in a western hotel, builds up a small fortune through side deals with farm machinery salesmen; thus she meets David Stone, the unsophisticated young son of Ezra, a wealthy wheat farmer, and leads him into falling in love with her. But her brother Mark comes to the city to save him from her intrigues, and enraged by his branding her a cheat, she plots revenge. When David proposes marriage, she accepts him. At the farm, Stone forces Mark to be polite, but Ezra is incensed to learn she does not love his son, and she exacts a price to leave them. Later, Ezra appears at her hotel, where she is holding a farewell party, and she begins to regret her action. When David begins to suffer from mental strain, Hallie returns the money, seeking his forgiveness, and they are reconciled. *Brothers. Farmers. Man-haters. Manicurists. Marriage. Revenge. Wheat.*

Note: While the 1930 English-language original, *The Devil's Holiday*, which was directed by Edmund Goulding and starred Nancy Carroll and Phillips Holmes, was made by Paramount in the U.S., all the foreign-language versions were produced at the Paramount studios in Joinville, France. In addition to the Spanish, German and Italian versions, which were released in the U.S., French and Swedish versions were also produced at Joinville, but no information concerning their release in the U.S. has been located.

The German version opened in San Francisco on 29 Jan 1931 under the title *The Devil's Holiday* translated into German. By the 13 Apr 1931 opening in Chicago, that version was entitled *Sonntag des Lebens*, the title used for later showings in New York and Berlin. The French version, entitled *Les vacances du diable*, was directed by Alberto Cavalcanti and starred Marcelle Chantal and Thomy Bourdelle; the Swedish version, entitled *En kvinnas morgondag*, was directed by Gustaf Bergman and starred Vera Schmiterlöw and Paul van der Osten.

Other language version(s):
Sonntag des Lebens (German language)
1931; San Francisco opening: 29 Jan 1931; Prod: at Paramount studios in Joinville, France. Sd (Western Electric); b&w. 6,743 ft. 77 min. German language.
Dir Leo Mittler. *Orig story and scr* Edmund Goulding. *Dial* Béla Balázs. *Prod mgr* Paul Reno.
German-language cast: Camilla Horn, Willy Clever, Oskar Marion, Leopold von Ledebour, Werner Kepich. [*German version not viewed*]

La vacanza del diavolo (Italian. language)
1931; New York opening: 19 Mar 1931; Prod: at Paramount studios in Joinville, France. 6,718 ft. 71 min. Italian. language.
Dir Jack Salvatori. *Orig story* Edmund Goulding. *Adpt and dial* Dino Falconi. *Photog* Enzo Riccioni.
Italian-language cast: Carmen Boni (*Lina Hobart*), Maurizio D'Ancora (*Robert Stone*), Camillo Pilotto (*Marc Stone*), Alfredo Robert (*Edward Stone*), Cesare Zoppetti (*Karl Thorn*), Oreste Bilancia (*Henry Carr*), Sandro Salvini (*Doctor Reynolds*), Armando Ansel (*May Connell*), Ada C. Almirante (*Bettina*), Mayo Moreno, Enzo Bozano. [*Italian. version not viewed*].
FD 22 Mar 1931, p. 11. Var 25 Mar 1931, p. 71. Var 29 Apr 1931, p. 50.

FIESTA TOWN *see* **THE GAY SENORITA**

FIFTY CANDLES (Chinese Americans)
Willat Productions. *Dist* W. W. Hodkinson Corp. 11 Dec **1921**. Si; b&w. 5 reels.
Dir Irvin V. Willat.
Source: Based on the novel *Fifty Candles* by Earl Derr Biggers (Indianapolis, 1926).
Cast: Bertram Grassby (*Hung Chin Chung*), Marjorie Daw (*Mary-Will Tellfair*), Ruth King (*Carlotta Drew*), Wade Boteler (*Mark Drew*), William Carroll (*Henry Drew*), George Webb (*Dr. Parker*), Dorothy Sibley (*Mah Li*), Edward Burns (*Ralph Coolidge*).
Mystery. Sentenced to be deported from Hawaii, Hung Chin Chung pledges twenty years of service to Henry Drew to escape the certain death that awaits him in China. Rage at his humiliation and inability to marry as a free man smolders in him throughout his servitude, near the end of which he sails to San Francisco with the Drew family. Also on board is Ralph Coolidge, who tries to retrieve from Drew his share of their gold mine, and who loves Drew's secretary, Mary-Will Tellfair. Shortly after their arrival, Henry Drew is murdered; suspicion falls on Ralph, the owner of the murder weapon, a curious Chinese dagger; but subsequent events lead Hung Chin Chung to confess to the crime. *Chinese Americans. Deportation. Hawaii. Indentured servants. Murder. San Francisco (CA). Secretaries.*
ETR 4 Feb 1922, p. 719. FD 8 Jan 1922. MPN 31 Dec 1921, p. 329. Var 6 Oct 1922, p. 43.

THE FIGHT NEVER ENDS (African Americans)
Alexander Productions. *Dist* Alexander Releasing Corp.; Lenox Pictures, Inc. Mar **1948**; World premiere in New York: 3 Mar 1948. Sd; b&w. 5,736 ft. 64 min.
Prod William Alexander. *Dir* Joe Lerner.
Song(s): "Let the Rest of the World Go By," music by Ernest R. Ball, lyrics by J. Keirn Brennan; "Call the Police," music and lyrics by Nat Cole; "The Joe Louis Punch Song," music and lyrics by Sidney and Max Rosenbaum; "Be Nice to Everyone," music and lyrics by Emmett "Babe" Wallace; and "Gone," composers undetermined.
Cast: Joe Louis (*Joe Louis, also known as "The Champ"*), Ruby Dee (*Janey*), The Mills Brothers, Harrel Tillman (*Jerry, also known as "The Caper"*), Elwood Smith (*Howard "Howie" Robinson*), William Greaves (*Frankie*), Emmett "Babe" Wallace, Milton Woods, Gwendolyn Tynes, Gilbert Whyte (*Spider*), William Leftwich (*Cricket*), Roger Furman, Katherine Byars, William Griffin, Bill Dillard, Theodore Eagan, Renaldo Jensen, Virgil Richardson, William Wilson, Archie Smith, Artie Sims and his band.
African American, Domestic, Crime, Drama, with songs. [*Not viewed*]. In Harlem, Howard "Howie" Robinson and boxer Joe Louis, also known as The Champ, admire the sight of their young friend Cricket riding a bike and singing a song that advertises Joe Louis Punch, the product he sells from his bicycle. Cricket offers the men a quick goodbye as he rushes away to attend the homecoming of his brother Jerry, who has just gotten out of the Army and returned from Florida. Cricket and his brother Spider arrive at the house at the same time, and notice a beautiful, new car parked in front. Inside, their sister Janey serves coffee and cake. Cricket and Spider beg to have coffee put in their milk, and, after much coaxing, Janey gives in. Jerry brings a lot of money and a pile of clothes for the family, and Janey's suspicions are confirmed when she sees his gun holster. Yelling at him that like their dead parents, she had hoped the Army would change him, Janey throws Jerry out. Spider, who sides with Jerry, also leaves, but Cricket remains with his sister and the two embrace tearfully. The next day, Cricket again rides his bike and sells punch, and when he sees Howie and The Champ, the two men encourage him to confide his family problems. Howie and The Champ realize that Jerry is none other than "The Caper," the newest racketeer in town. Cricket brings the two men to the warehouse where Spider and his gang of friends spend their time. The boys listen to a baseball game on a stolen radio, and Spider expresses second thoughts about joining his brother "The Caper," in his illicit schemes. Frankie, the toughest boy in the gang, believes that they should join Jerry, and when he calls Spider "yellow," the two come to blows. At that moment, the other boys scream in amazement to see The Champ arrive at the warehouse door. The Champ tells the boys to finish their fight cleanly and fairly, but when Janey arrives and is upset that The Champ has encouraged them to fight, he has to convince her of his good intentions. Howie, The Champ, and Janey try to convince Spider to go home with his family. They then get a projector and a film cannister out of the car and show the boys a movie, starring Joe Louis, on clean sportsmanship. Janey tries once more to encourage Spider, who refuses her entreaties, and she finally leaves. Howie follows her and apologes about Spider, while praising her for her child-rearing skills. Janey says, however, that she has failed in teaching them good morals, and Howie replies that with poverty as a factor, her job is a difficult one. Howie and Janey see Jerry enter the warehouse and secretly watch what happens next. Jerry tries to give the boys a cut of some stolen money, but Spider refuses, because another friend, Harry, was caught and has gone to jail. Jerry's girl friend Baby promises to have Harry released by virtue of her good connections at the police station. With this promise, the boys decide to go in on the robbery scheme, with Spider reluctantly joining them. At a fur warehouse, Spider and Frankie stand watch and when the signal is given, the other boys climb through a transom into the basement and begin to pack up the fur coats. Janey and Howie arrive and see Jerry and Baby outside. They enter the warehouse and secretly turn all the lights on. As all the boys scatter, Spider climbs up the ladder to the transom, but Frankie knocks it over, causing Spider to fall and injure himself. Even though Jerry hears a voice pleading for help, he leaves the scene of the crime anyway. Later, at the hospital, Spider's sprained ankle is bandaged as the police wait. Spider insists that he was hit by a car, and, when The Champ shows up, they release the boy. Spider arrives home, and a tearful Janey thanks The Champ but admits that his help is only a "flea speck" compared to the problem of kids turning delinquent, which she says is like a spreading cancer. The Champ decides to build a Boy's Club for the Boys of Harlem and a Boy's athletic club. As the boys prepare for a performance that will benefit the new club, Frankie goes into a small storage room in which he is helping Jerry hide. Soon detective Jack Billingsley stops by with a large donation of sports equipment and tells Spider that they are looking for Jerry because he killed a policeman as he was trying to escape. Meanwhile, the benefit concert begins. Billingsley sees Frankie guarding the storeroom, then sees Jerry slipping out. He takes aim, and when Janey tries to stop him, he pushes her aside and shoots Jerry dead. Frankie expects Billingsley to arrest him, but instead, the detective tells him to join the other boys. The Champ makes Janey take the stage and explain to the audience what has happened backstage and about the urgent need to end juvenile delinquency. *African Americans. Brothers and sisters. Juvenile delinquency. Joe Louis. New York City–Harlem. Racketeers. Boxers. Concerts. Fistfights. Hospitals. Moral reformation. Motion pictures. Orphans. Police detectives.*
Note: The above credits and plot synopsis were taken from contemporary reviews and a shooting script deposited with the NYSA. Although some modern sources list 1947 as the release year of the film, contemporary sources suggest that the film was not released until 1948. Official correspondence contained in the NYSA files indicates that the film was re-released in 1949 by Toddy Pictures, Inc. For additional films about boxing champion Joe Louis, please see the entry below for *Spirit of Youth.*
Box 6 Mar 1948. ExH 17 Mar 1948. New York Age 28 Feb 1948.

FIGHT THAT GHOST (African Americans)

Toddy Pictures Co. *Dist* Toddy Pictures Co. **1946?**. Sd; b&w. 5 reels, 4,933 ft.

Prod Ted Toddy. *Dir* Sam Newfield. *Asst dir* Thomas Darby. *Story and scr trmt* Sam Newfield and Ted Toddy. *Dir of photog* Jack Etra. *Asst of photog* Sol Wichuall. *Spec photog* Richard Marks. *Film ed* Elmer J. McGovern. *Sd eng* Nelson Minnerly. *Asst sd eng* J. Burgi Contner. *Makeup artist* R. J. Liszt. *Prod mgr* S. Hickman. *Scr ed* Violet Neufeld. *Eff eng* John Allsteadt.

Song(s): "Take Me," music and lyrics by Porter Grainger; "Hard Luck Blues" and "A Brown Skin Gal Is the Best Gal After All," music and lyrics by John "Rastus" Murray.

Cast: PIGMEAT "ALAMO" MARKHAM (*Pigmeat [Markham]*), John "Rastus" Murray (*Shorty [Murray]*), Percy Verwayne (*Moneybags Jim*), David Bethea (*Mr. Cook*), Alberta Pryne (*Sweet Sue*), Claire Leyba (*Honeychile Polly*), Bill Dillard (*Jim Brown*), George Wiltshire (*Lawyer Smith*), Wen Talbert (*James Henry*), Clarice Grayham (*Georgia Brown*), Ray Allen (*Fast Delivery Bill*), Rudolph Toombs (*John Mugger*), Milton Woods (*Bill White*), Sid Easton (*Spooky Lightning*).

African American, Comedy, with songs. [*Not viewed*]. Pigmeat Markham and Shorty Murray, proprietors of Pigmeat & Pigmeat & Shorty's Bootery and Tailor, are woken up one morning by their landlord, who loudly demands the rent. Shorty tries to trick the landlord by miscounting the money, but the man soon realizes he has been cheated and threatens to have the pair thrown in jail. With a sob story about his ninety-five year old grandmother, Pigmeat convinces him to wait a bit longer. At his shop, Pigmeat flirts mercilessly with all the women customers, driving them out, and when Mr. Cook comes in for a rush suit alteration and Pigmeat ruins it, Mr. Cook threatens to sue. With their problems multiplying, Shorty and Pigmeat decide to commit suicide by inhaling gas fumes. A lengthy series of last confessions, however, allows them to stall the final moment. Fortuitously, a telegram arrives, and its messenger lights a match that explodes the gas fumes, hurling the two onto the roof. The telegram announces that Pigmeat and Shorty are the beneficiaries of the will of Mr. Watkin Jones. Later, at the reading of will, Pigmeat and Shorty learn that, as the result of a favor they once did for Jones, they will each receive $2,500 and a house in Riverdale if they can spend one night alone in the dead man's bedroom. If not, the money goes to charity. The pair go to the Riverdale house and get locked inside a dark room. Strange occurrences begin to take place, including the appearance of mysterious hands offering Pigmeat a candle and a match. Pigmeat then hears a voice and notices that a man in a portrait has suddenly grown a beard. The two get into bed and again hear voices. Unknown to the pair, a gang of crooks who have been using the Jones Mansion as a hideout for the previous five years are trying to scare the wits out of the two so that they will never return. Pigmeat and Shorty eventually discover the ruse and slap the crooks in the dark, terrifying them. They decide to tie the crooks up and heroize themselves, until another strange noise causes them to flee. *African Americans. Bumblers. Haunted houses. Inheritance. Tailors. Attempted suicide. Explosions. Ghosts. Hideouts. Landlords. Ruses. Thieves.*

Note: The above credits and plot synopsis were taken from a shooting dialogue script deposited in the NYSA, which credits actor Dewey "Pigmeat" Markham as Pigmeat (Alamo) Markham. Regional censorship reports contained in the MPAA/PCA Collection at the AMPAS Library note that Maryland censors deleted lines containing the phrase "yellow gal" from the song "A Brown Skin Gal Is the Best Gal After All." The reports also indicate that between Apr 1946 and Jun 1947 the film was approved for exhibition in New York, Ohio and Pennsylvania without eliminations.

THE FIGHTER (Latino)

G-H Productions, Inc. *Dist* United Artists Corp. 25 May **1952**; Prod: late Dec 1951—mid-Jan 1952 at Motion Picture Center Studios [©G-H Productions, Inc.; 23 May 1952; LP1672]. Sd (RCA Sound System); b&w. 10 reels, 7,061 ft. 78 min. PCA cert no. 15743.

Pres ALEX GOTTLIEB. *Dir* Herbert Kline. [*Asst dir* Emmett Emerson]. *Scr* Aben Kandel and Herbert Kline. *Dir of photog* James Wong Howe. *Spec eff* Lee Zavitz. *Art dir* Daniel Hall. *Film ed* Edward Mann. *Men's ward* Izzy Berne. *Ladies' ward* Maria Donovan. *Mus comp and played by* Vicente Gomez. *Mus supv* Raoul Kraushaar. *Sd* Ben Winkler. *Makeup* Gus Norin. *Asst to prod* Rose Judell Reisman. *Prod supv* Maurie M. Suess. *Tech adv* Johnny Indrisano.

Music: "Vanessa" by Bennie Wayne.

Source: Based on the short story "The Mexican" by Jack London in *The Saturday Evening Post* (19 Aug 1911).

Cast: RICHARD CONTE [(*Felipe Rivera*)], Vanessa Brown [(*Kathy*)], Lee J. Cobb [(*Durango*)], Frank Silvera [(*Paulino*)], Roberta Haynes [(*Nevis*)], Hugh Sanders [(*Roberts*)], Claire Carleton [(*Stella*)], Martin Garralaga [(*Luis*)], Argentina Brunetti [(*Maria*)], Rodolfo Hoyos, Jr. [(*Alvarado*)], Margarita Padilla [(*Elba*)], Paul Fierro [(*Jose*)], Rico Alaniz [(*Carlos*)], Paul Marion [(*Rivas*)], Robert Wells [(*Tex*)].

Historical, Political, Drama. [*Print viewed*]. In 1910, after fleeing his native Mexico, Felipe Rivera settles in El Paso, Texas, hoping to join a group of Mexicans who are living in exile and planning to overthrow the dictatorial regime of President Porfirio Díaz Although Felipe shares the guerrillas' desire to create a democratic Mexico, he must first prove to them that he is not a spy. The only member of the group who does not question Felipe's allegiance is Kathy, an American widow whose husband was executed by Mexican Federales. While Felipe works as a sparring partner at a gymnasium operated by Roberts, a romance flourishes between him and Kathy. When Kathy asks Felipe about his past, he tells her the story of his life in Mexico, beginning when he was a fisherman on Lake Patzcuaro: One day, while he and his family are preparing for a fiesta, Felipe is visited by a wounded man, who reveals himself to be Durango, a guerrilla leader. Durango asks Felipe's help in hiding him from Col. Alvarado and his men, who are pursuing him. After helping Durango elude capture by Alvarado, Felipe escorts him to the mountains, where the guerrilla leader's allies await him. Felipe returns to the lake only to discover that his village has been set on fire by Alvarado, and that his fiancée and mother have perished. Felipe concludes his story by telling Kathy that his father, before dying, told him how the villagers tried in vain to defend themselves with only machetes. Time passes, and Felipe, now an established fighter, accepts a dangerous mission to go to Mexico to deliver a message to Durango. In Mexico, Felipe discovers that Durango is being held prisoner by Alvarado. After successfully rescuing Durango, Felipe abducts Alvarado and takes the colonel as a hostage. Durango then conducts an impromptu trial of Alvarado for the massacre at Felipe's village, with Felipe, the only surviving witness, giving testimony. Following Alvarado's conviction and death sentence, Felipe returns to El Paso and delivers Durango's request for additional weapons. When Kathy tells Felipe that there is no money to buy the guns that Durango needs, he decides to raise the money himself by fighting a champion boxer in a winner-take-all fight. Though he suffers a terrible beating at the hands of his opponent, Felipe eventually wins the match in a knockout. With the prize money, Felipe buys rifles for the guerrillas and delivers them to Durango, hopeful that his work will help bring about the end of the Diaz regime. *Boxers. Porfirio Díaz. Expatriates. Guerrilla warfare. Mexicans. Mexico–History. Politics. Abduction. Dictators. El Paso (TX). Engagements. Fiestas. Financial crisis. Gunrunners. Gunshot wounds. Jailbreaks. Massacres. Revenge. Romance. Traitors. Trials. Wagers. Widows.*

Note: The opening title card of the film reads: "Jack London's *The Fighter*." Although onscreen credits note "songs by Victor Cordero," there were no discernable songs sung in this picture. Porfirio Díaz was president of Mexico from 1877—1880 and again from 1884—1911. His regime, which was known for corruption and strong-arm tactics, was eventually ended when he resigned following a successful revolution led by Francisco Madero. Díaz died in exile in 1915.

The Fighter was the first independent film produced by former Warner Bros. producer Alex Gottlieb. According to a Feb 1952 *NYT* article, some background footage was filmed in the same area in Mexico that Herbert Kline had used for his 1941 film *Forgotten Village*. The article noted Kline's reluctance to name the exact locations in Mexico where he filmed *The Forgotten Village*, but Kline did indicate that for *The Fighter* he photographed fishing on Lake Patzcuaro and the bulk of the action in the village of Janitzio on Patzcuaro Island. Jack London's story also served as the basis for the 1944 Mexican film *El mexicano*, directed by Agustin P. Delgado and starring David Silva and Lupita Gallardo, and the 1977 Mexican film of the same name directed by Mario Hernandez and starring Jorge Luke and Pilar Pellicer.

Box 10 May 1952. *DV* 6 May 1952, p. 3. *FD* 13 May 1952, p. 12. *HR* 15 Nov 1951. *HR* 28 Dec 1951, p. 14. *HR* 11 Jan 1952, p. 15. *HR* 6 May 1952, p. 3. *MPHPD* 10 May 1952, p. 1357. *NYT* 10 Feb 1952. *NYT* 31 May 1952, p. 12. *Var* 7 May 1952, p. 6.

FIGHTING AMERICANS (African Americans)

Toddy Pictures Co. **1943**. Sd; b&w. 57 min.

Prod Ted Toddy. *Assoc prod* J. Richardson Jones. *Mus score* Harry Glass. *Tech adv* Sandra Hickman.

African American, World War II, Documentary. [*Not viewed*]. After the attack on Pearl Harbor, Americans from all walks of life

enlist in the armed forces. Aspects of the induction and training of many black men and women are shown. At a typical induction center, men are X-rayed, given overall physical examinations and participate in job classification interviews. Uniforms are handed out and the new soldier discovers the wonders of army cooking and the pleasures of the recreation center. However, endless drills are the new recruit's major occupation, preparing him for the day he will tramp down the streets of Berlin and Tokyo. Later, the men participate in simulated warfare exercises in Louisiana, and newspaper reporters from all over the United States are invited to observe the maneuvers. Brigadier General Benjamin O. Davis, Sr., the highest ranking African-American officer, is guest of honor. Truman K. Gibson, the acting civilian aide to the Secretary of War, and Lieutenant Carroll Fitzgerald are also present. While their men train to protect their homes and loved ones, the women of America are also playing their part, and many have joined the Women's Army Corps and have learned to perform a number of vital tasks, including driving and maintaining jeeps and other vehicles and the preparation of large quantities of meals. Other activities include a gas attack drill. Off-duty hours are devoted to letter writing, swimming, dances at the "Non-Com Club" and attending church services. Several WAC companies take part in a drill competition, and the winning company is congratulated by the battalion commander. The training of African-American cadets at the Tuskegee Army Flying School in Alabama is also shown. *African Americans. Air pilots, Military. Segregation. United States. Army. United States. Women's Army Corps. War preparedness. World War II. Cooks. Gas masks. Louisiana. Mechanics. Military bases. Military education. Military life. Tuskegee (AL). War games. Women military officers.*

Note: The plot summary was based on a dialogue and cutting continuity at NYSA. According to *Exb*, the film was made with the cooperation of the U.S. Government. A modern source states that the WACs sequences were shot at Fort Devens, Massachusetts.

Exb 23 Feb 1944, p. 1462.

FIGHTING BACK *see* **THE PRESCOTT KID**

FIGHTING CARAVANS (1934) *see* **WAGON WHEELS**

FIGHTING CARAVANS (Native Americans)
Paramount Publix Corp. *Dist* Paramount Publix Corp. 1 Feb **1931**; New York premiere: 23 Jan 1931 [©Paramount Publix Corp.; 13 Feb 1931; LP1977]. Sd (Western Electric); b&w. 10 reels, 8,280 ft. 91-92 min. Passed by the National Board of Review. PCA cert no. 3237-R [20 Mar 1937].
Dir Otto Brower and David Burton. *Adpt* Edward E. Paramore, Jr., Keene Thompson and Agnes Brand Leahy. *Photog* Lee Garmes and Henry Gerrard. [*Ed* William Shea]. [*Rec eng* Earl Hayman].
Source: Based on the novel *Fighting Caravans* by Zane Grey (New York, 1929).
Cast: Gary Cooper (*Clint Belmet*), Lily Damita (*Felice*), Ernest Torrence (*Bill Jackson*), Tully Marshall (*Jim Bridger*), Fred Kohler (*Lee Murdock*), Eugene Pallette (*Seth* [*Higgins*]), Roy Stewart (*Couch*), May Boley (*Jane*), Eve Southern (*Faith*), Frank Campeau (*Jeff Moffitt*), Charles Winninger (*Marshall*), Frank Hagney (*Renegade*), [James Farley], [James Marcus], [Donald MacKenzie], [E. Alyn Warren].
Western. [*Print viewed*]. During the Civil War, in Missouri, while preparing a caravan en route to California, frontier scouts Bill Jackson and Jim Bridger connive the drunken town marshal to release fellow scout Clint Belmet by coercing Felice, an orphan French girl, to pose as his bride. That night, as the caravan camps, the pioneers perform a ritual of chivalry on the "newlyweds" and Clint tries to coerce Felice into consummating the "marriage," but she rebuffs him. Next the caravan comes upon a stagecoach that has recently been ambushed and learns that the U.S. Cavalry has deserted its posts on the plains to join General Grant's army, leaving travellers unprotected. Despite the constant Indian menace, the settlers reach the Rocky Mountains, where the scouts find a deer killed with an arrow and begin to suspect Lee Murdock, the only survivor of an earlier Indian massacre, of siding with the Indians. Meanwhile, Felice falls in love with Clint, but her talk of home and marriage sends him into the woods alone, insisting he will always be a scout. There Clint spies Murdock conspiring with the Indians and, when Jim and Bill advise him to settle down because the railroad will make scouts obsolete, he confesses his love for Felice. As the three head back to camp, they hear Indians approaching and run to warn the settlers, who have

begun crossing the river. As women load guns, each family works to defend itself, while Jim and Bill compete to see who can kill the most Indians. When Murdock shoots Jim, Bill kills Murdock before dying himself from an arrow. Clint then ignites the kerosene wagon in the middle of the river and the Indians retreat. The caravan safely arrives in California and Clint and Felice marry. *Indians of North America. Railroads. Renegades. Scouts (Frontier). Settlers. Wagon trains. Marriage. Modernity. Rocky Mountains.* ·

Note: Zane Grey's novel was serialized in *Country Gentleman* (Nov 1928–Mar 1929). An ad for this film stated, "More money, time and talent lavished on this picture than any other on Paramount's great 1930-31 program!" Early scripts in the Paramount Script Collection at the AMPAS Library list Clifford Dempsey (*Couch*), Blanche Friderici (*Jane*) and Stanley Fields (*Lee Murdock*) in the cast, although they were later replaced. The first script was written by Arthur Caesar, although apparently none of his work was used in the final screenplay. Early scripts list Louis D. Lighton as production supervisor, although contemporary sources do not confirm his work on the production. The title card for this film was changed to *Blazing Arrows* for television release, although all contemporary sources verify its original title as *Fighting Caravans*. Modern credits in the opening frames of the television release print list Sid Saylor in the cast, but he is not in the cast credits from the original print that follow. A modern source lists Saylor's character name as "Charlie" and lists the following additional character names for actors in the cast: James Farley (*Amos*), James Marcus (*The Blacksmith*), Donald MacKenzie (*Gus*) and E. Alyn Warren (*Barlow*). In addition, modern sources list the following cast members: Jane Darwell (*Pioneer woman*), Irving Bacon (*Barfly*), Harry Semels (*Brawler*), Iron Eyes Cody (*Indian After Firewater*), Merrill McCormick, Tiny Sandford and Chief Big Tree. According to a modern source, portions of this film were shot in Sonora, CA. This film was remade by Paramount in 1934 as *Wagon Wheels* (see below). According to a modern source, so much footage was shot for *Fighting Caravans* that enough was left over to provide background shots for the remake.
FD 1 Feb 1931, p. 10. *MPH* 17 Jan 1931, pp. 59-60. *MPH* 24 Jan 1931, ad pp. 30-32. *NYT* 26 Jan 1931, p. 21. *Var* 28 Jan 1931, p. 15.

A FIGHTING COLLEEN (Irish Americans)
Vitagraph Co. of America. *Dist* Vitagraph Co. of America. 22 Nov **1919** [©Vitagraph Co. of America.; 27 Sep 1919; LP14244]. Si; b&w. 5 reels.
Dir David Smith. *Story and scen* Gerald C. Duffy.
Cast: Bessie Love (*Alannah Malone*), Ann Schaefer (*Mother Malone*), Charles Spere (*Jimmy Meehan*), Jay Marley (*Stanton Colby*), George Kunkel (*Mortimer Wall*), Beulah Clark (*Maggie O'Higgins*).
Drama. Alannah "Shrimpy" Malone, a spunky young Irish lady who has been in the United States for less than a year, sells newspapers to help her widowed mother support the family. Alannah knows that the woman in charge of the tenement house where she lives is a graft collector for the crooked mayor, so she helps the honest district attorney secure proof that the mayor is collecting bribes. As a reward, she and her boyfriend, Jimmy Meehan, are appointed superintendents of a municipal restaurant. *Evidence. Irish Americans. News vendors. District attorneys. Graft. Mayors. Restaurants. Rewards. Tenement-houses. Widows.*
Note: One source credits Sam Taylor as co-scenarist. The working title of the story was *Love at First Fight*.
ETR 20 Sep 1919, p. 1405. *ETR* 4 Oct 1919, p. 1601. *ETR* 15 Nov 1919, p. 2061. *MPN* 22 Nov 1919, p. 3789. *MPW* 22 Nov 1919, p. 455. *Var* 28 Nov 1919, p. 57. *Wid's* 16 Nov 1919, p. 23.

THE FIGHTING DEACON (African Americans)
Dist Theatrical Owners Booking Association. **1926**; Pittsburgh showing: 13 Sep 1926 [©Walk Miller; 3 Aug 1926; MU3529]. Si; b&w. 5 reels.
Prod Walk Miller. *Wrt* Walk Miller.
Cast: Theodore "Tiger" Flowers, Walk Miller.
African American, Boxing, Documentary. Episodes from the boyhood and early manhood of Theodore Flowers are presented, including his experiences in the United States Army during World War I. Flowers, formerly a porter, Flowers turns to boxing and, under the training of Walk Miller, becomes the middleweight champion, beating Harry Greb for the title. *African Americans. Boxers. Boxing managers. Deacons. Theodore Flowers. Harry Greb. Porters. World War I.*
Note: This film was also known as *The Life of Tiger Flowers*.
California Eagle 29 Oct 1926, p. 1. *PittsC* 4 Sep 1936, p. 10.

THE FIGHTING EDGE (Latino)

Warner Bros. Pictures, Inc. *Dist* Warner Bros. Pictures, Inc. 8 Jan **1926** [©Warner Bros. Pictures, Inc.; 7 Jan 1926; LP22238]. Si; b&w. 7 reels, 6,369 ft.

Dir Henry Lehrman. *Asst dir* Sandy Roth. *Adpt* Edward T. Lowe, Jr. and Jack Wagner. *Photog* Allan Thompson. *Addl photog* Robert Laprell. *Film ed* Clarence Kolster.

Source: Based on the novel *The Fighting Edge* by William MacLeod Raine (Boston & New York, 1922).

Cast: Kenneth Harlan (*Juan de Dios O'Rourke*), Patsy Ruth Miller (*Phoebe Joyce*), David Kirby (*Gilette*), Charles Conklin (*Chuck*), Pat Hartigan (*Taggert*), Lew Harvey (*Bailey*), Eugene Pallette (*Simpson*), Pat Harmon (*Hadley*), W. A. Carroll (*Joyce*).

Melodrama. A government agent named Joyce is imprisoned in a ranch house by a gang of smugglers. Juan O'Rourke, another agent, is then assigned to the case, going across the Mexican border disguised as a half-breed. He meets Joyce's daughter, Phoebe, and together they work their way into the smugglers' ranch house. With the aid of the cook, they free Joyce and make a break for the U. S. border. The smugglers follow, and the four take refuge in a deserted house. They are surrounded, but before they are finished off, the United States Army arrives and drives off the smugglers. Phoebe and Juan are married. *Cooks. Government agents. Impersonation and imposture. Indians of North America–Mixed blood. Mexican Americans. Mexican-American border region. Smuggling. United States. Army.*

Var 21 Apr 1926, p. 35.

FIGHTING FATHER DUNNE (Irish Americans)

RKO Radio Pictures, Inc. *Dist* RKO Radio Pictures, Inc. 19 Jun **1948**; Prod: 17 Mar–7 May 1947 [©RKO Radio Pictures, Inc.; 11 May 1948; LP1688]. Sd (RCA Sound System); b&w. 8,347 ft. 91-93 min. PCA cert no. 12333.

Exec prod Jack J. Gross. *Prod* Phil L. Ryan. *Dir* Ted Tetzlaff. *Asst dir* John Pommer and [John Temple]. *Dial dir* Eugene Busch. *Scr* Martin Rackin and Frank Davis. *Story* William Rankin. *Dir of photog* George E. Diskant. *Spec eff* Russell A. Cully. *Art dir* Albert S. D'Agostino and Walter E. Keller. *Film ed* Frederic Knudtson. *Set dec* Darrell Silvera and Adolph Kuri. *Mus dir* C. Bakaleinikoff. *Mus* Roy Webb. *Sd* Frank Sarver and Terry Kellum. *Makeup supv* Gordon Bau.

Cast: Pat O'Brien (*Father [Peter J.] Dunne*), Darryl Hickman (*Matt Davis*), Charles Kemper (*Emmett Mulvey*), Una O'Connor (*Miss O'Rourke*), Arthur Shields (*Mr. [Michael] O'Donnell*), Harry Shannon (*John [Tom] Lee*), Joe Sawyer (*Steve Davis*), Anna Q. Nilsson (*Mrs. Knudson*), Donn Gift (*Jimmy*), Myrna Dell (*Paula [Hendricks]*), Ruth Donnelly (*Kate Mulvey*), Jim Nolan (*Danny Briggs*), Billy Cummings (*Tony*), Billy Gray (*Chip*), Eric Roberts (*Monk*), Gene Collins (*Lefty*), Lester Matthews (*Archbishop [John Joseph Glennon]*), Griff Barnett (*Governor*), Jason Robards (*Sonin*), Rudy Whistler (*Soloist*), [Don Haggerty (*Gorilla Blake*)], [Ricky Berger, Albert Ray, Sonny Rees (*Boys*)], [Eugene Holland (*Art*)], [Bobby Frasco (*Pat*)], [George McDonald (*Mickey Polaski*)], [Vincent Graeff (*Petey Hendricks*)], [Paul Dunn (*Harry*)], [Leon Burbank (*Ed*)], [Tex Swan (*Driver*)], [Harry Harvey (*Dr. Adams*)], [Buddy Roosevelt (*Pedestrian*)], [Cedric Stevens (*Clerk*)], [Sedal Bennett, Florence Clayton (*Blowsy women*)], [Leo Kay, Tom Coleman (*Newspaper vendors*)], [Gerald Mackey (*Blackie*)], [Ernie Adams (*Man on loading dock*)], [Dot Farley (*Mrs. Flaherty*)], [Anne O'Neal (*Mrs. Monohan*)], [Broderick O'Farrell (*Butler*)], [Emmett Vogan (*Defense attorney*)], [Raymond Burr (*Prosecuting attorney*)], [Charles Miller (*Judge*)], [Harry Hayden (*Mr. Dunfee*)], [Freddie Chapman (*Roger Sylvester*)], [Phillip Morris (*Prison guard*)], [Frank Ferguson (*Colpeck*)], [Ellen Corby (*Colpeck's secretary*)], [Wesley Hopper (*Guard*)], [Perc Launders, Stanley Blystone (*Policemen*)], [Sid Wagner (*Swede*)], [Harold Smith (*Hoodlum*)], [Ralph Brooks (*Delivery boy*)], [Ray Walker (*Fred Carver*)], [Ralph Dunn, Chuck Flynn (*Workmen*)], [Timmy Hawkins (*Urchin*)], [Robert Bray, Robert Clarke (*Priests*)], [Jack Gargan].

Social, Biography. [*Print viewed*]. As two of his men are about to destroy the sidewalk outside St. Louis' rundown News Boys' Home and Protectorate, contractor Fred Carver asks that a piece of the sidewalk containing two sets of footprints be preserved. Fred explains to his workers that one set of footprints was made by him as a small boy, and the other belonged to Father Peter J. Dunne, the founder of the Home. Fred then recalls how Father Dunne became the "patron saint" of newsboys everywhere: In the winter of 1905, orphan

newsboys huddle together in the cold while waiting for newspapers to sell. During a grueling morning of work, two boys, Jimmy and Tony, go to see Father Dunne and tell him that Chip, another orphan newsboy, is sick. Concerned, Father Dunne asks Jimmy and Tony to take him to Chip's home, which turns out to be an unheated packing case. Father Dunne takes the ailing Chip to his sister Kate's house and calls a doctor. After the doctor prescribes bed rest for all three boys, Father Dunne convinces his reluctant brother-in-law, Emmett Mulvey, to sacrifice his only bed to the children. Father Dunne then informs his superior, Archbishop John Joseph Glennon, about the conditions under which the boys live and asks for help in creating a Home for them. Although the archbishop pledges to support Father Dunne's efforts, he also makes clear that the Catholic Church cannot donate any money to the cause. With that in mind, Father Dunne rents a shabby townhouse with help from lawyer Tom Lee and slowly begins to turn it into a home for Jimmy, Tony, Chip and two other boys. To supply the quickly expanding Home, the smooth-talking Father Dunne then cajoles various merchants into donating their goods to his cause. Father Dunne even talks Michael O'Donnell, a sour-faced businessman from Northern Ireland, into lending the Home his pony and cart, which some newsboys had earlier tried to steal. When one of the young thieves, Matt Davis, throws a brick through the Home's front window in order to "get in," Father Dunne welcomes him without question. Disturbed by the violence perpetrated on his boys by their older competitors, Father Dunne confronts Colpeck, the head of the *Herald Sun*'s circulation department, and his thug, "Gorilla" Blake. Although he is not intimidated by Colpeck and Blake, Father Dunne is unable to dissuade them from their strong-arm tactics. Taking Father Dunne's sermon on unity to heart, Matt, whose abusive, alcoholic father Steve has tried unsuccessfully to reclaim him, then organizes the boys into a group and uses O'Donnell's horse and cart to peddle their papers. Matt's strategy works at first, but Blake eventually orders several thugs to break up the group. During the ensuing mêlée, the horse is fatally injured and Jimmy's leg is crushed under the cart. After the guilt-ridden Matt runs away, Father Dunne asks O'Donnell, who owns the *Herald* building, to threaten the paper with eviction, and O'Donnell happily intimidates Colpeck into reforming. Months later, a still recuperating Jimmy beseeches Father Dunne to find Matt, and the priest agrees to search for him. Father Dunne locates Matt at his father's house, but is unable to break Steve's violent hold on the boy. Later, in an attempt to raise money to build a bigger Home, the priest hosts a "VIP" dinner. Because Father Dunne delivered the invitations at the last minute, however, only O'Donnell and Tom attend the function. Once again, O'Donnell comes to the priest's aid by offering to form a board of directors and use his financial clout to influence his peers. After the spacious, well-equipped new Home is built, a nattily dressed Matt returns for a visit. Although he claims to be doing well, Matt is nearly caught breaking into a store and runs to Father Dunne for help. Father Dunne encourages Matt to turn himself in, but a frightened Matt, imagining that the policeman in front of him is his drunken father, pulls a gun and shoots the officer. After Matt is sentenced to die, Father Dunne visits him in jail and listens to his pleas for mercy. Moved by the boy's words, the priest asks the governor to stop the impending execution, but the governor insists that justice be served. Although saddened by Matt's death, Father Dunne is comforted by the group of grateful boys who greet him later at the Home's door. *Charities. Father Peter J. Dunne. Newsboys. Poverty. Social reform. St. Louis (MO). United States-History–1901-1909. Alcoholics. Battered children. Brothers-in-law. Businessmen. Catholic Church. Dinners and dining. Executions. Fathers and sons. Fights. Governors. Horses. Irish Americans. Lawyers. Murder. Orphans. Physicians. Police. Priests. Robbery.*

Note: The working titles of this film were *Father Dunne's Newsboys Home* and *Father Dunne's Home*. The film's opening credits include the following written foreword: "This is a story about a man who lived in St. Louis. It is also a tribute to him and what he stood for. The conditions that Father Dunne helped alleviate no longer exist in St. Louis, or in any other city...." Excerpts from the songs "Rings on My Fingers" and "O, Lord, We Pray" are heard in the film. Although the character played by Harry Shannon is listed as "John Lee" in the onscreen credits, he is called "Tom Lee" in the film. According to *HR*, Ryan Productions, which was producer Phil L. Ryan's company, sold the rights to the film's story for $50,000, plus a percentage of the profits. RKO production files contained at the UCLA Arts Library—Special Collections note that Roddy McDowall tested for a role in the production. A Sep 1946 *LAEx* news item noted that producer Jack Gross was planning to shoot some scenes in St. Louis in Feb 1947, but no evidence that filming was done there has been found. Reviewers

noted the similarity between this film and M-G-M's 1938 hit movie *Boy's Town*, which chronicled the founding of Father Edward Flanagan's home for juvenile delinquents in Omaha, NE (see *AFI Catalog of Feature Films, 1931-40*; F3.0465). According to *LAT*, in Apr 1950, Matthew L. Davis of St. Louis lost a $300,000 lawsuit against RKO after a federal court decided that his reputation had not been damaged by this film. Davis lived at the News Boys' Home as a child and, after the picture was released, became jokingly known as "Killer Davis."

Box 15 May 1948. *DV* 12 May 1948, p. 3. *FD* 12 May 1948, p. 6. *HR* 11 Sep 1946, p. 1. *HR* 17 Mar 1947, p. 3. *HR* 8 May 1947, p. 16. *HR* 12 May 1948, p. 3. *HR* 28 Jun 1948, p. 5. *LAT* Sep 1946. *LAT* 14 Apr 1950. *MPHPD* 24 Apr 1948, p. 4139. *MPHPD* 15 May 1948, p. 4161. *NYT* 25 Jun 1948, p. 26. *Var* 12 May 1948, p. 20.

FIGHTING FOR GOLD (English Americans)

Fox Film Corp.; A Tom Mix Victory Picture. *Dist* Fox Film Corp. 30 Mar 1919 [©William Fox; 30 Mar 1919; LP13749]. Si; b&w. 5 reels.

Dir Edward J. LeSaint. *Scen* Charles Kenyon.

Source: Based on the novel *The Highgrader* by William MacLeod Raine (New York, 1915).

Cast: Tom Mix (*Jack Kilmeny*), Teddy Sampson (*Moya*), Sid Jordan (*Jim Bleyer*), Jack Nelson (*Curly Brandon*), H. Lounsdale (*Bobyan Verinder*), Robert Dunbar (*Lord Farquar*), Hattie Buskirk (*Lady Farquar*), Frank Clark (*Sheriff*), Lucille Young (*Pansy*).

Western. Jack Kilmeny, the heir to a dukedom, owns a valuable gold mine in the American West with his wayward partner, Curly Brandon, also from an English family. After Jack fights four men sent to take his claim by Lord Farquar, the owner of a British mining company, he falls in love with the Lord's daughter Moya, after saving her when his pet grizzly bear disrupts a picnic and frightens her horses, who carry her off in a wagon. Accused of theft when Curly, to please a dance hall girl, dresses in Jack's clothes and robs a man, Jack escapes the sheriff, finds Curly, and convinces him to leave the girl. After returning the money, Jack is permitted to go to his claim, which is threatened by Moya's suitor, Bobyan Verinder. Jack arrives to stop Verinder's hired men from attacking Moya. After Curly saves Jack, confesses the theft, and fulfills his ambition to die like a gentleman, Jack and Moya marry. *English. False accusations. Gold mines. Partnership. Rescues. Bears. Fights. Heirs. Impersonation and imposture. Nobility. Picnicking. Robbery.*

Note: The working title for this film was *The Highgrader*. *ETR* reviewer Helen Rockwell noted the film's depiction of "the silly-ass type of Englishman who is discomfited on every provocation."

ETR 12 Apr 1919, p. 1438. *MPN* 12 Apr 1919, p. 2353. *MPW* 12 Apr 1919, p. 270. *NYMT* 30 Mar 1919. *Var* 4 Apr 1919, p. 65.

THE FIGHTING GRINGO (Latino)

RKO Radio Pictures, Inc. *Dist* RKO Radio Pictures, Inc. 8 Aug 1939 [©RKO Radio Pictures, Inc.; 25 Aug 1939; LP9127]. Sd (RCA Victor Sound System); b&w. 59 min. PCA cert no. 5537.

[*Prod* Bert Gilroy]. *Prod exec* Lee Marcus. *Dir* David Howard. [*Asst dir* Harry D'Arcy]. *Scr and story* Oliver Drake. *Photog* Harry Wild. *Art dir* Van Nest Polglase. *Art dir assoc* Lucius Croxton. *Ed* Frederic Knudtson. *Mus dir* Roy Webb. *Rec* John C. Grubb.

Cast: GEORGE O'BRIEN [(*Wade Barton*)], Lupita Tovar [(*Nita Del Campo*)], Lucio Villegas [(*Don Aliso Del Campo*)], William Royle [(*Ben Wallace*)], Glenn Strange [(*Rance Potter*)], Slim Whittaker [(*Monty*)], LeRoy Mason [(*John Courtney*)], Mary Field [(*Sandra Courtney*)], Martin Garralaga [(*Pedro*)], Dick Botiller [(*Jose*)], Bill Cody, Sr. [(*Sheriff Warren*)], Cactus Mack [(*Utah Jones*)], Chris-Pin Martin [(*Felipe*)].

Western. [*Print viewed*]. Wade Barton is the leader of a band of trouble shooters who hire out their guns to the innocent and oppressed. When Wade and his buckaroos foil a stagecoach robbery, they meet Nita Del Campo, a passenger on the stage, who invites Wade to a festival at her father's ranch, El Rio Rancho. In town, Felipe, the barber, warns Wade that rancher John Courtney has designs on the Del Campo ranch. Courtney has bribed a surveyor to dispute the property line between his ranch and El Rio Rancho, thus ceding ownership to Courtney. At the Del Campo ranch that night, Courtney and his foreman, Ben Wallace, who is engaged to Courtney's sister Sandra, disrupt the fiesta to inform Don Aliso that the new survey proves that Courtney owns El Rio Rancho. In an ensuing struggle, Wallace shoots Courtney and frames Don Aliso for the murder. With the help of one of his ranch hands, Don Aliso escapes the clutches of the sheriff and becomes a hunted man. Meanwhile, Wade begins to suspect Wallace of Courtney's murder, and to gain his confidence, he agrees to evict Nita from the Del Campo ranch. Afterward, Wade tracks Don Aliso to a cantina and warns him that

Wallace's men are on their way, thus allowing him to escape. Wade then tricks Rance Potter, Wallace's right-hand man, into believing that Wallace is planning to double-cross him, thus eliciting a confession from Potter that Wallace killed Courtney. Wade passes this information along to the disbelieving Sandra. Wade's plan backfires, however, when Wallace and Potter discover his trickery, and at the Del Campo hacienda, Wade and his buckaroos shoot it out with Wallace and his men. As their guns blaze, Don Aliso and his men ride to the rescue, and when Potter confesses the truth to Sandra, she drops all claims against El Rio Rancho. *Frame-ups. Gunfighters. Land rights. Ranchers. Betrayal. Brothers and sisters. Confession (Law). Fathers and daughters. Festivals. Gunfights. Mexican Americans. Murder. Stagecoach robberies.*

Note: Modern sources add the following actors to the cast: Ben Corbett (*Shorty*), Forrest Taylor (*Jury foreman*) and Hank Bell (*Outlaw*).

FD 28 Nov 1939, p. 12. *HR* 23 Aug 1939, p. 3. *MPD* 25 Aug 1939, p. 7. *MPH* 5 Aug 1939, p. 86. *MPH* 26 Aug 1939, p. 57. *Var* 29 Nov 1939, p. 14.

THE FIGHTING HERO (Latino)

Reliable Pictures Corp. *Dist* State Rights; William Steiner. **1934**; New York opening: 1 Oct 1934. Sd; b&w. 55 min.

Prod Bernard B. Ray. *Dir* Harry S. Webb. *Scr* Rose Gordon and Carl Krusada. *Story* C. E. Roberts. *Dial* Carl Krusada. *Photog* J. Henry Kruse. *Film ed* Fred Bain. *Rec eng* Buddy Myers.

Cast: Tom Tyler (*Tom*), Renee Borden, Edward Hearn, Dick Botiller, Ralph Lewis, Murdock MacQuarrie, Nelson McDowell, Tom London, George Chesebro, Rosa Rosanova, J. P. McGowan.

Western. [*Not viewed*]. Tom, a fugitive with a price on his head, steps into a saloon and saves a young man from losing a payroll in a crooked card game, which has been engineered by the saloonkeeper. Tom next finds himself attending the trial of a young Mexican woman, who has been framed for murdering the town's leading citizen. The woman actually killed in self-defense, and Tom saves her from jail by abducting her from the street after she is convicted. Soon the woman and Tom fall in love. Tom then walks in on a gang as they plot to steal a shipment of gold. Believing that Tom is a fellow outlaw, the gang agrees to let him in on the robbery plot. Later, Tom finds the Mexican woman with the saloonkeeper and his cohort and concludes that she has betrayed him. After Tom leaves the saloon, the owner finds an identification card that reveals that the fugitive actually is a Wells Fargo express agent. The saloonkeeper joins forces with the outlaws, who seize the gold shipment. However, with the help of the sheriff and his men, who have been alerted by the Mexican woman, Tom reclaims the gold, routs the gang, and is happily reunited with his love. *Frame-ups. Fugitives. Mexicans. Murder. Outlaws. Undercover operations. Abduction. Betrayal. Cards. Gambling. Gold. Posses. Robbery. Romance. Saloon keepers. Sheriffs. Trials. Wells Fargo & Co..*

Note: According to a Jun 1934 *HR* news item, scenes for the film were shot in Newhall, CA. The same news item states that Al Greer, a "noted trick pistol shot," was injured during the location shooting. The exact nature of Greer's contribution to the production is not known. Although modern sources note that this film was the first of eighteen that Tom Tyler made with Bernard B. Ray and Harry S. Webb, contemporary sources suggest that at least two other Tom Tyler-Bernard B. Ray-Harry S. Webb titles, *Tracy Rides* and *Ridin' Thru*, were previously produced. Modern sources add Lew Meehan and Chuck Baldra (*Henchmen*) and Jimmie Aubrey (*Cowboy*) to the cast and list Harry S. Webb as associate producer. In addition, modern sources complete the above cast list with the following character names: Tom Tyler (*Tom Hall*), Renee Borden (*Conchita Alvarez*), Edward Hearn (*Bart Hawley*), Dick Botiller (*Dick*), Ralph Lewis (*The judge*), Murdock MacQuarrie (*Prosecutor*), Nelson McDowell (*Bailiff*), Tom London (*Sheriff*), George Chesebro (*Deputy*), Rosa Rosanova (*The aunt*) and J. P. McGowan (*Morales*). For more information on the Tom Tyler/Bernard B Ray series of westerns, see entry for *Ridin' Thru* (*AFI Catalog of Feature Films, 1931-40*; F3. 3757.

FD 17 Jul 1934, p. 6. *HR* 18 Jun 1934, p. 2. *MPD* 3 Oct 1934, p. 6. *Var* 9 Oct 1934, p. 18.

THE FIGHTING HOMBRE (Native Americans)

Bob Custer Productions. *Dist* Film Booking Offices of America. 1 May 1927 [©R-C Pictures Corp.; 16 Apr 1927; LP23875]. Si; b&w. 5 reels, 4,624 ft.

Pres Joseph P. Kennedy. *Supv* Jesse J. Goldburg. *Dir* Jack Nelson. *Scen* Evanne Blasdale and Madeline Matzen. *Cam* Ernest Miller.

Source: Based on the short story "Cherokee Rose" by Estrella Warde in *Ace-High Magazine*.

Cast: Bob Custer (*Bob Camp*), Mary O'Day (*Rose Martin*), Bert Sprotte (*Henry Martin*), David Dunbar ("*Goldstud*" *Hopkins*), Carlo Schipa (*Tony Mendoza*), Zita Makar (*Marie Mendoza*), Walter Maly (*Lone Badger*), Jack Anthony (*The Sheriff*).

Western. Bob Camp, a ranch foreman, saves his chore boy, Tony Mendoza, from a beating at the hands of gambler "Goldstud" Hopkins; Lone Badger, a renegade Indian, intervenes and holds them up, and Goldstud escapes. Having wronged Marie, Tony's sister, the gambler then attempts to win the favor of Rose Martin, daughter of the ranch owner, who is loved by Bob. While Bob is deputized to search for Lone Badger, Marie tries to induce Goldstud to marry her; when Tony attacks the gambler, Rose accidentally kills Goldstud. Bob suspects Marie, but he is interrupted by a battle between the posse and the cornered Lone Badger. Marie confesses to killing the unfaithful Goldstud, but she is freed by the "unwritten law." *Brothers and sisters. Cowboys. Indians of North America. Murder. Ranch foremen. Ranchers.*

Var 27 Jul 1927, p. 21.

THE FIGHTING IRISH *see* **KNUTE ROCKNE—ALL AMERICAN**

THE FIGHTING KENTUCKIAN (French Americans)
Republic Pictures Corp.; A John Wayne Production. *Dist* Republic Pictures Corp. 5 Oct **1949**; New York opening: week of 19 Sep 1949; Prod: early Mar—late Apr 1949 [©Republic Pictures Corp.; 9 Sep 1949; LP2570]. Sd (RCA Sound System); b&w. 100 min. Passed by the National Board of Review. PCA cert no. 13803.
Prod John Wayne. *Dir* George Waggner. [*Asst dir* Lee Lukather]. *Scr* George Waggner. *Dir of photog* Lee Garmes. [*Cam op* Harry Webb]. [*Gaffer* Vic Jones]. [*Stills* Don Keyes]. *Spec eff* Howard Lydecker and Theodore Lydecker. *Optical eff* Consolidated Film Industries. *Art dir* James Sullivan. *Film ed* Richard L. Van Enger. *Set dec* John McCarthy, Jr. and George Milo. *Cost des* Adele Palmer. *Uniforms* D. R. Overall-Hatswell. *Mus* George Antheil. *Orch* R. Dale Butts. *Sd* Dick Tyler and Howard Wilson. *Makeup supv* Bob Mark. [*Makeup* Webb Overland, Don Cash and Cecil Holland]. *Hair* Peggy Gray. [*Prod mgr* Kenny Holmes]. [*Scr supv* Dorothy Yutzi]. [*Grip* Benny Bishop].
Song(s): "Let Me Down, Oh Hangman" and "Kentucky Marching Song," music traditional, lyrics by George Waggner, arrangement by George Antheil.
Cast: John Wayne [(*John Breen*)], Vera Ralston [(*Fleurette DeMarchand*)], Philip Dorn [(*Col. Georges Geraud*)], Oliver Hardy [(*Willie Paine*)], Marie Windsor [(*Ann Logan*)], John Howard [(*Blake Randolph*)], Hugo Haas [(*Gen. Paul DeMarchand*)], Grant Withers [(*George Hayden*)], Odette Myrtil [(*Mme. DeMarchand*)], Paul Fix [(*Beau Merritt*)], Mae Marsh [(*Sister Hattie*)], Jack Pennick [(*Capt. Dan Carroll*)], Mickey Simpson [(*Jacques*)], Fred Graham [(*Carter Ward*)], Mabelle Koenig [(*Marie*)], Shy Waggner, Crystal White [(*Friends*)], [Albert Morin (*Pierre Le Brun*)], [Hank Worden (*Abner Todd*)], [Tony Travers (*Frenchman*)], [Charles Andre (*DeMarchand's servant*)], [Al Murphy (*Buck Skin*)], [Cliff Lyons (*Kentuckian*)], [Steve Darrell (*Gen. Jackson*)], [Ralph Dunn (*Riverman*)], [Michael Ross (*Sheriff*)], [Dave Anderson (*Giles*)], [Billy Green (*Bartender*)], [William Hawes], [Fred Libby].
Historical, Military, Western. [*Print viewed*]. In the early nineteenth century, after Congress has granted four townships in Alabama to a group of Napoleon's exiled soldiers, the men and their families settle Demopolis, a town two hundred miles from Mobile. One day in Mobile, at the end of the War of 1812, Kentucky soldier John Breen tries to evade the rest of his battalion, who are leaving for Demopolis. When he sees Gen. Paul DeMarchand's daughter Fleurette sitting in a carriage parked on the street, Breen immediately falls in love with her and asks her to pretend that they are together to fool his passing battalion. The battalion passes, and Breen believes that he is in the clear, until he sees his friend, Willie Paine, lagging behind. Sure that Willie will recognize him, Breen jumps aboard the carriage and begins driving around the square. After Fleurette's fiancé, Blake Randolph, and Col. Geraud report the apparent kidnapping, Sheriff George Hayden accompanies them on a search for Breen. They find the couple parked on a road outside of town, and Fleurette explains to Breen that the carriage belongs to Randolph. Hayden, however, reveals that Breen is wanted for assaulting a man at a tavern, but eventually decides to let him go. When the battalion arrives, Breen introduces everyone to his captain, Dan Carroll. Carroll recognizes Randolph as the man who refused to relinquish his river boat when he had tried to commandeer it during the war. At a soiree to celebrate Fleurette's engagement to Randolph, tensions rise between the French soldiers and the non-French rivermen. Later, Randolph conducts a contest to see who will win a gallon of rum. Willie steals

the prize, causing a brawl between the soldiers and the rivermen. Col. Georges Geraud then explains to Breen that while Randolph owns all the river boats, Hayden controls the workers. That evening, Breen tells Geraud that he plans to stay in Demopolis. Despite Breen's passionate kisses, Fleurette insists that she is going to marry Randolph and asks him to leave in the morning. Next morning, the battalion leaves without Breen or Willie, who has been instructed by Carroll to stay behind and keep Breen out of trouble. Later, Breen tries to visit Fleurette at home, but the butler turns him away. A few minutes later, Randolph calls, and Breen sees him admitted without hesitation. At the tavern, Hayden demands that Willie and Breen leave Demopolis, but Ann Logan, who works for Hayden, interrupts their dispute, pretending to know Breen. She tells Hayden that Breen is a surveyor and then delivers some surveying equipment to his cabin so that he can maintain this cover. Ann explains that the equipment belonged to her husband, who was murdered by Hayden after he discovered Hayden and Randolph's scheme to steal land for the French. After his death, Ann explains, she arrived to inspect the cabin that her husband had left her, but Hayden told her that it had accidentally burned down. She tells Breen that her friend, Beau Merritt, has agreed to help her find out the truth. When Ann asks him to help her spy on Hayden, he agrees to begin working for Hayden as a surveyor. The next morning, Breen takes the surveying equipment out to a field, and is followed by Beau, who shoots him in the wrist. After Beau escapes, Breen goes to a nearby cabin, where a young seamstress named Marie dresses his wound. Just then, Fleurette arrives to collect her wedding dress from Marie, and when Breen again asks for her hand in marriage, she accepts. Later, Breen overhears Ann and Beau planning to cheat Randolph out of $100,000. After Breen pulls his gun on them, Beau claims that the boundary markers have been moved so that the French now occupy land which does not belong to them. Beau then tells Breen that Hayden has rallied the riverboat workers to attack Demopolis in the morning. Shortly thereafter, Hayden and his men capture Breen and put him in jail. After Randolph admits to Ann that he and his men moved the stakes, he is found murdered. Breen escapes and is again shot, but this time Willie and the rest of the soldiers come to his rescue. Later, Breen and Fleurette are married. *Alabama. French Americans. Land claims. Officers (Military). Romantic rivalry. Butlers. Cabins. Contests. Eavesdropping. Engagements. Escapes. Fathers and daughters. Gunshot wounds. Impersonation and imposture. Jails. Kidnapping. Marriage. Prisoners. Proposals (Marital). Rescues. River boats. Robbery. Rum. Searches. Sheriffs. Surveyors. United States—History—War of 1812.*

Note: The working title of this film was *A Strange Caravan*. The opening credits note that the film was "Written and Directed by George Waggner." According to the *Var* review, the film's plot was based upon "a little known bit of American history, that Congress granted four townships of land in Alabama to French officers of Napoleon's defeated armies and their families." *HR* reported that the film was shot in Agoura, CA, and that a French cultural decoration, the Palms of the Officier d'Academy, was to be awarded to Donald Overall-Hatswell for his technical direction. His onscreen credit, however, was for uniforms. Modern sources include Chuck Roberson in the cast.

Box 17 Sep 1949. *Cue* 17 Sep 1949. *DV* 14 Apr 1949. *DV* 12 Sep 1949, p. 4. *FD* 15 Sep 1949, p. 5. *HR* 11 Mar 1949, p. 11. *HR* 8 Apr 1949, p. 7. *HR* 14 Apr 1949, p. 14. *HR* 22 Apr 1949, p. 15. *HR* 12 Sep 1949, p. 3, 4. *LAT* 30 Sep 1949, p. 8. *MPHPD* 17 Sep 1949, p. 18. *NYT* 19 Sep 1949, p. 18. *Var* 14 Sep 1949, p. 20.

FIGHTING PIONEERS (Native Americans, Crow)
Resolute Productions, Inc. *Dist* State Rights; Resolute Pictures Corp. **1935**; New York opening: 19 May 1935. Sd (Dramaphone Recording System); b&w. 54 or 60 min. Passed by the National Board of Review.
Supv Alfred T. Mannon. *Dir* Harry Fraser. [*Asst dir* Harry Knight]. *Story and scr* Harry Fraser and Chuck Roberts. *Photog* Robert Cline. *Ed* J. Logan Pearson. *Sd rec* Ralph G. Fear. *Prod* [*mgr*] Marion H. Kohn.
Cast: Rex Bell [(*Lieutenant Bentley*)], Ruth Mix [(*Wa-no-na*)], Buzz Barton [("*Splinters*")], Stanley Blystone [(*Hadley*)], Earl Dwire [(*Sergeant Luke*)], Chuck Morrison [(*Sergeant O'Shaughnessy*)], John Elliot [(*Major Denton*)], Roger Williams [(*Captain Burton*)], Chief Thunder Cloud [(*Eagle Feathers*)], Chief Standing Bear [(*Black Hawk*)], Guate Mozin [(*Crazy Horse*)].
Western. [*Print viewed*]. The elderly Crow Indian chief Black Hawk decides to lead an attack on a wagon train to prevent the loss of Indian land and buffalo to white men. After a wagon train scout intercepts a cavalry detachment under the command of Lieutenant Bentley and his men ride to protect the wagon train and defeat the Indians. Bentley allows the chief's daughter Wa-no-na to take her

mortally wounded father back to their village, and before dying he makes Wa-no-na the new leader of the tribe. Back at the fort, rifles captured from the Indians are discovered to be the cavalry's old model, some of which were stolen from the supply armory. Major Denton, the squadron commander, questions Bentley and another officer, Sergeant Luke, because they both had keys to the armory. Although Bentley and Luke deny complicity in the weapon theft, Luke clears himself and then casts suspicion upon Bentley. After being ordered to find the traitor, Bentley has Argo, an Indian who works in the fort, follow Luke and Hadley, a trader, to the Indian village, where Hadley demands advance payment from the Indians for a new shipment of rifles, with the intention of taking their money and leaving the area. However, Wa-no-na and her tribe have tired of Hadley's crooked dealings and take both he and Luke prisoner. Bentley enlists the aid of "Splinters," a young wagon train scout who wants to join the cavalry, and leaves the fort dressed in civilian clothes in order to investigate the dealings of Luke and Hadley and to clear himself. After Denton learns of Bentley's plan, he becomes suspicious and sends another officer, Captain Burton, to follow Bentley to the Indian encampment. Bentley sneaks into the Crow village and releases Hadley and Luke, but before they can escape undetected, an Indian guard sounds the alarm. The Indians pursue the escaping whites, and Wa-no-na succeeds in capturing Bentley, but does not kill him. Burton and his troops arrive, taking Wa-no-na prisoner, but Denton, refusing to believe Bentley's account of the incident, confines him to the stockade. One night Bentley manages to visit Wa-no-na, telling her that he regrets her confinement and asking her to reveal the identity of the gunrunner. Meanwhile, the Indians release Hadley after he promises to set Wa-no-na free, and once Wa-no-na has been released, he then takes Bentley back to the Indian village. There Wa-no-na releases Bentley, even though she is aware that her people will regard her as a traitor. Upon returning to the fort, Bentley finds Hadley and Luke quarreling and has them arrested, after which he alerts the cavalry to an upcoming Indian attack on a wagon train. Burton and his cavalry rescue the wagon train and win the battle, and Wa-no-na is forced to agree to a peace treaty, after which she bids farewell to Bentley. *Crow Indians. False accusations. Gunrunners. Traitors. Tribal chiefs. United States. Army. Cavalry. Buffalo (NY). Chases. Fathers and daughters. Forts. Prisoners. Rescues. Rifles. Scouts (Frontier). Thieves. Traders. Wagon trains.*

Note: Although the opening credits of the viewed print included a copyright statement, the title was not found in the copyright registry. According to modern sources, the cast also included Francis Walker, Bob Burns, Blackjack Ward and Barney Beasley.

FD 21 May 1935, p. 8. *MPD* 27 May 1935, p. 6. *Var* 29 May 1935, p. 34.

THE FIGHTING 69TH (Irish Americans)

Warner Bros. Pictures, Inc.; A Warner Bros.—First National Picture; Jack L. Warner in charge of prod. *Dist* Warner Bros. Pictures, Inc. 27 Jan **1940**; New York opening: 26 Jan 1940; Prod: late Sep—late Oct 1939 [©Warner Bros. Pictures, Inc.; 27 Jan 1940; LP9376]. Sd (RCA Victor System); b&w. 9 reels. 89 min. PCA cert no. 5756.

Exec prod Hal B. Wallis. *Assoc prod* Louis F. Edelman. *Dir* William Keighley. *Asst dir* Frank Heath. *Orig scr* Norman Reilly Raine, Fred Niblo, Jr. and Dean Franklin. *Photog* Tony Gaudio. *Spec eff* Byron Haskin and Rex Wimpy. *Art dir* Ted Smith. *Ed* Owen Marks. *Mus dir* Leo F. Forbstein. *Mus* Adolph Deutsch. *Orch arr* Hugo Friedhofer. *Sd* Charles Lang. *Makeup* Perc Westmore. *Tech adv* Captain John T. Prout, Mark White and [George Boothby].

Cast: JAMES CAGNEY (*Jerry Plunkett*), PAT O'BRIEN (*Father [Francis] Duffy*), GEORGE BRENT (*"Wild Bill" Donovan*), Jeffrey Lynn (*Joyce Kilmer*), Alan Hale (*Sergeant Big Mike Wynn*), Frank McHugh (*Crepe Hanger Burke*), Dennis Morgan (*Lieutenant Ames*), Dick Foran (*Lieutenant Long John Wynn*), William Lundigan (*Timmy Wynn*), Guinn Williams (*Paddy Dolan*), John Litel (*Captain Mangan*), Henry O'Neill (*The Colonel*), Sammy Cohen (*Mike Murphy*), Harvey Stephens (*Major Anderson*), Charles Trowbridge (*Chaplain Holmes*), DeWolf Hopper (*Private Turner*), Tom Dugan (*Private McManus*), Frank Wilcox (*Lieutenant Norman*).

War, **Drama**. [*Print viewed*]. In 1917, at Camp Mills, New York, Major "Wild Bill" Donovan swears in the new recruits of the fighting 69th New York regiment, among whom is Jerry Plunkett, an arrogant braggart who refuses to follow orders. Once sent overseas, Plunkett becomes even more belligerent, and not even the unit's beloved

Chaplain, Father Francis Duffy, can bring him back into the fold. Despised by the other men, Plunkett causes a massacre at Rouge Boquet when he disobeys orders and inadvertently incites the Germans to attack. Disgusted by Plunkett's behaviour, Donovan wants to transfer him out of the company, but Duffy convinces the Major to give him another chance. Although a bully in camp who brags about coming home "dripping with medals," Plunkett is a coward in battle, and after he becomes hysterical and alerts the Germans to the company's location, thus causing more deaths, he is court-martialed and sentenced to be shot. Meanwhile, the rest of the regiment is ordered on a suicide mission to take the sector at the Argonne without military support. As the regiment is besieged by shells, the jail in which Plunkett is imprisoned is bombed and he escapes. Dashing to the hospital, Plunkett witnesses Father Duffy leading the wounded in a recitation of the Lord's prayer, and discovers in himself the faith that the father had preached. Speeding to the front, Plunkett launches a daring attack with a trench mortar, blasting a hole through the barbed wire and thus allowing the regiment to capture their objective. In the attack, Plunkett is fatally wounded, but before he dies he is given the last rites and hailed as a hero. *Braggarts. Bullies. Cowardice. Father Francis Duffy. Faith. Irish Americans. Joyce Kilmer. Priests. Transformation. World War I. Argonne, Battle of the, 1918. Courts-martial and courts of inquiry. Escapes. France. Heroism. Military life. United States. Army.*

Note: According to a pre-production news item in *HR*, in Jun 1939, Fox announced that it was planning to make a film based on this story. In response, Warner Bros. claimed priority rights to the story. The working titles of this film were *The Old 69th* and *Father Duffy of the Fighting 69th*. Pre-production news items in *HR* note that Colonel Bill Donovan, the commander of the Irish 69th regiment, was hired as technical adviser for the film and George Boothby, the story adviser on the film, was written into the script. However, because the film credits Captain John T. Prout, a member of the original 69th regiment, as technical adviser, their participation in the final film has not been confirmed. Other pre-production news items in *HR* note that Warner Bros. decided to increase the budget for the film and replaced producer Bryan Foy with Lou Edelman. The studio built an exact replica of Camp Miles, the World War I training camp on Long Island, at Providencia Ranch, CA. Another item in *HR* adds that Jeffrey Lynn replaced John Payne in the role of "Joyce Kilmer" when Payne was dropped from the studio's contract list. According to news items in *HR*, the film, based on the exploits of the real Father Francis Duffy, featured actual war footage shot by Brendan. Joyce Kilmer was the author of the famous poem "Trees," and was killed in battle on 30 Jul 1918 above Ourcq, France. Kilmer served in the 165th regiment, however, not the 69th.

DV 3 Jan 1940, p. 3. *FD* 5 Jan 1940, p. 5. *FD* 25 Jan 1940, p. 9. *HR* 23 Mar 1939, p.1. *HR* 17 Jun 1939, p. 1. *HR* 20 Jun 1939, p. 4. *HR* 7 Aug 1939, p. 2, 7. *HR* 13 Sep 1939, p. 7. *HR* 16 Sep 1939, p. 2. *HR* 23 Sep 1939, pp. 6-7. *HR* 21 Oct 1939, pp. 3-4. *HR* 27 Jan 1940, p. 1. *HR* 4 Jan 1940, p. 3. *MPH* 25 Nov 1939, p. 35. *MPH* 13 Jan 1940, p. 36. *NYT* 27 Jan 1940, p. 9. *Var* 10 Jan 1940, p. 14.

THE FIGHTING SULLIVANS see THE SULLIVANS

FIGHTING THROUGH (Native Americans)

Willis Kent Productions. *Dist* State Rights. **1934**. Sd; b&w. 55 min.
Dir Harry Fraser. *Cam* James Diamond. *Film ed* Roy Luby. *Rec eng* Earl Crain.

Cast: Reb Russell (*Reb*), Lucille Lund (*Lucille*), Yakima Canutt (*Big Jack Thorpe*), Edward Hearn (*Lenihan*), Chester Gan (*Wong*), Steve Clemento (*Steve*), Bill Patton (*Bill*), Frank McCarroll (*Frank*), Benny Corbett (*Ben*), Hank Bell (*Hank*), Charles Whitaker (*Sheriff*), Jack Jones, Jack Kirk, Chuck Baldra (*Singers*), Nelson McDowell (*Parson*), Wally Wales, Rebel, a horse.

Western. [*Not viewed*]. Reb, a detective for the Cattlemen's Association, is sent to an area that has been plagued by a gang of cattle rustlers. Upon arriving at his assigned town, Reb learns from the local sheriff that the suspected gang leader is saloon keeper Lenihan. Posing as a cowboy, Reb goes to Lenihan's saloon, where Big Jack Thorpe, an Indian and former college football star, is engaged in a brawl. Big Jack began the fight after Wong, the servant to ranch owner Lucille, informed him that Lenihan had cheated him out of his money and his horse in a crooked card game. After the fight, Reb and Big Jack flee to Lucille's ranch, the Double Cross. Lucille recognizes Reb as a former Northwestern football star and offers both him and Big Jack jobs. While Reb is away from the ranch, Lenihan rides to the Double Cross and proposes to Lucille, who refuses him. Frustrated, Lenihan accuses Big Jack of horse stealing and prepares to lynch him. Reb returns to the ranch in time to save Big Jack, but Lenihan raids the ranch a second time. After stealing cattle, Lenihan and his men kill several of the ranch hands and kidnap Lucille. Reb and Big Jack trail the outlaws and eventually rescue Lucille. *Cowboys. Detectives.*

Ranchers. Rustlers. Undercover operations. Cards. Chinese. False accusations. Fights. Football players. Gambling. Indians of North America. Kidnapping. Lynching. Murder. Rescues. Saloon keepers. Servants. Sheriffs.

Note: Modern sources credit director Harry Fraser with the story and screenplay and add Lew Meehan to the cast.

FD 29 Aug 1934, p. 7.

FIND THE WOMAN (French Americans)

Vitagraph Co. of America; A Blue RIbbon Feature. *Dist* Greater Vitagraph, Inc. 10 Jun 1918 [©Vitagraph Co. of America; 3 Jun 1918; LP12490]. Si; b&w. 5 reels.

Pres Albert E. Smith. *Dir* Tom Terriss. *Scen* Stanley Olmstead. *Cam* Joe Shelderfer.

Source: Based on the short story "Cherchez la Femme" by O. Henry in *Roads of Destiny* (New York, 1909).

Cast: Alice Joyce (*Madeline Renard*), Walter McGrail (*Maurice Dumars*), Henry Houry (*Robbins*), Jessie Stevens (*Madame Tibault*), Jean Paige (*Nonette*), Arthur Donaldson (*Monsieur Morin*), Martin Faust (*Pierre*), Victor A. Stewart.

Drama. Madeline Renard, a singer with the French Opera Company in New Orleans, is loved by Maurice Dumars, a newspaper critic. When Madeline is awarded a starring role in *Faust*, she asks her old friend, Monsieur Morin, an expert gold worker, to make her a paste pearl necklace for the performance. He does this but suddenly is taken ill and dies. Morin had been guarding $20,000 in gold coins for Mme. Tibault, an innkeeper, and when the money is discovered missing from his safe, gossips soon convince the townspeople—including Maurice—that Madeline stole the money in order to buy her marvelous pearls. While visiting Mme. Tibault, Maurice learns that the simple innkeeper has unwittingly used as wallpaper the stock certificates that Maurice had purchased with her gold coins. The mystery cleared up, Madeline regains the affections of Maurice and her friends, and she, in turn, forgives them for their lack of faith. *French Americans. Goldsmiths. Gossip. Jewelry. Opera singers. Robbery. Stocks.* Critics. *Faust* (Opera). Gold. Innkeepers. New Orleans (LA). Safes. Wallpaper.

Note: The story was first published in *Ainslee's,* Mar 1903 written under the pseudonym, James L. Bliss. On the film's setting, *ETR* commented, "The atmosphere of old New Orleans is well taken care of," while *MPW* noted, "The entire atmosphere is French."

ETR 8 Jun 1918, p. 7. *ETR* 15 Jun 1918, p. 127. *MPN* 22 Jun 1918, p. 3739. *MPW* 15 Jun 1918, p. 1618. *MPW* 22 Jun 1918, p. 1754. *NYDM* 15 Jun 1918, p. 851. *NYDM* 29 Jun 1918, p. 925. *Var* 7 Jun 1918, p. 33. *Wid's* 9 Jun 1918, pp. 13-14.

FINNEGAN'S BALL (Irish Americans)

Graf Brothers Studio. *Dist* First Division Pictures. 15 Sep 1927. Si; b&w. 7 reels, 6,200-6,700 ft.

Supv Max Graf. *Dir* James P. Hogan. *Scen* Max Graf. *Photog* Blake Wagner.

Source: Based on the play *Finnegan's Ball* by George H. Emerick (ca 1894).

Cast: Blanche Mehaffey (*Molly Finnegan*), Mack Swain (*Patrick Flannigan*), Cullen Landis (*Flannigan, Jr.*), Aggie Herring (*Maggie Finnegan*), Charles McHugh (*Danny Finnegan, Sr.*), Westcott B. Clarke (*Lawyer O'Connell*), Kewpie Morgan (*Judge Morgan*), Mimi Finnegan (*Danny Finnegan, Jr.*).

Comedy. The Finnegans follow the Flannigans to America, Mr. Finnegan goes to work for Mr. Flannigan, and Molly and Jimmy are reunited. A feud between the families breaks out, however, which results in the Finnegans snubbing the Flannigans when the former fall heir to a fortune. But the inheritance proves to be an error, and the Finnegans are reduced to their earlier position. The Flannigans forgive them, and amity between the families is assured by the marriage of Molly and Jimmy. *Courtship. Family life. Feuds. Immigrants. Inheritance. Irish Americans. Wealth.*

Var 20 Oct 1927, p. 24.

THE FIREBRAND (Russian Americans)

Fox Film Corp.; A Fox Special Feature. *Dist* Fox Film Corp. 19 May 1918 [©William Fox; 26 May 1918; LP12487]. Si; b&w. 5 reels.

Dir Edmund Lawrence. *Scen* Adrian Johnson. *Story* E. Lloyd Sheldon.

Cast: Virginia Pearson (*Princess Natalya*), Victor Sutherland (*Julian Ross*), Carleton Macy (*Prince Andrei Rostoff*), Herbert Evans (*Boris Rostoff*), Jane Courtney (*Nasha*), Willard Cooley (*Leonid*), Nicholas Dunaew (*Dmitri*).

World War I, Drama. At the time of the Russian Revolution, the princess Natalya falls in love with Julian Ross, an American of Russian descent who has been imprisoned for writing revolutionary tracts. She has him released, telling him that she is a governess in the home of Prince Andrei Rostoff, who is actually her uncle. Natalya's brother is killed at the battle front because of the treachery of Rostoff and his son Boris, who, in league with the German Kaiser, had provided the Russian soldiers with faulty ammunition. For this, Julian assassinates the Rostoffs, and Natalya, in revenge, shoots the young American. Julian, only slightly wounded, produces a document proving the Rostoffs' connections with the Germans, whereupon Natalya forgives him and agrees to be his wife. *Americans in foreign countries. Assassination. Pamphleteers. Princes. Revenge. Revolutionaries. Russia–History–Revolution, 1917-1921. Russian Americans. Russians. Treachery. World War I. Germany. Governesses. Gunshot wounds.* Imprisonment. Ordnance. Russia. Army. Secret documents. Soldiers. Traitors. Uncles.

Note: The title of the scenario for this film included in the copyright descriptions was "Fires of Hate."

ETR 1 Jun 1918, p. 2084. *MPN* 1 Jun 1918, p. 3307. *MPW* 18 May 1918, p. 1040. *MPW* 1 Jun 1918, p. 1332. *NYDM* 1 Jun 1918, p. 776. *Wid's* 9 Jun 1918, pp. 11-12.

FIREKNIFE see THE YELLOW TOMAHAWK

THE FIRES OF JOHANNIS see THE FLAMES OF JOHANNIS

THE FIRES OF ST. JOHN see THE FLAMES OF JOHANNIS

THE FIRST BORN (Chinese Americans)

Hayakawa Feature Play Co. *Dist* Robertson-Cole Distributing Corp. 30 Jan 1921 Si; b&w. 5 or 6 reels.

Dir Colin Campbell. *Scen* Fred Stowers. *Photog* Frank D. Williams.

Source: Based on the novel *The First Born* by Francis Powers (New York, 5 Oct 1897).

Cast: Sessue Hayakawa (*Chan Wang*), Helen Jerome Eddy (*Loey Tsing*), "Sonny Boy" Warde (*Chan Toy*), Goro Kino (*Man Low Tek*), Marie Pavis (*Chan Lee*), Wilson Hummel (*Kuey Lar*), Frank M. Seki (*Hop Lee*).

Romance, Melodrama. Chan Wang, boatman on the Hoang-Ho, is forced to marry Chan Lee, when his beloved, Loey Tsing, is sold to Kuey Lar, a rich merchant in San Francisco. Soon a son, Chan Toy, is born to Chan Lee. In San Francisco, Wang meets his former sweetheart and arouses the jealousy of her owner, who entices Chan's wife and son to his home. There the child falls from a window and is killed. In revenge, Wang kills the abductor of his former love and the destroyer of his firstborn; then, in final submission, he returns to his native land with Loey Tsing. *Boatswains. China. Chinese. Chinese Americans. Marriage–Forced. Merchants. Murder. Revenge. San Francisco (CA). Unrequited love.* Accidental death. Falls from heights. Jealousy.

FD 6 Feb 1921. *NYT* 31 Jan 1921, p. 11. *Var* 4 Feb 1921, p. 21.

FISHERMAN'S WHARF (Italian Americans)

Principal Productions, Inc.; Bobby Breen Productions, Inc. *Dist* RKO Radio Pictures, Inc. 3 Feb 1939 [©Bobby Breen Productions, Inc.; 3 Feb 1939; LP8695]. Sd (RCA Victor System); b&w. 6,480 ft. 72 min. PCA cert no. 4879.

Prod Sol Lesser. *Dir* Bernard Vorhaus. *Asst dir* John Sherwood. [*Backgrounds dir* Al Raboch]. *Scr* Bernard Schubert, Ian Hunter and H. Clyde Lewis. [*Dial* Aben Kandel]. *Photog* Charles Schoenbaum. [*Background photog* William Dietz]. *Art dir* Lewis J. Rachmil. *Ed* Arthur Hilton. *Ward* Maurice Friedman. *Mus dir* Victor Young. *Mus supv* Abe Meyer. *Vocal arr* Max Terr. *Sd* Earl A. Wolcott.

Song(s): "Sell Your Cares for a Song," words and music by Victor Young and Charles Newman; "Songs of Italy," words and music by Frank Churchill and Paul F. Webster; "Fisherman's Chanty," words and music by Farlan Myers and William Howe.

Cast: Bobby Breen (*Tony Roma*), Leo Carillo (*Carlo Roma*), Henry Armetta (*Beppo*), Lee Patrick (*Stella*), Rosina Galli (*Angelina*), Tommy Bupp (*Rudolph*), George Humbert (*Pietro*), Leon Belasco (*Luigi*), Slicker, the seal (*Julius*), Dorr's St. Luke's Choristers, [Pua Lani, Leonard Kibrick, Jackie Salling, Ronald Paige, Milo Marchetti, Jr. (*Tony's gang*)].

Domestic, Drama, with songs. [*Print viewed*]. Carlo Roma, an Italian fisherman from San Francisco, is head of a happy family composed of his adopted son Tony, his helper Beppo, their housekeeper Angelina, and their pet seal Julius. The family's domestic bliss is disrupted when Carlo's widowed sister-in-law Stella arrives

with her spoiled young son Rudolph. Stella ensnares the financially successful Carlo, and then begins alienating his family one by one. Her first victim is Julius, whom she banishes from the house. Next, she offends the affable Beppo, making him feel unwelcome in Carlo's house. Then after deciding that Carlo is not making enough money from his three boats, Stella suggests that he demote his three helpers, Beppo, Luigi and Pietro, from equal partners to paid workers, and as a result, the three leave Carlo to work on their own. Angelina is the next to go when she quits and marries Beppo. Tony is the last victim when Rudolph cruelly informs him that he is illegitimate and that Carlo is not his father. Devastated by the news, Tony runs from the house after Carlo harshly reprimands him. While on the run, Tony visits Beppo, who tells Carlo of Rudolph's cruelty. Together, Beppo and Carlo sail after Tony, who has taken Carlo's boat, and after catching up to the boy, Carlo denounces the interlopers and begs Tony to return. As Stella and Rudolph set sail for Seattle, the Roma family is happily reunited. *Fathers and sons. Fishermen. Fortune hunters. Italian Americans. Sisters-in-law.* Adoption. Boats. Housekeepers. Parentage. Runaways. San Francisco (CA). Seals (Animals). Widows.

Note: According to an undated *HR* news item contained in the *AFI* Library, Vicki Brown was to have written the original story for this picture, but her participation in the final film has not been confirmed.

DV 24 Jan 1939, p. 3. *FD* 1 Mar 1939, p. 10. *HR* 24 Jan 1939, p. 3. *MPD* 31 Jan 1939, p. 4. *MPH* 10 Dec 1938, p. 41. *MPH* 28 Jan 1939, p. 33. *NYT* 24 Feb 1939, p. 15. *Var* 8 Feb 1939, p. 17.

FISHKA DER KRIMMER *see* THE LIGHT AHEAD

FIVE (African Americans)

Lobo Productions. *Dist* Columbia Pictures Corp. Oct **1951**; Los Angeles premiere: 28 Aug 1951 [©Lobo Productions; 24 Sep 1951; LP1169]. Sd (Western Electric Sound); b&w. 8,182 ft. 93 min. PCA cert no. 8359.

Prod Arch Oboler. *Dir* Arch Oboler. *Wrt* Arch Oboler. *Cine consultant* Louis Clyde Stoumen. *Prod des* Arch Oboler. *Film ed* John Hoffman. *Mus comp and cond* Henry Russell. *Orch* Charles Maxwell. *Mus ed* Betty Steinberg. *Sd* William Jenkins Locy. *Spec sd eff* Gus Bayz. *Photog, ed and prod asst* Sidney Lubow, Ed Spiegel, Louis Clyde Stoumen and Arthur L. Swerdloff. *Exec secy* Geraldine Klancke. [*Architect of*] "Cliff House" Frank Lloyd Wright.

Cast: William Phipps (*Michael [Rogin]*), Susan Douglas (*Roseanne*), James Anderson (*Eric*), Charles Lampkin (*Charles*), Earl Lee (*Mr. Barnstaple [Oliver Peabody Schaeffer]*).

Post-Apocalyptic, Drama. [*Print viewed*]. After a nuclear blast kills most of the world's population, Roseanne, a pregnant young woman, wanders through a small town, finding only the skeletal remains of the inhabitants. Traumatized, she makes her way to her aunt's country house but discovers that her aunt has died in the disaster and that a young man, Michael Rogin, is now living in the house. When Michael first appears, Roseanne screams and faints. As she wakes up, Michael declares that he recognizes her from photos he found at the house, and Roseanne later explains that the man seen with her in the photos is her husband. Michael tells her that he was operating an elevator at the Empire State Building when the blast occurred, and that he believed that he was the only one alive in all New York City. Roseanne explains that at the fateful moment, she was in the hospital getting x-rayed, and Michael surmises that the lead walls of the x-ray room saved her. The pair set up housekeeping, with Michael, a misanthropic ne'er-do-well from Dartmouth, exclaiming his satisfaction at having a chance to start his life over again close to nature. When Michael tries to kiss Roseanne, she sobs and informs him that she is pregnant. Just then, they hear a car horn honk and go out to meet Oliver Peabody Schaeffer, a banker, and Charles, a black bank cashier, who survived the blast because they were locked in the bank vault. Mr. Schaeffer is in a state of delirium, and eventually the telltale signs of radiation poisoning—purplish marks on the skin—become visible. Charles and Michael begin installing a generator and planting crops, and Mr. Schaeffer, his condition improving, begs that they take him to the seashore. At the beach, Michael imagines that he can see Coney Island, and just then, the body of a man, Eric, washes up on shore. Eric, an explorer who had been marooned atop Mt. Everest when the blast occurred, found his way across Asia and America by plane, and then finally ran out of gas and crashed. Mr. Schaeffer dies, and the group returns to the house. Eric explains that he wants to go to the city where there are food and luxury items, and

is disgruntled with the other men's insistence on living the primitive life. Eventually, Eric insists that they go back to the city as they all have a seeming immunity to the radiation, but Michael argues that Roseanne, nearing her term, is not well enough to travel. Eric then displays his virulent racism toward Charles, saying that he cannot stand being so close to a black man, and the two fight. After Roseanne gives birth, Charles offers to leave the house in order to keep the peace. Michael says that they cannot make the same mistakes as those did before them, and he goes to speak to Eric, who promises that his outburst was only the result of tension. Michael asks Eric to join in the work, and Eric agrees, but then sits in the sun smoking cigarettes instead of working. As Michael declares his love for Roseanne one morning, a buzzard flies over head. Charles appears and tells Michael that Eric sabotaged the crops, but Michael, wishing to protect his loved one, tells Roseanne that it was an animal. Sometime later, Roseanne and Michael kiss, and Roseanne accidentally calls him "Steven," her husband's name, and then runs away crying. That night, Eric goes to Roseanne's room and tells her that he is going to the city for a few days and that she should come with him to look for her husband. Roseanne hesitates but then decides to go, and the two plan to sneak out of the house and meet on the road. On his way out, Eric encounters a surprised Charles and stabs him to death. The next day, Michael discovers Charles' body, then finds the note that Roseanne left. In the city, Eric and Roseanne drive through burned-out streets, which are littered with skeletons. Roseanne goes first to her husband's former office, an architectural firm, and then to the waiting room at the hospital, where she was being x-rayed. There she discovers her husband's skeleton, shrieks in horror, and returns to Eric. After Eric announces that he has no intention of returning to the country house, he grabs Roseanne, who tries to flee. During the struggle, Eric notices signs of radiation poisoning on his arms and, howling in agony, runs away. Roseanne then makes her way back to the country house, and en route her baby dies. After Michael, who has gone out to search for Roseanne, finally catches up to her, they bury the infant. The couple goes back to the house, and Roseanne helps Michael to replant the crops and thus begin their new life together. *Atomic bomb. Cities and towns, ruined, extinct, etc.. City-country contrast. Racism. Radiation. Romance.* African Americans. Banks. Childbirth. Explorers. Infant death. Murder. Ne'er-do-wells. Pregnancy. Skeletons. Transformation. X-rays.

Note: According to onscreen credits, the film's subtitle was "A Story About the Day After Tomorrow." Lines from the poem "Creation" by Harlem Renaissance poet James Weldon Johnson appear in the opening credits, and a quote from Revelation 21 appears onscreen as well. Arch Oboler's first onscreen credit reads: "Produced, written and directed by Arch Oboler." Although Earl Lee's character is listed as "Mr. Barnstaple" in the cast credits, he is called "Oliver Peabody Schaeffer" in the film. Oboler also wrote a radio show similar in theme to *Five*, which featured Bette Davis. The film was shot at Oboler's 360-acre ranch in the Santa Monica Mountains, and "Cliff House," a Frank Lloyd Wright design, which was used in the film, was the Oboler family residence. According to correspondence on file in the MPAA/PCA Collection at the AMPAS Library, *Five* risked not receiving a code seal because of a "too graphic montage depicting the pangs and struggles of childbirth." No drafts of the script had been received by the PCA, and Oboler, who made the film as an independent venture, stated that, although he could re-edit the film, re-recording the soundtrack would prove too expensive. According to an 8 Feb 1951 PCA memo, Oboler agreed to distribute the film in the "'art circuit'" without a certificate. The childbirth scene was apparently edited down, but not entirely eliminated. A 14 Dec 1950 *HR* news item reported that *Five* was to have its first showing "in early January at Lake Success for a special committee of United Nations delegates," but it has not been confirmed that this screening took place. Oboler, a former radio writer, made *Bwana Devil*, the first 3-D movie, and also innovated a color process called Space-Vision. Ed Spiegel, Louis Clyde Stoumen and Arthur Swerdloff were all former USC students.

Box 5 May 1951. *DV* 25 Apr 1951, p. 4. *FD* 26 Apr 1951, p. 11. *HR* 14 Dec 1950. *HR* 25 Apr 1951. *LAT* 17 Dec 1950. *LAT* 29 Aug 1951. *MPD* 30 Apr 1951. *MPHPD* 15 Apr 1951, p. 802. *NYT* 31 Dec 1950. *NYT* 26 Apr 1951, p. 34. *Var* 25 Apr 1951, p. 6.

FIVE CENTS A GLASS *see* BEST OF ENEMIES

THE FIVE DOLLAR BABY (Jewish Americans)

Metro Pictures Corp. *Dist* Metro Pictures Corp. 4 Sep **1922**; New York premiere: ca25 Jun 1922 [©Metro Pictures Corp.; 29 Jul 1922; LP18123]. Si; b&w. 6 reels, 5,990 ft.

Prod Harry Beaumont. *Dir* Harry Beaumont. *Scen* Rex Taylor. *Story* Irvin S. Cobb. *Photog* John Arnold. *Art dir* A. F. Mantz. *Tech dir* A. F. Mantz.

Cast: Viola Dana (*Ruth*), Ralph Lewis (*Ben Shapinsky*), Otto Hoffman (*The Solitary Kid*), John Harron (*Larry Donovan*), Tom

McGuire (*Mr. Donovan*), Arthur Rankin (*Bernie Riskin*), Marjorie Maurice (*Esther Block*), Ernst Pasque (*Isadore*).

Comedy-drama. The Solitary Kid, a tramp, finds a waif, Ruth, on a doorstep with a note promising a rich reward when the child becomes eighteen. He "hocks" her for $5 with a Jewish pawnbroker, who rears her as his own daughter. When she becomes eighteen, The Solitary Kid learns that his reward is one that he will receive in heaven and tries to blackmail the pawnbroker. Ruth overhears the proposition and informs the police, The Solitary Kid is arrested, and Ruth marries an Irish youth who was her childhood sweetheart. *Blackmail. Irish. Jews. Pawnbrokers. Waifs.*

FD 4 Jun 1922. *MPW* 10 Jun 1922, p. 581. *Var* 30 Jun 1922, p. 33.

A FLAGPOLE NEEDS A FLAG *see* **BEHIND THE NEWS**

THE FLAMES OF JOHANNIS (Gypsies)

Lubin Mfg Co. *Dist* V-L-S-E, Inc. 10 Apr **1916** [©Lubin Mfg. Co.; 19 Apr 1916; LP8101]. Si; b&w. 5 reels.

Dir Edgar Lewis. *Scen* Alfred Hickman. *Cam* Edward C. Earle.

Source: Based on the play *Johannisfever* by Herman Sudermann (Germany, 1904).

Cast: Nance O'Neil (*Zirah/Marika*), George Clarke (*Mr. Vogel*), Eleanor Barry (*Mrs. Vogel*), Ethel Tully (*Gertrude*), Victor Sutherland (*George*), Irving Dillon (*Pastor Hoffner*), Mrs. Carr (*Kate*), James Cassady (*Paul*), Violet Axzell (*Little George*), Rosemary Carr (*Little Marika*).

Drama. On the same day that Vogel, a Pennsylvania farmer, adopts his dead brother's son George, he also buys a small girl, Marika, from Zirah, her gypsy mother. He and his wife raise the children together, and Marika and George quickly fall in love. The Vogels, however, want George to marry their daughter Gertrude. To please her foster parents, Marika begins keeping George at a distance, and so, feeling that he no longer loves her, he proposes to Gertrude. On the eve of the marriage, Marika, heartbroken, finally approaches George. They embrace, and he begs Marika to let him marry her. Once again thinking of the Vogels, however, she forces herself to refuse. Then, after the wedding, Marika goes to Zirah, whom she has found out is her mother, and stays with her until the old lady dies of alcoholism. *Adoption. Foster parents. Marriage–Arranged. Self-sacrifice. Alcoholics. Child selling. Farmers. Gypsies. Parentage. Pennsylvania. Weddings.*

Note: An American translation of the play, called *The Fires of St. John*, opened in New York on 28 Nov 1904, with Nance O'Neil as the star. The film was also called *The Fires of St. John* and *The Fires of Johannis*.

Motog 22 Apr 1916, p. 942. *MPN* 29 Apr 1916, p. 2555. *MPW* 22 Apr 1916, p. 644, 698. *NYDM* 15 Apr 1916, p. 28. *Var* 14 Apr 1916, p. 25. *Wid's* 20 Apr 1916, p. 525.

FLAMES OF WRATH (African Americans)

Western Film Producing Co. **1923**. Si; b&w. 5 reels.

Prod Maria P. Williams. *Scen* Samuel Ellison.

Cast: Roxie Mankins (*Pauline Keith*), John Burton (*William Jackson*), Charles Pearson (*Guy Braxton*), Anna Kelson (*Flora Fulton*), John Lester Johnson (*Frank Keith*), Frank Colbert (*C. Dates*), Maria P. Williams (*Prosecuting attorney*).

African American, Crime, Drama. After P. C. Gordon is murdered and robbed of a diamond ring that he brought as a birthday present for his wife, one of the thieves, C. Dates, is apprehended. A woman prosecuting attorney makes a compelling case against him, and he is given a ten-year penitentiary sentence. Dates escapes and heads for the vacant lot where he buried the ring. Meanwhile, a boy playing in the lot, digs up the ring and gives it to his older brother, Guy Braxton, a prosperous dry goods merchant. Guy shows it to William Jackson, an unscrupulous lawyer. When Pauline Keith, Jackson's young stenographer, learns of Jackson's scheme to steal the diamond, which also involves her own father, and a woman, Flora Fulton, she begins to investigate. After Jackson finds that several incriminating documents are missing, he fires Pauline. She immediately goes to work for Guy and prevents the theft of the diamond. Jackson is later elected district attorney and orders the arrest of Guy, but Pauline obtains evidence of Guy's innocence and saves him from a long prison term. After a $2,000 reward is issue for Dates, he turns himself in and is pardoned. *African Americans. Dismissal (Employment). District attorneys. Frame-ups. Lawyers. Merchants. Stenographers. Trials. Women lawyers. Brothers. Diamonds. Murder. Prison escapes. Rings. Robbery.*

Note: This film was also known as *The Flames of Wrath*. According to information in the George P. Johnson Collection at the UCLA Special

Collections Library, Maria P. Williams, the secretary and treasurer of Western Film Producing Co., was the first female African-American film producer in the U.S. The company was located in Kansas City, MO.

ChiDef 24 Mar 1923, p. 6.

THE FLAMING CRISIS (African Americans)

Monarch Productions. *Dist* Mesco Production. **1924?**. Si; b&w. 6 reels, 4,400 ft.

Prod Lawrence Goldman. *Dir* William H. Grimes.

Cast: Calvin Nicholson (*Newspaperman*), Dorothy Dunbar (*Tex Miller*), Talford White, Henry Dixon (*Mark Lethler*), Kathryn Sherman, Marie Chester, Arthur Yeargan, William Butler.

African American, Western. A young black newspaperman is convicted of murder on circumstantial evidence and sentenced to prison. He escapes and makes his way to the southwestern cattle country, where he falls in love with Tex Miller, a beautiful cowgirl. Having rid the territory of an outlaw band, he gives himself up to the law, thinking that he will be sent back to prison. After discovering that the real murderer has confessed, he returns to Tex and the country he has come to love. *African Americans. Circumstantial evidence. Fugitives. Injustice. Murder. Outlaws. Reporters.*

Note: According to information in the NYSA, an application for a license to be exhibited in New York State was submitted on 21 Aug 1924, although an exact release date has not been determined. Mesco Productions was located in Kansas City, MO. According to information in the George P. Johnson Collection at the UCLA Special Collections Library, producer Lawrence Goldman was a white former theater owner in Kansas City and head of the Motion Picture Exhibitors of Missouri. According to *Billboard*, the film was delayed for ten weeks for lead actor Calvin Nicholson to recover from injuries sustained during the filming of a cattle rush scene.

Billboard 19 Jan 1924, p. 55. *Billboard* 15 Mar 1924, p. 72. *Billboard* 24 May 1924, p. 46. *ChiDef* 23 Feb 1924, p. 7.

FLAMING FEATHER (Native Americans, Ute)

Nat Holt Pictures. *Dist* Paramount Pictures Corp. Feb **1951**; *Prod* mid-Nov–late Dec 1950 [©Paramount Pictures Corp.; 13 Dec 1951; LP1544]. Sd (Western Electric Recording); col (Technicolor). 9 reels, 6,992 ft. 77-79 min. PCA cert no. 15168.

Prod Nat Holt. *Assoc to the prod* Harry Templeton. *Dir* Ray Enright. *Asst dir* Clarence Eurist. *Story and scr* Gerald Drayson Adams. *Addl dial* Frank Gruber. *Dir of photog* Ray Rennahan. *Technicolor color consultant* Richard Mueller. *Art dir* John Goodman. *Film ed* Elmo Billings. *Set dec* Bert Granger. *Ward* Elmer Ellsworth. *Mus score* Paul Sawtell. *Sd rec* Harold Lewis and Gene Garvin. *Makeup artist* Norman Pringle.

Song(s): "There's No Ring on Her Finger," words and music by Frank Loesser and Manning Sherwin; "He Met Her on the Prairie," words and music by Ralph Rainger and Leo Robin; "You Can't Blame Polly," words and music by Lester Lee and Jerry Seelen.

Cast: Sterling Hayden [(*Tex McCloud*)], Forrest Tucker [(*Lt. Tom Blaine*)], Arleen Whelan [(*Carolina*)], Barbara Rush [(*Nora Logan*)], Victor Jory [(*Lucky Lee, also known as "The Sidewinder"*)], Richard Arlen [(*Showdown Calhoun*)], Edgar Buchanan [(*Sgt. O'Rourke*)], Carol Thurston [(*Turquoise*)], Ian MacDonald [(*Tombstone Jack*)], George Cleveland [(*Doc Fallon*)], [Bob Kortman (*Lafe*)], [Ethan Laidlaw (*Ed Poke*)], [Don Dunning (*Trooper Condon*)], [Paul Burns (*Prospector*)], [Ray Teal (*Brad Larkin*)], [Nacho Galindo (*Jose*)], [Gene Lewis (*Jeb Weaver*)], [Frank Lackteen (*Hopi Joe*)], [Donald Kerr (*Jubal Hite*)], [Bryan Hightower (*Black Cloud*)], [Herman Nowlin (*Stagecoach driver*)], [Larry McGrath (*Bartender*)].

Western, with songs. [*Print viewed*]. Between 1857 until 1877, a mysterious outlaw called The Sidewinder leads a group of renegade Utes in brutal attacks on Arizona settlers. When he destroys the Canyon Diablo ranch of Tex McCloud, the rancher determines to bring the killer to justice himself. One evening, while drinking at the Last Chance Saloon, Tex criticizes the Cavalry for letting The Sidewinder elude them for so many years. This provokes Lt. Tom Blaine into betting a year's salary that the Cavalry will beat Tex in finding the criminal. Carolina, an attractive saloon entertainer, offers to cover Tex's half of the bet, and later, she promises him a profitable mining stake in exchange for helping her to collect a debt from Lucky Lee, a wealthy mine owner in Fort Savage, who owes her $20,000. Carolina plans to have the handsome Tex capture the heart of Lucky's sweetheart, Nora Logan, then upon receipt of her money, she will guarantee Tex's departure from the scene. Tex rejects Carolina's offer and checks into a seedy hotel, where he encounters Nora. Distressed that her door lock is broken, Nora accepts Tex's offer to exchange

rooms. That night, however, gambler Showdown Calhoun and his partner Lafe break into Nora's room. Realizing that Carolina is behind the attack, Tex angrily orders them away at gunpoint, thereby earning Nora's gratitude. The next morning, Nora and Carolina both board the Fort Savage stagecoach. Upon learning that Showdown and his cohort left town earlier in the day, Tex leaps onto his horse and catches up with the stage just after the two men kidnap Nora. Tex rescues her and then accompanies the stage to Fort Savage. Nora introduces Tex to Lucky, who offers to repay the rancher for protecting his bride-to-be. Tex asks for a new rifle and returns to his room, where Carolina once again suggests that the two of them team up to collect the $20,000. Tex angrily rejects Carolina's advances and throws her out. The next day, Tex visits Lucky's trading post, where he learns that Nora, who had been kidnapped by The Sidewinder's men several years earlier, is marrying Lucky out of gratitude for his subsequent purchase of her freedom. While browsing in the trading post, Tex sees his own rifle for sale, and Lucky explains that his man, Hopi Joe, had earlier bought the Winchester from an outlaw named Tombstone Jack. Lucky suggests that Tombstone must be The Sidewinder, but later, he warns Tombstone that Tex is planning to kill him. When Tombstone attacks Tex that night, Tex injures him and accuses him of being The Sidewinder. Tombstone's friend Jeb Weaver however, claims that the outlaw was at his place when Tex's ranch was attacked. Carolina secretly kills Tombstone, and later, Showdown reminds her of her promise to marry him. Meanwhile, a young Ute woman named Turquoise threatens to reveal that Lucky is The Sidewinder if he refuses to abandon Nora and return to her. Lucky, his hands about her throat, states that a man in his position must marry one of his own kind. Frightened, Turquoise runs away. Tex, who is now the marshal, tells Blaine about Tombstone's alibi, whereupon both men decide to question Jeb. When Jeb is found dead, Tex accompanies Blaine's unit back to town to question their new prime suspect, Lucky. Bursting into Lucky's wedding, Tex and Blaine accuse him of being The Sidewinder. Lucky argues that his wealth makes criminal activities unnecessary, and to prove it, he offers to show them his hidden mine. That night, Lucky sends Turquoise to call his band of renegade Utes into action, and the next day, as Tex, the Cavalry and a group of townspeople are riding to Lucky's mine, the Utes attack them. During the battle, Carolina and Showdown are killed, and Lucky grabs Nora and escapes to his cliff-dwelling hideout. Tex and Blaine follow Lucky up the ladders to the cliff-dwelling, but as they fight, Turquoise finds a gun and kills Lucky. Tex, his arm around Nora, agrees that all bets on the capture of The Sidewinder are off. *Masked bandits. Ranchers. Renegades. Revenge. United States. Army. Cavalry. Wagers. Aged men. Arizona. Cliff-dwellings. Debt. False accusations. Gamblers. Gratitude. Gunfights. Jealousy. Kidnapping. Mine owners. Murder. Outlaws. Physicians. Raids. Romantic rivalry. Saloons. Shootouts. Singers. Trading posts. Unrequited love. Ute Indians. Weddings.*

Note: The working titles of this film were *Devil's Canyon* and *Fort Savage*. According to a Nov 1950 news item in *Par News*, contained in the production files at the AMPAS Library, Gail Russell was originally set to play the female lead. According to other *Par News* items, the film was shot on location around Oak Creek Canyon near Sedona, AZ, and at the Montezuma Castle National Monument near Sedona, an 800-year-old Indian cliff dwelling. According to a Jan 1952 *Par News* item, the local Yavapai Indians, who were employed as extras on the production, refused to enter the cliff-dwellings because they represented the "dwelling place of the dead," thus briefly halting production while a band of Navajos were brought in from a reservation 137 miles away to replace them. Modern sources add Forrest Taylor to the cast.

Box 22 Dec 1951. *DV* 14 Dec 1951, p. 3. *Exb* 19 Dec 1951, p. 3206. *FD* 26 Dec 1951, p. 10. *Har* 15 Dec 1951, p. 199. *HR* 17 Nov 1950, p. 12. *HR* 22 Dec 1950, p. 12. *HR* 14 Dec 1951, p. 4. *MPHPD* 22 Dec 1951, pp. 1161-62. *Var* 19 Dec 1951, p. 6.

THE FLAMING FOREST *see* **CALL OF THE FOREST**

THE FLAMING FRONTIER (Native Americans)
Universal Pictures Corp.; Universal-Jewel. 12 Sep **1926** [©Universal Pictures Corp.; 13 Feb 1926; LP22401]. Si; b&w. 9 reels, 8,828 ft.
Dir Edward Sedgwick. *Scen* Edward J. Montagne and Charles Kenyon. *Adpt* Raymond L. Schrock. *Story* Edward Sedgwick. *Photog* Virgil Miller.
Cast: Hoot Gibson (*Bob Langdon*), Anne Cornwall (*Betty Stanwood*), Dustin Farnum (*General Custer*), Ward Crane (*Sam Belden*), Kathleen Key (*Lucretia*), Eddie Gribbon (*Jonesy*), Harry Todd (*California Joe*), Harold Goodwin (*Lawrence Stanwood*), George Fawcett (*Senator Stanwood*), Noble Johnson (*Sitting Bull*),

Charles K. French (*Senator Hargess*), William Steele (*Penfield*), Walter Rodgers (*President Grant*), Ed Wilson (*Grant's secretary*), Joe Bonomo (*Rain in the Face*).
Western. Through the influence of Senator Stanwood, Bob Langdon, a Pony Express rider, is admitted to West Point. Bob falls in love with the senator's daughter, Betty, and, to protect the senator's son from a scandal involving a woman, Bob assumes the blame himself. Thrown out of the military academy, Bob returns to the command of General Custer. Custer is attacked at the Little Big Horn, and Bob rides for help. Bob later brings Belden, a crooked Indian agent, before the bar of justice and, his reputation cleared, returns to West Point. *General George Armstrong Custer. Ulysses Simpson Grant. Indian agents. Indians of North America. Little Big Horn, Battle of the, 1876. Pony Express. Sitting Bull. United States Military Academy. United States. Congress.*

FD 11 Apr 1926. *MPW* 17 Apr 1926. *NYT* 5 Apr 1926, p. 24. *Var* 7 Apr 1926, p. 36.

FLAMING FRONTIER (Native Americans, Dakota, Chippewa, Siksika)
Regal Films (Canada Ltd.); controlled by Regal Films, Inc. *Dist* Twentieth Century-Fox Film Corp. Aug **1958**; Prod: ended early Jan 1958 [©Twentieth Century-Fox Film Corp.; 26 Jun 1958; LP12206]. Sd (RCA Sound Recording); b&w; RegalScope. 8 reels, 6,280 and 6,284 ft. 70 min. PCA cert no. 18846. *Country of origin* Canada—U.S.
Prod Sam Newfield. *Dir* Sam Newfield. *Asst dir* Bert Marotta. *Wrt* Louis Stevens. *Dir of photog* Frederick Ford. *Art dir* Tom Kemp. *Film ed* Douglas Robertson. *Set dec* Danny Cassidy. *Ward* Sam Donaldson and Malabar. *Mus comp and cond* John Bath. *Sd* Ben Brightwell. *Makeup* Olga Mundick. *Prod mgr* Bert Sternbach. *Scr supv* Margaret Conolly. *Property master* Ollie Montgomery.
Cast: Bruce Bennett [(*Capt. James Huston*)], Jim Davis [(*Col. Hugh Carver*)], Paisley Maxwell [(*Felice Carver*)], Don Garrard [(*Sgt. Haggerty*)], Cecil Linder [(*Dan Carver*)], Peter Humphries [(*Sgt. Edmundson*)], Ben Lennick [(*Jeff Baxter*)], Larry Solway [(*Chief Little Crow*)], Bill Walsh [(*Gen. Dunn*)], Larry Mann [(*Bradford*)], Mike Fitzgerald [(*Maj. Franklin*)], Bob Vanstone [(*Capt. Carver's sentry*)], Shane Rimmer [(*Running Bear*)], Charles Kehoe [(*Soldier*)], Jeffrey Alexander [(*Army doctor*)], Brandon Dillon [(*Store clerk*)], Daryl Masters, [Allen Chrysler (*Capt. Leech*)], [Dave Wright (*2d clerk*)], [Elizabeth Beattie].
Historical, Western. [*Print viewed*]. During the Civil War, Captain James Huston, a half-Sioux, half-Danish Union officer, is sent to Fort Ridgely in Minnesota with a letter from President Abraham Lincoln giving him authority to take command. Huston's task is to stop Little Crow, the Sioux chief and Huston's boyhood friend, in his uprising against the whites. Lincoln is concerned that food supplies from Minnesota, needed by the Union Army, have stopped, and is worried that uprisings might spread to Idaho and the Dakota Territory. In Minnesota, Huston meets the commander, Colonel Hugh Carver, an Indian hater who believes that Little Crow does not want peace, and the colonel's brother, Dan Carver, an ambitious land dealer and owner of a trading post. With his partner, Jeff Baxter, Dan Carver wants to wipe out the Sioux, as they hope to become the wealthiest men in the state. Huston also meets the colonel's wife Felice, who, unhappy in her marriage, plans to return to St. Louis as soon as possible. When Running Bear, a Sioux brave, is captured during an ambush, the colonel prepares to whip him so that he will reveal the location of Little Crow's camp. Huston stops Colonel Carver, and with Sergeant Haggerty, who brought him to the fort, goes with Running Bear to meet Little Crow. On the way, the group is attacked by two Chippewa Indians, who shoot a poisoned arrow into Running Bear. During the fight, one Chippewa dies. Huston ministers to Running Bear, and Haggerty finds a document on the dead Chippewa that says dead soldiers are worth $100 at any agency store. Running Bear arranges for the soldiers to meet with Little Crow, and after the chief bests his old boyhood friend in a prolonged arm wrestling duel, he agrees to inform his council of Huston's promise that the Sioux will receive past due money payments and food on order at the trading post. When Sioux braves come to Carver and Baxter's trading post demanding food, Huston orders Baxter to fill their orders, then subdues him when Baxter tries to fight. Taking incriminating evidence, Huston orders Baxter to appear at a meeting of trading post owners to be held in eight days, at which a representative of Governor Ramsey will be present. That night, during a fight at the trading post, three whites, including Baxter's brother, and two Indians with food

orders are killed. Meanwhile, at the fort, when Huston notices a bruise on Felice's face, she confides in him. The fact that she is the daughter of a Frenchman and a Blackfoot Nation woman meant nothing to her husband when they married, but when he became commander of the fort and was promoted to colonel at the start of the war, his character changed as his desire for glory from fighting the Sioux grew into an obsession. When Colonel Carver refuses to hold the meeting and orders Huston to return Baxter's papers, Huston shows him the governor's letter and pulls rank. That night, Felice, her face covered with more bruises, warns Huston that Baxter and Dan Carver are out to kill him. Colonel Carver, drunk, catches them together and threatens to kill Huston, when news arrives that Indians are approaching the main gate. The Indians dump the mutilated bodies of the whites killed at the trading post, and Huston realizes it is an act of reprisal for breaking the agreement. Although the colonel wants to attack an Indian village at dawn, Huston convinces him to wait until he asks Little Crow for the men responsible for the killings to be tried in civil court. He is taken to see Little Crow, where he learns that soldiers have since plundered a Sioux village. Trying to avert a war, Huston blames evil white men who acted against the president's wishes. When Little Crow, speaking for the council, refuses to listen, Huston angrily takes a burning stick to the scar on his arm where, as boys, he and Little Crow became blood brothers, and ends their brotherhood. Battles ensue, and during an ambush, Colonel Carver is shot by Running Bear, who is then killed by Huston. Dying, the colonel tries to shoot Huston, but falls unconscious. Huston takes charge at the fort. The Sioux unsuccessfully storm the gate twice, then plan to attack that evening. After the colonel dies, Little Crow appears with a white flag and demands those guilty of starting the killing and cheating as his price for peace. Huston refuses, though he assures him they will be dealt with by the courts. Although the frightened settlers congregated in the fort want Baxter and Dan Carver to be turned over to the Sioux, Huston argues that if they give in now, Little Crow will destroy the fort. Later, when he learns that Baxter and Dan Carver have escaped, Huston goes with Haggerty to Little Crow's camp, where he finds the two men dead, tied to a tree. Little Crow, on his horse, breaks his war stick, then waves at Huston, who waves back. Little Crow then rides off with his braves. *Bigotry. Dakota Indians. Friendship. Greed. Indians of North America–Mixed blood. Megalomania. Officers (Military). Tribal chiefs. Battered women. Battles. Brothers. Chippewa Indians. Danish Americans. Drunkenness. Fights. French Americans. Abraham Lincoln. Marriage–Mixed. Minnesota. Nursing back to health. Poisoning. Self-mutilation. Settlers. Siksika Indians. Threats. Trading posts. United States–History–Civil War, 1861-1865.*

Note: This film was made by Regal Films (Canada) Ltd., a subsidiary of Regal Films, Inc. which undertook the production of features in Canada beginning in the summer of 1957. It originally was scheduled for national release in Apr 1958, but the release date was pushed back to Aug.

Box 14 Jul 1958. *Exh* 9 Jul 1958, p. 4487. *FD* 20 Jun 1958, p. 6. *Har* 7 Jun 1958, p. 91. *MPHPD* 30 Aug 1958, p. 961.

FLAMING HEART *see* **FLAMING STAR**

FLAMING LANCE *see* **FLAMING STAR**

FLAMING STAR (Native Americans, Kiowa)

Twentieth Century-Fox Film Corp. *Dist* Twentieth Century-Fox Film Corp. Dec **1960**; New York opening: 16 Dec 1960; Prod: 16 Aug–4 Oct 1960 [©Twentieth Century-Fox Film Corp.; 16 Dec 1960; LP18191]. Sd (Westrex Recording System); col (De Luxe). 8,263 ft. 92 or 101 min. PCA cert no. 19729.

Prod David Weisbart. *Dir* Don Siegel. *2d unit dir* Richard Talmadge. *Asst dir* Joseph E. Rickards. *Scr* Clair Huffaker and Nunnally Johnson. *Dir of photog* Charles G. Clarke. *Art dir* Duncan Cramer and Walter M. Simonds. *Film ed* Hugh S. Fowler. *Set dec* Walter M. Scott and Gustav Berntsen. *Cost des* Adele Balkan. *Mus* Cyril J. Mockridge. *Cond* Lionel Newman. *Orch* Edward B. Powell. *Dances staged by* Josephine Earl. *Sd* E. Clayton Ward, Warren B. Delaplain and E. C. Ward. *Makeup* Ben Nye. *Hair styles* Helen Turpin. *Tech adv* Col. Tom Parker.

Song(s): "Flaming Star," words and music by Sherman Edwards and Sid Wayne; "A Cane and a High Starched Collar," words and music by Sid Tepper and Roy Bennett; vocal accompaniment to Elvis Presley's songs by The Jordanaires.

Source: Based on the novel *Flaming Lance* by Clair Huffaker (New York, 1958).

Cast: ELVIS PRESLEY [(*Pacer Burton*)], Steve Forrest [(*Clint Burton*)], Barbara Eden [(*Roslyn Pierce*)], Dolores Del Rio [(*Neddy Burton*)], John McIntire [(*Sam Burton*)], Rudolph Acosta [(*Buffalo Horn*)], Karl Swenson [(*Dred Pierce*)], Ford Rainey [(*Doc Phillips*)], Richard Jaeckel [(*Angus Pierce*)], Anne Benton [(*Dorothy Howard*)], L. Q. Jones [(*Tom Howard*)], Douglas Dick [(*Will Howard*)], Tom Reese [(*Jute*)], Marian Goldina [(*Ph'Sha Knay*)], [Perry Lopez (*Two Moons*)], [Monte Burkhart (*Ben Ford*)], [Ted Jacques (*Hornsby*)], [Rodd Redwing, Lon Ballantyne, Pat Hogan, Foster Hood, Henry Amargo, Ray Beltram (*Indian braves*)], [Roy Jenson (*Matt Holcom*)], [Bob Folkerson (*Posseman*)], [Tom Fadden, Griswold Green, Tom Allen, Guy Way, Joe Brooks, William Herrin (*Men at crossing*), [Barbara Beaird (*Dottie Phillips*)], [Virginia Christine (*Mrs. Phillips*)], [Robert Adler (*Driver*)], [Sharon Bercutt (*Bird's Wing*)], [Larry Chance (*Indian chief*)].

Western. [*Print viewed*]. As Clint and Pacer Burton approach their Texas ranch on a moonlit night in 1878, they become worried by the silence that engulfs the house. They enter cautiously, and are surprised by family and friends who have come to celebrate Clint's birthday. Joining Sam Burton and his Kiowa wife Neddy are Will Howard and his family, along with the Pierces: Dred, Angus and Roslyn, who is Clint's sweetheart. After the party, the neighbors head home, but the Howards are attacked by Kiowa Indians, and everyone but Will is killed. The Burtons are concerned when the new Kiowa chief, the warlike Buffalo Horn, appears near the ranch, but it is not until the following day, when Clint and Pacer ride into town for supplies, that they learn about the massacre of the Howard family. Dred and Angus are hostile toward Pacer, who, as Neddy's son, is half Kiowa, and even though Clint, Sam's son from a previous marriage, is white, they hint that perhaps he, too, was somehow involved in the attack. Crushed by the news that her friends have been killed, Neddy wonders whether she and Sam did the right thing when twenty years before, they wed, but Sam assures her that the Burton family always will stick together. The family's strength is tested on the following night, when a gang of settlers questions their loyalty in the coming war with the Kiowas. When Matt Holcom insults Sam and Neddy, Clint wounds him with his gun, whereupon the settlers kill most of the Burtons' cattle. While Sam and Clint search for surviving livestock, Neddy and Pacer offer food to two hungry trappers, but one of the visitors forces himself on Neddy, and Pacer is forced to drive them away with his fists. Buffalo Horn asks Pacer to fight with his warriors as they attempt one last time to drive the whites from their land. Anxious to prevent unnecessary killing, Neddy decides to visit her family at the Kiowa camp, but although the men there treat Pacer as their brother, the women turn their backs on Neddy. Before the two leave, Buffalo denounces whites for moving more and more deeply into lands inhabited by Indians. Pacer's friend, Two Moons, accompanies them home, but as they approach the ranch, Will, maddened by the earlier massacre of his family, crawls from his hiding place and shoots Neddy. In the confusion, Two Moons is also shot, and Pacer kills Will. Clint and Sam arrive, and while Sam cares for his wife, who whispers that the flaming star of death is near, Clint and Pacer ride to town for Doc Phillips. The townspeople angrily send them away, but Pacer finally forces Phillips to accompany him. By the time the doctor, Roslyn and the two brothers return to the ranch, however, Neddy has risen from her bed, crawled toward the hills and died. Enraged, Pacer decides to join Buffalo Horn, and when Clint and Roslyn try to stop him, he threatens his brother with a gun. Sam gives Pacer his blessing but sadly observes as his son rides away that his efforts to build a family and a home have been in vain. Pacer takes the body of Two Moons back to the Kiowa camp, where he offers to take the warrior's place in battle. Meanwhile, while Clint delivers Roslyn to the crossing, a group of Kiowas, unaware of Buffalo Horn's promise to protect the Burton family, descends on the ranch and kills Sam. Alone now, Clint buries his father and rides off in search of revenge. As a war party rides by, Clint shoots at the chief, prompting the Indians, including Pacer, to give chase. When Clint is injured, Pacer takes him to a safe place and then leads the Indians in the other direction. Back at the ranch, Clint tells Pacer that Kiowas killed their father, whereupon Pacer, fed up, ties Clint to Roslyn's horse, sends the animal to the Crossing and prepares to meet the advancing Indians alone. Upon waking at the Pierce home on the following day, Clint

insists on returning to help Pacer, but as he stumbles out of the house, an injured man approaches on horseback. Slumped over the animal, Pacer reveals that he is dying. "You live for me, Clint," he urges. "Maybe someday, somewhere, people will understand folks like us." Then, following the flaming star of death, he rides toward the hills to die. *Family relationships. Indians of North America–Mixed blood. Kiowa Indians. Loyalty. Racism. Tribal chiefs. Ambushes. Birthdays. Death and dying. Fistfights. Gunshot wounds. Massacres. Murder. Neighbors. Parties. Ranchers. Revenge. Romantic rivalry. Settlers. Texas. Trappers.*

Note: The working titles of this film were *The Brothers of Flaming Arrow, Flaming Lance, Flaming Heart, The Brothers of Broken Lance, Black Star* and *Black Heart*. According to a May 1958 *HR* news item, Nunnally Johnson was initally slated to write, produce and direct the film. A May 1958 *DV* news item adds that Johnson wanted Marlon Brando and Frank Sinatra to play the brothers. A Jun 1960 *HR* news item credits Buddy Adler as executive producer, but the extent of his contribution to the released film has not been determined. Although an Aug 1960 *HR* production chart places Barbara Steele and Anne Seymour in the cast, their participation in the released film has not been confirmed.

According to an Aug 1960 *DV* news item, the picture was shot on location at the Conejo Ranch in Thousand Oaks, CA. A Nov 1960 *DV* news item notes that the two songs, "Britches" and "Summer Kisses, Winter Dreams," were cut from the film after a sneak preview. This may account for the variance in running times. Contemporary and modern critics praised Elvis' acting in the picture. The *NYT* review observed that the Indians "are not simply presented as 'heavies' but also as beleaguered men being ruthlessly deprived, in their view, of their lands....[The] unhappy ending...seems to underline the sadness of the period when the Indian began to vanish."

Box 26 Dec 1960. *DV* 27 May 1958. *DV* 16 Aug 1960. *DV* 29 Nov 1960. *DV* 19 Dec 1960, p. 3. *Exb* 11 Jan 1961, pp. 4781-82. *FD* 20 Dec 1960, p. 6. *Har* 24 Dec 1960, pp. 207-08. *HR* 7 May 1958. *HR* 13 Jun 1960. *HR* 26 Aug 1960. *HR* 23 Sep 960, p. 14. *HR* 19 Dec 1960, p. 3. *MPHPD* 24 Dec 1960, p. 964. *NYT* 17 Dec 1960, p. 19. *Var* 21 Dec 1960, p. 6.

FLESH (German Americans)

Metro-Goldwyn-Mayer Corp.; controlled by Loew's, Inc.; A John Ford Production. *Dist* Metro-Goldwyn-Mayer Distributing Corp. 8 Dec **1932**; Prod: 26 Sep—late Oct 1932 [©Metro-Goldwyn-Mayer Distributing Corp.; 12 Dec 1932; LP3472]. Sd (Western Electric Sound System); b&w. 10 reels. 95 min. Passed by the National Board of Review.

[*Prod* John W. Considine, Jr.]. *Dir* John Ford. [*Asst dir* Dave Taggart]. *Story* Edmund Goulding. *Adpt* Leonard Praskins and Edgar Allan Woolf. *Dial* Moss Hart. *Photog* Arthur Edeson. *Art dir* Cedric Gibbons. *Film ed* William S. Gray. *Rec dir* Douglas Shearer. *Sd* James Brock.

Cast: WALLACE BEERY (*Polikai*), Karen Morley (*Laura [Nash]*), Ricardo Cortez (*Nicky [Grant]*), Jean Hersholt (*Mr. Herman*), John Miljan ([*Joe*] *Willard*), Herman Bing (*Pepi, head waiter*), Vincent Barnett (*A waiter*), Greta Meyer (*Mrs. Herman*), Edward Brophy (*Dolan, referee*), [Ward Bond (*Wrestler Muscles Manning*)], [Nat Pendleton (*First opponent in America*)], [Charles Williams (*Sports reporter*)].

Drama. [*Print viewed*]. When American Laura Nash is released from a German prison, she is desperate to see her lover, Nicky, but cannot get the money to pay for his release from prison as well. At a beer garden, Karen can't pay for her meal, but is touched by the kindness of the Polikai, a waiter and wrestling champion, who settles the bill for her. Meeting again later that night, Polikai lets Karen stay at his place above the beer garden. Soon Polikai falls in love with her and proposes marriage, through his friend Herman, but Karen still yearns for Nicky, even though she is fond of Polikai. One night Polikai catches her trying to steal his money, but when she explains that she needs it to get her "brother" out of jail, he offers to help her. The next day Polikai brings Nicky back with him. Laura wants to leave with Nicky, but when she tells him that she is pregnant, he sneaks away after telling Polikai that he needs money to go to their sick mother in America. Karen marries Polikai and when her child is born, he thinks that he is the father. Because he is homesick for America, he takes her there, hoping to get the wrestling championship of the world. When Nicky comes into their lives again, Karen is at first cool to him. He sets up a series of crooked matches for Polikai, which he refuses but Laura talks him into it after Nicky slaps her into compliance. Soon Polikai has become a contender for the title, but begins to drink. Laura remorsefully tries to tell him the truth and begins to care for him, but when she tries to sober him up to win a match, Nicky begins to beat her. Just then Polikai wakes up and strangles Nicky. Polikai then wins the grueling match, after which he is arrested for Nicky's murder. Laura visits him in prison and tells him that everyone is behind him

and that the district attorney thinks that everything will be all right. She says that she will go away to prevent him from being hurt further, but as their hands clasp, he calls her "Liebchen." *Battered women. Deception. Ex-convicts. Fixed fights. Germany. Wrestlers and wrestling. Americans in foreign countries. Brothers and sisters. Drunkenness. German Americans. Hotels. Immigrants. Infants. Strangling.*

Note: According to pre-production news items in *HR*, Edmund Goulding was initally set to direct the picture. Several months after Goulding was announced as the director, *HR* had a news item reporting that Raoul Walsh was to direct the picture, however, one day later the paper published a correction, saying that Robert Z. Leonard, and not Walsh was set to direct. In Aug 1932, it was announced that Colleen Moore was to co-star with Wallace Beery, making her talking picture debut and her first film in three years. Moore did not make her first talking picture until 1933 when she appeared in the Fox picture *The Power and the Glory*. In Sep 1932 it was reported that Madge Evans would play the female lead opposite Beery, and finally, two days before production began, Karen Morley was named as the female lead. Other news items noted that writer Leonard Praskins was having a dispute with M-G-M, thus delaying the start of the picture for several months. A 29 Jul 1932 news item mentioned Milton Raison as co-adaptor with Praskins, however, the extent of his participation in the completed film has not been determined. *HR* also reported that Wladek Zybszko was to be in the cast, however, his appearance in the film cannot be confirmed. This was John Ford's first film for M-G-M. Character actor Nat Pendleton, who has a small part as a bumbling wrestler in the film, was actually an Olympic wrestler and was the World Champion in 1924.

FD 10 Dec 1932, p. 18. *HF* 1 Oct 1932, p. 16. *HF* 22 Oct 1932, p. 16. *HR* 10 Feb 1932, p. 7. *HR* 10 Jun 1932, p. 4. *HR* 11 Jun 1932, p. 3. *HR* 30 Jun 1932, p. 3. *HR* 28 Jul 1932, p. 3. *HR* 29 Jul 1932, p. 3. *HR* 19 Aug 1932, p. 3. *HR* 9 Sep 1932, p. 11. *HR* 20 Sep 1932, p. 2, 4. *HR* 24 Sep 1932, p. 3. *HR* 1 Dec 1932, p. 3. *MPH* 17 Dec 1932, p. 3. *NYT* 10 Dec 1932, p. 19. *Var* 13 Dec 1932, p. 14.

FLESH AND BLOOD (Chinese Americans)

Dist Western Pictures Exploitation Co. Jul **1922**. Si; b&w. 6 reels, 5,300 ft.

Pres Irving Cummings. *Dir* Irving Cummings. *Story* Louis Duryea Lighton.

Cast: Lon Chaney (*David Webster*), Edith Roberts (*The Angel Lady*), De Witt Jennings (*Detective Doyle*), Noah Beery (*Li Fang*), Ralph Lewis (*Fletcher Burton*), Jack Mulhall (*Ted Burton*), Togo Yamamoto (*The Prince*), Kate Price (*The Landlady*), Wilfred Lucas (*The Policeman*).

Drama. Unjustly imprisoned for fifteen years, David Webster, hoping to visit his wife, escapes; but he arrives in time only to see her funeral procession. The convict receives shelter from Li Fang, a Chinese politician; disguises himself as a crippled beggar to escape the police; and meets his daughter, the Angel Lady, to whom he does not reveal his identity. Determined to have revenge on Fletcher Burton, the man who sent him to prison, Webster finally corners his enemy and obtains a signed confession. At that moment, Webster's daughter enters the room, and he learns of her desire to marry Burton's son, Ted. In exchange for Burton's approval of the marriage Webster destroys the confession and returns to prison satisfied with the knowledge of his daughter's happiness. *Chinese Americans. Fatherhood. Handicapped. Prison escapes. Revenge.*

Note: "There is a bit of inserted action, illustrating a tale related to the impatient Webster by the philosophic Li Fang, which is told in color with Chinese players." (*ETR* 19 Aug 1922, p. 806.).

FD 27 Aug 1922. *MPN* 29 Jul 1922, p. 557. *MPW* 19 Aug 1922. *MPW* 16 Sep 1922.

FLESH AND FLAME see NIGHT OF THE QUARTER MOON

FLIGHT see DESPERATE

FLIGHT TO THE SUN (Native Americans)

Trans World Airlines. *Dist* Institute of Visual Training. **1948**. Sd; col. 16mm. 40 min.

Educational/Cultural. [*Not viewed*]. Scenes of Death Valley and the Grand Canyon, and of life in an Indian village of the Southwest are shown. *Death Valley (CA). Grand Canyon (AZ). Indians of North America.*

THE FLOWER OF DOOM (Chinese Americans)

Universal Film Mfg. Co.; Red Feather Photoplays. *Dist* Universal Film Mfg. Co. 16 Apr **1917** [©Universal Film Mfg. Co.; 6 Apr 1917; LP10517]. Si; b&w. 5 reels.

Dir Rex Ingram. *Scen* Rex Ingram. *Cam* Duke Hayward.

Cast: Wedgwood Nowell (*Sam Savinsky*), Yvette Mitchell (*Tea Rose*), Nicholas Dunaew (*Paul Rasnov*), M. K. Wilson (*Harvey Pearson*), Gypsy Hart (*Neva Sacon*), Tommy Morrissey (*Buck*), Frank Tokunaga (*Charley Sing*), Gordo Keeno (*Ah Wong*), Evelyn Selbie (*Arn Fun*).

Drama. Reporter Harvey Pearson becomes infatuated with cabaret dancer Neva Sacon. While showing Neva through Chinatown, Harvey pins a flower on her lapel that, unknown to him, is the symbol of a Tong. When Neva is spirited away by a member of a rival Tong and the efforts of the police to find her prove fruitless, Harvey turns to Charley Sing whom Harvey helped clear of a murder charge when he was writing an exposé of Chinatown. With Sing's help, they call at the opium den of Ah Wong and kidnap Tea Rose, a member of the Tong which is holding Neva prisoner. An exchange is then made between the two women, and Neva returns safely to Harvey. *Chinatowns. Chinese Americans. Opium dens. Tongs (Secret societies). Dancers. Infatuation. Reporters.*

ETR 21 Apr 1917, p. 1388. *MPN* 5 May 1917, pp. 2857-58. *MPW* 21 Apr 1917, pp. 487-88. *Wid's* 12 Apr 1917, p. 234.

FLOWER OF NIGHT (Latino)

Famous Players-Lasky Corp. *Dist* Paramount Pictures. 2 Nov **1925**; New York premiere: 18 Oct 1925 [©Famous Players-Lasky Corp.; 5 Nov 1925; LP21972]. Si; b&w. 7 reels, 6,374 ft.

Pres Adolph Zukor and Jesse L. Lasky. *Coöp* Mexican Government. *Dir* Paul Bern. *Scr* Willis Goldbeck. *Story* Joseph Hergesheimer. *Photog* Bert Glennon. *Gambling adv* Scott Turner.

Cast: Pola Negri (*Carlota y Villalon*), Joseph Dowling (*Don Geraldo y Villalon*), Youcca Troubetzkoy (*John Basset*), Warner Oland (*Luke Rand*), Edwin J. Brady (*Derck Bylandt*), Eulalie Jensen (*Mrs. Bylandt*), Cesare Gravina (*Servant*), Gustav von Seyffertitz (*Vigilante leader*), Helen Lee Worthing (*Josefa*), Thais Valdemar, Manuel Acosta, Frankie Bailey.

Melodrama. In the California of 1856, Don Geraldo y Villalon, descendant of Spanish grandees, has had the Flor de Noche gold mine wrested from him by dishonest Americans. Carlota, his daughter, falls in love with John Basset, the new assistant superintendent at the mine, and goes to a dance, against her father's wishes, to be near him. Mine superintendent Derck Bylandt, who has had too much to drink, dies of a heart attack when he tries to force Carlota to dance with him. Disgusted with the scene, Basset ignores her. She confesses to her father that she has disgraced the Villalon name, and he commits suicide. She then goes to San Francisco and becomes a dance hall girl. Stung by Basset's contempt, she accepts the offer of infatuated Luke Rand, the sinister head of the Vigilance Committee, to help her recover the mine. She recants when she realizes that Basset's life is in danger. In the end, Basset kills Rand; and he and Carlota realize their mutual love. *California. Dance hall girls. Mines. San Francisco (CA). Spaniards. Suicide. Vigilantes.*

Note: Musical theme and prolog entitled "Magic Love."

FD 25 Oct 1925. *MPW* 31 Oct 1925.

THE FLOWER OF NO MAN'S LAND (Native Americans)

Columbia Pictures Corp.; A Metro Wonderplay. *Dist* Metro Pictures Corp. 26 Jun **1916** [©Columbia Pictures Corp.; 27 Jun 1916; LP8590]. Si; b&w. 5 reels.

Dir John H. Collins. *Scen* John H. Collins. *Cam* Mr. Berkeley.

Cast: Viola Dana (*Echo*), Duncan McRae (*Roy Talbot*), Harry C. Brown (*Big Bill*), Mitchell Lewis (*Kahoma*), Fred Jones (*Pedro*), Nellie G. Mitchell (*Mrs. Talbot*), Eldine Steuart (*The Talbot child*), Marcus Moriarity (*Potter, the butler*).

Drama. Echo, the orphaned "flower of no man's land," has been raised by an Indian foster father, Kahoma. Then, when opera singer Roy Talbot goes West to recover his health, Echo falls instantly in love and forgets all about Big Bill, her cowboy sweetheart. Roy marries Echo and takes her back East, but soon after returning to his adoring public, he loses all interest in her. Finally, Echo leaves Roy and goes back to the wilderness, where she discovers that Roy had already been married when they met and had deserted his wife years before. For so deceiving his adopted daughter, Kahoma tracks Roy down and kills him, while Echo forgets about her big-city unhappiness and returns to Big Bill, with whom she makes plans to marry. *Bigamy. Fathers and daughters. Indians of North America. Opera singers. Revenge. Cowboys. Foster parents. Murder. Neglected wives. The West.*

Note: The cameraman for this film was listed only as Mr. Berkeley in *Wid's*. No information concerning his full name has been located.

MPN 8 Jul 1916, p. 104. *MPW* 8 Jul 1916, p. 261. *Var* 23 Jun 1916, p. 19. *Wid's* 6 Jul 1916, p. 703.

FLY AWAY HOME *see* DAUGHTERS COURAGEOUS

THE FLYING ACE (African Americans)

Norman Film Mfg. Co. **1926**; New York state license: 19 May 1928; Prod: at Norman Studios, Arlington, Florida. Sd; b&w. 6 reels, 5,600 ft.

Cast: [*In order of appearance:*] Boise De Legge (*Blair Kimball*), George Colvin (*Thomas Sawtelle*), Sam Jordan (*Dr. [A. G.] Maynard*), Harlod Platts (*Finley Tucker*), Lyons Daniels (*Jed Splivins*), Kathryn Boyd (*Ruth Sawtelle*), Dr. R. L. Brown (*Howard MacAndrews*), J. Lawrence Criner (*Billy Stokes*), Steve Reynolds (*Peg*).

African American, Aviation, Drama. [*Print viewed*]. On a sunny morning, Blair Kimball, paymaster of the M. N. & Q. Railroad, gets off the train at Mayport, Florida, the station at which passengers can change to the Eastern branch local. Finley Tucker, an aviator with a mysterious source of income, watches with Dr. A. G. Maynard, the local dentist, and Jed Splivins, the constable. Knowing that Kimball is not due to arrive until the next day, Finley wonders if he is carrying the payroll for employees of the Eastern branch in his satchel. After ascertaining that the connecting train will be late, Kimball waits in station master Thomas Sawtelle's office. Jed learns that Kimball is carrying $25,000 for the payroll and reports this to Finley and Maynard. Thomas' attractive daughter Ruth brings him lunch, and when Finley greets her, she asks him to take her for a ride in his new airplane. After the ride, he asks her for the hundredth time to marry him. She refuses, as usual, saying she is not certain she loves him. Alone, Finley vows that he will ask the next time in the plane, and she will say "yes" or "get out and walk on a cloud." At the railroad home office, Captain William "Billy" Stokes, known as the "Flying Ace" for his exploits in France bringing down seven German planes, visits the general manager, Howard MacAndrews, for whom he used to work as a detective. When Howard learns through a wire from Thomas that Kimball and the payroll have vanished, Billy accepts the offer of his old job back at double the pay, as the railroad tugs at his heart. Before flying to Mayport, he sends his one-legged mechanic "Peg" to hop a freight disguised as a tramp and arrive later. In Mayport, Thomas explains to Billy that while he was getting a wire, Kimball answered a knock. At the second knock, Thomas went to the door, and the next thing he remembers is waking up on the floor. Finley warns Ruth that Kimball's disappearance looks bad for Thomas, but says he will keep Billy occupied until Thomas can collect his wits. Finley offers five hundred dollars to stop his work for a day or two. When Billy refuses, Finley struggles with him, then asks why he will not arrest him for the murder. Billy says he has no proof, and Finley advises him to go to the swamp and look for buzzards swarming around Kimball's body. Billy finds Peg and tells him to stay around the station. At the railway express room, Billy finds a box sent from a book company to Maynard and discovers it has been freshly packed and made up to look like it just arrived. Billy then matches part of a vial he found outside Thomas' office with the spout of one that Peg found in a furnace and realizes they were part of a drug vial in which ethyl chloride was stored. Billy surmises that when the spout was broken, a whiff of the drug made Thomas unconscious. Billy finds cuts on Thomas' hands and believes they could have been caused by the broken vial. At the swamp, Peg shows Billy that buzzards have congregated in trees in the distance, and Billy learns from Maynard, who has come by in a wagon, that Thomas, who makes deliveries for extra money with a horse wagon, came there that morning. Seeing swamp mud on his back, Billy slaps handcuffs on the doctor, who admits he planted a hog in the swamp to throw guilt on Finley, who is trying to protect Thomas for Ruth's sake. Billy, however, accuses Maynard of hiding the payroll money in the book box. Meanwhile, Jed arrests Thomas, saying he found some of the missing money in his house with blood on it from the cut on his hand. Billy reveals to Finley that when they briefly fought, he smelled paper money clinging to his finger. He now accuses him of planning the murder and packing the money. As they brawl, Maynard escapes, but Peg runs him down and Billy subdues Finley. In the office, Billy handcuffs Jed, saying that when he sprayed the drug on Kimball, he spilled some on his finger. Peg brings in Finley and Maynard, then goes to get Kimball, and when he arrives, Billy explains the crime: Jed put the drug in Kimball's face when he answered the knock, and Maynard and Finley carried Kimball to a wagon and drove him to Finley's airplane, where Maynard placed him in a secret compartment he used to haul bootlegged liquor. Jed also

knocked Thomas out with the drug, and Finley then substituted the money for the books. As Billy talks, Jed unlocks his handcuffs with an extra key, while Maynard passes a vial to Finley. Jed shoots out the light, and during the subsequent struggle in the dark, Finley drugs Ruth with the vial, then carries her to his plane. Jed and Maynard escape in a car, and while Peg follows them on a bike, using his crutch to pedal, Billy pursues Finley. They fight, and Finley knocks Billy out with a log. He flies off with Ruth, but Billy revives and chases Finley in his plane. Peg, using a rifle he stuffed into his crutch, shoots the tire in the getaway car, forcing Jed and Maynard to stop in a field. Finley orders Ruth, who has revived, to kiss him, or "get out and walk on a cloud," but the plane catches fire. Billy drops a rope ladder to Ruth, who climbs into his plane. Failing to put out the fire, Finley dons a parachute and jumps. Peg tricks Jed and Maynard into attacking a bush on which he has put his hat, and they fight each other. After landing, Billy captures Finley, while Peg gets the others. Billy then plans to leave town until Peg sings a love song. Ruth looks at Billy shyly, and he says he'll stay and see if he can detect a way to make "Miss Sawtelle" let him call her "Ruth." She smiles demurely and turns away. *African Americans. Air pilots. Railroad detectives. Robbery. Chases. Constables. Crutches. Dentists. Drugging. False arrests. Fights. Fires. Florida. Handicapped. Impersonation and imposture. Kisses. Missing persons. Payrolls. Proposals (Marital). Railroad agents. Railroad stations. Railroad workers. Rescues. Swamps. Tramps. War heroes.*

Note: The opening credits for this film state: "Entire Cast Composed of Colored Artists." According to a pressbook for the film, a special "dummy" plane patterned after the Curtiss J.N.D. 4 was designed by Richard E. Norman, Sr., the owner of the company, for use in the production. The pressbook stated that the cost of the production went 75% over the original estimate and that Lawrence Criner and Ruth Sawtelle were in the Lafayette Players, Sam Jordan was from the vaudeville team of Jordan and Jordan, and Lyons Daniels was better known on stage as "Skunkum Bowser." The pressbook also made the following claim: "No Company making colored pictures have attempted and successfully made a picture like *The Flying Ace*. It even has situations in it which HAVEN'T BEEN SHOWN IN A WHITE PICTURE."

FLYING ROMEOS (Jewish Americans)

First National Pictures, Inc. *Dist* First National Pictures, Inc. 26 Feb **1928**. Si; b&w. 7 reels, 6,184 or 6,845 ft.

Prod E. M. Asher. *Dir* Mervyn LeRoy. *Story and scen* John McDermott. *Titles* Sidney Lazarus and Gene Towne. *Titles for Variety numbers* Jack Conway. *Photog* Dev Jennings. *Film ed* Paul Weatherwax.

Cast: Charlie Murray (*Cohan*), George Sidney (*Cohen*), Fritzi Ridgeway (*Minnie*), Lester Bernard (*Goldberg*), Duke Martin (*The Aviator*), James Bradbury, Jr. (*The Nut*), Belle Mitchell (*Mrs. Goldberg*).

Comedy. Barbers Cohen and Cohan both love their manicurist, who has a fondness for aviators. Therefore, they sign up for flying lessons and accidentally find themselves performing some fancy stunts in an airplane. Its impressed owner persuades the duo to make an overseas flight, which makes for more high jinks; on their return, Cohen and Cohan find their manicurist married to a pilot. *Air pilots. Airplanes. Barbers and barbershops. Irish. Jews. Manicurists. Stunt flying.*

FD 8 Apr 1928. *NYT* 3 Apr 1928, p. 33. *Var* 4 Apr 1928, p. 28.

FOLIES BERGÈRE DE PARIS (*foreign version*) *see* **L'HOMME DES FOLIES BERGÈRE**

FOLLOW THE GIRL (Swedish Americans)

Universal Film Mfg. Co.; A Butterfly Picture. *Dist* Universal Film Mfg. Co. 6 Aug **1917** [©Universal Film Mfg. Co.; 26 Jul 1917; LP11138]. Si; b&w. 5 reels.

Dir Louis William Chaudet. *Scen* Fred Myton.

Cast: Ruth Stonehouse (*Hilda Swanson*), Jack Dill (*Olaf*), Roy Stewart (*Larry O'Keefe*), Mrs. Witting (*Mrs. O'Keefe*), Claire Du Brey (*Donna*), Alfred Allen (*Martinez*), Harry Dunkinson (*Hong Foo*).

Espionage, Western. Orphan Hilda Swanson's prayers are answered when a Swedish-American colonization company agrees to send her to America. Aboard the steamer, she meets Olaf, a young Swede, and Donna, an enemy courier who is posing as a passenger. Learning that the secret service is on her trail, Donna sews secret documents into the hem of Hilda's skirt. She then sends a wire to her comrade Felix Martinez, notifying him to intercept the Swedish girl. Hilda and Olaf innocently evade Martinez and are sent West by

representatives of the colonization company. Missing their train at a stopover in cattle country, they are taken in by Larry O'Keefe, a big hearted rancher. Martinez finally tracks them down and arranges to have Hilda kidnapped by some Mexican cattle thieves who take the girl to their hut, only to discover that she no longer possesses the papers but has been given them to O'Keefe. Hilda escapes and meets Larry who has been searching for her. Meanwhile, Donna, unaware that she is being trailed by secret service agents, arrives at the O'Keefe ranch. The agents arrest both Martinez and Donna, and as Hilda hands over the papers, the agents assure the Swedish girl that she has done a great service for her new country. Larry then offers to marry Hilda, thus making her an official American citizen. *Citizenship. Foreign agents. Secret documents. Secret Service. Swedish Americans. Abduction. Orphans. Ranchers.*

ETR 11 Aug 1917, p. 785. *Motog* 25 Aug 1917, p. 423. *MPN* 18 Aug 1917, p. 1172. *MPW* 11 Aug 1917, p. 992. *MPW* 18 Aug 1917, p. 1083. *NYDM* 11 Aug 1917, p. 19. *Var* 3 Aug 1917, p. 24.

FOLLOWING THE FLAG IN MEXICO (Latino, Refugees)

Tropical Film Co. *Dist* State Rights; Feinberg Amusement Corp. Apr **1916** [©The Tropical Film Co.; 10 Apr 1916; MU579]. Si; b&w. 5 reels.

Documentary. At the northern Mexico border, General Francisco "Pancho" Villa poses. After Villa's raid on Columbus, New Mexico, dead men and horses lie in the streets, and ruins are in smoke. Major General Frederick Funston, of Fort Sam Houston, San Antonio, Texas, poses. American troops pass by the Alamo as they leave for the border. General Venustiano Carranza, Mexico's provisional president, sends a large army to cooperate with U.S. troops, led by General John J. Pershing, who poses at Columbus. Refugees crossing the Rio Grande are searched, vaccinated, and marched across the desert to internment camps at Fort Bliss, Texas. After some battles, Carranza triumphantly enters Mexico City. A federal soldier is captured and shot by a rebel firing squad. After a battle that lasts six days, Juarez is occupied by rebels. Street fighting occurs in Torréon. Villa's commanders are defeated. The American Red Cross treats wounded. Peaceful noncombatants, including an American and an Englishman, who were executed by Villa troops, hang in trees. Finally, a military funeral for American dead at Columbus is conducted. *Venustiano Carranza. Mexico. Mexico. Army. Revolutionaries. United States. Army. Francisco "Pancho" Villa. Alamo (San Antonio, TX). Columbus (NM). Firing squads. Fort Bliss (TX). Funerals. Juarez (Mexico). Mexico City (Mexico). John Joseph Pershing. Red Cross. Refugees. Political. Rio Grande. San Antonio (TX). Torréon (Mexico).*

Note: General Francisco "Pancho" Villa's attack on Columbus, New Mexico occurred on 9 Mar 1916. This film was also called *Following Villa in Mexico*. The copyright entry for the film lists Carl D. Pryer as the author. Because Pryer was the cameraman of another film produced by the Tropical Film Co., *Unites States Marines Under Fire in Haiti*, it is possible that he also shot this film.

MPN 15 Apr 1916, p. 2235. *MPW* 29 Apr 1916, p. 817, 825.

FOLLOWING VILLA IN MEXICO *see* **FOLLOWING THE FLAG IN MEXICO**

THE FOLLY OF REVENGE (Gypsies)

Nola Film Co. *Dist* State Rights. 9 Apr **1916**. Si; b&w. 5 reels.

Dir Walter Morton. *Cam* Norton Travis.

Cast: Warren E. Lyle (*Antonio Bordiga*).

Drama. When wealthy, dissolute William Baker meets the wife of sculptor Antonio Bordiga, he falls madly in love and kidnaps her. Antonio soon learns that his captive wife has committed suicide, so, after putting his infant daughter in a convent, he vows to catch up to Baker. When he does, after years of searching, he hires some gypsies to kidnap Baker's wife and then kill her. The gypsies make a mistake, however, and kidnap Antonio's daughter instead. Antonio manages to save her just as the gypsies are about to give her poisoned wine, and then, frenzied, he goes after Baker. He begins strangling him, but his daughter makes him stop, and convinces him to leave vengeance up to God. *Attempted murder. Fathers and daughters. Kidnapping. Mistaken identity. Revenge. Gypsies. Poisoning. Sculptors. Suicide.*

Note: *MPW* lists the release date as Mar 1916. The New York distributor of the film was The New York Film Co. The Nola Film Co. was located in New Orleans. Although *Wid's* credits George Travis as cameraman, this is probably an error, as Nola's cameraman at the time was Norton Travis.

MPW 15 Apr 1916, p. 403, 461, 518. *Var* 28 Jul 1916, p. 25. *Wid's* 27 Jul 1916, p. 750.

FOOLISH LIVES (African Americans)

Young Producers Filming Co. **1922**. Si; b&w. Length undetermined. [Feature length assumed.].

Cast: Frank Chatman, Henry Harris, Frank Carter, Jewell Cox, Marguerite Patton, Jonella Patton.

African American, Comedy. No information about the precise nature of this film has been found. *African Americans.*

Note: According to information in the George P. Johnson Collection at the UCLA Special Collections Library, this film was produced in Dallas, TX.

FOOLS' HIGHWAY (Jewish Americans)

Universal Pictures Corp.; Universal Super-Jewel. 3 Mar or 9 Mar **1924** [©Universal Pictures Corp.; 13 Feb 1924; LP19911]. Si; b&w. 7 reels, 6,800 ft.

Pres Carl Laemmle. *Dir* Irving Cummings. *Scen* Lenore J. Coffee and Harvey Gates. *Adpt* Emil Forst. *Photog* William Fildew.

Source: Based on the novel *My Mamie Rose; the Story of My Regeneration* by Owen Frawley Kildare (New York, 1903).

Cast: Mary Philbin (*Mamie Rose*), Pat O'Malley (*Mike Kildare*), William Collier, Jr. (*Max Davidson*), Lincoln Plummer (*Mike Flavin, The Boss*), Edwin J. Brady (*Jackie Doodle*), Max Davidson (*Old Levi*), Kate Price (*Mrs. Flannigan*), Charles Murray (*Mamie's father*), Sherry Tansey (*Ole Larsen*), Steve Murphy (*Chuck Connors*), Tom O'Brien (*Philadelphia O'Brien*).

Romance. Mike Kildare, a swaggering youth from New York City's Bowery at the turn of the century, loves Mamie Rose, a mender in a secondhand clothing shop. Mamie is fascinated by Kildare's brute strength, but she is also attracted to a kind and gentle Jewish boy. Kildare's gang, which he forsakes to prove his love to Mamie, waylays and beats Kildare in an underground den. He takes the severe punishment, reforms, wins Mamie, and joins the police force. *Clothing industry. Gangs. Irish. Jews. New York City–Bowery. Police. Seamstresses.*

MPW 15 Mar 1924. *Var* 2 Apr 1924, p. 23.

A FOOL'S PROMISE (African Americans)

White Film Corp. **1921**; Opened 15 Apr 1921 in Lynchburg, Virginia. Si; b&w. 5 reels.

Melodrama (?), African American. No information about the precise nature of this film has been found. *African Americans.*

Note: The White Film Corp. was located in Baltimore, MD.

FOR BETTER, FOR WORSE *see* **THE SAILOR TAKES A WIFE**

FOR FEAR OF LITTLE MEN *see* **THE LUCK OF THE IRISH**

FOR HIS MOTHER'S SAKE (African Americans)

Blackburn-Velde Pictures. *Dist* Fidelity Pictures. **1922**; Harlem premiere: 8 Jan 1922. Si; b&w. 5-6 reels, 5,400 ft.

Cast: Jack Johnson, Mattie Wilkes, Adrian Joyce, Jack Hopkins, Jack Newton, Dick Lee, Hank West, Everett Godfrey, Edward McGowan.

African American, Melodrama. When the youngest of two African-American brothers, who is the apple of his mother's eye, steals a valuable package from the express company for which he works, the older brother, employed by the same company, takes the blame, knowing his sacrifice will soften the blow to his mother. The older brother goes to Mexico and becomes a prizefighter. When he returns after winning of thousands of dollars, he pays back the theft and all ends happily. *African Americans. Boxers. Brothers. Mexico. Mothers and sons. Robbery. Self-sacrifice.*

Note: This film marked the fiction film debut of ex-heavyweight boxing champion Jack Johnson, who appeared in person at the film's opening in Harlem at the New Douglas Theater, of which he was said to be a partner, according to an unidentified news item in the George P. Johnson Collection in the UCLA Special Collections Library. The film was made at Cliffside, NJ, and at one point, a sheriff took possession of the negative for alleged non-payment of rent.

ChiDef 18 Feb 1922.

FOR SALE, A BABY *see* **SHOULD A BABY DIE?**

FOR THE DEFENSE (French Americans)

Jesse L. Lasky Feature Play Co. *Dist* Paramount Pictures Corp. 13 Mar **1916** [©Jesse L. Lasky Feature Play Co., Inc.; 2 Mar 1916; LU7746]. Si; b&w. 5 reels.

Dir Frank Reicher. *Scen* Hector Turnbull and Margaret Turnbull.

Cast: Fannie Ward (*Fidele Roget*), Jack Dean (*Jim Webster*), Paul Byron (*Richard Madison*), Horace B. Carpenter (*Henri*), Camille Astor (*Ninette*), James Neill (*Mr. Webster*), Gertrude Kellar (*Mrs. Webster*).

Drama. In New York en route from a French convent to one in Montreal, novice Fidele Roget is captured by a white slaver. During her escape, she witnesses a murder and then meets Jim Webster, who is about to commit suicide. She dissuades him, and he decides to help her get to Canada. On the way, however, he is arrested and ordered to stand trial for murder. Jim tells Fidele that he is being framed by his butler, who killed a man and then made all the evidence point to his employer. Fidele realizes that this is the murder she witnessed and decides to catch the real killer. Posing as a maid in the Webster household, she manages to trick the butler into a confession and then trades in a life devoted to the church for one devoted to Jim, whom she marries. *Frame-ups. Impersonation and imposture. Murder. Nuns. Attempted suicide. Butlers. Confession (Law). Escapes. French. Kidnapping. Maids. New York City. White-slave traffic.*

Note: The film's working title was *Fidele.*

Motog 25 Mar 1916, p. 709. *MPW* 25 Mar 1916, p. 2026. *NYDM* 1 Apr 1916, p. 28. *NYT* 13 Mar 1916, p. 5. *Var* 10 Mar 1916, p. 28. *Wid's* 16 Mar 1916, p. 436.

FOR THE LOVE OF MIKE (German Americans, Irish Americans, Italian Americans, Jewish Americans)

Robert Kane Productions. *Dist* First National Pictures, Inc. 31 Jul **1927** [©First National Pictures, Inc.; 1 Aug 1927; LP24252]. Si; b&w. 7 reels, 6,588 ft.

Pres Robert Kane. *Dir* Frank Capra. *Scen* J. Clarkson Miller and Leland Hayward. *Photog* Ernest Haller.

Source: Based on the story "Hell's Kitchen" by John Moroso (publication undetermined).

Cast: Claudette Colbert (*Mary*), Ben Lyon (*Mike*), George Sidney (*Abraham Katz*), Ford Sterling (*Herman Schultz*), Hugh Cameron (*Patrick O'Malley*), Richard "Skeets" Gallagher (*"Coxey" Pendleton*), Rudolph Cameron (*Henry Sharp*), Mabel Swor (*Evelyn Joyce*).

Comedy-drama. [*Not viewed*]. A not yet one-year-old boy, abandoned on a landing in a tenement house in New York's "Hell's Kitchen," is adopted by three men who live on that floor: German delicatessen owner Herman Schultz; Jewish tailor Abie Katz; and Irish street cleaner Patrick O'Malley. The men, although ignorant in the ways of infants, rear the child, whom they call "Mike." After the boy finishes high school, they plan to send him to college, but Mike wants to work rather than be a burden to them any longer. However, when Mary, their Italian-American neighbor who works as Herman's cashier, joins the men in trying to convince Mike otherwise, he agrees to go to Yale. On his twenty-first birthday, the three "fathers" have prepared a lavish banquet for Mike, now captain of the varsity crew and very popular, so that he could meet leading politicians, bankers and businessmen who might offer him a good job. Before going to the banquet, Mike gets drunk at a cocktail party to which he is lured by Evelyn Joyce, who is attracted to him. When he finally arrives at the banquet, the prominent people leave, insulted by his drunken behavior. When Mike later angrily turns against his three fathers, Patrick knocks him out. Back at college, Mike begins to gamble and gets in debt to Henry Sharp, a crooked gambler. Sharp threatens to have Mike arrested for writing a bad check unless he throws the upcoming Yale-Harvard crew race, but when Mike sees that his three fathers and Mary have come and are betting on him, he rows the team to victory. When Sharp threatens the fathers with sending Mike to jail, they push him overboard. Mike, now acclaimed by his school, forgiven by his fathers and loved by Mary, happily paddles to the crew house. *College life. Foundlings. German Americans. Irish Americans. Italian Americans. Jews. New York City–Hell's Kitchen. Tenement-houses. Yale University. Banquets. Delicatessens. Drunkenness. Gamblers. Parties. Romance. Rowing. Seduction. Street cleaners. Tailors. Wagers.*

Note: The film's working title was *Hell's Kitchen.* The above plot summary was based on press material in the copyright descriptions and reviews. Sources conflict concerning the scenarist: while information in the copyright descriptions, possibly taken from a print of the film, credits J. Clarkson Miller, the *FD* review credits Leland Hayward [although his name is mistakenly spelled "Heywood"]. According to *Var*, there were two shots in the film that may have come from newsreels: a "melting pot" shot at the beginning of the film; and an airplane shot of the regatta. This was Claudette Colbert's first film. According to modern sources, she starred in the Broadway play *The Barker* in the evenings during the production schedule and vowed not to make any more films afterward.

Modern sources also note that Benny Rubin stated he wrote gags for the film,

that the running time was 75 min. and that prints from the film no longer survive. In his autobiography, Capra states that Leland Hayward was the production manager and Joe Boyle the assistant director. He also notes that the film was shot at the Hearst-Cosmopolitan studio in New York and on location in Connecticut; that the budget was inadequate and he was not paid, due to financial difficulties of producer Robert Kane; and that because the film was a commercial failure, he returned to the Mack Sennett studio as a writer.

FD 4 Sep 1927, p. 27. *MPW* 2 May 1927, p. 829. *NYT* 24 Aug 1927, p. 27. *Var* 24 Aug 1927, p. 26.

FOR THE LOVE OF MIKE (Native Americans)

Shergari Corp. *Dist* Twentieth Century-Fox Film Corp. **1960**; Prod: early Feb—early Mar 1960 at Churubusco Azteca Studios, Mexico City [©Shergari Corp. & Twentieth Century-Fox Film Corp.; 9 Aug 1960; LP17056]. Sd (RCA High Fidelity); col (DeLuxe); CinemaScope. 10 reels, 7,563 ft. 84 or 87 min. PCA cert no. 19598.

Pres F. H. RICKETSON, JR. and TED R. GAMBLE. *Prod* George Sherman. *Asst to prod* Henry Spitz. *Dir* George Sherman. *Asst dir* Henry Spitz and Mario Cisneros. *Wrt* D. D. Beauchamp. *Photog* Alex Philips. *Art dir* Roberto Silva. *Ed supv* Fredrick Y. Smith. [*Film ed* Frank Gross]. *Mus* Raúl Lavista. *Sd supv* James L. Fields. *Sd* Manuel Topete. *Prod mgr* Antonio Guerrero Tello. *Scr supv* Bobbie Sierks.

Song(s): "Charro bravo," words and music by Rex Allen.

Cast: RICHARD BASEHART (*Father Phelan*), Stuart Erwin (*Doctor Mills*), Arthur Shields (*Father Walsh*), Armando Silvestre (*Tony Eagle*), Elsa Cárdenas (*Mrs. Eagle*), Michael Steckler (*Ty Corbin*), Rex Allen (*Himself*), and introducing Danny Bravo (*Michael [Little Bear]*).

Drama. [*Not viewed*]. On a warm and dusty afternoon in New Mexico, Father Phelan arrives at St. Joseph's parish to take over from his old friend, the ailing and much-loved Father Walsh. Father Phelan intends to pursue Father Walsh's pet project: building a new church for the poverty-stricken, mostly Indian parish. Just after his arrival, Father Phelan meets Michael Little Bear, a twelve-year-old orphan who lives at the rectory and cooks and cares for Father Walsh. Mike hopes one day to become a doctor and has a menagerie of animals whom he has saved, cured, and mended. Father Phelan brings Father Walsh back to St. Joseph's rectory to recover, and the elderly priest proves to be an uncooperative patient when the Protestant Doctor Mills tells him he must stay in bed and rest. Although Father Walsh complains that Doc Mills is working against the interests of the church, he actually respects and trusts the physician. Mike tells Father Phelan how much he hopes to give Father Walsh his church, and Father Phelan tries to let him know that the priest may die before the money can be raised and the church constructed. Mike prays to God for the money, and later sees a poster announcing a quarterhorse race with a $2,000 prize. Mike then announces to Doc his intention to enter his horse El Pueblo in the race, and Doc agrees to test the horse the next morning. Although the horse was once lame, Mike had set its leg carefully, and when the two friends test El Pueblo, the horse's speed surprises even Doc. Mike and Doc meet early every morning to practice El Pueblo, causing Father Walsh to become suspicious of the young Indian's whereabouts. After Father Phelan asks Doc about the horse and Mike's plan to race it, he gives Doc the church fund savings and asks him to "invest" it. Father Walsh then reveals to Father Phelan that he, too, knows about the race and would like his money "invested." At the racetrack, Doc encounters Rex Allen and Ty Corbin, a horse trainer and his assistant. Doc places a ten-to-one bet on El Pueblo to win, and as the horses and their riders line up, Rex recognizes El Pueblo as the offspring of his best stallion and a mare that ran away one night a few years before. El Pueblo and Mike enjoy a glorious victory, and Rex pays Doc $5,500 in winnings. When Rex asks Mike where he got the horse and then tries to buy it, Mike refuses and lies about the horse's origins. Later, Father Phelan tells Doc that Father Walsh wants to keep the money for Mike's education, and Rex calls and says that Mike's story that the government gave El Pueblo to the Indians was false. Father Walsh confronts Mike and he tells him the truth: He found the dying mare and colt in the hills, and knowing that the coyotes would get them, stayed with them for two days, then brought the colt back on a stretcher. When Rex and Ty show up at the rectory, Father Phelan reads them a letter he received from Mike, in which the boy apologizes and says that he had to leave with his dog because by lying he had brought shame upon his people. Rex offers to bring over horses for a search party, and Mike's old friend, Tony Eagle, a talented Indian scout, leads the group into an area called "Sangre de Christos," where he suspects Mike has sought

refuge. Tony's pregnant wife goes to stay with Father Walsh, and when she shows him Mike's letter, the priest begins to cry. Meanwhile, Mike is growing weary, and unknown to him, he is being stalked by a cougar. Father Phelan and Tony discuss Mike's lie, and Tony teasingly assures the priest that even though Mike lied, he also stole a horse from a white man, making him an Indian hero. By the time the search party arrives at Mike's deserted camp, night is approaching and all but Tony and Father Phelan decide to turn back. Mike, meanwhile, falls down a hill, and as he commands his horse to go home, he hears the cougar growling at him. The horse rears, alerting Tony and Father Phelan, who find a delirious Mike and carry him back to safety. Back at the rectory, Rex gives Father Phelan a blank check for the cost of the new church, and Mike apologizes. Rex tells Mike to keep the horse, but Mike refuses, and then Father Walsh strikes a compromise: the two will be partners, with half of the horse's winnings going for Mike's education. As they did at Father Walsh's homecoming, the group sings "Happy Birthday," the only happy song they all know. Churches. Horses. Indians of North America. Orphans. Priests. Catholics. Dogs. Gambling. Honor. Horse trainers. Horseracing. Invalids. Letters. New Mexico. Physicians. Protestantism. Pumas. Runaways. Searches.

Note: Although a print of this film was not viewed, the above credits and plot summary were taken from a cutting continuity contained in the Twentieth Century-Fox Produced Scripts Collection, located at the UCLA Arts—Special Collections Library. The working title of the film was *The Golden Touch*. The film was shot on location in Mexico City, at the Churubusco Azteca, S. A. Studios. The onscreen credits acknowledge the contribution of the Union of Motion Picture Workers of the Republic of Mexico. Actor Michael Steckler's name is listed as Stickler in the opening credits, but Steckler in the end credits. *HR* production charts list Danny Zaldiver as a cast member, but it is likely that Zaldiver was the real name of child actor Danny Bravo. According to a 2 Mar 1960 *HR* news item, Fredrick Y. Smith replaced editor Frank Gross following Gross's death.

Box 8 Aug 1960. *DV* 1 Aug 1960, p. 3. *FD* 2 Aug 1960, p. 6. *Exh* 3 Aug 1960, p. 4725. *Har* 6 Aug 1960, p. 127. *HR* 26 Feb 1960, p. 16. *HR* 2 Mar 1960, p. 3. *HR* 1 Aug 1960, p. 3. *MPD* 2 Aug 1960. *MPHPD* 6 Aug 1960, p. 796. *Var* 3 Aug 1960, p. 6.

FOR THE SERVICE (Native Americans)

Universal Productions, Inc.; A Buck Jones Production. *Dist* Universal Productions, Inc. 6 May **1936** [©Universal Productions, Inc.; 18 Mar 1936; LP6221]. Sd (RCA Victor "High Fidelity" Sound System); b&w. 7 reels. 64-65 min. PCA cert no. 2014.

Pres Carl Laemmle. *Dir* Buck Jones. *Asst dir* Les Selander and Harry Knight. *Orig story and scr* Isadore Bernstein. *Photog* Allen Thompson and Herbert Kirkpatrick. *Art dir* Ralph Berger. *Film ed* Bernard Loftus. *Sd supv* Bud Meyer.

Cast: BUCK JONES (*Buck O'Brien*), Clifford Jones (*George Murphy*), Edward Keene (*Captain Murphy*), Fred Kohler (*Bruce Howard*), Beth Marion (*Penny Carson*), Frank McGlynn, Sr. (*Jim*), Ben Corbett (*Ben*), Chief Thundercloud (*Chief Big Bear*).

Western. [*Print viewed*]. Dying cowboy Johnson, a former frontier scout, informs a trio of scouts, including Buck O'Brien and Ben, that the Bruce Howard gang has taken his stock and burned his ranch. While graves are dug for those who perished in the confrontation with Howard's gang, Buck pursues and shoots the rustlers. Buck reports to his superior, Captain Murphy, that Howard's white men have formed an alliance with renegade Indians by giving them "firewater" in Hell's Half-Acre. Later Murphy's son George, arrives from the East to carry on the family tradition as a scout. George has not seen Murphy since his mother and sister were massacred in front of him fifteen years earlier. For the pursuit, Buck asks to have George paired with him, and George is nervous when welcomed by a friendly Indian, Chief Big Bear, who dubs him Little Eagle. George falls instantly in love with Penny Carson, the daughter of the local storekeeper. The next day, as George and Buck search for a trail to Hell's Half-Acre, George expresses a general preference for white men over Indians, although Buck explains that whites such as Howard are far worse. When the pair is spotted by Indian guards, Buck shows the naïve George, who is unused to violence, how to trick the Indians and take their rifles without killing them. Once in Hell's Half-Acre, one white man kills another with a broken bottle, and Howard worries about his shortage of men and supplies. That night, Buck and George hear Indians attacking a wagon train, and while Buck helps bravely, George cowers, unable to move. Captain Murphy leads a rescue party and is wounded. Later, Sherman, leader of the wagon train, insists on giving George a gold watch as a token of gratitude. George feels humiliated and only Buck's urging keeps him from

revealing the truth. Realizing George and Penny are in love, and that George will never adapt to the West, Buck urges each of them separately to marry and leave the outpost for the East. However, before George can take Buck's advice, two men find the butchered bodies of two scouts, and Murphy orders his son to lead an assault on Hell's Half-Acre to massacre the gang. After observing the drunken nighttime revels of Howard's men, George suggests taking them prisoner, but the attack quickly becomes a shootout that the scouts win. However, George has been hit, and as he dies, he asks Buck to promise that no one will be shot in the back. George is buried with honors as the scouts and Chief Big Bear salute him. *Cowardice. Fathers and sons. Indians of North America. Scouts (Frontier).* Engagements. Liquor. Massacres. Racism. Ranches. Renegades. Rustlers. Self-sacrifice.

Note: *For the Service* was the first of three films in which Buck Jones directed as well as starred. The print viewed listed only Jones's name and the title; all other credits are from copyright records and reviews.
FD 19 May 1936, p. 7. *MPD* 21 May 1936, p. 6, 11. *Var* 3 Jun 1936, p. 54.

FOR THE SOUL OF RAFAEL (Latino)
Garson Studios, Inc. *Dist* Equity Pictures Corp. May **1920** [©Equity Pictures Corp.; 18 Apr 1920; LP15164]. Si; b&w. 7 reels, 7,090 ft.
Pres Harry Garson. *Dir* Harry Garson. *Scen* Dorothy Yost. *Adpt* Charles E. Whittaker. *Cam* Arthur Edeson. *Art dir* Ben Carré.
Source: Based on the novel *For the Soul of Rafael* by Marah Ellis Ryan (Chicago, 1906).
Cast: Clara Kimball Young (*Marta Raquel Estevan*), Bertram Grassby (*Rafael Artega*), Eugenie Besserer (*Dona Luisa*), Juan De La Cruz (*El Capitan*), J. Frank Glendon (*Keith Bryton*), Ruth King (*Ana Mendez*), Helene Sullivan (*Angela Bryton*), Paula Merritt (*Polonia*), Maude Emery (*Teresa*), Edward M. Kimball (*Ricardo*).
Drama. In old California, Marta Estavan is preparing to leave the convent where she has been reared when her guardian Dona Luisa Artega promises Marta in marriage to her son Rafael in hopes that marriage will tame her wild offspring. One night, Marta rescues Keith Bryton from his Indian captors and soon falls in love with him. Dona Luisa, desperate to break up their budding romance, tricks Bryton into believing that Marta has entered a convent and then lies to Marta that Bryton is dead. Bereft, Marta marries Rafael and pledges to Dona Luisa on her deathbed that she will reform him. Bryton returns, but Marta remains true to her vow. When in the course of eloping with another woman, Rafael is shot and killed by the bandit El Capitan, Marta is free to marry the man she loves. *California. Convents. Fidelity. Latino. Marriage–Arranged. Pledges. Wards and guardians. Bandits. Elopement. Indians of North America. Infidelity.*

Note: According to a news item, an advisory board of historians and technical experts was secured for consultation concerning the life and customs of early Californians, and many scenes were shot in the California locations mentioned in the novel, including many missions. Also, according to a news item, 200 Indians from the Soboba, Pima and Cocopah reservations near Los Angeles appeared in the film. The film had its premiere in Los Angeles on 21 Apr 1920, and was given a trade showing in New York on 26 May 1920.
ETR 5 Jun 1920, p. 54. *MPN* 12 Jun 1920, p. 4867. *MPW* 15 May 1920, p. 983. *NYMT* 30 May 1920. *Var* 28 May 1920, p. 27. *Var* 8 Oct 1920, p. 43. *Wid's* 30 May 1920, p. 6.

FOR THOSE WHO DARE *see* **LUST FOR GOLD**

FORBIDDEN PATHS (Japanese Americans)
Jesse L. Lasky Feature Play Co. *Dist* Paramount Pictures Corp. 5 Jul 1917 [©Jesse L. Lasky Feature Play Co.; 9 Jul 1917; LP11064]. Si; b&w. 5 reels.
Dir Robert T. Thornby. *Asst dir* Harry B. Haskins. *Scen* Beatrice C. de Mille and Leighton Osmun. *Story* Eve Unsell. *Cam* James C. Van Trees and Paul Perry.
Cast: Sessue Hayakawa (*Sato*), Vivian Martin (*Mildred Thornton*), Tom Forman (*Harry Maxwell*), Carmen Phillips (*Benita Ramirez*), James Neill (*James Thornton*), Ernest Joy (*American ambassador*), Paul Weigel (*Luis Valdez*).
Drama. When Mildred Thornton's father dies, he leaves the girl in the care of Sato, a Japanese American who enjoyed his fullest confidence during their business partnership. Although Mildred feels the deepest friendship towards Sato, she does not return the love he feels for her, preferring instead a young man named Harry Maxwell, who has been appointed ambassador to Mexico. In Mexico, Harry is roped into a hasty marriage by adventuress Benita Ramirez. Soon discovering his wife's true nature, however, Harry returns home and realizes that he actually loves Mildred. Soon after Benita comes to

seek her revenge on Harry. Sato, knowing that he can never have Mildred and that Benita stands in the way of her happiness, invites the adventuress on a boating trip. In mid-ocean, Sato scuttles the boat and both meet their deaths, freeing Harry to marry Mildred. *Fortune hunters. Japanese Americans. Marriage–Forced by circumstances. Revenge. Self-sacrifice. Wards and guardians. Ambassadors. Mexico.*

Note: Paramount studio records list Perry as cinematographer, but a contemporary review credits Van Trees.
ETR 30 Jun 1917, p. 266. *MPN* 7 Jul 1917, p. 118. *MPW* 7 Jul 1917, p. 78. *NYDM* 30 Jun 1917, p. 30. *NYDM* 7 Jul 1917, p. 2. *Var* 20 Jul 1917, p. 31. *Wid's* 28 Jun 1917, p. 405.

FOREIGN AGENT (German Americans, Italian Americans, Japanese Americans)
Monogram Picture Corp. *Dist* Monogram Pictures Corp. 9 Oct **1942**; Prod: 14 Jul—late Jul 1942 [©Monogram Pictures Corp.; 4 Sep 1942; LP11566]. Sd; b&w. 6 reels, 5,608 ft. 62 or 64 min. PCA cert no. 8694.
Prod Martin Mooney and Max M. King. *Prod supv* George Moskov. *Dir* William Beaudine. *Asst dir* Gerd Oswald. *Orig story* Martin Mooney. *Scr* Martin Mooney and John Krafft. *Cine* Mack Stengler. *Art dir* Dave Milton. *Film ed* Fred Baine. *Mus dir* Edward Kay. *Sd eng* Glen Glenn.
Song(s): "Down Deep in My Heart," words and music by Bill Mellette; "Taps for the Japs," words and music by Bill Anderson.
Cast: JOHN SHELTON (*Jimmy*), Gale Storm (*Mitzi [Mayo]*), Ivan Lebedeff (*Okura*), George Travell (*Nick*), Patsy Moran (*Joan*), Lyle Latell (*Eddie*), Hans Schumm (*Werner*), William Halligan ([*Bob*] *Davis*), Herbert Rawlinson (*Stevens*), Boyd Irwin (*Jennings*), Kenneth Harlan (*George McCall*), David Clarke ([*Carl*] *Beck*), Fay Wall (*Anna*), Edward Piel (*Nelson*), Paul Bryar (*Bartender*), Jack Mulhall (*Editor*), Anna Hope (*Flo*), Jimmy Starr (*Reporter*), Jack Raymond (*Little fellow*), Vince Barnett (*Drunk*), Rita Douglas (*Girl at bar*), Jean King (*Maid*).
Espionage, Drama, with songs. [*Print viewed*]. When a reporter learns that a body found in a Hollywood hotel has been identified as Mayo, a studio electrician who was working on an anti-aircraft device for the government, he concludes that the man was murdered. Later, a Nazi front group called the North American Peace Association, which is secretly headed by the Nazi spy Werner, searches for the blueprints for Mayo's invention, a filter that would allow a searchlight to expose enemy aircraft without visible light. During their search, the Nazis discover a picture of Mayo's daughter Mitzi and decide to try to get the plans from her. Meanwhile, Mitzi's boyfriend Jimmy tells her that he is joining the Army. When Mitzi's roommate Joan borrows her car for a date with her boyfriend Eddie, some of Werner's cronies follow them and steal Joan's diamond engagement ring and Mitzi's car. Near the waterfront, Carl Beck, a German-American member of Werner's group, and his girl friend haunt a bar hoping to pick up information from careless drinkers. Facts gleaned from a sailor's girl friend lead to the bombing of an American submarine. Soon after, Mitzi and Jimmy return to Mitzi's after a date, and discover that the house has been searched. She then tells Jimmy that she has her father's plans for the filter and asks him to keep them safe. Jimmy suggests that they show the plans to George McCall, an electrician at the studio where they both work, who might be able to build the filter. Later, Jimmy is asked to defer his plans to join the Army to help radio commentator Bob Davis investigate subversive groups and is assigned to watch Nelson and Jennings, the American figureheads of the North American Peace Association. Later, at the bar where Mitzi performs as a singer, Joan recognizes one of the men who stole her ring and calls Eddie. During the ensuing fight, one of the men drops his wallet, and the papers inside reveal his connection to Werner's group. Meanwhile, Davis discovers that his office is bugged and, with Jimmy's help, feeds the eavesdroppers false information. Jimmy then discovers the location of the spies' headquarters and sets up a system to tape their interactions. Later, Jimmy and Mitzi overhear Axis plans to bomb Los Angeles and turn the recordings over to the FBI. Meanwhile, Werner's men discover that they are being tapped and trace the tap to Mitzi's apartment. They capture Jimmy, Mitzi and Davis and take them and the recordings away. Jimmy plays them a recording that he and Mitzi made while pretending to be Werner and his mistress Anna and convinces the men that Werner is planning to double-cross them. During the ensuing confusion, U.S. government agents arrive and arrest Werner and his men. Later, Jimmy and Mitzi watch a demonstration of her father's invention, and Jimmy tells Mitzi

that he loves her. *Inventions. Spies. World War II–Collaborators. Bartenders. Fistfights. German Americans. Hollywood (CA). Kidnapping. Motion picture actors and actresses. Nazis. Proposals (Marital). Radio performers. Rings. Romance. Roommates. Singers. Wire-tapping.*

Note: This was the first Monogram film produced jointly by Martin Mooney and Max King.

Box 3 Oct 1942. *DV* 24 Jul 1942. *DV* 11 Sep 1942, p. 3. *FD* 21 Sep 1942, p. 6. *HR* 6 May 1942, p. 4. *HR* 10 Jul 1942, p. 8. *HR* 17 Jul 1942, p. 8. *HR* 24 Jul 1942, p. 6. *HR* 11 Sep 1942, p. 3. *MPHPD* 19 Sep 1942, p. 911. *Var* 28 Oct 1942, p. 8.

FOREVER YOURS *see* **THE AMAZING MRS. HOLLIDAY**

FORGED PASSPORT (Immigrants)

Republic Pictures Corp. *Dist* Republic Pictures Corp. 24 Apr **1939**; Prod: began 19 Dec 1938 [©Republic Pictures Corp.; 24 Feb 1939; LP8705]. Sd (RCA "High Fidelity" Recording); b&w. 7 reels, 5,582 ft. 60-61 or 64 min. Passed by the National Board of Review. PCA cert no. 5001.

Assoc prod John H. Auer. *Dir* John H. Auer. [*Asst dir* Phil Ford and George Blair]. *Scr* Franklin Coen and Lee Loeb. *Orig story* James Webb and Lee Loeb. *Photog* Jack Marta. *Art dir* John Victor Mackay. *Film ed* Edward Mann. *Supv ed* Murray Seldeen. *Cost* Irene Saltern. *Mus dir* Cy Feuer. *Prod mgr* Al Wilson.

Cast: Paul Kelly [(*Dan Frazer*)], June Lang [(*Helene*)], Lyle Talbot [(*Jack Scott*)], Billy Gilbert [(*Nick Mendoza*)], Cliff Nazarro [(*Shakespeare*)], Maurice Murphy [(*Kansas Nelson*)], Christian Rub [(*Mr. Nelson*)], John Hamilton [(*Jack Rogers, also known as Lefty*)], Dewey Robinson [(*Riley*)], Bruce MacFarlane [(*Buck*)], Ivan Miller [(*Captain Ellis*)], Frank Puglia [(*Chief Miguel*)].

Crime, Drama. [*Print viewed*]. Dan Frazer, a fiery-tempered but effective immigration officer stationed at the Mexican border, has earned the enmity of a smuggling ring, whose shipments of illegal aliens Dan has repeatedly stopped. Jack Scott, owner of a Tijuana nightclub and a member of the gang, warns Dan to be transferred. After Dan refuses to be intimidated, Scott receives orders from his boss, known only as Lefty, to set a trap for Dan. Imitating Dan's nightclub-owner friend, Nick Mendoza, to whom Dan owes money, Scott calls the station and demands that Dan settle the debt immediately. Dan sends new officer Kansas Nelson and realizes too late that it is a set-up. Dan rushes to the club, where Kansas has been shot in the back by Lefty, and Kansas dies in Dan's arms. Dan determines that the killer was left-handed and is discharged after taking complete responsibility for Kansas' death. Helene, an entertainer in Nick's club and Dan's girl friend, tries to persuade Dan to go to New York with her and get married, but Dan tells her that he must avenge Kansas' murder and help re-open Nick's club, which has been closed by Miguel, the Mexican police chief. Dan discusses the problem with his friend, Jack Rogers, an influential Chamber of Commerce member and rancher, who advises him to forget the matter. Dissatisfied, Dan goes to Nick and the pair open a gas station. Dan's plan is to pretend to be smuggling illegal aliens across the border, in the hopes of attracting Scott's gang. The plan soon works and Scott offers to take over Dan's operation, guaranteeing him a percentage of the earnings as well as fraudulent citizenship papers for the immigrants in San Diego. Dan agrees to the deal, which entails collecting $500 from each man shipped, but insists on sending his own load through that night. Nick supplies the money to Dan's men, and Dan follows the truck to a warehouse on the other side of the border. The next day, Dan intends to send five armed men in the shipment, but Nick does not have enough money to pay for them, so Dan goes to Rogers. He explains to Rogers that he has located the mysterious Lefty's headquarters in the warehouse and can capture him that night. Rogers gives Dan the money, but after Dan leaves, reveals himself to be Lefty when he orders Scott to place a time bomb in the truck with Dan's men. Scott does so, and also has Riley, a bouncer, guard Helene, who now works in his club. Scott inadvertently reveals that Rogers is behind the plot against Dan, and Helene cleverly passes the message on to Shakespeare, one of Dan's former co-workers, by discussing the story of one of Shakespeare's plays. Shakespeare and Helene escape and catch Dan after a mad chase. The bomb explodes on time, but the truck's passengers are long gone and Dan alerts Miguel. Dan and the others go to Rogers' house, where Dan tricks Rogers into revealing that he is left-handed. Rogers confesses to killing Kansas and is taken away by Miguel. Later, Nick's club re-opens and Dan and Helene sneak out together as Nick begins one of his long-winded stories. *Government officials. Mexican-*

American border region. Mexicans. Nightclubs. Revenge. Smuggling. Americans in foreign countries. Bombs. Chases. Confession (Law). Dancers. Debt. Dismissal (Employment). Duplicity. Escapes. Gas stations. Immigrants. Murder. Nightclubs. Partnership. Police chiefs. Ranchers. William Shakespeare. Tijuana (Mexico). Traps. Trucks. Warehouses.

Note: According to *HR* news items, Frances Langford was considered by Republic for the role of Helene, and Jimmy O'Gatty was set for an unspecified part. It is not known if O'Gatty appeared in the final film. *HR* news items also note that songwriter Eddie Cherkose was "given lines in the feature." According to pre-production news items, Cherkose and music director Cy Feuer composed the song "Una-Dos-Tres-Y," and Cherkose and William Lava wrote "So Far, So Good, So What," both of which were to be included in the film. Because no reviews or other sources mentioned the songs, and the print viewed was edited for television, it has not been determined if the songs were included in the final film. An *HR* production chart lists George Blair as the assistant director, while the *SAB* credits Phil Ford.

Box 11 Feb 1939. *DV* 2 Feb 1939, p. 3. *FD* 8 Feb 1939, p. 6. *HR* 7 Dec 1938, p. 1. *HR* 8 Dec 1938, p. 8. *HR* 12 Dec 1938, p. 6. *HR* 19 Dec 1938, p. 2. *HR* 20 Dec 1938, p. 7. *HR* 21 Dec 1938, p. 2. *HR* 24 Dec 1938, p. 6. *HR* 2 Feb 1939, p. 4. *MPD* 8 Feb 1939, p. 7. *MPH* 11 Feb 1939, p. 38. *Var* 22 Feb 1939, p. 12.

FORT APACHE (Native Americans, Apache)

Argosy Pictures Corp. *Dist* RKO Radio Pictures, Inc. **1948**; World premiere in Phoenix, AZ: 27 Mar 1948; Chicago premiere: 29 Mar 1948; Prod: 24 Jul—late Sep 1947 [©Argosy Pictures Corp.; 27 Mar 1948; LP1568]. Sd (Western Electric Recording); b&w. 11,493 ft. 127-128 min. PCA cert no. 12019.

Pres JOHN FORD and MERIAN C. COOPER. [*Exec asst* Jack Pennick]. *Dir* John Ford. *Asst dir* Lowell Farrell. [*2d asst dir* Frank Parmenter]. *Scr* Frank S. Nugent. *Cine* Archie Stout. [*Cam op* Eddie Fitzgerald]. [*Stills* Al St. Hilaire]. *Spec eff* Dave Koehler. *Art dir* James Basevi. *Film ed* Jack Murray. *Set dressings* Joseph Kish. *Props* Jack Galconda. *Ladies' ward* Ann Peck. *Men's ward* Michael Meyers. *Mus score* Richard Hageman. *Arr and cond* Lucien Cailliet. *Dance seq* Kenny Williams. *Sd* Frank Webster and Joseph I. Kane. *Makeup* Emile LaVigne. *Tech adv* Major Philip Kieffer, USA, Rtd. and Katharine Spaatz. *Cost research* R. O. Hatswell. *Research ed* Katherine Clifton. [*Prod mgr* Bernard McEveety]. [*Asst prod mgr* William Forsythe]. [*Scr supv* Meta Sterne]. [*Foreman* Robert Clark]. [*Grip* Carl Gibson]. [*Asst pub* Tom Wood]. [*Aerial liaison* Paul Mantz]. [*Auditor* Charles Quesnel]. [*Company clerk* William Ford]. [*Set doctor* Dr. James Green and Dr. Robert Nielson]. [*Stunt supv* Clifford Lyons]. [*Stunt rider* Ben Johnson].

Song(s): "Sweet Genevieve," words by George Cooper, music by Henry Tucker.

Source: Suggested by the short story "Massacre" by James Warner Bellah in *The Saturday Evening Post* (22 Feb 1947).

Cast: John Wayne [(*Capt. Kirby York*)], Henry Fonda [(*Lt. Col. Owen Thursday*)], Shirley Temple [(*Philadelphia Thursday*)], Pedro Armendariz [(*Sgt. "Johnny Reb" Beaufort*)], Ward Bond [(*Sgt. O'Rourke*)], George O'Brien [(*Capt. Sam Collingwood*)], Victor McLaglen [(*Sgt. Mulcahy*)], Anna Lee [(*Emma Collingwood*)], Irene Rich [(*Mrs. O'Rourke*)], Dick Foran [(*Tim Quincannon*)], Guy Kibbee [(*Dr. Wilkins*)], Grant Withers [(*Silas Meacham*)], Jack Pennick [(*Sgt. Dan Shatuck*)], Ray Hyke [(*Recruit*)], Movita [(*Guadalupe*)], Miguel Inclan [(*Cochise*)], Mary Gordon [(*Ma*)], Philip Kieffer [sic] [(*Reporter*)], Mae Marsh [(*Martha*)], Hank Worden [(*Southern recruit*)], and introducing John Agar [(*Lt. Michael Shannon O'Rourke*)], [Cliff Clark (*Stage driver*)], [Francis Ford (*Fink*)], [Frank Ferguson, William Forrest (*Reporters*)].

Historical, Western. [*Print viewed*]. In Arizona, after the Civil War, Lt. Col. Owen Thursday and his teenaged daughter Philadelphia stop at a rest station on the road to Fort Apache, where Thursday has just been reassigned as cavalry commander. Also on his way to Fort Apache is young West Pointer Lt. Michael Shannon O'Rourke, who is met by his godfather, the Irish Sgt. Mulcahy, and two other soldier friends. Philadelphia and Michael are immediately attracted to each other, but hide their feelings behind a facade of military decorum. Upon arriving at the fort, the exacting, strict Thursday is briefed about the Apache Indians by Capt. Kirby York and longtime acquaintance Capt. Sam Collingwood, the former commander of Fort Apache. Although Thursday, a demoted Eastern-bred Civil War general who resents his assignment to the remote fort, scoffs at reports of Apache insurrection, York, a seasoned frontier fighter, advises that the Apache threat be taken seriously. Later, Thursday confers privately with Collingwood, a fellow Civil War veteran who, unlike Thursday,

has enjoyed few promotions. After discussing Collingwood's upcoming transfer, Thursday talks privately with Michael's father, who is a noncommissioned sergeant at the fort. Thursday learns that Michael, whose professional demeanor has greatly impressed him, received his West Point commission because O'Rourke won the medal of honor during the Civil War. The next day, while Philadelphia, Collingwood's wife Emma and Mrs. O'Rourke turn the barren commander's quarters into a presentable home, Thursday receives word that a general alarm has been issued at neighboring Fort Grant. Despite the alarm, Michael takes Philadelphia riding the next morning, and the couple comes across the bodies of several massacred soldiers. After riding furiously back to Fort Apache with Philadelphia, Michael relates his findings to a worried Thursday. Although appreciative of Michael's detailed report, Thursday forbids the youth to see his daughter again and orders him to lead a small detail to retrieve the corpses. While Michael's detail picks up the slain bodies, Thursday, an avid, if unimaginative strategist, orders a platoon to follow the detail's wagons. As hoped, the wagons are attacked by gun-wielding Apaches, who are then chased off by the platoon. Later, Thursday and York angrily confront Silas Meacham, the local reservation agent, about selling "rotgut whiskey" and firearms to the Apaches. Although the greedy Meacham maintains his innocence, Thursday discovers that the general store's scales have been fixed and finds liquor where Bibles should be. Once back at the fort, York convinces Thursday to allow him and "Johnny Reb" Beaufort, a Spanish-speaking soldier, to approach Cochise, the leader of the rebel Apaches, alone and unarmed. While York and Beaufort ride across the Mexican border to the Apache camp, Philadelphia and her father argue about her future with Michael, who has just proposed to her. Thursday tells Philadelphia that, as the son of a non-commissioned officer, Michael can never marry her. He also informs her that he is sending her back East, where she must remain until she reaches legal age. Later, York and Beaufort interrupt a fort dance to report that, as arranged by York, Cochise is returning to Arizona to talk peace with Thursday and Meacham. Despite York's pleas that his promise to Cochise be honored, Thursday orders that the entire Fort Apache regiment report for battle. The regiment is quickly surrounded by Cochise's superior forces, however, and Thursday is forced to order York to negotiate a peaceful settlement. The proud Cochise, who is accompanied by Geronimo and other Apache leaders, demands that Meacham be ousted as a condition for peace, and threatens to "kill the whites" if this stipulation is not met by dawn. Outraged by Cochise's demands, Thursday decides to attack the Indians and orders his troops to ride into battle in groups of four. When York protests this strategy, which he calls "suicidal," Thursday relieves him of duty and orders that Michael and he man the supply wagons. As predicted by York, Thursday's approach proves disastrous to his troops, and he, too, is shot. After sending Michael to Fort Grant for help, York rescues Thursday, who insists on continuing, despite his wounds. Thursday joins his dug-in regiment and, while fighting alongside O'Rourke and Collingwood, who is unaware that he has just received the teaching commission he has longed desired, is attacked and killed by the Apaches. York and his contingency, the regiment's only survivors, then surrender to Cochise. Years later, after Philadelphia and Michael have married, York, now the highly decorated commander of Fort Apache, defends Thursday's reputation when questioned by reporters about the massacre. After stating that the spirit of Thursday's doomed regiment lives on in every new recruit, York rides off to face Geronimo in battle. *Apache Indians. Arizona. Fathers and daughters. Forts. Officers (Military). United States-History-Reconstruction, 1865-1898. United States. Army. Cavalry. Ambition. Class distinction. Cochise. Dances. Duplicity. Geronimo. Godparents. Indian agents. Indians of North America-Reservations. Irish Americans. Mexico. Military discipline. Proposals (Marital). Reporters. Riding. Traps.*

Note: The working title of this film was *War Party. Fort Apache* was the first film in what critics now refer to as director John Ford's "Cavalry trilogy." The second film, *She Wore a Yellow Ribbon*, was produced by Argosy Pictures and distributed by RKO in 1949, and the third, *Rio Grande*, was also produced by Argosy, but released by Republic Pictures in 1950 (see entries below). John Wayne starred in all three films, and Victor McLaglen played supporting roles in all three. Frank S. Nugent, a former *New York Times* film critic, made his screenwriting debut with this picture, and later wrote the screenplay for *She Wore a Yellow Ribbon*, as well as for Ford's 1956 picture *The Searchers.* Various sources contend that the film's portrayal of "Lt. Col. Owen Thursday" was inspired by General George Armstrong Custer and his ill-fated stand at Little

Big Horn. Unlike the Thursday character, however, Custer fought against the Sioux Indians in the Dakotas. According to modern biographical sources, Cochise, the chief of the Chiricahua Apaches in Arizona, led a band of followers into the Dragoon Mountains in 1861 and evaded capture until 1871, when he surrendered to General George Crook. In 1872, he fled the reservation until the government established a new Chiricahua reservation on Apache ancestral land. He surrendered a second time to Tom Jeffords and died in 1874. As depicted in *Fort Apache*, Geronimo was a member of the Apache warriors council under Cochise. In 1885, he began a campaign against the whites and was finally captured by General Crook in 1886. He escaped shortly afterward, was recaptured and eventually became a farmer.

HR news items add the following information about the production: Exteriors for the picture were shot in Monument Valley, twenty-two miles from the nearest telephone and town. (Modern sources note that because insurance was prohibitively expensive in Utah, filming was done on the Arizona side of the Valley.) Interiors were to be shot at Enterprise Studios in Hollywood, although no confirmation of this announcement has been found. (Modern sources contend that interiors were filmed at RKO's Pathe lot in Culver City.) At Monument Valley, director John Ford hired two doctors from Los Angeles to oversee his 600-person crew, which worked in 135 degree heat. The crew included at least ten stunt riders, including actor Ben Johnson, whom *HR* described as a "husky young cowboy from Pawhuska, Oklahoma." After his work on *Fort Apache*, Johnson was signed as a "termer" by Ford and Cooper and went on to appear in several other Ford westerns, including *Three Godfathers* and *She Wore a Yellow Ribbon* (see entries below). John Agar, a former serviceman who was married to co-star Shirley Temple at the time of production, made his screen debut in the film. He and Temple, both of whom RKO borrowed from David O. Selznick's company for the production, divorced in 1949. Although *HR* announced that Fernando Fernandez, "Mexico's Sinatra," was signed to a "singing role" in the film, his appearance in the final film has not been confirmed. Dick Foran sang the picture's only solo ("Sweet Genevieve"). In addition to "Sweet Genevieve," excerpts from the traditional song "The Girl I Left Behind Me" are also heard in the film. Technical adviser and bit player Major Philip Kieffer, whose name was misspelled in the cast list, was an army historian and "West Pointer."

Although RKO distributed Argosy's first production, *The Fugitive*, which was released in late 1947, United Artists was announced in Mar 1947 as this picture's distributor. In Jul 1947, however, just prior to the start of production on *Fort Apache*, *HR* reported that RKO was releasing the film because of United Artists' "unsettled status." According to *HR*, Argosy's deal with RKO included distribution rights to a second Ford film (*She Wore a Yellow Ribbon*). Although *MPA* lists the film's general release date as 9 Mar 1948, *HR* news items indicate that the world premiere took place in Phoenix, AZ, on 27 Mar 1948, and that a Chicago premiere occurred two days later. Proceeds from the picture's Chicago premiere, which was sponsored by the *Chicago Herald-American* newspaper, went to the newspaper's wounded soldier fund. In May 1948, *HR* announced that Argosy was planning to advertise *Fort Apache* and *The Fugitive* on KTLA, a newly formed, independent Los Angeles television station. Frozen assets from the British release of *Fort Apache* and *The Fugitive* were to be used to finance Ford's picture *The Quiet Man* (not made until 1952), according to an Apr 1948 *HR* news item.

Modern sources add the following information about the production: As preparation for writing the film's script, Ford had Nugent read fifty books about the story's period and setting and sent him to Arizona to study Apache culture. Nugent depicted the Apaches more sympathetically in his screenplay than Bellah did in his story. (In a Jan 1949 letter to Nugent, American historian Dee Brown complimented Nugent and Ford on their accurate, sensitive portrayal of the tribe.) The film's original budget was $2.8 million, and for their work, Temple, John Wayne and Henry Fonda were each paid $100,000, while McLaglen received $75,000. The parade ground exteriors were shot at Ray Corrigan's ranch near Chatsworth, CA. Cinematographer Archie Stout convinced Ford to shoot the exteriors on black-and-white infrared film, a film that produced superior day-for-night effects, but had been rarely used because of its tricky exposure requirements. Utilizing recently improved stock, Stout shot more infrared film than on any previous Hollywood picture. Production wrapped twenty-five days under schedule and $700,000 under budget. Modern sources credit William Clothier as second unit photographer, Eddie O'Fearna (Ford's older brother) as second assistant director, and Cliff Lyons as second-unit director. Modern sources add Harry Tenbrook (*Courier*), Fred Graham (*Cavalry man*), Mickey Simpson (*Noncom officer*), Archie Twitchell (*Stagecoach driver*), Dan Borzage (*Trooper*), Gil Perkins, Junior Hudkins and Hubie Kerns (*Cavalrymen/Stuntmen*) and Frank McGrath (*Bugler/Stuntman*) to the cast. In addition, modern sources note that Ford fired actor/director Paul Fix while the crew was filming in Monument Valley. The film earned $445,000 at the box office and was one of RKO's biggest moneymakers in 1948.

AmCin Aug 1948, p. 265, 289. *Box* 13 Mar 1948. *DV* 10 Mar 1948, p. 3. *FD* 10 Mar 1948, p. 8. *HR* 31 Mar 1947, p. 12. *HR* 26 May 1947, p. 10. *HR* 7 Jul 1947, p. 3. *HR* 10 Jul 1947, p. 4. *HR* 11 Jul 1947, p. 14. *HR* 22 Jul 1947, p. 11. *HR* 1 Aug 1947, p. 4. *HR* 29 Aug 1947, p. 20. *HR* 19 Sep 1947, p. 13. *HR* 5 Nov 1947, p. 14. *HR* 2 Dec 1947, p. 10. *HR* 10 Mar 1948, p. 3. *HR* 18 Mar 1948, p. 3. *HR* 25 Mar 1948, p. 11. *HR* 13 Apr 1948, p. 3. *HR* 5 May 1948, p. 12. *HR* 29 Jun 1948, p. 6. *MPHPD* 13 Mar 1948, p. 4094. *NYT* 25 Jun 1948, p. 26. *Var* 10 Mar 1948, p. 10.

FORT BOWIE (Native Americans, Apache)
Oak Pictures, Inc. *Dist* United Artists Corp. Feb **1958**; Prod: early May—mid-May 1957 [©Oak Pictures, Inc.; 6 Feb 1958; LP10302]. Sd (Westrex Recording System); b&w. 7,288 ft. 80-81 min. PCA cert no. 18663.

Prod Aubrey Schenck. *Dir* Howard W. Koch. *Asst dir* Paul Wurtzel and [John I. Schreyer]. *Scr* Maurice Tombragel. *Photog* Carl E. Guthrie. *Op cam* Nelson Cordes. *Photog eff* Jack Rabin and Lewis DeWitt. *Prod des* Jack T. Collins. *Supv ed* John F. Shreyer. *Ed* John A. Bushelman. *Prop master* Arden Cripe. *Ward* Wesley V. Jeffries and Angela Alexander. *Mus* Les Baxter. *Mus ed* Sam Waxman. *Sd mixer* Joe Edmondson. *Re-rec* Charles Cooper. [*Sd* Jack T. Collis]. *Makeup artist* Ted Goodley. *Hair styles* Mary Westmoreland. *Scr supv* George Rutter. *Key grip* Herschel Brown. *Lighting tech* Robert R. Farmer.

Cast: Ben Johnson [(*Capt. "Tomahawk" Thompson*)], Jan Harrison [(*Allison Garrett*)], Kent Taylor [(*Col. Jim Garrett*)], Jana Davi [(*Chenzana*)], Peter Mamakos [(*Sgt. Kukus*)], Larry Chance [(*Victorio*)], J. Ian Douglas [(*Maj. Wharton*)], Jerry Frank [(*Lt. Maywood*)], Barbara Parry [(*Mrs. Maywood*)], [Ed Hinton (*Gentleman*)], [Johnny Western (*Sergeant*)].

Western. [*Print viewed*]. During his first patrol, Major Wharton, an arrogant political appointee, slaughters a band of Apaches even though they are about to surrender. Watching in dismay, Capt. "Tomahawk" Thompson, named for the weapon he always carries, fears that Wharton's policy of annihilation will foment an Indian war. Upon returning to Fort Bowie, Wharton reports to his commanding officer, Col. Jim Garrett, who disagrees with Wharton's policies, but is unable to countermand him. When word comes that Victorio, the Apache leader, is rallying his braves, Garrett sends Thompson to escort the colonel's wife Allison back to the safety of the fort. That night, before he leaves, Chenzana, Victorio's spurned consort who works as a laundress at the fort, warns Thompson that Victorio is bent on revenge. Later, in Tucson, the glamorous Allison refuses to return to the fort with Thompson, so he tosses her into the back of a wagon. On the journey back to the fort, Allison makes romantic advances to Thompson, but he rejects her. After fending off an Indian attack, Thompson and Allison finally reach the fort. Disgusted by life on the frontier, Allison chastises her husband for not sacrificing his ideals to advance his political career. Then, to wound Garrett, Allison lies that Thompson made love to her. The next day, Garrett sends Wharton and his troops into the field to attack the Indians, assigning Thompson the suicidal task of convincing Victorio to surrender. As Thompson is about to depart on his mission with Sgt. Kukus, Allison warns him that her husband is trying to kill him, and Thompson assures her that Garrett's motives are purely tactical. Before leaving, Thompson requests the colonel to issue explicit orders to Wharton to hold back his troops until Thompson and Kukus are clear of the area. After Wharton and Thompson depart, Allison confesses to her husband that she lied about her affair and he contemptuously informs her that Thompson's death will be on her conscience. Led by Chenzana, Kukus and Thompson, meanwhile, meet with Victorio, who refuses to surrender. Spotting Wharton's troops snaking up the mountainside, Victorio takes Kukus and Thompson prisoner and then slaughters Wharton and his men. After ordering Thompson and Kukus left behind and tortured, Victorio rallies his braves and heads for the fort. Chenzana frees the captives and Thompson sends Kukus for reinforcements while he rides back to the fort. Just as Garrett is notified that he has been relieved of his command, the Apaches storm the fort. The Indians scale the walls, but Garrett, the women, and a handful of surviving troopers retreat to the mess hall. As Garrett fires at the marauders, Allison reloads his weapons and they reconcile. Just when all seems lost, Thompson charges the fort with his reinforcements. Victorio is about to bludgeon Allison when Thompson bursts into the room and fights him off with his tomahawk. As Thompson and Victorio grapple, Garrett fells the Apache with a bullet. After the colonel apologizes to Thompson for misjudging him, Thompson and Chenzana embrace. *Apache Indians. Forts. Jealousy. Massacres. Officers (Military). Raids. United States. Army. Cavalry. Axes. Duplicity. Laundresses. Marriage. Tucson (AZ).*

Note: According to a *LAT* news item, this picture was largely shot around Kanab, UT.

Box 10 Feb 1958. *DV* 31 Jan 1958, p. 3. *Exb* 19 Feb 1958, p. 4439. *FD* 26 Feb 1958, p. 6. *Har* 8 Feb 1958, p. 22. *HR* 10 May 1957, p. 13. *HR* 31 Jan 1958, p. 3. *MPHPD* 8 Feb 1958, p. 708. *Var* 5 Feb 1958, p. 20.

FORT DEFIANCE (Native Americans, Navajo)

Ventura Pictures Corp. *Dist* United Artists Corp. 9 Nov **1951**; Prod: Jun 1951 [©Ventura Pictures Corp.; 2 Nov 1951; LP1340]. Sd (Western Electric Recording); col (Cinecolor). 7,369 ft. 81 min.

Prod Frank Melford. *Assoc prod* Irving D. Koppel. *Dir* John Rawlins. *Asst dir* Charles Kerr and Eugene Anderson, Jr. *Scr* Louis Lantz. *Dir of photog* Stanley Cortez. *Col consultant* Wilton R. Holm and Clifford D. Shank. *Art dir* Lucius Croxton. *Film ed* Tom Pratt. *Ward* Frank Beetson. *Mus* Paul Sawtell. *Sd rec* W. John Myers. *Makeup* Louis Phillippi. *Tech dir* Iron Eyes Cody.

Cast: Dane Clark (*Johnny [Tallon]*), Ben Johnson (*Ben [Shelby]*), Peter Graves (*Ned [Tallon]*), Tracey Roberts (*Julie*), George Cleveland (*Uncle Charlie*), Ralph Sanford (*Stage coach driver*), Iron Eyes (*Brave Bear*), Dennis Moore (*Lt. Lucas*), Craig Woods (*Dave Parker*), Dick Elliott (*Kincaid*), Bryan Hightower (*Hankey*), David Rawlins (*Jaje*), Jerry Ambler (*Cheyenne*), Kit Guard (*Barfly*), Wesley Hudman (*Stranger*), Hugh Hooker (*Les*), [Duke York (*Doninger*)], [Lee Phelps (*Bartender*)].

Western. [*Print viewed*]. Civil War veteran Ben Shelby arrives at the Tallon ranch in the Arizona desert. After he saves blind Ned Tallon from being trampled by a spirited horse, he encounters Ned's uncle Charlie, who is suspicious of Ben's claim that he is a friend of Ned's brother Johnny. When Ben learns that Johnny is expected at the ranch soon, he offers to help Ned and Charlie while he waits for Johnny's arrival. As time passes, Ben and Ned become friends. Ned speaks with pride of his brother's medals and war honors, and Ben reveals that his younger brother was killed during the war. One day, Charlie returns from nearby Fort Defiance with news that the U.S. government intends to round up the local Navajos and move them to a reservation in the Oklahoma Territory. The angry Indians have hidden in the rugged canyons surrounding the area and are making raids on the white settlers. When Ned asks for news of Johnny, Charlie reluctantly discloses that he was killed during a bank robbery. Hearing that, Ben reveals that he came to Arizona to kill Johnny, whose surrender to the Confederates during the Battle of Tennessee Ridge caused the deaths of many soldiers. Ben, the only survivor, lost his brother. His illusions shattered, Ned asks Ben to stay, but he is eager to rejoin his wife, and rides into Fort Defiance. In the saloon, Ben starts to write his wife with details of Johnny's betrayal, then changes his mind and returns to the ranch to form a partnership with Ned and Charlie. Unknown to Ben, Dave Parker, whose brothers were also killed at Tennessee Ridge, has found his letter and is now determined to kill Ned in revenge. During a shootout at the ranch, Charlie sacrifices his life so that Ben and Ned can escape. While Ned and Ben hide in the canyons, Johnny, who is not dead, returns to the ranch. Learning what has happened, he and his friend Hankey track the two fugitives. When Johnny reaches the men, Ben, apprised of his identity, tries to kill him, but is disarmed by Hankey. Their skirmish is halted when they are forced to defend themselves against an Indian raiding party. Hankey is killed and the other three men decide to head for a little-known pass, hoping to escape further encounters with the Indians. The next day, however, they see a stagecoach under Indian attack and ride to help the passengers. That night, the Indians gather nearby. While the men prepare for a morning battle, passenger Julie, a disgraced dance-hall hostess on her way to San Francisco, talks with Ned. In the morning, the Indian attack is interrupted by the arrival of the Cavalry. Ben then tells Johnny that he will forget about seeking revenge for the death of his brother if he will allow Ned to remain with him. Johnny refuses, determined to take Ned to San Francisco for an eye operation. At Fort Defiance, however, Ned tries to kill Johnny, who realizes that he has lost his brother's love. Because Ned refuses to take any of the money Johnny stole to fix his eyes, Johnny forces Parker to buy the Tallon ranch. After giving the money to Ned, Johnny goes after Parker. During the gunfight, Johnny is killed along with Parker's men. Ben then kills Parker. Julie agrees to marry Ned and make a new start on the ranch. As they and Ben prepare to leave Fort Defiance, Ben's wife arrives on the stage to join them. *Arizona. Blindness. Brothers. Civil War veterans. Revenge. Dance hall girls. Forts. Fugitives. Gunfights. Murder. Navajo Indians. Ranchers. Romance. Self-sacrifice. Shootouts. Stagecoaches. Transformation. Uncles.*

Note: The picture was filmed on location in Gallup, NM. According to publicity material, Iron Eyes Cody's wife made the film's Navajo costumes. Some of the character names were unreadable in the viewed print and have been taken from a list supplied by the Call Bureau Cast Service.

Box 3 Nov 1951. *DV* 30 Oct 1951, p. 3. *Exb* 7 Nov 1951, p. 3187. *FD* 13 Nov 1951, p. 7. *Har* 3 Nov 1951, p. 176. *HR* 15 Jun 1951, p. 8. *HR* 22 Jun 1951, p. 10. *HR* 30 Oct 1951, p. 3. *MPHPD* 10 Nov 1951, p. 1102. *Var* 31 Oct 1951, p. 18.

FORT LARAMIE *see* **REVOLT AT FORT LARAMIE**

FORT MASSACRE (Native Americans, Apache, Pawnee, Piute)

The Mirisch Company, Inc. *Dist* United Artists Corp. May **1958**; Los Angeles opening: 14 May 1958; Prod: Oct 1957 [©Mirisch Co., Inc.; 2 May 1958; LP10473]. Sd; col (De Luxe); CinemaScope. 7,217 ft. 80 min. PCA cert no. 18849.

Prod Walter M. Mirisch. *Dir* Joseph M. Newman. *Asst dir* Jess Corallo. *Wrt* Martin M. Goldsmith. *Dir of photog* Carl Guthrie. *Spec eff* Danny Hayes. *Supv film ed* Richard V. Heermance. *Mus ed* Eve Newman. *Sd ed* Del Harris. *Ward* Bert Henrikson. *Mus* Marlin Skiles. *Rec eng* Frank McKenzie. [*Sd* B. F. Remington]. *Makeup artist* Emile LaVigne. *Hair styles* Alice Monte. *Prod mgr* Allen K. Wood. *Set cont* Frank Remsden. *Props* Ed Goldstein.

Cast: Joel McCrea (*Vinson*), Forrest Tucker (*McGurney*), John Russell (*Travis*), Susan Cabot (*Piute girl*), George N. Neise (*Pendleton*), Anthony Caruso (*Pawnee*), Robert Osterloh (*Schwabacker*), Denver Pyle (*Collins*), Francis J. McDonald (*Piute man*), Guy Prescott (*Tucker*), Rayford Barnes (*Moss*), Irving Bacon (*Charlie*), Claire Carleton (*Adele*), Larry Chance (*Moving Cloud*), [Walter Kray (*Chief*)], [Ben Rombouts, Bernie Grozier, Tom M'so, John Fritz (*Apache Indians*)].

Western. [*Print viewed*]. In 1879, in southwestern New Mexico, the 'C' Troop of the 6th Cavalry has been attacked by approximately seventy Apache Indians, whom they have driven off, but they have suffered very heavy casualties. As the troop captain has been killed, command of the troop falls to the only non-commissioned officer left alive, Sergeant Vinson. The few survivors include Travis, a college-educated drifter, and McGurney, an anti-authoritarian Irishman. Vinson, who has a great hatred for the Apaches, decides to head for Fort Crane, some hundred miles away, and hopes to meet up with the cavalry's main column en route. Travis and the troop's Indian scout, Pawnee, report that the Apache have occupied a waterhole up ahead and that there is no sign of the main column. As there is no other route except via the waterhole, Vinson decides to attack the Apache even though they are outnumbered four to one. After a long, brutal battle, the soldiers succeed in driving the Apache away. When Vinson kills an Apache as he appears to be about to surrender, the soldiers begin to think of him as a butcher. Later, they encounter Tucker and Moss, the only survivors of the massacre of the main column. Vinson elects to push on to the fort despite the main column's demise, but by a longer route. Travis learns from Vinson that, five years before, Vinson's wife and two children were ambushed by Apaches and that his wife, before she died, shot their children rather than have them taken alive. In an area normally out-of-bounds to the troops, they come upon an old couple, Charlie and Adele, who are trading with a young Apache brave, Moving Cloud. Vinson takes the brave as a hostage, hoping to guarantee their safe passage to the fort. He places Pawnee in charge of Moving Cloud, but they become involved in a knife fight in which the young Apache kills Pawnee then escapes. Farther on, the troop approaches a cliff dwelling, which is inhabited by an old Piute Indian and his seventeen-year-old granddaughter. Vinson tells Travis that he expects that the men will file charges against him when they reach the fort, but Travis says that he is proud to serve with him. After the grandfather warns Vinson that he can hear many horsemen headed their way, Vinson, fearing it may be an Apache scouting party, elects to stay where they are rather than be caught out in the open. Although the Piutes also fear the Apaches, Vinson will not permit them to leave, in case they alert the Apaches to the troop's whereabouts. The girl asks Travis for his help in leaving, but he refuses. When a small band of Apaches come to the stronghold, they are welcomed by the old Piute while the soldiers hide. The Apaches take the granddaughter prisoner, but even after more Apaches, including Moving Cloud, ride up, the grandfather does not reveal the soldiers' presence. Overcome by his hatred of Indians, Vinson opens fire on the Apaches, who then massacre all except Vinson, Travis and another trooper, Collins. Vinson orders the old Piute to ride to Fort Crane for help, but he accuses Vinson of shooting the Apaches when they were about to leave and says he will tell the truth about what happened. As Vinson moves to shoot the old man, Travis shoots and kills Vinson, then tells Collins that Vinson was as fine a man as he ever knew, and that although he fought to control the hate which festered within him, it finally overcame him. *Apache Indians. Officers (Military). Paiute Indians. Pawnee Indians. Racism. United States. Army. Cavalry. Battles. Cliff-dwellings. Grandfathers. Hostages. Irish Americans. Knife fighting. Massacres. New Mexico. Scouts (Frontier). Soldiers. Watches.*

Note: This was the first of many films made by the Mirisch Company for release by United Artists. According to the film's pressbook, the film was shot some thirty miles north of Gallup, NM, with twenty local Navajo Indians cast as Apaches. Actor George N. Neise is incorrectly listed as George W. Neise in the end credits. Tom M'so, a Navajo from Ramah, New Mexico, who plays a "Bad" Indian in the film, is quoted in the pressbook as enjoying the experience: "As long as Hollywood doesn't show the Indian as a coward, we do not mind....And we don't feel bad about movies in which the White Men are shown stealing our land and putting us on reservations. You see, we discovered Uranium on our reservation, and now our Navajo tribe is worth $35,000,000....Besides, in this picture, I play an Apache. And the Navajos never liked the Apaches anyway."

Box 28 Apr 1958. *DV* 25 Apr 1958, p. 3. *Exh* 30 Apr 1958, p. 4460. *FD* 1 May 1958, p. 6. *Har* 26 Apr 1958, p. 67. *HR* 11 Oct 1957, p. 13. *HR* 25 Oct 1957, p. 19. *HR* 25 Apr 1958, p. 3. *MPHPD* 26 Apr 1958, p. 809. *Var* 30 Apr 1958, p. 6.

FORT OSAGE (Native Americans, Osage)

Monogram Pictures Corp. *Dist* Monogram Pictures Corp. 10 Feb **1952**; Prod: Jul 1951 [©Monogram Pictures Corp.; 30 Dec 1952; LP1460]. Sd (Western Electric Recording); col (Cinecolor). 6,481 ft. 72 min. PCA cert no. 15469.

Prod Walter Mirisch. *Dir* Lesley Selander. *Asst dir* Edward Morey, Jr. *Dial dir* Stanley Price. *Story and Scr* Dan Ullman. *Photog* Harry Neumann. *Spec eff* Ray Mercer. *Color consultant* Wilton R. Holm and Clifford D. Shank. *Art dir* David Milton. *Film ed* Richard Heermance. *Set dresser* Vin Taylor. *Mus* Marlin Skiles. *Rec* Charles Cooper. *Prod mgr* Allen K. Wood. *Set cont* Wandra Ramsey.

Cast: ROD CAMERON [(*Tom Clay*)], Jane Nigh [(*Ann Pickett*)], Morris Ankrum [(*Arthur Pickett*)], Douglas Kennedy [(*George Keane*)], John Ridgely [(*Henry Travers*)], William Phipps [(*Nathan Goodspeed*)], Stan Jolley [(*Sam Winfield*)], Dorothy Adams [(*Mrs. Winfield*)], Francis McDonald [(*Osage chief*)], Myron Healey [(*Martin Christensen*)], Lane Bradford [(*Rawlins*)], Iron Eyes Cody [(*Old Indian*)], Barbara Woodell [(*Martha Woodling*)], [Anne Kimbell (*Emmy Winfield*)], [Hal Baylor (*Olaf Christensen*)], [Russ Conway (*Woodling*)], [Gregory Marshall (*Robert Woodling*)], [Fred Graham, Carol Henry, Marshall Reed, Lee Roberts, Glen McCarthy, Art Felix, Rocky Shahan, Chuck Hayward (*Henchmen*)], [Stanley Price (*Farmer*)], [George Deer, Carl Mathews (*Indians*)], [Al Eben (*Bartender*)], [Stanley Blystone (*Butcher*)], [Bill Chandler (*Stableman*)], [Lois Austin], [Gertrude Astor], [Paul Bryar], [Bob Peoples].

Western. [*Print viewed*]. Fort Osage, Missouri, gateway to the gold mines of California, is situated on the eastern edge of Osage Indian territory. Travelers from all over America stop in Fort Osage to prepare for the last leg of the overland journey west. Businessman Arthur Pickett and his partner, George Keane, provide emigrants with wagons, supplies, guides and armed guards, but their prices are unfairly high, and they often force delays in wagon train departures to enhance the profits of similarly greedy local shop owners. Pickett and Keane, whose Missouri Transit Company once gave the Osage Indians supplies in exchange for passage through Osage territory, decide in their greed to discontinue these supply shipments, believing that most of the tribe has settled in Oklahoma. When one family, unable to afford the high prices of Fort Osage, enters the territory alone, the angry Indians burn their wagon and kill them all. Tom Clay, who is on his way to Fort Osage to guide a Pickett wagon train that has been delayed for seven weeks, sees the attack and warns his employers that the Osages are on the warpath. Pickett, however, insists on sending out the wagon train. Furious that Pickett would charge high prices and then allow the emigrants to face certain death, Tom resigns. Keane sends a gunman to kill Tom, and although the plan goes awry, Tom is unable to discover who hired the killer. The smooth-talking Pickett, meanwhile, convinces his customers that the danger of Indian attack is minimal, and in their anxiety to reach California, they agree to continue the trip with a new wagon master. At the town dance, Tom tells Pickett's pretty daughter Ann that the Indians are decent and civilized people, and must have a reason for breaking the agreement. Later he kisses her. Impressed with Tom's integrity, Ann asks her father to meet with him. Tom offers to visit the Osage village and question the chief directly. Fearing that Tom will discover the cause of the tribe's anger, Keane sends several men to kill him on the way to the village, but Tom manages to escape. The chief tells Tom that when a party of braves went to meet the promised supply shipment, the men were brutally murdered. Tom, horrified and ashamed, vows that the treaty will be honored and that he, himself, will bring the supplies to the tribe. Meanwhile, Keane, who still believes that the Osages pose no threat, decides to frighten them

into submission by attacking the village. He and his men descend upon the unsuspecting Indians, killing many of them. One of the men escapes and rides to another Osage village for help. Unaware of this attack, Tom returns to Fort Osage and persuades Pickett to tell the truth about the Indian supply shipments. Tom organizes a party of emigrants to accompany the supply wagons to the village while Pickett, having offered to purchase the supplies himself, counts out the cash. When Keane realizes that Pickett has had a change of heart, he shoots his partner and knocks Ann unconscious. He and his men then steal the money and set out for California. Tom enters Pickett's office just as Ann is regaining consciousness, and soon afterward, they and the townspeople ride out in pursuit of Keane. The avenging Indians see Keane's gang from a distance but decide to attack Fort Osage instead. Soon they encounter Tom's party, and as they confiscate all the weapons, Tom tries to persuade the chief to join him in apprehending Keane. Because Tom is known and respected by the Osages, they agree to accompany him but hold Ann and the townspeople as hostages. Tom and the Osages soon overtake Keane's men, and a furious gun battle ensues. Most of Keane's henchmen are killed, and when Keane tries to escape, Tom leaps on him, and the two men fight. Tom finally kills Keane, and afterward shakes hands with the Osage chief. Back in town, Tom organizes the supply shipment and then, with Ann's help, guides the wagon train out of Fort Osage. *Fort Osage (MO). Greed. Osage Indians. Profiteering. Scouts (Frontier). Treaties. Wagon trains. Ambushes. Attempted murder. Chases. Fathers and daughters. Gold rushes. Gunfights. Hostages. Hypocrisy. Massacres. Missouri. Moral reformation. Murder. Partnership. Posses. Romance. Settlers. Tribal chiefs.*

Note: According to modern sources, Ray Jones was in the cast.

Box 26 Jan 1952. *DV* 16 Jan 1952, p. 6. *Exb* 27 Feb 1952, p. 3246. *Har* 19 Jan 1952, p. 11. *HCN* 12 Jan 1952. *HR* 5 Jul 1951, p. 12. *HR* 13 Jul 1951, p. 12. *HR* 20 Jul 1951, p. 12. *HR* 16 Jan 1952, p. 4. *LADN* 15 Feb 1952. *LAEx* 15 Feb 1952. *MPD* 18 Jan 1952. *MPHPD* 26 Jan 1952, p. 1215. *Var* 23 Jan 1952, p. 22.

FORT SAVAGE *see* **FLAMING FEATHER**

FORT TI (Native Americans, Ottawa)

Esskay Pictures Corp. *Dist* Columbia Pictures Corp. May **1953**; Prod: 16 Feb—4 Mar 1953 [©Columbia Pictures Corp.; 1 May 1953; LP2717]. Sd (RCA Sound System); col (Technicolor); Natural Vision 3-Dimension. 9 reels, 6,794 ft. 73 or 78 min. PCA cert no. 16394.

Prod Sam Katzman. *Dir* William Castle. *Asst dir* Jack Corrick. *Story and scr* Robert E. Kent. *Dir of photog* Lester H. White and Lothrop B. Worth. *Spec eff* Jack Erickson. *Technicolor color consultant* Francis Cugat. *Art dir* Paul Palmentola. *Film ed* William A. Lyon. *Set dec* Sidney Clifford. *Mus dir* Ross DiMaggio. *Sd eng* Josh Westmoreland. *Natural Vision 3-Dimension supv* M. L. Gunzburg. *Visual consultant* Julian Gunzburg, M.D. *Unit mgr* Herbert Leonard.

Song(s): "Le Batelier," lyrics by Tenis Chandler, music by Paul Mertz; "Alouette, Pretty Alouette," traditional.

Cast: George Montgomery [(*Capt. Jedediah Horn*)], Joan Vohs [(*Fortune Mallory*)], Irving Bacon [(*Sgt. Monday Wash*)], James Seay [(*Mark Chesney*)], Ben Astar [(*François Leroy*)], Phyllis Fowler [(*Running Otter*)], Howard Petrie [(*Major Robert Rogers*)], Cicely Browne [(*Bess Chesney*)], [Lester Matthews (*Lord Jeffrey Amherst*)], [George Leigh (*Capt. Delecroix*)], [Louis Merrill (*Raoul de Moreau*)], [Rusty Hamer (*Chesney child*)].

Historical, Drama. [*Print viewed*]. In 1759, during the French and Indian War, Captain Jedediah Horn and Sergeant Monday Wash of the irregular "Rogers' Rangers" fighting unit arrive in Albany, New York with a dispatch from their leader, English Major Robert Rogers, to General Lord Jeffrey Amherst. Rogers' dispatch calls for more men and reinforcements to keep the Indians out of the area until the army is ready to move north. Lord Amherst approves it because the entire campaign can collapse if the army is stopped in the north. Amherst warns Jed to be careful in Albany as the identity of French spy Raoul de Moreau has not been ascertained. Jed and Monday visit Jed's sister Bess, but arrive after Indians have kidnapped her and her two young sons and torched their cabin. Jed learns that Bess's husband Mark Chesney was not at the house at the time of the attack, and when Jed finds him in a tavern, he slugs Mark for running out on his family. Mark then visits Moreau, demanding to know the whereabouts of his wife and children. Moreau threatens to have Mark's family killed should he himself be harmed and says that they were kidnapped to keep Mark from deserting. Mark returns to Jed and confesses that four months earlier he agreed, in order to save his own life, to join various

committees to get information for the French, but that he told Moreau before his family was kidnapped that morning that he was through spying. Moreau, Mark reveals, now expects him to join up as one of the new Rogers' recruits and gather information on the number of men that the British plan to use and the route they plan to take on the march north to Ticonderoga and Quebec. Despite his inclination to shoot Mark as a spy, Lord Amherst agrees that he can earn his freedom by providing information that won't do any good nor harm to the French. On the march to meet Rogers' outfit, Jed and Monday rescue a woman from an Indian about to rip her blouse off. The woman, Fortune Mallory, says she is English and that she hasn't eaten for three days, having escaped from Fort Ticonderoga, but Jed is suspicious. They plan to put Fortune to work at the Leroy farm, where uniforms and supplies for the British troops are secretly made, and they isolate her so she cannot speak with Mark, whom they still suspect. In the middle of the night, Jed sees Mark wake her. Mark asks if she saw his wife and children at the fort, and she says they were alright. The next day, as Jed takes Fortune to the Leroy farm, he protects her during an Indian attack, then kills one Indian with a tomahawk throw. As another Indian is about to shoot him, the Indian is shot by French Canadian François Leroy, who then hugs Jed in friendship. Leroy's young Indian wife, Running Otter, kisses Jed passionately, not having seen him for four months, and Leroy explains to Fortune that she thinks of Jed as a father, as he had found her when she was orphaned and starving in the wood. Leroy, whose first wife was killed by Indians aligned with the French, brought Running Otter up like a white girl and later married the beautiful girl. At the farm, Fortune and Jed engage in a tender kiss, but when she says he needs a woman, he replies abruptly that he will think about what he needs only when the war is over. At night, back at the encampment, Wash, on patrol, sees Mark leave for Fort Ti and informs Jed. At the fort, Mark tells Moreau that, as it is now six weeks since the abduction, he wants some assurance that his wife and children are safe. Moreau promises that if Amherst's attack is crushed, using Mark's information, he will be able to join his wife before the summer is over. Mark then explains to Moreau and French General Montcalm that Amherst has brought in hundreds of engineers to build a road twenty miles east of Lake George; while a small force will use the lake in order to deceive the French, the bulk of the army will take the new road. Montcalm decides to concentrate his forces twenty miles east. Moreau then offers 5,000 English pounds if Mark will kill Rogers. When Jed sees Mark return, he questions him roughly until Rogers arrives. Mark relates that he gave Montcalm the information that Amherst asked him to relay. When Rogers learns from one of his scouts that the French have built defenses east of the river, he realizes that Mark has told the truth. During a raid, Jed rescues Mark as he is about to be killed. Jed then returns to the Leroy farm to tell them that supplies must be ready in three days, and Running Otter, oblivious to her husband, embraces Jed. At night, when Jed rejects Running Otter's advances, she accuses him of wanting a white woman instead, suspecting that he desires Fortune. Later, Running Otter witnesses Jed and Fortune exchange glances during a song by François, and when Jed is alone with Fortune, they kiss. Jed returns to his encampment, and after Running Otter visits Fort Ti, French troops raid the Leroy farm, and Running Otter accuses Fortune of being a French spy. Jed, Rogers and others successfully battle the French and disarm them. Fortune pleads innocence, but Jed does not believe her. François, who realizes that Running Otter betrayed them to the French, blames himself and tries to comfort his wife as she cries, but she tells him not to touch her, and as he kisses her, she takes his knife and stabs herself to death in the stomach. Rogers, Jed and the Rangers attack the French at the river. Afterwards, Jed, Fortune and Wash enter the fort, and Fortune leads them to Bess and her children. They escape the fort pursued by the French to an Indian burial cave. The next day, Jed and Wash defend the cave against the French and Indians, and as they are running out of ammunition, the cannon sounds of Lord Amherst cause the French to retreat. Soon, Mark is reunited with Bess and their children at the Rangers' camp. Montcalm has left for Quebec with his forces, and Jed kisses Fortune by a tree. *Deception. Espionage. Indians of North America. Major Robert Rogers. United States–History–French and Indian War, 1755-1763. Albany (NY). Ambushes. Jeffrey Amherst. Brothers and sisters. Caves. Children. Construction workers. English. False accusations. Farms. French. French Canadians. Governors. Impersonation and imposture. Jealousy. Kidnapping. Miscegenation.*

Personality change. Rescues. Romance. Stabbings. Suicide. Treason. Unrequited love.

Note: According to *DV*, this was the first Technicolor 3-D film to be released by a major company. *Var* stated that Columbia was rushing the film's release to beat that of Stanley Kramer's *The 5,000 Fingers of Dr. T. HR* commented that the film "depends more on the lure of 3-D for its grosses than it does on offering a sound, believable story." They commented that the 3-D process used showed a marked improvement, and that there were "only one or two moments of blur." *DV* noted that plans for stereophonic sound were dropped from the film's presentation.

Box 16 May 1953. *Cue* 30 May 1953. *DV* 11 May 1953, p. 3. *DV* 1 Jun 1953. *Exb* 20 May 1953, p. 3521. *FD* 19 May 1953, p. 6. *Har* 16 May 1953, p. 78. *HR* 11 May 1953, p. 3. *LADN* 29 May 1953. *LAEx* 29 May 1953. *MPD* 13 May 1953. *MPHPD* 16 May 1953, p. 1837. *NYT* 30 May 1953, p. 7. *Var* 13 May 1953, p. 6. *Var* 20 May 1953.

FORT YUMA (Native Americans, Membreno Apache)

Bel-Air Productions; A Bel-Air Production. *Dist* United Artists Corp. 4 Oct **1955**; Prod: late Apr—early May 1955 [©Camden Productions, Inc.; 4 Oct 1955; LP5535]. Sd (Western Electric Recording); col (Technicolor). 78 min. PCA cert no. 17569.

Exec prod Aubrey Schenck. *Prod* Howard W. Koch. *Dir* Lesley Selander. *Asst dir* Bud Andrews. *Scr* Danny Arnold. *Photog* Gordon Avil. *Cam op* William Margulies. *Spec eff* Milt Olsen. *Ed* John F. Schreyer. *Prop master* Arden Cripe. *Ward* Wesley V. Jefferies. *Mus* Paul Dunlap. *Sd mix* Joe Edmondson. *Sd* Sound Services, Inc. *Cast supv* John G. Stephens. *Light tech* Robert S. Comer.

Cast: Peter Graves (*Lt. Ben Keegan*), Joan Vohs (*Melanie Crowne*), John Hudson (*Sgt. Jonas*), Joan Taylor (*Francesca*), Wm. "Bill" Phillips (*Sgt. Milo Halleck*), James Lilburn (*Corp. Samuel Taylor*), Addison Richards (*Gen. Crooke*), Abel Fernandez (*Mangas Colorado*), Lee Roberts (*Capt. Santley*), Edmund Penney (*Pvt. Cassidy*).

Western. [*Not viewed*]. During peace negotiations at Fort Yuma, an elderly Apache chief is killed by a white settler and the chief's son, Mangas Colorado, declares a resumption of war. At Fort Apache, veteran officer Lt. Ben Keegan is given command of a cavalry column to escort ammunition and supplies to Fort Yuma. Keegan harbors an intense hatred for Apaches and is displeased at having an Apache, Sgt. Jonas, assigned as his scout, although he is secretly in love with Jonas's sister Francesca, who is accompanying missionary schoolteacher Melanie Crowne on her journey to the fort. Melanie is an Easterner with strong opinions about racial equality. The column leaves unaware that war has resumed and, during the journey, the Indians kill off the troopers by ones and twos and take their uniforms. Eventually, Keegan, Jonas and the two women are forced to take cover on a mountainside from where they can see the Apache, masquerading as cavalrymen, preparing a sneak attack on Fort Yuma. Francesca is mortally wounded while helping Keegan and dies in his arms. He and the others manage to thwart the attack on the fort, and the troopers win a fierce battle, during which Keegan kills Mangas Colorado in a fight pitting saber against war axe. Now contrite about his prejudice, Keegan rides off after placing a marker on Francesca's grave and wishing happiness to Melanie and Jonas, who share the same philosophy regarding Indian/white relations. *Apache Indians. Forts. Mangas Coloradas. Racism. United States. Army. Cavalry. Brothers and sisters. Deserts. Easterners. Fights. Gunfights. Impersonation and imposture. Missionaries. Peace conferences. Scouts (Frontier). Self-sacrifice. Teachers.*

Note: Although this film was not viewed, the credits were taken from a billing sheet in the PCA file at the AMPAS Library. This film was shot around Kanab, Utah. The film's pressbook lists John Picard and Stanley Clements in the roles of "Santley" and "Cassidy" while the "official" credits in the MPAA/PCA file in the AMPAS Library list Lee Roberts and Edmund Penney. Mangas Coloradas was an actual Apache chief; for additional information on his life, see entry below for *War Drums*.

Box 1 Oct 1955. *DV* 27 Sep 1955, p. 3. *Exb* 19 Oct 1955, p. 4047. *FD* 29 Sep 1955, p. 8. *Har* 1 Oct 1955, p. 159. *HR* 11 Apr 1955. *HR* 29 Apr 1955, p. 7. *HR* 27 Sep 1955. *MPHPD* 1 Oct 1955, p. 610. *Var* 28 Sep 1955, p. 9.

THE FORTY-NINERS (Native Americans)

Freuler Film Associates, Inc.; A Monarch Production. *Dist* Freuler Film Associates, Inc. 16 Oct **1932**. Sd; b&w. 5,000 ft. 49 or 52 min. Passed by the National Board of Review.

Supv Burton King. *Dir* John P. McCarthy. *Asst dir* William Nolte. *Story, cont and dial* F. McGrew Willis. *Photog* Edward Kull. *Film ed* Fred Bain. *Rec* International Recording Engineers, Ltd. *Sd tech* Homer Ackerman.

Cast: TOM TYLER (*Tennessee Matthews*), Betty Mack (*Virginia Hawkins*), Al Bridge (*O'Hara*), Fern Emmett (*Widow Spriggs*), Gordon Wood (*Jed Hawkins*), Mildred Rogers (*Lola*), Fred Ritter (*Tanner*), Frank Ball (*MacNab*), Florence Wells (*Tanner's wife*).

Historical, Western. [*Print viewed*]. In 1849, Jed Hawkins and his daughter Virginia wait with other settlers at Fort Laramie for a guide to lead them to Sacramento. Jed has a gold claim waiting for him, which he boasts about during his frequent drinking bouts, much to the dismay of his would-be paramour, Widow Spriggs. One afternoon, store owner MacNab tells Jed that guide O'Hara will be coming soon with a wagon train. The wagons arrive, and while Jed makes O'Hara's acquaintance, he once again boasts about his mine. O'Hara tells Jed they will leave in a few days, and MacNab tells Tanner, the wagon train's leader, that he will hold a dance to celebrate. At the dance, O'Hara and others vie for Virginia's attention, but she is captivated by Tennessee Matthews, a renowned buffalo trader. Their attraction is mutual, and after the dance, Tennessee escorts Virginia to her wagon, where she shows him the rose bush she is taking to California. Meanwhile, O'Hara goes to his cabin, where his Indian lover Lola waits for him. O'Hara cautions Lola never to let anyone into the cabin, where he hides loot he has stolen from his previous wagon trains, and orders her to instruct her tribe to meet him at a prearranged place to attack this new group of settlers. The next day, Virginia is sad to learn that they will be leaving the following morning, as Tennessee has stated that he will travel to his cabin in Yellowstone rather than join the wagon train. Virginia gives Tennessee a rose and they kiss goodbye, after which Virginia sees O'Hara beating Lola, and tenderly helps her. Virginia sees them and assumes that Lola belongs to Tennessee. The next morning, Tennessee sends a letter to the cavalry commander at Fort Collins, while O'Hara helps Virginia pack. Virginia dislikes O'Hara's advances but defends him out of spite when Tennessee, who is too much of a gentleman to mention O'Hara's relationship with Lola, attempts to force O'Hara away. The wagon train leaves, and as time passes, Widow Spriggs comforts Virginia while O'Hara plies Jed with drink in order to steal the map to his claim. Elsewhere, Tennessee waits for the wagon train to pass and, when it fails to show, he searches for it. He reaches the travelers and warns O'Hara that he is far off the trail and is heading deeper into Indian territory. O'Hara shoots Tennessee after he reveals that he has seen O'Hara's cabin and now knows why the other wagon trains O'Hara led disappeared. O'Hara tells the others he shot Tennessee in self-defense, and while the widow tends Tennessee, O'Hara asks Virginia to marry him. Virginia coldly informs him that she loves Tennessee, after which O'Hara meets Lola, who warns him that the cavalry found his cabin and is pursuing him. They plan the Indian attack for the next morning, and O'Hara orders two men to kidnap Virginia during the raid. The attack begins the next morning, and while the travelers defend themselves, Virginia is kidnapped. Tennessee rescues her, and Lola, who sees that O'Hara was doublecrossing her, shoots him. Tennessee then heads off a buffalo stampede as the cavalry arrive and saves the wagon train. The cavalry captain thanks Tennessee for alerting them, and the wagon train safely reaches California. Tennessee and Virginia bid farewell to Jed and Widow Spriggs, now Mrs. Hawkins, and head for Tennessee's cabin to begin their life together. *Duplicity. Fur traders. Guides. Indians of North America. Romantic rivalry. United States–History–19th century. Wagon trains. Battered women. Betrayal. Bison, American. California. Drunkenness. Fathers and daughters. Flowers. Fort Laramie (WY). Gold mines. Gunshot wounds. Kidnapping. Maps. Miscegenation. Proposals (Marital). Rescues. Stampedes. Thieves. United States. Army. Cavalry. Widows.*

Note: A *Var* preview review notes that William S. Hart can be seen in stock footage scenes of the wagon train. Although the viewed print included a copyright statement, the title was not found in copyright records.

FD 14 Dec 1932, p. 7. *Var* 20 Dec 1932, p. 16.

LA FOULE HURLE (French language)

Warner Bros. Pictures, Inc.; Warner Bros.—First National. *Dist* Warner Bros. Pictures, Inc.; The Vitaphone Corp. **1932**; Prod: in Germany. Sd; b&w. 81 min. French language.

Dir Howard Hawks and Jean Daumery. *Adpt and dial* Paul d'Estournelles de Constant.

Cast: Hélène Perdrière (*Anne*), Francine Mussey (*Lee Merrick*), Hélène Frédérick (*Mrs. Spud*), Jean Gabin (*Joe Greer*), Frank O'Neill (*Eddy Greer*), Henri Etiévant (*Mr. Greer*), Serjius (*Spud*).

Drama. [*Not viewed*]. [The following plot summary is based on the English-language version of this film, *The Crowd Roars*; character names refer to that version. For further information regarding the English-language version, please see the note below and the entry for *The Crowd Roars* in the *AFI Catalog of Feature Films, 1931-40*.] Racecar driver Joe Greer strongly believes that a family has no place in racing. For this reason, he refuses to marry his mistress, Lee Merrick, and tries to discourage his younger brother Eddie from taking up the sport. Once he learns that Eddie is determined to race and that he is good at it, however, Joe agrees to take him on the road, but tries to protect him from the less attractive side of racing. He keeps his relationship with Lee a secret, deeply wounding her by his actions. He completely breaks with Lee when he discovers Eddie having a drink with her and her friend, Anne Scott. Furious at the way her friend has been treated, Anne decides to seduce Eddie, but to her surprise, she falls in love with him. Joe, who is drinking heavily, and Eddie quarrel over Anne, parting bitterly. Joe's backup driver, Spud Connors, tries to separate the brothers in a race that night, and a drunken Joe drives him off the track to his death. His nerve broken by Spud's death, Joe starts losing races and ends up riding the rails as a hobo. Lee, who is still in love with Joe, borrows money to travel to Indianapolis for the 500 race, certain that Joe will be there. She meets him at the lunch stand where she is working and learns that he stopped drinking after Spud's death. During the race, when Eddie has a blowout and is injured, Joe takes over as relief driver, winning the race just before his car crashes. Joe is not badly hurt, and he and Eddie are reconciled. *Automobile racing. Brothers. Race car drivers. Alcoholism. Automobile accidents. Friendship. Guilt. Hoboes. Indianapolis (IN). Love affairs. Lunch stands. Mistresses. Regeneration. Seduction. Trains.*

Note: Some scenes from the English-language version, entitled *The Crowd Roars*, were used in this French version. Warner Bros. remade this film in 1939 as *Indianapolis Speedway* (see *AFI Catalog of Feature Films, 1931-40*; F3.2130). For information on the English-language version, which was directed by Howard Hawks and starred James Cagney and Joan Blondell, please see the entry for that film in the *AFI Catalog of Feature Films, 1931-40*; F3.0892.

FOUR FACES WEST (Latino)

Harry Sherman Pictures, Inc.; The Enterprise Studios. *Dist* United Artists Corp. 15 May **1948**; Prod: early May—mid-Jun 1947 at Enterprise Studios [©Harry Sherman Pictures, Inc.; 21 May 1948; LP1753]. Sd (Western Electric Recording); b&w. 10 reels, 8,070 ft. 90 min. Passed by the National Board of Review. PCA cert no. 12679.

Prod Harry Sherman. *Assoc prod* Vernon E. Clark. *Dir* Alfred E. Green. *Asst dir* Nathan Barrager. *Scr* Graham Baker and Teddi Sherman. *Adpt* William Brent and Milarde Brent. *Dir of photog* Russell Harlan. [*Cam op* George Clemens]. [*Stills* Charles "Scotty" Welbourne]. *Spec eff* Robert H. Moreland. *Prod des* Duncan Cramer. *Film ed* Edward Mann. *Set dec* Ray Robinson. *Ward* Alfred Berke. *Dir of mus* Rudolph Polk. *Mus comp and cond* Paul Sawtell. *Sd* Sound Services, Inc. *Sd eng* Frank Webster. *Makeup supv* Gustav Norin. [*Hair stylist* L. Lashin]. [*Prod mgr* Joseph C. Gilpin]. [*Scr supv* Marie Messinger]. [*Grip* Carl Gibson].

Source: Based on the novelette *Pasó Por Aquí* by Eugene Manlove Rhodes in *The Saturday Evening Post* (20 and 27 Feb 1926).

Cast: JOEL McCREA (*Ross McEwen*), FRANCES DEE (*Fay Hollister*), CHARLES BICKFORD (*Pat Garrett*), Joseph Calleia (*Monte Marquez*), William Conrad (*Sheriff Egan*), Martin Garralaga (*Florencio*), Raymond Largay (*Dr. Eldredge*), John Parrish (*Frenger*), Dan White (*Clint Waters* [*Garrett's deputy*]), Davison Clark (*Burnett*), Houseley Stevenson (*Anderson*), George McDonald (*Winston boy*), Eva Novak (*Mrs. Winston*), Sam Flint (*Storekeeper*), Forrest Taylor (*Conductor no. 2*).

Western. [*Print viewed*]. While the citizens of the New Mexico town of Santa Maria are welcoming their new U.S. Marshal, Pat Garrett, Ross McEwen, posing as Jefferson Davis, is holding up the local bank. After he gives banker Frenger an I.O.U. for the $2,000 he has demanded, Ross takes him out of town and leaves him shoeless and horseless. When Frenger eventually gets back to town, he offers a reward of $3,000 for Ross, dead or alive. Hoping to board a passing train, Ross, meanwhile, turns his horse loose and hides his saddle in some brush, where he is bitten by a rattlesnake. After making a tourniquet and sucking out the venom, Ross runs after the train and boards with the help of Mexican gambler Monte Marquez. On board, Fay Hollister, a railroad nurse from the East heading to a hospial in

Alamogordo, tends to his wound. When a posse discovers Ross's saddle near the railroad tracks, Garrett wonders if he may have escaped by train. Ross's escape is interrupted when news comes that the rail tracks have been washed out and all the passengers are forced to leave the train at Albuquerque, where a conductor advises them that the next train out may not arrive for a week but that a mail hack will be able to take a few passengers the next morning. Garrett, Ross, Fay and Monte decide to take the two-day mail trip, and make their first stop at a way-station near Inscription Rock. Monte translates the inscription made by conquistadores, as they journeyed by the rock: "Pasó por aquí"—"he passed this way." After their meal at the station, "wanted" posters for the Santa Maria bank robber arrive and Fay recalls that Ross boarded the train near there. Back on the train, as they are nearing Alamogordo, Fay tells Ross that if he is in any trouble, she would like to help. Ross writes a note to his father, which he sends on with the money he stole, then when the train reaches Alamogordo, he disembarks with Fay and they embrace. Monte, too, leaves the train and invites Ross to the Long Horn Saloon, which he co-owns with his cousins. Monte, who also suspects that Ross is the wanted man, helps him by introducing him to cattleman Burnett. Burnett hires him as top hand, and Ross continues to court Fay, who, aware that there is something in his past, urges him to clear himself with the law. Garrett and his deputy, Clint Waters, meanwhile, are on Ross's trail and when they reach Alamogordo, the sheriff tells them about the new man at Burnett's ranch. After Ross asks Monte to send some of his new earnings to the bank in Santa Maria and to say that it is from Jefferson Davis, Garrett comes to Monte's saloon. Although Ross is standing only a few feet away, Monte does not turn him in to Garrett. Ross then tells Fay that he must leave for a while, and presents her with a ring before riding away. Fay follows him and although he tells her about the robbery and urges her to go back, she stays with him. Garrett and a posse, as well as two bounty hunters, pursue the couple throughout New Mexico. Finally, when Ross will not give himself up, Fay leaves him and is captured by Garrett. To cross the White Sands desert, Ross exchanges his horse for a steer and, on the other side, attempts to acquire a horse at a small ranch. However, when Ross discovers that the Mexican rancher, Florencio, his wife and two sons all have diphtheria, he stays to help them. After trying a home remedy, Ross realizes that they need professional help, which is a two day ride away. In the hope of attracting someone's attention, Ross lights a fire, which is seen by Garrett and Clint. They find Ross in bad shape, so Garrett sends Clint to Alamogordo for a doctor while he stays to work alongside Ross. When Clint returns with a doctor, as well as Fay and Monte, Monte, who is Florencio's nephew, still does not identify Ross to Garrett and introduces Ross to Fay as if they had never met. Later, with Florencio and family recovering, Garrett rides off, leaving the way clear for Ross to escape. After Monte tells him that he will meet him with supplies at Inscription Rock, Ross takes off, but Garrett who has been waiting for Ross to leave, reveals that he knows who he is and talks him into giving himself up, promising to speak on his behalf. Before going with Garrett, Ross rides to Inscription Rock where he tells Fay that he is giving himself up but that they will be together soon. As a tribute to his friend's good deed, Monte tells Fay that Ross's name should be inscribed on the rock: "Ross McEwen, un caballero valiente, passed this way." *Bank robberies. Friendship. Fugitives. Gamblers. Mexican Americans. New Mexico. United States. Marshals. Alamogordo (NM). Bankers. Bounty hunters. Cattle. Cattlemen. Deserts. Diphtheria. Fires. Pat Garrett. El Morro National Monument (NM). Nurses. Posses. Railroads. Ranches. Saloons. Snake bites. Uncles.*

Note: This film's working title was *They Passed This Way*. The film begins with the following dedication: "Eugene Manlove Rhodes. He grew to manhood in this valley. Most of the stories which helped build his fame as a writer had their setting in southern New Mexico. One of the best known 'Pasó Por Aquí' was based on an actual occurrence at the Little Choza which his friends set aside as a monument to his memory. This is the story of 'Pasó Por Aquí.'" *Pasó Por Aquí* was published in book form with and under the title of another novelette *Once in the Saddle* (Boston, Apr 1927). According to a press release, shooting was done near Gallup and Alamogordo, in the town of San Rafael, and the White Sands National Monument, NM. Onscreen credits note that El Morro National Monument, (Inscription Rock), was photographed "by courtesy of National Park Service, Department of the Interior.".
Four Faces West was Harry Sherman's last film. He died on 25 Sep 1952. According to modern sources, Sherman, who had made his reputation as a producer of low budget Westerns, was particularly proud of the million-dollar *Four Faces West*. The picture, however, was a box office flop. Contemporary reviews commented favorably on the film's lack of violence and its attempt to portray the period authentically.

Box 22 May 1948. DV 10 May 1948, p. 3, 11. FD 10 May 1948, p. 10. HR 10 May 1948, p. 3. HR 9 Aug 1948, p. 6, 9. MPHPD 15 May 1948, p. 4162. NYT 4 Aug 1948, p. 18. Var 12 May 1948, p. 8.

FOUR MEN AND A PRAYER *see* **FURY AT FURNACE CREEK**

FOUR SHALL DIE (African Americans)

Million Dollar Productions, Inc. *Dist* State Rights. **1941**; New York opening: 12 Dec 1941; Prod: began 29 Sep 1940. Sd; b&w. 6,443 ft. 72 min. PCA cert no. 6773.

Exec prod and pres Harry M. Popkin. *Assoc prod* Sara Francis. *Prod* Clifford Sanforth. *Supv of prod* George D. Ringer. *Asst supv of prod* Arthur C. Ringer. *Dir* Leo C. Popkin. *Asst dir* George Hippard. *2d asst dir* Eddie Saeta. *Scr* Ed Dewey. *Photog* Marcel Picard. *Art dir* Paul Palmentole. *Film ed* Martin Cohen. *Prop master* Bill Billings. *Sd* Cliff Rubert and Earl Hiller. *Prod mgr* Alfred Westen. *Pub dir* Harry Levette.

Cast: Pete Webster (*Pierre Touissant*), Mantan Moreland (*Beefus*), Alfred Grant (*Roger Fielding*), Dorothy Dandridge (*Helen Fielding*), Vernon McCalla (*Doctor Ronald Webb*), Jesse Lee Brooks (*Doctor Hugh Leonard*), Reginald Fenderson (*Hickson*), Jack Carr (*Lew Covey*), Johnny Thomas (*Bill Summers*), Edward Thompson (*Sgt. Adams*), Earl Hall (*Jefferson*), Guernsey Morrow (*Attendant*).

African American, Horror. [*Not viewed*]. Helen Fielding, heir to the fortunes of the late millionaire Roger Fielding, Sr., has broken off her relationship with the unscrupulous Lew Covey to pursue a romance with reporter Bill Summers. Covey, determined to get at Helen's inheritance, vows to win her back. When Hickson, a friend of Helen's, tells Dr. Hugh Leonard and Covey about a visitation he had from his dead mother's spirit, Covey expresses disbelief and bets Hickson that he cannot prove the visitation took place. Hickson accepts the bet, and leads the men into Dr. Ronald Webb's spiritualistic parlor. There the voice of "Momba," an angry spirit, warns Covey that he will die later that night. The spirit also portends the deaths of Hickson and Leonard, telling them that they will die one day apart from each other following Covey's death. The ghost of Roger Fielding, Sr., the next apparition, tells his son, Roger Fielding, Jr., to prepare for his death. Later that night, Helen discovers Covey's dead body in her room. Bill is suspected as the killer, but Hickson believes that the spiritual portents drove the young man to suicide. Hickson, Bill and the others agree to keep the police ignorant of the death, and instead call on the famous detective Pierre Touissant and his assistant, Beefus, to help them solve the case. The following night, Hickson dies of a gunshot wound during a violent quarrel with a man named Jefferson. Hoping to flee from his predicted death, Roger takes the advice of Webb and sets sail for Argentina with a satchel containing $100,000. Touissant and Beefus prevent his departure, however, and return him to the Fielding home. There Touissant exposes Webb and his plot to get at the inheritance money by frightening Roger with fake apparitions and fake murders. A short time later, the police sergeant arrives with Covey and Hickson, who are very much alive, thus proving true Touissant's explanation. *African Americans. Ghosts. Heirs. Hoaxes. Scientists. Fathers and sons. Morgues. Murder. Police. Predictions. Private detectives. Reporters. Romance. Suicide.*

Note: The plot summary was taken from a synopsis contained in the file for the film in the MPAA/PCA Collection at the AMPAS Library. Some sources list actor Pete Webster as Peter or Neil Webster. According to a *HR* news item, "Pierre Touissant" was the name of the "grandson of Toussaint L'Overture, Haitian general who defied Napoleon."

HR 9 Sep 1940. HR 30 Sep 1940, p. 4. Los Angeles Eagle 1 Oct 1942, p. 2. New York Age 13 Dec 1941. NYP 13 Dec 1941.

FOUR WALLS *see* **STRAIGHT IS THE WAY**

FOX MOVIETONE FOLLIES *see* **STAND UP AND CHEER!**

THE FOXES OF HARROW (Irish Americans, Creoles, African
    Americans)

Twentieth Century-Fox Film Corp. *Dist* Twentieth Century-Fox Film Corp. 24 Sep **1947**; Prod: mid-Apr—18 Jul 1947 [©Twentieth Century-Fox Film Corp.; 1 Oct 1947; LP1437]. Sd (Western Electric Recording); b&w. 12 reels, 10,611 or 10,672 ft. 115 or 118 min. PCA cert no. 12357.

[*Exec prod* Darryl F. Zanuck]. *Prod* William A. Bacher. *Dir* John M. Stahl. [*Asst dir* Joseph Behm]. [*Dial dir* Michael Audley and Grace Bowman]. *Scr* Wanda Tuchock. [*Contr to dial* Dwight Taylor, Edwin Justus Mayer and Thomas Job]. *Dir of photog* Joe La Shelle. *Spec*

photog eff Fred Sersen. *Art dir* Lyle Wheeler and Maurice Ransford. *Ed supv* James B. Clark. *Set dec* Thomas Little and Paul S. Fox. *Cost des* Rene Hubert. *Ward dir* Charles LeMaire. [*Fitter* Lizzie Rogers and Zoya Nedzvejsky]. *Mus dir* Alfred Newman. *Mus* David Buttolph. *Orch arr* Maurice de Packh. *Sd* George Leverett and Roger Heman. *Makeup artist* Ben Nye. [*Casting dir* James Ryan]. [*Prod mgr* R. A. Klune]. [*Vocal coach* Jester Hairston]. [*Tech adv* Harry Mendoza and Aldo Nadi]. [*Tech adv for fencing* Ralph Faulkner]. [*Tech adv for jiu-jitsu* Galen Gough]. [*Research* Frances Richardson].

Song(s): "Pauv' Piti Mom'zelle Zizi" and "Musieu Bainjo," Creole folk songs; "Rye Whiskey," American folk song; "Erzilee," Voodoo chant, composed by Jester Hairston; "Wade in the Water" and "Soon—A Will Be Done," Negro spirituals.

Source: Based on the novel *The Foxes of Harrow* by Frank Yerby (New York, 1946).

Cast: Rex Harrison [(*Stephen Fox*)], Maureen O'Hara [(*Odalie D'Arceneaux Fox*)], Richard Haydn [(*Andre*)], Victor McLaglen [(*Mike Farrell*)], Vanessa Brown [(*Aurore D'Arceneaux*)], Patricia Medina [(*Desiree*)], Gene Lockhart [(*Vicomte D'Arceneaux*)], Charles Irwin [(*Sean Fox*)], Hugo Haas [(*Otto Ludenbach*)], Dennis Hoey [(*Master of Harrow*)], Roy Roberts [(*Tom Warren*)], [Marcel Journet (*St.-Ange*)], [Kenneth Washington (*Achille*)], [Helen Crozier (*Zerline*)], [Sam McDaniel (*Josh*)], [Libby Taylor (*Angelina*)], [Renee Beard (*Little Inch, age 6*)], [A. C. Bilbrew (*Tante Caleen*)], [Suzette Harbin (*Belle*)], [Jimmy Moss (*Etienne Fox, age 6*)], [William "Bill" Walker (*Ty Demon*)], [Mary Currier (*Mrs. Warren*)], [Clear Nelson, Jr. (*Little Inch, age 3*)], [James Lagano (*Etienne Fox, age 3*)], [Henri Letondal (*Maspero*)], [Jean Del Val (*Dr. Le Fevre*)], [Dorothy Adams (*Sara Fox*)], [Andre Charlot (*Dr. Terrebone*)], [Georges Renavent (*Priest*)], [Jasper Weldon (*Jode*)], [Celia Lovsky (*Minna Ludenbach*)], [Napoleon Simpson (*Georges*)], [Eugene Borden (*French auctioneer*)], [Joseph Crehan (*Captain of riverboat*)], [Ralph Faulkner (*Fencing instructor*)], [Randy Stuart (*Mother of Stephen Fox*)], [Lena Torrence (*Slave*)], [Jack Kirkwood, Robert Emmett Keane (*Auctioneers*)], [Maynard Holmes (*Fat man*)], [Louis Bacigalupi, Lennie Bremen, Russ Conklin, Wallace Scott, Al Sparlis, Juan Varro, John Bagni, John Doucette, Jim Toney, Cy Schindel (*Crew members*)], [Jessie Cryer, Frank "Billy" Mitchell, Tony Laurent, Ed Mundy, Peter Camlin, Emile Bejaut (*Vendors*)], [Gordon Clark (*Fop*)], [Bernard DeRoux (*Creole waiter*)], [Frederick Burton (*Creole gentleman*)], [Wee Willie Davis (*Sailor*)], [John Hamilton (*Auctioneer*)], [Jester Hairston Choir (*Voices in voodoo seq*)], [Jack Boyjan], [Manuel Paris], [Mayo Newhall], [Albert Morin], [Frank Dae], [Carlos Barbé], [John Dutriz], [Paul De Corday], [Maurice Marsac], [Andre Marsaudon], [Jean De Briac], [Leon Lenoir], [Paul Maxey], [Demetrius Alexis], [Perry Ivins], [Eddie Le Baron], [William Norton Bailey], [Jerry Miley], [Leo Galitzine], [William Schallert].

Historical, Social, Drama, with songs. [*Print viewed*]. In Ireland, in 1795, the master of the House of Harrow orders his servants, Sean and Sara Fox, to rear his daughter's illegitimate baby. The Foxes are paid well, and although the master admonishes Sean to mold the boy into a humble man, the grieving mother begs Sara to give him enough strength to leave Ireland. By 1827, Stephen, the Foxes' son, has grown into a charismatic man who lives by his wits as a gambler in America. Stephen's good looks intrigue Odalie D'Arceneaux, an aristocratic Creole, although she is shocked to learn that he has been accused of cheating at cards and is being cast off their riverboat onto a Mississippi River sandbar. Stephen connives his way off the sandbar onto the pigboat of the boisterous Mike Farrell, who takes him to New Orleans. There, Stephen befriends Andre, another upper-class Creole, who tells him of a charity ball being hosted by Odalie, her sister Aurore and their father, the Vicomte D'Arceneaux. Stephen again fascinates Odalie by donating one thousand dollars to her charity and then partnering Aurore when Odalie refuses his request for a dance. Later, Andre takes Stephen to *La Bourse de Maspero*, a combination slave market, stock market, gambling hall and restaurant. Stephen joins a blackjack game led by Otto Ludenbach, a German-American scoundrel who starved his family and slaves to acquire his rich plantation. Stephen wins the plantation from Ludenbach, then challenges him to a duel when he makes an insulting reference to Odalie. Ludenbach fires prematurely, wounding Stephen, but Stephen succeeds in killing him. Upon hearing of the duel, Odalie is furious that Stephen has linked his name to hers, but softens when she learns that he has given the grateful widow money

to start a new life. Soon Stephen is hard at work improving the plantation, which he renames "Harrow," and astutely building a financial empire. Stephen continues to work while Odalie visits Paris for a year, and upon her return, he invites her family to the grand opening of Harrow. At the celebration, Odalie is anxious about Stephen's possessiveness, but when he describes his humble birth and confesses that he built Harrow for her, she tells her father that she will marry Stephen. On their wedding night, Stephen and Odalie's passionate kiss is interrupted by the well wishes of a noisy group led by Farrell. Odalie refuses to acknowlege them, and so Stephen goes to drink with his friends. When he returns, Stephen finds the bedroom door locked and breaks it down. The next morning, distressed about the violent beginning of their marriage, Odalie declares that she will wear Stephen's jewels and preside at his table, but nothing more. Although he loves her, Stephen's own pride prevents him from pressing Odalie for her forgiveness, and he loses himself in gambling, drinking and hard work. One night, Stephen comes home to find Odalie watching a voodoo ceremony conducted by the slaves to ensure the safe birth of her son. Overjoyed that Odalie is pregnant, Stephen bears her continued coldness. When the child is due, the slave Achille comes to Stephen with the news that his wife, *La Belle Sauvage*, a proud slave newly arrived from Africa, has also given birth to a son. Stephen wants the boy to be his son's personal attendant, but Belle asserts that her son is a prince, not a slave, and attempts to drown him rather than subject him to a life of servitude. Stephen and Achille save the baby but Belle perishes in the river. Back at the house, Stephen and Odalie admire their new son, Etienne, although Stephen reacts angrily when the doctor states that the boy may grow up with a limp due to a turned-in foot. Later, on Etienne's third birthday, Odalie admires Stephen's plans for the boy's secure financial future, but over the next few years, worries as Stephen teaches the youngster fencing and horseback jumping. One night, she and Stephen have a heated argument over the rearing of Etienne, and when the lad hears them, he rushes down the stairs and falls. Etienne dies that night, and the grief-stricken Stephen yells at the assembled slaves, telling them that Harrow itself has died. Later, the economic crisis that Stephen had predicted strikes, and although Stephen succeeds in saving a few of his friends by buying their worthless stocks, he is destroyed financially. Determined to save Harrow, Odalie decides to strip the house of its furnishings and sell her jewels. She goes to talk to Stephen at the house of his mistress Desiree, but when she tells him of her plan and her wish to have another child with him, he states that he no longer wants her or Harrow. Odalie then returns to Harrow, but there finds that the furnishings and jewelry were not enough, and that the sugarcane must be harvested and sold immediately. As a storm approaches, the slaves hide in the fields and listen to the voodoo drums, which say that Stephen is dead. Odalie tries to convince the slaves to work but they refuse. Despairing, she goes to the house but then sees that Stephen has returned and is organizing the workers. After the storm has passed and the crop has been gathered, Odalie finds Stephen at Etienne's grave and tearfully embraces him when he declares that at least the ground in which Etienne lies will always be his. *African Americans. Ambition. Battle of the sexes. Children. Class distinction. Creoles. Marriage. Plantations. Accidental death. Aristocrats. Cardsharping. Dandies. Drunkenness. Duels. Fathers and daughters. Fathers and sons. Financial crisis. Gambling. German Americans. Handicapped. Illegitimacy. Irish Americans. Masked balls. Mississippi River. Mistresses. New Orleans (LA). Pride and vanity. Rape. Slavery. Stock market. Suicide. Voodoo.*

Note: Information in the Twentieth Century-Fox Records of the Legal Department at the UCLA Arts—Special Collections Library states that the studio paid author Frank Yerby $150,000 for the motion picture rights to *The Foxes of Harrow*, which was his first novel. A Dec 1947 *Ebony* article called the figure "the biggest bonanza ever pocketed by a colored writer" and stated that the book was "the first Negro-authored novel ever bought by a Hollywood studio." Yerby was quoted in the article as insisting as a condition of the purchase, "I won't stand to see any of the colored character debased. I painted them as they were—human beings with human qualities—and if it's filmed, they must remain that way." The magazine pointed out that the film version, however, bore "little resemblance to the original story and all controversial chapters [were] completely omitted from the screen script. The Negro movie-going public will be disappointed in *Foxes* because the most dramatic, most significant scenes about Negroes in Yerby's book are missing in the film." Mrs. A. C. Bilbrew, who played "Tante Caleen" is the film, noted in the magazine article that the character of "Desiree," a quadroon in the book with whom "Stephen Fox" lives, in the film "is not a colored girl. Little Inch [Achille's son,

who, in the book, becomes the New Orleans chief of police during Reconstruction] doesn't grow up at all." In addition, the book contains a scene involving ex-slave and abolotionist Frederick Douglass, and in general makes issues of race and slavery more prominent than they became in the film version.

In material in the Twentieth Century-Fox Produced Scripts Collection, also at UCLA, conference notes of studio production head Darryl F. Zanuck account for some of the changes. After the first treatment of the story was written by Jerome Cady, Zanuck, in notes dated 26 Jul 1946, stated that the film would have to concentrate on "the personal, emotional story" of the principal characters, and that it would be "practically impossible to take a book of this magnitude and tell everything in it within the confines of a screenplay." Concerning "Desiree," and the miscegenation aspect of the novel, Zanuck stated, "The Production Code will not permit us to use her in the story as now written; the Code would permit us to use her only if it could be made perfectly clear that nothing happened between her and Stephen, and that neither he nor she ever wanted anything to happen. Under these restrictions there doesn't seem to be much point in using the girl at all." Regarding "Tante Caleen," Zanuck noted, "Inasmuch as the Johnson Office [i.e., the PCA] would not permit us to show those scenes in which Caleen now plays a dominant part, she will have to be reduced to a part of less importance in the story." At this stage, Zanuck also was planning to omit the characters of "Achille," "Sauvage" and "Little Inch," but they were ultimately kept. Bilbrew, in the *Ebony* article, praised as "one of the high points of the picture... the story of the African princess Sauvage who commits suicide rather than raise a child in slavery." *Var*, in their review, speculated that this scene "is likely to run into difficulties in many Southern states."

According to a document in the legal records, Cady's work was not used by Wanda Tuchock in her final screenplay. According to *HR* news items, Gregory Peck was originally set to play "Stephen Fox." The legal records note that Dorothy Dandridge was originally cast in the role of "Zerline," and that Jimmy Moss replaced Billy Ward in the role of "Etienne" after Ward broke his arm. *HR* news items also note that Martin Wilkins and Alice Leone and their dance troupe were considered for the cast, which was to include Naomi Sakmar, Arline James, Libbey Wilcott and Joseph Hayden, but their participation in the final film has not been confirmed. The plantation scenes were shot on location in Sherwood Forest, CA, according to *HR*. *Ebony* related that the film cost $2,750,000 to produce, and studio publicity noted that Maureen O'Hara made her singing debut in the film. In Oct 1947, Fox took out an option to a sequel to be written by Yerby, but after he delivered the outline in Feb 1948, the studio decided against purchasing it. On 6 Dec 1948, *Lux Radio Theatre* broadcast a version of the story starring O'Hara and John Hodiak.

Box 27 Sep 1947. *Cue* 4 Oct 1947. *DV* 8 May 1946. *DV* 22 Sep 1947. *Ebony* Dec 1947, pp. 14-18. *FD* 23 Sep 1947, p. 8. *HR* 6 May 1946, p. 7. *HR* 6 Jun 1946, p. 4. *HR* 4 Feb 1947, p. 2. *HR* 25 Mar 1947, p. 11. *HR* 4 Apr 1947, p. 4. *HR* 11 Apr 1947, p. 15. *HR* 14 Apr 1947, p. 2, 4. *HR* 5 May 1947, p. 9. *HR* 26 May 1947, p. 11. *HR* 18 Jul 1947, p. 15. *HR* 22 Sep 1947, p. 3. *LAT* 11 Oct 1947. *MPHPD* 27 Sep 1947, p. 3849. *Newsweek* 6 Oct 1947. *New Yorker* 4 Oct 1947. *NYT* 25 Sep 1947, p. 35. *Var* 24 Sep 1947, p. 11.

FOXFIRE (Native Americans, Apache)
Universal-International Pictures Co., Inc. *Dist* Universal Pictures Co., Inc. Jul **1955**; New York opening: 13 Jul 1955; Los Angeles opening: 29 Jul 1955; Prod: 28 Jul—early Sep 1954 [©Universal Pictures Co.; 11 Apr 1955; LP4599]. Sd (Western Electric Recording); col (Technicolor); 1.85. 91-93 min. PCA cert no. 17280.

Prod Aaron Rosenberg. *Dir* Joseph Pevney. *Asst dir* Ronnie Rondell and [Phil Bowles]. [*Dial dir* Leon Charles]. *Scr* Ketti Frings. *Dir of photog* William Daniels. *Technicolor color consultant* William Fritzsche. *Art dir* Alexander Golitzen and Robert Clatworthy. *Film ed* Ted J. Kent. *Set dec* Russell A. Gausman and Ruby R. Levitt. *Gowns* Bill Thomas. *Mus* Frank Skinner. *Mus supv* Joseph Gershenson. *Sd* Leslie I. Carey and Robert Pritchard. *Hair stylist* Joan St. Oegger. *Makeup* Bud Westmore. *Jane Russell's hair stylist* Stephanie McGrew. *Jane Russell's make-up artist* Layne Britton. [*Unit prod mgr* Tommy Thompson].

Song(s): "Foxfire," music by Henry Mancini, lyrics by Jeff Chandler.

Source: Based on the novel *Foxfire* by Anya Seton (Boston, 1951).

Cast: JANE RUSSELL (*Amanda [Lawrence Dartland]*), JEFF CHANDLER (*Jonathan ["Dart"] Dartland*), Dan Duryea ([*Dr.*] *Hugh Slater*), Mara Corday (*Maria [Conchera]*), Barton MacLane (*Mr. [Jim] Mablett*), Frieda Inescort (*Mrs. Lawrence*), Celia Lovsky (*Saba [Dartland]*), Eddy C. Waller (*Old Larky*), Robert F. Simon (*Ernest Tyson*), Charlotte Wynters (*Mrs. Mablett*), Robert Bice (*Walt Whitman*), Arthur Space (*Foley*), [Lillian Bronson (*Mrs. Potter*)], [Phil Chambers (*Mr. Riley*)], [Guy Wilkerson (*Mr. Barton*)], [Mary Carroll (*Mrs. Riley*)], [Vicki Raaf (*Cleo*)], [Grace Lenard (*Rose*)], [Lisabith Fielding (*Mrs. Foley*)], [Dabbs Greer (*Bus driver*)], [Hal K. Dawson (*Tourists*)], Grace Hayle (*Tourists*)], [Charmienne Harker (*Rowena*)], [Beulah Archuletta (*Indian woman*)], [Billy Wilkerson (*Apache chief*)], [Chabon Jadi (*Bellhop*)], [R. H. Baldwin (*Hoist operator*)], [Manley Suathojame (*Indian husband*)], [Leon Charles, Jimmy Casino, Charles Soldani, Martin Cichy (*Miners*)].

Social, Drama. [*Print viewed*]. The beautiful and wealthy Amanda Lawrence gratefully accepts a ride from mining engineer Jonathan "Dart" Dartland and his alcoholic friend, Dr. Hugh Slater, when the car she has borrowed from the La Paz Guest Ranch breaks down in the Arizona desert. Although Hugh flirts with her, it is the handsome and reserved engineer who attracts her, and before saying goodbye, she invites the two to a dinner party in her mother's suite that evening. Dart arrives late, explaining as he walks with Amanda that he dislikes parties, people and mothers, particularly wealthy Eastern mothers with spoiled and beautiful daughters. Undaunted, Amanda kisses him and the two soon find that they are in love. Dart admits that his own mother is a Mescalero Apache, who settled on the local reservation following the death of his father, a Boston professor. Mortified at her earlier admission that Indians give her "the creeps," Amanda apologizes, and they kiss again. In the morning, Amanda dreamily informs her mother that they soon will have Indians in the family, whereupon Mrs. Lawrence books tickets for the flight back to New York. That afternoon, Amanda proposes to Dart, and on the following day, they are wed. The happy-go-lucky Amanda is unconcerned when Mrs. Mablett, the meddling wife of Dart's foreman, describes Apaches as "cruel, dangerous, and...tight-mouthed," but she is disturbed when Dart angrily sends her away from the mine, explaining that the Apache workers consider a woman in the underground tunnels a jinx. The newlyweds make up that evening, and Dart shows her the foxfire, a phosphorescent nighttime glow caused by the rotten timbers of the abandoned Foxfire mine, which he believes contains an undiscovered vein of gold. Over the next few months, Dart remains preoccupied with his work while Amanda develops an attachment to Hugh, which although understood by her as an innocent friendship, is taken more seriously by the lovesick doctor. Hugh's nurse, Maria Conchera, who is also part Apache, loves the doctor, and her jealous remarks fuel the town's appetite for gossip. Amanda opens Dart's foot locker and learns that his grandfather Tanosay was a respected Apache chief, but Dart is sensitive about his background and mistakes her interest for amusement. His anger and reticence cause Amanda to conceal her pregnancy from Dart, and the situation worsens when mine owner Ernest Tyson agrees to explore the Foxfire mine at Amanda's rather than Dart's prompting. While Dart gets the Foxfire project underway, Amanda visits the Apache reservation on a whim, and there she finally meets her mother-in-law, Princess Saba. She listens in bewilderment as Saba explains that Apache boys over the age of twelve are expected to leave their mothers, never again exhibiting tears or weakness. The child Amanda bears, she continues, will be of little concern to Dart before reaching that age. After explaining that her husband's death was almost too much to endure, she concludes that the Indian philosophy of love is the right one: love is only temporary. Meanwhile, Dart, unable to find his wife, joins Maria in assuming that she has "gone off somewhere" with Hugh. By the time Amanda returns to town, Dart is angry and drunk. Grabbing her roughly, he roars that Apache men tear out the hair of women who are unfaithful. Dart stays at the mine for several days, unaware that Amanda has suffered a miscarriage. When he finally learns the truth, he rushes to the hospital, but Amanda sends him away. Later, she tells Dart the marriage is over because he treated her "like a squaw." Obsessed with finding the lost Foxfire gold, Dart drives his men too hard, and one day, the mine collapses. After helping the men out, the injured Dart climbs into a newly opened tunnel, where he finds, along with some old Apache tools and wall paintings, a rich vein of gold. Tyson and Dart's Apache friend, Walt Whitman, are thrilled by the discovery, but Dart, his hands bandaged, thinks only of Amanda. Maria tells Amanda, who is about to leave for New York, about Dart's injury, and Amanda rushes back to her husband. Admitting that he needs her, Dart explains that he is slow at love, but is no longer afraid of it. They kiss as the new "Foxfire Gold Company" sign is put in place. *Apache Indians. Cultural conflict. Gold mines. Indians of North America–Mixed blood. Marriage–Mixed. Mescalero Indians. Socialites. Vocational obsession.* Alcoholics. Arizona. Deserts. Engineers. Gold miners. In-laws. Indians of North America–Reservations. Jealousy. Mine accidents. Mine foremen. Mine owners. Miscarriage. Mothers and daughters. Nurses. Physicians. Racism. Resorts. Small town life. Unrequited love.

Note: Although a 23 Jul 1954 *HR* production chart includes Linda Christian in the cast, she does not appear in the finished film. The onscreen credits note that "Miss Jane Russell's services" were provided "by courtesy of Russ-Field Corporation." According to studio publicity and a 27 Jul 1954 *HR* news item, the picture was filmed on location at Oatman and Kingman, AZ, and was the first

film in which husband and wife Barton MacLane and Charlotte Wynters appeared together. In the film, Jeff Chandler sings the theme song that he co-wrote with Henry Mancini. The *Saturday Review* critic remarked that the script "probes unusually deep in analyzing the position of women in an Apache tribe and their relation to their men, with one beautifully handled sequence in which the withered Indian mother explains by indirection the ways of her people to the bewildered young wife."

Box 25 Jun 1955. *DV* 14 Jun 1955, p. 3. *Exb* 15 Jun 1955, p. 3980. *FD* 22 Jun 1955, p. 10. *Har* 18 Jun 1955, p. 98. *HR* 23 Jul 1954, p. 10. *HR* 26 Jul 1954, p. 4. *HR* 27 Jul 1954, p. 8. *HR* 27 Aug 1954, p. 6. *HR* 14 Jun 1955, p. 3. *MPD* 14 Jun 1955. *MPHPD* 18 Jun 1955, p. 482. *NYT* 14 Jul 1955, p. 19. *Saturday Review* 30 Jul 1955. *Var* 15 Jun 1955, p. 6.

FRANK G. SLAUGHTER'S NAKED IN THE SUN *see* **NAKED IN THE SUN**

FRATE E SUORA *see* **COSÌ È LA VITA**

FREE AND EASY (*foreign version*, 1930) *see* **ESTRELLADOS**

FREE AND EASY (1935) *se* **PIERNAS DE SEDA**

FREE AND EQUAL (African Americans)
Thomas H Ince. *Dist* A H Woods. **1918**. Si; b&w. 5? reels.
Dir R. William Neill. *Story* R. Cecil Smith.
Cast: Charles K. French (*Judge Lowell*), Gloria Hope (*His daughter Margaret*), Jack Curtis (*Her fiancé*), Lydia Knott (*Mrs. Lowell*), Jack Richardson (*Alexander Marshall*), Thomas J. Guise (*Prosecuting attorney*), J. J. Dowling (*The Colonel*).
Social, Melodrama. Judge Lowell creates The Society for the Uplift of the Negro to satisfy his passion for the equality of the races and to further his own political ambitions. At Tuskegee Institute, Lowell meets Alexander Marshall, an extremely bright mulatto student. As Marshall shares Lowell's dream to see the intermarriage of the races result in equality, he becomes Lowell's private secretary and passes for the son of a wealthy Creole abolitionist in order to raise money for their organization. Lowell's daughter Margaret falls in love with Marshall, who satisfies his lustful "instincts" in brothels. After Margaret recoils from his advances, Marshall encounters Belle Andrews, a good-looking maid who earlier flirted with him, and kisses her against her will. Margaret comes to apologize and witnesses Marshall inadvertently kill Belle as he clasps her throat to stop her from shrieking. During Marshall's trial, Margaret admits that she married Marshall, but a young mulatto woman testifies that she is really Marshall's wife, and a black woman reveals that she is his mother. Lowell, horrified to learn of Marshall's marriage to Margaret, throws the book he had been writing, which advocates full equality, into the fire. Marshall is taken to prison, where he madly clutches the bars. *African Americans. Marriage–Mixed. Abolitionists. African Americans–Mixed blood. Bigamy. Brothels. Impersonation and imposture. Judges. Manslaughter. Secretaries. Trials. Tuskegee Institute.*

Note: According to a news item in *Photoplay*, Apr 1918, this film was produced by Thomas H. Ince at the Triangle studios in the summer of 1917. Ince, the item noted, did not want to release the film because it was not complimentary to blacks, so he let stage producer A. H. Woods exhibit it in Los Angeles in 1918. The news item further states that during the brief exhibition, the city authorities began litigation against the film. It was shelved until the Frequal Company, in which Woods was financially interested, presented it at the Astor Theatre in New York on 19 Apr 1925. This presentation included a staged prologue and epilogue written by Willard Mack. In the prologue, Jack Richardson, who played Alexander Marshall in the film, exhorts black singers and dancers by a levee to assert themselves as equals to whites. In the epilogue, it is revealed that the preceding film was Richardson's dream; he awakens and says that Booker T. Washington was right in stating that the Negro should stay in his place. The story by R. Cecil Smith was copyrighted in 1917 by Thomas H. Ince. Some of the story varies from the plot as reported by reviewers of the film in 1925. The film was not well received by critics in New York; *NYT* noted: "The story is as distasteful as it is ridiculous," while *Var* stated that it "is just so much junk." The *California Eagle*, a Los Angeles African-American newspaper, commented that "notice was posted backstage before the matinee [of 20 Apr] was finished to the effect that the show would close on Saturday. That information provided whatever pleasure came from the $1.10 spent on the show.... Just about all it accomplished was to tarnish the halo that colored people had long since placed upon the head of Al Woods whom they had come to know as a friend of the race. Mr Woods may not need this good will but it was genuinely his. It is reported that one of Mr. Woods' employees resigned his job on an elevator rather than work for a man who presented such a film." The newspaper was particularly critical of "performers who will prostitute their talents in any such propaganda against the race of which they are a part while there are dishes to wash, ditches to dig, streets to sweep or any other honorable job with which they might fend off starvation." According to information in the NAACP Papers at the Library of Congress, the National Office of the NAACP sent an official to the opening on 19 Apr 1925, after having received over a period

of a few months "more or less mysterious intimations" about the film "which was characterized as being much worse than *The Birth of a Nation*." The official judged the film to be "very offensive," and surmising that "the intimations sent us were a bid for publicity," the NAACP decided to take no action to protest the film. After a week in New York, it was withdrawn.

California Eagle 8 May 1925, p. 8. *NYT* 20 Apr 1925, p. 22. *Pboto* Apr 1918, p. 104. *Var* 22 Apr 1925, p. 34.

FREE CLINIC *see* **AM I GUILTY?**

FREEDOM *see* **MEN ARE SUCH FOOLS**

FRIENDLY ENEMIES (German Americans)
Belasco Productions, Inc. *Dist* Producers Distributing Corp. 16 Mar **1925** [©Belasco Productions, Inc.; 7 Apr 1925; LP21340]. Si; b&w. 7 reels, 6,288 ft.

Pres A. H. Sebastian. *Dir* George Melford. *Scen and titles* Alfred A. Cohn. *Adpt* Josephine Quirk. *Photog* Charles G. Clarke.

Source: Based on the play *Friendly Enemies* by Samuel Shipman and Aaron Hoffman (New York, 22 Jul 1918).

Cast: Lew Fields (*Carl Pfeiffer*), Joe Weber (*Henry Block*), Virginia Brown Faire (*June Block*), Jack Mulhall (*William Pfeiffer*), Stuart Holmes (*Miller*), Lucille Lee Stewart (*Hilda Schwartz*), Eugenie Besserer (*Mrs. Marie Pfeiffer*), Nora Hayden (*Nora*), Jules Hanft (*Frederick Schnitzler*), Fred Kelsey (*Adolph*), Johnny Fox (*Messenger boy*), Edward Porter (*Naval officer*).

Comedy. Carl Pfeiffer and Henry Block, who emigrated from Germany to the United States, have become prosperous and argumentative. When the World War breaks out, Henry is one hundred percent American while Carl's loyalties are divided between his adopted country and his native land. William Pfeiffer, Carl's son, enlists in the U. S. Army, deeply disturbing his father, who is persuaded by Miller, a German agent, to contribute money to the German cause. Miller uses the money to place a saboteur on the troopship to which William is assigned. The saboteur disables the ship, and Carl receives a report that as a consequence William has been killed. William turns up unharmed, however, and Carl and Henry set out to capture Miller with the help of Hilda Schwartz, a Secret Service agent. After Miller is finally captured, William marries June Block, Henry's beautiful daughter, with the happy consent of the old friends, who now agree completely in their loyalty to the United States. *German Americans. Immigrants. Patriotism. Sabotage. Secret service. Spies. Troop transports. World War I.*

FD 19 May 1925. *MPW* 16 May 1925. *NYT* 5 May 1925, p. 24. *Var* 6 May 1925, p. 46.

FRIENDLY ENEMIES (German Americans)
Edward Small Productions, Inc. *Dist* United Artists Corp. 26 Jun **1942**; New York premiere: 19 Jun 1942; Prod: 5 Feb—mid-Mar 1942 [©Edward Small Productions, Inc.; 10 Jun 1942; LP11368]. Sd; b&w. 10 reels, 8,580 ft. 95 min. PCA cert no. 8201.

Pres EDWARD SMALL. *Asst to prod* Grant Whytock. *Dir* Allan Dwan. *Asst dir* Sam Nelson. *Adpt for the screen by* Adelaide Heilbron. *Dir of photog* Edward Cronjager. *Spec eff ed* T. K. Wood. *Art dir* John DuCasse Schulze. *Supv film ed* Grant Whytock. *Film ed* William Claxton. *Set dec* Edward G. Boyle. [*Props* Ken Walton]. *Cost* Royer. *Mus dir* Lud Gluskin. *Mus score* Lucien Moraweck. *Sd* William Wilmarth. [*Sd rec* Jack Whitney and Sound Service, Inc.]. *Makeup* Don Cash. *Prod mgr* Max H. Golden.

Song(s): "My Country 'Tis of Thee," music by Henry Carey, lyrics by Samuel Francis Smith.

Source: Based on the play *Friendly Enemies* by Samuel Shipman and Aaron Hoffman (New York, 22 Jul 1918).

Cast: Charles Winninger (*Karl Pfeiffer*), Charlie Ruggles (*Henry Block*), James Craig (*William Pfeiffer*), Nancy Kelly (*June Block*), Otto Kruger (*Anton Miller [also known as George Stewart]*), Ilka Gruning (*Mrs. Pfeiffer*), Greta Meyer (*Gretchen*), Addison Richards (*Inspector McCarty*), Charles Lane (*Braun*), John Piffle (*Schnitzler*), Ruth Holly (*Nora*).

War, Comedy-drama. [*Print viewed*]. In the early days of World War I, Karl Pfeiffer, a German-born American who made his wealth in the brewery business in New York City, stands in opposition to President Woodrow Wilson's decision to send American troops to Europe. He fears that the people in his "Fatherland" will be obliterated by the Allied forces. Because Karl is excessively proud of his German heritage and has his own peculiar notions about how best to bring about peace in the world, he becomes susceptible to the manipulations of saboteur Anton Miller. Miller introduces himself to

Karl as "George Stewart" and convinces Karl to donate $50,000 to a supposed propaganda campaign designed to end the war. Karl tells Miller that he can pick up the check the following day at his Upper East Side apartment. That night, Maria, his wife of thirty years, and June Block, his soon-to-be daughter-in-law, are preparing a dinner for June's father, Henry Block. Henry is an assimilated German-American with political views that are in direct opposition to those held by Karl. As soon as the two men come together, their usual quarreling ensues. Karl's opinions and his explosive temper are familiar to all who know him, and it is because of this that his family has kept secret the fact that his son William has enlisted in the American army. The secret is soon out of the bag, though, when William arrives with news of his regiment's departure for Europe and requests that his family assemble for an early wedding. Karl is devastated by the news and angrily storms out of the apartment. He returns the next day and tries, unsuccessfully, to convince his son to reconsider his decision. When Miller collects the $50,000 check from Karl, he discovers that Karl is a friend of the wealthy Henry, and asks that he arrange a meeting with him. Soon after William boards his transport ship for Europe, Karl gets a telephone call from Miller, who informs him that his money was used to help sink the transport ship as it was leaving harbor. Now realizing that he was horribly misled by Miller, Karl vows revenge and plans to kill him. Henry's cool-headedness prevails, though, and the two decide to snare the saboteur instead. Soon after Miller arrives at Karl's to meet Henry, he is coaxed into revealing his true identity, at which point the police enter and arrest him. Karl's son, it turns out, did not perish in the ship tragedy and returns home safely. Reunited with his son, Karl vows to reject his earlier political beliefs and insists that henceforth his family refer to strudel as "apple pie." Karl then celebrates his newly found American patriotism by joining his family in a rousing chorus of "My Country 'Tis of Thee." *Assimilation (Sociology). Fathers and sons. German Americans. Patriotism. Sabotage. Bankers. Brewers and breweries. Debates. Germans. Impersonation and imposture. Military service, Compulsory. New York City. Propaganda. Rivalry. Secrets. Ships. Weddings. World War I.*

Note: The play on which this film is based was produced on Broadway by A. H. Woods and featured Louis Mann and Sam Bernard in the starring roles. The play ran two seasons on Broadway before it was taken on the road. Actor Charles Winninger appeared in the stage version of *Friendly Enemies* in 1918. A 6 Feb 1942 *HR* production chart lists Sharon Douglas in the cast, but her participation in the released film has not been confirmed. President Woodrow Wilson provided the foreword to this film, and according to the publicity material, it marked the first time that a picture featured a direct quote from a President of the United States regarding the subject matter of the film. Publicity material also relates the difficulties that properties man Ken Walton encountered in trying to procure a German-language newspaper as a prop for the film at a time when the FBI was enforcing strict bans on the printing of German publications. Walton, according to the publicity sheet, was granted access to an FBI-impounded German-language press in Los Angeles only after an FBI investigation into the matter was completed and after two affidavits were filed by the production company stating that no actual publications with German type would be distributed. The play was first adapted for the screen in 1925, when Producers Distributing Corp. released a version of *Friendly Enemies* directed by George Melford and starring Lew Fields and Joe Weber. *Friendly Enemies* was nominated for an Academy Award for Best Sound Recording.

Box 27 Jun 1942. *DV* 13 Feb 1942. *DV* 18 Jun 1942, p. 3. *FD* 24 Jun 1942, p. 5. *HR* 6 Feb 1942. *HR* 6 Mar 1942. *HR* 8 Jun 1942, p. 8. *HR* 18 Jun 1942, p. 3. *MPHPD* 27 Jun 1942, p. 738. *NYT* 22 Jun 1942, p. 19. *Var* 24 Jun 1942, p. 8.

THE FRIGHTENED CHILD *see* **THE HOUSE ON TELEGRAPH HILL**

THE FRISCO DOLL *see* **KLONDIKE ANNIE**

FRISCO LADY *see* **CHINATOWN SQUAD**

FRISCO NIGHTS *see* **CHINATOWN SQUAD**

FRISCO SALLY LEVY (Jewish Americans)
Metro-Goldwyn-Mayer Corp.; controlled by Loew's Inc. *Dist* Metro-Goldwyn-Mayer Distributing Corp. 2 Apr **1927** [©Metro-Goldwyn-Mayer Distributing Corp.; 2 May 1927; LP23919]. Si; b&w. 7 reels, 6,900 ft.

Dir William Beaudine. *Adpt* Vernon Smith. *Story* Lew Lipton. *Story and scen* Alfred A. Cohn. *Titles* Joe Farnham. *Photog* Max Fabian. *Art dir* Cedric Gibbons and David Townsend. *Film ed* Blanche Sewell. *Ward* René Hubert.

Cast: Tenen Holtz (*Isaac Solomon Lapidowitz*), Kate Price (*Bridget O'Grady Lapidowitz*), Sally O'Neil (*Sally Colleen Lapidowitz*), Leon Holmes (*Michael Abraham Lapidowitz*), Turner

Savage (*Isidore Patrick Lapidowitz*), Helen Levine (*Rebecca Patricia Lapidowitz*), Fido Rover (*Himself, a dog*), Roy D'Arcy (*I. Stuart Gold*), Charles Delaney (*Patrick Sweeney*).

Romantic comedy. Sally Colleen Lapidowitz, the daughter of an orthodox Jewish father and an intensely Irish mother, is the steady girl of Patrick Sweeney, a motorcycle cop. Sally becomes infatuated with Stuart Gold, a Jewish dandy, who, though he is approved by her father, soon proves himself to be a worthless cad. Patrick rescues her from the dandy, and all ends happily in the Hebrew-Irish family. *Cads. Courtship. Family life. Irish. Jews. Police. San Francisco (CA).*

Note: Copyrighted as 8 reels.
FD 17 Apr 1927. *MPW* 23 Apr 1927. *NYT* 13 Apr 1927, p. 29. *Var* 13 Apr 1927, p. 18.

FROM ACROSS THE BORDER (Latino)

Dist Methodist Board. 1942. Sd; b&w. 45 min.

Educational/Cultural. [*Not viewed*]. A Mexican boy comes with his mother to the United States to find work. A minister inspires him to go to school. After finishing his education, he becomes a successful pastor of an important Mexican church in Texas. *Immigrants. Mexican Americans. Ministers. Mothers and sons. Texas.*

Note: This film was listed in an educational film catalog, which stated that it was a true story.

FROM HERE TO VICTORY see MR. LUCKY

LAS FRONTERAS DEL AMOR (Spanish language)

Fox Film Corp. *Dist* Fox Film Corp. 1934; New York opening: 30 Nov 1934; Prod: Jun–Jul 1934 [©Fox Film Corp.; 7 Nov 1934; LP5080]. Sd; b&w. 9 reels, 7,355 ft. 82 min. PCA cert no. 198. Spanish language.

[*Prod* John Stone]. *Dirección* [*Dir*] Frank Strayer. [*Asst dir* Sam Schneider and Sol Michaels]. *Original de* [*Orig story*] Bernice Mason. *Adaptación cinematográfica* [*Scr*] Winifred Dunn. *Versión española* [*Spanish version*] Miguel de Zárraga. [*Photog* Arthur Martinelli]. [*Art dir* Duncan Cramer]. [*Ed* Ernest Nims]. [*Cost* Royer]. *Dirección musical* [*Mus dir*] Samuel Kaylin. [*Sd* Miguel de Zárraga, Jr.].

Song(s): "La donna è mobile" from the opera *Rigoletto*, music by Giuseppe Verdi, libretto by Francesco Maria Piave; "Te quiero dar mi vida," "¿Recuerdas?" and "La bola," music by Troy Sanders, lyrics by José Mojica; "Las mañanitas" and "Cielito lindo," folk songs, traditional lyrics adapted by José Mojica; "Estoy cantando," music by Troy Sanders, lyrics from the poem "Vida retirado" by Fray Luis De León; "Andar," music and lyrics by Ernesto Lecuona and Gustavo Garralaga; "The Minstrel," music by Easthope Martin, lyrics by Helen Taylor, Spanish translation of English lyrics by José Mojica; "Blanca palomita," composer undetermined.

Cast: José Mojica (*Miguel Segovia*), Rosita Moreno (*Alice Harrison*), Rafael Corio (*Gastón Garnier*), Juan Martínez Plá (*Tío Fred*), Alma Real (*Señora Harrison*), Rudolf Amendt (*Otto Van Ritter*), Chito Alonso (*José López*), Gloria de la Vega (*María*), Lola Montero (*Fermina*), Jesús Macías (*Pedro*).

Musical, Romance. [*Not viewed*]. The famous and much-loved opera singer, Miguel Segovia, has grown tired of the publicity tricks and the tour that his manager Harry has planned for him, so he returns to his ranch in Mexico. The ranch hands greet him excitedly, and the morning after an all-night party, he rides a horse to the cabin of the ranch's sheepherder José López. José, who has never met Segovia, tells the stranger that he needs to become a cowpuncher in order to marry his girl friend María, the daughter of the ranch's groom. Looking to get away from people, Segovia tells José to take his horse and promises to tend the sheep while José fulfills his wish. While Segovia is playing in a nearby field, a plane, sputtering from lack of gas, lands, and the pilot, Alice Harrison, of the high-society Harrisons in California, steps out. She tries to get Segovia, who says his name is José, to obtain fuel for her plane because her family will be worried if she does not return soon. He refuses but offers to let her stay in his cabin, which she declines, because it is too filthy, and walks back toward the plane. The real José, having been told who the stranger is, returns to his cabin only to be sent back for fuel by Segovia. Frightened by an animal's howling, Alice returns to the cabin, where she spends the night sleeping in a chair. The next day, Alice tries to bribe Segovia to go for fuel by offering him her Victrola. He is unimpressed until he tap-dances to one of her records. José returns with the fuel, but Alice fears it is too late in the day to leave, so she stays another night and falls in love with Segovia; however, because she believes that they are from different social classes, she leaves at

dawn before Segovia can stop her. In Los Angeles, an old beau, Otto Van Ritter, who does not know how to enjoy himself, proposes marriage, which Alice refuses. She confides to her Uncle Fred, who advises her to follow her heart. Meanwhile, Harry, having located Segovia, talks him into returning to the tour. Alice, having sent a letter to "José," receives an angry letter from María telling Alice of José's engagement to her. Otto proposes again and this time Alice accepts. Segovia reads about her engagement and goes to Alice's house, where he is told by her that it is none of his affair. Later, she overhears a radio broadcast of his concert and believing the voice to be José's, rushes to Mexico to follow her heart. Alerted to her trip by Uncle Fred, Segovia manages to delay her flight and reaches Mexico before her. When she arrives, he proposes to her; she accepts and José sings happily at their wedding. *Class distinction. Impersonation and imposture. Mexico. Opera singers. Ranchers. Romance. Cabins. Concerts. Engagements. Los Angeles (CA). Parties. Proposals (Marital). Publicity. Radio broadcasting. Ranches. Shepherds. Theatrical managers. Uncles. Upper classes. Weddings. Women air pilots.*

Note: The plot summary was based on a screen continuity in the Twentieth Century-Fox Produced Scripts Collection, and the onscreen credits were taken from a screen credits sheet in the Twentieth Century-Fox Records of the Legal Department, both of which are at the UCLA Theater Arts Library. The running time listed above was calculated from the footage given in NYSA records. Bernice Mason's original story was entitled "Enamorado" or "The Love Flight." The working titles of the film were *En alas del amor* and *El vuelo del amor.* The film was shown in Mexico under the title *¡Viva mi tierra!* According to information in the legal records, a Kellett Auto-Gyro flying machine was filmed at a location at or near Chatsworth, CA. In 1936, Twentieth Century-Fox remade this film as *Under Your Spell*, which was directed by Otto Ludwig Preminger and starred Lawrence Tibbett and Wendy Barrie (see *AFI Catalog of Feature Films, 1931-40*; F3. 4856).
CM Nov 1934, p. 614. *FD* 5 Dec 1934, p. 10. *NYT* 4 Dec 1934, p. 23.

FRONTIER DAYS (Native Americans)

Hall's Western Productions. 4 Jul **1920** [©Hall's Western Productions; 30 Oct 1920; MU1826]. Si; b&w. 5 reels.

Cam P. D. Hall and Glenn L. Hyder.

Cast: Mr. Tom L. Burnett, Mrs. Tom L. Burnett, Bryan Roach, Tommy Kirnan, Bey Kirnan, Fog Horn Clancy, Hugh Strickland, Leonard Stroud.

Western, Documentary. A roundup held in Tarrant County, Texas is shown in this documentary. Contestants are shown participating in roping, riding and other events. Indians perform native dances in authentic dress. *Cowboys. Rodeos. Roundups. Tarrant County (TX). Folk dancing. Indians of North America.*

Note: All of the persons in the film were actual contestants in the roundup.

FRONTIER FURY (Native Americans)

Columbia Pictures Corp. *Dist* Columbia Pictures Corp. 24 Jun **1943**; Prod: 14 Dec–22 Dec 1942 [©Columbia Pictures Corp.; 15 May 1943; LP12053]. Sd; b&w. 5,514 ft. 53 or 55 min.

Prod Jack Fier. *Exec prod* Irving Briskin. *Dir* William Berke. *Asst dir* William O'Connor. *Story and scr* Betty Burbridge. *Dir of photog* Benjamin Kline. *Art dir* Lionel Banks. *Assoc* Perry Smith. *Film ed* Jerome Thoms. *Int dec* Robert Priestley. *Sd eng* Lambert Day.

Cast: Charles Starrett (*Steve Langdon*), Arthur Hunnicutt (*Arkansas Tuttle*), Roma Aldrich (*Stella Larkin*), Clancy Cooper (*Dan Bentley*), I. Stanford Jolley (*Nick Dawson*), Edmund Cobb (*Tracy Meade*), Bruce Bennett (*Clem Hawkins*), Ted Mapes (*Jim Wallace*), Bill Wilkerson (*Chief Eagle Feather*), Stanley Brown (*Gray Bear*), Joel Friedkin (*Doc Hewes*), Jimmie Davis and his Singing Buckaroos, Jessie Arnold (*Minerva*), Elmo Lincoln (*Stewart*), Franklyn Farnum (*Homer*), Frank O'Connor (*Dan*), Frank LaRue (*Marshal*), Chief Yowlachie, Nuyaka, Jack Kirk (*Deputy*), George Russell (*Henchman*), Jack Rockwell (*Lane*), Eddie Borden (*Pop Barrows*).

Western, with songs. [*Not viewed*]. When Indian agent Steve Langdon and Gray Bear, the son of the chief, are sent to Independence, Kansas, to withdraw the Indians' funds from the bank, they decide to foil a planned robbery by sending an empty strong box on the freight stage and then stuffing the money into their saddlebags. Their plans go awry, however, and when the stage is attacked, Gray Bear is killed and the bandits escape with the footage found in their saddlebags. While fending off the outlaws, Steve notices a star tattooed on the leader's arm. As a result of the robbery, Steve is dismissed from his job and some innocent Indians are arrested when one of the stolen coins is found in their possession. Vowing to avenge Gray Bear's death and

bring the outlaws to justice, Steve decides to undertake his own investigation. While riding to the town in which one of the stolen coins has appeared, Steve is shot at by an unseen assailant. Soon after, Stella Larkin arrives in the town to meet her fiancé, who she discovers, has just been hanged as a bandit by the local vigilantes. When a collection is taken up for the bereaved Stella, Clem Hawkins, the stage driver, contributes one of the stolen coins. Under questioning, Clem admits that he informed the bandits about the money hidden in the saddlebags, but before he can go to trial, he is killed. When Stella appears once again, claiming that Clem was her fiancé, Steve exposes her ruse and forces her to admit that she is the sweetheart of bandit leader Dan Bentley, the man with the tattooed arm. In order to keep tabs on Stella, Steve arranges a job for her with a medicine show in town. One day, when she slips out to meet Dan, Steve follows her and walks into a trap. Experiencing a change of heart, Stella decides to help Steve and summons his friends. With their help, Steve captures the gang and recovers the stolen money. *Bandits. Indian agents. Indians of North America. Investigations. Robbery. Coins. False arrests. Impersonation and imposture. Medicine shows. Murder. Stagecoach drivers. Tattoos. Vigilantes.*

Note: A *HR* production chart places John Bond, Art Wenzel, Wes Tuttle and Ann Savage in the cast, but their appearance in the released film has not been confirmed. Although the *Var* review notes that several songs were performed in this picture, their titles and composers have not been determined. Modern sources add Lew Meehan to the cast.
Box 18 Sep 1943. *DV* 9 Jul 1943, p. 3. *FD* 22 Sep 1943, p. 8. *HR* 18 Dec 1942, p. 6. *HR* 9 Jul 1943, p. 3. *MPH* 17 Jul 1943. *MPHPD* 8 May 1943, p. 1305. *MPHPD* 17 Jul 1943, p. 1427. *Var* 15 Sep 1943, p. 10.

FRONTIER GUN (Native Americans)

Regal Films, Inc. *Dist* Twentieth Century-Fox Film Corp. Dec **1958**; *Prod:* early May—mid-May 1958 [©Twentieth Century-Fox Film Corp.; 23 Oct 1958; LP12673]. Sd; b&w; RegalScope. 8 reels, 6,302 ft. 70 min. PCA cert no. 19087.

Prod Richard E. Lyons. *Assoc prod* Maury Dexter. *Dir* Paul Landres. *Asst dir* Lou Perlof and [Clancy Herne]. *Wrt* Stephen Kandel. *Dir of photog* Walter Strenge. *Art dir* Edward Shiells. *Supv film ed* Robert Fritch. [*Film ed* Harry Gerstad]. *Mus ed* George Emick. *Set dec* Harry Reif. *Cost supv* Clark Ross. *Mus comp* Paul Dunlap. *Sd* Victor Appel. *Sd facilities* Glen Glenn Sound Co. *Makeup* Robert Littlefield. *Hair stylist* Lillian Shore. *Scr supv* Billy Vernon. *Prop master* Monroe Liebgold.

Cast: John Agar [(*Jim Crayle*)], Joyce Meadows [(*Peg Barton*)], Robert Strauss [(*Yubo*)], Barton MacLane [(*Simon Crayle*)], Lyn Thomas [(*Kate Durand*)], James Griffith [(*Cash Skelton*)], Morris Ankrum [(*Andrew Barton*)], Leslie Bradley [(*Rev. Jacob Hall*)], Doodles Weaver [(*Eph Loveman*)], Mike Ragan [(*Tanner*)], Tom Daly [(*Cowhand*)], Sammy Ogg [(*Virgil Barton*)], George Brand [(*Judge Ard Becker*)], Claire DuBrey [(*Bess Loveman*)], Daniel White [(*Sam Kilgore*)], Dan Simmons [(*Harry Corman*)], Sydney Mason [(*Doc Studdeford*)].

Western. [*Viewed print incomplete*]. In 1873, after Marshal Swain of Honcho, Texas is murdered, the town council contacts famous gunfighters, including Wild Bill Hickok, Bat Masterson and the Earp brothers, but all refuse to take the job. Saloon owner Yubo, a half-breed whose henchmen killed Swain, plans to put his own man in as marshal. Yubo hopes to run the town completely in ten years, so that he will not be "just another half-breed." The town's leading citizens, however, want Honcho, formerly just a crossroads, to grow into a safe place for "decent" people to live. Jim Crayle, son of one of the famous gunfighters who refused to come, rides to town and applies for the job. After he impresses the council with his marksmanship, he is given the badge. In Yubo's saloon, Yubo's mistress, Kate Durand, humiliates Jim by first kissing him, and then taking his gun. Jim bests Yubo's henchmen, Vince and Tanner, in a fight as the townsfolk watch, and after warning Yubo that he will throw out of town the next man who jumps him, he dumps Kate in a horse trough. Hotel owner Andrew Barton, impressed with Jim, invites him to supper at his large house on the hill up the main street. At the house, Barton's haughty daughter Peg tries to humiliate Jim, and during the meal, Jim drops a soup bowl. He apologizes to Peg, saying he's just a saddle tramp who has never had a home. She kisses him, but he rebukes her and says she is acting like a dance hall girl and that kissing has to be done with feeling. Jim's father Simon rides into town and rebukes his son for not facing up to the fact that he has an injured wrist and cannot draw fast enough to be a marshal. Jim blames his father for the accident that left

him injured and for the fact that the only thing he has ever wanted to be is a lawman. Their argument is interrupted by a fight that begins after a cowhand charges that the cards used in Yubo's saloon are marked. When Yubo threatens to draw on Jim if he looks at the cards, Jim shoves a table against Yubo to pin him to the wall. He finds that the deck is marked and gives Yubo until Monday morning to get out of town. Jim convenes a town council meeting and asks for twelve deputies, saying that Yubo will back down if they stand up to him, or take over the town if they don't. Jim succeeds in getting only three men, including Barton, to stand with him. Simon, suspecting that Peg is falling in love with Jim, tells her about the accident so she will intervene. Simon tells Jim that Peg cares for him and encourages him to listen to her. At the Barton house, Jim discourages Peg's younger brother Virgil when he says he wants to be his deputy by showing him up in a draw. Peg appreciates that, and when he says he will be nothing if he does not try to go against Yubo, she admits she loves him and cries. She tells him, though, that she doesn't want to change or weaken him and they kiss. A shot through the window grazes Peg's shoulder. Jim then tricks Vince, who fired the shot, and shoots him. Jim next sets fire to a haystack where Tanner lies in wait, forcing him out, then kills him. Simon advises Jim to arrest Yubo and then ride him until he goes for his gun, so that Jim could shoot him. Jim refuses the advice, though. When Cash Skelton, a drunk Yubo keeps in the saloon for amusement, tries to talk Kate into leaving town with him, Yubo overhears and beats Cash savagely. Insulted by Yubo, Kate tells Simon Yubo's plan to take over by luring Jim out of town. Simon finds Yubo on the road outside of town. but Yubo kills him and takes his gunbelt. At the church, as the reverend remonstrates his congregation, saying they must stand behind Jim, Yubo yells from outside for Jim to come out. Calling the townspeople cowards, Peg says Jim should not get himself killed for them. Only Barton, Virgil and the reverend accompany Jim to meet Yubo and his men. After they leave the church, however, the townsfolk decide to back them up, but Jim tells them to stay back. Yubo throws Jim Simon's belt "as a going away present," and they have a showdown. Yubo shoots Jim in the shoulder, and Jim shoots a bullet into Yubo's forehead. Jim sends the gang off, and the townspeople take Jim into the church. *Fathers and sons. Gunfighters. Indians of North America–Mixed blood. Megalomania. Saloon keepers. United States. Marshals. Alcoholics. Churches. Hotel owners. Mistresses. Reverends. Romance. Shootouts.*

Note: The print viewed was missing two reels; plot information for the missing reels was based on a continuity and dialogue deposited for copyright registration. *HR* stated that producer Richard E. Lyons said that he tried not to make a "psychological western." *MPD* noted that actor Robert Strauss "who usually plays a comedian, is unconventionally cast as a saloon owner and gambler." According to *HR*, the film had a seven-day shooting schedule.
Box 24 Nov 1958. *DV* 18 Apr 1958. *DV* 6 Nov 1958, p. 4. *Exb* 12 Nov 1958, p. 4530. *FD* 7 Nov 1958, p. 6. *Har* 15 Nov 1958, p. 182. *HR* 9 May 1958, p. 13. *HR* 16 May 1958, p. 8. *HR* 6 Nov 1958, p. 3. *MPD* 29 Oct 1958. *MPHPD* 8 Nov 1958, p. 44. *Var* 12 Nov 1958, p. 6.

FRONTIER SCOUT *see* **QUINCANNON, FRONTIER SCOUT**

THE FRONTIER TRAIL (Native Americans, Dakota)

Charles R. Rogers Productions, Inc. *Dist* Pathé Exchange, Inc. 20 Jun **1926** [©Pathé Exchange, Inc.; 17 May 1926; LU22729]. Si; b&w. 6 reels, 6,200 ft.

Pres Charles R. Rogers. *Dir* Scott R. Dunlap. *Story and scen* E. Richard Schayer and Basil Dickey. *Photog* Sol Polito.

Cast: Harry Carey (*Jim Cardigan*), Mabel Julienne Scott (*Dolly Mainard*), Ernest Hilliard (*Captain Blackwell*), Frank Campeau (*Shad Donlin*), Nelson McDowell (*Pawnee Jake*), Charles Mailes (*Major Mainard*), Harvey Clark (*Sergeant O'Shea*), Aggie Herring (*Mrs. O'Shea*), Chief Big Tree (*Chief Gray Wolf*).

Western. Dolly Mainard, en route to her father, a major at Fort Blaine, is escorted through dangerous Sioux territory by a cavalry detachment and Army scout Jim Cardigan. When Captain Blackwell offends some braves of Chief Gray Wolf's tribe, Jim is sent ahead to the Indian camp to ask for peace. Imprisoned by the Indians, he sends a message to Blackwell not to advance; Donlin, a renegade scout, tears the note in such a way that the message is distorted, and almost the entire force is killed. When Jim escapes, he is accused of treason by Blackwell, court-martialed, and sentenced to death; however, he escapes and rescues Dolly, her father, and Blackwell from Donlin's band of renegades. Jim discovers the missing portion of the note in Donlin's hat, proving his innocence, and Dolly remains to become his wife. *Capital punishment. Courts-martial and courts of inquiry. Dakota*

Indians. Forts. Scouts (Frontier). Secret documents. Traitors. United States. Army. Cavalry.

FD 4 Jul 1926. *MPW* 19 Jun 1926.

FRONTIER WOMAN (Native Americans)

Top Pictures. Jul **1956**. Sd; col (Eastman); Vistarama. 7,097 ft. 80 min.

Prod Lloyd Royal and Tom Garraway. *Dir* Ron Ormond. *Scr* Paul Piel. *Photog* Ted Allen. *Film ed* Hugh Winn. *Mus dir* Walter Greene.

Cast: Cindy Carson (*Polly*), Lance Fuller (*Catawampus Jones*), Ann Kelly (*Rosebud*), James Clayton (*Neshoba*), Rance Howard (*Prewitt*), Geneva Rush, Dan Jones, Pete Cunningham, Mario Galento, Sam Keller.

Western. [*Not viewed*]. Polly, the daughter of Davy Crockett, has been reared by an Indian woman in Tennessee. The woman's son Neshoba is secretly in love with Polly, who has only sisterly feelings toward him, while Rosebud, an Indian girl, is in love with Neshoba. An unscrupulous trader named Prewitt exploits Rosebud's jealousy of Polly in his scheme to seize the frontier settlers' land. At Prewitt's urging, Rosebud organizes a band of Indians, who launch a violent attack on the settlers. After Neshoba's mother is killed in a raid, another trader, Catawampus Jones, arrives with a memento for Polly from her late father, as well as the latest in firearms. While Catawampus is accompanying Polly and Neshoba to the settlement, they are attacked by Indians and Neshoba is killed. Polly and Rosebud fight. Polly wins but spares Rosebud's life, earning her gratitude. At the settlement, a fight breaks out between Catawampus and one of Prewitt's henchmen. Prewitt is about to shoot Catawampus when Rosebud shoots him with an arrow. Polly and Catawampus plan a future together. *Indians of North America. Jealousy. Massacres.* Davy Crockett. Fathers and daughters. Fights. Firearms. Gunfights. Mothers and sons. Settlers. Tennessee. Traders. Unrequited love.

Note: According to *MPHPD*, the film was subtitled *Daughter of Davy Crockett*. Modern sources include Curtis Dorsett and Indians from the Pearl River Reservation in the cast. The film was shot on the Chunky River in Mississippi.

Exb 9 Jan 1957. *Monthly Film Bulletin* Oct 1957, p. 127. *MPHPD* 6 Oct 1956, p. 99.

FRONTIERS OF '49 (Latino)

Larry Darmour Productions. *Dist* Columbia Pictures Corp. of California, Ltd. 19 Jan **1939**; Prod: 29 Oct—4 Nov 1938 [©Columbia Pictures Corp. of California, Ltd.; 27 Dec 1938; LP8544]. Sd (RCA Victor High Fidelity Sound System); b&w. 6 reels. 54 min. PCA cert no. 4933.

[*Prod* Larry Darmour]. [*Supv* J. A. Duffy]. *Dir* Joseph Levering. [*Asst dir* Carl Hiecke]. *Orig scr* Nate Gatzert. *Photog* James S. Brown, Jr. [*Film ed* Dwight Caldwell]. [*Mus dir* Lee Zahler]. [*Sd eng* Tom Lambert].

Cast: Bill Elliott (*John Freeman*), Luana De Alcaniz (*Dolores de Cervantes*), Charles King (*Howard Brunton*), Hal Taliaferro (*Kit*), Charles Whittaker (*Brad*), Octavio Giraud (*Don Miguel*), Carlos Villarias (*Padre*), Joe de la Cruz (*Romero*), Jack Walters (*Pete*), Al Ferguson (*Red*).

Western, Historical. [*Print viewed*]. In 1849, a struggle for control of land in California rages between the forces of America and Spain. One of the primary agencies of inequity is the Lower California Company, an agency headed by Howard Brunton, which has been commissioned by the American government to administer laws and collect taxes in the region. Instead of engaging in these legitimate practices, however, Brunton and his outlaws are levying exorbitant taxes on Spanish granted land and selling property to their own bidders for a pittance. These practices eventually begin to wreak havoc in the territory, forcing the U.S. government to send troops to retain order. In command of these troops is Major John Freeman, who slips into the territory disguised as a settler, accompanied by his scout Kit. John rides to the hacienda of Don Miguel Cervantes, where an auction is in progress. Brunton has just seized the estate, and the bidding has just begun on its assets. When John outbids Brunton's hirelings, the auctioneer postpones the sale for a week. Struck by the plight of Don Miguel and his beautiful daughter Dolores, John assures them that he is their friend and decides to help them keep their land. Hoping to learn more about Brunton's misdealings, John pretends to sympathize with the Lower California Co. by volunteering his services to Brunton. Brunton sees John as a threat to his enterprise, and though he pretends to hire him, he immediately instructs Brad, a henchman, to run him out of town. Meanwhile, in order to obtain the necessary

evidence to convict Brunton, John instructs Romero, a land holder who was evicted before his taxes were due, to ride to the town of Los Treos to have his last tax receipt notarized. On his way back, Romero is ambushed by Brunton's men and murdered. Enraged, John confronts Brunton and his gunman, Brad, but he is overpowered by Brunton's gang. Learning John's true identity, Brunton orders his men to rob the express office and make a getaway across the border. John escapes by cleverly outwitting his captors, and rides to his regiment, which has been waiting nearby. As the cavalry descends on the town of Los Treos, Brunton's men have just completed robbing the express office. Pursued by the troops, Brunton flees in a nearby stagecoach, in which Dolores has taken refuge from the shooting. John overtakes the coach, lassos Brunton and rescues Dolores. *California–History–1846-1850. Extortion. Impersonation and imposture. Land rights. Spaniards. Auctions.* Crime. Fistfights. Hostages. Murder. Officers (Military). Outlaws. Rescues. Robbery.

Note: A working title for this film was *California Cavalcade*, and it was reviewed as such in *MPH*. Modern sources list actors Kit Guard, Bud Osborne, Jack Ingram, Lee Shumway, Ed Cassidy and Tex Palmer in the cast, but their appearance in the released film has not been confirmed.

MPH 19 Nov 1938, pp. 56-57. *Var* 27 Feb 1939, p. 12.

THE FRONTIERSMAN (Native Americans, Creek)

Metro-Goldwyn-Mayer Corp.; controlled by Loew's Inc. *Dist* Metro-Goldwyn-Mayer Distributing Corp. 11 Jun **1927** [©Metro-Goldwyn-Mayer Distributing Corp.; 27 Jun 1927; LP24124]. Si; b&w. 5 reels, 4,982 ft.

Dir Reginald Barker. *Scen* L. G. Rigby. *Story* Ross B. Wills and Madeleine Ruthven. *Titles* Tom Miranda. *Photog* Clyde De Vinna. *Art dir* Edward Withers. *Film ed* Frank Sullivan. *Ward* André-ani.

Cast: Tim McCoy (*John Dale*), Claire Windsor (*Lucy*), Tom O'Brien (*Abner Hawkins*), Russell Simpson (*Andrew Jackson*), Lillian Leighton (*Mrs. Andrew Jackson*), Louise Lorraine (*Athalie Burgoyne*), May Foster (*Mandy*), Chief Big Tree (*Grey Eagle*), Frank Hagney (*White Snake*), John Peters (*Colonel Coffee*).

Historical, Drama. In 1813, Capt. John Dale and Sgt. Abner Hawkins, members of General Jackson's Tennessee Militia, attempt to make a peace treaty with the Creek Indians who threaten war with the whites, but White Snake resists. Later, Dale comes into conflict with army rivals for Athalie, over whom he engages in a duel. He is reprimanded by General Jackson, but he soon falls in love with Lucy, the general's ward. When Lucy is captured by the Indians during the uprising, Dale rescues her and the army subdues the Creeks. *Creek Indians. Horseshoe Bend National Military Park (AL). Andrew Jackson. Tennessee. United States–History–Indian campaigns.*

FD 6 Nov 1927. *Var* 26 Oct 1927, p. 22.

FROZEN JUSTICE (Native Americans, Native Alaskans)

Fox Film Corp. *Dist* Fox Film Corp. 13 Oct **1929** [©Fox Film Corp.; 4 Sep 1929; LP655]. Sd (Movietone); b&w. 9 reels, 7,170 ft. [Also si; 6,129 ft.].

Pres William Fox. *Dir* Allan Dwan. *Staged by* Elliott Lester. *Asst dir* William Tummel. *Scen* Sonya Levien. *Dial* Owen Davis. *Photog* Harold Rosson. *Film ed* Harold Schuster. *Sd* Edmund H. Hansen.

Song(s): "A Bird in a Gilded Cage," music by Harry von Tilzer, lyrics by Arthur J. Lamb; "Goodbye, Dolly Gray," by Will D. Cobb and Paul Barnes; "The Picture That Is Turned Toward the Wall," by Charles Graham; "The Right Kind of Man," music by Abel Baes, lyrics by L. Wolfe Gilbert.

Source: Based on the novel *Norden for lov og ret; en Alaska-Historie* by Ejnar Mikkelsen (Copenhagen, 1920).

Cast: Lenore Ulric (*Talu*), Robert Frazer (*Lanak*), Louis Wolheim (*Duke*), Ullrich Haupt (*Captain Jones*), Laska Winter (*Douglamana*), El Brendel (*Swede*), Tom Patricola (*Dancer*), Alice Lake (*Little Casino*), Gertrude Astor (*Mooseshide Kate*), Adele Windsor (*Boston school ma'm*), Neyneen Farrell (*Yukon Lucy*), Warren Hymer (*Bartender*), Lou Morrison (*Proprietor*), Charles Judels (*French sailor*), Joe Rochay (*Jewish character*), Meyers Sisters (*Harmony duo*), George MacFarlane (*Singer*), Landers Stevens (*Mate Moore*), James Spencer (*Medicine man*), Arthur Stone (*French Pete*), Jack Ackroyd (*English Eddie*), Gertrude Chorre (*Talu's mother*).

Melodrama. Talu, a half-caste born of an American father and an Eskimo mother, is torn between life with her Eskimo chief husband, Lanak, and the excitement that she imagines exists in Nome, the nearest town. Captain Jones, a ruthless trader whose ship crashes into

the ice near the Eskimo settlement, takes Talu to Nome in spite of his first mate's objections: Duke fears retaliation from Lanak. In Nome, Jones mistreats Talu, who sings in a saloon and wishes she were back in the settlement. Duke, having fallen in love with Talu, attempts to help her return to her husband, but Jones shoots him, forces Talu into a sled, and makes a break for it with Lanak in hot pursuit. They encounter a chasm and are thrown into a deep canyon. Jones is killed immediately; Talu, fatally injured, dies in her husband's arms. *Desertion (Marital). Indians of North America–Mixed blood. Native Alaskans. Nome (AK). Saloons. Shipwrecks. Singers. Traders.*

FD 27 Oct 1929. NYT 26 Oct 1929, p. 15. Var 30 Oct 1929, p. 25.

LA FRUTA AMARGA (Spanish language)

Metro-Goldwyn-Mayer Corp.; controlled by Loew's, Inc. *Dist* Culver Export, Inc. **1931**; New York opening: 13 Mar 1931; Prod: began mid-Dec 1930. Sd (Western Electric Sound System); b&w. 7 reels, 6,195 ft. 69 min. Passed by the National Board of Review. Spanish language.

[*Supv* Frank Davis]. *Dirigida por* [*Dir*] Arthur Gregor. [*Dial dir* José López Rubio]. [*Asst dir* José Dominguez]. *Escenificación y diálogo por* [*Scr and dial*] Frances Marion and Marion Jackson. *Versión española de* [*Spanish version*] Salvador de Alberich. *Diálogo adicional de* [*Addl dial*] Antonio de Lara. *Fotografiada por* [*Photog*] Clyde De Vinna. *Director artístico* [*Art dir*] Cedric Gibbons. *Editada por* [*Ed*] Carl L. Pierson. *Acústica* [*Sd*] Douglas Shearer.

Source: Based on the novel *Dark Star* by Lorna Moon (Indianapolis, 1929).

Cast: VIRGINIA FABREGAS (*Min*), Juan de Landa (*Bill*), María Luz Callejo (*Marga*), Elvira Morla (*Lulú*), Julio Peña (*Dick*), Juan Martínez Plá (*Agente*), Juan Costello (*Tony*), Alma Real (*Maestra*), Juan de Homs (*Maestro*), [Lucio Villegas (*Capitán*)].

Melodrama. [*Print viewed*]. [The following plot summary is based on the English-language version of this film, *Min and Bill*; character names refer to that version. For further information regarding the English-language version, please see the note below and the entry for *Min and Bill* in the *AFI Catalog of Feature Films, 1921-30*.] Min, a hard-boiled proprietress of a waterfront hotel, who has as her sweetheart Bill, a fisherman, brings up Nancy, a girl who was deserted by her own mother in infancy. Local authorities try to persuade Min that she is not a fit mother and that Nancy should be sent to school. Between the truant officer and prohibition officials, Min is forced to send her to live with the school principal's family, though Nancy insists that she would rather stay with Min. Meanwhile, Bella, Nancy's actual mother—now a down-and-out floozie—turns up, but Min sends her back to San Francisco. Min sacrifices to send Nancy to a proper boarding school, where she falls in love with Dick, a wealthy boy who loves her in spite of her background and plans to marry her. Bella, finding out about her daughter's good fortune, returns and tells Min she will reveal her identity so as to benefit from Dick's money. In a struggle, Min's face is burned, and she is forced to shoot Bella to stop her. Min is informed on by a jealous sailor; and as her daughter sails on her honeymoon, Min is led away by the police. *Courtship. Fishermen. Hotelkeepers. Manslaughter. Motherhood. Wards and guardians. Waterfronts.*

Note: The English-language version of this film, *Min and Bill*, released on 21 Nov 1930, was directed by George Hill and starred Marie Dressler and Wallace Beery (see *AFI Catalog of Feature Films, 1921-30*; F23632). The working title for the Spanish version was *Estrella negra*. The onscreen credits were taken from a studio cutting continuity. According to a modern source, actor Jack Castello is erroneously listed under the name "Juan Costello" in the onscreen credits, and noted Spanish director Luis Buñuel briefly appears as an extra in the film; this may have been his first work in the United States. Actors Juan Duval, Luis Orozco, Antonio Acosta and Luis Hickus are included in some sources, but their participation in the film has not been confirmed. Edgar Neville and Eduardo Ugarte may have contributed to the writing of the Spanish adaptation.

HF 20 Dec 1930, p. 24. HF 10 Jan 1931, p. 24.

LA FUERZA DEL QUERER (Spanish language)

James Cruze Productions, Inc. *Dist* Paramount-Publix Corp. Jun **1930**; Los Angeles opening: 21 Jun 1930; Prod: Mar—Apr 1930 at Educational Studios. Sd; b&w. Length undetermined. Spanish language.

Prod James Cruze. *Assoc prod* Gaston Glass. *Dir* Ralph Ince. *Scr* Walter Woods. *Span vers* Andrés de Segurola.

Source: Based on the play *The Big Fight* by Milton Herbert Gropper and Max Marcin (New York, 18 Sep 1928).

Cast: María Alba (*Shirley*), Carlos Barbé ("*The Tiger*"), Andrés de Segurola (*Chuck*), Vicente Padula (*Steve*), Tito Davison (*Lester*), Rita Royo (*Winnie*), Stepin Fetchit (*Spot*), Manuel Conesa (*Berelli*), Rafael Valverde (*Detective*).

Boxing, Crime, Drama. [*Not viewed*]. Shirley, girl friend of a boxer known as "El Tigre" ("The Tiger"), discovers that her brother Lester's life is in danger unless he pays his debts to Chuck, a gangster who uses a nightclub he operates as a front. Although the debt is considerable, "El Tigre" offers his savings to help Lester pay it off, but Shirley does not want to involve him in her family's problems. After Lester kills one of Chuck's henchmen, Chuck tries to come to an agreement with Shirley, suggesting that he will forget about his dispute with Lester if she can arrange for "El Tigre" to be drugged and lose his next fight on which he, Chuck, will bet heavily against the favorite. As Shirley will not go along with this, Chuck enlists the services of Steve, "El Tigre's" manager, who agrees to substitute drugged drinking water during the fight. However, the police have been tailing Chuck and his gang and, as the fight takes place, confront Chuck and shoot him. Meanwhile, "El Tigre" easily beats his opponent having accidentally replaced the drugged water with pure water. *Boxing. Brothers and sisters. Debt. Gambling. Gangsters. Boxing managers. Drugging. Nightclubs. Police.*

Note: This film was a Spanish-language version of the 1930 film *The Big Fight* (see *AFI Catalog of Feature Films, 1921-30*; F2.0394), which was directed by Walter Lang and starred Lola Lane and Ralph Ince. Ince, who played "Chuck," directed the Spanish version upon completing his role in the English version. After a private screening on 28 Apr 1930, the Spanish version premiered in Los Angeles as *La gran pelea* on 21 Jun. Although the English version was distributed in the U.S. by Sono Art, later in 1930, James Cruze Productions, Inc. made a deal with Paramount to distribute the Spanish version, as that company was handling a number of Spanish-language films internationally. Paramount changed the title to *La fuerza del querer*.

Cinl Jul 1930, p. 29.

THE FULL CUP *see* **THE GILDED SPIDER**

FULL OF LIFE (Italian Americans)

Columbia Pictures Corp. *Dist* Columbia Pictures Corp. Feb **1956**; Los Angeles showing: 25 Dec 1956; Prod: 2 May—20 Jun 1956 [©Columbia Pictures Corp.; 1 Mar 1957; LP8345]. Sd (RCA Sound Recording); b&w; 1.85. 10 reels, 8,183 ft. 91 min. PCA cert no. 18174.

Prod Fred Kohlmar. *Dir* Richard Quine. *Asst dir* Herb Wallerstein. *Scr* John Fante. *Dir of photog* Charles Lawton, Jr. *Art dir* William Flannery. *Film ed* Charles Nelson. *Set dec* William Kiernan and Louis Diage. *Mus* George Dunning. *Cond* Morris Stoloff. *Orch* Arthur Morton. *Rec supv* John Livadary. *Sd* Ferol Redd. *Makeup* Clay Campbell. *Hair styles by* Helen Hunt.

Source: Based on the novel *Full of Life* by John Fante (Boston, 1952).

Cast: Judy Holliday [(*Emily Rocco*)], Richard Conte [(*Nick Rocco*)], Introducing Salvatore Baccaloni [(*Papa Rocco*)], With Esther Minciotti [(*Mama Rocco*)], Joe De Santis [(*Father Gondolfo*)], Silvio Minciotti [(*Joe Muto*)], [Penny Santon (*Carla*)], [Arthur Lovejoy (*Mr. Jameson*)], [Eleanor Audley (*Mrs. Jameson*)], [Trudy Marshall (*Nora Gregory*)], [Walter Conrad (*John Gregory*)], [Sam Gilman (*Dr. Atchison*)], [Amanda Randolph (*Delia*)], [David McMahon (*Contractor*)], [Steve Benton (*Truck driver*)], [Audrey Swanson, Bobbie Collentine, Maggie Megennis (*Nurses*)], [Robert Mitchell (*Interne*)], [Richard Bull (*Doctor*)], [L. K. Smith (*Delivery man*)], [Jester Hairston (*Porter*)], [Dick Crockett (*Conductor*)], [Betsy Jones Moreland], [Cary Savage], [Theo Haran], [Charlotte Portney], [Naomi Perry], [Rube Schaffer], [Barbara Terry], [Ray Smith].

Domestic, Comedy-drama. [*Print viewed*]. As her pregnancy nears its eighth month, Southern Californian Emily Rocco, married seven years and about to have her first baby, experiences dissatisfaction with herself and her house. She is obsessed with cleanliness and with trying to understand her life through the philosophical books she reads. Her husband Nick tries to challenge her lapses into morbidity by saying their house will soon be full of life, with the babies they will have and books he will write. One day, the floor in the kitchen gives way from a termite infestation, and Emily falls in up to her waist. Although the doctor pronounces her fine, Emily moans that with her added weight she is a burden to Nick, and that as a pregnant woman, she is no longer attractive. Nick realizes they can't afford to fix the floor. Emily suggests they ask Nick's father Vittorio, a stonemason from Italy living in the

Sacramento Valley, and despite Nick's reservations, they fly to his parent's home. Vittorio graciously greets Emily, but is curt with his son. When Nick's mother has a fainting spell, Vittorio is unconcerned, and after a short rest, he orders her to get up and kill a chicken for supper. At the meal, Mama gives them garlic to wear so that they will have a boy. The next day, Vittorio takes Emily to a beautiful spot nearby for which he says he has paid a fifty-dollar deposit to a "paisano" so that he can build a stone house for her, Nick and the baby. Meanwhile, Nick has arranged for his mother to ask Vittorio to fix the hole. When Vittorio learns that they bought a house without telling him and that it is made of stucco, which he hates, he slaps his son, then goes off to drink in Sacramento. Emily tells Nick that she likes the area and thinks it will be good for children, but Nick doesn't feel he could write with his father nearby. That night, Mama gives Emily her wedding dress, insisting that they must have a church wedding despite the fact that they already were married in a civil ceremony. Emily reminds her gently that she is not a Catholic. Vittorio finally agrees to help with the hole, but upon arriving at the house, he immediately complains about smog, lack of shade and trees, and the grass. Rather than work on the floor, Vittorio wants to dictate a story to Nick about his Uncle Mingo and some pirates for his future grandson. Papa falls asleep from drinking as he tells the story, and Nick stays up until five in the morning finishing it. Neither Vittorio nor Emily want to read it though, and after a boy delivers liquor that Vittorio ordered, Nick yells at his father to fix the hole. Just then, Father Gondolfo from the neighborhood parish comes by in response to Vittorio's earlier request. When he questions Nick about the reason he has stopped going to church, Nick says that his thinking and the world have changed, while the church has not. Vittorio takes Nick away so that the priest can talk alone with Emily. Nick, to his father's distress, says he does not want the church, which does not allow birth control, to dictate his life. After the priest leaves, Emily tells Vittorio directly, yet kindly, that she cannot become a Catholic just because he wants her to be one. She says that she wants God in her home for herself and for her child, but that she cannot change overnight. Vittorio is worried that they will not have time to arrange a Catholic wedding before the baby comes, but Emily says that the priest told her they could be married in the rectory. Aghast, Nick refuses, saying he would have to go to confession before the sacrament. That night, he tells Emily he does not want to be pushed by his father and that he used to love the church until his father punished him if he stayed away. Emily points out that he never made an intellectual choice to leave the church, but that he left to rebel against his father; as an adult, if his wishes now coincide with his father's, she contends, he should be able to return. Papa begins to work on the hole, but when he notices their fake fireplace, he begins to knock out a wall. Emily is shocked at first, then laughs and joins him. Although Nick is upset when he comes home, he helps his father build a chimney and a beautiful fireplace of stone and bricks that Vittorio dedicates to his grandchild. After the wedding, Emily has labor pains and is taken to the hospital, but it is a false alarm. Later that night, Emily tells Nick it is time. At the hospital, Nick goes to see her while she is in pain, and she tells him to get out. He then goes to the chapel and prays on his knees. The next day, Vittorio finds him there asleep and leads him upstairs. He brings a telegram that *Saturday Evening Post* has bought the story about Uncle Mingo and the bandits for $5,000, and he and Nick hug. Nick is then called to the viewing room, and he and Vittorio, as they look at his son, notice red hair and big feet like Uncle Mingo had. When Vittorio says he will build a little fireplace for the baby, Nick says he is going back to Mama, who needs him, as he now has enough money to fix the hole. As he comes in to see his wife, Emily is putting on lipstick. They return home, where they find that the termite repair service truck has arrived. Authors. Fathers and sons. Fathers-in-law. Italian Americans. Pregnancy. Stonemasons. Catholic Church. Houses. Los Angeles (CA). Priests. Religion. Sacramento Valley (CA). Termites. Transformation. Weddings.

Note: The working titles of the film were *The Lady Is Waiting* and *The Family Way*. According to information in the MPAA/PCA Collection at the AMPAS Library, the novel by John Fante was originally to be called *The White Balloon* and was to be published by Viking and serialized in *Women's Home Companion*. In Sep 1950, Warner Bros. submitted a summary of the novel to the PCA, due to the interest of several of their producers. PCA officials responded that many aspects of the story would not be acceptable if put into a screenplay. They explained, "The problems lie in the many offensive anatomical details of pregnancy. In this respect the writer goes stark crazy.... One of the seizures which afflicts the wife is that she gets a burst of religion, out of fear of the oncoming childbirth. The process of being smitten by religion is handled in a smart-aleck, thoroughly repulsive manner, identifying the girl's panicky religiosity with the other queer things she is likely to do." The PCA also objected that the "seemingly innocuous title becomes unbelievably vulgar in its connection with the story. It refers to the huge stomach which the girl has in the latter stages of pregnancy, which the husband flippantly calls, 'her white balloon.' " [In the submitted synopsis, Emily undergoes a baptism and converts to Catholicism.] In Jun 1951, Warner Bros. having decided against production, the King Brothers submitted their version of the story to the PCA. The PCA demanded a number of omissions, including discussions about anatomical details of pregnancy and childbirth, fertility, syphilis and birth control. According to a PCA memo, Fante, working with the King Brothers, willingly accepted the PCA's suggestions. Concerning "Emily's" conversion, the PCA warns again against treating it as a peculiarity: "If this mood or flavor creeps into any finished product, it would be unacceptable, as being very damaging to religion. If it is treated with dignity and with the proper motivations, it would not only be acceptable but most desirable." At the time, Fante stated that the new title would probably be *Full of Life. HR* reported in Jul 1951 that the property had been purchased by the Stanley Kramer Co. for a Columbia release. In Dec 1951, according to *DV*, Kramer assigned it to Edward and Edna Anhalt to produce and Edward Dmytryk to direct. By Oct 1952, the film was scheduled to go into production soon, according to PCA material; however, in Nov 1952, the PCA judged the screenplay to be unacceptable, as it "plunges into the details of pregnancy with very little discretion and little exercise of good taste." Although the company agreed to a rewrite, production plans were halted until 1956.

This marked the screen debut of Metropolitan Opera basso Salvatore Baccaloni. *HR* praised him and the other Italian actors, stating, "The Italian-Americans in the picture are played by people who know to the smallest gesture how these people act and react." Reviewers were generally positive about the manner in which the film dealt with its adult subject matter. *HR* commented, "One of the nicer things about this picture is that it states its facts frankly and without subterfuge. Catholics are Catholics, pregnant women are pregnant; these are the facts of life that deserve to be dealt with in motion pictures. *Full of Life* actually is a realistic picture although the term 'realism' is usually reserved for less happy aspects of our current civilization." *LAT*, however, complained, "The film is handicapped by such a clinical treatment of the expectant motherhood situation as to verge at times on bad taste."

Box 22 Dec 1956. *Cue* 16 Feb 1957. *DV* 20 Dec 1951. *DV* 5 Mar 1956. *DV* 23 Aug 1956. *DV* 19 Dec 1956, p. 3. *Exh* 26 Dec 1956, pp. 4265-66. *FD* 19 Dec 1956, p.6. *Har* 22 Dec 1956, p. 202. *Holiday* Mar 1957. *HR* 31 Jul 1951. *HR* 22 Jun 1956. *HR* 23 Aug 1956. *HR* 19 Dec 1956, p.4. *LAEx* 26 Dec 1956. *LAT* 26 Dec 1956. *MPD* 20 Dec 1956. *MPHPD* 22 Dec 1956, p.193. *Newsweek* 18 Feb 1957. *New Yorker* 23 Feb 1957. *NYT* 13 Feb 1957, p. 38. *SatRev* 23 Feb 1957. *Time* 18 Feb 1957. *Var* 19 Dec 1956, p.6

FURIA *see* **WILD IS THE WIND**

THE FURIES (Latino)
Wallis-Hazen, Inc. *Dist* Paramount Pictures, Inc. Aug **1950**; Tucson, AZ premiere: 21 Jul 1950; Prod: 9 Nov 1949—23 Dec 1949; added scenes and retakes: 7 Jan 1950 [©Wallis-Hazen, Inc.; 28 Jun 1950; LP199]. Sd (Western Electric Recording); b&w. 9,771 ft. 107 or 109 min. Passed by the National Board of Review.

Prod HAL B. WALLIS. *Dir* Anthony Mann. *Asst dir* Francisco Day. [*2d asst dir* Mickey Moore]. [*Asst dir, location* Oscar Rudolph]. *Scr* Charles Schnee. *Dir of photog* Victor Milner. [*1st cam* Lee Garmes]. [*Cam, location* Irmin Roberts]. [*Cam op* Haskell Boggs]. [*Cam op, location* Otto Pierce]. [*Cam asst* J. Hawley]. [*Cam asst, location* J. Grant]. [*Stills* Malcolm Bullock]. *Spec photog eff* Gordon Jennings. *Process photog* Farciot Edouart. *Art dir* Hans Dreier and Henry Bumstead. *Ed* Archie Marshek. *Set dec* Sam Comer and Bertram Granger. [*Props* Art Camp]. [*Props, asst* C. Coleman]. *Cost* Edith Head. [*Ward* Ed Fitzharris and Grace Harris]. *Mus score* Franz Waxman. [*Dance dir* Josephine Earl]. *Sd rec* Hugo Grenzbach and Walter Oberst. *Makeup supv* Wally Westmore. [*Makeup artist* Hal Lierly, Bob Ewing and N. Vehr]. [*Hair* Dean Cole, Gertrude Read and S. Kirkpatrick]. [*Tech adv* Harry Mendoza]. [*Prod mgr* C. Kenneth DeLand and Herb Coleman]. [*Asst to prod* Jack Saper]. [*Scr supv* Irving Cooper]. [*Grip* Charles Sickler]. [*Gaffer* Earl Crowell].

Song(s): "The Great T. C. Roundup," music and lyrics by Jay Livingston and Ray Evans; "Ben Bolt (or, Oh! Don't You Remember)," music by Nelson Kneass, lyrics by Thomas Dunn English; "Trail to Mexico," traditional.

Source: Based on the novel *The Furies* by Niven Busch (New York, 1948).

Cast: BARBARA STANWYCK (*Vance Jeffords*), WENDELL COREY (*Rip Darrow*), WALTER HUSTON (*T. C. Jeffords*), Judith Anderson (*Flo Burnett*), Gilbert Roland (*Juan Herrera*), Thomas Gomez (*El Tigre*), Beulah Bondi (*Mrs. Anaheim*), Albert Dekker (*Mr. Reynolds*), John Bromfield (*Clay Jeffords*), Wallace Ford (*Scotty Hyslip*), Blanche Yurka (*Herrera mother*), Louis Jean Heydt (*Bailey*),

Frank Ferguson (*Dr. Grieve*), Charles Evans (*Old Anaheim*), Movita Casteneda (*Chiquita*), Craig Kelly (*Young Anaheim*), Myrna Dell (*Dallas Hart*), [Lou Steele (*Aguirre Herrera*)], [Pepe Hern (*Feliz Herrera*)], [Rosemary Pettit (*Carol Ann*)], [Arthur Hunnicutt, Douglas Grange, James Davies (*Cowhands*)], [Joe Dominguez (*Wagon driver*)], [Artie Del Rey (*Wagon driver's son*)], [Eddy C. Waller (*Old man*)], [Georgia Clancy (*Wedding guest*)], [Nolan Leary (*Drunk guest*)], [Sam Finn (*Dealer*)], [Baron Lichter (*Waiter*)], [Jane Novak], [Richard Kipling].

Western, with songs. [*Print viewed*]. In the 1870s, widowed rancher T. C. Jeffords returns from San Francisco to his ranch home "The Furies" in the New Mexico Territory. With him is bank appraiser Reynolds, whom he hopes will approve a loan request. Although T. C., who rules the territory like a king, disdains his son Clay, he admires his willful daughter Vance, who has followed in his footsteps. On behalf of the Anaheim Bank, Reynolds grants T. C. a $100,000 loan on condition that he will evict the squatters on his land. However, Vance insists that T. C. allow the Mexican-American Herrera family to remain, as Juan Herrera has been her best friend since childhood. T. C. then assures Vance that she will run the ranch after he returns to San Francisco, and offers to give her a $50,000 dowry if she marries someone of whom he approves. Instead, Vance falls in love with Rip Darrow, a mercenary saloon owner whose father was killed by T. C., and who is determined to regain the fertile land known as the "Darrow Strip," which T. C. won in a legal battle. Although Vance believes that she has seduced Rip, he accepts T. C.'s offer of her $50,000 dowry in exchange for leaving her. Rip then founds the Darrow Bank, and one year later, legally conducts Anaheim Bank's local business. When Anaheim and Darrow refuse to renew T. C.'s loan unless Vance finally drives off the squatters, she orders her ruthless ranch boss, El Tigre, to burn out everyone except the Herreras. Vance, however, still refuses to evict Juan, her only friend. T. C. then returns to The Furies with his fiancée, Flo Burnett, and Vance's jealousy of Flo erupts into rage when Flo announces that she has hired a manager to run the ranch and drive off the Herreras. Vance angrily hurls a pair of scissors at Flo, permanently disfiguring her, then rides to warn the Herreras. Vance stands by Juan as her father and his men attack the Herrera outpost. However, Juan, who is in love with Vance, surrenders when he realizes that she fears for T. C.'s life. Although T. C. agrees to let them leave peaceably, he insists on hanging Juan for stealing a Furies horse. Vance vows revenge and later travels throughout the Southwest to purchase all of T. C.'s IOUs, which he used more frequently than cash. When she returns to New Mexico, she and Rip ally themselves—Vance agrees to return the Darrow Strip to Rip, and in exchange, he lends her $50,000 and helps her retake the ranch. By now, T. C. is completely broke, and Flo, who has become an alcoholic, refuses to lend him money for fear that he will leave her because she is ugly. Vance convinces the Anaheims to extend T. C.'s loan, and then secretly buys 20,000 head of his cattle. When T. C. completes the cattle drive and arrives to collect his money, Vance pays him with his bought-out IOUs. Impressed by his daughter's acumen, T. C. accepts his defeat without a fight. Father and daughter reunite, and Rip makes his peace with T. C. and expresses his intention to marry Vance. As the three walk into town to celebrate, Juan's mother shoots T. C. in the back. As he dies, T. C. asks Rip and Vance to bury his name with him, as his powerful reputation would be a burden for an heir. However, after bringing T. C.'s body home to The Furies, Vance and Rip plan to name their son T. C. *Fathers and daughters. Mexican Americans. Ranchers. Reputation. Revenge. Alcoholism. Bankers. Cattle. Fathers and sons. Hanging. Loans. Murder. New Mexico. Ranch foremen. Romance. Saloon keepers. San Francisco (CA). Squatters. Weddings.*

Note: This film opens with the following written foreword: "This is a story of the 1870s...in the New Mexico territory...when men created kingdoms out of land and cattle...and ruled their empires like feudal lords. Such a man was T. C. Jeffords...who wrote this flaming page in the history of the great Southwest." *The Furies* marked actor Walter Huston's final film appearance. He died on 12 Apr 1950. The film was shot on location in Tucson, AZ.

Box 8 Jul 1950. *DV* 27 Jun 1950, p. 3. *FD* 29 Jun 1950, p. 7. *HR* 10 Nov 1949, p. 3. *HR* 29 Nov 1949, p. 10. *HR* 30 Nov 1949, p. 5. *HR* 9 Dec 1949, p. 4. *HR* 27 Jun 1950, p. 3. *HR* 7 Jul 1950, p. 7. *MPHPD* 1 Jul 1950, pp. 365-6. *NYT* 17 Aug 1950, p. 23. *Var* 28 Jun 1950, p. 6.

FURY AT FURNACE CREEK (Native Americans, Apache)
Twentieth Century-Fox Film Corp. *Dist* Twentieth Century-Fox Film Corp. May **1948**; Los Angeles opening: 30 Apr 1948; Prod: mid-Sep—mid-Nov 1947 [©Twentieth Century-Fox Film Corp.; 21 Apr 1948; LP2020]. Sd (Western Electric Recording); b&w. 9 reels, 7,906 ft. 88 min. PCA cert no. 12812.

[*Exec prod* Darryl F. Zanuck]. *Prod* Fred Kohlmar. *Dir* Bruce Humberstone. [*Asst dir* William Eckhardt, Stanley Hough and Paul Helmick]. [*Dial dir* Michael Audley]. *Wrt* Charles G. Booth. *Addl dial* Winston Miller. *Dir of photog* Harry Jackson. [*Cam op* Bud Mautino]. [*Stills* Ray Nolan]. *Spec photog eff* Fred Sersen. *Art dir* Lyle Wheeler and Albert Hogsett. *Film ed* Robert Simpson. *Set dec* Thomas Little. *Ward dir* Charles LeMaire. *Cost des* Rene Hubert. *Mus dir* Alfred Newman. *Mus* David Raksin. *Orch arr* Herbert Spencer and Maurice de Packh. *Sd* Eugene Grossman and Harry M. Leonard. *Makeup artist* Ben Nye and [George Lane]. [*Hair stylist* Peggy Adams]. [*Prod mgr* Sidney Bowen]. [*Asst prod mgr* R. L. Hough]. [*Script supv* Rose Steinberg]. [*Grip* Bruce Hunsaker].

Source: Based on the novel *Four Men and a Prayer* by David Garth (New York, 1937).

Cast: VICTOR MATURE [(*Cash Blackwell, also known as Tex Cameron*)], COLEEN GRAY [(*Molly Baxter*)], Glenn Langan [(*Rufe Blackwell, also known as Sam Gilmore*)], Reginald Gardiner [(*Captain Walsh*)], Albert Dekker [(*Leverett*)], Fred Clark [(*Bird*)], Charles Kemper [(*Peaceful Jones*)], Robert Warwick [(*General Fletcher Blackwell*)], George Cleveland [(*Judge*)], Roy Roberts [(*Al Shanks*)], Willard Robertson [(*General Leeds*)], Griff Barnett [(*Appleby*)], [Frank Orth (*Evans*)], [J. Farrell MacDonald (*Pops*)], [Charles Stevens (*Artego*)], [Jay Silverheels (*Little Dog*)], [Robert Adler (*Leverett henchman*)], [Harry Carter (*Clerk*)], [Mauritz Hugo, Howard Negley (*Defense counsels*)], [Harlan Briggs (*Prosecutor*)], [Si Jenks (*Jury foreman*)], [Guy Wilkerson (*Court clerk*)], [James Flavin (*Judge advocate*)], [Ralph Dunn (*Wagon master*)], [Fred Libby (*Lieutenant Ramsey*)], [Kermit Maynard (*Scout*)], [Paul Newlan (*Bartender*)], [Walter Soderling (*Undertaker*)], [Jerry Miley, Al Hill, George Chesebro (*Card players*)], [Al Thompson (*Waiter*)], [Virginia Engels (*Dance hall girl*)], [Herbert Heywood (*Luke*)], [Minerva Urecal (*Mrs. Crum*)], [Dick Rich (*Station agent*)], [Bob Cason (*Sgt. at arms*)], [Edmund Cobb (*Court clerk*)], [Thornton Edwards (*Hotel clerk*)], [Oscar O'Shea (*Jailer*)], [Alan Bridge (*Lawyer*)], [Ray Teal (*Sergeant*)], [James Harrison, Frank McCarroll (*Westerners*)], [Ted Mapes], [Ed Mundy], [Frederick Burton].

Western. [*Print viewed*]. In 1880, tensions between the whites and the Apache Indians escalate when the whites seek access to silver deposits in the Furnace Creek hills. While Captain Walsh of the U.S. Cavalry is escorting a supply wagon train to Fort Furnace Creek, he receives written orders to proceed immediately to Lordsburg, forcing the train to continue to the fort without an escort. Once the train is inside the fort, hordes of Indians emerge from the wagons, massacre the troops and burn the fort. Later, by government decree, the Apaches are driven out of the area and the territory thrown open to white settlers. General Fletcher Blackwell, under whose name the order to redirect the cavalry escort was issued, is court-martialed, even though the written order has been lost. Blackwell's son Rufe, a captain at West Point, refuses to believe his father gave such an order. During the court-martial proceedings, it is revealed that a mining syndicate began operation the day after the territory was opened up, and would have started only after the Apache had been expelled as a result of the massacre. An outraged General Blackwell denies any knowledge of this, and collapses on the witness stand and dies. Soon after, in a Kansas City jail, gambler Cash Blackwell, the general's other son, learns of his father's death from a newspaper story, which reports that evidence of the general's guilt was reputed to be overwhelming. Upon his release from jail, Cash sets out to clear his father's name and requests a transcript of the court-martial trial. He then begins a search for the now retired Captain Walsh and goes to Furnace Creek, which has become a boom town. There he makes friends with a local character named Peaceful Jones who, as punishment for his drunkenness, is chained to a portable tree trunk. At a saloon run by mining syndicate head Leverett, Cash then finds Walsh, who has become a drunk, and introduces himself to Walsh as Tex Cameron. Later, when Walsh is framed for cheating in a card game, Cash intervenes on his behalf and Leverett hires Cash as a bodyguard. During a visit to the ruins of Fort Furnace Creek, Cash

meets Molly Baxter as she tends the grave of her father, who died in the massacre. As they ride back to town, Molly, who is unaware of Cash's identity, tells Cash that she thinks General Blackwell sold out his own men. In Furnace Creek, Leverett announces that the 6th Cavalry is returning to supervise the territory. Little Dog, the chief of the Apaches, whom Leverett paid to raid the wagon train, now believes that Leverett double-crossed him. At the same time, Walsh who was also in the plot is desperate to leave Furnace Creek as he believes Leverett wants him dead. When Cash sees his estranged brother Rufe checking into the hotel under the name Sam Gilmore, he tells him that he has hopes of getting Walsh to talk. Later, at the café where she works, Molly hears from Peaceful that Cash is working for the syndicate, and decides to break off with him as she suspects that Leverett was involved in the massacre. After Rufe is recognized by an ex-soldier, Leverett assigns Cash to keep an eye on his brother. Walsh is then pursued by Artego, one of Leverett's henchmen, to Molly's café and is shot by Artego while he is writing a confession. Rufe finds the confession in Walsh's hand and learns that the captain and Leverett were involved in the massacre and that his father was innocent. After Cash tells Rufe that Leverett's men will be looking for him, he knocks him out and takes the confession. Leverett arrests Rufe for Walsh's murder, then arranges for a drunken, old judge to preside at Rufe's trial. Although Cash asks Molly not to testify that Walsh was writing when he was shot, she refuses, having guessed that Cash is Blackwell's other son. At the trial, the prosecutor suggests that Rufe came to Furnace Creek to kill the man who testified against his father. With Peaceful and Cash's help, Rufe escapes from the courtroom, but they are pursued by Leverett and his gang. While Cash acts as a decoy, Rufe sets off to take the confession to a federal marshal. Cash's horse goes down and he is shot in the thigh, but makes it to the fort. After he reveals his true identity to Leverett, Cash sets it up for Little Dog, who has been tracking Leverett, to shoot the white man. Back in town, Cash is recovering in bed when Molly brings him a newspaper with a front page story proclaiming that the War Department has exonerated his father. *Apache Indians. Brothers. Fathers and sons. Frame-ups. Military life. United States. Army. Cavalry. Alcoholism. Aliases. Betrayal. Confession (Law). Courts-martial and courts of inquiry. Forts. Frame-ups. Generals. Gunshot wounds. Judges. Massacres. Mines. Murder. Recognition. Syndicates (Finance).*

Note: According to information in the Twentieth Century-Fox Produced Scripts Collection at the UCLA Arts—Special Collections Library, Charles G. Booth's screenplay had various titles in pre-production: *Four Men and a Prayer*, *Silver Bullets* and *The End of the Trail*. It was shot under the title *The Ballad of Furnace Creek*. Filming began with approximately two weeks of location work near Kanab, Utah. According to a studio publicity release in the AMPAS Library, this was the first film on which the studio used planes, to ferry cast, crew and equipment from Hollywood to a distant location. An improvised landing field was created in the Utah badlands near where the fort set was constructed. *HR* news items of early Sep 1947 reported that George Montgomery had asked to be released from his contract to play Rufe Blackwell and was to be replaced by Glenn Langan. According to documents in the Twentieth Century-Fox Records of the Legal Department at the UCLA Arts—Special Collections Library, the role played by Frank Orth was all but eliminated from the final film. Characters portrayed by Robert Williams and Harry Seymour, who are listed in the *CBCS* also appear to have been cut. Fox first filmed Garth's novel in 1938 as *Four Men and a Prayer*. John Ford directed and Loretta Young and Richard Greene starred in the earlier version, which was set in India (see *AFI Catalog of Feature Films, 1931-40*; F3.1458). The novel had been serialized in *Hearst's International-Cosmopolitan* (Sep 1936—Jan 1937). An adaptation of *Fury at Furnace Creek* was broadcast on the *Screen Guild Players* radio program on 10 Feb 1949 and starred Victor Mature and Wendell Corey.

Box 10 Apr 1948. *DV* 7 Apr 1948, p. 3. *FD* 8 Apr 1948, p. 7. *HR* 11 Sep 1947, p. 1. *HR* 12 Sep 1947, p. 2. *HR* 7 Apr 1948, p. 3. *HR* 15 Jul 1948, p. 6. *MPHPD* 31 Jan 1948, p. 4039. *MPHPD* 10 Apr 1948, p. 4107. *NYT* 12 Jul 1948, p. 11. *Var* 7 Apr 1948, p. 10.

FURY AT SEA see **THIS WOMAN IS MINE**

FUZZ see **THIS REBEL BREED**

G. I. WAR BRIDES (English Americans, Immigrants)
Republic Pictures Corp. *Dist* Republic Pictures Corp. 12 Aug **1946**; Prod: mid-Apr—early May 1946 [©Republic Pictures Corp.; 8 Jul 1946; LP450]. Sd (RCA Sound System); b&w. 8 reels. 69 min. Passed by the National Board of Review. PCA cert no. 11702.

Assoc prod Armand Schaeffer. *Dir* George Blair. [*Asst dir* John Grubbs]. *Orig scr* John K. Butler. *Photog* Alfred Keller. [*2d cam* Al Myers]. *Spec eff* Howard Lydecker and Theodore Lydecker. [*Matte paintings* Lewis Physioc]. [*Transparency projection shots* Gordon Schaeffer]. *Art dir* Hilyard Brown. *Film ed* Tony Martinelli. *Set dec* John McCarthy, Jr. and Earl B. Wooden. *Mus dir* Morton Scott. *Mus score* Ernest Gold and [Joseph Dubin]. *Sd* Fred Stahl. [*Re-rec and eff mixer*] Thomas A. Carman and Howard Wilson. [*Sd* John Stransky, Jr. y Mus mixer]. *Makeup supv* Bob Mark. [*Tech adv* Barbara Walker]. [*Unit mgr* Mac D'Agostino].

Song(s): "Give Yourself a Pat on the Back," words and music by Ralph Butler and Raymond Wallace; "Auld Lang Syne," words by Robert Burns, music Scottish traditional.

Cast: Anna Lee [(*Linda Powell*)], James Ellison [(*Steve Giles*)], Harry Davenport [(*Grandpa Giles*)], William Henry [(*Capt. Roger Kirby*)], Stephanie Bachelor [(*Elizabeth Wunderlich*)], Doris Lloyd [(*Beatrice Moraski*)], Robert Armstrong [(*Dawson*)], Joseph Sawyer [(*Sgt. Frank Moraski*)], Mary McLeod [(*Kathleen Fitzpatrick*)], Carol Savage [(*Joyce Giles*)], Pax Walker [(*Margaret Lee*)], Helen Gerald [(*Ruth Giles*)], Pat O'Moore [(*Harold R. Williams*)], Maxine Jennings [(*Sgt. Polly Williams*)], Russell Hicks [(*Inspector Ramsaye*)], Francis Pierlot [(*Mr. Wunderlich*)], Pierre Watkin [(*Editor*)], Eugene Lay [(*Donnie*)], Lois Austin [(*Miss Nolan*)], Virginia Carroll [(*Helen Mayo*)], [Robert Bice (*Bill Sears*)], [Lester Dorr (*Steward*)], [Mary Newton, Beatrice Gray (*Red Cross workers*)], [Clarence Straight (*Immigration officer*)], [Guy Kingsford (*English radio announcer*)], [Gene Garrick, Dave Daggett, Michael Hughes (*M.P.s*)], [Fred Toones (*Pullman porter*)], [Pat Flaherty (*Lt. Cardigan*)], [Jack Norman (*Motorcycle cop*)], [Tristram Coffin (*Holliday*)], [Stephen Barclay (*Lt. Cooley*)], [Victor Sen Yung (*Chinese waiter*)], [Bruce Langley (*Photographer*)], [Charles Sullivan (*Brakeman*)], [David Reed (*Jimmy Fitzpatrick*)], [Jesse Graves (*Porter*)], [Ed Ramsey (*McDaniels*)], [Bob Wayne (*M.P. at depot*)], [Petra Silva (*Mexican shopkeeper*)].

Post-war life, Romance, with songs. [*Print viewed*]. At the United States Department of Justice's Immigration and Naturalization Service, an official shows the English-born war bride Beatrice Moraski a picture of another war bride, who claims to be Beatrice's sister, Joyce Giles, but who the inspector suspects is an impostor. When the inspector threatens to revoke Beatrice's right to live in the United States, she confesses that the woman in the picture is not her sister. Beatrice admits that she knows the pictured woman, Linda Powell, and tells the inspector that her sister forfeited her passage to the United States because she was not in love with her American husband Steve. Beatrice then tells the story of how she and Linda met and how she became involved in helping Linda travel in Joyce's stead: Moments before sailing for America, Joyce tells her sister that she does not wish to be reunited with a man she hardly knows, and refuses to make the voyage. When Beatrice finds Linda hiding in her ship cabin, Linda shows her a beautiful letter written by her American sweetheart, Capt. Roger Kirby. Realizing that Linda is truly in love, Joyce allows Linda to assume her identity for immigration purposes. During the ocean crossing, Dawson, a newspaper photographer who took a picture of Beatrice and Joyce at the English dock, suspects, but cannot prove, that Linda is not the same woman he photographed. Dawson believes he has stumbled upon a provocative story but decides to wait to expose the lie until his film is developed in New York. After arriving in New York, Linda passes through an immigration inspection with the help of Beatrice, who causes a diversion by feigning illness. En route to Los Angeles, Linda becomes worried when she learns that the war brides will not be free to go until their husbands sign for them. At the Los Angeles train station, under the watchful eye of Dawson and the immigration officials, Steve agrees to give Linda a welcoming hug and sign her release. Linda thanks Steve for helping her and immediately telephones Roger in San Francisco, unaware that he has forgotten her and has found another girl friend. Roger agrees to meet Linda, regardless, and takes the next train to Los Angeles. While waiting for Roger to arrive, Linda joins Steve on a sightseeing tour of Los Angeles, and they soon fall in love. Roger shows little interest in Linda when he arrives, and Linda soon realizes that Roger does not love her. Believing that the demise of her relationship with Roger will result in her deportation, Linda prepares to turn herself in to immigration officials. Beatrice concludes her story by telling the inspector that Linda was picked up by immigration officials on her way to turn herself in to them. The immigration inspector, aware of the unusual circumstances of Linda's presence in America, treats Linda with leniency and allows her to return to England without pressing charges against her. When Steve finds out about Linda's deportation, he races to the train station and proposes

to her. Linda accepts Steve's proposal and looks forward to a new life in America with the man she loves. *Aliens, Illegal. English in foreign countries. Immigrants. Impersonation and imposture. Romance. War brides. Children. Deportation. Los Angeles (CA). Photographs. Reporters. Self-sacrifice. Ships. Sisters. Stowaways. United States. Dept. of Immigration. United States. Women's Army Corps.*

Note: According to a 25 Feb 1946 *HR* news item, producer Armand Schaefer was to interview a group of war brides, who had recently arrived from England, about their experiences. Although Ernest Gold is credited onscreen with composing the film's music score, all other contemporary sources credit Joseph Dubin.

Box 24 Aug 1946. DV 7 Aug 1946, p. 3. FD 7 Aug 1946, p. 7. HCN 26 Apr 1946. HR 25 Feb 1946, p. 3. HR 16 Apr 1946, p. 3. HR 18 Apr 1946, p. 11. HR 19 Apr 1946, p. 21. HR 26 Apr 1946, p. 19. HR 1 May 1946, p. 17. HR 7 Aug 1946, p. 3. MPHPD 3 Aug 1946, p. 3127. MPHPD 17 Aug 1946, p. 3150. Var 7 Aug 1946, p. 15.

GAI, GAI DÉMARIONS-NOUS see **SOYONS GAIS**

GAI NGEO TIN XING see **JIA O TIEN CHEN**

GALAS DE LA PARAMOUNT (Spanish language)
Paramount Famous Lasky Corp. *Dist* Paramount Publix Corp. Aug **1930**; Buenos Aires, Argentina opening: 28 Aug 1930; Los Angeles opening: 12 Sep 1930. Sd (Movietone); b&w with col sequences (Technicolor). Length undetermined.

Supv Geoffrey Shurlock and Elsie Janis. *Dir* Dorothy Arzner, Otto Brower, Edmund Goulding, Victor Heerman, Frank Tuttle, Edwin H. Knopf, Rowland V. Lee, Victor Schertzinger, A. Edward Sutherland, Ernst Lubitsch and Lothar Mendes. *Dir of Spanish seq* Eduardo Venturini. *Spanish version* Josep Carner Ribalta. *Photog* Harry Fischbeck and Victor Milner. *Settings* John Wenger. *Dance dir* David Bennett.

Song(s): "Paramount on Parade," "Any Time's the Time To Fall in Love" and "I'm True to the Navy Now," words by Elsie Janis, music by Jack King; "Torna a Surriento," words by G. B. de Curtis, music by Ernesto de Curtis; "Dancing To Save Your Sole" and "Let Us Drink to the Girl of My Dreams," words by L. Wolfe Gilbert, music by Abel Baer; "All I Want Is Just One Girl," words by Leo Robin, music by Richard A. Whiting; "I'm Isadore, the Toreador," words and music by David Franklin; "Nichavo!" words by Helen Jerome, music by Mana-Zucca; "Sweeping the Clouds Away," words and music by Sam Coslow.

Cast: Ramón Pereda, Rosita Moreno, Barry Norton, Ernesto Vilches, Albertina Rasch, Juan Pulido, "La Argentinita", Luis Yance, Richard Arlen, Jean Arthur, Ludwig Berger, Clara Bow, Evelyn Brent, Mary Brian, Virginia Bruce, Nancy Carroll, Maurice Chevalier, Gary Cooper, Kay Francis, Skeets Gallagher, Harry Green, Mitzi Green, James Hall, Phillips Holmes, Dennis King, Abe Lyman and his Band, Nino Martini, Jack Oakie, Albertina Rasch dancers, Charles "Buddy" Rogers, Lillian Roth, Fay Wray.

Variety. [*Not viewed*]. After the opening "Showgirls on Parade" dance number in Technicolor, masters of ceremonies Ramón Pereda, Rosita Moreno and Barry Norton introduce themselves. Charles (Buddy) Rogers and Lillian Roth sing "Any Time's the Time to Fall in Love," then Spanish actor Ernesto Vilches demonstrates his versatility in extracts from his characterizations as "Mr. Wu," "Don Juan" and others. Maurice Chevalier and Evelyn Brent investigate the origins of the Apache dance, after which Nino Martini serenades Rosita Moreno from a Venetian gondola in a Technicolor sequence. The Albertina Rasch dancers perform, then Nancy Carroll and Abe Lyman and his band interpret "Dancing To Save Your Sole." Harry Green and Kay Francis follow with "I'm Isadore, the Toreador" in Technicolor, and Juan Pulido sings popular songs in Spanish. Chevalier returns as a French gendarme, patrolling a park, and sings "All I Want Is Just One Girl," after which Ramón Pereda introduces Mitzi Green who impersonates Chevalier and Charlie Mack. Richard Arlen, Jean Arthur, Mary Brian, Gary Cooper, James Hall, Fay Wray, Phillips Holmes and Virginia Bruce are featured in the Technicolor production number "Let Us Drink to the Girl of My Dreams." "La Argentinita," accompanied by guitarist Luis Yance, performs Spanish songs and dances. Clara Bow, Jack Oakie, Skeets Gallaher and a chorus of sailors sing "I'm True to the Navy Now," then Dennis King sings "Nichavo!" directed, onscreen, by Ludwig Berger in Technicolor. After Rosita Moreno performs a fado, Chevalier and the dancers appear as Parisian chimney sweeps in the Technicolor finale, "Sweeping the Clouds Away." *Actors and actresses. Apache dancers. Comedians. Dancers. Singers. Bullfighters and bullfighting. Chimney sweeps. Impersonations (Comic). Opera singers. Police. Sailors.*

Note: This film was a Spanish-language version of the 1930 film *Paramount on Parade* (see *AFI Catalog of Feature Films, 1921-30*; F2.4133). Contemporary sources indicate that the content and running order of the Spanish-version was considerably different in the various countries in which it was exhibited. However, the summary above, which was derived from an advertisement that appeared during the film's run in Mexico City, appears to reflect the most complete version.

Paramount made many foreign language versions of *Paramount on Parade*, but only the Spanish version appears to have been released in the U.S. The foreign versions all used most of the major musical sequences from the English original, but were introduced by onscreen hosts and hostesses speaking the language of the country in which the version was destined to be released. The hosts also performed in sequences that were substituted for most of the English sketches. At Paramount's Hollywood studio, Swedish singer Ernst Rolf and his Norwegian wife, Tutta Berntzen, filmed introductions and sequences for the Scandinavian version and Japanese comedian Suisei Matsui introduced and performed in the version released in his native land.

The majority of the foreign versions were prepared at Paramount's Joinville studio in Paris. Saint-Granier, Marguerite Moreno, Boucot fils and Charles de Rochefort were featured in the French version. De Rochefort directed the additional sequences and also directed Dina Gralla and Eugen Rex in their scenes for the German version. Theo Frenkel, Jr., Mien Duymaer van Twist and Louis Davids appeared in the Dutch version while Mira Ziminska and Mariusz Maszyński hosted the Polish version. Versions were also shot at Joinville for the Czech, Hungarian, Rumanian, Serbian and Italian markets, but the identities of the respective hosts have not been determined. The sequence featuring "La Argentinita" for the Spanish version was shot in New York on 10 Apr 1930.

THE GALLOPING KID (Latino)
National Pictures Corp. *Dist* Imperial Distributing Corp. **1932**. Sd; b&w. 5 reels, 4,600 ft.

Dir Robert Emmet. *Wrt* Robert Emmet.

Cast: LITTLE "BUCK" DALE (*Buck Parker*), Karla Cowan (*Mary Parker*), Al Lane (*Tom Farley*), Fred Parker, A. E. Anderson, H. B. Carpenter, Larry Warner, George Bates.

Western. [*Not viewed*]. Little Buck Parker leaves his sister Mary alone at their ranch to fend off the "Pedro" gang while he gets help from the sheriff. Mary is unable to hold them off, and Pedro Mario, Miguel, Jose and Juan break into the house and begin to search for a map. Mary is rescued from her predicament by Tom Farley, a passing stranger, who has the situation under control by the time Buck returns with Sheriff Blake. Blake arrests the gang and deputizes Tom. Although Blake is aware that the Pedro gang is working with Jack Ellis, who is after a map to a hidden gold mine that Buck's father drew just before he died, Blake is unable to prove any charges against the gang, and they are released. Tom spends a great deal of time at the Parker ranch, in an effort both to protect Mary and get to know her. When Ellis and Pedro engage rancher Fletcher in a game of poker during which he loses $15,000 and stands to lose his ranch, Tom intervenes and warns Fletcher that his opponents have been cheating. Fletcher is outraged, but is shot by Ellis. Ellis breaks jail and, after looting Mary's house once again to find the map, kidnaps Mary and intends to take her with him across the border. Ellis and Pedro separate, and while Buck captures Pedro, Tom captures Ellis, whom he is forced to kill. Pedro and the rest of the gang are arrested by the sheriff. With peace restored, Mary agrees with Tom that Buck would make a great brother-in-law. *Brothers and sisters. Maps. Mexican Americans. Outlaws. Ranchers. Chases. Deputies. Gold mines. Jailbreaks. Kidnapping. Murder. Poker (Game). Romance.*

Note: The above plot synopsis was taken from a studio dialogue continuity. No reviews for this film were found.

GALLOPING VENGEANCE (Native Americans)
Independent Pictures. *Dist* Film Booking Offices of America. 8 Mar **1925** [©R-C Pictures Corp.; 8 Mar 1925; LP21285]. Si; b&w. 5 reels, 5,095 ft.

Dir William James Craft. *Story* William Lester. *Cont* George H. Plympton. *Photog* Arthur Reeves.

Cast: Bob Custer (*Tom Hardy*), Mary Beth Milford (*Marion Reeves*), Ralph McCullough (*Jack Reeves*), Dorothy Ponedel (*Little Wolf*), David Dunbar (*Duke Granby*).

Western. Tom Hardy, a tough Texas Ranger, is ordered to find Big Wolf, an important leader of the Indians who is believed to have been kidnapped by the Granby gang. Little Wolf, who is helping Tom find Big Wolf, is wounded and taken to the Reeves ranch, where Tom first meets and falls in love with Marion Reeves, a beautiful girl who soon confides to him her concern for her brother, Jack, who is running with the Granby gang. Tom later discovers Jack in a saloon, drinking with the outlaws; there is a fight, and a man is killed, the blame being falsely laid on Jack, who runs to his sister for help, closely followed

by Tom. Marion holds Tom at the point of a gun while Jack escapes, hiding out in Granby's den; Little Wolf sees him and takes Tom there; Marion follows them; Jack and Granby fight. One of Granby's men blows up a dam, and the hideout is inundated. Tom saves Granby, who, with his dying words, exonerates Jack. Tom then saves Marion from the flood, permanently winning her love. *Bandits. Brothers and sisters. Dams. Floods. Indians of North America. Kidnapping. Revenge. Texas Rangers.*

MPW 28 Mar 1925.

THE GAMBLER OF THE WEST (Native Americans)
Biograph Co. *Dist* General Film Co. 17 Nov **1915** [©Biograph Co.; 10 Nov 1915; LP6939]. Si; b&w. 4 reels.
Source: Based on the play *The Gambler of the West* by Owen Davis (New York, 28 Jul 1906).
Cast: W. J. Butler (*Tom Grey*), Violet Reed (*Mrs. Grey*), Charles Perley (*Lucky Jack Gordon*), Robert Drouet (*Mike Clancy*), John Brammall (*Richard Kent, Jr.*), Charles H. West (*Dan Reardon*), Master A. Short (*Little Bear*), A. Hollingsworth (*Kansas Joe*), Linda Arvidson (*Mabel Grey*), Gertrude Robinson (*Cactus Kate*), Alfred Paget, Walter Lewis, Charles Gorman, E. Stone, Clara T. Bracey, George Pearce.
Western. While traveling west from Wyoming with his family, Tom Grey, a prospector, is killed by Indians and his son is taken captive. The widow remarries and inherits a stepson, Dick, who, at the urging of his half sister Mabel, sets off to find the missing son. Falling under the bad influence of Mike Clancy, the weak-willed Dick gambles away his allowance and tries to finagle money out of Mabel, who has joined Dick in the search. Taken with her earnest gentility, Jack Gordon, an honest gambler, aids Mabel in locating her lost brother, now called Little Bear. Dick also hears of Little Bear's identity and attempts to kill him to secure a larger share of the family inheritance, but Jack saves the Indian and foils the plot. Before Mabel and her brother are reunited, however, Dick and Mike kidnap each sibling separately and Jack, Mabel and Little Bear must then execute heroic rescues and battle angry Indians. *Brothers and sisters. Gamblers. Indians of North America. Missing persons. Moral corruption. Attempted murder. Fights. Greed. Inheritance. Kidnapping. Massacres. Prospectors. Rescues. Stepchildren. Wyoming.*

Motog 20 Nov 1915, p. 1099. *MPN* 13 Nov 1915, p. 108. *MPN* 20 Nov 1915, p. 85. *MPN* 4 Dec 1915, p. 105. *MPW* 13 Nov 1915, p. 1358. *MPW* 27 Nov 1915, p. 1664. *NYDM* 27 Nov 1915, p. 32.

GAMBLING HOUSE (Italian Americans, Polish Americans)
RKO Radio Pictures, Inc. *Dist* RKO Radio Pictures, Inc. Jan **1951**; Los Angeles opening: 23 Feb 1951; Prod: 3 Feb—13 Mar 1950, retakes and addl scenes: 8 May—13 May 1950 [©RKO Radio Pictures, Inc.; 18 Jan 1951; LP734]. Sd (RCA Sound System); b&w. 10 reels, 7,213 or 7,212 ft. 80 min. PCA cert no. 14420.

Exec prod Sid Rogell. *Prod* Warren Duff. *Dir* Ted Tetzlaff. [*Dir for addl scenes and retakes* Robert Stevenson]. [*Asst dir* Lloyd Richards]. [*Asst dir for addl scenes and retakes* A. Thompson]. *Scr* Marvin Borowsky and Allen Rivkin. *Based on a story by* Erwin Gelsey. [*Contr wrt* Warren Duff]. *Dir of photog* Harry J. Wild. [*Dir of photog for addl scenes and retakes* Leo Tover]. *Art dir* Albert S. D'Agostino and Alfred Herman. *Film ed* Roland Gross. *Set dec* Darrell Silvera and Jack Mills. *Gowns* Michael Woulfe. *Mus* Roy Webb. *Mus dir* C. Bakaleinikoff. *Sd* Phil Brigandi and Clem Portman. [*Sd for addl scenes and retakes* Frank McWhorter]. *Makeup artist* Mel Berns. *Hair stylist* Larry Germain. *Stand-in for Victor Mature* Robert St. Angelo. *Stand-in for Terry Moore* Mary Jane Carey.
Cast: VICTOR MATURE (*Marc Fury*), TERRY MOORE (*Lynn Warren*), WILLIAM BENDIX (*Joe Farrow*), Zachary A. Charles (*Willie*), Basil Ruysdael (*Judge Ravinek*), Donald Randolph (*Lloyd Crane*), Damian O'Flynn (*Ralph Douglas*), Cleo Moore (*Sally*), Ann Doran (*Della*), Eleanor Audley (*Mrs. Livingston*), Gloria Winters (*B. J. Warren*), Don Haggerty (*Sharky*), [William E. Green (*Doctor*)], Jack Kruschen (*Burly Italian*)], [Barry Brooks (*Guard*)], [Robert Cornthwaite (*Stefan, refugee at Ellis Island*)], [Leonidas Ossetynski (*Mr. Sobieski*)], [Loda Halama (*Mrs. Sobieski*)], [Delphine Hruby (*Sobieski daughter*)], [Stanley Price (*Apartment superintendent*)], [Victor Paul, Joseph Rogato, Guy Zanette (*Italian immigrants*)], [Stephan Chase (*Mr. Warren*)], [G. Pat Collins (*Jensen*)], [Tol Avery (*Adams*)], [Kirk Alyn (*F.B.I. man*)], [William Challee (*Parking attendant*)], [Robert St. Angelo, Jack Stoney (*Detectives*)], [Clark Howat (*Nick*)], [Jack Shea (*Wally*)], [Norman Field (*Cashier*)], [Betty

Underwood (*Wanda, performer*)], [Edward Clark (*Stage doorman*)], [Suzi Crandall (*Girl at theatre*)], [W. J. O'Brien (*Stage manager*)], [Vera Stokes (*Station wagon driver*)], [Homer Dickinson (*Doorman*)], [Forrest Burns (*Milkman*)], [Al Murphy (*Cab driver*)], [Gregg Barton, Gordon Wynne (*Police officers*)], [Tony Merrill (*Reporter*)], [Chester Jones (*Elevator attendant*)], [Carl Davis (*Big*)], [Art Dupuis (*Porter at dock*)], [Carl Sklover], [Eddie Fields], [Don Gazzaniga], [George Navarro], [Emilia Rivera], [Roland Jones], [Sherry Hall], [Bert Moorehouse].

Crime. [*Print viewed*]. Small-time gambler Marc Fury agrees to take the rap for gambling czar Joe Farrow, who has killed a man during an illegal crap game at which Marc was present, after Farrow and his lawyer, Lloyd Crane, offer Marc $50,000 and promise to help him further if anything goes wrong. As insurance, Marc takes Farrow's coded notebook. In a New York courtroom, Marc pleads self-defense and is found not guilty, but is immediately re-arrested by Immigration and Naturalization Service officials. As Marc enters Immigration headquarters, he passes Lynn Warren, an immigrant aid worker, and slips Farrow's notebook into her coat pocket. Inspector Ralph Douglas informs Marc that, according to their files, Marc was born Marcus Furioni in Lucania, Italy, and due to his lengthy criminal record, they intend to deport him as an undesirable alien. Marc claims to be an American citizen but cannot prove it. Until a hearing can be scheduled, Marc is detained on Ellis Island and, before Farrow bails him out, meets several potential immigrants. Marc goes to see Lynn at the Federated Assistance Leagues' office to recover Farrow's notebook, but she says she will bring it to him sometime later. He follows her to the docks, where due to a mixup, an immigrant Polish family, the Sobieskis, are to be housed in an inferior apartment. The person who sponsored their immigration to the U.S. cannot be found and may have died. Marc and Lynn then go to her apartment to get the notebook, and Marc kisses her but she resists him. At Marc's deportation hearing, Crane presents Marc's honorable discharge from the army and claims that he qualifies for citizenship under the G.I. Naturalization Act; however, the judge disqualifies Marc and orders him deported, then agrees to put off a final decision for two or three days. Marc goes to see Farrow and asks for the $50,000 he is still owed, but Farrow offers him only a few bills. Marc warns him that he had better pay up. When he leaves Farrow, Marc is mugged by Farrow's thugs. Lynn, who has changed her feelings about Marc, warns him not to go after Farrow, but Marc asks his friend Willie how he can set Farrow up, and Willie suggests a vulnerable gambling club Farrow operates in New Jersey. Marc accompanies Lynn when she has to pick up the Sobieski family whose residency has been denied for lack of a suitable sponsor and he begins to realize that the opportunities he has enjoyed have been denied to so many. While Lynn waits for him, Marc holds up Farrow and obtains his $50,000. Marc and Lynn are stopped by a police patrol car, and although Lynn provides Marc with an alibi, she later tells Marc she wants nothing more to do with him. While hiding out in in a cheap roominghouse, Marc gives Willie the cash to deposit in a bank and then write a check to Lynn to give to the Sobieskis. At Marc's final hearing, the judge asks Marc why he should not be deported, and in front of Willie, Lynn and one of Farrow's men, Sharky, Marc, as Willie hands Marc's check to Lynn, states that he would like to stay in America if he could know that he was wanted and that he belonged. He paraphrases a passage written by Thomas Wolfe on the virtues of America, which Lynn had given him. The judge rules that Marc not be deported and suggests that he apply for citizenship under the G.I. Naturalization Act. In his room, Marc receives a phone call from Willie and Lynn. Lynn is back in love with him, but Marc gives her a brush-off so that she will not be involved in what may happen next and asks Willie to tell her that if things work out, he will be seeing her. Later, Marc permits himself to be caught by Farrow and Sharky and sows seeds of doubt in Sharky's mind that Farrow intends to make him the fall guy for his murder. Sharky shoots Farrow, and after he is caught by police, whom Willie has tipped off, Marc walks off into the night. *Citizenship. Gamblers. Gangsters. Immigrants. Moral reformation. Social workers. United States. Dept. of Immigration. Arrests. Charities. Deportation. Gambling houses. Gunfights. Gunshot wounds. Italians. Judges. Lawyers. New York City. New York City–Ellis Island. Physicians. Poles. Police. Robbery. Romance. Self-sacrifice. Theaters. Trials. Thomas Wolfe.*

Note: Working titles of this film included *Alias Marc Fury, Alias Mike Fury, Mr. Whiskers* and *Walk Softly, Stranger.* According to documents in the RKO

Production Files at the UCLA Arts—Special Collections Library, the studio acquired the unpublished short story in or around 1941. Through the decade, various treatments and screenplays were written, including one screenplay by Samuel Fuller. According to an *HR* news item, Twentieth Century-Fox temporarily suspended Victor Mature when Mature failed to report for work on *Gambling House*. The item quoted Mature as saying that he didn't feel "the role was suitable for him." Fox agreed to loan their contract player Mature as part of a buy-out deal with RKO, to whom the actor owed two pictures. The passage by Thomas Wolfe quoted in the film comes from the last paragraph of "The Promise of America" in *You Can't Go Home Again* (New York, 1940): "So, then, to every man his chance/to every man, regardless of his birth, his shining golden opportunity/to every man the right to live, to work, to be himself, and to become whatever thing his manhood and his vision can combine to make him/this, seeker, is the promise of America."

Box 30 Dec 1950. *DV* 22 Dec 1950. *FD* 27 Dec 1950. *Har* 30 Dec 1950, p. 206. *HR* 19 Jul 1949, p. 2. *HR* 14 Dec 1949, p. 2. *HR* 22 Dec 1950. *LAT* 24 Feb 1951. *MPD* 22 Dec 1950. *MPH* 30 Dec 1950. *NYT* 19 Mar 1951. *Var* 27 Dec 1950, p. 6.

GANG SMASHERS (African Americans)

Million Dollar Productions, Inc. *Dist* Million Dollar Productions, Inc. 1 Jan **1939**. Sd; b&w. 6 reels, 5,800 ft. PCA cert no. 4847.

Prod Harry M. Popkin. *Assoc prod* George D. Ringer. *Supv* Arthur A. Brooks. *Dir* Leo C. Popkin. *Dial dir* Zella Young. *Adpt* Phil Dunham and Hazel Barnes Jamieson. *Photog* Robert Cline. *Art dir* E. H. Reif. *Ed* Bart Rauw. *Mus dir* Phil Moore. *Mus settings* Lou Frohman. *Sd eng* Glen Glenn. *Tech dir* Billy Myers. *Prod staff* Buck Jones and Halley Harding. *Public relations* Ralph G. Pollock.

Cast: Nina Mae McKinney, Mantan Moreland, Lawrence Criner, Monte Hawley, Reginald Fenderson, Eddie Thompson, Vernon McCalla, Phil Moore, and his Orchestra.

African American, Gangster, Drama. [*Not viewed*]. Racketeer Gat Dalton owns Harlem's Cellar Cabaret, and his chief lieutenant, Nick Crowder, is feared by all. With the help of his henchmen, Gloomy and Gopher, Gat runs the "Harlem Benevolent Protective Insurance League," which provides protection to merchants who pay him tribute money. Soon after storekeeper Sam Bowers tells Gloomy and Gopher that he refuses to pay tribute, his store is bombed and he is killed. Detective Captain Owens investigates the murder and rounds up a group of suspects, including Gat, but because the witnesses are afraid to testify against Gat, he is released. Later, when Gat proposes marriage to Laura, a former nurse and a singer at the Cellar, she refuses him. As part of an investigation into Gat's illicit activities, Police Lieutenant Sanders, posing as a fellow racketeer named Lefty Louis, infiltrates Gat's gang by acting tough and telling Gat that he was sent by a racketeer in Chicago. Gat's men, however, do not trust Lefty, so they follow him when he goes on a collection run. Although Gat's men are convinced that Lefty is legitimate when they witness him apparently murder a store manager, his cover is soon blown when Gat's friend in Chicago tells the gang leader that the real Lefty has been arrested. Gat and his men try to kill the impostor when the police arrive, and in the ensuing gun battle all of Gat's men are either killed or arrested. Sanders, who has been slightly wounded, is nursed back to health by Laura, who has returned to work at the hospital, and the two fall in love. *African Americans. Impersonation and imposture. Murder. New York City—Harlem. Police. Racketeers. Undercover operations. Cabaret performers. Cabarets. Convalescence. Explosions. Gunfights. Hospitals. Nurses. Police chiefs. Proposals (Marital). Romance.*

Note: According to modern sources, *Gang Smashers* was also known under the title *Gun Moll*. Modern sources also list actors Arthur Ray, Charles Hawkins and Neva Peoples in the cast.

Exh 14 Jun 1939, p. 331.

GANG WAR (African Americans)

Million Dollar Productions, Inc. *Dist* Sack Amusement Enterprises, Inc. **1940**; Harlem opening: week of 29 Mar 1940. Sd; b&w. 7 reels, 5,700 ft. 60 min.

Pres Harry M. Popkin. *Prod* Clifford Sanforth. *Exec prod* Harry M. Popkin. *Assoc prod* Sara Francis. [*Supv* Geo. D. Ringer]. *Dir* Leo C. Popkin. *Asst dir* Ben Chapman. *Scr* Lewis Sherman. *Orig story* Walter Cooper. *Photog* Marcel Picard. *Art dir* Paul Palmentola. *Film ed* Michael Luciano. *Music supv* Lou Porter. *Sd* Earl Cille and Lambert Day. *Prod mgr* Arthur C. Ringer. *Supv of prod* George D. Ringer.

Song(s): "Remember the Moon," music and lyrics by Lew Porter and Johnny Lange.

Cast: Ralph Cooper (*Bob "Killer" Meade*), Gladys Snyder (*Mazie ["Sugar"] Walford*), Reggie Fenderson (*Danny*), Lawrence Criner (*Lew Baron*), Monte Hawley (*Bill*), Jesse C. Brooks (*Lt. Holmes*), Johnny Thomas (*Phil*), Maceo Sheffield (*Bull Brown*), Charles Hawkins (*Pip*), Robert Johnson (*Waxy*), Henry Roberts (*Slim*), Harold Garrison (*Slicum*).

African American, Gangster, Drama. [*Print viewed*]. A fight in a diner over the claims of conflicting gangster factions reveals Bob "Killer" Meade as a rising lawbreaker in Harlem. A member of Bull Brown's gang, Bob soon takes over and orders Bull to be "given some air." Bob is indicted for his crimes, but witnesses are afraid to talk and he is found not guilty. At the courthouse, he meets Mazie "Sugar" Walford, who believes him innocent. Although Mazie is engaged to George Stevens, a member of a prominent local family, Bob falls in love and begins to court her, promising to lay Harlem at her feet. Bob decides to cut in on the juke box action of rival Harlem boss, Lew Baron, who sends several killers for him. However, Bob outsmarts them and demands half of Lew's take. In the ensuing gangland war, Bob and his men defeat Lew, taking over his machines. Lieutenant Holmes, a policeman who knew Bob as a boy, warns him about where his methods will lead. Lew calls to make a deal with Bob and learns that Bob and his men are celebrating the opening of Mazie's new show at a nightclub. During an African number, Lew's gang enters the club, and Bob and his company leave, prompting an automobile chase. Later, Bill, Lew's henchmen, goes to Mazie and forces her to sing her new song, "Remember the Moon," to Bob over the telephone. After the connection is broken, Bob finds the body of his old friend, Slicum, at his door with a note from Lew. With his other henchmen, Phil and Danny, Bob goes after Lew, catching and shooting him and his men as they are about to leave town. Mazie, who has warned Bob, tells Holmes of his actions, and the police surround Lew's hideout. Bob escapes to Mazie's but realizes it is too late to hide when Holmes comes to the door. Nonetheless, Bob makes a mad dash over the rooftops as the police pursue and finally shoot him, his corpse falling at the feet of Mazie and Holmes. *African Americans. Gangsters. Jukeboxes. New York City—Harlem. Rivalry. Automobile chases. Gunshot wounds. Hired killers. Newspapers. Nightclubs. Police. Romance. Rooftops. Singers. Telephone.*

Note: The film opens with a montage of long shots depicting violent gang warfare, followed by a newspaper headline that reads "Gang War—Local Police Seem Unable to Stem New Crime Wave." (This same headline reappears at the end of the picture.) An inset of presenter Harry M. Popkin against the newspaper comes next. The story opens with another montage of gang violence, and further montages of newspaper headlines show Bob's rise to criminal prominence. The picture also includes a collage of Harlem nightlife prior to the nightclub scene. The *Var* review comments that the use of numerous montages "seems a particularly bad technique in view of a prospective audience which is notoriously slow in reading and uninclined to it, while many Negroes in the South are actually unable to read." *Var* also notes that the picture deserves "a merit rating only in comparison with other output of the Negro picture makers." According to modern sources, *Gang War* was reissued in the 1940s by Toddy Pictures under the title *Crime Street*.

Var 3 Apr 1940, p. 16.

THE GANG'S ALL HERE (African Americans)

Sterling Productions. *Dist* Monogram Pictures Corp. 11 Jun **1941**; Prod: late Apr—early May 1941 [©Monogram Pictures Corp.; 11 Jun 1941; LP10672]. Sd; b&w. 6 reels. 63 min.

Prod Lindsley Parsons. *Dir* Jean Yarbrough. *Orig scr* Edmond Kelso. *Dir of photog* Mack Stengler. *Art dir* Charles Clague. *Film ed* Jack Ogilvie. *Settings* Dave Milton. *Mus dir* Edward Kay. *Sd dir* Glen Glenn. *Prod mgr* Glenn Cook.

Cast: FRANKIE DARRO (*Frankie*), Marcia Mae Jones (*Patsy* [*Wallace*]), Jackie Moran (*Chick*), Keye Luke (*George* [*Lee*]), Mantan Moreland (*Jeff*), Robert Homans (*Pop Wallace*), Irving Mitchell (*Saunders*), Ed Cassidy ([*Jack*] *Norton*), Pat Gleason (*Marty*), Jack Kenney (*Dink*), Jack Ingraham (*Matt*), Laurence Criner (*Ham Shanks*), [Paul Bryar (*Bob*)].

Crime, Comedy-drama. [*Print viewed*]. In Los Angeles, trucks operated by the Overland Transport Company are being sabotaged while making their interstate runs, and the drivers are frequently killed. Overland's owner, Pop Wallace, is unable to find new drivers because professional drivers are too scared to apply. Pop's daughter Patsy, meanwhile, hopes to marry the company's mechanic, Chick, and badgers him to be more assertive with her father. Loafer Frankie and his black friend, Jeff, read Pop's advertisement for drivers, and although Jeff is reluctant to work, they apply at the garage. Patsy, who sees in Frankie an opportunity to make Chick jealous, leads them to believe that Chick is the boss, and he hires them at her urging. Although Pop thinks Frankie is too young to handle the trucks, he

agrees out of fear of losing his business. Pop then calls his insurance agent, Saunders, with whom he has been secretly splitting the insurance reimbursements from the accidents, and begs him to stop rival truck business owner Norton's thugs from forcing his trucks off the road. Although Pop protests that the accidents were supposed to have been minor, Saunders refuses to recall Norton's men. As Frankie and Jeff return from Fresno, Norton's saboteurs attempt to force their truck off the road, but instead Frankie is stopped by the police for speeding. Frankie and Jeff bring their cargo in early, and Pop refrains from reprimanding him for his six speeding tickets because he has gotten a bonus from the shipper. Pop next hires Chinese American George Lee, the son of an old friend, who has asked to work gratis in order to learn the trucking business. Although he is friendly, George lurks around the garage eavesdropping on conversations and peering into packing crates, ostensibly to learn the job from the ground up. Frankie tries to teach Jeff how to drive, but he is resistant. On their next assignment, the saboteurs succeed in forcing Frankie off the road, and he and Jeff are taken hostage by Norton's men, Marty and Dink, who are reluctant to kill them because they are so young. Jeff and Frankie are kept under guard by the mechanic, Ham Shanks, at Norton's garage. Pop finds it odd that Saunders knows about Frankie and Jeff's disappearance before he does, and threatens to go to the police if his men do not return unharmed. George overhears his telephone conversation and reveals that he is actually an insurance investigator. Pop, who buckled under to threats by Saunders and Norton because his business was failing, refuses to identify them until Jeff and Frankie return, but agrees to cooperate with George. Norton plans to murder his hostages, but Frankie and Jeff escape from Ham Shanks and take their truck back to Pop's garage. When they discover that the crates are loaded with bricks rather than canned goods, Frankie goes into the office to confront Pop, but finds him lying unconscious on the floor. After taking the beaten Pop to the hospital, Frankie speculates that Pop was forced into the tire war for the insurance money, and everyone agrees to get evidence on Pop's behalf before calling the police. Chick and Patsy go to Saunders' apartment to seek his help, unaware that he is the mastermind. Frankie and Jeff take the truck back to Norton's garage and hide inside, and when Saunders arrives with Chick and Patsy as hostages, Frankie overhears him plotting with Norton. Frankie and Jeff are discovered and Chick and Patsy are thrown into the truck with them. Norton and Saunders drive the truck to a remote road, intending to get rid of their hostages, but are stopped by the police for speeding, and the delay permits George to catch up and have the criminals arrested. Patsy then yells at Frankie for allowing "her" Chick to be harmed. *Insurance fraud. Kidnapping. Murder. Sabotage. Trucking.* African Americans. Business rivals. Chinese Americans. Classified advertisements. Eavesdropping. Fathers and daughters. Insurance-Investigators. Los Angeles (CA). Mechanics. Police. Romance. Traffic violations.

Box 28 Jun 1941. *FD* 24 Jun 1941, p. 7. *HR* 25 Apr 1941, p. 12. *HR* 2 May 1941, p. 14. *HR* 4 Aug 1941, p. 3. *MPHPD* 31 May 1941, p. 146. *Var* 25 Jun 1941, p. 18.

THE GANG'S ALL HERE (Latino)
Twentieth Century-Fox Film Corp.; William Goetz in charge of production. *Dist* Twentieth Century-Fox Film Corp. 24 Dec 1943; *Prod*: 25 Apr–mid-Aug 1943; retakes late Sep 1943 [©Twentieth Century-Fox Film Corp.; 24 Dec 1943; LP12471]. Sd (Western Electric Recording); col (Technicolor). 11 reels, 9,288 ft. 103 min. PCA cert no. 9531.

Prod William LeBaron. *Dir* Busby Berkeley. [*Asst dir* Tom Dudley]. *Scr* Walter Bullock. *Based on a story by* Nancy Wintner, George Root, Jr. and Tom Bridges. *Dir of photog* Edward Cronjager. *Spec photog eff* Fred Sersen. *Technicolor dir* Natalie Kalmus. *Art dir* James Basevi and Joseph C. Wright. *Film ed* Ray Curtiss. *Set dec* Thomas Little. *Assoc* Paul S. Fox. [*Props* Mack Elliott]. *Cost* Yvonne Wood. *Mus dir* Alfred Newman and Charles Henderson. *Dances created and dir by* Busby Berkeley. *Sd* George Leverett and Roger Heman. *Makeup artist* Guy Pearce.

Song(s): "No Love, No Nothin'," "A Journey to a Star," "The Lady in the Tutti Frutti Hat," "The Polka Dot Polka," "You Discover You're in New York," "Paducah" and "Minnie's in the Money," music and lyrics by Leo Robin and Harry Warren; "Brazil," music and lyrics by Ary Barroso, English lyrics by S. K. Russell.

Cast: ALICE FAYE [(*Eadie Allen*)], CARMEN MIRANDA [(*Dorita*)], PHIL BAKER [(*Himself*)], BENNY GOODMAN AND HIS ORCHESTRA

[(*Himself*)], Eugene Pallette [(*Andrew J. "A. J." Mason, Sr.*)], Charlotte Greenwood [(*Blossom Potter*)], Edward Everett Horton [(*Peyton Potter*)], Tony De Marco [(*Himself*)], James Ellison [(*Sgt. Andrew J. Mason, Jr., also known as Sgt. Pat Casey*)], Sheila Ryan [(*Vivian Potter*)], Dave Willock [(*Sgt. Pat Casey*)], [The Banda Da Lua (*Carmen Miranda's orchestra*)], [Miriam Lavelle (*Specialty dancer*)], [Charles Saggau, Deidre Gale (*Jitterbug dancers*)], [George Dobbs (*Benson*)], [Leon Belasco (*Waiter*)], [June Haver (*Maybelle*)], [Frank Faylen (*Marine*)], [Russell Hoyt (*Sailor*)], [Virginia Sale (*Secretary*)], [Leyland Hodgson (*Butler*)], [Lillian Yarbo (*Maid*)], [Frank Darien (*Doorman*)], [Al Murphy (*Stage manager*)], [Hallene Hill (*Old lady*)], [Gabriel Canzona (*Organ grinder*)], [Fred Walburn (*Newsboy*)], [Virginia Wilson (*Dancing partner*)], [Billie Seward, Ruth Brady, Adele Jergens, Jean O'Donnell, Marion Rosamond, Lorraine Breacher, Blanche Taylor (*Dancers*)], [Lee Bennett], [Jeanne Crain], [Jo Carroll Dennison].

Musical. [*Print viewed*]. Wealthy businessman Andrew J. "A. J." Mason, Sr. takes his nervous partner, Peyton Potter, to the Club New Yorker for a celebratory evening with his son, Sgt. Andrew J. Mason, Jr., who is about to report for active duty in the Army. A. J. and Andy enjoy the show, which features master of ceremonies Phil Baker and dancer Tony De Marco, while Potter worries about what his wife Blossom would say if she knew he was there. While Potter is trapped into dancing with Brazilian sensation Dorita, Andy becomes intrigued by entertainer Eadie Allen. Phil warns Andy that because Eadie dances at the Broadway Canteen between shows, she will not go out on a date with him, but Andy follows her to the canteen and tells her that his name is Sgt. Pat Casey so that she will not be intimidated by his wealth. Despite her insistence that she cannot date servicemen outside the canteen, Eadie is charmed by Andy and agrees to meet him later when he pursues her to the nightclub. Eadie and Andy spend the evening talking and falling in love, and the next day, Eadie bids him farewell at the train station and promises to write every day. Andy distinguishes himself in battle in the South Pacific, and is granted a furlough after being awarded a medal. A. J. is thrilled and plans to throw a welcome home party for Andy at the Club New Yorker. Phil cannot accommodate his plans, however, as the club is closed for two weeks while the company rehearses a new show. Munificent as always, A. J. invites the performers to rehearse at his and Potter's homes, where they can throw a lavish garden party and war bond rally to welcome Andy. Potter is perturbed about the arrangements when he learns that Blossom knows Phil from her former days as an entertainer, and his chagrin grows when Tony's partner cannot perform and he asks Potter's daughter Vivian to dance with him. Hoping to persuade the stodgy Potter to allow Vivian to perform, Blossom tells him that Phil has threatened to reveal her wild past if Vivian is not in the show. Potter acquiesces, but his problems grow when he is pursued by the romantic-minded Dorita. When not chasing Potter, Dorita learns that Vivian has a boyfriend named Andy, and that he and Eadie's "Casey" are the same man. Complications arise as Dorita tries to keep Vivian and Eadie from discovering Andy's deception. When Andy and the real Pat Casey arrive at the club, however, Eadie learns the truth. Andy proclaims that he wants to marry her and not Vivian, but Eadie insists on breaking off their relationship, as she believes that Vivian really cares for him. During the show, however, Vivian tells Eadie that she is going to Broadway to perform as Tony's permanent partner, and reveals that she and Andy were never truly in love. As the show comes to a close, Eadie and Andy reconcile, and everyone joins in the final song. *Dancers. Deception. Romance. Singers. Soldiers.* Bananas. Band leaders. Brazilian Americans. Businessmen. Canteens (War-time, emergency, etc.). Comedians. Doughnuts. Fathers and daughters. Fathers and sons. Musical revues. New York City–Broadway. New York City–Staten Island. Nightclubs. Parties. Photographs. Propriety. War bonds. Wealth.

Note: The working title of this film was *The Girls He Left Behind*. According to a 7 Jan 1943 news item, composer Harry Warren was originally scheduled to work with lyricist Mack Gordon on the film's score, but Warren instead wrote the picture's songs with Leo Robin. A 30 Mar 1943 *HR* news item included "Pickin' on Your Momma" in the list of songs to be featured in the film. Modern sources note that the song, along with "Sleepy Moon" and "Drums and Dreams" were cut before the final release. According to *HR* news items and a studio press release, Linda Darnell was originally scheduled to play "Vivian Potter," which would have been her first dancing role in motion pictures. During dance rehearsals, however, Darnell sprained her ankle, and after her recovery, eloped with cinematographer Peverell Marley and asked Twentieth Century-Fox for an indefinite leave of absence. Darnell was replaced in the role by Sheila Ryan. Although Alice Faye did have a singing cameo in the 1944 film *Four Jills and*

a Jeep, this picture marked her last appearance in a musical film until the 1962 version of *State Fair*. Faye, who was pregnant with her second child during filming of *The Gang's All Here*, retired from the screen and only made one additional film, the 1945 drama *Fallen Angel* until 1962. *The Gang's All Here* marked the screen debuts of actresses June Haver, Jeanne Crain and Jo Carroll Dennison, who was Miss America of 1942. Director Busby Berkeley was borrowed from M-G-M for the production, although by the time additional scenes were shot in late Sep 1943, M-G-M had assigned his contract to Warner Bros.

The Gang's All Here was the first color film directed by Berkeley (although he did do the choreography for the 1930 two-strip Technicolor film *Whoopee*), and the extravagant production numbers were well received. While praising Berkeley's work, the *MPH* reviewer commented that the production numbers "are opulent in highly effective color combinations and are climaxed by a finale in the cubistic and modernistic tempo which is different from anything that has passed this reviewer's way since some of the abstract treatments employed by Walt Disney's *Fantasia*." Although some modern sources indicate that the film was banned in Brazil because of the giant bananas featured in "The Lady with Tutti-Frutti Hat" number, the film's file in the MPAA/PCA Collection at the AMPAS Library contained no information about censorship in Brazil and the film was approved for export to South American countries.

Box 11 Dec 1943. *DV* 26 Nov 1943, p. 3, 11. *FD* 29 Nov 1943, p. 5. *HR* 7 Jan 1943, p. 1. *HR* 1 Feb 1943, p. 8. *HR* 15 Feb 1943, p. 1. *HR* 16 Mar 1943, p. 3. *HR* 29 Mar 1943, p. 7. *HR* 30 Mar 1943, p. 6. *HR* 31 Mar 1943, p. 5. *HR* 6 Apr 1943, p. 4. *HR* 16 Apr 1943, p. 9. *HR* 21 Apr 1943, p. 1. *HR* 23 Apr 1943, p. 4. *HR* 25 Apr 1943, p. 11. *HR* 10 Jun 1943, p. 3. *HR* 2 Jul 1943, p. 11. *HR* 5 Aug 1943, p. 6. *HR* 27 Sep 1943, p. 12. *HR* 26 Nov 1943, p. 3. *HR* 27 Dec 1943, p. 7. *MPD* 29 Nov 1943. *MPH* 27 Nov 1943, p. 70. *MPHPD* 4 Dec 1943, p. 1653. *NYT* 16 May 1943. *NYT* 23 Dec 1943, p. 26. *Var* 1 Dec 1943, p. 10.

GANGS OF NEW YORK see **IT COULD HAPPEN TO YOU**

GANGWAY FOR TOMORROW (French Americans, Refugees)
RKO Radio Pictures, Inc. *Dist* RKO Radio Pictures, Inc. 1943; Brooklyn, New York opening: week of 16 Dec 1943; *Prod*: late Jun—mid-Jul 1943 [©RKO Radio Pictures, Inc.; 17 Nov 1943; LP12452]. Sd (RCA Sound System); b&w. 6,169 ft. 69 min. PCA cert no. 9489.

Prod John H. Auer. *Dir* John H. Auer. *Asst dir* Lloyd Richards. [*Dial dir* Dixie McCoy]. *Scr* Arch Oboler. *Orig story* Aladar Laszlo. *Dir of photog* Nicholas Musuraca. *Spec eff* Vernon L. Walker. *Art dir* Albert S. D'Agostino and Al Herman. *Ed* George Crone. *Set dec* Darrell Silvera and William Stevens. *Gowns* Edward Stevenson. *Mus dir* C. Bakaleinikoff. *Mus* Roy Webb. *Rec* Bailey Fesler. *Re-rec* James G. Stewart.

Cast: Margo [(*Lisette*)], John Carradine [(*Wellington*)], Robert Ryan [(*Joe Dunham*)], Amelita Ward [(*Mary Jones*)], William Terry [(*Bob Nolan*)], Harry Davenport [(*Fred Taylor*)], James Bell [(*Tom Burke*)], Charles Arnt [(*Jim Benson*)], Alan Carney [(*Swallow*)], Wally Brown [(*Sam*)], Erford Gage [(*Dan Barton*)], Richard Ryen [(*Colonel Mueller*)], Warren Hymer [(*Pete*)], Michael St. Angel, Don Dillaway [(*Mechanics*)], Sam McDaniel [(*Hank*)], John Wald [(*Radio announcer*)], [Leon Belasco (*French worker*)], [Gene Gary (*Russian worker*)], [Louis Donath (*Polish worker*)], [Bruce Edwards (*Rogan*)], [Carole Gallagher (*Peanuts*)], [Wheaton Chambers (*Priest*)], [Hope Landin (*Emma*)], [Earle Hodgins (*Constable*)], [Anne Kunde (*Sara Henry*)], [Theron Jackson (*Claremont*)], [Al Kunde (*Sam Kowalski*)], [Al Ferguson (*Ed Gilroy*)], [Elaine Riley (*Joe's girl*)], [Rita Corday (*Georgine*)], [Margaret Landry (*Yvette*)], [Robert Anderson (*Jean*)], [Richard Martin (*Jules*)], [Ida Shoemaker (*Grandma*)], [Jacques Lory (*François*)], [Alex Papana (*Paul*)], [Billy Roy (*George*)], [Louis Arco (*Squad officer*)], [Major Farrell (*Jacques*)], [Carl Ekberg (*Guard*)], [Egon Brecher (*Czech worker*)], [Dave Thursby (*Fogarty*)], [George Jackson (*Yugoslavian worker*)], [Gus Glassmire (*Employment clerk*)], [Bert Moorhouse (*Chairman of the board*)], [George Carleton (*Second boardman*)], [George Ford (*Naval recruiting officer*)], [David Newell (*Marine sergeant*)], [W. R. Denning (*Boardman*)], [Angelo Desfis, Kernan Cripps, Eddie Borden, Paul Lacy, Blanche Webb, Ben Watson, Charles Marsh, George Magrill, Harry Tenbrook, Lynton Brent, Bill Oakley, William J. O'Brien, James Farley, Bob Thom, Dick Rush (*Workers*)], [Leroy Strine (*Lieutenant*)], [Frank O'Connor (*Police officer*)], [Bob Evans, Josh Milton (*Soldiers*)], [Claire McDowell (*Old woman on street*)], [Babe Kane, June Booth (*Girls on street*)], [Lillian Elliott (*Burke's mother*)], [Edmund Glover, Robert Bice (*Stooges*)], [Edythe Elliott (*Mary's mother*)], [Hooper Atchley (*Desk clerk*)], [Don Kerr (*Bellhop*)], [John Sheehan (*Producer Bell*)], [Noelle DeLorme (*French girl in truck*)], [Frederick Brunn (*Sergeant*)], [George Melford, Chester Carlisle (*Judges*)], [Brandon Beach (*Worker/ Judge*)], [Jack Raymond (*Taxi driver*)], [Peggy Miller (*Girl*)], [Patti Brill (*Sis*)], [Gerald Pierce (*Messenger boy*)], [Bruce Cameron, Harro Meller, Harry Clay, John Bohn (*Officers*)].

Homefront, Drama. [*Print viewed*]. Jim Benson, the driver of a car carrying five defense workers to an aircraft manufacturing plant, invites his passengers home for dinner Sunday night and admits that he has made up fictional biographies about each of them in response to his wife's questions. Benson's story about Lisette, a French woman, triggers haunting memories of why she came to the United States: In Paris, during the war, Lisette used her work as a cabaret singer to hide her activities in the French underground. When Lisette and her freedom-fighter friends use a secret radio transmitter to interrupt Hitler's broadcast with a rendition of the "Marseillaise," a German colonel recognizes Lisette's voice, and she is arrested with the other members of her group. Betrayed by one of their own, the group is sentenced to die in front of a firing squad. After she accepts her life in exchange for entertaining the German troops, Lisette is loaded on a truck bound for prison. Lisette jumps from the rear of the truck, and returns to the radio transmitter where she broadcasts a warning about the traitor in their midst and memorializes her martyred friends. Coming out of her reverie, Lisette explains to Benson that after escaping from France, she came to America because her father was an American and she wanted to aid the war effort in any way possible.

Soon after Lisette finishes her story, Benson's car tire goes flat, and as the other passengers wait alongside the road, fellow defense worker Joe Dunham changes the tire. As he works, Joe remembers his pre-war life as a race car driver: Joe, who is planning to join the Air Corps after completing the Indianapolis race, is leading in the last lap when his tire blows and he loses control of his car. In the ensuing accident, Joe suffers injuries which render him ineligible for military service. His thoughts returning to the present, Joe finishes changing the tires, and the others climb back into the car.

The budding comraderie of his fellow passengers prompts Tom Burke to worry that he may have to recount his story: Before the war, Burke is a prison warden whose duties force him to supervise the execution of his younger brother, Dan Barton, an incorrigible criminal. As the hour of Dan's execution approaches, Burke reflects back to a year earlier, when he asked his brother to leave town before their mother discovered that her youngest son was a criminal. Dan defies his brother's request, and when their mother sees a newspaper headline identifying her son as the gunman who killed four men during a bank robbery, she dies, clutching Dan's photograph in her hand. Burke escorts Dan to the electric chair and is about to pull the switch when the phone rings. Ignoring the ringing phone, Burke electrocutes his brother and then answers the call from the governor pardoning Dan. Burke's thoughts return to the present when Wellington, another passenger in the car, asks him what he did before the war and he answers that he was in the legal business.

Benson's description of passenger Mary Jones as a "nice, pretty home girl" prompts her to think back to the triumphant night she won the Miss America pageant. No longer Miss Jones but Miss America, Mary foresakes her boyfriend, Bob Nolan, for her career. When Bob proposes, Mary insists upon postponing any thought of marriage until after she has completed her reign, and sets out to find fame in New York. Promised three song and dance numbers in a Broadway show, Mary sees her part reduced to a walk-on. Brokenhearted, Mary receives a letter from Bob, notifying her that he has enlisted in the Air Corps and is stationed in Australia. Benson's question about her boyfriend brings Mary back to the present, and she answers that he is still in Australia.

Benson's description of Wellington as an ex-banker prompts Wellington to reminisce about his travels as an erudite hobo. Arrested for vagrancy, Wellington is chastised by Judge Fred Taylor for failing to come to the defense of his country. Inspired by the judge's words, Wellington goes to work at the aircraft factory. As Wellington's thoughts return to the present, Benson's car arrives at the factory, and after agreeing to meet for dinner on Sunday, the workers link arms and enter the plant to the strains of "The Battle Hymn of the Republic." *Carpools. Defense plant workers. Aircraft industry. Automobile accidents. Beauty contests. Brothers. Executions. French. Hoboes. Miss America Beauty Pageant. Nazis. New York City–Broadway. Prison wardens. Race car drivers. Singers. Vocational obsession. War refugees. World War II–Resistance movements.*

Note: The working title of this film was *An American Story*. A *HR* production chart credits Les Milbrook as editor, but his participation in the completed film has not been confirmed. This was producer-director John Auer's first production for RKO. According to a news item in *HR*, the studio saved building material and labor by using the studio gate and machine shop as the setting for

the factory in the film. The *MPH* review commented that screenplay writer Arch Oboler, a prominent radio writer, employed radio dramatic techniques to great advantage in this film.

Box 6 Nov 1943. *DV* 2 Nov 1943, pp. 3-4. *FD* 3 Nov 1943, p. 7. *HR* 2 Jul 1943, p. 7. *HR* 7 Jul 1943, p. 6, 7. *HR* 16 Jul 1943, p. 6. *HR* 2 Nov 1943, p. 3. *MPH* 6 Nov 1943. *MPHPD* 2 Oct 1943, p. 1566. *MPHPD* 6 Nov 1943, p. 1614. *Var* 3 Nov 1943, p. 16. *Var* 22 Dec 1943, p. 12.

GAS HOUSE KIDS (Irish Americans, Italian Americans, Multi-ethnic)

Sigmund Neufeld Productions. *Dist* Producers Releasing Corp. 28 Oct **1946**; Prod: late Jul–mid-Aug 1946 [©Producers Releasing Corp.; 7 Oct 1946; LP685]. Sd (Western Electric Mirrophonic Recording); b&w. 66-68 min.

Series: Gas House Kids.

Prod Sigmund Neufeld. *Dir* Sam Newfield. *Asst dir* Stanley Neufeld and [Hack Kronish]. *Scr* Elsie Bricker, George Bricker and Raymond L. Schrock. *Original story* Elsie Bricker and George Bricker. *Dir of photog* Jack Greenhalgh. *Spec eff* Ray Mercer. *Art dir* Frank Sylos. *Film ed* Holbrook N. Todd. *Set dir* Elias H. Reif. *Master of props* Eugene C. Stone. *Mus dir* Leo Erdody. *Sd eng* John Carre. [*Sd* Charles Kenworthy]. *Dir of makeup* Tom McDonald. *Prod mgr* Bert Sternbach.

Cast: Robert Lowery [(*Eddie O'Brien*)], Billy Halop [(*Tony Albertini*)], Teala Loring [(*Colleen Flanagan*)], Carl Switzer [(*Sammy Levine*)], David Reed [(*Pat Flanagan*)], Rex Downing [(*One of the kids*)], Rocco Lanzo [(*One of the kids*)], Hope Landin [(*Mrs. O'Brien*)], Ralph Dunn [(*Police detective*)], Paul Bryar [(*Shadow Sorecki*)], Nanette Vallon, Charles Wilson.

Teenage, Drama. [*Print viewed*]. Everyone in Eddie O'Brien's neighborhood on the Lower East Side of New York City is excited when they hear that he is returning from World War II. Eddie's fiancée, Colleen Flanagan, however, is devastated when she learns from a letter that he wants to end their engagement. Mrs. O'Brien, Eddie's mother, consoles Colleen by insisting that she has misunderstood the letter and that Eddie certainly still loves her. Pat, Colleen's brother, overhears their conversation and tells the other members of his gang: Mickey Popopolous, Gus Schmidt, Sammy Levine and Tony Albertini. The boys still resent Eddie for his strict treatment of them when he was the neighborhood policeman, and now that they are convinced he has treated Colleen badly, they decide to ridicule him at his homecoming. They change their minds, however, when Eddie arrives permanently crippled by a war injury. Colleen persuades Eddie that his injury does not change her love for him, and he admits that he still loves her, but does not want to get married until he knows that he can support her. Colleen explains to Pat that she and Eddie had planned to buy a chicken farm in New Jersey, but they lack the money for a down payment. The boys then scheme to raise the needed funds, knowing that Eddie will not accept charity. After reading a newspaper story, one of the boys suggests that they try to capture bank robber Shadow Sorecki and collect a $10,000 reward. As this idea seems impractical, Pat proposes that Tony, who is an amateur boxer, try to fight K. O. Burke, a professional who has offered $200 to anyone who can last three rounds with him. That plan fails when Burke knocks Tony out in the second round. One day, Pat drives Colleen and Eddie to look at a farm for sale in New Jersey. The Jenkins, who own the farm, take to the couple and lower the asking price, but it is still too much for Colleen and Eddie. In New York, Tony gets into a dispute with Gaines, the rent collector. Later, Gaines tries to collect rent from tenants in the same building, who happen to be Sorecki's gang. Their last robbery attempt was thwarted by the police, and desperate for cash, the gang steals Gaines' rent money. In the ensuing struggle, the bag containing the money falls out the window to the alley below, and Gaines is killed by a blow to the head. Before the robbers can retrieve the money, Tony discovers it and tells the boys he found on the street three weeks earlier. The boys then open a bank account and write Mr. and Mrs. Jenkins a deposit check for the farm. When the boys return to New York, the gangsters corner Tony and demand the money, but when he recognizes Sorecki, they kidnap him. After dropping most of the gangsters at a hideout in the country, one drives Tony further into the country. Realizing that the man intends to kill him, Tony struggles with his captor and the car runs off a cliff. Meanwhile, Gaines' body is discovered and the police suspect Tony. Although Tony is missing, the rest of the boys are arrested. After hearing their story, Eddie offers to help them. Tony is finally discovered in a hospital where he has been unconscious. He

tells Eddie what happened and directs the police to Sorecki's hideout. The gang is rounded up, and Tony gets the reward money. Later, the judge paroles the boys to Eddie's custody, and he puts them to work on the farm. Criminals. Farms. Friendship. Handicapped. Veterans. Automobile accidents. Boxing. Brothers and sisters. Engagements. False accusations. Hospitals. Irish Americans. Italian Americans. Jews. Judges. Kidnapping. Landlords. Mothers and sons. Murder. New Jersey. New York City–East Side. Police. Rewards. War injuries.

Note: This film was the first in the "Gas House Kids" series. This series, like "The Little Tough Guys," "The East Side Kids" and "The Bowery Boys" series, which were produced from the late 1930s through the early 1950s, was loosely derived from "The Dead End Kids" series. The Dead End Kids first appeared in the 1938 Warner Bros. film *Crime School* (see *AFI Catalog of Feature Films, 1931-40*; F3.0873). Like the other series, "Gas House Kids" featured a gang of adolescent boys, living on New York City's East Side, who were not quite juvenile deliquents, but were frequently in trouble. Billy Halop, who stars in this film, had earlier appeared as one of the Dead End Kids and as one of the Little Tough Guys. Halop does not appear in the other Gas House Kids films, but Carl Switzer appears in all three. For more information on all of these series see the entry for *Crime School* in the *AFI Catalog of Feature Films, 1931-40*; F3.0873) and consult the Series Index under "The Dead End Kids," "The Little Tough Guys," "The East Side Kids," "The Bowery Boys" and "Gas House Kids."

DV 8 Oct 1946, p. 3. *FD* 9 Oct 1946, p. 8. *HR* 2 Aug 1946, p. 18. *HR* 9 Aug 1946, p. 18. *HR* 8 Oct 1946, p. 3. *MPHPD* 5 Oct 1946, p. 3238. *MPHPD* 12 Oct 1946, p. 3250.

GASHOUSE KIDS see **GAS HOUSE KIDS**

GATEWAY (Irish Americans)

Twentieth Century-Fox Film Corp.; Darryl F. Zanuck in charge of production. *Dist* Twentieth Century-Fox Film Corp. 5 Aug **1938**; Prod: 16 May–late Jun 1938 [©Twentieth Century-Fox Film Corp.; 5 Aug 1938; LP8344]. Sd (Western Electric Mirrophonic Recording); b&w. 8 reels, 6,657 ft. 73-74 min. PCA cert no. 4365.

Assoc prod Samuel G. Engel. *Dir* Alfred Werker. [*Asst dir* Charles Hall]. *Scr* Lamar Trotti. *Story* Walter Reisch. *Photog* Edward Cronjager. *Art dir* Bernard Herzbrun and Albert Hogsett. *Film ed* James B. Morley. *Set dec* Thomas Little. *Cost* Gwen Wakeling. *Mus dir* Arthur Lange. *Sd* Bernard Freericks and Roger Heman.

Cast: DON AMECHE (*Dick* [*Court*]), ARLEEN WHELAN (*Catherine* [*O'Shea*]), Gregory Ratoff (*Prince Michael Boris Alexis*), Binnie Barnes (*Mrs.* [*Fay*] *Sims*), Gilbert Roland (*Tony* [*Cadona*]), Raymond Walburn (*Mr.* [*Benjamin*] *McNutt*), John Carradine (*Leader of refugees*), Maurice Moscovich (*Grandpa Hlawek*), Harry Carey (*Commissioner Nelson*), Lyle Talbot (*Henry* [*Porter*]), Marjorie Gateson (*Mrs.* [*Arabella*] *McNutt*), Fritz Lieber [sic] (*Dr. Weilander*), Warren Hymer (*Guard-waiter*), Eddy Conrad (*Davonsky*), E. E. Clive (*Room steward*), Russell Hicks (*Ernest* [*Porter*]), Montague Shaw (*Captain*), Charles Coleman (*Purser*), Gerald Oliver Smith (*Englishman*), Albert Conti (*Count*), [George Du Count (*Pap Hlawek*)], [Angela De Witt (*Mama Hlawek*)], [Martha Bamattre (*Frau Hlawek*)], [Bobby Samrich, Tamara Ignation (*Hlawek children*)], [Virginia Brissac (*Friend of Mrs. McNutt*)], [William Wagner (*Friend of Mr. McNutt*)], [Joan Castle (*Sob sister*)], [Robert Lowery, Charles Tannen, Imboden Parrish, Robert Kellard, Robert Allen, Hal K. Dawson, Charles Williams, George Chandler (*Reporters*)], [Joan Carol (*Child*)], [Tom Ricketts (*Old man*)], [John Rogers, Larry Dodds (*Stewards*)], [Charles C. Wilson, Jack Stoney, Joseph Crehan, Davison Clark, Joe King, Selmer Jackson, Addison Richards (*Inspectors*)], [Hazel Keener (*Mother*)], [J. Anthony Hughes (*Irish inspector*)], [Rudolf Myzet, Nicholas Kobliansky (*Interpreters*)], [Egon Brecher (*Rabbi*)], [Freddie Walburn (*Boy*)], [Joseph De Stefani, Adolph Milar, Glen Cavender, Elisabeth Frohlich, Victor Delinsky, Dina Smirnova (*Immigrants*)], [C. Montague Shaw (*Captain*)], [Burr Caruth (*Old man*)], [Mary Gordon (*Scottish mother*)], [Henry Otho, Lee Shumway, Edward Gargan, Ralph Dunn, James Blaine, James Flavin, Eddie Hart (*Guards*)], [Lillian Harmer (*Matron*)], [Ben Welden, Edward Marr (*Motorboat men*)], [Helen Brown (*Nurse*)].

Social, Drama. [*Print viewed*]. Dick Court, a world-weary war correspondent traveling on an ocean liner to the United States, notices Catherine O'Shea below on the second-class deck dancing to music coming from the first-class area. Dick opens the gate separating the two classes and invites Catherine up. Although at first she refuses, they soon dance together. The next night, Catherine, in a dress borrowed from Dick's aunt, Fay Sims, accompanies Dick to dinner, where she confesses, to his chagrin, that she is coming to America from Dublin to be married. Benjamin McNutt, an American mayor, flirts with Catherine and then follows her to the deck for air. Shortly

thereafter, Dick and Fay find Catherine standing over McNutt's prone body. Catherine says that McNutt tried to kiss her and that she pushed him back, whereupon he slipped and hit his head. When he revives, McNutt, to protect himself, says that Catherine attacked him. The incident makes Walter Winchell's column, and when the boat approaches the Statue of Liberty, both Catherine and Fay, who had been denied admission several years earlier, are sent to Ellis Island for immigration hearings before a board of inquiry. At Ellis Island, Catherine tries to embrace her fiancé, Henry Porter, whom she met when he visited Ireland, but Henry pulls away and his suspicious brother Ernest tells of their family's displeasure with the publicity. Tony Cadona, an underworld figure under investigation, offers to help Catherine, but Dick, who knows that a woman friend of Tony's died supposedly from a fall from a window, warns him to lay off. At night, Catherine confesses to Fay that should her marriage plans fail, she could never go back to Dublin and face her family. At the inquiry, Dick, upon seeing the snooty Henry, talks about his own strong feelings for Catherine, and when Ernest then refuses to let his brother marry Catherine, the commissioner is forced to order her to return home on the boat the next day. Greatly upset with Dick, Catherine refuses to listen to his proposal of marriage. Hoping to change Henry's mind about her, Catherine accepts Tony's offer to help her illegally get into the country. Dick sees them together and, after another immigrant under investigation steals keys for him from a guard, he sneaks into Catherine's room and tries to convince her not to go with Tony. She calls a matron, and Dick is locked up with the "undesirables" who are awaiting deportation. When Fay learns that Catherine is planning to swim with Tony to a boat waiting in the fog, she convinces her to let her go with them so that she can stop her daughter from marrying someone whom she feels is no good. The leader of the deportees knocks Dick out and takes the keys from him, then leads the others out of their cells in an escape attempt. Because the riot attracts the police, Tony and Catherine do not swim to the boat, but Fay, unaware that the men in the boat have left because of the riot, dives in. Meanwhile, the leader of the revolt threatens to kill Dick and some guards if he is not let out. Dick knocks the leader down and fights him, but he himself is knocked out with a gun and taken to the hospital. The riot is quelled, and Tony is captured by guards and arrested on an income tax matter. He vows to Catherine that he will see that Dick is killed. Fay, who is rescued by a tugboat, tells Catherine that Tony means what he says, and Catherine visits Dick in the hospital to warn him. He says that he is not afraid and apologizes to her. When she kisses him goodbye, as she prepares to return to Ireland, they realize that they really love each other, and they soon marry and take the ferry to New York. *Deportation. Immigrants. Irish Americans. New York City–Ellis Island. Romance. Transformation.* Class distinction. Engagements. Escapes. Mayors. Ocean liners. Refugees, Political. Reporters. Riots. Russians. Scandal. Scientists. Walter Winchell.

Note: The onscreen credits list actor Fritz Leiber as "Fritz Lieber." The working title of this film was *Ellis Island.* According to a *HR* news item from Dec 1937, Twentieth Century-Fox purchased an original story entitled "Ellis Island" from "Prince" Michael Romanoff, known as an impostor who posed as a member of the Romanoff dynasty. In the late 1930s, he opened Romanoff's restaurant in Beverly Hills and became wealthy with a chain of restaurants. The story, according to the news item, was to star Annabella, Raymond Griffith was to produce, and Don Ettlinger and Karl Tunberg were assigned to write the screenplay. According to the Twentieth Century-Fox Produced Scripts Collection at the UCLA Theater Arts Library, Edith Skouras and Kathryn Scola, rather than Ettlinger and Tunberg, prepared a story outline, dated 17 Jan 1938. A 9 Feb 1938 *HR* news item states that the studio purchased an original story by Walter Reisch, also entitled "Ellis Island." That story, dated 29 Jan 1938, is in the Produced Scripts Collection. All subsequent work in the Produced Scripts Collection is by Lamar Trotti. It is not known if the story by Reisch, who received screen credit, was based on the story by Romanoff, or if any material contributed by Romanoff, Ettlinger, Tunberg, Skouras or Scola was included in the final film. *HR* production charts include Romanoff in the cast, but according to *NYT*, "Prince Mike, an old friend of the Bureau of Immigration, was going to play himself—that is, a bogus Russian nobleman. But Gregory Ratoff had to be substituted at the last minute because, it seems, Prince Mike wasn't bogus enough!"

According to a *HR* news item, Twentieth Century-Fox offered Maurice Conn, who produced a film entitled *Ellis Island* in 1936 for Invincible (see above), $7,500 for a release to the title, but Conn turned them down. Twentieth Century-Fox then offered $100 to anyone working at the studio who could come up with a suitable new title. According to a *HR* news item, after critics acclaimed Arleen Whelan for her performance in *Kidnapped* (see *AFI Catalog of Feature Films, 1931-40*;F3. 2279), her part was enlarged for this film. Gladys George, J. Edward Bromberg, George Barbier and Sidney Blackmer are

listed as cast members in *HR* production charts, but their participation in the final film is doubtful. According to modern sources, Ratoff directed the second unit, Leyland Hodgson played the ship's headwaiter, and James and Robert Haxton, Jr., seven-month-old twins, played the Hlawek baby. *FD* called the film a "Grand Hotel idea based on Ellis Island."

Box 6 Aug 1938. *DV* 29 Jul 1938, p. 3. *FD* 2 Aug 1938, p. 7. *HR* 14 Dec 1937, p. 1. *HR* 9 Feb 1938, p. 1. *HR* 16 May 1938, p. 13. *HR* 20 May 1938, p. 1. *HR* 23 Jun 1938, p. 4. *HR* 27 Jun 1938, p. 7. *HR* 29 Jul 1938, p. 3. *MPD* 5 Aug 1938, p. 5. *MPH* 2 Jul 1938, p. 29. *MPH* 6 Aug 1938, p. 46. *NYT* 8 Aug 1938, p. 9. *Var* 10 Aug 1938, p. 12.

GATLING GUN *see* **SIEGE AT RED RIVER**

GAUCHOS OF ELDORADO (Latino)

Republic Pictures Corp. *Dist* Republic Pictures Corp. 24 Oct **1941**; Prod: early Sep—mid-Sep 1941 [©Republic Pictures Corp.; 24 Oct 1941; LP10802]. Sd (RCA Sound System); b&w. 6 reels, 5,871 ft. 54 or 56 min. Passed by the National Board of Review. PCA cert no. 7718.

Series: The Three Mesquiteers.

Assoc prod Louis Gray. *Dir* Les Orlebeck. [*Asst dir* Harry Knight]. *Scr* Albert DeMond. *Story* Earle Snell. *Photog* Reggie Lanning. *Film ed* Charles Craft. *Mus dir* Cy Feuer. *Prod mgr* Al Wilson.

Song(s): "The Bird and the Wolf" by Jule Styne and Sol Meyer.

Source: Based on characters created by William Colt MacDonald.

Cast: Bob Steele (*"Tucson" Smith*), Tom Tyler (*"Stony" Brooke*), Rufe Davis (*"Lullaby" Joslin*), Lois Collier [(*Ellen*)], Duncan Renaldo [(*José Ojara, also known as The Gaucho*)], Rosina Galli [(*Isabella Ojara*)], Norman Willis [(*Bart Braden*)], William Ruhl [(*Samuel Tyndal*)], Tony Roux [(*Miguel*)], Raphael Bennett [(*Monk Stevens*)], Yakima Canutt [(*Snakes*)], [J. Merrill Holmes (*Casey*)], [Edmund Cobb (*Sheriff*)], [Casey Johnson (*Little José Ojara*)], [Bud Geary (*Tex*)], [Terry Frost (*Hank*)], [Eddie Dean (*Buck*)], [Earle S. Dewey (*Mayor*)], [John Merton (*The Curly Kid*)], [Roy Steele (*Madden*)], [Margaret Fealy (*Grandmother*)], [Eddie Cherkose (*Bank teller*)], [Virginia Farmer (*Agatha*)], [Si Jenks (*County clerk*)].

Western. [*Print viewed*]. After Bart Braden's gang robs a bank run by Samuel Tyndal, José Ojara, a gang member known as "The Gaucho," finds among the confiscated papers a mortgage for the Ojara ranch in Texas. José reminisces about his mother Isabella, the "madrecita" whom he has not seen for many years, and vows to pay the $5,000 due on her ranch. Meanwhile, Braden confers with cohort Monk Stevens about a geologist's report on the Ojara ranch, which has valuable bauxite deposits. After José steals $5,000 from Braden and escapes from the gang, he meets "Stony" Brooke, "Tucson" Smith and "Lullaby" Joslin, friends who are known as The Three Mesquiteers. The Mesquiteers share their dinner with José, who tells them that he is going to Black Rock to see his "sweetheart." As the gang approaches in the distance, José rides off, and when the Mesquiteers follow to help him, he draws the gang's fire as they are about to ambush the Mesquiteers. The gang is routed, but José is fatally injured. Before he dies, José asks them to take a medal to his sweetheart, and after finding the money and the mortgage papers, the Mesquiteers decide to carry on with José's mission. Upon arriving at the Ojara ranch, the Mesquiteers are dismayed to find that Isabella believes that Tucson is José, for he is carrying the medal given to José by his mother. Touched by Isabella's joy at finding her long-lost son, the Mesquiteers cannot bring themselves to tell her the truth, and so go to pay off the mortgage. Tyndal is upset, for he wanted to foreclose on the ranch and obtain rights to the bauxite, but when a clerk tells him that the Mesquiteers are using money stolen in the robbery, Tyndal has the Mesquiteers arrested. After explaining that they found the money, the Mesquiteers are released, and promise to pay off the mortgage and get enough money so that Isabella can reopen the bauxite mine. Meanwhile, Braden and Stevens make a deal with Tyndal to get the Mesquiteers out of the way in exchange for a half-interest in the mine once Tyndal forecloses on Isabella's land. When the Mesquiteers arrive in town, however, they capture Braden and turn him in for a $10,000 reward. Returning to the ranch, Tucson is amazed by the appearance of little José, whom José's sister-in-law has brought to live with him. Further complications ensue when the sheriff arrives to arrest the Mesquiteers for José's murder. Tucson explains to the sheriff and Isabella that he is not José, but that the Mesquiteers did not kill him. Escaping from the sheriff, who is working with Tyndal, the Mesquiteers cash the reward check and are about to pay off the mortgage when they learn that the gang has kidnapped little José and are demanding a $10,000 ransom. Despite a trap the gang has set up, the Mesquiteers rescue little José and

apprehend Tyndal, Braden and Stevens. With the mortgage paid and the mine reopened, all is well at the Ojara ranch as the Mesquiteers reassure Isabella of José's honesty and love for her, then set off in search of another adventure. *Bankers. Cowboys. Gangs. Mistaken identity. Mothers and sons.* Bank robberies. Bauxite. Children. Kidnapping. Long-lost relatives. Mines. Mortgages. Rescues. Rewards. Sheriffs.

Note: The opening title card to the film reads "Republic Pictures presents The Three Mesquiteers in *Gauchos of Eldorado*," followed by pictures of Bob Steele, Tom Tyler and Rufe Davis with their names and character names superimposed. Although *HR* news items stated that Anthony Coldway and Ivan Goff were working on the screenplay of this film, their contribution to the completed picture has not been confirmed. Modern sources include Ted Mapes, Bob Woodward, Horace Carpenter and Ray Jones in the cast. Between 1939 and 1940, Duncan Renaldo played one of The Three Mesquiteers in seven films, in which he was called "Renaldo" or "Rico." For more information about the series, consult the Series Index and the entry for *The Three Mesquiteers* in *AFI Catalog of Feature Films, 1931-40*; F3.4617.

Box 25 Oct 1941. *DV* 5 Dec 1941. *FD* 24 Oct 1941, p. 6. *HR* 2 Apr 1941, p. 5. *HR* 13 Aug 1941, p. 4. *HR* 5 Sep 1941, p. 10. *HR* 12 Sep 1941, p. 10. *MPH* 25 Oct 1941. *MPHPD* 25 Oct 1941, p. 330. *Var* 17 Dec 1941, p. 8.

THE GAY AMIGO (Latino)

Inter-American Productions, Inc. *Dist* United Artists Corp. 13 May 1949; Prod: late Jul—early Aug 1948 [©Inter-American Productions, Inc.; 13 May 1949; LP2484]. Sd; b&w. 5,794 ft. 61-62 or 64 min. PCA cert no. 13333.

Series: The Cisco Kid.

Prod PHILIP N. KRASNE. *Pres* PHILIP N. KRASNE. *Assoc prod* Duncan Renaldo. *Dir* Wallace Fox. [*Asst dir* Buddy Messinger and Larry Chapman]. *Orig scr* Doris Schroeder. *Cine* Ernest Miller. [*Cam op* Archie Dalzell]. [*Stills* Bill Crosby]. [*Art dir* Frank Dexter]. *Film ed* Martin Cohn. [*Set dec* Vin Taylor]. *Mus comp and dir* Albert Glasser. *Sd eng* Ferroll Redd. *Makeup* Ted Larsen. *Prod mgr* Dick L'Estrange. [*Scr supv* Boyd Blackburn]. [*Grip* Stanley Levin and Joe Carpenter].

Source: Based on the character created by O. Henry.

Cast: Duncan Renaldo ([*The*] *Cisco* [*Kid*]), Leo Carrillo (*Pancho*), Armida [(*Rosita*)], Joe Sawyer [(*Sergeant McNulty*)], Walter Baldwin [(*Stoneham*)], Fred Kohler, Jr. [(*Bill Brack*)], Kenneth MacDonald [(*Captain Lewis*)], George De Normand [(*Corporal*)], Clayton Moore [(*Lieutenant*)], Fred Crane [(*Duke*)], Helen Servis [(*Old maid*)], Beverly Jons [(*Girl*)], Bud Osborne [(*Driver*)], Sam Flint [(*Ed Paulsen*)].

Western. [*Print viewed*]. While riding near the Mexican border in the Arizona territory, two Mexican-Americans, Cisco and Pancho, hear gunshots. A short distance away, they see a cavalry platoon chase a gang of bandits into Mexico. Capt. Lewis orders his men to stop at the border and then notices Cisco and Pancho. Mistaking him for the gang's leader, Lewis directs his men to follow Cisco, but Cisco and Pancho escape. Later, Cisco and Pancho discover one of the slain bandits, who is dressed in Mexican clothes, and recognize him as an American named Pete Harmon. Pancho contemplates stealing Harmon's fancy belt, but Cisco talks him out of it. Later, in a nearby town, the captain sees Cisco, whom he recognizes as the infamous bandit known as "The Cisco Kid." He chases Cisco and Pancho into a cantina, where Rosita, the girl friend of Lewis' bumbling sergeant, McNulty, works as a waitress, and arrests them. Lewis takes them to cavalry headquarters, but is soon forced to release them due to lack of evidence. Believing that eventually Cisco and Pancho will lead them to the rest of the gang, the captain orders McNulty to follow them. Later, at the office of the *Arizona Globe*, the editor, Stoneham, writes an article demanding the bandits' immediate arrest. Cisco and Pancho eavesdrop on their conversation, then visit the cantina, where Pancho notices that Rosita is wearing Harmon's belt. When they ask her about the belt, Rosita tells them that blacksmith Bill Brack gave it to her. After news arrives that the bandits killed Stoneham's friend Ed Paulsen, McNulty arrests Cisco and Pancho. McNulty then takes them back to headquarters, but they quickly escape through the bathroom window. Later, Cisco and Pancho hold up a stagecoach and steal the passengers' jewelry and money. Then, Cisco enters the newspaper office with his gun drawn and orders the typesetter, Thompson, to take dictation, beginning with the headline "Mexican Bandits Strike Again." When Stoneham enters, Cisco grabs Stoneham's cache of stolen property and locks him and Thompson in a supply closet. Later, Brack asks Thompson for his share of the gang's latest haul, but Thompson explains that Cisco robbed them. The bandits then try to escape with large quantities of stolen gold, but are

detained by Cisco and Pancho. When the cavalrymen arrive and realize that the gang leaders are actually Stoneham and Brack, they offer their apologies and thanks to Cisco and Pancho. *Bandits. Editors. Mexican Americans. United States. Army. Cavalry. Arizona. Blacksmiths. Cantinas. Clothes. Corpses. Disguise. Eavesdropping. Escapes. False arrests. Gold. Gunshot wounds. Mexican-American border region. Mistaken identity. Newspapers. Officers (Military). Stagecoach robberies. Statehood (American politics). Waitresses.*

Note: The working title of this film was *Adventures of the Cisco Kid*. The opening title card reads: "Philip N. Krasne presents The Cisco Kid in *The Gay Amigo*." HR production charts include Barbara Billingsley, John Litel and Stanley Andrews in the cast, but their participation in the final film has not been confirmed. Modern sources include Al Ferguson and David Sharpe in the cast. This was the second film in United Artists' Cisco Kid series. For additional information on the series, please consult the Series Index and see the above entry for *The Cisco Kid*.

Box 28 May 1949. *DV* 6 May 1949, p. 3. *FD* 23 May 1949, p. 4. *HR* 30 Jul 1948, p. 13. *HR* 6 May 1949, p. 3. *MPHPD* 28 May 1949, p. 4627. *Var* 18 May 1949, p. 8.

THE GAY CABALLERO (Latino)

Twentieth Century-Fox Film Corp. *Dist* Twentieth Century-Fox Film Corp. 4 Oct 1940; Prod: 21 May—early-Jun and 5 Aug—13 Aug 1940 [©Twentieth Century-Fox Film Corp.; 4 Oct 1940; LP10085]. Sd (Western Electric Mirrophonic Recording); b&w. 6 reels, 5,050 ft. 57-58 min. PCA cert no. 6384.

Series: The Cisco Kid.

Assoc prod Walter Morosco and Ralph Dietrich. *Dir* Otto Brower. [*Asst dir* William Eckhardt]. *Scr* Albert Duffy and John Larkin. *Orig story* Walter Bullock and Albert Duffy. *Dir of photog* Edward Cronjager. *Art dir* Richard Day and Chester Gore. *Film ed* Harry Reynolds. *Set dec* Thomas Little. *Cost* Herschel. *Mus dir* Emil Newman. *Sd* Arthur von Kirbach and Harry M. Leonard. [*Publicity dir* Harry Brand]. [*Knife thrower* Steve Clemento].

Source: Based on the character "The Cisco Kid" created by O. Henry.

Cast: Cesar Romero (*The Cisco Kid*), Sheila Ryan [(*Susan Wetherby*)], Robert Sterling [(*Billy Brewster*)], Chris-Pin Martin [(*Gordito*)], Janet Beecher [(*Kate Brewster*)], Edmund MacDonald [(*Joe Turner*)], Jacqueline Dalya [(*Carmelita*)], [Montague Shaw (*George Wetherby*)], [Hooper Atchley (*Sheriff McBride*)], [George Magrill (*Deputy sheriff*)], [Jim Pierce, Ethan Laidlaw, John Byron (*Bandits*)], [Tom London (*Rancher*)], [Dave Morris (*Passenger*)], [Jack Stoney (*Stage guard*)], [Lee Shumway (*Stage driver*)], [LeRoy Mason (*Deputy*)], [Frank Lackteen (*Peon*)].

Western. [*Print viewed*]. While riding through the West in 1889, the Cisco Kid and his sidekick Gordito discover a grave with a headstone reading, "Here lies the Cisco Kid." Surprised to learn that he is dead, Cisco questions Carmelita, who is weeping by the grave. Carmelita, who works as a servant for rancher Kate Brewster, explains that the buried man was her fiancé Manuel, who was accused of being the notorious bandit and then killed by Kate's foreman, Joe Turner. Just then, Cisco and Gordito see three men try to rob the passengers of a covered wagon. After scattering the would-be thieves, Cisco finds out that the passengers are Englishman George Wetherby and his daughter Susan. The Wetherbys are on their way to the Brewster ranch, of which they are purchasing a parcel of from Kate. Cisco and Gordito accompany the Wetherbys to the ranch, where they hope to discover Turner's motive for framing and murdering Manuel. At the ranch, they meet Kate and her nephew Billy, who has just been made a sheriff's deputy. At dinner that night, Turner relates how the alleged Cisco Kid pillaged the land and livestock intended for the Wetherbys before Turner killed him. George is undeterred by the threat of bandits, and confides that he is investing all of his money in the land. The three men who tried to rob him then arrive at the ranch, and despite George's protests, Kate insists that they be allowed to stay, as her late husband always declared that the ranch was a sanctuary for any visitor. After dinner, Kate castigates Turner for allowing the three men, who are his henchmen, to come to the ranch. Kate and Turner are in league to rob George and drive him away, because selling the land, which George was mistakenly allotted by the bank, will divide Kate's ranch in two. While Kate and Turner scheme to rob the Wells Fargo stagecoach, which will be carrying George's money, Cisco realizes that they are behind the destruction of George's land and merely blamed it on the fake Cisco Kid as an alibi. Later, Kate reveals that she knows Cisco's real identity, even though he is using the name Señor Chiquelo, but he warns her that he will not desert the

Wetherbys. The next day, Sheriff McBride tries to arrest Cisco, but he claims the sanctuary of Kate's ranch. Billy and George, believing that Cisco is a truly dangerous desperado, turn against him, but Susan maintains that he is trustworthy. Later that night, Kate and Turner plan on setting Cisco up by luring him away from the ranch while Turner impersonates him and robs the stagecoach. The ruse works, and Cisco and Gordito return to the ranch after McBride is told of the robbery. Gordito is apprehended while Cisco escapes, but Cisco is captured the next day when he tries to free his friend. Cisco bests the deceitful Turner in a fair draw when he escapes later, then he and Gordito prevent Kate and her henchmen from stealing George's money, which was not taken in the stagecoach robbery. Kate is killed when her wagon overturns during the chase and crushes her. Cisco explains her schemes to George and Susan, but warns them not to tell the naïve Billy. He then escapes with Gordito as McBride's posse comes after them. *Bandits. English. Frame-ups. Fraud. Mexican Americans. Ranch foremen. Women ranchers. Accidental death. Aunts. Deputies. Fathers and daughters. Graves. Gunfights. Jailbreaks. Mistaken identity. Servants. Stagecoach robberies.*

Note: The end credits were missing from the print viewed. This film's working title was *Ghost of the Cisco Kid*. According to *HR* news items, the picture was partially filmed on location at Lone Pine, CA, and production was suspended for two months after Cesar Romero sustained a broken leg. According to a Twentieth Century-Fox publicity release, however, Romero was suffering from "para-typhoid" at the time of the film's suspension. Director Otto Brower acted as second unit director on *Brigham Young-Frontiersman* (see *AFI Catalog of Feature Films, 1931-40*; F3.0844) and directed *Youth Will Be Served* (see *AFI Catalog of Feature Films, 1931-40*; F3.5269) while Romero was recovering. According to a *HR* news item, Twentieth Century-Fox decided to drop the name "Cisco Kid" from the titles in the series in the belief that "the titles are often confusing to the public as to whether the picture is a different one from predecessors." For more information about the series, please consult the Series Index and see the entry above for *The Cisco Kid*.

Box 28 Sep 1940. *DV* 23 Sep 1940, p. 3. *FD* 28 Oct 1940, p. 5. *HR* 20 May 1940, p. 10. *HR* 12 Jun 1940, p. 1. *HR* 15 Jun 1940, p. 7. *HR* 19 Jun 1940, p. 3. *HR* 20 Jun 1940, p. 3. *HR* 29 Jul 1940, p. 9. *HR* 5 Aug 1940, p. 14. *HR* 14 Aug 1940, p. 2. *HR* 23 Sep 1940, p. 3. *MPD* 24 Sep 1940, p. 7. *MPH* 28 Sep 1940, p. 80. *Var* 25 Sep 1940.

THE GAY CAVALIER (Latino)

Monogram Pictures Corp. *Dist* Monogram Pictures Corp. 30 Mar **1946**; Prod: Dec 1945 [©Monogram Pictures Corp.; 15 Mar 1946; LP208]. Sd (Western Electric Mirrophonic Sound); b&w. 62 or 64-65 min. PCA cert no. 11455.

Series: The Cisco Kid.

Prod Scott R. Dunlap. *Dir* William Nigh. *Asst dir* Eddie Davis. *Orig story and scr* Charles S. Belden. *Foreword* Sidney Sutherland. *Dir of photog* Harry Neumann. [*2d cam* William Clothier]. [*Spec eff* Larry Glickman and Mario Castegnaro]. [*Art dir* Harry Hickson]. *Film ed* Fred Maguire. *Ward* Harry Bourne. *Mus dir* Edward Kay. *Rec eng* Frank McWhorter. [*Re-rec and eff mixer* Joseph I. Kane]. [*Mus mixer* William H. Wilmarth]. *Prod mgr* Charles Bigelow. *Tech dir* Ernest Hickson.

Song(s): "One Kiss" and "The Gay Caballero," music and lyrics by Ramsay Ames; "Ride, Amigo, Ride," music by Charles Rosoff, lyrics by Eddie Cherkose; and traditional Mexican songs.

Source: Based on the character created by O. Henry.

Cast: Gilbert Roland [(*The Cisco Kid*)], Martin Garralaga (*Don Felipe*), Nacho Galindo (*Baby*), Ramsay Ames (*Pepita*), Helen Gerald (*Angela*), Tristram Coffin (*Lawton*), Drew Allen (*Juan*), Iris Flores (*Fisherman's wife*), John Merton (*Lewis*), Frank La Rue (*Graham*), [Joseph Burlando (*Padre*)], [Pierre Andre, Iris Bocignon (*Dancers*)], [Ralph Johns, Dusty Rhodes, Bob Butt, Terry Frost, Delmar Costello, Alex Montoya, Mike J. Rodriguez, Jack La Tour, Artie Ortego (*Members of Cisco's gang*)], [Clem Fuller (*Driver of buggy*)], [Lynton Brent (*Guard*)], [Elvira Aldana (*Girl who bums*)], [Dorothy Michaels, Don Driggers (*Guests*)], [Ernie Adams, Larry Steers, Jack Cheatham (*Creditors*)], [Raphael Bennett (*Miguel*)], [Eddie Majors, Dee Cooper (*Bandits*)].

Western, Comedy-drama, with songs. [*Print viewed*]. In 1850 The Cisco Kid makes another annual pilgrimage to the California grave of his father, a former bandit. To atone for his father's crimes, Cisco has spent his life stealing from the rich to give to the poor. At a nearby ranch, Don Felipe is preparing for the marriage of his daughter Angela to a wealthy American businessman, Lawton. Although Angela is in love with Juan, she agrees to marry Lawton in the hope that he will pay Don Felipe's debts and save the ranch. On the road to the ranch, a stagecoach carrying money given by the poor

to build a new church is held up by bandits who claim to be the Cisco Kid's gang. Later, Cisco and his men find the injured driver and learn of the accusations against them. Before he dies, the driver also tells them that another injured man was taken to Don Felipe's ranch. When Lawton, the actual robber, arrives at the ranch, he spreads the rumor that Cisco was responsible for the theft. Pepita, Angela's sister, does not like Lawton and encourages Juan to fight for Angela. Later Cisco appears at the hacienda and encounters Pepita. Attracted to the dashing bandit, Pepita listens sympathetically when he tells her that Cisco's men would never steal money from the poor. Finding Lawton alone, Cisco tries to force him to confess, but they are seen by one of Lawton's men, who gives chase. Cisco escapes and hides in Pepita's room. Meanwhile, outside, an eavesdropping Juan learns where the stolen money is hidden. Juan follows Cisco to his camp and begs to join his fight against Lawton. Juan, Cisco, and Cisco's sidekick, Baby, sneak into the outlaw's hideout. Although one bandit escapes, the trio overcomes the others, and later Cisco returns the stolen money to the church. Alerted by the escaped bandit, Lawton tells Don Felipe that the money he was bringing for the ranch was stolen in the stagecoach robbery. Don Felipe then agrees to sign over the ranch without the money. When Cisco learns of the change in plans, he hurries to the hacienda with Juan. Cisco stops the wedding and engages Lawton in a sword fight. As Pepita watches breathlessly, Cisco overcomes Lawton. Now that he has made it possible for Angela to marry Juan, Cisco kisses Pepita and regretfully leaves the ranch for good. *Bandits. California–History–1846-1850. Marriage-Arranged. Churches. Fathers and daughters. Graves. Haciendas. Sisters. Spaniards. Stagecoach robberies. Sword fights. Womanizers.*

Note: The credits read: The Cisco Kid in *The Gay Cavalier*. The film begins with the following written foreword: "California—a new land of wealth and opportunity—of lovely women and gallant horsemen—of glamor, romance, mystery and—INTRIGUE!—Such was the California of 1850." Gilbert Roland was the fourth actor to play the part of "The Cisco Kid." The others were Warner Baxter, Cesar Romero and Duncan Renaldo. For more information on the series consult the Series Index and see the entry above for *The Cisco Kid*.

Box 6 Apr 1946. *DV* 10 Apr 1946, p. 3. *HR* 14 Dec 1945, p. 18. *HR* 21 Dec 1945, p. 16. *HR* 10 Apr 1946, p. 3. *MPHPD* 27 Apr 1946, p. 2963. *MPHPD* 15 Jun 1946, p. 3042.

THE GAY DECEIVER (*foreign version*) see SU ÚLTIMA NOCHE

THE GAY DEFENDER (Latino)

Paramount Famous Lasky Corp. 10 Dec **1927** [©Paramount Famous Lasky Corp.; 10 Dec 1927; LP24740]. Si; b&w. 7 reels, 6,376 ft.

Pres Adolph Zukor and Jesse L. Lasky. *Dir* Gregory La Cava. *Scen and adpt* Ray Harris, Sam Mintz and Kenneth Raisbeck. *Story* Grover Jones. *Titles* George Marion, Jr. and Herman Mankiewicz. *Photog* Edward Cronjager.

Cast: Richard Dix (*Joaquin Murrieta*), Thelma Todd (*Ruth Ainsworth*), Fred Kohler (*Jake Hamby*), Jerry Mandy (*Chombo*), Robert Brower (*Ferdinand Murrieta*), Harry Holden (*Padre Sebastian*), Fred Esmelton (*Commissioner Ainsworth*), Frances Raymond (*Aunt Emily*), Ernie S. Adams (*Bart Hamby*).

Romance. Joaquin Murrieta, son of Ferdinand, a Spanish land baron of California, falls in love with Ruth Ainsworth, daughter of the U. S. Land Commissioner. Bart Hamby is caught by Chombo, Joaquin's faithful servant, stealing gold from the Murrieta property, but the carefree Joaquin has him released. Jake, the villain's brother, decides to engage in a duel with Joaquin and steal the gold, but their meeting ends in a deadlock. Jake tries to persuade Ainsworth to aid him in illegal confiscation of gold lands; when he refuses, Jake shoots him with Joaquin's pistol. Joaquin seeks Ainsworth for consent to marry Ruth; set up through congratulatory drinks, he is framed for the murder, but he escapes and becomes a fugitive. The Hamby gang burns the hacienda and doubles the taxes, and Joaquin becomes a defender of the people, rescues Ruth from the villains, and takes revenge on Jake, the murderer of his father. *California. Duels. Frame-ups. Government officials. Land barons. Land rights. Murder. Revenge. Spanish Americans.*

FD 1 Jan 1928. *MPW* 31 Dec 1927. *NYT* 26 Dec 1927, p. 26. *Var* 28 Dec 1927, p. 16.

THE GAY NINETIES see SUNBONNET SUE

THE GAY SENORITA (Latino)

Columbia Pictures Corp. *Dist* Columbia Pictures Corp. 9 Aug **1945**; Prod: 19 Apr—11 May 1945 [©Columbia Pictures Corp.; 13 Jul 1945; LP13390]. Sd (Western Electric Mirrophonic Recording); b&w. 6,333 ft. 68-69 min. PCA cert no. 10976.

Prod Jay Gorney. *Dir* Arthur Dreifuss. [*Asst dir* Milton Feldman]. *Scr* Edward Eliscu. *Orig story* J. Robert Bren. *Dir of photog* Burnett Guffey. [*2d cam* Gert Andersen]. *Art dir* Jerome Pycha, Jr. *Film ed* Al Clark. *Set dec* Herman Schoenbrun. [*Mus mixer* Edwin L. Wetzel]. *Dances staged by* Antonio Triana. [*Sd eng* William Randall]. [*Research dir* Vera Mikol].

Song(s): "Buenas Noches," words and music by Serge Walter and Don George; "Juarez and Lincoln," words and music by Henry Myers, Edward Eliscu and Jay Gorney; "Tico-Tico no fuba," words and music by Zequinha de Abreu; "Cielito lindo" and "Allá en el Rancho Grande," traditional; "Jarabe tapatio," "Una linda mujer," "Samba alegre" and "Negra Leonor," composers undetermined.

Cast: Jinx Falkenburg [(*Elena Sandoval*)], Jim Bannon [(*Phil Frentiss, also known as Phil Dolan*)], Steve Cochran [(*Tomas Obrion, also known as Tim O'Brien*)], Corinna Mura [(*Corinna Mura*)], Isabelita [(*Chiquita*)], Thurston Hall [(*J. J. Frentiss*)], Isabel Withers [(*Kitty*)], Marguerita Sylva [(*Dona Maria Sandoval*)], [Luisita Triana (*Loreto*)], [Lola Montes (*Lola Montez*)], [Tommy Cook (*Paco*)], [Nina Bara (*Lupita*)], [Leander de Cordova (*Padre Anselmo*)], [Eddie Fields (*Pablo*)], [Antonio Triana (*Anastasio*)], [and The Tico Tico Guitars], [Frank Saucedo (*Carlos*)], [Antonio Arrias (*Manuelito*)], [Jose Alvarado (*Jose*)], [Charles Coleman (*Griggs*)], [George Lewis (*Torreon*)], [Alfred Sabato (*Allego*)], [Antonio Filauri (*Juan*)].

Comedy-drama, with songs. [*Print viewed*]. In the Mexican-American quarter of a large West Coast city, matriarch Dona Maria Sandoval hosts a fiesta to unveil her design for a street that will showcase Latin American crafts and culture. The day's festivities are darkened by a rumor concerning the plans of American businessman J. J. Frentiss, who wants to build a warehouse on the land intended for Sandoval Lane. The next day, Dona Maria and her nieces, Elena and Loreto, visit J. J. at his office to implore him to change his mind, but the hard-hearted businessman proclaims Sandoval Lane an impractical dream and refuses to abandon his plans. After the women angrily leave his office, J. J. asks his nephew Phil for help in convincing the women to sell their property. Accepting his uncle's challenge, Phil ventures to Sandoval Street but is denied admittance to the house because he lacks a proper introduction. While pondering his alternatives, Phil rests at the wishing well outside the gates of the house and soon sees his old college friend, Tim O'Brien, pass by. When Tim tells Phil that he is now known as Tomas Obrion, the leader of a popular society orchestra, Phil threatens to expose his friend's true identity unless he introduces him to the Sandovals. Following Tim's advice, Phil assumes the name of Dolan and serenades Elena from the street. When the mischievous Loreto throws a rose to Phil, Dona Maria invites the serenader into the house and introduces him to Elena. As Elena and Phil stroll through the garden, Elena confides her dream of Sandoval Lane and her anger at the Frentiss family. Phil begins to court Elena, and when J. J. flies to New York on business, he orders his nephew to have the land deal completed by the time he returns. When Phil absent-mindedly sketches a drawing of a building on a tablecloth, Elena guesses that he is an architect and insists on showing him the plans for Sandoval Lane. After Phil suggests several changes in the design, Elena hires him as the street's official architect and Dona Maria gives him the deed to her house as security for a bank loan. Meanwhile, in New York, J. J. is visited by several members of the Mexican Consulate, who have come to thank him for his commitment to Sandoval Lane. Furious, J. J. flies back to California and interrupts a fiesta in celebration of Sandoval Lane. When J. J. publicly reproaches his nephew, Phil admits that he is a Frentiss and is accused by Elena of betraying her family. The next day, Phil begs his uncle to return the Sandovals' deed. When J. J. refuses, Phil pleads for Elena's forebearance and then enlists his uncle's secretary and butler in a plot to convince the old man that he is suffering a nervous breakdown. When J. J. receives a mysterious call from his attorney's secretary, arranging a meeting at the Sandoval house, the old man catches on to his nephew's plot but agrees to attend the meeting anyway. At the Sandoval house, Elena and the others entertain J. J. with an elaborate song and dance number to convince him to change his mind, and at the end of their performance, he announces that he has decided to move his warehouse to the other side of the railroad tracks. *Businessmen. Impersonation and imposture. Land developers. Mexican Americans. Architects. Aunts. Band leaders. Courtship. Cultural conflict. Deeds. Nephews. Nieces. Uncles. Warehouses.*

Note: The working title of this film was *Fiesta Town*. The picture opens with architect Phil Frentiss narrating the story of the founding of Sandoval Lane. According to a Jun 1944 pre-production news item in *HR*, Sam White was initially slated to produce this picture, which was to feature Olvera Street, an old Mexican-themed street in Los Angeles, as its background. Although the film takes place on a Olvera-like street, the specific name is never mentioned. By Oct 1944, Jay Gorney was assigned to produce. Gorney, a well-known lyricist and composer, made his Columbia producing debut with this film and was also assigned to collaborate on the screenplay with Edward Eliscu. The extent of Gorney's writing contribution has not been determined, however.
Box 11 Aug 1945. *DV* 13 Aug 1945, p. 3. *FD* 21 Aug 1945, p. 6. *HR* 6 Jun 1944, p. 6. *HR* 26 Oct 1944, p. 1. *HR* 14 Nov 1944, p. 5. *HR* 9 Jan 1945, p. 3. *HR* 13 Aug 1945, p. 5. *MPHPD* 14 Jul 1945, p. 2543. *MPHPD* 25 Aug 1945, p. 2610.

GELEB UN GELAKHT *see* **LIVE AND LAUGH**

GEM FEN NGEI SENG *see* **GIN FEN NEE SHAAN**

GENERAL CUSTER AT LITTLE BIG HORN (Native Americans, Cheyenne, Dakota)
Sunset Productions. *Dist* Arthur C. Bromberg Independent Attractions. 15 Sep **1926**. Si; b&w. 6 reels, 5,094 ft. 76 min.
[*Prod* Anthony J. Xydias]. [*Dir* Harry L. Fraser]. [*Story* Carrie E. Rawles]. [*Photog* L. William O'Connell].

Cast: [Roy Stewart (*Lem Hawks*)], [Helen Lynch (*Betty Rossman*)], [John Beck (*General George Armstrong Custer*)], [Edmund Cobb (*Captain Page*)].

Historical, Western. [*Print viewed*]. Lem Hawks, a civilian scout attached to General George Armstrong Custer, is attracted to Betty Rossman, the daughter of a pioneer. Rivaling Lem for Betty's affections is Captain Page, who serves under Custer. Unknown to Custer, Cheyenne Chief Little Horse meets with Sioux leader Gall, who is wanted by the Army, and Sioux medicine man Sitting Bull, who is known as "the brains of the Sioux nation." Worried about the loss of their buffalo and lands, the Indian leaders form an alliance to fight the white man. Learning that Gall is in the area, Custer sends Lem to the warrior's encampment. Lem tries to persuade Gall to discuss peace with Custer, and although Gall adamantly refuses the offer, an Indian named Bear promises Lem that Gall will visit the general. Lem returns to Custer with the news, unaware that Page and his men have surrounded and bayoneted Gall. When he hears of Gall's injury, Custer is outraged, but Page replies, "A dead Indian is a good Indian." The attack on Gall rallies the Sioux to action, and they launch a series of attacks on homesteads and wagon trains. One evening, while Page romances a married woman at a dance, Lem enters with the news that the Indians are on the warpath. As Custer spreads word of the situation among his officers, Lem dances with Betty. This enrages Page, who blames Lem for the injury to Gall. The two men fight, but Custer, reporting that he has been ordered to pursue the Indians located by Major Reno's scouting party, urges them to put their argument aside. In the meantime, there is a war council between the Sioux and the Cheyenne. The whites must go, they maintain, so that the Indian can roam the plains freely. A war dance is then performed to the accompaniment of drum playing and singing, but later, having been notified that U.S troops are approaching, the Indians ride away. Back at the post, Page apologizes for having resorted to lying in his courtship of Betty. As she bids Lem farewell, Betty begs him to return to her. The troops depart, with Reno in the lead, Captain Benteen to the left, and Custer to the northern end of the Indian village. During the battle between Custer and the Indians, Page dies in Lem's arms. Lem rides to notify General Terry of their plight, but by the time Terry's advance guard reaches the battlefield, Custer and his men are dead. Sitting Bull is captured and confined to a reservation until his death. Lem then returns to Betty and they embrace. *Battles. Cheyenne Indians. General George Armstrong Custer. Dakota Indians. Little Big Horn, Battle of the, 1876. Officers (Military). Political alliances. Attempted murder. Dances. Heroism. Indians of North America–Social life and customs. Massacres. Medicine men. Montana. Moral reformation. Revenge. Rites and ceremonies. Romantic rivalry. Settlers. Sitting Bull. Tribal chiefs. United States–History–Indian campaigns. United States. Army. Cavalry.*

Note: The film was also known as *With Custer at Little Big Horn*. Modern sources add Arthur Morrison, Nora Lindley, Andre Farneur and Running Deer (*Chief Sitting Bull*) to the cast. Historically, it was the Oglala Teton leader Crazy Horse, not Little Horse, who participated in the events at Little Big Horn. For more information about Custer and the Battle of Little Big Horn, please see the entry below for *They Died With Their Boots On.*

Var 2 Nov 1927.

GENERAL SPANKY (African Americans)

Hal Roach Studios, Inc.; Metro-Goldwyn-Mayer Corp.; controlled by Loew's Inc. *Dist* Loew's Inc. 11 Dec **1936**; Prod: 22 Jul—late Aug 1936 [©Metro-Goldwyn-Mayer Corp.; 4 Dec 1936; LP6811]. Sd (Western Electric Sound System); b&w. 8 reels. 72-73 min. Passed by the National Board of Review. PCA cert no. 2480.

Pres HAL ROACH. [*Supv* S. S. Van Keuren]. *Dir* Fred Newmeyer and Gordon Douglas. *Orig story and scr* Richard Flournoy, Hal Yates and John Guedel. *Photog* Art Lloyd and Walter Lundin. *Photog eff* Roy Seawright. *Settings* Arthur I. Royce and W. L. Stevens. *Film ed* Ray Snyder. *Mus score* Marvin Hatley. *Sd* William Randall and [Elmer Raguse].

Cast: Spanky McFarland (*Spanky*), Phillips Holmes (*Marshall Vallent*), Ralph Morgan (*Yankee general*), Irving Pichel (*Captain Simmons*), Rosina Lawrence (*Louella [Blanchard]*), Billie "Buckwheat" Thomas (*Buckwheat*), Carl "Alfalfa" Switzer (*Alfalfa*), Hobart Bosworth (*Colonel Blanchard*), Robert Middlemass (*Overseer*), James Burtis (*Boat captain*), Louise Beavers (*Cornelia*), William Best (*Henry*), [Eugene "Porky" Lee, Harold Switzer, John Collum, Dickey Deneut, Flayette Roberts, Rex Haddon Downing, Jerry Tucker (*Gang kids in army*)], [Percy McPortland (*Second boat captain*)], [Jesse Graves (*Jesse, the butler*)], [Barney Carr (*Jeff*)], [Buddy Roosevelt (*Simmons' first lieutenant*)], [Dick Winslow (*Simmons' second lieutenant*)], [Carl Voss (*Simmons' third lieutenant*)], [Walter Gregory (*Captain Gary*)], [Jack Dougherty (*Captain Hayden*)], [Henry Hall, Frank LaRue (*Plantation owners*)], [Jack Clisby (*Stevedore*)], [David Worth, Larry Soule], [Nick Copeland, Nick Prather, Jeffrey Sayre (*Men at bulletin board*)], [Dave Pepper (*Colonel Baker*)], [Richard Neill (*Colonel Parrish*)], [Harry Strang, Bud Geary (*Sentries*)], [Freida Shaw's Etudes], [Elk Chanters].

Historical, Youth, Comedy-drama. [*Print viewed*]. Just before the start of the Civil War, six-year-old bootblack Spanky has to jump off a Mississippi River boat when his new little pal Buckwheat paints some of the passengers' shoes white to drum up business. Buckwheat, who is afraid he'll be shot as a runaway slave, soon follows, and the boys make their way to shore, then look food. Marshall Vallent, a kind man who had befriended Spanky on the boat, is against any war with the North, and is called a traitor by his friends. When Marshall encounters Spanky on shore, the boy convinces him that even though he is against war, he must stand by his friends. In gratitude for Spanky's advice, Marshall invites the boy to live with him and takes in Buckwheat as well, when he finds the hungry boy hiding under the dinner table. Some time later, the war between the North and South begins and Marshall, who has become a confederate officer, leaves Spanky in charge at home, and asks him to take special care of Marshall's sweetheart Louella, the daughter of elderly Colonel Blanchard. While the men are at war, Spanky, Buckwheat and their friend Alfalfa join other children in building a fort to protect the town. When some Yankee soldiers think that the fort is real, they fire upon it and make fools of themselves in front of their general when he arrives in time to see the "rebels" surrender. The bemused general commends the little soldiers for their bravery and calls Spanky "General Spanky." He then leaves the town in the care of Captain Simmons, who forcibly makes his headquarters in the Blanchard house. Meanwhile, Marshall has been wounded nearby and drags himself back to town where he is found by Spanky and his dog. They hide Marshall in their secret cave and summon Louella to help, but a suspicious Simmons follows Buckwheat to the cave and arrests Marshall. At a court-martial, Marshall is convicted as a spy and condemned to death, even though some members of the court think that the evidence is flimsy. When Marshall is sentenced to be shot, Spanky gets the idea to visit the Yankee general and ask for his help, as one general to another. After hearing Spanky's story, the Yankee general accompanies Spanky back to town, re-opens Marhsall's court-martial, apologizes to Colonel Blanchard for Simmons' behavior, then has Simmons arrested. The general then arranges for Marhsall to be included in an exchange of Northern and Southern prisoners of war if Marshall promises to return to civilian life. Finally, as a reward for his actions, the Yankee general is given an honorable induction into the children's army. *Children. Foundlings. Generals. Soldiers. United States–History–Civil War, 1861-1865. United States–South.* Adoption. African Americans. Bootblacks. Caves. Courts-martial and courts of inquiry. Dogs. Paddleboats. Parties. Romance. Singers. Slavery.

Note: The working title of this film was *Colonel Spanky*. Although Elmer A. Raguse, head of the sound department at Hal Roach Studies, was nominated for an Academy Award for Best Sound for this picture, only William Randall was credited onscreen. According to a news item in *HR* on 11 May 1936, co-director Fred Newmeyer was working with writer Richard Flournoy on the script, however, the extent of Newmeyer's contribution to the final script has not been determined. Portions of the film were shot on location on the Sacramento River, CA. This was the only "Our Gang" feature film and the only picture the characters made with an historical setting. *General Spanky* was also the first feature film directed by co-director Gordon Douglas. According to a *HR* news item, The Elk Chanters, a group that provided some musical backgrounds for the films, were affiliated with local Los Angeles Lodge 99 and were Elks Club national champions. Modern sources include the following additional cast members: Von the Dog, Hooper Atchley, Karl Hackett, Ernie Alexander, Jack Hill, Ham Kinsey, Jack Cooper, Slim Whittaker, Harry Bernard, Alex Finlayson, Richard Neill and Portia Lanning.

DV 23 Oct 1936, p. 3. *FD* 27 Oct 1936, p. 13. *HR* 11 May 1936, p. 3. *HR* 21 Jul 1936, p. 2. *HR* 27 Jul 1936, p. 6. *HR* 31 Aug 1936, p. 20. *HR* 19 Sep 1936, p. 5. *HR* 23 Oct 1936, p. 6. *MPD* 24 Oct 1936, p. 2. *MPH* 31 Oct 19361, p. 41. *Var* 3 Mar 1936, p. 14.

GENOVEFFA (Italian language)

Italian-American Photofilm Co. **1932**; Prod: at Newark Motion Picture Studio, Newark, NJ. Sd; b&w. 8 reels. Italian language.

Prod Giulio Amauli. *Dir* Giulio Amauli. *Mus score* Professor Giuseppe De Luca.

Cast: Giulio Amauli, Dina Lanza.

Historical, Drama. [*Not viewed*]. Genevieve and her loving husband, Count Siegfried, discuss impending war in the garden of their medieval castle. Golo, Siegfried's counselor, tells them that Captain Wolf has arrived with a message from the king calling him to defend France from invaders. Siegfried summons the castle's occupants to the main hall, where he announces that Golo will take command of the castle during his absence. As Siegfried and his soldiers disappear into the distance, Genevieve is overcome with grief and faints. Golo, eyeing her lustily, carries her to her room, and orders the servants to leave them alone. As he prepares to molest her, she wakes up suddenly, and demands that he leave. Meanwhile, Siegfried sends news of the war to his wife via messenger Drako. At the castle, Genevieve receives the letter, and asks Drako to tell her more about her husband. As they talk, Golo approaches and orders Drako to report to the guard for duty. When Genevieve protests, Golo declares his love for her, saying he is capable of doing anything to have her. In her room, Genevieve writes a letter to her husband telling him about Golo's behavior. Happening by, Golo sees the door guarded and becomes suspicious. He barges in, demanding that Drako give him the letter. When Drako refuses, Golo kills him, causing Genevieve to faint. Claiming that Genevieve and Drako have committed adultery, Golo has Genevieve imprisoned. Months later, Genevieve has endured the trials of prison life and given birth to a son. Golo continues to harass her, threatening her and her son with death. In a rage over the alleged adultery, Siegfried has sent an order from the front for both Genevieve and the baby to die. Although Golo offers Genevieve freedom if she will consent to his wishes, she says she prefers death. Berta, who has gained possession of the key to Genevieve's cell, tries to set her free. Genevieve, however, refuses to risk Berta's life, and instead, asks for a pencil and paper. She writes to her husband, explaining what has happened and begging him to treat Golo with mercy. The next morning, Kinz and Kunz, the executioners, take Genevieve and baby into the woods. Kinz begins to question the orders, and when Genevieve promises never to leave the forest, Kinz and Kunz decide to let them live. Genevieve runs into the forest, stopping to baptize the child in a stream. They make a home in a cave, and as the boy grows, Genevieve teaches him the story of Jesus. The war ends years later and Siegfried returns home unannounced. Siegfried interrupts one of Golo's sumptuous banquets, and a hush falls. Berta shows him Genevieve's letter, explaining that Golo is a scoundrel. Golo begs for death, but, respecting Genevieve's wishes, Siegfried imprisons him. Meanwhile, in the forest, Genevieve lies near death while her son attends to her. One day, while Siegfried is hunting in the woods, he happens upon the cave where Genevieve lies sleeping. He calls to his fellow hunters, who lead Genevieve and the boy back to the castle. The happy couple is united, and their son takes his rightful place as heir to the throne. *Infidelity. Lechery. Middle Ages. Self-sacrifice. Treachery.* Castles. Caves. Executions. Forests. Imprisonment. Infants. Letters. Maids. Missing persons, Assumed dead. Mothers and sons. Nobility. Reunions. Soldiers.

Note: The above plot synopsis is based on a dialogue continuity from NYSA. The script includes an English translation of the Italian dialogue and titles. According to *FD* news items, this film was a remake of a silent film released in New York in the 1920s. The film also had both English and Italian dialogue and titles, according to a *FD* news item. Although an exact release date has not been determined, the film was approved for release with eliminations by the New York State Censor in Nov 1932. At the time the film was submitted, its length was listed as 7,750 feet. *FD* lists the film's title in English as *Genevieve*.

FD 22 Aug 1932, p. 2. *FD* 30 Aug 1932, p. 10.

GENTE ALEGRE (Spanish language)

Paramount Publix Corp. *Dist* Paramount Publix Corp. **1931**; Los Angeles opening: 1 May 1931; Prod: 12 Jan–31 Jan 1931; addl shooting in Apr 1931. Sd; b&w. 10 reels, 8,302 ft. 92 min. Spanish language.

Supv Geoffrey Shurlock. *Dir* Eduardo Venturini. *Asst dir* Harry Ham and George Yohalem. *Story and scr* Henry Myers. *Spanish dial* Josep Carner Ribalta. *Photog* Henry Gerrard. *2d cam* Harry Merland and Roy Eslick. *Asst cam* Robert Rhea and Alfred Smalley. *Sd* Harry D. Mills. *Unit mgr* R. L. Johnston.

Song(s): "El espejo," words and music by Mario Alvarez; "Igual que tú" and other songs, composers undetermined.

Cast: Roberto Rey (*Raúl Roland*), Rosita Moreno (*Magda Martin*), Ramón Pereda (*Federico del Val*), Carmen Rodríguez (*Señora Morel*), Delia Magaña (*"Tilón"*), Mario Alvarez (*"Tilín"*), Vicente Padula (*Max*), María Calvo (*Felicia*), Chevo Pirrín (*Serafín*), Rafael Alvir, Luis Llaneza.

Romance, Musical. [*Not viewed*]. In a New York nightclub, beautiful singer and dancer Magda Martin falls in love with a young dashing tenor named Raúl Roland. Despite the machinations of the club's theatrical producer, Federico del Val, who has designs on Magda, and the show's financial backer, Señora Morel, who wants Raúl, the couple marries. Magda persuades Raúl to quit his job at the nightclub in order to avoid the designs of women such as Señora Morel, and he unhappily spends his days walking his dog, while del Val woos Magda. After del Val gives Magda an expensive bracelet, Raúl leaves Magda and returns to the café. Señora Morel, unaware that it is Raúl whom Magda married, excitedly convinces del Val to give Raúl the lead in the next musical. At first reluctant to be in one of del Val's shows, Raúl decides to join the cast on condition that Magda is fired. Señora Morel's financial power forces del Val to fire Magda, and in retaliation, Magda begins to encourage del Val's advances. Arriving at del Val's flat for a rendezvous, however, Magda realizes she is still in love with her husband and leaves. Raúl, too, has a change of heart and hurries to del Val's in a rage. Finding Magda's purse in his apartment, he beats up del Val, but Magda has since fled. On the opening night of the revue, Raúl nervously pines for Magda. When he sees her out front in a box seat, he approaches her, singing his love song, then joins her in the box, where they sing a duet. *Nightclubs. Romantic rivalry. Separation (Marital). Dancers. Infidelity. Marriage–Secret. Singers. Theatrical backers. Womanizers.*

Note: This film's working title was ¡*Arriba el telón!* Although contemporary sources state that this film was made in Jan 1931 and it is listed in a Paramount Studio records "route card" on 10 Jan 1931 (the date of the final script), according to files in the Paramount Script Collection at the AMPAS Library, the rights to Henry Myers' story were not purchased by Paramount until 20 Mar 1931. The film again appears on a studio "route card" on 27 Apr 1931, suggesting that some additional work was done in Apr. Some accounts of the shooting include Jack Castello in the film; however, his participation in the completed film has not been confirmed. Contemporary sources list Karl Hajos and Jay Gorney as contributing songs to this production.

CM Aug 1931, p. 635. *NYT* 19 Sep 1933, p. 26.

THE GENTLEMAN FROM CALIFORNIA *see* THE CALIFORNIAN

GENTLEMAN JIM (Irish Americans)

Warner Bros. Pictures, Inc.; A Warner Bros.–First National Picture. *Dist* Warner Bros. Pictures, Inc. 14 Nov **1942**; Prod: 20 May–23 Jul 1942 [©Warner Bros. Pictures, Inc.; 14 Nov 1942; LP11685]. Sd (RCA Sound System); b&w. 9,385 ft. 104 min.

Prod Robert Buckner. *Dir* Raoul Walsh. *Dial dir* Hugh Cummings. [*Asst dir* Russ Saunders]. *Scr* Vincent Lawrence and Horace McCoy. *Dir of photog* Sid Hickox. *Mont* Don Siegel and [James Leicester]. *Art dir* Ted Smith. *Film ed* Jack Killifer. *Set dec* Clarence Steenson. *Gowns* Milo Anderson. *Mus* H. Roemheld. *Orch arr* Ray Heindorf. *Mus dir* Leo F. Forbstein. *Sd* C. A. Riggs. *Makeup artist* Perc Westmore. *Tech adv* Ed Cochrane. [*Errol Flynn's trainer* Mushy Callahan]. [*Double for Errol Flynn* Fred Steele and Henry Ivliaigs].

Source: Based on the book *The Roar of the Crowd* by James J. Corbett (Garden City, NY, 1925).

Cast: ERROL FLYNN [(*James J. Corbett*)], ALEXIS SMITH [(*Victoria Ware*)], Jack Carson [(*Walter Lowrie*)], Alan Hale [(*Pat Corbett*)], John Loder [(*Clinton De Witt*)], William Frawley [(*Delaney*)], Minor Watson [(*Buck Ware*)], Ward Bond [(*John L. Sullivan*)], Madeleine Le Beau [(*Anna Held*)], Rhys Williams [(*Harry Watson*)], Arthur Shields [(*Father Burke*)], Dorothy Vaughn [(*Ma Corbett*)], James Flavin (*George Corbett*), [Pat Flaherty (*Harry Corbett*)], [Wallis Clark (*Judge Geary*)], [Marilyn Phillips (*Mary Corbett*)], [Art Foster (*Jack Burke*)], [Edwin Stanley (*President McInnes*)], [Henry O'Hara (*Colis Huntington*)], [Harry Crocker (*Charles Crocker*)], [Frank Mayo (*Governor Stanford*)], [Carl Harbough (*Smith*)], [Fred Kelsey (*Sutro*)], [Sammy Stein (*Joe Choynski*)], [Jean Del Val (*Renaud*)], [William Davidson (*Donovan*)], [Mike Mazurki (*Kilrain*)], [Joe King (*Colonel McLane*)], [Frank Hagney (*Mug*)], [Wedgwood Nowell, John Maxwell (*Brokers*)], [Syd Saylor (*Driver*)], [Leo White, Jack Wise (*Waiters*)], [Charles Marsh (*Station master*)], [Ed "Strangler" Lewis (*Riley*)], [Pat McKee (*Ticket taker*)], [Wee Willie Davis (*Flannagan*)], [Wade Crosby (*Manager*)], [Dick Wessel (*Referee*)], [Emory Parnell (*Simmons*)], [Bud McCallister (*Page boy*)], [Bert Hanlon (*Clerk*)], [John Merkyl (*Headwaiter*)], [Johnny Calkins (*Boy*)], [Charlotte Treadway (*Matron*)], [Georgia Caine (*Mrs. Geary*)], [George Lloyd (*Harrigan*)], [Joe Devlin (*Hogan*)], [Wade Boteler (*Policeman*)], [Peggy Diggins (*Beautiful actress*)], [Mary Gordon (*Irish woman*)], [Charles Wilson (*Gurney*)], [Emmet Vogan (*Stage manager*)], [Jack Gardner (*Usher*)], [Jack Roper (*Donaldson*)], [Davison Clark (*Auctioneer*)], [Dudley Dickerson (*Bellboy*)], [Hal Craig, Robert Fisko (*Telegraphers*)], [Dan Tobey (*Announcer*)], [Joe Crehan (*Duffy*)], [Lew Harvey, Lester Dorr, Victor Zimmerman (*Reporters*)], [Pat O'Malley, Lee Phelps (*Detectives*)], [Pat Moriarty (*Spectator*)], [Si Jenks], [Jack Mower], [Monte Blue], [Richard Kipling], [Hooper Atchley], [Joan Winfield], [Winifred Harris], [Charles Lang], [De Wolf Hopper], [Milt Kibbee], [Howard Mitchell], [George Sherwood], [Larry McGrath], [Frank Moran], [Herbert Heywood].

Boxing, Biography. [*Print viewed*]. In San Francisco, in 1887, an illegal boxing match is broken up by the police. Among those caught in the raid are two young bank employees, Jim Corbett and Walter Lowrie, and Judge Geary, a member of the bank's board of directors. Upset because boxing's bad reputation has resulted in a ban on the sport, Geary announces that as a member of the Olympic Club, he will arrange for matches involving young men from good families to be held there. The next day, when they see Geary enter the bank, Jim and Walter are convinced they are about to lose their jobs, but Geary is actually there to thank Jim for the story he told in court to explain their presence at the fight. When Victoria Ware, the daughter of Buck Ware, another Olympic Club member, comes to the bank to get a supply of coins for her poker-playing father, Jim insists on accompanying her back to the club. There he talks Vicki into giving him a tour of the club and having lunch with him. In the gym, Jim does a little boxing and so impresses the trainer that he is proposed for membership. Jim, whose father drives a hackney cab and whose brothers are longshoremen, becomes self-important after his election into the club. The other members, offended by his egotistical behavior, set up a match between Jim and Jack Burke, a former British heavyweight champion. To everyone's surprise, Jim's fancy footwork and quick punches win the match. At the ball afterward, a drunken Walter is asked to leave the club, and out of loyalty, Jim leaves with him. The next morning, Jim and Walter, painfully hungover, wake up in Salt Lake City. To earn the money to return to San Francisco, Jim boxes in a professional match and wins. With the help of manager Delaney, Jim turns professional and continues to win his fights. His successful fight against Joe Choynski takes place on a barge in an attempt to circumvent the laws which prohibit prizefights. Because of his elegant fighting style, and his penchant for fancy evening clothes, Jim is nicknamed "Gentleman Jim." Now that he is earning a lot of money, Jim moves his family to Nob Hill. Although Jim is attracted to Vicki, she dislikes his airs so much that she is eager to see him fail. In 1892, when Jim needs $10,000 to challenge heavyweight champion John L. Sullivan, Vicki anonymously puts up the money, hoping that Sullivan will knock the pride out of Jim. On the night of the fight, Vicki is in the audience to boo Jim, but he again resorts to his fancy footwork and, at the end of twenty-one rounds, wins the

championship. Even Vicki cheers the result, but she makes fun of Jim by buying him a huge hat to fit his swelled head. Sullivan comes to Jim's victory party to present him with his championship belt. They speak graciously of each other, and Jim expresses his deep appreciation of Sullivan's skills and place in history. Vicki is impressed with Jim's sensitivity and confesses that she loves him. When he proposes, she accepts. *Boxers. James J. Corbett. Egotists. Balls (Parties). Bank tellers. Drunkenness. Family relationships. Friendship. Gambling. Irish Americans. Police. Priests. Raids. Romance. San Francisco (CA). John L. Sullivan. Trains.*

Note: James John Corbett became world heavyweight boxing champion on 17 Mar 1897 when he knocked out John L. Sullivan in twenty-one rounds. He was the first successful fighter to use the Marquis of Queensberry rules. Good looks and a scientific method of boxing earned him the nickname "Gentleman Jim." After he quit boxing in 1903, Corbett starred in several plays, including *Gentleman Jack* and *The Naval Lieutenant,* and movies (see index to *AFI Catalog of Feature Films, 1911-20*). In 1886 Corbett married actress Olive Lake, and after their divorce, he married Jessie Taylor of Omaha. He died on 18 Feb 1933. Several reviews note discrepancies between the film *Gentleman Jim* and the actual events of Corbett's life. The *Var* review states:"...the heavyweight champ was a self-effacing, quiet personality so distinctly apart from the general run of mugg fighters of that day that the 'gentleman' tag was a natural....[He] was a revered member of the Olympic club to the very end.... Corbett fought most of his battles bareknuckle...and he first met Sullivan in a friendly sparring match at the Olympic club some years before their championship battle....Sullivan hated Corbett...[and] never gave Corbett his championship belt—that had been in the hock shops long before their battle...."

A 31 May 1940 *HR* news item notes that three major studios were interested in the screen rights to James J. Corbett's autobiography, which was previously serialized in *SEP* from 11 Oct—25 Nov 1924. Other *HR* news items add the following information about the production: Technical adviser Ed Cochrane was the sports editor of the *Chicago Herald-American* and an authority on James Corbett. Some scenes were filmed on location at the Baldwin Estate in Santa Ana, CA. A press release in the file on the film at the AMPAS Library announces the casting of Phil Silvers, but he does not appear in the film. A *NYT* article dated 31 May 1942 identifies Mushy Callahan, former junior welterweight champion, as one of Errol Flynn's trainers. According to information included in the file on the film at the USC Cinema-Television Library, Callahan also doubled for Errol Flynn in some of the shots showing "Corbett's" fancy footwork, although his name never appears in the daily production reports. Other information in the Warner Bros. Collection reveals that Lewis Milestone turned down an offer to direct the film because he did not like the script. Director Raoul Walsh wanted Barry Fitzgerald to play "Corbett's" father and was interested in either Ann Sheridan or Rita Hayworth for the role of "Vicki." Actors Mike Mazurki and Ed "Strangler" Lewis had been professional wrestlers. Shortly after the film's release, Flynn went on trial for statutory rape. Flynn was acquitted, and the highly publicized case apparently did not adversely affect his career.

Box 7 Nov 1942. *DV* 30 Oct 1942, p. 3. *FD* 30 Oct 1942, p. 7. *HR* 31 May 1940. *HR* 19 May 1942, p. 2. *HR* 28 May 1942, p. 3. *HR* 29 Jun 1942, p. 3. *HR* 30 Oct 1942, p. 4. *MPHPD* 31 Oct 1942, p. 981. *NYT* 31 May 1942. *NYT* 26 Nov 1942, p. 40. *Var* 4 Nov 1942, p. 8.

THE GENTLEMAN MISBEHAVES (French Americans, Refugees)
Columbia Pictures Corp. *Dist* Columbia Pictures Corp. 28 Feb 1946; Prod: 26 Oct—10 Nov 1945 [©Columbia Pictures Corp.; 28 Feb 1946; LP145]. Sd (Western Electric Mirrophonic Recording); b&w. 73 min. PCA cert no. 11354.

Prod Alexis Thurn-Taxis. *Dir* George Sherman. [*Asst dir* Chris Beute]. *Scr* Robert Wyler and Richard Weil. *Story* Robert Wyler and John B. Clymer. *Dir of photog* Philip Tannura. [*2d cam* Kenneth Green]. *Art dir* Jerome Pycha, Jr. *Film ed* Gene Havlick. *Set dec* James Crowe. *Gowns* Jean Louis. *Mus dir* Mario Silva. *Sd rec* Frank Goodwin. [*Re-rec and eff mixer* J. S. Westmoreland]. [*Mus mixer* Edwin Wetzel]. [*Res dir* Juanita L. Bell].

Song(s): "Thanks A Lot," words by Sammy Cahn, music by Jule Styne; "Home in Your Arms," words by Oscar Hammerstein II, music by Ben Oakland; "Where Am I?" and "I Knew," composers undetermined.

Cast: Robert Stanton [(*Edgar Raleigh*)], Osa Massen [(*Chinchilla, also known as Suzette Fleury*)], Hillary Brooke [(*Nina Mallory*)], Frank Sully [(*Taxi driver*)], Dusty Anderson [(*Marian Rand*)], Shemp Howard [(*Marty*)], Sheldon Leonard [(*Trigger Stazzi*)], Jimmy Lloyd [(*Jimmy Drake*)], [Chester Clute (*Quackenbush*)], [Ernie Adams (*Justice of the peace*)], [William Haade, Edgar Dearing (*Officers*)], [Jack George (*Boris*)], [Cy Shindell (*Stagehand*)], [Billy Benedict (*Bellboy*)], [Dan Stowell (*Fothergill*)], [George Eldredge (*Official*)], [Gladys Blake, Doris Houck (*PBX operators*)], [Jack Frack, Milt Kibbee (*Creditors*)], [P. J. Kelly (*Doorman*)], [Alphonse Martell (*Captain*)], [Mary Field (*Maid*)], [Earle S. Dewey (*Waldon*)], [Cy Malis (*Proprietor*)], [Charles Cane (*Immigration officer*)], [Alfred Allegro (*Author*)], [Victor Travers (*Doorman*)], [Virginia Vann (*Chorus girl*)].

Romance, Show business, Comedy, with songs. [*Print viewed*]. After his star Nina Mallory walks out of dress rehearsal because of his philandering, thus causing the critics to savage his new production, Broadway producer Edgar Raleigh finds himself in financial difficulty. Upon receiving a horseshoe from Nina, accompanied by a sarcastic note wishing him "better luck next time," Edgar hurls the horseshoe out the window of his hotel room, and it strikes Suzette Fleury, an innocent bystander on the sidewalk below. Chagrined, Edgar invites the injured Suzette to his room, and while he argues with Quackenbush, the hotel manager, over his bill, Suzette notices a stack of unpaid bills on the table. After Quackenbush leaves, Suzette offers Edgar $5,000 to marry her, explaining that as a French refugee, marriage to a U.S. citizen would allow her to remain in the United States. Observing that Suzette is wearing a chinchilla coat, Edgar assumes that she is wealthy and agrees to the bargain on the condition that she grant him an annulment after the ceremony. Edgar is astounded to discover after the ceremony that his bride is penniless except for her $20,000 coat. When a taxi driver takes the coat as collateral for their cab fare, Edgar determines to raise the money himself and takes off with the driver. As Suzette waits alone in her hotel room, Marty, an associate of gangster Trigger Stazzi, pulls open the door, tosses a satchel filled with the winnings from a crap game into the room and then runs away. Opening the bag, Suzette discovers that it is stuffed with cash and assumes that it is a present from her new husband. Edgar, meanwhile, has gone to the Coral Club in hopes of collecting some unpaid debts. Inebriated, Edgar sees Nina there and when the driver blurts out the news of Edgar's marriage, she becomes intrigued and accompanies the drunken Edgar home. When Edgar declares his love for Nina in front of his new wife, Nina is puzzled until Suzette explains the terms of their marriage. Fascinated, Nina makes a deal with Suzette: if Suzette keeps Nina's rival, Marian Rand, away from Edgar, Nina will appear in her new show. After Nina leaves, Edgar spies the pile of cash on the table and faints. The next morning, Marian phones Edgar and Suzette sweetly informs her that she is his new wife. Later, Edgar reads a newspaper account of a floating crap game at the hotel the previous night and realizes that the cash belongs to Trigger. Assuming the job of Edgar's secretary, Suzette uses the cash to pay Edgar's creditors, discards all perfumed letters addressed to him and refuses to allow Marian to speak to him. Deciding to teach the philandering Edgar a lesson, Suzette permits him and Nina to dine at the Coral Club, even though she knows that Marian will be performing there. That night, after a row between Nina and Marian, Edgar returns home from the club to find Suzette singing one of the numbers from his new production. When Suzette criticizes Edgar for his cavalier attitude toward women, they embrace and initiate a whirlwind romance. At rehearsal one day, Trigger and Marty come to the theater in search of their money and Suzette informs them that it has been invested in the show. Spotting Nina, Trigger is immediately smitten and offers to become Edgar's partner in the production. When the temperamental Nina becomes jealous of Suzette and announces that she is quitting, Trigger refuses to let her go until he learns of her affair with Edgar. Appalled by her lack of morals, Trigger fires Nina and replaces her with Suzette. During intermission on opening night, an immigration officer presents Suzette with deportation papers and informs her that the law granting citizenship to spouses has been repealed. When Suzette declares that she is pregnant, the officer leaves to discuss the issue with his superiors. After he departs, Edgar congratulates Suzette on her ingenuity and confides that he loathes children. Heartbroken because she really is pregnant, Suzette pens a farewell letter to Edgar and disappears immediately after the last act. When Trigger comes backstage to tell Edgar of his engagement to Nina and compliment him on the success of the show, they find Suzette's note. Discovering that Suzette has bought a steamship ticket home, Trigger intercepts her at the docks and takes her back to Edgar. *Actors and actresses. Aliens, Illegal. Citizenship. Financial crisis. French. Marriage of convenience. Philanderers. Romantic rivalry. Theatrical producers. Accidents. Drunkenness. Fur coats. Gangsters. Horseshoes. Hotel managers. Hotels. New York City–Broadway. Pregnancy. Taxicab drivers.*

Note: Working titles for this film were *Lullaby of Broadway* and *The Lady Misbehaves.*

Box 23 Feb 1946. *DV* 19 Jul 1946, p. 3. *FD* 6 Jun 1946, p. 8. *HR* 19 Jul 1946, p. 3. *MPHPD* 5 Jan 1946, p. 2792. *MPHPD* 27 Jul 1946, p. 3114.

GENTLEMAN'S AGREEMENT (Jewish Americans)

Twentieth Century-Fox Film Corp. *Dist* Twentieth Century-Fox Film Corp. Mar **1948**; New York opening: 11 Nov 1947; Prod: 24 May—19 Aug 1947 [©Twentieth Century-Fox Film Corp.; 11 Nov 1947; LP1777]. Sd (Western Electric Recording); b&w. 13 reels, 10,643 ft. 118 min. PCA cert no. 12488.

Pres DARRYL F. ZANUCK. *Prod* Darryl F. Zanuck. *Dir* Elia Kazan. [*Asst dir* Saul Wurtzel]. [*Dial dir* Michael Audley]. *Scr* Moss Hart. [*Revisions to scr* Elia Kazan]. *Dir of photog* Arthur Miller. *Spec photog eff* Fred Sersen. *Art dir* Lyle Wheeler and Mark-Lee Kirk. *Ed supv* Harmon Jones. *Set dec* Thomas Little. *Set des* Paul S. Fox. *Ward dir* Charles Le Maire. *Cost des* Kay Nelson. *Mus* Alfred Newman. *Orch arr* Edward Powell. *Sd* Alfred Bruzlin and Roger Heman. *Makeup artist* Ben Nye. [*Prod mgr* R. A. Klune].

Source: Based on the novel *Gentleman's Agreement* by Laura Z. Hobson (New York, 1947).

Cast: GREGORY PECK [(*Philip Schuyler Green*)], DOROTHY McGUIRE [(*Kathy Lacy*)], JOHN GARFIELD [(*Dave Goldman*)], Celeste Holm [(*Anne Dettrey*)], Anne Revere [(*Mrs. Green*)], June Havoc [(*Ethel Wales, also known as Estelle Walofsky*)], Albert Dekker [(*John Minify*)], Jane Wyatt [(*Jane*)], Dean Stockwell [(*Tommy Green*)], Nicholas Joy [(*Dr. Craigie*)], Sam Jaffe [(*Professor Lieberman*)], Harold Vermilyea [(*Jordan*)], Ransom M. Sherman [(*Bill Payson*)], [Roy Roberts (*Mr. Calkins*)], [Kathleen Lockhart (*Mrs. Minify*)], [Curt Conway (*Bert McAnny*)], [John Newland (*Bill*)], [Robert Warwick (*Irving Weisman*)], [Louise Lorimer (*Miss Miller*)], [Howard Negley (*Tingler*)], [Victor Kilian (*Olsen*)], [Frank Wilcox (*Harry*)], [Marilyn Monk (*Receptionist*)], [Wilton Graff (*Maitre d'*)], [Morgan Farley (*Clerk*)], [Mauritz Hugo (*Columnist*)], [Jack Conrad, Joseph Haworth, Lee MacGregor, Wally Scott (*Bellboys*)], [Grace Field, Stella Rae, Hallene Hill (*Old ladies*)], [Robert Karnes, Gene Nelson (*G.I.s*)], [Leo Kaye (*Porter*)], [Helen Gerald (*Page girl*)], [Marion Marshall (*Guest*)], [Jesse White (*Elevator starter*)], [Lew Leverett, Herbert Ratner (*Fathers*)], [Jane Earle (*Child*)], [Louise Buckley, Noel Mills (*Mothers*)], [Patty Robbins (*Receptionist*)], [George Leigh], [Federico Godoy], [Laura Treadwell], [Olive Deering], [Jane Green], [Virginia Gregg], [Adrienne Marden], [Barbara Wooddell], [Ray Largay], [Mary Worth], [Tom Handley], [Arthur Little, Jr.], [Henry Mowbray], [Monya Andre], [Patricia Cameron], [Irene Dehn], [Edna Holland], [Boyd Irwin].

Social, Drama. [*Print viewed*]. Philip Schuyler Green, a widowed journalist, arrives in New York from California with his son Tommy and his mother to work for *Smith's Weekly*, a leading national magazine. John Minify, the publisher, wants Phil to write a series on anti-Semitism, but Phil is lukewarm about the assignment. At a party, Phil meets Minify's niece, Kathy Lacy, a divorcee to whom Phil becomes attracted, and Kathy reminds her uncle that she suggested the series some time ago. Tommy asks his father about anti-Semitism, and when Phil finds it difficult to explain, he decides to accept the assignment. He is frustrated, however, at his inability to come up with a satisfactory approach, for he and Minify want the series to go deeper than just exposing the "crackpot" mentality. After trying to imagine how his Jewish boyhood friend, Dave Goldman, who is now overseas in the Army, must feel when he experiences bigotry, Phil decides to write from the point of view of a Jew. He continues to have difficulties writing, though, until he realizes that some things can never be known until one experiences them firsthand, and that the only way to get the necessary experience is to appear Jewish in the eyes of other people. When Minify announces the series to a luncheon group, Phil casually mentions that he is Jewish. Later, Phil learns from his new secretary that she was told there were no positions with the magazine when she applied under her real name of Estelle Walofsky, but when she reapplied using "Ethel Wales," she got the job. On his first day as a Jew, Phil becomes the target of slurs and learns of discriminatory rules at his apartment building. When he tells Kathy, with whom he has fallen in love, about his story "angle," she is at first confused that he might really be Jewish. The next day, the magazine's personnel director is reprimanded by Minify for his policy of not hiring Jewish secretaries and is told that every future ad must include the line, "Religion is a matter of indifference." When Miss Wales learns about the change of policy, however, her fear that a "kikey" Jew will ruin things for them prompts Phil to state that he hates anti-Semitism as much from her as from a gentile. Later, Kathy, to whom Phil is now engaged, tells Phil that her sister Jane in Darien, Connecticut has planned a party for them on the next Saturday, and Phil reluctantly agrees to allow Kathy to tell Jane about the ruse. When Kathy asks Phil not to discuss anti-Semitism at her sister's party, Phil refuses and and Kathy berates him for being argumentative. Soon after, Dave arrives in town on leave to look for a home, as he has been offered a job in the area. When Phil tells him about the series and says that, as a Jew, he is having his "nose rubbed in it and doesn't like the smell," Dave says he is just not "insulated" yet. Phil and Dave then meet Anne at a restaurant, where a drunken patron calls Dave a "yid, and Dave violently shoves the man away. Afterwards, Phil receives a call from Kathy, who says she is in Connecticut to confront Jane. When Phil arrives in Darien for Jane's party, he is surprised that the guests are interested in the series, but Kathy does not reveal that Jane screened the guests and only invited the "safe ones." Two days before Phil and Kathy's wedding, the couple learns from Anne that the Flume Inn, where they plan to honeymoon, is "restricted," meaning that Jews are not allowed, but when Phil's mother has a minor stroke, the wedding is postponed anyway. Dave, who has not been able to find a house, says he must return to his family and miss the wedding. Angered because he feels that Dave is being rejected because he is Jewish, Phil goes to the Flume Inn to confront the management. When he gets evasive answers to his queries, Phil raises his voice in anger and says he is Jewish, which disturbs some of the guests. Phil returns to Kathy and argues that she should help Dave find a home in Connecticut. When she reveals that the Darien citizens have a "gentleman's agreement" not to sell to Jews, Phil castigates her for not wanting to fight. Tommy, in tears, interrupts their quarrel and says that the kids at school called him a "dirty yid" and a "stinking kike." After Kathy tries to comfort the boy by saying that he is no more Jewish than she, Phil calms his son, then angrily lectures Kathy for instilling in Tommy a sense of superiority as a white Christian American. Phil contends that his biggest discovery has been that the "nice people," who are not anti-Semitic, sustain prejudice by not protesting against it. Kathy decides that they cannot marry due to Phil's temper and leaves despite his apologies. That night, Phil tells Dave about Tommy, and Dave says that he can now quit, as he has learned what it is like when anti-Semitism hits one's children. Phil delivers the first half of the series, entitled, "I Was Jewish for 8 Weeks," and announces that he is returning to California. Meanwhile, Kathy asks Dave to meet her at a restaurant, where she relates that earlier that night, a man told a bigoted joke, to which no one in her party objected, and that she felt ill about it. Dave's repeated question of "What did you do about it?" helps Kathy realize that she has been getting mad at Phil because he expected her to fight, but she should have been getting mad at those who help maintain bigotry. Dave advises that he has learned to "sock back" and that she might not feel ill if she had done so. When Kathy says she is not a fit wife for Phil, Dave contends that a man wants a wife who will go through the rough spots with him and feel that they are the same rough spots. Later, Phil's mother is reading his manuscript when Dave comes in and calls his boss to announce that he has found a house and will take the New York job. Dave explains that he will live at Kathy's Darien cottage, and that Kathy has decided to live with her sister and challenge the bigotry there. Thrilled that Kathy has changed, Phil embraces her. *Antisemitism. Engagements. Impersonation and imposture. Jews. Reporters. Transformation. Connecticut. Editors. Fathers and sons. Friendship. Houses. Inns. Magazines. New York City. Officers (Military). Physicians. Physicists. Secretaries. Sisters. Stroke. Widowers.*

Note: The best-selling novel *Gentleman's Agreement* was serialized in *Cosmopolitan* (Nov 1946—Feb 1947) before it being published in book form. In a Jul 1947 *Cosmopolitan* interview, author Laura Z. Hobson stated, "What did I try to do with the book? I think a woman who wrote to me put it in two wonderful sentences. She says, 'Villains aren't really frightening. It's the millions of nice people who do, and allow, villainous things.' I think that's the gist of what I was trying to say." Hobson noted that Darryl Zanuck, Fox's production head, who made the film his sole personal production of 1947, told her that if the film failed at the box office, it "would set Hollywood back twenty years in honest[ly] dealing with the problem of prejudice." The film marked the first time that noted playwright Moss Hart wrote directly for the screen. Director Elia Kazan, in his autobiography, states that Jewish heads of other major film studios held a meeting in which they urged Hart to convince Zanuck not to make the film because they did not want to stir up anti-Semitism. A *NYT* article from Mar 1947 noted, "A few objections [to the film] have come from Jews, who feel that the picture may increase rather than diminish intolerance, but a far larger proportion of Jewish opinion approves the venture, according

to Zanuck." In a *NYT* column from Nov 1947, reviewer Bosley Crowther mentioned a rumor that a "well-known Hollywood producer" tried to convince Hart that the film should not be made, a situation mirrored in the film itself, when a Jewish industrialist states, quoting Crowther, asserts, "You can't write it out of existence. The less talk about it, the better. Leave it alone!"

According to Twentieth Century-Fox legal records, scenes were shot at various locations in New York City, including Rockefeller Plaza and the NBC Building, and at Darien, CT. *DN* stated that John Garfield accepted his limited role in the film after Zanuck promised that the film would be faithful to Hart's script. Publicity for the film states that Zanuck paid Garfield "his full star's salary" for the role. *DV*, in reviewing the film, praised the acting of Garfield and Celeste Holm, stating, "This is one picture in which the performances of the supporting cast equal, or top, those of the two principals." Fox legal records report that Morris Carnovsky was originally hired to play "Professor Lieberman," but his contract was terminated by mutual agreement. Modern sources state that the film was Fox's top grossing picture of 1948, that it cost $2,000,000 to produce, and that it was the second largest grossing picture up to that time in the South. The film received the Academy Award for Best Picture, and Celeste Holm won for Best Supporting Actress. *Gentleman's Agreement* was also nominated for Academy Awards for Best Actor (Gregory Peck), Best Actress (Dorothy McGuire), Best Supporting Actress (Anne Revere), Writing—Screenplay (Moss Hart) and Film Editing (Harmon Jones). According to a *MPH* ad in Apr 1948, the picture won fifty-one film-related awards, including the New York Critics' Circle Award.

In a modern interview, Kazan stated about the film, "For the first time someone said that America is full of anti-semitism, both conscious and unconscious and among the best and most liberal people. That was then a much bolder statement than it is now.... It was saying to the audience: You are an average American and you are anti-semitic.'" In his autobiography, Kazan qualified his enthusiasm for the film by stating that it "doesn't have what would have made it lasting in its effect: the intimate experience of someone who had been through the bitter and humiliating experience." Reviewers gave the film high praise. *DN* lauded it for being "both daring and adult, a film that isn't afraid to call names or to depict a love affair whose conflicts, for once, are over ideas." *HR* called the film "the most spellbinding story ever put on celluloid." The Protestant Motion Picture Council challenged viewers that it will "take courage to see it. That is, to *really* see it, to face up to its personal implications, and then to 'do something about it.'"

Dialogue in the film refers to a number of then-prominent demagogic figures known for their bigotry, including U.S. Senator Theodore Gilmore Bilbo, from Mississippi, who advocated deporting all African Americans to Africa; Representative John Rankin, also from Mississippi, who in a statement from the House floor called broadcaster and columnist Walter Winchell "the little kike"; and Gerald L. K. Smith, a Christian Nationalist Crusade leader. In May 1947, Zanuck queried Fox legal counsel George Wasson on whether they were breaking any laws by making the references. After Wasson responded that no court would consider the references a violation of "right to privacy," and that there was only a slight risk of libel, Zanuck wrote, "Let them sue us. They won't dare and if they do nothing would make me more happy than to appear personally as a witness or a defendant at the trial." In Apr 1948, Smith did sue Twentieth Century-Fox in a Tulsa court to ban the film in Tulsa, his home for the previous six months. After a district judge refused to issue a restraining order, Smith took his complaint through the court system, suing the company for $1,000,000, but in Feb 1951, the case was dismissed.

In Sep 1948, the film was rejected for showing in Spain. The *NYT* reported that the ban was instigated "by order of the ecclesiastical member of the Film Censorship Board on moral grounds. According to a source close to the board, the banning order stipulated that while it was a Christian duty to 'stimulate love among individuals, societies, nations and peoples,' this should not extend to Jews." The report listed six points or "theological errors" of the film that warranted the ban, including that the film declared "that a Christian is not superior to a Jew" and that the film asserts that "for many Jews it is a matter of pride to be called Jews. Pride of what? The pride of being the people who put God to death? Of being perfidious, as they are called in Holy Scripture?" On 3 Oct 1948, according to *HR*, the President of the Board of Film Censors in Madrid, Gabriel Garcia Espina, called the statement reported in *NYT* to be a "calumny" and that the film was, in fact, banned because anti-Semitism was not an issue in Spain. Espina stated, "There is no racial problem in Spain. We do not know here the conflict of Semitism or anti-Semitism. And precisely because of the beautiful and traditional Spanish idea of human freedom, these anguishing racial differences that have disturbed so much, and apparently do disturb, the lives of the peoples, are alien to us and we want them to continue being alien to us." The film, however, was approved for showing in Spain on 12 Jan 1949 under the title *La Barrera Invisible*.

Lux Radio Theatre broadcast two radio versions of the story. The first show, starring Gregory Peck, Anne Baxter and Jeff Chandler, aired on 20 Sep 1948, and the second version, which starred Ray Milland, Dorothy McGuire and Shep Menken, was heard on 15 Mar 1955.

Box 22 Nov 1947. *Cosmopolitan* Jul 1947. *DN* 5 Jun 1947. *DN* 26 Dec 1947, p. 21, 23. *DN* 12 Feb 1948, p. 33. *DV* 10 Nov 1947. *FD* 11 Nov 1947, p. 8. *HR* 30 Dec 1946, p. 3. *HR* 3 Feb 1947, p. 2. *HR* 29 May 1947, p. 19. *HR* 15 Aug 1947, p. 13. *HR* 10 Nov 1947, p. 3. *HR* 17 Nov 1947, p. 14, 17. *HR* 5 Oct 1948. *LAT* 26 Dec 1947. *Life* 1 Dec 1947, pp. 95-96. *Look* 10 Jun 1947. *Look* 11 Nov 1947. *MPD* 10 Nov 1947. *MPH* 3 Apr 1948. *MPHPD* 15 Nov 1947, p. 3929. *NYT* 16 Mar 1947. *NYT* 12 Nov 1947, p. 36. *NYT* 16 Nov 1947. *NYT* 29 Sep 1948. *Tulsa Daily World* 10 Apr 1948, p. 1. *Var* 12 Nov 1947, p. 8.

GENTLEMAN'S FATE (Italian Americans)

Metro-Goldwyn-Mayer Corp.; controlled by Loew's, Inc. *Dist* Metro-Goldwyn-Mayer Distributing Corp. 7 Mar **1931**; Prod: began 24 Nov 1930 [©Metro-Goldwyn-Mayer Distributing Corp.; 19 Feb 1931; LP1991]. Sd (Western Electric Sound System); b&w. 10 reels. 90 or 93 min. Passed by the National Board of Review.

[*Supv* Harry Rapf]. *Dir* Mervyn LeRoy. *Dial cont* Leonard Praskins. *Photog* Merritt B. Gerstad. *Art dir* Cedric Gibbons. *Film ed* William S. Gray. *Ward* René Hubert. *Rec dir* Douglas Shearer.

Source: Based on the short story "A Gentleman's Fate" by Ursula Parrott in *Household* (Mar-Jul 1931).

Cast: JOHN GILBERT (*Jack Thomas,* [*also known as Giacomo Tomasulo*]), Louis Wolheim (*Frank* [*Tomasulo*]), Leila Hyams (*Marjorie* [*Channing*]), Anita Page (*Ruth* [*Corrigan*]), Marie Prevost (*Mabel*), John Miljan (*Florio*), George Cooper (*Mike*), Ferike Boros (*Angela*), Ralph Ince (*Dante*), Frank Reicher (*Francesco*), Paul Porcasi (*Mario* [*Giovanni*]), Tenen Holtz (*Tony*).

Crime, Drama. [*Print viewed*]. Wealthy gentleman Jack Thomas is engaged to Marjorie Channing, whom he plans to marry in one month. While planning his wedding and a European honeymoon, Jack is told by Mario, his guardian and financial adviser, that his name is really Giacomo Tomasulo and that he is not really an orphan. Mario also informs him that his father is on his deathbed and wants to see him. When Jack meets Frank Tomasulo, a brother he did not know that he had, at the Hotel Ritzi in Jersey City, he soon learns that his hard-boiled brother is a racketeer in the liquor-running business. Jack also realizes that Frank expects him to shed his high society ways and join the mob once his father dies. Jack eventually succumbs to his brother's pressure to join the mob, but insists that his fiancée be kept ignorant of his involvement. When Marjorie becomes entangled in a Tomasulo jewel robbery, however, she is prevented from leaving her hotel room and learns the truth about the family. Jack's first assignment in the gang is to take the rap for a jewel theft that has gone bad, which he does after Frank tells him that the money from the theft went to care for his ailing father. After he serves ten days in jail, the charges against Jack are dropped and he is freed. When he returns to the hotel, Jack punches Frank, and then reads a note from Marjorie, in which she informs him that she has decided to leave until the "unfortunate affair" has ended. Jack now realizes that he can never go back and live among the "swells," and when Frank offers him the opportunity to take over the Montreal end of the "booze" racket, he takes it. During a hijack attempt on Frank's goods by the rival Florio gang, Jack saves his brother's life by shooting Dante, one of Florio's henchmen. Several months later, at Florio's headquarters, Ruth, Dante's ex-moll, is sent by Florio to infiltrate the Tomasulo gang and take revenge on Jack for killing Dante. Jack meets Ruth at a banquet, which has been called to bring peace between the rival mobs. There, the drunken Florio insults Ruth and Jack punches him. The police arrive in time to prevent a gun battle from erupting and all are dispersed. After the raid, Jack tells Frank that he wants to quit the racket, and that he has been thinking about Marjorie. However, when Frank shows Jack a newspaper article announcing Marjorie's marriage to a man named Barlow, he is crushed. Jack soon concludes, though, that Ruth reminds him of Marjorie, so he marries her. Florio, angry at Ruth for having double-crossed him and still out to avenge Dante's murder, decides to kill both Ruth and Jack. When Florio and his men attempt to kill the couple, Ruth manages to shoot Florio. Jack, too, is shot in the mêlée, and dies. *Bootleggers. Brothers. Murder. Racketeers. Upper classes. Banquets. Drunkenness. Engagements. Fathers and sons. Frame-ups. Inheritance. Italian Americans. Jersey City (NJ). Molls. Montreal (Canada). Orphans. Parentage. Revenge. Rivalry. Robbery.*

Note: According to a *Var* obituary, this film was Louis Wolheim's last. He died on 18 Feb 1931 of cancer. Censorship records in the MPAA/PCA Collection at the AMPAS Library indicate that the Hays Office, after reading the script of *Gentleman's Fate*, warned M-G-M that the Code would not allow the showing of police as the "friends or protectors, rather than the enemies, of organized rum-running gangsters." The Hays Office also noted that the script "presents too attractively the activities of gangland" and suggested the elimination of the police entirely from the story. Following the release of the film, M-G-M responded to Hays Office accusations that the script called for too much drinking, by stating that "the drinking shown in the picture *is most certainly for proper characterization*—to say nothing of being an essential part of the plot." *Gentleman's Fate* was rejected by censors in India "on the grounds that it contains numerous scenes of excessive lawlessness and violence." The *Var* review notes that John Gilbert, whose career suffered greatly due to his first few talkies, "comes through very nicely. He talks in a strong tone and plenty." The reviewer went on to say that the film "was little good otherwise," even though it did prove "that Gilbert is allright on the audible screen if the story is right."

HR 3 Dec 1930, p. 2. *FD* 28 Jun 1931, p. 10. *MPH* 31 Jan 1931, p. 54. *MPH* 7 Mar 1931, p. 25. *NYT* 27 Jun 1931, p. 20. *Var* 25 Feb 1931. *Var* 30 Jun 1931, p. 15.

GEORGE WASHINGTON CARVER (African Americans)

Bryant Productions. *Dist* State Rights; St. George Motion Picture Supply Ltd. 16 Apr **1940**; New York premiere: 16 Apr 1940. Sd; b&w. 7 reels. 69 min. PCA cert no. 02815.

Pres Allen McDowell. *Prod* Ira Greene. *Assoc prod* Ernest St. George. *Dir* Ben Parker. *Orig scr* Robert Shurr. *Narr* John Martin.

Cast: Dr. George Washington Carver (*Himself*), Booker T. Washington III (*Booker T. Washington*), Milton Sprague (*Dr. Carver as a young man*), Ralph Edwards (*Dr. Carver as a boy*), Tim Campbell (*Friend of Dr. Carver*), Raye Gilbert (*His sweetheart*), Terressta Glasheri (*Manny, his boyhood guardian*), Tuskegee Choir.

African American, Biography, Documentary. [*Not viewed*]. This documentary on the eminent black scientist, George Washington Carver, opens with a brief history of black labor in the South. After examining some of the typical jobs of a black worker, including the tilling of soil, the cultivation of sugar and the gining of cotton, the film focuses on Carver, who, at age seventy-six, is teaching at the Tuskegee Institute in Alabama. When one of his young students approaches him with questions about what he will be able to do when he graduates, Dr. Carver relates his life story as an example: As an orphaned son of a slave woman, Carver is stolen from his owner by nightriders and ransomed for a racehorse. His interest in nature makes him determined to get an education, and through all the rebuffs and disappointments, he perseveres to become an agricultural specialist. Developing a scheme to raise peanuts on idle land not used for cotton crops, he creates an industry. His discovery of the many uses of the peanut plant helps to realize a source of income for the poor sharecroppers. Through his diligent research and unselfish devotion to his people, Dr. Carver serves as an example to all his students. *African Americans. African-American universities and colleges. Agriculture. George Washington Carver. Education. Tuskegee Institute. College students. Horses. Kidnapping. Peanuts. Poverty. Scientists. Sharecroppers. Slavery. United States–History–Reconstruction, 1865-1898. Booker T. Washington.*

Note: *MPH* suggested that this feature would not only be popular with black audiences, but also with "interracial betterment groups" and would be appreciated for the choral singing of the Tuskegee choir. Contemporary sources indicate that students and other faculty of Tuskegee appear in the film, and that it had its world premiere at Tuskegee. In 1938, M-G-M produced a short film entitled *The Story of Dr. Carver*, directed by Fred Zinneman.

Exb 1 May 1940, p. 519. *FD* 16 Apr 1940, p. 9. *HR* 12 Apr 1940, p. 6. *MPH* 20 Apr 1940, p. 35. *NYT* 17 Apr 1940, p. 26. *Var* 17 Apr 1940, p. 16.

GEORGE WASHINGTON COHEN (Jewish Americans)

Tiffany-Stahl Productions, Inc. 20 Dec **1928** [©Tiffany-Stahl Productions, Inc.; 19 Nov 1928; LP25850]. Si; b&w. 6 reels, 5,652 ft.

Dir George Archainbaud. *Adpt, cont and dial* Isadore Bernstein. *Photog* Harry Jackson. *Film ed* Robert Kern.

Source: Based on the novel *The Cherry Tree; Comedy in One Act* by Aaron Hoffman (c1915).

Cast: George Jessel (*George Washington Cohen*), Robert Edeson (*Mr. Gorman*), Corliss Palmer (*Mrs. Gorman*), Lawford Davidson (*Mr. Connolly*), Florence Allen (*Marian*), Jane La Verne (*Child*), Paul Panzer, Edna Mae Cooper.

Comedy-drama. George Washington Cohen, who is as honest as the day is long, finds a wallet thick with money and returns it to its owner, John Gorman, a wealthy Wall Street banker. Gorman is so impressed with George that he gives him a well-paying job as his private secretary. George soon discovers that Mrs. Gorman is having an affair with Connolly, and impulsively tells Gorman of his wife's infidelity. Gorman sues for divorce, and George is the chief witness; on the stand, George has a change of heart and deliberately perjures himself in order to keep the Gormans together for the sake of their child. Sentenced to jail, George is content in the knowledge that he has won for himself the love of Gorman's penniless ward, Marian. *Bankers. Divorce. Infidelity. Jews. New York City–Wall Street. Perjury. Secretaries. Self-sacrifice. Wards and guardians.*

FD 19 May 1929. *Var* 22 May 1929, p. 16.

GEORGIA ROSE (African Americans)

Aristo Film Corp. *Dist* Aristo Film Corp. **1930**; World premiere in Los Angeles: 30 May 1930; Prod: ended Apr 1930 at the Disney Mickey Mouse Studios. Sd; b&w. 7 reels, 6,600 ft.

Dir Harry A. Gant. *Story* Harry A. Gant. *Photog* Harry A. Gant.

Song(s): "You'll Never Tell Nobody," "You're Just a Rosebud from a Garden in Georgia" and "Come Back to Your Little Mama," by Fred C. Washington; "Will There Be Any Stars in My Crown," "I'll Go Where You Want Me To Go, Dear Lord" and "Little Georgia Rose," composers undetermined.

Cast: Clarence Brooks (*Ralph*), Irene Wilson (*Rose*), Evelyn Preer (*Grace*), Roberta Hyson (*Helen*), Allegretti Anderson (*Ethel*), Edward Thompson (*Bob*), Webb King (*Joe*), Spencer Williams (*Ezra*), Dora Dean Johnson (*Mary Barnett*), E. C. Dyer (*Reverend Hoskins*).

Musical comedy, African American. [*Not viewed*]. After his crops are destroyed by the boll weevil, a black parson from Georgia leads a small band of his followers to the Midwest, hoping to find better farming conditions there. They become the tenants of Mary Barnett, and the parson's daughter, Rose, falls in love with Ralph Barnett, Mary's son. Ralph works in the city and is part of a snobbish and elite social set led by Grace Dean, whose brother Bob sweet talks Rose into singing in a cabaret in the city. Ralph goes in search of Rose and finds her in time to prevent her corruption by cabaret life. They return to the Barnett farm, and Rose is forgiven by her father. *African Americans. Cabarets. Clergy. Cotton. Georgia. Singers. Tenant farmers. United States–Midwest. United States–South. Upper classes.*

Note: Writer-director Harry A. Gant and actor Clarence Brooks had worked together earlier for the Lincoln Motion Picture Co. In a letter dated 18 Aug 1930 to William G. Nunn of the *PittsC*, published in the 23 Aug issue of the newspaper, Gant takes issue with a review Nunn wrote concerning this film. Gant writes that his company made the film "primarily and principally for colored people."

Comparing this film to other black-cast films of the time, Gant, a white man, commented, "if Mr. Nunn's interpretation of the colored cast motion picture is to be along the lines of the white companies' productions such as *Hallelujah*, *Hearts in Dixie* and others of that type, Mr. Brooks and myself have been working in vain. We have tried, with our limited means, to make a picture with an all-Negro cast, showing the Negro as he really is in all walks of life....if we made pictures of the Negro singing spirituals, eating watermelon and shooting craps, as is generally done by white people, we could not possibly show them in colored houses and please colored audiences.... That the picture is below standard, from the angle of the big white producing companies, is right and because of the fact that they have 20,000 theaters in the United States to derive their income from against our 200, it is up to the colored people of the United States to overlook our shortcomings in the matter of cost of production and to give us their support or any other company that is sincerely endeavoring to make pictures to please the colored people, or they will be forced to have to sit and watch people of some other race enact the principal roles of the future moving picture." The *Chicago Whip* criticized the sound quality of the film: "Not one voice registers clearly even 'talkie clear,' while from where we sat the pause between conversation of the performers appeared entirely too lengthy at times." The name of the production and distribution company was also given as Rosebud Productions.

California Eagle 23 May 1930, p. 7. *California Eagle* 30 May 1930, p. 7, 10. *Chicago Whip* 13 Sep 1930. *Chicago Whip* 20 Sep 1930, p. 14. *ChiDef* 2 Aug 1930. *New York Age* 20 Sep 1930, p. 7. *PittsC* 3 May 1930, pt. II, p. 6. *Pittsburgh Courier* 16 Aug 1930, pt. II, p. 7. *Pittsburgh Courier* 23 Aug 1930, pt. II, p. 7.

GERONIMO (Native Americans, Apache)

Paramount Pictures, Inc. *Dist* Paramount Pictures, Inc. 12 Jan **1940**; Phoenix, AZ premiere: 26 Nov 1939; Prod: late Feb—late Mar 1939; additional scenes 14 Sep 1939 [©Paramount Pictures, Inc.; 21 Jan 1940; LP9339]. Sd (Western Electric Mirrophonic Recording); b&w. 10 reels. 89 min. PCA cert no. 5245.

[*Exec prod* William LeBaron]. *Dir* Paul H. Sloane. [*Asst dir* George Templeton]. *Scr* Paul H. Sloane. [*Orig story* Paul H. Sloane]. *Photog* Henry Sharp. *Photog eff* Farciot Edouart. *Art dir* Hans Dreier and Earl Hedrick. *Ed* John Link. *Int dec* A. E. Freudeman. *Mus score* Gerald Carbonara and John Leipold. *Sd rec* Harry Lindgren and Don Johnson.

Cast: Preston Foster [(*Captain Bill Starrett*)], Ellen Drew [(*Alice Hamilton*)], Andy Devine [(*Sneezer*)], William Henry [(*Lieutenant John Steele, Jr.*)], Ralph Morgan [(*General Steele*)], Gene Lockhart [(*Gillespie*)], Marjorie Gateson [(*Mrs. Steele*)], Pierre Watkin [(*Colonel White*)], Chief Thunder Cloud [(*Geronimo*)], [Kitty Kelly (*Daisy Devine*)], [Monte Blue (*Interpreter*)], [Addison Richards (*Frederick Allison*)], [Joseph Crehan (*President Grant*)], [Hank Bell (*Cherrycow*)], [William Haade (*McNeil*)], [Stanley Andrews (*Colombus Delano*)], [Ivan Miller (*Hamilton Fish*)], [Frank M. Thomas (*First politician*)], [Richard Denning (*Lieutenant Larned*)], [Syd Saylor (*Sergeant*)], [Gaylord Pendleton (*Private Young*)], [Eddy Waller (*Private*)], [Pat West (*Soldier*)], [Francis Ford (*First scout*)], [William Edmunds (*Second scout*)], [Russell Simpson (*Third scout*)], [Jack Chapin, Phillip Warren (*Orderlies*)], [Archie Twitchell (*General's orderly*)], [Harry Templeton (*Soldier Burns*)], [Cecil

Kellogg (*Soldier Kells*)], [José Domínguez (*Pedro*)], [Davison Clark (*Second politician*)], [Warren Dunaway (*Soldier Dunn*)], [James Glines (*Soldier Gaines*)], [Carl Sepulveda (*Soldier Jones*)], [Ted Wells (*Soldier Wall*)], [Frank Cordell (*Sergeant Cord*)], [Tommy Coats (*Corporal Coot*)], [Lee Shumway (*Captain Williams*)], [Chief Thunderbird (*Chief Eskiminzu*)], [Hooper Atchley (*George Boutwell*)], [Wheaton Chambers (*John A. Rawlins*)], [Edward Peil, Sr. (*John A. J. Cresswell*)], [John M. Sullivan (*Ebenezer Hoar*)], [Emmett Vogan (*Post doctor*)], [Harry Bailey (*Third politician*)], [Ted Oliver (*Officer*)], [Charles Stevens (*Indian*)], [Allen Fox (*Immigrants*)], [Ethel Clayton], [Gloria Williams], [Paula de Cardo].

Historical, Western. [*Print viewed*]. The bloody massacre of his family by the white man imbues the Indian leader Geronimo with a fanatical hatred and an obsessive desire to drive all "palefaces" from the Southwest. In his campaign, Geronimo is aided by Gillespie, a renegade white who supplies the Indians with rifles and ammunition. To cope with the Indian unrest, the United States Army sends General Steele to the fort in Grant, Arizona. Steele, a strict disciplinarian, insists that his troops be only comprised of seasoned soldiers, and consequently, when Jack, the son he has not seen since childhood is assigned to the general's command fresh out of West Point, the general gives the boy the cold shoulder. Although he is befriended by Captain Bill Starrett and Sneezer, the Indian scout, Lieutenant Steele rebels against his father and submits his resignation. Deciding to leave the army and go to California, the lieutenant sends for his sweetheart, Alice Hamilton, who is chaperoned by his mother. However, after Alice is wounded and Mrs. Steele killed when their coach is attacked by Indians, the lieutenant decides to single-handedly eliminate Geronimo. When Geronimo captures Jack, Starrett begs the general to let him lead a rescue mission, but Steele refuses. Defying orders, Starrett rides to free Jack and is himself captured by Geronimo. Back at the fort, a remorseful general finally realizes that he has failed his family and leads a small band of men to free his son. Learning that the general has left the protected fort, Geronimo leaves his prisoners behind in a trap to ambush the soldiers. After the detachment rescues Jack and Starrett, Geronimo and his men swoop down on them and in the ensuing gun battle, the general is wounded. Defying death, Starrett and Jack ride to the fort for reinforcements, but only Jack makes it alive. As Geronimo leads his massacre on the troops, Jack leads the reinforcements to the rescue. Not to be deprived of his prey, Geronimo, disguised as a soldier, is about to deal a death blow to the general when Jack pounces upon the renegade chief, and father and son are at last reconciled. *Apache Indians. Fathers and sons. Geronimo. Indians of North America. Revenge. United States–History–Indian Campaigns. United States. Army. Cavalry. Arizona. Engagements. Forts. Massacres. Renegades. Scouts (Frontier). Soldiers.*

Note: The working title of this film was *Great Enemy*. According to studio press releases, some backgrounds were shot at Fort Bliss, TX. The *Var* review notes that this picture marked the first use of a new fine-grain positive film, which was developed by Paramount engineers and produced by DuPont. The process lent a greater richness to the tone of the print. Although ads for the film and the *NYT* credit the role of "McNeil" to William Haade, the Paramount production files and other reviews credit Frank Cordell with the role. Cordell is credited on the CBCS with the role of "Sergeant Cord." A news item in *HR* adds that the production had to shoot around actress Kitty Kelly when Kelly spent three weeks in the hospital with a back injury. A modern source notes that writer Paul H. Sloane proposed the idea of producing this film to Paramount executives. Sloane's idea was to emulate the story of the studio's successful *Lives of a Bengal Lancer* and include footage from that film and other Paramount productions in order to make the film for a very low cost. Action sequences in the film also include footage from *Wells Fargo*, *The Plainsman*, *The Thundering Herd* and *The Texas Rangers*.

DV 16 Nov 1939, p. 3. *FD* 21 Nov 1939, p. 6. *HR* 13 Feb 1939, p. 1. *HR* 4 Apr 1939, p. 3. *HR* 14 Sep 1939, p. 2. *HR* 16 Nov 1939, p. 3. *HR* 25 Nov 1939, p. 2. *MPD* 20 Nov 1939, p. 2. *MPH* 25 Nov 1939, p. 40. *NYT* 8 Feb 1940, p. 18. *Var* 22 Nov 1939, p. 14.

GHOST MOUNTAIN *see* **ROCKY MOUNTAIN**

GHOST OF THE CISCO KID *see* **THE GAY CABALLERO**

THE GHOST OF TOLSTON'S MANOR *see* **A SON OF SATAN**

GHOST TOWN (1946) *see* **SINGIN' IN THE CORN**

GHOST TOWN (Native Americans, Cheyenne, Arapaho)
Bel-Air Productions; A Bel-Air Production. *Dist* United Artists Corp. Mar **1956**; Los Angeles opening: 7 Mar 1956 [©Sunrise Pictures, Inc.; 13 Feb 1956; LP6102]. Sd (Western Electric Recording); b&w. 75 min. PCA cert no. 17747.

Exec prod Aubrey Schenck. *Prod* Howard W. Koch. *Dir* Allen Miner. *Asst dir* Bud Andrews. *Story and scr* Jameson Brewer. *Photog* Joseph F. Biroc. *Ed* Mike Pozen. *Set des* Jack T. Collis. *Property master* Arden Cripe. *Ward* Wesley V. Jefferies and Angela Alexander. *Mus* Paul Dunlap. *Sd mix* Joe Edmondson. *Rec* Sound Services, Inc. *Hair styles* Mary Westmoreland. *Cast supv* Nina Vine. *Lighting tech* Bill Neff. *Key grip* Martin Kashuk.

Cast: Kent Taylor (*Anse Conroy*), John Smith (*Duff Dailey*), Marian Carr (*Barbara Leighton*), Serena Sande (*Maureen*), John Doucette (*Doc Clawson*), Joel Ashley (*Ben Dockery*), Gilman Rankin (*Simon Peter Wheedle*), Gary Murray (*Alex Dockery*), Edmund Hashim (*Dull Knife*), Chief Ted Nez (*Fire Knife*), William "Bill" Phillips (*Kerry McCabe*).

Western. [*Not viewed*]. A stagecoach traveling through Cheyenne country has four passengers: gambler Anse Conroy, veterinarian Doc Clawson, preacher Simon Peter Wheedle and Barbara Leighton, an apparently refined young lady. When the stage arrives at a way station, the passengers discover that it has been attacked by marauding Cheyennes, led by Dull Knife. They are met by gold prospectors Duff Dailey and Kerry McCabe. Duff, who is Barbara's fiancé, suggests that they all move on to the next station, but on the way they encounter Sgt. Ben Dockery and his son Alex, who inform them that the next station has also been wiped out. The group then heads north and comes upon a ghost town, where they decide to hide from the Indians with an old Cheyenne chief, Black Kettle, and his adopted Irish-Indian daughter Maureen, who are also in hiding there. Black Kettle is regarded as a traitor by his tribe, as several peace treaties he negotiated were followed by attacks by the U.S. Cavalry, and his people have removed his tongue. When the Cheyenne attack the town, preacher Wheedle, who believes in brotherhood with the Indians, attempts to talk with them but is killed. During the siege, the other passengers reveal their true characters and Conroy is discovered to have been selling guns to the Indians. After Dull Knife offers to let the others go free if Black Kettle surrenders, Barbara joins up with Conroy to steal Duff and Kerry's gold. Conroy double-crosses her and leaves without her, but returns when he discovers that the gold in the bags has been switched for dirt. As he has faith that Duff will try to bring justice to his tribe, Black Kettle saves them all by giving himself up for certain torture, and the attackers withdraw. Dockery, who has been fleeing from a court-martial, leaves with Conroy and Barbara to face trial, while Duff remains behind with his new love, Maureen, and old pal Kerry. *Cheyenne Indians. Ghost towns. Gold miners. Gunrunners. Preachers. Self-sacrifice. Adoption. Bigotry. Engagements. Irish Americans. Saloons. Sieges. Stables. Stagecoaches. Veterinarians.*

Note: This film was shot near Kanab, Utah.

Box 17 Dec 1955. *DV* 12 Dec 1955, p. 3. *Exh* 28 Dec 1955, p. 4079. *FD* 23 Dec 1955, p. 10. *Har* 24 Dec 1955, p. 207. *HR* 12 Dec 1955. *MPD* 8 Jun 1956. *MPHPD* 26 May 1956, p. 913. *Var* 21 Dec 1955, p. 16.

GHOSTS OF RIMROCK *see* **SECRET OF THE WASTELANDS**

GIANT (Latino)
Warner Bros. Pictures, Inc.; A George Stevens Production. *Dist* Warner Bros. Pictures, Inc. 24 Nov **1956**; New York opening: 10 Oct 1956; Los Angeles opening: 17 Oct 1956; *Prod:* mid-May—mid-Oct 1955 [©Giant Productions; 24 Nov 1956; LP9719]. Sd (RCA Recording); col (Warner Color); 1.66. 195 or 197-198 min. PCA cert no. 17675.

Prod George Stevens and Henry Ginsberg. *Dir* George Stevens. *Asst dir* Joe Rickards. *2d unit dir* Fred Guiol. *2d unit asst dir* Russ Llewellyn. [*1st asst dir* Dick Moder]. [*2d asst dir* Buddy Messenger, Rusty Meeks and Reed Killgore]. [*Dial dir* Robert Hinkle]. *Scr* Fred Guiol and Ivan Moffat. *Dir of photog* William C. Mellor. *2d unit photog* Edwin Dupar. [*Cam op* Frank Phillips and Wesley Anderson]. [*Asst cam* Jim Mathews, Eddie Alberts and Elmer Faubion]. [*Loc cam* Ted McCord]. [*Stills* Frank McCarthy]. [*Gaffer* Richard L. Wilson]. [*Spec eff* Ralph Webb]. *Prod des* Boris Leven. *Film ed* William Hornbeck. *Assoc film ed* Phil Anderson and Fred Bohanan. [*Film ed* Robert Lawrence]. *Set dec* Ralph Hurst. [*Drapery* Dean V. Lennon]. [*Prop master* John Moore]. [*Props* J. Leslie Asher and Weldon H. Patterson]. *Cost des* Marjorie Best. *Miss Taylor's cost des by* Moss Mabry. [*Men's ward* Victor Vallejo, Ted Kring and John Noble]. [*Women's ward* Sohia Stutz and Ann Landers]. *Mus comp and cond* Dimitri Tiomkin. *Sd* Earl Crain, Sr. [*Rec* Clifford Call]. [*Boom man* Samuel F. Good]. [*Cable man* James Alexander]. *Makeup supv* Gordon Bau. [*Makeup* Frank Prehoda and George Lane]. [*Hairdresser* Patricia

Westmore]. [*Body makeup* Edith Palmer]. *Prod mgr* Tom Andre. [*Asst prod mgr* Charles Greenlaw]. [*Unit mgr* Ralph Nelson]. [*Loc mgr* Carl Benoit]. [*Accounting* Harold Hourihan]. [*Scr supv* Sam Freedle]. [*Secy* Betty Coryell]. [*Casting* Hoyt Bowers]. [*Unit pub* Ted Ashton]. [*Greenman* George Stoltz]. [*Best boy* Warren E. Boes and Frank Lamber]. [*Grip* Charles Harris].

Song(s): "Giant" and "There's Never Been Anyone Else But You," music by Dimitri Tiomkin, lyrics by Paul Francis Webster; "Yellow Rose of Texas," traditional.

Source: Based on the novel *Giant* by Edna Ferber (New York, 1952).

Cast: Elizabeth Taylor [(*Leslie Lynnton Benedict*)], Rock Hudson [(*Jordan "Bick" Benedict, II*)], James Dean [(*Jett Rink*)], and presenting Carroll Baker [(*Luz Benedict, II*)], Jane Withers [(*Vashti Snythe*)], Chill Wills [(*Uncle Bawley*)], Mercedes McCambridge [(*Luz Benedict*)], Dennis Hopper [(*Jordan Benedict, III*)], Sal Mineo [(*Angel Obregon, III*)], Rodney Taylor [(*Sir David Karfrey*)], Judith Evelyn [(*Mrs. Horace Lynnton*)], Earl Holliman [(*Bob Dace*)], Robert Nichols [(*Pinky Snythe*)], Paul Fix [(*Dr. Horace Lynnton*)], Alexander Scourby [(*Old Polo*)], Fran Bennett [(*Judy Benedict*)], Charles Watts [(*Whiteside*)], Elsa Cardenas [(*Juana*)], Carolyn Craig [(*Lacey Lynnton*)], Monte Hale [(*Bale Clinch*)], Sheb Wooley [(*Gabe Target*)], Mary Ann Edwards [(*Adarene Clinch*)], Victor Millan [(*Angel Obregon, I*)], Mickey Simpson [(*Sarge*)], Pilar Del Rey [(*Mrs. Obregon*)], Maurice Jara [(*Dr. Guerra*)], Noreen Nash [(*Lona Lane*)], Ray Whitley [(*Watts*)], Napoleon Whiting [(*Swazey*)], [Felipe Turich (*Gomez*)], [Francisco Villalobos (*Mexican priest*)], [Tina Menard (*Lupe*)], [Anna Maria Majalca (*Petra*)], [Guy Teague (*Harper*)], [Natividad Vacio (*Desubio*)], [Max Terhune (*Dr. Walker*)], [Ray Bennett (*Dr. Borneholm*)], [Barbara Barrie (*Mary Lou Decker*)], [George Dunne (*Verne Decker*)], [Slim Talbot (*Clay Hodgins*)], [Tex Driscoll (*Clay Hodgins, Sr.*)], [Juney Ellis (*Essie Lou Hodgins*)], [Charles Meredith (*Minister*)], [Noreen Nash (*Lona Lane*)], [Rush Williams (*Waiter*)], [Bill Hale (*Bartender*)], [Tom Monroe, Marc Hamilton (*Guards*)], [John Wiley (*Asst. manager*)], [Martha Randall (*Young operator*)], [Claudia Bryar (*Older operator*)], [Carl Moore (*Toastmaster*)], [Paul Kruger (*General*)], [Ella Ethridge (*General's wife*)], [Eddie Baker (*Governor*)], [Ethel Greenwood (*Governor's wife*)], [Fernando Alvarado, Tony Morella (*Bus boys*)], [Julian Rivero (*Old man*)], [Maxine Gates (*Mrs. Sarge*)], [John Caler (*Driver*)], [Dan White, Jack Lomas (*Truck drivers*)], [Mitzi Sutherland, Pat Cortland, Vera Lee Friedman (*Vashti's daughters*)], [Richard Bishop, David Bishop (*Jordan, infant*)], [Steven Kay (*Jordan, age four*)], [Mary Ann Cashen, Georgann Cashen (*Judy, infant*)], [Dana Dillaway (*Judy, age four*)], [Christine Werner (*Luz, infant*)], [Judy Lent, Jill Lent (*Luz, age two*)], [John Garcia (*Angel, infant*)], [David Jiminez (*Angel, age five*)], [Colleen Crane, Marlene Crane], Wanda Lee Thompson (*Judy, II, age two*)], [Perfideo Aguilar, Margaret Trujillo (*Jordy, IV, infant*)], [Ramon Ramirez (*Jordy, IV, age two*)], [Ina Poindexter].

Historical, Drama. [*Print viewed*]. In the mid-1920s, Texas rancher Jordan "Bick" Benedict II goes to Maryland to buy "War Winds," a prized stallion, from Dr. Horace Lynnton. There Bick falls in love with Lynnton's spirited elder daughter Leslie. After Leslie breaks her engagement to Englishman Sir David Karfrey, they quickly marry and Bick brings Leslie back to his enormous ranch, Reata. When they arrive in the dusty, windswept town named after Bick's family, Leslie graciously greets their Mexican-American driver, Angel Obregon, and Bick admonishes her not to be too kind to "those people." Bick's tough, cattle-driving sister Luz throws a party for the newlyweds and Leslie faints when she is served a plate of barbequed calves' heads. Determined to become a real Texan, however, Leslie rises early the next morning and takes the breakfast duties away from Luz, who looks upon Leslie as a rival to her position as head of the household. While Luz, Bick, and Leslie are out driving cattle, Bick sends Leslie home with Jett Rink, a rough cowboy who is close to Luz, but clashes with Bick. On the way back to Bick's mansion, Leslie insists on stopping in Reata, where the poor Mexican laborers live. Leslie goes into one of the hovels and discovers that a mother, Mrs. Obregon, and her newborn, Angel III, are seriously ill. Returning home, Leslie learns that Luz has taken a serious fall while trying to break War Winds. After Luz dies, Leslie asks the doctor to go to the village to tend to the Obregons' sick baby, despite Bick's protests that their family physician should not tend to "those people." At the funeral, Bick, his lawyer and other friends tell Jett that Luz willed him

a piece of land, but encourage him to instead accept a cash settlement twice the value of the property. Jett declines the cash, and insists on taking the plot of land which he calls "Little Reata." Soon Leslie gives birth to twins, Jordan III and Judy. As the years pass, Bick continues to argue with her over her work at the migrant labor camps, where she has hired a new, Mexican-American physician, Dr. Guerra, to help improve living conditions. Leslie gives birth to another girl, whom they name Luz, and at the twins' fourth birthday party, Bick, who clearly favors his son, insists on forcing his frightened heir to ride a new pony. Bick's disappointment at Jordan's tears and Leslie's admonishment is further heightened when little Angel III skillfully rides the pony back to the corral. Uncle Bawley, Leslie's ally in her conflicts with Bick, tells her to continue rearing the children her way, as Bick knows no more about the job than his father. Realizing that their differences have caused too much friction in their marriage, Leslie decides to take the children for a long visit to Maryland. After a lonely Thanksgiving for both Bick and Leslie, Bick unexpectedly shows up at the wedding of Leslie's younger sister Lacey, who is marrying David. Bick takes Leslie back to Reata after she admits that she cannot change and he says Texans like vinegar with their greens. Meanwhile, Jett, who has found oil on Little Reata, becomes wealthy. His success enrages Bick, who forces Jett to stop using the name Reata, and the new company, Jettexas, becomes a multi-million dollar company. Years later, as the children approach adulthood, Judy wishes to go to college at Texas Tech to study animal husbandry, although Leslie wants her to go finishing school in Switzerland. Jordan, whom Bick has tried to groom since birth to be the heir to Reata, decides to become a doctor. At Christmas, just after the bombing of Pearl Harbor, Judy elopes with her sweetheart, Bob Dace, who has just been drafted. Angel Obregon brings Angel III to visit, proudly showing off his son's new soldier's uniform, and Jordan, who has received an over-sized cowboy hat from his father, meets Juana, a young nurse in training who has accompanied Dr. Guerra to the festivities. That afternoon, Bick gets drunk on eggnog, and tries to convince Jordan, and then Bob and Judy, to take the ranch when he retires, but they want to start a small ranch of their own. Jett, not realizing that it is Christmas, shows up and convinces Bick to allow an oil well to be drilled on Reata. After the war, all of the local ranchers, including Bick and Leslie, have become oil rich. At a pool party to celebrate the end of World War II, Leslie expresses disgust that the Texas oil barons are receiving a 27.5% tax exemption from the government. Jordan, who has just married Juana in a private, Mexican-Catholic ceremony, then announces his wedding, much to his father's anger. A short time later, Angel III is brought home in a casket and, at the funeral, after the attending soldiers give Angel's father the American flag in honor of his son's bravery, Bick gives the grieving Obregons a Texas flag from his own collection. Soon Judy and Bob, and Juana and Jordan have their first babies, both boys. Jett, now called "Mr. Texas," plans to have a huge celebration to commemorate the opening of his new airport and hotel in Hermosa, Texas. Luz, who has a crush on Jett, can think of nothing else, and Bick finally decides to attend "like the best of 'em," and even buys his own airplane to arrive in style. At a celebratory parade, Bick and Leslie are distressed to discover Luz riding a float as "Queen of the Parade." Later, in the hotel's quiet bar, Jett ignores his guests, gets drunk and proposes to Luz, who demurely declines, then leaves. At a cocktail party in the Benedict suite, Jordan arrives with their baby. When Juana goes to the hotel beauty salon to get her hair done for the banquet, they refuse service because they have orders from Jett not to do business with "her people." Jordan grows furious and breaks the salon's mirror. A short time later, Jett, almost stumbling from drunkenness, arrives late at the banquet, at which he is to give a speech. As he walks up to the podium, Jordan confronts him and the two exchange punches, until Jordan is carried out nearly unconscious. Bick then takes Jett into a store room and gives him a thrashing, after which the entire Benedict family and their close friends leave the banquet room. Jett finally arrives at his place on the dais and promptly passes out. Back in their suite, when Bick refers to Juana as a "fine little gal," Jordan becomes angry and accuses him of being as bad as Jett and argues that Bick only fought "Mr. Texas" because Jordan had disgraced the Benedict name by losing the fight. Luz is upset and wants to go to Jett, but her parents refuse. Uncle Bawley, for whom Leslie has always had a soft spot, convinces her to let him take Luz to Jett. They find him drunkenly sobbing in an empty

banquet room, rambling about his love for the beautiful Leslie. The next day, Bick sends the airplane back to Reata while he, Leslie, Luz, Juanna and the baby drive home. On the way, they stop at a roadside café where the waitress does not want to serve them because of Juana and the baby, but the owner acquiesces, realizing that Leslie and Bick are well-to-do. When an elderly Mexican husband and wife enter the café, however, the owner roughly tries to throw them out. Seeing this, Bick goes to their defense. Despite using his influence as "Bick Benedict," the owner refuses to change his mind and the two men engage in a brawl which ends in Bick's complete defeat. Back at Reata, Leslie reveals that Luz has forgotten about Jett and gone to Hollywood to become an actress. As she and Bick relax while babysitting their two grandsons, one white and one brown, Bick says that his grandson looks like a "wetback," but that men will just have to get over it. When he reflects that he is a failure, Leslie says that she realized what a great man he was when she saw him lying on the floor of the café after fighting for the rights of the downtrodden. The couple, finally content, gaze at the two boys, whose faces represent the future of Texas. *Family relationships. Marriage–Mixed. Mexican Americans. Migrant workers. Oil wells. Racism. Ranches. Texas. Businessmen. Cattle. Childbirth. Christmas. Cowboys. Drunkenness. Funerals. Horses. Lawyers. Parades. Physicians. Poverty. Thanksgiving Day. Twins. Wealth. World War II.*

Note: Edna Ferber's novel *Giant* was said to have been based on the life of Texas oil mogul Glen McCarthy. The film was shot on location in Marfa and Valentine, Texas, and Charlottesville, Virginia. The large Benedict home was built at the Warner Bros. prop department and shipped to the Worth Evans Ranch, twenty-one miles from Marfa, where the facade remains. The oil derricks seen in the film were also built in Hollywood and transported to the Texas film site. Valentine was the location of the film's Mexican village, and Charlottesville, the site of "Leslie Lynnton Benedict's's" Maryland family home. The Maryland sequences were shot on a seventeenth century estate. Production notes claim that of the hundreds of Texans hired to play extras in the film, ten were millionaires. Most of the extras appear in the film's barbeque scene. Other efforts to realistically render Texas included dialogue director Robert Hinkle's recording all the dialogue for the actors who played Texans and then having them listen to the tapes to learn the proper accents.

Contemporary reviews for the film praised its direct and unflinching portrayal of racism. Reviews singled out the scene in which patriarch "Bick Benedict," accompanied by his Mexican daughter-in-law and her son, brawls with a diner owner when he tries to defend a group of Mexicans who have been refused service. During the fight, the song "Yellow Rose of Texas" played on the diner's jukebox. After the film's release, that version of the song became a hit record. Hudson, in a later interview, claimed that when he viewed the film for the first time with an audience, he was booed throughout, but when the audience cheered him in the diner scene he realized the reaction was to his character and not to his abilities as an actor. The 10 Oct 1956 *HR* review stated that, due to its portrayal of race, the film "has the drumbeat of contemporary history," and the *DV* review noted that *Giant* demonstrates how racism against Mexicans in the Southwest is "as bad, and as wrong, as the Negro's situation in the Deep South and elsewhere." The review added the warning that the film's treatment of "tolerance" may create controversy in the South.

According to information in the file on the film in the MPAA/PCA Collection at the AMPAS Library, careful representation of ethnicity seemed to be the Code office's only concern. Geoffrey Shurlock requested that the producers of the film receive "adequate technical advice" in filming the Mexican wedding ceremony and burial ritual. The film received the following Academy Award nominations: Best Actor (James Dean, Rock Hudson), Supporting Actress (Mercedes McCambridge), Art Direction, Color (Boris Leven and Ralph S. Hurst), Costume Design, Color (Moss Mabry, Marjorie Best), Film Editing (William Hornbeck, Philip W. Anderson, Fred Bohanan), Best Scoring of a Dramatic or Comedy Picture (Dmitri Tiomkin), Best Adapted Screenplay (Fred Guiol, Ivan Moffat) and Best Picture. George Stevens alone won the award for Best Direction. *Giant* marked Carrol Baker's first major film role, the American film debut of Elsa Cardenas and James Dean's final screen performance. On 26 Sep 1955, four days after filming his final scenes, Dean was killed in a car crash near Salinas, CA. Many reviews singled Dean out for praise, and the *Var* review called Dean's performance "outstanding," and stated that "the film only proves what a promising talent has been lost."

According to modern and contemporary sources, Grace Kelly was sought for the role of Leslie Benedict. Modern sources claim that once her engagement to Prince Rainier of Monaco was announced, however, M-G-M decided not to loan her out for *Giant*. Elizabeth Taylor, who ultimately received the highly desirable role, was also a contract player with M-G-M, which loaned her out to Warner Bros. Modern sources also claim that Rock Hudson, when given the choice of his leading lady by Stevens, chose Taylor. Taylor, who had recently given birth to her second child, was apparently plagued with health problems during the shooting, a fact that did not help the troubled relationship between Taylor and director Stevens. Modern interviews with Hudson and Taylor reported that the day after Dean's death was announced, Stevens required a distraught and inconsolable Taylor to complete reaction shots for a scene she had played with Dean, and that the actress never forgave him. An Oct 1996 *AmCin* article includes Jack Trent (*Guest*) and Nick Adams (*Voice double for Dean in the banquet scene*) in the cast, and adds the following names to the

crew credits: *Spec visual eff* Jack Cosgrove; *Prod asst* George Stevens, Jr.; *Makeup* Bill Woods; *Hairdresser* Ruby Felkner; *Dance dir* Bob Osgood; and *Scr supv* Howard Hohler.

AmCin Mar 1956, pp. 158-9, 174-6. *AmCin* Oct 1996, pp. 86-92. *Box* 13 Oct 1956, p. 20. *Box* 27 Oct 1956, p. 3. *DV* 10 Oct 1956, p. 3. *FD* 10 Oct 1956, p. 7. *HR* 20 May 1955, p. 11. *HR* 7 Oct 1955, p. 17. *HR* 10 Oct 1956, p. 3. *LAEx* 8 Mar 1955. *LAMirror-News* 7 Jul 1955. *LAT* 25 Sep 1956. *LAT* 18 Oct 1956. *MPD* 10 Oct 1956. *MPHPD* 20 Oct 1956, p. 114. *NYT* 11 Oct 1956, p. 51. *Var* 10 Oct 1956, p. 6. *Var* 1 Aug 1957, p. 1, 6.

A GIANT OF HIS RACE (African Americans)

North State Film Corp. *Dist* Norman Film Mfg. Co. Sep **1921**; Chicago opening: 3 Sep 1921. Si; b&w. 7-8 reels, ca 6,300 or 8,000 ft.

Dir Ben Strasser.

Cast: Mr. Billopps, Miss Young, Mabel Holmes, Walter Holeby, Walter Long, Ruth Freeman (*Maid*).

African American, Historical, Drama. [*Not viewed*]. Munga, a faithful and optimistic African enslaved in the New World, dies of old age and leaves behind a son who had been brought with him from Africa and who bears his name. The young man, taking the name of Covington, works his way through medical school, and upon graduating, devotes his life to racial uplift. Sometime later, an epidemic known as the "yellow plague" is decimating the members of the black community where he has established a thriving practice. Covington spends hours in his laboratory trying to find a cure for the plague, and finally, when a young woman teacher offers herself as a subject for his experiments, he finds the cure and is awarded $100,000 for his discovery. Having saved his race from the horrible epidemic, Covington and the teacher fall in love and then marry. *Africa. African Americans. Ambition. Plague. Romance. Schoolteachers. Slavery.*

Note: The North State Film Corp. was located in Winston-Salem, NC. In an article in *Billboard*, African-American actor and director Leigh Whipper called this film the best Negro picture he had seen. The film had a pre-release show in Winston-Salem on 30 Aug 1921.

Billboard 1 Oct 1921, p. 47.

THE GILDED ROOSTER *see* **THE LAST FRONTIER**

THE GILDED SPIDER (Italian Americans)

Bluebird Photoplays, Inc. *Dist* Bluebird Photoplays, Inc. 8 May **1916** [©Bluebird Photoplays, Inc.; 15 Apr 1916; LP8083]. Si; b&w. 5 reels.

Dir Joseph De Grasse. *Scen* Ida May Park.

Cast: Louise Lovely (*Leonita/Elisa*), Lon Chaney (*Giovanni*), Lule Warrenton (*Rosa*), Gilmore Hammond (*Cyrus Kirkham*), Marjorie Ellison (*Mrs. Kirkham*), Hayward Mack (*Burton Armitage*), Jay Belasco (*Paul Winston*).

Drama. While traveling in Italy, Cyrus Kirkham, a dissolute American, kidnaps Leonita, but she kills herself rather than let him seduce her. Fifteen years later, Giovanni, Leonita's husband, arrives in the United States accompanied by his teen-age daughter Elisa. Giovanni holds a grudge against Americans that began with Leonita's death, so when Elisa falls in love with Paul Winston, an American artist, her father disapproves of the romance. When Cyrus sees Paul's portrait of Elisa, he decides to track her down and then brings her to a high society party. Giovanni finds out and breaks into the party intent on killing Cyrus. As soon as Cyrus sees him, however, and recognizes him as Leonita's husband, he drops dead from the shock. Then, convinced that his daughter's good name has been ruined, Giovanni kills himself, thus finally allowing Elisa and Paul to get married. *Cads. Fathers and daughters. Italians. Reputation. Suicide. Americans in foreign countries. Artists. Death by shock. Immigrants. Italy. Kidnapping. Parties. Portraits (Paintings). Recognition.*

Note: The title of the film was changed from *The Full Cup*.

MPN 6 May 1916, p. 2724. *MPW* 6 May 1916, p. 12. *MPW* 13 May 1916, p. 1228. *Var* 28 Apr 1916, p. 29. *Wid's* 27 Apr 1916, p. 536.

GIN FEN NEE SHAAN (Chinese language)

Grandview Film Co. **1947?**; Hong Kong showing: 1947? Sd; b&w. Length undetermined. Chinese language.

Dir Joseph Sunn.

Cast: Wong Hok-sing. [*Not viewed*]. [No information concerning the plot of this film has been located.].

Note: The Cantonese transliterated title is *Gem Fen Ngei Seng*. The English language title is *The Gold Braided Dress*. This film was probably made in the U.S.

GIN GUO CHIN YUAN (Chinese language)

Grandview Film Co. **1943**. Sd; b&w. Length undetermined. Chinese language.

Dir Joseph Sunn.

Cast: Wong Hok-sing. [*Not viewed*]. [No information concerning the plot of this film has been located.].

Note: The Cantonese transliterated title is *Kum Koh Tsen Yun*. The English language translation of the title is *Romance in the Golden Country*. This film was probably made in the U.S.

Chinese Times (San Francisco) 3 Feb 1943, p. 7.

THE GIRL FROM CHICAGO (African Americans)

Micheaux Pictures Corp.; Oscar Micheaux's Production. *Dist* Micheaux Pictures Corp. **1932?**. Sd; b&w. Length undetermined.

Pres A. BURTON RUSSELL. *Dir* Oscar Micheaux. *Asst dir* Vere E. Johns. *Story and adpt* Oscar Micheaux. *Photog* Sam Orleans. *Rec eng* Richard Halpenny.

Cast: Carl Mahon (*Alonso White*), Star Calloway (*Norma Shepard*), Alice B. Russell (*Miss Warren*), Eunice Brooks (*Mary Austin*), Minta Cato (*Her sister*), John Everett (*Jeff Ballinger*), Frank Wilson (*Wade Washington*), Cherokee Thornton (*A "snitch"*), Grace Smith (*Liza Hatfield*), Erwin Gary (*A numbers collector*).

African American, Crime, Drama. [*Print viewed*]. While returning from Europe, Alonso White, of the U.S. Secret Service, receives a telegram at sea telling him where to learn of his next assignment. Meanwhile, in "dear old Virginia," Norma Shepard graduates from high school, and Miss Warren arranges a teaching job for her with a friend in Batesburg. Norma finds her way to Mary Austin's boardinghouse, refusing the advances of Jeff Ballinger, the town boss, along the way. Mary is disturbed to find a note from Ballinger in which he expresses interest in Norma and states he will be around to see her. Wade Washington, a kind neighbor, introduces Alonso, who has just arrived at the roominghouse, as a new boarder. When Liza Hatfield, "Ballinger's woman," announces she is leaving, he shoots her. Arriving home an hour later, Washington, Liza's husband, finds her wounded. Although he tells her she deserves what has happened, he still loves her, but she hates him for not preventing her affair with Ballinger. While walking by a lake a few days later, Alonso and Norma realize they are in love, though he still remains reticent about discussing his job. Liza writes Washington a note announcing she is leaving him and Batesburg. Alonso finally reveals to Norma that he has been sent to investigate Ballinger. When Ballinger arrives to see Norma, a confederate at a window tries to warn him of Alonso's presence, but instead Ballinger shoots the confederate. Alonso takes the handcuffed Ballinger to jail and upon returning, learns that Mary has departed for New York to be with her sister, leaving Norma alone. Alonso proposes marriage to Norma, and after she accepts, they leave for Harlem. At the Radium Club, Norma recognizes Liza as an exotic singer. Liza is now married to Gomez, a Cuban who is head of the numbers racket. Mary has been spending all her money betting on the numbers and hating herself for it, because she needs $500 to pay for an operation for her sister. She places a large bet and wins, causing Gomez to flee. However, Liza catches and shoots Gomez, taking the money from him that belonged to her. Minutes later, Mary arrives to collect her winnings and, discovering Gomez's body, takes the $11,000 he owed her and leaves. Mary is prosecuted for the murder and sentenced to death, although Alonso still believes her innocent. On board a ship, Alonso locates Liza and, by seducing her, obtains a confession from her. With the case brought to a successful conclusion, Mary returns to Batesburg and the newly wed Whites take a honeymoon in Bermuda. *African Americans. Boardinghouses. Criminals. False arrests. Murder. Numbers racket. Secret Service. Confession (Law). Cubans. New York City–Harlem. Newlyweds. Nightclubs. Ocean liners. Operations, Surgical. Political bosses. Proposals (Marital). Seduction. Ships. Singers. Sisters. Teachers. Virginia. Wagers.*

Note: According to the onscreen credits, which are preceeded by the line "With a great COLORED CAST as follows," this film was based the short story "Jeff Bollinger's Woman," however, no information has been found as to the author of the story or its publication. The print viewed had numerous abrupt changes in locale and subplot, for which the narrative did not prepare the viewer. Four songs, two sung by Minta Cato, one sung by Frank Wilson and one sung by Grace Smith are heard in the film, although onscreen credits do not identify them. The titles indicate the film was copyrighted by the Micheaux Pictures Corp. of New York City in 1932, although no registration has been found. Modern sources give the length as 69 minutes, and list additional cast

members as "Slick" Chester, Juano Hernandez, Chick Evans, Bud Harris and the Rhythm Rascals. Although they are based on different literary sources, this film and the 1926 Micheaux film *The Spider's Web* (see *AFI Catalog of Feature Films, 1921-30*; F2.5320) have similar story lines.

THE GIRL FROM GOD'S COUNTRY (Native Americans)

Nell Shipman Productions, Inc. *Dist* F. B. Warren Corp. 18 Sep **1921** [©Nell Shipman Productions, Inc.; 25 Sep 1921; LP17007]. Si; b&w. 7 reels, 6,957 ft.

Pres W. H. Clune. *Dir* Nell Shipman and Bert Van Tuyle. *Story and scen* Nell Shipman. *Photog* Joseph Walker.

Cast: Nell Shipman (*Neeka Le Mort/Marion Carslake*), Edward Burns (*Owen Glendon*), Al Filson (*J. Randall Carslake*), George Berrell (*Pierre Le Mort*), Walt Whitman (*The old inventor*), C. K. Van Auker (*Otto Kraus*), Lillian Leighton (*Notawa*), L. M. Wells (*Sandy McIntosh*), Milla Davenport (*Mrs. Kraus*).

Melodrama. Carslake, a millionaire airplane manufacturer, his daughter, Marion, and her fiancé are on a hunting party in the North. There they meet Neeka, a half-breed girl who saves Carslake from the wrath of her grandfather, who recognizes him as the betrayer of her mother. Unaware that she is actually his daughter, Carslake adopts the girl and takes her to California. Otto Kraus, Carslake's competitor in a trans-Pacific flight, enlists Neeka's sympathies for his efforts when she and Marion quarrel over social blunders, and he obtains the secret of a "solidified gasoline," which Carslake himself has gained fraudulently from a demented inventor. The inventor's mind is restored when a hangar is set afire, and Neeka, realizing she has been duped, rescues him. Carslake's pilot is injured, but Neeka aids her sweetheart, a blinded aviator; Kraus is defeated in the competition and drowns after a fight with Neeka. *Aeronautics. California. Gasoline. Hunting. Indians of North Amerca–Mixed blood. Inventors. Millionaires. Parentage.*

FD 18 Sep 1921. *Var* 18 Nov 1921, p. 42.

GIRL FROM GOD'S COUNTRY (Native Americans, Native Alaskans)

Republic Pictures Corp. *Dist* Republic Pictures Corp. 30 Jul **1940**; Prod: 17 May–8 Jun 1940 [©Republic Pictures Corp.; 30 Jul 1940; LP9999]. Sd (RCA "High Fidelity" Sound System); b&w. 8 reels, 6,647 ft. 75 min. Passed by the National Board of Review. PCA cert no. 6369.

Assoc prod Armand Schaefer. *Dir* Sidney Salkow. [*Asst dir* Phil Ford]. *Scr* Elizabeth Meehan and Robert Lee Johnson. *Addl dial* Malcolm Stuart Boylan. *Photog* Jack Marta. *Art dir* John Victor Mackay. *Film ed* William Morgan. *Supv ed* Murray Seldeen. *Ward* Adele Palmer. *Mus dir* Cy Feuer. *Prod mgr* Al Wilson.

Source: Based on the short story "Island Doctor" by Ray Millholland in *The Saturday Evening Post* (29 Jul 1939).

Cast: Chester Morris [(*Jim Holden, previously known as Dr. Gary Currier*)], Jane Wyatt [(*Anne Webster*)], Charles Bickford [(*Bill Bogler*)], Mala [(*Joe*)], Kate Lawson [(*Koda*)], John Bleifer [(*Ninimook*)], Mamo Clark [(*Mrs. Bearfat Tillicoot*)], Ferike Boros [(*Mrs. Broken Thumb*)], Don Zelaya [(*Tom Broken Thumb*)], Clem Bevans [(*Ben*)], Ed Gargan [(*Poker player*)], Spencer Charters [(*Dealer*)], Thomas Jackson [(*Poker player*)], Vic Potel [(*Jake*)], Si Jenks [(*Trapper*)], Gene Morgan [(*Man at the dock*)], [Ace, a dog (*Blitzen*)].

Medical, Northwest, Drama. [*Print viewed*]. Jim Holden, a young doctor practicing in Alaska, eagerly awaits the arrival of his new nurse, Anne Webster. All of his previous nurses have been driven home within a few weeks by the rigors of the Alaskan winter, the primitive conditions and the surly disposition of their employer. Anne appears to be no exception, for after her first glimpse of her desolate new surroundings, she states that she will be returning home the next morning. Before she leaves, however, she witnesses Jim and his Eskimo assistant Joe deliver Mrs. Bearfat Tillicoot's baby by a Caeserian section. Anne is deeply impressed by Jim's dedication as he use his own blood to give Mrs. Tillicoot a life-saving transfusion. That night, Joe's wife Koda pleads with Anne to stay, but she remains firm in her resolve, even though she is again impressed by Jim's kindness to his patients. She watches as he refuses payment from a miner, whose dying partner was able to end his life quickly with the drugs that Jim left for him to use if he wished. The next day, Anne is about to leave when U.S. Marshal Bill Bogler arrives with Ninimook, an Eskimo Bogler arrested for fur theft. During their struggle, Bogler had fractured Ninimook's skull, and he now demands that Jim save the

man's life. Anne assists as Jim performs the dangerous brain surgery, but she leaves as Ninimook convalesces. After she is gone, Jim is needed to attend the Tillicoot baby, but is forced to stay with Ninimook. Jim warns Bogler that he will be held responsible if the Eskimo dies, but Ninimook soon recovers. As Bogler is praising Jim's surgical skill, he mentions a Dr. Gary Currier, a brilliant surgeon who fled Seattle five years earlier after being arrested for the euthanasic death of his terminally-ill father, who was also a prominent physician. Jim shrugs off Bogler's intimations, although he is in fact Currier, then goes to visit the Tillicoots. There he finds Anne, who, having chosen to say, has been tending the ill baby for two days. Jim is delighted to see her, and as the pair return to his house, their mutual attraction becomes obvious. When they arrive, Jim is forced to admit that he is Currier, and Bogler arrests him. Jim pleads with Anne to look after his patients until another doctor arrives, then leaves with Bogler. Joe and Anne follow them and help Jim escape with the aid of his lead sled dog, Blitzen. While Jim is in hiding, he reveals to Anne that his father committed suicide and that he accepted the blame in order to protect his father's reputation. Bogler is overcome by snow blindness while he is chasing Jim, and despite the danger to his own life and freedom, Jim tends to Bogler and restores his eyesight. Grateful for the doctor's help, Bogler grants Jim his freedom, and Jim and Anne celebrate with Joe and Koda. *Alaska. Euthanasia. False accusations. Fugitives. Native Alaskans. Nurses. Physicians. United States. Marshals. Blindness-Temporary. Childbirth. Dogs. Dogsledding. Drugs. Gratitude. Miners. Operations, Surgical. Romance. Self-sacrifice. Servants. Suicide. Vocational obsession.*

Note: According to *HR* news items from Oct and Nov 1939, Scott Darling was assigned to write the screenplay, but his contribution to the completed film has not been confirmed. Another *HR* news item noted that the title of Elizabeth Meehan and Robert Lee Johnson's screenplay was "All Night Long" when they sold it to Republic. According to *HR* production charts, Rosina Galli was in the cast, although her participation in the finished film has not been confirmed. This was Jane Wyatt's first film since *Lost Horizon* in 1937 (see *AFI Catalog of Feature Films, 1931-40*; F3.2576).

Box 27 Jul 1940. *DV* 17 Jul 1940, p. 3. *FD* 23 Jul 1940, p. 6. *HR* 31 Oct 1939, p. 1. *HR* 18 Nov 1939, p. 1. *HR* 26 Apr 1940, p. 4. *HR* 17 May 1940, p. 10. *HR* 18 May 1940, p. 6. *HR* 8 Jun 1940, p. 4. *HR* 19 Jul 1940, p. 3. *MPD* 23 Jul 1940, p. 6. *MPH* 27 Jul 1940, p. 35. *NYT* 9 Sep 1940, p. 18. *Var* 7 Aug 1940, p. 16.

THE GIRL FROM JONES BEACH (Immigrants)
Warner Bros. Pictures, Inc.; A Warner Bros.—First National Picture. *Dist* Warner Bros. Pictures, Inc. 16 Jul 1949; *Prod:* mid-May—1 Jul 1948 [©Warner Bros. Pictures, Inc.; 16 Jul 1949; LP2408]. Sd (RCA Sound System); b&w. 77 or 79 min.

Prod Alex Gottlieb. *Dir* Peter Godfrey. *Dial dir* John Maxwell. [*Asst dir* Art Lueker]. *Scr* I. A. L. Diamond. *Based on a story by* Allen Boretz. *Dir of photog* Carl Guthrie. *Spec eff* William McGann and Edwin DuPar. *Art dir* Stanley Fleischer. *Film ed* Rudi Fehr. *Set dec* William Kuehl. *Ward* Leah Rhodes. *Orch* Leonid Raab. *Mus* David Buttolph. *Sd* Dolph Thomas. *Makeup artist* Perc Westmore.

Cast: RONALD REAGAN [(*Bob Randolph*)], VIRGINIA MAYO [(*Ruth Wilson*)], EDDIE BRACKEN [(*Chuck Donovan*)], Dona Drake [(*Connie Martin*)], Henry Travers [(*Judge Bullfinch*)], Lois Wilson [(*Mrs. Wilson*)], Florence Bates [(*Emma Shoemaker*)], Jerome Cowan [(*Mr. Graves*)], Helen Westcott [(*Miss Brooks*)], Paul Harvey [(*Jim Townsend*)], Lloyd Corrigan [(*Mr. Evergood*)], Gary Gray [(*Woody Wilson*)], Myrna Dell [(*Lorraine Scott*)], [William Forrest (*Mr. Moody*)], [Mary Stuart (*Hazel*)], [Lennie Bremen (*News vendor*)], [Buddy Roosevelt (*Conductor*)], [Chester Clute (*Collection agent*)], [Dick Bartell (*Man at phone booth*)], [Billy Wayne (*Mac the bartender*)], [Richard Taylor, Dale Robertson (*Lifeguards*)], [Guy Wilkerson (*Janitor*)], [Angi O. Poulos (*Foreigner in hallway*)], [Antonio Filauri, Nick Thompson (*Italians*)], [Gregory Golubeff (*European*)], [Robert O'Neil (*Irishman*)], [Peter Camlin (*Frenchman*)], [Daniel de Jonghe (*Engstrand*)], [Sam Bernard (*Eschmann*)], [John Mylong (*Stravitch*)], [Nancy Valentine (*Margot*)], [Eve Whitney (*Penelope*)], [Lola Albright (*Vickie*)], [William Yetter (*Mr. Schwarzholz*)], [Sandra Gould (*Sylvia*)], [Alvin Hammer (*Charlie*)], [Patricia Northrop (*Emma Shoemaker, as a girl*)], [Bobby Barber (*Photographer*)], [Dolores Castle, Glen Gallagher (*Samba team*)], [Ray Montgomery (*Man dancing*)], [Creighton Hale (*Waiter*)], [John Marston (*Butler*)], [Eddie Garr (*Drunk*)], [Jack Gargan, Tony Merrill, Henry Iblings, Carey Harrison, Broderick O'Farrell, Raymond Bailey, Kay Mansfield, Grayce Hampton, Wally Dean (*Guests*)], [Anthony Jochim, Lute Crockett,

Henrietta Taylor, Philo McCullough, Jack Mower, Leah Baird (*Board members*)], [Oliver Blake (*Court clerk*)], [Maurice St. Clair, Grace Young (*Specialty dancers*)], [Carol Brewster, Joan Vohs, Betty Underwood, Alice Wallace, Joi Lansing, Lorraine Crawford, Vonne Lester, Karen Gaylord (*Models*)].

Comedy. [*Print viewed*]. Struggling New York City talent agent Chuck Donovan is hired by the producers of a television program to discover the identity of the model for "The Randolph Girl," a shapely woman drawn by commercial artist Bob Randolph. At Bob's studio, Miss Brooks, Bob's secretary, admits that even she does not know who the model is. Donovan then tries to convince Bob to reveal his secret, and while they are speaking, a man from a collection agency presents Bob with a bill for twelve gold bracelets. Later, a model arrives at the studio, and willingly admits to posing as the Randolph Girl. When Donovan confronts Bob with her statement, he confesses that the Randolph Girl is actually a composite of twelve different models, none of whom knows about the others. Thoroughly depressed, Donovan decides to kill himself. After sending a message to his girl friend, photographer Connie Martin, who always rescues him from his frequent suicide attempts, Donovan heads for Jones Beach, planning to drown himself. There, while searching for Connie through his binoculars, he spots a woman who is the perfect likeness of the Randolph Girl. By the time he rows ashore, however, she has vanished into the women's locker room, and he is unable to recognize her once she is fully dressed. Every day for a week, Donovan and Bob haunt the beach looking for the woman. Finally, Donovan guesses that Ruth Wilson is the mysterious woman and follows her home. He learns that Ruth is a schoolteacher who lives with her mother and younger brother Woody. Because she does not want a man to marry her for her looks, she purposely dresses in a dowdy style. Ruth teaches English to immigrants at night school, and Donovan persuades Bob to attend her class, posing as a recent immigrant from Czechoslovakia. Although Ruth is suspicious of Bob's mutating accent, she agrees to go out with him and gradually falls in love with him. When the newspapers announce that the Randolph Girl will be on television, all twelve of Bob's models expect to make an appearance. In the course of trying to mollify the women, Donovan accidentally drops Bob's address book at the home of one of the models. The next morning, all twelve of the models quit. Then Bob is spotted by Miss Brooks while he is with Ruth, and his real identity is revealed. Bob explains that after he saw Ruth at the beach, he wanted to meet her and thus enrolled in the class. He then adds that he is attracted to her mind, but perversely, Ruth wants him to admire her looks. Later, Bob refuses to attend a big party in honor of the Randolph Girl because he is in love with Ruth and wants to get married. The following day, Ruth asks Bob to meet her at Jones Beach. Donovan then phones Connie, planning to sneak a photograph of Ruth and leak it to the newspapers. When the picture runs, Emma Shoemaker, the dean of the school, asks for Ruth's resignation, and when she refuses, fires her. Ruth takes the school to court. Bob appears as a witness on her behalf and projects a film about bathing suits through the years. In one, a young Emma is seen being arrested for indecent exposure in the early 1900s. Then Ruth takes the stand in her bathing suit and states that her private life is none of the school's business. Ruth is reinstated, and she and Bob plan a double wedding with Donovan and Connie. *Commercial artists. Models. Romance. Schoolteachers. Talent agents. Attempted suicide. Bathing suits. Czechoslovakian Americans. Deans (in schools). Deception. Dismissal (Employment). Family relationships. Immigrants. Motion pictures. New York City–Jones Beach. Photographers. Propriety. Television programs. Trials.*

Note: According to a 19 Feb 1948 *NYT* news item, Julius J. and Philip G. Epstein were scheduled to work on the script of this film. On 14 Apr 1948, *HR* reported that Dennis Morgan had been assigned to star in the film. Lauren Bacall was suspended when she turned down a role in the film, according to a 19 Apr 1948 *HR* news item.

Box 25 Jun 1949. *DV* 21 Jun 1949, p. 3. *FD* 27 Jun 1949, p. 6. *HR* 14 Apr 1948. *HR* 19 Apr 1948, p. 1. *HR* 14 May 1948, p. 17. *HR* 2 Jul 1948, p. 7. *HR* 21 Jun 1949, p. 3. *MPHPD* 25 Jun 1949, p. 4658. *NYT* 19 Feb 1948. *NYT* 30 Jul 1949, p. 9. *Var* 22 Jun 1949, p. 6.

THE GIRL FROM MEXICO (Latino)
RKO Radio Pictures, Inc. *Dist* RKO Radio Pictures, Inc. 2 Jun 1939; *Prod:* early Mar—28 Mar 1939 [©RKO Radio Pictures, Inc.; 2 Jun 1939; LP8970]. Sd (RCA Victor System); b&w. 6,424 ft. 64, 69 or 71 min. PCA cert no. 5197.

Series: The Mexican Spitfire.

Prod Robert Sisk. *Prod exec* Lee Marcus. *Dir* Leslie Goodwins. [*Asst dir* Sam Ruman]. *Scr* Lionel Houser and Joseph A. Fields. *Story* Lionel Houser. *Photog* Jack MacKenzie. *Art dir* Van Nest Polglase. *Art dir assoc* Albert D'Agostino. *Ed* Desmond Marquette. *Ward* Renie. *Mus dir* Roy Webb. *Rec* John L. Cass.

Cast: LUPE VELEZ [(*Carmelita Fuentes*)], Donald Woods [(*Dennis Lindsey*)], Leon Errol [(*Uncle Matt*)], Linda Hayes [(*Elizabeth Price*)], Donald MacBride [(*Renner*)], Edward Raquello [(*Tony Romano*)], Elisabeth Risdon [(*Aunt Della*)], Ward Bond [(*Mexican Pete*)].

Comedy. [*Print viewed*]. Dennis Lindsey, an advertising executive, goes to Mexico to find a singer for one of his client's radio shows. There, he hears the hot-tempered Carmelita Fuentes sing, and after several incendiary confrontations with Dennis, Carmelita accedes to her family's wishes and signs a singing contract with him. After Dennis promises to look after her welfare in New York and invites her to stay with him, his aunt Della and uncle Matt, she decides to steal him from his fiancée, Elizabeth Price. Although she is told to stay home on the day before her audition, Carmelita persuades Uncle Matt to take her to a baseball game and a wrestling match, where she loses her voice cheering on wrestler Mexican Pete. At the audition, Carmelita croaks out her songs, causing the sponsor to cancel the show. To cover for Uncle Matt, Carmelita tells Dennis that she was out with an unnamed man, prompting Dennis to threaten to send her back to Mexico. An angry Carmelita blames Mexican Pete for her bad luck, and the wrestler offers her a job in his nightclub as compensation. That night, Dennis entertains a divorced client, Tony Romano, at the club, and Romano, impressed by Carmelita's performance, hires her to advertise his perfume. As the night progresses, Elizabeth becomes jealous of Dennis' concern for Carmelita, while Dennis becomes jealous of Romano's attention to Carmelita. After the performance, Uncle Matt and Carmelita stay out all night at the bike races, and Carmelita leads Dennis to believe that she was out with Romano. While at a photo session at Romano's house, Carmelita calls Dennis and tells him that she is moving in with Romano. When Dennis decides to leave his wedding rehearsal to rescue Carmelita, Elizabeth breaks their engagement and Dennis rushes to Romano's house, scoops up Carmelita and carries her to the altar. *Advertising. Engagements. Jealousy. Mexicans. Romantic rivalry. Singers. Tycoons. Auditions. Aunts. Baseball. Bicycle racing. Mexico. New York City. Nightclubs. Radio broadcasting. Radio sponsors. Uncles. Wrestlers and wrestling.*

Note: According to an article in *LAT*, this picture marked Lupe Velez's return to the screen after an eighteen month absence. A news item in *HR* adds that actress Linda Hayes, a former San Francisco hat check girl, was discovered in the Lasky "Gateway to Hollywood" contest. Modern sources note that this film was the prototype for the "Mexican Spitfire" series, which starred Velez, although RKO had no plans for the series when the picture was made. For more information about the series, consult the series index and see entry below for *Mexican Spitfire.*

DV 11 May 1939, p. 3. *FD* 17 May 1939, p. 5. *HR* 2 Mar 1939, p. 1. *HR* 18 Mar 1939, pp. 6-7. *HR* 29 Mar 1939, p. 2. *HR* 11 May 1939, p. 3. *LAT* 2 Feb 1939. *MPD* 18 May 1939, p. 3. *MPH* 20 May 1939, p. 48. *NYT* 8 Jun 1939, p. 31. *Var* 24 May 1939, p. 14.

THE GIRL FROM MONTERREY (Latino, Irish Americans)

PRC Pictures, Inc. *Dist* Producers Releasing Corp. 4 Oct **1943** [©PRC Pictures, Inc.; 19 Oct 1943; LP12330]. Sd (RCA Sound System); b&w. 5,337 ft. 58-60 min. PCA cert no. 9543.

Prod Jack Schwarz. *Assoc prod* Harry D. Edwards. *Dir* Wallace Fox. *Scr* Arthur Hoerl. *Orig story* George Green and Robert Gordon. *Dir of photog* Marcel LePicard. *Art dir* Frank Sylos. *Film ed* Robert Crandall. *Set dresser* Harry Rief. *Master of props* George Bahr. *Mus dir* Mahlon Merrick. *Mus supv* David Chudnow. *Sd eng* Hugh McDowell. *Prod mgr* Arthur Hammond.

Song(s): "Jive Brother Jive," "Last Night's All Over" and "Girl from Monterrey," music and lyrics by Louis Herscher.

Cast: Armida (*Lita* [*Valdez*]), Edgar Kennedy (*Doc Hogan*), Veda Ann Borg (*Flossie* [*Rankin*]), Jack La Rue ([*Al*] *Johnson*), Terry Frost (*Jerry O'Leary*), Anthony Caruso ([*Alberto*] *Baby* [*Valdez*]), Charles Williams (*Harry*), Bryant Washburn (*Commissioner*), Guy Zanett (*Perrone*), Wheeler Oakman (*Announcer*).

Boxing, Comedy-drama, with songs. [*Print viewed*]. In Mexico, dancer/singer Lita Valdez is fired from the cantina where she performs after she refuses to entertain a male customer at his table. When her younger brother Alberto, whom Lita calls "Baby," arrives to tell her that he has quit college in the United States to become a professional fighter, Lita insists that he knock down her boss. Instead,

Baby accidentally knocks out a customer, who happens to be a boxer. Fight promoter Doc Hogan is impressed with Baby's punch, and offers to represent him in New York City. There Lita is managing her brother's affairs while he is training when Hogan's other fighter, Jerry O'Leary, runs into her and the two are immediately attracted to each other. Baby then wins his first fight, and Lita watches all the fights to see the two men in her life, Baby and Jerry. One night at Perrone's nightclub, Baby meets Flossie Rankin, a singer, and falls in love. Jerry's manager, Al Johnson, arranges for Lita to sing with Flossie's band as a joke, but when she is a surprise hit with the audience, Perrone hires her and headlines her with Flossie. Baby, meanwhile, fights his way to the top of his rank, and despite Lita's protests, the boxing commission insists on matching Baby and Jerry in a fight. Al, hoping to make a bundle on a bet, spreads gossip that Baby is going to be the favorite, but plots with Flossie to interfere with Baby's training so that he loses the fight. One night after Baby comes home drunk, Lita confronts Flossie at her apartment. The women get into a furious fight, and Lita forces Flossie to admit her scheme to Baby. Baby absolves Flossie but rejects Lita because of her continual interference. Lita then refuses to see Jerry because she believes he was in on the set-up. Although Flossie seems to be playing along with Al, she has genuinely fallen in love with Baby and helps him train because he hopes that Jerry will return to studying medicine if he loses. Although the fight is difficult, Baby wins and Al loses his bet. Estranged from both men in her life, Lita continues performing at Perrone's. After several months, Flossie comes to see her at the nightclub and assures Lita that Jerry was never involved in the set-up. A delighted Lita then reunites with both Jerry and Baby, who have enlisted in the U.S. Army and Mexican Army, respectively, and are waiting for her in the club. *Boxers. Brothers and sisters. Fixed fights. Mexicans. Promoters. Boxing managers. Drunkenness. Mexico. New York City. Nightclubs. Singers. Wagers.*

Note: Although actor Anthony Caruso's name appears as "Athony" in the end credits, his name appears as "Anthony" in the opening credits.

Box 9 Oct 1943. *DV* 17 Sep 1943, pp. 3, 10. *FD* 27 Sep 1943, p. 4. *HR* 17 Sep 1943, p. 4. *MPH* 25 Sep 1943. *MPHPD* 28 Aug 1943, p. 1509. *MPHPD* 25 Sep 1943, p. 1554. *Var* 5 Jan 1944, p. 26.

GIRL FROM PANAMA *see* **THE FABULOUS SENORITA**

THE GIRL FROM POLTAVA *see* **NATALKA POLTAVKA**

THE GIRL FROM SAN LORENZO (Latino)

Inter-American Productions, Inc. *Dist* United Artists Corp. 24 Feb **1950**; Prod: Nov 1949 [©Inter-American Productions, Inc.; 24 Feb 1950; LP138]. Sd; b&w. 6 reels, 5,270 ft. 58-59 min. PCA cert no. 14290.

Series: The Cisco Kid.

Pres PHILIP N. KRASNE. *Prod* Philip N. Krasne. *Asst to prod* Mel Mark. *Dir* Derwin Abrahams. *Asst dir* Louis Germonprez. *Orig scr* Ford Beebe. *Dir of photog* Kenneth Peach. *Art dir* Fred Preble. *Film ed* Marty Cohn. *Set dec* Harry Rief [sic]. *Property master* Gene Stone. *Ward* Robert Harris. *Mus comp and cond* Albert Glasser. *Sd* Hugh McDowell. *Makeup artist* Arthur Dupuis.

Source: Based on the character created by O. Henry.

Cast: Duncan Renaldo ([*The*] *Cisco* [*Kid*]), Leo Carrillo (*Pancho*), Jane Adams [(*Nora Malloy*)], Bill Lester [(*Jerry Todd*)], Byron Foulger [(*Cal*)], Don Harvey [(*Kansas*)], Lee Phelps [(*Sheriff Ed Marlowe*)], Edmund Cobb [(*Wooly*)], Leonard Penn [(*Thomas McCarger*)], David Sharpe [(*Blackie*)], Wes Hudman [(*Rusty*)].

Western. [*Print viewed*]. After Mexican American cowboys The Cisco Kid and Pancho are falsely accused of a series of stage holdups, which are actually being perpetrated by two outlaws disguised to look like them, they escape from a sheriff and his posse and arrive in San Lorenzo, California. When Pancho receives a letter from someone claiming to be his ailing grandmother and pleading with him to come to Cactus Wells for a visit, Pancho tells Cisco that his grandmother is dead. They decide to go to Cactus Wells anyway to investigate the strange letter, but while riding down the street, they are shot at by a rancher named Thomas McCarger, who has been informed that Cisco murdered his brother. When bystander Nora Malloy sees McCarger draw his gun, she tries to grab it out of his hand. Later, Nora takes the stage to Cactus Wells, where she is to wed her fiancé, Jerry Todd. Cisco and Pancho, meanwhile, visit McCarger, who shows them a letter from Sheriff Ed Marlowe. The letter states that Cisco shot McCarger's brother during a stage holdup, but Cisco explains that he

has never been to Cactus Wells, then vows to go there to search for the real murderer. On their way, Cisco and Pancho see Rusty and Kansas, their impersonators, attacking a stagecoach. The outlaws shoot the driver and the guard before holding up the stage and escaping. Cisco aids the stage driver, who turns out to be Jerry, and he and Pancho take him to Nora's. When the sheriff and deputies arrive at Nora's to question them, Cisco and Pancho hide in the kitchen. Nora then grabs her gun and orders the lawmen to leave. Then, Rusty and Kansas burst in and lock the sheriff inside the cell, kidnap Cisco and Pancho and take them to the gang's hideout inside a cave in the mountains. After Cisco and Pancho fight with their captors and escape, Cisco holds up the stage and steals the express box. A short time later, Rusty and Kansas don their disguises and rob the stage, demanding the box. When the exasperated driver explains that he already gave it to them, the outlaws realize that Cisco and Pancho must have escaped. Cisco and Pancho break back into jail, release the sheriff and tell him about the impostors. That evening, at the newspaper office of the gang's leader, editor Ross, a rock is thrown through the window with the following note attached: "This is fair warning. I will come for the loot in your office safe before daylight. The Cisco Kid." Ross opens the safe to check on the loot, just as Cisco and the sheriff are arriving. After the rest of the outlaws show up and are arrested, Cisco asks the sheriff to send a letter to McCarger identifying his brother's murderer as Ross. Later, Cisco and Pancho accept the sheriff's thanks, then say farewell. *Cowboys. Frame-ups. Impersonation and imposture. Mexican Americans. Stagecoach robberies. Arrests. Brothers. Caves. Deputies. Engagements. Escapes. Guards. Hideouts. Jails. Kidnapping. Mountains. Posses. Ranchers. Safes. Sheriffs. Shootings.*

Note: The film's opening title card reads: "The Cisco Kid in The Girl from San Lorenzo." According to *HR* production charts, the picture was shot on location in Pioneertown, CA. Modern sources include Henry Wills in the cast. This was the last entry in the Cisco Kid series. For additional information on the series, please consult the Series Index and see the above entry for *The Cisco Kid*.

Box 25 Mar 1950. *DV* 2 Mar 1950, p. 3. *FD* 10 Mar 1950, p. 8. *HR* 1 Nov 1949, p. 4. *HR* 18 Nov 1949, p. 13. *HR* 25 Nov 1949, p. 13. *HR* 2 Mar 1950, p. 3. *MPHPD* 11 Mar 1950, p. 222. *Var* 8 Mar 1950, p. 6.

THE GIRL I LEFT BEHIND ME (Native Americans, Blackfoot, Siksika)

Box Office Attraction Co. *Dist* Box Office Attraction Co. Jan **1915** [©William Fox; 21 Jan 1915; LP5182]. Si; b&w. 5 reels.

Pres William Fox. *Dir* Lloyd B. Carleton. *Asst dir* Arthur Shaw Clifton.

Source: Based on the play *The Girl I Left Behind Me* by David Belasco and Franklyn Fyles (New York, 25 Jan 1893).

Cast: Robert Edeson (*Lieutenant Hawkesworth*), Stuart Holmes (*Lieutenant Parlow*), Irene Warfield (*Fawn Afraid*), Claire Whitney (*The general's daughter*), Walter Hitchcock (*The general*), J. Albert Hall.

Western. At a lonely army post in the West, a dance marking the engagement announcement of the general's daughter to Lieutenant Hawkesworth is interrupted when word arrives that the hostile Blackfoot tribe is on the warpath. Hawkesworth and the rival for his fiancée's affection, Lieutenant Parlow, are sent with the regiment to quell the uprising. Parlow turns out to be a coward at a critical moment, and after the regiment is routed, he blames Hawkesworth for the defeat. The general then orders his daughter to break her engagement and become Parlow's fiancée. The Blackfeet surround the fort, and Hawkesworth makes a daring ride through them to a neighboring fort. He brings the U.S. 6th Cavalry, who subdue the Blackfeet. Parlow's cowardice is then learned, and it is also revealed that earlier he eloped with the wife of an officer and then abandoned her. Hawkesworth and the general's daughter finally marry. *Cowardice. Military posts. Officers (Military). Rivalry. Siksika Indians. United States. Army. Duplicity. Fathers and daughters. Forts. Heroism. United States. Army. Cavalry. Uprisings.*

Note: According to reviews, some scenes were shot at Fort Assiniboine, Montana. *Var* noted, "The Indian tableaux deserves special mention."

Motog 13 Feb 1915, p. 266. *MPN* 6 Feb 1915, p. 46. *MPW* 20 Feb 1915, p. 1140. *Var* 29 Jan 1915, p. 24.

GIRL IN ROOM 20 (African Americans)

United Films. *Dist* State Rights. **1949?.** Sd (RCA); b&w. 5,694 ft. 63 min.

Dir Spencer Williams. *Cine* Frank Brodie and Jack Specht. *Ed* H. W. Kier. *Rec* Elmer Green.

Song(s): "Be Sweet to Me," music and lyrics by Roger Cockrell; "Swing Low, Sweet Chariot," and "God Will Take Care of You," spirituals.

Cast: Geraldine Brock [(*Daisy Mae Walker*)], July Jones [(*Dunbar Hamilton*)], Spencer Williams [(*Joe Phillips*)], [Myra Hemmings (*Mrs. Walker*)], [John Hemmings (*Jim Walker*)], [Margery Moore (*Mabel Walker*)], [Mrs. F. D. Benson (*Elviry Tatum*)], [Mamie Fisher (*Mamie Wilson*)], [G. T. Sutton (*Mr. Crowley*)], [Katherine Moore (*Clementine*)], [E. Celise Allen (*Duke Moody*)], [Howard Galloway (*Arnold Richardson*)].

African American, Show business, Melodrama, with songs. [*Viewed print incomplete*]. About to leave her placid hometown of Prairieville, Texas for New York City to seek success, talented singer Daisy Mae Walker is begged by sweetheart, Dunbar Hamilton, to stay and marry him. Though she is in love with Dunbar, Daisy Mae is determined to make enough money to pay for her sister's school and bids farewell to her friends and family. Dunbar is sad to see her go, but takes heart when Daisy's voice teacher reminds him of black singers such as Marion Anderson, Ella Fitzgerald and Lena Horne, who rose to fame because of their hard work and musical ability. When Daisy arrives in New York, she takes a taxi to a Mrs. Jones' residence hotel, only to discover that it is now a brothel run by a woman named Mamie Wilson. Taxi driver Joe Phillips takes a paternal interest in the naïve Daisy Mae and delivers her instead to the Crowley Hotel, where many theater people reside. Daisy Mae soon befriends members of Clementine's band and is invited to join their act at their upcoming Congo Club show. During rehearsal for the show, Daisy Mae catches the eye of the club's sleazy owner, Arnold Richardson, who invites her to attend his party at Mamie's Place. Joe follows Daisy Mae to the party and catches Mamie going through Daisy Mae's purse. Concerned for Daisy Mae's welfare in Richardson's hands, Joe telephones Dunbar and instructs him to come rescue his sweetheart. One day, while sitting in a beauty salon, Daisy Mae overhears two women gossiping about Richardson and learns that the newspapers have named her as his mistress. Later, Dunbar and Joe visit Daisy Mae just as a struggle has begun between her and Richardson. During the struggle, Mrs. Richardson enters the room and fires a shot at her husband, but the bullet accidentally strikes Daisy Mae. While Daisy Mae is treated at the Charity Hospital, her friends take up a collection to pay for her medical expenses. Soon after her recovery, Daisy Mae goes to the Crowley Hotel, where she sings for her sweetheart and her friends. To the relief of all the performers, who are now in desperate need of money, a telegram arrives requesting that the troupe perform at the Congo Club. Although the telegram also mentions that the troupe will have to provide its own costumes, a seemingly insurmountable obstacle, Dunbar steps forward and offers to pay for them. After the show, Dunbar takes Daisy Mae home to Prairieville as his bride and invites the troupe to join them. *African Americans. Bands (Music). Singers. Brothels. City-country contrast. Fistfights. Friendship. Gossip. Gunshot wounds. Hotels. Infidelity. Madams. New York City. Nightclub owners. Parties. Romance. Seduction. Self-sacrifice. Taxicab drivers. Texas.*

Note: Although modern sources claim that this film was released in 1946, it may not have been widely released until 1949, the year it was submitted for review to the New York State censors. Modern sources note that this film was shot in San Antonio, TX.

THE GIRL IN THE DARK (Chinese Americans)

Bluebird Photoplays, Inc. *Dist* Bluebird Photoplays, Inc. 4 Mar **1918** [©Bluebird Photoplays, Inc.; 20 Feb 1918; LP12095]. Si; b&w. 5 reels.

Dir Stuart Paton. *Adpt* Albert G. Kenyon. *Cam* B. C. "Duke" Hayward.

Source: Based on the novel *The Green Seal* by Charles Edmonds Walk (Chicago, 1914).

Cast: Carmel Myers (*Lois Fox*), Ashton Dearholt (*Brice Ferris*), Frank Tokanaga (*Ming*), Frank Deshon (*Lao Wing*), Harry Carter (*Strang*), Alfred Allen (*Struber, chief of police*), Betty Schade (*Sally*).

Mystery. Lois Fox, upon whose shoulder is branded a Chinese idiograph resembling the letters "A. Y.," is rescued from a gang of Chinese ruffians by Brice Ferris. His servant Ming, in attempting to steal from her finger a ring that bears a mysterious green seal, is

killed, and soon afterwards a stranger named Strang arrives, also in search of the girl. Despite Brice's efforts to protect her, Lois is abducted and taken to the headquarters of Lao Wing, the leader of a secret Chiense society known as the Tong. Ferris and chief of police Struber finally infiltrate the gang's headquarters and after a furious battle, Lois and Strang are freed. Strang, actually Lois' uncle, reveals that the sacred ring had belonged to an ancient Chinese order but had been stolen by Lois' father. *Chinese Americans. Gangs. Jewelry. Robbery. Secret societies.* Fights. Kidnapping. Long-lost relatives. Police chiefs. Rescues. Servants.

ETR 9 Mar 1918, p. 1142. *MPN* 23 Feb 1918, p. 1066. *MPN* 16 Mar 1918, p. 1612. *MPW* 9 Mar 1918, p. 1413. *MPW* 16 Mar 1918, p. 1556. *Var* 1 Mar 1918, p. 41. *Wid's* 14 Mar 1918, p. 1000.

THE GIRL OF MY HEART (Native Americans)
Fox Film Corp. *Dist* Fox Film Corp. Nov **1920** [©William Fox; 24 Oct 1920; LP15747]. Si; b&w. 5 reels, 4,340 ft ft.

Pres William Fox. *Dir* Edward J. Le Saint. *Scen* Edward J. Le Saint and Mildred Considine. *Cam* Friend Baker.

Source: Based on the novel *Joan of Rainbow Springs* by Frances Marian Mitchell (Boston, 1911).

Cast: Shirley Mason (*Joan*), Raymond McKee (*Rodney White*), Martha Mattox (*Prudence White*), Al Fremont (*Major Philips*), Cecil Van Auker (*Dr. Norman*), Calvin Weller (*Mona*), Hooper Toler (*Chawa*), Alfred Weller (*Pedro*).

Adventure. On Christmas Eve, Joan runs away from a cruel woman who had taken her from an orphanage and finds shelter at the White's mansion. Joan saves Rodney White from killing himself because he is a victim of the white plague. Impressed with Joan's faith, Rodney adopts her, taking her out West with his aunt in hopes of recovering his health. There, at an Indian settlement, they discover that Major Philips is selling whiskey to the Indians; Philips retaliates by hiring the Indian Chawa to kill Rodney and kidnap Joan. Rodney is only injured, however, and with the aid of the hermit Dr. Norman, recovers. They eventually rescue Joan from her kidnapper, Rodney learns that he is cured, and he and Joan fall in love. *Adoption. Attempted suicide. Indians of North America. Orphans. Runaways. Tuberculosis.* Abduction. Attempted murder. Christmas. Faith. Hermits. Hired killers. Liquor.

Note: The working title of this film was *Joan of Rainbow Springs*.

MPN 14 Aug 1920, p. 1373. *MPN* 18 Sep 1920, p. 2244. *MPN* 6 Nov 1920, p. 3565. *MPN* 20 Nov 1920, p. 3883. *MPN* 18 Dec 1920, p. 4677. *Var* 18 Feb 1921, p. 41. *Wid's* 12 Dec 1920, p. 23.

THE GIRL ON THE BRIDGE (Refugees)
Twentieth Century-Fox Film Corp. *Dist* Twentieth Century-Fox Film Corp. Dec **1951**; Prod: began late Nov 1950 [©Twentieth Century-Fox Film Corp.; 5 Dec 1951; LP1414]. Sd (RCA Sound System); b&w. 10 reels. 76 min. PCA cert no. 14999.

Prod Hugo Haas. *Assoc prod* Robert Erlik. *Dir* Hugo Haas. *Asst dir* Harry Franklin. *2d asst dir* Leonard Shapiro. *Orig story and scr* Hugo Haas and Arnold Phillips. *Dir of photog* Paul Ivano. *Spec eff* Harry Redmond. *Montages* Velma Ehlers. *Art dir* Rudi Field. *Ed* Merrill White and Albert Shaff. *Set const* Don Bruno. *Ward* Frank Beetson. *Mus by* Harold Byrns, *conducting the Los Angeles Chamber Symphony. Sd* Gary Harris. *Makeup* Harry Thomas. *Head elec* Don Stott. *Scr clerk* Bobbie Sierks. *Head grip* Carl Seawald.

Cast: Hugo Haas [(*David Toman*)], Beverly Michaels [(*Clara Barker*)], Robert Dane [(*Mario*)], Johnny Close [(*Harry*)], Anthony Jochim [(*Carl Cooper*)], Judy Clark [(*Blonde Doll*)], Darr Smith [(*Husband*)], Maria Bibikoff [(*Young woman*)], Richard Pinner [(*Prosecutor*)], [Al Hill (*Bartender*)], [Rose Marie Valenzuela (*Judy*)], [Joe Duval (*News vendor*)].

Drama. [*Not viewed*]. As David Toman, a lonely European refugee and watch maker, strolls upon a bridge one night, he encounters Clara Barker, an unwed mother and former dancer, as she contemplates ending her life in the dark waters beneath. The middle-aged David assures her that the morning will seem brighter, and in appreciation, Clara visits David's shop the next day with her infant daughter Judy. David immediately is taken with Judy, explaining that his own two sons and wife were killed by Nazis. Clara reveals to David that she was distraught the night before because her landlady, a drinker, had been taken away in an ambulance and would no longer be able to care for Judy while Clara was at work. David is surprised to learn that Clara is unmarried but, taken with the woman and her child, offers to babysit while Clara works. Some time later, Clara informs David that she has

been offered a job as a housekeeper in San Diego and that she and Judy will be moving. David, upset at the thought of Judy being so far away, offers to hire Clara as his own housekeeper, and Clara, initially unsure, finally agrees. Shortly after, Clara overhears Mrs. Cooper, the wife of David's best friend Carl, calling her a "floozy" and insisting that Judy is David's child. When Clara tells David about the accusations, he is pleased at the thought and proposes to Clara. Clara worries that she is not good enough for David, but eventually gives in and, soon after they are wed, becomes pregnant with his child. Meanwhile, Harry, a small-time hood and the cousin of Clara's former lover Mario, sees Clara in David's jewelry shop as he is picking up his shirts next door. The cousins have been out of town for some time, and when Harry tells Mario about Clara, Mario goes to the jewelry shop. Instead of Clara, Mario confronts David, whom he taunts with insults about his advanced age. However, when David begs and offers Mario money to leave them in peace, Mario, a good man at heart, promises to stop bothering them. Mario tells Harry the story, and Harry, believing that there is money to be made, tries to force him to go back to the shop and blackmail David. When Mario refuses and then threatens to kill Harry, the enterprising hood goes to the shop himself and tells David that Mario sent him for the money he had earlier offered. However, when David offers him $300, Harry laughs in his face and asks for $5,000. When Harry then tries to force his way into the apartment where Clara is sleeping, David hits him over the head with a heavy candlestick, killing him. David dumps Harry's body at the beach, where he hopes it will be washed away by the tides. When he returns home, Cooper, who saw him leave the night before, approaches him, and David confesses his crime. Cooper convinces David to go back for the body and call the police, but when they get to the beach, the body is already gone. Back at the shop, David sells the candlestick for a quarter of its worth, and then he reads in the paper that Mario has been apprehended for Harry's murder, as the night before he was overheard threatening to kill him. David decides that he will turn himself in only if Mario is convicted. As he awaits the verdict, however, his distress begins to drive him crazy. As he lies in bed ranting one evening, Cooper arrives to tell him that Mario was acquitted, and David, relieved, informs Clara that he would like to help Mario in some way. Unaware that David is his cousin's killer, Mario visits the jewelry store and tells him that he is leaving town but would appreciate receiving news of Judy's well-being from time to time. David, consumed by guilt, goes to the same bridge where he had earlier met Clara and, as he imagines Clara's voice praising him for his honesty, decency and respectability, decides to end it all. Clara wakes up and, noticing David gone, goes outside to see a crowd gathered around the bridge. Mario returns to comfort the now-widowed Clara, and as the two look into the waters, Mario asks if Clara will take him back on probation. When Clara protests that it is too late as she is carrying David's baby, Mario reminds her that David cared for his own child, and he would repay the favor. The couple smile at one another and walk away arm-in-arm. *Conscience. Justifiable homicide. Romance–Age difference. Unmarried mothers. Widowers.* Acquittals. Blackmail. Bridges. Clock and watch makers. Cousins. False accusations. Hallucinations. Housekeepers. Infants. Jewelry stores. Jews. Moral reformation. Neighbors. Pregnancy. Rumors. Suicide. War refugees.

Note: Although a print of this film was not viewed, the above credits and plot summary were taken from a cutting continuity contained in the Twentieth Century-Fox Produced Scripts Collection, located at the UCLA Arts—Special Collections Library. The working title of this film was *The Bridge*. According to a 10 Nov 1950 memo contained in the MPAA/PCA Collection at the AMPAS Library, PCA director Joseph I. Breen deemed the script "unacceptable under Code provisions" because "Clara" never shows "self-reproach or guilt" for her earlier misdeeds, presumably having a child out of wedlock. To make the story acceptable, Breen suggested that Clara "would have to recognize her wrongdoing as a sin." In the film, Clara indeed demonstrates remorse and shame about her past. Breen also complained about "David's" suicide, stating that it shows David "merely flee[ing] reality," instead of demonstrating that "his self destruction was the act of a deranged person." In the film, David's nationality is not specified, nor is he clearly identified as Jewish.

Exb 19 Dec 1951, p. 3207. *Box* 15 Dec 1951. *DV* 6 Dec 1951, p. 3. *FD* 26 Dec 1951, p. 10. *Har* 15 Dec 1951, p. 199. *HR* 13 Nov 1950. *HR* 6 Dec 1951, p. 3. *LAT* 6 Dec 1951. *MPH* 15 Dec 1951. *MPHPD* 15 Dec 1951, p. 1154. *Var* 12 Dec 1951, p. 6.

THE GIRLS HE LEFT BEHIND see **THE GANG'S ALL HERE**

GIRLS ON PROBATION see THE BELOVED BRAT

GIVE AND TAKE see STAND UP AND FIGHT

GIVE ME THE STARS see I AIM AT THE STARS; THE WERNHER von BRAUN STORY

GIVE US THIS DAY (Italian Americans)
Plantaganet Films, Ltd. *Dist* Eagle Lion Films, Inc. Jan **1950**; London opening: 14 Oct 1949; New York opening: 20 Dec 1949; Prod: at Denham Studios, London, England [©Plantaganet Films, Ltd.; 6 Jan 1950; LP35]. Sd (Western Electric Recording); b&w. 118 or 120 min. PCA cert no. 13967. *Country of origin* Great Britain.
Prod ROD E. GEIGER and N. A. BRONSTEN. *Dir* EDWARD DMYTRYK. *Dial dir* Phil Brown. *Asst dir* George Mills. *Scr* Ben Barzman. *Trmt* Pietro Di Donato. *Adpt* John Penn. *Dir of photog* C. Pennington Richards. *Cam op* Robert Day. *Spec eff* F. Carver, B. Warrington and S. Howell. *Art dir* A. Vetchinsky. *Research des* M. Corelik and R. McDonald. *Ed* John Guthridge. *Sd ed* Ken Heeley-Ray. *Set dec* Arthur Taksen. *Dress des* Eve Brierley. *Mus comp and cond* Benjamin Frankel. *Sd rec* John Cook and George Croll. *Makeup supv* Tony Sforzini. *Hairdressing supv* Vivienne Walker. *Administrator* [Plantaganet Films] Mark Rubens. *Prod supv* Kenneth Horne. *Cont* Barbara Cole.
Source: Based on the novel *Christ in Concrete* by Pietro Di Donato (Indianapolis, 1939).
Cast: Sam Wanamaker [(Geremio)], Lea Padovani [(Annunziata)], Kathleen Ryan [(Kathleen)], Bonar Colleano [(Julio)], Charles Goldner [(Luigi)], Sidney James [(Murdin)], Karel Stepanek [(Jaroslav)], William Sylvester [(Giovanni)], Rosalie Crutchley [(Julio's wife)], Nino Pastellides [(The Lucy)], Ina De La Haye [(Dame Katarina)], Philo Hauser [(Head of Pig)], [Ronan O'Casey (Bastian)], [Robert Rietty (Pietro)], [Charles Moffat (Pasquale)].
Social, Drama. [*Print viewed*]. When his wife Annunziata will not let him into their New York City apartment, Geremio, a second-generation Italian-American builder, breaks down the door. As their children watch, Annunziata angrily tells Geremio to return to his mistress, whereupon Geremio slaps her and rushes in despair to his lover Kathleen's apartment. There, Kathleen tries to comfort him while he thinks back to a time nine years earlier when he thought he knew what he wanted in life: In 1921, while Geremio is working as a bricklayer on a New York skyscraper, Murdin, a fellow worker, slips on some wet cement and nearly knocks Geremio to the floor below, but Geremio is saved by his friend Luigi, an older immigrant from Abruzzi. Frightened by the incident, Murdin quits, and Geremio and Luigi realize that should they die on the job, they would have no one to weep for them. Luigi shows Geremio a photograph of Philomena, a woman he loved in Abruzzi, and Geremio is taken with the face of Philomena's oldest sister, Annunziata. At Gennaro's tavern, Geremio dances with his girl friend, Kathleen, and shocks her when he proposes marriage. After Kathleen refuses to marry him unless he finds a "respectable" job, an insulted Geremio proudly declares his intention to remain in construction and tells Luigi that he wants to marry Annunziata. Some time later, as they wait for Annunziata's ship to dock, Geremio reveals to Luigi that after she had written to him, stating that he must own a home before she would marry him, he lied about being a homeowner. Luigi advises Geremio not to tell Annunziata the truth and adds that he will somehow obtain a house for them. At the wedding ceremony, Geremio, with Luigi's assistance, makes a deal with Jaroslav, a Slavic immigrant, to buy a house in Brooklyn for $1,000 by putting $25 down and moving in after he pays $750. Geremio rents the house for a three-day honeymoon, letting Annunziata think that it belongs to them. Once inside, Annunziata cries with joy, then gives "salt to the devil" by sprinkling salt in the corners to protect against evil. Annunziata and Geremio enjoy three days of bliss, but the honeymoon ends abruptly when Jaroslav arrives and Annunziata learns the truth about the house. Back in the city, at Geremio's noisy tenement, Annunziata makes her new husband promise that he will never lie to her again. The newlyweds then make plans to scrimp and save so that they can have the house in fifty-five weeks. At a new worksite, Murdin, now a foreman, offers a $100 bonus to the man who lays the most bricks and does the best work. Geremio wins the bonus and celebrates with his workmates at Gennaro's, where Kathleen confides to him that she is lonely. Geremio returns home drunk and he and Annunziata argue because of their frustration at how long it is taking to pay for the house.

Annunziata soon gives birth to a son, named Paul, and by 1928, the family includes two more sons and a daughter. When they are within a few weeks of having saved enough to move into the home, the stock market crashes and there is less work for Geremio. Jaroslav advises the couple that he must sell the house because he is desperate for money. Annunziata, extremely upset, gives him $100 of the last $125 that she and Geremio have, and Jaroslav agrees not to sell, no matter what. When Murdin asks Geremio to be the foreman on a new project on which he has bid, Geremio turns down the job out of safety concerns. Geremio eventually accepts the position, but when he shows the plans to his fellow workers, one of them notices that the demolition involved may be dangerous. The men hesitate at first to join up until Luigi declares that he trusts Geremio. As construction progresses, Geremio urges the men to work faster and harder. One day, after ordering the resting Luigi to go back to work or be replaced, Luigi is severely injured in an accident. Annunziata tries to comfort the guilt-ridden Geremio, but he treats her coldly and goes to the tavern, where his co-workers are hostile toward him. He then visits Kathleen, who consoles him, and they begin an affair. Later, Geremio, forgetting that the day is his birthday, tells Annunziata that he has to stay late again for another union meeting, but she urges him to come home for dinner. Geremio returns home late and drunkenly breaks down the door, slaps an angry, fed-up Annunziata and then heads for Kathleen's apartment. Having gone over the past nine years, Geremio tries to figure out why he is so unhappy. Kathleen criticizes Geremio's outlook on life, noting that in his world everything is either good or bad, while, for her, the world is divided into the strong and the weak. When Kathleen encourages Geremio to leave his family and go away with her, Geremio finally realizes that he desires more than the ostensible freedom that Kathleen offers. Geremio then returns home, where he falls to his knees in front of Annunziata and declares that they must never grow apart again. Back at the worksite on Good Friday, Geremio tells the men that, as it is the custom to wash one's soul clean on that day, he must confess that he has wronged them. Although one of the workers calls him the worst foreman he has ever had, they all forgive him. Geremio tells the men to work at their own pace and promises to do all he can to ensure their safety. They shore up the building with beams, and as the cement is being poured, Geremio insists on more shoring. Before this can be accomplished, however, a wall collapses, then a floor, and Geremio is knocked into a hole, which begins to fill up with cement. As he is being buried alive by the cement, Geremio hears voices from his past and dies after asking Annunziata to forgive him. Later, Annunziata is questioned by a governmental committee that will decide how much money she is to be paid as compensation for Geremio's death. When a priest tells her that the amount will be determined by how much Geremio would have earned during the rest of his life, Annunziata points out that they cannot place a value on his love and dreams. The committee decides to give her $1,000 in addition to monthly payments for the children, prompting Annunziata to declare that Geremio has at last bought them a house. *Accidental death. Brick layers. Conscience. Forgiveness. Friendship. Houses. Immigrants. Italian Americans. Marriage. Bars. Birthdays. Cement. Corruption. The Depression, 1929. Drunkenness. Foremen. Good Friday. Honeymoons. Infidelity. Installment plans. Live burial. Midwives. New York City. New York City–Brooklyn. Photographs. Priests. Proposals (Marital). Safety. Secrets. Self-sacrifice. Slavic Americans. Snow. Stock market crash of 1929. Superstition. Tenement-houses. Weddings.*

Note: The working title of the film, *Christ in Concrete*, was the title on the print viewed, although the title card appears to have been added subsequent to the film's initial release. The film opened in New York in Dec 1949 under its British title *Give Us This Day*, but by the time it played Los Angeles in Jun 1950, it had been retitled *Salt to the Devil*. The opening credits on the print viewed read, "A Geiger-Bronsten Production of Edward Dmytryk's *Christ in Concrete*." The novel was expanded from a short story, also entitled "Christ in Concrete," which was originally published in *Esquire* in Mar 1937
A *HR* news item of 16 May 1946 noted that American producer Rod E. Geiger had purchased the film rights to Pietro Di Donato's novel and planned to make the film with director Roberto Rossellini. A 1 Oct 1947 *FD* news item reported that Geiger had signed Luise Rainer for the role of "Annunziata." On 12 Feb 1948, *DV* reported that Geiger would start production on *Give Us This Day* at the Motion Picture Center Studios on 10 Mar, with a cast headed by Rainer, Sam Wanamaker, Albert Dekker, Karen Morley and J. Edward Bromberg. However, Geiger eventually made the film in Britain in 1949 with Wanamaker, director Edward Dmytryk and writer Ben Barzman, all of whom had been blacklisted as a result of the House Committee on Un-American Activities hearings. Although the film received excellent reviews in Europe and in New York, as Dmytryk

states in his book *A Memoir of the Hollywood Ten*, the then powerful American Legion picketed the U.S. screenings, causing the film to receive few bookings.

Box 17 Dec 1949. *DV* 12 Feb 1948, p. 2. *DV* 19 Jun 1950. *Exb* 21 Dec 1949, pp. 2768-69. *FD* 1 Oct 1947. *FD* 15 Dec 1949, p. 6. *Har* 17 Dec 1949, pp. 202-03. *HR* 16 May 1946. *HR* 19 Jun 1950, p. 3. *LAEx* 31 Jan 1948. *LAT* 8 Nov 1947. *LAT* 17 Jun 1950. *MPHPD* 17 Dec 1949, p. 122. *NYT* 21 Dec 1949, p. 41. *Var* 19 Oct 1949, p. 8. *Var* 7 Dec 1949.

THE GLACIER STORY see DANGEROUS MISSION

THE GLASS WALL (Italian Americans)

Shane-Tors Productions. *Dist* Columbia Pictures Corp. Apr **1953**; Prod: early May—mid-Jun 1952 at General Service Studios [©Columbia Pictures Corp.; 24 Mar 1953; LP2433]. Sd; b&w. 7,180 ft. 78 or 80 min. PCA cert no. 15884.

Prod Ivan Tors. *Assoc prod* Ben Colman. *Dir* Maxwell Shane. *Asst dir* Richard Dixon. *Asst dir, NY unit* Ben Berk. *Scr* Ivan Tors and Maxwell Shane. *Dir of photog* Joseph F. Biroc. *Spec eff* Jack Rabin, David Commons and Robert Jones. *Art dir* Serge Krizman. *Prod des* George Van Marter. *Supv film ed* Stanley Frazen. *Film ed* Herbert L. Strock. *Mus* Leith Stevens. *Sd* William H. Wilmarth.

Cast: Vittorio Gassman (*Peter Kuban*), Gloria Grahame (*Maggie*), Ann Robinson (*Nancy*), Douglas Spencer (*Inspector Bailey*), Robin Raymond (*Tanya*), Jerry Paris (*Tom*), Elizabeth Slifer (*Mrs. Hinckley*), Richard Reeves (*Eddie*), Joseph Turkel (*Freddie*), Else Neft (*Mrs. Zakolya*), Michael Fox (*Toomey*), Ned Booth (*Monroe*), Kathleen Freeman (*Fat woman*), Juney Ellis (*Girl friend*), Jack Teagarden (*Himself*), Shorty Rogers and His Band.

Drama. [*Not viewed*]. Peter Kuban, a European refugee, arrives in New York harbor as a stowaway. Peter tells the immigration officers that he helped the Allies after escaping from a concentration camp, and that he saved the life of an American paratrooper he knows only as Tom. He has no papers or proof of his actions, however, so he is denied entry. Desperate to avoid deportation, Peter jumps ship, breaking some ribs in the process, and sets off to look for Tom, who he knows is a clarinetist who works in Times Square. As Peter searches the streets of New York for Tom, the police begin to search for Peter. A photograph of Peter taken at his immigration hearing appears in the newspaper. In a cafeteria, Peter helps a down-on-her-luck woman, Maggie, escape from the police after he sees her try to steal a coat. She hides him in her room and tends to his broken ribs, but they go back on the run after Peter is forced into a fight with the landlady's son. The police catch up with them at the subway, but Peter escapes. Meanwhile, Tom has seen Peter's picture in the paper. After his nightclub performance with Jack Teagarden and his band, Tom goes to the authorities and convinces them that Peter is entitled to enter the country. However, Inspector Bailey explains that they must find Peter before morning, or he will automatically be labeled a criminal. Peter is befriended by Tanya, a kind-hearted burlesque dancer, but her brother throws him out, telling him to seek help from the United Nations Displaced Persons Commission. Peter is wandering through the empty United Nations building at dawn when the police finally track him down. Peter runs from them and, after staring down the building's massive glass wall, is about to jump off the roof when he hears Tom and Maggie calling to him. The police assure Peter that he will be allowed to stay. Chases. Immigrants. New York City. Police. Burlesque dancers. Cafeterias. Deportation. Escapes. Landladies. Musicians. Nightclubs. Photographs. Robbery. Searches. Stowaways. Subways. United Nations. Veterans. Wounds and injuries.

Note: Some scenes in this film were shot in New York City. According to *NYT*, *The Glass Wall* was the first film to use the newly constructed United Nations building as a location. Additional news items reported that director Maxwell Shane shot footage of people on the New York streets to make the film look more realistic. According to a *LADN* article, a subway motorman named Arnold Skeene was given a speaking part because of his authentic look. However, Skeene's participation in the final film has not been confirmed. The film originally was to be released by United Artists, according to news items. This was the first film Italian actor Vittorio Gassman made in the United States.

Box 7 May 1953. *DV* 10 Mar 1952. *DV* 4 Mar 1953, p. 4. *Exb* 25 Mar 1953. *FD* 2 Apr 1953. *Har* 7 Mar 1953. *HCN* 4 Apr 1953. *HR* 16 May 1952, p. 11. *HR* 6 Jun 1952, p. 15. *HR* 4 Mar 1953, p. 3. *LADN* 14 Jul 1952. *LADN* 4 May 1953. *LAEx* 4 Apr 1953. *MPHPD* 7 Mar 1953, p. 1750. *Newsweek* 20 Apr 1953. *NYT* 4 May 1952. *NYT* 8 Jun 1952. *Var* 4 Mar 1953, p. 6.

THE GLOBETROTTERS see THE HARLEM GLOBETROTTERS

THE GLORIOUS TRAIL (Native Americans)

Charles R. Rogers Productions, Inc. *Dist* First National Pictures, Inc. 28 Oct **1928** [©First National Pictures, Inc.; 11 Sep 1928; LP25611]. Si; b&w. 6 reels, 5,886 ft.

Pres Charles R. Rogers. *Supv* Harry J. Brown. *Dir* Albert Rogell. *Story* Marion Jackson. *Titles* Don Ryan. *Photog* Frank Good. *Film ed* Fred Allen.

Cast: Ken Maynard (*Pat O'Leary*), Gladys McConnell (*Alice Harper*), Frank Hagney (*Gus Lynch*), Les Bates (*Horse-Collar Keller*), James Bradbury, Jr. (*Bill Keller*), Billy Franey (*Jimmy Bacon*), Chief Yowlache (*High Wolf*).

Western. After a work crew stringing telegraph wires across the Great Plains is slaughtered by Indians, Pat O'Leary, the company superintendent, must take out another supply train to make the dangerous trip across open country. The Indians attack and are driven off. On the day the wires are finally strung, the settlers gather to hear the first message from the East. The Indians, incited by Lynch, a white renegade, attack the settlers, and Pat uses the telegraph to alert a nearby fort. The Indians are driven off, Lynch is killed, and Pat prepares to settle down with Alice Harper. *Frontier and pioneer life. Great Plains. Indians of North America. Settlers. Telegraph. Traitors.*

FD 14 Oct 1928. *Var* 17 Oct 1928, p. 24.

THE GLORY BRIGADE (Greek Americans)

Twentieth Century-Fox Film Corp. *Dist* Twentieth Century-Fox Film Corp. Jul **1953**; Prod: 15 Sep—20 Oct 1952 at Ft. Leonard Wood, Missouri; addl day at studio backlot on 27 Oct 1952 [©Twentieth Century-Fox Film Corp.; 10 Jun 1953; LP2910]. Sd (Western Electric Recording); b&w. 8 reels, 7,342 ft. 81-82 min. PCA cert no. 16116.

Prod William Bloom. *Dir* Robert D. Webb. *Asst dir* Eli Dunn. [*2d asst dir* Jack Sonntag and Paul Wurtzel]. *Wrt* Franklin Coen. *Dir of photog* Lucien Ballard. [*Cam op* Don Anderson and Arthur Lane]. [*Gaffer* Jack Brown]. *Spec photog eff* Ray Kellogg. *Art dir* Lyle Wheeler and Lewis Creber. *Film ed* Mario Mora. *Set dec* Fred J. Rode. [*Ward men* Reeder Boss and Jess Munden]. *Mus dir* Lionel Newman. *Choreography by* Matt Mattox. *Sd* W. D. Flick and Harry M. Leonard. [*Sd rec* Charles Cole]. [*Boom man* Paul Gilbert]. [*Cable man* Hal Lombard]. *Makeup artist* Ben Nye. [*Makeup* Ernie Park and Lynn Reynolds]. *Tech adv* [*on military details*] Captain William J. Knickerbocker, C.E., U.S.A. [*Tech adv on Greek speech and customs* James Harakas]. [*Unit prod mgr* Bill Eckhardt]. [*Auditor* Edward Arnold]. [*Loc mgr* Robert Sunderland]. [*Scr supv* Irving Cooper]. [*Explosives worker* Jess Wolf].

Cast: Victor Mature [(*Lt. Sam Prior*)], Alexander Scourby [(*Lt. Nikias*)], Lee Marvin [(*Corp. Bowman*)], Richard Egan [(*Sgt. Johnson*)], Nick Dennis [(*Corp. Marakis*)], Roy Roberts [(*Sgt. Chuck Anderson*)], Alvy Moore [(*Pvt. Stone*)], Russell Evans [(*Pvt. Taylor*)], Henry Kulky [(*Sgt. "Smitty" Smitowsky*)], Gregg Martell [(*Pvt. Ryan*)], [Lamont Johnson (*Capt. Adams*)], [Carleton Young (*Capt. Davis*)], [Frank Gerstle (*Maj. Sauer*)], [Stuart Nedd (*Lt. Jorgenson*)], [George Michaelides (*Pvt. Nemos*)], [John Verros (*Capt. Charos*)], [Alberto Morin (*Sgt. Lykos*)], [Archer MacDonald (*Sgt. Kress*)], [George Saris (*Medic*)], [Peter Mamakos (*Col. Kallicles*)], [Jonathan Hale (*Col. Peterson*)], [Father Patrinakos (*Chaplain*)], [Ray Harden (*New Zealand soldier*)], [Ricky La Ricos, Nico Minardos, David Gabbai, Peter Haramis, James George, George Conrad, Costas Morfis, John Haretakis (*Greek soldiers*)], [Matt Mattox, Jack Dodds (*Solo dancers*)].

War, Drama. [*Print viewed*]. In the United Nations campaign during the Korean War, Lt. Sam Prior leads his company of combat engineers in an operation to blow up a bridge that they think the enemy wants to use. Back at the base, Capt. Adams tells company commanders that the "Reds" are planning a big offensive within seventy-two hours in the area where the bridge was and that they believe the enemy is hiding something on the other side of the river. The division is sending a brigade of Greek infantrymen trained in guerrilla warfare on a reconnaissance of the area. When the bigoted platoon commander, Lt. Jorgenson, disdains conducting an operation with the Greeks, Sam, who says some of his best friends are Greeks, including his own father, volunteers his platoon to ferry them across the river. Sam's ranking officer, Major Sauer, warns that a lot of men share Jorgenson's attitude, but Sam assures him that his men know his name used to be Priopilis. Sam gives his men the choice to stay, but all are eager to go. When they come upon the camp of the Greek brigade, they find the men dancing to traditional music. While some of the Americans scoff, Sam, who is heartily welcomed by the brigade leaders, Capt. Charos and Lt. Nikias, proudly proclaims to his men that the Greeks have a tradition of being tough warriors and have never been beaten by any country of their own size. The plan is for

Sam to be in charge until they land, then Capt. Charos will take command of his men on their mission and return to the river in a reasonable time. Many of the platoon's rafts have been damaged by shrapnel from a mine, so Sam gives orders to abandon the machine guns and mortars, leaving the soldiers with only the weapons they can carry by hand. Before going across the river, a Greek chaplain leads his men in prayer, and the Americans join them. After the Greek brigade goes on their mission, the Americans are attacked by the enemy, but drive them off. Sam sends two men with the Greek translator, Corp. Marakis, to scout the woods, and they see that the enemy has taken about a dozen of the Greeks prisoners, seemingly without a fight. When the Americans learn what happened, they make disparaging comments about the Greeks and suggest that they leave because they have no heavy weapons. Sam sends the company back to get the weapons and remains behind with three of his men, Sgt. Chuck Anderson, Private Stone and Corp. Bowman, the demolitions expert, in addition to Corp. Marakis. As the sun begins to rise, the remaining men hear gunfire. They return to the river to find that all the men sent back have been massacred. As they are preparing the bodies for burial, a group of twenty-three Greeks return, and Lt. Nikias, leading them, reports that they were cut off from the rest of the brigade and jumped by the enemy. He says they had to fight hard to get through, but Sam angrily accuses them of not firing their guns or using their bayonets, which he sees are clean. Feeling responsible for getting his men killed because of his high regard for the Greeks, Sam now is ashamed of his heritage, believing that the Greek soldiers did not fight as his own men would have done. When they see an enemy tank, Sam tells Lt. Nikias to keep his men out of sight, then has Bowman lay dynamite to blow it up. After the charge stops the tank, Sam, risking his life, climbs to the top, opens the hatch and throws a grenade inside. When the lieutenant gives the command to return to the boats, Sam says they will instead go inland to learn what the enemy is hiding. Finding a hut that used to belong to an American company, Sam leads an attack to recover crates of ammunition hidden there. The Greeks fight fiercely and bravely, and Chuck notices that after the battle, they quickly clean their bayonets. He is told it is a national characteristic. Inside the hut, Lt. Nikias berates Sam for taking risky actions. He says Sam blames the loss of his men on the Greeks and himself, and now is trying to prove his own bravery. As the Greeks greatly outnumber the Americans, Lt. Nikias takes over the command, despite Sam's objections. A wounded New Zealand soldier found at the hut tells the men that he saw a concentration of enemy tanks and ground troops concealed about three miles back waiting for the Allied attack to smash their right flank. Realizing it is imperative for headquarters to get this information, Lt. Nikias sends two men ahead and orders that an old bulldozer be used to pull a transport to carry the wounded men. Sam, who has learned from Chuck about the Greek tradition of quickly cleaning their bayonets, now acknowledges that he approves of the lieutenant's taking command. After the bodies of the two messengers are found, a tank is spotted approaching. Spotting a container of "cugas," or "crazy gas" on the transport, Sam and Bowman get the idea to use it to set the tank aflame. The lieutenant calls it an excellent idea, and the gas, sent flying towards the tank by an explosive charge set by Bowman, destroys the tank. The lieutenant realizes that it will be suicide to continue with the slow bulldozer. He orders his men to move the wounded to the ridge, where they will fight it out with the enemy, and sends the four Americans back with the information. At the river, the Americans sees that the enemy has built an underwater bridge to transport tanks. They are ready to swim across, hoping one of them will make it alive with the information, when some Greek soldiers, who have escaped from the enemy, arrive and reveal that they and others have volunteered to surrender so that Captain Charos could slip the main group through. To protect the lives of his men, Sam decides to wait for Captain Charos to arrive at the river with his radio, by which they can contact their division. In the morning, Charos arrives with his brigade, and Sam, speaking Greek, contacts the Greek brigade headquarters with the radio. Division headquarters are notified and the commanders decide to use the underwater bridge themselves as a transport route. The Greek brigade and the Americans find Lt. Nikias and his men fighting the enemy from the ridge, and American planes drop explosives on the attacking enemy. Helicopters then rescue all the men, and as Sam and lieutenant, the last to go, fly off, Sam lights his cigarette from the lieutenant's pipe. *Cowardice.*

Cultural conflict. Greek Americans. Korean War, 1950-1953. Officers (Military). United States. Army. Corps of Engineers. Bigotry. Bridges. Bulldozers. Daredevils. Explosions. Grenades. Massacres. Munitions. Music. New Zealanders. Rescues. Rivers. Tanks (Military science). Translators. War injuries.

Note: The working title of this film was *Baptism of Fire.* The opening credits contain the following statement: "Appreciation is expressed to the Department of Defense, the Department of the Army, and the Corps of Engineers for their cooperation in the production of this film." It was shot for the most part at Ft. Leonard Wood, Missouri. Soldiers appeared as extras, and the Army Corps of Engineers built a 460-foot M-2 floating pontoon bridge for use in the film, according to studio publicity. Writer Franklin Coen served in the Signal Corps during World War II and wrote a number of engineering training scripts. According to *HCN,* crew member Jess Wolf died from injuries suffered while working on a dynamite blast for the film.

HR commented that the film was notable for attempting its "hitherto untouched subject of other nationalities in the UN struggle against the red." According to studio publicity, production head Darryl Zanuck ordered the production unit to fill every Greek role of the all-male cast with an actor of Greek parentage. These included Alexander Scourby, Nick Dennis, John Verros and Alberto Morin. The chaplain in the film was played by Rev. Dr. Nicon D. Patrinakos, priest of the St. Nicholas Greek Orthodox Church of St. Louis. The actor Henry Kulky was a wrestler known as Bomber Kulkowich.

Box 23 May 1953. *DV* 9 Feb 1953. *DV* 12 May 1953, p. 3. *Exh* 20 May 1953, pp. 3523-24. *FD* 28 May 1953, p. 6. *Har* 16 May 1953, p. 80. *HCN* 26 Sep 1952. *HR* 12 May 1953, p. 3. *LADN* 1 Aug 1953. *LAT* 1 Aug 1953. *MPD* 22 May 1953. *MPHPD* 16 May 1953, p. 1838. *NYT* 15 Aug 1953, p. 8. *Var* 13 May 1953.

THE GLORY ROAD *see* **THE BLOOD OF JESUS**

THE GLORY TRAIL (Native Americans, Dakota)
Crescent Pictures Corp. *Dist* Crescent Pictures Corp. 15 Sep **1936**. Sd; b&w. 64-65 min. PCA cert no. 2378.

Prod E. B. Derr. *Assoc prod* Bernard A. Moriarty. *Dir* Lynn Shores. *Asst dir* Fred Spencer and Jack Leonard. *Story and scr* John T. Neville. *Photog* Arthur Martinelli. *Art dir* F. Paul Sylos. *Film ed* Don Barrett. *Mus dir* Abe Meyer. *Rec* J. S. Westmoreland. *Prod mgr* Frank Melford.

Cast: TOM KEENE (*Captain John Morgan*), Joan Barclay (*Lucy Strong*), Captain E. H. Calvert (*Colonel Strong*), Frank Melton (*Lieutenant Gilchrist*), William Royle (*Captain Fetterman*), Walter Long (*Riley*), Allen Greer (*Indian Joe*), William Crowell (*Wainwright*), Harve Foster (*Hampton*), Ann Hovey (*Julie Morgan*), John Lester Johnson (*Toby*), Etta McDaniel (*Mandy*), James Bush (*David Kirby*).

Historical, Western. [*Not viewed*]. Following the Civil War, soldiers of the North and South head West on the Bozeman Trail into Sioux Indian country. Yankee lieutenant Gilchrist and his colonel's daughter, Lucy Strong, arrive at Fort Phil Kearny in Wyoming with a load of ammunition. There, they meet Confederate captain John Morgan. John's company of ex-rebels has refused to accept surrender and is determined to establish a Confederate colony along the Bozeman Trail. Renegade white Riley, who is traveling with his scout, Indian Joe, is aiding the Indians in their fight to deter the white man's encroachment on their land. After Riley helps the Sioux steal Gilchrist's ammunition wagon, John, who has been detaining Lucy at the rebel camp to get her to like him, is blamed. Determined to clear himself, John sets out to recover the ammunition. Gilchrist, meanwhile, incriminates the rebels to Union officer Captain Fetterman, who sends his soldiers to recover the ammunition. When the soldiers arrive at the rebel camp, they find John and his men celebrating the recovery of the ammunition. Fetterman places the rebels under arrest, but John refuses to recognize the colonel's authority and insists that he and his men return the ammunition to the fort themselves. After delivering the ammunition to Colonel Strong, John informs the officer that he and his men are planning to build a colony in the district of Powder River. Although Strong warns John about Chief Red Cloud, the Confederate soldiers build homes and plant crops in anticipation of the arrival of their families. John and Lucy, meanwhile, have fallen in love. Riley then frames Confederate lieutenant David Kirby for the murder of a Union soldier during an Indian attack. When Strong orders that Kirby be handed over to the Union soldiers for a trial, John is determined to have Kirby tried by his own men. Fearing Strong's retaliation on the new settlement, Kirby confesses, even though he is innocent; a jury of his own men finds him guilty and sentences him to death. As Kirby is shot down by a firing squad, a soldier confesses to John that Riley forced him to steal Kirby's sword so that he might be accused of murder. The soldier also warns John of Red Cloud's approach. A Union soldier then arrives at the settlement and tells John that all of Fetterman's cavalrymen who

were en route to arrest Kirby have been massacred by the Indians. Hope lies in the approaching wagon train, which is carrying more rifles. When thousands of Sioux Indians raid the caravan, Union and Confederate soldiers join forces under John and force the Indians to retreat. Following the death of John's sister Julie, who had just arrived, John recites marriage vows during a mass wedding between his men and their newly arrived brides, while Lucy repeats the vows at John's side. *Confederate States of America. Army. Dakota Indians. Fetterman Fight, 1866. Officers (Military). Renegades. Settlers. United States–History–Reconstruction, 1865-1898. Ammunition. Bozeman Trail (MT). Brides. Executions. William Judd Fetterman. Fort Phil Kearny (WY). Frame-ups. United States. Army. Wagon trains. Weddings.*

Note: This film was the first release of E. B. Derr's company, Crescent Pictures, and was the first in a series of Derr pictures that starred Tom Keene. *DV* 8 Jul 1936, p. 3. *FD* 10 Jul 1936, p. 8. *HR* 8 Jul 1936, p. 4. *MPD* 13 Jul 1936, p. 4. *MPH* 18 Jul 1936, p. 54. *Var* 21 Apr 1937, p 15.

GLOS SERCA see TODA UNA VIDA

GO DOWN, DEATH! (African Americans)

Sack Amusement Enterprises; A Harlemwood Studios production. *Dist* Sack Amusement Enterprises. **1946?**. Sd; b&w. 5,064 ft. 56 min.

Pres ALFRED N. SACK. *Dir* Spencer Williams. *Dial dir* Robert M Moscow. *Scr* Sam Elljay. *Story idea* Jean Roddy. *Photog* H. W. Kier. *Ed* L. J. Powell. *Sd eng* Bruce Jamieson.

Cast: *The Players*: Myra D. Hemmings, Samuel H. James, Eddye L. Houston, Spencer Williams, Amos Droughan, Walter McMillion, Irene Campbell, Charlie Washington, Helen Butler, Dolly Jones, [The Heavenly Choir], [Jimmie Green's Orchestra].

African American, Religious, Fantasy, Drama. [*Print viewed*]. When "Big Jim" Bottom, the head of all underworld activities in a Southern town, learns that Reverend Jasper Jones, the new minister, is threatening to clean up the town, Jim hopes to stop him by setting a "preacher trap." Jim plans to frame Jones in a sex scandal and sends three "fly chicks," Minnie, Mabel and Mae, to Jones's office with instructions to escort the reverend home after services. While the notorious women meet Jones in his office and feign interest in religion to gain his confidence, Jim's henchmen break into Jones's home and wait in hiding until he and the women arrive. Jones falls for the ruse and invites the women into his home to discuss their conversion to Christianity. The situation soon becomes odd, though, when Mabel seats herself on Jones's desk and hikes up her dress. A moment later, the women hand Jones a bottle of liquor and envelop him in a kiss while Jim's men take a picture of the scene. Things look bad for Jones until Aunt Caroline, who learned of the scheme from a young boy, enters the house and demands that Jim's men destroy the film. The men ignore Caroline, push her aside and leave with the film. Caroline then returns to her home and tells Jim, whom she adopted as a child after his parents were killed by a tornado, that she knows that he is behind the frame-up. She tries in vain to change Jim's ways, but he resents her meddling and hides the picture in his safe. That night, Caroline talks to a picture of Joe, her dead husband, and asks him to help her. At that moment, Joe's ghost appears and leads Caroline into the room where the safe is located. The ghost opens the safe and Caroline removes the picture, but Jim returns to the house and catches her in the act. In an ensuing struggle, Jim strikes Caroline and she collapses. Caroline's niece, Betty, who is Jones's fiancée, is awakened from her sleep by the commotion and rushes to Caroline's aid, but Caroline is dead. At Caroline's funeral, Jones gives his famous "Go Down, Death" sermon as her coffin is being lowered into the ground. The death of Caroline proves too much for Jim's conscience to bear, and the voices he hears drive him to run as far as he can. While trying to flee from his guilty conscience, Jim sees images of himself at the gates of Hell, followed by visions of devils torturing him and plunging him into the River Styx. The next day, Jim's body is found at the head of a deserted canyon. *Clergy. Crime. Frame-ups. Gambling. Ghosts. Guilt. Hell. Murder. Aunts. Death and dying. The Devil. Engagements. Flirts. Funerals. Heaven. Nieces. Orphans. Safes. Sermons.*

Note: A written foreword appears in the film following the opening credits: "This story of love and simple faith and the triumph of good over evil was inspired by the poem 'Go Down, Death!' from the pen of the celebrated Negro author James Weldon Johnson, now of sainted memory." Publicity material relating to the film lists the title as "Go Down Death! The Story of Jesus and the Devil." No contemporary reviews have been located for the film. It was approved for release with eliminations by NYSA in Dec 1947, and, according to

information contained in the MPAA/PCA Collection at the AMPAS Library, the film was completed by Jul 1946 when it was submitted for certification. The PCA file also reveals that regional censorship boards in Ohio and Maryland ordered a number of eliminations from the film, including scenes depicting Hell, the exposure of a naked breast and the scene in which "Mabel" pulls up her dress while talking to the preacher. In 1948, Ohio censors demanded the elimination of the sequence in which the devil is seen "chewing" a man. Modern sources list the running time as 54 minutes and indicate that it was made in 1944.

GO FOR BROKE! (Japanese Americans)

Metro-Goldwyn-Mayer Corp.; controlled by Loew's Inc. *Dist* Loew's Inc. 25 May **1951**; Los Angeles premiere: 9 May 1951; New York opening: 24 May 1951; Prod: 25 Sep—mid-Nov 1950 [©Loew's Inc.; 23 Mar 1951; LP891]. Sd (Western Electric Sound System); b&w. 10 reels, 8,154 or 8,270 ft. 90 or 92 min. Passed by the National Board of Review. PCA cert no. 15001.

Prod Dore Schary. *Dir* Robert Pirosh. [*Asst dir* Jerry Thorpe]. *Wrt* Robert Pirosh. *Dir of photog* Paul C. Vogel. *Spec eff* A. Arnold Gillespie and Warren Newcombe. *Art dir* Cedric Gibbons and Eddie Imazu. *Film ed* James E. Newcom. *Set dec* Edwin B. Willis. *Assoc* Alfred E. Spencer. *Mus* Alberto Colombo. *Rec supv* Douglas Shearer. [*Sd* John A. Williams]. *Make-up created by* William Tuttle. *Tech adv* Lt. Col. Thomas W. Akins Inf. *Spec consultant* Mike Masaoka. [*Acting coach* David Bradley]. [*Asst to tech adv* Frank Okada].

Song(s): "The Meaning of Love," words and music by Robert Pirosh, Alberto Colombo and Ken Okamoto.

Cast: Van Johnson (*Lt. Michael Grayson*), And the Heroes of the 442nd Regimental Combat Team: Lane Nakano (*Sam*), George Miki (*Chick*), Akira Fukunaga (*Frank*), Ken K. Okamoto (*Kaz*), Henry Oyasato ([*Takashi*] *Ohhara*), Harry Hamada (*Masami*), and Henry Nakamura (*Tommy* [*Kamakura*]), with Warner Anderson (*Col. Charles W. Pence*), Don Haggerty (*Sgt. Wilson I. Culley*), Gianna Canale (*Rosina*), Dan Riss (*Capt. Solari*), [George Tanaguchi (*Ohbara's brother*)], [Frank Okada (*Platoon leader*)], [Tommy T. Hirai (*Squad leader*)], [Ken Miwa (*Jeep driver*)], [Tsutomu Paul Nakamura (*Sergeant Major*)], [Edward Earle, Freeman Lusk (*Generals*)], [Richard Anderson (*Officer*)], [Harris Matsushige, Leo Tatara, Shigeru Jerry Endo, Robert Otoi, Frank Iwanaga, Paul Togawa, Ray Tamaki, Somita Nagafuchi, Luis Aihara, Thomas Matsuura, Bo Sakaguchi, Kenneth Fujioshi, George Shimizu (*Soldiers*)], [Robert Ward Wood (*First gunner*)], [Carmela Restivo (*Italian woman*)], [Ernesto Morelli (*Italian husband*)], [Frank Tarallo (*Italian boy*)], [George Waki (*Motorman*)], [Henry Guttman, John Banner (*German officers*)], [Tak Kobayashi (*Veteran*)], [Mario Siletti (*Italian farmer*)], [Lucia Tarallo (*Italian girl*)], [Jeanne Lafayette (*French girl*)], [Ann Codee (*Pianist*)], [Jack Reilly (*Texan*)], [Louis Mercier (*French farmer*)], [Michele Lange (*French bar girl*)], [Rollin Moriyama (*Nisei*)], [Paul Bannai (*Mail clerk*)], [Tony Christian (*German prisoner*)], [Toru Iura (*Interpreter*)], [Walter Reed (*Captain*)], [James Hamaji (*Sergeant*)], [Hugh Beaumont (*Chaplain*)], [Harris Yokei (*Gunner*)], [Frank Wilcox (*General*)], [Ned Roberts, William H. Yetter, Larry Winter, Albert d'Arno, Robert Boon (*German soldiers*)], [Ted Ohira (*Hula dancer*)], [Nori Sekino (*Sergeant*)], [Tennessee Jim, Joe Haworth, Mack Chandler, George Offerman, Jr., Eugene Gericke (*Texas soldiers*)], [Frank Francone, Anne Provincia, Richard Monda, Anthony La Morte (*Italian children*)], [Ray Hyke (*M.P.*)], [Roger Moore (*Major*)], [Josette Deegan, Gladys Holland, Monique Chantal, Andre Guy (*French girls*)], [Robert Spencer (*American officer*)], [Jerry H. Fujikawa (*Communications sergeant*)], [Jack George (*French priest*)], [Therese Plauzoles (*French woman*)], [Rene Deloffre, Claude Guy, Pierre Plauzoles (*French boys*)], [George Nakashima (*Nisei pilot*)], [Dan Aredas (*Masami's buddy*)], [Tad Imoto (*Nisei sergeant major*)].

World War II, Social, Drama. [*Print viewed*]. In 1943, Lieutenant Michael Grayson is dismayed when he finds that his first assignment as a lieutenant is to be the platoon leader at Camp Shelby, Mississippi of the 442nd Regimental Combat Team, a new outfit composed entirely of Japanese-American volunteers. When he requests a transfer to the 36th Division, his old Texas National Guard unit, Colonel Charles W. Pence refuses and dresses him down for using the word "Japs." Captain Solari, Grayson's superior officer, explains that the regimental slogan, "Go for Broke," is pidgin English for "shoot the works" and assures the suspicious lieutenant that none of the men are spies. In the barracks, Tommy Kamakura, an impetuous volunteer, and Sam, a soldier sending a package to his family in a relocation

camp, discuss the main reason they have volunteered—to show that they are good Americans, so that "relocations" will not happen again. As Grayson puts the men through much tough work, the unit becomes sharp. Tommy is anxious to fight in the Pacific, because his parents were killed in the attack on Pearl Harbor, but Sam tells him they will not be sent there because they might be mistaken for the enemy or thought to be spies. The men are shipped out on May 1, 1944 to Italy. After some time in Naples, they walk through the countryside to Rome. At a village town, a woman flirts with Grayson, and while he romances her in her home, the unit moves out. He interrupts the tryst when he learns that her recent "amico" was in the 36th Division, and excitedly leaves to try to find his friends. Captain Solari, who has covered up for Grayson, reprimands him for his attitude regarding the Japanese-American soldiers. When Tommy and Sam are invited by two soldiers of the 100th Infantry Battalion, the other Army unit composed of Japanese Americans, to partake of some wine they found in a vineyard, the four are shot at by a German officer and soldier in an observation post, and one of the soldiers from the 100th is killed. Tommy, Sam and the other soldier, Masami, blow up the Germans with grenades, and Tommy finds a baby pig, which he keeps as a pet. After reporting the incident, Grayson asks Colonel Pence again about the 36th Division, and the disgusted colonel says he will try to work up a transfer. Solari, who has become friendly with Grayson despite his bigoted views, argues that many in the Army have parents who were born in enemy countries, such as Italian Americans, like himself, and German Americans. Grayson says that the situation with the Japanese Americans is different, and Solari challenges him to state the reason, asking is it because of the shape of their eyes, or the color of their skin? The men are moved to another theater of operation, and during their march, a battle ensues among Roman ruins. Tommy is hit in the leg, but he courageously fires a mortar on target, and the unit captures a German stronghold. The German officers taken prisoner are shocked to see Japanese-American troops, and Grayson is won over by the men's courage. After landing in Marseilles, Grayson, though he objects, is finally transferred to act as a liaison officer at the headquarters of the 36th Division, to which the 442nd outfit is now attached. Back in Italy, Tommy, seeing the suffering and hunger of a poor family, sadly gives them his pet pig for food for the children. Grayson finds some of the 442nd at a bar, where his old platoon sergeant, Wilson I. Culley, is making racist slurs. Unknown to the 442nd, who think the two are buddies, Grayson fights Culley in an alley for calling him a "Jap-lover." Grayson is sent with Culley's unit to be with their artillery observer, and the unit is surrounded by Germans. Some of the 442nd, when they are told they are being sent to help, are upset, knowing of the unit's racism, but Tommy says this will be their chance to teach the Texans. As they approach, the 442nd begin to fire on the Texans, thinking they are Germans, until Grayson yells a Japanese word he does not understand, but which he has often heard. Culley, grateful for their arrival, reveals the fight he and Grayson earlier had, and Grayson learns that the Japanese word he used means, "You're a stupid jerk and a heel." He admits that was putting it mildly. The 442nd rescues the besieged Texans, and after winning the battle, the Japanese-American and Texan troops part amicably. The 442nd returns to America, where, in a ceremony on the White House lawn, President Harry S. Truman and General Mark W. Clark honor them, and they are cited for outstanding accomplishment in combat. The unit parades down Pennsylvania Avenue. *Americans in foreign countries. Officers (Military). Racism. United States. Army. 442nd Regimental Combat Team. War heroes. World War II. Battles. Fights. Hunger. Japanese Americans–Evacuation and relocation, 1942-1945. Military bases. Military discipline. Naples (Italy). Pigs. Ruins. Texans. Transformation. Harry S. Truman. United States. Army. 100th Infantry Battalion. United States. Army. 36th Division. War victims.*

Note: The film begins with a statement signed by Franklin D. Roosevelt: "The proposal of the War Deparment to organize a combat team consisting of loyal American citizens of Japanese descent has my full approval. The principle on which this country was founded and by which it has always been governed is that Americanism is a matter of the mind and heart. Americanism is not, and never was, a matter of race or ancestry." Following this, an introductory title card reads: "The 442nd Regimental Combat Team and the 100th Infantry Battalion were composed of American citizens of Japanese ancestry. *BATTLE RECORD:* 7 Major Campaigns in Europe; 9,486 Casualties; 18,143 Individual Decorations; 7 Presidential Unit Citations."

In his autobiography, Dore Schary, M-G-M's chief of production, states that he suggested to Robert Pirosh, the Academy Award-winning writer and associate producer of M-G-M's acclaimed 1950 release *Battleground*, that they make a

film about the internment camps used during World War II for Japanese-American citizens. While researching the camps, however, they decided instead to "latch onto a positive view of a negative fact," partly because of cold war tensions, and make a film about the 442nd combat unit. *NYT*, in a pre-production article, compared the planned film to recent Hollywood efforts to deal with bigotry: "Hollywood's current concern with the problem of racial and religious prejudice continues to lead movie-makers into new explorations of this apparently inexhaustible subject. Having investigated, in a succession of recent pictures, the plight of the Negro in a white society and dealt somewhat less fully with anti-Semitism and with alleged discrimination against Mexican-Americans in California, the screen now is about to speak in behalf of the Japanese-Americans, or Nisei."

According to news items in *DN* and *NYT*, Pirosh learned about the Japanese-American fighting units as he researched *Battleground*. Pirosh went to Hawaii and selected five veterans of the 442nd unit to play leading roles in the film. According to Schary, many of the stories included in the film were based on fact. David Bradley, recently hired by M-G-M as a fledgling director due to the interest in his 16mm student film *Julius Caesar*, was assigned to coach the non-actors in their performances. Mike Masaoka, the 442nd's first volunteer from the mainland, was hired as a consultant.

Director of photography Paul C. Vogel also shot *Battleground*, for which he won an Academy Award. Some scenes were shot in the Idyllwild Mountains in California. Reviews generally praised the film. *Var* commented, "The social angle is never overplayed and is effectively socked with a humorous touch." However, *HR* noted: "Underlying the action are strong pleas for racial tolerance which come a bit too frequently. Actually the case of the Nisei soldier's suffering from prejudice need be stated but once because his acts of valor are here on film to win anybody to his side who can be won. Anything more has the effect of shaming the audience, a vast majority of whom only recently disliked and mistrusted all Japanese for four years."

Box 31 Mar 1951. *Cue* 26 May 1951. *DN* 3 Oct 1950. *DV* 26 Mar 1951, p. 3. *Exb* 28 Mar 1951, p. 3050. *FD* 26 Mar 1951, p. 6. *Har* 31 Mar 1951, p. 51. *HCN* 11 May 1951. *HR* 29 Sep 1950. *HR* 26 Mar 1951, p. 3. *LADN* 10 May 1951. *LAEx* 10 May 1951. *LAT* 10 May 1951. *MGM News* 18 Aug 1950. *MPHPD* 31 Mar 1951, p. 785. *New Yorker* 2 Jun 1951. *NYT* 29 Jan 1950. *NYT* 17 Sep 1950. *NYT* 15 Oct 1950. *NYT* 25 May 1951, p. 31. *SatRev* 26 May 1951. *Time* 28 May 1951. *Var* 28 Mar 1951, p. 6.

GO LUI QING QIU *see* **BLOSSOM TIME**

GO MAN GO (African Americans, Jewish Americans)
Sirod Productions, Inc. *Dist* United Artists Corp. 22 Jan **1954**; World premiere in Manila, Philippines: 22 Dec 1953; Los Angeles opening: 20 Jan 1954; Prod: 16 Apr—early May 1953 at Fox Movietone Studios, NYC [©Sirod Productions, Inc.; 22 Jan 1954; LP3746]. Sd (Western Electric Sound System); b&w. 9 reels, 7,470 ft. 82-83 min. PCA cert no. 16840.

Prod Anton M. Leader. *Assoc prod* Michael Shore. *Dir* James Wong Howe. *Orig story and scr* Arnold Becker. *Dir of photog* William Steiner. *Prod des* Howard Bay. *Assoc* Carl Kent. *Film ed* Faith Elliott. *Mus comp and cond* Alex North. *Sd mixer* James Gleason. [*Makeup* Eddie Senz]. *Unit mgr* C. J. Di Gangi. *Tech adv* Harry Hannin.

Music: "Sweet Georgia Brown" by Ben Bernie, Maceo Pinkard and Kenneth Casey, Brother Bones recording by arrangement with Tempo Records.

Song(s): "Go Man Go," music by Sy Oliver, lyrics by Sy Oliver and Mike Shore, sung by Slim Gaillard.

Cast: Dane Clark [(*Abe Saperstein*)], Sidney Poitier [(*Inman Jackson*)], Pat Breslin [(*Sylvia Saperstein*)], Edmon Ryan [(*Zack Leader*)], Bram Nossen [(*Jack Willoughby*)], Anatol Winogradoff [(*Papa Saperstein*)], Celia Bodkins [sic] [(*Mama Saperstein*)], Ruby Dee [(*Irma Jackson*)], Lew Hearn [(*Appraiser*)], Slim Gaillard [(*Slim*)], Mort Marshall [(*MC*)], THE HARLEM GLOBETROTTERS: Stanley Burrell, Nat "Sweetwater" Clifton, Lee Garner, William "Pop" Gates, J. C. Gipson, Josh Grider, Robert Hall, Paul Hardy, Marques Haynes, Leon Hillard, Ducky Moore, George Moore, Ermer Robinson, Reece "Goose" Tatum, Sam Wheeler, Clarence Wilson, John Wilson, and William Wilson, [Carol Sinclair (*Fay Saperstein*)], [Ellsworth Wright (*Sam*)], [Frieda Altman (*Ticket seller*)], [Jean Shore (*Secretary*)], [Jule Benedic, Jerry Hauer (*Bathing beauties*)], [Marty Glickman, Bill Stern (*Announcers*)].

Sports, Biography, Comedy-drama. [*Print viewed*]. With the help of an old, tempermental car, basketball zealot Abe Saperstein and his all-black team, the Harlem Globetrotters, adhere to a rigid schedule of traveling, signing autographs, making appearances, and playing first-rate basketball against second-rate teams. They play in barns, community centers and high school gyms. Abe coaches the team and fills in as a substitute player, but he and loyal team members such as Inman Jackson are always searching for new talent. One such newcomer is Nat "Sweetwater" Clifton, who joins the Globetrotters when one of the players is forced to retire. By the end of the early season, each man has earned only about $650. Back home in Chicago,

Inman shares a meal with Abe's Jewish family and remarks that he soon plans to marry his sweetheart Irma. Hearing this, Abe's mother complains that her son's grueling road schedule prevents what she so dearly wants for him, a home and a wife. Abe, however, wants to discuss his hope of convincing promoter Jack Willoughby, "Mr. Professional Basketball," to help the talented Globetrotters attain big-league status. Soon afterward, Abe is disappointed when Willoughby instead offers him a job coaching another team. Declaring that the Harlem Globetrotters possess the best players in basketball, Abe promises Willoughby that his team "will show you how the game is played." Forced to continue their barnstorming, the players travel to Dubuque, where Abe befriends sports writer Zack Leader. He also adds a new player to the roster, Reece "Goose" Tatum, whose quick and intricate maneuvers impress not only his teammates, but also the spectators. By the end of the next season, the earnings per player have doubled. When Abe reports that Willoughby still refuses to support the team, Inman, now a husband and father, remarks, "We both know what the big hurdle is." The next season, the team, now equipped with a trailer, travels to Kenosha, where Abe falls in love with beauty contestant and ticket seller Sylvia Franklin. On the second day of their acquaintance, Abe proposes, adding, "Think about it. We have till five o'clock." After the two are married in a Jewish ceremony, the team continues its tour, and Sylvia, with the help of Abe's family, sets up an apartment in Chicago. Following Abe's arrival back home, Sylvia realizes the depth of her husband's love of basketball as he animatedly discusses the beauty and poetry of sports. During the next season's games, played before larger audiences, the Globetrotters begin to falter because of fatigue and injury. Abe suggests that each player should show off his own special "razzle-dazzle" for several moments during a game, thereby allowing the others to rest. Goose adds humor to his routine, and the rest of players follow suit. As a result, the crowd goes wild, and the Globetrotters win. Now based in a small office, with Sylvia as his secretary, Abe proposes that Zack's newspaper sponsor a basketball tournament for any qualifying professional team. He then meets with Willoughby, who offers him a job as Detroit's head coach and adds that the Globetrotters will never be accepted into the big league. Angry, Abe reminds Willoughby that the crowds love the Globetrotters, but later, the big arenas that had booked the team begin to cancel their appearances. Zack informs Abe that Willoughby secured the cancellations by describing the Globetrotters as a clown act, not a professional basketball team. When Abe learns that the team's application to play in the big tournament has been rejected, he loses hope and decides to quit the game. Inman warns Abe that without the faith he inspires, the team will fall apart, and Sylvia hints that by abandoning a life that makes him "crazy happy," Abe risks his identity as well as their marriage. Abe sells the team's bus and disappears, wiring only that he is in Detroit. Fearing that he has abandoned his principles to accept the Detroit job, Sylvia packs her bags and is about to return to Wisconsin when an agitated Zack, Inman and Pop Saperstein arrive at the apartment. Abe has wired Pop for money and seems to have borrowed against all their possessions. As the four argue, Abe appears and cheerfully announces that he has paid to schedule the Globetrotters into the biggest stadiums in the country, their games timed to compete with the big-league games. Afraid that the Globetrotters will steal big-league audiences, Willoughby allows the team to compete in the tournament but pits them, in their first game, against the powerful Washington Generals. Willoughby is astounded when the Globetrotters win, and later, he is even more surprised to find them playing in the championship game against the Chicago Majors. With Clifton and Tatum injured, the Globetrotters resort to a bit of clowning in order to give the other players needed rest, and in the final seconds, the team wins the game by a single point. Bursting with pride, Abe remarks that the success of the Harlem Globetrotters is only beginning. *African Americans. Basketball. Harlem Globetrotters (Basketball team). Promoters. Racism. Abe Saperstein. Athletic coaches. Beauty contests. Chicago (IL). Disillusionment. Dubuque (IA). Entertainers. Friendship. Gymnasiums. Jews. Kenosha (WI). Loyalty. Marriage. Sports reporters. Tournaments.*

Note: Onscreen credits include the following disclaimer: "With the exception of persons whose true names are used, the characters and events portrayed are fictional." Celia Boodkin's name is misspelled as "Bodkins" in the onscreen credits. Although most reviews and other contemporary sources list the film's title as either *Go, Man, Go* or *Go, Man, Go!* onscreen credits contain no punctuation. Abe Saperstein, who was born in London in 1902 after his parents migrated from Poland to England, grew up in Chicago and began coaching Negro basketball with the Giles Post American Legion Squad and the Savoy Big Five in 1926. The Harlem Globetrotters, so named by Saperstein because he wanted the public to know that the team was all-black, were formed principally from these two squads. As depicted in the film, the team performed for many years on the barnstorming circuit, but finally won the world professional tournament in Chicago in 1940. Later, however, the team switched their focus from competitive playing to showmanship and became enormously popular. The team continued its successful international tours after Saperstein's death in 1966. The players' comic warm-up routine is accompanied by the team's instrumental (and whistled) theme song, "Sweet Georgia Brown."

Go Man Go is a "prequel" to the 1951 Columbia release *The Harlem Globetrotters* (see entry below). Although contemporary sources indicate that Alfred Palca, the producer/writer of *The Harlem Globetrotters*, began as the producer/writer of *Go Man Go*, and had announced that *Go Man Go* was to be the initial production of Alfred Palca Enterprises, his name does not appear in the onscreen credits or in reviews, and his contribution to the final film cannot be confirmed. The film marked the directorial debut of James Wong Howe, one of the industry's most celebrated cinematographers. Although he co-directed *The Invisible Avenger* with John Sledge in 1958, *Go Man Go* was his only solo directing assignment. Pat Breslin made her screen acting debut in the picture. In addition to Fox's New York studio, filming took place at Madison Square Garden, and in Boston, MA, and Bergenfield, NJ, according to news items. As with *The Harlem Globetrotters*, reviewers commented on the film's subtle racial themes. The *LAEx* review noted that more than in the earlier film, *Go Man Go* concentrates on the "racial hurdles which the team has, in its history, overcome." The *DV* reviewer, however, added that "race is put over in the picture without direct mention or soapboxing of minority theme."

Box 23 Jan 1954. *DV* 5 Aug 1953. *DV* 14 Aug 1953. *DV* 14 Jan 1954, p. 3. *Exb* 27 Jan 1954, p. 3689. *FD* 20 Jan 1954, p. 10. *Har* 23 Jan 1954, pp. 14-15. *HR* 16 Dec 1953. *HR* 14 Jan 1954, p. 3. *LAEX* 21 Jan 1954. *MPHPD* 23 Jan 1954, p. 2157. *NYT* 5 Mar 1953. *NYT* 17 May 1953. *NYT* 10 Mar 1954, p. 29. *Var* 20 Jan 1954, p. 18.

GOD, MAN AND DEVIL (Yiddish language)

Aaron Productions, Inc. **1950**; New York opening: 21 Jan 1950 [©Aaron Productions, Inc.; 6 Feb 1950; LU2837]. Sd; b&w. 9,508 ft. 103 or 108 min. *Country of origin* Canada. Yiddish language.

Exec prod Daniel Silver and Sol C. Rynd. *Dir* Josef Zeiden. [*Scr* Isadore Frankel]. *Mus* Sholom Secunda.

Source: Based on the play *Got, Mentsh, un Tayvl* by Jacob Gordin (New York, 1900).

Cast: Michal Michalesko [(*Hershalle Debrovner*)], Berta Gersten [(*Pesye*)], Lucy Gehrman [(*Dobe*)], Gustav Berger [(*Satan/Uriel Mazik*)], Shifra Lehrer [(*Freide*)], Max Bozyk [(*Lazar Badkhn*)], Esta Salzman [(*Tsipe*)], Leon Schacter [(*Chatzkel Drakhmer*)], Joshua Zeldis [(*Motel*)].

Yiddish, Drama. [*Print viewed*]. In the clouds, God speaks with Satan, who reports that Adam's children are still doing the same foolish things. When God asks about Hershalle Debrovner, a religious and honest Jew who copies the Holy Scrolls for a pittance, Satan requests permission to tempt Hershalle with money to destroy his goodness. God sends him to try, while Satan brags that another of God's holy servants will be lost to him. On Earth, on the fifth night of Chanukkah, Hershalle's wife Pesye, their two nieces, Freide and Tsipe, whom they have reared since childhood, and his father Lazar, await Hershalle's arrival. Their neighbors, weaver Chatzkel Drakhmer, his wife Dobe and their son Motel, have come to celebrate the completion of the Torah that Hershalle has been copying for the past six months. Although the families plan for Motel and Freide to marry, she shyly avoids the subject. Hershalle arrives after having taken a ritual bath. He writes the last word of the Torah and praises God. During the gathering, a wolf howls, which Dobe calls a bad omen, and their lamp is extinguished. Satan enters, and after introducing himself as Uriel Mazik, which they know means "The Devil," he tempts Hershalle to take a lottery ticket with which he can win 50,000 rubles. While Hershalle maintains that he has no interest in winning, all the others encourage him, except Freide, who says that she has always been happy without money. After Hershalle wins the lottery, the family moves to a large new home, where their neighbors mock them. Lazar now complains of Hershalle's cold eyes and grand manner. Pesye is also unhappy, feeling that she and Hershalle were closer when they were poor. Hershalle spends much time with Mazik, with whom he is impressed, and is advised by him to open a prayer shawl, or "tallis," factory and force weavers to work cheaply. Mazik also encourages Hershalle to enjoy himself and marry Freide, reminding him it is a sin to live with a childless wife. Troubled by Freide's presence, Hershalle tells her that he must divorce Pesye, as rabbinical law forbids a childless marriage. Freide admits her attraction, but does not want to hurt Pesye. Hershalle assures her that if Pesye refuses the divorce, he will not insist. When

Chatzkel tells Hershalle that the local weavers have decided to manufacture prayer shawls in a cooperative and asks Hershalle for a loan to develop a patent that Berel, one of the weavers, has to make linen look like silk, Hershalle is about to agree. Mazik, however, dissuades him with a stern look, and Hershalle offers to hire them instead. Chatzkel is not interested, and when he asks about the engagement of Freide and Motel, Freide says she cannot marry Motel, who says he does not mind. Hershalle offers to provide the same dowry for Tsipe, who likes Motel, and announces that after twenty-two years of the childless marriage, he wants a divorce. Pesye, although shocked, agrees because of his piety. Then, when Freide says she will marry Hershalle, Pesye cries, seeing the look of desire between the two, and accepting her fate as God's will, goes to live with Tsipe. Hershalle, feeling guilty about his decision, admits to Pesye he is worse than she thought and asks for her forgiveness. Three years later, Freide, unhappy and bored, wishes she had a child. At a community meeting, when Hershalle is suggested for president of the synagogue, Chatzkel argues strenuously that he stole Berel's secret, is money mad, and has destroyed Pesye, who is now out of her mind, Meanwhile, Tsipe, who has lost her youthful glee, mocks her sister, who once had no interest in jewelry and fine clothes. Freide complains that the money has only brought her misery and a broken heart. Sometime later, Chatzkel and Motel again ask Hershalle's help to start a cooperative, saying they cannot earn a living, despite the fact that they work hard, and Motel explodes in anger over Hershalle's increased riches during hard times. Hershalle condescendingly offers them jobs as laborers, and Chatzkel accepts, as they must eat. Hershalle gives Freide new earrings from the big city, but as she looks in the mirror, she grows sullen. Hershalle, who wants to get back to work, callously suggests that in the summer they can visit a famous doctor in Vienna. She begs him to play his violin again, wanting to feel what she once felt when he played, but he says they were striving for happiness then and will not feel the same again. Sometime later, as Hershalle obsessively counts his beloved bills, Mazik demands that he sign a receipt for a valise of money, but Hershalle refuses. They struggle for the valise, and Mazik throws Hershalle down, then brandishes a knife. Freide witnesses Hershalle attack Mazik and cry out "My money!" as he gathers it up. Soon, Mazik recovers, and he and Hershalle become closer than before. Chatzkel, who had been made foreman by Hershalle, now works only part-time because he has refused to push the workers as Hershalle wanted. When Motel's hand gets caught in a wheel, Hershalle, who is standing nearby as his blood splashes out, remains unconcerned. Motel is brought home, where he is attended by Satan, disguised as a doctor. Hershalle, who has boarded his father with strangers because of his father's penetrating, cynical criticisms, now asks forgiveness, but Lazar says he feels more at home with the poor family with whom he now lives. Hershalle sadly recalls that God forgives sins through charity and forgiveness, but that the sins against fellow men cannot be erased by either. After Motel dies, Tsipe cries that God helps Mazik, but has taken her Motel, while Freide moans that the violin remains silent. When Chatzkel breaks the news to Hershalle that Motel died under the doctor's knife, Hershalle asks forgiveness of God. Chatzkel accuses him of making a mockery of God and throws Motel's blood-stained tallis on Hershalle's head. Hershalle now realizes that gold cannot cancel his smallest sin and that a rich man is really poor. When he plays his violin and sings a psalm, Freide hears and is overjoyed. Hershalle now puts on the bloody tallis and prays. He asks God how man can achieve purity, being impure, and bemoans a life of nothingness and emptiness, then resolutely knots the tallis and ties it around his neck. When Freide finds him hanged, she screams and cries. Satan, seeing that even though Hershalle had so much money, he chose not to live, admits he has lost. *The Devil. Family relationships. Jews. Lure of riches. Moral corruption. Nieces. Partnership. Religiosity. Tests of character. Accidental death. Business ethics. Childlessness. Cooperatives. Divorce. Engagements. Hanging. Hanukkah. Lotteries. Neighbors. Prayer. Religious articles. Suicide. Synagogues. Violinists.*

Note: The Yiddish-language title of this film is *Got, Mentsh, un Tayvl.* The film was released with English-language subtitles. After the opening credits, the following written introduction appears and is spoken: "The eternal struggle between God and Satan for the soul of man here evolves around a pious writer of Torah, Hershalle Debrovner. This simple man learns too late that power and wealth alone cannot buy the priceless beauties of man's existence. His way of life is changed when Satan takes control of him, body and soul." Aaron Productions, Inc. was located in Montreal, Canada and New York. Publicity for the film stated that "with the growing popularity of Foreign Language Films, Aaron Productions Inc. decided that a Yiddish-Language film could be produced which would take its place among the best in the foreign language picture field. *God, Man and Devil* will directly appeal to all." However, the *Var*, stated, "This pic[ture] is definitely limited to a Jewish-speaking following. Though English-titled, it will get best results from mid-week showings at Jewish neighborhood theatres." Although stating that the story "grows tiresome," the review also noted that there are some interesting characterizations and moments that will hit home with a number of Jewish viewers."

Exb 1 Mar 1950, p. 2805. *Var* 25 Jan 1950.

THE GODDESS OF LOST LAKE (Native Americans)
Louise Glaum Organization; Robert Brunton Productions. *Dist* W. W. Hodkinson Corp. 14 Oct **1918.** Si; b&w. 5 reels.

Prod Robert Brunton. *Dir* Wallace Worsley. *Scen* Jack Cunningham. *Story* M. Van de Water. *Cam* L. Guy Wilky.

Cast: Louise Glaum (*Mary Thorne*), W. Lawson Butt (*Mark Hamilton*), Hayward Mack (*Chester Martin*), Joseph J. Dowling (*Marshall Thorne*), Frank Lanning (*Eagle*).

Drama. Mary Thorne, a quarter-breed Indian, returns home from the East with a college degree and an air of refinement, although she relishes the freedom of her father Marshall's mountain cabin. When Mark Hamilton and Chester Martin visit the cabin on a hunting expedition, Mary, in a spirit of mischief, dons her Indian clothing and convinces them that she is full-blooded. Mark falls deeply in love with the girl, while Chester, contemptuous of her Indian background, though attracted to her, decides to possess her. While her father is hunting for gold at Lost Lake, Chester enters Mary's room and attacks her. Mark rescues her, after which he realizes, by the modern decor of her room, that Mary is a cultured young lady. Later, Marshall is killed by an Indian guard at Lost Lake, but Mary inherits the gold he discovered and marries Mark. *Impersonation and imposture. Indians of North America. Mountain life. Racism. Attempted rape. Gold. Hunting. Inheritance. Prospectors. Rescues.*

Note: *Var* calls this a Paralta film.

ETR 19 Oct 1918, p. 1705. *MPN* 5 Jun 1920, p. 4682. *MPN* 19 Oct 1918, p. 2598. *MPW* 28 Sep 1918, p. 1899. *MPW* 26 Oct 1918, p. 542. *MPW* 2 Nov 1918, p. 626. *NYDM* 28 Dec 1918, p. 998. *Var* 18 Oct 1918, p. 38.

GOD'S ANGRY MEN see SEVEN ANGRY MEN

GOD'S STEP CHILDREN (African Americans)
Micheaux Pictures Corp. *Dist* Micheaux Pictures Corp. **1938.** Sd (Wicmar and Blue Seal Noiseless Recording); b&w. 10 reels, 8,342 ft. 105 min.

Prod Oscar Micheaux. *Dir* Oscar Micheaux. *Photog* Lester Lang. *Ed* Patricia Rooney and Leonard Weiss. *Sd eng* E. A. Schabbehor, George Wicker, Ed Fenton and Nelson Minnerly.

Cast: Jacqueline Lewis (*Naomi, as a child*), Ethel Moses (*The teacher* [*Mrs. Cushinberry*]/*her daughter Eva, grown up*), Alice B. Russell (*Mrs. Saunders*), Trixie Smith (*A visitor*), Charles Thompson (*Jimmie, as a boy*), Carman Newsome (*Jimmie, the man*), Gloria Press (*Naomi, the woman*), Alec Lovejoy (*A "gambler"* [*Ontrue Cowper*]), Columbus Jackson (*His* [*Cowper's*] *associate*), Laura Bowman (*Aunt Carrie*), Sam Patterson (*A banker*), Charles Moore (*Sup. of schools*), Consuelo Harris, The Tyler Twins (*Muscle dancers*), Sammy Gardiner (*Tap dancer*), Leon Gross' Orchestra.

African American, Domestic, Drama, with songs. [*Viewed print incomplete*]. A stranger arrives at the home of widow Mrs. Saunders and begs her to adopt her baby daughter, whom she cannot afford to feed. After the stranger leaves, Mrs. Saunders, a black woman, realizes that the child is white, and is advised by her friend, Caroline Jones, to turn it over to the police. In the daylight, however, Mrs. Saunders sees that the child, which she has named "Naomi," is black, and believes that the girl will make a good playmate for her son Jimmie. Time passes, and Naomi, now a young schoolgirl, is thought by the other children to be aloof and is accused of not wanting to be black. When Naomi disappears on her way to school one day, Mrs. Saunders is told by Jimmie that Naomi deliberately avoided the black school she was supposed to attend and went to a white school. Naomi denies Jimmie's accusation and tells her mother that he is lying because he hates girls. When Mrs. Cushinberry threatens to give Naomi a beating for being insolent and mean, Naomi, in an angry outburst, tells the teacher that she hates her and all the other children because they are black. Naomi rejects Mrs. Cushinberry's insistence that "we're all God's children," and tells her that God "didn't make Negroes." That evening, Mrs. Cushinberry pays a visit to Mrs.

Saunders to tell her about Naomi's behavior, but when she realizes that Naomi has not told her mother about what happened that afternoon, she decides to remain silent. Naomi, however, has been eavesdropping, and when the teacher leaves, she begins to tell her mother that it was the teacher who was bad. Jimmie intervenes, however, and reveals the truth, that Naomi was whipped at school because was unruly and spit in the teacher's face. Mrs. Saunders then gives Naomi a beating. Later, Naomi starts a rumor that Mrs. Cushinberry has been having an affair with a married professor, and a riot at the school ensues. The angry crowd of students march to the school superintendent's house and demand that he fire both teachers. Mrs. Saunders, who has been told of the riot by Jimmie, rushes to the superintendent's office to dispel the rumor started by her daughter. While Naomi is sent to a convent, Jimmie, who has earned $6,700 by working as a Pullman porter, is approached by Ontrue Cowper, who tries to interest him in an investment in the numbers racket. Jimmie rejects Cowper's offer, and instead invests in a farm. After proposing marriage to his sweetheart Eva, Jimmie invites his mother to live on his new farm. Naomi, who has been reformed by her life at the convent, apologizes to her mother for being a bad child. When Jimmie meets his sister for the first time since her departure for the convent, his mother arranges to have him take her to the city for entertainment. Though things go well in the city, Eva's aunt Carrie does not trust Naomi's unnatural interest in Jimmie and believes that she should be watched. Aunt Carrie's suspicions prove to be well-founded as Naomi soon confesses her love for her adopted brother. When Jimmie, Eva and Naomi return to the country, Jimmie introduces Naomi to his friend, Clyde Wade, who immediately falls in love with her. Naomi, however, finds him repulsive and confesses to Jimmie that she has always wanted him to marry her. Realizing that Eva would be crushed by the loss of Jimmie, Naomi consents to marry Clyde. One year later, Naomi tells her mother that she is leaving Clyde and her newborn son and that she is also "leaving the Negro race." Naomi soon marries a white man, Andrew, who realizes that she is a mulatto when he notices her reaction to seeing her son and her mother. Naomi tries to lie about her past, but he sees through it and turns her out. After getting one last look at her family, Naomi drowns herself in the river. *Adoption. African Americans–Mixed blood. Brothers and sisters. Mothers and daughters. Racism. Transformation. Aunts. Cabarets. Convents. Desertion (Marital). Farmers. Jealousy. Marriage. Marriage–Forced. Miscegenation. Porters. Riots. Rumors. School attendance. Schools. Suicide. Superintendents. Tap dancing. Teachers. Widows.*

Note: The above credits were taken from the viewed print of the film. The plot summary was based on the viewed print and the original dialogue script contained in the New York State Archives. The original version of the film contained footage that was cut from the film soon after its release. No song titles for the film have been found. *Exb* review refers to this film as *All God's Stepchildren.* A trailer for the film contained the following title card: "God's Step Children, from the story 'Naomi Negress!' With an all star colored cast." "Naomi Negress!" may have been an original screen story written by the film's director and producer, Oscar Micheaux. The cover sheet of the dialogue script contains a "producers note," in which it is written that "all the characters appearing herein, regardless how bright in color they may seem, are all members of the Negro Race." The cover sheet also indicates that the picture was copyrighted in 1937; however, the film was not registered for copyright. According to a May 1938 *NYT* article, the film was "withdrawn from circulation" two days after its premiere at the RKO Regent theater in New York. The decision to withdraw the picture was the result of an unfavorable audience reaction to the film and a protest outside the theater. The article quoted Beatrice Godloe, head of the Young Communist Committee, which organized the picket, as saying that the film "slandered Negroes, holding them up to ridicule, playing light-skinned Negroes against their darker brothers." The film was eventually re-cut and the following scenes were removed from the print: The opening scene between the stranger and Mrs. Saunders in which the dialogue centers on "Naomi's" skin color; a portion of the scene in which "Naomi's" teacher says "we're all God's children" and Naomi responds "[God] didn't make the black ones"; a flashback scene in which Mrs. Cushinberry and her alleged paramour profess their love for each other; and a brief sequence at the end showing Naomi with a white husband, who asks her why she has become troubled after having peered into a house with "two Colored people and a boy." Following a meeting with producer Oscar Micheaux, members of various groups, including the National Negro Congress, the Harlem Teachers Union and the Workers Alliance, were guaranteed permission by the producer to preview his next two films, *Birthright* and *Swing*, before they were released. Actress Alice B. Russell was Micheaux's wife.

Exb 1 Apr 1938, p. 109.

GOING MY WAY (Irish Americans)

Paramount Pictures, Inc.; A Leo McCarey Production. *Dist* Paramount Pictures, Inc. **1944**; "The Fighting Front" premiere: 27 Apr 1944; New York premiere: 3 May 1944; Prod: 16 Aug—22 Oct 1943 [©Paramount Pictures, Inc.; 25 Feb 1944; LP13471]. Sd (Western Electric Mirrophonic Recording); b&w. 14 reels, 11,761 ft. 126-127 min. Passed by the National Board of Review.

[*Exec prod* B. G. DeSylva]. *Dir* Leo McCarey. [*Asst dir* Alvin Ganzer]. [*2d asst dir* H. Joslin and D. Keene]. *Scr* Frank Butler and Frank Cavett. *Story* Leo McCarey. *Dir of photog* Lionel Lindon. *Spec photog eff* Gordon Jennings. *Art dir* Hans Dreier and William Flannery. *Ed* LeRoy Stone. [*Set dresser supv* Sam Comer]. *Set dec* Steve Seymour. *Cost* Edith Head. *Mus dir* Robert Emmett Dolan. *Vocal arr* Joseph J. Lilley. *Mus assoc* Troy Sanders. [*Dance dir* Josephine Earle and Danny Dare]. [*Dance dir asst* A. Mann]. *Sd rec* Gene Merritt and John Cope. *Makeup artist* Wally Westmore. [*Hair supv* Leonora Sabine]. [*Opera tech adv* Armando Agnini]. [*Tech adv* Rev. John Devlin]. [*Unit mgr* E. Ralph]. [*Asst unit mgr* H. Brown]. [*Scr clerk* Nesta Charles]. *Double for Risë Stevens* Julie Gibson. *Double for Bing Crosby* John Skins Miller. *Double for Frank McHugh* Fred Stanley.

Song(s): "Habanera" and "First act finale" from *Carmen*, music by Georges Bizet, libretto by Henri Meilhac and Ludovic Halévy. "Going My Way," "The Day After Forever" and "Swinging on a Star," music by James Van Heusen, lyrics by Johnny Burke; "Silent Night, Holy Night," music by Franz Gruber, lyrics by Joseph Mohr; "Too-ra-loo-ra-loo-ral, That's an Irish Lullaby," music and lyrics by J. R. Shannon; "Adeste Fideles," music and lyrics by John Francis Wade; "Ave Maria," music by Franz Schubert, lyrics traditional; "Three Blind Mice," traditional.

Cast: Bing Crosby [(*Father Charles Francis Patrick O'Malley*)], Barry Fitzgerald [(*Father Fitzgibbon*)], Frank McHugh [(*Father Timothy O'Dowd*)], James Brown [(*Ted Haines, Jr.*)], Gene Lockhart [(*Ted Haines, Sr.*)], Jean Heather [(*Carol James*)], Porter Hall [(*Mr. Belknap*)], Fortunio Bonanova [(*Tomaso Bozanni*)], Eily Malyon [(*Mrs. Carmody*)], and Robert Mitchell Boychoir, Risë Stevens [(*Genevieve Linden*)], [George Nokes (*Pee-Wee Belknap*)], [Tom P. Dillon (*Officer Patrick McCarthy*)], [Stanley Clements (*Tony Scaponi*)], [Carl "Alfalfa" Switzer (*Herman Langerhanke*)], [Bill Henry (*Intern*)], [Hugh Maguire (*Pitch pipe*)], [Robert Tafur (*Don Jose*)], [Martin Garralaga (*Zuniga*)], [Sybyl Lewis (*Maid at Metropolitan Opera House*)], [George McKay (*Mr. Van Heusen*)], [William Frawley (*Max David*)], [Jack Norton (*Mr. Lilley*)], [Anita Bolster (*Mrs. Hattie Quimp*)], [Jimmie Dundee (*Fireman*)], [Julie Gibson (*Taxi driver*)], [Adeline deWalt Reynolds (*Mrs. Holly Fitzgibbon*)], [Constance Purdy], [Connie Leon], [Don Gallagher], [Cecil Weston], [Joe Mangum].

Religious, Comedy-drama, with songs. [*Print viewed*]. In New York City, mortgage broker Ted Haines, Sr. reluctantly tells elderly Irish priest Father Fitzgibbon that if the overdue payment on St. Dominic's church is not soon received, he will call in the mortgage. Haines's son Ted, Jr. urges leniency, but his father is adamant. Father Charles Francis Patrick O'Malley arrives in St. Dominic's neighborhood and makes a bad impression on a few neighbors because of his easy-going and unconventional manner. By the time Father O'Malley introduces himself to Father Fitzgibbon as his new curate, he has donned a sweatshirt and casual pants, and immediately puts the very traditional Fitzgibbon on his guard. The next day, O'Malley is visited by his childhood friend, Father Timothy O'Dowd, a jocular priest from the neighboring parish. Only O'Dowd is aware that O'Malley has been sent to take over the pastorship of St. Dominic's, which, in addition to being in financial trouble, is in a troubled neighborhood. When Ted, Jr. tries to evict Hattie Quimp, who initially found O'Malley to be a nuisance, O'Malley intercedes and promises that the church will guarantee her rent. As he is walking back to St. Dominic's, O'Malley sees teenagers Tony Scaponi and Herman Langerhanke stealing turkeys from a truck. The boys escape into the church garden where they encounter Fitzgibbon, to whom they give one of their stolen turkeys as a gift. That night over their turkey dinner, O'Malley suggests that the boys are delinquents, and Fitzgibbon defends the boys until he learns of their theft. Instead of punishing the boys, however, O'Malley takes them to a baseball game. One day, Officer Patrick McCarthy brings eighteen-year-old runaway Carol James to see O'Malley. O'Malley, who had had his own band and composed music before entering the priesthood, coaches Carol on

her singing, but when she rejects his offer of a housekeeping job at the church, he urges her to return home. Knowing she will not take his advice, O'Malley loans Carol ten dollars. After earning the trust of the boys's gang, O'Malley convinces them to train as a choir. When sounds of the boys rehearsing "Three Blind Mice" rise into the church from the cellar, Fitzgibbon loses his patience with O'Malley's unconventional methods and goes to see the bishop to ask for O'Malley's transfer. Fitzgibbon returns deflated, as he has learned that the bishop sent O'Malley there to take over for him. Distraught by his apparent retirement, Fitzgibbon runs away, but O'Malley puts McCarthy on the alert, and he returns late that evening with a storm-bedraggled Fitzgibbon, who is then coddled by O'Malley and the housekeeper, Mrs. Carmody. The two priests share a sip of whiskey, and Fitzgibbon confides his longing to see his ninety-year-old mother, who still lives in Ireland, after which O'Malley soothes him with an Irish lullaby. Not long after, O'Malley encounters another childhood friend, Metropolitan Opera star Genevieve Linden, who is surprised that her old flame "Chuck" has become a priest. When Mrs. Quimp informs Fitzgibbon that Carol has taken an apartment across from hers and is receiving visits from Ted, Jr., O'Malley is sent to "handle" the situation. O'Malley learns that Ted, Jr. and Carol met on the street and fell in love immediately, and that Ted, Jr. has let her live in a vacant apartment without his father's knowledge. Some time later, Jenny and O'Dowd visit St. Dominic's and make an appreciative audience when O'Malley rehearses the boys choir. O'Dowd reports that he has shopped around for publishers for O'Malley's original song, "Going My Way," but that publishers rejected the "schmaltzy" song. When Ted, Sr. comes to the apartment to discover why his son quit his job and has disappeared for two weeks, he discovers that Ted and Carol have married. The newlyweds are blissfully happy despite Ted, Sr.'s ire, but his anger soon dissipates when Ted, Jr. dons an Army Air Force uniform and, after bidding Carol a loving farewell, reports for service. O'Dowd, meanwhile, lures his friend, Max David, a music publisher, and Max's partners, to the Metropolitan Opera House, where Jenny has arranged for the orchestra and St. Dominic's boys choir to back her as she sings a classical arrangement of "Going My Way." The publishers gently reject the song as too highbrow, but are delighted by O'Malley's more upbeat song, "Swinging on a Star." Instead of paying O'Malley directly for the song, Max and his partners surreptitiously deposit a huge payment in the collection box during Fitzgibbon's Sunday sermon at O'Malley's suggestion. Fitzgibbon is elated by the generous donations of his parishioners, which is enough to make the mortgage payments, and he even accompanies O'Malley and O'Dowd when they play golf. Fitzgibbon's happiness comes to an abrupt end, however, when the church burns down. The elderly priest loses all hope and falls ill after he collects only thirty-five dollars from a neighborhood collection. O'Malley then tells Fitzgibbon that Ted, Jr. has had a minor jeep accident and will be returning home, and really lifts the pastor's spirits when he tells him that Jenny, who has taken the boys choir with her on a concert tour, has sent a $3,500 check from the proceeds. Construction soon begins on the new church, and O'Malley informs Fitzgibbon that he has been transferred to another church for the same type of assignment. Fitzgibbon, now fond of O'Malley, is sad to see him go and is chagrined when O'Dowd becomes his new curate. As Fitzgibbon praises O'Malley to his parishioners and informs them of his departure, Jenny brings in Fitzgibbon's elderly mother by arrangement with O'Malley. Fitzgibbon tearfully embraces his mother for the first time in forty-five years, and O'Malley walks away into the night. *Choirs (Music). Churches. Juvenile delinquents. Opera singers. Priests. Baseball. Bishops. Fathers and sons. Fires. Golf. Housekeepers. Irish. Marriage–Secret. Mothers and sons. New York City. Police. Publishers and publishing. Runaways. Sermons. Songwriters. Turkeys.*

Note: The working title of this film was *The Padre.* Risë Stevens' opening credit bills her as the "Famous Contralto of Metropolitan Opera Association." As Paramount officials were unable to get European copyright clearance for Georges Bizet's opera *Carmen,* they shot an additional sequence from Bedrich Smetana's *The Bartered Bride,* which replaced the *Carmen* sequence in foreign release. *HR* news items noted the following information about the production: Susan Hayward and Betty Rhodes were considered for roles in this film; Armando Agnini, the stage and technical director of the San Francisco Opera, supervised the staging, and used sets from the S.F. Opera's production of *Carmen* for this film. The opera sequences were shot at the Shrine Auditorium, and the golf sequence was shot on location at the Lakeside Golf Club in Los Angeles, CA. *HR* news items also reported that footage of the St. Louis Planter's Hotel and Duffy's restaurant was retained for possible use in the film, and that

director McCarey shot eighty-four-year-old Apache Joe Mangum as "Geronimo" for a scene at the St. Louis World Fair. Although no scenes of St. Louis landmarks appear in the film, it is possible that McCarey planned a St. Louis sequence, as it was "Father O'Malley's" hometown. News items also noted that composers Johnny Burke and Jimmy Van Heusen were working on a two-act operetta, and that a scene was planned between "street gamin and priest" in a New York hospital to introduce penicillin, the uses of which had only recently been discovered. Neither the operetta nor the hospital scene appear in the film.

Paramount arranged for the film's 27 Apr 1944 premiere to be shown to American troops at battlefronts across Europe. A *HR* article noted that "arrangement for the simultaneous world-wide showing to the troops in combat areas was made by the Army Pictorial Service," and that the film was shown "from Alaska to Italy, and from England to the jungles of Burma...." All in all, sixty-five prints were distributed for "The Fighting Front" premiere. A 16 Aug 1944 Hollywood premiere donated $10,500 in proceeds to the House of Nazareth orphanage. According to various contemporary news items, by Sep 1944, *Going My Way* had earned over $7,000,000 in gross revenue, with a total of $10,000,000 in foreign, thereby becoming Paramount's largest grossing film to date. New York Film Critics and the FDYB voted this the best film of the year. The film was nominated for Academy Awards in the categories of Cinematography, Lionel Lindon, and Film Editing, LeRoy Stone. *Going My Way* won Academy Awards in the following categories: Best Picture; Actor, Bing Crosby; Supporting Actor, Barry Fitzgerald; Direction, Leo McCarey; Writing (original story), Leo McCarey; Writing (screenplay), Frank Butler, Frank Cavett; Music (song), James Van Heusen and Johnny Burke for "Swinging on a Star." In 1945, RKO released *The Bells of St. Mary's,* in which Bing Crosby reprised his role as "Father O'Malley" (see above).

Box 4 Mar 1944. *DV* 28 Feb 1944, p. 3. *FD* 28 Feb 1944, p. 12 *HR* 25 May 1943, p. 2. *HR* 15 Jun 1943, p. 6. *HR* 8 Jul 1943, p. 9. *HR* 30 Jul 1943, p. 14. *HR* 10 Aug 1943, p. 18. *HR* 13 Aug 1943, p. 13. *HR* 30 Aug 1943, p. 2. *HR* 31 Aug 1943, p. 10. *HR* 1 Sep 1943, p. 3. *HR* 21 Sep 1943, p. 7. *HR* 30 Sep 1943, p. 11. *HR* 11 Oct 1943, p. 11. *HR* 15 Oct 1943, p. 3. *HR* 22 Oct 1943, p. 5. *HR* 28 Oct 1943, p. 8. *HR* 28 Feb 1944, p. 3. *HR* 15 Mar 1944, p. 1. *HR* 28 Mar 1944, p. 1. *HR* 18 Apr 1944, p. 1, 21. *HR* 9 May 1944, p. 12. *HR* 8 Jun 1944, p. 1. *HR* 17 Aug 1944, p. 4. *HR* 20 Feb 1945, p. 8. *HR* 3 Jul 1950. *LAT* 17 Aug 1944. *LAT* 16 Jan 1945. *MPH* 2 Sep 1944, p. 29. *MPH* 6 Jan 1945. *MPHPD* 19 Feb 1944, p. 1763. *MPHPD* 26 Feb 1944, p. 1773. *NYT* 5 Sep 1943. *NYT* 3 May 1944, p. 25. *NYT* 7 May 1944, p. 3 (sec 2.) *Var* 8 Mar 1944, p. 14.

GOING TO GLORY, COME TO JESUS (African Americans)

Royal Gospel Productions. *Dist* Toddy Pictures Co.; State Rights. **1947.** Sd; b&w. 8 reels, 7,325 ft. 79 min.

Song(s): "To Take My Troubles To," "I Don't Want a Body Without a Soul," "Keep Your Trust in the Lord," "Come to Jesus," "Where He Leads Me I Will Follow," "Take Me to the Water," "I Want to Go to Heaven," "Down by the Riverside," and "Lost Soul," spirituals; "Old Hundred(th) Doxology, or Praise God, from Whom All Blessings Flow," words from Psalm 134 of the Geneva Psalter, music by Louis Bourgeouis; "I Was Glad," "You'd Better Watch Out" and "Regardless," composers undetermined.

Source: Based on the play *Going to Glory, Come to Jesus* by Wesley Wilson and Leola Grant (production undetermined).

Cast: Irene Harper (*Lillie-Mae Scott*), Lloyd Howlett, Stella Van Derzee, Charles A. Freeman, John Watts, The Royal Gospel Choir, Sox Wilson, Irene Williams, Miss Coot.

African American, Religious, Drama, with songs. [*Not viewed*]. Outside a church, a young woman named Ethel is chatting with the congregation's reverend, Mr. Scott, when her old friend Bessie appears. Bessie is a wild girl who encourages Ethel to drink Manhattan cocktails and likes to talk about her boyfriend's zoot suit and wide-brimmed hat. Ethel then introduces Lillie-Mae Scott, the reverend's daughter, to Bessie. Although Bessie hopes to "hep" the straight-laced girl by criticizing her plain clothing and ugly face, Ethel assures Bessie that Lillie-Mae is a good, Christian child. A gospel singing group begins to perform in the church, and Ethel and Lillie-Mae are eager to listen. Bessie insists, however, that they go to the Half-Moon Jitterbug Club instead. Later, as Lillie-Mae gets ready for church, she thinks about Bessie's insults and feels a desire for new clothes and a life outside of the "amen-corner." She confesses her feelings to her mother, who tells her that she is a sick and sinful girl and promises to tell the reverend to pray for her. When her mother goes to church, Lillie-Mae thinks aloud that she would happily sell her soul to be beautiful. The Devil arrives and tries to tempt Lillie-Mae, but God's voice keeps her on the right path. When the reverend and his wife return home, they find their daughter in a delirium. Mrs. Scott believes Lillie-Mae to be sick and in need of a doctor, but the reverend tells her that the girl is a sinner and needs to pray. Mrs. Sharpe, a neighbor, fetches a doctor, despite Scott's insistence on prayer. After the doctor witnesses Lillie-Mae's mad ravings, he gives the girl a sedative and shows the Scotts out of the room. Just then, the Devil reappears and Lillie-Mae pledges her soul to him in exchange for beauty. Meanwhile, Joe, Bessie's boyfriend, tries to seduce Ethel.

When Bessie confronts him, he declares that she has been ruined now that she is "hep" and he now wants to find a marriageable girl. Although Azaline, Lillie-Mae's maid, assures her that she is the most beautiful person in the world, Lillie-Mae replies that she will never get married as it takes away one's pleasure. Just then, the Prince O'Hades arrives to take Lillie-Mae out on a date. Lillie-Mae is surprised to find that, when she tries to look at herself and the Prince in the mirror, he has no reflection. At the Cottage Inn Club, Lillie-Mae is introduced as the most beautiful girl in the world. Bessie shows up as a tramp selling flowers and Lillie-Mae calls her ugly and angrily sends her away. Bessie warns her that the Devil will get her just like he got Bessie. The Prince O'Hades begins to laugh diabolically and then Lillie-Mae sees that she has turned ugly again. As she hears the song "Where He Leads Me I Will Follow," she begs the Lord for mercy. Later, Lillie Mae is rebaptized in a river and begs God to take her back into the fold. Lillie-Mae then wakes up from a dream and tells her father that she dreamed of the Devil but now she wants to shout. The reverend joyously tells her to go ahead and shout, as she now has "got religion." *African Americans. The Devil. Ostracism. Religiosity. Transformation. Churches. Fathers and daughters. Materialism. Nightclubs. Orgies. Physicians. Preachers. Singers.*

Note: The above credits and plot synopsis were taken from a dialogue script and other material deposited at the NYSA in May 1947. According to publicity and advertising material contained at the NYSA, the film was made in 1946 over a six-month period and featured an "all colored cast of 30 and choir of 40." In addition to the above-listed songs, one other song was performed in the picture, but its title and composer have not been determined. Correspondence contained at the NYSA indicates that Royal Gospel Productions, which was located in New York City, had set for release two other all-black religious features entitled *Go Preach* and *Children of Jesus*. However, no further information has been found concerning Royal Gospel Productions or other films released by them. Regional censorship reports contained in the MPAA/ PCA Collection at the AMPAS Library indicate that censors in Ohio and Pennsylvania ordered some deletions to the film, including the cutting of the song "Regardless," which was sung by Irene Williams, and a musical number performed by "Miss Coot and Sox [Wilson]."

Exb 25 Jun 1947, p. 2187.

GOLD AND THE WOMAN (Native Americans)

Fox Film Corp. *Dist* Fox Film Corp. 13 Mar **1916** [©William Fox; 12 Mar 1916; LP7811]. Si; b&w. 6 reels.

Dir James Vincent. *Scen* Mary Murillo.

Cast: Theda Bara (*Juliet De Cordova*), Alma Hanlon (*Hester Gray*), H. Cooper Cliffe (*Colonel Ernest Dent*), Harry Hilliard (*Lee Duskara*), Carleton Macy (*Dugald Chandos*), Chief Black Eagle (*Chief Duskara*), Julia Hurley (*Duskara's squaw*), Carter B. Harkness (*Leelo Duskara*), Caroline Harris, Ted Griffin, Louis Stern, James Sheehan, Frank Whitson, Pauline Barry.

Drama. Generations after Dugald Chandos, an early settler, stole a thousand acres from Chief Duskara, Hester Gray, Dugald's descendant, is about to inherit the land. She wants to marry Lee Duskara, the chief's great-great-grandson, and so restore at least half the land to its rightful owner. Hester's guardian, Colonel Ernest Dent, has come under the influence of Juliet De Cordova, a Mexican adventuress, however, and she convinces Ernest to marry Hester himself, then shift the deed to the land from his wife to Juliet. Ernest forces Hester into the marriage but continues his affair with Juliet and keeps on taking orders from her. Finally, Hester discovers Ernest's double-cross and tries to commit suicide, but Lee saves her. Dent soon dies of dissipation, and Hester marries Lee, who in court, is awarded the rights to the land. *Adventuresses. Duplicity. Indians of North America. Land rights. Marriage–Forced. Attempted suicide. Dissipation. Hereditary tendencies. Infidelity. Inheritance. Marriage–Mixed. Mexicans. Officers (Military). Robbery. Settlers. Wards and guardians.*

MPN 4 Mar 1916, p. 1285. *MPN* 25 Mar 1916, p. 1775. *MPW* 18 Mar 1916, p. 1902. *MPW* 1 Apr 1916, p. 99, 105. *NYT* 13 Mar 1916, p. 5. *Var* 17 Mar 1916, p. 31. *Wid's* 23 Mar 1916, p. 459.

THE GOLD BRAIDED DRESS *see* GIN FEN NEE SHAAN

THE GOLD HUNTERS (Native Americans)

Guaranteed Pictures. *Dist* Davis Distributing Division. **1925** [©Davis Distributing Division; 28 Dec 1925; LP22186]. Si; b&w. 7 reels, 6,500 ft.

Dir Paul Hurst.

Source: Based on the novel *The Gold Hunters; a Story of Life & Adventure in the Hudson Bay Wilds* by James Oliver Curwood (Indianapolis, 1909).

Cast: David Butler (*Roderick Drew*), Hedda Nova (*Minnetake*), Mary Carr (*Mary McAllister*), Bull Montana (*"Hairy" Grimes*), Jimmy Aubrey (*Shorty*), Al Hallett (*Mukoki*), Noble Johnson (*Wabigoon*), Frank Elliott (*Hugh Beresford*), John T. Prince (*John Ball*), William Humphrey (*John McAllister*), Kathryn McGuire (*Miss Drew*).

Western. Roderick Drew, a wolf-hunter, discovers a birchbark map loosely gripped in the white fingers of a skeleton. Shortly thereafter, Roderick is almost killed by a golden bullet; he is then endangered by an unexpected avalanche. Roderick is preparing to see where the map leads when it is stolen by Hairy Grimes, a crook who has discovered the map's existence from Roderick's sweetheart, Minnetake. Minnetake tries to warn Roderick and is abducted by Grimes. Roderick learns of Minnetake's danger and goes after Grimes, defeating him and his gang with the help of an unknown ally. This ally turns out to be Minnetake's grandfather, and Roderick wins both the girl and her grateful grandfather's gold. *Abduction. Avalanches. Grandfathers. Hunters. Indians of North America. Secret documents. Treasure.*

Note: This picture was filmed on location in Sequoia National Park, according to contemporary sources.

THE GOLDBERGS *see* MOLLY

THE GOLDEN DOOR *see* HOLD BACK THE DAWN

THE GOLDEN EYE (Chinese Americans)

Monogram Pictures Corp. *Dist* Monogram Pictures Corp. 29 Aug **1948**; Prod: mid-Apr—late Apr 1948 [©Monogram Pictures Corp.; 22 Aug 1948; LP1857]. Sd (Western Electric Recording); b&w. 6,224 ft. 69 min. PCA cert no. 13185.

Series: Charlie Chan.

Prod James S. Burkett. *Dir* William Beaudine. *Asst dir* Wesley Barry. *Orig scr* W. Scott Darling. *Photog* William Sickner. [*Cam op* John Martin]. [*Stills* Al St. Hilaire]. *Art dir* Dave Milton. *Supv film ed* Otho Lovering. *Ed* Ace Herman. [*Set dec* Raymond Boltz, Jr.]. *Mus dir* Edward J. Kay. *Rec* Franklin Hansen. [*Sd* John Kean]. *Makeup* Webb Overlander]. [*Hair stylist* Lela Chambers]. *Prod supv* Allen K. Wood. [*Scr supv* Jules Levy]. [*Grip* Grant Tucker].

Source: Based on characters created by Earl Derr Biggers.

Cast: Roland Winters [(*Charlie Chan*)], Wanda McKay [(*Evelyn Manning*)], Mantan Moreland [(*Birmingham*)], Victor Sen Young [(*Tommy Chan*)], Bruce Kellogg [(*Talbot Bartlett*)], Tim Ryan [(*Lt. Mike Ruark*)], Evelyn Brent [(*Sister Teresa*)], Ralph Dunn [(*Driscoll*)], Lois Austin [(*Mrs. Margaret Driscoll*)], Forrest Taylor [(*Manning*)], Lee "Lasses" White [(*Pete*)], [Lee Tung Foo (*Wong Fai*)], [Michael Gaddis (*Pursuer*)], [Sam Flint (*Dr. Groves*)], [Geraldine Cobb (*Girl in riding clothes*)], [Mary Ann Hawkins, Aileen Babs Cox (*Bathing girls*)], [Edmund Cobb, John Merton (*Miners*)], [Jack Gargan (*Voice from darkness*)].

Detective. [*Print viewed*]. In San Francisco's Chinatown, Arizona mine owner Manning seeks help from famed private detective Charlie Chan, as someone is trying to kill him. Manning suggests that Chan pose as a tourist and check into the Lazy-Y Dude Ranch near his "Golden Eye" mine. Chan's son Tommy and chauffeur Birmingham accompany Chan to the ranch in Arizona, and when they arrive, Chan encounters San Francisco police lieutenant Mike Ruark, who is working undercover for the government. After Chan finds that their cases may be related, Mike tells Chan that Manning has just fallen down a mine shaft and has a possible skull fracture. Mike also informs Chan that, after many years of low ouput, the Manning mine has recently become one of the richest in the country. Claiming to be a dealer in oriental curios, Chan goes to the Manning home, where he meets Manning's daughter Evelyn, mine superintendent Driscoll and his wife, and local gold assayer Talbot Bartlett. Chan also sees Manning, but he is unconscious and his head is completely swathed in bandages. Back at the ranch, Chan finds Bartlett, who is the son of an old friend and has recognized him, waiting for him. Bartlett tells Chan that he is assaying some of the gold coming from the mine. Later, Evelyn, who is unaware of the mine's recent tremendous productivity, tells Bartlett that the nursing sister, whom Driscoll has hired from the nearby mission, is strange and uncommunicative. When Pete, an independent miner, who has gained access to the mine, brings a sample of ore for assaying, Bartlett tells him it is worthless. Chan then arranges for Pete to take him into the mine through a trapdoor in his shack, but when he, Tommy and

Birmingham show up, Pete is not there. However, they enter the mine and find Pete's body. After Mike tells Chan that he has learned that Driscoll has a criminal record, Chan discovers that Manning's nurse is a fake. Mike goes down the mine and is mugged, but escapes. Meanwhile, Chan finds out that Driscoll has been smuggling gold in from Mexico, where the price is much lower, and passing it off at a much higher value. Driscoll wants Manning and everyone else out of the way so that his operation can continue. When Chan, Tommy and Birmingham return to the mine, Chan finds another body with a bandaged head. They all return to the Manning house and Chan begins to remove the bandages from the patient's head. Sister Teresa rushes in, gun drawn, just as Chan reveals the patient to be Mrs. Driscoll. After Evelyn struggles with and subdues Teresa, Chan has to break the news to her that her father is dead. Driscoll enters and draws his gun, but Tommy outsmarts him and tells Chan that he has received a phone call from the Mexican police, who announce say that they have stopped the next shipment of gold at the border. Driscoll tries to escape but is shot by Bartlett, whom Chan captures and reveals to have been the brains behind the entire operation. *Arizona. Chinese Americans. Dude ranches. Gold. Murder. Private detectives.* African Americans. Assayers. Chauffeurs. Curio dealers. Dude ranches. Fathers and daughters. Fathers and sons. Gold mines. Gunfights. Mexican-American border region. Mine owners. Miners. Murder. Nurses. Physicians. Police. San Francisco (CA)–Chinatown. Smuggling. Superintendents.

Note: The working title of this film was *The Mystery of the Golden Eye.* The opening title card reads: "Charlie Chan in *The Golden Eye.*" The CBCS lists Herman Cantor and Sam McDaniel in the cast, but they were not seen in the print viewed. Copyright records list George L. Spaulding as "Dr. Groves," but the role was played by Sam Flint. Richard Loo, Barbara Jean Wong and Tom Tyler are also listed in the cast, but they did not appear in the print viewed. For additional information on the "Charlie Chan" series, please consult the Series Index and see the above entry for *Charlie Chan Carries On.*

DV 21 Oct 1948, p. 3. *HR* 21 Oct 1948, p. 3. *MPD* 12 Nov 1948. *MPHPD* 11 Sep 1948, p. 4311. *MPHPD* 25 Sep 1948, p. 4325. *Var* 22 Sep 1948, p. 8.

GOLDEN GATE GIRL (Chinese language, Chinese Americans)

Golden Gate Film Co. *Dist* Golden Gate Film Co. **1941**; San Francisco opening: week of 27 May 1941. Sd; b&w. 12 reels, 10,534 ft. 110 or 117 min. Chinese language.

Dir Esther Eng. *Scr and dial* Moon Quan. *Photog* J. Sunn. *Ed* Moon Quan.

Cast: Tso Yee Man (*Chain-Ying Ho/Lulu, also known as Loy Lo*), Wong Hok Sing (*Fay-Tien Wong, also known as Sing Kuo*), Moon Quan (*Jien-Sien Ho*), Liu Nom (*Duck Sook*), Luk Won Fee (*Mao Lee*), Far Sui Yung (*Sia-Lien Ho*), Chu Yut Hun (*Lulu as a child*), Chan Ligh Shun (*Midwife*), Lee Po (*Doctor*).

Drama, with songs. [*Not viewed*]. In San Francisco, widower Jien-Sien Ho, who is known to the Chinese community as Gin Man, worries that his sixteen-year-old daughter Chain-Ying spends too much time at the Chinese Opera. Nevertheless, Duck Sook, a salesman in Jien-Sien's shop, takes Chain-Ying to see Fay-Tien Wong, an actor from China, perform. After the show, Wong invites Chain-Ying to the Golden Gate Music Club for a party and the girl asks him for singing lessons. Chain-Ying and Wong begin to spend time together and Chain-Ying's friend, Sia-Lien Ho, tells Jien-Sien about his daughter's excursions with the actor and the fact that she has been missing school. Jien-Sien confronts Chain-Ying, who insists that in America, fathers have no rights over their daughters. When Chain-Ying says she loves Wong, Jien-Sien disowns her and then blames Duck Sook for his daughter's infidelity. Wong tells Chain-Ying that she must try to understand the old people's ways and then agrees to marry her, hoping that her father will now accept them. When Duck Sook tries to intervene on the couple's behalf, however, Jien-Sien says that he will never forgive them. The enraged father then goes to the theater owner and tells him to deport Wong, and the owner agrees not to renew the singer's contract, which is soon to expire. Several months later, Wong returns home one night and announces that he must return to China. Worried about his bride, who is now pregnant, he tells her that he will send for her when he has settled. Meanwhile, Duck Sook asks Jien-Sien to forgive his pregnant, lonely daughter, but he refuses. Mao Lee, Jien-Sien's cook, takes pity on Chain-Ying, gives her money and attends the birth of the baby girl. For his disloyalty, Jien-Sien fires Mao-Lee, who joins Duck Sook in taking over a Chinese laundry so that they can support Chain-Ying's baby after Chain-Ying's sudden death. Duck Sook and Mao Lee give the baby a Chinese name,

Loy Lo, and an American name, Lulu, and when the girl grows up, Duck Sook teaches her Chinese dances and instills in her a love of the theater. When a benefit concert and party is organized for Chinese war refugees, Lulu wishes to perform, and Duck Sook and Lulu both audition and receive parts. Lulu has a supporting role in an opera with a visiting star, Sing Kuo, but when Duck Sook must find the traditional dress that is required for her performance, he discovers that all the stores are sold out of it. Duck Sook steals a gown, and later encounters the woman from whom he stole it. She is understanding, however, and agrees to lend the garment to Lulu. During the show, it is revealed that Sing Kuo is really Wong, Lulu's father, and Duck Sook introduces the singer to his daughter and then to her grandfather, who has donated three-thousand dollars to the cause. Jien-Sien greets Lulu warmly and all shake hands and return to Jien-Sien's shop to celebrate their reunion. *Chinese Americans. Fathers and daughters. Immigrants. Opera. San Francisco (CA)–Chinatown.* Auditions. Benefit performances. Childbirth. Cooks. Employer-employee relations. Generation gap. Godparents. Grandfathers. Laundries. Reunions. Robbery. Romance. War refugees.

Note: The above plot summary and some credits were taken from an English language dialogue continuity deposited with the NYSA. The transliterated spelling of the actors' names varied from source to source; the above-spellings were taken from the *Var* review. Most of the transliterated spellings of the character names were taken from a modern translation of a Chinese-language summary which was included in playbills distributed to moviegoers in theater lobbies. The English-language continuity indicates that six songs were performed in the picture, although their titles are not listed. The *Var* review lists Moon Quan as co-director, in addition to writer and actor. The same review states that the film was the first production of the Golden Gate Film Co., and the first feature-length Chinese film made in San Francisco's Chinatown. An English-language version of the picture was "being readied" for release in May 1941, according to *Var*. The English-language continuity was submitted to New York censors in Aug 1941. Esther Eng was China's first woman film director. According to modern sources, she worked with Quan in Hong Kong, but the two fled to San Francisco when the Japanese were about to invade. Quan had worked in Hollywood prior to making *Golden Gate Girl*, and he is credited as a technical director on D. W. Griffith's *Broken Blossoms.*

Var 28 May 1941.

GOLDEN GLOVES *see* **WINNER TAKE ALL**

THE GOLDEN STALLION (Latino)

Republic Pictures Corp. *Dist* Republic Pictures Corp. 15 Nov **1949**; Prod: May 1949 [©Republic Pictures Corp.; 28 Oct 1949; LP2602]. Sd (RCA Sound System); col (Trucolor). 67 min. Passed by the National Board of Review. PCA cert no. 13900.

Assoc prod Edward J. White. *Dir* William Witney. [*Asst dir* Jack Lacey]. *Wrt* Sloan Nibley. *Dir of photog* Jack Marta. [*Cam op* Joe Novak]. [*Gaffer* Austin P. Herrick]. [*Stills* Mickey Marigold]. *Spec eff* Howard Lydecker, Theodore Lydecker and [Norman Skeet]. *Optical eff* Consolidated Film Industries. *Art dir* Frank Hotaling. *Film ed* Tony Martinelli. *Set dec* John McCarthy, Jr. and James Redd. *Cost supv* Adele Palmer. *Mus* Nathan Scott. *Orch* Stanley Wilson. *Sd* T. A. Carman. *Makeup supv* Bob Mark. [*Makeup* Steve Drumm]. [*Hair stylist* Louise Landmier]. [*Scr supv* Joan Eremin]. [*Grip* Garry Lambrecht].

Song(s): "The Golden Stallion" and "There's Always Time for a Song," music and lyrics by Sid Robin and Foy Willing; "Night on the Prairie," music and lyrics by Nathan Gluck and Anne Parentean, Spanish lyrics by Aaron Gonzales; "Down Mexico Way," music and lyrics by Eddie Cherkose, Sol Meyer and Jule Styne.

Cast: Roy Rogers [(*Roy Rogers*)], and Trigger, The Smartest Horse in the Movies, Dale Evans [(*Stormy Billings*)], Estelita Rodriguez [(*Pepita "Pepi" Valdez*)], Pat Brady [(*Sparrow Biffle*)], Douglas Evans [(*Jeff Middleton*)], Frank Fenton [(*Sheriff*)], Greg McClure [(*Ben*)], Dale Van Sickel [(*Ed Hart*)], Clarence Straight [(*Spud*)], Jack Sparks [(*Guard*)], Chester Conklin [(*Old man*)], Foy Willing, and The Riders of the Purple Sage, [Mauritz Hugo (*Holiday*)], [Buff Brady (*Rider*)].

Western, with songs. [*Print viewed*]. On the plains spanning the Mexican-American border region, a gang of smugglers tracks a herd of wild horses roaming freely across the border. They praise the lead horse, whom they call the "bell" mare, and then lasso another horse, which has been branded with a large "X." After they remove the horse's false horseshoe, they open it up and retrieve a small bag of diamonds inside. They then deliver the diamonds to their boss, Oro City Hotel proprietor Jeff Middleton. Meanwhile, rancher Roy Rogers and his men visit their friend, Stormy Billings, owner of the Circle B Ranch. Roy plans to lease the ranch, where he will train roping horses

for the local cattle companies, and reveals that he will draw his stock from the wild herd roaming the border. Later, when Roy and his men corner the herd in a canyon, Roy removes the saddle from his horse Trigger and sends him into the herd to calm the other horses. The gang attacks suddenly, however, and Trigger is swept away by the stampeding herd. Roy and his men return to the ranch and tell Stormy's friend, Pepita "Pepi" Valdez, that they are in no mood for the square dance that she has arranged for later. Before long, Trigger returns to the Circle B and coaxes the lead wild mare into the fenced yard. Overjoyed, Roy leads the mare into the stable, and the dance begins on a happy note. Soon, however, Middleton's henchman Art enters the stable and tries to grab the mare. The mare becomes frightened, knocks Art backward, killing him, and then gallops away. Roy discovers Art's corpse, and later, Middleton accuses Trigger of being the killer. When the authorities order that Trigger be destroyed, Roy "confesses" to killing Art in order to spare his companion. Roy is then ordered to pay a $5,000 fine and serve a number of years in jail, while the authorities auction off Trigger to the highest bidder: Middleton's henchman Ben. Some time later, the gang teaches Trigger to lead the wild herd back and forth across the border so that they can continue their diamond smuggling. Soon Stormy writes to tell Roy that after the "bell" mare gave birth to a colt, Trigger brought his offspring to live with them at the ranch. Since then, she says, the colt, which they named Trigger, Jr., has grown substantially. Three years later, when Roy is released on parole, the sheriff, who believes in Roy's innocence, agrees to help him stage his own escape and death. After the gang learns of Roy's "escape," they go to the ranch to wait for his arrival. From their hiding place, the gang sees Roy ride up, but before they can act, the sheriff also arrives and shoots at Roy with blanks. Satisfied that he is dead, the gang leaves, and later, captures the branded horse. Instead of the diamonds, however, the gang discovers sand inside. Then, to the gang's amazement, Roy appears, captures them and then lassos Trigger, taming him once again. *Diamonds. Horses. Outlaws. Ranchers. Smuggling. Animal culture. Animal trainers. Auctions. Canyons. Deception. Horseshoes. Hotelkeepers. Jails. Lassoes. Mexican Americans. Mexican-American border region. Parole. Sheriffs. Square dances. Stables. Stampedes.*

Note: According to a *Var* news item, dated 4 Sep 1946, the film's original story was written by James Macar, but he is not credited onscreen, and the extent of his contribution to the released film has not been determined. Modern sources include Karl Hackett in the cast.

Box 5 Nov 1949. *DV* 25 Oct 1949, p. 3. *FD* 26 Oct 1949, p. 8. *HR* 6 May 1949, p. 11. *HR* 20 May 1949, p. 3. *HR* 25 Oct 1949, p. 3. *MPHPD* 29 Oct 1949, p. 65. *Var* 4 Sep 1946. *Var* 26 Oct 1949, p. 18.

THE GOLDEN TIDE *see* **OH! SUSANNA**

THE GOLDEN TOUCH *see* **FOR THE LOVE OF MIKE**

THE GOLDEN WALL (French Americans)
World Film Corp. *Dist* World Film Corp. 15 Jul **1918** [©World Film Corp.; 11 Jul 1918; LU12641]. Si; b&w. 5 reels.
Pres William A. Brady. *Dir* Dell Henderson. *Adpt* Clara S. Beranger. *Cam* Louis Ostland.
Cast: Carlyle Blackwell (*Charles de la Fontaine, Marquis D'Aubeterre*), Evelyn Greeley (*Marian Lathrop*), John Hines (*Frank Lathrop*), Winifred Leighton (*Helen d'Aubeterre*), Madge Evans (*Madge Lathrop*), Jack Drumier (*Mr. Lathrop*), Kate Lester (*Countess d'Este*), George MacQuarrie (*Rudolph Miller*), Florence Coventry (*Mrs. Lathrop*), A. G. Corbell (*Monsieur Fremiere*), Louise de Rigny (*Mlle. Julie*).
Comedy-drama. After his father's death, Charles de la Fontaine, the Marquis d'Aubeterre, learns that the family is penniless and journeys to America to earn a living for himself and his sister Helen. The Countess d'Este secures him a position in the home of Lathrop, a millionaire, and the young nobleman instantly falls in love with Lathrop's pretty daughter Marian. Supposing that Charles is after her fortune, Marian avoids him and becomes engaged to the wealthy Rudolph Miller. Charles changes her opinion of him, however, when he and Marian are locked in an old tower, and, after swearing that he will only marry her when the two are equally wealthy, he makes a daring escape. Unknown to the Lathrops, Charles backs Marian's brother Frank in a financial venture, as a result of which the two young men become rich. Marian discovers that Rudolph is unfaithful, and with the "golden wall" of wealth that had separated them now obliterated, she and Charles wed. *French Americans. Immigrants.*

Millionaires. Nobility. Pledges. Wealth. Brothers and sisters. Escapes. Infidelity. Towers.

Note: Reviews and the copyright catalog note that the story was adapted "from an old French romance."

ETR 13 Jul 1918, p. 473. *MPN* 13 Jul 1918, p. 207, 253. *MPW* 13 Jul 1918, p. 249. *MPW* 27 Jul 1918, p. 591. *NYDM* 23 Mar 1918, p. 26. *NYDM* 20 Jul 1918, p. 89. *Var* 12 Jul 1918, p. 38.

THE GOLDEN WEST (Native Americans, Irish Americans, Jewish Americans)
Fox Film Corp. *Dist* Fox Film Corp. 30 Oct **1932**; Prod: 1 Aug—early Sep 1932 [©Fox Film Corp.; 24 Sep 1932; LP3331]. Sd (Western Electric System); b&w. 7 reels, 6,250 ft. 70 or 74 min. Passed by the National Board of Review. PCA cert no. 1276-R [21 Aug 1935].
Dir David Howard. [*Asst dir* Ad Schaumer]. *Scr* Gordon Rigby. [*Contr wrt* Sidney D. Mitchell]. *Photog* George Schneiderman. [*Cam op* Curtis Fetters]. [*Asst cam* James Gordon and Lou Kunkel]. *Art dir* Duncan Cramer. [*Film ed* Ralph Dietrich]. *Cost* David Cox. *Mus dir* Arthur Lange. *Sd rec* Bernard Freericks. [*Still photog* Bert Lynch]. [*Double for George O'Brien and stunts* Cliff Lyons].
Song(s): "Home Folks," music and lyrics by James F. Hanley.
Source: Based on the novel *The Last Trail* by Zane Grey (New York, 1909).
Cast: George O'Brien [(*David Lynch/Motano*)], Janet Chandler [(*Betty Summers/Betty Summers Brown*)], Marion Burns [(*Helen Sheppard*)], Arthur Pierson [(*Robert Summers*)], Onslow Stevens [(*Calvin Brown*)], Emmett Corrigan [(*Colonel Horace Summers*)], Bert Hanlon [(*Dennis Epstein*)], Edmund Breese [(*Sam Lynch*)], [Julia Swayne Gordon (*Mrs. Summers*)], [Dorothy Ward (*Mary Lynch*)], [Hattie McDaniel (*Mammy Lou*)], [Sam Adams (*Mike*)], [Eddie Dillon (*Pat*)], [George Rigas (*Black Wolf*)].
Western, Historical. [*Print viewed*]. In Kentucky, in 1847, David Lynch and Betty Summers, whose families are engaged in a feud, return from school after having met and fallen in love on the train. At a masked ball given in Betty's honor, she refuses to dance with Calvin Brown, a rising young engineer from Richmond, whom her family wants her to marry, and instead dances with someone whom no one knows. After her drunken brother Robert pulls off the mask of her partner, Colonel Horace Summers, Betty's father, is extremely upset to find Dave, a Lynch, in his house. Robert slaps Dave and challenges him to a duel when he sobers up. Insulted, Robert shoots at Dave and wounds him in the arm. Dave tries to take the gun away, but as they struggle, the gun goes off and kills Robert. Dave escapes on horseback and then doubles back and climbs up to Betty's window to say goodbye. He tells her that he may go West and agrees to send for her. The next morning, Dennis Epstein, a Jewish traveling merchant from Ireland, sees Dave about to fall off his horse. He hides him from Calvin and the colonel and tends to his wounds. They travel West together and join a wagon train to sell Dennis' wares. During a buffalo hunt, when the animals stampede, Dave rescues Helen Sheppard, an orphan traveling in the train. Colonel Summers and his party catch up with Dave, and the colonel challenges Dave to a duel. Dave does not shoot, and he is hit. After the colonel and the others ride off, Helen tends to Dave, and when they reach Fort Henry, Wyoming, the last outpost East of the Rockies, she remains to care for him. They marry and have a son named Davy. On Davy's birthday, Dennis arrives with a present, a music box from Switzerland, and Dave is affected as he associates its tune with Betty. Dennis relates that Betty, who married Calvin when she thought Dave had died, now has a cute daughter. During an Indian raid, Helen is killed, while Dave and the baby are captured. Twenty years later, the builders of the Union Pacific Railroad are harassed by Indians led by a mysterious white chief, Motano. The Indians conduct their attacks because they fear the railroad will bring more white men who will drive them out. Betty Brown, the daughter of Betty and Calvin, is in Wyoming with her father, now the chief engineer of the railroad. When Indians capture the stage Betty and Dennis are on, Motano rides up and takes her onto his horse. Dennis recognizes him as Dave Lynch's son. The Indians offer to return Betty if the work on the railroad will stop, but Calvin refuses. After a marriage ceremony, Motano takes Betty to his tepee, and in the morning, she tries to stab him, but he stops her. When Motano does not attack the railroad workers, his rival, Black Wolf, plans an attack and sends for all the mountain tribes to wage a war. Meanwhile, Motano gives Betty the music box, saying that it is the only thing he has always loved. She recognizes the tune as one her

mother used to sing. When she asks to be taken to her father, Motano agrees. Black Wolf and the others chase them to the railroad, where the battle begins. Motano joins the whites as the Indians encircle the train. When Black Wolf is about to get Betty, Motano fights him. Black Wolf is then shot with an arrow, and the Indians are driven off. Calvin accepts his daughter's newfound love for Motano, and the couple embraces. *Cultural conflict. Feuds. Indians of North America. Railroads. Unrequited love. The West. Abduction. Bison, American. Drunkenness. Engineers–Civil. Family relationships. Irish Americans. Jews. Kentucky. Marriage. Masked balls. Merchants. Music boxes. Nursing back to health. Raids. Recognition. Romance. Stagecoaches. Stampedes. Wagon trains. Wyoming.*

Note: The opening title card of this film reads, "Zane Grey's *The Golden West.*" According to information in the Twentieth Century-Fox Records of the Legal Department, author Zane Grey signed a contract with Fox to allow them to release a film based on the novel *The Last Trail*, which would not refer to the novel's title, but instead state that the film was "from an original story by Zane Grey." *MPH* speculates that "there are shots which appear to be from other big Fox pictures"; *Har* notes, "The scenes showing the settlers fighting off the Indians from a railroad train have been mixed with some scenes from an old picture." According to a *FD* news item, at the completion of shooting, George O'Brien presented cowboy hats to the members of the film unit. Fox earlier produced two films based on the same source, both of which were entitled *The Last Trail*: in 1921, directed by Emmett J. Flynn and starring Maurice B. Flynn; and in 1927, directed by Lewis Seiler and starring Tom Mix (see *AFI Catalog of Feature Films, 1921-30*; F2.2985 and F2.2986). In 1933, Fox produced another film based on the same source entitled *The Last Trail* (see *AFI Catalog of Feature Films, 1931-40*; F3.2395), also starring George O'Brien and directed by James Tinling.

FD 29 Oct 1932, p. 4. *FD* 3 Dec 1932, p. 4. *Har* 10 Dec 1932, p. 198. *HF* 3 Sep 1932, p. 12. *HR* 24 Sep 1932, p. 2. *IP* Nov 1932, p. 34. *MPH* 15 Oct 1932, p. 64.

GONE HARLEM (African Americans)

Dist Sack Amusement Enterprises, Inc. 15 Aug **1938**. Sd; b&w. Length undetermined.

African American, **Drama**. [*Not viewed*]. [No information on the plot of this film has been found.]. *African Americans.*

Note: A *MPH* release chart listed this film as a 1938 feature release. Although the exact length of *Gone Harlem* has not been determined, the picture is presumed to be a feature. According to modern sources, the cast included Jimmy Baskette, Ethel Moses, Florence Hill, Chuck Thompson and The Plantation Club Chorus. Modern sources list the release year as 1939 and the production company as the Creative Cinema Co.

GONE WITH THE WIND (African Americans)

Selznick International Pictures, Inc.; In Association with Metro-Goldwyn-Mayer Corp. *Dist* Loew's Inc. **1939**; World premiere at Loew's Grand Theater in Atlanta, GA, 15 Dec 1939; New York premiere: 19 Dec 1939; Los Angeles premiere: 28 Dec 1939; Prod: 10 Dec 1938; 26 Jan–15 Feb 1939; 2 Mar–1 Jul 1939; additional shooting, Jul–11 Nov 1939 [©Selznick International Pictures, Inc.; 31 Dec 1939; LP9390]. Sd; col (Technicolor). 20,300 ft. 220 min. PCA cert no. 5729.

Prod David O. Selznick. *Dir* Victor Fleming, [*Sam Wood and George Cukor*]. [*2d unit dir* William Cameron Menzies and Reeves Eason]. *Asst dir* Eric G. Stacey, Ridgeway Callow and Arthur Fellows]. [*Dir of Chico unit* Chester Franklin]. [*Dir of Southern backgrounds* James Fitzpatrick]. [*2d unit asst dir* Harve Foster, Ralph Slosser and John Sherwood]. *Scr* Sidney Howard. *Scen asst* Barbara Keon. [*Eastern story editor* Katharine Brown]. [*Script clerk* Lydia Schiller and Connie Earl]. [*Contr wrt* Ben Hecht, Oliver H. P. Garrett and Jo Swerling]. *Photog* Ernest Haller and Lee Garmes]. [*Cam op* Arthur Arling and Vincent Farrar]. *Technicolor assoc* Ray Rennahan and Wilfred M. Cline. [*Technicolor tests* Karl Struss]. *Spec photog eff* Jack Cosgrove. [*Mont dir* Peter Ballbusch]. [*Fire eff* Lee Zavitz]. *Technicolor Co. supv* Natalie Kalmus. *Prod des* William Cameron Menzies. *Art dir* Lyle Wheeler. *Supv film ed* Hal C. Kern. *Assoc film ed* James E. Newcom. [*Asst film ed* Richard Van Enger and Ernest Leadly]. *Int dec* Edward G. Boyle. *Int* Joseph B. Platt. [*Set dec* Howard B. Bristol]. [*Scenic dept. superintendent* Henry J. Stahl]. [*Prop mgr* Harold Coles]. [*Prop mgr on the set* Arden Cripe]. [*Greens* Roy McLaughlin]. [*Drapes* James Forney]. [*Spec properties made by* Ross B. Jackman]. [*Tara landscaped by* Florence Yoch]. [*Mechanical engineer* R. D. Musgrave]. [*Construction superintendent* Harold Fenton]. [*In charge of wardrobe* Edward P. Lambert]. [*Assoc* Marian P. Dabney]. *Cost* Elmer Ellsworth]. *Cost des* Walter Plunkett. [*Scarlett's hats by* John Frederics]. *Mus score* Max Steiner. *Asst mus dir* Lou Forbes. [*Dance dir* Frank Floyd and Eddie Frinz]. *Rec* Frank Maher. [*Hair styling* Mont Westmore]. [*Scarlett's hair styles* Sydney Guilaroff]. [*Wigs* Max

Factor]. [*Makeup* Mont Westmore]. [*Makeup and hair styling assoc* Hazel Rogers and Ben Nye]. *Tech adv* Susan Myrick and Will Price. *Prod mgr* Raymond A. Klune. [*Unit mgr* William J. Scully]. [*Chief elec* James Potevin]. [*Chief grip* Fred Williams]. [*Electrical superintendent* Wally Oettel]. *Historian* Wilbur G. Kurtz. [*Casting mgr* Charles Richards and Fred Schuessler]. [*Loc mgr* Mason Litson]. [*Still photog* Fred Parrish]. [*Publicity* Richard Birdwell]. [*Publicity for Atlanta and New York premieres* Howard Dietz]. [*Trailer supv* Frank Whitbeck]. [*Asst to Howard Dietz* William Hebert]. [*Stand-in for Vivien Leigh* Mozelle Miller].

Source: Based on the novel *Gone With the Wind* by Margaret Mitchell (New York, 1936).

Cast: *The Players: At Tara, The O'Hara Plantation in Georgia*: Thomas Mitchell (*Gerald O'Hara*), Barbara O'Neill [sic] (*Ellen, his wife*), *Their daughters*: Vivien Leigh (*Scarlett [O'Hara Hamilton Kennedy Butler]*), Evelyn Keyes (*Suellen [O'Hara]*), Ann Rutherford (*Carreen [O'Hara]*), *Scarlett's beaux*: George Reeves (*Brent Tarleton*), Fred Crane (*Stuart Tarleton*), *The house servants*: Hattie McDaniel (*Mammy*), Oscar Polk (*Pork*), Butterfly McQueen (*Prissy*), *In the fields*: Victor Jory (*Jonas Wilkerson, the overseer*), Everett Brown (*Big Sam, the foreman*), *At Twelve Oaks, the nearby Wilkes plantation*: Howard Hickman (*John Wilkes*), Alicia Rhett (*India [Wilkes], his daughter*), Leslie Howard (*Ashley [Wilkes], his son*), Olivia deHavilland (*Melanie Hamilton [Wilkes]*), Rand Brooks (*Charles Hamilton, her brother*), Carroll Nye (*Frank Kennedy, a guest*), *and a visitor from Charleston*: Clark Gable (*Rhett Butler*), *In Atlanta*: Laura Hope Crews (*Aunt Pittypat Hamilton*), Eddie Anderson (*Uncle Peter, her coachman*), Harry Davenport (*Dr. Meade*), Leona Roberts (*Mrs. Meade*), Jane Darwell (*Mrs. Merriwether*), Ona Munson (*Belle Watling*), Paul Hurst [(*A Yankee deserter*)], Cammie King [(*Bonnie Blue Butler*)], J. M. Kerrigan [(*Johnny Gallegher*)], Jackie Moran [(*Phil Meade*)], L. Kemble-Cooper [(*Bonnie's nurse*)], Marcella Martin [(*Cathleen Calvert*)], Mickey Kuhn [(*Beau Wilkes*)], Irving Bacon [(*The corporal*)], William Bakewell [(*A mounted officer*)], Isabel Jewell [(*Emmy Slattery*)], Eric Linden [(*An amputation case*)], Ward Bond [(*Tom, a Yankee captain*)], Cliff Edwards [(*Reminiscent soldier*)], Yakima Canutt [(*A renegade*)], Louis Jean Heydt [(*A hungry soldier*)], Olin Howland [(*A carpetbagger business man*)], Robert Elliott [(*The Yankee major*)], Mary Anderson [(*Maybelle Merriwether*)], Albert Morin (*René Picard*), [Terry Shero (*Fanny Elsing*)], [Billy McClain (*Old Levi*)], [Ed Chandler (*The sergeant*)], [George Hackathorne (*A wounded soldier in pain*)], [Rosco Ates (*A convalescent soldier*)], [John Arledge (*A dying soldier*)], [Tom Tyler (*A commanding offier*)], [Lee Phelps (*The bartender*)], [Ernest Whitman (*The carpetbagger's friend*)], [William Selling (*A returning veteran*)], [George Meeker, Wallis Clark (*Yankee major's poker-playing captains*)], [Adrian Morris (*A carpetbagger orator*)], [Blue Washington (*A renegade's companion*)].

Historical, **Romance**. [*Print viewed*]. In 1861, Scarlett O'Hara, the headstrong sixteen-year-old daughter of wealthy Georgia plantation-owner Gerald O'Hara, is sick of hearing talk about going to war with the North. She much prefers to have beaux like Brent and Stuart Tarleton talk about the next day's barbecue at Twelve Oaks, the neighboring Wilkes plantation. When the twins reveal the "secret" that Ashley Wilkes is planning to marry his cousin Melanie Hamilton from Atlanta, Scarlett refuses to believe it because she is in love with Ashley herself. Her father later confirms the news when he returns home to Tara, the O'Hara plantation, and advises Scarlett to forget about the serious-minded Ashley, because "like should marry like." At the barbeque, Scarlett acts coquettish with all of the young men, hoping to make Ashley jealous, then, during an afternoon rest, she sneaks into the library to see him. He says that he will marry Melanie because they are alike, but leads Scarlett to believe that he loves her instead of Melanie. When he leaves, Scarlett angrily throws a vase and is startled to discover Rhett Butler, a notorious rogue from Charleston, who has been lying unnoticed on a couch the entire time. She is angry at his seeming indifference to the seriousness of her feelings for Ashley and annoyed by his frank appreciation of her physical beauty. Later, when news arrives that war has broken out between the North and the South, Scarlett is stunned to see Ashley kiss Melanie goodbye as he leaves to enlist, and in a daze accepts the impulsive proposal of Melanie's brother Charles.

Just after Ashley and Melanie marry, Scarlett and Charles marry as

well, delighting Melanie, who tells Scarlett that now they will truly be sisters. Some time later, Scarlett receives word that Charles has died of the measles, and she is forced to don widow's black clothing and refrain from going to the parties she loves. Her understanding mother Ellen decides to let her go to Atlanta to stay with Melanie and her Aunt Pittypat, hoping that Scarlett will feel less restless there. At an Atlanta fundraising bazaar, Scarlett is so bored watching other girls dance, that when Rhett bids for her in a dance auction, she enthusiastically leads the Virginia Reel with him, oblivious to the outrage of the shocked local matrons. Rhett, who has become a successful blockade runner, continues to see Scarlett over the next few months and brings her presents from his European trips. As the war rages, Melanie and Scarlett receive word that Ashley will be returning home on a Christmas leave. Atlanta is now suffering the privation of a long siege, but the women manage to give Ashley a small Christmas feast. Before he returns to the front, Ashley tells Scarlett that the South is losing the war and asks her to stay by the pregnant Melanie.

Melanie goes into labor as Atlantans leave the city before Northern troops arrive. When Aunt Pitty leaves for Charleston, Scarlett desperately wants to go with her, but remembers her promise to Ashley, and remains with Melanie. Because Melanie's labor is difficult and the doctor is too busy attending wounded soldiers to come to her aid, Scarlett must attend her alone. After the baby is born, Scarlett sends her maid Prissy for Rhett, who reluctantly arrives with a frightened horse and a wagon. Though he thinks that Scarlett is crazy when she insists upon returning to Tara, he risks his life to drive the women and the infant through the now-burning city. Outside Atlanta, as Rhett and Scarlett see the decimated Southern army in retreat, he feels ashamed and resolves to join them for their last stand. Scarlett is furious with him, even after he admits that he loves her and gives her a passionate kiss before leaving. When the women finally arrive at Tara, the plantation is a shambles and the house has been looted. Scarlett's mother Ellen has just died of typhoid and her father's mind is gone. Desperate for something to eat, Scarlett first tries drinking whiskey, then goes into the fields. After choking on a radish, she vows that if she lives through this she will never go hungry again. [An Intermission divides the story at this point.]

Soon Scarlett bullies her sisters and the remaining house slaves into working in the fields. After she kills a Yankee scavenger and, with Melanie's help, hides the body, the contents of his wallet provide them with some money for food. When the war ends, Ashley returns and Scarlett goes to him for advice when Pork, one of the former slaves who has remained with the family, tells her that $300 in taxes are owed on Tara. Ashley offers no solution to her problem, but admits once again that he loves her, even though he will never leave Melanie. More determined than ever to obtain the money after Jonas Wilkerson, a ruthless Yankee who was once Tara's overseer, says that he is going to buy Tara when it is auctioned off for taxes, Scarlett decides to ask Rhett for the money. With no proper clothes to wear, Scarlett and her old governess, Mammy, use material from Tara's velvet drapes for a new dress. In Atlanta, they discover that Rhett has been imprisoned by the Yankees, but has charmed his way into their good graces. Scarlett tries to pretend that everything is fine at Tara, but Rhett soon sees her roughened hands and realizes what her situation is. Because he is under arrest and his money is all in an English bank, Rhett cannot help Scarlett, so she leaves, infuriated. That same day, she runs into Frank Kennedy, her sister Suellen's beau, and sees that he has become a successful merchant. Scarlett tricks Frank into marrying her by telling him that Suellen loves someone else, and is thus able to use his money to save Tara. Scarlett then moves to Atlanta to work at Frank's shop and to make his fledgling lumber business a success. She also uses an unwitting Melanie to help make Ashley come to work at the lumber mill. One day, Scarlett is attacked by scavengers while driving her carriage near a shanty town, but is saved by Big Sam, a former Tara slave. Scarlett is not physically harmed, but that night Frank, Ashley and some of the other men band together to "clear out" the shanty. While Scarlett, Melanie and the other women wait at Melanie's house, Rhett arrives to warn them that the Yankees are planning an ambush. Melanie tells him where the men have gone, and some time later, he prevents their arrest by pretending to the Yankees that they have all been drinking with him at the notorious Belle Watling's bordello. Ashley is wounded, but Frank has died on the raid.

A few weeks later, Scarlett, who is drinking heavily, is visited by

Rhett, who proposes to her and offers to give her everything she wants. Though she says that she does not love him, she agrees to marry him, and on their expensive honeymoon, he vows to spoil her to stop her nightmares of the war. A year later, Scarlett gives birth to a daughter, whom Melanie nicknames "Bonnie Blue." Though Rhett has never cared about Atlanta society, he now wants to ensure Bonnie's future. He begins to acquire respectability, and within a few years his charitable contributions and sincere devotion to Bonnie impresses even the hardest of Atlanta's matrons. Meanwhile, Scarlett still longs for Ashley and has told Rhett that she no longer wants him to share her bedroom. One day, Ashley's sister India and some other women see Scarlett and Ashley in an embrace. Though nothing improper happened, Scarlett is afraid to attend Melanie's birthday party for Ashley that night. A furious Rhett forces her to attend, though, then leaves. Melanie's open affection to her makes Scarlett ashamed, and when she returns home she sneaks into the dining room to drink. There she finds Rhett drunk and a violent quarrel erupts. After Scarlett calls Rhett a drunken fool, he grabs her and carries her upstairs, angrily telling her that this night there will not be "three in a bed." The next morning, Scarlett is happy, but when Rhett scoffs that his behavior was merely an indiscretion, her happiness turns to anger. Rhett then leaves for an extended trip to England and takes Bonnie with him.

Some months later, because Bonnie is homesick, Rhett returns to Atlanta and discovers that Scarlett is pregnant. She is happy to see Rhett, but his smirk of indifference and accusation about Ashley enrages her so that she starts to strike him and falls down the stairs. She loses the baby, and although she calls to him during her delirium, Rhett does not know and thinks that she hates him. After she recovers, he suggests that the anger and hatred stop for Bonnie's sake, and Scarlett agrees, but as they are talking, the headstrong Bonnie tries to make her pony take a jump and she falls and breaks her neck. Both are shattered by Bonnie's death, especially Rhett, who refuses to let her be buried because Bonnie was afraid of the dark. Only Melanie, to whom Rhett has always felt a closeness, convinces him to let the child go. After her talk with Rhett, Melanie, who has become pregnant despite the danger to her health, collapses and suffers a miscarriage. On her deathbed, Melanie asks Scarlett to take care of Ashley, but when Scarlett sees how much the distraught Ashley loves Melanie, she finally realizes how wrong she has been for years and knows that it is Rhett she truly loves. She rushes back home and tries to prevent him from leaving her, but he will not stay because it is too late for them. Scarlett tearfully asks him what she will do and as he leaves she answers, "Frankly, my dear, I don't give a damn." Through her sobs, Scarlett begins to think of Tara, from which she has always gained strength, and determines that she will return there and will think of a way to get Rhett back. She resolves to think about it tomorrow for, "after all, tomorrow is another day." *Death and dying. Flirts. Georgia. Lure of riches. Poverty. Servants. United States–History–Civil War, 1861-1865. United States–History–Reconstruction, 1865-1898. United States–South. Unrequited love. Accidental death. African Americans. Atlanta (GA). Balls (Parties). Barbeques. Blockades. Childbirth. Christmas. Clothes. Confederate States of America. Army. Convicts. Curtains. Dance parties. Drunkenness. Fires. Horses. Hospitals. Hunger. Infidelity. Ku Klux Klan. Lice. Lumber mills. Measles. New Orleans (LA). Overseers. Physicians. Plantations. Prostitution. Rescues. River boats. Self-defense. Self-sacrifice. Slavery. Stairs. Stores, Retail. Widows.*

Note: [*Note from the Editors*: the following information is based on contemporary news items, feature articles, reviews, interviews, memoranda and corporate records. Information obtained from modern sources is indicated. Some contemporary documents have been reproduced in modern sources. Because of the vast amount of material available, a comprehensive discussion of all aspects of *Gone With the Wind* is not possible here. Information included herein emphasizes the production of the film rather than the personalities of the filmmakers, the artistic reputation or cultural heritage of the film. The reader is advised to consult the Bibliography for titles of numerous books containing additional information on *Gone With the Wind*.] The opening credits read: "Selznick International in association with Metro-Goldwyn-Mayer has the honor to present its Technicolor production of Margaret Mitchell's Story of the Old South *Gone With The Wind*." Following the opening credits, a written prologue reads: "There was a land of Cavaliers and Cotton Fields called The Old South...Here in this pretty world Gallantry took its last bow...Here was the last ever to be seen of Knights and their ladies fair, of Master and of Slave...Look for it only in books for it is no more than a dream remembered. A Civilization gone with the wind." In the opening cast credits, actress Barbara O'Neil's surname is erroneously spelled "O'Neill."

The title *Gone With the Wind* is taken from the poem "*Non sum qualis eram*" by the eighteenth century poet Ernest Dowson, "I have been faithful to

thee, Cynara! in my fashion. I have forgot much Cynara! gone with the wind...." Margaret Mitchell's novel was published officially by the Macmillan Company on 30 Jun 1936, although advance reviews of the novel, which was at one time to bear the title *Tomorrow Is Another Day*, appeared as early as May 1936. The book immediately became a best seller, and many modern sources have cited it as the best-selling novel of all time. Magazines, newspaper articles and films of the time frequently alluded to the book, and characters and lines from the novel were well-known throughout the world. Producer David O. Selznick's Eastern Story Editor, Katherine "Kay" Brown, first became aware of the novel when she read it in galley form in May 1936 and brought it to Selznick's attention. A teletyped memo from Selznick to Brown, dated 25 May 1936 and reprinted in modern sources, indicates that Selznick initially considered *Gone With the Wind* "a fine story," but was reluctant to purchase it because his studio did not have a suitable female star under contract, and because he considered its Civil War setting "...very strongly against it." Selznick concluded his remarks by writing "most sorry to say no in face of your enthusiasm for this story."

A 26 May 1936 memo from Selznick to Brown stated "...the more I think about it, the more I feel there is excellent picture in it...." Additional memos and news items in trade papers between late May and late Jun 1936 indicate that Selznick's interest in the property increased, and by early Jul 1936, he had acquired the rights to the novel for $50,000. (Some news items erroneously reported the figure as $52,000.) Letters written by Mitchell, compiled in a modern source, indicate that Miss Annie Laurie acted as her literary agent and negotiated the sale to Selznick. Several letters also indicate that Mitchell was relatively distant from the actual negotiations, in part due to a severe eye problem that afflicted her at the time. Selznick memos and news items indicate that other studios were variously interested in the project but Selznick's firm offer was accepted by Laurie. In a letter from Mitchell to Harold Latham of the Macmillan Co., dated 13 Aug 1936, the author noted that "the deal was closed up about two weeks ago," after some changes in the contract involving rights and liabilities were made at her request.

In September 1936, Selznick had brought director George Cukor onto the project, and by late September Selznick had hired noted writer Sidney Howard to do a treatment and subsequent screenplay. Other early additions to the staff who were instrumental in the planning and production phases included production manager Ray Klune, production designer William Cameron Menzies, costume designer Walter Plunkett, art director Lyle Wheeler and former newsman Russell Birdwell, who was to publicize the film and has been credited in contemporary feature articles and modern sources with maintaining public enthusiasm for the project. The major aspects of the film's pre-production stage, conducted simultaneously from mid-1936 until late Jan 1939, were production design, screenplay and casting.

Contemporary memoranda and news items reveal that general discussion about the cast began immediately. Selznick memos prior to his purchase of the novel mention Ronald Colman as a potential "Rhett Butler," and either Miriam Hopkins or Tallulah Bankhead as a possible "Scarlett O'Hara." Around this time Selznick also mentioned M-G-M contract stars Clark Gable and Joan Crawford as potential leads. News items in trade papers appeared frequently from late summer 1936. Hundreds of news and feature stories appeared in newspapers and consumer magazines throughout the world, and the status of casting was a frequent topic on Hollywood-oriented radio programs. Numerous persons were mentioned in contemporary sources as potential cast members, and contemporary news items document the extraordinary interest among fans in the casting of the film.

Kay Brown traveled through the South on a highly publicized "scouting" trip in 1936, and the same year she and George Cukor conducted tests in New York City for Scarlett and other roles. Much of this early scouting, however, may have been conducted more for publicity purposes than actual talent searching. Among the first actresses seriously considered for the role of Scarlett was Tallulah Bankhead, who was photographically tested in New York in the autumn of 1936. A *HR* news item on 26 Oct 1936 stated that Bankhead had been tested in color, in anticipation of the picture being shot in Technicolor, however, surviving footage of the test is in black-and-white, and modern sources indicate that Paulette Goddard and Vivien Leigh were the only actresses tested in Technicolor for the role. Other actresses listed in Selznick International "daily reports," news items, the film's program and memoranda as tested or considered included Jean Arthur, Diana Barrymore, Joan Bennett, Marguerite Churchill, Claudette Colbert, Joan Crawford, Bette Davis, Frances Dee, Ellen Drew (using the name Terry Ray), Irene Dunne, Jean Harlow, Katharine Hepburn, Miriam Hopkins, Carole Lombard, Susan Hayward (under her real name, Edythe Marrener), Boots Mallory, Jo Ann Sayers, Norma Shearer, Margaret Sullavan, Margaret Tallichet, Lana Turner, Claire Trevor, Arleen Whelan and Loretta Young. Tests of many of the women considered have been included in documentaries on the film's production.

The names of other actresses mentioned in contemporary sources who were not seriously considered for the role included Marion Davies, Mrs. Jock Whitney, Betty Timmons (Margaret Mitchell's niece) and Lucille Ball. A Jun 1937 *Cinema Arts* article suggested that probably the only actresses not mentioned prominently in contention for the role of Scarlett were comedienne Martha Raye and child star Shirley Temple. News items and feature stories in contemporary magazines, as well as memoranda from Selznick and Brown prior to production, indicate that Norma Shearer was a serious contender for the role. News items in *NYT*, *DV* and *HR* throughout 1937 and 1938 indicate that Shearer was "signed" to play Scarlett, however, no contract was actually signed, and on 1 Apr 1937 *FD* reported that both Selznick and Shearer had issued statements "ending the possibility that the latter might play Scarlett O'Hara...." The statements apparently followed discussions by Kay Brown with Edwin Balmer, then editor of *Redbook* magazine, Lois Cole of the Macmillan Co. and "a rank outsider" about Shearer. In a memo from Brown to Selznick on 19 Mar 1937, Brown reported that, among other things, the consultants felt "Shearer does not seem to be associated with sex."

Of the many actresses under consideration, Bankhead, Hopkins and Arthur were variously said to be "signed" for the role and a 10 Nov 1938 *HR* news item reported that Arthur issued a statement saying that she had turned down the role because her contract with Columbia prevented her from making the future picture commitments with Selznick which he required. Corporate information indicates that while several actresses were serious contenders at various times, Goddard was apparently the leading candidate before Leigh, followed by Bennett and Arthur. According to memos and news items, Vivien Leigh tested for the role in mid-Dec 1938, a few days after Selznick met her on 10 Dec 1938, the night the "Burning of Atlanta" sequence was filmed. Her signing was announced to the press in early Jan 1939, at which time she was signed to a six-picture contract with Selznick. Modern sources note that several columnists decried the selection of Leigh, an Englishwoman, for the role. Shortly after the announcement, a Gallup Poll released on 21 Feb 1939 reported that 35% of those polled favored Leigh, 16% disapproved, 20% were undecided and 29% had not yet heard of her selection.

Selznick memoranda, daily reports, and trade paper news items confirm that Clark Gable was the most serious candidate for the role of Rhett, however, Warner Baxter, Ronald Colman, Gary Cooper, Fredric March and Errol Flynn were variously mentioned in news items as being considered, tested or even "signed" for the role. According to news items, Flynn was offered by Warner Bros. for Rhett, along with Bette Davis for Scarlett, in 1938 when the studio was negotiating for distribution rights to the picture. Gable was mentioned in many feature and news items as the "public's" strong choice to portray Rhett. Negotiations for Gable were also linked to distribution rights for the film. While news items in trade papers in mid-June 1938 reported that Selznick was to release *Gone With the Wind* through United Artists, with whom he already was committed to release two more films, and that he was negotiating with Samuel Goldwyn to borrow Cooper for the role, the M-G-M deal was announced in early August. By terms of the agreement, which was signed in front of the press on 24 Aug 1938, Selznick agreed to let Loew's, Inc. M-G-M's distribution arm) release the picture in exchange for Gable's services and an infusion of money into the project, which modern sources state was $1,250,000. Modern sources also note that in addition to a weekly salary of $4,500 for the film, Gable received a signing bonus of $50,000. In interviews Gable stated that he was reluctant to do the part, and in the film's program he was quoted as saying that he was "scared stiff" and "realized that whoever played Rhett would be up against a stumbling block...Miss Mitchell had etched Rhett into the minds of millions...It would be impossible to satisfy them all."

Modern sources have concluded that Gable was finally convinced to do the part for the bonus, which thus enabled him to divorce his estranged wife, Rhea Langham, and marry Carole Lombard. In regard to Gable, in a 25 Jul 1936 letter Margaret Mitchell wrote, "All of my friends are determined that he [Gable] should play the part, as tho [sic] what anyone thought could influence casting directors!" An exchange of letters between Mitchell and Kay Brown over the next eighteen months indicated that the author had no "inside" knowledge about the casting of Rhett or any other roles, but frequently related suggestions garnered from fellow Southerners and in Jul 1938 expressed the opinion that Gable was "not as popular here in the South as in other sections of the country...in looks and in conduct Basil Rathbone has been the first choice in this section." The most specific comments about Mitchell's own choices for roles concerned Miriam Hopkins as Scarlett, whom she felt "would be fine as Scarlett. She has the looks and, best of all, the voice."

Because of the world-wide popularity of the novel and the familiarity of the public with its characters, tests and interviews to fill several major roles took place over a long period of time. According to contemporary sources, actresses tested or rehearsed for "Melanie Hamilton" were Dorothy Jordon, Ann Dvorak, Frances Dee, Joan Fontaine (Olivia deHavilland's sister), Andrea Leeds, Marcella Martin and Anne Shirley. In addition, the program for the 1940 film *Our Town* noted that its star, Martha Scott, was almost rejected for the lead in that film because producers had seen her test for Melanie in *Gone With The Wind* and thought it was terrible. Actors tested and/or considered for the role of "Ashley Wilkes" included Melvyn Douglas, Ray Milland, Tyrone Power, Lew Ayres, Douglass Montgomery, Joel McCrea, Jeffrey Lynn and Alan Marshall. Selznick memos indicate that he thought positively of Milland at one point, despite his accent, and, though favorably impressed with Douglas' performance in a test, considered him physically wrong for the role. DeHavilland was signed for the role of Melanie and Howard was signed for Ashley in mid-Jan 1939. Modern sources indicate that deHavilland convinced Warner Bros. to loan her to Selznick for the role after an emotional appeal to Jack Warner's wife, and Howard's reluctance to take on the role of Ashley was overcome by Selznick's offer to allow the actor to produce as well as star in a film for Selznick International. (For information on that film, *Intermezzo*, released in 1939, see entry in (see *AFI Catalog of Feature Films, 1931-40*; F3.2140).

In addition to Hattie McDaniel, Hattie Noel was considered for "Mammy" and was tested with various actresses in the scene set in Scarlett's bedroom just prior to the barbeque sequence. Evelyn Brent, Estelle Taylor, June Compson and Eve Arden tested or interviewed for the role of "Belle Watling." Other actors and actresses who were tested for various roles in the film or were mentioned in contemporary sources as possible choices for roles in the film included Margaret Tallichet as "Carreen," Walter Connolly and Joseph Crehan as "Gerald O'Hara" and Conrad Nagel as "Frank Kennedy." A Selznick memo dated 26 Nov 1937 mentions a number of potential cast members for the film, including Lionel Barrymore as "Dr. Meade," Billie Burke as "Aunt Pittypat," and Judy Garland as "Carreen." News items in Oct and Nov 1937 in *HR* and *DV* stated that Tallichet and Connolly were respectively the first and second actors to be

"signed" by Selznick for the film. Tallichet was under contract to Selznick and tested for Scarlett and Melanie, but no available evidence confirms that she was specifically signed for a role in the film. News items about Connolly indicate that he was a strong possibility for "Gerald," but later reported that the role lessened in importance as the film approached production and hence Connolly's salary was deemed out of proportion to the size of the role and Thomas Mitchell was finally selected. Whether Connolly signed a general contract with Selznick and whether the de-emphasis of the role resulted in his being replaced has not been verified.

Following Sidney Howard's completion of a treatment of Mitchell's novel, several other writers worked on the project. Howard, who died during the film's production in an accident on his farm in 1939, is the only writer credited onscreen, but contemporary and modern sources credit writer Ben Hecht with significant contributions to story development and dialogue. In addition, Hecht wrote the opening prologue and the six other narrative title cards seen throughout the film. According to news items and memoranda, other writers who worked on the project at various times included Karl Van Druten, Oliver H. P. Garrett and Jo Swerling. News items in Jan 1939 note that novelist F. Scott Fitzgerald was hired to work on the screenplay, but, according to modern sources, he only worked for two or three weeks and none of his work was included in the film. According to various contemporary and modern sources, after considerable alteration of Howard's original work, Selznick went back to it, in part on Hecht's recommendation.

To design the "look" of the film, William Cameron Menzies created watercolor storyboard sketches for every scene of the picture. An article in *HR* on 15 Mar 1938 describes Menzies' use of watercolor for the storyboards and indicates that he had already completed some of the work by that date. A Selznick memo dated 1 Sep 1937 discusses Menzies' future role in the production: "Menzies may turn out to be one of the most valuable factors in properly producing this picture...I would probably give him some such credit as "Production Designed by William Cameron Menzies." This credit was also given to Menzies for his work on Selznick's 1938 picture *The Young in Heart* which, though shot and released prior to *Gone With the Wind*, was made after Selznick's decision to credit Menzies as production designer on the latter film. In addition to Menzies, art director Lyle Wheeler, costume designer Walter Plunkett and historian Wilbur Kurtz were instrumental in the overall "look" of the film and worked on the project from 1937 on. Hobe Erwin was hired for the picture's interior decoration in Mar 1938, but by the time the film went into production in late 1939, Erwin was no longer available and Joseph B. Platt and Edward G. Boyle replaced him. A number of other persons involved in various aspects of the film's art direction, and exterior and interior decoration were credited onscreen and in the official program. News items appeared in trade papers throughout 1937 and 1938 indicating various start dates for the production, but the various aspects of pre-production caused repeated delays.

The first shots were filmed on the evening of Saturday, 10 Dec 1938, when the "Burning of Atlanta" sequence was filmed on the Selznick International backlot in Culver City, CA. At that time, the casting of Scarlett and a number of other major characters had not yet been finalized. As noted above, Selznick was first introduced to Leigh during the filming, and the images of the characters Scarlett and Rhett were filmed only in long-shot. Because Scarlett had not yet been cast, modern sources note that the stuntwoman dressed as Scarlett had to be obscured to allow for any physical type. The structures burned during the sequence included sets from old RKO films that were shot on the lot when RKO was headquartered at the location. Among the sets burned, which can be identified in slow-motion and still photography, are the gates from *King Kong*, on which Selznick acted as executive producer (see *AFI Catalog of Feature Films, 1931-40*; F3.2288). According to modern sources, the fire was controlled by a series of dual pipes carrying water and oil that could be regulated to control the intensity of the flames. Lee Zavitz is credited in contemporary sources as the person in charge of "Fire effects," and according to modern sources created the pipe system. News items noted that seven Technicolor cameras were used for the sequence, which according to modern sources, included every Technicolor camera in existence in Los Angeles at the time.

Principal photography began officially on 26 Jan 1939, although modern sources note that the first day's production was largely ceremonial. At the time that the film began shooting, George Cukor was the director and Lee Garmes was the cinematographer. According to modern sources, professional relations between Cukor and Selznick had become strained as pre-production dragged on, and the cost of Cukor's exclusive services became a large financial burden. On 14 Feb 1939, news items in trade papers announced that Cukor and Selznick had issued a joint statement to the effect that Cukor was withdrawing from the film. The statement read: "Mr. Cukor suggested his withdrawal, but acquiesced to my [Selznick's] request that he continue shooting the picture until another director is selected...." As stated in news items, Cukor and Selznick had argued increasingly over the direction of the film. A letter from Selznick to Cukor dated 8 Feb 1939 alludes to disagreements between the men concerning Cukor's checking with Selznick on specific points and Selznick's visits to the set. In interviews in later years, both Selznick and Cukor stressed that their personal friendship remained throughout the years despite their disagreements over the picture. Numerous contemporary and modern sources have speculated on the reasons why Cukor was removed. Reasons cited for Cukor's removal include, among others, disagreements over "the birthing scene" to Cukor's slow and costly directing pace, to Gable's feelings that Cukor would give Leigh and the other women in the cast a better presentation in the picture than him.

Directors mentioned in news items as possible replacements for Cukor included King Vidor, Clarence Brown, Robert Z. Leonard and Jack Conway, who all worked at M-G-M at the time. On 17 Feb 1939, news items reported that Victor Fleming would be taking over the direction of *Gone With the Wind*

instead of completing work on M-G-M's *The Wizard of Oz* (see *AFI Catalog of Feature Films, 1931-40*; F3.5154). Although Selznick apparently planned to restart the production within a few days, it went on hiatus until 2 Mar. Some scenes shot by Cukor were later reshot, including the opening sequence of the film, but, according to a 22 Jan 1940 letter from Selznick to Frank Capra (then president of the Directors Guild) about the direction of the film, "three solid reels" of Cukor's work remained in the completed film. Shooting continued on the picture with Fleming as the director, and Menzies and Reeves "Breezy" Eason acting as second unit directors.

On 28 Apr 1939, however, news items reported that due to Fleming's "exhaustion" he would be leaving the production for about ten days. News stories also mentioned that M-G-M director Sam Wood was to replace Fleming in work with the principals while Menzies directed backlot exteriors, Chester Franklin directed location work in Chico (where the "shantytown" sequence was filmed), and Richard Rosson directed the battle scene sequences. Rosson is not mentioned in any other available sources after this date, and a Selznick International "Statistical Report of Completed Production" contained in the AMPAS Library file on the film does not include Rosson's name among the various directors, second unit or assistant directors. Rosson was a well-known second unit director at M-G-M during the 1930s, and it is possible that he was considered for a second unit position on *Gone With the Wind* but was unavailable. Later news items credit Eason with battle scene direction. When Fleming returned to the production in mid-May 1939, Wood continued to work for ten days. According to news items, upon Fleming's return the crew was then divided into five units to speed up production. The statistical report notes that of the three principal directors, Cukor worked for eighteen days, Fleming for ninety-three, and Wood for twenty-four, as of 1 Jul 1939, the end of principal photography. Fleming continued with retakes and, according to the film's program, the last shot was made by Fleming on 11 Nov 1939. In addition to location shooting in Chico, some exteriors were done at Busch Gardens in Pasadena, Malibu, Big Bear and Triunfo, CA, according to news items. Throughout the summer and early autumn of 1939, editing and post-production continued.

The first preview of the film was held in Riverside, CA on 11 Sep 1939. According to modern sources, the preview print was shown without completed titles and without special photographic effects. In interviews, film editor Hal Kern related that only he knew the location of the preview and kept the information secret even from Selznick. Editing continued on the film almost until the premiere. According to modern sources and interviews, Selznick, film editor Hal Kern, special effects man Jack Cosgrove and others worked continuously on the project, often for stretches of forty-eight hours or more without rest. Cosgrove and his crew created many exteriors in the film with matte shots. In the novel, Rhett's last words to Scarlett are, "My dear, I don't give a damn." In the film, his last words are, "Frankly my dear, I don't give a damn." According to Selznick memos, considerable time was spent by the producer and others to write another line for the film that did not use the word "damn" which was unacceptable by Production Code standards. By Sep 1939, Joseph I. Breen of the Hays Office had refused to grant the picture certification if the word "damn" was used. Permission was finally granted for the picture to receive a certificate by the Hays Office in late Oct 1939. A letter to Will H. Hays from Selznick, dated 20 Oct 1939 notes "It is my contention that this word as used in the picture is not an oath or a curse. The worst that could be said against it is that it is a vulgarism, and it is so described in the *Oxford English Dictionary*." According to modern sources Selznick was allowed to retain the word "damn" in the film after paying a $5,000 fine. The word "damn" had been used before the strict implementation of the Production Code in 1934. According to modern sources, the word was not used again until the 1941 Twentieth Century-Fox film *How Green Was My Valley*.

To ensure that the film was shown according to his precise specifications, Selznick had a special booklet prepared for exhibitors that gave a detailed description of how the film should be projected. Details included the screen's proper illumination level, sound intensity, care of the film and projector, and the length of the overtures. According to the instructions, before the film began, a decorative title card was projected while an overture, "carefully designed to establish a mood for the enjoyment of the film" was played for ten minutes, thirty-one seconds. Another title card was used during the film's intermission, which ran for seven minutes (or longer if theater managers desired to allow the audience more time during the intermission), and finally a four minute, fifteen second musical program ran at the end of the picture.

In preparation for the release of the film, Howard Dietz of M-G-M coordinated the national publicity campaign, and Frank Whitbeck, also of M-G-M, prepared and narrated the trailer. Unlike most film trailers of the era, *Gone With the Wind*'s did not include footage of the film. According to an exchange of memos between Dietz and Selznick, Selznick was adamant that the film not be promoted as an M-G-M picture, but as a Selznick International production and an M-G-M release. As part of the film's publicity, several national magazines featured cover stories on the picture, including the 25 Dec 1939 issue of *Time* magazine, which had a photograph of Vivien Leigh on the cover. In order to give the picture the earliest possible review, *Time*'s critic, Whittaker Chambers was even flown to Los Angeles for the 9 Dec press preview.

The world premiere of the picture was held on 15 Dec 1939 at the Loew's Grand Theater in Atlanta, GA. Leigh, Gable, deHavilland, Selznick and Margaret Mitchell were among the many celebrities who attended the premiere, parade and ball that took place in conjunction with the film. Contemporary news items estimated that the parade attracted as many as 1,500,000 people. The *AtlJ*, the newspaper on which Mitchell had once worked, devoted large sections of its issues to the festivities during the week of the premiere, and sold a special souvenir supplement edition on the film on 15 Dec. Premieres followed in New York on 19 Dec 1939 and in Los Angeles on 28 Dec, and the film opened at

roadshow engagements at a number of large cities over the following few weeks. *FDYB* and other contemporary sources printed a production breakdown on the picture that figures the total negative cost of the film at $3,957,000. Some modern sources have placed the total cost at $4,250,000. According to modern sources, the film grossed twenty million dollars by the end of May 1940 when the film completed its first run at roadshow prices. The picture was released nationally at "popular" prices on 17 Jan 1941. Many modern sources have indicated that *Gone With the Wind* is the highest grossing film ever, taking into consideration the original release, all re-releases, and factoring the difference between ticket prices in 1939 and current prices.

The film was nominated for thirteen Academy Awards and won eight of the nominated categories. Those awards included Picture, Director (Victor Fleming), Actress (Vivien Leigh), Supporting Actress (Hattie McDaniel), Screenplay (posthumously to Sidney Howard), Art Direction (Lyle Wheeler), Color Cinematography (Ernest Haller and Ray Rennahan), and Film Editing (Hal Kern and James Newcom). Other nominations included Actor (Clark Gable), Supporting Actress (Olivia de Havilland), Original Score (Max Steiner), Sound Recording (Thomas Moulton and the Samuel Goldwyn Studio Sound Department) and Special Effects (Jack Cosgrove and Frank Albin). An Oscar also went to William Cameron Menzies for "Outstanding achievement in the use of color for the enhancement of dramatic mood" in the film and to Don Musgrave and Selznick International Pictures for "pioneering use of coordinated equipment" on the picture. David O. Selznick also received the Irving G. Thalberg Memorial Award. McDaniel was the first black actor to win an Academy Award. Thomas Mitchell also won the Supporting Actor award the same year, but for his work in *Stagecoach* (see *AFI Catalog of Feature Films, 1931-40*; F3.4284). Though the film did win other awards, it was not honored in any category by the National Board of Review and only Vivien Leigh was honored by the New York film critics. The film did appear on the *NYT* "Ten Best" list, was *FDYB*'s top film of the year and was included in the *Var* list of the top twenty money-makers of the 1939-40 season.

Reviews were, for the most part, highly laudatory of the film. *HR* called it "more than the greatest motion picture which ever was made. It is the ultimate realization of the dreams of what might be done..." The *Var* reviewer said it "...appears finally as one of the screen's major achievements, meriting highest respect and plaudits, and poised for grosses which may be second to none in the history of the business." Consumer magazines and newspapers generally gave the picture excellent reviews, with many calling it the greatest film ever made. Some notable reviewers disagreed, among them Frank S. Nugent of the *NYT* who wrote, "Is it the greatest motion picture ever made? Probably, not, although it is the greatest motion mural we have seen," and John Mosher of *The New Yorker* described many moments in the film he didn't appreciate and concluded, "there might have been managed one full hour of superior material." Carlton Moss of *The Daily Worker* wrote, "Whereas *The Birth of a Nation* was a frontal attack on American history and the Negro people, *Gone With the Wind*...is a rear attack...sugar-smeared and blurred by a boresome Hollywood love story." Moss, a black playwright, entitled his review "An Open Letter to Mr. Selznick." Many contemporary and modern sources have noted that Moss's condemnation of aspects of the film reflected the feelings of black Americans about any romanticised or patronizing portrait of the Old South and slavery.

Since the film was first released, many popular polls have placed it as "the best" or "most popular" film of all time. A poll by the American Film Institute of its membership in 1977, and a *LAT* poll of its readers in 1978 both listed *Gone With the Wind* in first place, although the prestigious *Sight and Sound* poll of international film critics, conducted every ten years, has never included the picture in the top ten. Articles of the money the film has made in theaters, on television and video have overwhelmingly indicated that it has earned more money and been seen by more persons than any other film. The picture was rereleased on many occasions, most notably in 1947, 1954, 1967 and 1989. For the 1954 re-issue, the picture was shown in a "wide-screen" version to compete with the newly introduced CinemaScope process, and for the 1967 re-issue the film was blown up to 70mm. In 1989 a "Fiftieth Anniversary" of the picture was undertaken by Turner Entertainment to restore the picture to its original state while enhancing the sound and picture. A special video edition was subsequently released of the newly restored picture. Selznick sold the rights to the picture to Jock Whitney in 1942, and Whitney, in turn sold the rights to M-G-M in 1943. Turner Entertainment obtained the rights to *Gone With the Wind* and other M-G-M pictures when they purchased the M-G-M library in the early 1980s.

The possibility of a sequel to the story was raised even before the film was made. Margaret Mitchell emphatically rejected the idea of working on a sequel to her novel on numerous occasions. As early as Sep 1936, in a letter written in response to a reviewer's inquiry Mitchell stated, "...I am not writing a sequel. I have no intention of writing a sequel." According to modern sources this sentiment was repeated to Selznick in early 1941 when Selznick himself was considering a sequel tentatively entitled *The Daughter of Scarlett O'Hara*. For many years after Mitchell's death in Aug 1949, repeated speculation on a possible sequel, to be written by a writer selected by Mitchell's heirs surfaced. Various articles mentioned a possible television remake which, according to modern sources, was considered as a project by Selznick, who also tried to develop a Broadway musical version to be entitled *Scarlett O'Hara*. A screenplay was written by James Goldman for the the Zanuck Brown company in the early 1980s, but was not produced. Author Anne Edwards wrote a sequel to the novel entitled *Tara: The Continuation of Gone With the Wind*, and was mentioned in news items as the choice to write a screenplay based on her book, but the novel was never published. In 1991, Warner Books published a sequel authorized by the Mitchell estate, written by Alexandra Ripley and entitled *Scarlett*. That novel became an immediate best-seller (though not of the proportion of the original), and follows the characters of Scarlett and Rhett from the end of the original novel. Shortly after *Scarlett's* publication, film rights were sold to the Halmi Brothers, who turned the novel into a television mini-series of the same title, starring Joanne Whaley-Kilmer as Scarlett and Timothy Dalton as Rhett. The mini-series was broadcast on the NBC television network in 1994. Additional stories featuring characters from *Gone With the Wind* and *Scarlett* were announced by the author as future possibilities. The "phenomenon" of *Gone With the Wind* has made the film one of best known of all time. Satires on the film have appeared in print, motion pictures and television; lines from the film, such as "Frankly, my dear, I don't give a damn," are familiar throughout the world, as are visual images, such as Rhett's white suit and hat, Scarlett's white and green "barbecue" dress and Rhett carrying Scarlett up the stairs.

Marketing of characters from the story began as early as 1937 when Selznick International granted a license to the Madame Alexander Doll company for the exclusive manufacture of dolls based on the as-yet unproduced film. Licensing of the characters and images from the film has been almost continuous, with items as diverse as Scarlett O'Hara wedding dresses, paper dolls, limited edition plates, figurines and a 1989 U.S. Postal Service stamp featuring Rhett and Scarlett. Both contemporary and modern writers created puns, slogans and jokes about the vast production, as exemplified by a limerick printed in Irving Hoffman's "Tales of Hoffman" column in *HR* on 30 Dec 1939: "The Civil War was quite a fight and not a mere diversion; I never knew how tough it was before Dave Selznick's version."

AtlJ 15 Dec 1939. *AtlJ* 16 Dec 1939, p. 2. *Box* 16 Dec 1939, p. 16. *Box* 23 Dec 1939. *Box* 6 Jan 1940, p. 18. *DV* 15 Dec 1936, p. 1. *DV* 31 Jan 1938, p. 3. *DV* 10 Feb 1938, p. 4. *DV* 8 Mar 1938, p. 2 *DV* 15 Mar 1938, p. 7. *DV* 23 Mar 1938, p. 1. *DV* 28 Mar 1938, p. 3. *DV* 1 Jun 1938, p. 10. *DV* 10 Jun 1938, p. 1. *DV* 18 Jun 1938, p. 6. *DV* 23 Jun 1938, p. 1. *DV* 24 Jun 1938, p. 4. *DV* 1 Aug 1938, p. 1. *DV* 6 Aug 1938, p. 1. *DV* 27 Aug 1938, p. 1. *DV* 29 Aug 1938, p. 2. *DV* 8 Dec 1938, p. 6. *DV* 10 Dec 1938, p. 5. *DV* 12 Dec 1938, p. 1. *DV* 20 Dec 1938, p. 1. *DV* 21 Dec 1938, p. 1. *DV* 24 Dec 1938, p. 1. *DV* 28 Dec 1938, p. 1. *DV* 30 Dec 1938, p. 1. *DV* 4 Jan 1939, p. 3. *DV* 11 Jan 1939, p. 2, 5. *DV* 13 Jan 1939, p. 8. *DV* 14 Jan 1939, p. 1. *DV* 20 Jan 1939, p. 3. *DV* 24 Jan 1939, p. 1. *DV* 26 Jan 1939, p. 3. *DV* 28 Jan 1939, p. 5. *DV* 1 Feb 1939, p. 1, 3. *DV* 2 Feb 1939, p. 3. *DV* 8 Feb 1939, p. 6. *DV* 13 Feb 1939, p. 5. *DV* 14 Feb 1939, p. 1. *DV* 15 Feb 1939, p. 1. *DV* 16 Feb 1939, p. 1. *DV* 17 Feb 1939, p. 2. *DV* 18 Feb 1939, p. 3. *DV* 21 Feb 1939, pp. 1-2. *DV* 9 Mar 1939, p. 9. *DV* 10 Mar 1939, p. 1. *DV* 15 Mar 1939, p. 12. *DV* 24 Mar 1939, p. 3, 19. *DV* 30 Mar 1939, p. 1. *DV* 4 Apr 1939, p. 3. *DV* 5 Apr 1939, p. 9. *DV* 10 Apr 1939, p. 10. *DV* 11 Apr 1939, p. 6. *DV* 24 Apr 1939, p. 1. *DV* 28 Apr 1939, p. 19. *DV* 2 May 1939, p. 3. *DV* 3 May 1939, p. 2. *DV* 5 May 1939, p. 1. *DV* 9 May 1939, p. 3. *DV* 10 May 1939, p. 6. *DV* 12 May 1939, p. 1. *DV* 13 May 1939, pp. 1-2. *DV* 15 May 1939, p. 3. *DV* 17 May 1939, p. 4. *DV* 20 May 1939, p. 5. *DV* 27 May 1939, p. 2. *DV* 29 May 1939, p. 4. *DV* 2 Jun 1939, p. 5. *DV* 15 Sep 1939, pp. 1-2. *DV* 21 Sep 1939, p. 1. *DV* 27 Sep 1939, p. 3. *DV* 13 Oct 1939, p. 1. *DV* 19 Oct 1939, p. 4. *DV* 23 Oct 1939, p. 1. *DV* 24 Oct 1939, p. 2. *DV* 31 Oct 1939, p. 6. *DV* 1 Nov 1939, pp. 1-2. *DV* 4 Nov 1939, p. 6. *DV* 7 Nov 1939, p. 2. *DV* 17 Nov 1939, p. 2. *DV* 21 Nov 1939, p. 2. *DV* 22 Nov 1939, p. 4. *DV* 30 Nov 1939, p. 1. *DV* 5 Dec 1939, p. 2. *DV* 13 Dec 1939, pp. 2-3, 6 [Review, p. 3 & 6]. *DV* 16 Dec 1939, p. 2. *DV* 18 Dec 1939, p. 8. *DV* 23 Dec 1939, p. 1. *DV* 26 Dec 1939, p. 1. *DV* 29 Dec 1939, p. 1, 8. *DV* 4 Jan 1940, p. 2, 10. *DV* 17 Jan 1940, p. 2. *DV* 30 Jan 1940, p. 3. *DW* 9 Jan 1940 [Review]. *FD* 5 Dec 1936, p. 6. *FD* 3 Jan 1937, p. 10. *FD* 1 Apr 1937, p. 16. *FD* 19 Apr 1937, p. 2. *HR* 10 Jul 1936, p. 1. *HR* 17 Sep 1936, p. 1. *HR* 29 Sep 1936, p. 1. *HR* 9 Oct 1936, p. 14. *HR* 21 Oct 1936, p. 1. *HR* 26 Oct 1936, p. 1. *HR* 21 Dec 1936, p. 9. *HR* 23 Dec 1936, p. 16. *HR* 9 Feb 1937, p. 4. *HR* 23 Mar 1937, p. 1. *HR* 1 Apr 1937, p. 3. *HR* 8 Jun 1937, p. 1. *HR* 16 Jun 1937, p. 2. *HR* 22 Jun 1937, p. 1. *HR* 22 Oct 1937, p. 1. *HR* 23 Oct 1937, p. 3. *HR* 10 Nov 1937, p. 1. *HR* 22 Nov 1937, p. 3. *HR* 8 Dec 1937, pp. 1-8. *HR* 9 Dec 1937, p. 1. *HR* 10 Jan 1938, p. 2. *HR* 18 Jan 1938, p. 3. *HR* 2 Mar 1938, p. 9. *HR* 15 Mar 1938, p. 5. *HR* 8 Aug 1938, p. 1, 4, 8. *HR* 27 Aug 1938, p. 1. *HR* 22 Oct 1938, p. 1. *HR* 10 Nov 1938, p. 2. *HR* 22 Nov 1938, p. 1. *HR* 12 Dec 1938, p. 1. *HR* 31 Dec 1938, p. 1. *HR* 2 Jan 1939, p. 2. *HR* 5 Jan 1939, p. 1. *HR* 6 Jan 1939, p. 1. *HR* 9 Jan 1939, pp. 1, 3-4. *HR* 10 Jan 1939, p. 3. *HR* 12 Jan 1939, p. 4. *HR* 13 Jan 1939, p. 3. *HR* 14 Jan 1939, p. 1. *HR* 17 Jan 1939, p. 1. *HR* 29 Jan 1939, p. 4. *HR* 31 Jan 1939, p. 4 *HR* 13 Feb 1939, p. 11. *HR* 14 Feb 1939, p. 1. *HR* 15 Feb 1939, p. 1. *HR* 24 Feb 1939, p. 2. *HR* 2 Mar 1939, p. 4. *HR* 10 Mar 1939, p. 1. *HR* 18 Apr 1939, p. 1. *HR* 19 Apr 1939, p. 2. *HR* 22 Apr 1939, pp. 6-7. *HR* 25 Apr 1939, p. 1. *HR* 26 Apr 1939, p. 8. *HR* 28 Apr 1939, p. 1. *HR* 2 May 1939, p. 6. *HR* 3 May 1939, p. 2. *HR* 2 Dec 1939, p. 2, 5. *HR* 4 Dec 1939, p. 2. *HR* 5 Dec 1939, p. 2. *HR* 7 Dec 1939, p. 4. *HR* 8 Dec 1939, p. 4, 6. *HR* 9 Dec 1936, p. 3, 6. *HR* 12 Dec 1939, p. 1. *HR* 13 Dec 1939, p. 1, 3, 5 [Review p. 3]. *HR* 15 Dec 1939, p. 6. *HR* 18 Dec 1939, p. 2. *HR* 21 Dec 1939, p. 1, 3. *HR* 30 Dec 1939, p. 3. *HR* 2 Jan 1940, p. 2. *HR* 3 Jan 1940, p. 1, 4. *HR* 12 Jan 1940, p. 2. *HR* 16 Jan 1940, p. 7. *HR* 1 May 1940, p. 1. *HS* 23 Dec 1939, p. 11. *House and Garden* Nov 1939. *Liberty* 27 Jan 1940, p. 51. *Life* 18 Dec 1939, pp. 78-85. *Life* 25 Dec 1939, pp. 9-13. *Look* 18 Jul 1939, pp. 8-13. *MAD* Jan 1991, pp. 42-47. *MPD* 4 Feb 1938, p. 4. *MPD* 7 Jul 1938, p. 2. *MPD* 2 Aug 1938, p. 1, 4. *MPD* 5 Aug 1938, p. 1, 6. *MPD* 26 Aug 1938, p. 1, 13. *MPD* 13 Dec 1939. *MPH* 3 Sep 1938, p. 75. *MPH* 18 Feb 1939, p. 9. *MPH* 2 Dec 1939, p. 17. *MPH* 16 Dec 1939, p. 23, 29 [Review]. *MPH* 30 Dec 1939, p. 7. *MPH* 10 Feb 1940, p. 8. *MPH* 20 Jul 1940, p. 9. *NYT* 19 Mar 1937. *NYT* 24 Mar 1937. *NYT* 23 Apr 1939. *NYT* 24 Jun 1938. *NYT* 20 Dec 1939, p. 31 [Review]. *Photo* Mar 1937, pp. 21-24. *Time* 25 Dec 1939. *Var* 20 Dec 1939, p. 14 [Review]. *Woman's Home Companion* Feb 1940.

THE GOOD BAD GIRL (*foreign version*) *see* **EL PASADO ACUSA**

THE GOOD-BAD WIFE (French Amricans)

Vera McCord Productions, Inc. *Dist* State Rights. Oct **1920** [©Vera McCord Productions, Inc.; 7 Jun 1920; LP15224]. Si; b&w. 6 reels.

Supv Vera McCord. *Dir* Chester DeVonde. *Scen* Paul Price. *Cam* Abe Fried.

Source: Based on the short story "The Wild Fawn" by Mary Imlay Taylor in *Munsey's Magazine* (Sep 1919-Feb 1920).

Cast: Sidney Mason (*William Carter*), Dorothy Green (*Fanchon La Fare*), Moe Lee (*Toy To*), Leslie Stowe (*Johnson Carter*), Mathilde Brundage (*Mrs. Carter*), Albert Hackett (*Leigh Carter*), Pauline Dempsey (*Mirandy*), J. Wesley Jenkins (*Old Lucas*), Bessie Stinson, Erville Alderson, J. Thornton Baston, Beatrice Jordan, John Ardizoni.

Drama. William Carter, a young Virginian in Paris, becomes enchanted with music hall dancer Fanchon La Fare. After William reluctantly returns to America, Fanchon follows him, and when she is threatened with deportation because of an irregularity in her passport, William marries her. The marriage causes consternation in the upright Carter family, which is compounded when Fanchon performs one of her dances at a church benefit. At the conclusion of her dance, Fanchon sees a stranger in the audience and faints. Later, the same man appears at the Carter residence and demands to see her. Leigh Carter, William's younger brother, becomes angered and shoots the man. At the trial, Fanchon confesses that the stranger was her estranged husband whom she had been forced to marry when she was but a child. The crime thus clarified, Leigh is freed, and Fanchon, who had been expelled earlier from the Carter house, is welcomed back by her husband and his family. *Bigamy. Dancers. French. French Americans. Murder. Southerners. Americans in foreign countries. Brothers. Confession (Law). Marriage–Forced. Paris (France). Propriety. Trials. Virginia.*

Note: The story was also published as a novel in New York in 1920. The film was originally entitled *The Wild Fawn*. It was the first film made by Vera McCard Productions, Inc., and was produced at the Bacon-Backer studios in New York. Some sources credit Vera McCord with direction. The film was re-released by Federated Film Exchanges of America in 1921.

MPN 30 Oct 1920, p. 3451. *MPN* 13 Nov 1920, p. 3697. *MPW* 24 Aug 1920, p. 1020. *MPW* 30 Oct 1920, p. 1294. *Wid's* 24 Oct 1920, p. 6.

GOOD COMPANY *see* **A LADY'S PROFESSION**

THE GOOD-FOR-NOTHING (Native Americans)
Essanay Film Mfg Co.; Special Features Dept. *Dist* General Film Co. 8 Jun **1914**. Si; b&w. 4 reels.
Dir George M. Anderson.
Cast: George M. Anderson (*Gilbert Sterling*), Lee Willard (*Ralph Sterling*), Elsa Lorimer (*Gertrude Chapin*), Carl Stockdale (*John Sterling*), Evelyn Selbie (*Mrs. Sterling*), Victor Potel (*Old clerk*).
Comedy-drama. Gilbert Sterling, a drunkard and ne'er-do-well, is disowned by his wealthy father, over the protests of his indulgent mother. Years later, after Gilbert's brother Ralph has ruined the family in dishonest stock speculation, the Sterlings seek refuge in an almshouse. Meanwhile, Gilbert has become a changed man in a Western mining town where he saves an Indian who is suffering from smallpox from being lynched by vigilantes. Gilbert cares for the dying man and, in gratitude, the Indian leaves him a rich mine. Now wealthy, Gilbert returns East, takes his parents out of the poorhouse, and ruins Ralph on the stock exchange. Finally, he is reconciled with his brother and his parents and reestablishes the family business. *Bankruptcy. Brothers. Family honor. Family relationships. Moral reformation. Ne'er-do-wells. Disinheritance. Indians of North America. Inheritance. Lynching. Mines. Poorhouses. Smallpox. Stock market.*

Note: The film was shot at the Essanay studios in Niles, CA.
MPW 23 May 1914, p. 1092. *MPW* 6 Jun 1914, p. 1454. *NYDM* 18 Mar 1914, p. 33. *Var* 12 Jun 1914, p. 21.

GOOD LUCK HEBREWS *see* **MAZEL TOV YIDDEN**

GOOD LUCK, MR. YATES (German Americans, Greek Americans, Russian Americans)
Columbia Pictures Corp. *Dist* Columbia Pictures Corp. 29 Jun **1943**; Prod: 1 Mar—16 Apr 1943 [©Columbia Pictures Corp.; 21 Jun 1943; LP12101]. Sd (Western Electric Mirrophonic Recording); b&w. 6,339 ft. 68-69 min. PCA cert no. 9389.
Prod David J. Chatkin. *Dir* Ray Enright. [*Asst dir* Theodore Joos]. [*Dial dir* Harry Seymour]. *Scr* Lou Breslow and Adele Comandini. *Story* Hal Smith and Sam Rudd. *Dir of photog* Philip Tannura. *Art dir* Lionel Banks. *Assoc* Edward Jewell. *Film ed* Richard Fantl. *Set dec* Frank Tuttle. *Mus* John Leipold. *Mus dir* M. W. Stoloff. [*Sd eng* John Goodrich].
Cast: Claire Trevor [(*Ruth Jones*)], Jess Barker [(*Oliver Yates*)], Edgar Buchanan [(*"Jonesy" Jones*)], Tom Neal [(*Charlie Edmonds*)], Albert Basserman [(*Dr. Carl Hesser*)], Henry Armetta [(*Mike Zaloris*)], Scotty Beckett [(*Jimmy Dixon*)], Tommy Cook [(*Johnny Zaloris*)], [Frank Sully (*Joe Briggs*)], [Douglas Leavitt (*Monty King*)], [Rosina Galli (*Katy Zaloris*)], [Billy Roy (*Plunkett*)], [Conrad Binyon (*Bob Coles*)], [Bobby Larson (*Ross*)], [Rudy Wissler (*Wilson*)], [The Bob Mitchell Boy Choir], [The Sheriff's Boys Band], [Nan Wynn], [Barbara Brown (*Lucille Cosgrove*)], [Shimen Ruskin (*Peter Miliach*)], [Adia Kuznetzoff (*Gregory Rozniloff*)], [Edward Fielding

(*Col. Fredericks*)], [David Clyde (*Angus*)], [Dickie Meyers (*Norwaski*)], [Bobby Cooper (*Benson*)], [Harry McKim (*Rawlins*)], [George Magrill (*Soldier*)], [Hugh Beaumont (*Adjutant*)], [Horace MacMahon (*Truck driver*)], [Shirley Patterson (*Secretary*)], [David Alison, Bill Lally, Frank O'Connor (*Policemen*)], [Pat Flaherty (*Sgt. Moore*)], [Neil Reagan (*Enlistment officer*)], [Pierre Watkin (*Major*)], [Lewis Wilson (*Parkhurst*)], [Albert Ray, Dickie Dillon (*Cadets*)], [Douglass Drake (*Keeney*)], [William Forrest (*Thurston*)], [Robert Hill (*Myers*)], [Peggy Converse (*Amy Wallace*)], [John Hamilton (*Allison*)], [Jack Rice (*Steve*)], [Brian O'Hara (*Potts*)], Lew Harvey (*Bennie*), [Al Hill, Eddie Hall, Eddie Fetherston (*Workers*)], [Bud Geary (*Guard*)], [Eddy Chandler (*Riveter*)], [Mina Cunard, Adele Mara, Vi Athens, Neila Hart (*Welders*)], [Oscar Boetticher, Jr. (*Hocoy McManus*)], [Larry McGrath (*Referee*)], [Robert Perry (*Timekeeper*)], [Harvey Parry (*Standby*)], [Danny Mummert].

Homefront, **Drama**. [*Print viewed*]. Oliver Yates, a well-respected teacher at Carlyle Military Academy, realizes that he is losing the admiration of his pupils, who are disappointed that he has not quit teaching to enlist in the military. Yates asks Colonel Fredericks, the head of the school, to waive his essential status so that he can enlist, but Fredericks tells him that teaching is just as important as fighting, particularly when someone like Jimmy Dixon is depending upon him. Jimmy, a former juvenile delinquent, is now Yates's protege, and Yates is determined to see that Jimmy makes the most of his opportunities at Carlyle. Yates agrees to stay, but when Jimmy gets in a fight defending him against the other boys, who call him a draft dodger, Yates enlists despite Fredericks' objections. Jimmy is thrilled, and all of the boys join in a stirring ceremony to bid Yates farewell. After his physical, however, Yates is declared 4-F due to a perforated eardrum. Yates is devastated, but his old pal, Joe Briggs, whom he meets again at the induction center, takes him to Dr. Carl Hesser, a German refugee who states that he can repair the injury enough to change Yates's draft status. Joe, who convinces Yates not to tell the boys about the complications, as he intends to join the Army as soon as possible, then takes Yates to his boardinghouse, run by Greek-American Mike Zaloris and his wife Katy. Because Yates must stay in town for his ear treatments, he gets a job at the local shipyard, where most of the other boarders work. Yates meets the others, including would-be actor Monty King, boxer Charlie Edmonds, Ruth Jones and her father "Jonesy," and Russian-Americans Peter Miliach and Gregory Rozniloff. Despite his unfamiliarity with manual labor, Yates digs into his new job, earning the admiration of Ruth and the enmity of Charlie, who is also fond of Ruth. Meanwhile, Joe collects the mail that the unwitting boys have sent to Yates at the Army camp and gives it to Yates, who replies with Army-issued form letters supplied by Joe. The boys are thrilled with the letters they receive, but Charlie, hoping to find something to make Ruth dislike Yates, finds the letters addressed to him in the Army camp, and leads the other boarders to believe that he is a deserter. Matters worsen when the boys stop by the Army camp and learn that Yates was never inducted. Believing that Yates is missing, Fredericks initiates a search for him, while Yates, unaware of the uproar, presses Dr. Hesser to operate on him in order to hurry his treatments. When Dr. Hesser calls the boardinghouse to inform them that Yates will not be coming home that night, Charlie assumes that the doctor's thick German accent means that he is a Nazi, and that Yates is a spy working with him. Charlie whips the other boarders and shipyard workers into a frenzy against Yates, although Ruth still believes in him. When Yates returns to the boardinghouse after his surgery, about which he has told no one, he finds Jimmy waiting for him. Jimmy states that after two policemen confirmed Yates's address and civilian status, he had to see for himself why his teacher lied to him. Yates explains the situation to him, and Jimmy swells with pride at the thought of his important work in the shipyard. When Yates learns of Charlie's rumors, however, he rushes to the yard, where Charlie hits him without giving him a chance to explain. As the men fight, they break a pipe and start a fire in the hold of a ship being built, and at great peril to himself, Yates rescues Charlie and stops the fire from spreading to the other ships. Yates is declared a hero, and although his now-worsened ear injury will permanently prevent him from joining the Army, the boys are still proud of him. They ask him to return to the school, but Yates decides to stay with Ruth and continue his important work at the shipyard. *Deception. False accusations. Hero worship. Military service, Voluntary. Schoolteachers. Shipyards. 4-F. Adolescents. Boardinghouses. Boxers.*

Ears. German Americans. Greek Americans. Jealousy. Letters. Military schools. Missing persons. Patriotism. Physicians. Rescues. Rumors. Russian Americans. Ship fires.

Note: The working title of this film was *Right Guy*. Although a *HR* production chart places Constance Worth in the cast, her participation in the released film has not been confirmed. Although an Apr 1943 *HR* news item noted that The Three Stooges were to appear in the film, and The Stooges' names are listed in the CBCS, they did not appear in the viewed print, nor were they mentioned in any of the reviews.

DV 18 Oct 1943, p. 3. *HR* 3 Mar 1943, p. 7. *HR* 19 Mar 1943, p. 10. *HR* 2 Apr 1943, p. 3. *MPH* 19 Jun 1943. *MPHPD* 5 Jun 1943, p. 1351. *MPHPD* 19 Jun 1943, p. 1374. *Var* 21 Jul 1943, p. 22.

GOOD MORNING, MISS DOVE (Jewish Americans, Polish
    Americans)

Twentieth Century-Fox Film Corp. *Dist* Twentieth Century-Fox Film Corp. Nov **1955**; New York opening: 23 Nov 1955; *Prod:* 11 Jul—mid-Aug 1955 [©Twentieth Century-Fox Film Corp.; 10 Nov 1955; LP5864]. Sd (Western Electric Sound System); col (DeLuxe); CinemaScope; CinemaScope lenses by Bausch & Lomb. 12 reels, 9,668 ft. 107 min. PCA cert no. 17636.

[*Exec prod* Darryl F. Zanuck]. *Prod* Samuel G. Engel. *Dir* Henry Koster. *Asst dir* Ad Schaumer. *Scr* Eleanore Griffin. *Dir of photog* Leon Shamroy. *Spec photog eff* Ray Kellogg. *Color consultant* Leonard Doss. *Art dir* Lyle R. Wheeler and Mark-Lee Kirk. *Film ed* William Reynolds. *Set dec* Walter M. Scott and Paul S. Fox. *Ward dir* Charles LeMaire. *Cost des* Mary Wills. *Mus* Leigh Harline. *Cond* Lionel Newman. *Orch* Bernard Mayers. *Sd* Eugene Grossman and Harry M. Leonard. *Makeup* Ben Nye. *Hair styling by* Helen Turpin.

Source: Based on the novel *Good Morning, Miss Dove* by Frances Gray Patton (New York, 1954).

Cast: JENNIFER JONES [(*Miss Dove*)], Robert Stack [(*Tom Baker*)], Kipp Hamilton [(*Jincey Baker*)], Robert Douglas [(*John Porter*)], Peggy Knudsen [(*Billy Jean*)], Marshall Thompson [(*Mr. Pendleton*)], Chuck Connors [(*Bill Holloway*)], Biff Elliot [(*Alex Burnham*)], Jerry Paris [(*Maurice Levine*)], Mary Wickes [(*Miss Ellwood*)], [Ted Marc (*David Burnham*)], [Dick Stewart (*Dr. Temple*)], [Richard Deacon (*Mr. Spivey*)], [Than Wyenn (*Mr. Levine*)], [Leslie Bradley (*Alphonse Dave*)], [Edward Firestone (*Fred Makepeace*)], [Cheryl Callaway (*Annabel*)], [Mark Engel (*Marke*)], [Tim Cagney (*Bobsie*)], [Bill Walker (*Henry*)], [Robert Lynn, Sr. (*Dr. Hurley*)], [Kenneth Osmond (*Tommy Baker, age 9*)], [Paul Engle (*Alex Burnham, age 9*)], [Tiger Fafara (*Fred Makepeace, as a child*)], [John Hensley (*Bill Holloway, age 6*)], [Gary Pagett (*Bill Holloway, age 12*)], [Alfred Caizza (*Maurice, as a child*)], [Martha Wentworth (*Grandma Holloway*)], [Virginia Christine (*Mrs. Rigsbee*)], [Junius Matthews (*Mr. Pruitt*)], [Reba Tassell (*Polly Burnham*)], [Gary Diamond (*Harrison*)], [Myna Cunard (*Mrs. Aldredge*)], [A. Cameron Grant (*Mr. Prouty*)], [Janet Brandt (*Mrs. Levine*)], [Linda Brace (*Jacqueline Wood*)], [Ann Tyrell (*Mrs. Makepeace*)], [Nan Dolan (*Mrs. Wood*)], [Betty Caulfield (*Mother*)], [Elmore Vincent (*Mailman*)], [Vincent Perry (*Principal*)], [Steve Darrell (*Police captain*)], [Milas Clark, Leonard Ingoldsby, Tim Haldeman, Michael Gainey, Cary Savage (*Boys*)], [Ernest Dotson (*Boy at fountain*)], [Jo Gilbert (*Young matron*)], [Pamela Beaird, Carol Sydes, Lydia Reed (*Girls*)], [Jean Inness (*Night nurse*)], [Maude Prickett, Catherine Howard (*Nurses*)], [John Hiestand (*Prison guard*)], [Ed Mundy (*Hearse driver*)], [Tim Johnson (*Freshman*)], [Jean Andren (*Secretary to Mr. Dove*)], [Mae Marsh (*Woman in bank*)], [Sarah Selby, Mary Carroll (*Teachers*)], [Virginia Carroll (*Ann*)], [Elizabeth Flournoy (*Mildred*)], [George Dunn (*Janitor*)], [Herb Vigren (*Police surgeon*)], [Charles Webster, Richard Cutting (*Husbands*)], [Jane Crowley], [Eleanore Vogel], [Sam McDaniel], [William Hughes].

Domestic, Drama. [*Print viewed*]. In the small town of Liberty Hill, Miss Dove, a prim schoolteacher who is known as "terrible Miss Dove" because she is a strict disciplinarian, keeps a boy after class for swearing, but when she experiences sharp pains, sends him home to get his father, Dr. Tom Baker. As Miss Dove waits, she remembers years earlier when she first returned home from college: Miss Dove goes to see her father, the town banker, as soon as she arrives, and is warmly greeted by the bank's vice-president, John Porter. That night, her father dies suddenly after Miss Dove tells him that she is in love with an archaeologist named Pendleton. Miss Dove is startled to learn that her father had embezzled $11,000 from the bank, although John stresses that the money was merely "borrowed." To avoid a scandal, Miss Dove vows to repay the money by working as a schoolteacher.

Miss Dove then rejects Pendleton's marriage proposal and sacrifices her own happiness to work at the local elementary school. Back in class, Tom, one of Miss Dove's former pupils, insists that she be hospitalized. The attending nurse is another former student, Billy Jean, who is in love with her former classmate, policeman Bill Holloway, who reveres Miss Dove. Miss Dove recalls Bill as a child: Bill, a poverty-stricken orphan being raised by his alcoholic grandmother Annie, comes to class in filthy, ill-fitting clothes. Bill's ethics, however, outclass those of some of the wealthier students, and Miss Dove encourages him without showing undue affection. While maintaining her usual strict discipline, Miss Dove lavishes attention on Bill, allowing him to do yardwork at her house in exchange for lunch, and eventually buys him a graduation suit. Years later, after Annie dies, Miss Dove supports Bill, and when he returns from Marine service after World War II, she is the first person he visits. Miss Dove also recollects Tom's wife Virginia, who is now happily married and pregnant, but previously seemed misguided. Billy Jean, meanwhile, confesses that her own child is illegitimate, and that she claims to be a widow to protect her daughter. Billy Jean was severely disappointed because Bill broke their engagement when she admitted her transgression. The next morning, renowned playwright Maurice Levine, and convict Fred Makepeace, two more former pupils, come to visit Miss Dove. Miss Dove recalls when Maurice, then an eleven-year-old Polish refugee, first came to her class: Maurice is placed in the first grade so he can learn English, and she soon discovers he has a vivid imagination. However, his peers tease the bright Jewish boy, calling him "Rab," short for the word "rabbi." During geography lessons, Miss Dove instructs her class about the Jewish homeland, noting that "rabbi" is a term of respect. She then arranges for Maurice's family to host a special dinner for her class, in order to demonstrate that a Jewish family is the same as any other family. Miss Dove has since followed Maurice's career, and he thanks her for attending the opening night of his play. She then realizes that Fred has escaped from jail, and tactfully suggests that Bill go to lunch with Fred and Maurice, then escort Fred back to prison. Fred is grateful to Miss Dove, as is Bill after he hears her praise Billy Jean for being genteel. Not long after, John visits Miss Dove with news that the Board of Rotarians has elected to pay for her medical bills. John insists that it is not out of charity, but respect for her, as he feels indebted to her. Miss Dove then recalls years earlier when there was a run on the bank: A national scare causes anxious patrons to crowd the bank in order to withdraw their money before the bank closes. Although John tries to dispel rumors about the bank's closing, even loyal customers demand their money. Just a few minutes before closing, Miss Dove quietly makes her way through the throng and, with her usual air of authority, goes to the front of the line to make a deposit. When she tries to fill out a slip, she pretends that her pen is out of ink and asks for another. To further delay the process, Miss Dove calmly notes that the pen John gives her is also out of ink, once and, given another pen, slowly fills out the deposit slip. She finishes the transaction just at closing time, and reminds the protesting patrons that John is merely obeying federal law. John is still grateful for Miss Dove's action. Tom now reports that Miss Dove has a tumor on her spine which will require an operation. Miss Dove expresses her confidence in Tom's skill as a surgeon, and when he warns her the operation could be fatal, she gives him her father's pocketwatch, which he has always admired. The next day, after Tom begins surgery, the principal dismisses class for the day, while Fred escapes from jail again to go to Liberty Hill, and Bill reunites with Billy Jean. When Miss Dove finally awakens from her surgery, Tom returns the watch as a sign that all is well, and reports that Virginia has given birth to twins. The church bells chime as everyone gathers in the street below to celebrate the successful operation. In typical fashion, Miss Dove asks that the principal resume classes so that her students can study for an upcoming test. *Children. Debt. Ethics. Schoolteachers. Self-sacrifice. Small town life. Spinsters. Assimilation (Sociology). Bank failures. Bank presidents. Bigotry. Embezzlement. Fathers and daughters. Gratitude. Illegitimacy. Jailbreaks. Jews. Nurses. Operations, Surgical. Physicians. Playwrights. Police. Polish Americans. Poverty. Pregnancy. Proposals (Marital). War refugees. Watches.*

Note: Frances Gray Patton's novel incorporated three short stories that had previously appeared in *The Ladies Home Journal:* "The Terrible Miss Dove," "Miss Dove and Judgment Day" and "Miss Dove and the Maternal Instinct." According to information in the Twentieth Century-Fox Records of the Legal Department at the UCLA Arts—Special Collections Library, the studio paid

$52,500 for the rights to the novel. The Twentieth Century-Fox Produced Scripts Collection, also at UCLA, reveals that the Jewish family dinner portrayed in the film was originally written as a more extensive Passover seder.

AmCin Sep 1955, p. 508. *Box* 19 Nov 1955. *DV* 10 Nov 1955, p. 3. *Exb* 30 Nov 1955, p.4067. *FD* 22 Nov 1955, p. 6. *Har* 19 Nov 1955, p. 186. *HR* 8 Jul 1955, p. 13. *HR* 12 Aug 1955, p. 12. *HR* 10 Nov 1955, p. 3. *MPHPD* 19 Nov 1955, p. 673. *NYT* 24 Nov 1955, p. 41. *Var* 16 Nov 1955, p. 6.

THE GOOD PROVIDER (Jewish Americans)

Cosmopolitan Productions. *Dist* Paramount Pictures. 30 Apr **1922**; New York premiere: ca2 Apr 1922 [©International Film Service Co., Inc.; 19 Apr 1922; LP17819]. Si; b&w. 8 reels, 7,753 ft.

Dir Frank Borzage. *Scen* John Lynch. *Photog* Chester Lyons.

Source: Based on the short story "The Good Provider" by Fannie Hurst in *The Saturday Evening Post* (15 Aug 1914).

Cast: Vera Gordon (*Becky Binswanger*), Dore Davidson (*Julius Binswanger*), Miriam Battista (*Pearl Binswanger*), Vivienne Osborne (*Pearl Binswanger*), William (Buster) Collier, Jr. (*Izzy Binswanger*), John Roche (*Max Teitlebaum*), Ora Jones (*Mrs. Teitlebaum*), Edward Phillips (*Broadway sport*), Muriel Martin (*Flapper*), James Devine (*Mr. Boggs*), Blanche Craig (*Mrs. Boggs*), Margaret Severn (*Specialty dancer*).

Society, Melodrama. Working as a peddler in a small American town, Julius Binswanger, a poor Jewish immigrant, becomes prosperous; fifteen years later, great changes have transformed the community, and Binswanger finds difficulty in competing with the city trade. Since his daughter, Pearl, is in love with Max Teitlebaum, a wealthy New Yorker, and because his children chafe at small-town life, Binswanger, with the help of their mother, is persuaded to move to New York. Fast life at the Hotel Wellington, with exorbitant prices, appalls Julius; yet, he rejects his son Izzy's commercial ideas. Business troubles multiply, and when Izzy requests a loan to take over the business with Max, Julius passionately announces his bankruptcy and plans to take an overdose of sleeping powder. Max, however, explains to Pearl that he will ask no dowry from her and wishes to form a partnership with her father. Becky announces the good news to Julius, Max and Pearl are happily united, and the family returns home. *Bankruptcy. Immigrants. Jews. New York City. Small town life.*

ETR 22 Apr, 1922, p. 1519. *FD* 16 Apr 1922. *MPW* 22 Apr 1922. *MPW* 29 Apr 1922, p. 964. *Var* 14 Apr 1922, p. 39.

GOOD-BYE, BILL (German Americans)

Famous Players-Lasky Corp.; Robert Brunton Productions. *Dist* Famous Players-Lasky Corp.; Paramount Pictures. 15 Dec **1918** [©Famous Players-Lasky Corp.; 7 Dec 1918; LP13143]. Si; b&w. 5 reels, 4,854 ft.

Pres Adolph Zukor. *Dir* John Emerson. *Scen* John Emerson and Anita Loos. *Cam* Jacques Monteran.

Cast: Shirley Mason (*Elsie Dresser*), Ernest Truex (*Teddy Swift*), Joseph Allen (*Kaiser William the Nut*), Joseph Burke (*Herr Dresser*), Carl de Planta (*Prince Willie*), H. E. Koser (*Herr Tonik*), Herbert Frank (*Count Von Born Effry-Minutt*).

World War I, Comedy. During World War I, Herr Dresser, a German-American professor from West Hoboken, New Jersey, invents a "moustache fixer," which stiffens the whiskers, making the wearer look very fierce. Much to the consternation of Dresser's daughter Elsie, a patriotic American, Kaiser Wilhelm calls them to Berlin to begin mass production of the tonic for the German army. Elsie's boyfriend, Teddy Swift, is particularly disturbed by this turn of events and decides to earn enough money to follow her to Germany. When the United States joins the war, Teddy is among the first to enlist, and soon he finds himself in Berlin trying to help Elsie escape from prison. After several narrow escapes, the two make their way to the moustache factory and blow it up. Brought before the Kaiser, they are rescued when American troops storm the palace, and the Kaiser loses his moustache and the war. *Berlin (Germany). German Americans. Inventions. Loyalty. World War I.* Factories. Germany. Army. Imprisonment. Military service, Voluntary. Palaces. Prison escapes. Professors. Sabotage. Sieges. West Hoboken (NJ). Wilhelm II, German Emperor, 1859-1941.

Note: The title of the film was changed from *Gosh Darn the Kaiser.* An ad gave the title as *Good-bye Bill!*.

ETR 14 Dec 1918, p. 161. *ETR* 28 Dec 1918, p. 264. *MPN* 21 Dec 1918, p. 3769. *MPN* 4 Jan 1918, p. 3. *MPW* 14 Dec 1918, p. 1249. *MPW* 28 Dec 1918, p. 1558. *Var* 31 Jan 1919, p. 52. *Wid's* 8 Dec 1918, pp. 11-12.

GOODBYE MR. CREEPS *see* **PROFESSOR CREEPS**

GOSH DARN THE KAISER *see* **GOOD-BYE, BILL**

GOT, MENTSH, UN TAYVL *see* **GOD, MAN AND DEVIL**

LA GRAN JORNADA (Spanish language)

Fox Film Corp.; A Raoul Walsh Production. *Dist* Fox Film Corp. **1931**; New York opening: 13 Feb 1931; Prod: Nov—Dec 1930. Sd; b&w. Length undetermined. Spanish language.

Supv William Goetz. *Dir* David Howard. *Asst dir* Sam Schneider. *Story* Hal G. Evarts. *Spanish vers* Francisco Moré de la Torre. *Photog* Sidney Wagner. *Film ed* Jerry Webb. *Sd* Bernard Freericks.

Cast: Jorge Lewis (*Raúl Colman*), Carmen Guerrero (*Isabel Prados*), Roberto Guzmán (*Tomás*), Martín Garralaga (*Martín*), Allan Garcia (*Flack "El Rojo"*), Charles Stevens (*López*), Tito Davison (*Daniel*), Carlos Villarías (*Orena*), Adriana Délano (*Rosita*), Julio Villarreal (*Carson*), Lucio Villegas (*Sacerdote*), Renée Torres, Aurelio Manrique.

Western. [*Not viewed*]. [The following plot summary is based on the English-language version of this film, *The Big Trail*; character names refer to that version. For further information regarding the English-language version, please see the note below and the entry for *The Big Trail* in the *AFI Catalog of Feature Films, 1921-30.*] A wagon train of eastern pioneers leaves from Westport, Mississippi, to travel the Oregon Trail and to extend the boundaries of the American Republic to the Pacific Northwest. Their leader is scout Breck Coleman, who has pledged to avenge the death of a trapper friend. En route, the travelers experience a buffalo hunt, the treacherous fording of a river, a snowstorm, an Indian attack on the wagons, and the lowering of wagons, cattle, women, and children over a mountainside to pick up the trail to the West. Breck is enamored of Ruth Cameron, though he almost loses her to Bill Thorpe, and gradually establishes that Red Flack is the murderer of his friend. Thorpe, under Red's influence, tries to kill Breck but is himself shot. After reaching the Oregon country, Breck sets out in a snowstorm to avenge his pal's death and ultimately brings the villain to his end. *Bison, American. Blizzards. Courtship. Indians of North America. Mississippi. Oregon. Oregon Trail. Pioneers. Revenge. Scouts (Frontier).*

Note: Fox made four foreign-language versions of the 1930 film, *The Big Trail*, which was directed by Raoul Walsh and starred John Wayne and Marguerite Churchill (see *AFI Catalog of Feature Films, 1921-30*; F2.0416). In addition to versions in Spanish and French, German and Italian versions were also produced, but no record has been found of U.S. exhibitions of the French version. The Spanish version was released in Spain under the title *Horizontes nuevos.*

Other language version(s):
La piste des géants (French language)
1931. Sd; b&w. French language.
Dir Pierre Couderc.

Gaston Glass (*Pierre Calmin:* **French-language cast:**), Jeanne Helbling (*Denise Vernon*), Margot Rousseroy (*Yvette*), Raoul Paoli (*Flack*), Louis Mercier (*Lopez*), Jacques Vanaire (*Mayer*), Jacques Jou-Jerville (*Wellmore*), Frank O'Neill (*Lucien*), André Ferrier (*Blancart*), Emile Chautard (*Padre*), George Davis (*Pépin*), Jules Raucourt. [*French version not viewed*].
Die grosse Fahrt (German language)
1931; New York showing: 2 Jun 1932. German language.
Dir Lewis Seiler.
German-language cast: Theo Shall, Marion Lessing, Ulrich Haupt, Arnold Korff. [*German version not viewed*]
Il grande sentiero (Italian language)
1931; Los Angeles showing: 21 Feb 1931. Italian language.
Dir Louis Loeffler.
Italian-language cast: Franco Corsaro, Luisa Caselotti, Guido Trento, Franco Puglia, Agostino Borgato, Lucino Garuffi, Violet Galeotti. [*Italian version not viewed*].

CM Apr 1931, p. 327. *HF* 11 Oct 1930, p. 14. *HF* 8 Nov 1930, p. 14.

LA GRAN PELEA *see* **LA FUERZA DEL QUERER**

GRANADEROS DEL AMOR (Spanish language)

Fox Film Corp. *Dist* Fox Film Corp. **1934**; Santiago, Chile opening: 15 May 1934; New York opening: 31 Aug 1934; Prod: Dec 1933—Jan 1934 [©Fox Film Corp.; 12 Sep 1934; LP4946]. Sd (Western Electric Noiseless Recording); b&w. 8 reels, 7,184 ft. 80 min. Passed by the National Board of Review. Spanish language.

Supervisión de [*Supervised by*] John Stone. *Dirección de* [*Directed by*] John Reinhardt. *Original de* [*Original by*] William Kernell and John Reinhardt. *Versión española de* [*Spanish version by*] José López Rubio. [*Photog* Robert Planck]. *Dirección musical de* [*Musical director*] Samuel Kaylin. [*Sd* Al Bruzlin]. *Cuerpo de producción* [*Production staff*] Eugene Forde, Louis F. Moore and Lillian Wurtzel.

Song(s): "Qué es Hotcha-cha?" "Granaderos de Napoleón," "Babette," "La mujer fue inventada para obedecer" and "Bailemos, pues," music by William Kernell, lyrics by Raúl Roulien.

Cast: RAÚL ROULIEN (*Erich* [*Remberg*]/*Pierre* [*Laval*]), Conchita Montenegro (*Loni* [*von Keller*]), Valentín Parera (*Augusto*), Andrés de Segurola (*Barón von Keller*), Romualdo Tirado (*Peppi/Bombaste*), María Calvo (*Ana*), Carlos Villarías (*Empresario*), Lucio Villegas (*El Coronel* [*Dusac*]), Paco Moreno (*Burgomaestre*), Fred Malatesta (*Comandante*), [Tito Davison], [José María Sánchez García], [Francisco Marán], [Lita Santos], [José Peña "Pepet"], [Anita Camargo].

Historical, Musical, Drama. [*Print viewed*]. Author and actor Erich Remberg learns from his producer that his musical has been panned by the Viennese critics, who seem to prefer more romantic and less sexy productions these days. In order to find the inspiration to write an operetta, Erich goes with his friend Peppi to the von Keller castle in Tyrol. They are greeted by the eccentric Baron von Keller, who proudly shows them nonexistent antiques that only he can see. While investigating some strange noises he's heard in the middle of the night, Erich meets von Keller's daughter Loni, who is also curious about the room. She shows him a painting representing the Napoleonic invasion of Austria and tells him of her great-grandaunt, who scandalized the family. Erich imagines the scene with Loni playing the role of the baroness of the von Keller castle and himself as her French lover: Back in 1809, a French colonel insists on quartering at the von Keller home, and Loni dines with the invaders with reluctance. Lieutenant Pierre Laval approaches her later with romantic propositions, and she tells him that she will always be faithful to Augusto, an Austrian nobleman, who is away fighting the Napoleonic armies. However, she allows Pierre to woo her at a dance in the village, and when the French soldiers are ordered to retreat, Pierre chooses to stay behind with Loni. As the Austrians approach, Loni fears for Pierre's safety, and when Augusto and her father, the baron, arrive home, Pierre hides. Augusto proposes, but Loni is indifferent. Pierre disguises himself as the new butler and then convinces Loni to escape with him to the French encampment. The fleeing couple are caught trying to cross the Austrian lines, and Pierre reveals his true identity as one of Napoleon's men. Augusto orders Pierre's arrest, but two shots ring out, signalling a truce. The scene now shifts to a Viennese theatre, where Erich and Loni act out their roles in Erich's smash romantic musical. While taking their curtain calls, Erich and Loni joyfully announce their upcoming wedding to the audience. *Actors and actresses. Castles. French. Officers (Military). Playwrights. Romance. Tyrol (Austria)–History–Uprising of 1809. Vienna (Austria). Actors and actresses. Butlers. Dances. Desertion. Military. Dogs. Engagements. Escapes. Impersonation and imposture. Nobility. Paintings. Proposals (Marital). Theatrical producers.*

Note: The Twentieth Century-Fox Produced Scripts Collection at the UCLA Theater Arts Library contains a revised continuity by Paul Perez and Paul Schofield; however, it is not known if any of this material was used in the final film. The title was translated variously in reviews as "Love Grenadiers" and "Grenadiers of Love." The running time listed above was based on footage given in NYSA records.

CM May 1934, p. 246. *NYT* 4 Sep 1934, p. 23.

THE GRAND PARADE (Racial impersonation)

Pathé Exchange, Inc. *Dist* Pathé Exchange, Inc. 2 Feb **1930** [©Pathé Exchange, Inc.; 11 Mar 1930; LP1143]. Sd (Photophone); b&w. 8 reels, 7,450 ft.

Prod Edmund Goulding. *Dir* Fred Newmeyer. *Staged by* Frank Reicher. *Wrt* Edmund Goulding. *Photog* David Abel. *Art dir* Edward Jewell. *Set des* Ted Dickson. *Cost des* Gwen Wakeling. *Musical numbers* Richard Boleslavsky. *Rec eng* George Ellis and Cliff Stein. *Prod mgr* Gordon Cooper. *Props* Larry Haddock.

Song(s): "Moanin' for You," "Molly" and "Alone in the Rain," by Dan Dougherty and Edmund Goulding.

Cast: Helen Twelvetrees (*Molly*), Fred Scott (*Kelly*), Richard Carle (*Rand*), Marie Astaire (*Polly*), Russell Powell (*Calamity Johnson*), Bud Jamieson (*Honey Sullivan*), Jimmie Adams (*Jones*), Lillian Leighton (*Madam Stitch*), Spec O'Donnell (*Call Boy*), Sam Blum (*Sam*), Tom Malone (*Dougherty*), Jimmy Aubrey (*The Drunk*).

Romance. Kelly, a minstrel singer known as "Come-back" because of his weakness for liquor, degenerates because of his unhappiness with Polly Malone, a burlesque actress. He finds refuge in a cheap hotel, where he is cared for by Molly, a slavey. Rand, producer of the minstrel show to which Kelly was attached, induces him to return to work, and he finds success when he changes his song hit, "Polly," to "Molly." When Polly returns, Kelly introduces Molly as his wife, and she later consents to marry him. Molly joins the show and leads the grand parade at every performance. In Detroit, Kelly weakens and goes on a spree with Polly; rejected, Molly, who is pregnant, contemplates suicide. Realizing the truth, Kelly promises to go straight, and Molly beseeches God to help them both in their struggle. *Alcoholism. Burlesque. Courtship. Detroit (MI). Drudges. Marriage. Minstrel shows. Pregnancy. Religion.*

NYT 1 Feb 1930, p. 15. *Var* 5 Feb 1930, p. 24.

GRAND SLAM (Russian Americans)

First National Pictures, Inc.; controlled by Warner Bros. Pictures, Inc. *Dist* First National Pictures, Inc. 18 Mar **1933** [©First National Pictures, Inc.; 24 Feb 1933; LP3675]. Sd; b&w. 7 reels. 65 or 67 min. PCA cert no. 2612-R [3 Sep 1936].

Dir William Dieterle. [*Dial dir* Arthur Greville Collins]. *Scr* Erwin Gelsey and David Boehm. *Photog* Sid Hickox. *Art dir* Jack Okey. *Ed* Jack Killifer. *Gowns* Orry-Kelly. *Vitaphone Orch cond* Leo F. Forbstein.

Source: Based on the novel *Grand Slam: The Rise and Fall of a Bridge Wizard* by Benjamin Russell Herts (New York, 1932).

Cast: Paul Lukas (*Peter* [*Stanislavsky*]), Loretta Young (*Marcia* [*Stanislavsky*]), Frank McHugh (*Philip* [*also known as Speed*]), Glenda Farrell (*Blondie*), Helen Vinson (*Lola* [*Starr*]), Roscoe Karns (*Radio announcer*), Ferdinand Gottschalk (*Van Dorn*), [Walter Byron (*Barney*)], [Joseph Cawthorn (*Alex*)], [Paul Porcasi (*Nick*)], [Mary Doran (*Dot*)], [Lucien Prival (*Gregory*)], [Tom Dugan (*Artie*)], [Maurice Black (*Paul*)], [Lee Moran (*Harry*)], [Ruthelma Stevens (*Muriel*)], [Emma Dunn (*Sob sister*)], [Reginald Barlow (*Theodore*)], [Harry C. Bradley (*Referee*)], [Charles Levinson (*Ivan*)], [De Witt Jennings (*Detective Flynn*)], [George Cooper, John Sheehan (*Players*)], [Esther Howard (*Mary*)].

Comedy. [*Print viewed*]. Peter Stanislavsky works as a waiter in a Russian restaurant to support himself and his wife Marcia while he writes a serious novel. Although he thinks the game of bridge is supremely silly, Marcia forces him to learn the game. One evening, while he is catering a party of bridge players, the hostess, Lola Starr, drafts the attractive Peter to form a fourth at her table with bridge expert Van Dorn. Peter refuses to bid according to the Van Dorn system and to everyone's surprise wins the match. The next day, Philip, a ghost writer known as Speed, offers to write a book under Peter's name deliniating the Stanislavsky method. To promote the book, Peter and Marcia play in a variety of tournaments. They claim that because there are no rules in the Stanislavsky method, husbands and wives have no reason to fight with each other. In reality, Peter's criticisms of Marcia's bids cause quarrels between the two. Then when Lola asks Peter for private lessons, Marcia is convinced there is something between them, and she leaves Peter. Because he is in love with Marcia, Speed reveals that he wrote the book under Peter's name. Peter's waiter friends are angry because now they will lose the money they invested in the book. In order to pay them back, Peter approaches Van Dorn to propose a contest between the two of them. At the beginning of the contest, Peter is losing badly. Other players refuse to partner with Peter and it looks as though he will have to default until Marcia appears and offers to be his partner. An unbeatable team, they win the match and repair their marriage. *Bridge (Game). Contests. Marriage. Russian Americans. Acrobats. Authors. Boardinghouses. Detectives. Infidelity. Jealousy. Parties. Revenge. Waiters.*

Note: Onscreen director and cast credits appear on individual playing cards. *FD* notes that Alfred E. Green was originally announced as the director. Although screen credits list the name as "Philip," Frank McHugh's character is called "Speed" throughout the film. Contemporary sources note that the playoff between Peter and Van Dorn is a spoof of a match played between bridge experts Cuthbertson and Sidney S. Lenz. According to Warner Bros. production reports included in the file on the film in the AMPAS library, the film was shot over twenty-two days for a total cost of $164,000.

FD 23 Feb 1933, p. 7. *FD* 20 Oct 1933, p. 5. *HR* 5 Jan 1933, p. 3. *MPH* 14 Jan 1933, p. 30. *NYT* 22 Feb 1933, p. 25. *Var* 28 Feb 1933, p. 15.

LA GRANDE MARE *see* **THE BIG POND**

IL GRANDE SENTIERO *see* **LA GRAN JORNADA**

THE GRANDEE'S RING (Latino)

Interstate Feature Film Co. *Dist* Picture Playhouse Film Co. Nov 1915. Si; b&w. 5 reels.

Cast: Helene Wallace (*Shirley Saunders*), Kenneth MacDougall (*Carlos DeLaBarra*), Earl Beebe, A. Sears Pruden, H. Tudor Morsell.

Drama. While Professor Sinclair of Watson College in New England visits David Saunders and his daughter Shirley on their ranch at the Mexican border, the adventurous Shirley, despite warnings, rides near the Rio Grande and is captured by marauding Mexican bandits. After another prisoner, Carlos DeLaBarra, the scion of an old Castilian family, escapes from the bandits and rescues Shirley, an attachment develops between them. When Shirley and her father return East, they arrange for Carlos to be enrolled in Watson College, where, during the next four years, he and his roommate, Jack Foster, become baseball heroes and fall in love with Shirley. Although Jack bats in the winning run in the championship game, Shirley, who loves them both, is won by Carlos, because of a dream in which she learns about true love and the true character of both boys. *Aristocrats. Baseball. College life. Dreams. Latino. New England. Bandits. Baseball. Heirs. Kidnapping. Mexican-American border region. Professors. Rescues. Rio Grande. Roommates. Spaniards.*

Note: The Interstate Feature Film Co. was located in Middletown, CT.
MPW 20 Nov 1915, p. 1502, 1506-07. *MPW* 4 Dec 1915, p. 1912.

THE GRAY HORIZON (Japanese Americans)

Haworth Pictures Corp. *Dist* Robertson-Cole Co. through Exhibitors Mutual Distributing Corp. 18 Aug 1919 [©The Haworth Pictures Corp.; 5 May 1919; LU13671]. Si; b&w. 5 reels.

Dir William Worthington. *Story and scen* Clifford Howard. *Cam* Frank D. Williams.

Cast: Sessue Hayakawa (*Yano Masata*), Bertram Grassby (*John Furthman*), Eileen Percy (*Doris Furthman*), Mary Jane Irving (*Kenneth Furthman*), Tsuru Aoki (*O Haru San*), Andrew Robson (*Robert Marsh*).

Drama. Yano Masata, a struggling Japanese artist living in a mountainous area in America, refuses to tint counterfeit bonds for wealthy John Furthman. Yano's sister, O Haru San, comes from Japan to look for her husband who deserted her, and with the aid of a woman in the Japanese mission, finds Yano. When she recognizes Furthman as her husband, Furthman and Yano fight until Furthman's gun goes off, killing O Haru San, and Yano throws Furthman off a cliff. Later, Yano thanks the woman in the mission, and after they develop a friendship, he agrees to paint her husband's portrait from a photograph. The husband is Furthman and his wife thinks that his fall was an accident. After Yano paints the portrait, he destroys it in a moment of wrath and confesses the killing to Mrs. Furthman's financial adviser. Later, Yano burns the evidence of Furthman's crimes so that Mrs. Furthman and her son will remain unaware of Furthman's treachery and not be disgraced. The police then arrest Yano. *Brothers and sisters. Counterfeiters and counterfeiting. Fights. Friendship. Japanese Americans. Painters (Of paintings). Confession. Desertion (Marital). Evidence. Falls from heights. Missions. Murder.*

Note: This was partly filmed in the Sierra Nevada Mountains of CA.
ETR 16 Aug 1919, p. 905. *MPW* 16 Aug 1919, p. 1019. *Var* 22 Aug 1919, p. 76. *Wid's* 7 Sep 1919, p. 23.

THE GRAY TOWERS MYSTERY (Native Americans)

Vitagraph Co. of America. *Dist* Vitagraph Co. of America. 25 Oct 1919 [©Vitagraph Co. of America; 13 Sep 1919; LP14188]. Si; b&w. 5 reels.

Dir John W. Noble. *Scen* Sam Taylor and John W. Noble.

Source: Based on the novelette *Fate in the Balance* by Seward W. Hopkins (publication undetermined).

Cast: Gladys Leslie (*June Wheeler*), Frank Morgan (*Billy Durland*), Warner Richmond (*Jean Bautiste*), Warren Chandler (*Tom Makinnon*), Charles Craig (*Sam Bigby*), George Henry (*Mr. Orchard*), Marie Burke (*Mrs. Bigby*), Cecil Kern (*Miss Sutherland*), Miss Christensen (*Marie*).

Western. Orphan June Wheeler leaves Chicago when she inherits a vast ranch in the West. At the ranch, her foreman, half-breed Jean Bautiste, falls in love with her, while she falls in love with her wealthy neighbor, Billy Durland, who later is elected sheriff and accepts the position for the fun of it. June's cousin, Tom Makinnon, arrives claiming the rights to half the land. While they examine the estate on horseback, June slaps Makinnon after he gets aggressive with her and rides off, dropping her revolver. When Makinnon is found dead with June's gun nearby, she is arrested and sent to jail. Billy burns down the jail so that June can investigate the murder and while helping her, he is shot in the arm by Bautiste. After June forces Bautiste to confess that he murdered Makinnon out of jealousy, Bautiste throws himself over a gorge and June and Billy marry. *False arrests. Land rights. Murder. Ranches. Sheriffs. The West.* Chicago (IL). Cousins. Falls from heights. Firearms. Gunshot wounds. Indians of North America–Mixed blood. Inheritance. Jails. Jealousy. Orphans.

Note: The title of the film was changed from *Fate in the Balance*.
ETR 25 Oct 1919, p. 1799. *MPN* 25 Oct 1919, p. 3201. *MPW* 27 Dec 1919, p. 1192. *Var* 17 Oct 1919, p. 63. *Wid's* 2 Nov 1919, p. 11.

THE GREAT ADVISOR (Yiddish language)

Cinema Service Corp. *Dist* Cinema Service Corp. 13 Dec 1940. Sd; b&w. 7 reels, 6,479 or 6,500 ft. 75 min. Yiddish language with English subtitles.

Dir Josef Seiden. *Asst dir* H. Rosen. *Story* I. Frankel. *Photog* Don Malkames and Charles Levine. *Settings* J. Allstadt. *Songs and mus* Chiam Tauber, Fishel Kanapoff and Manny Fleishman. *Sd* M. Dichter and P. Jacobs.

Cast: IRVING JACOBSON [(*David Fish*)], YETTA ZWERLING [(*Sarah Flahm*)], Mae Schoenfeld [(*Shlime*)], Abraham Lox [(*Fischel Cookingspoon*)], Jacob Zanger [(*Boruch Dian*)], Chiam Tauber, Rose Greenfield, Muni Serebroff, Lazar Freed, Cantor Leibele Waldman, [Isidor Frankel (*Mr. Weiss*)], [Herman Rosen (*Brill*)], [Sylvia Fishman (*Mrs. Weiss*)], [Max Badin], [Helen Blay], [David Yonover], [Moishe Silverstein], [Miriam Grossman], [Dora Weissman].

Yiddish, Comedy, with songs. [*Print viewed*]. After Leibele Waldman, known as "America's Favorite Cantor," sings on a radio broadcast, announcer David the Trouble Fixer implores his audience to send him letters about their romantic problems. Some of his listeners make fun of him, calling him "David the Faker," and send him a phony letter, while others write to him in earnest seeking a match. Mrs. Sarah Flahm, a widow with $15,000, has not married again because she thinks that men are after her money. Following her uncle's advice, she writes to David as "The Lonesome Widow." While she rides in a carriage on the boardwalk at Coney Island, she passes the office of the Companion Friendship Bureau and meets the manager, shyster Boruch Dian. Later, on the boardwalk, Boruch sees David, whom he recognizes as David Fish from "the old country," and they discuss their similar avocations. Fischel Cookingspoon then introduces himself to them and tells of his scheme to sell lottery tickets to poor lovers and then keep ten percent of their winnings. Both David and Boruch are extremely interested and buy many tickets from him. David then meets a woman, Shlime, and proposes to her. Boruch invites them to his "rendezvous" of couples, which Mrs. Flahm also attends. When Shlime learns from Fishel that her cousin, Dr. Morris Shapiro, has just won $50,000 from an Irish sweepstakes ticket that he sold her, Shlime and David go to Shapiro's office and catch him in an embrace with a woman. Shapiro promises he will take care of them, but he fails to give them any of the money, and after a short period of time, David refuses to marry Shlime because she has no dowry. When he learns that Mrs. Flahm has $15,000, David brags about himself to her and talks against Boruch, then professes his love for her. Mrs. Flahm forcefully kisses him, and they plan to meet at midnight on the boardwalk. That night, as David and Mrs. Flahm ride in a carriage, Shlime spies them and replaces the man pushing the carriage. She then calls David her man, and the two women fight, then hit David and Boruch, who happens by. After David and Mrs. Flahm leave, Shlime cries to Boruch, who comforts her and vows to take David's place. He proposes to her and then plans a partnership to con together, hoping to make millions. Both couples attend Boruch's "rendezvous" and insult each other, but when Fischel proposes that they have a double wedding, they sing and kiss. *Confidence men. Jews. Matchmakers. Widows.* Cantors, Jewish. Cousins. Fistfights. Lotteries. New York City–Coney Island. Proposals (Marital). Radio broadcasting. Uncles.

Note: The Yiddish title of this film is *Der Groyser Eytse-Geber*. Although the film includes songs, no information concerning their identity has been located.
Exh 25 Dec 1940.

THE GREAT ALONE (Native Americans)

West Coast Films. *Dist* American Releasing Corp. 21 May **1922**. Si; b&w. 6 reels, 5,912 ft.

Pres Isadore Bernstein. *Dir* Jacques Jaccard and James Colwell. *Supv dir* Isadore Bernstein. *Asst dir* Justin H. McCloskey. *Story* Jacques Jaccard. *Photog* Frank B. Good.

Cast: Monroe Salisbury (*Silent Duval*), Laura Anson (*Nadine Picard*), Walter Law (*Winston Sassoon*), Maria Law (*Mary MacDonald*), George Waggoner (*Bradley Carstairs*), Richard Cummings (*MacDonald, the factor*).

Northwest, Melodrama. While attending Stanford University, Silent Duval, a half-breed Indian, is both a football star and the object of scorn by his fellow students—except Mary MacDonald. Duval leaves college in disgust and returns to his Northland home as a secret agent for MacDonald's business firm. Later, Duval learns that Mary has been lost in a violent snowstorm while searching for her father, and he defies death to repay her kindness by rescuing her and teaching her father's enemy, Winston Sassoon, a lesson in the law of the Yukon. Duval rewards the patience of Nadine Picard, also a half-breed, with his love. *Football. Indians of North America. Indians of North America-Mixed blood. Racism. Stanford University. Storms. Yukon Territory.*

Note: Some snow exteriors filmed at Blairsden, Feather River, California. *ETR* 24 Jun 1922, p. 243. *FD* 18 Jun 1922. *MPN* 24 Jun 1922, p. 3363. *MPW* 24 Jun 1922, p. 735. *Var* 7 Jul 1922, p. 59.

THE GREAT CARUSO (Italian Americans)

Metro-Goldwyn-Mayer Corp.; controlled by Loew's Inc. *Dist* Loew's Inc. 27 Apr **1951**; Prod: early Sep—mid-Oct 1950 [©Loew's Inc.; 12 Apr 1951; LP893]. Sd (Western Electric Sound System); col (Technicolor). 12 reels, 9,822 ft. 109-110 min. Passed by the National Board of Review. PCA cert no. 14927.

Prod Joe Pasternak. *Assoc prod* Jesse L. Lasky. *Dir* Richard Thorpe. [*Asst dir* Sid Sidman]. *Wrt* Sonya Levien and William Ludwig. *Dir of photog* Joseph Ruttenberg. *Spec eff* Warren Newcombe. *Mont seq* Peter Rallbusch. *Technicolor col consultant* Henri Jaffa and James Gooch. *Art dir* Cedric Gibbons and Gabriel Scognamillo. *Film ed* Gene Ruggiero. *Set dec* Edwin B. Willis. *Assoc* Jack D. Moore. *Women's cost* Helen Rose. *Men's cost* Gile Steele. *Operatic numbers staged and cond by* Peter Herman Adler. *Mus supv and background score* Johnny Green. *Rec supv* Douglas Shearer. *Hair styles des by* Sydney Guilaroff. *Makeup created by* William J. Tuttle. [*Voice double* Jacqueline Allen].

Song(s): "The Loveliest Night of the Year," music by Irving Aaronson, lyrics by Paul Francis Webster, adapted from "Over the Waves" by Juventino Rosas; "Magnificat," traditional; "A Marechiare," music by Francesco Paolo Tosti, lyrics by Di Giacomo; "A Vuccella," music by Francesco Paolo Tosti, lyrics by Gabriele D'Annunzio; "La Danza," music and lyrics by Gioacchino Rossini; "Celeste Aida," "Numi, Pieta," "Consecration Scene" and Trio Finale from the opera *Aida*, music by Giuseppe Verdi, libretto by Antonio Ghislanzoni; "La Donna è Mobile" and Quartet ("Bella Figlia dell'Amore") from the opera *Rigoletto*, music by Giuseppe Verdi, libretto by Francesco Maria Piave; "Miserere" ("Ah! Che la Morte Ognora") from the opera *Il Trovatore*, music by Giuseppe Verdi, libretto by Salvatore Cammarano; "E Lucevan le Stelle" and "Torture Scene" from the opera *Tosca*, and "Che Gelida Manina" from the opera *La Bohème*, music by Giacomo Puccini, libretto by Giuseppe Giacosa and Luigi Illica; "Brindisi" ("Viva il Vino Spumeggiante") and "Vilification Scene" from the opera *Cavalleria Rusticana*, music by Pietro Mascagni, libretto by Guido Menasci and Giovanni Targioni-Tozzetti; "Cielo e Mar" from the opera *La Gioconda*, music by Amilcare Ponchielli, libretto by Arrigo Boito; "Torna a Surriento," music by Ernesto de Curtis, lyrics by G. B. de Curtis; "La Mattinata," music and lyrics by Ruggiero Leoncavallo; "Recitativo" and "Vesti la Giubba" from the opera *Il Pagliacci*, music and libretto by Ruggiero Leoncavallo; "Sweethearts" from the operetta *Sweethearts*, music by Victor Herbert, libretto by Robert B. Smith; "Ave Maria," music by Charles Gounod, adapted from the First Prelude in The Well-Tempered Clavichord by Johann Sebastian Bach, French lyrics by Paul Bernard, English lyrics traditional; Sextet ("Chi mi Frena") from the opera *Lucia di Lammermoor*, music by Gaetano Donizetti, libretto by Salvatore Cammarano; "Because," music by Guy d'Hardelot, lyrics by Edward Teschemacher; Finale ("Qui Sola, Virgin Rosa") adapted from "The Last Rose of Summer," music based on "The Groves of Blarney" by Richard Alfred Milliken and "M'appari tutt'amor," from

the opera *Martha*, music by Friedrich von Flotow, libretto by Friedrich Wilhelm Riese; "Under the Bamboo Tree," music and lyrics by Robert Cole and J. Rosamond Johnson.

Source: Suggested by the book *Enrico Caruso, His Life and Death* by Dorothy Caruso (New York, 1945).

Cast: Mario Lanza (*Enrico Caruso*), Ann Blyth (*Dorothy Benjamin* [*Caruso*]), Dorothy Kirsten (*Louise Heggar*), Jarmila Novotna (*Maria Selka*), Richard Hageman (*Carlo Santi*), Carl Benton Reid (*Park Benjamin*), Eduard Franz (*Giulio Gatti-Casazza*), Ludwig Donath (*Alfredo Brazzi*), Alan Napier (*Jean de Reszke*), Paul Javor (*Antonio Scotti*), Carl Milletaire (*Gino*), Shepard Menken (*Fucito*), Vincent Renno (*Tullio*), Nestor Paiva (*Egisto Barretto*), Peter Edward Price (*Caruso, as a boy*), Mario Siletti (*Papa Caruso*), Angela Clarke (*Mama Caruso*), Ian Wolfe (*Hutchins*), Yvette Duguay (*Musetta Barretto*), Argentina Brunetti (*Mrs. Barretto*), Opera montage: Blanche Thebom, Teresa Celli, Nicola Moscona, Giuseppe Valdengo, Lucine Amara, and Marina Koshetz, [Gilbert Russell (*Arturo in sextet from "Lucia di Lammermoor"*)], [Robert Ebright (*Rhadames in Consecration scene from "Aida"*)], [Jacqueline Allen (*Soloist in "Magnificat"*)], [Olive Mae Beach (*Gilda in Quartet from "Rigoletto"*)], [Maurice Samuels (*Papa Gino*)], [Edit Angold (*Hilda*)], [Robert Sherwood (*Cub reporter*)], [Antonio Filauri (*Papa Riccardo*)], [Peter Brocco (*Father Bronzetti*)], [David Bond (*Father Angelico*)], [Charles Evans (*Finch*)], [Matt Moore (*Max*)], [Sherry Jackson (*Musetta as a child*)], [Mario DeLaval (*Ottello Carmini*)], [Martha Bamattre (*Midwife*)], [Anthony Mazola (*Fucito as a child*)], [Rudy Baron (*Gino*)], [Michael Frazco (*Young boy*)], [Dorothy Vaughn (*Housekeeper*)], [Hazel Dohlman (*Dowager*)], [Roddy McCaskill (*Small boy*)], [Tito Vuolo (*Pietro*)], [Minerva Urecal (*Carmelita*)], [Paul Harvey (*Band announcer*)], [John Hamilton (*Mr. DeWitt*)], [Jack George (*Promptor*)], [Harry Cody, Fred Hoose, Helen Dickson, Peggy Leon (*Guests*)], [Eula Guy (*Nurse*)], [Nino Pipitone (*Young man*)], [Dick Cogan (*Call boy*)], [Roger Moore (*Fireman in gallery*)], [Jack Gargan, Frank Pershing (*Ushers in gallery*)], [Bert Roach (*Electrician*)], [Thomas Quinn, Stuart Holmes (*Guests backstage at the Met*)], [Harold Miller, Nikki Juston (*Party guests*)], [Spec O'Donnell, Allan Ray, John Raven, Dario Piazza, Ernesto Morelli, Dino Bolognese, Henry DarBoggia (*Bellhops*)], [Douglas Carter (*Assistant in record shop*)], [Helen Reyes, Yolanda Mirelez (*Spanish girls*)], [German montage: John Piffle], [Esther Zeitlin], [Bob Lawrence], [Claude Cariguel], [William Yetter, Jr.], [and John Royce], [French montage: Manuel Paris], [Leo Mostovoy], [Viola Daniels], [and Charles Mauu], [Spanish montage: Danilo Valente], [Jose Portugal], [Albano Valerio], [Rod De Medici], [Renald DuPont], [and Blanche Franke], [Mario Cimino], [Zachary Yaconelli], [Michael Jordan], [George Restivo], [Richard LaMarr], [Maria Ganardi], [Nola Haines], [Mae Clarke], [Jewel Rose], [Tay Dunn], [Larry Williams], [Bess Flowers], [John Sheffield], [Eric Wilton], [William Nind], [Colin Kenny], [Philo McCullough], [Genevieve Bell], [St. Luke's Choristers].

Biography, Musical. [*Print viewed*]. In 1873, Enrico Caruso is born to humble parents in Naples, Italy. As a boy, he participates in the church choir, and one day, just before the start of a religious procession in which he is to sing, his mother falls gravely ill. Enrico wants to stay with her, but she persuades him to rejoin the procession. During the procession, Mama Caruso dies. When Enrico becomes a man, he sings for coins in local restaurants, and although he wants to marry the beautiful Musetta Barretto, her father finds such employment undignified. To please the old man, Enrico agrees to forsake his singing and become a merchant, but he is miserable. One of his deliveries takes him to the restaurant where he used to perform, and soon he is singing with his old friend Fucito. The great tenor Alfredo Brazzi, listening at a nearby table, is so impressed with Enrico's singing that he places him in the chorus for a performance of Giuseppe Verdi's *Aida*. Barretto, however, orders Enrico to keep away from his daughter. Enrico earns a bit part in *Tosca*, and makes his official debut in *Cavalleria Rusticana*. After topping the bill at the La Scala performance of *La Giaconda*, Enrico returns to his home town a great success. Everyone is impressed with the singer's fame and fine clothes, but Gino, the barber, finally reveals that Musetta has married someone else. Grateful to Gino for his honesty, Enrico asks his friend to accompany him to his debut in London's Covent Garden and there he proves a sensation in *Rigoletto*. His success is marred only by the outbursts of his temperamental co-star, Maria Selka, who despises Italian tenors, and the sadness of his mentor Brazzi, who has

lost his voice. Good-hearted and generous, Enrico hires Brazzi as his manager, and the party sets out for New York and Enrico's Metropolitan Opera debut. During rehearsal, Enrico and soprano Louise Heggar are taken with each other's singing, and as time passes, they become close friends. The effusive tenor does, however, unwittingly offend Park Benjamin, one of the Met's principal patrons. Later, while visiting the Benjamin home to make his apologies, Enrico meets and falls in love with the snobbish patron's lovely daughter Dorothy. During his first performance, Enrico is so nervous about impressing the "Diamond Horseshoe" of patrons and critics that he earns poor reviews and only polite applause. When Benjamin, disturbed by the attempt of an "Italian peasant" to portray a nobleman, attempts to have Enrico removed from the cast, the singer is deeply offended and declares, "I do not sing in America." Dorothy persuades him that if he performs for the people in the galleries, he will love and be loved by America. Before the next performance, Enrico clasps his good luck charm, prays to the Blessed Virgin, reminds himself that "I am no gentleman," and then entrances not only the gallery crowd but also famous tenor Jean de Reszke with his magnificent voice. Outside the theater, Enrico sings for an appreciative crowd of Italian immigrants before embarking on a triumphant world tour. Upon his return to the Met, he takes "Senorina Doro" to a small Italian restaurant, where he proposes. Dorothy happily breaks the news to her father and is disappointed when he, protesting that such a union would be "undignified," refuses his permission. The two are wed anyway, and Dorothy later surprises her husband by singing for him at his birthday party. Enrico is on stage when he learns of the birth of his daughter, whom he names Gloria Graziana Victoria America Caruso. The tenor's success continues, but one night, while singing a song to his daughter, he is overcome by a fit of coughing. When Dorothy discovers that he has been using an ether spray on his throat, she begs him not to appear in his scheduled performance of *Martha*, but he protests that he is well. That night, Caruso sings beautifully, but during the performance, he collapses on stage and dies. In the lobby of the Metropolitan Opera, admirers place a wreath at the bust of the great Caruso. *Enrico Caruso. Class distinction. Metropolitan Opera (New York City). Opera singers. Art patronage. Benefit performances. Bigotry. Christmas. Death and dying. Fame. Fathers and daughters. Italian Americans. Loyalty. Marriage. Mothers and sons. Naples (Italy). Opera. Restaurants. Snobs and snobbishness. Upper classes.*

Note: The working titles of this film were *Caruso Sings Tonight* and *The Life of Caruso*. Dorothy Caruso, who wrote the biography on which the film is based, was Enrico Caruso's wife. M-G-M purchased rights to the book from Jesse L. Lasky's company in 1949. As depicted in the film, Caruso was born in Naples in 1873 and sang in his church's choir as a young boy. After studying for three years with Guglielmo Vergine and Vincenzo Lombardi, Caruso made his official debut as a tenor in Naples on 16 Nov 1894. In 1898, he was engaged by the Teatro Lirico in Milan, and in 1901, he became a member of Milan's La Scala opera company. After triumphant appearances in Monte Carlo, Caruso was awarded contracts at Covent Garden in London and at the Metropolitan Opera in New York. On 23 Nov 1903, he made his American debut in the Met's production of *Rigoletto*, Although his initial performance received mixed reviews, he became the company's favorite singer by the end of the season. Caruso sang at the Met and other major opera houses for the next seventeen years, becoming the highest-paid and most beloved opera star in the world. At the Met, he sang in over 600 performances, in almost forty operas. He earned nearly two million dollars from his phonograph recordings.

Caruso appeared in two Famous Players-Lasky silent films, the 1918 *My Cousin*, (see entry below) and the 1919 *The Splendid Romance* (see *AFI Catalog of Feature Films, 1911-20*; F1.4213). On 11 Dec 1920, during a performance of *L'elisir d'amore* at the Brooklyn Academy, Caruso coughed blood and was later diagnosed with "intercostal neuralgia." His final appearance in an opera occurred on 24 Dec 1920, when he sang his favorite role in *La Juive*. On 2 Aug 1921, while in Naples recuperating from surgery and its complications, he died. According to a Sep 1950 *NYT* article, screenwriters Sonya Levien and William Ludwig never intended *The Great Caruso* as an authentic biography of the opera singer. In particular, they eliminated any reference to Caruso's common-law wife and his two illegitimate children by her. The *Var* reviewer noted that "there is nothing in the film to hint that Miss Benjamin was Caruso's second wife; that he had grown children and was middle-aged when he married her." According to a May 1955 *NYT* article, in addition to the biography, the writers had at their disposal notes from Caruso's secretary's journal.

In 1946, when Lasky was considering making Caruso's film biography, he planned to transfer recordings of the singer's voice to the picture's soundtrack, replacing the old orchestral accompaniment with an updated one. While many reviewers complained about the range of questionable accents displayed by the actors in *The Great Caruso*, most commented favorably on Mario Lanza's performance. Many of the singers in the opera montage were veteran performers of the Metropolitan Opera Company. The Metropolitan's mezzo-soprano Jarmila

Novotna, playing the diva "Maria Selka," did not sing in the picture. According to a May 1951 *LAEx* news item, much of Novotna's role was cut from the final film. Other arias recorded for the film's soundtrack album, but not included in the final film are "Questa o Quella" and "Parmi Veder Le Lagrime" from *Rigoletto*; "Reconditi Armonia" from *Tosca*; and "Una Furtiva Lagrima" from *L'Elisir D'Amour*. *The Great Caruso* was nominated for Academy Awards for Best Costume Design (color) and Best Scoring of a Musical Picture, and won the Oscar for Best Sound Recording. It was one of the four highest-grossing films of 1951. According to modern sources, it earned ten million dollars in its first year of release.

In early 1952, Caruso's Italian heirs, who had previously sued the makers of the Italian screen biography *Legend of Caruso* without success, sued M-G-M for not getting their consent to do the film and for taking liberties with Caruso's life. In late May 1955, *LAT* reported that the heirs had won an $8,000 suit against M-G-M, with the court ruling that the picture was "offensive to the honor and private and family life" of Caruso. M-G-M was ordered to pay all court expenses and withdraw all copies of the film from circulation in Italy. The heirs also protested the film's billboard advertising in Rome, which showed star Mario Lanza drinking Coca-Cola. The posters were ordered removed in Apr 1952. *The Great Caruso* was re-issued in 1963 and in 1970.

Box 21 Apr 1951. *DV* 15 Dec 1949. *DV* 13 Apr 1951, p. 3. *DV* 30 Apr 1952. *Exh* 25 Apr 1951, p. 3061. *FD* 16 Apr 1951, p. 6. *Har* 14 Apr 1951, p. 58. *HCN* 1 Feb 1946. *HR* 13 Apr 1951, p. 3. *HR* 16 Apr 1952. *HR* 24 Feb 1970. *LAEx* 30 May 1951. *LAT* 29 May 1955. *MPH* 6 Feb 1963. *MPHPD* 21 Apr 1951, p. 810. *NYT* 10 Sep 1950. *NYT* 11 May 1951, p. 32. *NYT* 8 May 1955. *Time* 21 May 1951. *Time* 5 May 1952. *Var* 18 Apr 1951, p. 6.

THE GREAT DIAMOND ROBBERY (Latino)

Playgoers Film Co. 23 Mar **1914**. Si; b&w. 6 reels.

Supv Daniel V. Arthur. *Dir* Edward A. Morange. *Picturized by* Herbert Hall Winslow.

Source: Based on the play *The Great Diamond Robbery* by Edward M. Alfriend and A. C. Wheeler (New York, 4 Sep 1895).

Cast: Wallace Eddinger (*Dick Brummage*), Gail Kane (*Maria*), Elita Proctor Otis (*Mother Rosenbaum*), Charles J. Ross (*Mr. Bulford*), Martin J. Alson (*Count Garbiadoff*), Purnell B. Pratt (*Maria's brother*), Stapleton Kent (*Don Plon*), Frank Hardy (*Mother Rosenbaum's son*), Herbert Barrington (*Frank Lavelot*), Dorothy Arthur (*Mary Lavelot*), R. E. Graham (*Grandfather Lavelot*), Phillip Sheffield (*Clerk*), Edward Gillespie (*Senator McSorker*), Percy Standing (*Crimp*).

Drama. While stealing the fabulous Romanoff diamonds, Brazilian adventuress Maria is surprised by her former accomplice Don Plon, who takes the jewels from her. Some time later, Maria marries wealthy New York banker Bulford whom Plon writes in the hopes of returning the diamonds to their rightful owner before his death. Accompanied by Dick Brummage, a detective, Bulford rushes to Plon's apartment but finds him dead, and the jewels gone. Without Bulford's knowledge, Maria has secured the jewels, but when he finds incriminating letters in Plon's apartment, he confronts her. During his rage, he has a seizure, which Maria pretends to calm with wine, actually laced with poison. She blames her husband's death on Frank Lavelot, a dismissed employee, whom she further implicates by kidnapping him with the help of her brother. Mary, Frank's sister and Dick's fiancée, obtains proof of Maria's guilt when she enters her employ disguised as a maid. Frank escapes, and Mary, whose life is jeopardized by Maria, is saved by Dick. At a reception, Maria triumphantly wears the stolen diamonds, but when confronted by Dick, she drinks poison and dies. *Diamonds. Frame-ups. Murder. Robbery. Suicide. Bankers. Disguise. Kidnapping. Letters. Maids. Poisoning. Private detectives. Rescues. South Americans.*

Note: This was the first production of the Playgoers Film Co.

Motog 4 Apr 1914, p. 238. *MPW* 28 Mar 1914, p. 1746. *MPW* 4 Apr 1914, p. 47, 86. *NYDM* 25 Mar 1914, p. 36. *Var* 27 Mar 1914, p. 17. *Var* 8 May 1914, p. 20.

GREAT ENEMY see GERONIMO

THE GREAT FLIRTATION (Hungarian Americans)

Paramount Productions, Inc.; A Charles R. Rogers Production. *Dist* Paramount Productions, Inc. 15 Jun **1934** [©Paramount Productions, Inc.; 13 Jun 1934; LP4769]. Sd (Western Electric Noiseless Recording); b&w. 8 reels. 70-71 min. Passed by the National Board of Review. PCA cert no. 1354-R [31 Aug 1935].

[*Exec prod* Emanuel Cohen]. *Assoc prod* Harry Joe Brown. *Dir* Ralph Murphy. *Scr* Humphrey Pearson. *Story* Gregory Ratoff. *Photog* Milton Krasner. *Cost des by* Travis Banton. [*Sd* Earl Hayman].

Cast: Elissa Landi (*Zita Marishka*), Adolphe Menjou ([*Stephan*] *Karpath*), David Manners (*Larry Kenyon*), Lynne Overman (*Joe Lang*), Raymond Walburn (*Henry Morgan*), Adrian Rosley (*Mikos*), Paul Porcasi (*Herr Direktor*), George Baxter (*Arpad*), Judith Vosselli (*Queen*), Akim Tamiroff (*Paul Wengler*), [Vernon Steele (*Bigelow*)].

Show business, Drama. [*Print viewed*]. In Budapest, Stephan Karpath is a reknown actor, but is pompous and egotistical from all the recognition. His lover, Zita Marishka, with whom he constantly feuds, yearns for fame. Although Stephan insists Zita is a terrible actress, she takes the female lead in a play with him. When he complains to the director, Zita is fired. Stephan insists on joining Zita when she rebelliously decides to go to New York and they are married on the ship. In New York, no one has heard of Stephan, and he and Zita live in poverty. When the female lead drops out of a show in which Stephan is acting, Zita decides to create the persona of a famous Russian actress for herself so she can get the part. Stephan reluctantly agrees to the ruse. They approach theatrical producer Henry Morgan, who is discussing the casting problem with the playwright, Larry Kenyon, and Joe Lang. All three men are completely smitten by Zita, who insists she is not married. Zita gets the part and is constantly wooed by Henry, Larry and Joe, but falls in love with Larry. In the meantime, she ignores Stephan, who is outraged at her insolence. When the lead male actor then quits the show, Stephan gets the part but, realizing he will lose Zita to Larry if the play is successful, does his best to act badly. The play is a huge success, however, and Stephan is lauded for his superb acting. When Stephan continues to denigrate Zita's acting and insists that she is simply the wife of a great actor, she tells him she has been unable to make their love scenes convincing any more because she is in love with Larry and leaves him. Seven months later, Zita stars in the premiere production of another play by Larry, and newspapers note the sudden disappearance of Stephan. In reality, Stephan is teaching acting in a hole of an apartment, his only companion his trusted manservant, Mikos. Mikos advises him to accept a job acting in his uncle's theater in North Dakota, and Stephan takes the part only so he can have enough money to see Zita's play. After the show, Larry invites Stephan backstage, but before Stephan goes in, Zita finally confesses to Larry that she has been married to Stephan all along. Recognizing the sad shape that Stephan is in, Larry agrees to step aside so she and Stephan can reunite. Zita tells Stephan she wants to return to him, but he realizes this is her best performance yet. He pretends that he is returning to Budapest and does not want her back, thereby sacrificing his happiness for hers. Afterward, he and Mikos head for North Dakota. *Actors and actresses. Egotists. Hungarian Americans. Impersonation and imposture. Romantic rivalry. Self-sacrifice. Budapest (Hungary). Confession. Envy. Infidelity. Marriage. New York City. Ocean liners. Playwrights. Poverty. Servants. Teachers.*

Note: Gregory Ratoff's unpublished story was called "I Love an Actress." The pre-release title of the film is *I Married an Actress*.

FD 23 Jun 1934, p. 4. *MPD* 4 Jun 1934, p. 5. *MPH* 26 May 1934, p. 32. *MPH* 9 Jun 1934, p. 47. *NYT* 22 Jun 1934, p. 16. *Var* 26 Jun 1934, p. 16.

THE GREAT JOHN L. (Irish Americans)

Bing Crosby Productions, Inc. *Dist* United Artists Corp. 25 May 1945; *Prod*: 28 Jun–2 Sep 1944 at General Service Studios [©Bing Crosby Productions, Inc.; 29 Jun 1945; LP13348]. Sd (Western Electric Recording); b&w. 8,668 ft. 96 min.

Prod Frank R. Mastroly and James Edward Grant. *Prod assoc* Milton Carter. *Dir* Frank Tuttle. *Asst dir* Jack Voglin. *Dial coach* Benno Scheider. *Orig scr* James Edward Grant. *Photog* James Van Trees. [*Second cam* John Russell]. [*Spec photog eff* Howard Anderson]. *Prod des* Bernard Herzbrun. *Film ed* Theodore Bellinger and [Elmo Veron]. *Set dec* Edward C. Boyle. *Cost consultant* Edward P. Lambert. *Women's cost* Odette. *Mus dir* Victor Young and [Lou Silvers]. [*Unit mixer* William H. Lynch]. [*Re-rec, eff and mus mixer* William H. Wilmarth]. *Makeup* H. C. Littlefield. *Hair styles* Scotty Rackin. *Exec prod mgr* Joe C. Gilpin. [*Boxing*] *contests staged by* John Indrisano. [*Pub* William J. Pierce, Jr.]. [*Singing voice double for Linda Darnell* Trudy Erwin].

Song(s): "A Friend of Yours" and "He was a Perfect Gentleman," music and lyrics by Johnny Burke and James Van Heusen; "We Will Always Be Comrades," music and lyrics by Lou Silvers; "When You Were Sweet Sixteen," music and lyrics by James Thornton; "Take Me Out to the Ball Game," music by Harry Von Tilzer, lyrics by Jack Norworth; "When You and I Were Young, Maggie," music by J. A. Butterfield, lyrics by George W. Johnson.

Cast: Linda Darnell [(*Anne Livingstone*)], Barbara Britton [(*Kathy Harkness*)], and introducing Greg McClure (*John L. Sullivan*), Otto Kruger [(*Richard Martin*)], Wallace Ford [(*McManus*)], George Matthews [(*John Flood*)], Robert Barrat [(*Billy Muldoon*)], J. M.

Kerrigan [(*Father O'Malley*)], Joel Friedkin [(*Michael Sullivan*)], Simon Semenoff [(*Monsieur Claire*)], Harry Crocker [(*Arthur Brisbane*)], Frank McCown, Fritz Feld [(*Claire's manager*)], Lee Sullivan (*Mickey* [*Steele*]), [Hope Landin (*Maura Sullivan*)], [Rory Calhoun (*James J. "Gentleman Jim" Corbett*)].

Biography, with songs. [*Print viewed*]. In 1880, young John L. Sullivan rejects an opportunity to play baseball for the Boston Red Soxes and instead chooses to become a boxer, much to the chagrin of his father Michael. At a church social, Father O'Malley, the parish priest, publicly questions the morality of professional boxing, but, privately, he fully supports John. That evening, John proposes to his childhood sweetheart, Kathy Harkness, but she questions their future together. After winning his first fight in New York City, John, called "The Boston Strong Boy" by the sportswriters, pronounces that "I can lick any man in the world." Richard Martin, a newspaper publisher, then arranges a match between the little-known John and top-ranked boxer John Flood, which the Boston fighter easily wins. While training for his championship fight against Paddy Ryan, John attracts the interest of Anne Livingstone, a singing star from the New York stage. Upon becoming the undisputed bareknuckle champion of the world, John returns to Boston, only to be rejected by Kathy, who openly questions his character. On the rebound, John marries Anne and begins drinking. Despite his new training companions—champagne and ale—John remains undefeated and travels to London, where he meets Edward, the Prince of Wales. Back at home, however, rumors persist about trouble in the Sullivan marriage, which Anne denies to Richard. John and Anne then travel to Paris, where he defeats Monsieur Claire, a French kickboxer, in a barroom fight. Back in Boston, the alcoholic John opens his own tavern, to the concern of Flood, who has become his friend and sparring partner. On his wedding anniversary, a palm reader tells John that he is "a very lonesome man," then privately tells a waiter that the boxer is in love with another woman. After finding a picture of John with Kathy, Anne, too, realizes that John is not in love with her, and after meeting Kathy, Anne offers to divorce John if Kathy agrees to marry him. Despite Kathy's refusal, Anne leaves John, and the fighter turns more and more to the bottle. John's alcoholism causes him to lose his championship to James J. "Gentleman Jim" Corbett, and he retires from the ring. Later, after failing as an actor and a boxing referee, a penniless John is sent by Richard to visit the dying Anne, who insists that he return to Boston and Kathy. When his saloon is repossed, Kathy proposes to John herself, but he rejects her, believing that she is asking out of pity. Having reached the bottom, John finally recognizes his drinking problem, "his personal demon" as Father O'Malley calls it, and swears off drinking. The ex-champion then becomes a speaker for the temperance movement and is reunited with Kathy. *Alcoholics. Boxers. Irish Americans. Singers. John L. Sullivan. Unrequited love. Actors and actresses. Americans in foreign countries. Boston (MA). Boxing. Boxing managers. Drunkenness. Edward VII, King of England, 1841-1910. Family relationships. London (England). Marriage. New York City. Paris (France). Priests. Proposals (Marital). Regeneration. Saloons. Temperance. Weddings. Zoos.*

Note: This was the first film produced by Bing Crosby Productions, Inc., an independent film production company owned by the noted performer. According to a May 1944 *HCN* news item, producer Frank R. Mastroly was once a New York City sportswriter who had written numerous columns about boxing champion John L. Sullivan. After purchasing the film rights to the boxer's life story, Mastroly convinced producer-writer James Edward Grant, a one-time Chicago sportswriter, to write the screenplay. Grant, in turn, showed the script to Crosby, his neighbor, who liked it so much that he formed his own company to produce it. According to *HR*, Phoenix financier Del Webb, a close friend of Crosby, was also involved in backing this production. A May 1944 *HR* news item announced that actor William Bendix was being considered for a role in the film. According to the *Var* review, Greg McClure was an unknown stage actor who was also working as a longshoreman and a day laborer when he was cast by Crosby in the lead, and that he was drafted into the U.S. Army upon the completion of *The Great John L.* According to *HCN*, actor-singer Lee Sullivan, a distant cousin of John L. Sullivan, who made his screen debut in this film, was cast after Crosby was told of his singing talent by fellow crooner Paul Whiteman.

HR news items include Alec Harford (*Bartender*), Leslie Denison (*King Edward VII*), Ben Carter, Marek Windheim Dick Curtis, Odette Myrtil, Eugene Borden, Brian O'Hara, Dewey Robinson, Edwin Maxwell, Wyndham Standing, Barry Norton, Frank Patrick Henry, Kenneth Gibson, William Nind, Leslie Sketchley, Jack Beery, Stuart Hall, Adrienne D'Ambricourt, Sherry Hall, Chester Conklin, Eddie Kain, Ray Cooper and Guy Bellis in the cast, but their appearances in the released film have not been confirmed. Fourteen "former ring stars"—Ace Hudkins, Frank Moran, Freddie Steel, Bob Perry, Charlie

Sullivan, Frankie Dolan, Phil Bloom, Larry Williams, Jack Perry, Bing Conley, John Condi, Bert Keyes, Sammy Shack and "Gentleman" George Delmont—also were cast, according to *HR*. *HR* production charts and news items also include Ed Gargan in the cast, but his participation in the released film is doubtful. According to a Jul 1944 *HR* news item, Art Foster was cast as English heavyweight champion Charlie Mitchell, but his scenes were cut from the released film. As depicted in the film, John L. Sullivan defeated Paddy Ryan in 1882 to win the undisputed bareknuckle championship of the world. Sullivan is credited by many sports historians for greatly improving boxing by touring the United States, fighting all challengers in regulated matches fought with gloves under the Queensberry rules. In 1892, Sullivan fought James J. "Gentleman Jim" Corbett for the world's heavyweight championship and lost in the 21st round by knockout. Though defeated, Sullivan retired having never lost a bareknuckled fight. Actor Ward Bond portrayed Sullivan in the 1942 Warner Bros. film *Gentleman Jim* (see entry above).

Box 9 Jun 1945. *DV* 4 Jun 1945, p. 3. *Down Beat* 1 Oct 1944, p. 7. *FD* 4 Jun 1945, p. 6. *HCN* 24 May 1944. *HCN* 20 Jul 1944. *HR* 17 Apr 1944, p. 2. *HR* 27 Apr 1944, p. 15. *HR* 12 May 1944, p. 4. *HR* 26 May 1944, p. 17. *HR* 26 Jun 1944, p. 5. *HR* 28 Jun 1944, p. 3. *HR* 30 Jun 1944, p. 19. *HR* 12 Jul 1944, p. 6. *HR* 17 Jul 1944, p. 7. *HR* 20 Jul 1944, p. 6. *HR* 27 Jul 1944, p. 9. *HR* 28 Jul 1944, p. 13. *HR* 3 Aug 1944, p. 44. *HR* 17 Aug 1944, p. 3. *HR* 21 Aug 1944, p. 4. *HR* 24 Aug 1944, p. 5. *HR* 28 Aug 1944, pp. 10-11. *HR* 5 Sep 1944, p. 13. *HR* 27 Sep 1944, p. 7. *HR* 5 Jun 1945, p. 3. *HR* 16 Jul 1945, p. 8. *MPHPD* 9 Sep 1944, p. 2093. *MPHPD* 9 Jun 1945, p. 2485. *NYT* 9 Jul 1945, p. 14. *Var* 6 Jun 1945, p. 12.

THE GREAT MEADOW (Native Americans, Shawnee)

Metro-Goldwyn-Mayer Corp.; controlled by Loew's, Inc. *Dist* Metro-Goldwyn-Mayer Distributing Corp. 24 Jan **1931**; *Prod:* early Sep—mid-Nov 1930 [©Metro-Goldwyn-Mayer Distributing Corp.; 2 Feb 1931; LP1946]. Sd (Western Electric Sound System); b&w. 9 reels, 7,242 ft. 80 min. Passed by the National Board of Review.

Dir Charles Brabin. [*Asst dir* Ben Taggert]. *Adpt* Charles Brabin and Edith Ellis. *Dial* Edith Ellis. *Photog* William Daniels and Clyde DeVinna. *Art dir* Cedric Gibbons. *Film ed* George Hively. *Ward* René Hubert. *Rec dir* Douglas Shearer. [*Rec eng* Ralph Shugart]. [*Tech adv* Chief Whitespear].

Source: Based on the novel *The Great Meadow* by Elizabeth Madox Roberts (New York, 1930).

Cast: John Mack Brown (*Berk Jarvis*), Eleanor Boardman (*Diony Hall*), Lucille LaVerne (*Elvira Jarvis*), Anita Louise (*Betty Hall*), Gavin Gordon (*Evan Muir*), Guinn Williams (*Reuben Hall*), Russell Simpson (*Thomas Hall*), Sarah Padden (*Mistress* [*Molly*] *Hall*), Helen Jerome Eddy (*Sally Tolliver*), [James Marcus (*James Harrod*)], [Gardner James (*Joe Tandy*)], [John Miljan (*Daniel Boone*)], [Andy Shuford], [Jack Winn], [Chief Whitespear], [William Bakewell].

Historical, Drama. [*Print viewed*]. In 1777, the Hall family of Virginia listens to a speech by Daniel Boone, the idol of Berk Jarvis, who is the eldest Hall daughter Diony's favorite beau. Impressed by Boone's descriptions of Kentucky's bounties, Berk, his brother Jack and their mother Elvira start a wagon train to be led by Berk. Berk asks Diony to marry him, and after the ceremony they set off. The journey to Kentucky is longer and more difficult than they had imagined, and Jack is killed during an Indian attack, but after six months the ragged little band reaches Ft. Harrod. The happy couple settle in, and are soon expecting a baby. One day, Diony and Elvira go outside the fort's walls to pick corn and are attacked by Black Fox, a Shawnee. Elvira bravely defends Diony and is killed and scalped. Black Fox is scared off before he can kill Diony, and everyone mourns the Jarvis' loss. Before long, however, Berk must leave to replenish the fort's supply of salt. Berk is gone for four months, during which time Diony gives birth to their son Tommy. On the night of Berk's return, the settlers have a celebration, which is interrupted by an attack by Black Fox and his warriors. Black Fox taunts Berk with Elvira's scalp, and the incident preys on Berk's mind until he tells Diony he must hunt down Black Fox and avenge Elvira. Diony tries to dissuade him, but acquiesces once she sees how determined he is. Berk leaves, and Diony and Tommy are taken care of by Evan Muir, one of Diony's former beaus from Virginia. Berk is captured by Indians, sold to the British and imprisoned for a year, but after he is freed, he continues his quest. He finds Black Fox and kills him, but is captured by the Shawnee. Evan receives news that Berk has been killed, and as time passes Diony's sorrow lessens and she marries Evan. Two years after Berk's departure, he escapes from the Shawnee, and returns to the fort. He finds Evan and Diony, who gently tells him that she married Evan, for she could not remain in the wilderness alone. The two men are on the verge of fighting when Diony reminds them of the wilderness law which says that if a man leaves his wife, and she thinks he is dead and remarries, it is for her to choose between the two men if her first husband returns. They agree to abide by her decision, and Diony tells them that although Berk is the great love of her life, she

cannot forget Evan's great kindness and devotion, and so she chooses Evan. Berk prepares to depart, but when Evan sees how Berk's attention to sleeping Tommy brings tears to Diony's eyes, he realizes that she and Berk belong together. Evan tells Diony how much he will treasure their time together and leaves the reunited couple to begin their life together again. *Family life. Marriage. Revenge. Settlers. Shawnee Indians. United States–History–Colonial period, ca. 1600-1775. Daniel Boone. Cabins. Childbirth. Dogs. Fort Harrod (KY). Motherhood. Murder. Sisters. Virginia. Wagon trains.*

Note: After the film's credits, a written statement reads: "America has enshrined in her soul those unlettered men and women whose courage and strength established her frontiers in 1777. They had but a glimpse of the mighty cause they served. Those devoted wives and sweethearts, who endured martyrdom for love's sake, lie quiet and unsung in the great meadow. Women of the Wilderness, we salute you!" According to the film's pressbook, Chief Whitespear, a Cherokee Indian, "was placed in charge" of the Indian actors, and led them in the film. According to *NYT* and the film's pressbook, scenes of the Indian attacks were filmed at "the 'Lake Sherwood' region or the old Canterbury Ranch," which was an 8,000 acre area located about fifty miles from Hollywood; and Fort Harrod was recreated on the 23,000 acre Russell Ranch, also located about fifty miles from Los Angeles. A *NYT* news item notes that director Charles Brabin and writer Edith Ellis consulted various southern Chambers of Commerce and historical organizations about the history of Fort Harrod, and also obtained authentic artifacts from them to use as props.

FD 15 Mar 1931, p. 10. *EXH* 6 Dec 1930, p. 27. *HF* 6 Sep 1930, p. 24. *HF* 22 Nov 1930, p. 24. *MPH* 9 May 1931, pp. 32-33. *NYT* 14 Mar 1931, p. 23. *NYT* 15 Mar 1931, p. 6. *NYT* 22 Mar 1931, p. 5. *NYT* 24 Apr 1932. *Var* 18 Mar 1931, p. 14.

THE GREAT SEIZER see **BAD LANDS**

THE GREAT SHADOW (Russian Americans)

Adanac Producing Co. *Dist* Republic Distributing Corp. Mar **1920** [©Republic Distributing Corp.; 21 Apr 1920; LU15067]. Si; b&w. 6 reels.

Dir Harley Knoles. *Story* Rudolph Berliner.

Cast: Tyrone Power (*Jim McDonald*), Donald Hall (*Donald Alexander*), Dorothy Bernard (*Elsie Alexander*), John Rutherford (*Bob Sherwood*), Louis Stern (*Klimoff*), E. Emerson (*Greek leader*), E. Hornbostell (*Frank Shea*).

Drama. Jim McDonald, the foreman of a shipbuilding plant and head of the labor union, strives to combat the anarchistic propaganda being put forth by Klimoff, the leader of a Bolshevik gang whose goal is to disrupt the country with strikes and anarchy. Despite McDonald's efforts, a strike is called, resulting in chaos. McDonald's child is knocked down by runaway horses abandoned by their striking driver, and dies. Mob scenes take place in America, as well as in Russia. Eventually, the unrest is quelled with an armistice called between Capital and Labor for a year, during which time wages are to be increased to reflect the cost of living, and leaders are to work out a common plan for their mutual advantage. The strikers now realize that they have been pawns of the Bolsheviks and call off the strike, agreeing to the plan. *Anarchists. Bolshevists and Bolshevism. Employer-employee relations. Labor leaders. Mobs. Russian Americans. Shipyards. Strikes and lockouts. Trade unions. Accidents. Children. Plant foremen.*

Note: Some of the subplots of the film cannot be summarized, as copyright information has deteriorated and reviews are inconclusive. Concerning the film's depiction of the Russian characters, *Var* commented, "No effort is spared to drive home the insidious methods of Russian aliens disseminating the gospel of Bolshevism among labor organizations in this country. The filthy, repulsive appearance of the Russian alien characters as depicted in the picture cause one to shrink and sudder."

MPN 6 Mar 1920, p. 2337. *MPW* 6 Mar 1920, p. 1656. *Var* 21 May 1920, p. 34.

THE GREAT SIOUX UPRISING (Native Americans, Dakota)

Universal-International Pictures Co., Inc. *Dist* Universal Pictures Co., Inc. Jul **1953**; *Prod:* early Oct—mid-Oct 1952 [©Universal Pictures Co.; 8 May 1953; LP2557]. Sd (Western Electric Recording); col (Technicolor). 7,213 ft. 79-80 min. PCA cert no. 16310.

Prod Albert J. Cohen. *Co-prod* Leonard Goldstein. *Dir* Lloyd Bacon. *Asst dir* Jesse Hibbs, [George Lollier and Rusty Meek]. [*Dial dir* Hugh Cummings]. *Scr* Melvin Levy, J. Robert Bren and Gladys Atwater. *Addl dial* Frank Gill, Jr. *Story* J. Robert Bren and Gladys Atwater. *Dir of photog* Maury Gertsman. *Technicolor color consultant* William Fritzsche. *Art dir* Alexander Golitzen, Alfred Sweeney and [Bernard Herzbrun]. *Film ed* Edward Curtiss. *Set dec* Russell A. Gausman and Joe Kish. *Cost* Bill Thomas. *Mus dir* Joseph Gershenson. *Sd* Leslie I. Carey and Glenn E. Anderson. *Hair stylist* Joan St. Oegger. *Makeup* Bud Westmore. [*Unit prod mgr* Art Siteman].

Cast: Jeff Chandler (*Jonathan Westgate*), Faith Domergue (*Joan Britton*), Lyle Bettger (*Stephen Cook*), Peter Whitney (*Ahab Jones*), Stacy S. Harris (*Uriah*), Walter Sande (*Joe Baird*), Stephen Chase (*Major McKay*), John War Eagle (*Red Cloud*), Glenn Strange (*Stand Watie*), Charles Arnt (*Gist*), Julia Montoya (*Heyoka*), Ray Bennett (*Sgt. Manners*), Dewey Drapeau (*Teo-Ka-Ha*), Boyd Red Morgan (*Ray*), Lane Bradford (*Lee*), Jack Ingram (*Sam*), Clem Fuller (*Jake*), [Virginia Mullen (*Madge Baird*)], [Monte Montague (*Tom*)], [George Taylor (*Simmons*)], [James Van Horn (*Cook's man*)], [Ed Rand], [Edmund Cobb], [Ned Davenport], [Kermit Maynard], [Carl Andre], [Philo McCullough], [Stanley Blystone], [Buddy Roosevelt], [Al Wyatt], [Earl Conner], [Duane E. Conner], [Howard B. Swartz], [Harvey Matlock], [Francis Shillal], [Gilbert E. Conner], [Mel Lambert].

Western. [*Print viewed*]. During the Civil War, livery stable owner Joan Britton learns that Union forces are in desperate need of horses and asks her cook, Heyoka, to help her find the great herds kept by the Sioux. On their way to the Sioux village, Joan and Heyoka are secretly tracked by horse trader Stephen Cook, who wants the valuable horses for himself. At the village, Chief Red Cloud tells Joan that the horses, a gift from the Nez Perce, are sacred and therefore not for sale. After eavesdropping from behind a tree, Cook decides to steal the horses, and returns later, with his men. The Indians try unsuccessfully to stop the thieves, and a horse and brave are shot in the skirmish. Then, physician Jonathan Westgate arrives in the Sioux village and helps Chief Red Cloud to heal the injured horse. Red Cloud explains that the tribe has elected not to pursue the horse thieves, fearing that the Cavalry might come and appropriate their remaining land. Red Cloud gives Jonathan a horse, and the physician promises to help locate the thieves. In town, Jonathan befriends blacksmith Ahab Jones and soon falls in love with Joan. Explaining that he gave up medicine because he was unable to help many dying Union soldiers, Jonathan sets up shop as the town veterinarian. That day, Cook arrives with three hundred horses, which he claims he bought from another dealer. Jonathan, however, removes an arrowhead from the horse of Cook's foreman and immediately suspects him in the horse theft. Later, Jonathan learns that the local horse ranchers are angry because Cook's men have been intimidating other horsemen attempting to sell to the Cavalry. Jonathan suggests that the ranchers journey to a nearby fort together to explain the situation to Major McKay, but Cook foils this plan by kidnapping Jonathan and persuading the ranchers to return home. When one of the ranchers defies him, Cook has one of his men stab him and carefully places Jonathan's scalpel near the body. Later, while he is being held captive at Cook's ranch, Jonathan performs an operation on Cook, saving his life. As soon as Jonathan is released, the townspeople brand him a murderer and try to hang him. Jonathan escapes and tells Red Cloud that he has seen a stolen Sioux horse at Cook's ranch. After Red Cloud agrees to help clear Jonathan of the murder charge, Cook discovers the doctor's plan and gets rid of the horse. Joan informs Red Cloud of this, but the chief accuses her of setting up the theft of the tribe's horses. The chief takes Joan and Jonathan to an Indian council, where Stand Watie, a Cherokee Confederate general, tries to convince Sioux, Oglala, Nez Perce, Cheyenne, Crow and Blackfoot leaders to join the Southern forces. As he is white, Jonathan is allowed to speak only after surviving a bludgeoning by a group of braves, and he expounds upon the Northern belief that no one is inferior because of skin color. Meanwhile, Cook and his men raid the remaining Sioux herd, killing a child in the process. Horrified, Red Cloud accuses Jonathan of treachery and sends his men to drive away the horse thieves. Hoping for assistance, Cook tells the fort that the Indians have raided a herd of horses that he purchased. After Joan and Jonathan escape from the Sioux village, Jonathan finds Cook and defeats him in a fistfight. Jonathan finally convinces McKay of Cook's guilt, after which the major promises Red Cloud that the Cavalry will punish the murderers and pay for the horses. Satisfied, Red Cloud agrees to maintain the peace. Later, Jonathan enlists in the Union army and promises to marry Joan upon his return. *Dakota Indians. Horse thieves. Physicians. Racism. Red Cloud. United States–History–Civil War, 1861-1865.* Blacksmiths. Cooks. Deception. Eavesdropping. Escapes. Forts. Frame-ups. Friendship. Heroism. Horse trading. Indians of North America. Kidnapping. Lynching. Military service, Voluntary. Murder. Reconciliation. Romance. Settlers. Tests of character. United States. Army. Cavalry. Veterinarians. Stand Watie.

Note: The working title of this film was *Sioux Uprising*. According to reviews, the film was shot on location in eastern Oregon. A 26 Jul 1952 *LAT* news item notes that Alexis Smith was originally scheduled to play the female lead. According to a preliminary Universal cast listing, Rosa Rey was to appear in the role of "Heyoka."

Stand Watie (1806-1871) was a Cherokee leader. During the early days of the Civil War, he sided with the Confederacy and commanded two regiments of the Cherokee Mounted Rifles. On 10 May 1864, he received the commission of brigadier general, becoming the first Native American so promoted. In 1865, after the U.S. government began building a road from Wyoming's Ft. Laramie to Montana, Red Cloud (1822-1909), chief of the Bad Face band of the Oglalas and leader of Sioux and Cheyenne bands, led his braves in attacks on U.S. forces designed to stop the flow of settlers. During the next two years, in what was dubbed Red Cloud's War, the warrior and his braves captured army construction troops on the Bozeman Trail and killed many whites. In 1868, Red Cloud agreed to have his people settled on the Red Cloud Agency in Nebraska.

Box 4 Jul 1953. *DV* 24 Jun 1953, p. 3. *Exb* 1 Jul 1953, p. 3549. *FD* 14 Jul 1953, p. 6. *Har* 27 Jun 1953, p. 104. *HCN* 1 Aug 1953. *HR* 3 Oct 1952, p. 23. *HR* 17 Oct 1952, p. 13. *HR* 24 Jun 1953, p. 3. *LAEx* 1 Aug 1953. *LAT* 1 Aug 1953. *MPD* 2 Jul 1953. *MPHPD* 27 Jun 1953, p. 1886. *NYT* 18 Jul 1953, p. 6. *Var* 24 Jun 1953, p. 6.

GREAT STAGECOACH ROBBERY (Native Americans)

Republic Pictures Corp. *Dist* Republic Pictures Corp. 24 Feb **1945**; Los Angeles opening: 15 Feb 1945; Prod: 6 Sep—mid-Sep 1944 [©Republic Pictures Corp.; 9 Feb 1945; LP13181]. Sd (RCA Sound System); b&w. 6 reels, 5,011 ft. 56 min. Passed by the National Board of Review. PCA cert no. 10455.

Series: Red Ryder.

[*Exec prod* William J. O'Sullivan]. *Assoc prod* Louis Gray. *Dir* Lesley Selander. *2d unit dir* Yakima Canutt. [*Asst dir* Roy Wade]. *Orig scr* Randall Faye. *Photog* Bud Thackery. [*2d cam* Maurice Kains]. [*Transparency projection shots* Gordon C. Schaefer]. *Art dir* Fred A. Ritter. *Film ed* Charles Craft. *Set dec* Charles Thompson. *Mus dir* Richard Cherwin. *Sd* Ed Borschell. [*Re-rec and eff mixer* John Stransky, Jr.]. [*Re-rec, eff and mus mixer* Howard Wilson].

Source: Based on the comic strip "Red Ryder" by Fred Harman (1938—1964), by special arrangement with Stephen Slesinger.

Cast: WILD BILL ELLIOTT (*Red Ryder*), Bobby Blake [(*Little Beaver*)], Alice Fleming [(*The Duchess*)], Don Costello [(*Jed Quinlan*)], Francis McDonald [(*Con Hollister*)], John James [(*Billy Hollister*)], Sylvia Arslan [(*Boots Hollister*)], Bud Geary [(*Joe Slade*)], Leon Tyler [(*Sneak kid*)], Freddie Chapman [(*Boy*)], [Dickie Dillon (*Small boy*)], [Bobby Dillon (*Boy on plank*)], [Raymond ZeBrack (*Last kid*)], [Patsy May (*Girl*)], [Chris Wren, Ginny Wren (*Twins*)], [Frederick Howard (*Saunders, banker*)], [Grace Cunard (*Mother*)], [Hank Bell (*Stagecoach driver*)], [Horace Carpenter].

Western. [*Print viewed*]. One afternoon in the small town of Blue Springs, schoolteacher Jed Quinlan breaks up a fight between tomboy Boots Hollister and Indian Little Beaver, who taunt each other with the names "Wildcat" and "Injun." Quinlan administers a hearty switching to both combatants, and later that afternoon, the children return to the schoolhouse accompanied by their guardians, Boots's older brother Billy, and Little Beaver's friend, Red Ryder. Billy does not disguise his antagonism toward Red, who, five years previously, sent Billy's father Con to prison for robbing his stagecoach line of $150,000. After settling the confrontation, Red goes to the stagecoach office, which he runs with his aunt, The Duchess, who is worried about a shipment of $150,000 that she is to receive the next day. Red assures her that the money will be safe, for while it is the same amount stolen by Con earlier, he is not due to be paroled for a few more days. Meanwhile, Quinlan meets with Con's former cohort, Joe Slade, who reveals that Con, who has reformed, was released weeks earlier. Quinlan, who is posing as a teacher to cover his many criminal activities, deduces that Con will be on the next day's stage, and that the upcoming shipment must be Con's old loot, which was never recovered. Quinlan and Slade then enlist the hot-tempered Billy in a robbery of the stage. Although he does not succeed in catching the outlaws, Red prevents the theft, then is pleasantly surprised to discover that Con, who is a passenger on the stage, has reformed and intends to return the money to the bank. Boots happily greets her father when he arrives home, but Billy is less pleased to see Con after he declares that the Hollister family is going to make a clean start. Billy runs off to join Slade, and Con and Boots go alone to town to seek a loan to rebuild their ranch. None of the locals are willing to give Con a second chance, although Red does his best to vouch for him. Bitter at seeing his father treated so shabbily, Billy agrees to Quinlan's plan to rob the bank. Red hears their gunshots, then chases the crooks as they attempt to escape and succeeds in shooting Slade

and wounding Quinlan. Quinlan eludes Red and rides Slade's horse to Con's barn, where he then hides. The horse and saddlebags, which contain the stolen money, are found by Con, whom Red suspects when he arrives shortly after. Determined to clear himself and help Billy, Con locks Red in a closet and sets off to find his son. Little Beaver frees Red and they ride in pursuit, after which Boots discovers the wounded Quinlan hiding in the barn. Boots realizes that Quinlan is one of the robbers, and shoots her with one of Red's pistols, which he had dropped while struggling with Con. When Con and Billy find Boots's body, Quinlan states that Red is the murderer, and Con holds Little Beaver captive in order to force Red into a fight. Upon his arrival at the Hollister house, Red deduces that Quinlan is the escaped robber and proves his guilt by comparing his wound to a bullet hole in the saddle bags, which he had been carrying over his shoulder. Red apprehends Quinlan, who is sentenced to hang after Billy testifies against him. In exchange for his testimony, Billy is paroled to Con's custody, and soon the father and son gratefully bid farewell to Red and Little Beaver. *Criminals–Rehabilitation. Frame-ups. Murder. Outlaws. Schoolteachers. Stagecoach lines. Aunts. Bank robberies. Brothers and sisters. Chases. Circumstantial evidence. Fathers and daughters. Fathers and sons. Feuds. Fights. Gunshot wounds. Horses. Indians of North America. Reputation. Stagecoach robberies. Tomboys. Wards and guardians.*

Note: Modern sources include Henry Wills, Robert Wilke and Tom London in the cast. For more information on the "Red Ryder" series, please consult the Series Index and see the entry below for *Tucson Raiders.*
DV 16 Feb 1945, p. 3. *HR* 16 Feb 1945, p. 4. *HR* 6 Sep 1945, p. 4. *HR* 8 Sep 1945, p. 13. *MPHPD* 2 Dec 1944, p. 2203. *MPHPD* 24 Feb 1945, p. 2330.

THE GREAT WHITE NORTH (Native Americans, Native Alaskans)
Dist Fox Film Corp. **1928** Sd eff and talking sequence (Movietone); b&w. 6 reels, 5,560 ft.
Dir Sydney Snow and H. A. Snow. *Story* Sydney Snow and H. A. Snow. *Titles* Malcolm Stuart Boylan and Barney Wolf. *Photog* Sydney Snow and H. A. Snow. *Film ed* Kenneth Hawks.
Cast: Vilhjalmur Stefanson (*Speaker in a short prolog to the film*).
Documentary. This film is a record of some aspects of life in the Arctic: a walrus hunt; a bear hunt that ends in the capture of the bear in nets; a conspectus of arctic bird life; and a whale hunt in which a whale is harpooned. The film concludes with scenes of Herald Island, where several members of the Stefanson Polar Expedition lost their lives. *Arctic regions. Birds. Explorers. Herald Island. Polar bears. Stefanson Polar Expedition. Walruses. Whales and whaling.*
Note: This film was also copyrighted and reviewed under the title *Lost in the Arctic.*

THE GREATEST LOVE (Italian Americans)
Select Pictures Corp. *Dist* Select Pictures Corp. Dec **1920**? [©Select Pictures Corp.; 28 Dec 1920; LP15978]. Si; b&w. 6 reels, 5,520 ft.
Pres Lewis J. Selznick. *Supv* Harry Rapf. *Dir* Henry Kolker. *Scen* Edward J. Montagne. *Story* Edward Dowling. *Cam* Jules Cronjager, Alfred Gandolfi and Philip E. Rosen.
Cast: Vera Gordon (*Mrs. Lantini*), Bertram Marburgh (*Mr. Lantini*), Yvonne Shelton (*Francesca Lantini*), Hugh Huntley (*Lorenzo Lantini*), William H. Tooker (*Mr. Manton*), Ray Dean (*Dorothy Manton*), Donald Hall (*Richard Sewall*), Sally Crute (*Mrs. Sewall*), Jessie Simpson (*Mrs. McCarthy*).
Drama. In 1905, the Lantinis and their children, Lorenzo and Francesca, emigrate to New York. Though poor, the family's situation begins to improve when Mr. Manton, a wealthy contractor, offers to provide Lorenzo with the opportunity for advancement, in gratitude for his having saved his daughter Dorothy in an accident. Fifteen years later, the Lantinis have advanced: Lorenzo is a successful architect, in love with Dorothy. At the Manton's party, Lorenzo and Francesca meet Richard Sewall, a theatrical magnate, for whom Lorenzo has designed a building. When Francesca meets with Sewall regarding some costumes, he seduces her. Lorenzo learns what has happened and goes to Sewall's office, only to find him dead, just as the police arrive. He is convicted of the crime, but his mother never doubts his innocence and seeks to prove it. By coincidence, she meets Sewall's wife, who confesses that she murdered Sewall because of his cruelty. Lorenzo is free, and the family reunited. *Architects. Immigrants. Italians. Murder. Seduction. Contractors. False arrests. Mothers and sons. New York City. Theater owners.*
Note: The working title of this film was *Mother Love.*

ETR 29 Jan 1921, p. 856. *MPN* 2 Oct 1920, p. 2661. *MPW* 29 Jan 1921, p. 594. *Var* 25 Feb 1921, p. 42. *Wid's* 30 Jan 1921, p. 3.

THE GREATEST LOVE OF ALL (Italian Americans)
George Beban Productions. *Dist* Associated Exhibitors, Inc. 1 Feb **1925** [©George Beban-Associated Exhibitors, Inc.; 31 Dec 1924; LU20975]. Si; b&w. 7 reels, 6,400 ft.
Dir George Beban. *Story* George Beban.
Cast: George Beban (*Joe, the iceman*), J. W. Johnston (*District Attorney Kelland*), Wanda Lyon (*Mrs. Godfrey Kelland*), Baby Evelyn (*Their daughter*), Nettie Belle Darby (*Marie Simpkin, the Maid*), O. Zangrilli (*The Cobbler*), Mary Skurkoy (*His daughter, Trina*), Maria Di Benedetta (*His "Sweetheart"*), William Howatt (*The Presiding Judge*), John K. Newman (*Attorney for the defense*), George Humbert (*Interpreter*), Robert M. Doll (*Court officer*).
Melodrama. Joe, a poor Italian iceman, saves enough money both to furnish a basement apartment in New York and to arrange passage to America from the old country for his mother. Joe is soon engaged to Trina, and Joe's mother secretly finds work doing laundry in the home of District Attorney Kelland, in order to help them save enough to be married. When a diamond bracelet belonging to Mrs. Kelland disappears, Joe's mother finds it in the dirty linen but, before she can return it, she is seen with it and arrested as a thief. She is tried, convicted, and sentenced to three years in jail. Joe is driven wild with anxiety and joins in a plot to kill the D. A. by putting high explosives in his golf ball. Joe relents and saves the D. A. when Trina proves that the Kellands' daughter was responsible for putting the bracelet in the wash. Joe's mother is released from jail, and she and the young lovers find happiness in a little home in the country. *Family relationships. Icemen. Immigrants. Injustice. Italian Americans. Laundresses. Motherhood. New York City.*
FD 23 Nov 1924. *MPW* 17 Jan 1925. *NYT* 11 Nov 1924, p. 14. *Var* 12 Nov 1924, p. 24.

THE GREATEST SIN (African Americans)
Trio Production Co. **1922.** Si; b&w. 4 reels.
Cast: Mae Evlyn Lewis, Victor Nix.
Melodrama (?), African American. No information about the precise nature of this film has been found. *African Americans.*
Note: Trio Production Co. was located in Dallas, TX.

THE GREATEST THING IN LIFE (French Americans, African Americans)
D. W. Griffith; Artcraft Pictures. *Dist* Famous Players-Lasky Corp. 8 Dec **1918** [©David W. Griffith; 15 Nov 1918; LP13064]. Si; b&w. 5-7 reels.
Pres D. W. Griffith. *Dir* D. W. Griffith. *Story and scen* Captain Victor Marier. *Cam* G. W. Bitzer.
Cast: Lillian Gish (*Jeanette Peret*), Robert Harron (*Edward Livingston*), Adolphe Lestina (*Leo Peret*), David Butler (*Monsieur Le Bebe*), Elmo Lincoln (*American soldier*), Edward Peil (*German officer*), Kate Bruce (*Jeanette's aunt*), Peaches Jackson (*Mlle. Peaches*), Ernest Butterworth.
World War I, Drama. Edward Livingston is the selfish, pampered scion of a wealthy New York family. To his chagrin, he finds that he is falling in love with the vivacious Jeanette Peret, who sells cigars in her father's Greenwich Village tobacco shop. Jeanette is attracted to Edward but soon becomes disillusioned by his condescending manner and his dislike of children. Jeanette's father Leo longs to visit his native land of France, and when Edward anonymously sends him a check for $1,000, he and his daughter make the journey to a small village on the Marne River. The young man follows, but because he cannot comprehend Jeanette's fondness for Monsieur Le Bebe, a common but goodhearted man, he returns to New York. With the outbreak of World War I, Edward fights with the American forces in the trenches of Europe, where he repeatedly witnesses selfless acts of courage. He is deeply moved when a young black soldier offers him his last drop of water. Soon afterwards, the soldier is shot, and as he lays dying and calling for his mammy, Edward kisses his cheek. Le Bebe is killed defending Jeanette, whose father's secret telephone has been traced by the Germans, and they are narrowly rescued by a detachment of Americans led by Edward. Having learned understanding and courage, Edward is united with Jeanette. *Courage. France. French Americans. Heirs. Snobs and snobbishness. World War I. African Americans. Espionage. Fathers and daughters. Germany. Army. Marne River (France). New York City. Soldiers. Telephone. Tobacconists. Trench warfare. United States. Army.*

Note: The working title of this film was *The Cradle of Souls*. Modern sources credit James Smith as film editor and give a length of 6,062 ft. Lengths noted in contemporary sources vary from five to seven reels. Some of the scenes were shot along the Marne River and Chateau Thierry in France. Captain Victor Marier, credited as the film's author, was the pseudonym of D. W. Griffith and S. E. V. Taylor. In her autobiography, Lillian Gish calls the film "one of Mr. Griffith's best films and one of his most neglected," states that she suggested the film's title. Modern sources state that the original title was *Cradle of Souls*. Gish also relates that portrait photographer Henrik Sartov shot close-ups of her for the film. According to modern sources, Griffith produced a stage prologue for the film's Los Angeles opening, which was directed by George Fawcett and featured, among others, Rudolph Valentino, Clarine Seymour and Carol Dempster.

ETR 14 Dec 1918, p. 88. *ETR* 4 Jan 1919, p. 425. *MPN* 4 Jan 1919, p. 149. *MPW* 28 Dec 1918, p. 1558. *MPW* 4 Jan 1919, p. 115. *NYT* 23 Dec 1918, 9:1. *Var* 3 Jan 1919, p. 38. *Wid's* 5 Jan 1919, p. 23.

GREED *see* **LUST FOR GOLD**

THE GREEN-EYED MONSTER (African Americans)
Norman Film Mfg. Co. **1921**; Chicago opening: 6 Jul 1921. Si; b&w. 8 reels.
Cast: Jack Austin, Louise Dunbar, Steve Reynolds.

Melodrama, African American. Two men, Negroes, both in love with the same girl, work for two different railroads that are competing for a contract to carry the Government Fast Mail. In order to establish a basis on which the contract can be awarded, a race is arranged between two trains. The winner of that race also wins the hand of his sweetheart. *African Americans. Jealousy. Postal service. Railroads. Romantic rivalry.*

Note: The Norman Film Mfg. Co. was located in Jacksonville, FL. Publicity for this film stated, "There is not a white man in the cast, or is there depicted in the entire picture anything of the usual mimicry of the Negro. This photoplay has been indorsed [sic] by the most prominent colored people of America." The publicity also stated that an $80,000 train wreck was filmed. A lobby card stated, "The characterizations in this spectacular production were enacted by colored people, chosen from many different walks of life. The Lawyer, Doctor, Banker and finished actor and actress portray this story which in a subtle way suggests the advancement of the colored race along educational and financial lines."

GREEN FIELDS (Yiddish language)
Collective Film Producers, Inc.; Kinotrade, Inc.; An Edgar G. Ulmer Production. *Dist* New Star Films, Inc. 11 Oct **1937**; Prod: began 5 Aug 1937 at Producers Service Studios Inc., Ridgefield, N.J. [©Collective Film Producers, Inc.; 22 Nov 1937; LP7634]. Sd (Variray Blue Seal Recording); b&w. 11 reels, 9,570 ft. 105 min. Passed by the National Board of Review. PCA cert no. 01839. Yiddish language with English subtitles.
Exec prod Roman Rebush. *Prod supv* Ludwig Landy. *Dir* EDGAR G. ULMER and Jacob Ben-Ami. *Asst dir* Louis Brandt and Sol Chodrow. *Adpt and dial* Peretz Hirshbein. *Scr* George G. Moskov. *English titles* Leon Dennen. *Cam* William Miller and J. Burgi Contner. *Landscapes and designs* Steve Goulding. *Ed* Jack Kemp. *Mus composition and arr* Vladimir Heifetz. *Clarinet solo* S. Bellison. *Rec* Edwin Schabbehar and Edward Fenton. [*Scr supv* Shirley Ulmer].
Song(s): "Di Nacht," words and music by Peretz Hirshbein; "Meid Lech," "A Malech Veint," "Es Lesht Zich Shtern," "Ohn Boiden Shloft der Dach" and "A Maisale," composer unknown.
Source: Based on the play *Grine Felder* by Peretz Hirshbein (New York, 1918).
Cast: Michael Goldstein (*Levy Yitzchok*), Helen Beverley (*Tzineh*), Izidor Casher (*Duvid Noiach*), Anna Appel (*Rochel*), Max Vodnoy (*Alkuneh*), Lea Noemi (*Gittel*), Dena Drute (*Stera*), Saul Levine (*Hersh-Ber*), Hershel Bernardi (*Avram-Yankov*), B. Arnon (*A yeshive bocher*).
Yiddish, Rural, Domestic, Comedy-drama. [*Print viewed*]. Sometime in the past, Levy Yitzchok, a young, restless *Talmudic* student in a city in Russia, leaves his *beth midrash*, or synagogue, after coming to the realization that one must search for truth. He wanders through the rural countryside, where he meets Avram-Yankov, a Jewish child. Meanwhile, Tzineh, Avram-Yankov's older sister, spies on her friend Stera, who has come to help Tzineh's family plant potatoes, and sees Stera kiss Tzineh's brother Hersh-Ber to his surprise. When Stera's mother Gittel says to Hersh-Ber's mother Rochel that Tzineh is spoiling Stera, Rochel, insulted, decides that she will be against a match between the children. As Tzineh teases Stera about the kiss, Avram-Yankov brings Levy Yitzchok to the farm, and the girls hide to look at the stranger. Impressed with Levy Yitzchok's thoughtful conversation, Tzineh's father Duvid Noiach

asks him to live with them and teach their children. Alkuneh, Gittel's husband, offers to chip in, and Levy Yitzchok, who has vowed to stop wherever he finds true Jews, accepts the offer. Tzineh is fascinated with the stranger. Envious that the scholar is staying with his neighbor, the blustery Alkuneh tells Stera not to see Hersh-Ber. After a month, Levy Yitzchok tells Avram-Yankov that he soon shall leave because he misses his books and the atmosphere of *Talmud* study. Avram-Yankov wants to go with him and become a rabbi also, but Levy Yitzchok says that it is also good to work the fields. When Levy Yitzchok tells Tzineh, whom he is uneasy around, that he may go because he thinks his presence at the farm is useless, she begs him to stay and asks him to teach her, but he says that it would not be proper. Alkuneh then tries to get Levy Yitzchok to come to his home, but Duvid Noiach, deeply upset, pleads with Levy Yitzchok not to disgrace him by leaving, as the other villagers are impressed that a scholar is staying at his house. Tzineh, alone with her mother, confesses that she wants to marry Levy Yitzchok and cries that she will die if he leaves. After Avram-Yankov shows Levy Yitzchok the beauty of the fields, he agrees to stay until after the holidays. As Duvid Noiach and his family help Alkuneh harvest his hay, Levy Yitzchok wistfully watches and asks Avram-Yankov to teach him to till the soil. When the potatoes are harvested, Levy Yitzchok, feeling useless, realizes that God desires both *Torah* study and labor from men. Tzineh falls from a tree, while getting apples for Levy Yitzchok. Touched by her effort, Levy Yitzchok is also happily suprised when she demonstrates that Avram-Yankov has taught her to write, but he is greatly flustered when she suddenly kisses him on the cheek and runs off. Alkuneh gruffly tells Duvid Noiach and Rochel that he wants the teacher, rather than Hersh-Ber, for a son-in-law and offends his neighbors when he and his wife contend that Tzineh is ruining Levy Yitzchok. Duvid Noiach then asks Levy Yitzchok not to go away, and Levy Yitzchok shocks him as he says he wants to be his son-in-law. Duvid Noiach readily agrees then calls Rochel to tell her the news, and she promises to be a mother to Levy Yitzchok, whose own parents died long ago. Alkuneh and Gittel interrupt the happy scene when they bring Stera to say that she does not want to see Hersh-Ber again. Stera denies this, and when Hersh-Ber sees her crying, he yells at Alkuneh then starts crying himself. Impressed by his passionate plea, Alkuneh is moved to tears himself, and he offers Hersh-Ber a dowry for Stera. Rochel tells Tzineh that she will be a bride, and Tzineh and Levy Yitzchok leave the joyful parents and walk hand-in-hand past a plow. *Family relationships. Farmers. Jews. Neighbors. Religiosity. Romance. Russia. Teachers. Wanderers. City-country contrast. Class distinction. Engagements. Envy. Feuds. Infatuation. Jealousy. Kisses. Orphans. Students.*

Note: The Yiddish title of this film was *Grine Felder*. This was the first film of Collective Film Producers, Inc., called, in a *HR* news item, a "co-operative outfit." Executive producer Roman Rebush earlier had handled distribution on the Ukrainian language film *Natalka Poltava* (see *AFI Catalog of Feature Films, 1931-20*; F3.3081), which had been directed by Edgar G. Ulmer. According to modern sources, Rebush had also been the head of Amkino, Inc. and Ludwig Landy had been a 16mm film distributor. Other films planned by Collective included *Yankel der Schmid* (see *The Singing Blacksmith* below) and three which were never made. *Uriel Acosta, Riverside Drive* and *Yankee Boile*, the latter two based on novels by Leon Kobrin. According to a modern interview with Ulmer, *Green Fields* was produced for $8,000 (which the producers raised from Household Finance by hocking their furniture) in a five-day shooting period, after six weeks of rehearsals. It was filmed on a farm in New Jersey and in Producers Service Studios, also in New Jersey, and only 15,000 feet of film (or approximately 166 minutes) was shot. Ulmer stated when that the lab that processed the film threatened to foreclose on the film because their bill had not been paid, he went to see Abraham Cahan of the Yiddish newspaper *Forverts*, who suggested he contact David Dubinsky, head of the International Ladies' Garment Workers' Union. Dubinsky liked the rough cut of the film and agreed to pre-purchase 75,000 tickets, which would allow Ulmer to pay off the lab and to finish post-production on the film.
Ulmer, in the modern interview, stated that he knew no Yiddish at the time of shooting. According to modern sources, writer Peretz Hirshbein allowed Collective to make the film under the condition that Jacob Ben-Ami, who played the *Talmud* student in the 1919 New York stage production and was one of the original members of Hirshbein's Theater Troupe in Odessa, play the same role in the film. However, because Ben-Ami's age would not have fit the role any longer, it was agreed that he would co-direct and oversee the acting and atmosphere to see that it was faithful to Hirshbein. According to the pressbook, many of the cast were members of the Artef Theatre or Maurice Schwartz's Yiddish Art Theatre. A pre-production news item stated that Ariane Roma was to be in the cast. No information regarding her participation in the final film has been located.
The plot summary in the pressbook ends with the following statement: "And thus *Green Fields* records a rapidly disappearing phase of Jewish life. For,

whether it be on the fields of Palestine or Biro-Bidjan [an area in the Soviet Far East that in 1934 was declared a Jewish autonomous region], the Jewish agricultural worker is no longer ignorant and superstitious, nor awestriken before the stoop-shouldered and world-weary symbol of the Jewish scholar. Moreover, in the fusion of [Levy Yitzchok] and Tzineh, the healthy and strong-willed peasant girl, the symbol of a new Jew is being born, a new Jew fighting for a new life." According to modern sources, Hirshbein attended the film's premiere and introduced it with the statement, "Twenty years ago, the play *Green Fields* marked the beginning of a better Yiddish theater in America. May the film *Green Fields* mark the beginning of a better Yiddish film." Most reviews hailed the film for its artistry. *FD* stated, "Here is an outstanding production that will find wide appeal outside of the Jewish race." *New York Post* remarked, "This is the best Jewish folk picture yet seen in New York." William Edlin, writing in the Yiddish newspaper *Der Tag*, commented, "This first venture may be pointed to as the first step to Jewish film industry. It is a happy thing to see that at last a Jewish movie has been made, which can be shown in all theatres throughout the world, just like all the well-made pictures of France, Czechoslovakia or Hungary." Edlin stated that this was "the first time one sees an excellent portrayal of the life of Jewish farmers in old Russia," and praised "the beautiful Yiddish one hears. It is not a literary Yiddish, but good, healthy Yiddish." In the Yiddish paper *Frebeit*, P. Novick commented, "This is the first time that we have a Jewish movie for which we do not have to find an excuse, for which we do not have to apologize....*Green Fields* is not a movie in the ordinary sense. The Hollywood laws of rapidity, tempo, are not contained here." Frank S. Nugent's mixed review in *NYT* was deemed "anti-Semitic" by Ulmer in the modern interview. In the review, Nugent wrote that the film is "a pastoral, moving with bovine complacence down the rural byway of gentle comedy." He remarked that the film's many conversational "thrusts and parries, although gayly received by those in the linguistic know, unfortunately sailed well above the goyishe kopf, for the English dialogue captions are the merest X-ray of a fatly worded script. When beard waggles at beard and farmers' wives stand chin to chin for a full two minutes, one is bound to feel like a tribal stepchild when the titled explanation proves to be 'You don't know what it means to have a man of learning in the family' or something equally incomplete. Peretz Hirshbein's folk tale has an ingenuous charm, however, even though it has, in this case, made its hero a rather ridiculous figure....The picture unquestionably would have profited by having a different leading man. Michael Goldstein carries Levy-Yitzchok's unworldliness to the point of imbecility—a better word for him, possibly, would be schlemiel. The others do more credit to the occasion...." Although Ulmer stated that *NYT* publisher Arthur Hays Sulzberger fired Nugent because of the review, this was not the case, as Nugent continued to write reviews for the paper, many of which were caustic and offensive to producers, until he left in 1940 to join Twentieth Century-Fox.

Detroit Jewish Chronicle 31 Dec 1937. *FD* 29 Jul 1937, p. 7. *FD* 20 Oct 1937, p. 6. *HR* 12 Jul 1937. *Jewish Independent* 7 Jan 1938. *MPD* 15 Oct 1937, p. 13. *MPH* 15 Jan 1938, p. 52. *NYT* 12 Oct 1937, p. 31. *Der Tag* Oct 1937.

THE GREEN PASTURES (African Americans)
Warner Bros. Pictures, Inc. *Dist* Warner Bros. Pictures, Inc. 1 Aug **1936**; New York opening: 16 Jul 1936; *Prod:* early Jan—early Mar 1936 [©Warner Bros. Pictures, Inc.; 15 Jul 1936; LP6463]. Sd (Western Electric Sound System); b&w. 10 reels. 90 or 93 min. PCA cert no. 1915.

[*Exec prod* Jack L. Warner and Hal B. Wallis]. [*Supv* Henry Blanke]. *Dir* Marc Connelly and William Keighley. [*Asst dir* Sherry Shourds]. [*Scr* Sheridan Gibney]. [*Contr to scr const* Marc Connelly]. *Photog* Hal Mohr. *Spec photog eff* Fred Jackman. [*Head gaffer* Larry Kennedy]. *Art dir* Allen Saalburg and Stanley Fleischer. *Film ed* George Amy. [*Cost* Milo Anderson]. *Chorale mus arr and cond by* Hall Johnson. [*Rec dir* Major Nathan Levinson]. [*Sd* Dave Forrest]. [*Scr clerk* Frank Fox]. [*Props* Maurice Golden]. [*Press agent* S. Charles Einfeld].

Source: Based on the play *The Green Pastures* by Marc Connelly (New York, 26 Feb 1930) and suggested by the book *Ol' Man Adam An' His Chillun* by Roark Bradford (New York, 1928).

Cast: Rex Ingram (*De Lawd/Adam/Hezdrel*), Oscar Polk (*Gabriel*), Eddie Anderson (*Noah*), Frank Wilson (*Moses*), George Reed (*Mr. Deshee*), Abraham Gleaves (*Archangel*), Myrtle Anderson (*Eve*), Al Stokes (*Cain*), Edna M. Harris (*Zeba*), James Fuller (*Cain the Sixth*), George Randol (*High Priest*), Ida Forsyne (*Noah's wife*), Ray Martin (*Shem*), Charles Andrews (*Flatfoot*), Dudley Dickerson (*Ham*), Jimmy Burress (*Japheth*), William Cumby (*Abraham/Head magician/King of Babylon*), George Reed (*Isaac*), Ivory Williams (*Jacob*), David Bethea (*Aaron*), Ernest Whitman (*Pharaoh*), Reginald Fenderson (*Joshua/Young soldier*), Slim Thompson (*Master of ceremonies*), Clinton Rosemond (*Prophet* [/*Hosea*]), The Hall Johnson Choir, [Freddie Archibald (*The gambler*)], [Bertha Wright (*Slender angel*)], [Leon Randall (*W. W. Whitfield*)], [Dolores Mae Lilly (*Carlotta Proback*)], [Florence Fields (*First cleaner*)], [Anna Mae Fritz (*Stout angel/Young gambler/Second cleaner*)], [Benevenita Washington (*Flashily dressed woman*)], [Rosina Weston (*Zipporah*)], [Fred "Snowflake" Toones (*Zubo*)], [John Larkin

(*Sexton*)], [Phillip Hurlic (*Carlisle Randall*)], [Louise Price (*Viney Proback*)], [Donald Brown (*Sexton's grandson*)].

African American, Religious, Allegory. [*Print viewed*]. One fine Sunday in the Louisiana delta, a black preacher, Mr. Deshee, tells Bible stories to his Sunday school class. In order to help the children visualize God and heaven, he describes them in terms of a Southern fish fry: De Lawd looks exactly like their preacher, and except for their wings, the angels look exactly like members of the congregation. De Lawd creates too much firmament one day, so he creates the sun and earth to drain it away. After realizing what good farmland he has made, De Lawd creates Adam and Eve to live on it. Sadly, De Lawd is disappointed by Adam and Eve's descendents. After punishing Cain for Abel's murder, De Lawd leaves the Earth alone for a while, but the next time he returns, he again finds a wicked world. Because he believes that Noah, a small town preacher, is an exception, De Lawd orders him to build an ark and then sends the rains down to destroy the rest of humanity. Soon, however, things have gotten bad again and De Lawd decides that man does not have enough to do, so he gives Abraham's descendents the land of Canaan and sends Moses to lead them out of Egypt. Moses and Aaron secure the release of the Hebrew slaves only after confounding the Egyptian pharoah with their magic tricks and killing his son. The Israelites reach the promised land, but De Lawd gets so disgusted with his children that he renounces them. Not even a delegation of angels can convince him to take them back. Yet a soft voice from Earth reaches De Lawd, and he realizes that mercy can be earned through suffering. De Lawd then wonders if this means that even God must suffer, and his question is answered by the life of Jesus Christ. Sunday school is over, and the children file out into the countryside that looks so much like heaven. *African Americans. Bible. Biblical characters. Preachers. Banjos. Children. Choirs (Music). Cooks. Dancers. Eden. Exile. Faith. Firearms. Floods. Gambling. Heaven. Hula. Jericho. Jews. Kings. Louisiana. Magicians. Moses. Prayer. Prophets. Shepherds. Slavery. Snakes. Storms.*

Note: The play on which this film was based won the 1930 Pulitzer Prize and ran on Broadway for five years and 1,779 performances. The Hall Johnson Choir sang portions of twenty-five spirituals in the film. The onscreen credits list Rex Ingram and William Cumby separately for each role they play. Although a *HR* production chart lists actor John Alexander in the cast, his appearance in the released film has not been confirmed. A *NYT* article notes that the cost of the film was in excess of $750,000. *Newsweek* indicates that Connelly was paid $100,000 and given a royalty guarantee for the screen rights to his play, and claims that it was the "highest price ever paid for screen rights." According to the file for the film in the MPAA/PCA Collection at the AMPAS Library, *The Green Pastures* was banned by censors in a number of countries, including Italy, Latvia, China, Palestine, Finland, Australia and Hungary. Censors in England reportedly inserted an explanatory foreword and eliminated many lines of dialogue. Contemporary sources indicate that the picture was one of the top moneymaking films of 1936 and was one of the top ten on the lists of both *FD* and *NYT*, as well as the National Board of Review's list of Best American Films. The play was presented on television three times during the 1950s.

DV 15 May 1936, p. 3. *FD* 19 May 1936, p. 7. *HR* 6 Jan 1936, p. 11. *HR* 2 Mar 1936, p. 11. *HR* 16 May 1936, p. 2. *MPD* 18 May 1936, p. 10. *MPH* 2 May 1936, pp. 16-17. *MPH* 30 May 1936, pp. 36-37. *MPSI* May 1936, p. 12. *Newsweek* 30 May 1936. *NYT* 17 Jul 1936, p. 20. *NYT* 31 Jan 1937. *Var* 22 Jul 1936, p. 17.

THE GREEN SHADOW see **MUSS 'EM UP**

GRETCHEN, THE GREENHORN (Dutch Americans, Italian Americans)
Fine Arts Film Co. *Dist* Triangle Film Corp. 3 Sep **1916**. Si; b&w. 5 reels.

Dir C. M. Franklin and S. A. Franklin. *Scen* Bernard McConville.

Cast: Dorothy Gish (*Gretchen*), Ralph Lewis (*John Van Houck*), Frank Bennett (*Pietro*), Eugene Pallette (*Rodgers*), Kate Bruce (*Widow Garrity*), George Stone, Violet Radcliffe, Carmen De Rue, Beulah Burns, Francis Carpenter, Tom Spencer (*The Garrity kids*).

Drama. When John Van Houck and his daughter Gretchen come to the United States from Holland, he resumes his profession as an engraver, while she falls in love with Pietro, an Italian immigrant living in their tenement. Recognizing John's skills, Rodgers, a criminal, tricks him into engraving a plate from which counterfeit money, indistinguishable from the real thing, can be made, and then convinces Gretchen to pass the phony bills. When Gretchen and John realize how they have been used, they make plans to expose Rodgers, but when he finds out, he drags them to his hideout and locks them in. The Garrity children, however, who live alongside Gretchen, witness the abduction and so alert Pietro. With the help of the police,

he captures Rodgers and then frees his sweetheart and her father, after which he and Gretchen get married. *Counterfeiters and counterfeiting. Duplicity. Dutch Americans. Engravers. Immigrants. Italian Americans. Kidnapping. Children. Fathers and daughters. Police. Tenement-houses.*
Motog 2 Sep 1916, p. 562. *MPW* 2 Sep 1916, p. 1533, 1599. *NYDM* 26 Aug 1916, p. 26. *Var* 25 Aug 1916, p. 23. *Wid's* 24 Aug 1916, p. 808.

GRIDIRON GRAFT *see* **WHILE THOUSANDS CHEER**

GRINE FELDER *see* **GREEN FIELDS**

THE GRIP OF JEALOUSY (African Americans)
Bluebird Photoplays, Inc. *Dist* Bluebird Photoplays, Inc. 28 Feb 1916 [©Universal Film Mfg. Co.; 31 Jan 1916; LP7535]. Si; b&w. 5 reels.
Dir Joseph De Grasse. *Scen* Ida May Park. *Mus accompaniment comp* M. Winkler.
Cast: Louise Lovely (*Virginia Grant*), Grace Thompson (*Beth Grant*), Jay Belasco (*Harry Grant*), Hayward Mack (*Phillip Grant*), Colin Chase (*Hugh Morey*), Harry Hamm (*Jack Morey*), Lon Chaney (*Silas Lacey*), Mr. Neff (*Harvey Lacey*), Walter Belasco (*Uncle Jeff*), Marcia Moore (*Lynda*), Dixie Carr (*Cora*).
Historical, Drama. In the deep South, before the Civil War, Lynda, a white girl, has been raised as a slave because she is believed to be the daughter of a black woman and Silas Lacey, the plantation owner who raped her. Only Virginia Grant knows that her sister Beth, who died in childbirth, is really the mother, and that the father is Jack Corey, who ran off with Beth and never returned. Virginia incorrectly believes, however, that Beth and Jack did not get married, and so she conceals Lynda's true identity in order to protect her sister's good name. Then, even though she loves Hugh Corey, Jack's brother, Virginia agrees to marry Harvey, Silas' loathsome son, as part of a deal in which Silas will free Lynda. Just before the wedding, however, Jack finally returns and discloses the true story of Lynda's birth, thereby freeing her from slavery and alleviating Virginia's fears about Lynda's legitimacy. As a result, Virginia walks out on Harvey and marries Hugh instead. *Family honor. Parentage. Plantations. Slavery–Emancipation. United States–South. Brothers. Marriage–Forced. Rape.*
Note: The original title of this film was *Love Thine Enemy.* Some exterior scenes were shot in San Francisco. Although this is a Bluebird Production, *Motog* refers to the actors as the "Rex Players."
Motog 25 Dec 1915, p. 1356. *Motog* 25 Mar 1916, p. 722. *MPW* 26 Feb 1916, p. 1372. *MPW* 4 Mar 1916, p. 1413, 1487. *Var* 18 Feb 1916, p. 22. *Wid's* 9 Mar 1916, p. 427.

DIE GROSSE FAHRT *see* **LA GRAN JORNADA**

DER GROYSER EYTSE-GEBER *see* **THE GREAT ADVISOR**

GRUMPY (*foreign version*) *see* **CASCARRABIAS**

GUH LU CHIN CHOW *se* **BLOSSOM TIME**

GUILE OF WOMEN (Swedish Americans)
Goldwyn Pictures Corp. **1921**; Los Angeles premiere: ca1 Jan 1921 [©Goldwyn Pictures Corp.; 26 Dec 1920; LP15975]. Si; b&w. 5 reels, 4,496 ft.
Dir Clarence Badger. *Asst dir* James Flood. *Cont* Edfrid A. Bingham. *Author* Peter Clark MacFarlane. *Photog* Marcel Picard.
Cast: Will Rogers (*Yal*), Mary Warren (*Hulda*), Bert Sprotte (*Skole*), Lionel Belmore (*Armstrong*), Charles A. Smiley (*Captain Larsen*), Nick Cogley (*Captain Stahl*), Doris Pawn (*Annie*), John Lince (*Butler*), Jane Starr (*Maid*).
Comedy-drama. Skole and Hjamlamar (better known as Yal) are sailors aboard the White Bear Line's oil steamer *Almaden.* Yal tells Skole of his unhappy experience with his sweetheart, Hulda, back in Sweden: five years ago he sent her $1,000 to come to America, but she never showed up. Despite this experience, Yal has a new girl, Annie, who is his partner in a delicatessen in San Francisco. When they arrive in port, Captain Larsen, president of the company, offers him a promotion and a chance to buy a share in a new ship, the *Hulda.* He goes to tell Annie the news and finds her in Skole's arms. Yal throws him out after a fight. When he tells her about his opportunity, Annie refuses to sell the shop—and he cannot prove that it was bought with his money. Dejected, Yal seeks the docks. Unknown to Yal, Hulda never received the $1,000 he sent her but came to San Francisco anyhow and has been adopted by the Larsens. They meet, and she persuades him to return to work, telling him she is only a maid in the Larsen household. When Larsen dies, she inherits the estate and Yal is made president of the company. *Delicatessens. Sailors. San Francisco (CA). Ships. Swedish Americans.*

ETR 5 Mar 1921, p. 1390. *FD* 6 Mar 1921. *MPN* 12 Mar *NYT* 28 Feb 1921, p. 16. *Var* 4 Mar 1921, p. 40.

THE GUILTY GENERATION (Italian Americans)
Columbia Pictures Corp. *Dist* Columbia Pictures Corp. 19 Nov **1931**; Prod: 17 Aug—12 Sep 1931 [©Columbia Pictures Corp.; 4 Nov 1931; LP2613]. Sd; b&w. 8 reels. 82 min.
Dir Rowland V. Lee. *Asst dir* William Crosby. *Adpt and dial* Jack Cunningham. *Photog* Byron Haskin. *Film ed* Otis Garrett. *Sd eng* George Cooper.
Source: Based on the play *The Guilty Generation* by Jo Milward and J. Kirby Hawkes (copyrighted as *The Windy City* 24 Sep 1928).
Cast: Leo Carrillo (*Mike Palmero*), Constance Cummings (*Maria Palmero*), Robert Young (*Marco Ricca, also known as Marco Smith*), Leslie Fenton (*Joe Palmero*), Boris Karloff (*Tony Ricca*), Emma Dunn (*Nina*), Jimmy Wilcox (*Don*), Elliott Rothe (*Benedicto Ricca*), Phil Tead (*Skid*), Frederic Howard (*Bradley*), Eddie Boland (*Willie*), William J. O'Brien (*Victor*), Ruth Warren (*Nellie*), Murray Kinnell (*Jerry*).
Gangster, Romance. [*Not viewed*]. A ruthless war takes place between the Palmero and Ricca gangs after the two leaders end a partnership. When two innocent children are killed in the conflict, the public outcry forces the gang leaders to flee the city. The socially ambitious Mike Palmero goes to Florida, where he attempts to finesse his way into high society after becoming wealthy through bootlegging. He still surrounds himself with bodyguards and continues to run his gang, while Tony Ricca runs his operation from the outskirts of Chicago. Mike's beautiful daughter Maria, who has been reared in a French convent, loathes her father's underworld activities, even though she knows the money he earns from them will raise her to social prominence. Mike hires a publicity woman and invites the well-known people of the city to a party in order to get Maria's picture in the newspapers. At the party, Maria meets handsome architect Marco Smith, who is actually Tony's son. Marco has disowned his father, however, and assumed the name of Smith to distance himself from Tony's lifestyle. Maria and Marco fall in love, but Maria is afraid to tell her father for fear of feuling the Palmero-Ricca feud. As members of the gangs continue to kill one another, Mike orders the murder of Benedicto, Tony's favorite son. Tony retaliates by having Maria's brother Joe killed in a hail of machine gun fire. While dying, Joe informs his father that Marco is also a Ricca. Meanwhile, Marco and Maria have eloped, and they return to tell her father. Mike plans to kill Marco but delays the murder in order to torture him with anxiety. Maria's grandmother Nina helps Marco escape, however, and kills her son rather than allow him to order the execution of Marco and Maria. The young lovers are thus free to build a new life together, while the rival gangs dwindle under the attrition of constant reprisals. *Family relationships. Feuds. Gangsters. Italian Americans. Murder. Rivalry. Romance. Architects. Bodyguards. Bootleggers. Chicago (IL). Elopement. Florida. Marriage–Secret. Mothers and sons. Newspapers. Parties. Publicists. Revenge. Social climbers.*
Note: According to the *Var* review, the scenes set in Florida and Leo Carrillo's Italian dialect suggest a comparison between the character "Mike Palmero" and to real life gangster Al Capone.
FD 22 Nov 1931, p. 10. *MPH* 28 Nov 1931, p. 45. *NYT* 21 Nov 1931, p. 20. *Var* 24 Nov 1931, p. 17.

THE GUN AND THE ARROW *see* **THUNDER IN THE SUN**

THE GUN AND THE CROSS *see* **SEVEN CITIES OF GOLD**

THE GUN AND THE GAVEL *see* **RAIDERS OF OLD CALIFORNIA**

GUN BATTLE AT MONTEREY (Latino)
Allied Artists Pictures Corp.; C. B. Pictures Corp. *Dist* Allied Artists Pictures Corp. 27 Oct **1957**; Prod: late Apr—mid-May 1957 [©Allied Artists Pictures Corp. & C. B. Pictures Corp.; 16 Oct 1957; LP9117]. Sd; b&w. 1.85. 6,079 ft. 67 min.
Exec prod D. Jersey Grut. *Prod* Carl K. Hittleman. *Dir* Carl K. Hittleman and Sidney Franklin, Jr. *Asst dir* Russell Ray Heinze. *2d asst dir* Sam Schneider. *Wrt* Jack Leonard, Lawrence Resner and David Lang. *Photog* Harry Neumann. *Spec eff* Milt Rice. *Art dir* David Milton. *Film ed* Harry Coswick. *Set dresser* Joseph Kish. *Props* Max Frankel and Frank Agnone. *Ward* Allan Sloane. *Mus dir* Robert Wiley Miller. *Sd rec* Ben Remington. *Sd mixer* Ralph Butler. *Makeup* Emile LaVigne. *Hairdresser* Alice Monte. *Prod mgr* Allen K. Wood. *Scr supv* Amalia Wade. *Constr* Jimmy West. *Head grip* Harry Lewis.

Cast: Sterling Hayden (*Jay Turner*), Ted de Corsia (*Reno*), Pamela Duncan (*Maria Salvador*), Mary Beth Hughes (*Cleo Winters*), Lee Van Cleef (*Kirby*), Charles Cane (*Mundy*), Byron Foulger (*Carson*), I. Stanford Jolley (*Idwall*), Pat Comiskey (*Frank*), Mauritz Hugo (*Charley*), Fred Sherman (*Abbott*), George Baxter (*Romero*), Michael Vallon (*Salvador*), John Dalmer (*Walt*), Felipe Turich (*Martin*), Rodolfo Hoyos, Steve Conte (*Possemen*), Richard Warren (*Bartender*), Frank Richards, Ralph Gamble, Charles Postal, Rick Warick, Chet Brandenburg.

Western. [*Not viewed*]. After holding up an express company, Jay Turner and Reno escape to a hideout near the ocean in Monterey, California. When Turner tells Reno he wants to move on alone, Reno shoots Turner and leaves him for dead. Turner is rescued by a Mexican American woman, Maria Salvador, who nurses him back to health. They fall in love, but Turner is obsessed with revenge and leaves Maria to track down Reno. He finds Reno running a successful gambling hall in Del Rey. Reno thinks he recognizes his former accomplice, but he cannot be certain since Turner has shaved off his beard. Reno considers having his hired gunman, Kirby, kill Turner, but finally decides to have his female dealer, Cleo Winters, ferret out the stranger's identity. When Cleo's efforts fail, Kirby eventually goads Turner into a gunfight. Turner defeats Kirby and throws him in jail, prompting the townspeople to make Turner their sheriff. A lynch mob comes after Reno, but Turner insists on taking him away, claiming that he is wanted by the law in another town. Turner then takes Reno back to Monterey, where he is wanted both for the express company robbery and Turner's murder. After turning Reno over to the sheriff, Turner returns to Maria, but she rejects him when she learns that he intends to let Reno hang for a crime he did not commit. Turner gives himself up and goes to jail, hoping to join Maria after he has served his time. *Bandits. False accusations. Gambling houses. Impersonation and imposture. Revenge. Robbery. Gunfights. Hired killers. Lynching. Mexican Americans. Monterey (CA). Moral reformation. Nursing back to health. Romance. Sheriffs.*

Note: The film's working title was *No Place to Die*. The studio production sheet lists David Lang as one of the film's three writers, although his name does not appear in any news item or review. The CBCS gives sole screenplay credit to John McGreevey, but his name does not appear anywhere else. McGreevey's contribution to the final film has not been determined.

Box 9 Nov 1957. *DV* 27 Feb 1957. *DV* 4 Nov 1957, p. 3. *Exb* 27 Nov 1957. *FD* 4 Nov 1957, p. 7. *Har* 9 Nov 1957. *HR* 26 Apr 1957, p. 13. *HR* 10 May 1957, p. 13. *HR* 27 Feb 1957. *HR* 6 Sep 1957. *HR* 4 Nov 1957, p. 3. *LAT* 15 Mar 1957. *MPHPD* 21 Dec 1957, p. 650. *Var* 6 Nov 1957, p. 6.

GUN FEVER (Native Americans, Dakota)

Jackson-Weston Productions, Inc. *Dist* United Artists Corp. Jan **1958**; Prod: late Mar–mid-apr 1957 [©Jackson-Weston Productions, Inc.; 9 Jan 1958; LP10094]. Sd; b&w. 8 reels, 7,450 ft. 81 or 83 min. PCA cert no. 18598.

Prod Harry Jackson and Sam Weston. *Co-prod* Edward L. Rissien. *Dir* Mark Stevens. [*Asst dir* Louis Germonprez]. *Scr* Stanley H. Silverman and Mark Stevens. *Story* Harry S. Franklin and Julius Evans. *Cam* Charles Van Enger. [*Art dir* Bob Kinoshite]. *Ed* Lee Gilbert. *Mus* Paul Dunlap. [*Sd* Jimmy Thompson].

Cast: MARK STEVENS (*Lucas Rand*), John Lupton (*Simon Waller*), Larry Storch (*Amigo*), Jana Davi (*Tanana*), Aaron Saxon (*Trench*), Jerry Barclay (*Singer*), Norman Frederic (*Charlie Whitman*), Clegg Hoyt (*Kane*), Jean Inness (*Martha Rand*), Russell Thorsen (*Thomas Rand*), Michael Himm (*Stableman*), Iron Eyes Cody (*Indian chief*), Eddie Little (*2d Indian chief*), Cyril Delavanti (*Jerry*), John Godard (*Lee*), Vic Smith (*Jack*), Robert Stevenson (*Fred Norris*), William Erwin (*Ed, the bartender*), George Selk (*Farmer*), David Bond.

Western. [*Viewed print incomplete*]. In the late 1860s, during a raid on a settler's shack that leaves a woman dead, Simon Waller waits outside while his father Trench and half-breed Charlie Whitman, commit the murder and theft. Simon tells his father he is quitting the gang, and when Trench moves menacingly toward him, Simon fires his pistol, deliberately hitting a nearby coffee pot, and then leaves without accepting his share of the take. Whitman's attempt to get Simon's share prompts a fight with Trench, who menacingly slides his knife across Whitman's face, then pushes him out of the cabin. In the next few years, Trench induces Indians to carry out many attacks on whites. When he learns that gold from a Virginia City strike is being shipped to a bank in the East, Trench convinces a band of Indians to help him steal the gold. Meanwhile, Simon has become partners in a prospecting venture with Lucas Rand, whose parents run a

waystation. With the gold they have mined and the money in the bank he has saved, Lucas plans to settle down in Arizona and become a cattleman. At his parents' waystation, Lucas reads in an old newspaper about Indian raids that have been breaking out sporadically, despite Washington's assurances that the situation with the Indians is all settled. Lucas' father Tom believes that if more honesty and humanity were used in dealing with the Indians, relations would improve, but Jerry, the family's handyman, calls the Indians "savages" and complains that the army will not act unless a full uprising occurs. Tom relates that most people believe that a white man is behind the recent attacks. That night, Indians led by Trench and his Mexican ally Amigo attack the waystation, where the stage carrying the Virginia City gold will stop. Tom, his wife Martha and Jerry are killed, and Lucas, after killing one of the Indians, is stabbed by Trench. The next day, Simon arrives at the station and revives Lucas. At the burial of his parents and Jerry, Lucas relates that his mother rode twenty miles one night to help an Indian woman give birth, then took care of the baby all winter. Recalling that his father used to say that Indians are human beings and should be treated as such, Lucas says he does not understand why they were killed and vows to kill the white man who led the Indians. He reveals to Simon that the white man had a scar down the left side of his face, and Simon realizes the man is his father, but does not tell Lucas. When Amigo tells Trench that he has heard talk that the army is coming into the territory, Trench decides to leave for California, where new gold fields are opening up. Trench plans to travel through the mountains, and they visit Whitman to hire him as a guide. Whitman's beautiful Indian wife Tanana refuses to respond when Trench demands that she brings him food, so he pours hot coffee on her arm, but Whitman still agrees to join them if they will give him half of the take. In town, where Whitman has gone for supplies, Simon witnesses Amigo shoot Whitman during a bar fight. Amigo then provokes Simon into a fight, and because Simon suffers a coughing fit, Amigo is able to to knock him down. Lucas arrives, however, and as Amigo goes for his gun, Lucas shoots him dead. When Simon revives, Lucas tells him he has learned that the white man behind the Indian raids is holed up in Sioux country and that there is talk of the army moving in. The next day, Simon helps Tanana bury Whitman, and she delivers a Christian prayer over the grave. She then agrees to take Simon to Trench's hideout. There, Trench stabs his son. Lucas arrives and kills several of Trench's gang, and just as Trench is about to kill Lucas, Simon, still alive, kills his father. Simon and Tanana, now in love, ride off together, leaving Lucas alone. *Fathers and sons. Indians of North America. Murder. Revenge. Bars. Burial. Gold miners. Indians of North America–Mixed blood. Mexicans. Miscegenation. Parricide. Partnership. Racism. Raids. Robbery. Romance. Scars. United States–History–Indian campaigns.*

Note: As the print viewed was missing the final reels, the conclusion of the above plot summary was based on reviews, and the credits were taken from contemporary sources. The working titles of this film were *Revenge!* and *Bitter Is the Ride*. According to information in the MPAA/PCA Collection at the AMPAS Library, when the script of this film was first presented to PCA officials, it was deemed "unacceptable" because of the excessive amount of brutal killings, but following two conferences, the altered script was approved. *HR* surmised that the producers tried "to do something off-beat and still commercial," but "they did not have the material to work with to achieve either aim completely." Several reviews commented on a scene made for the European version of the film (shown at the press screening), in which, according to *HR*, "the feminine lead takes a bath, dressing and undressing before the camera with only a few leafy branches as camouflage." The Protestant Motion Picture Council rated the film "Objectionable," stating, "The cruelty, senseless beatings and killings, the ugliness of the villains, the lack of motivation outside of vengeance and sheer desire for murder, the inducements offered to Sioux Indians to provoke them to robbing, raiding and massacre combine to produce a fearful, overdone, vicious, sinister, objectionable picture of the old West." In Jun 1958, Germany denied a license to the film due to extreme brutality. Jana Davi, who played Tanana, was the "Miss Ceylon" candidate in the "Miss Universe" pageant. This was her first film.

Box 13 Jan 1958. *DV* 9 Apr 1957. *DV* 6 Jan 1958, p. 3. *Exb* 8 Jan 1958, p. 4422. *FD* 24 Jan 1958, p. 8. *Har* 11 Jan 1958, p. 7. *HR* 29 Mar 1957, p. 54. *HR* 12 Apr 1957, p. 13. *HR* 6 Jan 1958, p. 3. *LAT* 12 Sep 1958. *MPHPD* 18 Jan 1958, p. 683. *Var* 15 Jan 1958, p. 7.

THE GUN FIGHTER (Native Americans)

New York Motion Picture Corp.; Kay-Bee. *Dist* Triangle Distributing Corp. 11 Feb **1917**. Si; b&w. 5 reels.

Supv Thomas H. Ince. *Dir* William S. Hart. *Story and scen* Monte M. Katterjohn. *Cam* Joe August. *Art dir* Robert Brunton.

Cast: William S. Hart (*Cliff Hudspeth*), Margery Wilson (*Norma Wright*), Roy Laidlaw (*El Salvador*), J. J. Dowling (*"Ace High" Larkins*), Milton Ross (*"Cactus" Fuller*), J. P. Lockney (*Col. Ellis Lawton*), George Stone (*Jimmy Wright*).

Western. Cliff Hudspeth, the leader of a band of outlaws in Arizona, has earned an infamous reputation as a gun fighter. Cliff's dominion is being challenged, however, by El Salvador, an outlaw half-breed and his gang. At the Golden Fleece saloon, Cactus Fuller, El Salvador's henchman, challenges Cliff to a shootout in which Cactus forfeits his life. Norma Wright, the town milliner, witnesses the gunfight and denounces Cliff as a cold-blooded murderer. Angered at Norma's accusation, Cliff seizes the girl and takes her to his cabin. There, drugged by whiskey, Cliff reviews his life and, confronted by the shades of his victims, he pledges to Norma that he will never kill again. Soon after, Cliff is offered a pardon if he will rid Arizona of El Salvador. Infuriated with Cliff's new appointment, El Salvador burns the town and drags Norma away to the mountains where Cliff rescues her and kills El Salvador, receiving a mortal wound in the battle. As Norma rides to safety, Cliff dies, consoled in the knowledge that his last killing was in her defense. *Gunfighters. Outlaws. Regeneration. Self-sacrifice. Abduction. Arizona. Gunfights. Indians of North America–Mixed blood. Milliners. Pardons. Rescues.*

ETR 10 Feb 1917, p. 705. *Motog* 17 Feb 1917, p. 373. *MPN* 17 Feb 1917, p. 1088. *MPW* 10 Feb 1917, p. 869. *MPW* 17 Feb 1917, p. 1082. *NYDM* 3 Feb 1917, p. 28. *Wid's* 1 Feb 1917, p. 72.

GUN MOLL *see* **GANG SMASHERS**

GUN RUNNERS *see* **GUN SMUGGLERS**

GUN SMUGGLERS (Latino)
RKO Radio Pictures, Inc. *Dist* RKO Radio Pictures, Inc. 28 Dec **1948**; Prod: 26 Jul—early Aug 1948 [©RKO Radio Pictures, Inc.; 9 Jan **1949**; LP2101]. Sd (RCA Sound System); b&w. 5,455 ft. 60-61 min. PCA cert no. 13335.
Prod Herman Schlom. *Dir* Frank McDonald. [*Asst dir* John Pommer]. *Orig scr* Norman Houston. *Dir of photog* J. Roy Hunt. [*Cam op* Eddie Pyle]. [*Stills* Rod Tolmie and Gaston Longet]. *Art dir* Albert S. D'Agostino and Feild Gray. *Film ed* Les Millbrook. *Set dec* Darrell Silvera and James Altwies. *Mus dir* C. Bakaleinikoff. *Mus* Paul Sawtell. *Sd* Phil Brigandi and Terry Kellum. *Tech adv* Col. Paul R. Davison, U.S.A., (Retired). [*Scr supv* Mercy Weireter]. [*Grip* Tom Clement].
Cast: TIM HOLT [(*Tim Holt*)], Richard Martin [(*Chito Rafferty*)], Martha Hyer [(*Judy Davis*)], Gary Gray [(*Danny Reeves*)], Paul Hurst [(*Sgt. Hasty Jones*)], Douglas Fowley [(*Steve Reeves*)], Robert Warwick [(*Col. Davis*)], Don Haggerty [(*Sheriff Shurlock*)], Frank Sully [(*Cpl. Clancy*)], Robert Bray [(*Dodge*)], [Steve Savage (*Tom*)], [Harry Harvey (*Doctor Quillen*)], [Al Ferguson (*Eddie, bartender*)], [Monte Montague (*Deputy*)].
Western. [*Print viewed*]. While picking up a shipment of Gatling guns in the town of Willcox, army sergeant Hasty Jones is questioned by a young boy named Danny Reeves. After he tells the curious Danny that the newly invented guns are to be taken to nearby Fort Winston, Hasty meets up with cowboy friends Tim Holt and Chito Rafferty. Tim and Chito have come to Willcox in response to a letter from Hasty and agree to become his partners in a ranch he has just purchased for his impending army retirement. While Tim and Chito ride to inspect Hasty's ranch, Hasty, his men and Judy Davis, the colonel's daughter, drive the loaded wagons toward Fort Winston. On the way, they are flagged down by Danny, who claims to be stranded and begs for a ride. At Judy's insistence, Hasty breaks army regulations and offers the boy a ride to his ranch. Soon after Hasty turns off the main road, however, the wagons are ambushed by a gang of gunrunners, with whom Danny is in cahoots. During the ensuing gunfight, Hasty is wounded and another soldier is killed. Hearing shots in the distance, Tim and Chito ride to the scene, but are unable to stop the gang from stealing the wagons. The gunrunners, who are led by Danny's older brother Steve and Steve's vicious partner Dodge, hide the wagons in a ranch barn. Later, in town, Tim and Chito learn of Danny's treachery and enlist the sheriff to form a posse to search for the stolen wagons. As they comb the canyon, Tim and Chito see Danny, who had been sent to Willcox to spy on them, riding nearby and follow him to the ranch hideout. After Danny reports the posse's activities to Steve, Tim and Chito stage a surprise attack, which leads to Steve's and Danny's arrest. When Steve refuses to reveal the guns's location, however, Tim convinces the sheriff to release Danny to his custody in the hope that he will reform once away from his brother's bad influence. At Hasty's ranch, Danny resists Chito's attempts to bathe him and refuses to say a word about the guns to Tim. Hasty, meanwhile, is court-martialed by Judy's father and is dishonorably discharged. Feeling responsible for Hasty's

plight, Judy denounces her father and declares that she is going to fight to have the sergeant re-instated. Later, she tells Tim that she has written to the Secretary of War, confessing her part in the ambush. Judy, Tim, Hasty and Chito then undertake to re-educate Danny and begin by forcing him into the bathtub. Danny's reformation becomes complete when, on his birthday, Hasty returns his favorite dog and horse to him and declares that keeping him on the "right trail" is most important job he could ever have. That same day, however, Dodge finds Danny at Hasty's ranch and tells him that Steve is being extradicted to Mexico and will be executed there. Dodge convinces the boy to intercept the stagecoach carrying Steve in order to say a final goodbye to him. As Danny embraces Steve in the road, Dodge and the gang attack the stage and free their leader. Later, a disconsolate Danny runs away from Hasty's ranch, but is followed by the gang's hideout by Tim, who then discovers the wagons in the barn. After Danny saves Tim from Dodge's bullet, he convinces the cowboy that he was an unwitting accomplice in Steve's escape. As Tim fights the gang from inside the barn, Danny is shot by Steve while riding for help. The wounded boy alerts Chito and the sheriff's posse, who then rescue Tim and arrest Steve. With the guns's return, Hasty is fully reinstated by Col. Davis, and a proud Danny declares that he wants to go to military school and be a soldier some day. *Brothers. Children. Cowboys. Firearms. Gunrunners. Moral reformation. United States. Army. Cavalry. Birthdays. Dogs. Fathers and daughters. Fights. Gunfights. Gunshot wounds. Hideouts. Horses. Mexican Americans. Ranches. Traps.*
Note: The working title of this film was *Gun Runners*. According to *HR*, exteriors were shot in Lone Pine, CA.
Box 1 Jan 1949. *DV* 23 Dec 1948, p. 3. *FD* 29 Dec 1948, p. 8. *HR* 21 Jul 1948, p. 1. *HR* 26 Jul 1948, p. 5. *HR* 6 Aug 1948, p. 13. *HR* 23 Dec 1948, p. 3. *MPHPD* 8 Jan 1949, p. 4450. *Var* 29 Nov 1948, p. 16.

THE GUN THAT WON THE WEST (Native Americans, Dakota)
Clover Productions, Inc. *Dist* Columbia Pictures Corp. Sep **1955**; Prod: 8 Oct–15 Oct 1954 [©Columbia Pictures Corp.; 8 Apr **1955**; LP4585]. Sd (RCA Sound Recording); col (Technicolor); 1.85. 8 reels, 6,273 or 6,277 ft. 69 or 71 min. PCA cert no. 17269.
Prod Sam Katzman. *Dir* William Castle. *Asst dir* Leonard Katzman. *Story and scr* James B. Gordon. *Dir of photog* Henry Freulich. *Technicolor color consultant* Henri Jaffa. *Art dir* Paul Palmentola. *Film ed* Al Clark. *Set dec* Sidney Clifford. *Mus cond by* Ross DiMaggio. *Sd* Virgil Smith. *Unit mgr* Leon Chooluck.
Cast: Dennis Morgan [(*Jim Bridger*)], Paula Raymond [(*Maxine Gaines*)], Richard Denning [(*Jack Gaines*)], Chris O'Brien [(*Sgt. Timothy Carnahan*)], Robert Bice [(*Chief Red Cloud*)], Michael Morgan [(*Afraid of Horses*)], Roy Gordon [(*Col. Henry Carrington*)], Howard Wright [(*General John Pope*)], [Dick Cutting (*Edwin M. Stanton*)], [Howard Negley (*General Carveth*)], [Kenneth MacDonald (*Col. E. M. Still*)].
Western. [*Print viewed*]. When Dakota Jack Gaines's Wild West Extravaganza comes to Washington, D.C., Jack's friend, Jim Bridger, with whom he served as a scout for Colonel Henry Carrington in the 18th Cavalry, goes on in a wig dressed like Jack because Jack, as frequently happens, has gotten drunk, to the dismay of his wife Maxine. General Carveth and Colonel E. M. Still come backstage to speak with Jack, and Max encourages Jim to continue to pose as Jack. The army officers relate that Colonel Carrington, under orders to erect a chain of forts along the Bozeman Trail in Wyoming, has asked the department to contract Jack and Jim to him because of their friendly dealings with Sioux chief Red Cloud. The railroad plans to go into Wyoming the next year and needs forts to protect the construction crews. Jim is skeptical about getting a new treaty with Red Cloud, but Max hopes this is just what Jack needs to put him on his feet again. Jim agrees to see Secretary of War Edwin McMasters Stanton, who tells him that the Springfield Rifle, which can be loaded and fired fifty times in three minutes, will soon be manufactured in quantity. Although he worries that Red Cloud may attack before the rifles are sent, Jim agrees to get the forts built. On the way to Fort Laramie, Jack sulks, angry that Max has sold the show out from under him and accuses Jim of trying to make his reputation by taking on the Sioux and Cheyenne, who together number 8,000. When a war party led by Red Cloud's right-hand man, Afraid of Horses, sees Jim, Jack, Max and Sgt. Timothy Carnahan approach, they attack. Jim shoots Afraid of Horses and the others leave, but he prevents Jack from killing him, so that Red Cloud will understand that they do not want

war. At Fort Laramie, Jim and Jack learn from Colonel Carrington that Red Cloud, who previously has refused to talk, will arrive the next day. Upset that work on the forts will begin before the rifles arrive, Jack refuses to meet with Red Cloud and drunkenly tries to scare him with talk about the new rifle. Red Cloud now realizes he must attack before the guns arrive. The colonel angrily places Jack under arrest and orders him to stay at the fort. Max decides to leave her husband and help with the expedition, as she believes he no longer loves her. Meanwhile, Red Cloud meets with other Sioux chiefs and relates that under the proposed peace treaty, lands previously belonging to the Sioux will be taken away; in exchange, he says, the whites claim that the "Iron Horse" will bring "new learning and days of plenty." He challenges his people to remain a nation on their own land, and they agree to join the Cheyenne to drive the white man off their land. As the expedition nears Sioux land, Jim and his scouting party see hundreds of Indians approach, so they take to the rocks, where they battle until Carrington leads his troops to drive the Indians away. The whites realize that the encounter has been a warning. Jim suggests they hide in the Big Horn mountain area until the rifles arrive. With that plan in mind, they feign a retreat, but head instead for the mountains. When Max tells Jim, who has become enamored of her, that she plans to leave Jack, he warns against their getting involved and advises her to return to the fort, but she decides to stay. Meanwhile, Carnahan, who has returned to the fort to confer with General John Pope, learns that the guns will arrive within five weeks. Jack, now sober, tells Carnahan to tell Max of his change only if he thinks she wants to hear about it. Sometime later, Sioux scouts locate the party in the mountains, and an arrow nearly hits Max. Carnahan seeing her with Jim, delivers Jack's message to Max, cautioning her not to get "careless" because of the nearness of death. Afraid of Horses, realizing that the whites did not return to Fort Laramie, advises Red Cloud to attack the fort, but the chief refuses to send his men against cannon. When the rifles arrive at the fort, Jack convinces General Pope to let him take one to Red Cloud to demonstrate it and discourage him from fighting. Jack is captured and taken to Red Cloud, who calls together the chiefs of the Sioux Nation to decide what to do. Although they decide against war, Red Cloud plans to kill Carrington and his men before the guns reach them. Jack knocks out Afraid of Horses and tries to escape, but he is shot as he rides off. On the way to Carrington, Jack kills three Indians, but a survivor returns to Red Cloud, who now orders his tribe to war. After Jack informs Carrington about the Sioux approach, Jim rides to General Pope to get his men with the rifles to intercept the Indians. Max realizes Jack's heroism. The Sioux are vanquished in the battle, and Jim drowns Afraid of Horses in the river. Later, Max and Jack ride off to start a ranch, leaving Jim behind. *Alcoholics. Dakota Indians. Friendship. Marriage. Moral reformation. Red Cloud. Rifles. Scouts (Frontier). United States–History–Indian campaigns. United States. Army. Cavalry. Unrequited love. Arrests. Bozeman Trail (WY). Col. Henry Carrington. Cheyenne Indians. Fort Laramie (WY). Heroism. Officers (Military). Separation (Marital). Edwin McMasters Stanton. Treaties. Washington (D.C.). Wild west shows.*

Note: According to *HR*, location shooting was done in Los Angeles' San Fernando Valley and in the canyons of Utah. Reviews criticized the extensive use of stock footage of Wild West shows, buffalo hunts and Indian fights. While onscreen credits list Ross DiMaggio for "Music conducted by," a Columbia production sheet credits Mischa Bakaleinikoff. Modern sources add Dennis Moore and Don Harvey to the cast.

Box 16 Jul 1955. *DV* 18 Jul 1955, p.3. *Exb* 27 Jul 1955, p.3997. *Har* 16 Jul 1955, p. 115. *HR* 21 Sep 1954. *HR* 15 Jul 1955, p.3. *LAEx* 24 Sep 1954. *MPD* 15 Jul 1955. *MPHPD* 16 Jul 1955, p. 514. *Var* 20 Jul 1955, p.6.

GUNFIRE AT INDIAN GAP (Latino)

Ventura Productions, Inc. *Dist* Republic Pictures Corp. **1958**; Prod: mid-Aug 1957 [©Republic Pictures Corp.; 19 Nov 1957; LP10404]. Sd; b&w; Naturama. 6,298 ft. 70 min. PCA cert no. 18774.

Prod Rudy Ralston. *Dir* Joe Kane. *Scr* Barry Shipman. *Photog* Jack Marta. *Art dir* Ralph Oberg. *Film ed* Fred Knudtson. *Set dec* John McCarthy, Jr. *Mus dir* Gerald Roberts. *Sd* Weldon Coe.

Cast: Vera Ralston (*Cheel*), Anthony George (*Juan Morales*), George Macready (*Pike, also known as Mr. Jefferson*), Barry Kelley (*Sheriff Harris*), John Doucette (*Loder*), George Keymas (*Scully*), Chubby Johnson (*Samuel*), Glenn Strange (*Matt*), Daniel White (*Moran*), Sarah Selby (*Bessie*), Joe Yrigoyen (*Bill*), Steve Warren (*Ed Stewart*), Chuck Hicks.

Western. [*Not viewed*]. When a stagecoach carrying a passenger named Pike and a large payroll is attacked by robbers, Sheriff Harris, who had been hiding on top of the stage, kills one of the bandits. The other two, Scully and Loder, escape after wounding the driver. While the stage is at the relay station, another stage arrives carrying Juan Morales, who became stranded in the desert after his horse broke a leg. When the sheriff, who suspects Juan of being one of the bandits, locks him in a bedroom, Cheel, a station employee with whom Juan has fallen in love, agrees to help Juan escape to Mexico. Before they can get away, however, Pike tells Juan that he is the leader of the outlaws, then forces Juan to take the payroll money, instructing Juan to wait for him at a mountain pass. Cheel, unaware that Juan has the stolen money, leaves with him. She later discovers the money, but Juan assures her that he plans to return it. Scully and Loder take the couple prisoner. When Pike arrives, he insists on giving Juan a cut of the money, to the outrage of Scully and Loder, who begin to plot against Pike and Juan. Pike kills Scully, but that night, Loder shoots Pike and leaves him for dead. Loder tries to force his attentions on Cheel, and he is about to shoot Juan when the wounded Pike kills him. The next morning, Juan confronts Pike and demands the money so he can return it to the sheriff. While Juan and Pike are shooting it out, the sheriff and his posse arrive. Pike attempts to shoot the sheriff, but Juan shoots Pike. The sheriff tells Juan that he got the real story from the dying Scully, and Cheel also vouches for Juan's honest intentions. With the money returned and their names cleared, Juan and Cheel ride away to start a new life. *Bandits. False accusations. Gunfights. Mexican Americans. Murder. Stagecoach lines. Arizona. Confession (Law). Money. Posses. Romance. Sheriffs. Stagecoach robberies.*

Note: The working title of the film was *Plunderers of Eldorado*. The character played by Vera Ralston is identified as "Lupe" in the copyright synopsis, but reviews list the character's name as "Cheel." Although most reviews identify Anthony George's character as Mexican, the *MPHPD* review identifies him as "of Mexican descent," and the copyright synopsis does not refer to his ethnicity at all.

Box 3 Feb 1958. *Exb* 22 Jan 1958. *FD* 27 Jan 1958, p. 6. *Har* 25 Jan 1958. *HR* 16 Aug 1957, p. 11. *HR* 23 Aug 1957, p. 9. *MPHPD* 1 Feb 1958, p. 698.

GUNMAN'S WALK (Native Americans, Dakota)

Columbia Pictures Corp. *Dist* Columbia Pictures Corp. Jul **1958**; Los Angeles opening: 23 Jul 1958; Prod: 10 Dec–23 Dec 1957 [©Columbia Pictures Corp.; 1 Jul 1958; LP11159]. Sd (RCA Sound Recording); col (Technicolor); CinemaScope. 11 reels, 8,527 ft. 90, 95 or 97 min. PCA cert no. 18907.

Prod Fred Kohlmar. *Dir* Phil Karlson. *Asst dir* Sam Nelson. *Scr* Frank Nugent. *From a story by* Ric Hardman. *Dir of photog* Charles Lawton, Jr. *Technicolor color consultant* Henri Jaffa. *Art dir* Robert Peterson. *Film ed* Jerome Thoms. *Set dec* Frank A. Tuttle. *Mus comp* George Duning. *Cond* Morris Stoloff. *Orch* Arthur Morton. *Rec supv* John Livadary. *Sd* Lambert Day. *Makeup* Clay Campbell. *Hair styles* Helen Hunt.

Song(s): "I'm a Runaway," music by Fred Karger, words by Richard Quine.

Cast: VAN HEFLIN [(*Lee Hackett*)], TAB HUNTER [(*Ed Hackett*)], Kathryn Grant [(*Cecily "Clee" Chouard*)], James Darren [(*Davy Hackett*)], Mickey Shaughnessy [(*Will Motely*)], Robert F. Simon [(*Sheriff Harry Brill*)], Edward Platt [(*Purcell Avery*)], Ray Teal [(*Jensen Sieverts*)], Paul Birch [(*Bob Selkirk*)], Michael Granger [(*Curly*)], Will Wright [(*Judge*)], [Chief Blue Eagle (*Black Horse*)], [Bert Convy (*Paul Chouard*)], [Paul E. Burns (*Cook*)], [Paul Bryar (*Bartender*)], [Everett Glass (*Rev. Arthur Stotheby*)], [Dorothy Adams (*Martha Stotheby*)], [Harry Antrim (*Doctor*)], [Ewing Mitchell (*Mr. Johnson*)], [Joseph Hamilton (*Storekeeper*)], [Bek Nelson, Peggy Whitman, Shirle Haven, Judy Cannon (*Dance hall girls*)], [John Cason, Walter La Rue, Jack Barry, Allen Pinson, Wayne Burson, Brett Halsey (*Wranglers*)], [Sam Flint, Watson Downs, Wheaton Chambers, Charles Heard, Pierce Lyden, Hal Taggart, Alan Reynolds (*Townsmen*)], [Irving Mitchell, Robert Malcolm, David McMahon, George Lewis, Russell Thorson (*Cattlemen*)], [Gloria Victor (*Girl*)], [Constance Cameron], [Lucille Vance].

Western. [*Print viewed*]. Davy Hackett and his older brother Ed arrive at an Indian agency in search of extra hands for their upcoming horse drive to Jackson City, Wyoming. Davy defends the beautiful Cecily "Clee" Chouard from his brother's disrespectful advances, and as he talks with her, he begins to fall in love. The two brothers hire two full-blooded Sioux Indians, Black Horse and Blue Eagle, along

with Clee's brother Paul, who like his sister was born to a Frenchman and his Sioux wife. Back at the Hackett ranch, Davy and Ed's father Lee reminisces with his friend, Bob Selkirk, about the days when they tamed the vast territory with their strength and guns. Lee insists that his sons continue to wear guns, but Davy protests that there is no longer any need to do so. Ed, who is as wild and proud as his father, however, enjoys displaying his prowess as a gunman. Determined to be considered the best horseman in the territory, Ed becomes upset when his father remarks that Paul is also good with horses. One day, Ed resolves to rope a beautiful white mare that has always eluded his capture, and soon, both he and Paul are racing along a steep cliff in pursuit of the horse. As Black Horse and Blue Eagle watch in horror, Ed, in attempting to charge ahead of his rival, pushes Paul over the cliff to his death. Ed describes Paul's death as an accident, but when Davy rides to the Indian agency to deliver the news to Clee, he learns from agent Purcell Avery that the two Sioux have charged Ed with murder. Meanwhile, Lee arrives in Jackson City with a large herd of horses. Openly disapproving yet secretly proud of Ed's behavior, Lee defends him when he learns about the murder charge. At the hearing, the judge, another of Lee's old cohorts, is about to charge Ed with murder on the testimony of the two Indians when an unknown horse trader named Jensen Sieverts suddenly claims that he saw Paul accidentally fall from the cliff. Later, Sieverts admits to Ed that he hopes to take some of Lee's finest horses with him when he leaves town. Lee asks Davy to keep an eye on Ed that night, but Davy, jealous of his father's legendary reputation, angrily dismisses his brother and is later arrested for drunkenness and fighting. He is furious when Lee bails him out. Davy visits Clee and declares that he wants to marry her, and despite the pain his family has caused her, she accepts his proposal. The next day, as Lee looks on glumly, Sieverts selects ten horses from his herd. Upon learning that the horse trader has taken his white mare, Ed shoots Sieverts in the middle of Jackson City's main street. At first, Ed refuses to surrender his gun even to his father, but finally allows himself to be jailed while protesting that he was right to shoot a horse thief. Lee quietly threatens to kill the wounded horse trader if he reveals the truth about Paul's death. Meanwhile, however, Ed kills the unarmed deputy and escapes into the countryside. Lee tries to find his son before the angry townspeople catch him, but Ed, hiding in the rocks, sees him approaching and threatens him with a gun. Ed complains that Lee did nothing but boast about his killings over the years. The older man admits his mistakes but declares, "I'll see you dead before I let you kill another man." The two men draw their weapons, but Lee is faster and Ed falls. Lee immediately drops his holster and gun and holds his son's lifeless body in his arms. Back in town, Lee asks Davy and Clee to accompany him and Ed's body back to the ranch, then breaks into tears. Davy and Clee support him, and the three walk toward their horses. *Brothers. Fathers and sons. Indians of North America–Mixed blood. Murder. Racism. Rivalry.* Bribery. Brothers and sisters. Dakota Indians. Deputies. Firearms. Gunfights. Horse owners. Horses. Jailbreaks. Judges. Loyalty. Perjury. Physicians. Ranchers. Romance. Saloons. Sheriffs. Wyoming.

Note: The film's working title was *The Slicks.* According to studio publicity materials, some scenes in the film were shot in and around Tucson, AZ.

Box 16 Jun 1958. *DV* 12 Jun 1958, p. 3. *Exb* 25 Jun 1958, p. 4481. *FD* 12 Jun 1958, p. 8. *Har* 14 Jun 1958, p. 96. *HR* 12 Jun 1958, p. 3. *MPHPD* 14 Jun 1958, p. 864. *Var* 18 Jun 1958, p. 6.

GUNMEN FROM LAREDO (Native Americans, Apache, Latino)

Allied Artists Productions, Inc.; Columbia Pictures Corp. *Dist* Columbia Pictures Corp. Mar 1959; *Prod:* began mid-Mar 1958 [©Columbia Pictures Corp.; 30 Dec 1958; LP12878]. Sd (Westrex Recording System); col (Columbia Color). 6,042 ft. 67 min. PCA cert no. 19058.

Prod Wallace MacDonald. *Dir* Wallace MacDonald. *Asst dir* Leonard Katzman. *Wrt* Clark E. Reynolds. *Dir of photog* Irving Lippman. *Color consultant* Henri Jaffa. *Art dir* Carl Anderson. *Film ed* Al Clark. *Set dec* Alfred E. Spencer. *Rec supv* John Livadary. *Sd* Lambert Day.

Cast: Robert Knapp [(*Gil Reardon*)], Jana Davi [(*Rosita*)], Walter Coy [(*Ben Keefer*)], Paul Birch [(*Matt Crawford*)], Don C. Harvey [(*Dave Marlow*)], Clarence Straight [(*Frank Bass*)], Jerry Barclay [(*Jordan Keefer*)], Ron Hayes [(*Walt Keefer*)], Charles Horvath [(*Coloradas*)], Jean Moorhead [(*Katy Reardon*)], [X Brands (*Delgados*)], [Harry Antrim (*Judge Raymond Parker*)], [Bob Cason (*Bob Sutton*)], [Hank Patterson (*Stableman*)], [Dan White (*Jury foreman*)], [Joseph Breen (*Walker*)], [Bill Hale (*Dodge*)], [Gil Perkins

(*Bowdrie*)], [Larry Thor (*Capt. Garrick*)], [Don Blackman (*Smoky*)], [Martin Garralaga (*Fierro*)].

Western. [*Print viewed*]. On their way from their ranch in Mexico to sell a herd of cattle in San Antonio, Gil Reardon, Katy, his wife of two years, and foreman Fierro cross the Rio Grande. When Katy asks the reason they don't go to Laredo, Gil relates that years earlier, he killed a man working for Ben Keefer, who runs Laredo's cattle market with his sons. The death occurred after a dispute in a fair fight, but Keefer didn't think so. That night, Keefer and his boys, lying in wait for Gil, attack Katy and Fierro while Gil is checking the softness of a creek bottom. Gil returns to help, but he is shot, and when he revives, he finds Fierro dead and Katy dying. He rides into Laredo to the gaming establishment run by Keefer. When one of Keefer's men, Bob Sutton, draws, Gil shoots and kills him. The next day, circuit judge Raymond Parker arrives in town with papers to give the district a U.S. Marshal, Matt Crawford. Parker conducts a jury trial, and Gil, who has no evidence to support his claim that Sutton went for his gun first, is found guilty and sentenced to 10-25 years in the New Mexico Territorial Prison. At the prison about four months later, two inmates file through Gil's leg irons, as Smoky, an African-American prisoner, sings a spiritual to hide the noise. When Gil asks Smoky to join them in their escape attempt, he says there is nothing on the outside for him. During a vicious rainstorm, the two other prisoners are shot at the prison wall, and although Gil escapes, a guard doubts that he can get through the desert, which is filled with Apaches. After the storm ends, Gil finds a woman tied to a tree. She proudly states she is a Mescalero Apache, but then admits she was born a Mexican and stolen by the Mescaleros as a child. Although the Indians call her Natana, she prefers Rosita. She explains that three days ago she was stolen by Delgados, the son of the chief of the Mescalero's enemies, the Chiricahua Apaches. Delgados returns from hunting and rushes Gil with a knife. Their fight ends when Delgados falls on his own knife and dies. Happy to be free of her abductor, Rosita wants to take Gil back to her family, but he orders her to guide him to Laredo despite her warning that Delgados' father, Coloradas, will follow their trail. As Gil and Rosita travel, she tries to discourage him from revenge, but he says he must deal with Keefer if he is going to live with himself. When she asks what he feels about being alone with her, he evades her question. She predicts that a *chisera*, a turbulent sandstorm, is coming soon, but he refuses to stop. After fighting the horrible storm, she leads them to a cave where they find refuge. As she cleans the sand from his eyes, they look deeply at one another, and he kisses her. She pulls back, saying she only wants to love once in her life, but when he tells her not to be afraid, she kisses him with passion. When Gil and Rosita reach the Texas foothills, he sends her away, but she returns. Their subsequent argument ends in an embrace, which is interrupted when Crawford and his two deputies, informed that Gil had broken out of prison, capture him and send her off. Coloradas and his braves chase Rosita back to Gil and the law officers, and the chief demands the couple. Gil taunts Coloradas, saying he is not a warrior like his ancestors if he will not fight him alone. Angered, Coloradas agrees to the Apache "Battle of the Warriors," a fight to the death in which one tomahawk is placed between the two men. During their battle, when Gil gets hold of the tomahawk, Coloradas calls to one of his men for another, but before he can use it, Gil throws his tomahawk into Coloradas' face. The saddened Indians take their leader away, and Gil, Rosita and the lawmen ride to Laredo. On the outskirts of town, Crawford, who believes Gil did not murder Sutton, allows him to grab his rifle and gives him ten minutes to take care of Keefer, who has been a menace to the town. When Keefer learns that Gil is coming, he sends his son Walt to the roof of a building with a rifle, then walks out to meet Gil with his other son Jordan. During the showdown, Gil notices Walt about to shoot and kills him. He then shoots Jordan. Gil orders Keefer to draw, but Keefer throws down his gun and asks what Gil's wife would think if he shot him in cold blood. As Gil hesitates, Keefer goes for Jordan's gun, and Gil shoots him. Crawford sends Gil and Rosita off to Gil's spread south of the border, and as the bodies of the Keefers are carried out, the lawmen make up a story about how Gil got away. *Apache Indians. Mexicans. Murder. Revenge. Romance.* African Americans. Cattle. Cattlemen. Caves. Deserts. Duels. False arrests. Fathers and sons. Gambling houses. Judges. Knife fighting. Laredo (TX). New Mexico. Prison escapes. Rainstorms. Rio Grande. Robbery. Sandstorms. Shootouts. Trials. Tribal chiefs. United States. Marshals.

Note: The working title of this film was *Chisera*. While the copyright register and *Exb* list the running time as 89 min., all other sources list 67 min. Morina Zoltah is listed as the female lead in a *HR* production chart and in material in the MPAA/PCA Collection at the AMPAS Library; in the *Har* review, while Jana Davi is listed at the top of the review, Morina Zoltah's name appears in the text of the review. It is possible that Davi changed her name to Zoltah temporarily during the film's production. The character "Coloradas" may have been loosely based on the real-life Apache Mangas Coloradas. For information on him, see entries above for *Fort Yuma* and below for *War Drums*.

Box 9 Mar 1959. *DV* 25 Feb 1959, p. 4. *Exb* 25 Feb 1959, p. 4561. *FD* 26 Feb 1959, p. 6. *Har* 28 Feb 1959, pp. 34-35. *HR* 25 Feb 1959, p. 3. *MPD* 26 Feb 1959. *MPHPD* 28 Feb 1959, p. 171. *Var* 25 Feb 1959, p. 6.

THE GUNS OF FORT PETTICOAT (African Americans, Cheyenne, Irish Americans, Latino, Native Americans)

Brown-Murphy Pictures, Inc. *Dist* Columbia Pictures Corp. Apr **1957**; Los Angeles opening: 3 Apr 1957; Prod: mid-Apr—mid-May 1956 [©Brown-Murphy Pictures, Inc.; 1 Apr 1957; LP8354]. Sd (Westrex Recording System); col (Technicolor). 9 reels, 7,315 or 7,432 ft. 80-83 min. PCA cert no. 18171.

Prod Harry Joe Brown. *Asst prod* David Breen. *Dir* George Marshall. *Asst dir* Abner E. Singer. *Scr* Walter Doniger. *Dir of photog* Ray Rennahan. *Technicolor color consultant* Henri Jaffa. *Art dir* George Brooks. *Film ed* Al Clark and [Gene Havelick]. *Set dec* William Kierman and Frank A. Tuttle. *Mus cond* Mischa Bakaleinikoff. *Rec supv* John Livadary. *Sd* Franklin Hansen, Jr.

Source: Based on the short story "Petticoat Brigade" by C. William Harrison in *Collier's* (25 Nov and 9 Dec 1955).

Cast: AUDIE MURPHY [(*Lt. Frank Hewitt*)], Kathryn Grant [(*Ann Martin*)], Hope Emerson [(*Hannah Lacey*)], Jeff Donnell [(*Mary Wheeler*)], Jeanette Nolan [(*Cora Melavan*)], Sean McClory [(*Emmett "Kettle"*)], Ernestine Wade [(*Hetty*)], Peggy Maley [(*Lucy Conover*)], Isobel Elsom [(*Mrs. Ogden*)], Patricia Livingston [(*Stella Leatham*)], Kim Charney [(*Bax*)], Ray Teal [(*Salt Pork*)], Nestor Paiva [(*Tortilla*)], James Griffith [(*Kipper*)], Charles Horvath (*Indian chief*)], [Ainslie Pryor (*Col. Chivington*)], [Dorothy Crider (*Jane Gibbons*)], [Madge Meredith (*Hazel McCasslin*)], [Pamela Beaird (*Nancy*)], [Evelyn Finley, Sharon Lucas, Helen Thurston (*Women soldiers*)], [Willard Willingham (*Medicine man*)], [Frank Hagney (*Blacksmith*)], [Hugh Sanders (*Sgt. Webber*)], [Charles Meredith (*Gen. Farwell*)], [Reed Howes (*Gen. Farwell's aide*)], [John Dierkes (*Proprietor*)], [Irene Barton (*Proprietor's wife*)], [Francis McDonald (*Captain*)], [Edwin Chandler (*Orderly*)], [Al Wyatt (*Sergeant*)], [Chief Geronimo Kuthlee (*Indian leader*)].

Western. [*Print viewed*]. At the close of the Civil War, Lt. Frank Hewitt, a Texan who has joined the U.S. Cavalry, encounters a band of Cheyenne Indians who have illegally left the Sand Creek Reservation on a trading expedition. Because the Indians are unarmed, Frank's detachment merely orders them to return home. After Frank reports the incident to his superior, Col. Chivington, however, Chivington orders an attack on Sand Creek. Worried about Indian reprisals in nearby Texas, which because of the war is occupied mostly by women and children, Frank deserts his post and heads south. Along the way, he witnesses the brutal massacre of the peaceful Cheyenne people at Sand Creek. In Texas, Frank's warnings of potential Indian attacks go unheeded because of the uniform he wears. Even his old flame, Stella Leatham, who has since married, calls him a "damned Yankee." After citizen Dora Hartley is attacked in her home, however, Frank is put in charge of defending the town. He names Hannah Lacey, a tough widow who can shoot, as his sergeant. Aided by the reluctant "Kettle," an Irish-American cowboy, he and Hannah begin to drill the new "soldiers." Among others, the soldiers-in-training include Mrs. Ogden, a haughty dowager from Charleston, her black maid Hetty, dance hall entertainer Lucy Conover, and Ann Martin, to whom Frank is secretly attracted. Although Kettle has convinced the women they must go to a safer location, Frank is certain they will all be killed if they leave and sets the horses free. Frank then catches Kettle trying to steal their one remaining horse and imprisons him. Speaking tenderly from his jail cell to his sweetheart, Mary Wheeler, who is pregnant with his child, Kettle promises to marry her if she will release him. After she does, Kettle shoves her to the ground and escapes to a ranch house some miles away. There he encounters one Mexican and two American outlaws, who force him to reveal the location of the women and their jewels and money. Then Kipper, the outlaws' leader, shoots Kettle, and the bandits ride out to a nearby mission. When the women see them, they raise their rifles and order the men to leave. The outlaws

ride into the countryside, encounter a large group of angry Indians and encourage them to attack the mission. The women hide on the roof, and the Indians, assuming the outlaws lied to them, fatally shoot the men. As the band rides away, however, young Bax stands up too soon and is spotted. Though short on ammunition, the women drive their attackers off. Later, Frank devises a plan and commands the women to place gunpowder "bombs" just outside the mission gates. The next morning, as the Indians attack, Sgt. Lacey and her troops fire their rifles at the bombs, causing them to explode and injure the Indians. In the resulting confusion, Frank finds the tribe's retreating medicine man and kills him, then returns to the mission with the corpse. Just as the ammunition runs out, the women hoist up the medicine man's body, causing the Indians to flee. Later, Frank returns to the Cavalry to face desertion charges, but Chivington refuses to believe that the women successfully defended themselves against hostile Indians. During the trial, Sgt. Lacey and her troops demand that Frank be released. The colonel is outraged, but the general states that the wrong man is on trial and arrests Chivington for his role in the Sand Creek massacre. As the women congratulate their former lieutenant, Ann approaches, and Frank embraces his new love. *Battles. Indians of North America. Outlaws. Texas. United States–History–Civil War, 1861-1865. United States–History–Indian campaigns. Women soldiers.* African Americans. Betrayal. Cheyenne Indians. Courage. Courts-martial and courts of inquiry. Dance hall girls. Desertion, Military. Dowagers. Indians of North America–Reservations. Irish Americans. Loyalty. Mexicans. Military education. Missions. Murder. Officers (Military). Pregnancy. Romantic rivalry. Sadism. Sand Creek Massacre, CO, 1864. Superstition.

Note: The working title of this film was *Petticoat Brigade*. According to contemporary sources, the film was based on C. William Harrison's 1955 short story "Petticoat Brigade," but Harrison also published a novel entitled *The Guns of Fort Petticoat* (New York, 1957). Historical sources note that in 1861, Cheyenne and Arapaho Indians were forced onto the desolate Sand Creek Reservation in southeastern Colorado when gold prospectors poured into the state. In retaliation, these tribes launched attacks on the stagecoach lines to Denver. However, it was a band of peaceful Cheyenne, led by Black Kettle, who were attacked without warning on 29 Nov 1864, when Col. John M. Chivington led volunteer Colorado militiamen in what is now known as the Sand Creek Massacre. As many as two hundred Cheyenne, many of them women and children, were killed during the massacre. Chivington was later investigated by Congress and forced to resign. According to a 7 Oct 1955 *HR* news item, writer Walter Doniger was originally scheduled to direct the film.

Box 23 Mar 1957. *DV* 13 Mar 1957, p. 3. *Exb* 20 Mar 1957, p. 4301. *FD* 22 Mar 1957, p. 9. *Har* 16 Mar 1957, pp. 42-43. *HR* 20 Apr 1956, p. 12. *HR* 11 May 1956, p. 20. *HR* 13 Mar 1957, p. 3. *MPHPD* 16 Mar 1957, p. 298. *Var* 13 Mar 1957, p. 6.

GUNS OF HATE (Latino)

RKO Radio Pictures, Inc. *Dist* RKO Radio Pictures, Inc. 18 Jun **1948**; Prod: 8 Dec—late Dec 1947 [©RKO Radio Pictures, Inc.; 27 May 1948; LP1649]. Sd (RCA Sound System); b&w. 5,548 ft. 61-62 min. PCA cert no. 12891.

Prod Herman Schlom. *Dir* Lesley Selander. [*Dial dir* Dan Ullman]. [*Asst dir* John Pommer and Harry Templeton]. *Scr* Norman Houston and Ed Earl Repp. *Story* Ed Earl Repp. *Dir of photog* George E. Diskant. *Spec eff* Russell A. Cully. *Art dir* Albert S. D'Agostino and Feild Gray. *Film ed* Desmond Marquette. *Set dec* Darrell Silvera and William Stevens. *Mus dir* C. Bakaleinikoff. *Mus* Paul Sawtell. *Sd* John L. Cass and Terry Kellum.

Cast: TIM HOLT [(*Bob Banning*)], Nan Leslie [(*Judy Jason*)], Richard Martin [(*Chito Rafferty*)], Steve Brodie [(*Morgan*)], Myrna Dell [(*Dixie*)], Tony Barrett [(*Matt Wyatt*)], Jim Nolan [(*Sheriff*)], Jason Robards [(*Ben Jason*)], Robert Bray [(*Rocky*)], Marilyn Mercer [(*Mabel*)].

Western. [*Print viewed*]. After out-of-work cowpunchers Bob Banning and Chito Rafferty fix the wagon wheel of Arizona miner Ben Jason, Ben gives them a gold nugget in thanks. In Rim Rock, Bob and Chito take the nugget to assayer Matt Wyatt, who eagerly gives them fifty dollars for it. As soon as the cowboys leave his office, Wyatt compares the nugget to an ore sample he keeps in a drawer and realizes that Ben has found the much sought-after "Lost Dutchman" mine. On the street, Wyatt then overhears Ben discussing his valuable claim with his niece Judy, who has just arrived in town, and sees him pocket a map to the place. Excited, Wyatt rushes to tell Morgan, the crooked Rim Rock saloon owner, about the mine and suggests that they steal the map and Ben's money belt before he can register his claim in nearby Trinity. Morgan agrees to the plan and takes Rocky, one of his men, to intercept Ben as he rides to Trinity. When Ben and

Judy become aware that they are being followed, Ben sends Judy ahead, while he stays to face the men. After a brief shootout, Morgan and Rocky kill Morgan, steal his map and money belt and ride off. At the same time, Bob and Chito are riding nearby and, hearing gun fire, rush to the scene. They arrive moments ahead of Judy and the sheriff and, despite their protests of innocence, are arrested for Ben's murder. While Bob and Chito sit in the Rim Rock jail, saloon girl Dixie, one of Chito's paramours, asks Morgan for an advance on her salary so that she can bail Chito out. Before Dixie can legally free Chito, however, Chito and Bob escape by setting a fire in their cell. Determined to clear themselves, Chito and Bob ride to the site of Ben's murder to search for his money belt, and run into Judy there. The cowboys eventually convince the wary Judy, who is also looking for her uncle's money belt, of their innocence. Realizing that Wyatt was the only other person who knew about the Ben's gold, Bob and Chito ride back to Rim Rock to question him. Although Wyatt, whom Morgan has double-crossed, denies any involvement in the crime, Bob senses his guilt and starts to beat him. When Chito alerts him to the sheriff's presence, Bob stops fighting, but spies on Wyatt as he runs to confront Morgan. Dixie then informs Bob that she saw Ben's money belt in Morgan's office, and he sneaks into Morgan's office just as Wyatt is forcing the saloon owner to open his safe. As Bob and Morgan then fight, Wyatt takes the map out of the money belt and flees with it. After Bob knocks Morgan out and out-manuevers Rocky and his cohorts, he instructs Dixie to take Ben's money belt to Judy, then hides from the sheriff and his posse. Morgan and Rocky also go to Judy's ranch and, holding her at gunpoint, demand that she reveal the location of the mine. Judy, who was told the mine's location by Ben, directs Morgan to the site, while Rocky stays behind to guard her and Dixie. Morgan finds Wyatt carrying bags of gold from the mine and kills him. Soon after, a group of Morgan's men ride up and begin collecting Ben's gold. Bob and Chito, meanwhile, arrive at Judy's and, following a brief gunfight with Rocky, rescue her and Dixie and head for the mine. After a fierce fight on a runaway wagon, Bob captures Morgan, while Chito joins the sheriff's posse in a gunfight with Morgan's men. With Morgan and the gang finally arrested, Judy is about to convince Bob to stay at her ranch when a terrified Chito races by on his horse and screams that Dixie has just proposed to him. *Betrayal. Cowboys. Gold mines. Greed. Murder. Robbery. Arizona. Assayers. Dance hall girls. Fistfights. Gunfights. Jailbreaks. Mexican Americans. Nieces. Prospectors. Romance. Saloon keepers. Sheriffs.*

Note: The working title of this film was *Guns of Wrath.* According to *HR,* some scenes in the picture were shot in Lone Pine, CA.

Box 15 May 1948. *DV* 13 May 1948, p. 3. *FD* 13 May 1948, p. 6. *HR* 2 Dec 1947, p. 1. *HR* 5 Dec 1947, p. 13. *HR* 9 Dec 1947, p. 2. *HR* 13 May 1948, p. 3. *MPHPD* 8 May 1948, p. 4155. *MPHPD* 15 May 1948, p. 4162. *Var* 12 May 1948, p. 20.

GUNS OF WRATH *see* **GUNS OF HATE**

THE GUNSAULUS MYSTERY (African Americans)
Micheaux Film Corp. **1921**; New York premiere: 18 Apr 1921. Si; b&w. 7 reels.
Pres Oscar Micheaux. *Prod* Oscar Micheaux. *Dir* Oscar Micheaux. *Wrt* Oscar Micheaux. *Photog* Leonard Galezio.
Cast: Lawrence Chenault (*Anthony Brisbane*), Evelyn Preer (*Ida May Gilpin*), Dick Abrams (*Sidney Wyeth*), Louis De Bulger (*Lem Hawkins*), Mattie Wilkes, Bessie Bearden,. Ethel Williams, Edward Brown, Mabel Young, Hattie Christian, E. G. Tatum, Ethel Watts, George Russel, W. D. Sindle, Alix Kroll, Inez Clough, Mr. Thomas.
African American, Legal, Drama. [*Not viewed*]. When Arthur Gilpin, a black night watchman, finds young Myrtle Gunsaulus mysteriously murdered in the basement of a factory, he is charged with the crime. His sister, Ida May, engages for his defense a young lawyer, Sidney Wyeth, who had once been in love with her but, falsely believing her to be immoral, had ended their courtship. The case is highly complicated and mysterious, with evidence including strange murder notes covered with a white substance and strands of the girl's hair scattered about the room. Although Lem Hawkins, a black janitor, is arrested, the police are unable to get much information from him. Suspicion is eventually directed to Anthony Brisbane, the superintendent and general manager of the factory. At the trial, Wyeth proves Gilpin's innocence and also gets Hawkins to make a confession, in which he claims that Brisbane is sexually perverted and killed Myrtle to try to hide his perversion. After his professional success, Wyeth writes a book in which he reveals a secret. Ida May, however, sees that Wyeth has some mistaken ideas and she sends him

a note clearing up all the earlier misunderstandings. *African Americans. Factory management. False arrests. Janitors. Lawyers. Murder. Sex crimes. Trials. Watchmen.*

Note: According to an unidentified news item from the African-American newspaper *ChiDef,* "the story is built around and about the famous Leo M. Frank trial which took place in Georgia some years ago...in which a member of the Jewish race was convicted of the murder of a young factory girl on the alleged confession of one of 'our folks,' who was employed by the same firm." A *ChiDef* ad for the film states that filmmaker Oscar Micheaux was in the courtroom during the Frank trial. After Frank was sentenced to death, Georgia Govenor John M. Slaton issued a stay of execution, but Frank was lynched by a mob after Slaton commuted his sentence to life imprisonment. On 11 May 1986, the state of Georgia issued a posthumous pardon for Frank. Other films based on the Frank trial include the 1915 Circle Film Corp. production *Thou Shalt Not Kill,* directed by Hal Reid and starring Rose and Charles Coghlan (see *AFI Catalog of Feature Films, 1911-20;* F.1445); a documentary short by Reid, also made in 1915 and entitled *Leo M. Frank;* the 1935 Micheaux Pictures Corp. production *Lem Hawkins' Confession,* directed by Oscar Micheaux and starring Clarence Brooks, which is a remake of this film (see below); the 1937 Warner Bros. production *They Won't Forget,* directed by Mervyn LeRoy and starring Claude Rains; and the 1988 NBC miniseries, *The Murder of Mary Phagan,* directed by Billy Hale and starring Jack Lemmon.

Billboard 7 May 1921, p. 257. *ChiDef* 26 Mar 1921, p. 5. *ChiDef* 25 Nov 1922, p. 7. *New York Age* 23 Apr 1921, p. 6.

GUON MIN GUH LU (Chinese language)
Grandview Film Co. **1944.** Sd; b&w. Length undetermined. Chinese language.
Cast: Wong Hok-sing. [*Not viewed*]. [No information concerning the plot of this film has been located.].
Note: The Cantonese transliterated title is *Kong Meng Chi Lou.* The English language translation of the title is *Road to Brightness.* This film was probably made in the U.S.
Chinese Times (San Francisco) 4 Sep 1944, p. 7.

THE GUTTERSNIPE (Irish Americans)
Universal Film Mfg. Co.; Universal Special. 30 Jan **1922** [©Universal Film Mfg. Co.; 10 Jan 1922; LP17449]. Si; b&w. 5 reels, 4,225 ft.
Pres Carl Laemmle. *Dir* Dallas M. Fitzgerald. *Scen* Wallace Clifton. *Story* Percival Wilde. *Photog* Milton Moore.
Cast: Gladys Walton (*Mazie O'Day*), Walter Perry (*Dennis O'Day*), Kate Price (*Mrs. O'Day*), Jack Perrin (*Tom Gilroy*), Sidney Franklin (*Sam Rosen*), Carmen Phillips (*Lady Clarissa*), Edward Cecil (*Lord Bart*), Hugh Saxon (*Angus*), Seymour Zeliff (*Red Galvin*), Eugene Corey (*Clarence Phillips*), Lorraine Weiler (*Sally*), Christian J. Frank (*Gregory*).
Romantic comedy. Mazie, a shop girl of New York City's Little Ireland, goes to the aid of a young man in formal attire involved in a street fight. Though badly beaten, he bears a strong resemblance to Lord Lytton, the hero of a magazine story Mazie is reading in installments. Although he is in reality a soda clerk, Mazie permits his attentions, and together they read the "Sloppy Stories" yarn about English nobility. When her beau is arrested as a counterfeiter, Mazie turns to the latest episode of the story for advice; and through this device the ending of their own love story is achieved. *Counterfeiters and counterfeiting. Irish Americans. Magazines. New York City. Saleswomen. Soda clerks.*

Note: Also known as *The Gutter Snipe.*
ETR 7 Jan 1922, p. 457. *FD* 1 Jan 1922. *Var* 3 Feb 1922, p. 42.

GYPSY *see* **RASCALS**

THE GYPSY TRAIL (Irish Americans)
Famous Players-Lasky Corp. *Dist* Famous Players-Lasky Corp.; Paramount Pictures. 17 Nov **1918** [©Famous Players-Lasky Corp.; 14 Sep 1918; LP12888]. Si; b&w. 5 reels.
Pres Jesse L. Lasky. *Dir* Walter Edwards. *Scen* Julia Crawford Ivers. *Cam* James C. Van Trees.
Source: Based on the play *The Gipsy Trail* by Robert Housum (New York, 4 Dec 1917).
Cast: Bryant Washburn (*Edward Andrews*), Wanda Hawley (*Frances Raymond*), Casson Ferguson (*Michael Rudder*), C. H. Geldart (*Frank Raymond*), Georgie Stone (*John Raymond*), Edythe Chapman (*Grandma*).
Comedy. Edward Andrews, a generous but faint-hearted young man, loves Frances Raymond, who fancies herself an incurable romantic. Edward realizes that Frances would love to be whisked off and romanced, but because he is too timid to abduct her himself, he hires Michael Rudder, a breezy young Irish reporter, to do the deed. Michael's dashing manner entrances Frances, but the Irishman prefers

the unencumbered life of a rover to that of a husband, and after he delivers her to the home of Edward's grandmother, he wanders away to a gypsy camp. Frances is so downhearted from losing Michael that the kindly Edward finds the reporter and convinces him to propose to the girl. Frances, however, moved by Edward's goodness, decides that he is the man she really loves and returns to him. *Abduction. Reporters. Timidity. Grandmothers. Gypsies. Irish Americans. Proposals (Marital).*

Note: The *Var* reviewer credits Frank Garbutt as cameraman, but materials in Paramount studio records credit Van Trees.

ETR 26 Oct 1918, p. 1771. *MPN* 2 Nov 1918, p. 2801. *MPW* 2 Nov 1918, p. 622. *NYDM* 23 Nov 1918, p. 774. *Var* 20 Dec 1918, p. 37.

HAI JEOW CHIN YUAN (Chinese language)

Grandview Film Co. 1947?; Hong Kong showing: 1947? Sd; b&w. Length undetermined. Chinese language.

Dir Jiang Wai-kwong. [*Not viewed*]. [No information concerning the plot of this film has been located.].

Note: The Cantonese transliterated title is *Hoi Gog Qing Yun*. This film was probably made in the U.S.

HAIR-TRIGGER CASEY (Chinese Americans)

Berke-Perrin Productions; Blue Ribbon. *Dist* Atlantic Pictures Corp. Feb? **1936**; Prod: began 16 Dec 1935. Sd; b&w. 60 min. PCA cert no. 1872.

[*Prod* William Berke]. *Dir* Harry Fraser. *Asst dir* William Nolte. [*Wrt*] *by* Monroe Talbot. *Cine* Robert Cline. *Ed* Arthur A. Brooks. *Mus eff* Lee Zahler. *Sd eng* T. T. Triplett.

Cast: JACK PERRIN (*Captain [Jim] Casey*), Betty Mack (*Jane Elkins*), Edward Cassidy (*Karney*), Snowflake (*Snowflake*), Wally Wales (*Dave Casey*), Phil Dunham (*Abner*), Robert Walker (*Colton*), Denny Meadows (*Brooks*), Victor Wong (*Lee Fix*), Starlight.

Western. [*Print viewed*]. Army Captain Jim Casey is called home to his ranch by border patrolman Colton to investigate strange happenings. On his way out of town, Casey finds his foreman Karney, who was nearly killed by a Chinese man's axe in Chinatown. When Casey arrives at the ranch he learns that his ranch hand, Slim Elkins, was killed the night before, when Karney was mysteriously absent. Casey's brother Dave had gone with Slim that night to investigate possible contraband being moved along the international road bordering the ranch. They had seen a car turn out its lights and shoot at them. Dave shot back and wounded one man, but Slim was killed. Karney then meets with bunkhouse cook Abner, who has been arranging the smuggling. Abner insists they run more contraband that night, even though Dave's "hair-trigger" shooting killed one of the outlaws the previous night. Jim finds a concha near the border and suspects the culprit is Mexican, and Colton reports that someone will be smuggling Chinese across the border that night. Jim then finds a Mexican named Jose in one of his cabins, where he is hiding three Chinese immigrants for which he was paid $150 each. Although Jose claims to be a rancher, Jim is suspicious and he and his men surround the cabin. One of the ranch hands fires a shot and Jose escapes onto the road, where he hides in Jane Elkins' car. Jim finds him and removes his disguise to discover that he is Karney. Jim then recollects the time he saved Karney's life in the war and is disappointed by Karney's ingratitude. Karney's ability to speak Spanish had made him able to implicate innocent Mexicans in the crime. Karney is holding up Jim and his men when the mysterious Chinese man, angry at Karney for taking his people's money, kills him with an axe and escapes. Jim, certain Colton will apprehend the killer, proposes to Jane, and his servant Snowflake plays the wedding march on his harmonica. *Chinese. Impersonation and imposture. Mexican-American border region. Officers (Military). Ranch foremen. Smuggling. Axes. Border patrols. Brothers. Chinatowns. Combat. Cooks. Disguise. Duplicity. Gunfights. Memory. Mexicans. Murder. Proposals (Marital). Ranchers. Rescues. Valets. World War I.*

Note: This film was reviewed in mid-Feb 1936 and a modern source gives a release date of 1 Mar 1936, although an exact release date has not been found. Although a 1936 copyright statement is listed on the viewed print, the title does not appear in U.S. copyright records. A 4 Dec 1935 *HR* news item states that Miller Easton was writing the script for this film, although he receives no credit on the screen.

DV 3 Dec 1935, p. 6. *FD* 19 Feb 1936, p. 4. *HR* 4 Dec 1935, p. 2.

THE HALF BREED (Native Americans)

Oliver Morosco Productions, Inc. *Dist* Associated First National Pictures. Jun **1922** Si; b&w. 6 reels, 5,484 ft.

Pres Oliver Morosco. *Dir* Charles A. Taylor. *Scen* Charles A. Taylor. *Photog* Charles G. Clarke and James C. Hutchinson. *Film ed* Elmer J. McGovern.

Source: Based on the play *Half-Breed; a Tale of Indian Territory* by H. D. Cottrell and Oliver Morosco (ca 1906).

Cast: Wheeler Oakman (*Delmar Spavinaw, the half-breed*), Ann May (*Doll Pardeau*), Mary Anderson (*Evelyn Huntington*), Hugh Thompson (*Ross Kennion*), King Evers (*Dick Kennion*), Joseph Dowling (*Judge Huntington*), Lew Harvey (*The Snake*), Herbert Pryor (*Ned Greenwood*), Sidney De Gray (*Leon Pardeau*), Nick De Ruiz (*Juan Del Rey*), Leela Lane (*Isabelle Pardeau*), Eugenia Gilbert (*Marianne*), Carl Stockdale (*John Spavinaw*), Evelyn Selbie (*Mary*), Dorris Deane (*Nanette*), Albert S. Lloyd (*Hops*), George Kuwa (*Kito*).

Western. Delmar Spavinaw, an educated half-breed, loves Evelyn Huntington, daughter of a racist judge. Evelyn's other suitor is Ross Kennion, a widower with one child, and owner of a vast tract of land which Spavinaw insists belongs to his Indian mother. Spavinaw seeks revenge when Judge Huntington decides to evict the squaw. Assisted by Juan Del Rey, a cattle rustler, Spavinaw steals the title to the land, wounds Kennion, stages a raid on the judge's cattle, and attempts to kidnap Kennion's son and Evelyn. The arrival of the sheriff forces him into flight across the border without his hostages. En route he meets Doll Pardeau, a school friend of Evelyn's, and together they ride for the Mexican border. Caught between a cattle stampede and a sheriff's posse, the couple catch a passing freight train, leaving calamity behind as the train slowly passes. *Indians of North America–Mixed blood. Indians of North America. Land rights. Racism. Squatters.*

ETR 1 Jul 1922, p. 305. *MPW* 1 Jul 1922. *MPW* 29 Jul 1922.

THE HALF-BREED (Native Americans)

Fine Arts Film Co. *Dist* Triangle Film Corp. 30 Jul **1916**. Si; b&w. 5 reels.

Dir Allan Dwan.

Source: Based on the short story "In the Carquinez Woods" by Bret Harte in his *In the Carquinez Woods and Other Tales* (London, 1883).

Cast: Douglas Fairbanks (*Lo Dorman*), Alma Reuben (*Teresa*), Sam De Grasse (*Sheriff Dunn*), Tom Wilson (*Curson*), Frank Brownlee (*Winslow Wynn*), Jewel Carmen (*Nellie*), George Beranger (*Jack Brace*).

Drama. Ostracized from white society, Lo Dorman, a half-breed, lives in the forest on the outskirts of town with his adopted Indian grandfather. While there, he meets another outcast, Teresa, who has run away from authorities after stabbing her unfaithful lover. Seeing her from a distance, Sheriff Dunn mistakes Teresa for Nellie, his sweetheart, and, believing that she has begun an affair with Lo, decides to kill him. Because she has gone through some of Lo's possessions, Teresa knows that Dunn is really his father, but as she tries to explain this to the sheriff, a forest fire breaks out. Lo tries to rescue both Teresa and Dunn, but finally must make a choice between them, and, unaware of their relationship, decides to leave Dunn to die. He is able to save Teresa, whom he later marries. *Fugitives. Indians of North America. Indians of North America–Mixed blood. Ostracism. Parentage. False accusations. Fires. Forests. Racism. Rescues. Sheriffs.*

Note: The working title for this film was *In the Carquinez Woods*. Some reviews refer to the film's title as *The Halfbreed*. Bluebird Photoplays, Inc. produced a film based on the same source in 1918 entitled *Tongues of Flame* (see below).

Motog 22 Jul 1916, p. 214. *MPN* 22 Jul 1916, p. 452. *MPW* 22 Jul 1916, p. 649. *MPW* 5 Aug 1916, p. 1002. *NYDM* 15 Jul 1916, p. 28. *NYT* 10 Jul 1916, p. 9. *Var* 14 Jul 1916, p. 19. *Wid's* 3 Jul 1916, p. 708.

THE HALF-BREED (Native Americans, Apache)

RKO Radio Pictures, Inc. *Dist* RKO Radio Pictures, Inc. May **1952**; Prod: early Mar—early Apr 1951 [©RKO Radio Pictures, Inc.; 9 May 1952; LP1719]. Sd (RCA Sound System); col (Technicolor). 9 reels, 7,329 ft. 81 min. PCA cert no. 15219.

Prod Herman Schlom. [*Exec prod* Sam Bischoff]. [*Prod* Irving Starr]. *Dir* Stuart Gilmore and [Edward Ludwig]. [*Asst dir* Max Henry]. *Scr* Harold Shumate and Richard Wormser. *Addl dial* Charles Hoffman. *Based on a story by* Robert Hardy Andrews. *Dir of photog* William V. Skall. *Technicolor color consultant* Morgan Padelford. *Art dir*

Albert S. D'Agostino and Ralph Berger. *Film ed* Samuel E. Beetley. *Set dec* Darrell Silvera and William Stevens. *Gowns* Michael Woulfe. *Mus* Paul Sawtell. *Mus dir* C. Bakaleinikoff. *Sd* John Cass and Clem Portman. *Makeup artist* Mel Berns. *Hair stylist* Larry Germain.

Song(s): "Remember the Girl You Left Behind," words and music by Harry Revel and Mort Greene; "When I'm Walking Arm in Arm with Jim," words by Harry Harris, music by Lew Pollack.

Cast: Robert Young [(*Dan Craig*)], Janis Carter [(*Helen Dowling*)], Jack Buetel [(*Charlie Wolf*)], Barton MacLane [(*Marshal Cassidy*)], Reed Hadley [(*Crawford*)], Porter Hall [(*Kraemer*)], Connie Gilchrist [(*Ma Huggins*)], Sammy White [(*Willy Wayne*)], Damian O'Flynn [(*Captain Jackson*)], Frank Wilcox [(*Sands*)], Judy Walsh [(*Nah-Lin*)], Tom Monroe [(*Russell*)], [Lee MacGregor (*Lt. Monroe*)], [Charles Delaney (*Sergeant*)], [Chief Thundercloud (*Sub-chief*)], [Caleen Calder (*Red head*)], [Jeane Cochran (*Maisie*)], [Robert Vera (*Mexican boy*)], [Herman Nowlin (*Stagecoach driver*)], [Ted Cooper (*Trooper*)], [Frank Tomlinson, Frank O'Connor (*Townsmen*)], [Chalky Williams, Allan Ray, Bob Robinson (*Bystanders*)], [Perry Ivans (*Veterinarian*)], [Phyllis Kennedy (*Bessie*)], [Al Cavens (*Clerk*)], [Al Hill (*Bartender*)], [Barry Brooks (*Deputy*)], [Chief Yowlachi (*Indian chief*)], [Stuart Randall (*Hawkfeather*)].

Western, with songs. [*Print viewed*]. In the year 1867, during America's expansion into Indian territory, the small Arizona town of San Remo comes under siege by an Apache war party led by Charlie Wolf, a "half-breed," who is protesting the corrupt Indian agency in charge of administering aid to Apaches. Dan Craig, a gambler passing through San Remo, takes an interest in the dispute when he suspects that San Remo's Marshal Cassidy is in league with Kraemer, the double-dealing Indian agency head. During his stay in San Remo, Dan also becomes involved with Helen Dowling, a pretty young singer who is planning to leave San Remo for San Francisco to further her career. The siege, which has been deliberately instigated by hotel owner Crawford and his men, who are planning to use the unrest as their excuse to make a claim on the gold buried under the Indian reservation, is momentarily suspended when Wolf enters Crawford's hotel with his gun lowered, asking for the surrender of Kraemer. While the townspeople view the proceedings in disbelief, Dan and Wolf begin negotiations. The temporary truce is soon broken, however, when Crawford starts a gun battle with the Apaches. Despite the attack by Crawford, Wolf sees a trustworthy friend in Dan and knows that he is sincere in his efforts to avert further bloodshed. As smoke signals emanating from the reservation tell of impending war, U.S. Cavalry troops under the command of Captain Jackson arrive in San Remo. At the captain's request, Dan relays a message to the Apaches that the government is willing to dismiss Kraemer from the agency in exchange for peace. The Apaches accept the offer, but as Dan and Wolf ride back to San Remo, Dan is wounded in an ambush. Soon after Dan and Wolf arrive in San Remo, Wolf meets Helen for the first time and falls instantly in love with her. Kraemer is later replaced by Dan as the local agency representative, and Wolf is made his assistant. The first attempt by the Apaches to get supplies in San Remo with Dan as head of the agency ends in tragedy, however, when Crawford's men ambush the caravan, steal their goods and kill many Indians. Later, when Dan finds Wolf forcing his attentions on Helen, the two men quarrel, and Wolf leaves San Remo. Hoping to prevent the Apaches from retaliating for the ambush, Dan promises to return their stolen goods and bring the culprit to justice. The fragile truce is further strained when Wolf's sister Nah-Lin is found murdered. One of Crawford's men, Russell, is arrested for the Nah-Lin's murder, but, faced with certain death at the hands of the Apaches, he names Crawford as the real culprit. Shortly after the admission, Crawford kills Russell. Dan chases after Crawford, kills him and delivers his body to the Apaches. Satisfied with the death of Nah-Lin's killer and the source of corruption in San Remo, the Apaches call off the war party and Wolf and Dan patch up their differences. Wolf decides to return to the reservation to help enlighten his people about the white man's ways. *Apache Indians. Arizona. Embezzlement. Indian agents. Indians of North America–Mixed blood. Land claims. Revenge. Ambushes. Confession (Law). Gamblers. Gold. Gunshot wounds. Murder. Rescues. Sheriffs. United States. Army. Cavalry.*

Note: According to an Apr 1950 *DV* news item, author Robert Hardy Andrews was signed by RKO executive producer Sid Rogell to write and produce this story. Although *HR* production charts indicate that filming began under the direction of Edward Ludwig, with Irving Starr producing, Ludwig was later replaced by Stuart Gilmore, and Starr was replaced by Herman Schlom. An early Feb 1951 *HR* news item noted that Ludwig was also set to work on the screenplay.

Box 19 Apr 1952. *DV* 12 Apr 1950. *DV* 16 Apr 1952, p. 3. *FD* 29 Apr 1952, p. 6. *HR* 6 Feb 1951. *HR* 2 Mar 1951, p. 12. *HR* 6 Apr 1951, p. 10. *HR* 16 Apr 1952, p. 3. *MPHPD* 19 Apr 1952, p. 1321. *NYT* 5 Jul 1952, p. 7. *Var* 16 Apr 1952, p. 6.

HALF PAST MIDNIGHT (Chinese Americans, Latino)

Twentieth Century-Fox Film Corp.; Sol M. Wurtzel Productions, Inc. *Dist* Twentieth Century-Fox Film Corp. Mar **1948**; Prod: early Nov—mid-Nov 1947 [©Twentieth Century-Fox Film Corp.; 19 Feb 1948; LP1891]. Sd (Western Electric Recording); b&w. 7 reels, 6,241 ft. 69 min. PCA cert no. 12859.

Pres SOL M. WURTZEL. *Dir* William F. Claxton. *Asst dir* Paul Wurtzel. *Story and Scr* Arnold Belgard. *Dir of photog* Benjamin Kline. [*Cam op* Perry Finnerman]. [*Stills* Buddy Longworth]. *Art dir* George Van Marter. *Film ed* Frank Baldridge. *Set dec* Al Greenwood. *Mus supv* David Chudnow. *Mus score* Darrell Calker. *Sd tech* Max M. Hutchinson. *Makeup artist* Lyle Dawn. *Hair stylist* Elaine Ramsey. *Prod asst* Clifford Gans. [*Scr supv* Sascha Laurence]. [*Grip* C. O. Morris].

Cast: Kent Taylor [(*Wade Hamilton*)], Peggy Knudsen [(*Sally Parker*)], Joe Sawyer [(*Joe Nash*)], Walter Sande [(*Lt. MacDonald*)], Martin Kosleck [(*Cortez*)], Mabel Paige [(*Hester Thornwall*)], Gil Stratton, Jr. [(*Chick Patrick*)], Jean Wong [(*Blossom*)], Jane Everett [(*Carlotta*)], [Damian O'Flynn (*Murray Evans*)], [Richard Loo (*Lee Gow*)], [Tom Dugan (*Barker*)], [Jean De Briac (*Alex*)], [Willie Best (*Andy*)], [Victor Sen Yung (*Sam*)], [George "Beetlepuss" Lewis (*Drunk in corridor*)], [George Meader (*Bascomb*)], [Tim Ryan (*Bartender*)], [Charles Williams (*Man in hallway*)], [Weaver Levy (*Chinese workman*)], [Gordon Clark (*Assistant manager*)], [Steve Darrell (*Plainclothesman*)], [Frank McGrath (*Taxi driver*)], [Mickey Simpson (*Husky man*)], [Eddie Lee (*Chinese man in alley*)], [Pat Goldin (*Waiter*)], [Max Wagner (*Mike*)].

Crime, Comedy-drama. [*Print viewed*]. Moments after arriving at the Los Angeles airport, playboy and trouble-making veteran Wade Hamilton grabs a woman waiting for her boyfriend and, pretending to have mistaken her for his sweetheart, gives her a passionate kiss. When the woman's boyfriend sees the two in an embrace, he punches Wade and walks off with the woman. Wade is then greeted by his pal Joe Nash, a police lieutenant, who asks Wade about newspaper reports that he challenged an irate husband to a duel in Hawaii. Joe knows that Wade has not reformed and suggests that he leave Los Angeles and return to San Francisco, but Wade assures him that he will only be staying a short time. Joe takes Wade to the Ambassador Hotel, where bellboy Chick Patrick, an old Army pal of Wade's, gives him a warm welcome. After overhearing Joe tell Wade that he will watching his every move, Chick telephones Joe, posing as Joe's sergeant, and gives him orders to go immediately to another location. Joe leaves Wade, but not before locking him in the bathroom and stealing his clothes. Chick then helps Wade escape to a nightclub, where he meets the alluring and aloof Sally Parker, who is at the club to see dancer Carlotta. Sally tells Wade that he is boring her, and is glad to see him leave her table to take a telephone call. While Chick warns Wade that Joe is after him and will be at the club soon, Sally barges into Carlotta's dressing room and tries to settle the dancer's blackmail demands by paying her $20,000. An argument ensues and Sally shoots Carlotta. Sally escapes with the gun, but mistakenly gets into the taxicab in which Wade is riding. Sally eventually realizes that she can trust Wade, and tells him that she was trying to get letters from Carlotta that her sister wrote to Carlotta's former dancing partner, Murray Evans. Wade is soon suspected of helping Sally escape, and a manhunt ensues. Sally asks Wade to help her find Evans, but he tells her that he must first save himself from the police. To that end, Wade goes to Chinatown, where he pays a visit to a former flame, Blossom, and her father, Lee Gow. Joe finds Wade there and helps him elude Lieutenant MacDonald in order to give him enough time to uncover evidence in the Carlotta murder case. Wade later questions Cortez, Carlotta's most recent dance partner, about the letters, and Cortez explains that Evans was jealous of her new partner and swore that he would not let them marry. Detectives arrive just as shots intended for either Cortez or Wade ring out, and Wade flees having gotten a tip about Evans' whereabouts. MacDonald finally captures Wade and insists that he tell him where Sally is. Chick, meanwhile, takes Sally to Evans, who is living in an apartment on Bunker Hill. When Evans starts to tell Sally who killed Carlotta, he is shot by Cortez, the real

murderer. Cortez then tries to flee, but Joe arrives in time to arrest him. *Fugitives. Murder. Playboys. Police. African Americans. Aged women. Aliases. Bellboys. Blackmail. Buses. Chases. Chinese Americans. Dancers. Impersonation and imposture. Los Angeles (CA). Los Angeles (CA)–Chinatown. Nightclubs.*

DV 11 Feb 1948, p. 3. *FD* 18 Feb 1948, p. 7. *HR* 11 Feb 1948, p. 3. *MPHPD* 31 Jan 1948, p. 4039. *MPHPD* 14 Feb 1948, p. 4059. *Var* 11 Feb 1948, p. 14.

HALF-WAY TO HEAVEN *(foreign version) see* **SOMBRAS DEL CIRCO**

THE HALFBREED (1916) *see* **THE HALF-BREED**

HALLELUJAH (African Americans)
Metro-Goldwyn-Mayer Corp.; controlled by Loew's Inc. *Dist* Metro-Goldwyn-Mayer Distributing Corp. 20 Aug **1929** [©Metro-Goldwyn-Mayer Distributing Corp.; 3 Sep 1929; LP652]. Sd (Movietone); b&w. 12 reels, 9,711 ft. [Also si; 6,579 ft.].
 Dir King Vidor. *Asst dir* Robert A. Golden and Harold Garrison. *Scen* Wanda Tuchock. *Story* King Vidor. *Trmt* Richard Schayer. *Dial* Ransom Rideout. *Titles* Marian Ainslee. *Photog* Gordon Avil. *Art dir* Cedric Gibbons. *Film ed* Hugh Wynn and Anson Stevenson. *Ward* Henrietta Frazer. *Rec eng* Douglas Shearer.
 Song(s): "Waiting at the End of the Road" and "Swanee Shuffle" by Irving Berlin.
 Cast: Daniel L. Haynes (*Zeke*), Nina Mae McKinney (*Chick*), William E. Fountaine (*Hot Shot*), Harry Gray (*Parson*), Fannie Belle De Night (*Mammy*), Everett McGarrity (*Spunk*), Victoria Spivey (*Missy Rose*), Milton Dickerson, Robert Couch, Walter Tait (*Johnson kid*), Dixie Jubilee Singers.
 Drama, African American. Zeke, a black tenant farmer, takes the family cotton crop to market and sells it for nearly one hundred dollars. Chick, a dance hall temptress, then uses her wiles to lure Zeke into a crap game with her lover, Hot Shot, who cheats Zeke out of his money with loaded dice. Zeke and Hot Shot fight, and Zeke gets possession of Hot Shot's gun, firing point blank into the crowd. The shot accidentally kills his younger brother, Spunk, and in repentance, Zeke becomes a preacher. He again meets Chick, and she gets religion, deserting Hot Shot to go with him. Zeke falls for Chick and jilts Missy Rose. Hot Shot returns, and the fickle Chick goes off with him. Zeke gives chase, and Chick is killed when Hot Shot's buggy overturns. Zeke then kills Hot Shot in a swamp, and, after serving time on the chain gang, returns home to the faithful Missy Rose. *African Americans. Brothers. Chain gangs. Cotton. Gamblers. Gambling. Preachers. Religion. Tenant farmers. Vamps.*
 Note: Several traditional Negro spirituals are used in the film, including "Goin' Home" and "Swing Low, Sweet Chariot."
 FD 25 Aug 1929. *NYT* 21 Aug 1929, p. 33. *Var* 28 Aug 1929, p. 18.

THE HALLIDAY BRAND (Native Americans)
Collier Young Associates, Inc. *Dist* United Artists Corp. Jan **1957** [©Collier Young Associates, Inc.; 16 Jan 1957; LP8173]. Sd (Westrex Recording System); b&w. 7,064 ft. 77 or 79 min.
 Prod Collier Young. *Assoc prod* Robert Eggen. *Dir* Joseph H. Lewis. *Asst dir* Louis Germonprez. *Wrt by* George W. George and George F. Slavin. *Dir of photog* Ray Rennahan. *Optical eff* Westheimer Company. *Art dir* David Garber. *Film ed* Michael Luciano. *Asst film ed* Stuart O'Brien. *Set dressing* Robert Bradfield. *Ward* Irving Levitt. *Mus comp and cond by* Stanley Wilson. [*Mus ed* Byron Chudnow]. *Sd* Fred Hynes and Earl Snyder.
 Cast: JOSEPH COTTEN [(*Daniel Halliday*)], VIVECA LINDFORS [(*Aleta Burris*)], BETSY BLAIR [(*Martha Halliday*)], WARD BOND [(*Big Dan Halliday*)], BILL WILLIAMS [(*Clay Halliday*)], Jay C. Flippen [(*Chad Burris*)], Christopher Dark [(*Jivaro Burris*)], Jeanette Nolan [(*Nante*)], Peter Ortiz, Glen Strange, John Dierkes, Stanford Jolley, John Ayres, Robin Short, Jay Lawrence, George Lynn, John Halloran, Michael Hinn, [Collier Young (*Undertaker*)].
 Western. [*Print viewed*]. When Clay Halliday tracks down his fugitive brother Daniel with a request from their dying father, Big Dan, to return home for a reconciliation, Daniel, who has come to loath his tyrannical father, refuses until his brother mentions that Big Dan has granted Clay permission to marry half-breed Aleta Burris. Believing that his father has changed, Daniel follows Clay home. Before entering his father's room, Daniel recalls the events that led up to their estrangement: Big Dan, the iron-willed sheriff of the territory, proudly presents Daniel, his favorite son, with a set of silver-plated

pistols and begs him to reconsider his decision not to become his deputy. Content to manage the family ranch, Daniel refuses, and Big Dan then recruits the weak-willed Clay for the post. When rumors begin to circulate that Jivaro Burris, the Halliday's head wrangler, has a mistress, Big Dan rides to investigate and enters Jivaro's cabin to find his daughter, Martha, embracing the wrangler. Outraged that a half-breed would dare fall in love with his daughter, Big Dan orders Jivaro to leave the ranch. Soon after, Jivaro becomes implicated in cattle rustling and murder when he tries to turn back a stampeding herd after a gang of cattle thieves murders a neighboring rancher. Despite Jivaro's pleas of innocence, Big Dan arrests him. As an enraged mob assembles outside the jailhouse, Big Dan rides off and leaves the jail unguarded, thus allowing the mob to break in and lynch Jivaro. Jivaro's hanging alienates both Martha and Daniel from their father, and after denouncing him, Daniel foresakes the ranch and rides to tell storekeeper Chad Burris of his son's death. While consoling Aleta, Jivaro's sister, Daniel begins to fall in love with her. Soon after Daniel rides off, Big Dan comes looking for his son. When Chad accuses him of murder, Big Dan goads him into drawing his gun and then shoots him down. Hearing gunfire, Daniel returns and vows vengeance on his father. Although Aleta attempts to calm him down and begs him to stay with her, Daniel, embittered and vengeful, departs. Deprived of all those dear to her, Aleta falls ill and Martha takes her home to nurse her back to health. At the ranch, Clay falls in love with Aleta, but she returns home once she has recovered. Meanwhile, to retaliate against his father, Daniel defies the law by stampeding cattle, torching buildings and robbing banks, declaring that he will not desist until his father resigns as sheriff. Although the townspeople beg for his resignation, Big Dan, obsessed with bringing his son to justice, refuses to abandon his quest and continues his search alone. Finally coming face to face, father and son engage in a violent fistfight in which Big Dan suffers a crippling stroke. As his thoughts return to the present, Daniel enters his father's bedroom and Big Dan pulls a gun from under the covers and aims it at his son. Martha, armed with her own pistol, pulls the weapon from her father's hand and slips it into a drawer. When Big Dan rescinds his permission for Clay to marry Aleta, declaring that it was just a ploy to bring Daniel home, all three children, now completely alienated from their father, turn their backs and leave him to die alone. Crawling from his bed, Big Dan retrieves his gun from the drawer and hobbles after them. When Daniel dares him to shoot, he collapses, unable to fire, and then dies. *Fathers and daughters. Fathers and sons. Indians of North America–Mixed blood. Revenge. Brothers. False accusations. Lynching. Murder. Stroke.*
 Note: According to a *HR* news item, this film was shot on location at Newhall, CA.
 Box 19 Jan 1957. *DV* 9 Jan 1957, p. 3. *Exb* 6 Feb 1957, pp. 4286-87. *FD* 16 Jan 1957, p. 6. *Har* 19 Jan 1957, p. 11. *HR* 16 Jul 1956. *MPHPD* 19 Jan 1957, p. 225. *Var* 16 Jan 1957, p. 18.

HAM AND EGGS AT THE FRONT (African Americans)
Warner Bros. Pictures, Inc. *Dist* Warner Bros. Pictures, Inc. 24 Dec **1927** [©Warner Bros. Pictures, Inc.; 14 Nov 1927; LP24662]. Si; b&w. 6 reels, 5,613 ft.
 Dir Roy Del Ruth. *Asst dir* Ross Lederman. *Scen* Robert Dillon and James A. Starr. *Story* Darryl Francis Zanuck. *Photog* Charles Clarke.
 Cast: Tom Wilson (*Ham*), Heinie Conklin (*Eggs*), Myrna Loy (*Fifi*), William J. Irving (*Von Friml*), Noah Young (*Sergeant*), Cameo (*Himself, a dog*).
 Comedy. Ham and Eggs, privates in an all-black regiment, become buddies in training camp and are stationed together in a small French village. The innkeeper, Friml, an enemy spy, desirous of learning the number of soldiers in the black regiment, has Fifi, his Negro waitress, flirt with the soldiers to get this information. Ham and Eggs fall for her and go to her house that night, each trying to outstay the other. An officer commands the two to force Fifi to disclose the location of Friml, and to shoot her if she refuses to talk; she escapes them, but they uncover a coded enemy message. When the pair are sent to the front, Ham is wounded. They are accidentally cast adrift in a balloon, and in parachuting to safety, they "capture" Friml. They are later decorated for their bravery. *African Americans. Balloons (Hot air). Dogs. France. Spies. United States. Army. World War I.*
 Note: This film was copyrighted under the title *Ham and Eggs*.
 Var 14 Mar 1928, p. 28.

HAMBRE (Spanish language)

1929. Sd; b&w. Length undetermined.

Cast: Olimpio Guillerme, Norma Gaytán, Vicente Padula, Alonso Machado, Lola Salvi. [*Not viewed*]. [No information concerning the plot of this film has been located.].

Note: An ad in *La Opinión* for *Hambre* (which is translated into English as "Hunger"), stated that it was to be shown at El Teatro Mexico in Los Angeles on 10 Oct 1929; however, listings for the theater on that date mention a different film. *Hambre* was advertised as being "Made in Hollywood," and the showing at El Teatro Mexico was to be the world premiere of the first synchronized Mexican film. No further information regarding the film has been located.

La Opinión 3 Oct 1929

HAMBURG SEVEN, SEVEN, SEVEN *see* **THE HOUSE ON 92ND ST.**

HAMPTON INSTITUTE: ITS PROGRAM OF EDUCATION FOR LIFE (African Americans)

The Harmon Foundation. **1941?**. Si; b&w and col. prints. 16mm. Length undetermined.

Dir Mr. Ray Garner and Mrs. Ray Garner. *Script* Evelyn S. Brown. *Photog* Mr. Ray Garner and Mrs. Ray Garner.

Documentary, **Educational/Cultural**. [*Print viewed*]. At Hampton Institute, Virginia, which has been an "important factor in the development of Negro citizenship" since 1868, one thousand students each year prepare to be artisans, teachers, businessmen and women, homemakers and farmers. The principle of "learning by doing" was inaugurated by the school's founder, General Samuel Chapman Armstrong. The college, while located in the South, attracts students from all over the United States, the West Indies, Africa and Canada. Scenes are shown of students, teachers, counsellors, doctors and nurses. Students are shown working to earn part of their expenses. They are also shown taking aptitude tests, preparing to be farm demonstration agents, teachers and scientific farmers; in business circumstances; and teaching in county schools. A chart shows the rise in the literacy rate for African Americans from 18.6 percent in 1868 to 83.7 percent in 1941. Library training is shown, as is instruction for women to become home economic teachers. Child development and family life is studied in a nursery school and a practice home. The college's thirteen trade schools are shown, including automobile mechanics; forging and welding; brickmasonry and plastering; electricity; cabinetmaking; upholstery; tailoring; dry cleaning; machine shop; plumbing and heating; sheetmetal and roofing; printing; and carpentry. In addition, activities of building construction and trade teaching are shown. Students are shown pursuing various artistic endeavors, including painting, ceramics, sculpture, weaving and African dance. The Hampton Choir, which has performed in Europe for royalty and for the president of the U.S., are shown performing, under the direction of Dr. R. Nathaniel Dett. The institute's regiment, which all men are required to join, is shown marching. The campus church, residences, social activities and sports program are shown. President Malcolm S. MacLean is shown talking with students in the Civil Aeronautics Authority training program and taking a ride with an advanced student pilot. Men from shipyards, naval bases, forts, camps and factories are sent to the school for training in defense skills. Graduates from the school are shown, and a chart shows the high percentage of graduates placed in jobs in various disciplines. The school's slogan, "Upward with Hampton for the Nation's Gain" is given. *African-American universities and colleges. Hampton Institute. Students. Virginia. Air pilots. Artists. Businessmen. Dancers. Teachers.*

Note: As noted in the film, the Hampton Institute, which is located in Hampton, VA, was founded in 1868 and chartered in 1870 for advanced education of African Americans.

THE HANDS OF NARA (Russian Americans)

Samuel Zierler Photoplay Corp. *Dist* Metro Pictures. 18 Sep 1922; Atlanta premiere: ca26 Aug 1922 [©Samuel Zierler Photoplay Corp.; 15 Sep 1922; LP18387]. Si; b&w. 6 reels, 6,000 ft.

Pres Harry Garson. *Dir* Harry Garson. *Photog* L. W. O'Connell.

Source: Based on the novel *The Hands of Nara* by Richard Washburn Child (New York, 1922).

Cast: Clara Kimball Young (*Nara Alexieff*), Count John Orloff (*Boris Alexieff*), Elliott Dexter (*Emlen Claveloux*), Edwin Stevens (*Connor Lee*), Vernon Steele (*Adam Pine*), John Miltern (*Dr. Haith Claveloux*), Margaret Loomis (*Emma Gammell*), Martha Mattox (*Mrs. Miller*), Dulcie Cooper (*Carrie Miller*), Ashley Cooper (*Gus Miller*), Myrtle Stedman (*Vanessa Yates*), Eugenie Besserer (*Mrs. Claveloux*).

Melodrama. Nara Alexieff, a Russian refugee from the Bolshevik revolution, comes to New York and is "taken up" by society woman Vanessa Yates. She meets Connor Lee, who convinces Nara that her hands have healing powers; sculptor Adam Pine; and Dr. Emlen Claveloux, who falls in love with Nara but rejects her when he suspects she is involved with Pine. Nara causes several cures, and, when the stories reach Emlen's father, the elder Dr. Claveloux begs Nara to help his wife. When she does so, Emlen reconsiders both his total reliance on science and his opinion of Nara, and they marry. *Physicians. Refugees, Political. Russian Americans. Sculptors. Spiritual healing.*

Note: This film was copyrighted at seven reels.

ETR 2 Sep 1922, p. 941. *FD* 13 Aug 1922. *MPW* 19 Aug 1922. *MPW* 23 Sep 1922. *Var* 22 Sep 1922, p. 41.

THE HANGING TREE (Swiss Americans)

Borada Productions, Inc. *Dist* Warner Bros. Pictures, Inc. Feb 1959; *Prod:* mid-Jun—early Aug 1958 [©Baroda Productions, Inc.; 21 Feb 1959; LP15455]. Sd (RCA Sound System); col (Technicolor); 1.85. 9,654 ft. 106 min.

Prod Martin Jurow and Richard Shepherd. *Dir* Delmer Daves. *Asst dir* Russell Llewellyn. *Scr* Wendell Mayes and Halsted Welles. *Dir of photog* Ted McCord. *Art dir* Daniel B. Cathcart. *Film ed* Owen Marks. *Set dec* Frank M. Miller. *Miss Schell's ward* Orry-Kelly. *Cost des* Marjorie O. Best. *Mus* Max Steiner. *Sd* Stanley Jones. *Makeup supv* Gordon Bau. *Unit prod mgr* Lew Leary.

Song(s): "The Hanging Tree," music by Jerry Livingston, lyrics by Mack David, sung by Marty Robbins.

Source: Based on the novelette *The Hanging Tree* by Dorothy M. Johnson (New York, 1957).

Cast: GARY COOPER [(*Dr. Joseph "Doc" Frail*)], MARIA SCHELL [(*Elizabeth Mahler*)], KARL MALDEN [(*Frenchy Plante*)], George C. Scott [(*George Grubb*)], Karl Swenson [(*Tom Flaunce*)], Virginia Gregg [(*Edna Flaunce*)], John Dierkes [(*Society Red*)], King Donovan [(*Wonder*)], and introducing Ben Piazza [(*Rune*)], [Stanley Rhodes, Carl Clark (*Guards*)], [Slim Talbot (*Older guard*)], [Annette Claudier, Rae M. Lee, E. Jane Maddux, Larrie L. Armstrong, Elsie Sanders (*Girls*)], [Guy Wilkerson, Harold Millen, George William Schrindel (*Sourdoughs*)], [Dorothy Klewer, Karen Norris (*Duck girls*)], [John V. Dale (*Man on a crutch*)], [Terrill Douglas (*Little girl*)], [Martin Eric (*Father*)], [Fern Barry (*Mother*)], [Joseph DuBuc (*Gaunt man on wagon*)], [Clarence Straight (*Dealer*)], [Cactus McPeters (*Player*)], [Billy Benedict (*Trapper*)], [Baron Lichter (*Tim, the piano player*)], [Dan Borzage (*Dan*)].

Western. [*Print viewed*]. After drifting into the goldrush town of Skull Creek, Montana, Dr. Joseph "Doc" Frail buys a cabin on the hill above town from a penniless prospector. Soon after, Rune, a young wanderer, tries to steal a gold nugget from a sluice box and is pursued by a bloodthirsty mob, guns ablaze. Hearing the injured Rune's cries for help, Doc rescues the boy and bandages his wound. In payment for his services, Doc demands that Rune become his bond servant, threatening to expose him as a thief if he refuses. Doc then sets up practice, and although he exhibits compassion for his patients, he can be imperious and severe when dealing with others, prompting Tom Flaunce, the town storekeeper and an old acquaintance, to comment that "Doc carries his soul in his doctor's bag." When Doc is assailed by George Grubb, a raving drunk who accuses him of being the devil, Doc, an expert marksman, drives Grubb off at gunpoint. While at the saloon one evening, Doc strikes a gambler who questions him about burning down a house in Illinois. One day, a stagecoach is attacked by a band of robbers, causing the horses to bolt and the carriage to careen over the side of a cliff. With his dying breath, the driver reveals that a woman passenger, the soul survivor, is trapped in the coach. Frenchy, a lecherous prospector, Rune and Flaunce head a search party for the woman. While camped around the fire for the night, Flaunce informs Rune that Frail is a name the Doc assumed because he felt that it described the state of mankind. Flaunce then relates the story of a doctor named Temple, who torched his grand house on the river after discovering the dead bodies of a man and a woman inside. The next day, Frenchy finds the missing woman, whom he dubs "Lost Lady." After they carry the unconscious woman to a shack in a nearby meadow, Doc examines her and declares that she is suffering from temporary blindness. He arranges for her to be transported to Flaunce's abandoned cabin, which is situated across from his own, and Rune volunteers to care for her. Three days later, the woman

regains consciousness, although she remains blind. After identifying herself as Elizabeth Mahler, she learns that her father was killed in the robbery. When Elizabeth tells Doc about emigrating from Switzerland to the "wonderous" America, Doc cautions her that she will find no glory in the wretched town of Skull Creek. Soon after, Flaunce's wife Edna, a mean-spirited, priggish woman, drives to the cabin to determine if Elizabeth is "decent," and is turned away by Doc. That night, after Doc leaves to play cards at the saloon, Frenchy sneaks into the cabin. When Elizabeth senses his presence, he claims that he has come for his canteen. As Frenchy is about to sexually attack the blind woman, Doc appears and orders him to leave. Later, at the saloon, Doc thrashes Frenchy and threatens to kill him if he ever returns to the cabin, and Frenchy vows revenge. As the days pass, Rune accuses Doc of trying to control people and objects to his isolation of Elizabeth. One day, Elizabeth is on the verge of recovering her eyesight when she lapses back into hysterical blindness. Doc inspires her to see again, but when she embraces him, he coldly informs her that she must leave the next day. Doc then gives Rune his freedom and presents him with a horse. The following morning, Rune and Elizabeth ride into town and Elizabeth shows Flaunce a brooch, an old family heirloom, and asks to use it as collateral for a grubstake. When Flaunce reports Elizabeth's request to Doc, Doc gives him the money to lend to her. Entering into partnership with Frenchy, Elizabeth and Rune establish the "Lucky Lady" mine. A month passes, and Doc continues to funnel money into the mine, unbeknown to Elizabeth. While out delivering a baby one day, Doc stops to say hello to Elizabeth. Jealous of Doc's intrusion, Frenchy manhandles Elizabeth and she decides to move into town. When Elizabeth comes to the store for another advance, Edna cruelly informs her that the brooch is worthless and accuses her of prostitution. Furious, Elizabeth accuses Doc of trying to play with people's lives and he admits that the rumor about the grand house on the river is true and that the man and woman were his wife and brother. In the midst of a violent rainstorm one day, a giant tree near the Lucky Lady is uprooted, revealing a pit filled with gold nuggets. To celebrate the strike, Frenchy plies the townsmen with liquor. While Elizabeth repairs to Doc's cabin with her sack of gold, the drunken revelers below turn mean and set the town on fire. Barging into Doc's cabin, Frenchy hurls Elizabeth onto the bed and assaults her. Doc returns to find the town in flames, then hurries to his cabin and throws Frenchy down the stairs. When Frenchy pulls his gun, Doc shoots him and then kicks his lifeless body over the hillside. Grubb seizes the opportunity to incite the frenzied crowd to lynch Doc, and as they place a noose around his neck, Elizabeth, bruised, hobbles down the hill and offers her gold in exchange for Doc's life. The greedy mob stampedes to the mine, leaving Doc behind. After Rune removes the noose from his neck, Doc bends down and caresses Elizabeth's face and they embrace. *Gold miners. Immigrants. Lechery. Mining towns. Physicians. Swiss. Attempted rape. Blindness-Temporary. Cabins. Drunkenness. Gambling. Gold. Indentured servants. Lynching. Mobs. Nursing back to health. Personality change. Prudes. Secrets. Stagecoach robberies. Storekeepers.*

Note: Although a Feb *LAEx* news item states that James Webb had written the script for this picture, the extent of his contribution to the released film has not been determined. Studio publicity materials contained in the AMPAS Library add that it was shot on location near Yakima, WA. This picture marked the screen debuts of George C. Scott and Ben Piazza and the initial effort of the producing team of Martin Jurow and Richard Shepherd. Modern sources add Guy Wilkerson and Bud Osborne to the cast.

AmCin Feb 1959, pp. 112-113, 130. *Box* 2 Feb 1959. *DV* 28 Jan 1959, p. 3. *Exb* 28 Jan 1959, p. 4555. *FD* 28 Jan 1959, p. 8. *Har* 31 Jan 1959, p. 19. *HR* 13 Jun 1958, p. 10. *HR* 8 Aug 1958, p. 8. *HR* 28 Jan 1959, p. 3. *LAEx* 22 Feb 1958. *MPHPD* 31 Jan 1959, p. 132. *NYT* 12 Feb 1959, p. 23. *Var* 28 Jan 1959, p. 6.

HAPPY ENDING *see* **HAPPY LANDING**

HAPPY LANDING (Norwegian Americans)
Twentieth Century-Fox Film Corp.; Darryl F. Zanuck, in charge of production. *Dist* Twentieth Century-Fox Film Corp. 28 Jan **1938**; New York opening: 21 Jan 1938; Prod: 18 Oct—mid-Dec 1937 [©Twentieth Century-Fox Film Corp.; 28 Jan 1938; LP7867]. Sd (RCA High Fidelity Recording); b&w. 12 reels, 9,200 ft. 102 min. PCA cert no. 3827.
Assoc prod David Hempstead. *Dir* Roy Del Ruth. [*Asst dir* Booth McCracken]. *Orig scr* Milton Sperling and Boris Ingster. *Photog* John Mescall. *Art dir* Bernard Herzbrun and Mark-Lee Kirk. *Film ed* Louis Loeffler. *Set dec* Thomas Little. *Cost* Royer. *Mus dir* Louis Silvers.

[*Vocal supv* Jule Styne]. *Dances staged by* Harry Losee. *Sd* Eugene Grossman and Roger Heman. [*Elec L. O.* James]. [*Publicity* Harry Brand].
Music: "War Dance of the Wooden Indians" by Raymond Scott.
Song(s): "Hot and Happy," "A Gypsy Told Me," "You Are the Music to the Words in My Heart" and "Yonny and His Oompah," music and lyrics by Sam Pokrass and Jack Yellen; "You Appeal to Me," music and lyrics by Walter Bullock and Harold Spina.
Cast: SONJA HENIE (*Trudy Ericksen*), DON AMECHE (*Jimmy Hall*), Jean Hersholt (*Herr [Lars] Ericksen*), Ethel Merman (*Flo Kelly*), Cesar Romero (*Duke Sargent*), Billy Gilbert (*Counter man*), Raymond Scott, Quintet (*Themselves*), Wally Vernon (*Al Mahoney*), Leah Ray, Condos Brothers (*Specialties*), El Brendel (*Yonnie*), Marcelle Corday (*Gypsy*), Joseph Crehan (*Agent*), Eddie Conrad (*Waiter*), Ben Weldon (*Manager skating rink*), [Alex Novinsky (*Count*)], [Harvey Parry, Matt McHugh (*Tough hecklers*)], [Otto Malde, Joe Hartman, Herbert H. Brodkin, Gene Mako (*Husbands*)], [Annabelle Brudie, Marianne Brudie, Gloria Brewster, Barbara Brewster (*Wives*)], [Louis Adlon (*Olaf*)], [Alex Schonberg, Victor Delinsky, Alex Palasthy, Bernard Siegel, Ralph Fitzsimmons, Paul Panzer, Hans Joby, Hans Tanzler, Bert Sprotte (*Cronies*)], [William B. Davidson (*Manager*)], [Marcel de Labrosse (*Rajah*)], [Norman Willis, Herbert Ashley (*Guards*)], [William Wagner (*Justice of peace*)], [George Offerman, Jr. (*Western Union messenger*)], [Eugene Borden (*Waiter*)], [John Hiestand (*Announcer*)], [Fredrik Vogeding (*Villager*)], [Adolph Milar (*Constable*)], [Syd Saylor (*Tuba player*)], [Billy Wayne, Ben Hendricks, Art Dupuis (*Mechanics*)], [Charles Tannen, Robert Lowery, Lon Chaney, Jr., Arthur Rankin, Harold Goodwin (*Reporters*)], [Fred Kelsey (*Turnkey*)], [June Storey (*Stewardess*)].

Musical comedy. [*Print viewed*]. As a publicity stunt, Duke Sargent, the famous bandleader, songwriter, nightclub star and ladies' man, is to fly the Atlantic to Paris to make a nightclub date. When he does not show up at the airport, Jimmy Hall, Duke's manager, locates him in the apartment of singer Flo Kelly, with whom he has fallen in love. Although Duke maintains that he does not want to make the flight, Jimmy convinces him to go by telling him of the thousands of other girls he may meet and the publicity the voyage will bring. Flo temporarily stops them when she reveals that she has recorded Duke's marriage proposal, but during a struggle, Jimmy breaks the record and manages to get Duke out. The plane is forced down near a small Norwegian village, where Duke becomes infatuated with Trudy Ericksen, who hopes to marry a wealthy, handsome, "princely" gentleman. He accompanies her to a dance, and when he asks her to dance for a second time, which, unknown to him, signifies a marriage proposal in Trudy's community, she readily accepts. Jimmy realizes that Duke unwittingly has become engaged and spirits him away in their plane. At Duke's club in Paris, he falls in love again with Flo, who is visiting with her new paramour, a wealthy count. Later in New York, Jimmy finds Trudy in their hotel lobby, and she tells him that she came to find Duke, whom she thinks Jimmy took from her. Jimmy convinces her that Duke does not care for her, but then Duke, who thinks Trudy's story would make good publicity, acts as if he is madly in love with her. Trudy now tells Jimmy that she hates him. At the Carleton Roof nightclub, Trudy witnesses Duke romance Flo, whose count has dropped her. When Jimmy learns that Duke plans to go with Flo to Florida, he quits and then finds Trudy outside the club, where she apologizes to him. They walk to Central Park, where Jimmy tries to give Trudy some "tips" at skating and learns that she is an expert. He then gets her work performing on ice, and soon she tours the country as the "Queen of the Silver Skates," the star of her own show. In Detroit, Jimmy is about to propose, when he receives a wire that the Carleton Roof is offering her $1,500 to appear for two weeks. Jimmy is disappointed to see Trudy's excitement at the anticipation that Duke now will have to take notice of her. Before Trudy's opening in New York, Jimmy finds a new manager for her and tells her he is leaving. Just then, he receives a desperate call from Duke in Florida, who pleads with him to come and help him escape the wrath of Flo, who is incensed at his new infatuation with a blonde. After Jimmy leaves, Trudy confesses to her cohort, Al Mahoney, that she loves Jimmy, and Al reveals that Jimmy loves her. He then wires Jimmy the news. In Miami, Flo and Duke make up, but she gets angry again when she learns about Duke's call to Jimmy and throws a vase at Jimmy, which hits Duke. Flo then tells reporters that Duke and Jimmy battled

over her and signs a warrant for Jimmy's arrest for assault and battery, and for allegedly poisoning her Pekinese. Meanwhile, Duke, who has flown back to New York, meets Trudy at the airport. Piqued after reading the newspaper accounts about the Florida incident, Trudy asks Duke to marry her. Unable to resist an attractive woman, Duke agrees. When Flo, who still loves Duke, reads about his wedding plans, she gets Jimmy out of jail to help. Flo has a retraction of the story printed, and then she and Jimmy return to New York, where Flo threatens Duke with another recording. Trudy sees that Jimmy is not in love with Flo, and she and Jimmy marry, as do Duke and Flo, after which Duke plays Flo's record and finds it to be a song. Back at Trudy's hometown, the happy couples skate to the song. *Band leaders. Ice skaters and ice skating. Infatuation. Norwegians. Philanderers. Romance. Singers. Theatrical managers. Airplanes. Dances. Detroit (MI). False arrests. Fathers and daughters. Fights. Gypsies. Miami (FL). Mirrors. New York City. New York City–Central Park. Nightclubs. Nobility. Norway. Paris (France). Ping-pong (Game). Proposals (Marital). Publicity. Recordings. Village life.*

Note: The working titles of this film were *Bread, Butter and Rhythm, Hot and Happy* and *Happy Ending*. This was Norwegian ice-skating Olympic champion Sonja Henie's third film. Henie had ranked as the eighth biggest money-making star in the 1937 *MPH* poll of exhibitors, and in 1938, she moved up to third. She also recently had been recognized by the Norwegian government with the Cross of the Order of St. Olaf. Studio head Darryl Zanuck was very involved in the development of this film, as is evidenced in notes from his conferences in the Twentieth Century-Fox Produced Scripts Collection at the UCLA Theater Arts Library. According to these notes, the character of the orchestra leader, although first suggested for Don Ameche, was later developed for Adolphe Menjou, and Ameche was given the role of Jimmy. At the beginning of the film, a newspaper headline announces that "Duke Sargent's" plane is to carry 100,000 ping pong balls on its Transatlantic flight, and "Jimmy" confirms a reporter's remark that the ping pong balls will keep the plane afloat if it is forced down. This scene is a reference to a recent flight by composer, singer, actor and aviator Harry Richman. In his conference notes, Zanuck states, "We are going to poke a little fun at Menjou in the light of Harry Richman and his Transatlantic trip—ping pong balls, et al....Menjou can use the line: 'In case we had come down in the water they would keep us afloat,' which is bound to be good for a laugh." Also, in these notes, Zanuck instructed his writers on the tone of the film, comparing it to other recent Twentieth Century-Fox musicals produced for Sonja Henie and others: "...you are to write it more low-down, so to speak, than *Thin Ice*. Avoid farce and make it real, solid comedy-drama on the order of *One in a Million* and *You Can't Have Everything* [see *AFI Catalog of Feature Films, 1931-40* for entries F3.4571, 3260, 5237 and 1835]." Also, according to the Produced Scripts Collection, there originally was to be a scene set at the Paris Exposition; the Frankfort set built for *Heidi* (see below) was to be used for the Norwegian village; and the Florida scenes originally were written to take place in Hollywood.

According to a *HR* news item, ski-jumping scenes were to be filmed in Truckee, CA. Publicity for the film noted that some scenes included a chorus of eighty-four skaters. *Var* and the studio trade advertising billing sheet included the Peters Sisters as performing a specialty number, but they are not listed in the screen credits, and their inclusion in the final film has not been confirmed. *MPH*'s "In the Cutting Room," lists Ted Harper as a specialty act, but his participation in the final film also has not been confirmed. According to a modern source, Henie requested Tyrone Power as her co-star, but Zanuck refused, and Belle Christy was in the chorus.

Box 29 Jan 1938. *DV* 22 Jan 1938, p. 3. *FD* 22 Jan 1938, p. 3. *HR* 25 Oct 1937, p. 7. *HR* 19 Nov 1937, p. 9. *HR* 13 Dec 1937, p. 15. *HR* 18 Dec 1937, p. 5. *HR* 31 Dec 1937, sect. II, p. 90. *HR* 22 Jan 1938, p. 3. *MPD* 19 Jan 1938, p. 8. *MPH* 27 Nov 1937, p. 51. *MPH* 29 Jan 1938, p. 53, 56. *NYT* 22 Jan 1938, p. 19. *Var* 17 Oct 1937. *Var* 26 Jan 1938, p. 14.

HARBOR OF MISSING MEN (Greek Americans)
Republic Pictures Corp. *Dist* Republic Pictures Corp. 26 Mar **1949**; Prod: Dec 1949 [©Republic Pictures Corp.; 31 Mar 1950; LP14]. Sd (RCA Sound System); b&w. 5,402 ft. 60 min. Passed by the National Board of Review. PCA cert no. 14354.

Assoc prod Sidney Picker. *Dir* R. G. Springsteen. [*Asst dir* Lee Lukather and Johnny Grubbs]. *Wrt* John K. Butler. [*Scr supv* Joan Eremin]. *Dir of photog* John MacBurnie. [*Cam op* Enzo Martinelli]. [*Stills* Don Keyes]. *Spec eff* Howard Lydecker and Theodore Lydecker. *Optical eff* Consolidated Film Industries. *Art dir* Frank Arrigo. *Film ed* Arthur Roberts. *Set dec* John McCarthy, Jr. and Charles Thompson. *Cost supv* Adele Palmer. *Mus* Stanley Wilson. *Sd* Dick Tyler. *Makeup supv* Bob Mark. [*Makeup* Howard Smit]. [*Hair stylist* Lynn Burke]. [*Gaffer* Babe Stafford].

Cast: Richard Denning [(*Jim "Brooklyn" Gannon*)], Barbra Fuller [(*Mae Leggett, also known as Miss Higgins*)], Steven Geray [(*Capt. Corcoris*)], Aline Towne [(*Angelike*)], Percy Helton [(*"Rummy" Davis*)], George Zucco [(*H. G. Danzinger*)], Paul Marion [(*Philip Corcoris*)], Ray Teal [(*Frank*)], Robert Osterloh [(*Johnny*)], Fernanda Eliscu [(*Mama Corcoris*)], Gregory Gay [(*Capt. Koretsky*)], Jimmie

Kelly [(*Carl*)], Barbara Stanley [(*Leodora*)], Neyle Morrow [(*Christopher*)], [Charles LaTorre (*John*)], [Rudy Rama (*Andros*)], [Basil Tellou (*Hector*)], [Theodore Rand (*Bannister*)], [Carlo Schipa (*Socrates*)], [Mary Bear (*Mrs. Henley*)], [Paul Maxey (*Mr. Henley*)].

Crime, Drama. [*Print viewed*]. In the Gulf of Mexico, off Florida's Key West, Jim "Brooklyn" Gannon, the owner of a fleet of rental fishing boats, smuggles valuable jewelry. After placing the jewelry into a hot water bottle, Brooklyn floats it out onto the water, where another boat quickly picks it up. Later, he returns to his shop and is kidnapped by some men working for gangster H. G. Danziger. They take him to Danziger's hideout, where the gangster offers him $2,000 to smuggle some machine guns onto a ship bound for Havana, Cuba. That evening, in the gulf, Brooklyn contacts Capt. Koretsky of the S.S. *Dardanelles* and boards his vessel. Koretsky gives Brooklyn an envelope containing $30,000 in cash, when suddenly, Danziger's secretary, Mae Leggett, who says that her name is "Miss Higgins," and her brother Frank step from their hiding place. They explain that Danziger has sent them to insure that the money reaches him safely. Mae, Frank and Brooklyn then return to Brooklyn's boat, where Mae and Frank take Brooklyn's wallet and demand at gun-point that he jump overboard. He does so, and Mae and Frank begin their journey back to Key West. Due to dense fog blanketing the Gulf, however, they become lost, while the boat is found beached some time later. The next morning, Brooklyn is rescued by boat owner Capt. Corcoris and his son Philip. They take him back to their home, Tarpon Springs, where he meets Mrs. Corcoris, Philip's sister Angelike, and his crippled brother Christopher. Later, Capt. Corcoris explains that Christopher suffered decompression sickness after he went sponge diving in the lagoon and was attacked by sharks. When Brooklyn phones his assistant "Rummy" Davis back in Key West, Rummy says that Danziger's men have been looking for him. In the meantime, Mae has hidden the money and told Danziger that Brooklyn is responsible for the theft. Later, Brooklyn and Philip decide to team up for a village contest, in which team members take turns diving for a solid gold crucifix after a member of the clergy tosses it into the bay. After Brooklyn wins the contest, Mrs. Corcoris gives him her crucifix pendant to wear for good luck. Back in Key West, Brooklyn is shot twice and, although one bullet enters his leg, Mrs. Corcoris's crucifix deflects the second one, saving his life. Brooklyn limps back to the boat where the Corcoris men are about to leave for two months of fishing. When Angelike, who was an army nurse during the war, sees Brooklyn's condition, she decides to join them on the trip so that she can remove the bullet. After they return, Brooklyn promises Angelike that he will return for her after he goes to see Danziger. When he phones Danziger and demands that he and his secretary meet with him, Mae becomes frightened and phones Frank. When Danziger and Mae arrive at the dock, Brooklyn orders them aboard his boat, and they depart. Once at sea, Brooklyn then tells Danziger that he has been double-crossed by Mae and that Capt. Koretsky, who is waiting in the gulf, will corroborate his story. When Danziger questions Mae, she confesses, but Frank suddenly appears and shoots Danziger. After Mae accidentally shoots Frank, Brooklyn returns to Tarpon Springs to be with Angelike. *Fishing boats. Robbery. Smuggling. Brothers and sisters. Bullets. Crucifixes. Decompression sickness. Divers and diving. Fathers and sons. Firearms. Fog. Gulf of Mexico. Havana (Cuba). Hot-water bottles. Jewelry. Key West (FL). Kidnapping. Lagoons. Miracles. Nurses. Operations, Surgical. Religiosity. Sea captains. Secretaries. Sponges. Tarpon Springs (FL).*

Note: A working title of the film was *Port of Missing Men*.

Box 22 Apr 1950. *DV* 17 Apr 1950, p. 5. *FD* 27 Apr 1950, p. 7. *HR* 9 Dec 1949, p. 11. *HR* 23 Dec 1949, p. 21. *HR* 17 Apr 1950, p. 3, 9. *MPHPD* 29 Apr 1950, p. 278. *Var* 19 Apr 1950, p. 8.

HARD AS NAILS *see* **TERROR IN A TEXAS TOWN**

HARD BARGAIN *see* **THIEVES' HIGHWAY**

HARLEM AFTER MIDNIGHT (African Americans)
Micheaux Pictures Corp. *Dist* Micheaux Pictures Corp. **1934?** [©Micheaux Pictures Corp.; 12 Mar 1935; LP5399]. Sd; b&w. 8 reels.
Dir Oscar Micheaux. *Wrt* Oscar Micheaux.

African American, Gangster, Drama. [*Not viewed*]. After her gangster husband Jerry Martin was sent to prison three years earlier, Vivian Poret began dating Nelson Gentry, the son of her employer, Charley. Nelson urges Vivian to get an annulment so that they can be married. When Jerry, known as Jerry "The Snitch," because he

snitched on his gang, escapes from prison, he learns that Vivian is living well in Harlem and decides to visit her. Although Vivian offers Jerry five hundred dollars, her life savings, to grant her a divorce, he refuses to cooperate and demands ten times that amount, which he tells her to get from the Gentrys. Meanwhile, Nelson ends his affair with Kate Elkins, a kept woman, and she determines to take revenge on him. Kate soon finds an opportunity to get her revenge when Vivian's younger sister, Sacha, comes to New York in the hope of becoming an entertainer. Kate and Jerry, united in their animosity towards Vivian, decide to have Jerry's pal Harold Stokes befriend Sacha and lead her astray. After gaining Vivian's trust, Harold takes Sacha out and offers to help further her career if she promises to keep subsequent meetings with him a secret from her sister. Harold is actually planning to sell her to an old man for his pleasure, but Sacha realizes her error in time and confesses to Vivian that she has learned her lesson. Kate knows that Jerry smokes marijuana and is a "reefer addict," and eventually becomes nervous when she learns that a man he informed on years earlier is now after him. The police are tipped off to raid Kate's, where Jerry has hidden Razoff, a wealthy Jew whom he kidnapped to collect a $10,000 reward. Jerry manages to avoid capture in the raid and tries, once again, to get money from Vivian, but she refuses. *African Americans. Ex-convicts. Gangsters. Informers. Marriage. New York City–Harlem. Revenge. Sisters. Adolescents. Blackmail. Dancers. Divorce. Drug addicts. Family relationships. Jews. Kidnapping. Marihuana. Mistresses. Pimps. Prison escapes. Stenographers.*

Note: Although the film was copyrighted in 1935, records from the New York Censor Board indicate that it was submitted for approval in Apr 1934. At that time, the Board approved the film "with eliminations." The exact date of the picture's release is not known. According to modern sources, the film was made early in 1933 and released in 1934, and the cast included Lorenzo Tucker as a gangster, Lionel Monagos, "Slick" Chester and possibly Dorothy Van Engle.

HARLEM BIG SHOT *see* THE BLACK KING

HARLEM FOLLIES (African Americans)
Futurity Film Corp. *Dist* Classic Pictures, Inc. **1949?** [©Futurity Film Corp.; 5 Jan 1955; LP4777]. Sd; b&w. 5 or 6 reels, 3,838 or 4,425 ft. 43 or 49 or 53 min.

Prod Arthur Jarwood. *Dir* Hugh Prince. *Asst dir* Tony Lo Presti. *Wrt* Hugh Prince. *Asst cam* Jack Martell. *Lighting eff* Walter Ruck. *Film ed* Vernon Lewis. *Mus arr* Edgar Battle. *Sd dir* Vernon Lewis. *Casting dir* Lew Perry.

Song(s): "Blues on Parade," "It Ain't No Sin" and "You Don't Care Anymore," music and lyrics by Hugh Prince.

Cast: "Chicago" Carl Davis, "Manhattan" Paul, Max Granville, Ruth Mason, "Fats" Noel, Clark Monroe, The Hip Paraders, Princess R'Wanda, Monique, Audrey Armstrong, Chicky Grimes, Los Avasiago, "Shootsie" Keith and the Savannah Club Chorus, Courtesy Savannah Club, N.Y.C.

African American, Show business, Drama, with songs. [*Viewed print incomplete*]. While rehearsing a musical number for his nightclub variety show, stage director Max Granville tells his dancers to "smile from the knees up" so that they are sure to impress "Manhattan" Paul, a backer who may finance the show. Desperate to get money for the show from Manhattan, Maxie urges his fiancée, singer Ruth Mason, to use her charms to help the deal along. Ruth objects to the set-up, as does her cousin, "Chicago" Carl Davis, who wants Maxie to reconsider putting Ruth in a costume that is a "skin-tight eye opener." After reassuring Chicago that Ruth is in no danger, Maxie tells the bartender, "Fats" Noel, to bring out his best champagne for Manhattan. Things look bad for Maxie as his money runs out and he finds himself unable to pay his bills. With only a short time left before the power is scheduled to be shut off at the club, Maxie begins a demonstration of his show for Manhattan. The performances dazzle the producer, and when he agrees to finance the show, Maxie realizes that his troubles are over. *African Americans. Dancers. Nightclubs. Singers. Theatrical backers. Theatrical directors. Bartenders. Cousins. Engagements. Financial crisis. Jazz music.*

Note: The above credits and summary were taken from a viewed print, which was 40 minutes in length, and a dialogue continuity deposited with the NYSA. Although no release date was found for the film, it was first submitted to the New York Censor Board sometime in 1949 and was approved with eliminations. The film's length in 1949 was listed at 4,425 feet, which would have been 49 minutes. On 23 May 1950, the film was rescreened by the Censor Board and additional eliminations were requested. According to correspondence included in the NYSA files, New York censors demanded cuts in the film because of

"indecent" dance footage. The film was listed at 3,838 feet (or 43 minutes) at that time. However, on 12 Jun 1950, Classic Pictures requested that the Censor Board allow ten minutes of new footage to be added, and when the film was copyrighted in 1955, the running time was listed as 53 minutes. The film was resubmitted to the Censor Board several times during the 1950s, and additional eliminations were demanded with each submission.

THE HARLEM GLOBETROTTERS (African Americans)
Columbia Pictures Corp.; Sidney Buchman Enterprises, Inc. *Dist* Columbia Pictures Corp. Nov **1951**; Prod: 12 Oct–24 Oct 1950; retakes 1 Dec 1950 [©Columbia Pictures Corp.; 19 Jul 1951; LP1058]. Sd (Western Electric Recording); b&w. 9 reels, 7,135 or 7,650 ft. 75 or 80 min. PCA cert no. 15014.

Prod Buddy Adler. *Assoc prod* Alfred Palca. *Dir* Phil Brown. *Dir of basketball seq* Will Jason. [*Asst dir* Gilbert Kay]. *Story and scr* Alfred Palca. *Dir of photog* Philip Tannura. *Art dir* Cary Odell. *Film ed* James Sweeney. *Set dec* David Montrose. *Mus score* Arthur Morton. *Mus dir* Morris Stoloff. [*Sd eng* George Cooper].

Music: "Sweet Georgia Brown" by Ben Bernie, Maceo Pinkard and Kenneth Casey, Brother Bones recording by arrangement with Tempo Records.

Cast: Thomas Gomez [(*Abe Saperstein*)], Dorothy Dandridge [(*Ann Carpenter*)], Bill Walker [(*Prof. Turner*)], Angela Clarke [(*Sylvia Saperstein*)], Peter Thompson [(*Martin*)], The Harlem Globetrotters: Billy Brown [(*Billy Townsend*)], Roscoe Cumberland, William "Pop" Gates, Marques Haynes, Louis "Babe" Pressley, Ermer Robinson, Ted Strong, Reese [sic] "Goose" Tatum, Frank Washington, Clarence Wilson, and Inman Jackson, [Steve Roberts (*Eddie*)], [Peter Virgo (*Rocky*)], [Ray Walker (*Jack Davidson*)], [Al Eben (*Charlie Peters*)], [Ann E. Allen (*Sara*)], [Tom Greenway (*Dave Barrett*)], [William Forrest (*Prof. Lindley*)], [Charles Marsh, Tom Daly (*Reporters*)], [John Duncan (*Attendant*)], [Martin Wilkins (*Justice of the peace*)], [Sydney Mason (*Doctor*)], [Robert A. Davis (*Frank*)], [Mildred Boyd (*Nurse*)], [Mack Williams (*McCleary*)], [Sam Balter (*Chicago radio announcer*)], [William H. Welsh (*Television announcer*)], [Tom Hanlon (*New York radio announcer*)], [Winfield Scott Welch (*Bus driver*)], [Bernard Hamilton (*Higgins*)].

Sports, Comedy-drama. [*Print viewed*]. In their run-down bus, the touring Harlem Globetrotters, the all-black "Magicians of Basketball," arrive for another sold-out game and immediately begin entertaining the audience with their comic warm-up routine. In the bleachers are All-American college basketball star Billy Townsend and his sweetheart, Ann Carpenter. After the game, which the Trotters win handily, Billy visits with Abe Saperstein, the team's coach and manager, and announces that he is available for the upcoming season. Having spoken to Billy's worried coach earlier in the evening, Saperstein thanks the confident young man for his offer but advises him to finish school before embarking on a career in professional basketball. His admonishment does not deter Billy, however, and at the next game, he tells Saperstein that he has just quit school and is determined to play for the Globetrotters because they pay "the highest salaries in the business." Saperstein reluctantly places Billy on the team, and when Billy returns to college to pack up his belongings, both Ann and Prof. Lindley, who considers Billy one of his finest chemistry students, express their disappointment in his decision. During his first day of practice, the veteran players run Billy ragged, but he remains annoyingly confident. Billy plays in his first game, but in his second, he scores only four points. On the bus ride to the team's first big season game with the New York Celtics, sports reporter Jack Davidson interviews Globetrotter stars Marques Haynes and Reece "Goose" Tatum, and then asks Saperstein about the origin of the comic routines. Saperstein explains that in the team's barnstorming days, some twenty-four years earlier, the players became fatigued by their seven-night-per-week schedule and realized that the clowning gave the players time to rest. When Billy tells Davidson that he wants more money, and then announces that he has hurt his leg, an alarmed Saperstein orders Billy to confine such remarks to the team. That night, Davidson raves about the Globetrotters in a radio broadcast, thereby prompting a gambler to bet thirty thousand dollars on the team. The all-white Celtics and the Globetrotters are equally matched, and the contest is close from beginning to end. Billy, sent in near the game's finish, scores several times. During the final thirty seconds, however, while the Globetrotters are trying to hold their one-point lead by running out the clock, he ignores Saperstein's directions and shoots. He scores, but Saperstein is angry and fines him for risking the team's victory.

The other players tease Billy, suggesting that perhaps they merely "get in his way." In Duluth, Billy starts the game, and Saperstein doubles his pay. Billy is the top scorer, but the opponents play roughly, and he is slightly injured. After the game, Prof. Turner, a chemistry instructor from an all-black state college in Baltimore, visits Billy, but the arrogant basketball star considers the institution too small, calling it a "jerkwater" school. During the hours before the team's second game against the Celtics, Billy secretly leaves his hotel and marries Ann in a civil service. Afterward, he is followed by one of the gambler's henchmen and crashes into a garbage can, thereby aggravating his knee injury. The gambler passes this news to the Celtics, who shadow Billy throughout the game. During the final seconds, his overworked knee slips, and he misses the critical last shot. Billy's nonchalance about the loss angers the other players, and when Billy shrugs off his coach's admonishments, Saperstein fires him. Later, Billy signs a contract with the New York Rams, on condition that he can rest his knee for several months. During that period, Prof. Turner convinces him to work toward his degree while teaching beginning chemistry at Baltimore State, but as the third and final Globetrotters-Celtics game approaches, Billy becomes distracted. Upon learning that the school's students, teachers and even the dean plan to attend, he complains to Ann, "You'd think it was their team." Ann argues that in a way, the Globetrotters *are* the black school's team and gently advises her husband to think of other people once in a while. Billy takes the suggestion to heart and when he discovers that a star Globetrotter is in the hospital, he risks losing his New York contract by offering to play for him in the Celtics game. Saperstein and the players gratefully accept his offer, and Billy again plays with the team. During the closing seconds of the agonizingly close game, Billy scores the winning basket but then has to be helped off the court. His knee again weak and his new contract lost, Billy plans to return to Baltimore State, but before he and Ann depart, the Globetrotters present him with a souvenir ball from the memorable game. African Americans. Athletic coaches. Basketball. Egotists. Harlem Globetrotters (Basketball team). Transformation. African-American universities and colleges. Baltimore State College. Chicago (IL). Contracts. Disillusionment. Dismissal (Employment). Entertainers. Gamblers. Gymnasiums. Loyalty. Marriage. New York Celtics (Basketball team). Professors. Radio broadcasting. Self-sacrifice. Sports reporters. Tournaments. Wounds and injuries.

Note: The film's working title was *The Globetrotters* (sometimes spelled as *The Globe Trotters*). Reece Tatum's name was spelled incorrectly as "Reese" in the onscreen credits. With the exception of Billy Brown, the Harlem Globetrotters portray themselves in the picture. As noted in the film, the Harlem Globetrotters were formed by Abe Saperstein in 1926 and began playing as a serious barnstorming team in 1927. In 1940, the team won the world professional tournament in Chicago. Later, however, the Globetrotters switched their on-court focus from competitive playing to showmanship, captivating fans around the world and drawing enormous crowds. (For more information on Abe Saperstein and the Globetrotters, see entry above for *Go Man Go*.) The players' comic warm-up routine is accompanied by the team's instrumental (and whistled) theme song, "Sweet Georgia Brown."

According to a Jan 1951 *DN* item, writer/producer Alfred Palca was inspired to undertake the film after he saw how enthusiastically theatergoers reacted to newsreel footage of the Globetrotters. The film was shot in twelve days at a reported cost of $250,000, according to the same item. Reviewers were generally impressed with *The Harlem Globetrotters*. *Har* called the film "one of the finest sport pictures ever produced," while the *Var* reviewer commented that Brown and Dorothy Dandridge, as well as Bill Walker "and the playing-themselves contributions of the Globetrotters, foster a very good impression for the Negro race." The *MPHPD* reviewer wrote: "It should be noted that no attempt is made to bring in any mention of race prejudice...it's simply a story of a great team with fine traditions." The *Box* reviewer added that the film "does not contain preachments along radical lines."

In a Feb 1951 *AmCin* article, director of photography Phil Tannura discussed the special latensification process used during the making of the picture. The process, which effectively stepped up the film's emulsion speed, intensified the latent image on the film. It was useful in lower budget films, in which the light level was not as high as in more costly productions. Tannura also noted that the stadiums in which over a quarter of the film was shot were located in Milwaukee, WI; Zion, Evanston and Chicago, IL; Hershey, Williamsport and Scranton, PA; and in Madison Square Garden, New York City. Release of the picture was delayed for almost a year so that it would coincide with the start of the basketball season, according to *DV*. In 1954, a "prequel" to *The Harlem Globetrotters*, *Go Man Go*, was released by United Artists (see above entry).

AmCin Feb 1951, pp. 54, 68-70. *Box* 27 Oct 1951. *DV* 17 Oct 1951, p. 3. *Exh* 7 Nov 1951, p. 3181. *FD* 24 Oct 1951, p. 6. *Har* 20 Oct 1951, p. 168. *HR* 20 Oct 1950, p. 14. *HR* 17 Oct 1951, p. 3. *LAT* 11 Oct 1950. *MPHPD* 27 Oct 1951, p. 1074. *Var* 17 Oct 1951, p. 20.

HARLEM IS HEAVEN (African Americans)

Lincoln Pictures, Inc. *Dist* Lincoln Pictures, Inc. **1932**; New York opening: 27 May 1932; Prod: at Ideal Studios (Hudson Heights, New Jersey). Sd (Moviegraph Sound System); b&w. 8 reels. 69 min.

[*Prod* Irving Yates and Tishman and O'Neal]. *Supv* Jack Goldberg. *Dir* Irwin R. Franklyn. *Asst dir* Harold Godsoe. *Wrt* Irwin R. Franklyn. *Chief cinematographer* Charles J. Levine. *Ed* Elmer J. McGovern. [*Special mus by* Porter Grainger, Joe Jordan, Shelton Brooks and Edgar Dorwell].

Cast: BILL ROBINSON (*Bill*), John Mason (*Spider*), Putney Dandridge (*Stage manager*), Jimmy Baskette (*Money Johnson*), Anise Boyer (*Jean Stratton*), Henri Wessell (*Chummy Walker*), Alma Smith (*Greta Rae*), Bob Sawyer (*Knobs Moran*), Eubie Blake, and his Orchestra, [Ferdie Lewis], [Myra Johnson], [Margaret Jenkins], [Jili Smith], ["Slick" Chester], [Thomas Moseley], ["Fullback"], [George Nagel], [Naomi Price], [Jackie Young].

African American, Musical. [*Print viewed*]. After praying at the famous Tree of Hope for a job, Jean Stratton asks people on the street how long she has to pray at the tree before she gets work. A crowd soon gathers, and a police officer begins to arrest Jean until the wealthy Money Johnson intercedes and offers her a job at his new Acme Theatre. The next day, Bill, one of Johnson's employees, begs for money for food from the stage manager, telling him that he lost all his money gambling. Meanwhile, in his office, Johnson dictates to his secretary, Miss West, a letter to a man named Wolf, which discusses the chiseling away of Johnson's Philadelphia business by a man named Moran in Harlem. After instructing Wolf to threaten the chisellers with death, Johnson eyes Miss West's legs and then makes a pass at her. Their subsequent kiss is interrupted by Jean, to whom Johnson relates the story of his rise to success. Johnson then warns Jean to never double-cross him and to always agree with him. When Jean is taken to meet Bill, she is introduced as Johnson's protégée. Bill and his pal, Chummy Walker, tell Jean that she must repay her debt to Johnson, and then take her to their boardinghouse, where she will be staying. On the day of the dress rehearsal, Johnson warns Walker to stay away from Jean and then sends out an invitation to her for a "private party" in his office. Meanwhile, in the dressing room, Bill brings Jean flowers and she kisses him. On his way out, Bill encounters Walker and tells him that Jean loves him, and Walker congratulates him. During a dance number, Johnson receives a telephone call from a woman named Greta Rae, who wants to see him. Johnson tells her that he does not have time for her, but when Greta threatens to go to the district attorney with information about his new policy racket, he changes his mind. Later, when Walker tells Jean that she is not safe under Johnson's supervision and that she should leave, she insists that she can take care of herself. Walker insists that she go and tells her that he cannot stand up to Johnson in a fight, which results in Jean calling him a coward and marching off to Johnson's office. In the office, Johnson makes advances toward Jean, but she resists. When Bill bursts into Johnson's office and demands that Jean leave with him, Johnson threatens him, and the two men fight. Bill wins and he and Jean leave. The next morning, after Bill and Jean are expelled from Johnson's club, they resolve to find other jobs. A month passes, during which Walker becomes a drunk and Bill and Jean live together. One day, Bill receives a letter from Walker, who writes that he "can't go on this way," and that he is leaving. Bill, who is now working at Moran's theatre, goes to a bar with his friend Spider, where he sees Walker, who is drunk, and they take him to Bill's home. Later, Johnson summons Walker to his office to let him in on his latest scheme, a new machine that takes the kink out of black people's hair. Johnson tells Walker that he wants to "float" the stock around Harlem first and then offers Walker stock and money to simply lend his name to the deal and not to mention Johnson's name at all. Walker agrees to do it and leaves. When Greta shows up at Johnson's office, her conversation with him reveals that he is trying to set up Walker because he thinks Walker is trying to take Jean away from him. Meanwhile, the district attorney begins an investigation into the hair kink racket, which results in Walker being indicted on charges of fraud. Upon learning this, Spider, to whom Walker sold a share of the stock, vows to get even with Walker. While visiting Walker at the police station, Jean learns that Johnson is behind the racket, but because Walker is afraid of Johnson, she decides to keep quiet. Later, Jean and Bill question Greta, hoping that she will implicate Johnson, but Greta does not cooperate with them until Jean forces her to do so

by fighting with her. Greta's statement results in Walker's vindication and Johnson's indictment. After Spider kills Johnson, Bill realizes that Jean and Walker are right for each other and leaves them to begin life anew. *Actors and actresses. African Americans. Frame-ups. New York City–Harlem. Racketeers. Singers. Theaters. Boardinghouses. Confession (Law). Dismissal (Employment). District Attorneys. Drunkenness. Employer-employee relations. Gangsters. Hair. Motion picture producers. Musicians. Nightclubs. Police. Prayer. Romance. Secretaries. Seduction. Self-sacrifice. Threats.*

Note: Although the onscreen credits contain a 1932 copyright statement, no indication of the film's registration for copyright has been found. Modern sources indicate that the picture was also known as *Harlem Rhapsody*. This film was the first produced by Lincoln Pictures, Inc., a company organized by producer Jack Goldberg in the early 1930s. Although it was run by whites, Lincoln specialized in films for black audiences. The company, which was also called Lincoln Productions, had no relation to the Lincoln Motion Picture Company. A 21 Mar 1932 *FD* item noted that the picture, which had been completed, was being edited at the H. E. R. Laboratories and would be ready for release on 31 Mar. According to the *Var* review, the picture, which cost less than $50,000 to make, made over $4,000 during its opening week at the Renaissance theater in Harlem and was held over. The *Var* review also notes that the "makers" of the picture were Irving Yates and the partnership of Tishman & O'Neal, former vaudeville agents, and that the picture was filmed in one week at the Ideal Studios in New Jersey and at various East coast theatres, including the Ideal Theater in Philadelphia and the R.K.O. Kenmore Theater in Brooklyn. The onscreen credits acknowledge the appearance of Boyer, Wessell, Smith, Sawyer, Baskette and Eubie Blake as having been "by special arrangement with 'The Cotton Club,' Harlem." According to the file for the film in the MPAA/PCA Collection at the AMPAS Library, *Harlem Is Heaven* was issued a tentative certificate number (02816) pending the production company's adherence to the Hays Office's demands regarding specific changes in the script.

FD 21 Mar 1932, p. 8. *Var* 7 Jun 1932, p. 20.

HARLEM ON PARADE (African Americans)
Hollywood Pictures Corp. 1946?. Sd; b&w. 4,931 ft. 55 min.
Prod Jack Goldberg and Dave Goldberg.
Music: "Boogie Woogie Dream" by Albert Ammons and Pete Johnson.
Song(s): "My New Gown," "Unlucky Woman," "Sermon on the Blues" and "Bugle Call Rhythm," composers undetermined.
Cast: Lena Horne, Albert Ammons, Pete Johnson, Del Casino, Edna Mae Harris, Alexander Brown, The Ebony Trio, Leo Reisman and His Band, Teddy Wilson and His Band, Lucky Millinder and His Band.
African American, Variety. [Not viewed]. This film is a musical revue with no story line or dialogue. While most of the songs are variations on the theme of romantic love, the film also features spirituals, a piano duet and a number about a dazzling tap dancer from Harlem who joins the Army. *New York City–Harlem. Pianists. Romance. Singers. Swing music. Tap dancing.*

Note: The film, which was composed mostly of unrelated musical numbers, may have been a compendium of "Soundies," short musical films which had originally been made for use in a "visual juke-box" format that was used in the late 1930s and early 1940s. Additionally, Lena Horne's two songs, "My New Gown" and "Unlucky Woman," in which she was accompanied by the Teddy Wilson band, as well as the Ammons/Johnson number "Boogie Woogie Dream," were taken from a 1944 short entitled *Boogie Woogie Dream*. The Ebony Trio's "Sermon on the Blues" was also featured in a short, *Bipp Bang Boogie*, produced by Alfred N. Sack. No release date information was found for *Harlem on Parade*, but NYSA records indicate that the film was submitted for censorship approval in Feb 1946.

HARLEM ON THE PRAIRIE (African Americans)
Associated Features, Inc. *Dist* Associated Features, Inc. 9 Dec **1937**; Prod: began: 18 Oct 1937 [©Associated Features, Inc.; 2 Feb 1938; LP7829]. Sd; b&w. 6 reels. 46, 54-55 or 57 min. PCA cert no. 3901.
Prod Jed Buell. *Assoc prod* Sabin W. Carr and Bert Sternbach. *Supv* Maceo B. Sheffield. *Dir* Sam Newfield. *Orig story and scr* Fred Myton. *Addl dial* Flournoy E. Miller. *Photog* William Hyer. *Film ed* Robert Jahns. *Dir of mus* Lew Porter. *Mus supv* Abe Meyer. *Sd eng* Hans Weeren.
Song(s): "Harlem on the Prairie," music and lyrics by Mary Schaeffer and Lew Porter; "Romance in the Rain," music and lyrics by Lyle Womack, Mary Schaeffer and Lew Porter; "There Is a New Range in Heaven," music and lyrics by Fred Stryker and Johnny Lange; "Polkadoo," music and lyrics by Lew Porter and Ira Hardin; "Albuquerque," music and lyrics by Don Swander and June Hershey; "Old Folks at Home" and "Swanee River," music and lyrics by Stephen Foster.

Cast: Herbert Jeffries (*Jeff Kincaid*), Flournoy E. Miller (*Crawfish, Short One*), Mantan Moreland (*Mistletoe, Tall One*), Connie Harris (*Carolina Clayburn*), Maceo B. Sheffield (*Wolf Cain*), Spencer Williams, Jr. (*Doc Clayburn*), George Randol (*Sheriff*), Nathan Curry (*Henchman*), Lucius Brooks, Rudolph Hunter, Leon Buck, Ira Hardin (*The Four Tones*), James Davis, Edward Brandon, Reginald Anderson, Jack Williams (*The Four Blackbirds*).
African American, Western, with songs. [Not viewed]. Doc Clayburn, formerly of the Ross outlaw gang, reformed his criminal ways when the group was nearly wiped out after robbing $50,000 in gold. Doc and his daughter Carolina now run a traveling medicine wagon with a minstrel show. Carolina convinces Doc to return to the area of the theft to return the gold, which he had hidden twenty years before, to its owners and ease his conscience. While escaping the law, outlaw Wolf Cain and his men recognize Doc, but he is protected by Jeff Kincaid, a wandering cowboy. After Jeff's departure, Wolf's men return, determined to get a map to where the gold is hidden. A fight ensues, and Doc is killed. Jeff, working for the sheriff, arrives in time for the dying Doc to beg him to return the gold and take care of Carolina. Jeff goes searching for the gold with Mistletoe and Crawfish, two amusing camp helpers, but they are trailed. Both Mistletoe and Crawfish become afraid while searching in a cave. Finding the treasure, they defeat two of the outlaws. However, upon returning, Jeff learns that Carolina has been abducted and is being held as ransom for the gold. Jeff surprises Wolf in his hideout, while Mistletoe and Crawfish lure his henchmen toward the sheriff. After returning the gold, Jeff and Carolina drive off together in the medicine wagon. *African Americans. Cowboys. Fathers and daughters. Outlaws. Treasure. Caves. Cowboys. Criminals–Rehabilitation. Gold. Hideouts. Kidnapping. Medicine shows. Minstrel shows. Ransom. Sheriffs. Wagons.*

Note: According to the *Var* review, the film's title was switched to *Bad Man of Harlem* for the first Broadway run. A Jan 1938 *HR* news item notes that the film was "the first 'all colored' picture to play on Broadway in a first run house." Some contemporary sources credit Mantan Moreland with the story. The songs "Harlem on the Prarie" and "Romance in the Rain" were performed by Herbert Jeffries and won praise from critics. Critics' estimates of the film's budget vary from under $20,000 to $50,000. *Var*, which mistakenly listed Spencer Williams' name as William Spencer, notes that this was the first black musical Western. In reviews, Maceo Sheffield is identified as a former Los Angeles policeman who purchased several nightclubs along Central Avenue in Los Angeles. Connie Harris was a nightclub entertainer along the same circuits, and *Time* notes that she worked in the Paradise Café in Yuma, AZ. The picture was intended principally for the eight hundred existing black theaters in the United States. Producer Buell, according to reviews, was to make between four and six similar films. However, the three follow-up black musical westerns with Jeffries were made by Richard Kahn for Hollywood Productions: *The Bronze Buckaroo* (see above), *Harlem Rides the Range* and *Two Gun Man from Harlem* (see below). Associated Features, Inc. was originally named Lincoln Pictures, Inc. The picture was filmed at N. B. Murray's black dude ranch near Victorville, CA, according to modern sources.

In a letter in the NAACP Collection at the Library of Congress, writer and actor Flournoy E. Miller asked the organization's help to have people "reserve criticisms" concerning the film. Miller wrote that "colored motion pictures are in an experimental stage due to the fact that you can only interest independent capital. I think that criticism of these pictures should be constructive rather than destructive.... major studios flatly refuse to give colored people a decent part or to produce a first class colored picture." Concerning the origin of the idea to do a Western with African-American cowboys, Miller stated, "why shouldn't we glorify Bill Pickett, Simeon Sheffield and other Negro ropers, bull doggers and bronco busters who inhabit Texas? We got the idea from a rodeo where a young Negro boy, Bob Scott, stole the show. In answer to our inquiries, Bob Scott told us that there were many more such colored boys who are adept riders and ropers."

DV 18 Oct 1937. *DV* 22 Nov 1937, p. 3. *FD* 5 Feb 1938, p. 4. *HR* 20 Jan 1938, p. 5. *HR* 22 Nov 1937, p. 2. *MPD* 24 Nov 1937, p. 5. *MPH* 27 Nov 1937, p. 54. *Time* 13 Dec 1937, p. 24. *Var* 9 Feb 1938, p. 14.

HARLEM RHAPSODY *see* **HARLEM IS HEAVEN**

HARLEM RIDES THE RANGE (African Americans)
Hollywood Productions. *Dist* Sack Amusement Enterprises, Inc. 1 Feb **1939**. Sd; b&w. 6 reels, 5,816 ft. 56 or 58 min.
[*Prod* Richard C. Kahn]. *Dir* Richard C. Kahn. *Scr* Spencer Williams, Jr. and F. E. Miller. *Story* Spencer Williams, Jr. *Photog* Roland Price and Clark Ramsey. [*Art dir* Vin Taylor]. *Mus* Lew Porter. *Sd eng* Cliff Ruberg. *Prod mgr* Dick L'Estrange.
Cast: Herbert Jeffrey (*Bob Blake*), Lucius Brooks (*Dusty*), F. E. Miller (*Slim Perkins*), Artie Young (*Miss [Margaret] Dennison*), Clarence Brooks (*Bradley*), Spencer Williams, Jr. (*Watson*), Tom Southern ([*Jim*] *Connors*), Leonard Christmas (*Dennison*), Wade

Dumas (*Sheriff*), John Thomas (*Cactus*), The Four Tones, [Stardusk, a horse].

African American, Western, with songs. [*Print viewed*]. Bradley and his henchman, Jim Connors, visit rancher Dennison to remind him that his mortgage is due and announces that they will either take a fifty-percent share of his mine or foreclose on him. When Bradley and Connors inform Dennison that they have stolen his radium samples, a struggle ensues and Dennison is apparently killed by Connors. Connors and Bradley quickly hide the body and flee. Later, two riders from Amarillo, Texas, Bob Blake and his lazy partner Dusty, enter the Dennison ranch hoping to find employment or dinner and discover blood on a table. After discouraging Dusty from stealing a tin of food, Bob sights a picture of a lovely girl and takes it. During target practice on the nearby Watson ranch, Mr. Watson agrees to hire Bob and Dusty for thirty dollars a month plus food. At Watson's ranch, Dusty recognizes Connors' horse as the one he saw fleeing the Dennison ranch and learns that Connors is the ranch foreman. Meanwhile, Cactus, a ranch hand, tells Watson that his buddy Tex has disappeared and leaves to look for him. Noticing Connors leaving late at night, Bob follows him into a trap, but bests him in a fistfight. The next morning, Watson fires Connors and makes Bob the new foreman. After Watson and Bob encounter Cactus burying Tex, they fetch the sheriff to pay a visit to the Dennison ranch. There they find a can of spilled tomato juice and believe that Bob and Dusty mistook it for blood. When Connors demands one hundred dollars from Bradley to keep quiet, Bradley kills him and throws suspicion on Bob. The sheriff arrests Bob, and Dusty insists on accompanying him to jail. When the sheriff tells Bradley that Watson has received a letter from Dennison's daughter Margaret saying that she will be arriving with $6,000 to pay off her father's debts, Bradley decides that she too must be killed. After escaping through the use of a rope trick, Bob sets out to rescue Margaret. Meanwhile, Cactus finds the sheriff locked up and shows him a letter that explains Bradley's duplicity. Bob and Margaret ride from the deserted train station to make their stand against Bradley's men. During the subsequent gun battle, Bob runs out of ammunition, but the sheriff, Watson and others ride up in time to capture Bradley and his men. Cactus then shoots Bradley to avenge Tex. Returning to the ranch, Bob and Dusty find that Dennison has recovered and has been hiding in his mine, and that it was he who spilled the tomato juice on the table. When Bob tries to return Margaret's photograph, she shows her affection for him by giving it back to him. *African Americans. Cowboys. Mines and mineral resources. Partnership. Ranch foremen. Arizona. Cooks. False arrests. Fathers and daughters. Fistfights. Frame-ups. Gunfights. Jailbreaks. Missing persons, Assumed dead. Mortgages. Murder. Photographs. Radium. Ranches. Revenge. Sheriffs. Thieves.*

Note: Although onscreen credits contain a copyright statement, no information concerning the film's registration for copyright has been located. The picture features two songs, the titles of which have not been determined. *Harlem Rides the Range* was the third black western directed by Richard C. Kahn and featuring Herbert Jeffrey as "Bob Blake." The first of the three films was *Two Gun Man from Harlem* (see below).

FD 20 Jun 1939, p. 14.

HARMONY LANE (Racial impersonation)

Mascot Pictures Corp. *Dist* Mascot Pictures Corp.; Republic Pictures Corp. 28 Aug **1935**; Prod: completed early Jul 1935 [©Mascot Pictures Corp.; 28 Aug 1935; LP5752]. Sd (RCA High Fidelity System); b&w. 9 reels, 7,641 ft. 84-86 min. Passed by the National Board of Review. PCA cert no. 1136.

Pres NAT LEVINE. [*Prod* Ralph De Lacy]. *Supv* Colbert Clark. *Dir* Joseph Santley. *Scr* Elizabeth Meehan and Joseph Santley. *Taken from the life and songs of Stephen Foster by* Milton Krims. *Photog* Ernest Miller and Jack Marta. *Film ed* Ray Curtiss. *Supv ed* Joseph H. Lewis. *Mus dir* Arthur Kay. *Mus assoc* Abe Meyer. *Sd eng* Terry Kellum. *Sd eff* Roy Granville.

Song(s): "Oh! Susanna," "Lou'siana Belle," "Old Folks at Home," "My Old Kentucky Home," "Old Black Joe," "Why No One to Love" and "Beautiful Dreamer," music and lyrics by Stephen Foster.

Cast: DOUGLASS MONTGOMERY (*Stephen Foster*), Evelyn Venable (*Susan Pentland*), Adrienne Ames (*Jane McDowall*), Joseph Cawthorne ([*Professor Henry*] *Kleber*), William Frawley ([*Edwin P.*] *Christy*), David Torrence [(*Mr. Pentland*)], Gilbert Emery [(*Mr. Foster*)], Lloyd Hughes [(*Andrew Robinson*)], Al Herman [(*Tambo*)], Cora Sue Collins [(*Marion Foster*)], James Bush [(*Morrison Foster*)],

Florence Roberts [(*Mrs. Foster*)], Ferdinand Munier [(*Mr. Pond*)], Clarence Muse [(*Old Joe*)], [Victor De Camp (*William Foster, Jr.*)], [Edith Craig (*Henrietta Foster*)], [Mildred Gover (*Delia*)], [James B. Carson (*Proprietor*)], [Rodney Hildebrand (*Mr. Wade*)], [Mary MacLaren (*Mrs. Wade*)], [Earl Hodgins (*Bones*)], [Hattie McDaniel (*Liza*)], [The Famous Shaw Negro Choir].

Biography, Musical. [*Print viewed*]. In the winter of 1848, Stephen Foster stands at the back of a black church, absorbing the melodies of the spirituals. With an idea for a song, he rushes to the home of his sweetheart, Susan Pentland, but he is expelled by her father, who disapproves of musicians, as does Stephen's own father. Ordered by his father to work in the Dunning Foster Steamship Co., Stephen becomes engaged to Susan, and he is inspired to complete his song "Oh! Susanna." However, although the song is internationally popular, Stephen is a failure in the family business, and Susan writes that she has married someone else. Depressed, Stephen is at a hofbrau with his friend, Professor Henry Kleber, a music teacher, when he meets Edwin P. Christy, an egotistical but likable leader of a minstrel show. Still heartbroken over Susan, Stephen is lured home by a family friend, Jane McDowall, and they are married in 1850. He sells "Old Folks at Home" to Christy for five hundred dollars, but Jane is dissatisfied, demanding a home of her own and spending money. Disapproving of minstrel shows, she walks out when Christy asks Stephen to give the first public performance of his song. Susan, who attends the show with her husband, Andrew Robinson, is touched by the song and invites the Fosters to visit them in Kentucky. There Stephen writes "Old Black Joe" and learns that Susan broke their engagement because of rumors told by Jane. From 1852 to 1857, he writes prolifically to support Jane and their daughter Marion, to whom he is devoted; however, one night he meets the drunken Christy singing "No One to Love" and brings him home, after which Jane announces she is leaving. Instead, Stephen leaves and moves to New York, where he turns out more music and begins to drink. Susan and Andrew visit him, but Stephen tells Susan he cannot bear to see her anymore. Soon he is beset by rejections from publishers, who no longer want "plantation songs," financial problems and alchoholism. In 1862, Stephen writes "Beautiful Dreamer," but sells it for only twenty-five dollars because he needs the cash. Kleber and Christy arrange a benefit performance, and Susan is sent to ask Stephen to attend. She is shocked at his aged, worn condition, miserable apartment and torn clothes. Although he promises to come, Kleber later finds Stephen dying, and Christy makes the announcement of his death. *Alcoholism. Composers. Stephen Collins Foster. Marriage. Minstrel shows. Musicians. Songs. Songwriters. African Americans. Businessmen. Engagements. Fathers and daughters. Kentucky. Publishers and publishing. Singers. United States–South.*

Note: Preceeding the credits is the following note: "This picture is dedicated to the memory of Stephen Collins Foster, one of America's never-to-be-forgotten sons. The man who wrote the songs which will forever live in our hearts." A news item in *HR* notes that William Frawley replaced George Jessel, who was unable to start filming on time. According to the *Var* review, this was the first film in which Frawley sang. As Republic took over Mascot in 1935, reviews of *Harmony Lane* list both companies as distributors. Other films based on Foster's life include Twentieth Century-Fox's 1940 release *Swanee River*, directed by Sidney Lanfield and starring Don Ameche (see *AFI Catalog of Feature Films, 1931-40*; F3.4420).

DV 5 Jul 1935, p. 2. *DV* 13 Aug 1935, p. 3. *FD* 15 Aug 1935, p. 4. *HR* 13 Jun 1935, p. 10. *HR* 13 Aug 1935, p. 4. *MPH* 31 Aug 1935, p. 50. *NYT* 24 Oct 1935, p. 19. *Var* 30 Oct 1935, p. 14.

HAROLD BELL WRIGHT'S THE CALIFORNIAN see THE CALIFORNIAN

A HARP IN HOCK (Jewish Americans)

De Mille Pictures Corp. *Dist* Pathé Exchange, Inc. 10 Oct **1927** [©Pathé Exchange, Inc.; 10 Oct 1927; LP24480]. Si; b&w. 6 reels, 5,996 ft.

Dir Renaud Hoffman. *Asst dir* Glenn Belt. *Scr* Sonya Levien. *Photog* Dewey Wrigley. *Art dir* Charles Cadwallader. *Film ed* Donn Hayes. *Cost* Gwen Wakeling.

Source: Based on the short story "A Harp in Hock" by Evelyn Campbell (publication undetermined).

Cast: Rudolph Schildkraut (*Isaac Abrams*), Junior Coghlan (*Tommy Shannon*), May Robson (*Mrs. Banks*), Bessie Love (*Nora Banks*), Louis Natheaux (*Nick*), Elsie Bartlett (*Mrs. Shannon*), Mrs. Charles Mack (*The Clock Woman*), Joseph Striker (*Dr. Franz Mueller*), Adele Watson (*Investigator*), Lillian Harmen (*Sourface*),

Clarence Burton (*Plainclothesman*), Bobby Heck (*Snipe Banks*).

Melodrama. Isaac Abrams, a lonely ghetto pawnbroker, is disliked by most of his neighbors; the only exceptions are Nora Banks, the landlady's charming daughter, and Mrs. Shannon, a poor scrubwoman saving to bring her son Tommy from Ireland. On the day the child arrives at Ellis Island, his mother is taken fatally ill, and Abrams is forced to take in the child. Tommy, who comes to love Abrams, is taught to care for the shop, barter with the customers, and study. When he beats Snipe Banks, the neighborhood toughie, Mrs. Banks vengefully reports Tommy to the authorities, who remove him to an orphanage and later to an Iowa family. Tommy escapes and returns to the pawnshop; when faced with another parting, Abrams plans to take him away. Abrams is denounced by Mrs. Banks, precipitating a riot, but Dr. Mueller, Nora's suitor, arrives to straighten out matters; Abrams is permitted to adopt the boy. *Adoption. Charwomen and cleaners. Iowa. Irish. Jews. New York City. New York City–Ellis Island. Orphans. Pawnbrokers.*

FD 30 Oct 1927. *MPW* 5 Nov 1927. *Var* 2 Nov 1927, p. 20.

HARPOON (Native Alaskans, Native Americans)
Danches Bros. *Dist* Screen Guild Productions, Inc. Nov **1948**; Premiere in New Bedford, Massachusetts: 20 Oct 1948.; Prod: late May—late Sep 1947 [©Danches Bros.; 16 Oct 1948; LP1940]. Sd (Western Electric Sound System); b&w. 9 reels, 7,533 ft. 84 min. PCA cert no. 12865.

Prod Ewing Scott. *Assoc prod* George Danches. *Dir* Ewing Scott. *Asst dir* Maurice M. Suess and [Jack Benson]. *Scr* Paul Gerard Smith and Ewing Scott. [*Story* Ewing Scott]. *Photog* Frederick Gately. [*Cam op* Harry Marble]. [*Cam op and stills* Andy McIntyre]. [*Stills* Ken Lobben]. *Spec eff* Ray Mercer. *Film ed* Robert O. Crandall. *Mus score* Lucien Cailliet. *Mus supv* David Chudnow. *Sd eng* William H. Lynch. [*Sd rec* Dean Spencer]. [*Makeup* Holly Bane]. *Prod supv* Ben A. Bradley. *Tech adv* Captain Jack Benson, U.S.N.R. [*Scr supv* Mildred Scott]. [*Grip* Earl Nickerel].

Song(s): "This Is Real," words and music by Doc Mason and Dok Stanford.

Cast: John Bromfield [(*Michael Shand*)], Alyce Louis [(*Kitty Canon*)], James Cardwell [(*Red Dorsett*)], Patricia Garrison [(*Christine McFee*)], Jack George [(*Rev. McFee*)], Edgar Hinton [(*Kurt Shand*)], Ruth Castle [(*Patsy*)], Hollis Bane [(*Kodiak*)], Grant Means [(*Swede*)], Lee Elson [(*Whaler*)], Gary Garrett [(*Prisoner*)], Frank Hagney [(*Red Dorsett, Sr.*)], Sally Davis [(*Sally*)], James Martin [(*Fuzzy*)], Alex Sharp [(*Whaler*)], Willard Jillson [(*Lockerby*)], Lee Roberts [(*Whaler*)].

Sea, Adventure. [*Viewed print incomplete*]. In 1882, Kurt Shand is shanghaiied from the streets of San Francisco by Red Dorsett to serve on his whaling ship. Kurt proves to be an inexpert harpoonist and, as he is frequently beaten, develops an intense hatred of Dorsett. Kurt jumps ship in Jabbertown, Alaska, but no ship will give him passage home as Dorsett has branded him a deserter. Kurt remains in Jabbertown, then marries Patsy, a local saloon girl, and fathers a son Michael. Twenty years later, Kurt, who reared the book-loving Mike to take vengeance on the Dorsett family, becomes involved in a fistfight with his son during a birthday party. Mike accidentally wounds Kurt mortally, and even though he had previously foresworn his father's plans of retribution, he swears to the dying man that he will take revenge against the Dorsetts. Although Dorsett has been dead for years, Mike finds his son, Red, Jr., at the Red Nugget Saloon in Jabbertown, and beats him up. Mike then takes over his boat, *The Chagnak*, and most of its crew. Kitty Canon, a saloon singer, whom Red brought to Alaska with the promise of marriage, also deserts him and becomes interested in Mike. Mike renames the boat "The Flying Kate" and sets out on a whaling expedition. However, when he attempts to harpoon a whale, he becomes entangled in the tow line and is believed to have drowned. Red's men, rowing in another boat, find him alive, but unconscious, and drag him on board. Red then orders his crew to put Mike in a skin boat and set him adrift. Two Eskimos find him and take him to the Point Hope Mission, run by Rev. McFee and his daughter Christine, where he recovers. Meanwhile, Mike's friend, Kodiak, explains to Kitty that Mike is dead and she takes over the ship, making Kodiak the skipper. Although the price being paid for whales is increasing when Mike eventually returns to Jabbertown, he appears to Kitty unwilling to go back to sea. Later, Chris becomes concerned because the Eskimos around the mission are starving, due to a shortage of seals and walrus that season. Aware that whales, which

Eskimos cannot capture on their own, have been spotted nearby, Chris decides to hold Mike to his promise that he would help them if needed and travels with several Eskimos in a long boat to Jabbertown. Kitty is jealous of Mike's friendship with Chris and, after he leaves, she tells Red about the whales's location. Red sets out after Mike, taking Kitty along as a prisoner. When Kodiak harpoons a whale, Red sends his crew out to take it. Meanwhile, Kitty escapes and Red boards Mike's main vessel. Mike's crew shoots a hole in Red's small boat with a harpoon gun and it capsizes. Red tries to attack Mike with a harpoon but Kitty pushes him away, after which Red gets caught in a rope and hangs himself. Kodiak brings in the whale, and later, Mike and Kitty are married on board the boat by Rev. McFee. *Alaska. Boats. Revenge. Sailors. Whales and whaling. Fathers and sons. Fistfights. Hanging. Harpoons. Jealousy. Missionaries. Native Alaskans. Romance. Sailors. Saloons. Scots. Shanghaiing. Singers.*

Note: The above credits and summary were taken from a cutting continuity prepared for the film's copyright registration and a print that was missing several reels. An opening title states that all scenes in the film, both exterior and interior, were photographed in Alaska on "the actual locale associated with the story." The cutting continuity lists the character name of "Mike Shand's" father as both "Kurt" and "Kirk." According to a *LAT* news item of 20 May 1947, producer Ewing Scott originally intended to make *Harpoon* for Universal-International. A 9 May 1948 *NYT* article stated that Scott, who had made the 1947 picture *Untamed Fury* with the Danches brothers (see below), finally convinced them to back a whaling story he had written. After the brothers purchased a four-year-old, 104-foot Army patrol craft, the cast and technicians, numbering twenty-six in all, left San Diego aboard the craft, which was outfitted as a floating studio, in late May 1947. According to the *NYT* article, Scott spent a month filming whaling scenes in the Bering Strait but that no actual killing would be seen in the picture, as government regulations prohibited such actions by private parties. Scott also filmed walrus hunts in Russian waters, but the cutting continuity indicates that these scenes were not used in the completed film. On Kodiak Island, according to the *NYT* article, actor Ernest Michens, who was first cast as "Red," suffered severe injuries when he fell through a rotting stairway, and had to be replaced. In addition, scratches on the negative necessitated costly retakes. All of the interiors were shot in Skagway in a real saloon and in the Pullen House, a Klondike museum. The company returned to California in late Sep 1947. The Danches brothers claimed that *Harpoon* cost $400,000 to make. Although this film was shot before John Bromfield's debut appearance in *Sorry, Wrong Number*, it was not released until after that film.

Box 27 Nov 1948. *DV* 22 Nov 1948, p. 3. *HR* 2 Oct 1947, p. 10. *HR* 22 Nov 1948, p. 3. *IP* Feb-Nov 1948. *NYT* 9 May 1948. *NYT* 9 Dec 1948, p. 48. *Var* 24 Nov 1948, p. 6.

HASHIMURA TOGO (Japanese Americans)
Jesse L. Lasky Feature Play Co. *Dist* Paramount Pictures Corp. 19 Aug **1917** [©Jesse L. Lasky Feature Play Co.; 1 Aug 1917; LP11164]. Si; b&w. 5 reels.

Dir William C. de Mille. *Asst dir* E. Traxler. *Scen* Marion Fairfax. *Cam* Charles Rosher.

Source: Based on the novel *Hashimura Togo* by Wallace Irwin (New York, 1914).

Cast: Sessue Hayakawa (*Hashimura Togo*), Florence Vidor (*Corinne Reynolds*), Mabel Van Buren (*Mrs. Reynolds*), Walter Long (*Carlos Anthony*), Tom Forman (*Dr. Garland*), Raymond Hatton (*Reporter*), Ernest Joy (*District Attorney*), Margaret Loomis (*O. Noto San*), Kuwuhara (full name unknown) (*Awoko*), Horin Konishi (*Nichi*).

Comedy. Bearing the burden of an accusation of a breach of diplomacy committed by his brother, Hashimura Togo leaves Japan in disgrace for the United States where he enters the employ of Mrs. Reynolds as a butler. Togo soon learns that Mrs. Reynold's daughter Corinne, although in love with Dr. Garland, is being coerced into marrying Carlos Anthony who, having appropriated all of her deceased father's funds, now promises to save the family from financial ruin in return for Corinne's hand in marriage. Enlisting the aid of a reporter, Togo succeeds in proving Anthony's duplicity in time to stop the marriage, thus freeing Corinne to marry Garland, and after a series of misadventures, returns home, his name cleared, to his sweetheart in Japan. *Japanese. Marriage–Forced. Reputation. Self-sacrifice. Upper classes. Brothers. Butlers. Duplicity. Immigrants. Japan. Physicians. Reporters.*

ETR 25 Aug 1917, p. 940. *MPN* 25 Aug 1917, p. 1275. *MPN* 1 Sep 1917, p. 1491. *MPW* 1 Sep 1917, p. 1386. *NYDM* 25 Aug 1917, p. 20. *Var* 17 Aug 1917, p. 25.

THE HATCHET MAN (Chinese Americans)
First National Pictures, Inc.; controlled by Warner Bros. Pictures, Inc. *Dist* First National Pictures, Inc.; The Vitaphone Corp. 6 Feb **1932**; Prod: ended late Nov 1931 [©First National Pictures, Inc.; 28 Jan 1932; LP2815]. Sd; b&w. 8 reels. 74 min.

Dir William A. Wellman. *Scr* J. Grubb Alexander. *Photog* Sid Hickox. [*2d cam* Richard Towers]. [*Asst cam* Wesley Anderson]. *Art dir* Anton Grot. *Ed* Owen Marks. *Gowns* Earl Luick. *Vitaphone Orch cond* Leo F. Forbstein. [*Sd* Robert B. Lee]. [*Still photog* John Ellis].

Source: Based on the play *The Honorable Mr. Wong* by Achmed Abdullah and David Belasco (production undetermined).

Cast: EDWARD G. ROBINSON [(*Wong Low Get*)], Loretta Young [(*Toya San*)], Dudley Digges [(*Nog Hong Fah*)], Leslie Fenton [(*Harry En Hai*)], Edmund Breese [(*Yu Chang*)], Tully Marshall [(*Long Sen Yat*)], J. Carroll Naish [(*Sun Yat Ming*)], Charles Middleton [(*Lip Hop Fat*)], E. Allyn Warren [(*The Cobbler, Soo Lat*)], Eddie Piel [(*Bing Foo*)], [Noel Madison (*Charles Kee*)], [Blanche Frederici (*Madame Si-Si*)], [Otto Yamaoka (*Chung Ho*)], [Evelyn Selbie (*Wah Li*)], [Willie Fung (*The notary, Fung Loo*)], [Anna Chang (*Sing girl*)], [Toshia Mori (*Miss Ling*)], [Gladys Lloyd (*Fan Yi*)], [Ralph Ince (*"Big Jim" Malone*)].

Drama. [*Print viewed*]. In the early part of the twentieth century, Wong Low Get, the hatchet man for the Lem Sing Tong in San Francisco, is responsible for dispatching justice with the stroke of his hatchet. When a Tong war erupts, he is ordered to kill his best friend, Sun Yat Ming. Though Wong tries to refuse, he knows his duty to the Tong and goes to visit his old friend. Before he dies, Sun makes his will in favor of Wong, giving him guardianship over his six-year-old daughter Toya and pledging her in marriage to Wong when she comes of legal age. Wong rears Toya in both traditional Chinese and modern American ways. When she is a grown woman, he asks her to marry him, rather than forcing her to honor her father's will. She agrees, out of respect for her father's wishes, and because Wong has been so kind to her. Soon after their marriage, another Tong war breaks out. Wong, now a successful businessman, calls for negotiation, but, as a precaution, Nog Hong Fah, the head of the Lem Sing Tong, hires some young Chinese gangsters from New York to act as bodyguards. One of Wong's bodyguards is Harry En Hai, a young man close to Toya's age who she had briefly met at a dance hall before her marriage to Wong. While Wong is in Sacramento killing "Big Jim" Malone, the white gangster who started the war, Harry and Toya go dancing together and fall in love. When Wong returns, he finds them in each other's arms and plans to kill Harry. Because he had vowed to Sun always to make Toya happy and she says that Harry will make her happy, Wong goes against tradition and lets them go after making Harry promise before Buddha to keep the same vow. Nog, who has observed Wong's actions, reports them to the Tong, and Wong is ostracized by his fellow Chinese. Soon his business fails, and he is forced to become a field worker. Some years later, Wah Li, Toya's old nurse, brings Wong a letter from China from Toya. In the letter, Toya says that she has been enduring a living death and begs his forgiveness, and also says that she has always loved him. After working his way to China shoveling coal on a steamship, Wong learns the location of the opium den where she is held prisoner after Harry sold her to the owner, Madame Si-Si, to pay his debts. When Wong and Toya are reunited, he is challenged for her by Madame Si-Si, but he tells her that ancient Chinese law commands that a wife belongs to her husband. When he reveals that he is a hatchet man, she does not believe him. Wong then throws one of his weapons at a dragon painting on the wall to demonstrate his hereditary skill, and does not realize that he has inadvertently hit Harry, who is sitting behind the wall. Free from their past, Toya and Wong leave to resume their marriage. When Madame Si-Si goes to berate Harry for the loss of Toya, he blankly nods his head, then falls dead, as the hatchet, which her servant has been removing from the wall, is revealed to have lethally struck Harry in the skull. *Chinese Americans. Cultural conflict. Pledges. Romance. Tongs (Secret societies). Bodyguards. Bracelets. Buddhism. Drug addicts. Farm hands. Friendship. Funerals. Gang wars. Gangsters. Hatchets. Infidelity. Marriage-Arranged. Murder. Opium. Revenge. Sacramento (CA). San Francisco (CA)-Chinatown. Wards and guardians. Wills.*

Note: *MPH* incorrectly credits Nat Pendleton with the role of "Big Jim" Malone. Some contemporary reviews incorrectly call J. Carroll Naish's character "Sun Yat Sen," the name of the actual Chinese revolutionary hero who died in 1926. In the film, Naish's character's name is both written and spoken as "Sun Yat Ming". Modern sources add James Leong to the cast. The film was released in Britain as *The Honourable Mr. Wong*.

FD 30 Nov 1931, p. 1. *FD* 7 Feb 1932, p. 10. *HR* 30 Dec 1931, p. 3. *IP* Mar 1932, p. 34. *MPH* 13 Feb 1932, p. 35. *NYT* 4 Feb 1932, p. 25. *Var* 9 Feb 1932, p. 15.

HAWAII (Hawaiians)

Burton Holmes Films, Inc. *Dist* Burton Holmes Films, Inc. **1940**. Silent; b&w. 3,758 ft. 42 min.

Travelogue. [*Not viewed*]. This film is a travelogue of Hawaii. [No information has been found about the exact contents of this film.]. *Hawaii.* Burton Holmes.

Note: No reviews of this film have been found. The film was submitted to the New York Censor Board in 1940. The running time was obtained by calculating the footage in NYSA. For more information on Burton Holmes and his production company see note for *Normandy and Brittany* in (see *AFI Catalog of Feature Films, 1931-40*; F3.3173).

HAWAII CALLS (Hawaiians)

Principal Productions, Inc.; Bobby Breen Productions, Inc. *Dist* RKO Radio Pictures, Inc. 11 Mar **1938**; Prod: 5 Nov—mid-Dec 1937. Sd (RCA Sound System); b&w. 71-73 min. Passed by the National Board of Review. PCA cert no. 4007.

Pres EDWIN SCHATZ. *Prod* Sol Lesser and [Barney Briskin]. *Dir* Edward F. Cline. *Asst dir* John Sherwood. *Scr* Wanda Tuchock. [*Contr to trmt* Dan Jarrett]. *Photog* Jack McKenzie. *Hawaiian backgrounds* [*photog by*] Paul Marques. *Art dir* Lewis J. Rachmil. *Film ed* Arthur Hilton. *Wardrobe supv* Waldron Johnson. *Mus score* Hugo Riesenfeld. *Mus supv* Abe Meyer. *Vocal supv* Max Terr. *Dance dir* Aggie Auld. *Sd eng* Hugh McDowell, Jr.

Music: "España" by Alexis-Emmanuel Chabrier.

Song(s): "Hawaii Calls" and "Down Where the Trade Winds Blow," words and music by Harry Owens; "That's the Hawaiian in Me," words and music by Johnny Noble and Margarita Lake; "Song of the Islands," words and music by Charles E. King; "Macushla," words and music by Josephine V. Rowe and Dermot MacMurrough.

Source: Based on the novel *Stowaways in Paradise* by Don Blanding (New York, 1931).

Cast: Bobby Breen (*Billy Coulter*), Ned Sparks (*Strings*), Irvin S. Cobb (*Captain O'Hare*), Gloria Holden (*Mrs. Milburn*), Warren Hull (*Commander [Joe] Milburn*), Mamo Clark (*Hina*), Raymond Paige (*Himself*), Aggie Auld (*Hula dancer*), Cy Kendall (*Hawaiian policeman*), Herbert Rawlinson (*Mr. Harlow*), William Harrigan (*Blake*), Juanita Quigley (*Doris Milburn*), Pua Lani (*Pua*), Dora Clement (*Mrs. Harlow*), Donald Kirke (*Regon*), Philip Ahn (*Julius*), Ward Bond (*Muller*), William Abbey (*Lonzo*), Birdie DeBolt (*Aunty Pinau*), [Larence Duran (*Banana*)], [Ruben Maldonado (*Solly*)], [Uilani Silva (*Hula dancer*)], [Jerry Mandy (*Taxi driver*)], [Ruben Duran (*Ka-ne*)].

Drama, with songs. [*Print viewed*]. When ocean liner stowaways Billy Coulter and Pua, a young Hawaiian, are caught in the cabin of Strings, a songwriter and ship musician, Captain O'Hare tells the orphan Billy that he will be sent back to San Francisco as soon as the boat docks in Honolulu. Although Billy's singing abilities impress the captain, he remains adamant about returning him, and consequently, when the ship lands, Billy and Pua dive overboard and swim to freedom on shore. In Honolulu, Pua takes Billy to his sister Hina, who shields him from the police. Concerned for Billy's safety, Hina then takes the boys to Maui, where Aunty Pinau lives, and is joined by Strings, who has violated his rule about not setting foot on the islands he writes about in order to search for the stowaways. After a few idyllic days on Maui, Billy is spotted by Navy commander Joe Milburn and his wife, former passengers on O'Hare's ship who are visiting the well-to-do Harlows. Unknown to Milburn, a group of foreign agents are plotting to steal secret government papers from him with the help of Julius, a trusted Harlow servant. That night, at Aunty Pinau's annual luau, Milburn confronts Billy and convinces him to return to Captain O'Hare to clear his name. On his way to the marina, Billy and chauffeur Julius are stopped and questioned by police about Milburn's stolen papers. Billy, remembering a conversation he overheard while exploring a cave with Pua, realizes that Julius is the thief and escapes from the car. Eventually, Billy and Pua lead Milburn and the police to the spies and are hailed as national heroes for their efforts. Billy then sings farewell to Hawaii as he and the Milburns set sail for San Francisco. *Espionage. Hawaii. Orphans. Stowaways. Chases. Foreign agents. Hawaiians. Luaus. Ocean liners. Officers (Military). Police. Sea captains. Secret documents. Singers. Songwriters. United States. Navy.*

Note: Don Blanding was Hawaii's "island poet," according to *MPH*. Onscreen credits state that the film's title was "inspired by Radio Station K.G.M.B." in Honolulu. Opening and closing onscreen credits vary in cast order. In the opening credits of the viewed print, Ward Bond and Mamo Clark are given top

billing, and Raymond Paige and His Orchestra are given a special mention on the title card. It is possible that the opening credits were changed for television broadcast. A *HR* news item adds Margaret Cole to the cast, but her participation in the final film has not been confirmed.

DV 24 Feb 1938, p. 3. *FD* 25 Feb 1938, p. 6. *HR* 30 Oct 1937, p. 5. *HR* 16 Nov 1937, p. 11. *HR* 6 Dec 1937, pp. 14-15. *HR* 24 Feb 1938, p. 3. *MPD* 24 Feb 1938, p. 8. *MPH* 4 Dec 1937, p. 38. *MPH* 5 Mar 1938, p. 37, 40. *NYT* 29 Apr 1938, p. 17. *Var* 2 Mar 1938, p. 15.

THE HAWK *see* **THE PHANTOM OF SANTA FE**

HAWK OF THE HILLS (Native Americans)
Pathé Exchange, Inc. 17 Mar **1929**. Si; b&w. 5 reels, 4,840 ft.
Dir Spencer Gordon Bennett. *Story, scen and titles* George Arthur Gray. *Photog* Edward Snyder and Frank Redman.
Cast: Allene Ray (*Mary Selby*), Walter Miller (*Laramie*), Robert Chandler (*Clyde Selby*), Jack Ganghorn (*Henry Selby*), Frank Lackteen (*The Hawk*), Paul Panzer (*Manson*), Wally Oettel (*Shorty*), Harry Semels (*Sheckard*), Jack Pratt (*Colonel Jennings*), J. Parks Jones (*Lieutenant MacCready*), Frederick Dana (*Larry*), John T. Prince (*The Hermit*), Chief Whitehorse, George Magrill, Evangeline Russell, Chief Yowlache (*Chief Long Hand*).
Western. The story line of this film is similar to that of the serial from which it was taken. The serial deals with the adventures of The Hawk, the half-breed leader of a band of Indians and renegade whites; prospectors, the objects of The Hawk's treachery; Mary Selby, the daughter of a prospector and the niece of an Indian agent; Laramie, who poses as an outlaw, becomes a member of The Hawk's gang, and finally reveals himself to be a government agent; and assorted Indians and troopers. *Gangs. Government agents. Indian agents. Indians of North Amerca–Mixed blood. Indians of North America. Prospectors. Traitors. United States. Army. Cavalry.*
Note: This film is a feature-length version of a ten-episode serial released by Pathé Exchange, Inc. in 1927.

THE HAWK'S NEST (Chinese Americans)
First National Pictures, Inc. *Dist* First National Pictures, Inc. 27 May **1928** [©First National Pictures, Inc.; 28 May 1928; LP25302]. Si; b&w. 8 reels, 7,426 or 7,433 ft.
Pres Richard A. Rowland. *Dir* Benjamin Christensen. *Scen* James T. O'Donohue. *Story* Wid Gunning. *Titles* Casey Robinson. *Photog* Sol Polito. *Art dir* Max Parker. *Film ed* Frank Ware.
Cast: Milton Sills (*The Hawk/John Finchley*), Montagu Love (*Dan Daugherty*), Mitchell Lewis (*James Kent*), Doris Kenyon (*Madelon Arden*), Stuart Holmes (*Barney McGuire*), Sojin (*Himself*).
Melodrama. Determined to find the murderer of McGuire, one of his employees, "The Hawk," owner of a Chinatown café, has plastic surgery on his scarred face and masquerades as Finchley, a Chicago gangster. He thus hopes to save the life of Kent, manager of his café, who is being framed on a murder charge. The Hawk gains the confidence of Dan Daugherty, owner of a rival café, whom he suspects to be the murderer, and Madelon Arden, a dancer in Daugherty's café. When he fails to prove Daugherty's guilt, the council of Chinatown, aware that Daugherty also caused the death of Ching Ling Fu, a Chinatown leader, forces Daugherty to confess to the other killing. The Hawk finds romantic interest in Madelon. *Cafes. Chinese Americans. Dancers. Frame-ups. Gangsters. Plastic surgery. San Francisco (CA)–Chinatown.*
FD 3 Jun 1928. *MPW* 16 Jun 1928. *NYT* 25 Jun 1928, p. 27. *Var* 27 Jun 1928, p. 34.

HAY QUE CASAR AL PRÍNCIPE (Spanish language)
Fox Film Corp. *Dist* Fox Film Corp. **1931**; New York and Los Angeles opening: 24 Jul 1931; Prod: May 1931. Sd; b&w. 8 reels, 6,903 ft. 73 min. Passed by the National Board of Review. Spanish language.
Pres WILLIAM FOX. *Dirección de* [*Directed by*] Lewis Seiler. [*Adpt and dial* William Kernell and Paul Perez]. [*Spanish translation* Matías Cirici-Ventalló]. [*Photog* Glen MacWilliams]. [*Art dir* William Darling]. [*Film ed* Fred Burnworth]. [*Sd* William R. Fox].
Song(s): "Paid to Love," "Mi libertad (Thru the Green Country Side)," "La canción de los gitanos (Gypsy Love Song)," "Mi sueño de amor (My Dream of Love Is True)," "En la vieja Sylvania" and "El regimento del amor (Regiment of Love,)" music by William Kernell, Spanish lyrics by José Mojica.
Source: Based on the film *Paid to Love*, story by Harry Carr, scenario by William Conselman and Seton I. Miller (Fox Film Corp., 1927).

Cast: José Mojica (*El Príncipe Alexis* [*/Teniente Eric Sandro*]), Conchita Montenegro (*Yvette*), José Alcántara (*El Príncipe Borio* [*Prince Borio*]), Miguel Ligero (*Mister Tomson*), Carlos Villarías (*Consejero* [*Counsellor*]), Manuel Arbó (*El Gran Duque Constantino* [*Grand Duke Constantino*]), Paco Moreno (*Sascha*), Rafael Calvo (*Coronel* [*Colonel*]).
Romance, Musical comedy. [*Not viewed*]. Tomson, a financial adviser, is called to the aid of the country of Sylvania by the Grand Duke Constantino, known as "Tino." Tomson refuses to aid Tino until the Duke's son Alexis is married. However, Alexis, a romantic, is not interested in the blue-blooded types that his father has selected for him. Instead he wants fate to intercede. Upon learning this, Tomson plans a wife-hunting trip to Paris, "the beauty mart of the world." Once in Paris, Tomson and Tino find a beautiful woman, Yvette, who, for a price, is willing to get the prince's attention without seeking marriage. A few days later, on her way to the palace, Yvette's car gets caught in a rain storm. Spying a lodge, she runs for help, but exhausted, she collapses into Alexis' arms. When Yvette awakens, Alexis, calling himself Lieutenant Eric Sandro, suggests that she continue her trip to the palace after the rain stops. She agrees, but when her visit exceeds three days, she decides to leave because he is too much of a temptation to her virtue. Alexis is intrigued and they agree to meet when her business at the palace is finished. Tomson and Tino plan for Yvette to meet Alexis at a charity festival the next day. At the festival's casino, the Duke's second son Borio, a spoiled prince, decides to play a trick on his father. Aware of Tino's plans, Borio tells Yvette that he is Alexis, which causes Yvette to flirt openly with him. Borio feigns boredom but agrees to meet Yvette the following day. She goes directly to Alexis' lodge, where he gives her a ring. When Borio sees the ring, he demands to know how she got it. Realizing what his brother has done, Borio exposes the ruse to Yvette, happily adding that a prince is not allowed to marry a commoner. At the officer's club, Alexis overhears Borio relating the sordid details to a large group of men. Yvette confirms that Borio's story is true, and a very confused Alexis seeks the help of his colonel, who advises Alexis to follow his heart even if it means standing up to Tino. Meanwhile, Yvette has informed Tino and Tomson of her and Alexis' love, but Tino is adamant that Alexis must marry a duchess. When it becomes apparent that Alexis plans to follow Yvette back to France, Tino, with Tomson's promise of financial aid, agrees to make Yvette a duchess. Following Yvette's trail in his sportscar, Alexis catches up with her when her car breaks down. She joins him, and as they pull away from her car, they kiss and sing a tribute to their love. *Class distinction. Impersonation and imposture. Mythical lands. Nobility. Paris (France). Princes. Romance. Brothers. Casinos. Clubs. Fathers and sons. Festivals. Hoaxes. Officers (Military). Palaces. Rainstorms.*
Note: The plot summary was based on a screen continuity in the Twentieth Century-Fox Produced Scripts Collection, and the onscreen credits were taken from a screen credit sheet in the Twentieth Century-Fox Records of the Legal Department, both of which are at the UCLA Theater Arts Library. This film was a remake of the 1927 Fox film entitled *Paid to Love*, directed by Howard Hawks and starring George O'Brien and Virginia Valli (see *AFI Catalog of Feature Films, 1921-30*; F2.4105). The story by Harry Carr that was the source of that film was entitled "A Royal Scandal."
CM Oct 1931, p. 750.

HAYNTIGE MAMES *see* **MOTHERS OF TODAY**

HE WAS A MAN *see* **HE WAS HER MAN**

HE WAS HER MAN (Portuguese Americans)
Warner Bros. Pictures, Inc. *Dist* Warner Bros. Pictures, Inc.; The Vitaphone Corp. 16 Jun **1934**; Prod: 5 Feb—mid-Mar 1934 [©Warner Bros. Pictures, Inc.; 21 May 1934; LP4705]. Sd; b&w. 7 reels. 70 min.
[*Prod* Robert Lord]. *Dir* Lloyd Bacon. *Scr* Tom Buckingham and Niven Busch. *Story* Robert Lord. *Photog* George Barnes. *Art dir* Anton Grot. *Ed* George Amy. *Gowns* Orry-Kelly. *Vitaphone Orch cond* Leo F. Forbstein.
Cast: James Cagney (*Flicker* [*Hayes, later known as Jerry Allen*]), Joan Blondell (*Rose* [*Lawrence*]), Victor Jory (*Nick* [*Gardella*]), Frank Craven (*Pop Sims*), Sarah Padden (*Mrs. Gardella*), Harold Huber ([*J. C.*] *Ward*), Russell Hopton (*Monk*), Ralfe Harolde [(*Red Deering*)], John Qualen [(*Dutch*)], Bradley Page [(*Dan*)], Samuel E. Hines [(*Gassy*)], George Chandler [(*Waiter*)], James Eagle [(*Whitney*)], [George Pat Collins].
Gangster, Romance. [*Print viewed*]. Recently released from jail, Flicker Hayes plans revenge on the men who were responsible for his

time in prison. He sets up a burglary and tips the police. In the ensuing encounter, a policeman is killed. When Red Deering, one of the gangsters, is sentenced to death, a contract is placed on Flicker's life. While hiding out in San Francisco under the alias Jerry Allen, Flicker is recognized by Pop Sims, but does not realize it. When he meets Rose Lawrence, a former prostitute who is leaving to marry Nick Gardella, a Portuguese fisherman in a small town to the south, Flicker invites himself along, thinking the town would be a good place to hide out. Pop learns Flicker's destination and, after transmitting the information to the gangsters, follows Flicker and Rose. Upon his arrival, Pop rents a room at the Gardellas'. Rose hopes that Flicker will leave, having delivered her to her destination, but the Gardellas invite him to stay for the wedding. Nick knows about Rose's past, but believes that they can start fresh after they are married. In spite of herself, Rose falls in love with Flicker and decides she cannot marry Nick. She intends to leave with Flicker; however, he has second thoughts. Discovering his gun is missing and Pop's bed is empty, Flicker sneaks out in the middle of the night. The gangsters arrive at the Gardellas', finding Rose alone in the house. They believe Rose knows more than she is saying and decide to use force on her to get her to talk. Waiting for the bus, Flicker learns that the gangsters are at the Gardellas' and plan to kill Rose because of him. When the bus arrives, Flicker does not leave, instead he returns to the Gardellas'. He convinces the gangsters that Rose knows nothing and also tells Rose that he has no intention of taking her with him. Not realizing that the gangsters intend to kill Flicker, Rose lets him go, believing that he no longer loves her. Before their wedding, Rose confesses her feelings about Flicker to Nick. But Nick repeats his belief that everything starts fresh with their wedding which then takes place as planned. *Fishermen. Gangsters. Revenge. Romance. Self-sacrifice. Frame-ups. Lodgers. Murder. Police. Portuguese Americans. Prostitution. Recognition. Robbery. San Francisco (CA). Weddings.*

Note: The film's working titles were *Without Honor* and *He Was a Man.* According to *HR*, the fishing village scenes were filmed in Monterey, CA. The film was placed on the Catholic Church's "condemned" list. Modern sources include Gino Corrado in the cast.

DV 5 Feb 1934, p. 3. *DV* 21 Feb 1934, p. 3. *DV* 13 Aug 1934, p. 6. *FD* 18 May 1934, p. 10. *HR* 5 Feb 1934, p. 7. *HR* 30 Mar 1934, p. 3. *MPD* 16 May 1934, p. 3. *MPH* 28 Apr 1934, p. 26. *MPH* 26 May 1934, p. 42. *NYT* 17 May 1934, p. 28. *Var* 22 May 1934, p. 15.

HEAD OVER HEELS (Italian Americans)

Goldwyn Pictures Corp. Apr 1922 [©Goldwyn Pictures Corp.; 20 Apr 1922; LP17763]. Si; b&w. 5 reels, 4,229 ft.

Dir Victor Schertzinger and Paul Bern. *Scen* Julien Josephson and Gerald C. Duffy. *Story* Nalbro Isadorah Bartley. *Photog* George F. Webber.

Cast: Mabel Normand (*Tina*), Hugh Thompson (*Lawson*), Russ Powell (*Papa Bambinetti*), Raymond Hatton (*Pepper*), Adolphe Menjou (*Sterling*), Lilyan Tashman (*Babe*), Lionel Belmore (*Al Wilkins*).

Comedy-drama. Sterling, a theatrical agent, hires Tina to come to the United States to perform when he sees her in an acrobatic act in Naples. Tina arrives ill-clad and plain. Her guardian, Papa Bambinetti, is "taken in" by Pepper, a press agent, who promises to make Tina a motion picture star. After they drag Tina into a beauty parlor, she emerges, to everyone's surprise, a beautiful young woman. Lawson, a member of the theatrical firm, falls in love with Tina, who cannot decide between him and her career. She decides against both and packs to return to Italy when she spies Lawson with another actress. But when Lawson repents, she chooses in his favor. *Acrobats. Italian Americans. Motion pictures. Naples (Italy). Press agents. Theatrical agents. Wards and guardians.*

ETR 17 Jun 1922, p. 189. *MPW* 6 May 1922, p. 89.

HEADLINE HUNTERS (Latino)

Republic Pictures Corp. *Dist* Republic Pictures Corp. 29 Sep **1955**; Los Angeles opening: 2 Sep 1955; Prod: mid-Apr—late Apr 1955 [©Republic Pictures Corp.; 3 Aug 1955; LP5863]. Sd (RCA Sound Recording); b&w. 6,301 ft. 70 min. PCA cert no. 17537.

Assoc prod William J. O'Sullivan. *Dir* William Whitney. *Asst dir* Roy Wade. *Scr* Frederic Louis Fox and John K. Butler. *Dir of photog* John L. Russell, Jr. *Spec eff* Howard Lydecker and Theodore Lydecker. *Optical eff* Consolidated Film Industries. *Art dir* Carroll Clark. *Film ed* Arthur E. Roberts. *Set dec* John McCarthy, Jr. and George Milo. *Cost supv* Adele Palmer. *Mus* R. Dale Butts. *Sd* Melvin M. Metcalfe, Jr. *Makeup supv* Bob Mark.

Cast: Rod Cameron [(*Hugh "Woody" Woodruff*)], Julie Bishop [(*Laura Stewart*)], Ben Cooper [(*Dave Flynn*)], Raymond Greenleaf [(*Paul Strout*)], Chubby Johnson [(*Ned Powers*)], John Warburton [(*Harvey S. Kevin*)], Nacho Galindo [(*Ramon*)], Virginia Carroll [(*Elsie*)], Howard Wright [(*Harry Bradley*)], Stuart Randall [(*Frank Hoffman*)], Edward Colmans [(*Rafael Garcia*)], Joe Besser [(*Coroner*)], [Tol Avery (*Examiner* reporter)], [Bob Carney (*Newsvendor*)], [Suzanne Cummings (*Receptionist*)], [Lou Krugman (*Star* reporter)], [Francis De Sales (*Tribune* reporter)], [Kenneth Chryson (*Bellboy*)], [Jack Dimond (*Office boy*)], [Howard Hoffman (*Evening Examiner* editor)], [Robert Foulk (*Daily Star* editor)], [Charles Evans (*Tribune* editor)], [Jonathan Hale (*Drunk*)], [Tom Black (*Detective*)], [Joe Dominguez (*Damasio Reyes*)], [Grandon Rhodes (*Magistrate*)], [Marc Hamilton (*Clerk*)], [Mike Ragan, Don C. Harvey (*Police officers*)], [John Daheim (*Nick*)], [Vicki Lee Churchill (*Girl*)], [Tyler MacDuff (*Young man*)].

Newspaper, Social, Drama. [*Print viewed*]. Dave Flynn, having recently graduated from the state school of journalism with a six-month scholarship to work at the *Daily Enquirer*, reports to managing editor Paul Strout, who assigns him to a story about the city's liquor commissioner, Frank Hoffman. Hoffman, who has received a death threat and is under police protection at his home, talks briefly with Dave, but as Hoffman leaves his house in his car, it explodes, killing him. Dave then reports to hard-drinking, veteran reporter Hugh "Woody" Woodruff, who is very cynical about the corruption in the city, but tells Dave that they can work together. Woody is courting Laura Stewart, who works for district attorney Harvey S. Kevin, who is running for re-election, and has received a number of story leads from her. A few days later, when Dave encounters Laura at a Mexican restaurant where she is waiting for Woody, she tells him that, due to the election, Kevin is anxious to convict someone for the Hoffman killing. She also confides to Dave that Woody used to be a much better reporter but is now very disgruntled and full of self-pity. When Woody arrives, Dave tells him that he has discovered that Hoffman had been taking bribes to provide liquor licenses. Spitefully, Woody sets Dave up with a phony story about the mayor being sued for divorce, and Dave is fired by Strout. When Dave confronts him, Woody says that he will get Dave his job back, but Dave chooses not to be indebted to him and looks for work on other newspapers. He soon finds that he has been "blackballed," but eventually is hired at *The Legal Ledger* and is assigned to check court activities. Dave is present when the district attorney sends over Damasio Reyes to be arraigned for the Hoffman murder. Reyes tells the judge, in Spanish, that he does not understand English, that he is from Mexico and has only been in the U.S. for three days. When told by the judge to ask Reyes how he pleads, Rafael Garcia, an interpreter assigned by Kevin, instead asks Reyes from which state he comes, but informs the judge that Reyes says that he pleads guilty. Dave, a fluent Spanish speaker, takes notes on all this and reports to *Ledger* publisher Harry Bradley that Reyes thought that he was in a deportation hearing and is obviously being framed for the Hoffman killing. Bradley feels, however, that without another witness, he could become involved in a libel suit and declines to print Dave's story. Although Dave tries to interest other newspapers, all the editors refuse to listen to him and print the "official" version. Dave tries to give the story to Woody, who declines it, thinking that Dave is trying to set him up to get revenge, but reveals that he got Dave the job with Bradley. Nonetheless, Dave accuses Woody of no longer being interested in reporting on issues affecting "the little guy." After Woody slugs him, Dave informs him that he used to be his hero but is no more. Later, after he falls out with Laura, Woody gets drunk and wakes up in Strout's office. Strout sobers him up, after which he goes to apologize to Laura and seek her help with information on the Reyes case. Laura also arranges a reconciliation between Woody and Dave, and they begin to work together on the Reyes story. Woody thinks that Hoffman may have been splitting payoffs with Kevin, and he, Dave and Laura manage to locate interpreter Garcia, who is working as a bartender. Dave tells him that he will testify that he lied in court and suggests to him that he may be murdered in order to silence him. As Garcia closes up the bar, two of Kevin's hoods show up and a brawl ensues, during which Garcia is shot in the shoulder. However, Woody and Dave overpower the thugs and, when the police arrive, Garcia agrees to confess. Woody phones in the story to Strout, giving the byline to Dave. Later, Woody and Laura become engaged and, as

another scholarship winner arrives, Dave is given a permanent job at the *Examiner*. Editors. Frame-ups. Mexican Americans. Mexicans. Murder. Political corruption. Reporters. Bartenders. Cynics. District attorneys. Drunkenness. Judges. Reconciliation. Restaurants. Romance. Scholarships. Transformation. Translators.

Note: This film's working title was *Deadline Alley*. It was a remake of the 1940 Republic film *Behind the News* (see above).

Box 19 Nov 1955. *DV* 6 Sep 1955, p. 3 *Exh* 2 Nov 1955, p. 4055. *MPHPD* 29 Oct 1955, p. 650.

A HEART IN PAWN (Japanese Americans)

Haworth Pictures Corp. *Dist* Robertson-Cole Co. through Exhibitors Mutual Distributing Corp. 10 Mar **1919** [©The Haworth Pictures Corp.; 5 Dec 1918; LU13103]. Si; b&w. 5 reels.

Dir William Worthington. *Scen* Frances Guihan and Thomas J. Geraghty. *Cam* Dal Clawson.

Source: Based on the play *Shadows* by Sessue Hayakawa (production undetermined).

Cast: Sessue Hayakawa (*Toyama*), Vola Vale (*Emily Stone*), Tsuru Aoki (*Sada*).

Drama. Toyama's wife Sada secretly earns money as a Geisha girl to finance his studies in America, but she says that the money comes from her deceased grandfather. In America, Toyama becomes an assistant to Dr. Stone, studying cures for inherited vices. When Toyama learns that Sada has been sentenced to death for murdering a prominent banker who attacked her, Toyama disappears and gives in to his hereditary tendency to drink until Dr. Stone cures him. Unknown to Toyama, Sada's sentence is commuted to life imprisonment when she gives birth to their daughter. Meanwhile, Toyama marries Stone's half-Japanese daughter Emily to fulfill Stone's dying request. In Japan, after Toyama lectures women prisoners and recognizes Sada, he discovers that the child he and Emily adopted is really his own daughter. When Sada escapes and finds Toyama, he decides to commit harakiri, but as the prison guards approach, Sada drowns herself to save him. Bigamy. Geishas. Hereditary tendencies. Japanese. Japanese Americans. Parentage. Self-sacrifice. Suicide. Alcoholism. Drowning. Escapes. Murder. Prison escapees. Students.

Note: The copyright records for this film are listed under the title *Shadows*. This title was not used because of another film made around the same time with that title. Sessue Hayakawa also starred in the stage production of *Shadows*. Some scenes were shot in the Japanese tea garden at Golden Gate Park in San Francisco.

ETR 15 Mar 1919, p. 1139. *MPN* 8 Mar 1919, p. 1533. *MPN* 15 Mar 1919, p. 1708. *MPW* 15 Mar 1919, p. 1529. *Var* 28 Feb 1919, p. 56.

THE HEART OF JACK JOHNSON *see* **AS THE WORLD ROLLS ON**

HEART OF MEXICO *see* **ON THE OLD SPANISH TRAIL**

THE HEART OF NEW YORK (Jewish Americans)

Warner Bros. Pictures, Inc. *Dist* Warner Bros. Pictures, Inc.; The Vitaphone Corp. 26 Mar **1932** [©Warner Bros. Pictures, Inc.; 6 Mar 1932; LP2910]. Sd; b&w. 8 reels. 65, 74 or 78 min.

Dir Mervyn LeRoy. *Adpt and dial* Arthur Caesar and Houston Branch. *Photog* James Van Trees. [*2d cam* Louis Jennings]. [*Asst cam* Vernon Larson]. *Art dir* Anton Grot. *Ed* Terry Morse. *Gowns* Earl Luick. *Vitaphone Orch cond* Leo F. Forbstein. [*Sd* Al Riggs]. [*Still photog* William Thomas].

Source: Based on the play *Mendel, Inc.* by David Freedman (New York, 25 Nov 1929).

Cast: Joe Smith [(*Sam Shtrudel*)], Charles Dale [(*Bernard Schnaps*)], George Sidney [(*Mendel*)], Ruth Hall [(*Lillian Mendel*)], Aline MacMahon [(*Bessie*)], Anna Appel [(*Mrs. Zelda Mendel*)], Donald Cook [(*Milton*)], Oscar Apfel [(*Gassenheim*)], Harold Waldridge [(*Jakie Mendel*)], Marion Byron [(*Mimi Mendel*)], George MacFarlane [(*Marshall*)], Ann Brody [(*Mrs. Nussbaum*)], Charles Coleman [(*The butler*)].

Domestic, Comedy. [*Print viewed*]. Mendel, who lives with his wife Zelda and children Mimi, Jakie and Lillian, on New York's Lower East Side, is too lazy to work as a plumber, his chosen occupation. Even though his children need shoes and his son needs his teeth fixed, Mendel's heart is in his inventions. Zelda, worried that her oldest daughter Lillian will never get married, asks her brother Bernard Schnaps to act as a matchmaker. He proposes a doctor. His friend, Sam Shtrudel, proposes a dentist, but Lillian has found her own boyfriend, a lawyer named Milton. Zelda is really worried when she discovers that the dentist, the doctor and the lawyer are all the same person;

Milton likes to study. Meanwhile, Mendel has invented a dishwasher, but no one believes in it except his neighbor Bessie. Nonetheless, he persists and his demonstration is a success. Schnaps and Shtrudel offer to take it to the landlord, Gassenheim, to see if he will produce it in his plant. Meanwhile, Mendel dreams of establishing a wonderful house on the Lower East Side with the profits from his invention. He returns home to find the landlord's agent waiting to serve an eviction notice. Schnaps and Shtrudel announce that the machine has broken all of Gassenheim's dishes and he is not interested in producing it. Zelda is so upset by Mendel's actions that she offers to trade places with him; she will work and he can take care of the house. Soon, however, Gassenheim announces he is ready to manufacture the machine. His cook figured out how to use it, and he thinks it is wonderful. Zelda and the children dream of moving uptown to a high class neighborhood, but when Mendel returns from signing with Gassenheim, he tells them he has purchased the building where they live. He builds a mansion on the site and hires someone to perform a rich man's duties, such as playing polo, while he sits at home, but Zelda and the family have moved out and do not see Mendel's improvements. Then Gassenheim stops sending checks, forcing Zelda and the children to return home, where they are surprised by how nice the house looks. Mendel learns that Gassenheim is behind the injunction that has stopped production on the machine, but Milton uses a lawyer's arguments to get around him. Everything is fine again, and Zelda and the children return home for good. Family life. Inventors. Jews. New York City–East Side. Cooks. Dishwashing. Eviction. Landlords. Lawyers. Laziness. Mansions. Matchmakers. Plumbers.

Note: The comedy team of Smith and Dale were also in the stage production. They were billed on screen as members of the Avon Comedy Four. Some scenes were shot on location in New York City. Before release, the film was entitled *Mendel, Inc.* and *East Side*.

FD 13 Dec 1931, p. 4. *FD* 31 Jan 1932, p. 4. *FD* 6 Mar 1932, p. 10. *HR* 20 Feb 1932, p. 2. *IP* May 1932, p. 34. *MPH* 12 Mar 1932, p. 55. *NYT* 2 Mar 1932, p. 15. *Var* 8 Mar 1932, p. 23.

THE HEART OF THE DESERT *see* **THE RED, RED HEART**

THE HEART OF THE IMMIGRANT *see* **CUORE D'EMIGRANTE**

THE HEART OF WETONA (Native Americans, Blackfoot)

Norma Talmadge Film Corp. *Dist* Select Pictures Corp. 5 Jan **1919** [©Norma Talmadge Film Corp.; 13 Dec 1918; LP13144]. Si; b&w. 6 reels, 5,265 ft.

Prod Joseph M. Schenck. *Dir* Sidney A. Franklin. *Scen* Mary Murillo. *Story* George Scarborough. *Cam* David Abel.

Cast: Norma Talmadge (*Wetona*), Fred Huntley (*Chief Quannah*), Thomas Meighan (*John Hardin*), Gladden James (*Tony Wells*), Fred Turner (*Pastor David Wells*), Princess Uwane Yea (*Nauma*), Charles Edler (*Comanche Jack*), White Eagle (*Nipo*), Black Wolf (*Passequa*), Black Lizard (*Eagle*).

Western. When Wetona, the half white, half Indian daughter of Chief Quannah of the Blackfoot tribe, tells her father that she would be an inappropriate choice to be the tribe's Vestal Virgin at the Corn Dance, the furious chief vows to kill her white lover. She goes to Government agent John Hardin for help, but her father sees them together and, speculating that Hardin has wronged her, demands that he marry her. Hardin agrees to the marriage to save her lover, whom he does not know is his friend and assistant Tony Wells. After Wetona learns that Tony was never sincere, she sees his cowardice during the Indian raid on Hardin's house. When the chief learns the truth, he stops the raid, apologizes to Hardin and shoots Tony as he flees. Quannah tells Wetona he will take her back, but since she and Hardin are now in love, they remain together. Indians of North America. Indians of North America–Mixed blood. Marriage–Forced. Virginity. Cads. Cowardice. False accusations. Government agents. Rites and ceremonies. Tribal chiefs.

Note: Princess Uwane Yea was the granddaughter of one of the chiefs who defeated Gen. George Custer. White Eagle, Black Wolf and Black Lizard were genuine chiefs of the Comanche tribe. Norma Talmadge was made an honorary Comanche princess during the filming.

ETR 28 Dec 1918, p. 345. *MPN* 4 Jan 1919, p. 146. *MPW* 4 Jan 1919, p. 114. *MPW* 11 Jan 1919, pp. 252-53. *NYT* 6 Jan 1919, p. 11. *Var* 10 Jan 1919, p. 45. *Wid's* 29 Dec 1918, p. 15.

HEART TROUBLE (German Americans)

Harry Langdon Corp. *Dist* First National Pictures, Inc. 21 Jul **1928** [©First National Pictures, Inc.; 17 Aug 1928; LP25537]. Si; b&w. 6 reels, 5,400 ft.

Dir Harry Langdon. *Scen* Earle Rodney and Clarence Hennecke. *Story* Arthur Ripley. *Titles* Gardner Bradford. *Photog* Frank Evans and Dev Jennings. *Film ed* Alfred De Gaetano.

Cast: Harry Langdon (*Harry Van Housen*), Doris Dawson (*The Girl*), Lionel Belmore (*Adolph Van Housen*), Madge Hunt (*Mrs. Adolph Van Housen*), Bud Jamieson (*Contractor*), Mark Hamilton, Nelson McDowell (*Conductors*).

Comedy. Harry Van Housen, the son of German immigrants, desperately wants to enlist in the United States Army during World War I in order to prove to his sweetheart that he is a true-blue American. Every time Harry volunteers for service, he is turned down for unfitness: he is underweight, four inches too short, nearsighted, flat-footed, and suffering from dandruff. Unwittingly, he comes across a German base being used to shuttle supplies to submarines off the United States coast; all unknowingly, he manages to free an American officer, blow up the base, and round up the spies. Harry is given a hero's welcome by his hometown, but he misses it, being too busy courting his girl to care about civic honors. *Civil defense. German Americans. Immigrants. Patriotism. Spies. World War I.*

FD 7 Oct 1928. *MPW* 19 May 1928. *MPW* 26 May 1928. *Var* 10 Oct 1928, p. 28.

HEARTACHES *see* SUM HUN

HEARTS IN DIXIE (African Americans)

Fox Film Corp. *Dist* Fox Film Corp. 10 Mar 1929; Los Angeles opening: 6 Mar 1929 [©Fox Film Corp.; 16 Mar 1929; LP234]. Sd; b&w. 8 reels, 6,444 ft.

Pres William Fox. *Dir* Paul Sloane. *Addl dir* A. H. Van Buren. *Scen, story and dial* Walter Weems. *Photog* Glen MacWilliams. *Film ed* Alexander Troffey. *Choreography* Fanchon & Marco. *Sd* Arthur L. von Kirbach.

Song(s): "Hearts in Dixie," music and lyrics by Walter Weems and Howard Jackson.

Cast: Clarence Muse (*Nappus*), Eugene Jackson (*Chiquapin*), Stepin Fetchit (*Gummy*), Bernice Pilot (*Chloe*), Clifford Ingram (*Rammey*), Mildred Washington (*Trailia*), Zack Williams (*Deacon*), Gertrude Howard (*Emmy*), Dorothy Morrison (*Melia*), Vivian Smith (*Violet*), Robert Brooks (*True Love*), A. C. H. Billbrew (*Voodoo woman*), Richard Carlyle (*White doctor*), Bilbrew Chorus.

African American, Comedy-drama. [*Not viewed*]. Nappus, an old black man who works a farm, despite his advanced years, has a daughter named Chloe who is married to Gummy, a shiftless young man who does nothing but sun himself while Chloe does both the housework and the manual labor. Gummy and Chloe have two children, Chiquapin and Trailia. Chloe and Trailia are taken ill, and instead of sending for the white doctor, Gummy sends for the voodoo woman. Both mother and daughter die, and Nappus sells his farm and his mule to raise enough money to send Chiquapin north to become a doctor, hoping that the boy will someday return south to help his people. *African Americans. Children. Farmers. Mules. Physicians. United States–South. Voodoo.*

Note: According to news items, Charles Gilpin was originally cast in the role of "Nappus." George Reed was next mentioned for the role, which eventually was given to Clarence Muse.

California Eagle 14 Dec 1928. *California Eagle* 21 Dec 1928. *ChiDef* 16 Mar 1929, pt. I, p. 6. *FD* 3 Mar 1929. *NYT* 28 Feb 1929, p. 30. *Var* 6 Mar 1929, p. 15.

HEARTS OF HUMANITY (Irish Americans, Jewish Americans)

Majestic Pictures Corp. *Dist* Majestic Pictures Corp. 1 Sep 1932. Sd; b&w. 56, 65 or 70 min.

Prod John Clein. *Dir* Christy Cabanne. *Asst dir* Jack Sullivan. *Story* Olga Printzlau. *Dial and scen* Edward T. Lowe. *Photog* Charles Stumar. *Art dir* Jack Schultz. *Ed* Don Lindberg. *Mus* Brown and Spencer.

Cast: Jean Hersholt (*Sol Bloom*), Jackie Searl (*Shandy*), J. Farrell MacDonald (*Tom O'Hara*), Claudia Dell (*Ruth Sneider*), Charles Delaney (*Tom Varney*), Lucille LaVerne (*Mrs. Sneider*), Dick Wallace (*Joey Bloom*), George Humbert (*Tony*), Betty Jane Graham (*Hilda*), John Vosburgh (*Dave Haller*), Tom McGuire (*Mr. Wells*).

Drama. [*Not viewed*]. Irish policeman Tom O'Hara is killed by a thief in Sol Bloom's antique store, but before he dies, he asks widower Sol to take care of his son Shandy, who will be arriving soon from Europe. Sol's own son Joey is streetwise and uncontrollable, although Sol has reared him lovingly. Sol adopts Shandy and treats him like his own son, and Shandy reciprocates with love and helpfulness. Shandy looks after Joey, who is continually getting into trouble. When Joey

steals a dollar from his father's cash register, Shandy pawns the harp his mother gave him to replace the money so Joey will not get into trouble. When Joey breaks a neighbor's window, Shandy offers to pay the owner ten dollars so he will not tell Sol, however he is unable to get his harp back because it has been sold. Desperate, Shandy asks the new owner to lend it to him, and then steals it when the owner refuses. He wins a ten dollar prize performing in an amateur night contest, but is so guilt-ridden about having stolen the harp that he wanders aimlessly in the rain. Shandy takes ill and is brought home by a policeman. Joey reforms and prays for Shandy's recovery. Joey's improvement bolsters Shandy, who recovers, and the harp's owner returns the harp to Shandy. *Adoption. Irish Americans. Jews. Moral reformation. Thieves. Widowers. Antique dealers. Contests. Fathers and sons. Guilt. Harps and Harpists. Pawnshops.*

Note: According to the *Var* review, this was filmed in six days at a cost of approximately $30,000.

FD 21 Sep 1932. *HR* 9 Sep 1932, p. 10. *MPH* 27 Aug 1932, pp. 48-49. *MPH* 24 Sep 1932, p. 34. *Var* 27 Sep 1932, p. 21.

HEARTS OF MEN (German Americans)

Charles K. Harris Feature Film Co. *Dist* World Film Corp. 19 Nov 1915 [©World Film Corp.; 3 Dec 1915; LU7145]. Si; b&w. 4 reels.

Dir Perry N. Vekroff. *Asst dir* Eddie James. *Scen* Charles K. Harris. *Cam* Harold Louis Miller.

Source: Based on the play *School Bells* by Charles K. Harris (New York, 1915).

Cast: Arthur Donaldson (*Fritz Wagner*), Beulah Poynter (*Hilda Wagner*), Frank Longacre (*Hans Wagner*), Ethelmary Oakland (*Amy Rapp*), Nicholas Long, Jr. (*Bad little boy*), Robert Fisher (*Adolph Rapp*), Jack McCauley, Florence [full name unknown] (*School children*), Gladys Peck.

Drama. Fritz Wagner develops a formula for a new scent in the German perfume factory where he and his best friend work. Slipping into the factory one night, the friend steals the formula and then disappears from the area. Years later, Fritz takes his family to America and sends his young son to a local school. Unable to speak proper English, Hans is aided in class by Amy, and the two children soon become close companions. By chance, Fritz meets up with his false friend, now a prominent figure in the American perfume business, and accuses him of the theft. During the ensuing argument, Fritz discovers that Amy is his rival's daughter and upon her next visit, he sends her away from his gate. On her way home, she is kidnapped by gypsies, but disobeying his father's orders, Hans takes off to find his friend and rescues her from her captors. The innocent bravery of the children finally reconciles the two fathers, restoring harmony in the hearts of men. *Betrayal. Children. Friendship. German Americans. Robbery. Factories. Germany. Gypsies. Immigrants. Kidnapping. Perfume. Rescues. Schools. Secret formulas.*

Note: The film was first titled *School Bells* and was made at the Kinemacolor studio in Whitestone, NY.

Motog 20 Nov 1915, p. 1088. *MPN* 20 Nov 1915, p. 84. *MPW* 20 Nov 1915, p. 1503. *MPW* 27 Nov 1915, p. 1732. *MPW* 14 Aug 1915, p. 1183. *MPW* 11 Sep 1915, p. 1854. *NYDM* 20 Nov 1915, p. 28. *Var* 12 Nov 1915, p. 22.

HEARTS OF MEN (Italian Americans)

A Hiram Abrams Production. *Dist* State Rights; Hiram Abrams. 27 Apr 1919. Si; b&w. 6 reels.

Pres Hiram Abrams. *Prod* George Beban. *Dir* George Beban. *Scen* Harvey Thew and Helen Filson. *Story* William M. McCoy. *Cam* William M. McGann.

Cast: George Beban (*Nicolo Rosetti*), Sarah Kernan (*Maria Rosetti*), George Beban, Jr. (*Beppo*), Mabel Van Buren (*Tina Ferronni*), Harry Rattenbury (*Judge Newcombe*), George Pierson (*Steve, the clerk*), Clarence Burton (*Buck Hughes*), Hop Sing (*Himself*).

Drama. Nicolo Rosetti leads a happy, if poor life growing flowers which his mother sells. When she becomes ill and the doctor prescribes a better climate, Nicolo buys land in Arizona which he finds is arid wasteland. A railroad construction gang, thinking that Nicolo is the forerunner of an influx of cheap Italian labor, tries to make him leave, but they are soon won over by Nicolo's motherless son Beppo and help Nicolo build a shack. When his mother dies, the men encourage Nicolo to remarry so that Beppo can have a mother. After he writes to a cousin in Italy, a bride, Tina Ferronni, arrives. Disappointed, Tina takes Beppo to Italy, ostensibly to visit his dying maternal grandmother, but in reality she is eloping with a clerk. After

she writes that Beppo has died, the men in Arizona secretly pay for an investigation. The day that Beppo returns, the grieving Nicolo strikes oil. Nicolo joyously receives Beppo and shares his newly found wealth with his friends. *Arizona. Duplicity. Fathers and sons. Friendship. Italian Americans. Land sales. Mothers and sons. Clerks. Elopement. Flower vendors. Oil. Railroad workers. Separation (Marital).*

Note: This film, the first Hiram Abrams production, was George Beban's first film as producer, director and star.

ETR 19 Apr 1919, p. 1519. *MPN* 19 Apr 1919, p. 2535. *MPW* 19 Apr 1919, p. 426. *MPW* 26 Apr 1919, pp. 480-83. *Var* 11 Apr 1919, p. 55. *Var* 20 Jun 1919, p. 53. *Wid's* 13 Apr 1919, p. 11.

HEARTS OF THE WOODS (African Americans)
Superior Art Productions Co. **1921**; Houston opening: 25 Dec 1921. Si; b&w. Length undetermined. [Feature length assumed.].
Dir Roy Calnek. *Photog* Jack Specht. *Art titles* J. O. Carlile.
Cast: Clifford Harris, Laurence McGuire, E. D. Pierson, Jr., Annie Lou Allen.
Drama, African American. [According to a review in an African-American newspaper, this film is about "the life of our people in the woods and around saw mills." The villain marries a girl in a church, then is denounced by his real wife. The ending is happy. No additional information about the plot has been found.]. *African Americans. Lumber mills. Marriage–Fake. Philanderers. Seduction.*

Note: Superior Art Productions Co. was located in Houston, TX. It was later called Superior Art Motion Pictures, Inc. Various sources list the director as Roy Calnek and R. E. Carlile. *ChiDef* reviewer D. Ireland Thomas wrote concerning the film, "This is according to my idea the poorest Race production ever made except *A Child in Pawn*."

ChiDef 4 Feb 1922, p. 8.

HEARTS UNITED (Native Americans)
Dist Sawyer, Inc. Oct **1914**. Si; b&w. 4 reels.
Cast: Edward Booth Tilton.
Drama. Professor Dodd, an anthropologist, hopes that his daughter Alma will marry Robert Harris, the son of a college friend, despite the fact that Alma loves Joe, the family chauffeur. Dodd invites Robert to visit, but unknown to the professor, Robert has died of heart failure and his place is taken by a gambler named Haines who is his exact double. Haines insinuates to Alma that Joe is married, after which the spurned Joe goes to the Northwest. When Alma discovers Haines's deception, she and Dodd follow Joe to the Northwest where the anthropologist intends to study Indians. Haines pursues them, disguised as a professor, and abducts Alma. Joe, having saved the Indian princess Water Lily, enlists her help and rescues Alma. In a final confrontation, Haines is killed. *Abduction. Chauffeurs. Impersonation and imposture. Professors. Rescues. Anthropologists. Doubles. Gamblers. Heart disease. Indians of North America. United States–Northwest.*

Motog 26 Dec 1914, p. 916. *MPN* 9 Jan 1915, p. 57.

HEAVEN FOR SALE see **TONIGHT WE SING**

HEAVEN WITH A BARBED WIRE FENCE (Latino)
Twentieth Century-Fox Film Corp. *Dist* Twentieth Century-Fox Film Corp. 3 Nov **1939**; Prod: 8 Jun—31 Jun 1939; addl scenes 20 Jul—26 Jul 1939 [©Twentieth Century-Fox Film Corp.; 3 Nov 1939; LP9458]. Sd (RCA High Fidelity Recording); b&w. 60-62 or 65 min. PCA cert no. 5488.
Exec prod Sol M. Wurtzel. *Dir* Ricardo Cortez. [*Dial dir* Arthur Berthelet]. [*Asst dir* Jasper Blystone and Jerry Braun]. *Scr* Dalton Trumbo, Leonard Hoffman and Ben Grauman Kohn. *Orig story* Dalton Trumbo. [*Contr to scr const* Sam Duncan]. *Dir of photog* Edward Cronjager. [*Cam op* Joe McDonald]. [*Asst cam* Henry Cronjager]. *Art dir* Richard Day and Chester Gore. *Film ed* Norman Colbert. *Set dec* Thomas Little. *Cost* Herschel. [*Ward* Sam Benson and Gladys Isaacson]. *Mus dir* Samuel Kaylin. *Sd* Joseph E. Aiken and William H. Anderson. [*Sd op* J. L. Sigler]. [*Boom man* Bob Bertrand]. [*Hair* Lydia Blythe]. [*Makeup* Gene Klum]. [*Prod mgr* William Koenig]. [*Unit mgr* Sam Schneider]. [*Scr clerk* Elena Torres]. [*Head grip* George Switzer]. [*Gaffer* Fred Kelly]. [*Best boy* Robert Campbell]. [*Props* Mack Elliot]. [*Location mgr* R. C. Moore]. [*Asst prop man* Charles Fremdling and Bob McLaughlin]. [*Follow-up* William Eull]. [*Still photog* Ray Nolan].
Cast: Jean Rogers (*Anita* [*Santos*]), Raymond Walburn (*The Professor* [*Townsend Thayer*]), Marjorie Rambeau (*Mamie*), Glenn Ford (*Joe* [*Riley*]), Nicholas Conte (*Tony* [*Casselli*]), Eddie Collins (*Bill*), Ward Bond (*Hunk*), Irving Bacon (*Sheriff* [*Clem Diggers*]),

Kay Linaker (*Nurse*), [Paul Hurst (*Guard*)], [Edward Gargan (*Truck driver*)], [Nick Copeland (*Brakeman*)], [George Melford (*Hobo*)], [Nigel De Brulier (*Russian priest*)], [Billy Wayne (*Bartender*)], [Dave Morris (*Farmer*)], [Fred Kelsey (*Detective*)], [Harry Strang, Paul Kruger (*Trainmen*)], [Otto Hoffman (*Station agent*)], [Paul Burns (*Railroad dispatcher*)], [Victor Potel (*Ranch hand*)].
Drama. [*Print viewed*]. At the Empire State Building, Joe Riley bids farewell to New York City as he prepares to head West to his ranch in Arizona. He dreams of his twenty acres of beautiful farmland called "Shady Acres" for which he has saved for six years. Hitchhiking across the country, Joe runs into a friendly drifter named Tony Casselli at a truck stop just outside of Cleveland. Tony tells Joe that the only way to travel cross-country is by rail, though Joe prefers to rely on his thumb. Joe jumps into a truck on its way to Cincinnati, but is discovered by the truck driver. Also discovered is another stowaway, Anita Santos, disguised as a boy. Anita follows Joe as he jumps onto a train, only to find Tony in the same car. Anita joins them, much to Joe's chagrin and Tony's pleasure. Forced off the train, the three discover a hobo camp. Leaving Anita in the woods for her safety, Tony and Joe go into the camp where they find Tony's old friend and traveling companion, The Professor. Hunk, the leader of the camp, watches Tony take Anita food, and later attacks her, with Joe coming to her defense. After The Professor knocks Hunk unconscious with a walking stick, the four hightail it out of the camp. Traveling cross country, Anita tells how her parents died during the Spanish Civil War and that she came to America to find her uncle in California. Although Joe constantly wants to leave Anita behind, the other two men become attached to her. When Tony receives a gunshot wound stealing food, The Professor pawns his prized pocket watch to get him medical attention. Although the three are told that Tony is fine and Tony, himself, promises to join them at Joe's ranch, Tony actually has lost his leg due to septic poisoning. After buying Anita new clothes, the three go into a bar where The Professor regains the acquaintance of old love Mamie. When the local sheriff comes in to question them on the origin of Tony's wound, he arrests Anita as an illegal alien and Joe for aiding and abetting her. The Professor convinces the sheriff to drop all charges on the condition that the two marry, which they do in an elaborate Russian Orthodox ceremony. When Joe tells Anita that he wants a divorce, however, she slips out of town during the reception. The next day, Joe tells The Professor and Mamie what has happened. The Professor has decided to stay behind with Mamie and run the bar, so Joe heads for Arizona alone. Finally there, Joe discovers his dream ranch is a nightmare, a broken down farm with nothing but bare ground. Anita arrives with supplies for the house, only to be met by a hostile Joe. Forced inside by a sudden rainstorm, Anita tells Joe how wonderful the ranch can be with a lot of hard work. As she prepares to leave, Joe stops her, telling her that they will build the ranch together. *Fugitives. Latino. Hoboes. Marriage–Forced by circumstances. Professors. Ranches. Trains. Arizona. Disguise. Empire State Building (New York City). Hitchhiking. Hospitals. Immigrants. New York City. Nurses. Oranges. Saloon Keepers. Sheriffs. Truck drivers. Watches. Weddings.*

Note: This picture marked Glenn Ford's feature film debut. According to a Twentieth Century-Fox press release, Jean Rogers worked on another film, *Stop, Look and Love*, simultaneous to the production of this film. The Twentieth Century-Fox Records of the Legal Department at the UCLA Theater Arts Library state that location filming was done in Thousand Oaks, Newhall, and Saugus, California. Press releases also reported that Nicholas Conte was signed by Twentieth Century-Fox for this film based on his screen test for the lead in Columbia Pictures' *Golden Boy*, a part he lost to William Holden.

Box 7 Oct 1939. *DV* 29 Sep 1939, p. 3. *FD* 26 Jan 1940, p. 10. *HR* 6 Jun 1939, p. 1. *HR* 7 Jun 1939, p. 2. *HR* 17 Jun 1939, p. 6. *HR* 1 Jul 1939, p. 2. *HR* 20 Jul 1939, p. 10. *HR* 26 Jul 1939, p. 2. *HR* 30 Sep 1939, p. 3. *MPD* 4 Oct 1939, p. 9 *MPH* 7 Oct 1939, p. 39. *Var* 6 Dec 1939, p. 14.

HEIL, JENNIE see **JENNIE**

DIE HEILIGE FLAMME see **LA LLAMA SAGRADA**

HELGA see **THREE WHO LOVED**

THE HELL CAT (Irish Americans, Native Americans)
Goldwyn Pictures Corp.; Diva Pictures, Inc. *Dist* Goldwyn Distributing Corp. 1 Dec **1918** [©Diva Pictures, Inc.; 25 Nov 1918; LP13070]. Si; b&w. 6 reels.
Dir Reginald Barker. *Story and scen* Willard Mack. *Cam* Percy Hilburn. *Asst cam* William B. Laub.

Cast: Geraldine Farrar (*Pancha O'Brien*), Tom Santschi (*Jim Dyke*), Milton Sills (*Sheriff Jack Webb*), William W. Black (*Pancha's father*), Evelyn Axzell (*Wan-o-mee*), Clarence Williams, George Hopkins, Clarence Snyder, Raymond Wallace, Monte Jarrett, Pete Nordquist, Jimmy Tuff, Dudley Smith, Charlie Black, Bryan Wangoman, Tommy Overstreet.

Western. Pancha O'Brien, the beautiful and spirited daughter of an Irish ranch owner, is loved by two men, Sheriff Jack Webb, whom she loves, and outlaw Jim Dyke, whose attentions she repeatedly rebuffs. Jim and his men attack Pancha's ranch, burning it to the ground and killing her father. The outlaw carries her to his cabin, where Wan-o-mee, his jealous squaw, tries to stab the girl. Pancha explains that she does not love Jim and sends Wan-o-mee to find Sheriff Jack. Stalling for time, Pancha agrees to marry Jim, and the two set out for Cheyenne. Jack and his posse overtake them on the road, but Pancha has already stabbed Jim, and he falls dead at the sheriff's feet. To protect Pancha, Jack claims that he killed the outlaw and then proposes to her. *Abduction. Indians of North America. Outlaws. Sheriffs. Unrequited love. Arson. Chases. Cheyenne (WY). Irish Americans. Posses. Ranchers. Ranches. Self-defense. Self-sacrifice.*

Note: According to publicity, the entire production of this film was shot in Wyoming near Cody. Some sources list the length as five reels. William B. Laub, a cinematographer who worked in the Goldwyn photographic department, is credited in a news item as having assisted in the production of this film. He may have worked in a capacity other than assistant cameraman.
ETR 7 Dec 1918, p. 65. *MPN* 14 Dec 1918, p. 3606. *MPW* 7 Dec 1918, p. 1118. *MPW* 14 Dec 1918, p. 1253. *NYDM* 7 Dec 1918, p. 847. *NYT* 25 Nov 1918, p. 11. *Var* 29 Nov 1918, p. 41. *Wid's* 8 Dec 1918, p. 3.

HELL TO ETERNITY (Japanese Americans)

Atlantic Pictures Corp.; Allied Artists Pictures Corp. *Dist* Allied Artists Pictures Corp. Aug 1960; Prod: late Feb—late Apr 1960 [©Atlantic Pictures Corp.; 1 Aug 1960; LP16594]. Sd (Westrex Recording System); b&w. 11,852 or 12,600 or 12,859 ft. 132 min. PCA cert no. 19675.

Prod Irving H. Levin. *Prod exec* Harry L. Mandell. *Assoc prod* Lester A. Sansom. *Dir* Phil Karlson. *Asst dir* Clark Paylow. *Scr* Ted Sherdeman and Walter Roeber Schmidt. *Story* Gil Doud. *Dir of photog* Burnett Guffey. [*Gaffer* David Curtis]. *Spec eff* Augie Lohman. *Art dir* David Milton. *Film ed* George White and Roy V. Livingston. *Mus ed* Aubrey C. Lind. *Sd ed* Charles Schelling. *Set dec* Joseph Kish. *Ward* Roger J. Weinberg, Wesley Jefferies, Norah Sharpe and Charles Arrico. *Mus comp and cond* Leith Stevens. *Dance seq staged by* Roland Dupree. *Sd ed* Ralph E. Butler and John Bury, Jr. *Makeup* Bob Mark. *Prod mgr* Edward Morey, Jr. and Harrold A. Weinberger. *Scr supv* Sam J. Strangis. *Constr supv* James West. *Props* Ted Mossman and Max Frankel. *Tech adv* David Foos, Jr., Clement J. Stadler and Guy Gabaldon.

Cast: Jeffrey Hunter [(*Guy Gabaldon*)], David Janssen [([Sgt.] *Bill* [*Hazen*])], Vic Damone [([Cpl.] *Pete Lewis*)], Patricia Owens [(*Sheila* [*Lincoln*])], Richard Eyer [(*Guy, as a boy*)], John Larch [(*Capt. Schwabe*)], Bill Williams [(*Leonard*)], Michi Kobi [(*Sono*)], George Shibata [(*Kaz Une*)], Reiko Sato [(*Famika*)], Richard Gardner [(*Sullivan*)], Bob Okazaki [(*Papa Une*)], George Matsui [(*George, as a boy*)], Nicky Blair [(*Semperi*)], George Takei [(*George Une*)], Miiko Taka (*Ester*), Tsuru Aoki Hayakawa (*Mother Une*), Sessue Hayakawa (*General Matsui*), [Paul Togawa (*Freddy*)].

World War II, Drama. [*Print viewed*]. In depression-era Los Angeles, young Guy Gabaldon's widowed mother is taken to the hospital, and the boy is left to fend for himself. After learning about Guy's predicament, school basketball coach Kaz Une takes him to live with his own parents, and when Guy's mother dies, the family adopts him. To comfort Guy, mother Une tells him the old Japanese tale of the Peach Boy, whose love for his parents is as precious as a great treasure, whereupon Guy tearfully embraces her. Years later, as Guy talks to Ester, his foster brother George's girl friend, a young white man calls Guy a "Jap lover" and accuses him of consorting with the enemy. Later that day, the family is distressed to learn that the United States has declared war against Japan. George wants to enlist immediately, but Kaz, who had tried to join up the day before, tells him that Japanese Americans, suspected of being spies, are being rejected from military service. Soon afterward, Guy's family and Japanese friends are taken to relocation camps. While George's parents and brothers go willingly, eager to help their government in any way they can, Guy is unwilling to betray the people he loves and refuses to enlist. Kaz and George finally do join up, and while they are

fighting in Italy, Guy travels to Camp Manzanar in California to visit his parents. When mother Une claims to be proud of her "All-American" sons, Guy realizes that she wants him to enlist. Soon afterward, Guy joins the Marines and, while in training at Camp Pendleton, befriends Sgt. Bill Hazen and Cpl. Pete Lewis. Before facing active duty, the three men visit a Honolulu nightclub called the Hawaiian Village, where they meet Famika, a stripper, Sono, a barmaid, and Sheila Lincoln, a reporter. Nicknamed the "Iron Petticoat" by the soldiers who have unsuccessfully attempted to seduce her, Sheila fumes as the men, now drinking at Sono's apartment, watch Famika perform a striptease. Too much whiskey and an attraction to Guy lead Sheila to perform a strip act of her own, after which each couple finds a private spot for lovemaking. Later, the Marines land on a well-defended beach in Saipan, and although he experiences conflicting emotions, Guy soon grows accustomed to the need to "kill or be killed." Because he speaks Japanese, Guy is able to persuade many of the starving local people to surrender their arms and emerge from the caves in which they have taken refuge. When Bill is killed, however, Guy is transformed by rage and massacres injured and unarmed Japanese soldiers who try to surrender. A letter from his mother soon softens his hatred, and he is appalled when he sees unarmed civilians, frightened at the prospect of becoming prisoners, leaping off steep cliffs to escape capture. On a scouting mission, Guy and another Marine overhear Japanese General Matsui ordering his sick and starving troops to prepare for a sudden, last-ditch attack on the Americans. The two Marines manage to capture Matsui and steal the attack plans, but Guy's partner is killed trying to warn the American troops. While Guy holds the general at gunpoint, he decries the fact that the Japanese commander would send injured soldiers, women and children into battle to face certain death against superior American forces, and then reveals that he was reared by a Japanese family. In a lengthy, emotional speech to his forces, Matsui orders his people to surrender, and as hundreds of prisoners accompany Guy back to the Marine encampment, the shamed general commits hara-kiri. *Guy Gabaldon. Japanese Americans. Patriotism. Racism. World War II. Adoption. Athletic coaches. Bars. Battles. Camp Manzanar (CA). The Depression, 1929. Family life. Friendship. Hara-kiri. Honolulu (HI). Honor. Japanese Americans–Evacuation and relocation, 1942-1945. Language and languages. Mexican Americans. Revenge. Saipan. Seduction. Strip-tease. Suicide. United States. Marine Corps. War heroes. War victims.*

Note: The working titles of this film were *Beyond the Call* and *Beyond the Call of Duty*. The closing credits include the following written acknowledgement: "We thank the Department of Defense, especially the Marine Corps. and its officers and men of the Third Marine Division on Okinawa, for the cooperation extended during the filming of the battle sequences of this motion picture." This was Tsura Aoki's first American film in thirty-five years.

The film is based on the true experiences of Marine hero Pfc. Guy Gabaldon, who was officially credited with taking "more than 1,000" Japanese soldiers during the Battle of Saipan, for which the eighteen-year-old Gabaldon was awarded the Silver Star. Many of the events of the film mirror Gabaldon's life: In Los Angeles, after his mother was hospitalized, the Mexican American Gabaldon was taken into several nisei homes, where he was reared in a traditional Japanese fashion. At the age of sixteen, he attempted to enlist in the Army, but was refused because of a punctured eardrum. After the attack on Pearl Harbor, Gabaldon tried the Marines, and although he was slightly under size, he was accepted because of his fluency in Japanese and assigned to an intelligence unit. While on the island of Saipan, Gabaldon repeatedly went behind enemy lines, talking many Japanese into surrendering. At first, Gabaldon persuaded small groups of Japanese to surrender, and eventually, single-handedly took 800 prisoners, a feat that required him to kill thirty-four civilians.

On 20 Jun 1957, *DV* reported that the screen rights to Gabaldon's life story, which had been featured on the NBC television show "This Is Your Life" the evening before, had been purchased by Gramercy Pictures. A 26 Oct 1960 *Var* news item then announced that the short-lived American Broadcasting-Parent Theatres company, which had been headed by producer Irving H. Levin, originated the project and provided a major portion of the financing for it. Press information contained in the copyright record notes that the Marine Corps. staged battle scenes on Okinawa with several hundred veterans of the Japanese Imperial Army appearing as extras.

According to information contained in the MPAA/PCA Collection at the AMPAS Library, strong objections were made to the scene in which "Famika" and "Sheila" perform a striptease. An 11 Jan 1960 letter from a PCA official to Allied Artists demanded that the suggestion of an illicit sexual affair between "Guy" and "Sono" be removed. In Feb 1960, the official informed the company that an altered version of the scene was still unacceptable, and on 7 Jun 1960, shortly after production was completed, studio official Gordon S. White agreed to reduce considerably the length of the scene, removing various sexually explicit shots. On 14 Jun 1960, the scene was accepted, and the script approved.

According to *HR* production charts, the film's production began in late Feb

1960. In late Mar 1960, however, the production was apparently suspended for approximately a week, finishing up in early May 1960. A 19 Sep 1961 *DV* news item reported that Gabaldon made personal appearances in connection with free screenings of the film in provincial areas of Mexico. The speech delivered by Sessue Hayakawa's character is spoken in Japanese. The story of Momotaro, the Peach Boy, is one of the best known folktales in Japan. Its principal character exemplifies kindness, courage and strength.

AmCin Jul 1960, pp. 412-414, 434, 436-38. *Box* 8 Aug 1960. *DV* 29 Jul 1960, p. 3. *DV* 19 Sep 1961. *FD* 29 Jul 1960, p. 6. *HCN* 1 Sep 1960. *HR* 26 Feb 1960, p. 16. *HR* 29 Apr 1960, p. 12. *HR* 29 Jul 1960, p. 3. *LAEx* 1 Sep 1960. *LAMirror-News* 16 May 1960. *LAMirror-News* 1 Sep 1960. *LAT* 7 Aug 1960. *LAT* 1 Sep 1960. *MPHPD* 6 Aug 1960, p. 796. *NYT* 1 May 1960. *NYT* 13 Oct 1960, p. 41. *Time* 31 Oct 1960. *Var* 3 Aug 1960, p. 7. *Var* 26 Oct 1960.

HELL VALLEY see OUT OF THE CRIMSON FOG

HELL'S ALLEY see OUT OF THE CRIMSON FOG

HELL'S END (Irish Americans)
Triangle Film Corp. *Dist* Triangle Distributing Corp. 14 Jul **1918**. Si; b&w. 5 reels.

Dir J. W. McLaughlin. *Scen* Charles J. Wilson, Jr. *Story* Anna Steese Richardson. *Cam* Steve S. Norton.

Cast: William Desmond (*Jack Donovan*), Josie Sedgwick (*Mary Flynn*), Bull Durham (*Hank Dillon*), Dorothy Hagar (*Belle Burns*), Charles Dorian (*Jimmie Flynn*).

Drama. Flynn becomes a millionaire and moves his family out of the tough New York tenement known as "Hell's End." As the years go by, Mary Flynn and her brother Jimmie lose track of their childhood friend, Jack Donovan, but on a slumming expedition, Mary renews her acquaintance with Jack, now the leader of a notorious group of gangsters and crooked politicians. Their conversation arouses the jealousy of Belle Burns, who is infatuated with him. She incites a fight between Jack and Hank Dillon, who is jealous of Jack's power, and in the brawl, Jack is seriously injured. After his release from the hospital, he helps Mary with her Red Cross work, and the two fall in love. Jack defeats his rival in a fight and regains his prestige, but soon he abandons the gangsters and finds happiness in the girl he loves in working to better the conditions in Hell's End. *Criminals–Rehabilitation. Gangsters. Irish Americans. Political corruption. Slums. Social reform. Fights. Hospitals. Jealousy. Millionaires. New York City. Politicians. Red Cross. Tenement-houses.*

Note: One source lists A. Steve Richardson as the author of the story.

MPN 20 Jul 1918, p. 361. *MPN* 27 Jul 1918, p. 642. *MPW* 20 Jul 1918, p. 407, 458. *MPW* 27 Jul 1918, p. 588. *NYDM* 3 Aug 1918, p. 164. *Var* 19 Jul 1918, p. 36. *Wid's* 14 Jul 1918, p. 15.

HELL'S HALF ACRE (Chinese Americans, Hawaiians)
Republic Pictures Corp. *Dist* Republic Pictures Corp. 1 Jun **1954**; Prod: mid-Aug—mid-Sep 1953 [©Republic Pictures Corp.; 7 Jan 1954; LP3259]. Sd (RCA Sound System); b&w. 9 reels, 8,153 ft. 91 min. PCA cert no. 16718.

Pres Herbert J. Yates. *Assoc prod* John H. Auer. *Dir* John H. Auer. *Asst dir* Herb Mendelson. *Wrt* Steve Fisher. *Dir of photog* John L. Russell. *Optical eff* Consolidated Film Industries. *Film ed* Fred Allen. *Cost supv* Adele Palmer. *Mus* R. Dale Butts. *Sd* T. A. Carman and Howard Wilson. *Makeup supv* Bob Mark. *Hair stylist* Peggy Gray. *Tech adv* Don the Beachcomber.

Song(s): "Polynesian Rhapsody" and "Lani," words and music by Jack Pittman.

Cast: Wendell Corey (*Chet Chester, previously known as Randy Williams*), Evelyn Keyes (*Dona Williams*), Elsa Lanchester (*Lida O'Reilly*), Marie Windsor (*Rose*), Nancy Gates (*Sally Lee*), Leonard Strong (*Ippy*), Jesse White (*Tubby Otis*), Keye Luke (*Chief Dan*), Philip Ahn (*Roger Kong*), Robert Shield (*Frank Ulman*), Clair Weidenaar (*Jamison*), Robert Costa (*Slim Novak*), Robert M. Luck (*Harry*), Beverly K. Rivera (*Girl*), Tiger Joe Marsh (*George*), Sun Lowe (*Croupier*), Daniel T. Aoki (*Native*), Akoroa Fukunaga (*Filipino*), Renny K. Brooks, John Kahaleva (*Hawaiians*), Frank Mullaney (*Music store manager*), Jimmy Walker (*Morgue keeper*), Kaumakapili Choir, Martha Hohu.

Crime, Melodrama. [*Not viewed*]. Chet Chester, an ex-racketeer, is now a respected Honolulu nightclub owner, but is being blackmailed by Slim Novak, one of his former criminal associates. While Chet is receiving plaudits for a Polynesian rhapsody he has composed, his Chinese girl friend Sally Lee shoots and kills Novak in the nightclub's office. Chet convinces Sally that he must stand trial for the murder. A few weeks later, in Los Angeles, Dona Williams hears a recording of Chet's rhapsody and recognizes the final line of

the lyric as being the same as an inscription on a photograph which her newlywed husband, Randy Williams, a former bank robber, gave her a few days before he was reported missing in the attack on Pearl Harbor. Frank Ulman, Dona's current beau, tries to talk her out of flying to Honolulu when she discovers that the song's composer is awaiting trial on a murder charge. Dona believes that the song could only have been written by her husband, but Frank feels that the use of the poetic lyric is simply a coincidence. Dona goes to Honolulu and contacts the Chinese police chief, determined to find out if Chet could be the husband she lost ten years earlier. Lida O'Reilly, an eccentric female taxi driver, takes Dona on a sight-seeing tour and points out Chet's house, which is currently being occupied by Sally. When Dona calls on Sally, she is met by Roger Kong, another of Chet's former partners in the rackets syndicate, who informs her that Sally is not at home. Roger has just accidentally killed Sally during a quarrel over whether to use Chet's money for his legal defense. When Chet learns about Sally's death, he escapes while being taken to police headquarters to meet Dona. Chet hides out in Hell's Half Acre, Honolulu's sordid, underworld neighborhood, and Dona poses as a taxi dancer to try to locate him. When they finally meet, Dona discovers that Chet is indeed Randy. However, Chet convinces her that Randy Williams should remain officially dead for the sake of their son Randy, Jr., of whose existence he has just learned. After Chet finds out that Kong killed Sally, he deliberately gives his own life while using himself as bait to help the police to trap Kong. Dona then returns to Los Angeles to marry Frank and to help Randy, Jr. keep alive his belief that his father died in the attack on Pearl Harbor. *Chinese Americans. Criminals–Rehabilitation. Hawaiians. Honolulu (HI). Racketeers. Self-sacrifice. Airports. Blackmail. Eccentrics. Escapes. Impersonation and imposture. Missing persons, Assumed dead. Morgues. Mothers and sons. Murder. Music stores. Nightclubs. Police. Shootings. Slums. Songs. Taxi dancers. Taxicab drivers.*

Note: According to the *Var* review, Steve Fisher collaborated with Jack Pittman on "Polynesian Rhapsody." Reviews and studio publicity reported that the film was shot in Honolulu.

Box 13 Feb 1954. *DV* 5 Feb 1954, p. 3. *FD* 19 Feb 1954, p. 6. *HR* 5 Feb 1954. *MPD* 5 Feb 1954. *MPHPD* 13 Feb 1954, p. 2183. *NYT* 27 Feb 1954, p. 11. *Var* 10 Feb 1954, p. 6.

HELL'S KITCHEN see FOR THE LOVE OF MIKE

HEN WEN SEN NENG see SING YUN SIN NIAN

HER AMERICAN HUSBAND (Japanese Americans)
Triangle Film Corp. *Dist* Triangle Distributing Corp. 27 Jan **1918**. Si; b&w. 5 reels.

Dir E. Mason Hopper. *Scen* E. Magnus Ingleton. *Cam* Friend F. Baker. *Cost* J. S. Fishenden. *Casting* Arthur Hoyt.

Cast: Teddy Sampson (*Cherry Blossom*), Darrell Foss (*Herbert Franklyn, "Mr. Butterfly"*), Leota Lorraine (*Miriam Faversham*), Thomas Kurihara (*Tokimasa*), Misao Seki (*Yoshisada*), Jack Abbe (*Kato Nakamura*), W. A. Jeffries (*Mason*), Arthur Millet (*Abott*), Ludwig Lowry (*Jessop*), Kathleen Emerson (*Dolly Varden*).

Drama. Herbert Franklyn, the son of a wealthy imported goods dealer, refuses to curb his appetite for gaiety and women after his engagement, with the result that his fiancée, Miriam Faversham, breaks off their relationship. On the firm's annual trip to Japan, Herbert meets Cherry Blossom, whose father Tokimasa wishes her to marry a Westerner. Despite her love for Kato Nakamura, Cherry Blossom complies with her father's wishes and departs for New Rochelle with her new husband. Soon after their arrival, Herbert resumes his old habits, neglecting his lonely bride. Kato has a vision of Cherry Blossom's unhappiness and comes to America with Tokimasa, who strangles Herbert and later commits suicide. *Japanese. Japanese Americans. Marriage–Arranged. Murder. Neglected wives. Playboys. Americans in foreign countries. Importers. Japan. New Rochelle (NY). Strangling. Suicide. Visions.*

Note: This film was also known as *Mr. Butterfly*. Several scenes were filmed in the Japanese Gardens, San Diego, CA.

MPW 2 Feb 1918, p. 684, 722. *NYDM* 26 Jan 1918, pp. 19-20. *Var* 25 Jan 1918, p. 45. *Wid's* 24 Jan 1918, p. 898.

HER DEBT OF HONOR (Native Americans)
Columbia Pictures Corp. *Dist* Metro Pictures Corp. 24 Jan **1916** [©Metro Pictures Corp.; 25 Jan 1916; LP7499]. Si; b&w. 5 reels.

Dir William Nigh. *Scen* William Nigh.

Cast: Valli Valli (*Marian Delmar*), William Davidson (*John Hartfield*), William Nigh (*Olin Varcoe*), J. H. Goldsworthy

(*Crawford Granger*), Frank Bacon (*Doctor Glade*), Mrs. M. Brundage (*Mr. Varcoe*), Ilean Hume (*Niatana*), Frank Montgomery (*Kalatin*), David H. Thompson (*Pierre Leroux*), R. A. Bresee (*Old Wolf*), Jack Murray (*Swiftwind*).

Drama. After her architect father dies, Marian Delmar receives a monthly allowance from Varcoe, another architect, until his own death. Over the objections of John Hartfield, her sweetheart, Marian decides to repay Varcoe by nursing back to health his dissolute son Olin, who is dying from hard living. While staying with Olin, at his estate on the St. Lawrence River at the Canadian border, she discovers papers explaining that her father had been the brains behind Varcoe's architectural success. Marian realizes that the monthly payments had indicated Varcoe's thanks as well as his guilty conscience. After Olin seduces an Indian girl working in the house, it is revealed that Olin's own mother had been an Indian and that the Indians who live in huts on the estate are the last members of his mother's tribe. Sensing that his various illnesses are irreversible, Olin throws one last wild party, where he tries to rape Marian. John and one of his Indian friends rescue her and wound Olin, who crawls to one of the huts. The father of a girl he had seduced shoots him, and Olin dies in the arms of his mother's father. Marian and her sweetheart now make plans for their marriage. *Architects. Canadian-American border region. Debt. Dissipation. Indians of North America. Nursing back to health. Orphans. Allowances. Attempted rape. Guilt. Incurable diseases. Parties. Secret documents.*

Note: *MPW* 5 Feb 1916 calls the film *The Debt of Honor*. The film was copyrighted as *A Debt of Honor*. *Var* noted that the moral of film "would seem to be that if a white man has an affair with an Indian woman, the offspring of such an alliance is apt to be a degenerate of the first rank."

Motog 29 Jan 1916, p. 266. *MPN* 29 Jan 1916, p. 558. *MPW* 15 Jan 1916, p. 494. *MPW* 5 Feb 1916, p. 791, 848. *NYDM* 5 Feb 1916, p. 28. *Var* 4 Feb 1916, p. 25.

HER GOD *see* **THE RED WOMAN**

HER HALF BROTHER *see* **PALS OF THE WEST**

HER MOMENT (Romanian Americans)
Author's Photo-Plays, Inc. *Dist* General Film Co. Jul **1918** Si; b&w. 7 reels.
Dir Frank Beal. *Story and scen* Samuel H. London.
Cast: Anna Luther (*Katinka Veche*), William Garwood (*Jan Drakachu*), Alida Jones (*Minka*), Ann Schaeffer (*Jan's mother*), Frank Brownlee (*Victor Dravich*), Bert Hadley (*Boris*), J. L. Franck (*Father Benoni*), William A. Lowery (*Ulaf*), William Bytell (*Sherwin Matthews*), Leon Kent (*Sando Gryj*), Eugene Owen (*Warren McLeod*), Scott R. Beal (*Roy Clint*), Murdock McQuarrie (*Mr. Johnson*).

Drama. In a small Romanian village, Katinka Veche, a peasant girl, falls in love with Jan Drakachu, a bright young man who spends his days studying. Jan wins a scholarship to an American university, graduates and becomes a successful engineer, while Katinka, left behind in the village, is sold into slavery by her cruel and dissolute father. Her owner, Victor Dravich, takes her to his gambling house in Syria, where he beats her and forces her to become his mistress. When the house is raided, Dravich takes her with him on his travels around the world until they finally settle in a small Arizona mining camp. Katinka sees Jan there but is too ashamed to speak to him. Broken, she sends for her old tutor Boris, who comes to Arizona and kills Dravich but then is shot by the sheriff. Katinka follows Jan to New York, where she is arrested, but he locates her in a girls' reclamation home and marries her. *Child selling. Immigrants. Mistresses. Murder. Romania. Romanian Americans. Arizona. Battered women. Gambling houses. Mining towns. New York City. Peasantry. Police raids. Reformatories. Sheriffs. Students. Tutors and tutoring.*

Note: The working title of this film was *Who's to Blame?* It was copyrighted under the title *Why Blame Me?*, shown at a press screening in New York in Feb 1918, and advertised as available for state rights exchanges, but no evidence of its public exhibition at that time has been located. In Jul 1918, General Film Co. released the film under the title *Her Moment*. Some sources credit Robert Brownlee as "Victor Dravich." The film was condemned by the Pennsylvania State Board of Censors.

ETR 2 Feb 1918, p. 721. *ETR* 16 Feb 1918, p. 915. *ETR* 22 Jun 1918, p. 156. *ETR* 10 Aug 1918, p. 835. *ETR* 7 Sep 1918, p. 1159. *MPN* 27 Jul 1918, p. 645. *MPW* 20 Jul 1918, p. 301, 464. *MPW* 27 Jul 1918, p. 589. *NYDM* 16 Feb 1918, p. 18. *NYDM* 17 Aug 1918, p. 239. *Var* 8 Feb 1918, p. 40. *Var* 15 Feb 1918, p. 54. *Var* 16 Aug 1918, p. 37. *Wid's* 21 Jul 1918, p. 2.

HER OWN PEOPLE (Native Americans)
Pallas Pictures. *Dist* Paramount Pictures Corp. 8 Feb **1917** [©J. C. Ivers; 22 Jan 1917; LP10107]. Si; b&w. 5 reels.
Dir Scott Sidney. *Scen* Gardner Hunting. *Story* Julia Crawford Ivers. *Cam* James C. Van Trees.
Cast: Lenore Ulrich (*Alona*), Colin Chase (*Frank Colvin*), Howard Davies (*John Kemp*), Adelaide Woods (*Eleanor Dutton*), Jack Stark (*Jimmie Pope*), Gail Brooks (*Morning Star*), Joy Lewis (*Myra Agnew*), William Winter Jefferson (*Blinn Agnew*), Ada Lewis (*Mrs. Colvin*), Mary Mersch (*Katherine Colvin*), William Gettinger (*Polsa Kar*).

Drama. Alona is the daughter of John Kemp, a wealthy aristocrat, and the Indian wife whom he married after renouncing his own society, following an unfortunate love affair. When his daughter reaches adulthood, Kemp realizes that he must provide for her future, and so sends Alona to a fashionable Eastern boarding school where she is snubbed by the other girls. She returns home to her own people after the death of her father, and there meets prospector Frank Colvin, her old sweetheart, who asks her to marry him. Alona, suspicious after her experiences back East, returns to the city and decides to test Frank by purchasing his mine through an agent. Frank, now wealthy, finds Alona again and, as he is about to offer his love, is shocked to discover that the poor Indian maid has been transformed into an heiress. Alona accepts his proposal, and they embark upon a happy life together. *Cultural conflict. Indians of North America. Indians of North America–Mixed blood. Love tests. Ostracism. Racism. Boarding schools. Heiresses. Marriage–Mixed. Mines. Prospectors. Real estate agents.*

Note: The working title of the film was *The Conflict*.
ETR 17 Feb 1917, p. 784. *MPN* 24 Feb 1917, p.1252. *MPW* 17 Feb 1917, p. 1083. *MPW* 24 Feb 1917, p. 1209. *NYDM* 3 Feb 1917, p. 24. *NYDM* 17 Feb 1917, p. 26. *Wid's* 15 Feb 1917, p. 106.

HER ROMANCE *see* **SILKS AND SATINS**

HER SECOND MOTHER (Yiddish language)
Cinema Service Corp. *Dist* Cinema Service Corp. 8 Nov **1940**. Sd; b&w. 9 reels, 7,964 ft. 89 min. Yiddish language with English subtitles.
Dir Josef Seiden. *Asst dir* H. Rosen. *Story* I. Frankel. *Photog* Don Malkames and Charles Levine. *Settings* J. Allstadt. *Mus* Sholom Secunda. *Sd* M. Dichter and P. Jacobs.
Cast: ESTA SALZMAN (*Surele [Polakoff]*), Max Badin (*Moishe [Polakoff]*), Rose Greenfield (*Esther [Polakoff]*), Margaret Schoenfeld (*Bella [Polakoff]*), Jacob Zanger (*Shimen [Kupperman]*), Yetta Zwerling (*Bruchi*), Muni Serebroff (*Juno*), Seymour Rechtzeit (*Nathan [Field]*), Dave Lubritsky (*Ben [Grossman]*), Herman Rosen (*Molinofsky*), Isidor Frankel (*Doctor*).

Yiddish, Domestic, Melodrama. [*Print viewed*]. Surele Polakoff, a stenographer in the office of Molinofsky & Son, asks bookkeeper Ben Grossman, whom she accuses of philandering, to stop his romance with her sister Bella. At home, Bella's mother Esther asks her to give up Ben, whom she calls a loafer. Upset that Surele has spoken against Ben, Bella complains that Esther loves Surele more than her even though Surele is not really her daughter by birth. Esther, who in a moment of weakness has revealed the secret of Surele's birth to Bella, pleads with her not to tell Surele. Three days later, Surele, learning that $25,000 is missing from the office safe, suspects Ben and fears that Bella will be implicated in the money's disappearance. Later, Ben visits Bella and, after saying that he just inherited $25,000, gives her $15,000 to hide and tells her to plan on getting married the next day, after which they will go to South America. When Bella asks Ben about Surele's accusation of his philandering, Ben states that Surele flirted with him. Extremely upset, Bella tells Surele that she is not really Esther and her husband Moishe's daughter. Surele then questions Esther and Moishe, who reveal that Surele's mother died during childbirth at their farm and that her father, in the midst of deserting her, was killed in an automobile accident. Esther and Moishe subsequently took care of Surele. Deeply upset, Surele decides to go to her mother's grave and try to find out who her parents were. When district attorney Nathan Field questions Bella about Ben, she claims that the reason he came to the house was to see Surele. To protect her sister, Surele lies, and when the money, which Bella has hidden in Surele's suitcase, is found, she is arrested. Although Nathan is convinced of Surele's innocence, he cannot get her to change her story. Surele tells Esther and Moishe that she is happy to be able to repay them by sacrificing herself for their daughter. Nathan convinces

the judge to hold the hearing in his chambers, and during the proceedings, Moishe tells the story of Surele's birth. The judge, whose name is Juno, is deeply affected by the story. He remembers that he and his wife Florence got caught in a storm, and when she became sick, he stopped by a farmhouse. The doctor announced that Florence was about to give birth, but that he needed his instruments or her life would be in danger. Juno volunteered to go to the doctor's village to get the instruments, but the roads were flooded and his car turned over. After the accident, Juno remembered nothing. Moishe then recognizes him as Surele's father. Bella admits that she put the money in Surele's valise; however, to protect Ben, Bella contends that she stole the money herself, until Nathan proves that Ben is married and the father of a child. A few years later, Juno and Moishe play with their grandchild, the son of Nathan and Surele, who have married. Bella has now just become engaged to Harry, a decent man, and the Polakoffs are now a happy family. *Family relationships. Foster parents. Frame-ups. Jews. Missing persons, Assumed dead. Parentage. Self-sacrifice. Amnesia. Bookkeepers. Death in childbirth. Deception. District Attorneys. Embezzlement. Jails. Judges. Rainstorms. Stenographers.*

Note: The Yiddish title of this film is *Ir Tsveyte Mame.* No reviews were located for this film. According to censorship records, the film was to be released in New York on 8 Nov 1940. While a print of the film states that it was copyrighted in 1940 by Cinema Service Corp., no record of its registration has been located.

HER STORY (Russian Americans)
Samuelson Film Manufacturing Co. *Dist* Second National Pictures Corp.; State Rights. 1920? [©Second National Pictures Corp.; 30 Mar 1922; LP17707]. Si; b&w. 5 reels.
Prod G. B. Samuelson. *Dir* G. B. Samuelson and Allyn B. Carrick. *Scen* William B. Laub. *Story* Dion Titheradge.
Cast: Madge Titheradge (*Betty Ashlyn*), C. M. Hallard (*Ralph Ashlyn*), Campbell Gullan (*Oscar Kaplan*).
Society, Drama. Shocked by a newspaper account of an escaped convict being discovered in his wife Betty's room, steel magnate Ralph Ashlyn hears, at her request, the story of her past. Alone in Russia after her father, a ship captain, dies at sea, the young Betty marries Russian agent Oscar Kaplan and moves to New York with him. Soon Kaplan begins to treat Betty cruelly and abandons her after taking up a life of crime. Betty takes a job in a department store that leads her to employment as a governess for Ashlyn's little girl. She sorrowfully declines Ashlyn's proposals of marriage until she discovers that her marriage to Kaplan was a fraud, after which she is finally persuaded to marry Ashlyn and enjoys five years of happiness. On a visit to Sing Sing prison, Betty recognizes Kaplan, now a convict. Later that weekend, Kaplan escapes and attacks Betty in her room at the country home at which she is a guest. Saved by the police, who chase Kaplan away, Betty rushes to her husband to explain. As Betty finishes her story, Ashlyn takes her in his arms. *Convicts. Governesses. Marriage–Fake. Reputation. Russia. Russian Americans. Attempted rape. Department stores. New York City. Prison escapes. Salesclerks. Sea captains. Sing Sing Prison (NY). Steel magnates.*

Note: British producer Samuelson made this film in America in the first half of 1920. It was released in England in mid-1920 but was probably not shown publicly in America until late 1921 or early 1922, when it was distributed by Second National. A mid-production trade article stated that Samuelson was directing the film, but a 1921 review lists Carrick as director, and several modern sources call Alexander Butler the director. A modern source states that the film was shot at Universal City. One contemporary trade article states that the film was adapted from a novel of the same name, but no evidence of the novel's existence has been discovered.
Bio 1 Jul 1920, p. 43. *MPN* 14 Feb 1920, p. 1722. *MPW* 4 Mar 1922, p. 85. *Var* 1 Sep 1921, p. 42.

HER WEDDING NIGHT (*foreign version*) see **SU NOCHE DE BODAS**

THE HERITAGE OF THE DESERT (Native Americans)
Famous Players-Lasky Corp. *Dist* Paramount Pictures. 20 Jan or 27 Jan 1924 [©Famous Players-Lasky Corp.; 30 Jan 1924; LP19874]. Si; b&w with col sequences (Technicolor). 6 reels, 5,785 ft.
Pres Adolph Zukor and Jesse L. Lasky. *Dir* Irvin Willat. *Adpt* Albert Shelby Le Vino. *Photog* Charles E. Schoenbaum.
Source: Based on the novel *The Heritage of the Desert* by Zane Grey (New York, 1910).
Cast: Bebe Daniels (*Mescal*), Ernest Torrence (*August Naab*), Noah Beery (*Holderness*), Lloyd Hughes (*Jack Hare*), Ann Schaeffer (*Mrs. Naab*), James Mason (*Snap Naab*), Richard R. Neill (*Dene*), Leonard Clapham (*Dave Naab*).

Western. Pioneer rancher August Naab finds easterner Jack Hare in the desert and takes him home. There, Mescal, Naab's Spanish-Indian ward, cares for and falls in love with Jack though she is betrothed to Naab's wayward son, Snap. To avoid marrying Snap, Mescal flees to the desert and there is captured by desert pirate Mal Holderness, a ruthless man who is seeking to control the water rights of the surrounding area by buying or seizing the local ranches. Because Naab has refused to sell, Holderness begins a feud, taking Mescal prisoner and killing Snap, the prospective bridegroom, who has followed Mescal into the desert. As the leader of the law-abiding community, Naab, with a group of sympathetic Indians, burns down the neighboring town serving as a hideout for Holderness and his gang. Mescal is rescued and returned to Jack. *Deserts. Indians of North America–Mixed blood. Indians of North America. Ranchers. Water-rights.*
FD 27 Jan 1924. *MPW* 2 Feb 1924. *NYT* 24 Jan 1924, p. 24.

THE HERO see **SATURDAY'S HERO**

HEROES IN BLUE (Irish Americans)
Duke Worne Productions. *Dist* Rayart Pictures. Nov 1927. Si; b&w. 5 reels, 4,936-5,076 ft.
Pres W. Ray Johnston. *Dir* Duke Worne. *Scen* George Pyper. *Story* Leota Morgan. *Photog* Walter Griffin.
Cast: John Bowers, Sally Rand, Gareth Hughes, Ann Brody, Lydia Yeamans Titus, George Bunny, Barney Gilmore.
Melodrama. "Around the Dugans and the Kellys is built this meller. Sally Rand of the 'Smoky' Dugan clan is opposite John Bowers, a young cop whose sire is a veteran flat-foot. The Dugan's stepson is a pyromaniac responsible for the series of incendiary fires and simultaneous robberies. A young member of the Kelly tribe, on the detective squad, is killed by the Dugan bad boy, as is Kelly pere. The double murder is avenged by her own father, 'Smoky' Dugan, who dies with the hoodlum in the punch conflagration of the footage." (*Var* 8 Feb 1928, p. 24.). *Firemen. Irish Americans. Murder. Police. Pyromania. Revenge.*
Var 8 Feb 1928, p. 24.

HEROES WITHOUT UNIFORMS see **ACTION IN THE NORTH ATLANTIC**

UNE HEURE PRÈS DE TOI (French language)
Paramount Publix Corp.; An Ernst Lubitsch Production. *Dist* Paramount Publix Corp. 1932; Paris opening: 1 Jun 1932. Sd; b&w. 78 min. French language.
Dir Ernst Lubitsch. *French script by* Léopold Marchand.
Song(s): French lyrics by André Hornez.
Source: Based on the play *Nur ein Traum (Only a Dream)* by Lothar Schmidt (Munich, 1909).
Cast: Maurice Chevalier (*Dr. Bertier*), Jeanette MacDonald (*Colette Bertier*), Lily Damita (*Mitzi Olivier*), Pierre Etchepare (*Adolphe*), Ernest Ferny (*Professor Kurt Olivier*), André Cheron (*Police commissioner*).
Romantic comedy, with songs. [*Not viewed*]. [The following plot summary is based on the English-language version of this film, *One Hour with You*; character names refer to that version. For further information regarding the English-language version, please see the note below and the entry for *One Hour with You* in the *AFI Catalog of Feature Films, 1931-40*.] In Paris in the spring, Dr. Andre Bertier and Colette, his wife of three years, live in a state of connubial bliss until Colette's flirtatious school chum, Mitzi Olivier, visits, and Andre is tempted to have an affair. Mitzi schemes to get Andre alone by feigning illness, and Colette urges him to visit Mitzi, believing Andre is reluctant because he doesn't like Colette's friend. At the Oliviers' apartment, Mitzi tries to seduce Andre, and Mitzi's husband, the professor, who has hired Detective Henri Pornier to find evidence of Mitzi's affairs, walks in on the doctor and his patient on the couch. When the Bertiers hold a dinner party, Andre switches place cards with Mlle. Marcel in order to avoid sitting next to Mitzi. Colette, believing Andre is having an affair with the mademoiselle, tells Mitzi, who spends the evening with Andre under the guise of saving Colette's marriage. When Andre meets Mitzi on the veranda, she unties his tie, and he is caught by Colette when the mademoiselle later reties it for him. After the party, Colette refuses to believe Andre's story about the mademoiselle, and he leaves to meet Mitzi in a waiting cab. Adolph, Andre's best friend, who has been pleading for Colette's affections all evening, then appears in her parlor and kisses

her before she orders him out. The next morning, Mitzi leaves for her mother's place in Lausanne, and Colette tries to guess who Mitzi's lover is. Next, Olivier confronts Andre with a minute-by-minute account of Andre's rendezvous with his wife, including nearly two hours—from 2:53 a.m. to 4:44—during which Mitzi and Andre were alone. When Andre receives a summons to appear as a witness at the Oliviers' divorce trial, he confesses his affair to Colette, and she tells him their marriage is over. Adolph then arrives, and although Andre believes his friend incapable of seducing Colette, she, with the help of Andre's amused promptings, forces a confession out of Adolph, making the husband and wife's infidelities equal. She then tells Andre, "An eye for an eye...an Adolph for a Mitzi." After they ask the rhetorical question, "What would you do?" the couple embraces. *Divorce. Infidelity. Love. Love affairs. Marriage. Romance. Sex. Deception. Detectives. Disease. False accusations. Friendship. Paris (France). Parties. Physicians. Spring.*

Note: An English-language version of Lothar Schmidt's play opened in New York on 29 Oct 1913. This film was a musical remake of Ernst Lubitsch's second American film, *The Marriage Circle* (also based on Lothar Schmidt's play *Only a Dream*), which Lubitsch directed for Warner Bros. in 1924, starring Florence Vidor and Monte Blue (see *AFI Catalog of Feature Films, 1921-30*, F2.3481). This French-language version of *One Hour with You* was shot simultaneously with the English-language version. For information on the English-language version, which also was directed by Lubitsch and also starred Maurice Chevalier and Jeanette MacDonald, please see the entry for that film in the *AFI Catalog of Feature Films, 1931-40*, F3.3257.

DI HEYLIGE SHVUE *see* **THE HOLY OATH**

HI, BEAUTIFUL (African Americans)

Universal Pictures Co., Inc. *Dist* Universal Pictures Co., Inc. 18 Dec 1944; Prod: 1 Jun—late Jun 1944 [©Universal Pictures Co., Inc.; 20 Nov 1944; LP12978]. Sd (Western Electric Recording); b&w. 5,771 ft. 64 min. PCA cert no. 10352.

[*Exec prod* Edward Dodds]. *Assoc prod* Dick Irving Hyland. *Dir* Leslie Goodwins. [*Asst dir* Seward Webb]. *Dial dir* Stacy Keach. *Scr* Dick Irving Hyland. *Orig story* Eleanore Griffin and William Rankin. *Dir of photog* Paul Ivano. *Art dir* John B. Goodman and Alexander Golitzen. *Film ed* Edward Curtiss. *Set dec* Russell A. Gausman and Victor A. Gangelin. *Gowns* Vera West. *Mus score and dir* Frank Skinner. *Songs cond by* H. J. Salter. *Dir of sd* Bernard B. Brown. [*Sd*] *tech* Robert Pritchard.

Song(s): "I Love to Whistle," words and music by Harold Adamson and Jimmy McHugh; "Singin' in the Rain" and "Everybody Sing," words by Arthur Freed, music by Nacio Herb Brown; "Tiger Rag," words by Harry DeCosta, music by the Original Dixieland Jazz Band; "Don't Sweetheart Me," words and music by Charles Tobias and Cliff Friend; "The Gal I Left at Home," composers undetermined.

Cast: MARTHA O'DRISCOLL (*Patty Callahan*), NOAH BEERY, JR. (*Jeff* [*Peters*]), Hattie McDaniel (*Millie*), Walter Catlett ([*Gerald*] *Bisbee*), Tim Ryan (*Babcock*), Florence Lake (*Mrs. Bisbee*), Grady Sutton (*Attendant*), Lou Lubin (*Husband* [*Louis*]), Virginia Sale (*Wife*), Tom Dugan (*Bus driver*), Dick Elliott (*Passenger*), James Dodd (*Soldier specialty*), [Barbara Perry (*Specialty dance*)], [Ida Moore (*Landlady*)], [Jimmy Aubrey (*Drunk*)], [Lester Dorr (*Conductor*)], [Charles Hall (*Milkman*)], [Julie Gibson (*Girl*)], [Gerald Perreau (*Boy*)], [Ruth Lee (*Mother*)], [Edna May Wonacott (*Young girl*)], [Gladys Blake (*Operator*)], [Jack Rice, Herbert Rawlinson, Forbes Murray, John Hamilton (*Board members*)], [Gerald Hamer, Alec Harford (*Bearded twins*)], [Max Wagner, Fred Steele (*Sailors*)], [Tom Brown (*Roger*)], [Patsy Patterson, Eva Lee Kuney (*Children*)], [Bea Roberts (*Hostess*)], [Arlene Harris (*Wacky woman*)], [Alice Draper], [Charles Sherlock].

Homefront, Comedy, with songs. [*Print viewed*]. Patty Callahan's routine life as the caretaker of a model home is disrupted when she discovers private Jeff Peters of the U.S. Army sleeping in the model's master bedroom. Jeff, unable to find a hotel room for his furlough, decides to move into the model, much to the chagrin of Patty and her maid, Millie. After Jeff rescues Patty from the amorous attentions of Babcock, her boss, Patty agrees to spend her Saturday afternoon with the soldier. When their bus driver quits in a dispute with another passenger, Patty takes the wheel and drives the bus to a nearby beach amusement park. Later, Patty and Jeff learn about a radio contest for which a $5,000 grand prize is being offered for the photograph of "the happiest G.I. couple." While Jeff wants to enter the contest, Patty feels that it would cheapen their relationship. Millie, however, is unaware of Patty's sentiments and sends in a

photograph of the couple. Jeff and Patty's photograph wins the contest, but the sponsors are given the mistaken impression that the couple is married. Feeling that she has been betrayed by Jeff, Patty orders him to leave, which he does before Millie has a chance to explain matters. As radio sponsor Gerald Bisbee has telephoned to announce that he and his wife plan to deliver the $5,000 check to the "happy" couple that night, Millie scrambles to reunite the couple. First, Millie finds Jeff at the local U.S.O. and tells him the truth, including the fact that she sent a note along with the photograph stating that Jeff and Patty have three children and a dog. Jeff then returns to the model home and convinces Patty to pretend to be his wife for a visiting "couple." With the help of some neighborhood children, Jeff and Patty successfully continue the charade for the Bisbees, until Babcock arrives and exposes them. Afraid of adverse publicity, Bisbee agrees to give the couple the prize money, and Babcock agrees to sell them the model home if they are married by the next day. Millie then tells Patty the truth about sending in the photograph, after which Jeff proposes marriage and Patty accepts. *Caretakers. Contests. Love. Model houses. Soldiers. United States. Army. African Americans. Amusement parks. Beaches. Bus drivers. Cats. Children. Dogs. Employer-employee relations. Harmonicas. Maids. Photographs. Proposals (Marital). Radio sponsors. Real estate agents. Stuttering. Telegrams. United Service Organizations.*

Note: The working title of this film was *Be It Ever So Humble*. According to the opening onscreen credits, the title of Eleanore Griffin and William Rankin's original story was "Be It Ever So Humble." Universal previously filmed Griffin and Rankin's original story in 1937 as *Love in a Bungalow*, starring Nan Grey and Kent Taylor and directed by Raymond B. McCarey (see *AFI Catalog of Feature Films, 1931-40*, F3.2598).

Box 30 Dec 1944. *DV* 17 Nov 1944, p. 3. *FD* 18 Dec 1944, p. 8. *HR* 1 Jun 1944, p. 6. *HR* 9 Jun 1944, p. 27. *HR* 16 Jun 1944, p. 10. *HR* 17 Nov 1944, p. 3. *MPHPD* 7 Oct 1944, p. 2131. *MPHPD* 25 Nov 1944, p. 2194. *Var* 29 Nov 1944, p. 18.

HI DE HO (African Americans)

All American News, Inc. *Dist* State Rights. May 1947; New York opening: 9 May 1947. Sd (RCA Sound System); b&w. 6,885 ft. 72 or 77 min.

Prod E. M. Glucksman. *Dir* Josh Binney. *Asst dir* Thomas Darby. *Orig story and scr* Hal Seeger. *Dir of photog* Don Malkames. *Cam* George Stoetzel, Sydney Zucker and Lester Lang. *Art dir* Frank Namczy. *Film ed* Louis Hess. *Cost* Eaves Costume Co. *Mus arr* Buster Harding. *Dance dir* Addison Carey. *Sd eng* Nelson Minnerly. *Makeup artist* Rudolph G. Liszt.

Song(s): "Don't Falter at the Altar," words and music by Cab Calloway, Hal Seeger and Buster Harding; "Hi De Ho Man," words and music by Cab Calloway and Jack Palmer; "We, the Cats Shall Hep Ya," words and music by Cab Calloway, Buster Harding and Jack Palmer; "Hey Now, Hey Now!" and "I Got a Gal Named Nettie," words and music by Cab Calloway and Elton Hill; "St. James Infirmary," words and music by Joe Primrose; "Open the Door, Richard," words by John Mason and Dan Howell, music by Jack McVea and Frank Clark; "Minnie's a Hepcat Now," "A Rainy Sunday," "Dawntime" and "Little Old Lady from Baltimore," composers undetermined.

Cast: CAB CALLOWAY AND HIS ORCHESTRA, Ida James (*Nettie*), Jeni Le Gon (*Minnie*), William Campbell (*Sparks*), Virginia Girvin (*His* [*Sparks's*] *fat friend*), George Wiltshire (*Boss Mason*), James Dunmore (*Mo, the Mouse*), Augustus Smith (*Preacher*), Edgar Martin (*Owner of Jive Club*), Leonard Rogers (*Ralph*), David Bethea (*Owner of Brass Hat*), Shepard Roberts (*Police sergeant*), Frederick Johnson (*Head waiter*), Peters Sisters, Miller Bros. & Lois.

African American, Show business, Variety, Drama. [*Viewed print incomplete*]. Singer Cab Calloway finds himself in trouble with his jealous sweetheart Minnie when she accuses him of having fallen for his new manager, Nettie. Minnie vows to kill Cab if he runs away with another woman, but Cab silences her rage by striking her. Later, at the Brass Hat Club, while Cab auditions for a spot in a show, Ralph, a booking agent and the owner of the club discuss the shiftlessness of their new competitor, Boss Mason. Ralph tells the owner that Mason is a tough racketeer who plans to open a New York-style club across the street from the Brass Hat. Minnie, meanwhile, plans to take revenge on Cab by enlisting the help of Mason to have him murdered. Mason likes the idea of cutting down his competition, but first tries to lure Cab away from the Brass Hat by pressuring him to sign a lucrative contract with him. Although Cab refuses the offer, Mason gives him half an hour to change his mind. While eavesdropping on a conversation between Nettie and Cab, Minnie realizes that his

relationship with his manager has been purely professional all along, and she immediately tries to warn Cab that his life is in danger. Cab, however, rushes off to his next performance before Minnie is able to warn him. Soon after the half-hour deadline expires, Mo, the Mouse, Mason's henchman, is sent to kill Cab, but Cab manages to foil the attempt by grabbing Mo's gun and forcing him out of his hotel room. Moments later, a second attempt is made on Cab's life by Mason, who has been hiding in the hallway. Mason fires his gun at Cab, but the bullet strikes Minnie as she tries to protect Cab. Mason is killed in his ensuing gunfight with the police, and Minnie later dies in Cab's arms. Time passes, and Cab takes the stage to sing a love song about his new romance with Nettie. At the end of the show, Cab announces that he is marrying Nettie, and a reverend appears on stage to perform an impromptu wedding ceremony in rhyming verse. *African Americans. Attempted murder. False accusations. Jazz music. Jealousy. Nightclubs. Singers. Auditions. Business rivals. Dancers. Death and dying. Gunfights. Hired killers. Jails. Racketeers. Reverends. Self-sacrifice. Talent agents. Theatrical managers. Threats. Weddings.*

Note: The viewed print of this film contained a copyright statement by All American News, Inc., but no record of such a copyright has been found. Although the *Exb* and *Var* reviews list "Dusty" Fletcher in the cast, he did not appear in the incomplete print viewed. *Var* notes that Fletcher performed his famous "Open the Door, Richard" routine in the film.

Exb 28 May 1947. *Var* 21 May 1947, p. 15.

HI-YO SILVER (Native Americans)

Republic Pictures Corp. *Dist* Republic Pictures Corp. 10 Apr **1940**; Prod: 1938 [©Republic Pictures Corp.; 10 Apr 1940; LP9575]. Sd (RCA High Fidelity Sound System); b&w. 7 reels. 69 min.

Assoc prod Sol C. Siegel. *Supv* Robert Beche. *Dir* William Witney and John English. *Asst dir* Louis Germonprez. *Orig scr* George Worthing Yates, Barry Shipman, Franklyn Adreon, Ronald Davidson and Lois Eby. *Photog* William Nobles. *Film ed* Helene Turner and Edward Todd. *Mus dir* Alberto Colombo. *Prod mgr* Al Wilson. *Unit mgr* Mack D'Agostino.

Source: Based on the radio series *The Lone Ranger* created by Fran Striker and George Trendle (30 Jan 1933—27 May 1955).

Cast: Lee Powell (*The Lone Ranger also known as Allen King*), Hi-Yo Silver (*Silver*), Chief Thundercloud (*Tonto*), Herman Brix (*Bert Rogers*), Lynne Roberts (*Joan Blanchard*), Stanley Andrews (*Jeffries, previously known as Smith*), George Cleveland (*Blanchard*), William Farnum (*Father McKim*), Hal Taliaferro (*Bob Stuart*), Lane Chandler (*Dick Forrest*), George Letz (*Jim Clark*), John Merton (*Kester*), Sammy McKim (*Sammy*), Tom London (*Felton*), Raphael Bennett (*Taggart*), Maston Williams (*Snead*), Frank McGlynn, Sr. (*Lincoln*), Raymond Hatton.

Historical, Western. [*Not viewed*]. As the Civil War comes to a close, the state of Texas is overrun with gangs of marauders, who take the law into their own hands to terrorize the honest ranchers and cattlemen. The leader of the most powerful of these gangs is an outlaw named Smith, who kills a special investigator from Washington named Jeffries and then assumes his identity in order to extort illegally high taxes from the helpless ranchers. Organizing a large, lawless band, Smith rules the territory until President Abraham Lincoln hears of the situation and appoints Blanchard as administrator of Texas. Blanchard and his daughter Joan soon arrive in Pecos, but after Joan's life is threatened, Blanchard signs his authority over to Smith. The Lone Ranger, the sole survivor of the disbanded Texas Rangers, whose real name is Allen King, learns of this injustice and reorganizes the Rangers with a nucleus of four trustworthy men and Tonto, his Indian friend. During their first skirmish with Smith's band, one of the Rangers is killed and buried in their cave hideout. Blanchard and Joan, now prisoners of Smith send word through the mission priest, Father McKim, that Smith is planning to steal a shipment of silver that has been collected as taxes. The Rangers, however, steal the silver before Smith can act and secret it in their mountain hideout. For their deed, the Rangers are captured and imprisoned at Fort Bentley, where they are to be tried. Knowing that the silver is not safe in the mountains, the Lone Ranger, with the assistance of Tonto, escapes from prison, returns the silver to the authorities and then helps the other Rangers to escape. Meanwhile, Smith learns that Joan and her father have discovered his true identity and plans to send them away. Joan sends word to the Lone Ranger of their danger, who rescues them and takes them to the cave, where they are attacked by Smith and his men. Riding for help, the Lone

Ranger gathers the ranchers together and after a bloody battle, captures the entire band of outlaws. After the fight, only one Ranger is left alive, the Lone Ranger, who reluctantly declines the honor of reorganizing the Rangers so that he may ride alone to aid those that need assistance. *Impersonation and imposture. Masks. Outlaws. Texas. Texas Rangers. United States–History–Reconstruction, 1865-1898. Fathers and daughters. Forts. Hideouts. Indians of North America. Jailbreaks. Abraham Lincoln. Mountains. Murder. Priests. Ranchers. Rescues. Silver. Thieves.*

Note: *The Lone Ranger* radio series, created by George Trendle and Fran Striker, was first broadcast on WXYZ in Detroit, MI, on 30 Jan 1933. It was then picked up by the Mutual Broadcast system. The film *Hi-Yo Silver* was a condensation of the fifteen chapter Republic serial *The Lone Ranger*, which was released in Mar 1938. According to the *Var* review of the feature, Raymond Hatton and "an unbilled youngster" were added to the cast of the feature and shown "In scenes whose purpose is to narrate the flashback around which the major story unfolds," however, Hatton is not otherwise billed in reviews or copyright records. Modern sources note that the "youngster" was played by Dickie Jones. On 25 Jan 1939, Republic released another fifteen part serial, *The Lone Ranger Rides Again*, which starred Robert Livingston as the Lone Ranger. On 15 Sep 1949 the Warner Bros. television series starring Clayton Moore as the Lone Ranger and Jay Silverheels as Tonto was first broadcast. That series continued until 1961. In 1956, Moore and Silverheels starred in the film *The Lone Ranger* for Warner Bros., and in 1958, the two starred in *The Lone Ranger and the Lost City of Gold*, a United Artists release. William A. Fraker directed *The Legend of the Lone Ranger* for Universal in 1981, starring Klinton Spilsbury in the title tole.

FD 16 Apr 1940, p. 7. *HR* 4 Jan 1939, p. 8. *HR* 10 Jan 1939, p. 7. *MPD* 16 Apr 1940, p. 4. *MPH* 20 Apr 1940, p. 35. *Var* 17 Apr 1940, p. 16.

HIAWATHA (Native Americans)

Frank E. Moore. *Dist* State Rights. Mar **1913**? [©F. E. Moore; 2 Apr 1913; LP586]. Si; b&w. 4 reels.

Pres The Indian Players. *Cam* Victor Milner.

Source: Based on the poem "The Song of Hiawatha" by Henry Wadsworth Longfellow (Boston, 1855).

Cast: Soon-goot (*Minnehaha*).

Drama. Years after Gitche Manito proclaims that a prophet will come to unite the Indian warriors, Hiawatha is born to Wenonah and the fickle Mudjekeewis. After Wenonah's death, her mother Nakomis adopts the child, announcing that he is the long-awaited prophet. Iagoo teaches Hiawatha to master the bow and arrow, and after he has slain his first deer, Hiawatha visits the arrow-maker across the lake. Smitten by the old man's daughter Minnehaha, Hiawatha soon marries her, and they live together happily until famine strikes the village. Following Minnehaha's death and burial, Iagoo announces the arrival of white men and tall ships. Hiawatha then greets the pale-faced Black Robe and proclaims that the real prophet has finally arrived. As the priest begins to preach, Hiawatha disappears into the sunset. *Christianity. Indians of North America. Prophets. Adoption. Famines. Hunters. Priests.*

Note: The film was copyrighted under the title *Hiawatha; the Indian Passion Play*. It featured a cast of 150 American Indians from New York, Canada and the Dakotas, and it was filmed in New York State and near Lake Superior. Before producing the film, F. E. Moore directed an open-air production of *Hiawatha* at parks and private estates throughout the United States. Other films based on Longfellow's poem include a 1903 British production, shot in Canada; a 1909 film produced by Imp; a two-reel Kinemacolor production, made in 1913; and the 1952 Monogram production (see below).

MPN 1 Mar 1913, p. 15. *MPW* 1 Mar 1913, ad following p. 906. *MPW* 8 Mar 1913, p. 962, 980. *NYDM* 2 Apr 1913, p. 27. *NYDM* 9 Apr 1913, p. 26, 31.

HIAWATHA (Native Americans, Chippewa, Ojibway, Illinois, Dakota)

Monogram Pictures Corp. *Dist* Allied Artists Productions, Inc. 28 Dec **1952**; Prod: Jun 1952 [©Monogram Pictures Corp.; 28 Dec 1952; LP2212]. Sd (Western Electric Sound System); col (Processing by Cinecolor Laboratories). 8 reels, 7,166 ft. 78-80 min. PCA cert no. 16068.

Prod Walter Mirisch. *Assoc prod* Richard Heermance. *Dir* Kurt Neumann. *Asst dir* Edward Morey, Jr. [*Dial dir* Clarence Marks]. *Scr* Arthur Strawn and Dan Ullman. *Photog* Harry Neumann. *Art dir* David Milton. *Film ed* Walter Hannemann. *Mus ed* Eve Newman. *Set cont* Ilona Vas. *Mus* Marlin Skiles. *Orch* Lloyd Basham. *Rec* Charles Cooper. *Sd* Sound Services, Inc. [*Makeup* Lou Phillipi]. *Prod mgr* Allen K. Wood.

Source: Based on the poem "The Song of Hiawatha" by Henry Wadsworth Longfellow (Boston, 1855).

Cast: Vincent Edwards [(*Hiawatha*)], Yvette Dugay [(*Minnehaha*)], Keith Larsen [(*Pau Puk Keewis*)], Gene Iglesias [(*Chibiabos*)],

Armando Silvestre [(*Kwasind*)], Michael Tolan [(*Neyadji*)], Ian MacDonald [(*Megissogwon*)], Katherine Emery [(*Nokomis*)], Morris Ankrum [(*Iagoo*)], Stephen Chase [(*Lakku*)], Stuart Randall [(*Mudjekeewis*)], [Richard Bartlett (*Chunung*)], [Michael Granger (*Ajawac*)], [Robert Bice (*Wabeek*)], [Gene Peterson (*Hikon*)], [Henry Corden (*Ottobang*)], [Bert Topper, Bernie Gozier (*Indian warriors*)], [Lou Ventre (*Drummer*)], [Gary Lee Jackson (*Child*)], [Belle Mitchell (*Mother*)], [Judy Walsh (*Bena*)], [Chabon Jadi (*Dancer*)], [Eula Morgan (*Mother of Chibiabos*)], [John Parrish], [Steve Conte], [Paul Stevens].

Drama. [*Print viewed*]. As Hiawatha and other members of the Ojibway tribe hunt for deer, they come across a hunting party of Illinois in their territory. Hiawatha removes his bow and arrow to talk to them in peace and the Illinois group leader begins to do the same, but Pau Puk Keewis, a hot-headed Ojibway, shoots the Illinois group leader, precipitating a battle. After the Illinois are run off, Pau Puk argues that he saved Hiawatha's life. At a village meeting, Pau Puk contends that the Illinois and Dakotah are planning a war. He is chosen to lead a scouting party to Illinois territory, but he objects to being accompanied by Hiawatha, saying he is not experienced or pure in Ojibway blood. Megissogwon, the chief, sends Hiawatha, who is puzzled by Pau Puk's remark, to scout Dakotah territory. Before he leaves, Hiawatha's grandmother Nokomis reveals that his father was a stranger from another tribe, whom his mother Winona chose to marry. After living together happily, Hiawatha's father left Winona while she was pregnant to return temporarily to his own people because his father, the chief, died. Winona died of grief while waiting for his return. Hiawatha now decides to kill his father, but Nokomis warns him to forget about vengeance. On the scouting trip, Hiawatha is attacked by a bear and rescued by Lakku, an arrow maker of the Dakotah. Lakku's beautiful daughter Minnehaha, obeying her father, nurses Hiawatha and they fall in love, despite her initial suspicions that he is a spy. Lakku tells Hiawatha that the Dakotah have no plans for war and gives him arrows as a gift for his chief, and he promises Minnehaha he will return before the leaves fall. On his way home, Hiawatha sees a war party of Illinois heading to Ojibway territory to avenge killings committed by Pau Puk. After killing an Illinois scout, Hiawatha warns his people, and the Ojibway repel the Illinois attack. Soon after, Hiawatha is welcomed to a place among the chieftains. When Hiawatha relates that he intends to marry a Dakotah maiden, Pau Puk, now also a tribal leader, encourages the council to ban him. Hiawatha vows to marry Minnehaha even if they have to live alone without a tribe, but the council gives their consent. Hiawatha returns for his bride and they build a lodge together in Dakotah territory, then return to Hiawatha's village for the marriage feast. The feast is disrupted when the body of Hiawatha's dear friend Kwasind is brought in. Pau Puk charges that he was killed by the Dakotahs, but Hiawatha refuses to blame the entire Dakotah Nation. Minnehaha is shunned by the Ojibway women, but she convinces Nokomis of her love for Hiawatha. As winter approaches, Pau Puk blames the poor corn harvest on the fact that Kwasind's murder has not been avenged. He encourages his people to raid the Dakotah buffalo and dried meat stores, but Minnehaha protests that her people would give the Ojibways food if they knew it was needed. Hiawatha proposes they send his friend Chibiabos to arrange a meeting between the two peoples, and Megissogwon agrees. On the way, however, Chibiabos is killed by Pau Puk with an arrow made by Lakku. The Ojibway now prepare for war, and when Hiawatha still does not given his consent, Nokomis reveals that the Dakotah chief, Mudjekeewis, is his father. Hiawatha then goes to kill his father. Brandishing a knife, Hiawatha awakens Mudjekeewis and they fight. The chief gets hold of the knife and prepares to kill Hiawatha, when Hiawatha reveal his identity and accuses him of killing his mother. Mudjekeewis explains that when he was made chief, the council would not permit him to return. He resolved to find a way, but gave up after learning of Winona's death. Mudjekeewis denies that his people killed Kwasind or Chibiabos and promises to give the Ojibway food. Hiawatha now realizes that Pau Puk killed his friends. As Pau Puk leads the Ojibway to attack, Hiawatha and the Dakotah approach unarmed. To prove Pau Puk's guilt, Hiawatha asks Pau Puk for the arrows he brought back from Lakku, and after Pau Puk says they were lost while hunting, they fight. Hiawatha kills Pau Puk with a knife and peace is achieved. *Chippewa Indians. Dakota Indians. Marriage–Mixed. Murder. Pacifism and pacifists. Romance. Tribal life. Bow and arrow. Fathers and sons.*

Grandmothers. Hunting. Illinois Indians. Ostracism. Parricide. Tribal chiefs.

Note: Lines from Longfellow's poem are read at the end of the film. The film contains only Indian characters, yet *Christian Science Monitor* noted concerning the film's actors, "The only Indians are in extra roles and battle scenes," and the Los Angeles Catholic newspaper *The Tidings* complained that the film "presents Hollywood Boulevard Indians, who, despite marked physical and historical attributes, never pass for redskin braves." *LAEx* criticized the stilted dialogue and commented that "makeup for the virtually non-Indian cast is applied too heavily and is obvious in the color film." *LAT* praised the depiction of tribal rituals "said to be authentic, including burial ceremonies, wedding and harvest feasts and war dances, all with their fascinating chants." *Cue* contended that the film "hasn't much to do with Longfellow," while *LAT* noted that while the film "does keep thoroughly in the spirit and feeling of the original," Longfellow's poem "doesn't have all the exciting doings of the picture play." This was Vince Edwards' first major film role. According to *Christian Science Monitor*, producer Walter Mirisch prepared the original outline for the film. Location shooting was done at Bass Lake in California.

In Sep 1950, according to *Time*, Monogram announced that the project was being shelved, as the pacifism advocated by the character "Hiawatha" was "too close, for current U.S. taste, to the Communist 'peace' line." Monogram president Steve Broidy, quoted in *LADN*, stated, "Because of the tremendous influence that the motion picture industry exerts internationally, producers are being extremely cautious in preventing any subject matter to (sic) reach the screen which might possibly be interpreted as Communistic propaganda to (sic) even the slightest degree. The *Hiawatha* screenplay, written by a scenarist (Arthur Strawn) whose Americanism is unquestioned, still left us with the feeling that Communistic elements might conceivably misinterpret the theme of our picture, despite its American origin, and that is why we have postponed its production." In Jan 1951, the film was put back on the production roster. At that time, president Broidy, as quoted in *Var*, explained that "the avalanche of editorial comment which greeted our announcement convinced us unquestionably that the American public would not be dupes for any Communist line, and that our *Hiawatha* picture could only serve the highest ends of education and entertainment." For information concerning other films based on Longfellow's poem, see the above entry for the 1913 version.

Box 13 Dec 1952. *Christian Science Monitor* 8 Jul 1952. *Cue* 27 Feb 1953. *DV* 8 Dec 1952, p.3. *Exh* 17 Dec 1952, p. 3430 *FD* 15 Dec 1952, p.6. *Har* 13 Dec 1952, p. 199. *HCN* 12 Feb 1953. *HCN* 17 Feb 1953. *HR* 29 May 1952, p. 13. *HR* 13 Jun 1952, p. 14. *HR* 8 Dec 1952, p.3. *HR* 23 Dec 1952. *LADN* 21 Sep 1950. *LAEx* 12 Feb 1953. *LAT* 15 Dec 1952. *LAT* 12 Feb 1953. *MPHPD* 29 Dec 1952, p. 1645. *NYT* 26 Dec 1952, p. 20. *The Tidings* 13 Feb 1953. *Time* 25 Sep 1950. *Var* 4 Jan 1951. *Var* 10 Dec 1952, p.6.

HIDDEN CHARMS (Irish Americans)
Argus Motion Picture Co. *Dist* State Rights; Film Market, Inc. **1920.** Si; b&w. 5 reels.
Dir Samuel Brodsky. *Story and scen* Robert McLaughlin. *Cam* Ernest Reynolds.
Source: Inspired by the poem "Believe Me If All Those Endearing Love Charms" by Thomas Moore in *Irish Melodies*, music arranged by Sir John Stevenson (London, 1807).
Cast: Daniel Kelly (*Daniel Manning*), Mrs. Charles Willard (*Margaret Manning*), Florence Dixon (*Mary Manning*), William Mortimer (*Judge Burke*), Robert Adams (*Jerry Burke*), Cecil Owens (*James Lacey*), George Fox (*Ryan, the gardener*).
Drama. Influenced by American politician James Lacey, Daniel and Margaret Manning forsake Dublin for the United States, disregarding the protests of their daughter Mary who is forced to leave her sweetheart Jerry Burke behind. Under Lacey's patronage, the Manning Contracting Company flourishes until the politician demands Mary's hand in marriage. Mary refuses his offer, and soon after, Jerry arrives from Ireland. In retaliation, the politician ruins Manning, and in order to save her family, Mary agrees to the marriage. The engagement brings a startling turn of events, because Mary, who knows that Lacey is attracted by physical charms only, becomes plainer in appearance. After an accident disfigures her face, Lacey foresakes his fiancée, thus freeing Mary to wed Jerry. However, the accident was all a ruse and Mary appears on her wedding day as beautiful as ever. *Immigrants. Irish Americans. Patronage. Political. Transformation. Accidents. Contractors. Disfiguration. Dublin (Ireland). Politicians.*
Note: This film was shot in Cleveland, OH and had a special premiere there on 7 Dec 1919. Although news items suggest that the production was completed and ready for distribution in Jan 1920, its general release date has not been determined. Some scenes for this film were shot at the estate of W. G. Marshall in Shaker Heights, Cleveland and inside the home of Horace Andrews. The offices of the *Cleveland Plain Dealer* were also used as a setting.
ETR 27 Dec 1919, p. 423. *ETR* 31 Jan 1920, p. 911. *MPN* 20 Mar 1920, p. 2727. *MPN* 1 May 1920, p. 3865.

THE HIDDEN CHILDREN (Native Americans, Iroquois, Mohegan)
Yorke Film Corp.; A Metro Wonderplay. *Dist* Metro Pictures Corp. 26 Mar **1917** [©Yorke Film Corp.; 28 Mar 1917; LP10469]. Si; b&w. 5 reels.

Dir Oscar C. Apfel. *Scen* Oscar C. Apfel. *Cam* Antonio Gaudio.
Source: Based on the novel *The Hidden Children* by Robert W. Chambers (New York, 1914).
Cast: Harold Lockwood (*Evan Loskiel*), May Allison (*Lois de Contrecoeur*), Lillian West (*Jeanne de Contrecoeur*), Henry Herbert (*Mayaro*), George MacDaniel (*Amochol*), Lester Cuneo (*Lieut. Boyd*), A. B. Ellis (*Calvert*), Lillian Hayward (*Mrs. Rannock*), Howard Davies (*General Sullivan*), Daniel Davies (*Hiatowoc*), Clara Lucas (*Marie Loskiel*), A. Allardt (*Capt. Jean de Contrecoeur*), Charles Cummings (*Guy Johnson*).
Historical, Drama. To save her son Evan from the St. Regis Indians, a dying Marie Loskiel, gives her little boy to English officer Guy Johnson who, with the help of Mayaro, Chief of the Mohicans, raises the boy. Similarly, Lois Contrecoeur becomes a "hidden child" when her mother Jeanne, held captive by the Indians, sends her daughter to a colonist named Calvert in order to prevent the child's sacrifice. Each year, her mother sends Lois a little pair of moccasins, and when she reaches adulthood, the girl becomes determined to locate her mother. Learning that her mother is in the village of Catherines-town in Iroquois territory, Lois follows Morgan's riflemen on their mission into the territory, hoping that they will blaze a trail to her mother. On her journey, Lois meets Evan Loskiel, who has become the chief scout for the division. Evan falls in love with Lois and eventually wins her confidence. They reach Catherines-town just in time to witness the execution of the White Sorceress, Jeanne de Contrecoeur, for interpreting ill fortune. Evan and Mayaro intervene and rescue Jeanne, finally reuniting mother and daughter. *Foundlings. Great Britain. Army. Iroquois Indians. Mothers and daughters. United States–History– Colonial period, ca. 1600-1775. Colonies. Executions. Missing persons. Mohegan Indians. Officers (Military). Rescues. Scouts (Frontier). Seers.*
ETR 14 Apr 1917, p. 1321. *Motog* 21 Apr 1917, p. 846. *MPN* 14 Apr 1917, p. 2365. *MPW* 10 Mar 1917, 1594. *MPW* 24 Mar 1917, p. 1854 (ad insert). *MPW* 31 Mar 1917, p. 2166. *MPW* 14 Apr 1917, p. 285. *NYDM* 7 Apr 1917, p. 27. *Var* 6 Apr 1917, p. 25. *Wid's* 5 Apr 1917, p. 222.

HIDDEN PEARLS (Hawaiians)

Jesse L Lasky Feature Play Co. *Dist* Famous Players-Lasky Corp.; Paramount Pictures. 18 Feb **1918** [©Jesse L. Lasky Feature Play Co., Inc.; 4 Feb 1918; LP12023]. Si; b&w. 5 reels.
Pres Jesse L. Lasky. *Dir* George H. Melford. *Asst dir* Claude Mitchell. *Story and scen* Beulah Marie Dix. *Cam* Paul Perry.
Cast: Sessue Hayakawa (*Tom Garvin*), Margaret Loomis (*Tahona*), Florence Vidor (*Enid Benton*), Theodore Roberts (*John Garvin*), James Cruze (*Koro Leon*), Noah Beery (*Teariki*), Clarence Geldart (*Capt. A. Todd*), Jack Holt (*Robert Garvin*), Gustav von Seyffertitz (*Senator Joseph Benton*), Henry F. Woodward (*Ensign Brooks*), John Burton.
Drama. The son of an American pearl trader and a Hawaiian island princess, knows nothing about life on his mother's island, having been reared and educated in America. He and Enid Benton are engaged, but when word comes that he has lost his family fortune, she informs him that she will not marry a poor man. In Honolulu, Tom's uncle, John Garvin, tells him that there is a rich store of pearls hidden on his mother's island, and the young man, now the island's rightful king, sails there immediately, where he is warmly greeted by the natives. The beautiful Tahona falls in love with Tom and shows him where the pearls are hidden. He escapes from the angry islanders with the pearls, but after his return to Honolulu, Enid's cold manner and his own conscience effect a change in him, and he soon catches a steamer back to the island. He and Tahona wed and rule the islanders as king and queen. *Hawaii. Hawaiians. Pearls. Poverty. Robbery. Tribal life. Guilt. Half-castes. Honolulu (HI). Royalty. Steamboats.*
Note: Many of the scenes were filmed in Hawaii. The Paramount press book credits John Burton with the role of Capt. Todd and lists Charles H. Geldert as Senator Benton.
MPN 23 Feb 1918, p. 1181. *MPW* 16 Feb 1918, p. 1003. *MPW* 23 Feb 1918, p. 1141. *NYDM* 16 Feb 1918, p. 18. *Wid's* 7 Feb 1918, pp. 930-31.

HIDDEN VALLEY (Native Americans)

Monogram Pictures Corp.; A Trem Carr Production. *Dist* Monogram Pictures Corp. 10 Oct **1932** [©Monogram Pictures Corp.; 15 Oct 1932; LP3385]. Sd (Balsley and Phillips); b&w. 6 reels.
Dir Robert N. Bradbury. *Story and adpt* Wellyn Totman. *Photog* Archie Stout. *Lighting eff* Edward Cox. *Settings* Ernest R. Hickson. *Ed* Carl Pierson. *Recordist* David Stoner. *Prod mgr* Paul Malvern.

Cast: BOB STEELE [(*Bob Harding*)], Gertie Messinger [(*Joyce Lanners*)], Francis McDonald [(*Frank Gavin*)], Ray Hallor [(*Jimmie*)], John Elliott [(*Judge*)], Arthur Miller [(*Sheriff Dave Bristow*)], V. L. Barnes [(*McCord*)], [George Hayes, Joe de la Cruz, Dick Dickinson (*Henchmen*)], [Captain Verner L. Smith (*Vern Smith, blimp pilot*)].
Western. [*Print viewed*]. In New Mexico, ranch foreman Bob Harding and Professor Anthony Woodridge are abandoned by their Indian guide while searching for a hidden valley, once home to an ancient civilization. The professor is shot and killed and the treasure map is stolen by unknown assailants, but an aged prospector believes Bob is the murderer and brings him back to town to stand trial. A jury finds him guilty, but Bob manages to escape from the courtroom, telling them the real murderer will have the map. Bob hides with his former employer Joyce Lanners, unaware that her naïve brother, Jimmie, was a member of the gang that killed Woodridge. Frank Gavin, leader of the gang, gives Jimmie the map to frame him and tells Joyce that Jimmie is the murderer. Bob emerges, fights with Gavin and then escapes again. The sheriff receives reports from various states which claim they have captured Bob, but Joyce convinces him of Bob's innocence and enlists the help of Vern Smith, pilot of the Goodyear Blimp, to fly over the desert and locate Bob. In the meantime, after having wandered the desert, Bob finds water and steals a horse, while Jimmy, having located the hidden valley, is captured by hostile Indians. Joyce and Smith find Bob, who climbs a ladder into the blimp and urges Smith to continue the search for the valley. Gavin and his gang find the valley and hide from the Indians while they perform a ceremony over Jimmie. Having seen the situation from above, Bob parachutes from the blimp and rescues Jimmie, who promises to confess although he did not actually kill Woodridge. Gavin and his gang shoot it out with Bob and Jimmie, who ride away from them and the attacking Indians and manage to climb aboard the blimp to safety. *False arrests. Indians of North America. Murder. Rescues. Airplanes. Brothers and sisters. Buried treasure. Deserts. Frame-ups. Maps. New Mexico. Professors. Prospectors. Sheriffs. Skydivers. Trials.*
Note: According to copyright records, Goodyear Rubber Co. loaned the blimp to Monogram, and it was flown by Captain Verner L. Smith. Copyright records also indicate that this film was shot on location near Lone Pine, CA. A modern source includes Tom London in the cast.
VarB 21 Oct 1932.

HIGH NOON (1949) *see* HOME OF THE BRAVE

HIGH NOON (Latino)

Stanley Kramer Productions, Inc. *Dist* United Artists Corp. 30 Jul **1952**; New York opening: 24 Jul 1952; Prod: 5 Sep–mid-Oct 1951 at Motion Picture Center [©Stanley Kramer Productions, Inc.; 30 Aug 1952; LP1846]. Sd (Western Electric Recording); b&w. 84-85 or 87 min. Passed by the National Board of Review. PCA cert no. 15653.
Dir Fred Zinnemann. *Asst dir* Emmett Emerson. *Scr* Carl Foreman. *Dir of photog* Floyd Crosby. *Prod des* Rudolph Sternad. *Art dir* Ben Hayne. *Ed supv* Harry Gerstad. *Film ed* Elmo Williams. *Mus ed* George Emick. *Set dec* Murray Waite. *Men's ward* Joe King. *Ladies' ward* Ann Peck. *Mus comp and dir* Dimitri Tiomkin. *Sd eng* Jean Speak. *Magnetic rec by* Sound Services, Inc. *Makeup* Gustaf Norin. *Hair stylist* Louise Miehle. *Prod supv* Clem Beauchamp. *Unit mgr* Percy Ikerd. *Head grip* Morris Rosen. *Scr clerk* Sam Freedle.
Song(s): "High Noon," music by Dimitri Tiomkin, lyrics by Ned Washington, sung by Tex Ritter.
Source: Based on the short story "The Tin Star" by John W. Cunningham in *Collier's* (6 Dec 1947).
Cast: GARY COOPER [(*Will Kane*)], Thomas Mitchell [(*Jonas Henderson*)], Lloyd Bridges [(*Harvey Pell*)], Katy Jurado [(*Helen Ramirez*)], Grace Kelly [(*Amy Kane*)], Otto Kruger [(*Judge Percy Mettrick*)], Lon Chaney [(*Martin Howe*)], Ian MacDonald [(*Frank Miller*)], Eve McVeagh [(*Mildred Fuller*)], Morgan Farley [(*Minister*)], Harry Shannon [(*Cooper*)], Lee Van Cleef [(*Jack Colby*)], Robert Wilke [(*James Pierce*)], Sheb Wooley [(*Ben Miller*)], [Tom London (*Sam*)], [Ted Stanhope (*Station master*)], [Larry Blake (*Gillis*)], [William Phillips (*Barber*)], [Jeanne Blackford (*Mrs. Henderson*)], [James Millican (*Baker*)], [Cliff Clark (*Weaver*)], [Ralph Reed (*Johnny*)], [William Newell (*Jimmy*)], [Lucien Prival (*Bartender*)], [Guy Beach (*Fred*)], [Howland Chamberlin (*Hotel clerk*)], [Virginia Christine (*Mrs. Simpson*)], [Virginia Farmer (*Mrs. Fletcher*)], [Jack Elam (*Charlie*)], [Paul Dubov

(*Scott*)], [Harry Harvey (*Coy*)], [Tim Graham (*Sawyer*)], [Nolan Leary (*Lewis*)], [Tom Greenway (*Ezra*)], [Dick Elliott (*Kibbee*)], [John Doucette (*Trumbull*)].

Suspense, Western. [*Print viewed*]. At 10:30 on a quiet morning in 1870, three outlaws ride into the western town of Hadleyville just as its marshal, Will Kane, is being married to a pretty Quaker named Amy Fowler. To please Amy, Will resigns his post immediately after the ceremony, but he is troubled because the new marshal has not arrived to take his place. Suddenly the station master rushes in with the terrible news that Frank Miller, a wild outlaw whom Will had arrested for murder five years earlier, recently received a pardon and is due to arrive in Hadleyville on the noon train. Three outlaws, Jack Colby, Ben Miller, and James Pierce, have ridden to the station and are awaiting Miller's arrival. Alarmed, the wedding guests urge Will and Amy to leave town immediately, but after several moments on the road, Will turns the wagon around and heads back. "I expect he'll come looking for me," Will replies when Amy asks for an explanation. Will's young wife begs him to leave with her, and when he protests that he has never run from anyone, she threatens to leave on the train whether or not he is with her. Will hurriedly begins to make plans for the town's defense, and he is surprised when Judge Percy Mettrick, who had sentenced Miller to be hanged, packs his belongings and flees. Will is relieved to see Harvey Pell, his deputy, still in town, but Harvey, angry that an outsider was hired to replace the retiring marshal, agrees to stay only if Will promises to support his bid for the post. Will refuses, whereupon Harvey removes his guns and walks out. Will visits his old flame, businesswoman Helen Ramirez, who had formerly been Miller's mistress. Will warns Helen about Frank, and she admits that she has sold her store and plans to depart on the noon train. In the saloon, men who enjoyed the rowdy times when Frank and his henchmen controlled the town celebrate his imminent return and refuse Will's request for help. Will then visits the home of his friend, Sam Fuller, but as Sam listens from the next room, his wife tells Will that he is not at home. Next, Will interrupts the church service to ask for deputies. Although several of the townspeople proclaim that it is Will who has made their town safe and decent, many of them also argue that Miller's impending arrival is not their problem. Finally, Mayor Jonas Henderson declares that a gunfight would hurt the town's image and that Will should have left when he had the chance. Stunned, Will leaves the church and asks his mentor, Martin Howe, for help. Howe, once the marshal himself, has become cynical, however, and after Will exits his home, he mumbles, "It's all for nothing, Will." Harvey, now drunk, tries to force Will to leave town, but Will refuses, and the two men fight until the marshal knocks his former deputy unconscious. As noon approaches, Amy visits Helen, who assures her that there is no longer anything between herself and Will. She also reproaches the young wife for not defending her husband, but softens after Amy reveals that both her father and brother were killed in a gunfight. In Will's office, the only citizen who had willingly pinned on a deputy's badge now backs out and goes home, leaving the marshal utterly alone. Will writes his last will and testament, then enters the deserted street as Amy and Helen drive a wagon toward the train station. The train arrives, and as Miller disembarks, the two women get on board. Miller straps on his gun, and the four outlaws walk toward the center of town, where Will awaits them. When one of the outlaws breaks a window, Will is able to duck inside a building and shoot him. Hearing the shot, Amy gets off the train and runs back to town. Will kills another of his attackers and takes cover in the livery stable, which the two remaining outlaws set on fire. As the frightened horses charge out, Will leaps on one and makes his escape, but falls after being shot in the arm. Amy shoots one of the gunmen in the back before he can shoot Will, but is captured by Miller, who uses her as a hostage. In response to Miller's threats, Will faces him in the street, but Amy pushes the outlaw, giving Will the chance to shoot him dead. Amy and Will embrace, and the townspeople rush into the street. Disgusted by the cowardice of his former friends, Will tosses his tin star in the dirt at their feet, then leaves with Amy. *Courage. Disillusionment. Loyalty. Marshals. Outlaws. Revenge. Wives. Churches. Clocks. Deputies. Duty. Fistfights. Friendship. Gunfights. Hotel clerks. Hypocrisy. Judges. Marriage. Mayors. Mexican Americans. Pacifism and pacifists. Quakers. Saloons. Small town life. Train stations.*

Note: *NYT* articles from spring 1949 indicate that producer Stanley Kramer's company Screen Plays Corp. was to produce the film and that Mark Robson, who had directed earlier Kramer pictures, might direct it. According to a 12 Mar 1949 *LAT* news item, Kirk Douglas and Lola Albright were originally set to star in the film. Modern sources note that John Wayne, Charlton Heston, Marlon Brando, Montgomery Clift and Gregory Peck were all considered to play "Will Kane" before Gary Cooper was signed for the role.

According to a 10 Jan 1953 *HCN* article, actors James Brown, Roberta Haynes and John Daheim, all of whom are listed on *HR* production charts, shot scenes for the film that were deleted before the final release. In the article, Brown describes the deleted scenes: "They were to be intercuts all through the picture, the idea being that Cooper says he knows he can count on Toby (his other deputy) if he gets there in time. The cuts show me taking my time with fights and drinking beer at a stage coach 'stop' with Roberta. In the scene she lets me know that if I stay, the time won't be wasted as far as our romance is concerned." A studio plot synopsis contained in the MPAA/PCA collection at the AMPAS Library lists Brown's character as "Toby," Daheim's character as "Peterson," and Haynes's character as "a seductive Mexican girl." In a modern interview, screenwriter Carl Foreman stated that the scenes with "Toby" were shot at the end of production, as insurance in case the film seemed too claustrophobic. The entire picture as released takes place only in the town of "Hadleyville." [According to a modern source, the extra sequences were deleted to help strengthen the film's use of "real time," in which the length of the story and the length of the film are approximately the same. After the picture's release, many reviewers praised its effective employment of real time.] A 4 Sep 1951 *HR* news item includes Marilee Phelps in the cast, but her participation in the completed film has not been confirmed. *HR* production charts note that the film was shot at the Motion Picture Center and on location at Sonora, CA. In a modern interview, Kramer and director Fred Zinnemann stated that they originally intended to photograph the film in color, but after some color sequences where shot, they switched to black and white for artistic reasons. Lee Van Cleef made his screen debut in the picture.

Many modern sources assert that *High Noon*'s plot and characters were a reflection of Foreman's experiences with the House Un-American Activities Committee and his subsequent blacklisting in the Hollywood community. The film, which garnered excellent reviews and was listed as a "box-office champion" by *MPH*, received Academy Award nominations for Best Film, Best Director and Best Screenplay. It won Oscars for Best Actor (Cooper), Best Song, Best Scoring of a Dramatic or Comedy Picture and Best Film Editing. Other awards included Golden Globes for Best Actor in a Drama (Cooper), Best Supporting Actress (Jurado) and Best Black-and-White Cinematography; inclusion on the National Board of Review's list of the ten best films of the year; Best Film and Best Direction awards from the New York Film Critics; and the Best-Written American Drama from the Writer's Guild of America. The film's ballad, "High Noon," was a huge hit both for Tex Ritter, whose singing is heard throughout the picture, and for Frankie Laine. In 1980, CBS televised *High Noon, Part II: The Return of Will Kane*, a made-for-television sequel that was directed by Jerry Jameson and starred Lee Majors in the title role.

Box 10 May 1952. *DV* 30 Apr 1952, p. 3, 7. *Exh* 7 May 1952, p. 3291. *FD* 30 Apr 1952, p. 6. *Har* 3 May 1952, p. 70. *HCN* 10 Jan 1953. *HR* 6 Jul 1948, p. 9. *HR* 12 Apr 1949, p. 2. *HR* 4 Sep 1951, p. 8. *HR* 5 Sep 1951, p. 8. *HR* 7 Sep 1951, p. 16. *HR* 12 Oct 1951, p. 14. *HR* 15 Oct 1951, p. 4. *HR* 30 Apr 1952, p. 4. *LAT* 12 Mar 1949. *MPHPD* 3 May 1952, p. 1349. *NYT* 10 Apr 1949. *NYT* 25 Jul 1952, p. 14. *NYT* 3 Aug 1952. *Var* 30 Apr 1952, p. 6.

HIGH PRESSURE (*foreign version*) *see* **LE BLUFFEUR**

THE HIGHGRADER *see* **FIGHING FOR GOLD**

EL HIJO DEL DESIERTO *see* **LA LEY DEL HAREM**

LOS HIJOS MANDAN (Spanish language)
Cobian Productions, Inc. *Dist* Twentieth Century-Fox Film Corp. 1939; San Juan, Puerto Rico opening: 4 Sep 1939; Los Angeles opening: 30 Apr 1940; Prod: Jan—Feb 1939 at the General Service Studios. Sd; b&w. 6,949 ft. 77 min. PCA cert no. 5133. Spanish language.

Prod Rafael Ramos Cobián. *Asst prod* Jack Boland. *Dir* Gabriel Soria. *Scr* Blanca de Castejón. *Story* Blanca de Castejón, Tommy A'Hearne and F. Maury Grossman. *Mus* Nilo Menéndez. *Mus cond* Elías Breeskin.

Source: Based on the play *El caudal de los hijos* by José López Pinillos (Madrid, 1921).

Cast: Blanca de Castejón, Fernando Soler, Arturo de Córdova, Julián Soler, Carmen Mora, Emilia Leovalli, Carlos Villarías, José Peña "Pepet", Rudy Cobián, Paul Ellis.

Drama. [*Not viewed*]. At the close of the nineteenth century, Francisca, the daughter of a provincial gentleman in Valencia, falls in love with Miguel, a young sculptor. When Miguel leaves for Paris to complete his studies, the lovers promise to wait for each other. During Miguel's absence, however, the Duke of Montesino calls on Francisca's father and asks for her hand in marriage. Her father, pressed for money because of gambling debts, agrees to the match. After Francisca and the Duke are married, they go to live in Madrid, where Francisca does her best to survive a loveless marriage. She gives birth to a son, and when the boy is five-years-old, Miguel returns from Paris and insists that Francisca run away with him. Although she resists him at first, she becomes overwhelmed by his pleas and agrees

to run away with him the following night after a party. Learning of the plot between Francisca and Miguel, the Duke reminds his wife of her duties as Duchess and mother, causing her to give up Miguel. Twenty years later, their son Alfonso leaves home to study at Oxford. While on vacation in Paris, he falls in love with Yvonne, a cabaret singer, marries her and brings her home to Madrid. The Duke is outraged and orders them out of the house, but Francisca insists that Yvonne be given a chance. A son is born to the young couple, and Yvonne begins to resent what she views as her mother-in-law's meddling. Deciding to run away, Yvonne sends a note to her former sweetheart. Learning of the plot, Francisca tells Yvonne her own story and convinces her to accept her responsibilities. As Francisca finishes her story, Yvonne's former lovers bursts into the room and insists that she leave with him. When Yvonne refuses, he pulls a gun and fires, but Francisca throws herself in front of the bullet, dying to preserve the Montesino family heritage. *Fathers and daughters. Fathers and sons. Honor. Marriage–Arranged. Mothers and sons. Self-sacrifice. Daughters-in-law. Gambling. Grandmothers. Nobility. Singers.*

Note: The running time listed above was calculated from footage found in NYSA records. This was Rafael Ramos Cobián's only Spanish-language picture to be released by Twentieth Century-Fox. Another item in *HR* adds that Cesar Romero was to have played the lead in this picture. An unidentified contemporary source in the AMPAS file on the film notes that the picture was financed by J. Cheever Cowdin, the head of Standard Capital Co. Some sources list the possible participation of Rafael Banquells.

HR 4 Nov 1938, p. 5. *HR* 19 Nov 1938, p. 3. *HR* 9 Jan 1939, p. 2. *HR* 11 Jan 1939, p. 7.

HILLS OF OLD WYOMING (Native Americans)

Harry Sherman Productions, Inc. *Dist* Paramount Pictures, Inc. 16 Apr **1937**; Prod: early Feb—early Mar 1937 at General Service Studios [©Paramount Pictures, Inc.; 16 Apr 1937; LP7083]. Sd (Western Electric); b&w. 8 reels. 78 min. Passed by the National Board of Review. PCA cert no. 3204.

Series: Hopalong Cassidy.

[*Pres* ADOLPH ZUKOR]. *Dir* Nate Watt. *Asst dir* D. M. Abrahams. *Scr and dial* Maurice Geraghty. *Photog* Archie Stout. *Spec eff* Mel Wolf. *Art dir* Lewis Rachmil. [*Ed* Robert Warwick]. *Ward* Al Kennedy. *Sd* Earl Sitar. *Prod mgr* Harry Knight.

Song(s): "Hills of Old Wyoming," music and lyrics by Leo Robin and Ralph Rainger.

Source: Based on the novel *The Round-Up* by Clarence E. Mulford (New York, 1933).

Cast: William Boyd (*Hopalong Cassidy*), George Hayes (*Windy*), Stephen Morris (*Andrews*), Russell Hayden ([*Mesquite*] *Lucky Jenkins*), Gail Sheridan (*Alice Hutchins*), John Beach (*Saunders*), Clara Kimball Young (*Ma Hutchins*), Earl Hodgins (*Thompson*), Steve Clemente (*Lone Eagle*), Chief Big Tree (*Himself*), George Chesboro (*Peterson*), Paul Gustine (*Daniels*), Leo McMahon (*Steve*), John Powers (*The cook*).

Western. [*Print viewed*]. Hopalong Cassidy, owner of the Bar Three ranch in Wyoming, and his neighboring ranchers around an Indian reservation, are suffering from cattle losses due to rustlers. Indians are suspected to be the culprits, but after several encounters with Andrews, the agent in charge of the reservation, Hoppy and his friends Windy and Lucky Jenkins suspect Andrews. Andrews, with the help of his Indian cohort Lone Eagle, frames Hoppy, but he evades arrest. Lone Eagle is found dead, and Andrews hopes the Indians will blame Hoppy for the murder. Hoppy brings Lone Eagle's body to the Indians and promises to return with the real killer. They allow him to leave accompanied by Indians, but keep Windy and Lucky hostage. Hoppy steals Andrews' rifle, which uses unusual bullets and proves to the Indian Chief Big Tree that the bullets in the rifle match those that killed Lone Eagle. The Indians release Windy and Lucky, and they all join together to get the rustlers. Andrews knocks out his superior officer Thompson, and escapes, but is caught by Hoppy. With the rustlers arrested, the Indians and Hoppy thank one another, and Windy and Lucky return to their romances with the general store owner and her daughter. *Cowboys. Frame-ups. Indian agents. Indians of North America–Reservations. Murder. Rustlers. Ambushes. Corpses. Evidence. Indians of North America. Romance. Storekeepers. Trading posts.*

Note: Clarence E. Mulford's story first appeared as a serial in *West Magazine* (6 Jul–17 Aug 1932). The title card of the film read "Clarence E. Mulford's *Hills of Old Wyoming.*" This picture marks Russell Hayden's screen debut. Publicity records note that the film is based on both Mulford's story and the song. According to a *HR* news item, Harry Sherman was hospitalized due to

injuries sustained while shooting at Kernville, CA. For more information on the series, see entry for *Hop-Along Cassidy* in *AFI Catalog of Feature Films, 1931-40*; F3.1990 and consult the Series Index.

FD 13 Apr 1937, p. 7. *HR* 5 Feb 1937, p. 2. *HR* 6 Mar 1937, p. 4. *HR* 9 Apr 1937, p. 3. *MPD* 19 Apr 1937, p. 4. *MPH* 10 Apr 1937, p. 45. *MPH* 17 Apr 1937, p. 46. *Var* 9 Jun 1937, p. 25.

HINTER SCHLOSS UND RIEGEL see PARDON US

HIS BIRTHRIGHT (Japanese Americans)

Haworth Pictures Corp. *Dist* Mutual Film Corp.; Mutual Star Productions. 8 Sep **1918** [©The Haworth Pictures Corp.; 4 Sep 1918; LU12808]. Si; b&w. 5 reels.

Dir William Worthington. *Scen* Frances Guihan. *Story* Sessue Hayakawa and Denison Clift. *Cam* Robert Newhard. *Art dir* Milton Menasco.

Cast: Sessue Hayakawa (*Yukio*), Marin Sais (*Edna Kingston*), Howard Davies (*Admiral John Milton*), Mary Anderson (*Helen Milton*), Tsuru Aoki (*Saki San*), Sidney De Grey (*James Barnes*), Harry Von Meter (*Admiral Von Krug*), Mayme Kelso (*Mrs. Harland Smith*).

Espionage, Drama. Yukio, the son of an American father, Admiral John Milton, and a Japanese mother, Saki San, is reared in Japan by an old man who tells him that Milton was responsible for Saki San's suicide. Determined to avenge her death, Yukio sails to America, where he becomes involved with a beautiful adventuress named Edna Kingston. Edna asks Yukio to obtain some papers from Milton in return for her love, but after he gives her the documents, she rejects him. His shame is heightened when he discovers that she heads a gang of German spies, and, in a furious struggle with the entire group, he retrieves the papers. Milton bursts into the room with the police and rescues his son, after which he welcomes the young man into his home. Milton explains that he always loved Saki San, and Yukio joins the army to fight for the American cause. *Adventuresses. Fathers and sons. Half-castes. Japanese. Japanese Americans. Spies. Germans. Japan. Officers (Military). Police. Rescues. Secret documents. Suicide. World War I.*

Note: This was the first release of Hayakawa's production company, Haworth Pictures Corp. Some news items state that the film was released 1 Sep 1918.

ETR 24 Aug 1918, pp. 1003-06, 1018. *ETR* 31 Aug 1918, p. 1087. *MPW* 24 Aug 1918, p. 1153. *MPW* 14 Sep 1918, p. 1612. *NYDM* 14 Sep 1918, p. 412. *Var* 20 Sep 1918, p. 45. *Wid's* 15 Sep 1918, pp. 23-24.

HIS BUTLER'S SISTER (Russian Americans, Swedish Americans)

Universal Pictures Co., Inc.; A Frank Borzage Production. *Dist* Universal Pictures Co., Inc. 26 Nov **1943**; Prod: 28 Jun—early Sep 1943 [©Universal Pictures Co., Inc.; 17 Nov 1943; LP12378]. Sd (Western Electric Recording); b&w. 8,424 ft. 92-93 min. PCA cert no. 9691.

Prod Felix Jackson. *Assoc prod* Frank Shaw. *Dir* Frank Borzage. *Asst dir* Lew Borzage. *Orig scr* Samuel Hoffenstein and Betty Reinhardt. *Dir of photog* Woody Bredell. *Spec photog eff* John P. Fulton. *Art dir* John B. Goodman and Martin Obzina. *Film ed* Ted Kent. *Set dec* R. A. Gausman and T. F. Offenbecker. *Gowns* Vera West. *Miss Durbin's gowns by* Adrian. *Song dir* Charles Previn. *Mus score* H. J. Salter. *Vocal coach* Andres de Segurola. *Sd dir* Bernard B. Brown. [*Sd*] *tech* Joe Lapis.

Song(s): "In the Spirit of the Moment," music by Bernie Grossman, lyrics by Walter Jurman; "When You're Away," music by Victor Herbert, lyrics by Henry Blossom; "Is It True What They Say About Dixie?" words and music by Irving Caesar, Sammy Lerner and Gerald Marks; selections from the opera *Turandot*, music by Giacomo Puccini, completed by Franco Alfano, libretto by Giuseppe Adami and Renato Simoni; medley of Russian songs, arranged by Max Rabinowitsh.

Cast: DEANNA DURBIN (*Ann Carter*), FRANCHOT TONE (*Charles Gerard*), PAT O'BRIEN (*Martin Murphy*), Akim Tamiroff (*Popoff*), Alan Mowbray ([*Buzz*] *Jenkins*), Walter Catlett ([*Mortimer*] *Kalb*), Elsa Janssen (*Severina*), Evelyn Ankers (*Elizabeth Campbell*), Frank Jenks (*Emmett*), Sig Arno (*Moreno*), Hans Conried (*Reeves*), Florence Bates (*Lady Sloughberry*), Roscoe Karns (*Fields*), Russell Hicks (*Sanderson*), Andrew Tombes (*Brophy*), Stephanie Bachelor (*Dot Stanley*), Marion Pierce (*Margaret Howard*), Iris Adrian (*Sunshine Twin*), Robin Raymond (*Sunshine Twin*), [Leo Mostovoy (*Headwaiter*)], [Halliwell Hobbes (*Willebrandt*)], [Joe King (*Conductor*)], [George Reed, Charles Hall (*Porters*)], [Paul Scardon (*Professor*)], [George Kirby (*Fat man*)], [Marie Osborne (*Kalb's secretary*)], [Alice Draper (*Spinster*)], [Blaney Lewis (*Boy*)], [Virginia Gardner (*Blonde*)], [Wilson Benge], [Jack George].

Comedy-drama, with songs. [*Print viewed*]. Broadway composer Charles Gerard is constantly harassed by stagestruck performers wanting to break into show business. When singer Ann Carter attempts to audition for him, she is sent to the wrong train compartment and ends up singing for a traveling girdle salesman instead. Ann then arrives in New York City and goes to Charles' estate, where she thinks her older half-brother Martin, who has told her he is a wealthy businessman, lives. In actuality, Martin is Charles's butler, and the composer mistakes Ann for the new maid. With the help of Severina, the cook, Ann forces her brother to hire her as a maid, and she immediately draws the attentions of Martin's friends: fellow butlers Popoff, Buzz Jenkins, Moreno, Reeves and chauffeur Emmett. That night, Charles has a dinner party whose guests include theatrical producer Mortimer Kalb, theatrical agent Fields, Lady Sloughberry and Elizabeth Campbell, Charles's socialite girl friend. Elizabeth, who disapproves of Charles' friends and associates, convinces him to stop working on his play and go with her to Maine. The next day, Charles gives Martin permission to fire Ann, so she decides to perform for the composer. Charles, however, mistakenly assumes her singing is coming from a nearby radio. Later, Ann tries to audition for Kalb, but he is more interested in her figure than her voice. Charles then arrives to tell Kalb that he is quitting the unfinished show, but Ann tells Charles that he will not be happy if he gives up his career. That night, Ann is invited to Popoff's birthday party at a Russian restaurant, where she is offered jobs in the households of her various servant suitors. Charles arrives at the restaurant just as Ann finishes singing a medley of Russian songs and tells her that he has decided to take her advice and finish Kalb's show. Charles and Ann quickly fall in love, but Martin fears that his employer is merely toying with his young sister. The overprotective brother tells Charles that the stagestruck Ann is only using him to advance her own career. Charles then breaks off his relationship with Ann and prepares to return to Elizabeth in Maine. Martin is fired as well, but convinces the heartbroken Ann to stay in New York with him, rather than return to their hometown in Indiana. The two go to the Butler's Ball that night, where Charles, as a non-servant, is refused entrance until he pretends to be Severina's cousin. The cook then informs her employer that Ann and Martin are siblings, and after hearing Ann sing, Charles realizes that hers is the voice he has been searching for, and the two are reunited. *Brothers and sisters. Butlers. Composers. Maids. Romance. Singers. Auditions. Balls (Parties). Birthdays. Class distinction. Cooks. Critics. Dismissal (Employment). Employer-employee relations. Gamblers. Mistaken identity. New York City. Restaurants. Romantic rivalry. Russian Americans. Socialites. Swedish Americans. Theatrical agents. Theatrical producers. Trains.*

Note: The working title of this film was *My Girl Godfrey*. The film's title initially was *His Butler's Sister*, but was changed to *My Girl Godfrey* while the film was in pre-production, then changed back to the original title once production began. In Mar 1941, *HR* announced that Universal was planning to make a film entitled *His Butler's Sister*, which was to star Deanna Durbin and be produced by Bruce Manning, directed by William Seiter, and written by Felix Jackson, who is credited as producer on the 1943 film. It has not been determined if any elements from the earlier, planned production were used in the released film. The film opens with the following written foreword: "The Food, Drinks, Clothes, Shoes, Rubber, Gas and other articles consumed or used in this picture are purely imaginary and have no relation to any actual Foods, Drinks, Clothes, Shoes, Rubber, Gas and other articles of today, rationed or unrationed. Any resemblance is purely accidental. This is a fable of the day before yesterday." According to Universal press materials, the Russian medley performed by Deanna Durbin included elements from the Russian folk songs "Yamschtschick," "Kalitka" and "Two Guitars." Bernard B. Brown was nominated for an Academy Award in the category of Sound Recording, but lost to E. H. Hansen's work on the Twentieth Century-Fox film *Wilson*. On 7 Feb 1944, Deanna Durbin, Pat O'Brien and Franchot Tone reprised their roles in a radio version of this film for the *Lux Radio Theatre*.

Box 13 Nov 1943. *DV* 9 Jul 1943. *DV* 5 Nov 1943, p. 3, 7. *FD* 9 Dec 1943, p. 8. *HR* 21 Mar 1941, p. 4. *HR* 24 Jun 1943, p. 9. *HR* 25 Jun 1943, p. 7. *HR* 5 Nov 1943, p. 4. *HR* 3 Jan 1944, p. 8. *HR* 13 Jan 1944, p. 30. *LAHE* 24 May 1943. *MPHPD* 25 Sep 1943, p. 1555. *MPHPD* 13 Nov 1943, p. 1625. *NYT* 30 Dec 1943, p. 13. *Var* 10 Nov 1943, p. 34.

HIS COUNTRY *see* A SHIP COMES IN

HIS DARKER SELF (African Americans)

G. and H. Pictures Corp. *Dist* W. W. Hodkinson Corp. 16 Mar **1924** [©G. and H. Pictures Corp.; 19 Mar 1924; LP20906]. Si; b&w. 5 reels.
Pres Albert L. Grey. *Dir* John W. Noble. *Story* Arthur Caesar. *Titles* Ralph Spence.
Cast: Lloyd Hamilton (*Claude Sappington*), Tom Wilson (*Bill Jackson*), Tom O'Malley (*Uncle Eph*), Lucille La Verne (*Darktown's*

Cleopatra), Edna May Sperl (*Bill Jackson's sweetheart*), Sally Long (*Claude's sweetheart*), Kate Bruce (*Claude's mother*), Warren Cook (*The Governor*).
Comedy. Thinking that he is hauling crates of bananas, Uncle Eph, an old black man working for the Sappington family, nightly carts contraband liquor to a dance hall run by Bill Jackson. When the revenue officers stage a raid on the dance hall, Jackson, believing that Eph has squealed, frames him for murder. Assuming that Eph is innocent, Claude Sappington, a mystery-story writer, sets out to prove it: disguised by blackface, he gets a job as a busboy in Jackson's dance hall. When Jackson's jealous girl friend catches the bootlegger visiting Darktown's Cleopatra, she accuses him of the murder for which Eph is charged; Claude overhears the angry remark and immediately tries to apprehend Jackson, who escapes in a speedboat. Claude gives chase and captures him, taking him to the governor in time to save Eph from hanging. While at the state capitol, Claude, who is in love with the governor's daughter, obtains his permission to marry her. *African Americans. Authors. Bootleggers. Capital punishment. Dance halls. Disguise. Frame-ups. Governors. Injustice. Murder. Racial impersonation. United States. Internal Revenue Service.*

FD 30 Mar 1924. *MPW* 5 Apr 1924. *NYT* 26 Mar 1924, p. 19. *Var* 26 Mar 1924, p. 27.

HIS DEBT (Japanese Americans)

Haworth Pictures Corp. *Dist* Robertson-Cole Co. through Exhibitors Mutual Distributing Corp. 25 May **1919** [©The Haworth Pictures Corp.; 8 Apr 1919; LU13575]. Si; b&w. 5 reels, 4,800 ft.
Dir William Worthington. *Scen* Frances Guihan. *Story* L. V. Jefferson. *Cam* Frank D. Williams.
Cast: Sessue Hayakawa (*Goro Mariyama*), Jane Novak (*Gloria Manning*), Francis MacDonald (*Blair Whitcomb*), Fred Montague (*J. P. Manning*).
Drama. Goro Mariyama, who uses the profits from his high-class honestly-run gambling house to help the poor, is shot by Blair Whitcomb, who earlier had accused Goro of cheating and then lost $10,000 to him over a cut of cards. Goro's lung is pierced and it is only through the efforts of nurse Gloria Manning, Blair's fiancée, that Goro pulls through. Goro tells Gloria that he loves her and is shocked to hear of her engagement. Demanding revenge, Goro forces Blair to come to his house to make good on his bounced $10,000 check. When Blair does this, Goro sends for the police. Gloria comes and pleads for Blair telling Goro that she loves Blair even though she knows he attempted murder and that she can never love Goro because of their difference in race. Goro lets Blair escape saying he is paying his debt to Gloria, whom he loves, for saving his life. *Debt. Gamblers. Japanese Americans. Nursing back to health. Racism. Unrequited love. Attempted murder. Charity. Gambling houses. Gunshot wounds. Nurses. Revenge.*

Note: While reviews call this film *His Debt*, the copyright records refer to it as *The Debt*. The film was shot in the Brunton studios by Hayakawa's own production company.

ETR 31 May 1919, p. 2021. *MPN* 31 May 1919, p. 3669. *Wid's* 25 May 1919, p. 19.

HIS FAMILY TREE (Irish Americans)

RKO Radio Pictures, Inc. *Dist* RKO Radio Pictures, Inc. 29 Sep **1935**; *Prod:* late Jun—mid-Jul 1935 [©RKO Radio Pictures, Inc.; 20 Sep 1935; LP5811]. Sd (RCA Victor System); b&w. 8 reels. 59 or 68-69 min. PCA cert no. 1102.
Assoc prod Cliff Reid. *Dir* Charles Vidor. *Scr* Joel Sayre and John Twist. *Photog* Lucien Andriot. *Art dir* Van Nest Polglase. *Art dir assoc* Perry Ferguson. *Ed* Jack Hively. *Cost* Walter Plunkett. *Mus dir* Alberto Colombo. *Rec* George D. Ellis.
Source: Based on the play *Old Man Murphy* by Patrick Kearney and Harry Wagstaff Gribble (New York, 16 May 1931).
Cast: James Barton [(*Patrick Murphy*)], Margaret Callahan [(*Elinor Murphy, also known as Elinor Murfree*)], Addison Randall [(*Mike Dononvan*)], Maureen Delany [(*Nellie Ouliban*)], William Harrigan [(*Charles Murphy, also known as Charles Murfree*)], Marjorie Gateson [(*Margaret Murphy, also known as Margaret Murfree*)], Clifford Jones [(*Dudley Weatherby*)], Ray Mayer [(*Terrance Gilligan*)], Herman Bing [(*Stonehill*)], Pat Moriarty [(*Bat Gilligan*)], Ferdinand Munier [(*Mayor John J. "Jolly John" Holtsapple*)], [Charles Coleman (*Hopkins*)], [Orville Caldwell (*Mayor's benchman*)], [William Lemuels (*Brannigan*)].
Political, Comedy. [*Print viewed*]. Because his son Charles has not responded to any of his letters, Patrick Murphy, an Irish boatswain

and pub owner, leaves his Kerry County home to find Charles in America. When Patrick arrives at his son's lavish house, he discovers that, at the insistence of Charles' ambitious, social-climbing wife Margaret, Charles has changed his name to Murfree and is running for mayor against the incumbent, John J. "Jolly John" Holtsapple. To protect Charles' campaign, only Margaret, his daughter Elinor and his campaign managers, Mike Donovan and Stonehill, are told of Patrick's presence. Soon after, however, Holtsapple's managers spread a rumor that Charles is not the descendent of the aristocratic Tennessee Murfree family, but is a common Irish immigrant named Murphy. These rumors cause widow Nellie Oulihan, the political leader of the Irish fourth precinct, to withdraw her support of Charles and to hold an "indignation meeting" above the Gilligan brothers' bar. The fun-loving Patrick, however, turns the meeting into a dance and, in front of Elinor and her fiancé, the snobbish Dudley Weatherby, convinces Nellie and her followers that Charles really is a Murfree. After Holtsapple's supporters send a spy to Tennessee to "dig dirt" on Murfree, Patrick sprays the portly candidate with a fire extinguisher as he concludes a particularly insipid radio speech. Disgusted by Patrick's display, Dudley ridicules him in front of Elinor, who in anger rejects him and reveals her grandfather's identity. Margaret then insults Nellie, who has fallen in love with widower Patrick, and causes Charles to lose the fourth precinct once again. Discouraged, Patrick gets drunk one evening and, as Holtsapple discloses in a rally that Charles' real name is Murphy, defiantly reveals his relationship to Charles. The news of Charles' deception sends his campaign into a tailspin, and desperate to prevent his defeat, Donovan and Elinor talk Patrick into campaigning. Aided by a plaster pig named "Johnny John," Patrick begins to turn the townspeople against Holtsapple. At the start of a crucial radio debate, however, the vengeful Dudley connives to have Patrick abducted and held prisoner in an apartment building so that Holtsapple can accuse Charles of turning on his own father. Using his boatswain's whistle, the bound and gagged Patrick alerts the Gilligan brothers to his whereabouts and is rescued in time to prevent Holtsapple from defaming Charles. After Charles wins the election as a Murphy, Elinor and Donovan, and Patrick and Nellie vote for marriage. *Family honor. Family relationships. Immigrants. Irish Americans. Political campaigns. Snobs and snobbishness. Abduction. Boatswains. Dances. Drunkenness. Engagements. Kerry County (Ireland). Meetings. Political corruption. Pubs. Radio broadcasting. Rallies. Rescues. Revenge. Social climbers. Speeches. Widows.*

Note: The working title of this film was *Old Man Murphy.*

DV 15 Aug 1935, p. 3. *FD* 17 Sep 1935, p. 6. *HR* 24 Jun 1935, p. 11. *HR* 9 Jul 1935, p. 10. *HR* 1 Jul 1935, p. 11. *HR* 15 Aug 1935, p. 3. *MPD* 16 Aug 1935, p. 12. *MPH* 5 Oct 1935, p. 42, 45. *Var* 12 Feb 1935, p. 18.

HIS FOREIGN WIFE (German Americans)

Pathé Exchange, Inc. *Dist* Pathé Exchange, Inc. 27 Nov **1927** [©Pathé Exchange, Inc.; 19 Jul 1927; LU24191]. Si; b&w. 5 reels, 4,890 ft.

Dir John P. McCarthy. *Scen* Albert De Mond. *Wrt* John P. McCarthy.

Cast: Greta von Rue (*Hilda Schultzenbach*), Edna Murphy (*Mary Jackson*), Wallace MacDonald (*Johnny Haines*), Charles Clary (*The Mayor*), Elsie Bishop (*Frau Schultzenbach*), Lee Shumway.

Society, Drama. When the United States is drawn into the European conflict, Joe and Johnny Haines enlist and are sent to the front. Joe is killed during the war; Johnny, who remains overseas with the United States Occupation Forces, falls in love with a German girl, marries her, and brings her to America. To his dismay, he finds that bitter prejudice against Germans makes his father hostile to his wife. When the father, a town official, is assigned to pin a decoration of bravery on his son, Johnny publicly denounces his father's sense of false patriotism and his inability to forget the past. Later, the father, realizing his error, forgives his son, and the family is happy once again. *Bigotry. Brothers. German Americans. Germans. Military occupation. War brides. World War I.*

FD 23 Oct 1927.

HIS GLORIOUS NIGHT (*foreign version*) see OLIMPIA

HIS GREAT CHANCE (African Americans)

Ben Strasser Productions. *Dist* North State Film Corp. 26 May **1923**. Si; b&w. 5 reels, 4,680 ft.

Dir Ben Strasser.

Cast: Sandy Burns (*The elder son*), Bobby Smart (*The younger son*), Tim Moore (*The father*), Gertrude Moore (*The mother*), Fred

Hart (*Theater magnate*), Fannetta Burns, Sam Russell, Mark Slater, Walter Long.

African American, Comedy-drama. [*Not viewed*]. Two African-American country boys with dancing talent are discovered by a theater magnate, who persuades them to leave the farm and try their luck on the stage. Initially seized by stage fright, the boys eventually become great successes. Back home, however, their parents, who are happy for their sons' good fortune, cannot help but feel neglected by them. At Christmas, the parents try to be merry, but miss their absent sons very much. Just then, the boys return home, full of good cheer for the holiday. The elder son, who has fallen in love with the theater manager's daughter, introduces his parents to his new bride and everyone is joyful. *African Americans. Brothers. City-country contrast. Dancers. Family relationships. Lure of the city. Christmas. Romance. Stage fright. Theatrical managers.*

Note: Leigh Whipper, reviewing the film in *Billboard*, called it "by far the best negro picture it has been my fortune to see" and commented, "I am very much of the opinion it will pave the way for a higher standard of films among us. It was entirely free from propaganda, totally devoid of any offensive features, and carried a smile and a tear with grace thruout."

Billboard 19 May 1923, p. 52. *ChiDef* 24 Mar 1923, p. 6.

HIS HARLEM WIFE *see* LIFE GOES ON

HIS LAST ADVENTURE *see* THE BATTLING BUCKAROO

HIS PARISIAN WIFE (French Americans)

Famous Players-Lasky Corp. *Dist* Famous Players-Lasky Corp.; Artcraft Pictures. 19 Jan **1919** [©Famous Players-Lasky Corp.; 31 Dec 1918; LP13271]. Si; b&w. 5 reels, 4,823 ft.

Pres Adolph Zukor. *Dir* Emile Chautard. *Scen* Eve Unsell.

Source: Based on the novel *The Green Orchard* by Andrew Soutar (London, 1916).

Cast: Elsie Ferguson (*Fauvette*), David Powell (*Martin Wesley*), Courtney Foote (*Tony Rye*), Frank Losee (*Thompson Wesley*), Cora Williams (*Mrs. Wesley*), Captain Charles (*Minister*), Louis Grizel (*Lawyer*).

Society, Drama. In Paris, American lawyer Martin Wesley meets Fauvette, a reporter, in a rainstorm. They share an umbrella, have tea, then dinner, and by eleven that night Martin proposes. After he brings his bride to live with his parents, a cold New England couple who hate anything from Paris, their disapproval gradually infects Martin. When his friend Tony Rye comes to dinner and Fauvette appears in a low-cut gown, Martin upbraids her. Their subsequent separation causes Martin to drink, while Fauvette thrives in New York as a famous author. When Martin hears this and also learns that Tony's sympathetic concern is becoming romantic, he smashes his liquor decanter and proves himself as a successful lawyer. After deciding to win Fauvette back, but then tell her to go to Tony, Martin sees her and realizes he loves her. When he pays off her money lender, Fauvette thinks he is trying to humiliate her, but soon he begs forgiveness and they start a new married life. *French Americans. Lawyers. Marriage. New England. Paris (France). Separation (Marital). Snobs and snobbishness. Americans in foreign countries. Authors. Drunkenness. Friendship. Rainstorms. Reporters.*

Note: One review referred to the title of this film as *The Parisian Wife.*

ETR 25 Jan 1919, p. 643. *MPN* 8 Feb 1919, p. 925. *MPW* 1 Feb 1919, p. 672, 677. *NYMT* 2 Feb 1919. *NYT* 20 Jan 1919, p. 13. *Var* 24 Jan 1919, p. 45. *Wid's* 19 Jan 1919, p. 7.

HIS PEOPLE (Jewish Americans)

Universal Pictures Corp.; Universal-Jewel. 27 Dec **1925**; New York premiere: 1 Nov 1925 [©Universal Pictures Corp.; 17 Nov 1925; LP22021]. Si; b&w. 9 reels, 8,983 ft.

Pres Carl Laemmle. *Dir* Edward Sloman. *Adpt* Charles E. Whittaker. *Adpt, cont and titles* Alfred A. Cohn. *Cont* Charles E. Whittaker. *Story* Isadore Bernstein. *Photog* Max Dupont. *Mus score* Edward Kilenyi.

Cast: Rudolph Schildkraut (*Rabbi David Cominsky*), Rosa Rosanova (*Rosie Cominsky*), George Lewis (*Sammy Cominsky* [*grown*]), Bobby Gordon (*Sammy Cominsky* [*child*]), Arthur Lubin (*Morris Cominsky* [*grown*]), Albert Bushaland (*Morris Cominsky* [*child*]), Blanche Mehaffey (*Mamie Shannon* [*grown*]), Jean Johnson (*Mamie Shannon* [*child*]), Kate Price (*Kate Shannon*), Virginia Brown Faire (*Ruth Stein*), Nat Carr (*Chaim Barowitz*), Bertram Marburgh (*Judge Nathan Stein*), Edgar Kennedy (*Thomas Nolan*), Charles Sullivan (*The Champion*), Sidney Franklin (*Levensky*).

Domestic, Melodrama. Rabbi Cominsky, the father of two sons, ekes out a living in New York's Lower East Side as a pushcart peddler.

He favors the studious and ambitious Morris, the elder, who wants to be a lawyer, rather than the loyal Sammy, who sells papers and who helps put his older brother through college. Cominsky finds out that Sammy has become a prizefighter under the name "Battling Rooney" and drives him out of the house. Morris demands that his father buy him a dress suit, so Cominsky pawns his overcoat to get one (which Morris throws in an ashcan) and becomes seriously ill from exposure to the cold. Cominsky passes the crisis but is told he must go to a warmer climate. Morris, meanwhile, has become engaged to marry Ruth Stein, his boss's daughter, but is ashamed of his parentage. Cominsky arrives at the engagement party, and Morris refuses to acknowledge his own father. Sammy, after winning the lightweight championship, faces up to his brother, denounces him, and drags him home. Morris, realizing his sin, begs and receives forgiveness. Cominsky acknowledges his gratitude to Sammy and gives his blessing to Sammy's Irish sweetheart, Mamie. *Boxers. Family life. Irish. Jews. New York City–Lower East Side. Peddlers and peddling. Rabbis.*

Note: This film was initially shown under the title *Proud Heart.* Its working title was *The Jew.*
FD 15 Nov 1925.

HIS SISTER'S CHAMPION *see* ROSIE O'GRADY

HIS SLAVE *see* THE BRIDE OF HATE

HIS SWEETHEART (Italian Americans)
The Oliver Morosco Photoplay Co. *Dist* Paramount Pictures Corp. 29 Jan **1917** [©Oliver Morosco Photoplay Co.; 13 Jan 1917; LP9991]. Si; b&w. 5 reels.

Pres Oliver Morosco. *Dir* Donald Crisp. *Story and scen* George Beban and Lawrence McCloskey. *Scen* John B. Clymer. *Cam* J. O. Taylor.

Cast: George Beban (*Joe, the Iceman*), Helen Jerome Eddy (*Trina Capino*), Sarah Kernan (*Joe's mother, Mama Mia*), Harry De Vere (*Godfrey Kelland*), Kathleen Kirkham (*Mrs. Kelland*), Peaches Jackson, Robert E. Rolson, J. N. Leonard, Cecil C. Holland, Charles Yorba.

Drama. Joe's sweetheart, his mother, comes to the United States from Italy expecting her son to be a wealthy American. Finding instead that he is a poor iceman, Mama Mia takes a position as a laundress for district attorney Kelland. As a prank, the Kelland's baby hides a valuable pin in a laundry basket and Mama Mia is arrested for theft. Under the district attorney's prosecution, Mama Mia is sent to prison, incurring Joe's wrath. Kelland's political enemies seize upon Joe's anger and involve him in a plot to kill the D. A. Joe is to substitute Kelland's golf ball with one filled with nitroglycerine. As Kelland is about to strike the ball, Joe watches in horror as the D. A.'s wife and daughter walk into range of the explosive. Rushing onto the course, Joe throws himself in front of the ball, saving Kelland. Mrs. Kelland then confesses her baby's part in the theft, Mama Mia is freed, and the family is happily reunited. *Attempted murder. False arrests. Immigrants. Italian Americans. Mothers and sons. Revenge. Children. Confession (Law). Conspiracy. District attorneys. Explosives. Golf. Icemen. Practical jokes.*

Note: The working title of this film was *Just an Old Sweetheart.* John B. Clymer is listed as author of a scenario for this film which was included in the Paramount studio records. His name was not included in the cutting continuity.
ETR 3 Feb 1917, p. 634. *Motog* 10 Feb 1917, p. 320. *MPN* 23 Dec 1916, p. 4028. *MPW* 10 Feb 1917, p. 868, 910. *NYDM* 20 Jan 1917, p. 30. *NYDM* 3 Feb 1917, p. 27. *Wid's* 1 Feb 1917, p. 70.

HIS UNOFFICIAL FIANCÉE *see* EL TANGO EN BROADWAY

HIS WIFE'S LOVER *see* ZEIN WEIB'S LUBOVNICK

HIS WIFE'S SWEETHEART *see* ZEIN WEIB'S LUBOVNICK

HISTORY OF THE AMERICAN INDIAN *see* LIFE OF AMERICAN INDIAN [*sic*]

HITLER'S CHILDREN (German Americans)
RKO Radio Pictures, Inc. *Dist* RKO Radio Pictures, Inc. 19 Mar **1943**; World premiere in Cincinnati, OH and surrounding cities: 14 Jan 1943; Prod: Oct 1942 [©RKO Radio Pictures, Inc.; 22 Jan 1943; LP11908]. Sd (RCA Sound System); b&w. 7,502 ft. 80 or 83 min. PCA cert no. 8878.

Prod Edward A. Golden. *Assoc prod* Robert S. Golden. *Dir* Edward Dmytryk and [Irving Reis]. *Asst dir* Sam Ruman. *Scr* Emmet Lavery. *Dir of photog* Russell Metty. *Spec eff* Vernon L. Walker. *Art dir* Albert S.

D'Agostino and Carroll Clark. *Ed* Joseph Noriega. *Set dec* Darrell Silvera and Harley Miller. *Gowns* Renie. *Mus dir* C. Bakaleinikoff. *Mus* Roy Webb. *Rec* Roy Meadows. [*Tech adv* Father Louis Pick].

Source: Based on the book *Education for Death: The Making of a Nazi* by Gregor Ziemer (London, 1941).

Cast: Tim Holt [(*Karl Bruner*)], Bonita Granville [(*Anna Muller*)], Kent Smith [(*Professor Nichols*)], Otto Kruger [(*Colonel Henkel*)], H. B. Warner [(*The bishop*)], Lloyd Corrigan [(*Franz Erhardt*)], Erford Gage [(*Dr. Schmidt*)], Hans Conried [(*Dr. Graf*)], Gavin Muir [(*Lieutenant and Commandant*)], Nancy Gates [(*Brenda*)], [Frank Eldredge, Nick Vehr, Richard Martin (*Gestapo men*)], [Bill Burrud (*Murph*)], [Jimmy Zaner (*Irwin*)], [Goetz Van Eyck (*German arresting officer*)], [John Stockton, John Merton (*Gestapo officers*)], [Max Lucke (*Plane dispatcher*)], [Anna Loos (*N.S.V. worker*)], [Bessie Wade (*German mother*)], [Harry McKim, Orley Lindgren, Billy Brow, Chris Wren (*Boys*)], [Egon Brecher (*Mr. Muller*)], [Elsa Janssen (*Mrs. Muller*)], [William Forrest (*American vice consul*)], [Rita Corday, Ariel Heath (*Young matrons*)], [Roland Varno (*Lieutenant*)], [Crane Whitley (*Whipping sergeant*)], [Edward Van Sloan (*Chief trial judge*)], [Douglas Evans (*German radio announcer*)], [Carla Boehm (*Magda*)], [Bruce Cameron (*Storm trooper*)], Betty Roadman (*First matron*)], [Kathleen Wilson (*Chief matron*)], [Joey Ray (*Person in labor camp*)], [Ann Summers], [Mary Stuart].

Exploitation, Youth, War preparedness, Drama. [*Print viewed*]. Professor Nichols, an American educator, recalls the halcyon days of 1933 Germany before the rise of Nazism: As a teacher at the American Colony School, "Nicky" encourages Anna Muller and his other students to question Germany's lust for land. Meanwhile, at the German school across the way, the stern Dr. Schmidt exhorts Karl Bruner and the other boys to consecrate their lives to Adolf Hitler. Karl, who is attracted to Anna, comes to the American school one day and strikes up a conversation with her. After he tells Anna that he is a German who was born in America, Anna responds that she is American born in Germany and is now living with her grandparents there. To nurture their friendship, Nicky invites Karl to join him and Anna on a picnic, and soon Karl is a regular participant in their weekly outings. While running through the woods one day, Anna sees a little boy bound and gagged, but when she tries to free him, Karl tells her that the boy is being tested for his fitness to join a Hitler Youth group. Nicky states that that was Karl's last picnic, for he became enveloped in the Nazi storm that was sweeping Germany. By 1939, the New Order is underway, and Anna is now Nicky's assistant. As the students at the American school gather to celebrate Memorial Day, the Gestapo arrives and demands custody of all Germans, Poles and Jews at the school. When Anna's name is called, Nicky objects and is taken to headquarters to speak to the lieutenant in charge. At headquarters, Nicky meets Lt. Karl Bruner, who asserts that as a German citizen, Anna is subject to German law. When Nicky's entreaties to the American Embassy prove fruitless, he turns to his friend, journalist Franz Erhardt, for help. Franz, who is intimidated by his own little Nazi sons, is afraid to help Nicky, although he does suggest that Anna is probably being held at a labor camp. Nicky then goes to the Ministry of Education to petition a visit to the camp. There, he sees Karl, who orders him to give up his search for Anna. When Nicky agrees to do so if Anna is happy at the camp, Karl informs him that Anna is an instructor at the camp and takes him to see her. After Anna learns of Nicky's plans to free her, she insists that she wants to stay at the camp out of fear for his safety. Karl, who believes that Anna is becoming a "true German," tells her that he has recommended that she be allowed to study at the University of Berlin. Anna rejects his offer, however, and denounces his world as evil and rotten. When Anna formally declines the offer and disparages the "diseased New Order," Colonel Henkel, Karl's superior officer, sentences her to toil for one year at a labor camp. Henkel orders that Anna be kept under surveillance, and when Karl withholds reports of her defiant behavior, Henkel begins to doubt his loyalty. To test Karl, Henkel invites him and Nicky on a tour of the Ministry. Taking them to a clinic where women deemed unfit to have children are sterilized, Henkel announces that Anna's name has been placed on the patient list. After leaving the clinic, Karl finds Anna at the camp, and after warning her of the danger, declares his love for her. When Anna confesses that she also loves him, he suggests placating the state by having a baby, but Anna refuses, saying that the child would not be hers, but Hitler's. That night, Anna runs away and seeks refuge in a

church. Soon after, the Gestapo arrives and orders the bishop to dismiss his parishioners so that they can find Anna. When, at the risk of his own life, the bishop defies their orders, Anna steps forward and surrenders. Ordering Anna publicly flogged and then sterilized, Henkel sends Karl to the flogging as his representative. Unable to bear Anna's pain, Karl seizes the whip from her tormentor's hands and, after proclaiming his love for her, admits that he was wrong. Later, Franz informs Nicky that Anna has been sentenced to death, but Karl has recanted and will denounce his sins against the state in a nationwide broadcast of their trial. As Nicky and Franz are about to tune in the broadcast, the Gestapo arrives and orders Nicky to leave for Paris on the next plane. At the airport, as Franz walks Nicky to his plane, the trial begins and is broadcast over loudspeakers on the airstrip. In his opening statement, Karl quotes a poem by Goethe about freedom and, after observing that the German people have relinquished their freedom, proclaims "long live the enemies of Nazi Germany." Henkel reacts by ordering Karl and Anna executed in the courtroom, and the sounds of gunshots are heard over the speakers. Nicky then boards his plane and addresses the audience, telling them that "they must ask themselves tonight, before they go home, can we stop Hitler's children before it is too late?" *Americans in foreign countries. Germany. Nazis. Personality change. Romance. Self-sacrifice. World War II. Americans in foreign countries. Bishops. Education. Flogging. German Americans. Gestapo. Labor camps. Picnicking. Reporters. Sterilization. Teachers. Trials.*

Note: This film opens with a picture of Gregor Ziemer's novel *Education for Death*. As the book begins to seep blood, the film's credits appear. Ziemer, a news commentator and analyst for radio station WLW in Cincinnati, worked as an American educator in Germany before the war, according to news items in *HR* and *PM* magazine. Another news item in *HR* notes that the Allies dropped flyers containing a condensed version of Ziemer's best-selling novel over the captured countries of Europe. A pre-production news item adds that Ziemer was initially slated to write the script for this film. In 1942, Disney produced a one-reel film, titled *Education for Death*, based on Ziemer's novel. According to pre-production news items in *HR*, Martha Scott, Anita Louise and June Lockhart were considered for roles in this film. A *HR* news item lists Lucy Daniel and Edgar Barrier in the cast, but their participation in the completed film has not been confirmed. Another *HR* news item notes that Edward Dmytryk took over the direction from Irvin Reis on 19 Oct 1942. According to a *NYT* article, Reis stormed off the set because of his inability to work with Tim Holt and Bonita Granville. *HR* news items add that the U.S. Army Air Force delayed Holt's induction so that he could finish this picture. The vestments worn by H. B. Warner in the cathedral scene were over 400 years old, according to another news item in *HR*. In CBCS, the character of Colonel Henkel is named Colonel Schwartz.

News items in *HR* offer the following information about the film's premiere: Prior to the Cincinnati premiere, RKO presented a special preview presentation in theaters across the country, donating the receipts to the League of Nations. The Cincinnati premiere was sponsored by radio station WLW and featured an appearance by Ziemer. Ticket sales for this film were three hundred percent above average, breaking all existing records and making it the champion "sleeper" in RKO history. Modern sources note that the film cost $205,000 to produce and returned $3,555,000 in film rentals. Bonita Granville's performance led to a new contract with the studio. According to the *Var* reviews, this was Edward Golden's first effort as a producer. A 1946 news item in *HR* reports that Golden rejected RKO's offer to buy his film rights for $500,000. Bonita Granville and Otto Kruger reprised their roles in a 24 May 1943 *Lux Radio Theatre* broadcast of the story.

Box 2 Jan 1943. *DV* 29 Dec 1942, p. 3. *FD* 6 Jan 1943, p. 5 *FD* 7 Jan 1943, p. 4. *FD* 15 Jan 1943, p. 2 *FD* 18 Jan 1943, p. 3. *FD* 22 Jan 1943, p. 2. *HR* 29 Jul 1942, p. 6. *HR* 3 Sep 1942, p. 3. *HR* 14 Sep 1942, p. 1. *HR* 15 Sep 1942, p. 4. *HR* 29 Sep 1942, p. 4. *HR* 9 Oct 1942, p. 7. *HR* 20 Oct 1942, p. 2. *HR* 23 Oct 1942, p. 9. *HR* 29 Oct 1942, p. 4. *HR* 11 Nov 1942, p. 1. *HR* 30 Dec 1942, p. 4. *HR* 13 Jan 1943, p. 1. *HR* 20 Jan 1943, p. 4. *HR* 3 Feb 1943, p. 4. *HR* 9 Feb 1943, p. 3. *HR* 1 Nov 1943, p. 1. *HR* 13 Jan 1946, p. 1. *MPH* 2 Jan 1943. *MPHPD* 12 Dec 1943, p. 1057. *MPHPD* 2 Jan 1943, p. 1089. *MPHPD* 24 Apr 1943, p. 1280. *PM* 3 Jan 1943. *NYT* 14 Feb 1943. *NYT* 25 Feb 1943, p. 27. *NYT* 2 Sep 1944. *Var* 30 Dec 1942, p. 16.

HITS AND BITS OF 1938 (African Americans)

International Road Shows, Inc. *Dist* International Road Shows, Inc. **1938**. Sd; b&w. 6 reels, 5,347 ft.

Song(s): "Deep River" and "Swing Low, Sweet Chariot," music and lyrics by Henry Thacker Burleigh; "Old Folks at Home," music and lyrics by Stephen Foster; "The Juba," music and lyrics by Leon and Otis René and Ben Ellison; "Tiger Rag," music by the Original Dixieland Jazz Band, lyrics by Harry DeCosta; "When Jesus Christ Was Born," "Wow, Wow, Wow, Wow, Wow, Baby," "Promised Land," "Shine On," "One Day Lord," "Lazy Bones," "When Ziekel Saw the Wheel," "I'll Be Ready," "While the Moon Is Shining," "Don't Close Them Gates," "Good News," and "Nobody Knows the Trouble I've Seen," composers undetermined.

Cast: Hampton University Choral Choir.

African American, Musical comedy. [*Not viewed*]. This film, which featured many popular songs and black spirituals, appears to have been a conceptualization of what the filmmakers imagined television programming would be like in the future. *African Americans. Television.*

Note: The description of the contents of this film was taken from a dialogue continuity of the film deposited at NYSA, which offers little indication as to the plot and action of the film. The continuity, which the NYSA received on 31 Dec 1937, bears the following inscription in what may have been the opening title card: "Bagdad in Harlem presents *Hits and Bits*. With a cast of millions (you count them)." The NYSA register of the continuity, as well as the PCA records, list the film as *Hits and Bits of 1938*, presumably the film's full title. Although the continuity notes that the Hampton University Choral Choir sang "When Jesus Christ Was Born," it is not known whether they sang the other songs in the film. The continuity contains no other legitimate credits, but it does feature the following mock credits: "We asked Cab Calloway of "hi-di-ho" fame to write the music. He suggested Beethoven and Liszt—felt they could handle the job better. Bill Robinson could not get released from his $5,000 a week contrack [sic] with 20th Century Fox to stage the dances—so the dancers staged their own. Dialogue and continuity by the Hit and Miss Boys. Scenery by Dame Mother Nature—and not in technicolor. Entire SUPER, COLOSSAL, TREMENDOUS, GIGANTIC production staged by Jumbo, now appearing in person with Ringling Bros. Barnum & Bailey Circus. Editor's Note: M-G-M gave us *Broadway Melody of 1938*, R-K-O gave us *Radio Revels of 1938*, Paramount gave us *Big Broadcast of 1938*. We, to be original, give you 'Television of 1937 [sic].' They tell us it's just around the corner ready for perfection. The same proverbial corner that prosperity is hiding behind. Let's take a look around that corner and see what we can see—and hear."

HITTING THE TRAIL (Multi-ethnic, Irish Americans, Italian Americans)

World Film Corp. *Dist* World Film Corp. 2 Dec **1918** [©World Film Corp.; 18 Nov 1918; LU13123]. Si; b&w. 5 reels.

Dir Dell Henderson. *Adpt* Harry O. Hoyt. *Story* Roy Somerville. *Cam* Louis Ostland and Lucien Tainguy.

Cast: Carlyle Blackwell (*Kid Kelly*), Evelyn Greeley (*Flo Haines*), Joseph Smiley (*Joe Carelli*), George MacQuarrie (*Rev. Thomas Roberts*), Mabel Bunyea (*Mamie*), Muriel Ostriche (*Annie*), Walter Green (*Tony*), Edward Elkas (*Goldberg*).

Drama. Kid Kelly, a gangster in New York's Lower East Side, attempts to rob the storeo of Goldberg the milliner. When the police arrive, Flo Haines, who had come to the building to look at an apartment, hides. When the police find her, they charge her with the crime, but the Kid turns himself over to the law instead. After his release, he again meets Flo, who works by day in an artifical flower factory and by night, in Reverend Roberts' relief mission, and soon falls in love with her. The Kid's jealous sweetheart Mamie tricks Flo into coming to her apartment, where she drugs the girl and turns her over to Joe Carelli, the lustful owner of the flower factory. The Kid saves Flo, but when Carelli is found murdered the next day, he is arrested for the crime. The confession of Annie, who had stabbed Carelli in a jealous rage, frees The Kid, who reforms himself and marries Flo. *Ex-convicts. Factory workers. Irish Americans. Italian Americans. Jealousy. Lechery. Murder. Clergy. Confession (Law). Criminals–Rehabilitation. Factory owners. False arrests. Gangsters. Jews. Missions. New York City–Lower East Side. Rescues. Self-sacrifice. Traps.*

Note: Sources vary concerning the cameraman. Information in the copyright descriptions and the *ETR* review credits Louis Ostland, while *Wid's* credits Lucien Tainguy. *MPN*, in their review, mentioned the film's depictions of "the quick wit of the Irish" and "a lustful Italian."

ETR 30 Nov 1918, p. 2079. *MPN* 30 Nov 1918, p. 3271. *NYDM* 14 Dec 1918, p. 880. *Var* 22 Nov 1918, p. 45. *Wid's* 8 Dec 1918, p. 9.

HJÄRTATS RÖST see TODA UNA VIDA

HOGAN'S ALLEY (Irish Americans, Jewish Americans)

Warner Bros. Pictures, Inc. *Dist* Warner Bros. Pictures, Inc. 12 Dec **1925** [©Warner Bros. Pictures, Inc.; 7 Nov 1925; LP21983]. Si; b&w. 7 reels, 6,875 ft.

Dir Roy Del Ruth. *Asst dir* Ross Lederman. *Adpt* Darryl Francis Zanuck. *Cam* Charles Van Enger. *Asst cam* Willard Van Enger. *Film ed* Clarence Kolster.

Source: Based on the short story "Hogan's Alley" by Gregory Rogers (publication undetermined).

Cast: Monte Blue (*Lefty O'Brien*), Patsy Ruth Miller (*Patsy Ryan*), Willard Louis (*Michael Ryan*), Louise Fazenda (*Dolly*), Ben Turpin (*A stranger*), Charles Conklin (*His friend*), Max Davidson (*Jewish clothier* [*Abie O'Murphy*]), Herbert Spencer Griswold ("*The Texas Kid*"), Frank Hagney (*Battling Savage*), Nigel Barrie (*Dr. Emmett Franklin*), Mary Carr (*Mother Ryan*), Frank Bond (*Al Murphy*).

Boxing, Drama. Lefty O'Brien, a pugilist, becomes engaged to ex-tomboy Patsy Ryan against the wishes of her father, Michael. They both live in an Irish-Jewish neighborhood on New York's East Side known as "Hogan's Alley." Lefty defeats Battling Savage for the championship, breaking his left hand and leaving his opponent close to death. Lefty seeks refuge from apprehension by the police, but Michael turns out both Lefty and Patsy. Patsy is injured, and Michael calls in wealthy Dr. Emmett Franklin, who takes more than a professional interest in Patsy. He invites Michael and Patsy to a dinner that turns into a wild party. Lefty breaks in, and Patsy returns his ring. The doctor invites father and daughter to his mountain lodge, but he leaves Michael stranded at the station. Michael and Lefty pursue the train in an automobile. The car and train collide, and the engineer abandons the train, leaving a part of it to run away. Lefty rescues Patsy with the aid of an airplane; the two settle down to married life and, to Michael's pleasure, make their fortune in plumbing. *Boxing. Irish. Jews. New York City–East Side. Physicians. Plumbers. Train wrecks.*

FD 29 Nov 1925. *NYT* 24 Nov 1925, p. 28. *Var* 25 Nov 1925, p. 39.

HOI GOG QING YUN *see* HAI JEOW CHIN YUAN

HOLD BACK THE DAWN (Immigrants)

Paramount Pictures, Inc. *Dist* Paramount Pictures, Inc. 26 Sep **1941**; New York premiere: 11 Sep 1941; Prod: 18 Feb–5 May 1941 [©Paramount Pictures, Inc.; 26 Sep 1941; LP10737]. Sd (Western Electric Mirrophonic Recording); b&w. 12 reels, 11,269 ft. 114-116 min. Passed by the National Board of Review. PCA cert no. 7139.

Prod Arthur Hornblow, Jr. *Dir* Mitchell Leisen. [*1st asst dir* Francisco Alonso]. [*2d asst dir* Harry A. Kaplan]. [*Loc dir* Cullen Tate]. *Wrt by* Charles Brackett and Billy Wilder. *Story* Ketti Frings. [*Contr to scr const* Richard Maibaum]. [*Contr wrt* Manuel Reachi]. *Dir of photog* Leo Tover. [*2d cam* Ernest Laszlo]. [*Asst to 2d cam* S. Burgess]. *Art dir* Hans Dreier and Robert Usher. *Ed* Doane Harrison. [*Asst ed* R. Farrell]. [*Int dec* Sam Comer]. [*Set dresser* G. Sawley]. [*Props* Art Camp and G. Daniels]. *Gowns* Edith Head. [*Ward* Clayton Brackett and Hazel Hagerty]. *Mus score* Victor Young. *Sd rec* Harold Lewis and John Cope. [*Makeup supv* Wally Westmore]. [*Makeup* K. House and J. Hadley]. [*Supv hair* Leonora Sabine]. [*Hair* Hedwig Mjorud and Lavaughn Speer]. [*Asst to prod* R. Blumenthal]. [*Tech adv* Ernesto Romero, Manuel Reachi and Padre Canseco]. [*Dial coach* Phyllis Laughton]. [*Loc mgr* N. Lacey]. [*Secy to prod* Estelle Newburgh and Virginia Keefer]. [*Secy to dir* Eleanor Broder]. [*Scr clerk* La Prele Jones]. [*Unit bus mgr* Charles Woolstenhulme]. [*Child welfare* worker Rachel Smith]. [*Stunts* Jimmy Dundee].

Song(s): "My Boy, My Boy," music by Fritz Spiehman, lyrics by Jimmy Berg, Fred Jacobson and Frank Loesser.

Cast: CHARLES BOYER (*George Iscovescu*), OLIVIA de HAVILLAND (*Emmy Brown*), PAULETTE GODDARD (*Anita Dixon*), Victor Francen (*Van Den Luecken*), Walter Abel (*Inspector Hammock*), Curt Bois (*Bonbois*), Rosemary DeCamp (*Berta Kurz*), Eric Feldary (*Josef Kurz*), Nestor Paiva (*Flores*), Eva Puig (*Lupita*), Micheline Cheirel (*Christine*), Madeleine LeBeau (*Anni*), Billy Lee (*Tony*), Mikhail Rasumny (*Mechanic*), Charles Arnt (*Mr. MacAdams*), Arthur Loft (*Mr. Elvestad*), Mitchell Leisen (*Mr. Saxon*), [Brian Donlevy, Richard Webb (*Actors*)], [Veronica Lake (*Actress*)], [Sonny Boy Williams (*Sam*)], [Edward Fielding (*American consul*)], [Don Douglas (*Joe*)], [Gertrude Astor (*Young woman at Climax Bar*)], [Jesus Topete, Tony Roux (*Mechanics*)], [Francisco Maran (*Mexican doctor*)], [Carlos Villarias (*Mexican judge*)], [June Pickrell (*Mrs. Brown*)], [Buddy Messinger (*Elevator boy*)], [George Anderson (*Emmy's doctor*)], [Pauline Wagner (*Nurse*)], [Harry Shannon (*American immigration official*)], [William Faralla (*Assistant director*)], [Henry Roquemore (*Driver of car*)], [Ella Neal (*Bride*)], [Antonio Filauri (*Mexican priest*)], [Placido Sigueiros (*Old peon*)], [Ray Mala (*Husky young Mexican bridegroom*)], [Soledad Jiménez (*Old peon's wife*)], [Daniel F. Rea (*Ox-cart driver*)], [Russ Clark, Alden Chase (*Cops in patrol car*)], [Jimmy Dundee (*Policeman*)], [Katharine Booth, Jean Phillips (*Girls at desk*)], [June Wilkins (*Miss Vivienne Worthington*)], [Harold F. Landon (*Studio guide*)], [Norman Ainsley (*Waiter with tray*)], [Frank Dae (*Elderly Kiwanis gentleman*)], [Mrs. Wilfrid North (*Elderly Kiwanis gentleman's wife*)], [Mitchell Ingraham (*One of Kiwanis group*)], [Leon Belasco (*Mr. Spitzer*)], [John Hamilton (*Mac*)], [Kitty Kelly (*American lady at bullring*)], [James Flavin (*First immigration guard*)], [Gordon De Main (*Second immigration guard*)], [Martin Faust (*Gas station attendant*)], [Chester Clute (*Man at Climax Bar*)], [Jay Tucker (*Suicide victim*)], [John Mari (*Corpse*)].

Romance. [*Print viewed*]. Roumanian immigrant George Iscovescu sneaks onto the Paramount studio lot in Hollywood to sell a story idea to director Saxon. Desperate for $500, George convinces Saxon to listen to the true story of George's life for the past year: At the outbreak of World War II, George flees from Europe to Mexico, from where he hopes to gain easy entry into the U.S. Due to the quota system, he is told that he must wait five to eight years to immigrate. Discouraged by this news, George checks into the dollar-a-day Esperanza Hotel in a border town. He meets his old flame and former dance partner, Anita Dixon, who tells him that she got citizenship by marrying an American and leaving him shortly thereafter. George, a gigolo and con man, immediately embarks on the same scheme, as many Americans have flooded into town for the Independence Day bullfight and celebration. George's victim is Emmy Brown, a naïve schoolteacher from Azusa, California, who is on a field trip. After George secretly sabotages the repair of the school bus, Emmy is forced to spend the night in the lobby of the Esperanza with her students. At first resistant to George's charm, Emmy soon falls for his artful words of love and they marry the next morning. Although Emmy has to return to Azusa with her students, George must wait four weeks before he will be allowed into the States. He immediately resumes his affair with Anita, and together they plan to go to New York after he leaves Emmy. To their surprise, Emmy reappears a week later, having been given leave by her school principal and been loaned the school bus with which to take her honeymoon. George is disconcerted by her presence and because immigration inspector Hammock is investigating suspicious marriages, he takes Emmy out of town immediately. After a long drive they end up in another small town that is celebrating multiple weddings. The high spirits of the place affect George and he falls in love with Emmy despite himself. Out of consideration for her, however, he pretends to have injured his shoulder on their honeymoon night so that she retains her innocence. After a week they return to the Esperanza where a jealous Anita discovers that George now intends to let Emmy down slowly. Anita reveals George's sordid past and his motives to Emmy, who is shocked but nonetheless protects George when Hammock interrogates her about their "quickie" marriage. Emmy blames herself for being duped and leaves for Azusa, but crashes her car along the way. News of her accident reaches George and he illegally drives across the border. George successfully evades the police and arrives at the hospital in time to restore Emmy's will to live. Knowing that she will recover, he escapes the police again and slips into the Paramount studios to tell Saxon his story, intending to repay Emmy's savings that she had given him with the money he earns from the studio. Hammock catches up with George at the studio and forcibly returns him to Mexico. One day, Hammock finds a dispirited George, who has broken off all relations with Anita, and informs him that he did not record his previous arrest and that he is free to enter the U.S. Hammock then leads George across the border, where Emmy waits to rejoin her true love. *Americans in foreign countries. Deception. Gigolos. Immigrants. Innocents. Marriage. Mexican-American border region. Automobile accidents. Automobile chases. Border patrols. Bullfighters and bullfighting. Children. Dancers. Gold diggers. Holidays. Honeymoons. Mechanics. Mexico. Moral reformation. Motion picture directors. Motion picture studios. Paramount Pictures Corp.. Pregnancy. Romanians. School buses. Schoolteachers. Suicide. Weddings.*

Note: The film opens with the following written prologue: "Perhaps the best way to begin this story is to tell you how it came to us. One day last August into the Paramount Studios in Hollywood walked a man...." The working titles of this film were *Ensenada*, *The Golden Door* and *Memo to a Movie Producer*. According to information in the Paramount Collection at the AMPAS Library, Paramount purchased a story by Ketti Frings titled "Memo to a Movie Producer" for $5,000. Her novel, *Hold Back the Dawn*, based on this story, was published before this film was released.

When this production was first announced in the trade papers, H. J. Anslinger, the United States Commissioner of Narcotics in the Treasury Department took an interest in the matter. Letters in the MPAA/PCA Collection at the AMPAS Library reveal that Anslinger advised the MPPDA that Ketti Frings's husband, Kurt Frings, on whose experiences her novel was based, was a "notorious international character" whose residency in the United States was then under consideration by the Congress. Anslinger stated that "in all probability, Kurt Frings related a story in which imagination played a greater part than fact..." and suggested that a film based on the novel would cause friction between the United States and Mexico. PCA Director Joseph I. Breen consulted with Paramount and noted in his response letter that "the studio...is rather startled by the quite patent inference set forth" in Anslinger's letter and would contact him for further discussion. The final outcome of this exchange was not included in any documentation in these files. However, modern sources report

by the quite patent inference set forth" in Anslinger's letter and would contact him for further discussion. The final outcome of this exchange was not included in any documentation in these files. However, modern sources report that Kurt Frings, a German championship boxer whom Ketti Frings met in Mexico while he was emigrating to the United States, threatened a lawsuit against Paramount after reading the screenplay based on his wife's story because the character of "Iscovescu" had become disreputable, and he feared that this might reflect on him and his wife. Producer Arthur Hornblow, however, accused Frings with theft of the script and threatened to have him deported and the lawsuit was not pursued.

Paramount proceeded to consult with the MPPDA on the script for *Hold Back the Dawn*. The MPPDA's overall estimation by Jan 1941 was that "the present version contains certain elements which seem to be unacceptable by reason of sex suggestiveness.... [I]t will not be acceptable to characterize your sympathetic lead as an immoral man, or to definitely indicate a sex affair between him and Tamara [the character who became "Anita" in the film]." In another letter, Breen told Paramount that "there must, of course, be no suggestion of a connecting door between their [Anita and George's] hotel rooms, as this would inevitably give the unacceptable flavor." Paramount got around this by carefully playing the scenes in the hotel room in a manner that Breen found acceptable.

According to contemporary and modern sources, the Mexican government was dissatisfied with the representation of their country and people in the screenplay and, through the State Department, requested various improvements. For example, as a result of their suggestions, Paramount recast the part of "Lupita," a comedy role, which was originally to be played by Jill Denet, with Eva Puig, the widow of a former Mexican Secretary of State, so that an American was not parodying a Mexican.

Modern sources indicate that further trouble occurred when actor Charles Boyer refused to perform a scene in which his character, dejected by being trapped in Mexico with no prospects of immigration, holds a one-way conversation with a cockroach in his hotel room. The scene was thrown out and because of further troubles with the screenplay, Brackett and Wilder diminished Boyer's role and strengthened de Havilland's, and chose to alter their screen credits from "Screenplay by" to "Written by" because they felt the screenplay was incomplete. Modern sources state that because of this incident, Wilder resolved to direct the films he wrote.

A news item and Paramount publicity information reveals that director Mitchell Leisen joined the Screen Actors Guild so that he could play the part of the director of *I Wanted Wings* in the sequence which was reshot specifically for inclusion in the Paramount lot sequence of *Hold Back the Dawn*. Leisen, who did direct *I Wanted Wings*, donated his bit player wages to charity. According to a *HR* news item, Leisen had initially intended to reshoot a scene with William Holden and Veronica Lake, both stars of *I Wanted Wings*; however, the scene was instead filmed with Lake, Brian Donlevy and Richard Webb.

Information in the Paramount Collection indicates that the Latin American release of the film included credits on the screen for assistant director Francisco Alonso and technical advisers Ernesto Romero (a former Mexican diplomatic attaché) and Padre Canseco. Olivia de Havilland was loaned by Warner Bros. for this film. According to a *HR* news item and information in the Paramount Collection, French actress Germaine Aussey tested for the role that Paulette Goddard ultimately played. This film marks the American film debuts of French actors Victor Francen, Micheline Cheirel and Madeleine LeBeau.

The following information is from Paramount Production Information at the AMPAS Library: The beach scene was filmed on location at Hueneme Beach in Oxnard, and the chase scene was filmed on a highway outside of San Clemente, CA. The band playing "La Marseillaise" was comprised of Hollywood American Legion musicians.

This picture was nominated for Academy Awards in the following categories: Best Picture; Actress (Olivia de Havilland); Best Writing (Screenplay), Charles Brackett and Billy Wilder; Cinematography (Black and White), Leo Tover; Music (Scoring of a Dramatic Picture), Victor Young; and Art Direction/Interior Decoration (Black and White), Hans Dreier and Robert Usher; Sam Comer. De Havilland's sister, actress Joan Fontaine, won the Academy Award for Best Actress for her role in *Suspicion*. Charles Boyer and Paulette Goddard reprised their roles in a *Lux Radio Theatre* broadcast on 10 Nov 1941.

Box 2 Aug 1941. *DV* 31 Jul 1941. *FD* 31 Jul 1941, p. 6. *HR* 4 Feb 1941, p. 8. *HR* 19 Feb 1941, p. 6. *HR* 12 Mar 1941, p. 7. *HR* 4 Apr 1941, p. 4. *HR* 31 Jul 1941, p. 3. *HR* 5 Sep 1941, p. 2. *LAT* 7 Jun 1940. *MPH* 2 Aug 1941. *MPHPD* 6 Sep 1941, p. 251. *NYT* 20 Apr 1941. *NYT* 2 Oct 1941, p. 29. *Var* 30 Jul 1941, p. 8.

HOLD 'EM YALE (Latino)

De Mille Pictures Corp. *Dist* Pathé Exchange, Inc. 14 May **1928** [©Pathé Exchange, Inc.; 14 Apr 1928; LP25186]. Si; b&w. 8 reels, 7,056 ft.

Dir Edward H. Griffith. *Asst dir* Richard Blaydon. *Scen and adpt* George Dromgold. *Scen* Sanford Hewitt. *Titles* John Krafft. *Photog* Arthur Miller. *Art dir* Anton Grot. *Film ed* Harold McLernon.

Source: Based on the play *Life at Yale* by Owen Davis (ca 1906).

Cast: Rod La Rocque (*Jaime Emmanuel Alvarado Montez*), Jeanette Loff (*Helen*), Hugh Allan (*Oscar*), Joseph Cawthorn (*Professor*), Tom Kennedy (*Detective*), Jerry Mandy (*Valet*).

Comedy. An Argentinian named Montez goes to Yale with his pet monkey and meets with great success, especially with one professor's daughter. He becomes a football hero by winning the game against

Princeton in the last few minutes of play. Throughout, a bumbling detective trails Montez because he believes Montez is wanted for something. *Argentines. Bumblers. College life. Detectives. Football. Monkeys. Princeton University. Yale University.*

Note: This film was also reviewed as *At Yale*.
FD 5 Aug 1928.

HOLD YOUR HORSES (Irish Americans)

Goldwyn Pictures Corp. Jan **1921** [©Goldwyn Pictures Corp.; 20 Dec 1920; LP15976]. Si; b&w. 5 reels.

Dir E. Mason Hopper. *Scen* Gerald C. Duffy. *Photog* John Mescall.

Source: Based on the short story "Canavan, the Man Who Had His Way" by Rupert Hughes in *The Saturday Evening Post* (11 Sep 1909).

Cast: Tom Moore (*Daniel Canavan*), Sylvia Ashton (*Honora Canavan*), Naomi Childers (*Beatrice Newness*), Bertram Grassby (*Rodman Cadbury*), Mortimer E. Stinson (*Jim James*), Sydney Ainsworth (*Horace Slayton*).

Comedy. Dan Canavan, a raw immigrant from Ireland, goes from street cleaner to husband of society belle Beatrice Newness. As a street cleaner he is trampled by horses drawing the Newness victoria. The accident leaves on his chest a scar in the shape of a horseshoe that perpetually brings him good luck. He finds he can control the world with the wave of a red flag. He makes this power the basis of his philosophy of life, and becoming a politician, he rises quickly to the position of czar of the city. He takes as his wife the woman whose horses once trampled him. When, however, she tires of his boorish, lower class manner and is about to leave him, he again waves the red flag and she is made to see his intrinsic worth beyond superficial manifestation. *Accidents. Horses. Immigrants. Irish Americans. Politicians. Socialites. Street cleaners. Talismans. Upper classes.*

Note: Rupert Hughes's story was also the basis for the 1915 film *The Danger Signal* (see above) and the 1936 film *It Had to Happen* (see below).
ETR 5 Feb 1921, p. 951. *FD* 6 Feb 1921. *Var* 28 Jan 1921, p. 39.

HOLIDAY INN (African Americans)

Paramount Pictures, Inc.; A Mark Sandrich Production. *Dist* Paramount Pictures, Inc. **1942**; New York premiere: 4 Aug 1942; Prod: 18 Nov 1941—30 Jan 1942 [©Paramount Pictures, Inc.; 12 Jun 1942; LP11636]. Sd (Western Electric Mirrophonic Recording); b&w. 11 reels, 9,044 ft. 100-101 min. Passed by the National Board of Review.

Prod Mark Sandrich. *Dir* Mark Sandrich. [*Asst dir* C. C. Coleman, Jr.]. [*2d asst dir* Oscar Rudolph]. *Scr* Claude Binyon. *Adpt* Elmer Rice. *Based on an idea by* Irving Berlin. [*Contr wrt* Ben Holmes, Zion Myers, Francis Swann and Bert Lawrence]. *Dir of photog* David Abel. *Art dir* Hans Dreier and Roland Anderson. [*Art dir asst* William Flannery]. *Ed* Ellsworth Hoagland. [*Set dresser* Sam Comer and Ray Moyer]. *Gowns* Edith Head. [*Ward des for chorus* Billy Livingston]. *Mus dir* Robert Emmett Dolan. *Mus asst* Arthur Franklin. *Specialty accompaniments* Bob Crosby's Band. [*Vocal arr* Joseph Lilley]. [*Orch scoring* Andrea Setaro]. *Dance ensembles staged by* Danny Dare. [*Dance dir* Sam Ledner]. [*Asst dance dir* George King and Bernard Pierce]. [*Dance staff* Al Mann]. *Sd rec* Earl Hayman and John Cope. *Makeup artist* Wally Westmore. [*Hair supv* Leonora Sabine]. [*Prod asst* Zion Myers]. [*Unit mgr* Charles Woolstenhulme]. [*Loc mgr* N. Lacey]. [*Pub* Jean Bosquet]. [*Stills* John Ellis]. [*Irving Berlin's secy* Eunice Douglas]. [*Scr clerk* Grace Dubray]. [*Secy and scr clerk* Trudy Wellman]. [*Dance secy* Hazel Noe]. [*Singing voice for Marjorie Reynolds* Martha Mears].

Song(s): "You're Easy to Dance With," "I'll Capture Her Heart Singing," "White Christmas," "Let's Start the New Year Right," "Happy Holiday," "Abraham," "Be Careful It's My Heart," "Plenty to Be Thankful For," "I Can't Tell a Lie," "Easter Parade," "Firecracker Song," "Song of Freedom" and "Lazy," music and lyrics by Irving Berlin.

Cast: Bing Crosby (*Jim Hardy*), Fred Astaire (*Ted Hanover*), Marjorie Reynolds (*Linda Mason*), Virginia Dale (*Lila Dixon*), Walter Abel (*Danny Reed*), Louise Beavers (*Mamie*), Irving Bacon (*Gus*), Marek Windheim (*Francois*), James Bell (*Dunbar*), John Gallaudet (*Parker*), Shelby Bacon (*Vanderbilt*), Joan Arnold (*Daphne*), [June Ealey, David Tihmar (*Specialty dancers*)], [Edward Emerson (*Man at Holiday Inn*)], [Leon Belasco (*Proprietor in flower shop*)], [Harry Barris, Ronnie Rondell (*Orchestra leaders*)], [Jacques Vanaire (*Assistant headwaiter*)], [Keith Richards, Reed Porter

(*Assistant directors*)], [Oscar G. Hendrian, Robert Homans (*Doormen*)], [Katharine Booth (*Hatcheck girl*)], [Judith Gibson (*Cigarette girl*)], [Barbara Slater, Alaine Brandes, Laurie Douglas, Louise LaPlanche (*Waitresses*)], [Lynda Grey (*Dancing girl*)], [Lora Lee (*Girl*)], [William Cabanne, Kenneth Griffith (*Boys*)], [Bud Jamison (*Santa Claus*)], [Muriel Barr, Patsy Bedell, Marion Colby, Loretta Barnett, Glen Forbes, Bob Locke Lorraine, Ross Murray, Don Brown (*Dancers*)], [Kitty Kelly], [Edward Arnold, Jr.], [Mel Ruick], [Anthony Nace].

Musical comedy, Romance. [*Print viewed*]. On Christmas Eve in New York, the performing trio of singer Jim Hardy, dancer Ted Hanover, and singer and dancer Lila Dixon, split up when Lila chooses to marry Ted and continue performing rather than marry fiancé Jim, who plans to quit performing to run a farm. After a year of struggling with farm work in Connecticut, and several weeks of recuperation in a sanitarium, Jim decides on a less exhausting occupation and opens Holiday Inn, a country-style inn which features live entertainment and is only open on holidays. As a way of stopping Linda Mason, an ambitious performer who works selling flowers, from pestering him, Ted's agent, Danny Reed, sends Linda to Connecticut to audition for Jim. The two are attracted to each other and Jim offers her a job. On New Year's Eve, after Lila jilts Ted so that she can marry a Texas millionaire, Ted travels to Holiday Inn to drown his sorrows. He arrives drunk, but immediately engages in a dance with Linda. The patrons all think that she is Ted's new dance partner and applaud as Ted collapses in a drunken stupor. In the morning, Ted cannot remember much about Linda but becomes determined to find her and make her his new dance partner. Jim does everything he can to thwart Ted's plans because he has fallen in love with Linda. Although Linda performs on Lincoln's birthday at the inn, Ted does not recognize her because Jim makes her wear blackface make-up for her number. Ted does find her on Valentine's Day, however, and insists that they perform together for Washington's birthday. Ted mercilessly pursues Linda to draw her away from Jim, and stays on at the inn through the next few holidays. When Jim overhears that Ted has brought two Hollywood film producers to see the Fourth of July show, he secretly asks his driver, Gus, who is picking Linda up at the train station, to make sure that she does not arrive in time for the show, and then invites Lila, who did not marry after all, to perform. Gus drives the car into a pond, and when Linda hitches a ride on the road, she is picked up by Lila. Unaware of Linda's identity, Lila tells Linda her story, and on the pretense of taking a shortcut, Linda makes sure Lila drives into the pond as well. Both women show up too late for the performance, but the producers offer to buy the idea of Holiday Inn to use as the basis of a musical. Having earned the enmity of all his friends because of his deception, Jim reluctantly agrees to the idea, but insists on remaining in Connecticut to write the music while Ted and Linda go to Hollywood. On Thanksgiving Day, when a lonely and dispirited Jim reads that Ted and Linda are engaged, his concerned housekeeper, Mamie, convinces him not to give up and to pursue Linda honestly. Jim arrives in Hollywood on Christmas Eve, just before Ted and Linda's wedding. Despite Ted and Danny's efforts, he manages to sneak onto a soundstage which has been set up like his Holiday Inn, and as Linda performs "White Christmas," the first song they ever sang together, Jim sings along and the two are happily reunited. Finally, on New Year's Eve, the two couples, Jim and Linda and Ted and Lila, perform together at Holiday Inn. *Dancers. Holidays. Nightclubs. Romantic rivalry. Singers. African Americans. Children. Christmas Eve. Deception. Drunkenness. Easter. Engagements. Farmers. Florists. Fourth of July. Gold diggers. Housekeepers. Inns. Laziness. Lure of the country. Motion picture producers. Motion picture studios. New Year's Eve. New York City. Proposals (Marital). St. Valentine's Day. Thanksgiving Day. Theatrical agents.*

Note: Opening credits read "Irving Berlin's *Holiday Inn*." Information in the Paramount Collection at the AMPAS Library reveals the following information about the production: Renie DeMarco, Richard Denning, Macdonald Carey, (erroneously called "Donald Carey") and Janet Blair were tested for roles in this film. Fred Astaire worked for two weeks without pay as a Christmas gift to Paramount. After three days of rehearsal, the firecracker dance sequence became the last scene to be shot and took two days to film. A *Paramount News* news item indicates that Julia Faye, Mildred Harris, Jane Novak and Ruth Clifford were slated to appear in the film. However, Clifford was not identified in the viewed print, and the participation of the other actresses in the film has not been confirmed. *HR* news items add the following information about the production: Paramount planned to include a special musical dance sequence to commemorate Navy Day, using a revamped version of an old Irving Berlin

song, "This Is a Great Country," but the number was dropped and was probably never shot. Plans for an elaborate opening in Los Angeles in Aug 1942 were abandoned due to wartime conditions on the Pacific coast. Proceeds from the New York premiere went to the Navy Relief Society. In Sep 1942, the shoes Fred Astaire wore in the firecracker sequence were sold at a Cleveland, OH, auction for $116,000 worth of war bonds, and then one shoe and both laces were later resold for another $22,000 worth of war bonds. According to modern sources, Berlin devised the concept for this film after he wrote the song "Easter Parade" for the 1933 Broadway play *As Thousands Cheer*, and subsequently planned a musical revue based on major American holidays. The musical play was never produced, but Berlin later pitched the idea to Mark Sandrich, who had worked with him on three Fred Astaire-Ginger Rogers pictures at RKO. A modern source notes that Berlin's contract stipulated that his music would not be altered once filming began, and lists Walter Scharf as a music arranger and director. Berlin won an Academy Award for his song, "White Christmas," and the film was nominated for Academy Awards in the following categories: Best Writing (Original Story), Irving Berlin; Best Music (Scoring of a Musical Picture), Robert Emmett Dolan. Berlin's "White Christmas" went on to become one of the most popular recorded songs in history. Although a 1960 article in *L.A. Mirror News* indicates that Berlin originally wrote "White Christmas" in 1938, a Berlin biography and other modern sources agree that the song was an original written for *Holiday Inn*. "White Christmas" was a favorite with homesick soldiers during World War II, and Crosby frequently sang it during USO tours. For many years it remained the largest-selling record in history. The Abraham Lincoln number is often cut from television prints due to the offensive nature of the performers in blackface. One of the notable dance numbers in the film was "Say It With Firecrackers," in which Astaire hurls firecrackers from his pocket and steps onto charges especially laid out in the floor to create small explosions in honor of Independence Day. Another number frequently shown in documentaries on Astaire is the "drunk dance," in which he appears to be drunk as partner Marjorie Reynolds helps him to stay upright. Bing Crosby and Fred Astaire again co-starred in the 1946 film *Blue Skies*, directed by Stuart Heisler, which also featured songs by Irving Berlin. In 1954, Paramount released the film *White Christmas*, which was loosely inspired by *Holiday Inn*. Robert Emmett Dolan produced the later film, which was directed by Michael Curtiz, starred Crosby and Danny Kaye, and featured songs by Irving Berlin, including the title song.

Box 13 Jun 1942. *DV* 15 Jun 1942, p. 3. *FD* 15 Jun 1942, p. 6. *HR* 13 May 1941, p. 1. *HR* 12 Jun 1941, p. 4. *HR* 20 Aug 1941, p. 4. *HR* 21 Aug 1941, p. 4. *HR* 28 Aug 1941, p. 1. *HR* 18 Sep 1941, p. 2. *HR* 14 Oct 1941, p. 4. *HR* 10 Nov 1941, p. 4. *HR* 14 Nov 1941, p. 2. *HR* 18 Nov 1941, p. 4. *HR* 4 Dec 1941, p. 3. *HR* 15 Dec 1941, p. 4. *HR* 23 Dec 1941, p. 1. *HR* 30 Mar 1942, p. 5. *HR* 8 Jul 1942, p. 2. *HR* 15 Jun 1942, p. 3. *HR* 22 Sep 1942, p. 6. *Down Beat* 15 Dec 1944, p. 7. *MPHPD* 13 Jun 1942, p. 713. *NYT* 5 Aug 1942, p. 16. *Var* 17 Jun 1942, p. 8.

HOLLYWOOD, CIUDAD DE ENSUEÑO (Spanish language)
Fenix Film Corp. *Dist* Universal Pictures Corp. **1932**; Havana, Cuba opening: 31 Dec 1931; San Juan, Puerto Rico opening: 11 Mar 1932; Los Angeles opening: 25 Dec 1933; Prod: Oct 1931 at International Film Studios. Sd; b&w. 8 reels. 68 or 72 min. Spanish language.

Dir George Crone. *Asst dir* Arthur Black. *Scr* Miguel de Zárraga. *Orig story* José Bohr. *Photog* Harry Jackson. *Mus dir* Carlos Molina.

Song(s): "Hollywood, ciudad de ensueño," "Si usted me pone a mí en el cine" and "Alice, I Love You," composed by José Bohr and Eva Bohr.

Cast: José Bohr (*José*), Lia Torá (*Helen Gordon*), Donald Reed (*Actor*), Nancy Drexel (*Alice*), Enrique Acosta (*Film director*), Elena Landeros, César Vanoni, Nicanor Molinare, Julia Bejarano, Myra Rayo, Luis Díaz Flores, Samuel Pedraza, Lloyd Ingraham.

Melodrama. [*Viewed print incomplete*]. After leaving a remote area of South America, José, a dreamer, comes to Hollywood seeking fame and fortune. Having taken the first step, José struggles to find his way in the movie business, and because he resembles a particular Hollywood star, he is given a chance by Helen Gordon, the hard-boiled head of a studio. As Helen's discovery, José becomes a success, while Helen, who has fallen in love with him, becomes jealous of the attention he receives from Alice, a blonde actress who tries to learn Spanish to communicate her passion to him. Eventually, José's love affair with Alice puts an end to his career. Defeated, José, who enjoyed for a moment the sweet sensation of success, returns to his country, older and completely disillusioned. *Disillusionment. Hollywood (CA). Motion picture actors and actresses. Motion pictures. City-country contrast. Envy. Jealousy. Motion picture producers. South America. Women in business.*

Note: The working title of this film was *Bajo el cielo de Hollywood*. The print viewed lacked two reels, including the first.
CM Feb 1932, p. 146. *FD* 10 Apr 1934, p. 6. *NYT* 4 Apr 1934, p. 26.

HOLLYWOOD, LA CIUDAD DE CARTÓN *see* LA CIUDAD DE CARTÓN

THE HOLY LIE see STAR FOR A NIGHT

THE HOLY MARTYR see YISKOR

THE HOLY OATH (Yiddish language)

Ray Film Co. *Dist* Ray Film Co. **1937**; Bronx opening: 24 Dec 1937; Prod: recorded at Reeves Sound Studio, Inc., New York. Sd; b&w. 6 reels, 5,100 ft. 57 min. Yiddish language with English subtitles.

Dir Henry Steward. *Asst dir* Abraham Appel. *Wrt* Henry Lynn. *Cam* J. Burgi Contner. *Mus dir* Jack Stillman. *In the Arabian "doine"* Dave Tarras. *Sd eng* Ernest Franck.

Cast: Morris Strassberg (*Abraham [Goldstein]*), Anna Appel (*The woman*), Lucy Levine (*The daughter*), Lazar Fried (*Rabbi*), Anna Weissman (*Golde [Goldstein]*), Murray White (*David [Herschberg]*).

Yiddish, Documentary, Drama. [*Print viewed*]. Golde Goldstein is dressed to go to a masquerade ball, but her boyfriend, David Herschberg, a lover of poetry, prefers to stay home. Golde's father Abraham, upon learning about the ball, suggests that they instead go with him to a Zionist meeting. David says that while growing up, he had no time for "cheder," Jewish schooling, because of public school and music lessons and calls the meeting a waste of time. Abraham then proceeds to tell them a story and promises that at the end, depending on David's response, either he, Abraham, will go with them to the ball, or David will go with him to the meeting. Abraham describes the creation of the earth and the Garden of Eden, later known as Palestine, a land flowing with milk and honey, which, he says, God gave to the people of Israel. Scenes are shown of Hebron, the town where Adam and Eve made their home, where Noah's children went following the flood, and which Joshua entered with the children of Israel from the wilderness. Hebron is shown in ruins, as is Jerusalem, now that the Jews have been driven out and it is inhabited by nomadic Bedouins. Abraham relates the holy oath that Jews took upon themselves when they were driven out: "If I should forget you, Jerusalem, let my right hand be forgotten." Abraham says that in the two thousand years since the Jews were driven out, they lived in many lands in which they were not allowed to even mention Palestine. A Jewish mother, seen with her crying child, asks the eternal question: "Why do they persecute us?" She then prays for guidance for their children and for the end of their troubles. As Abraham describes to Golde scenes of rioting in which Jews are shot by soldiers, these scenes are shown. Golde asks, "How can a people suffer so much?" Abraham replies that their children gave them courage. After scenes are shown of Arabs in Jerusalem and at the wailing wall, Abraham tells about the worldwide Jewish movement to get back the land and rebuild it, and thus keep the holy oath. He relates that fifty years earlier, Theodor Herzl first called on Jews to return to Palestine. The following scenes are shown of a new Palestine and Jerusalem: a new library with four million books; Hebrew University; the Nathan Straus Health Center; the National Fund Building, where land is bought for Jewish people; a Jewish shepherd; Jewish farmers working; Jewish daughters working the land, preparing wine at a vineyard, and breaking rocks for the building of roads; oranges being packed; factories; railroads; the Jordan river; a forest planted in honor of Lord Arthur James Balfour, who, as the British foreign secretary in November 1917, devised the Balfour Declaration, which lent British support to the establishment of a Jewish homeland in Palestine; the blooming colonies of Richon L'Zion, Nes Tziyono, Gdera and Eckron; a Jewish festival; streets in Tel Aviv; and the shores of Kinereth. Abraham states that the Jewish people will overcome hardships and win, and as the Jewish anthem "Hatikvah" is played, Jews march and the Jewish flag flies. *Jerusalem (Palestine). Jews–History. Palestine. Pledges. Regeneration. Religious persecution. Zionism. Arabs. Children. Creation. Factories. Farms. Theodor Herzl. Masked balls. Riots. Jordan River. Tel Aviv (Palestine). Vineyards.*

Note: The Yiddish title of this film is *Di Heylige Shvue*. No reviews were located for the film. While Ray Film Co. is listed as the manufacturer in NYSA records and as presenter in the onscreen credits, the credits open with a Star of David insignia, in which the word "Zion" is written in Yiddish. It is possible that "Zion" was the name of the production company. NYSA records list S & L Film Co. as the local exchange. Henry Lynn, who is credited as the writer of the film on an existing script, and Jack Stillman, credited onscreen as musical director, were co-producers of S & L's previous production, the 1935 Yiddish film *Bar-Mitzvah* (see above). The running time listed above was calculated from footage given in NYSA records. Although the screen credits state that the film was copyrighted in 1937, the film is not listed in the copyright register. The film contains footage of street fighting between soldiers and Jews from newsreels or other films. A modern source speculates that some dramatic footage in the film may have come from earlier Yiddish films. The film was re-released by Cinema Service Corp. An existing print is 42 minutes in length.

UN HOMBRE DE FRAC see UN CABALLERO DE FRAC

UN HOMBRE DE SUERTE (Spanish language)

Cinéstudio Continental; controlled by Paramount Famous Lasky Corp. *Dist* Paramount Famous Lasky Corp. **1930**; San Juan (Puerto Rico) opening: 13 Sep 1930; San Antonio (Texas) opening: 20 Sep 1930; Prod: Apr 1930. Sd; b&w. 8,607 ft. 96 min. *Country of origin* France. Spanish language.

Prod Robert T. Kane. *Dir* Benito Perojo. *Scr* René Barbéris. *Spanish adapt and dial* Pedro Muñoz Seca. *Photog* Harry Stradling. *Mus dir* José Sentis.

Source: Based on a play by Yves Mirande and Gustave Quinson (production undetermined).

Cast: Roberto Rey (*Lucano Barbosa/Lucas Gómez*), María Luz Callejo (*Urbana*), Valentín Parera (*Castrense*), Rosario Pino (*Doña Bermuda*), Carlos San Martín (*Don Digno Lesaca*), Joaquín Carrasco (*El jardinero*), Amelia Muñoz (*Isidra*), Helena D'Algy (*Salomé*).

Comedy. [*Not viewed*]. Lucano Barbosa, a young physician, opens a fully equipped medical practice in the center of Madrid to cure just about anything except his own lack of funds. Fortunately for him, news comes that a neighbor is near death from asphyxiation as a result of attempting to swallow an unshelled nut. Although he does not quite understand how he manages it, Lucano's first attempt saves the man. The patient can not pay him, but gives Lucano an old parchment that he says is valuable. On examining the parchment, Lucano discovers a map on the back detailing where a large quantity of gold coins are hidden. Eager to locate the fortune, Lucano takes a job as a chauffeur at a castle referred to in the map. However, Lucano does not anticipate that the spinster owner of the castle will attempt to seduce him or that he will be dismissed as an impostor. An enchanting niece, however, wants to share not only her heart with him, but also the treasure which she has already discovered. *Maps. Medical clinics. Physicians. Romance. Treasure. Asphyxia. Castles. Chauffeurs. Debt. Impersonation and imposture. Madrid (Spain). Nieces. Rescues. Seduction. Spinsters.*

Note: After the completion of the 1930 French production *Un trou dans le mur* (translated as *A Hole in the Wall*, but unrelated to the 1921 and 1929 American-made films of that title), Spanish and Swedish-language versions were shot. A *Var* review of the Swedish version's New York opening gives the running time as 101 min. The running time listed below was derived from the footage listed in NYSA censorship records. The film was advertised as the first 100% talking picture in Swedish. In an interview, Swedish director Edvin Adolphson stated that he traveled to London and Paris to learn techniques of sound film production. Adolphson also noted that the Paramount Joinville studio was not completed by the time production on the Swedish version had begun, so it was instead filmed at the Gaumont studio. To appeal to Danish and Norwegian audiences, actors Viking Ringheim and Else-Marie Hansen were hired. The Swedish-language version included the song "När rosorna slå ut," music by Sonja Sahlberg, lyrics by Nils Perne and George Eliasson.

Other language version(s):

Un trou dans le mur (French language)

1930; Paris opening: 6 Jun 1930; San Francisco opening: 5 Feb 1931. Sd; b&w. 83 min.; Country of origin: France. French language.

Prod Robert T. Kane. *Dir* René Barbéris. *Scr* René Barbéris.

French-language cast: Jean Murat (*André de Kerdrec*), Dolly Davis (*Lucie*), Léon Bélières (*Le comte de Corbin*), Marguerite Moreno (*Arthémise*), Pierre Brasseur (*Anatole*), Suzanne Dehelly (*La couturière*), Lucien Callamand (*Le jardinier*), Charles Lamy (*L'antiquaire*), Fanny Clair. [*French version not viewed*]

När rosorna slå ut (Swedish language)

1930; Stockholm opening: 30 Jul 1930; New York opening: 7 Feb 1931. Sd; b&w. 9,814ft. 109 min.; Country of origin: France. Swedish language.

Prod Robert T. Kane. *Dir* Edvin Adolphson. *Adpt and Swedish dial* Gösta Stevens and Edvin Adolphson.

Swedish-language cast: Karin Swanström (*Countess Charlotte*), Nils Wahlbom (*The Count*), Margita Alfvén (*Marguerite, the Count's daughter*), Sven Gustafsson (*Anatole, her fiancé*), Uno Henning (*André, attorney*), Anna-Lisa Baude (*Madame Jeanne*), Elsa de Castro (*Attorney's secretary*), Viking Ringheim (*Gardener*), Else-Marie Hansen (*Maid*). [*Swedish version not viewed*].

Var 18 Jun 1930.

EL HOMBRE MALO see THE BAD MAN

UN HOMBRE PELIGROSO (Spanish language)

Producciones Latinas, Ltd. *Dist* Criterion Pictures Corp. **1935**; New York opening: 11 Oct 1935; Prod: Jun 1935. Sd; b&w. 7 reels, 5,743 ft. 64 min. Spanish language.

Pres M. David Strong. *Dir* Richard C. Kahn. *Story* Richard C. Kahn. *Dial* Paul Ellis. *Photog* Leonard Poole and Victor Fisher. *Art ed* William Faris. *Mus supv* Alberto Corral and M. Camacho Vega. *Sd* Ralph G. Fear. *Sd eng* Floyd Campbell. *Prod mgr* B. W. Lamont.

Song(s): "Flores y manzanilla (Flowers and Wine)," "Camila mía (My Camila)" and "Paloma mía (My dove)," composers undetermined.

Cast: Anita Campillo (*Camila Castro*), Paul Ellis (*Juan Belgrano*), Carmen La Roux (*Carmen*), Jaime Devesa (*Miguel Farley*), Felipe Turich (*José Gomez*), Elena Madrigal, Daniel F. Rea.

Comedy-drama, with songs. [*Not viewed*]. In Mexico, at a picnic where children play and gypsies entertain, Juan Belgrano attempts to speak alone with the beautiful Camila Castro, with whom he is in love, but their conversation is interrupted by Camila's bossy aunt, who reminds Camila that she is engaged to Miguel Farley. Desperate to talk to Camila privately, Juan asks his friend José Gomez to divert the vain and gullible Mrs. Castro's attention from her niece by flirting with her and flattering her. After much pleading, Mrs. Castro convinces José, and Juan is able to take Camila away from the crowd, where he declares his love and begs her not to marry Farley. Camila replies that she is in love with Juan, but must marry Farley, who has threatened to reveal a dark secret about her father's past if she refuses. When Farley arrvies at the picnic, he roughs up Juan. Later, Camila has her palm read by the gypsy Carmen, who warns her of dire consequences if she marries Farley. That evening, Camila's family realizes that she has disappeared and, as they saw Farley leaving the picnic alone, they surmise that she has been kidnapped by the gypsies. Juan learns of Camila's disappearance and tracks down the gypsies' wagons, but they deny having Camila and a search turns up no trace of her. As Juan is leaving the camp, Carmen approaches him and tells h;m that Farley paid her father, the leader of the gypsies, to kidnap Camila and deliver her to him at a cabin in the remote Lost Canyon. At the cabin, Farley, furious over Camila's love for Juan, threatens to kill both Juan and her father if he refuses to cross the border and go with him to Chicago. Juan arrives at the cabin just in time to save Camila, and he bests Farley in a fight, although Camila accidently knocks him out in the confusion. When Juan comes to, Camila is at his side and a gleeful José is congratulating him on his newly acquired wealth. A confused Juan then learns that Farley was a wanted man and that there was a $10,000 reward for his capture. Juan then declares that his true reward will be Camila, and the couple embrace. *Blackmail. Gypsies. Marriage—Forced by circumstances. Romantic rivalry. Aunts. Fights. Fortune-tellers. Fugitives. Kidnapping. Picnicking. Rewards.*

Note: Some reviews translate the title as "A Dangerous Man." The plot synopsis was taken from a dialogue continuity deposited at the NYSA.

FD 17 Oct 1935, p. 4. *NYT* 14 Oct 1935, p. 21.

EL HOMBRE QUE ASESINÓ (Spanish language)

Paramount British Productions; controlled by Paramount Publix Corp. *Dist* Paramount Publix Corp. **1932**; Bilbao, Spain opening: 13 Jan 1932; San Juan, Puerto Rico opening: 12 Mar 1932; Los Angeles opening: 22 Sep 1932; Prod: May—Jun 1931 at British and Dominions Studios, Elstree, England. Sd; b&w. 7 reels, 6,200 ft. 69 min. *Country of origin* Great Britain. Spanish language.

Dir Dimitri Buchowetzki. *Dial dir* Fernando Gomis. *Scr* Reginald Denham. *Spanish vers* Carlos de Batlle.

Source: Based on the novel *L'homme qui assassina* by Claude Farrère (Paris, 1907) and the play of the same name by Pierre Frondaie (Paris, 19 Dec 1912).

Cast: Rosita Moreno (*Lady María Falkland*), Ricardo Puga (*Lord Archibald Falkland*), Carlos San Martín (*Colonel De Sevigné*), Helena D'Algy (*Lady Edith*), Gabriel Algara (*Príncipe Cernuvitz*), Luis Llaneza (*Mehemed Pachá*), Jesús Castro Blanco (*Narcise Boucher*), José Brujó (*Monsour*), José Argüelles (*Djelli*), Antonio Martiánez.

Drama. [*Not viewed*]. Colonel De Sevigné is invited to Istanbul by Marshal Mehemed Pachá, an old friend whose life he saved in battle and who is now chief of police. During his visit, De Sevigné falls in love with Lady María Falkland, a young English woman married to a neglectful husband and the mother of a young boy, who is the only consolation in her miserable marriage. Lord Falkland, who is having an affair with his wife's cousin, plans to put his wife in a compromising situation so that he can seek custody of their son when they divorce. However, before he can accomplish this, he is stabbed to death by the colonel. Although De Sevigné confesses to the police, Pachá destroys all the evidence that might incriminate his friend, and De Sevigné is freed. *Friendship. Istanbul (Turkey). Murder. Officers (Military). Police chiefs. Romance. Confession (Law). Cousins. English. Evidence. Frame-ups. Infidelity. Mothers and sons. Neglected wives. Nobility. Police. Stabbings.*

Note: No reviews were located for this film. The running time listed above was calculated from footage given in NYSA records. This was the Spanish-language version of the British-Paramount film *Stamboul*, which also was directed by Dimitri Buchowetzki, and starred Rosita Moreno and Warwick Ward. No information has been located concerning any showings of the English-language version in the U.S.

HOMBRES EN MI VIDA (Spanish language)

Columbia Pictures Corp. *Dist* Columbia Pictures Corp. **1932**; Los Angeles opening: 13 Feb 1932; Prod: Dec 1931—Jan 1932. Sd; b&w. 9 reels. Spanish language.

Dir David Selman. *Dial dir* Eduardo Arozamena. *Scr* Robert Riskin and Dorothy Howell. *Spanish dial* René Borgia.

Source: Based on the novel *Men in Her Life* by Warner Fabian (New York, 1930).

Cast: Lupe Vélez (*Julia Clark*), Gilbert Roland (*Jaime Gilman*), Ramón Pereda (*Andrés Brennon*), Carlos Villarías (*Bray, abogado defensor*), Paul Ellis (*Conde Ivan Karloff*), Luis Alberni (*Gaston*), Paco Moreno (*Criado Williams*), Virginia Ruiz, Marina Alcañiz.

Romance, Comedy-drama. [*Not viewed*]. [The following plot summary is based on the English-language version of this film, *Men in Her Life*; character names refer to that version. For further information regarding the English-language version, please see the note below and the entry for *Men in Her Life* in the *AFI Catalog of Feature Films, 1931-40*.] Julia Cavanaugh, a beautiful American socialite traveling alone in Europe, visits the small French town of St. Valery. There she meets the handsome Count Ivan Karloff, whose romantic, old-fashioned charm convinces her that he is different from her sophisticated but conventional suitors back home in New York. Believing herself to be in love with Karloff, she accepts his proposal of marriage. She discovers that her family fortune has been lost, but the count's ardor does not diminish and they are married immediately. The next day, Julia awakes to find that Karloff has left, taking her money and jewels and leaving her penniless. Julia is about to be evicted from the inn when Flashy Madden, a former New York racketeer and bootlegger, arrives and recognizes her. He pays her hotel bill and offers to drive her back to Paris, where she has friends. On the way, Flashy expresses his desire to acquire the manners of a gentleman and asks her to become his "social mentor." Julia accepts the unorthodox position, and Flashy's manners gradually improve during the next month in Paris, although he often reverts to his old ways. He falls in love with Julia and is about to propose when Dick Webster, the son of a United States senator, asks her to marry him, and Julia accepts, although she is thinking only of security and not of love. The couple returns to New York, and just before the nuptials, Flashy visits Julia to offer his best wishes. While Flashy is waiting to speak with her, Karloff arrives and tries to blackmail Julia by demanding $50,000 for the return of her letters. That night, Flashy again comes to Julia's rescue by tricking the count into surrendering the letters. Karloff pulls a gun on Flashy, however, and is killed in the ensuing struggle. The gallant Flashy telephones Julia to inform her that her letters have been destroyed, and then maintains complete silence about the nature of his quarrel with Karloff in order to protect Julia's name. Flashy's lawyer, Blake, tells Julia that Flashy's silence will mean a death sentence, and she agrees to testify on his behalf at the trial. Although Julia's testimony wins Flashy's acquittal, Dick decides that she is no longer good enough for his family because of her association with the former bootlegger. Undisturbed by Dick's lack of faith in her, Julia finally agrees to marry Flashy, the one true gentleman she has met during her travels. *Marriage. Racketeers. Romantic rivalry. Trials. Americans in foreign countries. Aristocrats. Bankruptcy. Blackmail. Bootleggers. Desertion (Marital). Engagements. Etiquette. Inns. Lawyers. Murder. New York City. Paris (France). Prisons. Socialites. Thieves.*

Note: For information on the English-language version, *Men in Her Life,*

which was directed by William Beaudine and starred Lois Moran and Charles Bickford, please see the entry for that film in the *AFI Catalog of Feature Films, 1931-40*; F3.2816. Adrienne D'Ambricourt and Antonio Vidal may have been in the cast of the Spanish-language version but their participation in the film has not been confirmed.

CM May 1932, p. 333.

HOME BEFORE DARK (Jewish Americans)

Warner Bros. Pictures, Inc.; A Mervyn LeRoy Production. *Dist* Warner Bros. Pictures, Inc. 22 Nov **1958**; Prod: 15 Jan—early Apr 1958 [©Warner Bros. Pictures, Inc.; 22 Nov 1958; LP15312]. Sd (RCA Sound Recording); b&w. 14 reels, 12,283 ft. 136-137 min. PCA cert no. 18922.

Dir Mervyn LeRoy. *Asst dir* Ivan Volkman. *Scr* Eileen Bassing and Robert Bassing. *Dir of photog* Joseph F. Biroc. *Art dir* John Beckman. *Film ed* Philip W. Anderson. *Set dec* Ralph Hurst. *Cost des* Howard Shoup. *Mus supv* Ray Heindorf. *Sd* Stanley Jones. *Makeup supv* Gordon Bau. [*2d asst to Mervyn LeRoy* John J. Kissel].

Song(s): "Home Before Dark," music by Jimmy McHugh, lyrics by Sammy Cahn.

Source: Based on the novel *Home Before Dark* by Eileen Bassing (New York, 1957).

Cast: JEAN SIMMONS [(*Charlotte Bronn*)], DAN O'HERLIHY [(*Arnold Bronn*)], RHONDA FLEMING [(*Joan Carlisle*)], EFREM ZIMBALIST, JR. [(*Jake Diamond*)], Mabel Albertson [(*Inez Winthrop*)], Steve Dunne [(*Hamilton Gregory*)], Joan Weldon [(*Frances Barrett*)], Joanna Barnes [(*Cathy Bergner*)], Kathryn Card [(*Mattie*)], Marjorie Bennett [(*Hazel Evans*)], Johnstone White [(*Malcolm Southey*)], Eleanor Audley [(*Mrs. Hathaway*)], [Tom Gleason (*Tony Barrett*)], [Rand Harper (*Joe Bergner*)], [Hal Taggart (*Professor Hathaway*)], [Bunny Waters (*Miss Helman*)], [Mary Alan Hokanson (*Dorothy Green*)], [Albert Godderis (*Dr. Von Linden*)], [Frieda Stoll (*Elsa Von Linden*)], [Walter Bacon (*Professor Dennison*)], [Mary Koval (*Mrs. Dennison*)], [Gail Bonney (*Clerk*)], [Lillian Culver (*Mrs. Franklin*)], [Ed Prentiss (*Dr. Collins*)], [Fred Blau, Jr. (*Male patient*)], [Chuck Hicks (*Male attendant*)], [Edna Holland (*Miss Angie*)], [Hart Sprager (*Teddy Brinker*)], [Edwin Jerome (*Dr. Beadley*)], [Stacey Marshall (*Buyer*)], [Evelyn Clarke (*Receptionist*)], [Joel Marston (*Frederic*)], [Susan Davis, Elizabeth Flournoy (*Salesladies*)], [Barbara Bell Wright (*Miss Evers*)], [Lillian West (*A fitter*)], [Betsy Duncan (*Girl vocalist*)].

Psychological, Drama. [*Print viewed*]. After a year's seclusion in Maraneck State Hospital in New England, twenty-six-year-old Charlotte Bronn is ready to return home. Her husband Arnold is warned by Dr. Collins that many patients come back within a year, because they return to the same situation that precipitated the breakdown. Collins worries that Charlotte holds a deep resentment towards her stepsister, Joan Carlisle, who lives with them, but Arnold assures him that they got along well before Charlotte's hospitalization. When the childlike Charlotte greets Arnold, he acts reserved. On the drive home to Cape Marble, Massachusetts, Arnold mentions they have a boarder, Jack Diamond, the first Jew on the faculty of the college where Arnold teaches. Arnold, who says he has always been against anti-Semitism, relates that some of the faculty members have been critical of Jake, as they do not want an influx of Jews. He also reveals that he hopes to be promoted to head of the philosophy department by ingratiating himself with Jake's sponsor. The next day, when Charlotte questions the reason Arnold did not sleep the previous night in their bedroom, he falsely tells her that Dr. Collins suggested she should sleep alone for awhile. At dawn one morning, Charlotte goes to the shore, where she finds Jake, who is doing a lobster run for an older man. He invites her for coffee, and they find that they both feel like outsiders in the town. As they walk, the wife of one of Arnold's colleagues notices them together. At a clothing store, Charlotte is humiliated when the proprietor makes her call Arnold to get his approval before she purchases a dress. When she asks Arnold to take a day off and spend it with her, he refuses. Jake decides not to go to a faculty gathering, and Arnold, offended and afraid Jake's behavior will bode ill for his chance at the promotion, characterizes him to Charlotte as a type who likes to sneer at others. That evening, Jake finds Charlotte, who also has refused to go to the gathering, asleep in the study. As he covers her, she touches his hand, then embraces and kisses him. Awakening, she pushes him away and he apologizes for accepting the kiss. When Arnold arrives home with Joan, Charlotte tries to kiss him, but he pulls away coldly. The next day, with a burst of energy, Charlotte announces she is joining Joan and her stepmother, Inez Winthrop, on a shopping trip to Boston. Joan runs into Hamilton Gregory, a former classmate, whom she rejected in favor of Arnold, who was then her professor. Hamilton, who has become an alcoholic, invites her to his apartment, where he indelicately implies that Arnold is having an affair with Joan. When her friend, Cathy Bergner, who is going through marital difficulties, asks Charlotte for advice concerning what she did when she learned about Arnold's affair with Joan, Charlotte is shocked, as Joan assured her recently that there had never been anything between her and Arnold. She walks five miles through the snow to Arnold's college, then interrupts a meeting and questions him to his discomfort. Charlotte protests to Arnold that if he wants her to get well the two of them should go away together, and he finally agrees to take her to Boston over the Christmas holidays, as he needs to see people at Harvard regarding the promotion. In Boston, Arnold loses his temper with Charlotte in their hotel room. She meets Hamilton, and when she tells him that she suspects Arnold is drugging her, he realizes something is wrong. He tries to set up an appointment for her with a psychiatrist, but she leaves him and goes instead to a beauty salon, where she has the owner make her into a blonde with braids in the back, like Joan has. She next sees a gown that looks like one of Joan's, and though it is much too large, she buys it and then meets Arnold and his guests in the hotel dining room. She introduces herself as Joan, then trips and loses a shoe, creating a scene. Arnold carries her to their room and cries when he is alone. Later that evening, Charlotte begs her husband to admit he doesn't love her, saying she can only save herself if she knows she is not deluded in that belief. When he calls her love an obsession, she bites his hand and he then acknowledges that he doesn't love her. Charlotte agrees to wait a month before seeking a divorce so there will be no scandal that could jeopardize his promotion. She finds Jake by the shore, and he relates that Arnold killed the last chance he had to stay at the college when he learned it was not to his advantage to support him. He says he has found a job in New York at a magazine and asks her to join him. Saying she is the last thing he or anybody needs, Charlotte refuses, but asks him to come to the New Year's dance for support. At the dance, people stare at the two of them together, and when Arnold insults her and looks longingly at Joan, Charlotte tells him to go to hell. She leaves with Jake, who kisses her and tells her he'll be at a hotel if she needs him. When Arnold and Joan return home, Charlotte confronts Joan for lying. She resolves, however, not to blame Arnold or Joan, or herself, for her breakdown, though she tells Arnold she doesn't love him and Joan that she hates her. She packs and calls Jake to ask him to drive her to Boston. She then calls Hamilton to have him find her a place to stay and make an appointment with a doctor. She tells Arnold she will file for divorce in Boston after the semester break, and that she expects him to move out of her house, as she is closing it down. Outside she cries, but Jake arrives and hugs her, and they drive off together. *Divorce. Infidelity. Marriage. Massachusetts. Mental Illness. Neglected wives. Professors. Small town life. Stepsisters. Alcoholics. Antisemitism. Beauty shops. Boston (MA). College life. Dances. Discrimination in employment. Dressmakers. Impersonation and imposture. Jews. Lobsters. Lodgers. Ostracism. Sanitariums. Snobs and snobbishness. Stepmothers.*

Note: Exteriors for the film were shot in Boston, Marblehead, Wakefield and Salem, Massachusetts, according to publicity for the film. The author of the best-selling novel, Eileen Bassing, formerly lived in Marblehead, which was the basis for the fictional "Cape Marble" of the book and film. Additional filming took place at the Crystal Room of the Beverly Hills Hotel, which was used for the hotel in Boston, and at Point Sequit on the coast at Malibu for the scenes by the lobster traps.

Box 20 Oct 1958. *Box* 27 Oct 1958. *Cue* 8 Nov 1958. *DV* 10 Oct 1958, p. 3. *Exh* 15 Oct 1958, p. 4523. *FD* 14 Oct 1958, p. 39 *Har* 11 Oct 1958, pp. 162-63. *HCN* 21 Nov 1957. *HR* 21 Nov 1957. *LAEx* 21 Nov 1958. *LAT* 20 Nov 1958 *MPD* 10 Oct 1958. *MPHPD* 11 Oct 1958, p. 4. *Newsweek* 10 Nov 1958. *NYT* 7 Nov 1958, p. 23. *SatRev* 29 Nov 1958. *Time* 10 Nov 1958. *Var* 15 Oct 1958, p. 6.

HOME OF THE BRAVE (African Americans)

Screen Plays II Corp. *Dist* United Artists Corp. May **1949**; World premiere in New York: 12 May 1949; Prod: late Feb—late Mar 1949 [©Screen Plays II Corp.; 17 Jun 1949; LP2476]. Sd (Western Electric Recording); b&w. 10 reels, 7,737 ft. 86 min. Passed by the National Board of Review. PCA cert no. 13715.

Prod Stanley Kramer. *Assoc prod* Robert Stillman. *Dir* Mark Robson. *Asst dir* Ivan Volkman. *Dial dir* Don Weis. *Scr* Carl Foreman. *Photog* Robert de Grasse. [*Cam op* Charles Burke]. [*Gaffer* Frank Uecker].

[*Stills* Scotty Welborne]. *Spec eff* J. R. Rabin. *Prod des* Rudolph Sternard. *Film ed* Harry Gerstad. *Set dec* Edward G. Boyle. *Ward* Joe King. *Mus comp and dir* Dimitri Tiomkin. *Sd eng* Jean Speak. *Sd rec* Sound Services, Inc. *Makeup supv* Gus Norin. *Prod mgr* Clem Beauchamp. *Head grip* Morris Rosen. *Poem* Eve Merriam.

Source: Based on the play *Home of the Brave* by Arthur Laurents (New York, 27 Dec 1945).

Cast: Douglas Dick (*Major Robinson*), Steve Brodie ([*Corporal*] T. J. [*Everett*]), Jeff Corey (*Doctor*), Lloyd Bridges (*Finch*), Frank Lovejoy (*Mingo*), James Edwards ([*Peter*] *Moss*), Cliff Clark (*Colonel*).

African American, World War II, Drama. [*Print viewed*]. During World War II, black soldier Peter Moss is admitted to a military hospital suffering from partial amnesia and paralysis. After the doctor finds no physical injury to account for his condition, the doctor asks Moss's superior, Maj. Robinson, to recount for him their recent reconnaissance mission: Robinson recalls that he had chosen his best men for a four-day mission to survey a Pacific island occupied by Japanese forces. Summoned to Robinson's office are Corp. T. J. Everett, a cartographer named Finch and another soldier named Mingo. When Moss arrives, Finch, his old school chum, is thrilled to see him, while Robinson expresses dismay. Robinson phones Col. Baker immediately to complain about Moss's race, but is told that he was the only surveyor to volunteer. Back at the hospital, the doctor begins a treatment called "narco-synthesis," in which drugs are used to trigger repressed memories. When the shot is administered, Moss recalls that after landing on the beach, the team buried their rubber dinghy in the sand. During their breaks from collecting data, Moss and Finch plan the restaurant and bar that they will open when they return home. After Moss and Finch become lost, however, Finch blames Moss and almost calls him "nigger." Just as a disappointed Moss is forced to acknowledge Finch's racist feelings, Finch is shot. Realizing that he is badly injured, Finch tells Moss to leave with the maps. Back in the hospital, Moss wakes up from his trance feeling that he was responsible for Finch's death. During a subsequent session, however, Moss recalls that he had asked Robinson for permission to return for Finch, but had been refused. From their position near the beach, the team listens to Finch's plaintive cries as he is tortured by Japanese soldiers. Robinson instructs T. J. to cross the beach and uncover the dinghy, instructing each of them to fire four quick shots if they encounter trouble. Moss volunteers to wait at the camp while the others go the beach to inflate the dinghy. Suddenly, he sees Finch crawl into a nearby clearing and die. Now finding that he is unable to walk, Moss fires four shots to summon the team, who must carry him to the dinghy. Back in the hospital, Moss awakens from his trance, and the doctor postulates that after seeing Finch shot, he experienced a momentary flash of relief that the bullet had wounded Finch, instead of him. This feeling of relief then led to guilt, the doctor explains, and the result was paralysis. To persuade Moss to try and walk, the doctor shouts, "Get up, you dirty nigger," which so angers Moss that he struggles to his feet and stumbles forward. By the time he has crossed the room, however, Moss's anger has subsided, and he gratefully embraces the doctor. The next day, shortly after he is discharged, Moss meets Mingo, who has lost an arm in battle. Moss repeats the doctor's explanation of his paralysis, and Mingo admits to feeling momentarily relieved after seeing a buddy shot. This admission consoles Moss, and he and Mingo decide to become partners in the restaurant and bar business. *African Americans. Combat. Psychosomatic illness. Racism. World War II. Beaches. Boats. Drugs. Friendship. Guilt. Gunshot wounds. Hospitals. Islands. Maps. Officers (Military). Physicians. Psychology. Soldiers. Surveyors.*

Note: The working title of this film was *High Noon*. In Arthur Laurents' play, the character played by James Edwards is Jewish, and the conflict revolves around antisemitism. The *Var* review commented that the thematic switch was made because antisemitism had already been depicted in previous Hollywood films and was therefore in danger of being "overplayed." A 20 Mar 1949 *NYT* news item notes that associate producer Robert Stillman "paid the entire cost of the picture with the help of his father without recourse to the banks, a startling departure from Hollywood custom." A 23 Mar 1949 *DV* news item reported that producer Stanley Kramer shot for two weeks on the picture before securing the legal rights to Laurents' play. According to a 28 Feb 1949 *HR* news item, some scenes in the film were shot in Malibu and Baldwin Hills, CA and government footage of fighting in the Pacific was to be included. On 21 Mar 1949, *HR* reported that background choral work would be performed by the Jester Hairston Choir, but their participation in the released film has not been confirmed. *HR* also noted on 30 Mar 1949 that Screen Plays had received a request for a print of the film from President Truman.

MPH called the film "the first picture dealing with anti-Negro prejudice."

Although initially banned in Southern Rhodesia by the South African government, the film was eventually approved for public screenings, excluding "children and natives." Despite early fears, the picture was not censored or protested in the South, although African Americans in Houston were allowed to attend only midnight screenings. *Parents Magazine* gave the picture a "special merit award," and Kramer was honored by the G. W. Carver Memorial Committee for his work on the film. *Home of the Brave* was one of several race-oriented films produced by various companies during the late 1940s, among them *Lost Boundaries* and *Pinky* (see entries below). Modern sources note that producer Stanley Kramer created a black press campaign and arranged for an opening of the film in Harlem, NY. Aside from this, one modern source notes, the film bore all of the marks of a typical Hollywood production: "the Breen office, the tradepapers, regional censors, preview respondents, distributor feedback, critics. In effect, the entire infrastructure of the industry signaled its readiness to resume the retailing of race-angled material."

Box 30 Apr 1949. *DV* 23 Mar 1949. *DV* 29 Apr 1949, p. 3. *DV* 1 Aug 1949. *DV* 29 Nov 1949. *FD* 29 Apr 1949, p. 8. *HR* 28 Feb 1949, p. 11. *HR* 4 Mar 1949, p. 13. *HR* 18 Mar 1949, p. 11. *HR* 21 Mar 1949, p. 7. *HR* 30 Mar 1949, p. 13. *HR* 18 Apr 1949, p. 12. *HR* 26 Apr 1949, p. 6. *HR* 29 Apr 1949, p. 3. *HR* 3 Aug 1949, p. 1. *HR* 1 Dec 1949. *HR* 19 Dec 1949, p. 6. *LADN* 11 Aug 1949. *MPHPD* 30 Apr 1949, p. 4590. *NYT* 20 Apr 1949. *NYT* 13 May 1949, p. 29. *Var* 4 May 1949, p. 11.

THE HOMESTEADER (African Americans, Scottish Americans)

Micheaux Book and Film Co.; Western Book Supply Co. Mar—Apr **1919**. Si; b&w. 7-8 reels.

Prod Oscar Micheaux. *Dir* Oscar Micheaux and Jerry Mills. *Scen* Oscar Micheaux.

Source: Based on the novel *The Homesteader* by Oscar Micheaux (Sioux City, 1917).

Cast: Charles D. Lucas (*Jean Baptiste*), Evelyn Preer (*Orlean*), Iris Hall (*Agnes Stewart*), Inez Smith (*Ethel*), Vernon S. Duncan (*N. Justine McCarthy*), Charles S. Moore (*Jack Stewart*), Trevy Woods (*Glavis*), William George (*Agnes's white lover*).

African American, Drama. Agnes Stewart, a Scottish girl who has come to South Dakota with her father, takes refuge in an isolated house during a blizzard. Hearing cries outside, she rescues Jean Baptiste, a black man who was in danger of freezing to death. Baptiste, who owns the house, falls in love with Agnes but despairs of overcoming the social barriers that prevent their union. He returns East to his people and marries Orlean, the daughter of preacher N. Justine McCarthy, a vain man who soon takes offense at Baptiste's refusal to praise him. Enlisting the aid of Orlean's sister Ethel and brother-in-law Glavis, McCarthy begins a campaign of persecution against Baptiste that Orlean is too weak-willed to battle. Finally Orlean goes insane, kills her father, and commits suicide. Baptiste returns to South Dakota and meets Agnes, who has discovered that she is really black. The two find happiness together at last. *African Americans. Fathers-in-law. Marriage. Miscegenation. Parricide. Racism. South Dakota. Suicide. Blizzards. Egotists. Fathers and daughters. Insanity. Preachers. Scottish Americans.*

Note: This was Oscar Micheaux's first film. Micheaux's company was located in Chicago. Contemporary sources disagree on whether Micheaux or Jerry Mills was the director. One contemporary source cites black film pioneer William Foster as doing "detailed service" on the production. Micheaux's production company was alternately called the Micheaux Book and Film Co. and the Micheaux Film Co. in ads. Modern sources call Evelyn Preer's character Orleans instead of Orlean. Some information in the plot synopsis comes from a 1927 interview with Preer. Micheaux's 1948 film *The Betrayal* is sometimes described as a loose remake of *The Homesteader* (see below).

ChiDef 22 Feb 1919, p. 14. *New York Age* 25 Dec 1920, p. 6.

LA HOMICIDA see LA INCORREGIBLE

L'HOMME DES FOLIES BERGÈRE (French language)

20th Century Pictures, Inc.; A Darryl Zanuck Production. *Dist* United Artists Corp. **1935**; New York opening: 18 Apr 1936; Prod: une production—Darryl Zanuck. Sd (Western Electric Noiseless Recording); b&w. 9 reels, 7,479 ft. 83 min. French language.

Pres JOSEPH M. SCHENCK. *Producteurs associés* [*Assoc prod*] William Goetz and Raymond Griffith. *Mise-en-scène de* [*Dir*] Roy Del Ruth and Marcel Achard. [*2d asst dir* Gabriel Scognamillo]. *Adpt* Jessie Ernst. *Scènario de* [*Scen by*] Marcel Achard, Bess Meredith and Hal Long. *Opérateur* [*Photog*] Barney McGill. *Photographie des danses par* [*Dances photog by*] Peverell Marley. *Montage* [*Film ed*] Allen McNeil and Sherman Todd. *Décors* [*Sets*] Richard Day. *Cost* Omar Kiam. *Chef d'orchestre* [*Mus dir*] Alfred Newman. *Danses crées par* [*Dances created by*] Dave Gould. *Ingénieurs de son* [*Sd eng*] Vinton Vernon and Roger Heman.

Song(s): "Au Revoir l'Amour," "C'Etait Ecrit," "La Romance de la Pluie" and "Le Chapeau de Paille," music by Jack Stern, French lyrics

by André Hornez; "Vous avez dit ce que j'allais dire," music by Burton Lane, French lyrics by André Hornez; "Valentine," by André Christine and Alfred Willemetz.

Source: Based on the play *The Red Cat* by Rudolph Lothar and Hans Adler (New York, 19 Sep 1934).

Cast: MAURICE CHEVALIER (*Deux roles, d'Eugene Charlier et Baron Cassini*), Natalie Paley (*La Baronne Cassini*), Sim Viva (*Mimi*), Jacques Louvigny (*Gustave Chatillard*), André Berley (*Pierre Baneffe*), Fernand Ledoux (*François*), André Cheron (*Morizet*), Ferdinand Gottschalk (*Perichot*), Ramsay Hill (*Christian de Guntherson*), Jules Raucourt (*Le ministre de finances*), Georges Renavent (*Le président du conseil*), Barbara Leonard (*Antoinette*), Pauline Garon (*Lulu*), [Eugene Borden (*Victor*)], [Albert Petit (*Joseph*)], [Fred Cavens (*Airport official*)], [Marcelle Corday (*Josephine*)], [Jacques Lory (*Stage manager*)], [Helen Mann, June Gale (*Cassini number*)].

Musical comedy. [*Not viewed*]. [The following plot summary is based on the English-language version of this film, *Folies Bergère de Paris*; character names refer to that version. For further information regarding the English-language version, please see the note below and the entry for *Folies Bergère de Paris* in the *AFI Catalog of Feature Films, 1931-40*.] After Eugene Charlier, star of the Folies Bergère in Paris, impersonates in his act the flirtatious Baron Cassini, the real baron, Fernand, goes backstage to congratulate Charlier and meets Charlier's lover Mimi, whom he tries to seduce. Meanwhile, Genevieve, the baroness, who is disillusioned with the baron's cheating and their passionless marriage, calls Charlier to her table, but she is taken aback when he flirts with her. When Henri Baneffe and Gustave Chatillard, the officials at the baron's bank, learn that the baron has gone to London to avoid bankruptcy by trying to get a loan to repay the twenty million francs he lost on the Nero mine in Mozambique, they hire Charlier to impersonate the baron during a reception for the premier of France. Genevieve plays along with the deception, although Charlier does not know that she knows he is not Fernand, and as a jest, she encourages his romantic inclinations. When Monsieur Paulet, the finance minister, asks to buy the baron's shares of stock in the Nero mine, Charlier unwittingly gets the price up to twenty-five million francs. Meanwhile, Mimi, angry at Charlier's absence, goes to visit the baron, whereupon Charlier, as the baron, kisses her to test her fidelity. She backs away until she recognizes the scratch marks she gave Charlier earlier, and then, to make him jealous, asks him to make violent love to her. Charlier slaps her, they argue and he leaves. The real baron returns and, having learned that Genevieve earlier had flirted with Charlier, tries to seduce her. Realizing the ruse, Genevieve kisses the baron passionately and leaves him thinking that she has betrayed him, but the next day, the baron, now aware of his wife's game, convinces her that he just arrived in town that morning. Ill with despair because she thinks that she earlier kissed Charlier, Genevieve learns the truth when he comes for a letter of recommendation. Although she tries to confuse the baron further, he kisses her passionately to prove that the earlier kiss was his. Later, he and the baroness watch Charlier, who has reconciled with Mimi, perform again in the Folies Bergère. Deception. Doubles. Entertainers. Flirtation. Folies Bergère. Impersonation and imposture. Marriage. Nobility. Ruses. Bankers. Bankruptcy. Loans. Mines. Paris (France).

Note: The onscreen credits for the French version of the film were taken from a screen credit sheet in the Twentieth Century-Fox Produced Scripts Collection at the UCLA Theater Arts Library. Reviews of the New York opening of the play *The Red Cat*, upon which this film was based, noted that it was presented with the backing of Twentieth Century Pictures. The *Var* reviewer of the film commented that the play was a flop. According to the *MPH* review of the play, the character of "Baron Cassini" was based on "a combination of Otto Kahn, Match King [Ivar] Kreuger, with a touch of the late Monsieur [Serge Alexandre] Stavisky."

According to a *DV* news item dated 20 Oct 1934, attorneys for the Folies Bergère in Paris attempted to halt production, charging that the film would cause the show irreparable damage. The studio, however, went ahead with the preparation and, according to the news item, photographed the theater from every angle. According to *Dancing Times*, Twentieth Century Pictures Vice-President in Charge of Production Darryl Zanuck, acquired in Paris the rights to use the title *Folies Bergère*.

According to a pressbook in the copyright descriptions, Maurice Chevalier had been a star of the Folies Bergère, where he gained fame as the partner of the renowned performer Mistinguette. Modern sources state that Charles Boyer was first offered the leading role, but because of his recent marriage to Pat Paterson, he declined and suggested Chevalier.

The French version was shot simultaneously with the English-language version, according to the call sheets in the Produced Scripts Collection.

Zanuck, in a letter in the MPAA/PCA Collection at the AMPAS Library, stated that for the French version, he brought over "the best known translators and adaptors headed by Mr. Marcel Achard" and that he "borrowed from the Theatre Française the leading actors and imported some of the best known screen names." The screen credits for the French version noted that actor Fernand Ledoux was from the Comédie Française. Gossip columnist Sidney Skolsky's column of 15 Jan 1935 in *DN* was devoted to the filming of a scene in the French version in which he was present on the set. As Skolsky described the scene, the camera followed Chevalier backstage to reveal an onstage tableau of "nude girls." Skolsky noted that the shooting of the scene drew many observers and that the scene was taken over and over again. He also stated that the members of the regular dancing chorus refused to work in the sequence, because they feared the harm that might come to their later careers because of the scene, should they become stars. The studio, according to Skolsky, was then forced to hire professional models. According to information in the MPAA/PCA Collection at the AMPAS Library, PCA Director Joseph Breen inquired of Zanuck about the scene, and Zanuck informed him that the director of the French version "permitted several of the stage girls to walk through the various scenes with their breasts uncovered" and that he, Zanuck, allowed the director "to uncover the breasts of some of the people that were merely used as atmosphere backstage inasmuch as this picture has not been made for exhibition in America or any English speaking countries." Following this exchange, Will H. Hays, President of the MPPDA, informed Schenck that under an agreement reached by the MPPDA Board, there could be no deviation from the principles of the Production Code in the making of any picture in an American studio, and thus that there could be no shot allowed in the French version that would be objectionable under the Production Code. Hays commented in a letter to Schenck, "It would do real harm, indeed, if they ever start making in Hollywood pictures of nude breasts." Zanuck responded with an angry letter to Breen, in which he began, "Hasn't Mr. Hays got enough troubles of his own without trying to find something else to worry about?" He conceded that several scenes "photographed as background atmosphere only" contained "several French chorus girls with their breasts uncovered. I have managed to eliminate them to the extent that they are quite inconspicuous." Zanuck went on to assure Breen, "Our French version could be seen tomorrow by any American audience and there would be nothing any more offensive in it than there is in the American version." In a letter dated 21 Mar 1935, Zanuck explained to Breen that he could not submit a print of the French version for review because the negative and only print had already been sent to France, where, because of an arrangement with the French United Artists Co., who financed the film, all further prints would be struck. However, Zanuck assured Breen that the French verison contained "no nude or undraped women—I saw to it that the one girl with her breasts uncovered was eliminated. You can assure the General [i.e. Hays] that he can sleep well; Hollywood has again upheld the true standards of France." On 9 Apr 1935, a contact in France wrote the Hays Office that he had viewed the film and "didn't see any naked breasts in it. All appear to be covered." When the French version played in New York in Apr 1936, *Var* commented, "Rumor lane had it that the French version had been made a good deal more risque than the original. If so, it doesn't show as screened here."

Modern sources list as additional cast members in the French version, Ferdinand Munier, Albert Pollet, Mario Dominici and Olga Borget. Twentieth Century-Fox remade the film twice: in 1941 as *That Night in Rio*, directed by Irving Cummings and starring Alice Faye and Don Ameche; and in 1951 as *On the Riviera*, directed by Walter Lang and starring Danny Kaye and Gene Tierney. For information on the English-language version, *Folies Bergère de Paris*, which was directed by Roy Del Ruth and starred Maurice Chevalier and Merle Oberon, please see the entry for that film in the *AFI Catalog of Feature Films, 1931-40*; F3.1414.

DN 15 Jan 1935. *NYT* 18 Apr 1936, p. 19. *Var* 22 Apr 1936, p. 19.

HONDO (Native Americans, Apache)

Wayne-Fellows Productions. *Dist* Warner Bros. Pictures, Inc. 4 Jan **1954**; New York opening: week of 26 Nov 1953; Los Angeles opening: 25 Dec 1953; Prod: early Jun—early Aug 1953 [©Wayne-Fellows Productions; 4 Feb 1955; LP4424]. Sd (RCA Sound System); col (WarnerColor); 3-D. 7,532 ft. 80 or 83-84 min. PCA cert no. 16575.

Prod Robert Fellows. *Dir* John Farrow. [*2d unit dir* John Ford]. *Asst dir* Nat Barragar. *Scr* James Edward Grant. *Photog* Robert Burks and Archie Stout. *Stills* Don Christie. *Spec eff* Al Gonzalez. *Art dir* Alfred Ybarra. *Ed* Ralph Dawson. *Property man* Joseph La Bella. *Ward* Carl Walker. *Mus* Emil Newman and Hugo Friedhofer. *Sd dial rec* Nicolas de la Rosa. [*Sd Ed* Borschell]. *Makeup artist* Web Overlander. *Prod mgr* Nate H. Edwards. *Unit prod mgr* Andrew McLaglen. *Tech adv* Major Philip Kieffer. *Scr supv* Sam Freedle.

Source: Based on the short story "The Gift of Cochise" by Louis L'Amour in *Collier's* (5 Jul 1952).

Cast: JOHN WAYNE [(*Hondo Lane*)], and introducing Geraldine Page [(*Angie Lowe*)], Ward Bond [(*Buffalo*)], Michael Pate [(*Vittoro*)], James Arness [(*Lennie*)], Rodolfo Acosta [(*Silva*)], Leo Gordon [(*Ed Lowe*)], Tom Irish [(*Lt. McKay*)], Lee Aaker [(*Johnny Lowe*)], Paul Fix [(*Major Sherry*)], Rayford Barnes [(*Pete*)].

Western. [*Print viewed*]. In the rugged Southwest of 1874, U.S. Cavalry dispatch rider Hondo Lane seeks refuge for himself and his

dog Sam at Angie Lowe's ranch, after losing his horse in a battle with Apache Indians. While offering Hondo her hospitality and a horse, Angie tells him that she and her young son Johnny are expecting her husband Ed to return home at any moment. Hondo, however, sees through her lie, and she later admits that Ed deserted her in the aftermath of an Indian uprising. After telling Angie that Apache Chief Vittoro has called a war council, Hondo tries to persuade Angie to leave the ranch before the next raid, but she refuses, insisting that the Apaches are friendly. Shortly after Hondo leaves Angie, Apaches surround her ranch and menace her. When Johnny tries to protect his mother by firing a gun at one of the Indians, Vittoro commends the boy's bravery and makes him a blood brother. Before leaving, Vittoro promises Angie that no harm will come to her now that Johnny is his blood brother. Meanwhile at the frontier post, Hondo is challenged to a fistfight by a poker player, who he later learns is Ed Lowe. Vittoro, who believes that Angie's husband is dead, returns to the Lowe ranch and demands that Angie choose one of his braves to be her new husband. Angie protests Vittoro's order, but the chief is determined to see Angie marry an Apache if her husband does not turn up. While Hondo makes his way back to the Lowe ranch, he discovers that Ed is following him. Hondo later saves Ed's life when they come under attack by the brother of Indian sub-chief Silva. Hondo kills Ed, however, when he tries to shoot him in the back. Hondo then resumes his journey, but not before taking a tintype of Johnny from the dead man. Back on the trail, Hondo is captured by the Indians, and is tortured by Silva. When Vittoro discovers the tintype, he believes that Hondo is Johnny's father and orders a halt to the torture. Before freeing Hondo, though, Vittoro orders that he engage Silva in a knife fight to give Silva the opportunity to avenge the killing of his brother. Hondo is injured in the fight, but is delivered to Angie, who tells the chief that he is her husband. Before leaving the Lowe ranch, Silva exacts his revenge on Hondo by killing Sam. When a Cavalry unit arrives at the Lowe ranch, Hondo keeps his promise to Vittoro and refuses to help the men save the remaining settlers. Vittoro is killed in a battle with the Cavalry, and afterward, Silva becomes the new Apache chief. After killing Silva, Hondo takes Angie and Johnny to his ranch in California to begin a new life. *Apache Indians. Desertion (Marital). Romance. United States. Army. Cavalry. Women ranchers. Attempted murder. Blood brotherhood. Dogs. Fistfights. Indians of North America–Mixed blood. Knife fighting. Marriage–Forced. Mistaken identity. Mothers and sons. Ne'er-do-wells. Photographs. Revenge. Widowers.*

Note: Louis L'Amour's short story was also published in a 1954 collection entitled *Bar 3; Round-up of Best Western Stories.* A novelization of the film, titled *Hondo,* was published in 1953 and released simultaneously with the picture. Information contained in the AMPAS Library file on the film indicates that the picture was nominated for an Academy Award as "Best Motion Picture Story," but that the nomination was disqualified by L'Amour, who asserted that his short story was not an original motion picture story. This picture marked Broadway actress Geraldine Page's first starring screen role. Although reviews claim that Page made her motion picture debut in *Hondo,* she had appeared in small parts in two previous films. Warner Bros. publicity materials note that John Ford directed second unit battle scenes. According to the *HR* review, some filming took place in Camargo, Mexico.

Modern sources add Chuck Roberson to the cast. Page was nominated for an Academy Award in the category of Best Supporting Actress. *Hondo* was televised in 1989 on a syndicated network as part of a benefit honoring the National Easter Seal Society's 75th anniversary. The film was shown in 3-D, with money from sale of special 3-D glasses donated to the Easter Seal Society. In 1991, a similar television airing of the film benefitted the Leukemia Society of America. In 1967, M-G-M made a television pilot inspired by L'Amour's story, titled *Hondo and the Apaches.* The pilot, which was directed by Lee H. Katzin and starred Ralph Taeger and Kathie Browne, never aired on American television, but was released theatrically overseas. Taeger and Browne also starred in *Hondo,* a television series based on L'Amour's story, which ran from 8 Sep—29 Dec 1967 and aired on the ABC network.

Box 28 Nov 1953, p. 34. *Box* 5 Dec 1953. *DV* 25 Nov 1953, p. 3. *DV* 2 Mar 1989. *FD* 27 Nov 1953, p. 4. *HR* 5 Jun 1953, p. 11. *HR* 31 Jul 1953, p. 9. *HR* 21 Oct 1953. *HR* 25 Nov 1953, p. 3. *HR* 16 May 1991. *MPHPD* 28 Nov 1953, p. 2085. *Var* 25 Nov 1953, p. 6.

HONEY (*foreign version*) *see* **CHÉRIE**

HONEYMOON HATE (foreign version) *see* **EL PRÍNCIPE GONDOLERO**

HONG YIEN FEI BO MING (Chiese language)
Grandview Film Co. **1947?**; Hong Kong showing: 1947? Sd; b&w. Length undetermined. Chinese language. [*Not viewed*]. [No information concerning the plot of this film has been located.].

Note: The Cantonese transliterated title is *Hung Ngan Fei Bog Ming.* This film was probably made in the U.S.

THE HONOR OF HIS HOUSE (Japanese Americans)
Famous Players-Lasky Corp. *Dist* Famous Players-Lasky Corp.; Paramount Pictures. 1 Apr **1918** [©Famous Players-Lasky Corp.; 25 Mar 1918; LP12217]. Si; b&w. 5 reels.
Dir William C. de Mille. *Asst dir* John Brown. *Story and scen* Marion Fairfax. *Cam* Charles Rosher.
Cast: Sessue Hayakawa (*Count Ito Onato*), Florence Vidor (*Lora Horning*), Jack Holt (*Robert Farlow*), Maym Kelso (*Mrs. Proudweather*), Tom Kurahara (*Sato*), Forrest Seabury (*Mr. Proudweather*).
Drama. While marooned on a desert island, Dr. Robert Farlow and wealthy toxicologist Count Ito Onato both fall in love with Lora, a beautiful Japanese-American girl. Lora prefers Robert but decides to reject him because of his excessive fondness for drinking. After their rescue, Lora marries Count Ito, but Robert, still in love and resolving to win her, abandons his drinking, and soon attains a reputation in medicine equalled only by the count's. When Robert again encounters Lora, he asks her to elope with him, but she refuses. The count, however, suspects that his wife has been unfaithful and poisons her. Upon learning that she is innocent, the count decides to give Lora a massive transfusion of his own blood, knowing that the operation will be fatal to him. Lora survives to give birth to Ito's son, and later, she marries the repentant Robert. *Alcoholics. Fidelity. Physicians. Regeneration. Self-sacrifice. Blood–Transfusion. Castaways. Islands. Japanese Americans. Nobility. Poisoning. Rescues. Toxicologists.*
ETR 13 Apr 1918, p. 1538. *MPN* 20 Apr 1918, p. 2420. *MPW* 6 Apr 1918, p. 135. *MPW* 20 Apr 1918, p. 430. *Wid's* 18 Apr 1918, pp. 1090-91.

THE HONORABLE FRIEND (Japanese Americans)
Jesse L. Lasky Feature Play Co. *Dist* Paramount Pictures Corp. 24 Aug **1916** [©Jesse L. Lasky Feature Play Co.; 9 Aug 1916; LP8894]. Si; b&w. 5 reels.
Dir Edward J. Le Saint. *Asst dir* B. L. Howard. *Scen* Eva Unsell. *Story* Elizabeth McGaffey. *Cam* Harold Rosson.
Cast: Sessue Hayakawa (*Makino*), Tsuri Aoki (*Toki-Ye*), Raymond Hatton (*Kayosho*), G. Kino (*Goto*), M. Matsumato (*Hana*), Billy Elmer (*Murphy*).
Drama. When Kayosho, a wealthy curio dealer in California, sees a photograph of Toki-Ye, the niece of Goto, his general manager, he forgets all about his engagement to Hana, Goto's daughter. He sends to Japan for Toki-Ye, but pretends that he is bringing her to California to marry Makino, who runs Kayosho's nurseries. When Toki-Ye arrives, she and Makino fall in love and are married in an American ceremony. Kayosho, however, soon discloses his intention of making Toki-Ye his wife and claims that only a Japanese marriage can be a legal one. Then, when Kayosho is found murdered shortly after making Toki-Ye a prisoner in his house, both she and Makino, each believing the other to be guilty, confess to the crime. Finally, however, it is discovered that Goto killed Kayosho because he had broken his engagement with Hana, and then, cleared of the murder charge, Toki-Ye and Makino begin living as husband and wife. *Duplicity. Japanese Americans. Marriage. Murder. Self-sacrifice. California. Curio dealers. Engagements. Fathers and daughters. Imprisonment. Photographs. Revenge. Social customs. Weddings.*
Motog 9 Sep 1916, p. 611. *MPW* 2 Sep 1916, p. 1603. *MPW* 9 Sep 1916, p. 1685. *NYDM* 2 Sep 1916, p. 26. *NYT* 28 Aug 1916, p. 7. *Var* 25 Aug 1916, p. 25. *Wid's* 31 Aug 1916, p. 830.

THE HONOURABLE GENTLEMEN *see* **PAGAN LOVE**

HOON SI GWAY LAI (Chinese language)
Grandview Film Co. **1947?**; Hong Kong showing: 1947? Sd; b&w. Length undetermined. Chinese language.
Cast: Wong Hok-sing. [*Not viewed*]. [No information concerning the plot of this film has been located.].
Note: The Cantonese transliterated title is *Wen Hei Quei Loi.* This film was probably made in the U.S.

HOP, THE DEVIL'S BREW (Chinese Americans)
Bluebird Photoplays, Inc. *Dist* Bluebird Photoplays, Inc. 14 Feb **1916** [©Universal Film Mfg. Co.; 18 Jan 1916; LP7443]. Si; b&w. 5 reels.
Dir Lois Weber and Phillips Smalley. *Scen* Lois Weber. *Cam* Al Siegler and Frank Williams. *Mus accompaniment selected and arr* R M. Winkler.

Cast: Phillips Smalley (*Ward Jansen*), Lois Weber (*Lydia Jansen*), Marie Walcamp (*Jane Leech*), Charles Hammond (*William Waters*), Juan De La Cruz (*Con Leech*), Ethel Weber.

Drama. While customs official Ward Jansen works in the Orient investigating opium smuggling, his wife Lydia, alone in San Francisco and despondent over the death of her child, becomes addicted to the drug. When Ward returns, he notices Lydia's strange behavior, but does not attribute it to opium. Then, Ward cracks down on a local gang of opium smugglers led by Lee Gow, who, with the help of Lydia's maid Jane, smuggles opium inside a fish from a ocean liner offshore. The opium is then hidden in playing cards and distributed to men in Chinatown who pay money for the cards. When Ward raids Lee Gow's opium den, he finds Lydia among the addicts, and learns that her father, William Waters, a respected city councilman, is the head of the smuggling operation. When William discovers that he has contributed to his own daughter's dependence on drugs, he kills himself, after which, with Ward's support, Lydia successfully rehabilitates herself. *Chinese Americans. Customs officials. Drug addicts. Opium. Police raids. Politicians. San Francisco (CA). Smuggling. Gangs. Political corruption. Regeneration. Suicide.*

Note: The film was made with the assistance of the United States Customs Service, and was shot primarily in San Francisco. According to an announcement in the copyright descriptions, "every episode of smuggling and distributing opium shown in this picture is based upon actual happenings since the law of 1909 went into effect." On 9 Feb 1909, Congress passed an act prohibiting importation of opium.

MPN 13 Nov 1915, p. 72. *MPN* 26 Feb 1916, p. 1171. *MPW* 19 Feb 1916, p. 1196. *MPW* 26 Feb 1916, p. 1308. *NYDM* 5 Feb 1916, p. 25. *NYDM* 11 Mar 1916, p. 31. *Var* 4 Feb 1916, p. 29.

HORIZONTES NUEVOS *see* LA GRAN JORNADA

HORROR HOUSE *see* SON OF INGAGI

A HORSE CALLED COMANCHE *see* TONKA

HORSIE *see* QUEEN FOR A DAY

HOT AND HAPPY *see* HAPPY LANDING

HOT BLOOD (Gypsies)

Columbia Pictures Corp.; A Howard Welsch Production. *Dist* Columbia Pictures Corp. Mar **1956**; Los Angeles opening: 7 Mar 1956; Prod: 21 Jul–24 Aug 1955 [©Columbia Pictures Corp.; 27 Mar 1956; LP6186]. Sd (Western Electric Recording); col (Technicolor); CinemaScope. 9 reels, 7,655 ft. 85 min. PCA cert no. 17750.

Prod Howard Welsch and Harry Tatelman. *Dir* Nicholas Ray. *Asst dir* Milton Feldman. *Scr* Jesse Lasky, Jr. *Based upon a story by* Jean Evans. *Dir of photog* Ray June. *Technicolor color consultant* Henri Jaffa. *Art dir* Robert Peterson. *Film ed* Otto Ludwig. *Set dec* Frank Tuttle. *Mus comp and cond* Les Baxter. *Choreography* Matt Mattox and Sylvia Lewis. *Rec supv* John Livadary. *Sd* Lambert Day. *Miss Russell's makeup* Layne Britton. *Miss Russell's hairdresser* Stephanie McGraw.

Music: "Whip Dance," by Les Baxter.

Song(s): "Gypsy," "Tsara, Tsara" and "I Could Learn to Love You," music by Les Baxter, lyrics by Ross Bagdasarian.

Cast: JANE RUSSELL [(*Annie Caldash*)], CORNEL WILDE [(*Stephano Torino*)], Luther Adler [(*Marco Torino*)], Joseph Calleia [(*Papa Theodore Caldash*)], Mikhail Rasumny [(*Old Johnny*)], Nina Koshetz [(*Nita Johnny*)], Helen Westcott [(*Velma*)], Jamie Russell [(*Xano*)], Wally Russell [(*Bombo*)], Nick Dennis [(*Korka*)], Richard Deacon [(*Mr. Swift*)], [Robert Foulk (*Desk Sgt. McGrossin*)], [John Raven (*Joe Randy*)], [Nefru Malouf, Jacqueline Auclair (*Young gypsies*)], [Joe Merrit (*Skinny gypsy*)], [Fred Darian, Inez Palange, Dorothea Wolbert (*Old gypsies*)], [Joe Palma, Mike Morelli, Faye Muell, Frank Mazzola (*Gypsies*)], [Franz Roehn, Manuel Paris (*Elders*)], [Joan Reynolds (*Girl*)], [John Indrisano (*Bartender*)], [Peter Brocco (*Doctor*)], [Les Baxter, Ross Bagdasarian (*Gas station attendants*)], [William Bagdad (*Knife sharpener*)], [Kay Koury], [Nadja Dubinsky], [Ethan Laidlaw].

Comedy-drama, with songs. [*Print viewed*]. In the gypsy quarters of Los Angeles, gypsy king Marco Torino urges his people to donate money to fund his search for "the promised land." Marco then visits the doctor who lives above his fortune-telling establishment, where he learns that what he had feared was true: he is incurably ill. Marco conceals this information, but realizes that if he is to see his rebellious younger brother Stephano take his place as king, he must

act quickly. First, he cunningly frightens away Stephano's prospective employer, Mr. Swift, the owner of a non-gypsy dancing school, by describing his brother as a "mostly reliable gypsy." Then he announces that he has arranged for Stephano to marry a beautiful gypsy from Chicago named Annie Caldash, a move that he hopes will cure the young man's restlessness. This, however, only infuriates Stephano, who accuses Marco of trying to run his life. Stephano tells Annie, her father Theodore and her brother Xano that the wedding is off. This angers Papa Caldash, who had planned to abscond with his daughter after accepting several thousand dollars in wedding settlement money from Marco. Annie, who is attracted to Stephano and tired of the fraudulent betrothals arranged for her by her father, describes a scheme that appeals to Stephano. During the ceremony, she will simply do as her father wishes: feign illness and run away with the dowry money. Believing that Marco will stop interfering in his life after enduring such humiliation, Stephano agrees to proceed with the wedding, but during the elaborate ceremony, Annie surprises him and Papa Caldash by allowing the ceremony to proceed without a hitch. As the guests feast, dance, and sing outside the couple's door, Stephano packs his bags while advising Annie to end the marriage with the traditional declaration, "there is no love." Annie rips his shirt and wrestles with her new husband, but to no avail: Stephano leaves with Velma, his blonde girl friend and proceeds directly to Swift's dance studio. Believing Swift failed to hire him due to prejudice against gypsies, Stephano hurls the bewildered man through a plate glass window and is arrested. Marco bails him out and later reveals to Annie the truth about his illness. Determined to win over her new husband, Annie seduces him, but just after he promises to stay with her, Marco enters and declares that he and Annie have won. Stephano assumes the two are in league together and once again leaves his wife. Velma gets him an interview with an agent, but Annie, disguised as a fortune-teller, enters the club and fights with her rival. Disgusted, Stephano signs the contract and leaves for San Diego, where he and Velma perform three nightly shows in a series of sleazy bars. After several months of this, Stephano realizes that he loves Annie and returns home. He is surprised to find her dancing with Marco and apparently enduring little unhappiness as a result of his absence. While Stephano dances with Annie, his grandfather, Papa Johnny, secretly prepares a brew that will make him sick and therefore likely to stay at home. To Papa Johnny's horror, Annie drinks the potion, and later, when Stephano tries to make love to her, she falls asleep. Annie's strange behavior causes everyone to gossip, and Stephano soon believes that his wife loves Marco. Stephano, seeing that Marco plans to leave town in a trailer upon which he has painted the words, "the promised land," mistakenly assumes his brother has not only stolen his wife but swindled thousands of dollars from his people. The two men fight with their belts, "like gypsies," and Marco is injured. Papa Johnny then tells Stephano about Marco's terminal illness. At the council meeting that evening, Marco names Stephano the new gypsy king. After Stephano accepts the king's staff, Annie asks him to approve the annulment of her marriage, publicly declaring that "my husband never wanted me." Stephano apologizes to her and to Marco for his behavior but grants the annulment. After collecting more money for Marco's trip to the "promised land," he runs after Annie's car, declaring his intention to be a good husband and king. Overjoyed, Annie falls into Stephano's arms as the gypsies sing and dance. *Brothers. Gypsies. Marriage–Arranged. Ruses. Assimilation (Sociology). Dancers. Family relationships. Fights. Fortune-tellers. Incurable diseases. Jealousy. Kings. Los Angeles (CA). Marriage–Annulment. Newlyweds. Potions. Romantic rivalry. Seduction. Swindlers and swindling. Transformation. Weddings.*

Note: The film's working title was *Tambourine*. Although the film is set in Los Angeles, a letter is shown during the picture that bears the address: "Marco Torino, Gypsy Quarters, New Market, PA." This was the last film of actor Mikhail Rasumny, who died on 22 Feb 1956, just before the film's Mar release. The *Var* reviewer noted that the film had "an occasional sociological note on the effect of city living on the free-souled gypsy...however...the footage is assembled to stress a charming, carefree, somewhat roistering existence." Modern sources add the following information about the film: Jean Evans was the pen name of Jean Abrams, director Nicholas Ray's first wife. In 1949, Ray wrote a treatment based on Evans' original research among the gypsies on New York City's Lower East Side and submitted it to RKO. In 1951, Ray worked with writer Walter Newman on a first draft of a script about urban gypsies which was then entitled *No Return*. Columbia finally agreed to make the film, but insisted that the script be re-written. Ray then collaborated with Jesse Lasky, Jr. on a new screenplay. Ray had wanted producer Gabriel Pascal to play "Marco Torino," the King of the Gypsies, but Pascal died before the film was made. According

to modern sources, Ray also considered Edward G. Robinson for the role. He then cast Luther Adler, a veteran of the Group Theater. Matt Mattox substituted for Cornel Wilde during the dances.

Box 3 Mar 1956. *DV* 24 Feb 1956, p. 3. *Exb* 7 Mar 1956, p. 4117. *FD* 27 Feb 1956, p. 6. *Har* 3 Mar 1956, p. 34. *HR* 24 Feb 1956, p. 3. *MPHPD* 3 Mar 1956, pp. 801-02. *NYT* 24 Mar 1956, p. 14. *Var* 29 Feb 1956, p. 6.

HOT MONEY see **DANGEROUS MONEY**

HOT RUBBER see **RUBBER RACKETEERS**

THE HOUSE BEHIND THE CEDARS (African Americans)
Micheaux Film Corp. **1924**; Prod: ended Mar 1923. Si; b&w. 9-10 reels.

Dir Oscar Micheaux.
Source: Based on the novel *The House Behind the Cedars* by Charles Chesnutt (Boston, 1900).
Cast: Andrew S. Bishop, Shingzie Howard, William Crowell, Lawrence Chenault, Douglas Griffin.

African American, Melodrama. [*Not viewed*]. Rena, a beautiful mulatto woman, who passes as white, receives a proposal from an aristocratic white millionaire who has fallen in love with her. Rena accepts without revealing the secret of her racial background. Unhappy, Rena returns to her former lover, Frank Fowler, a black man, who has risen to power despite his color. She tells him that although she has fooled the public, she has not fooled herself. *African Americans. African Americans–Mixed blood. Deception. Millionaires. Racial impersonation.*

New York Age 31 Mar 1923, p. 6.

THE HOUSE OF SCANDAL (Irish Americans)
Tiffany-Stahl Productions, Inc. 1 Apr **1928** [©Tiffany-Stahl Productions, Inc.; 16 Apr 1928; LP25154]. Si; b&w. 6 reels, 5,297 ft.

Dir King Baggot. *Scen* Frances Hyland. *Story* E. Morton Hough. *Titles* Viola Brothers Shore. *Photog* Barney McGill. *Art dir* Hervey Libbert. *Film ed* Desmond O'Brien.
Cast: Pat O'Malley (*Pat Regan*), Dorothy Sebastian (*Ann Rourke*), Harry Murray (*Danny Regan*), Gino Corrado (*Morgan*), Lee Shumway (*The Butler*), Jack Singleton (*"A Man About Town"*), Ida Darling (*Mrs. Chatterton*), Lydia Knott (*Mrs. Rourke*).

Melodrama. While Danny Regan, an Irish immigrant, is trying on his brother's police uniform, an automobile accident causes him to rush out of the house and into the street, where, naturally, he is mistaken for a police officer. He meets Ann, a young girl who is actually one of a group of jewel thieves. Danny's failure to arrest the thieves—when instructed to do so by a visiting jeweler who has been flimflammed—causes trouble for his brother, Pat. Attempting to clear Pat, Danny is shot by one of the crooks. Danny's courage inspires Ann to give herself up. After serving her prison sentence, she and Danny, now a full-fledged officer of the law, marry. *Automobile accidents. Brothers. Immigrants. Irish Americans. Jewelers. Mistaken identity. Police. Thieves.*

FD 15 Jul 1928.

HOUSE OF SOLOMON see **SOLOMON IN SOCIETY**

HOUSE OF SPIES see **NAZI AGENT**

HOUSE OF STRANGERS (Italian Americans)
Twentieth Century-Fox Film Corp. *Dist* Twentieth Century-Fox Film Corp. 1 Jul **1949**; Los Angeles opening: 30 Jun 1949; Prod: 21 Dec 1948—23 Feb 1949; retakes in Mar 1949 [©Twentieth Century-Fox Film Corp.; 30 Jun 1949; LP2467]. Sd (Western Electric Recording); b&w. 11 reels, 9,075 ft. 101 min. PCA cert no. 13652.

Prod Sol C. Siegel. [*Exec prod* Darryl F. Zanuck]. *Dir* Joseph L. Mankiewicz. [*Asst dir* William Eckhardt]. [*Dial dir* Tito Vuolo]. *Scr* Philip Yordan. [*Wrt of retakes* Joseph L. Mankiewicz]. *Dir of photog* Milton Krasner. [*Cam op* Paul Lockwood]. [*Gaffer* J. V. Brown]. [*Stills* Jerry Milligan]. *Spec photog eff* Fred Sersen. *Art dir* Lyle Wheeler and George W. Davis. *Set dec* Thomas Little and Walter M. Scott. *Ward dir* Charles LeMaire. *Mus* Daniele Amfitheatrof. *Orch* Maurice de Packh. *Sd* W. D. Flick and Roger Heman. *Makeup artist* Ben Nye. [*Makeup* Dick Smith]. [*Hair stylist* Irene Brooks and Stephan Garland]. [*Prod mgr* Sid Bowen and R. L. Hough]. [*Tech adv* Mushy Callahan]. [*Scr supv* Weslie Jones]. [*Grip* Logan Brown]. [*Double* Fred Lambert].
Music: "Overture" from the opera *Il barbiere di Siviglia* Gioacchino Rossini.

Song(s): "Largo al factotum" from the opera *Il barbiere di Siviglia*, music by Gioacchino Rossini, libretto by Cesare Sterbini; "M'Appari," aria from *Martha*, music by Friedrich von Flotow, libretto by Friedrich Wilhelm Riese; "La donna e mobile," aria from *Rigoletto*, music by Giuseppe Verdi, libretto by Francesco Maria Piave;"Can't We Talk It Over," music by Victor Young, lyrics by Ned Washington; "Please Don't Talk About Me When I'm Gone," music and lyrics by Sidney Clare, Sam H. Stept and Bee Palmer; "Was That the Human Thing to Do," music by Sammy Fain, lyrics by Joe Young.

Source: Based on the novel *I'll Never Go There Any More* by Jerome Weidman (New York, 1941).

Cast: EDWARD G. ROBINSON [(*Gino Monetti*)], SUSAN HAYWARD [(*Irene Bennett*)], RICHARD CONTE [(*Max Monetti*)], Luther Adler [(*Joe Monetti*)], Paul Valentine [(*Pietro Monetti*)], Efrem Zimbalist, Jr. [(*Antonio Monetti*)], Debra Paget [(*Maria Domenico*)], Hope Emerson [(*Helena Domenico*)], Esther Minciotti [(*Theresa Monetti*)], Diana Douglas [(*Elaine Monetti*)], Tito Vuolo [(*Lucca*)], [Sid Tomack (*Waiter*)], [Thomas Browne Henry (*Judge*)], [David Wolfe (*Prosecutor*)], [John Kellogg (*Danny*)], [Ann Morrison (*Woman juror*)], [Dolores Parker (*Nightclub singer*)], [Tommy Garland (*Pietro's opponent*)], [Charles J. Flynn, Howard Mitchell, Phil Tully, Gaza De Rosner, Peter Mamakos (*Guards*)], [Joseph Mazzuca (*Boy*)], [John Pedrini, George Magrill, Michael Stark, Charles McClelland, James Little (*Policemen*)], [Argentina Brunetti (*3rd applicant*)], [Bob Castro, Edward Saenz (*Preliminary fighters*)], [Dick Ryan (*Announcer*)], [Mushy Callahan (*Referee*)], [Herbert Vigran (*Neighbor*)], [Rhoda Williams (*Girl*)], [George Spaulding (*Doorman*)], [Donna La Tour, Maxine Ardell, Sally Yarnell, Jeri Jordan, Donna Hamilton, Marjorie Holliday (*Chorus girls*)], [William Janssen, Neil Carter (*Chorus boys*)], [John "Red" Kullers, Guy Thomajan (*Taxi drivers*)], [Scott Landers, Fred Hillebrand (*Detectives*)], [Arthur Space (*Bank examiner*)], [Roger Moore (*Architect*)], [Walter Lawrence, Joe Rubino (*Vendors*)], [John Butler (*Bartender*)], [Dolores Castle (*Secretary*)], [Lelia Goldoni (*Italian girl*)], [Russ Cheever (*Alto sax, offscreen*)], [Mario Siletti], [Maurice Samuels], [Frank Jacquet], [Larry Arnold], [Charles Faris], [Ford Rush], [Vickie Vann], [Tony Merlo], [Ernesto Morelli], [Nick Borgani], [Mike Macy], [Paul Bradley], [Steve Cavaliere], [Stephen Soldi], [Bob St. Angelo], [Martin Begley], [Carlo Tricoli], [Petra Silva], [Theresa Testa], [Rena Marlin], [Emma Palmese], [Frank Wilcox], [Gilda Oliva].

Domestic, Drama. [*Print viewed*]. In 1939, after serving seven years in prison, attorney Max Monetti returns to his deceased father Gino's trust and loan association in the East Side New York Italian neighborhood in which he grew up. His brothers, Joe, now the president of the bank, and Antonio and Pietro, the vice-presidents, welcome him with champagne, a cigar and a thousand dollars. Max refuses his brothers' offer of friendship and throws the money in the trash. After Max leaves, Tony is about to call a hit man, but Joe says they will keep it in the family. Max goes to the chic apartment of Irene Bennett, who is overjoyed when she comes home to find him in the shower. When she learns that he plans to carry out a vendetta against his brothers, however, Irene implores him to start over with her in San Francisco. The couple quarrel, after which Max returns to the old family house, where he sits beneath a portrait of Gino. As he plays his father's favorite opera record, Max remembers the past: In 1932, Gino acts like a beneficent despot to the neighborhood folk, making snap decisions concerning loans and terms of interest without maintaining sufficient written records. He treats Joe like a servant and insults the weak-willed Tony and Pietro, who works as a guard. During a family dinner, Max receives a call from Irene Bennett, a sultry new client who hired him that afternoon to take care of a matter involving an ex-lover. When she tells him it is an emergency, he goes to her apartment, where she attempts to get him to go to San Francisco with her. Although he is engaged to a beautiful Italian girl, Maria Domenico, Max soon begins an affair with Irene. When Maria's mother complains before the family about Max's affair, Gino counters that what a man does before marriage is nobody else's business. Maria vows never to marry anyone else and agrees to Gino's suggestion of a wedding the week after Easter, then kisses Max passionately. That night, Irene feels Max is preoccupied and tells him it will be their last night together. After not hearing from Irene for a week, Max goes to her apartment, where he meets Danny, to whom she has become engaged. Irene stops Danny and Max from fighting and tells Max that his father has been calling. At the bank, Gino tries to explain to a mob

of customers that the state has closed it because he did not require collateral for the loans he has made. Although he promises that they will get their money, he is beaten until Max arrives and hurries him into the building. Max learns that Gino could be indicted on twenty-two counts, each of which carries a one-year sentence, because he has not recorded many of his transactions. Gino vows to sell everything to pay back his customers, but Max says that will not be enough to clear him. Max gets the idea to divide responsibility for the bank between Gino and the other three brothers, so that nothing definite can be pinned on any of them. Joe bitterly complains that Gino has always treated him as a servant and refuses. Pietro, upset that Gino has always called him "dumbhead," and Tony, who does not want to stick his neck out, go along with Joe. Gino berates them and agrees with Max that he has a "house of strangers," not sons. In court, Max represents Gino, who loses his temper when the prosecutor calls him a "lecherous moneylender and a disgrace to decent Italian Americans." Later, Max gives Joe an envelope filled with money to bribe the one seemingly sympathetic juror, but Joe refuses. Afterwards, Irene tells Max that she does not love Danny and used him because she was hurt. Max kisses her and she drives him to the juror's apartment in a run-down part of town. The juror is tempted by the bribe, as she is a widow with children, but she ultimately refuses the envelope. As he walks out the door, Max is placed under arrest by police for attempted bribery. At the bank, Gino learns that his wife, to whom he signed the bank over for protection, has herself signed it over to the three brothers. When Joe laughs at him in derision, Gino tries to choke him, but Pietro pulls him off. Swearing a vendetta, Gino visits Max in prison and tells him that Joe informed the police about the bribe and that Tony now plans to marry Maria. Max then reluctantly agrees to Gino's pleas that he take revenge upon his brothers. When Gino dies in 1934, Max is given a pass to visit the house, where the family surrounds Gino's body as it lies in state. Under Gino's portrait, Max stares intently at Joe, then bites his thumb, the sign of the vendetta. Theresa rebukes him, saying she now has no husband or family, and in Italian orders him to go. His reminiscences ended, Max converses with Gino's portrait and suggests a way to get back at his brothers: he could entice Maria, who has married Tony, to leave him and take their child with her, then create a scandal at the bank so that Joe would be indicted. Joe's wife would then leave him and Pietro would be lost. Max decides, however, that Joe can have the bank, Tony can have Maria, and Pietro, his job, as Max now has Irene. Max calls Irene as she is preparing to go to the airport, and she cries when he asks her to pick him up so they can go together. The brothers then arrive and Joe says he does not want to live with the worry that Max will take revenge on their families or the business. On Joe's orders, Pietro brutally beats Max until Tony says to stop. Joe then has Pietro carry Max upstairs, saying he learned from Gino to finish off the other guy while he is down. When Joe orders him to throw Max off the balcony, however, Pietro hesitates. Joe repeatedly calls Pietro "dumbhead," until Pietro puts Max down and chokes Joe. Max convinces him not to force Joe over the side by saying that he will be doing what Gino wants if he kills Joe. Irene soon arrives and Max, smiling, gets into her convertible and they drive off. *Bankers. Brothers. Fathers and sons. Italian Americans. Lawyers. Revenge. Attempted murder. Bank failures. Bars. Boxers. Bribery. Class distinction. Death and dying. Engagements. Jealousy. Juries. Loans. New York City–East Side. Opera. Portraits (Paintings). Prisoners. Reconciliation. Seduction. Spaghetti. Transformation. Trials. Widows.*

Note: The working title of this film was *East Side Story*. In a modern source, producer Sol C. Siegel is quoted as saying that novelist Jerome Weidman had originally intended the family in the story to be a New York Lower East Side Jewish family, rather than Italian, but because Jews had criticized Siegel's earlier depictions in *I Can Get It for You Wholesale*, he changed the family's ethnicity. A 4 Nov 1941 *HR* news item announced that Warner Bros. had acquired the screen rights to the film, but a week later, it was stated that the rights were still available and that three companies were bidding for them. According to information in the Twentieth Century-Fox Records of the Legal Department at the UCLA Arts—Special Collections Library, Siegel took out a three-month option for Weidman's novel in Sep 1947. Jerome Cady prepared a story outline for Siegel in Oct 1947, but it is doubtful that he contributed to the finished film. Various Aug 1948 news items announced that Victor Mature was to star in the film. According to a modern source, Siegel had screenwriter Philip Yordan expand the role of "Max," the lawyer son, who was only involved in a small portion of Weidman's novel. Modern sources state that director Joseph Mankiewicz rewrote all of Yordan's dialogue, but this has not been confirmed. According to modern sources, the screen titles were to credit Yordan with the original story and both Yordan and Mankiewicz with the

screenplay, but Mankiewicz objected and ultimately was not listed in the credits for any writing duties.

According to information in the MPAA/PCA Collection at the AMPAS Library, the first screenplay submitted was deemed "unacceptable" because of the "illicit sex relation between the two leads, Irene and Max." Correspondence relates that the script was altered to indicate that "Irene" and "Danny" were not actually married. Concerned about the depiction of Italian Americans in the screenplay, PCA Director Joseph I. Breen wrote the following in a letter on the subject to MPAA head Eric Johnston on 8 Dec 1948: "In view of the great number of protests which, I understand, you are receiving at the present time, against the alleged unfavorable portrayals of Italians and Italian-Americans in motion pictures, I desire to direct your particular attention to a script which has been received from the Twentieth Century-Fox Corporation, carrying the title, 'East Side Story.' This is a low-pitched story of a family of Italian-Americans, residing in what is, suggestively, the east side district of New York City....Almost all the characters in the story are either Italians or Italian-Americans, who, when they are not characterized as definitely reprehensible people, are, at least, unsympathetic....With regard to the general overall unfavorable portrayal of the Italian-Americans, it is our thought that we have no way under the Code to correct this. It occurs to us that this picture, because of these Italian characteristics, may suggest a question of industry policy and, in accordance with our long-established procedure, we are referring this question to you." No information concerning any change in industry policy regarding the depiction of Italians or Italian Americans has been found.

In Mar 1949, Twentieth Century-Fox music director Alfred Newman secured permission from opera singer Lawrence Tibbett for background use of a recording he made of the aria "Largo al Factotum" from Rossini's *Il barbiere di Siviglia* (*The Barber of Seville*) for the 1935 Twentieth Century-Fox film *Metropolitan* (see *AFI Catalog of Feature Films, 1931-40*; F3.2843). Tibbett agreed in exchange for the right to use the *Metropolitan* soundtrack for a radio series he was planning. Tibbett wrote, "If the soundtrack is properly used in your picture I would want and expect due credit and billing since these are among my finest recordings." The studio agreed and Tibbett was given appropriate screen credit.

Publicity for the film stated that a number of supporting players came from the New York Italian theater, and commented, "The picture continued the trend toward the use of foreign language dialogue on the screen, if the part and situation call for it. At one time, Hollywood carefully deleted all phrases from the script that were not in English but *The Razor's Edge* broke away from the convention by permitting its French characters to speak French." Scenes were shot at a number of Manhattan locations, including the Second Avenue Baths and others in Little Italy. The Ocean Park Arena in Ocean Park, CA was used for the boxing scenes. Mushy Callahan, a former welterweight champion, played the referee in the film and trained Paul Valentine, who played "Pietro Monetti," and Susan Hayward, who in her role of "Irene" had to hit Richard Conte. Tommy Garland, who played "Pietro's" opponent in the ring, was a Los Angeles heavyweight boxer. Albert Morin played the role of "Vittoro," a man to whom "Gino" loaned money at a large rate of interest, but his appearance was cut from the final film. Edward G. Robinson was awarded the Best Actor award when the film was exhibited at the Cannes Film Festival.

According to a modern source, production head Darryl F. Zanuck wanted the family in the film to parallel the founders of the Bank of America, the Giannini family. The Gianninis objected, as did Twentieth Century-Fox's president, Spyros Skouras, who thought that his own family was the source of the "Monettis." *Lux Radio Theatre* presented a radio version of the film on 16 Oct 1950, starring Richard Conte, Anne Baxter and Hazel Shaw. A radio version was also broadcast by the *Screen Guild Players* on 25 Jan 1951, starring Victor Mature, Edward G. Robinson and June Havoc. In 1954, Twentieth Century-Fox based the film *Broken Lance* on Yordan's screenplay, without crediting Weidman. That film was directed by Edward Dmytryk and starred Spencer Tracy and Robert Wagner (see below). A television version, entitled "The Last Patriarch," was broadcast on the *20th Century Fox Hour* on 30 Nov 1956. It starred Walter Slezak, John Cassavetes and Vince Edwards. The 1961 Twentieth Century-Fox production *The Big Show*, directed by James B. Clark and starring Esther Williams, Cliff Robertson and Nehemiah Persoff, is said by modern sources to be based on the same novel.

Box 18 Jun 1949. *Cue* 2 Jul 1949. *DV* 15 Jun 1949, p. 3. *Down Beat* 27 Jan 1950, p. 8. *Exh* 22 Jun 1949, p. 2640. *FD* 16 Jun 1949, p. 7. *Har* 18 Jun 1949, p. 98. *HR* 4 Nov 1941. *HR* 12 Nov 1941. *HR* 9 Aug 1948. *HR* 17 Dec 1948. *HR* 14 Apr 1949. *HR* 15 Jun 1949, p. 3. *LAT* 2 Dec 1948. *LAT* 1 Jul 1949. *MPD* 15 Jun 1949, 1, 16. *MPHPD* 18 Jun 1949, 4649. *Newsweek* 1 Aug 1949. *New Yorker* 16 Jul 1949. *NYT* 9 Aug 1948, p. 11. *NYT* 2 Jul 1949, p. 8. *Time* 18 Jul 1949. *Var* 15 Jun 1949, p. 13.

HOUSE OF THE SEVEN TULIPS *see* **SEVEN SWEETHEARTS**

THE HOUSE ON CEDAR HILL (African Americans)
1926?. Si; b&w. Length undetermined. [Feature length assumed.].
Prod Carlton Moss. *Dir* Carlton Moss. *Wrt* Carlton Moss.
Biography. This film is based on the life of Frederick Douglass. *African Americans. Frederick Douglass. Slavery. United States–History–Civil War, 1861-1865.*

THE HOUSE ON 92ND ST. (German Americans)
Twentieth Century-Fox Film Corp. *Dist* Twentieth Century-Fox Film Corp. Oct **1945**; New York opening: 26 Sep 1945; Los Angeles opening: 18 Oct 1945; Prod: 16 Apr—late Aug 1945 [©Twentieth Century-Fox Film Corp.; 26 Sep 1945; LP45]. Sd (Western Electric Mirrophonic Recording); b&w. 10 reels, 7,900 ft. 88-89 min. PCA cert no. 10939.

[*Exec prod* Darryl F. Zanuck]. *Prod* Louis de Rochemont. *Dir* Henry Hathaway. [*Asst dir* Henry Weinberger and Johnny Graham]. [*2d asst dir* Joseph E. Rickards]. *Scr* Barre Lyndon, Charles G. Booth and John Monks, Jr. *Based on a story by* Charles G. Booth. [*Narr* John Stuart Martin]. *Dir of photog* Norbert Brodine. [*2d cam* George Stoetzel]. [*Cam asst* Bud Brooks]. [*Location cam* Larry Williams]. [*Location asst cam* Johnny Phipps]. [*Gaffer* Jack McEvoy]. [*Stills* Ed Bagley]. *Spec photog eff* Fred Sersen. *Art dir* Lyle Wheeler and Lewis Creber. *Film ed* Harmon Jones. *Set dec* Thomas Little. *Assoc* William Sittel, Jr. *Cost* Bonnie Cashin. [*Ward* Dave Preston]. *Mus dir* David Buttolph and Emil Newman. *Sd* W. D. Flick and Roger Heman. [*Rec* Chet Peck]. [*Sd maintenance* W. Kirkpatrick]. [*Mus mixer* Charles Althouse]. *Makeup artist* Ben Nye. [*Unit mgr* Gene Bryant]. [*Prod mgr* R. A. Klune]. [*Research dir* Frances C. Richardson]. [*Research asst* Gertrude Kingston]. [*Scr clerk* Stanley Scheure]. [*Grip* Leo McCreary]. [*Pub* Hugh Lester]. [*Casting dir* William Mayberry]. [*Double for Salo Douday and Charles Wagenheim* Nick Dennis]. [*Double for Leo G. Carroll* George Carroll].

Cast: William Eythe [(*Bill Dietrich*)], Lloyd Nolan [(*Inspector George A. Briggs*)], Signe Hasso [(*Elsa Gebhardt, also known as Mr. Christopher*)], Gene Lockhart [(*Charles Ogden Roper*)], Leo G. Carroll [(*Col. Hammershon*)], Lydia St. Clair [(*Johanna Schmidt*)], William Post [(*Walker*)], Harry Bellaver [(*Max Coburg*)], Bruno Wick [(*Adolphe Lange*)], Harro Meller [(*Conrad Arnulf*)], Charles Wagenheim [(*Gus Huzmann*)], Alfred Linder [(*Adolph Klaen*)], Renee Carson [(*Luise Vadja*)], [John McKee (*Dr. Arthur C. Appleton*)], [Edwin Jerome (*Major general*)], [Elisabeth Neumann (*Freda Kassel*)], [George Shelton (*Jackson*)], [Alfred Zeisler (*Colonel Felix Strassen*)], [Reed Hadley (*Narrator*)], [Rusty Lane (*Admiral*)], [Salo Douday (*Franz von Wirt*)], [Paul Ford (*Sergeant*)], [William Adams (*Customs officer*)], [Jay Eckels (*Policeman*)], [Tom Brown (*Intern*)], [Bruce Fernald, Jay Wesley (*FBI agents*)], [Benjamin Burroughs (*Aide*)], [Douglas Rutherford (*Colonel*)], [Frieda Altman, William Beach, Hamilton Benz, Henry Cordy, Mita Cordy, James J. Coyle, Hans Hansen, Kenneth Konopka, Scott Moore, Delmar Nuetzman, John Zak, Gertrude Wottitz (*Saboteurs*)], [George Brandt (*German*)], [Bernard Lenrow (*German saboteur*)], [Yoshita Tagawa (*Japanese man*)], [Sheila Bromley (*Customer*)], [Elmer Brown, Jack Cherry (*Scientists*)], [Victor Sutherland (*Toll guard*)], [Stanley Tackney (*Instructor*)], [Robert Culler, Vincent Gardenia, Carl Benson, Frank Richards, Ellsworth Glath, Edward Michaels, Harrison Scott, Anna Marie Hornemann, Sara Strengell, Eugene Stuckmann, Marriott Wilson, Harold Dyrenforth (*Trainees*)], [Frank Kreig (*Travel agent*)], [Antonio J. Pires (*Watchmaker*)], [Danny Leone (*Delivery boy*)], [Fred Hillebrand (*Policeman*)], [E. G. Marshall (*Attendant at morgue*)].

Espionage, Documentary. [*Print viewed*]. In 1939, due to increasing hostilities in Europe, the Federal Bureau of Investigation intensifies its observation of foreign nationals living in the United States. The F.B.I. finds a valuable ally in Bill Dietrich, a German-American college student who has been approached by a German Bund and promised a good job in Germany. When a suspicious Bill reports the incident to the F.B.I., Inspector George A. Briggs tells him to cooperate. After Bill is sent to Germany and enrolled in a specialized spy school, a hit-and-run automobile accident in New York City becomes the catalyst for one of the F.B.I.'s most complicated cases. In the morgue, the attendants discover that although the accident victim has a Spanish passport, he was carrying a notebook filled with German writing. The accident is reported to the F.B.I., which concludes that the man is German spy Franz von Wirt and then decodes a letter he was carrying. The letter, which states that "Mr. Christopher will concentrate on Process 97," alarms Briggs, for Process 97 is the U.S. military's most carefully guarded and important secret: the development of the atomic bomb. Briggs is instructed to make the Christopher case his top priority, and after Bill completes his training in Germany, he returns to New York, where Briggs helps him establish a decoy office. Bill contacts Elsa Gebhardt, a German agent posing as a couterier, at her house on 92nd Street. There, he also meets spies Max Coburg and Conrad Arnulf, and Gestapo agent Johanna Schmidt. Bill pretends to build a shortwave radio station, with which he is supposed to transmit Elsa's information to Hamburg. Actually, Bill's messages are relayed through an F.B.I. radio station, which keeps Briggs abreast of the latest developments. Elsa is suspicious of Bill's credentials, which were altered by the F.B.I. to state that he is authorized to contact all agents known to her, but because she cannot contact Hamburg directly for confirmation, she must trust him. Bill receives information from Col. Hammersohn, a professional spy, but he rebuffs Bill's attempt to learn the identity of Mr. Christopher. Hammersohn introduces Bill to Adolphe Klaen, another member of the spy ring, and Bill witnesses Johanna's ruthlessness when she orchestrates the murder of Klaen's drunken informant. While Bill continues his investigation, the F.B.I. intensifies its efforts after the attack on Pearl Harbor. Many suspected foreign agents are rounded up, although some, such as Elsa and Hammersohn, are allowed to go free in the hope that they will reveal Christopher's identity. Bill is able to obtain an important clue in the form a lipstick-stained cigarette left in Elsa's shop by an acquaintence of Christopher. The F.B.I. uses the clue to track down Luise Vadja, another German agent, who leads the federal agents to Charles Ogden Roper, a scientist working at the Appleton Laboratory, out of which the information is being smuggled. Briggs learns that Roper is a "memory artist" and has been memorizing complicated Process 97 plans and passing them to Christopher. When confronted, the naïve Roper confesses his complicity and says that one of his drop-off points is Adolphe Lange's bookshop. The F.B.I. establishes a surveillance operation opposite the bookstore and identifies Christopher as a man seen at Elsa's building. Meanwhile, Elsa receives a copy of Bill's credentials from Hamburg and thereby learns that the information he gave her was forged. He is brought to her house and is drugged, questioned and beaten by Elsa, Johanna and the others. Briggs and his men surround the house and order the spies to surrender, and when they refuse, they throw tear gas. During the ensuing confusion, Elsa removes her blonde wig and makeup, then dons the men's clothing she wears while enacting the role of Christopher. Due to the tear gas smoke, however, Arnulf does not recognize her, and, believing her to be a strange man, shoots and kills her. The federal agents enter the building and rescue Bill, then round up the rest of the spies. With Christopher's identity revealed and the case closed, Process 97 is safe and the F.B.I. continues its fight against foreign agents. *Atomic bomb. Espionage. Foreign agents. Germans. Undercover operations. United States. Federal Bureau of Investigation. Automobile accidents. Booksellers and bookselling. Cosmetics. Drugging. German Americans. Gestapo. Male impersonation. Memory. Microfilm. Motion pictures. Murder. New York City. Radio, Short wave. Scientific apparatus and instruments. Scientists. Surveillance devices. Tear gas. Washington (D.C.). Watches. World War II.*

Note: The working titles of this film were *Now It Can Be Told, Private Line to Berchtesgaden* and *Hamburg Seven, Seven, Seven.* After the opening credits, a written prologue reads: "This story is adapted from cases in the espionage files of the Federal Bureau of Investigation. Produced with the F.B.I.'s complete cooperation, it could not be made public until the first atomic bomb was dropped on Japan. The scenes in this picture were photographed in the localities of the incidents depicted—Washington, New York, and their vicinities; wherever possible, in the actual place the original incident occurred. With the exception of the leading players, all F.B.I. personnel in the picture are members of the Federal Bureau of Investigation."

Numerous contemporary sources note that J. Edgar Hoover gave approval for the film's production, and a 13 Sep 1945 *NYT* article reported that "one of Mr. Hoover's three principal assistants supervised the production to assure its authenticity." Hoover appears briefly at the beginning of the picture, which contains shots of his office and the Bureau's headquarters. According to a studio press release, the Bureau's cooperation included providing the production crew with a special surveillance vehicle from which they could film street scenes on location in New York City without attracting a crowd. A studio press release announced that before filming began, actors Lloyd Nolan and William Eythe spent a week at the F.B.I. Academy in Quantico, VA, where they attended classes with student agents and underwent basic physical training. As noted in the film's prologue, the picture was largely shot on location in New York City, Long Island and Washington, D.C. and contains much documentary footage, shot for this film, of federal agents at work in the Bureau's headquarters. The Bureau's fingerprint department is shown, as well as numerous scientific methods of analyzing evidence. The footage of employees entering and exiting the German Embassy in Washington, D.C. was also taken from Bureau photographic files. According to information in studio records, the Appleton laboratory scenes were shot at the Nassau Plant in Great Neck, Long Island. The plant was a top-secret war defense laboratory, and the film crew and cast had to be cleared by military authorities. The *Time* review noted that some sequences were shot at the California Institute of Technology. Footage of Hamburg, Germany, was taken from a film entitled *City of Hamburg*, which was in the possession of the U.S. Office of Alien Property Custodian, which regulated German-owned pictures located in the U.S. during the war.

According to information in the Twentieth Century-Fox Produced Scripts Collection and the Records of the Legal Department, both located at the UCLA Arts—Special Collections Library, this film was largely inspired by the F.B.I's

1941 arrest of thirty-three German and German-American spies. The spy ring, which was based in New York City, had been responsible for selling information about Norden bombsight, a valuable American military secret to Germany. Other military and defense secrets were sent to Germany by the spies, among whom Frederick Joubert Duquesne was the most famous. Duquesne had been a professional spy for over forty years at the time of his arrest. According to the studio records, Duquesne was the inspiration for "Col. Hammersohn" in the film. "Bill Dietrich" was based on William G. Sebold, a German-born, American citizen who infiltrated the spy ring with the aid of the F.B.I. and set up a shortwave radio station, as Dietrich does in the picture. Another spy convicted in the case, artist's model and socialite Lilly Stein, was the inspiration for "Elsa Gebhardt" (but not for "Mr. Christopher"). Hermann Lang, who memorized details of the Norden bombsight, was the inspiration for "Charles Ogden Roper." All thirty-three of the spies were convicted of espionage and failure to declare themselves as foreign agents. Duquesne was sentenced to eighteen years, Stein received a sentence of ten years and Lang received a sentence of eighteen years. Other F.B.I. cases were used in the film, and the script files reveal that as late as 2 Apr 1945, the name of the atomic bomb was not allowed to be printed in the studio's copy of the screenplay "until release from proper authority can be obtained." According to an 18 Aug 1945 *LAT* news item, if the atomic bomb had not been used by the U.S. during World War II, "the story of espionage and the work of the F.B.I. would have been given a different motivation before the picture was released." According to a 14 Aug 1945 *HR* news item, studio executives decided not to mention the atomic bomb in its advertising because they felt "the picture is too good to be tied into such exploitation."

The story records reveal that the role of "Elsa Gebhardt/Mr. Christopher" was originally to be played by a man, who would pretend to be a woman. Notes for a 9 Jan 1945 conference with production chief Darryl F. Zanuck report that Zanuck wanted Christopher to be "the one who is least suspected by the audience. Elsa should be Christopher—a man who poses as a woman. A German fairy. We want to cast a very good actor in this part—maybe someone from the stage, so that the audience will think it is a woman." In the finished picture, however, Elsa is a woman who impersonates a man. According to information in the legal records, Kurt Katch was originally signed to play "Col. Felix Strassen," and Charles Wallis was signed to play "Mr. X" and Fritz Pollard was signed to play "Julius." The latter two characters do not appear in the finished film. The picture marked the screen debuts of actors Vincent Gardenia, E. G. Marshall and Bruno Wick, and the American film debut of French actress Lydia St. Clair.

The House on 92nd Street, which garnered excellent reviews, received an Academy Award nomination for Charles G. Booth's original story. The picture was one of several semi-documentary, dramatic films produced by noted documentary filmmaker Louis de Rochemont, who created "The March of Time" newsreels in 1934. Other pictures directed by de Rochemont, which contained a similar blend of fact, real people, actors and fiction were *13 Rue Madeleine*, which was based on O.S.S. case files, and *Boomerang*. On 12 Oct 1945, William Eythe, Lloyd Nolan and Signe Hasso appeared in a radio version of the film, broadcast on the *This Is Your FBI* program. In Apr 1965, *DV* announced that de Rochemont had obtained screen rights to an espionage novel entitled *The House on 93rd Street*, but a film based on that book was not made.

Box 15 Sep 1945. *DV* 12 Sep 1945, p. 3. *FD* 13 Sep 1945, p. 6. *HR* 20 Jun 1944, p. 1, 14. *HR* 14 Aug 1944, p. 11. *HR* 9 Mar 1945, p. 1. *HR* 21 Mar 1945, p. 9. *HR* 4 Apr 1945, p. 3. *HR* 5 Apr 1945, p. 1. *HR* 17 Apr 1945, p. 3. *HR* 18 May 1945, p. 15. *HR* 11 Jun 1945, p. 8. *HR* 22 Jun 1945, p. 15. *HR* 13 Aug 1945, p. 1, 9. *HR* 14 Aug 1945, p. 5. *HR* 12 Sep 1945, p. 3. *HR* 28 Sep 1945, p. 1. *HR* 1 Oct 1945, p. 18. *HR* 2 Oct 1945, p. 1. *HR* 3 Oct 1945, p. 3. *HR* 5 Oct 1945, p. 4. *HR* 18 Oct 1945, p. 2. *HR* 19 Oct 1945, p. 3, 13. *HR* 24 Jan 1946, p. 19. *LAT* 22 Jul 1945. *LAT* 13 Aug 1945. *Life* 8 Oct 1945, p. 91-92, 94. *MPD* 12 Sep 1945. *MPHPD* 16 Jun 1945, p. 2499. *MPHPD* 15 Sep 1945, p. 2645. *NYT* 1 Apr 1945. *NYT* 12 Aug 1945. *NYT* 13 Sep 1945. *NYT* 27 Sep 1945, p. 24. *NYT* 30 Sep 1945. *Time* 8 Oct 1945. *Var* 12 Sep 1945, p. 16.

THE HOUSE ON TELEGRAPH HILL (Polish Americans)

Twentieth Century-Fox Film Corp. *Dist* Twentieth Century-Fox Film Corp. 12 May **1951**; *Prod:* late Aug—mid-Oct 1950 [©Twentieth Century-Fox Film Corp.; 12 May 1951; LP1101]. Sd (Western Electric Recording); b&w. 10 reels, 8,357 ft. 93 min. PCA cert no. 14810.

Prod Robert Bassler. *Dir* Robert Wise. [*Asst dir* Horace Hough]. [*Dial dir* Anthony Jowitt]. *Scr* Elick Moll and Frank Partos. [*Contr wrt* Robert Bassler, Robert Wise and Richard Murphy]. *Dir of photog* Lucien Ballard. *Spec photog eff* Fred Sersen. *Art dir* Lyle Wheeler and John De Cuir. *Film ed* Nick De Maggio. *Set dec* Thomas Little and Paul S. Fox. *Ward dir* Charles LeMaire. *Cost des* Renie. *Mus dir* Alfred Newman. *Mus* Sol Kaplan. *Orch* Edward Powell and Maurice de Packh. *Sd* George Leverett and Harry M. Leonard. *Makeup artist* Ben Nye. [*Tech adv* Allan A. Buchkantz].

Source: Based on the novel *The Frightened Child* by Dana Lyon (New York, 1948).

Cast: RICHARD BASEHART [(*Alan Spender*)], VALENTINA CORTESA [(*Victoria Kowelska*)], WILLIAM LUNDIGAN [(*Major Marc Bennett*)], Fay Baker [(*Margaret*)], Gordon Gebert [(*Chris*)], [Kei Thing Chung (*Kei, houseboy*)], [Steve Geray (*Dr. Burkhardt*)], [Herbert Butterfield (*Joseph C. Callahan*)], [John Burton (*Mr. Whitmore*)], [Katherine Meskill (*Mrs. Whitmore*)], [Mario Siletti (*Tony*)], [Charles Wagenheim (*Man at accident*)], [David Clarke

(*Mechanic*)], [Tamara Schee (*Maria*)], [Natasha Lytess (*Karin Dernakova*)], [Ashmead Scott (*Inspector Hardy*)], [Tom McDonough (*Farrell*)], [Henry Rowland (*Sergeant-Interpreter*)], [Les O'Pace (*UNRA sergeant*)], [Don Kohler (*Chemist*)], [Harry Carter (*Detective Ellis*)], [Spencer Chan (*Chinese cook*)], [Mari Young (*Chinese singer*)], [Jeffrey Sayre (*Police stenographer*)], [Roger McGee (*G.I.*)], [Eugene Porcheur (*Pole*)], [Florence Buzby], [Glen Walters], [Margaret Masters], [Sonia Charsky], [Eleanor Moore], [Jeraldine Jordan].

Suspense, Melodrama. [*Print viewed*]. The imposing Victorian house on Telegraph Hill overlooking San Francisco, where Victoria Kowelska once thought she would find peace and contentment, is now up for sale. Victoria begins her story eleven years earlier in 1939, when the German army left her beautiful home near Warsaw, Poland in ruins. Her husband died in the siege, and Vicky became one of thousands hoarded into concentration camps. At the camp at Belsen, Germany, Vicky becomes friends with another Pole, Karin Dernakova, a sickly, frail woman, who shares her life story with Vicky. Karin doubts that she will ever again see her son Christopher, whom she smuggled out of Poland to the United States just before the war began. After Vicky protects Karin from another prisoner's attempted theft, Karin invites her to San Francisco to live with her and Chris in the big house on the hill belonging to her aunt Sophie, a Polish noble who emigrated to the United States in 1904 to marry a wealthy shipbuilder. Karin had not seen her aunt since she was a little girl, Vicky decides to pose as Karin. At a displaced persons camp, Vicky sends a cable to Sophie, but receives a reply from Joseph C. Callahan, an attorney in New York, coldly informing her that Sophie is dead. Although her hopes are now nearly gone, Vicky perserveres, and in 1950 reaches New York on a United Nations refugee ship. At Callahan's office, she meets Alan Spender, a relative of Aunt Sophie by marriage, who adopted Chris after her death, believing that Chris's parents also had died. Callahan reveals that Sophie left her valuable estate to Chris, with Alan as guardian, and says he has doubts concerning Vicky's claim to be Karin. When Vicky vows to fight, Alan, admiring her resolve, invites her to dinner and during the next two weeks, woos her. Feeling that her best chance for safety is to be married to an American, Vicky accepts Alan's proposal and arrives in San Francisco as his wife. Vicky soon suspects that something is wrong in the house. Marc Bennett, a senior partner in the law firm representing the estate, recognizes Vicky as a refugee he questioned years earlier when he was in the army and offers himself as a friend. While playing catch with Chris, Vicky comes upon an abandoned playhouse that is damaged terribly. Vicky looks for Margaret, Chris's governess, to ask about the explosion and, not finding her in her room, starts to open a locked album, when Margaret discovers her. Margaret says coldly that Aunt Sophie gave her the album. During their subsequent argument, she calls Vicky an intruder. Vicky gives Margaret notice to leave, but when Alan returns home, he refuses to fire her. At the playhouse, Vicky discovers an extremely dangerous hole in the side and floor leading to a steep drop to a street below. Alan enters and as he chillingly questions her, she backs up in fear and falls through the hole, but he rescues her. Although he tries to comfort her, her suspicions about him increase. One day, as Vicky prepares to go with Chris to the store, Margaret stops them, saying that Chris has forgotten to clean his room. Vicky then leaves by herself, and when she steps on the brake while on a steep hill, she discovers she cannot stop her car. After narrowly avoiding other cars, she crashes into a construction site just in front of a wall leading to a steep drop below. She calls Marc and tells him that Alan tried to kill her and Chris so that he would get control of the estate. Marc doubts her, but promises to investigate. He confesses that he is in love with her, and she admits her real identity. Having seen Belsen himself, Marc understands her attempt to grab a chance for a better life, but feels that her own bad conscience has led her to magnify events into unwarranted suspicions about Alan. Later, while home alone, Vicky pries open the album in Margaret's room and finds a newspaper obituary for Aunt Sophie stating that the death occurred a few days after the date of the cable sent to her in 1945. Alan surprises her, and later that night, he removes the phone off the hook in the library. In the bedroom, Alan fixes a glass of orange juice for Vicky. When she starts to return to the library for a book, he goes instead, then, on returning to the bedroom, he encourages her to drink the juice. When she says that earlier it tasted bitter, he pours himself a glass from the pitcher and drinks it,

then says it tastes fine and she drinks hers. Vicky accuses him of killing Aunt Sophie, in addition to trying to kill her and Chris. Alan then admits that he has been hoarding doses of a sedative that the doctor has prescribed for Margaret's insomnia and has put all of it into her glass of orange juice. Aghast, Vicky informs Alan that he has drunk the contaminated juice himself; when he left to get her book, she poured herself a different glass and poured the juice from the first glass back into the pitcher. Now sweating profusely, Alan tells Margaret that Vicky has poisoned him and asks her to call for a doctor, explaining that the receiver in the library is off the hook. When Alan admits trying to kill Chris in the car, but says he did it so they could be together like old times, Margaret, who loves the boy, coldly informs him the line is dead. When the police arrive, Alan is dead. Vicky tries to defend Margaret for not calling a doctor, but the police plan to take her away for questioning. When they find Chris absent from his room, Vicky fears Margaret has left with him, but they discover her watching over the boy as he sleeps in her room. Vicky offers to be a witness for her, but Margaret replies that her conscience will be her witness. Marc takes Vicky and Chris away from the house to his mother's house, but before leaving she goes to Aunt Sophie's portrait. Marc says Aunt Sophie would approve, and Vicky replies that all she can do is thank her for everything. *Attempted murder. Impersonation and imposture. Inheritance. Marriage of convenience. Polish Americans. War refugees. Aunts. Automobile accidents. Bergen-Belsen (Germany: Concentration camps). Chinese Americans. Class distinction. Dismissal (Employment). Falls from heights. Friendship. Germany. Governesses. Houseboys. Jealousy. Lawyers. Mechanics. Officers (Military). Poisoning. Poland. Police inspectors. Portraits (Paintings). Sabotage. Telephone. World War II.*

Note: The working title of this film was *The Frightened Child*. The novel was purchased in Mar 1948 by Twentieth Century-Fox, prior to its serialization in *Harper's Magazine* in Apr 1948, and was assigned to producer Walter Morosco. According to information in the Twentieth Century-Fox Records of the Legal Department and the Produced Scripts Collection at the UCLA Arts—Special Collections Library, writers David Hertz, Irmgard Von Cube, Allen Vincent, Robert Hill and Karl Kamb worked on the film before Elick Moll and Frank Partos, who received screen credit, but Moll and Partos's work was not derived from the earlier efforts. In a conference in Oct 1949, production head Darryl Zanuck stated his desire to call the film *The House on Telegraph Hill* and situate it in San Francisco. Some filming was done at various locations in San Francisco, and the studio's art department converted the Julius Castle Restaurant, a well-known landmark, and its adjoining property into the exterior of the house used in the film.

According to information in the MPAA/PCA Collection at the AMPAS Library, PCA officials objected to the finale of an early script in which the character "Margaret" commits suicide, stating they could not approve the suicide of characters to escape the processes of the law. The PCA also objected to a subsequent script in which "Margaret" was allowed to go free, stating she should be held by the police for further questioning. In addition, they objected to the use of sleeping pills as the means to attempted murder, in an early draft, stating that such a detail could inspire imitation. Footage of displaced persons boarding an International Refugee Organization ship was included in the film at the request of the United Nations as a public service for "making the world conscious of the United Nations and its activities," according to a letter in the legal files.

AmCin Jul 1951, pp. 260-61, 274-75. *Box* 17 Mar 1951. *Cue* 19 May 1951. *DV* 6 Mar 1951, p. 3. *Exb* 14 Mar 1951, p. 308. *FD* 7 Mar 1951, p. 4. *Har* 10 Mar 1951, p. 40. *HR* 25 Aug 1950, p. 15. *HR* 13 Oct 1950, p. 15. *HR* 6 Mar 1951, p. 12. *LAEx* 9 Jun 1951. *LAT* 26 Mar 1948. *LAT* 9 Jun 1951. *MPHPD* 10 Mar 1951, pp. 749-50. *Newsweek* 28 May 1951. *NYT* 14 May 1951, p. 29. *Time* 18 Jun 1951. *Var* 7 Mar 1951, p. 6.

HOUSE-RENT PARTY (African Americans, Chinese Americans)

Toddy Pictures Co. *Dist* Toddy Pictures Co. **1946?**. Sd; b&w. 6 reels, 5,510 ft.

Prod Ted Toddy. *Dir* Sam Newfield. *Asst dir* Thomas Darby. *Story and scr trmt* Sam Newfield and Ted Toddy. *Dir of photog* Jack Etra. *Asst of photog* Sol Wichuall. *Spec photog* Richard Marks. *Film ed* Elmer J. McGovern. *Sd eng* Nelson Minnerly. *Asst sd eng* J. Burgi Contner. *Makeup artist* R. J. Liszt. *Prod mgr* S. Hickman. *Scr ed* Violet Neufeld. *Eff eng* John Allsteadt.

Song(s): "Yankee Dollar in Trinidad" and "Rockaway," music and lyrics by Rupert Grant; "The Rent Party (Mama's Got to Get That Rent)," music and lyrics by Porter Grainger.

Cast: PIGMEAT "ALAMO" MARKHAM (*Pigmeat*), John Rastus Murray (*Shorty*), Claude Demetri (*Mr. Johnson*), Rudolph Toombs (*Slippery Jim*), Bill Dillard (*Officer Jack*), David Beathea (*Nappy*), Lance Taylor (*Tough Guy Harry*), Alfred Cortez (*One Lung Lee*), Lou Swarz (*Mrs. Johnson*), Hannah Sylvester (*Mrs. Hannibel Shorty*), Kay Freeman (*Madame Crystal Ball*), James McNeely (*Police Sgt. Vim*), James Wilbur (*Jack Handy*), Roy Allen (*Bill Mountain*),

Dewey Wineglass (*Tough Greenbacks*), Willie Drake (*Master of ceremonies*), MacBeth's Calypso Band featuring The Lord Invador, Alberta Pryne (*Special singer*), Ozzy Mallon's Jitterbugs.

African American, Comedy, with songs. [*Not viewed*]. In Harlem, Shorty is thrown out of the house by his wife for sitting around reading detective stories and becoming an "IOU man" instead of collecting a real salary. When Shorty runs into Pigmeat, his pal and employer, on his way to Pigmeat's barber shop, he explains to him that his wife is making a fuss about his disappearing paycheck. In turn, Pigmeat explains to Shorty that his forty dollar salary is eaten up by taxes, insurance and vacation time, and that Shorty actually owes Pigmeat $1.25 at the end of each week, a sum the shop owner is kind enough to forget. Nappy, a customer, then arrives and asks for a hair straightening, Pigmeat's speciality. When Nappy complains about the heat from the chemicals, Pigmeat assures him that he has plenty of cold water waiting for him. However, the water company has turned off the water, and Pigmeat, in a panic, yells to Shorty to get a bucket of water from outside. After being doused with the water, Nappy at first declares that his hair has never felt cleaner, then realizes that he has lost it all. Later, Shorty reads about a $1,000 reward for the capture of jewel thief Slippery Jim, who has been operating in Harlem. Shorty decides that he and Pigmeat can become famous detectives using the knowledge that Shorty has gained reading detective novels. The pair plan to to disguise themselves and go to Miss Julie Jones's House Rent Party, where they are sure Slippery Jim will strike next. Before the party, Pigmeat goes to a Chinese laundry to pick up a new shirt, but has no money to pay for it, so he and One Lung Lee, the laundry proprietor, fight. Later, One Lung tries to use a laundry ticket to get in to the party, but is turned away before he has the clever idea of forging a press pass. He and Pigmeat then play dice, and Pigmeat tries to swindle One Lung, who claims to not know the game. One Lung, however, is merely playing the fool and ends up swindling Pigmeat. Slippery Jim enters with his girl friend, singer Alberta Pryne, and while Madame Crystal does a mind-reading act with the lights turned low, Lucy, a party goer, discovers that her necklace has been stolen. She accuses Shorty of the crime, and when the police arrive, Pigmeat, the actual thief, tries to give the stolen jewelry to his pal. Pigmeat then points Slippery Jim out to the police, who agree to look in his car for stolen jewels. Pigmeat gets the $1,000 reward and promises to share it with Shorty, but divides it up unequally. When a bill collector arrives and Pigmeat gives him both of their shares, saying that Shorty gets one-half of the bills, too, Shorty is unconcerned, noting that given the way Pigmeat was counting it out, he would have ended up with nothing anyway. *African Americans. Amateur detectives. Idlers. Jewel thieves. New York City—Harlem. Parties. Barbers and barbershops. Bill collectors. Chinese Americans. Craps (Game). Debt. Detective and mystery stories. Disguise. Finance-Personal. Hair. Laundries. Marriage. Mind-reading. Musicians. Police. Rewards. Robbery. Singers.*

Note: The above credits and synopsis were taken from a shooting dialogue script deposited with the NYSA; actor Dewey "Pigmeat" Markham was credited as Pigmeat (Alamo) Markham. Although the script, which was submitted for censorship approval in New York on 10 Apr 1946, indicates that a 1946 copyright disclaimer appeared in the screen credits, the film was never registered for copyright. Regional censorship reports contained in the MPAA/PCA Collection at the AMPAS Library indicate that the songs "Yankee Dollar in Trinidad" and "Rockaway" were cut from prints shown in the Ohio territory, and that Pennsylvania censors ordered the elimination of footage showing "Slippery Jim" sneaking up on women and removing their jewelry.

HOUSEBOAT (Italian Americans)

Scribe Productions. *Dist* Paramount Pictures Corp. Nov **1958**; New York opening: 13 Nov 1958; Prod: early Aug—mid-Oct 1957 [©Paramount Pictures Corp. & Scribe Productions; 17 Nov 1958; LP12426]. Sd (Westrex Recording System); col (Technicolor); VistaVision Motion Picture High-Fidelity. 110 or 112 min. PCA cert no. 18781.

Prod Jack Rose. *Prod assoc* Hal C. Kern. *Dir* Melville Shavelson. *Asst dir* Michael D. Moore. *Wrt* Melville Shavelson and Jack Rose. *Dir of photog* Ray June. *2d unit photog* Wallace Kelley. *Spec photog eff* John P. Fulton. *Process photog* Farciot Edouart. *Technicolor color consultant* Richard Mueller. *Art dir* Hal Pereira and John Goodman. *Ed* Frank Bracht. *Set dec* Sam Comer and Grace Gregory. *Cost* Edith Head. *Mus score* George Duning. *Sd rec* Hugo Grenzbach and Charles Grenzbach. *Makeup supv* Wally Westmore. *Hair style supv* Nellie Manley. [*Unit mgr* Charles Woolstenhulme].

Music: "That's Amore," by Harry Warren.

Song(s): "Almost in Your Arms," words and music by Jay Livingston and Ray Evans, sung by Sam Cooke, a Keen Records Artist; "Bing! Bang! Bong!" words and music by Jay Livingston and Ray Evans.

Cast: CARY GRANT [(*Tom Winston*)], SOPHIA LOREN [(*Cinzia Zaccardi*)], Martha Hyer [(*Carolyn Gibson*)], Harry Guardino [(*Angelo Donatello*)], Eduardo Ciannelli [(*Arturo Zaccardi*)], Murray Hamilton [(*Alan Wilson*)], Mimi Gibson [(*Elizabeth Winston*)], Paul Petersen [(*David Winston*)], Charles Herbert [(*Robert Winston*)], Madge Kennedy [(*Mrs. Farnsworth*)], John Litel [(*Mr. Farnsworth*)], Werner Klemperer [(*Harold Messner*)], [Peggy Connelly (*Elizabeth Wilson*)], [Kathleen Freeman, Helen Brown (*Women in laundromat*)], [Florence MacAfee (*Laundromat attendant*)], [Julian Rivero (*Spanish diplomat*)], [Ernest Brengk (*French diplomat*)], [Mary Forbes (*British society woman*)], [Richard Emory, Larry Carr, Gordon Wynn (*Young men at country club*)], [Richard Nelson (*Waiter*)], [William R. Remich (*Justice of the peace*)], [Wally Walker, Joe McTurk, Earl Spainard, Bob Scott, Brooks Benedict (*Pitchmen*)], [Gilda Oliva (*Pizza saleswoman*)], [Bill Hickman (*Handsome man*)], [Pat Moran (*Clown*)], [Marc Wilder (*Specialty dancer*)].

Comedy-drama, with songs. [*Print viewed*]. When Tom Winston, a government lawyer who, for several years, has been separated from his wife, takes charge of his three children—Elizabeth, David and Robert—following their mother's death, he is taken aback by their hostility toward him. Their aunt, the attractive but unhappily married Carolyn Gibson, explains that the loss of their mother has left the children with problems: None of them sleeps well, all three are melancholy, and little Robert, who claims to hate everyone, does nothing but play the harmonica. After first agreeing to let Carolyn and her parents adopt the children, Tom suddenly decides to take them to nearby Washington, D.C., where he rents a small flat. The children are unimpressed with their new home, and following an evening concert at the Watergate, Robert hides in a rowboat on the adjacent Potomac River. Also attending the concert is the beautiful but restless Cinzia Zaccardi, who is accompanying her father, a famous Italian conductor, on a tour of the United States. Cinzia longs for freedom and male companionship, but her father keeps a tight rein on her, and she escapes a stuffy society dinner only by climbing out a window and into Robert's rowboat. Cinzia dances with the child at a street carnival and later that evening takes him home. Tom threatens to spank the boy until Cinzia gently advises him to be "a parent, not a policeman." Seeing that all three children are taken with Cinzia, Tom, who believes that she is an abandoned "G.I. bride or something," offers her a job as their maid. Amused, Cinzia declines the job and returns to her father, but when he angrily vows never to let her out of his sight again, she decides to move with Tom and the children to Carolyn's guest house in nearby Virginia. When the guest house is accidentally demolished, an Italian-American storekeeper named Angelo Donatello offers to sell Tom his rickety houseboat. During the family's stormy first night on the boat, Cinzia sends a frightened Elizabeth to sleep with her father, who slowly begins to treat the child with warmth and affection. Carolyn reveals that she is divorcing her philandering husband and admits that she has always loved Tom. Meanwhile, Angelo invites Cinzia to the Fourth of July dance sponsored by the Sons of Italy. Cinzia and the children work hard to fix up the houseboat, and soon it is homey and charming. David, unhappy about his father's constant criticism, however, decides to run away one windy night. When David's rowboat capsizes, Tom leaps into the river and saves him. Cinzia tries to persuade Tom to be more accepting of David, and as the two talk, they find themselves nearly kissing. The next morning, Tom and David discuss death, and David teaches his father how to fish. Tom begins to date Carolyn, which so upsets Cinzia that she decides to leave. Tom buys her a dress and remarks that she has pulled his family together again. Just then, Carolyn and her friends arrive, and after one of them insults Cinzia, Tom orders them from the houseboat. He then takes Cinzia to the country club dance, and as they kiss at the end of the evening, he realizes he is in love with her. To Cinzia's surprise, the children, especially the jealous David, disapprove of their romance, and after explaining that she could never take their mother's place, she broken-heartedly returns to her father. Tom tracks her down and declares his love in the presence of Maestro Zaccardi, who, although approving of the union, warns Tom never to hurt his beloved daughter. The

children, however, do not come to terms with their father's remarriage until the wedding ceremony begins. After playing "The Wedding March" on his harmonica in the middle of the couple's vows, Robert smilingly approaches Cinzia, and the ceremony continues as the children join hands with the couple. *Family relationships. Fatherhood. Grief. Houseboats. Italians. Jealousy. Transformation. Widowers. Aunts. Carnivals. Concerts. Conductors (Music). Dances. Death and dying. Fathers and daughters. Fathers and sons. Fathers and sons. Harmonicas. Impersonation and imposture. Italian Americans. Lawyers. Maids. Potomac River. Rescues. Runaways. Unrequited love. Virginia. Washington (D.C.). Weddings.*

Note: Although contemporary news items note that the script was based on an unpublished story by B. Winkle (pseudonym of Cary Grant's then wife, actress Betsy Drake), onscreen credits and the SAB list Melville Shavelson and Jack Rose as sole writers. In Sep 1956, an *LAT* story reported that Rose and Shavelson had engaged Anna Perrott Rose to write the screenplay, but her contribution to the completed film has not been confirmed. The same news story asserted that the movie would be filmed on Lake Union in Seattle, WA. Other news items announced that the story was to be set in the Midwest. The film includes location shots of Washington, D.C., where part of the story is set. Other portions of the film were shot on location in Virginia and California. Rose and Shavelson's screenplay was nominated for an Oscar, as was the song "Almost in Your Arms."

Box 1 Sep 1958. *DV* 27 Mar 1956. *DV* 5 Sep 1958, p. 3. *Exh* 17 Sep 1958, p. 4514. *FD* 5 Sep 1958, p. 6. *Har* 6 Sep 1958, p. 143. *HR* 9 Aug 1957, p. 12. *HR* 18 Oct 1957, p. 10. *HR* 5 Sep 1958, p. 3. *LAEx* 14 Dec 1956. *LAT* 13 Sep 1956. *MPHPD* 6 Sep 1958, p. 967. *NYT* 14 Nov 1958, p. 24. *Var* 10 Sep 1958, p. 6.

HOW COULD YOU, JEAN? (Swedish Americans)

A Mary Pickford Production. *Dist* Famous Players-Lasky Corp.; Artcraft Pictures. 23 Jun 1918 [©Famous Players-Lasky Corp.; 4 Jun 1918; LP12496]. Si; b&w. 5 reels, 4,750 ft.

Dir William D. Taylor. *Asst dir* Frank Richardson. *Scen* Frances Marion. *Cam* Charles Rosher.

Source: Based on the novel *How Could You, Jean?* by Eleanor Hoyt Brainerd (Garden City, NY, 1917).

Cast: Mary Pickford (*Jean Mackaye*), Casson Ferguson (*Ted Burton, Jr.*), Spottiswoode Aitken (*Rufus Bonner*), Herbert Standing (*Burton, Sr.*), Fanny Midgley (*Mrs. Bonner*), Larry Peyton (*Oscar*), Zasu Pitts (*Oscar's sweetheart*), Mabelle Harvey (*Susan Cooper*), Lucille Ward (*Mrs. Kate Morley*), Emma Gerdes, Wesley Barry, Burwell Hamerick, Althea Worthley, Dorothy Rosher, Jack Herbert, Valeria Traxler (*The Morley kids*).

Comedy-drama. When Jean Mackaye, a pretty and resourceful young woman, discovers that she has lost her fortune, she dresses in Salvation Army clothing and secures a job in the Bonner home as a Swedish cook. Mr. and Mrs. Bonner, an elderly couple preoccupied with the study of insects, are too busy to notice that their Swedish hired man Oscar is falling in love with Jean. Soon, however, Ted Burton, the son of a cranky old millionaire, falls so deeply in love with her that he convinces Oscar to resign and applies for the position himself. Burton, Sr., anxious to discover the reason for his son's odd behavior, becomes a boarder in the house. Following a series of adventures in which Jean saves the old man's life, Burton blesses the union of his son and the "Swedish cook." *Aged persons. Cooks. Hired hands. Impersonation and imposture. Millionaires. Lodgers. Rescues. Salvation Army. Swedish Americans.*

Note: Sources call this a Mary Pickford production without specifying the exact name of her company. During 1918, Pickford's production company was called variously the Mary Pickford Film Co., and Pickford Film Corp. The novel *How Could You, Jean?* originally appeared in serial form in a popular magazine. Sources conflict concerning the name of the character played by Mabelle Harvey. According to reviews and Paramount publicity, the character was named "Susan Trent." However, the continuity in the Paramount studio records lists the character name as "Susan Cooper."

ETR 29 Jun 1918, p. 322. *MPN* 29 Jun 1918, p. 3874, 3945. *MPW* 29 Jun 1918, p. 1888, 1899. *NYDM* 29 Jun 1918, p. 927. *NYT* 1 Jul 1918, p. 9. *Var* 5 Jul 1918, p. 31. *Wid's* 16 Jun 1918, pp. 23-24.

HOW MOLLY MALONE MADE GOOD (Irish Americans)

Photo Drama Co. *Dist* Kulee Features, Inc. Nov **1915** [©Kulee Features, Inc.; 9 Oct 1915; LU6640]. Si; b&w. 6 reels.

Pres Lee Kugel. *Prod* William Steiner. *Dir* Lawrence B. McGill. *Scen* Burns Mantle.

Cast: Marguerite Gale (*Molly Malone*), Helen Hilton (*Hilton, a reporter*), John Reedy (*Reedy, a photographer*), William H. Tooker, W. A. Williams, Armand Cortes, James Bagley, Edward Sullivan, Madame Fjorde, Lulu Glaser, May Robson, Henry Kolker, Cyril Scott, Julian Eltinge, Charles J. Ross, Mabel Fenton, Robert Edeson, Leo Ditrichstein, Julia Dean, Henrietta Crosman (*Themselves*).

Melodrama. America-bound Molly Malone, from Ireland, strikes up an acquaintance with opera singer Madame Fjorde on the ocean liner the *Adriatic*. Upon landing, Molly learns that her brother, a *New York Tribune* reporter, went to the war two weeks earlier. After her request to work as a reporter is ridiculed, she hears Hilton, a woman reporter, refuse an interview assignment by claiming that Madame Fjorde was not on the *Adriatic*. When Molly proves her abilities by getting the reclusive singer's interview, the impressed editor sends her to interview ten stage stars in their country homes in only three days for the Sunday magazine section. First, she is to interview Lulu Glaser, from her get the next star's address and continue on to all ten. Although Hilton and Reedy, a discharged photographer, try to stop Molly by, among other things, stealing her interview cards and causing car and train wrecks, Molly travels throughout suburban New York and succeeds. From her last interview, she hires an airplane to reach the office by the deadline. Reedy and Hilton are arrested, and Molly falls in love with a helpful reporter. *Actors and actresses. Interviews. Irish. New York Tribune. Reporters. Airplanes. Automobile accidents. Editors. Immigrants. New York (State). Opera singers. Photographers. S.S. Adriatic. Train wrecks.*

Note: This film was also reviewed under the title *How Molly Made Good*. This was the first film released by Kulee Features. Burns Mantle, the scenarist, was at the time the dramatic critic for the *New York Evening Mail*. The film had its premiere on 1 Nov 1915 at the Metropolitan Opera House in Philadelphia. This was Marguerite Gale's first film. Madame Fjorde was a singer with the Royal Opera of Berlin. Some scenes in the film involving the famous stage stars who played themselves were shot at their summer houses in the following places: Mt. Vernon, NY, Sheepshead Bay, NY, Westchester County, NY, Bayside, Long Island, Harmon-on-the-Hudson, NY, Edgecliff, NJ, Asbury Park, NJ, Sag Harbor, Long Island, Stamford, CT, and Wilton, CT. According to the scenario in the copyright descriptions, George M. Cohan was to be the final star interviewed, and Mrs. Kugel, the wife of Lee Kugel, owner of Kulee Features, was to play Henry Kolker's maid. Charles J. Ross and Mabel Fenton were married. The families and pets of some of the stage stars also appeared in the film.

Motog 23 Oct 1915, pp. 863-64, 882. *Motog* 13 Nov 1915, p. 1000. *MPN* 16 Oct 1915, p. 68. *MPN* 23 Oct 1915, p. 46, 83. *MPN* 6 Nov 1915, p. 117. *MPN* 27 Nov 1915, p. 87. *MPW* 23 Oct 1915, pp. 626, 640, 672-73. *Var* 15 Oct 1915, p. 21. *Wid's* 14 Oct 1915.

HOW UNCLE SAM PREPARES (African Americans)

Hanover Film Co. *Dist* State Rights. Apr **1917**. Si; b&w. 4-5 reels.
Dir S. Grant and Charles E. Kimball.

World War I, **War preparedness**, **Documentary**. The film opens with a brief allegorical prologue in which Uncle Sam discusses the European War with Presidents Abraham Lincoln and Woodrow Wilson and awakens to the crisis after learning of the sinking of the *Laconia* and other misdeeds committed by the Prussians. Scenes showing American prosperity before the declaration of war are followed by shots of citizens, including Southern blacks, rallying to battle. The mustering of these raw recruits to the daily tasks of the seasoned soldiers are then depicted as the soldiers go through bayonet exercise, the maneuvers of field artillery and signal practice, and the basics of making camp. Also pictured are all-black regiments drilling in the same manner as the white regiments. The tasks of Navy seamen are reproduced as well. Various government officials, including Woodrow Wilson, appear in the film. *United States–Defenses. United States. Army. United States. Navy. World War I. African Americans. Military service, Voluntary. Sailors. Soldiers. Southerners.*

Note: This film was also known as *Uncle Sam Prepares*. Originally released as five reels, the film was later cut to four reels. According to a news item, it was produced under United States military supervision. In Jun 1917, Francis Holley, of the National Defense Division of the Bureau of Commercial Economics, Department of Public Instruction, requested that the film be shown in Washington, D.C. to various government officials and members of the U.S. Senate and House of Representatives. Modern sources state that immigrant soldiers are featured in the film as well as black recruits.

ETR 21 Apr 1917, p. 1362, 1391. *Motog* 28 Apr 1917, p. 905. *MPN* 28 Apr 1917, p. 2685. *MPN* 23 Jun 1917, p. 3916. *MPW* 28 Apr 1917, pp. 634-35. *MPW* 5 May 1917, p. 750. *Var* 20 Apr 1917, p. 23.

HUA CHIO JUH GUANG (Chinese language)

Grandview Film Co. **1940**. Sd; b&w. Length undetermined. Chinese language.
Dir Joseph Sunn. [*Not viewed*]. [No information concerning the plot of this film has been located.].

Note: The Cantonese transliterated title is *Wua Kio Tse Gon*. This film was probably made in the U.S.

HUCK AND TOM; OR, THE FURTHER ADVENTURES OF TOM SAWYER (Native Americans)

Famous Players-Lasky Corp.; Oliver Morosco Photoplay Co. *Dist* Famous Players-Lasky Corp.; Paramount Pictures. 4 Mar **1918** [©Oliver Morosco Photoplay Co.; 22 Jan 1918; LP12003]. Si; b&w. 5 reels.
Pres Jesse L. Lasky. *Dir* William D. Taylor. *Scen* Julia Crawford Ivers. *Cam* Homer Scott.

Source: Based on the novel *The Adventures of Tom Sawyer* by Mark Twain (San Francisco, 1896) and his novel *The Adventures of Huckleberry Finn* (New York, 1884).

Cast: Jack Pickford (*Tom Sawyer*), Robert Gordon (*Huck Finn*), George Hackathorne (*Sid Sawyer*), Alice Marvin (*Mary Sawyer*), Edythe Chapman (*Aunt Polly*), Frank Lanning (*Injun Joe*), Clara Horton (*Becky Thatcher*), Tom Bates (*Muff Potter*), Helen Gilmore (*Widow Douglas*), Antrim Short (*Joe Harper*), Jane Keckley (*Mrs. Thatcher*), John Burton (*Judge Thatcher*).

Comedy-drama. Intending to try out a magical cure for warts, Tom Sawyer and Huck Finn steal into a graveyard late one night carrying a dead cat. There they witness the murder of a grave robber, and although the boys swear an oath of secrecy to each other, Tom later testifies against half-breed Injun Joe, the murderer, in order to save the falsely accused old derelict, Muff Potter. Injun Joe escapes, but the boys discover him in an old haunted house as he is making plans to hide a chest of stolen money. A short time later, Becky Thatcher, with whom Tom is in love, gives a birthday picnic for her friends near the Painted Cave. While she and Tom are exploring, they become lost in the dark cavern, but Tom catches sight of Injun Joe just before a rescue party arrives. The following week, Tom learns that the cave has been sealed up and that Injun Joe has lost his life. Huck and Tom return to the cave, dig up the treasure, and then do their best to escape the doting attentions of the village ladies. *Country boys. Fugitives. Indians of North America–Mixed blood. Money. Murder. Rescues. Trials. Caves. Cemeteries. Cures. Escapes. False arrests. Grave robbers. Haunted houses. Picnicking. Robbery. Tramps.*

Note: Part one of this two-part series on Tom Sawyer also starring Jack Pickford and directed by William D. Taylor was released by Paramount on 2 Dec 1917. It was entitled *Tom Sawyer*. According to a news item, some scenes were filmed in Hannibal, MO, the setting of Mark Twain's stories. For information on other film versions of *The Adventures of Tom Sawyer* and *The Adventures of Huckleberry Finn*, see listings above for David O. Selznick's 1938 film *The Adventures of Tom Sawyer* and the 1960 M-G-M release *The Adventures of Huckleberry Finn*.

ETR 16 Mar 1918, p. 1229. *MPN* 16 Mar 1918, pp. 1613-14. *MPW* 9 Mar 1918, p. 1414. *MPW* 16 Mar 1918, p. 1558. *NYDM* 9 Mar 1918, p. 26. *Var* 8 Mar 1918, p. 42. *Wid's* 14 Mar 1918, p. 1011.

HUCKLEBERRY FINN (African Americans)

Famous Players-Lasky Corp. by arrangement with the Mark Twain Co.; A William D. Taylor Production; Mark Twain—Paramount-Artcraft Pictures. *Dist* Famous Players-Lasky Corp. 29 Feb **1920** [©Famous Players-Lasky Corp.; 30 Dec 1919; LP14604]. Si; b&w. 7 reels.
Pres Jesse L. Lasky. *Dir* William D. Taylor. *Scen* Julia Crawford Ivers. *Cam* Frank E. Garbutt.

Source: Based on the novel *The Adventures of Huckleberry Finn* by Mark Twain (New York, 1884).

Cast: Lewis Sargent (*"Huckleberry" Finn*), Katherine Griffith (*Widow Douglas*), Martha Mattox (*Miss Watson*), Frank Lanning (*Huck's father*), Orral Humphrey (*The Duke*), Tom D. Bates (*The King*), Gordon Griffith (*Tom Sawyer*), Edythe Chapman (*Aunt Polly*), Thelma Salter (*Becky Thatcher*), George Reed (*Jim*), L. M. Wells (*Judge Thatcher*), Harry Rattenbury (*Uncle Harvey*), Esther Ralston (*Mary Jane Wilks*), Fay Lemport (*Johanna*), Eunice Van Moore (*Mrs. Sally Phelps*), Charles Edler (*School teacher*).

Rural, **Comedy-drama.** Huckleberry "Huck" Finn is adopted by the Widow Douglas, who tries to "civilize" him. With Tom Sawyer, he decides to start a robber gang, but before they can organize, Huck is kidnapped by his shiftless father who is after the boy's money. Spirited away down the Mississippi in a raft, Huck finally escapes and is joined by Jim, a runaway slave. They pick up two actors calling themselves the Duke and the King, who sell Jim to a man named Phelps. Huck comes to his rescue and is aided by Tom, a relative of the Phelpses. Posing as Tom, Huck rescues Jim but Tom is shot in the leg during the escape. When the Phelpses learn the truth, they care for Tom, release Jim and assist Huck's return to the Widow Douglas.

Actors and actresses. Country boys. Etiquette. Friendship. Mississippi River. Rafts. Slavery. Slaves. Abduction. Adoption. Fathers and sons. Foster parents. Greed. Gunshot wounds. Impersonation and imposture. Runaways. Widows.

Note: According to a news item, Mark Twain's daughter Mrs. Ossip Gabrilowitsch viewed this film in a private Detroit screening. A special edition of the novel with stills from the movie was published by Harper & Bros. The film opened in New York on 22 Feb 1920. For information on other filmed versions of Mark Twain's novel, see entry above for the 1960 M-G-M release *The Adventures of Huckleberry Finn.*

ETR 24 Jan 1920, p. 807. *MPN* 31 Jan 1920, p. 1258. *MPN* 6 Mar 1920, p. 2393. *MPW* 17 Jan 1920, p. 323. *MPW* 21 Feb 1920, pp. 1290-91. *Var* 27 Feb 1920, p. 46. *Wid's* 29 Feb 1920, p. 3.

HUCKLEBERRY FINN (African Americans)

Paramount Publix Corp. *Dist* Paramount Publix Corp. 15 Aug **1931** [©Paramount Publix Corp.; 15 Aug 1931; LP2400]. Sd (Western Electric Noiseless Recording); b&w. 8 reels. 70 or 73 min. Passed by the National Board of Review. PCA cert no. 1392-R [31 Aug 1935].

Dir Norman Taurog. *Scr* Grover Jones and William Slavens McNutt. *Photog* David Abel. [*2d cam* Dan Fapp and Ernest Laszlo]. [*Asst cam* James King and Thomas Morris]. [*Sd rec* Gene Merritt]. [*Still photog* Gordon Head].

Source: Based on the novel *The Adventures of Huckleberry Finn* by Mark Twain (New York, 1884).

Cast: Jackie Coogan (*Tom Sawyer*), Junior Durkin (*Huckleberry Finn*), Mitzi Green (*Becky Thatcher*), Jackie Searl (*Sid Sawyer*), Eugene Pallette (*The Duke of Bilgewater,* [*Junior*]), Clarence Muse (*Jim*), Clara Blandick (*Aunt Polly*), Jane Darwell (*Widow Douglas*), Oscar Apfel (*The King,* [*Senior*]), Warner Richmond (*Pap,* [*Mr. Finn*]), Charlotte V. Henry (*Mary Jane*), Lillian Harmer (*Miss* [*Minnie*] *Watson*), Guy Oliver (*Judge Thatcher*), [Doris Short (*Ella*)], [Cecil Weston (*Mrs. Thatcher*)], [Aileen Manning (*Abigail Prentice*)], [Frank McGlynn (*Teacher*)].

Youth, Adventure, Historical. [*Print viewed*]. In the 1850's in St. Petersburg, Missouri, two mischievous boys, Tom Sawyer and Huckleberry Finn, find pirate's treasure while playing in a cave. Later, Huck goes to live in the house of the widow Douglas and makes an unsuccessful effort to adjust to school life. Tom, infatuated with Becky Thatcher, spends less time with Huck, who is about to run away when his drunken father kidnaps him and locks him in a shack. Overwhelmed by guilt for having let Huck down, Tom rescues Huck with the help of the widow Douglas' slave Jim, and the three decide to head south on the Mississippi River on a raft. Along the way, they encounter a pair of scoundrels, who command Tom's loyalty by pretending to be a king and duke. Tom and Huck, begging for food for the con men, meet a pair of recently orphaned sisters who await the arrival of two uncles from England, and the con men impersonate the uncles to steal the sisters' $14,000 legacy. Huck, however, is smitten with Mary Jane, the older sister, and at the last moment he and Tom foil the planned robbery. The three wanderers return home, and Huck cheerfully resumes school under Mary Jane's influence. *Country boys. Friendship. Impersonation and imposture. Runaways. Slavery. United States–History–19th century. Alcoholics. Battered children. Caves. Childhood sweethearts. Confidence men. Fathers and sons. Guilt. Kidnapping. Mississippi River. Orphans. Schools. Sisters. Thieves. Treasure. Widows.*

Note: For realism, the 1850s town of St. Petersburg, MO was reconstructed for a set, according to the pressbook. Mark Twain's novel has been the basis of many films. For information on other film adaptations of Mark Twain's novel, see entry above for the 1960 M-G-M release *The Adventures of Huckleberry Finn.*

FD 9 Aug 1931, p. 10. *HR* 23 Jul 1931, p. 3. *IP* Sep 1931, p. 29. *MPH* 1 Aug 1931, p. 30. *NYT* 2 Aug 1931, p. 3. *NYT* 8 Aug 1931, p. 16. *NYT* 16 Aug 1931, p. 3. *Var* 11 Aug 1931, p. 22.

HUDDLE (Italian Americans)

Metro-Goldwyn-Mayer Corp.; controlled by Loew's, Inc.; A Sam Wood Production. *Dist* Metro-Goldwyn-Mayer Distributing Corp. 14 May **1932**; Prod: began 11 Feb 1932 [©Metro-Goldwyn-Mayer Distributing Corp.; 26 May 1932; LP3056]. Sd (Western Electric Sound System); b&w. 11 reels. 103-104 min. Passed by the National Board of Review.

Dir Sam Wood. [*Asst dir* John Waters]. *Dial cont* Walton Hall Smith and C. Gardner Sullivan. *Adpt* Robert Lee Johnson and Arthur S. Hyman. *Photog* Harold Wenstrom. *Art dir* Cedric Gibbons. *Film ed* Hugh Wynn. *Gowns* Adrian. *Rec dir* Douglas Shearer. [*Sd* Charles

Wallace]. [*Technical detail by* Crilly Butler and Elbridge Anderson].

Song(s): "The Wiffenpoof Song," words by Meade Minnigeroode and George S. Pomeroy, music by Tod B. Galloway.

Source: Based on the novel *Huddle* by Francis Wallace (New York, 1931).

Cast: RAMON NOVARRO (*Tony* [*Amatto*]), Madge Evans (*Rosalie* [*Stone*]), Una Merkel (*Thelma*), Ralph Graves (*Coach Malcolm* [*Gale*]), John Arledge ([*Jim*] *Pidge* [*Pidgeon*]), Frank Albertson (*Larry* [*Wilson*]), Kane Richmond (*Tom Stone*), Martha Sleeper (*Barbara* [*Winston*]), Henry Armetta (*Mr. Amatto*), Ferike Boros (*Mrs. Amatto*), Rockcliffe Fellows (*Mr. Stone*), Joe Sauers (*Slater*), [Charley Grapewin (*Doctor*)], [Tom Kennedy (*Moving man*)].

Football, College, Drama. [*Print viewed*]. Italian-American steel worker Tony Amatto leaves his Gary, Indiana mill job when he gets a $2,000 scholarship to attend Yale. At school, he is reluctant to try out for the freshman football team, thinking it's frivolous, which puts him on the wrong side of the other boys, especially football hero Tom Stone, the son of the owner of the mill in which Tony worked. Tom also dislikes Tony because he thinks that he has insulted his sister Rosalie. During summer vacation, Tony again works at the mill to toughen himself for football, which he now knows will help his career, as well as get him even with Tom. Back at school, Tony helps popular student Jim "Pidge" Pidgeon during a town and gown riot, after which Pidge asks Tony to room with him. On the first day of football practice Tony accidentally breaks Pidge's leg and wants to quit, but Pidge convinces him to continue. Tony becomes a football star, but Tom still doesn't like him and is jealous because his girl friend, Barbara Winston, and Rosalie are both infatuated with him. Tony doesn't really care for Barbara, but she makes a play for him, and he spends a night in her train compartment. An increasingly conceited Tony then goes after Rosalie, who rejects him when he suggests that they spend the night in a private inn. Feeling like a heel, Tony shows up at Mory's Tavern drunk, but his teammates keep him from being seen by Coach Malcolm Gale. The next day, at the Yale-Dartmouth game, a hung-over Tony roughs up a tackler and is taken out of the game, then rushes back onto the field for an important tackle and is sent to the showers by the coach. At the fraternity rush, when Tony is not chosen because of his unsportsmanlike performance at the game, only Pidge stands by him. Tony then goes to the coach to quit, but, after resorting to fisticuffs, Malcolm teaches Tony a lesson about getting along with people and the two become friends. In the spring, Tony asks Rosalie's forgiveness for the way he acted and tells that he loves her. Rosalie returns his affection, but her father and brother are against their relationship, and Mr. Stone convinces Tony that Rosalie could not live in poverty while he struggles to the top. In Tony's junior year, Malcolm, now impressed by his dedication and hard work, puts Tony in the front line again. The night before the Harvard-Yale game, Rosalie comes to his room and tells him she loves him, and realizes what her father did. She tries to make Tony believe that she doesn't care about money, but he is worried that she will be found in his room and compromised. As she sneaks out, Tom sees her from the back and, thinking she is Barbara, starts a fight with Tony. Tony refuses to compromise anyone and claims that he had been smoking and drinking what was actually consumed by Rosemary. Tony, who has been having stomach pains, goes to see a doctor later and learns that he must have an emergency appendectomy, but he does not want to miss the game and leaves, even though he is warned about a possible burst appendix. Unknown to Tony, his parents come to the game as a surprise. Despite great pain, Tony plays the game, but when he is unable to do well, the coach replaces him. During half-time, Tony puts ice on his stomach in the locker room to deaden the pain, then begs the coach to let him play again. Though feverish and in extreme pain, Tony makes a touchdown, but is sent to the showers by Malcolm who suspects that Tony is ill. Tony hears in the locker room that at the last minute Yale tied the game, and is chastised by Tom, who thinks that Tony was just acting like a prima donna when he left the game, and slaps him. At a post-game party Tony's father tells Pidge that Tony's appendix has burst and he is gravely ill. Pidge then angrily denounces Tom and the others for being snobs, and tells them how much Tony really cares for the school. When Rosemary tells Tom that she was in Tony's room, he wants to apologize, but the coach makes him realize that Tony just wants to be one of the gang. In his senior year, a now recovered Tony is finally popular among the students, and at commencement, his parents sit with Mr. Stone and

Rosemary. *Brothers and sisters. Class distinction. College life. Football. Italian Americans. Yale University. Appendicitis. Drunkenness. Family relationships. Fistfights. Friendship. Gary (IN). Graduations. Mory's Tavern (New Haven, CT). Physicians. Reputation. Romance. Steel mills.*

Note: According to pre-production news items in *HR*, Robert Z. Leonard had tentatively been set to direct the film and Monte M. Katterjohn was to adapt the novel. Katterjohn was not mentioned in any sources after the film's production and it has not been determined if he did indeed write an adaptation or if any part of it was retained in the released film. A pre-production chart in *HF* credits Robert Shirley with sound, but production charts and *FDYB* only credit Charles Wallace. Another news item in *HR* mentioned that M-G-M decided to change the location from Notre Dame, which was the setting of the novel, to Yale, because Universal had recently released the film *Spirit of Notre Dame* with a similar theme. Some reviews also noted this change. *Var* said "Autumn stadium fans will recognize flashes of Albie Booth...and Barry Wood," popular college football players at the time, who appeared in footage of football games incorporated into the film. Some of the incidents of this film were recreated in the 1938 M-G-M British production *A Yank at Oxford* (see appendix), although neither the original Wallace novel, nor any of the screenwriters of *Huddle* were credited.

FD 29 May 1932, p. 10. *HF* 30 Jan 1932, p. 8. *HF* 13 Feb 1932, p. 8. *HR* 7 Jul 1931, p. 3. *HR* 21 Oct 1931, p. 4. *HR* 5 Nov 1931, p. 2. *HR* 12 Feb 1932, p. 3. *MPH* 25 Jun 1932, p. 28. *NYT* 17 Jun 1932, p. 24. *Var* 21 Jun 1932, p. 14.

HULDA FROM HOLLAND (Dutch Americans)

Famous Players Film Co. *Dist* Paramount Pictures Corp. 31 Jul **1916** [©Famous Players Film Co.; 14 Jul 1916; LU8683]. Si; b&w. 5 reels.

Dir John B. O'Brien. *Scen* Edith Barnard Delano. *Cam* Emmet Williams.

Cast: Mary Pickford (*Hulda*), Frank Losee (*John Walton*), John Bowers (*Allan Walton*), Russell Bassett (*Uncle Peter*), Harold Hollacher (*Little Yacob*), Charles E. Vernon (*The burgomaster*).

Drama. When Uncle Peter goes to pick up his niece Hulda, newly arrived in the United States from Holland, he is hit by a car and must be hospitalized. As a result, Hulda takes a room in a boardinghouse, where she falls in love with Allan, the artist son of John Walton, a railroad magnate who has been badgering Peter to sell him his land. Peter eventually recovers and Hulda goes to live with him, but Allan follows her and, at his father's request, keeps on suggesting that Peter sell his land to the railroad. Peter finally relents, after which Hulda and Allan get married. John attends the ceremony, and after the couple is married, there is a reconciliation between him and Peter. *Artists. Boardinghouses. Dutch Americans. Immigrants. Land sales. Railroads. Tycoons. Uncles. Automobile accidents. Weddings.*

Note: This film was re-issued by Famous Players-Lasky Corp. in their Success Series on 26 Apr 1919. The original title of the scenario was "Miss Jinny."

Motog 12 Aug 1916, p. 397. *MPN* 12 Aug 1916, p. 946. *MPW* 12 Aug 1916, p. 1102. *NYDM* 5 Aug 1916, p. 22. *NYT* 31 Jul 1916, p. 6. *Var* 4 Aug 1916, p. 29. *Wid's* 20 Jul 1916, p. 726.

HUMAN CARGO (Immigrants)

Twentieth Century-Fox Film Corp. *Dist* Twentieth Century-Fox Film Corp. 29 May **1936**; New York opening: 15 May 1936; Prod: 10 Feb-early Mar 1936 [©Twentieth Century-Fox Film Corp.; 29 May 1936; LP6418]. Sd (Western Electric Noiseless Recording); b&w. 7 reels, 6,000 ft. 65-66 min. PCA cert no. 2103.

Exec prod Sol M. Wurtzel. *Dir* Allan Dwan. *Asst dir* Samuel Schneider. *Scr* Jefferson Parker and Doris Malloy. [*Contr wrt* Allan Dwan, Hamilton MacFadden and Barry Trivers]. *Photog* Daniel B. Clark. *Art dir* Duncan Cramer. *Film ed* Louis Loeffler. *Cost* William Lambert. *Mus dir* Samuel Kaylin. *Sd* Alfred Bruzlin and Harry M. Leonard.

Source: Based on the novel *I Will Be Faithful* by Kathleen Shepard (New York, 1934).

Cast: Claire Trevor (*Bonnie Brewster*), Brian Donlevy ([*Patrick*] *Packy Campbell*), Alan Dinehart (*Lionel* [*"Bulldog"*] *Crocker*), Ralph Morgan (*District Attorney* [*Joe*] *Carey*), Helen Troy (*Susie*), Rita Cansino (*Carmen Zoro*), Morgan Wallace (*Gilbert Fender*), Herman Bing (*Fritz Schultz*), John McGuire (*"Spike" Davis*), Ralf Harolde (*Tony Sculla*), Wade Boteler (*Bob McSweeney*), Harry Wood (*Ira Conklin*), [Paul McVey (*Ship's officer*)], [Tom Ricketts (*Reporter*)], [Harry Semels (*Baretto*)], [Wilfred Lucas (*Detective lieutenant*)], [Stanley Blystone, Ivan "Dusty" Miller, Tom O'Grady, Pat Hartigan (*Detectives*)], [Edward Cooper (*Butler*)], [Fredrik Vogeding (*Captain*)], [John Rogers (*Foreigners' agent*)], [Arno Frey (*German husband*)], [Rosalie Hegedus (*German mother*)], [Hans Fuerberg, Milla Davenport (*German characters*)], [Otto H. Fries (*German cook*)], [Alphonse Martell (*Frenchman*)], [Hector V. Sarno (*Italian*)], [Lee Phelps, Alonzo Price (*Gangsters*)], [Eddie Buzard (*Copy boy*)], [Claudia Coleman (*Sob sister*)].

Crime, Social, Newspaper, Drama. [*Print viewed*]. A newspaper story by Patrick "Packy" Campbell reveals that 10,000 aliens are smuggled monthly across the borders into the United States, and that afterwards, the smugglers extort the illegals' salaries by threatening to turn them in. When Bonnie Brewster, the daughter of the newspaper's principal advertiser, arrives at the office hoping to become a reporter, Packy asks her to join him that evening to help get a story. At the 500 Club, during Latin dancer, Carmen Zoro's performance, Packy sends Bonnie up to Carmen's dressing room to look for Baretto, a gangster. She is trapped by Baretto, but the police are summoned and the criminal is shot. To get Carmen's story and to save her from reprisals, Packy hides her in his apartment with a ladies' editor to keep her company. However, Bonnie, whom Packy allowed to be arrested, brings District Attorney Joe Carey to take Carmen and Packy into custody. Now working for a rival newspaper, Bonnie convinces Carmen to tell her story, but as she is about to tell the name of the boss of the alien smuggling ring, Carmen is shot by mobster Tony Sculla. While Bonnie is upset, Packy telephones the story into their papers. They both then follow Carmen's lead to the *Northern Star* liner in Canada and pretend to be a French couple trying to enter the United States. They acquire passage and the bridal suite for $450, but the gang learns their true identity, and they are taken off the ship. Hauled away in a truck by Sculla, they manage to escape, and Packy takes the captured Sculla to the newspaper. Packy and his editor, Lionel "Bulldog" Crocker, scare the gangster by discussing the details of executions until Sculla names prominent civic leader Gilbert Fender as the leader of the mob. At the same time, Bonnie seeks Carey at the home of his friend, Fender. Waiting for Carey, she tells Fender what they have discovered, and she is tied up. When Packy, the police and Carey arrive at Fender's, Sculla recants his story at Carey's urging. However, Packy sees Bonnie's bracelet, and the gang is rounded up. *Aliens, Illegal. District Attorneys. Racketeers. Reporters. Rivalry. Smuggling. Women reporters. Boundaries. Canada. Dancers. Editors. Escapes. Extortion. Heiresses. Impersonation and imposture. Interrogation. Latin Americans. Ships.*

Note: The working title of this film was *I Will Be Faithful*. Eddie Bernard, Paul Stanton and Ford Sterling are listed as cast members in the *HR* production charts, but their participation in the final film has not been confirmed. According to a Nov 1935 *LAT* news item, a story with the title *Human Cargo*, which was to take place in Ethiopia and Egypt, was being adapted by Hamilton MacFadden. Although a treatment by MacFadden and a first draft screen adaptation by MacFadden and Barry Trivers are included in the file for the film in the Twentieth Century-Fox Produced Scripts Collection at the UCLA Theater Arts Library, it is uncertain whether any material from that story was used in this film.

Box 25 Apr 1936. *DV* 18 Apr 1936, p. 3. *FD* 21 Apr 1936, p. 5. *HR* 8 Feb 1936, p. 3. *HR* 10 Feb 1936, p. 15. *HR* 24 Feb 1936, p. 5. *HR* 2 Mar 1936, p. 11. *HR* 18 Apr 1936, p. 3. *LAT* 13 Nov 1935. *MPD* 20 Apr 1936, pp. 10-11. *MPH* 4 Apr 1936, p. 51. *MPH* 25 Apr 1936, p. 36. *NYT* 16 May 1936, p. 11. *Var* 27 May 1936, p. 15.

HUMORESQUE (Jewish Americans)

Cosmopolitan Productions; International Film Service Co. *Dist* Famous Players-Lasky Corp.; Paramount-Artcraft Pictures. 19 Sep **1920** [©International Film Service Co., Inc.; 29 Jun 1920; LP15323]. Si; b&w. 6 reels, 5,987 ft.

Dir Frank Borzage. *Scen* Frances Marion. *Cam* Gilbert Warrenton.

Source: Based on the story story "Humoresque" by Fannie Hurst in *Cosmopolitan* (Mar 1919).

Cast: Gaston Glass (*Leon Kantor, adult*), Vera Gordon (*Mama Kantor*), Alma Rubens (*Gina Berg*), Dore Davidson (*Abraham Kantor*), Bobby Connelly (*Leon Kantor, boy*), Helen Connelly (*Esther Kantor, girl*), Ann Wallick (*Esther Kantor, adult*), Sidney Carlyle (*Mannie Kantor*), Joseph Cooper (*Isadore Kantor, boy*), Maurice Levigne (*Isadore Kantor, adult*), Alfred Goldberg (*Rudolph Kantor, boy*), Edward Stanton (*Rudolph Kantor, adult*), Louis Stearns (*Sol Ginsberg*), Maurice Peckre (*Boris Kantor*), Ruth Sabin (*Mrs. Isadore Kantor*), Frank Mitchell (*Baby Kantor*), Miriam Battista (*Minnie Ginsberg*).

Drama. Mama Kantor is overjoyed when her young son Leon exhibits a great talent for playing the violin. After years of practicing, the adult Leon achieves fame and success as a violinist, enabling him to move his family from the Jewish ghetto to fashionable uptown quarters. He also proposes to his former childhood playmate, Minnie Ginsberg, now known as Gina Berg. At the pinnacle of his career, war breaks out; Leon enlists in the army and is sent to France where he right arm is seriously wounded. Convinced that he is crippled permanently and will never be able to play again, Leon breaks his

engagement to Gina. Heartbroken, the girl faints and Leon, rushing to her side, scoops her up in his arms. Realizing that his strength has returned, Leon reaches for the violin and begins to play again. *Cures. Jews. Mothers and sons. New York City. Violinists. War injuries. Children. France. Handicapped. Soldiers. World War I.*

Note: The film had a private showing in New York on 4 May 1920, and a prerelease run beginning 30 May 1920 at the Criterion Theatre in New York. It played for twelve weeks there and broke attendance records. Warner Bros. loosely remade *Humoresque* in 1947 with John Garfield and Joan Crawford in the lead roles. Clifford Odets and Zachary Gold re-adapted Hurst's story, and Jean Negulesco directed it.
ETR 15 May 1920, p. 2740. *MPN* 15 May 1920, p. 4231. *MPN* 18 Sep 1920, p. 2277. *MPW* 15 May 1920, p. 982, 1073. *NYMT* 9 May 1920. *NYT* 3 May 1920, p. 14. *Var* 4 Jun 1920, p. 27. *Wid's* 9 May 1920, p. 3.

HUMORESQUE (Jewish Americans)

Warner Bros. Pictures, Inc.; A Warner Bros.—First National Picture. *Dist* Warner Bros. Pictures, Inc. 25 Jan **1947**; New York opening: 25 Dec 1946; Prod: mid-Dec 1945—mid-Apr 1946 [©Warner Bros. Pictures, Inc.; 25 Jan 1947; LP793]. Sd (RCA Sound System); b&w. 11,210 ft. 123-124 or 126 min.
Exec prod JACK L. WARNER. *Prod* Jerry Wald. *Dir* Jean Negulesco. *Dial dir* Herschel Daugherty. [*Asst dir* Phil Quinn]. [*2d asst dir* Herbert Greene]. *Scr* Clifford Odets and Zachary Gold. *Dir of photog* Ernest Haller. [*2d cam* William Shurr]. [*Gaffer* James Geldenhar]. [*Stills* Jack Woods]. [*Stills gaffer* Ralph Burbank]. *Mont* James Leicester and David Forrest. *Spec eff dir* Roy Davidson. *Spec eff* Willard Van Enger. *Art dir* Hugh Reticker. *Film ed* Rudi Fehr. *Set dec* Clarence Steenson. [*Props* William Wallace and Levy Williams]. *Ward* Bernard Newman. *Miss Crawford's ward by* Adrian. [*Ward* Vic Vallejo, Ralph Hibbs, Janet Storke and Mary Deery]. *Mus adv* Isaac Stern. *Mus dir* Leo F. Forbstein. *Mus cond* Franz Waxman. *Sd* Robert B. Lee. *Makeup artist* Perc Westmore. [*Makeup* Ed Allen]. [*Hair* Gertrude Wheeler and Della Barnet]. [*Unit mgr* Lou Baum]. [*Unit pub* John Mitchell]. [*Pub* John Strauss]. [*Scr clerk* Alma Dwight]. [*Best boy* Paul Butler]. [*Grip* Stanley Young].
Music: "Humoresque" by Antonín Dvořák; selections from the opera *Carmen*, music by Georges Bizet; "Liebestod" from the opera *Tristan and Isolde* by Richard Wagner; "Zigeunerweise" by Pablo de Sarasate; selections from Violin Concerto in E minor by Felix Mendelsohn, Violin Concerto in D major by Peter Tchaikovsky, Violin Concerto in D minor, Opus 22 by Henryk Wieniawski, Sonata for Piano and Violin in A major by César Franck, *Symphonie Espagnole* by Édouard Lalo; Piano Concerto in A minor by Edvard Grieg; and Piano Concerto by Sergei Prokofieff; Polka by Dmitri Shostakovich; Waltz in A Flat by Johannes Brahms; Sonata in G minor by Johann Sebastian Bach.
Song(s): "Embraceable You," music by George Gershwin, lyrics by Ira Gershwin; "What Is This Thing Called Love?" and "You Do Something to Me," music and lyrics by Cole Porter.
Source: Based on the short story "Humoresque" by Fannie Hurst in *Cosmopolitan* (Mar 1919).
Cast: JOAN CRAWFORD (*Helen Wright*), JOHN GARFIELD (*Paul Boray*), Oscar Levant (*Sid Jeffers*), J. Carrol Naish (*Rudy Boray*), Joan Chandler (*Gina*), Tom D'Andrea (*Phil Boray*), Peggy Knudson (*Florence Boray*]), Ruth Nelson (*Esther Boray*), Craig Stevens (*Monte Loeffler*), Paul Cavanagh (*Victor Wright*), Richard Gaines ([*Frederick*] *Bauer*), John Abbott (*Rozner*), Bobby Blake (*Paul Boray, as a child*), Tommy Cook (*Phil Boray, as a child*), Don McGuire (*Eddie*), Fritz Leiber (*Hagerstrom*), Peg La Centra (*Nightclub singer*), Nestor Paiva (*Orchestra leader*), [Richard Walsh (*Teddy*)], [Sylvia Arslan (*Gina, as a girl*)], [Ann Lawrence (*Florence, as a girl*)], [Charles Kenworthy, Gary Armstrong (*Boys on street*)], [Creighton Hale, Leah Baird (*Professors*)], [Louis Quince (*Radio producer*)], [Leo Wonder (*Old violinist*)], [Monte Blue (*Furniture moving man*)], [Ramon Ros (*Engineer*)], [Janet Barrett (*Secretary*)], [Jane Harker (*Haughty blonde*)], [Ed Harvey (*Butler*)], [Angela Greene (*Blonde*)], [John Walsh (*Delivery boy*)], [Esther Michaelson (*Customer*)], [Frank Elliott (*Tailor*)], [Danny Dowling (*Tailor's assistant*)], [Patricia White (*Fitzie, telephone operator*)], [Paul Panzer (*Theater manager*)], [Joe Smith (*Man on beach*)], [Don Turner (*Man with dog*)].
Melodrama, with songs. [*Print viewed*]. After renowned violinist Paul Boray cancels his New York City performance, he tells Frederick Bauer, his manager, how much he wishes he were still the simple, happy child that he used to be: Paul first becomes interested in the

violin as a child on New York's East Side in 1920 and chooses the instrument, rather than a toy, for a birthday present. Encouraged by his mother Esther, Paul becomes proficient and attends music school. During the Depression of the 1930s, the family grocery store suffers. Phil, Paul's older brother, who is out of work, resents the fact that Paul spends his time practicing instead of working. Wounded by his brother's comments, Paul gets a job with a radio orchestra with the help of his friend, pianist Sid Jeffers, but is fired when he objects to the station's policy of cutting compositions to fit into an allotted time. Paul then decides that he is ready to make his concert debut. Sid suggests that he attend a party at the home of socialites Helen and Victor Wright, where he might meet people who will help him financially. Despite Paul's surly attitude, Helen is intrigued by his talent and offers to help him become established as an artist. She introduces him to Bauer and pays for his first public recital. Afterward, Paul's family has a small party in his honor, which he misses because he is celebrating with the Wrights. Esther warns Paul not to become involved with Helen and reminds him about Gina, a fellow student, who loves him. With Helen's aid, Paul becomes a successful performer, and eventually, he and Helen fall in love. When Victor offers Helen a divorce, she hurries to the hall where Paul is rehearsing to tell him, but he refuses to interrupt the rehearsal to talk to her. Helen feels that his dedication is a rejection and, as she often does, eases her pain by drinking. Later, Paul and Helen are reconciled and make plans to marry. Helen then attempts to make peace with Esther, who reminds Helen about her three previous marriages and begs her to consider the effect her drinking and need for attention will have on Paul's career. One night, while Paul performs on the radio, a drunken Helen realizes that she will never mean as much to Paul as his music and walks into the ocean to her death. Paul is devastated and cancels his concert appearances, but now knows that he must go on with his music. *Ambition. Art patronage. Mothers and sons. Violinists. Alcoholics. Brothers. Concerts. The Depression, 1929. Dismissal (Employment). Divorce. Fathers and sons. Grocers. Music schools. New York City. Parties. Pianists. Radio programs. Socialites. Suicide.*

Note: According to a 12 Mar 1945 studio memo from producer Jerry Wald to Warner Bros. executive Steve Trilling, reproduced in a modern source, large portions of Clifford Odets' script were originally written for the 1945 film *Rhapsody in Blue*, which was based on the life of George Gershwin (see below). Odets' script was not used in the final version of that film. In the Fanny Hurst story and its 1920 film screen adaptation *Humoresque*, the character of the violinist was Jewish, and that background was an integral part of the story. Although an undated studio memo to Wald, reprinted in a modern source, states that screenwriter Barney Glazer, who worked on an early version of the script, wanted "Paul Boray" to remain Jewish, his ethnic background was left unspecified in the finished film. Undated press releases included in the file on the film at the AMPAS Library announced that Irving Rapper was to direct the film, Waldo Salt to write it, James Wong Howe to photograph it, and Gig Young to star in it.
HR news items add that Eleanor Parker was first assigned to the female lead. *HR* also notes that some scenes were shot on location at Laguna Beach, CA. According to the *NYT* review, Peg La Centra sings "I Guess I'll Have to Change My Plan," but this song was not heard in the viewed film. According to Oscar Levant's autobiography, two violinists doubled off-camera for John Garfield: while one did the fingering, the second used the bow. Other modern sources state that Garfield did the fingering himself, after taking lessons from violinist Harry Zogan. Violinist Isaac Stern played the music heard on the soundtrack. Franz Waxman was nominated for an Academy Award for his musical score. The 1920 Famous Players-Lasky film *Humoresque* was directed by Frank Borzage and starred Gaston Glass and Vera Gordon (see above).
Box 26 Dec 1946. *DV* 23 Dec 1946, p. 3. *FD* 26 Dec 1946, p. 11. *HR* 10 Sep 1945, p. 2. *HR* 14 Dec 1945, p. 19. *HR* 22 Feb 1946, p. 3. *HR* 12 Apr 1946, p. 15. *HR* 23 Dec 1946, p. 3. *HR* 30 Dec 1946, p. 6. *MPHPD* 5 Jan 1946, p. 2786. *MPHPD* 14 Dec 1946, pp. 3363-64. *MPHPD* 28 Dec 1946, pp. 3385-86. *NYT* 26 Dec 1946, p. 28. *Var* 25 Dec 1946, p. 12.

THE HUN WITHIN (German Americans)

F-4 Picture Corp.; A Paramount-Artcraft Special. *Dist* Famous Players-Lasky Corp. 8 Sep **1918** [©Famous Players-Lasky Corp.; 6 Aug 1918; LP12734]. Si; b&w. 5 reels, 6,319 ft.
Supv D. W. Griffith. *Dir* Chet Withey. *Scen* Granville Warwick. *Story and scen* S. E. V. Taylor. *Cam* David Abel.
Cast: Dorothy Gish (*Beth*), George Fawcett (*Henry Wagner*), Charles Gerrard (*Karl Wagner*), Douglas MacLean (*Frank Douglas*), Bert Sutch (*Krippen*), Max Davidson (*Max*), Lillian Clarke (*Leone*), Robert Anderson (*Krug*), Eric von Stroheim (*Von Bickel*), Adolphe Lestina (*Beth's father*), Kate Bruce (*Frank's mother*).
Espionage, World War I, Drama. After the death of her father, Beth is adopted by Henry Wagner, a German who has made his fortune

in America. Beth believes herself in love with Wagner's American-born son Karl, although Frank Douglas, her school friend, is also in love with her. Following the United States' declaration of war against Germany, Karl returns home from Berlin where, in attending a German college, he had developed a strong loyalty to the German cause. When Karl drinks to the Kaiser's health, Henry denounces his son as a traitor, and later Beth overhears Karl making plans with Krug, a German spy, to blow up an American troop transport. While Krug plants a bomb on the ship, Karl imprisons Beth, but Frank, a Secret Service agent who has learned of the plot, fights off the band of spies and rescues her. The two wire the ship just in time to prevent the explosion, after which Karl and his cohorts are apprehended. Realizing that she has always loved Frank, Beth marries him. *German Americans. Germans. Sabotage. Treason. World War I. Adoption. Bombs. Fathers and sons. Fights. Imprisonment. Loyalty. Rescues. Secret Service. Ships. Spies.*

Note: Modern sources note that D. W. Griffith, under the pseudonym Granville Warwick, wrote the script with S. E. V. Taylor and set up an independent organization called the F-4 Company in order to finance and produce it. After its completion, Griffith sold the film to the Famous Players-Lasky Corp. Footage left over from Griffith's *Hearts of the World* was used in the film. (see *AFI Catalog of Feature Films, 1911-20*; F1.1829). The picture's working title was *F-4*. It was first shown publicly on 1 May 1918 in Pasadena, CA under the title *The Enemy Within*. This was the first Paramount-Artcraft Special.

ETR 18 May 1918, p. 1905. *ETR* 7 Sep 1918, p. 1166, 1177. *MPN* 7 Sep 1918, p. 1599. *MPW* 7 Sep 1918, p. 1434, 1459. *MPW* 28 Sep 1918, p. 1925. *NYDM* 7 Sep 1918, p. 371. *NYT* 26 Aug 1918, p. 9. *Var* 30 Aug 1918, p. 37. *Wid's* 1 Sep 1918, pp. 21-22.

HUNG NGAN FEI BOG MING *see* **HONG YIEN FEI BO MING**

THE HUNGER OF THE BLOOD (Native Americans)

William N. Selig Productions; Franklyn Farnum Series. *Dist* Canyon Pictures. Mar **1921** [©Canyon Pictures; 2 Mar 1921; LU16210]. Si; b&w. 5 reels.

Prod Col. William N. Selig. *Dir* Nate Watt. *Scr* William E. Wing. *Story* William C. Beale.

Cast: Franklyn Farnum (*Maslun*), Ethel Ritchie (*Margaret Kenyon*), Baby Jean O'Rourke (*Little Fawn*).

Western. Maslun, a half-breed, is entrusted with the tribal secret (that there is gold in Dead Man's Canyon on tribal land) just before his foster father, Chief Amek, dies. He finds and adopts a waif (a white girl), whom he names Little Fawn. She later goes into a trance in which the dead chief speaks through the child's lips and urges Maslun to find the gold for the tribe's sake. Maslun's attentions to Margaret Kenyon, a white girl who according to the white man's law owns the canyon, arouses the tribe's suspicions. Warriors kidnap Margaret, but she is rescued by Maslun. Little Fawn goes into another trance (which almost kills her) in which Amek informs Maslun of the gold's location. He goes to the canyon, is there attacked by his tribe, but is rescued by a band of cowboys. It is revealed that he is really a full-blooded white man, Margaret tells him of her love, and the gold is divided between the Indians and Margaret. *Cowboys. Gold. Indians of North America. Indians of North America–Mixed blood. Trance. Waifs.*

HUNGRY HEARTS (Jewish Americans)

Goldwyn Pictures Corp. 26 Nov **1922** [©Goldwyn Pictures Corp.; 1 Nov 1922; LP18529]. Si; b&w. 7 reels, 6,540 ft.

Dir E. Mason Hopper. *Scen* Julien Josephson. *Titles* Montague Glass. *Photog* Robert Newhard.

Source: Based on the novel *Hungry Hearts* by Anzia Yezierska (Boston, 1920).

Cast: Bryant Washburn (*David Kaplan*), Helen Ferguson (*Sara Levin*), E. A. Warren (*Abraham Levin*), Rosa Rosanova (*Hannah Levin*), George Siegmann (*Rosenblatt*), Otto Lederer (*Gedalyah Mindel*), Millie Schottland (*Mishel Mindel*), Bert Sprotte (*Cossack*), A. Budin (*Sopkin*), Edwin B. Tilton (*The Judge*).

Drama. The Levins come to the United States from Russia in hope of a better life but find it very difficult to make a living, even with everybody working. When Rosenblatt raises their rent, an enraged Hannah mutilates the walls, an act for which she must stand trial. Lawyer David Kaplan, who is Rosenblatt's nephew and Sara's sweetheart, successfully defends Hannah, marries Sara, and takes the Levin family out of the ghetto and into his suburban home. *Finance-Personal. Immigrants. Jews. Landlords. Lawyers. Russians.*

ETR 9 Dec 1922, p. 107. *FD* 3 Dec 1922. *MPW* 9 Dec 1922. *NYT* 27 Nov 1922, p. 18. *Var* 1 Dec 1922, p. 34.

THE HUNTRESS (Native Americans)

Associated First National Pictures, Inc. 20 Aug **1923** [©Associated First National Pictures, Inc.; 22 Aug 1923; LP19330]. Si; b&w. 6 reels, 6,236 ft.

Dir Lynn Reynolds. *Asst dir* Harry Welfer. *Adpt* Percy Heath. *Photog* James C. Van Trees. *Art dir* Milton Menasco.

Source: Based on the novel *The Huntress* by Hulbert Footner (New York, 1922).

Cast: Colleen Moore (*Bela*), Lloyd Hughes (*Sam Gladding*), Russell Simpson (*Big Jack Skinner*), Walter Long (*Joe Hagland*), Charles Anderson (*Black Shand Frazer*), Snitz Edwards (*Musq'oosis*), Wilfrid North (*John Gladding*), Helen Raymond (*Mrs. John Gladding*), William Marion (*William Gladding*), Lila Leslie (*Mrs. William Gladding*), Lawrence Steers (*Richard Gladding*), Helen Walron (*Mrs. Richard Gladding*), John Lince (*Butler*), Lalo Encinas (*Beavertail*), Chief Big Tree (*Otebaya*).

Melodrama. Bela, reared by Indians, learns that she is a white orphan and runs away from the Indian village to avoid marrying a brave from the tribe. She determines to marry land prospector Sam Gladding, who resists her advances but later falls in love with Bela when an Indian sage gives him some advice. *Indians of North America. Orphans. Parentage. Prospectors.*

FD 7 Oct 1923. *MPW* 13 Oct 1923. *Var* 11 Oct 1923, p. 30.

THE HURRICANE HORSEMAN (Latino)

Willis Kent Productions. *Dist* State Rights. **1931.** Sd; b&w. 59 min.

Pres WILLIS KENT. *Dir* Armand Schaeffer. *Asst dir* Wm. O'Connor and Melville Shyer. *Story* Douglas Dawson. *Cont and dial* Oliver Drake. *Photog* William Nobles. *Settings* Tec Art Studios. *Ed* Ethel Davey. *Rec* General Sound Engineers.

Cast: LANE CHANDLER (*"Gun" Smith*), Marie Quillan (*Tonita*), Walter Miller (*Pancho Gomez*), Yakima Cannutt (*Sheriff Jones*), Richard Alexander (*"Bull" Carter*), Lafe McKee (*Señor Roberto*), Charles Shafer (*"Cinco"*), Raven (*By himself*), [Robert Smith (*Rand*)].

Western. [*Print viewed*]. "Gun" Smith is traveling through the West on his horse, Raven, in search of work repairing revolvers, when he is warned by Sheriff Jones to be on the lookout for the notorious bandit Pancho Gomez. While Gun talks with Jones and his posse, they hear the sounds of Gomez and his gang holding up the pack train of wealthy gold mine owner Señor Roberto and his lovely daughter Tonita. Gun watches as the posse unsuccessfully chases the gang, which has kidnapped Roberto and Tonita. He then heads to the nearby town of Rawhide after commenting to Raven, "They sure ride straight and shoot crooked in this country, don't they?" At the gang's hideout, Roberto refuses to pay ransom to Gomez, who warns Roberto to do as he says if he values his daughter's life. Gomez sends Cinco and another of his bandits to Rawhide to find a gunsmith, since their guns are in such disrepair, and despite a fight Cinco picks with Gun, Gun agrees to help them and goes to the camp with them. At the camp, Gun quickly becomes enamored of Tonita, whom he protects from Cinco's brutality. Gun pretends to repair the outlaws' guns, while actually fixing them so they backfire or do not shoot straight. Gomez and his men, unaware of Gun's scheme, plan to hold a celebration that night and kill Gun in the morning. At the party, Gun and Tonita flirt as she teaches him to say "Yo te amo," but they are interrupted when Gomez threatens to shoot Roberto if Tonita does not dance for him. Gun is overpowered by the gang when he attempts to defend the prisoners, and he is tied to a wild horse and sent out into the desert to die. Raven comes to the rescue, however, and unties Gun, after which Gun attaches a note to Raven's bridle explaining his situation and sends him to Rawhide to find Jones. One of Gomez' men sees Raven and attempts to stop him, but Raven eludes him and reaches the sheriff, who immediately sets out with his posse to Gomez' camp. Gun infiltrates the hideout, although he is mystified by the sentries' reactions to the Spanish that Tonita has taught him, but he is captured and Gomez orders him to be shot by a firing squad. Gun is not worried, since he knows that their guns will be ineffective, but at the last moment, Gomez decides to shoot Gun himself with Gun's own pistol. Just then the posse arrives, and a shootout begins, with the posse triumphing thanks to Gun's ingenuity. Gun and Raven chase after Gomez and two of his men, and after Gun bests the other two, he knocks out Gomez as well, and returns to the camp. After Gun and Tonita inform the sheriff that from now on Gun can be reached at her ranch, Tonita explains to Gun that "Yo te amo" is Spanish for "I love

you." *Bandits. Deception. Gunsmiths. Horses. Kidnapping. Mexican Americans. Chases. Dancing. Firearms. Fistfights. Posses. Ransom. Rescues. Sheriffs.*

FD 11 Oct 1931, p. 10. *Var* 17 Nov 1931, p. 26.

HURRICANE ISLAND (Native Americans, Latino)

Columbia Pictures Corp. *Dist* Columbia Pictures Corp. Jul **1951**; Prod: 10 Oct–21 Oct 1950 [©Columbia Pictures Corp.; 16 Jul 1951; LP1049]. Sd; col (Super Cinecolor). 70-71 or 74 min. PCA cert no. 15011.

Prod Sam Katzman. *Dir* Lew Landers. [*Asst dir* Paul Donnelly]. *Wrt for the screen* David Mathews. *Dir of photog* Lester White. *Art dir* Paul Palmentola. *Film ed* Richard Fantl. *Set dec* Sidney Clifford. *Mus dir* Mischa Bakaleinikoff. [*Sd* Josh Westmoreland]. *Unit mgr* Herbert Leonard.

Cast: Jon Hall [(*Captain Carlos Montalvo*)], Marie Windsor [(*Jane Bolton*)], Romo Vincent [(*Jose*)], Edgar Barrier [(*Jose Ponce de Leon*)], Karen Randle [(*Maria*)], Jo Gilbert [(*Okahla*)], Nelson Leigh [(*Padre*)], [Marc Lawrence (*Angus Macready*)], [Marshall Reed (*Rolfe*)], [Don Harvey (*Valco*)], [Rick Vallin (*Coba*)], [Russ Conklin (*Owanga*)], [Alex P. Montoya (*Alfredo*)], [Lyle Talbot (*Physician*)], [Rusty Wescoatt (*Crandall*)], [Zon Murray (*Lynch*)].

Historical, Adventure. [*Print viewed*]. On Easter day, 1513, a Spanish expedition led by Jose Ponce de Leon, claims a coastal strip of land in the New World in the name of Spain. During the proclamation, the Spaniards are attacked by angry Indians and Ponce de Leon is injured by a poisoned arrow. The group leaves for Cuba to seek medical advice, and when the Spanish doctor is unable to help Ponce de Leon, he tells the commander's right-hand man, Captain Carlos Montalvo, to take his leader to the local witch doctor. The witch doctor says that Ponce de Leon is under the spell of "Hurricane," God of the Winds, and that he must return to the god's secret shrine, a golden fountain of youth, for the cure. Meanwhile, Jane Bolton, a notorious and beautiful pirate leader, learns about the Spaniards planned visit to the fountain of youth and assumes that it must be filled with gold. When Jane's men fail to steal the map to the fountain, she joins a group of women prisoners who Ponce de Leon's men have rounded up to help colonize the area for Spain. Jane flirts with Montalvo, hoping to gain access to the map, and as she locks him in a passionate kiss one evening, Jose, one of the crew, calls out that another ship has been spotted. Montalvo strips and swims to the strange vessel as its crew, led by Jane's lover, Angus Macready, climb into small boats. Montalvo torches the pirate ship and jumps into the water just before it explodes. After everyone has landed safely on shore, Macready and the pirates attack the Spanish encampment. During the scuffle, Jane grabs a gun and tries to force Jose to give her the treasure map, but Montalvo arrives and they put Jane in irons. The Indians, led by a young, belligerent warrior named Valco, watch the white men approach, and when Valco expresses the desire to attack them, Okahla, the tribe's leader and high priestess of Hurricane's fountain, insists that there will be no more bloodshed. Meanwhile, Jane tries to run away, but Montalvo captures her. During a wedding celebration for the Spaniards and their convict brides, Montalvo brings Jane food and she begins to admire the gallant Spaniard. When Montalvo goes to investigate strange noises in the jungle, Valco and his renegade braves take him prisoner. Returning with Montalvo to their village, the Indians demand that he show them the secret of the white man's power: firearms. Okahla is furious that Valco is challenging her peaceful rule, and then, to prove her power against the white man's weapon, she has Montalvo shoot her. Montalvo does not use bullets, and the pair successfully fools the Indians into believing that Okahla is invincible. Okahla takes Montalvo back to her tent and, in gratitude, offers to bring him to the fountain as long as he desires only a cure and not gold. Meanwhile, Valco approaches Macready and his pirates, and the two groups decide to join forces against Okahla's braves, who guard the fountain. At the idyllic fountain, Okahla offers Ponce de Leon a gold goblet filled with the fountain's waters, and he is miraculously cured. Just then, Macready, Valco and their men attack, and Okahla, believing that she has been double-crossed, calls on the god Hurricane to attack. When the winds begin to gust, Valco's men flee in terror and Macready and Montalvo have a sword fight, which Montalvo wins. As the rest of the men flee the hurricane winds, Montalvo forces a reluctant Okahla to leave the fountain. Okahla cannot live without the fountain's waters, however, and when the Spaniards put her into a life boat in the sea, she withers

and dies of old age before their eyes. The next day, which is clear and sunny, Ponce de Leon says that Okahla is not really gone because her philosophy of peace and wisdom will always remain with them. Montalvo and Jane, now in love, listen happily to the great explorer's words. *Explorers. Florida–History. Indians of North America. Pirates. Spaniards. Battles. Colonies. Cuba. Cures. Disguise. Expeditions. Explosives. Firearms. Gods. Gold. Hurricanes. Poison. Weddings. Women prisoners.*

Note: The following written prologue appears in the onscreen credits: "This story is based on history and a legend which has lived through centuries. To tell it, the language of the Indians and the Spaniards has been translated to that of our era." The 9 Jul 1951 *MPD* review responds to this prologue with the following: "In fashioning the screenplay, David Mathews seems to have slighted both history and legend, and relied instead on his own fertile imagination." In addition to Native Americans and Spanish Americans, the film includes English and Scottish nationals as characters.

Box 14 Jul 1951. *DV* 5 Jul 1951, p. 5. *Exh* 18 Jul 1951, p. 3109. *FD* 16 Jul 1951, p. 6. *Har* 7 Jul 1951, p. 106. *HR* 13 Oct 1950. *HR* 5 Jul 1951, p. 3. *MPD* 9 Jul 1951. *MPHPD* 7 Jul 1951, p. 922. *Var* 11 Jul 1951, p. 6.

HURRY, CHARLIE, HURRY (Native Americans)

RKO Radio Pictures, Inc. *Dist* RKO Radio Pictures, Inc. 13 Jun **1941**; Prod: 5 Mar–25 Mar 1941 [©RKO Radio Pictures, Inc.; 12 Jul 1941; LP10596]. Sd (RCA Sound System); b&w. 5,886 ft. 65 min.

Prod Howard Benedict. *Dir* Charles E. Roberts. [*Asst dir* Doran Cox]. *Scr* Paul Gerard Smith. *Story* Luke Short. *Dir of photog* Nicholas Musuraca. *Spec eff* Vernon L. Walker. *Art dir* Van Nest Polglase. *Art dir assoc* Albert D'Agostino. *Ed* George Hively. *Rec* Hugh McDowell, Jr. [*Stunt double* Bobby Rose and Teddy Mangean].

Cast: LEON ERROL [(*Daniel Boone Jennings*)], Mildred Coles [(*Beatrice Boone*)], Kenneth Howell [(*Jerry Grant*)], Cecil Cunningham [(*Mrs. Boone*)], George Watts [(*Horace Morris*)], Eddie Conrad [(*Wagon Track*)], Noble Johnson [(*Chief Poison Arrow*)], Douglas Walton [(*Michael Prescott*)], Renee Haal [(*Josephine Whitley*)], Georgia Caine [(*Mrs. Georgia Whitley*)], Lalo Encinas [(*Frozen Foot*)], [Chester Clute (*Cardwell*)], [Janette Fern (*Pain-in-the Neck*)], [Effie Anderson (*Servant*)], [Grady Sutton (*Dore Dare*)], [George McKay (*Vice President Quimby*)], [Connie Montoya (*Moaning Low*)], [Harry Harvey (*Railroad conductor*)], [William Haade (*Policeman*)], [Frank Yaconelli (*Peanut vendor*)], [Joe North (*Butler*)], [James Conlin (*Murphy*)], [Edwin Stanley (*Mr. Whitley*)], [Jason Robards (*F. B. I. agent*)], [Clive Morgan (*Major domo*)], [Dell Henderson (*Mayor*)], [Charles Ray (*Photographer*)], [Norman Mayes (*Railroad porter*)], [Douglas Spencer (*Reporter*)], [George Noisom (*Messenger boy*)].

Comedy. [*Print viewed*]. When business tycoon Daniel Boone Jennings bungles the elopement of his daughter Beatrice to bakery truck driver Jerry Grant, the snobbish Mrs. Boone is thrilled because she opposes the match. Mrs. Boone is determined to marry Beatrice to a member of the upper crust, and consequently, when Mrs. Georgia Whitley announces that she and her daughter Josephine are spending the weekend at the the country estate of Michael Prescott, she decides that the Boone family also should visit the country. To avoid spending time with the pompous Prescotts, Daniel pretends that a telegram he receives from his old friend, Horace Morris, inviting him to come fishing in Washington, Oklahoma, is really the Vice President summoning him to Washington, D.C. Daniel sets out for Washington wearing a top hat and fishing boots, and after he finds Chief Poison Arrow's son hiding in Horace's wagon, he is made an honorary member of the Indian tribe. Two weeks later, Daniel returns home and is greeted as a hero at the train station by reporters who think he was in Washington, D.C. discussing Indian affairs with Vice President Quimby. At the station, Mrs. Boone introduces her husband to their houseguest, the stodgy Michael Prescott, who she hopes will soon be her son-in-law. Upon arriving home, Daniel finds Poison Arrow and his companions, Wagon Track and Frozen Foot, smoking peace pipes in his study. They are followed by Horace, who has been sent to return the Indians to the reservation. When Mrs. Boone discovers her visitors, Daniel bluffs that the three were sent from Washington, D.C., prompting his wife to score a social coup by throwing a party for the Indians and Quimby. To placate his wife, Daniel dictates a telegram inviting Quimby to the party, then tears it up after she leaves his office. Unknown to Daniel, however, his secretary sends a copy of the invitation to Washington, D. C., Daniel plans to have Horace pose as Quimby, but when Horace is arrested on the night of the party, Jerry, who knows of the plan, decides to stand in for him. While Daniel goes

to post Horace's bail, Jerry arrives at the party disguised as Quimby and is introduced to Beatrice, who recognizes him. Soon after, Daniel and Horace return home, and Horace goes upstairs to tidy up his disguise. Before he can make his entrance, however, Horace becomes locked in the bathroom and climbs out through the window. Daniel, unable to find Horace, hurriedly dresses as Quimby just as the real Vice President arrives and is seated at the dinner table. When Quimby excuses himself to take a phone call from Washington, D.C., Daniel, disguised as the Vice President, comes down the stairs and sees Horace and Jerry. The three impostors are arrested by Quimby's guards and taken to the Vice President. Amused by the deception, Quimby appoints Daniel to the Committee on Indian Affairs. When Daniel sighs that the only thing he really desires is for Prescott to disappear, his "blood brothers" kidnap the prig, clearing the way for Beatrice and Jerry to elope. *Elopement. Impersonation and imposture. Indians of North America. Snobs and snobbishness. Tycoons. Fathers and daughters. Fishing. Mothers and daughters. Oklahoma. Parties. Telegrams. United States. Vice Presidents.*

Note: The working title of this picture was *Little White Father*. In the opening credits, star Leon Errol walks into the frame and comments disparagingly to the audience that there is no "Charlie" in the film. According to a news item in *HR*, Russell Gleason was forced to relinquish the role of "Jerry Grant" because of illness. Another news item in *HR* notes that this film marked director Charles Roberts' promotion from shorts to feature films.

Box 12 Jul 1941. *FD* 10 Jul 1941, p. 6. *HR* 6 Feb 1941, p. 1. *HR* 6 Mar 1941, p. 1. *HR* 18 Mar 1941, p. 2. *HR* 26 Mar 1941, p. 10. *HR* 8 Jul 1941, p. 3. *MPHPD* 17 May 1941, p. 135. *NYT* 12 Nov 1941, p. 31. *Var* 9 Jul 1941, p. 14.

HYPNOTIZED (African Americans)

M. H. S. Productions, Inc. *Dist* World Wide Pictures, Inc. 25 Dec 1932; Prod: 21 Jul–13 Aug 1932; inserts shot on 15 Aug 1932 at Mack Sennett Studios; music recorded on 24 Sep 1932 at Metropolitan Sound Studios [©M. H. S. Productions, Inc.; 25 Dec 1932; LP3565]. Sd (Western Electric Noiseless Recording); b&w. 7 reels, 6,313 ft. 65, 67 or 70 min. Passed by the National Board of Review.

Pres E. W. HAMMONS. *Dir* Mack Sennett. [*Asst dir* George Sherman]. [*2d asst dir* Gene Yarbrough]. *Scr* Mack Sennett and Arthur Ripley. *Adpt and dial* John A. Waldron, Harry McCoy and Earle Rodney. [*Contr wrt* Al Giebler, Felix Adler, Jack O'Donnell, Tom Geraghty, John Grey, Jeff Moffitt, Henry Johnson and Lew Foster]. *Photog* John W. Boyle and George Unholz. [*1st asst cam* Chuck Geisler]. [*2d asst cam* Eddie Cohen]. *Art dir* Ralph Oberg. *Settings* Harvey Gillette. *Film ed* William Hornbeck and Francis Lyon. [*Ward woman* Margaret Schuman]. *Mus score* Edward Ward. [*Sd*] *Tech* Paul Guerin and E. C. Sullivan. [*Sd crew* Frank Moran and George Lewin]. [*Mixer for music rec* Karl Zint]. [*Makeup* Bill Cooley]. [*Unit mgr* Babe Stafford]. [*1st grip* Dave Anderson]. [*2d grip* Glen De Vol]. [*Props* Billy Gilbert and Arden Cripe]. [*Dial clerk* Cliff Forester]. [*Action clerk* Ethel La Blanche]. [*Lion owner and trainer* Melvin Koontz]. [*Still photog* Roy Johnson]. [*Publicity dir* Jed Buell]. [*Double* Hubert Diltz].

Song(s): "Anywhere with You," "In a Gypsy's Heart" and "Love Bring Back My Love to Me," music by D. J. Vecsei, words by Bernie Grossman.

Cast: Moran & Mack [Charles Mack] (*Egbert Jackson*), [George Moran] (*Henry Johnson*), Ernest Torrence (*The hypnotist* [*Professor Horace S. Limberly*]), Charlie Murray (*Charles O'Brien*), Wallace Ford (*Bill Bogard*), Maria Alba ([*Princess*] *Mitzie*), Marjorie Beebe (*Pearl*), Herman Bing (*The captain* [*Otto Von Stromberg*]), Alexander Carr (*Abe Shapiro*), Matt McHugh (*Drummer*), Luis Alberni (*Consul*), Henry Schultz (*First mate* [*Ludwig*]), Mitchell Harris (*Ringmaster*), Nona Mozelle (*Captain's girl friend*), [Hattie McDaniel (*Ladies' room attendant*)], [Jackie, a lion], [Henry East (*Fritz, a dog*)], [Monica Bannister, Tepe Monaco, Joan Dix, Elsie Taylor, Alice Adair, Dixie Russell (*Bridesmaids*)], [Jean Lacy, Genee Boutell, Leta Howard, Estelle Essex, Alice Stombs, Anne Nagel, Eileen Taylor, Marion Weldon, Lorena Carr, Dorothy Stewart, Betty Collins, Madeline Carpenter, Pat Wing, Veleda Duncan (*Ballet girls and performers*)], [Teddy Mangean (*Fake bridegroom*)], [Fred Warren, Walter Lawrence (*Barkers*)], [Jack De Wees, George Ashforth, Al Mazzola, Charles Bimbo, Barney Hellum, Johnny Kacier, Larry Judd, Hubert Diltz (*Clowns*)], [Rex Robinson, Junior Fuller, Bob Haines (*Trapeze performers*)], [Ed Wolf (*Tall man*)], [Jack Murphy, Ernie Alexander, Neil Clyde (*Vendors*)], [Joe Bordeaux, Ted Stroback, Tom Forman (*Seamen and officers*)], [Spec O'Donnell (*Mess boy*)], [Francis Lyon, Roy Wade, Johnny Wilson, Ray Bensfield, Earle Davey,

George Abdul (*Men on boat*)], [Irene Thompson, Betty Collins, Myrtle Buckley, Betty Chisney, Lorena Carr, Geraldine Barton (*Women on boat*)].

Comedy, with songs. [*Print viewed*]. In Hoboken, New Jersey, circus elephant trainer Bill Bogard is in love with gypsy violinist Princess Mitzie, but is unable to declare his love because he is poor and she is wealthy. Mitzie, attracted to Bill, is furious when she thinks he is snubbing her. When Bill learns that he has won the grand prize of the Grand National Steeplechase derby sweepstakes, held in Aintree, England, he turns flips and cartwheels and promises to give ten percent to his friend, Egbert Jackson, a black porter. Egbert, however, has placed Bill's ticket stub for safekeeping in the pouch of a boxing kangaroo. After the stub is retrieved, Bill kisses Mitzie, who slaps him and breaks a violin over his head. When he continues, she knocks him out. Frantic that she may have killed the man she loves, Mitzie kisses him, but she is then angered when he revives and she thinks he is fooling with her. However, he convinces her that he is sincere, and they plan a wedding ceremony to go with her farewell performance, as she and her band are returning to Hungary. Bill, however, does not show up for the wedding. The attending audience becomes angry, as does circus owner Charles O'Brien, who had secured a $50,000 bond from Mitzie's father in exchange for finding her a husband. While returning to Europe on the *S.S. Austrilich*, Mitzie becomes distraught. Unknown to Mitzie, Bill and Egbert have been kidnapped by hypnotist Professor Horace S. Limberly, who has the ability perform his powers on "chumps," and has brought the two onboard the ship to assist him in his act. Bill and Egbert come out of their trance while they are out at sea, and the shock of their location is minimized by the discovery that Mitzie and Egbert's girl friend Pearl, a black maid, are onboard. When Limberly learns that Bill has won $500,000, he hypnotizes him and Egbert again and robs Bill. After O'Brien gets them out of the trance, they learn that a suicide note has been left by Limberly saying that he will jump overboard. At the captain's table, when a Russian nobleman's beard catches fire, the captain spritzes him, causing his beard and wig to fall off to reveal that he is really Limberly. He threatens to blow up the ship and throws an object that the others think is a grenade. Egbert catches it and tosses it to the captain, and it gets lodged in a chandelier, then falls into Egbert's pants and out his leg before it is discovered to be an avocado. Egbert upsets Pearl, who throws a knife at him and hits him over the head with a bowling pin. He unwittingly hides in a box to be used in a lion act and finds Limberly already in the box. The box is rolled onto the stage, and after it falls apart during the act, the lion bites Egbert in the pants, while Limberly tries to pull the lion away by the tail. Limberly bites the lion's tail, and the lion knocks Egbert down and lies on him, whereupon Egbert bites the lion's tail and they wrestle. Meanwhile, Mitzie has caught Bill in a compromising position with a woman clad only in a slip. When he kisses Mitzie, she curses him in Hungarian and slaps him. After he kicks her, she threatens him with a knife, but when he only laughs at her, she begins to cry. Egbert suggests to Limberly that he hypnotize the lion, but the professor says that the lion does not look like a chump. He succeeds, though only momentarily, before the lion breaks the spell and chases them through the crowd, causing pandemonium. The passengers scramble for lifeboats, and Mitzie refuses Bill's pleas that she get into one. O'Brien and Limberly disguise themselves as women to escape in a lifeboat, but they are found out. Soon sanity is restored, as the professor ends up washing dishes on the ship, Pearl revives Egbert, who almost drowns in the ship's swimming pool, and the captain marries Mitzie and Bill. *African Americans. Animal trainers. Circus performers. Gypsies. Hypnotists. Ocean liners. Porters. Romance. Chases. Circus owners. Disguise. Elephants. Female impersonation. Fires. Hoboken (NJ). Hungarians. Kangaroos. Kidnapping. Lions. Maids. Sweepstakes. Violinists. Wealth. Weddings.*

Note: The working title of this film was *Little Gypsy*. The opening credits introduce the film as "*Hypnotized* with Moran & Mack (The Two Black Crows)." George Moran and Charles Mack, two black-faced white comedians, became famous nationally in 1927 when they performed their "Two Black Crows" routine on a record. According to the *Var* obituary for Mack, who died in an automboile accident in 1934, the recording broke sales records and established a vogue for dialogue records. The team, which had been established in 1917 in vaudeville and burlesque, soon became headliners in the *Ziegfeld Follies*, *The Passing Show*, *George White's Scandals* and *Earl Carroll's Vanities* and made two films for Paramount, *Why Bring That Up?* in 1929 and *Anybody's War* (see above). The *Var* obituary for Moran, who died in 1949, stated, "Although their deliveries were in caricature vein, it never brought

criticism and they presumably had as many Negro fans as whites." In this film, Moran appears only in the beginning. In early drafts of the script in the Mack Sennett Collection at the AMPAS Library, there is no role for Moran, and Mack plays a character called "Henry Jackson," a name that by the final film was separated into "Egbert Jackson," Mack's role, and "Henry Johnson," Moran's brief role.

This was Mack Sennett's last feature-length film and his first since 1930. The pressbook in the copyright descriptions states that Sennett had made only eight features. According to information in the Sennett Collection, W. C. Fields was originally considered for the role of "Professor Limberly." Gene Towne is listed along with the three writers who received screen credit for adaptation and dialogue in an early mockup of screen credits in the Sennett Collection, but he is not listed in subsequent information nor included in a list of twelve writers (other than Sennett) in the pressbook. It is not known if Towne contributed anything to the final film. The film includes a sequence in which animated mice dance in the ship's stateroom; according to the Sennett Collection, Gus Meins was involved in the production of this sequence. According to the pressbook, actor Charlie Murray was in Sennett's original Keystone comedy company. Marjorie Beebe performs her role in blackface. According to news items, the film was originally intended as a fifteen-reel road show production. Although advertisements bill the film as being eight reels in length, copyright records list only seven reels. According to the pressbook, the S.S. *Emma Alexander* was chartered from Los Angeles to Ensenada, Mexico, for filming the ocean cruise sequences. *NYT* remarked concerning the scenes with the lion in the latter part of the film, "This animal submits to more literal tail-twisting than has any other lion in motion pictures. It seems miraculous that several of the players are not clawed and bitten, for this jungle beast is treated in a way that would cause any dog to use its teeth." *Var* rated the film as "among the very worst since the entrance of sound."

FD 20 Jun 1932, p. 6. *FD* 21 Jul 1932, p. 2. *FD* 30 Jul 1932, p. 5. *FD* 17 Oct 1932, p. 3. *FD* 7 Dec 1932, p. 2. *Har* 24 Dec 1932, p. 206. *HR* 16 Feb 1932, p. 3. *HR* 17 Aug 1932, p. 3. *HR* 22 Aug 1932, p. 7. *HR* 10 Dec 1932, p. 2. *MPH* 24 Dec 1932, p. 24. *NYT* 16 Jan 1933, p. 13. *Photo* Feb 1933, p. 118. *Var* 17 Jan 1933, p. 15. *Var* 16 Jan 1934. *Var* 3 Aug 1949.

THE HYPOCRITE (African Americans)
Micheaux Film Corp. Jun 1921. Si; b&w. 7 reels.
Melodrama (?), African American. No information about the precise nature of this film has been found. *African Americans. Hypocrisy.*

I AIM AT THE STARS: THE WERNHER VON BRAUN STORY (German Americans)
Morningside Worldwide Pictures, S.A.—FAMA; The Charles H. Schneer Production. *Dist* Columbia Pictures Corp. Oct **1960**; Prod: 12 Oct—16 Dec 1959 [©Columbia Pictures Corp.; 1 Oct 1960; LP18560]. Sd (Westrex Recording System); b&w. 12 reels, 9571-72 ft. 106-07 min. PCA cert no. 19572.
Prod Charles H. Schneer [*Co-prod* Friedrich Mainz]. *Dir* J. Lee Thompson. *Asst dir* Karl Elsner and Hans Sommer. *Scr* Jay Dratler. *Story* George Froeschel, U. Wolter and H. W. John. *Dir of photog* Wilkie Cooper. *Art dir* Hans Berthel. *Film ed* Frederick Wilson. *Mus* Laurie Johnson. *Sd eng* Walter Ruhland. *Prod supv* George von Block. *Tech adv* Paul F. Mertz, Maj. USA (S.C.). *Historical adv* Walt Wiesman.
Cast: CURT JURGENS [(*Wernher von Braun*)], VICTORIA SHAW [(*Maria von Braun*)], Herbert Lom [(*Anton Reger*)], Gia Scala [(*Elizabeth Beyer*)], James Daly [(*Maj. William Taggert*)], Adrian Hoven [(*Mischke*)], Gerard Heinz [(*Professor Hermann Oberth*)], Karel Stepanek [(*Captain Walter Dornberger*)], Peter Capell [(*Dr. Neumann*)], Hayden Rorke, Austin Willis [(*General John B. Medaris*)], Alan Gifford, Helmo Kindermann [(*General Kulp*)], Lea Seidl [(*Baroness von Braun*)], John Crawford, [Gunther Mruwka (*Wernher von Braun, as a child*)], [Arpad Diener (*Horst*)], [Hans Schumm (*Baron von Braun*)], [Eric Zuckmann (*Heinrich Himmler*)].
Biography, Drama. [*Print viewed*]. In Berlin, in the early 1920s, Wernher von Braun, the young son of a baron, enthusiastically experiments with rocket models. In the early 1930s, at the Space Rocket Society Ground, German Army Captain Walter Dornberger observes von Braun and his assistants, then offers to fund the society's further experiments under the auspices of the Army. During World War II, von Braun and his group work on rockets for the Army at Peenemünde Rocket Center. When von Braun realizes that the quality of steel used in the rockets is not good enough, he joins the Nazi Party to insure money and better materials for their work. A party official, unable to countenance their early failures, threatens to close Peenemünde in thirty days unless they have a successful landing. During their intense work, von Braun's secretary, Elizabeth Beyer, secretly photographs their plans for the Allies. The next test is a success, and the Nazis plan to mass produce V-2 rockets to launch

over London, hoping the resultant devastation will lead to the war's end. Heinrich Himmler, leader of the Schutzstaffel, or S.S., who is suspicious of the Army, asks von Braun to join his personal staff. When von Braun, who prefers to work under Dornberger, refuses, he is arrested and accused of working on a model for a spaceship to reach the moon in addition to working on weapons. After von Braun is heard in a tape recording referring to Adolf Hitler in an insulting manner, he is told he will be executed, but through Dornberger's influence, Hitler becomes convinced that von Braun's intellect puts him in a class of people too important to be executed. As they need von Braun to work on the V-2 rocket, Himmler is ordered to release him. Von Braun upsets his fiancée Maria with his attitude of indifference that his rockets may kill children in London. When London is bombed, the Allies decide to bomb Peenemünde. After receiving a call, Elizabeth hugs her lover, scientist Anton Reger, a colleague of von Braun's, and goes outside the city. Peenemünde is then hit with a bomb, which kills over 700 people. Elizabeth runs back to help, but is stopped by a guard. The next day, Anton finds a secret camera in her lipstick holder and accuses her of pretending passion to get information. She insists she was sincere with him and explains she became a spy after S.S. officers callously shot her husband, mistaking him for someone else. Although Anton strikes her in anger, he hides the camera to protect her. As Germany nears defeat and the Russians approach, von Braun encourages his colleagues to try to reach the Americans, so that they might be able to complete work on the spaceship. Outraged, Anton calls von Braun a traitor, but the others vote to join von Braun. After surrendering, von Braun refuses to consider himself a war criminal, but Major William Taggert, a former newspaperman whose wife and baby were killed in a London bombing, argues that because von Braun invented an infernal device to be used to support an iniquitous regime, he should be tried and killed. Taggert's ranking officer, however, tells von Braun that General Eisenhower has approved the continuation of his research with American resources and that he has been cleared, based on Elizabeth's report, to go to the U.S. for a probationary period of one year. Von Braun is warned, though, that he might face rebuke by the American public. Taggert seethes at the perceived immorality of using someone like von Braun, whom they fought to destroy. The scientists, along with Elizabeth, who is assigned to work with them, are sent to White Sands Proving Ground in New Mexico, where soldiers resent them. Taggert, the Special Intelligence Officer assigned to the group, blames von Braun for the death of his wife and child, and though Elizabeth, who has grown fond of Taggert, urges him to calm down, he rails against scientists who do not accept responsibility for the destruction that results from their work. After a year, when von Braun learns that Maria will soon arrive and that she may now choose to become a citizen, he realizes that America is "a hell of a country." Sometime later, after he and Maria are married, war breaks out in Korea and the scientists are sent to a new installation at Redstone Arsenal at Huntsville, Alabama to work on weapons. Incensed that von Braun is to work for the military, Taggert resigns to go back to work as a journalist. When Maria agrees with Taggert that von Braun should refuse to make rockets for war, he declares that he must continue his work. The Redstone rocket is successful, yet after the truce, Congress refuses to allocate money for space research. Von Braun goes on television in a debate with Taggert, who contends that human problems are more important to solve than scientific ones. Von Braun warns that mankind must learn to use atomic power sanely or it will perish. After the Navy wins an important commission over the Army to design a satellite, the Russians beat the Navy in launching the first satellite into space, and von Braun blames Taggert for holding the program back. In December 1957, after the Vanguard rocket explodes on lift-off at Cape Canaveral, Taggert lambasts von Braun's program "I Aim at the Stars" on television. As they watch, Maria asks von Braun if he now cares about the potential destruction that can result from his work, and he replies that he does. Worried about the loss of U.S. prestige, the Pentagon gives von Braun ninety days to get a satellite up. Taggert is among the press corps at the launch, and when another journalist accuses him of wanting it to fail and putting his own concerns above those of the country, he is reminded that this is the same accusation he once used against von Braun. After a suspenseful two hours, word arrives from stations around the world that the launch is a success. Later that evening, Taggert admits to von Braun that he has almost grown to like him. He asks what science has in place of human values,

and von Braun says it has a concern for the future and that the urge to explore is what makes man human. Taggert now wishes him good luck in exploring the universe. *Wernher von Braun. Conscience. German Americans. Germany–History. Germany. Army. Guilt. Nazis. Rocketry. Scientists. War crimes.* Bombing, Aerial. Cape Canaveral (FL). Debates. Walter Dornberger. Explorer (Artificial satellite). Heinrich Himmler. Korean War, 1950-1953. Love affairs. John Medariss. New Mexico. Officers (Military). Reconciliation. Reporters. Spies. Television programs.

Note: The film's working titles were *The Wernher von Braun Story, A Rocket and Four Stars* and *Give Me the Stars.* The opening credits contain the following acknowledgment: "to the Department of Defense and particularly the Department of the Army of the United States our sincere appreciation for their cooperation and assistance in the making of this film." News items concerning the projected film began appearing in the trade papers in Jun 1958, when producer Charles Schneer hired German writer George Froeschel. *Explorer I,* developed by von Braun's Development Operations Division of the Army Ballistic Missile Agency, had been launched five months earlier on 31 Jan 1958; it was called "the Free World's first scientific earth satellite" in a biography of von Braun issued by the U.S. Army Ordnance Missile Command Public Information office and included in a Columbia Pictures informational brochure. A Dec 1959 *Var* article states that Schneer had been in London when the Soviet Union launched the first Sputnik, and "he was depressed by the reaction of the British and European press which was calling the U.S. a second-class power." When *Explorer I* was launched, however, Schneer experienced "a sense of relief" and chose von Braun's life for the subject of a film. In the Columbia brochure, a corporate statement relates Schneer's reason for making the film: "The question he had determined to probe deeply and thoroughly was: 'How and why was it possible for a man who was known to have been a key scientist for the German Army during World War II to have become one of America's most honored citizens and a vitally valuable figure in the free world.'" The brochure promised, "The motion picture will reveal and re-enact the facts in a frank and forthright manner, with no punches pulled." Controversy about the film during pre-production centered on whether von Braun's Nazi past would be whitewashed. According to a *BHCN* article of Jul 1959, actor Curt Jurgens met with von Braun before accepting the part and convinced the scientist that the film should be frank about his role in the development of inventions used for the Nazi's war effort. Jurgens stated that "the first three scripts were pretty wishy-washy," but that after a lengthy meeting at Jurgens' home, von Braun agreed and later sent a letter acknowledging that his superiors at the missile agency in Huntsville, AL also agreed. The script, according to *LAT*, was written by German, British and American writers. According to *Var,* von Braun approved the screenplay, and in it he was "personally allowed to answer some of the charges leveled against him." British director J. Lee Thompson, who had flown RAF bomber missions over Germany during the war, was criticized for working on the film, according to *LAT.* In a *Newsweek* article, Thompson stated about von Braun, "To me he's a war criminal, and I believe that if he had surrendered to us instead of the Americans we should have hanged him." About the film, Thompson commented that he wanted to show "what some of these scientists have in place of a heart."

The film was produced in Munich at the Bavaria Studios with the British crew that Schneer used on his earlier production, *Gulliver's Travels.* (After labor disputes on that film, Schneer vowed never again to make a film in a British studio, according to *Var.*) Early pre-production news items stated that Schneer was producing the film in association with Friedrich Mainz of Rhombus Films, Germany. It is not known if Rhombus was involved in the actual production. According to news items, Schneer had a number of conferences with von Braun, with Major General John Medaris, commander of the Army Ballistic Missile Agency at Huntsville, and with Randy Morris, Chief of Technical Liaison, U.S. Army Ordnance Mission at White Sands Missile Range. Historical adviser Walt Wiesman, on leave from the Missile Agency, had worked with von Braun at Peenemünde, and production supervisor George von Block had been a former Luftwaffe pilot, according to *LAT.*

The film was greeted with demonstrations against von Braun at showings in Europe and New York, according to various news stories. Prior to the world premiere in Munich, von Braun and Jurgens held a press conference during which members of the Communist and British press hounded von Braun with humiliating questions and charges that the film whitewashed his war work. The press conference prompted von Braun to issue the following statement: "I have very deep and sincere regrets for the victims of the V-2 rockets, but there were victims on both sides. A war is a war, and when my country is at war, my duty is to help win that war." Later, a crowd of protesters mobbed the theater where the premiere was held. Demonstrators in London dropped anti-Nazi pamphlets onto theatergoers from a balcony. In New York, the film was picketed by an anti-Fascist youth organization. The film was previewed in Washington at the Senate Office auditorium, and its Oct 1960 opening in Washington was attended by First Lady Mamie Eisenhower and the chairman of the Joint Chiefs of Staff. The film was chosen to open the Edinburgh Film Festival, where it received a special diploma of merit.

Reviews in the U.S. were generally critical of the film. *HR* commented, "There is a tendency at the end to equate doubt about the morality of von Braun's position with lack of understanding, or even lack of patriotism. This film indicates von Braun was an unwilling Nazi. But it never suggests he regrets what he did for the Nazis. So the spectator must make his own choice." *NYT* stated that "the film is conspicuously fuzzy and takes its stand on the none too certain ground that Dr. von Braun's driving interest from boyhood was simply to develop rockets that could reach out into space. The possibility of reaching

intently into the depths of his scientist's mind and comprehending his certainly complex motivations is not achieved in this poorly written film." *Var,* while praising parts of the film, wrote that "several of the most vital junctures in von Braun's complicated life are sloughed over unsatisfactorily....from the point at which von Braun surrenders to U.S. authorities, an evasiveness is detectable." The character of Major William Taggert, said to be a composite character representing negative U.S. reaction to von Braun, according to *Var* "emerges [as] more of a symbolic device than a man as he leads a personal crusade against von Braun." A number of reviews characterized Jurgens' performance as "stolid."

BHCN 8 Jul 1959. *Box* 12 Sep 1960. *Cue* 22 Oct 1960. *DV* 16 Jun 1958. *DV* 22 Aug 1958. *DV* 27 Feb 1959. *DV* 8 Apr 1959. *DV* 16 Sep 1959. *DV* 22 Aug 1960. *DV* 24 Aug 1960. *DV* 7 Sep 1960, p. 3. *DV* 16 Sep 1960. *DV* 24 Oct 1960. *Exh* 14 Sep 1960, p. 4750. *FD* 29 Jun 1960. *FD* 7 Sep 1960, p. 6. *Har* 10 Sep 1960, p. 146. *HCN* 20 Oct 1960. *HR* 12 Jun 1958. *HR* 24 Feb 1959. *HR* 25 Feb 1959. *HR* 14 Apr 1959. *HR* 7 Sep 1960, p. 3. *HR* 16 Sep 1960. *LAEx* 16 Sep 1959. *LAEx* 29 Nov 1959. *LAEx* 21 Aug 1960. *LAT* 24 Sep 1958. *LAT* 29 Nov 1959. *LAT* 21 Aug 1960. *LAT* 11 Sep 1960. *LAT* 3 Oct 1960. *LAT* 20 Oct 1960. *LAT* 25 Nov 1960. *MPHPD* 10 Sep 1960, p. 835. *Newsweek* 3 Oct 1960. *Newsweek* 10 Oct 1960. *NYT* 20 Oct 1960, p. 42. *NYT* 23 Oct 1960. *Time* 17 Oct 1960. *Times (London)* 22 Sep 1959. *Var* 9 Dec 1959. *Var* 24 Aug 1960. *Var* 7 Sep 1960, p. 6.

I AM AN AMERICAN *see* **LET'S GET TOUGH!**

I AM JOAQUIN *see* **ROBIN HOOD OF EL DORADO**

I COME FROM HELL *see* **OLSEN'S BIG MOMENT**

I FOUND A DREAM *see* **IT HAD TO BE YOU**

I, JAMES LEWIS *see* **THIS WOMAN IS MINE**

I KILLED GERONIMO (Native Americans, Apache)

Jack Schwarz Productions, Inc. *Dist* Eagle Lion Films, Inc. 8 Aug 1950; Prod: early—mid-Jun 1950 [©Jack Schwarz Productions; 29 Jul 1950; LP352]. Sd; b&w. 7 reels, 5,609 or 5,611 ft. 61-63 min. Passed by the National Board of Review. PCA cert no. 14647.

Prod Jack Schwarz. *Assoc prod* Jack Rabin. *Dir* John Hoffman. *Asst dir* Arthur Hammond and [Mack Wright]. *Story and scr* Sam Neuman and Nat Tanchuck. *Photog* Clark Ramsey and Elmer Dyer. *Spec photog eff* I. A. Bloch. *Art dir* Ernie Hixon. *Film ed* Norman Colbert. *Set dec* Harry Reif. *Ward* Bob Lee Vanado. *Mus dir* Darrell Calker. [*Mus score* Darrell Calker]. *Sd eng* Harry Smith. *Makeup* Harry Thomas.

Cast: James Ellison (*Captain Packard* [*also known as Jeff Smith*]), Virginia Herrick (*Julie* [*Scott*]), Chief Thunder Cloud (*Geronimo*), Smith Ballew (*Lieutenant Furness*), Luther Crockett (*Major* [*Clem*] *French*), Jean Andren (*Mrs.* [*Martha*] *French*), Ted Adams ([*Walt*] *Anderson*), Myron Healy (*Frank* [*Cochran*]), Wesley Hudman (*Red*), Sam Wolfe (*Jennings*), Joseph J. Greene (*Paymaster*), Jack Kenney (*Sergeant Meade*), [Dennis Moore (*Luke*)], [Harte Wayne (*General Ives*)].

Western. [*Print viewed*]. In 1882, after Apache Indians terrorize innocent townspeople, Captain Jeff Packard of the U.S. Army, whose mother and father were killed by Apaches, is assigned to kill Apache warrior Geronimo. Packard takes the name "Jeff Smith," and travels to the town of Larksberg to meet his contacts, Frank Cochran and Fletcher. At the local gunsmith's shop, Packard poses as The Waco Kid, fooling outlaw Walt Anderson and his henchman, Jennings. Later, when he sees Luke, another Anderson henchman, attack a young woman named Julie Scott, Packard shoots him in the hand. Meanwhile, Major Clem French, concerned about Indian attacks, orders a military escort for a stagecoach carrying payroll funds. When Red, one of Anderson's gang, learns that The Waco Kid is actually in the penitentiary, he and Frank, who is also working secretly for Anderson, become suspicious of Packard. At the saloon, meanwhile, Packard asks Frank and Fletcher to intercept a shipment of guns at Fort Broken Bow so they will not fall into Geronimo's hands. Later, Fletcher takes Packard to a shack outside of town, and there they discover Frank's slain corpse. Red then kills Fletcher and escapes. The cavalry chases Anderson's men to the ranch owned by Julie's father Jason, and the outlaws take Jason hostage, placing him inside one of the wagons containing the guns. The cavalry stops to check the wagons for the guns, but are called away by Apache smoke signals before Jason or the guns are discovered. After Packard writes his name on a grave marker, the gang suspects that he is working for Army intelligence. Later, Packard creates a diversion to give Julie a chance to escape, but she is apprehended by Luke. The cavalry catches up to Packard and the gang, confiscates the guns and arrests them. Inside the jail at cavalry headquarters, Packard maintains his cover. To confuse Geronimo and his men, the cavalry moves the guns to another wagon, which is to be sent from Fort Broken Bow to Fort Apache. Later, Packard recommends that the cavalry arrange for Anderson to

escape so they can follow him to Geronimo. Once free, Anderson tells Geronimo what has happened, while Packard warns the major that the fort will be attacked unless they surrender the guns to Geronimo. While Anderson learns Packard's true identity, the major helps Julie and the major's wife Martha to board a stagecoach leaving the fort. After Packard tells him that the major wishes to negotiate at the fort, Geronimo demands three wagons full of guns in exchange for peace. When the major refuses, the Apaches attack. Later, Packard leaves the fort to warn the stagecoach not to continue. After Geronimo learns that the guns have been removed, he and his men kill the major. Geronimo then goes to Fort Apache to locate the guns, but when he realizes that they lack firing pins and are therefore useless, he kills Anderson. Packard reaches the stagecoach, but the Indians attack, and Martha is killed. After Packard grabs Geronimo's knife and stabs him in the back, he and Julie embrace. *Apache Indians. Firearms. Geronimo. Undercover operations. United States. Army. Cavalry.* Escapes. Espionage. Forts. Graves. Gunshot wounds. Gunsmiths. Impersonation and imposture. Knife wounds. Military intelligence. Officers (Military). Payrolls. Ranches. Saloons. Smuggling. Stagecoaches.

Note: Some events in this film were taken from the life of the much-feared Chiricahua Apache war chief Geronimo, who lived from 1829 until 1909. In 1876, following raids on Mexican settlements perpetrated by the Chiricahua, the Americans decided to move the tribe from Apache Pass to San Carlos. Only about half of the tribe made the move, however, while the rest, led by Geronimo, fled to Mexico. From there, they continued the raids, and in 1887, after a campaign against Geronimo's warriors led by Gen. George Crook, Geronimo was induced to surrender. He later embraced Christianity, joining the Dutch Reformed Church. Modern sources include Dennis Moore and Forrest Taylor in the cast. Before appearing in this picture, Chief Thunder Cloud played the title role in the 1939 Paramount film *Geronimo* (see entry above).
Box 19 Aug 1950. *DV* 10 Aug 1950, p. 3. *HR* 2 Jun 1950, p. 14. *HR* 9 Jun 1950, p. 12. *HR* 10 Aug 1950, p. 3. *MPHPD* 9 Dec 1950, p. 606. *Var* 29 Nov 1950, p. 14.

I LOVE A BANDLEADER (African Americans)
Columbia Pictures Corp. *Dist* Columbia Pictures Corp. 13 Sep **1945**; Brooklyn, NY opening: 9 Aug 1945; Prod: 1 May—25 May 1945 [©Columbia Pictures Corp.; 13 Sep 1945; LP13501]. Sd (Western Electric Mirrophonic Recording); b&w. 7 reels, 6,343 ft. 70 min. PCA cert no. 11013.
Prod Michel Kraike. *Dir* Del Lord. [*Asst dir* Ivan Volkman]. *Scr* Paul Yawitz. *Story* John Grey. *Dir of photog* Franz F. Planer. [*2d cam* Irving Klein]. *Art dir* Carl Anderson. *Film ed* James Sweeney. *Set dec* Albert Rickerd. *Mus dir* M. R. Bakaleinikoff and Paul Sawtelle. *Sd rec* Philip Faulkner. [*Mus mixer* Edwin L. Wetzel]. [*Research dir* Marianne Nussbaum].
Song(s): "Mister Beebe," words and music by Jule Styne, Sammy Cahn and Dudley Brooks; "My, My, Ain't That Somethin'," words and music by Harry Tobias and Pinky Tomlin; "That's What I Like 'Bout the South," words and music by Andy Razaf; "Poor Little Rhode Island," words by Sammy Cahn, music by Jule Styne; "The Darktown Poker Club," words by Jean Havez, music by Bert Williams and Will H. Vodery; "Counting the Days," words by Hy Zaret, music by Alex Kramer; "Good, Good, Good (That's You—That's You)," words and music by Allan Roberts and Doris Fisher; "Eager Beaver," words and music by Sammy Cahn and Jule Styne.
Cast: PHIL HARRIS [(*Phil Burton, also known as John Doe, also known as George Drake*)], ROCHESTER [(*Newton H. Newton*)], LESLIE BROOKS [(*Ann Stuart*)], Walter Catlett [(*B. Templeton Jones*)], Frank Sully [(*Dan Benson*)], James Burke [(*Gibley*)], Pierre Watkin [(*Dr. Gardiner*)], The Four V's [(*The Jordan Sisters*)], [Robin Short (*Edwin*)], [Philip Van Zandt (*Bill*)], [Nick Stewart (*Willie Winters*)], [Marilyn Johnson (*Madge*)], [Louise Franklin (*Miss Tilson*)], [Robert Williams (*Police officer*)], [John Tyrrell (*Cab driver*)], [Catherine York (*Big girl*)], [Barbara Ames (*Singer*)], [Jimmy Lloyd (*Assistant band leader*)], [Mike Lally, Joseph Palma, Roy Darmour (*Reporters*)], [Mildred Boyd (*Maid*)], [Anthony Caruso (*Ramon*)], [Vernon Dent (*Counter man*)], [Kernan Cripps].
Show business, Musical, Comedy. [*Print viewed*]. As house painters Newton H. Newton and Phil Burton remodel the Club Monterey on Broadway, owner Gibley auditions acts for his club's reopening. Theatrical agent B. Templeton Jones brings his client, aspiring singer Ann Stuart, to try out for a spot, and when Gibley doesn't hire her, Ann becomes discouraged. When Phil, who has watched Ann perform from his ladder, enters a dressing room and tries on a suit from the costume rack, Ann mistakes him for one of Gibley's partners and asks his help in winning a contract. Phil sympathizes with Ann, and when she runs off stage, he follows her,

trips and hits his head. After Phil awakens in a hospital room and discovers that he is suffering from amnesia, his physician, Dr. Gardiner, dubs him "John Doe" and suggests he return to the Club Monterey, where someone might recognize him. While seated at a table in the club, Phil begins directing the band, giving Gibley the idea to launch a publicity campaign exploiting Phil as an amnesiac band leader. Gibley's angle proves a huge success and Phil becomes a hit. When Newton rescues Phil from a group of adoring fans one day, the band leader hires him as his bodyguard. Although Phil reminds Newton of his old painting partner, Newton believes that his new employer really is a band leader. Now employed as a hat check girl at the Club Monterey, Ann checks Jones's hat, and when she recalls her earlier meeting with Phil, the agent informs Gibley. Recognizing a good publicity angle, Gibley decides to promote Ann as Phil's fiancé and hires her to sing in the club. Ann protests the ruse, but when reporters descend upon her and demand the name of her fiancée, she claims that he is George Drake from Buffalo. When Dr. Gardiner encourages Ann to continue the deception to help Phil's recovery, she agrees and soon finds herself falling in love with the band leader. Upon returning home from a date with Phil one evening, Ann finds Edwin, her former beau from Buffalo, waiting for her in the lobby. When Edwin demands an explanation for Ann's alienation of affection, she invites him to her room and tells him the whole story. Unknown to Ann, Phil is just outside her door, and when overhears her tale, he thinks that Ann doesn't love him and leaves, dejected. Later Phil tells Newton about Ann's story and announces that he plans to quit and leave town. Newton finally realizes that the band leader really is his former painting partner and hurries to Dr. Gardiner for advice. In Newton's absence, Phil disappears and Ann, feeling responsible for his misery, refuses to perform. After tracking Phil to the train station, Newton convinces two police officers to arrest the band leader for stealing a suit and deliver him to the Club Monterey. At the club, Jones tries to persuade Phil that Ann is in love with him, but when Phil refuses to believe the agent's story, Newton hits his old friend over the head with a brush. The blow brings back Phil's memory, and after he sees Ann, he remembers meeting her as an aspiring young singer, and the two embrace. *Amnesia. Band leaders. Entertainers. Publicity stunts. Romance.* African Americans. Bodyguards. Hat check girls. House painters. New York City–Broadway. Nightclub owners. Nightclubs. Physicians. Reporters. Ruses. Theatrical agents.

Note: Although a *HR* production chart places Carole Mathews in the cast, her participation in the released film has not been confirmed. Leslie Brooks's character is called "Ann Stuart" in the film, but both the CBCS and the *Var* review list her as "Ann Carter." Both Phil Harris and Eddie "Rochester" Anderson appeared as regulars on Jack Benny's radio show. This picture was filmed during the show's summer hiatus. "The Darktown Poker Club" and "That's What I Like 'Bout the South" were big hits for Harris, who did not make another picture until the 1950 Twentieth-Century Fox film *Wabash Avenue*. The composers of an additional ballad, which may be titled "Nothing At All" or "What Can I Do?," have not been determined.
Box 18 Aug 1945. *DV* 24 Jan 1946, p. 3. *Down Beat* 11 Feb 1946, p. 7. *HR* 11 May 1945, p. 10. *HR* 24 Jan 1946, p. 15. *MPHPD* 18 Aug 1945, p. 2597. *Var* 15 Aug 1945, p. 14.

I MARRIED A NAZI see **THE MAN I MARRIED**

I MARRIED AN ACTRESS see **THE GREAT FLIRTATION**

I PASSED FOR WHITE (African Americans)
Fred M. Wilcox Enterprises, Inc. *Dist* Allied Artists Pictures Corp. Mar **1960**; Prod: Nov 1959 [©Allied Artists Pictures Corp.; 7 Mar 1960; LP15537]. Sd; b&w; 1.85. 11 reels, 8,375 ft. 93 min. PCA cert no. 19518.
Prod Fred M. Wilcox. *Dir* Fred M. Wilcox. *Asst dir* Herb Mendelson and [Harry Slott]. *Scr* Fred M. Wilcox. *Dir of photog* George Folsey. [*Asst cam* Frank Gaudio and Jack Chandler]. [*Cam op* Jack Swain]. *Art dir* David Milton. *Film ed* George White. *Mus ed* Jerry Irvin. *Sd ed* Marty Greco. *Set dec* John Sturtevant. *Ward* Claire Cramer and Opal Vils. *Mus* Johnny Williams. *Dance dir* Phil Orlando. *Sd eng* Earl Snyder. *Makeup artist* Monte Westmore. *Hairdresser* Kay Reed. *Prod mgr* Edward Morey, Jr. *Dial coach* Patrick Westwood. *Property master* Ted Mossman. [*Constr* Howard Reed]. [*Scr supv* Judy Hart]. [*2d prop man* Max Frankel].
Source: Based on the novel *I Passed for White* by Mary Hastings Bradley (New York, 1955).
Cast: Starring and Introducing Sonya Wilde [(*Bernice Lee, also known as Lila Brownell*)], Also Starring James Franciscus [(*Rick Leyton*)], Featuring Pat Michon [(*Sally Roberts*)], Elizabeth Council

[(*Mrs. Leyton*)], Griffin Crafts [(*Mr. Leyton*)], Isabelle Cooley [(*Bertha*)], James Lydon [(*Jay Morgan*)], Thomas B. Henry [(*Dr. Merritt*)], Max Mellinger [(*Mr. Gordon*)], Phyllis Cole [(*Nurse*)], Calvin Jackson [(*Eddie, in dancing school*)], Lon Ballantyne [(*Chuck Lee*)], Temple Hatton [(*Eddie, friend of Bernice*)], Freita Shaw [(*Gram*)], Ed Hashim [(*Character*)], Ray Kellogg [(*Bartender*)], Elizabeth Harrower [(*Woman in employment office*)], [Charles Evans (*Minister*)], [Jackie Russell (*Stewardess*)], [Maila Nurmi (*Girl poet*)], [Mary Foran (*Female clerk*)], [William St. John (*Tom*)], [Patricia Knox (*Ethel*)], [John Indrisano (*Bartender*)], [Doug Williams (*Manager*)], [Henry Hunter], [Don Reardon].

Social, Drama. [*Print viewed*]. Bernice Lee, a light-skinned black student, attends a nightclub in Los Angeles where her dark-skinned brother Chuck performs in his own jazz group. Chuck gets into a fight when a white man calls him "Rastus" and insults Bernice, thinking she is a white girl dating Chuck. The next day, Bernice talks to her grandmother about the incident and about school, where she has been snubbed by both white and black children after a white girl, whom she thought was her friend, told everyone she was passing for white. Bernice wants to quit school and get a job, and she asks why she can't pass for white. Gram, whose husband was white, says that if she had to do it over, she would not intermarry because of the problems it creates for the children. Bernice assures her that she does not want to marry, but only get a job as a white girl. Gram still advises against living a lie. At an office building, Bernice is offered a job as an elevator girl and is told that if she had not written "Negro" as her race on her application form, she could have gotten secretarial work. She packs and flies to New York, where, using the name "Lila Brownell" and passing for white, she gets a job as a secretary for an ad agency. One night, she attends a company cocktail party and runs into Frederick "Rick" Leyton, who earlier tried to flirt with her on the plane. He admits he has tracked her down and they begin to date. Bernice soon learns that Rick is from a wealthy old New England family. During a dinner party with Sally Roberts, Bernice's co-worker, and Jay Morgan, Rick's friend, Bernice is overcome by her feelings for Rick, but when he calls at three in the morning to propose marriage, she tells him it is too soon and that there is much he does not know about her. In love with Rick, Bernice confides in Sally, who advises her not to tell Rick that she is black, because despite his feelings, he will have to tell his family, and they, Sally believes, will not allow the marriage. Bernice tries to avoid Rick, but he insists that what matters to him is whether she loves him, and she admits that she does. Bernice tells Rick's parents a number of lies about her family, who, she says, live in Richmond and cannot attend the wedding because they are leaving the country. After the wedding, Mrs. Leyton starts to suspect that Bernice has lied about her family. At a nightclub, Bernice nervously looks away after seeing that her brother Chuck is in the band. When Chuck approaches and takes her hand, Rick viciously hits him and orders him to take his hands off his wife. Bernice explains that Chuck is a musician she knew from school, but begins to cry when Rick argues that she left Richmond before the schools there were integrated. As she leaves the club, Chuck sadly shakes his head. When Bernice becomes pregnant, she worries that the baby will have brown or black skin. After her doctor prescribes exercise and even drink to calm her, she goes to a club with Rick and his parents and dances with a number of men. Rick explodes and berates her for acting like a "cheap dance hall dame," and when she acknowledges a black piano player, Rick says one would think she were friends with "those black cats." She now plans to go away with Sally to have the baby, and if the baby looks black, give Rick the opportunity to have nothing more to do with her or the baby; however, after she goes through a night of pain, she is taken to the hospital, where she delivers the baby. In a semi-delirious state, she asks the nurse if the baby is black, unaware that Rick is in the room. Rick then tells her that the baby did not live. Later, she is allowed to see the dead baby, which looks white. She explains to Rick that she was afraid the baby might have been black from choking, then cries hysterically. At home, Bernice learns from her black maid Bertha that Mrs. Leyton has discovered that the picture Bernice has identified as her mother, is a fake, and that Mrs. Leyton has also seen books on intermarriage in Bernice's dresser. Bertha reveals that she told Mrs. Leyton that the books are her own. Rick finds Bertha comforting Bernice and angrily orders her to take her hands off his wife and get out, then queries Bernice about her fascination with Negroes. He accuses her of having

slept with the black musician and violently throws her on the bed. She admits to lying, but says that the baby was Rick's. Unable to believe her, Rick leaves for town to stay overnight and think about their situation. Bernice goes to the airport with Sally and reasons it is just as well that the Leytons do not know the truth about her. Sally plans to visit her on her vacation. When Bernice arrives back home, she embraces Gram and Chuck. *African Americans. Class distinction. Marriage–Mixed. Pregnancy. Racial impersonation. Racism. Romance. Advertising agencies. Airplanes. Brothers and sisters. Dancing. Discrimination in employment. Fistfights. Friendship. Grandmothers. Jazz music. Los Angeles (CA). Maids. Miscarriage. Musicians. New Englanders. New York City. Ostracism. Secretaries.*

Note: While the novel was written by Mary Hastings Bradley under the pseudonym of Reba Lee, Bradley's own name appears in the screen credits of the film. *Var* called the film, "only a casual probing into the reasons and reactions of the Negro girl who 'passes.' It is actually a romantic melodrama in which racial problems are a factor. The approach, therefore, while tasteful, is superficial." *HR* commented, "There are thousands of mixed marriages in America, and while this film tries to avoid controversy by stating its qualified opposition to miscegenation (on the grounds of impracticality rather than morality), and supporting this viewpoint by finally separating the principals, it nevertheless contradicts itself on a deeper level.... The treatment of Negroes is dignified and respectful, but unfortunately one of the plot points unwittingly perpetuates an old wives' tale about genetic dominance. For much of the picture, she lives in fear of giving birth to a dark child." This was the first film of Fred W. Wilcox Enterprises, Inc., and Sonya Wilde's screen debut. According to reviews, producer-director Wilcox saw the Caucasian actress on Broadway in *West Side Story* and chose her because of her "Southern quality." In an interview in *LAMirror-News*, Wilde stated that the producers "couldn't find any light-skinned colored girls of the right age who had the acting qualifications, I guess." According to *LAMirror-News*, black actors were irritated by the casting.

According to *DV*, the film, which cost $250,000 to make, was refused ad space by newspapers, and radio and television advertising time, because of its title in a number of northern cities, including Providence, RI and Columbus, OH. After a number of first-run theaters and regional circuits in both the North and South were reluctant to book the film, fearing racial incidents, distributor Allied Artists released it to drive-ins and sub-run theaters. Subsequently, when no incidents were reported after more than 250 engagements, the first-run theaters and regional circuits booked the film in some cities.

Box 7 Mar 1960. *DV* 1 Oct 1959. *DV* 1 Mar 1960, p. 3. *DV* 5 Jul 1960, p. 1, 3. *DV* 13 Jul 1960. *Exh* 16 Mar 1960, p. 4685. *FD* 14 Mar 1960, p. 6. *Har* 13 Aug 1960, p. 130. *HR* 6 Nov 1959, p. 14. *HR* 20 Nov 1959, p. 14. *HCN* 16 Jun 1960. *HR* 1 Mar 1960, p. 3. *LAEx* 16 Jun 1960, sec. 2, p. 7. *LAT* 17 Jun 1960. *LAMirror-News* 9 Feb 1960. *MPHPD* 5 Mar 1960, p. 613. *NYT* 18 Aug 1960, p. 19. *Var* 2 Mar 1960, p. 6.

I REMEMBER MAMA (Norwegian Americans)

RKO Radio Pictures, Inc.; George Stevens' Production. *Dist* RKO Radio Pictures, Inc. 17 Mar **1948**; New York opening: week of 11 Mar 1948; Prod: 26 May—mid-Oct 1947 [©RKO Radio Pictures, Inc.; 11 Mar 1948; LP1606]. Sd (RCA Sound System); b&w. 12,081 ft. 134-135 or 137 min. PCA cert no. 12511.

Pres DORE SCHARY. *Prod* Harriet Parsons. *Exec prod* George Stevens. *Dir* George Stevens. *Asst dir* John H. Morse. *Scr* DeWitt Bodeen. *Dir of photog* Nicholas Musuraca. *Spec eff* Russell A. Cully and Kenneth Peach. *Art dir* Albert S. D'Agostino and Carroll Clark. *Film ed* Robert Swink. *Assoc ed* Tholen Gladden. *Set dec* Darrell Silvera and Emile Kuri. *Women's cost* Edward Stevenson. *Men's cost* Gile Stelle. *Mus dir* C. Bakaleinikoff. *Mus* Roy Webb. *Sd* Richard Van Hessen and Terry Kellum. *Makeup supv* Gordon Bau. *Hair stylist* Hazel Rogers. *Exec asst* Ivan Moffat.

Song(s): "Sovnen," Norwegian lullaby.

Source: Based on the play *I Remember Mama*, adapted by John van Druten (New York, 19 Oct 1944), which was based on the novel *Mama's Bank Account* by Kathryn Anderson McLean (New York, 1943).

Cast: IRENE DUNNE (*Mama* [*Marta Hanson*]), Barbara Bel Geddes (*Katrin* [*Hanson*]), Oscar Homolka (*Uncle Chris* [*Halvorsen*]), Philip Dorn (*Papa* [*Lars Hanson*]), Sir Cedric Hardwicke (*Mr.* [*Jonathan*] *Hyde*), Edgar Bergen (*Mr.* [*Peter*] *Thorkelson*), Rudy Vallee (*Dr. Johnson*), Barbara O'Neil (*Jessie Brown* [*Halvorsen*]), Florence Bates (*Florence Dana Moorhead*), Peggy McIntyre (*Christine* [*Hanson*]), June Hedin (*Dagmar* [*Hanson*]), Steve Brown (*Nels* [*Hanson*]), Ellen Corby (*Aunt Trina*), Hope Landin (*Aunt Jenny*), Edith Evanson (*Aunt Sigrid*), Tommy Ivo (*Cousin Arne*), [Lela Bliss, Louise Colombet, Constance Purdy (*Nurses*), [Eugene Holland (*Boy*)], [Art Dupuis, Lou Hicks (*Conductors*)], [Stanley Andrews (*Minister*)], [Ruth Tobey, Alice Kerbert, Peggy McKim, Peggy Kerbert (*Girls*)], [Cleo Ridgley (*Schoolteacher*)], [George Atkinson (*Postman*)], [Howard Keiser (*Bellboy*)], [Franklyn Farnum].

Domestic, Historical, Drama. [*Print viewed*]. Upon completing the last lines of her autobiographical novel, youthful Katrin Hanson reminisces about her family life: In 1910, in a modest San Francisco house, Katrin's Norwegian-born mother, Marta Hanson, computes the weekly budget with help from her husband Lars, daughters Katrin, Christine and Dagmar and son Nels. When the adolescent Nels declares his desire to attend high school, Marta is pleased, but realizes their "little bank" lacks sufficient funds to pay for his education. After each family member offers to make a monetary sacrifice so that Nels may continue his schooling, Trina, Marta's spinster sister, drops by to speak privately with Marta. To Marta's surprise, Trina announces that she is marrying Peter Thorkelson, a homely undertaker, and begs Marta to break the news to her sisters, Sigrid and Jenny, who Trina fears will laugh at her. As predicted, the bossy Jenny and whiny Sigrid laugh upon hearing of the engagement, but when Marta threatens to reveal embarrassing anecdotes about them to Trina, the sisters agree to keep quiet. Later that evening, Jonathan Hyde, the Hansons' erudite, penniless lodger, reads to them from Charles Dickens' *A Tale of Two Cities*, and the entire family, especially fledgling writer Katrin, is deeply moved by the story. Soon after, the family is visited by Marta's overbearing but big-hearted uncle, Chris Halvorsen, who drives into the city with his common law wife, Jessie Brown. When the lame Chris, whose loud, gruff ways strike fear in the Hanson children, learns that Dagmar, the youngest daughter, is severely ill with mastoiditis, he insists on driving her to the hospital. Because they disapprove of Jessie, Sigrid and Jenny attempt to stop Chris, but he bullies his way past them with Dagmar and Marta in tow. Then the meek Trina and Peter reveal their engagement to Chris, the family's head, and are relieved to receive his blessing. Although Dagmar's operation is a success, Marta is forbidden to see her by the hospital staff. At home, Marta, who promised Dagmar she would visit immediately after the operation, becomes increasingly agitated about the separation and begins scrubbing the floor nervously. Marta's scrubbing inspires a plan: Impersonating a floor-scrubbing maid at the hospital, Marta sneaks into Dagmar's ward and sings a Norwegian lullaby to help her frightened daughter fall asleep. Sometime later, when a recovered Dagmar returns home, she learns that her cat, Uncle Elizabeth, is very ill. Despite Dagmar's belief in her mother's curative powers, Marta feels helpless to save the wounded cat and sends Nels to buy some chloroform with which to kill it. The other children, meanwhile, see Mr. Hyde leaving the house with his suitcases, and Marta discovers that he has left them a check for his overdue rent, as well as his book collection. The family's joy at receiving Mr. Hyde's check is soon undone when Sigrid and Jenny inform them that their lodger has no bank account. Although Sigrid and Jenny are indignant over Mr. Hyde's deception, wise Marta declares that his gift of literature is payment enough. Marta then applies the chloroform to Uncle Elizabeth, but is astounded when, the next morning, an unsuspecting Dagmar marches off with a sleepy but very alive cat. Later, as Katrin nears her school graduation date, she brags to Christine that Marta is going to buy her a much-coveted dresser set as a present. Although the younger, envious Christine tells her that Marta is planning to give her their grandmother's brooch, Katrin does receive the dresser set. As Katrin is about to leave to perform "Portia" in her school's production of *The Merchant of Venice*, however, Christine informs her that Marta sold the beloved brooch in order to buy the dresser set. Crushed by this revelation, Katrin performs badly in the play, and later presents her mother with her brooch, which she exchanged for the dresser set. Touched by Katrin's gesture, Marta gives her the brooch and scolds Christine for telling. Then, to mark her entrance into adulthood, Katrin's father serves her coffee for the first time. Sometime later, Marta is notified that Uncle Chris is near death, and she takes Katrin to say goodbye to him at his ranch. The alcoholic but still feisty Uncle Chris reveals to Marta that he has no money to leave her, and confesses that he and Jessie have been married for years but have been silent about it because of his nieces' snubbing. After enjoying a last drink with Jessie and Marta, Uncle Chris dies. Marta then tells her sisters the truth about Jessie and that Uncle Chris had long been donating money to help poor lame children. Having "seen" death, Katrin returns to San Francisco with Marta and is devastated when she receives her first literary rejection letter. Determined to bolster Katrin's confidence, Marta takes some of her stories to renowned author Florence Dana Moorhead, who loves to eat, and convinces her to read one by offering to share a family

meatball recipe with her. Marta returns home to find Katrin destroying her writings and happily tells her that, while Moorhead agreed that her stories were lacking, she also felt that Katrin was a born author. Taking Moorhead's advice to write about "what she knows," Katrin submits a new story for publication and is overjoyed when she is paid $500 for her efforts. After announcing that some of the money is going to buy the winter coat that Marta has always longed for, Katrin confesses that her mother is the subject of her story and begins to read it aloud. The introduction of her story concludes with the line, "But first and foremost, I remember Mama." Authors. Family life. Motherhood. Norwegian Americans. San Francisco (CA). United States–History–1909-1919. Adolescents. Alcoholics. Cats. Death and dying. Engagements. Finance–Personal. Gifts. Handicapped. Hospitals. Intolerance. Jewelry. Lodgers. Marriage. Maturation. Physicians. Ranches. Recipes. Self-sacrifice. Sisters. Spinsters. Timidity. Uncles. Undertakers and undertaking.

Note: Contemporary news items add the following information about the production: Katherine Anderson McLean, whose pseudonym was Kathryn Forbes, published the first two chapters of her novel, "Mama's Bank Account" and "Mama's Roomer," in a national magazine in 1942. (Modern biographical sources note that, despite the seemingly autobiographical nature of the novel, McLean's actual family life only vaguely resembled that of her fictional characters.) RKO bought the rights to McLean's novel for $50,000. Later, RKO bought fifty percent of John van Druten's Broadway adaptation and made a deal with the play's producers, Richard Rodgers and Oscar Hammerstein II, to buy the screen rights to the play on a sliding price scale to be calculated at $2,500 for every week of the Broadway run, up to $150,000. The play ran for approximately twenty-one months. The deal with Rodgers and Hammerstein also stipulated that the studio could not begin production on the picture until the Broadway show had closed. Oscar Homolka was the only member of the Broadway show to revive his role on film. Mady Christians played "Mama" in the play, which also featured Marlon Brando as "Nels." To perform the role of Peter Thorkelson, popular ventriloquist Edgar Bergen appeared on screen for the first time without his dummy, Charlie McCarthy.

Some scenes in the picture were filmed in San Francisco, including Telegraph Hill, Russian Hill, the Ferry Building and Liberty Street, and at Agoura Ranch near Malibu, CA. Shortly after RKO acquired McLean's novel, producer Harriet Parsons approached Katina Paxinou, a Greek-born actress, to star as Mama and planned to change the nationality of the story's family from Norwegian to Greek. Modern sources note that Parsons also asked George Cukor to offer the role to Greta Garbo, who had retired by then, but she turned the part down. In addition, modern sources claim that Marlene Dietrich wanted to do the Mama role and had director Mitchell Leisen talk to RKO about casting her, but the studio rejected the idea because of Dietrich's racy image. A Mar 1948 *LAT* article states that after Parsons "got" Paxinou to play Mama, the project was "snatched away" from her. An article in *NYT* adds that, despite being ousted from the film, Parsons received an onscreen producing credit with director George Stevens because of her significant contributions to the final film. According to a *NYT* article, Paramount Pictures received twenty-five percent of the film's distribution gross because it had bought Liberty Films, a production company in which Stevens was part owner, in 1947. Modern sources note that, although it received excellent reviews, the picture lost money at the box office because of its big, $3,068,000, budget.

Irene Dunne was nominated for an Academy Award for her portrayal of "Marta," but lost to Jane Wyman in *Johnny Belinda*. Homolka was nominated as Best Supporting Actor, but lost to Walter Huston in *Treasure of the Sierra Madre*, and Barbara Bel Geddes and Ellen Corby were both nominated for Best Supporting Actress, but lost to Claire Trevor in *Key Largo*. Nicholas Musuraca was nominated for Best Cinematography. In addition to the John van Druten adaptation, McLean's novel was twice turned into a stage musical. The first, entitled *Mama*, was adapted by Neal Du Brock and John Clifton and opened in Buffalo, New York on 6 Jan 1972, with Celeste Holm as Mama. In 1979, Richard Rodgers wrote the music for the second musical version, also called *Mama*, for which Thomas Meehan wrote the book and Norwegian actress Liv Ullmann played Mama. Irene Dunne and Barbara Bel Geddes reprised their roles in a 30 Aug 1948 *Lux Radio Theatre* broadcast. McLean's book was also the basis for a television series, *I Remember Mama*, which was broadcast on the CBS network from 1 Jul 1949 to 17 Mar 1957. Peggy Wood starred as Mama in the popular show.

Box 13 Mar 1948. *DV* 9 Mar 1948, p. 3, 11. *FD* 9 Mar 1948, p. 6. *HR* 3 Jan 1947, p. 2. *HR* 31 Mar 1947, p. 14. *HR* 26 May 1947, p. 9. *HR* 27 May 1947, p. 6. *HR* 17 Oct 1947, p. 14. *HR* 9 Mar 1948, p. 3. *HR* 15 Mar 1948, p. 8. *LAT* 12 Mar 1948. *Life* 12 Apr 1948, pp. 61-62. *MPHPD* 28 Feb 1948, p. 4079. *MPHPD* 13 Mar 1948, p. 4093. *NYT* 6 Aug 1947. *NYT* 26 Oct 1947. *NYT* 12 Mar 1948, p. 29. *NYT* 21 Mar 1948. *NYT* 11 Apr 1948. *SF Chron* 9 Aug 1947. *Var* 10 Mar 1948, p. 10.

I WANT TO BE A MOTHER (Yiddish language)

Jewish Talking Picture Co. *Dist* Jewish Talking Picture Co. 26 Feb 1937; Prod: filmed in New York [©Jewish Talking Picture Co.; 11 Mar 1937; LU7016]. Sd; b&w. 8 reels, 7,697 or 7,850 ft. 84 or 87 min. Yiddish language with English subtitles.

Pres JOSEPH SEIDEN. *Dir* George Roland. *Author* Isidor Lash. *Photog* Joseph Freeman. *Asst photog* Irving Kleinerman. *Settings and art work* John J. Soble. *Choir leader* Joel Feig. *Rec eng* Murry Dichter. *Prod mgr* Herman Rosen.

Cast: Moishe Feder (*Jacob Goodman, a rabbi*), Rose Greenfield (*Bas Sheva, his wife*), Esta Salzman (*Celia, their daughter*), Hannah Hollander (*Amelia, Jacob's sister*), Leo Fuchs (*Benchik [Chiam] Bok, Bas Sheva's brother*), Yetta Zwerling (*Breina, his wife*), Muni Serebroff (*Aaron Waldman, a mine owner*), Dave Lubritzky (*Sol, his son*), Sam Gertler (*Eugene Guggenheim, Sol's friend*), Leibele Waldman (*The cantor*).

Yiddish, **Domestic**, **Melodrama**, **with songs**. [*Print viewed*]. As her family happily prepares for the wedding of her niece Celia, Amelia sits alone in her room playing a mournful phonograph record. Her sister-in-law, Bas Sheva, explains to a friend of Sol Waldman, the bridegroom, that Amelia was deceived in love twenty years earlier, after which she was taken to a hospital in critical condition. Following Celia's birth, Amelia never considered marriage and has loved Celia like a mother. Bas Sheva's husband Jacob, who has not spoken to his sister for twenty years, now goes into Amelia's room, and she cries in his arms. He insists that no one must know their secret, that Amelia, not Bas Sheva, is really Celia's mother, and orders Amelia, who is almost out of control with suffering, to give Celia her blessing at their home rather than at the synagogue, where the wedding is to take place. Amelia agrees, but during the ceremony, she rushes to the synagogue, where unseen by others, she watches Celia and Sol take their vows. Six months later, on the day before Sol is to graduate and become a full-fledged doctor, Celia, who is jealous of Sol's admiration for Amelia, overhears them innocently express their love for one another. Sol quells Celia's suspicions, but after he receives a telegram that his father from California, who had been unable to attend the wedding, will arrive the next day, Celia sees Sol and Amelia dancing in joy. Celia jealously tells Sol that either Amelia must leave or she will. Amelia sadly says goodbye to the family, but, unable to bear her suffering any longer, she tells Celia the truth. Jacob then explains to a shocked Bas Sheva that when Bas Sheva gave birth to a dead child, the doctor said that the death of the child would kill her. To save her life and Amelia from shame, he put the child just born to Amelia by Bas Sheva's side. Before Sol's father Aaron arrives, Celia embraces Amelia and, to her joy, calls her "mama." Aaron happily greets his daughter-in-law and her family, and upon learning that Jacob is a Russian from Suvalk, a city in Poland, he relates that twenty years earlier, while traveling there for an American oil company, he met a very learned woman and left her a book which he forgot to retrieve. Amelia recognizes Aaron as her long-ago lover and rebukes him. It appears that both Sol and Celia are Aaron's children, until later, he recovers from being confused and reveals that Sol was really the product of his deceased wife's first marriage. Aaron then proposes to Amelia, who returns the book and then agrees to go with it. *Aunts. Deception. Illegitimacy. Jews. Mothers and daughters. Parentage. Secrets. Books. Brothers and sisters. Incest. Jealousy. Physicians. Suwalki (Poland). Synagogues. Weddings.*

Note: The Yiddish title of this film is *Ikh Vil Zayn a Mame*. According to *Var*, comedian and dancer Leo Fuchs was misleadingly advertised as starring in this film, while his role was that of comedy relief. According to a modern source, producer Joseph Seiden released a fifteen-minute film entitled *I Want to Be a Boarder* (*Ikh Vil Zayn a "Boarder"*) from outtakes of Fuchs and his comedy cohort Yetta Zwerling. A press sheet for the re-release of *I Want to Be a Mother* lists its length as 75 minutes. Although the film includes songs, no information concerning their identity has been located.

Exh 15 Mar 1937, p. 36. *FD* 15 Mar 1937, p. 18. *Kansas City Jewish Chronicle* 9 Feb 1938. *Kansas City Jewish Chronicle* 2 Sep 1938. *Motion Picture Review Digest* 28 Mar 1937. *NYHT* 1 Mar 1937. *NYT* 27 Feb 1937, p. 9. *Var* 3 Mar 1937, p. 15. *Var* 26 Jul 1937.

I WANT TO FORGET (Austrian Americans)

Fox Film Corp. *Dist* Fox Film Corp. 15 Dec **1918** [©William Fox; 15 Dec 1918; LP13140]. Si; b&w. 5 reels.

Pres William Fox. *Dir* James Kirkwood. *Scen* James Kirkwood. *Story* Harry O. Hoyt and Hamilton Smith.

Cast: Evelyn Nesbit (*Varda Deering*), Russell Thaw (*Chauffeur's son*), Henry Clive (*Lieut. John Long*), Alphonse Ethier (*August Von Grossman*), William R. Dunn (*Helgar*), Jane Jennings (*Cordelia Deering*).

Espionage, **Drama**. Prior to the declaration of World War I, dancer Varda Deering was a member of the Austrian secret service, but later she becomes a loyal citizen of the United States. In America, she captivates many men but cares for none of them until she meets Lieut. John Long. The lieutenant regards Varda as little more than a social butterfly, but gradually he comes to recognize her goodness and falls in love with her. While John is away on a war-related diplomatic

mission, Varda agrees to aid the American secret service in procuring secret documents from August Von Grossman, an agent whom she had known in Austria. Von Grossman threatens to reveal Varda's past unless she accepts his lecherous attentions, and she pretends to accept his terms as she secures information for the government. When John finds Varda in the German's arms, he dismisses her as unfaithful, but later she helps him to penetrate the German spy headquarters. As they are escaping with the secret papers, the car carrying the pursuing spies is hit by an express train. Varda explains everything to John, who proves most understanding. *Austrian Americans. Blackmail. Secret documents. Secret Service. Spies. World War I.* False accusations. Germans. Lechery. Officers (Military). Train wrecks.

Note: Russell Thaw was actress Evelyn Nesbit's son. The story included in the copyright descriptions is entitled "The Fires of Redemption."

ETR 4 Jan 1919, p. 425. *MPN* 4 Jan 1919, p. 144. *MPW* 14 Dec 1918, pp. 1252-53. *MPW* 4 Jan 1919, p. 114. *Var* 20 Dec 1918, p. 35. *Wid's* 29 Dec 1918, pp. 9-10.

I WILL BE FAITHFUL *see* HUMAN CARGO

I WILL REPAY (African Americans)

Vitagraph Co. of America. *Dist* Greater Vitagraph (V-L-S-E). 12 Nov **1917** [©Vitagraph Co. of America; 6 Nov 1917; LP11689]. Si; b&w. 5 reels.

Dir William P. S. Earle. *Scen* William Addison Lathrop. *Cam* Jack Brown.

Source: Based on the short story "A Municipal Report" by O. Henry in *Hampton's Magazine* (Nov 1909).

Cast: Corinne Griffith (*Virginia Rodney*), William Dunn (*Steve*), George J. Forth (*Roger Kendall*), Mary Maurice (*Azalea Adair*), Arthur Donaldson (*Caesar*), Eulalie Jensen (*Beulab*).

Drama. Roger Kendall is sent to Nashville by the editor of his magazine to sign a contract for two cents a word with a woman writer named Azalea Adair. Once there, Kendall realizes that Azalea is very poor and is also the abused wife of Major Caswell, a drunkard who takes from Azalea every cent she earns. Kendall is able to piece their story together by following the movements of a torn dollar bill, which he gives to Azalea's former slave Caesar and which eventually winds up in Caswell's hands. In order to help Azalea, Kendall convinces his editor to increase her stipend to eight cents a word and also to advance her $30. At his hotel, Kendall meets Virginia Rodney, the semi-invalid daughter of a local judge and a good friend of Azalea. Later, Caesar, seeing Caswell violently take Azalea's advance from her, strangles the major. His part in the crime is covered up by Kendall and Virginia's father, however. Now free, Azalea goes to live with Virginia, who becomes engaged to Kendall. *Alcoholics. Authors. Battered women. Magazines. Poverty. African Americans. Editors. Hotels. Invalids. Judges. Nashville (TN). Strangling.*

Note: Many contemporary sources refer to Mary Maurice as "Mother" Maurice because she very frequently played the part of a mother in her films.

Motog 24 Nov 1917, p. 1113. *MPN* 24 Nov 1917, p. 3666. *MPW* 24 Nov 1917, p. 1186, 1228. *NYDM* 17 Nov 1917, p. 19. *Var* 23 Nov 1917, p. 44. *Wid's* 15 Nov 1917, pp. 729-30.

ICE-CAPADES (Swedish Americans, Immigrants)

Republic Pictures Corp. *Dist* Republic Pictures Corp. 20 Aug **1941**; Minneapolis premiere: 15 Aug 1941; Prod: skating seq: early Jun—mid-Jun 1941; dramatic seq began 26 Jun 1941 [©Republic Pictures Corp.; 20 Aug 1941; LP10735]. Sd (RCA Sound System); b&w. 9 reels, 7,945 ft. 88 min. Passed by the National Board of Review. PCA cert no. 7544.

Assoc prod Robert North. *Dir* Joseph Santley. [*Asst dir* George Blair]. *Scr* Jack Townley, Robert Harari and Olive Cooper. *Orig story* Isabel Dawn and Boyce De Gaw. *Addl dial* Mel Shavelson and Milt Josefsberg. [*Comedy seq for Barbara Jo Allen* Stanley Davis and Marvin Fisher]. *Photog* Jack Marta. *Art dir* John Victor Mackay. *Supv ed* Murray Seldeen. *Film ed* Howard O'Neill. *Ward by* Adele Palmer. *Mus dir* Cy Feuer. *Prod mgr* Al Wilson. *Skating seq staged by* Harry Losee.

Music: Selections from Symphony No. 5 by Dmitri Shostakovich; "Sophisticated Lady" by Duke Ellington.

Song(s): "Forever and Ever," music by Jule Styne, lyrics by Sol Meyer and George Brown.

Cast: Dorothy Lewis [(*Marie Bergen*)], James Ellison [(*Bob Clemens*)], Jerry Colonna [(*Colonna*)], Barbara Jo Allen [(*Vera Vague*)], Alan Mowbray [(*Pete Ellis*)], Phil Silvers [(*Larry Herman*)], Gus Schilling [(*Dave*)], Tim Ryan [(*Jackson*)], Harry Clark [(*Reed*)], Featuring the Ice-Capades Company with the Internationally Famous

Skating Stars: Belita, Lois Dworshak, Megan Taylor, Vera Rhuba [sic], Red McCarthy, Phil Taylor, Jackson and Lynam, The Benoits, Dench and Stewart, Al Surette, [Renie Riano (*Karen Vadja*)], [Carol Adams (*Helen*)].

Show business, Comedy-drama. [*Print viewed*]. When New York City newsreel cameraman Bob Clemens cannot get a plane to Lake Placid, he spends the night in a bar and misses his assignment to photograph Swiss ice skating star Karen Vadja. Bob's pal Colonna tries to help Bob come up with an excuse, but when Bob sees a woman skating on a Central Park pond, he decides to photograph her from a distance and state that the footage is of Vadja. Bob's hangover prevents him from doing the actual photography, and it is not until he is in a movie theater that he discovers that Colonna shot the woman in closeup. Also in the audience are Broadway impresario Larry Herman, his assistant Dave, and two Immigration Department officials, Jackson and Reed. While Larry, believing that the beautiful woman is Vadja, decides to star her in an Ice-capades show, Jackson and Reed recognize her as Marie Bergen, an illegal Swedish immigrant. Curious about why Marie is being billed as Vadja, Jackson and Reed question Bob at the newsreel office. Meanwhile, Marie auditions for Larry's show, and when she returns home, finds Jackson and Reed searching for her. Vera Vague, Marie's landlady, covers up for her while she escapes. As Marie is settling into a new apartment, Larry hosts a reception for Vadja, whom he meets for the first time. Larry is shocked to discover that Vadja is not the skater in the newsreels, and threatens to sue the newsreel company for misrepresentation. Bob's boss, Pete Ellis, is about to fire Bob and Colonna when Bob suggests that they find the skater and have her star in Larry's show. Larry agrees to the idea, and so the two friends begin their search. While Bob waits by the Central Park pond in case Marie appears, Colonna goes to Vera's house for a date, and when he sees a photograph of Vera and Marie, he realizes that they are friends. Colonna gets Marie's address and gives it to Bob, but Marie, believing that Bob is an immigration official, eludes him. The next day, the show is rehearsing when Bob tells Larry that he has not yet been able to locate Marie. Larry is about to cancel the show when Bob finds that Marie is one of the chorus girls and brings her to Larry's office. Marie is grateful for the opportunity, but, fearing the publicity, refuses to star in the show, and Larry cancels it. Larry sues the newsreel company, while Jackson and Reed reveal to Bob that Marie is about to be deported. Realizing that Marie can stay in the United States if she is married to a citizen, Pete tries to convince Bob to marry her, but Bob, a confirmed bachelor, refuses to go through with it. Bob finally admits to Pete that he cares for Marie and cannot marry her under such circumstances, so Pete tells Marie that Bob photographed her without her knowledge and will now go to jail unless she appears in the show. Her love for Bob overcoming her fear, Marie agrees, and soon opening night arrives. Jackson and Reed go backstage to arrest Marie, and when Bob finds out about Pete tricking Marie into appearing in the show, he punches Pete and tells Jackson and Reed that he will marry Marie. Larry promises to throw them a big wedding, and Marie then appears with the other Ice-capades stars in the big finale, "Legend of the Falls." *Ice skaters and ice skating. Mistaken identity. Newsreel cameramen. Romance. Beauty, Personal. Deportation. Employer-employee relations. Hangovers. Landladies. Lawsuits. Marriage of convenience. Misogyny. New York City–Central Park. Swedes. Theatrical producers. United States. Dept. of Immigration.*

Note: The working titles of this film were *Icecapades of 1941* and *Ice-capades of 1942*. In the onscreen credits, Barbara Jo Allen is listed as "Barbara Jo Allen (Vera Vague)." Vera Vague was Allen's radio character name. The film marked the screen debut of Vera Hruba, a Czechoslovakian ice skater whose surname is misspelled "Rhuba" in the onscreen credits. When the film was re-released in 1949 as *Music in the Moonlight*, Hruba was billed as "Vera Ralston," the name she assumed in 1946. In 1952, she married Herbert J. Yates, the chief executive of Republic. *HR* news items noted that Milt Gross was to work on the picture's screenplay with credited writer Jack Townley, but the extent of Gross's contribution to the released film has not been confirmed. According to *HR* news items, Belita, one of the stars of the Ice-capades touring company, was to star in the picture. Belita was replaced by fellow skater Dorothy Lewis, however, due to an "inability to get together with Republic executives regarding billing and script." On 12 Jun 1941, Belita agreed to appear in the picture, but by then, filming of most of the skating sequences had been completed and she was featured only in a specialty number. *HR* production charts include the Heasley Twins in the cast, but their participation in the finished picture has not been confirmed. Music director Cy Feuer was nominated for an Academy Award for Best Music (Scoring of a Musical Picture). In 1942, Republic released another film featuring the Ice Capades company entitled *Ice Capades Revue*.

Box 23 Aug 1941. *DV* 15 Aug 1941. *FD* 20 Aug 1941, p. 6. *HR* 8 Apr 1941, p. 1. *HR* 10 Apr 1941, p. 5. *HR* 14 Apr 1941, p. 4. *HR* 1 May 1941, p. 1. *HR* 12 May 1941, p. 8. *HR* 28 May 1941, p. 6. *HR* 2 Jun 1941, pp. 12-13. *HR* 5 Jun 1941, p. 1, 3. *HR* 13 Jun 1941, p. 4. *HR* 16 Jun 1941, p. 10. *HR* 19 Jun 1941, p. 6. *HR* 26 Jun 1941, p. 7. *HR* 1 Jul 1941, p. 9. *HR* 7 Jul 1941, p. 6. *HR* 31 Jul 1941, p. 13. *HR* 1 Aug 1941, p. 3. *HR* 8 Aug 1941, p. 4. *HR* 14 Aug 1941, p. 7. *HR* 15 Aug 1941, p. 3. *HR* 28 Aug 1941, p. 3. *MPH* 23 Aug 1941. *MPHPD* 23 Aug 1941, p. 219. *NYT* 25 Sep 1941, p. 29. *Var* 20 Aug 1941, p. 9.

ICE PALACE (Native Americans, Native Alaskans)

Warner Bros. Pictures, Inc. *Dist* Warner Bros. Pictures, Inc. 2 Jul **1960**; New York opening: 29 Jun 1960; Prod: 3 Aug—early Dec 1959 [©Warner Bros. Pictures, Inc.; 2 Jul 1960; LP20184]. Sd (Westrex Recording); col (Technicolor). 12,920 ft. 143 or 145 min. PCA cert no. 19414.

Prod Henry Blanke. *Dir* Vincent Sherman. *Asst dir* Russell Llewellyn and Gil Kissel. [*2d asst dir* Eddie Bernoudy]. *Scr* Harry Kleiner. *Dir of photog* Joseph Biroc. [*Cam op* George Nogie]. [*Asst cam* Elmer Faubien and J. B. Allim]. [*2d unit cam* Mark H. Davis]. [*2d unit cam op* Wally Meinardus]. [*2d unit asst cam* Albert Scheving]. [*Stills* Mac Julian]. [*Gaffer* Robert Farmer]. [*Spec eff* Dick Smith]. *Art dir* Malcolm Bert. *Film ed* William Ziegler. *Set dec* George James Hopkins. [*Props* Pat Patterson]. [*Asst props* Eugene Susman]. *Cost des* Howard Shoup. [*Men's ward* R. Richards]. [*Women's ward* Florence Crewell]. *Mus* Max Steiner. *Orch* Murray Cutter. *Sd* Stanley Jones. [*Boom man* E. Hughes]. [*Rec* William Lambert]. *Makeup supv* Gordon Bau. [*Scr supv* Meta Rebner]. [*Best boy* J. Monte]. [*Head grip* Ken Taylor]. [*2d grip* George Wilson]. [*Pub* Phil Gersdorf].

Source: Based on the novel *Ice Palace* by Edna Ferber (Garden City, NY, 1958).

Cast: Richard Burton [(*Zeb Kennedy*)], Robert Ryan [(*Thor Storm*)], Carolyn Jones [(*Bridie Ballantyne*)], Martha Hyer [(*Dorothy Wendt Kennedy*)], Jim Backus [(*Dave Husack*)], Ray Danton [(*Bay Husack*)], Diane McBain [(*Christine Storm*)], Karl Swenson [(*Scotty Ballantyne*)], Shirley Knight [(*Grace Kennedy, age 16*)], Barry Kelley [(*Einer Wendt*)], Sheridan Comerate [(*Ross Guildenstern*)], George Takei [(*Wang*)], Steve Harris [(*Christopher Storm, age 16*)], [Sheila Bromley (*Lucy Husack*)], [Sam McDaniels (*Porter*)], [Lennie Bremen, Charles Hicks, James Hope (*Doughboys*)], [Saul Gorss (*White checker*)], [John Pedrini (*Foreman*)], [Serge Maurier, Carl Ratcliff (*Fishermen and Kazatzka dancers*)], [William Yip (*Chinese maitre d'*)], [Chester Seveck (*Old Eskimo*)], [Dorcas Brower (*Una Storm*)], [Helen Seveck (*Old Eskimo woman*)], [I. Stanford Jolley (*Mr. Lawson*)], [Robert Griffin (*Engineer*)], [John Bleifer, David McMahon (*Fishermen*)], [Sal Ponti (*Jerry*)], [Maurice Wells (*Office manager*)], [Robert "Buddy" Shaw (*Room clerk*)], [S. John Launer (*Chairman*)], [Norma French (*Muriel*)], [Dorothy Partington (*Party guest*)], [Judd Holdren (*Muriel's escort*)], [Carol Nicholson (*Grace, age 7*)], [Alan Roberts Costello (*Christopher, age 7*)], [Ted du Domaine], [Clarence Straight], [Charles Fredericks].

Historical, Drama. [*Print viewed*]. The impulsive and volatile Zeb Kennedy arrives in his hometown of Seattle at the end of World War II and asks to resume his job at the Wendt Packing Co. Worried about his daughter Dorothy's abiding affection for this "troublemaker," however, his wealthy former boss, Einer Wendt, sends him away, whereupon Zeb signs up for a stint in an Alaskan cannery. Zeb loses that job after defending a mistreated Chinese worker named Wang, whom he had befriended during the boat trip to Alaska. He then meets Thor Storm, who offers him work on his salmon fishing boat, the *Bridie B.* During the voyage, the two men become friends, even though Thor, an idealist whose father was a missionary, seems an unlikely comrade for the bitter Zeb, whose ills can only be cured, he states, by money. Back in Thor's home port of Baranof, Zeb proposes that he and Thor open a cannery, but Bridie Ballantyne, Thor's part-Irish, part-Scottish fiancée, seems skeptical of the plan. While Thor sleeps off a large quantity of whiskey one night, Bridie admits to Zeb that what she actually fears is her intense attraction to him. Zeb is drawn to Bridie, too, and kisses her passionately, but because they do not want to hurt Thor, Zeb returns to Seattle to seek financial backing for the proposed cannery. There he learns from his old friend, Dave Husack, that Dorothy still loves him, and because he needs money, he marries her. The couple then returns to Baranof, but Bridie's distress at meeting Zeb's bride prompts Thor to question her. Horrified to learn of the mutual love between Zeb and Bridie, Thor punches his friend and flees Baranof in a dog sled. When he passes out in the snow far from town, an Eskimo family takes him in. Meanwhile, Zeb establishes a packing company in Baranof, hiring Dave as his foreman

and Wang as his house servant. Dorothy, now realizing that it is Bridie her husband loves, grows increasingly bitter despite the added wealth the cannery has brought her. Bridie delivers Dorothy's baby daughter because the doctor is away, but the experience is painful for both women, and Bridie decides to pursue a new life in Seattle. Before she leaves, however, she discovers that Thor has returned to Baranof with a baby son named Christopher. Because Thor's Eskimo wife died soon after the baby's birth, Bridie remains in Baranof to look after the child. Seven years later, little Grace Kennedy spends much of her time with Christopher and "Aunt Bridie" because her parents fight constantly. Zeb, too, seeks solace in Bridie's love, but she refuses to be his mistress despite her continuing love for him. Distressed at Zeb's salmon traps, which not only deprive the fishermen of their livelihoods but threaten to deplete salmon supplies, Thor asks him to discontinue their use, but Zeb angrily refuses. Moreover, when Zeb sees Grace with Christopher, he orders Thor to "keep that half-breed kid of yours away from her!" This so enrages Thor that he decides to organize both the fishermen and the Alaskan natives against Zeb. By the time Christopher and Grace have reached adulthood, Thor has become a candidate for the territorial legislature, calling for Alaskan statehood and railing against "Czar Kennedy." Unknown to their feuding fathers, Christopher and Grace have fallen in love, and when they secretly elope, Dorothy, after accusing Zeb of having neglected his daughter, suffers a heart attack and dies. The young couple lives happily with Christopher's maternal grandparents in the Eskimo village of Anavak, but Christopher insists that Grace have their baby in Baranof, and they begin the long journey by dogsled. When Thor learns that the two are missing, he, Zeb and Bridie launch a search. As Christopher is about to warm Grace, who has gone into labor, with the carcass of a freshly killed caribou, a bear appears and kills him. Thor, Zeb and Bridie shoot the animal, but their arrival is too late for Grace, and she dies giving birth to a baby girl. The child, named Christine, lives with Bridie for sixteen years, at which time she begins to stay with each of her still-feuding grandfathers for three-month stretches. When Zeb admits relief that his blonde granddaughter can pass for white, she angrily declares that prejudice is a cover-up for one's own inferiority. Thor, still fighting for Alaskan statehood, almost comes to blows with Zeb during congressional hearings, but later, Dave's son Bay, a lawyer, suggests that Zeb cultivate his own political allies for the inevitable day on which statehood is granted. Zeb suggests that Bay run against Thor, observing that the young man's marriage to Christine would downplay his connections to Zeb. Bay does propose to Christine, but during their engagement party, Bridie discovers Zeb's scheme and accuses him of having sold out everyone who was ever close to him. Shocked and hurt, Christine breaks off her engagement to Bay. Soon after, Ross Guildenstern, an Eskimo American who loves Christine, flies Thor to Juneau during a snowstorm and is forced to make a crash landing on a glacier. Bridie begs Zeb, an accomplished bush pilot, to rescue the men, and when he refuses, she leaves in disgust. Deeply affected by her anger, Zeb risks his life to save Ross and Thor. Thor goes on to Washington, where his passionate speeches prompt Congress to approve Alaska's statehood. Thor then gives a radio address, in which he thanks Zeb and urges the state's citizens to make Alaska "a shining demonstration of this faith in each other." *Alaska. Entrepreneurs. Family relationships. Feuds. Greed. Indians of North America–Mixed blood. Romantic rivalry. Statehood (American politics). Airplane accidents. Bears. Canneries. Childbirth. Chinese Americans. Death by animals. Death in childbirth. Dogsledding. Elopement. Fishermen. Fishing villages. Granddaughters. Heart disease. Hotelkeepers. Houseboys. Irish Americans. Lawyers. Loneliness. Marriage–Arranged. Native Alaskans. Neglected children. Neglected wives. Political candidates. Racism. Rescues. Salmon. Scottish Americans. Seattle (WA). Snow storms.*

Note: According to a 12 Dec 1957 *DV* news item, Warner Bros. acquired Edna Ferber's novel on a fifteen-year lease for $350,000, plus fifteen percent of the net profits. The novel, which noted that the town of Baranof is fictional, appeared as a serial in the *Ladies Home Journal* (5 Apr–9 Jun 1958). The film opens with a printed quotation from the Robert W. Service poem, "Alaska": "Wild and wide are my borders,/stern as death is my sway,/And I wait for the men who will win me/and I will not be won in a day;/And I will not be won by weaklings,/subtle, suave and mild,/But by men with the hearts of Vikings,/and the simple faith of a child." Although a 21 Jul 1958 *LAMirror-News* article stated that Art and Jo Napoleon, a husband and wife "writing and producing combo" were "preparing the film version" of Edna Ferber's novel, it is doubtful that they contributed to the finished film. According to a 24 Jul 1959 *DV* news item, Margaret O'Brien was a contender for a starring role in the picture, but she

did not appear in the released film. Although *HR* production charts include Eric Sherman in the cast, his participation in the released picture has not been confirmed. The film marked the screen debut of actor George Takei. Contemporary sources noted that location shooting was done in Petersburg, a salmon fishing center on Mitkof Island, Juneau and Fairbanks, Alaska. In 1959, Alaska became the forty-ninth state admitted to the Union.

Box 27 Jun 1960. *DV* 12 Dec 1957. *DV* 24 Jul 1959. *DV* 15 Jun 1960, p. 3. *Exb* 22 Jun 1960, pp. 4715-16. *FD* 15 Jun 1960, p. 8. *Har* 18 Jun 1960, p. 98. *HR* 31 Jul 1959, p. 13. *HR* 28 Aug 1959, p. 2. *HR* 4 Dec 1959, p. 16. *HR* 15 Jun 1960, p. 3. *LAMirror-News* 21 Jul 1958. *LAMirror-News* 4 Nov 1959. *MPD* 15 Jun 1960. *MPHPD* 18 Jun 1960, p. 740. *NYT* 27 Sep 1959. *NYT* 30 Jun 1960, p. 22. *Var* 15 Jun 1960, p. 6.

ICECAPADES OF 1941 *see* **ICE-CAPADES**

IF I DIE BEFORE I WAKE *see* **THE LADY FROM SHANGHAI**

IF I HAD MY WAY (Swedish Americans)
Universal Pictures Co., Inc. *Dist* Universal Pictures Co., Inc. 26 Apr **1940**; Prod: began early Feb 1940 [©Universal Pictures Co.; 6 May 1940; LP9621]. Sd (Western Electric Mirrophonic Recording); b&w. 10 reels. 93 min. PCA cert no. 6242.
Prod David Butler. *Dir* David Butler. *Asst dir* Joseph A. McDonough. *Orig story* David Butler. *Orig story and scr* William Conselman and James V. Kern. *Photog* George Robinson. *Art dir* Jack Otterson. *Art dir assoc* Richard H. Riedel. *Film ed* Irene Morra. *Set dec* R. A. Gausman. *Gowns* Vera West. *Mus dir* Charles Previn. *Orch* Frank Skinner. *Sd supv* Bernard B. Brown. [*Sd*] *tech* Charles Carroll. [*Makeup* Harry Ray].
Song(s): "Meet the Sun Halfway," "I Haven't Time to Be a Millionaire," "Pessimistic Character" and "April Played the Fiddle," words and music by James V. Monaco and Johnny Burke; "If I Had My Way," words and music by James Kendis and Lou Klein; "Little Grey Home in the West," words and music by Herman Lohr and D. Eardley-Wilmot; "Ida," words and music by Eddie Leonard; "Rings on My Fingers," words and music by Maurice Scott and Weston and Barnes.
Cast: BING CROSBY (*Buzz Blackwell*), GLORIA JEAN (*Patricia Johnson*), Charles Winninger (*Joe Johnson*), El Brendel (*Axel Swenson*), Allyn Joslyn (*Jarvis Johnson*), Claire Dodd (*Brenda Johnson*), Moroni Olsen (*Mr.* [*John*] *Blair*), Nana Bryant (*Marian Johnson*), Donald Woods (*Fred Johnson*), Kathryn Adams (*Miss Corbett*), Brandon Hurst (*Hedges*), Emory Parnell (*Gustav* [*Erickson*]), Verna Felton (*Mrs. DeLacey*), Barnett Parker (*Floorwalker*), Joe Whitehead (*Si*), Del Henderson (*Mrs. Harris*), Blanche Ring, Eddie Leonard [(*Themselves*)], Trixie Friganza, Julian Eltinge, Grace La Rue, Paul Gordon [(*Bike rider*)], Six Hits and a Miss, [Virginia Brissac (*Mrs. Blair*)], [Selmer Jackson (*Mr. Melville*)], [Joe King (*Bank guard*)], [Lee "Lasses" White (*Bus driver*)], [Richard Keene (*Soda clerk*)], [Rodney Cox (*Slim*)], [Edward Earle (*Headwaiter*)], [Louis Mercier (*Chef*)], [Rafael Corio (*Rhumba teacher*)], [Janet Waldo (*Miss Courtney*)], [Larry McGrath (*Waiter*)], [Lew Harvey (*G-man*)], [Alan Bridge (*Doorman*)], [Lillian West (*Saleslady*)], [Polly Vann Bailey].
Drama, with songs. [*Print viewed*]. On the eve of completing the final span of the Golden Gate Bridge, bridge builder Fred Johnson falls to his death, leaving his little daughter Patricia in the charge of his two best friends, Buzz Blackwell and Axel Swenson. Buzz and Axel take Pat to live with her social climbing uncle Jarvis Johnson in New York City, but he is too preoccupied with his social pursuits to rear a little girl. Consequently, Jarvis denies that he is her uncle and sends the trio packing to Joe and Marian Johnson, Pat's great uncle and aunt, retired vaudevillians who eagerly welcome the little girl into their home although they cannot afford to support her. As Buzz prepares to leave Pat in New York and return to San Francisco, an inebriated Axel uses their savings to buy his old friend Gustav Erickson's failing Swedish restaurant. With the help of the Johnsons' old vaudeville pals, Buzz decides to turn the restaurant into the Tin Type Club, and tricks Jarvis into buying some worthless shares of stock to finance the venture. Discovering that he has been fleeced, Jarvis visits the club on opening night and threatens to arrest Buzz for fraud. Fortunately, the club promises to become a financial success, prompting John Blair, the manager of the bank who is sympathetic to Pat's plight, to lend Buzz the money so that he can pay back Jarvis. With their financial future assured, the members of the Johnson clan reconcile their differences, and all ends happily. *Orphans. Social climbers. Uncles. Vaudevillians. Bankers. Falls from heights. Friendship. Golden Gate Bridge (San Francisco, CA). Loans. New York City. Nightclubs. Restaurants. Ruses. San Francisco (CA). Swedish Americans.*

Note: According to a *NYT* news item, this film was made as part of Bing Crosby's "one picture a year agreement" with Universal.

DV 25 Apr 1940, p. 3. *FD* 30 Apr 1940, p. 8. *HR* 10 Feb 1940, pp. 12-13. *HR* 17 Feb 1940, pp. 6-7. *HR* 20 Feb 1940, p. 6. *HR* 28 Feb 1940, p. 6. *HR* 25 Apr 1940, p. 3. *MPD* 1 May 1940, p. 9. *MPH* 20 Apr 1940, p. 39. *MPH* 4 May 1940, p. 36. *NYT* 24 Oct 1939. *NYT* 6 May 1940, p. 13. *Var* 1 May 1940, p. 18.

IGLOO (Native Americans, Native Alaskans)

Edward Small Productions, Inc. *Dist* Universal Pictures Corp. 14 Jul **1932**; Prod: Mar—Sep 1931 [©Universal Pictures Corp.; 7 Jul 1932; LP3134]. Sd (RCA Photophone System); b&w. 6 reels. 58 or 61 min.
Pres CARL LAEMMLE. *Prod* Edward Small. *Dir* Ewing Scott. [*Story* Ewing Scott]. *Narrative by* Edward T. Lowe and Wilfred Lucas. *Photog* Roy H. Klaffki. [*Asst cam* Ray Wise]. *Film ed* Richard Cahoon and Sidney Singerman. *Mus score* Val Burton and Edward Kilenyi. *Narr* Gayne Whitman.

Cast: Chee-ak (*The young hunter*), Kyatuk (*The girl*), Toyuk (*Her brother*), Lanak (*Her father*), Nahshook (*The medicine man*), and other Eskimo villagers and huntsmen of the Nuwuk tribe in the Arctic.

Drama, Educational/Cultural, Documentary. [*Print viewed*]. The Nuwuk, one of the rapidly vanishing Eskimo tribes, live above Pt. Barrow, Alaska in an ice-locked land. The tribe emerge from their igloos at the end of winter, as the temperature warms to thirty degrees below zero. The women prepare seal skins for clothing, while the men make harpoons and the children play. Kyatuk, the daughter of Lanak, the crippled chief, looks for food, but finds no seals to capture. Luckily for the tribe, Chee-ak, a hunter from a neighboring tribe who hopes to win Kyatuk, arrives with plenty of food. After the unmarried hunters make Chee-ak their leader, the tribe dances in his honor. Chee-ak gives Kyatuk a puppy, but she runs off. After the tribe have their feast of seal, Kyatuk joins a group playing a game, and she is tossed high in the air in a walrus-hide blanket. As a storm brews, Lanak appoints Chee-ak to lead the tribe, and he has them tie down their boats and get into their igloos. The storm lasts for weeks. On the verge of starvation, a man blows out his family's oil lamp and eats the seal oil from it, before giving some first to his dog and then to his sons, according to the tribe's ancient law, because of the importance of the leader and dog for the survival of the group. A mother nurses twins, one at each breast, but the father knows that only one can survive. The man takes one baby and wraps it in a blanket where it dies, then brings the corpse to the dogs, who devour the body. When Chee-ak sees that a hunter is about to kill a dog for food, he takes the man's knife away because dogs are more valuable than men. Despite protests, Chee-ak leaves the igloo in search of food, and when he returns, he tells the tribe they must move South. Before they leave, the medicine man invokes the tribal law which states that the helpless must be left behind. The oldest hunter is given a farewell and then sealed up inside an igloo. Lanak also is sealed up, but Kyatuk runs back, opens the igloo and refuses to leave her father. Chee-ak then carries Lanak to a sled in defiance of tribal superstition and provokes the anger of the tribe, who think he is offending the gods. Lanak's sled tips over as they travel, and after he falls down an embankment, he is covered by a small avalanche. Although Chee-ak digs him out, Lanak begs to be left to his fate. Kyatuk, however, clings to her father, and he is taken back to his sled. The others rebel, but Chee-ak, knowing the best way to the sea, prevails and continues to lead. At the sea, Chee-ak spies a whale and the tribe gives chase, but the whale escapes unharmed. As the ice melts, dangerous mountains of ice collapse killing some of the fleeing tribe. Chee-ak finds Lanak's canoe empty and sees Kyatuk chased by "Nanook," a hungry polar bear. Chee-ak harpoons the bear and kills it before rescuing Kyatuk. He then climbs a mountain of ice to ask forgiveness of the gods. Soon, schools of walruses appear, and Chee-ak leads the hunt. After the hunters kill a number of walruses and drink blood from their severed arteries, they celebrate the coming of Spring with a feast. Chee-ak taps Kyatuk's shoulder, she nods to him, and they walk to their kayak and paddle off. *Arctic regions. Courtship. Curses. Fathers and daughters. Hunger. Hunters. Native Alaskans. Rites and ceremonies. Survival skills. Tribal life. Aged persons. Blizzards. Brothers and sisters. Courage. Dogs. Handicapped. Ice floes. Igloos. Medicine men. Polar bears. Seals (Animals). Tribal chiefs. Walruses. Whales and whaling.*

Note: A note in the opening credits reads: "An authentic story based upon incidents in the life of the Primitive Eskimo in the Arctic Circle. Living among these people as a member of the tribe, Ewing Scott was able to faithfully record the courageous struggle for existence of those forgotten people." According to *MPH*, director Scott and his camera crew shot this film in the Arctic region

north of Point Barrow, AK, between Mar and Sep 1931. According to a *IP* article on the film, assistant cameraman Ray Wise, who was an Eskimo, played the lead role using his tribal name of "Chee-ak." Wise later played the lead role as a Polynesian in the 1935 M-G-M production *Last of the Pagans* (see *AFI Catalog of Feature Films, 1931-40*; F3.2386) using the name "Mala." Reviewers commented on the natural acting style of the "all-native" cast and noted that scenes showing details of every day Eskimo life were woven into the drama. According to *Var*, the film was shot silent but had added sound effects and narration. Although Scott is credited in reviews with the film's story, he did not receive screen credit.

The film was approved by the New York State censors on 6 May 1932 in a seven-reel version, submitted by Edward Small, who is listed as the manufacturer. The film was then reduced to six reels according to NYSA records dated 12 Jul 1932, which was two days before the film was released by Universal. It is not known if Small distributed the film in the longer version before 14 Jul 1932. Although *Var* credits Universal for both production and release, it is doubtful that they were involved in its production. In 1952, producer Boris L. Petroff turned the majority of *Igloo* into *Red Snow* in which Ray Wise (now using the name "Ray Mala") reappeared in a leading role. This is probably why, in 1952, the title of *Igloo* was changed to *Chee-ak*.

Har 2 Jul 1932, p. 106. *IP* Jun 1932, p. 6. *MPH* 16 Jul 1932, pp. 51-52. *NYT* 21 Jul 1932, p. 15. *Var* 26 Jul 1932, p. 17.

IKH VIL ZAYN A MAME see I WANT TO BE A MOTHER

ILLEGAL ENTRY (Immigrants)

Universal-International Pictures Co., Inc. *Dist* Universal Pictures Co., Inc. Jun **1949**; Prod: early Dec 1948—mid-Jan 1949 [©Universal Pictures Co., Inc.; 28 Apr 1949; LP2298]. Sd (Western Electric Recording); b&w. 83-84 min. PCA cert no. 13702.

Prod Jules Schermer. *Dir* Frederick de Cordova. *Dial dir* Jack Daniels. [*Asst dir* Fred Frank]. *Scr* Joel Malone. *Adpt* Art Cohn. *Based on a story by* Ben Bengal, Herbert Kline and Dan Moore. *Dir of photog* William Daniels. *Spec photog* David S. Horsley. *Art dir* Bernard Herzbrun and Richard H. Riedel. *Film ed* Edward Curtiss. *Set dec* Russell A. Gausman and John Austin. *Gowns* Yvonne Wood. *Mus arr and dir by* Milton Schwarzwald. *Sd* Leslie I. Carey and Joe Lapis. *Makeup* Bud Westmore. *Hair stylist* Joan St. Oegger.

Cast: HOWARD DUFF (*Bert Powers*), MARTA TOREN (*Anna Duvak* [*also known as Anna O'Neill*]), GEORGE BRENT (*Dan Collins*), Gar Moore (*Lee Sloan*), Tom Tully (*Nick Gruber*), Paul Stewart (*Zack Richards*), Richard Rober (*Dutch Lempo*), Joseph Vitale (*Joe Bottsy*), James Nolan (*Benson*), Clifton Young (*Billy Rafferty*), David Clarke (*Carl*), Robert Osterloh (*Crowthers*), Anthony Caruso (*Teague*), Donna Martell (*Maria*), [Tom Clark, Watson B. Miller (*Themselves*)], [Kenneth Tobey (*Dave*)], [Robert Bice (*Ken*)], [Peter Prouse (*Sanders*)], [Antony Bacchus (*Klinger*)], [Curt Conway (*Thin-faced man*)], [Eric Feldary (*Stephen Duvak*)], [William Forrest (*Ferguson*)], [Lester Sharpe (*Peter, a waiter*)], [Phil Tully (*Bartender*)], [Reuben Wendorff (*Frightened man*)], [Al Murphy (*Rick*)], [Walden Boyle (*Payson*)], [Will Kaufman (*Foreign man*)], [Rosa Turich (*Mexican woman*)], [Pierce Lyden, Lionel Dante (*Gunmen*)], [Edward Clark (*Paper man*)], [Jack Ingram (*Forest ranger*)], [Allan Ray (*Radio operator*)], [Sid Marion (*Clerk*)], [Alex Montoya, Eddie Randolph (*Waiters*)], [Vito Scotti (*Mexican youth*)], [Pilar Del Rey (*Mexican girl*)], [Frankie Van (*Man in apartment*)], [Joe Ploski, Alex Akimoff, Betty Chay (*Aliens*)], [Fraser McMinn (*Chula Vista radio operator*)], [Sam Finn (*Man on street*)], [Slim Crow (*Immigration officer*)], [Ray Flynn (*Bartender*)], [Paul Bradley], [Jack Chefe].

Crime, Drama. [*Print viewed*]. After a forest ranger finds an unidentifiable Polish survivor of the Dachau concentration camp dead in the wilderness of San Bernadino County, the matter is referred to Daniel Collins, the Los Angeles district chief for the U.S. Immigration and Naturalization Service. Collins places a photograph of the dead man in a local newspaper, which results in a call from the man's cousin, who states that he paid $2,000 to have the man brought into the country. The cousin is murdered, however, before he can tell Collins to whom he paid the money, saying only that the transaction took place at the Blue Danube Café. Collins then goes to Washington, D.C., where he asks that an undercover agent be assigned to the case, preferably Bert Powers, a friend of Wally O'Neill, the deceased husband of Anna Duvak, the German-American owner of the Blue Danube Café. Though initially reluctant, Bert, an Air Force veteran living in Amarillo, Texas, agrees to work for Collins and heads for Los Angeles. Pretending to be an out-of-work flyer, Bert quickly makes friends with Anna, and because she likes him, she tries to discourage him from seeing her, in hopes of keeping him out of the clutches of gangster Nick Gruber. Nevertheless, Bert is soon contacted by the

gangster's associates, who hire the flyer to smuggle an illegal alien into the United States from Mexico. Later, Nick hires Bert on a permanent basis, much to the annoyance of his more careful associate, Zack Richards. For the first few weeks, though, Bert is assigned to nothing more than routine cargo runs. Finally, he is assigned a smuggling flight from Mexico, and is met at the Ontario, California airport by Collins and his men. The plane is empty, however, as the smugglers threw all the immigrants out of the plane while over the Pacific Ocean, because they suspected one of being a government agent. Afterward, Dutch Lempo, the fugitive head of the smuggling organization, calls a meeting at his home in Mexico, and orders Nick to find the spy within their organization. They then set a trap for the infiltrator by having a seemingly drunk Richards falsely tell the flyers that Dutch is meeting with Nick at a downtown Los Angeles warehouse. Before Bert falls for the trap, however, Anna asks him out, and the two are accosted at a nearby bar by Lee Sloan, another flyer and a jealous, unwanted suitor of Anna's. Lee then inadvertently saves Bert's life by beating him to the warehouse, in hopes of telling Dutch that Anna is cheating on him, and is killed by the gangsters. The next day, Bert goes to see Anna, and she admits that she knows that he is the government agent and invited him out in order to keep him from Richards' trap. After learning that she is working for the smugglers only to protect her illegal immigrant brother Stephen, Bert agrees to help her smuggle Stephen out of Los Angeles. Stephen, however, thinks that he has only caused his sister more trouble, and commits suicide by hanging himself. When Anna refuses to go to work the next day, Dutch insists on being flown into Los Angeles to see her. Bert is assigned to Dutch's flight, but is caught by Joe Bottsy, one of Dutch's thugs, when he telephones Collins from Mexico. Though initially knocked unconscious by Bert, Joe manages to call Nick in Los Angeles, who radios Richards, the co-pilot on Dutch's flight, about Bert's true allegiance. Bert manages to knock Richards unconscious, however, so Dutch is forced to let him fly the plane into Los Angeles. Knowing that he will be killed as soon as he lands the plane, Bert executes a crash landing, which knocks the gun out of Dutch's hand. Though injured in the crash, Bert survives with minor injuries, while Dutch and his gang are arrested and later convicted on numerous smuggling charges. For her cooperation, all charges are dropped against Anna and she is released into Bert's "custody." *Aliens, Illegal. Gangsters. German Americans. Government agents. Smuggling. Undercover agents. United States. Dept. of Immigration.* Air lines. Air pilots. Airports. Bartenders. Blackmail. Brothers and sisters. Café owners. Drunkenness. Fights. Fugitives. Hanging. Hotels. Jealousy. Los Angeles (CA). Mexican Americans. Mexico. Murder. Poker (Game). Polish Americans. Suicide. Texans. Traps. Veterans. Waiters. Widows.

Note: The film contains the following written foreword: "We gratefully acknowledge the generous cooperation and assistance of the Immigration and Naturalization Service in the making of this picture." The film opens with statements about the Immigration and Naturalization Service spoken by Tom Clark, the United States Attorney General, and Watson B. Miller, the Commissioner of the Immigration and Naturalization Service. According to a *LAT* news item, portions of the picture were filmed along the Mexican border.

Box 18 Jun 1949. *DV* 8 Jun 1949, p. 3. *FD* 1 Jul 1949, p. 6. *HR* 10 Dec 1948, p. 15. *HR* 8 Jun 1949, p. 3. *LAT* 10 Dec 1948. *MPHPD* 11 Jun 1949, p. 4641. *NYT* 11 Jun 1949, p. 11. *Var* 8 Jun 1949, p. 18.

I'M NO COWBOY see SHUT MY BIG MOUTH

IMITATION OF LIFE (African Americans)

Universal Pictures Corp.; A John M. Stahl Production. *Dist* Universal Pictures Corp. 26 Nov 1934; Prod: 27 Jun—11 Sep 1934 [©Universal Pictures Corp.; 22 Nov 1934; LP5115]. Sd (Western Electric Noiseless Recording); b&w. 12 reels. 111 or 116 min. PCA cert no. 412.

Prod Carl Laemmle, Jr. [*Assoc prod* Henry Henigson]. *Dir* John M. Stahl. [*Asst dir* Scott Beal and Fred Frank]. *Scr* William Hurlbut. [*Addl dial* Victor Heerman and Finley Peter Dunne, Jr.]. [*Contr wrt* Arthur Richman, Preston Sturges, William Hurlbut, Walter Ferris, Bianca Gilchrist, Victor Heerman, Samuel Ornitz and Finley Peter Dunne, Jr.]. [*Contr to trmt* Sarah Y. Mason]. *Photog* Merritt Gerstad. [*2d cam* Alan Jones]. [*Asst cam* Paul Hill]. [*Gaffer* Warren Monroe]. [*Best boy* Murray Rock]. *Spec eff* John P. Fulton. *Art dir* Charles D. Hall. *Film ed* Philip Cahn and Maurice Wright. [*Supv film ed* Maurice Pivar]. *Mus dir* Heinz Roemheld. [*Sd supv* Gilbert Kurland]. [*Mixer* Joe Lapis]. [*Mike man* Jack Bolger]. [*Hair* Jane Romaine]. [*Makeup* William Ely]. [*Tech dir* Archie Hall]. [*Prod mgr* M. F. Murphy]. [*Grip* Fred Buckley, Jerry Vernon and George Schuman]. [*Props* Ernest M.

Smith]. [*Scr clerk* Cora Palmatier]. [*Secy* Bernice Boone]. [*Children's welfare worker* Mary West]. [*Stand-in for Louise Beavers* Etta McDaniel]. [*Stand-in for Rochelle Hudson* Emily Bolman]. [*Stand-in for Sebie Hendricks* Alma Johnson and Alameda Johnson]. [*Stand-in for Juanita Quigley* Barbara Boone].

Source: Based on the novel *Imitation of Life* by Fannie Hurst (New York, 1933).

Cast: CLAUDETTE COLBERT (*Beatrice Pullman*), WARREN WILLIAM (*Stephen Archer*), Rochelle Hudson (*Jessie Pullman*), Ned Sparks (*Elmer Smith*), Louise Beavers (*Delilah [Johnson]*), Fredi Washington (*Peola [Johnson]*), Baby Jane (*Baby Jessie*), Alan Hale ([*Martin,*] *the furniture man*), Henry Armetta (*The painter*), Wyndham Standing (*The butler*), [Marilyn Knowlden (*Jessie Pullman, aged 8*)], [Sebie Hendricks (*Peola Johnson, aged 4*)], [Dorothy Black (*Peola Johnson, aged 9*)], [Clarence Hummel Wilson (*Landlord*)], [Henry Kolker (*Doctor Preston*)], [G. P. Huntley, Jr. (*James*)], [Paul Porcasi (*Cafe manager*)], [Paullyn Garner (*Mrs. Ramsey*)], [Alice Ardell (*French maid*)], [Walter Walker (*Hugh*)], [Noel Francis (*Mrs. Eden*)], [Franklin Pangborn (*Mr. Carven*)], [Tyler Brooke (*Tipsy man*)], [William Austin (*Englishman*)], [Edgar Norton (*Butler*)], [Alma Tell (*Mrs. Carven*)], [Lenita Lane (*Mrs. Dale*)], [Barry Norton (*Young man*)], [Joyce Compton (*Young woman*)], [Reverend Gregg (*Black minister*)], [Edna Bowdoin (*Black secretary*)], [Daisy Bufford (*Black waitress*)], [Ethel Sykes, Monya Andre (*Party women*)], [Curry Lee (*Black chauffeur*)], [Claire McDowell, Norma Drew (*Teachers*)], [Madame Sul-te-wan (*Black cook*)], [Stuart Johnston (*Black undertaker*)], [Fred Toones, Hattie McDaniel, Hayes Robinson, Martin Turner, Libby Taylor, Elizabeth Jones, Bessie Lyle (*Persons at funeral*)], [Julius Molnar (*Footman*)], [William B. Davidson], [Gay Seabrook], [Bruce Warren].

Melodrama. [*Print viewed*]. After her husband's death, Beatrice Pullman continues his maple syrup business and hires Delilah Johnson to take care of her home and daughter Jessie. Delilah moves in with her daughter Peola, who, although she is light-skinned, is black like her mother. After tasting Delilah's delicious pancakes, made from a family recipe, Bea uses her gumption and ingenuity to open Aunt Delilah's Pancake House. The restaurant is a success and they are finally able to live comfortably, but Peola grows up resenting her heritage, as she feels it separates her from the rest of society. On the suggestion of vagrant Elmer Smith, Bea boxes the pancake mix, and hires Elmer as her manager. Bea prints Delilah's likeness on every box, and the business becomes a multimillion dollar corporation. Although she makes twenty percent of the profits, Delilah chooses to stay on as Bea's maid. At a party celebrating the tenth anniversary of the business, Bea meets ichthyologist Stephen Archer, who is a friend of Elmer. Bea and Stephen fall in love and make plans to marry, but decide to wait until Jessie meets him. Jessie returns home for a vacation from college, but Bea asks Stephen to look after her as she is compelled to go to Virginia with Delilah to find Peola, who has run away from college. In Virginia, Delilah finds Peola working at a restaurant that prohibits black customers. Peola bitterly denies knowing Delilah, and runs out of the restaurant. She returns home briefly, however, where she disowns Delilah so that she can lead a non-segregated life. In the meantime, Jessie has fallen in love with Stephen, although he has given her no encouragement, and thinks of her as a mere child. Peola's departure proves too much for Delilah, who becomes gravely ill. On her deathbed, Delilah asks Bea to take care of Peola should she ever return. Peola attends Delilah's funeral, and becomes overwhelmed by her own selfishness and the loss of her mother. Bea takes her home, and in time Peola agrees to return to college. Acknowledging Jessie's love for Stephen, Bea postpones their wedding indefinitely until Jessie no longer loves him, so that there will be no obstacles. Stephen promises to wait, and Bea and Jessie reminisce about the time when their beloved Delilah first arrived. *Maids. Mothers and daughters. Racial impersonation. Racism. Self-sacrifice. Women in business.* Death by shock. Engagements. Funerals. Generation gap. Ichthyologists. Maturation. Parties. Restaurateurs. Runaways. Schoolteachers. Self-reliance. Vagabonds. Wealth. Widows.

Note: Correspondence in the MPAA/PCA files at the AMPAS Library reveal that the AMPP was reluctant to approve Universal's original script because they felt that "the main theme is founded upon the results of sex association between the white and black race (miscegenation), and as such, in our opinion, it not only violates the Production Code but is very dangerous from the standpoint both of industry and public policy." Also objectionable was a lynching scene in the original script in which a young African-American man is nearly hanged for

approaching a white woman whom he believed had given him an invitation. In a memorandum for the files, the AMPP noted that they met with Carl Laemmle, Jr. and Universal Assistant General Manager Harry H. Zehner, and "emphasized the dangers involved in treating this story as regards to the possibilities having to do with negroes. It was our contention that this part of the plot—the action of the negro girl appearing as white—has a definite connection with the problem of miscegenation. We pointed out that not only from the picture point of view of the producer himself, but also from the point of view of the industry as a whole, this was an extremely dangerous subject and surely to prove troublesome, not only in the south, where it would be universally condemned, but everywhere else. The lynching scene in this story was discussed with the understanding that if used at all, would be considerably modified. The producer suggested that to avoid the inference that the leading character was a descendant of a white ancestor, they would definitely establish that her white skin was due to a rare but scientific fact that such a child might come of a line of definitely negro strain."

On 22 Mar 1934, AMPP director Joseph I. Breen sent a memo to Will H. Hays at the MPPDA updating him on *Imitation of Life*, and informing him that the studio was considering dropping the story. Breen sent the script to Maurice McKenzie, Executive Assistant to Hays, who, in addition to noting problems with words and phrases such as "nigger," "Mah Lo'dy" and "Lo'd help," disagreed that the film dealt with miscegenation as "the act of miscegenation has occurred so remotely in the ancestry of the characters that it need not concern us." Nonetheless, he continued that "We here share your concern over the attempt to discuss a racial problem of this nature on the screen, and it is our earnest hope that you will be able to persuade the company to abandon its plans for production." A 3 Jul memo reveals that Dr. James C. Wingate of the AMPP met again with Harry Zehner and John Stahl, who requested written approval of the script. Wingate demurred, as the AMPP still had not received a complete script and they felt that "the real problem involved in the script occurs in the last part of the story." He further noted that he "discussed with Mr. Stahl the word 'nigger.' He advised me he would not use the word, 'nigger,' with the possible exception of one or two places in the script, and there he will be fully protected. He intends to use the terms 'black'—'colored'—'darky'—and 'negro.'" Although by 17 Jul the picture had been shooting for two weeks, Breen continued to refuse to approve the script, stating that "it is our conviction that any picture which raises and elaborates such an inflammable racial question as that raised by this picture, is fraught with grave danger to the industry, and hence is one which we, in the dispensation of our responsibilities under the Resolution for Uniform Interpretation of the Production Code, may be obliged to reject."

Baby Jane changed her name to Juanita Quigley during production. According to a news item in *DV*, Paul Lukas was originally wanted for the role of "Stephen Archer," but Warren William was borrowed from Warner Bros. instead. A news item in *HR* noted that the film was doing a "stand-out business" at the Roxy theatre in New York, where "the Sunday jam resulted in a call for the police and fire departments to keep the waiting crowd in order." The *Var* review stated that the "most arresting part of the picture and overshadowing the conventional romance...is the tragedy of Aunt Delilah's girl born to a white skin and Negro blood. This subject has never been treated upon the screen before....It seems very probable the picture may make some slight contribution to the cause of greater tolerance and humanity in the racial question." The *Literary Digest* review notes that "In *Imitation of Life*, the screen is extremely careful to avoid its most dramatic theme, obviously because it fears its social implications....The real story [is]...that of the beautiful and rebellious daughter of the loyal negro friend....Obviously she is the most interesting person in the cast. They [the producers] appear to be fond of her mother, because she is of the meek type of old-fashioned Negro that, as they say, 'knows his place,' but the daughter is too bitter and lacking in resignation for them." *Imitation of Life* was nominated for Best Picture at the 1934 Academy Awards. Modern sources report that the African-American press viewed this film unfavorably, and that Louise Beavers was assisted by the NAACP in influencing the filmmakers to delete the word "nigger" from the screenplay. A modern source includes Dennis O'Keefe (then known as Bud Flanagan) as a dance extra. Universal released a remake in 1959 based on the same source, directed by Douglas Sirk, and starring Lana Turner, John Gavin, Sandra Dee and Susan Kohner (see below).

DV 24 Jul 1934, p. 1. *DV* 7 Aug 1934, p. 1. *DV* 13 Sep 1934, p. 6. *DV* 3 Nov 1934, p. 3. *DV* 22 Nov 1934. *FD* 23 Nov 1934, p. 10. *HR* 7 Jul 1934, p. 2. *HR* 10 Sep 1934, p. 3. *HR* 27 Nov 1934. *MPH* 1 Dec 1934, p. 39, 42. *MPSI* Feb 1935, p. 27. *NYT* 24 Nov 1934, p. 19. *Var* 27 Nov 1934, p. 15.

IMITATION OF LIFE (African Americans)

Universal-International Pictures Co., Inc. *Dist* Universal Pictures Co., Inc. Apr **1959**; New York opening: 17 Apr 1959; Prod: early Aug—early Oct 1958 [©Universal Pictures Co.; 24 Jun 1959; LP14526]. Sd (Westrex Recording System); col (Eastman Color by Pathe); CinemaScope. 11,155 ft. 124-25 min. PCA cert no. 19184.

Prod Ross Hunter. *Dir* Douglas Sirk. *Asst dir* Frank Shaw and [Wilson Shyer]. *Scr* Eleanore Griffin and Allan Scott. *Dir of photog* Russell Metty. *Spec photog* Clifford Stine. *Art dir* Alexander Golitzen and Richard H. Riedel. *Film ed* Milton Carruth. *Set dec* Russell A. Gausman and Julia Heron. *Gowns for Lana Turner* Jean Louis. *Miss Turner's jewels* Laykin et Cie. *Gowns* Bill Thomas. *Mus* Frank Skinner. *Mus supv* Joseph Gershenson. *Sd* Leslie I. Carey and Joe Lapis. *Makeup* Bud Westmore. *Hair stylist* Larry Germain. [*Prod mgr* Norman Deming].

Song(s): "Imitation of Life," music by Sammy Fain, lyrics by Paul Francis Webster, sung by Earl Grant; "Empty Arms," music by Arnold Hughes, lyrics by Frederick Herbert; "Trouble of the World," spiritual, sung by Mahalia Jackson.

Source: Based on the novel *Imitation of Life* by Fannie Hurst (New York, 1933).

Cast: LANA TURNER (*Lora Meredith*), JOHN GAVIN (*Steve Archer*), Sandra Dee (*Susie Meredith, age sixteen*), Susan Kohner (*Sarah Jane [Johnson], age eighteen*), Robert Alda (*Allen Loomis*), Dan O'Herlihy (*David Edwards*), Karin [sic] Dicker (*Sarah Jane [Johnson, age eight]*), Terry Burnham (*Susie [Meredith, age 6]*), Sandra Gould (*Receptionist*), and presenting Juanita Moore (*Annie Johnson*), Mahalia Jackson (*Choir soloist*), John Vivyan [(*Young man*)], Lee Goodman [(*Photographer*)], Ann Robinson [(*Show girl*)], Troy Donahue [(*Frankie*)], David Tomack [(*Burly man*)], Joel Fluellen [(*Minister*)], Jack Weston [(*Stage manager*)], Billy House [(*Fat man*)], Maida Severn [(*Teacher*)], Than Wyenn [(*Romano*)], Peg Shirley [(*Fay*)], [Cicely Evans (*Louise*)], [Bess Flowers (*Geraldine Moore*)], [Paul Bradley (*Preston Mitchell*)], [Napoleon Whiting (*Kenneth*)], [Nelson Leigh, John McNamara (*Doctors*)], [Lynne Hunter (*Schoolteacher*)], [Myrna Fahey (*Actress*)], [Ted Thorpe (*Dog owner*)], [Paul Levitt, Robert Darin (*Waiters*)], [Richard Collier (*McKinney*)], [Joe Mell (*Watchman*)], [Edwin Parker, Tedd Hadfield (*Policemen*)], [Fred Somers (*Truck driver*)], [George Barrows (*Furniture mover*)], [Chuckie Bradley], [Forbes Murray], [Leota Lorraine], [Jean Westmore], [Shep Houghton], [Norman Stevans], [John Marlowe], [Paul Gustine].

Melodrama. [*Print viewed*]. After frantically searching for her lost daughter Susie at Coney Island, an attractive widow named Lora Meredith finds her playing with Sarah Jane, a light-skinned black girl. Lora then meets Sarah Jane's single black mother, Annie Johnson, and a white photographer named Steve Archer, who takes some photographs of the girls. Lora discovers that Annie and Sarah Jane have no place to go, and although she is poor herself, having come to New York in search of an acting career, she invites the two to stay the night in her small apartment. In exchange for her small room, Annie offers to keep house and look after Susie while Lora seeks acting and modeling jobs. One evening, Steve comes by with the photographs, and the next day, he takes Lora to lunch, obviously smitten with her. Later, Lora invents a lie that gets her into the office of Allen Loomis, a well-known theatrical agent, but when he tries to make love to her, arguing that a successful actress must be willing to satisfy such requests, she angrily leaves. Back home, she sobs in frustration while Annie attempts to comfort and encourage her. One cold day, Annie brings Sarah Jane's galoshes to school, where she discovers that her daughter has been trying to conceal her race from her classmates. When Sarah Jane runs from Annie, her distressed mother turns to Lora and asks, "How do you explain to your child that she was born to be hurt?" Soon afterward, Steve, who has just been hired to promote a brand of beer, proposes to Lora, but she turns him down, saying that even though she loves him, marriage would prevent her from steadfastly pursuing a life in the theater. Just then, Loomis offers her a role in a new comedy by well-known writer David Edwards, but Steve forbids her to visit Loomis, prompting her to accuse him of settling for less in his own career. During her audition, Lora suggests that David rewrite portions of his play, and though angry at first, he soon realizes she is right. After Lora is cast and the play and its new leading actress are hugely successful, the papers report that "a new star is born" on Broadway. For the next ten years, Lora stars in one hit David Edwards play after another. The playwright wants to marry her, but as she admits one day to Annie, who still works for her, she does not really love him. Lora and David argue when she decides to appear in another writer's drama, but her performance is brilliant, and this play, too, becomes an instant hit. Surprised and overjoyed by a visit from Steve, Lora confesses she still loves him, and the two are reunited. Susie, who has suffered from her busy mother's lack of attention despite the material advantages Lora has provided her, looks forward to taking a trip with Steve and Lora, but the plans are canceled when Lora excitedly accepts a coveted role in an Italian film. Meanwhile, Sarah Jane tells Susie that she secretly has been seeing her white boyfriend, and that she would rather die than be considered black. When the young man learns that Sarah Jane's mother is black, however, he beats her. While Lora is filming in Italy, Steve looks after Susie, and the eager teenager soon falls in love with

him. Sarah Jane, meanwhile, claims to have accepted a job in a New York library, but Annie finds her singing and dancing in a seedy New York nightclub. Her mother's appearance gets Sarah Jane fired, and she again runs from her, causing Annie to faint. Back home, Annie tells Lora, who has just returned from Europe, that she will no longer interfere in her daughter's life, adding that she does hope to help her wayward daughter somehow. Steve, now a company vice-president, learns that Sarah Jane is working as a chorus girl in Los Angeles, and Annie, convinced she is dying, flies to California for one last look at her daughter. Sarah Jane is furious, exclaiming, "I'm somebody else, I'm white." Annie then introduces herself to Sarah Jane's white friend as Sarah Jane's former nanny and leaves, but not before Sarah Jane tearfully embraces her. Meanwhile, Lora and Susie argue over Steve. When Susie accuses Lora of loving her career more than her, Lora offers to give Steve up, but Susie has decided to go away to college. The two mothers are now alone in the house. One day, Annie tells Lora to make certain all her possessions are left to Sarah Jane and then, after reassuring her old friend that she is "going to glory," dies. Lora breaks down, but sees to it that Annie has the elaborate funeral she had requested. As the long cortege moves slowly along the street, Sarah Jane pushes through the crowds, flings herself on her mother's coffin, and weeps hysterically. Lora and Susie gently lead her into the hearse, where they reassure her that she did not cause her mother's death. As Steve looks on, the three women join hands in a gesture of comfort and love. *African Americans. Ambition. Friendship. Mothers and daughters. Neglected children. Racial impersonation.* Actors and actresses. Adolescence. Chorus girls. Funerals. Grief. Housekeepers. Infatuation. Maturation. New York City–Broadway. New York City–Coney Island. Photographers. Playwrights. Racism. Romance. Seduction. Spirituals (Songs). Theater. Theatrical agents. Vocational obsession. Widows.

Note: Actress Karen Dicker's name is misspelled as "Karin" in the onscreen credits. This picture, Douglas Sirk's last feature, was a remake of the 1934 Universal film of the same title directed by John M. Stahl and starring Claudette Colbert and Louise Beavers (see above). According to a 19 Jul 1956 *HR* news item, producer Ross Hunter originally planned to make a musical version of the story starring Shirley Booth and Ethel Waters. *HR* noted that in the novel on which the film is based, the character played by Lana Turner "combined her business acumen with a recipe for pancakes invented by a Negro woman and reaped a fortune. The characters lived together, loved one another and faced tragedy through their respective daughters. The plot formula would not have stood up in today's era of integration when a Negro who owned half a successful corporation could buy her own home in any area that pleased her." Of the change in plot, *Var* commented about the 1959 film, "While this device lends more scope, it also results in the over-done busy actress-neglected daughter conflict, and thus the secondary plot of a fair-skinned Negress passing as white becomes the film's primary force." A modern source reported that Sirk had read the novel before directing this film, but had not seen the 1934 film.

According to *DV*, Universal encountered some resistance to the promotion of the film and tailored its advertising campaign for the south, where, a studio representative said, "white southerners avoid films that are advertised as dealing with the race problem." On 2 Feb 1959, *HR* reprinted the following wire sent by *L.A. Tribune* editor Almena Lomac to numerous white publications: "*Imitation of Life*...is a libel on the Negro race. It libels our children and the Negro mother [and] should be banned in the interest of national unity, harmony, peace, decency and inter-racial respect. The *Tribune* is refusing all advertising of it and will picket it in the Los Angeles area and call upon the N.A.A.C.P. to condemn, oppose and picket it, too." The outcome of this boycott is not known. Juanita Moore and Susan Kohner both received Academy Award nominations for Best Supporting Actress, and Kohner won a Golden Globe in the same category.

Box 9 Feb 1959. Box 23 Feb 1959. DV 3 Feb 1959, p. 3. DV 1 Apr 1959. Exh 11 Feb 1959, pp. 4558-59. FD 3 Feb 1959, p. 6. Har 7 Feb 1959, p. 24. HR 19 Jul 1956. HR 8 Aug 1958, p. 8. HR 3 Oct 1958, p. 10. HR 2 Feb 1959. HR 3 Feb 1959, p. 3, 6. MPHPD 14 Feb 1959, p. 157. NYT 18 Apr 1959, p. 18. NYT 19 Apr 1959. Var 4 Feb 1959, p. 6.

THE IMMIGRANT (Russian Americans)

Jesse L. Lasky Feature Play Co. *Dist* Paramount Pictures Corp. 20 Dec **1915** [©Jesse L. Lasky Feature Play Co., Inc.; 8 Dec 1915; LU7165]. Si; b&w. 5 reels.

Pres Jesse L. Lasky. *Dir* George Melford. *Scen* Marion Fairfax.

Cast: Valeska Suratt (*Masha*), Thomas Meighan (*David Harding*), Theodore Roberts (*J. J. Walton*), Jane Wolf (*Olga*), Hal Clements (*John*), Ernest Joy (*Walton's partner*), Deane (full name unknown) (*Walton's secretary*), Mrs. Lewis McCord (*Stewardess*), Bob Flemming (*Officer on board ship*), Raymond Hatton (*Munsing, Harding's secretary*), Gertrude Kellar (*Walton's housekeeper*).

Drama. Masha, a young Russian emigrant traveling to America as a steerage passenger, is saved from an officer's advances by David

Harding, an American civil engineer and contractor riding in second class, who fights the officer. J. J. Walton, a self-made political boss and contractor traveling first class, notices Masha and, upon landing, pursues her to her sister Olga's house. Olga's brutish husband John forces Masha to accept Walton's offer to be his maid. After Walton breaks into Masha's room the first night, she leaves, but when Walton promises to marry and educate her, Masha becomes his mistress. Meanwhile, David wins a government contract over Walton's company to build a large dam in Arizona. Walton and his ring plan to dynamite it, and he uses Masha, by threatening to have Olga arrested for murder, to lure David from the dam. The dam bursts, but Walton dies when the subsequent flood destroys the house from which he watches. After David is knocked unconscious trying to save a little girl, Masha finds him, and they confess their mutual love. *Contractors. Engineers–Civil. Immigrants. Mistresses. Russian Americans. Sabotage.* Arizona. Business competition. Dams. Dynamite. Floods. Maids. Political bosses. Rescues. Traps.

Note: This was stage actress Valeska Suratt's first film. According to a news item, she designed the gowns which she wore in the film.

MPN 20 Nov 1915, p. 74. MPN 27 Nov 1915, p. 53, 79. MPN 18 Dec 1915, p. 68. MPN 1 Jan 1916, p. 79. MPW 25 Dec 1915, p. 2454. MPW 1 Jan 1916, p. 92. NYDM 1 Jan 1916, p. 28. Var 31 Dec 1916, p. 24.

THE IMMIGRANT (1932) see CUORE D'EMIGRANTE

THE IMMIGRANT (1936) see PADDY O'DAY

EL IMPOSTOR (Spanish language)

Fox Film Corp. *Dist* Fox Film Corp. **1931**; New York opening: 17 Apr 1931; Prod: Feb 1931. Sd; b&w. 9 reels. Passed by the National Board of Review. Spanish language.

Pres WILLIAM FOX. [*Dir* Lewis Seiler]. [*Scr* Garrett Fort]. [*Spanish version by* Matías Cirici-Ventalló]. [*Photog* Sidney Wagner]. [*Sd* Bernard Freericks].

Source: Based on the play *Scotland Yard* by Denison Clift (New York, 27 Sep 1929).

Cast: Juan Torena (*Sir Alfred Gray/Guilbert Donald*), Blanca Castejón (*Sandra*), Carlos Villarías (*Sir Arnold Bronson*), Julio Villarreal (*Harry Palmer*), Juan Aristi Eulate (*Capitán Lester*), André Cheron (*Doctor Dupont*), [Emma Roldán (*Marie*)], [Antonio Vidal (*Beverly*)], [Roberto Guzmán], [Rafael Alvir].

Drama. [*Not viewed*]. [The following plot summary is based on the English-language version of this film, *Scotland Yard*; character names refer to that version. For further information regarding the English-language version, please see the note below and the entry for *Scotland Yard* in the *AFI Catalog of Feature Films, 1921-30.*] Dakin Barrolles, attempting to elude Scotland Yard detectives, swims to the houseboat of Sir John Lasher, who is forced at gunpoint to shield the thief. Attracted to Lasher's bride, Xandra, Dakin takes a locket containing the couple's bridal photograph; but traced to his hideout, he is forced to join the army to escape. Dakin is badly wounded in action in France, and his face is restored by a plastic surgeon to resemble the features of Lasher on the locket. Xandra, hearing that her husband has been lost in action, takes Dakin to be Sir John, and he returns to England with her and plans, with his former partner, Fox, to rob the Lasher banking concern. His growing love for Xandra, however, dilutes his baser motives; and when he is found out by a Scotland Yard detective, he gives himself up but is placed in the custody of his "wife's" love. *Criminals–Rehabilitation. Detectives. Great Britain. Army. Impersonation and imposture. London (England). Plastic surgery. Scotland Yard (London, England). Thieves. World War I.*

Note: The onscreen credits were taken from a screen credit sheet in the Twentieth Century-Fox Records of the Legal Department at the UCLA Theater Arts Library. This is the Spanish-language version of Fox's 1930 English-language release of *Scotland Yard*, which was directed by William K. Howard and starred Edmund Lowe and Joan Bennett. This film was released in Santiago, Chile under the title *La mujer del otro*. Some sources indicate that Francisco Moré de la Torre was involved with the production, but it is not clear if he translated the dialogue into Spanish or if he supervised direction of the dialogue in Spanish. In 1941, Twentieth Century-Fox released another film entitled *Scotland Yard*, which was based on the play. It was directed by Norman Foster and starred Nancy Kelly, Edmund Gwenn and John Loder.

CM Jul 1931, p. 519.

IN HIGH GEAR (Chinese Americans)

Sunset Productions. *Dist* Aywon Film Corp. 1 Jul **1924**. Si; b&w. 5 reels, 4,737 ft.

Dir Robert North Bradbury. *Story and scen* Robert North Bradbury and Frank Howard Clark. *Photog* Bert Longenecker.

Cast: Kenneth McDonald, Helen Lynch.

Comedy. "Jack Holloway and Alice Cromwell each wealthy and bored with the sham of the exclusive Mirimar resort assume disguises as poor people, eventually meet and fall in love. Alice is kidnapped and thrown into Chinatown den where Jack rescues her after a series of thrilling fights. Real identities are revealed and a happy marriage follows." (*MPNBG* 7 Oct 1924, p. 29.). *Chinatowns. Chinese Americans. Disguise. Kidnapping. Resorts. Wealth.*

Note: Reissued Jan 1930.

FD 8 Feb 1925.

IN HOLLYWOOD WITH POTASH AND PERLMUTTER (Jewish
      Americans)

Goldwyn Pictures Corp. *Dist* Associated First National Pictures. Sep 1924 [©Samuel Goldwyn; 16 Sep 1924; LP20572]. Si; b&w. 7 reels, 6,685 ft.

Pres Samuel Goldwyn. *Prod* Samuel Goldwyn. *Dir* Alfred Green. *Adpt* Frances Marion. *Titles* Montague Glass. *Photog* Arthur Miller and Harry Hallenberger. *Art dir* Ben Carré. *Film ed* Stuart Heisler.

Source: Based on the play *Business Before Pleasure* by Montague Glass and Jules Eckert Goodman (New York, 15 Aug 1917).

Cast: Alexander Carr (*Morris Perlmutter*), George Sidney (*Abe Potash*), Vera Gordon (*Rosie Potash*), Betty Blythe (*Rita Sismondi*), Belle Bennett (*Mrs. Perlmutter*), Anders Randolph (*Blanchard*), Peggy Shaw (*Irma Potash*), Charles Meredith (*Sam Pemberton*), Lillian Hackett (*Miss O'Ryan*), David Butler (*Crabbe*), Sidney Franklin, Joseph W. Girard (*Film buyers*), Norma Talmadge, Constance Talmadge.

Comedy. Potash and Perlmutter give up their textile business to produce motion pictures. Though their initial effort is a failure, they interest a banker, Blanchard, in financing their productions, provided that they engage Rita Sismondi, an actress famous for vamp roles. She all but breaks up the homes of the partners. When they finally settle their differences, their new picture is a success and the vamp begins a romance with the director. *Actors and actresses. Hollywood (CA). Jews. Motion pictures. Textile mills. Vamps.*

FD 28 Sep 1924. *MPW* 20 Sep 1924. *NYT* 30 Sep 1924, p. 27.

IN JUDGMENT OF (Gypsies)

Metro Pictures Corp. *Dist* Metro Pictures Corp. 12 Aug 1918 [©Metro Pictures Corp.; 13 Aug 1918; LP12748]. Si; b&w. 5 reels.

Dir Will S. Davis. *Story and scen* George D. Baker. *Cam* William C. Thompson.

Cast: Anna Q. Nilsson (*Mary Manners*), Franklyn Farnum (*Dr. John O'Neill*), Herbert Standing (*Judge Brainard*), Edward Alexander (*Robert Brainard*), Lydia Knott (*Mrs. Manners*), Harry S. Northrup (*Andrew Vail*), Spottiswoode Aitken (*Mr. Manners*), Katherine Griffith (*Mrs. Brainard*), Robert Dunbar (*T. A. Adams*).

Drama. Mary Manners, a debutante, has inherited the power of mind reading from her gypsy ancestors. On a lonely country road, Dr. John O'Neill rescues Mary from a robber, and the two quickly become friends. John, whose father has supported but never identified himself to the young physician, visits Mary's home, where he meets Judge Brainard, the father of Mary's fiancé Robert. When Robert jealously complains of the doctor's presence, the judge admits that John is his son by a former marriage. Andrew Vail overhears the conversation and threatens to blackmail the old man. In a fierce struggle, Judge Brainard pushes Andrew over a cliff, but John is arrested for the crime on circumstantial evidence. Presiding over the trial, the judge maintains his silence as the jury pronounces his son guilty, but when he looks into Mary's knowing eyes, he breaks down and confesses his guilt. Because he acted in self-defense, the judge is acquitted, whereupon he takes his son and new daughter-in-law into his heart. *Confession (Law). Extrasensory perception. False arrests. Fathers and sons. Guilt. Hereditary tendencies. Judges. Long-lost relatives. Trials. Blackmail. Circumstantial evidence. Debutantes. Falls from heights. Fights. Gypsies. Jealousy. Physicians. Rescues. Self-defense. Stepbrothers. Thieves.*

Note: The picture's working title was *Judgment*.

ETR 17 Aug 1918, p. 882. *ETR* 24 Aug 1918, p. 1015. *MPN* 24 Aug 1918, p. 1214. *MPW* 17 Aug 1918, p. 1019. *MPW* 24 Aug 1918, p. 1154. *NYDM* 7 Sep 1918, p. 371. *Var* 30 Aug 1918, p. 38. *Wid's* 25 Aug 1918, pp. 23-24.

IN JUSTICE *see* **INJUSTICE**

IN OLD ARIZONA (Latino)

Fox Film Corp. *Dist* Fox Film Corp. 20 Jan **1929** [©Fox Film Corp.; 4 Feb 1929; LP75]. Sd (Movietone); b&w. 7 reels, 8,724 ft. 97 min.

Series: The Cisco Kid.

Dir Raoul Walsh and Irving Cummings. *Asst dir* Archibald Buchanan and Charles Woolstenhulme. *Scen, story and dial* Tom Barry. *Cam* Arthur Edeson. *Film ed* Louis Loeffler. *Sd* Edmund H. Hansen.

Song(s): "My Tonia," by Lew Brown, B. G. De Sylva and Ray Henderson.

Source: Based on the character created by O. Henry.

Cast: Edmund Lowe (*Sgt. Mickey Dunn*), Dorothy Burgess (*Tonia María*), Warner Baxter (*The Cisco Kid*), Farrell MacDonald (*Tad*), Fred Warren (*Piano player*), Henry Armetta (*Barber*), Frank Campeau, Tom Santschi, Pat Hartigan, Roy Stewart (*Commandant*), James Bradbury, Jr. (*Soldier*), John Dillon (*Second soldier*), Frank Nelson, Duke Martin (*Cowboys*), James Marcus (*Blacksmith*), Joe Brown (*Bartender*), Alphonse Ethier (*Sheriff*), Solidad Jiminez (*Cook*), Helen Lynch, Ivan Linow.

Western. The Cisco Kid is a gay caballero whose flair for dramatic thievery and penchant for dangerous trysts keep him just one step ahead of Sgt. Mickey Dunn. The Kid's reputation has preceded him when he approaches the local stagecoach, and he needs to fire only two warning shots to wrest the Wells Fargo box from the driver. His infatuation with a Mexican girl named Tonia María exposes him to near-capture, because of the se'norita's double-dealing association with Dunn. Eventually, a showdown becomes imminent, and the Kid exacts a final revenge by framing Tonia so that Dunn shoots her by accident, while the Kid rides laughing off into the sunset. *Arizona. Bandits. Mexicans. Robbery. United States. Army. Cavalry.*

Note: For information on other films featuring the character of The Cisco Kid, see entry above for *The Cisco Kid* and consult the Series Index.

FD 20 Jan 1929. *NYT* 21 Jan 1929, p. 18. *Var* 23 Jan 1929, p. 18.

IN OLD CALIENTE (Latino)

Republic Pictures Corp. *Dist* Republic Pictures Corp. 19 Jun **1939**; Prod: began 3 May 1939 [©Republic Pictures Corp.; 19 Jun 1939; LP8944]. Sd (RCA "High Fidelity" Recording); b&w. 6 reels. 57 min. PCA cert no. 5388.

Assoc prod Joseph Kane. *Dir* Joseph Kane. [*Asst dir* Tommy Flood]. *Scr* Norman Houston and Gerald Geraghty. *Orig story* Norman Houston. *Photog* William Nobles. *Film ed* Edward Mann. *Mus dir* Cy Feuer. *Prod mgr* Al Wilson.

Cast: ROY ROGERS [(*Roy Rogers*)], MARY HART [(*Jean*)], George "Gabby" Hayes [(*Gabby*)], Jack La Rue [(*Suguaro*)], Katherine De Mille [(*Rita*)], Frank Puglia [(*Don Jose*)], Harry Woods [(*Calkins*)], Paul Marion [(*Carlos*)], Ethel Wales [(*Felicia*)], Merrill McCormick [(*Pedro*)], [Trigger].

Historical, Western, with songs. [*Print viewed*]. In 1835, the newly annexed state of California sees an influx of American settlers moving West along the El Camino Real; these Americanos are perceived as a threat to the rancheros of the Spanish dons. Among the rancheros are Gabby and his niece Jean, who are leading a wagon train to meet their friend, Roy Rogers. Roy, a trusted hand on the ranch of Don Jose, is returning from a cattle drive with Carlos, son of the don, when he decides to ride ahead to the ranch, leaving Carlos behind with the wagon bearing the proceeds of the sale. On the ridge above the wagon awaits Suguaro, the half-breed foreman of Don Jose's ranch, who has led a band of "gringo" bandits to prey upon Carlos and the gold. When the bandits shoot Carlos and steal his gold, the clever Suguaro accuses the settlers of the crime, and when Roy protests, Don Jose banishes him from the ranch. After Roy joins Gabby and the wagons, he follows Suguaro to the bandits' cave hideout, but the clever Suguaro escapes Roy's trap and accuses Roy and Gabby of stealing the gold. When Don Jose orders the Americanos imprisoned, Jean pleads with the don to listen to their explanation. The don agrees, but before he can free Roy, Suguaro shoots him and frames Roy for the murder. Aided by Rita, the don's daughter, Roy and Gabby escape, but Carlos refuses to abandon the search for his father's killer. One night, Carlos follows Rita to Roy's grotto hideout, and Roy succeeds in convincing him that it was Suguaro who murdered his father. Together, they plan a massive cattle drive to tempt the bandits, and the trap works as Roy, Carlos and their men ambush Suguaro and

their band. Thus vindicated, Roy rides off to San Diego with Jean and the wagon train. *Bandits. California–History–To 1846. Frame-ups. Ranch foremen. Ranchers. Settlers. Spaniards. Wagon trains. Caves. Fathers and daughters. Hideouts. Murder. Nieces. Robbery. Traps. Uncles.*

Note: The working title of this film was *Road to Eldorado*. Although the character played by Jack La Rue is called "Saguaro" in the film, the reviews list his name as "Delgado." Similiarly, Frank Puglia is called "Don Jose" in the film, but the reviews list the character as "Don Miguel." Although the film features several songs, none of the song titles were identified.
FD 14 Jul 1939, p. 8. *HR* 1 May 1939, p. 1. *HR* 6 May 1939, pp. 6–7. *MPD* 14 Jul 1939, p. 5. *MPH* 22 Jul 1939, p. 50. *Var* 12 Jul 1939, p. 13.

IN OLD CALIFORNIA (Latino)
Audible Pictures. 1 Sep or 15 Oct 1929. Sd (Photophone); b&w. 6 reels, 5,400–5,500 ft. [Also si; 5,367 ft.].
Supv Lon Young. *Dir* Burton King. *Asst dir* Bernard F. McEveety. *Scen and dial* Arthur Hoerl. *Story* Fred Hart. *Photog* Charles Boyle. *Film ed* Earl Turner. *Rec eng* Ernest Rovere.
Cast: Henry B. Walthall (*Don Pedro DeLeón*), Helen Ferguson (*Dolores Radanell*), George Duryea (*Lieut. Tony Hopkins*), Ray Hallor (*Pedro DeLeón*), Orral Humphrey (*Ike Boone*), Larry Steers (*Ollie Radanell*), Richard Carlyle (*Arturo*), Harry Allen (*Sergeant Washburn*), Louis Stern (*Ramón De Hermosa*), Paul Ellis (*José*), Carlotta Monta (*Juanita*), Gertrude Short.
Historical, **Romance**. A flirtation begun in a California-bound stagecoach between Pedro DeLeón and Dolores Radanell is interrupted by bandits. The runaway horses are halted by Lieut. Tony Hopkins, who also shows an interest in Dolores. Inviting Dolores and her gambler father, Ollie Radanell, to a fiesta at his wealthy father's ranch, Pedro spends much of his time drinking and brooding over the lieutenant's obvious success with Dolores and his father's bitterness regarding Pedro's mother, Isabella. In the course of the evening, Don Pedro loses his ranch to Radanell in a card game, and a showdown between the two men reveals that Radanell took Isabella and Dolores away from Don Pedro—making Dolores Pedro's sister. Pedro defends his father in a final shooting match with Hopkins. *Bandits. Brothers and sisters. California. Gamblers. Ranchers.*

Note: The film's theme song was "Underneath a Spanish Moon."
FD 15 Sep 1929.

IN OLD CALIFORNIA (1936) *see* **ROBIN HOOD OF EL DORADO**

IN OLD CAPISTRANO *see* **THE MYSTERIOUS DESPERADO**

IN OLD CHICAGO (Irish Americans)
Twentieth Century-Fox Film Corp.; Darryl F. Zanuck's Production. *Dist* Twentieth Century-Fox Film Corp. 15 Apr 1938; World premiere in New York: 6 Jan 1938; Prod: mid-Jun—early Sep 1937 [©Twentieth Century-Fox Film Corp.; 24 Feb 1938; LP7943]. Sd (Western Electric Mirrophonic Recording); b&w. 12 reels, 10,002 ft. 115 min. PCA cert no. 3639.
Assoc prod Kenneth Macgowan. *Dir* Henry King. [*Dial dir* Edwin H. Curtis]. *Asst dir* Robert Webb. [*2d asst dir* Robert Herndon]. [*Asst dir for 2d unit* Ed O'Fearna]. *Scr* Lamar Trotti and Sonya Levien. *Story* Niven Busch. *Photog* Peverell Marley. [*Cam op* K. Green]. [*Asst cam* J. Van Wormer]. [*Gaffer* Eddie Petzoldt]. *Spec eff scenes staged by* Fred Sersen, Ralph Hammeras and Louis J. Witte. *Spec eff scenes dir by* H. Bruce Humberstone. *Spec eff scenes photog by* Daniel B. Clark. *Art dir* William Darling and Rudolph Sternad. *Film ed* Barbara McLean. [*Asst cutter* Richard Billings and Bobby Fritch]. *Set dec* Thomas Little. *Cost* Royer. [*Ward* Albert Conti]. [*Cost supv* Arthur M. Levy]. [*Ward man* Bob Lee]. [*Ward girl* Ollie Hughes]. [*Cost supplied by* Western Costume Co. and The United Costumers]. *Mus dir* Louis Silvers. [*Vocal supv* Jule Styne]. [*Mus casting* Frank Tresselt]. [*Dance dir* Jack Haskell, Geneva Sawyer and Nick Castle]. *Sd* Eugene Grossman and Roger Heman. [*Sd rec* W. R. Snyder]. [*Boom man* Bob Bertrand]. [*Cableman* H. Richards]. [*Hair* Gale Roe]. [*Makeup* Ben Nye]. [*Prod mgr* Ed. Ebele]. [*Unit mgr* Booth McCracken]. [*Scr clerk* Max Larey and Theresa Brachetto]. [*Grip* Jack Percy]. [*Asst grip* Al Bumpus and N. Hanley]. [*Props* Duke Abrahams]. [*Research work* Gene Fowler]. [*Script clerk for 2d unit* Rose Steinberg]. [*Asst prop* C. Fremdling]. [*Best boy* Clarence Collins]. [*Casting dir* Walter Whaley]. [*Supv of horses* Sid Jordan]. [*Press rep* Charles E. McCarthy]. [*Publicity dir* Harry Brand]. [*Stunts* Jack Raye].
Song(s): "In Old Chicago," music and lyrics by Mack Gordon and Harry Revel; "I'll Never Let You Cry," "I've Taken a Fancy to You"

and "Take a Dip in the Sea," music and lyrics by Lew Pollack and Sidney D. Mitchell; "Carry Me Back to Old Virginny," music and lyrics by James Bland.
Cast: Tyrone Power (*Dion O'Leary*), Alice Faye (*Belle Fawcett*), Don Ameche (*Jack O'Leary*), Alice Brady (*Molly O'Leary*), Andy Devine (*Pickle Bixby*), Brian Donlevy (*Gil Warren*), Phyllis Brooks (*Ann Colby*), Tom Brown (*Bob O'Leary*), Sidney Blackmer (*General Phil Sheridan*), Berton Churchill (*Senator Colby*), June Storey (*Gretchen*), Paul Hurst (*Mitch*), Tyler Brooke (*Specialty singer*), J. Anthony Hughes (*Patrick O'Leary*), Gene Reynolds (*Dion O'Leary, as a boy*), Bobs Watson (*Bob O'Leary, as a boy*), Billy Watson (*Jack O'Leary, as a boy*), Madame Sultewan (*Hattie*), Spencer Charters (*Beavers*), Rondo Hatton (*Body guard [Rondo]*), Thelma Manning (*Carrie Donahue*), Ruth Gillette (*Miss Lou*), Eddie Collins (*Drunk*), Scotty Mattraw (*Beef king*), Joe Twerp (*Stuttering clerk*), Charles Lane (*Booking agent*), Clarence Hummel Wilson (*Lawyer*), Frank Dae (*Judge*), Harry Stubbs (*Fire commissioner*), Joe King (*Ship's captain*), Francis Ford (*Driver*), Robert Murphy, Wade Boteler (*Police officers*), Gustav von Seyffertitz, Russell Hicks (*Men in Jack's office*), [Bess Flowers (*Woman with Senator Colby*)], [Harrison Greene (*Man with Senator Colby*)], [Rice and Cady (*Dutch comedians*)], [Jack Cheatham], [Eleanor Prentiss], [Jane Ray], [Muriel Scheck], [Louise Seidel], [Hope Taylor], [June Terry], [Valerie Traxler], [Lurline Uller], [Marion Weldon], [Dorothy White], [Mary Louise Kopp], [Billie Lee], [Patricia Lee], [Patsy Lee], [Mary Lorraine], [Patty Parrish], [Patsy Perrin], [Julie Cabanne], [Harriette Haddon], [Norah Gale], [Edna Mae Jones], [Jean Joyce], [Adelaide Kaye], [Crystal Keate], [Jacqueline Kopp], [Kathryn Barnes], [Sue Barstead], [Doris Becker], [Patsy Bedell], [Barbara Booth], [Dale Dee], [Jeanette Bates], [John Roy].
Historical, **Disaster**, **Drama**, **with songs**. [*Print viewed*]. In 1854, Irish immigrant Patrick O'Leary, traveling by covered wagon with his wife and three young sons to Chicago, is killed when he races a train and the wagon crashes down an embankment. Before he dies he tells his sons Jack, Dion and Bob to build and grow with Chicago, which he predicts will one day be the hub of the country. In the city, Patrick's wife Molly opens a successful French laundry. In 1867, her cow Daisy kicks Bob into an embrace with Gretchen, a servant girl, and they soon marry. Dion, a gambler, falls in love at first sight with Belle Fawcett, the newly arrived singer at The Hub, a saloon in the disreputable part of town known as The Patch. After several unsuccessful attempts to approach Belle, Dion appears in her dressing room, wrestles her to the ground, kisses her ear and succeeds in interesting her in his proposition that together they open up a saloon to rival The Hub. Their saloon, The Senate, proves to be very popular, and Gil Warren, the owner of The Hub, offers to close down and give Dion $10,000 for his support in his campaign for mayor. Dion, however, secretly organizes a committee to call upon his brother Jack, an idealistic lawyer, to run as a reform candidate. Jack accepts but warns Dion that if he wins, he will wipe out corruption in The Patch. To prevent Warren from winning, Dion arranges a brawl on election day so that Warren's repeat voters are locked up, and he forces Warren's unscrupulous poll watchers and judges to leave town for the day. Jack is elected, and he immediately declares war on The Patch, planning to have the area, which he calls a fire trap, condemned and torn down so that it can be rebuilt with steel. When Jack convinces Belle, who is now engaged to Dion despite Molly's spirited objections to her occupation, to help, Dion angrily reveals that he got Jack elected and tells Belle that if she is with the reformers, she will not be seeing much of him. The day before Belle is to testify against Dion, he proposes to her and convinces Jack to marry them that night. After the wedding, he states that now Belle cannot testify against her husband, whereupon Jack socks Dion and promises to ruin him. Meanwhile, at the O'Leary house, when Molly learns from Gretchen about the fight, she leaves Daisy nursing a heifer. Daisy responds to a sharp tug from the heifer by kicking over a lantern, and a fire starts in the barn. Because it has not rained in three months, the fire spreads quickly throughout the town, while rumors, fed by Warren, spread throughout The Patch that Jack has started the fire to burn The Patch out. After Bob tells Dion that Daisy caused the fire, they try to warn Jack of the mob that has formed to get him, and although Jack hits Dion upon seeing him, the three brothers are soon united in trying to keep the fire on the South side of the river away from the gas works. As Jack, defying the mob, lights a fuse to dynamite a building in The Patch and make a fire break,

Warren's bodyguard shoots him. The subsequent explosion causes the cattle to break out of the stockyards, and as they race through the streets, Warren is trampled. On the South shore of the river, among countless homeless people, Dion finds Belle, who has saved Molly. When Belle turns away from him, Molly berates her until Belle hugs him. As they watch the fire in the distance, Dion and Molly affirm that the dream of Patrick and Jack to see a great city built will be fulfilled.

Brothers. Chicago (IL)–History. Family life. Fires. Gamblers. Irish Americans. Reformers. Romance. Saloons. Singers. Cattle. Covered wagons. Death by animals. Elections. Explosions. Homelessness. Immigrants. Laundries. Marriage. Mayors. Mobs. Political corruption. Proposals (Marital). Rumors. Servants. Shootings. Stockyards. Weddings.

Note: After the opening credits, a title card reads: "We acknowledge with appreciation the assistance of the Chicago Historical Society in preparation of the historical background for this production." According to a *LAT* article, following the great success of M-G-M's *San Francisco* (see *AFI Catalog of Feature Films, 1931-40*; F3.3891), which featured a long sequence of earthquake and fire scenes, Darryl Zanuck, Twentieth Century-Fox's vice-president in charge of production, decided to make a film based on another historical disaster, the Chicago fire. According to a *NYT* article on the film, the Chicago fire, which occurred on 9 Oct 1871, burned four square miles of buildings, destroyed $2,000,000 worth of property and killed at least 300 people. According to information in the Twentieth Century-Fox Records of the Legal Department at the UCLA Theater Arts Library, soon after the fire started, Chicago businessman Charles H. Coles investigated the barn where the fire was rumored to have originated and found no evidence of an overturned lamp. Concerning the origination of the film's story, according to the legal records, Warner Bros. had registered two titles with the MPPDA title registration committee that pertained to the Chicago fire ahead of Twentieth Century-Fox; after Warners dropped *The Chicago Fire* in Oct 1936, Twentieth Century-Fox, which had that title on the reserve list, assigned two writers, Niven Busch and Richard Collins, to write separate story outlines under that title. According to *Var* and *LAT* news items, Collins' work was based on the novel *Barriers Burned Away* by E. P. Roe (New York, 1872). Although Gene Fowler sat in on some conferences with Busch and did some research work, he did no actual writing for this film. After Busch completed his original story, he worked with Sonya Levien on a treatment; Levien and Lamar Trotti then wrote a screenplay based on Levien and Busch's treatment. As the legal records state that nothing in the film was based on Roe's novel, it does not appear that any of Collins' work was used in the final film. Although Twentieth Century-Fox publicity stated that Busch's story was originally entitled "We the O'Learys," a communication in the legal records notes, "there never was a story 'We, the O'Learys' by Niven Busch nor by anybody else. The idea that Niven Busch had written an original story 'We the O'Learys' was developed by someone in our organization after the story and screenplay had been completely written, and this person or persons believed that it would be a clever idea to utilize the name of 'The O'Learys' and give Busch's original story a more catch title than 'The Chicago Fire.' "

According to information in the MPAA/PCA Collection at the AMPAS Library, when the final script was submitted to the PCA for approval, PCA Director Joseph Breen wrote a five page letter in which he detailed many "offensive or questionable details" that led him declare that the material "is not acceptable under the provisions of the Production Code." The major offending details that Breen listed concerned the depiction of prostitutes and "Miss Lou" as a madame and the description of "Belle's" apartment to suggest that she is a prostitute and that she uses her home "to ply her trade." Zanuck agreed to make Breen's changes and stated that it was never the studio's intention to characterize "Belle" as a prostitute.

The film was known as *Chicago* during pre-production, and in Jun 1937, Twentieth Century-Fox was granted the right by the MPPDA to use the title *In Old Chicago* over the protest of Columbia, which earlier had bought the rights to "Chicago" from Pathé, according to a *FD* news item. According to a *HR* news item dated 1 Jun 1937, M-G-M and Twentieth Century-Fox negotiated a swap to send Jean Harlow to Twentieth Century-Fox for the female lead in this film and Tyrone Power to M-G-M for *Madame X*. Harlow, however, died on 7 Jun 1937. According to *HR* news items, Janet Beecher tested for the role of "Mrs. O'Leary," and June Storey replaced Virginia Field, who was then able to play a more important role in *Ali Baba Goes to Town* (see *AFI Catalog of Feature Films, 1931-40*, F3.0056). According to a *HR* news item dated 13 Jul 1937, Jack Haskell resigned as dance director, and he was replaced by his assistants, Geneva Sawyer and Nick Castle. The news item noted that Sawyer was the only woman dance director in the studios. According to *HR*, Andy Devine and Alice Brady were borrowed from Universal, and the legal files note that location shooting was done at Oakdale, CA and near Yuma, AZ. Although the song, "Strolling with My Lady Love," by Lew Pollack and Sidney D. Mitchell, was submitted to the PCA for approval in connection with this film, it was not used in the final film.

NYT stated that this had the largest budget of any Twentieth Century-Fox film, and a review noted that the cost was about $2,000,000. The fire sequence, which, according to *Time*, at twenty-five minutes, was longer than the hurricane sequence in *Hurricane* (see *AFI Catalog of Feature Films, 1931-40*; F3.2034), cost $500,000, according to a press release. *NYT* notes that the wardrobe budget was $80,000. According to publicity for the film, Western Costume Co. could not supply all the costumes necessary, so the studio had to go to all the other costume companies in Los Angeles and even to some in New York. According to information in the legal files, a lantern manufacturer wrote

to the studio stating that the best authorities claim that it was a lamp, not a lantern, that the cow tipped over to start the Chicago fire and that a lantern would extinguish itself when tipped over. Herbert Levy, Walter Strohm and two assistants tested the claim, however, and found it false.

According to *Var*, the film was originally exhibited in two parts with an intermission after about eighty minutes, taking the story to the eve of the fire. According to information in the legal records, Philip Wylie wrote a serialization of the screenplay, which was published in newspapers including *DN* (L.A.) (3 Jan–25 Jan 1938), and a condensation of the screenplay was published in *The Ten Best Pictures of the Year* by Frank Vreeland. In addition, the first twenty-five sequences were published in a textbook for use in schools and colleges by The Macmillan Co. The film received Academy Awards for Supporting Actor (Alice Brady) and Assistant Director (Robert Webb), and nominations for Best Picture, Writing—Original Story (Niven Busch), Music—Best Score (Louis Stevens) and Sound Recording. The film ranked sixth on the *FD* poll of critics of America.

According to modern sources, Zanuck originally wanted Clark Gable for the male lead. Modern sources also state that although H. Bruce Humberstone, who received screen credit as the director of special effects scenes, took out ads in trade journals claiming that he directed the fire sequence, in reality, he directed the scenes of going to the fire, but not the actual fire scenes. Modern sources list the following additional cast members: Harry Hayden (*Johnson, Jack's secretary*), Vera Lewis (*Witness*), Minerva Urecal (*Frantic mother*) and Ed Brady (*Wagon driver*). Radio versions were broadcast on the Philip Morris Program (10 Dec 1943) and the Lux Radio Theatre (9 Oct 1944), and in 1957, Twentieth Century-Fox Television Productions produced "City in Flames," based on the same story and screenplay, as an episode for *The 20th Century-Fox Hour*; the program was produced by Sam Marx, directed by Albert S. Rogell and starred Anne Jeffreys, Jeff Morrow and Kevin McCarthy.

Box 8 Jan 1938. *DV* 31 Dec 1937, p. 3. *FD* 26 May 1937, p. 16. *FD* 26 Jun 1937, p. 1. *FD* 4 Jan 1938, p. 6. *HR* 14 May 1937, p. 3. *HR* 1 Jun 1937, p. 2. *HR* 16 Jun 1937, p. 1. *HR* 21 Jun 1937, p. 1. *HR* 28 Jun 1937, p. 23. *HR* 13 Jul 1937, p. 7. *HR* 30 Aug 1937, p. 19. *HR* 31 Dec 1937, sect I, p. 3; sect II, pp. 20-21, p. 90. *HR* 14 Jan 1938, pp. 4-5. *HR* 18 Jan 1938, pp. 5-21. *LAEx* 8 Jul 1937. *LAT* 12 Oct 1936. *MPH* 4 Sep 1937, pp. 48-49. *MPH* 8 Jan 1938, p. 48. *NYT* 27 Jun 1937. *NYT* 10 Oct 1937. *NYT* 19 Dec 1937. *NYT* 7 Jan 1938, p. 15. *Time* 17 Jan 1938, pp. 44-45. *Var* 12 Oct 1936. *Var* 21 Nov 1936. *Var* 5 Jan 1938, p. 16.

IN OLD LOUISIANA see LAZY RIVER

IN OLD NEW MEXICO (Latino)

Monogram Pictures Corp. *Dist* Monogram Pictures Corp. 15 May 1945 [©Monogram Pictures Corp.; 26 Mar 1945; LP13267]. Sd; b&w. 62-63 min. PCA cert no. 10413.

Series: The Cisco Kid.

Prod Philip N. Krasne. *Assoc prod* Dick L'Estrange. *Dir* Phil Rosen. *Asst dir* Seymour Roth. *Orig scr* Betty Burbridge. *Dir of photog* Arthur Martinelli. *Film ed* Martin G. Cohn. *Set dec* Ted Driscoll. *Mus dir* David Chudnow. *Mus score* Albert Glasser. *Dances created and staged by* Carlyle. *Sd rec* Glen Glenn.

Song(s): "Pooka Pooka," music and lyrics by Hershey Martin and Mayris Chaney.

Source: Based on the character created by O. Henry.

Cast: DUNCAN RENALDO [(*The Cisco Kid, also known as Juan Carlos Francisco Antonio*)], Martin Garralaga [(*Pancho*)], Gwen Kenyon [(*Ellen Roth*)], Pedro de Cordoba [(*Father Angelo*)], Aurora Roche [(*Dolores*)], Lasses White [(*Sheriff Clem Petty*)], Norman Willis [(*Will Hastings*)], Edward Earle, Donna Dax [(*Belle*)], John Laurenz [(*Brady*)], Richard Gordon [(*Tom Wills, previously known as Doctor Wills*)], Frank Jacquet, James Farley, Car-Bert Dancers, [Kenneth Terrell (*Cliff*)], [Harry Depp (*Printer*)].

Western. [*Print viewed*]. While robbing the Gilda stagecoach, The Cisco Kid, along with his friend Pancho, meets Ellen Roth, a registered nurse. Cisco abducts Ellen, knowing that she has been falsely accused of murdering her wealthy patient and benefactress, Mrs. Prescott. With the posse out looking for them, Cisco and Pancho then go into Gilda, where Cisco forces Pancho to return their booty to the empty sheriff's office. Afterward, Cisco waits at the post office to discover the owner of box seventeen, an address to which Mrs. Prescott had sent many letters. After Will Hastings, a saloon owner, removes a letter from the postal box, Cisco steals it and takes it to Ellen, who has sought sanctuary at the local mission. Though she has no further understanding of the letter than he, Ellen tells Cisco that Mrs. Prescott was administered a lethal overdose of sleeping pills by a "Dr. Wills," who claimed to be the new assistant of Mrs. Prescott's regular physician. As the letter has a reference to "Dolores," Cisco and Pancho go back into town to hunt for Dolores, who turns out to be a singer in Hastings' saloon. Dolores tells Cisco that Hastings recently returned to Gilda after a six-month absence and told her that he was about to come into "a great deal of money." After a brief fight with Hastings, Cisco is forced to make a hasty retreat from the saloon

when Sheriff Clem Petty arrives. Later, while the sheriff and his posse chase after Pancho, Cisco returns to town and confronts Hastings, who, he has learned, was Prescott's estranged nephew and next of kin. Cisco offers to turn Ellen over to Hastings for $10,000, and the crooked saloon owner quickly agrees to the bandit's terms, knowing that, upon Ellen's arrest and conviction, he will inherit his aunt's estate. After Ellen's arrest, Cisco and Pancho force the local printer to run a fake newspaper story, stating that Ellen has been exonerated and Tom Wills, alias "Dr. Wills," has been arrested for Mrs. Prescott's murder by the Denver police. Assuming that Ellen's testimony is the only evidence against Wills, Cisco offers to kill the nurse for Hastings. While Cisco fakes Ellen's murder, Wills arrives in town. The phony physician soon falls into Cisco's trap, and is taken unconscious to the mission. In the meantime, Hastings discovers Cisco's deception, but he, too, is captured by the bandit. When Wills awakens, he finds himself under the care of Ellen and confesses all, as Cisco, Pancho, Hastings and Sheriff Petty eavesdrop. Hastings and Wills are arrested for the murder of Mrs. Prescott, and Ellen offers her gratitude to Cisco. *Abduction. Bandits. False accusations. Mexicans. Murder. Nurses. Chases. Confession (Law). Dance hall girls. Escapes. Fights. Impersonation and imposture. Letters. Missions. New Mexico. Physicians. Poisoning. Posses. Post offices. Priests. Printers. Saloon keepers. Sheriffs. Singers. Stagecoach robberies. Traps.*

Note: The viewed print was a televison version of the theatrical film, which was entitled "Duncan Renaldo in *Old New Mexico*." The soundtrack of this print was re-dubbed and the characters of "The Cisco Kid" and "Pancho" are referred to as "Chico" and "Pablo." The film was also reviewed by contemporary sources under the title *The Cisco Kid in Old New Mexico*. Modern sources include Bud Osborne and Artie Ortego in the cast. For additional information about the series, consult the Series Index and see the entry above for *The Cisco Kid*.

DV 1 Aug 1945, p. 3. *HR* 1 Aug 1945, p. 3. *MPHPD* 10 Mar 1945, p. 2354. *MPHPD* 14 Jul 1945, p. 2542. *Var* 8 Aug 1945, p. 22.

IN OLD OKLAHOMA (Native Americans)

Republic Pictures Corp. *Dist* Republic Pictures Corp. 6 Dec **1943**; Prod: late Jul—early Sep 1943 [©Republic Pictures Corp.; 13 Oct 1943; LP12329]. Sd (RCA Sound System); b&w. 11 reels, 9,204 ft. 102 min. Passed by the National Board of Review. PCA cert no. 9542.

Assoc prod Robert North. *Dir* Albert S. Rogell. [*2d unit dir* Joe Kane]. [*Asst dir* Phil Ford]. *Orig story and adpt* Thomson Burtis. *Scr* Ethel Hill and Eleanore Griffin. *Photog* Jack Marta. *Spec eff* Howard Lydecker, Jr. *Art dir* Russell Kimball. *Film ed* Ernest Nims. *Set dec* Otto Siegel. *Cost* Walter Plunkett. *Mus score* Walter Scharf. *Sd* Dick Tyler and Howard Wilson. [*Loc mgr* Johnny Bourke].

Cast: JOHN WAYNE [(*Daniel Somers*)], MARTHA SCOTT [(*Catherine Allen*)], Albert Dekker [(*James E. Gardner*)], George "Gabby" Hayes [(*Desprit Dean*)], Marjorie Rambeau [(*Bessie Baxter*)], Dale Evans [("*Cuddles*" *Walker*)], Grant Withers [(*Richardson*)], Sidney Blackmer [(*Teddy Roosevelt*)], Paul Fix [(*The Cherokee Kid*)], Cecil Cunningham [(*Mrs. Ames*)], Irving Bacon [(*Ben, telegraph operator*)], Byron Foulger [(*Wilkins*)], Anne O'Neal [(*Mrs. Peabody*)], Richard Graham [(*Walter*)], [Pearl Early (*Mrs. Simpson*)], [Charles Arnt (*Conductor*)], [Bill Borzage, Jack Kenney, Lane Chandler, Mike Lally (*Oilers, Dan's men*)], [Bud Geary (*Oiler, Jim's man*)], [Dick Rich (*Brady, oiler*)], [Charles Jordan (*Crawford, oiler*)], [Dick Botiller (*Blake, oiler*)], [Eddie Chandler (*McCann, oiler*)], [Wade Crosby (*Corrigan, oiler*)], [Linda Brent, Rhonda Fleming, Wesley Brent, Mary Croft (*Dance hall girls*)], [Will Wright (*Doctor*)], [Edward Gargan (*Headwaiter*)], [Harry Woods (*Blackie Barton*)], [William Davidson (*Master of ceremonies*)], [Al Hill, Sr. (*Waiter*)], [Harry Shannon (*Charlie Witherspoon*)], [Myrna Dell (*Blonde*)], [Kenne Duncan (*Indignant businessman*)], [Jack Kirk (*Rowdy worker*)], [LeRoy Mason (*Beecher*)], [Larry Stewart (*Vendor*)], [Tom London (*Farmer*)], [June Terry Pickerell (*Farmer's wife*)], [Jack Raymond, Charles "Slim" Whitaker (*Oil workers*)], [Roy Barcroft (*Oil worker on train*)], [John Dilson (*Carlson, clerk*)], [Charles Bates (*Little Sun*)], [Gus Glassmire (*Secretary of the Interior*)], [Robert Warwick (*Chief Big Tree*)], [Emmett Vogan (*Secretary to Theodore Roosevelt*)], [Edmund Cobb (*Clerk*)], [Hooper Atchley (*Employee*)], [Stanley Andrews (*Mason, Indian agent*)], [Rebel Randall (*Woman on train*)], [Arthur Loft (*Fenton*)].

Western. [*Print viewed*]. In 1906, Easterner Catherine Allen scandalizes her community by writing a racy romance novel and deciding to quit her job as a schoolteacher to seek adventure in the West. As Catherine boards the train, she meets oilman James E.

Gardner, who immediately takes a liking to her. Believing her to be as experienced as her romantic heroine, Jim makes advances toward her, which Catherine indignantly spurns. The train stops when cowboy Daniel Somers flags it down, and Catherine gets him to sit near her to discourage Jim. Catherine intends to go to Kansas City, although Jim asks her to go to Sepulpa, Oklahoma, where he has discovered oil. Her choice is made for her when she is put off the train for being in Jim's private car. Dan also gets off the train and is greeted by his old pal, stagecoach driver Desprit Dean. Desprit warns Dan that their hometown of Sepulpa has changed drastically during Dan's absence, as Jim's oil discoveries have caused much dissension. Catherine also boards Desprit's coach, and Jim is picked up when his car breaks down. They then stop at one of Jim's oil rigs, and Catherine is impressed when the well comes in. Less happy is farmer Wilkins, who used to own the land on which the rig stands. Although Jim did buy the land, Wilkins feels that he has been cheated, and Dan is forced to stop them from fighting. Later, Jim asks Desprit to help him negotiate with Chief Big Tree, as the well's main oil pool lays underneath Indian lands. Dan also attends the next day's meeting, and when Jim offers Big Tree 12.5 percent of his profits, Dan advises the chief to refuse the deal. Jim is infuriated by Dan's interference, but the small ranchers and Indians oppose the greedy Jim and support Dan, asking him to go to Washington, D.C. to ask President Theodore Roosevelt for the oil rights. Dan at first refuses, as he is not an ambitious man, but when it becomes clear that Catherine is attracted to Jim's wealth and power, he decides to beat Jim at his own game in order to compete for her. Catherine does flirt with Dan, but hotel owner Bessie Baxter, Dan's friend, realizes that she is doing it only to make Jim jealous enough to propose. The factions travel to Washington, where Dan, who fought with Roosevelt in Cuba, reveals his plan to give the Indians a fifty percent share of the profits. Roosevelt gives Dan four months in which to deliver ten thousand gallons of oil to a Tulsa refinery, and if he does not make the deadline, the oil rights will go to Jim. Dan returns home and gets to work, but as his well nears completion, Jim's half-breed servant, The Cherokee Kid, deliberately sets off an explosion that kills a worker and destroys the rig. Catherine, who has fallen in love with Dan, pleads with Jim to leave Dan alone, but when Dan sees them together, he assumes the worst and breaks off his relationship with Catherine. Later, Dan and his men steal Jim's portable rig and bring in the well, but because Jim has bought the only pipeline to Tulsa, they must build giant barrels and race to the refinery to meet the deadline. The next day, Bessie brokers a reconciliation between Dan and Catherine during the massive campaign to get the oil to the refinery. Despite more sabotage by Jim and his men, Dan gets the oil to Tulsa on time, and after besting Jim in a fistfight, Dan embraces Catherine and begins plans to build their house. *Ambition. Indians of North America. Land rights. Oilmen. Romantic rivalry. Sabotage. Boom towns. Contracts. Easterners. Explosions. Fistfights. Hotels. Indians of North America–Mixed blood. Kansas. Loyalty. Oklahoma. Theodore Roosevelt. Schoolteachers. Trains.*

Note: The working title of this film was *War of the Wildcats*, which was also the title of the viewed print. According to *DV* and *HR* news items, the New York Theatre Guild sued Republic over the use of the title *In Old Oklahoma*, arguing that it was "unfair competition" for their musical *Oklahoma*. The case was settled when Republic agreed to withdraw the film from distribution in the United States by 1 Jan 1945, and not re-release it under the same title. *HR* also noted that Leonard Fields was originally scheduled to produce the picture and that Albert Dekker was borrowed from Paramount. News items about location shooting conflict, but an 18 Jun 1941 *HR* item stated that scenes would be shot in Cedar City, Kanab and Virginia Springs, UT and the Kaibob Forest of Arizona. Other possible locations mentioned in earlier *HR* items were Modesto, Bakersfield and Taft, CA. Although a 3 Jun 1941 *HR* item stated that real-life "early-day oil field characters" Tom Slick, Jake Hammond and J. B. Joyner would be portrayed in the film, they are not mentioned in the finished picture. Modern sources include the following actors in the cast: George Chandler, Curley Dresden, Yakima Canutt, Shirley Jean Rickert, Linda Scott, Jess Cavan, Pat Hogan, Charles Agnew, Fred Graham, Oril Taller, Juanita Colteaux, Bonnie Jean Harley, and Bob Reeves. A *Lux Radio Theatre* version of the story was broadcast on 13 Mar 1944 and starred Roy Rogers, Martha Scott and Albert Dekker.

Box 30 Oct 1943. *DV* 20 Oct 1943, p. 3, 6. *DV* 24 Dec 1943, p. 2. *FD* 25 Oct 1943, p. 12. *HR* 22 Dec 1941, p. 1. *HR* 22 Dec 1942, p. 2. *HR* 26 Feb 1943, p. 5. *HR* 24 Mar 1943, p. 10. *HR* 29 Mar 1943, p. 9. *HR* 1 Jun 1943, p. 3. *HR* 3 Jun 1943, p. 2. *HR* 18 Jun 1943, p. 4. *HR* 23 Jul 1943, p. 9. *HR* 12 Aug 1943, p. 2. *HR* 27 Aug 1943, p. 23. *HR* 30 Aug 1943, p. 6. *HR* 20 Oct 1943, p. 3, 6. *HR* 25 Oct 1943, p. 10. *HR* 26 Oct 1943, p. 2. *HR* 10 Nov 1943, p. 1. *HR* 24 Dec 1943, p. 9. *MPH* 23 Oct 1943. *MPHPD* 23 Oct 1943, p. 1593. *MPHPD* 11 Dec 1943, p. 1655. *NYT* 6 Dec 1943, p. 21. *Var* 27 Oct 1943, p. 10.

IN THE CARQUINEZ WOODS *see* **THE HALF-BREED** (1916)

IN THE CARQUINEZ WOODS *see* **TONGUES OF FLAME** (1918)

IN THE DAYS OF THE HEAD HUNTERS *see* **IN THE LAND OF THE HEAD HUNTERS**

IN THE DAYS OF THE MISSIONS *see* **A YOKE OF GOLD**

IN THE DAYS OF THE THUNDERING HERD (Native Americans)
Selig Polyscope Co.; Special Features Dept. *Dist* General Film Co. 30 Nov **1914** [©Selig Polyscope Co.; 12 Nov 1914; LP3756]. Si; b&w. 5 reels.
Dir Colin Campbell. *Story* Gilson Willets.
Cast: Tom Mix (*Tom Mingle*), Bessie Eyton (*Sally Madison*), Wheeler Oakman (*Chief Swift Wing*), Red Wing (*Starlight*).
Western. In 1849, Tom Mingle, a pony express rider, saves his sweetheart, Sally Madison, from a buffalo stampede. Later, when Sally's brother refuses to accompany her through Indian territory to the California gold fields to visit her ailing mother, Tom takes his place. The townspeople, hoping to strike-it-rich, form a wagon train and appoint Tom wagonmaster. When the train is attacked by Indians, only Sally and Tom survive. They are taken as prisoners to the Indians' village where Chief Swift Wind falls in love with Sally, and Starlight, Swift Wind's sister, becomes infatuated with Tom. Sally and Tom are able to escape to a buffalo hunter's encampment after which Sally slips away and summons help. Finally, in California, Sally is reunited with her parents and promises to marry Tom. *California. Gold rushes. Indians of North America. Massacres. Wagon trains. Bison, American. Engagements. Escapes. Hunters. Rescues. Reunions. Stampedes.*
Note: Some of the film was shot on location at the ranch of Pawnee Bill at Pawnee, OK. This film was re-issued in Aug 1915 under the title *The Thundering Herd*.
Motog 28 Nov 1914, p. 732. *Motog* 5 Dec 1914, p. 794. *MPN* 28 Nov 1914, p. 68. *MPW* 12 Dec 1914, p. 1506.

IN THE DEPTHS OF OUR HEARTS (African Americans)
Royal Gardens Film Co. of Chicago. Nov—Dec **1920**. Si; b&w. 7 reels, 7,000 ft.
Cast: Herman DeLavalade, Augusta Williams, Irene Conn, Virgil Williams, Charles Allen.
African American, Drama. [According to contemporary ads, the film's subject is "mother against son." Modern sources describe the plot as follows: The mother of a light-skinned black family raises her son and daughter to avoid the company of dark-skinned blacks. The son, who has a dark-skinned sweetheart, rebels, and his mother sends him to his uncle's Wisconsin farm, where he is mistreated. The boy flees to the city, where he prospers. On a visit to his home town, he meets his former sweetheart, who is a waitress in a restaurant. The two embrace upon meeting, and the restaurant owner, misinterpreting the gesture, fires the girl. Meanwhile, the boy's mother's health has failed, and his sister has been made unhappy by her love for the restaurant owner. The boy manages to get his sweetheart's job back and finally persuades his mother of the error of her ways.]. *African Americans. Employment. Mothers and sons. Racism. Farms. Mothers and daughters. Restaurants. Uncles. Waitresses. Wisconsin.*
Note: Scenes from this black independent production were shot on a Wisconsin farm. According to an ad, Virgil Williams, who appears in the film, was also the production company's president.
ChiDef 6 Nov 1920, p. 7. *ChiDef* 8 Jan 1921, p. 4.

IN THE LAND OF THE HEAD HUNTERS (Native Americans)
Seattle Film Co. *Dist* World Film Corp. 7 Dec **1914** [©Edward Sheriff Curtis; 7 Dec 1914; LU3709]. Si; b&w. 4 reels.
Dir Edward S. Curtis. *Scen* Edward S. Curtis.
Documentary, Drama. In Northern British Columbia and Southern Alaska, Motana, the son of Chief Kenada, competes with the sorcerer for the love of Naida. Waket, Naida's father, fearing the power of the sorcerer and his head-hunting warrior brother Yaklus, promises his daughter to the magician. In anger, Motana, Kenada, and their clan slay the sorcerer. Motana and Naida are married at a magnificent celebration. Seeking revenge, Yaklus slays travelers, clam diggers, fishermen, and Kenada. He also wounds Motana and abducts Naida. Restored to health by the medicine man, Motana rescues his wife. Yaklus and his party are drowned when their canoe overturns as they pursue Motana and Naida through a treacherous gorge. *Abduction. Headhunters. Indians of North America. Revenge. Sorcerers.*

Tribal life. Alaska. British Columbia (Canada). Canoes and canoeing. Chases. Drowning. Rescues. Weddings.
Note: According to contemporary news items about the film, Curtis' research was conducted under the patronage of the late financier J. Pierpont Morgan. The film cost $75,000 to produce. This film was reviewed in *Motog* on 2 Jan 1915 at six reels under the title *In the Days of the Head Hunters*. The scenario of the film was published as a short book in 1915. Modern sources list Edmund August Schwinke as the cameraman.
Motog 14 Nov 1914, p. 658. *Motog* 2 Jan 1915, p. 42. *Motog* 30 Jan 1915, p. 188. *MPW* 19 Dec 1914, p. 1685. *MPW* 26 Dec 1914, p. 1904.

IN THE LAND OF THE NAVAJO (Native Americans, Navajo)
Dist E. P. Hunt, Stanford University. **1941**. Si; col. 16mm. 90 min.
Educational/Cultural. [*Not viewed*]. "Natural color film of most remote and colorful parts of Navajo Indian reservation; home-life including all steps in making Navajo rugs, making bread, wedding games and contests. Navajo healing ceremony with rare sand painting pictures, story of the desert water hole, the trading done by the Navajos, their ceremonies. Without exception they are the best pictures covering the true life of the Southwest and the Southwestern scenery that I have ever seen. Your pictures are not only fascinating but are extremely educational."—Frank A. Kittredge. *Indians of North America–Reservations. Navajo Indians. Rites and ceremonies.* Contests. Healers. Paintings. Rugs. Traders. Weddings.
Note: This film was listed in an educational film catalog, which stated that revised versions were available in 1950 and 1952.

IN THE LAND OF THE SETTING SUN; OR, MARTYRS OF YESTERDAY (Native Americans, Cayuse)
Multnomah Film Corp.? **1919**? [©Raymond Wells and Multnomah Film Corp.; 11 Aug 1919; LU14047]. Si; b&w. Length undetermined.
Dir Raymond Wells. *Story* Raymond Wells.
Historical, Drama. In 1831, four Indians from Oregon set out to find the white race and bring back the "White Man's Book of Heaven." They are entertained in St. Louis by General Clark, of the Lewis and Clark expedition. After they return with gifts, but without their sought-after Bible, Dr. Marcus Whitman of New York learns about their visit and travels across the continent to establish a mission on the Walla Walla River, where he teaches Christianity, agriculture, reading and writing. Although the local war chief is interested in Christianity, Whitman's efforts at conversion are undermined by Joe Lewis, a Canadian half-breed, who says that Whitman and the other emigrants want to take the Indians' lands. In 1847, an emigrant train brings a measles epidemic. When Lewis convinces the Indians that Whitman is deliberately killing them with his medicine, they massacre Whitman and the other mission occupants, although the war chief stops Lewis' murder of the children. The resulting Cayuse Wars last for several years. After the war chief and three others surrender and are hanged, peace and prosperity are established. *Bible. Canadians. Cayuse Indians. Indians of North America. Indians of North America–Mixed blood. Massacres. Missionaries. Missions. Oregon. Tribal chiefs. Marcus Whitman. Christianity. George Rogers Clark. Epidemics. Executions. Gifts. Measles. Medicine. Religious conversion. St. Louis (MO). Walla Walla River (WA).*
Note: The working title of this film was *Martyrs of Yesterday*. A synopsis of the film and 47 still photographs were deposited with the Copyright Office when the film was copyrighted. Raymond Wells is listed in this material as the author. No other information has been located concerning this film. Raymond Wells directed films for various companies and organized the Historical Film Corp. of America to produce a series of films depicting stories of the Bible.

IN THE MEXICAN QUARTER *see* **BORDER CAFE**

IN THE RED *see* **DIPLOMANIACS**

IN THIS OUR LIFE (African Americans)
Warner Bros. Pictures, Inc.; A Warner Bros.—First National Picture. *Dist* Warner Bros. Pictures, Inc. 16 May **1942**; New York opening: 8 May 1942; Prod: late Oct—mid-Dec 1941 [©Warner Bros. Pictures, Inc.; 16 May 1942; LP11295]. Sd (RCA Sound System); b&w. 8,703 ft. 95 or 97-98 min. PCA cert no. 7856.
Exec prod Hal B. Wallis. *Assoc prod* David Lewis. *Dir* John Huston. *Dial dir* Edward Blatt. [*Asst dir* Jack Sullivan]. *Scr* Howard Koch. *Dir of photog* Ernie Haller. *Spec eff* Byron Haskin and Robert Burns. *Art dir* Robert Haas. *Film ed* William Holmes. *Gowns* Orry-Kelly. *Orch arr* Hugo Friedhofer. *Mus dir* Leo F. Forbstein. *Mus* Max Steiner. *Sd* Robert B. Lee. *Makeup artist* Perc Westmore.

Source: Based on the novel *In This Our Life* by Ellen Glasgow (New York, 1941).

Cast: BETTE DAVIS (*Stanley Timberlake*), OLIVIA DE HAVILLAND (*Roy Timberlake*), GEORGE BRENT (*Craig Fleming*), DENNIS MORGAN ([*Dr.*] *Peter Kingsmill*), Charles Coburn (*William Fitzroy*), Frank Craven (*Asa Timberlake*), Billie Burke (*Lavinia Timberlake*), Hattie McDaniel (*Minerva Clay*), Lee Patrick (*Betty Wilmoth*), Mary Servoss (*Charlotte Fitzroy*), Ernest Anderson (*Parry Clay*), William B. Davidson (*Jim Purdy*), Edward Fielding (*Dr. Buchanan*), John Hamilton (*Inspector*), William Forrest (*Forest ranger*), [Walter Huston (*Bartender*)], [Elliott Sullivan, Eddie Acuff, Alan Bridge, Walter Baldwin, Herbert Heywood (*Workers*)], [George Reed (*Butler*)], [Dudley Dickerson (*Waiter*)], [Walter Brooke (*Cab driver*)], [Ruth Ford (*Young mother*)], [Billy Wayne (*Customer*)], [Ira Buck Woods, Sam McDaniel, Billy Mitchell, Napoleon Simpson, Sunshine Sammy Morrison, Jester Harrison, Freddie Jackson (*Black men*)], [Fred Kelsey (*Guard*)], [Frank Mayo, Eddy Chandler (*Officers*)], [Lee Phelps (*Policeman*)], [Reid Kilpatrick (*Announcer*)], [Pat McVeigh], [Jack Mower].

Melodrama. [*Print viewed*]. Asa Timberlake has lost his money to William Fitzroy, his former partner in the tobacco business. His wife Lavinia, William's sister, and he have two daughters: Roy, who is married to Dr. Peter Kingsmill, and Stanley, engaged to be married to lawyer Craig Fleming. The selfish Stanley is the favorite of her uncle William, who showers her with expensive presents. The night before her wedding, Stanley runs off with Roy's husband. Roy wastes no time mourning, but continues with her decorating business and divorces Peter, leaving him free to marry Stanley. Sometime later, Roy encounters Craig in the park, and they begin to seeing each other. Craig hires Parry Clay, the son of the Timberlake maid, Minerva, to work in his law office to help Parry put himself through law school. William offers to make Craig his attorney if he will drop certain poorer clients, and when Craig refuses, Roy agrees to marry him as soon as possible. Meanwhile, in Baltimore, Stanley's marriage deteriorates: she spends too much money and Peter drinks too much. Finally, in desperation, Peter commits suicide, and Roy travels to Baltimore to bring her sister home. As soon as Stanley recovers, she resolves to win back Craig's affections. She visits Craig's office under the pretext of wanting information about Peter's insurance policy. Learning that Stanley wants money to leave town, Craig offers to arrange a loan. Stanley then asks him to dinner at a local tavern. When he does not appear, Stanley gets very drunk. Driving too fast, she hits and kills a child. Stanley's car is recognized, but when the police question her, she claims that Parry was driving her car that night and that he must have committed the crime. Roy is suspicious, however, and learns from Minerva that Parry was at home on the evening in question. Roy is convinced that Stanley is lying, but Craig is still unsure. He tricks Stanley into facing Parry, who is now in jail, but she still refuses to tell the truth. Craig reminds her that she had invited him to the tavern and when he tells her that he questioned the bartender, Stanley breaks down. Craig insists on taking her to the district attorney, but Stanley, under the guise of changing her clothes sneaks out. She drives to William's and begs him to save her from jail. William, who has just learned that he has only six months to live, is too stunned by the news to pay attention to his niece, however. The police, who have been summoned by Craig, arrive at the house and Stanley once again tries to escape. The police see her and chase the car. During the chase, Stanley crashes the car and dies. *Lawyers. Liars. Sisters. African Americans. Automobile accidents. Automobile chases. False accusations. Infidelity. Interior decorators. Lawyers. Manslaughter. Physicians. Suicide. Uncles.*

Note: Ellen Glasgow's novel won the 1942 Pulitzer Prize for Liberature. According to a *LAEx* news item dated 27 Feb 1941, the studio paid $40,000 for rights to the novel. A 27 Feb 1941 *HR* news item adds that the film was to star Olivia De Havilland and Errol Flynn. Warner Bros. was named to the Honor Roll of Race Relations of 1942 for making this film because of its dignified portrayal of an African-American, although, according to a 8 Sep 1942 *HR* news item, Warner Bros. cut scenes which treated Ernest Anderson's character in a "friendly fashion" in order to avoid offending viewers in the South. In 1943, when the film was examined by the Office of Censorship in Washington, D.C. prior to general export, it was disapproved because "only by the effort of a conscientious white man in whose law office a Negro boy is studying law is the young man saved from a charge of murder...recklessly made by a white woman....[who] claimed that the Negro and not she, was driving the car at the time of the accident and so strong is the race feeling in this Virginia community that the young Negro was practically condemned in advance. It is made abundantly clear that a Negro's testimony in court is almost certain to be disregarded if in conflict with the testimony of a white person." Actor Walter Huston, director John Huston's father, appears briefly in the film in a cameo role as a bartender. Modern sources erroneously note that Humphrey Bogart, Mary Astor, Sidney Greenstreet, Peter Lorre, Ward Bond, Barton MacLane and Elisha Cook, Jr. appear as uncredited bits in the bar scene in the tavern.

Box 11 Apr 1942. *DV* 7 Apr 1942, p. 3. *FD* 9 Apr 1942, p. 4. *HR* 27 Feb 1941, p. 1. *HR* 7 Apr 1942, p. 3. *HR* 5 May 1942, p. 1. *HR* 8 Sep 1942, p. 7. *HR* 18 Feb 1943, p. 6. *MPHPD* 11 Apr 1942, p. 597. *LAEx* 27 Feb 1941. *NYT* 9 May 1942, p. 10. *Var* 8 Apr 1942, p. 8.

LA INCORREGIBLE (Spanish language)

Films Paramount; controlled by Paramount Publix Corp. *Dist* Paramount Publix Corp. **1931**; Madrid, Spain opening: 17 Mar 1931; San Juan, Puerto Rico opening: 18 Jul 1931; Los Angeles opening: 31 Jul 1931; Prod: Dec 1930—Jan 1931 at Paramount studios in Joinville, France. Sd; b&w. 9-10 reels, 8,458 ft. 94 min. *Country of origin* France. Spanish language.

Dir Leo Mittler. *Scr* George Abbott. *Adpt and Spanish dial* José Luis Salado.

Source: Based on the novel *Manslaughter* by Alice Duer Miller (New York, 1921).

Cast: Enriqueta Serrano (*Evelyn*), Tony D'Algy (*Roy O'Bannon*), Gabriel Algara (*Mr. Albee*), Marita Angeles (*Elinor*), Ricardo Baroja (*Mason*), Carmen Muñoz (*Mary*), Francisco Gómez Ferrer (*Detective*).

Romance, Drama. [*Not viewed*]. [The following plot summary is based on the English-language version of this film, *Manslaughter*; character names refer to that version. For further information regarding the English-language version, please see the note below and the entry for *Manslaughter* in the *AFI Catalog of Feature Films, 1921-30*.] Lydia Thorne, a spoiled and selfish girl of wealth and position, meets Dan O'Bannon, a serious-minded district attorney, but their growing affection is disturbed by her thoughtlessness in speeding on the road and by a petty theft involving her maid, Evans. While being chased by a policeman for speeding, she causes the officer to be killed, and despite the efforts of an able defense lawyer, she is convicted of manslaughter and vows vengeance against O'Bannon. Prison discipline awakens her dormant kindness and generosity; meanwhile, O'Bannon resigns his position and leads an aimless, wild life, but eventually he manages to pull himself together. Released from prison, Lydia demands that O'Bannon's new employer discharge him. O'Bannon protests, claiming that he still loves her; and though he sends him away, later she finds happiness in his arms. *Automobiles. Courtship. District attorneys. Lawyers. Manslaughter. Prisons. Socialites.*

Note: This film was shown under the title *La homicida* in Mexico City beginning 10 Nov 1931. This was the Spanish-language version of the 1930 Paramount film *Manslaughter*, which was directed by George Abbott and starred Claudette Colbert and Fredric March. Although the English-language version was made in the U.S., the Spanish version, along with French, German and Swedish versions, was produced at the Paramount studios in Joinville, France. No information has been located concerning any exhibition of the French, German or Swedish versions in the U.S. The French version, entitled *La 'réquisitoire*, was directed by Dimitri Buchowetzki and starred Marcelle Chantal and Fernand Fabre; the German version, entitled *Leichtsinnige Jugend*, was directed by Leo Mittler and starred Camilla Horn and Walter Rilla; the Swedish version, entitled *Lika inför lagen*, was directed by Gustaf Bergman and starred Lillebil Ibsen and Karin Swanström. Some sources include as cast members in the Spanish version Antonia Arévalo, Antonio Gentil, Alfonso Granada, Rafaela Lozano and Manuel Bernardos, but their participation in the film has not been confirmed.

INDIAN AGENT (Latino, Native Americans)

RKO Radio Pictures, Inc. *Dist* RKO Radio Pictures, Inc. 11 Dec **1948**; Prod: 10 May—late May 1948 [©RKO Radio Pictures, Inc.; 12 Nov 1948; LP2011]. Sd (RCA Sound System); b&w. 5,812 ft. 63-65 min. PCA cert no. 13184.

Prod Herman Schlom. *Dir* Lesley Selander. [*Asst dir* John Pommer]. *Orig scr* Norman Houston. *Dir of photog* J. Roy Hunt. [*Cam op* Eddie Pyle]. [*Stills* Ollie Sigurdson]. *Art dir* Albert S. D'Agostino and Feild Gray. *Film ed* Les Millbrook. *Set dec* Darrell Silvera and Jack Mills. *Mus* C. Bakaleinikoff. *Sd* John Tribby and Terry Kellum. [*Hair stylist* Hazel Rogers]. [*Script supv* Dan Ullman]. [*Grip* Tom Clement].

Cast: TIM HOLT [(*Dave Taylor*)], Noah Beery, Jr. [(*Chief Redfox*)], Richard Martin [(*Chito Rafferty*)], Nan Leslie [(*Ellen Wheeler*)], Harry Woods [(*Carter*)], Richard Powers [(*M. Hutchins*)], Claudia Drake [(*Turquoise*)], Robert Bray [(*Nichols*)], Lee White [(*Inky*)], Bud Osborne [(*Sheriff*)], Iron Eyes Cody [(*Wovoka*)], [Steve Savage (*Chick*)].

Western. [*Print viewed*]. As the Carter Freighting Company wagons are crossing the arid southwestern range, an Indian warrior is spotted in the rocks overhead. Concerned, Carter speeds the wagons to his warehouse near the town of Boulder. Later, at the local Indian reservation, federal agent M. Hutchins is accosted by Chief Redfox, who threatens an uprising if his starving people do not receive their government rations soon. Hutchins denies any knowledge of the supply wagons, but immediately questions Carter, his partner-in-crime, about the missing goods. The greedy Carter insists that the supplies are to be sold at a gold prospecting camp, where a higher profit can be made, and convinces the nervous Hutchins to cooperate in the scheme. Carter then pays off two of his unsuspecting workers, Dave Taylor and Chito Rafferty, who plan to use their wages to buy cattle for their newly acquired ranch. As Dave and Chito head home, however, they see a small group of Indians descend on a wagon and ride to the rescue. Driving the wagon are editor Ellen Wheeler and her printer, Inky, who are on their way to Boulder to start a newspaper. Chito and Dave escort the grateful pair to town, then return to their ranch, where they discover an abandoned Indian baby in their bed. While the cowboys do their best to care for the hungry baby girl, whom they name Patchy, her parents, Redfox and Turquoise, are confronted by Hutchins at the reservation. The Indians, however, refuse to reveal the whereabouts of their baby, whom the starving Turquoise abandoned in the hope that she would be fed. Worried that the missing baby will cause the scheme to be exposed, Hutchins and his assistant, Nichols, trail Turquoise and soon discover the infant at Dave and Chito's ranch. Although unaware of Carter's duplicity, Dave and Chito refuse to turn the baby over to Hutchins, who then goes for the sheriff. Anxious to learn more about the child, Dave and Chito head for Boulder with her, but along the way, Dave senses that they are being followed. While Chito continues to town with Patchy, Dave ambushes the mistrustful Redfox to accompany him to town, but before they get far, Carter, who knows Patchy is in town, shoots the Indian in the back. After Carter flees the scene, Hutchins arrives with the sheriff, and Dave is arrested for the crime. Once Redfox's condition has stabilized, Dave is bailed out of jail by Ellen and heads for the reservation. There, as the tribal warriors perform a menacing war dance, the wounded Redfox and Turquoise tell Dave about the missing supplies. Dave vows to deliver the goods immediately and rides to Carter's freighter company with Chito. When Hutchins and Nichols arrive at Carter's office, demanding cavalry protection, Dave has Chito create a diversion so that he can steal Carter's signed requisition papers as proof of the scheme. The cowboys then escape with the papers and ride to town. Carter, meanwhile, murders Hutchins and, after making Nichols his new partner, tells the sheriff that Dave is the killer. Dave and Chito flee the sheriff, however, and intimidate Carter into revealing the location of the supplies by having the Indians threaten to burn him at the stake. Dave and Chito intercept the wagons before they reach the mining camp, but Nichols frees Carter from the Indians, and both men fight to reclaim the supplies. After the cowboys eventually defeat Nichols and Carter, Redfox and Turquoise, whose story has been published in Ellen's newspaper, are summoned to Washington, D.C. To Chito's surprise and delight, the Indians entrust Patchy to his care during their absence. *Duplicity. Freight lines. Indians of North America. Ranchers. Starvation. Bail. Editors. False arrests. Gunshot wounds. Indian agents. Indians of North America–Reservations. Infants. Jails. Mexican Americans. Murder. Newspapers. Rites and ceremonies.*

Note: According to *HR*, some scenes in the film were shot in Lone Pine, CA. *Box* 13 Nov 1948. *DV* 10 Nov 1948, p. 4. *FD* 19 Nov 1948, p. 6. *HR* 3 May 1948, p. 12. *HR* 7 May 1948, p. 9. *HR* 21 May 1948, p. 15. *HR* 10 Nov 1948, p. 3. *MPHPD* 6 Nov 1948, p. 4375. *MPHPD* 20 Nov 1948, p. 4390. *Var* 10 Nov 1948, p. 15.

INDIAN AMERICAN (Native Americans)

Cathedral Films, Inc. *Dist* Cathedral Films, Inc. 1955 [©Cathedral Films, Inc.; 1 Sep 1955; LP5331]. Sd; b&w. 16mm. 40 min.
Prod James K. Friedrich. *Dir* Jan Sadlo. *Scr* Donald H. Johnson. *Film ed* Thor Brooks.
Cast: Hugh Beaumont, Michael Whalen, Tom Selden, Charles Stevens, Jon Shepodd.
Religious, Social, Drama. [*Not viewed*]. A missionary at an Indian reservation brings the message of Christ to the Indians and to whites who seek to exploit the Indians. *Christianity. Indians of North America. Missionaries.*

Note: Advertising for this film included in the copyright materials calls it, "A significant film on the 1955-56 Home Mission theme" and comments, "The film makes a valuable contribution toward better understanding of the Indian and of the churches' responsibility in helping him to become both a good Christian and a good citizen."

THE INDIAN FIGHTER (Native Americans, Dakota)

Bryna Productions, Inc. *Dist* United Artists Corp. Dec **1955**; New York opening: 21 Dec 1955; *Prod:* late May—mid-Jun 1955 [©Bryna Productions, Inc.; 21 Dec 1955; LP5663]. Sd (Western Electric Recording); col (Eastman Color); CinemaScope; Print by Technicolor. 7,917 ft. 88 min. PCA cert no. 17674.
Prod William Schorr. *Assoc prod* Samuel P. Norton. *Dir* Andre de Toth. *Asst dir* Tom Connors, Jack Voglin and [Frank Mattison]. *Scr* Frank Davis and Ben Hecht. *Orig story* Ben Kadish. *Dir of photog* Wilfrid M. Cline. *Spec eff* Dave Koehler. *Art dir* Wiard Ihnen. *Film ed* Richard Cahoon. *Mus* Franz Waxman. *Sd rec* Joe Edmondson. *Prod mgr* Frank Mattison. *Cast supv* Anne Buydens.
Song(s): "The Indian Fighter" and "I Give It All to You," words and music by Irving Gordon and Franz Waxman.
Cast: KIRK DOUGLAS (*Johnny Hawks*), Introducing Elsa Martinelli (*Onahti*), Walter Matthau (*Wes Todd*), Diana Douglas (*Susan Rogers*), Walter Abel (*Captain Trask*), Lon Chaney (*Chivington*), Eduard Franz ([*Chief*] *Red Cloud*), Alan Hale (*Will Crabtree*), Elisha Cook ([*Jim*] *Briggs*), Ray Teal (*Morgan*), Frank Cady (*Trader Joe*), Michael Winkelman (*Tommy Rogers*), Harry Landers (*Grey Wolf*), Hank Worden (*Crazy Bear*), [William Phipps (*Lt. Blake*)], [Buzz Henry (*Lt. Shaeffer*)], [Lane Chandler (*Head settler*)].
Western, with songs. [*Print viewed*]. Johnny Hawks, a frontier scout who fought for the Confederacy in the recently ended Civil War, returns to the land of the Sioux, where his old friend, Chief Red Cloud, has been threatening a newly constructed fort along the trail to Oregon. Red Cloud's brother, Grey Wolf, greets Johnny with distrust, saying "There can be no friendship between red man and white." Red Cloud, although inviting Johnny to stay the night, is also suspicious, and Johnny soon discovers the reason for the chief's anger: With the discovery of gold on Sioux lands, white men have been giving his people whiskey in exchange for the precious metal. Fearing that gold will bring a flood of white men into Sioux territory, thereby devastating the land, Red Cloud proclaims that any Sioux who reveals the location of the gold or engages in secret deals with whites will be executed. As Johnny washes himself in the stream by the village, he observes that Red Cloud's daughter Onahti, whom he had known as a child, has grown into a beautiful woman. He grabs and kisses her, letting her go only after she threatens him with a knife. During the night, two men who are traveling with the wagon train Johnny has been hired to guide through Sioux territory, Wes Todd and his partner Chivington, attempt to bribe two Indians out of their gold with whiskey. When one of the Indians loudly refuses, Todd shoots him, but the village is awakened and the killer is caught. Todd blames the shooting on Chivington, who has escaped, but Grey Wolf prepares to burn the murderer alive. Johnny asks Red Cloud if he may take the prisoner to the fort, where government officials will bring him to justice, but Grey Wolf forces Johnny to fight for him. Johnny proves the stronger fighter, and as he rides to the fort with the prisoner, Todd admits that he and Chivington were after gold. When Johnny suggests that he knows where the gold is hidden, Todd invites him to become his partner. At the fort, Chivington has stirred the soldiers and settlers into a frenzy by claiming that Todd was scalped in an unprovoked attack. Todd soon appears in the saloon unharmed, and Capt. Trask has both men locked up. Johnny, who is respected as a knowledgeable Indian fighter, persuades Trask to meet with Red Cloud, and on the following day, the chief and his warriors are given a formal welcome. After Red Cloud signs a treaty, the fort's inhabitants celebrate with a spirited dance. Johnny dances with Susan Rogers, a widow whose little son Tommy is as fascinated with the Indians as the widow is with Johnny. The next morning, Johnny leads a train of about twenty wagons toward Oregon territory, where settlers have been promised free land. Todd and Chivington, having been released by the captain, ride along, as does a photographer who had apprenticed with Matthew Brady during the war. Sitting apart from the singers around the campfire that night, Susan and Johnny talk, and she suggests that he accompany them to Oregon as her husband. Johnny protests that he is not fit for marriage, and when he walks away, farmer Will Crabtree tries his hand at wooing Susan. The following days' journey

takes the wagon train deep into Sioux territory, and the travelers are unaware that Johnny has brought them there so that he may visit Onahti. Chivington tries to follow Johnny, thinking that the scout will head for the hidden gold, but Johnny sees him and slips away undetected. While Johnny makes love to Onahti, a group of Indians visit the camp intending to trade goods with the settlers. Nervous at first, the white travelers finally barter with the Sioux, but Todd and Chivington ply the feeble-minded Crazy Bear with so much whiskey that he reveals the location of the gold. Grey Wolf hears this, and as he angrily approaches, Todd stabs him. Chivington then shoots a white bystander, after which Todd shouts that the Indians have attacked the camp. Todd and Chivington send the settlers in a panic back toward the fort, while they ride off in search of the gold. When Johnny returns to camp, he finds Grey Wolf's body and then pursues the departed wagon train. Will and the other settlers assume Johnny had led them into a trap, and as he rides into the fort, they and Trask accuse him of betrayal. The men intend to lynch Johnny, but Trask orders them to prepare for the coming battle. Nevertheless, Johnny's admission that he abandoned his post to see a woman infuriates the captain, and he refuses to let Johnny search for Todd and Chivington. Red Cloud sends his warriors to attack the fort, and before nightfall, the Indians set fire to the wooden defenses and kill many soldiers. Certain that the fort will be obliterated in the morning, Johnny steals away and finds Onahti. Arguing that if the massacre is not prevented, the two of them will have no life together, he finally convinces her to lead him to the hidden gold. There he finds Todd and Chivington preparing to set off some dynamite. Johnny wants to deliver them to Red Cloud, but Todd jumps him, thereby setting off an explosion that kills Chivington. Todd tries to escape, but Onahti wounds him, and the three ride back to the village. Intent on avenging his brother's death, Red Cloud has Todd shot with a flaming arrow and then threatens to kill his daughter for revealing the tribe's secret. Johnny then declares that he loves Onahti. Back at the fort, the defenders prepare for battle, and they are surprised and greatly relieved when the approaching Indians suddenly turn away. With peace restored, the wagon train passes uneventfully through Sioux territory, but Johnny remains behind with Onahti. *Dakota Indians. Forts. Greed. Red Cloud. Romance. Scouts (Frontier). Settlers. Wagon trains. Battles. Camps. Children. Dances. Duplicity. Executions. Gold. Indians of North America. Justice. Liquor. Murder. Officers (Military). Panic. Racism. Revenge. Treaties. Tribal chiefs. United States. Army. Cavalry. Widows. Wyoming.*

Note: The picture, the first one produced by Kirk Douglas's independent company, Bryna Productions, was filmed entirely in Bend, Oregon. An written onscreen acknowledgement at the end of the film thanks the Bend, Oregon Chamber of Commerce and the U.S. National Forestry Service for their cooperation. Although an article in *AmCin* noted that the film was shot by Frank Daugherty, Wilfrid M. Cline is credited onscreen as director of photography; the extent of Daugherty's contribution to the released film, if any, has not been determined. According to a Feb 1955 *DV* news item, the film was to be based on a story by John Loring, but the extent of Loring's contribution to the released film has not been determined. Diana Douglas, who portrays "Susan Rogers," was Kirk Douglas's former wife. Anne Buydens, the picture's casting supervisor, was his current wife. The *Indian Fighter* marked the screen debut of international fashion model Elsa Martinelli.

During the years that followed the Civil War, many whites entered the Western mining territories of Colorado, Montana and California by way of the Bozeman Trail, which passed through Teton Sioux land. Red Cloud and his Oglala Tetons, along with other Teton bands, increased their raids on white migrants and military patrols. When the Army was ordered to build more forts to protect the trail, Red Cloud launched a two-year campaign against them. The 1868 Fort Laramie Treaty led to the evacuation of the forts in exchange for the cessation of these attacks, after which the Sioux burned the posts down.

AmCin Aug 1955, pp. 474-75, 488-89. *Box* 24 Dec 1955. *DV* 7 Feb 1955. *DV* 19 Dec 1955, p. 3. *Exb* 28 Dec 1955, p. 4079. *FD* 28 Dec 1955, p. 8. *Har* 24 Dec 1955, p. 207. *HR* 17 Jun 1955, p. 11. *HR* 19 Dec 1955, p. 3. *MPHPD* 24 Dec 1955, p. 713. *NYT* 22 Dec 1955, p. 2. *Var* 21 Dec 1955, p. 6.

INDIAN LIFE (Native Americans, Cheyenne, Crow, Dakota)

Northwestern Film Corp. **1918?** [©Northwestern Film Corp.; 24 Apr 1918; MP1207]. Si; b&w. 4 reels.
Dir Paul Powell. *Cam* John Leezer. *Mus accompaniment* Vern Elliott.

Documentary. Contemporary Indian life on the Crow, Cheyenne and Pine Ridge reservations in Wyoming, Montana and South Dakota is depicted. Indian farmers and ranchers are shown at work and play. In addition, Indian traditonal customs, the home life of the Indians, an Indian fair and an Indian vaudeville show are presented. *Cheyenne Indians. Crow Indians. Dakota Indians. Indians of North America. Indians*

of North America–Reservations. Pine Ridge Reservation (SD). Rites and ceremonies. Fairs. Farmers. Montana. Ranchers. South Dakota. Vaudeville. Wyoming.

Note: The Northwestern Film Corp. was located in Sheridan, WY. John E. Maple, the general manager of the company, obtained a special permit from the U.S. Department of the Interior to film on the Crow, Cheyenne and Pine Ridge reservations. Maple assembled a technical staff in Los Angeles, and had a laboratory built in Sheridan, but the company had no studio. Maple, who was adopted as a member of the Crow tribe, brought six reels of film to New York and arranged several private showings around the time of Apr 1918. In addition to four reels of documentary footage, Maple exhibited a two reel dramatic story, which was also copyrighted under the title *Indian Life*. *MPW* suggested that each reel of the documentary footage might be exhibited separately. No information has been located concerning the release of this film. The Community Motion Picture Bureau viewed the film on 12 Jun 1918. One modern source speculates that certain shots from the film were used in Maple's 1920 feature *Before the White Man Came* (see above).

MPW 20 Apr 1918, p. 370.

INDIAN TERRITORY (Native Americans)

Gene Autry Productions. *Dist* Columbia Pictures Corp. Sep **1950**; Prod: 28 Mar–8 Apr 1950 [©Gene Autry Productions; 1 Sep 1950; LP460]. Sd (RCA Sound System); b&w. 6,203 ft. 69-70 min.

Prod Armand Schaefer. *Dir* John English. [*Asst dir* Wilbur McGaugh and Donald Verk]. *Wrt* Norman S. Hall. *Dir of photog* William Bradford. *Art dir* Charles Clague. *Film ed* James Sweeney. *Set dec* David Montrose. *Mus supv* Paul Mertz. *Mus dir* Mischa Bakaleinikoff. [*Sd* Frank Goodwin].

Song(s): "Chattanoogie Shoe Shine Boy," words and music by Harry Stone and Jack Stapp; "When the Campfire Is Low on the Prairie," words and music by Sam H. Stept.

Cast: Gene Autry [(*Sgt. Gene Autry*)], Champion, World's Wonder Horse, Gail Davis [(*Melody Colton*)], Kirby Grant [(*Lt. Randolph Mason*)], James Griffith [(*The Apache Kid, also known as Johnny Corday*)], Philip Van Zandt [(*Curt Raidler*)], Pat Collins [(*Jim Colton*)], Roy Gordon [(*Major Farrell*)], Pat Buttram [(*Shadrach Jones*)], [Charles Stevens (*Soma*)], [Robert Carson (*Captain Wallace*)], [Boyd Stockman (*Kid's rider*)], [Sandy Sanders (*Andy*)], [Frank Ellis (*Tex*)], [Frank Marvin (*Hank*)], [John McKee (*Cowboy*)], [Bert Dodson (*Curley*)], [Nick Rodman (*Burns*)], [Wesley Hudman (*Cook*)], [Robert Hilton (*Rider*)], [Roy Butler (*Rancher*)], [Kenne Duncan (*Raidler man*)], [Chief Yowlachie, Frank Lackteen, Chief Thunder Cloud (*Chiefs*)], [Chief Thunder Sky (*Lookout*)].

Western, with songs. [*Print viewed*]. After the Civil War, only a few soldiers are assigned to police Indian territory. Many communities are thus left without law enforcement and at the mercy of unscrupulous white men, who take advantage of Indian discontent for their own purposes. Outside one Army fort, new officer Lt. Randolph Mason questions Sgt. Gene Autry, and when Gene does not stand at attention while he answers, arrests him. Later, at the fort, Capt. Wallace informs Randy that Gene was a captain in the Confederate Army and is now working undercover for the Chief of Indian Affairs. This information does not diffuse the bad feelings between the two men, so Wallace suggests they settle their disagreement with their fists. Gene, who has just returned from a parlay with the Apache chiefs, reports that the chiefs do not want to fight with the whites, but that many young braves, believing that the whites are exhausted from the war, are following The Apache Kid, who has promised them guns. The Kid, also called Johnny Corday, was Gene's courier during the war, and Gene is convinced that The Kid, who is half-Indian, is at the bottom of the troubles. In civilian dress, Gene arrives at Apache Springs and soon encounters The Kid. Gene learns that The Kid is working with a man named Curt Raidler, an Austrian who was thrown out of Quantrill's Raiders. Raidler and The Kid plot to drive rancher Jim Colton out of Hidden Valley because they want his land. Gene and his friend, Shadrach Jones, lose The Kid's trail, but discover Indian tracks and follow them just in time to help Colton and his daughter Melody drive away their Indian attackers. Later, Gene tells The Kid that he also intends to run cattle near Hidden Valley. When Gene and Shad return to their shack, they find Randy, who has been assigned to join them. Later, when the Colton camp is empty, The Kid and his men burn it down after killing the camp cook. Gene hears the shot and arrives in time to see The Kid riding away. Later, The Kid prevents Raidler from killing Gene and then tells him that he has repaid his debt and will kill him himself if he gets in the way. This does not stop Gene, who follows The Kid and learns that the guns are in a wagon train crossing the desert. Gene

signals the chiefs with smoke and instructs them to attack the wagon train. Furious, Raidler shoots The Kid and then fights with Gene. Before he dies, The Kid shoots Raidler for repeatedly calling him a savage, thus saving Gene's life. Summoned by Randy, the cavalry then arrives in Apache Springs. Later, Melody and Randy announce their plans to marry, and Randy and Gene finish their fight. *Indians of North America. Indians-Mixed blood. Undercover agents. United States-History-Reconstruction, 1865-1898. Austrian Americans. Cooks. Debt. Fathers and daughters. Fires. Fistfights. Gunrunners. Murder. Officers (Military). Ranchers. Romance. United States. Army. Cavalry. Wagon trains.*

Box 2 Dec 1950. *DV* 6 Sep 1950, p. 3. *FD* 8 Sep 1950, p. 4. *HR* 24 Mar 1950, p. 52. *HR* 31 Mar 1950, p. 10. *HR* 6 Sep 1950, p. 3. *MPHPD* 9 Sep 1950, p. 477. *Var* 6 Sep 1950, p. 8. *Var* 3 Jan 1951, p. 67.

INDIAN UPRISING (Native Americans, Apache)
Edward Small Productions, Inc. *Dist* Columbia Pictures Corp. Jan **1952**; Los Angeles opening: 26 Jan 1952; Prod: 13 Apr—7 May 1951; retakes 20 Jul 1951 [©Columbia Pictures Corp.; 31 Dec 1951; LP1408]. Sd (Western Electric Recording); col (Supercinecolor). 6,763 or 6,753 ft. 75 min. PCA cert no. 15296.

Prod Bernard Small. *Dir* Ray Nazarro. *Asst dir* Gilbert Kay and Milton Feldman. *Scr* Kenneth Gamet and Richard Schayer. *Story* Richard Schayer. *Dir of photog* Ellis Carter. *Art dir* Walter Holscher. *Film ed* Richard Fanti. *Set dec* James Crowe. *Mus dir* Ross Di Maggio. *Sd eng* Lodge Cunningham.

Cast: George Montgomery [(*Captain Case McCloud*)], Audrey Long [(*Norma Clemson*)], Carl Benton Reid [(*John Clemson*)], Eugene Iglesias [(*Sergeant Ramirez*)], John Baer [(*Lieutenant Whitley*)], Joe Sawyer [(*Sergeant Major Phineas T. Keough*)], Robert Dover [(*Tubai*)], Eddy Waller [(*Sagebrush*)], Douglas Kennedy [(*Cliff Taggert*)], Robert Shayne [(*Major Nathan Stark*)], Miguel Inclan [(*Geronimo*)], Hugh Sanders [(*Ben Alsop*)], [John Call (*Sergeant Timothy Aloysius Clancy*)], [Robert Griffin (*Dan Avery*)], [Hank Patterson (*Jake Wilson*)], [Fay Roope (*Major General Crook*)], [Peter Thompson (*Lt. Baker*)], [Ben Corbett (*Sergeant*)], [Selmer Jackson (*Commissioner of Indian Affairs*)], [Gayne Whitman (*Secretary of the Interior*)], [Charles Evans (*Secretary of War*)], [Grandon Rhodes (*Arizona delegate*)], [William E. Green (*Judge Barham*)], [Steve Pendleton (*Captain Denton*)], [Chuck Roberson, Guy Teague, Bob Wilke, Don Harvey, Reed Howes, Jack Low (*Taggert's men*)], [Chuck Hamilton (*Top sergeant*)], [Tris Coffin (*Major Kirby*)], [Kenne Duncan (*Lt. Richards*)], [Paul Campbell (*Signal man*)], [Bud Stark, Billy Williams (*sentries*)], [Thomas Jackson (*Sheriff*)], [George Chesebro, Bud Osborne, Ethan Laidlaw, Stanley Blystone (*Men on street*)], [Richard Fortune (*Signal Corp.*)], [Roque Ybarra (*Indian*)], [George Ford].

Western. [*Viewed print incomplete*]. In 1885, a small band of Apache Indians, led by Geronimo, are captured by U.S. Cavalry Captain Case McCloud, who respects the Apache and Geronimo, in particular. At Fort Steele, Arizona, Geronimo signs a peace treaty on the understanding that the land is to be given to white men. When three white men, Benjamin Alsop, Cliff Taggert and Dan Avery, promote gold mining in the mountains on the Indians' land, Case closes them down. Case is romantically involved with Norma Clemson, who intends to open a school on the reservation so that Indians can have the same opportunities as anyone else and can become useful citizens. Taggert and Avery attempt to bribe Case to permit mining on the reservation, but he throws them out. After anti-Indian political maneuvering in Washington results in Case being relieved of command, the miners resume operations and take Tubai, Geronimo's son, hostage and torture him. Case and several soldiers free Tubai. Major Nathan Stark, sent to replace Case, does not enforce the treaty for fear of censure by the citizens of nearby Tucson. Alsop and Taggert plan to murder a white man and make it appear to have been done by the Apaches so that warfare will erupt. Taggert kills an old miner, Sagebrush, with an Arapaho arrow and takes the body to the fort, where his gunmen kill Indians who have come there in peace. Case orders his soldiers to fire on Taggert and his men, and after several are killed, is arrested and relieved of duty. Geronimo attacks one of Major Stark's troops, trapping them. In the meantime, Case learns that Sagebrush was killed by an arrow from a distant tribe. After a young lieutenant allows Case to escape, he induces Avery to admit that Taggert has been in Arapaho country. Case then finds the bow and arrows in Alsop's office and takes him into the foothills.

Taggert shoots Alsop, but Case beats him up and takes him to where the soldiers are pinned down. Case reports to Stark and offers to talk with Geronimo and explain how he has been tricked into war. After Taggert has confessed to Stark that he killed Sagebrush and Alsop, Case shows his signed confession to Geronimo and asks him to meet with Stark. Geronimo asks Stark to swear that a new treaty will be kept, but the major refuses to do so. After cavalry reinforcements arrive from another fort, Geronimo is captured, and Stark reveals to Case that he was sent west specifically to accomplish this, and that Geronimo will be going to a prison in Florida. Later, Case resigns from the army and goes to see Geronimo, who is being held at the fort. He offers the chief his sword and tells him that he feels great dishonor. After Geronimo tells him that he should keep his sword, that his people will honor it as the only one raised in their defense by the white man, Case decides to remain in the army and plans to marry Norma. *Apache Indians. Geronimo. Gold miners. Indians of North America. Indians of North America-Reservations. Officers (Military). Treachery. Treaties. United States-History-Indian campaigns. United States. Army. Cavalry. Ambushes. Arizona. Bow and arrow. Confession (Law). Fathers and sons. Fistfights. Forts. Frame-ups. Gunfights. Hostages. Indians of North America-Reservations. Irish Americans. Massacres. Politicians. Saloon keepers. Schoolteachers. Torture. Tucson (AZ).*

Note: This film's working title was *War Cry.* As the print available for viewing was missing approximately 24 minutes, the summary was based on several additional contemporary sources. According to contemporary reports, Howard St. John was replaced by Robert Shayne in the role of "Major Nathan Stark." In the film, Geronimo speaks in Spanish which is translated for the whites by his son Tubai, who learned English at a missionary school. Geronimo surrendered for the last time in Sep 1886. He and several hundred Apaches were sent to prison in Florida and, later, in Alabama. Geronimo died, still a prisoner, in 1909.

Box 5 Jan 1952. *DV* 26 Dec 1951. *Exb* 2 Jan 1952, p. 3213. *FD* 15 Jan 1952. *Har* 29 Dec 1951, pp. 206-07 *HR* 20 Apr 1951, p. 10. *HR* 26 Dec 1951. *MPD* 3 Jan 1952. *MPHPD* 29 Dec 1951. *Var* 26 Dec 1951.

THE INDIAN WARS (Native Americans, Dakota)
Col. Wm. F. Cody (Buffalo Bill) Historical Picture Co.; Essanay Film Mfg Co. *Dist* State Rights. Aug **1914**. Si; b&w. 5 reels.

Dir Theodore Wharton and Vernon Day. *Cam* D. T. Hargan. *Tech adv* Lieutenant General Nelson Appleton Miles.

Cast: William F. Cody, Nelson Appleton Miles, Jesse M. Lee, Frank D. Baldwin, Marion P. Maus, Charles King, H. G. Sickles, Short Bull, Dewey Beard.

Biography, Documentary. This film recreates four key battles fought by the United States Cavalry and various tribes of the Sioux Indians. The Battle of Summit Springs (1869), the Battle of Warbonnet Creek (1876), the Battle of the Mission (1890) and the Battle of Wounded Knee (1890) are re-enacted along with the Campaign of the Ghost Dance or Messiah Craze War (1890-91) and the capture of Chief Big Foot. In addition, war dances of the Indians, the burning of camps and tepees by the soldiers, horse rustling and scalping are also depicted. The end of the film includes contemporary scenes of Indian children attending modern schools and Indian farmers bringing in their crops. *Dakota Indians. Indians of North America. United States-History-Indian Campaigns. United States. Army. Cavalry. Chief Big Foot. Farmers. Folk dancing. Mission, Battle of the, 1890. Rustlers. Schools. Summit Springs, Battle of, 1869. Warbonnet Creek, Battle of, 1876. Wounded Knee Creek, Battle of, 1890.*

Note: According to contemporary news reports, William F. Cody (Buffalo Bill) approached Secretary of War Lindley M. Garrison and Secretary of the Interior Franklin K. Lane about the making of this film, which was shot at the sites of the original battles between 26 Sep 1913 and 1 Nov 1913. Garrison supplied Cody with the necessary troops from the 12th U.S. Cavalry and Lane authorized the participation of over 1,000 Sioux Indians. Lieutenant General Nelson Appleton Miles was hired as a technical consultant as well as a cast member and made sure that the re-enactments were as accurate as possible. Colonel H. G. Sickles and Charles King recreated their parts in the original battles of Wounded Knee and Warbonnet Creek, respectively. The production, which boasted over 30,000 feet of film shot from the Bad Lands of South Dakota to the Black Hills of Wyoming, was plagued by blizzards and increasing costs and later required over six months of editing. On 27 Feb 1914, the finished film was screened for Secretary Lane and other members of Woodrow Wilson's cabinet. The film was released theatrically in Aug 1914, but according to modern sources played only in Denver and New York because of pressure from government forces, which disapproved of its content because it showed the Indians in a somewhat favorable light. In early 1917, after Cody's death, substantial footage from this film was used in *The Adventures of Buffalo Bill,* an homage to the late Western figure. According to news items from 1917, the original film was titled *Wars of Civilization* and was eight reels long. Modern

sources list alternate titles as *The Indian Wars Refought*, *The Last Indian Battles* or *From the Warpath to the Peace Pipe*, *The Wars for Civilization in America*, *Buffalo Bill's Indian Wars*, and *Indian War Pictures*. The production was co-owned by Cody's film company, by Essanay, and by the *Denver Post*. Another 1917 film, *The Buffalo Bill Show*, directed by John O'Brien and distributed by the Wild West Film Co., may have also used footage from this production. Modern sources credit Vernon Day as production manager and not co-director, Charles King as scenarist, and Conrad Luperti as co-cinematographer.

MPW 25 Oct 1913, p. 362. *MPW* 22 Nov 1913, p. 851. *MPW* 14 Mar 1914, p. 1370. *MPW* 15 Aug 1914, p. 849. *MPW* 22 Aug 1914, p. 1039. *MPW* 12 Sep 1914, p. 1500.

INDISCRETION OF AN AMERICAN WIFE (Italian Americans)

Selznick Releasing Organization, Inc.; A Vittorio De Sica Production. *Dist* Columbia Pictures Corp. May **1954**; *Prod*: 10 Oct—24 Dec 1952 in Rome, Italy [©Selznick Releasing Organization, Inc.; 30 Mar 1954; LP3528]. Sd (RCA Sound System); b&w. 6 reels, 5,695 or 5,794 ft. 63-64 min. PCA cert no. 16463.

Prod Vittorio De Sica. [*Exec prod* David O. Selznick]. *Assoc prod* Marcello Girosi and Wolfgang Reinhardt. *Dir* Vittorio De Sica. *Scr* Cesare Zavattini, Luigi Chiarini and Giorgio Prosperi. *Dial* Truman Capote. *Photographed in its actual settings by* G. R. Aldo. *Art dir* Virgilio Marchi. *Film ed* Eraldo Da Roma and Jean Barker. *Mus ed* Audray Granville. *Miss Jones' cost des by* Christian Dior. *Mus* Alessandro Cicognini. *Cond* Franco Ferrara. *Post-production audio* James G. Stewart. *Sd eng* Bruno Brunacci and Alberto Bartolome. *Tech assoc* Richard Van Hessen. *Prod mgr* Nino Misiano.

Cast: JENNIFER JONES [(*Mary Forbes*)], MONTGOMERY CLIFT [(*Giovanni Doria*)], Gino Cervi [(*Commissioner*)], Dick Beymer [(*Paul*)].

Romance, Drama. [*Print viewed*]. Mary Forbes, a married Philadelphia housewife and mother, falls in love with an Italian-American professor named Giovanni Doria while visiting her sister in Rome, Italy. Mary has a one-month romantic adventure with Giovanni, but is unable to continue the infidelity, and decides to leave Rome. She boards the first train to Paris, but before the train leaves the station, Mary catches sight of Giovanni, who has learned of her hasty departure from her sister. Giovanni asks Mary why she left without a word, but their conversation is interrupted by the arrival of Mary's young nephew, Paul. Paul leaves, and as the train pulls out of the station, Mary is transfixed by Giovanni's gaze and decides to postpone her departure so that she can explain her feelings. In a quiet corner of the station restaurant, Giovanni reminds Mary that she had told him only the day before that she loved him. Mary, however, cannot put the thought of her husband and young daughter Catherine out of her mind. When Giovanni tells Mary that he had dreams of a happy life with both she and Catherine in Pisa, he rekindles her passion. Giovanni persuades Mary to go with him to his apartment, but as they are leaving the terminal, she sees Paul. Flustered, Mary offers to buy a hot chocolate for the boy and sends him to the restaurant to wait for her. Mary then tells Giovanni that she feels that their relationship is doomed, and that they should part, but Giovanni, angered by her sudden change of heart, slaps her across the face and leaves. Paul waits with Mary for the next train, and they find a seat next to an Italian woman who has gone into labor. Mary helps the woman find a doctor and briefly watches her three children for her. Giovanni, meanwhile, becomes remorseful and returns to the station to find Mary. Giovanni eventually finds Mary, but is nearly struck by a passing train running to meet her. They embrace and make their way to darkened train compartment, where they engage in a passionate kiss. Giovanni begs Mary's forgiveness, but, moments later, the two are arrested for public lovemaking and taken before the police commissioner. The commissioner tells Mary and Giovanni that the charge requires a trial, but then decides to release Mary because she has a husband and child. Giovanni escorts Mary to the train, and the two bid each other a sad farewell. *Americans in foreign countries. Infidelity. Italian Americans. Rome (Italy). Train stations. Arrests. Children. Judges. Marriage. Nephews. Police commissioners. Pregnancy. Professors. Trains.*

Note: Released in the United States as *Indiscretion of an American Wife*, this picture was filmed in Italy as *Terminal Station* and was released in England as *Stazione Termini*, the Italian title of Cesare Zavattini's screen story. The film marked Italian director Vittorio De Sica's first English language picture, and, according to a *Var* pre-production news item, was originally slated as a French-Italian co-production to be directed by Claude Autant-Lara, with Marlon Brando starring. Actress Jennifer Jones was married to producer David O. Selznick. Although contemporary news items listed Italian actors Virgilio Riento and Giovanni Grazzo in the cast, their appearance in the released film has not been determined.

A Jun 1954 *Var* news item indicated that Columbia Pictures had paid Selznick $500,000 for the Western Hemisphere rights to the film. The film was shot in its entirety at the recently completed Stazione Termini in Rome, Italy. According to a Jul 1953 news item in *HCN*, filming took place at the station between the hours of midnight and 5 a.m., when the station was closed. Contemporary sources also note that initial showings of the picture were accompanied by a short film, an eight-minute "prologue," featuring Patti Page singing "Autumn in Rome" and "Indiscretion." The two songs, written by Sammy Cahn and Paul Weston, were based on Alessandro Cicognini's love theme from the film.

According to a Sep 1952 memo contained in the file for the film in the MPAA/PCA Collection at the AMPAS Library, an early version of the script was rejected for approval by the MPAA on the grounds that it was "an improper treatment of adultery." The memo noted that Selznick, during a meeting with MPAA officials, indicated he would change the story to one in which the Philadephia housewife "never committed adultery and at the end she would rejoin her husband and renounce the lover." A revised script later met with the approval of the MPAA and, in a Nov 1952 letter to an MPAA official, Selznick called the film "...probably the most moral picture ever to come out of Europe."

Modern sources add the following cast members: Paolo Stoppa (*Baggage clerk*), Mando Bruno (*Employee*), Clelia Mantania, Enrico Viarisio, Giuseppe Farelli, Enrico Olorio and Maria Pia Casillo-Ciro. Child actor Dick Beymer, who was later billed under the name Richard Beymer, made his motion picture debut in the film. According to modern sources, Columbia cut seventeen minutes from the picture's original eighty-minute running time. In 1983, the picture was restored to its original length and shown for the first time in the U.S. at that length. Modern sources also note that in addition to Truman Capote, Selznick employed writers Carson McCullers, Paul Gallico and Alberto Moravia to bolster the script.

Box 24 Apr 1954. *DV* 21 Apr 1954, p. 3. *FD* 30 Apr 1954, p. 6. *HCN* 31 Jul 1953. *HR* 21 Apr 1954, p. 3. *MPHPD* 24 Apr 1954, p. 2270. *NYT* 26 Jun 1954, p. 7. *Var* 10 Sep 1952. *Var* 30 Sep 1952. *Var* 20 Oct 1953. *Var* 21 Oct 1953. *Var* 22 Oct 1953. *Var* 21 Apr 1954, p. 6. *Var* 9 Jun 1954. *Var* 4 Aug 1983, p. 2.

THE INEVITABLE URGE see CHIJLKU WO MAWASURU CHIKARA

INJUSTICE (African Americans)

Democracy Film Co.; L-Ko Pictures Corp. *Dist* Bookertee Film Exchange. 20 Jul **1919**. Si; b&w. 6-7 reels.

Dir Capt. Leslie T. Peacocke. *Story and scen* Capt. Leslie T. Peacocke.

Cast: Thais Nehli-Kalini (*Irene Waterloo*), Maurice Stapler (*Count Bertrand Delande*), Vera Lavassor (*Gwendolyne Vanderbilt*), Dorothy Yvonne Dumont (*Minnie*), Sidney Preston Dones (*George Preston*), Ovid Scott (*Sgt. Chase*), Mrs. Wilhelmina Owens, Mrs. Hamer Burrell, Mrs. Seith Webb, Margaret Grace-Boon, Mrs. W. W. E. Gladden, Gwendoline Gordon, Mary Strange, Veronica Smith, Janette Criner, Mrs. James B. Seager, Mrs. Crystal Reed, Cora Reed, Miss Dreyfus, Mrs. Otis Banks, Chaplain W. W. E. Gladden, Robert Fortson, Lieut. Journee White, Eldridge Lee, Otis Banks, Robert C. Owens, Mr. Christian, Dr. W. A. Tarleton, Lieut. Clinton Ross, Lieut. Matthews, Lieut. Eugene Lucas, F. L. Banks, J. B. Bass, Harry Jones, Herbert Bost, J. W. Coleman, Julia Stuart, Lieut. Hankin, Lieut. Jackson.

African American, World War I, Drama. Wealthy society girl Irene Waterloo is courted by a designing nobleman, Count Bertrade Delande, who had previously pledged himself to Gwendolyne Vanderbilt. Gwendolyne and her socially ambitious mother uncover evidence that Irene is really black, and Irene, shocked by this revelation, goes to Europe. Eventually she finds happiness with George Preston, who was formerly her porter. [The film also treats the racism endured by blacks in Europe during World War I. No other verifiable information concerning the plot has been discovered.]. *African Americans. Europe. Parentage. Porters. Racism. Mothers and daughters. Nobility. Socialites. World War I.*

Note: The Democracy Film Co. which changed its name to the Loyalty Film Co. sometime in 1919 or 1920, included both blacks and whites in its management and produced films with black casts. During its opening run in Los Angeles, the film, which may have been made under the title *Democracy; or a Fight for Right*, was advertised and reviewed as *In Justice*, but later Democracy ads and most contemporary sources called the film *Injustice*. It is unclear whether the film was six or seven reels long at the time of its release. By late 1919 the film had been renamed *Loyal Hearts*, and it played in theaters under that title in late 1919 or early 1920, advertised variously as a five-reeler or a six-reeler. At about this time L-Ko contracted with Democracy to distribute the film; it cut the film to five reels, added titles in dialect, possibly added additional footage, and advertised the result as a comedy. Democracy brought suit against L-Ko, but the outcome of the dispute is unclear. It is also unclear whether *Loyal Hearts* was L-Ko's title for the film, whether the film had already been titled *Loyal Hearts* when L-Ko acquired it, or whether L-Ko released the film under yet another title. Modern sources state that Irene goes to Europe as a Red Cross nurse, is attacked and nearly raped by German soldiers there, and

is saved by George, now a soldier who is wounded in the fight. Scenes from the film may have been shot at the E&R Jungle Studio in Los Angeles.

LAEx 21 Jul 1919. *Los Angeles Leader* 3 Aug 1919, p. 1. *LAT* 21 Jul 1919. *MPW* 7 Jun 1919, p. 1491. *New York Age* 10 Apr 1920, p. 6.

LA INMACULADA (Spanish language)

Atalaya Films. *Dist* United Artists Corp. **1939**; Los Angeles opening: 19 Sep 1939; Prod: began 31 May 1939 at Grand National Studios. Sd; b&w. 8,855 ft. 98 min. PCA cert no. 5502. Spanish language.

Prod Maury M. Cohen and Fortunio Bonanova. *Dir* Louis Gasnier. *Dial dir* Adalberto Elías González. *Scr* Paul Perez. *Adpt* Gabriel Navarro. *Photog* Arthur Martinelli. *Art dir* F. Paul Sylos. *Film ed* Robert Warwick. *Gowns* Irene Saltern. *Mus dir* Albert Colombo. *Mus* Fortunio Bonanova, Pilar Arcos, Nilo Menéndez, Cecil Burleigh, Lorenzo Reyes Félix, Jr. and Ramiro Gómez Kemp. *Orch arr* Nilo Menéndez. *Sd* Ferol Redd. *Prod mgr* Melville Shyer.

Source: Based on the novel *La Inmaculada* by Catalina D'Erzell (Mexico City, 1920).

Cast: Fortunio Bonanova (*René*), Andrea Palma (*Consuelo*), Milissa Sierra (*Concha*), Tana (*María Luisa*), Luis Díaz Flores (*Luis Angel*), Daniel F. Rea (*Homobono*), Julia Montoya (*Severina*), Felipe Turich (*Nacho*), Raquel Turich (*Doña Rosa*), Carlos Villarías (*Dr. Torres*), Eva López, María Borello, Jesús Topete, Elena Madrigal, Matilde Liñán, Carmen Bailey, Elena Durán, José Peña "Pepet", Paco Moreno, Laura Puente, Luis Rojas.

Drama. [*Not viewed*]. In search of work to pay for the care of her sick mother, Consuelo, a country girl, moves to Mexico City where, with the help of her cousin Concha, she finds work in a stocking factory. There she meets René, the wealthy womanizer who owns the factory. René declares his love for Consuelo, and although at first she resists his charm, she eventually capitulates and the couple marry. Soon after the wedding, René becomes restless and resumes his liaison with his former mistress, María Luisa. When he squanders his wealth, however, María Luisa casts him aside and René suffers a stroke that paralyzes him. In disgrace, René is abandoned by all his friends, except for the faithful Consuelo, who is resigned to sharing his adversity. One day, Consuelo meets Luis Angel, a violinist, and falls in love with him. Luis begs her to divorce René and marry him, but Consuelo refuses, out of loyalty to René. When Consuelo refuses his proposal, Luis marries the girl his parents have picked out for him, and Consuelo, unseen, watches the ceremony. Meanwhile, René, overhearing the neighbors gossiping about Consuelo and Luis, realizes that he has wasted his life and throws away his life-maintaining medicine. *Infidelity. Marriage. Playboys. Self-sacrifice. Bankruptcy. Country girls. Cousins. Gossip. Marriage–Arranged. Mexico City (Mexico). Millionaires. Proposals (Marital). Stroke. Suicide.*

CM Oct 1939, p. 474. *DV* 14 Jul 1939. *FD* 19 Jul 1939, p. 19. *HR* 15 Apr 1939, p. 1. *HR* 20 May 1939, p. 4. *HR* 31 May 1939, p. 8. *HR* 15 Jul 1939, p. 3. *MPH* 22 Jul 1939, p. 52. *NYT* 28 Oct 1939, p. 11. *Var* 15 Jul 1939.

THE INNOCENT CHEAT *see* THE THIRD WOMAN

THE INNOCENT LIE (Irish Americans)

Famous Players Film Co. *Dist* Paramount Pictures Corp. 8 May **1916** [©Famous Players Film Co.; 21 Apr 1916; LU8124]. Si; b&w. 5 reels.

Dir Sidney Olcott. *Scen* Lois Zellner. *Story* Hugh Ford. *Cam* Alphonso Liguori.

Cast: Valentine Grant (*Nora O'Brien*), Jack J. Clark (*Terry O'Brien*), Morris Foster (*Pat O'Brien*), Hunter Arden (*Nora Owen*), Robert Cain (*Captain Stewart*), Frank Losee, William Courtleigh, Jr., Helen Lindroth, Charles Ferguson.

Drama. After Nora O'Brien comes to America from Ireland to see her brother, she suffers a concussion. She is then mistaken for another Irish Nora who had been planning to come to the United States to visit her seldom seen aunt, Mrs. Watson, but who decided, finally, to stay at home. A dazed Nora is taken to Mrs. Watson's home and treated like family, and then, when Mrs. Watson's son Jack returns from college he falls in love with his new cousin. Nora recovers from her injury and realizes that a mistake has been made, but she has been so impressed with the Watson's kindness that she does not want to confess that she is not related to them. Finally, however, the truth comes out, and because Nora already feels like a Watson, she eagerly consents to marry Jack in order to make her ties to the family completely legal and official. *Amnesia. Irish. Mistaken identity. Aunts. College students. Cousins.*

Note: This production was filmed in Bermuda.

Motog 20 May 1916, p. 1167. *MPN* 20 May 1916, p. 3090. *MPW* 20 May 1916, p. 1349. *NYDM* 20 May 1916, p. 25. *NYT* 8 May 1916, p. 7. *Var* 12 May 1916, p. 19. *Wid's* 11 May 1916, p. 567.

THE INSIDE OF THE WHITE SLAVE TRAFFIC (Immigrants)

Moral Feature Film Co. *Dist* Sociological Research Film Co. 8 Dec **1913** [©Samuel H. London; 31 Oct 1913; LU1508]. Si; b&w. 4 reels.

Pres Samuel H. London. *Dir* Frank Beal. *Asst dir* Abraham Canter. *Scen* Frank Beal. *Story* Samuel H. London.

Cast: Virginia Mann (*Victim*), Edwin Carewe (*Procurer*), Jean Thomas (*His sweetheart*), Ninita Bristow (*Immigrant*), Elinor O. Peterson.

Social, Drama. A white slaver who preys on unsuspecting immigrants catches sight of a pretty young woman, ordered from her house by her father and now wandering the streets of New York City. In order to make her acquaintance, the procurer orders his accomplice to insult the girl, whereupon the procurer gallantly comes to the rescue. The woman gratefully accompanies him to a nearby café, where he drugs her and then takes her to his apartment. Tricked by a staged marriage, the girl flees with her "husband" to New Orleans, where he sells her to a brothel. Disgusted, she escapes to Denver, but her poor reputation prevents her from finding a new life. Trapped in the trade, the young woman becomes a hopeless example of the tragedy of white slavery. *Brothels. Immigrants. Moral corruption. Pimps. Prostitution. Reputation. White-slave traffic.* Denver (CO). Drugging. Fathers and daughters. Marriage–Fake. New Orleans (LA). New York City.

Note: The film contains documentary footage shot in New Orleans, New York, and Denver. Samuel H. London reported on white slavery for the Rockefeller Commission after working for seven years as a secret service agent assigned to control the problem.

MPN 20 Dec 1913, p. 31. *NYDM* 24 Sep 1913, p. 31. *NYT* 9 Dec 1913, p. 8. *Var* 12 Dec 1913, p. 12, 25.

INSIDE THE MAFIA (Italian Americans)

Premium Pictures, Inc. *Dist* United Artists Corp. Sep **1959**; Prod: late Mar—mid-Apr 1959 at Paramount/Sunset Studio [©Premium Pictures, Inc.; 25 Sep 1959; LP14829]. Sd; b&w. 72 min. PCA cert no. 19342.

Prod Robert E. Kent. *Dir* Edward L. Cahn. *Asst dir* Herbert S. Greene. *Wrt* Orville H. Hampton. *Dir of photog* Maury Gertsman. *Art dir* Bill Glasgow. *Supv ed* Grant Whytock. *Eff ed* Henry Adams. *Mus ed* Robert Carlisle. *Set dec* Morris Hoffman. *Ward* Einar Bourman. *Mus* Albert Glasser. *Sd* Al Overton and Ryder Sound Services. *Makeup* Layne Britton. *Hairdresser* Frances Sperry. *Prod mgr* Joseph Small. *Cast dir* Betty Pagel. *Prop master* Max Frankel. *Scr supv* John Franco. *Chief tech* Buzz Gibson.

Cast: Cameron Mitchell (*Tony Ledo*), Robert Strauss (*Sam Galey*), Grant Richards (*Johnny Lucero*), Jim L. Brown (*Doug Blair*), Elaine Edwards (*Anne Balcom*), Edward Platt (*Dan Regent*), Richard Karlan (*Chins Dayton*), Ted de Corsia (*Augie Martello*), Louis Jean Heydt (*Rod Balcom*), Carol Nugent (*Sandy Balcom*), Frank Gerstle (*Julie Otranto*), Sid Clute (*Beery*), Steve Roberts (*Raycheck*), Hal Torey (*Molina*), Carl Milletaire (*Dave Alto*), Michael Monroe (*Buzz*), Jack Daley (*Joe, the barber*), Jim Bannon (*Corino*), Raymond Guth (*Morgan*), Anthony Carbone (*Kronis*), Jack Kenney (*Vince DeMao*), House Peters, Jr. (*Marty Raven*), Sheldon Allman (*Dyer*), Tony Warde (*Bob Kalen*), Donna Dale (*Manicurist*), John Hart (*Police sergeant*).

Gangster, Drama. [*Not viewed*]. Augie Martello, the leader of a group attempting to gain control of the East Coast Mafia, is shot in a New York barbershop by a rival faction. However, Martello survives and goes into hiding to recover. Tony Ledo, Martello's chief aide, tells him of a plan whereby they can still take over the syndicate. Johnny Lucero, a former Mafia boss who was deported, is returning in secret with the intention of reorganizing coast-to-coast, and Ledo plans to kill him as he steps off his plane and have Martello assume his role. To execute their scheme, Ledo and Sam Galey, a professional killer, take over the small emergency airfield where Lucero is scheduled to land and terrorize Rod Balcom, the manager, and his two daughters Anne and Sandy. However, while they are waiting for Lucero's plane, they hear a television newscast announcing Martello's death. Ledo suddenly switches plans and makes a deal with Lucero to spare his life, as proof of his loyalty, if he will force the Mafia council to let him take over Martello's spot. Ledo accompanies Lucero to a meeting of all the Mafia kingpins, but Lucero changes his mind and kills Ledo and

his supporters. The terrorized family outsmarts Galey, and the state police arrive to arrest the surviving Mafia members. *Airports. Gangsters. Gunfights. Italian Americans. Mafia. Murder. Barbers and barbershops. Fathers and daughters. Hired killers. Lodges. New York City. Police. Television.*

Note: Although this film was not viewed, the credits were taken from a billing sheet in the PCA file at the AMPAS Library. This film's working title was *Three Came to Kill.* According to publicity material, some scenes in the film were shot in Malibu, CA.

Box 28 Sep 1959. *DV* 24 Sep 1959, p. 3. *Exb* 23 Sep 1959, p. 4638. *FD* 24 Sep 1959, p. 6. *Har* 26 Sep 1959, p. 154. *HR* 27 Mar 1959, p. 12. *HR* 24 Sep 1959, p. 3. *MPHPD* 3 Oct 1959, p. 437. *Var* 30 Sep 1959, p. 6.

INTELLIGENCE *see* **AN ALIEN ENEMY**

INTO HER KINGDOM (Russian Americans)

Corinne Griffith Productions, Inc.; Asher-Small-Rogers Presents. *Dist* First National Pictures, Inc. 15 Aug **1926**; New York premiere: 8 Aug 1926 [©Corinne Griffith Productions, Inc.; 30 Jul 1926; LP22990]. Si; b&w. 7 reels, 6,447 ft.

Dir Svend Gade. *Adpt* Carey Wilson. *Titles* William Conselman. *Photog* Harold Wenstrom.

Source: Based on the short story "Into Her Kingdom" by Ruth Comfort Mitchell in *Red Book Magazine* (Mar 1925).

Cast: Corinne Griffith (*Grand Duchess Tatiana, at 12 and at 20*), Einar Hanson (*Stepan, son of a peasant, at 14 and at 22*), Claude Gillingwater (*Ivan, their tutor*), Charles Crockett (*Senov, a carnival fakir*), Evelyn Selbie (*Stepan's mother*), Larry Fisher (*A farmhand*), H. C. Simmons (*Czar Nicholas*), Elinor Vanderveer (*Czarina*), Byron Sage (*Czarevitch*), Tom Murray (*Bolshevik guard*), Marcelle Corday (*Tatiana's maid*), Maj. Gen. Michael N. Pleschkoff (*Court chamberlain*), Max Davidson (*Shoestring salesman*), Allan Sears (*American customer*), Mary Louise Miller (*Daughter of Stepan and Tatiana*), General Lodijensky, Maj. Gen. Ikanikoff, Maj. Gen. Bogomoletz, Lieut. George Blagoi, Lieut. Gene Walski, Feodor Chalyapin, Jr., George Davis (*Russian officers and court leaders*).

Romance. Stepan, a Russian peasant, is sent to Siberia for allegedly insulting the Grand Duchess Tatiana. Seven years later, upon his release, he joins the Bolsheviks who are plotting to execute the imperial family. Ivan, formerly his tutor as well as that of the royal family, persuades him to flee to America with Tatiana, now a beautiful young lady; though reluctant, he is at last won over by her beauty. Although she does not love the lowborn Stepan, Tatiana follows, and they settle in New Jersey as husband and wife. Clerking in a store, she tells stories to neighborhood children of the experiences of a princess, matching her story with facts of her early life; Stepan, realizing his inequality, pledges to return her to Russia. There he finds diplomatic agents eager for information of the supposedly massacred royal family, but Tatiana, having become a mother, enters Russia with her child, disclaims her royal birth, and is happily reunited with Stepan. *Bolshevists and Bolshevism. Immigrants. New Jersey. Nicholas II, Czar of Russia, 1868-1918. Refugees, Political. Romanov, House of. Royalty. Russia–History–Revolution, 1917-1921. Russian Americans. Russians.*

FD 22 Aug 1926. *NYT* 10 Aug 1926, p. 19. *Var* 11 Aug 1926, p. 14.

INTO THE CRIMSON WEST *see* **PRAIRIE SCHOONERS**

THE INTRUDER (1944) *see* **TOMORROW THE WORLD!**

INTRUDER IN THE DUST (African Americans)

Metro-Goldwyn-Mayer Corp.; controlled by Loew's Inc.; A Clarence Brown Production. *Dist* Loew's Inc. 3 Feb **1950**; Oxford MS premiere: 10 Oct 1949; Prod: late Feb—late Apr 1949 [©Loew's Inc.; 27 Sep 1949; LP2556]. Sd (Western Electric Sound System); b&w. 87 min. Passed by the National Board of Review. PCA cert no. 13920.

Prod Clarence Brown. *Dir* Clarence Brown. [*Asst dir* Melvin Stuart]. *Scr* Ben Maddow. *Dir of photog* Robert Surtees. [*Cam op* John Schmitz]. [*Stills* Jerome Hester]. *Art dir* Cedric Gibbons and Randall Duell. *Film ed* Robert J. Kern. *Set dec* Edwin B. Willis. *Assoc* Ralph S. Hurst. *Mus score* Adolph Deutsch. *Rec supv* Douglas Shearer. *Makeup created by* Jack Dawn. [*Prod mgr* Jay Marchant]. [*Scr supv* Eylla Jacobus]. [*Grip* Albert Hunter].

Source: Based on the novel *Intruder in the Dust* by William Faulkner (New York, 1928).

Cast: David Brian (*John Gavin Stevens*), Claude Jarman, Jr. (*Chick Mallison*), Juano Hernandez (*Lucas Beauchamp*), Porter Hall (*Nub Gowrie*), Elizabeth Patterson (*Miss [Eunice] Habersham*), Charles Kemper (*Crawford Gowrie*), Will Geer (*Sheriff Hampton*), David Clarke (*Vinson Gowrie*), Elzie Emanuel (*Aleck*), Lela Bliss (*Mrs. Mallison*), Harry Hayden (*Mr. Mallison*), Harry Antrim (*Mr. Tubbs*), [Dan White (*Will Legate*)], [Alberta Dishmon (*Paralee*)], [R. S. Williams (*Mr. Lilley*)], [Julia S. Marshbanks (*Molly Beauchamp*)], [Ephraim Lowe, Edmund Lowe (*Gowrie twins*)], [Jack Odom (*Truck driver*)], [Freddie B. Patton (*Barber*)], [W. P. Haley, Dr. Allison Busby (*Customers*)], [Harold Gean, John M. Keel (*Patrons*)], [W. G. Kimmons (*Deputy*)], [Robert Lee Young, C. E. Slough, Jack Bronfeld (*Men in crowd*)], [Noel Hodge, George T. Hemphill, Dewey McCoy (*Voices in crowd*)], [Eugene Roper (*Fraser's son*)], [John Morgan, James Kirkwood (*Black convicts*)], [Joyce Ann Baron (*Child with yo-yo*)], [Eylla Jacobus (*Fat woman*)], [Mrs. E. P. Lowe (*Woman in sunbonnet*)], [Guy Turnbowe (*Voice*)], [Ben J. Hilbun (*Attendant*)], [E. H. Windham], [George Winter], [John E. Avent], [Will Lewis], [E. P. Lowe], [Homer Arnold], [E. L. Hooker], [Tommy Bond], [Ann Hartsfield], [Howard Winters].

Crime, Rural, Drama. [*Print viewed*]. A short time after Vinson Gowrie, a white lumberman, is found murdered in a small town, Lucas Beauchamp, a black landowner, is arrested and charged with the killing. As Lucas is led by Sheriff Hampton through an angry crowd of people gathered at the jail house, he turns to Chick Mallison, a white youth he has befriended, and asks him to summon John Gavin Stevens, Chick's lawyer uncle, to his aid. Recalling the November day he first met Lucas, Chick later tells John the story of how he and the black man became friends: While on a rabbit-hunting expedition with his black friend Aleck, Chick falls into an icy river and nearly drowns, but is rescued by Lucas, who owns the land around the river. Lucas takes Chick to his home and gives him food and dry clothes, but Chick, who has not been taught to respect black people, does not know how to react to his generosity. One day, at Fraser's General Store, Chick witnesses a group of white men taunting Lucas, and sees Vinson attempt to strike Lucas on the head. While Chick watches in motionless silence, some of the men surround Vinson and prevent him from completing the assault. Chick concludes his story by telling John that, despite his silence, Lucas considers him to be his friend and has placed his trust in him. John reluctantly agrees to take the case, and when he and Chick visit Lucas in his jail cell, Lucas tells them that he was beaten by a white lumberman, who forced him to identify his business partner, Vinson, as the man who was stealing lumber from him. Lucas is cautious and refuses to tell John any more details about the incident, but he privately asks Chick to dig up Vinson's body to prove that the bullet that killed Vinson was not fired from his gun. Although John opposes Chick's plan to exhume Vinson's body, Chick later finds an ally in Miss Eunice Habersham, an elderly woman who believes that Chick may be on the trail of an important clue. Late one night, Miss Habersham, Aleck and Chick go to the chapel at which Vinson is supposed to have been buried and begin digging up the grave. When they open the coffin, however, they are surprised to discover that it is empty. The discovery of the missing corpse convinces John and the sheriff that Lucas is innocent, and they join Chick in his search for Vinson's body. With help from Nub Gowrie, Vinson's father, John, the sheriff and others follow a trail of footprints that lead to a patch of quicksand near a river. Vinson's body is retrieved from the quicksand, after which it is determined that the bullet that killed him could not have been fired from Lucas' gun. Back in town, an angry crowd of white men, led by Vinson's brother Crawford, surrounds the jail house and demands that Lucas be lynched. Meanwhile, inside the jail house, Lucas tells John and Chick that although he was present when Vinson was shot and can identify Vinson's business partner, he never saw the man who fired the gun. Concluding that Vinson's business partner must be the killer, and that he is trying to frame Lucas for the murder, the sheriff and John decide to set a trap for the killer. After announcing that Lucas has been released from jail, the sheriff waits for the killer to try to silence Lucas. The plan works, and the killer is revealed to be Crawford. Crawford is arrested, and as he is led into the jail house, the townspeople gathered outside the jail house disperse. *African Americans. Frame-ups. Friendship. Murder. Racism. United States–South. Adolescents. Aged women. Barbers and barbershops. Brothers. Bullets. Exhumation. Fathers and sons. Jails. Lawyers. Lumberjacks.*

Mobs. Partnership. Quicksand. Revenge. Searches. Small town life. Traps. Uncles.

Note: The working title of this film was *The Intruder*. The film marked the screen debut of former radio and stage entertainer Juano Hernandez. A Jul 1948 *HR* news item noted that M-G-M paid $50,000 for the film rights to William Faulkner's novel. A Feb 1949 *HR* news item indicates that Joel McCrea was considered for the part played by David Brian. Although late Mar and early Apr 1949 *HR* production charts list Albert Akst as the film editor, onscreen credits list Robert Kern. The film was shot on location in Oxford, MS. As the town was segregated at the time of production, Hernandez was forced to live apart from the rest of the film's cast and crew. According to an Apr 1949 *NYT* article, Hernandez stayed with a local black undertaker. According to a Dec 1949 *DV* news item, director Clarence Brown shot the picture without a sound track, and then dubbed the dialogue after the completion of camera work. Although the professional actors dubbed their own voices, Brown used radio actors' and extras' voices for those of the local Oxford people who appeared in the picture.
Box 15 Oct 1949. *DV* 4 Oct 1949, p. 7. *DV* 11 Oct 1949, p. 3. *DV* 28 Dec 1949, p. 2. *FD* 11 Oct 1949, p. 7. *HR* 13 Jul 1948, p. 1. *HR* 30 Aug 1948, p. 10. *HR* 24 Feb 1949, p. 3. *HR* 25 Feb 1949, p. 16. *HR* 25 Mar 1949, p. 44. *HR* 22 Apr 1949, p. 14. *HR* 29 Apr 1949, p. 12. *HR* 11 Oct 1949, p. 3. *MPHPD* 15 Oct 1949, p. 49. *NYT* 10 Apr 1949. *NYT* 23 Nov 1949, p. 19. *Var* 12 Oct 1949, p. 6.

THE INVADERS (Native Americans)
Big Productions Film Corp. *Dist* Syndicate Pictures. Oct **1929**. Sd eff and mus score; b&w. 7 reels, 6,200 ft. [Also si; 5 reels.].
Dir J. P. McGowan. *Scen* Walter Sterret. *Story* Sally Winters. *Titles* William Stratton. *Photog* Hap Depew.
Cast: Bob Steele, Edna Aslin, Thomas Lingham, J. P. McGowan, Celeste Rush, Tom Smith, Bud Osborne, Chief Yowlache.
Western. An Indian attack upon a wagon train kills all but two children. These siblings are soon separated; Major McLellan adopts the boy, while the girl is taken to live with Indians as Black Fawn. Years later, after the boy has joined the cavalry and fallen in love with the major's daughter, he shows his bravery during an Indian attack on the fort (perpetrated by plotting among treacherous white men and Indian braves). With the help of a squaw, he is then reunited with his sister. *Brothers and sisters. Indians of North America. United States. Army. Cavalry. Wagon trains.*
FD 24 Nov 1929. *Var* 20 Nov 1929, p. 33.

IR TSVEYTE MAME *see* **HER SECOND MOTHER**

IRENE (Irish Americans)
First National Pictures, Inc. *Dist* First National Pictures, Inc. 21 Feb **1926** [©First National Pictures, Inc.; 10 Feb 1926; LP22387]. Si; b&w with col sequences (Technicolor). 9 reels, 8,400 ft.
Pres John McCormick. *Dir* Alfred E. Green. *Scen* Rex Taylor. *Editorial dir, cont* June Mathis. *Comedy const* Mervyn LeRoy. *Titles* George Marion, Jr. *Photog* T. D. McCord. *Lighting eff* Lawrence Kennedy. *Art dir* John D. Schulze. *Film ed* Edwin Robbins. *Mus* Harry Tierney and Joseph McCarthy.
Source: Based on the musical *Irene* by James Montgomery (New York, 1 Nov 1919).
Cast: Colleen Moore (*Irene O'Dare*), Lloyd Hughes (*Donald Marshall*), George K. Arthur (*Madame Lucy*), Charles Murray (*Pa O'Dare*), Kate Price (*Ma O'Dare*), Ida Darling (*Mrs. Warren Marshall*), Eva Novak (*Eleanor Hadley*), Edward Earle (*Larry Hadley*), Laurence Wheat (*Bob Harrison*), Maryon Aye (*Helen Cheston*), Bess Flowers (*Jane Gilmour*), Lydia Yeamans Titus (*Mrs. Cheston*), Cora Macey (*Mrs. Gilmour*).
Romantic comedy. Irene O'Dare, a wistful Irish lass looking for a job in New York City, meets Donald Marshall, a wealthy aristocrat, who arranges for her to become a model in a new modiste's shop. But when the male proprietor, Madame Lucy, gives a fashion show, he leaves Irene behind to watch the shop. Donald finds her there and insists that she attire herself in a new French creation and accompany him to the fashion show. Irene is an immediate sensation with everyone there except Donald's mother, who hires a genealogist to report on the girl's ancestry. After being shown the report, Irene retreats to a fire escape, where Donald finds her lamenting her plight. Overhearing Irene profess love for him, Donald climbs through the window and embraces her. *Aristocrats. Couturiers. Family relationships. Fashion shows. Genealogy. Irish Americans. Models. New York City.*
FD 7 Mar 1926. *MPW* 13 Mar 1926. *NYT* 1 Mar 1926, p. 17. *Var* 3 Mar 1926, p. 34.

THE IRISH GRINGO (Irish Americans, Latino)
Keith Productions. *Dist* State Rights. **1935?**; *Prod:* began Sep 1935. Sd; b&w. Length undetermined.

[*Prod* Patrick Carlyle and William C. Thompson]. *Assoc prod* P. B. Mahoney and I. C. Overdorff. *Dir* Wm. C. Thompson. *Story* Patrick Petersalia, [Patrick Carlyle and William C. Thompson]. *Cine* Bert Longnecker. *Mus* Chito Montoya's Orchestra. *Music dir and comp* Manuela Budrow. *Dance dir* Anthony De Marlo. *Sd* Herbert Eicke. [*Prod mgr* Robert Farfan].
Cast: PAT CARLYLE [(*Don O'Brien, the Irish Gringo*)], William Farnum [(*Pop Wiley*)], Bryant Washburn, Elena Durán, Karlyn May, Olin Francis, Milt Morante, Don Orlando, Ace Cain, Rudolph Cornell, Marjorie Medford, [Joseph Swickard], [Kit Guard].
Western. [*Print viewed*]. After a gang of outlaws tortures a man named Taggart in order to force him to reveal the site of a legendary, hidden mine, known as the "Lost Dutchman," Taggart dies, and the gang soon realizes that they have confused him with Pop Wiley, a local rancher said to know the secret of the mine's location. When the gang notices a famous cowboy, dubbed the "Irish Gringo," ride by, they alert the sheriff and tell him that the Gringo is responsible for Taggart's death. In the meantime, Pop Wiley, realizing that the outlaws are aware of his knowledge of the mine, writes its location on his little granddaughter Sally's blouse and sends her into town to stay with a young woman named Anita. One of the outlaws overhears Wiley's instructions to Sally, however, and Sally witnesses him murder her grandfather. The Gringo and his cohorts, Pancho and Buffalo, manage to elude the sheriff's posse, and when they see a suspicious looking group of men ride away from the Wiley ranch, they go to investigate. At the ranch, they discover Sally sobbing and take the orphaned child into town for some milk. Ace Lewis, owner of the town saloon, crudely proposes marriage to Anita, but she is in love with a local boy named Jimmy Melton. When Jimmy tells her that he doesn't have enough money to marry her in the church, she replies that she would be willing to wed him under the trees and adds that "it's better to make a life than a living." The Gringo overhears her and becomes fond of both Anita and the saying, and he tells her that his real name is Don O'Brien and that he is half Mexican and half Irish. In addition to being a saloon owner, Ace, a murderer on the lam, is part of the gang searching for the Lost Dutchman. While a local woman named Carlotta, who is in love with the Gringo, knits a dress for Sally, she overhears the gang boasting that they framed the Gringo for Taggart's murder, and when he enters the saloon, the outlaws attempt to make a citizen's arrest. After a fight, the Gringo escapes with Carlotta, but when he stops to visit the minister to make arrangements for Anita's wedding, Carlotta misunderstands and becomes enraged with jealousy. After telling Ace all she knows, Carlotta goes to kill Anita, but finds her in Jimmy's arms and realizes her mistake. Carlotta warns the Gringo that the gang is after him, and he is ready to fight when they show up at Anita's wedding. Pancho shoots Ace, and the Gringo gives the blouse with the map, along with Sally, to the newlyweds, who already consider Sally as part of their family. As the Gringo rides away with Buffalo and Pancho, he believes that he has left the love-sick Carlotta behind, however she follows him. *Children. Cowboys. Good Samaritans. Irish Americans. Mexican Americans. Mines and mineral resources. Outlaws. Fights. Frame-ups. Grandfathers. Jealousy. Maps. Mistaken identity. Murder. Orphans. Posses. Ranchers. Saloon Keepers. Sheriffs. Torture. Unrequited love. Weddings.*
Note: Although a copyright statement appears in this picture's onscreen credits, its title is not listed in copyright register. No reviews were located for this film. According to a news item in *MPH*, this was the first of six outdoor pictures to star Pat Carlyle; however, no information concerning the production of subsequent films in the series has been found. Interiors were filmed in the Bryan Foy Studio. According to a Feb 1936 *HR* news item, creditors, including Western Film Lab and Agfa, foreclosed on the negative. The news item also states that Mrs. Alice Keith, a housewife, backed the film with a $2,500 investment. Modern sources indicate that Pat Carlyle was best known for his work in sex-exploitation pictures, and add Horace B. Carpenter and Foxy Callahan to the cast.
HR 29 Feb 1936, p. 8. *MPH* 28 Sep 1935, p. 349.

IRISH HEARTS (Irish Americans)
Warner Bros. Pictures, Inc. *Dist* Warner Bros. Pictures, Inc. 21 May **1927** [©Warner Bros. Pictures, Inc.; 14 May 1927; LP23958]. Si; b&w. 6 reels, 5,597 ft.
Dir Byron Haskin. *Asst dir* Gordon Hollingshead. *Scr* Bess Meredyth and Graham Baker. *Story* Melville Crossman. *Cam* Virgil Miller.
Cast: May McAvoy (*Sheila*), Jason Robards (*Rory*), Warner Richmond (*Emmett*), Kathleen Key (*Clarice*), Walter Perry (*Sheila's*

father), Walter Rodgers (*Restaurant proprietor*), Les Bates (*Taxi driver*).

Comedy-drama. Sheila, a happy and carefree colleen, loves Emmett, a shiftless Irish lad who goes to America to seek his fortune. While Sheila and her father are en route to join him, her father gives the steward her shamrock in payment for liquor, and she becomes wildly apprehensive. Learning Emmett has lost his job, Sheila is forced to work in a beanery, where she meets Rory, a poor American boy, who is attracted to her. Sheila is bitterly disappointed, however, when Emmett takes up with Clarice, a flashy flapper; she confides her troubles to Rory, who is currently employed as a section hand in a shipyard. When she is jilted by Emmett, missiles of food and crockery send the wedding party flying into the street. Rory finds the lost shamrock and looks forward to happiness with the triumphant Sheila. *Courtship. Flappers. Immigrants. Irish Americans. Shipyards. Talismans. Weddings.*
FD 29 May 1927. *MPW* 11 Jun 1927. *Var* 18 May 1927, p. 21.

THE IRISH IN US (Irish Americans)
Warner Bros. Pictures, Inc.; A First National Picture. *Dist* Warner Bros. Pictures, Inc.; The Vitaphone Corp. 3 Aug **1935**; *Prod*: began 25 May 1935 [©Warner Bros. Pictures, Inc.; 14 Aug 1935; LP5714]. Sd; b&w. 8 reels. 80 or 84 min. PCA cert no. 1049.
[*Prod* Sam Bischoff]. *Dir* Lloyd Bacon. [*Asst dir* Jack Sullivan]. *Scr* Earl Baldwin. *Story idea* Frank Orsatti. *Photog* George Barnes. *Art dir* Esdras Hartley. *Ed* James Gibbon. *Mus dir* Leo F. Forbstein.
Cast: James Cagney (*Danny O'Hara*), Pat O'Brien (*Pat O'Hara*), Olivia de Havilland (*Lucille Jackson*), Frank McHugh (*Mike O'Hara*), Allen Jenkins (*Carbarn [Hammerschlog]*), Mary Gordon (*Ma O'Hara*), J. Farrell McDonald [(*Captain Jackson*)], Thomas Jackson [(*Doc Mullins*)], Harvey Perry [(*Joe Delancy*)], [Mable Colcord (*Neighbor*)], [Edward Keane (*Doctor*)], [Herbert Heywood (*Cook*)], [Harry Seymour (*Announcer*)], [Sailor Vincent (*Chick*)], [Mushy Callahan (*Referee*)], [Jack McHugh (*Messenger boy*)], [Lucille Collins], [Edward Gargan], [Huntley Gordon], [Emmett Vogan], [Will Stanton].
Boxing, Comedy. [*Print viewed*]. Two of Ma O'Hara's three sons have solid jobs. Mike is a fireman and Pat is a policeman, but Danny, Ma's favorite because he is the youngest, is an occasional fight promoter who has never handled a successful boxer. Pat tries to talk Danny into taking the police exam, because he is planning to marry Lucille Jackson, his captain's daughter, and is worried that the family will not be able to get along without his salary. Danny is not interested, however, having discovered a new fighter, Carbarn Hammerschlog, who comes out slugging whenever he hears a bell. Anxious for Lucille to meet his mother, Pat asks her home to dinner, but Danny meets her first, by accident, when he and Carbarn help her change a flat tire. Lucille and Ma become friends right away, but Lucille causes her some distress when she admits that Pat has not asked her to marry him. When Pat tries to change out of his uniform, he discovers that Danny has loaned his best suit to Carbarn and then, to add insult to injury, he happens to be standing next to Carbarn when a bell rings and Carbarn knocks him out. With the dinner ruined, Danny offers to take Lucille home, and they stop along the way for an intimate dinner. Later, Lucille agrees to be Pat's date at the Fireman's Ball, but she cannot stay away from Danny. Pat sees them kissing and is so hurt that he plans to leave home until Danny moves out himself. Upset at having come between the two brothers, Lucille visits Danny at the gym to tell him she is not in love with him. Danny finally gets Carbarn a fight with the champion. Before the fight, Carbarn gets drunk while trying to kill a toothache with a bottle of gin, and Danny must go on in his place. He takes a beating, but keeps on fighting. At Ma's insistence, Pat gets into Danny's corner to tell him that Lucille does love him. Inspired, Danny defeats the champ and is reunited with his brother and Lucille. *Brothers. Family life. Irish Americans. Mothers and sons. Romantic rivalry. Boxers. Boxing. Dances. Drunkenness. Firemen. New York City. Police. Self-sacrifice. Toothache.*
Note: A modern source notes that publicity for this film focused on the fact that James Cagney did his own boxing. Modern sources add the following crew credits: *Gowns* Orry-Kelly; *Makeup artist* Perc Westmore; and *Unit mgr* Bob Fellows. Modern sources list Bess Flowers in the part of "Lady in ring."
DV 25 May 1935, p. 3. *DV* 10 Jul 1935, p. 3. *FD* 1 Aug 1935, p. 10. *HR* 10 Jul 1935, p. 4. *MPD* 11 Jul 1935, p. 8. *MPH* 13 Jul 1935, p. 68. *MPH* 20 Jul 1935, p. 88. *NYT* 1 Aug 1935, p. 15. *Var* 7 Aug 1935, p. 21.

IRISH LUCK (Irish Americans)
Famous Players-Lasky Corp. *Dist* Paramount Pictures. 7 Dec **1925**; New York premiere: 22 Nov 1925 [©Famous Players-Lasky Corp.; 8 Dec 1925; LP22093]. Si; b&w. 7 reels, 7,008 ft.
Pres Adolph Zukor and Jesse L. Lasky. *Dir* Victor Heerman. *Scr* Tom J. Geraghty. *Photog* Alvin Wyckoff. *Art dir* Walter E. Keller.
Source: Based on the novel *The Imperfect Imposter* by Norman Venner (New York, 1925).
Cast: Thomas Meighan (*Tom Donahue/Lord Fitzhugh*), Lois Wilson (*Lady Gwendolyn*), Cecil Humphreys (*Douglas*), Claude King (*Solicitor*), Ernest Lawford (*Earl*), Charles Hammond (*Doctor*), Louise Grafton (*Aunt*), S. B. Carrickson (*Uncle*), Charles McDonald (*Denis MacSwiney*), Mary Foy (*Kate MacSwiney*).
Melodrama. Tom Donahue, a New York traffic cop, wins a trip to Europe in a newspaper contest, and he decides to visit relatives in Ireland. Arriving in Dublin, he learns that he is an exact double for Lord Fitzhugh, a young Irish aristocrat with whom he becomes friends. The Earl of Killarney, Fitzhugh's uncle, who is on his deathbed, wishes to see his favorite nephew and wipe out past animosities. Fitzhugh, in the meantime, has disappeared, and his sister, Lady Gwendolyn, persuades Tom to take his place. Tom successfully impersonates Fitzhugh, thus assuring the latter's inheritance, and uncovers a conspiracy led by Douglas, another nephew, to kill Fitzhugh after the uncle's death and thus gain the estate. Fitzhugh is freed, and Tom wins the hand of Gwendolyn. *Aristocrats. Contests. Doubles. Dublin (Ireland). Impersonation and imposture. Inheritance. Ireland. Irish Americans. Police. Swindlers and swindling.*
Note: Most of the principal photography was done on location in Ireland.
FD 29 Nov 1925. *NYT* 24 Nov 1925, p. 28. *Var* 25 Nov 1925, p. 38.

THE IRON BEAST *see* AN ALIEN ENEMY

THE IRON MISTRESS (French Americans, Latino)
Warner Bros. Pictures, Inc.; A Warner Bros.—First National Picture. *Dist* Warner Bros. Pictures, Inc. 22 Nov **1952**; New York opening: week of 19 Nov 1952; *Prod*: early Apr–early Jun 1952 [©Warner Bros. Pictures, Inc.; 8 Nov 1952; LP2072]. Sd (RCA Sound System); col (Technicolor). 9,844 ft. 109-110 min. PCA cert no. 15877.
Prod Henry Blanke. *Dir* Gordon Douglas. *Asst dir* Oren Haglund. *Scr* James R. Webb. *Dir of photog* John Seitz. *Technicolor color consultant* Mitchell G. Kovaleski. *Art dir* John Beckman. *Film ed* Alan Crosland, Jr. *Set dec* George James Hopkins. *Ward* Marjorie Best. *Mus* Max Steiner. *Orch* Murray Cutter. *Sd* Stanley Jones. *Makeup artist* Gordon Bau.
Source: Based on the novel *The Iron Mistress* by Paul Iselin Wellman (Garden City, NY, 1951).
Cast: ALAN LADD [(*Jim Bowie*)], VIRGINIA MAYO [(*Judalon de Bornay*)], Joseph Calleia [(*Juan Moreno*)], Phyllis Kirk [(*Ursula de Veramendi*)], Alf Kjellin [(*Philippe de Cabanal*)], Douglas Dick [(*Narcisse de Bornay*)], Tony Caruso [(*"Bloody Jack" Sturdevant*)], Ned Young [(*Henri Contrecourt*)], George Voskovec [(*James Audubon*)], Richard Carlyle [(*Rezin Bowie*)], Robert Emhardt [(*Gen. Cuny*)], Donald Beddoe [(*Dr. Cuny*)], Harold Gordon [(*Andrew Marschalk*)], Gordon Nelson [(*Dr. Maddox*)], Jay Novello [(*Judge Crain*)], Nick Dennis [(*Nez Coupe*)], Sarah Selby [(*Mrs. Bowie*)], [Dick Paxton (*John Bowie*)], [George Lewis (*Col. Wells*)], [Edward Colmans (*Don Juan de Veramendi*)], [Daria Massey (*Teresa de Veramendi*)], [David Wolfe (*James Black*)], [Ramsey Hill (*Malot*)], [Eugene Borden (*Cocquelon*)], [Jean Del Val (*St. Sylvain*)], [Amanda Randolph (*Maria*)], [Wesley Gale (*Vendor*)], [Ann Codee (*Landlady*)], [Marcel De La Brosse (*Husband*)], [Juanita Moore, Frances Driver (*Maids*)], [Cecil Weston (*Seamstress*)], [Ivan Browning (*Butler*)], [Rudy Friml (*Orchestra leader*)], [Peter Camlin (*Croupier*)], [Victor Perrin (*Attendant*)], [Reed Howes, Dick Cogan (*Players*)], [Dave McMahon (*Waiter*)], [Charlita (*Girl*)], [Dick Bartell (*Starter*)], [Fred Rapport, Bill Griffith, Robert Strong (*Bettors*)], [Madge Blake (*Mrs. Cuny*)], [Stanley Fraser (*Al Blanchard*)], [Roger Cole (*Carey Blanchard*)], [Marshall Ruth (*Official*)], [Lawrence Marable (*Drummer*)], [Morris Buchanan (*Sam*)], [Harvey Parry (*Burke*)], [Louis Tomei (*Heacock*)], [Jack Carr (*Jake*)], [Roque Ybarra (*Postillion*)], [Alberto Morin (*Coachman*)], [Argentina Brunetti (*Duenna*)], [Frank Ferguson (*Doctor*)], [Oliver Blake (*Innkeeper*)], [Gabriel Peralta (*Butler*)], [Enrique Valadez, Juan Lopez, Primo Lopez, Gloria Varela, Dorita Pallais, Carmen Pallais (*Merrymakers*)],

[Ralph Smiley (*Latour*)], [Gayle Kellogg (*Payne*)], [W. Harry Brown (*Duran*)], [Ernest Anderson (*Cabin steward*)], [Carlo Tricoli (*Priest*)], [Salvador Baguez (*Mexican artist*)].

Historical, Western. [*Print viewed*]. In 1825, Jim Bowie journeys to New Orleans from his family's backwoods home in Bayou Sara to sell some lumber. His brothers caution Jim, a carefree young man whose only interest is in throwing knives, to hold out for a good price. In New Orleans, Jim makes the acquaintance of French painter James Audubon, who has angered the wealthy de Bornay family by painting birds instead of completing his portrait of the beautiful Judalon de Bornay. For verbally defending Audubon, Jim is challenged to a duel by Judalon's brother Narcisse. The challenge surprises Jim, who never intended to insult Narcisse, but Audubon explains that the upper classes of Louisiana's French-dominated society are strictly governed by "the code" of honor. Jim's use of gentle humor to prevent the duel charms Narcisse, and the two become friends. Narcisse worries, therefore, when Jim falls in love with Judalon, who is proud and spoiled. Judalon allows Jim to kiss her at a ball, but his passionate marriage proposal makes her angry, as Judalon has no intention of living on a bayou. Assuming that Jim has insulted Judalon, another suitor named Henri Contrecourt challenges him to a duel. Narcisse intervenes and is killed in the ensuing confrontation with Contrecourt. Jim then agrees to face Contrecourt, an excellent swordsman, armed only with his knife, and the two fight in a darkened chamber. To the surprise of the assembled crowd, Jim kills Contrecourt. He then sells the lumber mill and returns home with a plan to get rich by planting cotton in the bayou country. Over the next few years, the Bowies do become wealthy, but their business rivals, headed by Natchez cotton grower Juan Moreno, try to ruin them. Undeterred, Jim buys an unknown racehorse that defeats Moreno's steed in a race. Most of Moreno's cohorts pay Jim the money they bet, but Jim expects trouble and asks an expert blacksmith named Black to make him a strong knife. Black shapes a piece of a meteor into the knife, thereby making it unusually durable and sharp. Later, Jim discovers that Judalon has wed a New Orleans gentleman named Philippe de Cabanal, but after kissing Jim, she tells him that she is planning a divorce. Jim's brother suspects that she now wants to marry Moreno, but Jim is devoted to Judalon and refuses to listen. Following a duel, Moreno and his colleagues begin shooting at Jim and his friends, and after Moreno injures him, Jim stabs him to death. Judalon, unhappy because Moreno had promised to secure a bill of divorcement for her, promises to accompany Jim to a new home in Texas if he first has her husband released from a gambling debt to "Bloody Jack" Sturdevant. Jim defeats Sturdevant in a knife fight, but Judalon sends word that she has decided to remain with Philippe. En route to Texas, Jim is nearly killed by Sturdevant's men. He is found and nursed to recovery by Ursula de Veramendi, the Spanish daughter of the Texas vice governor. Jim soon proposes to Ursula, but she suspects he still loves Judalon. Jim returns to Louisiana to sell his lands, and on a steamboat, he encounters Judalon and Philippe. Jim learns that Philippe has lost all his money in a card game, but he exposes the gamblers as cheats and returns Philippe's money. After Judalon threatens to leave Philippe for her old admirer, the angry husband sneaks into Jim's room with a gun. At the same time, Sturdevant, seeking revenge for his earlier injury, hides in Jim's cabin, intending to kill him, but instead stabs Philippe by accident. Philippe shoots Sturdevant before dying himself, and Judalon's obvious glee at her husband's death stuns Jim. He leaves her, then drops his knife into the river and returns to San Antonio to marry Ursula. *James Bowie. Class distinction. Duels. Honor. Infatuation. Knife fighting. Pride and vanity. Social climbers. Attempted murder. John James Audubon. Bayous. Blacksmiths. Brothers and sisters. Business rivals. Cotton. Debt. Entrepreneurs. French Americans. Gamblers. Governors. Latino. Horseracing. Infidelity. Knife throwing. Knives. Marriage. New Orleans (LA). Painters (Of paintings). Portraits (Paintings). Revenge. Spanish Americans. Steamboats. Texas. Wagers.*

Note: The role of "Jim Bowie" was Alan Ladd's first under his contract with Warner Bros. As Bosley Crowther remarked in his *NYT* review, the film bears little resemblance to Paul Wellman's bestselling book, in which the legendary Bowie was portrayed as "something of a rascal in New Orleans in the days of Jean Lafitte." The real-life Jim Bowie was born in 1796, in either Georgia, Kentucky or Tennessee. As a young man, he moved to Texas, becoming a naturalized Mexican citizen, and in 1830, enlisted in the Texas Rangers. After fighting against the Indians, he joined the rebellion against Mexico and formed a small volunteer force. In Feb 1836, Bowie was designated the commander of the Alamo along with William B. Travis. When Bowie fell ill during the Mexican

siege of the Alamo, however, Travis took over as sole commander. The rebels were defeated by a superior Mexican force, and Bowie was killed during the battle on 6 Mar 1836. Bowie is credited with inventing the Bowie knife, a weapon widely used in the old West. According to Crowther, "the early career of Bowie is thoroughly fabled and carpentered" in the film. Although Richard Crane is listed in the role of "John Bowie" in CBCS, the part was actually played by Dick Paxton.

Box 25 Oct 1952. *DV* 16 Oct 1952, p. 3. *Exh* 22 Oct 1952, p. 3400. *FD* 20 Oct 1952, p. 6. *Har* 18 Oct 1952, p. 167. *HR* 4 Apr 1952, p. 11. *HR* 29 May 1952, p. 12. *HR* 16 Oct 1952, p. 3. *MPHPD* 18 Oct 1952, p. 1565. *NYT* 20 Nov 1952, p. 39. *Var* 22 Oct 1952, p. 6.

THE IROQUOIS TRAIL (Native Americans, Iroquois, Huron, Mohawk)

Edward Small Productions, Inc.; Reliance Pictures, Inc. *Dist* United Artists Corp. 16 Jun 1950; Prod: early Oct—early Nov 1949 at Motion Picture Center [©Reliance Pictures, Inc.; 16 Jun 1950; LP165]. Sd (RCA Sound System); b&w. 10 reels, 7,771 ft. 85-86 min. PCA cert no. 14258.

Pres EDWARD SMALL. *Prod* Bernard Small. *Dir* Phil Karlson. *Asst dir* Emmett Emerson. *Scr* Richard Schayer. *Dir of photog* Henry Freulich. *Art dir* Edward Ilou. *Film ed* Kenneth Crane. *Set dec* Robert Priestly. *Mus dir* Rudy Schrager. *Sd* Victor Appel and [Roger White]. *Makeup artist* Kiva Hoffman and George Bau. *Hair stylist* Carmen Dirigo. *Prod supv* Ben Hersh.

Source: Based on the novel *The Last of the Mohicans* by James Fenimore Cooper (Boston, 1826).

Cast: George Montgomery [(*Nat "Hawkeye" Cutler*)], Brenda Marshall [(*Marion Thorne*)], Glenn Langan [(*Capt. Jonathan West*)], Monte Blue [(*Sagamore*)], Paul Cavanagh [(*Col. Eric Thorne*)], Sheldon Leonard [(*Ogane*)], Reginald Denny [(*Capt. Brownell*)], Dan O'Herlihy [(*Lt. Blakeley*)], John Doucette [(*Sam Girty*)], [Don Gerner (*Sgt. Tom Cutler*)], [Marcel Gourmet (*General Montcalm*)], [Arthur Little, Jr. (*Adjutant Dickson*)], [Esther Somers (*Ma Cutler*)].

Historical, Military, Western. [*Print viewed*]. By 1755, fighting between England and France spills over into the New World and begins to affect the colonies. At the British headquarters in Albany, New York, near the southern edge of the ancient Indian war path known as the Iroquois Trail, Capt. Jonathan West delivers a dispatch to Col. Eric Thorne, the father of his onetime sweetheart Marion. Thorne summons all officers to Gen. Johnson's office, where they learn that French Gen. Montcalm's troops and his allies, the Huron Indians, have assembled at the border and threaten to attack their garrison at Crown Point. Thorne orders Sgt. Tom Cutler to deliver a dispatch to warn Crown Point of the impending attack and tells trail scout Sam Girty and his guide Ogane, a Huron chieftain impersonating a friendly Delaware Indian, to lead him to his mother's cabin, where he will be able to pick up the trail. They arrive, and when Tom says farewell and turns to enter the cabin, Girty shoots him in the back and steals the dispatch from his saddle bag. At that moment, Ma Cutler's other son Nat, whose scouting abilities have earned him the nickname "Hawkeye," arrives at the cabin with his Delaware Indian guide, Sagamore. Girty, meanwhile, tells Ogane to scalp Tom so that the Army will suspect that Indians killed him, but before he can do so, they see Nat running toward them firing his gun. After they escape, Girty instructs Ogane to deliver the dispatch to Montcalm, then lies to Lt. Blakeley, saying that Tom willingly gave the dispatch to a Huron. Meanwhile, at her cabin, Ma nurses Tom, who is drifting in and out of consciousness. Sometime later, Nat finds Girty at a tavern and shoots him, but he escapes on a horse. Later, Gen. Johnson receives word that an unsupported Crown Point has been attacked and assigns Jonathan to Fort Williams, near the Crown Point. Johnson then tells Marion, Jonathan and Sagamore to follow Ogane to Fort Williams, where they will arrive a couple of days ahead of the battalion. Nat and Sagamore are given permission to accompany them and help the party escape unharmed after they are attacked by Ogane's braves. Shortly after they arrive at the fort, Montcalm's forces attack, and a five-day siege ensues. When the fort runs short of gunpowder, Blakeley decides to send Ogane for reinforcements. Ogane leaves to meet secretly with Capt. Brownell, a French soldier spying in the British ranks, and Nat and Sagamore follow. Not realizing that Brownell is also a spy, Nat bursts in and exposes Ogane as a traitor. Brownell tries to draw his gun, but Nat does so first and shoots him, after which Nat and Sagamore are locked in the fort's jail. Ogane's braves break into the fort, kidnap Marion and take her back

to the Huron village, where Ogane plans to marry her. Before the ceremony is performed, Marion is rescued by Nat and Sagamore. While they are escaping, however, Sagamore is killed when a Huron throws a tomahawk into his back. Sometime later at headquarters, Jonathan celebrates his new assignment as battalion commander, while Nat eagerly accepts his assignment as a battalion scout. *Espionage. Forts. United States–History–French and Indian War, 1755-1763. United States. Army. Albany (NY). Cabins. Delaware Indians. Escapes. Family relationships. French Americans. Guides. Gunshot wounds. Huron Indians. Iroquois Indians. Jails. Kidnapping. Liars. Officers (Military). Saloons. Treason. Tribal chiefs. Villages.*

Note: This film was shot at Bartlett's Lake in Big Bear, CA, and marked Edward Small's last production for United Artists. For information on other filmed adaptations of James Fenimore Cooper's novel, see entry below for the 1936 United Artists production *The Last of the Mohicans.*

Box 10 Jun 1950. *DV* 5 Jun 1950, p. 3. *FD* 5 Jun 1950, p. 6. *HR* 8 Aug 1949, p. 2. *HR* 3 Oct 1949, p. 2. *HR* 7 Oct 1949, p. 11. *HR* 4 Nov 1949, p. 15. *HR* 5 Jun 1950, p. 3. *MPHPD* 10 Jun 1950, pp. 329-30. *Var* 27 Oct 1950, p. 24. *Var* 7 Jun 1950, p. 8.

IS EVERYBODY HAPPY? (Hungarian Americans)

Warner Bros. Pictures, Inc. *Dist* Warner Bros. Pictures, Inc. 19 Oct **1929** [©Warner Bros. Pictures, Inc.; 6 Oct 1929; LP749]. Sd (Vitaphone); b&w. 9 reels, 7,311 ft. [Also si.].

Dir Archie L. Mayo. *Story, scen and dial* James A. Starr and Joseph Jackson. *Titles* De Leon Anthony. *Photog* Ben Reynolds. *Film ed* Desmond O'Brien. *Dance dir* Larry Ceballos.

Song(s): "Wouldn't It Be Wonderful?" "I'm the Medicine Man for the Blues," "New Orleans" and "Samoa," by Grant Clarke and Harry Akst; "In the Land of Jazz" and "Start the Band," by Ted Lewis; "St. Louis Blues," by W. C. Handy; "Tiger Rag," music by The Original Dixieland Jazz Band, lyrics by Harry DeCosta.

Cast: Ted Lewis (*Ted Todd*), Alice Day (*Gail Wilson*), Ann Pennington (*Lena Schmitt*), Lawrence Grant (*Victor Molnár*), Julia Swayne Gordon (*Mrs. Molnár*), Otto Hoffman (*Landlord*), Purnell Pratt (*Stage manager*).

Domestic, Drama. Victor Molnár, an orchestra conductor in Budapest, retires and emigrates to the United States with his wife and young son, Ted, who takes with him a prized violin presented to him by Emperor Franz Joseph. They rent an inexpensive apartment in New York, and Ted looks up Lena, his former sweetheart, now a member of the Ziegfeld Follies. Ashamed of Ted's appearance, she greets him coolly. Ted is unable to find work with a symphony orchestra, and, faced with overdue rent, he borrows money on the precious violin, telling the family he has a job. Meanwhile, he practices the saxophone in the park, where he meets Gail, who is employed by a theatrical manager. When his parents discover him playing jazz in a Hungarian café, they are outraged and his father is heartbroken. Aided by Gail, Ted forms his own jazz band and becomes a star, and a family reconciliation takes place on Christmas Day. *Budapest (Hungary). Christmas. Conductors (Music). Family life. Francis Joseph I, Emperor of Austria, 1830-1916. Hungarians. Jazz music. Musicians. New York City. Saxophones. Violinists. Ziegfeld Follies.*

FD 10 Nov 1929. *NYT* 2 Nov 1929, p. 14. *Var* 6 Nov 1929, p. 19.

IS THIS LOVE? see SEI TU L'AMORE

ISLAND OF FORGOTTEN SIN see PRISONER OF JAPAN

IT COULD HAPPEN TO YOU (Immigrants)

Republic Pictures Corp. *Dist* Republic Pictures Corp. 28 Jun **1937**; *Prod:* Apr 1937 [©Republic Pictures Corp.; 28 Jun 1937; LP7334]. Sd (RCA Victor "High Fidelity" Sound System); b&w. 8 reels, 5,948 ft. 64 or 71 min. Passed by the National Board of Review. PCA cert no. 3355.

Assoc prod Leonard Fields. *Dir* Phil Rosen. *Asst dir* Phil Ford. *Scr* Samuel Ornitz and Nathanael West. *Story* Nathanael West. *Photog* Jack Marta. *Film ed* Ernest Nims. *Supv ed* Murray Seldeen. *Cost* Eloise. *Mus supv* Alberto Colombo. *Orch* Clarence Wheeler. *Sd eng* Terry Kellum.

Cast: Alan Baxter (*Bob Ames*), Andrea Leeds (*Laura Compton*), Owen Davis, Jr. (*Fred Barrett*), Astrid Allwyn (*Angela*), Walter Kingsford (*Professor Schwab*), Al Shean (*Max "Pa" Barrett*), Christian Rub (*Clavish*), Else Janssen (*Mrs. Clavish*), Edward Colebrook (*Pogano*), Stanley King (*Detective*), Nina Campana (*Italian woman*), Frank Yaconelli (*Greek*), John Hamilton (*Judge*), Paul Stanton (*District attorney*), Bob Murphy (*Moriarity*), Cy Kendall (*Detective*), Robert Anderson ("*Swede*"), Bert Sprotte

(*German*), Sada Simmons (*Swedish woman*), Hans Joby (*Small German*), Betty Holt (*Tessie*), Leonard Kibrick, Mickey Martin (*Boys*), Jack Carson, Yakima Canutt (*Truck drivers*), Leon Werner (*Russian singer*), Joan Havard (*Mickey*), Charles McAvoy, Rodney Hildebrand, Ed Schaefer (*Policemen*), Sam Flint (*President of faculty*), Grace Hayle (*Woman reporter*), Dirk Thane (*Chronicle reporter*), William Castle (*Dignified reporter*), Richard Beach (*Wrong reporter*), Robert Parrish, Rolf Ernest (*Runners*), George Magrill, Carleton Young, Frank Wayne (*Thugs*), Hans Von Morhart (*Purser*), Walter Thiele (*Steward*), Hedwiga Reicher (*German lady at boardinghouse*), James Sarno (*Clerk*), Jack Kenny (*Man on tree*), Harry Semels (*Fatso*), Adolph Milar, Max Etzkorn, Dina Smirnova, Victor De Linsky, Morgan Brown, Martha Bamattre, Harrison Greene.

Crime, Drama. [*Not viewed*]. Kindly Max Barrett, known to everyone as "Pa," is the proud owner of a candy store frequented by the other immigrants living in his New York East Side neighborhood. Pa's son Fred, an aspiring lawyer, has been reared with Bob Ames, an orphan whom Pa took in as a child. Bob works in a bookie's office with his former girl friend Angela, but aspires to a better life. When Professor Schwab announces that he is retiring from running the Foreign American institute, at which immigrants can learn how to become good American citizens, Bob sees his chance. In order to buy the school from Schwab, Bob attempts to pull a scam at the race track with Angela, but they are found out by their employer and dismissed. Desperate to obtain the money, Bob remembers the $600 showed to him by Pa, who has saved it to set up Fred in his own office. On the night of Fred's graduation from law school, Bob robs the candy store. Pa, who has forgotten his ticket to the commencement exercises, returns to the store and is killed by Bob, who does not recognize him until it is too late. The crime goes unsolved, but Laura Compton, Bob and Fred's childhood friend, with whom they are both in love, tells the police that one of the stolen bills was torn and repaired with tape. Schwab recognizes the bill as one with which Bob paid for the institute, and blackmails him into taking him on as a partner. Schwab then forces Bob to turn the school into a racket that threatens neighborhood immigrants with deportation if they do not attend the school and pay the five dollars-a-week tuition. The immigrants are furious with the deal, and Bob grows despondent over having to betray his lifelong friends. Tired of Angela, who is still in love with him, Bob tries to get Schwab to dismiss her, and she angrily tells the police the truth about Pa's murder. Refusing to believe that his friend could be guilty, Fred defends him and convinces the jury that the most damning evidence, Bob's fingerprints on the cookie jar containing Pa's money, is a natural result of Bob having grown up with the Barretts. After he is acquitted, Bob orders Schwab to leave the country, telling him that because he has been acquitted once, he cannot be tried again and is therefore free of Schwab's power over him. Schwab threatens to show the incriminating bill to Fred and Laura, and while the men argue, they are involved in a car accident, and Schwab is killed. Bob then goes to the institute, where he meets Fred and Laura. As they are talking, the angry students, fed up with the racket, storm the school and threaten to lynch Fred and Bob. Hoping to save Fred, Bob climbs to the roof and confesses that he murdered Pa and engineered the racket. The mob still threatens Fred, despite Bob's pleas that his friend is innocent, and so to convince them, Bob jumps from the building. Later, after Bob's funeral, Fred and Laura console each other with the knowledge that the school, now called the Max Barrett Institute, will be run legitimately. *Blackmail. Immigrants. Lawyers. Murder. Racketeers. Schools. Automobile accidents. Bookies. Candy. Evidence. Fingerprints. Foster parents. Jealousy. Jumps from heights. Lynching. Mobs. New York City–East Side. Romantic rivalry. Suicide. Trials.*

Note: The working titles of this film were *Gangs of New York* and *It Might Happen to You. Gangs of New York* was also the title of a 1938 Republic film, directed by James Cruze, that was about New York gangsters. Republic bought a novel by that title in Apr 1936 and some news items in late 1936 could be referring to either the 1937 film *It Could Happen to You* or the 1938 film *Gangs of New York* as both films were apparently known by the latter title during that period. According to the MPAA/PCA Collection at the AMPAS Library, the PCA rejected two early versions of the screenplay because they violated a resolution adopted by the PCA Board of Directors that prohibited portrayals of "the activities of American gangster armed and in violent conflict with the law, or law-enforcing officers." Once the gangster elements were removed and the violence toned down, the script was approved. A *HR* news item reported that "sideline musician" Harold Sorenson died while working on the picture.

DV 16 Jun 1937, p. 3. FD 18 Aug 1937, p. 1. HR 13 Nov 1936, p. 14. HR 18 Mar 1937, p. 3. HR 7 Apr 1937, p. 27. HR 8 Apr 1937, p. 2. HR 12 Apr 1937, p. 10. HR 19 Apr 1937, p. 6. HR 16 Jun 1937, p. 2. MPD 2 Jul 1937, p. 9. MPH 15 May 1937, p. 35. Var 7 Jul 1937, p. 13.

IT HAD TO BE YOU (Native Americans)

Columbia Pictures Corp.; A Don Hartman Production. *Dist* Columbia Pictures Corp. Dec **1947**; Prod: 6 May—15 Jul 1947 [©Columbia Pictures Corp.; 25 Nov 1947; LP1299]. Sd (Western Electric Recording); b&w. 98 min. PCA cert no. 12546.

Dir Don Hartman and Rudolph Maté. *Asst dir* Sam Nelson. *Scr* Norman Panama and Melvin Frank. *Story* Don Hartman and Allen Boretz. *Dir of photog* Rudolph Maté and Vincent Farrar. *Art dir* Stephen Goossón and Rudolph Sternad. *Film ed* Gene Havlick. *Set dec* Wilbur Menefee and William Kiernan. *Gowns* Jean Louis. *Jewels by* Lackritz. *Mus dir* M. W. Stoloff. *Sd rec* Jack Haynes. *Hair styles by* Helen Hunt. *Makeup* Clay Campbell. *Asst to the producer* Norman Deming.

Cast: GINGER ROGERS [(*Victoria Stafford*)], CORNEL WILDE [(*George McKesson/Johnny Blaine*)], Percy Waram [(*Ned Stafford*)], Spring Byington [(*Mrs. Stafford*)], Ron Randell [(*Oliver H. P. Harrington*)], Thurston Hall [(*Mr. Harrington*)], Charles Evans [(*Dr. Parkinson*)], William Bevan [(*Evans*)], Frank Orth [(*Conductor Brown*)], [Harry Hays Morgan (*George Benson*)], [Douglas Wood (*Mr. Kimberly*)], [Mary Forbes (*Mrs. Kimberly*)], [Nancy Saunders (*Model*)], [Douglas D. Coppin (*Boyfriend*)], [Michael Towne, Tom Daly, Fred Sears, George Riley (*Firemen*)], [Paul Campbell (*Radio announcer*)], [Carol Nugent (*Victoria, age six*)], [Jerry Hunt (*Indian boy*)], [Judy Nugent (*Victoria, age five*)], [Mary Patterson (*Victoria, age three*)], [Dudley Dickerson (*Porter*)], [Ralph Peters, Garry Owen, Ray Hyke (*Cab drivers*)], [Harlan Warde (*Atherton*)], [Myron Healy (*Standish*)], [Jack Rice (*Floorwalker*)], [Anna Q. Nilsson, Mary Emery (*Salesladies*)], [Gerald Fielding (*Peabody*)], [Robert Riordan, Sam Flint (*Business men*)], [Edward Harvey (*Dr. Thompson*)], [Ted Stanhope (*Drug store clerk*)], [Victor Travers (*Drug store manager*)], [Vernon Dent (*Man in drug store*)], [Jessie Arnold (*Woman in drug store*)], [Cliff Clark (*Fire chief*)], [Vera Lewis (*Mrs. Brown*)], [John Duncan (*Vendor*)], [David Polonsky, Vincent Graeff, Paul Graeff, Fred Chapman, Jerry Ryan (*Kid fans*)], [Bob Ryan (*Fight referee*)], [Joe Gray, Maurice Prince (*Prize fighters*)], [Joe Palma, Charles Hamilton, Raoul Freeman, Frank McClure, Cosmo Sardo, Charles Perry (*Prizefight fans*)], [Jack Chefe (*Waiter*)], [Oscar O'Shea (*Irish neighborhood watchman*)], [George Chandler], [Wally Rose], [Hurley Breen], [Ralph Volkie], [Carl Knowles], [Cy Malis].

Fantasy, Romantic comedy. [*Print viewed*]. Victoria Stafford, a pretty Fifth Avenue society girl, has made three unsuccessful attempts to marry, each time leaving her groom at the altar just as she is about to recite her vow. So infamous is Victoria's reputation at the altar, that the father of her next fiancé, the staid Oliver H. P. Harrington, demands that she take a month vacation alone to fully consider her decision. After a month of sculpting at her vacation home in Cape Cod, Victoria, now certain about her decision to marry Oliver, boards a train back to New York. En route, Victoria has a dream about an American Indian who, while breaking up her marriage to Oliver, insists that he is the one that she truly loves. When Victoria awakens, the Indian suddenly appears in the bunk above hers, explaining that his presence, though real, is merely a manifestation of her subconscious thoughts, and that she has dreamed of him on many occasions in the past. As the train pulls into Grand Central Station, Victoria attempts to flee from the Indian, but he appears at every turn. After exchanging his Indian garb for a business suit, the Indian makes a surprise appearance at the Stafford's as Victoria is nervously trying to explain the reason for missing Oliver at the train station. Searching for an excuse, Victoria explains that she instead drove from Cape Cod and that her visitor is her sculpting model. When asked the visitor's name, Victoria sees a picture of George Washington, then notices that the Indian is still wearing his moccasins, and thus derives the name "George McKesson." Mr. Stafford, Victoria's father, does not approve of his daughter's new live-in house guest, but when he tries to throw him out, George threatens to expose a past affair of his. With less than a week to go before the wedding, Victoria, now determined more than ever to marry Oliver, warns George not to follow her. When a man who looks just like George appears at the store in which Victoria is shopping, she calls the store detective to get rid him. The man, however, insists that he has never seen Victoria before. Back at home,

while watching home movies of herself as a child, Victoria suddenly realizes that George is really Johnny Blaine, a childhood sweetheart of hers who once dressed in an Indian costume. In an instant, Victoria also realizes that the man in the store was not George, but was in fact her dream man, Johnny Blaine, in the flesh. After getting Johnny's address from his store sales receipt, Victoria rushes to his home, only to discover that he lives and works at a fire station. Although Johnny is initially indifferent to Victoria, he soon becomes enamored of her when he realizes that they have much in common. While Victoria and Johnny find romance, George decides to help get rid of Oliver by planting evidence that his fiancée has deceived him. This, however, results in a misunderstanding on Johnny's part, and he, believing himself to be the one deceived, immediately breaks off his relationship with Victoria. The wedding day finally arrives, and Victoria, depressed and resigned to a loveless marriage with Oliver, glumly heads down the aisle for the fourth time. A final effort to reunite Victoria and Johnny succeeds, however, when George cleverly summons Johnny to the wedding by placing an emergency call to the fire department. Just as Victoria is about to take her vow, Johnny bursts into the Stafford home, throws Victoria over his shoulder and whisks her away. *Childhood sweethearts. Dreams. Indians of North America. Romance. Weddings. Baseball. Blackmail. Engagements. Firemen. Hallucinations. High society. Jealousy. Maine. Mistaken identity. New York City. Paranoia. Sculptors. Trains.*

Note: The working title for this film was *I Found a Dream*. The picture marked Ginger Rogers' first film for Columbia. Lucille Ball and Cornel Wilde played the leading roles in a CBS Screen Guild Players radio adaptation of the story that aired on 26 Apr 1948.

AmCin Jul 1947, p. 233. Box 25 Oct 1947. FD 27 Oct 1947. HR 20 Oct 1947, p. 3. IFJ 10 May 1947, p. 44. MPHPD 25 Oct 1947. NYT 8 Dec 1947, p. 35. Var 29 Oct 1947, p. 15.

IT HAD TO HAPPEN (Italian Americans)

Twentieth Century-Fox Film Corp.; Darryl F. Zanuck in charge of production. *Dist* Twentieth Century-Fox Film Corp. 14 Feb **1936**; Prod: 14 Nov—17 Dec 1935; added scenes 8 Jan-13 Jan 1936 [©Twentieth Century-Fox Film Corp.; 14 Feb 1936; LP6182]. Sd (Western Electric Noiseless Recording); b&w. 9 reels, 7,184 ft. 79-80 min. PCA cert no. 1825.

Assoc prod Raymond Griffith. *Dir* Roy Del Ruth. *Asst dir* Ben Silvey. *Scr* Howard Ellis Smith and Kathryn Scola. [*Writer of added scenes* Allen Rivkin]. [*Contr wrt* Aidan Roark, Norman Krasna and Gene Fowler]. *Photog* Peverell Marley. *Art dir* Hans Peters. *Settings* Thomas Little. *Film ed* Alan McNeil. [*Ed asst* Harry Reynolds and Wallace Grissell]. *Gowns* Gwen Wakeling. *Mus dir* Arthur Lange. *Sd* Eugene Grossman and Roger Heman. [*Prod mgr* Ed. Ebele].

Source: Based on the short story "Canavan, the Man Who Had His Way" by Rupert Hughes in *The Saturday Evening Post* (11 Sep 1909).

Cast: George Raft (*Enrico Scaffa*), Rosalind Russell (*Beatrice Newnes*), Leo Carrillo (*Giuseppe Badjagaloupe*), Arline Judge (*Miss Sullivan*), Alan Dinehart (*Rodman Drake*), Andrew Tombes (*Dooley*), Arthur Hohl (*John Pelkey*), Paul Stanton (*Mayor [Truddle] of New York*), Pierre Watkins (*District attorney*), Stanley Fields (*Mug*), George Irving (*Foreman of the jury*), Thomas Jackson (*Mayor's secretary*), [George Humbert (*Tony*)], [Nina Campana (*Tony's wife*)], [Margaret Bloodgood (*Mrs. Spears*)], [Harry C. Bradley (*Beatrice's secretary*)], [Clay Clement (*McCloskey*)], [John Sheehan (*Pelkey's secretary*)], [James Burke (*Foreman*)], [Frank Meredith (*Motor cop*)], [Frank De Voe, Gladden James, Bud Geary], [Torben Meyer (*Sign painter*)], [Robert Emmet O'Connor (*Policeman*)], [Selmer Jackson, Wallis Clark (*Immigration officer*)], [Matt McHugh (*Elevator man*)], [Michael Romano (*Santora*)], [Inez Palange (*Italian mother*)], [George Bookasta (*Italian boy*)], [Tommy Bupp (*Shine boy*)], [Raymond Turner (*Zeke*)], [Frank Moran, John Kelly (*Moving men*)], [Ben Taggart (*New York cop*)], [Harry Stubbs (*Bailiff*)], [John Dilson (*Juror*)], [Charles Lane (*Hilburn, state examiner*)], [Lloyd Whitlock, John Hyams (*Men in cafe*)], [Jack Hatfield, J. Anthony Hughes, Sam Ash, Cully Richards, Emmett Vogan, Franklyn Ardell (*Reporters*)], [Herbert Heywood (*Trainer*)], [Curtis Benton (*Radio announcer*)], [Edward Cooper (*Butler*)], [Pauline Garon (*French maid*)], [Edward Keane (*Bruce*)], [Paul Hurst, Ben Hendricks, Jack Curtis, James Dundee, Harry Woods, G. Pat Collins (*Workmen*)], [James C. Morton (*Bartender*)], [Loo Loy (*Chinese man*)], [Maxine Reiner].

Political, Drama. [*Print viewed*]. Disappointed at the opportunites for work afforded them, Italian immigrants Enrico Scaffa and Giuseppe Badjagaloupe get jobs as ditch diggers on a busy New York street. After the foreman gives Rico a red flag to stop traffic before an explosion, he begins to savor the taste of power that the flag gives him. Among the cars he enjoys stopping are the limousine of Beatrice Newnes, who complains that she is late for the races at Belmont, and that of the mayor, who becomes impressed with Rico's character and hires him as an assistant. Rico soon is feared as an unseen power, and when he learns that his district's branch of the Hudson Investment Trust is about to go under, he orders the district attorney to summon a special session of the grand jury to investigate because his people have their life savings invested there. Rico visits Rodman Drake, the head of the trust, who has married Beatrice, and tells him that the only way he can avoid the penitentiary is to give him four million dollars which, he says, he will see gets put back into the corporation before the examiner goes over the books. Drake agrees, but flies to Cuba in case there are problems. Rico, who says he has never had Beatrice out of his mind since he first saw her, persists in pursuing her and wagers a chance to take her to dinner that his horse, White Wing, will beat her horse, Lady Ann, in the upcoming race at Saratoga. After White Wing wins by a nose, Beatrice invites him to dinner, but after a romantic night, she finds that Drake has returned. She asks him for a divorce and says that she wants to marry Rico, but Drake begs her to remain because, he says, he needs her badly now. Beatrice and Rico agree not to see each other for two months. When one of the district attorney's men, John Pelkey, who has a grudge against Rico, tells Drake that Rico never deposited the four million dollars in the corporation, Drake agrees to cooperate in a grand jury investigation. Beatrice refuses to believe the accusation against Rico, and Drake orders her out of his house. After Rico tells Beatrice that he put the money into the trust, she agrees to marry him. Rico refuses to testify before the grand jury and thus implicate some innocent people who helped him secretly deposit the four million after the state examiner got hold the books so that Drake would not get caught. After his attorney advises him to leave the country until he can beat the indictment, Rico plans to go with Beatrice to Canada, where she can file for a divorce, but she walks out on him because she thinks he wants to run away like Drake instead of facing the charges like a man. Rico then grabs his red flag and interrupts the grand jury proceedings. He admits that he falsified records, but proves, through questioning Drake, that he did deposit the four million dollars. After he explains that he did it to avert a public scandal which threatened to undermine the confidence of depositors and investors, the district attorney concedes that he has been misled, and the proceedings are disbanded. Rico punches Pelkey and then awakens Beatrice, and still holding the red flag, tells her to get dressed and go to Reno for her divorce. He says he was to remain in town who accused him of taking a bribe, and after informing her that it is her job to love him until she dies, he orders her to kiss him, which she does again and again. *Class distinction. Flags. Government officials. Immigrants. Italian Americans. New York City. Romance. Bars. Bigotry. Construction foremen. Cowardice. District Attorneys. Divorce. False accusations. Fights. Grand juries. Horseracing. Mayors. Trusts and trustees.*

Note: The only screen credits on the print viewed were end credits listing actors and their roles; the above credits not in brackets were taken from company records listing screen credits in the Twentieth Century-Fox Records of the Legal Department at the UCLA Theater Arts Library. 20th Century Pictures, Inc. originally planned to produce this film, with Clark Gable and Constance Bennett, according to a *HR* news item. According to the *Var* review for the 1915 film *The Danger Signal*, produced by George Kleine, directed by Walter Irwin and starring Arthur Hoops, the original story was inspired by the life of former Tammany Hall boss Richard Croker (see above). Notes from Darryl F. Zanuck concerning *It Had to Happen*, which was called at the time *Canavan*, beginning 17 Sep 1934 and a script as late as 30 Mar 1935 give the main character as an Irish immigrant named Canavan. In a script of 8 Oct 1935, the main character is called Scaffa. At the beginning of a screenplay for the film in the Twentieth Century-Fox Produced Scripts Collection, also at UCLA, a quotation from the works of Friar Abbott (1659-1730) gives the source of the title: "Though there be the world between them, if it be ordained that this woman and this man are to be one, then so it will be; and no matter it take a lifetime ere these two can look upon each other in union—still, there can be no doubt, it had to happen."

According to information in the legal records, Edith Ellis was assigned as a writer on this film, but none of her material was used. Bert Glennon is listed for photography on an early advertising billing sheet, but it is not known if Glennon actually worked on any part of the film. According to a *HR* news item, director Roy Del Ruth called actor James Burke back in Jan 1936 for a week's

shooting to build up his part. According to *NYT*, a few years earlier, when the censors complained about crime pictures, George Raft was assigned by Paramount to dancing pictures, which were deadly for his career; this was his first crime film since the earlier period. According to information in the MPAA/PCA Collection at the AMPAS Library, Joseph Breen, the PCA director, objected to a scene in the final shooting script from which an adulterous situation involving the character "John Pelkey" was implied; appropriate lines were subsequently deleted. In addition to the 1915 George Kleine production mentioned above, another film based on the same source was produced in 1921 and entitled *Hold Your Horses*, which was directed by E. Mason Hopper and starred Tom Moore (see above).

DV 8 Nov 1935, p. 3. *DV* 27 Jan 1936, p. 3. *FD* 15 Feb 1936, p. 6. *HR* 14 Aug 1935, p. 3. *HR* 13 Jan 1936, p. 2. *HR* 27 Jan 1936, p. 3. *HR* 17 Oct 1936, sect. II, p. 69. *MPD* 28 Jan 1936, p. 8. *MPH* 15 Feb 1936, p. 44. *NYT* 15 Feb 1936, p. 18. *Var* 19 Feb 1936, p. 12.

IT HAPPENED TO ME *see* **CAUGHT IN THE ACT**

IT MIGHT HAPPEN TO YOU *see* **IT COULD HAPPEN TO YOU**

THE ITALIAN (Italian Americans)
New York Motion Picture Corp. *Dist* Paramount Pictures Corp. Jan **1915** [©New York Motion Picture Corp.; 7 Jan 1915; LP5156]. Si; b&w. 5-6 reels.

Prod Thomas H. Ince. *Dir* Reginald Barker. *Story* Thomas H. Ince and C. Gardner Sullivan.

Cast: George Beban (*Beppo Donnetti*), Clara Williams (*Annette Ancello*), J. Frank Burke (*Annette's father*).

Social, Drama. Venetian gondolier Pietro "Beppo" Donetti loves Annette Ancello, but Trudo, her father, prefers the wealthy merchant Roberto Gallia. After Trudo allows Beppo one year to make good, Beppo goes to New York and succeeds as a bootblack. Soon Annette comes and they marry. When their baby becomes ill during a heat wave, the doctor warns that he must have pasteurized milk. After Beppo is robbed of the money saved for the expensive milk and arrested for fighting his attackers, he appeals to the ward boss Corrigan that his baby's life is endangered. Corrigan rebuffs him, and Beppo is jailed for five days, while his baby dies. Vowing vengeance, Beppo soon learns that Corrigan's baby is ill. After entering Corrigan's house, Beppo overhears a doctor say that any sudden noise will kill the child. When he is about to break a glass shade, Beppo sees the baby make the same gesture his son did. Overcome with remorse, Beppo mourns at his baby's grave. *Infants. Italians. New York City. Political bosses. Revenge. Bootblacks. Conscience. Gondolas and gondoliers. Grief. Immigrants. Imprisonment. Milk. Physicians. Robbery. Venice (Italy).*

Note: The film was originally entitled *The Dago*. Some scenes in the film were shot in Venice, CA.

Motog 9 Jan 1915, p. 77. *MPN* 1 Jan 1915, p. 29. *NYDM* 30 Dec 1914, pp. 26-27. *Var* 1 Jan 1915, p. 29.

IT'S A BIG COUNTRY: AN AMERICAN ANTHOLOGY (Irish Americans, African Americans, Hungarian Americans, Greek Americans, Jewish Americans, Italian Americans)
Metro-Goldwyn-Mayer Corp.; controlled by Loew's Inc. *Dist* Loew's Inc. 4 Jan **1952**; Prod: early Apr—early Sep 1950 [©Loew's Inc.; 16 Nov 1951; LP1343]. Sd (Western Electric Sound System); b&w. 8,013 ft. 89 min. Passed by the National Board of Review. PCA cert no. 14770.

Prod Robert Sisk. *Seq [one] dir* Richard Thorpe. *Seq [two] dir* John Sturges. *Seq [four] dir* Charles Vidor. *Seq [five] dir* Don Weis. *Seq [six] dir* Clarence Brown. *Seq [seven] dir* William A. Wellman. *Seq [eight] dir* Don Hartman. *Story for picture* Dore Schary. *Episode one scr* William Ludwig. *Episode two scr* Helen Deutsch. *Episode three wrt* Ray Chordes. *Episode four scr* Isobel Lennart. *Episode five wrt for the screen by* Allen Rivkin. *From a story by* Lucile Schlossberg. *Episode six scr* Dorothy Kingsley. *Episode seven wrt* Dore Schary. *Episode eight scr* George Wells. *Dir of photog* John Alton, Ray June, William Mellor and Joseph Ruttenberg. *Spec eff* A. Arnold Gillespie and Warren Newcombe. *Art dir* Cedric Gibbons, Malcolm Brown, William Ferrari, Eddie Imazu, Arthur Lonergan and Gabriel Scognamillo. *Film ed* Ben Lewis and Frederick Y. Smith. *Set dec* Edwin B. Willis, Jack Bonar, Ralph S. Hurst, Arthur Krams, Fred MacLean and Alfred E.. Spencer. *Mus supv* Johnny Green. *Mus adpt* Alberto Colombo, Adolph Deutsch, Lennie Hayton, Bronislau Kaper, Rudolph G. Kopp, David Raksin and David Rose. *Rec supv* Douglas Shearer. *Hair styles des by* Sydney Guilaroff. *Make-up created by* William Tuttle.

Source: Based on the short stories "Interruptions, Interruptions" by Edgar Brooke in *Collier's* (28 Feb 1948); "Overlooked Lady" by

John McNulty in *The New Yorker* (10 Dec 1949); "Rosika the Rose" by Claudia Cranton in *Atlantic Monthly* (Jun 1930) and "Four Eyes" by Joseph Petracca in *Collier's* (24 Sep 1949).

Cast: With the following citizens: Ethel Barrymore [(*Mrs. Brian Patrick Riordan*)], Keefe Brasselle [(*Sgt. Maxie Klein*)], Gary Cooper [(*Texan*)], Nancy Davis [(*Miss Coleman*)], Van Johnson [(*Adam Burch*)], Gene Kelly [(*Icarus Xenophon*)], Janet Leigh [(*Rosa Szabo*)], Marjorie Main [(*Mrs. Wrenley*)], Fredric March [(*Papa Esposito*)], George Murphy [(*Mr. Callaghan*)], William Powell [(*Professor*)], S. Z. Sakall [(*Stefan Szabo*)], Lewis Stone [(*Sexton*)], James Whitmore [(*Traveler*)], Keenan Wynn [(*Michael Fisher*)], Leon Ames [(*Secret service man*)], Angela Clarke [(*Mama Esposito*)], Bobby Hyatt [(*Joseph Esposito*)], Sharon McManus [(*Sam Szabo*)], [Louis Calhern (*Narrator*)], [Elisabeth Risdon (*Woman in Episode one*)], [*Minor parts in Episode two*: Bill Baldwin (*Austin*)], [Mickey Martin (*Copy boy*)], [Ned Glass (*Receptionist*)], [William H. Welsh, Sherry Hall, Fred Santley, Henry Sylvester, Roger Moore, Roger Cole, Harry Stanton (*Officials*)], [*Minor parts in Episode four*: June Hedin (*Kati*)], [Luana Mehlberg (*Lenka*)], [Jeralyn Alton (*Yolande*)], [Jacqueline Kenley (*Margit*)], [Tony Taylor (*Baby-sitter*)], [Benny Burt (*Soda jerk*)], [George Economides (*Theodore*)], [Hal Hatfield, George Conrad, Richard Grindle, Anthony Lappas, Tom Nickols, Costas Morfis, David Alpert (*Greek athletes*)], [A. Cameron Grant (*Proprietor of inn*)], [*Minor parts in Episode eight*: Don Fields (*George*)], [Jerry Hunter (*Frank Grillo*)], [Don Gordon (*Mervin*)], [Lucile Curtis (*Miss Bloomburg*)], [Dolly Arriaga (*Concetta Esposito*)], [Elena Savanarola (*Amelia Esposito*)], [Carol Nugent (*Girl*)], [George McDonald, Charles Myers, David Wyatt, Mickey Little (*Boys*)], [Tiny Francone (*Girl in classroom*)], [Rhea Mitchell (*Schoolteacher*)].

Social, **Comedy-drama**. [*Print viewed*]. On a transcontinental train, a talkative traveler takes the seat next to a professor reading a book. The talkative man interrupts the professor with his continual boasting about how wonderful America is, until the professor asks, "Which America?" To the other man's befuddlement, the professor explains there are many kinds of America and that they are all changing. He mentions the political and historical America, the country as part of the world community, and the American personality, which includes immigrants and the American Indians. This quiets the talkative man, and in the dining room, when an elderly woman says she is proud to be a part of America, he asks, "Lady, which America?"

In Boston, Mrs. Brian O'Riordan, an elderly Irish American living in a modest house dwarfed among skyscrapers, is disturbed after reading in the newspaper that the 1950 census has been completed, and she realizes that she has not been counted. She takes a bus to see the managing editor of the newspaper, Mr. Callaghan, and complains that she is seventy-four, and that the next census will not be for another ten years. Callaghan takes her name and address, then sends reporter Michael Fisher to pose as a census official and get a human interest story from her, but Mrs. O'Riordan recognizes Fisher from the newsroom and reprimands him. Callaghan now sincerely tries to help, calling a number of census bureau officials, but they refuse to offer assistance. Indignant, he calls connections at Congress and the White House, and drives with Fisher to Mrs. O'Riordon's home with flowers to apologize. A man from the census bureau then arrives, saying his office received a call from Washington. The census taker becomes impatient when Mrs. O'Riordan is long-winded in answering the questions, but Callaghan, enjoying the bureaucrat's discomfort, advises her to answer in her own way, as they have all afternoon.

African-American military and civilian leaders are shown and lauded; persons shown include Brigadier General Benjamin O'Davis; his son, Lt. Col. Benjamin Davis; Jackie Robinson; Jesse Owens; Joe Louis; Sugar Ray Robinson; Levi Jackson; Lena Horne; the Perry brothers; Marian Anderson; Ethel Waters; Duke Ellington; Louis Armstrong; Eddie Anderson; Justice Francis Rivers of the City Court of New York; Judge Jane Bowland of the New York Court of Domestic Relations; noted radiologist Dr. Benjamin W. Anthony; Congressman Adam Clayton Powell, Jr.; the Right Reverend Bravid Harris; Irvin Molleson, appointed to the Federal Bench; Pauly Murray, former deputy attorney general of California; architect Paul Williams; the 1946 mother of the year, Mrs. Irma Clement; Dr. Ralph Bunche; and the late George W. Carver. A statue of Booker T. Washington is shown.

Hungarian-American Stefan Szabo raises a family of six daughters

while running a company that produces "Szabo's Best U.S. Hungarian Paprika." On the first day of summer, he complains that he will have no peace until his daughters marry. They respond that only that week he turned down proposals from five suitors for Rosa, the eldest, as he was unhappy with the "Smiths, Cohens and O'Rileys" who pursue her. He reserves his greatest dislike for Greeks, because, he says, Hungarians have hated Greeks for 500 years. As Rosa walks to the bus to go to business college, Icarus Xenophon pulls up his car alongside her, and they fall in love at first sight. He offers her a job and drives her to school, and she tells him that her father is afraid she will fall in love before she marries, which Hungarian girls are not allowed to do. Icarus confesses that he has never been in love before, and by the time they reach school, he proposes. When he shows her his confectionary store, he reveals he is Greek, and she says she cannot marry him because Hungarians, especially her father, hate Greeks. He convinces her, however, to stay and work for him. As she works, they stare at each other, then realize they cannot stand it any longer. When Rosa tells her father the name of her employer, he gets worried, but she quickly says that he has a pretty wife who works in the store. Sam, the youngest daughter, decides to investigate, and at the store, she sees Rosa and Icarus kissing. She tells Papa, and they collect all the family members to descend on the ice cream parlor. Papa accuses Icarus of being untrue to his wife, and Icarus protests his innocence. When patrons of the nearby Graeco-American Athletic Club arrive, they admire Rosa's sisters. Rosa then enters with groceries and shows her father her wedding ring. Everyone congratulates them, and Rosa tells her father, who sits forlornly at the counter, to get used to it. Icarus relates that when his father was upset, he used to make coffee. Papa vows never to drink Greek coffee, but when he is shown that the coffee offered is "Washington Post Coffee," he drinks it and embraces Rosa and Icarus.

It is stated that the fighting men of the United States are composed of all heritages and creeds. Following his term of duty in the Korean War, Maxie Klein rings the bell of Mrs. Wrenley and introduces himself as a buddy of her deceased son Jack. She is visibly upset when he mentions his Jewish name and says she does not recall Jack ever mentioning a "Maxie," but when she mentions he always wrote about "Jo-Jo," he says that is what Jack called him. He reads Mrs. Wrenley Jack's last letter, in which Jack writes that freedom, democracy and tolerance are not mere words, but are the real reason he is fighting. Mrs. Wrenley cries, as Jack, in the letter, calls Maxie "my kind of people" and his best pal. As Maxie prepares to go, Mrs. Wrenley says she would be glad to rent Jack's room to him, if he was not returning home, and that she'd like to write his mother about what a fine boy she has. Maxie kisses her, then leaves.

A Texan rolls a cigarette and talks about the "America of wide open spaces," and the "funny ideas" and exaggerations that people have about Texas. With tongue in cheek, he downplays the state's size, the ease of finding oil there, its large ranches, hospitality and pretty girls, and its independence from the rest of the country. He warns with a wink that people should not listen to the rumors about his state.

In 1944, Adam Burch, a new minister, is ordained to serve at St. Thomas Church in Washington, D.C., where the President of the United States attends when his schedule permits. Rev. Burch, somewhat overwhelmed at the prospect of preaching before the president, decides to prepare a sermon on "spiritual manifestations of our society as reflected in the war effort." The president does not show up, however, and Burch preaches to yawning parishioners. After five weeks of similarly high-minded sermons, Burch asks the sexton his opinion of the sermon he is preparing, and the sexton tells him he is not doing a good job. He points out that Burch has been preaching to one man, rather than to the whole congregation. In the reverend's next sermon, he admits he was in error and that he has learned that he must function as a minister for the entire congregation. Afterwards, a secret service man comes to his office to say that the president came into the church just as he began his sermon and listened from the back. The metallic sound of crutches is heard when the president, as just one of the flock, comes to the door.

In an elementary school in San Francisco, the teacher, Mrs. Coleman, calls on Joseph Esposito to do a division problem on the board, and when the boy says that the numbers are too small, she suggests he needs glasses. At home, Joey's father, a proud Italian-American immigrant, argues with his wife when Joey brings home a letter suggesting he should go to the optometrist, then goes to see the

teacher himself. He complains that glasses will make Joey different from his friends, but she contends that his schoolwork is suffering. Papa refuses to allow the glasses, but when Joey gets a headache from reading, his mother takes him to the optometrist. While playing with friends, Joey sees his father coming. He takes off his new glasses just as he is about to jump for a ladder and missing it, falls into a pile of bricks. As Joey recovers from his injury, Miss Coleman tutors him, and when she arrives for supper one night, Papa puts on glasses himself. Everyone looks surprised, then Joey puts his own on, and Papa tells him they look good. A narrator relates that ours is a big, wonderful country, proud of its past, strong in its present and confident in its future. It is one nation: the land of the free and home of the brave. *African Americans. Aged women. Antisemitism. Bigotry. Fathers and daughters. Fathers and sons. Greek Americans. Hungarian Americans. Immigrants. Irish Americans. Italian Americans. Jews. Ministers. Mothers and sons. Franklin Delano Roosevelt. Texans. Veterans. War victims.* Accidents. Boston (MA). Census. Coffee. Confectioners and confectionaries. Editors. Eyeglasses. Fathers and daughters. Friendship. Government officials. Impersonation and imposture. Korean War, 1950-1953. Letters. Marriage–Secret. Personality change. Professors. Reporters. San Francisco (CA). Schoolteachers. Secret Service. Sermons. Students. Trains. Washington (D.C.).

Note: The working titles of this film were *Big Country* and *My Country 'Tis of Thee.* In the Call Bureau Cast Service, and in other material on the film, the eight segments of the film are entitled, in the order of their appearance: "Interruptions, Interruptions"; "The Lady and the Census Taker"; "The Negro Story"; "Rosika, the Rose"; "Letter from Korea"; "Texas"; "Minister in Washington"; and "Four Eyes." According to a dialogue continuity in the copyright descriptions and information in reviews, the film begins with a shot of the Mt. Rushmore memorial and a title that reads, "This is a 'message' picture. The message is, Hurray for America!" This scene was missing from the print viewed. According to information in the MPAA/PCA Collection at the AMPAS Library, the first line of the statement was changed in Sep 1951, prior to release, from the line, "This is a propaganda picture." According to statements made by producer Robert Sisk in various articles about the film and in the film's pressbook, Dore Schary, when he became production head of M-G-M, suggested to Sisk that he make a film using short stories. In 1949, Schary had Sisk look at the short story anthology *Americans One and All*, about American minority groups, and from this, Sisk selected two stories for the proposed film. Sisk explained, in different articles, that the film aimed "at making moviegoers understand the melting pot that is America," that "the idea is to present comtemporary stories of the different kinds of people in this country," and to show "that the melting pot is *not* New York, but America, and that [America] is very nearly melted." Sisk stated that the episode "Four Eyes" would examine "old world versus new world ideology." An additional aim of the production, according to a *DV* article, was to keep M-G-M's major stars at work between their starring assignments. Directors also were assigned to the film between other assignments.

By Sep 1949, M-G-M had acquired the rights to the two stories in the *Americans One and All* anthology, "Rosika the Rose," by Claudia Crandall (which was used in the final film) and "Load," by Dudley Schnabel (which was not used), in addition to three other stories, "Standard of Living," by Dorothy Parker, in *The New Yorker* (20 Sep 1941), "Star in the Window," by Norman Katkov, in *The Saturday Evening Post* (23 Jul 1949) and "My Song, Yankee Doodle," by Carl Glick. None of the latter three stories were used in the final film. A screenplay for the Parker story was written by Marguerite Roberts. "Load," which originally appeared in *The Midland Magazine* (May 1931), concerned a Danish-American supervisor of electric power distribution in a large city; its screenplay was written by Luther Davis, and it was to star Marshall Thompson and Jean Hersholt, according to news items. "My Song, Yankee Doodle," which was published in *This Week* (13 Mar 1938), dealt with a Chinese-American boy who moves from San Francisco to the Bronx; Allen Rivkin wrote the screenplay. In a letter from 14 Apr 1950 in the MPAA/PCA Collection at the AMPAS Library, PCA head Joseph I. Breen wrote concerning this proposed episode, "we are quite concerned as to whether or not this may not contain incidents which will prove offensive to Chinese-Americans. Specifically, we question the use of such language as 'honorable father,' 'unworthy son,' etc., in this conversation between what is presumed to be a typical Chinese-American family. We are urging, therefore, that you get proper technical advice on this subject, to make certain that there is nothing in your finished picture that would be offensive to Chinese-Americans generally." It is not known if the objections raised by Breen led to the elimination of the episode. According to *DN*, an story written for the film dealing with "the problems of a Negro in the world of baseball" was also planned. Sisk stated that the story "will stress the avoidance of discrimination in baseball." This episode was never made; in its place, the third segment of the film deals in newsreel fashion with African-American achievements.

Another story, entitled "Wedding Plans," described in *DN* as a "filmic anecdote set in a catering establishment," also was never produced; it was presumably replaced by the anecdotal segment entitled "Texas." John McNulty, who wrote the story on which the episode "The Lady and the Census Taker" was based, was not included in the screen credits; it is possible that the episode in the film was not sufficiently similar to the story to warrant McNulty's credit. Other actors originally scheduled for the film who were not in it included

Walter Pidgeon as "The Professor" in the first episode, "Interruptions, Interruptions," June Allyson as "Rose" in "Rosika the Rose," Edmund Gwenn as the sexton in "Minister in Washington," Dean Stockwell as "Joey" in "Four Eyes," John Hodiak and Ann Sothern. Directors mentioned in news items as set for the film but who did not work on it included Robert Z. Leonard, George Cukor, Gerald Mayer, Ray Rowland, and the team of Norman Panama and Melvin Frank.

Reviews were heavily critical of the film. *HR,* in a thoroughly negative review, stated, "The average filmgoer will be disinclined to swallow its pointed preaching and editorializing as entertainment.... The film proves no new points about the American way of life.... It emerges as a hodge-podge, a film lacking strong continuity, a real conviction and dramatic purposes.... They are flimsy little vignettes, minus punch or authority—poor enough singly but which, when strung together, produce the woeful effect of an afternoon of soap opera radio....Briefly, *It's a Big Country* is a far cry from the definitive American appraisal it undoubtedly set out to be." *Var* commented that with the film, "Metro hops on the Americanism bandwagon.... Critically, there can be no quarrel with the idea behind the production; it is something about which a refresher course is never out of order. There can, and most likely will be, quibbles over the manner in which touchy subjects have been timidly kissed off."

A number of reviewers noted that the segment on African Americans was seemingly "segregated" from the rest of the film. *DV* commented, "there will undoubtedly be some reaction to the timid documentary handling of the place of the Negro in the community, since that phase of American life is crudely set apart by making it the only documentary portion of the entire film." They advised the studio to drop the episode completely "rather than set it apart by the documentary treatment." *LAEx* stated "the dignity of our Negro citizens can surely be dramatized, rather than brushed off with newsreel shots." Gilbert Seldes, in his *SatRev* review, commented that "the handling gives this picture the fairy-tale quality that is at once its charm and its fatal weakness.... I suspect that the producers thought they were presenting an important picture and may not know how they were trapped into making a trivial one. They were trapped by the laws of the movie-myth, which are inexorable.... The fatality comes when you touch a story not in the fairy-tales. You have no magic wand for the Negro in America....you fall back on a news-reel of Negro achievement, the Negro isolated from his fellow-citizens, Negro cadets, Negro women in uniform, distinguished and honored—and utterly segregated."

Box 1 Dec 1951. *Cue* 12 Jan 1952. *DN* 22 Mar 1950. *DV* 15 Sep 1949. *DV* 26 Nov 1951, p. 3. *Exh* 5 Dec 1951, p. 3197. *FD* 20 Nov 1951, p. 14. *Har* 24 Nov 1951, p. 186. *HCN* 1 Feb 1952. *HR* 15 Sep 1949. *HR* 14 Feb 1950. *HR* 7 Apr 1950, p. 10. *HR* 8 Sep 1950, p. 10. *HR* 1 Dec 1950. *HR* 8 Jan 1951. *HR* 26 Nov 1951, p. 3. *LADN* 1 Feb 1952. *LAEx* 2 Feb 1952. *LAT* 19 Dec 1949. *LAT* 15 Mar 1950, pt. III, p. 9. *LAT* 4 Apr 1950. *LAT* 10 Jun 1950. *LAT* 1 Feb 1952. *MGM News* 17 Apr 1950. *MGM News* 1 May 1950. *MPHPD* 24 Nov 1951, p. 1117. *Newsweek* 21 Jan 1952. *NYT* 18 Sep 1949. *NYT* 9 Jan 1952, p. 25. *SatRev* 5 Jan 1952. *Time* 28 Jan 1952. *Var* 15 Mar 1950. *Var* 28 Nov 1951, p. 6.

IT'S A GREAT LIFE (Italian Americans)

Eminent Authors Pictures, Inc. *Dist* Goldwyn Distributing Corp. 29 Aug **1920** [©Mary Roberts Rinehart; 26 Aug 1920; LP15480]. Si; b&w. 6 reels.

Dir E. Mason Hopper. *Asst dir* William A. Wellman. *Scen* Edward T. Lowe, Jr. *Cam* John Mescall.

Source: Based on the short story "Empire Builders" by Mary Roberts Rinehart in *The Saturday Evening Post* (20 May 1916).

Cast: Cullen Landis (*Stoddard*), Molly Malone (*Eloise Randall*), Clara Horton (*Lucille Graham*), Howard Halston (*The Wop*), Otto Hoffman (*Professor Mozier*), Tom Pearse (*Professor Randall*), Ralph Bushman (*Big Graham*), E. J. Mack (*Small*), John Lynch (*Watchman*).

Comedy. Stoddard and the Wop are the terrors of Pomptonvale prep school. One night, while eating in a restaurant, the Wop finds a pearl embedded in an oyster, which sparks visions of a trip to the Solomon Islands where treasures in the shape of pearls await them. Before they can embark upon their adventure, Stoddard succumbs to the charms of Eloise Randall, the schoolmaster's daughter. Attempting to find another pearl to present his new love, Stoddard consumes enough oysters to send him to the school infirmary. Several days later, his old sweetheart, Lucille Graham, pays Stoddard a visit in the hospital and Stoddard decides to remain in Pomptonvale, thus dispelling all dreams of a pearl empire. *Boarding schools. Oysters. Pearls. Students.* Italians. Solomon Islands.

Note: The working titles for this film were *The Empire Builders* and *This Is the Life.*

ETR 11 Sep 1920, p. 1618. *MPN* 29 May 1920, p. 4518. *MPN* 5 Jun 1920, p. 4658. *MPN* 26 Jun 1920, p. 109. *MPN* 11 Sep 1920, p. 2137. *MPW* 11 Sep 1920, p. 248. *NYDM* 11 Sep 1920, p. 472. *NYMT* 5 Sep 1920. *NYT* 30 Aug 1920, p. 12. *Var* 3 Sep 1920, p. 44. *Wid's* 5 Sep 1920, p. 9.

IT'S GREAT TO BE ALIVE (Latino)

Fox Film Corp. *Dist* Fox Film Corp. 2 Jun **1933**; Prod: Apr 1933 [©Fox Film Corp.; 23 May 1933; LP3912]. Sd (Western Electric Noiseless Recording); b&w. 8 reels, 6,210 ft. 68-70 min. Passed by the National Board of Review.

[*Prod* John Stone]. *Dir* Alfred Werker. [*Asst dir* Philip Ford]. *Adpt* Paul Perez. *Dial* Arthur Kober. [*Contr wrt* William Kernell and Donald W. Lee]. *Photog* Robert Planck. [*Cam op* Arthur Arling]. [*Asst cam* Maurice Kains and J. Van Wormer]. *Settings* Duncan Cramer. [*Film ed* Barney Wolf]. [*Ed asst* Bob Simpson]. *Frocks* Royer. *Mus dir* Samuel Kaylin. *Dance dir* Sammy Lee. *Sd rec* Alfred Bruzlin. [*Chief elec* H. David]. [*Grip* J. Murphy]. [*Props* Clarence Baker]. [*Still photog* Wallace Chewning].

Song(s): "Good Bye Ladies," "I'll Build a Nest," "Women," "It's Great to Be the Only Man Alive" and "World Congress," words and music by William Kernell.

Source: Based on the novelette *The Last Man on Earth* by John D. Swain in *Munsey's Magazine* (Nov 1923).

Cast: Raul Roulien (*Carlos Martin*), Gloria Stuart (*Dorothy Wilton*), Edna May Oliver (*Dr. Prodwell*), Herbert Mundin (*Brooks*), Joan Marsh (*Toots*), Dorothy Burgess (*Al Moran*), Emma Dunn (*Mrs. Wilton*), Edward Van Sloan (*Dr. Wilton*), Robert Greig (*Perkins*), [Gloria Roy (*Helen*)], [Elene Shannon, Beatrice Rossi, Margaret Rilling, Martha Reeves, Helen Pacino, Kathleen Ogilvie, Mona Munro, Helene Friend, Mildred Lewis, Liana Galen, Florence Kitzmiller, Zaruhi Elmassian, Emilia Da Prato, Josephine Campbell, Mary York, Betty Boldrick, Lorraine Bridges, Beatrice Becker, Mildred Carroll, Willow Wray, Lois Woody, Eleanor Wells, Gelal Talata, Alice Towne (*Singers*)], [Betty Keeler (*Singer "Cheko ambassadoress"*)], [Marjorie Seavey, Eva Sabenie, Ruth Moody, Harriet Mathews, Loraine Marshall, Lucille House, Dorothy Compton (*Dancers "Cheko girls"*)], [Marguerite Warner (*Singer "Dutch ambassadoress"*)], [Margaret Nearing, Ruth Jennings, Sugar Geise, Dixie Dean, Sally Haines, Audrene Brier, Betty Bryson, Mildred Clare (*Dancers "Dutch girls"*)], [Leonore La Hogue (*Singer and dancer "Cuban ambassadoress"*)], [Geneva Sawyer, Lucille Porcett, Patsy Lee, Peaches Jackson, Theo De Voe, Harriette Haddon, Marbeth Wright (*Dancers "Cuban girls"*)], [Florine McKinney (*American ambassadoress*)], [Lucille Miller, Gloria Fayth, Amo Ingraham, Edith Haskins, Sally Arden, Esther Brodelet, Bonita Barker (*Dancers "American girls"*)], [Gwen Seager, Bee Stevens, Margaret Harding, Lee Bailey, Georgia Clarke (*Dancers "Pages"*)].

Musical comedy, Fantasy. [*Not viewed*]. Carlos Martin, an irrepressible rake, must give up his slew of girl friends when he becomes engaged to his true love, Dorothy Wilton. After their engagement party at the Wilton house, to which he arrives late, delayed by a goodbye dinner for his various amours, a drunk Carlos stumbles into the bedroom of the slumbering Toots, who earlier flirted openly with him. When Toots screams and awakens the household, Dorothy breaks her engagement to Carlos, who, in his distraught condition, decides to make a dangerous flight over the Pacific. Dorothy listens on the radio to the progress of Carlos' flight, and Brooks, the butler, informs her that he accidentally led Carlos into Toots's room. Moments later, just as Carlos gives Dorothy a message over the radio, his plane goes down and he loses all contact with the outside world. Three years later, Dorothy's father, Dr. Wilton, and Dr. Ruth Prodwell continue to work on a cure for masculitis, a disease that kills only men. Another two years pass and the last man in the world has died as the women of the world, led by Dr. Prodwell, attempt to create a synthetic man. When the synthetic man blows up in a puff of smoke as he is being galvanized, an aviatrix comes to Dr. Prodwell's lab and informs her that she has found a man on a Pacific island. The women decide to keep the valuable discovery a secret, but Helen, assisting Dr. Prodwell, informs her gangster boss, "Al," about the last man's existence. The lady gangsters arrive on the island, find Carlos and bring him back to a stateside speakeasy where they attempt to auction him off to a rich woman. Before Carlos can be claimed, however, the police arrive with Dr. Prodwell, and Al is arrested for illegal possession of government property. Dorothy hears of Carlos' rescue and decides to claim her lost fiancé. Carlos is set up in a plush apartment where he is visited by adoring women, and attended to by a fleet of lovely females who flutter about, catering to his every whim. Dorothy gets Carlos alone and persuades him to run away with her, but refuses to bring the attendants with them, as Carlos requests. The police pursue the couple, who escape in Dorothy's plane, and call out the entire U.S. Navy and Air Force fleet to capture their valuable possession. Warships pick the couple up when they jump out of the plane in parachutes. A world congress is convened to decide the last man's fate where the nations plead their case for

Carlos' hand in marriage. Carlos, devoted to Dorothy, tries to convince them of his fidelity to his fiancée, and then, tired of their cajolery, threatens to kill himself, terrifying the female delegation. Dr. Prodwell agrees to the marriage of Carlos and Dorothy, and the couple kiss. *Engagements. Epidemics. Missing persons, Assumed dead. Playboys. Women physicians. Airplane accidents. Auctions. Chases. Drunkenness. Escapes. False accusations. Fidelity. Flirts. Islands. Skydivers. Speakeasies. Threats. Women gangsters.*

Note: The plot and onscreen credits were based on a screen continuity and credit sheets in the Twentieth Century-Fox Produced Scripts Collection and Records of the Legal Department at the UCLA Theater Arts Library. The working title of the Spanish language version was *El último de su sexo*. Fox produced the Spanish language version of this film before they made the English-language version. According to the legal records, Ray June, who photographed the Spanish version, was loaned from Feature Productions, Inc. According to *NYT*, the film included a scene at a "symposium attended by screen duplicates of Professors [Albert] Einstein and [Auguste] Piccard." *NYMirror* and *Chicago News* noted that Raul Roulien's voice and his manner of singing was in the style of Maurice Chevalier. *Philadelphia Inquirer* remarked that Fox "is pinning [upon Roulien] the badge of stardom and high hopes for the 'discovery' of a new screen personality....In all kindness, one would suggest that the Fox Company... let Mr. Roulien go back to his roles in pictures made wholly for Spanish-speaking audiences." According to information in the Fox legal files, some scenes were shot at the Grand Central Airport in Glendale, CA. The legal files also reveal that the title of the English-language version was taken from a song title written by Lew Brown and Ray Henderson. After an agreement was reached concerning the use of the title, Brown sent a telegram to Fox producer Sol Wurtzel which read, in part, "Accepting your offer of two hundred thousand dollars for title 'It's Great to Be Alive.' Hope this low figure will not establish a precedent for my future titles. Kindly send three dollars to cover this telegram and then you can disregard first part of this wire." According to a *FD* news item, this was the first film on which the prominent fashion designer Royer worked. A *HR* news item noted that Wurtzel tried to get actress Constance Cummings for this film.

According to information in the file on the film in the MPAA/PCA Collection in the AMPAS Library, the Hays Office objected to aspects of the screenplay of this film. Dr. James Wingate, director of the Studio Relations Committee of the AMPP, wrote to producer John Stone that the most serious problem with the film was the "overemphasis on sex as brought out through a situation wherein a world of sex starved females suddenly find one lone male whose presence brings about a series of humorous but nevertheless, rather baldly suggestive events." Stone thanked Wingate for his "constructive criticism" and replied that they "have since given the scenario a most careful overhauling, and eliminated the indicated—and other—objectionable points." After Wingate viewed a print of the film, he objected to a number of lines and bits of business, and the studio adhered to all the objections except a shot of "Toots" dropping a key into the bodice of her dress. Wurtzel noted that Wingate had not stated "definitely" that that should be eliminated. The shot remained in the film, and Wingate, in a letter to MPPDA secretary, Governor Carl E. Milliken, stated that "In the future I shall have to be more positive in my statements."

Fox also produced a film in 1924 based on the same source entitled *The Last Man on Earth*, directed by J. G. Blystone and starring Earle Foxe (see *AFI Catalog of Feature Films, 1921-30*; F2.2975).

Other language version(s):

El último varón sobre la Tierra (Spanish language)

1933; Madrid opening: 30 Jan 1933; San Juan, Puerto Rico opening: 18 Mar 1933; New York opening: mid-Jun 1933; Prod: began early Oct 1932. Sd; b&w. 7 reels. Passed by the National Board of Review. Spanish language.

Dirección de [*Directed by*] James Tinling. *Adaptación cinematográfica de* [*Screenplay by*] Paul Perez and William Kernell. *Versión española de* [*Spanish version by*] José López Rubio. [*Photog* Ray June].

Song(s): "Good Bye Ladies (Adiós a las mujeres)", "I'll Build a Nest (Un nido haremos, para los dos)", "Women (Mujeres)" and "It's Great to Be the Only Man Alive (Un moderno Barba Azul)", words and music by William Kernell, Spanish translation by Raúl Roulien and José López Rubio.

Raúl Roulien (*Ralph Martín*), Rosita Moreno (*Dolores Winkle*), Mimi Aguglia (*Al Bribona*), Carmen Rodríguez (*Doctora Prodwell*), Romualdo Tirado (*Belcher*), Hilda Moreno (*Toots*), Antonio Vidal (*Doctor Winkle*), Luz Segovia (*Señora de Winkle*), [Ligia de Golconda], [Lita Santos], [Blanca Vischer]. [*Spanish version not viewed*].

CM Feb 1933, p. 114. *Chicago News* 29 Aug 1933. *FD* 4 Oct 1932, p. 7. *FD* 5 Apr 1933, p. 6. *FD* 8 Jul 1933, p. 6. *HF* 8 Apr 1933, p. 3. *HF* 22 Apr 1933, p. 8. *HR* 14 Mar 1933, p. 1. *IP* Feb 1933, p. 33. *IP* Jun 1933, p. 34. *MPD* 8 Jul 1933, p. 4. *MPH* 1 Jul 1933, p. 25. *NYMirror* 8 Jul 1933. *NYT* 12 Jun 1933, p. 20. *NYT* 8 Jul 1933, p. 14. *Philadelphia Inquirer* 3 Jun 1933. *Var* 11 Jul 1933, p. 15.

JACK LONDON (African Americans)

Samuel Bronston Pictures, Inc. *Dist* United Artists Corp. 24 Dec **1943**; San Francisco, CA premiere: 24 Nov 1943; Prod: 14 Jul—21 Sep 1943 at Samuel Goldwyn Studios [©Samuel Bronston Pictures, Inc.; 8 Nov 1943; LP12434]. Sd (Western Electric Mirrophonic Recording); b&w. 8,412 ft. 92-94 min. PCA cert no. 9687.

Pres SAMUEL BRONSTON. *Prod* Samuel Bronston. *Assoc prod* Joseph H. Nadel. *Asst to prod* Albert de Courville. *Dir* Alfred Santell. *Asst dir* Sam Nelson. *Dial dir* Edward Padula. *Wrt for the screen by* Ernest Pascal. *Adpt* Ernest Pascal and Isaac Don Levine. *Dir of photog* John W. Boyle. *Spec eff* Harry Redmond. *Art dir* Bernard Herzbrun. *Film ed* William Ziegler. *Set dec* Earl Wooden. *Ward* Maria Donovan and Arnold McDonald. *Mus score* Frederic Efrem Rich. *Sd eng* Ben Winkler. *Unit mgr* Ben Berk. [*Tech adv* Charmian London].

Source: Based on the book *The Book of Jack London* by Charmian London (New York, 1921).

Cast: Michael O'Shea (*Jack London*), Susan Hayward (*Charmian Kittredge*), Osa Massen [(*Freda Maloof*)], Harry Davenport [(*Professor Hilliard*)], Frank Craven [(*Old Tom*)], Virginia Mayo [(*Mamie*)], Ralph Morgan [(*George Brett*)], Jonathan Hale [(*Kerwin Maxwell*)], Louise Beavers [(*Mammy Jenny*)], Leonard Strong [(*Capt. Tanaka*)], Regis Toomey [(*Scratch Nelson*)], Albert Van Antwerp [(*French Frank*)], Paul Hurst [(*"Lucky Luke" Lanigan*)], Lumsden Hare [(*Dick Davis, English correspondent*)], Hobart Cavanaugh [(*Mike*)], Sarah Padden [(*Cannery woman*)], Edward Earle [(*James Hare*)], Morgan Conway [(*Richard Harding Davis*)], Robert Homans [(*Capt. Allen*)], [Olin Howlin (*Mailman*)], [Ernie Adams (*Whiskey Bob*)], [John Kelly (*Red John*)], [Arthur Loft (*Fred Palmer*)], [Brooks Benedict (*American correspondent*)], [Mei Lee Foo (*Geisha dancer*)], [Robert Katcher (*Hiroshi*)], [Pierre Watkin (*American council*)], [Paul Fung (*Japanese general*)], [Charles Lung (*Interpreter*)], [Bruce Wong (*Japanese official*)], [Eddie Lee (*Japanese sergeant*)], [John Fisher ("*Spider*")], [Jack Roper (*Victor*)], [Sven Hugo Borg (*Axel*)], [Sid D'Albrook (*Pete*)], [Davison Clark (*Commissioner*)], [Harold Minjir, Roy Gordon, Torben Meyer (*Literary guests*)], [Charlene Newman (*Child*)], [Edmund Cobb (*Father*)], [Wallis Clark (*Theodore Roosevelt*)], [Charles Miller (*William Loeb*)], [Richard Loo (*Japanese ambassador*)], [Dick Curtis (*Cannery foreman*)], [Evelyn Finley (*Indian maid*)], [Rose Plumer (*Charmian's secretary*)], [Ace, a dog (*Buck*)].

Biography. [*Print viewed*]. In Oakland, California, in 1890, Jack London, who dreams of becoming a writer, quits his cannery job after a female employee's hands are crushed in a machinery accident. Mammy Jenny, Jack's maid and surrogate mother, lends him her savings so that he can buy a boat and earn his living hauling oysters from the San Francisco Bay. After he buys the boat from French Frank, who gets a cut of all his business, Jack discovers oyster pirate Mamie stowed aboard, and agrees to a partnership with her. They are later joined by a third partner, Scratch Nelson. Early one morning, the boat pulls into dock after a night's work of stealing from other traps and is fired at from the dock by the police. Scratch is killed, and although Mamie has fallen in love with him, Jack decides that oyster piracy is too dangerous a business and quits. Later, Jack signs on as an able-bodied seaman for a seven-month sealing trip. When his shipmates tease him about his reading habits, weathered sailor Old Tom comes to his defense, and the two become fast friends. One day Jack turns the tables on Red John, a rough practical joker who has harrassed him since his first day aboard ship, and proves his manhood once and for all in a fistfight with the sailor. That night, Jack writes about the sailor, calling him "the sea wolf," and is encouraged in his literary efforts by Old Tom. After his ocean adventures, self-educated Jack enrolls at the University of California at Berkeley. When a teacher selects one of his stories as an example of an overactive imagination, Jack defends his work, stating that having witnessed the vagaries of life, he only writes about cruelty with the hope of alleviating it. Realizing that formal training will not give him the education he craves, Jack leaves school and goes to Dawson City, Alaska, intending to capitalize on the gold strikes in the Yukon. One night in a saloon, Jack meets Greek singer Freda Maloof, and is delighted by her knowledge of Lord Byron's poetry. Although Freda falls in love with Jack, he leaves as soon as news spreads of a major gold strike eighty miles away, determined to earn enough money so that he can spend his time writing instead of working. Eventually Jack ensconces himself in a remote cabin in the wilderness with his German shepherd, Buck, and writes a novel about the dog titled *Call of the Wild*. Publisher George Brett pays Jack for his manuscript, and when Jack meets his secretary, Charmian Kittredge, he learns that she has already become smitten with him through his writing. Jack soon falls in love with Charmian, and on New Year's Eve, a newspaper publisher asks Jack to cover the Boer War for him. In keeping with her promise that she will never entrap Jack, Charmian encourages him to go. Jack returns, older and wiser, bearing many gifts for Charmian, who still wants to marry him. The next day Maxwell sends Jack to cover the burgeoning war between Japan and Russia, and Charmian again agrees to wait for him. Jack is one of many correspondents in Japan, most of whom believe that Russia will soon make peace with Japan. Jack, however, is suspicious of Japanese intentions, knowing that they are sending troops into Korea. When the Japanese refuse to allow correspondents to travel into Korea, Jack makes a bet with reporter Dick Davis, who is sure that Jack cannot cross the Korean border. Jack disguises himself as a Chinese worker, and gets passage on a "sampan" which crosses the Yellow Sea. Once there, he witnesses Japan's invasion of Korea firsthand. In Korea, Jack is befriended by Oxford-educated Captain Tanaka, who treats him as a guest and outlines for him Japan's plot to take over all of Asia, and ultimately, the world. Jack scoops all of the other papers and sends his report about the Japanese invasion of Korea. After some time, Jack is arrested as a Russian spy, and is thrown into prison with the Russian prisoners. Jack is horrified by the brutal treatment of the prisoners, who are denied water. When the dehydrated prisoners break free of their cell to slake their thirst at a well, the Japanese guards laugh as they gun them down. Davis learns of Jack's arrest and alerts the American government in Washington, D.C. President Theodore Roosevelt demands from the Japanese government Jack's immediate release, but upon his return home, he finds that no one believes his story of the Japanese plan to overtake the world, and is disappointed when Maxwell refuses to print his articles. As Jack and Charmian leave the publisher's office, Charmian reaffirms her love for Jack, and celebrates him for his courage and honesty. *Adventurers. Americans in foreign countries. Engagements. Jack London. Novelists. Reporters. African Americans. Bering Sea. California. University (Berkeley). Call of the Wild (Novel). Canneries. College students. Dance hall girls. Drunkenness. Fishermen. German shepherd dogs. Gold rushes. Housekeepers. Japanese. Korea–History–Japanese occupation, 1910-1945. Love affairs. Miners. Prisoners of war. Professors. Publishers and publishing. Theodore Roosevelt. Russians. Russo-Japanese War, 1904-1905. Sailors. Saloons. San Francisco (CA). The Sea Wolf (Novel). South African War, 1899-1902. Tokyo (Japan). Yukon Territory.*

Note: The working title of this film was *The Life of Jack London*. The film opens and closes with newsreel footage showing the christening of a ship named *Jack London*. As depicted in the film, Jack London (1876-1916) was a prolific American writer best known for his novels about the wilderness, including *Call of the Wild*, *White Fang* and *Burning Daylight*. Jack London's wife Charmian was a technical adviser on this film. *HR* news items report the following about the production: Cinematographer Lee Garmes was initially slated as photographer; some scenes were shot on location at Belden Falls, CA; filming was temporarily interrupted in late Aug 1943 after actor Michael O'Shea suffered a motorcycle accident. Bronston borrowed actress Susan Hayward from Paramount Studios. In Jul 1943, O'Shea, who was known on Broadway as Eddie O'Shea, had his name legally changed for films. This film marked Virginia Mayo's first onscreen credit. Mayo was married to O'Shea from 1947 until his death in 1973. *Jack London* was nominated for an Academy Award for Best Music (Scoring of a Dramatic or Comedy Picture).

Box 11 Dec 1943. *DV* 16 Jul 1943. *DV* 17 Sep 1943. *DV* 24 Nov 1943, pp. 3-4. *FD* 24 Nov 1943, p. 6. *HR* 6 Jul 1943, p. 9. *HR* 7 Jul 1943, p. 7. *HR* 12 Jul 1943, p. 4. *HR* 15 Jul 1943, p. 10. *HR* 3 Aug 1943, p. 13. *HR* 27 Aug 1943, p. 24. *HR* 17 Sep 1943. *HR* 21 Sep 1943, p. 6. *HR* 24 Nov 1943, p. 4. *HR* 26 Nov 1943, p. 2. *HR* 7 Mar 1944, p. 11. *MPH* 27 Nov 1943. *MPHPD* 27 Nov 1943, p. 1645. *NYT* 3 Mar 1944, p. 19. *Var* 24 Nov 1943, p. 18.

JACK LONDON'S NORTH TO THE KLONDIKE *see* **NORTH TO THE KLONDIKE**

JACK LONDON'S THE FIGHTER *see* **THE FIGHTER**

JACK MCCALL DESPERADO (Native Americans, Dakota)

Columbia Pictures Corp. *Dist* Columbia Pictures Corp. Apr **1953**; Prod: 1 May—13 May 1952 [©Columbia Pictures Corp.; 13 Mar 1953; LP2398]. Sd (RCA Sound System); col (Technicolor). 6,823 ft. 76 min.

Prod Sam Katzman. *Dir* Sidney Salkow. *Asst dir* Paul Donnelly. *Scr* John O'Dea. *Story* David Chandler. *Dir of photog* Henry Freulich. *Technicolor color dir* Francis Dugat. *Art dir* Paul Palmentola. *Film ed* Aaron Stell. *Set dec* Sidney Clifford. *Mus dir* Mischa Bakaleinikoff. *Sd eng* George Cooper. *Unit mgr* Herbert Leonard.

Cast: George Montgomery [(*JackMcCall*)], Angela Stevens [(*Rose Griffith*)], Douglas Kennedy [(*BillHickok*)], James Seay [(*Bat McCall*)], Eugene Iglesias [(*GreyEagle*)], William Tannen [(*Spargo*)], Jay Silverheels [(*RedCloud*)], John Hamilton [(*Colonel Cornish*)], Selmer Jackson [(*ColonelBrand*)], [Stanley Blystone (*Judge*)], [Gene Roth (*Attorney*)], [Alva Lacy (*Hisega*)], [Joe McGuinn (*U.S.Marshal*)].

Western. [*Print viewed*]. Jack McCall enters a saloon in Deadwood City, throws an Indian necklace on the table in front of Marshal Bill Hickok, and, when Hickok draws his gun, shoots him dead. Later, on trial for murder, McCall explains his reasons for killing Hickok: During the Civil War, McCall, a wealthy Southerner, joins a Union Army unit which includes his cousin Bat McCall, who envies McCall's wealth, and Hickok. Knowing that rebel soldiers are in the area, McCall, who grew up nearby, offers to meet the reinforcements that the unit anticipates and guide them past the rebels. Along the way, McCall meets some men in Union uniforms and draws them a map to headquarters on a scrap of paper. Unknown to McCall, the men are really Confederate spies and by the time he returns with the additional soldiers, headquarters is under attack. After the rebels are driven off, Hickok discovers the map, which has McCall's name on the back. Before he can explain, McCall is arrested for spying. Later, he escapes to his parents' plantation, but barely has time to relate the preceding events to his parents, before the Union soldiers, led by Bat, arrive. When McCall's father attempts to prevent the soldiers from searching his house, Hickok kills him. Bat then shoots blindly at an open door and kills McCall's mother, his aunt. Meanwhile, distrusted by both the Union and the Confederacy, McCall goes into hiding for the duration of the war, but continues to search for a southern soldier who can clear him of the charges against him. When the war ends, McCall learns that the man he seeks is named Spargo, but the former soldier refuses to testify until McCall offers him $1,000. On their way to the authorities, the men encounter Rose Griffith, a young woman whose horse has bolted, and McCall offers to escort her to town. When McCall turns off the road toward the plantation, however, Rose becomes extremely uneasy. The reason for her uneasiness soon becomes clear. Bat and Hickok have taken over the plantation and allowed drunks and rabble-rousers free reign. Upon their arrival, Rose is accused of theft. From Sam, an old retainer, McCall learns for the first time of his parents' deaths. When McCall demands the names of the killers, Hickok turns him over to the authorities and pays Spargo to change his story. Rose overhears the transaction and helps McCall escape. After robbing a stagecoach of money and clothing, McCall and Rose follow Bat and his men to Kansas City. There, McCall is about to confront Bat when the stagecoach arrives, and the passengers identify Rose as the woman who robbed them. McCall and Rose escape their pursuers and head for Deadwood City, which they have learned is Bat's final destination. Meanwhile, Hickok has become marshal and is plotting to take over gold fields belonging to the Sioux. When Red Cloud, the Sioux leader, complains to Hickok about raids by white men, Hickok advises him to sell the lands. A short time later, McCall and Rose witness a raid and rescue Gray Eagle, Red Cloud's son. Gray Eagle describes the situation and gives McCall a beaded necklace to show that he is a friend to the Indians. When McCall asks Hickok what he is doing to protect the Indians, Hickok deputizes him and assigns him to organize a Sioux attack against Bat's men. Although Red Cloud does not want to break his treaty with the U.S., he allows a few warriors to participate. Under Hickok's orders, the whites ambush the Indians, and during the ensuing battle, a dying Bat tells McCall that Hickok killed his father. When the battle is over, McCall confronts Hickok in the saloon and kills him. After he tells his story, McCall is acquitted. Later, McCall and his new wife Rose return to the plantation. *False accusations. Wild Bill Hickok. Jack McCall.* Ambushes. Battles. Cousins. Dakota Indians. Envy. Gold. Jailbreaks. Marshals. Murder. Plantation owners. Romance. Saloons. Servants. Soldiers. Spies. Stagecoach robberies. Trials. United States–History–Civil War, 1861-1865. United States–History–Reconstruction, 1865-1898. United States–South. The West.

Note: The historical Wild Bill Hickok was killed by Jack McCall in Deadwood, Dakota Territory. Most sources state that McCall shot Hickok in the back while Hickok was playing poker. For more biographical information on Hickok, please see the entry below for *The Plainsman*.

Exb 25 Mar 1953, p. 3485. *Har* 21 Mar 1953, p. 46. *Box* 21 Mar 1953. *FD* 18 Mar 1953, p. 4. *HR* 18 Mar 1953, p. 3. *MPHPD* 21 Mar 1953, p. 1765. *Var* 25 Mar 1953, p. 24.

THE JACKIE ROBINSON STORY (African Americans)
Jewel Pictures Corp. *Dist* Eagle Lion Films, Inc. 16 May 1950; Prod: began 10 Feb 1950 at Motion Picture Center [©Jewel Pictures Corp.; 19 May 1950; LP162]. Sd (RCA Sound Recording); b&w. 8 reels, 6,944 or 6,999 ft. 77 min. PCA cert no. 14466.
Pres WILLIAM JOSEPH HEINEMAN. *Prod* Mort Briskin. *Assoc prod* Joseph H. Nadel. *Dir* Alfred E. Green. *Dial dir* Ross Hunter. *Asst dir* Maurie M. Suess. *Wrt* Lawrence Taylor and Arthur Mann. *Dir of photog* Ernest Laszlo. *Prod des* Boris Leven. *Film ed* Arthur H. Nadel. *Set dec* Jack Mapes. *Cost* Maria Donovan. *Mus score* Herschel Burke Gilbert. *Orch arr* Joseph Mullendore. *Mus supv* David Chudnow. *Sd rec* Ben Winkler and Mac Dalgleish. *Makeup artist* Dave Grayson. *Tech supv* Arthur Mann.

Cast: Jackie Robinson (*Jackie Robinson*), Ruby Dee (*Rae Robinson [earlier known as Rae Isum]*), Minor Watson (*Branch Rickey*), Louise Beavers (*Jackie's mother*), Richard Lane ([*Clay Hopper*]), Harry Shannon (*Charlie*), Ben Lessy (*Shorty*), Bill Spaulding (*Bill Spaulding*), Billy Wayne (*Clyde Sukeforth*), Joel Fluellen (*Mack Robinson*), Bernie Hamilton (*Ernie*), Kenny Washington (*Tigers manager*), Pat Flaherty (*Karpen*), Larry McGrath (*Umpire*), Emmett Smith (*Catcher*), Howard Louis MacNeely (*Jackie, as a boy*), George Dockstader (*Bill*), [Dewey Robinson, Ben Welden, Joe Devlin (*Men in stands*)], [Dick Wessel (*Spike*)].

African American, Biography, Baseball, Drama. [*Print viewed*]. In 1928, Jackie Robinson, a young African-American boy who loves baseball, is given an old, worn out glove by a white man. Jackie keeps the glove as he grows up. In 1937, while representing Pasadena Junior College, Jackie breaks the national junior college broad jump record, which was previously held by his brother Mack. After Jackie leads his conference in touchdowns, UCLA football coach Bill Spaulding recruits him despite complaints from a colleague that "colored boys" have been getting too many athletic scholarships. Although Jackie receives Honorable Mention on the All-American team, he tells his girl friend, Rae Isum, that he wants to leave school and look for a full-time job so that they can get married. After discussing it with his mother, who wants him to graduate, Jackie talks with Mack, now a street sweeper despite his college degree. Jackie is skeptical about the value of a degree because schools are not hiring "colored coaches." Jackie remains in school, but his applications for college coaching positions are rejected. During World War II, he is drafted and becomes an athletic director in the army, while rising to the rank of lieutenant. After the war, Jackie plays baseball for the Black Panthers, a team in the Negro professional leagues and is soon introduced to the indignities of segregated life on the road. When Brooklyn Dodger scout Clyde Sukeforth asks Jackie to meet with the Dodgers, Jackie, not believing the man, fails to show up for the train he is to take to New York. Sukeforth finally convinces Jackie that his offer is real, and he travels to Brooklyn to meet with owner Branch Rickey. Rickey tells Jackie that because of setbacks caused by the war, he has sent scouts to look at players in Mexico, Cuba and in other Latin American countries, in addition to untapped sources in the U.S. Rickey warns Jackie that he will have to take insults, name-calling and dirty play, and not fight back, but do his job with hits, stolen bases and fielding. Jackie calls his mother in Pasadena, who suggests he seek a minister's advice. Reverend Carter, a black minister, encourages Jackie to accept the Dodgers' offer to join the Royals, their minor league club in Montreal, despite possible repercussions, and reminds Jackie that every step forward has meant a fight for their people. Jackie tells Rae that they can get married as soon as he succeeds, but Rae does not want to wait, and they decide to face the challenge together. At the Montreal spring training camp in Sanford, Florida, Jackie faces hostility from manager Clay Hopper and some of the players. Rae, having heard white men talk threateningly about Jackie, is afraid to go downtown or to the beach. When an exhibition game against the Dodgers is canceled because of a city ordinance prohibiting sports events between "white and colored," Jackie asks Rickey if he would like to call the experiment off, but Rickey refuses. On the day before the league opener in Jersey City, International League President Shaunnessy warns Rickey that having Robinson play may provoke racial fighting. Rickey replies that he believes that baseball teaches fair play and, if Shaunnessy's fears prove to be true, his whole life has been wasted. Boos greet Jackie when he bats the first time; however, he beats out a bunt, steals second, goes to third on a bad throw and then scores after provoking the pitcher to balk.

On his next turn at bat, Jackie hits a home run, and at the end of the game, Rickey proclaims Jackie's to be the best first game any ballplayer has ever had. The next week, after a game in a southern city, three white racists verbally abuse Jackie at the players' entrance, but his teammates walk him safely away. As he plays in other cities, Jackie experiences more abuse from spectators and opposing players, some of whom ask him for a shoeshine, call him "Sambo" and sloppily eat watermelon. At the end of the season, however, Shaunnessy asks Jackie to stay in Montreal, where he has drawn record crowds. Hopper, who initially viewed Jackie's entrance into baseball with racism and skepticism, now credits the team's victory in the Little World Series to him and calls him a gentleman and the greatest competitor he has ever seen. In Panama, where the Dodgers and Montreal team train together, Rickey meets with six Dodger players who have signed a petition saying they do not want Jackie in the club. Rickey castigates them for calling themselves Americans, reminding one of them, an Italian American, that no one stopped his immigrant parents from working at their jobs. He says he will fight for the American right to play a game that is supposed to represent democracy, principles of sportsmanship and fair play. Rickey then assigns Jackie to first base and challenges a bigoted Dodger pitcher to strike out Jackie if he wants to keep him with the team. After ducking a pitch, Jackie hits a home run. Later, at Ebbets Field, in his first time at bat as a Brooklyn Dodger, Jackie hits a triple. He then goes into a slump, due in part to problems playing in an unfamiliar position at first base. For the good of the team, the former first basemann gives Jackie a tip and ends his slump. When an opposing player starts a fight on the field, the Dodger bench piles out in Jackie's support. As a measure of his acceptance, Jackie is given a locker instead of being forced to use a hanger in the corner. After the Dodgers clinch the pennant with Jackie's help, he is invited to speak in Washington before the House of Representatives. He tells the congressmen and the American public that although life can be tough for people different from the majority, democracy works for those willing to fight for it and is worth defending. *African Americans. Baseball. Brooklyn Dodgers (Baseball team). Racism. Jackie Robinson. Brothers. California. University (Los Angeles). College sports. Democracy. Fights. Florida. Italian Americans. Marriage. Military service, Compulsory. Montreal (Canada). Mothers and sons. New York City–Brooklyn. Panama. Pasadena (CA). Reverends. Branch Rickey. Segregation. United States–South. United States. Congress. House of Representatives. Washington (D.C.).*

Note: Jackie Robinson (1919-1972), who joined the Brooklyn Dodgers in 1947, became the first African American to play for a Major League baseball team. He was chosen Rookie of the Year, and helped the Dodgers win the pennant that year. In 1949, he was voted Most Valuable Player after winning the batting championship. *NYT* commented that the film marked the first time a non-actor played a starring role as himself and noted that Dodger owner Branch Rickey did not give his approval to the film until the production company agreed to use Robinson and as many other ballplayers as possible.

According to information in the MPAA/PCA Collection at the AMPAS Library, an Italian-American organization in Jersey City, NJ, the 5th ward division of the John R. Longo Association, wrote to New Jersey's two U.S. senators in Aug 1950 to complain about the scene in the film in which an Italian-American player objects to Robinson playing on the team. Claiming that the film "smears and libels Americans of Italian extraction," the group in a resolution urged the senators to "launch an investigation to determine if a conspiracy exists in the movie industry to hold these decent Americans in such an unsavory light, and thereby perpetrating all phases of racial discrimination."

New Jersey Senator H. Alexander Smith then wrote to Senator Edwin C. Johnson, the Chairman of the Interstate and Foreign Commerce Committee: "As you have introduced legislation with regard to an investigation of the movie industry, I am wondering whether the legislation will cover the subject of this resolution." Senator Johnson subsequently wrote to Eric Johnston, president of the Motion Picture Association of America. Johnston had his New York office make a study of films released in the previous two years that contained depictions of Italians. He found that of 116 portrayals, 78 were sympathetic, 19 were unsympathetic and 19 were mixed or with no particular impact. Of the 50 prominent depictions among the 116, 34 were sympathetic, 11 unsympathetic and 5 mixed. Johnston then wrote to Senator Johnson that the same issue had been raised the previous year by the United Italian-American League of New York. At that time, Johnston supplied an editorial writer for the Italian-language newspaper, *Il progresso*, with information stating that motion picture producers routinely changed the names of unsympathetic Italian characters in plays and novels adapted for films and added sympathetic Italian characters where Italians originally had been cast as villains. Johnston wrote, "I've found from personal observation that Hollywood, in films dealing with different nationalities and groups, is guided by principles of fair play and justice, tolerance and understanding." Although he acknowledged the possibility of "errors and mistakes of judgment," he reiterated the Production

Code provision dealing with the issue: "The history, institutions, prominent people and citizenry of all nations shall be represented fairly." Joseph I. Breen, director of the Hollywood PCA office, also denied that Italian Americans were "smeared" in *The Jackie Robinson Story*, noting that later in the film, there is a scene in which the Dodgers are led by the Italian-American player as they rush out of the dugout in support of Jackie after he is threatened by a member of the opposing team.

HR praised the film stating, "There is no attempt to minimize the racial angle; yet this is not the essence of *The Jackie Robinson Story*. It happens to be an account of a great athlete and what must be a greater gentleman. The film is choppy, episodic, and sometimes its low budget shows at the seams. But director Alfred E. Green and his star maintain a serene dignity throughout it all." *Var* commented, "Robinson is a better baseballer than he is an actor, but still does rather well in a not too self-conscious portrayal of himself." *Fortnight* noted that the film "strives hard to be in line with the popular documentary technique of the moment." *HCN* criticized Robinson's performance and the film, stating "it strikes us more as a re-enactment of events rather than as a tremendous drama developing with all the psychological complexities mirrored before our eyes."

Amsterdam News (New York) 18 Feb 1948. *Box* 20 May 1950. *DV* 15 May 1950, p. 3, 10. *Exb* 24 May 1950, p. 2854. *FD* 16 May 1950, p. 5. *Fortnight* 23 Jun 1950. *Har* 20 May 1950, p. 79. *HCN* 15 Jul 1950. *HR* 30 Nov 1949. *HR* 10 Feb 1950, p. 20. *HR* 15 May 1950. *LAT* 15 Jul 1950. *MPD* 15 May 1950. *MPHPD* 20 May 1950, p. 301. *NYT* 30 Apr 1950. *NYT* 17 May 1950, p. 36. *Var* 17 May 1950, p. 6.

JACKPOT JITTERS *see* **JIGGS AND MAGGIE IN JACKPOT JITTERS**

JACOB THE BLACKSMITH *see* **THE SINGING BLACKSMITH**

THE JADE MASK (Chinese Americans)
Monogram Pictures Corp. *Dist* Monogram Pictures Corp. 26 Jan **1945**; Brooklyn, NY opening: week of 18 Jan 1945; Prod: Sep 1944 [©Monogram Pictures Corp.; 22 Nov 1944; LP13002]. Sd (Western Electric Recording); b&w. 64 or 69 min.
Series: Charlie Chan.
Prod James S. Burkett. *Dir* Phil Rosen. *Asst dir* Eddie Davis. *Orig scr* George Callahan. *Dir of photog* Harry Neumann. *Ed* John C. Fuller and [Dick Currier]. *Set dec* Vin Taylor. *Mus dir* Edward J. Kay. *Mus score* Dave Torbett. *Sd rec* Tom Lambert. *Prod mgr* Wm. Strohbach. *Tech dir* Dave Milton.
Source: Based on characters created by Earl Derr Biggers.
Cast: Sidney Toler [(*Charlie Chan*)], Mantan Moreland [(*Birmingham Brown*)], Edwin Luke [(*Eddie Chan*)], Hardie Albright [(*Walter Meeker*)], Frank Reicher [(*Harper*)], Janet Warren [(*Jean Kent*)], Cyril DeLevanti [(*Roth*)], Alan Bridge [(*Sheriff Mack*)], Ralph Lewis [(*Jim Kimball*)], Dorothy Granger [(*Stella Graham*)], Edith Evanson [(*Louise Harper*)], Joe Whitehead [(*Dr. Samuel R. Peabody*)], Henry Hall [(*Inspector Godfrey*)], Jack Ingram [(*Lloyd Archer*)], Danny Desmond, [Lester Dorr (*Michael Strong*)].
Detective, Drama. [*Print viewed*]. Disguised as a policeman, a murderer breaks into the mansion of Harper, a scientist, kills him and disposes of his body. Charlie Chan, the world famous Chinese-American detective now working as a government agent, is called to the case by police inspector Godfrey, who informs him that the scientist was working for the government to create a formula whereby wood could be made as strong as metal. At the scientist's mansion, Chan and Godfrey question, with the help of the local authority, Sheriff Mack, the inhabitants of the Harper household: Louise Harper, his sister; Jean Kent, his orphaned niece; Roth, his butler; Michael Strong, his mute chauffeur/handyman; and Walter Meeker and Stella Graham, his assistants. Chan quickly learns that all of them hated Harper, whose cruelty went so far as to force his relatives to work for him as servants. Meanwhile, Chan's two assistants—Eddie, his fourth son, and Birmingham Brown, his chauffeur—arrive at the Harper estate, having been thrown out of their hotel room. Later, Chan discovers the murdered Harper inside the scientist's gas chamber, and Meeker tells him that all of Harper's work will be rendered useless unless Chan can find the scientist's secret formula. After the local coroner, Dr. Samuel R. Peabody, declares that Harper died of "natural causes," Chan and Mack visit Peabody, who then discovers a poisonous dart inside the dead scientist's mouth. Later, Chan learns that Jim Kimball, a missing local policeman, was having a secret romance with Jean, but she insists that he was not the officer seen in the mansion at the time of Harper's disappearance. Roth is killed soon after he promises to tell Chan the name of the murderer. After examining the dead butler's quarters, Chan tells Mack that Roth was killed in his room, despite the fact that both Eddie and Birmingham saw the butler walking downstairs shortly before his death. Lloyd Archer, Harper's step-son, then arrives at the estate, claiming that

Harper's secret gas formula was stolen from his birth father. That night, Chan is nearly killed by a poisoned dart while searching for clues. The next morning, Louise discovers her brother's secret hiding place, but the vault itself can only be opened by Harper's voice speaking a coded message. Chan, realizing that someone inside is being gassed, opens the vault by playing a dictaphone recording of Harper. An unconscious Jean is then removed from the vault, but she later insists that she was not attempting to steal her uncle's formula. Michael is later killed after he writes Eddie a note, claiming to know who the murderer is. Kimball's dead body is then uncovered in the gas chamber by Birmingham, and Chan announces that all the murder victims were killed by an air gun hidden inside a ventriloquist's dummy, and that the dead Roth walked with the aid of puppeteer's strings. Knowing that Stella is a master puppeteer, Chan names her as the murderer's accomplice, then states that the life mask broken during Michael's murder was one of Meeker. The laboratory assistant attempts to escape, but is captured, after which Chan pulls a rubber mask from his face to show that he is really Archer, not Meeker, whose murdered body is later found in the basement. Chan then convinces Stella to tell all, and she states that Archer, a vaudevillian quick-change artist and impersonator, is actually her husband. With the case solved, Chan thanks his son for his assistance, though he is unsure of what assistance he was. *African Americans. Chauffeurs. Chinese Americans. Fathers and sons. Government agents. Murder. Brothers and sisters. Butlers. Coroners. Dictating machines. Disguise. Gases, Asphyxiating and poisonous. Hotels. Impersonation and imposture. Mansions. Marriage–Secret. Masks. Mutes. Nieces. Police. Puppeteers. Rescues. Scientists. Secret formulas. Secret passageways. Sheriffs. Vaults. Ventriloquists and ventriloquism.*

Note: The working title of this film was *Mystery Mansion*. The title card on the viewed print reads: "Charlie Chan in *The Jade Mask*." Early *HR* production charts include Russell Simpson in the cast, but it is unlikely that he appeared in the released film. The *Var* review mistakenly identifies Edwin Luke's character as "Tommy." Edwin Luke was the younger brother of actor Keye Luke, who had previously played Charlie Chan's son "Lee Chan" in numerous films in this series. For additional information about this series, consult the Series Index and see the entry above for *Charlie Chan Carries On*.

DV 21 Feb 1945, p. 3. *FD* 1 Feb 1945, p. 8. *HR* 1 Sep 1944, p. 12. *HR* 15 Sep 1944, p. 16. *HR* 21 Feb 1945, p. 4. *MPHPD* 7 Oct 1944, p. 2131. *MPHPD* 27 Jan 1945, p. 2290. *Var* 24 Jan 1945, p. 10.

JAKE THE PLUMBER (Jewish Americans)

R-C Pictures Corp. *Dist* Film Booking Offices of America. 16 Oct **1927** [©R-C Pictures Corp.; 16 Oct 1927; LP24637]. Si; b&w. 6 reels, 5,186 ft.

Pres Joseph P. Kennedy. *Dir* Edward I. Luddy. *Asst dir* Bill Dagwell. *Story* Edward I. Luddy. *Cont* James J. Tynan. *Photog* Phillip Tannura.

Cast: Jess Devorska (*Jake, the Plumber*), Sharon Lynn (*Sarah Levine*), Rosa Rosanova (*Mrs. Levine*), Ann Brody (*Mrs. Schwartz*), Bud Jamison (*Fogarty*), Carol Halloway (*Mrs. Levis*), William H. Tooker (*Mr. Levis*), Dolores Brinkman (*Sadie Rosen*), Eddie Harris (*Poppa Levine*), Fanchon Frankel (*Rachael Rosenblatt*).

Comedy-drama. Jake Schwartz, an apprentice for Fogarty, an Irish plumber, is forced to support his widowed mother on the miserly stipend of twelve dollars a week. He hopes eventually to be able to marry and support Sarah Levine, who supports *her* entire family by working in a garment factory. While on his way to work, Jake notices the careening automobile of Mrs. Sam Levis, wife of a retired manufacturer, who is subject to fainting spells; mistaking her falling arm as an invitation to ride, he hops in the front seat. Finding her unconscious, he takes the wheel and drives to his shop. Sarah, who has seen him from a streetcar, gives him the cold shoulder, plunging Jake into gloom, but Jake's mother and Mrs. Levis straighten out matters. All go as guests of Mr. Levis to the races. When Levis' jockey is discovered drugged, Jake agrees to ride in the race, which he wins by default. Three years later, Jake is found to be happily married to Sarah and the father of two children. *Clothing industry. Family life. Family relationships. Horseracing. Irish. Jews. Plumbers.*

FD 17 Oct 1927. *Var* 2 Nov 1927, p. 24.

JAMESTOWN (Native Americans)

The Chronicles of America Pictures Corp.; Chronicles of America Series. *Dist* Pathé Exchange, Inc. 4 Nov **1923** [©The Chronicles of America Pictures Corp.; 14 May 1923; LP18970]. Si; b&w. 4 reels.

Dir Edwin L. Hollywood. *Adpt* Roswell Dague.

Source: Based on the book *Pioneers of the Old South; a Chronicle of English Colonial Beginnings* by Mary Johnston (New Haven, 1918).

Cast: Dolores Cassinelli (*Pocahontas*), Robert Gaillard (*Sir Thomas Dale*), Harry Kendall (*Capt. George Yeardley*), Leslie Stowe (*The Reverend Richard Buck*), Paul McAllister (*Don Diego de Molina*), Leslie Austin (*John Rolfe*).

Historical, Drama. America's development at the time when England's control of Virginia was threatened by both the Indians and the Spanish is shown by describing Jamestown's Starving Time beginning in 1612. High Marshal Sir Thomas Dale holds Pocahontas as hostage in order to force Powhatan, her father, into joining the English colonists against the Spanish; but the marriage of John Rolfe to Pocahontas brings the groups together. *Thomas Dale. Indians of North America. Jamestown (VA). Pocahontas. Powhatan. John Rolfe. United States–History–War with Mexico, 1845-1848.*

MPW 3 Nov 1923.

[JAPANESE-AMERICAN FILM] (Japanese Americans, Japanese language)

Kato Ediguchi Productions. **1927**; Los Angeles showing: 24 May 1927. Si; b&w. 73 min. Japanese language.

Dir E. L. Zeer.

Cast: Harry Abbe (*The half-wit*), Tuki Mayeda (*The daughter*).

Drama. [*Not viewed*]. A Japanese father leaves his wife and daughter in Japan and takes his son to make their fortune in America. Years later, the father and son are prosperous farmers. The son has fallen in love with the sister of a white school friend, who lives on the adjoining land. The mother and daughter from Japan arrive in the U.S. with a half-wit, who is a friend of the family. After the half-wit is told to go, he strikes oil and returns with money. [No additional information has been located concerning the ending to the film]. *Family relationships. Farmers. Immigrants. Japanese Americans. Mentally handicapped persons. Miscegenation. Brothers and sisters. Oil.*

Note: The plot summary was based on a *Var* review of a Los Angeles showing of the film. The review noted that the film was untitled as yet, and that substantial cuts had made it unclear in spots. The reviewer speculated that the scenes dealing with the impending love affair between the Japanese boy and the white girl had been cut for the specific showing in a white neighborhood. Subtitles were in Japanese. During the presentation, the film was halted a number of times, and the actors from the film appeared on stage and performed parts of the story, as actor Harry Abbe provided a limited English translation. The ending was performed on stage, and Japanese instruments and singing accompanied the film. Some of the actors danced on stage, including Tuki Mayeda, a child actress, who performed a solo toe dance. *Var* suggested, "With entire revamping and expert cutting, this production should provide suitable program material for picture houses; particularly where Japanese settlements are in number."

Var 1 Jun 1927.

JAPANESE WAR BRIDE (Japanese Americans)

Bernhard Productions, Inc. *Dist* Twentieth Century-Fox Film Corp. Jan **1952**; New York opening: 29 Jan 1952; Prod: early Jun—early Jul 1951 [©Twentieth Century-Fox Film Corp.; 1 Jan 1952; LP1482]. Sd (RCA Sound System); b&w. 9 reels, 8,194 ft. 90-91 min. PCA cert no. 14517.

Prod Joseph Bernhard. *Co-prod* Anson Bond. *Dir* King Vidor. *Asst dir* Wilbur McGaugh. *Scr* Catherine Turney. *Story* Anson Bond. *Photog* Lionel Lindon. *Art dir* Danny Hall. *Film ed* Terry Morse. *Set dec* Murray Waite. *Ward* Izzy Berne and Adele Parmenter. *Mus* Emil Newman and Arthur Lange. *Sd* Vic Appel and Ed Borschell. *Makeup* Gene Hibbs. *Asst to prods* Paul Guilfoyle. *Prod mgr* Percy Ikerd. *Comptroller* Monte Kennedy. *Casting dir* Maxine Marlowe.

Cast: Shirley Yamaguchi (*Tae Shimizu*), Don Taylor (*Jim Sterling*), Cameron Mitchell (*Art Sterling*), Marie Windsor (*Fran Sterling*), James Bell (*Ed Sterling*), Louise Lorimer (*Harriet Sterling*), Philip Ahn (*Eitaro Shimizu*), Sybil Merritt (*Emily Shafer*), Lane Nakano (*Shiro Hasagawa*), Kathleen Mulqueen (*Mrs. Milly Shafer*), Orley Lindgren (*Ted Sterling*), George Wallace (*Woody Blacker*), May Takasugi (*Emma Hasagawa*), William Yokota (*Mr. Hasagawa*), Susie Matsumoto (*Tae's mother*), Weaver Levy (*Kioto*), Jerry Fujikawa (*Man at fish market*), Chieko Sato, Tetsu Komai (*Japanese servants*), Hisa Chiba (*Old Japanese woman*), David March (*Man at plant*).

Postwar life, Drama. [*Print viewed*]. Critically wounded while fighting in the Korean War, young American Army lieutenant Jim Sterling is transported to a Japanese hospital, where he is nursed back to health by a Japanese nurse named Tae Shimizu. Tae and Jim fall in love, and Jim later visits her grandfather Eitaro and asks him to bless their marriage. Eitaro objects to the marriage because he feels that

there are too many differences between the Anglos and the Japanese. Hoping to scare Jim off, Eitaro plays a trick on him, but Jim and Tae see through the ploy and insist on going through with the marriage. With his new bride at his side, Jim returns to his home in Salinas, California, and introduces her to his parents, his brothers, Art and Ted, and Art's wife Fran. Fran, who still carries a torch for Jim, becomes jealous of Tae. A short time later, Tae meets the Hasagawas, a second generation Japanese American family who own the land next to the Sterlings'. While trying hard to gain acceptance by the Sterlings, Tae falls victim to Fran's plots to discredit her. One day, Tae overhears Mrs. Sterling's friend, Milly Shafer, tell Mrs. Sterling that she is uneasy about Tae's presence because her son was killed in the war. Although Milly's remarks upset her, Tae decides to remain silent about the affair. The following day, while Tae and Ted are out picking mushrooms, Tae has a talk with Shiro Hasagawa, who tells her that his family was sent to an internment camp during World War II, and that the memory of the camp has embittered his father and made him resent all Anglo Americans. Later, Fran, still trying to make trouble for Tae, spreads word that she was seen alone with Shiro. Tae finds herself at the center of attention once again when, at a party, Jim's drunken friend, Woody Blacker, insults her by calling her a "geisha." Jim punches Woody, and a fistfight ensues. Time passes, and Tae, now pregnant, looks forward to starting a family in the house they plan to build on Sterling land. Soon after Tae gives birth to a baby boy, her troubles return when an anonymous and malicious letter is circulated through town claiming that the father of the child is Shiro. The accusations upset Jim, who makes plans to leave Salinas after telling Tae about the letter. Tae, however, is so devastated by the false accusations that she takes the baby and leaves without Jim. While Tae takes refuge at the Hasagawas, who later send her to live with relatives in Monterey, Jim concludes that Fran wrote the slanderous letter. Jim wrings a confession from Fran, after which Art strikes her. Jim then convinces Shiro that he is genuinely in love with Tae and that he wants to repair his marriage. As soon as Shiro tells him where he can find his wife, Jim sets out for Monterey. Tae tries to run away from Jim when she first sees him, and then contemplates jumping into the ocean from a nearby cliff. Jim prevents her from doing so, however, when he tells her that he truly loves her and is ready to start a new life in their new house. *Assimilation (Sociology). False accusations. Farmers. Japanese Americans. Korean War, 1950-1953. Miscegenation. Racism. Fistfights. Grandfathers. Japanese Americans–Evacuation and relocation, 1942-1945. Jealousy. Letters. Marriage. Nurses. Parties. Salinas (CA). Sisters-in-law. Veterans.*

Note: The working title for this film was *East Is East*. Shirley Yamaguchi, a popular Japanese actress, made her American film debut in the picture, according to *NYT. HR* production charts list the actress as Yoshiko Yamaguchi, and note that portions of the picture were filmed in Salinas, CA. According to a 1952 *HR* news item, a $75,000 plagiarism suit was filed against Twentieth Century-Fox, Bernhard Productions, and writers Anson Bond and Catherine Turney in May 1952 by Harold Nebenzal, who alleged that the story of the film was lifted from a treatment that he had submitted to Bernhard, through Bond, in 1949. The outcome of the suit is not known.

Box 12 Jan 1952. *DV* 19 Nov 1951. *FD* 21 Jan 1952, p. 7. *HR* 8 Jun 1951, p. 11. *HR* 29 Jun 1951, p. 11. *HR* 7 Jan 1952, p. 3. *HR* 6 May 1952. *MPHPD* 12 Jan 1952, pp. 1185-86. *NYT* 30 Jan 1952, p. 22. *Var* 9 Jan 1952, p. 6.

JASPER LANDRY'S WILL see UNCLE JASPER'S WILL

LA JAULA DE LOS LEONES (Spanish language)
Producciones Ci-Ti-Go. *Dist* J. H. Hoffberg Co. Aug **1930**; Los Angeles opening: 9 Aug 1930; Prod: Apr-May 1930 in Radiotone Studios. Sd; b&w. 8 reels. 74 min.

Supv Mateo Cicero. *Dir* Fred Balshofer. *Staging supv* Romualdo Tirado. *Orig scr* Romualdo Tirado. *Photog* W. C. Thompson. *Mus comp and dir* Ernesto González Jiménez. *Tech adv* Ricardo Bell, Jr.

Song(s): "Vals de amor," "Es por la mañana" and "Muñeca de oro," composers undetermined.

Cast: Romualdo Tirado (*El vagabundo*), Matilde Liñán (*La abuelita*), Amelia Bell (*Rosalinda*), Alicia Bell (*Rosalinda, de niña*), Luis Mendoza López (*Director empresario del circo*), José Peña "Pepet" (*Secretario*), Ramón Muñoz (*Domador*), Alfonso Pedroza (*Hércules*), Jesús Segovia (*Doctor*), Rosita Bell (*Camarera*), F. Meléndez del Valle (*Cantante*).

Drama, with songs. [*Not viewed*]. A hungry, despairing tramp comes to the aid of a poor old blind woman who has had an accident while taking a walk with her young granddaughter, Rosalinda, and, for the first time, discovers in their company a reason for living.

Motivated to find work, the tramp looks for a worthy job and without fully understanding the risks, temporarily substitutes for a lion tamer in a circus. To the amazement of all, he is a great success and is given the job permanently. Twelve years later, the grandmother dies and Rosalinda, now a young woman, marries a lad of her own age. However, the lion tamer, who has been secretly in love with Rosalinda, becomes profoundly depressed and carelessly falls victim to a fatal attack by one of his lions. *Circuses. Lion tamers. Lions. Tramps. Blindness. Circus performers. Death by animals. Depression, Mental. Granddaughters. Poverty. Unemployment. Unrequited love.*

Note: This film's working title was *La tragedia del circo*. Some contemporary sources list Romualdo Tirado as sole director. The *Var* and *FD* reviews incorrectly include María Alba in the cast.

FD 8 Mar 1931. *HF* 14 Jun 1930. *Var* 25 Feb 1931.

THE JAYHAWKERS! (French Americans)
Paramount Pictures Corp. *Dist* Paramount Pictures Corp. Oct **1959**; Prod: 10 Dec 1958—early Feb 1959 [©Paramount Pictures Corp. & Parkwood Enterprises, Inc.; 14 Oct 1959; LP14708]. Sd (Westrex Recording System); col (Technicolor). 100 min. PCA cert no. 19247.

Prod Norman Panama and Melvin Frank. *Asst to the prod* Doane Harrison. *Dir* Melvin Frank. *Asst dir* Daniel McCauley. *2d unit dir* Arthur Rosson. *Wrt* Melvin Frank, Joseph Petracca, Frank Fenton and A. I. Bezzerides. *Dir of photog* Loyal Griggs. *2d unit photog* Irmin Roberts. *Spec photog eff* John R. Fulton. *Process photog* Farciot Edouart. *Technicolor color consultant* Richard Mueller. *Art dir* Hal Pereira and Roland Anderson. *Ed* Everett Douglas. *Set dec* Sam Comer and Darrell Silvera. *Cost* Edith Head. *Mus* Jerome Moross. *Sd rec* Lyle Figland and Winston Leverett. *Makeup supv* Wally Westmore. *Hair style supv* Nellie Manley.

Cast: JEFF CHANDLER [(*Luke Darcy*)], FESS PARKER [(*Cam Bleeker*)], NICOLE MAUREY [(*Jeanne DuBois*)], Henry Silva [(*Lordan*)], Herbert Rudley [(*Governor William Clayton*)], Frank DeKova [(*Evans*)], Don Megowan [(*China*)], Leo Gordon [(*Jake*)], Shari Lee Bernath [(*Marthe*)], Jimmy Carter [(*Paul DuBois*)], Renata Vanni [(*Indian woman*)], Berel Firestone, Allan Wyatt, Charles Bail [(*Jayhawkers*)], Ned Glass [(*Storekeeper*)], Richard Shannon, Barbara Knudson, Max Power [(*Governor's aide*)], Joe Forte [(*Minister*)], Tony Regan [(*Bartender*)], Howard Joslin [(*Officer*)], John Wiley Rice [(*Jayhawker*)], [Courtland Shepard, Frank Hagney (*Jayhawkers*)], [Frank Wilcox (*Lieutenant*)], [Dean Stanton (*Smallwood*)], [Charles Boaz (*Gateman*)], [Kenneth MacDonald (*Rider*)], [Glenn Strange, Harry Clexx, James E. Hope (*Sheriffs*)], [Mike Mahoney (*Telegrapher*)], [George Barrows (*Captain*)], [Mitchell Kowal (*Governor's aide*)], [Polly Burson (*Schoolteacher*)], [Carole Conn (*Girl*)], [Paul McGuire (*Stationmaster*)], [Richard T. Adams (*Soldier*)], [William E. Green (*Mayor*)], [Jack Kruschen (*Cattleman*)], [Eric Alden (*Man with a whip*)], [Boyd Morgan (*Big guard*)].

Western. [*Print viewed*]. Just prior to the Civil War, Cam Bleeker breaks out of a Kansas Territorial prison because he cannot believe the news he has received telling him that his beloved wife is dead. After being injured during his escape, Cam arrives at his homestead in a state of delirium and is shocked to see that it is now inhabited by a French widow, Jeanne DuBois, and her two children, Paul and Marthe. The beautiful Jeanne tends his wounds and reluctantly shows him the grave of his wife. Her own husband, she explains, believed so strongly in freedom that he brought his family from France to the United States in order to help build the free, young nation. Shortly after they bought the Bleeker property, which had been seized by the government following Cam's imprisonment and Mrs. Bleeker's death, the Missouri Redlegs, a pro-slavery gang, raided the house and killed her husband. Now she hopes Cam will stay on to help her run the ranch, and after agreeing, Cam soon finds that he has become attached both to the children and to Jeanne. Before long, a posse arrives looking for Cam, and for the sake of the children's safety, he surrenders. He is brought before Governor William Clayton, who promises to return his freedom if he will find and capture Luke Darcy, the elusive leader of a powerful group of raiders called the Jayhawkers. Cam protests that he had led raiders of his own, an act that landed him in prison, merely to protect his home, and that he is unwilling to offer assistance either to the pro-slavery governor or his anti-slavery enemies. Clayton finally enlists Cam's cooperation by revealing that Darcy, after capturing Cam's wife during a raid, made love to the woman then abandoned her, whereupon she became an

alcoholic and a tramp. Poor and alone, she eventually died of pneumonia. Jeanne tells Cam that he has no right to seek revenge, but he leaves her and rides off in search of Darcy. Through one of his own former raiders, Cam soon locates this "backwoods Napoleon," who, although willing to kill any Jayhawker who violates his rules, is very charismatic, and even impresses Cam. Cam, in turn, impresses Darcy, and soon the escaped prisoner becomes the gang leader's right-hand man. One evening, Darcy admits that he had indeed loved Cam's wife but that their love had been a mistake. Cam is moved by Darcy's truthfulness, and when the Jayhawkers attack the next town, he saves Darcy's life. During a visit to Jeanne, Cam declares that he has joined the Jayhawkers, infuriating the Frenchwoman, who in her homeland had seen "big men" make empty promises similar to Darcy's. Meanwhile, Lordan, a Jayhawker who despises Cam, secretly sends a posse after him, but Cam gets away. Furious, Darcy almost kills Lordan for his act of betrayal. During a raid, Jeanne's little daughter Marthe runs after Cam and is nearly trampled to death by the Jayhawkers' horses. Cam delivers the injured child to Jeanne, who, by screaming that he is a murderer, finally persuades Cam to abandon the Jayhawkers. Cam discovers that wealthy cattle owners from several states soon will descend on Abilene for a huge cattle sale. By convincing Darcy that a raid on a scheduled train will yield enough money to secure Kansas for the Jayhawkers, Cam is able to organize an ambush. Unknown to Darcy, instead of a gold shipment, the train will carry Clayton's troops, and Darcy will be apprehended. Jeanne assists Cam with the plan, but Darcy's charm and gratitude make both her and Cam feel uneasy. Unknown to them, Lordan has discovered the plot and returned to Abilene with the news. At the last moment, Cam decides to warn Darcy about Clayton's impending attack, but Darcy, instead of fleeing from the approaching soldiers, angrily challenges Cam to a fight to the death. During the fight, Darcy gets Cam's gun away, but Cam retrieves it, and as Clayton's soldiers approach the saloon door and and prepare to hang Darcy, Cam challenges his friend to a duel. Darcy draws his gun, but Cam fires first and Darcy dies, saved from a hanging death he considered hideous and undignified. The governor agrees to pardon Cam, and as Darcy's body is borne away, Cam takes Jeanne's hand and looks on with sorrow and respect. *Betrayal. Dictators. Friendship. Kansas. Loyalty. Abolitionists. Ambushes. Children. Fistfights. French Americans. Gunfights. Immigrants. Raids. Revenge. Slavery. Undercover agents. United States–History–19th century. Widowers. Widows.*

Note: This film was very loosely based on the exploits of the "Jayhawkers," the name given to various groups, based in Kansas, some of whom were abolitionists, while others, under the guise of abolition, were bandits who raided their opponents in Kansas and neighboring states. Contemporary reviews noted that the film was filled with historical inaccuracies, and the *HR* critic commented: "The reason, in this case, for pointing out historical inaccuracies is not to strike a blow for pedantry but to emphasize that almost any valid tale of the Border War would have been better entertainment." Jeff Chandler was borrowed from Universal-International for the production, which, according to a *DV* news item, was partially shot on location at the Janss Ranch in Ventura County, CA.
Box 19 Oct 1959. *DV* 10 Dec 1958. *DV* 15 Oct 1959, p. 3. *Exh* 21 Oct 1959, p. 4646. *FD* 15 Oct 1959, p. 6. *Har* 17 Oct 1959, p. 166. *HR* 10 Dec 1958, p. 3. *HR* 12 Dec 1958, p. 12. *HR* 30 Jan 1959, p. 16. *HR* 15 Oct 1959, p. 3. *LAT* 6 Jan 1959. *MPD* 15 Sep 1959. *MPHPD* 17 Oct 1959, p. 451. *Var* 21 Oct 1959, p. 6.

THE JAZZ SINGER (Jewish Americans)

Warner Bros. Pictures, Inc.; The Vitaphone Corporation; A Warner Brothers Production. *Dist* Warner Bros. Pictures, Inc. 4 Feb **1928**; New York premiere: 6 Oct 1927 [©Warner Bros. Pictures, Inc.; 6 Oct 1927; LP24505]. Talking seq, mus score, and sd eff (Vitaphone); b&w. 9 reels, 8,117 ft. 90 min. Passed by the National Board of Review.

Dir Alan Crosland. *Asst dir* Gordon Hollingshead. *Adpt* Al Cohn. *Titles* Jack Jarmuth. *Photog* Hal Mohr. [*Engineering eff* Nugent Slaughter]. *Film ed* Harold McCord. *Mus score and Vitaphone orch dir* Louis Silvers. [*Sd* George R. Groves]. *Tech* Fred Jackman, Lewis Geib, Esdras Hartley, F. N. Murphy, "Alpharetta" and Victor Vance.

Song(s): "Mammy," by Sam Lewis, Joe Young and Walter Davidson; "Toot, Toot, Tootsie! by Gus Kahn, Ernie Erdman and Dan Russo; "Dirty Hands, Dirty Face," music by James V. Monaco, lyrics by Edgar Lewis, Grant Clarke and Al Jolson; "Blue Skies," by Irving Berlin; "Mother of Mine, I Still Have You," by Al Jolson, Louis Silvers and Grant Clarke; "Kol Nidre," traditional hymn.

Source: Based on the short story "The Day of Atonement" by Samson Raphaelson in *Everybody's Magazine* (Jan 1922) and his play *The Jazz Singer* (New York, 14 Sep 1925).

Cast: AL JOLSON (*Jakie Rabinowitz [also known as Jack Robin]*), May McAvoy (*Mary Dale*), Warner Oland (*The Cantor [Papa Rabinowitz]*), Eugenie Besserer (*Sara [Mama] Rabinowitz*), Bobby Gordon (*Jakie, at age 13*), Otto Lederer (*Moisha Yudelson [The Kibbitzer]*), Richard Tucker (*Harry Lee*), Cantor Josef Rosenblatt ([*Himself*] *Concert Recital*), [Nat Carr (*Levi*)], [William Demarest (*Buster Billings*)], [Anders Randolf (*Dillings*)], [Will Walling (*Doctor*)], [Roscoe Karns (*The agent*)], [Myrna Loy (*Chorus girl*)].

Melodrama, with songs. [*Print viewed*]. In New York City, at the turn of the century, Cantor Rabinowitz is determined that his thirteen-year-old son Jakie become the next in a long family line of cantors. On Yom Kippur, the Jewish Day of Atonement, he looks forward to the time when Jakie will take his place in the temple, but his loving wife Sara is concerned that their son wants to do something else. Meanwhile, Jakie is seen singing in a saloon by neighborhood kibbutzer Moishe Yudelson, who then rushes to inform the cantor. Jakie is then dragged home and given a whipping by his father. Later, Jakie tells his heart-broken mother that he is going to be on the stage, then runs away. Years later, in San Francisco, Jakie has become a singer performing at Coffee Dan's restaurant. When he sings the poignant song "Dirty Hands, Dirty Face" for the audience, followed by the jazz tune "Toot, Toot, Tootsie," vaudeville dancer Mary Dale, who is in the audience, is intrigued. She tells him that he has what other jazz singers do not, a tear in his voice, and helps him to get a job with her troupe. Some time later, while performing in Chicago, Jakie, who has changed his name to Jack Robin, goes to a concert of sacred songs given by famed Cantor Josef Rosenblatt, and is deeply moved. Through the years, Jack has sent letters home boasting of his success but has never reconciled with his father. Jack has grown to love Mary and is saddened when she leaves the troupe for a chance to appear in a Broadway show. A short time later, Jack is told by his agent that he, too, has been offered a part in a Broadway show, and he looks forward to a return home to New York and his mother. In the autumn of 1927, on Cantor Rabinowitz's sixtieth birthday, Jack pays a surprise visit home. Although Mrs. Rabinowitz is over-joyed to see her son, who promises to move them to a new house in the Bronx and buy her a new pink dress, Cantor Rabinowitz is furious to hear his son singing jazz music in the house. They have a violent argument over Jack's preference for show business over the family tradition of being a cantor, and Jack leaves after his father bitterly calls him a "jazz singer." On Yom Kippur, Cantor Rabinowitz is too ill to sing the *Kol Nidre* in the temple and dreams that his son will sing in his place. Yudelson goes to see Jack at the theater where *April Follies*, the show in which he is co-starring with Mary, is about to open, and asks him to sing in the temple. Although Jack is torn, he refuses. Just before Jack is to go on stage and perform his role in the dress rehearsal, Yudelson returns with Mrs. Rabinowitz, who begs her son to reconsider. Although Jack's heart is pulling at him, Mary reminds him of what he had just told her, that his career means everything to him. Jack refuses to leave the dress rehearsal and, seeing Jack on stage, Mrs. Rabinowitz realizes that her son no longer belongs to her and leaves. When his number is over, Jack is told by Mary that his mother realizes that his life is now show business, but Jack cannot deny what is in his heart, and rushes to see his father. Jack then goes to the temple and, after Cantor Rabinowitz hears his son singing the Kol Nidre, he dies in peace. Although the show's opening had to be canceled because of Jack, he is soon a Broadway star and sings "Mammy" as his mother and Yudelson proudly sit in the front row, and Mary happily watches from the wings. *Cantors, Jewish. Dancers. Fathers and sons. Jazz music. Jews. Mothers and sons. New York City–Broadway. Singers. Yom Kippur. Chicago (IL). Concerts. Death and dying. Racial impersonation. Railroad stations. San Francisco (CA). Theatrical agents.*

Note: The film opens with the following written prologue: "In every living soul, a spirit cries for expression—perhaps this plaintive, wailing song of Jazz is, after all, the misunderstood utterance of a prayer." According to modern sources, author Samson Raphaelson was inspired to write his short story "A Day of Atonement" after seeing Jolson perform "Where the Black-Eyed Susans Grow" on stage. In 1925, the short story was expanded into a novel (co-written with Arline De Haas) as well as a hit Broadway play, both titled *The Jazz Singer*. Although George Jessel starred in the Broadway show, Warner Bros. advertised the film as a "biography" of Jolson, whose father, a cantor, had initially opposed his show business career.

The film, which has dialogue and musical sequences, begins as a silent picture with background music. The first spoken dialogue occurs in the "Coffee Dan's" sequence, in which "Jakie Rabinowitz" (Al Jolson) sings the song "Dirty Hands, Dirty Face," after which the café's patrons show their

appreciation by striking little gavels on their tables. The first words are uttered by Jolson, who says, "Wait a minute, wait a minute. You ain't heard nothin' yet. Wait a minute I tell ya, you ain't heard nothin'. You want to hear 'Toot, Toot, Tootsie'?" Those words, which many contemporary and modern critics have likened to a metaphor for the birth of "talking" pictures, have frequently been repeated in documentaries about the history of motion pictures. Another sound sequence, in which "Jack" talks with his mother, then plays the piano and sings "Blue Skies," ends when "Cantor Rabinowitz" enters the room and shouts "Stop."

Experimental sound sequences, utilizing a variety of techniques, had been produced periodically, even before the beginning of the twentieth century. Among them was the 1926 Warner Bros. film *Don Juan*, which had musical accompaniment and sound effects. Although *The Jazz Singer* was not the first "talking picture," or the first to have some synchronized sound or dialogue segments, its enormous success was a significant factor in the rapid transition of the motion picture industry from silent to sound films.

The film received Academy Award nominations for Engineering Effects (Nugent Slaughter) and Adapted Screenplay (Al Cohn). Warner Bros., as the producers of the film, received a special Academy Award for "*The Jazz Singer*, the pioneer outstanding talking picture, which has revolutionized the industry." Jolson, who had been a long-standing star in vaudeville and the Broadway stage, made a number of additional films for Warner Bros. during the late 1920s and early 1930s and became one of the biggest stars of the early sound era.

The picture has had several "special anniversary screenings" since 1927, and was officially reissued in 1958. According to a 15 Oct 1958 *HR* news item, the film was to open at the Symphony Theatre, where it was to be "heftily exploited to cash in where possible on the 'novelty value' of the oldtimer." On 6 Oct 1977, the United States Postal Service issued a special commemorative stamp marking the fiftieth anniversary of talking pictures. At that time, according to a *LAT* article, the Los Angeles City Council member for Hollywood suggested that the old Warner Bros. Hollywood studio, where the picture was filmed and the home of television station KTLA and radio station KMPC, be turned into an official cultural monument; however, this apparently was not done.

Raphaelson's story was also the basis of a 1953 Warner Bros. picture (see below), a one-hour drama broadcast on NBC's *Ford Television Theater* on 13 Oct 1959, directed by Ralph Nelson and starring Jerry Lewis, and a 1980 film, also titled *The Jazz Singer*, directed by Richard Fleischer and starring Neil Diamond.

FD 23 Oct 1927. *HR* 15 Oct 1958. *LAT* 5 Sep 1977. *MPN* 28 Jan 1928. *MPW* 22 Oct 1927. *NYT* 7 Oct 1927, p. 24. *PM* 23 Jun 1946. *Var* 12 Oct 1927, p. 16. *Var* 6 May 1977 *Var* 7 May 1927.

THE JAZZ SINGER (Jewish Americans)

Warner Bros. Pictures, Inc.; A Warner Bros.—First National Picture. *Dist* Warner Bros. Pictures, Inc. 14 Feb **1953**; World premiere in Hollywood: 30 Dec 1952; New York opening: 13 Jan 1953; Prod: early Aug—early Oct 1952 [©Warner Bros. Pictures, Inc.; 3 Feb 1953; LP2286]. Sd (RCA Sound System); col (Technicolor). 9,595 ft. 106 or 108 or 110 min. PCA cert no. 16033.

Prod Louis F. Edelman. *Dir* Michael Curtiz. *Asst dir* Chuck Hansen. *Dial dir* Norman Stuart. [*2nd dir* Jimmy Petsch]. *Scr* Frank Davis, Leonard Stern and Lewis Meltzer. *Dir of photog* Carl Guthrie. [*Cam op* Richard Towers]. [*Cam tech* Paul Hill]. [*Cam asst* Stewart Higgs and Harry Marsh]. [*Stills* Jack Woods]. *Technicolor col consultant* Mitchell G. Kovaleski. *Art dir* Leo K. Kuter. *Film ed* Alan Crosland, Jr. *Set dec* George James Hopkins. [*Asst props* Morris Goldman]. *Ward* Howard Shoup. [*Men's ward* Jack Delaney and Gordon Murray]. [*Women's ward* Marguerite Royce]. *Vocal arr* Norman Luboff. *Mus numbers staged and dir by* LeRoy Prinz. *Mus dir* Ray Heindorf. *Sd* C. A. Riggs and David Forrest. *Makeup artist* Gordon Bau. [*Makeup* Henry Villardo]. [*Hair dresser* Tilly Starrett]. *Tech adv* Rabbi Morton A. Bauman. [*Scr supv* Meta Rebner]. [*Gaffer* Ralph Owen]. [*Best boy* William Studeman]. [*Grip* L. P. Maschmeyer].

Song(s): "Living the Life I Love," "I Hear the Music Now," "What Are New Yorkers Made Of," and "Lu Lulla Lu (Hush-a-Bye)," music and lyrics by Sammy Fain and Jerry Seelen; "Lover," music and lyrics by Richard Rodgers and Lorenz Hart; "Just One of Those Things," music and lyrics by Cole Porter; "I'll String Along with You," music and lyrics by Al Dubin and Harry Warren; "The Birth of the Blues," music and lyrics by B. G. DeSylva, Lew Brown and Ray Henderson; "This Is a Very Special Day," music and lyrics by Peggy Lee; "Kol Nidre," traditional Jewish hymn.

Source: Based on the short story "The Day of Atonement" by Samson Raphaelson in *Everybody's Magazine* (Jan 1922) and his play *The Jazz Singer*, as produced by Albert Lewis and Max Gordon, in association with Sam H. Harris (New York, 14 Sep 1925).

Cast: Danny Thomas [(*Jerry Golding*)], Peggy Lee [(*Judy Lane*)], Mildred Dunnock [(*Mrs. Ruth Golding*)], Eduard Franz [(*Cantor David Golding*)], Tom Tully [(*Dan McGurney*)], Alex Gerry [(*Uncle Louie*)], Allyn Joslyn [(*George Miller*)], Harold Gordon [(*Rabbi Roth*)], [Hal Ross (*Joseph*)], [Justin Smith (*Phil Stevens*)], [Anitra

Stevens (*Yvonne*)], [Murray Alper (*Cab driver*)], [Henry Slate (*Master of ceremonies*)], [Marcoreta Hellman (*Mrs. Robbins*)], [James Gonzalez (*Dance director*)], [Phil Arnold (*Stage hand*)], [Gayne Whitman (*Mr. Eskow*)], [Anthony Jochim (*Mr. Michton*)], [Vince Barnett (*Bartender*)], [Angi Poulos (*Club owner*)], [Dan Barton (*Ray Mullins*)], [Sam Wolfe (*Sammy*)], [Jimmy Ames (*Proprietor*)], [Charles Watts (*Leon Ballinger*)], [Harry Harvey (*Conductor*)], [Jimmy Conlin (*Mr. Demming*)], [Earl Lee (*Arthur*)], [Bill Schallert (*Assistant stage manager*)], [Joan Winfield (*Nurse*)], [David Leonard (*Dr. Johnson*)], [Bert Stevens (*Guest*)], [Fred Rapport, Frank Remsden (*Trustees*)], [Philip Rini (*Child singer*)], [Ezelle Poule (*Casting secretary*)], [Harry Harris], [Emilie Cabanne], [Roy Darmour], [George Hoagland], [Frank Peters].

Show business, Drama, with songs. [*Print viewed*]. Korean War veteran Jerry Golding returns to his home in Philadelphia in time to celebrate the Jewish New Year with his parents, Ruth and David, and other family members. Jerry's arrival coincides with David's announcement that he will be retiring as cantor at Temple Sinai. Later, at a nightclub, Jerry is reunited with Judy Lane, a U.S.O. singer he met while in Korea, and meets her producer, George Miller. Miller is impressed with Jerry's talents as a performer and offers him a spot in Judy's show, but David, without consulting his son, makes preparations for Jerry to take over as cantor. Jerry painfully breaks the news to his father that he does not want to be a cantor, and then goes to New York to begin rehearsing for the musical show "Top of the Town." The show opens to poor reviews and closes the same day, but critics praise Jerry's performance. Judy is given another assignment by her producer, but Jerry is left in New York without work. A theatrical booking agency books Jerry for one night at a bar in Hoboken, but cannot provide him with steady work. Judy tries to persuade her recording producer, Ray Mullins, to allow Jerry to accompany her on her next record, but he refuses, calling Jerry an "unknown." Jerry, meanwhile, takes a job as a disc jockey, but he is soon fired for being the wrong "type." One day, Jerry's uncle Louie visits him and sees that he has fallen on hard times. Louie delivers a prayer book from his father and urges him return home to Philadelphia for Passover. Jerry makes one more attempt to break into show business in New York and gets an audition for the lead in Judy's new show. Uncle Louie, who has gone into a partnership with the show's backers, is forced out before things get started, though, and Jerry finds himself back where he began. Dejected, Jerry returns to Philadelphia with Louie, and Judy, who is in love with Jerry, quits the show to join him. Jerry decides to turn his back on show business for good and resume his studies, but Judy returns to New York unconvinced that Jerry truly wants to be a cantor. David, however, is overjoyed by his son's decision, and immediately arranges to have him take over the choir. Time passes, and Jerry's increasing unhappiness leads him to leave the congregation. David, furious at his son's decision, strikes Jerry and throws him out of the house. Back in New York, Jerry resumes his romance with Judy and starts his show business career all over again. Jerry soon becomes a big hit and tours the country with his musical and comedy act. Miller later casts Jerry in the lead role of his next show, "Step This Way." Hours before the show is set to open, Jerry gets a telephone call from Louie, who summons him home to be with his ailing father. From his sickbed, David asks Jerry to forgive him for his stubbornness and then gives his son his blessing. To his father's delight, Jerry sings the "Kol Nidre" at the synagogue. David eventually makes a full recovery, and Jerry returns to Broadway and continues his successful rise to stardom with Judy at his side. *Cantors, Jewish. Comedians. Fathers and sons. Jazz music. Jews. Piety. Romance. Show business. Singers. Auditions. Birthdays. Disc jockeys. Korean War, 1950-1953. Mothers and sons. New York City. Nightclubs. Passover. Philadelphia (PA). Rosh Hashanah. Synagogues. Talent agents. Texans. Theatrical backers. Theatrical producers. Trains. Uncles. Veterans.*

Note: This film is a remake of the 1927 Warner Bros.' film *The Jazz Singer*, which was directed by Alan Crosland and starred Al Jolson, May McAvoy and William Demarest (see above entry). According to a *LAEx* item, Warner Bros. first announced plans to remake *The Jazz Singer* in Dec 1943 with Frank Sinatra as star. Two years later, executive producer Jack L. Warner announced he had selected actor Dane Clark for the Jolson role. Plans for what became the 1953 version were announced as early as Aug 1949. Studio publicity material, dated 31 Jul 1952, indicates that Jim Backus was originally slated for the part played by Allyn Joslyn. According to a contemporary article in *LADN*, crew members Herbert "Limey" Plews and Ralph Owen worked on both this film and the 1927 version. The article also noted that film editor Alan Crosland, Jr. was director

Crosland's son. *The Jazz Singer* was nominated for an Academy Award in the category of Best Scoring of a Musical Picture.

Box 17 Jan 1953. *DV* 29 Aug 1949. *DV* 31 Dec 1952, p. 3. *FD* 7 Jan 1953, p. 8. *HR* 1 Aug 1952, p. 11. *HR* 3 Oct 1952, p. 23. *HR* 30 Dec 1952. *HR* 31 Dec 1953, p. 3. *LADN* 2 Sep 1952. *LAEx* 27 Dec 1943. *MPHPD* 10 Jan 1953, p. 1677. *NYT* 14 Jan 1953, p. 27. *Var* 31 Dec 1952, p. 6.

JEALOUS HUSBANDS (Gypsies, Latino)

Maurice Tourneur Productions. *Dist* Associated First National Pictures. 12 Nov **1923** [©M. C. Levee; 14 Nov 1923; LP19606]. Si; b&w. 7 reels, 6,500 ft.

Pres M. C. Levee. *Dir* Maurice Tourneur. *Story and scen* Fred Kennedy Myton. *Photog* Scott R. Beal.

Cast: Earle Williams (*Ramón Martínez*), Jane Novak (*Alice Martínez*), Ben Alexander (*Bobbie, later called Spud*), Don Marion (*Sliver*), George Siegmann ("*Red" Lynch*), Emily Fitzroy (*Amaryllis*), Bull Montana ("*Portland Kid"*), J. Gunnis Davis ("*Sniffer Charlie"*), Carl Miller (*Harvey Clegg*), Wedgewood Nowell (*George Conrad*), Carmelita Geraghty (*Carmen Inez*).

Melodrama. Believing his wife, Alice, has been unfaithful, jealous husband Ramón Martínez condemns her and gives away their son, Bobbie, to some Gypsies. Alice is merely trying to protect Ramon's sister, Carmen, who is being blackmailed by a former lover, Harvey Clegg. Ramón and Alice separate; Carmen drowns in a shipwreck; but Bobbie, called Spud by the Gypsies, returns to prove his mother's innocence and thereby reunite his family. *Blackmail. Brothers and sisters. Children. Fatherhood. Gypsies. Latino. Infidelity. Jealousy.*

FD 3 Feb 1924. *MPW* 29 Dec 1923.

JEALOUSY (Refugees)

Gong Productions, Inc. *Dist* Republic Pictures Corp. 23 Jul **1945**; Prod: late Oct—late Nov 1944 [©Republic Pictures Corp.; 19 Jun 1945; LP13437]. Sd (RCA Sound System); b&w. 8 reels, 6,184 ft. 71 min. Passed by the National Board of Review. PCA cert no. 10678.

Exec prod Howard Sheehan. *Prod* Gustav Machaty. *Assoc prod* George Moskov. *Dir* Gustav Machaty. *Asst dir* Benjamin Kadish. *Scr* Arnold Phillips and Gustav Machaty. *Based on an orig idea by* Dalton Trumbo. *Photog* Henry Sharp. *Art dir* Frank Sylos. *Film ed* John Link. *Set dec* Glenn P. Thompson. *Cost* Maria Ray. *Orig mus score* Hanns Eisler. *Sd supv* Frank Butterworth. *Sd* Percival J. Townsend. *Tech supv* Martin Berliner.

Song(s): "Jealousy," music and lyrics by Rudolph Friml.

Cast: John Loder (*Dr. David Brent*), Jane Randolph (*Janet Urban*), Karen Morley (*Dr. Monica Anderson*), Nils Asther (*Peter Urban*), Hugo Haas (*Hugo Kral*), Herbert Holmes (*Melvyn Russell*), Michael Mark (*Shop owner*), Mauritz Hugo (*Bob*), Peggy Leon (*Secretary*), Mary Arden (*Nurse*), Noble "Kid" Chissell (*Expressman*), Dracula, a cat.

Drama. [*Not viewed*]. Peter Urban, a European refugee who once had a successful writing career in his homeland, is now an unemployed drunk who takes every opportunity to torment verbally his lovely wife Janet, whom he resents for supporting him by working as a taxi driver in Hollywood. One afternoon, Urban obtains a revolver and, after spending the evening drinking, attempts to kill himself. Janet stops him, despite his threats to kill her as well. Although she realizes that her marriage to Urban is probably doomed, Janet is determined to help him and pleads with him to seek employment, but he refuses. Sometime later, Janet gives a ride to Dr. David Brent, a handsome doctor, who immediately takes a liking to her. The couple meet several more times and begin to fall in love, despite themselves. Janet knows that Urban will never give her a divorce and so meets David secretly. David confesses his feelings for Janet to his partner, Dr. Monica Anderson, who has been secretly in love with him for many years. Monica is jealous but pretends to have friendly feelings for Janet, who accepts her as a confidante. Later, Urban is disturbed by Janet's happiness and suspects that she is having an affair. Determined to ruin Janet's life, a drunken Urban announces on Christmas Eve that he is going to sell the house and force her to move with him to Mexico City when his new book is published. Their subsequent argument is witnessed by Urban's friend, Hugo Kral, who hears Janet assert that she will leave him rather than move. After Janet storms out, Hugo also leaves the house as Urban's drunken ravings continue. At the cab company, Janet retrieves Urban's revolver, which she had hidden in her locker, and meets Monica, to whom she admits her fear of Urban. While the women are shopping, Janet loses her purse, which contains the revolver. Unable to find her purse, Janet

returns home, where she discovers that Urban has been shot and killed. The police rule his death a suicide, but Monica goads Hugo into revealing his suspicions about Janet to the police, who then arrest her. Janet is convicted of killing Urban and sentenced to twenty years in prison, but David, who believes her to be innocent, marries her the night before she is sentenced. When David tells Monica about his marriage, she faints, and David notices that she is wearing Janet's locket, which was in her lost purse along with the revolver. Monica confesses that she killed Urban in the hope of getting Janet out of the way and having David to herself. Monica is sent to prison, and Janet and David begin a new life together. *Frame-ups. Jealousy. Love affairs. Marriage. Murder. Physicians. Alcoholics. Attempted suicide. Authors. Firearms. Hollywood (CA). Taxicab drivers. Trials. War refugees. Women physicians.*

Note: According to information in the MPAA/PCA Collection at the AMPAS Library, the Breen Office rejected several early versions of the screenplay for this film because of "a non-acceptable treatment of marriage." The PCA objected to any inference that "David" and "Janet" were planning the breakup of her marriage to "Peter Urban," and stated: "we cannot approve a story in which one of the married parties is shown, definitely, to be in love with another man, and where the break-up of the marriage is made to appear, by the circumstances, as right and proper." The script was approved after the producers agreed that all references to divorce would be omitted and that David and Janet's relationship would remain platonic until after Urban's death. *Jealousy* was the only picture made by Gong Productions, and the last American film completed by writer, director and producer Gustav Machaty.

Box 4 Aug 1945. *DV* 23 Jul 1945, p. 3. *Exb* 8 Aug 1945. *FD* 26 Jul 1945, p. 6. *Har* 28 Jul 1945. *HR* 3 Apr 1944, p. 9. *HR* 27 Oct 1944, p. 11. *HR* 17 Nov 1944, p. 15. *HR* 23 Jul 1945, p. 3. *HR* 9 May 1945, p. 11. *HR* 10 May 1945, p. 14. *MPD* 1 Aug 1945. *MPHPD* 20 Jan 1945, p. 2279. *MPHPD* 28 Jul 1945, p. 2565. *Var* 25 Jul 1945, p. 20.

JEDE FRAU HAT ETWAS see CHÉRIE

JENG YIEN DOE LEE (Chinese language)

Grandview Film Co. **1948?**; Hong Kong showing: 1948? Sd; b&w. Length undetermined. Chinese language.

Cast: Wong Hok-sing. [*Not viewed*]. [No information concerning the plot of this film has been located.].

Note: The Cantonese transliterated title is *Zeng Yin Deo Lei*. The English language title is *Show Off Your Beauty*. This film was probably made in the U.S.

JENNIE (German Americans)

Twentieth Century-Fox Film Corp. *Dist* Twentieth Century-Fox Film Corp. 20 Dec **1940**; Prod: 7 Aug—27 Aug 1940 [©Twentieth Century-Fox Film Corp.; 20 Dec 1940; LP10153]. Sd (RCA Sound System); b&w. 8 reels, 6,991 ft. 75 or 78 min. PCA cert no. 6599.

Exec prod Sol M. Wurtzel. *Dir* David Burton. [*Asst dir* Jasper Blystone]. *Scr* Harold Buchman and Maurice Rapf. *Dir of photog* Virgil Miller. *Art dir* Richard Day and Lewis Creber. *Film ed* Al De Gaetano. *Set dec* Thomas Little. *Cost* Herschel. *Mus dir* Emil Newman. *Sd* E. Clayton Ward and Harry M. Leonard.

Source: Based on the short story "Heil, Jennie" by Jane Eberle in *Story* (Sep-Oct 1939).

Cast: Virginia Gilmore (*Jennie [Collins]*), William Henry (*George Schermer*), George Montgomery (*Franz [Schermer]*), Ludwig Stossel (*Fritz Schermer*), Dorris Bowdon (*Lottie [Schermer]*), Rand Brooks (*Karl [Schermer]*), Joan Valerie (*Clara [Schermer]*), Rita Quigley (*Amelia [Schermer]*), Hermine Stossel (*Mother Schermer*), Harlan Briggs (*Mr. Veitch*), Irving Bacon (*Real estate broker*), Almira Sessions (*Mrs. Willoughby*), Aldrich Bowker (*Dr. Hildebrand*), [Marie Blake, Effie Anderson (*Customer*)], [Harry Tyler], [William Wills], [Charles Tannen].

Domestic, Drama. [*Print viewed*]. Fritz Schermer, the stern patriarch of a German American Ohio family, will not allow his son Karl to accept a scholarship to study the violin with one of the finest teachers in Chicago because he wants him to work in the family shoe store when he finishes school. When George, Karl's older brother, announces that he would like to marry Jennie Collins, a cashier at the general store, Fritz agrees, but says that after the wedding, they should live with them. After they are married, Fritz becomes upset when Jennie encourages his third son Franz, a farmer, to grow flowers. Mother Schermer explains to Jennie that Fritz does not permit questioning of his authority and that it is best not to say anything. Later Jennie learns that Mother Schermer's family in Germany did not give her permission to marry Fritz because he was just a clerk at the time and have not communicated with her since. Jennie soon invites the Schermer daughters, Lottie, Clara and Amelia, to gossip at tea, but Fritz breaks up their fun and sends them to do

their work. When Jennie complains to George and asks that they move to their own home, he reveals that he receives no salary, only room and board, from his job at the shoe store. Jennie then tells Fritz that she is going to have a baby and that George needs at least fifteen dollars a week. Strutting in anticipation of becoming a grandfather, Fritz offers George a salary of five dollars, which Jennie, although disappointed at first, accepts. When Lottie returns home late one night after a date with her secret boyfriend and Fritz questions her, she talks back to him, and he tells her to get out. Jennie comforts Mother Schermer, but tells George she is glad that Lottie is on the road to freedom. Sometime later, Lottie returns ill, having gone to Philadelphia and married, only to be left by her husband. Fritz refuses to allow her to stay, however, and when Jennie offers to take Lottie to a hotel, he orders Jennie and George to leave as well. Before she goes, Jennie calls Fritz a little man and expresses the hope that the others also will leave him. Jennie makes a hard bargain with a real estate agent for a broken-down house for her, George and Lottie to live in and buys furniture on the installment plan, but George then informs her that he walked out of his job after a fight with his father and has not been able to get another. With only enough money to last a month, Jennie tries a plan to break Fritz's will by encouraging his family to leave him. She recommends Clara to Mrs. Willoughby, who is opening a dress shop, and after learning about a farm available for no cash down and easy payments, tries to convince Franz to buy it; however, neither Clara nor Franz respond. A few months later, after the real estate agent gives them a week to pay their overdue rent, George learns from the doctor that Jennie is pregnant, and he argues with her that they should go back to his father, while she wants to hold out. Just then, Clara and Franz tell Jennie that they have decided to leave Fritz, and Jennie tells them that they have saved her marriage. Jennie visits Fritz and, by suggesting that they may move to Toledo and have Mother Shermer visit them, gets Fritz to offer George ten dollars a week. She turns it down, then tells George, who wants to accept the offer, but when Jennie, Clara, Franz and Lottie urge him not to, he agrees. A letter comes from Fritz offering George fifteen dollars a week, but Jennie rips it up and sends an answer that they will not accept less than twenty-five. Later, Mother Shermer interrupts the children's meal with news that Fritz has suffered a heart attack. Jennie goes to see him and calls his bluff, accusing him of faking the attack because his old way of bullying his family no longer works. He finally agrees to pay the twenty-five dollar a week salary, buy a fur coat for Elsa, endorse notes for Franz's farm and to provide violin lessons for Karl. When she next asks for thirty dollars a week for George, he bellows for her to get out, but then calls her back and asks her opinion of him. She kisses his forehead and tells him she will keep her eyes on him and will tell him later. She then reports to the family that Fritz will live. Later, as the family sings at the piano, Fritz pounds with his cane on the floor. Thinking the music to be displeasing to him, Elsa runs to his bedside but he asks her to open the door so that he can hear, and she kisses him. *Bullies. Daughters-in-law. Family life. Fathers and daughters. German Americans. Marriage. Small town life. Cashiers. Farmers. Finance–Personal. General stores. Heart disease. Installment plans. Ohio. Pregnancy. Real estate agents. Shoe clerks. Violinists.*

Note: The working title of this film was *Heil, Jennie*. Executive producer Sol M. Wurtzel decided to drop the word "Heil," according to publicity for the film. According to *DV*, the film originally was to be an anti-Nazi picture. According to publicity, this marked the return of Dorris Bowdon to the screen following her marriage to writer and producer Nunnally Johnson.

DV 28 Nov 1940, p. 3. *HR* 7 Aug 1940, p. 1. *HR* 27 Aug 1940, p. 3. *HR* 28 Nov 1940, p. 3. *MPD* 4 Dec 1940, p. 5. *MPH* 7 Dec 1940, p. 43. *Var* 19 Mar 1941, p. 16.

JENNY LIND (French language)
Metro-Goldwyn-Mayer Corp.; controlled by Loew's, Inc. *Dist* Culver Export, Inc. **1931**; Prod: early Nov 1930. Sd; b&w. 11 reels. 92 min. Passed by the National Board of Review. French language.
Réalisation de [*Dir*] Arthur Robison. [*Asst dir* Al Shenberg]. *Scénario de* [*Scr*] Hans Kraly and Claudine West. *Dialogue de* John Meehan and Arthur Richman. *Adaptation française de* [*French adpt*] Jacques Deval. *Photographié par* [*Photog*] Norbert Brodine. *Décorateur* [*Art dir*] Cedric Gibbons. *Editeur* [*Ed*] Helene Warne. *Danses par* [*Dances staged by*] Sammy Lee. *Ingénieur du son* [*Sd eng*] Douglas Shearer.
Song(s): Musiques et paroles par [Music and lyrics by]: Carrie Jacobs Bond, Oscar Straus, Herbert Stothart, Clifford Grey, Arthur Freed and Harry Woods.

Source: Based on the novel *Jenny Lind* by Dorothy Farnum (publication undetermined).
Cast: GRACE MOORE (*Jenny Lind*), André Luguet (*Paul Brandt*), André Berley (*Barnum*), Mona Goya (*Selma*), Françoise Rosay (*Rosatti*), Georges Mauloy (*Garcia*), Paul Porcasi (*Maretti*), Giovanni Martino (*Zerga*), Adrienne d'Ambricourt (*Adèle*), Jean Diamond (*Louise*), Léo Klary (*L'aubergiste*), Marthe George (*La femme de l'aubergiste*).
Musical. [*Not viewed*]. [The following plot summary is based on the English-language version of this film, *A Lady's Morals*; character names refer to that version. For further information regarding the English-language version, please see the note below and the entry for *A Lady's Morals* in the *AFI Catalog of Feature Films, 1921-30*.] Paul Brandt, a young composer, falls hopelessly in love with the singer Jenny Lind, following her from city to city, hoping to impress her by his persistency. Jenny loses her voice while performing *Norma*, and in the chaos that ensues, Paul is struck on the head, gradually causing him to become blind. He is instrumental in bringing the songstress to a maestro who is able to restore her voice, thus proving his unselfish love. She returns with him to Sweden, still chaste and unstirred, but when it becomes evident that Paul is becoming blind, he leaves without explanation just as Jenny is beginning to respond to his love. She is about to make her American debut at the Castle Garden in New York under the direction of P. T. Barnum when she is happily reunited with Paul, now a wandering blind musician. *P. T. Barnum. Blindness. Composers. Courtship. Jenny Lind. Norma* (Opera). *Opera. Singers. Sweden.*

Note: The onscreen credits were taken from a studio cutting continuity. The English-language version of this film, *A Lady's Morals*, which was released on 8 Nov 1930, was directed by Sidney Franklin and starred Grace Moore and Reginald Denny. In the credits of the French version, Grace Moore was identified as "Prima donna du Metropolitan Opéra de New York."

HF 8 Nov 1930, p. 24.

THE JESTER (DER PURIMSPIELER) (Yiddish language)
Green-Film. *Dist* Sphinx Films Corp. **1937**; New York opening: 3 Dec 1937; Prod: in a Warsaw, Poland studio. Sd; b&w. 9 reels, 8,294 ft. 88 min. *Country of origin* Poland. Yiddish language with English subtitles.
Pres JOSEPH GREEN. *Dir* Joseph Green and Jan Nowina Przybylski. *Scenario* Joseph Victor. *English titles* Julian Leigh. *Dial* I. Manger. *Photog* Seweryn Steinwurcel. *Settings* Jacek Weinreich. *Cost* Fritz Kleinman. *Mus* Nikolaus Brodszky. *Lyrics* I. Manger.
Cast: Miriam Kressyn [(*Esther*)], Hymie Jacobson [(*Dick*)], Zygmunt Turkow [(*Getsel*)], Ajzyk Samberg [(*Reb Nukhem*)], Maks Bozyk [(*Grandfather*)], Berta Litwina [(*Tsippe*)], Eni Liton [(*Leah*)], Jakub Rajnglas [(*Helper*)], Maks Bryn [(*Caretaker*)], Samuel Landau [(*Rich man*)], Jakub Fiszer [(*Marriage broker*)].
Yiddish, Drama. [*Print viewed*]. Getsel, a Jewish wanderer, hears singing come from an orchard outside a little Galician town, and he is attracted to Esther, who is picking apples in a tree. She laughs at him and runs off, while her friend Leah gives him some goat milk. Getsel continues on to the *shtetl*, or Jewish village, where he has no luck finding work. Outside Nukhem's shoeshop, Nukhem's wife Tsippe accidentally throws a bowl of water into Getsel's face. Nukhem then invites Getsel in and asks him to stay and work for him. Seeing that Tsippe is against it, Getsel turns Nukhem down, until Esther, who is Nukhem's daughter, comes in and again laughs at him, whereupon Getsel decides to stay. Getsel seems to bring luck to Nukhem, who yearns to be rich, and he gets many orders for shoes to be repaired. As Getsel sits with Esther by a tree, he tells her that he once had been in love, but the woman married someone else before he confessed his love. As Esther talks of her dream "prince," Getsel imagines himself as a prince on horseback riding to Esther, but in his vision, she turns from him and walks away. On the Sabbath, as Nukhem sleeps in the afternoon, Getsel admits that he once played King Ahesuerus in a *Purim* play and accedes to the demands of Esther, Leah and Nukhem's father that he demonstrate. In so doing, he awakens Nukhem, who angrily rebukes the group, but they are interrupted by music from a traveling circus parading through the street. Esther goes out, and she is knocked down by a horse. Dick, one of the performers, helps her up and gives her two tickets for the evening's performance. Attracted to him, Esther goes with Leah, and Getsel follows them. When a magician asks for a volunteer, Getsel obliges and he gets soaked with water, as the crowd roars in laughter.

Humiliated, Esther leaves, and when Dick follows, she goes off with him. Getsel sadly watches them together, until Leah, who is in love with him, leads him away. After meeting Esther the next day, Dick tells a friend that he has changed from being a "skirt-chaser," now that he has met an "angel." He tells Esther that he must leave tomorrow and kisses her, but because Nukhem catches her returning home, he refuses to let her out the next day. Sometime later, Nukhem inherits a fortune. Nukhem and Tsippe hobnob with the wealthy in town, and through Faivel the matchmaker, Nukhem invites the wealthy Zeidmans for *Purim*, hoping to arrange a marriage between Esther and the Zeidmans' son Yossel, whom Esther considers to be a "dolt." During the *Purim* play, Getsel, as King Ahesuerus, makes fun of Yossel, and the Zeidmans, insulted, leave. Nukhem then orders Getsel out of town. Esther thanks Getsel and they leave together in the morning. They wander to a city, and when they pass a café, Esther, who had begun to be troubled, brightens immediately as she sees Dick performing inside. She and Dick dance together the whole night, and Getsel goes off. Later, Esther and Dick find Getsel and take him to an amusement park and then to a club. Esther becomes a singer and marries Dick. When Getsel leaves town, telling Dick that he is going to marry also, Esther knows he is lying, and they pursue him. Back in the town, some of the people threaten violence as they demand that Getsel tell them where Esther is, and Leah tries to protect him. Esther then appears and introduces Dick as her husband. After Nukhem accepts them, Getsel walks off alone and troubled, stares at the apple trees. *Actors and actresses. Bumblers. Family relationships. Galicia. Jews. Purim. Small town life. Unrequited love. Wanderers. Cafés. Circus performers. Circuses. Inheritance. Nouveaux riches. Runaways. Shoemakers. Singers. Sisters.*

Note: According to a *FD* news item, director Joseph Green signed Joseph Buloff, Hymie Jacobson and Miriam Kressyn from New York to be in the film and they planned to leave for Poland in May 1937. According to modern sources, Green replaced Buloff with Polish actor Zygmunt Turkow because Buloff withdrew to appear in a play. In an oral history conducted by the Hebrew University Oral History Department, Joseph Green stated that an imaginary town, consisting of a main street from a typical *shtetl* in Poland was built in a studio in Warsaw and that the latter part of the film was shot in Cracow and showed the famous Cracow church and synagogue. According to *MPD*, this was the first Yiddish film to play at the Cameo Theater in New York. According to modern sources, scenes of the *Purim* play were used in the notorious Nazi "documentary" *Der Ewige Jude.*
FD 12 May 1937, p. 11. *FD* 15 Dec 1937, p. 10. *MPD* 3 Dec 1937. *NYT* 6 Dec 1937, p. 19. *Var* 8 Dec 1937, p. 17.

THE JEW *see* **HIS PEOPLE**

A JEW IN EXILE *see* **THE WANDERING JEW**

THE JEW IN GERMANY *see* **THE WANDERING JEW**

A JEWEL IN PAWN (Jewish Americans)
Bluebird Photoplays, Inc. *Dist* Bluebird Photoplays, Inc. 16 Apr 1917 [©Bluebird Photoplays, Inc.; 23 Mar 1917; LP10434]. Si; b&w. 5 reels.
Dir Jack Conway. *Scen* Maie B. Havey. *Story* Constance Crawley and Arthur Maude. *Cam* Edward Kull.
Cast: Ella Hall (*Nora Martin*), Maie Hall (*Mrs. Martin*), Antrim Short (*Jimmy*), Walter Belasco (*Aaron Levovitch*), Jack Connolly (*Bob Hendricks*), George Pearce (*John Dane*), Marshall Mackaye (*The bully*).
Drama. Widow Martin struggles to rear her little daughter Nora amid the squalor of the slums yet imbue her with the refinement to which she had been accustomed in her girlhood. Fearing that she is losing the battle, Mrs. Martin decides to turn to her wealthy father, who had disowned her upon her marriage years earlier. To raise funds for the trip, she pawns Nora to Aaron Levovitch, an aged pawnbroker with a heart of gold under his gruff exterior. Upon reaching her father's house, Mrs. Martin falls ill and dies before she can relate her story, and Nora is raised by the pawnbroker until a reporter prints her human interest story of a "jewel in pawn." The girl's grandfather reads the article and claims Nora, then sends her to a fashionable boarding school. Nora longs for her home in the slums and her sweetheart Jimmy, however, and so returns to marry Jimmy in an elaborate traditional Jewish ceremony at the pawnbroker's home. *Grandfathers. Orphans. Pawnbrokers. Slums. Upper classes. Boarding schools. Disinheritance. Foster parents. Jews. Loans. Mothers and daughters. Newspapers. Reporters. Weddings. Widows.*

Note: The synopsis of this film included in the copyright descriptions was originally entitled "Pawned," and credits Mrs. McCollough with the role of "Mrs. Martin."
ETR 21 Apr 1917, p. 1391. *Motog* 28 Apr 1917, p. 901. *MPN* 28 Apr 1917, p. 2689. *MPW* 21 Apr 1917, p. 492. *MPW* 28 Apr 1917, p. 636. *NYDM* 21 Apr 1917, p. 26. *Var* 20 Apr 1917, p. 24. *Wid's* 19 Apr 1917, p. 255.

THE JEWISH CROWN (Jewish Americans)
Boris Thomashefsky Film Co. *Dist* Boris Thomashefsky. **1915?.** Si; b&w. Length undetermined.
Dir Sidney M. Golden.
Source: Based on a Yiddish play (production undetermined).
Cast: Boris Thomashefsky.
Drama?. [No information about the plot of this film has been located.]. *Jews.*
Note: The Boris Thomashefsky Film Co. was located in New York City and made films based on Yiddish plays. According to a news item, Thomashefsky, who was called "perhaps the best known Yiddish actor in the world," opened the first Yiddish theater in America some thirty years earlier. Although the news item stated that the film had been made, no information has been located concerning its release or length.
MPW 30 Jan 1915, p. 757. *MPW* 6 Feb 1915, p. 809.

JEWISH DAUGHTER *see* **A DAUGHTER OF HER PEOPLE**

JEWISH KING LEAR *see* **THE YIDDISH KING LEAR**

THE JEWISH MELODY (Yiddish language)
Cinema Service Corp. *Dist* Cinema Service Corp. **1940;** New York opening: Apr 1940. Sd; b&w. 8 reels, 7,841 or 8,272 ft. 89 min. Yiddish language with English subtitles.
Dir Josef Seiden. *Asst dir* H. Rosen. *Story* C. Tauber. *Photog* Don Malkames and Charles Levine. *Settings* J. Allstadt. *Mus* Sholom Secunda. *Sd* M. Dichter and P. Jacobs.
Cast: Izidor Casher (*Rev. David* [*Rosenschein*]), Lazar Freed (*Luigi Marbini*), Chiam Tauber (*Moishe* [*Rosenschein*]), Seymour Rechtzeit (*Martin*), Moishe Feder (*Samuel Boguslaffsky*), Rose Greenfield (*Pessah* [*Rosenschein*]), Dave Lubritsky (*Mendel*), Yetta Zwerling (*Genendel*), May Schoenfeld (*Freda* [*Boguslaffsky*]), Jacob Zanger (*Groinem*), Esta Salzman (*Esta* [*Rosenschein*]), Paula Klida (*Rosita*).
Yiddish, Domestic, Comedy-drama, with songs. [*Print viewed*]. When realtor Samuel P. Boguslaffsky, a millionaire and the president of the local synagogue, returns home to New York from Florida, he calls cantor David Rosenschein, whose son Moishe is to marry Sam's daughter Freda, to visit after supper. Despite his wife Pessah's view that Sam is the family's "guardian angel," David is upset because he feels that Sam has "bought" Moishe for his daughter by paying for Moishe to study music in Italy with the renowned Professor Luigi Marbini and by helping the Rosenscheins buy a home in Flatbush. Sam tells David that he is searching for a fifth wife and explains that three of his previous wives have died and one left with their baby daughter, then confesses that he wants David's daughter Esta for his bride. When David takes exception and points out that Esta is only a child, Sam threatens not to renew his contract as cantor, which expires in two weeks. David objects forcefully and leaves in a huff. When Sam discovers Freda in an embrace with his chauffeur Martin, whom she really loves, he indignantly fires Martin, who rebukes him. Meanwhile in Venice, Moishe has fallen in love with Rosita, the daughter of his teacher, but he is troubled because they are of different faiths. When Sam hears rumors about Moishe and Rosita, David contends that Moishe would never marry outside the faith and agrees to write to him to return. After Sam gives Esta a necklace as a present, David angrily tears it from her neck and falls stricken. The doctor warns David that he must have rest and quiet, and tells him that he will never sing again. Deeply upset, David hopes that Moishe will continue in his place. When Moishe receives a cablegram about his father's condition, he leaves for New York and promises to send for Rosita. Moishe admits to David that the rumors about his romance with Rosita are true, but vows that he'd sooner die than give up his faith. Freda is sent by Sam to see Moishe, and they are cold to each other until they learn that they each love someone else. Later, Luigi finds out from Rosita that Moishe's father will not allow him to return to Italy, so he brings her to America. Sam, meanwhile, arranges a double wedding for Moishe and Freda and himself and Esta, who is heartened when her meek cousin Mendel, who loves her, vows to knock out Sam's teeth. On the wedding day, Martin, a bit intoxicated, comes to fight Moishe, but Moishe confesses that he loves some one other than Freda, and they get drunk together. After most of the

wedding party leave for the synagogue, Luigi comes to the apartment and meets Pessah's brother Groinem. During their conversation, Luigi recognizes Sam's name. He then goes to the synagague with Rosita and reveals that she is Sam's daughter by his third wife, whom Luigi married after her divorce from Sam. When David learns that Rosita, thus, is Jewish and that Freda does not want to marry Moishe, he accepts the situation and blesses Moishe and Rosita. Moishe has Groinem bring Martin to marry Freda, and Genendel, Groinem's klutzy daughter, reminds him that Mendel loves Esta. Moishe then brings those two together, and Genendel, who has wanted to marry someone all along, vows to get Sam. Although at first Sam is taken aback because of Genendel's unsightly face, after a drink, he agrees to marry her. *Cantors. Jewish. Family relationships. Jews. Marriage–Arranged. Marriage–Mixed. Millionaires. Music students. Religion. Chauffeurs. Cousins. Dismissal (Employment). Drunkenness. Italians. Long-lost relatives. Music teachers. Necklaces. Nervous breakdown. New York City. Real estate agents. Threats. Venice (Italy). Weddings.*

Note: The Yiddish title of this film is *Der Yidisher Nign.* According to information at NCJF, the Maryland Board of Censors ruled that a "sacrificial scene" should be eliminated. In addition to Maryland, the film was submitted to censor boards in Ohio, Pennsylvania, New York and Chicago, but no reviews have been located. Modern sources state that Chiam Tauber was a radio star. Although the film includes songs, no information concerning their identity has been located.

JIA O TIEN CHEN (Chinese language)
Grandview Film Co. **1947?**; Hong Kong showing: 1947? Sd; b&w. Length undetermined. Chinese language.

Dir Joseph Sunn. [*Not viewed*]. [No information concerning the plot of this film has been located.].

Note: The Cantonese transliterated title is *Gai Ngeo Tin Xing.* This film was probably made in the U.S.

JIGGS AND MAGGIE IN BRINGING UP FATHER *see* **BRINGING UP FATHER**

JIGGS AND MAGGIE IN COURT (Irish Americans)
Monogram Pictures Corp.; A Barney Gerard Production. *Dist* Monogram Pictures Corp. 12 Dec **1948**; Prod: began early Sep 1948 [©Monogram Pictures Corp.; 12 Dec 1948; LP2014]. Sd (Western Electric Recording); b&w. 70-71 min. PCA cert no. 13489.

Series: Jiggs and Maggie.

Prod Barney Gerard. *Dir* William Beaudine and [Eddie Cline]. *Dial dir* Tim Ryan. *Asst dir* William Calihan. *Story and scr* Barney Gerard and Eddie Cline. *Photog* L. W. O'Connell. [*Cam op* Eddie Kearns]. [*Stills* Eddie Jones]. *Art dir* Dave Milton. *Supv film ed* Otho Lovering. *Film ed* Ace Herman. *Set dec* Raymond Boltz, Jr. *Mus dir* Edward J. Kay. *Sd tech* Buddy Myers. *Hairdresser* Charles Huber. *Hair* Lela Chambers. *Prod mgr* Allen K. Wood. *Chief elec* M. H. Serotte.

Song(s): "Laugh and the World Laughs with You (But It's Hard to Cry Alone)," music by Albert von Tilzer, lyrics by Barney Gerard.

Source: Based on the comic strip "Bringing Up Father" by George McManus, owned and copyrighted by King Features Syndicate, Inc. (12 Jan 1913—).

Cast: Joe Yule [(*Jiggs*)], Renie Riano [(*Maggie*)], the internationally known cartoonist George McManus [(*Himself*)], Tim Ryan [(*Dinty Moore*)], Pat Goldin [(*Dugan*)], June Harrison [(*Nora*)], Danny Beck [(*Danny Beckytype*)], Russell Hicks [(*Supreme Court judge*)], Cliff Clark [(*Judge Wilson*)], Grady Sutton [(*Mr. Twiddle*)], [Riley Hill (*Dennis Malone*)], [Robert Lowell (*Hardy Mercer*)], [Dick Ryan (*Grogan*)], [Jimmy Aubrey (*McGurk*)], [Jean Fenwick (*Mrs. Brinsley-Wellington-Fish*)], [Frank Austin (*Mr. Beaton, an attorney*)], [Sidney Marion (*Scotty*)], [Charles Middleton (*Mr. Burton, an attorney*)], [Richard R. Neill (*Mr. Bowton, an attorney*)], [Ken Britton (*Mailman Farley*)], [Francine Faye (*Accordionist*)], [Jimmy O'Brien (*Irish tenor*)], [Herman Cantor (*Court clerk*)], [Marie Harmon (*Alice, a salesgirl*)], [Baron Lichter (*Piano player*)], [Marcelle Imhoff (*Mrs. Baker, a grandmother*)], [Scott Clarke Taylor (*Little boy*)], [Sandra Kessler (*Little girl*)], [Angi O. Poulos (*Man in deep freeze*)], [Billy Curtis (*Little man*)], [Earle Hodgins (*Spectator*)], [Tom Kennedy (*Card player*)], [Sara Berner (*Mae West type voice*)], [Johnnie Morris (*Mr. Bagel, an attorney*)], [Bobby Hale (*Old Tad*)].

Domestic, Society, Comedy. [*Print viewed*]. Maggie, an aspiring New York socialite, is right at home examining an expensive Ming vase in a posh department store. Things quickly change, however, when she becomes enraged by comments made by some salespeople

and customers about her likeness to the George McManus comic strip shrew named Maggie. After breaking the Ming vase in a show of anger, Maggie goes to a bakery, where she again is met with comments about her likeness to the comic strip character. This time, the insulted Maggie starts a pie-throwing fight, which lands her in court to answer to charges of creating a public disturbance. Even the judge presiding over her trial cannot resist commenting on her likeness to the rolling pin-wielding, pie-throwing Maggie of the funny papers. When Maggie is sentenced to three months in jail, her milquetoast husband Jiggs and his tavern pal Dugan manage to convince the judge to put Maggie on probation instead. The change in sentence puts Maggie under the direct supervision of her husband, a situation that Jiggs is all too happy to exploit by going to his favorite watering hole, Dinty Moore's, whenever he likes. One day, Maggie is visited by an influential socialite who informs her that her application to join an exclusive social club has been rejected because of her recent court appearance. Unable to bear the stigma, Maggie marches over to George McManus' office and demands that he stop drawing her in his comic strip. Maggie is stunned when McManus readily signs a written agreement to stop using her likeness in his work. However, when she reads the fine print stating that the agreement does not take effect until 1999, she becomes enraged and plans a lawsuit against him. While Maggie concerns herself with her reputation, Jiggs throws a party at their apartment. During the party, Dinty is fooled into thinking that Jiggs, dressed in women's clothes, is Dinty's long-lost love. Maggie enters the apartment at the height of the merriment and both she and Dinty, who has discovered Jiggs's prank, attack him. Maggie's lawsuit against McManus results in a trial, which McManus wins by proving that Maggie could not possibly have been the model for his character because she is too young. After the trial, McManus makes amends with Maggie by showing her pictures of the women who inspired Maggie's character, which include pictures of Cleopatra, Madame de Pompadour and Marie Antoinette. *Cartoonists. Henpecked husbands. High society. Marriage. Social climbers. Trials. Bartenders. Cleopatra VII, Queen of Egypt, 69-30 B.C.. Contracts. Department stores. Dwarfs. Female impersonation. Flowers. Food fights. Marie Antoinette, Queen, consort of Louis XVI, King of France, 1755-1793. New York City–Park Avenue. Parties. Madame de Pompadour. Practical jokes. Salesmen. Sneezing. Transvestism.*

Note: Onscreen credits note that the "Bringing Up Father" comic strip appeared "regularly in *Puck*, the comic weekly." Although Eddie Cline is listed in copyright records, a Monogram studio production sheet and other contemporary sources as the film's co-director, only Barney Gerard is credited on screen. Contemporary sources offer conflicting information as to who played the "Bartender" and "Mr. Baker." While the Monogram production sheet and *DV* credit Chester Clute with the role of "Mr. Baker," the CBCS credits George Meader with the role. Similarly, the production sheet lists Fred Kelsey as "Bartender", while the CBCS credits Mike Pat Donovan with the role. This film was the third picture in Monogram's "Jiggs and Maggie" series. For more information on the series, consult the Series Index and see the entry above for *Bringing Up Father.*

Box 4 Dec 1948. DV 29 Nov 1948, p. 3, 14. FD 6 Dec 1948, p. 6. HR 10 Sep 1948, p. 13. HR 29 Nov 1948, p. 3. MPHPD 6 Nov 1948, p. 4375. MPHPD 4 Dec 1948, p. 4405.

JIGGS AND MAGGIE IN JACKPOT JITTERS (Irish Americans)
Monogram Pictures Corp.; A Barney Gerard Production. *Dist* Monogram Pictures Corp. 28 Aug **1949**; Prod: early Jun—21 Jun 1949 [©Monogram Pictures Corp.; 28 Aug 1949; LP2523]. Sd (Western Electric Recording); b&w. 6,025 ft. 67 min.

Series: Jiggs and Maggie.

Prod Barney Gerard. *Dir* William Beaudine. *Asst dir* Melville Shyer. *Dial dir* Tim Ryan. *Story and scr* Barney Gerard and Eddie Cline. *Dial dir* Tim Ryan. *Photog* L. W. O'Connell. *Art dir* Dave Milton. *Supv film ed* Otho Lovering. *Film ed* Roy V. Livingston. *Set cont* I. F. Vas. *Set dir* Raymond Boltz, Jr. *Mus dir* Edward J. Kay. *Sd dir* John Kean. *Makeup* Charles Huber. *Hairdresser* Lela Chambers. *Prod mgr* Allen K. Wood.

Source: Based on the comic strip "Bringing Up Father" by George McManus, owned and copyrighted by King Features Syndicate, Inc. (12 Jan 1913—).

Cast: Joe Yule [(*Jiggs*)], Renie Riano [(*Maggie*)], George McManus the internationally known cartoonist [(*Himself*)], Tim Ryan [(*Dinty Moore*)], Pat Goldin [(*Dugan*)], June Harrison [(*Nora*)], Sam Hayes, Joe Hernandez (*Race narrators*), [Joel Marston (*Dr. John Paxton*)], [Dick Ryan (*Grogan*)], [Jimmy Aubrey (*McGurk*)], [Tom Kennedy (*Murphy*)], [Betty Blythe (*Mrs. Van Belden*)], [Ed East (*Ron Dilson*)], [Earle Hodgins (*Joe Klink*)], [Willie Best (*Willie*)], [Joe

Devlin (*Danny*)], [Leon Belasco (*Composer*)], [Eddie Kane (*Conductor*)], [Walter G. McCarty], [Sid Marion], [Marcelle Imhoff], [Hank Mann], [Chester Conklin].

Domestic, Society, Comedy. [*Print viewed*]. While his wife Maggie, a desperate social climber suffering from sneezing fits, rides a stationary horse in their Park Avenue, New York apartment, Jiggs, who would rather climb onto a barstool than mix with the city's socialites, listens to a radio trivia contest. The two make so much noise that their upstairs neighbor is driven to distraction and jumps out of his window. When Jiggs learns that Maggie has bought her way into the socially prominent Northchester Hunt Club by sending them a check for $38,600, he decides to have payment on the check stopped before it is cashed. Maggie tries to prevent Jiggs from doing so by lassoing him and tying him up, but Jiggs manages to free himself. After tying the rope around Maggie, Jiggs takes care of the check. Jiggs then goes to Dinty's, his favorite tavern, where his pals and owner Dinty Moore snare him in a get-rich-quick scheme by convincing him that he will be able to square himself with Maggie by placing the highest bid at a racetrack horse auction. Meanwhile, Dr. John Paxton pays a visit to Maggie and tells her that her sneezing fits are a result of a rare allergy to horses and that she should avoid all contact with them. Later, as the *You Do or Your Don't Jackpot* program blares from their radio, Maggie sends Jiggs out to walk their dog and places the telephone under lock and key because of Jiggs' obsession with the radio contest. Unaware that representatives from the radio contest have been trying to call, Maggie ignores the ringing phone. However, Jiggs returns from his walk in time to unlock the phone and answer the contest question correctly. As winners of the contest, Jiggs and Maggie are presented with the prizes on a television show, which is broadcast from their living room. The prizes range from a luggage set to a horse, which immediately sends Maggie into a sneezing fit. Unable to control her sneezing, Maggie sends everyone out of the apartment and orders Jiggs to sell the horse. Maggie panics, though, when the Society of Thoroughbred Owners tells her that she has been granted membership into the prestigious social club because she is the new owner of the horse "Lord Chesterfield the Fifth." Maggie then instructs Jiggs to get the horse back. Although Jiggs retrieves "Lord Chesterfield" in time to enter it in a race, the horse finishes last. Determined to turn her horse into a winner, Maggie takes the horse's trainer's advice to move to California, where horses are better trained. With George McManus, who identifies himself as the creator of Jiggs and Maggie's cartoon characters, riding as a passenger, and with Dinty stowed away in the cattle car, Jiggs and Maggie board a train headed for California. En route, George tells Jiggs to bet on his horse "Maggie Jiggs" instead of Lord Chesterfield. Jiggs bets on McManus' horse and saves himself and Maggie from ruin when Maggie's horse loses again. "Lord Chesterfield" is eventually retired from racing and is relegated to the task of pulling a carriage. *High society. Horseracing. Horses. Social climbers. Allergy. California. Cartoonists. Contests. New York City–Park Avenue. Saloons. Television programs. Trains. Wagers.*

Note: Onscreen credits note that the "Bringing Up Father" cartoon strip appeared "regularly in *Puck* the comic weekly." *Jiggs and Maggie in Jackpot Jitters* was part of Monogram's series of "Jiggs and Maggie" films starring Joe Yule and Renie Riano. For additional information on the series, please consult the Series Index and see the entry for *Bringing Up Father* (above).

Box 3 Sep 1949. *DV* 29 Aug 1949, p. 4. *FD* 6 Sep 1949, p. 9. *HR* 10 Jun 1949, p. 10 *HR* 17 Jun 1949, p. 16. *HR* 29 Aug 1949, p. 4. *MPHPD* 3 Sep 1949, p. 1-2.

JIGGS AND MAGGIE IN SOCIETY (Irish Americans)

Monogram Pictures Corp.; A Barney Gerard Production. *Dist* Monogram Pictures Corp. 12 Dec **1947**; *Prod:* mid-Sep—late Sep 1947 [©Monogram Pictures Corp.; 15 Dec 1947; LP1383]. Sd (Western Electric Recording); b&w. 61, 65 or 67 min. PCA cert no. 12776.

Series: Jiggs and Maggie.

Prod Barney Gerard. *Dir* Eddie Cline. *Asst dir* Theodore Joos. *Dial dir* Edward Colebrook. *Orig story and scr* Eddie Cline and Barney Gerard. *Photog* L. W. O'Connell. *Art dir* Dave Milton. *Film ed* Ace Herman. *Set dec* Raymond Boltz, Jr. *Stylist* Lorraine MacLean. *Men's ward* Sid Mintz. *Furs by* William H. George. *Mus dir* Edward J. Kay. *Sd tech* Earl Sitar. *Makeup* Harry Ross. *Prod mgr* Glenn Cook.

Source: Based on the comic strip "Bringing Up Father" by George McManus, owned and copyrighted by King Features Syndicate, Inc. (12 Jan 1913–).

Cast: Joe Yule [(*Jiggs*)], Renie Riano [(*Maggie*)], Tim Ryan [(*Dinty Moore*)], Wanda McKay [(*Millicent Parker*)], Lee Bonnell [(*Van de Graft*)], Pat Goldin [(*Dugan*)], Herbert Evans [(*Jenkins*)], June

Harrison [(*Nora*)], Scott Taylor [(*Tommy*)], Jimmy Aubrey [(*McGurk*)], Thayer Roberts [(*Pete*)], Richard Irving [(*Al*)], Wm. Cabanne [(*George Austin*)], Dick Ryan [(*Grogan*)], Constance Purdy [(*Mrs. Blackwell*)], Edith Leslie [(*Mary*)], Helena Dare [(*Aggie*)], Lesley Farley [(*Mimi*)], Betty Blythe [(*Mrs. Vacuum*)], Marcelle Imhof [(*Mrs. Gabydame*)], and introducing Dale Carnegie, Arthur Murray, Sheilah Graham (*Who appear as themselves*), [Tommie Menzies (*Ambrose*)], [James Mobley, Judy K. Schenz, Gary Zekley (*Children*)], [Ken Christy (*McDermott*)], [Lou Marcelle (*Radio voice*)], [Robert Earle (*Waiter in cocktail bar*)], [Effie Laird (*Mrs. Heveydoe*)], [Jack Mower (*Officer at party*)], [Edna Nelson (*Annie*)], [Ted Stanhope (*Dan Wiley*)], [Danny Beck (*Pianist*)], [Jerry Franks (*Flute player*)], [Phil Arnold (*Harp player*)], [Dulce Daye (*Miss Jones*)].

Domestic, Society, Comedy. [*Print viewed*]. Maggie, a Park Avenue social climber, will do anything to get her name into the *Blue Book* of the New York elite. Her husband Jiggs, however, is a construction contractor and a simpleton who would rather have his name permanently engraved on his bar stool at Dinty Moore's saloon than see it in a social register. When Maggie learns that Mr. Van de Graft, a confidence artist posing as a genealogist, has found her family's coat of arms, and that he is coming to her apartment with her family tree, she quickly sees to it that the apartment is in order. Maggie fears that her husband and her visiting sister's brood of children will make a bad impression on Van de Graft, but he arrives before she can send them away. The family tree, Maggie believes, is the one item she needs to have "every socialite in town bowing and scraping" before her. Complications soon arise, however, when Jiggs mistakes Van de Graft for an intruder and tries to throw him out of the apartment. When Maggie finds an advertisement in the newspaper for Dale Carnegie's courses in "How to Advance Socially," she decides that the courses will help refine her husband's tastes and improve his social skills. Carnegie, however, first tackles Maggie's problems and tells her that she must learn how to control her temper. Later, Van de Graft returns to Jiggs and Maggie's apartment and tells Maggie that she must redecorate it to make it fit for entertaining society. While Van de Graft is making decorating suggestions, Maggie looks out the window and sees Jiggs arriving at the building in the company of a young blonde woman. Distracted by what she thinks is an infidelity on her husband's part, Maggie inadvertently gives Van de Graft *carte blanche* to do with the apartment whatever he wishes. When Jiggs enters the apartment, she nearly clobbers him with a chair, but at the last moment she remembers Carnegie's advice and decides to "kill him with kindness" instead. To Maggie's delight, her first plunge into the world of society comes when she is introduced to Arthur Murray, founder of the Arthur Murray Dance School. Her mood quickly changes, though, when she sees Jiggs watching his female companion modelling a coat for him. Maggie returns home to find the police investigating the disappearance of her little nephew Tommy. The police bring Jiggs to the apartment for questioning, and the blonde, Millicent Parker, is brought in with him. Maggie is about to tear into Millicent when Van de Graft convinces her to be kind to the woman because she can help her rise in society. Maggie hides her disgust and accepts an invitation from Millicent to a *soiree* at her house. Soon after meeting Van de Graft, Millicent becomes wise to her family tree scheme. At Millicent's *soiree*, Van de Graft argues with his jewel-thieving pals and warns them not to spoil his plans. When the jewel theft is discovered, Jiggs's saloon pal, Dugan, is accused of the crime. Dugan is about to be escorted to the police by the real thieves when Dinty pulls a gun on them and makes a citizen's arrest. After Van de Graft's scheme is exposed, Maggie learns that Jiggs was only interested in Millicent because she was Maggie's size and could model the coat that was to be her birthday present. *Confidence games. Impersonation and imposture. Social climbers. Socialites. Cartoonists. Children. Dance teachers. False accusations. False arrests. Genealogy. Irish Americans. Jewel thieves. Missing persons. New York City–Park Avenue. Parties. Psychology. Radio announcers.*

Note: *Jiggs and Maggie in Society* was the second film in Monogram's "Jiggs and Maggie" series starring Joe Yule and Renie Riano. According to *Var*, Constance Purdy's role was a parody of well-known society party giver Elsa Maxwell. Sheilah Graham, who appeared as herself in the film, was a popular gossip columnist and radio personality. Arthur Murray owned a chain of dance studios, and Dale Carnegie, who lectured and taught on the subject of public speaking, was the author of many self-help books, including the best-selling *How to Win Friends and Influence People*. For additional information on the "Jiggs and Maggie" series please consult the Series Index and see the entry for *Bringing Up Father*.

Box 14 Feb 1948. *DV* 4 Feb 1948, p. 3. *FD* 18 Feb 1948, p. 7. *HR* 12 Sep 1947, p. 18. *HR* 17 Sep 1947, p. 16. *HR* 4 Feb 1948, p. 3. *MPHPD* 21 Feb 1948, p. 4066-67. *Var* 11 Feb 1948, p. 14.

JIGGS AND MAGGIE OUT WEST (Irish Americans)

Monogram Pictures Corp.; A Barney Gerard Production. *Dist* Monogram Pictures Corp. 23 Apr **1950**; Prod: mid-Jan—early Feb 1950 [©Monogram Pictures Corp.; 23 Apr 1950; LP170]. Sd (Western Electric Recording); b&w. 6,109 or 6,111 ft. 66 or 68 min. PCA cert no. 14434.

Series: Jiggs and Maggie.

Prod Barney Gerard. *Dir* William Beaudine, Sr. *Asst dir* Melville Shyer. *Dial dir* Tim Ryan. [*Dir, 2d unit* Vernon Keays]. *Story* Barney Gerard and Eddie Cline. *Scr* Barney Gerard and Adele Buffington. *Photog* L. W. O'Connell. *Art dir* Dave Milton. *Supv film ed* Otho Lovering. *Film ed* Roy V. Livingston. *Set cont* Grace Baughman. *Set dir* Raymond Boltz, Jr. *Mus dir* Edward J. Kay. *Sd dir* John Kean. *Makeup* Charles Huber. *Hair dresser* Clara Holgate. *Prod mgr* Allen K. Wood.

Source: Based on the comic strip "Bringing Up Father" by George McManus, owned and copyrighted by King Features Syndicate, Inc. (12 Jan 1913—).

Cast: Joe Yule [(*Jiggs*)], Renie Riano [(*Maggie*)], George McManus the internationally known cartoonist [(*Himself*)], Tim Ryan [(*Dinty Moore*)], Jim Bannon [(*Snake Bite Carter*)], Riley Hill [(*Bob Carter*)], Pat Goldin [(*Dugan*)], June Harrison [(*Nora*)], Wrestlers in main event: "Bomber" Kulkowich [sic], and Terry McGinnis [(*Cyclone*)], [Billy Griffith (*Lawyer Blakely*)].

Domestic, Fantasy, Society, Comedy. [*Print viewed*]. When New York social climber Maggie is proclaimed the official heir of her Grandpa J. P. MacGillacudy's fortune, her thirty-seven year struggle to obtain her rightful inheritance comes to an end. Soon after learning that she has inherited her grandfather's Gower Gulch mansion and gold mine, Maggie is visited by his ghost, who tells her to go to Gower Gulch and prevent the property from being bulldozed. Unnerved by the apparition, Maggie arms herself with a rolling pin and wastes no time in getting her husband Jiggs and daughter Nora out of their Park Avenue apartment and onto a train bound for Jackass Junction, the nearest stop to Gower Gulch. No sooner do Jiggs, Maggie and Nora approach Gower Gulch than they are greeted by flying bullets from Snake Bite Carter and his henchmen, who try to scare them off. When their stagecoach driver flees, Maggie takes over the reins and drives the coach until they are rescued by Bob Carter, Snake Bite's kind half brother. Snake Bite tells Maggie that the rivalry between the Carters and the MacGillicudys, two of the most powerful clans in Gower Gulch, has been renewed by his outlaw brother, who is trying to get the MacGillicudy gold mine for himself. Arriving in Gower Gulch, Maggie and her family are disappointed to find that the town is a ghost town and that the mansion is old and run-down. Later, Maggie is visited once again by her grandfather's ghost and is warned about the Carters. Bob, who has become smitten with Nora, calls his brother the blacksheep of the family, prompting Snake Bite to challenge him to a gunfight. Jiggs, meanwhile, starts a gold rush to Gower Gulch when he sends his friend, Dinty Moore, a telegram telling him to come out. Dinty brings many of Jiggs's pals with him, including Dugan, who is made sheriff of the town. When it is learned that Maggie is wandering through the nearby hills alone, and that Snake Bite and his men have gone after her, a posse is formed to rescue her. Snake Bite gets to her first, though, and instead of harming her, takes her to George McManus, the creator of her comic strip character. McManus tells Maggie that he put her and Jiggs in the country just to see how they would act in Western surroundings, and she is furious. *City-country contrast. Ghosts. Inheritance. Socialites. Abduction. Cartoonists. Feuds. Ghost towns. Gold mines. Gold rushes. Gunfights. Half brothers. Irish Americans. New York City–Park Avenue. Saloons. The West. Wrestlers and wrestling.*

Note: Wrestler Bomber Kulkavich's surname is misspelled "Kulkowich" in the onscreen credits. Kulkavish also acted under the name Henry Kulky. *Jiggs and Maggie Out West* was the last picture of actor Joe Yule, who died at the age of fifty-six, three weeks before the film was released. It was also the fifth and final picture in Monogram's "Jiggs and Maggie" series. For additional information on the series, please consult the Series Index and see the entry for *Bringing Up Father* (above).

Box 25 Mar 1950. *DV* 20 Mar 1950, p. 3. *HR* 27 Jan 1950, p. 18. *HR* 3 Feb 1950, p. 16. *HR* 20 Mar 1950, p. 3. *MPHPD* 25 Mar 1950, p. 237. *Var* 22 Mar 1950, p. 20.

JIGSAW (African Americans, Jewish Americans)

Tower Pictures, Inc. *Dist* United Artists Corp. 11 Mar **1949**; Prod: at Eastern Sound Studios [©Tower Pictures, Inc.; 11 Mar 1949; LP2158]. Sd (Western Electric Sound System); b&w. 8 reels, 6,480 ft. 70 min. Passed by the National Board of Review. PCA cert no. 04682.

Pres EDWARD J. DANZIGER and HARRY LEE DANZIGER. *Prod* Edward J. Danziger and Harry Lee Danziger. *Dir* Fletcher Markle. *Asst dir* Sal J. Scoppa, Jr. *Scr* Fletcher Markle and Vincent McConnor. *From an orig story by* John Roeburt. *Dir of photog* Don Malkames. *Film ed* Robert Matthews. *Mus score* Robert W. Stringer. *Rec dir* David M. Polak. *Makeup created by* Fred Ryle. *Unit mgr* William L. Nemeth.

Cast: Franchot Tone (*Howard Malloy*), Jean Wallace (*Barbara Whitfield*), Myron McCormick (*Charles Riggs*), Marc Lawrence (*Angelo Agostini [also known as "The Angel"]*), Winifred Lenihan (*Mrs. [Grace] Hartley*), Betty Harper (*Caroline Riggs*), Hedley Rainnie (*Sigmund Kosterich*), Walter Vaughn (*District Attorney Walker*), George Breen (*Knuckles [also known as Miller]*), Robert Gist (*Tommy Quigley*), Hester Sondergaard (*Mrs. Borg*), Luella Gear (*Pet shop owner*), Alexander Campbell (*Pemberton*), Robert Noe (*Waldron*), Alexander Lockwood (*Nichols*), Ken Smith (*Wylie*), Alan Macateer (*Museum guard*), Manuel Aparicio (*Warehouse guard*), Brainard Duffield (*Butler*), [Burgess Meredith (*Bartender*)], [Henry Fonda (*Waiter*)], [John Garfield (*Man with newspaper*)], [Marlene Dietrich, Fletcher Markle (*Nightclub patrons*)], [Marsha Hunt (*Secretary*)], [Leonard Lyons (*Columnist*)].

Drama. [*Print viewed*]. After New York City printer Max Borg is murdered, District Attorney Walker, who is assigned to the case, learns that Borg, who had recently been exposed as the printer of propaganda posters for a race hate group called "The Crusaders," was apparently silenced by them. When an article about the group appears in a local newspaper, Walker's deputy, Howard Malloy, visits the author, Charles Riggs, who is also his sister Caroline's fiancé. Later, Charlie is followed home by a mysterious figure, who knocks him unconscious and pushes him out of his high-rise window. After Caroline finds a propaganda poster inside Charlie's room and shows it to Howard, he notices the words "Sigmund Kosterich, Rembrandt Studios" printed on the back. Howard goes to Kosterich's shop, posing as a potential customer, but Kosterich insists he does not print posters. Before leaving, Howard admires Kosterich's painting of a lovely singer named Barbara Whitfield. When a man follows Howard home, Howard draws his gun, grabs the man's wallet and learns that his name is Miller. Inside the wallet, he finds a newspaper advertisement for Barbara's nightclub act and a card with an address and the words "See the Angel" printed on it. Howard goes to the address, which turns out to be the headquarters of the Mohawk Political Club. There, he introduces himself to "The Angel," Angelo Agostini, who offers to help him win a promotion to special prosecutor. Later, when Howard's friend, socialite Grace Hartley, hears Howard's name linked to Angel's, she warns him against associating with unsavory characters. Howard attends a party at Grace's house, then leaves after receiving a message from his partner, Tommy Quigley. After her show at the Blue Angel nightclub, Barbara meets Howard, and although she is Angel's sweetheart, Howard kisses her. When Angel sees Barbara with Howard, he becomes jealous and orders her to break it off with him. Later, Barbara tells Howard about The Crusaders' racist agenda, and when he tries to kiss her, she surmises that he is only after information and pushes him off the couch. Howard is knocked unconscious when his head hits the coffee table, and while he is unconscious, Grace, the secret head of The Crusaders, arrives, shoots Barbara to death and escapes. Howard revives, and when Kosterich shows up, Howard assumes he is the murderer. Kosterich blames Grace, who unknown to him, is eavesdropping in the hallway outside, then tells Howard that he found evidence of her involvement with The Crusaders while painting a portrait at her house. When Grace overhears Kosterich say that he has hidden the evidence behind one of his paintings at the museum, she rushes out, followed by Angel and Miller, who is also known as "Knuckles." At the museum, Grace knocks out the night watchman, while Howard phones Quigley and tells him to come to the museum. After Howard and Kosterich arrive and find the watchman, Howard goes after Angel, while Kosterich creeps up behind Grace. Howard then shoots Angel, and Grace shoots Kosterich. When Miller arrives and fires at Howard, Kosterich grabs Howard's gun and shoots Grace. Just then, several squad cars arrive at

the scene, and Caroline is so relieved to see that her brother is unhurt that she kisses him. *Clubs. District attorneys. Investigations. Racism. Secret societies. Advertisements. Bribery. Brothers and sisters. Eavesdropping. Engagements. Escapes. Falls from heights. German Americans. Italian Americans. Jealousy. Kisses. Murder. Museums. New York City-Brooklyn. Newspapers. Nightclubs. Painters (Of paintings). Parties. Printers. Propaganda. Reporters. Romantic rivalry. Shootings. Singers. Socialites. Undercover operations. Watchmen.*

Note: The opening credits identify the nightclub used for location shooting as the Blue Angel Night Club in New York City. The closing credits include the following acknowledgement: "This picture was filmed with the obvious good will of many famous stars. The producers wish to thank them." A 28 Mar 1949 *HR* news item noted that producer Harry Lee Danziger and the staff at Eastern Sound Laboratories in New York City "devised a collapsible dolly and special hangers for lights" for interior shooting. According to a Dec 1948 article in *AmCin*, the picture was shot entirely without sound. Danziger and his brother, Edward J. Danziger, had been using a highly successful technique of sound dubbing to dub foreign films and decided to use it for *Jigsaw*, their first feature production. The *HCN* noted "a recording defect which makes the sound fuzzy, occasionally unintelligible, and frequently out of synchronization with the players' lips." *AmCin* reported that the producers' search for "natural settings" led them to New York, where "not a single set was built for the entire production. Even the props were those found on the locations." Locations included the interior of the Brooklyn Museum, a Fifth Avenue pet shop, a night club, a large restaurant "of unique design," an apartment house interior and a warehouse. *Jigsaw* marked the screen directing debut of Fletcher Markle, who, along with Winifred Lenihan and many other cast members, had worked mainly in radio. Franchot Tone and Jean Wallace were married at the time of the production, but divorced shortly thereafter.

AmCin Dec 1948, p. 412, 427-428. *Box* 19 Mar 1949. *DV* 8 Mar 1949, p. 3, 10. *FD* 11 Mar 1949, p. 5. *HCN* 30 Mar 1949. *HR* 15 Dec 1948, p. 4. *HR* 8 Mar 1949, p. 4. *HR* 25 Mar 1949, p. 9. *HR* 28 Mar 1949, p. 12. *LAMirror* 30 Mar 1949. *MPHPD* 12 Mar 1949, p. 4530. *NYT* 30 May 1949, p. 9. *Var* 9 Mar 1949, p. 6.

JIM THORPE—ALL-AMERICAN (Native Americans)

Warner Bros. Pictures, Inc.; A Warner Bros.—First National Picture. *Dist* Warner Bros. Pictures, Inc. 1 Sep **1951**; New York opening: 24 Aug 1951; Prod: late Aug—late Nov 1950 [©Warner Bros. Pictures, Inc.; 21 Aug 1951; LP1135]. Sd (RCA Sound System); b&w. 9,634 ft. 107 min. PCA cert no. 14872.

Prod Everett Freeman. *Dir* Michael Curtiz. *Dial dir* Norman Stuart. *2d unit and montage dir* David C. Gardner. [*Asst dir* Sherry Shourds]. [*2d asst dir* Russ Llewellyn]. *Scr* Douglas Morrow and Everett Freeman. *Addl dial* Frank Davis. *Scr story* Douglas Morrow and Vincent X. Flaherty. *From the biography by* Russell J. Birdwell. *In collaboration with* James Thorpe. *Dir of photog* Ernest Haller. [*2d cam* Eli Fredericks]. [*Asst cam* Larry Cairen]. [*Still man* Mac Julian]. [*Gaffer* V. Johnson]. *Art dir* Edward Carrere. [*Supv art dir* Bertram Tuttle]. *Film ed* Folmar Blangsted. *Set dec* William Wallace. *Ward* Milo Anderson and [Vic Vallejo]. [*Ward set* R. Hibbs and Marie Pickering]. *Orch* Murray Cutter. *Mus dir* Max Steiner. *Sd* Oliver S. Garretson. *Boom boy* J. Jensen. *Makeup artist* Gordon Bau. [*Hair* Agnes Flanagan and J. Marvin]. [*Makeup* Al Greenway]. *Tech adv* Jim Thorpe. [*Script supv* Irva Ross]. [*Props* L. Plews]. [*Asst* L. Williams]. [*Best boy* C. Swanner]. [*Grip* Warren Yaple]. [*Publicity* Harry Friedmen].

Cast: Burt Lancaster [(*Jim Thorpe*)], Charles Bickford [([*Glenn S.*] *Pop Warner*))], Steve Cochran [(*Peter Allendine*)], Phyllis Thaxter [(*Margaret Miller*)], Dick Wesson [(*Ed Guyac*)], Jack Bighead [(*Little Boy*)], Suni Warcloud [(*Wally Denny*)], Al Mejia [(*Louis Tewanema*)], Hubie Kerns [(*Ashenbrunner*)], [Nestor Paiva (*Hiram Thorpe*)], [Jimmie Moss (*Jim Thorpe, Jr.*)], [Billy Gray (*Jim Thorpe, as a boy*)], [Nick Rodman (*Frant Mr. Pleasant*)], [Eula Morgan (*Charlotte Thorpe*)], [Bob Williams (*Lafayette coach*)], [Sarah Selby (*Miss Benton*)], [J. Thornton Baston (*King Gustav*)], [Frank McFarland (*Chairman*)], [Joseph Kerr, Phil Tead (*Board members*)], [Roy Gordon (*Coach McGraw*)], [Ralph Montgomery, Tim Graham (*Photographers*)], [Norman Phillips (*Reporter*)], [Mary Alan Hokanson (*Operator*)], [Jimmy Ogg (*Bellboy*)], [Robert Harrison (*Locker room boy*)], [Hal Fieberling, Alex Sharpe, Charles Horvath, John Close, Chester Hayes (*Players*)], [Matt Willis (*Michael*)], [Mike Ragan (*Lacey*)], [Ken Swanson (*Wildcat*)], [Edwin Max (*Manager*)], [Max Wagner (*Coach*)], [Sam Hayes (*Announcer*)], [Max Terhune (*Farmer*)], [Tom Greenway (*Coach Howard*)], [Joe Haworth (*Indian*)], [Chris Munson (*Indian athlete*)], [George Spalding (*Doctor*)], [Dewey Robinson (*Bartender*)], [Charles Wagenheim (*Briggs*)], [Buddy Shaw, Jack Perrin, Joe Gilbert (*Spectators*)], [Carl Saxe (*Quarterback*)], [Robert Simpson (*New player*)], [Charles O'Brien (*Owner*)], [Frank Pharr (*Attendant*)], [Barry Regan (*Ticket taker*)], [Timmy Hawkins, Jimmy Hawkins, Nicky Sardegna, Lew Fay,

Anthony Mazola, Charles Finney, Peter Roman, Richard Mazola, Bobby Taylor (*Young boys*)], [Dale Van Sickle (*Cop*)], [Billy Wayne].

Biography, Sports, Drama. [*Print viewed*]. Jim Thorpe, a young boy born on the Sac and Fox Indian reservation in Oklahoma, rejects his father's repeated attempts to place him in school because he is unaccustomed to the confines of a classroom. No sooner does his father drop him off at a new school than Jim rushes home, running the entire twelve-mile distance and arriving before his father. Although running is Jim's passion, his father tries to instill the value of a good education in Jim so that he can find a better life off the reservation. In time, Jim fulfills the promise he made to his father and attends the Carlisle Indian School in Pennsylvania. There he captures the attention of Glenn S. "Pop" Warner, the Director of Athletics, who sees Jim run and realizes that he can be an asset to the school track team. Pop's assessment of Jim's skills proves true when he leads the Carlisle team to many victories. While Jim makes fast friends with students Ed Guyac and Little Boy, he also stirs the interest of Margaret Miller, a fellow student who takes pleasure in sewing Jim's college letter onto his sweater. Realizing that he must vie with the captain of the football team to win Margaret's affection, Jim decides to go out for football and show off his prowess. Pop attempts to dissuade Jim from playing football because he fears that Jim's precious running legs might be injured, but Jim insists on joining. Game after game, Jim finds himself relegated to the bench, until the day of the game against Harvard, when Pop sends him onto the field. With the game tied, Jim manages to score a seemingly impossible touchdown, winning the game for Carlisle. From then on, Jim leads the team to one victory after another. As the football season comes to a close, Jim decides that his life ambition is to be a football coach, and that he wants to marry Margaret. Margaret does not return the following term, however, because she is not an Indian and is ashamed that she let Jim assume that she was. When Pop sees how despondent Jim is over losing Margaret, he gets her a job in the school infirmary, and the couple reunite, declaring that their love is more important than their different backgrounds. Jim continues his athletic success at Carlisle but is unable to get the coaching job he so desperately wants. To further prove his prowess, Jim enters the 1912 Olympic games in Stockholm, where he wins two gold medals. Soon after returning to the United States and marrying Margaret, Jim is accused by the Olympic Committee of breaking the rules and accepting money for playing on a minor league baseball team during one summer. Although he was unaware of the rule, Jim is stripped of his gold medals and, because of the resultant bad publicity, his career as an amateur is ruined. Jim then turns professional and enjoys careers in both baseball and football. He is devoted to his young son, and the boy's unexpected death sends Jim into a deep depression. Unable to endure Jim's drinking and aimless wandering from team to team, Margaret finally leaves him. Years pass, and in 1932, Pop gives Jim a ticket to the Los Angeles Olympics. Attending the event reminds Jim of his earlier ambitions and gives his life new meaning. On his way home, Jim accidentally drives over a football, and when he goes to return it to the neighborhood boys, he suddenly finds himself doing what he loves most, coaching. Many years later, Jim is honored by the American press as the greatest athlete in the first half of the century. *Carlisle (PA). United States Indian School. College life. Football. Indians of North America. Racism. Romance. Jim Thorpe. Track and field athletics. Alcoholism. Baseball. Death and dying. Depression, Mental. Fathers and sons. Football coaches. Governors. Indians of North America–Reservations. Marriage. John McGraw. Oklahoma. Olympic games. Reputation. Romantic rivalry. Scandal. Separation (Marital).*

Note: The working title for this film was *The All-American*. The onscreen credits contain the following acknowledgement: "Our grateful appreciation to Bacone College for its aid and cooperation in making this picture possible." Contemporary *HR* news items note that two weeks of filming took place at Bacone College, which is located in Muskogee, OK.

As depicted in the film, Jim Thorpe, a Sac and Fox Indian, was born in Oklahoma on 28 May 1888. As a boy, Thorpe, whose Indian name, Wa-tho-huck, meant Bright Path, disliked school, and his father would enrolled him in schools an increasing distance away from home to discourage him from running away. In 1904, however, Thorpe's educational experiences changed dramatically when he began attending the famed Carlisle Indian School in Pennsylvania. The school was founded in 1879 by Lt. Richard Pratt, an Army officer who was interested in improving the educational opportunities of Indians. The institution, which was the first off-reservation school funded by the U.S. government, was a vocational school rather than a college, and the length of attendance varied upon the course of study. Pratt, determined to help the Indian students adapt to white culture, initiated an "outing" system in

which students would spend their holidays working for white families or employers rather than going home. The school, which closed in 1918, was well-known for the athletic prowess of its students. The most famous Carlisle coach was Glenn S. "Pop" Warner (1871–1954), who guided Thorpe in college football and track-and-field. During Warner's college coaching career, which spanned over forty years, his record-making teams included those of Carlisle, the University of Pittsburgh, Stanford and Temple University. Warner was renowned for his innovative plays and ability to mold strong teams. Thorpe started under Warner's tutelage in track-and-field, then moved onto football and was twice named All-American. In 1912, Thorpe participated in the Olympic games in Stockholm, where he won gold medals in the pentathlon and decathlon. Thorpe's astonishing performance moved King Gustav of Sweden to declare him "the greatest athlete in the world." In 1913, the International Olympic Committee discovered that Thorpe had broken the rules governing amateur standing by receiving payment for two summers of play in a minor league baseball team. Thorpe maintained that he had not been aware of the rules, but the committee nonetheless stripped him of his medals and expunged his achievements from official record books. Following the loss of his amateur status, Thorpe enjoyed careers in both professional baseball and football. After his retirement from professional sports in 1929, Thorpe was employed in a variety of jobs, including occasional extra and bit player work in Hollywood films. He appeared in a wide variety of films, including *King Kong* (1933), *She*, (1935), and finally *Wagonmaster*, (1950). Thorpe's private life was more complicated than depicted in the film, which portrayed only one of his three wives. His first wife was a white student at Carlisle, and their son, James, Jr., died of infantile paralysis when he was three years old, but the couple also had three daughters. Thorpe had four sons with his second wife, and was living with his third wife at the time of his death of a heart attack on 28 Mar 1953. In 1982, the International Olympic Committee restored Thorpe's medals [reproductions of the medals were presented to his children in Jan 1983] and re-entered his achievements in the official record books. Modern sources indicate that while filming *Jim Thorpe—All-American*, Burt Lancaster was personally involved in trying to restore Thorpe's medals. In a biography of Thorpe, Lancaster noted that "there was a strong attempt on the part of Warner Bros. to try to get his medals back. They were hoping to be able to do that as the finish for the picture." In addition to his Olympic honors, Thorpe was elected to the college and professional football halls of fame, as well as the track-and-field hall of fame, and in 1950, was voted the greatest athlete of the first half-century in a poll of sports writers conducted by The Associated Press.

According to a 1951 *Var* article on the thirty-year development history of the film, Thorpe's life story had been suggested a number of times by various individuals. The article notes that in the early 1930s, Thorpe and noted publicist Russell J. Birdwell collaborated on an unpublished biography entitled *Red Sons of Carlisle*, the film rights to which were immediately purchased by M-G-M. M-G-M shelved the story, but in 1943, when Thorpe's friends, sports writer Norman Sper and *Var* columnist Frank Scully, wrote a piece about Thorpe for *Reader's Digest*, interest in the athlete's life story was renewed. According to an article by Scully in *Var*, M-G-M took another look at *Red Sons of Carlisle*, only to discover that all the legal rights to details not covered in the book had been acquired by Sper. Scully also notes that he and Sper were offered $25,000 for the rights to their *Reader's Digest* piece by an RKO producer, and attributes the demise of the deal to an argument Scully and Sper had over the fee for rewriting the script. According to a biography of director Michael Curtiz, in May 1949, following M-G-M's failure to negotiate legal details with Thorpe's wife, who possessed her husband's power of attorney, the studio released its option on the film rights to *Red Sons of Carlisle*. The rights were then picked up by Monogram producer Lindsley Parsons, who planned to produce a film based on an original story that was written by sportswriter Vincent X. Flaherty. According to the Curtiz biography, after Warner Bros. successfully negotiated the film rights with Mrs. Thorpe, producer Everett Freeman considered Kirk Douglas for the lead. A Jul–Aug 1996 *FIR* article noted that Curtiz and Thorpe first met at the 1912 Stockholm Olympics, in which Curtiz participated on the Hungarian fencing team.

The *Var* review noted that stock footage of the 1912 and 1924 Olympic Games were used in the film. The film was released in Britain as *Man of Bronze*. According to an Oct 1988 *LAHE* news item, Richard Leary was to write a screenplay of Thorpe's life to be filmed by Englander Productions, but the picture was not made.

Box 16 Jun 1951. *DV* 14 Jun 1951, p. 3. *FD* 18 Jun 1951, p. 22. *FIR* Jul–Aug 1996, pp. 4-19. *HR* 3 Aug 1950. *HR* 25 Aug 1950, p. 15. *HR* 8 Sep 1950, p. 11. *HR* 20 Oct 1950, p. 15. *HR* 17 Nov 1950, p. 13. *HR* 14 Jun 1951, p. 3. *LAHE* 7 Oct 1988. *LAEx* 27 Sep 1948. *MPHPD* 16 Jun 1951, p. 885. *NYT* 12 Jun 1949. *NYT* 25 Aug 1951, p. 7. *Var* 20 Jun 1951, p. 6. *Var* 29 Aug 1951.

JIVIN' IN BE-BOP (African Americans)

Alexander Productions. *Dist* Alexander Distributing Co. **1947**; New York opening: 29 Jul 1947. Sd (RCA Sound System); b&w. 5,261 ft. 58-59 min.

Pres WILLIAM D. ALEXANDER. *Prod* William D. Alexander. *Dir* Leonard Anderson. *Scr* Powell Lindsay. *Photog* Don Malkames. *Film ed* Gladys Brothers. *Sd* Nelson Minnerly. *Makeup* Fred Ryle and Dave Gaston.

Music: "Shaw 'Nuff," by Charlie Parker and Dizzy Gillespie; "A Night in Tunisia," by Dizzy Gillespie and Frank Paperelli; "One Bass Hit" and "Things to Come," by Dizzy Gillespie and Gil Fuller; "Ornithology," by Charlie Parker and Benny Harris; "Boogie in C," "Grosvenor Square," "Knocking at the Pearly Gates," "Scales,"

"Ray's Idea," "Dynamo A," and "Boogie on the Milky Way," composers undetermined.

Song(s): "Salt Peanuts" and "I Waited for You," music and lyrics by Dizzy Gillespie; "Oooh Baba Leba," music and lyrics by Dizzy Gillespie and John Brown; "Oop Bop Sh'Bam," music and lyrics by Gil Fuller, Dizzy Gillespie and Roberts [given name undetermined]; "He Beeped When He Shoulda Bopped," music and lyrics by Dizzy Gillespie, Gil Fuller and John Brown; "Crazy About a Man," composers undetermined.

Cast: Dizzy Gillespie and His Orchestra, Helen Humes, Ray Sneed, Sahji, Freddie Carter [(*"Peanut Head" Jackson*)], Ralph Brown, Dan Burley, and Johnny Taylor, Phil and Audrey, Johnny and Henny, Daisy Richardson, Pancho and Dolores, [The Hubba Hubba Girls], [Ray Brown (*Himself, bass player*)], [Kenny Clarke (*Himself, drummer*)], [John Lewis (*Himself, pianist*)], [Milt Jackson (*Himself, vibes player*)].

African American, Variety, with songs. [*Print viewed*]. At a black variety show, master of ceremonies "Peanut Head" Jackson introduces Dizzy Gillespie and His Orchestra. The show features the talent of many "bebop" jazz musicians and many dancers. After the first number, Dizzy and the emcee tell jokes until singer Helen Humes, joining in the fun and pretending to be Peanut Head's wife, interrupts them and sings a song. Dizzy's orchestra provides the musical accompaniment for all the specialty acts to follow, including dance numbers performed by Johnny and Henny, Daisy Richardson, Sahji, Ralph Brown, Ray Sneed and Phil and Audrey. The show also features the talent of singers Helen Humes, Kenny "Pancho" Hagood and Dolores Brown. *African Americans. Concerts. Dancers. Jazz music. Musicians. Singers. Comedians. Orchestras. Tap dancing.*

Note: Although there is a copyright statement on the film, dated 1947 for producer William D. Alexander, the picture is not in the copyright registry. Modern sources note that Spencer Williams co-directed this film. Modern sources include Dave Burns and James Moody in the cast.

JO AND JOSETTE see **JOSETTE**

JOAN OF RAINBOW SPRINGS see **THE GIRL OF MY HEART**

JOB see **SINS OF MAN**

JOE DAKOTA (Native Americans)

Universal-International Pictures Co., Inc. *Dist* Universal Pictures Co., Inc. Sep **1957**; *Prod*: 12 Nov–3 Dec 1956 [©Universal Pictures Co.; 30 Apr 1957; LP8589]. Sd (Westrex Recording System); col (Eastman Color). 79 min. PCA cert no. 18418.

Prod Howard Christie. *Dir* Richard Bartlett. *Asst dir* Frank Shaw and Wilbur Mosier. *Wrt* William Talman and Norman Jolley. *Dir of photog* George Robinson. *Art dir* Alexander Golitzen and Bill Newberry. *Film ed* Fred MacDowell and [Russell Schoengarth]. *Set dec* Russell A. Gausman and Ray Jeffers. *Gowns* Marilyn Sotto. *Mus supv* Joseph Gershenson. *Sd* Leslie I. Carey and Joe Lapis. *Makeup* Bud Westmore. [*Hair stylist* Virginia Jones]. [*Unit prod mgr* Sergei Petschnikoff].

Song(s): "The Flower of San Antone," music by Ray Joseph, lyrics by Mack David.

Cast: Jock Mahoney (*The Stranger* [*Joe Dakota*]), Luana Patten (*Jody Weaver*), Charles McGraw (*Cal Moore*), Barbara Lawrence (*Myrna Weaver*), Claude Akins (*Aaron Grant*), Lee Van Cleef (*Adam Grant*), Anthony Caruso (*Marcus Vizzini*), Paul Birch (*Frank Weaver*), George Dunn (*Jim Baldwin*), Steve Darrell (*Sam Cook*), Rita Lynn (*Rosa Vizzini*), Gregg Barton (*Tom Jensen*), Anthony Jochim (*Claude Henderson*), Jeane Wood (*Bertha Jensen*), Juney Ellis (*Ethel Cook*).

Western. [*Print viewed*]. While Joe Dakota is searching for his friend, whom he calls The Old Indian, he rides into the seemingly abandoned town of Arborville, California. When he goes to visit the nearby farm owned by the Indian, he witnesses an oil well being dug. Cal Moore, the leader of the enterprise, allows Joe to watch the proceedings, but when Joe enters a cabin on the land, Cal gets angry and his men push Joe into the oil pool. Joe goes back to Arborville, where Jody Weaver, a young woman he had met upon his arrival, gives him fresh clothes. When he inquires about The Old Indian, she insists that his name was Joe Dakota, but refuses to say much more. While Joe is taking a bath in the town's horse trough, the townspeople return from the well and are outraged. Joe asks about the Indian, but like Jody, the people refuse to talk. Later, the townspeople meet in Marcus

Vizzini's saloon to discuss the day's proceedings, and Cal suggests that "the stranger" is a "wildcat." When Joe returns from another investigation of the cabin, Myrna, Jody's sister and Cal's girl friend, alerts the men. Joe goes to Marcus' saloon, where a fight breaks out between Joe and the town's two bullies, brothers Aaron and Adam Grant. Joe reveals his identity and claims that the property on which the well is being dug belongs to him. Cal insists that the Indian signed the land deed over to him, but Joe nonetheless establishes himself at the cabin. Joe then goes to the local barber, Jim Baldwin, and discovers that Cal recently arrived in Arborville after a career as a wildcat, and that he accidentally found the oil well after buying the Indian's land for farming purposes. After Jody goes to see Joe at the cabin and demands to know his identity, Joe explains that The Old Indian had telegrammed him for help and was using Joe's own name. Jody claims that the Indian was hanged because he tried to rape her one night, but Joe accuses her of lying, and Jody leaves in anger. After Joe goes to the Indian's grave and leaves a cross on it, he returns to the cabin to find Jody waiting for him. Joe explains that the Indian, who had been his scout during his Army days, had used his name because it was the only thing he could write, and therefore, Cal's paper must be a fake. Jody insists that the townspeople were not aware of the well's existence until after the hanging took place and tells Joe the story of the attempted rape. Joe makes her realize that the attack, which happened in the dark, could not have been perpetrated by the Indian because she remembers feeling a rough beard and Indians do not have whiskers. Cal, meanwhile, returns to Arborville and convinces the townspeople to fight against Joe, and they all go to the oil well just as a gusher starts to blow. After Jody tells her story to the group, Cal knocks Joe out, then holds his gun on the group and makes them work to stop the gusher. Just then, Joe revives and attacks Cal, knocking him out after a fight. As the people leave the oil well, Marcus throws a torch and burns it so that they will have a friendly town once again. Later, Joe and Jody go to The Old Indian's grave, and Joe places his own name on the cross. *Frame-ups. Indians of North America. Land rights. Oil prospectors. Oil wells. Attempted rape. Brothers. California. Drunkenness. Fistfights. Forgers and forgery. Graves. Greed. Impersonation and imposture. Italian Americans. Saloon keepers. Small town life. Veterans.*

Note: The Native American character, referred to throughout the film as "Joe Dakota" or "The Old Indian," appears in one flashback sequence, but the actor who plays the role is not listed in the credits or in any contemporary source.

Box 15 Jun 1957. *DV* 4 Jun 1957, p. 3. *Exh* 26 Jun 1957, p. 4344. *FD* 6 Jun 1957, p. 6. *Har* 8 Jun 1957, p. 91. *HR* 4 Jun 1957, p. 3. *MPD* 17 Jun 1957. *MPHPD* 8 Jun 1957, p. 410. *Var* 5 Jun 1957, p. 6.

THE JOE LOUIS STORY (African Americans)

Federated Films, Inc. *Dist* United Artists Corp. 18 Sep **1953**; *Prod:* early Feb—mid-May 1953. Sd (RCA Sound System); b&w. 7,864 ft. 88 min. PCA cert no. 16654.

Pres WALTER CHRYSLER, JR. *Prod* Stirling Silliphant. *Assoc prod* William F. Joyce. *Dir* Robert Gordon. *Asst dir* Isaac Jones and George Ackerson. *Orig scr* Robert Sylvester. *Dir of photog* Joseph Brun. *Op cam* Moe Hartzband. *Film ed* David Kummins. *Set des* Robert Gundlach. *Ward* Florence Transfeld. *Mus comp and cond* George Bassman. *Sd eng* James Shields. *Makeup* Herman Buchman. *Hairstyles* Helen Grizuk. *Cont* Roberta Hodes. *Tech adv* Mannie Seamon. *Production management and operations by* Motion Picture Techniques, Inc. *Unit mgr* Thomas Whitesell. *Asst unit mgr* Dorothy Bohen. *Bus mgr* Philip Donoghue. [*Pub* Kay Norton and Richard Condon].

Song(s): "I'll Be Around," music and lyrics by Alex Wilder.

Cast: Introducing Coley Wallace (*Joe Louis*), Paul Stewart (*Tad McGeehan*), Hilda Simms (*Marva [Trotter] Louis*), James Edwards (*[Jack] "Chappie" Blackburn*), John Marley (*Mannie Seamon*), Dotts Johnson (*Julian Black*), Evelyn Ellis (*Mrs. Barrows*), Carl Rocky Latimer (*Arthur Pine*), John Marriott (*Sam Langford*), Isaac Jones (*Johnny Kingston*), P. Jay Sidney (*John Roxborough*), Royal Beal (*Mike Jacobs*), Herbert Ratner (*Newspaperman*), Ruby Goldstein (*Himself*), Norman Rose (*Lieutenant*), David Kurlan (*Bartender*), Ralph Stanley (*Nick, the announcer*), Shorty Linton (*Himself*), Anita Ellis [(*Singer*)], Ellis Larkins Trio (*Themselves*), [Joe Louis (*Himself*)].

African American, Sports, Biography. [*Print viewed*]. Having followed the career of world-famous boxing champion Joe Louis from the time he began fighting in Detroit, sportswriter Tad McGeehan sadly writes the story about his friend's final defeat in New York in 1951. His story begins in 1932, when Joe, known then as Joseph Louis Barrow, was a teenager living in Detroit: One day, while walking home from his violin lesson, Joe's pal, Johnny Kingston, talks him into using the money for his violin lessons to take boxing lessons. Though he comes home with a black eye after his first boxing lesson, Joe returns for more lessons, and soon shows great promise as a fighter. Joe's mother eventually discovers that he is not using the money she gives him for violin lesson, but she gives him her blessing to continue boxing when he promises to study it with all his heart. In 1934, after winning the Golden Gloves title in Detroit and Chicago, Joe is signed to a contract by manager Julian Black. In the same year, Joe begins training with Jack "Chappie" Blackburn, who puts him on a rigorous training program and teaches him the fighting techniques he will need to be a champion boxer. Following a string of winning fights, Joe returns to Detroit, where promoters Mike Jacobs and Johnson, who represent Madison Square Garden, compete for his contract. Joe shows little interest in the contract negotiations, as he is distracted by the beauty of Marva Trotter, a young woman from Chicago. Joe is introduced to Marva, and she tells him to look her up the next time he visits Chicago. After signing with Jacobs, Joe arrives in New York for his first fight there. A romance blossoms between Joe and Marva, and they are soon married. The wedding celebration is cut short, however, when Chappie reminds Joe that he must fight Max Baer. Joe wins by a knockout in the fourth round then takes his earnings and goes on a wild spending spree. Joe's overspending soon leads to mounting debts, and his new cockiness eventually shows its ill effects in the ring. After a loss to German fighter Max Schmeling leaves Joe badly beaten, he shamefully admits that he did not do his best to prepare for the fight. He vows to resume his training and spends the next two years preparing for a re-match with Schmeling. Joe is further motivated to claim a victory over Schmeling when McGreehan tells him that Hitler is counting on Schmeling's win to support his theory of Aryan superiority. Joe finally gets his wish in June 1938, when he knocks out Schemling only minutes into their fight. Six years after their wedding, Marva, unable to bear being married to the big-time fighter, sues Joe for divorce. Joe, however, refuses to grant Marva a divorce, and instead works to repair their broken marriage. In the years that follow, Joe fights his way from one victory to another, and when war breaks out, he joins the Army as a private. Joe suffers an enormous loss when Chappie dies, and he names Mannie Seamon to replace him as his trainer. Following the war, Joe returns home to Marva and their new daughter, only to discover that he owes thousands of dollars in back taxes. Forced to return to the ring to pay his debts, Joe again loses the love of Marva, who files for divorce. After finally paying off his debts, Joe announces his retirement from the ring, but rumors soon circulate that he is planning a comeback. McGeehan urges Joe not to return, and tells him that he would only suffer embarrassing losses if he did. Joe ingores McGeehan's sage advice and, in 1951, returns to the ring for one last fight. Rocky Marciano's victory over Joe serves as the last episode in McGeehan's story about the champion fighter's career. *Boxing. Boxing managers. Joe Louis. Neglected wives. Boxing trainers. Debt. Detroit (MI). Divorce. Germans. Golf. Grief. Madison Square Garden (New York City). Military Service, Voluntary. Mothers and sons. Parenthood. Singers. Sports reporters. Weddings.*

Note: This picture marked former Twentieth Century-Fox publicity manager Stirling Silliphant's first film as a producer, and was the first film to be produced under Silliphant's Federated Films, Inc. banner. The film also marked the screen debut of championship heavyweight fighter Coley Wallace, who, according to contemporary news items, was paid $17,500 for appearing in the title role. Joe Louis, born Joe Louis Barrow, in Lafayette, Alabama, in 1914, was the longest-reigning world heavyweight champion in boxing history.

Nicknamed the "Brown Bomber," he turned professional in 1934 after winning the Amateur Athletic Union light-heavyweight title. His most notable defeat came in 1936, when he lost to Germany's Max Schmeling in a nontitle fight. In 1937, he won the heavyweight title by knocking out James J. Braddock in eight rounds. He avenged his loss to Schmeling in 1938, knocking him out in the first round. He retired as champion in 1949 after holding the title for almost twelve years and defending it a record-breaking 25 times. As depicted in the film, he returned to the ring in 1950 because of financial problems, and lost a 15-round decision to Ezzard Charles in another title bout. He retired permanently the following year, after being knocked out in a bout with Rocky Marciano.

According to a Nov 1953 *DV* article, the picture, which was originally budgeted at $298,000, ran into financial difficulties three weeks into production, when some of the film's investors failed to make payments. At that point, production on the film was halted, and Silliphant and Joe Louis, who was

partnered with the producer for an equal share of the profits, reportedly gave up much of their interest to raise more money for the film. Filming eventually resumed when Silliphant brought in Walter Chrysler Jr. and William Zeckendorf as principal investors. The *DV* article also noted that, in addition to his financial problems, Silliphant encountered resistence to the film from Southern exhibitors, and was warned repeatedly that his film would not get booked into many "white" houses. The article quoted Silliphant as saying that "the only one who seemed to have faith in us was United Artists."

According to a Jan 1953 *NYT* news item, Art Smith was originally slated for the part played by John Marley. Joe Louis appears in the film in a number of scenes taken from actual footage of his professional fights. Contemporary news items indicate that filming took place in Detroit, Michigan, and in locations around New York State, including New York City, Liberty and the Catskills. According to *Var*, the final cost of the picture was $311,000. In Feb 1954, according to a *Var* news item, a $745,000 lawsuit was filed against United Artists and a group of exhibitors by Laura Blackburn Shaw, the widow of boxer Jack "Chappie" Blackburn, who claimed that her late husband was portrayed in the film without her written consent. A May 1954 *HR* news item notes that the suit was settled out of court for $20,000 and a percentage of the picture's future television grosses. The settlement was reached shortly after a judge ruled that the name and picture of Jack Blackburn were property rights that belonged to his estate. For information about other films based on Joe Louis' life, see the entry below for *Spirit of Youth*.

Box 3 Oct 1953. *DV* 30 Sep 1953, p. 3. *DV* 18 Nov 1953. *FD* 5 Oct 1953, p. 6. *HR* 29 Apr 1953. *HR* 22 May 1953. *HR* 30 Sep 1953, p. 4. *HR* 23 May 1954. *Look* 3 Nov 1953, p. 86. *MPHPD* 3 Oct 1953, p. 2013. *NYT* 18 Jan 1953. *NYT* 4 Nov 1953, p. 29. *Var* 13 May 1953. *Var* 30 Sep 1953, p. 6. *Var* 18 Nov 1953. *Var* 3 Mar 1954.

JOHANNA ENLISTS (German Americans)

Pickford Film Corp. *Dist* Famous Players-Lasky Corp.; Artcraft Pictures. 29 Sep **1918** [©Pickford Film Corp.; 5 Sep 1918; LP12832]. Si; b&w. 5 reels, 4,388 ft.

Dir William D. Taylor. *Asst dir* Frank Richardson. *Scen* Frances Marion. *Cam* Charles Rosher. *Art dir* Wilfred Buckland.

Source: Based on the short story "The Mobilization of Johanna" by Rupert Hughes in *Hearst's* (Sep-Oct 1917).

Cast: Mary Pickford (*Johanna Renssaller*), Anne Schaefer (*"Maw" Renssaller*), Fred Huntley (*"Paw" Renssaller*), Monte Blue (*Private Vibbard*), Douglas MacLean (*Capt. Archie Van Rensaller*), Emory Johnson (*Lieutenant Frank Le Roy*), John Steppling (*Major Wappington*), Wallace Beery (*Colonel Fanner*), Wesley Barry (*Johanna's brother*), June Prentis, Jean Prentis (*Johanna's twin sisters*).

World War I, Comedy-drama. Johanna Renssaller, who lives on a Pennsylvania Dutch farm with her parents, brother, and twin sisters, dreams of having a "beau" who will bring romance and excitement into her dreary life. Her wish is more than fulfilled when an entire regiment of World War I recruits encamps on her father's farm. Suddenly the center of attention, Johanna decides to beautify herself by taking a milk bath in the dairy, but while she is bathing, young Lieutenant Le Roy suddenly bursts in. Her screams attract Private Vibbard, who insults the lieutenant and subsequently is arrested. Both men are in love with Johanna, but at the court-martial she meets and falls in love with Captain Van Rensaller. Le Roy drops the charges against Vibbard, and Johanna rides away with her captain to be married. *Baths. Courts-martial and courts of inquiry. Farms. Milk. Officers (Military). Pennsylvania Dutch. Soldiers. World War I. Dairy farms. Family life.*

Note: The pre-release title of the film was *Mobilizing of Johanna*. The film, according to *MPN*, was "...produced with the co-operation of the 143d Artillery Regiment, under the command of Captain Faneuf, and of which Miss Pickford is an honorary Captain."

ETR 17 Aug 1918, p. 925. *ETR* 14 Sep 1918, p. 1261. *MPN* 14 Sep 1918, p. 1754, 1762. *MPW* 14 Sep 1918, p. 1610. *MPW* 28 Sep 1918, p. 482. *NYDM* 28 Sep 1918, p. 482. *NYT* 16 Sep 1918, p. 9. *Var* 13 Sep 1918, p. 45. *Wid's* 8 Sep 1918, pp. 27-28.

JOHN AND MARY *see* THE SAILOR TAKES A WIFE

JOHN BARLEYCORN (African Americans)

Bosworth, Inc. *Dist* State Rights; W. W. Hodkinson. Jul **1914** [©Bosworth, Inc.; 26 Jan 1914; LU2033]. Si; b&w. 6 reels.

Dir Hobart Bosworth and J. Charles Haydon. *Scen* Hettie Gray Baker.

Source: Based on the novel *John Barleycorn* by Jack London in *The Saturday Evening Post* (New York, 1913).

Cast: Elmer Clifton (*Jack, 3rd period*), Antrim Short (*Jack, 2nd period*), Matty Roubert (*Jack, 1st period*), Viola Barry (*Haydee*), Hobart Bosworth (*Scratch Nelson*), Joe Ray.

Drama. Aboard his yacht *The Roamer*, author Jack London recounts his lifelong struggle with alcoholism. At age five, as a California farmboy, Jack drinks some beer from an overflowing pail intended for his father and falls down drunk. Several times during his youth he has encounters with drunkenness, while a San Francisco newsboy, an oyster pirate, an explorer, and a seal hunter. Jack's staunchest supporter is his black nursemaid. Eventually Jack meets and marries Haydee, who helps him overcome his addiction. *Alcoholism. Regeneration.* African Americans. Beer. California. Country boys. Explorers. Farms. Fishermen. Hunters. Marriage. Newsboys. Nursemaids. San Francisco (CA).

Note: The novel serialized in *The Saturday Evening Post* between 15 Mar 1913 and 3 May 1913, and the film, are based on incidents from Jack London's own life. According to items contained in the Jack London collection, exteriors for the film were shot in San Francisco and Oakland, CA areas. Additional information in the collection shows that the film opened in San Francisco on 15 Feb 1914 but was exhibited infrequently until Jul 1914. Ads in contemporary trade journals confirm that W. W. Hodkinson assumed the film's distribution at that point. Items in the London collection, supported by trade journal articles, relate that a group of liquor companies, worried about the effect that the film would have on upcoming referenda on prohibition, offered Bosworth, Inc. $25,000 to delay the film's release until after the elections in six particular states. Bosworth declined the offer, but the film's release was delayed by Pennsylvania censor J. Louis Breitinger, and controversy arose over Breitinger's professional connections to several breweries. Exhibitors showed the film in defiance of Breitinger, but censors eventually required cuts in the film in both Pennsylvania and Ohio, where scenes of children drinking alcohol were excised. One pre-release item in the London collection lists Helen Walker, Lincoln Helt (probably Elmo Lincoln, working under his real name, Lincolnhelt), Dick La Reno, and Rhea Haines as additional cast members. Most contemporary sources cite Bosworth as director, but J. Charles Haydon is listed in the 1918 *MPSD* as the director. One modern source claims that Lois Weber wrote the scenario, but this is probably an error.

LAEx 2 Mar 1914. *MPN* 25 Jul 1914, p. 65. *MPN* 8 Aug 1914, pp. 17-18. *MPW* 18 Jul 1914, p. 386, 406. *NYDM* 7 Jan 1914, p. 29. *NYDM* 11 Feb 1914, p. 38. *NYDM* 29 Aug 1914, p. 24. *NYDM* 19 Aug 1914, p. 22. *NYDM* 31 Mar 1915, p. 32. *Newark News* 16 May 1914. *SFChron* 16 Feb 1914. *Var* 17 Jul 1914, p. 17.

JOHN BROWN'S RAIDERS *see* SEVEN ANGRY MEN

JOHN ERMINE OF THE YELLOWSTONE (Native Americans, Crow)

Universal Film Mfg. Co.; A Butterfly Feature. *Dist* Universal Film Mfg. Co. 5 Nov **1917** [©Universal Film Mfg. Co.; 26 Oct 1917; LP11632]. Si; b&w. 5 reels.

Dir Francis Ford. *Asst dir* Joseph A. McDonough. *Scen* Maud Grange.

Source: Based on the novel *John Ermine of the Yellowstone* by Frederic Remington (New York, 1902) and the play of the same name by Louis Evan Shipman (New York, 2 Nov 1903).

Cast: Francis Ford (*John Ermine*), Mae Gaston (*Katherine Searles*), Mark Fenton (*Colonel Searles*), Duke Worne (*Lieut. Butler*), Burwell Hamrick (*White Weasel*), William Carroll (*Crooked Bear*), Joe Flores (*Wolf Voice*), Elsie Ford (*Mrs. Searles*), John Darkcloud (*Fire Bear*).

Western. As a baby, John Ermine is stolen from a wagon train by the Crow Indians, and is adopted by Chief Fire Bear. John grows to manhood, ignorant that he is a white man until his parentage is disclosed to him by Crooked Bear, a white hermit who is on friendly terms with the Crows. Crooked Bear teaches John the language and customs of the white man's civilization, impressing upon him that it is his sacred responsibility to keep peace between the white men and the Indians. Later, John is sent to the Yellowstone army post on a scouting mission and, while there, falls in love with Katherine Searles, the daughter of company Colonel Searles. Katherine, believing John to be a halfbreed, takes his declaration of love as an insult, as does her father and Lieutenant Butler, her suitor. Rejected, John returns to his tribe. When news comes that the fort has been attacked by hostile Indians, the Crows come to the rescue in the nick of time, but John falls in battle while protecting his beloved Katherine. *Crow Indians. Cultural conflict. Parentage. Racism. Settlers.* Abduction. Adoption. Hermits. Military posts. Officers (Military). Scouts (Frontier). Self-sacrifice. Sieges. United States. Army. Wagon trains. Yellowstone National Park (WY).

Note: According to publicity for the film, John Darkcloud, called "Tahamount" in his own language, was a model for Remington, an artist noted for his themes of the American West, for more than nineteen years. Before appearing in this film, Darkcloud, a chief of the Algonquins, graduated from Carlisle University and became a lecturer. Director Ford allowed Darkcloud to arrange anything which had to do with Indians in his own way.

MPN 17 Nov 1917, p. 3445, 3487. *MPW* 10 Nov 1917, p. 911. *MPW* 17 Nov 1917, p. 1031.

JOHN PAUL JONES (Scottish Americans)

John Paul Jones Productions, Inc. *Dist* Warner Bros. Pictures, Inc. Aug **1959**; Prod: 17 Apr—early Oct 1958 [©John Paul Jones Productions, Inc.; 8 Aug 1959; LP16791]. Sd; col (Technicolor); Technirama. 13 reels, 11,323 ft. 126 min. PCA cert no. 19223.

Pres SAMUEL BRONSTON. *Prod* Samuel Bronston. *Assoc prod* Barnett Glassman. *Dir* John Farrow. *Asst dir* Frank Losee. *Scr* John Farrow and Jesse Lasky, Jr. *Chief cine* Michel Kelber. *Spec eff* Rosco S. Cline. *Prod des* Franz Bachelin. *Film ed* Eda Warren. *Sd eff ed* Winston Ryder. *Set dresser* Dario Simoni. *Cost des* Phyllis Dalton. *Cost* Nathans. *Mus* Max Steiner. *Orch* Murray Cutter. *Choreographer* Hector Zaraspe. *Sd rec* Charles Knott. *Makeup artist* Neville Smallwood. *Hair stylist* Joan Smallwood. *Prod adv* Victor Oswald. *Prod mgr* Emmett Emerson. *Tech adv* Rear Admiral J. L. Pratt, U.S.N. (R.E.T.). *Master of sail* Alan Villiers. *Prod assoc* Alan Brown. *Unit publ* Phil Gersdorf. *Tech consultant* Donald Hatswell. *Scr supv* June Faithfull. *Prod filmed with the collaboration of* Suevia Films and Cesareo Gonzales. *European unit mgr* Cecil R. Foster Kemp. *Asst prod mgr* Donald Wyman. *Prop master* Stan Detlie. *Coordinator* Carl Gibson. *Casting dir* Robert Lennard. *The frigates "Bonhomme Richard" and "Serapis" converted by* cooperativa construzioni Navali. *Naval architect* Enrico Fea. *Supv [of frigate construction]* Oscar Brazzi. *Assistance* Registro Italiano Navale.

Cast: Starring: Robert Stack [(*John Paul Jones*)], Marisa Pavan [(*Aimee de Tellison*)], Charles Coburn [(*Benjamin Franklin*)], Erin O'Brien [(*Dorothea Danders*)], With Guest Stars: MacDonald Carey [(*Patrick Henry*)], Jean Pierre Aumont [(*Louis XVI*)], David Farrar [(*John Wilkes*)], Peter Cushing [(*Captain Pearson*)], Susan Canales [(*Marie Antoinette*)], Jorge Riviere [(*Russian chamberlain*)], Featuring: Tom Brannum [(*Peter Wooley*)], Bruce Cabot [(*Gunner Lowrie*)], Thomas Gomez [(*Commodore Esek Hopkins*)], Bob Cunningham [(*Marine Lt. Wallingsford*)], Eric Pohlmann [(*King George III*)], John Crawford [(*George Washington*)], Frank Latimore [(*Lt. Richard Dale*)], Bruce Seton [(*Scottish bagpiper*)], Basil Sydney [(*Sir William Young*)], Archie Duncan [(*Duncan MacBean*)], Judson Laire [(*Mr. Danders*)], John Charles Farrow [(*John Paul*)], Pepe Nieto [(*Red Cherry*)], Patrick Villiers [(*Ensign*)], Ford Rainey [(*1st Lt. Thomas Simpson*)], Paul Curran [(*John Younger*)], George Rigaud [(*Franklin's secretary*)], Nicholas Brady [(*Lt. Trumble*)], Christopher Rhodes [(*Ringleader*)], John Phillips [(*John Hancock*)], Mitchell Kowal [(*Capt. Saltonstall*)], Charles Wise [(*Scipio*)], Alfred Brown [(*Lt. Landais*)], Phil Brown [(*Sentry*)], Rupert Davies [(*British naval captain*)], Robert Ayres [(*John Adams*)], Macdonald Parke [(*Arthur Lee*)], David Phethean [(*English officer*)], Reed De Rouen [(*Joseph Hewes*)], Archie Lyall [(*Steward*)], Randolph McKenzie [(*Cato*)], Félix de Pomés [(*French chamberlain*)], *And a special appearance by* Bette Davis (*Catherine the Great*).

Historical, Drama. [*Print viewed*]. On a large Navy frigate, an officer tells new seamen of the legacy of the man who commanded the first ship to carry the U.S. flag into a European port, John Paul Jones. In 1759, at age twelve, John, from the poor Scottish Paul family, witnesses an English officer disperse townspeople playing the bagpipes, which are viewed as an instrument of war music. The officer also insults the group by calling the kilt, forbidden by law, a "skirt." John, in hiding, hits the officer in the face with an egg. Desiring to be master of a ship, John goes to sea and by age seventeen is skilled in navigation. Seeking further experience, he serves on all manner of ships, including slavers, but decides that trafficking, while lucrative, is not for him. In 1773, John is master of a ship in the West Indies, but when a mutinous crew member dies from a cracked skull after John subdues him in a fight, the governor of Tobago suggests John change his name and leave. Complying, John adds the name "Jones" to his own and goes to Fredericksburg, Virginia to visit his brother William. John learns from William's clerk and accountant, young Peter Wooley, that his brother died from an illness three months earlier. When John finds that two slave boys, Scipio and Cato, whom his brother planned to free, are in danger of being sold, John vows to see that they will be freed. Wooley suggests that John get Patrick Henry, a friend of William's, as his lawyer. At a dance, when a British lieutenant haughtily condemns colonial courage as being no better than the virtue of colonial women, John slugs him. The lieutenant's commanding officer Pearson apologizes for his conduct. John attempts to flirt with socialite Dorothea Danders, whom Henry is courting, but she warns against a "sudden and swift attack." Taken

with Dorothea, John now decides to stay in Virginia and buy a farm, but he does not take well to farm life, and Dorothea's father, who is in the resistance with Henry, rejects John as a suitor because of their illustrious ancestors and John's questionable past. When the war begins, John joins the Continental Navy and, as second-in-command on a battleship in the Bahamas, presents a novel plan to surprise attack British troops in Nassau with Marines. After the Declaration of Independence is signed, John is assigned his first independent command. He learns that Tories have burned and destroyed his farm and carried off his servants to be sold in Jamaica; however, his Scottish friend, Duncan MacBean, with his bagpipes, and Scipio and Cato, playing fife and drums, join Peter in coming to John's ship. Near Newfoundland, John captures eighteen ships, then gives supplies intended for the wintering General Burgoyne to Washington's army. After he learns that he no longer can command a ship because he is ranked low among captains, John goes to Valley Forge to deliver his resignation personally to General Washington. When John complains of favoritism and corruption, Washington, whose army suffers from hunger, mutiny and frostbite, castigates him. John then volunteers to serve in any capacity, and Washington sends him to France, hoping that a French alliance could break a possible blockade of the coasts. Washington suggests he steal the British ship *Ranger* at Portsmouth, New Hampshire, and gather whatever crew he can get. The ship, on its arrival at Brest, is greeted by the first French cannon fire salute ever given to a ship flying the United States flag. In the company of Benjamin Franklin, John is celebrated in Paris as a hero. Aimee de Tellison, secretly the illegitimate daughter of the king, Louis XVI, acts as John's guide to the city. Franklin encourages John to take over a frigate built in Holland and invade the British Isles, hoping that the English people will then protest the war and that insurance rates will rise. After burning the ships and destroying the cannon at the harbor of Whitehaven, John speaks to the citizenry and relates that George III has likewise raided American shores. He vows not to harm any home or person if they make no attempt to fight, and a citizen leader lets them through. After the raid, Lloyd's of London increases its rates on insuring ships, and members of the House of Commons decry the war. John is feted in Versailles, but at a meeting of the Marine Commission, the *Ranger* is ordered home as the result of a false report that John couldn't handle his men, sent by an aristocratic underling whom John had humiliated. After Franklin convinces John to remain without a ship, Aimee, moved by John's determination to build a new naval power, gives his proposal for financing a frigate to the queen, Marie Antoinette. When Franklin points out that the Crown would benefit from fleets John might capture, Louis agrees to the proposal if the ship sails under the American flag and uses as its name *Le Bonhomme Richard*, the French title of Franklin's most popular work, *Poor Richard's Almanac*. During the subsequent battle with Captain Pearson's new ship, *The Serafis*, the traitorous commander of a ship allied with Jones fires on *Le Bonhomme Richard*. As John's men are dying, Pearson asks if he is surrendering, and John calls out, "No sir, I have not yet begun to fight!" Though MacBean, Scipio, and many others on the ship die, Pearson ultimately surrenders because of a fire underneath the magazine. John is awarded a medal and sword at Versailles, but he learns that because Aimee's father is of royal blood, she has been sent away. After the peace treaty is signed, John is told that present finances will not permit him to form an adequate sea force. While waiting for funds to be granted, he goes to Russia in 1790, as Empress Catherine has applied for the loan of his services. At St. Petersburg, Catherine tempts him with dancing girls, then, convinced of his sense of duty, assigns him to the Black Sea, where ships and crews are in bad condition. After John wins the battle against the enemy's ships and fort, Louis bestows on him the rank of chevalier, which could allow him to marry Aimee, but he becomes very ill. He travels to Paris, where Aimee writes his last letter for him in which he dictates the qualities needed in a naval officer: he must be a gentleman, have a liberal education, fine manners, courtesy, sense of personal honor, tact, fairness and justice. The naval commander on the frigate finishes his tale, saying that John's spirit continues to serve and inspire the Navy. *Class conflict. English. John Paul Jones. Naval maneuvers. Officers (Military). Scottish Americans. Ships. United States–History–Revolutionary War, 1776-1783. United States. Navy. African Americans. Ambition. Bagpipes. Black Sea. Brest (France). Catherine II, Empress of Russia, 1729-1796. Clerks. The Declaration of Independence. False accusations. Farmers. Fights. Fires.*

Benjamin Franklin. Fredericksburg (VA). Great Britain. Parliament. Patrick Henry. Lloyd's of London (England). Louis XVI, King of France, 1754-1793. Marie Antoinette, Queen, consort of Louis XVI, King of France, 1755-1793. Mutiny. Newfoundland (Canada). Paris (France). Portsmouth (NH). Scotland. Slaves. Socialites. St. Petersburg (Russia). Valley Forge (PA). Versailles (France). Virginians. George Washington. West Indies.

Note: The opening credits contain the following statements: "This production is dedicated to Fleet Admiral Chester M. Nimitz, U.S.N., able inheritor of the John Paul Jones tradition. To him we owe much gratitude for his unflagging encouragement and inspiration. We thank the Department of Defense and the officers and men of the United States Navy for their cooperation: also the Government of Spain. We thank too, Mr. Victor Oswald, Production Adviser, for his many services." According to Warner Bros. production notes and statements made in articles during the production, Samuel Bronston had the idea to make a film about John Paul Jones in 1946 and found that other studios had registered the title since the late 1930s, but those companies dropped the idea because of expense and the lengthy screen time necessary to adequately cover the subject. According to various news items, in 1939, Warner Bros. bought the rights to Clements Ripley's biographical novel about Jones, entitled *Clear for Action*, which was serialized later in 1939 in *The Saturday Evening Post* before being published as a book in 1940. James Cagney was to star in the Warner production with his brother, William Cagney, producing, and Michael Curtiz directing. In 1946, a *LAT* news item stated that Jack Warner gave Jerry Wald and Delmer Daves the "green light" for the project. In 1949, according to *DV*, the film was going to be produced by Lou Edelman with Cagney starring. In Dec 1955, according to *DV*, Warner assigned the production rights to Admiralty Pictures Corp., a newly-formed company of which Bronston was president. According to *HR*, Warner gave the property to Bronston in return for the rights to make a film about Charles Lindbergh, to which Bronston had a claim. The chairman of the board of Admiralty (a precursor to John Paul Jones Productions, Inc., the film's ultimate producer) was R. Stuyvesant Pierrepont, Jr. In addition to Pierrepont, the company was backed by Laurence and Nelson Rockefeller, the Charles Dana, Jr. family, James Watriss, Pierre DuPont III, Ernest Gross, C. D. Jackson, Frederick Stern and others, representing General Motors, Firestone Tire and Rubber Co., Eastman Kodak, Time, Inc., a Swiss banking firm and other industrial organizations. The backers were able to use assets frozen in Spain, France and Italy, according to news items, because filming was to be done in Europe, primarily in Spain. Bronston claimed that this film opened up an avenue for financing films that had been previously unavailable.

Jesse L. Lasky, Jr. was signed to do the screenplay in Dec 1955. According to *HR* and *DV*, he conducted extensive research with Navy officials in Washington and wrote a screenplay in 1956 based on the Ripley book. Later, when John Farrow was hired to direct, Farrow, who liked Lasky's screenplay, asked him to collaborate on a rewrite, but Lasky was unable to work on it at that time. In Dec 1958, while the film was in post-production, Lasky saw ads listing Farrow as sole writer and heard that Farrow was to get sole screenplay credit. Lasky filed a protest with the Writers Guild of America and ultimately received equal billing with Farrow for the screenplay. Ripley's name, however, does not appear on the film. According to a *DV* news item, in Jul 1956, Bronston signed Ben Hecht to write the script, but no information regarding his actual work on the script has been located. At that time, William Dieterle, who had established a reputation for making biographical films, was assigned to direct. In 1956, Richard Todd and Richard Basehart were both considered for the title role, along with John Miljan for the role of George Washington and John Lupton for that of a French naval officer.

In Mar 1958, prior to shooting, the Hollywood American Federation of Labor Film Council, representing more than 24,000 members of film unions and guilds, threatened to boycott the film if it was to be shot totally abroad, as was then planned. The group also vowed to protest to President Eisenhower and Congress the Navy's cooperation with the producers, who, they claimed, planned to shoot abroad such historical scenes as the signing of the Declaration of Independence, Washington at Valley Forge, and a ball in Fredericksburg, Virginia. They stated, "We are not protesting the filming abroad of scenes legitimately laid abroad. But we do not think the American public will approve the photographing in Spain of the signing of the Declaration of Independence and other historical American events, especially when such foreign production deprives American craftsmen of sorely needed work." According to a *DV* article, the Council previously boycotted the film *Daniel Boone* because it was filmed in Mexico, although its setting was American, and claimed that the boycott was responsible for that film being withdrawn from release. *HR* stated that the group in the previous two years had made numerous motions for a consumer boycott of films made abroad by U.S. firms. *HR* speculated that "the tinder which sparked" this protest was the Warner Bros. publicity campaign for the film, which noted that the production hired 150 Spanish women for the roles of "Virginia belles," planning to have the women wear blonde wigs. The Council also threatened to contact the Daughters of the American Revolution and the American Legion concerning their protest. In Apr 1958, *DV* reported that Bronston had agreed to shoot some scenes in Virginia, Maryland and Pennsylvania in response to the Council's action. Nevertheless, in Oct 1958, after shooting was completed, the Council voted to conduct a nationwide boycott upon the film's release and complained to the Navy concerning the use of Navy equipment and U.S. Marines in scenes depicting a beach landing filmed in Spain, according to *HR*. Bronston stated at the time that although they had planned to use Marines, he hired local extras instead when the Marines were sent to Lebanon unexpectedly. Bronston also said that twenty of the cast and twenty-two of the crew members, along with some of their families, were brought to Europe from the U.S. for the production. He claimed that had the film been made in the U.S., the cost would have been $10,000,000, rather than the actual production cost of $4,000,000.

According to news items and publicity for the film, shooting was done in Spain at the CEA Studio in Madrid, and at outdoor locations in Galicia, Andalusia, Rota, Benidorm and Denia. Sets for the Scottish village, Whitehaven, a wharf in Delaware and a dock site in Portsmouth, NH were constructed in and around Denia. Shooting was also done in Scotland, at the palace at Versailles, Parliament and King James's Palace in London, the Royal Palace in Madrid, where the throne rooms of Catherine the Great and of Louis XVI were shot, the summer palace at Aranjuez, and state buildings in La Granja, Spain. The film was edited, dubbed and scored in London. Fleet Admiral Nimitz was an adviser and consultant. Rear Admiral J. L. Pratt returned to active duty to act as a technical adviser. Director Farrow had been a Navy commander and had directed a number of previous sea adventure films. His cousin, Alan Villiers, a British Navy officer during World War II, who also had been the captain of the *Mayflower II* (a replica of the original ship) on a recent transatlantic voyage, remembered seeing hulks of old sailing ships in Sicily during the war. Villiers oversaw the refurbishment of two of these ships in Ostia, Italy, and was an adviser during filming. Another ship built in Barcelona was also used in the film. According to *NYT*, ships from this film were later used in the 1962 film, *Billy Budd*. John Charles Farrow and Patrick Villiers, two sons of Farrow and his wife, Maureen O'Hara, were in the cast. While production notes state that Bette Davis was paid $25,000 for four days' work, Louella Parsons related that she was to be paid $50,000. An early plan to have Hollywood celebrities who had served in the Navy, Marines or Coast Guard portray seamen of the past did not come to fruition.

In the latter part of 1958, Bronston and Barnett Glassman, who received associate producer credit on the film, traded charges in press and in court regarding ownership of the production company and Glassman's credit for the film. In Dec 1958, *Var* reported that nineteen litigations were pending regarding the company. The two men had worked together on earlier films. No information regarding the outcome of any of the suits has been located. After production, Bronston and Farrow formed a new company to make three films abroad, but this was Farrow's last film.

For its release in France, the film was called *Le capitaine Paul*, which was the title of a novel by Victor Hugo about Jones. *HR*, in its review, criticized the portrayal of Jones, saying that the film's writers used "only those rumors as were flattering to their subject" while ignoring "other sources that were salty with accounts of brawls, love affairs and humor." Jones, according to *HR*, actually killed two mutineers in the West Indies. *HR* went on to state: "The film makes no effort to clear up some of the most fascinating enigmas about Jones. Was he, as he sometimes implied, the illegitimate son of the Earl of Selkirk? Why did he send a shore party for the *Richard* to raid Selkirk Hall and steal the silver? Why did he return this loot with a baffling letter to Lady Selkirk? Why did the imperial Catherine use the notorious Koltzwarthen woman in an attempt to ensnare him in an obvious badger game? More daring dramatists might have sought some answers. At times, the picture is a bit too accurate. Continental Marines wore green uniforms. Jones dressed his in British scarlet to fool the spyglasses of his opponents. Since the picture doesn't explain his crafty reason for this, it occasionally confuses the audience." *Var* was critical of the portrayal of historical characters, stating, "They end, as they begin, as historical personages rather than human beings."

BHCN 29 Jun 1959, p. 5. *Box* 15 Jun 1959, p. 3. *Box* 22 Jun 1959, p. 6. *DV* 2 Mar 1949. *DV* 23 Dec 1955, p. 1, 4. *DV* 22 Feb 1956. *DV* 24 Jul 1956. *DV* 27 Jul 1956. *DV* 31 Mar 1958. *DV* 21 Apr 1958. *DV* 11 Jun 1959, p. 3. *Exb* 17 Jun 1959, pp. 4598-99. *FD* 9 Mar 1939. *FD* 11 Jun 1959, p. 6. *Har* 13 Jun 1959, p. 94. *HR* 7 Mar 1939. *HR* 18 Sep 1939. *HR* 10 Jul 1940. *HR* 19 Dec 1957. *HR* 31 Mar 1958. *HR* 2 May 1958, p. 9. *HR* 22 Aug 1958. *HR* 10 Oct 1958, p. 9. *HR* 3 Nov 1958. *HR* 12 Nov 1958. *HR* 8 Dec 1958. *HR* 11 Jun 1959, p. 3. *LAEx* 4 Mar 1939. *LAEx* 16 Aug 1957. *LAEx* 1 Mar 1959, sec. 5, p. 6, 8. *LAEx* 9 Jul 1959. *LAT* 9 Feb 1939. *LAT* 5 Sep 1946. *LAT* 11 Jan 1956. *LAT* 17 Feb 1956. *LAT* 7 Mar 1956. *LAT* 24 Jul 1956. *LAT* 11 Sep 1956. *LAT* 8 Dec 1956. *LAT* 24 Oct 1957. *LAT* 27 Oct 1958. *LAT* 21 Jun 1959. *LAT* 9 Jul 1959. *MPHPD* 13 Jun 1959, p. 300. *NYT* 7 Sep 1956. *NYT* 17 Aug 1958. *NYT* 17 Jun 1959, p. 39. *SatRev* 20 Jun 1959. *Time* 29 Jun 1959. *Var* 21 Feb 1949. *Var* 8 Oct 1958. *Var* 17 Dec 1958. *Var* 17 Jun 1959, p. 6.

JOHN STEINBECK'S TORTILLA FLAT *see* TORTILLA FLAT

JOHNNY ANGEL (French Americans)

RKO Radio Pictures, Inc. *Dist* RKO Radio Pictures, Inc. **1945**; Los Angeles opening: week of 25 Oct 1945; Prod: 27 Nov 1944—mid-Jan 1945 [©RKO Radio Pictures, Inc.; 24 Aug 1945; LP13631]. Sd (RCA Sound System); b&w. 7,127 ft. 76 or 79 min. PCA cert no. 10627.

Prod William L. Pereira. *Exec prod* Jack J. Gross. *Dir* Edwin L. Marin. *Asst dir* Sam Ruman. *Scr* Steve Fisher. *Adpt* Frank Gruber. *Dir of photog* Harry J. Wild. *Spec eff* Vernon L. Walker. *Mont* Harold Palmer. *Art dir* Albert S. D'Agostino and Jack Okey. *Ed* Les Millbrook. *Set dec* Darrell Silvera and William Stevens. *Gowns* Renie. *Mus dir* C. Bakaleinikoff. *Mus* Leigh Harline. *Rec* John Cass. *Re-rec* James G. Stewart.

Song(s): "Memphis in June," music by Hoagy Carmichael, lyrics by Paul Francis Webster.

Source: Based on the short story "Mr. Angel Comes Aboard" by Charles Gordon Booth in *Liberty* (22 Jan—4 Mar 1944).

Cast: GEORGE RAFT [(*Johnny Angel*)], CLAIRE TREVOR [(*Lilah Gustafson*)], SIGNE HASSO [(*Paulette Gerard*)], Lowell Gilmore [(*Sam Jewell*)], Hoagy Carmichael [(*Celestial O'Brien*)], Marvin

Miller [(*George "Gusty" Gustafson*)], Margaret Wycherly [(*Miss Drumm*)], J. Farrell MacDonald [(*Captain Angel*)], Mack Gray [(*Bartender*)], [Jason Robards, Marc Cramer (*Officers*)], [Bill Williams (*Big sailor*)], [Robert Anderson (*Reporter*)], [Chili Williams (*Redhead*)], [Rusty Farrell (*Blonde*)], [Virginia Belmont (*Cigarette girl*)], [Rosemary La Planche (*Hat check girl*)], [Bryant Washburn, Russell Hopton, Carl Kent (*Reporters*)], [Ann Codee (*Charwoman*)], [Wade Crosby (*Watchman*)], [O. M. Steiger (*French person*)], [Eddie Hart (*Seedy sailor*)], [Johnny Indrisano (*Al*)], [Jack Overman (*Biggsy*)], [Bert Holm (*Isherwood*)], [Eddie Lewis (*Black boy*)], [Aina Constant (*Secretary*)], [Ed Dearing (*First police officer*)], [Louis Mercier (*Cigar maker*)], [Philip Morris (*Second police officer*)], [Theodore Rand (*Headwaiter*)], [James Flavin (*Mate*)], [Don Brodie (*Clerk on Putnam*)], [Kernan Cripps (*First official*)], [Perc Launders (*Second official*)], [John Hamilton (*Ship's captain*)], [Marcel De La Brosse (*French civilian*)], [Al Rhein (*Checker*)], [Joey Ray (*Third mate*)], [Leland Hodgson (*Paul Jewell*)], [Alf Haugan, Charles Sullivan, Jimmy O'Gatty (*Sailors*)], [Ernie Adams (*Leslie*)], [Al Murphy (*Lookout*)], [George Magrill].

Sea, Mystery. [*Print viewed*]. When sea captain Johnny Angel finds the vessel piloted by his father abandoned and adrift in the fog, he senses that his father has perished. After towing the ship to port in New Orleans, Johnny visits his employer, George "Gusty" Gustafson, the owner of the Gustafson Steamship Line. There Johnny questions Gusty, a milquetoast caught between the demands of Miss Drumm, his former nursemaid who now functions as his overbearing secretary, and his wife Lilah, a hard-boiled gold digger. When Gusty pleads ignorance about Captain Angel's fate, Johnny returns to the ship in search of clues and finds a woman's shoe and a French newspaper. After a dockhand informs him that a woman left the ship, Johnny meets Celestial O'Brien, an enigmatic cab driver, who takes him to the French Quarter to search for the missing woman. At a bar there, Johnny meets a French woman and, suspecting that she is the woman from the boat, begins to question her. Becoming frightened by Johnny's aggressiveness, the woman, Paulette Gerard, runs upstairs to her room. Johnny follows her and slips the shoe on her foot. When the bouncer appears at the door and orders Johnny to leave the two men begin to struggle. Paulette grabs her suitcase and flees, leaving behind a page from the phonebook with the address of the Jewell Box Café circled. Following Paulette there, Johnny finds Lilah Gustafson seated at a table with Sam Jewell, the suave owner of the café. After Sam excuses himself, Lilah, who was Johnny's former sweetheart, tries to rekindle their romance. When Johnny shows no interest in her, Lilah leaves, and Johnny then sees Paulette walking down the sidewalk. As she approaches the café, an unseen gunman begins to shoot at her, and Paulette takes refuge in a deserted shop. Johnny runs to her aid, but is knocked unconscious by her assailant. He is revived by the police and Sam, but Paulette is nowhere to be found. Unknown to Johnny, Celestial has taken her to safety at a boardinghouse owned by his cousin Hugh. The next morning, Celestial drives Johnny to see Paulette and after she bursts into tears, Johnny feels sorry for her and takes her for a walk in the country. As they stroll, Paulette confirms that Captain Angel is dead and recounts the following story: Angel's ship is transporting five billion dollars in gold bullion from Casablanca to New Orleans. The bullion, entrusted to Paulette's father, was stolen and her father murdered and framed for the theft. To clear his name, Paulette begs Captain Angel, an old family friend, to grant her passage to America. When the ship reaches the Gulf of Mexico, three crew members, abetted by an unidentified stowaway, mutiny and murder the crew. Hiding in her stateroom, Paulette overhears the muntineers say that Paul Jewell, Sam's brother, plans to transport the gold ashore aboard his boat, *The Dolphin*. Pursued by the mutineers, Paulette pretends to jump overboard and then hides in a lifeboat. As she watches, the men load the gold onto Jewell's boat, and when they speed away, the stowaway shoots his accomplices. As Paulette completes her tale, Johnny realizes that he has fallen in love with her and warns her to stay out of sight until he can uncover the murderer and *The Dolphin*. Johnny's search is cut short, however, when Gusty orders him to ship out. When Gusty refuses to change Johnny's assignment, a sympathetic Miss Drumm arranges for his cargo to be transferred to another ship, thus freeing Johnny to continue his quest. That night, Johnny meets Lilah for dinner and, pretending to be jealous of Sam, questions her about *The Dolphin*. To prove her love to Johnny, Lilah offers him a fortune in gold, but

before she is able to divulge the details, Gusty and Miss Drumm enter the restaurant and Johnny arranges to meet her later that night at a bar. There Lilah assures Johnny that Gusty has gone out of town on business and invites him to her house. At the house, as Lilah demands evidence of Johnny's love, Gusty enters the room and angrily fires him. Meanwhile, two of Sam's thugs locate Paulette and escort her to Sam's office. There Sam questions Paulette about Captain Angel's death, and Celestial, who had witnessed her entering the Jewell Box, informs Johnny of her peril. Back at the club, Paulette blurts out the news of Paul Jewell's demise, and as Sam begins to menace her, Johnny bursts in and comes to the rescue. Meanwhile, at the Gustafson house, the humiliated Gusty begs Lilah to come to bed and, after secreting a dagger in her sleeve, she joins him. The next morning, Lilah appears on the deck of Johnny's ship and offers to drive him to the deserted island that harbors *The Dolphin* and her cargo of gold. Suspecting that Sam is Lilah's accomplice, Johnny anticipates finding him waiting in ambush. Instead, he finds Gusty, staggering from knife wounds inflicted by Lilah, and carrying a gun in his hand. After accusing Lilah of betrayal, Gusty confesses that he was the stowaway, having acquiesced to murder and robbery to satiate his wife's desires. As Gusty trains his gun on Lilah, Miss Drumm enters the room and shoots him. With his father's murder solved, Johnny returns to Paulette, and after he comforts her, the two embrace. *Greed. Infidelity. Murder. Sea captains.* Brothers. Fathers and sons. French. Missing persons, Assumed dead. Mutiny. New Orleans (LA). Nightclub owners. Robbery. Secretaries. Ship owners. Stowaways. Taxicab drivers. Witnesses.

Note: According to a pre-production news item in *HR*, Roy Enright was initially slated to direct this film. A news item in *HR* notes that RKO borrowed Signe Hasso from M-G-M to appear in this film. An item in *LAex* adds that although RKO originally brought Hasso over from Sweden in the early 1940s and had her under contract for two years, she never appeared in a single RKO film under that contract. According to *HR*, Eric Feldary tested for a leading role in this film. This picture marked William Pereira's debut as a producer.

Box 4 Aug 1945. *DV* 1 Aug 1945, p. 3. *FD* 2 Aug 1945, p. 8. *HR* 24 Jul 1944, p. 7. *HR* 27 Nov 1944, p. 3. *HR* 19 Jan 1945, p. 14. *HR* 1 Aug 1945, p. 3. *LAex* 7 Nov 1944. *MPHPD* 6 Jan 1945, p. 2259. *MPHPD* 4 Aug 1945, p. 2577. *NYT* 28 Dec 1945, p. 12. *Var* 1 Aug 1945, p. 16.

THE JOINT IS JUMPIN' (African Americans)
All American News, Inc. *Dist* State Rights. 1949?. Sd; b&w. 6 reels. 64 min.

Prod E. M. Glucksman. *Dir* Josh Binney. *Asst dir* I. Keim. *Orig story* Hal Seeger. *Photog* Ray Soitz. *Art dir* B. Bernard. *Film ed* F. Hafferkamp. *Cost* Lester, Ltd. *Mus arr* G. Lawson. *Sd eng* Lawrence Gianneschi. *Makeup artist* Alvin Kerr.

Song(s): "Casey Jones," music by Eddie Newton, lyrics by T. Lawrence Seibert; "That's My Desire," music and lyrics by Carroll Loveday and Helmy Kresa; "Danny Boy," lyrics by Frederick Edward Weatherly (based on "Londonderry Air," traditional); "Bully-Wully Boogie," music and lyrics by Hadda Brooks; "I've Got the Blues So Bad" ("Dead Man Blues"), music and lyrics by Shifte Henri; "The Animal Fair," music and lyrics by Frederick Johnson, Harry La Forrest and Harley Russo; " 'Taint Yours," music by Una Mae Carlisle, lyrics by Barney Young; "Oh My Deedle Dee Dum Dum Dee," composer undetermined.

Cast: John Mason, Charles Ray, J. Patrick Patterson, Mattie Weaver, Mildred Kirk, Jimmy Short, Barbara Browning, Charles Weaver, Specialties: Una Mae Carlisle, Eddie South, The Jubilaires, Hadda Brooks, Phil Moore Four, Olivette Miller, Slick and Slack, Gertrude Saunders, Rozelle Gayle, John Oscar, Frog Edwards, Doris Ratliff, George Lawson and His Band, The All American Girl Band, [Bob Howard].

African American, Comedy, with songs. [*Viewed print incomplete*]. When Jimmy informs his friend Spider that Mattie and Sally, two women they met the previous summer in Atlantic City, are in town for the evening, Spider is distressed because he and Jimmy are flat broke. Jimmy, however, has a plan. They will invite the girls to the restaurant, eat and drink all they want, and when the check comes, they will pretend to fight over who is going to pay for it. The fight will become so ferocious that the men will be thrown out for disturbing the other guests and the check will be forgotten. When Sally and Mattie arrive at the restaurant, they order enough food to feed an army, and in dismay, Jimmy orders only a "subway cocktail," a glass of water with a dime in it. Spider orders two quarts of 125 proof whiskey so he won't have to remember the events of the

evening. When Dan, the waiter, brings the order, he joins the party for a drink, and the five share a round of amusing toasts. After all the merriment, however, the check arrives, and Spider insists that Jimmy has already paid it. Spider fights with Dan, injuring the waiter so badly that he has to go to the hospital, leaving Spider in charge of the restaurant. Customers begin to demand service and Spider fills their requests, angering one couple when he refuses to grant their requests for hamburgers, insisting they must order cheeseburgers. When they finally agree to the cheeseburgers, Spider informs them that the kitchen is out of cheese. Later that evening, a television salesman brings in an example of his product, and Spider believes that he is watching midgets perform in a box. The salesman switches channels and together they watch a variety of singers and dancers on the different channels. When John Mason, also known as "The Famous Spider Bruce," appears, Spider claims never to have heard of the man. The salesman becomes angry after he learns that Spider is not really the restaurant manager, and when he begins to remove the set, the customers beg him to stay. The band leader then suggests that they put on a show of their own. John Oscar and Frog Edwards perform a comedy act, and Jimmy does the "Rope Dance." Dan eventually returns and threatens to thrash Spider, who then alerts him to the crowd of customers assembled in his restaurant. Spider boasts about all the great acts that performed there that night, neglecting to mention that they were on the television. When Dan hears that "Spider Bruce" John Mason was there in his underwear, he is especially excited and reveals that he himself is none other than John Mason. *African Americans. Impersonation and imposture. Restaurants. Ruses. Singers. Swing music. Comedians. Drunkenness. Fistfights. Jazz music. Salesmen. Tap dancing. Television. Waiters.*

Note: The above credits were taken from an incomplete print of the film. The synopsis was based on the original dialogue continuity contained in the NYSA. Although the screen credits contain a 1948 copyright disclaimer, the film was not registered for copyright. Although exact release date information was not found, the film was submitted to the New York State Censor Board for approval in Aug 1949, according to NYSA records. It was accepted for exhibition "with eliminations" at that time. In addition to the songs listed above, the film contains other compositions that have not been identified. According to NYSA records, the state of New York ordered the elimination of the "Shake Dance" performed by Doris Ratliff on the grounds that it was "indecent." Actor Jimmy Short is credited twice in the onscreen credits; his second credit appears under the heading "Specialties," after Ratliff's credit. The sequences with Una Mae Carlisle, Bob Howard, Phil Moore and Eddie South appear to have been borrowed from the same producer's earlier film *Stars on Parade* (see below).

JOLSON SINGS AGAIN (Jewish Americans)

Sidney Buchman Enterprises, Inc. *Dist* Columbia Pictures Corp. Feb **1950**; Prod: 11 Nov–24 Dec 1948 [©Columbia Pictures Corp.; 20 Sep 1949; LP2520]. Sd (Western Electric Recording); col (Technicolor). 8,584 ft. 95-96 min.

Prod Sidney Buchman. *Dir* Henry Levin. *Asst dir* Milton Feldman. *Wrt* Sidney Buchman. *Dir of photog* William Snyder. *Mont dir* Lawrence W. Butler. *Technicolor color dir* Natalie Kalmus. *Assoc* Francis Cugat. *Art dir* Walter Holscher. *Film ed* William Lyon. *Set dec* William Kiernan. *Gowns* Jean Louis. *Orch* Larry Russell. *Mus score* George Duning. *Mus adv* Saul Chaplin. *Mus dir* Morris Stoloff. *Dial rec* George Cooper. *Mus rec* Philip Faulkner. *Re-rec* Richard Olson. *Makeup* Clay Campbell. *Hair styles* Helen Hunt. *Songs staged by* Audrene Brier.

Song(s): "Is It True What They Say About Dixie?" words and music by Irving Caesar, Sammy Lerner and Gerald Marks; "For Me and My Gal," words by Edgar Leslie and E. Ray Goetz, music by George W. Meyer; "Back in Your Own Backyard," words and music by Al Jolson, Billy Rose and Dave Dreyer; "I Only Have Eyes for You," words by Al Dubin, music by Harry Warren; "Sonny Boy," words and music by Al Jolson, B. G. DeSylva, Lew Brown and Ray Henderson; "Toot, Toot, Tootsie!" words and music by Gus Kahn, Ernie Erdman and Dan Russo; "Rock-a-bye Your Baby with a Dixie Melody," words by Sam M. Lewis and Joe Young; music by Jean Schwartz; "California, Here I Come," words and music by Al Jolson, B. G. DeSylva and Joseph Meyer; "You Made Me Love You," words by Joseph McCarthy, music by James V. Monaco; "Ma Blushin' Rosie (Ma Posie Sweet)," words by Edgar Smith, music by John Stromberg; "My Mammy," words by Sam M. Lewis and Joe Young, music by Walter Donaldson; "Anniversary Song," words by Al Jolson and Saul Chaplin, based on a theme by Iosif Ivanovici; "Learn to Croon," words by Sam Coslow, music by Arthur Johnston.

Cast: Larry Parks [(*Al Jolson*)], Barbara Hale [(*Ellen Clark*)], William Demarest [(*Steve Martin*)], Ludwig Donath [(*Cantor Yoelson*)], Bill Goodwin [(*Tom Baron*)], Myron McCormick [(*Col. Ralph Bryant*)], Tamara Shayne [(*Mama Yoelson*)], [Eric Wilton (*Henry*)], [Robert Emmett Keane (*Charlie*)], [Peter Brocco (*Captain of waiters*)], [Dick Cogan (*Soldier*)], [Martin Garralaga (*Mr. Estrada*)], [Michael Cisney, Ben Erway (*Writers*)], [Helen Mowery (*Script girl*)], [Morris Stoloff (*Orchestra leader*)], [Philip Faulkner, Jr. (*Sound mixer*)], [Virginia Mullen (*Mrs. Bryant*)], [Nelson Leigh (*Theater manager*)], [Margie Stapp (*Nurse*)], [Evelyn Keyes (*Julie Benson*)], [Eleanor Marvak], [Frank McClure], [Jock O'Mahoney], [Betty Hill], [Charles Regan], [Charles Perry], [Richard Gordon], [David Newell], [Joe Gilbert], [David Horsley], [Wanda Perry], [Louise Illington], [Gertrude Astor], [Steve Benton].

Show business, **Biography**. [*Print viewed*]. At the request of his wife, Julie Benson, entertainer Al Jolson had retired from show business, but when she hears him sing at a nightclub, she realizes that he loves singing and can never give it up and leaves him. Al does not understand why she would leave and flies to New York to bring her home, but by the time he arrives, Julie has disappeared. When Al's friend and former manager, Steve Martin, joins him, Al asks Steve to find him a job. Al starts performing again, but when he learns that Julie has gotten a divorce, he leaves the show. Even though the country is at war, Al tries to forget his troubles by traveling, buying racehorses and prizefighters, and dating many different women. When Mrs. Yoelson, Al's mother, becomes ill with pneumonia, it takes so long to find Al that she dies before he can return home. After Al finally comes home, his father gently makes it clear that he disapproves of the way Al is spending his time now that the country is at war. Later, Steve reveals that he has taken a job booking talent to entertain the troops, and Al signs up, although he is afraid that the young soldiers will not remember him. In Alaska, he meets Col. Ralph Bryant, a movie producer in civilian life, who remembers him from his childhood in Duluth, Minnesota. His warm regard gives Al the boost he needs, and his tour is very successful. Eventually, Al collapses with a fever and wakes up in a hospital, attended by attractive nurse Ellen Clark, who comes from Arkansas. Ellen's down-to-earth, Southern manner charms both Al and his father, who is visiting the hospital. On her last night before transferring to an Arkansas hospital, Ellen has dinner with Cantor Yoelson, who tells her how much he appreciates her advice to Al to relax and enjoy life. Although he is not well enough to entertain the troops, Al now performs at hospitals, traveling around the world until he arrives at the Arkansas hospital where Ellen is working. Al and Ellen start to fall in love, even though Ellen is much younger than Al. She encourages him to go back on stage, but urges him to get more out of life than just singing. In California, Al collapses again and undergoes an operation on his lungs. Ellen hurries to his side, and they are married. Because Ellen wants Al to face his past, the couple moves into the Encino house that he shared with Julie. They are happy together, but Ellen realizes that Al wants to go back to work. When she asks Steve to find him some work, however, Steve confesses that no one on Broadway wants to hire Al. After Cantor Yoelson arrives for a long visit, Ellen talks a reluctant Al into singing at a Community Chest benefit. The organizers of the benefit reluctantly include him, but put him last on the program. Although many people have already left by the time Al sings, he is a hit with those who remain. In the audience is Bryant, who is again working as a producer, and he decides to approach Al with an idea for a movie based on his life. The following day, Bryant proposes that Al sing new versions of his famous songs, which would then be dubbed over the actor who would play him in the film. The new recordings are well-received, and young actor Larry Parks is chosen to play Al in the film. At the preview, Al is so nervous that he almost passes out from an overdose of tranquilizers, but the film is a great success. Al's records are again popular, and he is given a radio program. When the next benefit is held, Al is one of the featured performers, and is watched by his proud father and a radiant Ellen. *Entertainers. Al Jolson. Marriage. Benefit performances. Cantors. Jewish. Divorce. Encino (CA). Fathers and sons. Fever. Hospitals. Jews. Lungs–Diseases. Mothers and sons. Motion picture producers. Motion pictures. New York City. Nurses. Pneumonia. Romance–Age difference. Soldiers. Southerners. Vocational obsession. World War II.*

Note: Sidney Buchman's credit reads: "Written and produced by Sidney Buchman." The scene in the nightclub with "Julie Benson" was taken from the

1946 Columbia film *The Jolson Story* (see below). During World War II, Jolson contracted malaria while entertaining the troops in North Africa and eventually lost his left lung. He met his fourth wife, Erle Chennault Galbraith, in a Hot Springs, AR, hospital in 1944. For more information about Al Jolson's life, see entry below for *The Jolson Story*. The *Var* review notes that producer Sidney Buchman, like the fictional "Ralph Bryant," came from Duluth. The reviewer also points out that Jolson was billed last at a Hillcrest Country Club benefit in Los Angeles, not a Community Chest benefit, as depicted in the film. Portions of the following songs are heard in medleys: "I'm Looking Over a Four-Leaf Clover," "Red, Red Robin," "Give My Regards to Broadway," "Chinatown, My Chinatown," "I'm Just Wild About Harry," "Baby Face," "After You're Gone" "Swanee," "Quarter to Nine," "The World Was in Bloom," "Waiting for the Robert E. Lee," "April Showers," "Pretty Baby" and "Carolina in the Morning."

A 25 Oct 1947 *LAEx* news item notes that Larry Parks was not expected to star in the sequel because his testimony before the House Un-American Activities Committee revealed that he had been a member of the Communist party. According to a 20 Sep 1948 *DV* news item, however, the main barrier to Parks performing the role was a suit he brought against Columbia asking to be released from the contract he signed before he made *The Jolson Story*. When the suit was settled, Parks was hired for the part. Before the suit was settled, the filmmakers considered having Jolson play himself in the film, according to a 27 Jul 1948 *DV* news item. Although Columbia originally intended to produce the sequel, a 6 Apr 1948 *DV* news item reported that Jolson had made an agreement with M-G-M to make the sequel at that studio. At that time, Gene Kelly was proposed as the star, and Clark Gable and Greer Garson were considered for other parts. Eventually, the film went into production at Columbia. Tamara Shayne, Ludwig Donath and William Demarest reprised the roles they played in *The Jolson Story*. As in the earlier film, Al Jolson's voice is heard on the soundtrack singing the songs.

Lux Radio Theatre presented a version of this story, starring Al Jolson, Barbara Hale and William Demarest, on 22 May 1949. William Snyder received an Academy Award nomination for Best Color Cinematography for his work on the film, while Sidney Buchman was nominated for Best Story and Screenplay, and Morris Stoloff and George Duning were nominated for Best Musical Score.

Box 20 Aug 1949. *DV* 11 Dec 1947. *DV* 6 Apr 1948. *DV* 27 Jul 1948. *DV* 20 Sep 1948. *DV* 12 Aug 1949, p. 3, 6. *FD* 12 Aug 1949, p. 5. *HR* 12 Aug 1949, p. 3. *LAEx* 25 Oct 1947. *MPHPD* 13 Aug 1949, p. 4713. *NYT* 18 Aug 1949, p. 16. *Var* 17 Aug 1949, p. 8.

THE JOLSON STORY (Jewish Americans)

Columbia Pictures Corp. *Dist* Columbia Pictures Corp. Jan **1947**; World premiere in New York: 10 Oct 1946; Prod: 24 Oct 1945—15 Mar 1946 (©Columbia Pictures Corp.; 12 Sep 1946; LP732]. Sd (Western Electric Recording); col (Technicolor). 11,648 ft. 128 min. PCA cert no. 11154.

Prod Sidney Skolsky. *Assoc prod* Gordon S. Griffith. *Dir* Alfred E. Green. *Prod numbers dir by* Joseph H. Lewis. *Asst dir* Wilbur McGaugh. [*Dial dir* Roy Hamilton]. *Scr* Stephen Longstreet. *Adpt* Harry Chandlee and Andrew Solt. *Dir of photog* Joseph Walker. [*2d cam* Victor Scheurich]. *Mont dir* Lawrence W. Butler. [*Matte paintings cam* Don Glouner]. *Technicolor col dir* Natalie Kalmus. *Assoc* Morgan Padelford. *Art dir* Stephen Goossón and Walter Holscher. *Film ed* William Lyon. *Gowns* Jean Louis. *Mus dir* M. W. Stoloff. *Vocal arr* Saul Chaplin. *Orch arr* Martin Fried. *Dances staged by* Jack Cole. *Sd rec* Hugh McDowell. *Re-rec* Richard Olson. *Mus rec* Edwin Wetzel. *Makeup* Clay Campbell. *Hairstyles* Helen Hunt. [*Tech adv* Robert Gordon]. [*Research dir* Thelma Hoover]. [*Voice double for Larry Parks* Al Jolson].

Song(s): "Let Me Sing and I'm Happy," music and lyrics by Irving Berlin; "Kol Nidre," traditional Jewish hymn; "On the Banks of the Wabash," music and lyrics by Paul Dresser; "Ave Maria," music by Franz Schubert, lyrics, traditional; "When You Were Sweet Sixteen," music and lyrics by James Thornton; "After the Ball," music and lyrics by Charles K. Harris; "By the Light of the Silvery Moon," music by Gus Edwards, lyrics by Edward Madden; "Bluebell," music by Theodore M. Morse, lyrics by Edward Madden and Dolly Morse; "Ma Blushin' Rosie (Ma Posie Sweet)," music by John Stromberg, lyrics by Edgar Smith; "I Want a Girl Just Like the Girl Who Married Dear Old Dad," music and lyrics by William Dillon and Harry Von Tilzer; "My Mammy," music by Walter Donaldson, lyrics by Sam M. Lewis and Joe Young; "I'm Sittin' on Top of the World," music by Ray Henderson, lyrics by Sam Lewis and Joe Young; "You Made Me Love You," music by James V. Monaco, lyrics by Joseph McCarthy; "Swanee," music by George Gershwin, lyrics by Irving Caesar; "Toot, Toot, Tootsie!," music and lyrics by Gus Kahn, Ernie Erdman and Dan Russo; "The Spaniard Who Blighted My Life," music and lyrics by Billy Merson; "April Showers," music by Louis Silvers, lyrics by B. G. DeSylva; "California, Here I Come," music and lyrics by B. G. DeSylva, Al Jolson and Joseph Meyer; "Liza," music by George Gershwin, lyrics by Ira Gershwin; "There's a Rainbow 'Round My Shoulder," music and lyrics by Al Jolson, Billy Rose and Dave Dreyer; "She's a Latin from

Manhattan" and "About a Quarter to Nine," music by Harry Warren, lyrics by Al Dubin; "Anniversary Song," music by J. Ivanovici, lyrics by Al Jolson and Saul Chaplin; "Waiting for the Robert E. Lee," music by Lewis F. Muir, lyrics by L. Wolfe Gilbert; "Rock-a-bye Your Baby With a Dixie Melody," music by Jean Schwartz, lyrics by Sam M. Lewis and Joe Young.

Cast: Larry Parks [(*Al Jolson [assumed name of Asa Yoelson]*)], Evelyn Keyes [(*Julie Benson*)], William Demarest [(*Steve Martin*)], Bill Goodwin [(*Tom Baron*)], Ludwig Donath [(*Cantor Yoelson*)], Scotty Beckett [(*Al Jolson, as a boy*)], Tamara Shayne [(*Mrs. Yoelson*)], Jo-Carroll Dennison [(*Ann Murray*)], John Alexander [(*Lew Dockstader*)], Ernest Cossart [(*Father McGee*)], Mitchell "Boychoir", [William Forrest (*Dick Glenn*)], [Ann Todd (*Ann Murray, as a girl*)], [Edwin Maxwell (*Oscar Hammerstein*)], [Emmett Vogan (*Jonsey*)], [Coulter Irwin (*Young priest*)], [Jimmy Lloyd (*Roy Anderson*)], [Adele Roberts (*Ingenue*)], [Bob Stevens (*Henry*)], [Dan Stowell (*Ticket seller*)], [Charles Marsh (*Man at theater*)], [Harry Shannon (*Policeman*)], [John Tyrrell (*Man in line*)], [Joseph Palma (*Brakeman*)], [Ted Stanhope (*Electrician*)], [P. J. Kelly (*Doorman*)], [Buddy Gorman (*Call boy*)], [Charles Jordan, Eddie Featherstone (*Assistant stage managers*)], [Eddie Kane (*Ziegfield*)], [Pierre Watkin (*Architect*)], [Eugene Borden (*Headwaiter*)], [Eddie Rio (*Master of ceremonies*)], [Will Wright (*Sourpuss*)], [Arthur Loft (*Stage manager*)], [Ed Keane (*Director*)], [Bill Brandt (*Orchestra leader*)], [Pat Lane (*Cameraman*)], [Ralph Linn (*Recorder*)], [Mike Lally (*Lab manager*)], [George Magrill (*Stage gaffer*)], [Helen O'Hara (*Dancer and actress*)], [Jessie Arnold (*Wardrobe woman*)], [Donna Dax (*Publicist*)], [Louis Traeger (*Boy*)], [Fred Sears (*Cutter*)], [Fred Howard], [Lillian Bond].

Show business, Biography, Musical. [*Print viewed*]. In Washington, D.C., at the turn of the century, twelve-year-old Asa Yoelson, the son of Cantor Yoelson, dreams of a life in show business. While attending a burlesque show with his friend, Ann Murray, Asa sings aloud with the music and catches the attention of comedian Steve Martin. Later, Steve visits the Yoelsons and offers Asa a part in his burlesque act, but Asa's father refuses to allow his son to sing outside of the synagogue. Determined to sing with Steve, Asa runs away from home and boards a train for Baltimore, where the burlesque troupe is performing its next show. No sooner does Asa arrive in Baltimore than he is picked up as a runaway and placed in St. Mary's Home for Boys. There Asa joins the church choir until Father McGee, the head of St. Mary's, reunites him with his parents. With help from Steve, Asa manages to persuade his parents to allow him to join him on tour, and Asa is cast as a "stooge" who sings from his seat in the audience. When Asa's adolescent voice starts to change during a performance, he begins to whistle instead and is such a hit that Steve decides to alter the act and have Asa work with him onstage. As the years pass and the act continues on the road, Asa decides to change his name to "Al Jolson." His parents have accepted their son's desire to remain in show business and follow his career, but Al's visits home are infrequent. When Al is a grown man, he realizes that his singing voice is better than ever. He begs Steve to let him sing onstage, but Steve wants to wait until they have time to re-work the act. The next day, when Al realizes that one of his fellow performers, Tom Baron, is too drunk to perform his blackface routine, he takes Tom's place. As soon as the stage manager realizes that Al is taking over Tom's routine, he orders the curtains closed, but Al goes through the curtains and jokingly tells the audience "You ain't heard nothin' yet." The performance, which is a hit with the audience, is seen by minstral-show producer Lew Dockstader, who later offers Al a part in his show. Out of loyalty to Steve, Al is reluctant to accept, but Steve encourages him to move on. Al joins the minstrel troupe, but soon tires of Dockstader's traditional songs. While in New Orleans, Al hears jazz music for the first time and tries to convince Dockstader to include some new arrangements in the show. Dockstader is uninterested in jazz and the two men agree that Al should move on. While visiting his family in Washington, Al receives a telephone call from Tom, now a director, who offers him a spot at the Winter Garden in New York City. Al accepts the job and is an instant hit. He keeps Tom's show running in New York for two years, and hires Steve as his manager. Al enjoys his success and works constantly, disregarding the pleas of his parents and Steve, refuses to take a vacation or even a day off. In 1927, at the peak of his career, Al announces that he is leaving the stage to appear in the first sound motion picture. During his

farewell show, Al meets and falls instantly in love with dancer Julie Benson. Later that night, Julie rejects Al's marriage proposal, but keeps in touch with him through long-distance telephone calls. When Julie opens on Broadway in the play *Liza*, Al surprises her by attending the performance and sings to her from the audience. After completing his role in the film *The Jazz Singer*, Al returns to New York, where the film's premiere creates a sensation. He soon marries Julie, promising that he will stop working so hard and build her a home in the country. More films, both for Al and for Julie, constantly delay their plans, however. Despite her own success, Julie continues to long for a life in the country and threatens to leave Al if he does not quit show business. Al eventually grants Julie's wish and retires from the limelight to a country home near Los Angeles, where he, Julie and Steve live a quiet life. Not wanting to lose Julie, Al refuses to sing for over two years. Although she is glad that Al has retired, she worries that he is not happy. When Mr. and Mrs. Yoelson come for a visit on their anniversary, Al reluctantly sings for them, then agrees to go to a nightclub to celebrate. When asked to come onstage, Al at first refuses, then relents, and after his first song, recites his popular phrase, "You ain't heard nothin' yet," and continues to sing. Watching Al's happiness while performing, Julie tells Steve that she was wrong to ask him to give up his career and walks out of the nightclub, leaving her husband to the audiences he loves. *Actors and actresses. Fathers and sons. Al Jolson. Singers. Theatrical troupes. Burlesque. Cantors, Jewish. Childhood sweethearts. Choirs (Music). Dancers. Oscar Hammerstein. Hollywood (CA). Jews. Marriage. Motion pictures–History. New York City–Broadway. Nightclubs. Police. Priests. Proposals (Marital). Racial impersonation. Retirement. Romance. Runaways. Self-sacrifice. Theatrical managers. Washington (D.C.). Wedding anniversaries.*

Note: Working titles for this film were *The Life of Al Jolson, The Al Jolson Story* and *The Story of Al Jolson*. Al Jolson's rendition of "Let Me Sing and I'm Happy" is an early example of a song being performed over the opening credits. In addition to the songs listed above, excerpts from many well-known numbers are also heard in the film, including "When the Red, Red Robin Comes Bob, Bob, Bobbin' Along," "We're in the Money" and "Forty-Second Street." Jolson was born Asa Yoelson in Russia on 26 May 1886. Around 1895, his parents emigrated to Washington, D.C., where his father worked as a cantor. As depicted in the film, Jolson, who sang with his father during services, left home as a young man to start a career in show business. He first appeared with a circus, then was hired as a burlesque and vaudeville singer. As a minstrel show singer, he appeared in blackface, a theatrical convention with which he became strongly associated. In 1911, he was cast in his first important role in the Broadway show *La Belle Paree*. In 1923, film director D. W. Griffith hired him for *Mammy's Boy*, but the picture was never made. Jolson sang three songs in Warner Bros.' 1926 experimental sound short *Al Jolson in A Plantation Act sings "April Showers" (and other songs)*, and was subsequently cast in the studio's ground-breaking 1927 "talkie" *The Jazz Singer* (see entry above). After starring in many successful film musicals during the 1930s, Jolson's popularity began to wane. His career was somewhat revived when he went on tour entertaining troops during World War II. Jolson died from a heart attack on 23 Oct 1950, shortly after returning from a tour entertaining troops in Korea. He was awarded the Congressional Medal of Merit posthumously in recognition of his many goodwill tours.

In Aug 1945, according to pre-production news items in *HR*, Columbia borrowed Bruce Humberstone from Twentieth Century-Fox to direct *The Jolson Story*. Subsequent *HR* news items indicate that Humberstone returned to his home studio two months later, after encountering too many script delays. Columbia replaced Humberstone with Alfred E. Green, who was assigned to the film two days prior to the picture's Oct 24 start date. The extent of Humberstone's contribution to the final film has not been determined.

In a 1975 *LAHEx* interview, Humberstone claimed that Columbia production executive Harry Cohn, while explaining the reasons for the script delay, indicated that the film had no real producer assigned to it. According to Humberstone's recollection of Cohn's statements, producer Sidney Skolsky, a former assistant at Warner Bros., contributed nothing more to the film than the basic idea, which was offered in exchange for a screen credit. When Humberstone suggested that Cohn hire producer Sidney Buchman to oversee the production, Cohn told him that the decision required the approval of Jolson, who held a fifty percent controlling interest in picture. According to Humberstone, both Jolson and Cohn agreed to give up ten percent of their shares and offered them to Buchman to produce the film. The interview also indicates that Jolson gave a ten percent share to Humberstone for his "spunk" in suggesting the plan. Buchman was reportedly unaware that Humberstone had arranged his hiring. One week after Buchman took over the production, Humberstone quit, complaining that he could not work with a script that was being written only a few pages each day, and with a producer who was always on the set. Although Buchman did not receive screen credit for his contribution to *The Jolson Story*, he went on to produce the film's sequel, *Jolson Sings Again* (see above entry).

According to modern sources, Warner Bros. head Jack Warner, who initially rejected Skolsky's proposal to film Jolson's story, tried to beat Columbia to it when he learned that Cohn was planning a Jolson film. Warner reportedly

offered Jolson $200,000 for the rights to film his story and engaged the services of director Michael Curtiz before Jolson ended up signing a contract with Cohn. The modern source also claims that Cohn considered a number of actors to play the part of Jolson before he eventually settled on Parks. After offering the role to James Cagney, who refused the part, Cohn offered the role to Danny Thomas. Although Thomas reportedly refused the role when Cohn asked him to undergo an operation to reduce the size of his nose, he later played Jolson's role in Warner Bros.' 1953 remake of *The Jazz Singer* (see above entry). Other actors considered for the title role were José Ferrer and Richard Conte, according to modern sources.

According to a Sep 1946 *Cue* article, Columbia made repeated recordings of Jolson singing his most popular songs, in order to get the best possible versions. Parks then matched as exactly as possible Jolson's mouth, head and body movements. According to the article, this method created the most convincing dubbing on screen to date. One of the film's songs, "Anniversary Song," was popularized by the film and was named the number one song on *Billboard* magazine's 1947 Honor Roll of Hits. *Cue* also noted that Parks prepared for his role by spending three months with Jolson, listening to his recordings and watching his films. Jolson himself appears in the film in a long shot, during the "Swanee" number. Modern sources also credit Rudy Wissler as Scotty Beckett's vocal double.

Jolson's third wife, singer, actress and dancer Ruby Keeler, was portrayed in the film as the character "Julie Benson." According to an Oct 1946 article in *Time* magazine, Keeler was paid $25,000 for her cooperation on the production, but refused to allow her name to be used in the film. Actor William Demarest, who plays "Steve Martin" in the film, played a somewhat similar character in the 1927 film *The Jazz Singer*. [According to a modern source, author Samson Raphaelson was inspired to write his short story "A Day of Atonement," on which *The Jazz Singer* is based, after seeing Jolson perform "Where the Black-Eyed Susans Grow."] Columbia borrowed Demarest from from Paramount for this production. Dialogue director Robert Gordon also appeared in *The Jazz Singer*. Contemporary sources note that the final cost of the film was $2,500,000.

In Aug 1946, the film had a preview screening in Santa Barbara, CA. According to the *Cue* article, Jolson, who attended the preview, overheard an audience member comment that it was "too bad that Jolson isn't alive to see this picture." The film was a box office hit, especially in New York, where it was booked as a special engagement. Prior to its Jan 1947 general release, the picture was booked on a "day and date" basis in various cities around the country.

In Mar 1947, a *HR* news item reported that the Shubert family had filed a $500,000 lawsuit against Columbia, charging the studio with using the Shubert name and filming shots of the Shubert-owned Winter Garden Theatre without permission. The suit was heard in New York's Supreme Court, where lawyers representing Columbia claimed that the use of the Winter Garden was only incidental in the telling of Jolson's story. The suit was dismissed in Jun 1947, when the judge presiding over the case ruled that the Shuberts did not have claim to any property rights in the name of their theater. The ruling was appealed by the Shuberts in 1948, but the case was again dismissed.

In Feb 1948, according to a *HR* article, Larry Parks filed suit against Columbia, claiming that in 1945, he was pressured by Cohn into signing an "unsatisfactory" contract. Parks further alleged that Cohn gestured with a riding crop while demanding that the actor choose between a stint in Columbia's "B" pictures, or a weekly salary of eight hundred dollars. According to the article, the attorney representing Columbia responded to the accusations by denying any duress, and stating that Parks had received a $10,000 bonus for his work on *The Jolson Story*. Parks claimed that the bonus amount was to have been $25,000, and that it was cut to $10,000 when he refused to extend his contract for one more year. On 3 Mar 1948, according to *HR*, the judge presiding over Parks's case ruled that even though Parks had been subjected to undue duress, he had waited too long before seeking reparations, and was, therefore, still subject to the terms of his contract. In May 1948, Parks made a public announcement in the press stating that he would immediately cease to honor the contract he made with Columbia in 1945. The day after Parks made his announcement, the studio released a statement in which it condemned the actor's "habit of trying his case in the newspapers," and warned that Columbia would use every legal means in its power to prevent Parks from abrogating his contract. By Sep 1948, according to *HR*, Parks and Columbia had settled their differences and announced their collaboration on a planned sequel to *The Jolson Story*, which was eventually released in 1950 under the title *Jolson Sings Again*.

The Jolson Story received Academy Awards for Best Music and Best Sound Recording, and was nominated for awards in the categories of Best Actor (Larry Parks), Best Supporting Actor (William Demarest), Best Cinematography and Best Film Editing. Parks reprised his Jolson role for the sequel and also portrayed the singer in a *Lux Radio Theatre* dramatization of *The Jolson Story*, which aired on 16 Feb 1948. *The Jolson Story*, which had grossed $8,000,000 by Aug 1953, was re-released in 1954 in widescreen format with stereophonic sound. According to a May 1954 *Var* news item, four minutes were cut from the original film for the re-release version. On 14 Aug 1969, a re-issued version of the film in 70mm format began a roadshow engagement in London. The 70mm re-issue had its American premiere in Aug 1975.

Box 28 Sep 1946. *DV* 16 Sep 1946, p. 3. *FD* 16 Sep 1946, p. 6. *HR* 17 Jan 1945, p. 4. *HR* 27 Aug 1945, p. 1. *HR* 30 Aug 1945, p. 3. *HR* 2 Oct 1945, p. 3. *HR* 3 Oct 1945, p. 5. *HR* 6 Oct 1945, p. 5. *HR* 19 Oct 1945, p. 2. *HR* 22 Oct 1945, p. 1. *HR* 24 Oct 1945, p. 2. *HR* 6 Nov 1945, p. 9. *HR* 18 Jan 1946, p. 12. *HR* 30 Jan 1946, p. 9. *HR* 16 Sep 1946, p. 3, 12. *HR* 14 Oct 1946, p. 10. *HR* 20 Feb 1947, p. 4. *HR* 25 Mar 1947, p. 2. *HR* 9 Jun 1947, p. 1. *HR* 25 Feb 1948, p. 8. *HR* 27 Feb 1948, p. 2. *HR* 3 Mar 1948, p. 12. *HR* 4 Mar 1948, p. 1. *HR* 10 May 1948, p. 1. *HR* 11 May 1948, p. 3. *HR* 4 Jun 1948, p. 9. *HR* 21 Sep 1948, p. 10.

MPH 15 Mar 1947. *MPHPD* 9 Mar 1946, p. 2883. *MPHPD* 21 Sep 1946, p. 3209. *Newsweek* 17 Mar 1947. *NYT* 11 Oct 1946, p. 28. *Var* 18 Sep 1946, p. 16. *Var* 19 Aug 1953. *Var* 21 Apr 1954.

JOSEPH IN THE LAND OF EGYPT (Yiddish language)

Guaranteed Pictures Co. *Dist* Guaranteed Pictures Co. **1932**; Prod: Mar 1932; synchronization at the Atlas Soundfilm Recording Studios in New York completed Apr 1932 [©Guaranteed Pictures Co., Inc.; 1 Jun 1932; LP3066]. Sd; b&w. 8 reels, 6,588 ft. 80 min. Yiddish language with English subtitles.

Pres Mortimer D. Sikawitt and Samuel Goldstein. *Dir* George Roland. *Dial* Michael Goldberg. *Ed* Jean Roland. *Mus arr* I. J. Hochman. *Rec eng* Lyman J. Wiggin.

Source: Based on the Biblical drama "Joseph and His Brethren."

Cast: Ben Adler (*Jacob*), Joseph Greenberg (*Joseph*), Sigmund Zuckerberg, Herman Serotsky, Wolf Goldfaden, Joseph Schwartzberg, Wolf Barzell, Ida Adler, Gertrude Levitan, Sonya Adler.

Yiddish, **Historical**, **Drama**. [*Not viewed*]. In the land of Canaan, Jacob's twelfth son Benjamin is born when Jacob is an old man, and during the birth, Jacob's wife Rachel dies. Leah, Jacob's first wife, finishes making a coat of many colors for Joseph, Jacob's other son by Rachel, and Jacob prophesies that Joseph will be famous and powerful someday. Joseph's brothers are jealous of him, and their anger is increased when Jacob says that Joseph will be the superintendent over them. Joseph tries to tell his brothers two dreams he has had, which he interprets to mean that his whole family will bow before him in the future, but his brothers don't want to listen. After his brothers leave Canaan, Joseph goes in search of them. They plot to kill Joseph, until Reuben, one of the brothers, pleads that they should not shed blood, but only cast Joseph into a pit. The brothers carry out Reuben's plan, but when they see Ishmaelites on their way to Egypt, Simeon convinces his brothers to sell Joseph as a slave. Afterward, they slay a goat and smear its blood on Joseph's coat, which they bring back to Jacob, who deduces that a wild animal devoured him. Meanwhile, a merchant sells Joseph to Lord Potiphar, who soon makes Joseph overseer of his household. Potiphar's wife tries to seduce Joseph, but when he refuses her, she claims that he attacked her and made violent love to her. Joseph is put into prison, where he impresses Pharoah's butler with his ability to interpret dreams that predict the future. When Pharoah's astrologers fail to satisfy him with their interpretations of his dreams, the butler remembers Joseph, and Joseph interprets the dreams as a prophesy that Egypt will face seven years of rich harvests, followed by seven years of famine. He advises Pharoah to select a wise man to store food for the famine years, and Pharoah chooses Joseph, proclaiming him ruler of all save himself. During the famine, Jacob sends all his sons except Benjamin to Egypt to buy food. The ten sons are brought to Joseph as spies, and Joseph, whom they do not recognize, has them imprisoned. He secretly puts money in their sacks of grain, then frees all except Simeon and tells them he will hold Simeon prisoner until they bring their youngest brother. Jacob refuses to let Benjamin return with his brothers, but when they run out of food, he relents. Joseph weeps when he sees Benjamin. Joseph has his cup hidden in Benjamin's sack of grain and instructs his men to bring back the stolen cup. Joseph then makes Benjamin his slave and tells the other brothers they can go, but Reuben says that the loss of Benjamin will kill their father, whereupon Joseph reveals his identity. As they all bow, Joseph says that his dreams have come true. Joseph sends his brothers to bring Jacob, and on the way, God tells Jacob that he will make of him a great nation. Joseph greets his father and presents him to Pharoah, who gives Jacob the land of Goshen, the best in Egypt, for his people. Jacob, however, wants to be buried in Canaan, where his grandfather and grandmother, Abraham and Sarah, lie buried. Before he returns there, Jacob predicts that after his death, his people will become slaves in Egypt and that later, they will spread over the earth among all the peoples. At a future date, a messiah will deliver them into their own nation, where they will become a mighty and honored nation. He urges Joseph to remember the value of peace, and Joseph says a blessing in Hebrew. Biblical characters. Brothers. Dreams. Egypt– History. Fathers and sons. Jews–History. Prophets. Coats. Deception. False arrests. Famines. Jealousy. Merchants. Nobility. Prisons. Revelation (Theology, inspiration). Seduction. Slavery.

Note: The Yiddish title of this film is *Yoysef in Mitsraim*. The working title was *Joseph and His Brethren*. In an oral history conducted by the Hebrew University Oral History Department on 16 Apr 1979, Joseph Green, who is credited in reviews as Joseph Greenberg, relates that Guaranteed Pictures

bought an old Italian film, dubbed it into Yiddish and produced this film, which was a big success in the United States and in Poland. Green states that with the money he made from this film, he was able to finance *Yiddle with His Fiddle*, which he later produced in Poland (see above). In addition to dubbing the silent film, director George Roland filmed some new scenes, and a musical score was added. While modern sources have identified the silent film as the 1914 Italian production *Joseph in Egypt*, the existence of which has not been confirmed, it is more likely that the silent film to which Green refers was really the 1914 U.S. production *Joseph in the land of Egypt*, which was produced by Thanhouser Film Corp., directed by Eugene Moore and starred James Cruze and Marguerite Snow (see *AFI Catalog of Feature Films, 1911-20*; F1.2296). According to a Mar 1932 news item, this film was planned to be released during Passover in the New York area. An ad for the film claims that 5,000 people were in the cast.

FD 7 Mar 1932, p. 2. *FD* 20 Mar 1932, p. 5. *FD* 10 Apr 1932, p. 4. *FD* 22 May 1932, p. 10.

JOSETTE (French Americans)

Twentieth Century-Fox Film Corp.; Darryl F. Zanuck in charge of production. *Dist* Twentieth Century-Fox Film Corp. 3 Jun **1938**; Prod: 20 Dec 1937—mid-Jan 1938; early Apr—mid-Apr 1938 [©Twentieth Century-Fox Film Corp.; 3 Jun 1938; LP8340]. Sd (RCA High Fidelity Recording); b&w. 8 reels, 6,624 ft. 70 or 74 min. PCA cert no. 3995.

Assoc prod Gene Markey. *Dir* Allan Dwan. [*Asst dir* William Forsyth]. *Scr* James Edward Grant. *Photog* John Mescall. *Art dir* Bernard Herzbrun and David Hall. *Film ed* Robert Simpson. *Set dec* Thomas Little. *Cost* Royer. *Mus dir* David Buttolph. [*Vocal supv* Jule Styne]. *Sd* W. D. Flick and Roger Heman.

Song(s): "May I Drop a Petal in Your Glass of Wine?" "In Any Language It's Love," and "Where in the World," music and lyrics by Mack Gordon and Harry Revel.

Source: Based on the play *Jo and Josette* by Paul Frank and Georg Fraser (production undetermined), which was based on a short story by Ladislaus Vadnai (publication undetermined).

Cast: DON AMECHE (*David Brossard, Jr.*), SIMONE SIMON (*Renee Le Blanc*), ROBERT YOUNG (*Pierre Brossard*), Joan Davis (*May Morris*), Bert Lahr (*Barney Barnaby*), Paul Hurst (*A. Adolphus Heyman*), William Collier, Sr. (*David Brossard, Sr.*), Tala Birell (*Mlle. Josette*), Lynn Bari (*Mrs. [Elaine] Dupree*), William Demarest (*Bill*), Ruth Gillette (*Belle*), Armand Kaliz (*Thomas*), Maurice Cass (*Furrier*), [Raymond Turner (*Mose*)], [George H. Reed (*Butler*)], [Billy Baxter (*Messenger boy*)], [Paul McVey (*Hotel manager*)], [Fred Kelsey (*Hotel detective*)], [Lillian Porter (*Cigarette girl*)], [Alice Armand (*Toinette*)], [Antonio Filauri (*Waiter*)], [James C. Morton (*Bartender*)], [Edward Keane (*Doorman*)], [Hank Mann (*Janitor*)], [Robert Kellard (*Reporter*)], [Robert Lowery, Lon Chaney, Jr. (*Boatmen*)], [Slim Martin (*Orchestra leader*)], [Ruth Peterson (*Switchboard operator*)], [June Gale (*Girl in cafe*)], [Jayne Regan], [Brooks Benedict], [John Donaldson], [Harry Denny], [Harold Foshay].

Romantic comedy, **with songs**. [*Print viewed*]. In New Orleans, strait-laced, business-oriented David Brossard, Jr. and his playboy brother Pierre own a cannery and fishing fleet, which they inherited from their father. Brossard, Sr., who, like Pierre, is quite the ladies' man, constantly gets involved with women who mistakenly think he still owns the business, while in reality he receives an allowance from his sons. After the sons get a telegram from their father vacationing in Havana, informing them that he will soon wed French cabaret singer Josette, they trick their father, who has returned to New Orleans with Josette, into taking a business trip to New York to get him out of the way so that they can buy off Josette. Unknown to Pierre and David, Josette has left for New York along with their father. At the Silver Moon Café, where Josette is supposed to perform, wardrobe mistress Renee Le Blanc, who wants to be a singing star, impersonates the chanteuse. After her first performance, the owner, Barney Barnaby, who thinks she is better than Josette, convinces her to continue the impersonation, but she is recognized as a phony by a drunken man who saw the real Josette perform in Havana. Barnaby, however, manages to keep the man well supplied with liquor to stop him from calling the police. Thinking that Renee is Josette, Pierre decides to romance her in order to keep her away from his father. After Pierre gets Renee to go sailing with him, David, who is suspicious of his brother's scheme, stows away on the boat, and then Renee, attracted to David, hides in his car after the trip. Despite getting the car stuck in the mud and becoming soaked in a rainstorm, David and Renee have a wonderful time together and they kiss as they part when they return to the club. Renee wants to quit the impersonation, so as not to deceive David, but Barnaby convinces her to continue for just one

more night to avoid having the club taken over by a bank. Meanwhile, the elder Brossard, who was deserted by Josette when she learned his true financial status, returns home feeling foolish and tells David that Josette was only after his money. David gets drunk and rages at Renee, and she leaves with the sweet-talking Pierre. When the real Josette returns to the Silver Moon and discovers that someone has been impersonating her, a reporter overhears her and calls in the story to his newspaper. By the time David discovers the truth, Renee has left with Pierre on his yacht. Wanting to apologize and tell Renee that he loves her, David follows in a boat with Renee's friend, May Morris. On the yacht, Pierre chases Renee until she locks herself in a storage cabin. Pierre then tricks her into coming out, but as David and May arrive, Renee attacks Pierre and swims for shore. David dives in after her. Later, at the café, Renee sings as herself. David sits with Pierre, whose leg is in a cast, and after Renee sings "I love you" to David, Pierre trips him as he attempts to go to Renee. *Brothers. Fathers and sons. Gold diggers. Impersonation and imposture. Mistaken identity. New Orleans (LA). Romance. Singers. Cafés. Canneries. Drunkenness. New York City. Nightclub owners. Reporters. Restaurateurs. Seduction. Yachts and yachting.*

Note: The working title of this film was *Jo and Josette.* Sam Hellman is listed as a contributing writer in a SAB Notice of Tentative Credits, but his name is missing from a subsequent listing entitled "Confirmation that contributing writers have agreed on screen credits." Hellman's contribution, if any, has not been determined. According to a *HR* news item, Sidney Lanfield was originally scheduled to direct, but he was hospitalized and replaced by Allan Dwan a week before shooting began. *HR* news items also report that production was halted in Jan 1938 with eight days remaining and did not resume until Apr because of Simone Simon's long illness. According to a *HR* news item, Robert Young was borrowed from M-G-M. Modern sources list Zeffie Tilbury and Harry Holman as additional cast members.

Box 4 Jun 1938. *DV* 11 Jun 1938, p. 3. *FD* 11 Jun 1938, p. 3. *HR* 28 Oct 1937, p. 2. *HR* 14 Dec 1937, p. 8. *HR* 17 Dec 1937, p. 1. *HR* 20 Dec 1937, p. 15. *HR* 31 Dec 1937, sect. II, p. 90. *HR* 17 Jan 1938, p. 39. *HR* 4 Apr 1938, p. 7. *HR* 11 Apr 1938, p. 7. *HR* 27 May 1938, p. 3. *MPD* 31 May 1938, p. 4. *MPH* 29 Jan 1938, pp. 39-40. *MPH* 4 Jun 1938, p. 32. *NYT* 11 Jun 1938, p. 9. *Var* 1 Jun 1938, p. 12.

JOURNEY TO FREEDOM (Bulgarian Americans)

Apostolof Productions. *Dist* Republic Pictures Corp. Jun **1957** [©Republic Pictures Corp.; 8 May 1957; LP9467]. Sd (RCA Sound System); b&w. 5,402 ft. 60 min. PCA cert no. 18521.

Prod Stephen C. Apostolof. *Assoc prod* Stafford B. Harrison. *Dir* Robert C. Dertano. *Dial dir* George Graham. *Scr* Herbert F. Niccolls. *Orig story* Stephen C. Apostolof and Herbert F. Niccolls. *Dir of photog* William C. Thompson. *Paris photog* Stephane Grouef. *Opt eff* Consolidated Film Industries. *Film ed* Bob Dertario. *Set dec* Lyle B. Reifsneider. *Ward supv* Charles Arrico. *Mus* Josef Zimanich. *Sd* Dale Knight. *Makeup* Armand Delmar. *Prod supv* Ed F. Finney. *Casting* Bill Crewe.

Cast: Jacques Scott (*Stephan Raikin*), Geneviv Aumont (*Nanette*), George Graham (*James Wright*), Morgan Lane (*Nick Popov*), Jean Ann Lewis (*Mary Raikin*), Peter E. Besbas (*Pete*), Don McArt (*Louie*), Dan O'Dowd, Barry O'Hara (*Pals*), Tor Johnson (*Giant Turk*), Fred Kohler, Miles Shepard (*Detectives*), Don Marlowe (*Lt. Wilson*).

Drama. [*Not viewed*]. Stephan Raikin, a Bulgarian journalist, is captured by the Communist Party Police and imprisoned for his underground activities against the Party. Tortured and beaten, Stephan escapes from prison with the help of the underground resistance organization. With his friend Pete, Stephan flees to Turkey, but the Communists track him down there and kill Pete. In terror, Stephan seeks refuge in France, where he meets Nanette and falls in love. His spirit rekindled by love, Stephan redoubles his efforts against the Communists, attacking them in printed articles and in his broadcasts over Radio Free Europe. Unrelenting, the Communist Secret Police makes another attempt on Stephan's life. Barely managing to escape, Stephan flees to the United States, where he works hard to establish himself. While laboring on a construction job one day, Stephan is injured in an accident and hospitalized. In the hospital, Stephan meets Mary, a nurse, and begins to court her. After Stephan and Mary are wed, they have a baby daughter and move to Los Angeles, where Stephan continues his crusade against Communism. Stephan's speeches are broadcast over the pro-democracy Voice of America, and win him much acclaim. One night, after celebrating an honorary award presented to him for his valiant efforts, Stephan's car strikes and kills a man, and Stephan is arrested for manslaughter. Although the evidence is strongly against Stephan, his lawyer discovers that the accident was a frame-up by Nick Popov, an alleged

friend of Stephan's who is really working as an undercover agent for the Communist party. Unmasked, Popov tries to escape justice and is killed by the police. Once exonerated, Stephan becomes an American citizen and is happily reunited with his family. *Bulgarians. Communists. Frame-ups. Refugees, Political. Reporters. Undercover agents. Betrayal. Citizenship. France. Hospitals. Lawyers. Murder. Nurses. Radio Free Europe. Torture. Turkey. Voice of America (Radio program).*

Note: The working titles of this film were *Escape to Freedom* and *The New Refugee.* *HR* production charts include Pete Welkoff in the cast, but his participation in the released film has not been confirmed. According to the *Exh* review, the picture includes "scenic shots of Istanbul, Paris and American cities."

Exb 10 Jul 1957, p. 4351. *HR* 31 Aug 1956, p. 14. *HR* 21 Sep 1956, p. 16. *HR* 8 Nov 1957. *MPD* 22 Oct 1957. *MPHPD* 2 Nov 1957, p. 587.

JUDGE HARDY AND SON (Italian Americans)

Metro-Goldwyn-Mayer Corp.; controlled by Loew's Inc. *Dist* Loew's Inc. 22 Dec **1939**; *Prod:* began mid-Sep 1939; retakes Oct 1939 [©Loew's Inc.; 16 Dec 1939; LP9304]. Sd (Western Electric Sound System); b&w. 9 reels. 88 min. PCA cert no. 5802.

Series: The Hardy Family.

[*Prod* Lou Ostrow]. *Dir* George B. Seitz. [*Asst dir* Tom Andre]. *Orig story and scr* Carey Wilson. *Dir of photog* Lester White. [*2d cam* Roy Clark]. [*Asst cam* Bob Gough]. *Art dir* Cedric Gibbons. *Art dir assoc* Wade B. Rubottom. *Film ed* Ben Lewis. [*Asst cutter* Ira Hyman]. *Set dec* Edwin B. Willis. [*Wardrobe woman* Vicki Nichols]. *Mus score* David Snell. *Rec dir* Douglas Shearer. [*Mixer* William Steinkamp]. [*Makeup* Neil Wakeman]. [*Unit mgr* Arthur Rose]. [*Scr clerk* Frank Myers]. [*Head grip* H. E. Franzen]. [*Props* Charles Ryan]. [*Gaffer* Robert Worl]. [*Stage mgr* William Edmondson]. [*Still photog* Milton Brown].

Source: Based on characters created by Aurania Rouverol.

Cast: LEWIS STONE (*Judge [James] Hardy*), MICKEY ROONEY (*Andy Hardy*), CECILIA PARKER (*Marian Hardy*), FAY HOLDEN (*Mrs. [Emily] Hardy*), Ann Rutherford (*Polly Benedict*), Sara Haden (*Aunt Milly*), June Preisser (*Euphrasia Clark*), Maria Ouspenskaya (*Mrs. [Judith] Volduzzi*), Henry Hull (*Dr. Jones*), Martha O'Driscoll (*Elvie Horton*), Leona Maricle (*Mrs. Horton*), Margaret Early (*Clarabelle Lee*), George Breakston (*"Beezy"*), Egon Brecher (*Mr. [Anton] Volduzzi*), Edna Holland (*Nurse Trowbridge*), Marie Blake (*Augusta*), [Milton Parsons (*Florist*)], [James B. Carson (*Mogilby, tailor*)], [Joe Yule (*Munk, tire man*)], [William Tannen (*Officer*)], [Ernie Alexander (*Court clerk*)], [Erville Alderson (*Bailiff*)], [Jack Mulhall (*Intern*)], [Eddie Marr (*Second clerk*)].

Domestic, Teenage, Comedy-drama. [*Print viewed*]. Touched by the plight of the Volduzzis, an elderly destitute couple who are in danger of losing their house, Judge James Hardy agrees to look into their case. Sensing that the Volduzzis might have a daughter who could provide them financial support, the judge enlists Andy's help in locating her. Andy, who is desperately in need of money to fix his jalopy in time to take Polly Benedict to the Fourth of July fireworks, eagerly accepts his father's offer of a reward and begins to interview the girls in his school with the middle initial V. His search leads him to the Horton estate, where he meets daughter Elvie, who is writing an essay on Alexander Hamilton for a Fourth of July competition. After learning about the competition's fifty dollar prize, Andy decides to enter the contest himself, and begins to charge flowers, clothes and tires against his anticipated winnings. When he then discovers that the cash prize is only offered to girls, Andy convinces Euphrasia Clark to enter his essay in her name. Andy's plan backfires, however, when Euphrasia threatens to use his proposal to blackmail him into taking her to the fireworks show. Andy's girl and money problems pale when his mother becomes seriously ill with pneumonia. The family is brought closer together while they await the doctor's prognosis, and after a harrowing night, Mrs. Hardy recovers. Relieved, Andy pays another visit to Elvie, who confesses that she hates her mother and wants to win the essay contest for her own self-respect. When Andy offers her the best part of his essay, Elvie tells him that her mother's maiden name was Volduzzi. Armed with this piece of information, Judge Hardy pays Mrs. Horton a visit and learns that the frightened woman is ashamed of what her new husband will think of her immigrant parents. The judge counsels Mrs. Horton to confess all to her husband and reconcile with her parents, and she agrees to do so. All ends happily as the judge offers to help Andy with his debts, and a grateful Elvie lends Andy her limousine to take Polly to the

fireworks show. *Family life. Fathers and sons. Fourth of July. Impersonation and imposture. Parentage.* Blackmail. Contests. Courtship. Debt. Immigrants. Italian Americans. Judges. Mothers and daughters. Physicians. Pneumonia. Poverty. Wealth.

Note: The CBCS incorrectly credits Brandon Tynan with the role of Dr. Jones; that role was actually played by Henry Hull. For additional information about the series, consult the Series Index and see *A Family Affair* in *AFI Catalog of Feature Films, 1931-40;* F3.1269.

DV 12 Dec 1939, p. 3. *FD* 15 Dec 1939, p. 4. *HR* 16 Sep 1939, pp. 6-7. *HR* 12 Dec 1939, p. 3. *MPD* 19 Dec 1939, p. 6. *MPH* 18 Nov 1939, p. 41. *MPH* 16 Dec 1939, p. 25. *NYT* 8 Jan 1940, p. 27. *Var* 13 Dec 1939, p. 11.

JUDGE PRIEST (African Americans)

Fox Film Corp. *Dist* Fox Film Corp. 28 Sep **1934**; Prod: early Jun—18 Jul 1934 [©Fox Film Corp.; 28 Sep 1934; LP4979]. Sd (Western Electric Noiseless Recording); b&w. 8 reels, 7,220 ft. 79-80 min. PCA cert no. 111.

Prod Sol M. Wurtzel. *Dir* John Ford. [*Asst dir* Ed O'Fearna]. *Scr* Dudley Nichols and Lamar Trotti. *Photog* George Schneiderman. *Settings* William Darling. [*Film ed* Paul Weatherwax]. *Gowns* Royer. *Mus dir* Samuel Kaylin. *Sd* Albert Protzman. [*Still photog* William Thomas].

Song(s): "Massa Jesus Wrote Me a Note" and "Aunt Dilsey's Song," music by Cyril J. Mockridge, lyrics by Dudley Nichols and Lamar Trotti.

Source: Based on the character created by Irvin S. Cobb.

Cast: WILL ROGERS (*Judge [William Pitman] Priest*), Tom Brown (*Jerome Priest*), Anita Louise (*Ellie May Gillespie*), Henry B. Walthall (*Rev. Ashby Brand*), David Landau (*Bob Gillis*), Rochelle Hudson (*Virginia Maydew*), Roger Imhof (*Billy Gaynor*), Frank Melton (*Flem Talley*), Charley Grapewin (*Sergeant Jimmy Bagby*), Berton Churchill (*Senator Horace Maydew*), Brenda Fowler (*Mrs. Caroline Priest*), Francis Ford (*Juror No. 12*), Hattie McDaniels (*Aunt Dilsey*), Stepin Fetchit (*Jeff Poindexter*), [Paul McAllister (*Doc Lake*)], [Matt McHugh (*Gabby Rives*)], [Louis Mason (*Sheriff Birdsong*)], [Hy Meyer (*Herman Felsberg*)], [Grace Goodall (*Mrs. Maydew*)], [Ernest Shield (*Milan*)], [Vester Pegg (*Joe Herringer*)], [Paul McVey (*Trimble*)], [Winter Hall (*Judge Fairleigh*)], [Duke Lee (*Deputy*)], [Gladys Wells, Beulah Hall Jones, Melba Brown, Thelma Brown, Vera Brown (*Black singers*)], [May Rousseau (*Guitar player*)], [Harry Tenbrook, Pat Hartigan, Harry Wilson, Frank Moran, Constantine Romanoff (*Townsmen in saloon*)], [Margaret Mann (*Governess*)], [George H. Reed (*Black servant*)].

Rural, Comedy-drama. [*Print viewed*]. In an old Kentucky town in 1890, Judge William Pitman Priest reads the comics, and confederate veterans argue about their battles as ex-State Senator Horace Maydew tries to prosecute Jeff Poindexter, a sleeping black man, for stealing chickens. After the judge questions Jeff about his favorite fishing spot, he and Jeff go fishing, and Jeff subsequently becomes a part of the judge's household. When the judge's nephew Jerome, "Rome" for short, returns after getting a law degree, he is disappointed that the girl next door, Ellie May Gillespie, whom he loves, wants to end their courtship because Rome's mother Caroline objects that Ellie May's mother died in childbirth and no one knows the identity of her father. When Flemming Talley, an uncouth barber, visits Ellie May, the judge scares him away and encourages Rome to court her. Feeling lonely, the judge visits his wife's grave and sees Bob Gillis, an uncommunicative blacksmith, place flowers on the grave of Ellie May's mother. After Gillis punches Talley for making jokes about Ellie May's background and character, Talley and two others attack him with pool cues. Gillis cuts Talley with his knife, and Talley takes Gillis to court for starting the fight. Rome represents Gillis, and Maydew, who is running for circuit court judge against Judge Priest, demands an impartial judge. The judge, hurt and upset, steps down, and during the trial, Gillis' refusal to mention Ellie May hurts his chances to win. After Reverend Ashby Brand, who knows Gillis' past, confides in Judge Priest, the judge joins the defense and has the reverend testify that during the "war for the Southern confederacy," he recruited Gillis, a chain-gang prisoner, who fought nobly. The reverend's recitation of Gillis' heroic deeds builds to an emotional peak and climaxes when he reveals that Gillis, Ellie May's father, has secretly paid him to provide for her education. The courtroom explodes with adulation, Caroline wants to be Ellie May's mother, and during the veteran's parade that day, Gillis is asked to carry the confederate flag. *Civil War veterans. Courtship. False accusations. Fathers and daughters. Judges. Kentucky. Parentage.*

Small town life. Trials. War heroes. African Americans. Barbers and barbershops. Blacksmiths. Candy. Croquet (Game). Knife wounds. Lawyers. Nephews. Parades. Reverends. Senators. United States-History-Civil War, 1861-1865. Widowers.

Note: The working title of this film was *Old Judge Priest.* According to information in the Twentieth Century-Fox Records of the Legal Department at the UCLA Theater Arts Department, Fox purchased the motion picture rights to three "Judge Priest" stories for this film from Irvin S. Cobb: "A Treeful of Hoot Owls," which was first published in *Hearst's International-Cosmopolitan,* Aug 1930; "Br'er Fox and the Brian Patch," which was first published under the title "Br'er Rabbit, He Lay Low," in *Hearst's International-Cosmopolitan,* May 1931; and "Words and Music," which was first published in *The Saturday Evening Post,* 28 Oct 1911. The first two stories were included in the collection *Down Yonder with Judge Priest and Irwin S. Cobb* (New York, 1932), while the third story was included in the collection *Back Home* (New York, 1912). The publishers of the first collection, Ray Long and the R. R. Smith Corp., sued Twentieth Century-Fox and Cobb in 1938 because they received no compensation for the use of the stories, and in 1939, the studio settled with them for $2,000.

When Cobb learned that Fox planned to use in their screen credits for the film the statement, "Based on the Judge Priest stories by Irvin S. Cobb," he objected that the statement would not be accurate, as at the time he had written over seventy "Judge Priest" stories and planned to write still more, and that the statement might mitigate against future sales of his stories. He suggested a number of alternative statements, including the one used in the final credits, "Based on Irvin S. Cobb's character of 'Judge Priest'." Included in the legal records is a statement by Cobb in which he notes that the writers of the screenplay "practically created a new and different story from the material [i.e. the three "Judge Priest" stories] turned over to them" and that many of the characters in the film, including "Ellie May Gillespie," "Jerome Priest" and "Virginia Maydew" were not his creations. At a later date, Twentieth Century-Fox officials determined that a fourth "Judge Priest" story, entitled "The Mob from Massac," which was also included in the collection *Back Home,* provided the basis for one of the sequences in the film, but that the studio never purchased the rights to that story.

The character played by Frank Melton, although called "Flem Talley" during most of the film, is called "Flem Jones" in the courtroom scene. In the screen credits, Stepin Fetchit's name, although listed last, is in larger letters than the other cast members' except for Rogers'.

According to modern sources, a lynching scene was originally shot for the film, but was excised by the studio. The first draft screenplay, dated 12 Apr 1934, in the Twentieth Century-Fox Produced Scripts Collection, also at UCLA, contains a scene in which a mob of townsfolk are fixing to lynch "Jeff," the character who in the film was played by Stepin Fetchit. Having blood on his hands from some beef liver that had been eaten by dogs, Jeff is mistaken for another black man suspected of assault. The mob storms tries to storm the jail, but Judge Priest is summoned, and he sends them home. No information has been located to confirm that this scene was actually shot. Modern sources also list Robert Parrish as a cast member and note that the film was one of 1934's top grossing films. In a 1972 interview, John Ford noted that *Judge Priest* was his favorite picture of all time. In 1953, Ford directed another film, entitled *The Sun Shines Bright,* based on three of Irvin S. Cobb's "Judge Priest" stories, one of which was the above mentioned "The Mob from Massac." That film was produced by Argosy Productions, released by Republic, and starred Charles Winninger, Arleen Whelan and Stepin Fetchit (see below).

Box 20 Oct 1934. *DV* 18 Jul 1934, p. 4. *FD* 18 Aug 1934, p. 4. *Har* 25 Aug 1934, p. 134. *HF* 9 Jun 1934, p. 8. *HF* 30 Jun 1934, p. 8. *HR* 4 May 1934, p. 7. *HR* 4 Aug 1934, p. 3. *IP* Jul 1934, p. 16. *MPD* 6 Aug 1934, p. 8. *MPH* 11 Aug 1934, p. 31. *NYT* 12 Oct 1934, p. 33. *Var* 16 Oct 1934, p. 12.

JUDGMENT *see* IN JUDGMENT OF

JUEGO, AMOR Y SANGRE *see* EL CUERPO DEL DELITO

JUKE GIRL (Greek Americans)

Warner Bros. Pictures, Inc.; A Warner Bros.—First National Picture. *Dist* Warner Bros. Pictures, Inc. 30 May **1942**; Prod: early Oct—12 Dec 1941 [©Warner Bros. Pictures, Inc.; 30 May 1942; LP11373]. Sd (RCA Sound System); b&w. 8,095 ft. 90 min.

Exec prod Hal B. Wallis. *Assoc prod* Jerry Wald and Jack Saper. *Dir* Curtis Bernhardt. *Dial dir* Hugh Cummings. [*Asst dir* Jesse Hibbs]. *Scr* A. I. Bezzerides. *Adpt* Kenneth Gamet. *Dir of photog* Bert Glennon. *Art dir* Robert Haas. *Film ed* Warren Low. *Gowns* Milo Anderson. *Mus dir* Leo F. Forbstein. *Mus* Adolph Deutsch. *Sd* Charles Lang. *Makeup artist* Perc Westmore.

Song(s): "Found Me a Bluebell," "No One Talks to No One No More" and "Slaphappy Pappy," music and lyrics by M. K. Jerome and Jack Scholl.

Source: Based on the article "Land of the Jook" by Theodore Pratt in *The Saturday Evening Post* (26 Apr 1941).

Cast: ANN SHERIDAN (*Lola Mears*), RONALD REAGAN (*Steve Talbot*), Richard Whorf (*Danny Frazier*), George Tobias (*Nick Garcos*), Gene Lockhart (*Henry Madden*), Alan Hale (*Yippee*), Betty Brewer (*Skeeter*), Howard da Silva (*Cully*), Donald MacBride ("*Muckeye*" *John*), Willard Robertson (*Mister Just*), Faye Emerson

(*Violet "Murph" Murphy*), Willie Best (*Jo-Mo*), Fuzzy Knight (*Ike Harper*), Spencer Charters (*Keeno*), William B. Davidson (*Paley*), Frank Wilcox (*Truck driver*), William Haade (*Watchman*), [Eddy Waller (*Man in car*)], [Paul Burns (*Ed*)], [Clancy Cooper, Hank Mann, Jack Mower, Don Turner, Cliff Saum, Paul Panzer, Glen Cavender, Forrest Taylor, Pat McVeigh (*Farmers*)], [Frank Darien], [Pat Flaherty (*Mike*)], [William Edmunds (*Travitti*)], [Dewey Robinson, Kenneth Harlan (*Dealers*)], [James Flavin (*Officer*)], [Jean Fitzgerald (*Juke girl*)], [Sol Gorss, William Gould (*Deputies*)], [De Wolfe Hopper (*Clerk*)], [Frank Mayo (*Detective*)], [Alan Bridge], [Jack Gardner], [Fred Kelsey], [Frank Pharr], [Ray Teal], [Bill Phillips], [Guy Wilkerson], [Milt Kibbee], [Ed Peil, Sr.], [Victor Zimmerman], [Glen Strange].

Rural, Drama, with songs. [*Print viewed*]. Steve Talbot and Danny Malone, two itinerant farmworkers, join the crowd streaming into Cat-Tail, Florida to work the crops. On the way, they encounter Skeeter, a young girl who has become expert in scavenging for her family, as well as Lola Mears and Violet "Murph" Murphy two "juke girls" who entertain at roadhouses known as "juke joints." Steve wants to work the crops, but Danny insists that they try for higher paying jobs at Henry Madden's packing plant. By eliminating his competition, Madden has forced the farmers to accept his low prices for their produce, which so angers Greek American farmer Nick Garcos that he refuses to sell to Madden. When a fight breaks out between Nick and Madden's foreman, Cully, Steve fights on Nick's side. Consequently, Cully refuses to hire either Steve or Danny. Yippee, a worker at the plant, offers to let the two men share his shack in nearby Tent City where Skeeter, Lola and Murph live also. That evening, while Steve and Danny relax at "Muckeye" John's juke joint, Nick, having tried unsuccessfully to sell his crops outside of town, agrees to accept Madden's offer, but Madden, who had surreptitiously prevented the sale, offers Nick an even lower price than before. Furious, Nick again attacks Madden, and this time, Danny, hoping to get in with Madden, joins on Madden's side. Steve comes to Nick's aid, which impresses Lola, who has taken a job at Muckeye's. After the fight, Lola and Steve walk back to Tent City together and discover that they are both from the Midwest where Steve's farmer father was put out of work by the drought. Eager to leave the farm where she grew up, Lola has never wanted to put down roots anywhere else. Steve and Lola check on Nick's progress and learn that he plans to take his crop of tomatoes to Atlanta, hoping to sell them before they rot. Realizing that Nick's truck will never make it that far, Steve and Lola plot to steal one of Madden's trucks, but the theft is discovered, and Nick's tomatoes are destroyed by Madden's men, including Danny. At Lola's suggestion, a devastated Steve helps Nick plant his new crop. Although Danny warns Steve that Madden plans to interfere with the farmers, Nick, Steve and Lola manage to convince the pickers to work for the promise of payment when the crops are sold. Afterward, an angry Madden forces Muckeye to fire Lola, and Steve, who has fallen in love with her, takes her to Nick's to stay. Madden does everything he can to prevent Nick from selling his crops in Atlanta, but the farmers succeed despite his efforts. The footloose Lola runs away in Atlanta and a jubilant Nick and a disheartened Steve return to Florida. That night a drunken Nick tries to patch things up with Madden and when Madden rebuffs his overtures Nick attacks him. In self defense, Madden hits Nick on the head and kills him. He then hides the body and frames Steve and Lola for the murder. When Skeeter tells Danny that Cully is trying to foment a lynch mob, he and Yippee force Madden to confess, and the mob turns on him. Danny leaves town for new territory and Steve and Lola plan to work Nick's farm. *Farm hands. Farmers. Murder. Drunkenness. Fistfights. Florida. Frame-ups. Friendship. Greek Americans. Lynching. Migrant workers. Roadhouses. Romance. Tomatoes. Trucks.*

Note: A Warner Bros. press release included in the file on the film at the AMPAS Library announced that Ida Lupino was to star in the film. News items in *HR* add the following information: Some scenes were shot on location in Florida. Fuzzy Knight and Betty Brewer were to sing three songs but do not appear in the film. A juke house was the name given to a cheap roadhouse. The term also refers to the music played in these roadhouses and in brothels.

Box 11 Apr 1942. *DV* 7 Apr 1942, p. 3. *FD* 8 Apr 1942, p. 8. *HR* 8 Sep 1941, p. 1. *HR* 24 Sep 1941, p. 13. *HR* 17 Oct 1941, p. 15. *HR* 12 Dec 1941, p. 2. *HR* 7 Apr 1942, p. 6. *MPHPD* 11 Apr 1942, p. 597. *NYT* 20 Jun 1942, p. 9. *Var* 8 Apr 1942, p. 8.

JUKE JOINT (African Americans)

A Bert Goldberg Production. *Dist* Sack Amusement Enterprises. 1947; Prod: at Harlemwood Studios. Sd; b&w. 6,090 ft. 68 min.

Pres ALFRED N. SACK. *Dir* Spencer Williams. *Orig story* True T. Thompson. *Dir of photog* George Sanderson. *Asst cam* William Gullette. *Prop master* Arthur Kendall. *Cost* Julian Jullienne. *Mus dir* George Randolf. *Sd eng* Richard E. Byers. *Makeup and coiffure* Farilla McGowan. *Tech adv* True T. Thompson.

Cast: Spencer Williams ([*Bad News Johnson, also known as*] *Whitney Vanderbilt*), July Jones ([*July Jones, also known as*] *"Cornbred" Green*), Inez Newell ([*Louella*] *"Mama Lou" Holiday*), Leonard Duncan (*"Papa Sam" Holiday*), Dauphine Moore (*Honey Dew Holiday*), Melody Duncan (*Melody Holiday*), Katherine Moore (*Florida Holiday*), Tilford Patterson (*Jefferson Lee*), Albert Smith (*"High Life" Harris*), Howard Galloway (*"Juke Joint" Johnny*), Clifford Beamon (*Bartender*), Frances McHugh (*Waitress*), Entertainers Mac and Ace, Kit and Kit, The Jitterbug Johnnies (*Specialties*), Don Gilbert (*Master of Ceremonies*), Duncan's Beauty Show Girls, Red Calhoun and His Orchestra.

African American, Domestic, Comedy, with songs. [*Viewed print incomplete*]. Having fled Memphis, Tennessee, to start a new life, smalltime fugitive Bad News Johnson and his slow-witted companion, July Jones, arrive in Dallas with no place to stay and only twenty-five cents to their name. Johnson explains to July that they are taking the advice of the great thinker Horace Greeley, who said, "Go west young man, and do your best; then come east and spend your grease." When Johnson realizes that July does not understand the quote, he tells July that he is so dumb that he probably thinks that "Veronica Lake is some kinda' summer resort." Using his charm and graciousness, mixed in with a touch of pure deception, Johnson procures a room for himself and July at the home of the Holiday family. Mrs. Louella "Mama Lou" Holiday is at first reluctant take in two strangers as boarders, but when Johnson, who has introduced himself as Mr. Whitney Vanderbilt, impresses her as a great "thespian," she, in the hope that he will tutor her daughter Honey Dew in poise, decides to give them a room. Johnson and July, who is now known as Mr. Green, gladly accept the offer. Meanwhile, Mama Lou's lazy husband, Papa Sam, who was sent by his wife on an errand to the market, is instead at Johnny's Juke Joint playing poker with his pals. Papa Sam's daughter Florida, also at the juke joint, is being pursued by Johnny, the owner of the establishment, who wants to take her to Chicago. When Papa Sam returns home without the food he was sent to get, Mama Lou scolds him until Honey Dew breaks up the fight. Back at the juke joint, while Florida considers Johnny's offer, he calls his wife and tells her that he will be home late. After Johnson and July enjoy their first dinner at the Holidays, Johnson gives Honey Dew lessons on how to carry herself at the beauty contest she has entered, while Florida is told to do the dishes. Johnson's lessons are proven valuable when Honey Dew wins first prize in the contest. Backstage at the contest, Papa Sam's buddy, "High Life" Harris, suggests that Honey Dew be taken to the juke joint to celebrate her success, and Papa Sam agrees. When Mama Lou returns home to find that her husband and Florida, who was given the responsibility of preparing the house for a party, are missing, she marches over to Johnny's with an umbrella in hand and takes swings at Harris, Johnny and Florida. Mama Lou then discovers Papa Sam kissing a waitress outside the juke joint and pounces on him. At home, Mama Lou gives Florida one last beating to punish her for her actions as Johnson and July watch through a keyhole. *Acting–Study and teaching. African Americans. Boardinghouses. Family life. Idlers. Impersonation and imposture. Roadhouses. Beauty contests. Dancers. Fugitives. Henpecked husbands. Jukeboxes. Philanderers. Seduction. William Shakespeare. Strangers.*

Note: Although the viewed print contained a copyright statement for the year 1947, it was not included in the copyright registry. The viewed print was missing approximately ten minutes of the story. The film was Spencer Williams' last as a director. Modern sources note that filming took place in two Texas "juke joints": Dallas' Rose Room and Don's Keyhole in San Antonio. *Juke Joint* was considered a lost film for many years, until 1983, when a print was discovered in a Tyler, TX warehouse and identified by film historian G. William Jones.

LAT 6 Feb 1985.

JULIETA COMPRA UN HIJO (Spanish language)

Fox Film Corp. *Dist* Fox Film Corp. **1935**; New York opening: 22 Mar 1935; Prod: began 3 Dec 1934 [©Fox Film Corp.; 12 Jan 1935; LP5388]. Sd; b&w. 8 reels, 6,709 ft. 74 min. Passed by the National Board of Review. PCA cert no. 542. Spanish language.

[*Assoc prod* John Stone]. *Dirección de* [*Directed by*] Louis King. *Supervisión y dirección de diálogo* [*Supervision and dialogue direction*] Gregorio Martínez Sierra. *Adaptación cinematográfica por* [*Screenplay by*] José López Rubio. [*Photog* Daniel Clark]. *Dirección musical* [*Musical director*] Samuel Kaylin. [*Sd* E. Clayton Ward].

Source: Based on the play *Julieta compra un hijo* by Gregorio Martínez Sierra and Honorio Maura (published in Madrid, 1927).

Cast: CATALINA BÁRCENA (*Julieta Albornoz*), Gilbert Roland (*Jack Aranda*), Luana Alcañiz (*Cecilia*), Julio Peña (*Guillermo*), Soledad Jiménez (*Duquesa de Solsona*), Barbara Leonard (*Ketty*), Antonio Vidal (*El médico*), Tina Menard (*La nurse*), Agostino Borgato (*Matías*), Rosa Rey (*Soledad*), José Peña Pepet (*Un campesino*), Filomena Liñán (*Una campesina*), [Patrick Michael Cunning (*Antonio*)], [Anita Campillo (*Isabel*)], [Lucio Villegas (*Best man*)], [Jaime Devesa (*The butler*)].

Drama. [*Not viewed*]. On her wedding day, Julieta Albornoz reveals that she has waited her whole life to wed because men in the past have always desired her for her money. When another woman, Isabel, arrives to inform Julieta that Antonio, Julieta's fiancé, has fathered her child and promised to continue to support them with his wife-to-be's money, a despondent Julieta runs off on a cruise with her friend Cecilia. While she pedals an exercise bike on deck, she meets Jack Aranda, and the two are instantly drawn to each other, though they do not exchange names. Jack's aunt, a duchess, discovers that the rich Julieta is on the ship and encourages her nephew to woo her, as he has fallen into financial hard times. Jack admits that he has fallen in love with another, but agrees to his aunt's plan nonetheless. When Jack and his younger cousin Guillermo approach Julieta and Cecilia at a masquerade ball with the intention of seducing the rich young woman, Julieta tells Jack that he has mistaken her for Cecilia, who has money. Jack then approaches Cecilia with the same words of love, and Julieta rebukes him for his greed, but later invites him to her cabin with a business proposition. She offers Jack a sum to marry her and to help her conceive a son, after which they would divorce. Jack reluctantly agrees and hopes that the two will love each other eventually and have a real marriage. Julieta treats Jack coldly throughout their honeymoon in Biarritz, and when she suspects erroneously that he is having an affair, she asks that he take her away somewhere. At his family's home in the province of Burgos, he insists that she pretend to be his happy bride, but when he tells her that he loves her, she demands that they leave the house. Their car crashes, and they are placed in the same bed in order to recover. Months later, Julieta has a daughter and asks Jack to go away now that he has fulfilled his contract. Jack, who shows extraordinary devotion and love to his child, tells Julieta that the contract is not binding as she had a daughter, and he must help her to have a son. He returns to her the uncashed check that she had originally given to him in payment for his services, declares his devotion and promises to stay with her until she has a son. Julieta agrees, and the two spend the night together like a happily married couple, Julieta finally finding a man whose love is not self-interested. *Contracts. Fatherhood. Marriage of convenience.* Aunts. Automobile accidents. Biarritz (France). Burgos (Spain). Cousins. Honeymoons. Masked balls. Nobility. Ocean liners. Weddings.

Note: The plot summary was based on a dialogue continuity in the Twentieth Century-Fox Produced Scripts Collection, and the onscreen credits were taken from a screen credit sheet in the Twentieth Century-Fox Records of the Legal Department, both of which are at the UCLA Theater Arts Library. The title was translated variously as *Juliet Buys a Son* and *Juliet Buys a Baby*. The running time was calculated based on the footage as given in NYSA records. According to information in the legal records, Helen Logan and Robert Ellis completed a continuity based on the screenplay in Jan 1935, after shooting was completed. It is not known if this work was for a proposed English-language version. Also, according to the legal records, Elena Durán was originally cast as "La nurse."

CM Apr 1935, p. 214. *DV* 3 Dec 1934, p. 3. *FD* 27 Mar 1935, p. 6. *NYT* 25 Mar 1935, p. 12.

JUNCTION 88 (African Americans)

Century Theatrical Productions. *Dist* Sack Amusement Enterprises. **1948?**. Sd; b&w. 4,457 ft. 50 min.

Prod D. J. Mastrony. *Dir* George P. Quigley. *Asst dir* J. De Lacey. *Cam* Don Malkames and John Visconti. *Ed* Mavis Lyons. *Sets* Frank Mansey. *Original songs and music played by Noble Sissel's Orchestra. Sd* Robert Rosien.

Song(s): "Junction 88," "Somewhere Happy with You," "Where Does the Wind Go?" "Eagle Eye Blues," "Walking with Caroline," "Off Beat Rhythm" and "Get Your House in Order," music and lyrics by J. Augustus Smith and Herbert Junior; "My Country 'Tis of Thee," words by Samuel Francis Smith, music based on "God Save the Queen" by Henry Carey; "Poor Lulu." composers undetermined.

Cast: Bob Howard (*Bob Howard*), "Pigmeat" Markham (*Piggy*), Noble Sissel (*Noble Sissel*), Wyatt Clark (*Buster [Jenkins]*), Marie Cooke (*Lolly [Simpson]*), Gus Smith (*Pop [Simpson]*), Abbey Mitchell (*Mom [Simpson]*), Artie Belle McGinty (*Mrs. Jenkins*), George Wiltshire (*Rev. Juniper*), Herbert Junior (*Onnie*), Alonzo Bosan (*Charlie*), Maude Simmons (*Lady*), Al Young (*Old man*), Augustus Smith, Jr. (*Chinka Pin*), *Choir* Eugene Thompson, Rumena Matson, Mable Berger, Dephine Roach, Henry Nelson.

African American, Musical, Comedy. [*Print viewed*]. In the small town of Junction 88, young black musician Buster Jenkins plays a love song on the piano for his sweetheart, Lolly Simpson. Meanwhile, out on the Simpsons' porch, Lolly's father, "Pop" Simpson, tells "Mom" Simpson and Buster's mother that he will not give his consent for his daughter to marry Buster because he believes that the struggling musician will not be able to make a decent living. Although the mothers defend Buster as a good, God-fearing, churchgoing boy, Pop continues to favor the hard-working, hard-drinking Onnie as his future son-in-law. Miles away from Junction 88, music agent Bob Howard and his colleague Piggy discover in their mail what they believe will be a hit song. Determined to sign the song's composer, "Hewlett Green," Bob and Piggy set out for Junction 88, the town from which the song was sent. When they arrive, Bob and Piggy are amazed to discover that no one in Junction 88 has ever heard of Hewlett Green. Bob and Piggy continue their fruitless search for Hewlett Green and enlist the help of a young boy named Chinka Pin, who spends much of his time singing at the town barber shop. Later, Bob and Piggy meet Lolly, who introduces them to her friend Caroline. Bob falls instantly in love with Caroline, and the four attend a benefit concert that Buster has organized at the church. Before the concert begins, Lolly introduces Bob and Piggy to Buster, and they are granted permission from Buster to perform in the concert. Noble Sissle and his orchestra play after Chinka Pin sings the National Anthem. Bob and Piggy close the concert with three songs. Lolly notices that Buster is upset about something, but he keeps his troubles to himself and tells her that he is not ready to reveal what is upsetting him. Bob and Piggy put the word out that they want to sign Hewlett Green to a long-term contract. The search quickly comes to an end, however, when Buster steps forward in church and reveals that he has been writing songs under the assumed name of Hewlett Green. After signing a contract with Bob and Piggy, Buster takes Lolly's hand in marriage. *African Americans. Aliases. Churches. Composers. Musicians. Swing music. Theatrical agents.* Barbers and barbershops. Family life. Marriage. Reverends. Romantic rivalry. Searches. Singers. Small town life.

Note: Onscreen credits of the viewed print do not credit a writer for this film, and none was identified in other available contemporary sources. Although no reviews of this film have been found, the release year was determined from records of the NYSA.

THE JUNGLE (Immigrants, Lithuanian Americans)

All Star Feature Corp. *Dist* State Rights. 25 May **1914**. Si; b&w. 5 reels.

Dir Augustus Thomas, George Henry Irving and John H. Pratt. *Scen* Benjamin S. Kutler. *Mus accompaniment comp* Manuel Klein.

Source: Based on the novel *The Jungle* by Upton Sinclair (New York, 1906).

Cast: George Nash (*Jurgis Rudkus*), Gail Kane (*Ona*), Julia Hurley (*Elzbieta*), Robert Cummings (*Connor*), Alice Marc (*Marija*), Robert Payton Gibbs (*Antanas*), Clarence Handyside (*John Durham*), Ernest Evers (*Freddy Durham*), George Henry Irving, Harold Vermilye, Maxine Hodges, May McCabe, Nickelas Sinnerella.

Drama. In a prologue, author Upton Sinclair describes his methods of researching *The Jungle*. A panoramic view of the Chicago stockyards is also shown. In the main story, Lithuanian immigrant Jurgis Rudkus arrives in Packingtown and through the efforts of his friend Jokubas, secures a job in the stockyards. Soon Jurgis is able to marry Ona, thus saddening Marija, an immigrant girl who loves him. At Jokubas' urging, Jurgis buys a house and is plunged into debt. Meanwhile, stockyard owner John Durham, outraged by the extravagances of his wife and worthless son Freddy, orders a large wage reduction for his workers. During a strike, Ona's stepfather, Antanas, becomes ill, the family is evicted, her sister Katrina dies of industrial poisoning, and Marija is drugged and raped by Durham's Freddy. Ona then has sex with foreman Connor in exchange for money to feed her starving child, only to learn of the infant's death. When Ona tells Jurgis, he throws Connor into a cattle pen where the foreman is killed. Ona later dies and Jurgis is imprisoned. Upon his release, Jurgis, unable to find the rest of his family attends a Socialist Party rally, where he is inspired to champion their cause. When he saves a woman from drowning herself, he finds that she is Marija, now a prostitute. Together they then work for the establishment of a "cooperative commonwealth." *Authors. Chicago (IL). Employer-employee relations. Immigrants. Lithuanian Americans. Meatpackers and meatpacking. Upton Sinclair. Socialism. Attempted suicide. Debt. Marriage. Murder. Prostitution. Rape. Self-sacrifice. Strikes and lockouts.*

Note: Although *MPW* lists a W. Vermilyea in the cast, Harold Vermilye includes this title in his 1918 *MPSD* credits.

Motog 25 Dec 1913, p. 22. *Motog* 4 Jul 1914, pp. 21-22. *MPW* 2 May 1914, p. 680. *MPW* 13 Jun 1914, p. 1553. *MPW* 20 Jun 1914, p. 1675. *NYDM* 15 Apr 1914, p. 35. *NYDM* 10 Jun 1914, p. 34. *Var* 26 Jun 1914, p. 19.

JUST AN OLD SWEETHEART *see* HIS SWEETHEART

JUST JIM (Chinese Americans)
Universal Film Mfg. Co.; A Broadway Universal Feature. *Dist* Universal Film Mfg. Co. 16 Aug **1915** [©Universal Film Mfg. Co.; 29 Jul 1915; LP5959]. Si; b&w. 4 reels.

Dir O. A. C. Lund. *Scen* O. A. C. Lund.

Cast: Harry D. Carey (*Jim*), Jean Taylor (*Rose*), William Crinley, Mr. Edmundson, Duke Worne, Olive Golden.

Drama. When Jim is released from prison, he returns to his Chinatown neighborhood determined to lead a virtuous life. While walking, he hears a woman's cries issuing from a house and enters to investigate. In her delirium, the dying woman mistakes Jim for Tom, her nephew, and entrusts him to deliver a package to her daughter Rose. Later, the scheming nephew finds Jim's forgotten hat and follows him West. Jim goes to the saloon where Rose was last seen, but before he can find her, Tom has him arrested. On the way to the jail, the coach crashes in a storm and Jim escapes. Finally locating Rose, Jim hands over the package, which contains papers that identify the governor as her father. To complete his task, Jim takes Rose to her father and then quietly departs, only to be shanghaied by Chinese smugglers. After thwarting the smugglers, Jim passes a final test of character devised by the governor and is rewarded with Rose's hand in marriage. *Criminals–Rehabilitation. Ex-convicts. False arrests. Parentage. Tests of character. Accidents. Chinese Americans. Governors. Kidnapping. Nephews. San Francisco (CA)–Chinatown. Secret documents. Smuggling. Stagecoaches.*

Note: Some scenes for this film were shot along the waterfront and in Chinatown in San Francisco, and in Oxnard, CA, Yosemite National Park and the Mojave Desert.

Motog 21 Aug 1915, pp. 369-70, 389. *MPN* 5 Jun 1915, p. 47. *MPN* 19 Jun 1915, p. 47. *MPN* 26 Jun 1915, p. 52. *MPN* 7 Aug 1915, p. 76. *MPN* 21 Aug 1915, p. 102. *MPN* 16 Oct 1915, p. 74. *MPW* 14 Aug 1915, p. 1227. *MPW* 21 Aug 1915, p. 1318. *Var* 20 Aug 1915, p. 21.

JUST SQUAW (Native Americans)
Beatriz Michelena Features. *Dist* Robertson-Cole Co. through Exhibitors Mutual Distributing Corp. 11 May **1919**. Si; b&w. 5 reels.

Supv George E. Middleton. *Prod* George E. Middleton. *Dir* George E. Middleton. *Story and scen* Earle Snell.

Cast: Beatriz Michelena (*Fawn*), William Pike (*The stranger*), Andrew Robson (*Snake Le Gal*), Albert Morrison (*The half-breed*), D. Mitsoras (*Romney*), Jeff Williams, Katherine Angus.

Western. Before she dies, an Indian woman asks her half-breed son never to tell his sister Fawn that her mother was white. Years later, when Fawn falls in love with a stranger who loves her even though he thinks she's a half-breed, her brother, now a fugitive known as the Phantom, warns her not to marry. After the stranger identifies himself as the son of the murdered Sheriff Hollister and leads a posse to the Phantom's cave, thinking he killed a man during a stagecoach robbery, Snake Le Gal, responsible for stealing Fawn from her father, Jimmy Dorr, killing Sheriff Hollister, and robbing the stage, stabs Romney, his cohort and the real killer, because they both desire Fawn. When Romney confesses to stop the Phantom's lynching, the Phantom races to Le Gal's cabin and saves Fawn from rape. Dorr then shoots Le Gal, who, before he dies, confesses that Fawn "is all white." She and Hollister can now marry. *Brothers and sisters. Fugitives. Indians of North America–Mixed blood. Parentage. Strangers. Attempted rape. Caves. Confession. Lynching. Murder. Posses. Rescues.*

Note: The film was made at Beatrice Michelena's studio in San Rafael, and other Northern California locations in 1917. The publicity for the film states that no artificial lighting devices were used. Title cards in this film included a picture of the head of the character speaking in the left corner.

ETR 17 May 1919, p. 1831. *MPN* 10 May 1919, p. 3095. *MPN* 17 May 1919, pp. 3229-30. *MPW* 10 May 1919, pp. 934-5.

JUSTICE OF THE FAR NORTH (Native Americans, Native Alaskans)
Columbia Pictures Corp. *Dist* C.B.C. Film Sales Corp. **1925** [©C.B.C. Film Sales Corp.; 3 Apr 1925; LP21323]. Si; b&w. 6 reels.

Dir Norman Dawn. *Story* Norman Dawn. *Photog* Tony Mormann and George Madden.

Cast: Arthur Jasmine (*Umluk*), Marcia Manon (*Wamba*), Laska Winter (*Nootka*), Chuck Reisner (*Mike Burke*), Max Davidson (*Izzy Hawkins*), George Fisher (*Dr. Wells*), Katherine Dawn (*Lucy Parsons*), Steve Murphy (*Broken Nose McGee*), Ilak the Wolf Dog (*Himself*).

Northwest, Melodrama. Umluk, an Eskimo chief, falls into a crevice while hunting and is rescued by Dr. Wells, a distinguished Arctic explorer and scientist. Umluk returns to his igloo, where he finds Mike Burke, an ex-whaler who runs a trading post in partnership with Izzy Hawkins; Burke has been attempting to win the favor of Umluk's promised bride, a Russian half-breed Eskimo named Wamba, by giving her trinkets and treating her like a white woman. Umluk forces Burke to leave, but the trader returns later and takes the willing Wamba away with him, forcing Wamba's sister, Nootka, to go with them as their cook and drudge. Umluk learns from Hawkins just what has happened and gives chase to the party in a light sled. Umluk soon catches sight of the three travelers, but an unlucky accident to his sled prevents him from catching them. Umluk eventually finds them in a rough settlement, and, after trials and tribulations, returns to his icy home with the faithful Nootka, leaving the degraded Wamba behind. *Abduction. Arctic regions. Cooks. Dogs. Explorers. Indians of North America–Mixed blood. Native Alaskans. Scientists. Trading posts. Whales and whaling.*

Var 3 Nov 1926, p. 20.

JUVENILE JUNGLE *see* THIS REBEL BREED

THE KAISER'S FINISH (German Americans)
Warner Brothers. *Dist* State Rights; Warner Brothers. Nov **1918** [©A. Warner; 2 Nov 1918; LP13026]. Si; b&w. 6-8 reels.

Pres A. Warner. *Supv* William Nigh. *Prod* S. L. Warner. *Dir* John Joseph Harvey. *Asst dir* Clifford P. Saum. *Story* John Joseph Harvey and Clifford P. Saum. *Cam* Rial Schellinger. *Ed* William Nigh.

Cast: Earl Schenck (*Robert Busch/Crown Prince*), Claire Whitney (*Emily Busch*), Percy Standing (*Richard Busch*), Louis Dean (*The Kaiser*), John Sunderland (*Lieut. Patin*), Fred G. Hearn (*Carl Von Strumpf*), Charles T. Parr (*Lewis Keene*), Philip Van Loan (*A Blue Devil*), Billie Wagner (*Little French girl*), Vic De Linsky (*Butler*).

World War I, Drama. In pre-World War I Germany, Kaiser Wilhelm fathers a number of illegitimate children and sends them to various parts of the world to be raised by his loyal agents. Under the guardianship of Dr. Carl Von Strumpf, one of these children, Robert Busch, grows up believing that he is the son of wealthy German-American Richard Busch, but in reality, Strumpf and Busch are servants of the Kaiser. When the United States declares war on Germany, Robert expresses his earnest desire to enlist in the American army, much to the delight of his patriotic sister Emily. Before he can do so, however, Strumpf tells Robert the secret of his parentage, believing that the young man now will be eager to fight for Germany's cause. Robert feigns enthusiasm but secretly offers his services to the U.S. government, and with the passport provided him by the Pan-German league, he goes to Germany and kills the crown

prince. Next, he shoots the Kaiser and blows up the entire palace, thus sacrificing his life for the principles of democracy. *Assassination. German Americans. Germany. Illegitimacy. Parentage. Patriotism. Secret agents. Self-sacrifice. Wilhelm II, German Emperor, 1859-1941. World War I.* Brothers and sisters. Explosions. Military service, Voluntary. Passports. Wards and guardians. Wilhelm, Crown Prince of Germany, 1882-1951.

Note: The film contains newsreel footage of Kaiser Wilhelm and the Crown Prince Wilhelm as well as actual warfare scenes.

ETR 5 Oct 1918, pp. 1472-73. *ETR* 19 Oct 1918, p. 1699, 1770. *MPN* 12 Oct 1918, p. 2409, 2443. *MPN* 26 Oct 1918, p. 2704. *MPW* 19 Oct 1918, pp. 343-44, 445-46. *MPW* 9 Nov 1918, pp. 694-95. *NYDM* 14 Dec 1918, p. 880. *Wid's* 15 Dec 1918, p. 13.

KATHLEEN MAVOURNEEN (Irish Americans)

Tiffany Productions, Inc. 20 Jun **1930** [©Tiffany Productions, Inc.; 5 Jun 1930; LP1344]. Sd (Photophone); b&w. 6 reels, 5,196 ft.

Dir Albert Ray. *Adpt and dial* Frances Hyland. *Photog* Harry Jackson.

Source: Based on the play *Kathleen Mavourneen* by Dion Boucicault (production date undetermined).

Cast: Sally O'Neil (*Kathleen*), Charles Delaney (*Terry*), Robert Elliott (*Dan Moriarity*), Aggie Herring (*Aunt Nora Shannon*), Walter Perry (*Uncle Mike Shannon*), Francis Ford (*Butler*).

Melodrama. Kathleen, an Irish lassie, comes to New York to marry Terry, a plumber. At a celebration in her Aunt Nora's flat, she meets Dan Moriarity, a political boss whom she regards as a "great gentleman." He invites her to his home on Long Island, and his attentions cause Terry to treat her with a jealous protectiveness. But Moriarity proposes marriage to her and informs Terry that they are to wed. At the wedding, however, a man accuses Moriarity's men of a gang killing; Moriarity shoots him in the back before Kathleen and tells the butler to dispose of the body. Terrified, and stopping only long enough to return her wedding ring, Kathleen rushes from the room and finds consolation in the arms of Terry. *Courtship. Irish Americans. Murder. New York City. Plumbers. Political bosses.*

Note: In 1913, a one-reel film of "Kathleen Mavourneen" was produced by Thomas A. Edison, Inc. and a three reel film was produced by Imp and released by Universal Film Mfg. Co. Fox produced a version in 1919 that starred Theda Bara and was directed by Charles J. Brabin (see *AFI Catalog of Feature Films, 1911-20;* F1.2334). A British version, also starring Sally O'Neil and directed by Norman Lee, was made in 1937. However, some of these films are based on source material other than the play, and some of their plots vary.

FD 20 Jul 1930.

KATIE FOR CONGRESS see THE FARMER'S DAUGHTER

KEEP MOVING see BREAKING THE ICE

KEEP PUNCHING (African Americans)

M. C. Pictures, Inc. *Dist* State Rights. **1939**; World premiere at the Apollo Theatre in Harlem: 8 Dec 1939. Sd (Blue Seal Recording); b&w. 81 min.

Pres EDWARD MEAD. *Prod* John Clein. *Dir* John Clein. *Scr* Marcy Klauber. *Story* J. Rosamund Johnson. *Photog* J. Burgi Contner and Jay Rescher. *Film ed* Al. Harburger. *Mus score* Lee Norman. *Sd eng* N. Dean Cole.

Song(s): "Lazy Moon," music by J. Rosamund Johnson, lyrics by Bob Cole; "Comes Love Again," music and lyrics by Herbert Goodwin; "Lift Every Voice and Sing," music and lyrics by James Weldon and J. Rosamund Johnson.

Cast: HENRY ARMSTRONG (*Henry Jackson*), Willie Bryant (*Frank Harrison*), Mae Johnson (*Jerry [Jordan]*), Hamtree Harrington (*"Windy" Butler*), Francine Everett (*Fanny Singleton*), Canada Lee (*Speedy*), Lionel Monagos (*Ed. Watson*), Arthur "Dooky" Wilson (*Baron Skinner*), Hilda Offley (*Mrs. Jackson*), Walter Robinson (*Mr. Jackson*), J. Rosamund Johnson (*The minister*), George Wiltshire (*Hemingway*), Lee Norman's Orchestra, [Whitey's Savoy Lindy Hoppers].

African American, Boxing, Drama. [*Print viewed*]. At the Lincoln Prep School graduation ceremony, Henry Jackson is the pride of the community. Although his teachers and girl friend, Fanny Singleton, want Henry to enter college to become a lawyer, Ed Watson and Speedy, who have noticed the young man's athletic prowess in school, want him to go to New York and box. Henry prefers to become a prizefighter, and he persuades his family to support his decision. With Watson as his manager, Henry goes to New York with Fanny and soon becomes a success. Henry is introduced to Hemingway, who backs him as he breaks into the big time and helps

to arrange a championship bout with Pedro Lopez. As Henry trains with Speedy, he meets an old friend from his hometown, Frank Harrison, who has become a corrupt boxing operator. Frank takes Henry to Baron Skinner's Sunset Club and presents him to his associate, Miss Jerry Jordan, whom he calls the "most beautiful girl in New York." Henry also meets an honest friend, "Windy" Butler, who is now known as "Dynamite." Later, Henry is asked to present an award at the club's beauty contest while Windy wins a prize for his jitterbugging. When Watson learns that Henry is out when he should be quietly preparing for his fight, he argues with Henry and leaves him. Meanwhile, the Jacksons prepare to travel to New York to see Henry's fight with Pedro. Frank, who is betting against Henry, tries to lure him with Jerry, but Henry remains sincere and loyal and tells Jerry about his love for Fanny. Desperate, Frank forces Jerry to put a knockout drug into Henry's drink, but Windy sees the scheme and takes the drug himself to save his friend. At the fight, Watson reappears, but Henry is battered during the early rounds. Jerry, unaware of Windy's action, leaves the stadium and wanders into a church, where she prays for Henry and her own redemption. After overhearing the newspaper boys announce the headline that Henry has won in a knockout, Jerry returns to Frank's apartment to pack her things to leave. Meanwhile, Frank, who has lost all his money betting on Pedro, is killed by angry creditors. Everyone is proud of Henry, and with his family, Fanny and Windy, he returns to Frank's apartment for a party, unaware of what has happened to Windy, who has since recovered from drinking the poison. At the party, Fanny meets Jerry, and although at first she suspects the worst, she is soon relieved when Jerry tells her how lucky she is to have Henry. Fanny and Henry resolve never to be apart, and Henry says that he will probably go back to college. *African Americans. Boxers. Loyalty. Moral corruption.* Beauty contests. Boxing managers. Churches. Colleges. Drugging. Friendship. Lure of the city. Moral reformation. Murder. New York City. Nightclubs. Parties. Politicians. Prayer. Preparatory schools. Self-sacrifice. Small town life.

Note: According to the onscreen credits, this picture was copyrighted in 1939; however, no information concerning its registration for copyright has been located. *Keep Punching* marked the film debut of world welterweight champion Henry Armstrong. According to an article in the *New York Age,* the film was produced in Harlem. According to modern sources, the cast also included Alvin Childress, and the production company was Film Art Studios, Inc.

Exb 13 Dec 1939, p. 443. *HR* 5 Dec 1939, p. 1. *New York Age* 2 Dec 1939. *New York American* 2 Dec 1939.

KEEP TO THE RIGHT see WHO'S YOUR BROTHER?

KELLY THE SECOND (Irish Americans)

Hal Roach Studios, Inc.; Metro-Goldwyn-Mayer Corp.; controlled by Loew's Inc. *Dist* Loew's Inc. 21 Aug **1936**; Prod: 15 Jun—late Feb 1936 [©Metro-Goldwyn-Mayer Corp.; 27 Jul 1936; LP6500]. Sd (Western Electric Sound System); b&w. 7 reels. 70-71 min. Passed by the National Board of Review. PCA cert no. 1961.

Dir Gus Meins. [*Asst dir* Harold Graham]. *Scr* Jeff Moffitt and William Terhune. *Adpt* Jack Jevne and Gordon Douglas. *Dial* Tom Bell and Arthur V. Jones. *Photog* Art Lloyd. [*Asst cam* Bernie Gusty]. *Photog eff* Roy Seawright. *Film ed* Jack Ogilvie. *Mus dir* Marvin Hatley. *Sd* William Randall.

Song(s): "The Irish Washerwoman," traditional.

Cast: Patsy Kelly (*Mollie [Patricia Kelly]*), Guinn "Big Boy" Williams (*Cecil Callahan*), Charley Chase (*Dr. J. Willoughby Klum*), Pert Kelton (*Gloria*), Edward Brophy (*Ike Arnold*), Harold Huber (*Spike*), Max Rosenbloom (*Butch Flynn*), De Witt C. Jennings (*Judge*), Billy Gilbert (*Fur trader*), Syd Saylor (*Dan*), [Carl "Alfalfa" Switzer (*Boy with stomach ache*)], [Robert E. O'Connor (*Policeman*)].

Comedy. [*Print viewed*]. Mollie Patricia Kelly is rushing to her job as the lunch counter manager at Dr. J. Willoughby Klum's drugstore when her car accidentally latches onto a passing truck that drags her through half of New York. When the truck finally stops, she starts yelling at its driver, Cecil Callahan, and their arguing results in a free-for-all fight among bystanders. The police are used to Cecil's fighting and alert the station house, which dispatches a paddy wagon. When Mollie accidentally hits a radio, causing it to play "The Irish Washerwoman," however, Cecil quickly bests his opponents and the two flee. After driving Mollie to work, Cecil finally has to face the police, who spot his truck outside. Because Mollie and Dr. Klum try

to hide Cecil, they are also brought into court, but are set free. Feeling sorry for Cecil, Dr. Klum offers to help and inadvertently winds up posting his store as a bond to ensure that the pugnacious Cecil will never fight again. Realizing that Cecil can't live without fighting, Mollie decides to turn him into a boxer, with Klum as manager and herself as trainer. On the night of his first fight, Cecil is a few pounds underweight, so Mollie stuffs him with bananas just before the match. Meanwhile, Klum is seated next to gangster Ike Arnold and unwittingly gets Arnold to bet $1,000 on Cecil when the two men find they have a common interest in astrology. When Cecil is quickly knocked out because of his upset stomach, Arnold thinks he has been duped and the frightened Klum rushes back to the drug store, closely followed by Arnold and his gang. Because he saw Cecil slug his opponent for real in the dressing rooms, Arnold knows that he can fight and proposes a partnership with Klum. Soon Mollie and Cecil go to train in the country and Cecil begins to win. Within a few months, he has won nineteen fights and is scheduled to oppose the heavyweight champion, Butch Flynn. At a party, Mollie becomes jealous of Gloria, Arnold's girl friend, when she thinks that Cecil prefers her. That same night, Gloria becomes angry at Arnold because he tries to palm a rabbit coat off as ermine, so she decides to make a play for Cecil. Cecil and Mollie argue, and when Gloria invites him to her apartment, he goes. On the night of the fight, neither Mollie nor Klum can find Cecil until their assistant Dan tells Mollie that he is in a nightclub with Gloria. Mollie goes to get him, but when he drunkenly says he is going to marry Gloria, she leaves. When Cecil finally comes back, Klum tries to sober him up, but Arnold sees him and secretly decides to bet on Flynn. When the fight starts, Cecil tries to win, but can't, because he misses Mollie. She, meanwhile, has disguised herself in a long beard and glasses and is watching the fight from the audience. When she hears Gloria tell Arnold that she wasn't fooling around with Cecil, and all he talked about was Mollie, Mollie rushes to the ring and encourages him to win. She uses a hatpin to stick him when he falls down, but when even this doesn't help, she asks Klum to play "The Irish Washerwoman" on a hurdy gurdy. Cecil then jumps into action until a nervous Arnold has the hurdy gurdy smashed. Now desperate, Mollie rushes into the audience, and after asking for Irishmen, gets them to sing the song. Soon the entire audience joins in and Cecil bests his opponent. Finally free from worries, Klum says that Cecil and Mollie can now get married, and after a few verbal punches, they agree. *Boxers. Gangsters. Irish Americans. Romance. Automobile accidents. Bananas. Farms. Fistfights. Fox hunts. Hurdy-gurdies. "The Irish Washerwoman" (Song). Jealousy. Judges. New York City. Pharmacists. Police. Trucks. Waitresses.*

Note: Preview running times for the film were 82 and 85 minutes. The *Var* review noted that the film was trimmed "about fifteen minutes" from its original release. It has not been determined if it was released in some places at the preview length. According to *MPSI*, Paul Gustine was in the cast, but his participation in the released film has not been confirmed. According to reviews, this was Patsy Kelly's first starrring role in a feature after starring in many short films.

Box 25 Apr 1936. *DV* 18 Apr 1936, p. 3. *FD* 21 Apr 1936, p. 5. *HR* 14 Jan 1936, p. 2. *HR* 18 Jan 1936, p. 6. *HR* 18 Apr 1936, p. 6. *MPD* 20 Apr 1936, pp. 10-11. *MPH* 10 Oct 1936, p. 21. *MPSI* May 1936, p. 36. *NYT* 3 Oct 1936, p. 21. *Var* 7 Oct 1936, p. 15.

A KENTUCKY CINDERELLA (African Americans)
Bluebird Photoplays, Inc. *Dist* Bluebird Photoplays, Inc. 25 Jun 1917 [©Bluebird Photplays, Inc.; 26 May 1917; LP10851]. Si; b&w. 5 reels.
Dir Rupert Julian. *Scen* Elliott J. Clawson. *Story* Steve Rounds.
Source: Based on the short story "A Kentucky Cinderella" by Francis Hopkinson Smith in *The Other Fellow* (Boston, 1899).
Cast: Rupert Julian (*John Silverwood*), Ruth Clifford (*Nannie*), Harry Carter ("*Kentuck*" *Windfield Gordon/Henry Gordon*), Aurora Pratt (*Mrs. Morgan*), Emory Johnson (*Tom Boling*), Eddie Polo (*Ed Long*), Frank Lanning (*Frank Long*), Zoe Rae (*Zoe*), Lucretia Harris (*Aunt Chlorindy*), Myrtle Reeves (*Rachel*), Gretchen Lederer (*Miss Morgan*), Elsie Jane Wilson (*Henry's wife*).
Drama. When the Long brothers try to jump the gold claim owned by "Kentuck" Windfield Gordon and John Silverwood, Kentuck is killed while defending his property and Silverwood sends Kentuck's orphaned daughter Nannie back to her Uncle Henry in Kentucky. When she arrives, Uncle Henry is away on business, leaving Nannie at the mercy of Henry's second wife, who mistreats the girl as a poor relation and resents the competition she presents to her own daughter, Rachel. Aunt Chlorindy, the mammy who helped raise

Nannie, protects her, and when the girl is driven out of the house by Mrs. Gordon, Aunt Chlorindy finds her refuge with Mrs. Morgan, a wealthy widow living nearby. There Nannie meets Tom Boling, a rich young bachelor who falls in love with her. Justice is served when Tom marries Nannie rather than Rachel as Mrs. Gordon had planned, and Silverwood returns for the ceremony, rich from striking gold, and falls in love with Mrs. Morgan. *Battered children. Class distinction. Foster parents. Kentucky. Orphans. African Americans. Aunts. Brothers. Claim jumpers. Gold. Murder. Nursemaids. Rivalry. Upper classes. Weddings. Widows.*

ETR 30 Jun 1917, p. 270. *Motog* 30 Jun 1917, p. 1392. *MPN* 7 Jul 1917, p. 116. *MPW* 30 Jun 1917, p. 2155. *MPW* 7 Jul 1917, p. 75. *NYDM* 30 Jun 1917, p. 30. *Var* 22 Jun 1917, p. 26. *Wid's* 28 Jun 1917, p. 411.

KENTUCKY RIFLE (Comanche, Native Americans)
Howco Productions, Inc. *Dist* Howco Productions, Inc. Jul **1955**; Prod: early Nov—mid-Nov 1954 at KTTV Studios [©Howco Productions, Inc.; 15 Apr 1956; LP4614]. Sd; col (Pathé Color). 9 reels, 7,243 ft. 80 or 82 min. PCA cert no. 17387.
Pres J. Francis White and JOY HOUCK. *Prod* CARL K. HITTLEMAN. *Assoc prod* Ira S. Webb. *Dir* Carl K. Hittleman. *Asst dir* Austen Jewell. *Orig story* Carl K. Hittleman and Lee J. Hewitt. *Scr* Francis Chase, Jr., Lee J. Hewitt and Carl K. Hittleman. *Dir of photog* Paul Ivano. *Spec eff* Ray Mercer. *Prod des* Ray Heinze. *Film ed* Hugh Winn. *Ward* Wesley Jefferies. *Mus comp and dir* Irving Gertz. *Rec* Jack Solomon. *Sd* Glen Glenn Sound Co. *Makeup artist* Eddie Polo. *Hair stylist* Sally Berkeley. *Prop master* Max Frankel. *Co-ordinator* Tom Kemp. *Dial coach* Stanley Price. *Scr supv* Connie Earle. *Casting* Yolanda McGinnis.
Song(s): "Sweet Betsy from Pike," traditional.
Cast: Chill Wills (*Tobias Taylor*), Lance Fuller (*Jason Clay*), Cathy Downs (*Amy Connors*), Sterling Holloway (*Lon Setter*), Henry Hull (*Preacher Bently*), Jeanne Cagney (*Cordie Hay*), Jess Barker (*Daniel Foster*), John Pickard (*Reuben Hay*), John Alvin (*Luke Thomas*), I. Stanford Jolley (*Jed Williams*), Rory Mallinson (*Indian chief*), George Keymas (*Interpreter*), Clyde Houck (*Clyde Thomas*), Alice Rolph (*Mrs. Thomas*).
Western. [*Print viewed*]. When the wheel on Daniel Foster's wagon breaks, once again delaying the wagon train's long journey across the western plains, he argues that the weight of the rifles he is hauling for gunmaker Jason Clay is to blame. Jason responds that his fine Kentucky rifles protect the entire party from the Indians, but Dan is furious and refuses to listen. Jason's poorly concealed interest in Dan's fiancée, Amy Connors, heightens the tension, and when Jason discovers that the wheel's axle is broken, the two men almost come to blows. As the wagon train continues, several of the travelers, including Amy, Jason, his friend, Tobias Taylor, Preacher Bently, Lon Setter, Luke Thomas, Reuben Hay, and his expectant wife Cordie, reluctantly decide to stay behind until the wagon is repaired. While riding into the hills to look for sturdy timber, Tobias encounters angry Comanches, and when he reports this to the others, Luke worries that his wife and child may be attacked with the wagon train. Despite Jason's warnings, Luke rides out to warn the wagon train during the night, and the next morning, Jason and Tobias find his body hanging from a tree. Three Comanches, including a chief and an interpreter, then interrupt Luke's burial service, demanding gifts in exchange for safe passage through their territory. Dan insists on giving the Indians all of their goods, including the rifles, but Jason and Tobias forbid him. Although Jason earns the respect of the chief by defeating the interpreter in hand-to-hand combat, the chief, warns him that his warriors have many cunning arrows and shoots an arrow into Luke's grave marker. After praying for help, Tobias shoots his rifle, "Sweet Betsy," at the arrow and hits it, and the Indians leave. The men then make a new axle, and by nightfall, the wagon is ready to travel. During the night, however, several Indians shoot arrows into the camp, narrowly missing the frightened Lon. Jason sneaks into the darkness and kills the attackers, but when he returns with an arm wound, Amy insists on nursing him. Increasingly attracted to Jason, Amy finally kisses him. Later that night, Dan steals away from camp to make a deal with the Comanches. In the morning, Jason pursues him and finds him as he is promising the Indians their rifles. Furious, Jason protests that the Indians, armed with rifles, will kill not only their party, but many of the settlers who plan to journey across the plains. The Indians threaten to kill Dan, whereupon Jason, believing that Amy still loves her fiancé, returns to his group for a vote. Tobias argues against the

deal, but the rest of the men vote to give the guns to the Comanches. The chief promises Jason that his people will allow the wagon to pass in safety, but when Jason leaves to fetch the rifles, the Indians gleefully prepare for battle. Dan leaps on a horse and returns to the wagon to warn the others, but he is seriously injured by an arrow. Soon after he arrives, the Indians appear, but the men, armed with their sturdy rifles, drive them off. One of the warriors charges the wagon, killing Dan, but the other Comanches retreat, and the wagon continues its journey. Cordie, now in labor, moans in pain as the wagon approaches a narrow pass in the hills. Although the hills are full of Indians, the chief, admitting the superiority of the white man's weapons, states that the wagon may pass through. Just as the wagon emerges from the pass, one bloodthirsty Comanche shoots an arrow into Tobias' back. The cries of Cordie's new baby fill the air as Tobias, praising his Kentucky rifle as a "thing of beauty," dies in Jason's arms. *Comanche Indians. Rifles. Settlers. Wagons. The West.* Battles. Bow and arrow. Burial. Childbirth. Cowardice. Fights. Gunsmiths. Indians of North America. Prayer. Preachers. Romantic rivalry. Translators. Treachery. Tribal chiefs. Wagon trains.

Exb 8 Aug 1956, p. 4201, 4203. *HR* 12 Nov 1954, p. 7. *HR* 19 Nov 1954, p. 7. *MPD* 24 Aug 1956, p. 6. *MPHPD* 1 Sep 1956, p. 50.

KEY LARGO (Italian Americans, Native Americans, Seminole)
Warner Bros. Pictures, Inc.; A Warner Bros.—First National Picture. *Dist* Warner Bros. Pictures, Inc. 31 Jul **1948**; New York opening: 16 Jul 1948; Prod: late Dec 1947—mid-Mar 1948 [©Warner Bros. Pictures, Inc.; 31 Jul 1948; LP1750]. Sd (RCA Sound System); b&w. 100 min.

Prod Jerry Wald. **Dir** John Huston. [*Asst dir* Art Lueker]. [*2d asst dir* John Prettyman]. **Scr** Richard Brooks and John Huston. **Dir of photog** Karl Freund. [*2d cam* Ellie Fredericks]. [*Asst cam* Wally Meinardus]. [*Stills* Mac Julian]. [*Gaffer* Lee Wilson]. **Spec eff dir** William McGann. **Spec eff** Robert Burks. **Art dir** Leo K. Kuter. **Film ed** Rudi Fehr. **Set dec** Fred M. MacLean. [*Props* Bud Friend and George Sweeney]. **Ward** Leah Rhodes, Ted Shultz and Marie Blanchard]. **Mus** Max Steiner. **Orch** Murray Cutter. **Sd** Dolph Thomas. **Makeup artist** Perc Westmore. [*Makeup* Frank McCoy]. [*Hair* Betty Delmont]. [*Unit mgr* Chuck Hansen]. [*Scr supv* Jean Baker]. [*Grip* E. F. Dexter]. [*Best boy* Burt Jones].

Song(s): "Moanin' Low," words by Howard Dietz, music by Ralph Rainger.

Source: Based on the play *Key Largo* by Maxwell Anderson, as produced by The Playwrights Company (New York, 27 Nov 1939).

Cast: HUMPHREY BOGART [(*Frank McCloud*)], EDWARD G. ROBINSON [(*Johnny Rocco*)], LAUREN BACALL [(*Nora Temple*)], Lionel Barrymore [(*James Temple*)], Claire Trevor [(*Gaye Dawn*)], Thomas Gomez [(*Curly Hoff*)], Harry Lewis [(*Toots*)], John Rodney [(*Deputy Clyde Sawyer*)], Marc Lawrence [(*Ziggy*)], Dan Seymour [(*Angel*)], Monte Blue [(*Ben Wade*)], William Haade [(*Henchman*)], [Jay Silverheels, Rodric Redwing (*Oceola brothers*)], [Joe P. Smith (*Bus driver*)], [Albert Marin (*Skipper*)], [Jerry Jerome, John Phillips, Lute Crockett (*Ziggy's henchmen*)], [Felipa Gomez (*Old Indian woman*)], [Pat Flaherty].

Crime, Drama. [*Print viewed*]. Disillusioned veteran Frank McCloud arrives on the island of Key Largo, Florida to visit the family of George Temple, who died under his command in Italy during World War II. At the rundown Hotel Largo where George's wheelchair-bound father James lives with George's widow, Nora, Frank encounters Curly Hoff, Toots, Angel and Gaye Dawn in the bar. Learning from them that the hotel is closed for the off-season, Frank searches out the Temples, who greet him warmly and insist that he stay the night. Nora explains that their guests offered her father-in-law so much money to open the hotel for them, that he could not turn them down. Later, a hurricane warning is issued and as Nora fastens the shutters in preparation, the telephone rings. Curly tells the caller that the Temples are not around and adds that Sawyer, the local police officer, has not been seen either. When Temple objects, the men pull their guns. In response to the activity, the men's leader comes downstairs for the first time since Frank's arrival, and Frank recognizes him as deported gangster Johnny Rocco. Rocco has entered the country illegally from Cuba in order to make a delivery of counterfeit money, but his contacts have been delayed by the approaching storm. Meanwhile, he and his men have captured and beaten Sawyer, who was searching for the Oceola brothers, Seminoles who had escaped from jail. When Rocco, impressed by Nora's feisty

spirit, makes a pass at her, she spits in his face, and Frank stops him from killing her with some fast talking. Mocking Frank's heroics, Rocco throws him a gun and, holding his own gun on Frank, tells him that he can rid the world of Rocco if he is willing to die in the process. To the disappointment of both Nora and Temple, Frank refuses to shoot. He throws the gun down and Sawyer grabs it and tries to escape. Rocco kills Sawyer, revealing that the other gun was not loaded, a fact that Frank had no way of knowing. Rocco then demands that Gaye, his alcoholic former mistress, sing a song before she can have a drink. She is too desperate to sing well, and when Rocco still refuses to give her a drink because her singing was "rotten," Frank takes pity on her. Rocco slaps him and once again, Frank does nothing. The full force of the hurricane then hits, terrifying Rocco and giving Nora a chance to challenge Frank about his disillusionment. After the storm passes, Rocco discovers that his boat has disappeared. He orders Frank to take Temple's boat and transport him to Cuba. Before they can leave, a second police officer comes looking for Sawyer and finds his body on the shore, where it washed up during the storm. Rocco blames the murder on the Oceola brothers, who are on the island to turn themselves in on Temple's advice, and when the Indians try to escape, the officer murders them. As the gangsters prepare to leave, Gaye begs Rocco to take her along, and while she clings to him, she grabs his gun from his jacket pocket and slips it to Frank. After he sets course for Cuba, Frank maneuvers the boat to knock one man overboard and shoots the others, including Rocco. Although he has been wounded, Frank radios his position and then calls the hotel to tell Nora and Temple that he is coming back home. *Disillusionment. Gangsters. Hotels. Key Largo (FL). Veterans.* Alcoholics. Boats. Brothers. Fathers-in-law. Firearms. Handicapped. Hurricanes. Mistresses. Murder. Police. Psychological torment. Seminole Indians. Widows.

Note: The film begins with the following foreword: "At the southernmost point of the United States are the Florida Keys, a string of small islands held together by a concrete causeway. Largest of these remote coral islands is Key Largo." According to a 6 Nov 1947 *HR* news item, some scenes were filmed on location in Key West, FL, although Huston stated in a modern interview that it was shot mostly in the studio. A 13 Jan 1948 *HR* news item reported that director of photography Karl Freund shot a three-minute continuous sequence using two dollies and a new light-weight camera. The shot begins when Humphrey Bogart and Thomas Gomez are in a bathroom and moves through a room into the hallway, down two flights of stairs, through another hallway and onto a porch. A modern source notes that Huston drew on his 1944 war documentary *San Pietro* when writing the scenes in which "Frank" tells "Nora" and "Temple" about his dead friend. This was Huston's last film for Warner Bros., and the last film that Bogart and Bacall made together. Claire Trevor won the Academy Award for Best Supporting Actress. Edward G. Robinson and Claire Trevor reprised their roles for a *Lux Radio Theatre* broadcast on 28 Nov 1947.

Box 10 Jul 1948. *DV* 7 Jul 1948, p. 3. *FD* 7 Jul 1948, p. 14. *HR* 6 Nov 1947, p. 4. *HR* 26 Dec 1947, p. 13. *HR* 13 Jan 1948, p. 6. *HR* 12 Mar 1948, p. 17. *HR* 7 Jul 1948, pp. 3-4. *HR* 20 Jul 1948, p. 6. *MPHPD* 3 Jul 1948, p. 4226. *MPHPD* 10 Jul 1948, p. 4233. *NYT* 17 Jul 1948, p. 6. *Var* 7 Jul 1948, p. 6.

KEY WITNESS (African Americans, Latino)
Avon Productions, Inc.; Metro-Goldwyn-Mayer Corp.; controlled by Loew's Inc.; A Pandro S. Berman Production. *Dist* Loew's Inc. Oct **1960**; Prod: late Sep—10 Nov 1959 [©Loew's Inc. & Avon Productions, Inc.; 3 Mar 1960; (copyright number not known)]. Sd (Westrex Recording System); b&w; CinemaScope; Photographic lenses by Panavision. 9 reels, 7,239 ft. 81 min. PCA cert no. 19514.

Prod Kathryn Hereford. **Dir** Phil Karlson. **Asst dir** Donald C. Klune. **Scr** Alfred Brenner and Sidney Michaels. **Dir of photog** Harold E. Wellman. **Art dir** George W. Davis and Malcolm Brown. **Film ed** Ferris Webster. **Set dec** Henry Grace and Fay Babcock. **Women's cost** Kitty Mager. **Mus** Charles Wolcott. **Rec supv** Franklin Milton. **Makeup** William Tuttle.

Source: Based on the novel *Key Witness* by Frank Kane (New York, 1956).

Cast: Jeffrey Hunter [(*Fred Morrow*)], Pat Crowley [(*Ann Morrow*)], Dennis Hopper [("*Cowboy*" *William L. Tompkins*)], Joby Baker [("*Muggles*")], Susan Harrison [(*Ruby*)], Johnny Nash [("*Apple*")], Corey Allen [("*Magician*")], Frank Silvera [(*Detective Rafael Torno*)], Bruce Gordon [(*Arthur Robbins*)], Terry Burnham [(*Gloria Morrow*)], Dennis Holmes [(*Phil Morrow*)], [Harry Lauter (*Hurley*)], [Eugene Iglesias (*Emelio*)], [Will J. White (*Deputy*)], [Carlos Rivera (*Mr. Sanchez*)], [Fred Coby, James Gavin, John Damler (*Policemen*)], [Rodney Bell, John Zaremba, Mary Alan Hokanson (*Reporters*)], [Owen McGiveney (*Pedestrian*)], [Hilda Haynes

(*Apple's mother*)], [John Close (*Detective*)], [Ted Knight (*Lawyer*)], [William Keene (*Judge*)], [Jack Daly (*Recorder*)], [Morgan Jones (*Deputy*)], [Harry Hines (*Blind man*)], [Julia Montoya (*Mrs. Sanchez*)].

Crime, Social, Youth, Drama. [*Print viewed*]. Fred Morrow, a Los Angeles real estate agent, gets off the freeway in an East L.A. neighborhood and makes a phone call at a café frequented by teenagers. While on the phone, he witnesses the fatal stabbing of Emelio Sanchez by gang leader William L. Tompkins, known as "Cowboy," who found Emelio dancing with his flirtatious girl friend Ruby. When none of the many neighborhood witnesses offer information to the police, Fred steps forward and relates Emelio's dying words, "Cowboy did it." At police headquarters, Fred identifies Cowboy's mug shot to Detective Rafael Torno, who is fearful he will lose Fred's cooperation once he discovers the possible consequences of being the only witness to the murder. At the gang's hangout in a garage, Cowboy becomes frantic when he learns from a newspaper that Emelio has died and that the district attorney has a mystery witness. After Ruby relates that she saw police officer Hurley write down Fred's name and address, "Muggles," a beat-talking drug addict, comes up with a plan to get Hurley's notebook. In Hurley's sight, "Apple," an African-American member of the gang, and the only one who was visibly pained when Emelio was stabbed, attacks Ruby and takes her purse, then runs into an alley and hides. When Hurley follows, Cowboy knocks him over the head with a pipe, and they get Hurley's notebook and gun. Cowboy calls Fred's home and learns from his young daughter that he and his wife Ann have gone to the supermarket. Apple tries to talk Cowboy out of killing Fred, but Cowboy orders him to go away and keep his mouth shut. The gang rams Fred and Ann in their car after they leave the supermarket and pushes them through an intersection, nearly causing an accident. Muggles then pulls a gun on Ann, while Cowboy warns Fred to tear up the affidavit. Fred reports the incident to Torno, who arranges police protection for the Morrows. In the evening, Cowboy phones and gives Fred until midnight to rip up the affidavit, or else, he says, his wife and children will die. When a note tied to a rock is thrown through their living room window, Fred prepares to take his crying children and Ann to a motel, but they find that their car has been vandalized and the tires slashed. When the police arrive, Fred throws a tantrum. Meanwhile, Torno goes to see Apple, whom he once arrested with Cowboy, but Apple denies being with Cowboy that day. At ten minutes to twelve, Cowboy phones Fred, who tells him to go to hell. Ann becomes hysterical, yelling that the gang will slit their throats. As Cowboy and the gang prepare to torch the Morrows' house with kerosene, Apple comes to the garage asking for money so that he can leave town. Torno and the police, who have followed Apple, surprise the gang, but Cowboy escapes in a stolen Jaguar and leads the police on a chase through Los Angeles streets and freeways. After eluding them by turning the wrong way up an exit ramp, Cowboy drives over an embankment. Torno catches him on foot and subdues him. Meanwhile, Apple's mother interrupts him as he is packing to tell him that Muggles, Ruby and another gang member, "Magician," have come for him. When Apple tells his mother that he is leaving to take a job in San Diego, she indignantly says that although she scrubs floors for a living, she is not a fool, but he asks her to believe him and she says she does. Magician, a racist, hits Apple, whom they accuse of purposely leading the police to the garage. When Muggles pulls a gun on him, Ruby takes it away, saying she believes Apple. That night, Fred identifies Cowboy through a one-way glass at the police station. The next day, Ruby decides they will kidnap the Morrows' children. Apple is aghast, but the others agree to her plan. As Fred is about to testify, Ruby attacks Ann in the courthouse hallway. When Fred learns about the attack, he testifies he was mistaken in his identification of Cowboy. Meanwhile, on the playground at the childrens' school, Muggles locates the Morrows' son and pulls a gun. Apple hits his arm as Muggles shoots, wounding the boy. As they drive off, Apple rolls out of the moving car. Muggles sees him run to Fred's house and tells Cowboy, now free on bail. Finding Apple at his home, Fred socks him and makes a racist remark, then tries to get him to fight. Apple asks help to reach Torno, but Fred taunts him, saying facetiously that he should tell the newspapers he is underprivileged, fatherless, hungry, lonely or mentally ill, so that they will protect him. When Fred calls him "boy," Apple goes to leave, but the gang shows up. Cowboy pulls a switchblade, and Fred tries to protect Apple. The gang make a circle

around the two, and Cowboy asks Fred why he is risking his life for a "nigger." After another racist remark, they fight, and Fred knocks the knife away. Torno then arrives with the police, who capture the gang. Fred tells him that now he has two key witnesses. *African Americans. Courage. Family life. Fear. Gangs. Latino. Racism. Threats. Witnesses. Youth. Arrests. Chases. Dancing. Drugs. Flirts. Garages. Grocery stores. Kidnapping. Los Angeles (CA). Mothers and sons. Murder. Police. Police detectives. Real estate agents. Telephone booths. Trials.*

Note: Although the film is listed in the copyright register under the number "LP15382," that number is incorrect, and the correct number has not been identified. The opening credits contain the following statement: "The story you are about to see is fictional; but all good fiction is based on some truth; and the truth of this story is, that it may happen every day throughout the entire world. It can happen to you now in your town. If you fail to give your support to the laws you make; give your strength to justice, to decency and to the innocent. Law without enforcement is only a word. Enforcement without your help is not possible." The statement ends with the signature of Stanley Mosk, Attorney General, State of California.

According to information in the MPAA/PCA Collection at the AMPAS Library, when M-G-M submitted material on the proposed film to the PCA in Apr 1958, PCA officials stated "we do not feel that we can approve a picture based on this material. A year ago... we agreed that this office would not approve any more sadistically conceived juvenile delinquency pictures, which were filled with violence and savagery. We so informed producers generally, and since then there have been no pictures of this type presented." A script dated 3 Sep 1959 was similarly rejected as "unacceptable under the Code," and PCA officials informed the studio, "this story is filled with an accumulation of violence, savagery, and sadism to such a degree as to seem almost orgiastic." They warned of "an ominous background of public wrath" against such pictures and stated they "cannot approve a film even remotely containing the amount of arrogant aggressiveness and anti-social violence which this script contains." The PCA demanded that "some scenes of the innate health and weight of society would have to be developed so that it would not seem to be ineffectual or easily violable by insolent, psychotic hoodlums as in the present script." Among other desired changes, the PCA asked the studio not to dramatize the first killing, to eliminate an attempt by the gang to run down "Apple" with a car, and to cut out a telephone threat to "sexually abuse Morrow's daughter." The studio complied with all these requests. In addition, PCA officials objected to the depiction of "Muggles" as a "dope addict" and the portrayal of "Ruby" as "a shameless little nymphomaniac," commenting, "The description of the way she dresses, walks, provokes men sexually, and particularly how she throws herself on the back seat of the automobile with her legs deliberately open in coaxing Cowboy, is nothing short of abominable." On 2 Oct 1959, following the first three days of rushes, although a number of changes had been made or promised, the PCA warned M-G-M that they still could not guarantee that the final film would be acceptable and cautioned, "Proceeding with it under these conditions is a gamble pure and simple on the part of the Studio."

According to *HR*, at the time of production, Pandro S. Berman was listed as producer, but when the film was released a year later, Kathryn Hereford, "for many years [Berman's] girl Friday," who married Berman following the film's completion, received the credit. *HR* reported in Sep 1958 that Larry Marcus was to do the screenplay, but Marcus' participation in the final film has not been confirmed. According to the pressbook, the freeway scenes were shot in five nights between 8 p.m. and 4 a.m. on an unopened segment of the Santa Ana Freeway. Reviews generally praised the film highly. *NYT* called it "fast, tough, tight, sickeningly real to watch and wonderfully well put together." *MPH* described it as "taut with terror almost to the breaking point." *HR*, however, was critical, stating "the total effect... is to have the spectator make a silent vow never, never to be a police witness for anything." *HR* and *Var* criticized the element of racism in the film. *HR* stated, "It is done pointlessly and to no particular advantage." *Var* commented, "Only important flaw is an unnecessary scene in which references are made to Nash's race, Negro. It's been established earlier that the Negro's the only decent one in the gang, so adding the realtor's racial prejudices into the conflict then promptly resolving them—all in a few final minutes—is dramatically unsound."

Box 3 Oct 1960. *DV* 17 Sep 1958. *DV* 27 Sep 1960, p. 3. *Exh* 14 Sep 1960, p. 4750. *FD* 27 Sep 1960, p. 10. *Har* 1 Oct 1960, p. 158. *HCN* 13 Oct 1960. *HR* 9 Aug 1960. *HR* 20 Sep 1960. *HR* 27 Sep 1960, p. 3. *LAEx* 13 Oct 1960. *LAT* 14 Oct 1960, pt. 11, p. 8. *MPD* 23 Oct 1960. *MPHPD* 1 Oct 1960, p. 860. *NYT* 12 Nov 1960, p. 15. *Var* 28 Sep 1960, p. 6.

DEM KHAZNS ZUNDL *see* **THE CANTOR'S SON**

THE KIBITZER (Jewish Americans)
Paramount Famous Lasky Corp. 11 Jan **1930** [©Paramount Famous Lasky Corp.; 8 Jan 1930; LP980]. Sd (Movietone); b&w. 9 reels, 7,273 ft. [Also si; 6,569 ft.].

Dir Edward Sloman. *Scen* Marion Dix. *Adpt and dial* Sam Mintz and Viola Brothers Shore. *Photog* Alfred Gilks. *Film ed* Eda Warren. *Rec eng* Harry D. Mills.

Song(s): "Just Wait and See Sweetheart," music by Richard A. Whiting, lyrics by Leo Robin.

Source: Based on the novel *The Kibitzer* by Joseph Swerling and Edward G. Robinson (New York & Los Angeles, 1929).

Cast: Harry Green (*Ike Lazarus*), Mary Brian (*Josie Lazarus*), Neil Hamilton (*Eddie Brown*), Albert Gran (*James Livingston*), David Newell (*Bert Livingston*), Guy Oliver (*McGinty*), Tenen Holtz (*Meyer*), Henry Fink (*Kikapoupolos*), Lee Kohlmar (*Yankel*), E. H. Calvert (*Westcott*), Thomas Curran (*Briggs*), Eddie Kane (*Phillips*), Henry A. Barrows (*Hanson*), Paddy O'Flynn (*Reporter*), Dick Rush (*Mullins*), Eugene Pallette (*Klaus*).

Comedy-drama. Ike Lazarus, a Jewish tobacconist, does his kibitzing nightly when his friends gather at the store for pinochle. Josie, his daughter, who is engaged to Eddie Brown, goes with Bert, a financier's son, to a horse race. They are followed there by Ike and Eddie, and Eddie loses his money on a "hot tip" given him by Ike. When Josie threatens to elope with Bert, her father goes to Livingston, Bert's father, and thwarts the plot. As a reward, Livingston gives Ike some shares in American Steel. The market rises, then falls, but Ike's brother unwittingly sells the stock at its peak value. With the fortune he has acquired, Ike finances a garage for Eddie, who is happily reunited with Josie. *Garages. Horseracing. Jews. Pinochle (Game). Speculation. Tobacconists.*

FD 22 Dec 1929. *NYT* 21 Dec 1929, p. 17.

KID MONK BARONI (Italian Americans)

Jack Broder Productions. *Dist* Realart Exchange. May **1952**; Prod: Jan 1952 at General Service Studios. Sd; b&w. 7,171 ft. 79-80 min.

Prod Jack Broder. *Assoc prod* Herman Cohen. *Dir* Harold Schuster. *Asst dir* Ben Chapman. *Scr* Aben Kandel. *Photog* Charles Van Enger. *Art dir* James Sullivan. *Film ed* Jason Bernie. *Mus dir* Herschel Burke Gilbert. *Sd* Vic Appel.

Cast: Richard Rober (*Father Callahan*), Bruce Cabot (*Mr. Hellman*), Allene Roberts (*Emily Brooks*), Mona Knox (*June Travers*), Leonard Nimoy (*Paul [Kid] "Monk" Baroni*), Jack Larson (*Angelo*), Budd Jaxon (*Knuckles*), Archer MacDonald (*Pete*), Kathleen Freeman (*Maria Baroni*), Joseph Mell (*Gino Baroni*), Paul Maxey (*Mr. Petry*), Stuart Randall (*Mr. Moore*), Chad Mallory (*Joey*), Maurice Cass (*Pawn broker*), Bill Cabanne (*Seattle Wildcat*), Ted Avery.

Boxing, Drama. [*Not viewed*]. Kid "Monk" Baroni, leader of "The Billy Goats," a gang of teenaged hoodlums from New York's Little Italy, is so sensitive about his disfigured face that he flies into an animal-like rage at any mention of it. Father Callahan, the new parish priest, induces Monk and his gang to use the church gymnasium, and gradually teaches Monk how to box without having to fight like a beast. Under Callahan's influence, Monk learns to control his temper and becomes interested in the church's social programs, especially after he meets Emily Brooks, who helps with the programs. One night, Monk's old gang starts a fight with him, and Callahan, while attempting to stop it, is accidentally knocked unconscious by Monk. Ashamed to face the priest after this accident, Monk leaves the neighborhood and becomes a professional fighter. His new manager, Mr. Hellman, makes a deal with a boxing syndicate to build up Monk as a "killer" because of his animal-like fighting in the ring. Under Hellman's guidance, Monk becomes a top fighter and earns a considerable amount of money. One day, Monk encounters the priest, who forgives him and persuades him to attend a church dance, where he renews his interest in Emily. Realizing that Monk is still ashamed of his face, Emily convinces him to have plastic surgery. The surgery not only gives him a new face, but also a hard, self-centered outlook on life. Monk begins to ignore Emily and takes up with gold digger June Travers, who abandons him as soon as he has spent all his money on her. Meanwhile, Monk loses match after match because of his new defensive style of fighting, which he developed to protect his face. When the syndicate decides to drop Monk, Hellman persuades him to revert to his old killer style for just one more bout, promising to contribute his share of the winnings to the priest for a new recreational center. Monk tries hard to win the fight, but is beaten by a superior opponent. His loss turns out to be his gain, however, for his donation to the church puts him back in the good graces of his family and friends. Monk then marries Emily and is appointed the physical education director of the new recreation center. *Boxers. Juvenile delinquents. Maturation. New York City–Little Italy. Priests.* Boxing managers. Charities. Churches. Gold diggers. Italian Americans. Plastic surgery. Romance.

Note: A Nov 1951 *HR* news item stated that this was to be the first entry in a proposed "Billy Goat" film series.

HR 23 Nov 1951. *HR* 4 Jan 1952, p. 9. *HR* 11 Jan 1952, p. 15. *Box* 26 Apr 1952. *DV* 17 Apr 1952, p. 3. *Exh* 7 May 1952, p. 3293. *FD* 30 Apr 1952, p. 6. *Har* 26 Apr 1952, p. 67. *HR* 17 Apr 1952, p. 3. *MPHPD* 26 Apr 1952, p. 1329. *Var* 23 Apr 1952, p. 6.

THE KILLER see MYSTERY RANCH

KILLER DILLER (African Americans)

All American News, Inc. *Dist* State Rights. **1948**. Sd (RCA Sound System); b&w. 6,616 ft. 73 min.

Prod E. M. Glucksman. *Dir* Josh Binney. *Asst dir* Walter Sheridan. *Story and scr* Hal Seeger. *Dir of photog* Lester Lang. *Art dir* Sam Corso. *Film ed* L. Hesse. *Draperies* Frank W. Stevens. *Cost* Mme. Bertha & Eaves Costume Co. *Mus arr* Rene J. Hall. *Dance dir* Charles Morrison. *Sd eng* Harold Vivian. *Makeup artist* Doc Liszt.

Music: "Breezy and the Bass" by Nat Cole and Johnny Miller; "Basie Boogie" by Count Basie; "Gator Serenade" and "Apollo Groove," composers undetermined.

Song(s): "Ooh, Kickeroonie," words and music by Nat Cole; "Now, He Tells Me!" words and music by Don Wolf and Alan Brandt; "If I Didn't Care," words and music by Jack Lawrence; "I Believe," words by Sammy Cahn, music by Jule Styne; "Ain't Misbehavin'," words by Andy Razaf, music by Thomas "Fats" Waller and Harry Brooks; "I Don't Want to Get Married," "It Ain't Nobody's Business What I Do" and "Don't Sit on My Bed!" composers undetermined.

Cast: Dusty Fletcher (*Dusty*), George Wiltshire ([*Mortimer*] *Dumdone, the manager*), Butterfly McQueen (*Butterfly, his secretary*), Nellie Hill (*Lola, his fiancee*), Freddie Robinson (*Sarge*), William Campbell, Edgar Martin, Sid Easton (*Policemen*), Gus Smith (*Stage band*), Jackie Mabley (*Vaudeville star*), Ken Renard (*Voodoo Man, a magician*), King Cole Trio, Andy Kirk and His Orchestra, Beverly White, Clark Bros., Four Congaroos, Patterson & Jackson, Varietiettes Dancing Girls from the Katherine Dunham School of Dancing.

African American, Variety. [*Print viewed*]. Mortimer Dumdone, the manager of a variety show, is distressed to learn from Butterfly, his secretary, that the show's magician has disappeared and, therefore, a replacement must quickly be found. When Lola, Dumdone's glamorous fiancee, enters the office, Dumdone presents her with an expensive pearl necklace. As Lola leans forward to give Dumdone a kiss of gratitude, a strange man appears, seemingly out of nowhere, and she mistakenly kisses him instead. A furious Dumdone prepares to punch the intruder, but refrains when the stranger introduces himself as Dusty, a magician, and requests an audition for the open spot. After enclosing Lola and her necklace in one of two large cabinets placed on the stage, Dusty succeeds in making her disappear, but is unable to bring her back. Dumdone calls the police and they catch Dusty flirting with Butterfly back in the office. The police sergeant suggests that Dusty reenact the trick using the policemen as subjects, so Dusty obliges, making the four officers disappear and reappear in his cabinet. Dumdone demands that the police arrest the fleeing Dusty, and the bumbling officers head after him, tripping over one another at regular intervals. Declaring that the show must go on, Dumdone makes preparations for that night's variety show. Dusty returns briefly to a now-lovesick Butterfly, then heads down to the basement to hide from the police. In front of a packed house, the variety show opens with a number by Andy Kirk and his orchestra. Next, Beverly White sings two numbers, followed by the hefty singing and tapdancing duo of Patterson and Jackson. Jackie "Moms" Mabley does her stand-up comedy routine, and the Clark Bros. tapdance and impersonate the Ink Spots, after which the King Cole Trio performs. As the Four Congaroos dance troupe do their act, the police continue to chase Dusty through the basement and up onto the roof. Dumdone, still desperate for a replacement magician, asks Moms to entertain the crowd until Dusty can be located. As Moms stands on stage, Dusty runs by, followed by the clumsy policemen. Dusty then begins his act and encloses himself in the first cabinet. After a trap door dumps Dusty into the basement, the policemen follow. However, Moms succeeds in making the policemen and the long-lost Lola reappear on stage. The missing magician, known as "Voodoo Man," is revealed to be the culprit behind Lola's disappearance when he shows up on stage attempting to sell her necklace. After Voodoo Man is hauled off by the police, the show closes with a dance number by the eight Varietiettes. Backstage, Dusty becomes a prisoner of a different sort when he finds himself handcuffed to the infatuated Butterfly. *Magicians. Theatrical managers. Vaudevillians.* Engagements. Impersonations (Comic). Infatuation. Necklaces. Police. Secretaries. Thieves.

Note: Although the print viewed contained a 1948 copyright statement, no record of such a copyright has been found.
Exb 7 Jul 1948.

THE KINDLING (German Americans)

Jesse L. Lasky Feature Play Co., presented by arrangement with Edward J. Bowes. *Dist* Paramount Pictures Corp. 12 Jul **1915** [©Jesse L. Lasky Feature Play Co., Inc.; 15 Jul 1915; LU5831]. Si; b&w. 4-5 reels.

Pres Jesse L. Lasky. *Dir* Cecil B. DeMille.

Source: Based on the play *The Kindling* by Charles A. Kenyon.

Cast: Charlotte Walker (*Maggie Schultz*), Thomas Meighan (*Heine Schultz*), Raymond Hatton (*Steve Bates*), Mrs. Lewis McCord (*Mrs. Bates*), Billy Elmer (*Rafferty*), Lillian Langdon (*Mrs. Burke-Smith*), Florence Dagmar (*Alice Burke-Smith*), Tom Forman (*Dr. Taylor*).

Social, Drama. Maggie Schultz is a cheery tenement dweller whose two clean rooms contrast with the Hell's Kitchen slum in which she lives. She happily expects her first child until her husband Heine, an honest and hard-working stevedore, unknowingly remarks that he would kill any child of his rather than raise it in such a "hell-hole" which, he says, consumes children like fire burns kindling. After settlement worker Alice Burke-Smith, whose heartless mother, although a "reformer," owns the Schultz's tenement, gets Maggie a job sewing for her mother at five dollars per week, a neighbor, Steve Bates, offers Maggie $100 to arrange for him to burgle the Burke-Smith home. When she realizes that $100 will allow her and Heine to purchase a homestead out West, and she sees Mrs. Burke-Smith lavish luxuries on her dog, Maggie agrees. After she is caught, Heine upbraids her but takes the blame. Thinking that her baby will be born in jail, Maggie curses Mrs. Burke-Smith, who then realizes her wrongs. Maggie and Heine are exonerated and, with loans from the Burke-Smiths, go West. *Hypocrisy. Poverty. Robbery. Transformation. Upper classes. Burglars. German Americans. Laborers. Seamstresses. Self-sacrifice. Settlement workers. Slums. Tenement-houses.*

Note: This was Charlotte Walker's first film. According to modern sources, DeMille also produced, wrote the scenario and edited the film; Alvin Wyckoff was the cameraman; and Wilfred Buckland was the art director.

Motog 31 Jul 1915, pp. 232-33. *MPN* 19 Jun 1915, p. 48. *MPN* 24 Jul 1915, p. 71. *MPW* 17 Jul 1915, p. 568. *MPW* 24 Jul 1915, pp. 665-66. *NYDM* 21 Jul 1915, p. 24. *Var* 16 Jul 1915, p. 17.

KING OF CHINATOWN (Chinese Americans)

Paramount Pictures, Inc. *Dist* Paramount Pictures, Inc. 17 Mar **1939**; Prod: mid-Aug—early Oct 1938 [©Paramount Pictures, Inc.; 17 Mar 1939; LP8727]. Sd (Western Electric Mirrophonic Recording); b&w. 6 reels. 57 or 60 min. Passed by the National Board of Review. PCA cert no. 4746.

[*Exec prod* William Le Baron]. [*Assoc prod* Stuart Walker]. *Dir* Nick Grinde. [*Asst dir* George Templeton and Alvin Ganzer]. *Scr* Lillie Hayward and Irving Reis. *Story* Herbert Biberman. [*Contr to scr const* Gladys Unger, Stuart Anthony and Robert Yost]. *Photog* Leo Tover. *Art dir* Hans Dreier and Robert Odell. *Ed* Eda Warren. *Int dec* A. E. Freudeman. *Cost* Edith Head. *Mus dir* Boris Morros. [*Sd* Richard Olson]. *Sd rec* Charles Hisserich and Glenn Rominger.

Cast: Anna May Wong (*Dr. Mary Ling*), Akim Tamiroff (*Frank Baturin*), J. Carrol Naish (*The Professor*), Sidney Toler (*Dr. Chang Ling*), Philip Ahn (*Robert "Bob" Li*), Anthony Quinn (*Mike Gordon*), Bernadene Hayes (*Dolly Warren*), Roscoe Karns (*Rep Harrigan*), Ray Mayer (*Potatoes*), Richard Denning (*Interne*), Archie Twitchell (*2nd interne*), Edward Marr (*Bert, fight trainer*), [George Anderson (*Detective*)], [Charles B. Wood (*1st gangster*)], [George Magrill (*2nd gangster*)], [Charles Trowbridge (*Dr. Jones*)], [Lily King (*Chinese woman*)], [Wong Chung (*Chinese man*)], [Chester Gan (*Mr. Foo*)], [Pat West (*Announcer at fight*)], [Guy Usher (*Investigator*)], [Alex Pollard (*Heath*)], [Sam Ash (*Barber*)], [Pierre Watkin (*District Attorney Phillips*)], [Larry McGrath (*Referee*)], [Jimmy Vaughn (*Slugger Grady*)], [Charles Lee (*Tommy Wu*)], [Ivan Miller, Ben Taggart (*Investigators*)], [Grace Lem (*Chinese woman*)], [David Dong (*Chinese boy*)], [Robert Homans (*Pat, the doorman*)], [Gloria Williams (*Scrubwoman*)], [Marie Burton, Sheila Darcy, Judith King, Dolores Casey (*Nurses*)], [Luana Walters (*Check room girl*)], [Dorothy Dayton], [Paula de Cardo], [Harriette Haddon], [Helaine Moler], [Norah Gale], [Gwen Kenyon], [Joyce Mathews], [Dorothy White], [Ethel Clayton], [Florence Wix].

Drama. [*Print viewed*]. Frank Baturin, called "The King of Chinatown," has all the rackets in the palm of his hand. After Baturin

loses $20,000 in a benefit boxing match, he hires hit man Rep Harrigan to kill his rival, Mike Gordon. Gordon has won the loyalties of Baturin's lieutenant, an ex-convict called "The Professor," however, who orders Rep to warn Gordon instead of killing him. As a result, Baturin is shot by Gordon in front of a pharmacy owned by Dr. Chang Ling, who refuses to join the Merchant's Protection Association, which has been extorting money from the local merchants. Baturin is found by Ling's daughter, Dr. Mary Ann Ling, who, believing that her father shot the racketeer to stop his threats against the Chinese merchants, comes to the aid of the wounded man. Because of Baturin's extended convalescence, Mary is forced to relinquish her fundraising activities to establish a Red Cross nursing unit in war-torn China. During his weeks of recovery, Baturin falls in love with Mary, despite her involvement with lawyer Bob Li, and is determined to reform. Although the Professor had hoped to succeed Baturin in running the mob, Gordon takes over, and a reign of terror follows in Chinatown. The Professor visits Mary to try to intimidate her into allowing Baturin to die or else her father will be killed. Learning of the Professor's threats to Mary, Ling hires an attorney to frame the Professor. Rep then tells Mary that Gordon was Baturin's would-be assassin. When District Attorney Phillips confronts the Professor, he names Gordon as Baturin's attacker, and Gordon confesses. Meanwhile, Ling visits Baturin's to take Mary home, and she hopes to convince Ling that Baturin is a reformed man. Rep then calls Baturin to warn him that the Professor is en route to his home to kill him and Ling. Baturin successfully disarms the Professor, but is mortally wounded. The police then arrest the Professor. Before dying, Baturin bequeaths Mary a healthy endowment for her nursing unit. She marries Bob and leaves for China, secure in the knowledge that her father had no hand in the violence. *Chinatowns. Chinese Americans. Extortion. Moral reformation. Nurses. Nursing back to health. Racketeers. Benefactors. Bombs. Boxing. Confession. District Attorneys. Fathers and daughters. Hired killers. Lawyers. Merchants. Murder. Rivalry. Wagers.*

Note: The cast credits on the viewed print were cut off after Edward Merr, and it is possible that several additional names followed.

DV 15 Mar 1939, p. 3. *FD* 21 Mar 1939, p. 4. *HR* 20 Aug 1938, p. 8. *HR* 1 Oct 1938, pp. 8-9. *HR* 15 Mar 1939, p. 3. *MPD* 21 Mar 1939, p. 6. *MPH* 18 Mar 1939, pp. 52-53. *NYT* 16 Mar 1939, p. 27. *Var* 22 Mar 1939, p. 20.

KING OF JAZZ (Multi-ethnic)

Universal Pictures Corp. *Dist* Universal Pictures Corp. 17 Aug **1930**; New York premiere: 2 May 1930 [©Universal Pictures Corp.; 17 May 1930; LP1318]. Sd (Western Electric Sound System); col (Technicolor). 12 reels. 98 min.

Pres Carl Laemmle. *Prod* Carl Laemmle, Jr. *Devised and dir by* John Murray Anderson. *Asst dir* Robert Ross. [*Scr* Edward T. Lowe, Jr.]. *Comedy sketches* Harry Ruskin. [*Dial* Charles MacArthur]. *Cine* Hal Mohr, Jerome Ash and Ray Rennahan. *Settings* Herman Rosse. *Asst art dir* Thomas F. O'Neill. *Film ed* Robert Carlisle. *Supv film ed* Maurice Pivar. *Anim cartoons* Walter Lantz and Bill Nolan. *Cost* Herman Rosse. *Orch* Ferde Grofé. [*Mus arr* James Dietrich]. *Dance dir* Russell E. Markert. *Rec supv* C. Roy Hunter. [*Monitor* Harold I. Smith].

Music: "Rhapsody in Blue," music by George Gershwin.

Song(s): "Music Hath Charms," "My Bridal Veil," "A Bench in the Park," "Happy Feet," "I Like to Do Things for You" and "Song of the Dawn," music by Milton Ager, lyrics by Jack Yellen; "It Happened in Monterey," music by Mabel Wayne, lyrics by Billy Rose; "Ragamuffin Romeo," music by Mabel Wayne, lyrics by Harry De Costa; "So the Bluebirds and the Blackbirds Got Together," music by Harry Barris, lyrics by Billy Moll; "Mississippi Mud," music and lyrics by Harry Barris and James Cavanaugh; "La paloma," music by Yradier, lyricist undetermined; "Cielito lindo," traditional.

Cast: PAUL WHITEMAN AND HIS BAND, John Boles, Laura La Plante, Jeanette Loff, Glenn Tryon, William Kent, "Slim" Summerville, Merna Kennedy, The Rhythm Boys, [Bing Crosby], [Harry Barris], [and Al Rinker], Kathryn Crawford, Beth Laemmle, Stanley Smith, Charles Irwin, George Chiles, Jack White, Frank Leslie, Walter Brennan, Churchill Ross, Johnson Arledge, Al Norman, Jacques Cartier, Paul Howard, Nell O'Day, and The Tommy Atkins Sextette, Marion Stattler, Don Rose, Russell Markert Girls, [Jeanie Lang], [Roy Bargy], [The Sisters G], [The Brox Sisters], [Nancy Torres], [Grace Hayes], [Yola D'Avril], [Willie Hall], [George Sidney].

Variety, Musical. [*Print viewed*]. Charles Irwin introduces items from the Paul Whiteman scrapbook. In an animated cartoon

sequence, Whiteman is "crowned" the "King of Jazz" by animals in the African jungle. Whiteman then introduces members of his band and the chorus girls. In the "My Bridal Veil" number, featuring Jeanette Loff and Stanley Smith, a young woman conjures up visions of bridal costumes through the ages. A "blackout" sketch, "Ladies of the Press," written by William Griffith, presents Laura La Plante, Jeanie Lang, Merna Kennedy, Grace Hayes and Kathryn Crawford. The Rhythm Boys (Bing Crosby, Harry Barris and Al Rinker) perform "So the Bluebirds and the Blackbirds Got Together." "It Happened in Monterey" features John Boles, Jeanette Loff, The Sisters G, George Chiles and the Russell Markert Girls, and includes a passage of "La Paloma," sung in Spanish by Nancy Torres and Loff. "In Conference," another very brief comedy sketch, presents Laura La Plante, Glenn Tryon and Merna Kennedy. Jack White performs a comedy number about wanting to own a fish store. Jeanette Loff, Stanley Smith, The Brox Sisters and The Rhythm Boys appear in the production number "A Bench in the Park." "Another Quickie—Springtime" with Slim Summerville, Yola D'Avril and Walter Brennan follows. A sketch, "All Noisy on the Eastern Front," features Walter Brennan, Paul Whiteman and others. Willie Hall performs "Pop Goes the Weasel" on a violin and finishes by playing "Stars and Stripes Forever" on a bicycle pump. In an opulent production number, Roy Bargy plays George Gershwin's "Rhapsody in Blue" on the piano, accompanied by The Sisters G and Jacques Cartier. A comedy sketch, "Oh! Forevermore" with William Kent and Walter Brennan follows. A production number, "My Ragamuffin Romeo," presents Jeanie Lang, George Chiles and dancers Don Rose and Marion Stattler. A "blackout" about a pantomime horse features Walter Brennan and Slim Summerville. In another "blackout," a couple, Glenn Tryon and Kathryn Crawford, discover that they are not legally married. "Happy Feet," a production number, features The Rhythm Boys, The Sisters G and Al Norman. Slim Summerville and George Sidney appear in a brief sketch in which Summerville seeks permission to marry Sidney's daughter. "I Like to Do Things for You," is performed by Jeanie Lang, Grace Hayes, William Kent and dancers Nell O'Day and The Tommy Atkins Sextette. "Has Anyone Seen Our Nelly?," a comedy song utilizing magic lantern slides follows. John Boles performs "The Song of the Dawn." The finale, "The Melting Pot of Music," features most of the cast and shows that in America, music from various countries, including England, Italy, Scotland, Ireland, Mexico, Russia and France, is fused into one great new rhythm, Jazz. *Africa. Bands (Music). Jazz music. Mexicans. Musical revues. Russians. Scots. Brides. Drunkenness. Jungles. Magic lanterns. Parks. Police. Women reporters. World War I.*

Note: The main title credits Paul Whiteman and his Band as "Exclusive Columbia Phonograph Artists." Universal produced several versions of the film for different countries, each with its own master and mistress of ceremonies speaking the appropriate language. The foreign-language versions may have featured only the musical numbers and none of the sketches. The Spanish version, *El rey del jazz*, which was supervised by Paul Kohner and featured "maestros de ceremonias," Lupita Tovar and Martín Garralaga, under the direction of Kurt Neumann, was probably exhibited in the U.S. although exact release information has not been located. Other versions that were probably also supervised by Kohner and appear to have had no U.S. exhibition include: the German, *Der Jazzkönig*, introduced by Arnold Korff and Paula Wedekind, under Neumann's direction; the French, *La féerie du Jazz*, introduced by André Cheron and Georgette Rhodes; the Portuguese *O rei do Jazz*, presented by Olimpio Guillerme and Lia Torá and the Italian, *Il re del Jazz*, presented by Allesandro Giglio and Nella Nelli. The Japanese and Czech versions, the titles of which are undetermined, were introduced by Tetsu Komai and Iris Yamaoka, and Antonin Vaverka, respectively. Modern sources suggest that a Hungarian version may have been introduced by Bela Lugosi.

Contemporary information suggests that some sketches were shot for the English-language original but were subsequently dropped. Files at the USC Cinema-Television Library includes stills of a sketch for the film in which George Sidney appears with Charlie Murray. Some sources also include John Fulton and Otis Harlan in the cast, but their appearance in the released film is unconfirmed. In 1933, Universal reissued the film in a reduced, eight-reel version, largely to exploit the increased popularity of Bing Crosby.

FD 30 Mar 1930. *NYT* 23 Nov 1930, p. 6. *Var* 7 May 1930, p. 21. *Var* 7 Jan 1931, p. 36.

KING OF THE BANDITS (Latino)

Monogram Pictures Corp. *Dist* Monogram Pictures Corp. 8 Nov 1947; New York opening: week of 30 Dec 1947; Prod: mid-May—late May 1947 [©Monogram Pictures Corp.; 8 Nov 1947; LP1357]. Sd (Western Electric Recording); b&w. 65-66 min. PCA cert no. 12518.

Series: The Cisco Kid.

Prod Jeffrey Bernerd. *Prod supv* Glenn Cook. *Dir* Christy Cabanne. *Tech dir* Ernest Hickson. *Asst dir* Eddie Davis. *Scr* Bennett R. Cohen.

Orig story Christy Cabanne. *Addl dial* Gilbert Roland. *Dir of photog* William Sickner. *Film ed* Roy Livingston. *Set dec* Vin Taylor. *Mus dir* Edward J. Kay. *Rec eng* Tom Lambert. *Makeup* Harry Ross.

Source: Based on the character created by O. Henry.

Cast: Gilbert Roland [(*The Cisco Kid, also known as Chico Villa*)], Angela Greene [(*Alice Mason*)], Chris Pin Martin [(*Pancho*)], Anthony Warde [(*Smoke Kirby*)], Laura Treadwell [(*Mrs. Mason*)], William Bakewell [(*Capt. Mason*)], Rory Mallinson [(*Burl*)], Pat Goldin [(*Pedro Gomez*)], Cathy Carter [(*Connie*)], Boyd Irwin [(*Col. Wayne*)], Antonio Filauri [(*Padre*)], Jasper Palmer [(*U.S. marshal*)], Bill Cabanne [(*Orderly*)], [Frank Marlo, Guy Teague (*Henchmen*)], [James Harrison (*Leader*)], [George Douglas (*Guard*)], [Douglas Aylesworth (*Trooper*)], [Jack O'Shea (*Bartender*)], [Bill Neff (*Captain*)].

Western. [*Print viewed*]. Pancho, the lifetime companion of kind Mexican bandit Chico Villa, dreams that he and Chico are shot in Arizona, and later warns Chico not to go there. Despite Pancho's advice, Chico takes Pancho to Arizona, where they rescue Pedro Gomez, a saddlemaker, from a lynch mob that believes he has been aiding an impostor Chico Villa in a series of robberies. Chico next saves Alice Mason and her mother when their coach, which was ambushed by the robbers, runs out of control. Chico inquires about the robbery in town and discovers that local outlaw Smoke Kirby ambushed the coach. After Chico retrieves Alice's stolen locket from a saloon girl, he accompanies Alice and her mother to Fort Roberts to meet Alice's brother Frank. Meanwhile, Frank gets orders to lead a group of cavalrymen to arrest Chico. Kirby follows Chico and demands a duel, but when Kirby cheats, Chico mercifully spares his life. When Frank arrives on the scene, Kirby accuses Chico of being Chico Villa. Chico is then arrested after Alice's locket is found on him. With Pedro's help, Chico and Pancho escape by holding up Frank, and Frank is accused of setting them free out of sympathy for Alice, who has fallen in love with Chico. Believing that Alice devised the escape, Frank accepts a court-martial to protect her. Chico eventually gets a signed confession from Kirby stating that he posed as Chico Villa and turns it over to Frank's superior officer, who exonerates him. Chico later tells Alice that while he will always think of her, he must remain a wanderer. After giving Pedro gold to buy his own saddleshop and wishing him "many children," Chico rides out of Arizona with Pancho. *Bandits. False arrests. Impersonation and imposture. Mexicans. Vigilantes. Arizona. Brothers and sisters. Confession (Law). Courts-martial and courts of inquiry. Dreams. Duels. Lockets. Lynching. Mothers and daughters. Officers (Military). Outlaws. Rescues. Saddlery. Self-sacrifice. Stagecoach robberies. United States. Army.*

Note: According to a pre-production *HR* news item, Jeffrey Bernerd took over producing duties on the picture after Scott Dunlap was promoted to executive assistant. For more information on the series, consult the Series Index and see the entry above for *The Cisco Kid*.

DV 8 Oct 1947, p. 3. *HR* 6 Jan 1947, p. 2. *HR* 9 May 1947, p. 20. *HR* 8 Oct 1947, p. 3. *MPHPD* 29 Nov 1947. *Var* 7 Jan 1948, p. 56.

KING OF THE RITZ see A NIGHT AT THE RITZ

KING OF THE STALLIONS (Native Americans)

Edward F. Finney Productions. *Dist* Monogram Pictures Corp. 11 Sep **1942**; Prod: 11 Jun—late Jun 1942 [©Monogram Pictures Corp.; 14 Aug 1942; LP11560]. Sd; b&w. 6 reels, 5,729 ft. 63 min. PCA cert no. 8253.

Prod Edward Finney. *Dir* Edward Finney. *Asst dir* Don Verk. *Exec asst* Samuel Wallis. *Scr* Arthur St. Claire and Sherman Lowe. [*Orig story* Roger Merton]. *Photog* Marcel LePicard. *Film ed* Fred Bain. *Mus score and dir* Frank Sanucci. *Sd* Ben Winkler. *Prod aide* Aaron Klein. [*Trainer* Frank Sanders and Curly Twiford].

Cast: Chief Thundercloud (*Habawi*), Ric Vallin (*Little Coyote*), Princess Bluebird (*Telenika*), Dave O'Brien (*Steve Mason*), Chief Yowlache (*Chief Matapotan*), Thunder (*Black stallion [Nakoma]*), Paint (*Killer stallion*), Ted Adams (*Barlow*), Sally Cairns (*Lucy Clark*), Gordon DeMain (*Pop Clark*), Forrest Taylor (*Hinshaw*), Joe Cody (*Manka*), [Bill Wilkerson (*Tonga*)].

Western. [*Print viewed*]. Indians are blamed for the work of horse rustlers, who are led by Barlow, a foreman who has been stealing horses from his employer, rancher Pop Clark. Clark culls his horses from the wild, and then sells them to the army. When Indian Little Coyote returns to his tribe after several years of formal education, he is rejected by the tribe because he is unable to master a reputedly evil

wild black stallion known to be the leader of the wild horse herds. The black horse escapes and Little Coyote wanders in the forest until he encounters Hahawi, another exile. Hahawi teaches Little Coyote how to be one with the creatures of the forest. Clark, meanwhile, is murdered by Barlow after he discovers his foreman's treachery, and when his body is found by cowboy Steve Mason, who defended the Indians to Clark when he accused them of rustling, Barlow shoots him as well. Steve survives, however, and is rescued by Hahawi and Little Coyote, while Barlow tells Clark's daughter Lucy that her sweetheart Steve is responsible for her father's death. Barlow, in the meantime, is paid by the Army for the delivery of Clark's horses. Hahawi and Little Coyote recapture some of Clark's stolen horses from the wild herd and also capture the black stallion. This time, however, Little Coyote is successful in befriending the horse and, discovering that he is not evil after all, names him Nakoma, which means "King of the Stallions." Little Coyote and Hahawi survive an ambush by Barlow and his men and return the stolen ponies to the Clark ranch, and whereby Steve regains Lucy's trust. Lucy learns that Barlow is responsible for her father's death and the rustled horses, and all watch as Nakoma battles with Paint, a killer horse who has been assisting Barlow in rustling the wild horses. Nakoma wins the battle and is reunited with his mate, while Little Coyote and Hahawi are welcomed back into their tribe. *Frame-ups. Horses. Indians of North America. Murder. Rustlers. Ambushes. Fathers and daughters. Ostracism. Ranchers.*

Note: *HR* production charts include I. Stanford Jolley in the cast, however, his appearance in the final film has not been confirmed. Onscreen credits note that this picture was filmed on location in Crater Canyon, CA and Monument Valley, AZ.

Box 5 Sep 1942. *DV* 19 Jun 1942. *DV* 21 Aug 1942, p. 3. *FD* 25 Aug 1942, p. 6. *HR* 21 Aug 1942, p. 3. *MPHPD* 29 Aug 1942, p. 870.

KING OF THE WILD HORSES (Native Americans, Navajo)

Columbia Pictures Corp. *Dist* Columbia Pictures Corp. 10 Nov **1933**; Prod: 15 Aug—7 Sep 1933 [©Columbia Pictures Corp.; 23 Oct 1933; LP4200]. Sd; b&w. 7 reels. 60-61 or 65-66 min.

Supv George B. Seitz and Ben Pivar. *Dir* Earl Haley. *Asst dir* Edward Bernoudy. *Scr* Fred Myton. *Story* Earl Haley. *Photog* Benjamin Kline. *Film ed* Clarence Kolster. *Sd eng* Dean Daily.

Cast: Rex (*Rex, the hero*), Lady (*Lady, the heroine*), Marquis (*Marquis, the villain*), William [Preston] Janney (*Red Wolf*), Dorothy Appleby (*Wanima*), Wallace MacDonald (*Clint Bolling*), Harry Semels (*Big Man*), Ford West (*Davidson*), Art Mix (*Cowboy*).

Animal, Western. [*Not viewed*]. In an attempt to steal thousands of horses from a Navajo tribe in Arizona, outlaw Clint Bolling pretends to be a government inspector assigned to weed out the tribe's diseased animals. Bolling's forged documents allow him and his gang access to the herd, which is led by the magnificent stallion "Rex." While Bolling trains his horse, "Marquis," to lead the horses into a trap, the Indians hold a high council to celebrate the coming of age of Red Wolf. Big Man, Red Wolf's father, was once the most celebrated member of the tribe, and he decides that in order to prove his manhood, his son must capture and tame Rex. Red Wolf trails Rex into the desert and finally captures him in quicksand. Red Wolf becomes obsessed with training the beautiful animal, and even forgets Wanima, the beautiful maiden who loves him. Desperate to get rid of Rex so that Marquis can take control of the herd, Bolling goes to the corral under the pretense of inspecting Rex's health, although he really intends to kill him. Bolling torments the spirited animal until Rex, filled with hatred, escapes in pursuit of Bolling after the impostor is forced to leave the corral. News arrives from Washington that Bolling is a fake, and the tribe also searches for him. As they arrive at his hiding place, Marquis is leading the horses into a trap, but Rex suddenly appears. After a desperate fight with Marquis, Rex kills the other horse and sends his herd to safety. Rex then finds Bolling cowering in a crevice and tramples him with his hooves. Red Wolf proudly ties Rex beside Wanima's hogan, thereby indicating that the couple is engaged, and Wanima's father and Big Man begin bargaining over whether the dowry shall be forty or fifty sheep. *Death by animals. Horses. Impersonation and imposture. Navajo Indians. Revenge. Rites and ceremonies. Arizona. Deserts. Dowry. Gangs. Indians of North America–Reservations. Manhood. Traps.*

Note: The working title of this film was *Wild Horse Stampede*. According to press information, the film was shot entirely on location at the Navajo and Hopi reservations in AZ. Publicity information also noted that various Indian ceremonies were captured on film, and approximately 2,000 Indians appear as extras. The film was also released as *Rex, King of the Wild Horses*, and was re-

released in Jun 1938. The picture was remade by Columbia in 1947 as *King of the Wild Horses*, directed by George Archainbaud and starring Preston Foster and Gail Patrick.

DV 31 Oct 1933, p. 3. *FD* 21 Mar 1934, p. 10. *FD* 7 Jun 1938, p. 9. *Var* 27 Mar 1934, p. 12.

KING OF THE ZOMBIES (African Americans)

Sterling Productions. *Dist* Monogram Pictures Corp. 14 May **1941**; Prod: 28 Mar—early Apr 1941 [©Monogram Pictures Corp.; 14 May 1941; LP10469]. Sd (Western Electric Mirrophonic Recording); b&w. 7 reels, 6,060 ft. 67 min. PCA cert no. 7290.

Prod Lindsley Parsons. *Dir* Jean Yarbrough. *Scr* Edmond Kelso. *Photog* Mack Stengler. *Art dir* Charles Clague. *Settings* Dave Milton. *Film ed* Richard Currier. *Mus score and dir* Edward Kay. *Sd dir* William Fox and Glen Rominger. *Prod mgr* Mack Wright.

Cast: Dick Purcell [(*James "Mac" McCarthy*)], Joan Woodbury [(*Barbara Winslow*)], Mantan Moreland [(*Jefferson Jackson*)], Henry Victor [(*Dr. Sangre*)], John Archer [(*Bill Summers*)], Patricia Stacey [(*Alyce Sangre*)], Guy Usher [(*Admiral Wainwright*)], Marguerite Whitten [(*Samantha*)], Leigh Whipper [(*Momba*)], Madame Sul-te-Wan [(*Tahama*)], Lawrence Criner [(*Zombie*)], [Jimmy Davis (*Lazarus*)].

Horror, Comedy-drama. [*Print viewed*]. Pilot James "Mac" McCarthy goes off course somewhere between Cuba and Puerto Rico and is unable to pick up any radio transmissions. When he and his passengers, Bill Summers and his black valet, Jefferson Jackson, hear a lone transmission in a foreign language, they crash land the plane on the island below. The lost men discover themselves in a graveyard, and follow the sound of drums to a nearby mansion. There they are greeted by Viennese Dr. Sangre, who treats Mac's minor head wound with the warning that untreated injuries are easy prey for evil spirits. Sangre says there are no radios on the island and allows the men to spend the night as his guests, although he insists that Jeff stay in the servants quarters in the basement. Jeff becomes alarmed when the maid, Samantha, and the cook, Tahama, call forth two "zombies," but when he runs upstairs to tell his boss, Sangre dismisses the idea as ludicrous. Sangre's wife Alyce also appears to be in a trance-like state, which Sangre attributes to jungle fever. Sangre appears surprised when Bill tells him about American Admiral Wainwright, whose plane disappeared in the same location. Sangre then tells the men that no one in his family, which includes his beautiful niece, Barbara Winslow, can leave the island because they are Austrian refugees lacking passports. Later that night, Jeff confides in Samantha that Bill is a government agent on a secret mission. Sangre's butler, Momba, Samantha and Tahama leave Jeff alone in the kitchen just before midnight, with the admonition not to pay notice to anything unusual. When two zombies nearly attack Jeff, he runs to Bill and Mac's room for safety. Jeff is later awakened by the appearance of a woman who seems to come and go through a wall, and when he awakens Bill and Mac, they believe him only after finding an earring. The three men split up to search the house, and Bill finds Barbara in the library reading a book on hypnotism. Barbara says that she is reading the book to help her aunt, who has been in the trance-like state since arriving at the island, and Bill confides his belief that Sangre is hiding a radio. Bill and Mac finally believe Jeff's stories about zombies after Mac is attacked by one. The next morning, Mac and Bill discover a freshly dug grave in the cemetery, and that someone has stolen the plane's radio. Mac goes in search of a generator, while Bill returns to the house, unaware that the admiral is being held hostage in a cellar and that Tahama is trying to pry military secrets from him with the use of voodoo. After Sangre calls in a report to his German allies, Mac disappears. Sangre then lures Jeff into the cellar, where he hypnotizes him into believing that he is a zombie. While Bill is searching for Mac, he finds Barbara using hypnotism on her aunt, and assumes that she is collaborating with Sangre, despite her protests that she is trying to restore her aunt's memory. Mac returns in a zombie-like state, and a physician called by Sangre says that he has been dead for hours. When Momba receives orders by radio for Sangre to transmit the stolen military information, he and Tahama prepare a special ceremony to wrest the information from the admiral. Jeff lines up with the other zombies for dinner, but Samantha breaks his spell. Jeff then meets with Bill and moments later, they hear a woman's scream and find Alyce dead. Bill and Jeff follow the sound of drums into the cellar, where Sangre is holding a ceremony during which the admiral's thoughts are to be transmitted into Barbara's brain. Bill breaks up the

ceremony and when Sangre orders the zombies to attack Bill, they instead follow Mac, and turn on Sangre. Sangre shoots Mac and, while backing away from the zombies, falls to his death into a firepit. After Wainwright phones the Coast Guard, and Mac's injuries are treated, Wainwright tells Bill that Sangre forced his plane to land with a false radio signal, then killed his crew and tortured him for Canal Zone fortification plans. When his torture did not work, he used Alyce and Barbara as test subjects with other methods. *African Americans. Air pilots. Americans in foreign countries. Hypnotism. Nazis. Voodoo. Airplane accidents. Attempted murder. Cemeteries. Falls from heights. Islands. Mansions. Missing persons. Nieces. Radios. Rites and ceremonies. Secret Service. Servants. Wives. World War II. Zombies.*

Note: *HR* news items reported the following information about the production: Bela Lugosi was initially considered for the role of "Dr. Sangre," and Monogram later hoped to obtain Peter Lorre for the cast. The filmmakers planned for the "zombies" to sing "The Grave Digging Song" in the film. Although a chant is heard in the film, it has not been confirmed as "The Grave Digging Song." A *HR* news item also noted that producer Lindsley Parsons intended this film to be a "satirical" treatment of the typical "zombie" film. This film was nominated for an Academy Award for Scoring of a Dramatic Picture.
Box 17 May 1941. *DV* 7 May 1941. *FD* 9 May 1941, p. 7. *HR* 20 Jan 1941, p. 5. *HR* 27 Mar 1941, p. 6. *HR* 28 Mar 1941, p. 14. *HR* 4 Apr 1941, p. 10. *HR* 7 May 1941, p. 3. *MPH* 10 May 1941.

THE KING'S GAME (Russian Americans)
Pathé Exchange, Inc.; Gold Rooster Plays. *Dist* Pathé Exchange, Inc. 7 Jan **1916** [©Pathé Exchange, Inc.; 27 Mar 1916; LU7914]. Si; b&w. 5 reels.

Prod Arnold Daly. *Dir* Ashley Miller. *Story* George Brackett Seitz.

Source: Based on the play *The King's Game* by George Brackett Seitz (New York, 26 Dec 1910).

Cast: George Probert (*Philip, Grand Duke of Kiev/Perciley*), Pearl White (*Catherine Dardinilis*), Sheldon Lewis (*Count Sergius Dardinilis*), Nora Moore (*Lady Dardinilus*), George Parks (*Chief Wolcott*).

Comedy-drama. Although he prefers partying to politics, Philip, the Grand Duke of Kiev who lives in New York, nonetheless has been targeted for assassination by a group of nihilists. Perciley, the man chosen to kill Philip, looks exactly like his intended victim, and so, after the police have arrested the would-be killer, the nihilists mistake the Grand Duke for their fellow traveler and instruct him in precisely how the murder should be committed. Then, Philip falls in love with the daughter of Dardinilis, the man who heads the nihilists. As a result, Philip, always the good sport, convinces the police to leave the nihilists alone, and then marries Dardinilis' daughter, after which he gives Dardinilis himself a commission in the Russian Royal Hussars. *Assassination. Doubles. Mistaken identity. Nihilists. Nobility. Russian Americans. Russians. Kiev (Ukraine). New York City. Police. Russia. Army.*

Note: Some sources credit Arnold Daly with the direction of this film.
Motog 22 Jan 1916, p. 190. *MPN* 22 Jan 1916, p. 393. *MPW* 25 Dec 1915, p. 2450. *MPW* 8 Jan 1916, pp. 194-95, 300. *MPW* 15 Jan 1916, p. 435. *NYDM* 15 Jan 1916, p. 28. *Var* 14 Jan 1916, p. 19.

KINGS GO FORTH (African Americans)
Frank Ross-Eton Productions. *Dist* United Artists Corp. Jul **1958**; New York opening: 3 Jul 1958; Prod: late Aug—mid-Sep 1957 in France; early Nov—mid-Dec 1957 in California [©Frank Ross-Eton Productions; 14 Jun 1958; LP12937]. Sd (Westrex Recording System); b&w. 9,902 ft. 109 min. PCA cert no. 18926.

Prod Frank Ross. [*Assoc prod* Richard Ross]. *Dir* Delmer Daves. *Asst dir* Edward Denault. *Scr* Merle Miller. *Dir of photog* Daniel L. Fapp. *Art dir* Fernando Carrere. *Ed supv* William B. Murphy. *Set dec* Darrell Silvera. *Cost des* Leah Rhodes. *Mus* Elmer Bernstein. *Orch* Leo Shuken and Jack Hayes. *Sd rec* Francis J. Scheid. *Sd ed* Bert Schoenfeld. *Makeup* Bernard Ponedel. *Prod mgr* Richard McWhorter. [*Army tech adv* Major Vincent Marcheselli]. [*Pub* A. S. Young].

Source: Based on the novel *Kings Go Forth* by Joe David Brown (New York, 1956).

Cast: FRANK SINATRA [(*Lt. Sam Loggins*)], TONY CURTIS [(*Britt Harris*)], NATALIE WOOD [(*Monique Blair*)], Leora Dana [(*Mrs. Blair*)], Karl Swenson [(*Colonel*)], Ann Codee [(*Mme. Brieux*)], Edward Ryder, Jacques Berthe [(*Jean Francoise*)], [Marie Ismond (*French woman*)], [Red Norvo, Pete Candoli, Mel Lewis, Richie Kamuca, Red Wooten, Jimmy Weible (*Members of bistro band*)].

World War II, **Drama**. [*Print viewed*]. In 1944, while Allied troops attempt to remove German occupation forces from the mountains of southern France, a brash and wealthy young radio technician named Britt Harris joins the battle-weary platoon of Lt. Sam Loggins. The lieutenant is puzzled by his new corporal, who, having tried to bribe his way out of military service, soon demonstrates a heroic willingness to rescue soldiers injured in a mine-littered apple orchard. Upon learning that Loggins' men have been under fire for many months, the colonel in charge begins issuing them weekend passes to Nice, a coastal resort on the Riviera that has been supplied with every amenity for the admired American liberators. One afternoon, Sam drives his jeep out of town, where he meets the beautiful Monique Blair, who was born and reared in France, but whose family is American. In Mme. Brieux's cozy restaurant, Sam discusses his past, and Monique, in turn, describes the wisdom and goodness of her deceased father. Sam wants to see Monique again, but although she likes him, she states clearly that she has no interest in a romantic relationship. Disappointed, Sam returns to the business of flushing out Germans. After Britt risks his life to secure a strategically placed bunker for the platoon, Sam overcomes his envy of Britt's wealth and good looks and gives the young soldier a promotion. On Saturday night, Sam returns to the little restaurant, where he meets Monique's mother, who invites him to dine at their villa. Monique explains that her father, who had died two years earlier, had taken orphans and refugees into the house during the worst days of the occupation. She then lets Sam kiss her. Sam begins to spend all of his weekend passes with Monique and her mother, and one evening, he confesses his love to Monique. Again declaring that she wants only his friendship, Monique reveals something she earlier had been afraid to admit: Her father was black. "I guess 'nigger' is one of the first words you learn in America, isn't it?" she asks, and when Sam fails to respond, she bursts into tears. Monique's mother explains that although she and her husband Fred had lived together proudly in Philadelphia, they moved to France before their daughter's birth because of its "blindness to color." Sam, who had been on "the opposite side" when he lived near Harlem as a child, struggles with Monique's revelation throughout the following week and finally decides to renew their friendship. Thrilled, Monique accompanies him to a jazz club in Nice. Sam is surprised when Britt performs a stirring trumpet solo with the band, and is disheartened when he immediately captures Monique's admiration. While the soldiers occupy the captured bunker later that week, Britt admits that he likes Monique, but before he can react to the news of her father's race, a bomb lands nearby. Determined to find the source of the heavy German artillery that has halted their advance, Sam and Britt request permission to scan the area from a bell tower behind enemy lines. After one of his evenings with Monique, Britt announces that he has proposed, whereupon Sam, skeptical of Britt's intentions, practically forces the corporal to submit a marriage application. Several months later, on the day on which Sam learns that their mission has been approved, he also hears that Britt has quietly withdrawn his marriage application, calling the whole matter a gag. That night, Sam forces Britt to reveal this to Monique and her mother. Britt, admitting that the affair was just a "new kick" for him, callously insults Monique's racial background. Hysterical, Monique runs away, and later that night, Sam learns that she has tried to kill herself. As he and Britt begin their dangerous nighttime mission, Sam angrily vows to kill the young soldier. Nevertheless, the two steal into a German-held village and position themselves atop the church bell tower. With illumination provided by assisting Allies, the men radio the positions of German troops and ammunition supplies back to base, whereupon the Allies immediately bomb those positions. As they work, Britt apologizes repeatedly for hurting Monique, explaining that unlike Sam, he has no character. The two finally instruct the Allies to bomb their own position, but as they run to escape the coming explosions, Britt is killed by a German soldier. Sam loses an arm, and after four months in a French hospital, he decides to quit brooding and return to his business in Los Angeles. On his way home, he visits Monique, whose mother has recently died. He finds the villa transformed into a school for war orphans, as Monique has resolved to carry her burden with dignity. As the children sing, Monique smiles bravely at her old friend. *African Americans–Mixed blood. France–German occupation, 1940-1945. Miscegenation. Philanderers. Romantic rivalry. Unrequited love. World War II. Alps. Amputees. Attempted suicide. Bombing, Aerial.*

Friendship. Heroism. Jazz music. Mediterranean Sea. Mines, Military. Mothers and daughters. Munitions. Nice (France). Nightclubs. Officers (Military). Orphans. Racism. Radio operators. Resorts. Restaurants. Riviera (France). Soldiers. United States. Army. War injuries. War victims.

Note: Pre-release items include Zina Provendie, Romney Brent and Lili Valenty in the cast, but their participation in the released film has not been confirmed. The pickup band in the film's bistro scenes featured several well-known jazz musicians. According to the film's pressbook, some exterior scenes were filmed on location in Nice and along the Cote d'Azur, France, and film comedian Harold Lloyd's Southern California estate, Greenacres, was used as the set of the "Blair" villa. Some combat scenes were filmed near Carmel, CA, according to a Dec 1957 *NYT* article. In that article, producer Frank Ross revealed that "the film had drawn considerable interest from the Negro community." Ross who admitted in the article that "he was not in favor of miscegenation," explained his decision to cast white actress Natalie Wood in the role of the half-black "Monique," by stating that " 'the picture would lose its dramatic kick if the girl were Negro.' "

Although Ross asserted that he and distributor United Artists did not plan to exploit the interracial love theme in the film's advertising, some ads did exploit it. One ad included the line: "Last night she was good for you...last night her skin was white enough for you." A. S. Young, the film's publicist, was the first African American press agent to work on a Hollywood production, according to the Dec 1957 *NYT* article. According to the film's pressbook, Frank Sinatra recorded a special spot announcement aimed at African American audiences. The film had its world premiere in Monte Carlo on 14 Jun 1958, according to modern sources. *Kings Go Forth* was awarded the 1958 Los Angeles Urban league Award as the "motion picture that does most for the promotion of better race relations and understanding."

Box 23 Jun 1958. *DV* 13 Jun 1958, p. 3. *Exb* 25 Jun 1958, p. 4483. *FD Har HR* 30 Aug 1957, p. 13 *HR* 13 Sep 1957, p. 17. *HR* 8 Nov 1957, p. 9. *HR* 13 Dec 1857, p. 16 *HR MPHPD NYT* 15 Dec 1957. *NYT* 4 Jul 1958, p. 15. *Var*

KISMET (German language)

First National Pictures, Inc.; controlled by Warner Bros. Pictures, Inc. *Dist* First National Pictures, Inc. **1931**; Berlin opening: 23 Jun 1931. Sd; b&w. Length undetermined. German language.

Dir Wilhelm Dieterle. *Scr* Howard Estabrook, Ulrich Steindorff and Karl Etlinger. *Photog* Sid Hickox.

Source: Based on the play *Kismet* by Edward Knoblock (London, 19 Apr 1911).

Cast: Gustav Fröhlich, Dita Parlo, Vladimir Sokoloff, Anton Pointner, Karl Etlinger.

Adventure. [*Not viewed*]. [The following plot summary is based on the English-language version of this film, *Kismet*; character names refer to that version. For further information regarding the English-language version, please see the note below and the entry for *Kismet* in the *AFI Catalog of Feature Films, 1921-30*.] Hajj, beggar and thief, schemes with a guide to obtain gold from the famous bandit, the White Sheik, who is searching for his long-lost son; but Hajj recognizes the White Sheik as his enemy, Jawan, and refuses the guide his share; and the guide has Hajj arrested. Mansur, the Wazir of Police, offers Hajj the choice of losing his hand and his daughter, Marsinah, or assassinating the caliph. Saved from Hajj's dagger by his coat of mail, the caliph sends the beggar to prison, where he encounters Jawan, kills his enemy, exchanges clothing, and is released. Hajj is soon again in Mansur's clutches for trying to spirit his daughter from the wazir's harem, but Hajj kills Mansur (Jawan's son) just as the caliph enters. Rather than receiving further punishment, Hajj is released—for the caliph, who has disguised himself as his gardener's son, is about to marry Marsinah. *Assassination. Beggars. Disguise. Family relationships. Harems. Police. Prisons. Revenge. Royalty. Thieves.*

Note: The 1930 English-language version was directed by John Francis Dillon and starred Otis Skinner and Loretta Young (see *AFI Catalog of Feature Films, 1921-30*; F2.2888). Other films based on the play include the 1920 Waldorf Film Corp. production, which was directed by Louis J. Gasnier and also starred Otis Skinner, with Rosemary Theby (see *AFI Catalog of Feature Films, 1911-20*; F1.2361); a 1944 M-G-M production, with songs by Harold Arlen and E. Y. Harburg, which was also directed by Wilhelm Dieterle and starred Ronald Colman and Marlene Dietrich; and a 1955 M-G-M musical, based on the Broadway musical by Charles Lederer and Luther Davis. The latter film was directed by Vincente Minnelli and starred Howard Keel and Ann Blyth.

THE KISS (Latino)

Universal Film Mfg. Co. 4 Jul **1921** [©Universal Film Mfg. Co.; 22 Jun 1921; LP16706]. Si; b&w. 5 reels, 4,488 ft.

Dir Jack Conway. *Scen* A. P. Younger and George Pyper. *Photog* Bert Glennon.

Source: Based on the short story "Little Erolinda" by Johnston McCulley in *Adventure Magazine* (Feb 1916).

Cast: George Periolat (*Don Luis Baldarama*), William E. Lawrence (*Audre Baldarama*), J. P. Lockney (*Selistino Vargas*), Carmel Myers (*Erolinda Vargas*), J. J. Lanoe (*Carlos*), Harvey Clarke (*Miguel Chavez*), Jean Acker (*Isabella Chavez*), Ed Brady (*Manuel Feliz*).

Melodrama. At the harvest fiesta, Don Luis expects to announce the betrothal of his son, Audre, to Isabella, the daughter of a neighboring don, but Audre plans to elope with Erolinda, the daughter of the ranch superintendent. They are surprised by Vargas, who believes that his daughter has been dishonored and shoots Audre. The latter's vaqueros, believing him to be murdered, storm the house, but Erolinda holds them at bay. Audre pacifies his men, then kisses Erolinda in their sight, thus claiming her as his bride. *California-History–To 1846. Honor. Ranch foremen. Ranches.*

Note: Some sources give George Pyper co-authorship credit for scenario; Universal records credit A. P. Younger.

FD 3 Jul 1921. *Var* 8 Jul 1921, p. 27.

KISS OF FIRE (1950) *see* THE TOAST OF NEW ORLEANS

KISS OF FIRE (Native Americans, Comanche, Paiute, Latino)

Universal-International Pictures Co., Inc. *Dist* Universal Pictures Co., Inc. Oct **1955**; New York opening: 23 Sep 1955; Prod: early Nov–late Dec 1954 [©Universal Pictures Co.; 27 Jul 1955; LP5321]. Sd (Western Electric Recording); col (Technicolor). 7,851 ft. 87 or 89 min. PCA cert no. 17379.

Prod Samuel Marx. *Dir* Joseph M. Newman. *Asst dir* Marshall Green and [Gordon McLean]. *Scr* Franklin Coen and Richard Collins. *Dir of photog* Carl Guthrie. *Technicolor color consultant* William Fritzsche. *Art dir* Alexander Golitzen and Robert Boyle. *Film ed* Arthur H. Nadel. *Set dec* Russell A. Gausman and Julia Heron. *Cost* Jay A. Morley, Jr. *Mus supv* Joseph Gershenson. *Sd* Leslie I. Carey, Joe Lapis and [Corson Jowett]. *Makeup* Bud Westmore. *Hair stylist* Joan St. Oegger. [*Unit prod mgr* Foster D. Thompson].

Source: Based on the novel *The Rose and the Flame* by Jonreed Lauritzen (Garden City, NY, 1951).

Cast: JACK PALANCE (*El Tigre*), BARBARA RUSH (*Princess Lucia*), Rex Reason (*Duke of Montera*), Martha Hyer (*Felicia*), Leslie Bradley ([*Baron*] *Vega*), Alan Reed (*Diego*), Lawrence Dobkin (*Padre Domingo*), Joseph Waring (*Victor*), Pat Hogan (*Pahvant*), Karen Kadler (*Shining Moon*), Steven Geray (*Ship captain* [*Bellon*]), Henry Rowland (*Acosta*), [Bernie Gozier (*Roderico*)], [Dave Kashner (*Machado*)], [John Mansfield (*Messenger*)], [David Alpert (*Mate*)], [Charles Horvath (*Guard*)], [Shooting Star (*Indian*)], [Robert Hoy, Paul Marion (*Soldiers*)].

Adventure. [*Print viewed*]. In 1700, the beautiful Princess Lucia of Spain, while dining in her Santa Fe, New Mexico, villa with her guardian, the Duke of Montera, and her cousin Felicia, learns that because King Charles II is dying, she must return to the court to assume the throne. Concerned not only about the trek to Monterey, California, a land unfamiliar to their party, as well as the treachery of others who would like to inherit the crown, the Duke of Montera summons a former Spanish soldier called El Tigre to guide and protect them on their journey. The Viceroy of Spain, who wants to see Leopold of Bavaria on the throne, tries to have El Tigre killed, but the dashing rogue outwits the viceroy's men, arriving in Santa Fe to announce his lack of interest in helping the future queen. That night, however, as he watches Lucia worriedly contemplating the days to come, El Tigre falls deeply in love with her, and the next morning, he begins to organize the expedition to Monterey. Unknown to Lucia, the Baron Vega and a nobleman named Acosta support the viceroy and are determined to have her killed before she reaches Spain. Soon after the party sets out, two disloyal soldiers sneak away from camp to deliver a message to the co-conspirators at a nearby fort. El Tigre and his cohort Diego unsuccessfully pursue them, and the next day, the travelers learn that soldiers from the fort were planning to ambush them. Montera whips one of the traitorous soldiers to death, an act that sickens both Lucia and El Tigre. Later Montera proposes to Lucia, but because he bases his case not on love but on the nobility of his blood, she refuses him. Later, Montera is attacked by Comanches and nearly dies, but following Padre Domingo's last rites, he begins to recover. When Paiutes visit their camp, Chief Pahvant tells El Tigre that a contingent of Spanish soldiers is following them. El Tigre asks the Paiutes to see them safely to Monterey, but that hope is dashed when Vega, misunderstanding a Paiute custom, stabs Pahvant. Montera then discovers that Vega is a traitor and kills him in a sword

fight. Fearing that their party will be wiped out the next day by either attacking Paiutes or Acosta's soldiers, or both, Lucia abandons propriety and dances with El Tigre, and later, they kiss. During the night, however, El Tigre learns through Paiute drums that the Indians mistakenly think the travelers have joined with Acosta's men. El Tigre's plan to lure the soldiers into battle with the Indians is successful, but Montera uses deceit to escape the battle and spirit Lucia away. She now argues that she wishes to avert the killing and give up the throne, but the duke ignores her, saying, "We both have our duty." El Tigre pursues them to Monterey, where he finds Lucia locked in a stateroom of the French ship on which Montera has secured passage to Spain. The men fight, but as he is about to deliver the lethal blow, El Tigre shows Montera mercy and releases him to Felicia's care. As the ship carries Montera and Felicia back toward Spain, Lucia returns to the California shore with El Tigre, happy to exchange the old world for the new. *California–History–To 1846. Cultural conflict. Expeditions. Guides. Spaniards. Spanish Americans. Comanche Indians. Indians of North America. Monterey (CA). Nobility. Paiute Indians. Princesses. Romantic rivalry. Santa Fe (NM). Ships. Soldiers. Spain. Sword fights. Traitors. Tribal chiefs. Wards and guardians. Whips and whippings.*

Note: The working title of this film was *The Rose and the Flame*. Although a *HR* production chart places Rhonda Fleming in the cast, she does not appear in the released print. According to materials contained in the MPAA/PCA files at the AMPAS Library, this picture was shot on location in the Nevada desert. A modern source notes that Mary Tyler Moore appeared as a dance hall girl in this film.

Box 3 Sep 1955. *DV* 26 Aug 1955, p. 3. *Exh* 7 Sep 1955, pp. 4026-27. *FD* 29 Aug 1955, p. 6. *Har* 27 Aug 1955, p. 138. *HR* 5 Nov 1954, p. 10. *HR* 17 Dec 1954. *HR* 26 Aug 1955, p. 3. *MPHPD* 27 Aug 1955, p. 570. *NYT* 24 Sep 1955, p. 11. *Var* 31 Aug 1955, p. 6.

THE KISSING BANDIT (Latino)
Metro-Goldwyn-Mayer Corp.; controlled by Loew's Inc. *Dist* Loew's Inc. Jan **1949**; Prod: mid-May—early Aug 1947; added scenes began mid-Mar 1948 [©Loew's Inc.; 10 Nov 1948; LP1942]. Sd (Western Electric Sound System); col (Technicolor). 11 reels, 9,025 ft. 99-100 or 102 min. Passed by the National Board of Review. PCA cert no. 12671.
Prod Joe Pasternak. *Dir* Laslo Benedek. [*Asst dir* Marvin Stuart]. *Orig scr* Isobel Lennart and John Briard Harding. *Dir of photog* Robert Surtees. [*Cam op* Al Lane]. [*Stills* J. Frank Shugrue]. *Spec eff* A. Arnold Gillespie. *Technicolor col dir* Natalie Kalmus. *Assoc* Henri Jaffa. *Art dir* Cedric Gibbons and Randall Duell. *Set dec* Edwin B. Willis. *Assoc* Jack D. Moore. *Cost des* Walter Plunkett. *Mus dir* Georgie Stoll. *Arr* Leo Arnaud. *Fiesta dance specialty created by* Robert Alton. *Dance dir* Stanley Donen. *Rec dir* Douglas Shearer. [*Sd* Wilhelm Brockway]. *Hair styles designed by* Sydney Guilaroff. *Makeup created by* Jack Dawn. [*Prod mgr* Sergei Petschnikoff]. [*Scr supv* Florence Swan]. [*Grip* Albert Hunter]. [*Guitar playing double for Frank Sinatra* Bob Bain].
Music: "Dance of Fury" by Nacio Herb Brown.
Song(s): "Tomorrow Means Romance," music by Nacio Herb Brown, lyrics by William Katz; "What's Wrong with Me?" "Love Is Where You Find It," and "Señorita," music by Nacio Herb Brown, lyrics by Earl Brent; "I Steal a Kiss," music by Nacio Herb Brown, lyrics by Edward Heyman.
Cast: FRANK SINATRA (*Ricardo*), KATHRYN GRAYSON (*Teresa*), J. Carrol Naish (*Chico*), Mildred Natwick (*Isabella*), Mikhail Rasumny (*Don Jose*), Billy Gilbert (*General [Felipe] Torro*), Sono Osato (*Bianca*), Clinton Sundberg (*Colonel Gomez*), Carleton G. Young (*Count [Ricardo] Belmonte*), Edna Skinner (*Juanita*), Vicente Gomez (*Mexican guitarist*), [Ricardo Montalban, Ann Miller, Cyd Charisse (*Fiesta specialty dance*)], [Henry Mirelez (*Pepito, 8 years*)], [Nick Thompson (*Pablo*)], [José Domínguez (*Francisco*)], [Albert Morin (*Lotso*)], [Michael Kostrick (*Juan*)], [Fred Gillman (*Pedro*)], [Pedro Regas (*Esteban*)], [Leo Mostovoy, Gero Maly, Wilson Wood (*Advisors*)], [Margaret Martin (*Rosita*)], [Carl Pitti (*Whip expert*)], [Captain Garcia (*Coachman*)], [Carlos Albert (*Footman*)], [Julian Rivero (*Postman*)], [Mitchell Lewis (*Fernando*)], [Byron Foulger, Jack Manolas (*Grandees*)], [Linda Howard, Nora Christy, Norma Gentner, Ginny Jackson (*Convent girls*)], [Susan Hoyt (*Tiny girl*)], [Nana Bryant (*Nun*)], [Alex Montoya (*Bandit*)], [Suzanne Ridgway (*Guest*)].
Historical, Musical, Romantic comedy. [*Print viewed*]. In 1830, when California was a colony of Spain, Chico, an innkeeper and former cohort of the fugitive outlaw known as the Kissing Bandit,

learns that the bandit's son Ricardo will be visiting from Boston. In a letter to Chico, Ricardo has written that he has been attending college and intends to help Chico with his "business," but Chico misinterprets the letter and believes that the young man is coming to help him return to banditry. Chico and many of his pals eagerly await the arrival of Ricardo, whom they expect will be as brave and cunning as his father, but their excitement soon turns to disappointment when Ricardo approaches them too quickly, loses control of his horse and crashes through the window of Chico's inn. Ricardo, who knows nothing of his father's criminal legacy and has been told that Chico was a former associate of his father's, faints when Chico tells him the truth. Ricardo balks at Chico's expectation that he will become the new bandit chief, and instead insists that he has come to California to help Chico operate his inn. Determined to make a bandit leader out of Ricardo, Chico disregards Ricardo's objections and dresses the young man in his father's clothes. Although Ricardo proves that he is worthless as a holdup man during the first attempt to lead a stagecoach robbery, the other bandits decide to keep him in the gang and use him to distract the women they are robbing with kisses. During the robbery of a stagecoach carrying Teresa, the daughter of Governor Don Jose, Ricardo, stricken by the young woman's beauty, is unable to leave her with a cheap kiss. Teresa returns home dejected, and mistakenly concludes that she was not kissed because the bandit found her unattractive. In love with Teresa, Ricardo later serenades her, but as soon as he finishes singing, he is shot at by Don Jose's guards and forced to flee. Don Jose, who believes that the Kissing Bandit insulted his daughter by refusing to kiss her, orders the arrest of the young trespasser and sends Colonel Gomez to find him. Later, Spanish tax collectors Count Ricardo Belmonte and General Felipe Torro, who are en route to the governor's hacienda, rent a room at Chico's inn. When Belmonte catches Chico stealing money from the sleeping Torro, a fistfight ensues. After subduing Belmonte and tying both tax collectors to their beds, Chico and Ricardo discover that the men are important officials and that they are carrying a letter of introduction to Don Jose. Ricardo and Chico steal the letter and disguise themselves as the tax collectors to gain entry to the governor's hacienda. At Don Jose's hacienda, Ricardo resumes his romantic pursuit of Teresa, and Chico begins romancing Isabella, the governor's sister. While Chico and Ricardo continue to deceive the governor at a fiesta held in honor of the visiting tax collectors, the real tax collectors escape from Chico's inn and make their way to the governor's. By the time they arrive there, however, Chico and Ricardo have revealed their true identities to Don Jose and have won his friendship. After sending Torro and Belmonte back to Spain, the governor asks Ricardo to stay at the hacienda and gives his blessing to their romance. *Bandits. California–History–To 1846. Legendary characters. Romance. Spanish Americans. Colonies. Dancers. Fathers and daughters. Fiestas. Fistfights. Governors. Haciendas. Impersonation and imposture. Innkeepers. Inns. Kisses. Singers. Spaniards. Taxation.*

Note: According to an Aug 1944 *HR* news item, this film was to mark the screen debut of soprano Marion Bell, who was set for the leading female role. In Dec 1944, another *HR* news item announced that Frank Morgan and Lina Romay would appear in major roles. Although *HR* news items in Apr and late Aug 1945 listed John Carroll in the title role, an early Aug 1945 *HR* news item listed Morgan, Romay, Bell and John Hodiak in the top spots. The starring lineup was changed again in May 1946, when *HR* announced that Kathryn Grayson and Tony Martin were assigned the leads. Martin was later replaced by Frank Sinatra. In Jan 1947, a *HR* news item noted that Robert Z. Leonard was set to direct, but he did not participate in the final film. A *HR* news item notes that portions of the film were shot on location in Sonora, CA.
The Kissing Bandit marked the first feature film directed by Hungarian-born Laslo Benedek, although he previously had directed retakes for the 1944 M-G-M film *Song of Russia*. Subsequent to the release of *The Kissing Bandit*, the film became jokingly known as one of M-G-M's biggest "flops" and an acknowledged lowpoint in the careers of Sinatra and Grayson.

Box 20 Nov 1948. *DV* 18 Nov 1948, p. 5. *Down Beat* 25 Feb 1949, p. 8. *FD* 18 Nov 1948, p. 6. *HR* 24 Aug 1944, p. 15. *HR* 5 Dec 1944, p. 4. *HR* 8 Feb 1945, p. 3. *HR* 6 Apr 1945, p. 10. *HR* 12 Apr 1945, p. 2. *HR* 3 Aug 1945, p. 8. *HR* 22 Aug 1945, p. 8. *HR* 29 Aug 1945, p. 2. *HR* 14 May 1946, p. 13. *HR* 25 Nov 1946, p. 2. *HR* 15 Jan 1947, p. 1. *HR* 20 Jan 1947, p. 4. *HR* 16 May 1947, p. 20. *HR* 6 Jun 1947, p. 10. *HR* 1 Aug 1947, p. 14. *HR* 17 Mar 1948, p. 8. *HR* 18 Nov 1948, p. 3, 9. *MPHPD* 27 Nov 1948, p. 4397. *NYT* 19 Nov 1948, p. 35. *Var* 17 Nov 1948, p. 13.

KIT CARSON (Native Americans, Blackfoot, Siksika)
Paramount Famous Lasky Corp. 23 Jun **1928** [©Paramount Famous Lasky Corp.; 21 Aug 1928; LP25550]. Si; b&w. 8 reels, 7,464 ft.
Dir Alfred L. Werker and Lloyd Ingraham. *Scen* Paul Powell. *Story* Frank M. Clifton. *Titles* Frederick Hatton. *Photog* Mack Stengler. *Film ed* Duncan Mansfield.

Cast: Fred Thomson (*Kit Carson*), Nora Lane (*Josefa*), Dorothy Janis (*Sings-in-the-Clouds*), Raoul Paoli (*Shuman*), William Courtright (*Old Bill Williams*), Nelson McDowell (*Jim Bridger*), Raymond Turner (*Smokey*).

Western. In a saloon in Taos, Kit Carson gets into a fight with Shuman over a Spanish dancer who has taken Kit's fancy. The following day, both men, who are part of a government peace-keeping mission ordered into the troubled Blackfeet country, ride north. On the way, Kit encounters Sings-in-the-Clouds, the daughter of the Blackfeet chief, rescuing her from an attacking bear. This single brave act establishes peaceful relations between the whites and the Indians. These relations are almost broken, however, when Shuman attacks the Indian girl with a knife; Kit shoots him in the hand and sends him packing. Shuman later attacks the girl in the desert and causes her death. Kit goes after him and throws him from a cliff into the Blackfeet circle of death. With peace established, Kit returns to Taos. *Bears. Kit Carson. Dancers. Scouts (Frontier). Siksika Indians. Taos (NM).*

FD 23 Sep 1928.

KIT CARSON (Native Americans, Latino, Shoshoni)
Edward Small Productions, Inc. *Dist* United Artists Corp. 30 Aug 1940; Denver opening: 26 Aug 1940; Prod: began May 1940 [©Edward Small Productions, Inc.; 6 Sep 1940; LP9897]. Sd (Western Electric Sound System); b&w. 11 reels. 97 min. PCA cert no. 6527.

Pres EDWARD SMALL. *Dir* George B. Seitz. *2d unit dir* Arthur Rosson. *Asst dir* John Burch. *Orig scr* George Bruce. *Story* Evelyn Wells. *Photog* John Mescall and Robert Pittack. *Spec eff* Howard A. Anderson. *Photog eff* Jack Cosgrove. *Art dir* John DuCasse Schulze. *Film ed* Fred R. Feitshans, Jr. and William Claxton. *Set dec* Edward Boyle. *Cost* Edward Lambert. *Mus* Bob Wright, Carlos Ruffino, Edward Ward and Chet Forrest. *Sd* Earl Sitar. *Rerecording ed* Richard Heermance. *Makeup* Don Cash. *Prod mgr* Val Paul. *Asst to prod* Grant Whytock. [*Stand-in for Jon Hall* Buell Bryant]. [*Stand-in for Lynn Bari* Marie Toomey]. [*Stand-in for Dana Andrews* Jack Hendricks]. [*Stand-in for Ward Bond* Carl Sepulveda]. [*Stand-in for Harold Huber* Ben Corbett]. [*Stand-in for Harry Strang* Curley Gibson].

Song(s): "Sail Along Prairie Schooner," words by Chet Forrest and Bob Wright, music by Edward Ward; "With My Concertina," English lyrics by Bob Wright and Chet Forrest, Spanish lyrics by Carlos Ruffino, music by Edward Ward.

Cast: Jon Hall (*Kit Carson*), Lynn Bari (*Dolores Murphy*), Dana Andrews (*Captain John C. Fremont*), Harold Huber (*Lopez*), Ward Bond (*Ape*), Renie Riano (*Miss Pilchard*), Clayton Moore (*Paul Terry*), Rowena Cook (*Alice Terry*), Raymond Hatton (*Jim Bridger*), Harry Strang (*Sergeant Clanahan*), C. Henry Gordon (*General Castro*), Lew Merrill (*General Vallejo*), Stanley Andrews (*Larkin*), Edwin Maxwell (*John Sutter*), Peter Lynn (*James King*), Charley Stevens (*Ruiz*), William Farnum (*Don Miguel Murphy*), [Blaney Harris (*Second Lieutenant*)], [Al Kikume (*Indian Chief*)], [Harry Semels (*Pioneer*)].

Historical, Western. [*Print viewed*]. Fearless frontier scout and Indian fighter Kit Carson and his friends, Ape and Lopez, narrowly escape an attack by a tribe of gun-toting Shoshone Indians as they ride to Fort Bridger, the gateway to the Oregon Trail. After safely arriving at the fort, Kit is asked by wagon leader Paul Terry to guide his train south along the Oregon Trail to California. Kit at first refuses on the grounds that the trip is too dangerous, but when Terry and the wagons make arrangements to ride with Captain John Fremont and his cavalry troops, Kit reconsiders and agrees to lead the train. He soon finds himself in competition with Fremont for the leadership of the train as well as the attentions of Dolores Murphy, a young California beauty on her way to her father's hacienda in Monterey. Meanwhile, General Castro, the Mexican Governor General of California, arms the Indians in an effort to keep the Americans out of California. As the rivalry between Kit and Fremont mounts, Fremont insists upon leading his troops through a canyon, thus exposing them to the danger of ambush, while Kit insists upon leading the wagons along a safer route. As Fremont leads his men into the narrow pass, half the Indians dynamite the entrance, thus trapping the soldiers, while the other half of the tribe attacks the wagons. Kit blasts the entrance open in time to free the soldiers and rescue the wagons, and they continue on to Monterey. As Dolores and the others celebrate their safe passage at the Murphy hacienda, Castro plots the demise of the Americans. Kit

discovers his plans when he sees some Mexican army wagons carrying guns to the general and learns of his plans to destroy the hacienda. As the Americans rally at the Murphy hacienda to raise the flag of the California Republic, Kit orchestrates the forces to defeat Castro. After successfully routing Castro and his troops, Kit is appointed colonel in the United States Army and bids Dolores farewell as he rides off to defend the California Republic. *California–History. Kit Carson. Rivalry. Scouts (Frontier). Wagon trains. John Fremont. Indians of North America. Mexicans. Mexico. Army. Monterey (CA). Officers (Military). Oregon Trail. Territorial governors. United States. Army. Cavalry.*

Note: According to a news item in *HR*, Randolph Scott was originally slated to play the role of Kit Carson. This picture was filmed on location at Cayente, AZ. The 1936 Universal film *Sutter's Gold* (see below) and the 1939 Universal film *Mutiny on the Blackhawk* (see below) also featured the character of Kit Carson.

FD 27 Aug 1940, p. 6. *HR* 1 May 1940, p. 3. *HR* 15 May 1940, p. 2. *HR* 18 May 1940, p. 1. *HR* 27 Aug 1940, p. 3. *MPD* 27 Aug 1940, p. 1, 4. *MPH* 31 Aug 1940, p. 52. *NYT* 15 Nov 1940, p. 25. *Var* 28 Aug 1940, p. 16.

KIVALINA OF THE ICE LANDS (Native Americans, Native Alaskans)
B. C. R. Productions, Inc. **1925** [©B. C. R. Productions, Inc.; 25 Jun 1925; LP21670]. Si; b&w. 6 reels, 5,946 ft.

Dir Earl Rossman. *Titles* Katherine Hilliker. *Photog* Earl Rossman. *Film ed* Katherine Hilliker.

Cast: Kivalina (*The Heroine*), Aguvaluk (*The Hero*), Nashulik (*Witch doctor*), Tokatoo (*Kivalina's brother*), Nuwak (*The Master Hunter*).

Drama. Aguvaluk, a great Eskimo hunter, plans to marry Kivalina and goes to the witch doctor for his consent. The witch doctor tells Aguvaluk that he may not marry until he has discharged all of his father's debts by bringing back the hides of 40 seals. The great hunter accomplishes this incredible feat and returns with the hides only to be told that, in order to pay off the interest on the debt, he must also bring in the hide of a silver fox. After great privation, Aguvaluk captures the fox, but before he can return to safety, he is caught in a fierce storm. He builds an ice shelter that protects him from the bitter cold and the following morning kills a small reindeer, satisfying his hunger with the meat and using the hide to make a small sled. Finally reaching home, Aguvaluk prepares to marry Kivalina, and there is a great feast. *Foxes. Native Alaskans. Seals (Animals). Storms. Witch doctors.*

FD 5 Jul 1925. *MPW* 11 Jul 1925. *NYT* 23 Jun 1925, p. 24. *Var* 1 Jul 1925, p. 32.

DIE KLATCHE *see* **THE LIGHT AHEAD**

KLONDIKE ANNIE (Chinese Americans)
Paramount Productions, Inc. *Dist* Paramount Productions, Inc. 21 Feb **1936**; Prod: began 25 Sep 1935 [©Paramount Productions, Inc.; 21 Feb 1936; LP6201]. Sd (Western Electric Noiseless Recording); b&w. 78, 80 or 85 min. Passed by the National Board of Review. PCA cert no. 1857.

Pres ADOLPH ZUKOR. *Prod* William LeBaron. [*Exec prod* Henry Herzbrun]. *Dir* Raoul Walsh. [*Asst dir* David MacDonald]. *Story* Marion Morgan and George B. Dowell. *Scr and dial* Mae West. *Material suggested by* Frank Mitchell Dazey. [*Contr to spec seq* Boris Petroff and Bert Hanlon]. *Photog* George Clemens. *Art dir* Hans Dreier and Bernard Herzbrun. *Ed* Stuart Heisler. *Int dec* A. E. Freudeman. *Sd rec* Harold Lewis and Louis Mesenkop.

Song(s): "Occidental Woman" and "Cheer Up, Little Sister," music and lyrics by Gene Austin; "Mr. Deep Blue Sea" and "Little Bar Butterfly," music and lyrics by Gene Austin and Jimmie Johnson; "Auld Lang Syne," words by Robert Burns, music Scottish traditional; "A Hot Time in the Old Town," words by Joe Hayden, music by Theodore M. Metz; and other songs.

Cast: MAE WEST ([*Rose Carleton*] *The Frisco Doll*), Victor McLaglen ([*Captain*] *Bull Brackett*), Phillip Reed ([*Inspector*] *Jack Forrest*), Helen Jerome Eddy (*Annie Alden*), Harry Beresford (*Brother Bowser*), Harold Huber (*Chan Lo*), Lucille Webster Gleason (*Big Tess*), Conway Tearle (*Vance Palmer*), Esther Howard (*Fanny Radler*), Soo Yong (*Fah Wong*), John Rogers (*Buddie*), Ted Oliver (*Grigsby*), Lawrence Grant (*Sir Gilbert*), Gene Austin (*Organist*), Vladimar Bykoff (*Marinoff*), [George Walsh (*Quartermaster*)], [James Burke (*Bartender*)], [Chester Gan (*Ship's cook*)], [Jack Daley (*Second mate*)], [Jack Wallace (*Third mate*)], [Carl Harbaugh, George MacQuarrie (*Port officers*)], [Wong Chung, Paul Fung (*Tong men*)], [Mrs. Chan Lee (*Blind woman*)], [Otto

Heimel (*Cocoa*)], [Gladys Gale, Edna Bennett, Pearl Eaton, Kathleen Key, Ilean Hume, Marie Wells (*Dance hall girls*)], [Howard Lang, Eddie Allen, Dick Allen (*Miners*)], [Katherine Clare Ward (*Miner's wife*)], [Jackson Snyder (*Little boy*)], [D'Arcy Corrigan, Arthur Turner Foster, Nell Craig, Nella Walker (*Missionaries*)], [Homer Dickinson (*Dress man*)], [Philip Ahn (*Wing*)], [William Norton Bailey (*Mission man*)], [Polly Vann (*Mission woman*)], [Mrs. Wong Wing (*Ah Toy*)], [Maidel Turner (*Lydia Bowley*)], [Huntly Gordon (*Clinton Reynolds*)], [Paul Kruger (*First sailor*)], [Edward Brady (*Second sailor*)], [John Lester Johnson (*Third sailor*)], [Frank C. Baker, George Burton (*Port officials*)], [Jim Thorpe], ["Beans" Reardon], [Hank Hankinson], ["Dink" Templeton], [Billy McGowan], [Kathryn Bates], [Marcel Ventura], [Guy D'Ennery], [Laura Treadwell].

Comedy-drama, **with songs**. [*Print viewed*]. In San Francisco's Chinatown of the 1890s, Rose Carleton, the "Frisco Doll," is Chan Lo's kept woman at his extravagant gambling house, where she is also a singer. When Chan Lo intercepts a note to Doll being carried by her faithful servant, Ah Toy, he tortures Ah Toy to determine the note's origins. Doll meets her friend Vance Palmer in the gambling house and he informs her that he has secretly arranged passage for her on a ship to Nome, Alaska, where Doll hopes to take advantage of the gold strike. Vance gives Doll a farewell kiss, which inspires the jealous Chan Lo to threaten Doll. Late that night, Doll is forced to kill Chan Lo in self-defense, and she and a young servant, Fah Wong, board the ship *Java Maid*. The *Java Maid*'s captain, Bull Brackett, falls in love with Doll, and gives her his cabin. Bull agrees to drop Fah Wong off in Seattle, although it is out of his way, and there he learns that Doll is wanted for the murder of Chan Lo, however, he loves Doll in spite of her reputation. Settlement worker Sister Annie Alden boards the boat in Seattle, and although she is dismayed by Doll's loose morals, when Annie falls ill, Doll nurses her and is impressed by Annie's sincerely charitable nature. Annie dies just as Inspector Jack Forrest boards the boat off the coast of Alaska, intending to arrest Doll, so she impersonates Annie, and she and Bull convince Jack that the deceased Annie is actually Doll. Still impersonating Annie in Alaska, Doll revives membership in the settlement workers' Alaskan Settlement House for which Annie was headed by aiming her appeal to the dance hall crowd and conducting rousing meetings. A romance arises between Doll and Jack, but one day he overhears her conversation with Bull in which he hears that she is the Doll. Jack is willing to give up his career to be with Doll, and she is forced to make a decision between him and Bull. Doll realizes that she cannot allow Jack to ruin his career because of the murder charge against her and, having successfully gotten the town to close on Sundays and raised enough to pay off the settlement's debts, Doll gives up the missionary life. Before she leaves, she bids brother Bowser to build a bigger settlement house dedicated to Sister Annie Alden. After she leaves the settlement house, she is nearly killed by a knife thrown by one of Chan Lo's avengers, however, she drops her Settlement Book, and the knife misses her as she bends over to pick it up. As she has had a dream in which Annie bids her to return to face trial, Doll returns to Bull and asks him to take her to San Francisco, where she will face the murder charges with faithful Bull at her side. *Chinese Americans. Impersonation and imposture. Mistresses. Murder. Police inspectors. Reformers. Alaska. Boats. Chinatowns. Conversion (Religious). Dance halls. Death and dying. Missionaries. Proposals (Marital). San Francisco (CA). Sea captains. Settlers.*

Note: The opening credits of the film read, "From a play by Mae West, a story by Marion Morgan and George B. Dowell and material suggested by Frank Mitchell Dazey." According to *SAB*, Mae West's unpublished and unproduced play was called *Frisco Kate*. *SAB* also indicates that Morgan and Dowell's unpublished story was called "Hallelujah, I'm a Saint," and Dazey's suggested material was actually an unpublished story called "Lulu Was a Lady." Pre-release scripts at the AMPAS Library are titled *The Frisco Doll* and *Klondike Lou*. The original story in the script files is titled "Hallelujah! I'm a Saint! or How About It, Brother?" According to a Jan 1936 news item in *HR*, Paramount was considering dropping Mae West as a contract star because of the "production turmoil entailed in working with the temperamental star" and the high cost of their production. The article notes that the approximate cost of *Klondike Annie* was $1,000,000, $200,000 of which went to West for her performance and writing. Paramount threatened to halt filming of *Klondike Annie* and sue West for the cost of production; however, by late Jan 1936, West and Paramount came to an agreement, the production continued, and her contract was renewed for another feature. A Sep 1935 news item in *HR* indicates that cameramen Victor Milner and Ted Tetzlaff were slated to work on the film, but were replaced by George Clemens when Mae West insisted on a new cameraman. *DV* news items noted that assistant director James Dugan also left

the production due to "difficulties" with West, and was replaced by David MacDonald. According to *NYT*, Dugan directed the poker scenes.

The MPAA/PCA Collection at the AMPAS Library reveal that Will H. Hays, president of the MPPDA, was adamant that the character of Annie never appear as an actual "religious worker," or that the film make any actual religious references. In 1935, the first script, *Klondike Lou*, was rejected for this reason. A Sep 1935 letter from the Hays Office regarding the second submitted script noted that Annie's clothing "ought not to have about it any definite suggestion of her religious work." In addition, the lines, "There are souls to be saved everywhere," and "We have a mission at Nome," were recommended to be changed to "There are souls to be rescued" and "We have a settlement at Nome." Hays's concern over the possible religious content of the film continued into Feb 1936, when he stated in an interoffice letter to Joseph I. Breen, director of the PCA, "My worst worry is not the alleged salaciousness, but is in the producer's failure to avoid the impression that it is a *mission* house picture and that "The Doll" was masquerading as a missionary. The effort to avoid this is to me unconvincing." Nonetheless, with alterations the film was approved and released.

Local censors almost unanimously deleted the scene in which Chan Lo is stabbed by Doll, in addition to the scenes in which Ah Toy is tortured, and various scenes of intimacy between Doll and her lovers were also deleted. The Hays Office came under fire from various organizations for approving the release of *Klondike Annie*, and newspapers owned by Paul Block and William Randolph Hearst launched a vigorous campaign against the promotion of the film. In a May 1936 letter to Paramount from the president of the San Francisco Motion Picture Council, the president condemned the film because "it presents its heroine as a mistress to an Oriental, then as a murderess, then as a cheap imitator of a missionary—jazzing religion—[it] is not in harmony with other education forces of our social set-up. And these elements are particularly objectionable when they are interspersed with smutty wise-cracks." The Atlanta Better Films Committee also condemned the film because of its topic. The Paul Block newspapers published an editorial that suggested that the Hays Office would "serve the American public as well as the whole film industry to better purpose if they were to outlaw indecent and immoral pictures such as the film *Klondike Annie*. Here is a picture which lauds disreputable living and glorifies vice. Censors may cut out a few of the worst scenes in some states. But they cannot clean it up, for the whole story is on the lowest possible level. It is humiliating that a film of this kind can be presented to the public in the guise of entertainment." Hearst's papers banned all advertisements for *Klondike Annie*; however, Paramount managed to get around this by placing the following advertisement in the trade papers: "Important feature. For information call VA-2041." The National Legion of Decency published a proclamation against the film in several publications. An article in the *Herald* claimed the film was "an affront to the decency of the public." According to contemporary articles, the *National Police Gazette* filed a libel suit against Paramount for using a facsimile of the magazine in the film during a scene in "a bawdy house." The film was banned in Australia. Despite the negative press, *MPH* reported that *Klondike Annie* grossed "$2500 to $8500 over average per box office."

According to the pressbook, some Chinese musicians from Los Angeles appear in the film. Malamutes appearing in the film were owned by Carl Stecker. Although *FD* credits Sam Coslow with music and lyrics, his contribution to the final film has not been confirmed. *NYT* reports that Victor McLaglen earned $87,500 for this film. Modern sources add Philo McCullough to the cast.

DV 3 Nov 1935, p. 1. *DV* 15 Nov 1935, p. 1. *FD* 26 Oct 1935, p. 7. *FD* 10 Feb 1936, p. 3. *FD* 21 Feb 1936, pp. 9-12. *HR* 26 Sep 1935, p. 6. *HR* 16 Jan 1936, p. 1. *HR* 18 Jan 1936, p. 3. *HR* 5 Feb 1936, p. 3. *HR* 16 May 1936, p. 4. *MPH* 28 Dec 1935, p. 49. *MPH* 15 Feb 1936, p. 44. *MPH* 7 Mar 1936. *NYT* 12 Mar 1936, p. 18. *Var* 26 Feb 1936. *Var* 4 Mar 1936. *Var* 18 Mar 1936, p. 17. *Var* 27 Oct 1937.

DI KLYATSHE *see* **THE LIGHT AHEAD**

KNICKERBOCKER HOLIDAY (Dutch Americans)
Producers Corp. of America. *Dist* United Artists Corp. 17 Mar **1944**; Prod: mid-Sep—mid-Nov 1943 [©Producers Corp. of America; 17 Mar 1944; LP12615]. Sd (Western Electric Mirrophonic Recording); b&w. 7,693 ft. 82 or 85 min.

Prod Harry Joe Brown. [*Assoc prod* Stanley Logan]. *Dir* Harry Joe Brown. *Asst dir* Raoul Pagel. *Scr* David Boehm, Rowland Leigh and Harold Goldman. *Adpt* Thomas Lennon. *Dir of photog* Philip Tannura. *Prod des* Bernard Herzbrun. *Supv film ed* John F. Link. *Asst* Walter Hannemann. *Set dec* Julia Heron. *Cost des* Walter Plunkett. *Mus dir* Jacques Samossoud. *Mus score* Werner R. Heymann. *Sd rec* Ben Winkler. *Makeup* Steve Drum. *Hair stylist* Nina Roberts. *Prod mgr* Sid Brod.

Music: Additional musical numbers by Theodore Paxson.

Song(s): "There's Nowhere to Go But Up," "It Never Was You," "The One Indispensable Man" and "September Song," music by Kurt Weill, lyrics by Maxwell Anderson; "Love Has Made This Such a Lovely Day" and "One More Smile," music by Sammy Cahn, lyrics by Jule Styne; "Oh Woe!" and "Holiday," words and music by Nelson Eddy; "Let's Make Tomorrow Today," music and lyrics by Werner R. Heymann and Forman Brown; "Sing Out," music and lyrics by Franz Steininger and Forman Brown.

Source: Based on the play *Knickerbocker Holiday* book and lyrics by Maxwell Anderson, music by Kurt Weill, as produced by Playwrights Company (New York, 19 Oct 1938).

Cast: Nelson Eddy [(*Brom Broeck*)], Charles Coburn [(*Peter Stuyvesant*)], Constance Dowling [(*Tina Tienhoven*)], Ernest Cossart [(*Tienhoven*)], Shelley Winter [(*Ulda Tienhoven*)], Johnny Davis [(*Tenpin*)], Percy Kilbride [(*Jailer*)], Otto Kruger [(*Roosevelt*)], Fritz Feld [(*Poffenburgh*)], Richard Hale [(*Tammany*)], and Carmen Amaya and Her Company, [Chester Conklin (*Town caller*)].

Historical, Musical comedy. [*Print viewed*]. In 1647, the citizenry of New Amsterdam eagerly await the arrival of their new governor, Peter Stuyvesant. Meanwhile, Tienhoven, the head of the city council, convenes a meeting to order the arrest of crusading newspaper publisher Brom Broeck, who has accused the council of being scoundrels and thieves. Upon hearing the news, Tina, Tinhoven's daughter and Brom's sweetheart, hurries to the newspaper officer to warn Brom of his impending arrest. There, Tina chides Brom for failing to settle down and marry her. Soon after, Tienhoven and the jailer arrive and usher Brom to the stockades. After they leave, Tina organizes Brom's supporters to demonstrate at the stockades. When Stuyvesant arrives, Tina escorts him to the townsquare, where Brom is confined. Stuyvesant, a shrewd manipulator who regards his silver peg leg as a symbol of power and authority, realizes that Brom is being made into a martyr and orders his release. Stuyvesant then promises to abolish bribery and corruption, thus tricking the population into believing that he is their friend. To silence Brom, Stuyvesant offers him the job of "Secretary of Printing," and Brom naïvely accepts so that he can earn enough money to marry Tina. After confiscating the concilmen's property and businesses, the greedy Stuyvesant placates them with slick words and medals. Enchanted by Tina, Stuyvesant decides to eliminate Brom as his rival and slyly convinces the idealistic young man to leave New Amsterdam and travel to the colonies to promote unity. Agreeing to postpone his marriage for the good of his country, Brom departs on his mission. In his absence, Stuyvesant begins to woo Tina, who regards him as "an old pot roast." By the time Brom finally returns home, Tina is furious with him for leaving her. At the governor's ball, Tienhoven announces his daughter's engagement to Stuyvesant, and Tina, blaming Brom for her predicament, storms out. Later, at the barbershop, Brom threatens Tienhoven with the blade of a razor and insists that he break Tina's engagement. Meanwhile, at the Tienhoven house, Stuyvesant is pressing Tina to agree to an early wedding date. As Tina begs for more time, Brom and Tiehoven burst into the room. After Brom apologizes and kisses Tina, she forgives him, and Stuyvesant sentences him to spend five years in jail for his impertinence. Sneaking into the jail house, Tina jumps through the bars and into Brom's cell, ripping her skirts in the process. When Brom's Indian friends come to his cell window, Brom fashions a rope with Tina's skirts, ties it around his cell bars and asks Big Muscle, an Indian strongman, to yank the bars from the window. Brom then escapes into the woods, and when Tienhoven and Stuyvesant find Tina, the jilted Stuyvesant bribes her father into consenting to an immediate wedding. Meanwhile, Brom and his assistant, Tenpin, launch a campaign against the tyranny of the governor and call for a meeting of the colonists to overthrow the government. When Stuyvesant learns about the planned assembly, he schedules a fair on the day of the meeting and offers a large reward for Brom's arrest. On the day of the fair, Tenpin and Brom, wearing disguises, pass out pamphlets opposing the governor's policies, while Tina sneaks into the mansion and steals Stuyvesant's silver peg leg. Unable to leave the palace without his leg, Stuyvesant devises a plan to lure Brom there by announcing that the wedding is to be held at noon. Brom outsmarts Stuyvesant by diverting the crowd to the stockade, where he calls for a rebellion against the governor's policies. Brom's plan backfires, however, when the crowd erupts into an angry mob. Realizing that only Stuyvesant's slick words can calm the mob, Brom goes to the palace and offers the governor a chance to become an honest man by instituting order and democracy. Brom then returns Stuyvesant's peg leg, now stripped of its silver plating, and Stuyvesant welcomes the colonists as partners in the union. Brom and Stuyvesant shake hands, inaugurating a new political era. *Governors. New York City–History. Newspaper publishers. Political corruption. Reformers. Romantic rivalry. United States–History–Colonial period, ca. 1600-1775. Balls (Parties). Democracy. Dutch Americans. Engagements. Fairs. Fathers and daughters. Indians of North America. Jailbreaks. Mobs. Prostheses and artificial limbs.*

Note: The film opens with the following written prologue: "Little Old New York in 1647—when it was ruled by the Dutch and called New Armsterdam for short. Any similiarity between the two towns is purely coincidental and unintentional." According to a pre-production *HR* news item, Walter Huston, who appeared in the Broadway production, was originally to appear as "Peter Stuyvesant," and Marta Eggerth was to play the female lead. Although a *HR* production chart places Charles Judels, Dick Baldwin, Ferninand Munier and Percival Vivian in the cast, their participation in the released film has not been confirmed. Although Theodore Paxson is credited with additional musical numbers, his exact contribution is not known. This was the initial production of Producers Corporation of America, headed by former agent and publicity man Sid Shlager. On 17 Nov 1950, NBC broadcast a televised version of the Maxwell Anderson musical, directed by William Brown, Jr. and starring Dennis King, John Raitt and Doretta Morrow.

Box 4 Mar 1944. *DV* 22 Feb 1944, p. 3. *FD* 29 Feb 1944, p. 7. *HR* 29 Jun 1943, p. 1. *HR* 17 Sep 1943, p. 9. *HR* 12 Nov 1943, p. 9. *HR* 22 Feb 1944, p. 3. *HR* 24 Apr 1944, p. 12. *MPHPD* 4 Mar 1944, p. 1781. *NYT* 20 Apr 1944, p. 22. *Var* 1 Mar 1944, p. 20.

THE KNIFE *see* **BLACK HAND**

KNOCK ON ANY DOOR (Italian Americans, Latino, African Americans, Slavic Americans)

Santana Pictures, Inc. *Dist* Columbia Pictures Corp. Apr **1949**; New York opening: 22 Feb 1949; Prod: 2 Aug–17 Sep 1948 [©Santana Pictures, Inc.; 21 Feb 1949; LP2162]. Sd (Western Electric Recording); b&w. 98 or 100 min.

Prod Robert Lord. *Assoc prod* Henry S. Kesler. *Dir* Nicholas Ray. *Asst dir* Arthur S. Black. *Scr* Daniel Taradash and John Monks, Jr. *Dir of photog* Burnett Guffey. *Art dir* Robert Peterson. *Film ed* Viola Lawrence. *Set dec* William Kiernan. *Gowns* Jean Louis. *Mus score* George Antheil. *Mus dir* M. W. Stoloff. *Sd eng* Frank Goodwin. *Makeup* Clay Campbell. *Hair styles* Helen Hunt. *Tech adv* National Probation and Parole Association.

Source: Based on the novel *Knock on Any Door* by Willard Motley (New York, 1947).

Cast: HUMPHREY BOGART [(*Andrew Morton*)], George Macready [(*District attorney Kerman*)], Allene Roberts [(*Emma*)], Susan Perry [(*Adele Patterson*)], Mickey Knox [(*Vito*)], Barry Kelley [(*Judge Drake*)], And introducing John Derek (*Nick Romano*), [Dooley Wilson (*Piano player*)], [Cara Williams (*Nelly*)], [Jimmy Conlin (*Kid Fingers*)], [Sumner Williams (*Jimmy*)], [Sid Melton (*Squint*)], [Pepe Hern (*Juan Rodriguez*)], [Dewey Martin (*Butch*)], [Robert A. Davis (*Sunshine*)], [Houseley Stevenson (*Junior*)], [Vince Barnett (*Bartender*)], [Thomas Sully (*Officer Hawkins*)], [Florence Auer (*Aunt Lena*)], [Pierre Watkin (*Purcell*)], [Gordon Nelson (*Corey*)], [Argentina Brunetti (*Ma Romano*)], [Dick Sinatra (*Julian Romano*)], [Carol Coombs (*Ang Romano*)], [Joan Baxter (*Maria Romano*)], [Evelyn Underwood, Mary Emery, Franz Roehn, Betty Hall, Jack Jahries, Rose Plumer, Mabel Smaney, Sidney Dubin, Homer Dickinson, Netta Packer, Joy Hallward, John Mitchum (*Jury members*)], [Frank Arnold (*Artist*)], [Ann Duncan, Lorraine Comerford (*Bobby soxers*)], [Chuck Hamilton, Frank Marlo, Ralph Volkie (*Bailiffs*)], [Joe Palma, Eddie Randolph, Eda Reiss Merin, Joan Danton, Dick Bartell (*Reporters*)], [Donald Kerr (*Court clerk*)], [Myron Healey (*Assistant district attorney*)], [Jane Lee (*Lunch woman*)], [Dorothy Vernon (*Knitter*)], [Blackie Whiteford (*Tattoo artist*)], [Ned Glass (*Fiddler*)], [Brick Sullivan (*Policeman on street*)], [Bill Haade (*Policeman with Hawkins*)], [Charles Sullivan (*Telescope man*)], [Jack Clisby (*Black policeman*)], [Glen Thompson, Paul Baxley, Lee Phelps (*Policemen*)], [Dudley Dickerson (*Bootblack*)], [Garry Owen (*Larry*)], [George Chandler (*Cashier*)], [George Hickman (*Pool player/detective*)], [Chester Conklin (*Barber*)], [Jeff York (*Hawkins partner*)], [Frank Pharr (*Old man*)], [Wesley Hopper (*Boss*)], [Paul Kreibich (*Headwaiter*)], [Sid Tomack (*Duke*)], [Charles Camp (*Waiter*)], [Frank Hagney, Peter Virgo (*Suspects*)], [Saul Gross, Al Hill, Phillip Morris (*Detectives*)], [Sam Flint (*Warden*)], [Helen Mowery (*Miss Holiday*)], [Jody Gilbert (*Gussie*)], [Curt Conway (*Elkins*)], [Edwin Parker, Al Ferguson (*Guards*)], [John Indrisano], [Ray Johnson], [Jack Perry], [Joe Brockman], [Franklyn Farnum], [Connie Conrad], [Anne Cornwall], [Beulah Parkington], [Betty Taylor], [Hazel Boyne], [Tex Swan], [Harry Wilson], [Eddie Borden], [Theda Barr], [Cliff Heard], [Charles Colean], [Roberta Haynes].

Crime, Social, Teenage, Drama. [*Print viewed*]. When young Nick Romano is arrested for the murder of a policeman during a robbery, he begs lawyer Andrew Morton to defend him. Andy reluctantly agrees to take the case after Nick swears that he is innocent and, although a bartender insists that he saw Nick running

away from the scene of the crime, Nick's friends, Sunshine and Butch, confirm his alibi. In his opening speech at the trial, Andy, who left the slums to become a lawyer, tells the jury about Nick's background: Andy met Nick six years earlier after his father was jailed for killing someone in self-defense. Despite Andy's efforts to have him released from jail, Nick's father dies in jail of a heart attack. Because the family now has no income, they are forced to move to a bad neighborhood, and Nick joins some of the other boys in petty thievery. Later, Nick is arrested for stealing a car and is sentenced to a brutal reform school, where his friend dies of pneumonia after being punished. After his release, Nick meets Emma, a poor but respectable girl who lives with her alcoholic aunt, and starts dating her. Eventually, he falls in love with her, but refuses to become involved with her as he does not want to ruin her life. Nick is arrested again, and social worker Adele Patterson begs Andy to help him. Andy befriends Nick, but Nick, feeling resentful about what he believes to be charity, steals money from Andy and angers him. After Nick and Emma marry, Andy again tries to help him go straight, but Nick's quick temper and disreputable background cause him to be fired from a succession of jobs. Finally, after Emma reveals that she is pregnant, Nick bitterly advises her to give the baby away. His motto, he tells her, is "live fast, die young and have a good-looking corpse." Convinced that Nick no longer loves her, Emma kills herself. A few months later, Nick is charged with murder. Back in the courtroom, the prosecution presents its case, and Andy first casts doubt on the bartender's identification of Nick by proving that his memory is not reliable. He then attacks the credibility of subsequent witnesses. The prosecution then calls Juan Rodriguez, a friend of Nick, who previously stated that Nick had committed the murder. On the witness stand, however, Juan claims that the police threatened him with deportation unless he swore that Nick was guilty. During the defense's presentation, District Attorney Kerman is able to create uncertainty about Nick's ailbi. Andy then calls Nick to the stand. At first, Nick's testimony holds up, but after intense badgering by Kerman, Nick finally breaks down and admits his guilt. Before sentencing, Andy makes one last statement on Nick's behalf, condemning society for his crimes, and begs the court for mercy. Although moved, the judge sentences Nick to death. Before Nick's execution, Andy promises to help other boys like him. *Italian Americans. Juvenile delinquents. Lawyers. Trials. African Americans. Alcoholics. Alibi. Aunts. Bartenders. Criminals–Rehabilitation. District attorneys. Fistfights. Funerals. Juries. Marriage. Murder. Police. Pregnancy. Reformatories. Robbery. Slums. Social workers. Suicide.*

Note: According to an 8 Sep 1947 *LAEx* news item, Willard Motley's novel was first purchased by producer Mark Hellinger, who died on 21 Dec 1947. Motley was a black writer who had been involved with the Federal Writers' Project in Chicago. This film was the first production of Santana Pictures, Inc., a company formed by Humphrey Bogart, his business manager, A. Morgan Maree, and producer Robert Lord. This was John Derek's first starring role; he had previously had small parts in two other films. The *Var* review called him "a new bobbysoxer dream and a personality who will click with the femmes, motherly or otherwise."

Box 26 Feb 1949. *DV* 21 Feb 1949, p. 3, 11. *FD* 21 Feb 1949, p. 7. *HR* 13 Aug 1948, p. 14. *HR* 10 Sep 1948, p. 12. *HR* 21 Feb 1949, p. 4. *LAEx* 8 Sep 1947. *LAT* 9 Mar 1949. *MPHPD* 26 Feb 1949, p. 4513-14. *NYT* 23 Feb 1949, p. 31. *Var* 23 Feb 1949, p. 10.

KNUTE ROCKNE—ALL AMERICAN (Norwegian Americans)

Warner Bros. Pictures, Inc.; A Warner Bros.—First National Picture; Jack L. Warner in charge of production. *Dist* Warner Bros. Pictures, Inc. 5 Oct **1940**; World premiere at South Bend, IN: 4 Oct 1940; Prod: began 2 Apr 1940 [©Warner Bros. Pictures, Inc.; 5 Oct 1940; LP9953]. Sd (RCA Victor Sound System); b&w. 11 reels. 97 min. PCA cert no. 6204.

Exec prod Hal B. Wallis. *Assoc prod* Robert Fellows. *Dir* Lloyd Bacon. [*Asst dir* Jesse Hibbs, Don Alvarado and Frank Anthony]. *Orig scr* Robert Buckner. *Dir of photog* Tony Gaudio. *Spec eff* Byron Haskin and Rex Wimpy. *Art dir* Robert Haas. *Film ed* Ralph Dawson. *Gowns* Milo Anderson. *Mus dir* Leo F. Forbstein. *Orch arr* Ray Heindorf. *Sd* Charles Lang. *Makeup* Perc Westmore. *Tech adv* Nick Lukats and J. A. Haley.

Cast: Pat O'Brien (*Knute Rockne*), Gale Page (*Bonnie Skiles Rockne*), Ronald Reagan (*George Gipp*), Donald Crisp (*Father John Callahan*), Albert Basserman (*Father Julius Nieuwland*), John Litel (*Committee chairman*), Henry O'Neill (*Doctor*), Owen Davis, Jr. (*Gus Dorais*), John Qualen (*Lars Knutson Rockne*), Dorothy Tree (*Martha Rockne*), John Sheffield (*Knute, age 7*), The Moreau Choir of Notre Dame, *The Four Horsemen*: Nick Lukats [(*Harry Stuhldreher*)], Kane Richmond [(*Elmer Layden*)], William Marshall

[(*Don Miller*)], William Byrne [(*James Crowley*)], Howard Jones, Glenn "Pop" Warner, Alonzo Stagg, William "Bill" Spaulding, [Billy Sheffield (*Knute, age 4*)], [Ruth Robinson (*Gipp's mother*)], [Cliff Clark (*Paymaster*)], [Richard Clayton, George Haywood (*Students*)], [Carlyle Moore, Jr., George Reeves, Peter Ashley, Michael Harvey, Gaylord Pendleton (*Players*)], [George Irving, Harry Hayden, Charles Trowbridge (*Professors*)], [Charles Wilson (*Gambler*)], [John Ridgely, Jeffrey Sayre, Joe Cunningham, De Wolfe Hopper, David Bruce, Frank Mayo (*Reporters*)], [Dutch Hendrian (*Hunk Anderson*)], [Robert O. Davis, Egon Brecher, Fred Vogeding (*Elders*)], [Phil Thorope (*Boy center*)], [Dickie Jones (*Boy quarterback*)], [George Billings (*Boy quarterback*)], [William Haade, Eddy Chandler, Pat Flaherty (*Workers*)], [Creighton Hale (*Secretary*)], [John Gallaudet (*Harper*)], [Lee Phelps, James Flavin (*Army coaches*)], [Tommy Bennett (*O'Reilly*)], [Donald Curtis (*Army player*)], [Robert Winkler, Danny Jackson, Gary Watson, Harry Harvey, Jr. (*Boys*)], [Ruth Toby (*Isobel*)], [Dudley Dickerson (*Porter*)], [Wade Boteler (*Trainer*)], [Pierre Watkin, Ed Stanley (*Board members*)], [Frank Coghlan, Jr. (*Messenger*)], [Owen King (*Telegraph clerk*)], [Edgar Dearing (*Friend*)], [Erville Alderson (*Kansas farmer*)], [Maris Wrixon, Lucille Fairbanks (*Telephone operators*)], [Tommy Baker (*Newsboy*)], [Peter B. Good (*Bill Rockne, age 2*)], [Bunky Fleischman (*Bill Rockne, age 5*)], [David Dickinson (*Bill Rockne, age 10*)], [Jack Grant, Jr. (*Bill Rockne, age 14*)], [David Wade (*Knute Rockne, Jr., age 7*)], [Billy Dawson (*Knute Rockne, Jr., age 12*)], [Billy Gratton (*Jackie Rockne, age 4*)], [Patricia Hayes (*Jeanne Rockne, age 10*)].

Biography, **Drama**. [*Print viewed*]. In 1892, Lars Knutson Rockne leaves Norway for America, in search of a better life for his family. The Rockne family settles in Chicago, where little Knute becomes fascinated by football. Years later, now grown to manhood, Knute finally saves enough money to enroll in Notre Dame, where he excels in chemistry and football. With his roommate Gus Dorais, Knute develops the famous football strategy of the forward pass and defeats the Army team. After graduation, Knute stays on at Notre Dame, teaching chemistry and coaching football to earn enough money so that he can marry his sweetheart Bonnie Skiles. After three years, Knute decides to give up chemistry and make coaching his life work. The legendary Notre Dame team finally comes together when Knute finds his half-back in freshman George Gipp. However, tragedy dims the team's triumph when Gipp is stricken with a fatal illness. After Gipp's death, Knute revolutionizes football with the backfield shift of his "Four Horsemen," thus winning further glory for his school. Later, crippled by phlebitis, Knute is forced to coach from a wheel chair, but never loses his team spirit. The real threat that Knute must face is not his phlebitis but the allegation of scholastic favoritism in college football. While flying to a hearing in California to defend his beloved sport, Knute tragically loses his life in a plane crash, but his good works live on in the sport that he strove so hard to build. *Athletic coaches. College sports. Football. Football players. Knute Rockne. University of Notre Dame. Airplane accidents. Chemists. Chicago (IL). College life. Family life. Immigrants. Incurable diseases. Norwegians. Roommates. Sportsmanship. Teachers.*

Note: The working titles of this picture were *All American, The Spirit of Knute Rockne, The Story of Knute Rockne, The Fighting Irish, Laughing Irish Hearts* and *The Life of Knute Rockne.* The opening credits read "Based upon the private papers of Mrs. Rockne and the reports of Rockne's associates and friends." The *Var* review notes that football coaches Howard Jones, Glenn "Pop" Warner, Alonzo Stagg and William Spaulding, who appeared as themselves in the film, were friends of Rockne. According to news items in *HR,* John Payne was originally considered for the lead role. William K. Howard began the direction of the film, but was replaced by Lloyd Bacon because of a difference of opinion with Warner Bros. over the treatment of the story. Modern sources suggest that these differences centered around a death scene in which Howard wanted Rockne to convert to Catholicism. *HR* items add that technical adviser Nick Lukats was a former Notre Dame football star and that the film was shot on location at Notre Dame at South Bend, IN. The line "win just one for the Gipper" that is spoken by Ronald Reagan, who plays George Gipp in the film, became Reagan's trademark and he often mentioned it during his presidency. The entire speech reads, "Some day when the team's up against it...breaks have beaten the boys...ask them to go in there with all they've got...win just one for the Gipper. I don't know where I'll be then but I'll know about it. I'll be happy." In 1940, Pat O'Brien and Ronald Reagan starred in a Lux Radio Theatre version of the story. The 1931 Universal film, *The Spirit of Notre Dame,* was also based on the life of the athletic coach (see *AFI Catalog of Feature Films, 1931-40;* F3.4259), produced by M-G-M TV.

DV 7 Oct 1940, p. 3. *FD* 7 Oct 1940, p. 8. *HR* 16 Feb 1940, p. 4. *HR* 25 Mar 1940, p. 9. *HR* 3 Apr 1940, p. 7. *HR* 12 Apr 1940, p. 1. *HR* 15 Apr 1940, 1. *HR* 4 May 1940, p. 8. *HR* 21 Aug 1940, p. 2. *HR* 7 Oct 1940, p. 3. *MPD* 7 Oct 1940, p. 1, 5. *MPH* 12 Oct 1940, p. 46. *NYT* 19 Oct 1940, p. 21. *Var* 9 Oct 1940, p. 16.

DIE KÖNIGSLOGE (German language)

Warner Bros. Pictures, Inc.; A Warner Bros. and Vitaphone Production. *Dist* Warner Bros. Pictures, Inc. Nov **1929**; Berlin, Germany, opening: 21 Nov 1929; New York opening: 24 Dec 1929.; Prod: mid-May—late Jun 1929 [©Warner Bros. Pictures, Inc.; 6 Oct 1930; LP1629]. Sd; b&w. 9 reels, 7,464 ft. 76 or 83 min. German language.

Dir Bryan Foy. *Asst dir* Phil Quinn. *Scr* Murray Roth. *Adpt* Edmund Joseph and Arthur Hurley. *German trans* Dr. Arthur Rundt. *Photog* E. B. Du Par and Ray Foster. *Art dir* Frank Namczy and Tom Darby. *Mus dir* Harold Levy.

Source: Based on the play *The Royal Box* by Charles Coghlan (New York, 21 Dec 1897), an adaptation and translation of the French play *Kean* by Alexandre Dumas (Paris, 1836).

Cast: Alexander Moissi (*Edmund Kean*), Camilla Horn (*Alice Doren*), Lew Hearn (*Salomon*), Elsa Ersi (*Countess Toeroek*), Egon Brecher (*Count Toeroek*), William F. Schoeller (*H.R.H. the Prince of Wales*), Leni Stengel (*Lady Robert*), Carlos Zizold (*Lord Melvill*), Greta Meyer (*Mrs. Barker*), William Gade (*Tommy Widgetts*), Siegfried Rumann (*Bailiff*).

Romance, Biography, Drama. [*Not viewed*]. In 1810, Edmund Kean, the famous British actor, is at the peak of his career when he falls in love with the Countess Toeroek, wife of the Hungarian ambassador. However, the Prince of Wales, Kean's friend and patron, is also pursuing the countess. Alice Doren, a wealthy young English girl who is being forced by her guardian to marry the impoverished Lord Melvill, solely to acquire his title, becomes romantically interested in Kean, and a false rumor is spread that she and Kean have eloped to America. Later, at a dinner party given by the ambassador and his wife, Kean pointedly relates a story about how an actor, who wanted the wife of a prominent person to visit him, told her that a certain theater box had a door leading backstage to his dressing room and thus a rendezvous was arranged. The countess takes the hint and promises to visit Kean. After he rescues Alice from the clutches of Lord Melvill, Kean promises to help her to become an actress and arranges for her to appear as "Ophelia" to his "Hamlet" in a benefit performance of scenes from his most famous plays. Just before the performance, the countess visits Kean's dressing room, but she has to leave hurriedly when her husband and the Prince of Wales are announced, and forgets her fan. The count recognizes it and takes it with him. In a private audience, the prince forbids Kean to see the countess again. Kean becomes very angry and slightly demented, to the extent that his portrayal of "Hamlet" is a disaster. He mumbles, forgets his lines, and has to be prompted, then finally rushes down to the footlights and wildly denounces the prince, seated in the royal box, as being a false, perfidious friend. As a result, the prince withdraws his patronage and banishes the actor from London. As bailiffs remove Kean's furniture for non-payment of debts, the countess asks to have some letters returned. Kean informs her that her husband has found her fan in his dressing room. However, the prince arrives with a duplicate of the fan, which he gives to her, and they leave together. Even Alice abandons Kean, preferring to continue her theatrical career in London. Ten years later, Kean, now a shabby, bent old man, encounters a young actor who has no knowledge of the great actor. *Actors and actresses. Ambassadors. George IV, King of England, 1820-1830. Great Britain–History–19th century. Great Britain–History–Social life and customs. Infidelity. Edmund Kean. Royalty. Theaters. Bailiffs. Courtship. Debt. Fans (Clothing accessory). Hamlet (Play). Hungarians. Ingenues. London (England). Nobility. Patronage, Political. Wards and guardians.*

Note: *Die Königsloge*, which was reviewed under its English-language title *The Royal Box*, was shot in Vitaphone's New York studio and was the first American-made, foreign-language feature to be released. In 1914, the Selig Polyscope Co. copyrighted a four-reel version of Coghlan's play. Alexander Moissi, who played Edmund Kean, was Italian by birth, but had spent many years playing major roles in Max Reinhardt's legendary theater company in Germany. According to the *NYT* review, the lounge of the Fifth Avenue Playhouse, where the film opened in New York, "has been turned into a tiny replica of a German beer garden and patrons are served with near-beer and pretzels." This film marked the screen debut of Siegfried Rumann, who was later known as Sig Ruman.

NYT 15 Dec 1929. *NYT* 25 Dec 1929. *Var* 1 Jan 1930. *Wisconsin News* 22 Feb 1930.

KOL NIDRE (Yiddish language)

Cinema Service Corp. *Dist* Cinema Service Corp. **1939**; New York opening: 7 Sep 1939; Prod: Aug 1939 at Cinema Studios in Palisades, NJ [©Cinema Service Corp.; 16 Oct 1939; LU9179]. Sd; b&w. 9 reels, 8,061 ft. 85 or 90 min. Yiddish language with English subtitles.

Dir Joseph Seiden. *Story* Ben Gitlitz. *Photog* Don Malkames. *Mus* Sholem Secunda.

Cast: Joseph Sheongold (*Moishe Dorfman*), Bertha Hart (*Sarah, his wife*), Lili Liliana (*Jenny, their daughter*), Menasha Oppenheim (*Jack Grossman*), Leon Liebgold (*Rabbi Joseph Goldstein*), David Lederman (*Shmelke Shmelkevitz*), Yetta Zwerling (*Chasie, his wife*), Leibele Waldman (*Himself*), Chaim Tauber (*Himself*), Zish Kac, Joel Feig, Choir.

Yiddish, Melodrama, with songs. [*Not viewed*]. Joseph Goldstein wants to be a rabbi when he grows up. His classmate, Jack Grossman, whose father is rich, hates all the other kids and thinks they hate him. The two boys almost come to blows over Jenny Dorfman, the daughter of a poor, but devout man. However, Jenny gets them to shake hands, and they all make a vow to remain loyal to each other. Ten years later, Jack and Jenny, in love with each other, have just finished college, while Joseph has just graduated from Yeshiva College and is about to become the rabbi of Jenny's father's synagogue. When Jenny's father Moishe sees Jenny with Jack, he rebukes her for running around with a loafer and mentions Joseph as a real match for her. She replies that American children today do what they want; that she does not want to be a rabbi's wife; that she likes Jack because he is rich and has a nice car; and that the sooner Jews assimilate, the better it will be for them. When Jenny tells Jack about the argument with her father, he suggests that they elope and get married. She accedes to his wishes and afterward has to hide the marriage from her family. After some urging, Jenny's mother persuades her to join them to hear Joseph speak at the synagogue. His lecture relates incidents in Jewish history to the problem of the current younger generation of Jews who deny their heritage. After the talk, Joseph speaks with Jenny and expresses his love for her, but she stops him. Later, when Moishe admonishes Jenny for meeting Jack in the park, Jenny, who now suspects that Jack is seeing other women, admits that they are married and that she is pregnant. Moishe rages at her and, after sending her out of their house and saying that she is dead to them, has a stroke. Two years later, while Jack cavorts for two days with another woman, Jenny faces dispossession for failure to pay rent and cannot buy milk for her baby. When Jack returns, they argue and separate. Meanwhile, the doctor has told Joseph that if Moishe, who repeatedly calls out deliriously for a wedding, sees Jenny, perhaps his health will be restored. On the eve of *Yom Kippur*, the Day of Atonement, Jenny hears the choir at the synagogue sing the traditional *Kol Nidre* prayer and asks forgiveness for the sin she is about to commit. She is then saved from killing herself and her baby by a policeman, after which a social worker, Miss Brown, is assigned to help her. After Jack, in a drunken state, kills himself and his lover in a car accident, Miss Brown tells Joseph about Jenny, and Joseph takes over her treatment. Jenny recovers and accepts Joseph's proposal, then goes to visit her father. Jenny asks for forgiveness, and Moishe, recovering, gives it. *Assimilation (Sociology). Family relationships. Jews. Rabbis. Attempted murder. Attempted suicide. Automobile accidents. Drunk driving. Elopement. Infidelity. Marriage–Secret. Romantic rivalry. Separation (Marital). Sermons. Social workers. Stroke. Synagogues. Yom Kippur.*

Note: This film starred members of "The Yiddishe Bande," a cabaret troupe from Poland, who, according to *Exb*, had toured in the Eastern United States in the spring. A scene of this film was cut by New York State censors because of its alleged sacrilegious nature. The film was later reissued in a 82 minute version. Although the film includes songs, no information concerning their identity has been located.

Exb 20 Sep 1939. *HR* 22 Aug 1939, p. 7.

KONG MENG CHI LOU *see* GUON MIN GUH LU

KOSHER KITTY KELLY (Jewish Americans)

R-C Pictures Corp.; Gold Bond Series. *Dist* Film Booking Offices of America. 5 Sep **1926** [©R-C Pictures Corp.; 5 Sep 1926; LP23124]. Si; b&w. 7 reels, 6,103 ft.

Pres Joseph P. Kennedy. *Dir* James W. Horne. *Scen* Gerald C. Duffy. *Photog* Allan Siegler.

Source: Based on the play *Kosher Kitty Kelly* by Leon De Costa (New York, 15 Jun 1925).

Cast: Viola Dana (*Kitty Kelly*), Tom Forman (*Officer Pat Sullivan*), Vera Gordon (*Mrs. Feinbaum*), Kathleen Myers (*Rosie Feinbaum*), Nat Carr (*Moses Ginsburg*), Stanley Taylor (*Morris Rosen*), Carroll Nye (*Barney Kelly*), Aggie Herring (*Mrs. Kelly*).

Comedy-drama. Kitty Kelly, her brother Barney, and Mrs. Kelly are neighbors of Rosie Feinbaum and her mother, who live over the delicatessen of Moses Ginsburg on New York's East Side. Rosie is in love with young Morris Rosen, a hospital intern; Kitty loves Officer Pat Sullivan. With a gang, Barney attempts to hold up Ginsburg, and Officer Pat, pursuing the gang, wounds Barney in the shoulder. Although Kitty pleads with him, Pat places duty above love and takes Barney to a waiting ambulance. En route to the hospital, Kitty is comforted by Morris; Pat and Rosie, believing the other two to be on intimate terms, team up together. Mrs. Kelly is infuriated, and a dispute with the Feinbaums develops into a neighborhood battle. Pat withdraws from the alderman race to assure Barney's parole, the boy sets out to get revenge, and Ginsburg's shop is set afire during a battle; Morris saves Rosie, and Pat saves Kitty. The original lovers are united, along with Ginsburg and Mrs. Feinbaum. *Aldermen. Courtship. Delicatessens. Gangs. Interns (Medicine). Irish. Jews. New York City–East Side. Police.*

FD 26 Sep 1926. NYT 28 Sep 1926, p. 30. Var 29 Sep 1926, p. 14.

DI KRAFT FUN LEBN *see* **THE POWER OF LIFE**

KREUTZER SONATA (Jewish Americans)

William Fox Vaudeville Co. *Dist* Fox Film Corp. Mar **1915** [©William Fox; 1 Mar 1915; LP6156]. Si; b&w. 5 reels.

Pres William Fox. *Dir* Herbert Brenon. *Scen* Herbert Brenon. *Cam* Philip E. Rosen.

Source: Based on the play *The Kreutzer Sonata* by Jacob Gordin (New York, 13 Aug 1906).

Cast: Nance O'Neil (*Miriam Friedlander*), Theda Bara (*Celia Friedlander*), William E. Shay (*Gregor Randar*), Mimi Yvonne.

Drama. Miriam Friedlander, the daughter of an Orthodox Jew, falls in love with Count Belusoff, an army captain. They cannot marry, however, because consent of the parents is necessary in Russia, and Belusoff's father will not allow a mixed marriage, while Miriam's will not let her convert. After Belusoff kills himself, Miriam tells her father that she is pregnant. Friedlander convinces Gregor Randar, the conceited, pampered son of a bandleader, to marry Miriam for a sum of money, and the couple goes to New York, where the child is born. Later, Friedlander and his family move to a farm in Connecticut. After Miriam's sister Celia runs away to Miriam, she and Gregor, who quarrels with Miriam and beats the child, carry on a flirtation, which later is consummated. After Celia goes West to give birth to a child, which is placed in an orphanage, Miriam learns about the romance and in a mad rage, kills both Gregor and Celia, before shooting herself. *Family relationships. Infidelity. Jews. Murder. Russians. Suicide. Battered children. Connecticut. Farms. Immigrants. Marriage–Arranged. Marriage–Mixed. New York City. Nobility. Pregnancy. Russia. Sisters.*

Note: The book, *The Kreutzer Sonata*, written by Count Leo Nikolayevich Tolstoy, published in 1890, figures in the story in that Count Bresuloff and Miriam read it together. He gives the book to her, along with a photograph and letter, before he kills himself. She later reads it during various crises and Celia taunts Miriam that she does not have the courage to follow the example in the book. Advertisements for the film stated that it was based on Tolstoy's *The Kreutzer Sonata*. According to the copyright entry, however, the film was based on the Jacob Gordin version of *The Kreutzer Sonata*. There was a trade showing of the film in New York on 2 Mar 1915. One review refers to the character played by William E. Shay as "Gregor Moskowitz."

Motog 27 Mar 1915, pp. 508-09. MPN 13 Mar 1915, pp. 10-11. MPN 17 Apr 1915, p. 5. MPW 27 Mar 1915, p. 1934.

KUAN FONG LANG TYEH (Chinese language)

Grandview Film Co. **1944.** Sd; b&w. Length undetermined. Chinese language.

Dir Joseph Sunn.

Cast: Wong Hok-sing. [*Not viewed*]. [No information concerning the plot of this film has been located.].

Note: The Cantonese transliterated title is *Kung Fong Lon Dih*. The English language translation of the title is *Wild Bees, Promiscuous Butterfly*. This film was probably made in the U.S.

Chinese Times (San Francisco) 9 Oct 1944, p. 7.

KUANG FENG JUU YIEN FAY (Chinese language)

Grandview Film Co. **1948?**; Hong Kong showing: 1948? Sd; b&w. Length undetermined.

Dir Joseph Sunn. [*Not viewed*]. [No information concerning the plot of this film has been located.].

Note: The Cantonese transliterated title is *Kung Fong Juu Yin Fei*. This film was probably made in the U.S.

KUM KOH TSEN YUN *see* **GIN GUO CHIN YUAN**

KUNG FONG JUU YIN FEI *see* **KUANG FENG JUU YIEN FAY**

KUNG FONG LON DIH *see* **KUAN FONG LANG TYEH**

LADDIE (English Americans)

Gene Stratton Porter Productions. *Dist* Film Booking Offices of America. 26 Sep **1926** [©Gene Stratton Porter, Inc.; 15 Jul 1926; LP22917]. Si; b&w. 7 reels, 6,931 ft.

Pres Joseph P. Kennedy. *Dir* James Leo Meehan. *Asst dir* Charles Kerr. *Adpt* Jeanette Porter Meehan. *Photog* Allen Siegler.

Source: Based on the novel *Laddie; a True Blue Story* by Gene Stratton Porter (Garden City, New York, 1913).

Cast: John Bowers (*Laddie*), Bess Flowers (*Pamela Pryor*), Theodore von Eltz (*Robert Paget*), Eugenia Gilbert (*Shelley Stanton*), David Torrence (*Paul Stanton*), Eulalie Jensen (*Mrs. Stanton*), Arthur Clayton (*Mahlon Pryor*), Fanny Midgley (*Mrs. Pryor*), Aggie Herring (*Candace*), Gene Stratton (*Little Sister*), John Fox, Jr. (*Leon*).

Romance. Laddie, son of the Stantons, an Ohio pioneer family, falls in love with Pamela Pryor, daughter of a neighboring aristocratic English family, though the Pryors adopt a condescending attitude toward the Stanton family. Through the efforts of Little Sister, who knows of Laddie's love, the two secretly communicate, and Mr. Pryor takes a liking to Laddie when he tames a wild horse for him. Meanwhile, Shelley, a Stanton girl, falls in love with city lawyer Robert Paget; when he leaves her under mysterious circumstances, she returns home heartbroken. The Pryors, disgraced because of a false accusation against their son in England, are at length forced to accept Laddie. It develops that Paget is actually the banished son of the Pryors; after a strained crisis Pryor forgives his son, and Laddie and Pamela, Robert and Shelley, and the Stantons and the Pryors are happily united. *Children. Courtship. English. Exile. Family life. Ohio. Pioneers.*

FD 22 Aug 1926. MPW 4 Sep 1926.

LADIES' DAY (Latino)

RKO Radio Pictures, Inc. *Dist* RKO Radio Pictures, Inc. 9 Apr **1943**; New York opening: 26 Mar 1943; Prod: mid-Jul—early Aug 1942; addl scenes began 20 Jan 1943 [©RKO Radio Pictures, Inc.; 1 Jan 1943; LP11954]. Sd (RCA Sound System); b&w. 5,581 ft. 62 min. PCA cert no. 8692.

Prod Bert Gilroy. *Dir* Leslie Goodwins. *Asst dir* Ruby Rosenberg. *Scr* Charles E. Roberts and Dane Lussier. *Dir of photog* Jack Mackenzie. *Art dir* Albert S. D'Agostino and Feild M. Gray. *Ed* Harry Marker. *Set dec* Darrell Silvera and Harley Miller. *Gowns* Renie. *Mus* Roy Webb. *Rec* John E. Tribby.

Source: Based on a play by Robert Considine, Edward Lilley and Bertrand Robinson (production date undetermined).

Cast: Lupe Velez [(*Pepita Zorita*)], Eddie Albert [(*Wacky Waters*)], Patsy Kelly [(*Hazel Jones*)], Max Baer [(*Hippo Jones*)], Jerome Cowan [(*Updyke*)], Iris Adrian [(*Kitty McLoan*)], Joan Barclay [(*Joan*)], Cliff Clark [(*Dan Hannigan*)], Carmen Morales [(*Marianna D'Angelo*)], George Cleveland [(*Doc*)], Jack Briggs [(*Marty Samuels*)], Russ Clark [(*Smokey Lee*)], Nedrick Young [(*Tony D'Angelo*)], Eddie Dew [(*Spike McLoan*)], Tom Kennedy [(*Dugan, house detective*)], [Richard Martin, Russell Wade, Wayne McCoy, Bud McTaggart (*Ball player*)], Mal Merrihugh, Charles Russell, Jack Shea, Jack Gargan, Cy Malis (*Ball players*)], [Rube Schaffer (*Runner*)], [Mary Stuart, Ariel Heath, Mary Halsey, Ann Summers (*Wives*)], [Sally Wadsworth (*Cute blonde*)], [Jack Carrington (*Announcer on field*)], [Eddie Borden (*Man on field*)], [Don Kerr (*Pepita's assistant*)], [Frank Mills, Ralph Sanford, Kernan Cripps, Bud Geary (*Umpires*)], [George O'Hanlon (*Young rube*)], [Earle Hodgins (*Old man customer*)], [Russell Hoyt (*Assistant director*)], [Henry Hall (*Dr. Adams*)], [Wesley Barry (*Reporter*)], [Ted O'Shea (*Attendant at airport*)], [John Sheehan (*Producer*)], [Jack Arnold (*Director*)], [Allen Wood (*Locker boy*)], [Norman Mayes (*Pullman porter*)], [Teddy

Mangean (*Upstair's bellhop*)], [Barrie Millman (*Baby*)], [Fred Carpenter (*Bellhop*)], [Jack O'Connor (*Cab driver*)], [Jack Stewart (*Doorman*)], [George Noisom (*Mess boy at airport*)], [Marten Lamont].

Baseball, Comedy-drama. [*Print viewed*]. Women are the downfall of Wacky Waters, the crack pitcher of the Sox baseball team; whenever Wacky falls for a female, his pitching average also falls. Consequently, when movie star Pepita Zorita visits the game to sell kisses for War Bonds, Dan Hannigan, the Sox's manager, becomes concerned. After savoring $300 worth of kisses from the glamorous Pepita, Wacky proceeds to lose the game to the opposing team. When Updyke, the representative of the bank that owns the team, arranges for Pepita to accompany the Sox on the road as a publicity stunt, Hazel Jones, the wife of player Hippo Jones, determines to keep Wacky and Pepita apart in the interests of the team. Despite the combined efforts of Hazel and the other wives, Pepita and Wacky sneak away one day and are secretly married. Wacky's marriage intitiates a losing streak for the pitcher, and the team sees their penant hopes evaporate. The Sox and their wives are relieved when Pepita accepts a starring role in Hollywood, but when she finishes production early to hurry back to her husband, Hazel decides to take action. When, in the middle of the World Series, Pepita calls Wacky to arrange a meeting in Kansas City, Hazel, accompanied by fellow baseball wives Kitty McLoan and Joan, beat Wacky to the airport and kidnap Pepita. The three women hold Pepita hostage in a Kansas City hotel room, sending Wacky nightly telegrams from his loving wife. Pepita's continual shrieks bring house detective Dugan to investigate, but Hazel placates him with a story about her ventriloquist sister. Hazel's plan works until the second to the last game of the series, when Kitty is listening to the game on the radio and hears that her husband Spike is kissing a blonde. Kitty becomes furious, and in the ensuing chaos, Pepita steals a bellboy's uniform and escapes the hotel to return to Wacky. With one game remaining, Hazel schemes to keep the newlyweds apart. As Pepita awaits Wacky in the bridal suite, Hazel pretends to make amends by spraying her with perfume. The atomizer holds red dye, however, and after Pepita's face is covered with red spots, a phony doctor hired by the team diagnoses that she has a rare rash and must be quarantined. The next day, as Wacky pitches the final game in the series, the Sox are losing until Pepita enters the stadium and cheers their husband to victory. *Abduction. Baseball. Newlyweds. Wives.* Detectives. Kansas City (KS). Motion picture actors and actresses. Quarantine. Romance. Ruses. War bonds. World Series (Baseball).

Box 20 Mar 1943. *DV* 16 Mar 1943, p. 3. *FD* 24 Mar 1943, p. 8. *HR* 17 Jul 1942, p. 9. *HR* 7 Aug 1942, p. 9. *HR* 20 Jan 1943, p. 3. *HR* 16 Mar 1943, p. 3. *MPH* 20 Mar 1943. *MPHPD* 17 Oct 1942, p. 962. *MPHPD* 20 Mar 1943, p. 1213. *NYT* 26 Mar 1943, p. 14. *Var* 17 Mar 1943, p. 8.

LADIES LOVE BRUTES (Italian Americans)
Paramount Famous Lasky Corp. 26 Apr **1930** [©Paramount Publix Corp.; 25 Apr 1930; LP1256]. Sd (Movietone); b&w. 10 reels, 7,171 ft.
Dir Rowland V. Lee. *Adpt and dial* Waldemar Young and Herman J. Mankiewicz. *Photog* Harry Fischbeck. *Film ed* Eda Warren. *Rec eng* J. A. Goodrich.
Source: Based on the play *Pardon My Glove* by 'Zo'e Akins (production date undetermined).
Cast: George Bancroft (*Joe Froziati*), Mary Astor (*Mimi Howell*), Fredric March (*Dwight Howell*), Margaret Quimby (*Lucille Gates*), Stanley Fields (*Mike Mendino*), Ben Hendricks, Jr. (*Slattery*), Lawford Davidson (*George Wyndham*), Ferike Boros (*Mrs. Forziati*), David Durand (*Joey Forziati*), Freddie Burke Frederick (*Jackie Howell*), Paul Fix (*Slip*), Claude Allister (*The Tailor*), Crauford Kent, E. H. Calvert (*Committeemen*).

Society, Melodrama. Joe Forziati, an Italian immigrant who has battled his way to success as a New York building contractor, decides to embark on a social career. Wyndham, his lawyer, arranges for him to be a guest at the home of socialite Mimi Howell, but his son Joey and his grandmother view his flashy new wardrobe dubiously. Mimi, who is on the verge of a divorce from her husband, Dwight, falls under the spell of Joe. Mike Mendino, a labor agitator whom Joe has defeated, plots revenge by arranging for Slip, one of his gang, to become Joe's chauffeur. Mimi breaks off their relationship because of their unequal social positions, but Joe has Slip kidnap her child so that he may return the boy himself. His own son is kidnapped by the

gang, but after a battle with them, the child is retrieved. Mimi is reunited with her husband, and Joe, realizing the impossibility of his aspirations, returns home with his son. *Children. Contractors. Courtship. Gangsters. Immigrants. Italian Americans. Kidnapping. Lawyers. New York City. Socialites.*

FD 18 May 1930. *Var* 21 May 1930, p. 25.

LADY FROM FRISCO *see* **REBELLION**

LADY FROM LOUISIANA (French Americans)
Republic Pictures Corp. *Dist* Republic Pictures Corp. 22 Apr **1941**; *Prod*: 3 Mar—late Mar 1941 [©Republic Pictures Corp.; 22 Apr 1941; LP10455]. Sd (RCA Sound System); b&w. 9 reels, 7,418 ft. 82 min. Passed by the National Board of Review. PCA cert no. 7207.
Assoc prod Bernard Vorhaus. *Dir* Bernard Vorhaus. [*Asst dir* Phil Ford]. *Scr* Vera Caspary, Michael Hogan and Guy Endore. *Orig story* Edward James and Francis Faragoh. *Photog* Jack Marta. *Art dir* John Victor Mackay. *Supv ed* Murray Seldeen. *Film ed* Edward Mann. *Ward* Adele Palmer. *Mus dir* Cy Feuer. *Prod mgr* Al Wilson.
Song(s): "*Très Bien*," music and lyrics by Jule Styne and Eddie Cherkose.
Cast: John Wayne [(*John Reynolds*)], Ona Munson [(*Julie Mirbeau*)], Ray Middleton [(*Blackburn Williams*)], Henry Stephenson [(*General Anatole Mirbeau*)], Helen Westley [(*Blanche Brunot*)], Jack Pennick [(*Cuffy Brown*)], Dorothy Dandridge [(*Felice*)], Shimen Ruskin [(*Gaston*)], Jacqueline Dalya [(*Pearl*)], Paul Scardon [(*Judge Wilson*)], Major James H. MacNamara [(*Senator Cassidy*)], James C. Morton [(*Littlefield*)], Maurice Costello [(*Edwards*)].

Drama. [*Print viewed*]. When New England lawyer John Reynolds travels by steamboat to New Orleans in the late 1800s, he falls in love with Julie Mirbeau, whose name he does not learn until they reach the dock. Julie is greeted by her father, General Anatole Mirbeau, and his right-hand man, Blackburn "Blackie" Williams. John is met by reformer Blanche Brunot, who has hired him to stop Mirbeau's lottery and its resultant corruption. Although the lovers are dismayed to learn that they are on opposite sides of the issue, they meet later that night to celebrate Mardi Gras. They attend the lottery drawing, which is won by one of John's new acquaintances, restaurateur Gaston. The lottery appears legitimate, and before they part, Julie becomes convinced that John will support her father. Later that night, however, John searches for Gaston, who has been forced by Blackie's thugs to go to the notorious Parisian Palace in Frenchtown and gamble away his winnings. Learning that John is searching the area, the men murder Gaston to keep him quiet. The next day, John arrives at the Mirbeau house to discuss Julie with the general, but when Mirbeau assumes that John will now come to work for him for Julie's sake, John announces that he will investigate the connection between Gaston's murder and the lottery. Furious at John's accusations, Julie tells him that their relationship is over. Soon after, Mirbeau genially fires Blackie, who has been covertly collecting protection money from the Frenchtown businesses and embezzling lottery profits intended for Mirbeau's various charities. Determined to regain control of the lottery, Blackie hires fighter Cuffy Brown, who shoots and kills Mirbeau during a reform league demonstration, thereby making it seem as if one of the reformers is responsible. When John, who has been appointed special city attorney, comes to Julie to pay his respects, she accuses him of indirectly causing her father's death, and determines to keep the lottery going strong. Blackie steps up the seamier sides of the business, although Julie remains ignorant of what she is protecting when she influences various political figures to favor the lottery over the reformers. John is stymied in his efforts to expose the protective racket until he and Blanche steal the records of the lottery's bribes to high officials. That same night, Julie goes to warn Blackie, to whom she has become engaged, about the theft and finds him in the Parisian Palace embracing Pearl, the owner. As John and the police arrive, the extent of Blackie's corruption and his participation in her father's death become clear to Julie, and she tries to testify against the lottery when John brings the case to trial. The trial is interrupted, however, when a rainstorm sweeps through the area, and the levee, which was to have been cared for by the Mirbeau charities, breaks. The courthouse is destroyed, and in the ensuing chaos, John pursues Blackie onto a steamboat while Julie and Blanche try to find shelter on a nearby rooftop. During a fight, John knocks Blackie into the water, then orders the steamboat captain to block the

hole in the levee with the boat. The plan works and the flooding is stopped. Later, Blanche and her friends wave goodbye as John and Julie leave for their honeymoon. *Lawyers. Lotteries. New Orleans (LA). Protection racket. Reformers. Romance. African Americans. Boxers. Bribery. Fathers and daughters. Floods. French. Judges. Levees. Mardi Gras. Murder. New Englanders. Police raids. Political corruption. Rainstorms. Servants. Southerners. Steamboats. Trials.*

Note: The working titles of this film were *Lady from New Orleans* and *Lady of New Orleans.* Although a *HR* news item asserted that the film was the "most postponed picture in Republic's history," after having been on and off the studio's production schedule for three years, other news items indicate that pre-production on the film began in mid-to-late 1939. In May 1939, *HR* announced that Republic had purchased a novel entitled *The Lady from New Orleans*, written by Beth Brown, but it does not appear to have been the basis for this picture. Among the writers listed by *HR* as working on the screenplay in 1939 were Jan Fortune, Joseph Moncure March and Garrett Fort, but their contribution to the completed film has not been confirmed. *HR* news items also noted that Sol Siegel and Armand Schaefer were set at various times to produce the picture, and that Heinie Conklin was to be included in the cast, although Conklin's participation in the finished picture has not been confirmed. *DV* reported that Ray Middleton was to sing a song in the picture, although he did not. *DV* also reported that "femme barker" Peggy Lynn was to make her film debut, but her participation in the completed picture has not been confirmed.

Box 17 May 1941. *DV* 12 Mar 1941, p. 7. *DV* 19 May 1941, p. 3. *FD* 30 Apr 1941, p. 18. *HR* 8 May 1939, p. 1. *HR* 4 Aug 1939, p. 3. *HR* 30 Nov 1939, p. 1. *HR* 7 Oct 1940, p. 11. *HR* 17 Sep 1940, p. 1. *HR* 28 Feb 1941, p. 27. *HR* 3 Mar 1941, p. 3, 6. *HR* 21 Mar 1941, p. 8. *HR* 19 May 1941, p 4. *MPD* 30 Apr 1941. *MPH* 3 May 1941, p. 40. *NYT* 15 May 1941, p. 27. *Var* 21 May 1941, p. 18.

LADY FROM NEW ORLEANS *see* **LADY FROM LOUISIANA**

THE LADY FROM SHANGHAI (Chinese Americans)
Columbia Pictures Corp. *Dist* Columbia Pictures Corp. May **1948**; Prod: 2 Oct 1946—27 Feb 1947 [©Columbia Pictures Corp.; 14 Apr 1948; LP1559]. Sd (Western Electric Recording); b&w. 7,864 ft. 86-87 min. PCA cert no. 12111.

Prod Orson Welles. *Assoc prod* Richard Wilson and William Castle. *Dir* Orson Welles. *Asst dir* Sam Nelson. *Scr* Orson Welles. *Dir of photog* Charles Lawton, Jr. [*Fill-in dir of photog* Rudolph Maté]. [*Cam op* Irving Klein]. [*Asst cam* Donald Ray Cory]. [*Stills* Eddy Cronenweth]. *Art dir* Stephen Goosson and Sturges Carne. *Film ed* Viola Lawrence. *Set dec* Wilbur Menefee and Herman Schoenbrun. *Gowns* Jean Louis. *Mus score* Heinz Roemheld. *Mus dir* M. W. Stoloff. *Sd rec* Lodge Cunningham. [*Hair stylist* Helen Hunt]. [*Scr supv* Dorothy Cormack]. [*Grip* Don Murphy].

Song(s): "Please Don't Kiss Me," music and lyrics by Allan Roberts and Doris Fisher.

Source: Based on the novel *If I Die Before I Wake* by Raymond Sherwood King (New York, 1938).

Cast: RITA HAYWORTH [(*Elsa Bannister*)], ORSON WELLES [(*Michael O'Hara*)], Everett Sloane [(*Arthur Bannister*)], Glenn Anders [(*George Grisby*)], Ted de Corsia [(*Sidney Broome*)], Erskine Sanford [(*Judge*)], Gus Schilling [(*Goldie*)], Carl Frank [(*District attorney*)], Louis Merrill [(*Jake*)], Evelyn Ellis [(*Bessie*)], Harry Shannon [(*Cab driver*)], [Won Show Chong (*Li*)], [Sam Nelson (*Yacht captain*)], [Edythe Elliott, Dorothy Vaughn (*Old women*)], [Peter Cusanelli (*Bartender*)], [Joseph Granby (*Police lieutenant*)], [Al Eben, Norman Thomson, Eddie Coke, Steve Benton, Milt Kibbee, Harry Strang (*Policemen*)], [Gerald Pierce (*Waiter*)], [Maynard Holmes (*Truck driver*)], [Jack Baxley, Ed Peil, Heenan Elliott (*Guards*)], [Philip Morris (*Port steward/Policeman/Peters*)], [Phil Van Zandt (*Toughie/Policeman*)], [William Alland, Alvin Hammer, Mary Newton, Robert Gray, Byron Kane (*Reporters*)], [John Elliott (*Clerk*)], [Charles Meakin (*Jury foreman*)], [Jessie Arnold (*Schoolteacher*)], [Doris Chan, Billy Louie (*Chinese girls*)], [Joe Recht (*Garage attendant*)], [Jean Wong (*Ticket seller*)], [Wong Artarne (*Ticket taker*)], [Grace Lem (*Chinese woman*)], [Preston Lee (*Chinese man*)], [Joseph Palma (*Cab driver*)], [Tiny Jones], [Mabel Smaney], [George "Shorty" Charello], [Vernon Cansino].

Film noir. [*Print viewed*]. In New York City's Central Park, Michael O'Hara, an Irish merchant sailor, rescues the beautiful Elsa Bannister from a group of thieves who are attempting to rob her. After fighting off the three attackers, Michael escorts Elsa to safety, and later learns that she is married to the renowned lawyer Arthur Bannister. The following day, Arthur, a cripple, offers Michael a job working on his yacht, and Michael reluctantly accepts the offer. The yacht sets sail from New York to San Francisco with Michael, the Bannisters, Arthur's partner, George Grisby, and a small crew. During the trip, Michael

falls in love with Elsa, and learns that she agreed to marry Arthur only after he threatened to expose her shady past in Shanghai. Soon after the yacht reaches the Mexican coast, Michael and Elsa realize that they are being watched by the yacht's steward, Sidney Broome, who is actually a detective hired by Arthur to keep watch over Elsa. In Acapulco, Grisby tells Michael that he intended to disappear on the voyage so that his wife could collect his life insurance money. After explaining his plans to stage his own murder, Grisby offers Michael $5,000 to confess to killing him. Grisby assures Michael that he cannot be convicted of murder because there will be no corpse to prove his guilt. The voyage ends in San Francisco, where Michael, hoping that the $5,000 will buy Elsa's freedom from Arthur, agrees to sign a confession admitting that he murdered Grisby. Later, Grisby shoots Broome when Broome accuses him of planning the staged murder as part of a ploy to kill Arthur. The wounded Broome then finds Elsa and tells her that Arthur is about to be killed by Grisby. Meanwhile, Grisby and Michael enact the murder plot at the waterfront, where Michael fires three shots into the air, and Grisby speeds away on a motor boat. A short time later, Broome reports to Michael with his dying breath that Grisby arranged the phony murder to frame him for the murder of Arthur. Believing that Arthur has been murdered, Michael is surprised when he learns that Grisby has been killed. When the police find Michael's signed confession, they arrest him and charge him with the murder of Grisby. While visiting Michael in his jail cell, Elsa tells him that Arthur has volunteered to defend him. Though he distrusts Arthur, Michael is left with no alternative but to accept his help. Arthur deliberately presents a losing defense case, and, during the jury's deliberation, tells Michael that he hopes to send him to the gas chamber. When Arthur admits to Michael that it was he who killed Grisby, Michael creates a diversion in the courtroom by grabbing a handful of sedative pills and swallowing them. After punching Arthur and two bailiffs, Michael escapes and takes refuge in a Chinatown theater. Elsa finds him there, arranges to have her Chinese servant hide him, and promises to help him by looking for the gun that was used in the murder. While discussing the arrangement with Elsa, Michael accidentally discovers the missing gun hidden in Elsa's purse, and immediately realizes that Elsa is the one who murdered Grisby. When the pills he took begin to take effect, Michael loses consciousness and is taken by Elsa's servant to an amusement park fun house. Michael regains consciousness in a hall of mirrors, where he witnesses a gun duel between Elsa and Arthur. The Bannisters mortally wound each other in the duel, during which Arthur reveals that he sent a letter to the district attorney establishing Elsa's guilt. After Elsa and Arthur die, Michael leaves the amusement park, certain that the letter will exonerate him. *Femmes fatales. Frame-ups. Lawyers. Marriage—Forced by circumstances. Murder. Trials. Yachts and yachting. Acapulco (Mexico). Amusement parks. Automobile accidents. Chinatowns. Confession (Law). Drunkenness. Escapes. Fistfights. Gunfights. Handicapped. Hired killers. Irish. Jealousy. Mirrors. New York City. New York City–Central Park. Private detectives. Rescues. Robbery. Romance. Sailors. San Francisco (CA). San Francisco (CA)–Chinatown. Servants.*

Note: Working titles for this film were *Black Irish, If I Die Before I Wake* and *Take This Woman.* Orson Welles's onscreen credit reads: "Screenplay and Production Orson Welles." Many of the actors appearing in the film were performers in Welles's Mercury Theatre stage and radio shows. The picture marked the screen debut of Carl Frank, a veteran radio star and member of the Mercury Theatre. A Dec 1946 *HR* news item indicates that cinematographer Rudolph Maté temporarily took over for Charles Lawton, Jr. when Lawton fell ill. According to a Jun 1946 *HR* news item, co-producer William Castle was under consideration as Welles's co-director. An Oct 1946 *HR* news item notes that assistant cameraman Donald Ray Cory died of heart failure while filming on location in Acapulco, Mexico. Information contained in the MPAA/PCA Collection at the AMPAS Library indicates that the third draft of the screenplay was deemed "unacceptable" by the PCA because of a scene in which the character played by Hayworth commited suicide to escape justice. Some contemporary reviews, including the *Var* review, which called the script "wordy and full of holes," criticized the film's confusing story.

According to modern sources, Ida Lupino was originally set for the role played by Hayworth. Modern sources also note the following about the production: Welles wrote the first draft of the screenplay adaptation in a seventy-two hour period while he was staying at a hotel on Catalina Island. In his contract with Columbia, Welles was to be paid $2,000 for a week for his acting, an additional $100,000 after the studio recouped its costs, and fifteen percent of all the profits generated by the film. Although the novel on which the film is based was set in New York City and Long Island, Welles moved the main setting of the story to Mexico and Sausalito, CA. Hayworth and Welles, who married in 1943, were estranged at the time Welles cast her in the film.

Hayworth reportedly accepted the assignment in the hope that her daughter Rebecca would benefit from Welles's profits from the film after their divorce. The divorce was finalized a short time after the filming of the picture was completed.

An interview with Welles quoted in a modern source indicated that the script was originally written for actress Barbara Laage. According to a biography of Welles, Welles had limited control over the editing of the film and was displeased with many aspects of the final picture. Welles criticized much of the completed film, which, he claimed, was significantly altered by Columbia production head Harry Cohn and editor Viola Lawrence. Chief among Welles's criticisms were the overpunctuated score, the reduction of approximately twenty percent of the film, and the addition of a less ambiguous ending. The Welles biography also notes that Cohn delayed the release of the picture for nearly a year in an unsuccessful attempt to have it released after *The Loves of Carmen*, a film in which Hayworth, one of his most valuable stars, had a more flattering role. Some filming took place on location in Acapulco, Mexico, and in California at the Columbia Ranch, and in San Francisco and Sausalito. The picture's hall of mirrors sequence, which has been imitated and parodied in many films, including the 1993 Woody Allen directed film *Manhattan Murder Mystery*, starring Allen, Diane Keaton, Alan Alda and Angelica Huston.

AmCin Jun 1948, p. 200-01, 213. *Box* 17 Apr 1948. *DV* 9 Apr 1948, p. 3, 10. *FD* 9 Apr 1948, p. 4. *HR* 6 Jun 1946, p. 3. *HR* 27 Sep 1946, p. 1. *HR* 3 Oct 1946, p. 13. *HR* 4 Oct 1946, p. 2. *HR* 16 Oct 1946, p. 13. *HR* 18 Dec 1946, p. 10. *HR* 9 Apr 1948, p. 3. *HR* 14 Jun 1948, p. 6, 10. *MPHPD* 21 Feb 1948, p. 4069. *MPHPD* 17 Apr 1948, p. 4125. *NYT* 10 Jun 1948, p. 28. *Var* 14 Apr 1948, p. 8.

THE LADY IS WAITING *see* **FULL OF LIFE**

LADY, LET'S DANCE! (Refugees)

Scott R. Dunlap Productions. *Dist* Monogram Pictures Corp. 11 Apr **1944**; World Premiere in San Francisco: 5 Apr 1944; Prod: Sep 1944 [©Monogram Pictures Corp.; 29 Jan 1944; LP12611]. Sd; b&w. 7,396 ft. 86 or 88 min. PCA cert no. 9769.

Exec prod Trem Carr. *Prod* Scott R. Dunlap. *Supv* William D. Shapiro. *Dir* Frank Woodruff. *Asst dir* William Strohbach and Eddie Davis. *Orig scr* Peter Milne and Paul Gerard Smith. *Story* Scott R. Dunlap and Bradbury Foote. *Photog* Mack Stengler. *Tech dir* Ernest Hickson. *Film ed* Richard Currier. *Mus dir* Edward Kay. *Danced staged by* Dave Gould. *Ballet staged by* Mischa Panaieff. *Sd rec* Virgil Smith and Tom Lambert. *Prod mgr* Charles J. Bigelow. *Supv acquacade sequence* Olive Hatch.

Music: "Symphony No. 5," by Ludwig van Beethoven.

Song(s): "Lady Let's Dance," "Dream of Dreams," "Days of Beau Brummel," "Happy Hearts" and "Ten Million Men and a Girl," words and music by David Oppenheim and Ted Grouya; "Silver Shadows and Golden Dreams," words and music by Lew Pollack and Charles Newman; "Solamente una vez," by Augustín Lara; "Rhumba, Rhumba," words and music by Castro Valencia and Jose Pafumy; "Hot Lips," words by Henry Lange and Lou Davis, Eugene Mikeler.

Cast: Belita (*Belita*), James Ellison (*Jerry Gibson*), Walter Catlett (*Timber Applegate*), Frick (*Frick*), Frack (*Frack*), Lucien Littlefield (*Snodgrass*), Maurice St. Clair (*Manuelo*), Emmett Vogan (*Stack*), Harry Harvey (*Fraser*), Jack Rice (*Given*), Barbara Wooddell (*Dolores*), Eugene Mikeler (*Eugene*), Henry Busse (*Henry Busse*), Henry Busse Orchestra, Eddie LeBaron Orchestra, Mitch Ayres Orchestra, Lou Bring Orchestra.

Show business, Drama, with songs. [*Not viewed*]. When rumba dancers Manuelo and Dolores, the star attraction at the Indian Springs Hotel, are forced to break up after Dolores becomes pregnant, promoter Jerry Gibson promises Snodgrass, the manager of the hotel, that he will find a new dancer for the show, which is scheduled to open in two days. After Manuelo and Timber Applegate, the old westerner who is part owner of the hotel, discover that Belita, one of the waitresses, was a well-known dancer in Europe before the war, they press her into service. On opening night, Belita makes a hit with the audience and recognizing her great talent, Jerry sends her to Chicago to join Henry Busse and his show, pretending that Busse has forwarded money for her expenses. After joining Busse's show, Belita discovers that he did not send for her, but she nevertheless rises to stardom. Back at the hotel, Jerry has been fired for allowing Belita to leave, and drifts from one bad job to another. Timber finally locates him for Belita, but he refuses to contact her, drops from sight and joins the army. Months later, Timber finds Jerry wounded in a nearby hospital and takes Belita to his bedside. After Jerry and Belita reconcile, Timber accompanies Jerry to the theater, where Belita dances a special skating number for Jerry, who sits in his wheelchair, watching proudly from the wings. *Dancers. Ice skaters and ice skating. Waitresses. War refugees.* Band leaders. Dismissal (Employment). Hotels. Reconciliation. War injuries.

Note: Although a Mar 1943 *HR* news item stated that Paul Whiteman and Kenny Baker were cast in this picture, it is doubtful that they appeared in the completed film. A *HR* production chart places Jimmy Alexander in the cast, but his participation in the released film has not been confirmed. Other *HR* news items noted that Olive Hatch, who supervised the aquacade routine, was an Olympic swimming champion. The item adds that the number was filmed at the Arrowhead Springs Hotel in Lake Arrowhead, CA. Choreographer Mischa Panaieff was a star of the Russian ballet and Belita's dancing partner in Paris and London. Post-production *HR* news items add that Monogram dubbed this film into Spanish for Spanish-speaking countries. This was the first Monogram film that featured a dubbed foreign language soundtrack, according to the *HR*. This picture was nominated for an Academy Award for Best Score and the song "Silver Shadows and Golden Dreams" was nominated as Best Song.

Box 5 Feb 1944. *DV* 19 Jan 1944, pp. 3-4. *FD* 26 Jan 1944, p. 6. *HR* 1 Mar 1943, p. 3. *HR* 10 Sep 1943, p. 10. *HR* 22 Sep 1943, p. 6. *HR* 27 Sep 1943, p. 11. *HR* 1 Oct 1943, p. 8. *HR* 25 Jul 1944, p. 1. *HR* 1 Nov 1944, p. 11. *MPHPD* 29 Jan 1944, p. 1735. *Var* 26 Jan 1944, p. 12.

THE LADY LIES (*foreign version*) *see* **DOÑA MENTIRAS**

LADY LUCK *see* **LUCKY GHOT**

THE LADY MISBEHAVES *see* **THE GENTLEMAN MISBEHAVES**

LADY OF NEW ORLEANS *see* **LADY FROM LOUISIANA**

A LADY TO LOVE (Italian Americans)

Metro-Goldwyn-Mayer Corp.; controlled by Loew's Inc.; A Victor Seastrom Production. *Dist* Metro-Goldwyn-Mayer Distributing Corp. 8 Mar **1930**; New York premiere: 28 Feb 1930 [©Metro-Goldwyn-Mayer Distributing Corp.; 10 Mar 1930; LP1138]. Sd (Movietone); b&w. 10 reels, 8,898 ft. 99 min.

Prod Victor Seastrom. *Dir* Victor Seastrom. *Scen* Sidney Howard. *Dial* Sidney Howard. *Photog* Merritt B. Gerstad. *Art dir* Cedric Gibbons. *Film ed* Conrad A. Nervig and Leslie F. Wilder. *Gowns* Adrian. *Rec eng* J. K. Brock and Douglas Shearer.

Source: Based on the play *They Knew What They Wanted* by Sidney Howard (New York, 24 Nov 1924).

Cast: Vilma Banky (*Lena*), Edward G. Robinson (*Tony*), Robert Ames (*Buck*), Richard Carle (*Postman*), Lloyd Ingraham (*Father McKee*), Anderson Lawler (*Doctor*), Gum Chin (*Ah Gee*), Henry Armetta (*Angelo*), George Davis (*Giorgio*).

Romance. [*Not viewed*]. Tony, a prosperous Italian vineyardist in California, advertises for a young wife, passing off a photograph of his handsome hired man, Buck, as himself. Lena, a San Francisco waitress, takes up the offer, and though she is disillusioned upon discovering the truth, she goes through with the marriage because of her desire to have a home and partially because of her weakness for Buck, whose efforts to take her away from Tony confirm her love for her husband. *California. Italian Americans. Marriage. San Francisco (CA). Waitresses. Wine and wine making.*

Note: The credits for the German version were derived from a studio cutting continuity. Vilma Banky appeared "by arrangement with Samuel Goldwyn." An earlier adaptation of Sidney Howard's play was released in 1928 as *The Secret Hour* and starred Pola Negri and Jean Hersholt under Rowland V. Lee's direction (see below). It was remade in 1940 as *They Knew What They Wanted* starring Carole Lombard and Charles Laughton, directed by Garson Kanin (see below). The 1956 Broadway musical, *The Most Happy Fella* was also based on Howard's play.

Other language version(s):
Die Sehnsucht Jeder Frau (German language)
Eine Victor Seastrom Produktion [A Victor Seastrom Production]. **1930**; Chicago opening: 21 Feb 1931. Sd (Western Electric Sound System); b&w. 11 reels, 9,336 ft. 104 min. German language.

Prod Victor Seastrom. *Regie* [*Dir*] Victor Seastrom. *Bearbeitung und dialog* [*Adpt and dial*] Sidney Howard. *Deutscher Beirat* [*German asst*] Frank Reicher. *Deutscher Dialog* [*German dial*] Hans Kraly. *Photographie* [*Photog*] Merritt B. Gerstad. *Bauten* [*Art dir*] Cedric Gibbons. *Filmschnitt* [*Film ed*] Conrad A. Nervig. *Kostume* [*Ward*] Adrian.

German-language cast: Vilma Banky (*Mizzi*), Joseph Schildkraut (*Buck*), Edward G. Robinson (*Tony*), William Bechtel (*Der Pfarrer*), Frank Reicher (*Der Doktor*), Conrad Seidemann (*Der Landbrieftraeger*), Henry Armetta (*Angelo*), George Davis (*Georgio*), Gum Chin (*Ah Gee*). [*German version not viewed*].

FD 2 Mar 1930. *NYT* 1 Mar 1930, p. 23. *Var* 5 Mar 1930, p. 21.

A LADY WITHOUT PASSPORT (Austrian Americans, Refugees)

Metro-Goldwyn-Mayer Corp.; controlled by Loew's Inc. *Dist* Loew's Inc. 18 Aug **1950**; Prod: early Jan—late Feb 1950 [©Loew's Inc.; 12 Jul 1950; LP241]. Sd (Western Electric Sound System); b&w. 6,444 ft. 72 min. Passed by the National Board of Review. PCA cert no. 14465.

Prod Sam Marx. *Dir* Joseph H. Lewis. [*Asst dir* Reggie Callow and Sid Sidman]. *Scr* Howard Dimsdale. *Adpt* Cyril Hume. *Suggested by a story by* Lawrence Taylor. *Dir of photog* Paul C. Vogel. [*Asst cam* Harry Stradling, Jr.]. [*Cam op* James Harper]. [*Stills* S. C. Manatt]. *Spec eff* A. Arnold Gillespie. *Art dir* Cedric Gibbons and Edward Carfagno. *Film ed* Frederick Y. Smith. *Set dec* Edwin B. Willis. *Assoc* Ralph S. Hurst. *Mus* David Raksin. *Rec supv* Douglas Shearer. [*Sd* Conrad Kahn]. *Hair styles des by* Sydney Guilaroff. [*Hair styles* Jane Roberts]. *Makeup created by* Jack Dawn. [*Makeup* Gene Hibbs]. *Tech advice and assistance* Raymond F. Farrell and Cecil W. Fullilove. [*Prod mgr* Charley Hunt]. [*Scr supv* Eyla Jacobus]. [*Grip* Hank Forester]. [*Gaffer* Chet Davis]. [*Unit mgr* Serge Petschnikoff].

Cast: HEDY LAMARR (*Marianne Lorress*), JOHN HODIAK (*Pete Karczag*), James Craig (*Frank Westlake*), George Macready (*Palinov*), Steven Geray (*Frenchman*), Bruce Cowling (*Archer Delby James*), Nedrick Young (*Harry Nordell*), Steven Hill (*Jack*), Robert Osterloh (*Lt. Lannahan*), Trevor Bardette (*Lt. Carfagno*), Charles Wagenheim (*Ramon Santez*), Renzo Cesana (*A. Sestina*), Esther Zeitlin (*Beryl Sandring*), Carlo Tricoli (*Mr. Sandring*), Marta Mitrovitch (*Elizaveth Alonescu*), Don Garner (*Dimitri Matthias*), Richard Crane (*Navy flyer*), Nita Bieber (*Dancer*), [Mario Siletti (*Proprietor*)], [Robert Foulk (*Vice consul*)], [Al Hill, Rudolpho Hoyos, Jr., Martin Garralaga (*Policemen*)], [King Donovan (*Surgeon*)], [Tom Greenway (*Sergeant*)], [Paula Drew (*Stewardess*)], [Jay Barney (*Chemist*)], [Paul Picerni (*Italian*)], [Angela Carabella (*Italian wife*)], [David Bond (*Nick*)], [Frank Francone (*Child*)], [Michael Dugan (*Embassy official*)], [Jay Lawrence (*Bartender*)], [Nacho Galindo (*Vendor*)], [Ann Codee (*Maria*)], [Lillian Molieri (*Girl*)], [Movita (*Lorena*)], [Harry Lang (*Clerk*)], [David Cota (*Bellboy*)], [Carl Milletaire (*José*)], [Phyllis Graffeo (*Woman with musician*)], [George Derrick (*Waiter*)], [Dan White (*Dispatcher*)], [Arthur Loew, Jr. (*Sam*)], [Gaylord Pendleton (*Joe*)], [Bret Hamilton, David Clarke (*Operators*)], [Julia Montoya (*Charwoman*)], [José Domínguez (*Flower vendor*)], [Eddie LeBaron (*Guide*)], [Felipe Turich (*Slinky man*)], [George Ramsey, Barry Brooks, Norma Topaz, Ellen Charlesworth (*Tourists*)], [Tom Hern (*Sketch artist*)], [Tony Roux (*Jolly motorman*)], [Gary Jackson (*Italian boy*)], [Rico Alaniz (*Young Cuban man*)], [Nina Bara (*Young Cuban girl*)], [Pilar Del Rey (*Spanish girl*)], [Paul Fierro (*Alien*)].

Crime, Romance. [*Print viewed*]. Following the murder of a Cuban man on a busy street in New York City, Frank Westlake, the chief patrol inspector for the United States Department of Immigration, begins an investigation into the crime and its connection to an illegal alien smuggling racket headed by a man known as Palinov. Meanwhile, in Havana, Cuba, immigration detective Pete Karczag dedicates himself to the capture of Palinov. Posing as a Hungarian refugee desperate to gain entry into the United States, Pete befriends Palinov and offers him money to secure his passage to America. While waiting for Palinov to introduce him to a smuggler, Pete meets Marianne Lorress, a refugee from Vienna who survived internment in a German concentration camp. Late one night, Pete walks by a nightclub just as Marianne is being arrested for taking employment there without working papers. Thinking fast, Pete wins Marianne's release by posing as her husband. When one of Palinov's henchmen, Harry Nordell, discovers that Pete is really an American agent, he knocks him unconscious and reports his discovery to Palinov. Though Palinov later tells Pete that he knows who he is, Pete vows to continue his search for evidence. Later, however, Pete, having fallen deeply in love with Marianne, makes plans to resign from his job so that he may stay in Cuba and continue his romance. Marianne leaves Pete when Palinov tells her that he is an American immigration agent. Harry is given orders to kill Pete, but Pete manages to overpower him and then forces him to confess that a man named Archer Delby James is the pilot who will be flying Palinov's plane to the United States later that night. After informing Westlake about the illegal flight and its pilot, Pete returns to the United States to help plan the interception of the airplane. Meanwhile, Palinov, realizing that immigration officials are closing in on him, decides to flee Cuba with the next group that James will be smuggling to the United States. Among the six passengers whom Palinov is smuggling is Marianne, but Palinov plans to make her his captive once they arrive in America. As American Navy planes follow the smugglers, Pete, aware that Marianne is on the airplane, monitors the flight's progress with apprehension. When Palinov and James spot the Navy planes, they attempt to escape capture by crash-

landing the plane in the Florida Everglades. After they kill one passenger and abandon the others, Palinov and James take Marianne and attempt a getaway on a small life raft. While Westlake rescues the abandoned airplane passengers, Pete takes a motor boat to the site of the crash and finds Marianne with Palinov. Aware that the gas tank is empty and that Palinov will not be able to escape, Pete then trades his boat for Marianne. Once safely in Pete's custody, Marianne accepts the penalty for entering the country illegally, but looks forward to a happy future with Pete. *Aliens, Illegal. Impersonation and imposture. Romance. Smuggling. Undercover agents. United States. Dept. of Immigration. Airplane accidents. Boats. Dancers. Escapes. Everglades (FL). Havana (Cuba). Hostages. Hungarians. Murder. Refugees, Political. Rescues. Snakes. Traps.*

Note: The working title of this film was *Visa*. The onscreen credits for technical assistance read: "The Technical Advice and Assistance of Raymond F. Farrell, Assistant Commissioner, and Cecil W. Fullilove, Investigator, and the U.S. Immigration and Naturalization Service are gratefully acknowledged." Early Jan 1950 *HR* production charts list James Whitmore in the cast, but he did not appear in the released film. A Dec 1949 *DV* news item notes that Peter Coe was to appear in a featured role, his participation in the released film has not been confirmed. Although a 26 Jan 1950 *DV* news item notes that locations were to be shot in Havana, Cuba, this has not been confirmed.

Box 15 Jul 1950. *DV* 13 Sep 1949, p. 11. *DV* 23 Dec 1949, p. 2. *DV* 27 Dec 1949, p. 10. *DV* 26 Jan 1950, p. 3. *DV* 13 Jul 1950, p. 3. *FD* 3 Jul 1950, p. 7. *HR* 6 Jan 1950, p. 10. *HR* 13 Jan 1950, p. 3, 10. *HR* 20 Jan 1950, p. 18. *HR* 24 Feb 1950, p. 12. *MPHPD* 15 Jul 1950, p. 390. *NYT* 4 Aug 1950, p. 13. *Var* 19 Jul 1950, p. 6.

A LADY'S MORALS *(foreign version) see* **JENNY LIND**

A LADY'S PROFESSION (English Americans)
Paramount Productions, Inc. *Dist* Paramount Productions, Inc. 3 Mar **1933** [©Paramount Productions, Inc.; 2 Mar 1933; LP3696]. Sd (Western Electric Noiseless Recording); b&w. 7 reels. 65 or 72 min. Passed by the National Board of Review. PCA cert no. 2078-R [2 Mar 1936].

Dir Norman McLeod. *Scr* Walter DeLeon and Malcolm Stuart Boylan. *Story* Nina Wilcox Putnam. *Photog* Gilbert Warrenton.

Cast: Alison Skipworth (*Lady Beulah Bonnell*), Roland Young (*Sir Reginald Withers*), Sari Maritza (*Cecily Withers*), Kent Taylor (*Dick Garfield*), Roscoe Karns (*Tony*), Warren Hymer (*Nutty Bolton*), George Barbier (*James Garfield*), De Witt Jennings (*Mr. Stephens*), Billy Bletcher (*Keyhole McKluskey*), Dewey Robinson (*The Colonel*), Edgar Norton (*Crotchett*), [Ethel Griffies (*Lady McDougal*)], [Claudia Craddock (*Miss Snodgrass*)], [James Burke (*Mulroy*)], [Jackie Searl (*The Bad Boy*)].

Comedy. [*Print viewed*]. While Lady Beulah Bonnell of Twicket on Topping, Sussex, goes bankrupt, her niece Cecily Withers receives flowers from Dick Garfield, son of an American billionaire. Beulah and her brother, Sir Reginald Withers, sail to America to find work. On board the boat, Dick proposes to Cecily, but she refuses him. In America, Reginald is tricked into buying a speakeasy and names it Little Twicket on Topping. Bootleggers Nutty Bolton and Keyhole McKluskey then insist that Reginald pay for his quota of liquor by 10:30 that night. Before the deadline, Reginald pays people to come to his club in the hope of selling his investment to unsuspecting capitalist Mr. Stephens. He mistakes Stephens for a policeman, however, and when Beulah tells him American cops must be bought off, Reginald tells Stephens the crowd is fake so as to pay less for police protection. Stephens, who was about to buy the club, rips up his check and leaves laughing. Garfield, in attendance with Dick and Cecily, gives Reginald $500 just minutes before 10:30. When he learns Reginald owns the place, however, Garfield accuses him of being a fortune hunter and is thrown out of the club. While the families feud, Beulah insults Dick in order to get him to fight for Cecily. Meanwhile, Beulah has transformed the club into the respectable Boots and Saddle. When Reginald refuses to buy Bolton's cheap liquor, the bootleggers fill ginger ale bottles with liquor and deliver cases of them. That night, the club is filled with upper class clientele whom Beulah has invited. Garfield arrives to get Dick, but gets very drunk on "ginger ale," allowing Dick and Cecily to escape and elope. The married couple returns when they learn the police are about to raid the place. Just after Beulah sells to Stephens, the police arrive, and Dick confesses he actually bought the club for Cecily. At the police station, they find out the bootleggers framed them, after which the police escort Cecily and Dick to their honeymoon. *Aristocracy. The Depression, 1929. English in foreign countries. Nightclubs. Prohibition. Speakeasies. Abduction. Bankruptcy.*

Bootleggers. Businessmen. Class distinction. Drunkenness. Elopement. Gangsters. Horses. Idle rich. Mistaken identity. Nieces. Police raids. Pride and vanity. Proposals (Marital). Reputation. Ships.

Note: This film's working title was *Good Company*.

DV 17 Feb 1933, p. 3. *FD* 25 Mar 1933, p. 3. *HR* 6 Jan 1933, p. 2. *MPH* 25 Feb 1933, p. 40. *NYT* 25 Mar 1933, p. 13. *Var* 28 Mar 1933, p. 15.

LAFITTE THE PIRATE *see* **THE BUCCANEER**

LAKE OF FIRE *see* **THE LONE RANGER AND THE LOST CITY OF GOLD**

LAKE PLACID SERENADE (Czech Americans)
Republic Pictures Corp. *Dist* Republic Pictures Corp. 23 Dec 1944; Prod: 1 Aug–late Sep 1944 [©Republic Pictures Corp.; 13 Dec 1944; LP13066]. Sd (RCA Sound System); b&w. 10 reels, 7,668 ft. 85 min. Passed by the National Board of Review. PCA cert no. 10420.

Assoc prod Harry Grey. *Dir* Steve Sekely. [*Asst dir* Harry Knight]. [*Ice dir* Arthur Vitarelli]. *Scr* Dick Irving Hyland and Doris Gilbert. *Orig story* Frederick Kohner. *Photog* John Alton. [*2d cam* Al Keller]. *Spec eff* Howard Lydecker and Theodore Lydecker. [*Transparency Projection shots* Gordon C. Schaefer]. *Art dir* Russell Kimball. *Film ed* Arthur Roberts. *Set dec* Earl Wooden. *Cost supv* Adele Palmer. *Mus dir* Walter Scharf. [*Dance dir* Jack Crosby]. *Sd* Dick Tyler and Howard Wilson. [*Re-rec and eff mixer* John Stransky, Jr.]. [*Unit mgr* Joseph Popkin]. [*Tech adv* Harry Owens].

Music: "Deep Purple," by Peter DeRose; "L'amour de l'apache," by Jacques Offenbach; "My Isle of Golden Dreams," by Walter Blaufuss; "National Emblem March," by E. E. Bagley; "A Love Story—Intermezzo," by Heinz Provost; "Serenade," by Riccardo Drigo; "The Moldau" by Frederick Smetana; "When the Citrus Is in Bloom," composer undetermined.

Song(s): "Winter Wonderland," music by Felix Bernard, lyrics by Dick Smith; "Waiting for the Robert E. Lee," music by Lewis F. Muir, lyrics by L. Wolfe Gilbert; "While Strolling Through the Park One Day," music and lyrics by Ed Haley and Robert A. Keiser; "Hej Slovane," composer undetermined.

Cast: VERA HRUBA RALSTON [(*Vera Haschek*)], Eugene Pallette [(*Carl Cermak*)], Vera Vague [(*Countess*)], Robert Livingston [(*Paul Jordan*)], Stephanie Bachelor [(*Irene Cermak*)], Walter Catlett [(*Carlton Webb*)], Lloyd Corrigan [(*Jaroslav "Papa" Haschek*)], Ruth Terry [(*Susan Cermak*)], William Frawley [(*Jiggers*)], John Litel [(*Walter Benda*)], Ludwig Stossel [(*Mayor of Lany*)], Andrew Tombes [(*Skating club head*)], and Ray Noble and Orchestra, Harry Owens and His Royal Hawaiians, Ice Specialties: McGowan and Mack, Twinkle Watts, The Merry Meisters, and *Guest Star*: Roy Rogers King of the Cowboys, [Marietta Canty (*Priscilla, the maid*)], [Janina Frostova, Felix Sadovsky (*Specialty dancers*)], [Janet Martin (*Specialty singer*)], [Jo Ann McGowan (*Skater*)], [Mike Macy, Erno Kiraly, Hans Herbert (*Judges*)], [Sewall Shurtz (*Apprentice boy*)], [Janna De Loos (*Friend at lake*)], [Demetrius Alexis (*Tourist*)], [Ferdinand Munier (*Kris Kringle*)], [Nora Lane (*Benda's secretary*)], [John Dehner (*Radio announcer*)], [Frank Mayo, Pat Gleason, Dick Scott, Ernie Adams, Charles Williams (*Reporters*)], [Ruth O. Warren (*Cleaning woman*)], [Bert Moorehouse (*Photographer*)], [Eric Alden, Stewart Hall, Craig Lawrence (*Candidates*)], [Geoffrey Ingham (*Good-looking man*)], [Eddie Kane (*Desk clerk*)], [John Hamilton (*Hopkins*)], [Chester Clute (*Haines*)], [Stanley Andrews (*Executive*)], [Virginia Carroll (*Receptionist*)].

Comedy-drama, with songs. [*Print viewed*]. Ice skater Vera Haschek lives with her godfather, Jaroslav "Papa" Haschek, in a small Czechoslovakian village, where she diligently practices for the country's championship skating match. The night before the competition, superstitious Papa presents Vera with a pair of silver skates that he has made for her by hand. Vera triumphs at the match and is crowned the Czechoslovakian champion, thereby drawing the attention of three visiting Americans who are seeking a star for their new ice show. The group consists of the rich Countess, impressario Carlton Webb and press agent Jiggers. Before they can approach Vera, however, she receives an invitation to appear at the Lake Placid Ice Carnival as a special guest. Papa and the other villagers bid Vera farewell at the train station, and one friend gives her a porcelein doll, which is supposed to summon the love of Vera's life. During the journey, Vera resists attempts by the Countess, Webb and Jiggers to sign her to a contract, and in Lake Placid, Vera is a hit in the show. Vera's happiness is destroyed though, by the news that Germany is

about to invade Czechoslovakia. Vera rushes to New York, where she meets with Walter Benda, the Czech consul. Benda informs her that he has not been able to contact her godfather and advises her to find her uncle, Carl Cermak, who moved to the United States many years previously. Carl is now a successful businessman, and although they have never met before, he welcomes her to his home. There, Vera gets a mixed reception from Carl's daughters. Susan is friendly, but snobbish Irene is annoyed by her cousin's simple clothes and manners. In order to escape Irene, Vera practices skating on the backyard ice pond, and falls down just as Paul Jordan, Carl's junior partner, passes by. Vera, believing that Paul is the man sent by her porcelein doll, is immediately smitten, as is Paul with her. Paul promises to give her a skating lesson on Christmas Eve but must leave before learning her name or telling her his. Unknown to Vera, Irene is infatuated with Paul and calls him her fiancé, even though he has not proposed. Time passes as Carl grows more attached to Vera, who awaits the return of her mysterious suitor. On Christmas Eve, the family opens their presents, and Irene states that she is giving an expensive pipe to her fiancé. Vera then waits by the ice pond where Paul, who has returned from his business trip, arrives and greets her enthusiastically. The couple begins to skate, but when Vera sees the pipe fall from Paul's pocket, she realizes who he is and runs off without an explanation. Vera returns to Lake Placid, and there she and cowboy star Roy Rogers are crowned the queen and king of the winter carnival. Susan, who has deduced that Vera and Paul have fallen in love, arranges for them to meet, but when Paul declares his affection, Vera again disappears, although she accidentally leaves one of her handmade skates. Vera agrees to sign with the Countess and Webb, but only if her real name is not advertised, so Jiggers devises a campaign whereby she is billed as "The Cinderella Girl." After a number of successful shows, Jiggers engineers a publicity stunt whereby dozens of young men with skates will go to Madison Square Gardens during Vera's appearance there. Carl sees the newspaper ad for the show, which includes a photograph of Vera, and arranges for the attendance of Paul and Papa, who has been located and sent for by Carl. Vera is thrilled to see Papa, and after her show, Papa reveals that Paul is the one who found her skate. Irene apologizes for her earlier jealousy, and the happy Paul and Vera embrace. *Czechoslovakian Americans. Ice shows. Ice skaters and ice skating. Placid, Lake (NY). Romance. African Americans. Americans in foreign countries. Christmas Eve. Cinderella (Fictional character). Contracts. Cousins. Czechoslovakia. Dolls. Gifts. Godparents. Impresarios. Jealousy. Music boxes. Press agents. Publicity stunts. Superstition. Uncles.*

Note: The working title of this film was *Lake Placid*. According to a Mar 1944 *HR* news item, George Sherman was set to direct the picture, and a 4 Aug 1944 *LAEx* item reported that Brad Taylor was set for the lead. Although Taylor is listed on *HR* production charts, he was replaced by Robert Livingston. Production charts also include Laurie Haile in the cast, but her participation in the completed film has not been confirmed. Copyright materials noted that twelve-year-old Jo Ann McGowan, was the daughter of ice skaters Everett McGowan and Ruth Mack. Background scenes were shot on location at Lake Placid, NY, according to *HR*, which also noted that Vera Hruba Ralston and Roy Rogers were to be crowned King and Queen of Winter during Lake Placid's annual winter carnival, after the film's release there on 28 Dec 1944. In 1953, the picture was re-edited and re-released as *Winter Serenade*.

Box 30 Dec 1944. *DV* 20 Dec 1944, p. 4. *FD* 21 Dec 1944, p. 8. *HR* 20 Mar 1944, p. 1. *HR* 21 Mar 1944, p. 19. *HR* 31 Jul 1944, p. 9. *HR* 4 Aug 1944, p. 47. *HR* 17 Aug 1944, p. 8. *HR* 18 Sep 1944, p. 8. *HR* 22 Sep 1944, p. 15. *HR* 20 Dec 1944, p. 4, 9. *LAEx* 4 Aug 1944. *MPHPD* 14 Oct 1944, p. 2142. *MPHPD* 23 Dec 1944, p. 2239. *NYT* 25 Dec 1944, p. 15. *Var* 20 Dec 1944, p. 8.

LAM WU BIG YUG *see* **LANG HU BEE YUH**

THE LAMB (Native Americans, Yaqui)
Fine Arts Film Co. *Dist* Triangle Film Corp. 7 Nov 1915 [©Triangle Film Corp.; 1 Nov 1915; LP7887]. Si; b&w. 5 reels.

Supv D. W. Griffith. *Dir* W. Christy Cabanne. *Cam* William E. Fildew.

Cast: Douglas Fairbanks (*Gerald*), Seena Owen (*Mary*), William E. Lowery (*Yaqui Indian Chief*), Lillian Langdon, Monroe Salisbury, Kate Toncray, Alfred Paget, Eagle Eye.

Adventure, Comedy. Gerald, the weakling son of a wealthy New York family, loses his fiancée Mary after he is shown up by Bill, an enormous Arizonian, during a beach bathing accident. Disgusted by Gerald's "yellow streak," Mary goes to visit friends in Arizona with Bill but is followed by a determined Gerald. On the train West, Gerald disembarks to buy trinkets and is captured by Yaqui Indians and taken

to Mexico. Later, Mary is also kidnapped and ends up next to Gerald. While the less-than-heroic Bill runs back across the border to secure help for Mary, Gerald locates an abandoned Mexican rapid-fire cannon that the Yaquis won in a battle with the Mexicans. Gerald uses the cannon, which the Indians regarded as junk, to begin an assault on them. After a long and heated battle, the battered but victorious Indians close in on Gerald, intending to cut out his heart, but both he and Mary are saved by American troopers. Convinced of her companion's bravery and manliness, Mary reunites with Gerald. *Abduction. Cowardice. Heroism. Arizona. Manhood. Mexico. New York City. Ordnance. Trains. United States. Army. Cavalry. Yaqui Indians.*

Note: This film, which featured Douglas Fairbanks in his first starring screen role (according to a *NYT* review, *The Martyrs of the Alamo* was the first film in which he acted, though it was released after *The Lamb*), was part of the first Triangle Film Corp. program and was re-issued on 2 Sep 1917. Copyright submissions state that *The Lamb* was based on *The Man and the Test*, a novel by Granville Warwick, D. W. Griffith's pseudonym. According to modern sources, however, Griffith wrote an original scenario for the film but was encouraged by Harry Aitken, head of the Triangle Film Corp., to allow his name to be used as the author of various non-existent novels that were cited as the literary sources for some Fine Arts productions. Griffith later denied any contribution on the film beyond the scenario.

Motog 9 Oct 1915, p. 715. *Motog* 20 Nov 1915, p. 1106. *MPN* 11 Sep 1915, p. 13. *MPN* 18 Sep 1915, p. 91. *MPN* 25 Sep 1915, p. 58. *MPN* 9 Oct 1915, p. 84. *MPN* 30 Oct 1915, p. 112. *MPW* 9 Oct 1915, p. 233, 340. *MPW* 13 Oct 1917, p. 298. *Var* 1 Oct 1915, p. 18.

THE LAND OF HOPE (Polish Americans)
Realart Pictures Corp. Jul **1921** [©Realart Pictures Corp.; 23 May 1921; LP16574]. Si; b&w. 5 reels, 4,964 ft.
Dir Edward H. Griffith. *Scen* Fred Myton. *Story and scen* Robert Milton, Frederick Hatton and Fanny Hatton. *Photog* Gilbert Warrenton.
Cast: Alice Brady (*Marya Nisko*), Jason Robards (*Sascha Rabinoff*), Ben Hendricks, Jr. (*Jan*), Schuyler Ladd (*Serge Kosmanski*), Laurence Wheat (*Stephen Ross*), Martha McGraw (*Sophia*), Betty Carsdale (*Mildred St. John*), Fuller Mellish (*Josef Marinoff*).
Melodrama. On her voyage to the United States, Marya Nisko falls in love with another Polish immigrant, Sascha Rabinoff. Arriving and discovering her sister's poverty, she fails as a lady's maid and then arranges an introduction to a theatrical manager, though Sascha is opposed to her becoming a professional dancer. She obtains an engagement through Stephen Ross, who arranges for her training. Meanwhile, unable to pursue his education and reduced to the breadline, Sascha attracts the attention of a wealthy philanthropist, Josef Marinoff, who takes an interest in his idea for a home for immigrants, and through Marinoff's aid he and Marya are reunited. *Dancers. Immigrants. Philanthropists. Polish Americans. Theater.*

ETR 6 Aug 1921, p. 681.

LAND OF HUNTED MEN (African Americans)
Range Busters, Inc.; A George W. Weeks Production; William L. Nolte in Charge of Production. *Dist* Monogram Pictures Corp. 26 Mar **1943** [©Range Busters, Inc.; 5 Feb 1943; LP11866]. Sd; b&w. 5,192 ft. 57 min. PCA cert no. 9077.
Series: The Range Busters.
Dir S. Roy Luby. *Orig story* William L. Nolte. *Cont* Elizabeth Beecher. *Photog* James Brown. *Film ed* Roy Claire. *Mus dir* Frank Sanucci. *Sd* Lyle Willey. *Asst prod mgr* Clark L. Paylow.
Song(s): "The Trail to Mexico (Bury Me Not on the Lone Prairie)," traditional.
Cast: RAY "CRASH" CORRIGAN [(*Crash*)], DENNY MOORE (*Denny Moore*), MAX "ALIBI" TERHUNE AND ELMER [(*Alibi*)], Phyllis Adair (*Dorrie*), Charles King (*Faro* [*Wilson*]), John Morton (*Pelham*), Ted Mapes (*Piebald*), Frank McCarrol (*Tabasco*), Forrest Taylor (*Dad* [*Oliver*]), Steve Clark ([*Sheriff Andy*] *Wallace*), Fred Toones (*Snowflake*).
Western. [*Print viewed*]. While trying to capture stagecoach robbers, Range Buster Denny Moore is shot in the arm. Denny then joins up with his fellow Range Busters, Crash and Alibi, and hides at a line shack belonging to their friend, rancher "Dad" Oliver. Vigilantes led by businessman Faro Wilson claim that Denny is a robber, but cannot find him. While Denny recuperates, Crash sends their black cook, Snowflake, to work undercover and gather information about Faro. Crash and Alibi, meanwhile, go to meet with Sheriff Andy Wallace at his office, and overhear mine manager Pelham threatening Andy if he does not find the outlaws who stole the mine

payroll. Andy maintains that Faro has impeded his progress. Crash and Alibi then pose as cattle buyers and meet Snowflake, who is now working at Faro's saloon. When Crash starts winning at cards, Snowflake overhears Faro making plans to get the money back by accusing Crash of cheating. Snowflake warns Crash, who then fights his accuser. Crash and Alibi soon escape and spend the night at the Oliver farm. Later, Faro's thugs come gunning for Crash and Alibi at the line shack, and Denny fends them off until Crash and Alibi can chase them away. That night at the Olivers', Crash and Denny compete for the affection of Dad's daughter Dorrie, and Snowflake brings over the money that Crash won during the card game, which he retrieved from the floor during the fight. After Crash asks Snowflake to have Andy check the serial numbers on the bills at the bank, Pelham arranges for another payroll to be shipped by buckboard and guarded by Andy and his deputy. When Snowflake overhears Pelham plotting with Faro to rob the buckboard and keep the payroll, Snowflake warns Andy about Pelham's duplicity. Andy and Crash realize that Faro is the leader of the outlaws when the bank confirms that the serial numbers on Crash's winnings are the same as the bills stolen from the stagecoach. The next day, the Range Busters watch the progress of the buckboard from afar, and emerge only after Faro and his gang attack it. The Range Busters round up the outlaws, and turn them over to Andy for arrest. Their work completed, the Range Busters ride off for their next adventure. *Duplicity. Marshals. Outlaws. Stagecoach robberies. African Americans. Deputies. Farms. Fathers and daughters. Fistfights. Gunshot wounds. Mines. Money. Payrolls. Romantic rivalry. Saloons. Sheriffs. Ventriloquists and ventriloquism. Vigilantes.*

Note: The title card reads "*Land of Hunted Men—Another Adventure with the Range Busters.*" Opening credits include the following statement: "Featured Song 'The Trail to Mexico' sung by Phyllis Adair" and "Photographed on Ray Corrigan's Ranch" in Simi Valley, CA. Modern sources include Carl Sepulveda, Tex Palmer, Augie Gomez, Al Haskell and Ray Jones to the cast. For further information on the "Range Busters" series, see the entry for *The Range Busters* in *AFI Catalog of Feature Films, 1931-40*; F3.3620 and consult the Series Index.

DV 16 Apr 1943, p. 3. *HR* 16 Apr 1943, p. 3. *MPH* 24 Apr 1943. *MPHPD* 24 Apr 1943, p. 1274.

LAND OF LIBERTY (African Americans, Latino, Native Americans)
Motion Picture Producers and Distributors of America, Inc. *Dist* Loew's Inc. 24 Jan **1941**; World premiere at the New York World's Fair and Golden Gate International Exposition, San Francisco: 15 Jun 1939; Prod: assembly of footage began Dec 1938 [©Motion Picture Producers and Distributors of America, Inc.; 1 Jan 1941; LP10199]. Sd (Western Electric Mirrophonic Recording; RCA Victor High Fidelity Sound); b&w with col seq. 14 reels. 138 min. PCA cert no. 5400.
Ed Cecil B. DeMille. *Narr wrt by* Jeanie MacPherson and Jesse L. Lasky, Jr. [*Ed*] *asst* Herbert L. Moulton and William H. Pine. [*Ed asst* Francis S. Harmon and Arthur H. DeBra]. *Historical consultant* James T. Shotwell.
Song(s): "Old Man River," words by Oscar Hammerstein II, music by Jerome Kern; "My Country 'Tis of Thee," words by Samuel Francis Smith, music based on "My Country 'Tis of Thee," music by Henry Carey, lyrics by Samuel Francis Smith.
Compilation, Historical, Documentary. [*Print viewed*]. Through the use of footage taken from Hollywood feature and short films, the history of the United States is traced and recreated. After hearing President Franklin Roosevelt call America "the land of the second chance," the picture shows new colonial settlers arriving in America, seeking an escape from European tyranny. In the English colonies, a revolt begins over repressive taxation, with Patrick Henry declaring, "Give me liberty or give me death!" The American Revolutionary War begins, lasting five years and ending in American independence. Without a strong central government, however, the new country begins to fall apart, and war hero George Washington is brought in for leadership. There is a call for a Constitutional Convention, which meets in Philadelphia in 1787. In 1789, the first Congress meets in New York, and the Bill of Rights is signed into law. 1801 sees greater westward movement, led by such explorers as Daniel Boone. With the Spanish defeat by the French in Europe, Napoleon takes control of the Louisiana Territory. President Thomas Jefferson, seeking a peaceful annexation of this area, sends James Monroe to France to negotiate its purchase. Told to spend only two million dollars, Monroe makes the Louisiana purchase for fifteen million, which adds fifteen more stars to the American flag. When the British begin kidnapping American

seamen for its war against Napoleon, the War of 1812 erupts between the United States and England, which leads to the burning of Washington. After this war, the U.S.-Canadian border is disarmed to prevent further outbreaks. When Mexican government rejects Texas' request for representation, the Texans declare their independence, which leads to the battle of the Alamo. Following nine years of independence, Texas joins the Union in 1845. After a border war with Mexico, the United States gains California, as well as the Oregon territories. Gold is discovered at Sutter's Mill in California, leading to the Gold Rush of 1849. The dispute over slavery leads to the Civil War, as the Southern states seek to withdraw from the Union. During the Civil War, the Northern naval blockade of the South almost results in another war with England. After the war, Lincoln is assassinated, leading to the mistreatment of the defeated South during the Reconstruction period, which then encourages the formation of the Klu Klux Klan. In the West, the first Trans-Continental Railroad is completed, leading to more westward movement of settlers and the Indian wars, which include the battle of Little Big Horn. With the turn of the century comes the Spanish-American War, Walter Reed's cure for yellow fever in Cuba, and the great San Francisco earthquake. The Panama Canal is completed in 1914, as World War I breaks out in Europe. President Woodrow Wilson first declares the United States neutral, but with the sinking of the *Lusitania* by the Germans, two million Americans enter the war. After the war, the ill-fated League of Nations is formed, in hopes of world peace. The twentieth century sees America becoming the land of ingenuity, with inventors such as Thomas Edison and Alexander Graham Bell, and such black luminaries as Booker T. Washington and George Washington Carver. As the United States celebrates its 150th year of central government, the film proclaims that the great challenge of the time is peace. The film ends with a color montage showing American landmarks, such as Mount Rushmore and the Grand Canyon, while "Let Freedom Ring" plays in the background. *Motion pictures. United States–History. African Americans. Alexander Graham Bell. George Washington Carver. Thomas Alva Edison. Gold rushes. Grand Canyon (AZ). Patrick Henry. Indians of North America. Thomas Jefferson. Abraham Lincoln. Little Big Horn, Battle of the, 1876. Mexican Americans. James Monroe. Napoleon I, Emperor of the French, 1769-1821. Railroads. Major Walter Reed. Franklin Delano Roosevelt. Theodore Roosevelt. San Francisco earthquake, 1906. United States–History–Civil War, 1861-1865. United States–History–Colonial period, ca. 1600-1775. United States–History–Indian campaigns. United States–History–Reconstruction, 1865-1898. United States–History–Revolutionary War, 1776-1783. United States–History–War of 1812. United States–History–War of 1898. United States–History–War with Mexico, 1845-1848. United States. Army. United States. Congress. United States. Supreme Court. Booker T. Washington. George Washington. Woodrow Wilson. World War I.*

Note: [Although released nationally on 24 Jan 1941, this film was first shown in 1939 and the entry is reprinted from the *AFI Catalog of Feature Films, 1931-40*; F3.2367.] The above summary was based on a print of the 1939 original version. The film begins with the following proclamation: "The motion picture you are about to witness constitutes the Industry's exhibit at the New York World's Fair and the Golden Gate International Exposition. It is composed exclusively of material taken from one hundred and twenty-six feature films and short subjects, as well as scores of newsreel clips and stock shots. Not a single scene was specially filmed for this production. The Motion Picture Industry is proud of the fact that in providing entertainment for the millions, it has drawn so frequently upon the dramatic events of American history for themes and background and that film material could be thus assembled in historical continuity." The film is also subtitled "A Cavalcade of American History Drawn from Film Classics Produced During the Past Quarter-Century." The film contains the following written prologue: "America's history is a saga of struggle and achievement by millions of men and women who courageously labored to build a home for Freedom....a Bulwark of Democracy......wherein all, regardless of race, creed, color or position, might continue to enjoy a priceless heritage..LIBERTY!" The end credits state the following: "This motion picture is composed of sequences from MOTION PICTURE ENTERTAINMENT FILMS produced for the theatre and made available by the following...Artcinema Associates, Inc.; Astor Pictures Corp.; Audio Productions, Inc.; Al. O. Bondy; Bray Pictures Corp.; Caddo Company, Inc.; Cinema Corp. of America; Columbia Pictures Corp.; Commonwealth Pictures Corp.; Cosmopolitan Corp.; Cecil B. DeMille Productions, Inc.; Eastman Kodak Company; Walt Disney Productions, Ltd.; Educational Pictures, Inc.; Electrical Research Products, Inc.; First National Pictures, Inc.; Fitzpatrick Pictures, Inc.; Fox Movietone News; Gaumont British Picture Corp. of America; Samuel Goldwyn, Inc., Ltd.; Grand National Pictures, Inc.; D. W. Griffith, Inc.; Inspiration Pictures, Inc.; Loew's, Inc.; March of Time, Inc.; Monogram Pictures Corp.; News of the Day; Paramount News; Paramount Pictures Inc.; Pathé Film Corp.; Pioneer Pictures Corp.; Principal Pictures Corp.; Progress Films, Inc.; RCA Manufacturing

Company, Inc.; Reliance Pictures, Inc.; Republic Pictures Corp.; RKO-Pathé News; RKO Radio Pictures, Inc.; Hal Roach Studios, Inc.; Selznick-International Pictures, Inc.; Edward Small Productions, Inc.; Stone Film Library, Inc.; Syndicated Pictures Exchange; Technicolor, Inc.; Terrytoons, Inc.; Twentieth Century-Fox Film Corp.; United Artists Corp.; Universal Newsreel; Universal Pictures Company, Inc.; Vitagraph, Inc.; Vitaphone Corp.; Walter Wanger Pictures, Inc.; Warner Bros. Pictures, Inc. Motion Picture Producers and Distributors of America, Inc. acknowledges with appreciation the cooperation of all those individuals and organizations which contributed facilities, properties, time and creative effort to the making of this historical picture."

According to the *Var* review and the program notes contained in the production files for the film at the AMPAS Library, the picture, which originally ran 138 minutes, was produced by the MPPDA at the request of civic leaders and educators for exhibition at the New York World's Fair and the San Francisco Exposition of 1939. It had its premiere at both expositions in Jun 1939 and was shown daily throughout the expositions. According to modern sources, producer-director Cecil B. DeMille was asked to oversee the production without salary, as the film was originally budgeted at a modest $25,000. *Var* notes that DeMille, his staff and Hays Office experts spent six months examining 2,000,000 feet of film from shorts, features and newsreels provided by fifty-three motion picture companies before choosing the footage that finally went into the film. Two months more were then spent compiling the footage. According to modern sources, DeMille telegrammed Will Hays in Oct 1938, stating that the film needed to be restructured to "personalize our story." It was decided to incorporate new footage into the film of a "typical American family gathered around the radio listening to the history of America." At an additional cost of $27,658, Malcolm St. Clair directed this sequence for six days with a cast that included Spring Byington, John Litel, Lynne Overman, Virginia Grey, Billy Lee, Richard Cromwell, Florence Roberts and Mischa Auer. It was later decided, however, that this sequence did not work, and it was deleted in favor of existing footage and voice-over narration.

The program notes state that James T. Shotwell, the historical consultant for the film, was Bryce Professor of International Relations at Columbia University, Chairman of the American National Committee on Intellectual Cooperation and Director of Economics and History of the Carnegie Endowment for International Peace. To work on the film, Shotwell made two trips to Hollywood; the first was in Jan 1939, when he explained his ideas to the studios on the scope of the film's story. In May 1939, he returned to work with DeMille as DeMille edited and assembled the film. For its initial release at the New York World's Fair, the film included excerpts of notable performances by the following actors: Walter Huston in United Artist's 1930 film *Abraham Lincoln*; Clark Gable and Jeanette MacDonald in M-G-M's 1936 film *San Francisco*; Richard Dix and Irene Dunne in RKO's 1931 epic *Cimarron*; Anna Neagle in the 1937 RKO film *Victoria the Great*; Don Ameche and Henry Fonda in Twentieth Century-Fox's 1939 film *The Story of Alexander Graham Bell*; Robert Montgomery and Lewis Stone in M-G-M's 1938 film *Yellow Jack*; Bette Davis, Henry Fonda and George Brent in Warner Bros. 1938 film *Jezebel*; Paul Robeson in Universal's 1936 film *Showboat*; and Basil Rathbone in M-G-M's 1935 film *A Tale of Two Cities*.

After the film's opening, it was cut at various times for further showings in 1939 and 1940 at the fairs. For the 1940 showings, clips from a number of recently released films were included. Also, the 1940 versions contained references to recent international events not mentioned in the 1939 versions. According to a news item in *MPD*, in 1941, the film was cut to 98 minutes and released nationally by Loew's, Inc. on a non-profit basis. The box office earnings from the film were donated to the Red Cross and other war relief agencies. A 1959 news item in *Var* states that Henry S. Noerdlinger, a longtime associate of DeMille's, was hired by Teaching Film Custodians, Inc. to re-edit the film. According to a *Var* review, Noerdlinger's film was released as a 22-minute short by Teaching Films Custodians in 1959. Modern sources state that the film's final budget was approximately $100,000 and include the following additional credits: *Narr* Gayne Whitman; *Mus* Rudolph Kopp; *Ed* Anne Bauchens, Ray Curtiss, Jerry Hopper, and George Dutton; and *Tech* James Wilkinson.

AmCin Mar 1991, pp. 34-40. *FD* 14 Jun 1939, p. 6. *LAT* 10 Jun 1939. *MPD* 8 Jan 1941. *MPH* 17 Jun 1939, p. 50. *Var* 21 Jun 1939, p. 14. *Var* 5 Feb 1959.

LANG HU BEE YUH (Chinese language)
Grandview Film Co. 1949?; Hong Kong showing: 1949? Sd; b&w. Length undetermined. Chinese language.

Dir Ng Kam-ha. [*Not viewed*]. [No information concerning the plot of this film has been located.].

Note: The Cantonese transliterated title is *Lam Wu Big Yug*. Director Ng Kam-ha was also known as Esther Eng. This film was probably made in the U.S.

LARAMIE (Native Americans)
Columbia Pictures Corp. *Dist* Columbia Pictures Corp. 19 May **1949**; Prod: 11 Oct—19 Oct 1949 [©Columbia Pictures Corp.; 19 May 1949; LP2302]. Sd (RCA Sound System); b&w. 6 reels. 55 min. PCA cert no. 13557.
Series: The Durango Kid.
Prod Colbert Clark. *Dir* Ray Nazarro. *Asst dir* Earl Bellamy. *Scr* Barry Shipman. *Dir of photog* Rex Wimpy. *Art dir* Charles Clague. *Film ed* Paul Borofsky. *Set dir* James Crowe. *Sd eng* Lodge Cunningham.
Cast: Charles Starrett (*The Durango Kid, also known as Steve Holden*), Smiley Burnette (*Smiley Burnette*), Fred Sears (*Col. Dennison*), Tommy Ivo (*Ronald Dennison, Jr.*), Elton Britt

(*Sergeant*), Bob Wilke (*Cronin*), George Lloyd (*Sergeant Duff*), Myron Healey (*Lt. Reed*), Shooting Star (*Chief Eagle*), Jay Silverheels (*Running Wolf*), Jim Diehl (*Brecker*), Bob Cason (*Pete*), Rod Redwing (*Indian lookout*), Nolan Leary (*Senator Briggs*).

Western. [*Not viewed*]. In 1868, government agent Steve Holden, who is a member of a peace commission that is attempting to avert an Indian uprising, pays a surprise visit to Colonel Dennison, an old friend, and is introduced to Cronin, the regiment scout. During a meeting at the fort between Steve, his friend Chief Eagle, the chief's son Running Wolf and Dennison, the chief is shot by a gunman hiding outside the room. Steve runs after the culprit, who eludes him. When he returns to the fort, Steve discovers that the chief is dead and Running Wolf has been taken prisoner. Steve tries to convince Dennison that war will break out if Running Wolf does not return to his people, but Dennison sends the Indian to the guardhouse. That night, Steve, dressed as the masked avenger The Durango Kid, releases Running Wolf. The next day, Steve notices a distinctive boot print near a window and asks traveling shoemaker Smiley Burnette to watch for anyone who gives him boots with that mark to repair. Meanwhile, Cronin, who is attempting to stir up an Indian war in order to sell guns to the Indians, tries to turn Running Wolf against all other white men. By accident, Smiley discovers that the boots belong to Cronin and gets the information to Steve. With the help of Dennison's son Ronald, Jr., Cronin is finally captured. Steve proves to the Indians that Cronin is Chief Eagle's killer, and war is prevented. *Disguise. Government agents. Indians of North America. Uprisings.* Boots. Fathers and sons. Firearms. Forts. Jailbreaks. Murder. Scouts (Frontier). Shoemakers. Tribal chiefs. United States. Army.

Note: For additional information about "The Durango Kid" series, consult the Series Index.

Box 4 Jun 1949. *DV* 10 Jun 1949, p. 3. *HR* 10 Jun 1949, p. 3. *MPHPD* 29 Oct 1949, p. 66. *Var* 19 Oct 1949, p. 18.

THE LARIAT THROWER see **CROSS ROADS**

LASCA (Latino)
Universal Film Mfg. Co. *Dist* Universal Film Mfg. Co. 8 Dec **1919** [©Universal Film Mfg. Co.; 25 Nov 1919; LP14473]. Si; b&w. 5 reels.
Dir Norman Dawn. *Scen* Clifford Howard. *Adpt* Percy Heath. *Cam* Thomas Rea.
Source: Inspired by the poem "Lasca" by Frank Desprez (publication undetermined).
Cast: Frank Mayo (*Anthony Moreland*), Edith Roberts (*Lasca*), Arthur Jasmine (*Ricardo*), Veola Harty (*Clara Vane*), Lloyd Whitlock (*John Davis*).
Western. The fiery, impulsive, yet purehearted Lasca lives in a Mexican settlement near the Rio Grande with her twin brother Ricardo and their aunt. She falls in love with cattle rancher Anthony Moreland, whose teasings bring out her jealous temper, but Moreland, although fond of Lasca, thinks of her as a child. Seeing the flirtatious, though engaged, Clara Vane fall in love with Anthony, Lasca, in a vicious fit, stabs his wound and begs forgiveness. When Clara's fiancé, John Davis, angered by the flirtation, bribes one of Anthony's men to allow his cattle to stampede during the Texas "norther" blowing in, Lasca warns Anthony. After trying to head off the stampede, Lasca lies on Anthony and dies protecting him from the cattle onslaught. For revenge, Ricardo leaves Davis to die in quicksand. Anthony, crushed in spirit, buries Lasca, builds a shrine, and remains faithful to her the rest of his life. *Brothers and sisters. Fidelity. Flirtation. Jealousy. Mexican Americans. Self-sacrifice. Stampedes.* Bribery. Cattlemen. Knife wounds. Quicksand. Revenge. Shrines. Twins.

Note: In addition to this version of Desprez's poem, Universal made the two reel *Lasca* in 1913, the one reel *The Mad Stampede* in 1917, and the feature *Lasca of the Rio Grande*, starring Leo Carrillo and directed by Edward Laemmle, in 1931 (see below).

ETR 22 Nov 1919, p. 2139. *MPN* 29 Nov 1919, p. 3976. *MPW* 22 Nov 1919, p.455. *NYMT* 16 Nov 1919, p. 62. *Var* 5 Dec 1919, p. 62. *Wid's* 23 Nov 1919, p. 25.

THE LASH (Latino)
First National Pictures, Inc. *Dist* First National Pictures, Inc. 14 Dec **1930** [©First National Pictures, Inc.; 28 Dec 1930; LP1910]. Sd (Vitaphone); b&w; Vitascope. 65mm. 9 reels, 7,169 ft.
Dir Frank Lloyd. *Scr* Bradley King. *Photog* Ernest Haller. *Film ed* Harold Young. *Rec eng* Oliver S. Garretson.
Source: Based on the novel *Adiós* by Lanier Bartlett and Virginia Stivers Bartlett (New York, 1929).

Cast: Richard Barthelmess (*Francisco Delfino*), Mary Astor (*Rosita García*), Fred Kohler (*Peter Harkness*), Marian Nixon (*Dolores Delfino*), James Rennie (*David Howard*), Robert Edeson (*Don Marino Delfino*), Arthur Stone (*Juan*), Barbara Bedford (*Lupe*), Mathilde Comont (*Concha*), Erville Alderson (*Judge Travers*).
Romance. Returning from the university in Mexico to California around 1850, Don Francisco Delfino finds his native land in the hands of unscrupulous Americans, his family estate in shambles, and his loved ones living in fear. Anger drives Francisco to stampede a herd of cattle he is delivering to Peter Harkness, the crooked land commissioner, and still obtain his money—thus earning him the name "El Puma." Don Francisco and others start making Robin Hood-type bandit raids, one of which leads to Francisco's rescue by Sheriff David Howard, their subsequent friendship, and David's love for Francisco's sister, Dolores. Finally avenging his father's murder by killing Harkness, Francisco must leave not only California but also his faithful love, Rosita, and his sometime sweetheart, Lupe; however, David gives him a head start, and Rosita promises to meet him in Mexico. *Bandits. California. Land grants. Mexicans. Murder. Revenge. Sheriffs. Stampedes.*

Note: This film was originally titled and reviewed as *Adiós*.

FD 1 Jan 1931, p.13. *NYT* 1 Jan 1931, p. 31. *Var* 17 Dec 1930, p. 13.

THE LAST ANGRY MAN (Jewish Americans)
Fred Kohlmar Productions, Inc. *Dist* Columbia Pictures Corp. Nov **1959**; Prod: 10 Nov 1958—19 Feb 1959; addl scenes 4 May—14 May 1959 [©Fred Kohlmar Productions, Inc.; 1 Oct 1959; LP14704]. Sd (Westrex Recording System); b&w. 8,978 ft. 100 min. PCA cert no. 19274.
Prod Fred Kohlmar. *Dir* Daniel Mann. *Asst dir* Irving Moore. *Scr* Gerald Green. *Adpt* Richard Murphy. *Dir of photog* James Wong Howe. *Art dir* Carl Anderson. *Film ed* Charles Nelson. *Set dec* William Kiernan. *Gowns* Jean Louis. *Mus comp by* George Duning. *Cond* Morris Stoloff. *Orch* Arthur Morton. *Rec supv* John Livadary. *Sd* Harry Mills. *Makeup supv* Clay Campbell. *Hair styles by* Helen Hunt.
Source: Based on the novel *The Last Angry Man* by Gerald Green (New York, 1956).
Cast: PAUL MUNI [(*Dr. Sam Abelman*)], DAVID WAYNE [(*Woodrow Wilson Thrasher*)], Betsy Palmer [(*Anne Thrasher*)], Luther Adler [(*Dr. Max Vogel*)], Claudia McNeil [(*Mrs. Quincy*)], Joby Baker [(*Myron Malkin*)], Joanna Moore [(*Alice Taggart*)], Nancy R. Pollack [(*Sarah Abelman*)], Billy Dee Williams [(*Josh Quincy*)], Robert F. Simon [(*Lyman Gattling*)], Dan Tobin [(*Ben Loomer*)], [Cicely Tyson (*Attacked woman*)], [Godfrey Cambridge (*Nobody Home*)], [David Winters (*Lee Roy*)], [Helen Chapman (*Miss Bannahan*)], [Paul Langton (*Jack Vickery*)], [Charles Herbert (*Woody Thrasher, Jr.*)], [Anatol Winogradoff (*Pomerantz*)], [Daniel Ocko (*Agitator*)], [Pat de Simone (*Gang member*)], [James O'Rear (*Dexter Daw*)], [Elimelech Solomon (*Elderly man*)], [Martin Garralaga (*Angelo Traficanti*)], [Rev. Solomon J. Gottesman (*Rabbi Piltz*)], [Harry Davis (*Dannenfelser*)], [Alma Murphy (*Secretary*)], [William Quinn (*Andrew Bain Lloyd*)], [Edna M. Holland (*Gattling's secretary*)], [Ned Glass (*Butcher*)], [Joseph Sullivan, Edward "Skipper" McNally, Jack Kenney (*Policemen*)], [Louis Lettieri (*Boy*)], [George Selk (*Peddler*)], [David Wanger (*Engineer*)], [Jordan "Smoki" Whitfield (*Ambulance attendant*)].
Medical, Show business, Drama. [*Print viewed*]. One night in the Brownsville section of Brooklyn, delinquent teenager Josh Quincy and his gang leave a brutally attacked young black woman on the doorstep of Dr. Sam Abelman. Sam, a physician dedicated to helping his neighbors regardless of their ability to pay, arranges for the girl to be taken to a hospital. The next day, Sam's nephew, Myron Malkin, a copyboy, convinces his editor to publish an article in which he dubs Sam a "Good Samaritan of the slum." Woodrow Wilson Thrasher, a harried producer for a national television network, reads the article over his breakfast of Dexedrine pills and conceives of a plan to feature Sam in his new series on America's "unsung heroes," and tie in the pharmaceutical company that sponsors the show. Woody goes to Brooklyn but fails to interest Sam in his proposition. While he is there, one of Sam's black neighbors, Mrs. Quincy, brings in her son Josh, who has been suffering from convulsions and is terrified of the doctor. Woody and Myron peek through a curtain and observe as Sam skillfully calms Josh, who threatens him with a knife. Woody makes his proposal to the television show's sponsor, Lyman Gattling, who approves of connecting his company with an altruistic physician.

Although Myron promises to obtain Sam's consent, Sam proves intransigent. At Myron's suggestion, Woody contacts Sam's best friend, Max Vogel, a wealthy specialist, with whom Sam consults on Josh's case. Woody surreptitiously meets with Max while he is fishing, but Max, protective of his self-sacrificing friend, refuses to help him unless the network offers Sam compensation. At Max's suggestion, Woody convinces Gattling to purchase a small house for Sam in a better neighborhood, which the physician has had his eye on for some time. As Sam has already put a down payment on the house, Woody makes arrangements for the real estate agent to refund the down payment, without Sam's knowledge, and keep the network's purchase a secret. Woody plans to shoot the show at Sam's house, and brings a film crew to interview neighbors and rehearse. Sam, however, departs suddenly when he learns that Josh has had another attack. Woody accompanies him to the market where Josh lies temporarily paralyzed, but the teenager runs away after he recovers, and Sam sadly realizes that he has a brain tumor. When Woody asks why Sam is loyal to an "ingrate" like Josh, Sam replies "because he is my patient." Woody's wife Anne, meanwhile, becomes increasingly distraught over her husband's obsession with financial success no matter the cost. The next day, the entire neighborhood gathers at Sam's house as they shoot a rehearsal, and when the camera is turned on Sam, he gives his frank opinion about commercialism and the medical profession. Shortly after, Woody's boss insists that Woody curb Sam's opinions, and tells him that slips will be inserted into all Gattling products so that "Mr. and Mrs. America" can pay for Sam's house. Woody realizes that Sam will be publicly humiliated by the new plan, and tells Sam the truth. Sam is outraged that Woody and the studio have tried to "buy" him, as it runs counter to his high ethical standards, and cancels the show. Woody's boss immediately fires him for losing Sam, but Gattling is impressed by Sam's honesty, and insists that Woody obtain Sam's approval to do the show without compensation. Sam consents, but just before shooting begins, he is called to the police station, where Josh has been taken, having stolen and crashed a car following surgery. Sam tends to Josh and lectures him on personal responsibility, but the youth is unresponsive. Sam, disheartened, leaves, but turns back when Josh calls out an apology as he struggles out of his cell, which has been left open. Sam heads up the stairs toward Josh, but is felled by a heart attack. Woody brings Sam home and cancels the show, after which Max hooks Sam up to an electrocardiograph machine. Woody experiences a moral reawakening and finally embraces Sam's philosophy. Anne joins him in Brooklyn, and he tells her he is leaving his job to return to a less competitive environment. Sam dies, and as Max writes the cause of death as coronary occlusion, he mutters to himself that Sam really died from winning other people's battles. *Ambition. Ethics. Moral reformation. Physicians. Self-sacrifice. Television producers. African Americans. Aged men. Brain surgery. Death and dying. Editors. Electrocardiography. Employer-employee relations. Fishing. Heart disease. Jews. Juvenile delinquents. Nephews. New York City–Brooklyn. Poverty. Real estate agents. Reporters. Television sponsors. Henry David Thoreau. Wives.*

Note: Gerald Green's novel, although a work of fiction, was based on the life of his father, a Brooklyn physician. In an *LAT* article, director Daniel Mann noted that while the novel covers the entire life of the fictional character "Sam Abelman," the film only focuses on his last days. Mann hoped that the film would "illuminate...the meaning of the book." A 1956 *LAEx* news item reported that Columbia studio head Harry Cohn paid $250,000 for the film rights to Green's manuscript, and that Marlon Brando was initially offered the lead role. 1957 *LAEx* news items reported that Cohn was considering producing a stage version of the novel starring Paul Muni before making the film, and that Vera Caspary had written a screenplay for Columbia based on the novel. The play was never produced, however, and Caspary's contribution to the final film has not been determined.

This film was shot on location in Brooklyn, NY. Various reviews praised the film for its ethical content and fine performances. The Legion of Decency gave the film its highest rating, and added the following notation: "The self-sacrifice and dedication to humanity which characterized the life of the protagonist are intellectually rewarding as well as heartwarming. The film can serve as an inspiration to people of all races and creeds." The *Har* review, while praising the film for its morality, noted that "There are some who have said, because the film deals with the death of a Jewish doctor, and lacks the exploitation values so common in today's market, that the film will have little box office potential." The film, unlike the novel, does not overtly state that "Dr. Sam Abelman" and his family are Jewish, however, the characters do state that they are Russian immigrants. "Dr. Sam Abelman" marked Paul Muni's first American film role since 1946, and his final screen performance before his death in 1967. This film also marked the screen debuts of Billy Dee Williams, Cicely Tyson,

Godfrey Cambridge and Claudia McNeil. The film was nominated for an Academy Award in the category of Best Actor (Paul Muni), and Best Art Direction (black & white). On 24 Apr 1974, the ABC network aired a television version of the novel, also titled *The Last Angry Man*, written by Green, and starring Pat Hingle.

DV 30 Sep 1959. *Box* 12 Oct 1959. *DV* 9 Oct 1959, p. 3. *Exh* 21 Oct 1959, p. 4645. *FD* 9 Oct 1959, p. 6. *Har* 10 Oct 1959, p. 161, 164. *HR* 20 Feb 1959. *HR* 9 Oct 1959, p. 3. *LAEx* 20 Oct 1956. *LAEx* 20 Feb 1957. *LAEx* 11 May 1957. *LAT* 14 Jan 1959. *MPHPD* 10 Oct 1959, p. 444. *NYT* 23 Nov 1958. *NYT* 23 Oct 1959, p. 24. *Var* 9 Nov 1958. *Var* 14 Oct 1959, p. 6.

THE LAST COMMAND (Latino)

Republic Pictures Corp. *Dist* Republic Pictures Corp. 3 Aug **1955**; Prod: 1 Mar—11 Apr 1955 [©Republic Pictures Corp.; 12 Jul 1955; LP5862]. Sd (RCA Sound Recording); col (Trucolor by Consolidated); 1.66-1. 12 reels, 9,856 ft. 110 min. PCA cert no. 17500.

Pres HERBERT YATES. *Assoc prod* Frank Lloyd. *Dir* Frank Lloyd. *Asst dir* Herb Mendelson. *Scr* Warren Duff. *Story* Sy Bartlett. *Dir of photog* Jack Marta. [*2d unit dir of photog* Ellis Carter]. *Spec eff* Howard Lydecker and Theodore Lydecker. *Optical eff* Consolidated Film Industries. *Art dir* Frank Arrigo. *Film ed* Tony Martinelli. *Set dec* John McCarthy, Jr. and George Milo. *Cost des* Adele Palmer. *Mus* Max Steiner. *Sd* Dick Tyler, Sr. and Howard Wilson. *Makeup supv* Bob Mark. *Tech adv* Capt. John S. Peters, U.S.A., Ret.

Song(s): "Jim Bowie," music by Max Steiner, lyrics by Sidney Clare and Sheila MacRae, sung by Gordon MacRae, a Capitol Recording Artist; "Yo Me Alegro de haber sido," based on several old Spanish melodies.

Cast: Sterling Hayden [(*James Bowie*)], Anna Maria Alberghetti [(*Consuela*)], Richard Carlson [(*William Travis*)], Arthur Hunnicutt [(*Davy Crockett*)], Ernest Borgnine [(*Mike Radin*)], J. Carrol Naish [(*General Antonio López de Santa Anna*)], Ben Cooper [(*Jeb Lacey*)], John Russell [(*Lt. Dickson*)], Virginia Grey [(*Mrs. Dickinson*)], Jim Davis [(*Evans*)], Eduard Franz [(*Lorenzo de Quesada*)], Otto Kruger [(*Stephen Austin*)], Russell Simpson [(*The parson*)], Roy Roberts [(*Dr. Sutherland*)], Slim Pickens [(*Abe*)], Hugh Sanders [(*Sam Houston*)], [Morris Ankrum (*Juan Bradburn*)], [Vincent Padula (*General Cos*)], [Don Kennedy (*Bonham*)], [Cheryl Callaway (*Dickinson child*)], [Argentina Brunetti (*Maria*)], [Alex Montoya (*Mexican colonel*)], [Edward Colmans (*Seguin*)], [Pepe Hern (*Seguin's son*)], [Rico Alaniz (*Tomas*)], [George Navarro (*Mexican lieutenant*)], [Fernando Alvarado (*Groom*)], [Abel Fernandez (*Soldier*)], [Charles Stevens (*Peon*)], [Robert Burton (*Business man*)], [Tom Hernandez (*Aide*)], [Alberto Morin (*Official*)], [Tyler MacDuff (*Rider*)], [Evelyn Rudie (*Little girl*)], [Harry Woods], [Steve Darrell], [Walter Reed], [Jack O'Shea], [Frank Hagney].

Western. [*Print viewed*]. In the 1830s, Texas is a part of the Mexican republic north of the Rio Grande, populated by Indian tribes, a smattering of Mexican citizens and American settlers given land by the Mexican government to speed development of the territory. Colonel James Bowie, who has fought with General Antonio López de Santa Anna, the current Mexican president, stops in the town of Anahuac, where he meets a young American, Jeb Lacey, who tells him that Santa Anna has been oppressing the American settlers, and that William Travis, the spokesman for the Americans, has been arrested. After Jim arranges for Travis' release, they visit the home of Lorenzo de Quesada, a Mexican citizen of Spanish heritage, who sides with the American colonists because Santa Anna has been moving toward despotism. Travis and Mike Radin want to create a militia, but Quesada urges them to proceed with caution, not wanting to cause a break in friendship with the proud Mexican people. Jim, who is married to a Mexican woman and holds Mexican citizenship, takes no side in the discussion. That night, Quesada's niece Consuela asks Jim why he did not fight Travis and Radin, and he explains that killing solves nothing. Radin challenges Jim to a knife fight, which Jim wins, earning Radin's admiration. Riding to his village, Jim is intercepted by soldiers and taken to Santa Anna, who informs Jim that his wife and children have died from a plague. Although he orders his brother-in-law, General Cos, to release American prisoner Stephen Austin, Santa Anna later has Cos garrison the town of San Antonio, making all who have arms surrender them. Austin now believes the only course open is to fight, but Jim refuses to join the rebels. Sometime later, Jim and a group of twenty-five are riding behind a hundred Mexican soldiers when they learn from Jeb that Texas militia in Concepcion have Cos and his men cornered. Realizing that the soldiers they have followed

are reinforcements, Jim and the Texans attack and defeat them. Following the victory over Cos, Travis is confident because, although he knows Santa Anna will attack, the famous Davy Crockett of Tennessee will soon arrive with a thousand men. Consuela, who is now nearly nineteen, stops a fight between Travis and Jim over the question of Jim's allegiance, and Jim tells her she reminds him of his deceased wife. As the Mexican soldiers approach, the men then elect Jim as their leader, and he asks Travis to command jointly with him. The grizzled, jovial Crockett arrives with only twenty-nine men, and the Texans then move to a broken-down fort known as the Alamo. Santa Anna and his troops arrive outside the Alamo, and the general asks Jim to convince the Texans to put down their arms, explaining that he cannot accept the insult they inflicted when they attacked Cos's troops. Jim refuses and returns to the fort, while Consuela and other women tend to the wounded in the chapel. Jim is seriously injured during the seige, and he asks Travis to take command. Jim overhears Jeb tell Consuela that he wants to speak to her uncle about marrying her, but she gently refuses. After the Texans learn from a rider who breaks through that reinforcements will not arrive, Travis gives the Texans permission to surrender, but encourages them to fight and kill as many of Santa Anna's men as possible. All the men decide to stay. While Jim writes a letter to Jeb, encouraging him to be patient in winning Consuela's love, Travis writes of the men's decision in a letter to General Sam Houston. Jim then insists that Travis send Jeb with the letter, and he gives him Jeb own letter to read later. The Texans fight fiercely, but the Mexican soldiers invade the fort. Radin is shot, then Travis, and as Crockett is about to be besieged, he lights an explosive and blows himself and his enemies to bits. Jim is stabbed, then dies after killing a number of soldiers entering his room. Following the battle, Houston announces that Santa Anna's strength has been weakened and that the battle has bought them the time necessary to conquer. Jeb, who has reached Houston, learns that the women of the Alamo are arriving. He finds Consuela dazed and depressed, but when he touches her hand and looks at her, she cries and embraces him. *Alamo (San Antonio, TX). James Bowie. Loyalty. Mexicans. General Antonio López de Santa Anna. Sieges. Texans. Texas–History. Stephen Austin. Davy Crockett. Sam Houston. Knife fighting. Mexico City (Mexico). Rivalry. Romance. San Antonio (TX). William Travis. Uncles. Widowers.*

Note: The working titles of this film were *Men Who Dared*, *Texas*, *Alamo*, *San Antonio de Bexar* and *The Texas Legionnaires*. The opening credits include the following written statement: "This picture was produced in Texas, U.S.A. by the Republic Studio Organization." According to *LAT* and *DV*, John Wayne had wanted to make this film for Republic three years earlier, but because he wanted to shoot it in Mexico and Republic head Herbert Yates wanted it shot in Texas, Wayne left the company and Yates refused to sell him the property. Wayne subsequently produced, directed and starred in his own version, entitled *The Alamo*, which was released in 1960. According to publicity for the film, the set of the fort was built at Fort Clark in southwest Texas.

In the publicity material, director Frank Lloyd states his view concerning the use of fiction in the making of films based on fact: "The addition of fiction to fact is permissible and often dramatically desirable so long as the fiction does not contradict the fact, but is presented as a logical and reasonable development. It is the perversion of facts, not their augmentation, that destroys authenticity." *LAEx* praised the film's treatment of the subject matter, stating that it "makes a serious attempt to provide a sympathetic understanding of the clash that led to the Alamo." The article also applauded the depictions of the historic figures, commenting, "The character of Bowie is an adult one, and Crockett himself emerges as a human as well as heroic figure." According to a modern source, Kermit Maynard was also in the cast.

John Wayne's 1960 film *The Alamo* was the largest production centering on the seige of the Alamo, but the 1953 Budd Boetticher-directed Universal picture *The Man from the Alamo*, starring Glenn Ford (see below) and *Davy Crockett, King of the Wild Frontier*, directed by Norman Foster for Walt Disney, starring Fess Parker (see above), also centered portions of their plots on the seige.

AmCin Apr 1955, p. 188. *Box* 30 Jul 1955. *DV* 17 Dec 1954. *DV* 8 Feb 1955. *DV* 21 Jul 1955, p. 3. *Exb* 10 Aug 1955, pp. 4006-07. *FD* 5 Aug 1955, p.8. *Har* 30 Jul 1955, p. 123. *HR* 8 Apr 1955. *HR* 21 Jul 1955, p. 3. *LAEx* 18 Nov 1955. *LAT* 14 Jan 1955. *LAT* 13 Oct 1955. *MPHPD* 30 Jul 1955, p. 537. *Newsweek* 3 Oct 1955. *Var* 27 Jul 1955, p. 6.

THE LAST DANCE (Irish Americans)
Audible Pictures. 8 Mar **1930**. Sd (Photophone); b&w. 5,825-6,500 reels. [Also si.].
Supv Lon Young. *Dir* Scott Pembroke. *Story, scen and dial* Jack Townley. *Photog* M. A. Anderson. *Film ed* Scott Himm. *Sd* Lester E. Tope.
Song(s): Theme Song: "Sally, I'm Lovin' You, Sally," by Haven Gillespie and Neil Moret.

Cast: Vera Reynolds (*Sally Kelly*), Jason Robards (*Tom Malloy*), George Chandler (*Sam Wise*), Gertrude Short (*Sybil Kelly*), Harry Todd (*"Pa" Kelly*), Lillian Leighton (*"Ma" Kelly*), Miami Alvarez (*"Babe" LaMarr*), Lynton Brent (*Jones*), James Hertz (*Edgar*), Henry Roquemore (*Lucien Abbott*), Fred Walton (*Weber*).
Drama. Sally Kelly, taxi dancer at the Bon Ton Ballroom, dreams of escaping the Bronx, her Irish family, and Sammy, her conceited, saxophone-playing beau; she intends to marry a wealthy man and live on Park Avenue. Purchasing a large diamond ring on credit, Sally tells her family that she is engaged to Tom Malloy of the Malloy Tea Co. The word spreads to the newspapers, and Tom takes his friends to the Bon Ton to see Sally. Coincidence piles on complication before Sally realizes Tom's identity, but by then they have fallen in love, and Tom forgives Sally's pretensions. They have only to weather a phony breach-of-promise suit cooked up by Sammy before their happiness is complete. *Breach of promise. Irish Americans. Mistaken identity. Musicians. New York City–Bronx. Saxophones. Taxi dancers. Tea. Upper classes. Wealth.*
Var 2 Apr 1930.

THE LAST FRONTIER (Native Americans, Dakota)
Metropolitan Pictures Corp. of California. *Dist* Producers Distributing Corp. 16 Aug **1926** [©Metropolitan Pictures Corp. of California; 6 Aug 1926; LP23026]. Si; b&w. 8 reels, 7,800 ft.
Pres John C. Flinn. *Dir* George B. Seitz. *Adpt* Will M. Ritchey. *Photog* C. Edgar Schoenbaum.
Source: Based on the novel *The Last Frontier* by Courtney Ryley Cooper (Boston, 1923).
Cast: William Boyd (*Tom Kirby*), Marguerite De La Motte (*Beth*), Jack Hoxie (*Buffalo Bill Cody*), Junior Coghlan (*Buddy*), Mitchell Lewis (*Lige*), Gladys Brockwell (*Cynthia Jaggers*), Frank Lackteen (*Pawnee Killer*).
Western. Impoverished by the Civil War and eager to replenish his fortune in the West, Colonel Halliday, his wife, and his daughter, Beth, proceed toward Salina, Kansas by wagon train, at the persuasion of Tom Kirby, a government scout and Beth's fiancé. Although Bill Hickok, Tom's friend, and a company of cavalry are in charge, Pawnee Killer, chief of the Sioux, attacks the wagon train, and Halliday and his wife are killed. Bill rides to Salina for help and to deliver the news to Buffalo Bill Cody. Beth, now hostile to Kirby, joins the household of Lige Morris, a trader in Salina, and, at the suggestion of Bill, Kirby joins General Custer's scouting expedition. Lige tells Beth that Kirby is suspected of being in league with Pawnee Killer, but she learns from the post adjutant's daughter that he loves her. Beth seeks out Kirby just as the Sioux stampede a herd of buffalo through the town, and together they find refuge. Custer gives battle to the Indians, Pawnee Killer slays Lige, and the lovers are reconciled. *Bison, American. Buffalo Bill Cody. General George Armstrong Custer. Dakota Indians. Wild Bill Hickok. Salina (KS). Scouts (Frontier). Stampedes. Traders. United States. Army. Cavalry. Wagon trains.*
Note: The initial project was conceived by Thomas H. Ince, then turned over to Hunt Stromberg, who later sold the rights to Metropolitan Pictures to complete the film.
Var 20 Oct 1926, p. 67.

THE LAST FRONTIER (Native Americans, Dakota)
Columbia Pictures Corp. *Dist* Columbia Pictures Corp. Jan **1956**; New York opening: 7 Dec 1955; Prod: began late Mar 1955 [©Columbia Pictures Corp.; 5 Jan 1956; LP5725]. Sd; col (Technicolor); CinemaScope. 97-98 min.
Prod William Fadiman. *Dir* Anthony Mann. *Asst dir* Sam Nelson. *Scr* Philip Yordan and Russell S. Hughes. *Dir of photog* William Mellor. *Technicolor color consultant* Henri Jaffa. *Art dir* Robert Peterson. *Film ed* Al Clark. *Set dec* James Crowe. *Orch* Arthur Norton. *Mus comp* Leigh Harline. *Mus cond* Morris Stoloff. *Rec supv* John Livadary. [*Sd*] Jean Valentino]. *Makeup* Clay Campbell. *Hair stylist* Helen Hunt.
Song(s): "The Last Frontier," music by Lester Lee, lyrics by Ned Washington, sung by Rusty Draper; "Do They Miss Me at Home?" music by S. M. Grannis, lyrics by Mrs. Caroline A. Mason; "Me and My Dreams," music and lyrics by Morris Stoloff, Fred Karger, Allan Roberts and Lester Lee.
Source: Based on the novel *The Gilded Rooster* by Richard Emery Roberts (New York, 1947).
Cast: VICTOR MATURE [(*Jed Cooper*)], GUY MADISON [(*Capt. Riordan*)], ROBERT PRESTON [(*Col. Frank Marston*)], James

Whitmore [(*Gus*)], Anne Bancroft [(*Corinna Marston*)], Russell Collins [(*Capt. Clarke*)], Peter Whitney [(*Sgt. Major Decker*)], Pat Hogan [(*Mungo*)], Manuel Donde [(*Chief Red Cloud*)], Guy Williams [(*Lt. Benton*)], Mickey Kuhn [(*Luke*)], William Calles [(*Spotted Elk*)], [Jack Pennick (*Corporal*)], [William Traylor (*Soldier*)], [John Cason, Robert St. Angelo, Allen Pinson, Reg Parton, Terry Wilson (*Sentries*)], [Bill Hale].

Western, with songs. [*Print viewed*]. In order to save their lives, a trio of rugged, Wyoming fur trappers—Jed Cooper, Gus and Mungo, an Indian—have to give up their horses to Chief Red Cloud and his band of Sioux Indians. Red Cloud explains that whites are no longer welcome in their territory because the "blue coats," members of the U.S. Cavalry, have been cutting down too many trees. Undaunted, the trappers march straight to Fort Shallan to get new horses, which they believe the Army rightfully owes to them. Capt. Riordan, the commanding officer, instead persuades them to take jobs as scouts, though Gus, the elder of the group who mistrusts progress and all civilizing efforts, fears they are walking into a trap. The trappers get drunk on whiskey, and while looking for more, Cooper barges into the home of Corinna Marston, the lovely wife of Col. Marston, who is away building the new Fort Medford. When Cooper informs her that her husband is a dead man if he is working in Red Cloud's territory, Corinna throws him out. Cooper then finds out from Riordan that Gus and Mungo were sent on a scouting mission in the area of Fort Medford and, furious, sets out to retrieve his friends. He finds Gus and Mungo camping out with Marston and his company, who fled the fort when it was burnt down by the Indians. Marston demands that Cooper return to the captain and bring back reinforcements, but Cooper refuses. Just then, the warring Indians arrive, and during the subsequent attack, Gus is injured. The surviving troops return to Fort Shallan, but Marston, who is a violent and bitter man, is determined to return to the frontier with all available troops to teach Red Cloud a lesson. When Riordan refuses to participate, Marston pulls rank on him, and Cooper is sent to scout Red Cloud's village, reporting back that several tribes have joined forces with him. Marston insists on going out anyway, and Capt. Clarke, a doctor, tells Marston to recount to Riordan, Cooper and Corinna the story of Shiloh, a Civil War battle in which Marston sent 1,500 men to their deaths. After Corinna, upset, leaves the room, Cooper finds her, kisses her and takes her to his room, telling her that he wants to "make her his woman." Later, Marston brings his men out to scout Red Cloud's camp, and when he falls into a bear trap, Cooper refuses to release him until he promises to leave the chief alone. Cooper refuses to capitulate, so Cooper returns to the fort, where Corinna and Riordan denounce his treatment of Marston. Cooper rescues Marston, who immediately orders the entire company attired. Marston attempts to deliver a rousing speech to the men, but is heckled by a drunken Cooper, who has donned a stolen Army coat. Cooper runs from the fort and jokingly calls on Red Cloud, and when he tries to return to the fort's gates, he is attacked by Indians. After Cooper makes it back to the fort, Marston urges his sergeant to go to Cooper's room and attack him. The two fight, and Cooper pushes the sergeant off the roof to his death. When Marston announces his intention to hang him for the "crime," Cooper flees. Riordan confines Marston to his quarters, having requested his arrest from the chief officer of the area, but when Mungo returns with the dispatch, Riordan learns that his request has been denied. Mungo leaves the fort and finds a disgruntled Cooper in the woods. The troops headed by Marston enter Red Cloud's territory, and Cooper watches from the safety of the trees as scores of camouflaged Indians lie in wait. When Gus is sent ahead to scout, however, Cooper shoots a brave as he is about to kill the trapper. In the fighting that ensues, both Gus and Marston are shot and killed, and Cooper tells the surviving troops to run back to Fort Shallan. There, artillery fire is used on the Indians, who finally retreat. Later, Cooper is made sergeant, and now that he is civilized enough to be her man, he takes his hat off to Corinna. *Dakota Indians. Fur trappers. Romantic rivalry. Scouts (Frontier). United States–History–Indian Campaigns. United States. Army. Cavalry. Animal traps. Battles. Drunkenness. Falls from heights. Forts. Heroism. Indians of North America. Mental illness. Raids. Red Cloud. Self-defense. Shootings. War crimes. Wyoming.*

Note: The working title of this film was *The Gilded Rooster*. The title card of the viewed print reads: "Columbia Pictures Corporation presents *Savage Wilderness* (formerly titled *Last Frontier*)." According to modern sources, *Savage Wilderness* was the film's television release title. *HR* production charts list Kathryn Grant in the cast, but her participation in the final film is doubtful.

Reviews note that location shooting took place in Popocatepetl, Mexico.

According to information in the file on the film in the MPAA/PCA Collection at the AMPAS Library, a scene in which Anne Bancroft's character repeatedly stabbed an Indian was considered too brutal and was eliminated from the final film. Contemporary reviews unanimously praised the film's beautiful outdoor scenery, but found the story and characters problematic. In particular, the *HR* review complained that the film marked the second time that Manuel Donde, who plays "Red Cloud," had been made "to look like a lunkhead by the Columbia scenario department" even though the Sioux chief was a "Native American genius." For more about Red Cloud, see above entry for *The Indian Fighter*.

Box 10 Dec 1955. *DV* 7 Dec 1955, p. 3. *Exb* 28 Dec 1955, pp. 4077-78. *FD* 27 Dec 1955, p. 7. *Har* 10 Dec 1955, p. 198. *HR* 18 Mar 1955, p. 8. *HR* 25 Mar 1955, p. 18. *HR* 7 Dec 1955, p. 3. *MPHPD* 17 Dec 1955, p. 706. *NYT* 8 Dec 1955, p. 45. *Var* 14 Dec 1955, p. 6.

THE LAST HUNT (Native Americans, Dakota)

Metro-Goldwyn-Mayer Corp.; controlled by Loew's Inc. *Dist* Loew's Inc. 24 Feb **1956**; Los Angeles opening: 22 Feb 1956; Prod: mid-Jul—early Sep 1955 [©Loew's Inc.; 23 Jan 1956; LP6176]. Sd (Western Electric Sound System); col (Eastman Color). 12 reels, 9,315 ft. 103 or 108 min. Passed by the National Board of Review. PCA cert no. 17729.

Prod Dore Schary. *Dir* Richard Brooks. *Asst dir* Robert Saunders. *Scr* Richard Brooks. *Dir of photog* Russell Harlan. *Spec eff* Warren Newcombe. *Col consultant* Charles K. Hagedon. *Art dir* Cedric Gibbons and Merrill Pye. *Film ed* Ben Lewis. *Set dec* Edwin B. Willis and Fred MacLean. [*Spec cost* Joe De Yong]. *Mus* Daniele Amfitheatrof. *Rec supv* Dr. Wesley C. Miller. [*Sd* Lowell Kinsall]. *Makeup created by* William Tuttle.

Source: Based on the novel *The Last Hunt* by Milton Lott (Boston, 1954).

Cast: Robert Taylor (*Charles Gilson*), Stewart Granger (*Sandy McKenzie*), Lloyd Nolan (*Woodfoot*), Debra Paget (*Indian girl*), Russ Tamblyn (*Jimmy* [*O'Brien*]), Constance Ford (*Peg*), Joe DeSantis (*Ed Black*), Ainslie Pryor (*1st buffalo hunter*), Ralph Moody (*Indian agent*), Fred Graham (*Bartender*), Ed Lonehill (*Spotted Hand*), [Terry Wilson (*2nd buffalo hunter*)], [Dan White (*Deputy*)], [Jerry Martin (*Barber*)], [Steve Darrell (*Wells Fargo man*)], [Joe Balch (*Barfly*)], [Roy Barcroft (*Major*)], [William "Bill" Phillips], [Dick Rich], [Casey MacGregor], [Rosemary Johnston], [Gerald Millard].

Western. [*Print viewed*]. When a huge buffalo herd charges directly through his Dakota grazing lands, Sandy McKenzie can only watch helplessly as all of his cattle are killed in the stampede. Buffalo hunter Charles Gilson asks Sandy to join him in hunting buffalo, but Sandy, an ex-buffalo hunter who had abandoned the trade after growing weary of all the killing, is anything but eager to return to that line of work. Charley, a dark and volatile character, remarks that killing, as he learned during the war, is both natural and pleasurable. Realizing he has little choice, Sandy finally agrees to become Charley's partner, and in town, he hires two men to round out the party: Jimmy O'Brien, a red-headed "half-breed" who has decided to leave the reservation and live as a white man, and Woodfoot, a peg-legged alcoholic who once was known as the best mule skinner in the territory. Before the men depart, however, their mules are stolen. Charley pursues and kills the Sioux thief and his companion, then takes a beautiful woman who was with the men and her infant son back to camp, where he orders her to prepare a meal and later kisses her roughly. On the following day, Charley locates a herd of grazing buffalo and, from his position on the nearby hill, shoots until the meadow is filled with carcasses. Sandy kills even more of the magnificent beasts, but he spares a white buffalo because the animal is sacred to the Sioux. Charley, however, nonchalantly kills the beast, and when the Sioux woman sees the slaughter, she bitterly declares, "You take away our food and now you kill our religion." Unperturbed, Charley leads the woman into his shack for the night, upsetting Sandy, who loves her. The next day, Jimmy's friend Spotted Hand offers to trade his horses for the buffalo hide, but Charley refuses and then challenges the young man to a gun battle. Spotted Hand is killed, and that night, the woman secretly gives Jimmy the sacred hide. At some distance from the camp, Jimmy uses the hide in a burial ritual for his friend. Later, Sandy asks why the woman remains with Charley, and she replies that because her people are starving, she must do whatever is required to keep the child alive. Feeling jealous of Charley and guilty at his own role in the killing of the buffalo, Sandy rides into town to sell the hides. He then gets drunk and starts a fight in the saloon, and later he inadvertently insults Peg, the dance hall girl, by suggesting that she is part Indian. Upon his

return to camp, Sandy tells Woodfoot of his intention to free the Sioux woman. Several days pass, but few buffalo appear. Driven half-crazy by his desire to kill more animals, Charley mistakes the sounds of a passing thunderstorm for pounding buffalo hooves and sets out in pursuit of his prey. That night, Woodfoot gets Charley so drunk that Sandy is able to ride quietly away with the woman, but when daylight comes, Charley goes after them in a rage. Woodfoot drives Charley's horse away, an act that prompts Charley to kill him. After arriving at the reservation, Sandy learns that the Army never delivered a promised shipment of food and supplies to the Indians who live there. He and the Sioux woman ride to town for the supplies just as bitterly cold weather sets in. In town, Charley nearly kills Jimmy for refusing to speak ill of Sandy, and soon afterward, Jimmy sees Sandy and warns him of Charley's presence. Sandy, Jimmy and the woman drive a supply-laden wagon and a small herd of cattle back toward the reservation. The cold drives them into a cave for the night, but Charley arrives and shouts that when morning comes, he will kill them. The blizzard worsens, and Charley kills a buffalo and wraps himself in the hide for warmth. In the morning, however, Sandy emerges from the cave to find that Charley has frozen to death. *Bison, American. Dakota Indians. Dakota Territory. Hunting. Indians of North America–Mixed blood. Racism. Sadism. Blizzards. Chases. Cruelty to animals. Cultural conflict. Dance hall girls. Drunkenness. Fistfights. Guilt. Gunfights. Hypothermia. Indians of North America–Reservations. Infants. Insanity. Murder. Romantic rivalry. Stampedes. Starvation.*

Note: The film's opening credits include the following written acknowledgement: "The M-G-M Studio is grateful to the officials of Custer State Park, the U.S. National Monument at Badlands and to Governor Joe Foss of South Dakota for their full-hearted cooperation in the making of this film. The area in which this picture was filmed maintains the largest buffalo herd in America. An annual thinning of the herd is required. We were permitted to photograph this necessary process. The shooting of the buffalo is the assignment of expert government riflemen who worked with us in the filming of the picture."

According to information in the MPAA/PCA files at the AMPAS Library, despite the above explanation, the Humane Society received some letters protesting the film's buffalo slaughtering scene. Rutherford T. Phillips, the executive director of the Los Angeles chapter of the SPCA, responded to the complaints by saying that the slain buffalo had been earmarked for destruction because of their physical condition and were killed by a single gunshot fired by expert marksmen. Reviewers also commented on the brutality of the slaughter scene. The *NYT* review described the scene as "startling and slightly nauseating," but added that it was dramatically necessary because the film "aimed to display the low and demoralizing influence of a lust for slaughter upon the nature of man." In addition to the above-acknowledgement, the film includes a written forewdord, stating that, due to reckless slaughter "by hunters and Indians," the number of buffalo in America had been reduced from sixty million in the 1850s, to 3,000 in the 1880s, and 500 by 1900.

MPAA/PCA records also indicate that in mid-May 1955, the PCA pressured producer Dore Schary and writer/director Richard Brooks to remove any suggestion that "Charley" rapes the Indian woman, a plot element apparently included in late drafts of the script. Although *HR* production charts list Anne Bancroft in the cast, she did not appear in the final film. M-G-M borrowed Debra Paget from Twentieth Century-Fox for the production. According to a studio pressbook contained at the AMPAS Library, Joe De Yong, a painter and expert on early western life, designed the hunter and Indian costumes for the film. The pressbook also notes that Gerald Millard, a two-year-old Native American, was reportedly found by Brooks on the Rosebud Sioux Indian Reservation and cast in the picture, as were descendants of Sitting Bull and his followers, who were discovered on the Rapid City and Pine Ridge Reservations. Les Price, the superintendent of Custer State Park, helped organize the location filming, according to the pressbook. A Jun 1955 *HR* news item announced that filming would take place at five locations in the Black Hills and one in the Badlands. Four cameras were used to shoot the buffalo stampede, which employed 1,000 animals herded by a flotilla of jeeps and wranglers, according to the pressbook. Some modern critics consider Robert Taylor's performance in the film as one of his best.

AmCin Mar 1956, pp. 148-49, 172-74. *Box* 18 Feb 1956. *DV* 14 Feb 1956, p. 3. *Exh* 22 Feb 1956, p. 4110. *FD* 16 Feb 1956, p. 6. *Har* 25 Feb 1956, p. 31. *HR* 16 Jun 1955. *HR* 2 Sep 1955. *HR* 14 Feb 1956, p. 3. *MPHPD* 18 Feb 1956, p. 786. *NYT* 1 Mar 1956, p. 37. *Var* 15 Feb 1956, p. 6.

THE LAST HURRAH (Irish Americans)

Columbia Pictures Corp.; A John Ford Production. *Dist* Columbia Pictures Corp. Nov **1958**; Los Angeles opening: 29 Oct 1958; Prod: 24 Feb—24 Apr 1958 [©Columbia Pictures Corp.; 1 Nov 1958; LP12756]. Sd (RCA Sound Recording); b&w. 12 reels, 12,000 ft. 120-122 min. PCA cert no. 19086.

Prod John Ford. *Dir* John Ford. *Asst dir* Wingate Smith and Sam Nelson. *Scr* Frank Nugent. *Dir of photog* Charles Lawton, Jr. *Art dir* Robert Peterson. *Film ed* Jack Murray. *Set dec* William Kiernan. [*Master prop* Charles Granucci]. [*Gowns* Jean Louis]. *Rec supv* John Livadary. *Sd* Harry Mills. *Hair styles* Helen Hunt.

Source: Based on the novel *The Last Hurrah* by Edwin O'Connor (Boston, 1956).

Cast: SPENCER TRACY [(*Frank Skeffington*)], Jeffrey Hunter [(*Adam Caulfield*)], Dianne Foster [(*Maeve Caulfield*)], Pat O'Brien [(*John Gorman*)], Basil Rathbone [(*Norman Cass, Sr.*)], Donald Crisp [(*Cardinal Martin Burke*)], James Gleason [(*Cuke Gillen*)], Edward Brophy [(*Ditto Boland*)], John Carradine [(*Amos Force*)], Willis Bouchey [(*Roger Sugrue*)], Basil Ruysdael [(*Bishop Gardner*)], Ricardo Cortez [(*Sam Weinberg*)], Wallace Ford [(*Charles J. Hennessey*)], Frank McHugh [(*Festus Garvey*)], Carleton Young [(*Mr. Winslow*)], Frank Albertson [(*Jack Mangan*)], Bob Sweeney [(*Johnny Degnan*)], William Leslie [(*Dan Herliby*)], Anna Lee [(*Gert Minihan*)], Ken Curtis [(*Monsignor Killian*)], Jane Darwell [(*Delia Boylan*)], O. Z. Whitehead [(*Norman Cass, Jr.*)], Arthur Walsh [(*Frank Skeffington, Jr.*)], [Edmund Lowe (*Johnny Byrne*)], [Charles Fitzsimmons (*Kevin McCluskey*)], [Helen Westcott (*Mrs. McCluskey*)], [Ruth Warren (*Ellen Davin*)], [Mimi Doyle (*Mamie Burns*)], [Dan Borzage (*Pete*)], [James Flavin (*Police captain*)], [William Forrest (*Doctor*)], [Frank Sully (*Fire captain*)], [Charlie Sullivan (*Chauffeur*)], [Bill Henry, Rand Brooks, Harry Lauter, William Neff, John Bryant, William Hudson (*Young politicians*)], [Jack Pennick (*Riley*)], [Ruth Clifford (*Nurse*)], [Richard Deacon (*Club secretary*)], [Harry Tyler (*Elderly retainer*)], [Robert Levin (*Jules Kowalsky*)], [Julius Tannen (*Mr. Kowalsky*)], [Hal K. Dawson, Joe Forte (*Managing editors*)], [Harry Tenbrook (*Footsie*)], [Clete Roberts (*News commentator*)], [Tommy Earwood (*Gregory McCluskey*)], [Harriet Wollis, Helaine Wollis (*McCluskey twins*)], [Debbie Cooney (*McCluskey daughter*)], [Sam Harris, Frank Baker, Raoul Freeman (*Bankers*)], [Jimmy Murphy (*Office boy*)], [Joe Forte (*Managing editor*)], [Helen Gereghty, Millie Fitzgerald (*Carmichael sisters*)], [Molly Roden, Eve March (*Neighbor women*)], [Edward "Skipper" McNally (*Ward heeler*)], [Bobette Bentley, June Kirby (*Blondes*)], [Roy Jenson, Charles Hicks (*Fighters*)], [Edward Featherstone], [Frank Marlowe], [Jack Henderson], [Gail Bonney], [Dick Ryan], [Ted Stanhope], [Joe McGuinn], [George Spaulding], [Joe Devlin], [Tommy Jackson], [Harry Strang], [Brian O'Hara], [Frank Scannell], [Phil Tully], [Charles Trowbridge], [Charles Anthony Hughes], [Edmund Cobb], [Dick Keene], [William H. O'Brien], [Webster La Grange], [Wilbur Mack], [Stuart Holmes], [Clint Dorrington], [Victor Romito], [Buck Russell], [Johnny Leone], [Alex Akimoff], [Rolland Jones], [Emma Palmese], [Cosmo Sardo], [Chuck Howard], [Frank Magrin], [Charles Cirillo], [Mike Jeffers], [Phillip Adams], [Bud Cokes], [James Dime], [Stephen Soldi], [Lenny Smith], [Richard Dale Clark], [John Deauville], [William Janssen], [George Ford], [Bob Perry], [Jordan Shelley], [Dick Cherney], [Hank Mann], [Anna Stein], [Sue Shannon], [Fred Kennedy], [Harvey Perry], [Steve Benton], [Claire Dellatorre].

Political, Comedy-drama. [*Print viewed*]. Frank Skeffington, the Irish-American mayor of a large New England city, descends his staircase, pausing, as he does every morning, to place a fresh rose by the portrait of his deceased wife. At the bottom of the stairs wait his secretary, the city wardheelers and various aides, and outside the office door is the usual crowd of noisy constituents. Skeffington's staff notes that Amos Force's newspaper opposes the mayor's recently announced bid for a fifth term, even though the two major opposing candidates are unimpressive: Charles J. Hennessey, a longtime but harmless opponent, and Kevin McCluskey, a young naval hero with few ideas of his own. In Force's newsroom, the sour old publisher is planning a series of articles in support of McCluskey, not because he respects the younger candidate but because he despises Skeffington. Adam Caulfield, the writer of the paper's popular sports column and Skeffington's nephew, asks his uncle why Force so dislikes him. Skeffington reveals that his own mother, once a maid in the home of Force's father, was humiliated and then fired by the elder Force for stealing two overripe bananas and a small apple, a "crime" usually accepted by the wealthy Yankees who employed poor Irish immigrants. The Force family had never forgiven their maid's son for becoming mayor of the city and governor of the state. During this conversation, Skeffington asks Adam to cover his re-election campaign "from the inside." Uninterested in politics, but fascinated by his sometimes unethical but always humane uncle, Adam agrees, much to the chagrin of his wife Maeve and her father, Roger Sugrue. Nevertheless, Adam's respect and affection for his uncle, emotions not expressed by Skeffington's playboy son "Junior," increase as he

attends rallies and other campaign events. At the wake of Knocko Minihan, for example, Adam is at first outraged when Skeffington fills the widow's house with his supporters, who hand out cigars while conducting ward business. Skeffington's manager, John Gorman, however, explains that while admittedly trying to promote his campaign, Skeffington has nonetheless succeeded in packing the wake of the universally disliked Minihan with well-wishers, a fact that deeply touches the grieving widow. When Adam later hears Skeffington threaten to take greedy undertaker Johnny Degnan before his licensing board unless he reduces the high cost of the services, Adam becomes his uncle's avid supporter. After the funeral, Skeffington learns that the city's bankers have decided not to provide the loan needed to clean up one of the city's worst slums. Furious, he and his cronies invade the exclusive Plymouth Club, where banker Norman Cass, Sr. is lunching with a group of Skeffington detractors, among them Force and Bishop Gardner. Skeffington begs the men not to use the housing project as a political football, but Cass and his associates remain adamant. That afternoon, Skeffington flatters Cass's simpering son into becoming the fire commissioner. The next day, the mayor shows the elder Cass a photograph of his son, looking particularly foolish in his fireman's helmet, and asks, "Do I announce the appointment?" Cass agrees to provide the loan in exchange for the embarrassing photograph. Soon the Plymouth Club becomes the site of McCluskey's campaign headquarters, and the young candidate begins to make numerous television appearances. On the night before the election, Skeffington has dinner with Adam and Maeve and finally succeeds in charming the young woman. After the couple votes, however, she smilingly refuses to reveal her choice to her husband. As the returns begin to come in, Skeffington's campaign headquarters is noisy and upbeat, but it soon becomes apparent that McCluskey has won the election by a landslide. After hearing the television reporter describe the election as the biggest political upset in the city's history, Skeffington warmly congratulates his opponent and announces that he now plans to run for governor. The mayor then walks home alone as McCluskey's raucous victory parade fills the streets. Shrugging sheepishly at the portrait of his wife, Skeffington begins to climb the stairs but suddenly suffers a heart attack and collapses. The next day, as Skeffington rests in bed, scores of well-wishers appear outside the mayor's residence. Though his doctor orders him to see no one, Skeffington insists on saying goodbye to his old friends. Sugrue disdainfully asserts that if he had it to do over again, Skeffington would surely live his life differently. Barely able to open his eyes, Skeffington exclaims, "Like hell I would!" and dies. *Class distinction. Irish Americans. Mayors. New England. Political bosses. Political campaigns. Bankers. Bigotry. Blackmail. Catholic Church. Clergy. Clubs. Elections. Fathers and sons. Graft. Heart disease. Idle rich. Jews. Loyalty. Nephews. Newspaper publishers. Playboys. Political corruption. Reporters. Television. Undertakers and undertaking. Upper classes. Urban life. Wakes. Widows.*

Note: Edwin O'Connor's novel was loosely based on the life of Boston's Irish-American political boss, James M. Curley, 1874-1958. Colorful and shrewd, Curley was the four-term Democratic mayor of Boston, the governor of Massachusetts, and a two-term Congressman. Even though he was convicted of mail fraud in 1947, he continued to serve as mayor, and in 1950 received a full pardon from President Harry S. Truman. O'Connor's novel was allegedly based on Curley's failed 1949 mayoral campaign. The publication of the novel generated considerable controversy and a lawsuit. In Aug 1958, *LAT* reported that Curley filed a lawsuit against Columbia, arguing that the film would constitute an invasion of privacy, as well as damage the prospects of any film adaptation of his autobiography, *I'd Do It Again*. According to *Var*, Columbia argued in court that it had a signed and notarized agreement with Curley releasing the studio from any liability in connection with the film in exchange for $25,000. Curley denied signing the agreement, and both the notary and Curley's agent, James E. Sullivan, to whom the studio made the payment, had disappeared. In its review, *MPHPD* pointed out that the two sides later settled the lawsuit out of court. According to *DV*, the film was produced for $2,500,000. Modern sources include James Waters in the cast. O'Connor's novel was also the basis for a 1977 television film of the same name, starring Carroll O'Connor and directed by Vincent Sherman.

Box 20 Oct 1958. *DV* 3 Sep 1958. *DV* 12 Sep 1958. *DV* 15 Oct 1958, p. 3. *Exb* 15 Oct 1958, p. 4521. *FD* 17 Oct 1958, p. 6. *Har* 18 Oct 1956, pp. 166-67. *HR* 15 Oct 1958, p. 3. *LAT* 20 Aug 1958. *MPHPD* 25 Oct 1958, p. 29. *NYT* 27 Apr 1958. *NYT* 24 Oct 1958, p. 40. *Var* 10 Sep 1958. *Var* 15 Oct 1958, p. 6.

THE LAST INDIAN BATTLES OR FROM THE WARPATH TO THE PEACE PIPE *see* THE INDIAN WARS

THE LAST OF HIS PEOPLE (Native Americans)

Select Pictures Corp. *Dist* Select Pictures Corp. 20 Dec **1919** [©Select Pictures Corp.; 20 Nov 1919; LP14465]. Si; b&w. 5 reels, 5,195 ft.

Dir Robert North Bradbury. *Story and scen* Robert North Bradbury and Frank Howard Clark. *Cam* L. W. McManigal.

Cast: Mitchell Lewis (*Lone Wolf, later known as Wolf Briggs*), Harry Lonsdale (*Anthony Briggs*), Yvette Mitchell (*Na-ta-le*), Catherine Van Buren (*Yvonne Lacombe*), J. J. Bryson (*Robert Lacey*), Eddie Hearn (*Reynard Lacey*), Joseph Swickard (*Baron Bonart*).

Northwest, Drama. Young chief Lone Wolf and his sister Na-ta-le, whose people died of "spotted sickness," are adopted by woodsman Anthony Briggs, who lives in isolation in the Canadian North Woods. Briggs's wife left with the lumber camp foreman, Robert Lacey, for New York, where she died in poverty. Years later, Briggs's daughter, Yvonne Lacombe, an artist and heartbreaker of the Bohemian set, returns with a hunting party, including her fiancé, Lacey's son Reynard. When Wolf helps Yvonne after an accident, she accepts a wager that she can capture Wolf's heart. She paints his portrait and wins the bet, leaving Wolf brokenhearted. After Reynard betrays Na-ta-le, Wolf interrupts the wedding of Reynard and Yvonne, demanding satisfaction. He pursues Reynard, who goes to Na-ta-le's cabin, and while he and Briggs fight, Na-ta-le is accidentally shot and killed. As Wolf pursues Reynard, Yvonne discovers that she is Briggs' daughter and is part Indian. After Wolf hurls Reynard over a precipice during a knife fight, he returns to discover Yvonne waiting. *Brothers and sisters. Canada. Flirts. Indians of North America. Painters (Of paintings). Parentage. Wagers. Woodsmen. Accidental death. Bohemians and Bohemianism. Class distinction. Falls from heights. Hunting. Knife fighting. Seduction. Weddings.*

Note: Some scenes were filmed at Big Bear Lake, CA.

ETR 27 Dec 1919, p. 425. *MPN* 27 Dec 1919, p. 270. *MPW* 27 Dec 1919, p. 1187. *Var* 9 Jan 1920, p. 53. *Wid's* 21 Dec 1919, p. 21.

LAST OF THE BUCCANEERS (French Americans)

Columbia Pictures Corp. *Dist* Columbia Pictures Corp. Oct **1950**; Prod: 14 Mar—29 Mar 1950 [©Columbia Pictures Corp.; 1 Oct 1950; LP967]. Sd; col (Technicolor). 7,080 ft. 78-79 min.

Prod Sam Katzman. *Dir* Lew Landers. *Asst dir* Jack Corrick. *Wrt for the scr by* Robert E. Kent. *Dir of photog* Vincent Farrar. *Technicolor col consultant* Francis Cugat. *Art dir* Paul Palmentola. *Film ed* Henry Batista. *Set dec* Sidney Clifford. *Mus dir* Mischa Bakaleinikoff. *Sd eng* Josh Westmoreland. *Unit mgr* Herbert Leonard.

Song(s): "Pirate from Kentucky," composers undetermined.

Cast: Paul Henreid (*Jean Lafitte*), Jack Oakie (*Sergeant Dominick*), Karin Booth (*Belle Summers*), Mary Anderson (*Swallow*), Edgar Barrier (*George Mareval*), John Dehner (*Sergeant Beluche*), Harry Cording (*Cragg Brown*), Eugene Borden (*Captain Perez*), Jean Del Val (*Sauvinet*), Pierre Watkin (*Governor Claiborne*), Sumner Getchell (*Paul DeLorie*), Paul Marion (*Jose Cabrillo*), Rusty Wescoatt (*Colonel Parnell*).

Historical, Sea, Swashbuckler, Drama. [*Print viewed*]. During the War of 1812, pirate Jean Lafitte helps General "Stonewall" Jackson defeat the British and endears himself to Belle Summers, the beautiful niece of wealthy shipowner George Mareval. Later, when the governor of Louisiana refuses to return his ships to him, Lafitte captures a recently provisioned ship belonging to Mareval. He then offers his services to the consul of Venezuela, whose country is at war with Spain. Knowing that as long as he loots only Spanish ships, the American authorities will leave him alone, Lafitte promises to return for Belle and takes to the seas. As the months pass, Lafitte and his buccaneers establish a kingdom on the island of Galveston in the Gulf, and Lafitte builds a castle, which he names the Maison Rouge. The spoils from his raids are kept in tunnels which, if threatened, can be destroyed by a pulling a secret lever. When pirate Cragg Brown attacks an American ship against Lafitte's express orders, he is hanged. In New Orleans, the news that one of Lafitte's ships has plundered an American vessel angers the people. Belle is convinced that Lafitte is innocent and offers to prove it. Under safe conduct from the authorities, Lafitte takes Belle to Galveston, where she plans to prove that the bills of lading for the goods in his warehouse do not correspond with those from the missing American ship. Shortly before her wedding day, however, Belle finds a document that proves that Lafitte does have the loot from the American ship. Not knowing that

Lafitte has hanged the responsible man, she gives the authorities in New Orleans information that will enable them to capture Galveston. Just before the soldiers arrive, Belle learns the truth about the capture of the ship, but it is too late to stop the invasion. When the soldiers are about to search the tunnel, Swallow, the daughter of one of Lafitte's loyal workers, pulls the secret lever, and the treasure is buried forever. Lafitte forgives Belle, and the two lovers escape in a fishing boat. *Galveston (TX). Jean Lafitte. Pirates. United States–History–1815-1861. Betrayal. Castles. Governors. Hanging. Islands. Jealousy. New Orleans (LA). Romance. Ship owners. Ships. Treasure. Uncles. United States–History–War of 1812.*

Note: Jean Lafitte was a French pirate who headed a band of privateers and smugglers outside New Orleans, LA, and was also involved in the slave trade. During the War of 1812, when the British asked for his help in an attack on New Orleans, he revealed their plans to the American authorities. During the Battle of New Orleans in late 1814, Lafitte was put in charge of American artillery. After the end of the war, Lafitte returned to piracy and established his headquarters at Galveston, TX. His headquarters were raided and destroyed after he scuttled an American merchant ship in 1820. He continued his pirate raids on the Spanish high seas until he disappeared around 1825. Lafitte was also the main character in two Cecil B. De Mille films, both called *The Buccaneer*. The 1938 Paramount film starred Fredric March as the pirate (see above). The 1958 film the role was performed by Yul Brynner.

Box 14 Oct 1950. *DV* 13 Oct 1950, p. 3. *FD* 18 Oct 1950, p. 6. *HR* 13 Oct 1950, p. 3. *MPHPD* 14 Oct 1950, p. 518. *NYT* 15 Dec 1950, p. 43. *Var* 18 Oct 1950, p. 6.

LAST OF THE COMANCHES (Native Americans, Cheyenne, Comanche, Kiowa)

Columbia Pictures Corp. *Dist* Columbia Pictures Corp. Jan **1953**; Los Angeles opening: 28 Jan 1953; Prod: 27 Nov 1951—3 Mar 1952 [©Columbia Pictures Corp.; 5 Nov 1952; LP2039]. Sd (Western Electric Recording); col (Technicolor). 9 reels, 7,588 ft. 85 min. Passed by the National Board of Review. PCA cert no. 15709.

Prod Buddy Adler. *Dir* Andre De Toth. *Asst dir* James Nicholson. *2d unit dir* Yakima Canutt. *Wrt for the screen by* Kenneth Gamet. *Dir of photog* Charles Lawton, Jr. and Ray Cory. *Technicolor col consultant* Francis Cugat. *Art dir* Ross Bellah. *Film ed* Al Clark. *Set dec* Frank Tuttle. *Mus dir* Morris Stoloff. *Mus score* George Duning. *Sd eng* George Cooper.

Cast: Broderick Crawford [(*Sgt. Matt Trainor*)], Barbara Hale [(*Julia Lanning*)], Johnny Stewart [(*Little Knife*)], Lloyd Bridges [(*Jim Starbuck*)], Mickey Shaughnessy [(*Rusty Potter*)], George Mathews [(*Romany O'Rattigan*)], Hugh Sanders [(*Denver Kinnaird*)], Ric Roman [(*Martinez*)], Chubby Johnson [(*Henry Ruppert*)], Martin Milner [(*Billy Creel*)], Milton Parsons [(*Prophet Satterlee*)], Jack Woody [(*Cpl. Floyd*)], John War Eagle [(*Black Cloud*)], [Carleton Young (*Maj. Lanning*)], [William Andrews (*Lt. Floyd*)], [Jay Silverheels, Rod Redwing (*Indians*)], [Harry Harvey (*Civilian*)], [Bud Osborne (*Wagon driver*)], [George Chesebro (*Pete*)].

Western. [*Print viewed*]. In August 1876, Black Cloud and his elusive renegade Comanches, the only Indians not at peace with the white inhabitants of the Southwest, attack a scouting patrol seeking the Comanche chief as it stops for water at the desert town of Dry Buttes. During the night, Black Cloud sends a stampede of horses into the town, followed by overwhelming numbers of Comanches. The town is burned to the ground, and all but six cavalrymen are killed. These survivors, led by flinty Sgt. Matt Trainor, head into the desert for the one-hundred-mile trek back to Fort Macklin. Not long after their departure, they encounter a stagecoach driven by Romany O'Rattigan and carrying three passengers—argumentative whiskey salesman Henry Ruppert, former scout Prophet Satterlee, and elegant Julia Lanning, the sister of Fort Macklin's commander, Maj. Lanning. The threat of Comanche attack unites the two parties, and the thirsty soldiers are relieved to see that O'Rattigan carries a large water barrel on the coach. When a group of Comanches later attacks the coach, however, the water barrel is shot full of holes. Sgt. Trainor takes the offensive and the Indians retreat, but Trainor now believes that the only safe route to the fort is through the hills. Because this route will add miles to the trip, they decide to take Satterlee's advice and visit an abandoned trading post in search of water. On the way, they encounter a man who identifies himself as a cattle buyer but whom trooper Jim Starbuck recognizes as a murderer named Denver Kinnaird. Sgt. Trainor places Kinnaird under arrest, and the party moves on to the trading post. There they learn, to their dismay, that the well Satterlee described has gone dry. Buried in the sand are quantities of carefully wrapped guns that look just like the ones Black Cloud has been using, and Trainor realizes that the weapons were

placed there by the gunrunner who has been supplying the Comanches. Not knowing what else to do, Trainor rations the rest of the water. While on night watch, young soldier Billy Creel worries that they will all die soon. His friend, Rusty Potter, tries to distract him with stories, but to no avail. The next day, the group comes upon a Kiowa boy named Little Knife, who attends a reservation school but was captured by Black Cloud while hunting. Little Knife, having chewed through his bindings and escaped, asserts that Black Cloud hates all Indians who are at peace with the white man, but Trainor distrusts the boy and leaves him behind. Julia argues that the boy deserves at least a drink, but Trainor relents only after seeing him running to catch up with the stagecoach. An old soldier named Floyd, who was injured in the Dry Buttes battle, passes out from lack of water, but there is none left, and he dies. Little Knife then remembers that during dry spells, his people got water at an old mission some miles away. At the mission, Little Knife locates the well, but finds that the water only drips from its source. The party catches the precious drops in buckets, but it takes hours to fill each container. The travelers take cover among the ruins of the mission as two Comanches approach. The soldiers capture them, and one of the Indians admits that the rest of the Comanches under Black Cloud are on their way to the mission to find water. Seeing a way to stop Black Cloud for good, the sergeant suggests that they send a messenger to the fort for troops, while they stall Black Cloud at the mission. Starbuck considers this plan suicidal, but the group nonetheless votes to attempt it. Because of his small size, Little Knife is given a horse and sent to Fort Macklin. When the Indians arrive, there are so many of them that Trainor is forced to light the dynamite the men have placed around the mission. The explosions are forceful enough to drive the attackers off, but trooper Martinez is killed. Little Knife, meanwhile, rides until his horse drops and then continues the journey on foot. At the mission, Black Cloud meets Trainor under a flag of truce, but because the chief will not surrender his guns, the sergeant refuses to give the Indians the many gallons of water he claims they have stocked at the mission. During another battle that night, Ruppert, who has done little else but complain, sacrifices his life to save Satterlee. The next day, O'Rattigan, dressed in his finest clothes, again tries to offer Black Cloud water in exchange for Comanche guns. Black Cloud rejects the offer, and O'Rattigan is shot in the back as he returns to the mission. Meanwhile, Little Knife, having long since run out of water, crawls slowly across the sand. The next night, as Julia watches over the wounded O'Rattigan, Starbuck sees a bill of sale in Kinnaird's gear and realizes that he is the gunrunner. Kinnaird runs from the mission, but Starbuck pursues and shoots him. The Comanches shoot Starbuck, and later, Rusty is killed while again trying to comfort Billy. Stunned, Billy pours the last of the water into the dead man's mouth, and just then, Black Cloud launches another attack. This time the Indians penetrate the mission, but as they begin to jump through windows and over walls, Maj. Lanning and his troops arrive from the fort. The cavalry finally defeats Black Cloud, after which Billy, Satterlee, Trainor, O'Rattigan, Julia and Little Knife are honored and thanked by the commander. Trainor declares that those who died gave their lives for something worthwhile. *Battles. Comanche Indians. Deserts. Missions. Thirst. Tribal chiefs. United States. Army. Cavalry. Children. Courage. Fear. Gunrunners. Indians of North America. Loyalty. Massacres. Military discipline. Renegades. Rescues. Self-sacrifice. Soldiers. Stagecoach drivers. Stagecoaches. United States–Southwest. Water. Wells.*

Note: The film's working titles were *Trails Westward* and *The Sabre and the Arrow*. Although the picture depicts the final surrender of the Comanches as a violent affair occurring in 1876, the actual surrender was peaceful and took place on 2 Jun 1875. The last of the Comanches, led by Quanah Parker, came into Fort Sill in Oklahoma under a flag of truce and thereafter lived on the reservation. According to contemporary sources, the film was shot on location near Yuma, AZ. Modern sources note that *Last of the Comanches* was loosely based on the 1943 Columbia film *Sahara*, a World War II drama directed by Zoltan Korda and starring Humphrey Bogart. Lloyd Bridges, who plays "Jim Starbuck" in *Last of the Comanches*, also appeared in *Sahara*.

Box 27 Dec 1952. *DV* 17 Mar 1952. *DV* 24 Dec 1952, p. 4. *Exb* 31 Dec 1952, p. 3437. *FD* 30 Dec 1952, p. 6. *Har* 3 Jan 1953, p. 2. *HR* 24 Dec 1952, p. 4. *MPHPD* 3 Jan 1953, p. 1669. *Var* 24 Dec 1952, p. 14.

LAST OF THE DUANES (*foreign version*) *see* **EL ÚLTIMO DE LOS VARGAS**

THE LAST OF THE MAFIA (Italian Americans)

Neutral Film Co. *Dist* State Rights. Mar **1915** [©David Krakauer; 24 Feb 1915; LU4520]. Si; b&w. 5 reels.

Dir Sidney M. Goldin. *Scen* Sidney M. Goldin.

Cast: Jack Clark, Catherine Lee, William Conrad.

Crime, Drama. The famous Italian detective Guila Ferrati is sent by the Italian government to trail members of the Mafia who have landed in America. After these two resume their criminal activities in New York, a bootblack named Tony overhears the Chief Inspector of the police talking to Ferrati. Tony goes to the Mafia's den and reports that Ferrati is in town. After Ferrati visits a saloon frequented by the Mafia, he is lured to a secluded house and killed. Meanwhile, Aramatti Lattori, a wealthy Italian merchant, receives letters from the Black Hand threatening the kidnapping of his child unless he delivers a large sum of money to them. The subsequent kidnapping climaxes into a series of incidents, including the throwing of a bomb, which sets the city in an uproar. Then, through clever ruses and daring exploits, Detective Lieutenant Cavanaugh, of Italian parentage, rescues the child and rounds up the gang, and the two Mafia members are delivered to representatives of the Italian government for extradition. *Detectives. Kidnapping. Mafia. New York City. Bombs. Bootblacks. Italians. Merchants. Murder. Ransom. Rescues.*

Note: This was the first film of the Neutral Film Co.

Motog 27 Mar 1915, p. 510. *MPW* 20 Mar 1915, p. 1784.

THE LAST OF THE MOHICANS (Native Americans, Delaware, Huron, Mohegan)

Maurice Tourneur Productions, Inc. *Dist* Associated Producers, Inc. 21 Nov **1920** [©Maurice Tourneur; 16 Nov 1920; LP15837]. Si; b&w. 6 reels.

Pres Maurice Tourneur. *Dir* Maurice Tourneur and Clarence L. Brown. *Scen* Robert A. Dillon. *Cam* Philip R. Dubois and Charles Van Enger. *Art dir* Floyd Mueller. *Mus accompaniment comp* Arthur Kay.

Source: Based on the novel *The Last of the Mohicans* by James Fenimore Cooper (Boston, 1826).

Cast: Wallace Beery (*Magua*), Barbara Bedford (*Cora Munro*), Albert Roscoe (*Uncas*), Lillian Hall (*Alice Munro*), Henry Woodward (*Major Heyward*), James Gordon (*Colonel Munro*), George Hackathorne (*Captain Randolph*), Nelson McDowell (*David Gamut*), Harry Lorraine (*Hawkeye*), Theodore Lerch (*Chingachgook*), Jack F. McDonald (*Tamenund*), Sydney Deane (*General Webb*), Joseph Singleton.

Historical, Drama. During the French and Indian War, Cora Munro and her younger sister Alice are on their way to Fort Henry, unaware that the fort, under the command of their father Colonel Munro, is besieged by Indians in league with the French. Leading the girls is Magua, a heinous Indian who has been cast out from the Huron tribe. En route, they meet Uncas, Chingachgook and the scout Hawkeye. Realizing Magua's identity, Hawkeye attempts to capture him, but the scoundrel eludes him. Next morning, the group is captured, but Uncas, Chingachgook and Hawkeye escape and rescue their party. Just as they approach the fort, Colonel Munro is forced to surrender with the agreement that the women and children be spared. Meanwhile, the Hurons, incited by Magua, attack the fort and a terrible massacre ensues. Magua takes Cora and Alice prisoner in the Delaware Indian camp. Soon after, Uncas arrives and reveals himself to be the "last of the Mohicans" and therefore a royal member of the Delawares. Attempting to accommodate royalty, a compromise is reached among the Indians: Cora is to go with Magua and Alice is to be freed. Later, Magua murders both Cora and Uncas but is felled by a bullet from Hawkeye. The Delawares then lament the passing of the Last of the Mohicans. *Frontier and pioneer life. Huron Indians. Massacres. Mohegan Indians. Royalty. Scouts (Frontier). Sieges. United States–History–French and Indian War, 1755-1763. Delaware Indians. French. Parentage. Sisters.*

Note: This was Tourneur's first film for Associated Producers. Clarence Brown, Tourneur's assistant, took over direction when Tourneur was injured during shooting. According to modern sources, Boris Karloff had a small role in this film as a marauding Indian. A pre-production news item states that Omar Whitehead was to play the role of Hawkeye. For information on the many other film adaptations of Cooper's novel, see entry below for the 1936 United Artists production of *The Last of the Mohicans*.

MPN 4 Sep 1920, p. 1915. *MPN* 16 Oct 1920, p. 3038. *MPN* 23 Oct 1920, p. 3238. *MPN* 30 Oct 1920, p. 430. *MPN* 27 Nov 1920, p. 4124. *MPN* 4 Dec 1920, p. 4343. *MPW* 4 Dec 1920, p. 589. *MPW* 11 Dec 1920, p. 771. *NYMT* 28 Nov 1920. *Wid's* 28 Nov 1920, p. 2.

THE LAST OF THE MOHICANS (Native Americans, Mohegan)

Reliance Productions of California; An Edward Small Production. *Dist* United Artists Corp. 4 Sep **1936**; World premiere at Saratoga Springs (NY): 13 Aug 1936; New York premiere: 19 Aug 1936; Prod: began early May 1936 at RKO Pathé Studios [©Reliance Production of California; 18 Aug 1936; LP6529]. Sd; b&w. 10 reels. 91 min. PCA cert no. 2345.

Pres HARRY M. GOETZ. [*Supv* Ken Goldsmith]. *Dir* George B. Seitz. *Assoc dir* Wallace Fox. *Asst dir* Clem Beauchamp. *Scr* Philip Dunne. *Adpt* John L. Balderston, Paul Perez and Daniel Moore. *Photog* Robert Planck. [*Dir of photog and spec eff cam* Paul Eagler]. [*2nd unit cam* Edward Snyder]. *Art dir* John Ducasse Schulze. *Film ed* Jack Dennis and Harry Marker. *Gowns* Franc Smith. [*Cost supplied by* Western Costume Company]. *Mus dir* Roy Webb. *Rec* John L. Cass. [*Prod mgr* Emile de Ruelle]. *Research dir* Edward P. Lambert. [*Prod processed by* Consolidated Film Industries, Inc.]. [*"Whoops" stand-in for Phillip Reed* Harvey Shepard].

Source: Based on the novel *The Last of the Mohicans* by James Fenimore Cooper (Boston, 1826).

Cast: Randolph Scott (*Hawkeye*), Binnie Barnes (*Alice [Munro]*), Henry Wilcoxon (*Major [Duncan] Hayward*), Bruce Cabot (*Magua*), Heather Angel (*Cora [Munro]*), Phillip Reed (*Uncas*), Robert Barrat (*Chingachgook*), Hugh Buckler (*Colonel Munro*), Willard Robertson (*Captain Winthrop*), William Stack (*General Montcalm*), Lumsden Hare (*General Abercrombie*), Frank McGlynn, Sr. ([*David*] *Gamut*), Will Stanton (*Jenkins*), William V. Mong (*Sacham*), Art Du Puis (*DeLevis*), Ian MacLaren (*William Pitt*), Reginald Barlow (*Duke of Newcastle*), Olaf Hytton (*King George II*), Lionel Belmore (*Patroon*), Claude King (*Duke of Marlborough*).

Historical, Adventure, Drama. [*Print viewed*]. In 1757, during the French and Indian War, British Colonel Munro and his daughters, Alice and Cora, are stationed at Fort William Henry, New York. Major Duncan Hayward, who is in love with Alice, arrives with orders to march against the French, but Magua, an Indian Army scout who is actually a French spy, sabotages the march and kidnaps Alice, Cora and Duncan. Hawkeye, a skillful Colonial scout who was reared by Mohawks, saves them with the help of Uncas and Chingachgook, the last men of the Mohican tribe. Uncas falls in love with Cora at first sight, while Hawkeye earns Alice's respect. When the group reaches the fort, they discover it is under attack by the French. Uncas is wounded attempting to get through enemy lines, and when some of the Colonialists desert, Hawkeye is unjustly jailed as a traitor. Just as the British reach honorable terms for surrender with the French, Magua leads an Indian attack and Colonel Munro dies nobly in the battle. Alice and Cora are captured by Magua, who wants Cora as his squaw and plans to burn Alice at the stake. Uncas frees Cora, but while being pursued by Magua, he falls from a cliff. Cora leaps after him, joining him in death. At the Indian camp, Hawkeye and Duncan are captured when they try to save Alice, and Magua offers Alice's life in exchange for Hawkeye's. Duncan disguises himself as Hawkeye, but is discovered, and the real Hawkeye is tied to the stake. The army arrives and Hawkeye is freed to face a court-martial, but the charges are dismissed when his true loyalty is disclosed. Hawkeye, now in love with Alice, returns to his duty with new purpose. *Duty. False arrests. Mohegan Indians. Officers (Military). Spies. United States–History–French and Indian War, 1755-1763. Accidental death. Canoes and canoeing. Courts-martial and courts of inquiry. Disguise. English. Falls from heights. Firearms. Fires. Fort William Henry (NY). French. George II, King of England, 1683-1760. Impersonation and imposture. Kidnapping. Loyalty. Miscegenation. William Pitt, the Elder, 1st Earl of Chatham. Romance. Scouts (Frontier). Self-sacrifice. Trappers.*

Note: The title card for the viewed print reads: "Harry M. Goetz Presents an Edward Small Production of James Fenimore Cooper's Classic of Early America." *FD* reported on 12 Aug 1936 that in honor of this film's world premiere at Saratoga Springs, New York, George H. Bull, president of the Saratoga Racing Association, named various races after characters in the film, including Uncas, Hawkeye, the Mohican Handicap, the Chingachgook Handicap and the Magua Handicap. *FD* also reported that the Loew's theater circuit opened the film on 14 Aug 1936. This film was shot at RKO-Pathé Studios as part of RKO's arrangement with United Artists. Location shooting included a principal unit under George Seitz at Sherwood Forest, CA, and a second unit, under the direction of Wallace Fox, in northern California and later at Cedar Lake in Big Bear, CA. According to *HR*, an Eagle Boy Scout was hired to accompany the crew to Sherwood Forest, where he instructed Indian extras on how to start fires with flint and steel. *HR* also states that actor Phillip

Reed persuaded Harry Goetz to allow Harvey Shepard to act as his "whoops" stand-in after being advised by his vocal instructor that the raucous war whoops were injuring his voice.

A *HR* ad for this film credits Paul Eagler, not Robert Planck, as both director of photography and special effects cameraman, and lists Roy Webb, who is credited on the film as music director, with the musical score. Copyright records list Nathaniel Shilkret as music director. Both of these men were musical directors at RKO at the time of this production. Ken Goldsmith was on leave from Republic at the time of this production, while George Seitz was under contract to M-G-M at the time. Early *HR* production charts list Ralph Block with Philip Dunne as screenwriter, but Block does not appear in later production charts. According to *HR*, Merle Oberon was originally set to star in this film. Juvenile actor David Scott, who was placed under contract to Edward Small in Oct 1935, was also scheduled to appear in this film; however, no information has been found to confirm his appearance in the final film. According to a *LAT* news item on 23 Aug 1935, this film was originally going to be shot in Technicolor. According to an article in *NYT*, Randolph Scott, who was borrowed from Paramount, tried to get out of playing Hawkeye because he believed it improbable that his character would speak the "flowery Cooper dialogue" called for in the script; Scott reportedly balked at the line, "I take my leave when the sun goes down behind yon hill," and finally was allowed to change some of his dialogue. According to *DV*, assistant director Jack Boland sued Reliance, Harry Goetz, Edward Small, Morris Small and research director Ed Lambert for $2,000, which he claimed was due as salary for his directing services following a fifty percent paycut of his $250 weekly salary during production. No other sources verify Boland's work on this production, however, and it is unclear what, if any, contributions he made to the film.

A *NYT* article notes that Lambert relied on the Remington Schuyler painting "Custer's Last Stand," which portrays several scalpings in progressive stages, to make the scalping scenes as authentic as possible. Lambert is quoted as saying, "There is nothing facetious in this matter...the action must necessarily be correct in every detail in order to stave off the hordes of boner-hunters all over the country." Lambert also consulted the descendants of what *NYT* referred to as "this country's outstanding scalpers." According to *FD*, Goetz offered a personal prize of one-hundred dollars for the best exploitation campaign for this film. A news item in *FD* on 25 Aug 1936 states that B. E. Fry of the Loew's Vendome theater in Nashville hired two Western Union boys to carry a six-foot telegram addressed to the mayor, inviting him to the film's opening, through the city's streets to City Hall.

Cooper's novel was also the source of the following productions: the 1920 Maurice Tourneur film of the same title, directed by Tourneur and Clarence L. Brown, and starring Wallace Beery and Barbara Bedford (see above); a 1947 Columbia film entitled *Last of Redmen*, directed by George Sherman and starring Jon Hall (see above); a 1950 United Artists production entitled *The Iroquois Trail*, directed by Phil Karlson and starring George Montgomery and Marian Thorne (see above); an eight-part BBC production aired in 1971, directed by David Maloney and starring Patricia Maynard, Tim Goodman and Kenneth Ives; a 1977 television movie, directed by James L. Conway and starring Steve Forrest and a 1992 Twentieth Century-Fox release, directed by Michael Mann, and starring Daniel Day-Lewis and Madeleine Stowe. The 1992 film was partially based on Philip Dunne's screenplay.

DV 9 May 1936, p. 3. *DV* 8 Aug 1936, p. 3. *FD* 12 Aug 1936, p. 9, 15. *FD* 13 Aug 1936, p. 2. *FD* 25 Aug 1936, p. 6. *HR* 4 Mar 1935, p. 1. *HR* 30 Oct 1935, p. 11. *HR* 7 Mar 1936, p. 2. *HR* 22 Apr 1936, p. 3. *HR* 4 May 1936, p. 25. *HR* 11 May 1936, p. 2. *HR* 12 May 1936, p. 9. *HR* 21 May 1936, p. 2. *HR* 8 Aug 1936, p. 3. *HR* 14 Aug 1936, pp. 5-16. *HR* 28 Sep 1936, p. 4. *MPH* 18 Jul 1936, pp. 16-17. *MPH* 15 Aug 1936, p. 54, pp. 63-64. *NYT* 24 May 1936. *NYT* 3 Sep 1936, p. 17. *NYT* 15 Nov 1936. *Var* 9 Sep 1936, p. 16.

LAST OF THE REDMEN (Native Americans, Iroquois)

Columbia Pictures Corp. *Dist* Columbia Pictures Corp. Aug **1947**; Los Angeles opening: 10 Jul 1947; Prod: 3 Sep—3 Oct 1946 [©Columbia Pictures Corp.; 15 Aug 1947; LP1198]. Sd (Western Electric Recording); col (Cinecolor). 77-78 min. PCA cert no. 11991.

Prod Sam Katzman. *Dir* George Sherman. [*Asst dir* Leonard Shapiro and Mike Eason]. *Scr* Herbert Dalmas and George H. Plympton. *Photog* Ray Fernstrom and Ira H. Morgan. *Art dir* Paul Palmentola. *Film ed* James Sweeney. *Set dec* Sidney Clifford. *Mus dir* Mischa Bakaleinikoff. [*Sd tech* Hugh McDowell]. *Prod mgr* Mel Delay.

Source: Based on the novel *The Last of the Mohicans* by James Fenimore Cooper (Boston, 1826).

Cast: JON HALL (*Major [Duncan] Heywood*), MICHAEL O'SHEA (*Hawk-Eye*), Evelyn Ankers (*Alice Munro*), Julie Bishop (*Cora Munro*), Buster Crabbe (*Magua*), Rick Vallin (*Uncas*), Buzz Henry (*Davy [Munro]*), [Guy Hedlund (*General [Alexander] Munro*)], [Frederick Worlock (*General Webb*)], [Emmett Vogan (*Bob Wheelwright*)].

Historical, Adventure. [*Print viewed*]. In 1757, during the French and Indian War, British forces at Fort William Henry and Fort Edward in New York prepare for an imminent attack by French forces from the north. As the French forces, under the command of General Montcalm, and their Iroquois Indian allies move down from Canada, Magua, an Iroquois Indian scout serving the British, tells General Webb, the British commander at Fort Edward, that he has spotted Iroquois approaching from the south, not the north. Webb, who is expecting the arrival of the two daughters and young son of the commander at Fort Henry, General Alexander Munro, fears that the English visitors may have come under Iroquois attack en route to the fort, and sends troops to find them. Major Duncan Heywood, who is escorting Munro's daughters, Alice and Cora, and their brother Davy, arrive safely at camp a short time later. Hawk-Eye, a white scout, warns Webb that Magua, whom Munro had flogged earlier in the year, is a traitor and that he lied about the position of the attacking forces. Webb, however, refuses to believe that Magua is disloyal, and ignores Hawk-Eye's warning. The following day, Webb sends his men to the south to intercept the French and Indians before they attack, and arranges to have Cora, Alice and Davy sent north to be with their father at Fort Henry. Meanwhile, General Munro tries to warn Webb that the Iroquois are to the north of Fort Edward, but the Indian messenger carrying the warning is killed in an ambush en route to the fort. As Heywood and his charges travel northward, Hawk-Eye and his friend, the Mohican Chief Uncas, find the dead messenger and try to warn Heywood of the danger ahead. After Hawk-Eye wins the trust of Heywood, he is placed in charge of delivering the Munros to safety. Magua eventually reveals his true loyalties when he flees from the group during an Iroquois attack. Heywood chases Magua into a lake, where the two battle each other. When Magua and Heywood reach the shore, Magua's Iroquois compatriots surround Heywood and chase him back into the lake. Heywood swims to an island in the lake while Hawk-Eye wards off the Indians by shooting at them. The travelers rest in a cave on the island, and Hawk-Eye soon realizes that the Iroquois are planning to take Cora and Alice hostage. While guarding the Munros, Heywood is injured in the battle with some Iroquois warriors who have landed on the island, leaving only Hawk-Eye and Uncas to defend the group. Surrounded by Iroquois, Hawk-Eye devises a plan to trap the Iroquois by allowing them to capture Cora, Alice and Davy, and then following them to Magua's village. The scheme goes as planned when Magua abducts the Munros and Heywood, and takes them to his chief. At the Iroquois village, Uncas tells Magua's chief that the Munros are his prisoners, and that Magua stole them from him. When Davy sets off firecrackers to divert the Iroquois' attention, Hawk-Eye effects a daring rescue of Cora and Alice, and they continue their journey to Fort Henry. While crossing a hill, the travelers spot General Munro and his weary soldiers in the distance and race to meet them. Davy, Cora and Alice are reunited with their father, who has lost his fort to the Iroquois, and Magua and his warriors observe the reunion from afar. Sensing an imminent attack by the Iroquois, Hawk-Eye urges the British to circle their wagons and prepare for a gun battle. During the fierce Iroquois attack, Uncas kills Magua in a hand-to-hand battle, and then leads British reinforcements to the site of the battle. The reinforcements arrive in time to rout the Iroquois warriors, but Alice and Uncas are killed in the bloody battle. *Iroquois Indians. Mohegan Indians. Officers (Military). Spies. Traps. United States–History–French and Indian War, 1755-1763. Brothers and sisters. Canoes and Canoeing. Caves. Fort William Henry (NY). Great Britain. Army. Gunfights. Irish. Islands. Kidnapping. Lakes. Rescues. Revenge. Romance. Scouts (Frontier). Trappers.*

Note: The working title for this film was *Last of the Mohicans*. Columbia borrowed actor Jon Hall from Samuel Goldwyn's company. According to *HR* news items, some filming took place at Mount Wilson, CA, and at Ray Corrigan's ranch near Calabasas, CA, and at the Providencia Ranch. For information on other adaptations of James Fenimore Cooper's novel, see entry above for the 1936 United Artists production, *The Last of the Mohicans*.

Box 2 Aug 1947. *DV* 10 Jul 1947. *HR* 21 Jun 1946, p. 2. *HR* 22 Aug 1946, p. 6. *HR* 16 Sep 1946, p. 7. *HR* 24 Sep 1946, p. 14. *HR* 10 Jul 1947, p. 3. *IFJ* 12 Oct 1946, p. 40. *MPHPD* 29 Nov 1947. *NYT* 30 Aug 1947, p. 8. *Var* 16 Jul 1947, p. 20.

THE LAST OUTPOST (Native Americans, Apache)

Paramount Pictures Corp. *Dist* Paramount Pictures Corp. May **1951**; Prod: mid-Oct—mid-Nov 1950 [©Paramount Pictures Corp.; 11 May 1951; LP910]. Sd (Western Electric Recording); col (Technicolor). 10 reels, 8,010 ft. 87-89 min. Passed by the National Board of Review. PCA cert no. 14971.

Prod William H. Pine and William C. Thomas. *Dir* Lewis R. Foster. [*Asst dir* Howard Pine]. *Wrt for the screen by* Geoffrey Homes, George Worthing Yates and Winston Miller. *Suggested by a story by* David Lang. *Dir of photog* Loyal Griggs. *Technicolor col consultant* Robert Brower. *Art dir* Lewis H. Creber. *Film ed* Howard Smith. *Set dec* Alfred Kegerris. *Cost for Miss Fleming* Edith Head. *Ward* Charles Keehne. *Mus score* Lucien Cailliet. *Sd rec* Harold C. Lewis. *Makeup*

artist Errol K. Silvera and Paul Stanhope. *Hair stylist* Kay Shea. [*Prod mgr* Doc Norman]. [*Tech adv* Col. James P. Owens].

Cast: Ronald Reagan [(*Capt. Vance Britton*)], Rhonda Fleming [(*Julie McQuade*)], Bruce Bennett [(*Col. Jeb Britton*)], Bill Williams [(*Sgt. Tucker*)], Noah Beery [(*Sgt. Calhoun*)], Peter Hanson [(*Lt. Crosby*)], Hugh Beaumont [(*Lt. Fenton*)], Lloyd Corrigan [(*Delacourt*)], John Ridgely [(*Sam McQuade*)], [Charles Evans (*Chief Grey Cloud, previously known as Maj. Gen Harrison Page*)], [James Burke (*Gregory*)], [Richard Crane (*Lt. McReady*)], [Ewing Mitchell (*Maj. Thomas Riordan*)], [War Eagle (*Geronimo*)].

Western. [*Print viewed*]. In 1862, Union forces drive the Confederate Army of the Southwest into Texas, a development that renders the Santa Fe Trail a supply line to the Union's "bleeding troops." Hindering the delivery of the supplies, however, is a brash, cigar-smoking rebel captain named Vance Britton, who with his crack troop of Texas dragoons captures most of the Union wagons before they are able to reach Fort Point. Trader Sam McQuade, who supplies the nearby Apache Indians with dangerous guns and bad liquor, is disappointed when Col. Jeb Britton, Vance's brother, who has been assigned to put an end to the Confederate raids, arrives at the fort with only a small detachment of Union soldiers. McQuade believes that the government should enlist the aid of the Apaches in subduing the rebels, but Jeb, who is certain the Indians would indiscriminately kill Confederate soldiers as well as settlers, rejects the idea. That evening, Jeb meets McQuade's wife Julie, who recognizes him as the brother of her ex-fiancée, Vance. Believing that it was Jeb whom his wife loved, Sam tries to humiliate them both, prompting Julie to leave her husband and take up residence in the nearby town of San Gil. Jeb attempts to set a trap for the rebels, but his plan backfires, and he finds that his own brother is leading the plunderers. Vance steals Jeb's horses, boots and supplies, and when the embarrassed colonel returns to the fort, he learns that Sam has persuaded officials in Washington to negotiate with the Apaches. Soon afterward, Sam is attacked by Apaches and killed. Vance finds his body and discovers through a letter in the dead man's pocket that Maj. Thomas Riordan is on his way from Washington to meet with the Apache chiefs. Vance waylays Riordan, dons his uniform, and visits the Apaches himself, along with his men, sergeants Tucker and Calhoun. Vance is surprised to find that Chief Grey Cloud is actually Maj. Gen. Harrison Page, a white man who chose the Indian life in part because he married an Apache and also because of the government, which continually broke promises he himself had made to the Indians. Grey Cloud and three other chiefs decide to stay out of the white man's war, but just then word comes that a group of Apaches led by young Chief Geronimo has been arrested for McQuade's murder. Vance promises to get the Indians released, realizing that failure to do so will lead to battle. In San Gil, Vance, still posing as the Union major, encounters Julie, who angrily refuses to believe that he left her at the start of the Civil War to save her the pain of possible widowhood. He also visits the imprisoned Geronimo, who defends McQuade's murder by claiming that the trader's guns and liquor brought death to his people. Vance tries to discourage Delacourt, a bureaucrat newly arrived from Washington, from arming the Indians. Unsuccessful, he then decides to release the Apaches to appease Grey Cloud and also plots to steal a shipment of Union gold that has just arrived in San Gil. Jeb appears, however, and although he is inclined to let Vance go free, he pulls a gun on him when he learns of Vance's robbery plan. Vance escapes anyway, and after he returns to his troops, they decide to head south, despite Vance's concern for the safety of the woman he still loves. Meanwhile, Grey Cloud accompanies a force of Apaches to San Gil, offering, under a flag of truce, to remain neutral if the Apache prisoners are released. An angry citizen insults and shoots Grey Cloud, and a fierce battle ensues. Vance and his men witness the attack on the town as they ride away, and the young captain orders his men to offer assistance. With the help of the Confederates, San Gil is saved. Julie returns to Baltimore, but promises to reunite with Vance after the war. Jeb then gives Vance a cigar, and after the two brothers shake hands, the Confederate soldiers ride away. *Apache Indians. Battles. Brothers. Impersonation and imposture. United States–History–Civil War, 1861-1865. Cigars. Confederate States of America. Army. Forts. Geronimo. Government officials. Indians of North America. Jealousy. Loyalty. Miscegenation. Mobs. Murder. Officers (Military). Political alliances. Racism. Raids. Reconciliation. Rescues. Revenge. Santa Fe Trail. Separation (Marital). Texas. Tribal chiefs. United States. Army. Cavalry.*

Note: The working title of this film was *The Apache Outpost*. The picture was filmed on location in Tucson, AZ. Although Rhonda Fleming's and John Ridgely's character's surname is listed as "McCloud" in reviews and other sources, they are called "McQuade" in the film. According to a studio publicity item, Arizona governor Dan E. Garvey was cast in the picture as a soldier. His participation in the final film has not been confirmed, however. A modern source includes Iron Eyes Cody in the cast. Although a modern source claims that this film is a remake of a 1935 Paramount film of the same title, the two pictures are not related. Modern sources note that *The Last Outpost* was Ronald Reagan's first full-fledged Western.

Box 14 Apr 1951. *DV* 9 Apr 1951, p. 3. *Exb* 25 Apr 1951, p. 3062. *FD* 17 Apr 1951, p. 6. *Har* 14 Apr 1951, p. 60. *HR* 13 Oct 1950, p. 12. *HR* 10 Nov 1950, p. 12. *HR* 9 Apr 1951, p. 3. *MPHPD* 14 Apr 1951, p. 802. *NYT* 22 Jun 1951, p. 16. *Var* 11 Apr 1951, p. 6.

THE LAST ROUND-UP (Native Americans)

Gene Autry Productions. *Dist* Columbia Pictures Corp. 5 Nov **1947**; Prod: 16 May–7 Jun 1947 [©Gene Autry Productions; 28 Oct 1947; LP1258]. Sd (Western Electric Recording); b&w. 76-77 min. PCA cert no. 12552.

Prod Armand Schaefer. *Dir* John English. [*Asst dir* Earl Bellamy]. *Scr* Jack Townley and Earle Snell. *Story* Jack Townley. *Dir of photog* William Bradford. *Art dir* Harold MacArthur. *Film ed* Aaron Stell. *Set dec* Frank Tuttle. *Mus supv* Paul Mertz. *Mus dir* Mischa Bakaleinikoff. [*Sd tech* Hugh McDowell].

Song(s): "The Last Round-Up," music and lyrics by Billy Hill; "You Can't See the Sun When You're Crying," music and lyrics by Allan Roberts and Doris Fisher; "A Hundred and Sixty Acres," music and lyrics by David Kapp; "An Apple for the Teacher," music by James V. Monaco, lyrics by Johnny Burke; "She'll Be Comin' Round the Mountain," traditional.

Cast: Gene Autry [(*Gene Autry*)], Champion, Jean Heather [(*Carol*)], Ralph Morgan [(*Charlie Mason*)], Carol Thurston [(*Lydia Henry*)], Mark Daniels [(*Matt Mason*)], Bobby Blake [(*Mike*)], Russ Vincent [(*Jeff Henry*)], The Texas Rangers, [George "Shug" Fisher (*Marvin*)], [Trevor Bardette (*Indian chief*)], [Lee Bennett (*Goss*)], [John Halloran (*Taylor*)], [Sandy Sanders (*Jim*)], [Roy Gordon (*Smith*)], [Silverheels Smith (*Sam Luther*)], [Frances Rey (*Cora Luther*)], [Bob Cason (*Carter*)], [William P. Wilkerson (*Indian herder*)], [George Carleton (*Doctor*)], [Don Kay (*Indian boy*)], [Nolan Leary (*Jake*)], [Jack Baxley (*Bill*)], [Ted Adams (*Harris*)], [Steve Clark (*Larry*)], [Edward Peil, Sr. (*Carl*)], [Charles Hamilton (*Harry*)], [Bud Osborne, Frank Marvin, Kernan Cripps (*Ranchers*)], [Jose Alvarado (*Bobby*)], [Arline Archuletta (*Helen*)], [Louis Crosby (*Radio announcer*)], [Virginia Carroll (*Saleslady*)], [Brian O'Hara (*Johnson*)], [Rod Redwing, J. W. Cody, Iron Eyes Cody, Alex Montoya (*Indians*)].

Western, with songs. [*Print viewed*]. When government officials in Mesa City announce plans to build an aqueduct on a river bordering a nearby Indian reservation, some of the Indians on the reservation assemble a war party and threaten an attack. The news of the aqueduct plan also angers cattle rancher Gene Autry, who is a friend of the Indians. In the hopes of averting a war between the ranchers and the Indians, Gene proposes a compromise calling for the Indians to be moved to better land in Cedar Valley, and for the ranchers to relinquish their water rights to the city. A short time later, Gene meets Carol Taylor, a schoolteacher at the Indian school, and falls instantly in love with her. Gene's compromise wins the support of the ranchers, who plan to use the money promised to them by the government to pay their debts to financier Charlie Mason. Charlie and his son Matt, however, are conspiring to force the ranchers further into debt so that they can repossess their land. Gene later engages Matt in a fistfight when Matt falsely accuses Gene of working for the Mesa City aqueduct builders. Carol, too, begins to question Gene's motives, and later urges her father, a rancher, to oppose the deal. To counter the growing Indian opposition to the deal, Gene appears on a local television program and reassures the Indians that they will be given fertile land in Ceder Valley. The television program restores Carol's faith in Gene, and their romance blossoms. A short time later, Charlie tries to sabotage the aqueduct project by staging a fake accident, in which many Indians are injured. By spreading lies about Gene's motives, Charlie's men succeed in destroying the friendship between Gene and Jeff Henry, an influential Indian. When Charlie begins to foreclose on the land he sold to the ranchers, Gene persuades the ranchers to sell their cattle to raise enough money to defend themselves against Charlie's scheme. No sooner do the ranchers head out for the cattle market than they are ambushed by Jeff and some Indian warriors. Jeff is killed in a shootout with Matt, after

which Gene captures Matt and brings him to justice. With the end of the Mason family's control of the ranchers, life on the mesa returns to normal. *Cattlemen. Duplicity. Indians of North America. Ranchers. Water-rights. Aqueducts. Cattle. Debt. False accusations. Fathers and sons. Foreclosure. Funerals. Gunfights. Murder. Romance. Schoolteachers. Stampedes. Television.*

Note: This film marked Gene Autry's initial production under his Gene Autry Productions banner. Modern sources list actors Dale Van Sickle, Blackie Whiteford and Robert Walker in the cast. A May 1947 *HR* news item indicates that some filming took place in Tucson, AZ.

Box 11 Oct 1947. *FD* 6 Oct 1947, p. 8. *HR* 15 May 1947, p. 4. *HR* 3 Oct 1947, p. 3. *IFJ* 24 May 1947, p. 50. *MPHPD* 11 Oct 1947. *Var* 8 Oct 1947, p. 8.

THE LAST SLAVER see SLAVE SHIP

LAST TRAIN FROM GUN HILL (Native Americans)

Paramount Pictures Corp. *Dist* Paramount Pictures Corp. Jul **1959**; Prod: 31 Mar–21 May 1958; addl scenes, 28-29 May 1958 [©Hal B. Wallis & Joseph H. Hazen; 8 Jul 1958; LP13941]. Sd (Westrex Recording System); col (Technicolor); VistaVision. 8,477 ft. 94 min. PCA cert no. 19095.

Prod HAL B. WALLIS. *Assoc prod* Paul Nathan. *Dir* John Sturges. *Asst dir [and 2d unit dir]* D. Michael Moore. *[Asst dir* Danny McCauley]. *[2d asst dir* Lloyd Allen and Ralph Axness]. *Scr* James Poe. *Story* Les Crutchfield. *[Contr to scr constr* Edward Lewis]. *[Contr wrt* Edmund North]. *Dir of photog* Charles Lang, Jr. *[Cam* Wallace Kelley and Paul Uhl]. *[Cam op* Guy Bennett, Frank Dugas and Kyme Meade]. *[1st asst cam* Jim Hawley and James Grant]. *[Gaffer* Pat Drew]. *[Cam asst* Ed Wahrman]. *[Cam loader* Terry Meade]. *[Stills* Bud Fraker and Malcolm Bulloch]. *Spec photog eff* John P. Fulton. *Process photog* Farciot Edouart. *Technicolor color consultant* Richard Mueller. *Art dir* Hal Pereira and Walter Tyler. *Ed supv* Warren Low. *Set dec* Sam Comer and Ray Moyer. *Cost* Edith Head. *[Ladies' cost* Grace Harris]. *[Men's cost* John Anderson]. *[Ward* Bud Clark]. *Mus comp and cond* Dimitri Tiomkin. *Sd rec* Harold Lewis, Winston Leverett and [R. D. Cook]. *[Sd boom man* Bud Parman]. *[Sd cableman* N. Gerolimates]. *Makeup supv* Wally Westmore. *[Makeup* Frank Westmore and Harry Ray]. *Hair style supv* Nellie Manley. *[Hair* Hedy Mjorud]. *Prod in association with* Bryna Productions, Inc. *[Asst to prod* Jack Saper]. *[Prod mgr* Frank Caffey]. *[Asst prod mgr* Curtis Mick]. *[Unit prod mgr* Richard Blaydon]. *[Casting dir* Eddie Morse]. *[Casting* William Cowitt]. *[Outer casting* Bill Greenwald]. *[Casting dir secretary* Alice Moriarty]. *[Scr supv* Marvin Waldon]. *[Constr* Gene Lauritzen]. *[Transportation* Al Latta and L. D. McKnight]. *[Co. grip* Ed Crowder]. *[Mike grip* Hayden Hohstadt]. *[Best boy* Warren Hoag]. *[Grip* William Collins, Archie Gardner, Cecil Gardner, D. Seminero, Herb Welts and Rollie Lilly]. *[Elec* Joe Schuster, Thomas "Pep" Lee, Loren Netten and Dave Perry]. *[Wrangler* Bob Miles]. *[Livestock* Bill Hurley]. *[1st propman* Robert McCrellis]. *[2d propman* Dwight Thompson]. *[Prop shop* Cline Jones and R. Birkmeyer]. *[Cam mechanic* Howard Cashion]. *[Generator op* Walter Sullivan]. *[Staff shop* Manuel Vasquez]. *[Staff* Pedro Regaldo]. *[Loc auditor* Bill Gray]. *[Publicity* Art Sarno]. *[Craft serviceman* Dick Rabis]. *[Standby painter* Dee Turner]. *[Double for Ziva Rodann* Polly Burson]. *[Double for Earl Holliman* Jerry Gatlin]. *[Double for Brian Hutton* Erwin Neal]. *[Double for Lars Henderson, Jr.* Ann Duncan].

Cast: KIRK DOUGLAS [(*Matt Morgan*)], ANTHONY QUINN [(*Craig Belden*)], Carolyn Jones [(*Linda*)], Earl Holliman [(*Rick Belden*)], Brad Dexter [(*Beero*)], Brian Hutton [(*Lee Smithers*)], Ziva Rodann [(*Catherine Morgan*)], Bing Russell [(*Skag*)], Val Avery [(*Bartender*)], Walter Sande [(*Sheriff Bartlett*)], [Lars Henderson, Jr. (*Petey*)], [Henry Wills (*Jake*)], John R. Anderson (*Salesman at Horseshoe bar*)], [William Newell (*Hotel clerk*)], [Len Hendry (*Craig's man in lobby*)], [Dabbs Greer (*Andy*)], [Mara Lynn (*Minnie*)], [Raymond A. McWalters (*Wounded gunman, Craig's man*)], [Eric Alden, Carl H. Saxe, Frank Hagney (*Craig's men*)], [Dante Charles Stradella, Michael Bachus (*Townsmen*)], [Kym Lesli, Vera Denham (*Townswomen*)], [Sid Tomack (*Roomer*)], [Charles Stevens (*Keno*)], [Julius Tannen (*Cleaning man*)], [Ken Becker, Courtland Shepard, Ty Hardin (*Cowboys*)], [Frank Carter (*Cowboy on train*)], [Glenn Strange (*Bouncer*)], [Jack Lomas (*Charlie*)], [Tony Russo (*Pinto*)], [Rickey Kelman, Alan Roberts, Rusty Havens, Robin L. Warga (*Boys*)], [Walter "Tony" Merrill, Bob Scott (*Conductors*)], [Dick Haynes, Hank Mann (*Storekeepers*)], [Mike Maloney (*Drummer on train*)], [Harriette Tarler (*Townswoman, B-girl*)], [Fred Coby (*Luke*)], [William Benedict], [Baron Lichter], [P. Bradley].

Western. [*Print viewed*]. While traveling home to Pawlee by cart with her nine-year-old son Petey, after visiting her parents on their reservation, a young Indian woman is raped by two drunken white youths. Petey escapes on one of their horses and rides to his father, Marshal Matt Morgan, who returns to the crime scene to find his wife dead. After recognizing the saddle on the horse Petey rode as belonging to Craig Belden, a former close friend from his outlaw days who once saved his life, Matt discourages his wife's father from coming with him, as the old man wants to kill the perpetrator slowly, "the Indian way." Matt boards a train for Gun Hill, where Craig has become a cattle baron and major power. Meanwhile, Rick Belden, Craig's only son, who was one of the attackers, tells his autocratic father that his horse was stolen while he and his pal Lee were in a Pawlee saloon. Craig orders his son to bring back the saddle. Craig then greets his old friend Matt and offers to help find his wife's killer, but when Matt reveals that Petey saw his mother strike one of her attackers with her whip across his face, Craig realizes that the killers are Rick and Lee, as Rick returned with his face badly cut. From Craig's reaction, Matt realizes Rick is guilty, and when he vows to bring him to justice, Craig orders Matt to leave town by the next train. Matt says he'll leave by the last train that night, but that he'll have two prisoners with him. Craig interrogates his son, who says that the woman was nobody—"just an Indian squaw"—and quotes his father as saying there's nothing prettier than a Cherokee squaw. Outraged by his son, Craig informs him that the woman was Matt's wife. After the local law officers refuse to help, Matt surprises Rick in the hallway of a bordello and knocks him out, then, with gun drawn, carries him to his hotel room. Craig's men surround the hotel and snipers fire through the window, but Matt moves the bed, to which Rick is handcuffed, near the window to stop the shooting. When Craig's mistress Linda, whom Matt met on the train to Gun Hill, comes to Matt's room to get him to let the boy go, Matt asks her to bring him a shotgun. That night, Lee tells Linda what occurred, and when he makes bigoted remarks about the dead woman, she throws her drink in his face. Rick arouses Matt's ire by saying that it isn't his fault Matt married "some damn squaw." Matt vows that Rick will die slowly, not the Indian way suggested by his father-in-law, but the white man's way—after a trial and a hanging, which he describes in gruesome detail. Craig comes to the room to talk, but two of his men follow and Matt kills them, then tells Craig they are even, as he refrained from killing him also because Craig once saved his life. Linda then smuggles a shotgun to Matt, and after one of Craig's men sets fire to the back of the hotel, Matt, with the shotgun planted under Rick's chin, walks to the train, threatening to blow Rick's head off. At the station, Lee shoots at Matt and hits Rick, killing him, before Matt shoots and kills Lee. Craig, broken by his son's death, challenges Matt, who demands Craig draw first, and Matt kills him in their gunfight. He then boards the train and exchanges a glance with Linda as he returns home. *Fathers and sons. Indians of North America. Murder. Racism. Rape. Revenge. United States. Marshals. Arson. Brothels. Cattlemen. Hotels. Mistresses. Shootouts.*

Note: The working titles of this film were *Last Train from Harper's Junction, Last Train from Laredo, One Angry Day* and *Showdown at Gun Hill*. The original motion picture story by Les Crutchfield, a television writer, was entitled "Showdown." According to a *DV* news item, it was purchased by Hal Wallis in Mar 1954 as a possible starring vehicle for Burt Lancaster or Charlton Heston. Studio publicity noted that the film was patterned in some ways after *Gunfight at the O.K. Corral*, a 1957 Western, which also was produced by Wallis, directed by John Sturges, shot by Charles Lang, Jr. and starred Kirk Douglas. One week of location shooting was done near Tucson, AZ. The town was created on the Paramount backlot, and additional shooting was done at the Monogram Ranch. According to publicity, actress Ziva Rodann, who played the Indian woman who is attacked, was an Israeli actress and ex-soldier, whom Wallis saw on the "Groucho" television show on which she appeared while vacationing in the U.S. Bing Russell was a former professional basketball player. Ty Hardin, who played a bit role as a cowboy, had become a television star in the series *Cheyenne* and *Bronco* by the time this film was released. A title song was written by Dimitri Tiomkin and Paul Webster, and sung by Kitty White, but it was ultimately dropped from the film. *Var* praised the cinematography of Charles Lang, Jr. commenting, "Lang has one technique, opening on a background with a medium shot and then pulling back to bring in the scene's central character, that seems fresh and effective. Lang also employs an unusual number of very long shots in his sun-baked exteriors, with the human figures barely discernible black miniatures on the raw, yellow landscape. None of this is conspicuously 'arty,' but acts as an imperceptible aid in heightening tension and involvement." *HR* speculated concerning Anthony Quinn's portrayal of "Craig Belden", "Though it never is stated, there are many subtle touches that make one believe he, himself, may have Indian blood in his veins." The film was reissued by Paramount in 1963.

AmCin Sep 1959, pp. 544-45, 560, 562. *Box* 27 Apr 1959. *Cue* 1 Aug 1959. *DV* 25 Mar 1954. *DV* 7 Jun 1956. *DV* 15 Apr 1959, p. 3. *Exb* 22 Apr 1959, p. 4578. *FD* 16 Apr 1959, p. 11. *Har* 18 Apr 1959, p. 62. *HCN* 16 Jul 1959. *HR* 25 Mar 1958. *HR* 15 Apr 1959, p. 3. *LAEx* 16 Jul 1959. *LAEx* 16 Jul 1959. *LAT* 16 Jul 1959. *MPHPD* 24 Apr 1959, p. 237. *Newsweek* 3 Aug 1959. *New Yorker* 8 Aug 1959. *NYT* 30 Jul 1959, p. 31. *NYT Magazine* 10 May 1959. *Time* 10 Aug 1959. *Var* 15 Apr 1959, p. 6.

THE LAST VOYAGE (African Americans)

Andrew L. Stone, Inc.; An Andrew & Virginia Stone Production. *Dist* Loew's Inc. Feb **1960**; Los Angeles opening: 24 Feb 1960; Prod: mid-May—late Jun 1959 [©Loew's Inc. & Andrew L. Stone, Inc.; 18 Jan 1960; LP15352]. Sd (Ryder Sound Services, Inc.); col (Metrocolor). 10 reels, 8,195 or 8,210 ft. 91 min. Passed by the National Board of Review. PCA cert no. 19361.

Dir Andrew L. Stone. *Asst dir* Harrold A. Weinberger. *Wrt* Andrew L. Stone. [*Photog* Hal Mohr]. *Spec eff* A. J. Lohman and [Robert Bonning]. *Film ed* Virginia L. Stone. *Mus arr and cond* Rudy Schrager. *Sd mix* Philip N. Mitchell. *Prod mgr* Harrold A. Weinberger. [*Tech adv* Cmdr. Francis Douglas Fain, USN (Ret.)].

Cast: Robert Stack [(*Cliff Henderson*)], Dorothy Malone [(*Laurie Henderson*)], George Sanders [(*Capt. Robert Adams*)], Edmond O'Brien [(*Second Engineer Walsh*)], Woody Strode [(*Hank Lawson*)], Jack Kruschen [(*Chief Engineer Pringle*)], Joel Marston [(*Third Officer Ragland*)], George Furness [(*First Officer Osborne*)], Richard Norris [(*Third Engineer Cole*)], Andrew Hughes [(*Radio operator*)], Marshall Kent [(*Quartermaster*)], Robert Martin [(*Second Mate Mace*)], Bill Wilson [(*Youth*)], and introducing Tammy Marihugh (*Jill [Henderson]*), [Esther Maloney (*Passenger*)].

Disaster, **Drama**. [*Print viewed*]. During one of her last scheduled crossings, a fire breaks out in the boiler room of the huge old luxury liner, the *Claridon*. The fire soon spreads to a dining room, but although some of the officers want to alert the passengers to the potential danger of the situation, Capt. Robert Adams insists that they act as though nothing has happened. Meanwhile, Cliff and Laurie Henderson and their young daughter Jill are enjoying their first ocean voyage, a trip occasioned by Cliff's job transfer to Tokyo. The fire is put out, but the next day, crew members notice that boiler pressure has greatly increased and that because of the fire, several safety valves have been fused shut. Chief Engineer Pringle orders the crew members out of the boiler room, knowing that if he is unable to release the safety valves, the resulting explosion will lead to his death. As he strains to pry open a valve, a huge explosion rips through the boiler room and many of the decks situated above it, killing Pringle and several passengers. Laurie is pinned beneath a fallen steel beam that Cliff is unable to move, and little Jill finds herself trapped on the far side of their cabin. While trying to rescue her, Cliff nearly falls through the gaping hole in the cabin floor. On the bridge, the captain ignores the warnings of First Officer Osborne and decides that as long as the bulkhead holds, the passengers are in no danger. Cliff eventually rescues his terrified daughter, and as the captain finally sends out an S.O.S., he leaves his trapped wife to find help. Cliff tries to locate an acetylene torch with which he may free his wife, but the crew members are too occupied with the task of shoring up the bulkhead to be of any help. Eventually Cliff encounters Hank Lawson, a black member of the boiler room crew. Hank agrees to help Cliff, but they are unable to locate an acetylene torch. The bulkhead finally blows apart, and a number of Engineer Walsh's men are killed. Laurie tries to convince Cliff to take Jill and get off the ship, but although he agrees to put the child on a lifeboat, he insists on remaining by his wife's side. When Laurie learns that the ship is being abandoned, she asks Hank to help her commit suicide, but he refuses. Hank finally puts Jill, who is screaming wildly for her mother, on a lifeboat, asking the passengers to send a torch back after the approaching Hawaiian fishing boat picks them up. Capt. Adams orders Walsh to help Cliff, but the engineer, whose father died on the *Titanic*, decides to save his trapped men instead. Walsh accuses the captain of sacrificing lives in order to secure his own promotion, because he knows that if the ship had reached its destination intact, the captain would have been proclaimed a hero. This accusation breaks the captain, and he retreats to his office, where he is killed by a falling smokestack. As water fills Laurie's cabin, the lifeboat returns with the acetylene torch, and Hank, Walsh and Cliff begin to cut through the metal that has pinned her to the floor. She is freed just as the water covers her head. All of them reach the upper deck just as the ship is slipping under. After climbing into the lifeboat, Cliff extends his hand to Hank, declaring, "This is one guy I'm going to help aboard personally!" *Disasters*.

Heroism. Ocean liners. Rescues. Ship crews. Shipwrecks. African Americans. Attempted suicide. Drowning. Explosions. Family relationships. Fear. Fires. Lifeboats. Panic. Sea captains.

Note: Andrew L. Stone's onscreen credit reads: "Written and Directed by Andrew L. Stone." Harrold A. Weinberger's onscreen credit reads: "Assistant Director & Production Manager...Harrold A. Weinberger." According to a Jan 1959 *DV* item, the film was originally to have been shot in CinemaScope, off the coast of England. Reviews and news items note that the film was photographed almost entirely in the Sea of Japan, off Osaka, using the retired French luxury liner *Il de France*. Fearing negative publicity, the French company that built the liner initially attempted to block Stone's purchase of the ship, but finally acquiesced when M-G-M agreed to change the name of the vessel and not publicize the sale. During filming, Stone blew up the interior of the ship piece by piece, flooded parts of it and toppled one smokestack. The *Var* review noted that in addition to the real setting, natural sound and natural lighting were used in the picture. According to a Jan 1960 *HR* news item, the crew was forced to shoot the final lifeboat scene in Santa Monica, CA, because there were too many poisonous jellyfish in the Sea of Japan. The same item claimed that part of the film's story was based on the real-life experiences of a woman passenger on the ill-fated ocean liner *Andrea Doria*. Tammy Marihugh, a regular on the television program *The Bob Cummings Show*, made her screen acting debut in the film. *The Last Voyage* marked the third pairing of stars Dorothy Malone and Robert Stack. [Their previous pictures were *Written on the Wind* and *Tarnished Angels*.] Malone's mother, Esther Maloney, appears in the picture as a boat passenger, according to studio publicity material.

AmCin Jun 1959, p. 338. *Box* 25 Jan 1960. *DV* 14 Jan 1959. *DV* 28 Apr 1959. *DV* 16 Jul 1959. *DV* 20 Jan 1960, p. 3. *Exb* 20 Jan 1960, p. 4669. *FD* 22 Jan 1960, p. 6. *Har* 23 Jan 1960, pp. 14-15. *HR* 20 Jan 1960, p. 3. *MPHPD* 23 Jan 1960, p. 564. *NYT* 28 Jun 1959. *NYT* 20 Feb 1960, p. 14. *Time* 15 Jun 1959. *Var* 20 Jan 1960, p. 6.

THE LAST WAGON (Native Americans, Apache, Comanche)

Twentieth Century-Fox Film Corp. *Dist* Twentieth Century-Fox Film Corp. Sep **1956**; Prod: mid-Apr—early Jun 1956 [©Twentieth Century-Fox Film Corp.; 28 Aug 1956; LP7346]. Sd (Westrex Recording System); col (Deluxe); CinemaScope; Lenses by Bausch & Lomb. 98-99 min. PCA cert no. 18072.

Prod William B. Hawks. *Dir* Delmer Daves. *Asst dir* Joseph E. Rickards. *Scr* James Edward Grant, Delmer Daves and Gwen Bagni Gielgud. *Story* Gwen Bagni Gielgud. *Dir of photog* Wilfrid Cline. *Spec photog eff* Ray Kellogg. *Col consultant* Leonard Doss. *Art dir* Lyle R. Wheeler and Lewis H. Creber. *Film ed* Hugh S. Fowler. *Set dec* Walter M. Scott and Chester Bayhi. *Exec ward des* Charles LeMaire. *Cost des* Mary Wills. *Mus* Lionel Newman. *Orch* Edward B. Powell. *Sd* Bernard Freericks, Harry M. Leonard and [William Buffinger]. *Makeup* Ben Nye. *Hair styles* Helen Turpin.

Cast: RICHARD WIDMARK [(*Comanche Todd*)], Felicia Farr [(*Jenny*)], Susan Kohner [(*Jolie*)], Tommy Rettig [(*Billy*)], Stephanie Griffin [(*Valinda*)], Ray Stricklyn [(*Clint*)], Nick Adams [(*Ridge*)], Carl Benton Reid [(*General Howard*)], Douglas Kennedy [(*Col. William Normand*)], George Matthews [(*Sheriff Bull Harper*)], James Drury [(*Lt. Kelly*)], Ken Clark [(*Sergeant*)], [Tim Carey (*Cole Harper*)], [George Ross (*Sarge*)], [Juney Ellis (*Mrs. Clinton*)], [Abel Fernandez (*Apache Medicine Man*)], [Cleis Coburn].

Western. [*Print viewed*]. Comanche Todd, a white man reared by Comanche Indians, is captured by Sheriff Bull Harper, who has accused Todd of murdering three of his brothers. As the sheriff drags Todd along by a rope, they encounter a wagon train of teenagers and children, led by Col. William Normand of the Union Army. The wagon train is on its way to Tucson through the dangerous Canyon de la Muerte, and Harper warns Normand about the imminent danger posed by the Apache Indians. Harper decides to ride along with the train, and, as the group rests for mealtime, he ties Todd to a wagon wheel. Although the sheriff has refused to allow his prisoner to eat or drink, Billy, a young boy traveling to Tucson with his sister Jenny, brings the nearly starving Todd a plate of food anyway. When Harper shoots at Billy, Normand intervenes, telling the sheriff that they are Christian people, and demanding that he untie and feed the prisoner. Later, when another teenager gives Todd a puff of his tobacco pipe, the sheriff almost shoots the young man, but Todd manages to throw an ax at Harper's chest, killing him. Normand is furious and warns Todd not to try to escape, as they plan to turn him over to the law. Later that night, one of the teenage boys encourages some of the children to go for a midnight swim, including Normand's two motherless daughters—Jolie, from his first marriage to an Indian woman, and Valinda, the offspring of his second marriage to a white woman. When the group returns, they discover that an Indian ambush has taken place and that their families have been killed. Todd, who had been left on guard by the teens, is the only one found alive, and while Billy and Jenny greatly admire Todd for his bravery, the other half of the

group thinks he is an Indian-loving murderer. Jolie decides, along with Billy and Jenny, to trust Todd, but Valinda loathes the man and believes all Indians to be dirty savages, including her own sister whom she deeply resents. Todd's first order, much to the teenagers' shock, is that they cannot bury their dead relatives, as the graves would signal to the Indians that some of the camp was left alive. That night Todd witnesses the gathering of Apaches, who are planning to retaliate for an attack on them, which left many women and children dead. Todd returns to the camp and says the group must move fast to avoid the warring Indian bands. During the journey, Billy and Todd become fast friends. One day, as Todd teaches Billy how to trap a rabbit, an Indian appears with bow and arrow, but Todd shoots him before he kills the boy. Valinda is then bitten by a rattlesnake, and Todd saves her, despite her bad temper and screaming, which he fears will alert the Indians to their presence. Later, two Apaches appear, and Todd challenges them to hand-to-hand combat, killing them and saving the group from an Indian attack. While recovering from her snakebite, Valinda begins to soften and offers Todd the key to his shackles, which he has worn around his wrists for the entire journey. Todd then hears Indian drums and discovers hundreds of Indians gathered. He tells the group that he will keep watch from a cliff, but at the sound of his signal, they must ride fast to the west. Believing it might be her last night alive, Jenny goes to sleep with Todd, who kisses her and then offers to share his life with her. The next morning, when a group of Cavalry scouts arrive, Todd deduces who the Indians are targeting. When the soldiers ask if they have seen Comanche Todd, the group stands by their new friend and says that Todd is "Mr. Putnam," husband of Jenny and father of Billy. Todd is disappointed to learn that there are only eight Cavalry men, as three hundred Indians have been tracking them and are ready to attack. When the Indians do attack, Todd and the soldiers manage to trick the Indians and make it out alive. During the battle, however, one of the soldiers sees Harper's sheriff's star, which Todd had taken from Harper as a memento. Now aware of Todd's true identity, the Cavalry men take him to Redrock Bluff, where Todd is tried by the Bible-reading General Howard, a Civil War hero and famed Indian fighter. Todd explains that he killed the four men in retaliation for the murder of his wife and sons. Then Jenny gives a speech about how Todd saved them all, and each of the adolescents recounts what Todd did for them. After Howard gives Jenny and Billy custody of Todd, the wagon train moves on to Tucson and the new family, Todd, Jenny and Billy, ride away. *Adolescents. Ambushes. Apache Indians. Arizona. Children. Comanche Indians. Wagon trains. Christianity. False accusations. Half sisters. Indians of North America–Mixed blood. Judges. Justifiable homicide. Officers (Military). Racism. Rattlesnakes. Revenge. Sheriffs. Trials. United States. Army. Cavalry.*

Note: *The Last Wagon* was filmed on location in Sedona, AZ, at the mouth of Oak Creek Canyon. In an article in the *NYT*, director Delmer Daves described the difficulty he had in finding a pristine location for the film, as his previous western, *Broken Arrow*, had popularized the region.

DV 27 Aug 1956. *HR* 24 Oct 1955. *HR* 13 Apr 1956, p. 13. *HR* 1 Jun 1956, p. 10. *HR* 27 Aug 1956. *LAT* 20 Sep 1956. *MPD* 28 Aug 1956. *NYT* 1 Jul 1956. *Var* 29 Aug 1956.

LAUGH YOUR BLUES AWAY *see* **LET'S HAVE FUN**

LAUGHING BILL HYDE (Native Americans)
Rex Beach Pictures; Star Series. *Dist* Goldwyn Distributing Corp. 30 Sep 1918 [©Goldwyn Pictures Corp.; 30 Sep 1918; LP15678]. Si; b&w. 6 reels, 5,790 ft.
Dir Hobart Henley. *Asst dir* Walter Sheridan. *Scen* Willard Mack. *Cam* Arthur Cadwell. *Art dir* Hugo Ballin.
Source: Based on the short story "Laughing Bill Hyde" by Rex Ellingwood Beach in *Laughing Bill Hyde and Other Stories* (New York, 1917).
Cast: Will Rogers (*Laughing Bill Hyde*), Anna Lehr (*Ponotah*), John M. Sainpolis (*Black Jack Burg*), Mabel Ballin (*Alice*), Clarence Oliver (*Dr. Evan Thomas*), Joseph Herbert (*Joseph Wesley Slayforth*), Robert Conville (*Denny Slevin*), Dan Mason (*Danny Dorgan*).
Northwest, Drama. Convict Bill Hyde and his friend, Danny Dorgan, break out of prison, but in running from the guards, Danny is mortally wounded. The local doctor, Evan Thomas, tries so hard to save Danny that later, when Bill and the doctor meet in Alaska, the two become friends. A dying man gives his mine to the doctor, but upon discovering that it is worthless, Bill sells it to a crook named John Wesley Slayforth for $50,000. Slayforth attempts to cheat

Ponotah, a part Indian woman who owns another mine in which he has an interest, and Bill secures employment in the mine in order to investigate. When he learns that the superintendent is systematically stealing gold from the mine, Bill in turn robs him and buries the money near his cabin. Most of the gold he gives to Ponotah, who accepts his marriage proposal, while the $50,000 goes to the doctor, enabling him to return home and wed the girl of his heart. *Alaska. Convicts. Friendship. Gold mines. Indians of North America. Indians of North America–Mixed blood. Physicians. Prison escapes. Fraud. Gold. Mine foremen. Miners. Robbery. Thieves.*

Note: This was Will Rogers' first feature film. It had a pre-release showing in New York in 22 Sep 1918.

ETR 21 Sep 1918, p. 1345. *ETR* 28 Sep 1918, p. 1369. *ETR* 5 Oct 1918, p. 1521. *MPN* 5 Oct 1918, p. 2245. *MPW* 5 Oct 1918, p. 120, 127. *NYDM* 5 Oct 1918, p. 516. *NYT* 23 Sep 1918, p. 7. *Var* 27 Sep 1918, p. 45. *Wid's* 29 Sep 1918, p. 32.

LAUGHING BOY (Native Americans, Navajo, Paiute)
Metro-Goldwyn-Mayer Corp.; controlled by Loew's Inc.; A W. S. Van Dyke Production. *Dist* Loew's Inc. 13 Apr **1934**; Prod: mid-Nov 1933–31 Jan 1934 [©Metro-Goldwyn-Mayer Corp.; 7 Apr 1934; LP4617]. Sd (Western Electric Sound System); b&w. 8 reels. 78-79 min. Passed by the National Board of Review.
Prod Hunt Stromberg. *Dir* W. S. Van Dyke. [*Asst dir* Les Selander]. *Scr* John Colton and John Lee Mahin. *Photog* Lester White. *Art dir* Arnold Gillespie. *Film ed* Blanche Sewell. *Int dec* Edwin B. Willis. *Ward* Dolly Tree. *Mus score* Herbert Stothart. *Rec dir* Douglas Shearer. [*Prod mgr* Bud Barsky].
Source: Based on the novel *Laughing Boy* by Oliver La Farge (Boston, 1929).
Cast: RAMON NOVARRO (*Laughing Boy*), Lupe Velez (*Slim Girl, [also known as Lily]*), William Davidson ([*George*] *Hartshone*), Chief Thunderbird (*Laughing Boy's father*), Catalina Rambula (*Laughing Boy's mother*), Tall Man's Boy (*Wounded Face*), F. A. Armenta (*Yellow Singer*), Deer Spring (*Jesting Squaw's son*), Pellicana (*Red Man*), [Chief Meyers (*Crooked Nose*)], [Sidney Bracy (*White Father*)], [Standing Bear (*Quiet Hunter*)], [Ki Yellowhorse, Night Hawk (*Indian boys*)], [Ferdinand Munier (*Fred*)], [Anita Sheldon (*Yellow Singer's wife*)], [Grace Hayle (*Mabel*)], [Dora Clement (*Mother*)], [Joseph William Cody (*Leader of horsemen*)], [Carol Flores (*Rosie*)], [Julius Bogua (*Jesting Squaw's son*)], [Dennett Dell (*Gossip*)], [Romiere Darling (*Dancing girl*)], [Anna Dupea (*Older wife*)], [Aphed Elk (*Younger wife*)], [Walks Alone, White Flower (*Indian girls*)], [White Dove, Agnes Norcha, Clara Hunt (*Young married women*)], [Winona Nora, Glympia Houten (*Married gossips*)], [William Steele (*Guide*)], [Edward Hearn, Ruth Channing, Carl Stockdale (*Tourists*)], [James Mason (*Cowboy*)], [Tito H. Davison (*Navajo*)], [Katherine Sheldon, Nora Cecil (*Teachers*)], [Frances Gillman (*Dancer*)], [Bill McSwain (*Peanut vendor*)].
Romance, Western. [*Print viewed*]. Newly arrived to the southern section of the Navajo nation, Laughing Boy, an expert silversmith, attends the annual Great Sing Dance at T'si Lani and there meets the beautiful Slim Girl. Reared by whites, the orphan Slim Girl, whose "town" name is Lily, is ostracized by the conservative Navajos and is denounced as a prostitute. Although confused by Slim Girl's overtly seductive behavior, Laughing Boy is nonetheless drawn to her and is goaded by her to compete in a horse race. During the race, for which Laughing Boy has offered his most coveted bracelet as a prize, Red Man, a Pauite, causes Laughing Boy's horse to fall. Laughing Boy loses the race but, determined to win back his bracelet and impress Slim Girl, immediately challenges Red Man to a wrestling match. After Laughing Boy defeats Red Man in the match, he confesses his love to an admiring Slim Girl. Although his strict father refuses to sanction a union with Slim Girl, Laughing Boy leaves with her that night. While camping, Slim Girl seduces the inexperienced Laughing Boy with "moonshine" and flirtation, but finds herself alone the next morning, abandoned by the now-ashamed Navajo. Crushed, Slim Girl returns to her shabby life as mistress to George Hartshone, a brutish but well-to-do rancher. Soon, however, her yearning for Laughing Boy overcomes her, and sensing that he is near, she rides to the hills to find him. Once reunited, the couple marry and join Laughing Boy's family tribe. In spite of her efforts to work and behave like a traditional Navajo wife, Slim Girl is criticized by her in-laws and is labeled as weak and unfit. Overwhelmed with loneliness and rejection, Slim Girl suggests to Laughing Boy that they move to their own hogan and support themselves by trading his silver jewelry for money to buy and raise

goats. Slim Girl then convinces her husband that she must go to town alone to do the trading. Eventually, however, Slim Girl's repeated absences from home drive Laughing Boy to distraction, and during Fourth of July celebrations, he rides to town to find her. After searching the town, Laughing Boy is directed to Slim Girl's house, unaware that she has been staying there with Hartshone. When he finds Slim Girl in Hartshone's arms, Laughing Boy shoots an arrow at his rival but strikes his wife in the chest instead. As she dies in his arms, Slim Girl begs Laughing Boy to forgive her, then promises to wait for him in heaven. *Cultural conflict. Infidelity. Marriage. Navajo Indians. Revenge. Romance. Accidental death. Bracelets. Contests. Drunkenness. Fourth of July. Goat ranchers. Horseracing. In-laws. Liquor. Mistresses. Ostracism. Paiute Indians. Ranchers. Rites and ceremonies. Seduction. Silversmiths. Wrestlers and wrestling.*

Note: According to *Var*, M-G-M purchased the rights to Oliver La Farge's novel from Universal. Onscreen credits refer to the work as "the Pulitzer Prize novel." A Jun 1932 *HR* news item announced that Richard Arlen had tested "in Indian makeup" for the lead in the film. In late Aug 1932, *HR* announced that the production had been postponed because a suitable lead had not been found. Scenes for the film were shot on an Arizona Navajo reservation and near Cameron and Flagstaff, AZ. According to *DV*, director W. S. Van Dyke, production manager Bud Barsky and star Ramon Novarro were made honoray chiefs of the Navajo tribe during filming. A Jun 1933 *HR* article states that Lynn Riggs was assigned to write a screen treatment for this film. This writer's contribution to the production, if any, has not been determined. The *Var* reviewer noted that, because of objections from the New York censor board, parts of the film, including the scene in which "Slim Girl" and "Laughing Boy" camp out together, were deleted for screenings in that state. *Var's* running time for the picture was only 75 minutes.

DV 13 Nov 1933, p. 7. *DV* 2 Dec 1933, p. 3. *DV* 16 Dec 1933, p. 3. *FD* 12 May 1934, p. 4. *HF* 25 Nov 1933, p. 12. *HR* 29 Jun 1932, p. 1. *HR* 22 Aug 1932, p. 3. *HR* 9 Jun 1933, p. 2. *HR* 1 Feb 1934, p. 2. *MPD* 18 May 1934, p. 18. *MPH* 30 Jun 1934, p. 53. *Var* 15 May 1934, p. 14.

LAUGHING GRAVY (*foreign version*) *see* **LOS CALAVERAS**

LAUGHING IRISH EYES (IrishAmericans)

Republic Pictures Corp. *Dist* Republic Pictures Corp. 15 Mar **1936**; Prod: began 18 Jan 1936 [©Republic Pictures Corp.; 4 May 1936; LP6329]. Sd (RCA Victor "High Fidelity" Sound System); b&w. 8 reels, 6,338 ft. 70 or 73 min. Passed by the National Board of Review. PCA cert no. 1981.

[*Prod* Nat Levine]. *Supv* Colbert Clark. *Dir* Joseph Santley. [*Asst dir* Mack Wright]. *Scr* Olive Cooper, Ben Ryan and Stanley Rauh. *Orig story* Sidney Sutherland and Wallace Sullivan. *Photog* Milton Krasner and Reggie Lanning. *Film ed* Murray Seldeen. *Supv ed* Joseph H. Lewis. *Mus supv* Harry Grey. *Sd eng* Terry Kellum.

Song(s): "Bless You, Darlin' Mother," music and lyrics by Sam H. Stept; "All My Life" and "Laughing Irish Eyes," music by Sam H. Stept, lyrics by Sidney Mitchell; "Londonderry Air," Irish folk song.

Cast: Phil Regan [(*Danno O'Keefe*)], Walter C. Kelly [(*Pat Kelly*)], Evalyn Knapp [(*Peggy Kelly*)], Ray Walker [(*Eddie Bell*)], Mary Gordon [(*Mrs. O'Keefe*)], Warren Hymer [(*Tiger O'Keefe*)], Betty Compson [(*Molly*)], J. M. Kerrigan [(*Tim*)], Herman Bing [(*Weisbacher*)], Raymond Hatton [(*Gallagher*)], Clarence Muse [(*Deacon*)], Russell Hicks [(*Silk Taylor*)], Maurice Black [(*Tony Martin*)], John Sheehan [(*Joe Cronin*)], Robert E. Homans [(*Announcer*)], [John Indrisano (*Fight trainer*)], [Ritchie McCarron (*Dynamite O'Reilly*)], [Jimmy O'Gatty (*Killer O'Kearny*)], [Don LaRue (*Kid Campo*)], [Charles Randolph (*Referee*)], [Ray Brown (*Editor*)].

Boxing, Comedy-drama, with songs. [*Print viewed*]. Pat Kelly, a fight promoter and head of the Irish-American Athletic Club, bets his crooked partners, Silk Taylor and Tony Martin, $10,000 and his interest in the club that he can find an Irish boxer who can become a contender to the title within six months. Kelly's reputation has been sullied in part by the radio broadcasts of sports announcer Eddie Bell, who is in love with Pat's daughter Peggy, but nonetheless discredits Pat on the radio. Pat and Peggy go to Dublin, where Pat is to negotiate with trainer Joe Cronin for the contract of middleweight boxer Tiger O'Keefe, who is also a heavyweight drinker. While Pat waits at a tavern for Tiger, Peggy meets singing blacksmith Danno O'Keefe, with whom she goes to the Cork County Fair. She encourages him to enter a singing contest, which he wins, although his prize, a new car, is wrecked soon after when Danno, distracted by kissing Peggy, does not see it roll down a hill. The couple then go back to the tavern where Pat is still waiting. Danno bids Peggy goodbye, but outside the tavern, he bumps into Tiger and they begin to fight. Pat watches as

Danno knocks out Tiger, and Cronin then convinces Danno to pass himself off as Tiger, whom Pat has not yet met, so that he can go to America while Cronin keeps his commission. On board the ship to the United States, Peggy finds out that Pat thinks Danno is Tiger, but Danno promises her that he will fight and not disgrace her father. When they arrive, however, Peggy uses her influence with Eddie to get Danno a singing job on the radio. The same night Danno is to begin his show, however, he is scheduled to fight his first bout, and the distraught Peggy confides in Eddie that Danno is not a professional boxer. Eddie then convinces Silk and Tony that if they arrange for Danno to win a few fights, they can make a mint betting against him later. Silk and Tony bribe Danno's first opponent, Kid Campo, to take a dive, as well as his next one, Battling Winters. Soon Danno is set to fight the contender, K. O. Schultz, and Pat bets Silk more money and his interest in Danno that the Irishman will win in six rounds. Meanwhile, Peggy tells Eddie that she and Danno are to be married directly after the fight. Jealous, Eddie feels that he has been used, so he reveals the secret of Danno's identity over the radio. Danno confronts Eddie, who then tells him that Peggy betrayed him, and Danno tries to leave for Ireland hours before the fight. Peggy locates Danno on the dock, exposes Eddie's duplicity and assures him of her love. Determined to help Pat, Danno enters the ring at Madison Square Garden and, after a fierce struggle, wins the fight. He then retires from boxing, happy with his new radio contract and beautiful Peggy. *Boxers. Boxing managers. Duplicity. Fixed fights. Impersonation and imposture. Irish. Irish Americans. Singers. Americans in foreign countries. Automobiles. Blacksmiths. Contests. Cork County (Ireland). Drunkenness. Dublin (Ireland). Fairs. Fathers and daughters. Gymnasiums. Hotels. Jealousy. Madison Square Garden (New York City). Mistaken identity. Radio broadcasting. Reputation. Romantic rivalry.*

Note: According to *HR* and *FD* news items, this picture was originally to star Guy Robertson. *HR* news items noted that Charles A. Logue and Mary McCarthy were scheduled to work on the screenplay, but their participation in the completed film has not been confirmed. This was the first film Phil Regan, who was a Brooklyn police officer prior to becoming an actor, made for Republic.

Box 21 Mar 1936. *DV* 5 Mar 1936, p. 3. *FD* 21 Oct 1935, p. 10. *FD* 4 Mar 1936, p. 5. *HR* 20 Jul 1935, p. 4. *HR* 14 Nov 1935, p. 3. *HR* 18 Jan 1936, p. 3. *HR* 20 Jan 1936, p. 18. *HR* 5 Mar 1936, p. 3. *MPD* 4 Mar 1936, p. 29. *MPH* 14 Mar 1936, p. 58. *NYT* 4 Apr 1936, p. 11. *Var* 8 Apr 1936, p. 16.

LAUGHING IRISH HEARTS *see* **KNUTE ROCKNE—ALL AMERICAN**

LAUGHTER (*foreign version*) *see* **LO MEJOR ES REÍR**

THE LAUREL-HARDY MURDR CASE (*foreign version*) *see* **NOCHE DE DUENDES**

LAW AND LAWLESS (Latino)

Majestic Pictures Corp. *Dist* Majestic Pictures Corp. 30 Nov **1932**. Sd; b&w. 62 min.

Prod Henry L. Goldstone. *Dir* Armand Schaefer. [*Wrt*] by and dial Oliver Drake. *Photog* Wm. Nobles. *Film ed* Roy S. Luby. *Rec* International Recording Engineers, Ltd. *Sd eng* Earl N. Crane.

Cast: JACK HOXIE [(*Montana*)], Hilda Moreno [(*Rosita Lopez*)], Julian Rivero [(*Pancho Gonzales*)], Yakima Canutt [(*Tex Barnes*)], Jack Mower, Wally Wales [(*Buck Daggett*)], J. Frank Glendon, Edith Fellows [(*Betty Kelly*)], Bob Burns, Helen Gibson [(*Molly*)], Dynamite, the Wonder Horse, [Fred Burns (*Blane*)], [Alma Rayford], [Joe de la Cruz], [Elvira Sanchez], [William Quilan], [Al Taylor], [Dixie Star].

Western. [*Print viewed*]. After the notorious "Wolf" gang burns the Kelly family's cabin, the Kellys give general store proprietor Cash Hopton the claim on their homestead to pay off their debt to him. Meanwhile, wandering gunslinger Montana and his pal, Pancho Gonzales, rescue Don Roberto Lopez and his daughter Rosita when their horses are spooked by the gang, who are chasing one of their members, Brown because they suspect he has leaked information about their activities. Montana and Pancho escort the Lopezes into town, where Roberto deeds one quarter of his land to Cash to pay off his own debts. While Roberto is explaining to Pancho that he is having financial difficulty because rustlers are stealing his cattle, Montana is hired by Buck Daggett, the foreman of the Lazy Y. Pancho tells Montana that he has already hired both of them out to Roberto, after which Montana informs Buck that he cannot work for him. The furious Buck starts a brawl that Montana and Pancho quickly finish. Later, Pancho tries to teach Roberto's Mexican ranch hands how to

shoot, and Roberto informs his ranch manager, Tex Barnes, that Pancho and Montana are there to stop the rustlers. Steve, the foreman, and Montana arrive after inspecting the cattle, and Rosita makes it plain that she does not trust gunfighters, and Montana in particular. Tex goes to the town café, where Molly, the waitress, tells him to expect trouble from Buck, who runs the wolf gang for a mysterious boss. Meanwhile, Pancho tells Rosita, who has confessed that she is interested in Montana after all, that he is a terrible womanizer with six wives. When Montana returns to the ranch, he cannot understand Rosita's coldness to him, but his attempts at romance are interrupted by Roberto's announcement that Brown has been murdered. Fearing that Roberto will be the gang's next target, Montana stands guard that night, but Tex lets the horses loose from the corral to distract Montana while the gang rustles more of the Lopez cattle. Steve fires Montana and Pancho after Tex accuses them of freeing the horses, but Roberto rehires them the next day. That night, Tex murders Steve and pins the blame on Montana. Montana and Pancho are taken to jail, but with the help of Montana's horse, "Dynamite," they break out and force Tex to take them to the gang's meeting place while Rosita gets the sheriff. Montana and Pancho battle the gang until Roberto and the sheriff arrive with their men. Tex reveals that Cash is the secret leader of the gang, and that he terrorized the homesteaders in order to obtain their land when they were forced to leave. The gang is rounded up, and Rosita, who now knows the truth about Montana, rewards him with a kiss. *Gunfighters. Mexicans. Outlaws. Ranchers. Rustlers. Storekeepers. Cafés. Debt. Deception. Fights. Fires. Homesteaders. Horses. Jailbreaks. Murder. Ranch foremen. Romance. Waitresses.*

Note: According to modern sources, Larry Darmour was the producer of *Law and Lawless*, and the following players were in the cast: Ben Corbett, Slim Whitaker, Hank Bell and Gracia Granadas' Orchestra.

FD 12 Apr 1933, p. 8.

LAW AND LEAD (Latino)

Colony Pictures, Inc. *Dist* State Rights. 1937; New York opening: 17 Apr 1937. Sd; b&w. 5,474 ft. 57 or 60 min. Passed by the National Board of Review. PCA cert no. 2912.

Prod Arthur Alexander and Max Alexander. *Dir* Bob Hill. *Asst dir* Jack Korrick. *Scr* Basil Dickey. *Story* Rock Hawkey. *Cam* Bob Cline. *Film ed* Charles Henkel. *Sd* Hans Wearen [sic].

Cast: REX BELL (*Jimmy Sawyer*), Wally Wales (*Steve [Bradley]*), Harley Wood (*Hope Hawley*), Earl Dwire (*Hawley*), Solidad Jiminez (*Señor [a] Gonzales*), Donald Reed (*Pancho Gonzales*), Roger Williams (*Jeff*), Lane Chandler (*Ned Hyland*).

Western. [*Print viewed*]. Cattlemen's Association agent Jimmy Sawyer successfully wraps up another case and is about to take a well-deserved vacation when he finds out that another agent, Ned Hyland, is investigating a bandit called the Juarez Kid. Jimmy is stunned, because he himself captured and reformed the Juarez Kid, who is now known as Pancho Gonzales, three years before. Jimmy takes over the case and goes to visit Pancho. Pancho, meanwhile, is himself greatly upset by the bandit, who has falsely assumed his former name, and swears to his mother that he will discover the scoundrel's identity. Jimmy arrives at the ranch of Hawley and his daughter Hope, who treats Jimmy with suspicion. She warms up once he tells her that he is not a law agent, and she tells him that her father was wounded in the Juarez Kid's latest stagecoach robbery. Pancho, on the trail of the false Juarez Kid, is shot by him and is eventually found by Jimmy, who was following Pancho's dog, "Friday." Friday carries a mysterious note that appears to be meant for the bandit, and after Jimmy helps Pancho, he follows Friday again to find the note's recipient. Back on the Hawley ranch, Hope discusses Jimmy with hired hand Steve Bradley, who proposes to her and intimates that her father is the outlaw. Friday comes to Steve and Hope, and while Steve follows the dog, Hope goes home even more suspicious of her father, as Friday was headed toward their ranch. Steve goes to the saloon owned by Pancho and his mother, Señora Gonzales, and talks with the señora. Steve tells her that all is going according to plan, with Hope suspecting her father of the crimes. The señora protests that even though Steve is her nephew and she must therefore help him, she is worried about Pancho. Steve tells her she must obey him and leaves. The señora then finds the injured Pancho and tends to him until Jimmy arrives. Jimmy questions Pancho about Steve and the Hawleys, while at their ranch, the Hawleys read a newspaper article identifying Jimmy. Jimmy goes to the ranch, and after Hope bitterly accuses him of being a spy, she tells him that her father has disappeared. After

Hope leaves to search for Hawley, Jimmy sees Steve prowling in the house, and after a fight, Steve escapes dressed in his bandit costume. At Pancho's saloon, Hawley finally convinces Hope of his innocence, while in the back, the señora meets Steve. Jimmy sneaks up on them and captures Steve, and after Steve agrees not to implicate the señora, Jimmy tells him that he will try to help him. Hope apologizes to Jimmy, and he tells her he will be back during his vacation. *Bandits. Disguise. Fathers and daughters. Frame-ups. Impersonation and imposture. Undercover agents. Cattlemen's associations. Dogs. Gunshot wounds. Mexicans. Mothers and sons. Nephews. Ranchers. Romance. Saloons.*

Note: Although there is a copyright statement on the opening title card of the film, the title is not listed in the copyright catalog. Solidad Jiminez's character is incorrectly listed as "Señor Gonzales" in the onscreen credits and in the *Var* review. Sound engineer Hans Weeren's name is spelled Wearen in the onscreen credits. Although the *Var* lists Republic Pictures Corp. as the film's distributor, Republic most likely served only as the local New York exchange and not as the nationwide distributor. Modern sources note the film's release date as 15 Nov 1936 and include the following actors in the cast: Lloyd Ingraham, Karl Hackett, Ed Cassidy and Lew Meehan.

MPD 22 Oct 1937, p. 8. *Var* 21 Apr 1937, p. 15.

THE LAW AND MARTIN ROME *see* CRY OF THE CITY

LAW OF THE TONG (Chinese Americans)

Willis Kent Productions. *Dist* State Rights; Syndicate Pictures Corp. 15 Dec **1931**; *Prod:* at Tec-Art Studios. Sd; b&w. 52 or 56 min.

Dir Lew Collins. *Orig story* Orville Drake. *Photog* William Nobles.

Cast: Phyllis Barrington (*Joan*), John Harron (*Denny*), Jason Robards (*Charlie Wong*), Frank Lackteen (*Yuen Lee*), Mary Carr (*Mother McGregor*), Dot Farley (*Madame Duval*), William Mahlen (*Captain McGregor*), Richard Alexander (*Davy Jones*).

Drama. [*Not viewed*]. Joan works in a waterfront dive in San Francisco as a dance hall hostess. She is befriended by Denny, who encourages her to leave the place. After Joan leaves, Charlie Wong, a Tong gang leader, finds her wandering the streets of Chinatown and takes her to the Salvation Army, where she again meets Denny. Joan learns that Denny is a government agent who has been assigned to capture Wong. Both Denny and Joan are captured by the Tong and are condemned to death. At the price of his own life, Wong allows Joan to escape and bring the police, who rescue Denny. *Chinese Americans. San Francisco (CA)–Chinatown. Self-sacrifice. Tongs (Secret societies). Undercover agents. Dance hall girls. Police. Sailors. Salvation Army.*

Note: The film was also reviewed as *Law of the Tongs*.

FD 20 Dec 1931, p. 10. *HR* 12 Oct 1931. *MPH* 9 Jan 1932, p. 40. *Var* 22 Dec 1931, p. 21.

THE LAW RIDES AGAIN (Native Americans)

Monogram Pictures Corp. *Dist* Monogram Pictures Corp. 30 Jul **1943**; *Prod:* began 22 Apr 1943 [©Monogram Pictures Corp.; 18 Jun 1943; LP12103]. Sd; b&w. 5,055 ft. 55-56 or 58 min. PCA cert no. 9393.

Series: The Trail Blazers.

Prod Robert Tansey. *Dir* Alan James. *Asst dir* Robert Emmett. *Orig scr* Frances Kavanaugh. *Cine* Marcel LePicard. *Film ed* Carl Pierson. *Mus dir* Frank Sanucci. *Sd eng* Lyle Willey. *Prod mgr* Fred Hoose.

Cast: KEN MAYNARD [(*Ken*)], HOOT GIBSON [(*Hoot*)], Jack LaRue [(*Duke Dillon*)], Betty Miles [(*Betty Conway*)], Emmett Lynn [(*Eagle Eye*)], Ken Harlan [(*John Hampton*)], Chief Thundercloud [(*Thunder Cloud*)], Chief Many Treaties [(*Barking Fox*)], Bryant Washburn [(*Commissioner Lee*)], Fred Hoose [(*Hank*)], Ken Duncan, Roy Brent, John Bridges [(*Jess*)], John Merton, Hank Bell [(*Sheriff*)], Charles Murray, Jr. [(*Marshal*)], Steve Clark, Bud Buster.

Western. [*Print viewed*]. Near Preston, Arizona, Indians are making repeated raids on wagon trains and stagecoaches. Marshals Hoot and Ken are commissioned to determine why the Indians are breaking their treaty. Hoot gets the idea to enlist the aid of recently convicted killer Duke Dillon to finger the man responsible for inciting the Indians, as Dillon is likely to know the culprit. Hoot and Ken arrange to have Dillon released from custody as soon as he arrives in Preston. When Hoot and Ken learn that the stagecoach on which Dillon is riding with a marshal is likely to be attacked by Indians, they ride ahead and defend the coach from the attack. During the furor, Dillon kills the marshal and escapes, and the stage driver, Betty Conway, pulls the stagecoach safely into Preston with Ken and Hoot as her escorts. Hoot and Ken are arrested for the marshal's murder, but they

escape from jail and track Dillon to a remote cabin. Although Dillon double-crossed them, they still enlist his help, and take him to Preston. Dillon immediately goes to the office of the Indian agent, John Hampton, who has been cheating the Indians of their government-alloted cattle with the help of a trusting tribe member, Barking Fox. When Hampton learns that Eagle Eye, a scout, has made arrangements for Chief Thunder Cloud to meet with Hoot and Ken, Hampton plans to sabotage the meeting. Dillon confronts Hampton, who took over his business when he left, and demands to be paid off. Ken follows Dillon into Hampton's office, while Hoot gets the sheriff, but Dillon disappears into a secret passage and Hampton claims not to know of him. While Hoot goes to meet with Thunder Cloud, and Betty meets with her fiancé, the captain of the cavalry, Ken sneaks into Hampton's office and obtains his receipts. Hoot returns and says that Thunder Cloud has received about 30 head of cattle, although Hampton's receipts show that he delivered 600. Barking Fox overhears their conversation and angrily accuses Hampton of stealing from his people, but Hampton has him taken away. Hampton decides to make an escape while he still can, but when he takes the money from his safe, Dillon shoots him and escapes through the secret passageway. Ken and Hoot chase Dillon into the hills, and are followed by Hampton's gang, who are led by Dillon's cohort Spike. Hoot shoots Spike and Dillon, both of whom have tried to kill Ken, and Spike falls from the cliff where he was fighting with Ken. The cavalry arrives as arranged by Betty, and shortly after, the Indian tribe arrives to help in the gunfight. Dillon dies and the thieving gang is rounded up. *Ex-convicts. Fraud. Indian agents. Indians of North America. Marshals. Ambushes. Arizona. Gunfights. Murder. Robbery. Secret passageways. Sheriffs. Stagecoach drivers.*

Note: For further information on the "Trail Blazers" series, consult the Series Index.

Box 21 Aug 1943. *DV* 13 Aug 1943, p. 3. *FD* 5 Aug 1943, p. 10. *HR* 21 Apr 1943, p. 1. *HR* 13 Aug 1943, p. 3. *MPH* 21 Aug 1943. *MPHPD* 29 May 1943, p. 1339. *MPHPD* 21 Aug 1943, p. 1496. *Var* 11 Aug 1943, p. 10.

THE LAWLESS (Latino)

Pine-Thomas Productions, Inc. *Dist* Paramount Pictures, Inc. Jul **1950**; San Antonio, TX opening: late Jun 1950; Prod: late Oct—late Nov 1949 [©Paramount Pictures, Inc.; 4 Jun 1950; LP223]. Sd (Western Electric Recording); b&w. 9 reels, 7,472 ft. 81-82 min. Passed by the National Board of Review. PCA cert no. 14310.

Prod William H. Pine and William C. Thomas. *Dir* Joseph Losey. [*Asst dir* Howard Pine]. *Wrt for the screen by* Geoffrey Homes. *Dir of photog* Roy Hunt. *Art dir* Lewis H. Creber. *Ed* Howard Smith. *Set dec* Alfred Kegerris. *Mus supv* David Chudnow. *Mus score* Mahlon Merrick. *Sd rec* John Carter.

Cast: MacDonald Carey (*Larry Wilder*), Gail Russell (*Sunny Garcia*), John Sands (*Joe Ferguson*), Lee Patrick (*Jan Dawson*), John Hoyt (*Ed Ferguson*), and introducing Lalo Rios (*Paul Rodriguez*), and Maurice Jara (*Lopo Chavez*), Walter Reed (*Jim Wilson*), Guy Anderson (*Jonas Creel*), Argentina Brunetti (*Mrs. Rodriguez*), William Edmunds (*Mr. Jensen*), Gloria Winters (*Mildred Jensen*), John Davis (*Harry Pawling*), Martha Hyer (*Caroline Tyler*), Frank Fenton (*Mr. Prentiss*), Paul Harvey (*Chief of Police Blake*), Felipe Turich (*Mr. [Juan] Rodriguez*), Ian MacDonald (*Al Peters*), Noel Reyburn (*Fred Jackson*), Tab Hunter (*Frank O'Brien*), Russ Conway (*Eldredge*), Robert Williams (*Boswell*), James Bush (*Anderson*), Julia Faye (*Mrs. Jensen*), Howard Negley (*Pete Cassell*), Gordon Nelson (*Cadwallader*), Frank Ferguson (*Carl Green*), Ray Hyke (*Motorcycle officer*), Pedro de Cordoba (*Mr. Garcia*).

Social, Drama. [*Print viewed*]. In Santa Marta, California, Mexican-American fruit picker Paul Rodriguez dreams of owning a small farm, but his friend, Lopo Chavez, has become embittered by poverty and the prejudice he has faced since returning from World War II. One day while driving through town, Lopo accidentally runs a stop sign and has a minor accident with another car. The driver, Harry Pawling, and his passenger, Joe Ferguson, make a racial slur against Lopo, who responds with his fists. A policeman breaks up the fight and sends Harry and Joe home, and after fining Lopo for running the stop sign, helps him push his disabled car to the side of the road. Lopo then visits Sunny Garcia, whose father publishes the Spanish weekly newspaper *La Luz*, and makes sure she is going to the Good Fellowship dance that night. Paul, meanwhile, goes home to his shanty and tells his parents about the incident. When his father Juan warns him against spending time with "Americans," Paul protests that

he is an American. At the same time, Joe is reprimanded by his wealthy father Ed, who regrets that his son has grown into a bigot. That night, *The Union* newspaper's new owner/editor, Larry Wilder, a former big city journalist known for his provocative exposés, meets Sunny while waiting in line at the dance. Larry acknowledges that he is there because he anticipates a brawl, but Sunny insists that the Mexican gangs have made peace. Joe, Harry and their friend, Frank O'Brien, show up at the dance, and when Joe starts to harass a young woman, Paul comes to her defense. Joe throws the first punch and a brawl erupts and spills out of the hall. Paul runs away after accidentally striking policeman Al Peters, and escapes in a stolen ice cream truck. Larry's reporter, Jonas Creel, calls in the story to a larger newspaper in Stockton, and exaggerates the fight as a riot. Paul, terrified, then steals a car as the police chase him, but finally gives up and allows himself to be arrested. Peters angrily starts to beat Paul, but his partner, Boswell, insists that he restrain himself. Of the participants that night, Joe is the only white man arrested, and Sunny resents Joe's guilt-ridden father paying the bail for the poor Mexican boys because they cannot afford a lawyer to prove their innocence. When Boswell tries to stop Peters from roughing up Paul in the back of the police car, he loses control of the car and crashes. Boswell is killed in the accident, and Paul runs away from Peters because he blames him for the death. Later, Stockton reporter Jan Dawson arrives at Larry's office and shows Larry her paper, which has already printed a sensationalized headline reading "Fruit Pickers Riot." Meanwhile, Paul is hiding out in a barn and when he startles teenage farm girl Mildred Jensen, she hits her head on a board and is knocked unconscious. Encouraged by Jan, Mildred later tells police that Paul assaulted her, and news of the attack is reported on television, and Paul is made out to be a dangerous "gangster." Larry wants to publish interviews with Harry, Joe and Frank, but is threatened by all of their fathers, except Ed. Paul is finally tracked to an area near a quarry by another farmer, and a dragnet is formed. Larry manages to find Paul first and protects the frightened, sobbing boy while he is arrested. Sunny implores Larry to print the truth about Paul to counter the vicious lies that have already been published, but Larry fears disrupting the town's peaceful lifestyle. Larry's conscience nags him, however, and he writes a sympathetic article about Paul and publicly asks for money for his defense. The article incites the townspeople, and because Larry stated that Mildred could not know the truth because she was unconscious, her father and his friend try to assault him in his office, then attack Lopo and two friends in their car. Although Lopo's friends escape, he is brutally beaten and left behind. Jensen directs an angry mob to lynch Paul at the jail, but Larry arrives first and convinces the sheriff to take Paul elsewhere. Jensen then leads the mob to Larry's office, where Lopo has taken refuge with Sunny. The mob ignores Lopo's pleas for peace, and after he is battered by stones, they storm the offices and destroy everything. When the police finally arrive with Larry, an ambulance takes Lopo away, and Larry finds Sunny, with whom he has fallen in love, crumpled in a heap on the floor. Sunny revives and is unharmed, but Larry is so revolted by the destruction that he plans to leave town immediately. After Ed puts up Paul's bond, the boy tells Larry that he knew he could trust him because he sees his own brother, who died in the battle at Normandy, in Larry's eyes. Larry is deeply moved by Paul's faith, and instead of bidding Sunny farewell, he proposes they put out a weekly newspaper called *The Union* on her modest press. *False accusations. Fathers and sons. Lynching. Mexican Americans. Newspaper publishers. Racism. Automobile accidents. Bail. California. Chases. Dances. Disillusionment. Family relationships. Farm hands. Fistfights. Fugitives. Mobs. Police. Rape. Romance. Television. Veterans.*

Note: The working titles of this film were *The Big Showdown, Outrage, The Dividing Line* and *Voice of Stephen Wilder*. The film opens with the following written foreword: "This is the story of a town and of some of its people, who, in the grip of blind anger forget their American heritage of tolerance and decency, and become the lawless."

Information in the MPAA/PCA Collection at the AMPAS Library provides the following information about the production: After reading an early draft of the script, the PCA recommended changing any references to the alleged rape of "Mildred Jensen," such as eliminating the word "rape," and eliminating the line, "What they holdin' back the doctor's report on what he done to her for," as well as the following line: "and I thought of those hands mauling the lovely little body of Mildred Jensen." Although the PCA determined that the script was basically acceptable under the guidelines of the Production Code, PCA director Joseph I. Breen issued the following statement in a 5 Oct 1949 letter to Paramount: "The shocking manner in which the several gross injustices are heaped upon the head of the confused, but innocent young American of

Mexican extraction, and the willingness of so many of the people in your story to be a part of, and to endorse, these injustices, is, we think, a damning portrayal of our American social system. The manner in which certain of the newspapers are portrayed in this story, with their eagerness to dishonestly present the news, and thus inflame their readers, is also, we think, a part of a pattern which is not good. The over-all effect of a story of this kind made into a motion picture would be, we think, a very definite disservice to this country of ours, and to its institutions and its ideals....This whole undertaking seems to us to be fraught with very great danger." Paramount evidently held similar reservations about the film, as noted in Paramount representative Luigi Luraschi's response to the PCA, in which he noted that, "Unfortunately, the script you received did not reflect all of the changes we hope Pine-Thomas will make." In the film, it is not explicitly stated that "Paul" raped "Mildred"; it is reported that she was "attacked."

The Lawless marked a departure for producers William H. Pine and William C. Thomas, who were known for making low-budget action melodramas for Paramount. In a *Time* magazine interview, Pine commented that he and Thomas had wanted to do a serious story about a journalist for years, but were unable to conceive of a suitable screenplay until they started working with writer Geoffrey Homes, pseudonym of Daniel Mainwaring. Pine also noted in the interview that Paramount, which was not known for producing controversial films, was hesitant to make a picture with such a touchy theme, and that they had difficulty finding a Mexican actor for the lead. They finally hired Lalo [Edward] Rios, who was not a professional actor at the time. In addition to Rios and Maurice Jara, Tab Hunter made his screen debut in the picture. In a 5 Mar 1950 *NYT* article, Homes wrote a detailed description of the film's production, noting that "though it is true that discrimination against guys named Garcia and Chavez is more prevalent in the Texas and California border towns and in Los Angeles, it exists wherever there is a Mexican community. This I wanted to say on film."

The film was shot in eighteen days on location in Marysville and Grass Valley, CA, areas which were home to many migratory workers. In the *NYT* article, Homes noted that many local citizens participated in the film and appear as the angry mob in one scene. "Of course, no one ever said what the picture was about. That may have been why they were so amiable." A May 1950 *ParNews* item quoted a *LADN* article, which stated that "this film...points up eloquently, and with great feeling and understanding, the problem that has developed in California as a result of Mexican persons and those of other nationalities trying to adjust themselves to each other. It demonstrates that the fault is on both sides but mainly on the side of those of us of Anglo-Saxon traditions."

Paramount held the film's premiere in late Jun 1950 in San Antonio, TX, assisted in part by The Lulacs, an organization which promoted "loyal, united Latin-American society." According to a *DV* news item, Pine and Thomas received an award from the Los Angeles Urban League for "outstanding achievement in developing better racial understanding through the production of their film, *The Lawless*." A *LAT* review stated that "Geoffrey Homes, in one of the most cleverly balanced scripts yet written for a controversial theme, (all racial themes, unhappily, seem to be controversial), has found direction to match in Joseph Losey's dynamic use of camera and speech." Losey was blacklisted by the HUAC in 1951. For more information on this aspect of his career, see the entry above for *The Boy with Green Hair*. In a modern interview, Losey noted that he worked with John Hubley on the production design for this film, however, Hubley was not credited onscreen.

Box 8 Apr 1950. *DV* 7 Apr 1950, p. 3, 14. *DV* 9 Mar 1951. *FD* 12 Apr 1950, p. 6. *HR* 7 Apr 1950, pp. 3-4. *HR* 10 May 1950, p. 8. *LAT* 28 Jul 1950. *MPHPD* 8 Apr 1950, p. 253. *NYT* 29 Jan 1950. *NYT* 5 Mar 1950. *NYT* 23 Jun 1950, p. 29. *Time* 3 Jul 1950. *Var* 12 Apr 1950, p. 6.

THE LAWLESS EIGHTIES (Native Americans, Dakota)

Ventura Productions; Republic Pictures Corp. *Dist* Republic Pictures Corp. 31 May 1957 [©Republic Pictures Corp.; 10 May 1957; LP9662]. Sd (RCA Sound Recording); b&w; Naturama. 7 reels, 6,302 ft. 70 min. PCA cert no. 18569.

Prod Rudy Ralston. *Dir* Joe Kane. *Asst dir* Virgil Hart. *Scr* Kenneth Gamet. *Photog* Jack Marta. *Optical eff* Consolidated Film Industries. *Art dir* Ralph Oberg. *Film ed* Joseph Harrison. *Set dec* John McCarthy, Jr. *Cost supv* Alexis Davidoff. *Mus supv* Gerald Roberts. *Sd* Roy Meadows. *Makeup supv* Bob Mark.

Source: Based on the book *Brother Van, a Biography of the Rev. William Wesley Van Orsdel* by Alson Jesse Smith (Nashville, 1948).

Cast: Buster Crabbe [(*Link Prescott*)], John Smith [(*William Van Orsdel, "Brother Van"*)], Marilyn Saris [(*Lynn Sutter*)], Ted de Corsia [(*Grat Bandas*)], Anthony Caruso, John Doucette, Frank Ferguson [(*Owen Sutter*)], Sheila Bromley, Walter Reed, Buzz Henry, Will J. White, Bob Swan.

Western. [*Print viewed*]. In the period after the Civil War, circuit rider William Van Orsdel, known as Brother Van, is entrusted by the Indian bureau of the federal government to distribute seeds of wheat and corn to the Indians of the frontier and teach them to be farmers. When he sees white men rob some Sioux of their cattle and shoot one brave, Van rides to help the wounded man, Little Wolf, son of leader Wolf Chief. The Sioux leader expresses little interest in the seeds and warns that if the cavalry do not protect their cattle, as agreed upon by their treaty, there will be war. Learning that the Indians got the cattle

from Indian agent Grat Bandas, Van rides to see him. Bandas, who routinely cheats the Indians out of supplies, plans to start an Indian war so that the cavalry will open the land to settlers; as he has regularly been stealing cattle belonging to the Indians, he plans to have one of the biggest cattle spreads in the territory. Van explains to Bandas that he is not an ordained minister, but that he has dedicated his life to missionary work and wants to teach the fallacy of war and violence, and the benefits of working the land. After Van leaves for the nearby town of Deadwood, Bandas sends two of his men, Art Corbin and Magee, to kill him. Corbin shoots Van in the shoulder from a distance, but a lone rider, Link Prescott from Texas, sees the attack and shoots Magee in the shoulder, driving them off. Link takes Van to the ranch of Owen and Myra Sutter, and their attractive daughter Lynn, of whom Captain Ellis North of the cavalry is fond. At supper, Van relates that he became a preacher after witnessing, at age fifteen, the horrors of the battle of Gettysburg. Link believes that Van's words have no place on the frontier unless they are backed up with a gun and advises him to go. Aware of Link's reputation as a crack shot, Bandas hires him for protection in case of Indian raids. Bandas' men catch Little Wolf, whom Bandas has accused of horse stealing, and Corbin ties him up, planning to cripple, then shoot him, Link objects, saying he should be brought in for trial. A fire begins from Corbin's cigarette stub that threatens to engulf Little Wolf, and when Link tries to put it out, the others grab him. Watching from afar, Van stampedes wild horses in front of the outlaws and unties Little Wolf, who, before riding off, gives beads to Van. When Corbin is about to hit Van, Link stops him, saying the valley people would run them out of the country if Van were harmed. Link warns Van not to lose the beads, which will allow him to travel safely through Indian country. Later, when Lynn rebuffs Link's pleasantries, Van tells her that Link allowed him to release Little Wolf, and she agrees to invite him to the dance next Sunday to raise money for the church. At the dance, Captain North jealously watches Lynn dance with Link. In the midst of the party, they notice smoke coming from the nearby Bowers ranch, where Bandas' men are shooting flaming arrows taken earlier from Little Wolf. Corbin shoots Andy Bowers, hoping to start a war with the Indians. When Bandas admits to Link that it was his idea to provoke a war, Link quits. Corbin shoots Link in the arm and is about to finish him off, when they hear riders approach and hide Link in the shed. Sutter, Van, North and his troops arrive to question Bandas about the raid, and Bandas says that Little Wolf is the ringleader of the rebellious Indians. Van asks if he could go to Wolf Chief to try to persuade him to bring those renegades responsible for the raid to Deadwood, and Captain North allows him. Meanwhile, Link revives and rides off. He hides his horse and saddle at the Sutter ranch, and when Corbin and his cohort arrive to search, Lynn hides Link in her room. After they leave, Link tells the Sutters that Bandas and his men plan to start a war. They suggest he hide at an old mine opening on the ridge. Van meets with Wolf Chief, who agrees to bring any guilty Indians to Deadwood the next day; however, when he arrives, he relates that none of the Sioux had left the territory, and that Little Wolf, who did not steal a horse, had his bow and arrows taken from him. Captain North orders Bandas to bring back the arrows that he took and says he must hold Wolf Chief in jail until he finds out who is lying. In response, Indians carry Lynn off, thinking she is Captain North's girl, and threaten to kill her if they do not release Wolf Chief. North leaves to get a squadron sent to the area and holds Bandas responsible for Wolf Chief's safety. Saying that Lynn is dead, Bandas goads the townspeople into wanting to lynch Wolf Chief and gives them the keys to the jail. Just as they are about to lynch him, Van stops them and says he believes that if Wolf Chief is released, he will set Lynn free. He accuses Bandas' men of shooting Andy Bowers, and while he and Bandas argue, Wolf Chief escapes and rides off. Bandas and his men chase Wolf Chief, and when Link, now recovered, arrives, he and Van pursue them. During a battle, Van tackles Corbin as he tries to get a clear shot at Link. Link kills Bandas in a shoot-out and then wounds Corbin, who is about to shoot Van. Wolf Chief, wounded in the fight, agrees to release Lynn. The Indians ride off, and Link now offers his services to Captain North, who congratulates him and Lynn. *Dakota Indians. False accusations. Indian agents. Missionaries. Murder. Pacifism and pacifists. Rustlers. Tribal chiefs. United States–History– Indian campaigns. Dances. Fathers and sons. Fires. Gunshot wounds. Kidnapping. Lynching. Ranchers. Rescues. Romance. Sharpshooters. Stampedes. Texans. United States. Army. Cavalry.*

Note: The working titles of this film were *Brother Van* and *Showdown in Deadwood*. According to a *DV* news item, Republic purchased the book in Feb 1950. *FD* noted that William Van Orsdel, known as "Brother Van," was a "Pennsylvania evangelist who preached in Montana is the 1870's." According to information in the MPAA/PCA Collection at the AMPAS Library, the first script submitted for approval was dated 6 Jan 1954. *HR* stated that the filming was set to begin on 20 Feb 1954. No information has been located concerning the reason the project was halted at that time. In 1955, a *HR* news item noted that Warren Duff was assigned to write the script, but no information has been located to determine if any of Duff's material was used in the final film. In Oct 1955, a PCA official urged Republic Pictures to contact George A. Heimrich, of the National Council of Churches Film and Broadcasting Commission "to make certain that there will be nothing in your finished picture which might give any possible offense to Protestants." Heimrich responded to the studio, complaining that the script for the film made Brother Van "a secondary character" to Link Prescott. Heimrich urged the studio to make Van "as least as important" as Link, "and try to minimize his tendency to be naïve in things practical as regards human relations."

DV 15 Feb 1950. *Exb* 30 Oct 1957, p. 4396. *FD* 13 Mar 1950. *HR* 22 Aug 1950. *HR* 28 Oct 1953. *LAT* 16 Mar 1957. *MPD* 12 Aug 1957. *MPHPD* 20 Jul 1957, p. 458.

LAWLESS PLAINSMEN (Native Americans, Pima)
Columbia Pictures Corp. *Dist* Columbia Pictures Corp. 12 Mar **1942**; Prod: 6 Nov—18 Nov 1941 [©Columbia Pictures Corp.; 12 Mar 1942; LP11238]. Sd (Western Electric Mirrophonic Recording); b&w. 5,344 ft. 59 min.
Prod Jack Fier. [*Exec prod* Irving Briskin]. *Dir* William Berke. [*Asst dir* Milton Carter]. *Orig scr* Luci Ward. *Dir of photog* Benjamin Kline. *Art dir* Lionel Banks. *Assoc* Perry Smith. *Film ed* William Lyon. [*Sd eng* Frank Goodwin].
Song(s): "Lady Luck" and "Ridin', Just Ridin' On," composers undetermined.
Cast: CHARLES STARRETT (*Steve Rideen*), RUSSELL HAYDEN ("*Lucky*" *Bannon*), Luana Walters (*Baltimore Bonnie*), Cliff Edwards (*Harmony Stubbs*), Raphael Bennett (*Seth McBride*), Gwen Kenyon (*Madge Mason*), Frank LaRue (*Bill Mason*), Stanley Brown (*Tascosa*), Nick Thompson (*Ochella*), Eddie Laughton (*Slim*), [Francis Walker (*Abbott*)], [Steve Clark (*Sheriff*)], [Kermit Maynard (*Barlow*)], [Forrest Taylor (*Kit Carson*)], [Al Seymour (*Indian lookout*)], [Carl Mathews (*Keller*)].
Western, with songs. [*Print viewed*]. On a cattle drive from Texas to Arizona, Steve Rideen, the foreman, and "Lucky" Bannon, the son of ranch owner Mike Bannon, stop at a cow town. There, Steve meets his old friend, Bill Mason, and Bill's daughter Madge, who are leading a wagon train to Tucson. At Baltimore Bonnie's saloon, meanwhile, Bonnie, the proprietor, chides Harmony Stubbs for peddling worthless land to her customers, then retreats to her office. Bonnie is surprised to find her ex-husband, Seth McBride waiting for her, and after Seth claims that he is entitled to half of her money, Bonnie throws him out. Returning to the gambling tables, Bonnie engages Lucky in a hand of blackjack. As Bonnie deals the cards, McBride instructs his henchman, Keller, to create a disturbance while he sneaks into Bonnie's office and robs her safe. In the ensuing scuffle, Lucky is injured and Madge takes him to her wagon to recuperate. When the sheriff arrives at the saloon to investigate the incident, Keller accuses Bonnie of cheating him, and the sheriff orders her to leave town that day. Soon after, Steve comes to the saloon in search of Lucky, and Harmony tells him that Lucky has pulled out with the wagon train. After directing his cowhands to continue the drive without him, Steve and Harmony catch up to the wagons and find Lucky riding with Madge and Bonnie. In the lead wagon, meanwhile, McBride demands that Mason cede him half interest in the wagon train and Mason refuses. Soon after, Mason is shot and his terrified horses bolt. Steve pursues the runaway team, and after he frees the horses, the wagon plunges over a cliff, sending Mason to his death. Feeling responsible for the now leaderless settlers and determined to bring Mason's killer to justice, Steve agrees to accompany the wagons to Tucson. As they near Indian territory, Steve glimpses smoke signals in the hills and orders the wagons to keep moving through the night. McBride, who is in league with the Indians to plunder the wagons, balks at Steve's command and insists upon stopping for the evening. As the wagons continue, the Indians attack, but Steve and the others fend them off. The next day, while scouting for water, Harmony, Lucky and Steve come upon several Indians beating a helpless man. Riding to the captive's rescue, the three chase away the Indians. Their victim then introduces himself as Tascosa, the son of Pima chief Ochella, and explains that his assailants were Apaches, an enemy of his people and members of the tribe that attacked the wagons the

previous evening. After sending Lucky to Fort Grant for reinforcements, Steve and Harmony return to camp with Tascosa. McBride, who has since rejoined the train, objects to the presence of the Indian, and asserts that the Pima tribe was responsible for the raid. Claiming that the Apaches are using the white man's bullets and guns, Tascosa offers to ride back to his tribe and assemble an escort of Pima warriors to protect the wagon train. Determined to eliminate Tascosa before he returns with help, McBride follows him. As soon as McBride departs, Bonnie goes to his wagon to look for her stolen money. Keller tries to stop her, but when Steve learns of her suspicions, he searches the wagon and finds Bonnie's strong box as well as a cache of guns and ammunition. Intimidated, Keller confesses McBride's plan to murder Tascosa as he did Mason. Steve, Harmony and Bonnie pursue McBride, catching up to him just after he has shot Tascosa. Steve knocks McBride off his horse, and in the ensuing fight, McBride pulls his gun on Steve, forcing Steve to shoot in self-defense. After sending Harmony and Bonnie back to the wagons, Steve journeys to the Pima camp to deliver Tascosa's lifeless body to his father. Lucky, meanwhile, meets Kit Carson, who volunteers to convey the message to Fort Grant so that Lucky can return to the wagon train. Upon reaching the wagons, Lucky learns of Steve's peril and rides out to help him. At the Pima camp, meanwhile, Ochella blames Steve for his son's death and orders his execution. As the war drums beat, Lucky sneaks into the tent in which Steve is being held captive and frees him. When the Indians discover that Steve is missing, they jump on their horses, bent on revenge. Lucky and Steve gallop back to camp, followed by the Indians, who swiftly surround the camp and open fire. At that moment, the cavalry comes to the rescue and chases away the Indians. Upon reaching Tucson, Bonnie and Madge open a general store, while Lucky and Steve, their mission completed, ride back to the Bannon ranch in Texas. Duplicity. Indians of North America. Murder. Wagon trains. Kit Carson. Cattle drives. Cowboys. Ex-spouses. False accusations. Fathers and daughters. Fathers and sons. Gambling. Raids. Rescues. Robbery. Saloons. Settlers. Sheriffs. Tucson (AZ).
Box 23 May 1942. *FD* 10 Jun 1942, p. 5. *MPHPD* 13 Jun 1942. *Var* 10 Jun 1942, p. 8.

LAZY RIVER (Cajuns, Chinese Americans)
Metro-Goldwyn-Mayer Corp.; controlled by Loew's, Inc. *Dist* Metro-Goldwyn-Mayer Corp. 16 Mar **1934**; Prod: 23 Jan—10 Feb 1934 [©Metro-Goldwyn-Mayer Corp.; 7 Mar 1934; LP4549]. Sd (Western Electric Sound System); b&w. 8 reels. 75 or 77 min. Passed by the National Board of Review.
Prod Lucien Hubbard. *Dir* George B. Seitz. [*Asst dir* Red Golden]. [*Dir of background photog* Tod Browning]. *Scr* Lucien Hubbard. *Photog* Gregg Toland. [*Background photog* Clyde De Vinna]. [*Background photog asst* William Snyder, Robert Hoag and Cecil Wright]. *Art dir* James Havens. *Film ed* William LeVanway. *Ward* Dolly Tree. *Mus score* Dr. William Axt. *Rec dir* Douglas Shearer. [*Mixer* William Steinkamp].
Song(s): "Fifi from Fontenoy" and "Cajun Love Song," words and music by Dr. William Axt.
Source: Based on the play *Ruby* by Lea David Freeman (production undetermined).
Cast: Jean Parker (*Sarah* [*Lescalie*]), Robert Young (*Bill* [*Drexel*]), Ted Healy ([*William*] *Gabby* [*Stone*]), Nat Pendleton ([*Alfred*] *Tiny* [*Smith*]), C. Henry Gordon (*Sam Kee*), Ruth Channing (*Ruby*), Maude Eburne (*Miss Minnie* [*Lescalie*]), Raymond Hatton (*Captain* [*Herbert*] *Orkney*), Irene Franklin (*Suzanne*), Joseph Cawthorn (*Ambrose*), Erville Alderson (*Sheriff*), George Lewis (*Armand* [*Lescalie*]), [Ben Hendricks (*Mate*)], [Charles Dunbar (*Chauffeur*)], [Maurice Brierre (*Ettiene*)], [Purnell B. Pratt (*Lawyer*)], [Chris Pin Martin (*Raoul*)], [Lee Beggs (*Detective*)], [Bud Fine (*C. P. O. officer*)], [Bobby Burns (*Slim*)], [Walter Long (*Buck*)], [John Larkin (*Negro*)], [Lee Shumway (*Sailor*)], [Donald Douglas (*Officer*)].
Rural, **Drama**, with songs. [*Print viewed*]. Because they refused to participate in a prison escape, in which a fellow convict, Armand Lescalie, was killed, William "Gabby" Stone and Alfred "Tiny" Smith receive commendations from the Alabama governor and are freed. A few weeks later, Bill Drexel, another reluctant escapee, also is released and off. The next day, while scouting tracks his ex-convict friends to a horse stable in New Orleans. Although Bill discourages Gabby and Tiny from pursuing a robbery and horse-betting scheme, he feels no compunction about looking up Miss Minnie, Armand's supposedly rich mother, in a Louisiana shrimping village. When Bill arrives in the small, impoverished Cajun village, he is dismayed to learn from Sarah, Miss

Minnie's daughter, that not only is the widowed Miss Minnie not rich, but her shrimping business is on the verge of a hostile takeover by the shrewd half-Chinese smuggler and racketeer, Sam Kee. Before the disappointed Bill leaves the village, however, Tiny and Gabby show up, hungry and pursued, having failed at both their robbery and betting schemes. While Tiny and Gabby search for food, the village is stirred by the arrival of Ambrose, the Lescalies' old friend, whom Miss Minnie had contacted for financial help. After a night of festivities, Ambrose promises to return with the needed money, but is seen leaving by Kee and is killed. The next morning, as the village sheriff is about to auction off Miss Minnie's business to a cohort of Kee, Tiny spots a safe in Kee's boat and, with Gabby's help, steals enough cash for Bill to buy the business himself. Gabby then pickpockets more money from one of Kee's henchmen, and as her partner, Bill is able to revitalize Miss Minnie's sabotaged shrimping operation. Four weeks later, Bill discovers that he has fallen in love with Sarah and tells her about his troubled life, which includes a disapproving father in Boston and an alcohol-induced marriage to a gold-digging waitress. Sarah is heartbroken by the news and is even more stunned when Ruby, Bill's wife, suddenly arrives in the village. Depressed that Ruby refuses to divorce him, Bill takes a late-night walk on the village pier and is kidnapped by Kee and his men. Gabby and Tiny, however, see Kee rowing Bill to his boat and pursue him in their own rowboat. At the same time, the Coast Guard, suspicious that Kee is using the village to smuggle Chinese refugees in from Mexico, confront Kee's ship with warning gun fire. Before the Coast Guard boards his ship, however, Kee disposes of his illegal cargo by throwing the bound-and-gagged Chinese refugees and Bill overboard. After Tiny executes an underwater rescue of Bill, the three men board Kee's ship and beat and tie up their foes. When Bill returns to shore, he is met by Lodge, his father's lawyer. As a joyful Sarah listens, Lodge informs Bill that his father is anxious for a reconciliation, and that, after he was sent to prison, Ruby had divorced him. Finally free of his past, Bill embraces Sarah. Cajuns. Criminals–Rehabilitation. Extortion. Fishing villages. Louisiana. Romance. Smuggling. Alabama. Auctions. Chinese Americans. Divorce. Ex-convicts. Fights. Gambling. Gold diggers. Hunger. Kidnapping. Lawyers. Murder. Parties. Pickpockets. Prison escapes. Refugees. Political. Safecrackers. Sea rescues. Sheriffs. Thieves. United States. Coast Guard. Widows.

Note: The working titles of this film were *Ruby, Dance Hall Daisy, Bride of the Bayou, Louisiana Lou, In Old Louisiana* and *Louisiana*. According to studio records, Lea David Freeman's play was also titled *Dance Hall Daisy* and is referred to in early news items by that title. Studio records note that the play was purchased in May 1933 and the following writers were assigned to work on the project between Mar and Oct 1933: Harry Hervey, Lucien Hubbard, Raymond Schrock, Chandler Sprague, Leon Gordon, Jules Furthman, John Colton, William Faulkner, Erskine Caldwell and Arthur Caesar.

According to studio records, Faulkner arrived in Louisiana on 26 Apr 1933 to work on the script with Tod Browning, who was the film's original director. However, studio records state: "Faulkner did not do the Basic Material....None of his material on this [film] was ever in Script Dept. files. Perhaps no material was turned in." In a modern interview, Faulkner describes his experience on the production: "I arrived at Mr. Browning's hotel about six p.m. and reported to him. A party was going on. He told me to get a good night's sleep and be ready for an early start in the morning. I asked him about the story. He said, 'Oh, yes. Go to room so and so. That's the continuity writer. He'll tell you what the story is.' I went to the room as directed. The continuity writer was sitting in there alone. I told him who I was and asked him about the story. He said, 'When you have written the dialogue I'll let you see the story.' " After viewing potential locations in Grand Isle sometime later, Browning informed Faulkner that he had been fired by the studio, but before Browning could do anything about it, he was also fired. Although studio records indicate that Faulkner left Louisiana on 9 May 1933, news items suggest that Browning was still directing the project as late as mid-Jun 1933. According to *IP*, cinematographer Clyde De Vinna was shooting backgrounds in Louisiana with Browning in Jun 1933. A mid-Jul 1933 news item in *MPH* noted that the film was being shot in the "shrimp camps of Lake Baratria and the land of the Louisiana Cajuns." Joan Crawford, Alice Brady, Lionel Barrymore and Madge Evans were all announced as stars of the picture in various mid-1933 news items.

In Jan 1934, *HR* announced that M-G-M was taking *Lazy River* "off the shelf." *DV* notes that when the project was revived, director George Seitz and producer Hubbard rewrote the story from scratch. It is not known how much of Browning's background footage was used in the final film. *HR* news items from Jan 1934 state that Lupe Velez, Warner Oland and Isabel Jewell were assigned to play parts in the film. None of these actors, however, appears in the finished film. May Robson also was announced as a cast member, but according to *HR*, she withdrew from the picture because her part, presumably that of "Miss Minnie," was too small. According to a Mar 1934 *HR* news item, the film was to have its premiere in New Orleans one week prior to the general release date, but a 3 Apr 1934 news item in *FD* suggests that the Louisiana opening may have taken place after the general release.

DV 12 Jan 1934, p. 8. *DV* 23 Jan 1934, p. 2. *DV* 10 Feb 1934, p. 4. *DV* 24 Feb 1934, p. 3. *FD* 20 May 1933, p. 4. *FD* 17 Jan 1934, p. 8. *FD* 23 Jan 1934, p. 5. *FD* 3 Apr 1934, p. 1. *HF* 27 Jan 1934, p. 8. *HR* 12 Jun 1933, p. 3. *HR* 10 Jan 1934, p. 3. *HR* 18 Jan 1934, p. 3. *HR* 22 Jan 1934, p. 7. *HR* 2 Mar 1934, p. 7. *HR* 24 Feb 1934, p. 3. *IP* Jun 1933, p. 25. *MPD* 2 Mar 1934, p. 10. *MPH* 15 Jul 1933, p. 61. *MPH* 24 Feb 1934, p. 63. *MPH* 10 Mar 1934, p. 49, 52. *NYT* 4 Apr 1934, p. 26. *Var* 10 Apr 1934, p. 13.

LEAVE IT TO THE IRISH *see* **THE LUCK OF THE IRISH**

DER LEBEDIKER YUSEM *see* **MY SON** (1939)

LEGACY *see* **ADAM HAD FOUR SONS**

LA LEGIÓN EXTRANJERA *see* **DE LA SARTÉN AL FUEGO**

LEM HAWKINS' CONFESSION (African Americans)
Micheaux Pictures Corp. *Dist* Micheaux Pictures Corp. **1935** [©Micheaux Pictures Corp.; 23 Aug 1935; LP5763]. Sd; b&w. 10 reels. 98 min.
Pres A. BURTON RUSSELL. [*Prod* Oscar Micheaux]. [*Dir* Oscar Micheaux]. [*Wrt* Oscar Micheaux]. *Photog* Chas. Levine. *Art dir* Tony Continenta. [*Cabaret seq wrt and dir by* Clarence Williams]. *Rec eng* Harry Belock and Armond Schettin. *Prod mgr* Chas. B. Nason.
Song(s): "Harlem Rhythm Dance" and "Ants in My Pants," music and lyrics by Clarence Williams.
Cast: Clarence Brooks (*Henry Glory*), Dorothy Van Engle (*Claudia Vance*), Andrew Bishop (*Brisbane*), Alec Lovejoy (*Lem Hawkins*), Laura Bowman (*Mrs. Epps*), Bee Freeman (*The Catbird*), Lionel Monagas, Alice B. Russell [(*Mrs. Vance*)], Sandy Burns, Lea Morris, Joie Brown, Jr., Eunice Wilson, Henrietta Loveless, Lorenzo McClane, Helen Lawrence, David Hanna, "Slick" Chester [(*Detective*)], [Oscar Micheaux (*Second detective*)], [Ei Pugh], [Byron Shore].
African American, Mystery, with songs. [*Print viewed*]. When a watchman at National Chemical Laboratories, Inc. finds the body of Myrtle Stanfield, he calls the police, who find two mysterious notes near the body that implicate the watchman. Three years earlier, door-to-door salesman Henry Glory sells a novel to a young woman named Claudia Vance, who lives with her mother. When Henry delivers the book a few days later, he is told by Claudia's neighbor that Claudia is a woman of ill-repute and is known as "Catbird." Soon after meeting Henry, Claudia coaxes Henry into admitting that he wrote the novel himself, anonymously, and that he will be using the profits from the sales to put himself through law school. Henry is immediately smitten with Claudia and the next day, tells Claudia's neighbor that he intends to tell Claudia at 8:30 that evening that he loves her. Meanwhile, two white men are seen plotting something that will take place at 8:30 p.m. That night, Henry arrives at Claudia's but is knocked out by a man who comes up behind him and mistakes him for the intended victim. Now, three years later, in 1934, after Henry reads the headlines announcing Myrtle's murder, Claudia shows up at his office and tells him that the accused watchman is her brother Harper, and asks him to take his case. Henry accepts the case, and after interviewing Harper, realizes that he was not at the factory at the time the murder took place. At the trial, Brisbane, the plant boss, takes the witness stand and states that, at noon, Myrtle and Harper entered a back room at the plant. Harper, however, denies that he ever saw Myrtle. Next, Myrtle's mother Stella testifies that Myrtle's boyfriend, George Epps, went to the chemical plant to get his paycheck and that she never saw her daughter again after that. Later, Henry and Claudia deduce that Brisbane, who has a perfect alibi, committed the murder and that he is trying to blame it on her brother. The following night, Catbird, who is actually Claudia's criminal neighbor, greets Lem Hawkins at a nightclub, and Claudia, who is also there, gets Hawkins drunk. Hawkins soon admits to Claudia that Harper is being "railroaded" and that Brisbane is bribing him to keep quiet. The next day, Hawkins is arrested and tells how the murder happened: Brisbane tried to make love to Myrtle in the back room but she resisted, hit her head after being pushed to the ground by him and was knocked unconscious. Believing that she had been badly hurt, Brisbane sent Hawkins to bring Myrtle to the front of the building, but she had died. Brisbane, who intended to frame Hawkins, instructed him to write incriminating notes, but decided to frame Harper instead when Hawkins bungled the story. Later, Claudia finds a witness, a young boy, who told his mother that George became angry after seeing Myrtle and Brisbane kissing in the back room and wanted to kill them both. When he found Myrtle unconscious, George killed her by strangling her with a rope and then fled. The case is solved, and after Henry discovers Claudia is not Catbird, he kisses her and

promises to take her away from the "Catbird's nest." *African Americans. Frame-ups. Lawyers. Murder. Trials. Authors. Books. Brothers and sisters. Drunkenness. Jews. Laboratories. Law students. Mistaken identity. Neighbors. Nightclubs. Police. Seduction. Students. Vamps. Watchmen.*

Note: According to the onscreen credits, the story on which this film was based was entitled "The Stanfield Murder Case." The title of the film on the viewing print was *Murder in Harlem*, which may have been a later release title. A modern source lists the title of the film as *Brand of Cain*, although it has not been determined when that title was used. Publicity material preserved in the copyright records labeled the picture "Society's Strangest Triangle—The Story of a Jew, a Gentile—and a Negro!" The film was a remake of Micheaux' 1921 silent film, *The Gunsaulus Mystery* (see above), which was based on the true case of Leo Frank, a Jewish man wrongfully accused and convicted of killing a girl in Atlanta. Although the governor of Georgia, John M. Slaton, commuted Frank's death sentence to life imprisonment, Frank was lynched by a mob on 16 Aug 1915. On 11 Mar 1986, the state of Georgia issued a posthumous pardon for Frank. Other films that were based on the Frank trial include *Thou Shalt Not Kill*, directed by Hal Reid and starring Rose Coghlan and Charles Coghlan (see *AFI Catalog of Feature Films, 1911-20*; F1.4445); a documentary short entitled *Leo M. Frank* also made in 1915 by Reid; and the 1937 Warner Bros. production, *They Won't Forget*, directed by Mervyn LeRoy and starring Claude Rains (see *AFI Catalog of Feature Films, 1931-40*; F3.4570). The NBC network aired a made-for-television film of the Leo Frank story, entitled *The Murder of Mary Phagan*, on 24 Jan 1988. The telefilm was directed by Billy Hale and starred Jack Lemmon and Richard Jordan.

THE LEOPARD MAN (Latino)
RKO Radio Pictures, Inc. *Dist* RKO Radio Pictures, Inc. 8 May **1943**; Prod: 9 Feb—8 Mar 1943 [©RKO Radio Pictures, Inc.; 19 May 1943; LP12246]. Sd (RCA Sound System); b&w. 5,940 ft. 59 or 65-66 min. PCA cert no. 9179.

Prod Val Lewton. [*Supv* Lou Ostrow]. *Dir* Jacques Tourneur. *Asst dir* William Dorfman. *Scr* Ardel Wray. *Addl dial* Edward Dein. *Dir of photog* Robert de Grasse. *Art dir* Albert S. D'Agostino and Walter E. Keller. *Ed* Mark Robson. *Set dec* Darrell Silvera and Al Fields. *Mus dir* C. Bakaleinikoff. *Mus* Roy Webb. *Rec* J. C. Grubb.

Source: Based on the novel *Black Alibi* by Cornell Woolrich (New York, 1942).

Cast: Dennis O'Keefe [(*Jerry Manning*)], Margo [(*Clo-Clo*)], Jean Brooks [(*Kiki Walker*)], Isabel Jewell [(*Maria*)], James Bell [(*Dr. Galbraith*)], Margaret Landry [(*Teresa Delgado*)], Abner Biberman [(*Charlie How-Come*)], Tula Parma [(*Consuelo Contreras*)], Ben Bard [(*Chief Roblos*)], [Ariel Heath (*Eloise*)], [Fely Franquelli (*Rosita*)], [Richard Martin (*Raoul Belmonte*)], [Robert Anderson (*Dwight Brunton*)], [Jacqueline de Wit (*Helene Brunton*)], [Robert Spindola (*Pedro Delgado*)], [William Halligan (*Brunton*)], [Sid D'Albrook, John Eberts (*Waiters*)], [David Cota (*Boy singer*)], [Kate Lawson (*Senora Delgado*)], [Jacques Lory (*Philipe*)], [Tola Nesmith (*Senora Contreras*)], [Marguerita Sylva (*Marta*)], [Charles Lung (*Manuel*)], [John Dilson (*Coroner*)], [Mary MacLaren (*Nun*)], [Tom Orosco (*Window cleaner*)], [Eliso Gamboa (*Senor Delgado*)], [Joe Dominguez (*Police officer*)], [Belle Mitchell (*Senora Calderon*)], [Betty Roadman (*Clo-Clo's mother*)], [Rosa Rita Varella (*Clo-Clo's sister*)], [John Piffle (*Flower vendor*)], [Rosita Delva, Jose Portugal (*Young lovers*)], [Bob O'Connor, Ed Agresti (*Mexican police officers*)], [Manuel Paris (*Man blowing smoke*)], [Rene Pedrini (*Frightened waiter*)], [Brandon Hurst (*Gatekeeper*)], [Rose Higgins (*Indian weaver*)], [George Sherwood (*Police lieutenant*)], [Juan Ortiz (*Plainclothesman*)], [John Tettemer (*Minister*)], [Russell Wade], [Dora Leyva].

Psychological, **Horror**. [*Print viewed*]. At a nightclub in a small New Mexican town, Clo-Clo, an exotic Latin dancer, upstages the performance of Kiki Walker. To draw attention to his client, Kiki's press agent, Jerry Manning, rents a black leopard for her to use in the act. As Kiki leads the leopard onstage, however, it becomes frightened by the sounds of Clo-Clo's castanets and escapes. That night, as Clo-Clo walks home from the club, she passes the Delgado house. Inside, Mrs. Delgado orders her daughter Teresa to go to the store, and when the little girl protests that she is terrified to go outside because of the leopard, her mother pushes her out the door. Upon finding the village store closed for the evening, Teresa is forced to cross the arroyo to shop at another store. On her way home, the leopard emerges from the shadows and attacks her. Running home, Teresa cries for her mother to open the door, but when the lock becomes stuck, Mrs. Delgado can only watch in horror as her daughter's blood seeps under the door. The next day, the sheriff, Chief Roblos, organizes a posse to search for the beast, and during the hunt, Jerry meets Dr. Galbraith,

the curator of an Indian museum. That night, at the club, a fortune-teller reads Clo-Clo's cards and foretells that the dancer will receive a sum of money from a rich man, after which the "black card of death" will follow. The next morning at a flower vendor, Clo-Clo meets Rosita, the maid to Consuelo Contreras, a young noblewoman. Rosita brings flowers to her mistress in honor of her birthday, and later that afternoon, Consuelo visits a cemetery to keep a secret rendezvous with her lover, Raoul Belmonte. When Raoul is late for their meeting, Consuelo is locked within the cemetery walls by the gatekeeper. As night falls and the wind begins to howl, Consuelo calls for help and is answered by a man who promises to return with a ladder. Before he comes back, however, Consuelo hears a rustling in the trees and screams in terror. The next day, when Consuelo's body is found clawed to death, Galbraith and Roblos are certain that she was assaulted by the leopard. Jerry begins to have doubts, however, and goes to speak with the cat's owner, an Indian named Charlie How-Come. After Charlie, who rented the animal to Jerry, assures him that the cat is not vicious, Jerry takes Charlie to the museum to consult with Galbraith. When Jerry proposes that Consuelo's assailant was human, Galbraith suggests that Charlie could have killed the girl when he was drunk. Fearful that Galbraith might be right, Charlie insists upon being jailed for murder. That night at the club, Clo-Clo meets a wealthy old man who gives her a $100 bill. On her way home, she visits the fortune-teller, who once again uncovers the black card of death. After arriving safely home, Clo-Clo discovers that she has lost her money and ventures back onto the street to retrieve it. There, after hearing the shuffle of footsteps, Clo-Clo stares in horror as her attacker lunges from the dark. After Clo-Clo's death, Roblos sends for the state hunter and Charlie is exonerated. Jerry and Kiki plan to leave for Chicago, but when Galbraith sends Kiki a farewell bouquet of flowers, she feels compelled to place them at the site of Consuelo's murder in the cemetery. There, Kiki confesses her love to Jerry and insists upon staying in town to catch the killer. When Charlie finds his leopard dead, lying by the side of the arroyo, Jerry remembers that he saw Galbraith enter the arroyo and tells Roblos that the curator killed the animal. Roblos refuses to arrest Galbraith without evidence, however, and so Jerry seeks Raoul's help in exposing the murderer. That night, during the rites of a religious procession, Galbraith walks along the street toward the museum. As he passes the cemetery, he hears a woman's screams followed by the clicking of castanets. Panicking, Galbraith rushes to the museum, and soon after, Kiki arrives to watch the procession pass. When she insists upon turning off the lights to better see the procession, Kiki drops a pair of castanets, causing Galbraith to flee and join the marchers. Jerry and Raoul follow and subdue Galbraith, who then confesses to murdering Consuelo and Clo-Clo after watching the leopard maul Teresa. Out of revenge for his lost love, Raoul shoots Galbraith, and later, outside the funeral parlor, Jerry and Kiki reaffirm their love for each other. *Frame-ups. Leopards. Murder. New Mexico. Cemeteries. Children. Curators. Dancers. Fortune-tellers. Indians of North America. Leopards. Mexican Americans. Museums. Nightclubs. Press agents. Sheriffs.*

Note: According to a pre-production news item in *HR*, producer Val Lewton initially assigned DeWitt Bodeen to write the screenplay for this film. Another *HR* pre-production news item notes that Rita Corday was to play a lead in the film. Corday does not appear in the released film, however, and the extent of Bodeen's contribution to the screenplay has not been determined. A news item in *LAT* adds that RKO negotiated with Lon Chaney, Jr. to appear in this picture. According to an RKO Legal Files memo from Lewton to Wynn Rocamora, the agent for the actress Margo, Lewton offered to restructure Cornell Woolrich's novel to expand the part of "Clo-Clo," the role that Lewton wanted Margo to play. According to a contemporary interview with writer Ardel Wray as reprinted in a modern source, the film exteriors were shot around Santa Fe, New Mexico. This was director Jacques Tourneur's third and last picture for Lewton. It also marked Ben Bard's first screen appearance since the 1934 film *The White Parade* (see *AFI Catalog of Feature Films, 1931-40*; F3.5084).

Box 8 May 1943. *DV* 4 May 1943, p. 3. *FD* 11 May 1943, p. 12. *HR* 21 Aug 1942, p. 10. *HR* 13 Nov 1942, p. 4. *HR* 22 Feb 1943, p. 3. *HR* 4 May 1943, p. 4. *HR* 14 May 1943, p. 3. *LAT* 9 Apr 1942. *MPH* 8 May 1943. *MPHPD* 3 Apr 1943, p. 1241. *MPHPD* 8 May 1943, p. 1303. *NYT* 20 May 1943, p. 26. *Var* 5 May 1943, p. 16.

LET FREEDOM RING (Immigrants)
Metro-Goldwyn-Mayer Corp.; controlled by Loew's Inc. *Dist* Loew's Inc. 24 Feb **1939**; Prod: 25 Nov 1938—13 Jan 1939 [©Loew's Inc.; 23 Feb 1939; LP8675]. Sd (Western Electric Sound System); sepia. 9 reels. 85 or 87 min. Passed by the National Board of Review. PCA cert no. 5064.

Prod Harry Rapf. *Dir* Jack Conway. [*2d unit dir* John Waters]. [*Asst dir* Horace Hough]. *Scr* Ben Hecht. *Orig story* Ben Hecht. *Photog* Sidney Wagner. *Montage* John Hoffman. *Art* Cedric Gibbons. *Art dir assoc* Daniel B. Cathcart. *Film ed* Frederick Y. Smith. *Set dec* Edwin B. Willis. *Women's cost* Dolly Tree. *Men's cost* Valles. *Mus dir* Arthur Lange. *Orch arr* Leonid Raab. *Rec dir* Douglas Shearer. *Makeup* Jack Dawn.

Song(s): "Dusty Road," music and lyrics by Otis René and Leon René; "When Irish Eyes Are Smiling," music by Ernest R. Ball, lyrics by Chauncey Olcott and George Graff; "Pat, Sez He," music by Phil Ohman, lyrics by Marty Symes; "Where Else But Here," music by Sigmund Romberg, lyrics by Edward Heyman; "Home, Sweet Home," music by H. R. Bishop, lyrics by John Howard Payne; "My Country 'Tis of Thee," music by Henry Carey, lyrics by Samuel Francis Smith; "Love's Serenade," music by Riccardo Drigo, lyrics by Bob Wright and Chet Forrest; "The Star-Spangled Banner," music and lyrics by Francis Scott Key; "I've Been Working on the Railroad," music and lyrics by Bob Wright and Chet Forrest.

Cast: Nelson Eddy (*Steve Logan*), Virginia Bruce (*Maggie Adams*), Victor McLaglen (*Chris Mulligan*), Lionel Barrymore (*Thomas Logan*), Edward Arnold (*Jim Knox*), Guy Kibbee (*[Judge] David Bronson*), Charles Butterworth (*The Mackerel*), H. B. Warner (*Rutledge*), Raymond Walburn (*Underwood*), Dick Rich (*"Bumper" Jackson*), Trevor Bardette (*Gagan*), George F. Hayes (*[Jerry] "Pop" Wilkie*), Louis Jean Heydt (*Ned Wilkie*), Sarah Padden (*"Ma" Logan*), Eddie Dunn (*"Curly"*), C. E. Anderson, Captain (*Sheriff [Hicks]*), [Philo McCullough, Harry Fleischmann, Ralph Bushman (*Gagan henchmen*)], [Maude Allen (*Hilda*)], [Adia Kuznetzoff (*Pole*)], [Luis Alberni (*Tony*)], [Emory Parnell (*Swede*)], [Tenen Holtz (*Hunky*)], [Mitchell Lewis (*Joe*)], [Victor Potel (*2nd Swede*)], [Constantine Romanoff (*Russian*)], [Lionel Royce (*German*)], [Billy Bevan (*Cockney*)], [Syd Saylor (*1st surveyor*)], [Ted Thompson (*2nd surveyor*)].

Drama, with songs. [*Print viewed*]. As the railroad blazes its way across the country, the town of Clover City is scheduled to become an important junction on the line. Railroad tycoon Jim Knox will stop at nothing to acquire the land he needs to build the railroad, and hires a gang of cutthroats to burn down the homes of the ranchers whose property lies on the right of way. The beleaguered ranchers are led by Thomas Logan, whose son Steve is returning home after finishing his law studies at Harvard. When Jerry "Pop" Wilkie's house is burned down, Rutledge, a local resident, shoots Gagan, who was working with Knox and was responsible for the blaze. Later, Maggie Adams, Steve's old sweetheart, warns Knox that Steve will lead the embittered town in bringing him to justice. After evaluating the situation, however, Steve decides that the best way to combat the railroad king is to pretend to be his ally. Disowned by his family and friends for his apparent allegiance to Knox, Steve secretly circulates a newspaper in which he accuses the tycoon of stealing property. He also preaches the principles of free choice and democracy to the railroad construction gang, which is composed mainly of immigrants. Steve befriends Knox' construction foreman, Chris Mulligan, and convinces him that his boss is a swindler and a crook. Maggie, thinking that Steve has abandoned her as well as his morals, becomes furious with him and, out of spite, agrees to marry Knox to make him jealous, but her plan fails. Realizing that Knox is preoccupied with his underground newspaper, Steve convinces the tycoon to start his own newspaper, and when Knox purchases the equipment, Steve steals the new press for his own use. Tension is heightened when Tom is shot and his house is set ablaze, and when Knox tries to prevent Steve from rescuing his father from the fire. After revealing his plan to win Knox' confidence to his father and Maggie, Steve makes an appeal to the townspeople by speaking against tyranny, while Knox stands at the opposite end of the stage and makes threats against him. Things look bad for Steve until Maggie saves the day by leading everyone in the song, "My Country 'Tis of Thee." As a result, the townspeople show their solidarity with Steve, and Knox is overthrown. Having restored the tenets of democracy to the town of Clover City, Maggie and Steve reunite. Ethics. Heroes. Land rights. Newspapers. Railroad companies. Railroads. Ranchers. Arson. Construction workers. Democracy. Employer-employee relations. Fathers and sons. Gunshot wounds. Immigrants. Impersonation and imposture. Irish Americans. Jealousy. Lawyers. Romance. Songs. Speeches. Thieves.

Note: Working titles for this film were *The Dusty Road* and *Song of the West.* A *HR* pre-release news item indicates that Allen Jenkins was originally set

for the comedy lead that was taken over by Victor McLaglen in the film. Although a *HR* pre-release news item lists actor Francis X. Bushman, Jr. in the cast, his appearance in the released film has not been confirmed. *HR* news items also note that exteriors were filmed in Arizona at Keene Camp and in the San Jacinto Mountains, CA., and that a desert sequence was filmed on a studio sound stage that housed the studio ice rink. Some actors reportedly complained of cold feet while performing on the sand-covered ice rink. Studio records note that McLaglen injured himself while filming a scene in which he was to tackle a mule after it kicked him. The mule bit McLaglen, and when he tried to bite the mule back, McLaglen slipped and pulled a ligament. According to information contained in the MPAA/PCA Collection at the AMPAS Library, German censors "deleted the song praising America as a land of freedom," a reference to one of the characters as an "Irish windmill," and a fight between "Mulligan" and "Steve." Censors in Estonia deleted the line: "You Germans, Italians, Jews...All you who are oppressed...here you are free." *Var* commented that this film is "the first in the cycle of film offerings to stress the American type of democracy and freedom for the classes and masses." They praised the presentation of film's message, stating, "Showmanship is apparent in selecting historical background and episodes in which to stress the freedom of America and its advantages. Message is brought home through patriotic appeals to gang of more than 200 hunkies, and picture nicely stresses the nationalities represented in that group which came to America to enjoy the advantages of this country."

DV 15 Feb 1939, p. 3. *FD* 20 Feb 1939, p. 9. *HR* 25 Nov 1938, p. 3. *HR* 26 Nov 1938, p. 2. *HR* 29 Nov 1938, p. 3. *HR* 1 Dec 1938, p. 2. *HR* 6 Jan 1939, p. 4. *HR* 11 Jan 1939, p. 7, 8. *HR* 15 Feb 1939, p. 2. *MPD* 20 Feb 1939, p. 5. *MPH* 14 Jan 1939, p. 36. *MPH* 18 Feb 1939, p. 42. *NYT* 10 Mar 1939, p. 19. *Var* 22 Feb 1939, p. 12.

LET US BE GAY (*foreign version*) see **SOYONS GAIS**

LET'S FALL IN LOVE (Swedih Americans)

Columbia Pictures Corp.; Harry Cohn, President. *Dist* Columbia Pictures Corp. 26 Dec 1933; *Prod*: 23 Oct–18 Nov 1933 [©Columbia Pictures Corp.; 5 Jan 1934; LP4387]. Sd (Western Electric Noiseless Recording); b&w. 7 reels. 67 or 73 min. PCA cert no. 6222-R [1 Apr 1940].

[*Assoc prod* Felix Young]. *Dir* David Burton. [*Asst dir* Arthur Black]. *Story and scr* Herbert Fields. *Photog* Benjamin Kline. *Film ed* Gene Milford. *Mus dir* Bakaleinikoff. [*Sd eng* George Cooper].

Song(s): "Let's Fall in Love" and "Love Is Love Anywhere," music and lyrics by Harold Arlen and Ted Koehler.

Cast: Edmund Lowe (*Ken [Lane]*), Ann Sothern (*Jean [Kendall, also known as Sigrid Lund]*), Miriam Jordan (*Gerry [Marsh]*), Gregory Ratoff (*Max [Hooper]*), Greta Meyer (*Lisa [Bjorkman]*), Betty Furness (*Linda*), Arthur Jarrett (*Composer*), Anderson Lawler (*Allen [Foster]*), Tala Birell ([*Hedwig*] *Forsell*), Ruth Warren (*Nellie*), Marjorie Gateson (*Agatha [Holmes]*), [John Qualen (*Svente Bjorkman*)], [Niles Welch (*Archie Frost*)], [Kane Richmond (*Ray*)], [Ethel Clayton (*Star*)], [Lorin Raker (*Secretary*)], [Selmer Jackson (*Barton*)], [Charles Giblyn (*Garland*)], [Michael Visaroff (*Trent*)], [Edwin Stanley (*Roland Markwell*)], [Consuelo Baker (*Mildred*)], [Sven Hugo Borg (*Eric*)].

Show business, Comedy-drama, with songs. [*Print viewed*]. On a sound stage at Premier Pictures in Hollywood, successful film director Ken Lane is preparing to shoot the next scene of his new production, a five-year-old pet project set in Sweden. Tempestuous star Hedwig Forsell, whom Ken discovered, becomes irritated with her maid for a small oversight, then stalks off the set after claiming that the script is "bunk" and vowing to return home. Despite producer Max Hooper's efforts to defuse the situation, Ken refuses to play "wet nurse to a flat-footed Swede." When Max suggests replacing Hedwig with an American, Ken insists that his film needs a Swedish actress who can sing well. The New York office pressures Max to shut down the production, but Ken keeps hoping to discover his elusive star. When Ken and his fiancée, Gerry Marsh, visit a circus, Ken is taken with the beautiful Jean Kendall, a sideshow concession worker with a fake French accent. Although she does not initially believe Ken's promise to make her a movie actress, he convinces her to give it a try. Ken places Jean in the home of Lisa and Svente Bjorkman, from whom she learns the customs and language of Sweden. Ken is able to stall Max's cancellation of the project for another five weeks, and after Jean successfully passes herself off to a group of Lisa's friends, Ken believes that she is ready for Max. Jean, who has fallen in love with Ken, is disappointed to learn that he is engaged. Consoled by Lisa, Jean nonetheless hopes that one day Ken will love her. Ken tells Max about Jean, whom he has renamed Sigrid Lund, and convinces him that she is reluctant to become an actress. Max invites Jean to lunch and believes, after much effort, that he has convinced her to sign a seven-year contract with his studio. After Jean performs a love scene with Ken as a screen test, Gerry views the developed footage

and becomes convinced that Jean, whom she recognizes from the circus, is too realistic in her performance. As the publicity for the new star fills headlines across the country, Max invites the press and representatives of the film industry to meet Jean at his home in Santa Monica. As Sigrid begins to sing at the party, the drunken and jealous Gerry exposes the scam and walks out on Ken. Max, infuriated with Ken for not telling him of his decision to cast an American instead of a Swede, lashes out at the director, who resigns the next morning. After Jean disappears, the public swamps theater owners with letters demanding that her film be released. Max, realizing that it was a mistake to lose the star and her director, offers to renegotiate with Ken, who will return to the studio only if Jean is found. Learning from Lisa that Jean has returned to the circus, Ken trails her to Kansas City, where the reunited couple declare their love. *Hollywood (CA). Impersonation and imposture. Motion picture actors and actresses. Motion picture directors. Publicity. Circuses. Contracts. Deception. Engagements. Jealousy. Letters. Motion picture producers. Parties. Santa Monica (CA). Swedish Americans.*

Note: Although contemporary reviews list only two songs, "Let's Fall in Love" and "Love Is Love Anywhere," modern sources list two additional songs, "Breakfast Ball" and "This is Only the Beginning," which were not included in the final print. The story was remade by Columbia in 1949 under the title *Slightly French*, directed by Douglas Sirk and starring Dorothy Lamour.

DV 6 Jan 1934, p. 3. *FD* 20 Jan 1934, p. 3. *MPD* 9 Jan 1934. *MPH* 13 Jan 1934, p. 39. *NYT* 22 Jan 1934, p. 12. *Var* 23 Jan 1934, p. 13.

LET'S GET TOUGH! (Japanese Americans, Chinese Americans)

Banner Productions. *Dist* Monogram Pictures Corp. 29 May **1942**; Prod: 31 Mar—mid-Apr 1942 [©Monogram Pictures Corp.; 22 May 1942; LP11456]. Sd; b&w. 7 reels, 5,572 ft. 62 min. PCA cert no. 8317.

Series: The East Side Kids.

Prod Sam Katzman and Jack Dietz. *Assoc prod* Barney A. Sarecky. *Dir* Wallace Fox. *Asst dir* Arthur Hammond and Gerald Schnitzer. *Orig story and scr* Harvey Gates. *Photog* Arthur Reed. *Art dir* David Milton. *Film ed* Robert Golden. *Sd eng* Glen Glenn. [*Prod mgr* Ed Rote].

Cast: Leo Gorcey (*Muggs*), Bobby Jordan (*Danny*), Huntz Hall (*Glimpy*), Gabriel Dell (*Fritz Heinbach*), Tom Brown (*Phil*), Florence Rice (*Nora Stevens*), Robert Armstrong (*Pop Stevens*), David Gorcey (*Peewee*), Sunshine Sammy Morrisson (*Scruno*), Bobby Stone (*Skinny*), Sam Bernard (*Heinbach Sr.*), Phil Ahn (*Joe Matsui*), Jerry Bergen (*Music master*).

Youth, Comedy-drama. [*Print viewed*]. The Eastside Kids, a gang of tough but honest youth in New York City, are frustrated that their age keeps them from serving in the army during World War II, so they wage a private war at home. Their first target is a storekeeper whom they believe to be Japanese, and they pelt his store with rotten vegetables. When they enter the store to smash the curios, they discover the owner has been stabbed to death. The Kids are questioned and released by the police. Learning that the owner was actually Chinese, the Kids make a heartfelt apology to his widow. Their curiosity is then aroused when a supposed patron, Joe Matsui, steals a pen from the store's desk. After they steal the pen from Joe, the Kids discover a piece of paper hidden inside it, which reveals Japanese writing when a light is held near it. Muggs, the leader of the East Side Kids, takes the note to the Matsui tea shop and asks Joe's father to interpret it. When the elder Matsui snatches the note, Muggs grabs it back, and Matsui commits suicide. The Kids drag policeman Pop Stevens to the scene, but Joe disguises himself as his own father to allay suspicions about his father's death. Danny, a member of the gang, is surprised by the appearance of his brother Phil in the tea shop. Phil has been dishonorably discharged from the Navy for sabotage, and his covert actions now seem suspicious to the Kids. They steal a bag containing a white substance hidden in the tea shop and take it home. When the bag explodes on the stove, Stevens helps them put out the fire and identifies the substance as magnesium, a valuable wartime resource which he suspects is being illegally supplied by a local storekeeper named Heinbach. Muggs gives the Japanese note to Nora, Phil's girl friend and Stevens' daughter, to be translated, but when she takes it to her old high school friend, Joe, he and Heinbach's son Fritz hold her hostage. The Kids now become convinced that a spy ring is operating in their neighborhood and break into the tea shop and infiltrate a clandestine meeting of fifth columnists wearing hoods and gowns. After Phil is revealed as a member, the Kids are discovered and a brawl ensues. Phil, who has

actually been working undercover for the U.S. government, rounds up the spies, including Matsui and Heinbach, Sr., with the help of the Eastside Kids, the spies are arrested by the police. Phil and Nora marry, but he is forced to report back to the Navy before they can go on their honeymoon. *Bigotry. Japanese. Juvenile delinquents. Murder. Nazis. Spies. Brothers. Chinese. Curio dealers. Fathers and sons. Fights. Magnesium. New York City. Police. Suicide. Undercover agents. World War II.*

Note: The opening title card reads "The Eastside Kids in *Let's Get Tough!*" The working titles of this film were *Little MacArthurs*, *I Am an American* and *Little Americans*. *Little MacArthurs* was announced in *HR* as the first film title to mention General Douglas MacArthur by name. For additonal information on the series, consult the Series Index and see entries for *Crime School* and *Little Tough Guy* in *AFI Catalog of Feature Films, 1931-40*; F3.0873 and F3.2534.

Box 16 May 1942. *DV* 16 Mar 1942. *DV* 11 May 1942. *FD* 13 May 1942, p. 6. *HR* 5 Mar 1942, p. 3. *HR* 10 Apr 1942, p. 4. *HR* 11 May 1942, p. 3. *MPHPD* 16 May 1942, p. 662.

LET'S HAVE FUN (Russian Americans)

Columbia Pictures Corp. *Dist* Columbia Pictures Corp. 4 Mar **1943**; Prod: 7 Jul—25 Jul 1942 [©Columbia Pictures Corp.; 16 Feb 1943; LP11884]. Sd (Western Electric Mirrophonic Recording); b&w. 5,863 ft. 63 or 66 min. PCA cert no. 8636.

Prod Jack Fier. *Dir* Charles Barton. [*Asst dir* Rex Bailey]. *Story and scr* Harry Sauber. *Dir of photog* Philip Tannura. *Art dir* Lionel Banks. *Assoc* Paul Murphy. *Film ed* William Claxton and [James Sweeney]. *Mus dir* M. W. Stoloff. *Dance dir* Robert Priestley. [*Sd eng* John Haynes].

Song(s): "On the Road to Siberia" and "I Like This Loving You," words and music by Sammy Cahn and Saul Chaplin.

Cast: Margaret Lindsay (*Florence Blake*), John Beal (*Richard Gilbert*), Leonid Kinskey (*Gregory Loosnikoff*), Sig Arno (*Ivan Bloosnikoff*), Dorothy Ann Seese (*Toni Gilbert*), Bert Gordon (*"The Mad Russian"* [*Boris Raskolnikoff*]), [Constance Worth (*Diana Crawford*)], [Edward Keane (*J. H. Bradley*)], [Ernest Hilliard (*"Pepe" J. Morgan*)], [John Tyrrell (*Jimmy Wood*)], [Netta Packer (*Miss Berkley*)], [Louise Squire (*Burlesque queen*)], [John T. Murray (*Legitimate actor*)], [Walter Baldwin (*Hotel clerk*)], [Shirley Patterson (*Girl*)], [Jayne Hazard (*Norma*)], [Edward Kane (*Norton*)], [Beryl Wallace (*Sonia*)], [Reginald Simpson, Ray Johnson, Wedgwood Nowell (*Reporters*)], [Dick Rush (*Doorman*)], [Pat McVey (*Bates*)], [Hallene Hill], [James Morton], [Al Herman], [Gwen Seager], [Joe Novak].

Show business, Comedy-drama, with songs. [*Print viewed*]. Unemployed theatrical director Boris Raskolnikoff, unemployed actor Richard Gilbert and Gilbert's little daughter Toni all share a suite at the Hotel Montrose. When their rent falls in arrears, Richard decides to take a job as a taxi driver to support them. Richard's decision spurs Boris into action, and he talks his friends, Russian restauranteurs Gregory Loosnikoff and Ivan Bloosnikoff, into investing in his play *The Road to Siberia*. After the production fails miserably, Boris moves to the Bronx. Before leaving Manhattan, he admonishes Richard's agent and sweetheart, Florence Blake, to prevent Richard from abandoning his career in the theater. After Boris departs, Richard and Toni leave the hotel and rent an inexpensive apartment. Hoping to promote Richard's career, Florence visits producer J. H. Bradley, who is in the process of assembling a cast and crew for a production backed by the rich boyfriend of his temperamental star, Diana Crawford. When Florence shows Diana Richard's photograph, the man-hungry actress inquires if he is married. After Florence responds in the negative, Diana offers Richard the part of her leading man. Florence also convinces Bradley to hire Boris as his dance director, and Boris returns from his exile in the Bronx. At the start of rehearsals, Diana begins her seduction of Richard. Boris, meanwhile, decides to surprise Richard by moving back into their old Montrose Hotel suite, and organizes a party to celebrate the occasion. As the hour grows late, Richard fails to appear and Toni goes to bed, disappointed. When Richard finally returns home tipsy after a night of party-hopping with Diana and her fancy friends, Boris rebukes him. Concerned that Richard has become smitten by the superficial Diana, Boris asks Florence to help bring him to his senses. To thwart Richard's budding romance, Boris invites Toni to rehearsals, and when Diana learns that Richard has a daughter, she discharges both him and Boris. Fed up with Diana's temper tantrums, Bradley fires her, even though it means losing the financial backing of her rich boyfriend. After Richard and Boris reconcile, Boris decides to ask the Russian restauranteurs to invest in Bradley's play.

Before Boris arrives at the restaurant, a representative from an advertising agency offers the Russians $10,000 for the rights to *The Road to Siberia*. When they read the play's contract, however, they discover that Boris owns the rights. Soon after, Boris enters the restaurant and the Russians eagerly offer to buy his rights to the play. When Boris counters their offer with a deal to produce Bradley's play, the three Russians proceed to the advertising agency and collect a check for $10,000, which they invest in the drama. After Boris hires a new, married, leading lady, rehearsals begin, and the production becomes a smash hit. *Actors and actresses. Financial crisis. New York City–Broadway. Seduction. Theatrical directors. Advertising agencies. Drunkenness. Fathers and daughters. Flirts. Plays. Russians. Theatrical agents. Theatrical backers. Theatrical producers. Unemployment.*

Note: The working titles of this film were *Laugh Your Blues Away* and *Shall I Tell 'Em?*. Early *HR* production charts list James Sweeney as editor, although William Claxton is listed in that position in the onscreen credits.

Box 20 Feb 1943. *DV* 22 Apr 1943, p. 3. *HR* 17 Jul 1942, p. 9. *HR* 22 Apr 1943, p. 3. *MPH* 1 May 1943. *MPHPD* 1 May 1943, p. 1290.

LET'S SING AGAIN (Italian Americans)
Principal Productions, Inc.; Bobby Breen Productions, Inc. *Dist* RKO Radio Pictures, Inc. 12 Jun 1936; Prod: 11 Jan—late Feb 1936 at RKO Pathé Studios. Sd (RCA Victor System); b&w. 67 or 70 min. PCA cert no. 2152.
Prod Sol Lesser. *Dir* Kurt Neumann. *Asst dir* Fred Tyler. *Scr* Don Swift and Dan Jarrett. *Story* Don Swift. *Story supv* Harry Chandlee. *Photog* Harry Neumann and [Frank Good]. *Art dir* Ben Carre. *Film ed* Robert Crandall. *Mus setting conceived and dir by* Hugo Riesenfeld. *Assoc* Abe Meyer. *Sd eng* Richard E. Tyler and [Hal Baumbaugh]. *Prod mgr* Edward Gross.
Song(s): "Let's Sing Again," words and music by Jimmy McHugh and Gus Kahn; "Lullaby," words and music by Hugo Riesenfeld and Selma Hautzik; "Farmer in the Dell," words and music by Samuel Pokrass and Charles O. Locke.
Cast: Bobby Breen (*Billy Gordon*), Henry Armetta (*Joe Pasquale*), George Houston (*Leon Alba*), Vivienne Osborne (*Rosa Donelli*), Grant Withers [(*Jim "Diablo" Wilkins*)], Inez Courtney [(*Margie Wilkins*)], Richard Carle [(*Carter*)], Lucien Littlefield [(*Superintendent Henry Perkins*)], Ann Doran [(*Alice Alba*)], Clay Clement [(*Jackson*)].
Drama, with songs. [*Print viewed*]. Tired of her life of poverty in Naples, Alice Alba leaves her aspiring opera singer husband Leon and returns to America with their baby son. Years later, the now orphaned boy, Billy Gordon, lives at the Mapleton Orphanage in Connecticut, unaware of his parentage. When Carter's Traveling Theatre rolls into town, Billy sneaks in to see the show and meets Joe Pasquale, a former opera star and teacher, now reduced to playing the singing buffoon. Taken with Joe, Billy hides in a basket in his trailer, where he is discovered by the singer the next morning, far away from the orphanage. Although he is at first reluctant to allow Billy to stay, Joe eventually makes him a member of the troupe and begins to develop the boy's superior young voice. At the same time, Jim "Diablo" Wilkins, the show's misanthropic trapeze artist, sees Billy as a way out of his penny ante life and wires the orphanage with an offer to adopt the boy. As Diablo and the orphanage authorities are about to grab Billy, Billy and Joe escape and head for New York, where Joe, sick with fever, arranges a meeting with his ex-pupil, Rosa Donelli, a successful soprano. Concerned for Joe's health, Rosa brings Joe and Billy to stay at her lavish home, unaware that her friend, Leon Alba, who has been searching vainly for his long-lost wife and son, is Billy's father. Diablo and the police soon track Billy to Rosa's, but before they can lay claim to him, Leon, who is giving a concert there, begins to sing the lullaby that he wrote for Billy as a baby. Recognizing the tune that his mother taught him, Billy joins in, and father and son are at last reunited. *Italian Americans. Long-lost relatives. Opera singers. Orphans. Reunions. Adoption. Aerialists. Concerts. Connecticut. Desertion (Marital). Escapes. Naples (Italy). New York City. Orphanages. Police. Sideshows.*

Note: The working title of this film was *The Show Goes On*. Bobby Breen, the "Wonder Boy," a popular eight-year-old radio performer and a protégé of Eddie Cantor's, made his screen debut in this film. After the success of *Let's Sing Again*, Principal Productions made seven other "Bobby Breen" movies for RKO, which touted Breen as its resident child star. Other songs performed in part by Breen were the aria "La donna e mobile" from Giuseppe Verdi's opera *Rigoletto*, and the Italian folk song "Oy, Marie." According to a *HR* news item, producer Sol Lesser tried to cast opera star Marion Talley in the "Rosa Donelli"

role, but was "unable to get together" with her on a salary. Because of a delay in the start of production, Kurt Neumann had to replace Arthur Greville Collins as director, according to *HR*. *HR* also noted that during production, Breen had an emergency appendectomy, which delayed production for about two weeks. As indicated by *HR* production charts, after filming resumed, Harry Neumann replaced Frank Good as photographer and Richard E. Tyler replaced Hal Baumbaugh as sound engineer. *HR* production charts add Spencer Charters and Renee Whitney to the cast, but their participation in the final film has not been confirmed. Although the viewed print of the film included a copyright statement for Variety Film Distributors, no record of such a copyright has been found. It is presumed that Variety was a television distributor.

DV 15 Apr 1936, p. 3. *FD* 17 Apr 1936, p. 4. *HR* 6 Jan 1936, p. 3. *HR* 10 Jan 1936, p. 2. *HR* 13 Jan 1936, p. 2. *HR* 30 Jan 1936, p. 5. *HR* 17 Feb 1936, p. 2. *HR* 15 Apr 1936, p. 3. *MPH* 25 Apr 1936, pp. 36-37. *NYT* 9 May 1936, p. 11. *Var* 13 May 1936, p. 14.

THE LETTER (*foreign version*) see **LA CARTA**

LETTER FROM THE PRESIDEN see **MY MAN AND I**

A LETTER TO MAMA see **A BRIVELE DER MAMEN**

LEWIS AND CLARK see **THE FAR HORIZONS**

LA LEY DEL HAREM (Spanish language)
Fox Film Corp. *Dist* Fox Film Corp. 1931; Los Angeles opening: 9 Oct 1931; Prod: Jul—Aug 1931. Sd; b&w. 8 reels, 6,903 ft. 77 min. Passed by the National Board of Review. Spanish language.
Dir Lewis Seiler. [*Scen* Paul Perez and William Kernell]. [*Spanish version* Matías Cirici-Ventalló]. *Photog* Sidney Wagner. *Film ed* Jerry Webb. *Sd* Bernard Freericks. [*Tech adv* Jamiel Hasson].
Song(s): "Alah, oye nuestra canción," "Nocturno," "Grito de guerra," and "Mi Serenata (Serenata veneciana)" by William Kernell and José Mojica; "Cuento," by Troy Sanders and José Mojica.
Source: Based on the novel *L'insoumise* by Pierre Frondaie (Paris, 1922).
Cast: José Mojica (*El príncipe Al-Hadi*), Carmen Larrabeiti (*Renée Duval*), María Alba (*Fátima*), Ralph Navarro (*Fredy Clavering*), Julio Villarreal (*Hassan*), Rafael Calvo (*Muezzin*), Raúl Figarola (*Achmed*), Miguel Ligero (*Alberto Herbert*), Virginia Arbo (*Mary Herbert*), [Paco Moreno (*Primer eunuco*)], [Alfredo del Diestro (*Segundo eunuco*)].
Romance, Adventure, Musical. [*Not viewed*]. Al-Hadi, an Arabian prince, returns from a successful hunt only to learn that a caravan has been ambushed by his traditional enemies, the Kababish. Al-Hadi and his warriors ride out after the bandits and discover, hidden in the ruins of the caravan, Renée Duval, a Frenchwoman who had been on her way to Venice via her yacht on the Red Sea. Al-Hadi captures the bandit chieftain and orders that Renée be escorted to a nearby railroad to head for home. After Renée is taken away, the bandit's head is chopped off, but not before the appropriate prayers are said. Al-Hadi returns to his harem, where Fátima, a concubine, tries to charm him. He is cold, however, and not even a pillow fight between the concubines and the eunuchs cheers him up. Fátima's father, Grand Vizier Hassan, wants Al-Hadi and Fátima to wed so that he can increase his own personal power. Hassan convinces the local holy man, the Muezzin, to suggest the marriage to Al-Hadi, but the prince replies that he first has a long journey to make. He goes to a party in Venice, where Renée's boyfriend, Fredy Clavering, presses her to marry him. Fredy becomes perturbed at the attention Renée showers on the dashing prince. Renée and Al-Hadi take a gondola ride, and they kiss after the prince serenades her. The two then elope to Paris, where they are married. There they enjoy the life of the rich, until Al-Hadi becomes sick of European ways and, despite her resistance, takes Renée back to his kingdom. During the next six months, Renée is miserable and uncooperative, while Hassan and the Muezzin try to convince Al-Hadi to get rid of her and take Fátima as his wife. When Al-Hadi refuses, Fátima wants to kill Renée with a dagger, but her father comes up with a scheme to solve the problem. He convinces Renée that she is in great danger and provides her with a guide, money, and horses to get away. Hassan then shoots the guide and, after he has Renée captured, accuses her of theft. Al-Hadi believes the charge and imprisons her until she tells who helped her attempt the escape. After Hassan quotes an ancient law, "The woman who has abandoned her husband's household shall be condemned to death by torture," Renée is sentenced to die at dawn. Al-Hadi then denounces the law, and he is seized as a traitor. He fights his captors, then jumps through a window, takes a horse and rides off into the desert. Finding a tribe of his nomadic followers, Al-Hadi convinces them to aid him in rescuing Renée. Hassan has a brazier of hot coals placed in her cell

and promises to begin the torture in one hour. Al-Hadi and his men then burst into the city and fight their way toward the prison. Just as Hassan is about to brand Renée with a hot iron, Al-Hadi crashes through the door and shoots the villain dead. The couple escape back into the desert, where Al-Hadi acknowledges that he has been mistreating Renée and offers to let her go home alone. She refuses and they agree to find a distant land where they can both be happy together. *Arabs. Bandits. Cultural conflict. Deserts. French. Marriage. Princes. Rescues. Romance. Romantic rivalry. Branding. Caravans. Concubinage. Decapitation. Elopement. Escapes. Eunuchs. False arrests. Fathers and daughters. Gondolas and gondoliers. Harems. Nomads. Paris (France). Parties. Red Sea. Torture. Venice (Italy).*

Note: The plot summary was based on a screen continuity in the Twentieth Century-Fox Produced Scripts Collection at the UCLA Theater Arts Library. The working titles of this film were *En los brazos de ella* and *El hijo del desierto*. In 1928, Fox produced a film based on the same source entitled *Fazil*, which was directed by Howard Hawks and starred Charles Farrell and Greta Nissen (see *AFI Catalog of Feature Films, 1921-30*; F2.1670).

    CM Nov 1931, p. 828. *FD* 20 Jun 1933, p. 4. *NYT* 17 Jun 1933, p. 16.

LI TING LANG (Chinese Americans)

Haworth Pictures Corp. *Dist* Robertson-Cole Distributing Corp. Jul 1920 [©Haworth Pictures Corp.; 15 Jul 1920; LU15398]. Si; b&w. 5 reels, 4,700 ft.

Dir Charles Swickard. *Scen* E. Richard Schayer. *Cam* Frank D. Williams.

Source: Based on the short story "Li Ting Lang, Chinese Gentleman" by Howard P. Rockey in *The Green Book Magazine* (Dec 1916).

Cast: Sessue Hayakawa (*Li Ting Lang*), Allan Forrest (*Rob Murray*), Charles E. Mason (*Red Dalton*), Doris Pawn (*Marion Halstead*), Frances Raymond (*Priscilla Mayhew*), Marc Robbins (*Prince Nu Chang*).

Drama. College student Li Ting Lang is a favorite of his friends until his attentions toward socialite Marion Halstead bring forth protests on all sides. In defiance, Marion announces her engagement to Li Ting Lang. Gradually, she becomes socially isolated and Li, realizing that she will be friendless, releases her from her commitment. Soon after, an emissary to America arrives with instructions to compel Li to return to his native land and administers a drug to Li, who awakens aboard a ship bound for China, while back in America, his friends believe that he has committed suicide. Li arrives in the middle of a revolution and becomes a great military leader. Years later, while visiting the Orient on her honeymoon, Marion sees Li and recognizes him. Venturing to his house, she is followed by one of his enemies who plans to kill the girl and throw the guilt on Li, thereby ruining him. When the plotters arrive, Li defends Marion singlehandedly until a rescue party of his old college chums comes to his aid. After a warm reunion among old friends, Marion departs with her husband, and Li is sadly left alone once again. *China. Chinese. Miscegenation. Officers (Military). Ostracism. Racism. Revolutions. Students. College life. Drugs. Friendship. Kidnapping. Socialites.*

Note: This film was copyrighted under the title *Traditions Altar*.
    ETR 24 Jul 1920, p. 843. *MPN* 24 Jul 1920, p. 857. *MPW* 24 Jul 1920, p. 505. *NYMT* 11 Jul 1920, p. 9. *Var* 23 Jul 1920, p. 33. *Wid's* 11 Jul 1920, p. 9.

THE LIAR (African Americans)

Fox Film Corp. *Dist* Fox Film Corp. 18 Aug 1918 [©William Fox; 18 Aug 1918; LP12769]. Si; b&w. 5 reels.

Dir Edmund Lawrence. *Story* Katherine Kavanaugh.

Cast: Virginia Pearson (*Sybil Houston*), Alexander Frank (*Hugh Houston*), Edward F. Roseman (*Franklin Harvey*), Victor Sutherland (*John Carter*), Eugene Borden (*Jimmie Marsh*), Albert Roccardi (*Sam Harris*), Liane Held Carrera (*Mary Elliott*), Myra Brooke (*Mammy Lou*), Matilda Brundage (*Mrs. Elliott*).

Drama. Sam Harris, a black worker on the sugar plantation of Hugh Houston in Puerto Rico, is crippled for life when Houston beats him. Huston silences Harris with money and promises him a monthly allotment for the rest of his life. Houston's secretary, Franklin Harvey, is puzzled by Harris' regular appearances at Houston's office. When Houston's daughter Sybil, who lives in Boston, visits her father, she so enchants Harvey that he becomes fiercely determined to marry her. Sybil repulses Franklin's attentions, and after her father dies, Franklin tries to prevent her marriage to the man she loves, John Carter, by falsifying Houston's marriage certificate, substituting the name of Harris' mother for that of Sybil's own. When he threatens to reveal to

John that Sybil is part black, she orders him to leave but is later haunted by the fear that her child will be born black. Franklin angrily tells his story to John, and while the two men fight, Sybil rushes into the next room and apparently shoots herself. Remorseful at the thought that Sybil killed herself because of him, Franklin confesses his lie, but Sybil appears at the door unharmed and says she knew he was lying. *African Americans. Blackmail. Boston (MA). Forgers and forgery. Racism. Secretaries. Unrequited love. Confession (Law). Fear. Fights. Plantations. Puerto Rico.*

Note: The copyright entry attributes the scenario to Adeline Leitzbach. The story by Katherine Kavanaugh included in the copyright descriptions was originally entitled "The Alien Strain." On the cover sheet of the story, George Scarborough's name as story writer seems to be partially scratched out or erased.

    ETR 3 Aug 1918, p. 747. *ETR* 31 Aug 1918, p. 1089. *MPN* 31 Aug 1918, p. 1367. *MPW* 16 Feb 1918, p. 1008. *MPW* 31 Aug 1918, p. 1302. *NYDM* 31 Aug 1918, p. 319. *Var* 13 Sep 1918, p. 44.

THE LIE *see* **THE SIGN OF THE POPPY**

LIEBE AUF BEFEHL *see* **DON JUAN DIPLOMÁTICO**

LIEBE UND LEIDENSCHAFT *see* **LOVE AND SACRIFICE**

THE LIFE AND DEATH OF LIEUTENANT PETROSINO *see* **THE ADVENTURES OF LIEUTENANT PETROSINO**

LIFE BEGINS IN COLLEGE (Native Americans)

Twentieth Century-Fox Film Corp.; Darryl F. Zanuck in charge of production. *Dist* Twentieth Century-Fox Film Corp. 1 Oct 1937; New York opening: week of 24 Sep 1937; Prod: 12 Jul—early Sep 1937 [©Twentieth Century-Fox Film Corp.; 1 Oct 1937; LP7520]. Sd (Western Electric Mirrophonic Recording); b&w. 11 reels, 8,493 ft. 94 min. PCA cert no. 3641.

Assoc prod Harold Wilson. *Dir* William A. Seiter. *Asst dir* Charles Hall. *Story* Karl Tunberg and Don Ettlinger. *Photog* Robert Planck. *Art dir* Hans Peters. *Film ed* Louis Loeffler. *Set dec* Thomas Little. *Cost* Royer. *Mus dir* Louis Silvers. [*Vocal supv* Jule Styne]. [*Dance dir* Geneva Sawyer and Nick Castle]. *Sd* Arthur Von Kirbach and Roger Heman.

Song(s): "Big Chief Swing It," "Our Team Is on the Warpath," "Fair Lombardy" and "Why Talk About Love?" music and lyrics by Lew Pollack and Sidney D. Mitchell; "Sweet Varsity Sue," music and lyrics by Charles Tobias, Al Lewis and Murray Mencher; Ritz Brothers Specialties by Samuel Pokrass, Sid Kuller and Ray Golden.

Source: Suggested by short stories by Darrell Ware (publication undetermined).

Cast: RITZ BROTHERS (*Themselves*), Joan Davis (*Inez*), Tony Martin (*Band leader*), Gloria Stuart (*Janet O'Hara*), Fred Stone (*Coach [Tim] O'Hara*), Nat Pendleton (*George Black*), Dick Baldwin (*Bob Hayner*), Joan Marsh (*Cuddles*), Jed Prouty (*Oliver Stearns, Sr.*), Maurice Cass (*Dean Moss*), Ed Thorgersen (*Radio announcer*), Marjorie Weaver (*Miss Murphy*), Robert Lowery (*Sling*), Lon Chaney, Jr. (*Gilks*), J. C. Nugent (*T. Edwin Cabot*), Fred Kohler, Jr. (*Bret*), Elisha Cook, Jr. (*Ollie Stearns*), Charles Wilson (*Coach Burke*), Frank Sully (*Acting captain*), Norman Willis (*Referee*), [Dixie Dunbar (*Polly*)], [Dick Klein, Ron Cooley (*Cheerleaders*)], [Jim Pierce, Jeff Cravath (*Coaches*)], [Hal K. Dawson (*Graduate manager*)], [Sarah Edwards (*Teacher*)], [Robert Murphy (*Rooter*)], [Spec O'Donnell (*Ugly student*)], [Jan Duggan (*Telephone operator*)], [Edmund Jones, Lester Wilkins, Ben Green, Roy Glenn (*Singing porters*)], [Martin Turner (*Pullman porter*)], [Frank Melton (*Customer*)], [Edward Arnold, Jr., Thomas Kellard, Grant Peters (*Huskies*)], [Ernie Alexander, William Moore (*Score markers*)].

College, Football, Musical comedy. [*Print viewed*]. Little Black Cloud, who calls himself "George Black," is the first Indian in recent times to enroll at Lombardy College, which was founded in 1847, according to a plaque, "to give the Indian nations of North America access to higher education." Upon George's arrival, football star Bob Hayner and his fraternity pals blindfold George and dress him in a nightgown, then encourage him to go into a women's physical science class and give a "war whoop." George obeys and the girls convulse in laughter. After Janet O'Hara, who owns the nightgown that the pranksters used, is drenched with a bucket of water meant for George, she berates Bob. Humiliated, George decides to leave, but he first takes his ripped trousers to the "Klassy Kampus Kleaners," which is run by the Ritz Brothers. Seeing that George carries a lot of money, the brothers convince him to stay in school. Meanwhile,

Janet's father, Coach Tim O'Hara, is asked to resign because of his age by a committee of which Bob is a member. Bob, who is attracted to Janet, tells her that he has convinced the committee to change their minds, but at a dance, the dean announces her father's resignation, whereupon Janet slaps Bob. George, whom Janet has helped escape from Inez, a love-struck student, tells the Ritz Brothers that he would like to help the coach, but that he does not want to use his money, which he gets from oil wells in Oklahoma, because he wants people to like him for himself. The brothers offer to spend the money for him, and after purchasing massages, manicures, shoeshines, new clothes and cars, they give the college $50,000 on the condition that O'Hara be reinstated and that they be allowed to play on the football team. At practice, George tackles Bob, who makes a bigoted remark regarding him. George then runs back a punt for a touchdown and knocks Bob over. When Bob slugs George, O'Hara makes George the first-string quarterback. With George in command, Lombardy begins to win all their games by wide margins, despite the efforts of the Ritz Brothers, who invariably, though unintentionally, score points for the other side. At a victory bonfire before the big game with Midwestern, George, annoyed by Inez, tells her that in order to marry him, she must have a tattoo of a snake on her arm. Janet becomes convinced that Bob really did try to help, but she is dismayed when she sees him with his former girl friend Cuddles, who forces him to take her home by threatening to reveal that George used to play football in Oklahoma for an oil company team and therefore, because he was a professional, cannot play in college. On the train to Midwestern, Cuddles sees Bob with Janet and, using Bob's name, sends a wire to the Midwestern coach about George's past. When questioned, George admits playing for the oil team, but he says that he did it for fun and gave the money away. Nevertheless, he is deemed ineligible to play. The coach is about to kick Bob off the team for sending the wire, but Bob denies the charge and George says he believes him, so the coach relents. Bob makes an eighty-two-yard run to score a touchdown and then blocks extra point kicks, so that with five minutes remaining, the score is twelve to seven with Midwestern leading. After Bob collapses with a broken collarbone, the Ritz Brothers sneak onto the field and then proceed to commit penalties which drive their team back to their own six-yard line. Harry Ritz, however, catches his own pass and scores a touchdown just as the gun to end the game goes off. After Cuddles confesses, Janet kisses Bob, who is recovering. Inez shows George that she has the tattoo on her arm, but when George then ferociously kisses her, she tries to rub the tattoo off. *Brothers. College life. College students. Football. Indians of North America. College deans. Dances. Dry cleaning. Fathers and daughters. Football coaches. Fraternities. Infatuation. Jealousy. Racism. Tattoos.*

Note: The working titles of this film were *1937 Pigskin Parade, Pigskin Parade of 1937* and *Pigskin Parade of 1938.* This was the Ritz Brothers' first starring picture and Dick Baldwin's first film. According to *NYT,* Baldwin, whom they called "a Zeppo to the Ritz brothers," won the male lead opposite Simone Simon in *Love and Hisses* (see *AFI Catalog of Feature Films, 1931-40;* F3.2587) because of his success in this film. According to a *Var* news item, George Marshall was originally scheduled to direct. *FD* noted that Sid Kuller wrote material for the Ritz Brothers before they entered films. According to news items, Ed Thorgersen was the sports announcer for the "Fox Movietone News." George Murphy and Phyllis Brooks are listed as cast members in early *HR* production charts, but it is unlikely that they were in the final film. According to *Liberty* and *HR* production charts, the Brewster Twins were in the cast, but their participation in the final film has not been confirmed. *HR* production charts list Barney McGill as cameraman, but his participation in the film has not been confirmed. According to *Box* and *DV,* the running time of the preview was 80 minutes. The character of "George Black" contains some similarities to the great American football player and athlete Jim Thorpe, who was predominantly of American Indian descent and who was deprived of his gold medals for winning the decathlon and pentathlon in the 1912 Olympics because he played 2 summers of minor league baseball in 1910 and 1911.

Box 9 Oct 1937. *DV* 25 Sep 1937, p. 3. *FD* 15 Jun 1937, p. 10 *FD* 28 Sep 1937, p. 8. *HR* 12 Jul 1937, p. 11. *HR* 7 Sep 1937, p. 19. *HR* 22 Sep 1937, p. 5. *HR* 31 Dec 1937, sect. II, p. 90. *Liberty* 13 Nov 1937. *MPD* 24 Sep 1937, p. 6. *MPH* 2 Oct 1937, p. 38. *NYT* 3 Oct 1937. *NYT* 9 Oct 1937, p. 16. *Var* 2 Jun 1937. *Var* 23 Jun 1937. *Var* 29 Sep 1937, p. 14.

LIFE GOES ON (African Americans)

Million Dollar Productions, Inc. *Dist* Million Dollar Productions, Inc. 1 Apr **1938**; World Premiere in Baltimore, MD: 7 Jan 1938. Sd; b&w. 6,403 ft. 71 min. PCA cert no. 3856.

Exec prod Harry M. Popkin. *Assoc prod* Leo C. Popkin. *Dir* William Nolte. *Asst dir* Herman Webber. *Scr* Phil Dunham. *Cam* Robert Cline. *Art dir* Vin Taylor. *Cost* Bruce Randall. *Rec eng* Glen Glenn. *Makeup* Steve Calentzos. *Prod mgr* Halley Harding.

Cast: Louise Beavers (*Sally Weston*), Edward Thompson (*Bob Weston*), Reginald Fenderson (*Henry Weston, later known as Monte Howard*), Lawrence Criner (*Bull Connors*), Monte Hawley (*District attorney*), Hope Bennet (*Betty*), Jesse Brooks (*Officer James*), Mae Turner (*Lou Minters*), Artie Brandon (*Alice*), Edward Robertson (*Bob, as a boy*), Oliver Farmer (*Henry, as a boy*), Eloise Witherspoon (*Young Alice*), Lillian Randolph (*Cinthy*).

African American, Melodrama. [*Not viewed*]. Sally Weston, a widow with two sons, Bob and Henry, leaves her native small Southern town for Harlem to provide better educational opportunities for her boys. Once in Harlem, however, Sally realizes that the city is a cold and friendless place, and because she has difficulty finding work, her savings begin to dwindle. Time passes, and after working at many low-paying and back-breaking jobs, Sally finally has saved enough money to open a coffee shop. While Sally is delighted with Bob, who is enthusiastic about his studies and wants to be a lawyer, she despairs over Henry, who soon turns to delinquency. As Bob becomes an honor student and captain of the football team, Henry continues on a downward spiral into gambling and petty crimes. Following his graduation from college, Bob marries his coed sweetheart Betty and passes his bar examinations. Henry, meanwhile, is expelled from school. During this time, Sally's best friend, Police Officer James, proposes marriage to her, but she refuses, declaring that she must devote her attention to her boys. Bob and Betty eventually move into a beautiful apartment and invite Sally to live with them. Henry gets deeper into trouble after falling in with a group of gamblers in the employ of Bull Connors, a gambling house owner. When Connors tries to involve Bob in his illicit activities, Bob refuses and punches him. Connors vows revenge, and when he learns that Henry is Bob's brother, he makes Henry the club manager moments before a police raid, thus setting him up to take the punishment and bringing disgrace on the Weston family. One evening, when safecracker Slug Finney, one of Connors' men, attempts to break into his boss's safe in a darkened room, he is caught and killed by an unseen gunman. Later, one of Connors' men finds Henry standing over Finney's body holding a gun, and calls the police. After Henry, who now calls himself Monte Howard, is taken into custody, Bob is deputized as public defender and assigned to handle Howard's case, unaware that Howard is his brother. Bob is shocked when he discovers who he has been assigned to defend. During the trial, as things begin to look bad for Henry, Bob cross-examines Connors and reveals him as the real murderer. Following Connors' confession, Henry is vindicated, and he vows to reform his life. Realizing that his mother was happier in her old home in the South, Bob buys it for her and takes her back to live there. *African Americans. Brothers. Frame-ups. Juvenile delinquents. Mothers and sons. Revenge. Self-sacrifice. Trials. Coffee shops. Confession (Law). Crime. Education. Expulsion. Fistfights. Gambling. Gangsters. Lawyers. Lure of the city. Moral reformation. Murder. New York City–Harlem. Police raids. Proposals (Marital). Revenge. Safecrackers. Superstition. Trials. United States–South. Widows.*

Note: A working title for the film was *My Sons.* According to the file for the film in the MPAA/PCA Collection at the AMPAS Library, in Sep 1937 the PCA informed Ralph Cooper of Million Dollar Pictures, Inc. that "because of the suicide of a criminal," this story was not acceptable under the Production Code. Elaborating on this, the PCA wrote Cooper that the Code prohibited the showing of "a murderer escaping justice through suicide." According to the pressbook for the film, this was "Louise Beavers' first all-Negro picture." *Life Goes On* was re-released in the late 1940s by Toddy Pictures under the title *His Harlem Wife.*

FD 24 Feb 1938, p. 10. *PittsC* 8 Jan 1938, p. 20.

LIFE IS LIKE THAT see **COSÌ È LA VITA**

THE LIFE OF AL JOLSON see **THE JOLSON STORY**

LIFE OF AMERICAN INDIAN [SIC] (Native Americans)

1915?. Si; b&w. Length undetermined.

Cam Harry Keepers.

Documentary. [No specific information about the plot of this film has been located.]. *Indians of North America.*

Note: Very little information from contemporary sources has been located on this film. Cameraman Harry Keepers lists it in both 1916 studio directories, stating that it was made for the "Wanamaker Expeditions," was "recorded in" the Smithsonian Institution and was a first-prize winner at the 1915 Panama Expo. According to modern sources, Rodman Wanamaker, as a police commissioner, led a 1913 expedition to the Crow Reservation near Sheridan, WY, during which director Rollin S. Dixon took footage of the tribe that was

edited into a thirteen-reel film in 1915. This film, referred to in modern sources as *History of the American Indian*, is probably the same as *Life of American Indian*. The intention of the filmmakers was to record for posterity ancient tribal customs, rites and ceremonies, including the ceremonial steam bath and the use of the medicine stick, as well as combat techniques, as demonstrated in staged battles. Another part of the documentary featured a more contemporary view of reservation life and included scenes of Indians participating in a cattle round-up. No further information on the production, including its exact connection to the Smithsonian Institution, has been discovered.

THE LIFE OF BUFFALO BILL *see* **THE ADVENTURES OF BUFFALO BILL**

THE LIFE OF CARUSO *see* **THE GREAT CARUSO**

THE LIFE OF JACK LONDON *see* **JACK LONDON**

THE LIFE OF KNUTE ROCKNE *see* **KNUTE ROCKNE—ALL AMERICAN**

THE LIFE OF SAM DAVIS: A CONFEDERATE HERO OF THE SIXTIES (African Americans)
1915? [©James Henry Ragsdale; 7 May 1915; LU6232]. Si; b&w. Length undetermined.
Historical, Drama. Sam Davis, the son of a Tennessee farmer, leaves his rural home to attend military school in Nashville and is called to the front at the outbreak of the Civil War. In the Union army camp, officers draw up plans for various maneuvers and then leave for dinner. While they are out, Tom, a black slave, steals the plans while cleaning the officers' quarters with his lover. To protect Tom, the black woman denies any knowledge of the missing documents, and suspicion begins to spread throughout the camp. Tom delivers the papers to Esquire English, a Confederate sympathizer, who hands them over to Captain Shaw, a Rebel spy disguised as a Union doctor. In turn, Shaw entrusts the plans to Sam Davis with instructions to rush them to the front. On his way, Sam is ambushed by Union soldiers, who later question him in an attempt to discover the traitor's name. When Sam refuses again and again to reveal his sources, he is tried and hanged, but dies a hero in the eyes of his comrades. *Sam Davis. Espionage. Tennessee. United States–History–Civil War, 1861-1865. War heroes. African Americans. Couriers. Executions. Impersonation and imposture. Military schools. Nashville (TN). Physicians. Trials.*

Note: Although the exact length of this film is not known, the copyright submission includes a four-act outline. This film may be the same as another 1915 film, *Sam Davis, the Hero of Tennessee*, copyrighted in Jul 1915, but as they were both based on actual persons and events whose fiftieth anniversary was being celebrated at that time, it is possible that more than one film on the subject may have been produced.

THE LIFE OF TIGER FLOWERS *see* **THE FIGHTING DEACON**

LIFEBOAT (African Americans, Multi-ethnic)
Twentieth Century-Fox Film Corp.; Alfred Hitchcock's Production. *Dist* Twentieth Century-Fox Film Corp. 28 Jan **1944**; New York opening: 11 Jan 1944; Prod: 3 Aug—17 Nov 1943 [©Twentieth Century-Fox Film Corp.; 28 Jan 1944; LP12521]. Sd (Western Electric Recording); b&w. 11 reels, 8,711 ft. 96-98 min. PCA cert no. 9598.
[*Exec prod* Darryl F. Zanuck and William Goetz]. *Prod* Kenneth Macgowan. *Dir* Alfred Hitchcock. [*Asst dir* Saul Wurtzel]. *By* John Steinbeck. *Scr* Jo Swerling. [*Orig story idea* Alfred Hitchcock]. *Dir of photog* Glen MacWilliams and [Arthur Miller]. [*Cam op* Paul Lockwood]. [*Loc cam* Harry Jackson]. *Spec photog eff* Fred Sersen. [*Backgrounds* James Havens]. *Art dir* James Basevi and Maurice Ransford. *Film ed* Dorothy Spencer. *Set dec* Thomas Little. *Assoc* Frank E. Hughes. *Cost* Rene Hubert. *Mus* Hugo W. Friedhofer. *Mus dir* Emil Newman. *Sd* Bernard Freericks and Roger Heman. *Makeup artist* Guy Pearce. *Tech adv* Thomas Fitzsimmons and [Robert Nelson Adrian]. [*Dial coach* Queenie Leonard and Eugen Sharin]. [*Unit prod mgr* Ben Silvey]. [*Prod mgr* R. L. Hough].
Music: "Preislied" by Richard Wagner.
Song(s): "Don't Sit Under the Apple Tree (With Anyone Else But Me)," music and lyrics by Lew Brown, Charlie Tobias and Sammy Stept; "Heidenröslein," music by Franz Schubert, lyrics by Johann Wolfgang von Goethe; "Du, Du, Liegst Mir im Herzen" and "Treue Liebe," traditional German folksongs.
Cast: Tallulah Bankhead [(*Constance Porter*)], William Bendix [(*Gus Smith*)], Walter Slezak [(*Willi, the German*)], Mary Anderson [(*Alice Mackenzie*)], John Hodiak [(*Kovac*)], Henry Hull [(*C. J. "Ritt" Rittenhouse*)], Heather Angel [(*Mrs. Higley*)], Hume Cronyn [(*Stanley "Sparks" Garrett*)], Canada Lee [(*Joe Spencer*)], [William Yetter, Jr. (*German sailor*)].

Sea, **World War II**, Drama. [*Print viewed*]. As an Allied freighter sails from New York to London, it is attacked by a German submarine. While the freighter's crew retaliates, the submarine shells the passengers as they struggle to board lifeboats. After the battle has ceased and both vessels have been sunk, renowned journalist and cynic Constance Porter is alone in a lifeboat when Kovac, an oiler from the freighter, pulls himself aboard. Kovac accidentally knocks Connie's 16-mm camera overboard while pulling Stanley "Sparks" Garrett, a English radio operator, into the boat, infuriating Connie. Both men then assist Army nurse Alice Mackenzie, wounded seaman Gus Smith and passenger C. J. "Ritt" Rittenhouse into their craft. Connie is glad to see Ritt, a wealthy industrialist who is an old friend. She is also pleased to hear the yell of black steward Joe Spencer, who put her in the lifeboat and is now attempting to rescue Mrs. Higley and her baby. After the others help Joe and Mrs. Higley aboard, Alice discovers that the infant is dead, and Sparks explains that Mrs. Higley is an English shell shock victim who is returning to Bristol. Mrs. Higley does not realize that her baby is dead, and the group's attention is distracted by the arrival of another survivor: a German who does not appear to speak English. Connie translates his declarations that he is an ordinary seaman and is sorry for the attack. Kovac, a Czechoslovakian-American, wants to throw the German overboard, but Gus, a German-American who changed his name from Schmidt to Smith out of shame, insists that a "guy can't help being born who he is." Ritt asserts that they cannot kill the German according to international law, and the majority votes to keep him as a prisoner. Soon after, Joe says a prayer as they bury the baby at sea, and that night, they tie Mrs. Higley to a chair to keep her from committing suicide. The next morning, however, they discover that she has jumped overboard. Ritt tries to cheer the survivors by taking stock of their small store of provisions and organizing jobs for everyone. When Ritt follows the German's advice about setting a course, Kovac accuses him of electing himself captain. Connie tricks the German into revealing his true rank when she calls him *Kapitän* and he reacts. Although she believes that the German is best qualified to run the lifeboat, Kovac angrily proclaims himself captain and orders them to follow Sparks's course to Bermuda, which is the opposite of the German's. As they sail, Gus's wounded leg becomes infected, and after the German states that he was a surgeon in civilian life, Alice assists as he amputates the leg. Later, having gained their trust, the German, whose name is Willi, tells the others to change direction. Kovac, hoping to save Gus's life, reluctantly accepts Willi's advice. That night, however, as Sparks is at the tiller, the stars show him that they are heading away from Bermuda, not toward it. The next morning, the group urges Joe, a reformed pickpocket, to search Willi, and Joe finds a compass that Willi had secretly been using to steer them toward a German supply ship. Kovac is about to stab the German when a huge storm strikes, and Willi, who reveals that he speaks English, brings the group safely through the storm. At the storm's end, the survivors have lost all of their food and water, and with the boat's mast gone, Willi rows them toward the German ship. Kovac laughs about their "prisoner" taking control, but Willi asserts it is the logical thing to do now that the storm has blown them off course. As time passes, all of the group grow weak except Willi. Despite their suffering, Connie and Kovac become romantically involved, as do Alice and Sparks. Gus's thirst causes him to hallucinate, but one morning, he sees Willi drinking water. Hoping to keep his water supply a secret, Willi pushes Gus overboard, but Gus's weak, drowning cries reach Sparks. After the group realizes that Willi is sweating, which requires hydration, Joe grabs a water flask from Willi's shirt. The flask is broken, and Willi admits that he has been subsisting on hoarded water and energy tables. With their nerves finally broken, Alice leads the others in an attack on Willi. All participate except Joe, who watches with horror and sadness as they beat Willi and force him overboard. Later, the survivors are bemoaning their fate when Connie, who has become less selfish and haughty, yells at them for being quitters. She gives Kovac her diamond bracelet to use as a lure, and he catches a fish with it. Just as they are pulling the fish in though, Joe spots a ship. The ship is the German vessel that Willi was trying to reach, but before it can pick them up, it is attacked by an American warship. The German ship is sunk, and as the group awaits rescue by the Americans, a young German sailor climbs aboard the lifeboat. Swayed by his youth, the women want to save him, but Ritt declares that Germans cannot be

treated as human beings. The sailor brandishes a pistol at them, but Joe disarms him. When the youth asks if they are going to kill him, Kovac wonders what can be done with such people, and Connie replies that maybe Mrs. Higley and Gus could answer him. *Despair. Germans. Lifeboats. Self-reliance. World War II. African Americans. Atlantic Ocean. Bracelets. Cards. Cigars. Class distinction. Compasses. Cynics. Czechoslovakian Americans. English. German Americans. Hallucinations. Industrialists. Merchant Marine. Nurses. Operations, Surgical. Romance. Sea battles. Sea captains. Sea rescues. Shell shock. Storms. Suicide. Tattoos. Thirst. Women reporters.*

Note: The film's opening title card reads: "Twentieth Century-Fox Presents Alfred Hitchcock's Production of *Lifeboat* By John Steinbeck." According to a 16 Nov 1942 *HR* news item, Twentieth Century-Fox obtained Hitchcock's directorial services in a deal whereby the studio purchased from David O. Selznick the rights to three story properties and the services of several actors and technicians. The news item stated that Hitchcock would direct two films for Twentieth Century-Fox; however, he did not direct a second film for the studio. [Modern sources assert that the contract remained unfulfilled because of the studio's dissatisfaction with the length of production on *Lifeboat*.] A 28 Dec 1942 *HR* news item announced that Hitchcock's first film for his new studio would be based on an original idea by himself, and would star an all-male cast. Information in the Twentieth Century-Fox Produced Scripts Collection and the Records of the Legal Department, both contained at the UCLA Arts—Special Collections Library, confirms that the original idea for the film was Hitchcock's. The collections further reveal that Hitchcock first considered asking A. J. Cronin or James Hilton to write the screenplay, but no evidence was found confirming an offer to either author. The studio records contain a 30 Dec 1942 telegram from Hitchcock to Ernest Hemingway, requesting his assistance in preparing the screenplay. Hemingway declined, citing pressures from his own work, after which Hitchcock turned to Steinbeck.

Lifeboat marked the first time that Steinbeck wrote a fictional story directly for the screen. [His first screenplay was for *The Forgotten Village*, a 1941 documentary.] *HR* news items indicate that Steinbeck originally intended to publish his story as a novel, to which the studio would then purchase the screen rights. Steinbeck's screen story was never published, however, and the studio paid him $50,000 for his novella, according to studio records. According to a 13 May 1943 memo from producer Kenneth Macgowan to Hitchcock, contained in the legal files, Steinbeck's literary agent, Annie Laurie Williams, and Pat Covici "felt that *Lifeboat* was very inferior Steinbeck, however good it might be for pictures, and they decided it would be a great mistake for him to publish at this time another 'little' book, and one rather inferior." A condensation of the story appeared in *Collier's* (13 Nov 1943) with the credits "By Alfred Hitchcock and Harry Sylvester. Based on an original screen story by John Steinbeck for 20th Century-Fox." According to the legal records, Hitchcock declined an onscreen credit for his contribution to the film's screenplay, although Steinbeck's contract with the studio stipulated that Hitchcock would receive the credit "based on a story idea by Alfred Hitchcock."

A comparison of Steinbeck's novella and later drafts of the screenplay, included in the scripts collection, reveals that much of Steinbeck's work was altered by subsequent writers or by Hitchcock. For example, in Steinbeck's story, the German character is a physically weak man with a broken arm, whom "Joe" attempts to save after the others push him overboard. According to the studio records, Alma Reville [Mrs. Hitchcock], MacKinlay Kantor, Patricia Collinge, Al Mannheimer and Marian Spitzer worked on drafts of the screenplay, but the extent of their contribution to the completed picture has not been determined. A 27 Jan 1943 studio press release indicated that Macgowan would write the screenplay version of Steinbeck's book. According to a 1 Feb 1943 *HR* news item, during the writing of the story, Hitchcock and Steinbeck conferred with "the Maritime Commission, which is interested in the picture as a morale builder."

According to an 18 Feb 1943 *HR* news item, Hitchcock was planning to shoot the picture in Technicolor and use only eight male characters. A 29 Apr 1943 *HR* news item stated that, "following his usual procedure," Hitchcock would try to "cast as many unfamiliar faces as expedient" in the film and planned to "use unknowns for all principal roles." Stage actor Canada Lee was the first actor cast, according to a 22 Jun 1943 *HR* news item. Tallulah Bankhead, who was paid $75,000 for her performance according to modern sources, had not made a film since the 1932 M-G-M production *Faithless*, except for a cameo appearance in *Stage Door Canteen*. *HR* news items indicate that Hitchcock tested Barbara Booth, Ron Randall and Eve March for parts in the film and note that William Bendix replaced Murray Alper in the role of "Gus Smith" when Alper fell ill after the start of filming. A 28 Jul 43 *HR* news item noted that it was crucial for all of the actors to be cast before filming began because Hitchcock intended to shoot in sequence. A 15 Oct 1943 *HR* news item stated that Patricia Knox was to be included in the cast as a "vision" seen by William Bendix, but Knox does not appear in the completed film.

An 18 May 1943 *HR* news item noted that during pre-production, Hitchcock and Macgowan used a miniature lifeboat and model figures to plan camera angles, as well as "official British lifeboat manuals" for authenticity in the script. According to a 13 Aug 1943 *HR* news item, four lifeboats were used during the production: one for rehearsals, one for close-ups, another for long shots and the last was kept floating on the "studio lake," or tank. *HR* news items note that background shots, supplied by a camera crew led by James Havens, were taken near Miami, the Florida Keys and San Miguel Island, CA. According to a studio press release, director of photography Glen MacWilliams replaced Arthur Miller after the first two weeks of filming when Miller became ill. The strenuous production, which often resulted in the actors being soaked with

water and oil, led to two cases of pneumonia for Bankhead, a serious illness for actress Mary Anderson and two cracked ribs for actor Hume Cronyn, according to his autobiography. Filming was suspended for several days due to Bankhead and Anderson's illnesses, according to Nov 1943 *HR* news items.

Hitchcock made his trademark appearance in the film in a newspaper advertisement for a fictional diet aid called "Reduco." The ad features "before and after" photographs of Hitchcock, who had recently gone on a rigorous diet. In the 2 Dec 1950 issue of *The Saturday Evening Post*, Hitchcock stated that the ad in *Lifeboat* was his favorite "role," and that he had had "an awful time thinking it up." He also commented that, after the film's release, he was besieged by letters from fans requesting information about "Reduco." Some modern sources erroneously state that Hitchcock appeared in the film as a dead body floating in the water. Although Heather Angel's character is often referred to as "Mrs. Higgins" by contemporary and modern sources, she is called "Mrs. Higley" in the film.

Lifeboat generated much controversy upon its release, as some critics were angered by the character of "Willi." Political columnist Dorothy Thompson and film critic Bosley Crowther were among the influential writers who accused Steinbeck and Hitchcock of glorifying the German character while presenting the "Allied" characters as negative. The irate Thompson gave the film "ten days to get out of town," while Crowther professed to having a "sneaking suspicion that the Nazis, with some cutting here and there, could turn *Lifeboat* into a whiplash against the 'decadent democracies.' And it is questionable whether such a picture, with such a theme, is judicious at this time." The criticism led Steinbeck, who had previously been accused of being pro-Nazi with reference to his German characters in the novel and film *The Moon Is Down*, to disassociate himself from *Lifeboat*. *Life* magazine noted that Steinbeck "disclaimed any responsibility for Director Hitchcock's and Scenarist Jo Swerling's treatment of his material." Upon learning of Steinbeck's discontent with the film, Crowther wrote an article for the *NYT* detailing the differences between Steinbeck's original story and the film, and stating that Hitchcock and Macgowan had "pre-empted" Steinbeck's "creative authority." In a telegram to Annie Laurie Williams, reprinted in a modern source, Steinbeck requested that she tell Twentieth Century-Fox to remove his name "from any connection with any showing of this film." Some critics also complained about the portrayal of "Joe," who they felt was too stereotyped. In a 26 Dec 1943 *NYHT* interview, actor Lee stated that he had tried to "revise the part" by cutting out some dialogue and action that he found to be demeaning. On 15 Mar 1945, in a deposition given for a pending lawsuit concerning the film (described below), Lee voiced his disappointment over the released picture. Lee stated that he had thought the character of Joe would be "a variation from any other Negro that was ever on the screen," but instead the filmmakers "stunk it up somehow or other, and it turned out to be the same old stereotyped Negro."

Hitchcock, Macgowan and Bankhead all defended the picture in print. Hitchcock maintained that he had intended the film to show how the Allies must stop bickering amongst themselves and unite in order to win the war. In a 19 Mar 1944 *LAT* article, Hitchcock defended his protrayal of "Willi" by stating, "I always respect my villain, build[ing] him into a redoubtable character that will make my hero or thesis more admirable in defeating him or it." Bankhead supported Hitchcock in a 6 Feb 1944 *NYHT* interview, in which she declared that "Hitchcock's a genius, a real genius. He wanted to teach an important lesson. He wanted to say that you can't trust the enemy....in *Lifeboat* you see clearly that you can't trust a Nazi, no matter how nice he seems to be." In a letter to the screen editors of the *NYT*, Macgowan noted that the chief objective of the filmmakers had been to shape "a film with as much excitement and reality as we could summon under challenging technical limitations."

Lifeboat, a box-office failure, was the last film produced by Macgowan for Twentieth Century-Fox. The film did receive much critical praise, with some critics asserting that it was a powerful piece of propaganda, capable of demonstrating that the united Allies could defeat Germany. The acting was lauded, as was Hitchcock's direction, which was challenged by the limiting set. The absence of background music was also noted and praised. [Although there is music during the picture's opening, it ends when the dramatic action begins.] Bankhead was chosen as the best actress of the year by the New York Film Critics, and *FD* and the National Board of Review named the picture as one of the ten best films of the year. Steinbeck received an Academy Award nomination for Best Original Story, and Glen MacWilliams received a nomination for Best Black And White Cinematography. Hitchcock was awarded his second Academy Award nomination for Best Director.

In Jan 1945, playwright Sidney Easton filed suit against Twentieth Century-Fox, claiming that the studio had plagiarized his unpublished play, *Life Boat No. 13*. The studio legal records contain a great deal of information about the suit, in which Easton alleged that he had given a copy of his play to actor Leigh Whipper, who in turn gave it to Steinbeck and the studio. Easton alleged that Steinbeck and the studio then stole his storyline and characters. Reports detailing the studio's internal investigation of the claim reveal that Hitchcock consulted many factual accounts of shipwreck survivors during the film's pre-production. Whipper denied having received the play from Easton, and both he and Steinbeck asserted that they had never met. In his deposition for the lawsuit, screenwriter Jo Swerling said, "After the first reading that I gave to the Steinbeck story, I never again referred to it, nor did anybody else working on the picture. We just didn't use it." On 31 Oct 1947, Easton agreed to drop his claim against the studio, in exchange for which he received nine thousand dollars.

On 16 Nov 1950, an hour-long version of *Lifeboat* was broadcast by NBC on the *Screen Director's Playhouse* radio show. The broadcast was directed by and featured Hitchcock, with Bankhead reprising her role as "Constance Porter." Other cast members included Jeff Chandler and Sheldon Leonard. In 1993, the Fox television network broadcast a remake of the film entitled *Lifepod*.

Directed by and co-starring Ron Silver, the remake starred Robert Loggia and CCH Pounder, and was set aboard a lifepod that escapes from an exploding rocket in the year 2169.

Box 22 Jan 1944. *DV* 19 Oct 1943, p. 13. *DV* 16 Nov 1943, p. 1. *DV* 12 Jan 1944, p. 3, 33. *FD* 12 Jan 1944, p. 29. *HR* 16 Nov 1942, p. 1, 6. *HR* 28 Dec 1942, pp. 1-2. *HR* 22 Jan 1943, p. 10. *HR* 1 Feb 1943, p. 1. *HR* 18 Feb 1943, p. 3. *HR* 15 Apr 1943, p. 3. *HR* 29 Apr 1943, p. 8. *HR* 13 May 1943, p. 3. *HR* 18 May 1943, p. 6. *HR* 16 Jun 1943, p. 6. *HR* 22 Jun 1943, p. 2. *HR* 19 Jul 1943, p. 6. *HR* 20 Jul 1943, p. 6. *HR* 22 Jul 1943, p. 4, 9. *HR* 28 Jul 1943, p. 9. *HR* 2 Aug 1943, p. 3. *HR* 6 Aug 1943, p. 7. *HR* 9 Aug 1943, p. 3. *HR* 13 Aug 1943, p. 12. *HR* 14 Oct 1943, p. 4. *HR* 15 Oct 1943, p. 4. *HR* 29 Oct 1943, p. 14. *HR* 2 Nov 1943, p. 3. *HR* 5 Nov 1943, p. 1. *HR* 12 Nov 1943, pp. 8-9. *HR* 16 Nov 1943, p. 3. *HR* 18 Nov 1943, p. 11. *HR* 10 Jan 1944, p. 1. *HR* 12 Jan 1944, p. 3. *HR* 17 Jan 1944, p. 4. *HR* 25 Jan 1944, p. 1, 3. *HR* 24 Mar 1944, p. 1. *LAT* 19 May 1944. *Life* 31 Jan 1944, pp. 76-81. *MPD* 12 Jan 1944. *MPHPD* 15 Jan 1944, p. 1713. *New Yorker* 5 Feb 1944. *NYHT* 26 Dec 1943. *NYHT* 2 Jan 1944. *NYHT* 6 Feb 1944. *NYT* 13 Jan 1944, p. 17. *NYT* 23 Jan 1944. *NYT* 6 Feb 1944. *SEP* 2 Dec 1950. *Var* 12 Jan 1944, p. 24.

LIFE'S SHOP WINDOW (English Americans, Native Americans)

Box Office Attraction Co.; A Fox Special. *Dist* Box Office Attraction Co. 20 Oct **1914** [©William Fox; 2 Nov 1914; LP5056]. Si; b&w. 5 reels.

Dir J. Gordon Edwards. *Synopsis* Mary Asquith. *Cam* Harry A. Fishbeck.

Source: Based on the novel *Life's Shop Window* by Victoria Cross (New York, 1907).

Cast: Claire Whitney (*Lydia Wilton*), Stuart Holmes (*Bernard Chetwin*).

Drama. Lydia Wilton, an impoverished English orphan, is the overworked servant of Mr. and Mrs. John Anderson and their spoiled daughter Bella. Lydia meets Bernard Chetwin and secretly marries him, and then meets and is befriended by Eustace Pelham, a wandering philosopher who expounds his theory of "life's shop window," that, like children's toys, destinies are chosen for brilliance and superficiality rather than real merit. Bernard leaves England to establish a home for himself, Lydia, and their expected child, in Arizona. After giving birth, Lydia joins Bernard in Arizona, but he is so absorbed with his farm that he neglects her. When Eustace visits the Chetwins, he falls in love with Lydia and persuades her to elope with him. Lydia, however, is convinced by her Indian servant of her child's dependency on her and returns to Bernard without consummating her relationship with Eustace. In time, she earns Bernard's forgiveness and devotion. *Immigrants. Infatuation. Motherhood. Arizona. Elopement. England. Farm life. Indians of North America. Marriage–Secret. Philosophers. Servants.*

Note: Production information on a theatrical version of the novel which pre-dates the film is unknown. Modern sources credit either Herbert Brennon or Harry Belmar with direction.

Motog 28 Nov 1914, p. 762. *MPN* 21 Apr 1914, p. 40. *MPN* 17 Apr 1915, p. 5. *MPN* 12 Jun 1915, pp. 10-11. *MPW* 10 Oct 1914, p. 142. *Var* 14 Nov 1914, p. 25.

LIFTING SHADOWS (Russian Americans)

Léonce Perret Productions. *Dist* Pathé Exchange, Inc. 4 Apr **1920** [©Pathé Exchange, Inc.; 8 Mar 1920; LU14827]. Si; b&w. 6 reels, 5,486 ft.

Dir Léonce Perret. *Scen* Léonce Perret. *Story* Henri Ardel. *Cam* Alfred Ortlieb.

Cast: Emmy Wehlen (*Vania*), Stuart Holmes (*Clifford Howard*), Wyndham Standing (*Hugh Mason*), Julia Swayne Gordon (*Countess Vera Lobanoff*), F. French (*Gregory Lobanoff*), R. Bongini (*Serge Ostrowski*).

Drama. Vania, the daughter of Russian revolutionary Serge Ostowski, escapes to America when her father is blown up by one of his own bombs. There she marries Clifford Howard, a drug-ridden man whom she comes to despise. One night while in a drunken rage, Howard attacks her, and Vania shoots and kills him. Her attorney, Hugh Mason, believing her innocent, falls in love with his client. Vania does not tell him the truth for fear of losing his love. Meanwhile, revolutionaries have pursued Vania to America to obtain her father's papers. In defense, Hugh hires detectives to protect her. One night, a revolutionary breaks into her house and is shot by the detective. Before dying, he confesses that it was he who fired the shot that killed Vania's husband, thus freeing her to accept Hugh's love. *Drug addicts. Immigrants. Lawyers. Revolutionaries. Russian Americans. Russians. Self-defense. Bombs. Detectives. Drunkenness. Explosions. Russia–History–Revolution, 1917-1921.*

ETR 3 Apr 1920, p. 2005. *MPW* 3 Apr 1920, p. 139. *MPN* 27 Mar 1920, p. 2864. *MPN* 3 Apr 1920, p. 3171. *NYMT* 28 Mar 1920. *Var* 9 Apr 1920, p. 61. *Wid's* 28 Mar 1920, p. 9.

THE LIGHT AHEAD (Yiddish language)

Cinema Repertory; Carmel Productions, Inc. *Dist* Ultra Film Distributors. **1939**; World premiere in Detroit: 8 Sep 1939. Sd; b&w. 12 reels, 9,910 ft. 110 min. Yiddish language with English subtitles.

Pres CINEMA REPERTORY. *Assoc prod* Peter E. Kassler. *Dir* Edgar G. Ulmer. *Dial dir* Izidore Cashier. *Asst dir* Wolf Mercur and Fred Kassler. *Scr* Sherle Ulmer and Edgar G. Ulmer. *Adpt and dial* Chaver Paver. *English titles* Julien Leigh. *Cam* J. Burgi Contner and Edward Hyland. *Ed* Jack Kemp. *Landscapes and settings* Edgar G. Ulmer and Robert Benney. *Cost* Aaron Mensch. *Sd* N. Dean Cole. *Makeup* Edward Zenz. [*Prod mgr* Gustav H. Heimo]. [*Scr supv* Shirley Ulmer].

Source: Based on the short stories "Di Klyatshe," "Fishke der Krumer," "Di Takse" and "Der Prisiv" by Mendele Moicher Sforim (publication undetermined).

Cast: DAVID OPATOSHU (*Fishke*), Izidor Cashier (*Mendele Moicher Sforim*), Helen Beverley (*Hodel*), Rosetta Bialis (*Drabke*), Tillie Rabinowitz (*Neche*), Anna Gushkin (*Gitel*), Celia Budkin (*Chaye*), Jenny Cashier (*Dobe*), Yudel Dubinsky (*Isaak*), Misha Fishson (*Reb Aaron*), Leon Seidenberg ([*Reb*] *Alter Yaknehose*), Wolf Mercur (*Getzel Ganev*), Leon Shachter (*Frechman*), Wolf Goldfaden (*Wecker*), Israel Mandel (*Yisrolick*), Nuchim Brind (*Chaim Shuster*), Morris Shorr (*Hershl Kremer*), Zishe Katz (*Badchen*), Benny Adler, Misha Budkin, Helen Beda, Charles Cohen, Abraham Fishkind, Isaac Gladstone, Solomon Krause, Saul Nagoshiner, Isaak Rothblum, Ben-Zion Shoenfeld, Louis Weisberg.

Yiddish, Rural, Drama. [*Print viewed*]. In the late nineteenth century Russian countryside, two sleeping Jewish men in horse-drawn carts awaken and almost come to blows when they find that each of their horses are eating hay from the other's cart. When the men recognize each other, Mendele Moicher Sforim, a bookseller, gets into Reb Alter Yaknehose's cart, and they head back to the small town of Glubsk. On the road, they see Fishke, a lame man from town, walking alone on his way to Odessa, a city in which he hopes to be successful as a beggar. Concerned that Fishke has left his companion Hodel, a blind girl, Mendele urges him to return. Although Fishke calls Glubsk a terrible place and painfully relates that Hodel called him "Fishke the cripple," he accepts Mendele's invitation to return with him. In Glubsk, Hodel, who vows never to beg as long as she can earn money in other ways, cries when she learns from the widow Drabke that Fishke left town. Fishke returns and sees her cry, then sits beside her and vows never to leave her again. Fishke then listens as a number of men argue about the power of God. Mendele complains that schoolboys may catch cholera from swimming in a contaminated river and argues for the need of a doctor in the town, while Hershl Kremer, another townsperson, maintains that only God, not a doctor, can decide who will live or die. Getzel Ganev, a thief, proposes to Dobe, a hunchback, but she tells him that she prefers Fishke. Getzl then proposes to Hodel, and when she refuses him, he tells her that Fishke has been running after Dobe. Hodel accuses Fishke of walking with Dobe, but he denies it, and she vows never to quarrel again. When Fishke sees Hodel with six other girls go bathing in the river, he warns them about the danger of cholera, but they ignore him. After the community argues about the need for a hospital, Gitel, one of the girls, dies. During a town meeting, Mendele pleads for the townspeople to use their money to make the river and streets clean and to pay for a hospital. When a woman suggests that the children are dying of cholera because they profaned the Sabbath, the townspeople decide to follow a superstition and marry the poorest boy and girl, Fishke and Hodel, in the cemetery. Reb Alter tells Fishke of the town's decision, and he refuses to marry, as does Hodel, when she is told by the women, but they finally go through with the wedding, although they are ashamed to be the "cholera bride and groom." They then leave the town, with the help of Mendele, to go to a large city not beset by superstition, where, Mendele hopes, Hodel might be made to see again. They walk off hand-in-hand as Mendele speaks to his mare of the wonderful people of Israel with their eternal hope and belief in a new dawn. He wishes joy and peace to all "Fishkes" and "Hodels," to all Israel and to all mankind. *Beggars. Blindness. Booksellers and bookselling. Cholera. Handicapped. Jews. Marriage–Forced by circumstances. Small town life. Superstition. Cemeteries. Disease. False accusations. Hunchbacks. Meetings. Proposals (Marital). Rivers. Swimming. Thieves. Widows.*

Note: The film was also released with the Yiddish title *Di Klyatshe*. It was called *Die Klatche* and *Die Kliatche* in Yiddish reviews. The print viewed was

entitled *Fishka der Krimmer*. According to modern sources, the film was lost for a number of years, and the prints now in circulation, which are twenty to thirty minutes shorter than the original prints, were made from a print found in the 1960s. It is possible that the prints in existence are from a re-release, and that the companies listed were involved in the re-release. While the film was based on several stories by Mendele Moicher Sforim, according to the review in the Yiddish newspaper *Der Tag*, practically none of the content of the stories is included in the film. Sforim, one of the leading Yiddish writers of the nineteenth century, was born Sholom Yakov Abramowitz. Modern sources state that screenwriter Chaver Paver based his work on his own unproduced play entitled *Fishke der Krumer*, which itself was based on Sforim's stories. According to a news item, the supporting cast had either 300 or 500 players, 53 in speaking roles. According to *NYT* and information in *NYSA*, the film was produced in New Jersey. Shirle Castle was the pseudonym of Shirley Ulmer, the director's wife.

Box 7 Oct 1939. *Danny Grey Report* 20 Nov 1940. *Detroit Jewish Chronicle* 8 Sep 1939. *Exb* 4 Oct 1939. *FD* 12 Oct 1939, p. 5. *HR* 20 Dec 1939, p. 8. *NYT* 23 Sep 1939, p. 22. *Der Tag* 28 Sep 1939. *World Telegram* 23 Sep 1939.

LIGHT AT DUSK (Russian Americans)

Lubin Mfg Co. *Dist* V-L-S-E, Inc. 31 Jul **1916** [©Lubin Mfg. Co.; 20 Jul 1916; LP8846]. Si; b&w. 6 reels.

Dir Edgar Lewis. *Scen* Anthony P. Kelly. *Cam* Edward C. Earle. *Art dir* Anton Grot.

Cast: Orrin Johnson (*Vladimir Krestovsky/Mr. Krest*), Mary Kennavan Carr (*Nataska*), Sally Crute (*Mrs. Krest*), Hedda Kuszewski (*Olga*), Robert W. Frazer (*Nicholas*), Evelyn Terrill (*Frances Farrell*).

Drama. Eager for success, Russian peasant Vladimir Krestovsky leaves his wife Nataska and daughter Olga and goes to the United States. In just a few years, Vladimir moves from steel mill worker to financial magnate, and then, after changing his name to the more "American" sounding Krest, he marries into a socially prominent family. When his new wife dies, however, a suddenly reflective Vladimir has a vision of Christ and realizes that he has been consumed by his desire to make money and has turned his employees into virtual slaves. Vladimir vows to change his philosophy, after which Nataska and Olga, having arrived in America, find jobs in his plant. Vladimir finally recognizes them, and the family is reunited just as he institutes a series of reforms to help his workers. *Bigamy. Employer-employee relations. Immigrants. Moral reformation. Russian Americans. Steel magnates. Greed. Jesus Christ. Peasantry. Social climbers. Steel workers. Visions.*

MPN 5 Aug 1916, p. 788. *MPW* 5 Aug 1916, p. 941, 1006. *NYDM* 29 Jul 1916, p. 22. *Var* 4 Aug 1916, p. 30. *Wid's* 3 Aug 1916, p. 762.

THE LIGHT IN THE FOREST (Native Americans)

Walt Disney Productions. *Dist* Buena Vista Film Distribution Co. 10 Jul **1958**; World premiere in Harrisburg, PA: 9 Jul 1958; Prod: 9 Jul 1957—20 Sep 1957 [©Walt Disney Productions; 12 Mar 1958; LP10641]. Sd (RCA Sound Recording); col (Technicolor). 10 reels, 8,373 ft. 93 min. PCA cert no. 18820.

Pres WALT DISNEY. *Dir* Herschel Daugherty. *Asst dir* Robert G. Shannon. [*2d unit dir* Peter Ellenshaw]. [*2d asst dir* Jack Cunningham, Cliff Reid and Bill Sheehan]. *Scr* Lawrence Edward Watkin. *Photog* Ellsworth Fredricks. [*Cam op* Jack Whitman, Sr.]. [*Asst cam* Robert McGowan and Jack Whitman, Jr.]. *Matte eff* Peter Ellenshaw. *Art dir* Carroll Clark and [James Mainsbridge]. *Film ed* Stanley Johnson. *Mus ed* Evelyn Kennedy. *Set dec* Emile Kuri and Fred MacLean. [*Prop maker* Roy Bolton]. [*Prop master* Jack Golconda]. [*Props* Jack Boss]. [*Asst props* Charles Chrisman]. *Cost* Chuck Keehne and Gertrude Casey. [*Ward* Beau Van Den Ecker, Leonard Harris, Elmer Ellsworth and Esther Kress]. *Mus* Paul Smith. *Orch* Franklyn Marks. *Sd supv* Robert O. Cook. *Sd rec* Dean Thomas. [*Rec* Lou Skelton]. [*Boom man* Tom Goldrick]. [*Cable man* Malcolm Rennings]. *Makeup* Pat McNalley. [*Key makeup* John Holden and Jack Stone]. [*Makeup crew* Willon Fields and Tom Bartholomew]. *Hair stylist* Ruth Sandifer. [*Hair* Hazel Thompson, Lillian Lashin and Fae Smith]. [*Key hair* Linda Cross]. *Tech adv* Iron Eyes Cody, [Jack Pennick and Yewas Parker]. [*Unit mgr* Virgil Hart]. [*Prod mgr* John Grubbs]. [*Asst prod mgr* Bill Sheehan]. [*Scr supv* Donna Norridge]. [*Head grip* Bruce Hunsacher]. [*Grip* Ren Daw]. [*Best boy* Walter Lea]. [*Elec* John Collins, Millard Holmes and Knox Kelly]. [*Ramrod* Bill Jones]. [*Greensman* Abe Siegel]. [*Radioman* James Lester Gear]. [*Pub* Leonard Shannon]. [*Location casting dir* Ted Kehoe]. [*Driver* Captain Thornsberry]. [*Fight stunt double for James MacArthur* Harvey Perry]. [*Fight stunt double for Wendell Corey* Al Wyatt]. [*Stand-in* Tom Collins, Joe De Angelo, Walt Davis, Carlos Albert, R. Terry,

William Angelo, Russell Meeker, B. Spencer, B. Brady, Colin Kenny, D. Green, C. Sullivan, A. Vaughn, V. Hall, Ann Gardner, J. McKinney, C. MacAllister and T. Morales].

Song(s): "The Light in the Forest," music and lyrics by Gil George and Paul Smith; "I Asked My Love a Favor," music and lyrics by Lawrence Edward Watkin and Paul Smith.

Source: Based on the novel *The Light in the Forest* by Conrad Richter (New York, 1953).

Cast: Fess Parker [(*Del Hardy*)], Wendell Corey [(*Wilse Owens*)], Joanne Dru [(*Milly Elder*)], James MacArthur [(*True Son, also known as Johnny Butler*)], Jessica Tandy [(*Myra Butler*)], John McIntire [(*John Elder*)], Joseph Calleia [(*Chief Cuyloga*)], and Introducing Carol Lynley [(*Shenandoe Hastings*)], Rafael Campos [(*Half Arrow*)], Frank Ferguson [(*Harry Butler*)], Norman Fredric [(*Niskitoon*)], Marian Seldes [(*Kate Owens*)], Stephen Bekassy [(*Col. Henry Bouquet*)], Sam Buffington [(*George Owens*)], [Iron Eyes Cody (*Blackfish*)], [George Keymas (*Trader*)], [Eddie Little (*Little Crane*)], [Joyce Vanderveen (*Little Crane's bride*)], [Gloria Castillo (*Regina*)], [Robert Anderson (*Capt. Grant*)], [Jack Lorenz (*Guard*)], [Kevin Hagen, Kay Kuter (*Fiddlers*)], [Myrna Sahey (*Hannah Moore*)], [Pat Brady, Jack Hill (*Musicians*)], [Nancy Crawford, Noralee Norman, Don Washbrook (*Teenagers at party*)].

Historical, Drama. [*Print viewed*]. In 1764, after an outbreak of Indian attacks on white settlers, Colonel Henry Bouquet marches the 1,500 soldiers of the Royal American Regiment one hundred miles down the Ohio River from Fort Pitt. Cuyloga, chief of the Delaware Indians, presents a belt to Colonel Bouquet, saying it is the will of the Great Spirit that there be peace. When the colonel castigates Cuyloga for the murder of people on the frontier, Cuyloga contends that the Paxton Boys, vigilantes from the Paxton township, attacked their village first and murdered helpless Indian women and children, scalping them and committing indecencies. When Bouquet promises that no white man will settle on the Indians' lands and that there will be no further attacks, Cuyloga agrees to return all the white prisoners. When Half Arrow, the chief's son, asks his friend, True Son, a white teenager captured as a child and raised by Cuyloga, if he will leave, True Son defiantly asserts that he is an Indian, not a white. The council of chiefs votes to respect the existing treaty, however, and Cuyloga tells all the white children that they must leave. Along the march to Pennsylvania, True Son attempts to kill himself by eating a mandrake root, but scout Del Hardy, the colonel's interpreter, who lived among the Delaware himself as a child, makes him spit it out. After Half Arrow brings True Son a message from Cuyloga telling him not to fight back, True Son says he will bear his disgrace like an Indian. When True Son meets his real parents, Harry and Myra Butler, he refuses to speak English. Myra is stern with him, insisting that he realize he is not an Indian and demanding that he speak his English name, Johnny, and he finally gives in. Colonel Bouquet, sensing that Johnny's presence in the community may stir up conflicts with the Paxton Boys, asks Del to remain at Fort Pitt. Del learns that the commander of the Paxton Boys, John Elder, is considered to be a fine man, but that he oversees some hotheads. At a party in Johnny's honor, Del meets Elder and his daughter Milly. Wilse Owens, Myra's brother, who is one of the "hotheads," taunts Johnny by calling the Indians "devils." When Johnny denies that Indians have attacked white women and children, Wilse introduces his indentured servant, Shenandoe Hastings, a teenager who testifies that her mother, father and little sister were scalped. Wilse takes pride in the Paxton Boys' massacre of Indians and slaps Johnny when the boy calls him a butcher. Del responds by threatening Wilse. As Myra begins to get to know her son, she asks him to teach her the Delaware language. When Johnny sees that his Indian clothes have been put on a dummy at which Wilse and his friends are shooting, he runs to the target. Del stops Wilse from shooting at Johnny by knocking his gun away, and after challenging Wilse to a shooting contest, shoots the weather vane off Wilse's barn. As Del gets to know Milly, he admits he might be willing to leave the army to become a farmer. Johnny talks to Shenandoe about the deaths of her family and suspects the perpetrators were Wyandots. At a dance, when Johnny is told to give a ring he finds in a piece of cake to the one he likes most, he presents it to Shenandoe. He is told to kiss her, but he says Indians do not kiss. Outside, Wilse, who earlier tried to grab Shenandoe in a barn, hits Johnny, warning him to keep his "snake eyes" off her. Johnny vows to Shenandoe that he will kill Wilse, but she goes off exasperated,

fearing he will grow up to be like Wilse. Del soon leaves to rejoin Colonel Bouquet, but promises to stake Johnny's claim of Piney Woods Mountain, a beautiful wooded area by a waterfall, which Johnny and Shenandoe found one day. After Del goes, Johnny proposes to Shenandoe and they kiss. In the midst of their embrace, gunshots are heard, and Johnny finds Half Arrow, who has come with a message that tribesman Little Crane has been killed for trying to visit his "white squaw," who had been returned to the whites because of the treaty. When Wilse finds them together and fights them, Half Arrow is about to take Wilse's scalp, but Johnny stops him. Afraid he will be killed if he stays, Johnny returns to the Delaware. The tribe's council decides that twenty scalps will avenge Little Crane's death. Meanwhile, Del tells Colonel Bouquet of his decision to leave the army and become a farmer, but he agrees to help stop settlers from taking lands from the Indian side of the Ohio. Del and his men find a burned village and signs of the Delaware war party. Little Crane's brother, Niskitoon, reports to Cuyloga with fifteen scalps, including some children's, which saddens the chief. When they see a settlers' boat approach, Niskitoon gives white clothes to Johnny so that he can lure them close. Dressed in the clothes, Johnny tells the settlers he is starving. Before they reach him, however, Johnny warns them it is an ambush, and they escape unharmed. In the Indian camp, as Niskitoon is about to burn Johnny, Cuyloga takes the blame for Johnny's treachery and rules that Little Crane's death is avenged. He cuts Johnny loose and sadly tells him to go and that if they meet in battle he must kill him. Del finds Johnny, who disconsolately says that he now has no people. Del compares Niskitoon and Wilse, and says that there are good and bad on both sides. They return to Fort Pitt, and when Wilse calls Johnny a savage beast, Del blames Wilse for the killing that led to the death of the fifteen settlers. As the whole town watches, Johnny and Wilse have a fistfight. With instructions from Del and encouragement from Shenandoe, Milly and Harry, Johnny beats Wilse, who afterwards smiles and says Johnny has now become white. As Milly hugs and kisses Del, Shenandoe and Johnny run off to the waterfall. *Delaware Indians. Family relationships. Racism. Scouts (Frontier). United States–History–Colonial period, ca. 1600-1775. Youth. Ambushes. Attempted suicide. Henry Bouquet. Dances. Fathers and daughters. Fistfights. Friendship. Indentured servants. Kisses. Massacres. Murder. Officers (Military). Ohio River. Orphans. Ostracism. Parties. Pittsburgh (PA). Prisoners of war. Proposals (Marital). Revenge. Romance. Scalping. Self-sacrifice. Settlers. Sexual harassment. Treaties. Tribal chiefs. Vigilantes. Waterfalls.*

Note: According to a *NYT* news item, although Walt Disney bought the rights to the novel by Pulitzer Prize-winning author Conrad Richter in Jun 1953, a month after its publication, he did not plan to put it into production until 1957. The *NYT* review noted that the ending of the film was changed from the book. Location shooting was done at Massengale Point, TN and along the Tennessee River, about twenty miles from Chattanooga. The Rowland V. Lee Ranch, about fifty miles from the Disney studio in Burbank, was used for the Indian village, and the "Piney Woods Mountain" scenes were shot at the Rainbow Angling Club in Azusa, CA.

According to news items and publicity for the film, *The Light in the Forest* was James MacArthur's second film. Disney signed him after seeing his first film, *The Young Stranger*. MacArthur, the adopted son of Helen Hayes and Charles MacArthur, was a student at Harvard at the time, and his contract stated that he would work only during the summer break from school. The picture marked Carol Lynley's screen debut. Disney signed Lynley, who had been an actress and model since age ten, after seeing her picture on the cover of *Life*, but she agreed only to a one-year contract.

According to reviews and news items, Iron Eyes Cody, who played the role of "Blackfish" and acted as technical adviser, designed and made over thirty-five costumes for the film with his wife, Yewas Parker. In addition, Cody translated the Delaware dialogue and helped the cast speak the language. *HR* noted that the actors playing Delawares, "speak in the language of the Hurons, to which linguistic group they belonged." According to the pressbook, the Penomsquat Indians in Oldtown, ME made a twenty-foot war canoe for the film, which was to go to Disneyland following production. Disney himself came to the Tennessee location for three days, according to news items. The film's premiere at Harrisburg, PA was to benefit community charities.

Var, in its review, commented, "Like most Disney productions, it is pastoral in quality, almost fable-like in its gentle approach to some basically bitter situations." *HR* noted, "Volumes of fan mail praising authenticity have convinced [Disney] that meticulous research has given his studio tremendous prestige in educational circles and this is of real commercial advantage." The film was telecast in two parts on 12 Nov and 19 Nov 1961 as "True Son" and "True Son's Revenge" on *Walt Disney's Wonderful World of Color.*

Box 5 May 1958. *DV* 29 Apr 1958, p.3. *Exh* 30 Apr 1958, p. 4457. *FD* 2 May 1958, p.5. *Har* 3 May 1958, p. 70. *HCN* 14 Jul 1958. *HCN* 24 Jul 1958. *HR* 16 Jun 1953. *HR* 29 Apr 1958, p.3. *LAHE* 24 Jul 1958. *LAT* 24 Jul 1958. *MPHPD* 3 May 1958, p.816. *Newsweek* 14 Jul 1958. *NYT* 21 Jun 1953. *NYT* 11 Jul 1958, p. 15. *Time* 4 Aug 1958. *Var* 30 Apr 1958, p.6.

THE LIGHTNING RIDER (Latino)

Stellar Productions, Inc. *Dist* W. W. Hodkinson Corp. 18 May **1924** [©Stellar Productions, Inc.; 18 May 1924; LP20431]. Si; b&w. 6 reels, 5,771 ft.

Pres Hunt Stromberg. *Pers supv* Hunt Stromberg. *Dir* Lloyd Ingraham. *Adpt* Doris Dorn. *Story* Shannon Fife. *Titles* Walter Anthony. *Art titles* Edward Withers. *Photog* Sol Polito. *Film ed* Laurence Creutz.

Cast: Harry Carey (*Philip Morgan*), Virginia Brown Faire (*Patricia Alvarez*), Thomas G. Lingham (*Sheriff Alvarez*), Frances Ross (*Claire Grayson*), Leon Barry (*Ramon Gonzales*), Bert Hadley (*Manuel*), Madame Sul-Te-Wan (*Mammy*).

Western. The California border town of Caliboro appears to be menaced by a bandit known as The Black Mask. The real culprit, Gonzales, causes deputy sheriff Philip Morgan to lose his job, thus provoking Morgan to track down the bandit in his own disguise. *Bandits. Disguise. Mexican-American border region. Sheriffs.*

MPW 21 Jun 1924.

LIGHTS OF OLD BROADWAY (Irish Americans)

Cosmopolitan Productions. *Dist* Metro-Goldwyn Distributing Corp. 18 Oct or 8 Nov **1925**; New York premiere: 1 Nov 1925 [©Metro-Goldwyn-Mayer Corp.; 5 Nov 1925; LP22049]. Si; b&w. 7 reels, 6,595 ft.

Dir Monta Bell. *Scen and adpt* Carey Wilson. *Photog* Ira H. Morgan.

Source: Based on the play *Merry Wives of Gotham; or, Two and Sixpence* by Laurence Eyre (New York, 16 Jan 1924).

Cast: Marion Davies (*Fely/Anne*), Conrad Nagel (*Dirk De Rhondo*), Frank Currier (*Lambert De Rhondo, his father*), George K. Arthur (*Andy*), Charles McHugh (*Shamus O'Tandy*), Eleanor Lawson (*Mrs. O'Tandy*), Julia Swayne Gordon (*Mrs. De Rhondo*), Mathew Betz (*Baby Blue*), Wilbur Higby (*Fowler*), Bodil Rosing (*Widow Gorman*), George Bunny (*Tony Pastor*), George Harris (*Joe Weber*), Bernard Berger (*Lew Fields*), Frank Glendon (*Thomas A. Edison*), Buck Black (*Young Teddy Roosevelt*), Karl Dane (*Roosevelt's father*), William De Vaull (*De Rhondo's butler*).

Romance. Fely and Anne are twins orphaned when their mother dies en route from Ireland to America. Fely is adopted by the O'Tandys, who live in New York's Shantytown, and Anne is adopted by the wealthy De Rhondos. Fely grows up without knowing her sister and becomes a dancer in Tony Pastor's theater. Dirk De Rhondo, Anne's stepbrother, is attracted to Fely, and after protecting her during the great Orangemen's riot falls in love with her. She consents to his proposal but later retracts when Dirk's father dispossesses her family. Fely's father, however, becomes wealthy when his investment in Edison's incandescent light pays off, but Dirk's father is ruined. Fely saves De Rhondo's bank from a run by making a large deposit, thus winning over Dirk's family and paving the way for their marriage. *Adoption. Dancers. Thomas Alva Edison. Electricity. Lew Fields. Irish Americans. New York City–Broadway. Orangemen. Orphans. Tony Pastor. Theodore Roosevelt. Sisters. Twins. Wealth. Joe Weber.*

Note: The working title of this film was *Merry Wives of Gotham.*
NYT 2 Nov 1925, p. 20. *Var* 4 Nov 1925, p. 42.

LIGHTS OUT see BRIGHT VICTORY

LILI SCARLET see DUEL ON THE MISSISSIPPI

LIMEHOUSE BLUES (Chinese Americans)

Paramount Productions, Inc. *Dist* Paramount Productions, Inc. 9 Nov **1934** [©Paramount Productions, Inc.; 9 Nov 1934; LP5089]. Sd (Western Electric Noiseless Recording); b&w. 7 reels, 5,916 ft. 63 or 65-66 min. Passed by the National Board of Review. PCA cert no. 300.

Pres ADOLPH ZUKOR. *Prod* Arthur Hornblow, Jr. [*Exec prod* Emanuel Cohen]. *Dir* Alexander Hall. [*2d unit dir* William Shea]. *Scr* Cyril Hume and Arthur Phillips. *Orig story* Arthur Phillips. [*Contr to trmt* Philip MacDonald and Idwal Jones]. [*Contr to scr const* Grover Jones]. *Photog* Harry Fischbeck. [*Art dir* Hans Dreier and Robert Usher]. [*Ed* William Shea]. [*Makeup* Wally Westmore]. [*Stand-in for Jean Parker* Lillian Kilgannon].

Song(s): "Limehouse Nights," music and lyrics by Sam Coslow.

Cast: George Raft (*Harry Young*), Jean Parker (*Toni [Talbot]*), Anna May Wong (*Tu Tuan*), Kent Taylor (*Eric Benton*), Montagu Love (*Pug Talbot*), Billy Bevan (*Herb*), Robert Loraine (*Inspector Sheridan*), John Rogers (*Smokey*), E. Alyn Warren (*Ching Lee*), Wyndham Standing (*Commissioner Kenyon*), Louis Vincenot

(*Rhama*), [Forrester Harvey (*McDonald*)], [Robert Adair (*Alfred*)], [Keith Kenneth (*Policeman in Pug's house*)], [Colin Kenny (*Davis*)], [Eric Blore (*Slummer*)], [Desmond Roberts (*Constable*)], [Tempe Pigott (*Maggie*)], [Colin Tapley (*Man fighting with wife*)], [Rita Carlisle (*His wife*)], [Eily Malyon (*Woman who finds Pug*)], [Elsie Prescott (*Woman employment agent*)], [Joe May (*Taxi driver*)], [Otto Yamaoka (*Chinese waiter on boat*)], [Dora Mayfield (*Flower woman*)], [Angelo Bianchi (*Street organist*)], [Joe Glick].

Crime, Romance. [*Print viewed*]. On London's Limehouse Causeway, a riverfront slum, Chinese-American Harry Young runs a smuggling business out of his club, The Lily Gardens. In his short time on Limehouse, Harry has overtaken all of ruffian Pug Talbot's business. Pug takes his anger out on his beautiful daughter Toni, whom he has reared as a pickpocket. After Harry saves Toni from arrest, she develops a fondness for him. Pug tries to foil one of Harry's pick-ups by alerting the police, but Toni warns Harry and he evades the law. When Harry finds out later that Pug beat Toni for helping him, he vows revenge. Harry sends Herb, his right-hand man, to make an appointment to meet with Pug. Pug accepts the key to Harry's apartment, unaware that he is being set up. When Pug arrives for his meeting, he is stabbed to death, and his body is left in the alley. After her father's death, Toni agrees to be Harry's "watchdog," in exchange for room and board. Harry's jealous Chinese lover, Tu Tuan, knows that Harry is in love with Toni and warns him that the "white girl" cannot give him what he wants. To protect Toni from Tu Tuan, Harry fires her, but gives her an allowance. In Piccadilly, Toni meets Eric Benton, who owns a pet shop, and after spending many afternoons together, they fall in love. Toni does not want to accept Harry's charity, but he prevents her from getting a job so he will not lose her. Tu Tuan warns Harry that Toni is in love with someone else and, after deriding him for being in love with a white woman, leaves him. Toni finally confesses her sordid background to Eric and abandons him, but he finds the Lily Gardens and makes an appointment with Harry, who gives him the infamous key. That night, Harry takes Toni with him on his pick-up at Ching Lee's ship, unaware that Tu Tuan informed on him to the police and then killed herself. Harry realizes Toni's deep love for Eric when she becomes hysterical upon discovering his murder plans. Willing to sacrifice his own happiness for hers, Harry leaves Ching Lee's to try and stop the killing. He is chased by the police and shot, but arrives in time to save Eric. Harry clears Toni's name before he dies, leaving Toni and Eric to return to the West End to find happiness together. *Chinese Americans. Cultural conflict. London (England). Murder. Self-sacrifice. Smuggling. Unrequited love.* Battered children. Confession. Dismissal (Employment). Fathers and daughters. Gunshot wounds. Informers. Jealousy. Moral reformation. Nightclubs. Pet shops. Pickpockets. Police inspectors. Prayer. Revenge. Romance. Sailors. Salvation Army. Slums. Suicide.

Note: The working title of the film was *Limehouse Nights*. According to a *DV* news item, Sylvia Sidney was originally cast to play "Toni," but upon her refusal, Heather Angel was tested for the role. M-G-M loaned Jean Parker for this film. *DV* news items also note that scenes filmed at San Pedro Harbor, CA, were directed by William Shea; and, that when retakes required the presence of Anna May Wong in Oct 1934, the studio recorded her speaking her lines over the telephone from New York. The pressbook for this film gives Grover Jones a screenplay credit. While most contemporary sources credit Hans Dreier and Robert Usher, one source credits Dreier and Roland Anderson with the art direction. The pressbook credits importer and actor Tom Gubbins as providing the Oriental artwork appearing in the film. An early script in the Paramount script files at the AMPAS Library dated 20 Aug 1934 lists James Wing playing the character of "Ching Lee." The film was later released as *East End Chant*.

DV 15 Aug 1934, p. 1 *DV* 21 Aug 1934, p. 2. *DV* 15 Sep 1934, p. 2. *DV* 11 Oct 1934, p. 1. *FD* 11 Dec 1934, p. 6. *MPH* 22 Dec 1934, p. 35, 38. *NYT* 12 Dec 1934, p. 28. *Var* 18 Dec 1934, p. 13.

THE LITTLE AMERICAN (German Americans)
Mary Pickford Film Corp. *Dist* Artcraft Pictures Corp. 2 Jul **1917** [©Artcraft Pictures Corp.; 28 Jun 1917; LP11016]. Si; b&w. 6 reels.
Dir Cecil B. DeMille. *Asst dir* Cullen Tate. *Scen* Cecil B. DeMille. *Story and scen* Jeanie Macpherson. *Cam* Alvin Wyckoff. *Scenic artist* Wilfred Buckland. *Tech adv* Ian Hay Beith.
Cast: Mary Pickford (*Angela Moore*), Jack Holt (*Karl Von Austreim*), Raymond Hatton (*Count Jules de Destin*), Hobart Bosworth (*German colonel*), Walter Long (*German captain*), James Neil (*Senator John Moore*), Ben Alexander (*Bobby Moore*), Guy Oliver (*Frederick Von Austreim*), Edythe Chapman (*His American wife*), Lillian Leighton (*Angela's great-aunt*), De Witt Jennings (*English barrister*), Robert Gordon.

World War I, Drama. Karl Von Austreim, a German-American living in the United States, bids farewell to his sweetheart, Angela Moore, and returns to Germany at the outbreak of World War I to fight for his native country. Count Jules de Destin of the French embassy, a rival for Angela's hand, also leaves, and shortly afterwards, Angela is called to France to care for her dying aunt. Her ship, the *Veritania*, is torpedoed, but she is rescued and finally arrives in France to find her aunt dead and the old chateau converted into a hospital. Having angrily forsaken her position of American neutrality, Angela agrees to conceal a telephone by which she may contact the retreating French, and after the Germans arrive, she begins sending messages to the Allies. Karl, transformed by the war, attacks Angela in the dark, but when the German colonel orders her to be shot as a spy, her former lover denounces the Kaiser and joins her before the firing squad. An attack by the French saves them, and they escape to a church, where Jules, as a reward for Angela's bravery, gives Karl his freedom and grants them both safe passage to America. *France. Heroism. Patriotism. Self-sacrifice. World War I.* Americans in foreign countries. Churches. Diplomats. Escapes. Firing squads. German Americans. Germany. Army. Hospitals. Rivalry. Sea rescues. Ships. Telephone. Torpedoes.

Note: Cecil B. DeMille in his autobiography stated that Ramon Novarro, Wallace Beery and Sam Wood acted in this film. Other modern sources credit DeMille as film editor and list Colleen Moore, Norman Kerry and Gordon Griffith as appearing in the film. Some sources list Artcraft as the producing company. The film was shot at the Lasky studio in Hollywood.

ETR 14 Jul 1917, p. 416. *Motog* 28 Jul 1917, p. 208. *MPN* 21 Jul 1917, p. 432, 890. *MPW* 21 Jul 1917, p. 471, 542. *NYDM* 14 Jul 1917, p. 2, 16. *Var* 6 Jul 1917, p. 24. *Wid's* 12 Jul 1917, pp. 440-41.

LITTLE AMERICANS *see* **LET'S GET TOUGH!**

THE LITTLE ANGEL OF CANYON CREEK (Native Americans, Immigrants)
Vitagraph Co. of America; A Broadway Star Feature. *Dist* General Film Co.; Special Features Dept by arrangement with Broadway Star Features Co. Dec **1914** [©Vitagraph Co. of America; 14 Dec 1914; LP21807]. Si; b&w. 5 reels.
Dir Rollin S. Sturgeon. *Scen* Col. Jasper Ewing Brady. *Cam* William Stephen Smith, Jr.
Source: Based on the novel *The Little Angel of Canyon Creek* by Cyrus Townsend Brady (New York, 1914).
Cast: Gertrude Short (*Olaf Tryggvesson*), George Stanley (*Parson Bill*), George Holt (*Dead Shot Jackson*), William V. Ranous ("*Four Eyes," the sheriff*), Otto Lederer (*Doc Casey*), George Streaton (*Blue Wing*), Anne Streaton (*Jennie Morrison*), William Weston (*Edward Morrison*), Violet Malone (*Mary Morrison*), Charles Hutchinson (*Bishop Mills*).

Western. Olaf Tryggvesson, a ten-year-old immigrant orphan, is sent West from New York on a train transporting a party of waifs. When the train stops, Olaf leaves and is befriended by an Indian who takes the child to his camp. Later, Dead Shot Jackson kills the Indian and his wife over a disputed card game. During the fray, Jackson's partner is also killed and Blue Wing, an Indian boy, is knocked unconscious. Unaware that Olaf has witnessed the murder, Jackson accuses Blue Wing of the crime, but Olaf exonerates him and Jackson flees. Olaf is then befriended by Parson Bill and by the Morrison family, the founders of the Canyon Creek Sunday School. Jackson takes a shot at the Parson during services one Sunday, but Olaf blocks the bullet. Jackson is apprehended and sentenced to hang, but the wounded Olaf convinces the townspeople to spare his life. Finally, Parson Bill and Mary Morrison wed and their child becomes Olaf's companion. *Indians of North America. Murder. Orphans. Self-sacrifice. The West.* Capital punishment. Cards. Clergy. False accusations. Immigrants. New York City. Trains. Waifs.

Note: This film opened at the Vitagraph Theatre in New York on 2 Nov 1914.
Motog 28 Nov 1914, p. 730. *Motog* 26 Dec 1914, p. 915. *MPN* 9 Jan 1915, p. 62. *NYDM* 11 Nov 1914, p. 32. *Var* 7 Nov 1914, p. 23. *VLP* Dec 1914, p. 32.

LITTLE BIG HORN (Native Americans)
Lippert Pictures, Inc. *Dist* Lippert Pictures, Inc. 18 Jun **1951**; *Prod*: mid-Feb—early Mar 1951 [©Bali Films, Inc.; 27 Jun 1951; LP997]. Sd; b&w. 7,729 ft. 86 min. PCA cert no. 15249.
Pres ROBERT L. LIPPERT. *Prod* Carl K. Hittleman. *Dir* Charles Marquis Warren. *Asst dir* Ira Webb. *Scr* Charles Marquis Warren. *Based on a story by* Harold Shumate. *Dir of photog* Ernest W. Miller. *Spec eff* Ray Mercer. *Art dir* F. Paul Sylos. *Film ed* Carl Pierson. *Mus ed* George C. Emick. *Sd ed* John Hall. *Set dec* Theodore Offenbecker.

Prop master Leigh Carson. *Ward* Alfred Berke. *Mus comp and cond by* Paul Dunlap. *Sd eng* John Carter and Virgil Smith. *Makeup artist* Paul Stanhope. *Prod supv* William Magginette. *Scr supv* Emily Ehrlich.

Song(s): "On the Little Big Horn," music and lyrics by Stanley Adams, Maurice Sigler and Larry Stock, from an original arrangement and recording by Ralph Flanagan.

Cast: John Ireland (*Lt. John Haywood*), Lloyd Bridges (*Capt. Phillip Donlin*), Marie Windsor (*Celie Donlin*), Reed Hadley (*Sgt. Maj. [Peter] Grierson*), Jim Davis (*Cpl. Doan Moylan*), Wally Cassell (*Pvt. Danny Zecca*), Hugh O'Brian (*Pvt. Al DeWalt*), King Donovan (*Pvt. James Corbo*), Richard Emory (*Pvt. Mitchell Shovels*), John Pickard (*Sgt. "Vet" McCloud*), Robert Sherwood (*Pvt. David Mason*), Sheb Wooley (*Quince*), Larry Stewart (*"Bugler" [Steve] Williams*), Rod Redwing (*Cpl. Arika*), Richard Paxton (*Pvt. Ralph Hall*), Ted Avery (*Pvt. Tim Harvey*), Gordon Wynne (*Pvt. Arndst Hofstetter*), Barbara Woodell [(*Mrs. Margaret Owens*)], Anne Warren [(*Anne*)].

Western. [*Print viewed*]. In Jun 1876, at Fort Abraham Lincoln in the Montana Territory, Celie Donlin, the neglected wife of Capt. Phillip Donlin of the U.S. Cavalry, tries to convince her lover, Lt. John Haywood, to resign his commission and leave the army with her. Unknown to them, Phil has returned early from his patrol and has heard everything. The unrepentant Celie tells Phil that she no longer loves him and the heartbroken captain leaves the next morning on another patrol. After three weeks, Phil tells his exhausted men that they must keep up their grueling pace in order to arrive at Camp Yellowstone and warn General George Armstrong Custer of the large buildup of Sioux Indians before he leads the Seventh Cavalry to the Little Big Horn river. While resting at a water hole, Phil's unit is joined by John and his unit, who have been sent to recall Phil to Fort Lincoln. Told that Custer has already left for Little Big Horn, Phil decides to disregard his orders and attempt to warn the general. John argues that such a mission would be suicide and refuses to subject his men to such a hazard, so Phil lets John's detail return to the fort, but orders the lieutenant to join his patrol as second-in-command. With only three days to cover two hundred and fifty miles, the patrol goes on a forced march through hostile Indian territory. After one of the over-anxious soldiers fires on a Sioux lookout as the unit travels through a narrow ravine, John is sent up the ridge to kill the brave in hand-to-hand combat. He does so, only to have his own life saved by Quince, the unit scout, who kills a second Indian. Afterwards, John gives Phil a picture of Celie, stating that it is the only thing he has of her. John does not tell Phil, however, that he had earlier ended his relationship with Celie, knowing that she still loves her husband. Worried about his pregnant wife, Pvt. Arndst Hofstetter convinces young Pvt. Tim Harvey to desert the unit and return to the fort with him, but the two are soon ambushed by a group of Sioux. Hofstetter is saved from certain death by John, though Tim falls prey to a Sioux arrow. With their presence now known, the patrol attempts to quicken their pace. While riding point, Cpl. Arika, a Crow Indian, and Pvt. Doan Moylan, a thief, discover Quince nailed to a stake. Arika is killed attempting to rescue the scout, who dies soon thereafter. While John continues to worry about the men in their dwindling patrol, Phil reminds him that they are only a few men, trying to save the lives of hundreds. With John missing while on point, the enlisted men threaten to mutiny against Phil, only to have the lieutenant return and report that the Sioux have gathered in wait for Custer. Seeing the threat to his authority, Phil challenges John to a fistfight, which ends in a draw. The patrol then heads out, only to discover an ambushed wagon train. The patrol is soon attacked by the Sioux, and Phil is the first to fall. Learning that Custer has yet to arrive at Little Big Horn, the dying commander puts John in charge. He then leads the remnants of the patrol on a direct assault, but badly outnumbered, no one survives. *Officers (Military). Self-sacrifice. Soldiers. United States. Army. Cavalry. Crow Indians. Dakota Indians. Desertion. Military. Fistfights. Infidelity. Little Big Horn, Battle of the, 1876. Military life. Montana. Rescues. Revenge. Romantic rivalry. Thieves.*

Note: The film begins with the following written foreward: "This is a story based upon a strange and little known incident in America's history. From such incidents has risen the greatest fighting force in the world today—The United States Army—to which this picture is respectfully dedicated." The film ends with the following written statement: "Months after Custer made his last stand—and less than six miles from the actual spot—nine graves were found. Although marked unknown, they are generally believed to be the graves of the patrol

commanded by Capt. Philip Donlin and Lt. John Haywood, whose real names were: Capt. Frederic K. Giddleren and Lt. Charles Larin, United States Cavalry." For more information about Custer and the Battle of Little Big Horn, please see the entry below for *They Died With Their Boots On*. A *DV* news item states that Lippert Prod. purchased an original screenplay entitled *Little Big Horn* from Sydney Byrd in Jan 1950, but it has not been determined if any materials from that work were used in the production of this film. According to *HR*, Joanne Dru, then the wife of John Ireland, was tested for the starring female role in the film, which was played by Marie Windsor. News items also state that writer Harold Shumate, credited with the film's story, was originally slated to direct the film. Instead, screenwriter Charles Marquis Warren made his directing debut. In a letter found in the file on the film in the MPAA/PCA Collection at the AMPAS Library, Harold Mantell, Secretary of the National Film Committee for the Association of American Indian Affairs, Inc., complained about "the distortion and callousness evident in the story-line and advertising of *Little Big Horn*." Modern sources give the alternate title of *The Fighting 7th*.

Box 2 Jun 1951. *DV* 9 Jan 1950. *DV* 26 Jan 1951. *DV* 23 May 1951, p. 4. *FD* 29 May 1951, p. 6. *HR* 1 Sep 1950. *HR* 16 Feb 1951, p. 12. *HR* 2 Mar 1951, p. 12. *HR* 25 May 1951, p. 3. *MPHPD* 2 Jun 1951, p. 869. *NYT* 27 Jul 1951, p. 15. *Var* 30 May 1951, p. 6.

THE LITTLE BOY SCOUT (Latino)

Famous Players Film Co. *Dist* Paramount Pictures Corp. 28 Jul **1917** [©Famous Players Film Co.; 25 Jun 1917; LP11009]. Si; b&w. 5 reels.

Dir Francis J. Grandon. *Story and scen* Charles Sarver. *Cam* William Marshall.

Cast: Ann Pennington (*Justina Howland*), Owen Moore (*Thomas Morton*), Fraunie Fraunholtz (*Miguel Alvarez*), Marcia Harris (*Elizabeth Howland*), George Burton (*Luis Alvarez*), Harry Lee (*Sergeant Jones*).

Drama. After the death of her American father and Mexican mother, Justina Kneeland lives in Mexico with her mother's brother, who plans to marry the girl to his son in order to gain control of the rich mines that the orphan will inherit. To avoid the marriage, Justina runs away and starts for the home of her Aunt Elizabeth who lives in Lowell, Massachusetts. Detained at the border by American troops, Justina is befriended by Lieutenant Thomas Morgan, who helps her to reach her aunt's house. The uncle pursues her to Lowell, and in order to escape being taken back to Mexico, Justina disguises herself as a boy scout and joins the troop, now under the command of Lieutenant Morton, who has also come to Lowell. When the uncle overtakes the scouts and tries to force Justina to go with him, he discovers that he is too late because Justina has become Mrs. Thomas Morton. *Escapes. Inheritance. Marriage–Arranged. Mexican Americans. Orphans. Uncles. Aunts. Boy Scouts. Lowell (MA). Male impersonation. Marriage. Mexican-American border region. Mexico. Officers (Military). United States. Army.*

Note: One review calls the character played by Ann Pennington, "Justina Kneeland," and that played by Marcia Harris, "Elizabeth Kneeland."

ETR 14 Jul 1917, p. 416. *Motog* 21 Jul 1917, p. 156. *MPN* 21 Jul 1917, p. 434. *MPW* 28 Jul 1917, p. 652, 695. *NYDM* 14 Jul 1917, p. 17. *Var* 13 Jul 1917, p. 26. *Wid's* 12 Jul 1917, p. 444.

LITTLE CAESAR (Italian Americans)

First National Pictures, Inc.; controlled by Warner Bros. Pictures, Inc. *Dist* First National Pictures, Inc.; The Vitaphone Corp. 25 Jan **1931**; New York premiere: 9 Jan 1931 [©First National Pictures, Inc.; 29 Dec 1930; LP1912]. Sd; b&w. 8 reels, 7,300 ft. 77 or 80 min.

Dir Mervyn LeRoy. *Scr version and dial* Francis Faragoh. *Cont* Robert N. Lee. *Photog* Tony Gaudio. *Art dir* Anton Grot. *Ed* Ray Curtiss. *Gen mus dir* Erno Rapee.

Source: Based on the novel *Little Caesar* by W. R. Burnett (New York, 1929).

Cast: Edward G. Robinson (*Little Caesar "alias Rico"* [*Enrico Cesare Bandello*]), Douglas Fairbanks, Jr. (*Joe Massaro*), Glenda Farrell (*Olga Strassoff*), William Collier, Jr. (*Tony Passa*), Sidney Blackmer (*Big Boy*), Ralph Ince ([*Diamond*] *Pete Montana*), Thomas Jackson (*Sergeant Flaherty*), Stanley Fields (*Sam Vittori*), Maurice Black (*Little Arnie Lorch*), George E. Stone (*Otero*), Armand Kaliz (*De Voss*), Nick Bela (*Ritz Colonna*), [Lucille La Verne (*Ma Magdalena*)], [Landers Stevens (*Gabby*)].

Gangster, Drama. [*Print viewed*]. After robbing a gas station, Enrico Cesare Bandello, known as Rico, leaves his small town for the city with his friend Joe Massaro. Joe wants to find work as a dancer, but Rico admires the front page notoriety that gangster Diamond Pete Montana receives. He joins Sam Vittori's gang, one of the two biggest gangs in town, working directly under Montana, chief lieutenant to Big Boy, the head of the city's underworld. The other gang is headed by Little Arnie Lorch, who owns a gambling salon. Joe has a job as a dancing partner to Olga Strassoff at Lorch's establishment. Rico plans a New Year's Eve raid on Lorch's club and convinces Joe to act as the

front man. During the raid, Rico kills McClure, the crime commissioner, who is a guest that night. After that, Rico and Sam compete for leadership of the gang and Rico wins. Lorch tries to kill Rico, and after he fails, Rico hunts him down and drives him out of the city. Soon afterward, Big Boy offers Rico Montana's territory, and Rico begins to dream of heading the underworld in place of Big Boy. Joe, meanwhile, plans to leave the gang at Olga's urging. Rico cannot bear to let Joe go, however, and in turn, demands that he leave Olga, threatening to kill her when Joe refuses. To save them both, Joe decides to turn state's evidence. Rico intends to kill Joe to stop him from talking, but he cannot pull the trigger. After his failed assassination attempt, Rico flees, hiding out from the police. Hoping to goad Rico into revealing himself, Sergeant Flaherty tells the newspapers that Rico was a coward. Rico reacts by phoning the police, and the call is traced to his hiding place, where the police hunt him down and shoot him. Rico dies beneath a poster advertising the dancing team of Joe and Olga. *Ambition. Crime. Egotists. Friendship. Gangsters. Italian Americans. Murder. Attempted murder. Banquets. Dancers. Funerals. Love affairs. Loyalty. Machine-guns. Mothers and sons. New Year's Eve. Rivalry.*

Note: *MPH* notes that the opening weekend of this film's release broke the all-time attendance record for Warner Bros.' Strand Theater in New York, grossing $50,000 in eleven performances. Both Edward G. Robinson and Douglas Fairbanks, Jr. made personal appearances at the New York premiere, for which the top ticket prices were two dollars. According to his biography, Jack Warner wanted Clark Gable for the role of Rico. According to modern sources, the character of Massara was based on actor George Raft, who was associated with Owney Madden, the man who organized the taxi racket in New York City. Although *The Doorway to Hell*, a gangster film released by Warner Bros. in 1930 (see *AFI Catalog of Feature Films, 1921-30*; F2.1414) was a big hit at the time, most sources consider *Little Caesar* to be the film which started a brief craze for the genre in the early 1930s. *Little Caesar* was Robinson's first starring role and won him wide public attention, typecasting him for a while in gangster roles. The MPAA/PCA collection at the AMPAS library include a letter from MPPDA official Maurice McKenzie to Colonel Jason S. Joy reporting New York Congressman F. H. LaGuardia's strenuous objections to the portrayal of Caesar as an Italian. McKenzie wrote, "...he is going to publicly denounce Mr. Hays as a hypocrite, and the picture business as a bad business...[he states that] Mr. Hays would not dare to produce such a picture with a Jew as that character—he would lose his job if he did...." According to modern sources, in some release prints, Rico's last words, "Mother of God, is this the end of Rico?" were changed to "Mother of mercy, is this the end of Rico?" to avoid objections from the United Council of Churches. The film was budgeted at $700,000 according to modern sources. Modern sources list additional credits as Al Hill (*Waiter*), Ernie Adams (*Cashier*), Larry Steers (*Café guest*) and George Daly (*Machine gunner*).

FD 16 Nov 1930, p. 11. *FD* 25 Jan 1931, p. 4. *MPH* 17 Jan 1931, p. 34, 60. *NYT* 10 Jan 1931, p. 19. *Var* 14 Jan 1931, p. 12.

THE LITTLE CHEVALIER (French Americans)

Thomas A Edison, Inc.; Conquest Pictures. *Dist* K-E-S-E Service. 11 Aug **1917** [©Thomas A. Edison, Inc.; 31 Jul 1917; LP11157]. Si; b&w. 4 reels.

Dir Alan Crosland. *Scen* E. Clement D'Art. *Cam* Philip Tannura.

Source: Based on the novel *The Little Chevalier* by Mary Evelyn Moore Davis (New York, 1903).

Cast: Shirley Mason (*The Little Chevalier/Diane de la Roche*), Ray McKee (*Henri Valdeterre*), Richard Tucker (*Delaup*), Joseph Burke (*Chapron*), William Wadsworth (*Dominick*).

Historical, Drama. A duel in France in which the Chevalier de la Roche kills the Vicomte de Valdeterre, results in an ongoing feud between the two families. Years later, in New Orleans, Valdeterre's son Henri arranges a duel with the son of the Chevalier de la Roche, known as the Little Chevalier. Overwhelmed at the swordsmanship of the Little Chevalier, Henri faints and, upon regaining consciousness, leaves the de la Roche estate. Later, at a ball held at the governor's mansion, Henri meets Diane, the daughter of the late Chevalier and, smitten, begins to court her. This arouses the jealousy of Delaup, who is the governor's secretary and an ardent suitor of Diane's. Delaup discovers a royal proclamation sent to Henri, granting him the power to seize the de la Roche estate, and attempts to use the document to force Diane to marry him. In response, Diane sends for Henri, and when he arrives, he finds the Little Chevalier waiting to duel. Henri's refusal to fight is met with the Little Chevalier removing his cloak to reveal that he is really Diane. The long term feud between the two families is then ended with Diane and Henri's marriage. *Duels. Feuds. Male impersonation. New Orleans (LA). United States–History–Colonial period, ca. 1600-1775. Balls (parties). Extortion. France. French Americans. Jealousy. Nobility. Secret documents. Secretaries. Sword fights. Territorial governors.*

MPN 1 Sep 1917, p. 1490. *MPN* 21 Apr 1917, p. 2493. *MPW* 18 Aug 1917, p. 1122. *NYDM* 25 Aug 1917, p. 21.

THE LITTLE COLONEL (African Americans)

Fox Film Corp.; A B. G. DeSylva Production. *Dist* Fox Film Corp. 22 Feb **1935**; Prod: late Nov 1934—9 Jan 1935 [©Fox Film Corp.; 22 Feb 1935; LP5464]. Sd (Western Electric Noiseless Recording); b&w with col seq (Technicolor). 8 reels, 7,345 ft. 80 min. PCA cert no. 596.

Dir David Butler. [*Asst dir* Ad Schaumer]. *Scr and adpt* William Conselman. [*Contr to scr constr* David Butler]. *Photog* Arthur Miller. *Color photog* William Skall. *Color dir* Natalie Kalmus. *Art dir* William Darling. *Cost* William Lambert. *Mus dir* Arthur Lange. *Mus adpt* Cyril J. Mockridge. *Sd* S. C. Chapman.

Song(s): "The Old Woman (Love's Young Dream)," Irish folksong; "God's Gwinter Trouble De Water," Negro spiritual; "Moaning," music by Louis de Francesco; "Sun Shines Brighter," words by William Kernell, music by Louis de Francesco; "Little Colonel Improvisation," words and music by Cyril J. Mockridge.

Source: Based on the novel *The Little Colonel* by Annie Fellows Johnston (New York, 1895).

Cast: SHIRLEY TEMPLE (*Lloyd Sherman*), LIONEL BARRYMORE (*Colonel Lloyd*), Evelyn Venable (*Elizabeth*), John Lodge (*Jack Sherman*), Sidney Blackmer (*Swazey*), Alden Chase (*Hull*), William Burress (*Dr. Scott*), Frank Darien (*Nebler*), Robert Warwick (*Colonel Gray*), Hattie McDaniel (*Mom Beck*), Geneva Williams (*Maria*), Avonne Jackson (*May Lily*), Nyanza Potts (*Henry Clay*), Bill Robinson (*Walker*), [David O'Brien (*Frank Randolph*)], [C. E. Anderson, Captain (*Overseer*)], [Lillian West (*Neighbor woman*)], [Lucille Ward (*Aunt Sally*)], [Frank Hammond (*Carriage driver*)], [Ford West (*Village hanger-on*)], [Vester Pegg, Marty Faust (*Frontiersmen*)], [John Ince (*Sheriff*)], [Arthur Stuart Hull (*Passerby*)], [Frank O'Connor (*Aide*)], [Roland Hamblen (*Card manipulator*)], [Charles C. Wilson (*Higgins*)], [Harry Strang (*Sergeant*)].

Youth, Historical, Comedy-drama, with songs. [*Print viewed*]. In Lloydsburg, Kentucky, in the 1870's, Colonel Lloyd tries to stop his granddaughter Elizabeth from eloping with Jack Sherman, who fought for the North. When he fails to dissuade her, he warns that should she leave, she will never be welcome in his house. The couple elopes, and after six years of life in Philadelphia, they come West to seek their fortune. At a frontier outpost, their daughter Lloyd is declared an honorary colonel. Jack goes off to prospect for gold, while Elizabeth, with Lloyd, returns to the cottage her mother left her in Lloydsburg. Colonel Lloyd, upon learning that he has a new neighbor, brings flowers as a welcoming gift, but when he sees that the neighbor is his daughter, he throws the flowers down and leaves without a word. After she sees her mother crying, Lloyd learns about the past from the cook, Mom Beck, who points out that all the Lloyds are stubborn. As Lloyd makes mud pies with two black children on the colonel's property, he pokes her with his stick. She then gets angry and throws mud on his white suit. The colonel chases her, and she hides behind Mom Beck, who tells him that she is Lloyd Sherman. Colonel Lloyd then apologizes, and Lloyd calls him "grandfather." Meanwhile, Swazey, who encouraged Jack in his quest for gold, shoots some gold from a rifle into a rock and then convinces Jack to buy the land on which the rock sits. After seeing a baptism, Lloyd steals some sheets from the colonel's bed and baptizes her young black friend. The colonel comes upon them and takes her to his house to get her clothes dried. Lloyd dresses in a fancy Southern dress from a trunk in the attic, and as she sings a song which her mother taught her that her grandmother used to sing, the colonel imagines his deceased wife accompanying her on the harp. During a Civil War game that they play with toy soldiers, the colonel and Lloyd argue about which salute is the proper one, Union or Confederate. As the argument gets heated, the colonel knocks Lloyd's soldiers off the table, and Lloyd knocks the table over. He then warns her that unless she learns to control her temper she will face much unhappiness, and she agrees to try if he will. Jack returns broke and ill with a fever. The doctor convinces Elizabeth to overcome her pride and send Lloyd to live with the colonel until Jack gets well, but after a confrontation with her grandfather, Lloyd wants to go home. When a representative from the Union Pacific Railroad visits Jack and offers $5,000 for the right-of-way through his property, Jack excitedly sends Elizabeth to the bank to get the deed. Swazey and his partner Hull arrive while she is away and try to buy the deed for what Jack paid them. Jack refuses and they wait for Elizabeth's return. Lloyd comes back to the house and

overhears Swazey threaten to kill her father. She then runs through the scary woods to find her grandfather at the overseer's house, but he refuses to help until she calls him a wicked, hateful old man and says that she never wants to see him again. He then rides back with her, and they arrive just as Swazey gets the deed from Elizabeth. The colonel shoots a gun out of Hull's hand and turns the pair over to the sheriff. He then hugs his daughter and shakes hands with Jack. At a celebration that follows, Lloyd gives the colonel the Confederate salute, and he returns the Union one. *Children. Civil War veterans. Kentucky. Pride and vanity. Southerners. African Americans. Baptism. Cooks. Deception. Deeds. Elopement. Gold. Land rights. Railroads. Sheriffs. Soldiers. Songs. Threats. United States–History–Reconstruction, 1865-1898. Visions.*

Note: According to *DV*, Irving Cummings was set to direct this film, but he instead was assigned to direct retakes of *East River*, which was released as *Under Pressure* (see *AFI Catalog of Feature Films, 1931-40*; F3.4845), and David Butler replaced him shortly before production began. According to *FD*, because of his work in this film, Bill Robinson was later assigned to *In Old Kentucky* (see *AFI Catalog of Feature Films, 1931-40*; F3.2119). The final sequence of this film, the celebration, was shot in Technicolor. According to *NYT*, the sequence, which appears to have been photographed outdoors, but actually was shot in an enclosed stage, presented a problem in that Shirley Temple's dress seemed to change color as she moved across the stage.

Box 23 Feb 1935. *DV* 20 Nov 1934, p. 1. *DV* 9 Jan 1935, p. 3. *DV* 6 Feb 1935, p. 3. *FD* 11 Mar 1935, p. 7. *FD* 22 Mar 1935, p. 7. *HF* 1 Dec 1934, p. 8. *HR* 6 Feb 1935, p. 3. *MPD* 7 Feb 1935, p. 8. *MPH* 26 Jan 1935, p. 56. *MPH* 16 Feb 1935, p. 46. *NYT* 17 Feb 1935. *NYT* 22 Mar 1935, p. 26. *Var* 27 Mar 1935, p. 15.

THE LITTLE DIPLOMAT (African Americans)
Diando Film Corp. *Dist* Pathé Exchange, Inc. 15 Jun **1919** [©Pathé Exchange, Inc.; 24 May 1919; LU13750]. Si; b&w. 5 reels, 4,620 ft.
Dir Stuart Paton. *Story and scen* Emma Bell Clifton.
Cast: Baby Marie Osborne (*Little Marie*), Lydia Knott (*Mrs. Bradley West*), William Welsh (*Bradley West*), Jack Connolly (*Trent Gordon*), Murdock MacQuarrie (*Raymond Brownleigh*), Velma Clay (*Hulda*), Al MacQuarrie (*Kendall*), Betty Compson (*Phyllis Dare*), Little Sambo (*George Washington Jones, Jr.*).
Comedy-drama. Bradley West, an antique collector, agrees to adopt Little Marie, a French war orphan, to please his wife. Marie and a servant's son, George Washington Jones, Jr., get into mischief, irritating West, until Hulda, a new maid, objects to Marie playing with a black boy. Marie then whitewashes George and shocks the guests at a tea party when she introduces him. After Marie becomes friends with Trent Gordon, West's nephew and secretary, she confuses Trent's sweetheart, Phyllis Dare, when her doll is mistakenly sent to Phyllis by Trent instead of flowers. Meanwhile, crooks desiring a sacred Hindu idol that West has obtained, drug Trent. When he refuses to give West's safe combination and is allowed to return, Phyllis mistakes his drugged state for drunkenness. When the burglars break into the safe, with Hulda's help, they awaken Marie, who locks the leader in the safe until Trent comes and captures them. Marie now becomes West's object of affection. *Adoption. Antiques. Collectors and collecting. Foster children. Nephews. Orphans. African Americans. Drugging. Hindus. Maids. Parties. Racism. Safecrackers.*

ETR 31 May 1919, p. 2015. *MPN* 31 May 1919, p. 3664. *MPW* 31 May 1919, p. 1395, 1397. *Wid's* 25 May 1919, p. 13.

LITTLE DYNAMITE *see* **RASCALS**

LITTLE GYPSY (1932) *see* **HYPNOTIZED**

LITTLE GYPSY (1938) *see* **RASCALS**

THE LITTLE IMMIGRANT *see* **PADDY O'DAY**

THE LITTLE IRISH GIRL (Irish Americans)
Warner Bros. Pictures, Inc. *Dist* Warner Bros. Pictures, Inc. 6 Mar **1926** [©Warner Bros. Pictures, Inc.; 8 Mar 1926; LP22472]. Si; b&w. 7 reels, 6,667 ft.
Dir Roy Del Ruth. *Asst dir* Sandy Roth. *Adpt* Darryl Francis Zanuck. *Photog* Lyman Broening. *Addl photog* Willard Van Enger. *Film ed* Clarence Kolster.
Source: Based on the short story "The Grifters" by C. D. Lancaster (publication undetermined).
Cast: Dolores Costello (*Dot Walker*), John Harron (*Johnny*), Matthew Betz (*Jerry Crawford*), Lee Moran (*Mr. Nelson*), Gertrude Claire (*Granny*), Joseph Dowling (*Captain Dugan*), Dot Farley (*Gertie*), Henry Barrows (*Bankroll Charlie*).

Melodrama. Dot Walker, a come-on girl for grifters operating a crooked card game in San Francisco, uses her considerable charms on Johnny, a young fellow who has come to the city in an attempt to sell his grandmother's hotel. Johnny loses all his ready cash and then invites the fellows to return to his hometown to buy the hotel. They go with Johnny and attempt to swindle Granny out of $8,000. She is too smart for them, however, and instead swindles *them*. Dot reforms and wins Johnny's love. *Confidence men. Criminals–Rehabilitation. Grandmothers. Hotels. Irish Americans. San Francisco (CA). Small town life.*

FD 23 May 1926. *NYT* 11 May 1926, p. 24. *Var* 12 May 1926, p. 13.

LITTLE ITALY (Italian Americans)
Realart Pictures Corp. Jul **1921** [©Realart Pictures Corp.; 16 Jul 1921; LP16767]. Si; b&w. 5 reels, 4,875 ft.
Dir George Terwilliger. *Scen* Peter Milne. *Story* Frederic Hatton and Fanny Hatton. *Titles* Tom McNamara. *Photog* Gilbert Warrenton.
Cast: Alice Brady (*Rosa Mascani*), Norman Kerry (*Antonio Tumullo*), George Fawcett (*Marco Mascani*), Jack Ridgway (*Father Kelly*), Gertrude Norman (*Anna*), Luis Alberni (*Ricci*), Marguerite Forrest (*Bianca*).
Domestic, Melodrama. Rosa Mascani disobeys her father's command that she marry Ricci, and she is banished from home. Later she makes a vow to marry the first man she meets, who happens to be Antonio Tumullo, a truck farmer, leader of a family with whom the Mascanis have a deadly feud. Antonio's attempts to win the love of his wife are in vain, and she goes to live with her cousin in the Bronx, where her child is born. In an hour of distress when the baby is ill, Rosa realizes her love for Antonio and, seeking his forgiveness, returns to him. *Family relationships. Feuds. Italian Americans. New York City–Bronx. New York City–Little Italy. Truck farmers.*

ETR 30 Jul 1921, p. 606. *FD* 24 Jul 1921. *Var* 22 Jul 1921. p. 36.

THE LITTLE JEWESS (Jewish Americans)
Kinetophote Corp. 21 Dec **1914**. Si; b&w. 3-4 reels.
Drama. When the ship in which they are sailing to America founders, Jewish emigrant Isaac Zangwill, his wife Sarah, and their eight-year-old daughter Rebecca, are separated. While Isaac is rescued by a Jewish millionaire bound for Paris on his yacht, Sarah and Rebecca board a ship continuing on to the United States. Years later, Rebecca is a renowned detective who enters the Secret Service. While working on a case, she happens upon her father, now a distinguished diamond merchant visiting New York City. Rebecca prevents him from being misled by confidence man Jim Dayton and his accomplice, Eva Lumley, who claims to be Isaac's long-lost daughter. Finally, Rebecca arrests the pair of crooks and reunites her parents. *Confidence games. Detectives. Fathers and daughters. Jews. Merchants. Reunions. Shipwrecks. Diamonds. Immigrants. Impersonation and imposture. New York City. Sea rescues. Secret Service.*

Motog 21 Nov 1914, p. 719. *MPN* 9 Jan 1915, p. 57. *MPW* 14 Nov 1914, p. 988.

LITTLE MACARTHURS *see* **LET'S GET TOUGH!**

LITTLE MEENA'S ROMANCE (German Americans)
Fine Arts Film Co. *Dist* Triangle Film Corp. 9 Apr **1916** [©Triangle Film Corp.; 9 Apr 1916; LP9541]. Si; b&w. 5 reels.
Supv D. W. Griffith. *Dir* Paul Powell. *Story* F. M. Pierson.
Cast: Dorothy Gish (*Meena Bauer*), Owen Moore (*Count Fredrich von Ritz*), Fred J. Butler (*Matthew Bauer*), Robert Lawler (*Jacob Kunz*), Alberta Lee (*Jacob's mother*), Mazie Radford (*Jacob's sister*), George Pierce (*Jacob's father*), Fred A. Turner (*Meena's uncle*), Kate Toncray (*Meena's aunt*), Margaret Marsh, James O'Shea (*Meena's cousins*), William H. Brown (*The butler*).
Comedy-drama. The German monarchy having fallen upon hard times, Count Fredrich von Ritz comes to the Pennsylvania Dutch country as a clothes wringer salesman. He soon falls in love with Meena Bauer, who knows nothing of his royal status, but before the romance can develop fully, Fredrich receives some money from the family estate, and uses it to move to New York. A few months later, after her father has died and left her a fortune, Meena also goes to New York, where she once again meets Fredrich. Each remains unaware of the other's social position, however, as he believes that Meena is working as a servant, and she is certain that Fredrich has gone from peddling wringers to selling books. They fall in love all over again, and then, after their wedding, Meena discovers that she has become

a countess, while a delighted Fredrich realizes that he has married a millionaire. *German Americans. New York City. Nobility. Pennsylvania Dutch. Salesmen. Inheritance. Pennsylvania.*

Motog 1 Apr 1916, p. 763. *MPN* 1 Apr 1916, p. 1917. *MPW* 1 Apr 1916, p. 101. *MPW* 29 Apr 1916, p. 868. *NYDM* 8 Apr 1916, p. 30. *NYT* 3 Apr 1916, p. 11. *Var* 7 Apr 1916, p. 23. *Wid's* 13 Mar 1916, p. 454.

LITTLE MISS HAWKSHAW (Irish Americans)

Fox Film Corp. *Dist* Fox Film Corp. 23 Aug 1921 [©William Fox; 25 Sep 1921; LP17113]. Si; b&w. 5 reels, 4,106 ft.

Pres William Fox. *Dir* Carl Harbaugh. *Story* Carl Harbaugh. *Photog* Otto Brautigan.

Cast: Prolog: Eileen Percy (*Patricia*), Eric Mayne (*Sir Stephen O'Neill, her father*), Leslie Casey (*Her husband*), **Cast—New York Sequence:** Eileen Percy (*Patsy*), Francis Feeney (*Arthur Hawks*), Frank Clark (*Mike Rorke*), Vivian Ransome (*Miss Rorke*), J. Farrell MacDonald (*Inspector Hahn*), Fred L. Wilson (*J. Spencer Giles*), Glen Cavender (*Sock Wolf*).

Melodrama. Stephen O'Neill's daughter, Patricia, secretly marries a poor chap against her father's wishes and leaves for America when her husband is imprisoned on false charges. She dies en route, after giving birth to a daughter. Eighteen years later Patsy, the daughter, is living in the Bowery with the family of Mike Rorke and works at his newsstand. Meanwhile, Patsy's grandfather sends his nephew, Arthur Hawks, to America to find his daughter. Hawks acquires the services of J. Spencer Giles, a private detective who has incurred the enmity of Inspector Hahn. The inspector, hearing of the lost heiress, persuades Patsy to impersonate Sir Stephen's granddaughter; and Sir Stephen, struck by her resemblance to her mother, proves that she is actually the heiress. Hawks finds himself in love with the girl, and they are destined for a happy future. *Detectives. Heiresses. Impersonation and imposture. Irish Americans. New York City–East Side. News vendors.*

ETR 29 Oct 1921, p. 1555. *FD* 9 Oct 1921.

LITTLE MISS ROUGHNECK (Latino)

Columbia Pictures Corp. of California, Ltd. *Dist* Columbia Pictures Corp. of California, Ltd. 23 Feb 1938; Prod: 18 Oct–12 Nov 1937 [©Columbia Pictures Corp. of California, Ltd.; 14 Feb 1938; LP7812]. Sd; b&w. 6 reels. 64 min. PCA cert no. 3860.

Exec prod Irving Briskin. *Assoc prod* Wallace MacDonald. *Dir* Aubrey Scotto. *Asst dir* Bob Farfan. *Scr* Fred Niblo, Jr., Grace Neville and Michael Simmons. *Story* Fred Niblo, Jr. and Grace Neville. *Photog* Benjamin Kline. *Art dir* Stephen Goosson. *Film ed* James Sweeney. *Gowns* Kalloch. *Mus dir* Morris Stoloff. *Sd eng* George Cooper.

Song(s): by Ben Oakland and Milton Drake.

Cast: Edith Fellows (*Foxine LaRue*), Leo Carillo (*Pascual Orozco*), Scott Colton (*Al Partridge*), Jacqueline Wells (*Mary LaRue*), Margaret Irving (*Mrs. Gert LaRue*), Inez Palange (*Mercedes Orozco*), George McKay (*Phil Edwards*), Thurston Hall (*Joe Crowley*), Frank C. Wilson (*DeWilde*), John Gallaudet (*Joe Larkin*), Walter O. Stahl (*Von Hemmer*), Ivan Miller (*Yerkes*), Alan Bridge (*Sheriff*), Wade Boteler (*Inspector Carr*), Guy Usher (*Captain Dorn*), Phillipe Turick (*Tonio*), George Mori (*Serafina*), Gilbert Enriquez (*Pepe*), Eddie Laughton (*Master of ceremonies*), Ernest Wood (*Publicity director*), George Lloyd (*Mob leader*), George C. Pearce (*Proprietor of store*), Jack Daley (*Desk sergeant*), Eddie Fetherston, Neal Burns (*Assistant directors*), Iris Meredith, Ann Doran (*Girls*), Ben Crawford (*Juggler*), Frances Morris (*Mae*), Leona Valde (*Receptionist*), J. G. MacMahon (*Waiter*), Cyril Ring (*Ward*), Gene Stone (*Headwaiter*), Ed Coxen (*Bearded man*), Bud Geary (*Buckaroo*), Oscar G. Hendrian (*Truck driver*), Larry Fisher (*Blacksmith*), Earl Bunn (*Hank*), Bill Lally (*Mechanic*), Al Rhein (*Village citizen*), Harry Hollingsworth (*Deputy sheriff*), Harry Tenbrook, Cy Schindell, Jack Lowe, Robert Wilber (*Prisoners*), Chuck Hamilton (*Turnkey*), Dick Rush (*Sergeant*), Bert Moorhouse, Walter Anthony Merrill (*Reporters*), Ralph McCullough (*Fingerprint man*), Harry Strang (*Detective*), Dick Curtis, Bud Jamison, Vernon Dent, Bill Irving, Bert Starkey, George Hoey.

Show business, Drama. [*Not viewed*] Ten-year-old Foxine LaRue is being groomed for the vaudeville stage by her mother Gertrude, while her older sister, Mary, makes many personal sacrifices to support the family. During one of Foxine's performances, Hollywood agent Al Partridge takes an interest in Mary, and later goes backstage seeking an introduction to her. When Al learns that Foxine is Mary's

sister, he immediately feigns interest in the child star in order to get closer to Mary, and sees his chance with her in having the whole family join him on a train ride to Hollywood. Soon after arriving at the International Studios in Hollywood, Foxine gets herself into trouble and is ejected from one studio lot after another. Hoping to generate some much-needed publicity for her daughter, Gertrude concocts a plan in which Foxine is to be the victim of a fake kidnapping. After leaving evidence in her room to suggest a struggle, Foxine, dressed in boys' clothes, mails a ransom note and steals away on a freight train. The next day, as police scour the area looking for Foxine, Mary accuses her mother and Al of staging the kidnapping, and the police overhear her. While Al and Gertrude are arrested for the hoax, Foxine meets a Mexican man named Pascual Orozco, who takes her into his family. Gertrude and Al are later released when the police mysteriously receive a second ransom note. Realizing that he cannot keep her, Pascual drives Foxine to the orphanage she said she was from, but the girl manages to escape en route by stealing his car. Police soon capture Foxine, and later arrest Pascual when they find him mailing a letter that the girl had given him, not realizing that it is a ransom note. Al, Mary and Gertrude all arrive at the jail to take Foxine home, but Foxine refuses to go until they stop a lynch mob from storming the jail and attacking Pascual, who has been accused of the kidnapping. Although Foxine confesses her hoax to the crowd, her fans forgive her and she soon appears in her first film. *False accusations. Hoaxes. Kidnapping. Mothers and daughters. Prodigies. Vaudeville. Dismissal (Employment). Hollywood (CA). Mexican Americans. Mobs. Motion picture studios. Motion pictures. Police. Publicity. Self-sacrifice. Sisters. Talent agents. Trains.*

Note: The working title of this film was *Wonder Child.*

DV 2 Apr 1938, p. 3. *FD* 1 Jul 1938, p. 4. *HR* 2 Apr 1938, p. 3. *MPD* 5 Apr 1938, p. 2. *MPH* 4 Dec 1938, p. 38. *Var* 9 Mar 1938, p. 14.

LITTLE MISS SMILES (Jewish Americans)

Fox Film Corp. *Dist* Fox Film Corp. 15 Jan 1922 [©William Fox; 15 Jan 1922; LP17483]. Si; b&w. 5 reels, 4,884 ft.

Pres William Fox. *Dir* Jack Ford. *Scen* Jack Strumwasser and Dorothy Yost. *Photog* David Abel.

Source: Based on the novel *Little Aliens* by Myra Kelly (New York, 1910).

Cast: Shirley Mason (*Esther Aaronson*), Gaston Glass (*Dr. Jack Washton*), George Williams (*Papa Aaronson*), Martha Franklin (*Mama Aaronson*), Arthur Rankin (*Davie Aaronson*), Alfred Testa (*Louis Aaronson*), Richard Lapan (*Leon Aaronson*), Sidney D'Albrook ("*The Spider*"), Baby Blumfield (*Baby Aaronson*).

Domestic melodrama. The Aaronson family, who live in a New York tenement, suffer many hardships according to their station in life, but their worst sorrow occurs when Mama Aaronson is diagnosed as going blind. While Davie wishes to become a prizefighter, his parents strenuously object to his ambition. On the other hand, their cheerful young daughter Esther is beloved by a popular young doctor, Jack Washton. Davie falls into bad company and shoots a gangster who insults his sister; he is eventually cleared of the crime, however, and Esther marries Dr. Jack. *Blindness. Boxers. Brothers and sisters. Family life. Gangsters. Jews. New York City. Physicians. Tenement-houses.*

ETR 18 Feb 1922, p. 867. *FD* 22 Jan 1922. *MPW* 28 Jan 1922, p.428. *MPW* 11 Feb 1922 p. 656. *Var* 10 Feb 1922, p. 34.

LITTLE MISTER JIM (Chinese Americans)

Metro-Goldwyn-Mayer Corp.; controlled by Loew's Inc. *Dist* Loew's Inc. Apr 1947; Prod: 8 Oct 1945—early Jan 1946; retakes mid-Feb—early Mar 1946 [©Loew's Inc.; 10 May 1946; LP318]. Sd (Western Electric Sound System); b&w. 8,308 ft. 92 min. Passed by the National Board of Review. PCA cert no. 11378.

Prod Orville O. Dull. *Dir* Fred Zinnemann. [*Asst dir* Horace Hough]. *Scr* George Bruce. *Dir of photog* Lester White. [*2d cam* David Ragin]. *Art dir* Cedric Gibbons and Hubert Hobson. *Film ed* Frank Hull. *Set dec* Edwin B. Willis. *Assoc* Ralph S. Hurst. *Cost supv* Irene. *Assoc* Howard Shoup. *Mus score* George Bassman. *Rec dir* Douglas Shearer. [*Unit mixer* Lowell S. Kinsall]. [*Re-rec and eff mixer* James Z. Flaster, Ralph A. Pender, Robert W. Shirley, Newell Sparks, William Steinkamp, Michael Steinore, Don T. Whitmer and John A. Williams]. [*Mus mixer* M. J. MacLaughlin and William Saracino]. *Tech adv* Lt. Col. Felix Hardison, Air Corps A.U.S. [*Research dir* George Richelavie]. [*Asst research dir* Paul Wrangell].

Source: Based on the novel *Army Brat* by Tommy Wadelton (New York, 1943).

Cast: Jackie "Butch" Jenkins (*Little Jim Tukker*), James Craig (*Capt. Big Jim Tukker*), Frances Gifford (*Jean Tukker*), Luana Patten (*Missey Choosey*), Spring Byington (*Mrs. Starwell*), Chingwah Lee (*Sui Jen*), Laura La Plante (*Mrs. Glenson*), Henry O'Neill (*Chaplain*), Morris Ankrum (*Colonel Starwell*), Celia Travers (*Miss Martin*), Ruth Brady (*Miss Hall*), Sharon McManus (*Elsie*), Buz Buckley (*Ronnie*), Carol Nugent (*Clara*), Jean Van (*Mary*), [William Tannen (*Sergeant*)], [Les Fong, Spencer Chan, Weaver Levy, Gee Wee, Wong Artarne (*Chinese clerks*)], [H. T. Tsiang (*Proprietor*)], [Timmie Hawkins, Gary Gray, Charles Bates, Billy Gray (*Boys*)], [Doris Chan, Shirley Lew (*Chinese girls*)], [Castle McCall (*Girl*)].

Domestic, **Drama**. [*Print viewed*]. In 1938, at the United States Military Reservation at Fort Carroll, Little Jim Tukker, the seven-year-old son of Capt. Big Jim Tukker, is reported missing by Sui Jen, the Tukkers' Chinese house servant. Big Jim and others search for Little Jim and his dog Wolf, but it is Little Jim's mother Jean who finds him in the nearby wilderness and takes him home. The following day, Big Jim tells his son that he will soon have a baby brother or sister with whom to play, and Little Jim immediately tells friends the exciting news. Little Jim's friends, hoping to win the privilege of playing with the baby when it arrives, give Little Jim special consideration. When Jean goes into a difficult labor, she is taken to an off-base hospital, where Sui Jen and Big Jim anxiously await news of her condition. Little Jim, meanwhile, is taken to the home of their friends the Glensons and is shielded from the truth about his mother. When Jean dies in childbirth, Sui Jen gently prepares Little Jim for tragic news, and helps him accept the loss by telling him a Chinese myth about the disappearance of a woman. Meanwhile, Big Jim, devastated by the death of his wife, grows increasingly reclusive and begins drinking heavily. Three months pass, and some of the neighborhood women decide to help Big Jim by finding him a new wife. Gossip about the plans to remarry Big Jim eventually reach some of Little Jim's friends, who taunt him with the news. Angered, Little Jim engages Ronnie, one his pals, in a fistfight and goes home with a blackened eye. When Sunday school teacher Miss Martin, the wife of Col. Starwell and Miss Hall visit the Tukkers, they show their displeasure at Little Jim's lack of conventional religious schooling and decide that Sui Jen is a poor influence on the boy. Sui Jen eventually assumes some of the responsibilities of caring for Little Jim, and takes him to visit the base chaplain for a religious consultation. Although Little Jim recites in Chinese the only prayer he knows, the chaplain realizes that Sui Jen has taught Little Jim religious beliefs that are universally true, and gives Sui Jen his blessing to continue educating Little Jim. Sui Jen then gets an idea to help Big Jim by dressing Little Jim in Chinese garb, hoping that the sight of his son dressed as a Chinese boy will shock Big Jim into realizing that he has been neglecting his son. The plan works, and when Big Jim sees his son in his new clothes, he angrily demands to take over Little Jim's upbringing. Big Jim eventually quits drinking, and resumes his role as a father. A short time later, after Little Jim is enrolled in military school, the Tukkers discover that Sui Jen is a former Chinese army general, and that he has been asked to return to China to lead the army in its fight against the Japanese. *Death and dying. Fathers and sons. Grief. Military life. Officers (Military). Regeneration. Alcoholics. Birthdays. Cards. Chaplains. Children. Chinese. Death in childbirth. Dissipation. Dogs. Fistfights. Generals. Gifts. Philosophers. Pregnancy. Racism. Religion. Servants.*

Note: The working title for this film was *Army Brat*. Some contemporary reviews list the film as *Little Mr. Jim*. Contemporary reviews indicate that the film was set for a mid-1946 release, but, for reasons that have not been determined, it was not released until Apr 1947. A Feb 1945 *HR* news item noted that Joseph Harrington was set to adapt the novel for the screen, but his contribution to the final film has not been determined. According to contemporary news items in *HR*, some filming took place at Fort Douglas, UT, and in Chatsworth, CA. *HR* news items also note that ten days of retakes were shot following an unfavorable audience reaction to a preview showing of the film in mid-Feb 1946.

Box 15 Jun 1946. *DV* 5 Jun 1946, p. 3. *Exb* 12 Jun 1946 *Exb* 5 Mar 1947. *FD* 10 Jun 1946, p. 8. *HR* 8 Feb 1945, p. 1. *HR* 3 Oct 1945, p. 5. *HR* 3 Dec 1945, p. 11. *HR* 4 Jan 1946, p. 14. *HR* 8 Feb 1946, p. 3, 13. *HR* 22 Feb 1946, p. 7. *MPHPD* 6 Apr 1946, p. 2926. *MPHPD* 8 Jun 1946, p. 3030. *Var* 5 Jun 1946, p. 13.

LITTLE MOTHER see MAMELE

LITTLE NELLIE KELLY (Irish Americans)
Metro-Goldwyn-Mayer Corp.; controlled by Loew's Inc. *Dist* Loew's Inc. 22 Nov **1940**; Prod: 29 Jul—19 Sep 1940 [©Loew's Inc.; 13 Nov 1940; LP10064]. Sd (Western Electric Sound System); b&w. 10 reels.

96 or 98 min. Passed by the National Board of Review. PCA cert no. 6612.

Prod Arthur Freed. *Dir* Norman Taurog. [*Asst dir* Marvin Stuart]. *Scr* Jack McGowan. *Photog* Ray June. *Art dir* Cedric Gibbons. *Art dir assoc* Harry McAfee. *Film ed* Fredrick Y. Smith. *Set dec* Edwin B. Willis. *Women's cost* Dolly Tree. *Men's cost* Gile Steele. *Mus dir* George Stoll. *Mus adpt* Roger Edens. [*Dance dir, waltz teacher to Douglas McPhail* Eleanor Walsh]. *Rec dir* Douglas Shearer. *Make-up created by* Jack Dawn.

Song(s): "Nellie Kelly I Love You," music and lyrics by George M. Cohan; "It's a Great Day for the Irish" and "A Pretty Girl Milking Her Cow," music and lyrics by Roger Edens; "Singin' in the Rain," music by Nacio Herb Brown, lyrics by Arthur Freed; "Danny Boy," music and lyrics by Fred E. Weatherly, adapted from a traditional Irish air.

Source: Based on the musical *Little Nellie Kelly* by by George M. Cohan (New York, 13 Nov 1922).

Cast: Judy Garland (*Nellie Kelly/Little Nellie Kelly*), George Murphy (*Jerry Kelly*), Charles Winninger (*Michael Noonan*), Douglas McPhail (*Dennis Fogarty*), Arthur Shields (*Timothy Fogarty*), Rita Page (*Mary Fogarty*), Forrester Harvey (*Moriarty*), James Burke (*Sergeant McGowan*), George Watts (*Keevan*), [Addison Richards (*Judge*)], [Sidney Miller (*Boy at dance*)], [Robert Homans (*Dooley*)], [Thomas P. Dillon (*Father Malone*)], [Henry Blair (*Dennis, as a child*)], [Frederick Worlock (*Lord Cavelstoke*)], [Charles McAvoy (*Cop*)], [Milton Kibbee (*Clerk*)], [George Guhl (*Postman*)], [Joseph Crehan (*O'Brien*)], [Margaret Bert (*Miss Deane*)], [Barbara Bedford (*Miss Wilson*)], [Robert Emmett Keane (*Dr. Walton*)], [John Raitt (*Intern*)], [Almira Sessions (*Baby nurse*)], [Catherine Lewis (*W.U. girl*)], [Pat Moriarity (*Workman*)], [George McKay (*Bill*)], [Lee Phelps (*Barter*)], [Howard Mitchell (*Boyd*)], [Charles Halton (*Judge*)], [Pat O'Malley (*Mounted cop*)], [Edward Hearn (*Court clerk*)], [John Power, Will Armstrong, Frank O'Connor, Bob Ingersoll, Larry Clifford (*Ireland cronies*)], [Vondell Darr (*Girl dancer*)], [Robert Bradford, Earl Covert, Hubert Head, Norman Nielson (*Solos in "Little Nellie Kelly" number*)].

Musical. [*Print viewed*]. Irishman Michael Noonan does his best to avoid work of any kind, even though his beloved daughter Nellie tries her best to convince him to do some. When Nellie and her sweetheart, Jerry Kelly, marry over Michael's petty objections, he vows never to speak to Jerry, even though he reluctantly agrees to accompany the pair to America. After several years in New York, the three become citizens and Jerry becomes a policeman, but Michael still will not speak to him. When Nellie dies giving birth to a baby daughter, Michael again refuses to make peace with Jerry, even though he continues to live with him and take care of the baby. Many years later, Jerry has risen to the rank of police captain, and the baby, also named Nellie, has grown into a young woman who is the image of her mother, and like her mother is torn by her love for both Michael and Jerry. Their daily squabbling becomes more serious when Nellie takes an interest in young Dennis Fogarty, the son of Michael's old friend Timothy. Michael makes unreasonably objections against Dennis, while Jerry tries to make Nellie realize that Michael is using her devotion to him for selfish reasons. She continues to see Dennis, but is heartbroken when Michael leaves home after a fight over Dennis. Some time later, at the Policeman's Ball, Nellie and Dennis decide to take a walk in the park, and discover that Michael has finally gotten a job as a handsome cab driver. Despite his inability to control the horse, he seems to be suited for the job and all ends happily as the three generations are reconciled. *Family relationships. Immigrants. Irish Americans. Police. Reconciliation. Balls (Parties). Childbirth. Citizenship. Hansom cabs. New York City. St. Patrick's Day. Widowers.*

Note: Although the film was based on George M. Cohan's musical comedy of the same name, little of the original plot was transferred to the screen. Judy Garland's "swing" rendition of "Singin' in the Rain" was among the musical numbers featured in the 1974 M-G-M compilation picture, *That's Entertainment*. "Nellie Kelly" was the first adult role played by Garland. Actor John Raitt, who appeared in a small role as an "Intern" in the film, became a well known Broadway singing star. This was apparently his first motion picture.

DV 19 Nov 1940, p. 3. *FD* 15 Nov 1940, p. 8. *HR* 30 Jul 1940, p. 1. *HR* 2 Aug 1940, p. 38. *HR* 20 Sep 1940, p. 1. *HR* 18 Nov 1940, p. 4. *MPD* 13 Nov 1940, p. 4. *NYT* 25 Dec 1940, p. 33. *Var* 20 Nov 1940, p. 18.

LITTLE OLD NEW YORK (Irish Americans)
Cosmopolitan Pictures. *Dist* Goldwyn-Cosmopolitan Distributing Corp. 4 Nov **1923** [©William Randolph Hearst; 21 Sep 1923; LP19451]. Si; b&w. 11 reels, 10,366 ft.

Dir Sidney Olcott. *Adpt* Luther Reed. *Photog* Ira H. Morgan and Gilbert Warrenton. *Cost* Gretl Urban.

Source: Based on the play *Little Old New York* by Rida Johnson Young (New York, 8 Sep 1920).

Cast: Marion Davies (*Patricia O'Day*), Stephen Carr (*Patrick O'Day*), J. M. Kerrigan (*John O'Day*), Harrison Ford (*Larry Delavan*), Courtenay Foote (*Robert Fulton*), Mahlon Hamilton (*Washington Irving*), Norval Keedwell (*Fitz-Greene Halleck*), George Barraud (*Henry Brevoort*), Sam Hardy (*Cornelius Vanderbilt*), Andrew Dillon (*John Jacob Astor*), Riley Hatch (*Mr. DePuyster*), Charles Kennedy (*Reilly*), Spencer Charters (*Bunny*), Harry Watson (*Bully Boy Brewster*), Louis Wolheim (*Hoboken Terror*), Charles Judels (*Delmonico*), Gypsy O'Brien (*Ariana DePuyster*), Mary Kennedy (*Betty Schuyler*), Elizabeth Murray (*Rachel Brewster*), Thomas Findlay (*Chancellor Livingston*), Marie Burke (*Mrs. Schuyler*).

Historical, Romance. Patricia O'Day comes to America to claim a fortune left to her brother, who has died en route. In that circumstance the fortune should revert to the stepson, Larry Delavan, but disguised as Patrick, her brother, Patricia gets the inheritance and wins the friendship of Larry Delavan when she assists him in financing Robert Fulton's steamship venture. During a riot Patricia reveals her true identity; she and Delavan marry and go to Ireland. *John Jacob Astor. Loenzo Delmonico. Robert Fulton. Fitz-Greene Halleck. Immigrants. Impersonation and imposture. Inheritance. Irish. Irish Americans. Washington Irving. New York City. Steamboats. Cornelius Vanderbilt, Jr..*

FD 5 Aug 1923. *MPW* 18 Aug 1923. *NYT* 2 Aug 1923, p. 10. *Var* 9 Aug 1923, p. 26.

LITTLE PEPPINA *see* **POOR LITTLE PEPPINA**

LITTLE RED DECIDES (Chinese Americans)
Triangle Film Corp. *Dist* Triangle Distributing Corp. 24 Feb **1918**. Si; b&w. 5 reels.

Dir Jack Conway. *Scen* Jack Cunningham. *Cam* Elgin Leslie.

Source: Based on the short story "Little Red Decides" by William M. McCoy in *American Magazine* (Dec 1917).

Cast: Barbara Connolly (*Little Red*), Goro Kino (*Duck Sing*), Frederick Vroom (*Col. Ferdinand Aliso*), Jack Curtis (*Tom Gilroy*), Walter Perry (*Two Pair Smith*), Jean Hersholt (*Sour Milk*), Frank MacQuarrie (*Parson Jones*), Nellie Anderson (*Mrs. Jones*), Margaret Cullington (*Miss Hanly*), Alice Davenport (*Widow Bolton*), Maude Handforth (*Eliza Squires*), Percy Challenger (*Little Doc*), George Pearce (*Dr. Kirk*), Curley Baldwin (*Foreman*), Betty Pearce (*Miss Wattles*).

Western, Comedy-drama. Upon learning that the parents of "Little Red" have died, the cowboys of Colonel Ferdinand Aliso's ranch adopt the boy. Parson Jones and his church committee protest that the child should be brought up in more refined surroundings, but the cowboys, particularly Duck Sing, Aliso's Chinese cook, are so enamored of Little Red that they donate their poker money to the church in order to placate the congregation. After Little Red catches pneumonia and nearly dies, however, Dr. Kirk insists that the boy either live with the minister or acquire a mother through the marriage of one of the cowboys. While Little Red is recuperating at the parson's home, ranch hand Tom Gilroy courts the only marriageable women in town—a widow and two spinsters—but much to his relief, they all turn him down. In the end, Duck Sing, whom the child much prefers to the parson, kidnaps Little Red, after which the colonel legally adopts him. *Adoption. Children. Cowboys. Orphans. Ranches. Chinese Americans. Clergy. Cooks. Kidnapping. Officers (Military). Physicians. Pneumonia. Poker (Game). Spinsters. Widows.*

Note: In praising the actor Goro Kino, who played "Duck Sing," *Var* commented, "His smile and understanding of his role fixes him as a screen figure which undoubtedly will be seen more often."

ETR 23 Feb 1918, p. 994. *MPN* 2 Mar 1918, p. 1318. *MPW* 2 Mar 1918, p. 1274. *NYDM* 23 Feb 1918, p. 20. *Var* 8 Mar 1918, p. 42. *Wid's* 28 Feb 1918, p. 973.

THE LITTLE RUNAWAY (Irish Americans)
Vitagraph Co. of America; A Blue Ribbon Feature. *Dist* Greater Vitagraph, Inc. 6 May **1918** [©Vitagraph Co. of America; 30 Apr 1918; LP12350]. Si; b&w. 5 reels.

Dir William P. S. Earle. *Scen* George H. Plympton. *Story* Paul West.

Cast: Gladys Leslie (*Ann*), Edward Earle (*Lord Killowen*), Jessie Stevens (*Ann's aunt*), Mary Maurice (*Ann's grandmother*), William Dunn (*Peter Dowd*), Betty Blythe (*Eileen Murtagh*), William Calhoun (*Harvey Dowd*).

Comedy-drama. Lord Killowen, the landlord of a little village in Ireland, employs Harvey Dowd and his worthless son Peter to collect the rents. When Peter arrives at the modest home of Ann, a young lace maker who lives with her aunt and blind grandmother, he makes improper advances towards her, but Killowen, who is motoring through the area, rescues her. Without leaving her a receipt, Peter absconds with the rent money to America, and Ann's family is evicted. Determined to recover her money, Ann follows Peter to New York, where she is befriended by a policeman, who informs her that Killowen has come to America to court the wealthy Eileen Murtagh. Lord Killowen takes Ann to Eileen's home, but the latter, in a fit of jealousy, orders the girl to leave. When Ann returns during Eileen's engagement party, Killowen realizes that he prefers the little lace maker and proposes to her. *Collection agents. Eviction. Ireland. Irish. Landlords. Ne'er-do-wells. Nobility. Robbery. Attempted rape. Aunts. Blindness. Grandmothers. Jealousy. New York City. Parties. Police. Village life.*

Note: The working title of this film was *Ann Acusbla..*

ETR 4 May 1918, p. 1721. *ETR* 11 May 1918, p. 1847. *MPN* 18 May 1918, p. 2956, 3003. *MPW* 11 May 1918, p. 901. *MPW* 18 May 1918, p. 1033. *NYDM* 18 May 1918, p. 704. *Var* 3 May 1918, p. 39.

THE LITTLE SAMARITAN (African Americans)
Erbograph Co. *Dist* Art Dramas, Inc. 27 Aug **1917**. Si; b&w. 5 reels.

Dir Joseph Levering. *Scen* Rev. Clarence J. Harris.

Cast: Marian Swayne (*Lindy Gray*), Carl Gerard (*Reverend*), Lucile Dorrington, Sam Robinson, Bernard Niemeyer, Charles MacDonald, Mrs. Allen Walker, Olive Corbett.

Drama. Lindy Gray, a little orphan who lives with her grandmother, is ostracized by the townspeople because of the uncertainty of her birth. In spite of cruel treatment by her neighbors and the threat of foreclosure on her grandmother's home, Lindy maintains a cheerful optimism. One day, a new minister comes to town and befriends Lindy, recognizing her virtue. Lindy convinces him to hire Noah, an old black man who is Lindy's only other friend, as the church sexton. When the collection money is missing the day after Lindy's grandmother's mortgage is due, the townspeople accuse the little girl of robbery. To save her friend, Noah confesses to the crime. The minister suspects that neither one is guilty, however, and uncovers evidence that proves that Jim, the son of the town snob, is the thief. After a stirring sermon in which he chastises his congregation for their narrow-mindedness, the minister proposes to Lindy. *Clergy. False accusations. Orphans. Ostracism. Robbery. African Americans. Churches. Foreclosure. Grandmothers. Mortgages. Parentage. Self-sacrifice. Sermons. Snobs and snobbishness.*

Motog 8 Sep 1917, p. 530. *MPW* 8 Sep 1917, p. 1523. *NYDM* 1 Sep 1917, p. 19. *Var* 14 Sep 1917, p. 38.

A LITTLE SISTER OF EVERYBODY (Immigrants)
Anderson-Brunton Co. *Dist* Pathé Exchange, Inc. 30 Jun **1918** [©Pathé Exchange, Inc.; 21 Jun 1918; LU12565]. Si; b&w. 5 reels.

Dir Robert T. Thornby. *Scen* Charles Sarver. *Story* William Addison Lathrop.

Cast: Bessie Love (*Celeste Janvier*), George Fisher (*Hugh Travers, Jr.*), Joseph J. Dowling (*Nicholas Marinoff*), Hector Sarno (*Ivan Marask*).

Social, Comedy-drama. Celeste Janvier lives in an East Side tenement with her immigrant grandfather, Nicholas Marinoff, an old philosopher, socialist and humanitarian. Like Marinoff, Celeste is a kindhearted soul, whose friendly nature earns her the epithet, "the little sister of everybody." When several undesirable men court her, however, she is forced to turn them down. Meanwhile, Hugh Travers, Jr., whose father, a factory owner, has died suddenly, poses as a laborer in order to understand why his workers are threatening to strike. While working at the factory, he meets and falls in love with Celeste, and soon he secures a better job for her. When Celeste learns that anarchist Ivan Marask plans to kill Travers, she hurries to warn her employer and is astonished to learn that he is the poor laborer whom she loves. Marask comes to respect Travers, who agrees to improve conditions at the factory and finds happiness with Celeste. *Employer-employee relations. Factory owners. Factory workers. Impersonation and imposture. New York City–East Side. Anarchists. Attempted murder. Grandfathers. Immigrants. Philosophers. Socialism. Tenement-houses.*

ETR 29 Jun 1918, p. 323. *MPN* 29 Jun 1918, p. 3874, 3950. *MPW* 29 Jun 1918, p. 1891. *MPW* 6 Jul 1918, p. 114. *NYDM* 10 Aug 1918, p. 200. *Var* 9 Aug 1918, p. 33. *Wid's* 23 Jun 1918, pp. 3-4.

LITTLE TOKYO, U.S.A. (Japanese Americans)

Twentieth Century-Fox Film Corp. *Dist* Twentieth Century-Fox Film Corp. 14 Aug **1942**; Prod: 11 May—early Jun 1942 [©Twentieth Century-Fox Film Corp.; 14 Aug 1942; LP12024]. Sd (Western Electric Mirrophonic Recording); b&w. 7 reels, 5,723 ft. 64 min. PCA cert no. 8516.

[*Exec prod* William Goetz]. *Prod* Bryan Foy. *Dir* Otto Brower. [*Asst dir* Sam Schneider]. *Orig scr* George Bricker. *Dir of photog* Joseph MacDonald. *Art dir* Richard Day and Maurice Ransford. *Film ed* Harry Reynolds. *Set dec* Thomas Little. *Cost* Herschel. *Mus dir* Emil Newman. *Sd* Bernard Freericks and Harry M. Leonard. [*Pub dir* Harry Brand].

Cast: Preston Foster (*Michael Steele*), Brenda Joyce (*Maris Hanover*), Harold Huber ([*Ito*] *Takimura*), Don Douglas (*Hendricks*), June Duprez (*Teru*), George E. Stone (*Kingoro*), Abner Biberman (*Satsuma*), Charles Tannen (*Marsten*), Frank Orth (*Jerry*), Edward Soo Hoo (*Suma*), Beal Wong (*Shadow*), Daisy Lee (*Mrs. Satsuma*), Leonard Strong (*Fujiama*), J. Farrell MacDonald (*Captain Wade*), Richard Loo (*Oshima*), Sen Yung (*Okono*), Melie Chang (*Mrs. Okono*), [Millard Mitchell (*George "Sleepy" Miles*)], [Tom Tucker (*Boy*)], [Emmett Vogan, Mel Ruick, John Wald (*Announcers*)], [Lester Dorr (*Clerk*)], [James Farley (*Police sergeant*)], [Emory Parnell (*Slavin*)], [William Forrest (*District attorney*)], [Nino L. Pipitone (*Japanese consul*)].

Espionage, Drama. [*Print viewed*]. On 1 November 1941, American-born Japanese businessman Ito Takimura meets with Japanese spies in Tokyo. Takimura is welcomed into the Black Dragon Society and urged to use his importing business as a front for gaining information about Pacific Coast industries and defense plans. When Takimura returns to his home in the Little Tokyo section of Los Angeles, he organizes his compatriots, Kingoro, Satsuma and German-American spy Marsten. As the weeks pass, police detective Michael Steele becomes suspicious that there are spies in the area, but Takimura assures him that he is mistaken. Mike's suspicions are heightened, however, when he stops two boys from fighting and one of them, Satsuma's son Suma, brags that his father talks to Tokyo every night on a radio. Mike asks an old friend, Oshima, to investigate Satsuma, then goes to the radio station, where his girl friend, Maris Hanover, works as a commentator. Maris derides Mike's fears of espionage, but later that night, after Oshima fails to meet them, she accompanies Mike to Oshima's apartment, where they discover that the Okono family has moved in and claim no knowledge of Oshima's whereabouts. Mike rushes to Satsuma's house to search for the radio, but finds no transmitting devices or evidence concerning Oshima's disappearance. Satsuma introduces Mike to Teru, a beautiful young woman Satsuma claims is his daughter, but who is really the mistress of Hendricks, Maris' boss. The German-American Hendricks is secretly in league with Takimura and the others, and allows them to use the radio station's transmitter to relay signals to Japanese ships late at night. After leaving Satsuma's home, Mike goes to the morgue, where his pal Jerry shows him a decapitated corpse. Mike recognizes the body as Oshima's from a scar on his shoulder and realizes that the mode of killing indicates that his friend was murdered by the Black Dragon Society. On 4 December 1941, police captain Wade informs Mike that pressure from prominent Japanese businessmen has resulted in his transfer to another precinct, to take effect in four days. Mike asserts that the transfer proves he is close to catching the spies, and his refusal to cease his investigation prompts Takimura to use Teru as bait in a trap. On the night of 6 December, Teru invites Mike to Satsuma's house, where she drugs him. As Mike sleeps, Hendricks and Takimura kill Teru and make it look as if Mike murdered her while trying to assault her. Mike is arrested for the murder, and the next morning, is in prison when he learns of the Japanese attack on Pearl Harbor. Mike then escapes from jail and soon discovers where Takimura, Hendricks and the others meet. With Maris' help, Mike tricks the spies into revealing their activities while the police listen, and soon the gang is rounded up. After Japanese Americans on the West Coast are taken to internment camps, Little Tokyo becomes a ghost town, and Maris comments on her radio show that loyal Japanese Americans must suffer along with the disloyal in the interest of national security. She then reads an excerpt of Robert Nathan's poem "Watch America," and urges Americans to maintain their vigilance against espionage. *Foreign agents. Japanese Americans. Los Angeles (CA)–Little Tokyo. Police detectives. World War II.* Battered children. Black Dragon Society. Decapitation. Frame-ups. German Americans. Japanese Americans–Evacuation and relocation, 1942-1945. Morgues. Murder. Pearl Harbor (HI), Attack on, 1941. Radio announcers. Radio broadcasting. Temptresses.

Note: After the film's opening credits, a spoken prologue states: "For more than a decade, Japanese mass espionage was carried on in the United States and her territorial outposts while a complacent America literally slept at the switch. In the Philippines, in Hawaii, and on our own Pacific Coast, there toiled a vast army of volunteer spies, steeped in the traditions of their homeland: Shintoists, blind worshippers of their Emperor....This film document is presented as a reminder to a nation, which until December 7, 1941, was lulled into a false sense of security." The prologue is spoken over shots of Japanese people photographing U.S. military installations and industrial factories. According to a studio press release, the film was based on actual incidents of Japanese espionage in the Los Angeles area, as described in government records. The *HR* review and the studio story files note that the opening credits include a statement claiming that "All of the incidents in this motion picture having to do with espionage are based on facts." The statement was not in the print viewed, however.

According to *HR* news items, the film was originally to be directed by Eugene Forde. A 30 Apr 1942 studio press release announced that John Shepperd and Nancy Kelly would have the leading roles. Although a 6 Mar 1942 *HR* news item stated that the film would be set on Terminal Island near San Francisco, an 11 Mar 1942 *HR* news item noted that producer Bryan Foy had sent a camera crew to the First and Los Angeles streets area in Los Angeles because he had realized that "the local little Tokyo may soon look like a deserted village when the Japanese are removed." According to a studio press release, by the time production actually began, Little Tokyo was too deserted to be used as a location, and so the picture was partially shot on location in Los Angeles' Chinatown. After the picture had completed shooting, a 5 Jun 1942 *HR* news item commented that "some fast scoring and editing" was being done to finish the film in order "to get the picture before the public before the evacuation of Japanese fades from the front pages." While praising the timeliness of actual footage of the evacuation of Japanese Americans from Los Angeles, some contemporary reviews dismissed the film as a routine spy melodrama. The *NYT* reviewer commented, "the film as a whole is so larded with hackneyed plot devices and stock Nipponese characters that it smacks more of the conventional spy story than anything else." None of the actors in the film were Japanese, which the *HR* review noted when it praised the performances of the "occidentals who play amazingly realistic Orientals" and "the group of Chinese actors who do not mind defaming Japanese."

Box 11 Jul 1942. *DV* 8 Jul 1942, p. 3. *FD* 8 Jul 1942, p. 7. *HR* 6 Mar 1942, p. 1. *HR* 11 Mar 1942, p. 6. *HR* 11 May 1942, p. 4. *HR* 22 May 1942, p. 9. *HR* 29 May 1942, p. 15. *HR* 5 Jun 1942, p. 6. *HR* 8 Jul 1942, p. 4. *LAT* 2 Feb 1942. *LAT* 2 May 1942. *MPD* 8 Jul 1942. *MPHPD* 11 Jul 1942, p. 766. *NYT* 7 Aug 1942, p. 13. *Var* 8 Jul 1942, p. 8.

LITTLE WHITE FATHER see HURRY, CHARLIE, HURRY

THE LITTLEST REBEL (African Americans)

Photoplay Productions Co. *Dist* State Rights. Sep **1914**. Si; b&w. 6 reels.

Dir Edgar Lewis. *Cam* Philip Rosen.

Source: Based on the play *The Littlest Rebel* by Edward Peple (New York, 14 Nov 1911).

Cast: E. K. Lincoln (*Capt. Herbert Carey*), William J. Sorelle (*Lt. Col. Morrison*), Estelle Coffin (*Mrs. Carey*), Mimi Yvonne (*Virgie*), Elaine Ivans (*Sally Ann*), Martin Reagan (*Uncle Billy*), Fred Fleck (*Lieutenant Harris*), Bert S. Frank (*Jim Dudley*), Paul Pilkerton (*Joe Dudley*).

Historical, Drama. Herbert Carey, the owner of a Southern plantation, fires Joe and Jim Dudley, after which they join the Union army. Carey entrusts his wife and little daughter Virgie to his slaves Uncle Billy and Sally Ann and becomes a captain in the Confederate army. When Union soldiers under the command of Lieutenant-Colonel Morrison invade the Carey home, Jim Dudley attempts to rape Mrs. Carey. Morrison punishes him, but in revenge, Jim sets fire to the house. Morrison shoots him, thus evoking a vow of revenge from Joe. With the loss of their home, Mrs. Carey and Virgie seek shelter in the overseer's shack where the mother dies. Later, Captain Carey, disguised as a Union officer, comes to see Virgie. They try to escape to Richmond but are intercepted by Morrison who, moved by Virgie's pleas, gives them a pass. Later, Joe causes both Carey and Morrison to be arrested for treason and sentenced to death. Virgie then pleads to General Grant, who pardons them both. Morrison returns to his company and the Careys are given safe passage to Confederate lines. After the war, the Morrisons and the Careys join hands over Mrs. Carey's grave. *Fathers and daughters. Impersonation and imposture. Revenge. Soldiers. Treason. United States–History–Civil War, 1861-1865.* African Americans. Attempted rape. Frame-ups. Ulysses Simpson Grant. Pardons. Plantations. Slaves. Southerners.

Note: This was the first feature of the Photoplay Productions Co. of New York. It was shot on location in Augusta, GA. The film was remade by Fox in 1935, with Shirley Temple as star and David Butler directing (see below).

Motog 18 Apr 1914, p. 278. *Motog* 27 Jun 1914, p. 484. *Motog* 29 Aug 1914, pp. 297-98. *MPN* 22 Aug 1914, p. 46. *MPW* 30 May 1914, p. 1277. *MPW* 5 Sep 1914, p. 1381. *MPW* 12 Sep 1914, p. 1562. *NYDM* 8 Apr 1914, p. 32, 33.

THE LITTLEST REBEL (African Americans)

Twentieth Century-Fox Film Corp.; Darryl F. Zanuck in charge of production. *Dist* Twentieth Century-Fox Film Corp. 27 Dec **1935**; New York opening: 19 Dec 1935; Prod: mid-Sep—late Oct 1935 [©Twentieth Century-Fox Film Corp.; 27 Dec 1935; LP6082]. Sd (Western Electric Noiseless Recording); b&w. 8 reels, 6,618 ft. 73 min. PCA cert no. 1727.

Assoc prod B. G. DeSylva. *Dir* David Butler. *Asst dir* Booth McCracken. *Scr* Edwin Burke and [Harry Tugend]. *Photog* John Seitz. [*Spec eff tech* James Donlan]. *Art dir* William Darling. *Film ed* Irene Morra. [*Ed asst* Eleanor Morra and Mary Crumley]. [*Scenery* Thomas K. Little]. *Cost* Gwen Wakeling. *Mus arr* Cyril Mockridge. *Sd* S. C. Chapman and Roger Heman.

Song(s): "Dixie," words and music by Dan D. Emmett; "Believe Me If All Those Endearing Young Charms," words by Thomas Moore, music by anonymous; "Polly Wolly Doodle" and "My Lodging Is on the Cold Ground," traditionals.

Source: Based on the play *The Littlest Rebel* by Edward Peple (New York, 14 Nov 1911).

Cast: SHIRLEY TEMPLE (*Virgie Cary*), John Boles (*Captain Herbert Cary*), Jack Holt (*Colonel Morrison*), Karen Morley (*Mrs. Cary*), Bill Robinson (*Uncle Billy*), Guinn Williams (*Sergeant Dudley*), Willie Best (*James Henry*), Frank McGlynn, Sr. (*Abraham Lincoln*), Bessie Lyle (*Mammy*), Hannah Washington (*Sally Ann*).

Youth, **War**, **Drama**. [*Print viewed*]. During his six-year-old daughter Virgie's birthday party, Captain Herbert Cary of the Confederate Army gets word that Fort Sumter has been fired upon and that war has been declared. The men in attendance get ready to report to their Richmond regiment, and the children are sent home. Virgie asks the black house slave Uncle Billy about the war, and he tells her that he has heard that a man up North wants to free the slaves, although he admits he does not know what that means. After the men parade off to war, the Union troops arrive at the Cary plantation, and Virgie hits the commander, Colonel Morrison, with a rock shot from her slingshot. Although he admires her spunk, he warns her not to use the slingshot again. As he leaves, she tauntingly sings "Dixie." With the plantation in enemy controlled territory, Cary, now a scout for General Lee, has to sneak through enemy lines to visit his family. At the end of one short visit, a Yankee troop led by the gruff Sergeant Dudley arrives looking for him. After the soldiers find the family's hidden food and valuables, and Dudley chases Virgie upon discovering that she has covered her face with boot polish out of fear for what the soldiers would do to whites, Dudley struggles with Mrs. Cary, who is trying to protect her daughter, and he shoves her down some stairs. Morrison arrives, and after ordering the men to return the loot, he sends Dudley to get twenty-five lashes and apologizes to Virgie and her mother. When three gunshots are fired to signal that Cary has safely gotten through lines, Morrison leaves, but not before Virgie hits him with another rock shot from her slingshot. Later, as the battle rages in front of the Cary house, Mrs. Cary and Uncle Billy take Virgie into the woods, where, during a violent rainstorm, Mrs. Cary covers Virgie in her cloak. A month later, Uncle Billy arrives at Cary's camp to tell him that his wife is extremely ill. They return to the plantation where Mrs. Cary, now in Uncle Billy's cabin because the house has been burned down, dies after seeing that her husband will take care of Virgie. After the funeral, the Union troops arrive, and Cary hides in a garret attic. Morrison discovers him, but when he learns that Cary was not on a scouting trip and that he was planning to take Virgie to his sister in Richmond, Morrison, who has a daughter the same age as Virgie, tells Cary where he has left a Yankee uniform at a nearby plantation to be mended and writes him a pass to allow him and Virgie to travel to Richmond. Cary, dressed in the Yankee uniform, and Virgie are questioned as they pass through a Union camp, and Dudley overhears Virgie's voice. Cary whips him, and he and Virgie try to escape in their carriage, but the soldiers surround them. Both Cary and Morrison are court-martialed and sentenced to be hanged. A major, sympathetic to their plight, gives Uncle Billy a letter to take to a judge in Washington, D.C. To procure funds for the train trip, Uncle Billy and Virgie dance in the public square. Uncle Billy and Virgie see President Abraham Lincoln, after the judge writes him about the case, and as the president shares an apple with Virgie, she

tells him the story. After she relates that her father instructed her that she was "honor-bound" not to tell anyone in Richmond about what she saw while they were traveling, because of a promise he made to Morrison, the president is convinced that the men are not spies and instructs his secretary, John Hay, to rush a pardon for them to General Grant. Virgie hugs the president. Later, back at the Union barracks, Virgie sings "Polly Wolly Doodle" with the Union soldiers and hugs her two "fathers," Cary and Morrison. *Fathers and daughters. Honor. Soldiers. Southerners. United States–History–Civil War, 1861-1865. African Americans. Birthdays. Courts-martial and courts of inquiry. Dancing. Death and dying. John Hay. Impersonation and imposture. Abraham Lincoln. Pardons. Plantations. Racial impersonation. Rainstorms. Ruses. Slavery.*

Note: *Var* noted that there is "no trace of the Edward Peple play in the [Edwin] Burke film version" and that the play introduced Mary Miles Minter to the stage. According to a *HR* news item, two actors in the cast were replacements. Stepin Fetchit was originally cast in the role of "James Henry," but he was replaced by Willie Best after he claimed that the set lights were affecting his eyes; one hour's shooting on opening day apparently was lost because of this. Also, Charles Bickford was originally cast for the role of "Colonel Morrison," but he was replaced by Jack Holt because he was mauled by a lion during the filming of *East of Java* (see above). According to another *HR* news item, special effects technician James Donlan rescued Bill Robinson after Robinson was knocked unconscious during a scene with John Boles in which they crossed a stream on a log. The log unexpectedly turned over, and as they went under, Robinson struck his head on the log. Jule Styne, in his autobiography, states that he was Shirley Temple's vocal coach for this film. In 1914, Photoplay Productions Co. produced a film based on the same source which was directed by Edgar Lewis and starred E. K. Lincoln, William J. Sorelle and Mimi Yvonne (see above).

Box 7 Dec 1935. *DV* 19 Nov 1935, p. 3. *FD* 22 Nov 1935, p. 8. *HF* 26 Oct 1935, p. 8. *HR* 19 Sep 1935, p. 2. *HR* 1 Oct 1935, p. 1. *HR* 24 Oct 1935, p. 10. *HR* 19 Nov 1935, p. 3. *HR* 17 Oct 1936, sect. II, p. 69. *MPD* 20 Nov 1935, p. 8. *MPH* 30 Nov 1935, p. 58. *NYT* 20 Dec 1935, p. 30. *Var* 25 Dec 1935, p. 15.

LIVE AND LAUGH (Yiddish language)

Jewish Talking Picture Co. *Dist* Jewish Talking Picture Co. Dec? **1933** [©Jewish Talking Picture Co.; 2 Jan 1934; LU4417]. Sd; b&w. 6 reels, 5,400 ft. 60 min. Yiddish language with English subtitles.

Dir Max Wilner. *Author* Max Wilner. *Ed* Sam Rosen. *Rec eng* Murray Dichter.

Cast: Max Wilner (*Master of ceremonies*), Pincus Lavenda, Yudel Dubinsky, Celina Breene, Seymour Rechtzeit, Hymie Jacobson, Miriam Kressyn, Chaim Tauber, Mae Simon, Eddie Friedlander, Eva Miller, Cantor Josef Rosenblatt, Tamara, Menashe Skulnick, Joseph Buloff, Boris Rosenthal, Jack Shargel, Meyer Machtenberg, Sadie Banks.

Yiddish, **Compilation**, **Musical comedy**. [*Not viewed*]. A married couple from the Yiddish stage argue because the husband has been hired to act as master of ceremonies at an all-Jewish vaudeville show and the wife wants to assist him. At the theater, the wife makes the husband promise to let her participate in the show before she allows him to begin. As the husband introduces the subsequent acts, the wife continually butts in to inquire when she is to go on. Finally the husband allows the wife on the stage, and she introduces an act. However, from the wings, the husband and wife continue their quarrel. The wife introduces another act, and at the end of the show, they think they have done well and close singing a duet. *Jews. Marriage. Vaudeville.*

Note: The Yiddish title of this film is *Geleb un Gelakht*. This was called "the first all-Yiddish musical revue" by *FD*. The film contains portions of short films made in 1930 by Judea Films, which was owned by Joseph Seiden, who also owned Jewish Talking Pictures, the producer of this film. The Judea films were directed by Sidney Goldin. The following acts are included in this film: a sailor song and dance (possibly from the two-reel film *Sailor's Sweetheart*, which starred Hymie Jacobson and Miriam Kressyn); a Russian song entitled "Natascha," sung by Pincus Lavenda from the two-reel film of the same name; an unidentified prohibition song done by Yudel Dubinsky; child star Celina Breene (possibly in the one-reel film *The Broken Doll*); the song "Land of Freedom," done by Seymour Rechtzeit from the two-reel film of the same name; an unidentified musical comedy scene by Hymie Jacobson and Miriam Kressyn (possibly from the two-reel film *The Jewish Gypsy*); a clown scene by Chaim Tauber; a scene entitled "Yiddish Mamma," with Mae Simon and Eddie Friedlander as her son, who sings the *Kaddish*, or mourning hymn, on the death of his father (possibly from the four-reel film *Mayne Yidishe Mame*); a song done by Eva Miller (possibly from the one-reel film *An Evening in a Jewish Camp*); a scene entitled "The Shoemaker's Romance" from the two-reel film *Shuster Libe*, starring Josef Buloff; Cantor Josef Rosenblatt, who died in 1933, singing with an ensemble of eleven in a Wailing Wall presentation (possibly filmed for the 1934 *My People's Dream*, see *AFI Catalog of Feature Films, 1931-1940*; F3.3034); a pinochle game scene; Tamara singing "A Day in a

Gypsy Camp"; a comedy scene entitled "Oy! Doctor" from the two-reel film of the same name, starring Menashe Skulnick; and a musical comedy scene with a chorus. The film was released in Maryland in 1936 in a two-reel version. According to modern sources, Sadie Banks does an imitation of Mae West in the film, and some of the scenes were included in the 1941 *Mazeltov, Yidn* and the 1950 films *Borsht Belt Follies* and *Monticello, Here We Come!* (see below).

FD 8 Dec 1933, p. 6.

THE LIVING ORPHAN *see* **MY SON** (1939)

LJUBAV I STRAST (Yugoslavian Americans, Croatian language)
Yugoslavian Pictures, Inc. *Dist* Yugoslavian Pictures, Inc. **1932**; United States premiere in New York: 15 Dec 1932; Prod: completed early Nov 1932 at Royal Studios, Grantwood, NJ. Sd; b&w. 6 reels, 5,878 ft. 60-61 min. Croatian language.
Supv Ben Berk. *Dir* Frank Melford. *Story* George Moskov and Frank Melford. *Adpt and dial* Eve Ettinger. *Cam* William Steiner, Frank Zucker and Sam Levitt. *Ed* Edna Hill. *Prod mgr* Joseph Nadel.
Cast: Raquel Davidovitch (*Helen*), Ivan Plemic (*Richard*), Zorka Bregovska (*Mother*), Rajner Hlaca (*Jeweler*), Yucca Salamonic (*John*), Olga Adamovic (*Kitty*), Obren Stajica (*Doctor*), Captain Ribic (*Judge*), John Ribio (*District attorney*), Slavko Kranjcina (*Butler*).
Romance, Drama. [*Not viewed*]. Helen, a beautiful Yugoslavian stenographer living in New York's Lower East Side, is pursued by her boss, wealthy Yugoslavian lawyer, Richard. Unknown to Helen, Richard has bet his friend $5,000 that he will win her love. Richard truly falls in love with Helen, however, and intends to propose marriage, but Helen finds out about his wager and rejects him. Helen is arrested for theft, and after Richard clears her of the charges, they marry. *Class distinction. Employer-employee relations. Proposals (Marital). Stenographers. Wagers. Yugoslavian Americans. False arrests. Lawyers. New York City–East Side. Romance.*
Note: *FD* and *NYT* reviews note that this is the first release in the U.S. of a film in the Yugoslavian language with native-speaking actors. *FD* pre-release news items gave the English language title as *Born to Kiss*. Reviews note that the film's English title is *Love and Passion*.
FD 11 Nov 1932. *FD* 23 Nov 1932, p. 4. *FD* 6 Dec 1932, p. 2. *FD* 7 Dec 1932, p. 6. *FD* 10 Dec 1932, p. 2. *NYT* 16 Dec 1932, p. 25. *Var* 20 Dec 1932, p. 16.

LA LLAMA BLANCA *see* **NADA MÁS QUE UNA MUJER**

LA LLAMA SAGRADA (Spanish language)
Warner Bros. Pictures, Inc. *Dist* Warner Bros. Pictures, Inc. **1931**; Los Angeles opening: 30 Jan 1931; Prod: Sep—Oct 1930. Sd; b&w. 7 reels, 5,716 ft. 64 min. Spanish language.
Supv Henry Blanke. *Dir* William McGann. *Dial dir* Guillermo Prieto Yeme. *Asst dir* Louis Marlowe. *Scr* Harvey Thew. *Spanish version* Alvaro Jimeno. *Photog* Frank Kesson. *Film ed* George Amy.
Source: Based on the play *The Sacred Flame* by W. Somerset Maugham (New York, 19 Nov 1928).
Cast: Elvira Morla (*Señora de Taylor*), Martín Garralaga (*Mauricio Taylor*), Luana Alcañiz (*Estela*), Guillermo del Rincón (*Carlos Taylor*), Juan de Homs (*El Mayor*), Antonio Vidal (*Doctor Hart*), Carmen Rodríguez (*Enfermera Wayland*).
Melodrama. [*Not viewed*]. [The following plot summary is based on the English-language version of this film, *The Sacred Flame*; character names refer to that version. For further information regarding the English-language version, please see the note below and the entry for *The Sacred Flame* in the *AFI Catalog of Feature Films, 1921-30*.] On the same day that Col. Maurice Taylor of the Royal Flying Corps is married to Stella Elburn, his back is injured in an airplane accident, rendering him an invalid. Three years later, after he has clung to life out of devotion to his wife, his younger brother, Colin, returns from South America and at Maurice's request takes Stella out, resulting in their gradually falling in love. When Maurice dies, Nurse Wayland accuses Colin of murdering him with an overdose of sleeping powder; but Mrs. Taylor, who realized that Stella planned to elope, confesses that she administered the fatal overdose so that her son would never know that his wife left him. *Accidents. Air pilots. Brothers. Infidelity. Invalids. False accusations. Mothers and sons. Nurses. Sleeping potions.*
Note: The working title of the Spanish-language version of this film was *Amor contra amor*. The 1929 English-language version, entitled *The Sacred Flame*, was directed by Archie L. Mayo and starred Pauline Frederick and Conrad Nagel (see *AFI Catalog of Feature Films, 1921-30*; F2.4751). Although a German-language version was also produced, no information has been located concerning any exhibition of that version in the U.S. Some sources list Gaby Arnold as a cast member of the Spanish version, but the actor's participation in

the film has not been confirmed. Alvaro Jimeno, the adapter of the Spanish version, and Guillermo Prieto Yeme, dialogue director, are the same person.
Other language version(s):
Die heilige Flamme (German language)
1931. Berlin opening: 13 Apr 1931; Sd. b&w. German language.
Dir Berthold Viertel and Wilhelm Dieterle. *German adpt* Berthold Viertel and Heinrich Fraenkel. *Photog* Frank Kesson.
German-language cast: Gustav Fröhlich, Dita Parlo, Hans Heinrich von Twardowski, Salka Steuermann, Charlotte Hagenbruch, Wladimir Sokoloff, Hubert von Meyerinck, Anton Pointner. [*German version not viewed*].
CM Feb 1931, p. 151.

LO MEJOR ES REÍR (Spanish language)
Films Paramount; controlled by Paramount Publix Corp. *Dist* Paramount Publix Corp. **1931**; Panama opening: 1 Sep 1931; San Juan, Puerto Rico opening: 12 Sep 1931; Los Angeles opening: 1 Sep 1932; Prod: Mar 1931 at Paramount studios in Joinville, France. Sd; b&w. 10 reels. *Country of origin* France. Spanish language.
Dir E. W. Emo. *Dial dir* Florián Rey. *Scr* Benno Vigny. *Story* Harry d'Abbadie D'Arrast and Douglas Doty. *Adpt and Spanish dial* Pedro Muñoz Seca.
Song(s): "Lo mejor es reír," "Yo siempre te esperé" and "Un hombre busco yo," composers undetermined.
Cast: Imperio Argentina (*Gaby*), Tony D'Algy (*Paul Moret*), Rosita Díaz Gimeno (*Margarita*), Manuel Russell (*Charles Lagrange*), Carlos San Martín (*Henri Gilbert*), José Brujó (*Bernard*), Marguerite Moreno (*Bijou*).
Comedy. [*Not viewed*]. [The following plot summary is based on the English-language version of this film, *Laughter*; character names refer to that version. For further information regarding the English-language version, please see the note below and the entry for *Laughter* in the *AFI Catalog of Feature Films, 1921-30*.] Peggy Gibson, a former Follies beauty, forsakes her life of carefree attachments to marry C. Mortimer Gibson, an elderly but very wealthy broker. A year later, three significant events occur almost simultaneously: Ralph Le Saint, a young sculptor, still in love with Peggy, plans his suicide in a mood of bitterness; Paul Lockridge, a pianist, also in love with her, returns from Paris and offers her his companionship as a diversion from her stuffy life; and Gibson's daughter, Marjorie, returns from schooling abroad. Marjorie is paired with Ralph, and their escapades result in considerable trouble for the old gentleman, while Paul implores Peggy to go to Paris with him, declaring "You are rich—dirty rich. You are dying. You need laughter to make you clean," but she refuses. When Marjorie plans to elope with Ralph, Peggy exposes the sculptor as a fortune hunter, and dejected, he commits suicide. As a result, Peggy confesses her unhappiness to Gibson, then joins Paul and laughter in Paris. *Brokers. Desertion (Marital). Fortune hunters. Marriage. Pianists. Sculptors. Suicide.*
Note: This was the Spanish-language version of the 1930 Paramount film *Laughter*, which was directed by Harry D'Abbadie D'Arrast and starred Nancy Carroll and Fredric March. Although the English-language version was produced at Paramount's studios in Astoria, New York, the Spanish version, along with French and German versions, were made at the company's studios in Joinville, France. No information has been located concerning any showings in the U.S. of the French or German versions. The French version, entitled *Rive gauche*, was directed by Alexander Korda and starred Henri Garat and Meg Lemonnier; the German version, entitled *Die Männer um Lucie*, was also directed by Korda and starred Liane Haid and Walter Rilla.

LOCAL BOY MAKES GOOD (*foreign version*) *see* **L'ATHLÈTE INCOMPLET**

LOCKED LIPS (Japanese Americans)
Universal Film Mfg. Co. *Dist* Universal Film Mfg. Co. 28 Apr **1920** [©Universal Film Mfg. Co.; 8 Apr 1920; LP14992]. Si; b&w. 5 reels.
Dir William C. Dowlan. *Scen* Violet Clark.
Source: Based on the short story "Blossom" by Clifford Howard (publication undetermined).
Cast: Tsuru Aoki (*Lotus Blossom*), Stanhope Wheatcroft (*Parker, later known as Harvey Stanwood*), Magda Lane (*Audrey*), Jack Abbe.
Drama. Upon returning home from school one day, Lotus Blossom, a Japanese orphan who lives on the island of Hilo in Hawaii and teaches at a native school, discovers Parker, nearly dead from hunger. Believing his story of a shipwreck, Lotus nurses him back to health and then, mistaking loneliness for love, agrees to marry her patient.

Soon tiring of her, Parker deserts her and assumes a new identity. Later, Lotus falls in love with Komo, a visiting Japanese artist, and follows him to America. There she accepts a job as a companion to Mrs. Stanwood. When Mr. Stanwood returns from a business trip, Lotus is shocked to discover that he is her former husband but decides to remain silent. Stanwood, distrusting her silence, attempts to kill her by poisoning her incense. Before Lotus succumbs to the deadly fumes, Komo arrives, and in the ensuing fight, Stanwood is locked in Lotus' room and dies by the deadly smoke that he had intended for Lotus. *Bigamy. Desertion (Marital). Japanese Americans. Poisoning. Artists. Fights. Hawaii. Schoolteachers. Starvation.*

ETR 24 Apr 1920, p. 2416. *MPN* 24 Apr 1920, p. 3741. *MPW* 24 Apr 1920, p. 601. *NYMT* 18 Apr 1920. *Var* 28 May 1920, p. 43. *Wid's* 18 Apr 1920, p. 16.

LOCURAS DE AMOR (Spanish language)

Hal Roach Studios, Inc.; Metro-Goldwyn-Mayer Corp.; controlled by Loew's, Inc. *Dist* Metro-Goldwyn-Mayer Distributing Corp. **1930**; Santiago, Chile opening: 2 Sep 1930; Buenos Aires, Argentina opening: 23 Oct 1930; Barcelona, Spain opening: 12 Dec 1930; San Juan, Puerto Rico opening: 24 Jun 1931. Sd; b&w. 5 reels, 4,080 ft. 45 min. Passed by the National Board of Review. Spanish language.

Prod Hal Roach. *Dir* James W. Horne. [*Scr* Leo McCarey]. [*Orig story* Leo McCarey]. *Dial* H. M. Walker. *Photog* Art Lloyd. *Film ed* Richard Currier. *Sd* Elmer Raguse.

Cast: Charley Chase (*Carlos*), Carmen Guerrero (*La novia*), Enrique Acosta, Alfonso Pedroza, Arturo Turich.

Comedy. [*Not viewed*]. Carlos, who is very ambitious, works as a driver in his father's taxi business. He wants to marry the daughter of a banker, although she will not consider marriage without her father's approval. An escaped patient from the mental asylum collides with the banker, who gives the patient his business card in case of claims for damages. Later, the patient collides with Carlos and gives him the banker's card as if it were his own. Carlos recognizes his girl friend's father's name, and thinking the patient to be the banker, invites him to dine, but the asylum attendants arrive and take the patient back to the asylum. Having cleared up that confusion, Carlos encounters the banker, who offers his card. Carlos, however, does not believe that he is the banker, and thinking that the previous incident could repeat itself, grabs the banker and throws him into a fountain. The daughter arrives to find her father humiliated, and she flies into a temper and shoves Carlos into the water. The patient then shows up again, and after he rushes the girl, everyone ends up soaked. *Mistaken identity. Romance. Taxicab drivers. Ambition. Automobile accidents. Bankers. Fathers and daughters. Fathers and sons. Insane asylums. Mentally handicapped persons.*

Note: This film was an expanded, Spanish-language version of the two-reel 1930 English-language film *Fast Work*, which was directed by James W. Horne and starred Charley Chase, June Marlowe, Dell Henderson and Charles K. French. The Spanish version played in Buenos Aires under the title *¡Ay amor, cómo me has puesto!* It is probable that some actors who were in the English-language version were also in the Spanish version, but the complete composition of the Spanish cast has not been ascertained.

LOLA'S MISTAKE *see* **THIS REBEL BREED**

THE LONE DEFENDER (Latino)

Mascot Pictures Corp. *Dist* State Rights. **1934**. Sd (Disney Recording System; Powers Cinephone Sound System); b&w. 6 reels.

Pres Nat Levine. *Dir* Richard Thorpe. *Story and dial* William Burt and Ben Cohn. *Photog* Ernest Miller. *Ed* Fred Baine.

Cast: Rin Tin Tin (*Rinty*), Walter Miller (*Ramon [Roberto]*), June Marlowe (*Dolores Valdez*), Joseph Swickard (*Juan Valdez*), Buzz Barton (*Buzz*), Lee Shumway (*Amos Harkey*), Julia Bejarano (*The duenna [Maria]*), Lafe McKee (*Sheriff Billings*), Arthur Morrison (*Limpy*), Frank Lanning (*Burke*), Robert Kortman (*Jenkins*), Victor Metzetti (*Red*), Otto Metzetti (*Butch*).

Western. [*Print viewed*]. Blind Juan Valdez assures his daughter Dolores that he and his friend, Burke, will be safe while traveling to their unclaimed gold mine, whose secret location he has marked on a map he keeps in his pocket watch. Unknown to Juan, however, greedy Amos Harkey, the local cantina owner, is aware of his plans and is sending his men to ambush him. While a terrified Burke watches, Juan is killed in the desert during a ferocious sand storm, but the brave fighting of "Rinty," Juan's devoted dog, prevents the outlaws from obtaining Juan's watch. Later at Harkey's cantina, Rinty recognizes the killer outlaw and attacks him. When the outlaw starts to get the better of Rinty, Ramon, a mysterious stranger dressed like

a Mexican bandit, intercedes on his behalf. While Sheriff Billings worries about apprehending the Cactus Kid, a stagecoach robber whose "wanted posters" are being systematically cut up by a man dressed like a bandit, Harkey orders his men to capture Rinty because he believes the dog can lead him to the gold mine. Aided by Ramon and Buzz, a young cowboy, Rinty escapes from Harkey. When Rinty is later found lying next to a dead colt, however, he is accused of its killing and is sentenced to be destroyed by the sheriff, who is unaware that the colt was actually killed by a wolf. Once again, however, Ramon comes to Rinty's rescue, and the two of them flee from town together. Dolores, meanwhile, is harassed by Harkey's men, who lurk around her ranch house and try to steal her father's watch, using trap doors and secret tunnels to facilitate their actions. After a series of near disasters, including a fire in a powderhouse in which Dolores is nearly killed, Harkey forces Burke, whose memory and sanity were damaged in the sand storm, to take him to the mine. At the same time, Rinty leads Ramon to the mine, while Dolores and Buzz follow close behind. As they all reach the mine, another sand storm blows in, and Harkey and Buzz find themselves in a race to the recorder's office. Harkey apparently arrives at the claim office first and signs his name to the mine. Soon after, officers of the border patrol arrive in town and announce that a photograph of the real Cactus Kid is coming in on the next stagecoach. Confident that the Cactus Kid will hold up the stage for the photograph, the patrol lies in wait for him. As expected, the Cactus Kid tries to rob the stage but, although wounded by the patrol, eludes capture. At the same time, Rinty is seen fighting with the killer wolf by passing ranch hands and is cleared of all guilt. The border patrol follows the bandit into town, where Ramon eventually tracks him and reveals him to be Harkey in disguise. After Rinty attacks Juan's killer again, Burke's memory is jogged, and he is able to identify the criminal. Finally, Ramon confesses to Dolores that he is Ramon Roberto, a Justice Department agent, and that Buzz is his faithful assistant. Ramon then tells Dolores that Buzz actually won the race to the recorder's office and gives her the page from the recorder's book that Harkey had ripped out in order to sign his name. Safe at last, Dolores and Rinty express their gratitude to their hard-working friend, Ramon. *Bandits. Dogs. False accusations. Gold mines. Impersonation and imposture. Mexican Americans. Murder. Thieves. Amnesia. Blindness. Border patrols. Deserts. Disguise. Escapes. Fathers and daughters. Fights. Fires. Horses. Insanity. Mexican-American border region. Mining claims. Recognition. Rescues. Saloon Keepers. Sandstorms. Secret passageways. Sheriffs. Stagecoach robberies. Traps. Tunnels. United States. Federal Bureau of Investigation. Watches. Wolves.*

Note: *The Lone Defender* was first seen in 1930 as a twelve chapter serial. In 1934, a feature version of the serial was released. No reviews or precise release date information have been found for the feature. The above credits and plot summary were taken from a print of the serial and a dialogue script for the feature, which was submitted to the New York State Censor Board on 6 Jun 1934. Paul N. Robins, who is credited on the serial as presenter but is not credited on the feature dialogue script, appears on screen at the start of each episode of the serial. Although the onscreen credits of the serial included the word "copyrighted," no copyright entry was found for this title. Modern sources add Bob Irwin (*Deputy sheriff*), Arthur Metzeth (*Dutch*) and Billy McGowan (*Henchman*) to the cast of the serial.

FD 5 Jun 1934, p. 4.

THE LONE RANGER (Native Americans)

Jack Wrather Productions. *Dist* Warner Bros. Pictures, Inc. 25 Feb **1956**; New York opening: 10 Feb 1956; Prod: early Aug—early Sep 1955 [©Lone Ranger Pictures, Inc.; 25 Feb 1956; LP7854]. Sd; col (WarnerColor). 7,759 ft. 86 min. PCA cert no. 17676.

Prod Willis Goldbeck. *Dir* Stuart Heisler. *Asst dir* Robert Farfan. *2d asst dir* Allen Pomeroy, C. M. Folorance and Edward Roden. *Scr* Herb Meadow. *Dir of photog* Edwin DuPar. *Cam op* Lew Jennings. *Asst cam* Henry Kruse and Walter Robinson. *Photog* Jack Woods. *Art dir* Stanley Fleischer. *Film ed* Clarence Kolster. *Asst cutter* Ed Schroeder. *Set dec* G. W. Berntsen. *Prop master* Weldon H. Patterson. *Asst props* Charles McLaughlin. *Ladies' wardrobe* Peg McKeon. *Men's wardrobe* Gene J. Martin. *Mus* David Buttolph. *Sd* M. A. Merrick. *Boom* John Jensen. *Makeup supv* Gordon Bau. [*Makeup* Al Greenway]. *Hair stylist* Alice Monte. *Scr supv* Meta Rebner. *Gaffer* Victor Johnson. *Best boy* Claude Swanner. *Grip* Nicholas Thoeson. *Pub* Jack Casey. *Auditor* Glen Roswold. *First aid* Ardon Faught.

Cast: Clayton Moore (*The Lone Ranger*), Jay Silverheels (*Tonto*), Lyle Bettger (*Reece Kilgore*), Bonita Granville (*Welcome Kilgore*),

Perry Lopez (*Pete Ramirez*), Robert Wilke (*Cassidy*), John Pickard (*Sheriff Kimberly*), Beverly Washburn (*Lila Kilgore*), Michael Ansara (*Angry Horse*), Frank De Kova (*Red Hawk*), Charles Meredith (*The governor*), Mickey Simpson (*Powder*), Zon Murray (*Goss*), Lane Chandler (*Whitebeard*), Lee Roberts (*John Muller*), Edward Colemans (*The padre*), Bill Schallert (*The governor's secretary*), Russell Simpson (*Kimberly's father*), Rush Williams (*Knuckles*), Malcolm Atterbury (*Storekeeper*), Elmore Vincent (*Abernathy*), Bob Williams (*Marshal*), Paul Power, Robert Filmer (*Businessmen*), Robert Malcolm (*Rancher*).

Western. [*Not viewed*]. After being secretly assigned by the governor to investigate unrest that has been festering between the Indian and white people of the territory, the masked rider known as the Lone Ranger and his faithful Indian companion Tonto head for the cow town of Brasada. On the outskirts of town, they witness a band of Indians attack rancher Pete Ramirez and come to his rescue. After ruefully recounting how the Indians slaughtered his small herd of cattle, Ramirez warns the masked man to steer clear of the town. The next day, the governor comes to Brasada, posing as a guest of wealthy rancher Reece Kilgore, so that he can meet covertly with the Lone Ranger. At a mission church, the governor keeps his appointment with the Lone Ranger, who, disguised as an old prospector, shows him a silver bullet, the mark of the Lone Ranger. After conferring with the governor, the Lone Ranger and Tonto proceed to the Indian reservation, where Chief Red Hawk promises to keep the peace and confides that his braves are furious because of the spurious accusations of the whites. In Brasada, meanwhile, Cassidy, Kilgore's foreman, assembles a crew to drive the herd to Abilene, and Ramirez reluctantly joins them. En route to Abilene, Cassidy rustles the herd owned by Sheriff Kimberly's father and shoots the old man. Upon reaching Abilene, Ramirez notices a shipment of dynamite addressed to Kilgore and soon after, is murdered in his room. When Ramirez fails to return with the others, the Lone Ranger sends Tonto into Brasada to inquire about him. Seeing Tonto, an Indian, wearing a gun, Kilgore attacks him. Although he fights valiantly, Tonto is captured by Kilgore, but manages to send his riderless horse back to the Lone Ranger, who rides to town and frees Tonto, thus saving him from a lynching. Disguised once again as the old prospector, the Lone Ranger travels to Abilene and there discovers the dynamite shipment and Ramirez' murder. He and Tonto then return to the reservation, where they find the Indians, led by Angry Horse, who has taken control from the ailing Red Hawk, preparing for war. While riding back to their camp, they spot four Indians burning a rancher's field and capture them and take them to Kimberly's office. When the Indians are unmasked as white men working for Kilgore, the Lone Ranger sends the sheriff to the governor's office to arrange for Kilgore's arrest. Kilgore, meanwhile, is inciting the ranchers to war against the Indians. He sends his daughter Lila to safety, but refuses to permit his wife Welcome to accompany her because he hates her for failing to bear him a son. Shortly after Lila departs, an arrow bearing her scarf is shot into Kilgore's door. Learning of the child's abduction, the Lone Ranger goes to the reservation and battles Angry Horse. After winning the fight, the Lone Ranger rescues Lila and takes her to her mother, who tells him of Kilgore's treachery. While the townspeople gather at Pilgrim's Crossing, Kilgore goes to Spirit Mountain to obtain dynamite to use against the Indians. Alone, the Lone Ranger attempts to stop him and his men, but Kilgore wounds him and flees, leaving the dynamite behind on a pack mule. Soon after, Tonto locates his wounded friend and the two discover that the mountain is laden with silver, and that Kilgore has been fomenting unrest to gain control of the mountain. Together, they take the dynamite to a narrow pass leading to the reservation, and keep the warring factions apart by hurling dynamite sticks at them. Kimberly, leading a cavalry troop, finally arrives with a warrant for the arrest of Kilgore and Cassidy. When accused of murdering Ramirez, Kilgore turns on Cassidy, who shoots him. Cassidy attempts to flee, but the Lone Ranger pursues and apprehends him. Several weeks later, the Lone Ranger goes to visit the mission church where Lila and Welcome have sought refuge. As Welcome swears to absolve the name of Kilgore, the Lone Ranger and Tonto depart before she can thank them. *Frame-ups. Impersonation and imposture. Indians of North America. Ranchers. Bullets. Dynamite. Fathers and daughters. Government agents. Governors. Hostages. Indians of North America-Reservations. Masks. Mothers and daughters. Murder. Prospectors. Ranch foremen. Rustlers. Sheriffs. Silver.*

Note: Although the *NYT* review states that this film was made in CinemaScope, no other source mentions the process. According to an Aug 1954 *DV* news item, Jack Wrather paid $3,000,000 for the rights to this property. Included in the deal were 130 television programs, 1,500 radio transcriptions, as well as all merchandising and cartoon contracts. Wrather also received control of all stock in Lone Ranger, Inc., owned by George Trendle, who created the Lone Ranger radio series with Fran Striker. According to a *HR* production chart, this film was shot on location in Kanab, Utah. *The Lone Ranger* marked Bonita Granville's last appearance before retiring from the screen to marry Wrather. For additional information on other films featuring the character of "The Lone Ranger," please consult the Series Index and see the entry above for *Hi-Yo Silver*.

Box 7 Jan 1956. *DV* 3 Aug 1954. *DV* 4 Jan 1956, p. 3. *Exh* 11 Jan 1956, p. 4087. *FD* 9 Jan 1956, p. 8. *Har* 7 Jan 1956, p. 2. *HR* 9 Feb 1955. *HR* 5 Aug 1955, p. 13. *HR* 2 Sep 1955, p. 13. *HR* 4 Jan 1956, p. 3. *MPHPD* 7 Jan 1956, p. 729. *NYT* 11 Feb 1956, p. 12. *Var* 11 Jan 1956, p. 6.

THE LONE RANGER AND THE LOST CITY OF GOLD (Native Americans)

Jack Wrather Productions. *Dist* United Artists Corp. Jun **1958**; Prod: early Nov—late Nov 1957 [©Lone Ranger Pictures, Inc.; 4 Jun 1958; LP10701]. Sd (Westrex Recording System); col (Eastman Color). 7,307 ft. 80 min. PCA cert no. 18863.

Prod Sherman A. Harris. *Prod supv* Hugh McCollum. *Dir* Lesley Selander. *Asst dir* Willard M. Reineck. *Wrt* Robert Schaefer and Eric Freiwald. *Dir of photog* Kenneth Peach. *Art dir* James D. Vance. *Film ed* Robert S. Golden. *Set dec* Charles Thompson. *Mus* Les Baxter. *Sd* Ryder Sound Service and Philip Mitchell. *Makeup supv* Layne Britton.

Music: Overture to the opera *William Tell* by Gioacchino Antonio Rossini.

Song(s): "Hi Yo Silver," music and lyrics by Lenny Adelson and Les Baxter.

Source: Based on the television series *The Lone Ranger*, created by Fran Striker and George Trendle (15 Sep 1949—1952; 1954—1957) and the radio series of the same name, created by Fran Striker (30 Jan 1933—27 May 1955).

Cast: Clayton Moore (*The Lone Ranger, also known as Bret Reagan*), Jay Silverheels (*Tonto*), Douglas Kennedy [(*Ross Brady*)], Charles Watts [(*Oscar Matthison*)], Noreen Nash [(*Frances Henderson*)], Ralph Moody [(*Padre Vicente Esteban*)], Lisa Montell [(*Paviva*)], John Miljan [(*Tomache*)], Norman Fredric [(*Dr. James Rolfe*)], Maurice Jara [(*Redbird*)], Bill Henry [(*Travers*)], Lane Bradford [(*Wilson*)], [Belle Mitchell (*Caulama*)].

Western. [*Print viewed*]. The Lone Ranger, formerly a Texas Ranger, fights outlaws with the aid of Tonto, his faithful Indian companion. Riding through some Arizona hills, the two unsuccessfully pursue six hooded outlaws who have just killed an Indian. They take a baby that the Indian had hidden safely in the rocks to the mission of Padre Vicente Esteban, who remarks that the raiders have been killing and plundering for several months. A beautiful young Indian woman named Paviva is entranced with the child and decides to care for him. Concerned about the baby's health after his ordeal, Tonto tries to fetch Dr. James Rolfe from the nearby saloon, but the bartender, who also happens to be Sandorio's sheriff, has some roughnecks badly beat the "redskin" for daring to enter a white establishment. Later, near a body of water known as the Lake of Fire, Tonto and the Lone Ranger learn from a young man named Redbird the significance of the five-day torch-lighting ceremony just begun by the Indians: Many years earlier, a huge ball of fire had destroyed the camp of the Spanish soldiers who were planning to attack the Indian village. The Lone Ranger remarks that the ball of fire was undoubtedly a meteorite, but Redbird declares that it was dropped "by someone above." At the well-appointed ranch of respected widow Frances Henderson, Ross Brady, one of the hooded raiders, gives her the medallion he took from the murdered Indian's neck. She pieces it together with a previously stolen medallion, but complains that she cannot yet make out the message inscribed on the original silver plaque, broken into five sections centuries ago. She and her deceased husband had discovered through years of research that the plaque revealed the location of Cibola, one of the fabled seven cities of gold that so intrigued the Spanish explorer Francisco Coronado. Convinced that Fran knows something about the murders, the Lone Ranger pays her a visit disguised as southern bounty hunter Bret Reagan. Declaring that he is after the reward money she has offered for the capture of the criminals, "Bret" flirts with Fran until Brady roughly reminds her, "You're my woman!" At the mission, Paviva begs James to admit he is an Indian, but he argues that concealing his

ancestry is the only way he can make enough money to build a hospital for the Indians. Paviva, who loves the doctor, cries, "You were born a red man, and you will die that way." When an old Indian is killed, the Lone Ranger and Tonto visit Chief Tomache, who sadly reveals that he had found the silver medallions years before in the canyon, and that the men to whom he had given the pieces were now being killed. One of the recipients would arrive soon for the ceremony, and another was his long-lost grandson. The Lone Ranger and Tonto save the arriving visitor, although the Indian's medallion is stolen. Redbird captures one of the outlaws, and just after the man whispers his employer's name, Brady, hidden behind a tree, shoots him. After learning about Brady's involvement, "Bret" again visits Fran, claiming that he is in possession of the fifth medallion. The next day, the Lone Ranger rides to the nearest town for help, and while he is away, Tonto watches as Paviva stands up to the sheriff's insults in the street. When he tries to help her, the sheriff shoots Tonto in the back. Furious, James proudly admits to everyone present that he is Tomache's grandson and shows them the medallion the chief gave him years before. As he heads toward Tomache's village with Paviva and the baby, Brady organizes his raiders, and Tonto struggles onto his horse to warn the unsuspecting doctor of the danger. Tonto leads James, Paviva, and the baby to a safe spot in the village and tries to distract the raiders away from them. After shooting one of the murderers, Tonto collapses, but the Lone Ranger arrives and drags him to safety. Brady finds the doctor, steals the medallion, and takes the baby as hostage. The Lone Ranger's horse, Silver, chases Brady, who sets the baby down and rides back to Fran's ranch. Ignoring Brady's wound, Fran eagerly assembles the now complete set of medallions. Brady angrily grabs them, but as he is leaving, Fran kills him with a hatchet. Just then, the Lone Ranger arrives and Fran is apprehended. At Tomache's village, James, Paviva, and Redbird use the plaque to locate a tunnel hidden behind some rocks. This leads to a cave filled with gold, which, as James remarks to his beloved Paviva, will enable him to build the much needed hospital. Padre Vicente and the Indians turn to thank Tonto and the Lone Ranger, but the two men have left the cave and mounted their horses. The Indians wave gratefully as the Lone Ranger calls, "Hi yo, Silver, away!" *Cibola, Seven Cities of. Greed. Indians of North America. Masked bandits. Racial impersonation. Texas Rangers. Arizona. Chases. Gold. Infants. Legends. Long-lost relatives. Missions. Murder. Orphans. Physicians. Priests. Racism. Rescues. Rites and ceremonies. Self-sacrifice. Texas. Treasure. Tribal chiefs.*

Note: An early working title for the film was *Lake of Fire.* The opening title card reads "The Lone Ranger and the Lost City of Gold Starring Clayton Moore as The Lone Ranger, Jay Silverheels as Tonto." Onscreen credits also include the statement "Based on the Lone Ranger legend." Contemporary sources note that the film was partially shot on location in Tucson, AZ. This was the second of two Lone Ranger features starring Clayton Moore and Jay Silverheels that were produced to capitalize on the success of the popular *Lone Ranger* television series. For additional information on films featuring the characters of The Lone Ranger and Tonto, see entry above for *Hi-Yo Silver.*

Box 23 Jun 1958. *DV* 13 Nov 1957. *DV* 29 May 1958, p. 3. *Exh* 11 Jun 1958, p. 4479. *FD* 3 Jun 1958, p. 6. *Har* 7 Jun 1958, p. 92. *HR* 27 May 1958. *HR* 29 May 1958, p. 3. *MPHPD* 31 May 1958, p. 849. *Var* 4 Jun 1958, p. 6.

LONE STAR (Native Americans)
American Film Co.; A Mutual Star Production. *Dist* Mutual Film Corp. 23 Nov **1916**. Si; b&w. 5 reels.
Dir Edward Sloman. *Story* Kenneth B. Clarke.
Cast: William Russell (*Lone Star*), Charlotte Burton (*Helen Mattes*), Harry Von Meter (*John Mattes*), Alfred Ferguson (*Jim Harper*), Ashton Dearholt (*Jefferson Mattes*).
Drama. Disgusted by the brutal and archaic "healing" methods of the Indians, Lone Star decides to study medicine as practiced by white men. He goes East to become a doctor, and soon begins a romance with a nurse, Helen Mattes, who rejected her family's world of high society in order to tend to the sick. Before they can get married, however, Helen's slumlord father raises stern objections to having an Indian for a son-in-law. Then, while Helen wavers between her love for Lone Star and her loyalty to her father, she is seriously injured in an accident in one of the cheaply installed elevators in her father's tenement. Performing delicate surgery, Lone Star saves Helen, thereby forcing her father to reject his notion of Indian inferiority. However, Lone Star himself realizes that while the white man's medicine can be of use in the Indian world, a white woman will always be out of place there, and so he returns alone to his village. *Indians of North America.*

Landlords. Medical students. Medicine. Miscegenation. Nurses. Operations, Surgical. Physicians. Racism. Accidents. Elevators. Fathers and daughters. Slums.

Motog 2 Dec 1916, p. 1252. *MPN* 9 Dec 1916, p. 3669. *MPW* 25 Nov 1916, p. 1223.

THE LONE WAGON (Native Americans)
Sanford Productions. 15 Nov **1923**; New York showing: 4 Mar 1924. Si; b&w. 5 reels, 4,800-5,009 ft.
Dir Frank S. Mattison. *Wrt* Frank S. Mattison. *Photog* Elmer G. Dyer.
Cast: Matty Mattison, Vivian Rich, Lafayette McKee, Earl Metcalf, Gene Crosby.
Western. "... dealing with adventures of Southern family in going west. The hero, a Spaniard, is hired as guide. Daughter falls in love with him but family interferes. He saves the party from various Indian attacks, and finally the lovers are united." (*MPNBG* 6 Apr 1924, p. 43.). *Frontier and pioneer life. Guides. Indians of North America. Spaniards.*

FD 9 Mar 1924. *Var* 12 Mar 1924, p. 26.

THE LONELY GUN *see* **MAN FROM DEL RIO**

LONELY HEART (Native Americans)
Dist Affiliated Distributors. Dec **1921**. Si; b&w. 5 reels, 5,054 ft.
Dir John B. O'Brien. *Photog* Lawrence E. Williams.
Cast: Robert Elliott, Kay Laurell.
Drama. Indian drama of the oil fields. *Indians of North America. Oil fields.*

Var 9 Sep 1921, p. 45.

THE LONESOME TRAIL (Native Americans, Apache)
L. & B. Productions. *Dist* Lippert Productions, Inc. 1 Jul **1955**; Prod: began 4 Feb 1955 [©Intercontinental Pictures, Inc.; 4 Sep 1955; LP5339]. Sd; b&w. 8 reels, 6,574 ft. 73 min. PCA cert no. 17462.
Prod Earle Lyon. *Assoc prod* Ian MacDonald. *Dir* Richard Bartlett. *Scr* Richard Bartlett and Ian MacDonald. *Addl dial* J. A. Wenzel. *Dir of photog* Guy Roe. *Lighting* Vaughn Asher. *Exteriors* Joseph Stanley. *Supv ed* Merrill White. *Asst ed* James Mitchell. *Set des* Gene Kelly. *Set dec* Harry Reif. *Mus comp and cond* Leon Klatzkin. *Sd* Ollie Garretson. *Makeup* Roland Ray. *Prod mgr* William Calihan. Carl Brainard.
Source: Based on the short story "Silent Reckoning" by Gordon D. Shirreffs in *Real Western Stories* (Dec 1954).
Cast: Wayne Morris, John Agar [(*Johnny Rush*)], Margia Dean [(*Pat Wells*)], Edgar Buchanan [(*Dan Wells*)], Adele Jergens, Douglas Fowley [(*Crazy Charley*)], Earle Lyon [(*Harold "Hal" Brecker*)], Ian MacDonald [(*Gonaja*)], Richard Bartlett, Diane DeLaire, Bill Anders, Helen Jay, Earl Hansen, Dave Tomack, Kit Carson, Leonard Tarver, [Betty Blythe].
Western. [*Not viewed*]. Johnny Rush returns to Lonesome Valley after working for the Army chasing Apaches back to their reservation in the South. Johnny finds his property has been burned to the ground by the current owner of Lonesome Valley, Harold "Hal" Brecker of McKane Surveyors. Adding insult to injury, some of Hal's men shoot at Johnny as he stands at the ruins. Johnny's old friend, Crazy Charley, who lives in a dugout near the Indian reservation, explains that old man Brecker died before he could change the Lonesome Valley survey to make sure that Johnny, Charley, and Dan Wells did not lose their properties; young Hal stepped in, told Charley to get out and, along with his deputies, has been making all the laws ever since in nearby Tyrone. When Johnny asks the Wells family to join him to fight against Hal, Dan, confined to a wheelchair, angers Johnny when he explains that he is allowing Hal to marry his daughter Pat in exchange for allowing his family to remain on the property. Pat explains that striking such a deal was the only way her parents would be allowed to stay. Johnny tries to understand, and then shows her the Indian brooch he found in the smoky debris of his house. The brooch belonged to his mother, who died when he was born. In Tyrone, Johnny throws one of Hal's men, Larry Baker, out of a saloon. After Hal calls Johnny a "half-breed" and orders him out of town, a gunfight ensues, and Johnny shoots Hal's cohort, Walt Driscoll, then leaves town. Baker follows and shoots Johnny, then leaves him for dead. The Indian Gonaja finds Johnny and takes him to Charley's place, where Charley bandages Johnny's injured shoulder. Charley asks Gonaja why he would rescue an Indian chaser like Johnny, and Gonaja explains that he discovered the brooch, which he had made long ago for a young Apache Indian girl named Morning Star, who left the

reservation and married a white man; when he found Johnny with the brooch, Gonaja realized that Morning Star was his mother. As he is slow with his gun because of his injury, Johnny decides to let Charley teach him to use a bow and arrow, hoping to rehabilitate his arm. Johnny asks Gonaja to give Pat the message that "two alone are not lonely," which will let her know that he is alive. Meanwhile, Dan, beginning to reconsider the deal he made with Hal, tries to convince Pat that he and her mother will be fine without her marrying Hal, then goes to Tyrone to tell Hal himself. Despite a bond that is beginning between Johnny and Gonaja, Johnny, ignoring Charley's warning, leaves to see Pat and then confront Hal. Mrs. Wells tell Johnny that Pat has gone to find her father. In Tyrone, Hal's girl friend Mae gets into a fight with Pat. As he rides into town, Johnny sees one of Hal's men, Jed Hartel, dragging Dan's body from his horse and kills Jed. Charley forces Hal at gunpoint to sign a contract transferring ownership of the land back to Charley, Johnny and Dan, then rides off with the contract inside a Bible. Driscoll chases him down and shoots Charley, then takes the Bible and leaves Charley for dead. Johnny finds him, and when Pat comes upon them, Johnny tells her that Dan has been killed. He instructs her to stay with Charley and rides back to town with Charley's bow and arrow. After shooting Driscoll and Baker with arrows and retrieving the Bible, Johnny fights Hal, bow and arrow against a gun, and Johnny kills him. Gonaja comes into town carrying Charley, accompanied by Pat. As the townspeople gather, Charley says to Johnny as he dies to tell Pat that "there's nothing wrong with being part Indian." Johnny acknowledges he's known that he is part Indian for a long time and that he is now happy and proud of it. Johnny gives Pat the brooch, and she says with understanding that two alone are not lonely. *Apache Indians. Bow and arrow. Indians of North America–Mixed blood. Bible. Contracts. Fathers and daughters. Gunfights. Jewelry. Marriage–Forced by circumstances. Nursing back to health. Romance. Wheelchairs.*

Note: The onscreen credits and plot summary were derived from a dialogue and cutting continuity submitted for copyright. According to a *HR* production chart, this film was shot in Chatsworth, CA.

Exh 7 Sep 1955, p. 4023. *HR* 4 Feb 1955. *LAT* 20 Jan 1955. *MPD* 29 Sep 1955. *MPHPD* 17 Sep 1955, p. 594.

THE LONG FIGHT *see* **THE CAPTAIN OF THE GRAY HORSE TROOP**

THE LONG GRAY LINE (Irish Americans)
Columbia Pictures Corp.; Rota Productions, Ltd. *Dist* Columbia Pictures Corp. Feb **1955**; New York opening: 10 Feb 1955; Prod: 15 Mar—17 May 1954 [©Rota Productions, Ltd.; 31 Dec 1954; LP4353]. Sd (RCA Sound Recording); col (Technicolor). 16 reels, 12,314 ft. 135 or 138 min. PCA cert no. 17118.
Prod Robert Arthur. *Dir* JOHN FORD. *Asst dir* Wingate Smith and Jack Corrick. *Scr* Edward Hope. *Dir of photog* Charles Lawton, Jr. *Technicolor color consultant* Francis Cugat. *Art dir* Robert Peterson. *Film ed* William A. Lyon. *Set dec* Frank Tuttle. *Gowns* Jean Louis. *Mus supv and cond* Morris Stoloff. *Mus adpt* George Duning. *Sd* John Livadary and George Cooper. *Re-rec* Richard Olson. *Makeup* Clay Campbell. *Hair styles* Helen Hunt. *Tech adv* Lt. Col. George McIntyre and Maj. George Pappas.
Source: Based on the book *Bringing Up the Brass: My Fifty-Five Years at West Point* by Marty Maher and Nardi Reeder Campion (New York, 1951).
Cast: TYRONE POWER [(*Martin Maher*)], MAUREEN O'HARA [(*Mary O'Donnell Maher*)], Robert Francis [(*James "Red" Sundstrom, Jr.*)], Donald Crisp [(*Martin Maher, Sr.*)], Ward Bond [(*Capt. Herman J. Koehler*)], Betsy Palmer [(*Kitty Carter Sundstrom*)], Phil Carey [(*Charles Dotson*)], William Leslie [(*James "Red" Sundstrom*)], Harry Carey, Jr. [(*Dwight D. Eisenhower*)], Patrick Wayne [(*Cherub Overton*)], Sean McClory [(*Dinny Maher*)], Peter Graves [(*Cpl. Rudolph "Rudy" Heinz*)], Milburn Stone [(*Capt. John Pershing*)], Erin O'Brien Moore [(*Mrs. Koehler*)], Walter D. Ehlers [(*Mike Shannon*)], Willis Bouchey [(*Maj. Thomas*)], [Don Barclay (*McDonald*)], [Martin Milner (*Jim O'Carberry*)], [Chuck Courtney (*Whitey Larson*)], [Major Philip Kieffer (*Superintendent*)], [Norman Van Brocklin (*Gus Dorais*)], [Elbert Steele (*President*)], [Diane DeLaire (*Nurse*)], [Donald Murphy (*Army captain*)], [Lisa Davis (*Eleanor*)], [Dona Cole (*Peggy*)], [Pat O'Malley, Harry Denny (*Priests*)], [Robert Knapp (*Lieutenant*)], [Denny Niles, Gene Whittington, Mark Andrews, Jim Moloney, Don Oreck, Harry McKim (*Cadets*)], [Robert Roark (*Cadet Pirelli*)], [Robert Hoy (*Cadet Kennedy*)], [Robert Ellis (*Cadet Short*)], [Mickey Roth (*Cadet Curly*

Stern)], [Tom Hennessy (*Peter Dotson*)], [John Herrin (*Cadet Ramsey*)], [James Lilburn (*Cadet Thorne*)], [Jack Pennick (*Recruiting sergeant*)], [Peter Ortiz (*Chaperon*)], [William Boyett (*Major*)], [Mimi Doyle (*Nun*)], [James Sears (*Knute Rockney*)], [Mickey Simpson (*New York policeman*)], [Ken Curtis (*Specialty*)], [Norma La Roche], [Pat Harding], [Jean Moorhead], [Dorothy Ann Seese], [Mary Benoit], [Fritz Apking], [Chester Jones], [Hubert Kerns], [David Armstrong], [Erwin Neal], [Jack Mower], [Jack Del Rio], [Raoul Freeman], [Jack Ellis], [Barry Regan], [Joe Brooks], [Guy Way], [Leon C. McLaughlin].

Comedy-drama. [*Print viewed*]. In a specially arranged meeting with President Dwight D. Eisenhower, Army officer Martin Maher complains that the United States Military Academy at West Point, where he has served for fifty years, is forcing him into retirement. Protesting that he is perfectly healthy, Marty remembers his first day at the Academy: Having just arrived from County Tipperary, Ireland, Marty reports to West Point to begin his job as a waiter. Unimpressed with military discipline, and too much the exuberant Irishman to maintain a silent and respectful demeanor, Marty gets himself into trouble from the very beginning. His salary proves insufficient to pay for the dishes he constantly breaks, and when he realizes that enlisted men receive better treatment than do hired laborers, he immediately joins up. Mistakenly believing that Cpl. Rudolph Heinz betrayed a cadet, Marty fights the officer, and is placed in the guardhouse. Upon his release, he learns that Capt. Herman J. Koehler was impressed with his boxing skills and wants him to assist in athletics instruction. Soon after Marty begins teaching boxing classes, he meets Mrs. Koehler's cook, Mary O'Donnell, an attractive young woman who has just arrived from County Donegal. It is love at first sight for Marty, but Mary refuses to speak to him. Exasperated, Marty finally proposes and is astonished when Mary says yes. Capt. Koehler, she explains, had advised her to remain silent because to speak to an argumentative Irishman would have invited an immediate fight. The two do fight but are married nonetheless. Over the following few years, Marty becomes a corporal, and Mary saves enough money to bring his father and brother Dinny to America. Dinny becomes a successful businessman, and although Mary loves West Point, Marty decides to quit the military and join his brother's firm. When Mary becomes pregnant, however, he re-enlists. The baby, named Martin Maher, III, dies only hours after his birth, and Mary learns that she may never have another child. The cadets, who cherish the couple's friendship, however, remain with them during their grief. One of these cadets is James "Red" Sundstrom, who worries that he will be dismissed because of his poor grades. Marty and Mary introduce him to Kitty Carter, who tutors Red and, after several years, becomes his bride. As time passes, Marty continues to earn the love and respect of cadets such as Omar Bradley, James Van Fleet, George Patton and Eisenhower. When the U.S. enters the war in 1917, both Marty and his father try to join the troops at the front, but Koehler, now a colonel, argues that they are needed at the Academy. Soon after the armistice is signed, Marty hears that Red has been killed, and in pain and disgust, he again decides to leave the Academy. Kitty receives Red's posthumously awarded medal of honor, along with an honorary West Point appointment for her baby son. When she reacts with bitterness, it is Marty who reminds her how important military service was to Red. Years later, Marty is still at West Point, and James "Red" Sundstrom, Jr., along with the sons of others whom Marty had trained, is becoming a cadet. News of Japan's attack on Pearl Harbor is announced, whereupon Red, Jr. makes a confession to Marty: He has broken the Academy's code of honor by secretly marrying and then having the marriage annulled. Because Red, Jr. is like a son to her, Mary begs Marty to keep quiet about the incident, but the breach of honor so disturbs him that he decides to retire. During their conversation, Red, Jr. and Kitty arrive. Red, Jr. has resigned from the Academy, enlisted in the Army, and is being shipped overseas. Beaming with pride, Marty watches him depart. Later, Mary attempts to view one of the parades she so loves, but her health is too poor and she is forced to watch the proceedings from her own porch. As Marty is fetching her shawl, she quietly dies. On Christmas Eve, Marty returns home alone. He begins to prepare a poor supper for himself but is interrupted by a group of lively cadets. Suddenly Kitty arrives with Red, Jr., who has earned his captain's bars on the battlefield and wants Marty to pin them on. By Eisenhower's desk, Marty completes his reminiscences, adding that West Point "has been my whole life."

Eisenhower contacts West Point, and when Marty returns to the Academy, the cadets arrange for a full dress parade in his honor. As the band plays a series of Irish tunes, all the people Marty loves, both living and dead, join the marching cadets on the field. *Irish Americans. Military life. Military schools. Physical education and training. United States Military Academy. United States–History–Social life and customs. Aging. Boxing. Cadets. Christmas. Courtship. Death and dying. Dwight David Eisenhower. Football. Friendship. Grief. Honor. Infant death. Love. Marching bands. Marriage. New York (State). Officers (Military). Parades. Retirement. Swimming. Widows. World War I. World War II.*

Note: The working title of this film was *Mister West Point.* The film begins with the following written foreword: "The United States Military Academy at West Point is 153 years old. This is the *true story* of an enlisted man who was there for 50 of those years. His name is Marty Maher." The phrase "the long gray line" refers to the succession of officers who have been educated at the United States Military Academy at West Point, NY, many of them sons and grandsons of earlier graduates. It also refers to the line of cadets, who wear grey uniforms. In May 1947, *LAT* reported that Robert Fellows was planning to produce a film set at West Point entitled *The Long Gray Line* for Paramount, but it has not been determined if that project is related to this film. According to *NYT*, producer Jerry Wald had originally wanted to produce a film adaptation of Maher's life story while under contract to RKO. The studio, however, refused to purchase the rights, and after his production company, Wald-Krasna, was dissolved, Wald took an executive producer position at Columbia. He then convinced that studio to purchase the book and assigned Robert Arthur to produce. After casting problems delayed the production, Arthur left Columbia for Universal-International. Later, when Tyrone Power was hired to star and John Ford to direct, Arthur was borrowed back from Universal-International to produce the film. According to *MPHPD*, portions of the film were shot at West Point. This was the first CinemaScope picture to be directed by Ford and was his first film after a nearly one-year layoff due to eye surgery.

Box 12 Feb 1955. *DV* 9 Feb 1955, p. 3. *Exb* 9 Feb 1955, pp. 3913-14. *FD* 9 Feb 1955, p. 6. *Har* 12 Feb 1955, p. 26. *HR* 9 Feb 1955, p. 3. *LAT* 15 May 1947. *MPHPD* 12 Feb 1955, p. 321. *NYT* 18 Apr 1954. *NYT* 11 Feb 1955, p. 19. *Var* 9 Feb 1955, p. 10.

LOOK OUT, MR. MOTO *see* MR. MOTO TAKES A CHANCE

LOOK YOUR BEST (Italian Americans)

Goldwyn Pictures Corp. 18 Feb 1923 [©Goldwyn Pictures Corp.; 25 Jan 1923; LP18641]. Si; b&w. 6 reels, 5,304 ft.

Dir Rupert Hughes. *Asst dir* James Flood. *Story and cont* Rupert Hughes. *Photog* Norbert Brodin. *Art dir* Cedric Gibbons. *Dance supv* Ruth St. Denis.

Cast: Colleen Moore (*Perla Quaranta*), Antonio Moreno (*Carlo Bruni*), William Orlamond (*Pietro*), Orpha Alba (*Nella*), Earl Metcalfe (*Krug*), Martha Mattox (*Mrs. Blitz*), Francis McDonald (*Alberto Cabotto*).

Comedy-drama. Perla Quaranta, a half-starved "daughter of Little Italy," is given the place in Carlo Bruni's "Butterfly Act" that is vacated by a chorus girl who has grown too fat. Although Perla becomes friendly with Krug, the wire-man, she rejects him as a suitor, and in revenge Krug causes Perla's wire to break, hoping she will be fired for gaining weight. Instead, Bruni thrashes Krug, a felony for which he spends thirty days in jail. When freed, Bruni produces a new and successful dance act with Perla as the star, and the couple marry, each encouraging the other in his struggle against food. *Acrobats. Aerialists. Dancers. Diets. Italian Americans. Obesity.*

Note: The working title of this film was *The Bitterness of Sweets.*
MPW 14 Apr 1923.

LOOKOUT SISTER (African Americans)

Astor Pictures Corp. *Dist* Astor Pictures Corp. **1949**; World premiere in N.Y.: 17 Dec 1948; Prod: mid-Mar 1948. Sd; b&w. 5,851 ft. 65 min.

Pres R. M. SAVINI. *Prod* Berle Adams. *Dir* Bud Pollard. *Asst dir* Willard Sheldon and [Mike Agins]. *Orig scr story* John E. Gordon. *Addl dial* Will Morrissey. *Photog* Carl Berger. *Mont and spec eff* Nat Sobel. *Ed* Bud Pollard. *Cost* Western Costume Co. *Sd rec* Glen Glenn and Harry Eckles. *Chief grip* Wm. Johnson.

Music: "Turkey in the Straw," by Otto Bonnell.

Song(s): "Jack, You're Dead!" music by Dick Miles, lyrics by Walter Bishop; "Caldonia," music and lyrics by Fleecie Moore; "We Can't Agree" and "Boogie in the Barnyard," music and lyrics by Wilhelmina Gray; "Early in the Mornin'," music and lyrics by LeRoy Hickman, Louis Jordan and Dallas Bartley; "Lookout Sister," music and lyrics by Louis Jordan; "A New Ten-Gallon Hat," music and lyrics by Bob Wills, Smiley Burnette and Lee Penny; "Don't Burn the Candle at Both Ends," "Chicky Mo," "You're Much Too Fat" and "Roamin' Blues," composers undetermined; additional songs by Don Wilson,

Sid Robins (sic), Benny Carter, Irving Gordon, Ben Lorre and Jeff Dane.

Cast: LOUIS JORDAN and his Tympany Band:, Aaron Izenhall (*Trumpet*), Paul Quinchette (*Tenor saxophone*), Wm. Doggett (*Piano*), Wm. Hadnott (*Bass*), Chris Colombus (*Drums*), James Jackson (*Guitar*), Suzette Harbin (*Betty Scott*), Monte Hawley (*Mack Morgan*), Glenn Allen (*Billy*), Tommy Southern (*Cactus*), Jack Clisby (*Pistol Pete*), Maceo Sheffield (*Officer Lee/The sheriff*), Peggy Thomas (*Dancer*), Louise Franklin (*Bathing beauty*), Anice Clark, Dorothy Seamans (*Girl exhibition divers*), and introducing The Champion Cowboy Bob Scott.

African American, Musical, Western. [*Print viewed*]. Louis Jordan is hospitalized with a physical breakdown after a long road tour with his band and is forced to lay off for a year or so. Theatrical agent Mack Morgan phones Louis' manager to complain that he has Louis booked for ten weeks and will lose a lot of money due to the cancellations. He also feels that Louis has been playing too many benefits. Louis is confined to a sanatorium where he meets Billy, a young boy on crutches, who would like to become a cowboy. Louis tells nurse Betty Scott that he is going to try to find a way to help the boy achieve his goal. After taking some medication, Louis falls into a deep sleep and has a dream which includes some of the people from his life. In the dream, Louis and his band go to a convalescent ranch in Lookout, Arizona. A neighboring ranch owner, Mack Morgan, tells Betty Scott that the Health and Happiness Ranch, which she and her brother Bob have recently inherited, is too big for her to run and that she appears to be getting into debt. However, Betty intends to keep the ranch going so that adults and children can come there to recuperate. When Morgan tells her that the mortgage he gave her father is due, but that he is willing to forget the debt if Betty marries him, she protests that she does not love him. Bob informs Morgan that a rich former patient, a banker, is returning and will help them to keep the ranch going. Morgan, however, informs them that unless he gets his money he will foreclose on the mortgage. Later, while Louis and his band perform at the ranch, Morgan and his henchman Cactus send a fake telegram from the county health commissioner to the banker advising him to cancel his visit due to a strange epidemic. Morgan wants to run Betty and Bob off the ranch as he has discovered oil on it. Later, after Bob performs some horse riding and rodeo tricks, Louis is persuaded to have a go but is quickly bucked off his horse. After Morgan shows Bob and Betty a newspaper story about the banker vacationing elsewhere, he demands his money by the following evening. When Louis learns of their dilemma, he tells Betty and Bob that he will wire stars of stage, screen and radio and that they will fix up everything. Morgan overhears Louis, draws a gun on him and advises him to leave. Later, when Billy invites Louis to a range for some shooting practice, Louis accidentally shoots a jar containing a sample oil deposit and realizes that the oil is the reason Morgan wants to get rid of Betty and Bob. Cactus witnesses Louis's discovery and informs Morgan, who then decides to frame Louis for horse-stealing. However, Billy spots Cactus leaving a stolen horse in the ranch's barn, and when Morgan brings the sheriff to arrest Louis, Bob, tipped off by Billy, comes to Louis' defense. A fistfight breaks out and Bob and Louis escape on horseback, pursued by Morgan and the sheriff's posse. During a long chase, Morgan shoots at Louis, who returns fire, knocking Morgan off his horse. Just as the posse catches up with him, Louis wakes up in his hospital bed and tells Billy that he knows just the place where he can go to get well and learn to be a cowboy—The Health and Happiness Ranch. Louis phones his manager and asks him to wire many stars to attend the opening of his new ranch in Lookout. Nurse Betty thinks that this is a great idea and kisses him. *African Americans. Bands (Music). Cowboys. Dreams. Hospitals. Ranches. Singers. Swing music. Brothers and sisters. Chases. Convalescence. Crutches. Divers and diving. Fistfights. Frame-ups. Musicians. Nurses. Oil. Riding. Romance. Sheriffs. Telegrams. Theatrical agents.*

Note: This film's working title was *The Dude Ranch.* A biography of Louis Jordan states that some of the film was shot at his home in Phoenix, Arizona. The onscreen credits list Don Wilson, Sid Robins (sic), Benny Carter, Irving Gordon, Ben Lorre and Jeff Dane as additional composers but the titles of their numbers have not been determined and it is possible that they wrote some or all of the songs listed without composers.

Down Beat 11 Mar 1949, p. 8. *HR* 24 Mar 1948, p. 12. *HR* 7 Feb 1949, p. 3. *Var* 22 Dec 1948, p. 18.

LOOSER THAN LOOSE (*foreignversion*) *see* **UNA CANA AL AIRE**

LORD EPPING OUT WEST *see* **MEXICAN SPITFIRE OUT WEST**

LORD EPPING SEES A GHOST *see* **THE MEXICAN SPITFIRE'S BABY**

LORD LOVELAND DISCOVERS AMERICA (English Americans)
American Film Co.; Mutual Masterpictures De Luxe Edition. *Dist* Mutual Film Corp. 27 Jan **1916**. Si; b&w. 5 reels.
Dir Arthur Maude. *Asst dir* F. Harmon Weight.
Source: Based on the novel *Lord Loveland Discovers America* by Charles Norris Williamson and Alice Muriel Livingston Williamson (New York, 1910).
Cast: Arthur Maude (*Lord Loveland*), Constance Crawley (*Leslie Dearmer*), William Carroll (*Bill Willing*), Charles Newton (*Major Hunter*), William Frawley (*Tony Kidd*), George Clancy (*Alexander the Great*), Nell Franzen (*Izzy*).
Comedy-drama. Besieged by British creditors, Lord Loveland brings his title, but no money, to the United States and starts hunting for an American heiress. To support himself, he gets a job as a waiter, and while at the restaurant, he renews an acquaintance with Leslie Dearmer, a playwright whom he met on the ship from England. Leslie tries to help Loveland, but she loses touch with him when he joins a barnstorming theater troupe. Then, when the actors perform one of Leslie's plays without her permission, she tracks them down in order to stop them. Leslie is surprised and pleased to see Loveland once again, and immediately gives him a job as her chauffeur. Although Loveland is still determined to marry a millionaire, he cannot help falling in love with his new employer. Thus, when she tells him that she is an heiress, the last shred of Loveland's reluctance vanishes and he and Leslie get married. *English. Fortune hunters. Heiresses. Nobility. Playwrights. Actors and actresses. Chauffeurs. Debt. Theatrical troupes. Waiters.*
Motog 29 Jan 1916, p. 260. *MPN* 29 Jan 1916, p. 564. *MPW* 15 Jan 1916, p. 362. *MPW* 22 Jan 1916, p. 665. *MPW* 5 Feb 1916, p. 799. *NYDM* 5 Feb 1916, p. 28.

THE LORD LOVES THE IRISH (Irish Americans)
Robert Brunton Productions. *Dist* W. W. Hodkinson Corp. through Pathé Exchange, Inc. 14 Dec **1919**. Si; b&w. 5 reels, 4,900 ft.
Pres Robert Brunton. *Dir* Ernest C. Warde. *Scen* Monte M. Katterjohn. *Story* Monte M. Katterjohn. *Cam* Arthur Todd.
Cast: J. Warren Kerrigan (*Miles Machree*), Aggie Herring (*Mother Machree*), James O. Barrows (*Timothy Lynch*), Fritzi Brunette (*Sheila Lynch*), William Ellingford (*Malachi Nolan*), Wedgwood Nowell (*Allyn Dexter*), Joseph J. Dowling (*Dr. Leon Wilson/Hugo Strauss*).
Comedy-drama. Miles Machree is content to live with his mother, brothers, and sisters, tilling the soil in Glengarry, Ireland, until he meets attractive Sheila Lynch, touring with her father, a bank president in New York, who years earlier left the village. Because she chides him for not having ambition, and encourages him to come to America, Miles follows Sheila home and soon, with the help of his uncle, Malachi Nolan, a saloon keeper and alderman, becomes a policeman. Although he is disappointed to learn of Sheila's engagement to her father's secretary, Allyn Dexter, when Miles overhears Dexter and Dr. Leon Wilson discussing a scheme to substitute counterfeit money for bank bills, Miles tries to protect Dexter for Sheila's sake. After Sheila is lured to the counterfeiter's den, Miles rescues her and, during a scuffle involving the Secret Service, Dexter is killed. The counterfeiters are captured, and Miles becomes Lynch's private secretary and son-in-law. *City-country contrast. Counterfeiters and counterfeiting. Immigrants. Ireland. Irish Americans. Police. Aldermen. Bank presidents. Engagements. Farmers. Saloon keepers. Secret Service. Secretaries. Uncles.*
ETR 20 Dec 1919, p. 267. *MPN* 27 Dec 1919, p. 272. *MPW* 20 Dec 1919, p. 104. *NYMT* 14 Dec 1919. *Var* 19 Dec 1919, p. 44.

LOS QUE DANZAN (Spanish language)
Warner Bros. Pictures, Inc.; First National Pictures, Inc. *Dist* Warner Bros. Pictures, Inc. Dec **1930**; New York opening: 5 Dec 1930; Prod: Aug—Sep 1930. Sd; b&w. 7 reels, 6,665 ft. 74 min. Spanish language.
Supv Henry Blanke. *Dir* William McGann. *Asst dir* Louis Marlowe. *Dial dir* Alfredo del Diestro. *Scr* Joseph Jackson. *Story* George Kibbe Turner. *Spanish version* Baltasar Fernández Cué. *Photog* Ernest Haller. *Film ed* Hugh Bennett.

Cast: Antonio Moreno (*Daniel Hogan, also known as Frank "Cicatriz" Tunner*), María Alba (*Nora Brady*), Pablo Alvarez Rubio (*Juan*), Teresa Renner (*Nelly*), Tito Davison (*Chico Brady*), Alfredo del Diestro (*Benson*), Martín Garralaga (*Pat Hogan*), José Soriano Viosca (*Capitán O'Brien*), Juan Duval (*Tomás*).
Gangster, Melodrama. [*Not viewed*]. After a warehouse on the Hudson River in New York is robbed, the police arrest Chico Brady and charge him with killing a worker when he tried to sound the alarm. A watchman at the building, in league with the thieves, confirms the accusation in order to protect Juan, the gang's leader. When Chico is sentenced to death for a crime he did not commit, his sister Nora does all in her power to prove his innocence, seeking help from Juan and, later, from the police who assign the case to detective Daniel Hogan, brother of the man killed. Posing as a gangster known as Frank "Scarface" Tunner, Hogan infiltrates the gang and finds the proof that reveals the real culprit. Chico's scheduled execution is halted at the last moment, and Dan and Nora make plans to start a new life together. *Brothers and sisters. False accusations. Gangsters. Impersonation and imposture. Murder. Frame-ups. New York City. Robbery. Romance. Watchmen.*
Note: The 1930 film *Those Who Dance*, which was directed by William Beaudine and starred Monte Blue and Lila Lee, was also made in Spanish, German and French versions. All the foreign versions were filmed simultaneously. No evidence has been located to indicated that the French version, entitled *Contre-enquête*, had U.S. screenings. An earlier film based on the same story was produced, in 1924, by Thomas H. Ince (see *AFI Catalog of Feature Films, 1921-30*; F2.5646 and F2.5647).
Other language version(s):
Der Tanz geht weiter (German language)
1930. Berlin opening: 3 Nov 1930; New York opening: 5 Jan 1931; Los Angeles opening: 30 May 1931; Sd. b&w. 7,183 ft. 72 or 80min. German language.
Supv Henry Blanke. *Dir* Wilhelm Dieterle. *German adpt* Heinrich Fraenkel. *Photog* Sid Hickox. *Film ed* Edward Schroeder. *Mus arr* Ernö Rapée.
German-language cast: Wilhelm Dieterle (*Dan*), Lissi Arna (*Elly*), Anton Pointner (*Joe*), Carla Bartheel (*Kitty*), Werner Klinger (*Tim*), John Reinhardt (*Pat*), Lothar Mayring, Paul Panzer, Adolph Miller. [*German version not viewed*].
FD 11 Jan 1931, p. 10. *Cinl* Dec 1930, p. 30. *CM* Dec 1930, p. 1,210. *NYT* 6 Jan 1931, p. 25. *Var* 26 Nov 1930, p. 19. *Var* 24 Dec 1930, p. 29.

LOST AT THE FRONT (German Americans, Irish Americans)
John McCormick Productions. *Dist* First National Pictures, Inc. 29 May **1927** [©First National Pictures, Inc.; 12 May 1927; LP23955]. Si; b&w. 6 reels, 5,254 or 5,559 ft.
Pres John McCormick. *Prod* Frank Griffin. *Dir* Del Lord. *Scen* Hampton Del Ruth. *Wrt* Frank Griffin. *Comedy const* Clarence Hennecke. *Titles* Ralph Spence. *Photog* James Van Trees.
Cast: George Sidney (*August Krause*), Charlie Murray (*Patrick Muldoon*), Natalie Kingston (*Olga Pietroff*), John Kolb (*Von Herfiz*), Max Asher (*Adolph Meyerburg*), Brooks Benedict (*The Inventor*), Ed Brady (*Captain Kashluff*), Harry Lipman (*Captain Levinsky*), Nita Martan, Nina Romano (*Two Russian girls*).
Comedy. Patrick, a New York Irish policeman, and August, a German barkeeper, are the best of friends, though both are rivals for Olga, a sculptress whose studio is nearby. When August is called to the front as a German reservist, he takes a wireless which he believes will help Germany in the war. Patrick and Olga decide they must confiscate the invention before it destroys the United States Army; Pat enlists in the Russian Army, as he is too old to join that of the United States. The friends meet on the Russo-German front, where Pat takes August prisoner; they engage in a game of dodging both armies, disguising themselves as women, and get into a Russian Battalion of Death. In their subsequent attempt to escape, news of the Armistice arrives. Returning home, they find that Olga has married in their absence. *Bartenders. Friendship. German Americans. Irish Americans. Police. Radio operators. Russia. Sculptors. World War I.*
MPW 25 Jun 1927. *Var* 15 Jun 1927, p. 21.

THE LOST BATTALION (Chinese Americans, Multi-ethnic)
MacManus Corp. *Dist* W. H. Productions Co.; State Rights. 8 Sep **1919** [©MacManus Corp.; 6 Sep 1919; LP14170]. Si; b&w. 6-8 reels.
Supv Edward A. MacManus. *Prod* Edward A. MacManus. *Dir* Burton King. *Asst dir* Leander De Cordova, John Coleman and Frederick F. McGuirk. *Scen* Charles A. Logue. *Cam* A. A. Cadwell, William Reinhart, Roy Vaughan, William Tuers and A. Fried.

Cast: Major-General Robert Alexander (*Himself*), Lt. Col. Charles W. Whittlesey (*Himself*), Major George McMurtry (*Himself*), Captain William J. Cullen (*Himself*), Lt. Arthur F. McKeogh (*Himself*), Lt. Augustus Kaiser (*Himself*), Private Abraham Krotoshinsky (*Himself*), Helen Ferguson (*The stenographer*), Marion Coakley (*Nancy Crystal*), Mrs. Stuart Robson (*The landlady*), Blanche Davenport (*The mother*), Lt. Jordan (*Himself*), Bessie Lern (*The girl next door*), Sydney D'Albrook (*The burglar*), Gaston Glass (*Harry Merwin*), Jack McLean (*The kicker*), William H. Tooker, Stephen Grattan, J. A. King.

World War I, **Drama**. The men in the 308th Regiment's 77th Division, have been drafted from diverse ethnic, economic, and social groups in New York. Two men are fighting Chinatown tongs, one is a burglar, another is a wealthy merchant's son in love with his father's stenographer, who dreams of becoming the greatest movie actress, another is a private in love with the merchant's ward, and finally there is "the Kicker," who finds fault with everything. After training in Yaphank and in France, the 463 men advance under the command of Lt. Col. Charles W. Whittlesey into the "Pocket" of the Argonne Forest, to help break down the supposedly impregnable German defense. Cut off from Allied troops and supplies, and surrounded by the enemy, the Division, nicknamed "The Lost Battalion," withstands six days without food or water. When the German commander asks for their surrender, Whittlesey replies, "Tell them to go to hell!" The Chinese rivals fight bravely side-by-side, while the burglar dies heroically. After their rescue, the survivors are given a parade in New York, and are reunited with their families and sweethearts. *American Expeditionary Force. Argonne Forest (France). Combat. France. The Lost Battalion. Military service, Compulsory. Officers (Military). War heroes. War victims. World War I. Burglars. Chinese Americans. Germany. Army. New York City. Parades. Tongs (Secret societies).*

Note: Pre-release showings were given on 1 Jul 1919 in Washington and on 2 Jul 1919 in New York. The film premiered in Hartford on 28 Jul 1919. The film was authorized by the United States Government and included scenes shot by the U. S. Signal Corps. Lt. Augustus Kaiser used his own pictures which he drew of men under fire in drawing the title card decorations. Actual maps documents, and the German note asking for surrender were used in the film.

ETR 19 Jul 1919, p. 571. *MPN* 20 Sep 1919, p. 2469. *MPW* 20 Sep 1919, pp. 1867-68. *NYMT* 6 Jul 1919. *NYT* 3 Jul 1919, p. 16. *NYT* 8 Sep 1919, p. 16. *Wid's* 6 Jul 1919, p. 3.

LOST BOUNDARIES (African Americans)

RD-DR Corp.; A Louis de Rochemont Production. *Dist* Film Classics, Inc. 5 Aug 1949; World premiere in New York City: 30 Jun 1949; Prod: completed late Apr 1949 [©RD-DR Corp.; 22 Jun 1949; LP2414]. Sd (RCA Sound System); b&w. 97 or 99 min. PCA cert no. 13889.

Assoc prod Borden Mace and Lothar Wolff. *Dir* Alfred L. Werker. *Asst dir* George Ackerson, Horace Hough and John Gerstad. *Scr adpt* Charles Palmer. *Scr* Virginia Shaler and Eugene Ling. *Addl dial* Maxime Furlaud and Ormonde de Kay. *Dir of photog* William J. Miller. *Art dir* Herbert Andrews. *Chief film ed* David Kummins. *Film ed* Angelo Ross. *Props* Fred Ballmeyer. *Mus dir* Jack Shaindlin. *Mus score* Louis Applebaum. *Sd* Hugh McDowell. *Makeup* Fred Ryle. *Unit mgr* Percy Ikerd. *Chief elec* Arthur Maher. *Head grip* William Nallon.

Song(s): "I Wouldn't Mind," music and lyrics by Carleton Carpenter; "Guess I'm Thru with Love," music and lyrics by Albert C. Johnston, Jr.; and other songs by Herbert E. Taylor.

Source: Based on the article "Document of a New Hampshire Family" by William L. White in *Reader's Digest* (1947).

Cast: BEATRICE PEARSON [(*Marcia Carter*)], MEL FERRER [(*Scott Carter*)], Susan Douglas [(*Shelly Carter*)], Rev. Robert A. Dunn [(*Rev. John Taylor*)], And introducing Richard Hylton [(*Howard Carter*)], Grace Coppin [(*Mrs. Mitchell*)], Seth Arnold [(*Clint Adams*)], Parker Fennelly [(*Alvin Tupper*)], William Greaves [(*Arthur Cooper*)], Leigh Whipper [(*Janitor*)], Maurice Ellis [(*Dr. Cashman*)], Edwin Cooper [(*Baggage man*)], Carleton Carpenter [(*Andy*)], Wendell Holmes [(*Morris Mitchell*)], Ralph Riggs [(*Loren Tucker*)], Rai Saunders [(*Jesse Pridham*)], Morton Stevens [(*Dr. Walter Brackett*)], Alexander Campbell [(*Mr. Bigelow*)], Royal Beal [(*Detective Staples*)], and Canada Lee [(*Lt. Thompson*)], [Peggy Kimber (*Joan*)], [Emory Richardson (*Dr. Charles Frederick Howard*)], [Patricia Quinn O'Hara (*Mrs. Taylor*)], [Margaret Barker (*Nurse Richmond*)], [Valerie Black (*Receptionist*)], [John Glendinning (*Lt. Lacey*)], [John Gerstad (*George Turner*)], [Peter Hobbs (*Eddie Clark*)], [Horace Mitchell (*Horace Durgin*)], [William G. Wendell (*Mr. Parsons*)], [Lee Nugent (*Nurse Sullivan*)], [Nancy Heyl (*Mrs. Compton*)].

Biography, **Social**, **Drama**, with songs. [*Print viewed*]. In 1922, at the Chase Medical School outside Chicago, Scott Carter graduates at the top of his class, with members of his black fraternity. That afternoon, Scott marries his girlfriend, Marcia, and they leave for his internship at a Georgia hospital. The internship was arranged by Scott's good friend, Dr. Charles Frederick Howard, a prominent black physician. When the hospital administrator sees that Scott is light-skinned, he tells him that he can only accept Southern applicants. Consequently, Scott and Marcia are forced to move in with her parents, Mr. and Mrs. Morris Mitchell, in Brookline, Massachussetts, where they live among white people, and where Marcia, who is also light-skinned, has never been identified as a black. At a dinner party at Dr. Howard's, Scott is advised by his black friends to act white in order to get employment. After Marcia gets pregnant, Scott acquiesces and accepts an internship at a white hospital. One weekend, Scott saves a New England doctor named Walter Brackett from complications from a bleeding ulcer, and the doctor befriends him. Brackett later offers Scott his father's family practice in the small town of Keenham, New Hampshire, where he had practiced for fifteen years before his death the previous fall. When Scott confesses that he is black, Brackett advises him to be practical and build a reputation first, then later reveal his ethnicity. In 1924, Scott and Marsha move into the old Brackett home, and are soon accepted fully into the community, where they raise their son Howard and daughter Shelley as whites. Scott, meanwhile, secretly practices one day a week at Dr. Howard's clinic in Boston with his friend from college, Jesse Pridham. One weekend, young Howard, a composer, brings home a black friend named Arthur "Coop" Cooper, and Shelley, embarrassed by the presence of a black man in her house, calls him a "coon" and is sternly upbraided by her father. Later, Howard goes to bootcamp, and Scott applies for a Navy commission. Coop, meanwhile, is denied a commission because he is black. Scott is made a lieutenant-commander in the Navy, but on the night of his farewell parade, which the townspeople have organized, he is visited by an agent of Navy Intelligence. After Scott is forced to confess that he is black, his commission is revoked. Scott finally tells Howard, who is on leave from bootcamp, the truth, and, devastated, Howard runs away to New York City to live among blacks in Harlem. Before he leaves, Howard breaks up with his white girl friend, and Shelley sadly breaks up with her white boyfriend. Scott, meanwhile, bravely waits three days at the Navy Yard for an assignment before he is turned down; he then goes to stay at the Howard clinic. Meanwhile, in New York, Howard intervenes in a tenement brawl to save a man and is arrested, but refuses to reveal his identity. A black policeman gently coaxes Howard's story from him, and defends his parents' actions. Coop's father is a well-known judge, and soon Howard is released into Coop's custody. Later, Howard is reconciled with his father at the Howard clinic, and they go home together. At a Sunday church service, Reverend John Taylor, a loyal friend of the Carters, preaches against ignorance and racial prejudice, encouraging the Carters to stay in Keenham. An announcement is then made that the U. S. government has declared that commissions in the Navy will be extended to all men, regardless of color or creed. Shelley exits the church alone. *African Americans. Physicians. Racial impersonation. Racism. Chicago (IL). Composers. Family relationships. Georgia. Hospitals. Massachusetts. Medical clinics. Medical colleges. New York City–Harlem. Police. Reverends. Small town life. United States–South. United States. Navy.*

Note: The film's working title was *The White Piano*. The title card on the viewed print reads: "A Drama of Real Life from the *Reader's Digest*, the Louis de Rochemont Production of *Lost Boundaries*." The film opens with a shot of the Brackett home in the fictional town of Keenham, New Hampshire, and a voice-over narration alluding to a legend that haunts the mansion. The film ends with a voice-over narration which states that the "Carters" still live in Keenham and "Scott Carter" is still the town physician. The character of Scott Carter was based on Dr. Albert C. Johnston, a black radiologist, who graduated with honors from the University of Chicago's Rush Medical School and passed as white in the 1930s. Johnston's black ancestry was disclosed when the United States Navy refused him a commission in 1940 because he admitted to being part black. Johnston continued to work in Keene, New Hampshire (which was called Keenham in the film) until the mid-1960s, when he moved to Kauai, Hawaii with his wife, Ihyra Baumann, who was of mixed parentage. He died in Honolulu on 23 Jun 1988 at the age of eighty-seven. As depicted in the film, Johnston's son, Albert, Jr., became a composer and wrote songs for this picture. The *HR* review of the film stated: "It is seldom written about, yet it is estimated that some 8,000,000 Negroes accomplish the deception [of 'passing' as whites] successfully," but that statistic has not been verified by any contemporary or

modern source.

According to one modern source, the idea for the film began when, while in his home town in New Hampshire, producer Louis de Rochemont met a light-skinned student (presumably Albert C. Johnston, Jr.), who confessed to having recently learned of his black ancestry. De Rochemont reportedly took the story to *Reader's Digest*, where it was written into a magazine article (and later a book) by William L. White. The same source states that Fredi Washington, who had starred in Universal's 1934 film about "passing," Fanny Hurst's *Imitation of Life* (see above), interviewed for a role in the film.

This film marked the screen debut of Reverend Robert A. Dunn, an Episcopal clergyman from Portsmouth, New Hampshire. As reported in a *NYT* article, de Rochemont, who had a producing contract with M-G-M, was forced to produce the film independently after M-G-M canceled the project because of economic restrictions, and because the studio was planning two other films "dealing with other Negro questions": *Intruder in the Dust* (see above) and *Stars in My Crown* (see below).

The name of the film's production company, RD-DR Corp., was an acronym for Reader's Digest—de Rochmont. De Rochemont was known for creating (along with Roy E. Larsen of Time, Inc.) the popular *March of Time* newsreel series, which won an Academy Award in 1936. In a 15 Feb 1948 memo to de Rochemont from scenarist Charles "Cap" Palmer included in the MPAA/PCA files at the AMPAS Library, Palmer states that he tried to "handle the story so that it avoids the pitfall of becoming a clinical study of the negro problem, and becomes a story of a *guy*, with the hell of a *universal* human problem." Scripts in the Charles Palmer Collection at the AMPAS Library reveal that Palmer's original ending showed "Shelley" standing alone on the green outside the church as her family attends services inside. A production note written by Palmer states that he wrote this ending to avoid "any peaches-and-cream feeling of a completely happy ending on a problem which is still unsolved generally."

On 18 Nov 1949, RD-DR Corp. and Film Classics filed a federal lawsuit against Atlanta, Georgia after city censor Christine Smith banned all screenings of *Lost Boundaries* because of its racial theme. As noted in *Var*, Smith's decision was in accordance with a city ordinance that empowered her to bar any picture which would "adversely affect the peace, health, morals and good order of the city." As reported in *Newsweek*, in Oct 1949, local censor Lloyd T. Binford banned the film in Memphis theaters, giving the reason: "In passing as white the Negro doctor in the film had slurred his own race by proving himself 'an impostor and a liar.'" Citing the First and Fourteenth Amendments, former Justice Samuel Rosenman, the prosecuting attorney in the Atlanta case, stated in Nov 1949 trade papers that he hoped the suit would show deprivation of freedom of expression without due process of law, thereby testing the constitutionality of all censorship of motion pictures prior to public showing. As reported in *DV*, during the 6 Feb 1950 opening arguments in the U.S. district court, Assistant City Attorney J. M. B. Bloodworth, arguing the censors' side, alluded to a 1916 U.S. Supreme Court decision that films, as "spectacles," do not come under the First Amendment. Rosenman responded: "Films are no longer a spectacle but a medium of information and opinion, as much or more than they are mere amusement. Our interests go beyond those of my client and of the motion picture industry. They should be of concern to all Americans interested in their freedom." The case eventually went before the Fifth Circuit Court of Appeals, where the Atlanta censor's decision was upheld. In Oct 1950, the U. S. Supreme Court refused to hear an appeal of the case.

According to *HR*, this film, which was shot in Massachusetts, Portsmouth, NH and Harlem, NY, won best scenario for 1949 at the Cannes film festival. Additionally, the film marked Richard Hylton's screen debut.

Box 2 Jul 1949. *DV* 20 Jul 1949, p. 3, 8. *DV* 9 Nov 1949. *DV* 21 Nov 1949, p. 10. *DV* 7 Feb 1950. *DV* 1 Jun 1950. *DV* 29 Sep 1950. *FD* 28 Jun 1949, p. 7. *HR* 31 Jan 1949, p. 5. *HR* 18 Apr 1949, p. 4. *HR* 15 Jun 1949, p. 12. *HR* 20 Jul 1949, p. 3. *HR* 28 Jul 1949, p. 4. *HR* 9 Sep 1949, p. 1. *HR* 21 Nov 1949. *HR* 17 Oct 1950, p. 5. *LAT* 2 Jul 1988. *MPHPD* 2 Jul 1949, p. 4665-66. *MPH* 2 Sep 1950. *Newsweek* 10 Oct 1949. *Newsweek* 2 Jan 1950. *NYT* 14 Nov 1948. *NYT* 1 Jul 1949, p. 14. *NYT* 28 Jun 1988. *Var* 19 Jun 1949, p. 14. *Var* 8 Feb 1950. *Var* 4 Oct 1950.

LOST IN THE ARCTIC *see* **THE GREAT WHITE NORTH**

LOST IN TRANSIT (Italian Americans)
Pallas Pictures. *Dist* Paramount Pictures Corp. 3 Sep 1917 [©Julia Crawford Ivers; 15 Aug 1917; LP11278]. Si; b&w. 5 reels.
 Prod J. C. Ivers. *Dir* Donald Crisp. *Scen* Gardiner Hunting. *Story* Kathlyn Williams. *Cam* Faxon M. Dean.
 Cast: George Beban (*Niccolo Darini*), Helen Jerome Eddy (*Nita Lapi*), Pietro Sosso (*Lapi*), Vera Lewis (*Mrs. Flint*), Henry Barrows (*Mr. Kendall*), Frank Bennett (*Paolo Marso*), Bob White (*Baby*).
 Drama. Mr. Kendall, a wealthy man who had sent his infant son to a home after the death of his mother at birth, decides that it is time for his son to come home. On his carriage ride to the father he has never seen, however, the boy mysteriously disappears. At the same time, a woman deposits a little boy on the cart of Italian junkman Niccolo Darini, and then disappears. Niccolo becomes strongly attached to the waif, and although his neighbors advise him to take the child to the police, he refuses. Kendall posts a reward notice in the paper for the return of his son, and when Niccolo's rival for the hand of the beautiful Nita Lapi reads the notice, he tells the police of Niccolo's ward. Niccolo is forced to give up his little charge, which breaks his heart. However, the Kendall's rightful heir is found when

a beggar, run over by a car, confesses on his death bed that the child with him is really the Kendall boy. Niccolo's beloved ward is then returned to him, along with a check from Kendall for $5,000 dollars. Niccolo's happiness is made complete when Nita agrees to marry him. *Foundlings. Heirs. Italian Americans. Junk trade. Missing persons. Beggars. Carriages and carts. Classified advertisements. Confession. Parentage. Police. Rewards. Rivalry.*
 Note: The title of the original story was "Partners."
 Motog 6 Oct 1917, p. 740. *MPW* 22 Sep 1917, p. 1858. *NYDM* 15 Sep 1917, p. 19. *Var* 14 Sep 1917, p. 34. *Wid's* 13 Sep 1917, p. 593.

LOTUS BLOSSOM (Chinese Americans)
Wah Ming Motion Picture Co. *Dist* National Exchanges. 1 Dec **1921** [©Wah Ming Motion Picture Co.; 2 Nov 1921; LU1715 ·j. Si; b&w. 7 reels.
 Dir Frank Grandon and James B. Leong. *Scen* George Yohalem and Charles Furthman. *Story* James B. Leong. *Photog* Ross Fisher.
 Cast: Lady Tsen Mei (*Moy Tai*), Tully Marshall (*Quong Foo*), Noah Beery (*Tartar Chief*), Jack Abbe (*Quong Sung*), Goro Kino (*The Emperor*), James Wang (*Prof. Lowe Team*), Chow Young (*Tsze Sin*).
 Drama. Chong, inventor of the first clock that would eliminate the use of the village's sacred bell, is sentenced to life imprisonment by the emperor. The philosopher-inventor is concealed by Quong Foo and his little daughter, Moy Tai, who gives him a lotus flower. Time passes, and Moy Tai is soon a beautiful girl loved by Quong Sung, whom her father adopted as a boy. He is sent away to complete his studies and falls under the spell of a light woman, Tzse Sin. When the sacred bell cracks, Foo is commisssioned by the emperor to cast a new one, but the metals refuse to mingle and he is threatened with death. In a Tartar attack, Quong Sung is killed; Moy Tai learns from Chong that the metals will fuse only with the addition of a human sacrifice. She sacrifices herself for her father's honor, and the new bell is cast. *Bells. China. Clocks. Human sacrifice. Inventors. Philosophers.*
 Note: According to a modern source, the working title of this film was *The Lotus Flower*. The Wah Ming Motion Picture Co. was also known as James B. Leong Productions. It was established in Los Angeles and financed by Chinese businessmen to make Chinese stories using Chinese actors. This may have been the company's only film. While *Picture Play* states that Leong directed the film, reviews list Frank Grandon.
 Picture Play Jan 1922, p. 84.

LOUISIANA (International Stageplay Pictures, Inc., 1934) *see* **DRUMS O' VOODOO**

LOUISIANA (M-G-M, 1934) *see* **LAZY RIVER**

LOUISIANA GAL *see* **OLD LOUISIANA**

LOUISIANA LOU *see* **LAZY RIVER**

THE LOUISIANA PURCHASE (1937) *see* **OLD LOUISIANA**

LOUISIANA PURCHASE (Austrian Americans)
Paramount Pictures, Inc. *Dist* Paramount Pictures, Inc. 25 Dec **1941**; Prod: 11 Jul—late Aug 1941 [©Paramount Pictures, Inc.; 24 Nov 1941; LP10946]. Sd (Western Electric); col (Technicolor). 11 reels, 8829 ft. 95 or 98 min. PCA cert no. 7578.
 [*Exec prod* B. G. DeSylva]. *Assoc prod* Harold Wilson. *Dir* Irving Cummings. [*Asst dir* Charles Coleman]. *Scr* Jerome Chodorov and Joseph Fields. [*Contr to dial* Barney Dean and Louis S. Kaye]. *Dir of photog* Ray Rennahan and Harry Hallenberger. *Technicolor color dir* Natalie Kalmus. *Assoc* Morgan Padelford. *Art supv* Hans Dreier and Robert Usher. *Ed* LeRoy Stone. *Settings* Raoul Pène duBois. [*Int dec* Stephen A. Seymour]. [*Props* Tommy Plews]. *Cost des* Raoul Pène duBois. *Mus dir* Robert Emmett Dolan. *Mus asst* Arthur Franklin. [*Dance dir* Eddie Prinz]. [*Dance supv* Sam Ledner]. *Sd rec* Earl Hayman and Walter Oberst. *Makeup artist* Wally Westmore.
 Song(s): "Louisiana Purchase," "You're Lonely and I'm Lonely," "It's a Lovely Day Tomorrow" and "You Can't Brush Me Off," music and lyrics by Irving Berlin.
 Source: Based on the musical comedy *Louisiana Purchase*, score by Irving Berlin, book and lyrics by Morrie Ryskind (New York, 28 May 1940), which was based on a story by B. G. DeSylva.
 Cast: Bob Hope (*Jim Taylor*), Vera Zorina (*Marina Von Minden*), Victor Moore (*Senator Oliver P. Loganberry*), Irene Bordoni (*Madame Bordelaise*), Dona Drake (*Beatrice*), Raymond Walburn (*Colonel Davis, Sr.*), Maxie Rosenbloom (*The Shadow*), Phyllis Ruth

(*Emmy Lou*), Frank Albertson (*Davis, Jr.*), Donald MacBride (*Captain Whitfield*), Andrew Tombes (*Dean Manning*), Robert Warwick (*Speaker of the House*), Charles LaTorre (*Gaston*), Charles Laskey (*Danseur*), Emory Parnell (*Lawyer*), Iris Meredith (*Lawyer's secretary*), Catherine Craig (*Saleslady*), [Sam McDaniel (*Sam*)], [Kay Aldridge, Katharine Booth, Alaine Brandes, Barbara Britton, Brooke Evans, Blanche Grady, Lynda Grey, Margaret Hayes, Louise LaPlanche, Barbara Slater, Eleanor Stewart, Jean Wallace (*Louisiana belles*)], [Edgar Dearing (*House detective*)], [William Wright (*Ambulance driver*)], [Floyd Shackelford (*Doorman at club*)], [Tom Patricola (*Cabby*)], [Aileen Haley (*Lady in waiting*)], [Jack Chefe, Albert Pollet, André Cheron, Albert Godderis, George Mardelli, Constant Franke (*French chefs*)], [Dave Willock (*Bellhop*)], [Jetsy Parker, Maxine Ardell (*Drum majorettes*)], [Jack Norton, Donald Kerr, Joy Barlowe, Patsy Mace (*Jesters*)], [Patricia Carey, Ruth Swanson (*Sailorettes*)], [Douglas Dean (*Fuschia man*)], [Arlyne Varden, Jean Phillips (*Ladies in green*)], [Lillian West (*Special lady*)], [Harold De Garre (*Man on stilts*)], [John Hiestand (*Radio commentator*)], [Joseph Siegel (*Man at Mardi Gras*)], [Richard Kipling (*Club member*)].

Comedy. [*Print viewed*]. Film studio lawyer Sam Horowitz reads the book for the Broadway musical comedy *Louisiana Purchase* and advises the studio that they cannot produce the show unless they make all the characters fictional. As a result, the lyrics sung by the performers on stage introduce the film noting that everything is fictional except the name of the state: Louisiana state representative Jim Taylor is framed by his four business partners, Colonel Davis, Sr., Davis, Jr., Captain Whitfield and Dean Manning, to take the rap for a graft investigation that Senator Oliver P. Loganberry, New England Republican, is launching against their Louisiana Purchasing Company. Although Jim is president of the company, he is a mere figurehead appointed by the four guilty partners and is innocent of graft. Jim unsuccessfully tries to distract the prudish and befuddled Loganberry from his investigation. He then enlists the help of Madame Bordelaise, a notorious New Orleans restaurateur, who hires Marina Von Minden, a beautiful young emigrant from Austria who boards with her, to ruin Loganberry's reputation. Marina, who is desperate to earn enough money to bring her mother to the U.S., goes along with the ploy in a private room at the restaurant. Disguised as a waiter, Jim tricks the teetotaler Loganberry into getting drunk, and then the four partners photograph him in compromising positions with Marina. When the evidence is presented to Loganberry, Marina defends him by claiming that they are engaged, as he has promised to use his influence to get her mother into the country. Jim, who has fallen in love with Marina, feels betrayed by her and convinces Madame Bordelaise to use her own vast experience to get Loganberry to drop the investigation. Her ruse only results in her marrying Loganberry, and Jim's partners desert him. To save himself, Jim, inspired by the film *Mr. Smith Goes to Washington*, creates a filibuster in the House of Representatives by reading *Gone With the Wind* and other enormous novels. When he collapses, Loganberry receives a telegram revealing that Jim is innocent and that the corrupt business partners have been arrested. The House members applaud and Jim and Marina kiss. *Frame-ups. Investigations. Louisiana. Romance. African Americans. Austrians. Ballet. Blackmail. Drunkenness. Filibusters. Gone With the Wind* (Novel). *Graft. Immigrants. Impersonation and imposture. Mardi Gras. Models. Mr. Smith Goes to Washington* (Motion picture). *Musical revues. New Orleans (LA). Partnership. Photographs. Prudes. Restaurateurs. Senators. Teetotalers. United States. Congress. House of Representatives.*

Note: Actors Vera Zorina, Irene Bordoni, Victor Moore, Charles Laskey and Lynda Grey appeared in the original stage production of the play, which had been produced by Paramount production head B. G. DeSylva. According to a *NYT* news item, Paramount purchased the rights to the hit play for $150,000. *Var* notes that except for a new finish, the film was "an almost literal translation from the stage." *HR* news items indicate the following: Ethel Merman was initially considered for a leading role in the film; New York fashion model Laurie Douglas was cast, but her appearance in the final film has not been confirmed; the airport scene was filmed on location at Lockheed Airport in Los Angeles, CA. This film marked the motion picture debut of actress Jean Wallace. *Louisiana Purchase* was nominated for Academy Awards in the following categories: Cinematography (Color); Harry Hallenberger and Ray Rennahan; and Art Direction/Interior Decoration (Color), Raoul Pène du Bois/Stephen A. Seymour.

Box 6 Dec 1941. *DV* 28 Nov 1941. *FD* 1 Dec 1941, p. 12. *HR* 29 May 1941, p. 2. *HR* 10 Jun 1941, p. 9. *HR* 23 Jun 1941, p. 7. *HR* 14 Jul 1941, p. 4. *HR* 22 Jul 1941, p. 4. *HR* 30 Jul 1941, p. 4. *HR* 28 Nov 1941, p. 4. *Life* 19 Jan 1942. *MPHPD* 29 Nov 1941, p. 385. *NYT* 26 Feb 1941. *NYT* 1 Jan 1942, p. 37. *New Yorker* 10 Jan 1942. *Var* 26 Nov 1941, p. 9.

LOUISIANA STORY (Cajuns)

Robert J. Flaherty Productions, Inc. *Dist* Lopert Films, Inc. 28 Sep **1948** [©Robert J. Flaherty Productions, Inc.; 28 Sep 1948; LP2093]. Sd (Western Electric Recording); b&w. 77 min.

Prod Robert Flaherty. *Assoc prod* Richard Leacock and Helen Van Dongen. *Dir* Robert Flaherty. *Story* Frances Flaherty and Robert Flaherty. *Photog* Richard Leacock. *Ed* Helen Van Dongen. *Ed asst* Ralph Rosenblum. *Mus* Virgil Thomson. [*Mus*] *performed by* Members of the Philadelphia Orchestra. *Cond* Eugene Ormandy. *Tech asst for mus* Henry Brant. *Sd* Benjamin Doniger. *Sd asst* Leonard Stark. *Mus rec* Bob Fine. *Re-rec* Dick Vorisek and Reeves Sound Studios.

Cast: Joseph Boudreaux (*The boy [Alexander Napoleon Ulysses LaTour]*), Lionel LeBlanc (*His father [Jean LaTour]*), Mrs. E. Bienvenu (*His mother*), Frank Hardy (*The driller [Tom]*), C. P. Guedry (*His boilerman*).

Documentary. [*Print viewed*]. As a young boy named Alexander Napoleon Ulysses LaTour plays with his pet raccoon among the bayous of Petit Anse, Louisiana, oil prospectors set up a derrick and begin drilling in the marshlands. Although the boy's father, Jean, thinks the men have little chance of locating oil, he cheerfully gives them permission to drill. The driller, Tom, and his boilerman befriend Alexander, who tells them that he always carries a bag of salt to ward off the evil spirits of the bayous. One day, Alexander's raccoon is chased by an alligator, and the boy, believing the " 'gator ate his 'coon," spits on his bait for luck and catches the alligator. He and his father then proudly show the skin to the oilmen. Soon, the wildcat rig blows, shooting up gas and salt water, and eventually has to be capped. After the men abandon the well, Alexander pours his "magic" salt and spits into it, then tells the men that the evil "things" of the marshes are preventing them from striking oil. Later the men angle their drilling, bypassing the pressure area, and strike oil. The derrick is removed, and the well is topped with the usual metal cap, called a "Christmas tree." When Tom thanks Jean for his lease, Alexander tells Tom he knew he would strike oil. With profits from the well, Jean buys presents for his wife and son. As he tries out the new rifle his father gave him, Alexander finds his raccoon in a tree. The oil workers then depart on a barge with all of their equipment, and Alexander sits with his raccoon on top of the "Christmas tree" and waves goodbye. *Cajuns. Children. Louisiana. Oil prospectors. Oil wells. Alligators. Fathers and sons. Fishing. Hunting. Raccoons. Superstition.*

Note: The film's title card reads: "*Louisiana Story* being an account of certain adventures of a cajun (Acadian) boy who lives in the marshlands of Petit Anse Bayou in Louisiana." The onscreen credits offer "deep thanks for [the] help and cooperation" of the following people: E. A. McIlhenny and family, Avery Island; Lucy Benjamin Lemann, New Orleans; W. B. Cotten, Jr., Baton Rouge; Mr. and Mrs. Larry Jordan, Weeks Island; and to the officials and crew of the Humble Derrick No. 1 on Petit Anse Bayou. According to a modern source, the native Louisiana Cajun boy, Joseph Boudreaus, was discovered by cameraman Richard Leacock and Flaherty's wife Frances. *Louisiana Story* was the first film that Flaherty, whom the *NYT* called the "father of documentary," made following a six-year absence from the screen. His previous picture, *The Land*, was released in 1942. As noted in the *Var* review, Standard Oil of New Jersey contributed $200,000 to the film's production. The review states that although the company had no rights and no identification in the film, it stood "to get across the idea that oil companies are beneficently public-spirited, their employees honest, industrious and amiable, and their operations productive and innocuous." According to a modern source, Flaherty's contract with Standard Oil insured that all of the film's profits went to him. A *NYT* article on the production notes that filming took place over a fifteen month period (beginning in May 1946, according to modern sources), and out of the 300,000 feet of exposed negative that was shot, only 8,000 were used in the final film. Robert and Frances Flaherty were nominated for an Academy Award for Best Writing (Motion Picture Story) for the film. Although the *HR* review called Virgil Thomson's musical score "static...florid and out of place," Thomson, a music critic for the *NYHT*, was awarded a Pulitzer Prize for the score. According to *HCN*, Thomson's Pulitzer was the first given for music connected to a motion picture. As noted in *HR*, in Oct 1948, Film International of America acquired worldwide distribution rights to the film. According to modern sources, the film was re-released in 1952 under the title *Cajun* and was shown as a second feature with Armand Denis' *Watussi*. *Louisiana Story* was Flaherty's last completed picture. He died in 1951.

Box 2 Oct 1948. *DV* 15 Dec 1948, p. 4. *DV* 3 May 1949. *FD* 20 Sep 1948, p. 6. *HCN* 3 May 1949. *HR* 29 Oct 1948. *HR* 15 Dec 1948, p. 3. *MPHPD* 2 Oct 1948, pp. 4333-34. *NYT* 26 Sep 1948. *NYT* 29 Sep 1948, p. 36. *Var* 22 Sep 1948, p. 8.

LOVE AMONG SKYSCRAPERS *see* **EL TANGO EN BROADWAY**

LOVE AND DEATH *see* **AMORE E MORTE**

LOVE AND PASSION *see* **LJUBAV I STRAST**

LOVE AND SACRIFICE (Yiddish language)

Jewish Talking Picture Co. *Dist* Jewish Talking Picture Co. Apr **1936**; New York opening: 7 Apr 1936; Prod: Mar 1936 at Seiden Studios of the Talking Picture, New York [©Jewish Talking Picture Co.; 6 May 1936; LU6337]. Sd; b&w. 8 reels, 7,200 or 7,239 ft. 75 or 80 min. Passed by the National Board of Review. Yiddish language with English subtitles.

Pres JOSEPH SEIDEN. *Dir* George Roland. *Asst dir* Herman Rosen. *Screen adpt* A. Armband and M. Kenig. [*Contr wrt* Joseph Seiden]. *Photog* Joseph Freeman and Irving Kleinerman. *Settings* Frank Brownlow and Jack Sobel. *Mus* Abe Schwartz. *Rec* Murray Dichter.

Source: Based on the novel *Liebe und Leidenschaft* by Isidore Zolotarefsky (Poland, 1936).

Cast: Lazar Freed (*Bernard Steinfield*), Rose Greenfield (*Ray [Steinfield]*), Esta Salzman (*Alice*), Robert Bennett (*Dave*), Anna Thomashefsky (*Molka*), Louis Kramer (*Moilich*), Anne Loeb (*Florence*), Willie Schwartz (*Edward*), Ray Schnier (*Mme. Edelstam*), Sam Kravitz (*Rosenheim*), Arthur Winters (*James*), Jacob Wexler, Leible Waldman (*The cantor*).

Yiddish, Domestic, Melodrama, with songs. [*Print viewed*]. During a birthday party in New York City for her six-year-old daughter Alice, Ray Steinfield tells her that her father Bernard is delayed on a business trip in Cleveland and won't be home until next week. On the day Bernard is to return home, Florence Ehrlich, his cousin, who desires him, visits his partner, Julius Rosenheim, who has designs on Ray, and recognizes Rosenheim's butler and chauffeur James as "Kid Shy Bloom," her former criminal cohort. James, who has escaped prison, threatens to shoot Florence, who has gone straight, if she squeals. Florence and Rosenheim scheme to cause Ray and Bernard to divorce. As part of the plan, James phones Ray and tells her to come to Rosenheim's hotel room because Rosenheim, who, James says, has suffered a heart attack, must give her important papers for Bernard. When Bernard returns and learns from Florence that Ray went to see Rosenheim, he gets angry and takes off after her. In his hotel, Rosenheim tries to embrace Ray and locks the door. She grabs a gun, which James has left, and when Bernard knocks, Rosenheim tells her that if she doesn't hide in the other room, Bernard could divorce her and take the children. Bernard sees Ray's coat and hat, and Rosenheim says that she is sleeping in his bedroom and that he loves her. Ray then comes out with the gun and orders Rosenheim to tell the truth. When he continues to lie, she shoots him. Ray is found guilty of murder in the second degree and is sentenced to twenty years in the state prison. She implores Bernard to tell their children, Alice and David, that she is dead. Twelve years later, Bernard, now married to Florence, has changed his name to Stone. Alice is engaged to Edward Edelstein, whose mother, a social worker, takes them to prison to speak with the warden about a woman inmate for whom she has developed a concern. The woman turns out to be Ray, although Alice has no knowledge that she is her mother. Mrs. Edelstein wants to appeal to the governor for Ray's freedom, but Ray does not care to be free. When Alice asks Ray if she isn't anxious to see her children, Ray says that she would give her life for a glimpse of them, but that she mustn't be freed. Haunted by her encounter with Ray, Alice convinces Edward that they must do something for her. Meanwhile, James, who went back to prison after Florence squealed on him, confesses to the warden about the plan to separate Alice and Bernard. The warden arranges a meeting between Ray and James, who begs forgiveness. When she learns that Florence is now Bernard's wife and that her name is now Stone, she surmises that Alice is her daughter. At Alice and Edward's wedding, Alice waits nervously for Mrs. Edelstein to bring Ray's sister, a rich woman from South Africa, whom they have never seen. Ray, who impersonates this "aunt," does not reveal her identity, saying that she looks just like her sister. She holds Dave and Alice and, after explaining that she lost her own two children through a misfortune, asks if they will allow her to take their mother's place at the wedding. After the ceremony, Florence, fearing the "aunt" will open old wounds, tells Alice that her mother is alive in prison for killing the man she loved. Alice doesn't believe her, but tells Edward, so that he will have the choice to divorce her if he wants. Edward, however, is indignant to Florence. Ray brings in detectives, and they

arrest Florence, who the Chicago police have sought for eighteen years. Ray then takes off her wig and reveals to Alice and Dave that she is their mother. Ray tells Bernard that she feels the situation was not his fault, and Bernard vows to start life anew with her. *Convicts. Family relationships. Jews. Long-lost relatives. Marriage. Ruses. Butlers. Chauffeurs. Confession. Cousins. Detectives. Fugitives. Impersonation and imposture. Murder. New York City. Partnership. Prison wardens. Prisons. Seduction. Shootings. Social workers. Weddings.*

Note: *Var* reviewed this film under the title *Liebe und Leidenschaft*. In an article in the *Brooklyn Daily Eagle*, producer Joseph Seiden states that three weeks before Passover, the best season of the year for his company to release a film, he still did not have an idea for a film until he found a Polish booklet entitled *Love and Passion* in a small bookstore. According to Seiden, he wrote the scenario in two days, cast the film, and also cut it. No editor was credited in the screen credits, and A. Armband and M. Kenig were credited with the screen adaptation, rather than Seiden. The article also states that the film took two weeks to make, cost $3,000, and that it was shot at the Seiden Studios of the Talking Picture in Manhattan. The *Var* review states that the film was shot in three days. Although the film includes songs, no information concerning their identity has been located.

Brooklyn Daily Eagle 7 Apr 1936. *FD* 10 Apr 1936, p. 12. *Var* 15 Apr 1936, p. 23.

LOVE AND THE LAW (German Americans)

Edgar Lewis Productions. *Dist* William L. Sherry Service through Film Clearing House Exchanges. 2 Mar **1919** [©Edgar Lewis; 6 Mar 1919; LP13478]. Si; b&w. 6 reels.

Pres Edgar Lewis. *Dir* Edgar Lewis.

Source: Based on the short story "The Troop Train" by William Hamilton Osborne in *The Saturday Evening Post* (11 May 1918).

Cast: Glen White (*Karl "Curly" Casterline*), Josephine Hill (*Mina*), Arnold Storrer (*Kleinfeldt*), Paul Ker (*Baudenistel*), W. T. Clark (*Herman Lindig*), Tom Williams (*McIlvaine*), Arthur Bauer (*Adolf Bauerle*), Louis Stern (*Mr. Kurz*), Curt Karpe.

Espionage, World War I, Drama. Karl "Curly" Casterline, a New York cop discharged after a "public-minded" citizen sees him playfully shooting craps for pennies, becomes a hired hand on a northern Midwest farm to help the war effort. While he is attracted to Mina, the niece of his boss, Adolf Bauerle, Curly suspects that Bauerle and a cohort Kurz plan to blow up a troop train. Curly hides and kills Kurz and Bauerle when they each try to throw the switch, creating a delay that allows the train to pass unharmed. After Curly is jailed and roughed up by Sheriff Lindig, Mina praises Curly for preventing her uncle from murdering thousands of soldiers. When a German jury sentences Curly to death, and the Governor refuses to pardon him, the case becomes celebrated nationwide. After the armistice, the Governor explains that he refused the pardon to enlighten the public to the danger of German propaganda. After he pardons Curly and enlists him as an officer to protect the State from its enemies, Curly, who married Mina in jail, escorts Lindig and his cohorts to Leavenworth. *German Americans. Police. Treason. United States–Midwest. Dismissal (Employment). Farms. Governors. Pardons. Sabotage. Sheriffs. Trials. Troop transports. Uncles. World War I.*

Note: This film may have had a pre-release title of *The Troop Train*. The film contains footage of New Yorkers crowding the streets to celebrate the end of the war.

ETR 15 Feb 1919, p. 830, 847. *MPN* 1 Feb 1919, p. 739. *MPN* 7 Jun 1919, p. 3748.

THE LOVE GIRL (East Indian Americans)

Bluebird Photoplays, Inc. *Dist* Bluebird Photoplays, Inc. 10 Jul **1916** [©Bluebird Photoplays, Inc.; 16 Jun 1916; LP8523]. Si; b&w. 5 reels.

Dir Robert Z. Leonard. *Scen* Robert Z. Leonard.

Cast: Ella Hall (*Ambrosia*), Adele Farrington (*Her aunt*), Betty Schade (*Her cousin*), Harry Depp (*The boy next door*), Grace Marvin (*The maid*), Wadsworth Harris (*Swami*).

Drama. After her mother dies, Ambrosia goes to live with her austere, unloving aunt, whose only eccentricity is her devotion to an Indian swami. As a result, she naturally enlists the swami's aid when her daughter decides to marry a man who has no money. The swami hypnotizes the daughter and orders her to break the engagement; and then, seeing a chance to collect a fortune, he kidnaps her. Ambrosia, however, with the help of the boy next door, discovers where the daughter is being held captive, after which she turns the swami over to the police. Aware of how Ambrosia has helped her, the aunt becomes loving and, after accepting her niece into the family, finally consents to her daughter's marriage. *Aunts. East Indians. Hypnotism. Hypnotists. Kidnapping. Neighbors.*

Note: The original title of the film was *Ambrosia*.
MPN 8 Jul 1916, p. 103. *MPW* 8 Jul 1916, p. 265, 308. *Var* 30 Jun 1916, p. 19.

LOVE IN THE MOUNTAINS *see* **AMOR IN MONTAGNA**

LOVE, LIVE AND LAUGH (Italian Americans)
Fox Film Corp. *Dist* Fox Film Corp. 3 Nov **1929** [©Fox Film Corp.; 28 Oct 1929; LP795]. Sd (Movietone); b&w. 10 reels, 8,090 ft.
Pres William Fox. *Dir* William K. Howard. *Staged by* Henry Kolker. *Asst dir* Phil Ford. *Scen* Dana Burnet. *Dial* Edwin Burke and George Jessel. *Cam* Lucien Andriot. *Asst cam* Walter Scott. *Film ed* Al De Gaetano. *Settings* William S. Darling. *Cost* Sophie Wachner. *Sd* Al Protzman.
Song(s): "(A Song of) Margharita," "Two Little Baby Arms" and "If You Believe in Me," music by Abel Baer, lyrics by L. Wolfe Gilbert.
Source: Based on the play *The Hurdy-Gurdy Man* by Leroy Clemens and John B. Hymer (ca 1922).
Cast: George Jessel (*Luigi*), Lila Lee (*Margharita*), David Rollins (*Pasquale Gallupi*), Henry Kolker (*Enrico*), John Loder (*Dr. Price*), John Reinhardt (*Mario*), Dick Winslow Johnson (*Mike*), Henry Armetta (*Tony*), Marcia Manon (*Sylvia*), Jerry Mandy (*Barber*).
Drama. Luigi, an Italian immigrant, settles down in Little Italy in New York City and falls in love with Margharita, whose uncle gives him a job in his music store. Luigi is recalled to Italy by his father's illness, and, becoming embroiled in the early stages of the war, goes to the Austro-Italian front. During the war, he is blinded and spends three years in a prison camp; returning to the United States, he finds that Margharita, thinking Luigi killed, has married her employer, Dr. Price. An operation by the doctor cures Luigi's blindness, and the girl plans to tell her husband of her love for Luigi. Luigi, however, realizing that the revelation would destroy her happiness, goes to live with his friend Pasquale. Blindness. Courtship. Eye surgery. Hurdy-gurdies. Immigrants. Italian Americans. Italy. Army. New York City–Little Italy. Prisoners of war. World War I.
FD 10 Nov 1929. *NYT* 2 Nov 1929, p. 14. *Var* 6 Nov 1929, p. 19.

THE LOVE MART (African Americans)
First National Pictures, Inc. *Dist* First National Pictures, Inc. 18 Dec **1927** [©First National Pictures, Inc.; 12 Dec 1927; LP24753]. Si; b&w. 8 reels, 7,388 ft.
Pres Richard A. Rowland. *Dir* George Fitzmaurice. *Adpt* Benjamin Glazer. *Titles* Edwin Justus Mayer. *Cam* Lee Garmes. *Film ed* Stuart Heisler. *Cost* Max Ree.
Source: Based on the novel *The Code of Victor Jallot* by Edward Childs Carpenter (Philadelphia, 1907).
Cast: Billie Dove (*Antoinette Frobelle*), Gilbert Roland (*Victor Jallot*), Raymond Turner (*Poupet*), Noah Beery (*Captain Remy*), Armand Kaliz (*Jean Delicado*), Emil Chautard (*Louis Frobelle*), Boris Karloff (*Fleming*), Mattie Peters (*Caresse*).
Melodrama. Antoinette Frobelle, reigning belle of the South, is accused of having Negro ancestry and is sold as a slave to Victor Jallot, a young adventurer. He frees her, makes Captain Remy confess to his responsibility for the lie about her parentage, and then weds the girl. In 1808, after Congress passes a law against the importation of slaves into the U.S., slave-running or smuggling, becomes a frequent practice especially along the Louisiana coast. Victor Jallot, a penniless Creole aristocrat, and his black servant Poupet arrive at an old inn near New Orleans, which serves as a rendezvous point for smugglers. In a card game, Victor acquires the deed to an establishment which he is led to believe is a fencing academy. That night, Victor meets Antoinette Frobelle, the daughter of a New Orleans ship merchant, and carries her across a muddy street, to the displeasure of her companion, Creole dandy Jean Delicado. Victor soon discovers that the "academy" is really an abandoned barber shop, where fencing is also taught. Nevertheless, Victor and Poupet go into business as a fencing teacher and assistant. At a café, after Antoinette invites Victor to join her at her table, Delicado contends he is only a barber and she insults Victor. Although she later tries to apologize, he spurns her. When Antoinette's father Louis cannot repay money he has used that belongs to slave runner Captain Remy, the captain confronts him with a charge that Antoinette is really an octoroon, and not his daughter. Louis is unable to refute Remy's information, and Antoinette is summarily placed on the auction block with slaves. Victor, having pawned his jewels, buys her, then gives her the assignment and sets her free. Although she goes off with Louis, she later returns to Victor,

saying she cannot accept her freedom. Victor tells her he believes that she is fully white and confesses he loves her. They are interrupted as Remy and Delicado enter the barber shop intoxicated. As Victor begins to shave Remy, he threatens to slit his throat with his razor unless he tells the truth about Antoinette, and Remy confesses that she is white and of aristocratic birth. The Creoles then beat Remy for his effrontery, and Antoinette hugs Victor, telling him she'll be his slave forever. African Americans. Parentage. Slavery–Emancipation. United States–South.
FD 1 Jan 1928. *MPW* 25 Jun 1927. *NYT* 26 Dec 1927, p. 16. *Var* 28 Dec 1927, p. 18.

LOVE O' MIKE *see* **THE TROUBLE BUSTER**

LOVE ON APPROVAL *see* **OUTSIDE OF PARADISE**

LOVE REDEEMED *see* **A FALLEN IDOL**

A LOVE SUBLIME (French Americans, Greek Americans)
Fine Arts Film Co. *Dist* Triangle Distributing Corp. 11 Mar **1917**. Si; b&w. 5 reels.
Dir Wilfred Lucas and Tod Browning. *Scen* Wilfred Lucas and Tod Browning.
Source: Based on the short story "Orpheus" by Samuel Hopkins Adams in *Collier's Weekly* (11 Nov 1916).
Cast: Wilfred Lucas (*Philip*), Carmel Myers (*Toinette*), Fred A. Turner (*The professor*), Alice Rae (*The sculptress*), George Beranger (*Her husband*), Jack Brammall (*Piney the Rat*), James O'Shea (*The policeman*), Bert Woodruff (*The Little Red Doctor*), Mildred Harris (*Eurydice*).
Drama. Philip, a powerfully built Greek, falls in love with Toinette, a French girl whom he meets when she is injured in an auto accident. Later, as a result of the accident, she is hospitalized and operated upon and then recovers. A hospital attendant misinforms Philip that Toinette has died, however; and the Greek, keeping a pledge to his love, continues to sing beneath her hospital room window every night at midnight. Meanwhile, a gang has been terrorizing a park near the hospital, and one night during a confrontation with the police, the leader is knifed and taken to the same doctor who has arranged for Toinette to enter the hospital. While at the hospital, the leader recognizes Philip as the person who slipped him a pack of cigarettes when he was hospitalized earlier, during Toinette's stay. The gangster informs Philip that his love is alive and well. The Greek rushes to Toinette, who had been told that Philip had returned to Greece, and the lovers are reunited. French Americans. Gangsters. Greek Americans. Hospitals. Automobile accidents. Fights. Knife wounds. Operations, Surgical. Orderlies (Hospital). Parks. Physicians. Police.
Note: The film's working title was *Orpheus*. Some contemporary sources cite Browning as the film's sole director, while others give Browning and Lucas joint directing credit. Alice Rae, also known as Alice Wilson, married Browning in the summer of 1917. Trade articles from early in the production credit Elmer Clifton and Alexander McClure as cast members, but it is unclear whether they appear in the finished film. One scene was shot at a confectionary store in Los Angeles.
ETR 17 Mar 1917, p. 1042. *Motog* 17 Mar 1917, p. 587. *MPN* 31 Mar 1917, p. 2030. *MPW* 3 Feb 1917, p. 6930. *MPW* 24 Feb 1917, p. 1195. *MPW* 17 Mar 1917, p. 1760, 1828. *NYDM* 10 Mar 1917, p. 29. *Tri* 3 Mar 1917, p. 3. *Var* 9 Mar 1917, p. 22. *Wid's* 22 Mar 1917, pp. 184-85.

LOVE THINE ENEMY *see* **THE GRIP OF JEALOUSY**

LOVER COME BACK *see* **NEW MOON**

LOVE'S LAW (Polish Americans)
Gail Kane Productions. *Dist* Mutual Film Corp. 1 Sep **1918** [©Mutual Film Corp.; 15 Sep 1918; LP13145]. Si; b&w. 5 reels.
Dir Francis J. Grandon. *Scen* J. Clarkson Miller. *Story* Joseph Franklin Poland. *Cam* Jake Badaracco.
Cast: Gail Kane (*Sonia Marinoff*), Courtenay Foote (*Andrew Hamilton*), Reed Hamilton (*John Lorimer*), Frederick Jones (*Alexis Khalkoff*), Augusta Perry (*Olga Jandoroff*), Walter Deming (*Ivan Jandoroff*), Mathilde Baring (*Mrs. Grey*), Emile La Croix (*Kalma*), Frank Lenox.
Drama. Sonia Marinoff, a young Polish American whose deceased parents were famous musicians, exasperates her poverty-stricken guardian, Ivan Jandoroff, with her dreams of becoming a great violinist. When his employer, Andrew Hamilton, threatens to lower the wages at his steel mill, Ivan orders Sonia to work in the mill and then pawns her violin. The outraged Sonia soon learns that Andrew

has purchased the instrument and visits the millionaire's home to demand its return. Upon hearing her play, Andrew offers to finance Sonia's musical education, but following her successful debut, he suggests that she offer herself to him to cancel the debt. Sonia tearfully smashes the violin and then returns to the factory, where she nurses the sick laborers through an epidemic and prevents a strike that would have ruined Andrew. Realizing his injustices to his workers and the woman he loves, Andrew promises to improve conditions at the mill and later proposes to Sonia. *Art patronage. Employer-employee relations. Factory workers. Millionaires. Polish Americans. Steel magnates. Steel mills. Violinists. Violins. Epidemics. Musicians. Poverty. Strikes and lockouts. Wards and guardians.*

Note: The character names vary among the reviewers as do several points concerning the plot. Several reviewers include Walter Downing, rather than Walter Deming, in the cast. This was the first film made by Gail Kane Productions. According to information in the copyright descriptions, *Love's Law* was to be the working title. Suggested titles given were "The Great Test" and "The Greater Test."

ETR 21 Sep 1918, p. 1333. *MPN* 7 Sep 1918, p. 1597. *MPW* 6 Jul 1918, p. 76. *MPW* 7 Sep 1918, p. 1465. *Var* 6 Sep 1918, p. 37. *Wid's* 8 Sep 1918, pp. 19-20.

LOVE'S PLAYTHING (French Americans)

Radin Pictures, Inc. *Dist* State Rights. 15 Jan **1921**. Si; b&w. 6 reels. *Dir* Walter V. Coyle. *Ed* Maurice Pivar.

Cast: William Cavanaugh (*Julian La Rue*), Claire Collinge (*Josephine Rambeau*), Glenn White.

Melodrama. During the Mardi Gras in New Orleans, Julian La Rue rescues Josephine Rambeau from a ruffian. After they fall in love, they discover that each possesses half of a wedding ring passed down through three generations of their families. Julian's foster grandfather was in love with Josephine's grandmother in the early nineteenth century, but the latter was forced to marry a nobleman who arranged to have the former kidnapped and set adrift at sea. Stranded on a desert island, Julian's foster grandfather discovered a chest of gold and made his way back to New Orleans with the help of a courageous cabin boy, whom the older man later adopted. The older man died of a broken heart after discovering his sweetheart's marriage, and the younger man, Julian's father, eventually fell in love with Josephine's mother. This romance also was doomed by circumstance, and Julian's father moved away and married the daughter of a well-to-do Southerner. Julian and Josephine, more fortunate than their ancestors, marry. *French Americans. Grandfathers. Grandmothers. Heredity. Mardi Gras. New Orleans (LA). Southerners. Adoption. Cabin boys. Castaways. Jewelry. Marriage–Forced. Nobility. Treasure.*

Note: The director's name is spelled Walter V. Cole in several contemporary sources. According to an ad in *ETR* 1 Jan 1921, this film, which was then playing for one week at the Newark Theatre, was to be released to Greater New York and Northern New Jersey on 15 Jan 1921. One review lists the female lead as Cora Collins.

ETR 18 Dec 1920, p. 227. *ETR* 1 Jan 1921, p. 450. *MPW* 21 May 1921, p. 326.

LOVE'S TRAGEDY *see* **SENZA MAMMA E'NNAMURATO**

LOYAL HEARTS *see* **INJUSTICE**

LUAN FENG HEH MING (Chinese language)

Grandview Film Co. **1947?**; Hong Kong showing: 1947? Sd; b&w. Length undetermined. Chinese language.

Dir Jiang Wai-kwong. [*Not viewed*]. [No information concerning the plot of this film has been located.].

Note: The Cantonese transliterated title is *Luin Fung Heb Ming*. This film was probably made in the U.S.

LAS LUCES DE BUENOS AIRES (Spanish language)

Films Paramount; controlled by Paramount Publix Corp. *Dist* Paramount Publix Corp. **1931**; Buenos Aires opening: 23 Sep 1931; Los Angeles opening: 30 Oct 1931; Prod: May—Jun 1931 at the Paramount studios in Joinville, France. Sd (Western Electric); b&w. 9 reels, 7,643 ft. 85 min. *Country of origin* France. Spanish language.

Dirección de [*Dir*] Adelqui Millar. [*Asst dir* Manuel Romero]. *Basada en la obra original de* [*Based on the original work by*] Manuel Romero and Luis Bayón Herrera. *Fotografía de* [*Photog*] Ted Pahle. *Música típica de* [*Traditional music by*] Matos Rodríguez. *Mus dir* Julio de Caro.

Song(s): "Tomo y obligo," music by Carlos Gardel, lyrics by Manuel Romero; "El rosal," "La provinciana" and "Canto por no llorar," by Matos Rodríguez.

Cast: Carlos Gardel [(*Anselmo*)], Sofía Bozán [(*Elvira del Solar*)], Gloria Guzmán [(*Rosita*)], Pedro Quartucci [(*Pablo Soler*)], Carlos Baena [(*Empresario*)], Kuindós [(*Alberto Villamil*)], Marita Angeles [(*Lily*)], Vicente Padula [(*Ciriaco*)], Jorge Infante [(*Romualdo*)], José Agüeras [(*Secretario*)], y las 16 bellezas criollas [and 16 Argentinian beauties], [María Estheer Gamas], [Elena Bozán].

Melodrama, with songs. [*Print viewed*]. Near a ranch in the Argentine pampas, the car belonging to an important theatrical impresario gets stuck. Elvira, the girl friend of the ranch's owner, sings for the ranch hands, ignoring the criticism of her sister Rosita, who thinks she should save her voice for more important occasions. After revealing her talent to the impresario, Elvira moves to Buenos Aires in search of fame and fortune. Rosita also seeks a career as a dancer, although she is not very good. She does, however, win the love of the theater's star. Anselmo, Elvira's spurned boyfriend, learns of her fame in the newspapers and leaves for Buenos Aires to look for her. There, Elvira regards him as a bumpkin and Anselmo returns to his ranch. However, two of his ranch hands go to the theater, lasso Elvira off the stage and deliver her back to Anselmo at the ranch, where she decides to remain. *Argentina. City-country contrast. Fame. Ranchers. Singers. Sisters. Buenos Aires (Argentina). Dancers. Impresarios. Pampas (Argentina).*

Note: Some scenes were shot at Evreux in France. Some sources stated that Antoñita Colomé appeared in the film, but her participation has not been confirmed. *Var* noted that the "cast consists of Argentine artists."

CM Jan 1932, p. 6. *Var* 10 Nov 1931, p. 23.

LUCIA *see* **THE TELL-TALE STEP**

THE LUCK OF THE IRISH (Irish Americans)

Mayflower Photoplay Corp.; Allan Dwan Productions. *Dist* Realart Pictures Corp. Feb **1920** [©Mayflower Photoplay Corp.; 31 Dec 1919; LP14704]. Si; b&w. 7 reels.

Prod Allan Dwan. *Dir* Allan Dwan. *Cam* H. Lyman Broening and Glen MacWilliams. *Art dir* Charles H. Kyson. *Art titles* Nell Walker.

Source: Based on the novel *The Luck of the Irish* by Harold MacGrath (New York, 1917).

Cast: James Kirkwood (*William Grogan*), Anna Q. Nilsson (*Ruth Warren*), Harry Northrup (*Richard Camden*), Ward Crane (*Norton Colburton*), Ernest Butterworth (*The Kid*), Gertrude Messenger (*The Kid's romance*), Madame Deione (*The Malay Street woman*), Louise Lester (*The landlady*).

Drama. One day in New York City, Irish-American plumber William Grogan, who meets the outside world only through the little basement window of his plumbing shop, sees and falls in love with a pretty pair of feet. The owner is Ruth Warren, a schoolteacher who is lusted after by Norton Colburton, a dissolute playboy. Ruth is about to marry Colburton, but at the last minute runs away and decides to take a Cook's tour. On the boat, she meets Grogan, who has inherited a fortune, and recognizing the feet, he falls in love with their owner. Meanwhile, Colburton sends a henchman to locate Ruth. In various foreign cities, Grogan is attacked and Ruth is accosted by Colburton, who has followed her. Finally, Ruth is imprisoned in a house of prostitution, Grogan comes to her rescue, and the two are married. *Irish Americans. Kidnapping. Lechery. Plumbers. Schoolteachers. Tourists. Americans in foreign countries. Boats. Brothels. Criminals. Inheritance. Playboys. Rescues.*

Note: This film had a pre-release showing in Los Angeles on 31 Jan 1920. It was given pre-release showings in New York during the week of 8 Feb 1920. According to *MPN*, special efforts were made by the distributor Realart to have exhibitors run the film on St. Patrick's Day. The demand was heavy for bookings in Boston that day, due to the large Irish population there. *ETR* advised exhibitors to "Circularize your Irish societies. Solicit the aid of the Knights of Columbus. The title will be strong enough to interest them. Inform them that your offering shows some of the dominant personalities of the Irish race."

ETR 31 Jan 1920, p. 899. *MPN* 17 Jan 1920, p. 840. *MPN* 24 Jan 1920, p. 1125. *MPN* 7 Feb 1920, p. 1537. *MPN* 27 Mar 1920, p. 2953. *MPN* 17 Apr 1920, p. 3408. *MPW* 31 Jan 1920, p. 774. *MPW* 14 Feb 1920, p. 1032. *NYMT* 25 Jan 1920. *Var* 31 Jan 1920, p. 56. *Wid's* 25 Jan 1920, p. 29.

THE LUCK OF THE IRISH (Irish Americans)

Twentieth Century-Fox Film Corp. *Dist* Twentieth Century-Fox Film Corp. Sep **1948**; Los Angeles opening: 3 Sep 1948; Prod: late Jan—late Mar 1948 [©Twentieth Century-Fox Film Corp.; 1 Sep 1948; LP2113]. Sd (Western Electric Recording); b&w. 11 reels, 8,931 ft. 99 min. PCA cert no. 12958.

[*Exec prod* Darryl F. Zanuck]. *Prod* Fred Kohlmar. *Dir* Henry Koster. [*Asst dir* Joseph Behm]. *Scr* Philip Dunne. [*Addl dial* J. M.

Kerrigan]. *Dir of photog* Joseph LaShelle. [*Cam op* Don Anderson]. [*Stills* Jerry Milligan]. *Spec photog eff* Fred Sersen. *Art dir* Lyle Wheeler and J. Russell Spencer. *Film ed* J. Watson Webb, Jr. *Set dec* Thomas Little and Paul S. Fox. *Ward dir* Charles LeMaire. *Cost des* Bonnie Cashin. *Mus* Cyril Mockridge. *Mus dir* Lionel Newman. *Orch arr* Herbert Spencer and Maurice de Packh. *Sd* George Leverett and Roger Heman. *Makeup artist* Ben Nye and [Harry Maret]. [*Hair stylist* Lillian Hokom]. [*Prod mgr* Max Golden]. [*Scr supv* Doris Drought]. [*Dial coach* J. M. Kerrigan]. [*Grip* Harry Jones].

Song(s): "The Rose of Tralee," music by Charles W. Glover, lyrics by C. Mordaunt Spencer.

Source: Based on the novel *There Was a Little Man* by Guy and Constance Jones (New York, 1948).

Cast: TYRONE POWER [(*Stephen "Fitz" Fitzgerald*)], ANNE BAXTER [(*Nora*)], Cecil Kellaway [(*Horace*)], Lee J. Cobb [(*D. C. Augur*)], James Todd [(*Bill Clark*)], Jayne Meadows [(*Frances Augur*)], J. M. Kerrigan [(*Taedy*)], Phil Brown [(*Higginbotham*)], Charles Irwin [(*Cornelius*)], [Louise Lorimer (*Augur's secretary*)], [Tim Ryan (*Clancy the cop*)], [Harry Antrim (*Senator Ransom*)], [Margaret Wells (*Mrs. Augur*)], [John Goldsworthy (*Butler*)], [Dorothy Neumann (*Employment agency manager*)], [Ruth Clifford, Marion Marshall (*Secretaries*)], [Douglas Gerrard (*Manager*)], [Tito Vuolo (*Vendor*)], [Tom Stevenson (*Gentleman's gentleman*)], [Norman Leavitt (*Milkman*)], [Frank Mitchell (*Irish dancer*)], [Bill Swingley (*Terrance Flaherty*)], [Hollis Jewell (*Cab driver*)], [Ann Frederick (*Hat check girl*)], [Eddie Parks (*Pickpocket*)], [John Roy (*Subway guard*)], [Claribel Bressel (*Bride*)], [Lee MacGregor (*Groom*)], [Jimmy O'Brien (*Singer*)], [George Melford (*Doorman*)], [Robert Karnes, Robert Adler, John Davidson, Wilson Wood, Don Brodie, Gene Garrick (*Reporters*)], [Albert Morin].

Comedy, Fantasy. [*Print viewed*]. On their way by car to Shannon Airport in Ireland, freelance American newspaperman Stephen "Fitz" Fitzgerald and his European editor Bill Clark, get lost in the countryside. When their car sinks after breaking through the floor of an old wooden bridge, Fitz leaves to seek help. Beside a waterfall, in the middle of a wood, Fitz encounters Horace, an old shoemaker sporting a green coat with brass buttons. Horace gives him directions to the village of Ballynabun, where Fitz and Bill take rooms at the Kittiwake Inn. As the village is sealocked, they must wait for a trawler to transport them to their destination. Fitz mentions having been at the waterfall to Taedy, the innkeeper, who is amazed to hear about the old shoemaker and tells him that there is no waterfall and that the man he met was a leprechaun. Later that night, Fitz sees Horace come for a bottle of whisky Taedy has left out for him and follows him. When Fitz catches Horace and asks to see his fabled "pot o' gold," Horace reluctantly digs it up for him. Fitz discovers that the coins are genuine and gives them back to Horace, who, out of gratitude, presents him with one of the coins as and then disappears behind the waterfall. The next morning, Fitz wakes up and wonders if he dreamed about the meeting with Horace. Nora, who works at the inn, also tells Fitz that there is no waterfall, so he takes her to the spot, but finds only woods. After they spot the trawler approaching, Fitz tosses Horaces's coin for luck, and Nora identifies it as a sixteenth century Spanish doubloon, which she claims are quite common in the area. Later Nora and Bill say goodbye to Fitz, who is headed for a new job in New York. There Fitz reports to D. C. Augur, the head of New Era Publications, who intends to run for the U.S. Senate and assigns him to write his speeches. Fitz then rekindles his romance with Augur's daughter, Frances. Soon after, Horace shows up at Fitz's apartment, which Augur has leased for him, in the guise of a man servant, and claims to have been sent by an employment agency engaged by Augur. Horace denies that he and Fitz have met before even after Fitz shows him the doubloon. When Horace is driving Fitz to an appointment, the car mysteriously breaks down and Fitz is forced to take the subway, where he loses his wallet to a pickpocket and encounters Nora. She thinks he is broke and invites him to lunch at an Irish tavern. There she explains that a relative of Taedy's has died in New York and she is there to straighten out the estate for him. Later, Augur asks Fitz to recant an earlier article he has written, which he feels is not in accord with his political stance, but Fitz, who is becoming disenchanted with Augur, refuses to compromise. Augur orders him to do it, however, and as Fitz begins to write, Horace explains the master/servant relationship to him. Feeling exploited, Fitz tells Frances he is going to quit, but she advises him that if her

father's campaign is successful, he will need someone to run the publishing business, and Fitz finds the prospect appealing. Having received a cable from Nora that Fitz needs a job, Bill offers him an assignment in Italy and is disappointed to learn that Fitz is still working for Augur. Fitz goes to explain his situation to Nora at the tavern where a traditional Irish wedding is taking place. After he discovers that she is returning to Ireland the next day, he gets involved in a brawl with her escort, Terrance Flaherty, who knocks him out. When he comes to, he finds Nora caring for him and they embrace, but he later confesses that he is supposed to marry Frances in a month's time. Fitz then returns to his apartment to find Horace making shoes and asks him to explain how the doubloon in his pocket has turned into a pebble. Horace finally confesses that he is indeed a leprechaun and that he joined Fitz in New York out of gratitude for his not having taken the pot o' gold. During a major speech at the Journalists' Club, Augur announces that, if he is elected, he will resign from running his publishing company and appoint Fitz as his successor. As Fitz prepares to respond, he sees the room fill with "Horaces," and then declines the offer, saying Augur needs someone who agrees with him. When asked about his future plans, Fitz replies that he is going to sit under a waterfall with an old friend. Later, back in Ireland, Fitz, who has married Nora and lives at the inn, where Horace can keep an eye on them, argues with Bill over his latest article. *Ireland. Irish Americans. Journalistic ethics. Leprechauns. Reporters. Americans in foreign countries. Coins. Editors. Engagements. Fistfights. Forests. Impersonation and imposture. Inns. New York City. Pickpockets. Political campaigns. Publishers and publishing. Romance. Servants. Speeches. Subways. Treasure. Weddings.*

Note: This film had several working titles including *That Old Magic*, *The Shamrock Touch* and began shooting as *For Fear of Little Men*, changing to *Leave It to the Irish* towards the end of production. According to information in the Twentieth Century-Fox Records of the Legal Department and the Twentieth Century-Fox Produced Scripts Collection at the UCLA Arts—Special Collections Library, the studio purchased Guy and Constance Jones's unpublished novel *For Fear of Little Men* in Jul 1947 for $50,000. The novel was published in Mar of the following year under the title *There Was a Little Man*. Peggy Cummins was an early contender for the role of "Nora," and Barry Fitzgerald and Scottish actor Will Fyffe were considered for the role of "Horace." Dublin-born actor J. M. Kerrigan, who contributed dialogue revisions for the film, also functioned as dialogue coach. The *CBCS* lists J. Farrell MacDonald as appearing in a bit part as a Captain but his role was cut before the film's release. In addition to "The Rose of Tralee," the film's score included excerpts from a number of Irish traditional airs including "Norah O'Neale," "The Leprechaun," "The Foggy Dew," "Garryowen," and "Irish Washer Woman". For the film's initial release, the Irish sequences were printed on green-toned stock. Cecil Kellaway was nominated for an Oscar in the Best Supporting Actor category. In an oral history for the Screen Directors' Guild, Henry Koster described an atmospheric sequence he designed and shot in which he introduced "Horace," but this was cut by studio head Darryl Zanuck, who felt that it slowed down the beginning of the film. A *Lux Radio Theatre* version of the screenplay was broadcast on 27 Dec 1948 and starred Anne Baxter and Dana Andrews.

Box 4 Sep 1948. *DV* 1 Sep 1948, p. 3, 11. *FD* 1 Sep 1948, p. 7. *HR* 1 Sep 1948, p. 3. *HR* 21 Sep 1948, p. 5, 9. *MPHPD* 31 Jul 1948, p. 4258. *MPHPD* 4 Sep 1948, p. 4301. *NYT* 16 Sep 1948, p. 34. *Var* 15 Sep 1948, p. 15.

LUCKY BOY (Jewish Americans)

Tiffany-Stahl Productions, Inc. 2 Feb **1929** [©Tiffany-Stahl Productions, Inc.; 4 Feb 1929; LP100]. Talking sequences and mus score (Photophone); b&w. 10 reels, 8,708 ft.

Dir Norman Taurog and Charles C. Wilson. *Dir sd seq* Rudolph Flothow. *Story* Viola Brothers Shore. *Cont* Isadore Bernstein. *Dial and titles* George Jessel. *Titles* Harry Braxton. *Photog* Harry Jackson. *Addl photog* Frank Zucker. *Art dir* Hervey Libbert. *Film ed* Desmond O'Brien and Russell Shields. *Set dresser* George Sawley. *Mus score* Hugo Riesenfeld. *Mus cond* Sacha Bunchuk.

Song(s): "Lucky Boy" and "My Mother's Eyes," by L. Wolfe Gilbert and Abel Baer; "Old Man Sunshine," "My Real Sweetheart" and "Bouquet of Memories," by Lewis Young and William Axt; "My Blackbirds Are Bluebirds Now," by Irving Caesar and Cliff Friend; "California Here I Come," by Al Jolson, B. G. De Sylva and Joseph Meyer.

Cast: George Jessel (*Georgie Jessel*), Gwen Lee (*Mrs. Ellis*), Richard Tucker (*Mr. Ellis*), Gayne Whitman (*Mr. Trent*), Margaret Quimby (*Eleanor*), Rosa Rosanova ("*Momma*" *Jessel*), William Strauss (*Jacob Jessel*), Mary Doran (*Becky*).

Comedy-drama. Georgie Jessel, a Jewish jeweler's son from the Bronx, wants to break into show business. After being turned down by several theatrical managers, he makes plans to put on a show of his

own by renting a neighborhood theater for one night. Georgie sells tickets to friends and neighbors, but there is not enough money to pay the full rent and he must call off the show. Humiliated, Georgie goes to San Francisco, where he becomes a success singing in a nightclub and falls in love with Eleanor Ellis. When his mother falls ill, Georgie returns to the East and becomes a star in a Broadway musical comedy. After a special kindness to Eleanor's mother, Georgie receives her long-withheld permission to marry Eleanor, thereby making his happiness complete. *Family relationships. Jewelers. Jews. New York City–Broadway. New York City–Bronx. Nightclubs. San Francisco (CA). Singers. Theater. Theatrical managers.*
FD 26 Jan 1929. *NYT* 25 Feb 1929, p. 16.

THE LUCKY BRIDE *see* SING YUN SIN NIAN

LUCKY CISCO KID (Latino)
Twentieth Century-Fox Film Corp. *Dist* Twentieth Century-Fox Film Corp. 28 Jun **1940**; Prod: 26 Feb–mid-Mar 1940 [©Twentieth Century-Fox Film Corp.; 28 Jun 1940; LP9749]. Sd (RCA High Fidelity Recording); b&w. 7 reels, 6,089 ft. 67-68 min. PCA cert no. 6129.
   Series: The Cisco Kid.
   [*Exec prod* Sol M. Wurtzel]. *Assoc prod* John Stone. *Dir* H. Bruce Humberstone. [*Asst dir* Aaron Rosenberg]. *Scr* Robert Ellis and Helen Logan. *Orig story* Julian Johnson. [*Contr wrt* Lee Loeb]. *Dir of photog* Lucien Andriot. *Art dir* Richard Day and Chester Gore. *Film ed* Fred Allen. *Set dec* Thomas Little. *Cost* Helen A. Myron. *Mus dir* Cyril J. Mockridge. *Sd* Bernard Freericks and William H. Anderson.
   Source: Based on the character created by O. Henry.
   Cast: Cesar Romero ([*The*] *Cisco Kid*), Mary Beth Hughes (*Lola*), Dana Andrews (*Sergeant Dunn*), Evelyn Venable (*Mrs. [Emily] Lawrence*), Chris-Pin Martin (*Gordito*), Willard Robertson (*Judge McQuade*), Joseph Sawyer ([*Bill*] *Stevens*), John Sheffield (*Tommy Lawrence*), William Royle (*Sheriff*), Francis Ford (*Court clerk*), Otto Hoffman (*Storekeeper* [*Ed Stoke*]), Dick Rich (*Stagecoach driver* [*Tex*]), [Bob Hoffman (*First soldier*)], [Harry Strang (*Corporal*)], [Boyd Morgan (*Second soldier*)], [Gloria Roy (*Dance hall girl*)], [Lillian Yarbo (*Queenie*)], [Adrian Morris, Jimmie Dundee, William Pagan (*Passengers in stagecoach*)], [Lew Kelly (*Stage dispatcher*)], [Milton Kibbee (*Wells Fargo man*)], [Sarah Edwards (*Spinster*)], [Ethan Laidlaw (*Henchman*)], [Frank Lackteen (*Bandit*)], [Thornton Edwards, James Flavin (*Ranch foremen*)], [Henry Roquemore (*Proprietor*)], [Syd Saylor (*Hotel clerk*)], [Spencer Charters (*Hotel guest*)], [Charles Tannen], [Pat O'Malley], [Sid Jordan].
   Western. [*Print viewed*]. The Cisco Kid and his pal Gordito attempt to board a stagecoach but are stopped by a group of drunken passengers. Even the driver, Tex, refuses to let Cisco and Gordito on, but the pair of jovial bandits soon hijack the coach. Pursued by soldiers led by Sergeant Dunn, they abandon the vehicle before arriving in a small Arizona town. Cisco and Gordito split up, and while Cisco makes the acquaintance of Dunn's girl friend, saloon singer Lola, Gordito sings with a religious group to avoid detection. After Gordito and Cisco meet in a saloon, they listen to leading citizen Judge McQuade proclaim that the soldiers are useless and that the town needs a vigilante committee to catch the dreaded Cisco Kid. As the outlaw's crimes are listed, Cisco realizes that someone is impersonating him and committing crimes of a nature that he himself would never do. Tex recognizes Cisco and Gordito and demands their arrest. Just then, little Tommy Lawrence rushes in and pleads for help in driving the Cisco Kid and his gang away from his mother Emily's ranch. The men ride to the ranch, where they discover that a gang has burned the barn and killed the cattle. After the gang is routed, Cisco and Gordito offer to work for Emily, who is a widow struggling to keep her ranch despite the large sum of money she owes to McQuade. The next day, Cisco and Gordito go to Ed Stoke's store to get supplies and discover that the store is owned by McQuade, who has been charging Emily twice what he charges other customers. Later, McQuade and Dunn discuss the next arriving stagecoach, which will carry a Wells Fargo strongbox, while Cisco goes for a ride with Lola and gives her his monogrammed handkerchief. They return to the saloon, where Cisco tangles with tough Bill Stevens, who is another of Lola's suitors. Late that night, Cisco and Gordito watch as the stagecoach is robbed despite an escort of soldiers, and Cisco is wounded in the confusion. Emily hides them when they return to the ranch, for Cisco's handkerchief was found at the scene of the robbery and the soldiers are looking for him. In the morning, Cisco discovers

from Lola that Bill took his handkerchief, but he is captured before he can find Bill. Bill is also apprehended when Lola finds the strongbox money in his saddlebags, and both men are brought before McQuade. Just as Cisco is about to be taken away by Dunn, Gordito enters with proof from McQuade's safe that McQuade and Bill are in league together. While Bill has impersonated Cisco and terrorized the local ranchers, McQuade has driven them into debt, and thus they have been obtaining the ranchers' lands cheaply when the people have fled. Cisco gives Lola the reward money for Bill's capture, and she persuades Dunn to let Cisco and Gordito go. As the laughing bandits ride off, Gordito reveals to Cisco that he has kept half of the reward money. *Duplicity. Frame-ups. Impersonation and imposture. Judges. Mexicans. Outlaws. Singers. Soldiers. Arizona. Baths. Chases. Drunkenness. Fires. Fortune hunters. Gangs. Handkerchiefs. Ranches. Rewards. Romantic rivalry. Saloons. Stagecoach drivers. Stagecoach robberies. Storekeepers. Vamps. Widows.*
   Note: The working title of this film was *Rogue of the Rio Grande*, and it first appeared on a *HR* production chart as *Cisco Kid No. 3*. Modern sources include Blackie Whiteford in the cast. For more information on the series, please see the entry above for *The Cisco Kid*.
DV 23 May 1940, p. 3. *FD* 28 Jun 1940, p. 5. *HR* 24 Feb 1940, p. 7. *HR* 7 Mar 1940, p. 14. *HR* 16 Mar 1940, p. 7. *HR* 23 May 1940, p. 3. *MPD* 29 May 1940, p. 7. *MPH* 13 Apr 1940, p. 46. *MPH* 1 Jun 1940, p. 41. *NYT* 24 Jun 1940, p. 19. *Var* 29 May 1940, p. 14.

LUCKY DAY *see* SPEED TO BURN

LUCKY GHOST (African Americans)
Dixie National Pictures, Inc. *Dist* Consolidated National Film Exchanges; Dixie National Film Exchanges, Inc.; Toddy Pictures Co. 10 Feb **1942**. Sd; b&w. 6 reels, 5,489 ft. 67-68 min. Passed by the National Board of Review. PCA cert no. 6533.
   Prod Jed Buell. *Assoc prod* Maceo B. Sheffield. *Dir* William X. Crowley. *Asst dir* Edwin Monfort. *Story* Lex Neal and Vernon Smith. *Story ed* Josephine Wickland. *Dir of photog* Robert Cline. *Art dir* Eugene Stone. *Film ed* Robert Crandall. *Mus dir* Don Swander and Lorenza Flennoy. *Sd* Hans Weeren. *Prod mgr* Peter Jones.
   Song(s): "If Anybody Cares," "When You Think of Loving, Think of Me" and "Can't Use it Anymore," music and lyrics by Don Swander and June Hershey; "In Old Darktown," music and lyrics by McClure Morris.
   Cast: Mantan Moreland (*Washington [Delaware Jones]*), F. E. Miller (*Jefferson*), Maceo B. Sheffield (*Dr. Brutus Blake*), Arthur Ray (*Blackstone*), Florence O'Brien (*Hostess*), Harold A. Garrison (*Brown*), Jessie Cryer (*Dawson*), Nappie Whiting (*Chauffeur*), Jessie Brooks (*Door man*), Ida Coffin (*Hat check girl*), Nathan Curry (*Farmer*), Millie Monroe (*First waitress*), Louise Franklyn (*Second waitress*), Lucille Battles (*Third waitress*), Aranelle Harris (*Fourth waitress*), Monty Hawley (*Masher*), Vernon McCella [sic] (*First man guest*), Harry Lavette [sic] (*First man diner*), Henry Hastings (*Uncle Ezra's ghost*), Florence Field (*Mrs. Ezra's ghost*), John Lester Johnson (*First ghost*), Eddie Thompson (*Second ghost*), Leonard Christmas (*Third ghost*), Reggie Finderson (*Dealer*), [Buck Woods].
   African American, Comedy, Fantasy, with songs. [*Print viewed*]. After being ordered by a judge to get out of town, ne'er-do-well Washington, Delaware Jones and his pal Jefferson hit the road in search of a new home. While travelling, they discuss the possibility of getting white-collar jobs. Because they are both hungry, Washington and Jefferson decide to pursue careers as food tasters. They begin training for the profession by posing as food inspectors and stealing chickens from a chicken coop. The duo then come across a wealthy man named Brown, stranded on a country road because his car has run out of gas. While Brown's chauffeur is off looking for gas, Washington and Jefferson engage Brown and his friend Dawson in a dice game. After winning all of Dawson's and Brown's money, Washington and Jefferson take their car and instruct the chauffeur to drive them to Dr. Brutus Blake's Sanitarium and Country Club. When Washington and Jefferson arrive at Blake's elegant but crooked establishment, Blake thinks that they are rich and plans to fleece them in a fixed crap game. While Washington and Jefferson settle into the sanitarium, Blake and his partner, Blackstone, become embroiled in a bitter argument. The argument eventually leads Blackstone to threaten Blake with informing on his activities. Later, when Blake sees Washington dancing with the hostess, he flies into a jealous rage and picks a fight with him. Blake is knocked unconscious in the fight when a punch he intends for Washington lands on a wall and dislodges a hanging plate over his head. Calm is soon restored,

however, when the hostess reminds Blake that Washington and Jefferson are wealthy and that he needs their money. While Washington and Jefferson are graciously escorted into Blake's gambling room, the ghosts of Blake's dead relatives discuss their regret at having bequeathed the place to him. Because they feel that Blake has turned the sanitarium into a sinful place, the ghosts send the ghost of Ezra Dewey, Blake's uncle, to straighten out the situation. The invisible Ezra arrives at the sanitarium just as Blake has lost the place in a bet to Washington and Jefferson. Much to the dismay of the ghosts, the sanitarium under the management of Washington and Jefferson remains a sinful place. Ezra is now joined by the other ghosts in his effort to rid the property of all the noise and sinful activity. Meanwhile, Blake and Blackstone make plans to regain control of the sanitarium by having the sheriff arrest Washington and Jefferson on trumped-up charges. The scheme is soon thwarted by Ezra, who overhears the plans and spooks Blake by telling him that his dead relatives are ashamed of him. The ghosts then scare away Jefferson, Washington and the others by haunting the sanitarium. After handing over their dice and money to a piano-playing skeleton, Washington and Jefferson run away. *African Americans. Gambling. Ghosts. Ne'er-do-wells. Sanitariums.* Blackmail. Casinos. Chauffeurs. Craps (Game). Dice. Fistfights. Frame-ups. Hostesses. Jazz music. Jealousy. Nouveaux riches. Parties. Singers. Skeletons.

Note: The onscreen credits incorrectly spell actor and newspaper columnist Harry Levette's name "Lavette." Actor Vernon McCalla's surname is misspelled "McCella." The *MPH* review notes that this film was the second of seven films planned for production by Jed Buell. *Lucky Ghost* is a follow-up to the 1940 Buell film *Mr. Washington Goes to Town*, which also starred Mantan Moreland and F. H. Miller and featured the characters "Brutus Blake" and "Blackstone" (see below). *Lucky Ghost* was originally titled *Lady Luck*. Material contained in the MPAA/PCA Collection at the AMPAS Library indicates that the film underwent a title change in late 1941 or early 1942. The reason for the change in title is not noted in the records.

Exh 25 Feb 1942. *MPHPD* 21 Feb 1942, p. 518.

LUIGI LA VOLPE *see* **MONSIEUR LE FOX**

LUIN FUNG HEH MING *see* **LUAN FENG HEH MING**

LULLABY OF BROADWAY *see* **THE GENTLEMAN MISBEHAVES**

THE LUNATIC *see* **WHAT A MOTHER-IN-LAW!**

THE LURE OF A WOMAN (African Americans)
The Afro-American Film Exhibitors Co. of Kansas City, Missouri; Progress Picture Association. **1921**; Kansas City opening: 21 Aug 1921. Si; b&w. 5 reels.
Dir J. M. Simms. *Asst dir* Mrs. Osborne. *Wrt* J. M. Simms. *Photog* Howard Curtis.
Cast: Regina Cohee, Charles H. Allen, Dr. A. Porter Davis, Mrs. J. D. Brown, Roberto Taylor, Leonore Jones, John Cobb, Alonzo Dixon, Susie Dudley, Veronica Miller, Emily Gates, Alice Johnson.
Melodrama (?), African American. No information about the precise nature of this film has been found. *African Americans.*

Note: According to an information in the George P. Johnson Collection at the UCLA Special Collections Library, this was the first release of The Afro-American Film Exhibitors Co. of Kansas City, Missouri. An ad called the film "The first Negro production ever made in Kansas City" and stated, "All the cast in this production are Kansas City Negroes. All the scenes were taken about the city." Charles H. Allen, the male lead, was the general manager and treasurer of the company. They planned a series of eight films that would be released in Central and South America, as well as in the U.S., and boasted of a distribution policy "that will enable it to overcome some of the difficulties usual to colored pictures." Their second release was to be called *The Human Devil*. No additional information concerning the company has been located.

ChiDef 20 May 1922, p. 7.

THE LURE OF LOVE (Russian Americans)
Pictures in Motion. *Dist* Ace-High Productions. 28 Apr **1924**. Si; b&w. 5 reels, 4,600 ft.
Dir Leon E. Dadmun.
Cast: Zena Keefe, Edward Earle.
Melodrama. "Concerns young Russian exiled from homeland by officer who desires hero's sister. In America he works in a steel mill and makes his way up the ladder, defeating a plot to undermine his prestige with the workmen. He also wins the love of the daughter of steel mill owner and eventually locates his sister and brings her from Russia." (*MPNBG* 8 Apr 1925, p. 58.). *Brothers and sisters. Exile. Immigrants. Russian Americans. Russians. Steel industry.*

THE LURE OF NEW YORK (German Americans)
New York Film Co. *Dist* State Rights. Nov **1913**? [©Abraham J. Danziger; 30 Oct 1913; LU1497]. Si; b&w. 4 reels.
Scen Abraham J. Danziger.
Social, Drama. Hearing that their inn is to be closed for non-payment, young Regina Muller bids her mother farewell and leaves her Bavarian home to seek her fortune in America. On the ship to New York, Regina meets a woman who invites the girl to live in the Bowery with her and her husband, Gentleman Joe, but after her arrival, the couple forges a letter informing Regina that her mother is dead. When Gentleman Joe, actually a vicious criminal, starts a fight in Chinatown, Regina becomes suspicious of her new "parent," but after she fights off his lustful attack, she decides to make her escape. Regina eludes her underworld pursuers with the help of a policeman's son, but the next day, her adventures continue as she is struck by Madame Du Pont's car. Charmed by the young immigrant, Madame Du Pont adopts her and introduces her to society life. Meanwhile, Mrs. Muller arrives in New York to search for her daughter. By chance, she is hired as Madame Du Pont's servant, and mother and daughter are finally reunited. *Criminals. Debt. German Americans. Immigrants. Letters. Mothers and daughters. New York City—Bowery.* Adoption. Attempted rape. Automobile accidents. Bavaria (Germany). Dowagers. Escapes. Servants. Ships.

Note: The director was probably George K. Rolands. Exterior scenes were filmed on location in New York City.

MPW 8 Nov 1913, p. 618, 649. *MPW* 15 Nov 1913, p. 790.

THE LURE OF WOMAN (Native Americans)
World Film Corp.; Armstrong. *Dist* World Film Corp. 27 Sep **1915** [©World Film Corp.; 30 Sep 1915; LU6642]. Si; b&w. 5 reels.
Source: Based on the play *The Renegade* by Paul Armstrong (New York, ca. 1910).
Cast: Alice Brady (*Katie O'Day*).
Western. John Found, a well-educated American Indian, works as an interpreter on an army post in the West. Although John Lane, a post officer, loves Katie O'Day, a rancher's daughter, he becomes the amorous target of the widowed Mrs. Van Allen. To rid herself of Katie, Mrs. Van Allen starts a rumor that Lane has a wife in an insane asylum. In spite of Katie's sudden cold behavior, Lane spurns Mrs. Van Allen, who then turns her attentions on John Found. Found proposes to the widow but is rejected with a brutal racial slur. Humiliated, Found uses his position to incite the local Indians. After attacking the O'Day ranch, the Indians besiege the unguarded post, and Found drags Mrs. Van Allen through the post by her hair, eventually causing her to die of fright. Entreated by Startled Fawn, his Indian lover, to flee, Found escapes unharmed, and the army troops defeat the remaining Indians. Lane convinces Katie of his bachelorhood, and they happily reunite. *Indians of North America. Jealousy. Military posts. Uprisings.* Racism. Ranches. Rumors. Translators. United States. Army. Widows.

Motog 2 Oct 1915, p. 706. *MPW* 30 Oct 1915, p. 1034, 1036.

LUST FOR GOLD (Latino, Native Americans, Apache, German Americans)
Columbia Pictures Corp. *Dist* Columbia Pictures Corp. Jun **1949**; Prod: 25 Oct–13 Dec 1948 [©Columbia Pictures Corp.; 27 May 1949; LP2301]. Sd (Western Electric Recording); b&w. 89-90 min.
Prod S. Sylvan Simon. *Assoc prod* Earl McEvoy. *Dir* S. Sylvan Simon. *Asst dir* James Nicholson. *Scr* Ted Sherdeman and Richard English. *Dir of photog* Archie Stout. *Art dir* Carl Anderson. *Film ed* Gene Havlick. *Set dec* Sidney Clifford. *Miss Lupino's ward by* Jean Louis. *Mus* George Dunning. *Mus dir* M. W. Stoloff. *Sd eng* Lodge Cunningham. *Makeup* Clay Campbell. *Hair styles* Helen Hunt.
Source: Based on the book *Thunder God's Gold* by Barry Storm (Tortilla Flat, AZ, 1945).
Cast: IDA LUPINO [(*Julia Thomas*)], GLENN FORD [(*Jacob Walz*)], Gig Young [(*Pete Thomas*)], William Prince [(*Barry Storm*)], Edgar Buchanan [(*Wiser*)], Will Geer [(*Deputy Ray Covin*)], Paul Ford [(*Sheriff Lynn Early*)], [Jay Silverheels (*Walter*)], [Eddy Waller (*Coroner*)], [Will Wright (*Parsons*)], [Virginia Mullen (*Matron*)], [Antonio Moreno (*Ramon Peralta*)], [Arthur Hunnicutt (*Ludi*)], [Myrna Dell (*Lucille*)], [Tom Tyler (*Luke*)], [Elspeth Dudgeon (*Mrs. Martha Bannister*)], [Paul E. Burns (*Bill Bates*)], [Hayden Rorke (*Floyd Buckley*)], [Fred Sears (*Hotel clerk*)], [M. G. Fain (*Gambler*)], [Robert Malcolm (*Bartender*)], [Virginia Farmer (*Clerk*)], [Jack Kay (*Piano Player*)], [Billy Gray (*Little boy*)], [Harry

Cording (*Butcher*)], [Baynes Barron (*Sharp man*)], [Phil Tully (*Anxious man*)], [William J. Tannen (*Eager fellow*)], [Si Jenks (*Bright man*)], [Alvin Hammer (*Husband*)], [Anne O'Neal (*Mrs. Butler*)], [Karoline Grimes (*Little girl*)], [Percy Helton (*Barber*)], [Arthur Space (*Old man*)], [Richard Alexander], [Dorothy Vernon], [Edmund Cobb], [George Chesebro], [Howard Negley], [John Doucette], [Paul Bryar], [Tom Daly], [Eddie Fetherston], [Kermit Maynard], [Trevor Bardette], [Billy Engle], [Guy Beach], [Louis Mason], [Maudie Prickett], [Nita Mathews], [George Morrell], [Nora Bush].

Western, Drama. [*Print viewed*]. Barry Storm, the grandson of Jacob Walz, who in 1880 was the owner of the Lost Dutchman mine, surreptitiously follows Floyd Buckley as he searches for the mine in Arizona's Superstition Mountains. When Buckley is murdered by a sniper, Barry hikes back to town to report his death. The sheriff tells Barry that twenty-one men have been murdered while searching for the mine, and Buckley is the fourth to have been shot in the same area with the same gun. Barry knows that one hundred years earlier the Peralta brothers: Pedro, Ramon and Manuel, discovered the mine: After Ramon returns home, the other miners are attacked by an Apache. The brothers cover the entrance to the mine and attempt to escape, but are killed by the Indian. After he reflects on the past, Barry takes deputy sheriff Ray Covin to the place where Buckley was killed and then stays behind to continue his search for the mine. He accidentally stumbles on an ancient rifle, which he believes might have belonged to Walz. Sheriff Lynn Early sends Barry to an old folks home near Phoenix, and there, Mrs. Martha Bannister and Bill Bates tell Barry what they know about his grandfather: Walz encounters Ramon Peralta and Ludi, his American companion, in a small town near the Superstitions and, with his friend Wiser, follows them through the mountains. One night, Peralta and Ludi wait for moonlight to strike a certain spot, then start digging. Walz kills all the others and then fills his own pockets with gold. After Walz returns to town with the gold, Julia Thomas, who owns the bakery, becomes determined to get the gold and leave her fugitive husband Pete. Chance favors her plans when a drunken Walz collapses in front of her shop. She puts him to bed, and in the morning, pretends disinterest in his gold. When Walz learns that Julia speaks German, he begins to court her. No one dares to tell the quick-tempered Walz that Julia is already married, but Julia offers the information herself, explaining that she no longer loves her husband. After Walz offers to pay Pete to divorce her, he accidentally learns that Julia is not separated from Pete as he has told him, and becomes convinced that Julia is after his money like everyone else. Later, Walz gives Julia a map of the mine and asks her to meet him there. When Julia and Pete reach the mine, Walz hides their burros and supplies and watches from a hiding place as they grow weak from hunger and thirst. A desperate Julia kills Pete with a knife and begs Walz to help her. Walz shows her no sympathy, and later, an earthquake buries Julia and the mine. When Barry's research confirms some of the details of this story, he becomes convinced that he can discover the buried mine. Once again, he explores the Superstitions and finally locates one of the landmarks. Covin, who has been looking for the mine for twenty years, tries to shoot Barry, as he has the other treasure hunters. He then struggles with Barry, but falls to his death after he is bitten by a rattlesnake. Early, who suspected that Covin was the murderer, arrives, having followed Covin at a distance. Together, Barry and Early wait for the moon to rise, but quickly realize that unless they know the exact date on which the moonlight will hit the entrance to the mine, they will never find it. *Duplicity. Gold. Lure of riches. Murder.* Aged persons. Apache Indians. Bakers and bakeries. Brothers. Deputies. Earthquakes. Falls from heights. Fugitives. German Americans. Grandsons. Mexicans. Rattlesnakes. Romance. Sheriffs.

Note: The film's working titles were *Superstition Mountain, Greed,* and *Bonanza. HR* reviewed the film under the title *For Those Who Dare.* On 2 Sep 1948, *LAT* announced that George Marshall was to direct the film. Later, he was replaced by S. Sylvan Simon. Barry Storm's book was a documentary account of the actual Lost Dutchman mine and the cruel fates of those who tried to find it. He was not related to Jacob Walz. In 1955, according to a 29 Nov *HR* news item, Storm, the *nom de plume* of John Griffith Climenson, sued Columbia for libel, stating that he was falsely portrayed in the film as the "illegitimate grandson of an Arizona frontier character, Jacob Walz." According to a modern source, the suit was settled out of court.

Box 28 May 1949. *DV* 17 May 1949, p. 3. *FD* 31 May 1949, p. 6. *HR* 16 May 1949, p. 4. *HR* 29 Nov 1955. *MPHPD* 28 May 1949, p. 4625. *NYT* 4 Jul 1949, p. 9. *Var* 25 May 1949, p. 8.

THE LUST OF THE RED MAN (Native Americans)
Albuquerque Film Mfg Co. *Dist* Warner's Features, Inc. Jun **1914?**. Si; b&w. 4 reels.
Dir Gilbert P. Hamilton. *Scen* Dot Farley.
Cast: Dot Farley.
Drama. Indians terrorize a settler and his wife, who almost lose their faith in God. They are rescued by the U.S. Cavalry. *Faith. Indians of North America. Rescues. Settlers. United States. Army. Cavalry.*
MPN 8 Aug 1914, p. 68. *MPW* 20 Jun 1914, p. 1691.

LYING LIPS (African Americans)
Dist Sack Amusement Enterprises, Inc. **1939**. Sd; b&w. 8 reels, 7,590 ft.
Pres ALFRED N. SACK. *Dir* Oscar Micheaux. *Dir of dial* John Kollin. *Wrt by* Oscar Micheaux. *Photog* Lester Lang. *Ed* Leonard Weiss. *Mus dir* Jack Shilkret. *Rec* Nelson Minnerly.
Song(s): "Beautiful Baby," music and lyrics by James F. Hanley; "I've Got a Heartful of Rhythm," composer undetermined.
Cast: Edna Mae Harris (*Elsie Bellwood*), Carman Newsome (*Benjamin Hadnott*), Earl Jones (*Detective Wanzer*), Frances Williams (*Elizabeth Green*), Cherokee Thornton (*"John"*), "Slim" Thompson (*"Clyde"*), Gladys Williams (*Aunt Josephine*), Juano Hernandez (*Reverend Bryson*), Henry "Gang" Gines (*"Ned" Green*), Don Delese (*Farina*), Charles Latorre (*Garotti*), Robert Paquin (*District attorney*), George Reynolds (*Lieutenant of police*), Amanda Randolph (*Matron*), Teddy Hall (*Boy*).
African American, Crime, Drama, with songs. [*Print viewed*]. Black nightclub singer Elsie Bellwood refuses to go out with two Italian customers who want to sponsor a party with some of the showgirls, despite the urgings of her white boss, Farina. Farina decides to call on her black manager, Benjamin Hadnott, to try to convince her, but Ben refuses and quits his job. That evening, Elsie has dinner with Ben, who tells her that he has been studying to become a detective. Believing he is trying to conceal his unemployment, Elsie decides to take care of Ben until he gets a new job. One evening, Elsie is summoned to her Aunt Josie's, only to find that Josie has been killed. When the police arrive, the white police lieutenant decides to arrest Elsie, even though black detective Wanzer believes she is innocent. Desperate, Elsie gives Ben's address to Wanzer, and he and Ben agree to do what they can to help her. Elizabeth Green, Elsie's cousin, suggests a possible motive for the murder when she tells the police that Elsie had taken out a large insurance policy on her aunt. Meanwhile, Elsie's cousins, "John" and "Clyde," who have been hired by Farina to replace Ben, claim they saw Elsie leave the club for a half hour around the time of the murder. Although she denies their statement, Elsie is convicted of the murder. When Ben and Wanzer learn that "Ned" Green, Elizabeth's husband, was in love with Josie, they question Reverend Bryson, a longtime friend of the family, who tells them the story of Ned: Elizabeth forced Ned to marry her by tricking him into believing that she was pregnant. When Ned found out that she had lied, he left her without waiting for an annulment. Elizabeth and her unscrupulous brothers then followed Ned to the north, where he went to be near his true love, Josie. John and Clyde eventually found Ned and forced him to return to Elizabeth. Now, years later, Ned has disappeared again, and to help find him, Ben suggests that he and Wanzer abduct John and tell him they are taking him for a ride to haunted Tolston Manor. When they accuse John of killing Josie, he admits that he lied to shift the blame to Elsie. Ned, it is learned, decided he would kill Josie if she did not run away with him. When the police realize that the frame-up was planned in order to get the insurance money from Elsie, Elsie is released from prison. Once reunited with Ben, Elsie gives him the money, which he puts into a trust fund for their "children." *African Americans. Detectives. Frame-ups. Insurance. Murder. Singers.* Aunts. Children. Confession (Law). Cousins. Haunted houses. Italians. Jails. Nightclub owners. Nightclubs. Parties. Racism. Reverends. Theatrical managers.

Note: Although an onscreen statement claims that the picture featured "an All-Star Colored Cast," the actor who played nightclub owner "Farina" was white, as were a number of actors in the roles of policemen. According to modern sources, Hubert Fauntleroy Julian produced the film, and Frank Costell and J. Louis Johnson were in the cast.

McFADDEN'S FLATS (Irish Americans, Scottish Americans)

First National Pictures, Inc.; Asher-Small-Rogers Present. *Dist* First National Pictures, Inc. 6 Feb **1927** [©First National Pictures, Inc.; 26 Jan 1927; LP23593]. Si; b&w. 8 reels, 7,846 ft.

Prod Edward Small. *Dir* Richard Wallace. *Scen* Charles Logue. *Adpt* Jack Wagner, Jack Jevne and Rex Taylor. *Photog* Arthur Edeson.

Source: Based on the play *McFadden's Row of Flats* by Gus Hill (London, 22 Oct 1896).

Cast: Charlie Murray (*Dan McFadden*), Chester Conklin (*Jock McTavish*), Edna Murphy (*Mary Ellen McFadden*), Larry Kent (*Sandy McTavish*), Aggie Herring (*Mrs. McFadden*), De Witt Jennings (*Patrick Halloran*), Cissy Fitzgerald (*Mrs. Halloran*), Dorothy Dwan (*Edith Halloran*), Freeman Wood (*Desmond Halloran*), Dot Farley (*Bridget Maloney*), Leo White (*Hat salesman*), Harvey Clark (*Interior decorator*).

Comedy-drama. McFadden, an Irish contractor, and McTavish, a Scottish barber, become fast friends, and McTavish's son, Jock, meets and falls in love with Mary Ellen, McFadden's daughter. McFadden, having increased his store of worldly goods, sends his daughter to a finishing school, to the dismay of young Jock. McFadden also provokes frequent outbursts from McTavish, whose outlook on life is the antithesis of his own. McFadden's ambition to complete a flat building is well underway when he suddenly finds himself in financial straits; when McTavish secretly helps him out, all eventually works out well for the friends and the young lovers. *Barbers and barbershops. Boarding schools. Contractors. Irish Americans. Scottish Americans. Wealth.*

Note: For information on a 1935 adaptation of the play, please see entry below.

MPW 12 Feb 1927. *NYT* 13 Feb 1927, p. 7.

McFADDEN'S FLATS (Irish Americans, Scottish Americans)

Paramount Productions, Inc. *Dist* Paramount Productions, Inc. 29 Mar **1935**; New York opening: week of 12 Mar 1935 [©Paramount Productions, Inc.; 28 Mar 1935; LP5429]. Sd (Western Electric Noiseless Recording); b&w. 7 reels. 65 min. Passed by the National Board of Review. PCA cert no. 585.

Pres ADOLPH ZUKOR. *Prod* Charles R. Rogers. [*Exec prod* Emanuel Cohen]. *Dir* Ralph Murphy. *Scr* Arthur Caesar and Edward Kaufman. *Adpt* Casey Robinson. *Addl dial* Andy Rice. [*Contr to trmt* Seena Owen]. *Photog* Ben Reynolds. [*Ed* Joseph Kane]. [*Rec eng* Earl Hayman].

Source: Based on the play *McFadden's Row of Flats* by Gus Hill (London, 22 Oct 1896).

Cast: Walter C. Kelly (*Dan McFadden*), Andy Clyde (*Jock MacTavish*), Richard Cromwell (*Sandy MacTavish*), Jane Darwell (*Nora McFadden*), Betty Furness (*Molly McFadden*), George Barbier (*Mr. Hall*), Phyllis Brooks (*Mary Ellen Hall*), Howard Wilson (*Robert Hall*), Nella Walker (*Mrs. Hall*), Frederick Burton (*Jefferson*), [Esther Michelson], [Anna Demetrio], [Mary Forbes], [Lee Kohlmar], [Pat Moriarity].

Comedy. [*Print viewed*]. Dan McFadden builds an apartment house in a working-class neighborhood on New York's East Side called "McFadden's Flats." At the same time, Dan and his wife Nora send their tomboyish daughter Molly to an expensive girls' school to teach her etiquette. Molly only agrees to go after her sweetheart, Sandy MacTavish, convinces her she should. When Dan is unable to complete the apartments because of a lack of money, Sandy's father Jock, a Scottish barber and Dan's best friend, secretly backs Dan's loan at the bank, even though Jock is known for his penny-pinching ways. When Jock mistakenly shaves off a clump of hair from the back of Dan's head, however, then wants to charge him for the cut, Dan ends their friendship. With Jock's loan, Dan finishes his tenement, while Molly spends the summer at her classmate Mary Ellen Hall's estate outside Chicago. Molly, who has turned into a lady and has fallen for Mary Ellen's brother Robert, denies her working-class background. Mr. Hall, head of a major construction firm, offers to go into business with Dan after he opens a New York office and is eager to meet him. Dan is elected president of the hod-carriers union and gets to lead the Labor Day Parade. Molly happens to be in town for the event with the Halls, who view the parade with haughty eyes from a hotel balcony. When Dan recognizes his daughter, he proudly blows her a kiss from the street, but she pretends not to know him, breaking his heart. Later, at home, Dan scolds Molly for her behavior, and she apologizes, but convinces her father to transform their flat into a fancy, modern

apartment in time for Halls' return from Boston. The McFaddens then host a housewarming party, sending invitations to all their neighbors. The night of the party, Mary Ellen calls and Dan spontaneously invites the Halls. Robert arrives drunk and makes a pass at Molly, after telling her his mother has forbidden him to marry her and insulting her father. Sandy, who was broken-hearted to find Molly so attentive to the Halls, hits Robert for accosting Molly. Mr. Hall and Dan, meanwhile, have been getting drunk together and have discovered they are from the same neighborhood, where they both started out as bricklayers. During their drunken reverie, they have a contest to see who can first complete a wall made out of books. Mrs. Hall leaves in a huff, calling the McFaddens "riff-raff," and Dan is sure he has lost his chance to do business with Hall. Dan then learns it was Jock who guaranteed his loan, which is overdue, and reaffirms their friendship, while Sandy and Molly kiss. Hall then returns and congratulates Sandy for hitting Robert, something, he says, he should have done years ago, and assures Dan the deal will take place. *Brick layers. Class distinction. Fathers and daughters. Friendship. Irish Americans. New York City–East Side. Scottish Americans. Tenement-houses. Barbers and barbershops. Boarding schools. Construction foremen. Debt. Guilt. Interior decorators. Loans. Misers. Neighbors. Parties. Partnership. Pride and vanity. Romantic rivalry. Self-sacrifice. Snobs and snobbishness. Social climbers. Tomboys. Trade unions.*

Note: Gus Hill's play was the basis for the 1927 Asher-Small-Rogers film *McFadden's Flats*, which was distributed by First National Pictures. The 1927 film was directed by Richard Wallace and starred Charlie Murray and Chester Conklin (see above).

FD 12 Mar 1935, p. 8. *HR* 27 Feb 1935, p. 3. *MPD* 2 Mar 1935, p. 3. *MPH* 26 Jan 1935, p. 54. *Var* 13 Mar 1935, p. 27.

MACHETE (Latino)

J. Harold Odell Productions, Inc. *Dist* United Artists Corp. Dec **1958**; *Prod*: early–late Dec 1957 [©J. Harold Odell Productions, Inc.; 3 Dec 1958; LP12928]. Sd; b&w. 75 min. PCA cert no. 18938.

Exec prod Jack H. Odell, Lawrence Rapport and David Odell. *Assoc prod* Victor Carrady. *Prod* Kurt Neumann. *Dir* Kurt Neumann. *Asst dir* Henry Hartman and Richard Diaz. *Wrt* Carroll Young and Kurt Neumann. *Dir of photog* Karl Struss. *Film ed* Jodie Copelan. *Mus* Paul Sawtell and Bert Shefter. *Sd* Howard Warren and Hector Moll. *Rec* Glen Glenn Sound Company. *Makeup* Lydia Rodriquez. *Prod mgr* Harold Winston.

Cast: Mari Blanchard (*Jean Montoya*), Albert Dekker (*Don Luis Montoya*), Juano Hernandez (*Bernardo*), Carlos Rivas (*Carlos*), Lee Van Cleef (*Miguel*), Ruth Cains (*Rita*), Ulysses Brenes, Richard Verney.

Drama. [*Not viewed*]. When Don Luis Montoya, an elderly planter and long-time bachelor, returns from New York to his sugar plantation in Puerto Rico, he brings with him his enticing young bride, Jean. Although Jean is fond of Don Luis, she has married him only for security. This is immediately evident to Don Luis' household, which includes Carlos, Don Luis' handsome young protégé and manager, whom he has reared since childhood; Bernardo, the old majordomo; Bernardo's assistant Rita, who is in love with Carlos; and Miguel, Don Luis' sponging cousin. At a dinner to celebrate the wedding, Miguel drunkenly berates Don Luis for denying him his inheritance and becomes so insulting toward Jean that Carlos slaps him. Miguel then goes berserk with a machete, accidentally wounds Don Luis and is banished from the plantation after being beaten up by Carlos. With the marriage still unconsummated due to Don Luis's injury, Jean seeks relief from her boredom with Carlos and falls in love with him, but he rebuffs her and remains loyal to his sweetheart Rita and benefactor Don Luis. However, Miguel arouses Don Luis' suspicions, and he finds Jean and Carlos in a compromising situation which she has deliberately contrived. Despite Carlos' protestations of innocence, Don Luis thrashes him and that night forcibly consummates the marriage. Later, Jean agrees to renounce all claims to the Montoya estate, in exchange for Miguel's help in an escape plan. While the cane fields are being burned, Miguel arranges for Jean and Carlos to meet at an abandoned sugar mill, then informs Don Luis that they are running away. Don Luis, drunk and enraged, takes his machete, the symbol of his honor, and sets out after the couple. Miguel traps him in an isolated field and sets it afire. As Carlos is about to leave, he sees the peril Don Luis is in and rescues him, only to be attacked by Miguel, whom he kills with Luis' machete. Carlos and Luis are unable to save Jean from being burned to death, and

Carlos returns to his sweetheart Rita. *Fires. Infidelity. Marriage. Plantations. Puerto Ricans. Seduction. Sugar. Arson. Cousins. Drunkenness. Rape. Romance–Age difference. Servants. Traps.*

Note: Although this film was not viewed, the credits were taken from a billing sheet in the PCA file at the AMPAS Library. Exteriors for the film were shot in Aguirre, Puerto Rico.

DV 5 Dec 1958, p. 3. *Exb* 10 Dec 1958, p. 4542. *FD* 10 Dec 1958, p. 6. *Har* 6 Dec 1958, p. 194. *HR* 13 Dec 1957, p. 12. *HR* 20 Dec 1957. *HR* 5 Dec 1958, p. 3. *MPH* 7 Feb 1959. *Var* 10 Dec 1958, p. 6.

MAD HOLIDAY (Chinese Americans)

Metro-Goldwyn-Mayer Corp.; controlled by Loew's Inc. *Dist* Loew's Inc. 13 Nov 1936; Prod: 26 Aug–15 Sep 1936 [©Metro-Goldwyn-Mayer Corp.; 3 Dec 1936; LP6863]. Sd (Western Electric Sound System); b&w. 8 reels. 68 or 71-72 min. Passed by the National Board of Review. PCA cert no. 2779.

Prod Harry Rapf. *Dir* George B. Seitz. [*Asst dir* Dolph Zimmer]. *Scr* Florence Ryerson and Edgar Allan Woolf. *Photog* Joseph Ruttenberg. *Art dir* Cedric Gibbons. *Art dir assoc* Stan Rogers and Edwin B. Willis. *Film ed* George Boemler. *Ward* Dolly Tree. *Mus score* Dr. William Axt. *Rec dir* Douglas Shearer.

Source: Based on the novel *Murder in a Chinese Theatre* by Joseph Santley (publication undetermined).

Cast: Edmund Lowe (*Philip Trent*), Elissa Landi (*Peter Dean*), ZaSu Pitts (*Mrs. [Fay] Kinney*), Ted Healy (*Mert Morgan*), Edmund Gwenn (*Williams*), Edgar Kennedy ([*Sergeant*] *Donovan*), Soo Yong (*Li Tai*), Walter Kingsford (*Ben Kelvin*), Herbert Rawlinson (*Captain Bromley*), Raymond Hatton ("*Cocky Joe*" *Ferris*), Rafaela Ottiano (*Ning*), Harlan Briggs (*Mr. [Bertie] Kinney*), Gustav von Seyffertitz (*Hendrick Van Mier*), [Charles Trowbridge (*Doctor*)], [Russell Hicks (*Chief Gibbs*)], [Richard Loo (*Li Yat*)], [Sherry Hall (*Radio operator*)], [Chester Gan (*Vendor*)], [Adrian Rosley (*Official guide*)], [Wilbur Mack (*Mayor Howell*)].

Mystery, Comedy. [*Print viewed*]. Movie star Philip Trent, tired of playing "Selby James the Super Sleuth" and thinking that the Peter Dean novels featuring the detective are unbelievable trash, decides to take a cruise, much to the chagrin of his studio. His vacation starts off badly when he is mobbed by fans at the dock and asked for autographs on board. Then, in his cabin, Philip is approached by a beautiful blonde claiming to be pursued by a man with a gun. While he fixes her a drink, she sneaks out of his cabin with a letter opener. He looks for her in the fog, but returning to his cabin, he finds a body, dripping with blood. After summoning ship's captain Bromley and a detective, Sergeant Donovan, Philip returns to the cabin, but finds a blonde curl instead of a body. Donovan thinks it's all a publicity stunt, which is confirmed by the arrival of Mert Morgan, the studio press agent, and by Peter Dean, who turns out to be a beautiful woman, the same one who wore a blonde wig earlier. Finally realizing it was all a joke, Philip later tells "Pete" what tripe she writes, but when they return to his cabin they find the corpse of passenger Hendrick Van Mier. Trent summons Donovan again, who doesn't believe him, but when he finally examines the body he discovers that Van Mier's valuable White Dragon diamond has been stolen. As the ship is being searched, Philip wants to let Donovan handle the case while Pete wants to trace clues herself, especially those involving a Chinese woman, Li Tai, whose family had once owned the diamond. When Mert finds a bloody hand print, made by a man with a scar, they realize that it was made by "Cocky Joe" Ferris, whom Pete hired to play the corpse, and whom Donovan knows is a jewel thief. Donovan then leaves Pete and Philip handcuffed together and while they discuss the case, a masked man comes in with a gun demanding the diamond. Recognizing the set-up from one of her stories, Pete and Philip overtake the gunman, but when the lights go out he escapes and in the confusion, Pete accidentally knocks Philip unconscious. Helping Philip recuperate in her cabin, Pete prepares a drink for the two of them which turns out to have been drugged. Next morning, while everyone searches for the missing Donovan, Van Mier's valet, Williams, comes to Pete's cabin and brings Philip clothes to prevent gossip, after which Philip hires Williams. Before the boat docks in San Francisco, the diamond has been found and Trent is given credit, even though he doesn't want it. The diamond is switched for a hunk of coal, though, and the absent Donovan is revealed as a fake who has stolen the real diamond. Because the newspapers make Philip a laughing stock, Pete advises him to find the real murderer, whom she is certain is not Donovan. They find the body of Cocky Joe outside his

room, but soon discover that he is only wounded and Joe tells Pete that Donovan is hiding in Chinatown, trying to sell the diamond. Chief Gibbs of the San Francisco police refuses to listen to Philip's new story, so Philip joins in on Pete's plan and talks to Donovan on the telephone, disguising his voice as Li Yat, the famous Chinese actor and husband of Li Tai. They arrange to meet Donovan at the Chinese theater at which Li Yat is playing. Meanwhile, the real Li Yat gets a note signed "Donovan" to meet him in the prop room. Donovan's dead body is later found by Philip and Pete in the prop room. It is finally revealed that Williams is the murderer and only posed as an English valet to get the diamond. With the help of Li Yat and his costumes, Philip is able to disarm Williams and, like the end of all his movies, ends up in the arms of the beautiful girl. *Amateur detectives. Authors. Detective and mystery stories. Motion picture actors and actresses. Murder. Ships. Chinese Americans. Corpses. Diamonds. Drunkenness. Impersonation and imposture. Jewel thieves. Maids. Police. Press agents. Romance. San Francisco (CA). San Francisco (CA)–Chinatown. Theaters. Valets. Wagers.*

Note: According to a news item in *Var* an early working title of the film was *The Cock-Eyed Cruise.* *HR* production charts also list the film as *The White Dragon.* *HR* charts include E. E. Clive and Hobart Cavanaugh in the film, and a news item includes King Baggott in the cast as a director, but they were not in the viewing print and their participation in the completed film has not been confirmed.

Box 14 Nov 1936. *DV* 5 Nov 1936, p. 3. *FD* 30 Nov 1936, p. 8. *HR* 25 Aug 1936, p. 7. *HR* 31 Aug 1936, p. 19. *HR* 8 Sep 1936, p. 6. *HR* 5 Nov 1936, p. 3. *MPD* 6 Nov 1936, p. 9. *MPH* 14 Nov 1936, p. 58. *NYT* 26 Nov 1936, p. 39. *Var* 9 Oct 1936. *Var* 2 Dec 1936, p. 38.

MME. McCOY AND THE PIRATE see **BUCCANEER'S GIRL**

MADAME X (*foreign version*) see **LA MUJER X**

MLLE. FROUFROU see **THE TOY WIFE**

MADE IN HEAVEN (Irish Americans)

Goldwyn Pictures Corp. May 1921 [©Goldwyn Pictures Corp.; 17 Apr 1921; LP16546]. Si; b&w. 5 reels, 4,684 ft.

Dir Victor Schertzinger. *Scen* Arthur F. Statter. *Story* William Hurlbut. *Photog* Ernest Miller. *Art dir* Cedric Gibbons.

Cast: Tom Moore (*William Lowry*), Helene Chadwick (*Claudia Royce*), Molly Malone (*Elizabeth Royce*), Kate Lester (*Mrs. Royce*), Al Filson (*Mr. Royce*), Freeman Wood (*Davidge*), Charles Eldridge (*Lowry, Sr.*), Renée Adorée (*Miss Lowry*), Herbert Prior (*Leland*), Fronzie Gunn (*Ethel Hadden*), John Cossar (*Mr. Hadden*).

Romantic comedy. William Lowry, an Irish immigrant, rescues Claudia Royce from a burning building, and upon hearing that her parents are trying to force her to accept millionaire Leland, whom she does not love, he proposes a marriage of convenience to himself. She accepts, and Bill arranges a fake ceremony; but when she falls in love with Davidge, Bill refuses her a "divorce." Later, Bill gets rich in the manufacture of a patented fireman's pole, and when he buys a house for Claudia she realizes her love for him and they are legally married. *Fire departments. Immigrants. Irish Americans. Marriage of convenience. Marriage–Fake. Millionaires.*

ETR 30 Apr 1921, p. 1934. *FD* 1 May 1921. *Var* 22 Apr 1921, p. 41.

MADELON OF THE REDWOODS see **FALSE EVIDENCE**

LA MADRE ADOPTIVA see **TRES AMORES**

MAGGIE AND JIGGS IN JACKPOT JITTERS see **JIGGS AND MAGGIE IN JACKPOT JITTERS**

THE MAGIC LAND see **AN AMERICAN ROMANCE**

THE MAGNIFICENT YANKEE (Jewish Americans)

Metro-Goldwyn-Mayer Corp.; controlled by Loew's Inc. *Dist* Loew's Inc. Feb 1951; World premiere in Los Angeles: 20 Dec 1950; Prod: late Jun—late Jul 1950 [©Loew's Inc.; 2 Dec 1950; LP550]. Sd (Western Electric Sound System); b&w. 9 reels, 7,955 or 7,961 ft. 89-90 min. Passed by the National Board of Review. PCA cert no. 14787.

Prod Armand Deutsch. *Dir* John Sturges. [*Asst dir* Perry Thorpe]. *Wrt* Emmet Lavery. *Dir of photog* Joseph Ruttenberg. *Spec eff* A. Arnold Gillespie and Warren Newcombe. *Art dir* Cedric Gibbons and Arthur Lonergan. *Film ed* Ferris Webster. *Set dec* Edwin B. Willis. *Assoc* Jack D. Moore. *Cost des* Walter Plunkett. *Mus* David Raksin. *Rec supv* Douglas Shearer. [*Sd* Joe Edmondson]. *Makeup created by* William J. Tuttle. *Hairstyles des by* Sydney Guilaroff.

Source: Based on the play *The Magnificent Yankee* by Emmet Lavery, as produced and staged by Arthur Hopkins (New York, 22 Jan 1946), which was based on the book *Mr. Justice Holmes* by Francis Biddle (New York, 1942).

Cast: Edith Evanson (*Annie Gough*), James Lydon (*Clinton*), Richard Anderson (*Reynolds*), Guy Anderson (*Baxter*), Ian Wolf (*Adams*), Philip Ober (*Owen Wister*), Eduard Franz (*Louis Brandeis*), Ann Harding (*Fanny Bowditch Holmes*), Louis Calhern ([*Oliver Wendell Holmes, Jr.*] *The Magnificent Yankee*), [Robert Sherwood (*Drake*)], [Hugh Sanders (*Parker*)], [Harlan Warde (*Norton*)], [Charles Evans (*Chief Justice Fuller*)], [John R. Hamilton (*Justice White*)], [Dan Tobin (*Dixon*)], [Robert E. Griffin (*Court crier*)], [Stapleton Kent (*Clerk of court*)], [Robert Malcolm (*Marshall*)], [Everett Glass (*Justice Peckman*)], [Hayden Rorke (*Graham*)], [Marshall Bradford (*Headwaiter*)], [Holmes Herbert (*Justice McKenna*)], [Selmer Jackson, William Johnstone (*Lawyers*)], [George Spaulding (*Justice Hughes*)], [Todd Karns, Robert Board, Wilson Wood, James Horne, Gerald Pierce, Lyle Clark, David Alpert, Tommy Kelly, Bret Hamilton, Jim Drum (*Secretaries*)], [David McMahon (*Workman*)], [Freeman Lusk (*Announcer*)], [Fred Gillman (*Driver*)], [Sherry Hall, Jack Gargan, Dick Cogan, Tony Merrill (*Reporters*)], [Wheaton Chambers, Gayne Whitman (*Senators*)].

Biography, Historical, Drama. [*Print viewed*]. Novelist Owen Wister, tells the life story of Oliver Wendell Holmes, Jr., and begins his tale in 1902, when Holmes left his home in Boston to serve as a Supreme Court judge in Washington, D.C.: Soon after Holmes and his wife Fanny settle into their new home, Fanny tells her husband that she sees herself as a lesser wife because she is unable to bear him any children. Holmes, a loving husband, reassures her that he has little interest in producing heirs. Following his swearing-in ceremony, Holmes and his fellow jurists debate the significance of the Fourteenth Amendment to the Constitution, and later hear arguments both for and against the Sherman Anti-Trust Act. When Holmes indicates his opposition to the anti-trust act, President Theodore Roosevelt, a supporter of the act, launches a personal attack on Holmes, saying that he could "carve a judge with more backbone out of a banana." Though the act is voted into law by a majority of five to four, Roosevelt continues his grudge against Holmes and vows to have him thrown out of the White House if he ever catches him there. Managing his staff with unyielding authority, Holmes issues an order prohibiting his aides from marrying while in his service. The edict is put to a test when Baxter, one of the judge's aides, resigns so that he can marry his sweetheart. Fanny, who is opposed to her husband's harshness, urges him to reconsider his rule and reject Baxter's resignation. Holmes eventually concedes that Fanny is right and decides to keep Baxter. During a great battle over the Supreme Court nomination of Holmes's friend, Judge Louis Brandeis, Holmes defends the nominee and facilitates his confirmation. Seventeen years after his arrival in Washington, Holmes, now a distinguished judge, celebrates his eightieth birthday with his many assistants, whom he calls his "sons." Despite his seniority and his reputation as "The Great Dissenter," Holmes is passed over for the appointment to Chief Justice. In 1929, just before her death, Fanny secures a promise from her husband that he will continue his work on the court after her death. Holmes remains on the court until he reaches the age of ninety, and announces his retirement soon after the election of Franklin Delano Roosevelt. In one of the proudest moments of his life, Holmes is visited by the new president, who has come to honor the departing justice. *Oliver Wendell Holmes. Judges. United States. Supreme Court. Aged persons. Antisemitism. Louis Brandeis. Feuds. Fires. Infertility. Justice. Law (Concept). Law students. Marriage. Patriotism. Pledges. Reporters. Retirement. Romance. Franklin Delano Roosevelt. Theodore Roosevelt. The Sherman Anti-Trust Act of 1890. Washington (D.C.). Wills.*

Note: The order of the onscreen cast credits that appear at the end of the film differ from the opening credits, which list the stars of film, Louis Calhern and Ann Harding, first. According to a Dec 1950 *LAT* news item, this film was originally scheduled for a Feb 1951 general release, but had its premiere and limited release in Dec 1950 to qualify for the 1950 Academy Awards. The play on which this film was based starred Louis Calhern in the title role and Dorothy Gish as "Fanny Holmes." Contemporary sources note that Francis Biddle, the biographer who provided the "source material" for the play, served as one of Justice Oliver Wendell Holmes, Jr.'s young Harvard Law School assistants. Material in the M-G-M Story Department's Index Files contained at AFI's Louis B. Mayer Library indicates that in 1943, M-G-M producer Voldemar Vetluguin wrote a screen treatment of Biddle's book of essays, *Mr. Justice Holmes*, and submitted it to the Hays Office for review. According to a 1947 *LAEx* news

item, United Artists producer Benedict Bogeaus purchased the screen rights to Emmet Lavery's play with the intention of casting "a younger actor" than Calhern in the leading role. A Jul 1947 *HR* news item noted that Bogeaus had actor Gregory Peck in mind for the title role at the time he purchased the film rights.

A Jun 1949 *DV* news item stated that Twentieth Century-Fox writer and director Shepard Traube optioned the film rights to the play. A *NYT* article noted that on 29 Oct 1947, Lavery was placed on a "contempt list" of the House Subcommittee on Un-American Activities and was called to testify against Hollywood figures purported to be Communists. Lavery refused to "name names" and questioned the committee's Constitutional right to ask such questions. After assuring the committee that he himself was not a Communist, Lavery suggested that a better approach to curtailing the rise of Communism in the United States might be to "dramatize the American way of life," like showing "how good Mr. (Justice Oliver Wendell) Holmes was than how bad Mr. Stalin is." (For more information on the House Subcommittee on Un-American Activites hearings, see above entry for *Crossfire*.) A *Hallmark Hall of Fame* television production of Lavery's play, which aired on 4 Feb 1965 and starred Alfred Lunt and Lynn Fontanne, received a Gavel Award from the American Bar Association. Calhern and Ann Harding reprised their roles for a *Lux Radio Theatre* version of the story, which aired on 19 May 1962.

Box 18 Nov 1950. *Box* 25 Nov 1950. *DV* 15 Jun 1949. *DV* 15 Nov 1950. *FD* 15 Nov 1950, p. 8. *HR* 1 Jul 1947, p. 1. *HR* 30 Jun 1950, p. 8. *HR* 21 Jul 1950, p. 10. *HR* 15 Nov 1950, p. 3. *LAEx* 16 Jun 1947. *LAT* 14 Dec 1950. *MPHPD* 18 Nov 1950, pp. 569-70. *NYT* 30 Oct 1947. *NYT* 19 Jan 1951, p. 21. *Var* 15 Nov 1950, p. 6.

MAID OF SALEM (African Americans)
Paramount Pictures, Inc. *Dist* Paramount Pictures, Inc. 12 Feb **1937**; Prod: late Aug—early Nov 1936 [©Paramount Pictures, Inc.; 19 Feb 1937; LP6932]. Sd (Western Electric Noiseless Recording); b&w. 9 reels. 85-86 min. Passed by the National Board of Review. PCA cert no. 2715.

Pres ADOLPH ZUKOR. *Prod* Howard Estabrook. [*Exec prod* William LeBaron]. *Dir* FRANK LLOYD. *Asst dir* William Tummel. [*Unit casting dir* John Zinn]. *Scr* Walter Ferris, Bradley King and Durward Grinstead. *Story* Bradley King. [*Contr to dial* Harlan Ware]. *Photog* Leo Tover. *Art dir* Hans Dreier and Bernard Herzbrun. *Ed* Hugh Bennett. *Int dec* A. E. Freudeman. *Cost des* Travis Banton. *Mus dir* Boris Morros. *Orig mus* Victor Young. *Sd rec* Gene Merritt and Louis Mesenkop. [*Tech res* Lance Baxter].

Song(s): "Bid Me But Live," traditional.
Cast: CLAUDETTE COLBERT (*Barbara Clarke*), FRED MacMURRAY (*Roger Coverman, of Virginia*), Harvey Stephens (*Dr. John Harding*), Gale Sondergaard (*Martha, his wife*), Louise Dresser (*Ellen Clarke, Barbara's aunt*), Bennie Bartlett (*Timothy, her son*), Edward Ellis (*Elder [Nathaniel] Goode*), Beulah Bondi (*Abigail, his wife*), Bonita Granville (*Virginia, their daughter*), Virginia Weidler (*Nabby, their daughter*), Donald Meek (*Ezra Cheeves*), E. E. Clive ([*Thomas Ezekiel*] *Bilge*), Halliwell Hobbes (*Jeremiah [Adams]*), Pedro de Cordoba (*Mr. Morse*), Madame Sul-te-wan (*Tituba, a slave*), Lucy Beaumont (*Rebecca Nurse*), Henry Kolker (*Crown Chief Justice Laughton*), William Farnum (*Crown Justice Sewall*), Ivan Simpson (*Rev. [Samuel] Parris*), Brandon Hurst (*Tithing man*), Sterling Holloway (*Miles Corbin, cow herder*), Zeffie Tilbury (*Goody Hodgers*), Babs Nelson (*Baby Mercy Cheeves*), Mary Treen (*Susy Abbott*), J. Farrell MacDonald (*Captain of ship*), Stanley Fields (*First mate*), Lionel Belmore (*Tavern keeper*), [Tom Ricketts (*Giles Cory*)], [Guy Bates Post (*Governor*)], [Kathryn Sheldon (*Mrs. Deborah Cheeves*)], [Rosita Butler (*Mary Watkins*)], [Madge Collins (*Elizabeth*)], [Amelia Falleur (*Sarah*)], [Clarence Kolb (*Town crier*)], [Russell Simpson (*Village marshal*)], [Colin Tapley (*Roger's friend*)], [Chief Big Tree, White Bird (*Indians*)], [Harold Entwistle (*Court clerk*)], [Harold Nelson (*Judge*)], [Hayden Stevenson (*Deputy marshal*)], [Thomas L. Brower (*Salem town marshal*)], [Edwin Mordant (*Elder*)], [Howard Davies, Ray Hanford (*Bailiffs*)], [Wade Lane (*Clerk*)], [John Power (*Minister*)], [James Marcus (*Sea captain*)], [Jack Deery, Clive Morgan (*Non-commissioned officers*)], [Colin Kelly, Sidney D'Albrook (*Hunters*)], [Hal Cooke (*Horseman*)], [Joseph Tozer (*Clergyman*)], [Dave Dunbar (*Man in montage*)], [John Spacey (*Business man*)], [Harry Cording (*Guard*)], [Grace Kern (*Convict*)], [Wally Albright (*Jasper*)], [Jack H. Richardson (*Sheriff*)], [Jack Daley (*Hangman*)], [George Magrill (*Sailor*)], [Charles McAvoy (*Father*)], [Vangie Beilby (*Mother*)], [Tommy Bupp], [Ricca K. Allen], [Agnes Ayres], [Wilson Benge], [Sidney Bracy], [Fritzi Brunette], [Herbert Evans], [Fryda Gagne], [Edith Hallor], [Frank H. Hammond], [Carol Holloway], [Harold Howard], [Ward Lane], [Stella Le Saint], [Ralph Lewis], [Vera Lewis], [Anne O'Neal], [Rita Owin], [Audrey Reynolds], [Allen D. Sewall], [Walter Soderling], [Al Stewart], [William Wagner], [Elsie Prescott].

Historical, Drama. [*Print viewed*]. In 1692, in a milieu of Puritan ethics which are strictly enforced by church elder Nathaniel Goode, the women of Salem, Massachusetts become fascinated with stories about Satan told to them by Tituba, a slave in the Goode household. Meanwhile, Barbara Clarke, who lives with her widowed Aunt Ellen and her son Timothy, meets fugitive Roger Coverman, who fled Virginia after being pronounced a traitor for resisting taxation. In love with Roger's free spirit, Barbara continues to meet him in secret. As the town's fear of the occult grows, two women are arrested for witchcraft at Cape Ann. Virginia Goode then steals her father's book on witchcraft, and, caught by Tituba, she is punished by her father and schemes for vengeance against Tituba. During the height of the town's hysteria and paranoia, Virginia feigns a hallucinating fever which convinces the parish elders that she is also a victim of Tituba's witchcraft. The slave is arrested and forced to confess, implicating two other town innocents as well. Barbara boldly moves to defend Tituba until Aunt Ellen reveals that Barbara's mother was accused of witchcraft and hanged in England. To escape the frenzy of Salem, Roger leaves with his recluse uncle, Jeremiah Adams, for Florida (which is under Spanish rule) via Boston, but Jeremiah is killed by seamen who seek the reward for Roger's arrest, and he is put in jail. Back in Salem, when a harmless old woman named Rebecca Nurse is sentenced to die at "Gallows Hill" by the Cheeves, a couple who carries an old grudge against her, Barbara defends her and is accused of being a witch herself. Timothy, who saw Barbara kiss Roger good-bye in the night, tells the court Barbara had assured him she was with "no man" and the judge twists his testimony into an admission of Barbara's consorting with the Devil. Meanwhile, Roger escapes from prison, ironically on the day the new governor of Virginia arrives with his pardon, and makes his way to Salem, where fifteen people have now been hanged for witchcraft. During Barbara's trial, she refuses to confess to being a witch, but, because she must protect Roger's anonymity, is unable to prove that she was not with Satan. When Barbara's friend John rises to defend her, his wife Martha, fearing it was John whom Barbara was with, reveals the truth about the death of Barbara's mother, sealing her fate. As Barbara is about to be hanged, Roger finally arrives, solving the mystery of Barbara's lover. Virginia then admits that it was spite that made her incriminate Tituba. Finally realizing that all were wrongfully accused, Crown Justice Sewall appeals to the governor to abolish the trial for witchcraft. As Barbara is let out of prison, she and Roger embrace. The governor then orders that the tree at Gallows Hill be burned, and the villagers set fire to it. *The Devil. Executions. Hysteria (Social psychology). Puritans. Salem (MA)–History. United States–History–Colonial period, ca. 1600-1775. Witchcraft. African Americans. Confession (Law). False accusations. Florida. Fugitives. Governors. Hereditary tendencies. Injustice. Misogyny. Mistaken identity. Murder. Mysticism. Nieces. Rescues. Revenge. Rewards. Romance. Salem (MA). Samuel Sewall. Slavery. Small town life. Taxation. Trials. Virginians. Widows.*

Note: A written prologue that opens the film states that the story was based on "authentic records of the year 1692." According to the film's pressbook, the sermon preached by Rev. Samuel Parris was taken "almost wholly" from a rare collection of sermons by Reverend Deodat Lawson, who served with Parris at Salem Village. As reported in the pressbook from information found in the Essex Museum in Salem, in Puritan days, there were two Salems: Salem Town, on the seacoast, which is now modern Salem; and Salem Village (now called Danvers), a farming community located seven miles inland, where most of this film is set. The film was shot on location on a farm four miles outside of Santa Cruz, CA, where Paramount reproduced the Salem countryside on forty acres of land. A sailor's shanty was built on a bluff overlooking the Pacific Ocean at Carmel, CA. According to the pressbook, the British Museum supplied two ancient songs for the film: a sea chanty written in 1530 and a ballad, "Bid Me But Live," ca. 1630, which was sung by Fred MacMurray in the picture. According to a 26 Jan 1937 news item in *HR*, an eight-hundred foot trailer was being prepared featuring director Frank Lloyd in the cutting room. "Action" scenes shot through the Moviola were also included.
According to files in the MPAA/PCA Collection at the AMPAS Library, on 14 May 1936, Joseph I. Breen, Director of the PCA, wrote to Paramount distribution executive John Hammell with his reaction to an outline of Bradley King's story, which was called "Between Two Worlds." Breen requested that Hammell have his research department verify whether alleged witches were actually burned in Salem. Breen wrote, "It is our impression that there were no burnings—rather was the alleged punishment confined to hangings." The film's program included the following note: "The widely held belief that there were witch burnings doubtless arises from witchcraft annals in England and France (most notably Joan of Arc) where there were many burnings. This, however, was never true in America." In reference to a kiss between Roger and Barbara, the PCA cautioned the filmmakers in a letter dated 27 Aug 1936: "they should, of course, not be lying on the ground." Further caution was expressed about the

portrayal of the clergy: "While there is of course ample historical grounds to prove that many of the clergy were caught up in the hysteria of the time, it might be well to counter-balance this in your picture by introducing briefly another minister [besides Reverend Samuel Parris] who will typify the more rational element among the clergy." On 28 Aug 1936, Breen wrote to Hammell, quoting the Production Code, "Ministers of religion in their characterizations of ministers should not be used in comedy, villains, or as unpleasant persons," and warning Hammell to "make definite changes in your script RE: Rev. Parris to bring picture in compliance with above Code provisions." An inter-office memo dated 31 Aug 1936 from Geoffrey Shurlock, Breen's assistant, outlines Hammell's response to the previous letter. The memo states: [director Frank] "Lloyd aware of danger in portrayal of the minister. Rev. Parris, played by [Ivan] Simpson, will portray him as stern upright minister, but with no tinge of the blue nose about it. They are also cutting out most, if not all, of the scenes in which minister is shown (in script) actually connected with the witch-hunting. [They also will be] introducing the character of another minister who will represent the liberal viewpoint, and who will protest against the witch-hunting hysteria of the time."
According to a news item in *HR* on 29 Dec 1936, following a sneak preview of the film, Paramount decided to revise the ending, and recalled the company back for a few days of retakes. A script dated 15 Oct 1936 in the Paramount Script Collection at the AMPAS Library indicates that in the preview version, after Roger saves Barbara from being hanged, Sewall calls an end to the witchhunt, and Barbara collapses into Roger's arms. Elder Goode then realizes Virginia has lied, and Sewall prays to God for forgiveness. A member of the mob then calls for the burning of the tree at Gallows Hill, and the film ends. In the script to the revised final reel dated 29 Dec 1936, the governor signs a decree abolishing the trial for witchcraft and orders the tree at Gallows Hill to be burned. (The signing of a proclamation that freed prisoners of the witchhunt appeared in an early script, but had been removed by 1 Sep 1936.) Later Barbara emerges from her dungeon cell, where she embraces Roger. The tree is then burned. In an early script dated 22 Aug 1936, John is struck by a soldier while defending Barbara at her hanging and dies. According to contemporary news items, this film was screenwriter Howard Estabrook's first producing assignment for Paramount. Some reviews erroneously credit Russell Simpson as "Rev. Samuel Parris." Russell appears as "Village marshal," and Ivan Simpson appears as "Rev. Samuel Parris."

DV 21 Jan 1937, p. 3. *FD* 26 Jan 1937, p. 8. *HR* 31 Aug 1936, p. 20. *HR* 2 Nov 1936, p. 14. *HR* 26 Oct 1936, p. 6. *HR* 29 Jun 1936, p. 3. *HR* 29 Dec 1936, p. 2. *HR* 21 Jan 1937, p. 3. *HR* 26 Jan 1937, p. 4. *MPD* 22 Jan 1937, p. 12. *MPH* 19 Dec 1936, p. 42, 47. *MPH* 30 Jan 1937, p. 47. *MPSI* Jul 1937, p. 11. *NYT* 4 Mar 1937, p. 27. *Var* 10 Mar 1937, p. 14.

LA MAISON DE LA PEUR see **NOCHE DE DUENDES**

MALAVITA see **PARIGI AFFASCINA; OVVERO, MALAVITA**

MAM LEI TSUN FU see **WON LEE SHUEN FU**

MAMÁ (Spanish language)
Fox Film Corp. *Dist* Fox Film Corp. **1931**; New York opening: 25 Sep 1931; Prod: 29 Jun—17 Jul 1931. Sd; b&w. 9 reels, 7,240 ft. 80 min. Passed by the National Board of Review. Spanish language.
Supervisión y dirección de [*Supv and dir*] Gregorio Martínez Sierra and Benito Perojo. [*Addl dir* Bert E. Sebell]. [*Screen adpt* José López Rubio]. [*Photog* Sidney Wagner and Daniel Clark]. [*Film ed* Dorothy Spencer]. [*Makeup* Jack Dawn].
Source: Based on the play *Mamá* by Gregorio Martínez Sierra (Spain, 1913).
Cast: CATALINA BÁRCENA (*Mercedes*), Rafael Rivelles (*Santiago*), María Luz Callejo (*Cecilia*), Julio Peña (*José María*), José Nieto (*Alfonso* [*de Heredia*]), Andrés de Segurola (*Fernando*), Félix de Pomés (*Mauricio*), José Alcántara (*Julio*), Ralph Navarro (*Carlos*), Rafael Calvo (*Velasco*), Enriqueta Soler (*Juana*), [Carmen Jiménez], [Alma Real].
Domestic, Comedy. [*Not viewed*]. Mercedes, a socialite who is married to Santiago, one of the richest men in Madrid, gambles with friends and loses 23,000 pesatas, which she borrowed from her friend Alfonso. Unknown to Mercedes, Alfonso is pretending to fall in love with her in order to leech off her husband's fortune. When she arrives home late, Santiago informs her that their children, José María and Cecilia, will be coming home from college the next day. She excitedly tells him that she will face her familial duties with zest on the day following their arrival, as she has several pressing social engagements. On the train, José and Cecilia chatter happily about their mother and the prospect of being a family for the first time in many years. That evening at Cecilia's debut ball, Alfonso propositions Mercedes. She declines his offer but pointedly promises to repay her gambling debt. Determined to swindle the family, Alfonso flirts with Cecilia and wins her affection. The next morning, after asking her father Fernando, who cannot help, for the money she owes Alfonso, Mercedes is forced to seek Santiago's aid. Assuming that the money will be spent on her father's escapades, Santiago refuses to give her any. She leaves his office and finds Alfonso waiting to speak with her.

José walks in on them, which causes Alfonso to leave, and Mercedes then tells her son the truth about her debt. The next morning, Alfonso, arriving to take Cecilia out, is greeted by José, who gives him the money owed by his mother and asks Alfonso to stay away from the family. José is summoned to his father's office, where Santiago accuses him of stealing money from his office and, although he knows the money is for Mercedes, tells José he wishes never to see him again. When José comes home to pack, he tells Mercedes, who is touched by his act. On her way to confront Santiago, Mercedes spies Alfonso and Cecilia in the garden, and she exposes Alfonso's treachery, causing Cecilia to flee in tears and forcing Alfonso to leave. She then goes to Santiago's office and berates him for his behavior. She says that he has made all of the decisions in their marriage, including sending the children away to school, which she now realizes created a void in her life that she filled with a busy social schedule. Shocked by her outburst, Santiago asks her forgiveness, and when José comes in, he and Santiago embrace. Mercedes and Santiago both cancels plans to go out separately that evening, and Mercedes, desiring a "homey" atmosphere, has a servant light a fire. She happily proclaims that her new family life shall begin immediately. *Family relationships. Marriage. Neglected wives. Socialites. Balls (Parties). Debt. False accusations. Gambling. Madrid (Spain). Seduction. Swindlers and swindling.*

Note: The onscreen credits were taken from a print, and the plot summary was based on a screen continuity in the Twentieth Century-Fox Produced Scripts Collection at the UCLA Theater Arts Library. According to a contemporary source, Bert E. Sebell took over as director after production began.

CM Nov 1931, p. 828. *FD* 20 Jul 1933, p. 6. *NYT* 8 Jul 1933, p. 14.

MAMA RAVIOLI see **EAST OF THE RIVER**

MAMELE (Yiddish language)

Green-Film. *Dist* Sphinx Films Corp. Jan **1939**; New York opening: 23 Dec 1938; Prod: ended early Aug 1938 in a Warsaw, Poland studio. Sd; b&w. 10 reels, 9,180 ft. 102-103 or 109 min. PCA cert no. 02411. *Country of origin* Poland. Yiddish language with English subtitles.

Pres JOSEPH GREEN. *Assoc prod* Bernard J. Weinberg. *Dir* Joseph Green and Konrad Tom. *Scenario* Konrad Tom. *English titles* Julian Leigh. *Photog* Seweryn Steinwurcel. *Art dir* Jacob Kalish. *Mus* Abe Ellstein.

Song(s): "Mazel," "Ich Sing" and "Abi Geziunt Ken Men Sliklach Sain," words by Molly Picon, music by Abraham Ellstein.

Source: Based on the play *Mamele* by Meyer Schwartz (New York, Feb 1927).

Cast: MOLLY PICON [(*Chavchi Samet, also known as Mamele*)], Edmund Zayenda [(*Schlesinger*)], Max Bozyk [(*Berel Samet*)], Gertrude Bullman [(*Bertha Samet*)], Simche Fostel [(*Naderman*)], Ola Shlifko [(*Yetka Samet*)], Menashe Oppenheim [(*Max Katz*)], Carl Latowich [(*Zeisher*)], Max Pearlman [(*David Samet*)], Ruth Turkow [(*Bailchi*)], Lew Schriftzecer [(*Konchicker*)], Max Brin.

Yiddish, Domestic, Comedy-drama, with songs. [*Print viewed*]. In Lodz, Poland, Chavchi Samet is the "mamele," or little mother, to her widowed father, three brothers and two sisters, none of whom appreciate the hard work she does to keep their lives orderly, except the two youngest boys, Zimke and Avremel. When Max Katz, an underworld figure with whom Chavchi's sister Bertha is involved, comes to take Bertha away for *Sukkoth*, a Jewish holiday, Chavchi's father, a layabout, is impressed with Katz. Chavchi, however, is suspicious of him, and she insists that she go along as a chaperone, but Bertha and Katz leave without her. That night, Chavchi hears from across the courtyard, her neighbor Schlesinger, in whom she has tried to get Bertha interested, play the violin, and she sings from her window. Meanwhile, Zimke, who has received some money from Katz to deliver a message to two of his comrades in a club, gets drunk with them. Finding Zimke's bed empty, Chavchi goes to the club and locates him, and when she sees a note with a floor plan and address, she surmises that Katz is a criminal. The next day, on *Sukkoth*, as the neighbors come for a feast, Chavchi serves Schlesinger, as she urges her neighbor Bailchi to serve her brother David, whom she would like Bailchi to marry. Two men come for Zimke, and Chavchi overhears them talk about a planned robbery. She follows them and sees them make a hole in the wall, then she falls on a ladder, which collapses on them. She takes Zimke home, where she applies bandages to his head. When Katz visits, Chavchi locks him in and, by threatening to shoot him with a fake gun, makes him write a

letter to Bertha saying that he never loved her, that the police are after him for a theft, and that he is leaving the country. When Bertha reads the letter, she runs from their room in tears. Chavchi is successful in bringing Bailchi and David together, and Bailchi's parents prepare a meal to celebrate their upcoming wedding. Schlesinger, noticing Chavchi's absence, finds her alone paging through a scrapbook of photographs of her grandmother. As she cries because, she says, no one ever has a good word for her, Schlesinger promises that her day will come. Chavchi now begins to dress up, and when Schlesinger invites her to the opera, she accepts. When Bertha learns that Schlesinger is to be the first violinist and concert master in Chekhotsinek, she asks Chavchi to act as a matchmaker for them. Later, Bertha learns that Chavchi forced Katz to write the letter, and the whole family berates Chavchi. Having had enough of their ingratitude, Chavchi leaves to stay with Schlesinger and his mother at their country home. Without Chavchi, the Samet house quickly becomes a mess, while Chavchi enjoys herself with the Schlesingers. As Schlesinger is about to propose one evening, the Samets turn up and plead for Chavchi to return, but she refuses; however, when Zimke says that he hasn't gone to Hebrew school, and Chavchi sees Avremel's filthy face and neck, she agrees to return for the children's sake. Later, at the wedding feast for Chavchi and Schlesinger, Chavchi, still the "mamele" of the family, makes sure everything is in order and even pours milk for her kitty, before going off with Schlesinger. *Drudges. Family life. Gratitude. Jews. Lodz (Poland). Self-sacrifice. Criminals. Drunkenness. Letters. Matchmakers. Neighbors. Nightclubs. Opera. Romance. Sukkoth. Threats. Violinists. Weddings. Widowers.*

Note: The play was reviewed in *NYT* under the English title *Kid Mother. NYT* and *Var* give *Little Mother* as the English translation of the title. Some scenes in this film were shot in Kazimierz, Poland a suburb outside of Warsaw, in Lodz and in the Warsaw film studios, which were subsidized by the government. This was the third film that Green-Film produced in Poland. According to modern sources, Jacob Kalish, Molly Picon's husband, had unsuccessfully tried in 1932 to get Columbia Pictures to produce an English-language film based on the play, in which Picon starred in the 1920s. Modern sources state that the play takes place in New York's Lower East Side; that Lodz, Poland, where the film version is set, was producer Joseph Green's hometown; that some scenes were shot in Ciechocinek in Poland; that J. M. Neuman did the adaption with Konrad Tom, who received screen credit; and that Jacek Rotmil and Stefan Norris were the designers.

Box 21 Jan 1939. *Exh* 11 Jan 1939. *FD* 18 Jan 1939, p. 6. *MPD* 4 Aug 1938, p. 2. *MPD* 29 Dec 1938, p. 7. *NYT* 26 Dec 1938, p. 29. *Var* 11 Jan 1939, p. 13.

THE MAN ABOVE THE LAW (Native Americans, Navajo)

Triangle Film Corp. *Dist* Triangle Distributing Corp. 6 Jan **1918**. Si; b&w. 5 reels.

Dir Raymond Wells. *Scen* Lanier Bartlett. *Cam* Pliny Horn.

Cast: Jack Richardson (*Duke Chalmers*), Josie Sedgwick (*Esther Brown*), Claire McDowell (*Natchah*), May Giraci (*Tonah*).

Western. Having been unlucky in love, Duke Chalmers renounces civilization and moves to New Mexico, where he establishes himself as an illicit whiskey trader. Although he does not really love her, Duke marries Natchah, a Navaho Indian, who bears him a daughter, Tonah. When Esther Brown arrives from the East and opens a school in the small New Mexican settlement, Duke denies Tonah permission to attend, but Esther refuses to abandon her interest in the child and soon grows to love her. Duke rescues Esther from a pair of drunken Mexicans, after which he falls in love with her. Esther, however, reminds him of his duty toward his wife and daughter, whereupon Duke closes his shop and takes his family to a new life in the Far West. *Family life. Indians of North America. Settlement workers. Traders. Unrequited love. Drunkenness. Mexicans. New Mexico. Rescues.*

ETR 12 Jan 1918, p. 520. *MPN* 12 Jan 1918, p. 294. *MPW* 12 Jan 1918, p. 241. *Var* 4 Jan 1918, p. 40. *Wid's* 3 Jan 1918, p. 844.

MAN AND HIS ANGEL (Russian Americans)

Triumph Film Corp. *Dist* Equitable Motion Pictures Corp. released through World Film Corp. 13 Mar **1916** [©Triumph Film Corp.; 14 Feb 1916; LP7748]. Si; b&w. 5 reels.

Dir Burton King. *Story* Stanley Dark. *Cam* Henry G. Frommer.

Cast: Jane Grey (*Sonia Dimitri*), Willard Deshielle (*Paul Dimitri*), Edward MacKay (*Schuyler*), Robert Lee Hill (*Arthur Sutton*), Henri Bergman (*David Tryne*), Mayme Kelso (*Kitty Fish*), Adolphe Menjou.

Drama. Exiled from Russia, nobleman Paul Dimitri comes to New York, opens a book store, and raises his daughter Sonia without telling her about her royal heritage. Paul's employee, David Tryne, a

hunchback, falls in love with Sonia and, after Paul dies, does his best to end her engagement to Schuyler. To effect a breakup, David spreads the rumor that Sonia was born out of wedlock, even though he knows about her ancestry. Schuyler nevertheless reasserts his eagerness to marry her, but Sonia feels herself unworthy of him, and ends their romance. Then, however, tormented by his actions, David impulsively reveals the truth about Sonia, after which she and Schuyler are married. *Hunchbacks. Illegitimacy. Immigrants. Nobility. Reputation. Rumors. Russian Americans. Booksellers and bookselling. Exiles. Guilt. New York City. Russia.*

Motog 18 Mar 1916, p. 649. *MPN* 25 Mar 1916, p. 1772. *MPW* 25 Mar 1916, p. 2024, 2090. *NYDM* 18 Mar 1916, p. 33. *Wid's* 16 Mar 1916, p. 444.

THE MAN BEHIND THE GUN (Latino)

Warner Bros. Pictures, Inc.; A Warner Bros.—First National Picture. *Dist* Warner Bros. Pictures, Inc. 13 Jan **1953**; Prod: early Dec 1951—early Feb 1952 [©Warner Bros. Pictures, Inc.; 28 Dec 1952; LP2201]. Sd (RCA Sound System); col (Technicolor). 7,413 or 7,596 ft. 82 or 84-85 min. PCA cert no. 15756.

Prod Robert Sisk. *Dir* Felix Feist. [*Asst dir* Frank Mattison]. *Scr* John Twist. *Story* Robert Buckner. *Dir of photog* Bert Glennon. *Technicolor color consultant* Mitchell Koyaleski. *Art dir* Douglas Bacon. *Film ed* Owen Marks. *Set dec* William Wallace. *Ward* Milo Anderson. *Mus* David Buttolph. *Orch* Maurice De Packh. *Sd* Leslie G. Hewitt. *Makeup artist* Gordon Bau. [*Whips* David Kashner].

Song(s): "La Paloma," music and lyrics by Sebastian Yradier; "Some Sunday Morning," music by M. K. Jerome and Ray Heindorf, lyrics by Ted Koehler; "Adios, mi amor," "Adios, Mama Carlotta" and "Jarabe tapatio," composers undetermined.

Cast: RANDOLPH SCOTT [(*Maj. Ransome Callicut* [*also known as Rick Bryce*)], Patrice Wymore [(*Lora Roberts*)], Dick Wesson [(*"Monk" Walker*)], Philip Carey [(*Capt. Roy Giles*)], Lina Romay [(*Chona Degnon*)], Roy Roberts [(*Sen. Mark Sheldon*)], Morris Ankrum [(*Bram Creegan*)], Katharine Warren [(*Phoebe Sheldon*)], Alan Hale, Jr. [(*Olaf Swenson*)], Douglas Fowley [(*Buckley*)], Tony Caruso [(*Vic Sutro*)], Clancy Cooper [(*Kansas Collins*)], Robert Cabal [(*Joaquin Murietta*)], [James Brown (*Lt. Catliff*)], [Ralph Gibson (*Water seller*)], [Reed Howes (*Dude*)], [Rory Mallinson, John Logan, Lee Morgan, Ray Spiker (*Troopers*)], [Ed Hearn (*Traveler*)], [Terry Frost (*Citizen*)], [Charles Horvath (*Hoodlum*)], [Art Millan (*Waiter*)], [Rex Lease (*Lookout*)], [Jack Parker (*Horseman*)], [James Bellah (*Gunman*)], [Billy Vincent (*Henchman*)], [Albert Morin (*Pico*)], [Edward Colemans (*Carillo*)], [Herbert Deans (*Nichols*)], [Nestor Amaral (*Musician*)], [Vicki Raaf].

Western, with songs. [*Print viewed*]. In 1853, Maj. Ransome Callicut and his old Army buddy, "Monk" Walker, arrive in the port of San Pedro, California, which Callicut describes as a "maze of intrigue." Although Callicut is unable to disclose his secret mission to anyone, he enlists the aid of another former Army comrade, Olaf Swenson, who now drives a stagecoach in Southern California. Before boarding Olaf's stage to Los Angeles, Callicut informs his two friends that his undercover name is Rick Bryce. The other passengers include attractive and strong-minded schoolteacher Lora Roberts; state senator Bram Creegan, who believes that Southern California should become a separate, slave state; Sen. Mark Sheldon, who strongly disagrees with Creegan; and notorious gunman Vic Sutro. When Sutro tries to rob the stagecoach, Callicut outmaneuvers him, and later turns the outlaw over to U.S. Army captain Roy Giles in Los Angeles. Callicut then learns that Lora has come to Los Angeles to marry the captain and surmises that she is the teacher he has been sent to replace. Giles, however, identifies Callicut and accuses him of being wanted by the Army for desertion and murder. Later, Callicut, still posing as Bryce, visits Sen. Mark Sheldon and his sister Phoebe. Sheldon plans to have the state indict Creegan for charging excessive fees for irrigation and drinking water. Callicut then visits Sheldon's guest, Lora, who tells him that Sheldon is investigating Buckley's Palacio, a local dance hall frequented by secessionists. At the Palacio that night, Olaf pretends to lift a 1,300-pound rock to win a $1,500 prize, while in the basement, Monk and Callicut use a post to surreptitiously lift the rock. After Creegan threatens Sheldon, the senator is shot dead just as the post breaks. Monk and Olaf are locked up in the garrison, while Callicut, who remains in the basement, discovers a cache of guns. Callicut hides in the room of singer and secessionist Chona Degnon. As he enters, he finds Giles kissing Chona but promises to keep silent if Giles releases Monk and Olaf. After

Giles's departure, Callicut returns the prize money and then joins Chona in watching as Creegan is rescued from hanging by a gang of armed men. The next day, Chona offers the impressive new "schoolteacher" a high position in the growing secessionist army, explaining that its major objective is to control the water supply. She is about to reveal the names of the movement's leaders when Callicut unknowingly drops a card identifying himself as an undercover agent. Callicut realizes that Chona is now aware of his mission and is prepared when outlaw Joaquin Murietta, who has been dealing weapons for Chona, arrives to kill him that night. Callicut persuades the young outlaw to become his spy, then reveals his mission to Lora. The following day, Giles releases Monk and Olaf, and Callicut reveals to him that the man he is wanted for killing was a spy and that he is not a fugitive. Later, Callicut accuses Giles of conspiring with the traitors, but after Sutro fires at him and is shot to death, Callicut's trust in Giles is renewed. During the night, Sheldon, who faked his death, kidnaps Lora and takes her to the rebels' camp. Back at the Palacio, Chona sings "Adios, Mi Amor," signaling to the revolutionaries that it is time to take control of the reservoirs. In the basement, however, Murietta sets off a series of explosions which destroy the rebels' gun supply. Tipped off by a remark made by Sheldon's sister Phoebe, Callicut digs up the senator's grave and finds Creegan's corpse inside. Later, Chona meets Sheldon at his ranch, where Murietta promises to deliver more arms. After Lora unwittingly reveals that Murietta is secretly working for Callicut, Murietta escapes from the ranch and reports Lora's kidnapping to Callicut. On the way to Sheldon's camp, Callicut and Murietta encounter Buckley, who informs them of the new rebel plan: to dam the river canyon and dry up all the reservoirs. In the morning, Olaf and Monk, disguised as a settler and his wife, approach the mountain camp, while Callicut rides quietly behind their wagon. The disguise enables them to distract the lookouts so that Giles and his troops can surprise Sheldon in his headquarters. Just before Giles attacks, Chona threatens Lora with a knife, and the two fight. Lora finally gasps that she no longer loves Giles, and that if Chona testifies against Sheldon, she can have the captain. Sheldon overhears this, kills Chona and, realizing that his forces face defeat, tries to flee the scene, but is captured by Callicut. Later, Los Angeles celebrates the defeat of the secessionists with a big fiesta, while Lora welcomes her new pupils, and Callicut kisses her. *California–History–1846-1850. Insurgency. Los Angeles (CA). Secession. Undercover agents. Water. Bandits. Chases. Dance halls. Exhumation. Explosions. Female impersonation. Fistfights. Gunfighters. Gunrunners. Hostages. Impersonation and imposture. Jealousy. Lynching. Mexican Americans. Joaquin Murieta. Parties. Prizes and trophies. Rescues. Romantic rivalry. San Pedro (CA). Schoolteachers. Senators. Singers. Slavery. Swedish Americans. Swindlers and swindling.*

Note: Working titles of this film included *City of the Angels* and *Man with a Gun.* According to information contained in the copyright record of the film, Lina Romay's father was the Mexican vice-consul in Los Angeles at the time of the picture's production. The real Joaquin Murieta, whose name is spelled "Murietta" in reviews, was a famous bandit who was born in Mexico around 1830. In 1849, Murieta came to California, and in 1853, was killed by Rangers serving under Capt. Harry S. Love. This film bears little resemblance to Murieta's actual life.

Box 20 Dec 1952. *DV* 18 Dec 1952, p. 3. *Exh* 31 Dec 1952, p. 3440. *FD* 29 Dec 1952, p. 6. *Har* 20 Dec 1952, p. 204. *HR* 21 Dec 1951, p. 19. *HR* 1 Feb 1952, p. 11. *HR* 18 Dec 1952, p. 3. *MPHPD* 27 Dec 1952, p. 1662. *Var* 24 Dec 1952, p. 14.

A MAN CALLED PETER (Scottish Americans)

Twentieth Century-Fox Film Corp. *Dist* Twentieth Century-Fox Film Corp. Mar **1955**; World premieres in New York and in Glasgow, Scotland: 31 Mar 1955; Prod: late Sep—late Nov 1954 [©Twentieth Century-Fox Film Corp.; 1 Apr 1955; LP4990]. Sd (Western Electric Recording); col (De Luxe); CinemaScope; Lenses by Bausch & Lomb. 13 reels, 10,727 ft. 119 min. PCA cert no. 17246.

[*Exec prod* Darryl F. Zanuck]. *Prod* Samuel G. Engel. *Dir* Henry Koster. *Asst dir* David Silver. [*2d unit dir* James D. Clark]. *Scr* Eleanore Griffin. [*Consultant and tech adv* Catherine Marshall]. *Dir of photog* Harold Lipstein. *Spec photog eff* Ray Kellogg. *Color consultant* Leonard Doss. *Art dir* Lyle Wheeler and Maurice Ransford. *Film ed* Robert Simpson. *Set dec* Walter M. Scott and Chester Bayhi. *Ward dir* Charles LeMaire. *Cost des* Renie. *Mus* Alfred Newman. *Orch* Edward B. Powell. *Voc supv* Ken Darby. *Sd* Bernard Freericks and Warren B. Delaplain. *Makeup artist* Ben Nye. *Hair stylist* Helen Turpin. [*Unit mgr* William Eckhardt]. [*Stand-in for Jean Peters* Marion McDonough].

Source: Based on the biography *A Man Called Peter* by Catherine Marshall (New York, 1951).

Cast: Richard Todd [(*Peter Marshall*)], Jean Peters [(*Catherine Marshall*)], Marjorie Rambeau [(*Miss Laura Fowler*)], Jill Esmond [(*Mrs. Findlay*)], Les Tremayne [(*Senator Willis K. Harvey*)], Robert Burton [(*Mr. Peyton*)], Gladys Hurlbut [(*Mrs. Peyton*)], Richard Garrick [(*Col. Evanston Whiting*)], Gloria Gordon [(*Barbara Tremaine*)], Billy Chapin [(*Peter John Marshall*)], [Sally Corner (*Mrs. Whiting*)], [Voltaire Perkins (*Senator Wiley*)], [Edward Earle (*Senator Prescott*)], [Marietta Canty (*Emma*)], [Peter Votrian (*Peter Marshall, as a boy*)], [Arthur Tovey (*Usher*)], [Mimi Hutson, Janet Stewart (*College girls*)], [Sam McDaniel (*Maitre D'*)], [Dorothy Neumann (*Miss Crilly*)], [Oliver Hartwell (*Janitor*)], [Doris Lloyd (*Miss Hopkins*)], [William Forrest (*Seminary president*)], [Barbara Morrison (*Miss Standish*)], [Betty Caulfield (*June Whitney*)], [Ann Davis (*Ruby Coleman*)], [Carlyle Mitchell (*Dr. Milton Black*)], [Emmett Lynn (*Mr. Briscoe*)], [William Walker (*Butler*)], [Charles Evans (*President of Senate*)], [Larry Kent (*Chaplain at Naval Academy*)], [Ruth Clifford (*Nurse*)], [Ben Wright (*Mr. Findlay*)], [Bruce Underhill (*Georgia Tech. player*)], [Sam Gilman, Richard Collier (*Parking lot attendants*)], [Jim Murphy (*Boy*)], [John Intlekafer (*Baseball player*)], [Robert Lynn, Jr. (*Ensign*)], [Ashley Cowan (*Soldier*)], [Robert Lynn, Steve Darrell (*Doctors*)], [Tom Selden (*Sailor*)], [Marjorie Hellen (*Young girl*)], [Barry Bernard, Charles Keane (*Stevedores*)], [Dayton Lummis (*Scottish policeman*)], [Ed Mundy (*Old man*)], [Roy Glenn, Sr.], [Amanda Randolph].

Biography, **Religious**, **Drama**. [*Print viewed*]. As a boy in Coatbridge, Scotland, in 1915, Peter Marshall makes several attempts to run away to sea from the docks in nearby Glasgow. Peter's stepfather, Mr. Findlay, tells him that he will have to find a job, and he goes to work in the tube mills, but continues his education at night school. Seven years later, while returning from school one night, Peter finds himself on a foggy patch of land. He thinks he hears a voice, then trips and narrowly misses falling into a quarry. Peter feels that it was God's voice and tells his mother that he intends to become a minister and that God is sending him to America. After three years of working double shifts at the mill, Peter saves enough to buy passage to America. With faith and trust in his heart, he arrives and awaits further "orders from the Chief." Peter works in a variety of jobs before he is led by God, he believes, to the Columbia Theological Seminary in Decatur, Georgia. He graduates *summa cum laude* and is offered two positions, one at a large church in Atlanta, the other in a little town, Covington. Peter asks the Lord for advice and selects Covington, but later moves to the Atlanta church where he encounters an indifferent congregation, encumbered by debt. However, Peter's stimulating sermons draw large crowds, and many young people from nearby colleges attend, among them Catherine Wood, a senior at Agnes Scott College. Catherine attends Sunday service for two years without summoning up the courage to talk with Peter, with whom she has fallen in love. However, her college receives an invitation from Peter to send a student to speak at a temperance youth rally and Catherine is selected. The audience is mostly composed of rowdy young people, but Catherine talks about the role of women in religious and social history, quoting from Peter's sermons, and wins the crowd over. After the rally, Peter drives her back to the college and tells her that he fully expects that the Lord will select his wife for him, but asks if he might see her again. A week later, their date ends with Peter realizing that Catherine is to be his wife and he proposes. That fall, they marry and during their honeymoon in Cape Cod, Peter tells Catherine that he has accepted a call to the New York Avenue Presbyterian Church in Washington, D.C., the church of the presidents. On their arrival, they are invited to a dinner party, given by Col. Evanston Whiting, president of the church's board of trustees, at which they learn that the church's first minister, in the early 1800's, was also a Scot. Peter's first sermon to a half-filled church is not well received, particularly by Miss Laura Fowler, an elderly member of Washington society, who feels that Peter, as an immigrant, has no right to invite just anybody to attend the church. However, Peter's blunt, popular approach attracts many young people to the church and his sermons become very well attended. Four years pass, and Senator Willis K. Harvey, an early supporter of Peter, comes to him with the moral dilemma of being forced by the political machine back home to vote against his

conscience on a land bill; however, after talking with Peter, he casts the deciding defeating vote. On December 7, 1941, Catherine gives birth to a son, Peter John. Later that day, after preaching at the Annapolis Naval Academy, Peter hears the news on his car radio of the Japanese attack on Pearl Harbor. During the war years, Peter, with Catherine's and the congregation's help, operates a canteen for the Armed Forces in the church's basement. However, when Miss Fowler discovers a sailor and a girl necking in Lincoln's parlor, she initiates a campaign to have the canteen closed, as she abhors Peter's apparent disregard for her church's traditions and history. Peter explains that the couple were on their two-hour honeymoon; he had married them earlier that day and the sailor was shipping out that evening. Peter threatens to leave unless the canteen stays open, and he prevails. Later, Catherine learns that she has contracted non-communicable tuberculosis and will have to remain in bed for three or four months. When Catherine does not improve after many months, Peter feels that his relationship with God is failing. He wonders if he has become egotistical, and Catherine feels equally lost and abandoned by God. However, during a radio broadcast of one of Peter's sermons, both become revitalized and Catherine experiences a partial recovery. The doctors recommend continued rest and a change of scenery, so Peter buys a small house on Cape Cod for the summer months. Peter and Peter John build a boat together and the family adopts a puppy, Jeff. Back in Washington, as Peter is delivering a sermon, he collapses, suffering a coronary thrombosis, and is given less than a fighting chance of survival. Many pray for his recovery and the crisis passes. Although the doctors tell him not to preach for at least a year, Peter returns to work immediately. Over the years, Peter has won over Miss Fowler, and after his first service back, she presents him with a family heirloom: a button from the jacket of a another Scottish immigrant, John Paul Jones. On the tenth anniversary of his becoming an American citizen, Peter is invited to become Chaplain to the United States Senate. Catherine and Senator Harvey, fearing the additional strain on him, try to dissuade him from accepting but have to relent. One night, however, Peter experiences great pain and as he is taken to hospital tells Catherine, "See you darling, see you in the morning." In the morning, Catherine learns that Peter has died. Senator Harvey reads Peter's last prayer to the Senate. In the summer, Catherine, Peter John and Jeff return to Cape Cod where they find solace on the boat Peter John and his father built. *Clergy. Marriage. Peter Marshall. Presbyterians. Religion. Scottish Americans. Sermons. United States. Congress. Senate. Atlanta (GA). Canteens (War-time, emergency, etc.). Cape Cod (MA). Chaplains. College students. Decatur (GA). Docks. Dogs. Faith. Glasgow (Scotland). Heart disease. Immigrants. John Paul Jones. Mills. Parenthood. Physicians. Prayer. Quarries and quarrying. Romance. Rowboats. Sailors. Scotland. Senators. Soldiers. Temperance. Theological seminaries. Trusts and trustees. Tuberculosis. United States Naval Academy. Washington (D.C.). World War II.*

Note: In Catherine Marshall's book, *To Live Again* (New York, 1957), she devotes many pages to an account of her involvement in the production of *A Man Called Peter*. She relates that Twentieth Century-Fox writer-producer Lamar Trotti, who had recently suffered the loss of a son in an automobile accident, was drawn to the book and made extensive notes on it. However, Trotti was stricken by a fatal heart attack in Aug 1952, and his notes passed into the hands of fellow producer, Samuel G. Engel. The studio purchased an option to the book in Nov 1952, and Sylvia Richards was assigned to write the screenplay. Richard Burton and Jean Peters were suggested for the roles of Peter and Catherine Marshall. The following summer, the studio exercized its option and purchased rights to the book for $30,000. In Nov 1953, Eleanore Griffin was given the screenplay assignment, and Catherine Marshall was engaged as technical adviser for the screenplay. In her book, Mrs. Marshall notes that it proved necessary to make a few modifications to the actual events; "For example, in real life Peter and I had spent our honeymoon in New York, not on Cape Cod; in the script there was the necessity of introducing Cape Cod early in the story. In real life Peter John was born on January 25, 1940, not in December of 1941. Yet this time shift simplified the Annapolis sequence in the movie.... Changes of this sort did not bother me, because they did no violence to the spirit of the truth."

In Twentieth Century-Fox publicity material, Engel commented on his decision to include in the film lengthy scenes of Marshall delivering sermons: "The sermons are wonderfully imaginative and interesting and what gives the Marshall character its dimensions. But nobody had ever put as much as 20 minutes of sermons into a film. Maybe nobody should try. I tried to figure out ways of presenting them in scenes. Finally, one day I said to myself, 'Look, if you were making *The Jolson Story* you wouldn't try to do it without songs would you? If you are afraid of the sermons, forget the picture!' Mr. Zanuck backed me on this 100 percent." Reviews lauded the filmmakers for these scenes. *Var* commented, "Again and again, the camera picks up Richard Todd as Peter Marshall mounting the pulpit to deliver the sermons for which he was famous

and which drew over-flow crowds Sunday after Sunday to the New York Ave. Presbyterian Church in Washington. These sermons are things of beauty and Koster and Engel deserve kudos for allowing them to run on for serveral minutes at a time.... Todd does such a masterful job of preaching the sermons, the camera staying on him most of the time, they're almost the best thing in the picture." As Richard Burton proved to be unavailable, the role of Peter Marshall was offered to Richard Todd, who, as he had personal doubts regarding his ability to do the role justice, asked if he might shoot a test of himself delivering one of Marshall's sermons. This was shot, very successfully, in England, and on seeing it, studio head Darryl F. Zanuck wrote to Engel saying, "I was simply mesmerized. I couldn't believe this was something on film." Although Jean Peters was originally announced to play Catherine, other actresses including Eva Marie Saint, Elizabeth Taylor, Jean Simmons, Dorothy McGuire and Donna Reed were considered, but Peters was assigned to the part just six days before shooting started.

Filming began with second unit work in Atlanta, Decatur and Covington, GA, then moved to Washington, D.C. and thence to the U.S. Naval Academy at Annapolis, MD. Although the New York Avenue church had been torn down shortly after Marshall's death, the new church built on the site was sufficiently like the old one that its exterior could be used. The manse, however, had undergone more radical changes, and a suitable house was found near Capitol Hill. Interiors for the church and manse were built at the studio. According to her book, Mrs. Marshall was not present when any of the film was shot. On 24 Jan 1955, eighty clergymen—Catholic, Jewish and Protestant—saw a rough-cut version of the film at a special screening at the studio. Their reaction was overwhelmingly positive. When Catherine Marshall saw the final cut, shortened by about fifteen minutes, at the studio's New York screening room on 7 Mar, she felt that "some memorable scenes had been sacrificed to length," but knew that "whatever small faults the picture had, it was all right." She wired Engel, in part, "Peter's spirit and personality come through with complete integrity. Even the most emotional scenes have the restraint of real artistry. May the picture become a milestone both in motion picture history and in the spiritual life of the nation."

Previews were held in Richmond, VA and in Miami, FL. Simultaneous world premieres were held on the night of 31 Mar 1955 at the Roxy in New York and at the La Scala in Glasgow, Scotland. Catherine Marshall and Richard Todd attended the New York premiere, whose proceeds went to the Highland Fund of North America and the Caledonian Hospital of Brooklyn. The premiere was preceded by a parade of Scottish War Veterans and the Canadian Legion, nurses from the Caledonian Hospital and a seventy-man color guard. After opening to slow business, word-of-mouth built the film into a box-office success. *Life* magazine gave the film a six-page spread but criticized the film's promotion which included, "He was a lovin' kind of guy.... He was God's kind of guy."

While Marshall was a Presbyterian minister, the film's producer and director were Jewish, and the screenplay writer, Catholic. In an article in *HCN* of 19 May 1955 producer Samuel Engel stated, "No one [involved in the production] stopped to think whether he was a Christian or a Jew, or whether he was a Catholic or a Protestant. All fell into step because each in his way wanted to have a hand in the making of this picture.... I had not the remotest notion when I was sitting at the feet of my maternal grandfather, who was a rabbi, and learning the eternal truths of the Torah and the brilliant interpretations of the Talmud that one day I would be a writer and producer of films in Hollywood. Certainly, I never dreamed that the long years devoted to gaining a Hebrew education would stand me in good stead in my professional career.... Only in a free country like ours could the son of a poor Jewish immigrant still carry the Star of David in his heart and at the same time be given the opportunity and privilege of bringing the life of one of Christ's foremost disciples to the screens of the world." The following actors appeared in scenes cut before the film's release: Agnes Bartholomew, Rick Kelman, Luis Torres, Jr., Bob Hunter, David Wood, Alex Campbell, Jonathan Hole and Maudie Prickett. Alfred Newman's score includes a reprise of his main theme for *Young Mr. Lincoln* (1939). *A Man Called Peter* was nominated for an Academy Award for best Color Cinematography.

Box 26 Mar 1955. *Christian Science Monitor* 5 Apr 1955, p. 11. *DV* 3 Dec 1952. *DV* 19 Nov 1953. *DV* 7 Dec 1953. *DV* 23 Mar 1955, p. 3. *Exh* 6 Apr 1955, p. 3944. *FD* 23 Mar 1955, p. 6. *Har* 26 Mar 1955, p. 50. *HCN* 19 May 1955. *HR* 15 Sep 1953. *HR* 23 Mar 1955, p. 3. *Life* 4 Apr 1955, pp. 115-120. *MPD* 23 Mar 1955. *MPHPD* 26 Mar 1955, p. 377. *NYT* 1 Apr 1955, p. 22. *Var* 23 Mar 1955, p. 6.

MAN FROM DEL RIO (Latino)

Robert L. Jacks Productions, Inc. *Dist* United Artists Corp. Oct 1956; *Prod*: mid-Mar—early Apr 1956 [©Robert L. Jacks Productions, Inc.; 26 Oct 1956; LP8031]. Sd (RCA Sound Recording); b&w; 1.85. 9 reels, 7,421 ft. 82 min. PCA cert no. 17996.

Prod Robert L. Jacks. *Assoc prod* Richard Carruth. *Dir* Harry Horner. *Orig story and scr* Richard Carr. *Photog* Stanley Cortez. *Film ed* Robert Golden. *Sd ed* Wayne Fury. *Set dec* Mowbray Berkeley. *Ward* Frank Beetson and Opal Vils. *Mus* Frederick Steiner. *Sd* Jack Solomon. *Makeup artist* Louis Hippe. *Hair stylist* Kay Shea. *Prod supv* Frank Parmenter. *Scr supv* Mary Gibsone. [*Tech adv on shooting scenes* Fred Carson].

Cast: ANTHONY QUINN [(*David Robles*)], Katy Jurado [(*Estella*)], Peter Whitney [(*Ed Bannister*)], Douglas Fowley [(*Doc Adams*)], John Larch [(*Bill Dawson*)], Whit Bissell [(*Breezy Morgan*)], Douglas Spencer [(*Jack Tillman*)], [Guinn "Big Boy" Williams (*Fred Jasper*)], [Marc Hamilton (*George Dawson*)], [Adrienne Marden (*Mrs. Tillman*)], [Barry Atwater (*Dan Ritchy*)], [Carl Thayler ("*The Kid*," *Danny Sheridan*)], [William Erwin (*Roy Higgens*)], [Otto Waldis (*Tom Jordan*)], [Paul Harber (*Mr. Brown*)], [Jack Hogan (*Boy*)], [Frank Richards (*Stableman*)], [Donald Covert (*Gunman*)].

Western. [*Print viewed*]. When gunfighter Dan Ritchy rides into the quiet town of Mesa, he finds a lone Mexican-American man waiting for him. The man, David Robles, reminds Ritchy that they met five years earlier when Ritchy and three cohorts shot up David's town of Del Rio. David says he now has learned to use a gun and has killed the other three men. In a shoot-out, David kills Ritchy and suffers a wound himself. After Doc Adams determines that he only has a flesh wound, the doc's assistant, Estella, an attractive Mexican-American woman, tends to David's wounds despite her contempt for gunfighters. Saloon owner Ed Bannister, an ex-gunfighter himself, welcomes David, saying that he had invited Ritchy to town, but now is happy to have David instead. When three other gunfighters, the Dawson brothers and Fred Jasper, arrive in town, they drink with David, impressed that he gunned down Ritchy. The friendliness amongst the gunslingers evaporates instantly when David expresses the wish to go see a girl, and Bannister says that there are no decent "white" women in the vicinity. David repays Estella for bandaging him, then tries to kiss her, but she threatens him with a scissors. They are interrupted by the sound of gunfire and find that the Dawsons and Jasper have strung up sheriff Jack Tillman and have begun to drunkenly fire at him as he swings from a rope. When David does nothing, Estella intercedes. One of the Dawson brothers grabs her and calls her "Chiquita," and when Jasper calls David "Pancho," David shoots him and one of the brothers, while the other rides off in fright. Bannister tells David of his plan to make Mesa a wide-open town where cowherders from Texas could spend their trail money at saloons and dancehalls without interference from the law. When he says he needs David's fast gun to back him up, David replies he does not like him. David tries to romance Estella again, but she rebuffs him saying that her deceased husband was a gunfighter and that his death left her alone with a daughter, who now lives with in-laws in Wichita. She says it has taken her four years to establish herself in Mesa. Having witnessed the prejudice there, David questions whether she has been accepted, and she contends that she has earned the town's respect. David is offered $100 a month plus a room to be the town's new sheriff, and he accepts. When Estella taunts him, he says he has won the respect of the town in one day, while it took her four years. She retorts that it is only his gun that is respected. Snubbed by some of the townsfolk, David gets drunk in the street with Breezy Morgan, an alcoholic. Estella encourages him to leave town, and he confesses that he took the job not because of the money but because of her. When she laughs that he only wants her for another notch in his gun, he slaps her and accuses her of trying to forget how she feels, and she cries. David gets into a fight with Bannister and wins, but when he learns from Doc Adams that he has broken his wrist, he is terrified that he can no longer be a gunfighter. Doc Adams warns him to leave town, but David convinces him not to tell anyone about his wrist. The next morning, David orders Bannister to get out of town by noon. When a young gunslinger new to town refuses to leave, David challenges him to draw, then slaps him down until the boy grabs at his arm. The doc, seeing David's pained look, takes David into his office, where Breezy overhears David say that because of his broken wrist, he plans to leave town once Bannister goes. Breezy relates this to Bannister, who now challenges David to meet him in the street in ten minutes. When Estella suggests they leave town and make a home together with her daughter, he kisses her and tells her to have the horses saddled up; however, when he steps onto the street and Bannister taunts him, he rolls up his sleeve and unravels his bandage. David challenges Bannister to draw, but Bannister, suspecting David paid Breezy to give him false information so that he could gun him down, allows David to take his gun. Estella now looks at David with pride, and they walk together past the horses that were waiting to take them out of town. Bigotry. Gunfighters. Mexican Americans. Pride and vanity. Romance. Saloon keepers. Sheriffs. Small town life. Widows. Alcoholics. Dances. Drunkenness. Fistfights. Gunshot wounds. Megalomania. Ostracism. Physicians. Revenge. Shootouts.

Note: The working title of this film was *The Lonely Gun. HR* called the film an "unusual and rather artistic western." According to modern sources, Katherine DeMille, who was married to Anthony Quinn at the time, had a small role in the film.

Box 20 Oct 1956. *DV* 3 Oct 1956, p. 3. *Exb* 17 Oct 1956, p. 4239. *FD* 9 Oct 1956, p. 8. *Har* 6 Oct 1956, p. 158. *HR* 8 Dec 1955. *HR* 16 Mar 1956, p. 11. *HR* 30 Mar 1956, p. 17. *HR* 9 May 1956. *HR* 3 Oct 1956, p. 3. *LAEx* 1 Nov 1956. *LAT* 1 Nov 1956. *MPD* 8 Oct 1956. *MPHPD* 6 Oct 1956, p. 98. *Newsweek* 22 Oct 1956. *Time* 31 Dec 1956. *Var* 3 Oct 1956, p. 26.

MAN FROM MONTEREY (Latino)

Warner Bros. Pictures, Inc.; A Four Star Western. *Dist* Vitagraph, Inc. 15 Jul **1933** [©Vitagraph, Inc.; 10 Jun 1933; LP4004]. Sd (Western Electric Noiseless Recording); b&w. 5,294 ft. 56-57 or 59 min. Passed by the National Board of Review. PCA cert no. 2660-R.

Pres LEON SCHLESINGER. *Assoc prod* Sid Rogell. *Dir* Mack V. Wright. *Scr and dial* Lesley Mason. *Photog* T. D. McCord. *Film ed* Wm. Clemens. *Mus score* Leo F. Forbstein.

Song(s): "Forget Me Not," composer unknown.

Cast: JOHN WAYNE [(*Captain John Holmes*)], DUKE [(*A horse*)], Ruth Hall [(*Dolores Castanares*)], Luis Alberni [(*Felipe*)], Donald Reed [(*Don Luis Gonzales*)], Nina Quartero [(*Anita Garcia*)], Francis Ford [(*Don Pablo Gonzales*)], Lafe McKee [(*Don Jose Castanares*)], Lillian Leighton [(*Juanita*)], Charles Wittaker [(*Jake Morgan*)], [Chris-Pin Martin].

Historical, Western. [*Print viewed*]. After it acquires the California territory from Spain, the United States government requires the holders of Spanish land grants to register their land or the land will become public domain. Don Pablo Gonzales, eager to acquire the lands of Don Jose Castanares, misleads Don Jose into believing that he should refuse to register. At the same time, Don Pablo's son Luis is pursuing Dolores, Don Jose's daughter. She does not love him, however, preferring to find a man of action. American soldier Captain John Holmes is dispatched to convince the land owners to register. On the way to Don Jose's, he rescues Dolores from her runaway coach. Luis is furious, as he instigated the attack so he could rescue Dolores and prove his manhood. By defending them, John acquires some allies in Felipe, a fortune-teller, and in Jake Morgan's gang. Dolores introduces John to her father as the man who saved her life. John explains the land registration to Don Jose, who agrees to register his land the next day. When Don Jose leaves home, however, Don Pablo kidnaps him and Dolores promises to marry Luis in order to free her father. After learning that Luis is engaged to Anita Garcia, the daughter of the saloon owner, John plans to have her substituted for Dolores before the wedding. He sends his horse, Duke, with a message for Morgan's men, and when they arrive, Don Pablo's duplicity is revealed. Dolores is now free to marry John with her father's blessing. *California–History–1846-1850. Duplicity. Latino. Land claims. Ranchers. Soldiers. Fortune-tellers. Jealousy. Kidnapping. Marriage–Forced. Mistaken identity. Sword fights. Transvestism. Weddings.*

Note: According to press releases in the copyright records, most of the scenes were shot on the former ranch La Providencia, where the Warner Bros. studio was located.

FD 16 Aug 1933, p. 7. *HR* 8 Apr 1933, p. 2. *MPD* 16 Aug 1933, p. 2. *MPH* 26 Aug 1933, p. 79. *Var* 22 Aug 1933, p. 22.

THE MAN FROM TEXAS (African Americans)

Ben Roy Productions. **1921**. Si; b&w. 5 reels.

Prod Ben D. Wilson. *Dir* Ben D. Wilson.

Western, African American. [No information about the plot of this film has been located.]. *African Americans. Texans.*

Note: According to information in the George P. Johnson Collection at the UCLA Special Collections Library, Ben Roy Productions was located in Houston, TX, and the film was shot at a large ranch near Dallas.

THE MAN FROM THE ALAMO (Latino)

Universal-International Pictures Co., Inc. *Dist* Universal Pictures Co., Inc. Aug **1953**; Prod: 25 Aug—mid-Sep 1952; late Oct 1952 [©Universal Pictures Co.; 8 May 1953; LP2848]. Sd (Western Electric Recording); col (Technicolor). 7,134 ft. 79 min. PCA cert no. 16344.

Prod Aaron Rosenberg. *Dir* Budd Boetticher. *Asst dir* Tom Shaw, [Marshall Green and Phil Bowles]. [*Dial dir* Harold Clifford]. *Scr* Steve Fisher and D. D. Beauchamp. *Based on a story by* Niven Busch and Oliver Crawford. *Dir of photog* Russell Metty. *Technicolor col consultant* William Fritsche. *Art dir* Alexander Golitzen and Emrich Nicholson. *Film ed* Virgil Vogel. *Set dec* Russell A. Gausman and Ruby R. Levitt. *Cost* Bill Thomas. *Mus* Frank Skinner. [*Mus dir* Joseph Gershenson]. *Sd* Lslie I. Carey and Corson Jowett. *Hair stylist* Joan St. Oegger. *Makeup* Bud Westmore.

Cast: GLENN FORD (*John Stroud*), JULIA ADAMS (*Beth Anders*), Chill Wills (*John Gage*), Hugh O'Brian (*Lt. [Tom] Lamar*), Victor

Jory (*Jess Wade*), Neville Brand (*Dawes*), John Day (*Cavish*), Myra Marsh (*Ma Anders*), Jeanne Cooper (*Kate Lamar*), Mark Cavell (*Carlos*), Edward Norris (*Mapes*), Guy Williams (*Sergeant*), [George Eldredge (*Sheriff Kohl*)], [Dan Poore (*Cobby*)], [Erik Nielsen (*Lamar son*)], [Patricia Weil (*Lamar daughter*)], [Fred Coby, Robert Hoy, Emile Avery, John Phillips, Carl Andre (*Soldiers*)], [Evan Loew (*Mrs. Mapes*)], [Helen Gibson, Polly Burson (*Women in wagon train*)], [Dennis Weaver (*Reb*)], [Stuart Whitman (*Orderly*)], [Charles Hand (*Courier*)], [Alberto Morin (*Trooper*)], [Trevor Bardette (*Davy Crockett*)], [Walter Reed (*Billings*)], [Howard Negley (*General Sam Houston*)], [Stuart Randall (*James Bowie*)], [Arthur Space (*Lt. Col. Travis*)], [Smokey Whitfield (*Sam*)], [Guy Wilkerson (*Rifleman*)], [John McKee (*Kaye*)], [Chuck Hamilton (*Mose*)], [Bob Smiley (*Hayworth*)], [Frank Wilcox], [Robert Carson], [Raymond Bond], [Hugh Prosser], [Dick Cutting], [Monte Montague], [Phil Chambers], [Ken MacDonald], [Edwin Parker], [Harte Wayne], [Ethan Laidlaw], [Roy Butler], [Felice Richmond], [Frank Ellis], [Walter Lawrence].

Historical, Western. [*Print viewed*]. In 1836, following the election of General Santa Anna to the Mexican presidency, the people of the free state of Texas find themselves faced with the unhappy prospect of a military rule by the new Mexican government. Leading the opposition to the new regime is General Sam Houston, who believes that a military force should be assembled to protect Texas' status as an independent republic. When word reaches Houston that Santa Anna has occupied San Antonio, and that Lt. Col. Travis, with only two hundred soldiers, has retreated across the Sabine River to the Alamo, he quickly assembles a militia. As the battle to save the Alamo rages on, a group of soldiers from Ox Bow, fearing for the safety of their families, draw lots and select John Stroud as the man to go back to the town to protect the women and children. Stroud reaches Ox Bow in the aftermath of a bloody massacre, and finds that his wife and son are among the dead. When the sole survivor of the massacre, a young Mexican boy named Carlos, tells Stroud that the killings were carried out by white men disguised as Mexicans, Stroud vows to hunt down the killers. Meanwhile, the Alamo has fallen into the hands of the Mexicans, who are now poised to charge across Texas. Under the leadership of Lt. Tom Lamar, the women, elderly and children of Franklin, Texas are evacuated. Stroud arrives in Franklin during the evacuation, and leaves Carlos in the care of one of the evacuees, Beth Anders. When Lamar recognizes Stroud as the man who left the Alamo before its fall, the entire town surrounds and taunts him. Just as Stroud is about to leave Franklin, Carlos tells him that a drunken man leaving the saloon is one of the men who massacred the people at Ox Bow. Stroud tries to approach the man, but the townspeople warn him to leave and attempt to lynch him. Jailed for his own protection, Stroud shares a cell with Dawes, a member of a renegade gang supporting the Mexicans. Hoping to infiltrate the gang, Stroud expresses his interest in its cause, and when gang leader Jess Wade breaks Dawes out of jail, Stroud goes with him. Wade later decides to go after the wagon train for its bankroll, and accepts Stroud as one of the gang. While waiting in a gorge, ready to ambush the wagon train as it passes, Stroud fires his gun at one of the gang members, Cobby, in a deliberate attempt to warn the approaching wagon train of the impending raid. Stroud's plan works, and the shots send the wagons scurrying for safety. Wounded in a gun battle with Wade and left behind to die, Stroud is found by Carlos and is brought back to the wagon train. There, Beth, the only person who believes that he was not a part of the renegade gang, nurses him back to health. Stroud makes a full recovery, and when Lamar receives orders from Houston to report his regiment to San Jacinto for the final assault on the Mexican army, Stroud is appointed the new leader of the wagon train. Stroud steers the wagon train southward and, after outrunning Wade's gang, sets a trap for them. As Wade's gang approaches, the old men and women of the wagon train, fully armed, defeat them in a fierce gun battle. After killing Wade in a hand-to-hand fight and avenging the murder of his family, Stroud leaves the wagon train to join Houston at San Jacinto. *Alamo (San Antonio, TX). False accusations. Mexicans. Renegades. Texas–History. United States–History–19th Century. Ambushes. Chases. Cowardice. Disguise. Drunkenness. Evacuations. Fistfights. Gunshot wounds. Sam Houston. Jailbreaks. Lynching. Massacres. Officers (Military). Orphans. Revenge. Romance. General Antonio Lopéz de Santa Anna. Soldiers. Wagon trains. Wards and guardians.*

Note: According to an Oct 1951 *Var* news item, John Ford and John Wayne protested Universal's use of the word "Alamo" in the title, noting that they had

already registered the title *The Alamo*. After the matter went to arbitration, however, Wayne and Ford conceded that they had no exclusive right to the word "Alamo." The same item announced that Jeff Chandler was being considered for the starring role in the film. According to a *DV* news item, Glenn Ford suffered three broken ribs during production when he was thrown against a tree by a horse. Filming was suspended for approximately five weeks.

Box 18 Jul 1953. *DV* 10 Jul 1953, p. 3. *Exb* 15 Jul 1953, p. 3560. *FD* 20 Jul 1953, p. 10. *Har* 11 Jul 1953, p. 111. *HR* 22 Aug 1952, p. 10. *HR* 19 Sep 1952, p. 15. *HR* 24 Oct 1952, p. 13. *HR* 10 Jul 1953, p. 3. *MPHPD* 18 Jul 1953, p. 1918. *NYT* 12 Sep 1953, p. 13. *Var* 31 Oct 1951. *Var* 15 Jul 1953, p. 6.

THE MAN I MARRIED (German Americans)

Twentieth Century-Fox Film Corp. *Dist* Twentieth Century-Fox Film Corp. 2 Aug **1940**; Prod: 4 May—mid-Jun 1940 [©Twentieth Century-Fox Film Corp.; 2 Aug 1940; LP10157]. Sd (Western Electric Mirrophonic Recording); b&w. 6,940 ft. 65 or 76-77 min. PCA cert no. 6331.

Prod Darryl F. Zanuck. *Assoc prod* Raymond Griffith. *Dir* Irving Pichel. [*Asst dir* Booth McCracken]. *Scr* Oliver H. P. Garrett. *Dir of photog* Peverell Marley. *Art dir* Richard Day and Hans Peters. *Film ed* Robert Simpson. *Set dresser* Thomas Little. *Cost* Travis Banton. *Mus dir* David Buttolph. *Sd* Joseph E. Aiken and Roger Heman.

Source: Based on the novel *Swastika* by Oscar Schisgall (New York, 1939).

Cast: JOAN BENNETT (*Carol [Hoffman]*), FRANCIS LEDERER (*Eric Hoffman*), LLOYD NOLAN (*Kenneth Delane*), ANNA STEN (*Freda Heinkel*), Otto Kruger (*Heinrich Hoffman*), Maria Ouspenskaya (*Frau Gerhardt*), Ludwig Stossel (*Dr. Hugo Gerhardt*), Johnny Russell (*Ricky [Hoffman]*), Lionel Royce (*Herr Deckart*), Fredrik Vogeding (*Traveler*), Ernst Deutsch (*Otto*), Egon Brecher (*Czech*), William Kaufman (*Conductor*), Frank Reicher (*Friehof*), [Charles Irwin (*English newspaperman*)], [Lillian Porter (*Receptionist*)], [Lillian West (*Secretary*)], [Walter Bonn (*Customs official*)], [Glen Cavender (*Petty official*)], [Hans Von Morhart, William Yetter, Carl Freybe (*Gestapo officers*)], [Ragnar Qvale (*Freibof's older son*)], [Rudy Frolich (*Freibof's son*)], [John Stark, Tom Mizer (*Storm troopers*)], [Hans Schumm (*First storm trooper*)], [Robert O. Davis (*Second storm trooper*)], [Greta Meyer (*Hausfrau*)], [Albert Geigel (*Boy*)], [Eleanor Wesselhoeft (*Old lady*)], [Diane Fisher (*Young girl*)], [John Hiestand, Leyland Hodgson, Arno Frey, Eugene Borden (*Announcers*)], [Harry Depp].

Political, Drama. [*Print viewed*]. In July 1938, *The Smart World* magazine art critic Carol Hoffman prepares to leave New York with her husband Eric on a trip to Germany. Eric must go to Germany to help his father with the family business, but both he and Carol see the trip as an extended vacation. Dr. Hugo Gerhardt arrives at Carol's office to ask a favor. His brother, the renowned philosopher Hans Gerhardt of Berlin University, has been taken to the Dachau concentration camp. Hugo has raised $500 in bribe money and asks Carol and Eric to deliver it for him. Arriving by boat in Bremerhaven, Eric tells Carol he feels like a tourist, not a tourist. On the train to Berlin, Eric reads a German newspaper to Carol, telling her how, according to the journal, there is no unemployment in Germany and how German radios and cars are cheaper, yet superior, to their American counterparts. Seeing a train of prisoners, Eric and Carol are informed by a fellow traveler that they are Austrian forced labor. The traveler also comments on how inferior German products really are. At the Berlin train station, the couple is met by Freda Heinkel, Eric's old flame. Once at home, Eric's father Heinrich explains that the old Germany he knew is gone and that Eric must now either take over the family business or sell it. At a large military rally, Eric begins to feel that Germany is "alive, exciting," much to Carol's chagrin. Then, at a dance, Eric confesses to Carol that he wants to stay in Germany and run the family factory. Freda arrives and tells Carol that they cannot give the money to Hans Gerhardt, as he is a traitor to his country. Carol, despite this, vows to deliver the money as promised. At the *Overseas News Service*, Carol meets American reporter Kenneth Delane. When Carol asks about Hans, Ken tells her that Gerhardt died in Dachau of "acute appendicitis." Ken suggest that Carol give the money to Gerhardt's family. On the way to see the Gerhardts, Carol and Ken run into a Storm Trooper patrol, which is making Czech women and children pick up garbage in the streets. At the Gerhardt home, Frau Gerhardt thanks Ken and Carol, but refuses their offer to send her to America. When told the official cause of her husband's death, Frau Gerhardt informs them that Hans had his appendix removed twenty years earlier. After Carol returns home, Eric

dismisses what she has seen as isolated incidents. When he informs Carol that he is having dinner with Freda and some Nazi officials, Carol calls Hitler "Schickelgruber" (his real name), a comment that Eric declares is grounds for divorce. That night, Carol attempts to help their neighbor Friehof hide his eldest son, who has just escaped from a concentration camp. When the Gestapo arrives, however, Friehof's youngest son turns them in. At Gestapo headquarters, Carol is interrogated by Herr Deckart, but Ken, using the power of the American press, gets her released. At Hitler's speech at the Berlin Sportspalast, Eric fully absorbs the Nazi idea, to Carol's horror. The next morning, Eric reveals to Carol that he has decided to stay in Germany permanently. When Carol protests, Eric admits that he has joined the Nazi party and is in love with Freda. Carol agrees to a divorce, but Eric refuses to let her take their son Ricky back to America with her. Ken offers his help in sneaking Ricky out of Germany, but Eric foils the plan. Heinrich confronts his son, however, telling him that the boy belongs with his mother. When Eric, with Freda's support, still refuses to give up Ricky, Heinrich tells him that his mother was Jewish. Repulsed, Freda leaves and Heinrich informs the shattered Eric that now he will have to suffer what he would have done to others. At the train station, Carol and Ricky leave Germany, as Ken tells them that he will be staying in Germany for the duration. *Fascism. Fathers and sons. German Americans. Germany. Marriage. Nazism. Politics. Reporters. Appendicitis. Berlin (Germany). Betrayal. Bribery. Concentration camps. Czechs. Dances. Deception. Fugitives. Gestapo. Joseph Paul Goebbels. Adolf Hitler. Interrogation. Jews. Political prisoners. Rallies. Speeches. Torture. Trains.*

Note: The working title of this film was *I Married a Nazi*. Many contemporary sources indicate that Oscar Schisgall's novel *Swastika* was first published as a serialized story in *Liberty* magazine. George Sanders and Richard Greene were cast in the film at the start of production. According to a Twentieth Century-Fox press release, Saunders, originally cast in the "Eric Hoffman" role, was still acting in *Foreign Correspondent*, which had gone over schedule, and was forced to give up his role in this film. Greene, cast as "Kenneth Delane," was replaced after he became bed-ridden for two weeks with the flu. *HR* production charts list William Gargan in the cast, but his participation in the final film has not been confirmed. Press releases report that over "two hundred" applicants were seen for the role of Adolf Hitler in this film. Carl Ottman was finally cast in the role, but his performance was cut from the film. In the scene at the Berlin Sportspalast, Hitler's actual voice was used. Press materials also indicate that actual Nazi propaganda was used in the set design of the film. In addition, press releases note that 1,000 Nazi uniforms were used in this film, though they were shared with another Twentieth Century-Fox film, *Four Sons*. The following was reported by Twentieth Century-Fox press materials: during a scene that required fifty young boys to dress in Nazi uniforms, eight boys walked off the set, unable to play their characters. A new type of set construction was featured in this film, in which canvas, instead of wood, was used, which led to a twenty-five per cent savings in construction costs. For the scene in which storm troopers forced Czechs to pick up garbage in the street, there was not enough garbage available at the Twentieth Century-Fox cafeteria, so trucks were sent out to collect garbage from nearby Beverly Hills housewives. A *NYT* article states that this film, along with other anti-Nazi propaganda films from Hollywood did not perform well at the box office. The article speculated that audiences were either bored by the constant Nazi depravities or objected to "having a philosphic attitude rammed down their throats." An undated *HR* clipping from the AFI Mayer Library states that Twentieth Century-Fox and the German consul had heated discussion over this film, with the German consul threatening to refuse distribution of Twentieth Century-Fox films in his country. According to modern sources, the film was pulled shortly after its release in an attempt to stay neutral in the then-European conflict and so as not to offend "a friendly foreign country." Thus, the working title was changed and few prints of the film were struck.

Box 20 Jul 1940. *DV* 12 Jul 1940, p. 3. *FD* 16 Jul 1940, p. 5. *HR* 4 May 1940, p. 2. *HR* 15 Jul 1940, p. 3. *MPH* 20 Jul 1940, p. 26. *NYT* 3 Aug 1940, p. 9. *NYT* 18 May 1941. *Var* 17 Jul 1940, p. 16.

THE MAN IN BLUE (Irish Americans, Italian Americans)

Universal Pictures Corp.; Universal-Jewel. 21 Jun **1925** [©Universal Pictures Corp.; 25 Feb 1925; LP21189]. Si; b&w. 6 reels, 5,634 ft.

Dir Edward Laemmle. *Scen* E. Richard Schayer. *Photog* Clyde De Vinna.

Source: Based on the short story "The Flower of Napoli" by Gerald Beaumont in *Red Book* (Mar 1924).

Cast: Herbert Rawlinson (*Tom Conlin*), Madge Bellamy (*Tita Sartori*), Nick De Ruiz (*Gregoria Vitti*), Andrí de Beranger (*Carlo Guido*), Cesare Gravina (*Tony Sartori*), Jackie Morgan (*Pat Malone*), Dorothy Brock (*Morna Malone*), D. J. Mitsoras (*Cesare Martinelli*), Carrie Clark Ward (*Mrs. Shaughnessy*), C. F. Roark (*Mr. Shaughnessy*), Martha Mattox (*Bendetta*).

Melodrama. Tom Conlin, an Irish cop walking a beat in an Italian neighborhood, falls in love with Tita Sartori, the daughter of a florist. Tita returns Tom's affection but keeps him at a distance, believing him to be married; Tita is also wooed by an unscrupulous politician of considerable wealth. This politician is responsible for the death of an Italian youth, who was also in love with Tita. He later kidnaps Tita, confining her to his apartment. She is rescued by Tom, who captures the murderer after a brutal battle in a restaurant. Tita learns that Tom is single, and she admits her love for him. *Florists. Irish Americans. Italian Americans. Kidnapping. Murder. Police. Politicians.*

FD 22 Feb 1925. MPW 28 Feb 1925.

MAN IN THE SHADOW (Latino)

Universal-International Pictures Co., Inc. *Dist* Universal Pictures Co., Inc. Dec **1957**; Prod: mid-Oct—early Nov 1956 [©Universal Pictures Co.; 20 Nov 1957; LP10526]. Sd; b&w; Cinemascope. 7,204 ft. 79 min.

Prod Albert Zugsmith. *Dir* Jack Arnold. *Asst dir* David Silver. *Wrt* Gene L. Coon. *Dir of photog* Arthur E. Arling. *Art dir* Alfred Golitzen and Alfred Sweeney. *Film ed* Edward Curtiss. *Set dec* Russell A. Gausman and John P. Austin. *Gowns* Bill Thomas. *Mus supv* Joseph Gershenson. *Sd* Leslie I. Carey and Joe Lapis. *Makeup* Bud Westmore.

Cast: JEFF CHANDLER (*Ben Sadler*), ORSON WELLES (*Virgil Renchler*), COLLEEN MILLER (*Skippy Renchler*), BEN ALEXANDER (*Ab Begley*), Barbara Lawrence (*Helen Salder*), John Larch (*Ed Yates*), James Gleason (*Hank James*), Royal Dano (*Aiken Clay*), Paul Fix (*Herb Parker*), Leo Gordon (*Chet Huneker*), Martin Garralaga (*Jesus Cisneros*), Mario Siletti (*Tony Santoro*), Charles Horvath (*Len Brookman*), William Schallert (*Jim Shaney*), Joseph J. Greene (*Harry Youngquist*), Forrest Lewis (*Jake Kelley*), Harry Harvey, Sr. (*Dr. Creighton*), Joe Schneider (*Juan Martin*), Mort Mills (*Gateman*).

Western. [*Print viewed*]. When Mexican American laborer Jesus Cisneros witnesses his fellow brasero, Juan Martin, beaten to death by foreman Ed Yates in the toolshed of Virgil Renchler's Golden Empire ranch, he timidly reports the murder to sheriff Ben Sadler. At first reluctant to confront Renchler, the most powerful man in the county, Ben finally decides that it is his duty to investigate the charges, even though his deputy, Ab Begley, tries to dissuade him. After ascertaining that Cisneros will seek refuge at his friend Aiken Clay's ranch, Ben drives to the Golden Empire to question Renchler. Ben is met with hostility by the arrogant Renchler, who belittles his concern for a "wetback" and implies that the sheriff's job will be in jeopardy if Ben continues his investigation. After Ben leaves, Yates admits to Renchler that he killed Martin, and Renchler then phones Herb Parker, the county commissioner. Soon after, Chet Huneker, an employee of the Golden Empire, comes to Ben's office and claims that he hit Martin with his car. At the ranch, meanwhile, Skippy Renchler, Virgil's attractive young daughter, questions her father about the sheriff's visit and recalls hearing a blood curdling scream the previous night. After declaring that she was only dreaming, Renchler orders Skippy to her room and posts a guard outside her door. Defying her father, Skippy slips out the window. At the office of coroner Jake Kelley, Cisneros, meanwhile, identifies Martin's body. When Ben tells Cisneros Chet's story about hitting Martin with his car, Cisneros claims that Chet helped Yates beat Martin to death. After imploring Ben to drop his investigation, Kelley phones Renchler to apprise him of the situation. Upon returning to his office, Ben finds Skippy waiting. When she learns of Martin's death, Skippy asserts that Yates killed Martin because he was jealous of his friendship with her and reveals that she heard a man's scream on the night of the murder. Their conversation is interrupted by Herb, who demands that Ben immediately cease his investigation. Ignoring Herb's threats, Ben obtains a warrant to search the Renchler ranch. At the ranch, Ben goes directly to the tool room, where he finds a patch of blood embedded on a board. As Ben slices the blood from the board, Yates, outside, loosens the lugs on the wheel of the sheriff's car. While driving home, Ben's car wheel falls off, but he is thrown from the vehicle before it crashes into a tree. Upon regaining consciousness, Ben is driven back to town by a passing motorist. There, he finds a drunken Ab, who admits to telling Renchler that Cisneros is at the Clay ranch. Realizing that Cisneros is in danger, Ben speeds to the ranch but arrives too late, for Cisneros has been mortally wounded. At home, Ben receives threatening phone calls, and a rock is hurled through his window. As his wife Helen pleads with him to drop his investigation, Herb, Kelley

and the other town officials meet to force Ben from office. When an anonymous caller promises to divulge the truth about the murders if Ben will agree to meet at a deserted shack on the outskirts of town, Ben drives off to the meeting despite the warning of his only ally, barber Tony Santoro. At the shack, Yates and Chet beat Ben unconscious, tie him to the back of their truck and drag him through the town streets as they drunkenly shoot out the shop windows. After Ben is freed and bandaged, he wrathfully pulls a rifle from the gun rack in the sheriff's office, rips off his badge, denounces the town and vows to bring Renchler to justice. Joining Ben on his quest, Clay crashes his truck through Renchler's gate. When Ben proclaims that he is taking Renchler into custody, Renchler unleashes his vicious watchdog on the sheriff, and Chet hurls a knife into Clay's chest. Just as Renchler and his thugs are about to silence Ben forever, the townsfolk arrive, guns in hand. After a violent skirmish, Ab arrests Renchler and his men and then returns the sheriff's badge to Ben. *Corruption. Laborers. Mexican Americans. Murder. Ranchers. Sheriffs. Small town life.* Automobile accidents. Barbers and barbershops. Coroners. Deputies. Drunkenness. Fathers and daughters. Fights. Foremen. Jealousy. Ranches. Sabotage.

Note: The working title of this film was *Pay the Devil*. The onscreen credits begin after the sequence showing the beating of the Mexican laborer at the Renchler ranch.

Box 7 Dec 1957. DV 26 Nov 1957, p. 3. Exh 11 Dec 1957, pp. 4414-15. FD 5 Dec 1957, p. 9. Har 30 Nov 1957, p. 191. HR 12 Oct 1956, p. 16. HR 9 Nov 1956, p. 10. HR 26 Nov 1957, p. 3. MPHPD 7 Dec 1957, p. 633. Var 27 Nov 1957, p. 6.

A MAN IS TEN FEET TALL *see* EDGE OF THE CITY

MAN OF BRONZE *see* JIM THORPE—ALL-AMERICAN

MAN OF CONQUEST (Native Americans, Cherokee)

Republic Pictures Corp. *Dist* Republic Pictures Corp. 15 May **1939**; New York opening: week of 28 Apr 1939; Prod: 6 Jan—13 Mar 1939 [©Republic Pictures Corp.; 15 May 1939; LP8942]. Sd; b&w. 11 reels. 96-97 min.

Assoc prod Sol C. Siegel. *Dir* George Nicholls, Jr. *Asst dir* Kenneth Holmes. *Scr* Wells Root, E. E. Paramore, Jr. and Jan Fortune. *Orig story* Harold Shumate and Wells Root. *Photog* Joseph H. August and Ernest Miller. [*Fill-in photog* Frank Redman]. *Spec eff* Howard Lydecker. *Art dir* John Victor Mackay. *Film ed* Edward Mann. *Supv ed* Murray Seldeen. *Cost* Adele Palmer. *Gowns* Edith Head. *Mus score* Victor Young. *Sd rec* Richard Tyler. *Prod mgr* Al Wilson.

Cast: Richard Dix (*Sam Houston*), Gail Patrick (*Margaret Lea*), Edward Ellis (*Andrew Jackson*), Joan Fontaine (*Eliza Allen*), Victor Jory (*William B. Travis*), Robert Barrat (*David Crockett*), George Hayes (*Lannie Upchurch*), Ralph Morgan (*Stephen Austin*), Robert Armstrong (*James Bowie*), C. Henry Gordon (*Santa Ana*), Janet Beecher (*Mrs. Lea*), Pedro de Cordoba (*Oolooteka*), Max Terhune (*Deaf Smith*), Kathleen Lockhart (*Mrs. Allen*), Ferris Taylor (*Jonas Lea*), Leon Ames (*John Hoskins*), Francis Sayles (*President James Van Buren*).

Biography, Historical, Drama. [*Print viewed*]. After spending much of his youth among the friendly Cherokee Indians, Sam Houston enlists with General Andrew Jackson and is severly wounded while leading a charge at the battle of Horseshoe Bend. Jackson commends Houston for his gallantry and a lifelong friendship is formed. Soon after, Jackson is elected to the Presidency and Houston becomes governor of Tennessee. On the eve of Houston's reelection, he marries Eliza Allen, but the demur Eliza is unable to adjust to life as the wife of a boisterous politician, and she leaves Sam. The scandal of their divorce forces Sam to resign as governor and sends him back to the Cherokees, accompanied by his friend, Lannie Upchurch. As Ambassador to the Cherokee Nation, Houston goes to Washington to protest the government's treatment of the Indians, and there he meets Margaret Lea at the Presidential Ball. After Jackson accedes to his demands, Houston joins Margaret on a stagecoach headed for Texas. On their way West, the two fall in love, but Houston foresakes his love for Margaret for his quest to free Texas from Mexico. In Texas, Houston is opposed by the peace-loving colonist Stephen Austin, who refuses to enter into war with Mexico. When word comes that Santa Ana is marching his army across Texas, killing and pillaging all in his path, Austin realizes that war is inevitable, and Jackson persuades Houston to fight for the statehood of Texas. Appointed head of the army, Houston leads his handful of troops to relieve the garrison at the Alamo. Arriving too late, Houston retreats before the advancing

Mexican army and, at San Jacinto, launches the strategic attack that routs the Mexican forces and frees Texas. As Texas is admitted into the Union, a dying Jackson praises his old friend for scoring a victory for the principles of Jacksonian democracy. *Sam Houston. Texas. United States–History–War with Mexico, 1845-1848.* Alamo (San Antonio, TX). Ambassadors. Stephen Austin. Balls (Parties). James Bowie. Cherokee Indians. Davy Crockett. Divorce. Elections. Governors. Indians of North America. Andrew Jackson. Patriotism. Politicians. Romance. Santa Ana (CA). Scandal. Tennessee. United States–History. Washington (D.C.).

Note: Sam Houston (1793-1863) was an American general and political leader and the president of the Republic of Texas from 1836-38 and 1841-44. The production credits were missing from the print viewed. The working title of this film was *Wagons Westward*. An early *HR* production chart lists Ernest Miller as photographer, although he is not credited on reviews. According to a news item in *HR*, Max Terhune replaced Guinn Williams in the role of Deaf Smith because Williams was working on the Warner Bros. film *Juarez*. News items in *HR* reveal the following members of the production were plagued by various illnesses. When C. Henry Gordon, who replaced Victor Jory in the role of "William Travis" because Jory was busy working on *Juarez*, fell ill with appendicitis, Jory stepped in to take over the part. Gordon appeared in the completed film as "Santa Ana." Richard Dix, who played "Sam Houston," fractured two bones during a fight scene, forcing a week delay in the production. Photographer Joseph H. August was hospitalized during the last week of filming and was replaced by Frank Redmond. The film was shot on location at Sonora, CA. At the time of its production, this picture was the costliest film Republic had made and was awarded the most expensive advertising campaign in the studio's history. Other news items in *HR* add that after the film was released, Republic was sued by author Marquis James, who claimed that the studio had plagiarized his book *The Raven*, a biography of Sam Houston. In 1917, Fox made *The Conquerer*, which was also based on the life of Sam Houston, starring William Farnum and directed by R. A. Walsh (see above).

DV 7 Apr 1939, p. 3. *FD* 10 Apr 1939, p. 6. *HR* 28 Nov 1938, p. 2, 3. *HR* 6 Jan 1939, p. 7. *HR* 7 Jan 1939, p. 2. *HR* 16 Jan 1939, p. 6. *HR* 17 Jan 1939, p. 3. *HR* 11 Feb 1939, pp. 5-6. *HR* 23 Feb 1939, p. 6. *HR* 25 Feb 1939, p. 4. *HR* 28 Feb 1939, p. 8. *HR* 1 Mar 1939, p. 3. *HR* 8 Mar 1939, p. 12. *HR* 14 Mar 1939, p. 1. *HR* 7 Apr 1939, p. 3. *HR* 10 Apr 1939, pp. 5-12. *HR* 24 Feb 1940, p. 5. *MPD* 2 May 1939, pp. 4-5. *MPD* 10 May 1939, pp. 4-5. *MPH* 28 Jan 1939, p. 40. *MPH* 15 Apr 1939, p. 57. *NYT* 28 Apr 1939, p. 31. *Var* 21 Apr 1939, p. 25.

A MAN OF SORROW (Gypsies)

Fox Film Corp. *Dist* Fox Film Corp. 20 Mar **1916** [©William Fox; 23 Apr 1916; LP8137]. Si; b&w. 5 reels.

Dir Oscar C. Apfel. *Asst dir* Ray S. Comstock. *Scen* Oscar C. Apfel. *Cam* A. Gandolfi.

Source: Based on the play *Hoodman Blind* by Henry Arthur Jones and Wilson Barrett (New York, 30 Nov 1885).

Cast: William Farnum, Dorothy Bernard, Willard Louis, Mary Ruby, Fred Huntley, Harry DuRoy, Henry J. Herbert, William Burress, H. A. Barrows, Thelma Burns, William Scott, Robert Wayne, Mildred Halsey, Jacob Abrams.

Drama. When a husband sees his wife with another man, he abandons her and soon decides to drown himself. At the pier, he watches a woman attempt suicide by jumping into the ocean, and then he dives in to save her. She looks exactly like his wife, and before she dies, she recognizes him, and tells him that she is his wife's gypsy half sister, about whom the wife had never known. A man who loved the wife had hired the gypsy to impersonate her and flirt with a stranger, and so convince the husband of her unfaithfulness. The husband then seeks out the man and beats him, and, because he is wanted for a murder, turns him over to the police. Afterward, the husband's wife warmly welcomes him back when he explains his mistake and apologizes for it. *Attempted suicide. Doubles. Gypsies. Impersonation and imposture. Infidelity. Drowning. Sisters.*

Note: The film was copyrighted at six reels, but all trade journals list it at five.

Motog 25 Mar 1916, p. 722, 725. *MPN* 4 Mar 1916, p. 1285. *MPN* 13 May 1916, p. 2913. *MPW* 13 May 1916, p. 1175. *NYT* 24 Apr 1916, p. 11. *Var* 28 Apr 1916, p. 28. *Wid's* 27 Apr 1916, p. 539.

MAN OF THE PEOPLE (Italian Americans)

Metro-Goldwyn-Mayer Corp.; controlled by Loew's, Inc. 29 Jan **1937**; Prod: 19 Dec–6 Jan 1937 [©Metro-Goldwyn-Mayer Corp.; 26 Jan 1937; LP6888]. Sd (Western Electric Sound System); b&w. 8 reels. 80-81 min. Passed by the National Board of Review. PCA cert no. 3003.

Prod Lucien Hubbard. *Dir* Edwin L. Marin. [*Asst dir* Tom Andre]. *Orig story and scr* Frank Dolan. *Photog* Charles Clarke. *Art dir* Cedric Gibbons. *Art dir assoc* Eddie Imazu and Edwin B. Willis. *Film ed* William S. Gray. *Mus score* Edward Ward. *Rec dir* Douglas Shearer.

Cast: Joseph Calleia (*Jack Moreno*), Florence Rice (*Abbey [Reid]*), Thomas Mitchell ([*William J.*] *Grady*), Ted Healy (*Joe, the glut [Dwire]*), Catharine Doucet (*Mrs. Reid*), Paul Stanton (*Stringer*), Jonathan Hale (*Carter Spetner*), Robert Emmett Keane (*Murphy*), Jane Barnes (*Marie Rossetti*), William Ricciardi ("*Pop*" *Rosetti*), Noel Madison ("*Dopey*" *Benny*), Soledad Jiminez (*Mrs. Rosetti*), Edward Nugent (*Edward Spetner*), Donald Briggs (*Baldwin*), [Clarence Wilson (*Sulker*)], [Heinie Conklin (*Hot Clam Harry Foster*)], [Frank Reicher (*Distrist Attorney Robinson*)], [Selmer Jackson (*Governor*)], [Charles Trowbridge (*Man in courtroom*)], [Russ Powell (*Manager of brewery*)], [Eddie Dunn (*Kitty Horse*)], [Claire DuBrey (*Mrs. Segon*)], [Jack Baxley (*Duffy*)], [Genaro Spagnoli, Hector Sarno, Agostino Borgato (*Italian men*)], [Walter Soderling (*Flaherty*)], [Marty Faust, Frank Bruno (*Hoodlums*)], [Nina Campana, Ines Palange, Belle Mitchell (*Italian women*)], [Eddie Shubert (*Tough guy*)], [Earl Seaman (*Bailiff*)], [Hal Cooke (*Clerk of Court*)], [Al Herman, Edward LeSaint (*Foremen of jury*)], [William Worthington, Frank H. LaRue (*Judges*)], [Charles King (*Announcer*)], [Harry Lash (*Friend of drunk*)], [Louis Natheaux (*Hard-faced gambler*)], [Don Brody (*Pool player*)], [Dick Kipling (*Newspaper man*)], [Clark Marshall (*Miley*)], [Sherry Hall (*First clerk*)], [Alonzo Price (*Second clerk*)], [Mary Loos (*Mannish girl*)], [Lee Phelps (*Relative*)], [Claudia Coleman (*Society woman*)], [Wilson Benge (*Evening butler*)], [Harry B. Stafford, Phillips Smalley (*Society men*)], [Hank Mann (*Watchman*)], [John Ardizoni (*Guierpe*)], [Polly Bailey (*Crying mother*)], [General Savitsky (*Russian doorman*)], [Constantine Romanoff, Budd Fine, Paul Newland (*Bums*)], [Edwin J. Brady, Pat Moriarity, Jimmy O'Gatty (*Tramps*)], [Richard Cramer (*Heckler*)], [Drew Demorest (*Cab driver*)], [Ivar McFadden (*Bearded bum*)], [Ernest Morrelli], [Frank Marlowe], [Lauretta Parillo], [Ray Cooke], [James Quinn], [Elsie Wicks], [Mimi Lawler], [Nick Copeland], [Ernie Adams].

Drama. [*Print viewed*]. On the day that Jack Moreno sets up his law practice in New York's Little Italy, society girl Abbey Reid accidentally hits a neighborhood child with her car. Though the child is not hurt, Abbey feels faint after the incident, and Jack invites her to a party in his honor. As the weeks pass, Jack's practice languishes and he soon is visited by Joe "The Glut" Dwire, an underling of district ward boss William J. Grady. When Joe tells Jack that he can't survive without Grady's help, Jack refuses and says that he is his own man. When Joe later tells this to Grady, Grady decides to pressure Jack by seeing to it that he loses all of his cases. Finally realizing that he cannot survive alone, Jack decides to accept Grady's "help," and his practice soon prospers. Meanwhile, Abbey and a society admirer, Edward Spetner, attend a dinner party at which Edward's father Carter offers stock in a company called La Paz that is marketing a device that purportedly can find gold. When she becomes bored with Edward's talk on the machine, Abbey sneaks away and invites Jack out. When they meet at a Russian restaurant he likes, they begin to fall in love. The next day, unknown to Abbey or Jack, Carter Spetner goes to visit Grady, an old business acquaintance, who promises to help Spetner sell stock in La Paz. Soon, when people in the neighborhood begin buying shares, Jack becomes suspicious. When he assumes a position as assistant district attorney, which he has gotten through Grady's political help, Jack is angry that his boss, Stringer, refuses to allow him to investigate phony securities cases. A short time later, when Ice Wagon, a known criminal, is tried for first degree murder, Jack refuses to reduce the charge, thus angering Grady, who secretly decides to get rid of him. At the ward picnic, Abbey comes with Jack, who anticipates that Grady will announce that Jack is his candidate for District attorney in the next election. Instead of announcing Jack, however, Grady endorses his crony, Joseph B. Murphy. Jack then jumps up on the podium, resigns his job and announces himself as an independent ticket candidate who will expose local corruption. The crowd is against Jack, however, and only Joe and Abbey stay by him. During the campaign, hecklers and agitators disrupt all of Jack's speeches. On election day, Grady follows a "bearded man" strategy, whereby he bribes beared men to vote three times: once with full beard, once with a moustache and once clean-shaven, and Murphy wins. Abbey goes to see Jack that night and they realize they are in love, but he is despondent because he is ruined and an honest man has lost to criminals. Just then, Jack gets a telegram from the governor congratulating him on his defeat and asking him to head a unit to investigate phony securities. "The Moreno Commission" is

successful, then, when Abbey learns that Jack will be investigating La Paz, she asks him to get off the case because her mother is on the board. He refuses, and she angrily leaves. At the hearings, Jack successfully uses magnets to prove that the La Paz gold machine is a scam, then leaves the commission, certain that he has lost Abbey forever. He then returns to his old neighborhood to practice law and enthusiastically goes to the Russian Restaurant when Abbey calls him to meet her there. *Class distinction. Italian Americans. Lawyers. New York City–Little Italy. Political corruption. Romance. Alibi. Beards. Confidence men. Contests. District Attorneys. Elections. Fish. Gluttony. Gold. Governors. Irish Americans. Jews. Judges. Mothers and daughters. Political bosses. Restaurants. Robbery. Trials. Unrequited love.*

Note: Some reviews noted a preview running time of either 85 or 86 minutes for the film. The working title of the picture was *To the Victor.* The *MPH* review and the Call Bureau Cast Service incorrectly refer to Joseph Calleia's character as "Joe" rather than "Jack." According to news items in *HR* and *MPH*, a plagiarism suit was filed against M-G-M and screenwriter Frank Dolan by Henry Rose. Rose's suit claimed that the film plagiarized his play *Burrow, Burrow.* The suit was settled in Jan 1939. Although no details on the amount of the settlement have been located, an additional news item in Apr 1939 noted that Henry M. Schiffer, an agent for Rose and his attorney, George E. Carmody, had filed suit against them for ten percent of the settlement. The outcome of that suit has not been determined.

Box 30 Jan 1937. *DV* 18 Jan 1937, p. 3. *FD* 25 Feb 1937, p. 10. *HR* 21 Dec 1936, p. 18. *HR* 28 Dec 1936, p. 6. *HR* 6 Jan 1937, p. 4. *HR* 18 Jan 1937, p. 3. *HR* 10 Feb 1938, p. 2. *HR* 12 Jan 1939, p. 2. *HR* 5 Apr 1939, p. 7. *MPD* 19 Jan 1937, p. 12. *MPH* 23 Jan 1937, p. 47. *MPH* 30 Jan 1937, p. 50, 52. *MPH* 21 Aug 1937, p. 52. *NYT* 23 Feb 1937, p. 25. *Var* 3 Mar 1937, p. 14.

MAN ON A STRING (Russian Americans)
RD-DR Corp. *Dist* Columbia Pictures Corp. May **1960**; Prod: 31 Mar—27 May 1959 [©RD-DR Corp.; 1 May 1960; LP16664]. Sd (Westrex Recording System); b&w. 10 reels, 8,320 or 8,374 ft. 92 min. PCA cert no. 19491.

Prod Louis De Rochmont [sic] *Assoc prod* Louis De Rochmont [sic] III and Lothar Wolff. *Dir* Andre De Toth. *Asst dir* Eddie Saeta and Jean Hoerler. *Scr* John Kafka and Virginia Shaler. *Dir of photog, Hollywood* Charles Lawton, Jr. *Dir of photog, Berlin, Germany* Albert Benitz. *Dir of photog, New York* Gayne Rescher. *Dir of photog, Moscow, Russia* Pierre Pioncarde. *Art dir* Carl Anderson. *Film ed* Al Clark. *Set dec* James M. Crowe. *Mus comp* George Duning. *Cond* Morris Stoloff. *Orch* Arthur Morton. *Sd* Lambert Day. *Narr* Clete Roberts.

Source: Based in part on the book *My Ten Years as a Counterspy* by Boris Morros in collaboration with Charles Samuels (New York, 1959).

Cast: Ernest Borgnine [(*Boris Mitrov*)], Kerwin Mathews [(*Robert Avery*)], Colleen Dewhurst [(*Helen Benson*)], Alexander Scourby [(*Vadja Kubelov*)], Glenn Corbett [(*Frank Sanford*)], Vladimir Sokoloff [(*Papa*)], Friedrich Joloff [(*Nikolai Chapayev*)], Richard Kendrick [(*Inspector Jenkins*)], Ed Prentiss [(*Adrian Benson*)], [Holger Hagen (*Hans Gruenwald*)], [Robert Iller (*Hartmann*)], [Reginald Pasch (*Otto Bergman*)], [Carl Jaffe (*People's judge*)], [Eva Pflug (*Rosnova*)], [Michael Mellinger (*Detective*)].

Espionage, Drama. [*Print viewed*]. The "Central Bureau of Intelligence," a network formed to consolidate activities of several American spy agencies, learns that one of their agents, who was close to infiltrating the Kremlin, has been thrown off a train in Switzerland and killed. In Washington, Inspector Jenkins tells agent Frank Sanford that the director wants them now to develop as an agent Boris Mitrov, a well-known Russian-born American musician and Hollywood producer, who has been secretly conspiring with the Soviet Union. For more than eighteen months, the Bureau has been watching Boris, his Russian contact, Colonel Vladimir "Vadja" Kubelov, who is the ranking KGB officer in Washington, and an American multi-millionaire banker and his wife, Adrian and Helen Benson, both of whom are Communists. While a squad of agents spy upon Boris' luxurious Beverly Hills home, Boris brings home his elderly father, a dissident who has just been released from Russia. Vadja interrupts the reunion bringing papers for Boris to sign that will give Adrian control of Boris' film studio. Boris had agreed to this in order to get his father out, and Vadja now tells him that the fate of his brothers, still in Russia, will depend upon his future work. Sometime later, Boris is visited by Frank and Inspector Jenkins, who bring proof that Boris is working for Russian intelligence. Ashamed, Boris explains he began a friendship with Vadja ten years earlier at a time when he felt the

effects of prejudice because of his identity as a Russian. He denies taking money, but admits accepting gifts for acting as a liaison between Communist agents and acquaintances in the U.S., and allowing his business to be used as a coverup for espionage. Boris' father, having overheard the conversation, berates his son for betraying his country, and reveals that his other sons have been killed by the Soviets. Boris now agrees to help the Bureau, and they send him to Berlin, ostensibly to make documentary films for the U.S. government. When Boris learns that his supposed close friend and assistant, Robert Avery, will be the special agent assigned to accompany him, he is deeply upset at Robert's deception, but later, Robert conveys his sympathy for Boris' situation, and Boris thanks him. When Vadja tells Helen Benson, with whom he is having an affair, that the Russian embassy has recalled him, she implores him to take her with him to Moscow. She returns reluctantly, however, to Adrian, who has discovered that their home and studio are bugged, and they quickly leave for Mexico to get asylum. In a Berlin nightclub, Boris meets Rosnova, an attractive female Russian agent, who brings him to a trial in East Berlin, in which Otto Bergman, a concentration camp survivor who works at Boris' studio, is being accused of crimes against East Germany. Bergman's earlier warning to Boris about former Gestapo informer Hans Gruenwald, who now works for the Russian secret police, had been overheard by an informer. To protect his own espionage work, Boris reluctantly testifies against Otto. After the Bureau supplies Boris with inocuous information to give to Vadja, he is invited to Moscow. Robert gives him a cigarette lighter containing an electric pistol that shoots tiny cyanide bullets, and they decide that the code word "Cinerama" in a message will signal that he is in danger. In Moscow, General Nikolai Chapayev, director of the KGB, tells Boris that he is considering putting him in charge of several new American espionage units. At Moscow University, Boris attends a class for students who plan to infiltrate communities in America and other countries posing as citizens. Vadja reveals that in an emergency, every agent could carry a bomb. Meanwhile, the Bensons arrive in Berlin, where Helen tells Robert of her husband's plan to destroy Vadja by denouncing Boris as a counterspy. Robert sends Boris a telegram that he must return to Berlin for an important Cinerama conference. The next day, as Boris lands at the East Berlin airport, Chapayev learns of Adrian's suspicions and orders checkpoints to West Berlin closed. After Boris shoots a police officer who has handcuffed him with the lighter filled with cyanide bullets, he escapes to West Berlin. At his hotel, Robert instructs him to immediately talk about everything he has learned in Moscow, as their conversation is being recorded. Boris recalls the code names and descriptions of the agents who have been sent to various parts of the U.S., as a sniper fires through Boris' window and two KGB agents kick in the door. Robert shoots one before he is wounded by Gruenwald, then Boris savagely beats Gruenwald over the head with the handcuffs. Boris' information leads to arrests at the Los Angeles airport of the new Russian agents. Boris, who now considers the U.S. his home, is awarded a special commendation in Congress for his services. *Espionage. Loyalty. Boris Morros. Russia. Russian Americans. Traitors. Transformation. Airports. Bankers. Berlin (Germany). Beverly Hills (CA). Birthdays. Boats. Cigarette lighters. Dances. Eavesdropping. Fathers and sons. Hotels. Infidelity. Kremlin (Moscow). Los Angeles (CA). Mexican-American border region. Millionaires. Moscow (Russia). Motion picture producers. Motion picture studios. New York City. Nightclubs. Ruins. Russians. Switzerland. Taxicabs. Trains. Universities. Washington (D.C.).*

Note: The working title of this film was *Ten Years a Counterspy.* The character "Boris Mitrov" was based on Boris Morros, who was identified by the U.S. government as a counterspy in 1957. According to articles appearing in 1957 and 1958, Morros, a child prodigy musician in czarist Russia, came to the U.S. in 1922. While Morros and many sources state that he came here as music director of the French revue *Chaive-Souris* and that he wrote a popular song in the revue, "Parade of the Wooden Soldiers," this was disputed by the widow of Nikita Balieff, the show's producer. In an autobiographical article, Morros states that in 1933, while he was supervisor for the stage shows of the Paramount theaters in New York, a Russian trade official offered to help facilitate the sending of food packages to his parents in the Soviet Union and to arrange for his father to visit in return for an agreement that he not book Leon Trotsky for the shows. As Morros had no interest in booking Trotsky, he agreed. In 1936, while Morros was general musical director of Paramount in Hollywood, a Russian official convinced him to sign an affidavit stating that the official was working as a talent scout for the studio so that he could work in Germany surreptitiously against the Nazis. Morros later became a producer for Paramount, and in 1938, resigned to form Boris Morros Productions. During the

war, he produced training films for the Army, and in 1945, organized an independent company with William LeBaron. Morros was the producer of the critically acclaimed *Carnegie Hall*, and also made *Tales of Manhattan* and *The Flying Deuces*. In 1943, the FBI began surveillance of Morros, who had been meeting with West Coast Soviet consular officials and spy boss Vassily Zubilin. That year, Morros was able to get his father, the former conductor of the Imperial Symphony Orchestra, into the U.S. with the help of Soviet officials. Morros soon became part of a Soviet spy ring, but by 1947, he had become a counterspy for the FBI.

Morros' role seems to have been that of a courier of written and verbal information. His testimony as a witness in 1957 was responsible for indictments against three groups of spies. In Jan 1957, Jack Soble, an appointee of former Soviet spy chief Lavrenty P. Beria, Soble's wife Myra, and Jacob Albam were arrested and later indicted and sentenced for 23 "overt acts" of espionage over a ten-year period, involving the passing of U.S. military and economic secrets to Soviet agents in New York, Paris, Vienna and Zurich. Morros, named as an "unknown individual" involved in 14 of the acts, was identified publicly at that time after the Sobles' lawyer demanded that his identity be revealed. The story of his career as a spy and counterspy was first made public on 25 Feb 1957. Later in 1957, a 38-count indictment was issued against George Zlatovski, a Russian-born engineer and former U.S. Army intelligence officer, and his wife Jane Foster Zlatovski, a former O.S.S. employee. The couple, who worked under Soble, were charged with having conspired since December 1940 with Soviet agents in New York, Washington, Paris, Austria and Switzerland to obtain and transmit defense and intelligence information to Russia, along with compromising information on the sexual and drinking habits of Americans assigned to Austria.

By the time of the indictment, the Zlatovskis had been given political asylum in Paris. In Aug 1957, Morros testified before the House Un-American Activities Committee that Martha Dodd Stern, daughter of distinguished historian and former ambassador to Germany, William E. Dodd, and her husband, Alfred K. Stern, a former New York investment banker and Illinois housing commissioner, were also involved in the ring. The Sterns became the models for the fictional couple the "Bensons" of the film. Before their indictment, they had gone to Mexico, and they later surfaced in Moscow. Morros related that once while he was meeting with Beria in Moscow, word arrived from Mrs. Stern that he was a counterspy, but he was able to convince the Soviets that her charge was based solely on jealousy. Morros also testified that Zubilin once drove him to the Sterns' exclusive Ridgefield, Connecticut home, where Stern agreed to provide $130,000 to set up a movie company as a cover for espionage activities. Both of these incidents are dramatized in the film.

Morros had been shunned by the film industry during the early 1950s when he paid $60,000 in cash to the Soviet Union for the rights to the Russian musical *Marika*, despite the official U.S. policy of discouraging trade with Russia involving dollars. He died in 1963 at age 73 of cancer and was called a "patriot" in his obituaries. Location shooting for the film was done in Moscow and Berlin. Cliff Robertson was originally cast in the role of the FBI agent.

Box 11 Apr 1960. *Chicago Daily Tribune* 3 Jan 1958. *Cue* 4 Jun 1960. *DV* 22 Dec 1958. *DV* 23 Dec 1958. *DV* 9 Apr 1959. *DV* 8 Apr 1960, p. 3. *Exb* 13 Apr 1960, p. 4693. *FD* 8 Apr 1960, p. 6. *FIR* May 1960, pp. 289-90. *Har* 9 Apr 1960, p. 58. *HCN* 9 Jul 1957. *HCN* 9 Jan 1963. *HR* 13 Aug 1957. *HR* 21 Apr 1957. *HR* 27 Apr 1959. *HR* 8 Apr 1960, p. 3. *LAEx* 26 Feb 1957. *LAEx* 9 Jul 1957. *LAEx* 4 Apr 1957. *LAEx* 6 Dec 1957. *LAEx* 22 Dec 1958. *LAEx* 10 Jan 1963. *LAT* 26 Feb 1957. *LAT* 13 Aug 1957. *LAT* 21 Oct 1960. *Look* 26 Nov 1957. *MPD* 11 Apr 1960. *MPHPD* 16 Apr 1960, p. 661. *Newsweek* 4 Mar 1957. *NYT* 21 May 1960, p. 15. *NYT* 10 Jan 1963. *Time* 26 Aug 1957. *Var* 13 Apr 1960, p. 6.

MAN ON THE TRAIN *see* THE TALL TARGET

MAN TSO TEH HOW SIN *see* MIN JOK JAY HUNG SING

THE MAN WHO CAME BACK *(foreignversion) see* DEL INFIERNO AL CIELO

THE MAN WHO DARED (Italian Americans)

Fox Film Corp. *Dist* Fox Film Corp. 29 Aug **1920** [©William Fox; 29 Aug 1920; LP15585]. Si; b&w. 6 reels, 6,320 ft.

Dir Emmett J. Flynn. *Story and scen* Julius G. Furthman. *Cam* Clyde De Vinna.

Cast: William Russell (*Big Jim Kane*), Eileen Percy (*Mamie Lee*), Frank Brownlee (*Ed Cass*), Fred Warren (*Sam Corwin*), Lon Poff (*Long John*), Joe Ray.

Drama. When Mamie Lee's father, Sam Corwin, is sentenced to jail for forgery, the sheriff, Ed Cass, offers to cover the debt in return for Mamie Lee's hand in marriage. The distraught daughter agrees, and Cass robs the saloon to obtain the money, framing Jim Kane, his rival for Mamie's affections, for the crime. Jim is sent to jail an embittered man. In the adjacent cell he watches an Italian stonecutter, a condemned murderer, spend the night before his execution chiseling a figure of Christ. After the sculptor collapses from exhaustion, Jim is astounded to see the spirit of Christ appear and minister to the condemned man. His religious experience converts Jim to Christianity. Meanwhile, Mamie Lee discovers a confession to the robbery written by Cass and brings it to the judge. Realizing that he is doomed, the sheriff kills himself, thus freeing Jim to begin life anew with Mamie Lee. *Frame-ups. Jesus Christ. Religious conversion.*

Sculpture. Sheriffs. Christianity. Confession (Law). Debt. Executions. Forgers and forgery. Ghosts. Italian Americans. Miracles. Rivalry. Robbery. Sculptors. Suicide.

Note: According to a news item, some scenes were shot in a lumber camp in California's redwood country.

MPN 10 Apr 1920, p. 3328. *MPN* 28 Aug 1920, p. 1692. *MPN* 4 Sep 1920, p. 1828. *MPW* 14 Aug 1920, p. 932. *NYMT* 1 Aug 1920. *Wid's* 8 Aug 1920, p. 14.

THE MAN WHO DARED: AN IMAGINATIVE BIOGRAPHY (Czech Americans)

Fox Film Corp. *Dist* Fox Film Corp. 14 Jul **1933**; Prod: began mid-May 1933 [©Fox Film Corp.; 30 Jun 1933; LP4005]. Sd (Western Electric Noiseless Recording); b&w. 8 reels, 6,200 ft. 72 or 75 min. Passed by the National Board of Review. PCA cert no. 3320-R [15 Apr 1937].

[*Prod* Sol M. Wurtzel]. *Dir* Hamilton MacFadden. [*Asst dir* Ed O'Fearna]. *Orig scr* Dudley Nichols and Lamar Trotti. *Photog* Arthur Miller. [*2d cam* Joe La Shelle]. [*Asst cam* Bill Abbott and Milton Gold]. *Settings* Duncan Cramer. [*Film ed* Al DeGaetano]. *Cost* Royer. *Mus dir* Samuel Kaylin. *Sd* E. F. Grossman.

Cast: Preston Foster (*Jan Novak*), Zita Johann (*Teena Pavelic*), Joan Marsh (*Joan* [*Novak*]), Irene Biller (*Tereza Novak*), Clifford Jones (*Dick*), June Vlasek (*Barbara* [*Novak*]), Leon Wykoff (*Yosef Novak*), Douglas Cosgrove (*Dan Foley*), Douglas Dumbrille (*Judge Collier*), Frank Sheridan (*Senator* [*John*] *McGunness* [*McGuinness*]), Leonid Snegoff ([*Victor*] *Posilipo*), Elsie Larson (*Ruzena* [*Novak*]), Lita Chevret (*Miss Rainey*), Vivian Reid (*Ronda*), Matt McHugh (*Karel*), Jay Ward (*Jan Novak, the boy*).

Biography, **Drama**. [*Print viewed*]. In 1871, Bohemian immigrants Yosef and Tereza Novak bring their infant son Jan to the United States. On their way to Chicago, a man swindles them by selling them fake citizenship papers, and further misfortune strikes when their train cannot stop in Chicago because of a huge fire. On the advice of the conductor, the Novaks settle in nearby Braidwood, where Yosef becomes a coal miner. In 1880, Yosef advises Jan to study hard so that he can take advantage of the opportunities provided by America. Later that day, however, Yosef is killed in a mine explosion, and Jan is forced to work to support his mother and two sisters, Ruzena and Katie. Twelve years later, Jan is fired for asking for a raise, after which he walks to Chicago to begin a new life. Jan works hard and, while becoming a successful peddler, makes the acquaintence of Teena Pavelic, a waitress in the café of Viktor Posilipo. Viktor helps Jan defeat his rivel, Karel, in their struggle for Teena's affections, and soon the young couple are wed. Their first daughter is born at the time of the Spanish-American War, and while the Novaks are celebrating, local Senator John McGuiness worries about garnering the immigrant vote. One of his men, Dan Foley, suggests that he cultivate Jan, who is a leader in the Bohemian community. McGuinness and Foley persuade Jan to work for their party and, after Jan helps defeat Judge Collier, a McGuinness rival, he becomes an important district leader. Later, around the time of the assassination of President William McKinley, Jan is elected state senator and runs afoul of other political leaders when he refuses to introduce martial law to suppress a miners' strike. Jan fights for the miners and enables them to win the right to have their dispute settled by arbitration. In 1912, after President Woodrow Wilson is elected president, McGuinness reprimands Jan for not supporting his bill to repeal the civil service, but Jan declares that the civil service should be reformed instead. Jan's liberal views keep him in constant conflict with his former cronies, but his family life continues to bring happiness as his daughter Joan marries her sweetheart Dick. Dick fights in World War I, and while the war is being waged, Jan fights against Prohibition, which he believes is not fair to enact while the soldiers are gone and cannot vote and will lead to a rise in organized crime. Although Jan loses the election for United States Senator, he eventually becomes the first foreign-born mayor of Chicago. Tragedy strikes, however, when Teena dies on the night of the election. Jan then devotes all of his energy to rid Chicago of crime and to prepare the city for the next world's fair. He reminisces about going with Teena to the previous Chicago world's fair, forty years earlier, and decides to invite President-Elect Franklin Delano Roosevelt to the festivities. Jan travels to Miami to meet with Roosevelt, and there he is shot by an assassin who is attempting to kill the president-elect. As Jan lays dying, he tells Roosevelt that he is glad it was himself who was shot, rather than the leader of his adopted country. *Assassination.*

Chicago (IL). Czechoslovakian Americans. Marriage. Mayors. Patriotism. Vocational obsession. Cafés. Childbirth. Coal miners. Fairs. Family life. Immigrants. William McKinley. Miami (FL). Peddlers and peddling. Picnicking. Political bosses. Prohibition. Rivalry. Franklin Delano Roosevelt. Soldiers. Swindlers and swindling. Temptresses. United States–History–20th century. United States–History–War of 1898. Women's suffrage. World War I.

Note: The working title of this film was *The American*, and it was based on the life of Anton Cermak. Cermak, an immigrant from Bohemia, was Chicago's first foreign-born mayor. He was shot by Italian anarchist Giuseppe Zangara on 15 Feb 1933, when Zangara attempted to assassinate President-Elect Franklin Delano Roosevelt in Miami. When Cermak died nineteen days later, Zangara was sentenced to the electric chair and was executed on 20 Mar 1933. The film's file in the MPAA/PCA Collection at the AMPAS Library contains a review by PCA staff member Vincent G. Hart, who stated: "Mr. Cermak's life is not overdone, and care has been taken not to emphasize the fatal shooting, which is a duplicate of the newsreels of the tragedy. The use of the President in this scene has been very carefully handeled, and only the hands of the imaginary President are shown, which takes care of any objection."
The Man Who Dared was the first screenplay written by Lamar Trotti, who was formerly the aid of Colonel Jason S. Joy of the MPAA. It was also the first of seven scripts on which Trotti and former *New York World* reporter Dudley Nichols collaborated. Plans for this biography were announced as early as 10 Mar 1933 by producer Sol Wurtzel, who stated that Nichols and Trotti had been working on the script since the shooting occurred. The part of "Jan Novak" was originally assigned to Spencer Tracy. According to a *LAT* news item, Tracy asked to be removed from the cast so that he could instead star in *The Power and the Glory* (see *AFI Catalog of Feature Films, 1931-1940*; F3.3506). The news item also noted that Victor Jory was to have been in the cast, but was instead placed by Fox in *The Devil's in Love* (see *AFI Catalog of Feature Films, 1931-1940*; F3.1039). A *FD* news item announced that Frank Conroy was signed for a role in the picture, but his participation in the completed film has not been confirmed. An earlier assassination plot against Cermak was the subject of a two-part episode of the ABC television series *The Untouchables*, which was broadcast in the 1959-1960 season.
FD 15 Apr 1933, p. 3. *FD* 10 May 1933, p. 10. *FD* 9 Sep 1933, p. 4. *HH* 11 May 1933, p. 14. *IP* Jun 1933, p. 25. *LAT* 11 Mar 1933, p. 7. *LAT* 3 May 1933, p. 7. *MPD* 9 Sep 1933, p. 2. *MPH* 15 Jul 1933, p. 71. *NYT* 9 Sep 1933, p. 9. *Var* 12 Sep 1933, p. 17.

MAN WITH A GUN *see* **THE MAN BEHIND THE GUN**

MAN WITH A SHOVEL *see* **ACCENT ON LOVE**

THE MAN WITH TWO MOTHERS (Irish Americans)
Goldwyn Pictures Corp. Feb **1922** [©Goldwyn Pictures Corp.; 11 Feb 1922; LP17543]. Si; b&w. 5 reels, 4,423 ft.
Dir Paul Bern. *Scen* Julien Josephson. *Story* Alice Duer Miller. *Photog* Percy Hilburn.
Cast: Cullen Landis (*Dennis O'Neill*), Sylvia Breamer (*Claire Mordaunt*), Mary Alden (*Widow O'Neill*), Hallam Cooley (*Richey*), Fred Huntly (*Butler*), Laura La Varnie (*Mrs. Bryan*), Monte Collins (*Tim Donohue*), William Elmer (*Clancy*).
Comedy-drama. Dennis O'Neill comes to America from Ireland at the request of his wealthy aunt, who intends to make him heir to the family fortune accrued from a junk business, but Mrs. Bryan objects to the presence of his widowed mother, who reminds her of their humble origins. Claire, niece of Mrs. Bryan, supports Dennis in his determination not to abandon his mother, and he installs Mrs. O'Neill in a nearby apartment of Tim Donohue, a friend from the old country, from whose window she can signal to Dennis. Dennis discovers that Hansen, manager of the junk firm, and his assistant, Richey, a suitor of Claire's, are padding the payroll. He finds that his affections for Claire are reciprocated, but Richey informs her that he is keeping another girl in the Donohue apartment. Dennis produces his mother, takes vengeance on Richey, and wins Claire—all to the satisfaction of Mrs. Bryan. *Family relationships. Inheritance. Irish Americans. Junk trade.*
ETR 29 Apr 1922, p. 1599. *FD* 4 Jun 1922. *Var* 16 Jun 1922, p. 42.

MANDARIN'S GOLD (Chinese Americans)
World Film Corp. *Dist* World Film Corp. 10 Feb **1919** [©World Film Corp.; 16 Jan 1919; LU13418]. Si; b&w. 5 reels, 4,877 ft.
Dir Oscar Apfel. *Scen* Lucien Hubbard. *Story* Philip Lonergan. *Cam* Lucien Tainguy. *Cost* Madame Simon.
Cast: Kitty Gordon (*Betty Cardon*), Irving Cummings (*Blair Cardon*), George MacQuarrie (*Geoffrey North*), Marguerite Gale (*Susan Pettigrew*), Veronica Lee (*Cherry Blossom*), Warner Oland (*Li Hsun*), Joseph Lee (*Wu Sing*), Marion Barney (*Mrs. Stone*), Tony Merlo (*Bertie Standish*), Charles Fang, Alice Lee.
Drama. In China, a boy reads a legend about a mysterious woman's power over a wealthy Mandarin prince. In New York, Betty Cardon, a social butterfly, disregards her husband Blair's order to stop gambling their money at bridge, and finds herself in debt to Geoffrey North, who, encouraged by her flirting, now wants sexual payment. Cherry Blossom, a Chinese girl who refuses to be sold by her father to the brutal Li Hsun, a wealthy Mandarin, hides in Betty's home after Betty's friend, Susan Pettigrew, a mission worker, introduces them. Panicked and distraught, Betty accepts Li Hsun's gold for Cherry Blossom. She guiltily follows them and witnesses Cherry Blossom's torture to force her to give up her lover. Both are killed when she refuses. Blair arrives with the police who shoot Li Hsun trying to escape. After Blair denounces Betty, she awakens to discover she dreamed she accepted Li Hsun's offer. She then confesses to Blair and vows to stop gambling. *Chinese Americans. Dreams. Gambling. Guilt. New York City–Chinatown. Princes. Socialites. Bridge (Game). China. Confession. Debt. Flirtation. Marriage. Murder. Settlement workers. Torture.*

Note: Scenes in this film were shot in New York's Chinatown.
ETR 8 Feb 1919, p. 775. *MPN* 8 Feb 1919, p. 929. *MPW* 8 Feb 1919, pp. 805-06. *NYMT* 9 Feb 1919. *Var* 31 Jan 1919, p. 53. *Wid's* 16 Feb 1919, p. 15.

THE MANDARIN'S SECRET *see* **SHADOWS OVER CHINATOWN**

MANHATTAN FOLKSONG *see* **MUSIC MAN**

MANHATTAN MERRY-GO-ROUND (Italian Americans)
Republic Pictures Corp. *Dist* Republic Pictures Corp. 26 Nov **1937**; Prod: began 4 Aug 1937 at Biograph Studios, New York; added scenes: 22 Sep—23 Sep 1937 [©Republic Pictures Corp.; 13 Nov 1937; LP7597]. Sd (RCA Victor "High Fidelity" Sound System); b&w. 10 reels. 78 or 82 min. Passed by the National Board of Review. PCA cert no. 3734.
Assoc prod Harry Sauber. *All mus seq supv* Harry Grey. *Dir* Charles F. Riesner. *Asst dir* George Sherman. [*Dir of New York seq* John H. Auer]. *Scr* Harry Sauber. *Photog* Jack Marta. *Art dir* John Victor Mackay. *Ed* Ernest Nims. *Supv ed* Murray Seldeen. *Cost* Eloise. *Furs by* Willard H. George. *Jewelry by* Mauboussin, Trabert & Hoeffer, Inc. *Miss Geva's wardrobe by* Muriel King. *Mus dir* Albert Columbo. *Mus supv* Harry Grey.
Song(s): "Have You Ever Been in Heaven," "I Owe You" and "All Over Nothing at All," music and lyrics by Peter Tinturin and Jack Lawrence; "Mama, I Wanna Make Rhythm," music and lyrics by Walter Kent, Jerome Jerome and Richard Byron; "It's Roundup Time in Reno," music and lyrics by Jack M. Owens and Gene Autry, additional lyrics by Jack Lawrence; other songs by Sammy Cahn and Saul Chaplin.
Source: Based on the musical *Manhattan Merry-Go-Round* by Frank Hummert (production undetermined).
Cast: PHIL REGAN [(*Jerry Hart*)], LEO CARRILLO [(*Tony Gordoni*)], ANN DVORAK [(*Ann Rogers*)], Tamara Geva [(*Charlizzini*)], James Gleason [(*Danny the Duck*)], Ted Lewis and His Orchestra [(*Themselves*)], Cab Calloway and His Cotton Club Band [(*Themselves*)], Kay Thompson and Her Radio Choir [(*Themselves*)], Joe DiMaggio [(*Himself*)], Henry Armetta [(*Spadoni*)], Luis Alberni [(*Martinetti*)], Max Terhune [(*Himself*)], Smiley Burnette [(*Frog, accordian player*)], Louis Prima, and His Band [(*Themselves*)], Gene Autry [(*Himself*)], [Selmer Jackson (*J. Henry Thorne*)], [Eddie Kane (*McMurray*)], [Moroni Olsen (*Jonathan*)], [Nellie V. Nichols (*Momma Gordoni*)], [Gennaro Curci (*Michael Angelo*)], [Sam Finn (*Speed*)], [Al Herman (*Blackie*)], [Robert E. Perry (*Baldy*)], [Jack Adair (*Eddie*)], [Jack Jenny, and His Orchestra (*Themselves*)], [The Lathrops (*Themselves*)], [Rosalean and Seville (*Themselves*)], [Thelma Wunder (*Dorothy*)], [Ralph Edwards (*Radio man*)].
Musical. [*Viewed print incomplete*]. Italian mobster Tony Gordoni buys the Associated Recording Company and acquires recording contracts with Ted Lewis, Kay Thompson and Cab Calloway. When his mother accuses him of being ashamed of his Italian heritage, Gordoni forces singer Jerry Hart to charm the hot-tempered opera star Charlizzini into making a record. Jerry, however, has just proposed to Associated secretary Ann Rogers, who had convinced Gordoni to record Jerry after he lost his job at the Manhattan Merry-Go-Round nightclub, and balks at the idea. Gordoni threatens to harm Ann if Jerry does not meet Charlizzini that evening, the night of Ann and Jerry's wedding. While Ann waits at the church, Jerry, along with Gordoni's thug, Danny the Duck, sings for Charlizzini and convinces her an album would make her a benefactor to shut-ins around the

world. The next few days, Charlizzini monopolizes Jerry's time, insisting he call her "Charlie," and he is unable to explain to Ann. After opera impresario Martinetti refuses to allow Charlizinni to record, Gordoni takes her to a Long Island estate with Jerry to make it look as though she has been kidnapped. He then promises Martinetti he will return her if he allows her to record, and Martinetti acquiesces. Meanwhile, the police go to the estate and Charlizinni admits the abduction was a hoax to control Martinetti. Back at the studio, Ann refuses to speak to Jerry, and when Charlizzini throws a tantrum, Jerry scoffs at her and disappears. Danny locates Jerry on Gene Autry's ranch, singing with the Cowboy Band. By convincing Autry's group to record at Associated, Gordoni gets Jerry back to the studio. Meanwhile, Charlizzini and Gordoni fall in love and explain all to Ann. After Ann records a reconciliation speech, which they play for Jerry, the reunited couple embraces. *False accusations. Gangsters. Italian Americans. Recordings. Singers. Brides. Cowboys. Family honor. Fidelity. Hoaxes. Kidnapping. Long Island (NY). Love tests. Mothers and sons. Opera singers. Police. Proposals (Marital). Radio broadcasting. Ranches. Romantic rivalry. Television. Timidity. Weddings.*

Note: In the opening credits, Gene Autry's photograph appears over the words "and introducing that cowboy singing star Gene Autry," however Autry had appeared in a number of films previous to this. The title *Metropolitan Merry-Go-Round* was announced in the 1935 *Film Daily Product Guide* as part of Republic's upcoming 1935-36 season, and contemporary news items from Jun and Nov 1935 list Pinky Tomlin and Roger Pryor in the cast. Production on *Manhattan Merry-Go-Round* did not start until early Aug 1937, however, and it is unclear whether *Metropolitan Merry-Go-Round* was an early title for this film. According to a news item in *HR* on 4 Aug 1937, the day shooting began at Biograph Studios in New York, John Auer was set to direct ten days of shooting there. While a *HR* production chart from day seven lists Auer as the New York director (with credited director Charles F. Reisner listed as director of the entire production), Auer is not credited on the screen or in reviews. The production note also lists Harry Grey as New York producer (with credited producer Harry Sauber listed as the film's general producer), but Grey receives screen credit as the supervisor of all musical sequences. On 22 Sep 1937, Phil Regan returned to Republic for two days of added scenes. According to a Sep 1937 letter to AMPAS, the film's official billing below the title was changed from "with James Gleason—Tamara Geva" to "with Tamara Geva—James Gleason." The film contains newsreel footage of the homerun that Joe DiMaggio hit for the New York Yankees in the 1936 World Series. Although some sources include the Cab Calloway/Irving Mills song "Minnie the Moocher" in the credits, only the last few bars of the song were included in the film. In a nightclub sequence, Calloway ends the song, then tells the audience that they have just heard about Minnie the Moocher, and will now hear about a man named "Jasha." He and his orchestra then perform the song "Mama, I Want to Make Rhythm." According to a 1937 *HR* announcement, Virginia Dabney was cast in this film, although her appearance in the final film has not been confirmed.

DV 5 Nov 1937, p. 3. *FD* 11 Nov 1937, p. 12. *FD* 16 Nov 1937, pp. 10-11. *HR* 4 Aug 1937, p. 17. *HR* 9 Aug 1937, p. 14. *HR* 22 Sep 1937, p. 7. *HR* 5 Nov 1937, p. 2. *MPD* 8 Nov 1937, p. 7. *MPH* 23 Oct 1937, p. 49. *MPH* 13 Nov 1937, p. 42. *NYT* 31 Dec 1937, p. 3. *Var* 10 Nov 1937, p. 18.

THE MANICURE GIRL (Italian Americans)

Famous Players-Lasky Corp. *Dist* Paramount Pictures. 6 Jul **1925** [©Famous Players-Lasky Corp.; 11 Jul 1925; LP21646]. Si; b&w. 6 reels, 5,959 ft.

Pres Adolph Zukor and Jesse L. Lasky. *Dir* Frank Tuttle. *Scr* Townsend Martin. *Story* Frederick Hatton and Fanny Hatton. *Photog* J. Roy Hunt. *Art dir* Julian Boone Fleming.

Cast: Bebe Daniels (*Maria Maretti*), Edmund Burns (*Antonio Luca*), Dorothy Cumming (*Flora*), Hale Hamilton (*James Morgan*), Charlotte Walker (*Mrs. Morgan*), Ann Brody (*Mother Luca*), Marie Shotwell (*Mrs. Wainright*), Mary Foy (*Mrs. Root-Chiveley*).

Romance, Drama. Maria Maretti, a manicurist in the beauty shop of a large metropolitan hotel, is engaged to Antonio Luca, an electrician who operates a small radio repair business. At the hotel, Maria meets James Morgan, a wealthy guest who, when Maria will not go out with him, sends her ten dollars for theater tickets. Over Antonio's objections, Maria does not return the money; instead she and Antonio go to a play. After the performance, Antonio is too niggardly to hire a taxi; and while he is chasing his hat down a windy street, Maria accepts a ride with Morgan. Later, she and Antonio fight, and she goes to Morgan for consolation, belatedly discovering that he is married. Maria reunites Morgan with his wife, then gladly returns to the penitent Antonio. *Beauty shops. Electricians. Hotels. Italian Americans. Manicurists. Marriage. Radios.*

FD 5 Jul 1925. *NYT* 15 Jun 1925, p. 10. *Var* 17 Jun 1925, p. 35.

A MAN'S DUTY (African Americans)

Lincoln Motion Picture Co. **1919**; Premiere in Omaha, Nebraska: 3 Sep 1919; Prod: 15 Jun—7 Jul 1919. Si; b&w. 5 reels.

Dir Harry A. Gant and D. Ireland Thomas. *Cam* Harry A. Gant.

Cast: Clarence Brooks (*Richard Beverly*), Webb King (*Hubert Gordon*), Tasmania Darden, Ethel Gray, Eva Johnson, Anita Thompson, W. H. Sanders, Mrs. Connors, Frank White, Gennette Criner.

African American, Drama. Socialite Richard Beverly and Hubert Gordon are rivals for the affections of Myra Lewis. A drunken revel, contrived by Hubert to embarrass Richard in public, ends with the two spending the night at a bordello. Learning of the trick the next day, Richard fights Hubert, who hits his head on a rock after Richard fells him. Richard, thinking that he is a murderer, flees and becomes a dissipated drunk in a distant city, where he meets Merriam Givens, an unmarried woman with a child. Hoping to clear himself of disgrace so that he can marry Merriam, he writes home and learns that, although Hubert survived the accident, the prostitute Helen is pregnant as a result of their night together. Richard confides to Merriam, who tells him that the child she has raised is not hers and that he should return home to marry Helen. Upon his return he learns that Hubert, who has married Myra, is really the father of Helen's unborn child. Richard summons Merriam to his home to join in a joyous family reunion. *African Americans. Dissipation. Illegitimacy. Moral reformation. Pregnancy. Romantic rivalry. Brothels. Drunkenness. Fights. Parentage. Socialites. White-slave traffic.*

Note: This was the first feature-length production of the Lincoln Motion Picture Co., one of the leading black independent companies of the period. Contemporary sources disagree as to whether Gant or Thomas directed the film. Anita Thompson is also identified as Anita DeBois by contemporary sources.

ChiDef 7 Aug 1920, p. 4. *NYN* 24 Jul 1919. *Omaha Monitor* 28 Aug 1919.

MANSLAUGHTER (*foreign version*) see LA INCORREGIBLE

MANTAN MESSES UP (Africa Americans)

Lucky Star Production Co. *Dist* Toddy Pictures Co. **1946**. Sd; b&w. 5 reels, 3,902 ft. 43 min.

[*Prod* Ted Toddy].

Song(s): "That's My Hap-Hap-Happiness," words by Howard Johnson and Charles Tobias, music by Al Sherman, and other songs.

Cast: Mantan Moreland (*Office boy* [*also known as Mantan*]), Monte Hawley (*Office manager, Mr. Hawley*), Jo Rhetta (*Secretary*), Doryce Bradley (*Dancer*), Lola Carrington (*Wife*), Raymond Harris (*Actor*), *Special added cast*: Lena Horne, Eddie Green, Buck and Bubbles, Nina Mae McKinney, Red Caps, Neva Peoples, Bo Jinkins, Delia White, Four Tones.

African American, Comedy, with songs. [*Not viewed*]. Mantan, who is looking for a job, wanders into the See-All, Know-All television station that has just televised its very first broadcast, a singing performance. As the station's secretary asks Mantan about his experience, the prospective office boy persists in asking her for a date, but she responds that she has five children and is married to a policeman. When the office manager, Mr. Hawley, appears, he offers to interview Mantan, even though Mantan would prefer to join the secretary on her lunch break. During the interview for the office boy position, Mr. Hawley explains how television works, as Mantan must be disabused of his notion that a television is like a telescope. After the interview, the boss himself goes for lunch with the secretary and leaves Mantan in charge of the station. Mantan pretends that he is the office manager and a parade of people pass through the studio, including a Shakespearean actor and Mantan's wife, who is impressed at her husband's new role as the big boss. Next, a dancer arrives looking for work, and Mantan tells her she will be on television if she can fit into the costume. In order to do so she must strip off a few articles of clothing, and Mr. Hawley walks in, shocked to see the young woman auditioning in his office. Eventually the dancer returns in order to get paid, but the boss tells her that they do not pay for auditions. A big kiss from the dancer convinces the boss otherwise, and he then fires Mantan. While bemoaning his fate to his wife, Mantan accidentally wanders onto the stage and, to his shock, sees himself on television. *Flirts. Television programs. Unemployment. Auditions. Dancers. Dismissal (Employment). Marriage. Secretaries. Singers.*

Note: The above credits and plot summary were based on a dialogue continuity deposited with the NYSA. According to the continuity, the film was copyrighted in 1945 by Toddy Pictures Company, but the film is not included

in U.S. Copyright records. The opening credits included the following written prologue: "Instead of radio, this is what you will see in your homes in the future. NO FOOLIN.' Television." The continuity contains the lyrics to several songs, but their titles and composers have not been determined.

MANTAN RUNS FOR MAYOR (African Americans)

Lucky Star Production Co. *Dist* Toddy Pictures Co. **1947**. Sd; b&w. 5 reels, 5,340 ft.

Cast: Mantan Moreland (*Mantan*), Flournoy E. Miller (*Alex*), Johnny Lee (*Johnny Lee, Mantan's opponent*).

African American, Comedy. [*Not viewed*]. After collecting his usual meager paycheck, Mantan, a part time janitor at the local courthouse, commiserates with his ne'er-do-well friend Alex, who is similarly poorly paid. Since Mayor Henry Corbit has been arrested for drunken driving and sentenced by the famous "poetical" judge, Alex comes upon the idea of having Mantan run for mayor, with Alex serving as his campaign manager. Mantan and Alex then go over to Susie Que's Restaurant, where Alex orders up a feast, figuring that Mantan will pay the bill. Aware that Susie has plenty of money, Alex encourages Mantan to flirt with her, but Mantan is frightened of the hefty Susie, who towers over him. Nevertheless, Susie is smitten with Mantan and agrees to finance his mayoral campaign. Johnny Lee, Mantan's opponent, becomes angry when his posters are replaced by Mantan's and criticizes Mantan as an upstart who knows nothing about politics. In the meantime, Alex tries to teach Mantan how to be a public speaker, but spends most of his time spending Susie's money on expensive cigars and suits. Lee approaches Mantan in order to make a deal whereby one would sell the other his votes, but neither candidate has any money, so Lee suggests a crap game as a means of settling the question. Lee confuses Mantan's ignorance of dice games with cheating and, frustrated, leaves the game in a huff. At Mantan's big rally, Lee claims that Mantan gambled him out of votes, while Mrs. Johnson, Mantan's and Alex's landlady, shows up demanding three months back rent. The police remove the heckling Lee from the audience, after which Susie shows up for Mantan's speech and quickly learns that Mantan has been showering his campaign secretary with flowers and candy paid for by Susie. Mantan begins his speech, promising two chickens for every pot, while Lee sneaks back into the hall, using Susie's ample girth as a cover. As Mantan tries to finish his speech, Susie loudly announces that she will no longer finance Mantan's campaign. Then, with Lee's help, she removes Mantan's expensive suit, leaving him at the podium in his underwear. Now back to where they began, Alex reminds Mantan that he owes him five bucks. *African Americans. Ne'er-do-wells. Partnership. Political campaigns. Cigars. Craps (Game). Drunkenness. Flirtation. Janitors. Judges. Landladies. Rallies. Restaurants. Secretaries. Speeches. Unrequited love.*

Note: The plot summary for this film is based on a dialogue continuity deposited with the NYSA. Although the continuity contains a copyright statement by Toddy Pictures Company dated 1947, it was not registered for copyright.

MARCHING HERDS *see* **THE TEXANS**

MARCHING ON! (African Americans)

Sack Amusement Enterprises. *Dist* Astor Pictures Corp. **1943**; World premiere in San Antonio, Texas: mid-Mar 1943. Sd (RCA High Fidelity Recording); b&w. 6,317 ft. 70 min.

[*Prod* H. W. Kier]. *Dir* Spencer Williams, Jr. *Wrt* Spencer Williams, Jr. *Photog* Clark Ramsey. *Rec* H. W. Kier.

Cast: Emmet Jackson (*Sergeant* [*Robert L.*] *Keen*), George T. Sutton (*Grandpa Tucker*), L. K. Smith (*Rufus*), Myra J. Hemming (*Mama T.*), Hugh Martin (*Rodney Tucker, Jr.*), Georgia Kelly (*Martha Adams*), Clarissa Deary (*Jenny*), Lawrence "Pepper" Neely (*Wash*), Estrica McZekkashing (*Wimpy*), J. W. Hemming (*The hobo*).

African American. [*Print viewed*]. Sergeant Robert L. Keen, an officer of the African-American 25th Regiment, is sent to many Northern states and all over the deep South on a recruitment tour. In Texas, at a family meal, Rodney Tucker, Jr. becomes upset when his cousin Jenny and his grandfather, who dresses in his old army uniform, talk about the coming war. Rodney's mother, Mama T., a religious woman, tries to comfort him by saying that she will be filled with concern when he joins the Army, but he walks off annoyed when she shows him a picture of his father, who she says was a good soldier. Sergeant Keen comes to town in search of recruits, and Martha Adams, Rodney's fiancée, sings at the recruiting drive. She berates Rodney when he calls Keen a "tin soldier," insisting that he lacks the courage

to join up. When Rodney accuses her of wanting him in the Army so that she can go after Keen, she slaps him and returns his engagement ring. Rodney wanders to a poolroom, where a man talks, to his displeasure, about volunteering to help the country in the impending war. He next goes to a cigar store, where he hears an announcer on the radio relate the Japanese attack on Pearl Harbor. Soon after, Mama T., who now sews for the Red Cross, tells Jenny, now a junior air raid warden, that she hopes the army will bring out the man in Rodney, who has not left the house since Martha went away after war was declared. The mail brings Rodney's draft notification and a letter from Martha wishing him luck. At Fort Watchuka, a training camp in the Arizona mountains, an officer tells the new recruits that the country faces the greatest crisis in its history. Rodney scoffs in disbelief and says that whites should do their own fighting, but another black soldier tells him that the country is as much theirs as anybody else's. When Rodney sleeps through reveille, he is assigned to K.P. duty. The recruits are taught field maneuvers and how to shoot rifles and clean a cannon. Rodney is reprimanded when he fires the cannon by accident. Officers comment that Rodney, who takes no interest in anything except athletics, has the potential to be a great soldier, and he is made to do cleaning chores. Meanwhile, Grandpa packs his old car with his war souvenirs to take to Rodney's camp in Arizona, hoping to inspire him and the other recruits. At the camp, Rodney meets up with Keen, who despite Rodney's resentment, invites him to his quarters one night. Keen turns on the radio, knowing that Martha will be singing from a camp in Texas, and when Martha dedicates a song to Keen, Rodney hits him. Although Keen tries to make little of it, Rodney is ordered to stay in his barracks. When he learns that Martha has arrived in town and that Keen is planning to bring her to the camp, he blames Keen for provoking the fight so that he would be stuck in his barracks when she arrived. Rodney goes AWOL and jumps a train heading east. He awakens in a boxcar and finds a tramp, who is unable to remember anything about himself before 1919 but believes that he was once a soldier. One night, the tramp, who walks in his sleep, falls off the moving train, and Rodney gets off and finds him. The injured man, his memory jogged by the fall, tells Rodney that he has to get home to find his wife Ellen and his baby boy, Rodney Tucker, Jr., who was born while he was fighting in France. The tramp dies and Rodney finds in his pocket a photograph of Ellen, his own mother, Mama T. Rodney realizes that the tramp was his father and that he never came home because he lost his memory in a traffic accident. As he buries his father, Rodney vows not to go back to the Army, then wanders through the desert. Meanwhile, Grandpa's old car is stopped by a motorcycle officer, who asks if he has seen any "Japs" in the vicinity. As Rodney walks, he imagines scenes of war, then collapses from exhaustion. Grandpa finds him and revives him with water. Rodney tells Grandpa about meeting up with his father, Grandpa's son, and confesses that he has deserted. He now realizes that he has everything—family, home, freedom and democracy—for which to fight, and vows to prove, if he is given another chance, that he is a red-blooded American like his father and the others who have fought for their country. Later, when they need water for the car radiator, Grandpa points out the entrance to what was once Geronimo's stronghold in the nearby cliffs, where a spring of water is located. As they climb, two Japanese with a radio transmitter, hear them and hide. Rodney and Grandpa find their hideout, and a fight ensues. Rodney fights both of them until a number of jeeps full of soldiers arrive and notice them fighting. Before he dies from injuries, Grandpa thanks God for letting him fight once more for his country. For his bravery in fighting the Japanese, Rodney is now given the chance to fight with his grandfather's regiment, the 25th. Martha, who has read about his heroism and is now in the Women's Army Auxiliary Corps, asks if he still has the engagement ring. He puts it on her and they kiss. *African Americans. Desertion, Military. Fathers and sons. Grandfathers. Long-lost relatives. Military posts. Slackers. Soldiers. Amnesia. Arizona. Automobiles. Cousins. Death and dying. Deserts. Engagements. Fights. Heroism. Japanese. Military service, Compulsory. Mothers and sons. Prayer. Radio broadcasting. Religiosity. Singers. Somnambulism. Texas. Trains. Tramps. United States. Women's Army Corps. Veterans. Visions.*

Note: The print viewed was entitled *Where's My Man To-Nite*, and contained the following credits, which were not on the original print: "A Bourgeois-Jenkins Picture"; "Featuring the Original 'Brownskin Models'." According to a *Box* news item, John Jenkins and O. K. Bourgeois of Astor Pictures acquired the world rights to the film in Mar 1943 following the world premiere in San

Antonio, where the film was produced. According to a dialogue continuity at NYSA, the picture began with an announcer relating a history of African-American soldiers. The print viewed was missing this narration and also a few additional segments present in the continuity. *Where's My Man To-Nite* includes a twenty-three minute segment that is not in the NYSA continuity. The segment consists of a music performance, a comedy act and dancers called the "Brownskin Models." Most likely, the segment was added by Bourgeois-Jenkins.

Box 20 Mar 1943.

MARCUS GARLAND (African Americans)

Micheaux Film Corp. 1925. Si; b&w. Length undetermined. [Feature length assumed.].

Cast: Salem Tutt Whitney, Amy Birdsong.

Melodrama (?), African American. No information about the precise nature of this film has been found. *African Americans.*

Note: The indicated release year is approximate.

MARGIN FOR ERROR (Jewish Americans)

Twentieth Century-Fox Film Corp. *Dist* Twentieth Century-Fox Film Corp. 19 Feb **1943**; Prod: late Sep–3 Nov 1942; additional scenes began 16 Dec 1942 [©Twentieth Century-Fox Film Corp.; 19 Feb 1943; LP12212]. Sd (Western Electric Recording); b&w. 6,686 ft. 74 min.

[*Exec prod* William Goetz]. *Prod* Ralph Dietrich. *Dir* Otto Preminger. [*Asst dir* Percy Ikerd]. *Scr* Lillie Hayward. *Dir of photog* Edward Cronjager. [*Photog* Lucien Andriot]. *Art dir* Richard Day and Lewis Creber. *Film ed* Louis Loeffler and [Fred Allen]. *Set dec* Thomas Little and Al Orenbach. *Cost* Earl Luick. *Mus* Leigh Harline. *Mus dir* Emil Newman. *Sd* Eugene Grossman and Harry M. Leonard.

Source: Based on the play *Margin for Error* by Clare Boothe (New York, 3 Nov 1939).

Cast: Joan Bennett [(*Sophie Baumer*)], Milton Berle [(*Moe Finkelstein*)], Otto Preminger [(*Karl Baumer*)], Charles Esmond [(*Max von Alvenstor*)], Howard Freeman [(*Otto Horst*)], Poldy Dur [(*Frieda*)], Clyde Fillmore [(*Dr. Jennings*)], Ferike Boros [(*Mrs. Finkelstein*)], [Joseph Kirk (*Officer Solomon*)], [Hans von Twardowski (*Fritz*)], [Ted North, Elmer Jack Semple, J. Norton Dunn (*Saboteurs*)], [Hans Schumm (*Moeller*)], [Edward McNamara (*Captain Mulrooney*)], [Selmer Jackson (*Coroner*)], [Eddie Dunn (*Desk sergeant*)], [Barney Ruditsky (*Policeman*)], [Don Dillaway (*Reporter*)], [Dick French (*Photographer*)], [Ruth Cherrington (*Dowager*)], [Byron Foulger (*Drugstore clerk*)], [Emmett Vogan (*Fingerprint expert*)], [David Alison (*Jacoby*)], [Allan Nixon, Malcolm McTaggart, Tom Seidel (*Soldiers*)], [John Wald, Gary Breckner (*American announcer*)], [Louis Donath (*Hitler's voice*)], [Wolfgang Zilzer].

Mystery, Comedy-drama. [*Print viewed*]. Despite his best efforts to avoid the assignment, police officer Moe Finkelstein is ordered by the mayor of New York City to guard the life of German Consul Karl Baumer. Moe turns in his badge when he realizes that he has been assigned to protect a Nazi, but the mayor refuses to accept his resignation. The mayor tells Moe that although he is opposed to Adolf Hitler's Nazi regime, he is under special orders from Berlin to halt demonstrations in New York against Nazi sympathizers and organizers. The mayor tells Moe that he has decided to abide by the wishes of the Berlin government in order to teach the Nazis the difference between the American system of democracy and their fascism. Soon after he arrives at the Consul's residence, Moe discovers that Baumer is in trouble with Berlin for having squandered money meant for sabotage. Meanwhile, Baumer's secretary, Baron Max von Alvenstor, has become disenchanted with Baumer and the Nazi cause and refuses to abide by Baumers's orders to stall the delivery to Berlin of a damaging finiancial report. Sophie, Baumer's Czechoslovakian-born wife, confesses to Moe that she despises her husband and that she married him only to get her father out of prison. Moe comes to truly hate Baumer, and unable to contain his anger one day, flies into a rage and insults the Consul. Moe's temper eventually subsides as he begins a romance with Frieda, the Consul's maid, whom he takes on a date to see the film *Confessions of a Nazi Spy*. Also at odds with Baumer is Otto Horst, the bumbling leader of the American bund, who is ordered by the Consul to procure false identification cards for a group of German saboteurs being sent to blow up an American port. In order to protect himself from Berlin's harsh reprimands, Baumer tells Max that he has information that his ancestors are Jewish and that he will use it against him unless he stalls the financial report. Under orders from Berlin to dispense of Horst's services, Baumer

arranges an eloborate scheme to frame Max for Horst's murder. Baumer then tries to enlist the help of his wife in the scheme, but she refuses and warns Horst of the plan. Horst decides to defend himself against the attack by carrying his gun to his next visit with the Consul. Meanwhile, the saboteurs have rigged a bomb to explode at an American port at the moment Hitler concludes his radio broadcast. While listening to the broadcast with Horst, Max and Dr. Jennings, Sophie, transfixed by the sight of Horst's gun, grabs it and shoots her husband. A loud noise in the radio broadcast coincides with the gunshot, and it takes a moment before Max notices that Baumer is dead. Max quickly whisks Sophie out of the room before anyone sees her, and tells her to flee. When Moe discovers the body, he rounds up all the possible suspects, including Sophie, who readily confesses to killing her husband. To protect her, though, Max insists that he was the one who killed the Consul. All are dumbstruck when Moe reveals that Baumer was not only shot but stabbed as well. Furthermore, following Dr. Jennings' examination of the body, it is determined that Baumer was poisoned, too. Max, meanwhile, rushes to the ship where the saboteurs are hiding and orders them to dismantle the bomb before it detonates. With only minutes to spare, the bomb is dismantled and the saboteurs are captured. Back at the Consul's house, Max identifies Horst as an accomplice to the sabateurs, and Horst is arrested. Max is cleared of murder charges when the coroner's report reveals that Baumer died of poisoning by his own hand. The poison, it seems, was intended for Max, but the glasses got switched and Baumer accidentally took his own poison. *Bodyguards. Consuls. Germans. Murder. Sabotage. Antisemitism. Birds. Blackmail. Confession (Law). Corruption. Frame-ups. Gunshot wounds. Adolf Hitler. Jews. Marriage–Forced by circumstances. Mayors. New York City. Poison. Police. Radio programs.*

Note: The opening credits for the film read: "Twentieth Century-Fox presents *Claire Booth's Margin for Error*." Otto Preminger directed and starred in the Broadway run of Boothe's play. According to a *NYT* news item, Twentieth Century-Fox purchased the rights to the play for $25,000 in the spring of 1941. The article notes that the property was temporarily shelved because the studio felt that Boothe's "statement of the opposition between fascism and democracy had become self-evident to the point of banality." The article also states that the character of the bund leader (Nazi organizer) in the play was eliminated for the film, and that the scene depicting the rescue of a prisoner from a concentration camp was dropped. In reference to the concentration camp rescue scene, Preminger is reported to have said that the situation, as it existed in the story, was "implausible." Although a 14 Oct 1941 news item noted that director, producer and screenwriter Arch Oboler had worked on the script for ten weeks, just prior to his departure from the studio, and although a Sep 1942 *HR* news item noted that Arthur Kober was set for a writing assignment on the picture, the extent of their contribution to the final film has not been determined.

Actor Charles Esmond, who was credited onscreen as such, was better known as Carl Esmond. *HR* production charts and studio publicity materials list Lucien Andriot as the photographer, although Edward Cronjager is listed on the film. Actor Howard Freeman was loaned to Fox from M-G-M. While the film does not clearly identify the character of the New York City mayor as Fiorello La Guardia, the *Var* review suggests that La Guardia was indeed the model for the story's unnamed mayor.

A biography of Preminger notes that Twentieth Century-Fox initially offered Preminger only a starring role in the film, and that when he responded to the offer with a request to direct the film, it was flatly denied. Preminger eventually struck up a compromise with the studio, which allowed him to direct the film at no pay, and allowed the studio to release him as the director after a one-week trial period if his work was not satisfactory. According to modern sources, before shooting began on the film, Preminger hired writer Sam Fuller to do a last-minute re-write of the script.

Box 16 Jan 1943. *DV* 8 Jan 1943, p. 3, 9. *FD* 8 Jan 1943, p. 5. *HR* 14 Oct 1941, p. 4. *HR* 3 Sep 1942, p. 2. *HR* 2 Oct 1942, p. 7. *HR* 30 Oct 1942, p. 4, 8. *HR* 4 Nov 1942, p. 4. *HR* 15 Dec 1942, p. 5. *HR* 8 Jan 1943, p. 3. *MPH* 9 Jan 1943. *MPHPD* 7 Nov 1942, p. 995. *MPHPD* 9 Jan 1943, p. 1101. *NYT* 8 Nov 1942. *NYT* 25 Jan 1943, p. 10. *Var* 13 Jan 1943, p. 8.

LA MARI DE LA REINE *see* ECHEC AU ROI

MARIDO Y MUJER (Spanish language)

Fox Film Corp. *Dist* Fox Film Corp. **1932**; Los Angeles opening: 22 Feb 1932; Prod: Oct 1931. Sd; b&w. 10 reels. Passed by the National Board of Review. Spanish language.

Dirección de [*Dir*] Bert E. Sebell. [*Spanish dial* José López Rubio].

Source: Based on the novel *Bad Girl* by Eugene Delmar and Viña Delmar (New York, 1928) and the play of the same name by Viña Delmar and Brian Marlowe (New York, 2 Oct 1930).

Cast: CONCHITA MONTENEGRO (*Clare Haley*), JORGE LEWIS (*Eddie Collins*), Rosita Granada (*Jennie Driggs*), Allan Garcia (*Doctor Burgess*), José Nieto (*Jim Haley*), Mimi Aguglia (*Señora Gordon*), [José López Rubio (*Father of twins*)].

Domestic, **Drama**. [*Print viewed*]. [The following plot summary is based on the English-language version of this film, *Bad Girl*; character names refer to that version. For further information regarding the English-language version, please see the note below and the entry for *Bad Girl* in the *AFI Catalog of Feature Films, 1931-40*.] While being fitted for a wedding gown, dress model Dorothy Haley complains to another model that she always falls prey to lecherous men like her boss, Mr. Cochran, who tries to get her to go on a drive with him. To ward off her unwanted suitors, Dorothy tells them that her husband is a jealous prizefighter. One day, at an amusement park, Dorothy's friend Edna Driggs introduces her to Eddy Collins, a radio salesman whom Edna considers a rarity among the male species, in that he does not flirt with every woman he sees. After meeting Dorothy, the disaffected Eddy tells her that "if you don't want guys to salute you, take down your flag." Intrigued by Eddy, Dorothy tries to woo him by playing the ukelele for him, but he shows little interest in her and claims that "if a guy makes a pass at you, you call the police; if he doesn't, you call out the army." Eventually, Eddy and Dorothy end up dating, but when Eddy discovers that Dorothy lives in a crowded tenement, he snobbishly tells her that he is not geared for a life of scrimping. Later, Eddy brags to his co-workers that he will never marry and that he plans to own his own store. After spending a late evening out with Eddy, Dorothy returns home to face the admonition of her strict brother Jim, who is the orphaned girl's guardian. When Dorothy accepts Eddy's marriage proposal without consulting her brother, Jim angrily kicks her out of the house. Dorothy goes to Eddy's for refuge, but is shocked when she discovers that he has moved out of his boardinghouse, and that he is no longer employed at his job. Eddy later finds Dorothy and tells her that any wife of his will have to quit her job because he wants to be the sole breadwinner. Dorothy consents to his terms, but soon decides that she wants to go back to work. Eddy surprises Dorothy one day when he takes her on a tour of a beautiful apartment and then tells her that he spent all his money to buy the place for them. Dorothy then surprises Eddy when she tells him that she is going to have a baby. Determined to provide only the best for his new wife and the baby-to-come, Eddy seeks the services of Dr. Burgess, a renowned physician, to care for his wife during her pregnancy. Eddy, however, is unable to afford Dr. Burgess' expensive fees, and decides to ask his pal Joe to fix him up in a fight in order to make some extra money. Exhausted from working nights and fighting fights for ten dollars a round, Eddy pleads with his opponent, Mike, not to knock him out because his wife is expecting a child. Mike, who has two children of his own, empathizes with Eddy and takes the fall himself. Because Eddy is busy making extra money, he is not at home when Dorothy goes into labor, and as a result, Dorothy thinks he does not care about her. When Eddy finally shows up at the hospital, Dorothy immediately thinks that he has been beaten up in a barroom brawl and scorns him. Following Dorothy's delivery of a baby boy, Dr. Burgess announces that he will donate his services to the young couple, and starts a fifty-dollar savings account for the infant. Later, Dorothy becomes hysterical when she cannot find her child in the hospital. As soon as the baby is found, however, Dorothy realizes that Eddy also loves the baby and the two reconcile. *Brothers and sisters. Class distinction. Marriage. Poverty. Pregnancy. Self-sacrifice. Boxing. Childbirth. False accusations. Flirtation. Hospitals. Models. Orphans. Physicians. Salesmen. Snobs and snobbishness. Tenement-houses.*

Note: The file for *Bad Girl*, the English-language version of this film, in the MPAA/PCA Collection at the AMPAS Library, contains an evaluation of the novel on which the film is based, dated 16 Nov 1928, by Hays Office official Lamar Trotti, who said: "'Bad Girl' might be produced as a sex hygiene picture called 'Motherhood.' It is simply the story of girl who is 'bad' for one night, marries the boy the next day, and then has a baby." Trotti called the novel a "nauseating story of doctors, illnesses, etc." and said that the book "disgusted" him and was "cheap and shoddy writing about cheap and shoddy people." The MPAA/PCA file also indicates that prior to Fox's purchase of the rights to the story, a number of motion picture companies, including Pathé, M-G-M and Universal, had considered but ultimately declined to produce the film. Correspondence between the Hays Office and various producers between 1929 and 1930 indicates that the companies were strongly urged not to make a film based on the Delmar story and play because it would undoubtedly be "too censorable." By May 1931, however, Fox presented the Hays Office with a treatment of the story that apparently met with its approval, for only a handful of relatively minor changes were suggested. In Jul 1931, Trotti, after seeing a preview of the completed film, said that it was the "best picture since sound came in...it is a marvelous job and will do the industry untold good." According to contemporary news items in *FD*, a lawsuit was filed against Fox in Aug 1931 by stage producer Robert V. Newman, who claimed that he sold Fox the rights to the story with the stipulation that the picture not be released until 1 Sep 1931.

Newman also sued the Roxy Theatre, where the film had its premiere and first run. The injunctions were eventually denied by the Supreme Court, which said that "no substantial damage" had been done by releasing the film earlier.

Martín Garralaga, Alfredo del Diestro, Antonio Cumellas and Roberto Guzmán may have been in the Spanish-language version. *Bad Girl* was nominated for an Academy Award for Best Picture of 1931. Frank Borzage won an Academy Award for Best Direction, and Edwin Burke received an award for his screen adaptation. *Bad Girl* was also voted one of the Ten Best Pictures of 1931 by *FD*'s nationwide poll of film critics. A 1940 Twentieth Century-Fox remake of *Bad Girl*, entitled *Manhattan Heartbeat*, was directed by David Burton and starred Robert Sterling and Virginia Gilmore (see *AFI Catalog of Feature Films, 1931-40*; F3.2732.) A 1948 *LAT* news item announced that actors Dan Dailey and Jeanne Crain were set to star in a remake of this film, but it was never made. For further information on the English-language version, which was directed by Frank Borzage and starred James Dunn and Sally Eilers, please see the entry for that film in the *AFI Catalog of Feature Films, 1931-40*; F3.0217.

FD 9 Aug 1931, p. 10. *FD* 18 Aug 1931, p. 1. *FD* 20 Aug 1931, p. 1. *HF* 6 Jun 1931, p. 20. *HF* 4 Jul 1931. *HR* 9 Jul 1931, p. 4. *IP* 31 Oct 1931, p. 28. *MPH* 18 Jul 1931, p. 38. *MPH* 26 Sep 1931, p. 27. *NYT* 15 Aug 1931, p. 18. *Var* 18 Aug 1931, p. 30.

MARIONS-NOUS *see* **SU NOCHE DE BODAS**

MARJA OF THE STEPPES *see* **SOLD FOR MARRIAGE**

MARJORIE MORNINGSTAR (Jewish Americans)
Warner Bros. Pictures Inc.; Beachwold Pictures, Inc. *Dist* Warner Bros. Pictures Inc. 5 Apr 1958; Prod: mid-Aug—early Nov 1957 [©Beachwold Pictures, Inc.; 5 Apr 1958; LP14508]. Sd (RCA Sound Recording); col (Warnercolor). 11,430 ft. 123 or 125 min. PCA cert no. 18772.

Prod Milton Sperling. *Dir* Irving Rapper. *Asst dir* Don Page. *Scr* Everett Freeman. *Dir of photog* Harry Stradling. *Art dir* Malcolm Bert. *Film ed* Folmar Blangsted. *Set dec* Ralph Hurst. *Cost consultant* Howard Shoup. *Mus comp* Max Steiner. *Mus supv* Ray Heindorf. *Vocal arr* Lyn Murray. *Orch* Murray Cutter and Gus Levene. *Dances and mus numbers staged by* Jack Baker. *Sd* Stanley Jones. *Makeup supv* Gordon Bau. *Dial supv* Burt Steiner. [*Tech supv* Rabbi Max Vorspan and Max Helfman]. [*Gene Kelly's stand-in* Bob Koblan].

Song(s): "A Very Precious Love," music by Sammy Fain, lyrics by Paul Francis Webster.

Source: Based on the novel *Marjorie Morningstar* by Herman Wouk (New York, 1955).

Cast: Gene Kelly [(*Noel Airman, also known as Noel Ehrman*)], Natalie Wood [(*Marjorie Morningstar, also known as Marjorie Morgenstern*)], Claire Trevor [(*Rose Morgenstern*)], Everett Sloane [(*Arnold Morgenstern*)], Marty Milner [(*Wally Wronken*)], Carolyn Jones [(*Marsha Zelenko*)], George Tobias [(*Mr. Greech*)], Martin Balsam [(*Dr. David Harris*)], Jesse White [(*Lou Michaelson*)], Edward Byrnes [(*Sandy Lamm*)], Paul Picerni [(*Philip Berman*)], Alan Reed [(*Puddles Podell*)], Ruta Lee [(*Imogene Norman*)], Ed Wynn (*Uncle Samson* [*Morgenstern*]), [Howard Bert (*Seth Morgenstern*)], [Patricia Denise (*Karen*)], [Lester Dorr (*Elevator operator*)], [Carl Sklover (*Leon Lamm*)], [Jean Vachon (*Mary Lamm*)], [Elizabeth Harrower (*Miss Kimble*)], [Guy Raymond (*Mr. Klabber*)], [Edward Foster (*Carlos*)], [Leslie Bradley (*Blair*)], [Maida Severn (*Tonia Zelenko*)], [Fay Nuell (*Helen Harris*)], [Fred Rapport (*Nate*)], [Harry Seymour (*Frank*)], [Shelley Fabares (*Seth's girl friend*)], [Walter Clinton (*Mr. Zelenko*)], [Pierre Watkin (*Civil official*)], [Reginald Sheffield (*Clerk*)], [Sandy Livingston (*Betsy*)], [Peter Brown (*Alec*)], [Gail Ganley (*Wally's girl friend*)], [Russell Ash (*Harry Morgenstern*)], [Rad Fulton (*Romeo*)], [Efraim Wolff (*Boy at Seder*)], [Lana Wood].

Drama. [*Print viewed*]. Sweet old Samson Morgenstern visits his nephew Arnold Morgenstern, a businessman whose success has allowed him to move his family out of the Bronx into a lovely new West Side apartment. The Morgensterns are celebrating the bar mitzvah of young Seth, who happily accepts when Samson gives him a tallis, the prayer scarf that is worn by adult Jewish men. Seth's beautiful older sister Marjorie is uncertain of her love for wealthy Sandy Lamm, even though her mother Rose is thrilled to learn that he has proposed to her daughter. Marjorie, a drama student at Hunter College, finally persuades her mother to let her think things over while working at a girls' summer camp with her college friend, Marsha Zelenko. Across the lake from the camp is South Wind, a brilliantly lit resort. One night, Marsha and an unwilling Marjorie sneak into the resort, and while her more worldly friend pursues a musician, Marjorie meets and quietly falls for social director Noel Airman, a performer whose talent and looks deeply impress the young women. Noel's assistant, a writer named Wally Wronken, is smitten

with Marjorie, but she is too entranced with Noel's singing to notice him. She is about to be thrown out by the resort's owner when Noel, whose real name is Noel Ehrman, saves her from humiliation by offering her a job. Noel calls her "Marjorie Morningstar" as he says good night, and she is so taken with the name that she adopts it. Soon Uncle Samson, who has been sent by the Morgensterns to keep an eye on Marjorie, takes a job in the resort's kitchen, and his arrival comes none too soon, as Noel has invited Marjorie to his cabin for an intimate supper. Samson's concern for Marjorie's welfare touches Noel, and he tries to drive her away, but fails. He is so deeply in love that even the disapproval of her visiting parents hardly phases him. Samson then suffers a fatal heart attack while clowning for the guests during a skit. Afterward, Marjorie returns to college and begins to date Dr. David Harris. Months after Marjorie's graduation, Noel reveals that he now has a respectable job in an advertising firm. The two begin to discuss marriage, and one night, after the Morgenstern family Seder, Noel remarks that he now values family, faith and tradition, all the things he once ridiculed. When Wally becomes an admired Broadway playwright, however, Noel becomes jealous of his former protégé's success and disappears from sight. Marjorie soon finds that he has left his job, begun to drink, and has become intimate with a blonde named Imogene Norman. Shocked, she leaves Noel again, but some time later, when a teary Marsha, who is about to marry a wealthy, cigar-chomping older man, calls her a fool for abandoning such an intense love, Marjorie becomes confused. At the wedding, Noel appears and announces to Marjorie that the musical he has worked on for years is nearly complete, and begs her to return to him. This time, Marjorie gives herself to Noel completely. At Marjorie's urging, Marsha's husband finances a Broadway production of Noel's play, *Princess Jones*, even after Noel insults him. The play is a disaster, and once again, Noel disappears. Ignoring his written request to be left alone, Marjorie searches for her lover all over Europe. Wally eventually informs her that Noel has returned to South Wind, where he finally has found happiness. Despite Wally's warning, Marjorie immediately returns to the resort. Through the window, she sees Noel contentedly performing his song, "A Very Precious Love," for a group of ardent young admirers. Realizing at last that their love is not good for either of them, Marjorie quietly boards a departing bus and is surprised to see that Wally, whom her mother has long admired, is waiting for her. *Bohemians and bohemianism. Family relationships. Love affairs. Maturation. Resorts. Self-respect.* Actors and actresses. Adirondack Mountains. Advertising agencies. Bar mitzvah. Camps. Friendship. Heart disease. Jews. Musical revues. New York City. New York City–Broadway. Playwrights. Premarital sex. Seder (Jewish holiday). Songwriters. Theatrical backers. Uncles. Unrequited love. Weddings.

Note: According to onscreen credits, some exterior scenes were photographed at Scaroon Manor and Camp Cayuga Boys and Girls Camp, at Schroon Lake in the Adirondack Mountains, New York. Other scenes were shot at Bellevue Hospital, Central Park West, Greenwich Village and Radio City Music Hall in New York City, according to a Jun 1957 *NYT* article. The *LAT* reported on 24 Oct 1955 that Jack Warner, the head of Warner Bros. Studios, paid Herman Wouk one million dollars, "probably the highest price ever paid for any story," for the screen rights to the author's best-selling novel. Other sources, however, claim that Wouk received no cash up front, but negotiated for 50 percent of the film's profits.

Contemporary sources note that Wouk served in a supervisory capacity during the two-year pre-production period, overseeing the screenplay and casting, and also supervised filming at Scaroon Manor. Information included in the PCA files reveals that the PCA wanted the producers to make sure that the illicit affair between Noel and Marjorie was compensated for by the characters' acknowledgement of their wrongdoing. According to a 30 Jun 1957 article in *NYT*, Edward G. Robinson and Bette Davis were considered to play "Marjorie's" parents, and Conrad Janis and Norma Crane were tested for other roles. The *Var* reviewer complained that in the film version the "Jewish flavor" of the novel was "watered down." The *LAEx* reviewer also noted the picture's "Lack of stress on the Jewish faith...so important in the book." The *HR* reviewer, however, called the film "beautifully produced and magnificently acted," and "an act of brotherhood." According to modern sources, Jack Warner wanted Danny Kaye to play "Noel," but Kaye refused.

Box 17 Mar 1958. *Box* 24 Mar 1958. *DV* 24 Oct 1955. *DV* 11 Mar 1958, p. 3. *Exb* 19 Mar 1958, p. 4447. *FD* 11 Mar 1958, p. 6. *Har* 15 Mar 1958, p. 42. *HR* 24 Oct 1955. *HR* 16 Aug 1957, p.10. *HR* 8 Nov 1957, p. 8. *HR* 11 Mar 1958, p. 3. *LAEx* 29 Mar 1958. *LAT* 24 Oct 1955. *MPHPD* 15 Mar 1958, p. 756. *NYT* 30 Jun 1957. *NYT* 25 Apr 1958, p. 32. *Var* 12 Mar 1958, p. 6.

MARK OF THE APACHE *see* **TOMAHAWK TRAIL**

THE MARK OF THE RENEGADE (Latino)
Universal-International Pictures Co., Inc. *Dist* Universal Pictures Co., Inc. Aug **1951**; World premiere in Los Angeles: 24 Jul 1951; Prod: mid-Oct—late Nov 1950 [©Universal Pictures Co.; 28 Jun 1951; LP1011]. Sd (Western Electric Recording); col (Technicolor). 7,298 ft. 81 min. PCA cert no. 15036.

Prod Jack Gross. *Dir* Hugo Fregonese. [*Asst dir* William Holland, George Lollier and Bill Cody]. *Scr* Louis Solomon and Robert Hardy Andrews. *Story* Johnston McCulley. *Dir of photog* Charles P. Boyle. *Technicolor color consultant* William Fritzsche. *Art dir* Bernard Herzbrun and Robert Boyle. *Film ed* Frank Gross. *Set dec* Russell A. Gausman and Ruby R. Levitt. *Cost* Leah Rhodes. *Mus* Frank Skinner. *Dances staged by* Eugene Loring. *Sd* Leslie I. Carey, Richard De Weese and [Glenn E. Anderson]. *Makeup* Bud Westmore. *Hair stylist* Joan St. Oegger. [*Prod mgr* Dewey Starkey].

Cast: Ricardo Montalban [(*Marcos Zappa*)], Cyd Charisse [(*Manuella de Vasquez*)], J. Carrol Naish [(*Luis*)], Gilbert Roland [(*Pedro Garcia*)], Andrea King [(*Anita Gonzales*)], George Tobias [(*Captain Bardoso*)], Antonio Moreno [(*José de Vasquez*)], Georgia Backus [(*Doña Concepcion*)], Robert Warwick [(*Colonel Vega*)], Armando Silvestre [(*Miguel de Gandara*)], [Bridget Carr (*Rosa*)], [Alberto Morin (*Cervera*)], [Renzo Cesana (*Father Juan*)], [Robert Cornthwaite (*Innkeeper*)], [Edward C. Rios (*Paco*)], [David Wolfe (*Landlord*)], [Peter Mamakos (*Pirate*)], [Felipe Turich, Mario Silveira (*Servants*)], [Pilar Del Rey, Vida Aldana (*Señoritas*)], [Alex Montoya (*Gatekeeper*)], [Carlos Albert (*Card dealer*)], [Charles Soldani, Ethan Laidlaw (*Grandees*)], [Michael Zaccone (*Guitar player*)], [Rod Normond], [Paul Levitt].

Historical, **Adventure.** [*Print viewed*]. In the early 1800's, as California became a territory of the newly born Republic of Mexico, many sought to take over the rich land for themselves. In 1825, Mexican Marcos Zappa comes ashore on the coast of California from a pirate ship under the command of Captain Bardoso and is taken to meet Pedro Garcia, who tells him that he knows that Marcos has been found guilty of disloyalty to the Republic and banished into exile. Marcos always wears a bandana across his forehead to conceal the area where he was branded with the letter "R" for renegade; in California, he will be instantly killed if the mark is seen. Garcia, who intends to become emperor of California, blackmails Marcos into helping him, then buys him new clothes and sends him to meet his rival, José de Vasquez, leader of the party for the Republic in California. Marcos is to court de Vasquez's daughter Manuella and marry her, thus providing Garcia with direct access to the current ruler of California and enabling him to control de Vasquez by threatening to reveal that his daughter is married to a renegade. Manuella already has a fiancé, Miguel de Gandara, so Garcia orders Marcos to initiate a quarrel with Miguel and kill him. Garcia sends Bardoso and Luis, one of his henchmen, to accompany Marcos to the pueblo of Los Angeles, where Marcos and Bardoso go to a gambling house run by Anita Gonzales, who tries to seduce Marcos. When a fight breaks out among the gamblers, Marcos and Bardoso escape but are later spotted by soldiers. Marcos, who had met de Vasquez, Manuella and Miguel earlier when he helped to foil a staged holdup of their carriage, receives an invitation to a fiesta at the de Vasquez home, where they will raise the flag of the Republic for the first time in California. Garcia, whom Manuella previously rejected as a suitor, is also invited. Manuella shows interest in Marcos, finding him mysterious, and he tells her that, under different circumstances, he may be able to say that he loves her, then shows her the brand mark. When Marcos later falls from a horse, he insists that he only be attended by Father Juan, a Franciscan priest. Garcia gives Marcos a deadline by which he must become engaged to Manuella or be exposed as a renegade. Garcia also orders Bardoso to bring his pirates to attack Los Angeles, so that he, Garcia, can appear to save the population and enhance his plan to dominate the state. Manuella thinks that Marcos is involved with Anita, who is in league with Garcia, but Marcos swears that he is in love with her, Manuella. After Manuella visits Marcos in his room one night, her father accuses Marcos of bringing shame on his family and insists that they marry. At the wedding ceremony, Miguel challenges Marcos to a pistol duel, but Marcos shoots into the ground as Colonel Vega and his troops arrive. Vega confronts Garcia with Bardoso, whom he has arrested along with his men. Bardoso confesses that he had been ordered by Garcia to raid and loot Los Angeles. Anita identifies Marcos as a renegade, but Manuella states that she has known this for

some time. However, Father Juan reveals a major surprise as he removes Marcos' "brand" with some wine and relates that, in Mexico City, after his Order had informed the government of a plot to take over California, they decided to send a secret emissary to investigate. Marcos was chosen and voluntarily accepted disgrace and exile so that he could join the pirates and discover the mastermind behind the plot, Garcia. Marcos and Garcia engage in a sword fight, and after Marcos kills him, Manuella and Marcos marry. *California–History–To 1846. Conspiracy. Los Angeles (CA). Megalomania. Mexicans. Renegades. Romance. Undercover agents.* Blackmail. Branding. Broken limbs. Dances. Duels. Engagements. Escapes. Fathers and daughters. Fiestas. Franciscans. Gamblers. Impersonation and imposture. Pirates. Pistols. Priests. Rescues. Riding accidents. Self-sacrifice. Sword fights. Territorial governors. Weddings.

Note: This film's working title was *Don Renegade.* The consul-general of Mexico attended the film's premiere, which benefitted Los Angeles Mexican charities.

Box 4 Aug 1951. *DV* 24 Jul 1951, p. 3. *Exb* 1 Aug 1951, p. 3119. *FD* 27 Jul 1951, p. 6. *Har* 28 Jul 1951, p. 119. *HR* 13 Oct, 1950, p. 13. *HR* 24 Jul 1951, p. 3. *LAT* 25 Jul 1951. *MPHPD* 28 Jul 1951, p. 945. *NYT* 7 Sep 1951, p. 24. *Var* 25 Jul 1951, p. 6.

THE MARK OF ZORRO (Latino)

Douglas Fairbanks Pictures Corp. *Dist* United Artists Corp. 5 Dec **1920** [©Douglas Fairbanks Pictures Corp.; 22 Nov 1920; LP15847]. Si; b&w. 8 reels.

Prod Douglas Fairbanks. *Dir* Fred Niblo. *Asst dir* Theodore Reed. *Scen* Eugene Miller. *Cam* William McGann and Harry Thorpe. *Art dir* Edward Langley.

Source: Based on the serial story *The Curse of Capistrano* by Johnston McCulley in *All-Story Weekly* (9 Aug–6 Sep 1919).

Cast: Douglas Fairbanks (*Don Diego Vega/Señor Zorro*), Noah Beery (*Sergeant Pedro*), Charles Hill Mailes (*Don Carlos Pulido*), Claire McDowell (*Doña Catalina, his wife*), Marguerite De La Motte (*Lolita*), Robert McKim (*Captain Juan Ramon*), George Periolat (*Governor Alvarado*), Walt Whitman (*Fra Felipe*), Sidney De Grey (*Don Alejandro*), Tote du Crow (*Bernardo*), Noah Beery, Jr., Charles Belcher, Albert McQuarrie, Charles Stevens, John Winn.

Historical, Adventure. When Don Diego Vega returns to Old California from school in Spain, he discovers the tyrannical governor Alvarado in power. Assuming the persona of an effeminate fop while secretly masquerading as Zorro, a masked California Robin Hood, Diego attempts to restore justice. His true identity known only to his faithful servant Bernardo, Zorro outwits his enemies, wins over the soldiers to his case, forces the governor to abdicate and wins the affections of Lolita, a lovely aristocrat who is delighted to discover that her foppish fiancé Diego, whom she scorns, is actually a dashing hero. *Aristocrats. California–History–To 1846. Dandies. Disguise. Heroism. Impersonation and imposture.* Abduction. Juan Bautista Alvarado. Governors. Servants.

Note: The working title of this film was *The Curse of Capistrano.* While one contemporary source credits Eugene Miller with the adaptation, modern sources credit Elton Thomas, which was Douglas Fairbanks' pseudonym. McCulley's story was published in book form under the title *The Mark of Zorro* in 1924. Some scenes in the film were shot in the San Fernando Valley in CA, where a set representing Los Angeles during the period of 1840 was built. M. Harry Uttenhover of Belgium, thrice the world's champion fencer, was hired to instruct cast members Noah Beery and Robert McKim. The film opened in New York at the end of Nov 1920. Among the many other films based on McCulley's story or using the character of Zorro are: the 1925 United Artists release *Don Q, Son of Zorro,* starring Douglas Fairbanks and Mary Astor and directed by Donald Crisp (see above); the 1936 Republic film *The Bold Caballero* (see above), starring Robert Livingston and directed by Wells Root; a series of Republic serials in the thirties and forties, including 1939's *Zorro's Fighting Legion,* starring Reed Hadley and directed by William Witney and John English; the 1940 Twentieth Century-Fox film *The Mark of Zorro,* starring Tyrone Power and directed by Rouben Mamoulian (see below); the 1957 ABC-TV series *Zorro,* starring Guy Williams and produced by Walt Disney; the 1975 Italian film *Zorro,* starring Alain Delon and directed by Duccio Tessari; and the 1981 Twentieth Century-Fox release *Zorro the Gay Blade,* starring George Hamilton and directed by Peter Medak.

ETR 11 Dec 1920, p. 108. *MPN* 13 Nov 1920, p. 3729, 3779. *MPW* 11 Dec 1920, p. 719. *NYT* 29 Nov 1920, p. 20. *Wid's* 5 Dec 1920, p. 3.

THE MARK OF ZORRO (Latino)

Twentieth Century-Fox Film Corp. *Dist* Twentieth Century-Fox Film Corp. 8 Nov **1940**; Cincinnati opening: 1 Nov 1940; Prod: 25 Jul—12 Sep 1940 [©Twentieth Century-Fox Film Corp.; 8 Nov 1940; LP10310]. Sd (Western Electric Mirrophonic Recording); b&w. 8,409 ft. 93 min. PCA cert no. 6597.

[*Exec prod* Darryl F. Zanuck]. [*Assoc prod* Raymond Griffith]. *Dir* Rouben Mamoulian. [*2d unit dir* Lynn Shores]. [*Asst dir* Bill Weenberger and Sidney Bowen]. *Scr* John Taintor Foote. *Adpt* Garrett Fort and Bess Meredyth. *Dir of photog* Arthur Miller. *Art dir* Richard Day and Joseph C. Wright. *Film ed* Robert Bischoff. *Set dec* Thomas Little. *Cost* Travis Banton. *Mus* Alfred Newman, [David Buttolph, Hugo Friedhofer and Cyril Mockridge]. *Sd* W. D. Flick and Roger Heman. [*Tech adv* Ernesto Romero].

Source: Based on the serial story *The Curse of Capistrano* by Johnston McCulley in *All-Story Weekly* (9 Aug–6 Sep 1919).

Cast: TYRONE POWER (*Diego* [*Vega*]), Linda Darnell (*Lolita Quintero*), Basil Rathbone (*Capt. Esteban Pasquale*), Gale Sondergaard (*Inez Quintero*), Eugene Pallette (*Fray Felipe*), J. Edward Bromberg (*Don Luis Quintero*), Montagu Love (*Don Alejandro Vega*), Janet Beecher (*Señora Isabella Vega*), Robert Lowery (*Rodrigo*), Chris-Pin Martin (*Turnkey*), George Regas (*Sergeant Gonzales*), Belle Mitchell (*Maria* [*de Lopez*]), John Bleifer (*Pedro*), Frank Puglia (*Proprietor*), Eugene Borden (*Officer of the day*), Pedro De Cordoba (*Don Miguel*), Guy D'Ennery (*Don Jose*), [Fred Malatesta, Fortunio Bonanova, Jean Del Val, Joseph Villard (*Sentries*)], [Harry Worth, Gino Corrado, George Sorel, Lucio Villegas (*Caballeros*)], [Paul Sutton, Art Dupuis (*Soldiers*)], [Ralph Byrd (*Officer-student*)], [Ted North (*Michael*)], [Rafael Corio (*Manservant*)], [Franco Corsaro (*Orderly*)], [William Edmunds (*Peon selling cocks*)], [Hector Sarno (*Peon at inn*)], [Charles Stevens (*Jose*)], [Stanley Andrews (*Commanding officer*)], [Victor Kilian (*Boatman*)], [Andre Cuyas, Frank Yaconelli, George Chermanoff (*Servants*)], [Francisco Maran (*Officer*)], [Paco Moreno (*Peon*)], [Bob Cautiero (*Groom*)], [Robert Conway].

Historical, Adventure. [*Print viewed*]. In the early 1800's, when Diego Vega, one of the best swordsmen in all of Spain, is unexpectedly summoned home to California by his father, Don Alejandro, he returns to find that his father has been deposed as alcalde and the peasants crushed beneath the yoke of tyranny under Don Luis Quintero and his soldiers, who are led by the sword brandishing Captain Esteban Pasquale. With the odds against an uprising because of the sheer number of soldiers under Pasquale's command, Diego becomes the scourge of the oppressors by acting as the masked bandit Zorro by night while impersonating a foppish dilettante by day. As Zorro, he falls in love with Quintero's beautiful niece Lolita, while as Don Diego, he flirts with Quintero's conceited wife Inez, thus earning the ire of Pasquale, her other suitor. When Zorro orders that Quintero return to Spain and appoint Don Alejandro as his successor, Pasquale cleverly proposes an alliance between the Vega and Quintero families through a marriage between Diego and Lolita. At first repulsed, Lolita embraces Diego after she discovers that he is the dashing Zorro. However, Diego's masquerade is exposed when his accomplice, Fray Felipe, is arrested by Pasquale and Diego challenges the smug captain to a duel. When Diego kills his opponent, he attracts the suspicion of Quintero, who arrests him and sentences him to death. As Fray Felipe and Diego await the firing squad, Diego outwits the guard, breaks out of jail and leads the peasants and caballeros in a rebellion against the soldiers. With Quintero and his men defeated, Don Alejandro takes over as alcalde, and peace is restored to the village of Los Angeles. *California–History–To 1846. Despotism. Impersonation and imposture. Masked bandits. Uprisings.* Fathers and sons. Flirtation. Fops. Mayors. Nieces. Peasantry. Romance. Soldiers. Spain. Sword fights.

Note: The working title of this film was *The Californian.* According to an item in *LAEx,* Douglas Fairbanks sold Fox his rights to the Johnston McCulley story, which was published in book form in 1924 as *The Mark of Zorro.* Materials contained in the Twentieth Century-Fox Records of the Legal Department at the UCLA Theater Arts Library add that McCulley retained author's rights to the character of Zorro and wrote several other Zorro stories. As a result, Fox did not control the rights to the Zorro character, thus enabling Republic to make *The Bold Caballero* in 1936 (see above). The legal files also add that William A. Drake and Dorothy Hechtlinger worked on treatments for the film. Materials contained in the Twentieth Century-Fox Produced Scripts Collection at the UCLA Theater Arts Library note that Darryl Zanuck suggested that Richard Greene test for the role of Zorro. The film had its premiere in Cincinnati, the home town of star Tyrone Power. It was nominated for an Academy Award for Best Original Score. The 1981 Fox release *Zorro, the Gay Blade,* starring George Hamilton and directed by Peter Medak, was dedicated to director Rouben Mamoulian. For more information on other Zorro films, see entries above for *The Bold Caballero* and the 1920 *The Mark of Zorro.*

DV 4 Nov 1940, p. 3. *FD* 6 Nov 1940, p. 5. *HR* 12 Jul 1940, p. 6. *HR* 25 Jul 1940, p. 4. *HR* 26 Jul 1940, pp. 8-9. *HR* 6 Aug 1940, p. 9. *HR* 12 Sep 1940, p. 2. *HR* 10 Oct 1940, p.

1. *HR* 28 Oct 1940, p. 9. *HR* 4 Nov 1940, p. 3. *LAEx* 20 May 1939. *MPD* 6 Nov 1940, p. 6. *MPH* 9 Nov 1940, p. 35. *NYT* 4 Nov 1940, p. 33. *NYT* 10 Nov 1940, p. 5. *Var* 6 Nov 1940, p. 16.

MARK TWAIN'S THE ADVENTURES OF HUCKLEBERRY FINN *see* THE ADVENTURES OF HUCKLEBERRY FINN

MARKED CARDS (Irish Americans)
Triangle Film Corp. *Dist* Triangle Distributing Corp. 14 Jul **1918**. Si; b&w. 5 reels.

Dir Count H. D'Elba. *Scen* Lanier Bartlett. *Story* Adela Rogers St. Johns. *Cam* Elgin Leslie.

Cast: Margery Wilson (*Ellen Shannon*), Wallace MacDonald (*Ted Breslin*), Jack Curtis (*Pat Shannon*), Rae Godfrey (*Janet Breslin*), Harvey Clark (*"Poker" LeMoyne*), Joe Bennett (*Don Jackson*), Lillian Langdon (*Mrs. J. De Barth Breslin*), Lee Phelps (*Wesley Cutting*), Anne Kroman (*Winona Harrington*), Ben Lewis (*Arnold Heath*), E. J. Brady (*John Acton*).

Drama. Ellen Shannon, the daughter of self-made Irish politician Pat Shannon, is engaged to Ted Breslin, but because Pat began his career as a menial laborer, Ted's mother, Mrs. J. De Barth Breslin, refuses to sanction the marriage. Heartbroken, Ted takes up drinking and gambling with "Poker" LeMoyne and Don Jackson, while Ellen attends a finishing school hoping to improve herself. While trying to elude her chaperone, Ellen unwittingly dashes into a man's hotel room, and from the window, she witnesses Don and "Poker" playing cards, while Ted lies unconscious from too much drink. When the two gamblers quarrel, Don kills "Poker," but Ted is accused of the crime. Fearing a scandal, Ellen maintains her silence, but on the final day of the trial, she enters the courtroom and testifies, thereby saving Ted from the gallows. Deeply grateful, Mrs. Breslin now welcomes Ellen into the family. *Engagements. Evidence. False accusations. Irish Americans. Mothers and sons. Murder. Snobs and snobbishness. Drunkenness. Finishing schools. Gambling. Trials.*

ETR 13 Jul 1918, p. 470. *MPW* 20 Jul 1918, p. 459. *MPW* 27 Jul 1918, p. 588. *NYDM* 27 Jul 1918, p. 126. *Var* 26 Jul 1918, p. 32.

MARSE COVINGTON (African Americans)
Rolfe Photoplays, Inc. *Dist* Metro Pictures Corp. 12 Jul **1915** [©Metro Pictures Corp.; 12 Jul 1915; LP6430]. Si; b&w. 5 reels.

Dir Edwin Carewe. *Scen* George Ade.

Source: Based on the play *Marse Covington* by George Ade (production undetermined, 1906).

Cast: Edward Connelly (*Captain Covington Halliday, also known as "Marse Covington"*), Louise Huff (*Martha Halliday*), John J. Williams (*Uncle Dan*), Lyster Chambers (*Walter Lewis*), Howard Truesdell (*Edward Bantree*), Paul Dallzell (*Jim Daly*).

Drama. Proud Confederate Captain Covington Halliday refuses to allow his daughter Martha to marry Yankee lawyer Walter Lewis. Covington relates to her his life before, during and after the Civil War. As a boy, Covington was given the black servant Dan who called him "Marse Covington." After the war, Dan refused his freedom and shared Covington's misfortunes. Jim Daly, who holds the mortgage to Halliday House, also wants to marry Martha. He schemes with Yankee gambler Edward Bantree to fix a horse race in which Covington has wagered all his property on his beloved horse Bess. After Bess loses and Covington refuses to influence Martha, who spurns Daly, Covington, Martha and Dan move to New York. Their savings soon run out and Covington is forced to stand in bread lines. After Dan becomes Bantree's servant, he learns about the fix and tells Walter. When Bantree kills Daly in a fight over cards, Walter's charge for defending him is the Halliday House deed. Covington returns with Dan, and allowing that Walter was born just three miles into the North, he happily agrees to the marriage. *Northerners. Racism. Rivalry. Southerners. African Americans. Deeds. Fraud. Gambling. Horseracing. Lawyers. Mortgages. Murder. New York City. Officers (Military). Poverty. Servants. Slavery. United States–History–Civil War, 1861-1865. Wagers.*

Note: According to *Motog*, Adelle Barker played the role of Martha. *MPW* referred to the granddaughter as "Miss Carol."

Motog 31 Jul 1915, pp. 214-15, 233. *MPN* 17 Apr 1915, p. 55. *MPN* 31 Jul 1915, p. 76. *MPW* 31 Jul 1915, p. 832. *MPW* 14 Aug 1915, p. 1231. *NYDM* 21 Jul 1915, p. 27.

MARSHAL OF CRIPPLE CREEK (Native Americans)
Republic Pictures Corp. *Dist* Republic Pictures Corp. 15 Aug **1947**; Prod: late Oct—mid-Nov 1946 [©Republic Pictures Corp.; 28 Jul 1947; LP1210]. Sd (RCA Sound System); b&w. 58 min. Passed by the National Board of Review. PCA cert no. 12134.

Series: Red Ryder.

Assoc prod Sidney Picker. *Dir* R. G. Springsteen. [*Asst dir* Eddie Stein]. *Orig scr* Earle Snell. *Photog* William Bradford. *Set dec* Howard Lydecker and Theodore Lydecker. *Art dir* Frank Arrigo. *Film ed* Harold R. Minter. *Set dec* John McCarthy, Jr. and Helen Hansard. *Mus dir* Mort Glickman. *Sd* Victor B. Appel. *Makeup supv* Bob Mark.

Source: Based on the comic strip "Red Ryder" by Fred Harman (1938–1964), by special arrangement with Stephen Slesinger.

Cast: Allan Lane [(*Red Ryder*)], Bobby Blake [(*Little Beaver*)], Martha Wentworth [(*The Duchess*)], Trevor Bardette [(*Tom Lambert*)], Tom London [(*Baker*)], Roy Barcroft [(*Link*)], Gene Stutenroth [(*Long John Lacey*)], William Self [(*Dick Lambert*)], Helen Wallace [(*Mae Lambert*)], [Budd Buster (*Citizen*)], [Roy Bucko, Art Dillard, Herman Hack, Silver Harr, George Russell, Jack Sparks, Leonard Wood (*Deputies*)], [Frank O'Connor].

Western. [*Print viewed*]. After wandering cowboy Red Ryder witnesses a wagon being hijacked near the gold rush town of Cripple Creek, Wyoming, he captures one of the outlaws with the help of his pal, Little Beaver. At a ranchers' meeting at Long John Lacey's saloon, a miner named Baker is nominated for the job of marshal. Long John, who co-owns a gold mine with Baker, offers to contribute to the new marshal's salary. Just then, Little Beaver enters with news of the captured outlaw, and the citizens persuade Red to act as marshal until a permanent one can be found. Later, at the saloon, when a gambler named Billy loses a game of cards to dealer Link, Billy accuses him of stacking the deck. After the saloon has closed, outlaw Tom Lambert breaks in, planning to rob it, but is seen by Baker, who offers him $500 to stock his mine with gold ore. Later, Link and the bandits rob the wagon carrying Baker's gold shipment, and after Tom warns the bandits that Red is bringing a posse to look for them, the gang decides to ambush the men in a ravine. During the attack, Tom is shot, and the gang flees without him. While the doctor tends to Tom's wound, Tom's wife Mae and their son Dick arrive at the saloon, where they are greeted by Red and The Duchess. Tom recovers, and is sentenced to life in prison. While Tom is in prison, Long John recruits Dick to join the gang. When Red sees Dick inside the saloon, he orders him out because he is underage, and Link and Red fight. Red then discovers that Dick has been cheating at cards and is forced to arrest him. At the jail, however, Long John announces that the charges against Dick have been dropped, and the boy is released. After Link gets drunk and shoots at Red, he is sentenced to the state penitentiary, where he is given the cell next to Tom's. During their stay at the penitentiary, Link convinces Tom that Red has singled Dick out for harassment. Later, Mae and The Duchess visit Dick at Baker's mine, where he has taken a job. Tom escapes from prison and returns to Cripple Creek to look for Red. When he finds Red, Tom pulls a gun, but Little Beaver knocks it out of Tom's hand. He and Red hog-tie Tom until Mae arrives and sets him free. Meanwhile, Red plans to hide inside one of the wagons carrying the gold ore. When Tom offers to help the gang with the robbery, Long John tells him to go with Dick to the lookout point. Once alone, Tom chastises Dick for his life of crime and tells him to quit the gang immediately. The gang then hijacks the wagon and takes it to the mine, where Red jumps out and attacks Tom. As he tries to escape with Red, Tom is shot in the back by Baker. Baker warns Long John that Red is coming to arrest him, and when Red arrives, Baker is poised to shoot him. Again, Little Beaver comes to the rescue, breaking a bottle over Baker's head, who is then placed in custody. After Baker is sent to jail, Red is forced to quit his marshal's job because there is no more crime in Cripple Creek. *Deputies. Fathers and sons. Outlaws. United States. Marshals. Arrests. Cards. Cripple Creek (WY). Drunkenness. Firearms. Gambling. Gold mines. Gunshot wounds. Hijackers. Posses. Prisons. Robbery. Saloons. Wagons. Wyoming.*

Note: *Marshal of Cripple Creek* was the last entry in Republic's "Red Ryder" series. In 1949, Equity Pictures released four films starring Jim Bannon as "Red." For more information on the "Red Ryder" series, please consult the Series Index and see the entry below for *Tucson Raiders*.

Box 23 Aug 1947. *DV* 18 Aug 1947. *FD* 18 Aug 1947, p. 6. *HR* 1 Nov 1946, p. 17. *HR* 8 Nov 1946, p. 21. *HR* 18 Aug 1947, p. 3. *IFJ* 9 Nov 1946, p. 43. *MPHPD* 23 Aug 1947. *Var* 20 Aug 1947, p. 18.

MARSHAL OF RENO (Native Americans)
Republic Pictures Corp. *Dist* Republic Pictures Corp. 2 Jul **1944**; Los Angeles opening: 29 Jun 1944; Prod: early Mar—mid-Mar 1944 [©Republic Pictures Corp.; 22 May 1944; LP12700]. Sd (RCA Sound System); b&w. 6 reels, 5,031 ft. 54 or 58 min. Passed by the National Board of Review. PCA cert no. 10067.

Series: Red Ryder.

Assoc prod Louis Gray. *Dir* Wallace Grissell. [*Asst dir* Joe Dill]. *Orig story* Anthony Coldewey and Taylor Caven. *Scr* Anthony Coldewey. *Photog* Reggie Lanning. *Art dir* Gano Chittenden. *Film ed* Charles Craft. *Set dec* George Milo. *Mus score* Joseph Dubin. *Sd* Tom Carman.

Source: Based on the comic strip "Red Ryder" by Fred Harman (1938–1964), by special arrangement with Stephen Slesinger.

Cast: WILD BILL ELLIOTT (*Red Ryder* [*also known as Reno*]), George "Gabby" Hayes [(*Gabby*)], Bobby Blake [(*Little Beaver*)], Alice Fleming [(*The Duchess*)], Herbert Rawlinson [(*John Palmer*)], Jay Kirby [(*Danny Boyd*)], LeRoy Mason [(*Faro Carson*)], Blake Edwards [(*Lee Holden*)], Fred Graham [(*Drake*)], Jack Kirk [(*Kellogg*)], Kenne Duncan [(*Adams*)], Bud Geary [(*Ward*)], Tom Steele [(*Crane*)], Tom London [(*Sheriff Walker*)], Tom Chatterton [(*Judge Holmes*)], [Edmund Cobb (*Bob Wendell*)], [Hal Price (*Joe Richards*)], [Al Taylor (*Brown*)], [Marshall Reed (*Wilson*)], [Bob Wilke (*Deputy*)], [Ken Terrell (*Waiter*)], [Charles Sullivan (*Bartender*)].

Western. [*Print viewed*]. In 1895, the citizens of Blue Springs are competing with their neighbors in Rockland for the honor of having their town named county seat. An outbreak of lawlessness has hurt Blue Springs's reputation, however, and when the stagecoach carrying Judge Holmes is attacked and the judge is wounded, things look bleak for the townsfolk. Sheriff Walker organizes a posse to find the two bandits, who also stole the coach's money bags. In order to escape, the bandits, meanwhile, swap their distinctive horses with those of two unsuspecting young men from the East. Leading citizen Red Ryder, his Indian ward Little Beaver, and their friend Gabby find the criminals and retrieve the loot, but not before the posse has caught the two Easterners. Kellogg, a member of the posse, is the henchman of the secret leader of the bandits' gang, John Palmer, a newspaper publisher who hopes to make a fortune by promoting the interests of Rockland. In order to prevent the two Easterners, Danny Boyd and Lee Holden, from identifying the bandits, Kellogg tricks Lee into trying to escape, then shoots him. The posse is about to lynch Danny when Red arrives and proves his innocence. Danny vows revenge for Lee's death, and despite Red's attempts to placate him, Danny captures three members of the posse that evening and threatens to kill them if they do not reveal who murdered Lee. Red stops Danny and urges him to make a fresh start in Rockland, where Palmer offers him a job. Judge Holmes, who is convalescing at the ranch owned by Red's aunt, The Duchess, believes Red's assertion that he will bring law and order to Blue Springs, and so, in order to stir up more trouble, Palmer orders his men to kill the posse members one by one. When posse member Brown is killed, Red trails the shooter to the Rockland saloon, which is run by Faro Carson, Palmer's right-hand man. Carson does not recognize Red, who has been away for a long time, and when Red claims to be an outlaw named Reno, Carson offers him a job. Red thus infiltrates the gang, and he, Carson and henchman Adams begin a crime spree. Red warns the intended victims in advance, but the townspeople believe that they have been shot, and the "killings" are blamed on Danny. Palmer is about to publish an article naming Danny as the murderer when Gabby confides that he has "inside information" to prove Danny's innocence. Palmer prints the story anyway, and an infuriated Danny, who has been working at a nearby ranch, confronts him. That same day, Palmer meets Red in the saloon, and the unsuspecting Red tells Palmer about his undercover investigation. Fearing that Carson will kill Danny, whom he is now holding captive, Red asks Palmer to alert Sheriff Walker. Palmer instead warns Carson that Red is the former marshal of Reno, and then tells Walker that Danny is gunning for him. Meanwhile, Red tells Danny to find Walker, who will protect him, then frees him. The gang captures Red and Gabby, but Little Beaver helps them escape, and they ride to Blue Springs. Danny has already reached the town and is bewildered when the sheriff arrests him. As Danny is trying to explain, Carson and his men enter the sheriff's office and steal forty thousand dollars, which The Duchess had left for safekeeping. Danny chases Adams as he is trying to escape with the loot, but Palmer convinces the gathering crowd that Danny is the perpetrator, and a posse pursues him. Red then joins the posse, which has trapped Danny on a rocky hillside, but Danny refuses to believe Red's assurances that no one will hurt him. Although Palmer orders Kellogg to kill Danny before he and Red can deduce the truth, Danny

is only wounded in the shoulder, and Red, Gabby and Little Beaver are able to round up the gang. Later, Palmer and his men are convicted of their crimes and Blue Springs is made the county seat. *Bandits. Cowboys. False accusations. Newspaper publishers. Tenderfoots. Undercover operations. Aliases. Aunts. Chases. Duplicity. Escapes. Gamblers. Horses. Indians of North America. Judges. Murder. Posses. Saloons. Sheriffs. Wards and guardians. Women ranchers.*

Note: A 10 Mar 1944 *HR* production chart erroneously lists Spencer Bennet as the director of this film. Modern sources include the following actors in the cast: George Chesebro, Augie Gomez, Pascale Perry, Jim Corey, Fred Burns, Jack O'Shea, Carl Sepulveda, Horace B. Carpenter and Roy Barcroft. For more information on the "Red Ryder" series, please consult the Series Index and see the entry below for *Tucson Raiders*.

DV 30 Jun 1944, p. 3. *HR* 10 Mar 1944, p. 7. *HR* 17 Mar 1944, p. 19. *HR* 30 Jun 1944, p. 3. *MPHPD* 3 Jun 1944, p. 1923. *MPHPD* 8 Jul 1944, p. 1981.

MARTY (Italian Americans)

Hecht-Lancaster Productions. *Dist* United Artists Corp. Mar **1955**; *Prod:* began 7 Sep 1954 in the Bronx; late Oct 1954–Feb 1955 at Goldwyn Studios in Hollywood [©Steven Productions; 11 Apr 1955; LP4751]. Sd (Western Electric Recording); b&w; 1.85. 8,032 ft. 89 min. PCA cert no. 17297.

Prod Harold Hecht. *Assoc prod* Paddy Chayefsky. *Dir* Delbert Mann. *Asst dir* Paul Helmick. *Story and scr* Paddy Chayefsky. *Photog* Joseph LaShelle. *Art dir* Edward Haworth and Walter Simonds. *Ed supv* Alan Crosland, Jr. *Mus eff ed* Robert Carlisle. *Set dec* Robert Priestley. *Cost des* Norma. *Mus* Roy Webb. *Addl mus* George Bassman. *Sd rec* John Kean and Roger Heman. *Makeup* Robert Schiffer. *Hair styles* Agnes Flanagan. *Casting supv* Betty Pagel.

Song(s): "Marty," music by Harry Warren, words by Paddy Chayefsky.

Source: Based on the teleplay *Marty* by Paddy Chayefsky, on *Goodyear Television Playhouse* (NBC, 24 May 1952).

Cast: Ernest Borgnine (*Marty* [*Piletti*]), Betsy Blair (*Clara* [*Snyder*]), Esther Minciotti (*Mrs.* [*Teresa*] *Piletti*), Augusta Ciolli (*Aunt Catherine*), Joe Mantell (*Angie*), Karen Steele (*Virginia*), Jerry Paris (*Tommy*), [Frank Sutton (*Ralph*)], [Walter Kelley (*The Kid*)], [Robin Morse (*Joe*)].

Domestic, Drama. [*Print viewed*]. Marty Piletti, a stocky, homely thirty-four-year-old Bronx butcher, good-naturedly dismisses the nagging of his customers, who want to know when he will get married now that the last of his unmarried siblings has wed. After work, Marty goes to Michael's restaurant, where he "hangs out" with his best friend Angie. With nothing to do that night, Angie tries to get Marty to call Mary Feeney, a girl they met a month before at a movie theater, but he refuses, saying that he is tired of looking for a girl. At his home, which Marty shares with his Italian-born mother Teresa, Marty's cousin Tommy and his wife Virginia complain that Tommy's mother Catherine is not getting along with Virginia and ask Teresa if Catherine, her sister, can move in with her. Marty and Teresa agree, and Marty makes an appointment to talk with Tommy, an accountant, about the feasibility of his buying his boss's butcher shop. Marty then calls Mary and asks her out, but she rejects him. Later, during dinner, Teresa asks Marty why he does not go to the Starlight Ballroom, which she has learned from Tommy, is "loaded with tomatoes." Although Marty laughs at first, he blows up when she prods him and cries out that he does not have what women want and does not want to get hurt anymore. When she warns that he will die without a son, he yells that he is a fat, ugly man, but finally agrees to go to the ballroom. There, a man offers him five dollars to take home a blind date whom the man does not like, but Marty angrily refuses him. The man finds someone else to accept the money, but the woman, Clara Snyder, a twenty-nine-year-old high school chemistry teacher from Brooklyn, announces that she is going home alone. She then walks out to the fire escape and cries. Marty follows her and after asking her to dance, assures her that she is not the "dog" she thinks she is and confesses that he himself has suffered from rejection. As Marty and Clara walk from the dance hall, he talks excitedly about his life. He explains that he waited for his sisters to marry, according to the Italian tradition, and at times has thought of suicide, a terrible sin for a Catholic. When he tells Clara about his desire to buy the butcher shop, she encourages him. Clara then admits that she has a chance to take an advanced position outside the city, and Marty advises her not to be afraid to leave her family. As they talk, Marty's buddy Ralph calls him over to a car in which he and their friend Leo are sitting with three nurses. Ralph asks Marty if he wants to join them, saying the third

nurse is like "money in the bank," but Marty refuses to leave Clara. Upon arriving at his house, Marty senses that Clara is nervous and offers to take her home, but while helping her on with her coat, he impulsively tries to kiss her. She struggles and pulls away, but after he cries out that he only wanted a kiss, she confesses that she simply did not know how to handle the situation. As Marty sulks, Clara says she would like to see him again, calling him the kindest man she has met. They make plans to see a movie the next night, and when he also asks her out New Year's Eve, they hug and kiss. Just then, Teresa returns from a visit with Catherine and explains her sister's situation to Clara. Clara upsets Teresa when she asserts that she does not think it is good for parents to live with their married children and that they should not depend on children for rewards in life. While Marty is walking Clara to the subway, he runs into Angie, who barely acknowledges Clara. After saying goodnight at Clara's door, Marty is exuberant. The next morning, Tommy and Virginia, arguing bitterly over his mother, arrive at Marty's with Catherine. Marty tries to ask Tommy's advice about buying the store, but a distraught Tommy questions why Marty, a single man, would want to saddle himself with a mortgage and expenses. Upon learning that Marty has met a girl, Catherine, meanwhile, tells Teresa that college girls are "one step up from the street" and warns that Marty will soon suggest they move to a small apartment, where Teresa will be just an old lady sleeping on a couch in her daughter-in-law's apartment. As if on cue, Marty comes in and, noticing some fallen plaster, casually suggests they sell the house. Just before Mass, a now-worried Teresa tells Marty not to bring Clara to the house again, saying there are plenty of nice Italian girls. Later, at Michael's, Ralph, in a state of satiation, stares dumbfounded when Marty declares that he enjoyed just talking with Clara, whom Angie has described as a "dog." After his buddies, who quote Mickey Spillane and gaze at girlie magazines, inform him that it is bad for his reputation to go out with "dogs," Marty gives in to peer pressure and does not phone Clara. As he and his friends face another tedious night at Michael's, however, Marty explodes, calling them miserable, lonely and stupid. Marty then announces that if he continues to have good times with Clara, he will beg her to marry him. He then goes to call Clara, and when Angie follows, he asks his pal when he is going to get married. *Bachelors. Butchers. Courtship. Dance halls. Friendship. Italian Americans. Mothers and sons. New York City–Bronx. Widows. Accountants. Aunts. Catholic Church. Cousins. The Ed Sullivan Show (Television program). Immigrants. Marriage. Mothers-in-law. Nurses. Restaurants. Schoolteachers. Sisters. Mickey Spillane.*

Note: According to reviews, *Marty* was the first feature-length film to be based on a television play. The television production, which was directed by Delbert Mann and starred Rod Steiger, won the Donaldson and Sylvania awards for best drama. Author Paddy Chayefsky related in a *NYT* article that the character of "Marty" was based on a friend, "this lonely bachelor, a nice guy, not so young." In addition, Chayefsky had lived in the area of the Bronx where *Marty* is set and utilized his knowledge of the setting while writing the script. Chayefsky sold the film rights to Norma Productions (later called Hecht-Lancaster Productions), because he wanted a small company to make the film and Norma co-owner Harold Hecht had once been his agent. Norma bought the screen rights in Sep 1953 and signed a deal in Feb 1954 with United Artists to release it. In a Jan 1956 *NYT* article, Chayefsky wrote that, during production, he was "consulted on every aspect of the picture, even those not relevant to the actual screen play." According to a Sep 1954 *NYT* news item, Chayefsky insisted that Delbert Mann also direct the film. This marked Mann's film debut.

Reviews made note of the fact that Marty was Ernest Borgnine's first major, sympathetic film role. According to the *HR* review, Norma co-owner Burt Lancaster had wanted to cast Borgnine, with whom he had made *From Here to Eternity*, in one of his company's pictures and after Hecht saw the television production, he concluded that Borgnine was right for the role. In the pressbook for the film, Hecht stated, "We departed from the old pattern...by gambling with unknown names. They've been doing it in Europe and it pays off." Esther Minciotti, who played "Teresa" in the television production, reprised her role in the film. Location shooting was done in the Bronx, while interiors were shot in Hollywood at Goldwyn studios. News items stated that the film had a negative cost of $343,000, though *Var* noted that "there is no evidence of any stinting in the production values, a factor the industry will note." A year after its release, the company had spent over $400,000 on advertising, according to *HR*.

The film opened in New York at the Sutton Theatre, traditionally, according to *Var*, "an outlet for offbeat and 'art' merchandise." In other areas, according to a *NYT* article, the film was screened intensely two weeks prior to its opening for community "opinion-makers," including ministers, shopkeepers and physicians. Many reviewers commented on the universal appeal of the film's story. *HR* stated, "The story is a genre study of second generation and foreign-born Americans. It has the sharp true observation of life that was to be found in *Studs Lonigan* without its bitterness. And the compassionate understanding

of an *I Remember Mama*. Since there are thousands of Americans descended from ancestors who came over in the steerage for every one who had an ancestor on the Mayflower, the film offers opportunities for recognition and self-identification that should appeal to almost everybody." While the film did little business in some areas, including Memphis, New Orleans and Bridgeport, within six months, it had branched out to 500 theaters and had grossed $800,000.

Marty won Academy Awards for best picture, director, actor and writer. In addition, it received Academy Award nominations for best supporting actor (Joe Mantell), best supporting actress (Betsy Blair), art direction (black and white) and cinematography (black and white). The film received the New York Film Critics award for best picture and actor, and was the first American film to win the Golden Palm grand prize at the Cannes Film Festival. It is the only film ever to win both the Academy Award for best picture and the Golden Palm. Sergei Yutkevich, a Russian film director on the jury at Cannes, stated in a *Pravda* review, "It truly depicts the life of simple folk in America." The film opened in Moscow on 10 Nov 1959 as the first in a series of ten American films purchased by the Soviet Union as part of a cultural exchange with the U.S. According to *NYT*, *Marty* was the first major U.S. film to be screened there following World War II.

In Oct 1996, *Var* reported that a musical version of *Marty*, starring Jason Alexander, was being prepared for a Broadway opening during the 1998-99 season.

Box 26 Mar 1955. *Box Office Digest* 31 Oct 1955. *Cosmopolitan* May 1955. *Cue* 16 Apr 1955. *DV* 21 Mar 1955, p. 3. *Exb* 6 Apr 1955, p. 3945. *FD* 21 Mar 1955, p. 6. *Har* 26 Mar 1955, p. 51. *HCN* 16 Jul 1955. *HR* 12 Apr 1954. *HR* 21 Mar 1955, p. 3. *HR* 14 Nov 1955. *HR* 22 Dec 1955. *HR* 14 Mar 1956. *HR* 12 Nov 1959. *LAT* 20 Feb 1955. *MPHPD* 26 Mar 1955, p. 377. *New Yorker* 23 Apr 1955 *NYT* 20 Sep 1953. *NYT* 8 Feb 1954. *NYT* 12 Sep 1954. *NYT* 10 Apr 1955. *NYT* 12 Apr 1955, p. 25. *NYT* 17 Apr 1955. *NYT* 31 May 1955. *NYT* 14 Sep 1955. *NYT* 8 Jan 1956. *NYT* 11 Nov 1956. *NYT* 13 Nov 1956. *SatRev* 26 Mar 1955. *Time* 19 Mar 1956. *Var* 11 Nov 1953. *Var* 23 Mar 1955, p. 3, 6, 15. *Var* 17 Oct 1996.

THE MARTYRED MOTHER *see* **AMOR IN MONTAGNA**

MARTYRS OF YESTERDAY *see* **IN THE LAND OF THE SETTING SUN; OR, MARTYRS OF YESTERDAY**

MARUSIA (Ukrainian language)
Ukrafilm Corp. *Dist* Ukrafilm Corp. 8 Dec **1938**; Prod: 26 Jun—31 Jul 1938 at Eastern Service Studios, Inc.. Sd; b&w. 95 or 105 min. Ukrainian language.
Dir Leo Bulgakov. *Scr* Vladimir Kedrowsky and Andrei Kist. *Photog* George Hinners and Edward Hyland. *Ed* Leon Levy. *Mus score* Professor Roman Prydatekych. *Choral and vocal mus* Dr. Alexander Koshetz. *Dance dir* Andrei Kist.
Source: Based on the folk play *Marusia* by M. Staritsky (1872).
Cast: Stephania Melnyk (*Marusia*), Nicholas Stehnitzky (*Hyrtz*), Peter Chorniuk (*Khoma*), Donia Stephania Werbowetzka (*Daryna*), Halia Troitzka (*Halyna*), Mykola Novak (*Potap*), Michael Skorobohach (*Dmytro*), Fedor Braznyk, Anton Kulyk, Halia Troyan, K. Hupalowa, Maria Skubowa, Teklia Kobzar, S. Besruchko, F. Kotowych.
Drama. [*Not viewed*]. Marusia and her lover Hyrtz are betrothed and plan to marry when Hyrtz has enough money. Their happiness is marred, however, when Khoma, a hunchback warped in mind as well as body and the richest man in the village, plans to separate the lovers and win Marusia for his own. To accomplish this, Khoma causes Hyrtz to quarrel with his best friend Potap and then induces him to insult Marusia and leave the village for good. Khoma then succeeds in placing Marusia's parents under financial obligation to him. Meanwhile, Marusia, perplexed and pining for Hyrtz, slowly succumbs to Khoma's courtship. Hyrtz returns just in time to prevent the marriage between Marusia and Khoma. When the love between Marusia and Hyrtz rekindles, Khoma arranges for the lovers to be poisoned. After his treachery is exposed, Khoma flees the vengeance of the village, but perishes in the river after Potap throws him from a cliff. *Hunchbacks. Poisoning. Romantic rivalry. Treachery. Ukrainians. Engagements. Falls from heights. Friendship. Rivers. Village life.*
Note: According to a news item in *HR*, this Ukrainian dialogue film was produced with a budget of $45,000. The *MPH* review adds that the footage was shot in New York State, New Jersey and Long Island.
FD 16 Dec 1938, p. 10. *HR* 27 Jun 1938, p. 3. *HR* 1 Aug 1938, p. 5. *MPH* 31 Dec 1938, p. 54. *Var* 21 Dec 1938, p. 15.

MARY O'ROURKE *see* **A BACHELOR'S WIFE**

MASK OF THE DRAGON (Chinese Americans)
Spartan Productions, Inc. *Dist* Lippert Pictures, Inc. 10 Mar **1951** [©Spartan Productions, Inc.; 10 Apr 1951; LP840]. Sd; b&w. 6 reels, 4,807 ft. 52, 54-55 or 60 min. PCA cert no. 15041.
Prod Sigmund Neufeld. *Dir* Samuel Newfield. *Asst dir* Stanley Neufeld. *Scr* Orville Hampton. *Dir of photog* Jack Greenhalgh. *Spec*

eff Ray Mercer. *Film ed* Carl Piersonn. *Set dec* Harry Reif. *Ward* Al Berke. *Handknits and fashions* Diane. *Mus* Dudley Chambers. *Sd* Glen Glenn. *Makeup artist* Paul Stanhope. *Prod mgr* Bert Sternbach. *Set construction* Tom Kemp.

Cast: Richard Travis [(*Phil Ramsey*)], Sheila Ryan [(*Ginny O'Donnell*)], Sid Melton [(*Manchu Murphy*)], Michael Whalen [(*Major Clinton*)], Lyle Talbot [(*Lt. "Mack" McLaughlin*)], Dee Tatum [(*Terry Newell*)], Richard Emory [(*Dan Oliver*)], Jack Reitzen [(*Kim Ho*)], Mr. Moto [(*Moto*)], Karl Davis [(*Kingpin*)], John Grant [(*Announcer*)], Curt Barrett and The Trailsmen, [Eddie Lee (*Chen Koo*)], [Ray Singer (*Grantland*)], [Carla Martin (*Sarah*)], [Dick Paxton], [Barbara Atkins].

Detective. [*Viewed print incomplete*]. With his tour of duty in Korea about to end, Lt. Dan Oliver stops in at Chen Koo's curio shop. Chen Koo asks Dan to take a jade dragon with him, promising that he will be paid generously for delivering it to the Jade Lotus curio shop in Los Angeles. Dan, whose concealed camera has been photographing various objects in the shop, agrees. When Dan arrives in Los Angeles, he goes straight to the detective agency that he operates with his old friend and fellow World War II veteran Phil Ramsey, unaware that he is being followed by two thugs, Manchu Murphy and Kingpin. Phil is at his girl friend Ginny O'Donnell's apartment when Dan calls to ask if they have received an important package that he sent them. Before Dan can explain, Manchu and Kingpin sneak up and kill him. They then rifle through Dan's suitcase but do not find what they are looking for. Phil and Ginny, who works in the police crime lab, rush over to the agency and find Dan's body. While Ginny calls her colleague, Lt. "Mack" McLaughlin, a homocide detective, Phil finds a folder containing an ad for the Jade Lotus curio shop in Chinatown. At the crime lab, Mack enters with Terry Newell, a singer who met Dan when she was entertaining the troops in Korea. Terry is eager to know if Dan had something for her in his bags, and she invites Phil to visit her at the television station where she records a nightly program. They are joined by Major Clinton, who is representing the Army in the investigation of Dan's murder. Phil is offended by Major Clinton's suggestion that Dan was involved in something shady, and he decides to investigate the crime himself. At the Jade Lotus curio shop, Manchu, who is dressed in Chinese garb, notes Phil's arrival suspiciously. Phil watches as the proprietor, Kim Ho, completes several furtive transactions involving small figurines of the Eight Immortals, symbols of the Taoist sect. Kim Ho tells Phil that the political turmoil in China has made it difficult to import art objects, so his agent in Korea sometimes engages American soldiers as couriers. He assures Phil that the pieces are not valuable enough to cause a murder. As soon as Phil leaves the shop, he is ambushed by Manchu and Kingpin and taken to a hotel room, where he is beaten by Judo expert Moto. After Manchu and Kingpin leave, Moto opens the door for an unseen female visitor, who knocks him out and unties Phil, leaving before he can remove the blindfold. Phil goes to see Terry at the television station and says he can tell by her perfume that she was the one who rescued him. Terry tells Phil that she is in trouble, and Phil convinces her to go with him to police headquarters after the broadcast. While she is waiting for her cue, however, she is stabbed to death by Manchu and Kingpin, who had sneaked into the studio. At the homocide office, Mack complains that Phil has been watching too many movies that glamorize private detectives and make it look as if they do all the police's work for them. Major Clinton comes in and requests information on Terry's death, arousing Phil's anger and suspicion. Meanwhile, Ginny has received a package from Dan containing the jade dragon. She wants to call the police, but Phil refuses and insists on returning to the Jade Lotus. After he leaves, Mack calls with the news that "Kim Ho" is actually the alias for a dangerous criminal. At the curio shop, Kim Ho offers to buy the jade dragon, but Phil demands a steep price. Kim Ho goes to find Manchu and Kingpin, and Phil hides in the back room, where Moto catches him. While they are struggling, Clinton enters and tries to kill Phil. Mack and Ginny arrive with the police in time to rescue Phil and arrest Kim Ho, Major Clinton and their accomplices. Later, it is revealed that the curio shop was a front for a smuggling ring that was bringing in uranium from the Orient by concealing it in the figurines. Mack admits that Phil did a good job of cracking the case. *Chinese Americans. Curio dealers. Espionage. Impersonation and imposture. Private detectives. Smuggling. Art objects. Chinatowns. Forensics. Hired killers. Judo. Los Angeles (CA). Murder. Officers (Military). Partnership.*

Police. Racial impersonation. Singers. Spies. Television. United States. Army. Veterans.

Note: The only print available for viewing was a shortened television version titled *Oriental Clue*. The above plot and credits were taken from a copyright cutting continuity deposited in Apr 1951. The television version, which ran approximately 26 minutes, contained a different ending and other footage not found in the continuity. Although the *Var* review and other contemporary sources identify the character played by the actor Mr. Moto as "Simo," in the cutting continuity he is referred to only as "Moto." According to information contained in the file on the film in the MPAA/PCA Collection at the AMPAS Library, the Breen Office objected to the story's implication that the jade dragon and Eight Immortals figurines were being used to smuggle opium. Lippert Productions was required to eliminate all references to drugs, and to insert a newspaper headline establishing that the substance being smuggled was uranium.

DV 19 Mar 1951, p. 5. *Exh* 28 Mar 1951, p. 3045. *Har* 28 Apr 1951, p. 66. *HR* 19 Mar 1951, p. 3. *LAT* 17 Mar 1951. *Var* 12 May 1951, p. 12.

THE MASK OF ZORRO see **THE BOLD CABALLERO**

DIE MASKE FÄLLT (German language)
First National Pictures, Inc.; controlled by Warner Bros. Pictures, Inc. *Dist* First National Pictures, Inc. **1931**; Berlin opening: 2 Mar 1931.; Prod: Oct 1930. Sd; b&w. 7 reels. German language.
Prod Heinz Blanke. *Dir* Wilhelm Dieterle. *Scr* Bradley King. *Photog* Sid Hickox.
Source: Based on the novel *Syndafloden* by Henning Berger (publication undetermined).
Cast: Lissy Arna, Anton Pointner, Karl Etlinger, Carla Bartheel, Ulrich Steindorff, Salka Steuermann, Charlotte Hagenbruch, Leon Janney, Paul Weigel, Arno Frey, Anders Van Haden, Leo White, Lew King, Pat O'Malley.
Melodrama. [*Not viewed*]. [The following plot summary is based on the English-language version of this film, *The Way of All Men*; character names refer to that version. For further information regarding the English-language version, please see the note below and the entry for *The Way of All Men* in the *AFI Catalog of Feature Films, 1921-30*.] The plot is similar to that of the 1926 silent version, *The Sin Flood*, also directed by Frank Lloyd. *Actors and actresses. Bartenders. Brokers. Cafes. Chorus girls. Death and dying. Engineers. Floods. Lawyers. Mississippi River. Preachers. Regeneration. Tramps.*
Note: The 1930 English-language version, entitled *The Way of All Men*, was directed by Frank Lloyd and starred Douglas Fairbanks, Jr. and Dorothy Revier. The German version was approved for showing by the New York State censors in 1931. In 1922, Goldwyn Pictures released a film entitled *The Sin Flood*, which was based on the same source. That film was also directed by Frank Lloyd and starred Richard Dix and Helene Chadwick (see *AFI Catalog of Feature Films, 1921-30*; F2.5088).

MASKED EMOTIONS (Chinese Americans)
Fox Film Corp. *Dist* Fox Film Corp. 23 Jun 1929 [©Fox Film Corp.; 18 Jun 1929; LP483]. Mus score and sd eff (Movietone); b&w. 7 reels, 5,419 ft. [Also si; 5,389 ft.].
Pres William Fox. *Dir* David Butler and Kenneth Hawks. *Asst dir* Ad Schaumer. *Scen* Harry Brand and Benjamin Markson. *Titles* Douglas Z. Doty. *Photog* Sidney Wagner.
Source: Based on the short story "A Son of Anak" by Ben Ames Williams in *The Saturday Evening Post* (13 Oct—10 Nov 1928).
Cast: George O'Brien (*Bramdlet Dickery*), Nora Lane (*Emily Goodell*), J. Farrell MacDonald (*Will Whitten*), David Sharpe (*Thad Dickery*), James Gordon (*Captain Goodell*), Edward Peil, Sr. (*Lee Wing*), Frank Hagney (*Lagune*).
Melodrama. Thad Dickery, the younger brother of Bram Dickery, falls into the clutches of Lee Wing when he is discovered aboard a ship that harbors smuggled Chinese. The ship is owned by Captain Goodell, the father of Bram's sweetheart, Emily. When Bram discovers that his brother has been stabbed by the smugglers, he vengefully attacks Lee Wing and his confederate, causing the drowning of the former. Relieved that Emily is not involved in the conspiracy, he rushes Thad to the mainland, where he is treated for his wounds. Bram is subsequently reunited with his sweetheart. *Brothers. Chinese Americans. Kidnapping. Smuggling.*
FD 28 Jul 1929. *Var* 24 Jul 1929, p. 39.

MASKED RAIDERS (Latino)
RKO Radio Pictures, Inc. *Dist* RKO Radio Pictures, Inc. 15 Oct **1949**; Prod: 29 Apr—mid-May 1949 [©RKO Radio Pictures, Inc.; 23 Sep 1949; LP2599]. Sd (RCA Sound System); b&w. 5,413 ft. 59-60 min. PCA cert no. 13821.

Prod Herman Schlom. *Dir* Lesley Selander. [*Asst dir* John E. Pommer]. *Wrt* Norman Houston. *Dir of photog* George E. Diskant. [*Cam op* Emmett Bergholz]. [*Gaffer* S. H. Barton]. [*Stills* Oliver Sigurdson]. *Art dir* Albert S. D'Agostino and Feild Gray. *Film ed* Les Millbrook. *Set dec* Darrell Silvera and Jack Mills. *Mus* Paul Sawtell. *Sd* John Cass and Clem Portman. [*Makeup* Jack Barron]. [*Hair stylist* Fae Smith]. [*Scr supv* William Hole]. [*Grip* Frank Williams].

Cast: TIM HOLT [(*Tim Holt*)], Richard Martin [(*Chito Rafferty*)], Marjorie Lord [(*Gale Trevett*)], Gary Gray [(*Artie Trevett*)], Frank Wilcox [(*Corthell*)], Charles Arnt [(*Doc W. J. Nichols*)], Tom Tyler [(*Trig*)], Harry Woods [(*Marshal Tom Barlow*)], Houseley Stevenson [(*Uncle Henry*)], Clayton Moore [(*Matt*)], Bill George [(*Luke*)], [Jason Robards (*Capt. Cummings*)], [George Magrill (*Saloon keeper*)].

Western. [*Print viewed*]. After his business in Willcox, Texas, is robbed many times by a gang of masked bandits led by The Diablo Kid, banker Corthell wires the Texas Rangers in Pinecrest for help. Former cowboys Tim Holt and Chito Rafferty are assigned to the case and ride north for Willcox. Outside of town, Tim and Chito remove their Ranger badges to hide their identity and then accosted by a group of gun-wielding men, who force them to ride to a nearby ranch. After Tim and Chito convince the ranch's suspicious owner, Gale Trevett, that they are out-of-work cowboys, Gale advises them to head west to find jobs. Tim and Chito continue to Willcox, however, and soon after, Corthell's bank is again robbed by The Diablo Kid's gang. As the outlaws are making their escape, Tim jumps The Diablo Kid, but is shot from behind by the town doctor, W. J. "Doc" Nichols. The Diablo Kid flees and is pursued by Marshal Tom Barlow, while Tim is taken to Doc for treatment. Aware only that his attacker fired a rifle at him, the slightly wounded Tim questions Doc about the assault. As Doc counsels Tim not to be too curious about The Diablo Kid, the gang, which is actually comprised of Gale, her uncle Henry and her cousins, count their stolen loot. Gale, who has been disguising herself as The Diablo Kid in order to rob the greedy, corrupt Corthell, divides the money up according to the specific needs of her neighboring ranchers. She then entrusts Artie, her young brother, to deliver the money, which she has placed in his lunch box, to Doc. While looking for Doc in Willcox, Artie runs into Chito and inquires about Tim's wound. Suspicious, Chito follows the boy into the town saloon, where he and one of Corthell's men both discover the contents of the lunch box and start to brawl. In the confusion, Artie escapes with the box and rushes to Doc's office. Corthell's man, meanwhile, shows the banker and Marshal Barlow a bill he snatched from Artie's box, and they both recognize it as part of the stolen cash. Barlow and Corthell intercept Doc and Artie as they are leaving town and, after finding the box and a note written by Gale, try to beat Doc into revealing her identity. Alerted by Artie, Tim and Chito stop the beating and expose themselves as Rangers. Reluctantly, Tim arrests Doc, but also fires Barlow and takes the money as evidence. Later, the Rangers question Artie about the money, but he maintains that he found it on the road. Acting on Tim's suggestion, Gale then starts to write Doc a testimonial, unaware that the Ranger actually wants a sample of her handwriting to compare with the note from the box. Before Tim can make the comparison, however, his pockets are picked, and the note is taken. Later, at the town jail, Tim again questions Doc about The Diablo Kid, but is told only that, like Robin Hood, the bandit robs from the rich and gives to the poor. As Doc is about to leave for Pinecrest with Chito, Tim and the money, Barlow, who is angry over his firing, poses as the masked bandit in order to steal back the cash for Corthell. At the same time, Gale dons her Diablo Kid mask, hoping to free Doc. Barlow and his men reach Doc first, however, and, after demanding the money, shoot and wound Doc before he identifies them as impostors. While pursuing Barlow, Tim meets up with Gale and finally exposes her as the bandit. Gale explains that she began her impersonation after Corthell and Barlow conspired to rob and kill her father as soon as he had finally saved up enough money to repay the banker's unreasonable loan demands. Doc then tells Tim and Chito that he recognized Barlow's horse during the ambush and sends them to the marshal's ranch. There, Tim and Chito engage in a gun battle with Barlow after he shoots Corthell in cold blood. The Trevett clan then comes to the Rangers' aid, and Tim arrests Barlow. Later, Chito and Doc head for Pinecrest, while Tim stays behind to obtain a deposition from a grateful Gale. *Bankers. Marshals. Masked bandits. Ranchers. Texas Rangers. Bank robberies. Brothers and sisters. Chases. Children. Cousins. Debt. Dismissal*

(Employment). *Escapes. Fights. Gunshot wounds. Male impersonation. Mexican Americans. Money. Physicians. Posses. Robin Hood (Legendary character). Saloons. Uncles. Women outlaws.*

Note: The working titles of this film were *Trouble in Texas* and *Miss Robin Hood.* According to *HR*, because of the popularity of John Huston's 1948 film *The Treasure of the Sierra Madre*, in which Tim Holt had a supporting role, the budgets for Holt's RKO Westerns, beginning with *Masked Raiders*, were to be increased. According to modern sources, exteriors for the picture were filmed at the Jack Garner ranch in Idyllwild, CA.

Box 1 Oct 1949. *DV* 22 Sep 1949, p. 3. *FD* 3 Oct 1949, p. 5. *HR* 21 Apr 1949, p. 2. *HR* 22 Apr 1949, p. 8. *HR* 22 Sep 1949, p. 3. *MPHPD* 1 Oct 1949, p. 34. *Var* 28 Sep 1949, p. 6.

MASSACRE (Native Americans, Dakota)
First National Pictures, Inc.; controlled by Warner Bros. Pictures, Inc. *Dist* First National Pictures, Inc.; The Vitaphone Corp. 20 Jan **1934** [©First National Pictures, Inc.; 16 Jan 1934; LP4411]. Sd; b&w. 8 reels. 69-70 or 74 min. PCA cert no. 2621-R [3 Sep 1936].

Dir Alan Crosland. *Scr* Ralph Block and Sheridan Gibney. *Story* Robert Gessner. *Photog* George Barnes. *Art dir* John Hughes. *Film ed* Terry Morse. *Gowns* Orry-Kelly. *Vitaphone Orch cond* Leo F. Forbstein.

Cast: RICHARD BARTHELMESS (*Joe Thunder Horse*), Ann Dvorak (*Lydia*), Dudley Digges (*Elihu P. Quissenberry*), Claire Dodd (*Norma*), Henry O'Neill (*Mr. Dickinson*), Robert Barrat (*Dawson*), Arthur Hohl (*Dr. Turner*), Sidney Toler (*Thomas Shanks*), Clarence Muse [(*Sam*)], Charles Middleton [(*Scatters*)], Tully Marshall, Wallis Clark [(*Cochran*)], Wm. V. Mong [(*Mr. Grandy*)], De Witt Jennings [(*Sheriff*)], Juliet Ware, James Eagles [(*Adam*)], Frank McGlynn, Sr. [(*Missionary*)], Agnes Narcha [(*Jenny*)], [Douglass Dumbrille (*Chairman*)], [William Davidson (*Senator Beale*)], [Henry Kolker (*Senator Woolsey*)], [George Blackwood], [Samuel Hinds].

Social, Drama. [*Print viewed*]. Joe Thunder Horse makes a lot of money stunt riding at the Chicago World's Fair and, when not working, lives a modern life. He becomes aware of how little he knows about his Sioux background when his white girl friend Norma proudly shows him Indian artifacts that she has purchased as decorations. Joe, learning that his father is dying, returns to the reservation where he finds that his father is not receiving medical care. Lydia, a college-educated Indian, warns Joe that life on the reservation is not what he thinks. Joe slowly realizes that the white leadership of the reservation is corrupt. Doctor Turner never treats the sick, and Elihu P. Quissenberry, the agent, and Shanks, the undertaker, are running a racket to get Indian lands from the families of the dead. When Joe's father dies, Joe refuses to allow Shanks to bury him, choosing instead to hold a traditional Indian funeral. At the funeral, Shanks rapes Joe's sister Jenny. After he learns what happened, Joe drags Shanks behind his car, severely injuring him. Quissenberry arrests Joe for attempted murder, and his court appointed lawyer pleads him guilty. Lydia sneaks Joe a set of car keys, and he escapes to Washington, D.C., where he tells the whole story to J. R. Dickinson, head of the Bureau of Indian Affairs. Dickinson agrees to help Joe fight for Indian rights. Shanks dies and Joe is arrested for murder. Quissenberry's men kidnap Jenny to keep her from testifying. Once again, Joe escapes from jail to find her. After she is found, Quissenberry reveals his corruption and is removed from office. Dickinson offers Joe a job, which frees Joe to ask Lydia to marry him. *Dakota Indians. Family relationships. Indians of North America–Reservations. Political corruption. Racism. Reformers. African Americans. Automobile chases. A Century of Progress International Exposition, 1933-1934 (Chicago, IL). Cultural conflict. False arrests. Funerals. Gunshot wounds. Indian agents. Jailbreaks. Kidnapping. Lawyers. Physicians. Rape. Rites and ceremonies. Trials. United States. Bureau of Indian Affairs. Washington (D.C.).*

DV 18 Jan 1934, p. 3. *FD* 18 Jan 1934, p. 8. *MPD* 18 Jan 1934, p. 11. *MPH* 27 Jan 1934, p. 41, 44. *NYT* Jan 18 1934, p. 19. *Var* 23 Jan 1934, p. 13.

MASSACRE CANYON (Native Americans, Apache)
Columbia Pictures Corp. *Dist* Columbia Pictures Corp. May **1954**; *Prod:* mid-Oct 1953 [©Columbia Pictures Corp.; 30 Mar 1954; LP3557]. Sd (Western Electric Recording); b&w; 1.85. 5,925 ft. 66 min. PCA cert no. 16803.

Prod Wallace MacDonald. *Dir* Fred F. Sears. *Asst dir* Abner Singer. *Story and scr* David Lang. *Dir of photog* Lester H. White. *Art dir* George Brooks. *Film ed* Aaron Stell. *Set dec* Frank Tuttle. *Mus dir* Mischa Bakaleinikoff. *Sd eng* George Cooper.

Cast: Phil Carey [(*Lt. Richard Faraday*)], Audrey Totter [(*Flaxey*)], Douglas Kennedy [(*Sgt. James Marlowe*)], Jeff Donnell [(*Cora*)], Guinn Williams [(*Pvt. Archibald "Peaceful" Allen*)], Charlita [(*Gita*)], Ross Elliott [(*George Davis*)], Ralph Dumke [(*"Parson" Canfield*)], Mel Welles [(*Gonzales*)], [Chris Alcaide (*Running Horse*)], [Steve Ritch (*Black Eagle*)], [John Pickard (*Lt. Ridgeford*)], [James Flavin (*Col. Joseph Tarant*)], [Bill Hale (*Lt. Farnum*)], [Frank Sully (*Schmitt*)], [Robert B. Williams (*Borapsy*)], [Post Park (*Shotgun*)].

Western. Sgt. James Marlowe of the U.S. Cavalry is assigned to pose as a civilian wagon train driver in order to transport a cargo of rifles through dangerous Apache territory. With the two men under his command, Pvts. Archibald "Peaceful" Allen and George Davis, Marlowe stops at a trading outpost in Spanish Bit, which is run by Gita, an Apache, and Gonzales, her abusive husband. Traveling salesman "Parson" Canfield becomes suspicious of Marlowe and, with Gita, who is secretly aligned with the renegade Apache Black Eagle, he lures Marlowe and his men away from their wagons by offering to introduce them to his passengers, Flaxey and Cora, who have come out West in search of husbands. The soldiers' cover is blown when Cora recognizes Peaceful as her missing boyfriend and, despite Peaceful's protestations to the contrary, loudly insists that he is a soldier. Willing to betray the soldiers for gold, Canfield asks Gita to take him to the Apaches, but Gita stabs him in the back and then leaves Spanish Bit to alert Black Eagle herself. As Marlowe and his men prepare to leave, a drunken brawl breaks out between Gonzales and a stranger who has spent the last several days drinking whiskey at the outpost. Much to his disgust, Marlowe soon learns that the drunken man is Lt. Richard Faraday, who is on his way to Fort Collins to assume the post to which Marlowe had hoped he would be promoted. Because he is outranked, a disgruntled Marlowe must take Faraday with him to Fort Collins, together with Flaxey and Cora, who refuse to stay in Spanish Bit once Canfield's body is discovered. As they ride to a rendezvous with soldiers escorting two additional wagons full of rifles, Marlowe makes no secret of his contempt for Faraday and later throws out Faraday's supply of whiskey. Before Marlowe can reach them, the other soldiers are massacred by Black Eagle's warriors, who were alerted by Gita, and their cargo of rifles is stolen. Faraday and Marlowe have a heated argument over the best strategy for getting through Apache territory alive, and Flaxey, who is attracted to the sensitive and troubled Faraday, later learns that he was drinking to forget his dead fiancée. The following day, the group stops to pick up a wounded Apache lying in the road and takes him prisoner, unaware that he has been placed in their path by Black Eagle. That night, Davis, who was demoted to private after a mishap occurred under his command, is assigned by Marlowe to the most important watchman post because Marlowe, whose own father was falsely accused of wrongdoing by the military, wants to give him a chance to prove himself. Once everyone is asleep, the Apache, Running Horse, breaks free of his bonds and throws Davis unconscious into a ditch, then pokes holes in all of the water jugs, forcing the group through Massacre Canyon in order to reach the nearest water supply. Unable to find Davis, Marlowe and Faraday set off for Massacre Canyon, sending Flaxey and Cora, escorted by Peaceful, on a different, less dangerous route. Peaceful and the women find a severely injured Davis lying in the road, and he tells them that he has overheard Black Eagle's and Gita's plan to trap the soldiers in Massacre Canyon. In order to clear his name, the dying Davis begs Peaceful to bring him to Marlowe so that he can warn him himself, and Peaceful acquiesces. Although Marlowe and Faraday are already under fire when Peaceful arrives with Davis in tow, Davis dies a hero. Flaxey, Cora and Peaceful help defend the wagons against the Apaches, but they are vastly outnumbered. However, Marlowe remembers a nearby tunnel through which to escape. As Marlowe and Faraday guide the wagon through the narrow tunnel, Flaxey, Cora and Peaceful throw dynamite in the path of the Apaches. After they make it safely to the other side, the tunnel collapses in a final explosion, killing Black Eagle, Gita and their warriors. Through their travails, Faraday and Marlowe earn each other's respect and become friends, while Cora and Peaceful are reunited, and Flaxey looks forward to her new life at Fort Collins with Faraday by her side. *Apache Indians. Firearms. Heroism. Impersonation and imposture. Traps. United States. Army. Cavalry. Betrayal. Drunkenness. Dynamite. Massacres. Rivalry. Romance. Spies. Traveling salesmen. Tunnels. Wagon trains.*

Note: The working title of this film was *Massacre at Moccasin Pass*. A *DV* news item dated 6 May 1953 reported that the film was to be based on an original story by Tom Reed, who had also been hired to write the screenplay; however, Reed is not credited onscreen or in reviews, and his contribution to the finished film has not been determined. A modern source indicates that *Massacre Canyon* was tinted using the "Sepiatone" process.

Box 17 Apr 1954. *DV* 6 May 1953. *DV* 7 Apr 1954, p. 3. *Exb* 21 Apr 1954, pp. 3733-34. *FD* 3 Jun 1954, p. 10. *Har* 10 Apr 1954, p. 59. *HR* 9 Oct 1953, p. 10. *HR* 7 Apr 1954, p. 3. *MPD* 9 Apr 1954. *MPHPD* 10 Apr 1954, p. 2254. *Var* 14 Apr 1954, p. 6.

MASSACRE RIVER (Native Americans)

Windsor Pictures Corp. *Dist* Allied Artists Productions, Inc. 1 Apr **1949**; Prod: early Sep—mid-Oct 1948 at Monogram Studios [©Windsor Pictures Corp.; 1 Apr 1949; LP2412]. Sd (Western Electric Sound System); sepia. 6992 ft. 75 or 77-78 min.

Prod Julian Lesser and Frank Melford. *Dir* John Rawlins. *Asst dir* Clem Beauchamp and [Bert Briskin]. *Orig scr* Louis Stevens. [*Addl dial* Otto Englander]. *Dir of photog* Jack MacKenzie. *Cam movements* Charles Straumer and Morris Rosen. *Photog eff* Jack R. Glass. *Art dir* Lucius O. Croxton. *Supv film ed* Richard Cahoon. *Assoc ed* W. J. Murphy. *Set dec* John Sturtevant. *Men's ward* Frank Beetson. *Gowns* Ann Peck. *Mus dir* Lud Gluskin. *Mus score* Lucien Moraweck and John Leipold. *Sd* Jean L. Speak. *Makeup* Norbert Miles. *Hair stylist* Gale McGarry. *Prod mgr* Harry S. Franklin. *Military adv* Col. Henry J. Matchett, U.S.A. [*Grip* Morris Rosen].

Source: Based on the novel *When a Man's a Man* by Harold Bell Wright (New York, 1916).

Cast: GUY MADISON (*Larry Knight*), RORY CALHOUN (*Phil Acton*), Carole Mathews (*Laura Jordon*), Cathy Downs (*Kitty Reid*), Johnny Sands (*Randy Reid*), Steve Brodie (*Burke Kimber*), Art Baker (*Col. James Reid*), Iron Eyes Cody (*Chief Yellowstone*), Emory Parnell (*Sgt. Johanssen*), Queenie Smith (*Mrs. Johanssen*), Eddie Waller (*Joe*), James Bush (*Eddie*), John Holland (*Roberts*), Douglas Fowley (*Simms*), Harry Brown (*Piano player*), Kermit Maynard (*Scout*), Gregg Barton (*Frank*), [Olin Howlin (*Circuit rider*)], [J. W. Cody].

Military, Western. [*Print viewed*]. At an Army post near the Wachupi River, Chief Yellowstone visits Col. James Reid to discuss their new treaty. Just as the chief is urging Reid to respect their agreement, a lieutenant enters with news that a group of white buffalo hunters has been found scalped near the Wachupi, which has become known as "Massacre River" for the many bloody clashes that have occurred there. When Reid asks the chief what he knows about these killings, he explains that his rebellious braves are anxious for war. Later, soldiers Phil Acton and Larry Knight, two suitors for the hand of Reid's daughter Kitty who are also best friends, learn from her brother Randy that she will be hosting a party that evening before her departure for St. Louis. At the party, Phil asks Kitty to marry him, but she tells him that she loves Larry. Later, Reid sends Phil and Larry, out on patrol but warns them not to cross the Wachupi into Indian territory. When the stagecoach arrives at the fort, passenger Sgt. Johanssen explains that the suitcase he is carrying belongs to Laura Jordon, the woman with whom he had shared the stagecoach. Laura states that she inadvertently left the suitcase on board and asks Phil to take it to her at the Blue Star Hotel. Meanwhile, Laura tells Blue Star owner Burke Kimber that her deceased husband left his stake in the hotel to her. When Burke insists that he is the sole owner of the hotel, the sheriff shows him the deed proving her claim. Later, while out on patrol, Randy becomes separated from his unit and is shot by Indian braves, who then quickly return to their side of the Wachupi. He struggles back to the fort, where Laura removes the bullet and dresses the wound. Later, Larry arrives and tells Laura that he loves Kitty. In the hotel saloon, Larry overhears Laura talking about their love triangle and realizes that he actually loves her. When Phil senses Larry's change of heart, he visits Laura and tries to seduce her to prove that she is a tramp, but Laura perceives his purpose and asks him to leave. Later, Burke arrives and asks her to sell her interest in the hotel, but she declines. Out of desperation, Burke threatens to kill her, and when Larry arrives, the two men grab their guns. Larry, however, is quicker on the draw and shoots Burke first. When Reid tries to question Larry about the incident, he does not respond except to say that he is resigning from the Army. Randy then finds Phil with Laura and fires at them, but Larry shoots Randy, killing him, and reports to Reid that he shot Randy in self-defense. Larry tells Laura that he killed Randy, and she reaffirms her feelings for him and warns him to avoid Phil. Larry and Laura then elope, and Phil tracks them for days. He

finally catches up to them and begins fighting with Larry. Just then, the entire tribe attacks, and Laura is shot and killed. Some time later, after Laura is buried and Larry has left the fort, Kitty and Phil are married. *Forts. Friendship. Indians of North America. Officers (Military). Romantic rivalry. United States. Army. Brothers and sisters. Chases. Deeds. Eavesdropping. Elopement. Fathers and daughters. Gunshot wounds. Hotel owners. Hunters. Inheritance. Luggage. Parties. Proposals (Marital). Saloons. Scalping. Seduction. Self-defense. Sheriffs. Shootings. Stagecoaches. Threats. Treaties. Tribal chiefs.*

Note: The working title for this film was *When a Man's a Man.* The opening credits include the following written acknowledgement: "The exterior scenes of this motion picture were photographed thru the courtesy and cooperation of the U.S. Department of the Interior, the National Park Service and the Office of Indian Affairs." The *LAT* review mistakenly credits Harry S. Franklin as director. According to *HR* production charts, interiors were shot at Monogram Studios. A *HR* production news item indicated that portions of the film were shot in Canyon de Chelly National Monument in Northern Arizona. A *HR* news item dated 6 Oct 1948 reported that two endings of the film were to be shot and shown to test audiences to determine which to use.

Box 9 Apr 1949. *DV* 29 Mar 1949, p. 3. *FD* 7 Apr 1949, p. 5. *HR* 10 Sep 1948, p. 12. *HR* 6 Oct 1948, p. 3. *HR* 15 Oct 1948, p. 16. *HR* 29 Mar 1949, p. 3. *MPHPD* 9 Apr 1949, p. 4566. *NYT* 15 Jul 1949, p. 17. *Var* 6 Apr 1949, p. 8.

THE MATCH KING (Swedish Americans)

First National Pictures, Inc.; controlled by Warner Bros. Pictures, Inc. *Dist* First National Pictures, Inc.; The Vitaphone Corp. 31 Dec **1932**; Prod: 29 Aug—early Oct 1932 [©First National Pictures, Inc.; 9 Dec 1932; LP3467]. Sd; b&w. 9 reels. 70, 72 or 79 min. PCA cert no. 2632-R [3 Sep 1936].

Dir Howard Bretherton and William Keighley. *Scr* Houston Branch and Sidney Sutherland. *Photog* Robert Kurrle. [*2d cam* Al Green]. [*Asst cam* John Shepek]. *Art dir* Anton Grot. *Ed* Jack Killifer. *Gowns* Orry-Kelly. *Vitaphone Orch cond* Leo F. Forbstein. [*Sd* Bill Walling, Jr.]. [*Still photog* Dolph Thomas].

Source: Based on the novel *The Match King* by Einar Thorvaldson (New York, 1932).

Cast: Warren William (*Paul Kroll*), Lily Damita (*Marta Molnar*), Glenda Farrell (*Babe*), Juliette Compton (*Sonia* [*Lombard*]), Claire Dodd (*Ilse* [*Wagner*]), Harold Huber (*Scarlatti*), John Wray (*Foreman*), Spencer Charters (*Oscar*), Murray Kinnell (*Nyberg*), Hardie Albright (*Erik* [*Borg*]), Alan Hale (*Borglund*), Edmund Breese (*Christofsen*), Robert McWade (*Larsen*), [Greta Meyer (*Trudi, the Maid*)], [Harry Beresford (*Christian Hobe*)], [George Meeker (*Erickson*)], [De Witt Jennings (*Rodensky*)], [Alphonse Ethier (*Uncle Gustav*)], [Bodil Rosing (*Frau Necher*)].

Drama. [*Print viewed*]. During his time in Chicago, Swedish immigrant Paul Kroll aquires a small sum of money by cheating his friends and fellow workers. The people at home in Sweden believe that Paul is a successful businessman, so when the local match factory has business troubles, Kroll's uncle begs him to return home and help them. After stealing the money that his girl friend Babe had saved, Kroll buys a first-class passage and sails home. There, he bluffs the bank into financing a merger between the small plant and a more modern one. In order to maintain his initial success, he continues to borrow more money and ultimately buys all the match factories in the country. After he promotes superstitions such as the belief that it is bad luck to light three cigarettes on a match in order to increase sales, he plots to take over match factories throughout Europe. Soon, by using blackmail and other underhanded methods, the Kroll Match Co. obtains the European monopoly on matches. While on business in Germany, Kroll becomes infatuated with beautiful actress Marta Molnar. He sends her a diamond bracelet and invites her to dinner. When she turns him down, he pursues her doggedly. Eventually she succumbs to his entreaties, and he neglects his business during the romance. Kroll's friend, Erik Borg, suggests that he is wealthy enough to give up business altogether. Kroll's business is so deeply in debt, however, that he cannot stop. When he learns of the invention of an everlasting match, he has the inventor, Christian Hobe, committed to an insane asylum. After the stock market crashes, Kroll's bank loan is not renewed, so he borrows money on fraudulent stock and murders the forger. With the money, he intends to leave the business and marry Marta, who is now working in Hollywood. She has fallen in love with someone else, however, and when the forgery is revealed, Kroll sees no choice but to kill himself. *Entrepreneurs. Fraud. Match industry. Moral corruption. Sweden. Actors and actresses. Bankruptcy. Chicago (IL). Confidence men. Debt. Forgers and forgery. Immigrants. Inventions. Loans. Murder. Romance. Stock market crash of 1929. Suicide. Swedish Americans.*

Note: According to *Var*, the novel and film are based on the life of Swedish industrialist Ivar Kreuger who swindled thousands after developing an international match monopoly. According to *Var*, the character of Marta Molnar is based on Swedish actress Greta Garbo. According to *HR*, Warner Bros. tried to borrow Garbo from M-G-M for the role. Before the credits roll, shots of people around the world using matches are seen to suggest a worldwide reliance on them. A Nov 1934 article in *NYT* notes that the Polish government complained that two of the disreputable characters in the story had the names of Polish national heroes. Production records contained in the film on the film at the AMPAS Library note that the production took twenty-five shooting days for a total cost of $165,000.

FD 3 Oct 1932, p. 6. *FD* 9 Dec 1932, p. 5. *HR* 15 Aug 1932, p. 1. *HR* 24 Aug 1932, p. 1. *HR* 4 Nov 1932, p. 3. *IP* Dec 1932, p. 36. *MPH* 17 Dec 1932, p. 35, 38. *NYT* 8 Dec 1932, p. 25. *NYT* 4 Nov 1934. *Var* 13 Dec 1932, p. 15.

THE MATING CALL (Russian Americans)

Caddo Co. *Dist* Paramount Pictures. 21 Jul **1928** [©Caddo Co.; 4 Sep 1928; LP25596]. Si; b&w. 7 reels, 6,352 ft.

Pres Howard Hughes. *Prod* Howard Hughes. *Dir* James Cruze. *Adpt* Walter Woods. *Titles* Herman J. Mankiewicz. *Photog* Joseph Morgan. *Film ed* Walter Woods.

Song(s): "The Mating Call," by Frances Ring and Martin Roones.

Source: Based on the novel *The Mating Call* by Rex Beach (New York, 1927).

Cast: Thomas Meighan (*Leslie Hatton*), Evelyn Brent (*Rose Henderson*), Renée Adorée (*Catherine*), Alan Roscoe (*Lon Henderson*), Gardner James (*Marvin Swallow*), Helen Foster (*Jessie*), Luke Cosgrave (*Judge Peebles*), Cyril Chadwick (*Anderson*), Will R. Walling.

Drama. After the Armistice, Leslie Hatton, a Florida farmer, returns home to discover that his wife, Rose, has had their marriage annulled in order to marry wealthy Lon Henderson. Leslie returns to farming for solace, and Rose, quickly disillusioned by Henderson's infidelity, again offers herself to Leslie. He wants no part of her, however, and goes instead to Ellis Island, where he persuades Catherine, an aristocratic Russian immigrant, to marry him in return for a home in the United States. Jessie Peebles, a young girl disillusioned by an affair with Henderson, drowns herself in a pond on Leslie's farm, and Henderson, head of the local Ku Klux Klan, orders Leslie tried before a Klan tribunal. Leslie is found not guilty when letters are produced that link Henderson with the dead girl. Leslie's ordeal has had a good side, however, for he and Catherine have realized that what was to have been a marriage of convenience has become a marriage of love. *Aristocrats. Farmers. Florida. Immigrants. Ku Klux Klan. Marriage of convenience. Marriage–Annulment. New York City–Ellis Island. Russian Americans. Suicide. Veterans.*

FD 14 Oct 1928. *NYT* 8 Oct 1928, p. 14. *Var* 10 Oct 1928, p. 15.

MAYN ZUNDELE see **MY SON** (1939)

MAZEL TOV (Yiddish language)

Judea Films, Inc. *Dist* Judea Films, Inc. **1932**; New York opening: 10 May 1932; Prod: original 1923 film produced by Listo-Film and Picon-Film in Vienna, Austria; 1932 additions produced in New York. Sd (Seiden Sound System); b&w. 8 reels, 7,700 ft. 86 min. *Country of origin* Austria. Yiddish language with English subtitles.

[*In charge of prod* Sam Rosen]. *New version under dir* Solomon Krause and Abraham Armband. *Dir* [*of 1923 film*] S. M. Goldin. *Film ed* Sam Rosen. *Sd eng* Leonard A. Herzig.

Cast: [*1923 film:*] Molly Picon [(*Mollie*)], Jacob Kalich [(*Jacob, later known as Ben Alli*)], [Sidney M. Goldin (*Morris Brown, formerly "Brownstein"*)], [Saul Natan (*Mottel Brownstein*)], [Laura Glucksman (*Old Mrs. Brownstein*)], [Eugen Neufeld (*Alfred Freed*)], [Johannes Roth], *Prologue Cast:* Madam Bertha Gutentag, Bennie Schechtman, Simon Schechtman, Frankie Schechtman, Hilda Reiber, Gertrude Krause, Gertrude Bercowich, Sylvia Weinthal, Baby Celina Breene, [Art Shryer].

Yiddish, Comedy. [*Print viewed*]. An elderly woman tells the following story to a group of children at a party: Morris Brown, a wealthy, Jewish clothing manufacturer in New York, who has changed his name from "Brownstein," travels to Galicia with his rambunctious daughter Mollie to attend the wedding of his brother Mottel's daughter Zelda. Mottel, who is a well-off merchant, supports Jacob, a poor *Talmud* student, as is the custom. Also in Mottel's household are Shabse, a servant, and Mochel, whom Shabse considers an idler. During *Yom Kippur*, the Day of Atonement, Mollie secretes an English language book inside her prayer book. Famished, she sneaks into the kitchen during the religious service, and although

fasting is expected on the solemn day, she gorges herself on chicken, bread and apples, which is being kept for the evening when the fast is to be broken. At the end of the day, Mochel discovers a cat and dog eating the remains of the food. He accuses Mollie, and Morris sends her to her room. Upset at Mochel, Mollie dons boxing gloves and challenges him to a bout. After she knocks him down, Morris slaps and spanks her. Before Zelda's wedding, Mollie shows the boys how to do the latest American dance, and Jacob's thoughts wander from the *Talmud* to Mollie. When Mollie gets on a table to demonstrate, the cantor brings Morris, who drags her down. On the evening before the wedding, Mollie, with bobbed hair, dresses as a boy to be with the men, but Shabse tells Morris, and he spanks her in front of everyone. Later, when Mollie sees Zelda in her wedding dress, Mollie tries on the headpiece and suggests that they go through a mock marriage for fun. Jacob is dragged in to play the groom, and Mochel, who plays the rabbi, gives him a ring, but warns him not to put it on Mollie's finger. Jacob, however, puts the ring on her finger, and the cantor says that according to Jewish law, Jacob and Mollie are now married. During Zelda's wedding, as everyone else dances, Mollie cries in her room. Morris then comforts her and dances with her. Afterward, at the rabbi's home, Jacob is asked to give Mollie her freedom, but he refuses, saying that he loves her. Jacob is called an infidel by the other students, and after his uncle in Vienna, wealthy manufacturer Alfred Freed, invites him to live with him, Jacob tells the rabbi that he is going away and that if Mollie still wants a divorce in five years, he will give it. When Jacob arrives at his uncle's home, he is at first thrown out by the gardener. After Alfred realizes he has come and sends the servants for him, Jacob runs from them, but they capture him and bring him to the house. At night, Jacob thinks of love. Meanwhile, Morris takes Mollie sightseeing. Jacob soon discovers the books in his uncle's library and goes to a barber shop, where his beard is shaved off. Near the end of the five years, Jacob has turned into the author "Ben Alli," and he gives a reading at the Oriental Academy, where he is made an honorary member. Mollie and her father attend the reading and do not recognize him. Mollie is attracted to "Ben Alli," and when he begins to court her, she worries that she is still married. After the five years are over, Jacob dons a false beard and affects the stooped stance of his former self, and when Mollie visits Freed's home and sees him in this guise, she almost has a heart attack. Morris berates Jacob and says that he had to remain in Europe for five years away from business because of him. When Morris threatens to hit Jacob unless he gives Mollie her freedom, Jacob hands over a divorce paper, which says "Ben Alli is only Jacob in the guise of greater fame, but Jacob surely loves you so what is in a name." He then takes off his beard and asks Mollie if she still wants a divorce. She says no, then has everyone turn away and kisses Jacob. *Cultural conflict. Galicia. Jews. Marriage. Students. Tomboys. Transformation. Aged women. Authors. Boxing. Brothers. Cantors, Jewish. Children. Dances. Disguise. New York City. Ostracism. Parties. Rabbis. Rites and ceremonies. Romance. Uncles. Vienna (Austria). Weddings. Yom Kippur.*

Note: This film was a re-release of a 1923 Austrian film that was called, variously, *Mizrekh un Mayrev*, *Mazeltoff*, *East and West* and *Ost und West*, with a framing sequence and dubbed Yiddish narration shot in New York in 1932. The framing sequence consists of an elderly woman telling the story to a group of children at a party and includes some singing by the children. These scenes cut into the original approximately seven times. The original film was made by Listo-Film and Picon-Film, which were located in Vienna. According to modern sources, the 1923 film was 2,380 meters in length and written by director Sidney M. Goldin and Eugen Preis. That film, according to modern sources, was originally condemned by the New York State censors for sacrilegious and indecent content before it was passed with a number of eliminations. For the 1932 version, the New York State censors again insisted that a number of scenes were sacrilegious and demanded that they be eliminated for exhibition in that state. Specifically, the scenes of "Mollie" with her "dime novel" in the prayer book and those of her eating in the kitchen and returning to the synagogue after having broken her fast were judged to be sacrilegious.

FD 8 May 1932, p. 5. *Var* 3 Sep 1924, p. 22.

MAZEL TOV YIDDEN (Jewish Americans, Yiddish language)
Jewish Talking Pictures. *Dist* Cinema Service Corp. **1941.** Sd; b&w. 8,151 ft. 89 min. Yiddish language.
Dir Joseph Seiden. *Mus dir* Sholom Secunda and Alexander Olshanetsky.
Song(s): "My Country 'Tis of Thee," words by Samuel Francis Smith, music by Henry Carey; "Motel the Operator," composer undetermined; and other songs.

Cast: Michel Rosenberg (*Master of ceremonies*), Victor and Shirley, Annie Thomashefsky, Louis Kramer, Cantor Leibele Waldman, Seymour Rechtzeit, Yetta Zwerling, Gustave Berger, Jacob Zanger, Hannah Hollander, Dave Lubritsky, Esta Salzman, Leon Leibgold, Leo Fuchs, Chaim Tauber, Lili Liliana, Leo Fuchs, Menashe Oppenheim, Harry Feld.
Yiddish, Musical, Comedy. [*Not viewed*]. Comedian Michel Rosenberg tells jokes and stories, and introduces various Jewish singers and comedians performing skits and singing songs. *Jews. Musical revues.*

Note: This film was advertised as "A Jewish Vaudeville Talkie." According to a dialogue continuity contained in NYSA, duets in the film are performed by Annie Thomashefsky and Louis Kramer, Seymour Rechtzeit and an unidentified woman, Dave Lubritsky and Esta Salzman, Leo Fuchs and Yetta Zwerling, and Lili Liliana and Menashe Oppenheim. Cantor Leibele Waldman sings two times, as does Gustave Berger. Berger's numbers are accompanied by orchestra director Alexander Orshanetsky. In addition to appearing with Fuchs, Yetta Zwerling performs another skit and song with an unidentified actor. It is very likely that some, if not all, of the performances were excerpted from other films. The title is translated on the NYSA continuity as *Good Luck Hebrews*.

MAZELTOFF *see* **MAZEL TOV**

ME AND MY GAL (Irish Americans)
Fox Film Corp.; Raoul Walsh Production. *Dist* Fox Film Corp. 4 Dec **1932**; *Prod*: 22 Sep—late Oct 1932 [©Fox Film Corp.; 5 Nov 1932; LP3444]. Sd (Western Electric System); b&w. 8 reels, 7,295 ft. 79 min. Passed by the National Board of Review.
Dir Raoul Walsh. [*Asst dir* Horace Hough]. *Scr* Arthur Kober. *Story* Philip Klein and Barry Conners. [*Contr wrt* Frank J. Dolan, Philip Dunne, Charles Vidor and Al Cohn]. *Photog* Arthur Miller. [*Cam op* Joe La Shelle]. [*Asst cam* Billy Abbott, Clarence Slifer and Don Anderson]. *Art dir* Gordon Wiles. [*Film ed* Jack Murray]. *Ward* Rita Kaufman. *Mus dir* George Lipschultz. *Sd rec* George Leverett. [*Still photog* Roy Johnson]. [*Publicist* Albert A. Price].
Song(s): "Oleo the Gigolo," music by James F. Hanley, lyrics by Val Burton.
Cast: Spencer Tracy [(*Danny Dolan*)], Joan Bennett [(*Helen Riley*)], Marion Burns [(*Kate Riley*)], George Walsh [(*Duke Castenega*)], J. Farrell MacDonald [(*Pop Riley*)], Noel Madison [(*Baby Face*)], Henry B. Walthall [(*Sarge*)], Bert Hanlon [(*Jake*)], Adrian Morris [(*Al*)], George Chandler [(*Eddie Collins*)], Will Stanton [(*Drunk*)], [Hank Mann (*Hank*)], [Emmett Corrigan (*Police captain*)], [Lemist Ester (*Doctor*)], [Jesse De Vorska (*Jake*)], [Frank Moran].
Police, Romance, Comedy-drama. [*Print viewed*]. After Danny Dolan, a police officer newly assigned to the harbor precinct, rescues a drunk who has fallen into the water at New York's Pier 13, Danny is promoted to detective. The detective who was with Danny at the time, Al, is reprimanded because after he fell into the water as Danny was rescuing the drunk, some mobsters whom Al was sent to watch got away. Duke Castenega, the leader of the gang, visits his ex-lover, Kate Riley, at the bank where she works, and although he is about to be married, she realizes that she still loves Duke, who plans to get a list of combination numbers for safe deposit boxes from her. Kate's sister Helen, who works at a chowder house by the pier, has enjoyed bantering with Danny since he began his beat. After Kate marries Eddie Collins, and Duke is arrested, Duke's brother Baby Face visits Kate and urges her to give him the list of numbers. Danny and Al come to the wedding party because of complaints of noise, and Danny is greatly relieved to learn that it was Helen's sister, and not Helen, who got married. Duke is sent to prison, and when Eddie has to go to Cuba, Baby Face tries to force Kate to give him the numbers, but she refuses. During a date with Helen, Danny turns out the lights and tries to kiss her, but she slaps him and he leaves in a huff. Later, Danny apologizes to Helen, and he confesses that things are hard for men: if they don't try to neck, he says, women will think they are too slow; while if they do, they think they are fresh. She says it is the same for a woman: if she lets a guy "maul" her, he will think she's no good; while if she doesn't, he will think she's old-fashioned. They realize that they have fallen in love and kiss. After Duke escapes from prison, Danny's captain offers a promotion, and the newspapers offer a $10,000 reward for Duke's capture. Duke hides in Kate's attic, and Eddie's father Sarge, a paralytic who can only blink to communicate, sees them together. After Helen agrees to marry Danny, Sarge tries to communicate that Duke is in the attic. Danny and Helen plan to get a Morse code book the next day to see what he is trying to tell them.

Duke and his gang invade the home of a family living just above a bank, and after drilling through their floor, and using a blow torch to blast through the bars, iron vault and safe deposit boxes, they escape with $87,000. Meanwhile, Helen deciphers Sarge's message and runs to Kate's home. Danny finds a carbon of the message and follows. After Helen orders Duke to leave, Danny arrives. She pleads with him not to arrest Duke in the house to protect her sister, but he angrily refuses, upset that she wasn't "square" with him. Duke hides in the attic, but Danny breaks through the skylight and shoots him as he tries to escape. Danny then tells his captain that he chased Duke from Pier 13, and that Duke broke into Kate's apartment. Kate cries as she thanks Duke, and he warns her to stick to Eddie. After Helen and Danny marry, they escape the celebration and head to the pier, where they plan to leave for Bermuda. Eddie, Kate, Pop Riley and Sarge follow, however. Danny, who shares the reward money with Sarge, tells him it is nice that he did not tip off Eddie about Kate. *Piers. Police. Romance. Sisters. Waitresses. Alcoholics. Attics. Bank robberies. Detectives. Dogs. Family relationships. Fights. Gangsters. Irish Americans. Morse code. New York City. Paralysis. Rescues. Shootouts. Weddings.*

Note: The working title of this film was *Pier 13*. According to information in the Twentieth Century-Fox Records of the Legal Department at the UCLA Theater Arts Library, the story was based in part on an episode in the 1920 Fox film entitled *While New York Sleeps*, original story by Charles J. Brabin and Thomas F. Fallon (see *AFI Catalog of Feature Films, 1911-20*; F1.4915). The episode, entitled "A Tragedy of the East Side," is about a married woman who hides her lover, a gangster, in the attic of her home as her father-in-law, a paralytic who cannot speak, watches. The legal files and news items indicate that William K. Howard, Alfred Werker and Marcel Varnel were set to direct *Me and My Gal* at various times before it went into production and that director Raoul Walsh completed the film in nineteen shooting days. The *HR* review noted, "The rowdy, ribald humor in which Raoul Walsh specializes... marks his direction." The film includes a parody of *Strange Interlude*, the film version of Eugene O'Neill's play, produced by M-G-M also in 1932, in which the thoughts of the characters were spoken aloud. On Danny's date with Helen, he mentions that he saw "a swell picture" last night called "Strange Inner Tube or something." In the following scene, the thoughts of both Danny and Helen are spoken in addition to their dialogue. *Var* notes that the actor playing the drunk, whom they could not identify, did "one of the best stews of late on the screen." The actor, Will Stanton, soon became well-known for his portrayals of drunks. Actor George Walsh was the brother of the director. In her autobiography, Joan Bennett remarks that this was the only film of the six she made at Fox in 1932 that was not "unmemorable." A biography of Spencer Tracy notes that Tracy liked the story, which apparently was being developed for James Dunn and Sally Eilers, and requested that he and Bennett play the leads.

Included in the files for the film in the MPAA/PCA Collection at the AMPAS Library is a letter from the Cincinnati Better Motion Picture Council which complained of a number of scenes in the film, including the bank robbery scene, which they called "a facsimile of a recent outrage perpetrated in Chicago, in which occupants of an apartment building were terrorized by bandits in order to effect entry into the vaults below." No information has been located concerning the Chicago bank robbery. On 30 Oct 1935, after corresponding with the Hays Office, Twentieth Century-Fox withdrew their application for PCA certification for a reissue of the film. Twentieth Century-Fox produced a remake of this film in 1940 entitled *Pier 13*, which was directed by Eugene Forde and starred Lynn Bari and Lloyd Nolan (see *AFI Catalog of Feature Films, 1931-40*; F3.3460).

FD 10 Dec 1932, p. 18. Har 24 Dec 1932, p. 207. HF 22 Oct 1932, p. 16. HR 2 Aug 1932, p. 1. HR 1 Sep 1932, p. 1. HR 22 Sep 1932, p. 3. HR 27 Sep 1932, p. 4. HR 26 Oct 1932, p. 1. HR 4 Nov 1932, p. 3. IP Dec 1932, p. 36. LAT 17 Dec 1932, pt. I, p. 7. MPH 17 Dec 1932, pp. 34-35. NYT 12 Dec 1932, p. 18. Var 13 Dec 1932, p. 15. VarB 4 Nov 1932.

ME UND GOTT (German Americans)

Romayne Super-Film Co. *Dist* State Rights. Aug **1918** [©Romayne Super-Film Co.; 9 Jul 1918; LU12665]. Si; b&w. 6 reels.

Dir Wyndham Gittens. *Story* Wyndham Gittens.

Cast: Paul Weigle (*The Kaiser*), Robert N. Dunbar (*The father*), Gertrude De Vere (*The daughter*), Frank Brownlee (*The butler/ August Weber*), James T. Welch (*Von Hollweg*), Jack McCready (*Irish*), Betty Burbank (*Hilda*), Fred Bond (*Herman Weber*), Nigel De Brullier (*The pacifist*), Josephine Crowell (*Nanette*), Adeline M. Alvord (*The mother*), Ray Eberle (*Fifine*).

World War I, Drama. A symbolic prologue dramatizes the invasion of an American home by German troops who are admitted to the house by a butler who has bound his master and abused the master's daughter. In the main story, the American-born son of an ex-Prussian officer wants to atone for the wrongs done by people of his own blood when he realizes what America means to him. *German Americans. Patriotism. World War I. Butlers. Germany. Army. Military invasion.*

Note: The copyright directory gives the film's title as *Me und Gott; or, When America Awoke*. There were trade showings in Chicago on 15 Jul 1918 and 16 Jul 1918 and in New York on 25 Jul 1918.

ETR 20 Jul 1918, p. 516. ETR 17 Aug 1918, p. 925. MPW 17 Aug 1918, p. 922. MPW 7 Sep 1918, p. 1463.

THE MEANEST MAN IN THE WORLD (African Americans)

Twentieth Century-Fox Film Corp. *Dist* Twentieth Century-Fox Film Corp. 12 Feb **1943**; Prod: 22 Jul—early Sep 1942; retakes early Nov—10 Nov 1942 [©Twentieth Century-Fox Film Corp.; 11 Sep 1942; LP12084]. Sd (Western Electric Recording); b&w. 6 reels, 5,139 ft. 57 min. PCA cert no. 8661.

[*Exec prod* William Goetz]. *Prod* William Perlberg. *Dir* Sidney Lanfield. [*Dir of retakes* Ernst Lubitsch]. [*Asst dir* Aaron Rosenberg]. *Scr* George Seaton and Allan House. [*Contr wrt* Morrie Ryskind]. [*Comedy wrt* Wilkie Mahoney]. *Dir of photog* Peverell Marley. *Art dir* Richard Day and Albert Hogsett. *Film ed* Robert Bischoff. *Set dec* Thomas Little and Paul S. Fox. *Cost* Earl Luick. *Mus* Cyril J. Mockridge. *Mus dir* Emil Newman. *Sd* W. D. Flick and Roger Heman. *Makeup artist* Guy Pearce.

Source: Based on the play *The Meanest Man in the World* by Augustin MacHugh, as produced by George M. Cohan (New York, 12 Oct 1920).

Cast: JACK BENNY [(*Richard Clarke*)], PRISCILLA LANE [(*Janie Brown*)], Rochester [(*Shufro*)], Edmund Gwenn [(*Frederick P. Leggitt*)], Matt Briggs [(*Brown*)], Anne Revere [(*Miss Crockett*)], Margaret Seddon [(*Mrs. Frances H. Leggitt*)], Helene Reynolds [(*Wife*)], [Jackie Averill (*Boy with lollypop*)], [Lyle Talbot (*Bill Potts*)], [Don Douglas (*Husband*)], [Harry Hayden (*Mr. Chambers*)], [Arthur Loft (*Mr. Billings*)], [Andrew Tombes (*Judge*)], [Paul Burns (*Farmer*)], [Ralph Byrd (*Reporter*)], [Frank Orth (*Bartender*)], [Mae Marsh (*Old lady*)], [Chester Clute (*Lawyer*)], [Robert Emmett Keane (*City editor*)], [Ed Gargan, Ed Dearing (*Detectives*)], [William Newell, Hal K. Dawson (*Photographers*)], [Bud McCallister (*Bellboy*)], [Nicodemus Stewart (*Elevator boy*)], [Gary Gray, Conrad Binyon, Harry McKim, Gerald Mackey, Freddie Walburn (*Boys*)], [Dave Morris (*Blind man*)], [Margaret McWade (*Lady with umbrella*)], [Mary Currier (*Relief worker*)], [Frank Jaquet (*Client*)], [Harold Minjir (*Hotel clerk*)], [Sam Hayes, John Hiestand (*Announcers*)], [Tor Johnson (*Vladimir Pulaski*)], [Philo Reh (*Newsboy*)], [Frank Ferguson, Milt Kibbee (*Tellers*)], [Will Wright (*Pawnbroker*)], [Gladden James (*Clerk*)], [Edward Clark (*Jury member*)], [Besse Wade (*Farmer's wife*)], [Tom Dugan (*Policeman*)].

Comedy. [*Print viewed*]. Lawyer Richard Clarke has a small legal practice in Pottsville, New York, but as his black assistant, Shufro, points out, Clarke is just too nice to make any money, for he refuses to charge his poor clients or accept morally questionable clients. Clarke is in love with pretty Janie Brown, whose successful father wants her to marry wealthy Bill Potts. One afternoon, Janie and Brown visit Clarke's office, and after Brown leaves, his car is hit by a truck-driving farmer. Hoping to impress Brown, Clarke takes the case to court and sues the farmer for damages. Upon learning how impoverished the farmer is, however, Clarke gets the case dismissed. Brown pretends to be pleased with Clarke's ability to temper justice with mercy and encourages him to go to New York City to make a name for himself. Oblivious to the fact that Brown actually is trying to get rid of him, Clarke, accompanied by Shufro, gamely makes the move. Four months pass as Clarke's bills accumulate and not a single client comes through his door. One day, Clarke receives word that Janie and Brown, who think he lives in luxury on Park Avenue, are coming to visit, and in a panic, he and Shufro try to find a suitable apartment. While visiting one ritzy building, they hear a husband and wife arguing, and after the couple leave, Shufro installs Clarke in their apartment. Clarke brings along Brown and Janie, who wants to marry the lawyer immediately. Clarke insists that they wait for one month, and when the arguing couple return to the apartment, Clarke hustles Brown and Janie out for a tour of nightclubs. The next day, Clarke admits to his secretary, Miss Crockett, that the club hopping used up the last of his money, and Shufro urges him to become meaner to attract clients. Determined to practice being mean, Clarke goes for a walk, during which he steals a little boy's lollypop. A passing photographer snaps a picture of the act, which is then immortalized in the next day's newspaper with the headline "Meanest Man In The World Takes Candy From Baby!" Clarke is mortified, but soon feels better when billionaire Frederick P. Leggitt, who is looking for an unscrupulous attorney, arrives at his office. Clarke accepts a large retainer from Leggitt, then begins his first assignment, which is to evict Leggitt's elderly sister-in-law Frances. Shufro arranges for a

photographer to get a picture of Clarke dispossessing Frances, and the publicity brings him even more clients. Unknown to the public, who fear that Frances has committed suicide, Clarke installs Frances in his new apartment. Soon after, Clarke is telling Leggitt about the eviction when Janie arrives to plan their wedding. Horrified to learn of Clarke's apparent change in character, Janie breaks off their engagement. While Clarke is getting drunk in a hotel bar, a body, presumed to be Frances', is found in a river. A reporter calls Clarke's apartment for a comment, and when Frances answers, she refuses to give her name and says only that she lives with Clarke. Meanwhile, Clarke has met the equally drunk Janie in the bar, and when she hears a radio report that he is living in a love nest with an ex-Follies star, she slaps his face. A photographer captures the moment and it is published in the newspaper with a caption identifying Janie as Clarke's love nest partner. An infuriated Brown abducts Clarke and takes him to Janie's apartment, and after the couple are tied up, a Pottsville judge persuades Brown to allow him to marry them. Brown also agrees to get Clarke a job as attorney for the Pottsville bank, where he can reform and become a good husband. The delighted Janie then reveals that Shufro and Frances have already told her the truth about Clarke's "mean streak." *African Americans. Engagements. Ethics. Lawyers. Scandal. Transformation. Aged women. Ambulance chasing. Apartments. Children. Debt. Drunkenness. Eviction. Farmers. Judges. Marriage-Forced. New York (State). New York City. Photographers. Pigeons. Racial impersonation. Secretaries. Trials.*

Note: A 1 Nov 1939 *LAT* news item reported that Universal was trying to purchase the rights to Augustin MacHugh's play. According to a 13 May 1942 *LAEx* news item, Walter Lang was originally scheduled to direct this film, and Maureen O'Hara was cast as "Janie Brown." On 17 Jun 1942, *HR* noted that due to his illness, Lang was being replaced as director by Sidney Lanfield. Priscilla Lane was borrowed from Warner Bros. for the film, while Eddie "Rochester" Anderson was borrowed from Paramount and Anne Revere and Edmund Gwenn were borrowed from M-G-M.

The film's troubled production history is detailed in *HR* news items, which reported that the story, purchased on the strength of Jack Benny's success in the 1941 film *Charley's Aunt*, went through numerous rewrites. According to the Twentieth Century-Fox Records of the Legal Department, located at the UCLA Arts Library, Benny, who had script, director and co-star approval, postponed the start of shooting several times. On 8 Jul 1942, both *HR* and *DV* reported that the production, which was due to begin filming soon, had been called off by the studio, despite an investment of $150,000 up to that time. The screenplay had not met with Benny's approval, and on 9 Jul 1942, *HR* noted that "one of the main difficulties in the controversy was Benny's objection to a part of the script that seemed to him to be too juvenile."

The film's problems continued after a sneak preview on 25 Sep 1942 in Huntington Park, CA, when it was decided to reshoot some of the scenes. A 2 Nov 1942 *HR* news item commented that Morrie Ryskind, who had worked on early versions of the screenplay, was being called in to write material for ten days of retakes to be directed by Ernst Lubitsch. According to the news item, Twentieth Century-Fox stated that Lubitsch was replacing Lanfield as director because of Lanfield's commitment to Paramount, but the latter studio asserted that Lanfield was not needed at that time. Many contemporary reviews commented on how the production problems affected the finished film, especially in regard to its length. The *NYT* reviewer noted: "Twentieth Century-Fox had more trouble than it bargained for in making the film, according to reports out of Hollywood, and the difficulties are apparent in the finished work." The *MPHPD* reviewer called the picture "a problem for showmen" due to its short running time, and termed it Benny's "most perplexing contribution to the theatre man's flow of screen ware."

After the film was released, another problem arose when a group of lawyers in New Haven, CT, filed suit to prevent the film from being exhibited because they believed that it "showed the legal profession in a disreputable light," according to a 29 Mar 1943 *FD* news item. The next day, *FD* reported that Superior Court Judge Patrick O'Sullivan denied the lawyers' plea for an injunction, stating that they had "no standing to obtain such relief." O'Sullivan did, however, commend "the plaintiffs' zeal in attempting to safeguard the profession." MacHugh's play was the basis for two other works, both entitled *The Meanest Man in the World*: in 1923, Principal Pictures produced a film directed by Edward F. Cline and starring Bert Lytell and Blanche Sweet (see *AFI Catalog of Feature Films, 1921-30*; F2.3536); and on 6 Jul 1955, a one-hour version of the play, directed by Sidney Lumet and starring Wally Cox and Josephine Hull, was televised by the CBS network on the *U.S. Steel Hour.*

AmCin May 1943, p. 186. *Box* 16 Jan 1943. *DV* 30 Jan 1942. *DV* 8 Jul 1942. *DV* 8 Jan 1943, p. 3, 9. *FD* 15 Jan 1943, p. 6. *FD* 29 Mar 1943, p. 8. *FD* 30 Mar 1943, p. 1, 8. *HR* 30 Jan 1942, p. 1. *HR* 16 Mar 1942, p. 1. *HR* 11 Jun 1942, p. 3. *HR* 17 Jun 1942, p. 1. *HR* 8 Jul 1942, p. 1, 10. *HR* 9 Jul 1942, p. 1. *HR* 23 Jul 1942, p. 10. *HR* 24 Jul 1942, p. 7. *HR* 27 Jul 1942, p. 7. *HR* 28 Aug 1942, p. 11. *HR* 2 Nov 1942, p. 4. *HR* 11 Nov 1942, p. 2. *HR* 8 Jan 1943, p. 3. *LAEx* 13 May 1942. *LAT* 1 Nov 1939. *MPH* 9 Jan 1943. *MPHPD* 17 Oct 1942, p. 962. *MPHPD* 16 Jan 1943, p. 1115. *MPHPD* 29 May 1943, p. 1341. *NYT* 25 Feb 1943, p. 27. *Var* 13 Jan 1943, p. 8.

A MEDAL FOR BENNY (Latino)

Paramount Pictures, Inc. *Dist* Paramount Pictures, Inc. 29 Jun **1945**; New York opening: 23 May 1945; Prod: early Jun—late Jul 1944 [©Paramount Pictures, Inc.; 16 Apr 1945; LP13352]. Sd (Western Electric Recording); b&w. 7,139 ft. 77 or 79 min. Passed by the National Board of Review. PCA cert no. 10249.

Assoc prod Paul Jones. *Dir* Irving Pichel. [*Asst dir* Oscar Rudolph]. *Scr* Frank Butler. *Addl dial* Jack Wagner. *Story* John Steinbeck and Jack Wagner. *Dir of photog* Lionel Lindon. [*2d cam* Neal Beckner]. *Process photog* Farciot Edouart. [*Asst spec photog eff* Wallace Kelley and Harry Perry]. *Special photog eff* Gordon Jennings. [*Asst spec photog eff, Matte paintings* Jan Domela]. *Art dir* Hans Dreier and Hal Pereira. *Ed* Arthur Schmidt. *Set dec* Steve Seymour. *Cost* Edith Head. *Mus score* Victor Young. *Sd rec* Stanley Cooley and Joel Moss. [*Mus mixer* Philip Wisdom]. *Makeup supv* Wally Westmore.

Cast: DOROTHY LAMOUR [(*Lolita Sierra*)], ARTURO DE CORDOVA [(*Joe Morales*)], J. Carrol Naish [(*Charley Martin*)], Mikhail Rasumny [(*Raphael Catalina*)], Fernando Alvarado [(*Chito Sierra*)], Charles Dingle [(*Zack Mibbs*)], Frank McHugh [(*Edgar Lovekin*)], Rosita Moreno [(*Toodles Castro*)], Grant Mitchell [(*Pantera's mayor, Smiley*)], Douglass Dumbrille [(*The general*)], [Nestor Paiva (*Frank Alviso*)], [Eva Puig (*Mrs. Catalina*)], [Isabelita Castro (*Luz*)], [Pepito Perez (*Pamfilo Chavez*)], [Minerva Urecal (*Mrs. Chavez*)], [Frank Reicher (*Father Bly*)], [Robert Homans (*Chief of police*)], [Edward Fielding (*The governor*)], [Max Wagner (*Jake*)], [Joe Dominguez, Lupe Puig, Frances Dominguez, Dario Piazza, Martin Garralaga, Julian Rivero, Chico Sandoval, Charles Stevens (*Paisanos*)], [Oliver Prickett, Victor Potel, Harry Hayden (*Pepsters*)], [Jack Gardner (*Cameraman*)], [Eddie Chandler (*Bank guard*)], [Tom Fadden (*Eddie Krinch*)], [Alice Fleming (*Dowager*)], [Jack Gardner (*Red*)], [Maxine Fife (*Telephone operator*)], [Jimmie Dundee (*Policeman*)].

Rural, Drama. [*Print viewed*]. In 1942, in Pantera, a small town in California, ne'er-do-well Joe Morales buys a fishing boat with Charley Martin's money in order to make a living so that he may marry Lolita Sierra. Lolita, however, is promised to Benny Martin, Charley's thieving son, who was exiled from town after a fracas in which he bit off and swallowed the end of a policeman's gun. After the boat sinks, Charley, who has been desperate for rent money since Benny left, is threatened with eviction. Lolita has not heard from Benny in months, but remains loyal to him and refuses Joe's affections. After Lolita's little brother Chito tells Joe that Benny was always buying Lolita gifts, Joe swindles the naïve Charley out of twenty-five dollars he needs for rent. He then buys Lolita a dress for the town dance, but she refuses it when she learns how he got it. At the dance, Joe arrives with a tough-talking woman named Toodles Castro, who claims to know Benny. When Lolita sees Toodles wearing the dress bought for her as well as Lolita's father's wedding ring that she had given to Benny, she fights Toodles, and Joe leaves humiliated. Lolita suddenly realizes she loves Joe and goes to him. When Charley attempts to use his animals as collateral for a bank loan, he is ignored. Meanwhile, the news wire reports that Benny Martin of Pantera is a war hero and is about to be awarded a Congressional Medal of Honor by President Franklin D. Roosevelt for single-handedly killing one hundred Japanese soldiers in the Philippines. Joe, who meanwhile has sold the boat back to its original owner, returns Charley's money to Lolita. The mayor arrives to tell Charlie that his son is a hero, but sadly informs him that the medal is to be awarded posthumously by the governor and an army general. The chamber of commerce uses the event as a publicity stunt and sets Charley up in a beautiful house to avoid the embarrassment of showing him in his humble home. When Charley realizes the scheme, however, he refuses to go to the rally, and the general presents the medal at Charley's home. In his speech, Charley says that Benny will live on in his and Lolita's hearts. She then tells Joe that she cannot marry him yet, because it might break Charley's heart, so Joe volunteers for the army. *California. Fathers and sons. Mexican Americans. Romantic rivalry. Small town life. War heroes. Dances. Exiles. Fishermen. Loyalty. Ne'er-do-wells. Poverty. Publicity. Robbery. United States. Army. World War II.*

Note: The working title of this film was *Benny's Medal*. A written foreword to the film states: "Pantera in the spring of 1942—a small California town which pretends for its own pride that it is a city. In the old part of town are the Paisanos—Americans of mixed Indian and Spanish blood. A simple, friendly people, they have been here for more than a hundred years, and are the original

California settlers. This is a story of these people, but in particular the story of—-*A Medal for Benny.*" The character of Benny is never seen onscreen, but is only referred to in the story. Dorothy Lamour appeared in a *Lux Radio Theatre* broadcast of *A Medal for Benny* on 15 Oct 1945. This film was nominated for Academy Awards in the following categories: Best Supporting Actor, J. Carroll Naish; and Best Writing (Original Story), John Steinbeck and Jack Wagner. Rosita Moreno, who portrayed "Toodles Castro" in the film, should not be confused with actress Rita Moreno (b. 1931) who also acted under the name Rosita Moreno early in her career.

Box 7 Apr 1945. *DV* 9 Apr 1945, p. 3. *FD* 16 Apr 1945, p. 6. *HR* 9 Jun 1944, p. 26. *HR* 21 Jul 1944, p. 8. *HR* 9 Apr 1945, p. 3. *HR* 28 May 1945, p. 8. *MPHPD* 9 Sep 1944, p. 2093. *MPHPD* 14 Apr 1945, p. 2401. *NYT* 25 Jun 1944. *NYT* 24 May 1945, p. 15. *Var* 11 Apr 1945, p. 14.

MEDIA HORA see EL SECRETO DEL DOCTOR

THE MEDICO RIDES see THUNDER OVER THE PRAIRIE

MEET THE PRINCE (Russian Americans)
Metropolitan Pictures Corp. of California. *Dist* Producers Distributing Corp. 9 Aug 1926 [©Metropolitan Pictures Corp. of California; 16 Jun 1926; LP22819]. Si; b&w. 6 reels, 5,929 ft.

Dir Joseph Henabery. *Adpt* Jane Murfin and Harold Shumate. *Photog* Karl Struss.

Source: Based on the short story "The American Sex" by Frank R. Adams in *Munsey's Magazine* (Jun 1925).

Cast: Joseph Schildkraut (*Prince Nicholas Alexnov*), Marguerite De La Motte (*Annabelle Ford*), Vera Steadman (*Cynthia Stevens*), Julia Faye (*Princess Sophia Alexnov*), David Butler (*Peter Paget*), Helen Dunbar (*Mrs. Gordon McCullan*), Bryant Washburn, Bessie Love.

Comedy. Prince Nicholas Alexnov falls asleep on the fire escape of an East Side tenement in New York and dreams of his elegant palace in Russia: *An old servant tries to rouse him, but he will not wake up even though a revolution is imminent; at a conference held in the drawing room, the Princess Sophia, among others, is excited over the threatening labor strikes; a wounded footman staggers in shouting "Revolution"; and after killing a ruffian who pursues his sister, Nicholas escapes with her.* Wakened by a broken milk bottle, the prince finds himself in the shabby milieu of his sister and his faithful friends. Nicholas goes to pawn a plaque but instead buys a painting from Annabelle Ford, in his pride pretending to be a collector. At a party given by wealthy Cynthia Stevens, Nicholas ignores the hostess in favor of Annabelle, who is courted also by Peter Paget. Nicholas then poses as a butler at Paget's country home to be near her. Ultimately, Paget is united with Sophia, and Nicholas carries off the rebellious Annabelle. *Butlers. Dreams. Immigrants. Impersonation and imposture. New York City–East Side. Royalty. Russia–History–Revolution, 1917-1921. Russian Americans. Russians.*

Note: Copyrighted as 7 reels.
FD 18 Jul 1926. *MPW* 3 Jul 1926.

MELODÍA DE ARRABAL (Spanish language)
Films Paramount; controlled by Paramount Publix Corp. *Dist* Paramount Publix Corp. 1933; Buenos Aires, Argentina opening: 5 Apr 1933; San Juan, Puerto Rico opening: 17 Jun 1933; New York opening: 4 Aug 1933; Prod: Nov 1932 at Paramount studios in Joinville, France. Sd; b&w. 8,421 ft. 94 min. *Country of origin* France. Spanish language.

[*Supv* Florián Rey]. *Dirección de* [*Dir*] Louis Gasnier. *Escenario de* [*Scr*] Alfredo Le Pera. *Fotografía de* [*Photog*] Harry Stradling. *Mus accompaniment* Juan Cruz Mateo, Orchestra.

Song(s): "Melodía de arrabal" and "Mañanita de sol," music by Carlos Gardel, lyrics by Alfredo Le Pera and Mario Battistella; "Cuando tú no estás," music by Carlos Gardel and Marcel Lattés, lyrics by Alfredo Le Pera and Mario Battistella; "Silencio," music and lyrics Carlos Gardel, Alfredo Le Pera and Horacio Pettorossi; "No sé por qué," music and lyrics by José Sentís; "Evocación," music and lyrics by Raoul Moretti; "Batallón, a pelear" and "Te llevaste mi fe," composers undetermined.

Cast: Imperio Argentina (*Alina*), Carlos Gardel (*Roberto Ramírez*), Vicente Padula (*Gutiérrez*), Jaime Devesa (*Rancales*), Helena D'Algy (*Marga*), Felipe Sassone (*Empresario*), Manuel París (*Maldonado*), José Argüelles (*Julián*), [Josita Hernán (*Singing student*)].

Musical, Melodrama. [*Print viewed*]. At nightfall, various shady characters, drunks and women of easy virtue congregate at a café, "La Estrella," in the old district of Buenos Aires. Even though he has a fine singing voice, Roberto Ramírez plays cards there with people unacquainted with his trickery. Roberto gets to know Alina, a young voice teacher and occasional talent scout, who predicts a great future for him as a tango singer. In front of Inspector Maldonado, the card sharks at "La Estrella" conceal the cheating, except for Rancales, who, but for Roberto's intervention, would have shot the policeman. Roberto's future lies between the profitable business of card games and the uncertainty of the world of the tango, but Alina's enthusiasm for her protégé resolves the dilemma, and with the help of an impresario, she launches him on the road to fame. Although Roberto has forsaken gambling, Rancales seeks a large pay-off from him not to reveal his past. Roberto and Rancales fight, a gun goes off and Rancales dies. Maldonado finds evidence that Roberto has killed the blackmailer but, realizing that Roberto is the man who saved his life, lets him go free. Roberto makes his professional concert debut, and is successful in song and in love. *Buenos Aires (Argentina). Romance. Singers. Talent scouts. Vocal instructors. Accidental death. Cafés. Cardsharping. Concerts. Evidence. Fights. Impresarios. Police inspectors. Tango (Dance).*

Note: *FD* and *NYT*, reviewing the New York showing of this film, gave the English translation as "Suburban Melody." Some sources list Juanita Bianco as a cast member, but she was not included in the film's credits.
FD 9 Aug 1933. *NYT* 5 Aug 1933, p. 9.

LA MELODÍA PROHIBIDA (Spanish language)
Fox Film Corp. *Dist* Fox Film Corp. 1933; Los Angeles opening: 13 Sep 1933; Prod: 21 Feb—11 Mar 1933. Sd (Western Electric Noiseless Recording); b&w. 8 reels. Passed by the National Board of Review. Spanish language.

[*Prod* John Stone]. *Dirección* [*Dir*] Frank Strayer. *Adaptación cinematográfica de* [*Scr*] Paul Perez and Enrique Jardiel Poncela. [*Cont* William Kernell]. [*Orig story* Eve Unsell]. [*Photog* Harry Jackson]. [*2d cam* Jack Greenhalgh]. [*Asst cam* Russell Hoover]. *Dirección musical* [*Mus dir*] Samuel Kaylin.

Song(s): "Pais ideal (The Islands Are Calling Me)," "Siempre (Till the End of Time)," "La canción del paria (Derelict Song)" and "La melodía prohibida," music by Harry Akst, lyrics by L. Wolfe Gilbert, Spanish translation by José Mojica and Enrique Jardiel Poncela; "Como tú y yo" and "Cuando me vaya (When I Go Away)," music and lyrics by María Grever.

Cast: JOSÉ MOJICA (*Kalu*), Conchita Montenegro (*Tuila*), Mona Maris (*Peggy*), Romualdo Tirado (*Al Martin*), Juan Martínez Plá (*Bob Grant*), Carmen Rodríguez (*Tía Olivia*), Antonio Vidal (*El gobernador*), Ralph Navarro (*Tom Nichols*), [Agostino Borgato (*Win Ta Tu*)], [Soledad Jiménez (*Fa Uma*)], [Charles Bancroft (*Ricky Doyle*)].

Island, Musical, Drama. [*Not viewed*]. On the morning of their wedding, Kalu and Tuila romp joyously on their secluded South Pacific island. A pleasure yacht arrives, and the island's colonial governor invites the tourists to the solemn nuptials, where Kalu performs the "Forbidden Melody," a song which a man sings to his beloved only once in his life. In the jungle, Kalu meets Peggy, who arrived on the yacht, and commends her for her dancing skills, which she admirably displayed at the primitive wedding the night before. She asks him to sing the "Forbidden Melody," but he tells her that to do so would be taboo. A village child tells Tuila that Kalu was seen with a white woman in his arms, and Tuila finds Peggy to warn her to leave alone the innocent native boy, who is a diversion for Peggy at best. Kalu meets Peggy's entourage, including Bob Grant, a nightclub promoter who compliments him on his singing and offers him a contract to perform at his cabaret in San Francisco. Peggy later finds Kalu in the Thunder God's cave, where he pays obeisance. Peggy insists on entering the holy place despite Kalu's protests, and she convinces him that the Thunder God approves of their love. In San Francisco, Kalu sings his "Forbidden Melody" to jazz accompaniment. Peggy, already bored with her latest project of "civilizing the savage," flirts with a pro football player in the audience. At a party at Peggy's house, Kalu expresses his disappointment that he can never see her alone, and Peggy admits that she doesn't love him. Kalu, despondent, goes to a sleazy bar and gets drunk. When he hears his "Forbidden Melody," on the radio, he cries out and runs outside. Believing that he's heard Tuila's love call, he runs into the street, but the call was a siren from a fire engine and it strikes and kills him. Back on the island, the governor listens sadly to a recording of the dead prince singing an exotic song on the radio.

Cultural conflict. Innocents. Rites and ceremonies. Seduction. Socialites. Songs. South Sea islands. Tribal life. Accidental death. Bars. Caves. Dancing. Drunkenness. Fire-engines. Football players. Jazz music. Promoters. Radio broadcasting. San Francisco (CA). Tourists. Weddings. Yachts and yachting.

Note: The plot summary was based on a dialogue continuity and a script in the Twentieth Century-Fox Produced Scripts Collection, and the onscreen credits were taken from a screen credit sheet in the Twentieth Century-Fox Records of the Legal Department, both of which are at the UCLA Theater Arts Library. The title was translated in reviews as "Forbidden Melody." The film showed in Los Angeles under the title *La canción probibida*. The *NYT* review credits Tom Patricola as a cast member; however, no information in the studio records or in other reviews confirms his participation in the film.

FD 28 Mar 1934, p. 9. IP Mar 1933, p. 21. NYT 4 Oct 1933, p. 27.

THE MELODY MAN (Austrian Americans)

Columbia Pictures Corp.; Columbia Pictures Corp. 15 Jan **1930** [©Columbia Pictures Corp.; 18 Feb 1930; LP1090]. Sd (Movietone); b&w. 7 reels, 6,386 ft. [Also si.].

Prod Harry Cohn. *Dir* R. William Neill. *Asst dir* Sam Nelson. *Dial dir* James Seymour. *Cont and dial* Howard J. Green. *Cam* Ted Tetzlaff. *Asst cam* Henry Freulich. *Art dir* Harrison Wiley. *Film ed* Leonard Wheeler. *Sd eng* John P. Livadary. *Sd mix eng* G. R. Cooper.

Song(s): "Broken Dreams, " by Ballard MacDonald, Arthur Johnston and Dave Dreyer.

Source: Based on the play *The Melody Man* by Herbert Fields, Richard Rodgers and Lorenz Hart (New York, 13 May 1924).

Cast: William Collier, Jr. (*Al Tyler*), Alice Day (*Elsa*), John St. Polis (*Von Kemper*), Johnny Walker (*Joe Yates*), Mildred Harris (*Martha*), Albert Conti (*Prince Friedrich*), Tenen Holtz (*Gustav*), Lee Kohlmar (*Adolph*), Bertram Marburgh (*Van Bader*), Anton Vaverka (*Franz Josef*), Major Nichols (*Bachman*).

Drama. Earl von Kemper, a famous Viennese composer, has scored a great success with his *Dream Rhapsody* at a concert for the emperor and empress, but when he finds the woman he loves entertaining Crown Prince Friedrich in her boudoir, he shoots and kills him and escapes to the United States with his daughter. Fifteen years later, in New York, the musician is earning his living by playing his violin, with Gustav and Adolph, at a small restaurant. Elsa, his talented daughter, becomes acquainted with Al Tyler, a young jazz musician, and secretly arranges scores for his band; when they replace Kemper's trio at the café, he refuses to let his daughter associate with the jazz artists. Al happens to hear *Dream Rhapsody*, and Elsa arranges a jazz version that Al makes famous; but Baden, the Austrian Minister of Police, hears and recognizes it. Kemper, about to be apprehended, leaves the young lovers on the pretext of returning for a European engagement. Austrian Americans. Composers. Courtship. Family relationships. Francis Joseph I, Emperor of Austria, 1830-1916. Fugitives. Jazz music. Murder. Musicians. New York City. Royalty. Vienna (Austria).

FD 16 Feb 1930. Var 26 Feb 1930, p. 29.

MELODY ROUNDUP see WILD WEST

MELODY TRAIL (Gypsies)

Mascot Pictures Corp.; A Nat Levine Mascot Production. *Dist* Republic Pictures Corp. 21 Oct **1935**; Prod: ended 26 Aug 1935 [©Republic Pictures Corp.; 14 Oct 1935; LP5858]. Sd; b&w. 6 reels, 5,470 ft. 61 min. Passed by the National Board of Review.

Supv Armand Schaefer. *Dir* Joseph Kane. [*Asst dir* George Sherman]. *Scr* Sherman Lowe. *Story* Sherman Lowe and Betty Burbridge. *Photog* Ernest Miller. [*Asst cam* Bill Bradford]. *Film ed* Lester Orlebeck. *Supv ed* Joseph H. Lewis. *Sd eng* Terry Kellum. *Sd eff* Roy Granville.

Song(s): "Western Lullaby," "Where Will the Wedding Supper Be?," "Hold on Little Dogies, Hold On," and "A Lone Cowboy on the Lone Prairie," words and music by Gene Autry and Smiley Burnette; "My Neighbor Hates Music," "Way Down on the Bottom" and "Melody Trail," words and music by Smiley Burnette.

Cast: GENE AUTRY [(*Gene Autry, also known as Arizona*)], Ann Rutherford [(*Millicent Thomas*)], Smiley Burnette [(*Frog Millhouse*)], Wade Boteler [(*Timothy Thomas*)], Champion [(*Gene's horse*)], Buck [(*Souvenir*)], Willy Castello [(*Frantz*)], Al Bridge [(*Matt Kirby*)], Fern Emmett [(*Nell*)], Marie Quillan [(*Perdita*)], Gertrude Messinger [(*Cuddles*)], Tracy Layne [(*Slim*)], Abe Lefton (World Famous Rodeo Announcer), [Lord A. Shah (*Baby Rica*)], [George De Normand (*Pete*)], [Marion Dowling (*Sally*)], [Ione Reed (*Mamie*)], [Jane Barnes (*Helen*)].

Western, with songs. [*Print viewed*]. Gene Autry, radio and phonograph star, and his friend, comedian Frog Millhouse, attend a rodeo where Gene falls for a spectator, Millicent Thomas. Millicent, who is being harassed by her father's former ranch hand, Matt Kirby, is delighted when Gene sings for the crowd, then beats Matt in a bucking bronco competition. That night, however, as Gene dreams of Millicent, his $1,000 in rodeo winnings are stolen by the gypsy Frantz, the husband of Perdita, a fortune-teller. The next day, while Millicent goes into town with her father, rancher Timothy Thomas, her dog, Souvenir, a compulsive thief, takes a detour into the gypsy camp and steals a basket containing Frantz and Perdita's baby daughter Rica. Millicent later discovers the infant and takes her in, not knowing who her parents are, and Frog and Gene, who end up going to work as cooks on the Thomas ranch, assume the baby to be hers. Gene, using the moniker "Arizona," captures two wild stallions to impress Millicent and the cowgirls she has hired to replace Matt and his men, who have defected. However, after Souvenir steals Gene's cookbook, his efforts in the kitchen are far less successful, and the meal that he and Frog prepare for the cowgirls makes them all ill. In the meantime, Matt plots to rustle the Thomas' cattle, and while the cowgirls bathe in a pond, he steals their clothes in order to prevent them from protecting the herd. Frantz, searching for Baby Rica, recovers her from Millicent, but Gene pursues him, believing him to be a kidnapper. Gene captures and ties up Frantz, and Frantz returns the money he earlier stole from Gene, after explaining that Rica is his daughter. Gene then sees Matt and his men stealing the cattle and apprehends all eight of them, including Matt, single-handedly. After Gene saves the ranch, he and Millicent, and Frog and Cuddles, one of the cowgirls, are wed in a large, musical ceremony along with the other cowboys and girls, but the wedding is interrupted by the realization that Souvenir has stolen all their wedding rings. Cooks. Dogs. Ranchers. Singers. Thieves. Cattle. Comedians. Cowgirls. Fathers and daughters. Fortune-tellers. Gypsies. Infants. Kidnapping. Rodeos. Rustlers. Weddings.

Note: Buck, a St. Bernard dog, appeared earlier in 1935 in *The Call of the Wild* (see *AFI Catalog of Feature Films, 1931-40*; F3.0568).

FD 24 Sep 1935, p. 12. HR 26 Aug 1935, p. 3. HR 19 Sep 1935, p. 3. MPD 20 Sep 1935, p. 10. MPH 19 Oct 1935, p. 87. Var 11 Dec 1935, p. 34.

THE MELTING POT (Jewish Americans, Russian Americans)

Cort Film Corp. *Dist* State Rights. 30 May **1915**. Si; b&w. 5-6 reels.

Prod Gerald F. Bacon. *Dir* James Vincent and Oliver D. Bailey. *Scen* Catherine Carr and Oliver D. Bailey.

Source: Based on the novel *The Melting Pot* by Israel Zangwill (London and New York, 1908) and his play of the same name (New York, 6 Sep 1909).

Cast: Walker Whiteside (*David Quixano*), Valentine Grant (*Vera Ravendal*), Fletcher Harvey (*Baron Ravendal*), Henry Bergman (*Mendel Quixano*), Julia Hurley (*Frau Quixano*), Harold Crane (*Quincy Davenport*), Henry Leone (*Herr Papelmeister*).

Social, Drama. Young violinist David Quixano witnesses the slaughter of his family in the Easter morning pogrom at Kishineff, Russia, which is being conducted by Baron Ravendal to carry out the Czar's decree to massacre one-third of the Jews in Russia, baptize another third and exile the rest. The baron's daughter Vera, imprisoned by the Czar's spies when she aids victims, escapes and goes to New York, where she falls in love with David, who plays in East Side concert halls to survive. After David interests a German music master in promoting his symphony to symbolize the amalgamation of races and religions in America's "melting pot," the baron arrives to reproach Vera. Although Vera subdues his protests, David declares that rivers of blood separate them. The baron penitently offers his life and David is about to kill him, when a broken violin string reminds him of his symphony's ideals. When the symphony is performed, a giant crucible is shown to convert people from all races and countries into American citizens. After David is proclaimed a genius, he and Vera marry. Idealists. Music. Religious persecution. Composers. Easter. Imprisonment. Jews. Kishinev (Russia). Massacres. New York City–East Side. Nobility. Self-sacrifice. Violinists.

Note: This was the first film of the Cort Film Corp. It was produced at the Centaur Film Co., Bayonne, NJ. Walker Whiteside, who played the role of David on stage, made his screen debut in this film. The film had its premiere at the Hippodrome in New York, for which a special orchestration was prepared. Some sources indicate that James Vincent was the sole director. Some sources also indicate that Catherine Carr was the sole scenarist.

Motog 17 Apr 1915, p. 592. *Motog* 1 May 1915, p. 689. *Motog* 8 May 1915, p. 736. *Motog* 22 May 1915, p. 856. *Motog* 5 Jun 1915, p. 918. *Motog* 12 Jun 1915, p. 973. *Motog* 3 Jul 1915, p. 32. *MPN* 24 Apr 1915, pp. 94-95. *MPN* 1 May 1915, p. 15. *MPN* 8 May 1915, p. 54, 89. *MPN* 15 May 1915, p. 54. *MPN* 22 May 1915, p. 62. *MPN* 5 Jun 1915, p. 56. *MPN* 12 Jun 1915, p. 48, 69. *MPW* 22 May 1915, p. 1340, 1342. *MPW* 12 Jun 1915, p. 1786. *NYDM* 9 Jun 1915, p. 28. *Var* 4 Jun 1915, p. 18.

THE MEMBER OF THE WEDDING (African Americans)

Stanley Kramer Co. *Dist* Columbia Pictures Corp. Mar **1953**; Los Angeles opening: 25 Dec 1952; New York opening: 30 Dec 1952; Prod: 18 Jun—25 Jul 1952 [©Stanley Kramer Co.; 3 Feb 1953; LP2392]. Sd (Western Electric Recording); b&w. 8,236 ft. 88 or 91 min. PCA cert no. 16047.

Assoc prod Edna Anhalt and Edward Anhalt. *Dir* Fred Zinnemann. *Asst dir* Sam Nelson. *Scr* Edna Anhalt and Edward Anhalt. *Dir of photog* Hal Mohr. *Prod des* Rudolph Sternad. *Art dir* Cary Odell. *Ed supv* Harry Gerstad. *Film ed* William A. Lyon. *Set dec* Frank Tuttle. *Mus score* Alex North. *Mus dir* Morris Stoloff. *Sd eng* Lambert Day. *Makeup* Clay Campbell. *Hair styles by* Helen Hunt. *Prod mgr* Clem Beauchamp. [*Dir of pub* George Lait].

Song(s): "His Eye Is on the Sparrow," music and lyrics by Charles H. Gabriel and Mrs. C. D. Martin.

Source: Based on the novel *The Member of the Wedding* by Carson McCullers (Boston, 1946) and her play of the same name, as produced by Robert Whitehead, Oliver Rea and Stanley Martineau (New York, 5 Jan 1950).

Cast: Ethel Waters [(*Berenice Sadie Brown*)], Julie Harris [(*Frances* ["*Frankie*"] *Addams*)], Brandon de Wilde [(*John Henry*)], Arthur Franz [(*Jarvis Addams*)], Nancy Gates [(*Janice*)], William Hansen [(*Mr. Addams*)], James Edwards [(*Honey Camden Brown*)], Harry Bolden [(*T. T. Williams*)], Dick Moore [(*Soldier*)], [Charlcie Garrett (*Aunt Pet*)], [Danny Mummert (*Barney MacKean*)], [June Hedin (*Helen*)], [Ann Carter (*Doris*)], [Harry Richards (*Organ grinder*)], [Hugh Beaumont (*Minister*)], [Wheaton Chambers (*Man who gives bride away*)], [Helen St. Rayner (*Organist*)], [Gil Perkins (*Moving man*)], [Ralph Montgomery (*Tractor man*)], [Ivan Browning (*Black porter*)], [Paul Brinegar (*Gas station attendant*)], [Howard Negley (*Bus station clerk*)], [Henry Sylvester], [Jack Gargan], [Al Ferguson], [Rhea Mitchell], [Alma Mansfield], [Ella Ethridge], [Margaret Bert], [Jeanne Blackford], [Mary Emery], [Charles Perry], [Gail Bonney].

Domestic, Teenage, Drama. [*Print viewed*]. On a steamy southern afternoon, Jarvis Addams and his fiancée Janice visit the Addams home to discuss their upcoming wedding. Jarvis' twelve-year-old sister Frankie is deeply disturbed by restlessness, loneliness and the conflicting emotions of becoming an adolescent, and her thoughts become fixated on the happy couple. Several days before the wedding, Frankie tells Berenice Sadie Brown, the housekeeper, and John Henry, Frankie's younger cousin, that she plans to leave town and live with the couple after the wedding. Berenice is a practical but softhearted widow who, since the death of Frankie's mother, has offered the girl guidance and companionship. She describes her own sadness at the loss of her first husband in order to warn Frankie that she will end up with a broken heart if she imposes herself on the couple. Frankie refuses to listen, however, and during the ceremony, sneaks into the couple's car with her suitcase. When the newlyweds, followed by their families and friends, approach the car, they are stunned to see Frankie in the back seat. Janice gently explains to Frankie that she and her husband wish to be alone on their honeymoon, but Frankie refuses to leave and is dragged screaming from the car. Her father, Berenice and John Henry all try to comfort the girl, but their efforts are fruitless. That night Frankie types her father a farewell letter and runs away. After wandering aimlessly through a disreputable part of town, she enters a bar and meets a drunken soldier. When he tries to kiss her, she breaks free and runs toward home. Meanwhile, Berenice learns that her foster brother Honey, a restless musician who is frequently drunk, has become involved in a hit-and-run accident with a stolen car. She gives him all her money and helps him make his getaway. Later, when Frankie arrives home, she learns that Berenice is nursing John Henry, who has become gravely ill. Several months pass, and Frankie, who has made a new friend and is much more confident, enters the room to say goodbye to Berenice. John Henry has died, and because Frankie's family is moving in with the boy's mother, they no longer need a housekeeper. Berenice muses sadly on both the death of John Henry and on Honey's ten-year prison sentence, but Frankie, her mind on the handsome boy down the street, brightly delivers her farewell and

skips out of the house. With tears in her eyes and a sad smile on her face, Berenice hums quietly to herself. *Adolescents. African Americans. Nannies. Obsession. Southerners.* Automobile accidents. Bars. Children. Clubs. Cousins. Death and dying. Drunkenness. Fathers and daughters. Fugitives. Georgia. Infatuation. Letters. Loneliness. Musicians. Racism. Runaways. Self-sacrifice. Sisters. Small town life. Soldiers. Weddings. Widows.

Note: The onscreen credit for Hal Mohr, director of photography, notes that Garutso Balanced Lenses were used. Director Fred Zinnemann, in his autobiography, states that the new lenses gave an enormous depth of focus. The play, which was directed by Harold Clurman, won the New York Drama Critics Circle and Donaldson awards as best play for the 1949-50 season. According to news items, in Feb 1951 Stanley Kramer paid $100,000 for the screen rights to the play. Ethel Waters, Julie Harris, Brandon de Wilde, William Hansen and Harry Bolden recreated their Broadway stage roles for the film. Reviews remarked on the film's faithfulness to the play, and *NYT* noted that one scene, where "Frankie" wanders through a disreputable part of town, was taken from the novel rather than the play. Harris, who played the twelve-year-old "Frankie," was actually twenty-six at the time of filming. *NYT* commented that in close-up, Harris' face was that "of a woman that is mature in expression and form." Zinnemann, in his autobiography, states that location shooting was done in Colusa, CA near the Sacramento River.

Harris received an Academy Award nomination for Best Actress. Brandon de Wilde won a Golden Globe award for best juvenile actor. In Jun 1958, NBC broadcast a television version of the play, on the *DuPont Show of the Month*, which was produced by David Susskind, directed by Robert Mulligan, and starred Claudia McNeil, Collin Wilcox and Dennis Kohler. In Dec 1982, *NBC Live Theatre* broadcast another version, which was directed by Delbert Mann and starred Pearl Bailey, Dana Hill, Howard Rollins and Benjamin Bernouy. In 1986, the publishing house Stock, which owned the French-language adaptation rights to the novel, alleged that the novel was adapted without permission to provide the scenario for the French film *L'Effrontée*, produced by Oliane Productions and directed by Claude Miller. No further information concerning this has been located. A television version, starring Anna Paquin, was planned for 1996.

Box 20 Dec 1952. *Cue* 3 Jan 1953. *DV* 13 Feb 1951. *DV* 15 Dec 1952, p. 3. *DV* 14 Jan 1986, p. 14. *Exb* 31 Dec 1952, p. 3437. *FD* 18 Dec 1952, p. 6. *Har* 20 Dec 1952, p. 203. *HR* 15 Dec 1952, p. 3. *LADN* 26 Dec 1952. *LAEx* 13 Feb 1951. *LAT* 16 Dec 1952. *LAT* 25 Dec 1952, pt. II, p. 12. *MPHPD* 20 Dec 1952, pp. 1645-46. *Newsweek* 12 Jan 1953. *New Yorker* 3 Jan 1953. *NYT* 31 Dec 1952, p. 10. *SatRev* 10 Jan 1953. *Time* 29 Dec 1952. *Var* 17 Dec 1952, p. 6.

MEMO TO A MOVIE PRODUCER *see* **HOLD BACK THE DAWN**

THE MEN (Latino)

Stanley Kramer Productions. *Dist* United Artists Corp. 25 Aug **1950**; New York opening: 20 Jul 1950; Prod: early Nov—early Dec 1949 at Motion Picture Center [©Stanley Kramer Productions; 25 Aug 1950; LP329]. Sd (Western Electric Recording); b&w. 7,760 ft. 85-86 min. Passed by the National Board of Review. PCA cert no. 14228.

Prod Stanley Kramer. *Assoc prod* George Glass. *Dir* Fred Zinnemann. *Asst dir* Lloyd Richards. *Dial dir* Don Weis. *Story and scr* Carl Foreman. *Photog* Robert de Grasse. [*Cam op* Charles Burke]. [*Stills* Scotty Welborne]. *Lighting eff* James Potevin and Ted Anderson. *Prod des* Rudolph Sternad. *Film ed* Harry Gerstad. *Set dec* Edward G. Boyle. *Men's ward* Joe King. *Ladies' ward* Ann Peck. *Mus comp and dir* Dimitri Tiomkin. *Sd eng* Jean Speak. *Magnetic rec by* Sound Services, Inc. *Makeup* Gus Norin. *Hair stylist* Hollis Barnes. *Prod mgr* Clem Beauchamp. *Head grip* Morris Rosen. *Tech adv* Pat Grissom and Herbert Wolf. [*Scr supv* Don Wise].

Song(s): "Love Like Ours," music by Dimitri Tiomkin, lyrics by John Lehmann.

Cast: MARLON BRANDO (*Ken* ["*Bud*" *Wilocek*]), TERESA WRIGHT (*Ellen*), Everett Sloane (*Dr. Brock*), Jack Webb (*Norm* [*Butler*]), Richard Erdman (*Leo*), Arthur Jurado (*Angel*), Virginia Farmer (*Nurse Robbins*), Dorothy Tree (*Ellen's mother*), Howard St. John (*Ellen's father*), Nita Hunter (*Dolores*), Patricia Joiner (*Laverne*), John Miller (*Mr. Doolin*), Cliff Clark (*Dr. Kameran*), Ray Teal (*Man at bar*), Marguerite Martin (*Angel's mother*), And forty five of the men of Birmingham Veterans Administration Hospital:, [Obie Parker (*The lookout*)], [Ray Mitchell (*Thompson*)], [Pete Simon (*Mullin*)], [Paul Peltz (*Hopkins*)], [Tom Gillick (*Fine*)], [Randall Updyke III (*Baker*)], [Marshall Ball (*Romano*)], [Carlo Lewis (*Gunderson*)], [and William Lea, Jr. (*Walter*)], [Dr. Norman Karr (*Doctor*)], [Helen Winston (*Physical therapist*)], [Rhoda Cormeny, Eunice Newberry (*Nurses*)], [Polly Bergen (*Nightclub singer, off screen*)].

Postwar life, Drama. [*Print viewed*]. After he is paralyzed from the waist down while serving during World War II, Army Lt. Ken "Bud" Wilozek is sent to the paraplegic ward at a hospital in his hometown. When Bud's fiancée Ellen meets the ward physician, Dr. Brock, she tells him that since his injury, Bud has become depressed and broken

their engagement. Brock asks Ellen to give Bud some time to adjust to his paralysis, but while other patients at the hospital make friends, Bud remains bitter and withdrawn. Later, Brock tells Bud about his conversation with Ellen, but Bud reacts angrily, declaring that he does not wish to see her. Brock later instructs Nurse Robbins to take Bud to the exercise room, where he is forced to interact with the others. There, Bud meets fellow patients Leo, Norm Butler, and a Mexican American named Angel. At Ellen's urging, Brock decides to let her in to see Bud, who has refused to cooperate with his rehabilitation. Brock instructs her to come to the ward the following evening, when everyone else will be attending a wedding. The next evening, after Ellen finds Bud lying alone in the darkness, he shouts at her to leave and then begins weeping when his call for a nurse goes unanswered. Eventually, Bud befriends Angel, who persuades him to fight back against his condition and begin training to build his upper body strength. Soon, Norm starts seeing a woman named Laverne and brings her to the hospital to meet the others. Soon after, Angel dies suddenly of spinal meningitis, and Bud is thrust back into depression. Nevertheless, he perseveres and begins to see Ellen again. When Ellen pleads with Bud to marry her, he agrees to give marriage a try. Norm, meanwhile, returns to the ward after an evening of drinking and tells Bud that Laverne stole $900 from him and fled to Canada. In the weeks before the wedding, Bud trains vigorously, hoping to be able to pull himself up and stand for his vows by holding onto a railing. On the big day, Bud manages to stand, but when he lets go of the rail to put the ring on Ellen's finger, he slumps helplessly to the floor. Bud is so wounded by this humiliation, that when they return home from the ceremony on their wedding night, he is cruel and argumentative. When Ellen admits that she is unhappy, Bud decides to return to the ward in the car that she had customized for his use. Later, Leo persuades Bud to sneak out for a drink at a local bar, after which Bud wrecks his car. The next day, a report of the crash appears in the newspaper, and the head of the hospital comes down hard on Bud for his behavior. Brock, however, convinces the administrator to allow the Paralyzed Veterans Association, the ward's self-governing body, to decide on Bud's punishment. When she reads about the crash, Ellen rushes to the hospital to apologize and asks Bud to return home, but he refuses. After the association votes to discharge Bud, Brock urges him to give his marriage another try. With a renewed appreciation for life, Bud drives his damaged car home, where Ellen is waiting to help him up the front steps. *Hospitals. Marriage. Paraplegics. Veterans.* Automobile accidents. Bars. Depression. Mental. Engagements. Exercise. Jewelry. Meningitis. Mexican Americans. Nurses. Physical therapy. Physicians. Polish Americans. Psychological torment. Rites and ceremonies. Thieves.

Note: The working title of this film was *The Courage of Ten.* The film's opening credits include the following written dedication: "In all wars, since the beginning of history, there have been men who fought twice. The first time they battled with club, sword or machine gun. The second time they had none of these weapons. Yet, this by far was the greatest battle...This is the story of such a group of men. To them this film is dedicated." The film opens with voice-over narration by Marlon Brando, who made his motion picture debut in *The Men.*

In Aug 1949, *HR* reported that Kirk Douglas was being considered for the lead role. According to a 26 Oct 1949 *DV* news item, three paralyzed veterans—Herb Wolf, Pat Grissom and Ted Anderson—who were living at Birmingham Hospital in Van Nuys, CA, where the film was shot, were to serve as technical advisers on the production. Only Wolf and Grissom received onscreen credit, however. In addition to Arthur Jurado, a real-life paraplegic who was given a sizable speaking role, many others from Birmingham Hospital were added to the cast, including Dr. Norman Karr, physical therapist Helen Winston and nurses Rhoda Cormeny and Eunice Newberry. A 16 Oct 1949 *NYT* news item reported that in preparation for his role as a paraplegic, Brando moved into the hospital for an entire month before filming began in order to learn how to maneuver a wheelchair effectively. An unidentified news item contained in the MPAA/PCA Collection at the AMPAS Library, dated Nov 1949, noted that "use of paraplegics to play themselves was made necessary after it was found that it would take weeks to train actors in the wheelchair technics of paraplegics." The *NYT* article also reports that screenwriter Carl Foreman and director Fred Zinnemann spent more than a month studying patients in the paraplegic ward of the hospital. In Jan 1950, *NYT* published an article by Zinnemann in which he states that "all of the situations and dialogue in the script...were written by Carl Foreman from material he picked up from the men themselves." Sources disagree on the spelling of the last name of Brando's character.

According to a 28 Jun 1950 *DV* news item, British censors banned *The Men,* citing a speech given to a group of wives and mothers by Everette Sloane's character in which he tells them that their paralyzed men may be unable to have children. A 10 Nov 1949 *HR* news item noted that a one-reel trailer, featuring Brando touring Hollywood landmarks, was produced by Stanley Kramer to advertise the film on television. Kramer also arranged pre-release showings of

the film in Jul 1950 in New York City, Chicago, Boston, Atlantic City and San Francisco. On 11 May 1950, *HR* reported that a pre-release press screening, scheduled for 17 May 1950 in Los Angeles, would be attended by the Reserve Officers Association of the United States, whose military display would honor the wounded veterans memorialized in the film. A forty-piece Marine Corps band from Camp Pendleton, honor guards, color guards and others participated in the event. In 1950, Foreman was nominated for an Academy Award for his work on the film.

Before starring in the picture, Brando had appeared in the Broadway play *A Streetcar Named Desire,* receiving rave reviews for his performance. He had been scheduled to make his screen debut in *St. Benny the Dip,* which George Auerbach was to produce, but the deal collapsed according to an Aug 1949 *HR* news item. Of his performance in *The Men,* *NYT* stated: "Mr. Brando as the veteran who endures the most difficult time is so vividly real, dynamic and sensitive that his illusion is complete." The *HR* review called him "an amazingly life-like actor, a performer who seems to live rather than play his role...Whatever the individual opinion, Brando is an important new star in the Hollywood horizon." *DV* noted that Brando "plays his role realistically, often without sympathy" and hailed him as "a new type of leading man, and as such must be accepted." The *Var* review, however, complained that "Brando fails to deliver with the necessary sensitivity and inner warmth which would transform an adequate portrayal into an expert one. Slight speech impediment which sharply enhanced his 'Streetcar' role jars here. His supposed college graduate depiction is consequently not completely convincing." Modern sources include the working title *Battle Stripe.*

Box 27 May 1950. *DV* 26 Oct 1949. *DV* 19 May 1950, p. 3. *DV* 28 Jun 1950, p. 1, 4. *FD* 19 May 1950, p. 7. *HR* 7 Jul 1949, p. 7. *HR* 11 Aug 1949, p. 1. *HR* 25 Aug 1949. *HR* 4 Nov 1949, p. 15. *HR* 8 Nov 1949. *HR* 10 Nov 1949, p. 12. *HR* 25 Nov 1949, p. 13. *HR* 31 Jan 1950, p. 5. *HR* 28 Mar 1950, p. 3. *HR* 6 Apr 1950, p. 8. *HR* 5 May 1950, p. 2. *HR* 11 May 1950, p. 5. *HR* 19 May 1950, p. 3, 8. *MPHPD* 20 May 1950, p. 301. *NYT* 16 Oct 1949. *NYT* 8 Jan 1950. *NYT* 21 Jul 1950, p. 15. *Var* 24 May 1950, p. 6.

MEN ARE SUCH FOOLS (Italian Americans)

Jefferson Pictures Corp. *Dist* RKO Radio Pictures, Inc. 18 Nov **1932** [©RKO Radio Pictures, Inc. & Jefferson Pictures Corp.; 31 Oct 1932; LP3401]. Sd (RCA Photophone System); b&w. 8 reels. 64-65 min.

Prod Joseph I. Schnitzer and Samuel Zierler. *Dir* William Nigh. *Asst dir* Bernard McEveety. [*2nd asst dir* Samuel Schnitzer]. *Story* Thomas Lloyd Lennon. *Adpt and dial* Viola Brothers Shore. *Cont* Ethel Doherty. *Cine* Charles Schoenbaum. [*Cam op* Earl Stafford]. [*Asst cam* Bernard Moore]. *Art dir* Edward C. Jewell. *Film ed* Viola Lawrence. *Dir of mus* Bakaleinikoff. *Rec* Lambert Day and [Lodge Cunningham]. [*Still photog* Fred Archer].

Cast: Leo Carrillo (*Antonio* [*"Tony"*] *Mello*), Vivienne Osborne (*Lilli Arno*), Una Merkel (*Molly*), Tom Moore ([*Tom*] *Hyland*), Joseph Cawthorn (*Werner*), Earle Fox ([*Joe*] *Darrow*), J. Farrell MacDonald (*Randolph*), Paul Hurst (*Stiles*), Albert Conti (*Kraus*), Paul Porcasi (*Klepak*), Eddie Nugent (*Eddie* [*Martin*]), Lester Lee (*Giuseppe*).

Prison, Melodrama. [*Print viewed*]. Italian-born Antonio "Tony" Mello plays second violin in a Viennese café and is in love with aspiring singer Lilli Arno. Lilli pressures Tony to introduce her to the café's owner, Klepak, and after promising to sing in a seductive manner, she is given a chance to perform and soon becomes the café's star entertainer. As she grows more successful, however, she begins to lose interest in Tony and resents his covetous manner. When two American tourists flirt provocatively with her in the café, Tony flies into a rage and knocks out one of the offending men. Lilli is fired over the incident and is about to break with Tony when he announces his intention to go to America and try his hand at composing. Her own ambitions aroused, Lilli agrees to marry Tony, and they emigrate to San Francisco. In San Francisco, Tony's old friend, Werner, gets Tony a job playing second violin in his club's orchestra and introduces the couple to Molly, a hat check girl, Tom Hyland, a detective, and Joe Darrow, the owner of a rival nightclub. Darrow, a notorious playboy whose previous romantic involvement resulted in his jilted lover's suicide, becomes infatuated with Lilli and, over Tony's objections, induces her to sing in his club. Lilli soon gives in to Darrow's advances, and an affair quickly progresses. Then one night, Tony, having grown suspicious of Lilli's new jewelry collection, makes an unexpected visit to the club and finds Lilli in Darrow's arms. Enraged with jealousy, Tony assaults Darrow and, because he refuses Hyland's request to implicate Lilli and Darrow in an affair, is sent to San Quentin Prison. While in prison, Tony composes several marches and teaches his fellow inmates to play classical music. Although ridiculed by his mates for his enduring faith in Lilli, Tony dreams of their reunion and savors letters he believes are from Lilli but are actually written by a sympathetic Molly. Later, Tony is scheduled to conduct the prison orchestra before an audience of distinguished musicians, but receives his parole just before the performance. As soon as he is

released, Tony rushes to find Lilli, but discovers that she committed suicide after being cast off by Darrow. Overwhelmed by anger, Tony tracks down Darrow and kills him. Back in prison on a life sentence, Tony falls into a lifeless depression, and the initial efforts of his cellmate Stiles, Molly, Hyland, the warden and Werner to restore his vigor fail. When the prison band begins to perform one of his marches and deliberately plays it badly, however, Tony leaps to the podium and begins to lead the band with joyful abandon. Finally in his element, Tony faces his future, which may include parole and a romance with Molly, with hope. *Composers. Infidelity. Italian Americans. Murder. Revenge. San Quentin Federal Penitentiary (CA). Cafés. Conductors (Music). Depression, Mental. Detectives. Dismissal (Employment). Fights. Hat check girls. Jealousy. Musicians. Nightclub owners. Nightclubs. Parole. Prison life. Prison wardens. San Francisco (CA). Singers. Suicide. Tourists. Vienna (Austria). Violinists.*

Note: The working titles of this film were *Freedom* and *Second Fiddle.* Producer Joseph Schnitzer was a former president of RKO Radio Pictures. *Men Are Such Fools* was the first production of his independent film company, Jefferson Pictures Corp. Second assistant director Samuel Schnitzer was Joseph's son. A *FD* news item adds Dorothy Vernon and Lyle Tayo to the cast, but their participation in the final film has not been confirmed.

FD 13 Aug 1932, p. 8. FD 22 Aug 1932, p. 3. FD 26 Aug 1932, p. 8. FD 9 Sep 1932, p. 6. FD 13 Mar 1933, p. 4. Var 14 Mar 1933, p. 15.

MEN IN HER LIFE (*foreign version*) *see* **HOMBRES EN MI VIDA**

MEN OF THE NORTH (*foreign version*) *see* **MONSIEUR LE FOX**

MEN WHO DARED *see* **THE LAST COMMAND**

THE MENACE *see* **SCARFACE**

MENDEL, INC. *see* **THE HEART OF NEW YORK**

THE MERRY WIDOW (*foreign version*) *see* **LA VEUVE JOYEUSE**

MERRY WIVES OF GOTHAM *see* **LIGHTS OF OLD BROADWAY**

METROPOLITAN MERRY-GO-ROUND *see* **MANHATTAN MERRY-GO-ROUND**

MEXICAN QUARTER *see* **BORDER CAFE**

MEXICAN SPITFIRE (Latino)
RKO Radio Pictures, Inc. *Dist* RKO Radio Pictures, Inc. 12 Jan 1940; Prod: began late Sep 1939 [©RKO Radio Pictures, Inc.; 12 Jan 1940; LP9358]. Sd; b&w. 67 min. PCA cert no. 5781.
Series: The Mexican Spitfire.
Prod Cliff Reid. *Prod exec* Lee Marcus. *Dir* Leslie Goodwins. [*Asst dir* James Anderson]. *Scr* Joseph A. Fields and Charles E. Roberts. *Story* Joseph A. Fields. *Photog* Jack MacKenzie. *Art dir* Van Nest Polglase. *Art dir assoc* Albert D'Agostino. *Ed* Desmond Marquette. *Gowns* Renie. *Mus dir* Paul Sawtell. *Rec* Bailey Fesler.
Cast: LUPE VELEZ [(*Carmelita*)], Leon Errol [(*Uncle Matt Lindsey/ Lord Basil Epping*)], Donald Woods [(*Dennis Lindsay*)], Linda Hayes [(*Elizabeth Price*)], Elisabeth Risdon [(*Aunt Della*)], Cecil Kellaway [(*Chumley*)], Charles Coleman [(*Butler*)].
Comedy. [*Print viewed*]. When Dennis Lindsay returns home from Mexico with his new bride Carmelita, his marriage is met with consternation by his aunt Della and his former sweetheart, Elizabeth Price. Consequently, Aunt Della, who would have preferred Elizabeth and her Plymouth Rock ancestry for a niece, schemes with Elizabeth to break up Dennis's marriage. Dennis has cut short his honeymoon to consumate an important contract with Lord Epping, and when Dennis invites his client to dinner, Elizabeth insists that she would be a better hostess than Carmelita, who Epping thinks is Dennis's secretary. Consequently, she pretends to be Dennis's wife at dinner. To thwart Elizabeth, Carmelita persuades Della's husband Matt to impersonate Lord Basil Epping. Complications arise when the real Epping arrives for dinner, and in the confusion, he is insulted and leaves without signing the contract. Carmelita, feeling responsible for the disaster, decides to leave Dennis and is joined by Uncle Matt, who thinks that he is wanted by the police for false impersonation. The pair seek refuge in Mexico, where they both file for divorce. Matt, still thinking that he is being pursued by the police, dons his Lord Epping disguise and meets Chumley, Epping's associate. Chumley, believing that Matt is Epping, tells him that he must sign the contract. The phony Epping agrees and tells Chumley to turn the signed contract over to Uncle Matt for delivery. Thus, Uncle Matt and Carmelita return to New York with contract in hand. They arrive on

the eve of Dennis' marriage to Elizabeth, and Dennis, meeting Carmelita again, realizes that he still loves her. A telegram from the Mexican police notifies Carmelita that her divorce is invalid, and the next day at Elizabeth's wedding, Carmelita announces that she and Dennis are still married. Carmelita's announcement starts a food fight between the man-stealing Elizabeth and Carmelita. *Contracts. Impersonation and imposture. Marriage. Mexican Americans. Mistaken identity. Romantic rivalry. Aunts. Divorce. Fights. Mexico. New York City. Nobility. Snobs and snobbishness. Uncles. Weddings.*

Note: This picture, inspired by the success of RKO's *The Girl from Mexico,* was the first in the *Mexican Spitfire* series. Including *The Girl from Mexico,* Lupe Velez starred as "Carmelita" and Leon Errol as "Uncle Matt" in eight *Mexican Spitfire* films for RKO, from 1939-1943. In addition to his role as "Uncle Matt", Errol also impersonated a member of British nobility in these films. The last film in the series was 1943 film *Mexican Spitfire's Blessed Event.* For additional information about the series, consult the Series Index. A *HR* production chart lists Ward Bond in the cast, but his participation in the final film has not been confirmed. Modern sources add Lester Dorr to the cast.

DV 7 Dec 1939, p. 3. FD 14 Dec 1939, p. 8. HR 30 Sep 1939, pp. 6-7. HR 7 Dec 1939, p. 3. MPD 12 Dec 1939, p. 5. MPH 16 Dec 1939, p. 25. NYT 10 Jan 1940, p. 16. Var 13 Dec 1939, p. 11.

MEXICAN SPITFIRE AND THE GHOST *see* **MEXICAN SPITFIRE SEES A GHOST**

MEXICAN SPITFIRE AT SEA (Latino)
RKO Radio Pictures, Inc. *Dist* RKO Radio Pictures, Inc. 13 Mar 1942; Prod: mid-Oct—early Nov 1941 [©RKO Radio Pictures, Inc.; 1 Jan 1942; LP11057]. Sd (RCA Sound System); b&w. 6,557 ft. 72 or 76 min. PCA cert no. 7836.
Series: The Mexican Spitfire.
Prod Cliff Reid. [*Exec prod* J. R. McDonough]. *Dir* Leslie Goodwins. [*Asst dir* Bill Dorfman]. *Orig scr* Jerry Cady and Charles E. Roberts. *Dir of photog* Jack MacKenzie. *Art dir* Albert S. D'Agostino and Walter E. Keller. *Ed* Theron Warth. *Gowns* Edward Stevenson. *Mus dir* C. Bakaleinikoff. *Rec* Earl A. Wolcott.
Cast: LUPE VELEZ [(*Carmelita Lindsey*)], LEON ERROL [(*Uncle Matt Lindsey/Lord Basil Epping*)], Charles "Buddy" Rogers [(*Dennis Lindsey*)], ZaSu Pitts [(*Miss Emily Pepper*)], Elisabeth Risdon [(*Aunt Della Lindsey*)], Florence Bates [(*Mrs. Baldwin*)], Marion Martin [(*Fifi*)], Lydia Bilbrook [(*Lady Ada Epping*)], Eddie Dunn [(*George Skinner*)], Harry Holman [(*Joshua Baldwin*)], Marten Lamont [(*Purser*)], [John Maguire (*Ship's officer*)], [Ferris Taylor (*Captain Nelson*)], [Richard Martin, Wayne McCoy (*Stewards*)], [Warren Jackson], Julie Warren (*Maid*)], [Lou Davis (*Ship's waiter*)], [Mary Field (*Elizabeth's maid*)].
Domestic, Comedy. [*Print viewed*]. Dennis Lindsey and his hot-tempered wife Carmelita set sail on a cruise to Hawaii that Carmelia believes is their "delayed" honeymoon. In reality, Dennis and his uncle Matt and aunt Della have booked the cruise in hopes of winning an advertising contract from the social climbing Baldwins. Also on the voyage is Dennis' business riva, George Skinner. To prevent the snobbish Baldwins from signing with Skinner, Dennis has promised to introduce them to Lord and Lady Epping at a party that night. When Carmelita learns of her husband's motive for their trip, she angrily shoves him out of their cabin and into the neighboring cabin of Fifi, an old girlfriend of Dennis'. Mr. Baldwin walks by at that moment, and seeing Dennis in Fifi's room, assumes that she is Mrs. Lindsey and invites her to the party. Aunt Della, who despises Carmelita, thinks that Fifi would make a splendid Mrs. Lindsey and persuades Dennis to continue the deception for business reasons. After berating her husband, a remorseful Carmelita begs uncle Matt to impersonate Lord Epping and induce Dennis to reconcile with her. Meanwhile, Lady Epping has decided to travel incognito, and the real Lord Epping, unable to locate his wife's stateroom, meets Skinner while he is wandering the ship's hallways. To conceal Epping from Dennis, Skinner offers him refuge in his own cabin. As Lord Epping drinks in Skinner's cabin, Dennis is deceived by uncle Matt's impersonation of the Englishman and takes him to meet Mr. and Mrs. Baldwin, who request that he bring Lady Epping to the party that evening. Carmelita, who is unaware that the real Eppings are on the ship, convinces a reluctant Matt to attend the party and recruits Miss Emily Pepper, an amateur playwright and actress, to play the part of Lady Epping. To continue his charade, uncle Matt as Lord Epping insists that Matt Lindsey not be invited to the gathering. Meanwhile, Carmelita, still fuming, meets Skinner and tells him about Dennis' "fake wife." Skinner proposes that she even the score by attending

the Baldwin party as his fiancée. At the soirée that night, Miss Pepper, pretending to be Lady Epping, begins to read her play, but becomes perplexed when the guests start shouting and making faces at her because Matt has told them that she is deaf. When Matt loses his Lord Epping mustache in a cocktail glass, he runs out of the room, and the real Lord Epping then enters. Miss Pepper, thoroughly confused, flees the party, and Lord Epping follows, angry because his friend Matt has not been invited. Carmelita and Skinner then join the group, and Matt, having found his mustache, returns. Meanwhile, Lady Epping, who has read about the party in the ship's bulletin, enters, and Matt denies that she is his wife. To break the streak of bad luck that Mrs. Baldwin sees plaguing her party, she suggests that Carmelita and Skinner wed immediately, and Carmelita agrees after Baldwin offers her the contract as a reward. As Carmelita stalls the ceremony, Matt sets off the ship's rescue alarm, leading the passengers to believe that the ship is sinking. Chaos ensues as everyone runs to their cabins to don lifejackets, but all ends happily on deck when Carmelita presents Dennis with the Baldwin contract. *Contracts. Cruises. Impersonation and imposture. Mistaken identity.* Actors and actresses. Aunts. Business competition. Disguise. Nobility. Parties. Plays. Social climbers. Uncles.

Note: A news item in *HR* notes that the studio cast contract players Rosemary Coleman, Frances Neal, Lee Bonnell, Jane Woodworth, Marten Lamont, Walter Reed, Wayne McCoy, Richard Martin and Linda Rivas in this picture to "test them under fire." The participation of Coleman, Neal, Bonnell, Woodworth, Reed and Rivas in the final film has not been confirmed. Actress ZaSu Pitts also appeared in the previous "Mexican Spitfire" film, *The Mexican Spitfire's Baby* (see below). For additional information about the series, consult the Series Index and see the above entry for the 1939 film *Mexican Spitfire.* 1931-40; F3.2846.

Box 10 Jan 1942. *DV* 6 Jan 1942, p. 3. *FD* 8 Jan 1942, p. 6. *HR* 16 Oct 1941, p. 4. *HR* 17 Oct 1941, p. 17. *HR* 7 Nov 1941, p. 8. *HR* 6 Jan 1942, p. 4. *MPHPD* 10 Jan 1942, p. 450. *NYT* 26 Jun 1942, p. 16. *Var* 7 Jan 1942, p. 45.

MEXICAN SPITFIRE OUT WEST (Latino)

RKO Radio Pictures, Inc. *Dist* RKO Radio Pictures, Inc. 29 Nov 1940; Prod: mid-Jul—13 Aug 1940 [©RKO Radio Pictures, Inc.; 15 Nov 1940; LP10065]. Sd (RCA Sound System); b&w. 8 reels, 6,840 ft. 75-76 min. PCA cert no. 6535.

Series: The Mexican Spitfire.

Prod Cliff Reid. *Exec prod* Lee Marcus. *Dir* Leslie Goodwins. [*Asst dir* Kenneth Holmes]. *Scr* Charles E. Roberts and Jack Townley. *Story* Charles E. Roberts. *Dir of photog* Jack MacKenzie. *Spec eff* Vernon L. Walker. *Art dir* Van Nest Polglase. *Art dir assoc* Albert D'Agostino. *Ed* Desmond Marquette. *Cost* Renié. *Mus score* Roy Webb. *Rec* Richard Van Hessen.

Cast: LUPE VELEZ [(*Carmelita Lindsay*)], LEON ERROL [(*Uncle Matt Lindsay/Lord Basil Epping*)], Donald Woods [(*Dennis Lindsay*)], Elisabeth Risdon [(*Aunt Della*)], Cecil Kellaway [(*Chumley*)], Linda Hayes [(*Elizabeth*)], Lydia Bilbrook [(*Lady Epping*)], Charles Coleman [(*Ponsby*)], Charles Quigley [(*Roberts*)], Eddie Dunn [(*Skinner*)], Grant Withers [(*Withers*)], Tom Kennedy [(*Taxi driver*)], [Gus Schilling (*Desk clerk*)], [Ferris Taylor (*Thorne*)], [Dick Hogan (*Bellhop*)], [Jack Arnold (*Brown*)], [Charles Hall (*Elevator boy*)], [Youda Hays (*Maid*)], [Frank Orth (*Window cleaner*)], [Rafael Storm (*Travel clerk*)], [Rita Owin (*Public stenographer*)], [Teddy Mangean (*Page boy*)], [Lester Dorr (*Harry*)], [Warren Jackson (*Stranger*)], [Carl Freemanson (*Bartender*)], [Sammy Stein (*Cowboy*)], [Paul Everton (*Dignitary*)], [Herta Margot (*Beauty contest winner*)], [John Sheehan (*Janitor*)], [Jan Buckingham (*Secretary*)], [Fred Kelsey, Kernan Cripps (*Cops*)], [Jane Woodworth].

Comedy. [*Print viewed*]. Dennis Lindsay, a busy advertising executive, will go to great lengths and do almost anything to secure a business agreement with English distiller Lord Basil Epping. As soon as Epping arrives in New York, Lindsay foils an attempt by Mr. Skinner, his chief competitor, to approach him, and then takes him to his home for safe keeping. There, he instructs his butler, Ponsby, to hide Epping's suitcase to prevent him from leaving. In order to devote all of his attention to Epping, Lindsay neglects his wife Carmelita, who soon becomes jealous over her husband's attentions to Elizabeth, the woman that his Aunt Della wanted him to marry. Upset, Carmelita goes to Reno to get a divorce, and sends Lindsay a telegram hoping that he will follow her out there to stop her. Meanwhile, when Skinner learns that Epping is at the Lindsays', he tries to call him there. Uncle Matt answers the phone, however, and while impersonating Epping, he tells Skinner that he is a "nuisance" and that he does not wish to do business with him until he gets back from

Reno. Hoping to find Epping in Reno, Skinner leaves for Nevada, while Uncle Matt goes there to save Lindsay's marriage. Back at the Lindsays', Epping manages to escape by getting drunk with a window cleaner and exchanging clothes with him, and then goes to Skinner's office, where he learns that Skinner has left for Reno. In Reno, when Uncle Matt overhears Skinner and Brown talking about Epping, he successfully impersonates the English distiller once again, thereby preventing Skinner from doing business with the real Epping. When Lindsay discovers that Epping has escaped, he and Aunt Della make haste for Reno. Shortly after, Lady Epping, the distiller's wife, who has come from England to join her husband, is told that he is in Reno, and she too heads for Nevada. There, she and all the others become entangled in a complicated web of mistaken identity. Chaos ensues until Lindsay's marriage is saved and Uncle Matt's identity is disclosed. *Business competition. Distillers. Divorce. Impersonation and imposture. Mexican Americans. Mistaken identity. Uncles.* Abduction. Aunts. Butlers. Drunkenness. English. Hotels. Jealousy. Mothers and sons. Neglected wives. Nephews. Nobility. Reno (NV). Window washers.

Note: The working title for this film was *Lord Epping Out West.* Although the picture may not have been originally intended to be a part of the "Mexican Spitfire" series, it followed *Mexican Spitfire* (see above) in the series. Although *HR* production charts list actress Jane Patten in the cast, her appearance in the released film has not been confirmed. According to a Nov 1940 *HR* news item, the favorable audience response to the picture prompted RKO to seek contracts with Lupe Velez and Leon Errol for future "Mexican Spitfire" films. For more information on the series, consult the catalog entry for *Mexican Spitfire* above.

DV 3 Oct 1940, p. 3. *FD* 9 Oct 1940, p. 13. *HR* 8 Jun 1940, p. 4. *HR* 19 Jul 1940, p. 6. *HR* 14 Aug 1940, p. 6. *HR* 3 Oct 1940, p. 4. *HR* 8 Nov 1940, p. 4. *MPD* 7 Oct 1940, p. 8. *MPH* 12 Oct 1940, p. 49. *NYT* 30 Oct 1940, p. 29. *Var* 30 Oct 1940, p. 14.

MEXICAN SPITFIRE SEES A GHOST (Latino)

RKO Radio Pictures, Inc. *Dist* RKO Radio Pictures, Inc. 26 Jun 1942; Prod: 28 Jan—mid-Feb 1941 [©RKO Radio Pictures, Inc.; 28 May 1942; LP11390]. Sd (RCA Sound System); b&w. 6,722 ft. 69-70 min. PCA cert no. 8100.

Series: The Mexican Spitfire.

Prod Cliff Reid. *Dir* Leslie Goodwins. [*Asst dir* Bill Dorfman]. *Orig scr* Charles E. Roberts and Monte Brice. *Dir of photog* Russell Metty. *Art dir* Albert S. D'Agostino and Carroll Clark. *Ed* Theron Warth. *Gowns* Renie. *Mus dir* C. Bakaleinikoff. *Rec* John E. Tribby.

Cast: LUPE VELEZ [(*Carmelita Lindsey*)], LEON ERROL [(*Uncle Matt Lindsey/Lord Basil Epping*)], Charles "Buddy" Rogers [(*Dennis Lindsey*)], Elisabeth Risdon [(*Aunt Della Lindsey*)], Donald MacBride [(*Percy Fitzbadden*)], Minna Gombell [(*Edith Fitzbadden*)], Don Barclay [(*Fingers O'Toole*)], John Maguire [(*Luders*)], Lillian Randolph [(*Hyacinth*)], Mantan Moreland [(*Lightnin'*)], Harry Tyler [(*Bascombe*)], Marten Lamont [(*Harcourt*)], [Jane Woodworth, Julie Warren (*Secretaries*)], [Richard Martin (*Chauffeur*)], [Mary Stuart], [Linda Rivas], [Sally Wadsworth].

Comedy. [*Print viewed*]. When Lord Basil Epping receives a telegram from his old flame, Edith Fitzbadden, notifying him that she and her nervous brother Percy are coming to visit, Epping's business partner, Dennis Lindsey, hopes that Percy will infuse their business with working capital. Epping decides to go hunting rather than meet his guests, however, and instructs Dennis to entertain the Fitzbaddens at his country house. When Dennis' snobby aunt Della warns him to keep his hot-tempered wife Carmelita away from the Fitzbaddens, Dennis takes her advice and drives to the country with Della as his hostess. They are met by Bascombe, the "real estate agent," who informs them that the servants have deserted. In reality, Bascombe is the leader of a band of gangsters who are making nitroglycerin in Lord Epping's basement. After Della calls home to instruct her husband Matt to pick up the Fitzbaddens, Matt and Carmelita pretend to be Epping's servants, Hubble and Maria, and deliver the Fitzbaddens to the country house. Upon discovering that their host is away on a hunting trip, the Fitzbaddens decide to leave until Carmelita convinces Matt to impersonate Lord Epping. Meanwhile, the real Lord Epping returns to New York and decides to join the Fitzbaddens in the country. Back at the country house, Edith flirts with Matt, posing as Epping, while Percy challenges him to a high-stakes poker game. Matt leaves the card table just as the real Epping arrives and takes his place at the table. After Epping excuses himself, Matt, as Epping, returns to the table, and Percy decides to cash in his chips. When the poker stake, which has been stolen by one of the gangsters, is discovered missing, the Fitzbaddens insist upon searching the servants, and Matt quickly hides his Lord Epping hairpiece and reappears as Hubble. After Edith

searches him, Matt discovers that his hairpiece has been stolen by a dog, and he and Carmelita pretend to be cats to lure the dog from its hiding place. Shocked by the servants' caterwauling, Percy and Edith demand to see Lord Epping, so Matt dons his wig. Della watches as Matt disguises himself as Epping, and when the real Epping comes downstairs, she thinks that he is Matt and insults him. Meanwhile, Bascombe, who has been summoned by Edith to investigate the stolen money, appears and sparks an argument between Epping and Percy over Epping's ancestors, and Percy announces that he plans to leave in the morning. That evening, Epping, dressed in his nightshirt, is accosted by Della who, thinking that he is Matt, orders him to take off his "outfit" and accuses him of being crazy. Della's outburst is witnessed by the increasingly incredulous Fitzbaddens. Plotting to scare the visitors from the house, one of the gangsters dresses in armor and clanks through the hallways, driving Carmelita and Matt to visit their spouses' bedrooms and incensing the Fitzbaddens, who still believe that the two are servants. Later, Dennis tells Matt about Epping's argument with Percy, and Matt, posing as Epping, apologizes to Percy and convinces him to sign the business contract. After signing the contract, Percy meets the real Epping, who orders him out of the house. In response, Percy declares that he is leaving before he "blows up," and at that moment, the nitroglycerin in the basement explodes, prompting Matt to observe that Percy is a man of his word. *Gangsters. Impersonation and imposture. Marriage. Mistaken identity. Partnership. Brothers. Contracts. Explosives. Ghosts. Nobility. Poker (Game). Servants. Sisters.*

Note: The working title of this film was *Mexican Spitfire and the Ghost*. A *HR* production chart adds Barbara Moffett to the cast, but her participation in the final film has not been confirmed. This was producer Cliff Reid's final picture for RKO. For additional information about the series, consult the Series Index and see the entry above for the 1939 film *Mexican Spitfire*.

Box 16 May 1942. *FD* 6 May 1942, p. 6. *HR* 29 Jan 1942, p. 3. *HR* 30 Jan 1942, p. 11. *HR* 5 May 1942, p. 6. *MPHPD* 9 May 1942, p. 646. *NYT* 31 Jul 1942, p. 11. *Var* 13 May 1942, p. 8.

THE MEXICAN SPITFIRE'S BABY (Latino)
RKO Radio Pictures, Inc. *Dist* RKO Radio Pictures, Inc. 28 Nov 1941; Prod: 21 May—11 Jun 1941 [©RKO Radio Pictures, Inc.; 24 Sep 1941; LP10773]. Sd (RCA Sound System); b&w. 6257 ft. 69-70 min. PCA cert no. 7417.
Series: The Mexican Spitfire.
Prod Cliff Reid. *Dir* Leslie Goodwins. [*Asst dir* Doran Cox]. *Orig scr* Jerry Cady and Charles E. Roberts. *Dir of photog* Jack MacKenzie. *Art dir* Van Nest Polglase. *Art dir assoc* Carroll Clark. *Ed* Theron Warth. *Gowns* Renie. *Mus dir* C. Bakaleinikoff. *Rec* Corson J. Jowett.
Cast: LUPE VELEZ [(*Carmelita Lindsey*)], LEON ERROL [(*Uncle Matt Lindsey/Lord Basil Epping*)], Charles "Buddy" Rogers [(*Dennis Lindsey*)], ZaSu Pitts [(*Miss Pepper*)], Elisabeth Risdon [(*Aunt Della Lindsey*)], Fritz Feld [(*Lieutenant Pierre Gaston de la Blanc*)], Marion Martin [(*Fifi*)], Lloyd Corrigan [(*Chumley*)], Lydia Bilbrook [(*Lady Ada Epping*)], Jack Arnold [(*Hotel clerk*)], [Tom Kennedy (*Sheriff*)], [Max Wagner (*Bartender*)], [Jane Patten (*Dennis' stenographer*)], [Jack Briggs (*Orchestra leader*)], [Jane Woodworth (*Cashier*)], [Ted O'Shea (*Manager*)], [Jack Grey, Buddy Messinger, Jack Gardner, Jimmy Harrison, Don Kerr (*Reporters*)], [Dick Rush (*Policeman*)], [Chester Tallman (*Photographer*)].
Domestic, Comedy. [*Print viewed*]. When Carmelita Lindsey threatens to divorce her husband Dennis on their first wedding anniversary because of his preoccupation with business, uncle Matt Lindsey decides to reconcile the quarrelling couple by bringing an infant into their lives. Consequently, Matt cables his friend, Lord Basil Epping, to arrange for Dennis and Carmelita to adopt a French war orphan. Lord Epping adopts an orphan from the wrong war, however, and arrives in New York with Fifi, a blonde French bombshell. To keep his new "daughter" secret from Carmelita, Dennis orders Matt to take Fifi out of town, and they hide out at the Bide A While Inn at Lake Cherokee. Soon after, Fifi's fiancée, Lieutenant Pierre Gaston de la Blanc, visits the Lindsey apartment in search of Fifi, leading Aunt Della to think that Carmelita is having an affair with him. After Pierre leaves, Aunt Della hears a radio broadcast from Lake Cherokee announcing that advertising executive Matt Lindsey is dancing with Fifi at the resort, and she insists upon immediately driving to the lake. Meanwhile, at the resort, Miss Pepper, the hotel manager, has become suspicious of Matt and Fifi's relationship and hides under Matt's bed to discover if he is an adulterer. Aunt Della, Carmelita, Dennis and Lord Epping then arrive at the lake, and after accusing Carmelita of

adultery, Della bursts into Matt's room, where she finds Miss Pepper hiding under the bed. At that moment, Matt, who has been fixing a leaky faucet in Fifi's room, returns to his roo, and Della instructs Miss Pepper to call the police. When Della refuses to believe the truth about Fifi, Matt says that she is Lord Epping's fiancée, and Carmelita persuades Matt to pose as Epping and tell Della that he plans to divorce Lady Ada Epping. Lady Epping then arrives at the resort in search of her husband, and is greeted by Della who offers her sympathy. Marital woes abound when Carmelita overhears Fifi call Dennis "daddy," and she demands a divorce. Soon after, Pierre arrives at the hotel looking for Fifi, and Miss Pepper informs him that she has registered with Matt. Pierre declares that he intends to duel Matt for his honor, until he overhears Miss Pepper confide to the desk clerk that Lord Epping is divorcing his wife to marry Fifi. Matt, who has disguised himself as Lord Epping to hide from Pierre, is astonished when the Frenchman challenges him to a duel at dawn and Carmelita chooses knives as his weapon. As dawn approaches, Carmelita calls the sheriff to stop the duel. Before the sheriff can put on his jacket, Miss Pepper, who has observed Matt donning his Lord Epping disguise, phones and announces that Lord Epping is an impostor. The duel begins, and as Matt uses his sword as a bat to fend off Pierre's knives, the sheriff arrives. Miss Pepper then unmasks Matt, but when the real Lord Epping enters the hotel lobby, she faints. *Impersonation and imposture. Infidelity. Mistaken identity. Adoption. Advertising. Divorce. Duels. English. False accusations. French. Hotel managers. Hotels. Marriage. Nobility. Radio broadcasting. Resorts. Sheriffs.*

Note: The working title of this film was *Lord Epping Sees a Ghost*. This was the third in RKO's "Mexican Spitfire" series, which began in 1939 with *Mexican Spitfire*. The series was sometimes referred to as the "Lord Epping" series. For additional information about the series, see the Series Index and consult the above entry for the 1939 film *Mexican Spitfire*.

Box 6 Sep 1941. *DV* 4 Sep 1941. *FD* 4 Sep 1941, p. 4. *HR* 22 May 1941, p. 5. *HR* 11 Jun 1941, p. 4. *HR* 4 Sep 1941, p. 7. *MPH* 6 Sep 1941. *MPHPD* 13 Sep 1941, p. 261. *Var* 10 Sep 1941, p. 16.

MEXICAN SPITFIRE'S BLESSED EVENT (Latino)
RKO Radio Pictures, Inc. *Dist* RKO Radio Pictures, Inc. Jul **1943**; Prod: 24 Mar—14 Apr 1943 [©RKO Radio Pictures, Inc.; 11 Jul 1943; LP12245]. Sd (RCA Sound System); b&w. 62-63 min. PCA cert no. 9273.
Series: The Mexican Spitfire.
Prod Bert Gilroy. *Dir* Leslie Goodwins. *Asst dir* James Casey. *Scr* Charles E. Roberts and Dane Lussier. *Story* Charles E. Roberts. *Dir of photog* Jack MacKenzie. *Art dir* Albert S. D'Agostino and Walter E. Keller. *Ed* Harry Marker. *Set dec* Darrell Silvera and Harley Miller. *Gowns* Renie. *Mus dir* C. Bakaleinikoff. *Rec* Richard Van Hessen.
Cast: LUPE VELEZ [(*Carmelita Lindsey*)], LEON ERROL [(*Uncle Matt Lindsey/Lord Basil Epping*)], Walter Reed [(*Dennis Lindsey*)], Elisabeth Risdon [(*Aunt Della Lindsey*)], Lydia Bilbrook [(*Lady Ada Epping*)], Hugh Beaumont [(*George Sharpe*)], Aileen Carlyle [(*Mrs. Pettibone*)], Alan Carney [(*Bartender*)], Marietta Canty [(*Verbena*)], [Ruth Lee (*Mrs. Walters*)], [Wally Brown (*Desk clerk*)], [Robert Anderson (*Captain Rogers*)], [George Plues (*Driver*)], [Eddie Dew (*Sheriff Walters*)], [George Rogers, Dorothy Rogers, Don Kramer (*Dancers*)], [Billy Edward Reed (*Attendant*)], [Charles Coleman (*Parkins*)], [Eddie Borden (*Messenger boy*)], [June Booth (*Nurse*)], [Anne O'Neal (*Matron at orphanage*)], [Joan Barclay], [Patti Brill], [Margaret Landry], [Margie Stewart], [Barbara Hale], [Rita Corday], [Mary Halsey], [Ann Summers], [Rosemary La Planche].
Comedy. [*Print viewed*]. While on a two-week leave from the Merchant Marine, Dennis Lindsey, accompanied by his uncle Matt Lindsey and Matt's wife Della, visits Lord Basil Epping at his hunting lodge in Canada, where the Lindseys hope to convince Epping to sign an advertising contract with their firm. Their efforts are jeopardized by the arrival of George Sharpe, a business competitor. Epping decides to award the contract to the Lindseys, however, after Dennis receives a telegram from his wife Carmelita notifying him that "his little kitten has become a mama." The message from Carmelita, who is vacationing at a dude ranch in Arizona, refers to their pet ocelot, but Epping misunderstands and announces that Dennis, as a new father, deserves the contract. When Sharpe suggests that Epping see the baby before signing the contract, they all pack up and head for Arizona. After Carmelita shows Matt her "blessed event," Matt realizes that their contract is in jeopardy and stalls for time by reporting that the doctor has ordered that no one can see the baby for twenty-four hours. After Dennis and Aunt Della discover the truth about

Carmelita's blessed event, Della accuses her of ruining her husband's career. Meanwhile, Sharpe questions the hotel doctor about the Lindsey baby, and when the doctor denies any knowledge about the infant, Epping announces that if there is no baby, there is no contract. Plotting to keep Sharpe away from Epping, Carmelita convinces Uncle Matt to pose as Epping and buys him a toupe. In the hotel bar, Carmelita sees Epping and, thinking that he is Matt, begins to flirt with him. When Sharpe leaves Epping's side to get a copy of the contract, Lady Epping comes to escort her husband to lunch and Matt takes his place. Sharpe returns, and when Matt's toupe is blown off his head by a draft from the fan, he quickly dons Sharpe's hat and runs out of the room, announcing that he is sick. The real Epping then enters the bar, and when a befuddled Sharpe questions him about his health, he impatiently proclaims that he wishes Dennis had a baby so that he could award him the contract. This prompts Carmelita to pose as a nurse and borrow the baby of a hotel guest. Carmelita shows "baby Basil" to Epping, who immediately makes the contract out to "Basil Lindsey." Carmelita, delighted, leaves the baby with Epping while she goes to tell Dennis the good news. Meanwhile, the baby's mother has discovered that the nurse is an impostor, and demands that Epping return her child. Epping refuses and takes the baby to Carmelita, who then wheels the baby's carriage back to his mother's room. As Matt and Carmelita scheme to get Epping to change the name on the contract to Dennis Lindsey, Sharpe overhears them and watches as Matt dons his Epping disguise. Sharpe then informs the sheriff, who is the baby's father, that Epping is Matt Lindsey in disguise. When the real Epping enters the lobby, Sharpe kicks him in the pants. After the sheriff begins to question him about the baby, Epping runs out of the lobby and is lassoed by the sheriff and his men. Sharpe urges dunking Epping in the well until he tells the truth, and when Matt appears, a chagrinned Sharpe pulls a soaking Epping out of the well. All ends happily, however, as Epping awards Dennis his contract, the mother finds her baby, the doctor announces that Carmelita is pregnant and Matt pushes Sharpe into the well. *Business competition. Contracts. Impersonation and imposture. Infants. Arizona. Canada. Dude ranches. Lodges. Mistaken identity. Nobility. Physicians. Sheriffs. Telegrams. Uncles. Wigs.*

Note: A *HR* production chart places Erford Gage in the cast, but his participation in the completed film has not been confirmed. The *Var* review incorrectly identifies this film as *Mexican Spitfire's Baby*, the title of a 1941 "Mexican Spitfire" film. This was the eighth and final film in the series. The *HR* review and a news item in *HR* note that the studio announced its intentions to produce a new series based on the "Lord Epping" character, but that series was never made. In *HR* news items, the "Mexican Spitfire" series was occasionally referred to as the "Lord Epping" series. For additional information about the series, consult the Series Index and see the above entry for *Mexican Spitfire*.

Box 17 Jul 1943. DV 15 Jul 1943, p. 3. HR 13 Aug 1942, p. 3. HR 24 Mar 1943, p. 4. HR 26 Mar 1943, p. 10. HR 9 Apr 1943, p. 6. HR 14 Apr 1943, p. 4. HR 15 Jul 1943, p. 3. HR 6 Oct 1943. MPH 17 Jul 1943. MPHPD 3 Jul 1943, p. 1402. MPHPD 17 Jul 1943, p. 1426. Var 21 Jul 1943, p. 22.

MEXICAN SPITFIRE'S ELEPHANT (Latino)

RKO Radio Pictures, Inc. *Dist* RKO Radio Pictures, Inc. 11 Sep **1942**; Prod: Jun 1942 [©RKO Radio Pictures, Inc.; 11 Sep 1942; LP11640]. Sd (RCA Sound System); b&w. 5,736 ft. 63-64 min. PCA cert no. 8508.

Series: The Mexican Spitfire.

Prod Bert Gilroy. *Dir* Leslie Goodwins. *Asst dir* Ruby Rosenberg. *Scr* Charles E. Roberts. *Story* Charles E. Roberts and Leslie Goodwins. *Dir of photog* Jack MacKenzie. *Art dir* Albert S. D'Agostino and Feild M. Gray. *Ed* Harry Marker. *Set dec* Darrell Silvera and Harley Miller. *Gowns* Renie. *Mus dir* C. Bakaleinikoff. *Rec* Roy Meadows.

Cast: LUPE VELEZ [(*Carmelita Lindsey*)], Leon Errol (*Uncle Matt Lindsey/Lord Basil Epping*), Walter Reed [(*Dennis Lindsey*)], Elisabeth Risdon [(*Aunt Della Lindsey*)], Lydia Bilbrook [(*Lady Ada Epping*)], Marion Martin [(*Diana Decaro*)], Lyle Talbot [(*Reddy Madison*)], Luis Alberni [(*Luigi*)], Arnold Kent [(*Alamos*)], [George Cleveland (*Chief inspector*)], [Marten Lamont (*Arnold*)], [Jack Briggs (*Operative*)], [Max Wagner (*Head waiter*)], [Tom Kennedy, Neely Edwards (*Bartenders*)], [Harry Harvey (*Ship steward*)], [Jack Briggs (*Lewis*)], [Lloyd Ingraham (*Doorman*)], [Jack Arnold (*Hotel manager*)], [Don Barclay (*Mr. Smith*)], [Keye Luke (*Magician*)], [Ann Summers, Mary Stuart (*Maids*)], [Don Kerr (*Hotel clerk*)], [Ronnie Rondell (*Emcee*)].

Domestic, Comedy. [*Print viewed*]. To divert the customs agents, diamond runners Diana Decaro and Reddy Madison decide to use Lord Basil Epping, a fellow passenger on their cruise ship, to smuggle a

gem into the country. Pretending to know Epping, Diana presents him with an elephant trinket in which the diamond is hidden. Lord Epping and his wife Ada are traveling to New York to assist in a benefit for Della Lindsey's Women's War Relief organization. Della, who detests her nephew Dennis' wife Carmelita, excludes the hot-tempered Latin from the Eppings' welcoming party. Dennis and Della greet the Eppings at dockside, and when Diana asks Lord Epping to return her elephant, he responds that he has locked it in his trunk. Diana follows them to the Hotel Regal where, to avoid trouble with his wife, Lord Epping introduces her as Dennis' friend. Della's husband Matt and Carmelita are attending a meeting at the hotel, and when Carmelita sees Dennis in the elevator with Diana, she accepts a job dancing at the café Villa Luigi to spite him. The next night, Diana meets Lord Epping at the café and asks him for the elephant. As Reddy Madison then approaches their table and demands the trinket, Carmelita witnesses them threatening Lord Epping convinces Matt to impersonate the lord to discover what Diana and Reddy are plotting. After Epping leaves the table to go to the bar, Matt takes his place, and when Reddy gives him two hours to return the elephant, Matt, taking his threat literally, tells Carmelita to borrow an elephant. Carmelita delivers the elephant to the café, causing a tipsy Lord Epping to think that he is hallucinating. In hopes of reconciling Carmelita and Dennis, Matt convinces Lady Epping to include Luigi's dancers in the charity show. At the club, Carmelita, determined to unravel the mystery of the elephant, instructs Matt to tell Reddy that he has given the trinket to her because he has fallen in love with her. Posing as Epping, Matt meets Reddy and informs him that Carmelita has the elephant. Matt then leaves the table and the real Lord Epping, who has come to audition the dancers, takes his place. Carmelita, thinking that he is Matt, begins to kiss him. Lady Epping and Della then arrive at the café, and when Della spies Matt removing his Lord Epping disguise, she complains to Luigi about him. When Reddy threatens Carmelita, Matt dons a police uniform and chases him away while Della orders the bouncer to eject Epping, who she thinks is Matt. At curbside, Della pushes Epping into a puddle just as Matt and Carmelita walk out the stage door. Lord Epping, furious, refuses to attend the benefit the next evening and Carmelita convinces Matt to impersonate the lord once again. As they walk past the hotel desk, the clerk hands Matt the elephant trinket that the cleaners found in his jacket pocket. At the performance, a mind reader picks Matt as his subject and produces the elephant. After leaving the stage, Matt goes to Carmelita's dressing room, where he finds Reddy and Diana holding her captive. Just as they take the elephant from Matt, the customs agents break in and Reddy slugs Dennis while trying to escape. After the agents seize the smugglers and the diamond, Carmelita takes pity on her injured husband and forgives him. Meanwhile, Matt, still dressed as Lord Epping, chastises Della for her behavior, but when she realizes that he is really her husband in disguise, she chases him into the hotel lobby with an umbrella. There she sees the real Epping and, mistaking him for Matt, whacks him. *Impersonation and imposture. Mistaken identity. Smuggling. Benefit performances. Dancers. Diamonds. Elephants. Hotels. Marriage. Mexican Americans. Mind-reading. New York City. Nightclubs. Nobility. Ships. Socialites. Uncles.*

Note: Cliff Reid replaced Bert Gilroy as the producer of the "Mexican Spitfire" series with this film. A news item in *HR* noted that the picture marked the film debut of Arnold Kent, a former dance teacher at the Arthur Murray studio. For additional information about the series, consult the Series Index and see the entry above for *Mexican Spitfire*.

Box 8 Aug 1942. DV 4 Aug 1942, p. 3. FD 5 Oct 1942, p. 6. HR 12 Jun 1942, p. 7. HR 15 Jun 1942, p. 4. HR 19 Jun 1942, p. 9. HR 4 Aug 1942, p. 4. MPHPD 8 Aug 1942, p. 827. NYT 18 Sep 1942, p. 25. Var 5 Aug 1942, p. 27.

MI HERMANO ES UN GANGSTER *see* **NO MATARÁS**

MI PRIMER AMOR *see* **MIS DOS AMORES**

MI SEGUNDA MUJER *see* **SEÑORA CASADA NECESITA MARIDO**

MI ÚLTIMO AMOR (Spanish language)

Fox Film Corp. *Dist* Fox Film Corp. **1931**; Los Angeles opening: 28 Nov 1931; Prod: Sep 1931. Sd; b&w. 9 reels. Passed by the National Board of Review. Spanish language.

[*Supv* John Stone]. *Dirección de* [*Dir*] Louis Seiler. *Según la adaptación inglesa de* [*From the English adaptation by*] Leon Gordon. [*Spanish translation* José López Rubio].

Song(s): "Song of the Fisher Maidens," "I Love the Last One Best of All (Mi último amor)," "Hold My Hand (Dame tu mano)," "Little

Flower of Love'' and ''Wedding Song,'' music by William Kernell, Spanish lyrics by José Mojica; ''Fiesta Song,'' words and music by José Mojica; ''La cucaracha,'' traditional.

Source: Based on the book *Basquerie* by Eleanor Mercein (New York, 1927).

Cast: José Mojica (*Fernando Urrutia*), Ana María Custodio (*Diana Carter*), Mimi Aguglia (*Betsy*), Andrés de Segurola (*Lord Harry*), Carmen Rodríguez (*Doña Cristina*), Elvira Morla (*Tía Susana*), Nancy Torres (*Lupe*), Robert Cartier (*Juanito*), Paco Moreno (*Criado*).

Romance, Melodrama. [*Not viewed*]. [The following plot summary is based on the English-language version of this film, *Their Mad Moment*; character names refer to that version. For further information regarding the English-language version, please see the note below and the entry for *Their Mad Moment* in the *AFI Catalog of Feature Films, 1931-40*.] American Suzanne Stanley, who is nearly broke, has taken her stepdaughter Emily to Biarritz to look for a wealthy husband. Emily agrees to end a short-lived romance with a Basque boatman, Esteban Cristera, and accept the marriage proposal from a man she does not love, Sir Harry Congers, whom she considers to be sweet, but pompous. Annoyed with Sir Harry, she goes to her hotel room, where Esteban enters through a window. He asks her to be his wife and come to his hacienda in the mountains to meet his grandmother, who is the head of his clan. While Dibbs, Emily's cousin, encourages her to go, Emily confesses that although she loves Esteban, she hasn't the courage to accept him as he is; however, when Suzanne rebukes her for associating with a peasant, Emily resolves to accompany Esteban and, in her words, live her whole lifetime in the next few days before her wedding to Sir Harry. On the mountain roads during a rainstorm, Emily hits her head on the windshield when the car skids. Esteban takes her to an inn, and because there are no women to help, he assists her in removing her soaked clothing. When she learns that a woman in his village, Stancia, is in love with him, she encourages him to stay the night with her, but he leaves the room, saying that he loves her and that he is afraid of himself. At the hacienda, Esteban's grandmother cautions him that Emily is not of their kind, but he reminds her of his own mother, also not of their kind, whom ''Grand Mere'' loved. Grand Mere warns Emily of the hardness of a Basque woman's life, and when Stancia describes this life of work, scrubbing, feeding the men and bearing children, Emily says she envies a woman like Stancia, who welcomes such a life with Esteban. Feeling out of place, Emily sneaks away at night and drives back to Biarritz. Esteben defends her to Grand Mere and Stancia and blames himself for not being satisfied to take romance as he finds it. On the day that her wedding to Sir Harry is to take place, Emily, upset that he vows to teach her to hunt despite her assertion that she does not like to kill, leaves the hotel for one last hour of freedom. Esteban finds her in a park, and when she explains that she believes love to be a luxury she cannot afford, he frightens her with a description of the lonely life of those who live without love. He says he will not let her go, and overcome, she asks him to take her back to the mountains; however, he vows to take her to another place, but will not say anymore, and she agrees to go. Esteban rows her in his boat to a yacht on which they set sail for England. Dibbs, Suzanne and Sir Harry, after watching them through binoculars from the hotel, learn that Esteban made a fortune in America and that he is back in Spain for his usual return to his home for the harvest. As Dibbs, who is tickled by the irony, takes a last look, the happy couple sails away. *Basques. Cultural conflict. Marriage–Forced by circumstances. Romance. Spain. Automobile accidents. Cousins. Finance–Personal. Grandmothers. Harvest festivals. Hotels. Inns. Jealousy. Nobility. Parks. Rainstorms. Snobs and snobbishness. Stepmothers. Yachts and yachting.*

Note: The plot summary was based on a screen continuity in the Twentieth Century-Fox Produced Scripts Collection, while the screen credits were taken from credit sheets in the Twentieth Century-Fox Records of the Legal Department, both of which are at the UCLA Theater Arts Library. Although the screen credits state that the film was ''From the novel *Basquerie* by Eleanor Mercein,'' the book was actually a collection of six short stories, all of which were appeared originally in *The Saturday Evening Post*, beginning with the story ''Basquerie'' in the 3 Jul 1926 issue, and ending with the story ''Nostalgia'' in the 13 Aug 1927 issue. The working title of this Spanish-language version was *Momento loco*, and *NYT* reviewed the Spanish language version in 1933 under the title *Su último amor*. The setting of the Spanish language version was Baja California. It is possible that Paul Perez was involved in the adaptation of the Spanish version, and some sources mention the participation of Eduardo Ugarte in the Spanish adaptation, but this is very unlikely. According to a news

item, Twentieth Century-Fox planned to remake the film in 1941 as a Walter Morosco production, and Harold Buchman and Lee Loeb were to write it, but that film was never made. For information on the English-language version, *Their Mad Moment*, which was directed by Chandler Sprague and starred Dorthy Mackaill and Warner Baxter, please see the entry for that film in the *AFI Catalog of Feature Films, 1931-40*; F3.4546.

NYT 19 Aug 1933, p. 14.

MIDDLE OF THE STREET *see* **RIDE A CROOKED TRAIL**

THE MIDNIGHT ACE (African Americans)
Dunbar Film Corp. *Dist* Dunbar Film Corp. 30 Apr **1928**; Pittsburgh opening: 30 Jul 1928; Prod: 1 Mar—1 Apr 1928 at Warner Bros. studio in Brooklyn, NY. Si; b&w. 7 reels, 6,500 ft.
Supv of prod Swan E. Micheaux, Jr. *Dir* John H. Wade. *Story* Jack Harrison.
Cast: A. B. De Comathiere (*''The Midnight Ace''*), Mabel Kelly, Oscar Roy Dugas, Walter Cornick, Susie Sutton, William Edmonson, Roberta Brown, Bessie Givens, Anthony Gaytzera, Pete Smith, Edward Day, Clarence Penalver.

African American, Crime, Drama. [*Not viewed*]. A young black girl falls in love with a master criminal, believing him to be a good and decent man. The criminal and his gang's many robberies leave the city gripped in terror. After the criminal calls the police to direct them to the sight of the latest robbery, a black detective finds a playing card, the ace of spades, at the scene of the crime. The detective is hopelessly in love with the girl who loves the criminal. After the detective finds another clue leading to the identification of the criminal, he informs the girl that the man she loves is a crook and a philanderer. After the criminal's wife finds a photograph of the girl in her home, she horsewhips her husband, who then beats her and leaves her to die after turning on the gas in their kitchen. The girl saves the wife, and they go to the scene of the next robbery, where the criminal and his gang are apprehended. At the trial, as he is being sentenced, the criminal escapes from the courtroom and makes a break for freedom. The stolen car in which he flees goes over a cliff, however, and carries him to a rocky death. The detective and the girl find love and happiness with each other. *African Americans. Deception. Detectives. Gangs. Infidelity. Philanderers. Robbery. Trials. Attempted murder. Chases. Falls from heights. Gases, Asphyxiating and poisonous. Whips and whippings.*

Note: According to a May 1928 article in *PittsC*, *The Midnight Ace* was the first production of the Dunbar Film Corp., which was located in New York City. Swan E. Micheaux, Jr., who previously had worked for eight years with his brother, noted African-American filmmaker Oscar Micheaux, interested white investors in the formation of the company. While the president of the company, Peter Eckert, and the secretary and treasurer, Bertha Elwald, were white, the director of the film, John H. Wade, was black. Swan Micheaux was responsible for booking, buying and supervising the production. The article noted that the Micheaux brothers were the only African Americans producing films at that time. The film's production cost was $8,000. An unidentified news item in the George P. Johnson Collection at the UCLA Special Collections Library noted: ''While it [the film] was only fair it is a slight improvement on his [Swan Micheaux's] brother Oscar.'' According to a *ChiDef* news story, Swan Micheaux secured the film rights to twelve stories by Jack Harrison, who wrote the story of this film.

ChiDef 31 Mar 1928. *PittsC* 5 May 1928, sec. II, p. 3.

THE MIDNIGHT GIRL (Russian Americans)
Chadwick Pictures Corp. 15 Feb **1925** [©Chadwick Pictures Corp.; 17 Mar 1925; LP21256]. Si; b&w. 7 reels, 6,300 ft.
Dir Wilfred Noy. *Adpt* Wilfred Noy and Jean Conover. *Story* Garrett Fort. *Photog* G. W. Bitzer and Frank Zukor.
Cast: Lila Lee (*Anna*), Gareth Hughes (*Don Harmon*), Dolores Cassinelli (*Nina*), Charlotte Walker (*Mrs. Schuyler*), Bela Lugosi (*Nicholas Schuyler*), Ruby Blaine (*Natalie Schuyler*), John D. Walsh (*Victor*), William Harvey (*Nifty Louis*), Sidney Paxton (*Joe*), Signor N. Salerno (*Manager*).

Melodrama. Anna, a Russian with a beautiful voice, comes to the United States and experiences great difficulty in becoming established as a singer. She meets and falls in love with Don Harmon, orchestra leader and the son of an opera impresario. The elder Harmon's leading singer, a temperamental diva named Nina, is losing her voice, and Harmon dismisses her. Don then gives Anna a job dancing in a production number, ''The Midnight Girl,'' that is part of the floor show at the café where he works. A theatrical agent working for Don's father discovers Anna and arranges for the girl to see him. The elder Harmon makes a pass at her, and she takes a shot at him, inadvertently wounding Nina, who is hiding behind the curtain in

Harmon's study. The accident brings him to his senses, and he is reconciled to his former star. Don marries Anna, and the happy bride becomes a star in the Harmon opera. *Conductors (Music). Dancers. Impresarios. Opera. Russian Americans. Singers.*

FD 12 Jul 1925. *MPW* 28 Mar 1925.

THE MIDNIGHT PATROL (Chinese Americans)

Thomas H Ince, Inc.; A Select Special. *Dist* Select Pictures Corp. Nov **1918** [©Thomas H. Ince; 25 Oct 1918; LP13002]. Si; b&w. 5 reels.

Supv Thomas H. Ince. *Prod* Thomas H. Ince. *Dir* Irvin V. Willat. *Scen* Julien Josephson and Denison Clift. *Cam* Dwight Warren.

Cast: Thurston Hall (*Terence Shannon*), Rosemary Theby (*Patsy O'Connell*), Kino (*Wu Fang*), Charles French (*Jim Murdock*), Marjorie Bennett (*Minnie*), Harold Holland (*Michael O'Shea*), William Musgrave (*"Chink" Ross*), Yamamatto (*Sing Bok*), Harold Johnstone (*Sergt. Joe Duncan*).

Drama. Wu Fang rules the Chinese underworld with the aid of crooked politician Jim Murdock, who shields the criminal from the police in exchange for a share of the profits. When Wu Fang kills Sergt. Joe Duncan, however, Patrolman Terence Shannon decides to conduct a raid. Wu Fang, who is expecting to receive a large shipment of opium, kidnaps Chinatown mission worker Patsy O'Connell and threatens to harm her if the police interfere in the drug smuggling operation. Although Terence is attracted to Patsy, he places duty before his own feelings and goes ahead with the raid but is captured by Wu Fang. Patsy and Terence are about to be thrown into a rat-infested pit when Officer Michael O'Shea and his men arrive, and in the ensuing battle, Wu Fang is killed and Murdock arrested. Chinatown having been made safe, Patsy agrees to be the wife of the new police chief, Terence. *Chinatowns. Chinese Americans. Graft. Opium. Police raids. Smuggling.* Abduction. Criminals. Murder. Police. Political corruption. Rats. Settlement workers.

Note: The working title of this film was *The Dragon's Shadow*.

ETR 2 Nov 1918, p. 1821. *MPN* 15 Feb 1918, p. 1061. *MPN* 22 Feb 1918, p. 1224. *MPW* 7 Dec 1918, p. 1124. *Var* 27 Dec 1918, p. 182.

MIDNIGHT PHANTOM (*foreign version*) see EL CRIMEN DE MEDIA NOCHE

MIDNIGHT SHADOW (African Americans)

George Randol Productions. *Dist* Sack Amusement Enterprises, Inc. **1940.** Sd; b&w. 57 min. PCA cert no. 5479.

Prod George Randol. *Dir* George Randol. *Asst dir* Charles Hawkins. *Photog* Arthur Reed. *Film ed* Robert Jahns. *Mus dir* Johnny Lange and Lew Porter. *Sd eng* Corson Jowett. *Prod mgr* Wilfred Black.

Cast: Frances Redd (*Margaret Wilson*), Buck Woods (*Lightfoot*), Richard Bates (*Jr. Lingley*), Clinton Rosemond (*Mr. [Dan] Wilson*), Jesse Lee Brooks (*Sergeant Ramsey*), Edward Brandon (*Buster [Barnett]*), Ollie Ann Robinson (*Mrs. [Emma] Wilson*), John Criner (*Prince Alihabad*), Pete Webster (*Mr. [John] Mason*), Ruby Dandridge (*Mrs. Lingley*), Napoleon Simpson (*Mr. [Ernest] Lingley*).

African American, Mystery. [*Print viewed*]. Over her mother Emma's objections, Margaret Wilson, an impressionable small-town beauty, encourages the romantic interests of the refined Prince Alihabad and rejects her longtime admirer, the sincere but poor Buster Barnett. Unknown to Margaret, Alihabad is a charlatan from the vaudeville circuit, whose interest in the East Texas oil field that her father Dan has set aside for her wedding present appears to be more than passing. After Dan shows him where the oil land deed is kept, Alihabad asks Margaret to leave with him on an extended overseas trip. While Margaret debates and finally rejects Alihabad's dubious invitation, a man watches her house. Later the man breaks into the Wilsons' home and, after drugging Emma and Dan, steals the deed. Margaret discovers her father dead the next morning and telephones Ernest Lingley, whose bumbling son Jr. is an aspiring private detective. While Jr. and his equally ineffectual partner, Lightfoot, rush to the crime scene, homicide detective Sergeant Ramsey questions Buster, who casts suspicion on Alihabad. Ramsey, who had learned that Dan had contacted an oil developer in Shreveport, Louisiana, about his land, orders his men to locate Alihabad, Jr. and Lightfoot take off for Shreveport. There they inform John Mason, the oil company agent, to expect a man to approach him with the Wilson deed. Mason notifies the local police, while Jr. and Lightfoot cover the train depot. Later that night, the killer shows up at Mason's office,

presents the stolen deed, then demands cash for it at knifepoint. At the same time, Jr. and Lightfoot, having spent the day in fruitless pursuit, return to Mason's office just in time to alert the police and apprehend the killer. The mystery of Dan's death solved, Ramsey then corners Alihabad, who reveals his fakery and loses Margaret to the deserving, faithful Buster. *African Americans. Charlatans. Deeds. Murder. Private detectives. Thieves.* Bumblers. Drugging. Family relationships. Fortune hunters. Impersonation and imposture. Land developers. Oil fields. Partnership. Police detectives. Princes. Romantic rivalry. Shreveport (LA). Small town life.

Note: Although the film's onscreen credits indicate that the film was copyrighted in 1939, it was not registered for copyright. The onscreen foreword of the film includes the following statement: "Here in certain communities, the life of which is found no where else in all the world, these people of darker hue have demonstrated their abilities in self-government by the orderly processes of law of which they are capable when unhampered by outside influences." A modern source states that the picture was filmed at International Studios, Hollywood.

Exb 2 Oct 1940, p. 614.

THE MIDNIGHT STORY (Italian Americans)

Universal-International Pictures Co., Inc. *Dist* Universal Pictures Co., Inc. Aug **1957**; New York opening: 4 Jul 1957; Los Angeles opening: 14 Aug 1957; Prod: mid-Jul—mid-Aug 1956 [©Universal Pictures Co.; 5 Jun 1957; LP8674]. Sd (Westrex Recording System); b&w. 8,048 ft. 87 or 89 min. Passed by the National Board of Review. PCA cert no. 18247.

Prod Robert Arthur. *Dir* Joseph Pevney. *Asst dir* Joseph E. Kenny and [Wilbur Mosier]. [*Dial dir* Leon Charles]. *Scr* John Robinson and Edwin Blum. *Story* Edwin Blum. *Dir of photog* Russell Metty. *Spec photog* Clifford Stine. *Art dir* Alexander Golitzen and Eric Orbom. *Film ed* Ted J. Kent. *Set dec* Russell Gausman and Ray Jeffers. *Gowns* Bill Thomas. *Mus supv* Joseph Gershenson. *Sd* Leslie I. Carey and Frank H. Wilkinson. *Makeup* Bud Westmore. *Hair stylist* Joan St. Oegger and [Merle Reeves]. [*Unit prod mgr* Lewis Leary].

Cast: Tony Curtis (*Joe Martini*), Marisa Pavan (*Anna Malatesta*), Gilbert Roland (*Sylvio Malatesta*), Jay C. Flippen (*Sgt. Jack Gillen*), Argentina Brunetti (*Mama Malatesta*), Ted de Corsia (*Lt. Kilrain*), Richard Monda (*Pietro ["Peanuts"] Malatesta*), Kathleen Freeman (*Rosa Cuneo*), Herbert Vigran (*Charlie Cuneo*), Peggy June Maley (*Veda Pinelli*), John Cliff (*Father Giuseppe*), Russ Conway (*Det. Sergeant Sommers*), Chico Vejar (*Frankie Pellatrini*), Tito Vuolo (*Grocer*), Helen Wallace (*Mother Catherine*), James Hyland (*Frank Wilkins*).

Crime, Drama. [*Print viewed*]. When Father Tomasino, a much-loved priest, is stabbed to death in a dark alley, the Italian-American community of North Beach in San Francisco is stunned. No one is more shocked and angry, however, than traffic officer Joe Martini, a former orphan whom Father Tomasino had guided into adulthood. Explaining that the priest was the closest thing he had to family, Joe asks homicide detective Lt. Kilrain if he may assist with the murder investigation. Kilrain impatiently sends him away, and after Joe reveals that a man named Sylvio Malatesta was enduring "the tortures of the damned" during the funeral, and should therefore be considered a suspect, the lieutenant angrily threatens to fire him. Determined to discover the truth, Joe resigns from the force and visits Sylvio at his waterfront restaurant. Joe introduces himself as a friend of Father Tomasino's and explains that the priest thought Sylvio might be able to give him a job. Sylvio treats Joe kindly and invites him home for dinner, and Joe is touched by the jocularity and affection that fills Sylvio's home. It soon becomes apparent that Sylvio, his mother, and his younger brother "Peanuts" are earnestly seeking a husband for Sylvio's pretty cousin Anna, who recently has come from Italy to live with the family. Sylvio takes a liking to Joe and convinces him to move in with his family. Joe soon finds that he, along with so many others in the neighborhood, is becoming fond of the generous and good-natured Sylvio, although because Sylvio restlessly paces the floor at night, his suspicion lingers. Anna explains that Sylvio lost the woman he loved while fighting in Europe during World War II, and that he has been tormented by this ever since. Soon Joe and Anna fall in love, and when Joe becomes convinced that Sylvio was playing cards at the Vallejo Club on the night of the murder, he forgets his suspicions and proposes to her. During their festive engagement party, Sgt. Jack Gillen, Joe's old friend from the police force, beckons Joe into his car. Gillen and Detective Frank Wilkins warn Joe that Sylvio's alibi was a lie.   On the night of the murder, Sylvio

accompanied his friend, Charlie Cuneo, to the Horizon Club, where Charlie had arranged to meet a married woman named Veda Pinelli for a date. Charlie and Veda then departed, leaving Sylvio alone for the evening. Later that night, Anna demands to know what is gnawing at Joe, but he remains silent. Visiting the orphanage the next day, Anna learns that Joe was once a policeman, but at the station, Gillen refuses to tell her why her fiancé left the force. Upstairs, Joe and Kilrain learn from Veda that Sylvio had been absent from the Horizon Club when Father Tomasino was killed. Joe persuades Kilrain to let him probe Sylvio for a motive before making an arrest. Returning home, Joe seems desperate but refuses to tell the tearful Anna what is wrong. He visits Sylvio at the darkened restaurant and delivers a story intended to test his friend's innocence: The police believe that Joe is the priest's killer. The man who can destroy his alibi is blackmailing him, and he plans to kill him. Sylvio warns Joe not to commit this crime, as it will eat away at him. Sylvio then confesses that because his previous sweetheart had planned to leave him, he killed her. Realizing that Sylvio must have confessed his sin to Father Tomasino, Joe finally accuses Sylvio of the priest's murder. Sylvio admits to killing Father Tomasino, whose gentle, knowing eyes tormented him, but explains that he was only trying to protect his family. Sylvio attacks Joe, but when the young man gasps that he, too, would do anything to protect his family, Sylvio throws down his knife and rushes into the street. A truck hits him, and as he lays dying, Sylvio asks for and receives Joe's forgiveness. Later, Joe tells Gillen and Kilrain that he was unable to confirm that Sylvio was the murderer, and then attempts to console his new family. *Family relationships. Friendship. Guilt. Impersonation and imposture. Murder. Romance. Accidental death. Alibi. Confession (Law). Engagements. Family honor. Infidelity. Investigations. Italian Americans. Neighbors. Orphanages. Parties. Police. Priests. Private detectives. Restaurateurs. San Francisco (CA)–North Beach.*

Note: The working titles of this film were *The Eyes of Father Tomasino* and *Appointment with a Shadow. The Midnight Story* was a working title for a 1955 Universal film, *The Price of Fear,* but the two pictures are unrelated. According to contemporary news items, Mark Stevens Productions purchased the screen rights to Edwin Blum's unproduced script *The Eyes of Father Tomasino* in early Aug 1955 and announced that it would present the drama first on *Lux Video Theatre,* as a kind of preview for the feature production. Buzz Kulik directed Keefe Brasselle in the broadcast, which aired on the NBC television network on 22 Sep 1955. In Mar 1957, Stevens sold the screen rights to Universal. According to information in the film's file at the AMPAS Library, the Academy categorized the script as an adaptation, although the studio had identified it as a screen original. Reviews note that some scenes in the picture were shot in North Beach, the Italian-American section of San Francisco.

Box 22 Jun 1957. *DV* 11 Jun 1957, p. 3. *Exh* 26 Jun 1957, p. 4344. *FD* 24 Jun 1957, p. 8. *Har* 15 Jun 1957, p. 95. *HR* 9 Aug 1955. *HR* 17 Aug 1956. *HR* 8 Jan 1957. *HR* 19 Mar 1957. *HR* 11 Jun 1957, p. 3. *MPHPD* 15 Jun 1957, p. 418. *NYT* 5 Jul 1957, p. 14. *Var* 12 Jun 1957, p. 6.

THE MIGHTY McGURK (English Americans)

Metro-Goldwyn-Mayer Corp.; controlled by Loew's Inc. *Dist* Loew's Inc. Jan 1947; *Prod:* mid-Apr–mid-Jun 1946 [©Loew's Inc.; 10 Oct 1946; LP645]. Sd (Western Electric Sound System); b&w. 9 reels. 85 or 87 min. Passed by the National Board of Review. PCA cert no. 11814.

Prod Nat Perrin. *Dir* John Waters. [*Asst dir* Tom Andre]. *Orig scr* William R. Lipman, Grant Garrett and Harry Clork. *Dir of photog* Charles Schoenbaum. *Art dir* Cedric Gibbons and Hubert Hobson. *Film ed* Ben Lewis. *Set dec* Edwin B. Willis. *Assoc* Alfred E. Spencer. *Cost supv* Irene. *Cost des* Howard Shoup. *Men's cost* Valles. *Mus score* David Snell. *Rec dir* Douglas Shearer. *Makeup created by* Jack Dawn. *Tech adv* Lloyd Doctor.

Song(s): "New York Town," music and lyrics by Jay Gorney.

Cast: WALLACE BEERY (*Roy "Slag" McGurk*), Dean Stockwell (*Nipper*), Edwardu Arnold (*Mike Glenson*), Aline MacMahon (*Mamie Steeple*), Cameron Mitchell (*Johnny Burden*), Dorothy Patrick (*Caroline Glenson*), Aubrey Mather (*Bruno Milbane*), Morris Ankrum (*Fowles*), Clinton Sundberg (*Flexter*), Charles Judels (*First brewer*), Torben Meyer (*Second brewer*), [Stuart Holmes (*Sightseer*)], [Edward Earle (*Martin*)], [Tom Kennedy (*Man at punching machine*)], [John Berkes (*Man at bar*)], [Tom P. Dillon (*Moriarty*)], [George Humbert (*Tony*)], [Al Hill (*Acme agent*)], [Joe Yule (*Irish immigrant*)], [Trevor Tremaine (*Cockney*)], [Lee Phelps (*Cop*)], [Wheaton Chambers (*Customs official*)], [Milton Parsons (*Man at funeral parlor*)], [Joe Devlin (*Dog man*)], [Tom Dugan (*Conductor*)], [Larry McGrath (*Man at table*)], [Celia Travers

(*Secretary*)], [Guy Stockwell (*Kid*)], [Harry Tyler (*Shopkeeper*)], [James Flavin (*Clancy*)], [Del Henderson (*Man at Childrens Society*)], [Jane Green, Rhea Mitchell (*Women at Childrens Society*)], [Vince Barnett (*Tailor*)], [Harry Lamont (*Unshaven derelict*)], [Tom Pilkington, Skeets Noyes, Frank Pharr, Alan Bridge (*Toothless derelicts*)], [Jack Overman (*Bucktooth man*)], [Bing Conley, Al Ferguson (*Hecklers*)], [Bill Wolfe (*Thin man*)], [Pete Cusanelli (*Fat man*)], [Oliver Blake (*Bass drummer*)], [Jimmy Dundee (*Tough*)], [Mitchell Lewis, Robert Emmet O'Connor (*Bartenders z*)], [Ruth Brady, Ernie Adams, Eddie Chandler (*Singers*)], [Sailor Vincent (*Big-nosed derelict*)], [Frank Mayo, Fred Gillman, Lew Smith (*Agents*)], [Mike Tellegen (*Man put out*)], [John Kelly (*Punchdrunk fighter*)], [Dewey Robinson].

Historical, Comedy-drama. [*Print viewed*]. In New York City's Bowery in the early 1900s, former world heavyweight champ Roy "Slag" McGurk wonders why Johnny Burden, the boy he "brought out of the gutter" and trained to be middleweight champion of the world, has turned his back on boxing and joined the Salvation Army. While Slag works at Mike Glenson's saloon bouncing some of the neighborhood's roughest customers, Johnny devotes his life to "saving souls" in the Bowery. Johnny also devotes himself to continuing his romance with Glenson's daughter Caroline, even though her hard-nosed father disapproves of him and the Salvation Army. Glenson rents out part of his building to the Salvation Army, which refuses to move, and sees the organization and Johnny as obstacles to his expansion plans. To prevent Johnny from resuming his romance with Caroline, who is returning to New York from London, Glenson sends Slag to Ellis Island to be the first to greet her. Slag remains loyal to Johnny, however, and tips him off about Caroline's arrival. At Ellis Island, Slag inadvertently becomes the temporary guardian of a young English orphan named Nipper, who has been sent to America to live on Madison Avenue with his wealthy uncle. As the boy has lost his uncle's address, Slag consents to help him find his new home, hoping to collect a generous reward for his efforts. Back in the Bowery, Glenson threatens to expose Slag's false claims as a fighter unless he agrees to incite a riot in front of the Salvation Army. Nipper, meanwhile, has grown fond of Slag and asks to stay with him permanently, but Slag eventually discovers that the boy's uncle is Bruno Milbane, Vice President of Milbane Investment Co., and resolves to deliver the boy to his rightful guardian. Milbane and his associates, Fowles and Flexter, are actually underworld figures who are skipping town and want nothing to do with the boy, so they promise Slag a cash allowance to keep the boy for a time. Slag accepts the offer because he is desperate for money to buy back his fight belt from his old sweetheart, Mamie Steeple, who runs a pawnshop in the Bowery. Later, Johnny tells Slag that he will withhold his recommendation of him to be the boy's guardian to the Childrens Protective Society until he vows to stop drinking and brawling, and until he joins the Salvation Army. Still hoping to profit from keeping Nipper for Milbane, Slag immediately gives up his vices and joins the Salvation Army. When Slag learns that Milbane and his associates are broke and do not want Nipper, he loses interest in the boy and takes him to the Salvation Army. There Nipper tells Mamie that Slag only kept him because he was promised a reward, which angers Mamie and prompts her to upbraid Slag. Slag then has a change of heart and, after confessing to everyone in the saloon that he won the heavyweight championship only after his opponent took a fall, he leads the fight against those attempting to start a riot at the Salvation Army. Slag wins back the respect of those he loves and Johnny recommends him for Nipper's adoption. While Caroline and Johnny resume their romance undisturbed, Slag and Mamie look forward to rearing Nipper together. *Boxers. New York City–Bowery. Orphans. Romance. Saloons. Salvation Army. Wards and guardians. Blackmail. Bouncers. Bribery. Child custody. English. Fathers and daughters. Fistfights. Gangsters. New York City–Ellis Island. Parades. Pawnshops. Regeneration. Riots. Uncles.*

Note: This film marked the last production assignment for screenwriter Nat Perrin.

Box 12 Apr 1947. *DV* 14 Nov 1946, p. 3. *FD* 29 Nov 1946, p. 6. *HR* 26 Apr 1946, p. 18. *HR* 7 Jun 1946, p. 18. *HR* 14 Nov 1946, p. 3. *MPHPD* 29 Jun 1946, p. 3066. *MPHPD* 23 Nov 1946, p. 3321. *NYT* 4 Apr 1947, p. 19. *Var* 20 Nov 1946, p. 22.

EL MILAGRO DE LA CALLE MAYOR *see* **MIRACLE ON MAIN STREET**

THE MILLION DOLLAR MYSTERY (Russian Americans)
Thanhouser Film Corp. *Dist* State Rights; Randolph Film Corp. through Arrow Film Corp. Jun **1918**. Si; b&w. 6 reels.

Dir Howell Hansell. *Scen* Lloyd Lonergan. *Story* Harold MacGrath. *Cam* George Webber. *Loc* Daniel Keleher.

Cast: Sidney Bracey (*John Hargreaves/The butler*), Marguerite Snow (*Countess Olga*), Florence La Badie (*Florence Hargreaves*), James Cruze (*Jim Norton*), Mitchell Lewis (*Gang leader*), Frank Farrington (*Braine*), Lila Chester (*Susan*), Irving Cummings.

Mystery. In his youth, John Hargreaves joins the Black Hundred, a Russian secret service organization, but later he abandons the group, moves to the United States, and earns a fortune. To protect his little daughter Florence, he places her in a boarding school but sends for her when she reaches the age of seventeen. When Hargreaves learns that several Black Hundred agents are after him, he withdraws a million dollars from various banks and prepares to flee. The Russian agents, led by Countess Olga, decide to secure the money, and to this end, they kidnap and threaten Florence. In the end, however, she is saved by newspaper reporter Jim Norton, who helps to round up the gang and reunites Florence with her father. *Fathers and daughters. Immigrants. Kidnapping. Russia. Secret Service. Russian Americans. Boarding schools. Nobility. Reporters. Rescues.*

Note: Originally released as a 23-chapter serial in 1914 and 1915, the picture was edited, and re-issued with new titles by the Randolph Film Corp. as a state rights feature in 1918. Some of the 23 episodes were copyrighted in 1914. One review credited Philip Lonergan rather than Lloyd Lonergan with the scenario. The film was remade in 1927 by Trem Carr Productions with James Kirkwood starring and Charles J. Hung directing. (See *AFI Catalog of Feature Films, 1921-30*; F2.3622.).

ETR 8 Jun 1918, p. 51. *MPN* 8 Jun 1918, p. 3455. *MPW* 11 May 1918, p. 880. *MPW* 8 Jun 1918, pp. 1473-74. *MPW* 29 Jun 1918, p. 1895.

THE MILLIONAIRE (African Americans)
Micheaux Film Corp. **1927**; Philadelphia showing: 28 Nov 1927 [©Oscar Micheaux; 15 Feb 1928; LU24983]. Si; b&w. 7 reels.

Prod Oscar Micheaux. *Dir* Oscar Micheaux. *Wrt* Oscar Micheaux.

Cast: Grace Smith (*Celia Wellington*), Lionel Monagas (*Pelham*), J. Lawrence Criner, Cleo Desmond, William Edmonson, Vera Bracker, S. T. Jacks, E. G. Tatum, Robert S. Abbott, Mrs. Robert S. Abbott.

Melodrama, African American. Pelham Guitry, a black soldier of fortune, goes to Argentina, where, after fifteen years of hard work, he makes his fortune. Returning to New York, he meets Celia Wellington, a woman controlled by the underworld, and she tries to trap him into marriage. Pelham defeats the forces of crime and reforms the girl, who learns to take pleasure in her beauty and especially in her talents. *African Americans. Argentina. Criminals–Rehabilitation. Millionaires. New York City. Soldiers of fortune. South America.*

Note: According to a review and information in the George P. Johnson Collection at the UCLA Special Collections Library, this film was produced in Chicago. Robert S. Abbott, the editor and publisher of the African-American newspaper *ChiDef*, and his wife played roles in the film.

ChiDef 26 Nov 1927, p. 6.

MILLIONAIRES (Jewish Americans)
Warner Bros. Pictures, Inc. *Dist* Warner Bros. Pictures, Inc. 13 Nov **1926** [©Warner Bros. Pictures, Inc.; 3 Nov 1926; LP23289]. Si; b&w. 7 reels, 6,903 ft.

Dir Herman C. Raymaker. *Asst dir* Ted Stevens. *Scr* Raymond L. Schrock. *Adpt* Edward Clark and Graham Baker. *Cam* Byron Haskins. *Asst cam* Frank Kesson.

Source: Based on the novel *The Inevitable Millionaires* by Edward Phillips Oppenheim (Boston, 1925).

Cast: George Sidney (*Meyer Rubens*), Louise Fazenda (*Reba*), Vera Gordon (*Esther Rubens*), Nat Carr (*Maurice*), Helene Costello (*Ida*), Arthur Lubin (*Lew*), Jane Winton (*Lottie*), Otto Hoffman (*Detective*), William Strauss (*Helper in Meyer's tailor shop*).

Comedy-drama. Meyer Rubens, a poor Jewish tailor on New York's East Side, is constantly reproached by his wife, Esther, whose sister, Reba, has made a wealthy marriage. Reba's unscrupulous husband, Maurice, persuades Meyer to buy some apparently worthless oil stock that reaps a fortune. With great wealth at their command, Meyer and Esther move to Fifth Avenue and live in luxury; Meyer, however, finds himself in constant difficulty because of his ignorance of social

graces. At Reba's suggestion, Esther decides to get a divorce. Maurice employs Lottie to flirt with Meyer and create a case against him, but his plan fails. Ida, who is in love with Meyer's son, Lew, informs Esther that Meyer is actually adored by the society set, while she herself is merely tolerated. As a result she returns to Meyer, and Lew and Ida are happily married. *Family life. Jews. Millionaires. New York City–East Side. New York City–Fifth Avenue. Nouveaux riches. Tailors. Upper classes. Wealth.*

FD 14 Nov 1926. *MPW* 20 Nov 1926. *Var* 4 May 1927, p. 24.

MIN AND BILL (*foreign version*) *see* **LA FRUTA AMARGA**

MIN JOK JAY HUNG SING (Chinese language)
Grandview Motion Picture Co. *Dist* Grandview Motion Picture Co. **1941**. Sd; b&w. 4,451 ft. min. Chinese language.

Supv Joseph Sunn. *Dir* Tong Hill Dong. *Photog* John B. Law. *Sd* Dai Jin Lo. *Production* Harry Jue.

Cast: Jung Ying (*Lui Pan*), Bill Fung (*Clan Dai*), Chan Tien Chung (*Hor Bak Hung*), Look Suit Far (*Mrs. Hor*), Wong Anug (*Ah Ying*), Ng Wui (*Lo Eng*), Fun Fong (*Hor Sheung*), Ko Lo Chuen (*Captain Tong*), Tso Dak Wah (*Duck*).

War, **Drama**. [*Not viewed*]. During the Japanese invasion of China, a group of refugees travel by foot to Hong Kong and carry with them their worldly possessions. Once in Hong Kong, Hor Bak Hung, a wealthy man, and his wife reunite with their son. Hor explains to his son the hardships the family endured on the road, but the son is only interested in acquiring some of his father's money. Later, Mrs. Hor catches her son trying to seduce Ah Ying, a poor young Chinese woman who has been hired as a servant. Although Mrs. Hor knows that Ying is innocent, she fires her. While looking for a job, Ying meets three young men from the refugee group, who invite her to move into their humble household, where the walls are covered with nationalist epithets and slogans. They all pool their meager resources, and when one of the members wishes to give up, Lui Pan, the scholar of the group, says that they must fight like Sun Yat Sun, the founder of a Chinese republic. Lui takes odd jobs as a laborer and gives street-corner lectures to his fellow refugees about the current situation in China as well as the country's heroic past. One day, when Hor, the owner of the building at which Lui gives his lectures on nationalist revolution, tries to force Lui to stop speaking, the crowd turns on the wealthy man with fury. Sang, a young man who had carried Hor's luggage during the flight to Hong Kong, is especially incensed. Hor treats Sang rudely, but Lui makes Sang's acquaintance and gains another disciple for his cause. One day, as Sang, a hotel bellhop, is at work, he notices Hor meeting with a businessman named Captain Tong. The two men have benefitted from the war, and Sang discovers evidence of their plan to sell the enemy the rare and valuable tungsten ore that is needed for bombers and weapons. Sang tells Lui of the treacherous plan and it is decided that one of the members of the group, Tai, will go to the commander of the guerilla forces in China and inform him of the plot. Meanwhile, Hor, owner of the Far East Knitting Factory where Ying has found a job, slashes the employees' pay by twenty percent in order to pay for a lavishly expensive wedding celebration for his spoiled son. The employees, including Ying, who has learned much from Lui about workers' rights, go on strike. Sometime later, Lui gathers together a group of discontents outside the building where the Hor wedding is taking place. He then reads a newspaper article implicating Hor in the sale of tungsten ore to the enemy and stating that Tong has already been executed for his crimes against China. Shortly thereafter, a servant at the wedding announces the scandal, and the bride loudly expresses her disapproval of her new father-in-law. Just as Hor manages to get his agitated guests to relax, he receives a phone call informing him of the strike at his factory. The strike representatives demand their old salary, money for board, and the assurance that Hor will not use enemy materials, and Hor is forced to capitulate to their demands. When Tai returns from China, he brings news of the guerilla commander's lack of pretension and the new sense of brotherly love that is sweeping the invaded country. He tells the group that every man in China is being educated and has learned to grow his own vegetables. Heeding the call of their nation, the small group of refugees decide to return to their country with the knowledge that if China's four-hundred and fifty million people unite, they will never again lose their freedom. *Chinese. Hong Kong. Nationalism. Sino-Japanese Conflict, 1937-1945. Traitors. War refugees. Bellboys.*

Businessmen. Communal living. Education. Employer-employee relations. Factory workers. Family relationships. Guerrilla warfare. Laborers. Ne'er-do-wells. Poverty. Servants. Speeches. Strikes and lockouts. Weddings.

Note: The above credits and plot summary were taken from a translated dialogue continuity deposited with the NYSA. The Mandarin transliteration of the Chinese-language title is *Min Tsu Teb Ho Sheng*, and the Cantonese transliteration is *Man Tso Teb How Sin*. The English-language translation of the was *Roar of the Nation*. The film included at least one song, but titles and composers could not be verified. Exact release date information was not found; the film was submitted to the New York Censor Board on 28 Jul 1943.

Chinese Times (San Francisco) 22 Dec 1941, p. 3.

THE MINE WITH THE IRON DOOR (Native Americans)
Sol Lesser Productions. *Dist* Principal Pictures. 2 Oct **1924**. Si; b&w. 8 reels, 6,180 ft.

Dir Sam Wood. *Scen* Arthur Statter and Mary Alice Scully. *Adpt* Hope Loring and Louis D. Lighton. *Photog* Glen MacWilliams.

Source: Based on the novel *The Mine With the Iron Door* by Harold Bell Wright (New York, 1923).

Cast: Pat O'Malley (*Hugh Edwards*), Dorothy Mackaill (*Marta*), Raymond Hatton (*Bill Jansen*), Charlie Murray (*Thad Grove*), Bert Woodruff (*Bob Hill*), Mitchell Lewis (*Sonora Jack*), Creighton Hale (*Dr. James Burton*), Mary Carr (*Mother Burton*), William Collier, Jr. (*Chico*), Robert Frazer (*Natachee*), Clarence Burton (*Sheriff*).

Western. Bob Hill and Thad Grove, two prospectors, find a small child in the desert cabin of bandit Sonora Jack. The little girl, Marta, who has been kidnapped by Jack, is taken by the men, who vainly attempt to find her parents. Marta grows to womanhood and falls in love with Hugh Edwards, a young fugitive from justice. Edwards saves Natachee, an educated Indian, from the depredations of a bandit gang, and in return the grateful Indian shows Edwards the location of the "mine with the iron door," a hidden and extremely rich gold mine. Sonora Jack returns and kidnaps Marta, offering to exchange her for knowledge of the location of the "mine with the iron door." Edwards and Natachee go after the bandit and kill him while saving Marta. Edwards is proved to be innocent of the charge of embezzlement placed against him, and he and Marta are married. *Bandits. Fugitives. Gold mines. Indians of North America. Injustice. Kidnapping. Prospectors.*

FD 21 Dec 1924. *Var* 29 Oct 1924, p. 30.

MINSTREL MAN (Racial impersonation)
PRC Productions, Inc. *Dist* Producers Releasing Corp. 1 Aug **1944**; New York opening: week of 15 Jul 1944; Prod: 31 Jan–14 Feb 1944, 16 Mar–late Apr 1944 [©Producers Releasing Corp.; 30 Jun 1944; LP428]. Sd (Western Electric Mirrophonic Recording); b&w. 5,996 ft. 67 or 69 min.

Prod Leon Fromkess. *Assoc prod* Harry Revel. *Dir* Joseph H. Lewis and [Wallace Fox]. *Asst dir* Don Verk. *Scr* Irwin R. Franklyn and Pierre Gendron. *Orig story* Martin Mooney and Raymond L. Schrock. *Dir of photog* Marcel Le Picard. *Art dir* Paul Palmentola. [*Prod des* Edgar Ulmer]. *Film ed* Carl Pierson. *Set dresser* Glen P. Thompson. *Master of prop* Charles Stevens. *Ward* James H. Wade. *Mus arr* Ferde Grofe. *Mus dir* Leo Erdody. *Dance dir* Johnny Boyle. *Sd eng* Wm. H. Lynch. [*Prod mgr* C. A. Beute].

Song(s): "Cindy," "Remember Me to Carolina," "I Don't Care If the World Knows About It," "Shaking Hands with the Sun" and "My Bamboo Cane," music by Harry Revel, lyrics by Paul Webster; "My Melancholy Baby," words and music by George A. Norton and Ernie Burnett.

Cast: BENNY FIELDS (*Dixie Boy Johnson* [*later known as Jack Carter*), GLADYS GEORGE (*May White*), Alan Dinehart (*Lew Dunn*), Roscoe Karns ([*Lee*] *"Lasses" White*), Judy Clark (*Dixie Girl Johnson* [*Caroline at age 15*]), Jerome Cowan (*Bill Evans*), Molly Lamont (*Caroline Johnson*), John Raitt (*John Raitt*), Lee "Lasses" White, Eddie Kane [(*Booking agent*)], The Anestos, [Gloria Petroff (*Caroline at age 5*)].

Show business, Drama, with songs. [*Print viewed*]. Over the years, minstrel singer Dixie Boy Johnson has risen from the boards of vaudeville to the lights of Broadway. On the night that Dixie is to open in his own show, *Minstrel Man*, his beloved wife Caroline goes into labor with their first child. Dixie's producer, Lew Dunn, insists that Dixie go on with the show rather than comfort his wife at the hospital, and when Dixie steps off the stage, he learns that Caroline died shortly after giving birth to a baby girl. Shattered by his loss,

Dixie abruptly closes the show, entrusts his daughter, whom he has named Caroline, to his friends, May and Lasses White, and travels to Europe. Five years later, Dixie returns to New York and is warmly welcomed back by his audience. When he goes to reclaim his daughter, however, May castigates him for abandoning the girl and informs him that Caroline believes that she and Lasses are her parents. Remorseful over his neglect of Caroline, Dixie determines to leave the city and asks his agent, Bill Evans, to find him an out-of-town booking. Dixie travels to Havana, but one night, when he is asked to sing the song he wrote for his wife, he breaks into tears and runs offstage. Deciding that it is time to return home, Dixie books passage on a steamer bound for New York. When the ship sinks, Dixie is listed among the casualties. Blaming herself for Dixie's death, May finally tells Caroline the truth about her parentage. When Dixie reads the report of his death in the paper, he resolves to disappear and assumes the name Jack Carter. Years later, Caroline celebrates her fifteenth birthday with a party and invites Lew to the event, hoping to convince him to produce a minstrel show on Broadway. Impressed by Caroline's prodigious talent, Lew decides to revive *Minstrel Man* with Caroline starring as "Dixie Girl Johnson." Dixie, meanwhile, is playing the piano and singing for tips in a shabby San Francisco nightclub. One night, Bill, who has been searching for Dixie, appears at the club to tell him about the revival of *Minstrel Man*. Hungry for a percentage, Bill reminds Dixie that he still owns the show and urges him to return to New York and seize ownership of the production from Lew. Dixie arrives in New York just as the show has completed rehearsals and begins to have doubts about creating problems for the production. On opening night, Dixie is standing backstage when Caroline, wearing blackface, asks him to help hook up her dress. After Caroline takes the stage, May notices Dixie and asks his forgiveness. As Caroline sings the song that her father made famous, Dixie changes his mind about stopping the show and shakes hands with Lew. When May and Lew insist that he stay for the end of the performance, Dixie applies his blackface and joins Caroline onstage for the finale. *Entertainers. Fathers and daughters. Minstrel shows. New York City–Broadway. Parentage. Widowers. Adolescents. Birthdays. Conscience. Grief. Havana (Cuba). Missing persons, Assumed dead. Nightclubs. San Francisco (CA). Shipwrecks. Songs. Theatrical agents. Theatrical producers.*

Note: *HR* news items yield the following information about this production: Veteran minstrel comic Lee "Lasses" White was hired to assist in the making of the film, as well as appear in it. The production was shut down for over a month when director Wallace Fox and actress Gerra Young, who originally portrayed the role of the teenage "Caroline" became ill. In mid-Feb 1944, Young contracted chicken pox, thus delaying the shooting for several weeks. In early Mar, when the Board of Health refused to allow Young to perform any dance scenes because it felt the exertion might cause her to have a relapse, the studio replaced her with Judy Clark. At that time, all the musical scoring had to be scrapped because it had been pitched to Young's voice. As a result of the delay and necessary re-shooting, the insurance firm Lloyd's of London was forced to pay PRC $150,000 in losses incurred from Young's illness. The insurance company then refused to insure anyone under the age of eighteen. When production began again in mid-Mar 1944, Joseph H. Lewis took over direction from Fox, who had fallen ill with the flu. Binnie Barnes, who had been cast as "May White", had to leave the film because the production delays conflicted with her previous commitments. Although a 28 Jan *HR* production chart lists William Frawley in the cast, he does not appear in the released print. That production chart also credits Jackson Rose with photography, but the extent of his contribution to the released film has not been determined. Although a *HR* news item announced that Chuy Reyes and his band were to appear in the film, their participation in the released film has not been confirmed. In a letter written by producer Leon Fromkess in 1969, the producer stated that director Edgar Ulmer began principal photography on the film, but after four or five days of production, the direction was turned over to Lewis. Ulmer then was assigned to direct the stage sequences, according to Fromkess.

Box 24 Jun 1944. *DV* 14 Jun 1944, p. 12. *FD* 21 Jun 1944, p. 12. *HR* 8 Nov 1943, pp. 6-8. *HR* 27 Dec 1943, p. 6. *HR* 28 Jan 1944, p. 14. *HR* 31 Jan 1944, p. 17. *HR* 2 Mar 1944, p. 2. *HR* 8 Mar 1944, p. 4. *HR* 31 Mar 1944, p. 3. *HR* 14 Jun 1944, p. 3. *HR* 26 Jun 1944, p. 7. *HR* 24 Jul 1944, p. 6. *MPHPD* 1 Jul 1944, p. 1970. *NYT* 17 Jul 1944, p. 18. *Var* 19 Jul 1944, p. 13.

MIO FIGLO *see* **CUORE D'EMIGRANTE**

IL MIO PASSATO *see* **AMOR IN MONTAGNA**

MIRACLE IN HARLEM (African Americans)
Herald Pictures, Inc. *Dist* Screen Guild Productions, Inc. 29 Nov **1948**; World premiere in New York: 6 Aug 1948; Prod: began 18 Sep 1947 at Filmcraft Studios, NY [©Herald Pictures, Inc.; 28 May 1948; LP192]. Sd; sepia. 6,401 ft. 69-70 or 72 min. PCA cert no. 04434.

Prod Jack Goldberg. *Dir* Jack Kemp. *Dial dir* James Light. *Orig story and scr* Vincent Valentini. *Dir of photog* Don Malkames. *Art dir* Frank Namezy. *Ed* Don Drucker. *Ward* Ann Blazier. *Mus supv* John Gluskin. *Mus dir* Jack Shaindlin. *Sd eng* Nelson Minnerly. *Creator of makeup* Dr. Rudolph G. Liszt. *Tech adv* J. M. Lehrfeld.

Song(s): "I Want to Be Loved (But Only By You)," words and music by Savannah Churchill; "Patience and Fortitude," words and music by Blackie Warren and Billy Moore Jr.; "Swing Low, Sweet Chariot," spiritual; "John Saw the Number," "Chocolate Candy Blues" and "Watch Out," composers undetermined.

Cast: Hilda Offley (*Aunt Hattie*), Sheila Guyse (*Julie Weston*), Kenneth Freeman (*Jim Marshall*), William Greaves (*Bert Hallam*), Sybyl Lewis (*Alice Adams*), Creighton Thompson (*Reverend Jackson*), Lawrence Criner (*Albert Marshall*), Jack Carter (*Phillip Manley*), Milton Williams (*Wilkinson*), Monte Hawley (*Lt. Renard*), Ruble Blakey, Alfred Chester (*Detectives*), *Specialties*: Savannah Churchill ([*Performer of*] *"I Want to Be Loved"*), Lavada Carter ([*Performer of*] *"John Saw the Number"*), Norma Shepherd ([*Performer of*] *"Patience and Fortitude"*), Juanita Hall ([*Performer of*] *"Chocolate Candy Blues"*), Lynn Proctor Trio ([*Performers of*] *"Watch Out"*), The Juanita Hall Choir, and Stepin Fetchit.

African American, Mystery, with songs. [*Print viewed*]. Aunt Hattie, a deeply religious, elderly black woman who operates a candy factory from her kitchen in Harlem, eagerly awaits the arrival of Bert Hallam, her adopted son, who is returning from the Army to study for the ministry. Bert is in love with Julie Weston, Hattie's niece, who will soon be taking over control of the candy factory. At the same time, Lt. Renard of the police homicide bureau begins a search for Phillip Manley, a confidence artist who is wanted for murder and is known to have been involved in a Chicago check swindling operation with Jim Marshall, the ne'er-do-well son of candy manufacturer Albert Marshall. During a police interview, Albert informs detectives that he sent his son to Chicago to study chemistry, and that his son was not interested in the candy business. Back at Hattie's home, the old woman tells Bert and Julie that she has had a premonition of her impending death and begins rehearsing for her funeral. When Jim makes an unexpected visit to his father's office, Albert cuts off his money supply and tells him that his reckless living is the result of his mother's death. To spite his father, Jim vows to work for Albert's rival candy company and make them a better business competitor by modernizing their equipment. Albert likes the idea, though, and instead of opposing his son, decides to use his idea to swindle Hattie out of her business. Acting anonymously through an employee named Wilkinson, Albert convinces Hattie to sign her company over to him by pledging to upgrade and expand her factory. Julie and Hattie fall for Albert's trick, but when Jim accuses her father of stealing her idea, Albert puts him in charge of Hattie's factory. Jim and Julie soon fall in love, and one day, Bert catches Jim making a pass at her. A short time later, however, Jim rejects Julie's romantic overtures and tells her that Albert is actually the owner of Hattie's factory. Bert punches Jim when he catches him trying to coerce Julie into yielding to his affections. When Albert double-crosses Wilkinson, Wilkinson sends him a box of poisoned chocolates. Albert eats the chocolate and dies, after which Julie is arrested on suspicion of murder. Julie proclaims her innocence and tells police that Alice, Albert's secretary, and Jim had better motives to kill Albert. Julie is released by the police, but when she returns home, Jim tries to kill her. During the struggle, a mysterious man enters the darkened room and kills Jim. Julie is arrested again and placed in a police line-up. A break in the case finally comes when Bert recalls Jim's association with Manley. A trap is then set for Manley, and he is arrested following a full confession of his crimes, which includes the killing of Jim. After Alice confesses that she murdered Albert, she attempts suicide but is stopped and later is sent to die in the electric chair. With the racketeering operation exposed, Julie and Bert resume their romance, and Hattie decides to give up her obsession with her impending death. *African Americans. Business competition. Candy. Fathers and sons. Murder. Racketeers. Aged women. Attempted suicide. Blackmail. Confession (Law). Death and dying. Electric chair. Fistfights. Foster children. Ne'er-do-wells. New York City–Harlem. Nieces. Poisoning. Revenge. Reverends. Romance. Swindlers and swindling. Traps.*

Note: Unidentified contemporary news items in the George P. Johnson Collection at UCLA note that *Miracle in Harlem* was filmed at twenty locations in New York City's Harlem, and that some filming took place at Filmcraft Studios in the Bronx.

Box 14 Aug 1948. *FD* 11 Aug 1948, p. 5. *HR* 22 Oct 1947, p. 7. *MPD* 13 Aug 1948. *MPHPD* 14 Aug 1948, p. 4274. *NYT* 24 Oct 1949, p. 19. *Var* 11 Aug 1948, p. 8.

THE MIRACLE MAKERS (Chinese Americans)

Leah Baird Productions. *Dist* Associated Exhibitors, Inc. 14 Oct 1923 [©Associated Exhibitors, Inc.; 9 Nov 1923; LU19582]. Si; b&w. 6 reels, 5,834 ft.

Dir W. S. Van Dyke. *Story* Leah Baird. *Photog* André Barlatier.

Cast: Leah Baird (*Doris Mansfield*), George Walsh (*Fred Norton*), Edith Yorke (*Mrs. Emma Norton*), George Nichols (*Capt. Joe Mansfield*), Edythe Chapman (*Mrs. Martha Mansfield*), Richard Headrick (*The Boy*), Mitchell Lewis (*Bill Bruce*).

Melodrama. Bill Bruce, smuggler of Chinese laborers into the country, captures Doris Mansfield and forces her to marry him. Later, he is apprehended and sent to prison, but Doris, who was engaged to air coast patrolman Fred Norton before her marriage, does not explain her situation to her fiancé. He, thinking she no longer loves him, signs up for duty in France. Years later, Bruce, released from prison, seeks out his wife, who has had a child, and tries to make amends, but he falls into a well and suffers a fatal injury. Fred Norton, who has returned from France, marries Doris. *Chinese Americans. Immigrants. Marriage. Smuggling. United States. Coast Guard. World War I.*

MPW 22 Dec 1923.

THE MIRACLE OF LIFE see OUR DAILY BREAD

THE MIRACLE OF THE BELLS (Polish Americans)

Jesse L. Lasky Productions, Inc. *Dist* RKO Radio Pictures, Inc. 27 Mar **1948**; World premiere in New York: 16 Mar 1948; Prod: 14 Jul—late Sep 1947 [©Jesse L. Lasky Productions, Inc.; 16 Mar 1948; LP1605]. Sd (RCA Sound System); b&w. 10,781 ft. 118 or 120 min. PCA cert no. 12607.

Prod Jesse L. Lasky and Walter MacEwen. *Dir* Irving Pichel. *Asst dir* Harry D'Arcy. *Scr* Ben Hecht and Quentin Reynolds. [*Contr to scr constr and spec seq* DeWitt Bodeen]. *Dir of photog* Robert de Grasse. [*Cam op* Charles Burke]. [*Stills* Rod Tolmie]. *Spec eff* Russell A. Cully and Clifford Stine. *Art dir* Albert S. D'Agostino and Ralph Berger. *Film ed* Elmo Williams. *Set dec* Darrell Silvera and Harley Miller. *Ward* Renié. *Mus dir* C. Bakaleinikoff. *Mus* Leigh Harline. [*Dance dir* Charles O'Curran]. *Sd* Philip N. Mitchell and Clem Portman. *Church bell eff* Liberty Carillons. *Makeup supv* Gordon Bau. [*Makeup* Karl H. Herlinger, Jr.]. [*Hair stylist* Annabelle Levy]. [*Casting dir* Eddie Ryan]. [*Prod mgr* Fred Fleck]. [*Scr supv* J. Davies]. [*Grip* Ralph Wildman].

Song(s): "Ever Homeward," music and lyrics by Jule Styne and Sammy Cahn, adapted from the Polish folk song "Powrot," music and lyrics by Kasimierz Lubomirski; "The Miracle of the Bells," music by Pierre Norman, lyrics by Russell Janney.

Source: Based on the novel *The Miracle of the Bells* by Russell Janney (Garden City, NY, 1946).

Cast: Fred MacMurray (*Bill Dunnigan*), Valli by arrangement with David O. Selznick (*Olga* [*Treskovna, previously known as Olga Trocki*]), Frank Sinatra (*Father Paul*), Lee Cobb (*Marcus Harris*), Harold Vermilyea ([*Nick*] *Orloff*), Charles Meredith (*Father* [*J.*] *Spinsky*), Jim Nolan (*Tod Jones*), Veronica Pataky (*Anna Klovna*), Philip Ahn (*Ming Gow*), Frank Ferguson ([*Mike*] *Dolan*), Frank Wilcox (*Dr. Jennings*), [Quentin Reynolds (*Radio announcer*)], [Ray Teal (*Koslick*)], [Dorothy Sebastian (*Katie*)], [Billy Wayne (*Tom Elmore*)], [Syd Saylor (*Freddy Evans*)], [Thayer Roberts (*Earl of Warwick in Joan of Arc*)], [Franz Roehn (*Cauchon in Joan of Arc*)], [Herbert Evans (*Nobleman in Joan of Arc*)], [Pat Davis, Jack Gargan (*Assistant directors*)], [Ned Davenport, Charles Miller (*Priests*)], [Robert Bacon, Duncan MacDonell, Roger Creed, Jim Pierce (*Soldiers*)], [George Cathrey, Roy Darmour, Bill Wallace, Mel Wixon, Peter Erickson, Hamilton Warren, Mike Sandler, Bob Thom (*Reporters*)], [Tom Stevenson (*Milton Wild*)], [Michael Raffetto (*Harold Tanby*)], [Ian Wolfe (*Grave digger*)], [Dorothy Neumann (*Miss Milkhouser*)], [Al Eben, Ken Terrell, Jerry Jerome, Al Murphy, David Perry, Jack Stoney, Alonzo Price, David McMahon, Ralph Stein (*Miners*)], [Maxwell Hamilton (*Ray Tanner*)], [Charles Wagenheim (*Kummer*)], [Bert Davidson (*Bob Briggs*)], [Oliver Blake (*Slenzka*)], [George Chandler (*Max*)], [Max Wagner (*Baggage man*)], [Perry Ivans (*Druggist*)], [Jack Lindquist (*Boy*)], [Richard Mickelsen, Bill Clauson (*Bellringer's sons*)], [Frank Pharr (*Bellringer*)], [Franklyn Farnum, Snub Pollard, Beth Taylor (*Worshippers*)], [Brooks Benedict, Maxine Johnston (*Drunken couple*)], [Eula Guy], [Fred Grahame], [Bertha Ledbetter], [Will Van Vleck], [Art Dupuis], [Sam Lufkin], [Bob

Robinson], [Sedal Bennett], [Phil Solomon], [Lynne Terrell], [Ray Toones], [Jean Ransome], [Ted Deputy], [Albert Pollet], [Paul Lacy], [Arthur Flavin], [Sid D'Albrook], [Edward Peil, Sr.], [Clarence Hennecke], [Donald Kerr], [Bobby Barber], [Lyle Tayo], [Patsy O'Byrne], [Dorothy Dell], [Mary Henderson], [Arlene Bletcher], [Mary Scheue], [Lillian Clayes], [Maude Hume], [Jean Spangler], [Frank Beauregard], [Budd Fine], [Mable Colcord], [Regina Wallace].

Drama. [*Print viewed*]. As soon as Hollywood press agent Bill Dunnigan returns the body of his dear friend, actress Olga Treskovna, to her home in Coaltown, Pennsylvania, he is barraged with money demands from local funeral director Nick Orloff. While driving with Orloff to the funeral parlor, Bill remembers his first meeting with the young Polish beauty: Olga is about to be fired from the chorus line of a burlesque show when Bill, a theater publicist who has been observing the rehearsal, convinces the show's choreographer to give her another chance. Although Bill is deeply attracted to Olga, he leaves without seeing her perform. Back in Coaltown, Bill tries to locate friends of Olga's dead, alcoholic father to act as pallbearers for her funeral but, as the greedy Orloff had predicted, the only men who accept the job demand two dollars for their efforts. Disgusted, Bill begins to reminisce about his reunion with the kindhearted Olga: On a snowy Christmas Eve, while waiting for a train in a small town, Bill discovers that Olga is acting in a cheap touring show. Bill and Olga are delighted to see each other after a year's separation and dine together at a Chinese restaurant. There, the sagacious owner, Ming Gow, treats the couple to a feast and suggests that their reunion was predestined. Afterward, Olga, who is plagued by a hacking cough, points out the star that her father "gave" her as a child and offers Bill half of it. Bill is touched by the gift, but says goodbye to Olga once more and returns to the East. Coming out of his reverie, Bill goes to see Father Paul, the priest at Coaltown's impoverished St. Michael's church, where Olga had asked to be buried. Bill is impressed by Father Paul's generous, warm nature, and after arranging for Olga's funeral, he tells the priest about Olga's days in Hollywood: As a press agent for movie producer Marcus Harris, Bill once again runs into Olga after the temperamental star of Harris' latest epic, *Joan of Arc*, is fired. Olga has been working as the star's stand-in and when she sees Bill on the set, she invites him to dinner in her one-room apartment. During the evening, Bill gets the idea to cast Olga as "Joan" and has her perform a scene from the movie for him. Impressed, Bill then convinces Harris to test her for the role, and she easily wins the part. Olga soon becomes the talk of Hollywood, but while she is filming *Joan of Arc*, her cough grows worse. Concerned about her health, Bill goes to see her doctor and learns that, as a result of being exposed to coal dust as a child, she has developed tuberculosis and will die without immediate treatment. Despite Bill's warnings, Olga insists on finishing the last, dramatic scene of the picture. Her performance is inspired, but when she dies a day after filming is completed, Harris decides to shelve the project rather than release the film with a dead, unknown star. After relating this story to Father Paul, Bill is suddenly inspired with an idea for a publicity stunt. Writing a series of bad checks, Bill pays every church in Coaltown to ring their bells for three days and nights in honor of Olga's passing. He then wires Harris and, assuring him that he has found a way to release *Joan of Arc*, asks him to send $10,000. After the bells begin to ring, reporters appear in Coaltown, and to convince them of his sincerity, Bill relates Olga's dying moments: On her deathbed, Olga tells Bill that she was driven to become a movie star as a way of fulfilling the lost dreams of the poor people of Coaltown. Sure that her appearance in *Joan of Arc* will bring hope to her hometown, Olga declares her "job" done and dies. The reporters are moved by Bill's words and print Olga's story in newspapers across the country. Despite the instant publicity, the skeptical Harris still refuses to release *Joan of Arc*, fearing that Olga's notoriety will be short-lived. At the same time, the owner of the biggest mine in Coaltown is threatening to silence the bells, and Father J. Spinsky, of the well-to-do St. Leo's church, is threatening to arrest Bill for writing bad checks unless he agrees to hold Olga's funeral in his parish. Although Harris wires Bill enough money to cover his debts, he insists on re-shooting *Joan of Arc* with another star. Thus defeated, Bill wanders into St. Michael's church, which is packed with worshippers anxious to see the now-famous Olga. Suddenly, two large religious statues begin to turn on the altar until they are facing Olga's casket. Bill rushes to see Father Paul, who has already deduced that the

statues moved because the weight of the crowd caused the pillars on which the statues were mounted to shift slightly. Although Father Paul is reluctant to describe the movement as a miracle, Bill convinces him to tell the people of Coaltown that divine intervention played some part in the event. The statues' turning is picked up by the press, and after listening to a radio report about its effect on Coaltown, Harris flies to the town and announces that he is releasing *Joan of Arc*. He also offers to build a hospital in Olga's name, which would be dedicated to finding a cure for the lung disease that killed the star. As Bill says a final farewell to his beloved Olga, reborn worshippers flood the streets of Coaltown. *Ambition. Faith. Funerals. Miracles. Motion picture actors and actresses. Press agents. Small town life. Bells. Catholic Church. Chinese Americans. Chinese restaurants. Chorus girls. Christmas Eve. Churches. Coal miners. Dismissal (Employment). Greed. Joan, of Arc, Saint, 1412-1431. Lungs–Diseases. Motion picture producers. Pennsylvania. Physicians. Polish Americans. Poverty. Priests. Publicity stunts. Statues. Tuberculosis.*

Note: The opening credits of the film read: "Jesse L. Lasky Productions, Inc. presents *Russell Janney's The Miracle of the Bells*." Contemporary news items add the following information about the production: Lasky and co-producer Walter MacEwen purchased Janney's novel in Oct 1946 for $100,000 plus five percent of the producers' gross up to the first $4,000,000. After $4,000,000, Janney was to receive ten percent of the producers' gross, with no maximum limit set. Four other parties negotiated for the book's screen rights, including William Cagney, who wanted the property as a vehicle for his brother, James Cagney. At that time, Lasky and MacEwen reportedly made James Cagney a "percentage offer" to play the part of "Bill Dunnigan." Janney was announced as the picture's screenwriter at that time. Clark Gable and Cary Grant were also considered for the lead male role. Many actresses were considered for the part of "Olga," including Barbara Bel Geddes, Ingrid Bergman, Jennifer Jones, Joan Fontaine and Greer Garson. In 1946, Bergman appeared as "Joan of Arc" in the Maxwell Anderson stage play *Joan of Lorraine*. (Ironically, shortly after the release of this film, RKO distributed *Joan of Arc*, Walter Wanger's screen adaptation of Anderson's play, starring Bergman.) Lasky and MacEwen also considered casting an unknown actress in the part and tested Jana Garth, who also had played "Joan of Arc" on stage, and Ricky Soma, an eighteen-year-old New York ballerina. Maxwell Hamilton, who plays a reporter in the picture, was the editor of *Motion Picture* magazine.

In Feb 1947, John Cromwell was announced as the film's director, but he was replaced by Irving Pichel. Lasky borrowed Pichel from Paramount for the production. Lasky and MacEwen considered doing the picture in Technicolor, but eventually concluded that the story would "work better" in black and white. A reproduction of a Pennsylvania mining town was built at RKO's Forty Acres ranch in Culver City. *HR* announced in Jun 1947 that a featurette about the making of the film was to be shot and used in movie theaters to advertise the multi-million dollar production. Although the national release of the film coincided with Easter week of 1948, *HR* announced in Oct 1947 that the film was to be shown in Los Angeles in Dec 1947 in order to qualify for the 1947 Academy Awards. The picture did not receive any Academy Award nominations, however.

In Mar 1948, *NYT* reported a rumor that the actual contribution of radio personality Quentin Reynolds, who is credited onscreen with Ben Hecht as a screenwriter, was "reading the novel and reporting its contents to Mr. Hecht, the latter having taken the assignment of writing the screenplay on the provision that he didn't have to read the book." According to *NYHT*, Hecht, a declared Anglophobe, had his name removed from British release prints of the film. In Aug 1948, Raymond Polniaszek, an undertaker from Glen Lyon, Pennsylvania, sued RKO for $500,000 in damages on the grounds that he had been caricatured as "Nick Orloff" in the film, according to a *DN* article. Polniaszek claimed that he participated in a number of real-life events that were depicted in both the novel and the film, including the burial of a woman named Olga Trotski. The disposition of that suit has not been discovered.

Modern sources add the following information about the production: Before casting Frank Sinatra in the role of "Father Paul," Lasky sought approval from the Catholic Church, which voiced no objections to the performer. Sinatra, who had actively sought the part, then announced his intention to donate his acting salary to the Church. Sinatra's scenes were written by DeWitt Bodeen. Reviewers commented on Sinatra's simple, *a capella* rendition of the song "Ever Homeward."

Box 6 Mar 1948. *DN* 11 Aug 1948. *DV* 2 Mar 1948, p. 3. *FD* 2 Mar 1948, p. 7. *HR* 31 Oct 1946. *HR* 6 Dec 1946, p. 1. *HR* 8 Jan 1947, p. 12. *HR* 9 Jan 1947, p. 13. *HR* 6 Feb 1947, p. 1. *HR* 26 Mar 1947, p. 3. *HR* 23 Apr 1947, p. 4. *HR* 29 May 1947, p. 3. *HR* 10 Jun 1947, p. 10. *HR* 16 Jun 1947, p. 9. *HR* 17 Jun 1947, p. 13. *HR* 14 Jul 1947, p. 11. *HR* 17 Jul 1947, p. 3. *HR* 20 Aug 1947, p. 2. *HR* 28 Aug 1947, p. 10. *HR* 4 Sep 1947, p. 12. *HR* 19 Sep 1947, p. 13. *HR* 2 Mar 1948, p. 3. *HR* 19 Mar 1948, p. 8, 10. *LAT* 21 Oct 1946. *MPHPD* 28 Feb 1948, p. 4079. *MPHPD* 6 Mar 1948, p. 4085. *NYHT* 16 Sep 1948. *NYT* 17 Mar 1948, p. 30. *NYT* 21 Mar 1948. *Var* 3 Mar 1948, p. 8.

MIRACLE ON MAIN STREET (Latino, Spanish language)
Arcadia Pictures Corp. *Dist* Columbia Pictures Corp. 29 Oct **1939**; *Prod:* 17 Apr—May 1939 at Grand National Studios [©Columbia Pictures Corp.; 27 Oct 1939; LP9207]. Sd (Western Electric Mirrophonic Recording); b&w. 9 reels. 78 min. PCA cert no. 5437.
Prod Jack Skirball. *Dir* Steven Sekely. *Asst dir* Gordon Griffith. *Scr* Frederick Jackson. *Orig story* Samuel Ornitz and Boris Ingster.

Photog Charles Van Enger. *Art dir* Ralph Berger. *Ed* Barney Rogan. *Set dresser* Glenn P. Thompson. *Cost* Irene Saltern. *Mus dir* Hans J. Salter. *Orig mus* Walter Jurmann. *Sd* Buddy Myers. *Prod mgr* Fred Scheld.

Song(s): "City of Angels" and "Lullabye," music and lyrics by Walter Jurmann and Ralph Freed.

Cast: Margo (*Maria [Porter]*), Walter Abel (*Jim [Foreman]*), William Collier, Sr. (*Doctor [Miles]*), Jane Darwell (*Mrs. Herman*), Lyle Talbot (*Dick [Porter]*), Wynne Gibson (*Sade [Blake]*), Veda Ann Borg (*Flo*), Pat Flaherty (*Detective*), George Humbert (*Pepito*), Jeanne Kelly (*Nina*), Susan Miller (*Singer*), Willie Best (*Duke*), Dorothy Devore (*Woman in church*), Ottola Nesmith (*Welfare worker*), [Jean Louise Grandpre, Jackie Taylor, Larry Augustine, James Clemons, Jr. (*Babies*)].

Melodrama. [*Print viewed*]. Maria Porter, a striptease dancer in a carnival side show in the Mexican quarter of Los Angeles, is unhappily married to Dick, a carnival barker with a criminal nature. Attempting to drum up business on Christmas Eve, the pair try to rob an undercover policeman disguised as a lecherous drunk, and when the officer announces that they are under arrest, they flee. Maria joins a crowd entering a church, where she finds an abandoned infant in the Christ child's manger. As a disguise, she picks up the baby and carries it to her boardinghouse. To avoid the police, Dick leaves Maria to fend for herself and disappears. The deserted Maria is helped by Dr. Miles and her landlady, Mrs. Herman, and soon finds herself unable to part with the infant. To support herself, Maria takes a job sewing so that she can stay home with the baby, but she is unable to earn enough money to pay her bills. When Mrs. Herman urges her to return to dancing, Maria goes to Pepito's nightclub to ask for work. At the club, Jim Foreman, a lonely, recently divorced rancher, overhears Maria imploring Pepito for a job and, taking pity on her, invites her for a drink. Their drink initiates a courtship, and Maria, with Jim's support, becomes a fashion designer. Jim falls in love with Maria, but his proposal of marriage puts her into a quandary about revealing her sordid past. Just as she is about to confess all to Jim, Dick returns and offers to get out of his wife's life for a price. To prevent Dick from extorting money from Jim, Maria pretends that she still loves the man who caused her such anguish. In revenge, Dick tells the welfare department that Maria is an unfit mother. All ends happily, however, when Dick is killed in an attempted robbery, and Jim returns to take care of Maria and the baby. *Adoption. Carnivals. Criminals-Rehabilitation. Dancers. Infants. Mexican Americans. Child custody. Christmas. Churches. Couturiers. Extortion. Fiestas. Landladies. Los Angeles (CA). Nightclubs. Physicians. Ranchers. Revenge. Seamstresses. Welfare workers.*

Note: According to materials contained in the Production Files at the AMPAS Library, this picture was made in 1939 under the Arcadia Production banner as a possible Grand National release. After the demise of Grand National, it was picked up by Columbia. Twentieth Century-Fox released the Spanish language version, which was filmed simultaneously with the English language version. The Spanish version was entitled *Quiso ser madre* when it was shown in Santiago, Chile on 26 Dec 1939. Some sources also credit Luis Alberni as a cast member in the Spanish-language version, but his participation has not been confirmed. A news item in *HR* adds that Maurice Moscovitch was set to take over William Collier's role, but Collier remained in the picture. This picture was Hungarian director Steven Sekely's first American film. According to the pressbook in the copyright materials, scenes of the film were shot in the Mexican quarter of Los Angeles, including Olvera street, using Hispanic players in bit and extra roles; some scenes of a Mexican fiesta and Christmas procession were included.

Other language version(s):
El milagro de la Calle Mayor (Spanish language)
1940; Buenos Aires opening: 8 Sep 1939; Los Angeles opening: 23 Dec 1940; Prod: Apr—May 1939 at Grand National Studios. Sd; b&w. 9 reels, 7,537 ft. 84 min. Spanish language.
Prod Jack H. Skirball. *Dir* Steven Sekely. *Asst dir* Gordon Griffith. *Dial dir* N. A. Cuyás. *Scr* Frederick Jackson. *Orig story* Samuel Ornitz and Boris Ingster. *Spanish dial* Enrique Uhthoff. *Literary supv* Miguel de Zárraga. *Photog* Charles Van Enger. *Film ed* Barney Rogan. *Prod mgr* Fred Scheld. *Cost* Irene Saltern.
Song(s): "En tu boca una flor," "Canción de cuna," "Berceuse" and "Luego, luego me voy," words and music by Walter Jurmann, Ralph Freed and Cesar Miró.
Margo (*María*), Arturo de Córdova (*Carlos*), José Crespo (*Dick*), Pilar Arcos (*Doña Nicolasa*), Carlos Villarías (*El médico*), Tana (*Sade*), José Luis Tortosa (*McNeil*), Robina Duarte (*Nina*), Romualdo

Tirado (*Pepito*), Juan Duval (*Bartender*), Carmela Peña (*Welfare worker*), Carmen de Miró (*Woman in church*), Adelina García (*Singer*), Cesar Miró, Lorenzo Félix, José Nieto (*Members of trio*), Carmen Mora (*Flo*). [*Spanish version not viewed*].

CM Sep 1939, p. 435. *FD* 2 Jan 1940, p. 10. *HR* 9 Feb 1939, p. 7. *HR* 11 Apr 1939, p. 4. *HR* 14 Mar 1940, p. 3. *HR* 13 Apr 1939, p. 20 *HR* 14 Apr 1939, p. 2. *HR* 20 Apr 1939, p. 4.

MIRELE EFROS (Yiddish language)
Credo Pictures, Inc.; A Josef Berne Production. *Dist* Credo Pictures, Inc. 19 Oct **1939**. Sd (Variray Blue Seal Recording); b&w. 8 reels, 7,810 ft. 87 or 90 min. Passed by the National Board of Review. Yiddish language with English subtitles.
Prod Roman Rebush. *Dir* Josef Berne. *Asst dir* Louis Brandt. *Scr* Ossip Dymow and Josef Berne. *English titles* Julian Leigh. *Photog* J. Burgi Contner. *Art dir* Sam Corso. *Ed* Leslie Vidor. *Costumes for Miss Gersten* Madam Anna Kay. *Orig mus* Vladimir Heifetz. *Sd eng* Edward Schabbehar. *Tech adv* Jacob Mestel. *Prod mgr* George Moskov. *Special asst* Lewis Jacobs.
Source: Based on the play *Mirele Efros* by Jacob Gordin (1898).
Cast: BERTA GERSTEN [(*Mirele Efros*)], Michael Rosenberg (*Nuchumtze Chana-Dvoire's*), Ruth Elbaum (*Shaindel*), Albert Lipton (*Yosel*), Sarah Krohner (*Chana-Dvoire*), Moishe Feder (*Shalmon*), Louis Brandt (*Donya*), Paula Walter (*Machle*), Jerry Rosenberg (*Shloimele*), Ella Brouner (*Dina*), Rubin Wendroff (*The Badchen*), Jacob Mestel (*Pogorelsky*), Moishe Schorr (*Coachman*), Eugene Sigaloff (*Peasant*), Clara Deutchman (*Barwoman*).

Yiddish, Domestic, Melodrama. [*Print viewed*]. In 1899, in Grodno, a region in Poland, Mirele Efros, a wealthy widow who has built a flax business from scratch, is one of the most respected persons. When her son Yosel is about to marry Shaindel, who is from a poor but good family of the town of Slutsk, Mirele travels to meet the bride's family. Mirele is offended by the demand of Shaindel's pushy mother Chana-Dvoire that Mirele give them money for a fancy wedding before the ceremony. Mirele orders her bookkeeper Shalmon to pack and return to Grodno, but she later relents, and the wedding proceeds. Sometime later, Shaindel demands that Yosel be given his share of his inheritance from his father. Mirele then relates that when her husband died sixteen years earlier, she turned down offers to marry again so that she could rear her two children and share their joys. No one but Shalmon knew that her husband died bankrupt, owing 60,000 rubles. Through hard work, Mirele paid the debts and made the fortune that she now controls. She says, however, that if it will make her son and daughter-in-law happy, they can take control of the business. Despite Shalmon's objections, Mirele signs away all her wealth and property. After Shalmon is let go, Shaindel's father Nuchumtze replaces him as manager. Nuchumtze is sent to buy flax, but because he waits to receive a rabbi's blessing before the purchase, the flax rots in the rain. The Polish peasants from whom he agreed to buy the flax insist that he pay them, and when he returns and reports the incident, the family castigates him for losing 4,000 rubles. Meanwhile, Shalmon brings two men, who represent a committee that plans to build a hospital, to Mirele, who now spends her time making preserves and feeding ducks. The men complain that her family will not honor her previous commitment to renew contracts with them. Seeing her shame, Shalmon offers the committee 5,000 rubles, which he falsely says was lent to him by Mirele years earlier to buy a house. After the men leave, Mirele calls the family together and demands money to repay Shalmon and, when they refuse, pleads with them to loan it to her. When Shaindel, to whom Yosel has signed over the property, refuses entreaties from both Mirele and Yosel, Mirele leaves the home she came to twenty-five years earlier and goes to Shalmon to ask for work. Shalmon confesses that since his wife died, he has come to think of Mirele as more than an employer, but Mirele's shocked silence causes him to abandon his romantic entreaty. Shalmon suggests that they become partners, but as she does not want to compete with Shaindel, she agrees only to keep his books. As time passes, Shalmon's business increases, and the money Mirele makes goes to the hospital, while Shaindel's tyrannical nature causes her business to lose money each year. When Yosel and Shaindel's child Shloimele has his *bar mitzvah*, or confirmation, Mirele gives Yosel a watch for the boy, but refuses to come to the ceremony. After a fight between Yosel and Shaindel, she visits Mirele and tells her that she provoked the split in the family because she wanted Yosel to break loose from Mirele. Because their marriage is in danger, she now begs

Mirele to return, but Mirele pridefully refuses. Shloimele then tells Mirele that he had to fight boys in the street because the story has spread that his grandmother had been kicked out of the house. When Mirele still refuses to return, Shloimele gives back the watch, calls her a "bad grandma" and leaves. At the *bar mitzvah*, Mirele appears in the doorway. The family gathers around her as she sits in her chair. She tells them that whether they are good children or bad children, they are children after all and grasps their hands. *Daughters-in-law. Family life. Jews. Poles. Pride and vanity. Women in business. Bar mitzvah. Bookkeepers. Class distinction. Family honor. Flax. Grandsons. Hospitals. Mothers and sons. Poland.*

Note: The screen credits began with the words "Commemorating the thirtieth anniversary of the death of the celebrated Jewish playwright Jacob Gordin" appearing over a statue of Gordin. A modern source states that the play most likely has been the most widely performed Yiddish play. The screen credits called the film "A New Version by Ossip Dymow." Ruth Elbaum's screen credit states that she is appearing "by courtesy of *Pins and Needles*," a Broadway play in which she was acting. According to news items, Roman Rebush organized Credo Pictures, Inc. and planned this film as the first of four Jewish films. This, however, was the only film produced by that company. This film was re-issued in 1949. An earlier film version of the play was made in 1912 in Poland.
Daily News 8 Mar 1949. *FD* 1 Nov 1939, p. 7. *HR* 10 Aug 1939, p. 10. *MPD* 15 Jun 1939. *MPH* 4 Nov 1939. *NYT* 21 Oct 1939, p. 12. *New York World Telegram* 1 Sep 1939. *Var* 25 Oct 1939, p. 23.

MIS DOS AMORES (Spanish language)

Cobian Productions, Inc. *Dist* Paramount Pictures, Inc. **1938**; New York preview: 11 Aug 1938; San Juan, Puerto Rico opening: 4 Oct 1938; Los Angeles opening: 9 May 1939; Prod: began Jun 1938 at the General Service Studios. Sd; b&w. 8 reels. 75 or 80 min. PCA cert no. 4465. Spanish language.

Prod Rafael Ramos Cobián. *Assoc prod* Lester P. Sussman. *Dir* Nick Grindé. *Scr* Milton Raison. *Orig story* José Antonio Miranda. *Spanish dial* Miguel de Zárraga and Miguel de Zárraga, Jr. *Photog* Arthur Martinelli. *Art dir* Ralph Berger. *Ed* Martin G. Cohn. *Cost* William Bridgehouse. *Mus dir* Ernesto González Jiménez. *Makeup supv* Max Factor.

Song(s): "Madre," "Ouiubo ouiubo?" "Jalando jalando," "Mis dos amores," "Tú nada más para mí" and "Mi primer amor," music by Tito Guízar, lyrics by Nenette Noriega; "Rosas y mujeres" and "Vuélveme a besar," music and lyrics by Leopoldo González.

Cast: Tito Guízar (*Julio Bertolin*), Blanca de Castejón (*Rita Santiago*), Emilia Leovalli (*Mercedes Bertolin*), Romualdo Tirado (*Rafael Bertolin*), Juan Torena (*District attorney José Miranda*), Carolina Segrera (*Ana Celia Ramos*), Carlos Villarías (*Don Antonio Santiago*), Evelyn Del Rio (*Anita Ramos*), Paul Ellis (*"El Chato"*), Martín Garralaga (*Alfonso Hernández*), José Peña "Pepet" (*Manuel Paniagua*).

Drama, with songs. [*Not viewed*]. Rita Santiago's father, Don Antonio, stubbornly refuses to give permission for her to marry Julio Bertolin, a struggling medical student, because he wants his daughter to marry a rich Brazilian. Because of this, Julio leaves medical school and determines to gain wealth and position for himself by becoming a singer. He soon moves to Los Angeles and becomes a popular singer in a Latin American cabaret owned by "El Chato." A dancer at the cabaret, Ana Celia Ramos, falls in love with Julio, and angers El Chato, who is in love with her and extremely jealous. When he confronts Ana about her feelings for Julio, El Chato becomes so enraged that he accidentally kills her, then places the blame on Julio. Julio is then arrested for the crime, but is eventually cleared of the crime by Anita, Ana's six-year-old daughter. The girl reveals that just before Ana died, she told her daughter her killer's identity. *Latino. Los Angeles (CA). Medical students. Murder. Nightclubs. Romantic rivalry. Singers. Accidental death. Brazilians. Dancers. District Attorneys. False accusations. Fathers and daughters. Fights. Jealousy. Mothers and daughters. Nightclub owners. Unrequited love.*

Note: The working title of this film was *Mi primer amor*. *MPH* refers to it by the English translation of the Spanish title, "My Two Loves." The *MPH* review also notes that the picture's producer, Rafael Ramos Cobián, had recently signed a contract with Twentieth Century-Fox to make four Spanish-language pictures a year. Reviews and news items note that *Mis dos amores* was the first of a new series of films aimed at the Spanish-language markets in the United States, Central and South America that would star Tito Guízar, who was playing his first dramatic starring role in a North American film. The *MPH* and *Var* reviewers both wrote favorably about the film and predicted that it would do well in all Spanish-language markets. The *Var* review incorrectly credits costumer William Bridgehouse with the cinematography.

DV 13 Aug 1938, p. 3. *HR* 13 Aug 1938, p. 3. *MPD* 1 Sep 1938, p. 15. *MPH* 20 Aug 1938, p. 47, 50. *Var* 17 Aug 1938, p. 23.

MISS ROBIN HOOD *see* **MASKED RAIDERS**

MISSING MEN *see* **BORDER PATROL**

MISSING SUBMARINE *see* **SUBMARINE RAIDER**

MISSISSIPPI WOMAN *see* **BABY DOLL**

THE MISSOURIANS (Polish Americans)

Republic Pictures Corp. *Dist* Republic Pictures Corp. 25 Nov **1950**; Prod: mid-Aug—late Aug 1950 [©Republic Pictures Corp.; 30 Nov 1950; LP568]. Sd (RCA Sound System); b&w. 5,399 ft. 60 min. Passed by the National Board of Review. PCA cert no. 14809.

Assoc prod Melville Tucker. *Dir* George Blair. [*Asst dir* John Grubbs and Herb Mendelson]. *Wrt* Arthur E. Orloff. *Dir of photog* John MacBurnie. [*Cam op* Enzo Martinelli]. [*Gaffer* Wilbur Kinnett]. [*Stills* Don Keyes]. *Spec eff* Howard Lydecker and Theodore Lydecker. *Optical eff* Consolidated Film Industries. *Art dir* Frank Arrigo. *Film ed* Robert M. Leeds. *Set dec* John McCarthy, Jr. and Charles Thompson. *Mus* Stanley Wilson. *Sd* T. A. Carman. *Makeup supv* Bob Mark. [*Makeup* Dan Greenway]. [*Hair stylist* Hazel Keithley]. [*Scr supv* Joan Eremin]. [*Grip* Whitey Lawrence].

Song(s): "Roll Along Wagon Wheels," composer undetermined.

Cast: Monte Hale [(*Marshal Bill Blades*)], Paul Hurst [(*John X. Finn*)], Roy Barcroft [(*Nick Kovacs*)], Lyn Thomas [(*Peg*)], Howard J. Negley [(*Lucius Paul Valentine*)], Robert Neil [(*Steve Kovacs*)], Lane Bradford [(*Stash*)], John Hamilton [(*Mayor McDowell*)], Sarah Padden [(*Mother*)], Charles Williams [(*Postmaster Walt Williams*)], Perry Ivins [(*Judge*)], [Wade Crosby (*Butcher*)], [Bud Osborne (*Driver*)], [Joe McGuinn (*Townsman*)].

Western. [*Print viewed*]. When a notorious Missouri outlaw known as "Stash" reads a newspaper article crediting Marshal Bill Blades with the exceptionally low crime rate in Dorado, Texas, his partner, Polish American Nick Kovacs, mentions that his mother and brother Steve live there. The outlaws decide to visit Dorado, where they meet a shopkeeper, who tells Bill, a lawyer named John X. Finn, and one of Kovacs's henchmen, that Steve has recently stolen some goods from his shop. When Mayor McDowell suggests that Steve return to his native Poland, John defends Steve's rights as an American. Later, the gang goes to the Kovacs' cabin and pressures Steve to join them. The gang learns that the town has raised ten thousand dollars toward a new church, and Kovacs forces Steve to reveal which road he thinks the wagons carrying the church building supplies will take into town. The gang rides out to the road, and when Steve tries to warn the wagon train of the impending attack, Kovacs knocks him unconscious. Bill interrupts the robbery, but before escaping, the gang shoots his horse so that he cannot follow them. After Bill meets Lucius Paul Valentine, one of Kovacs' henchmen who claims to be the director of a Shakespeare company, he notices a dazed Steve wandering nearby. When Steve is questioned, he refuses to incriminate his brother, which prompts the mayor to demand his arrest. Later, John and Bill stuff the town's money into a shoe box, which they mail immediately for fear of being caught with the money. At the post office, they send the package to Bill's home via registered mail and are given a receipt in exchange. As they are leaving, however, Kovacs and the gang steal the receipt from them. A few days later, Postmaster Walt Williams attempts to deliver the package to Bill's home. There Bill's friend Peg has received a visit from Valentine, ostensibly to promote his company. When Valentine and Peg explain that Bill is out, Walt decides to wait for him. Kovacs and Valentine eventually knock out Walt, stealing both the package and a poster announcing Kovacs's fugitive status. Walt says he is sure Steve was behind the attack, as he saw the assailant wearing Steve's distinctive plaid shirt. Later, Kovacs, who stole Steve's shirt in order to frame him, forces his brother to confess publicly. While an angry lynch mob gathers outside, Bill and John find the remains of the poster, which has been burnt, and make out Kovacs's name on it. Suddenly, Kovacs and Valentine break into the jail, shoot the mayor and then escape. Valentine then lures Steve into the mayor's office, where Peg is treating the mayor's wounds. Through the window, Kovacs sees Steve enter the office, and after firing a shot at the mayor, drops the gun into the room to implicate Steve. Upon Bill's request, Steve reingratiates himself with the gang, to see what he can discover about them. Later, Steve tells Valentine that he has just learned about

a shipment of gold to be made from a previously dormant mine. At the mine, however, the wagon is loaded with empty boxes, and when the gang attacks, Bill is poised to arrest them. The citizens build their church, and on the next Sunday morning, they gather for worship. *Brothers. Marshals. Outlaws. Robbery. Cabins. Churches. Confession (Law). Escapes. Frame-ups. Fugitives. Gold mines. Gunshot wounds. Jails. Lawyers. Marshals. Mayors. Mobs. Money. Mothers and sons. Newspapers. Polish Americans. Postmasters. Storekeepers.*

Note: *HR* production charts list Gilbert Kay in the cast, but his participation in the released film has not been confirmed.

Box 9 Dec 1950. *DV* 28 Nov 1950, p. 4. *FD* 4 Dec 1950, p. 4. *HR* 28 Nov 1950, p. 4. *MPHPD* 2 Dec 1950, p. 598. *Var* 29 Nov 1950, p. 14.

MISTAKEN IDENTITY (African Americans)

Century Productions. *Dist* Sack Amusement Enterprises; State Rights. **194-**. Sd; b&w. 5,211 ft. 58 min.

Prod George P. Quigley and Arthur Leonard. *Dir* George P. Quigley and Arthur Leonard. *Scr* Victor Vicas and Norman Borisoff. *Based on story by* George Freeland. *Photog* George Webber. *Orig mus* Skippy Williams. *Sd rec* Robert E. Rosien.

Music: "Jam Session," by Skippy Williams.

Song(s): "Can't Help It," music and lyrics by Skippy Williams, "I'm a Cute Little Banji from Ubangi" and "That's the Cheese You Gotta Squeeze," composers undetermined.

Cast: Nelle Hill (*Lola*), George Oliver (*Hal*), Bill Dillard (*Mike*), Ruth Cobbs (*Mary Smith*), Ken Renard (*Bill Smith*), Andrew Maize (*Jerry* [*O'Hara*]), Bob Brown (*Editor*), Pinky Williams (*Lewis*), Alston and Young (*Dance team*), Skippy Williams (*Band*), [Marjorie Oliver (*Secretary*)].

African American, Crime, Drama, with songs. [*Print viewed*]. While auditioning at a black nightclub owned by former detective Bill Smith, Lewis, a piano player, is struck and killed by a knife flying across the room. Hal, a reporter, immediately telephones the news to his editor, explaining how his activities during the previous night provide valuable information about the crime: At singer Lola's apartment, Hal is watching a television program featuring black dancers when Lola's husband Mike, a prison escapee, returns home. Hal hides in a closet and listens as Mike demands that Lola go away with him and stop seeing Hal. Mike and Lola then plan a trip to Bill's apartment, hoping to borrow new clothes for Mike so that he can change out of his prison uniform. His curiosity piqued, Hal goes to Bill's apartment and hides there, waiting to see what will happen. Bill and his wife Mary return home drunk later that night, and when Bill goes out to find his cat, he is mistaken for Mike and, unknown to Mary, is arrested. The arresting officer, Jerry O'Hara, stays at Bill's apartment after Bill is taken away. From jail, Bill places a number of telephone calls to his apartment, hoping to clear up the confusion and win his release, but his calls go unanswered as Lola's seductive singing is distracting the officer. As partygoers arrive at Bill's apartment, Mike secretly ushers them to a closet and hides them from Jerry's view. Finally, to get out of jail, Bill calls his secretary, who arranges for him to be released. The following day, the band is performing in Bill's nightclub when Mary enters and sees Bill and Lola together. Mary, unaware that Bill spent the night in jail, becomes jealous and suspects that he is having an affair with the singer. That night, the piano player is murdered and Bill begins an investigation. He soon discovers that Hal is the culprit, and that Hal, who was in love with Lola, hoped to eliminate both rivals at once by killing Lewis and framing Mike for the murder. Hal is sent to prison, and Bill and Mary are reconciled after Mary learns that Bill was in jail and not with Lola. *African Americans. Murder. Nightclub owners. Reporters. Singers. Auditions. Bands (Music). Eavesdropping. Editors. Frame-ups. Jails. Jazz music. Jealousy. Mistaken identity. Nightclubs. Parties. Pianists. Police. Prison escapees. Secretaries. Tap dancing. Television.*

Note: This film was re-released in 1948 as *Murder with Music*. The re-released film contained added footage, additional characters and new musical numbers. The onscreen credits for *Murder with Music* were identical to those of *Mistaken Identity*, with the following exceptions: *Murder with Music* did not contain Arthur Leonard's co-producer and co-director credit; John Visconti was credited as co-photographer; Gus Smith was credited, along with Victor Vicas and Norman Borisoff, for writing the screenplay; Sidney Easton and Gus Smith replaced Skippy Williams in the "Original Music" credit (although Williams was credited as having written the numbers used from *Mistaken Identity*). The dance team of "Johnson and Johnson" and Noble Sissle and His Orchestra were also added to the cast; Marjorie Oliver, as the "Secretary," received an onscreen credit in the 1948 release.

In the earlier release, Bob Brown is credited with the part of the "Editor," but

in the 1948 re-release he was replaced by Bob Howard in newly shot footage in which his character tells reporter "Ted," played by Milton J. Williams, what happened to "Hal." Howard also performed a song with the Sissle band. The cast list in the onscreen credits of the re-released version was re-ordered, with Howard's name appearing first, followed by Williams Williams, Nelle Hill, George Oliver, Bill Dillard, Marjorie Oliver, Ruth Cobbs, Ken Renard, Andrew Maize, Pinky Williams and Skippy Williams. Ken Renard also appeared in a brief climactic scene with Howard in the re-issue. As indicated in the credits of the re-released film, *Murder with Music* featured the following two additional songs and two instrumentals, all by Sidney Easton and Gus Smith: "Too Late Baby," "Hello Happiness," "Geeshee" and "Running Around." No contemporary information was found regarding the release date of *Mistaken Identity*, but it is presumed to be the early 1940s. Modern sources list the release year as 1941. *Mistaken Identity* contained a scene in which "Lola" and "Hal" watch a musical number being performed on television.

MISTER ANTONIO (Italian Americans)

Tiffany-Stahl Productions, Inc. 1 Oct or 15 Oct **1929** [©Tiffany-Stahl Productions, Inc.; 23 Sep 1929; LP742]. Sd (Photophone); b&w. 8 reels, 6,978 ft. [Also si; 5,362 ft.].

Dir James Flood and Frank Reicher. *Scen, dial and art titles* Frederick Hatton and Fanny Hatton. *Photog* Ernest Miller. *Film ed* Arthur Roberts.

Source: Based on the play *Mister Antonio* by Booth Tarkington (New York, 18 Sep 1916).

Cast: Leo Carrillo (*Antonio Camaradino*), Virginia Valli (*June Ramsey*), Gareth Hughes (*Joe*), Frank Reicher (*Milton Jorny*), Eugenie Besserer (*Mrs. Jorny*), Franklin Lewis (*Earl Jorny*).

Comedy-drama. Antonio Camaradino, florist and street musician, befriends a man robbed of his overcoat and money in a disreputable bar. Tony recognizes the man as Jorny, mayor of Avalonia, a straitlaced town where Tony was once arrested for playing his hurdy-gurdy. After this meeting, Tony's travels take him again to Avalonia. Camped on the outskirts of town, he meets June Ramsey, a cousin of the mayor's wife, ejected from town by the mayor because his reelection campaign is jeopardized by her having been seen in a roadhouse. Under considerable pressure because he wishes to conceal his previous encounter with Tony from the opposition, Jorny returns Tony's favor by asking June's forgiveness and inviting her to return to Avalonia. June accepts his apologies; she then follows Tony, with whom she has fallen in love. *Florists. Hurdy-gurdies. Italian Americans. Mayors. Political campaigns. Reputation. Street entertainers.*

Var 11 Dec 1929, p. 39.

MR. BUTTERFLY see HER AMERICAN HUSBAND

MR. JONES GOES TO TOWN see MR. WASHINGTON GOES TO TOWN

MR. KOPOLPECK see TAXI

MR. LEMON OF ORANGE (Swedish Americans)

Fox Film Corp. *Dist* Fox Film Corp. 22 Mar **1931**; Prod: 17 Dec 1930—late Jan 1931 [©Fox Film Corp.; 14 Feb 1931; LP2030]. Sd (Western Electric System); b&w. 8 reels, 6,331 ft. 67 or 72 min. Passed by the National Board of Review.

Pres WM. FOX. *Dir* John Blystone. [*Asst dir* Jasper Blystone]. *Dial* Eddie Cantor and Edwin Burke. *Photog* Joseph August. *Settings* Jack Schultze. *Film ed* Ralph Dixon. *Cost* Sophie Wachner. *Sd rec* W. W. Lindsay, Jr.

Song(s): "My Racket Is You," words and music by James F. Hanley.

Source: Based on the play *Mr. Lemon of Orange* by Jack Hays (copyrighted 5 Apr 1930).

Cast: EL BRENDEL [(*Oscar Lemon/Silent McGee*)], FIFI D'ORSAY [(*Julie La Rue*)], William Collier, Sr. [(*Mr. Blake*)], Donald Dillaway [(*Jerry*)], Joan Castle [(*June Blake*)], Ruth Warren [(*Hilda Blake*)], John Rutherford (*Castro*)], [Eddie Gribbon (*Waiter*)], [Nat Pendleton (*Gangster*)], [Lew Meehan (*Policeman*)].

Gangster, Comedy. [*Print viewed*]. Oscar Lemon, a bumbling Swedish immigrant fond of practical jokes, lives in Orange, New Jersey with his adoring sister, Hilda Blake, his less hospitable brother-in-law and their daughter June. Oscar is fired from his job at a toy shop for taking too much pleasure in amusing his juvenile customers with gag tricks. Meanwhile, gangster Silent McGee, a dead ringer for Lemon and a master of disguise, plans with his henchman, Smithy, to steal a truckload of liquor belonging to rival gang leader Pierre La Rue. During the heist, Oscar passes the crime scene and is mistaken for McGee, the first of many such mix-ups. Moments later, La Rue's limousine is showered with bullets, and his sister, the lovely Julie La

Rue, vows to avenge her brother's death. Julie and Tony, La Rue's right-hand man, encounter Oscar walking down the street and believe that he is McGee disguised as a Swede. Julie lures Oscar to the Golden Slipper, a speakeasy where she sings, and tries to seduce him into revealing the whereabouts of the truck before bumping him off. Failing to procure the information, Julie tries to coerce a now drunken Oscar into a phone booth, the appointed place for the hit. Instead, Oscar wanders into the ladies' dressing room, where he swallows a miniature harmonica and subsequently squeaks whenever squeezed. Julie finally extorts with kisses and pleas the truck's whereabouts that Oscar, who saw after it broke down near his home earlier, innocently reveals. Jerry, June's boyfriend and a junior reporter, arrives at the Golden Slipper and warns Oscar about the gangsters' error in identification. Oscar, finally realizing what is going on, tries to disguise himself and then escapes through a trapdoor in the phone booth only to learn that Julie has been taken hostage by McGee's men pending McGee's return. Oscar, now consciously assuming his disguise as McGee, rescues Julie with Jerry's help, just as the real McGee arrives. After a riotous chase, the doubles meet on the Blakes's front porch for a final duel. The police arrive and offer Oscar a $10,000 reward for McGee's capture, and Julie, relieved that Oscar is not really McGee, squeezes her brave Swede, whose swallowed harmonica squeaks one last time. *Bumblers. Doubles. Gangsters. Impersonation and imposture. Mistaken identity. Swedish Americans. Bootleggers. Brothers and sisters. Brothers-in-law. Dismissal (Employment). Harmonicas. Hostages. Reporters. Revenge. Rewards. Romance. Seduction. Speakeasies. Telephone booths. Toys. Waiters.*

Note: In a 1971 interview, Leonard Spigelgass stated: "The worst picture that I ever made was *Mr. Lemon of Orange.*" Although no contemporary information about his involvement with the film has been found, it is likely that he worked on the picture as a writer.

FD 29 Mar 1931, p. 10. *MPH* 24 Jan 1931, p. 44, 47. *MPH* 7 Mar 1931, p. 61. *NYT* 28 Mar 1931, p. 15. *Var* 1 Apr 1931, p. 16.

MR. LUCKY (Greek Americans)
RKO Radio Pictures, Inc. *Dist* RKO Radio Pictures, Inc. 28 May 1943; Prod: 28 Oct 1942—5 Jan 1943 [©RKO Radio Pictures, Inc.; 28 May 1943; LP12109]. Sd (RCA Sound System); b&w. 8,987 ft. 96 or 99-100 min. PCA cert no. 9950.

Prod David Hempstead. *Dir* H. C. Potter. *Asst dir* Harry Scott. *Scr* Milton Holmes and Adrian Scott. *Story* Milton Holmes. [*Contr wrt* Charles Brackett, Dudley Nichols, Kenneth Earl, M. M. Musselman and Edmund Joseph]. *Dir of photog* George Barnes. *Spec eff* Vernon L. Walker. *Art dir* Albert S. D'Agostino and Mark-Lee Kirk. *Prod des* William Cameron Menzies. *Ed* Theron Warth. *Set dec* Darrell Silvera and Claude Carpenter. *Gowns* Renie. *Mus dir* C. Bakaleinikoff. *Mus* Roy Webb. *Rec* Richard Van Hessen. *Re-rec* James G. Stewart. [*Stand-in for Cary Grant* Mel Merrihugh]. [*Stand-in* M. Webb, D. Lawrence, F. Henry, Leo Snell, G. Wainwright, E. Cheatham, D. Dean, Y. Hays, L. Kelly, P. Patrick, C. Hiby, E. Rochelle, Sam Lufkin and Lynn Craft].

Source: Based on the short story "Bundles for Freedom" by Milton Holmes in *Cosmopolitan* (Jun 1942).

Cast: CARY GRANT [(*Joe "the Greek" Adams/Joe Bascopolous*)], Laraine Day [(*Dorothy Bryant*)], Charles Bickford [(*Hard Swede*)], Gladys Cooper [(*Captain Steadman*)], Alan Carney [(*The Crunk*)], Henry Stephenson [(*Mr. Bryant*)], Paul Stewart [(*Zepp*)], Kay Johnson [(*Mrs. Ostrander*)], Erford Gage [(*Gaffer*)], Walter Kingsford [(*Commissioner Hargraves*)], Florence Bates [(*Mrs. Van Every*)], [Edward Fielding (*Foster*)], [Vladimir Sokoloff (*Greek priest*)], [J. M. Kerrigan (*McDougal*)], [Al Rhein, Sammy Finn, Al Murphy, Fred Rapport (*Gamblers*)], [John Bleifer (*Siga*)], [Juan Varro (*Bascopolous*)], [Frank Mills (*Slot machine workman*)], [Mary Forbes (*Grim-faced woman*)], [Don Brodie (*Dealer*)], [Kernan Cripps, Joe Crehan (*Plainclothesmen*)], [Art Yeoman, Jack Gargan (*Reporters*)], [Ray Flynn, Dick Rush (*Policemen*)], [Hal K. Dawson (*Draft board director*)], [Robert Strange (*Costello*)], [Frank Henry (*Reporter on street*)], [Charles Cane (*Comstock*)], [Budd Fine (*Stevedore*)], [Hilda Plowright (*Maid*)], [Lloyd Ingraham (*Chauffeur*)], [Emory Parnell (*Dock watchman*)], [Isabel Withers, Daphne Moore (*Nurses*)], [Mary Stuart], [Rita Corday], [Ariel Heath].

Romance, World War II. [*Print viewed*]. As the lone figure of a woman paces the New York docks one foggy night, Hard Swede, a sailor, tells the night watchman about her. Swede, the former captain of the gambling ship *Fortuna*, explains that the woman is waiting for the return of the ship and its owner, gambler Joe "the Greek" Adams,

but adds that the ship will never return because it is sitting on the bottom of the Atlantic Ocean. Swede then relates the following story: Just prior to America's entry into World War II, the *Fortuna* is about to sail for Havana when Joe and his partner, Zepp, receive their draft notices. Protesting that he fought his war by crawling out of the gutter, Joe decides to circumvent the draft by assuming the identity of petty criminal Joe Bascopolous, a dying sailor who has been classified 4-F. Joe and Zepp, who has also been classified 1-A, roll the dice for the ownership of the boat and Bascopolous' 4-F card, and after Joe wins the roll, Zepp goes to the draft board and is himself classified as physically unfit to serve because of a heart condition. Joe is searching for a way to raise money to sail when socialite Dorothy Bryant approaches him on the street and asks him to buy a ticket to the War Relief charity ball. Realizing that the ball offers a perfect way for him to raise the money, Joe visits the all female War Relief office and suggests that a gambling concession at the ball could easily raise $100,000 to send medical supplies to Europe. Captain Steadman, the head of the organization, is charmed by Joe and his idea, but Dorothy protests that gambling is illegal. After leaving the draft board, Zepp, meanwhile, returns to the ship and finds a letter from the parole board addressed to Bascopolous, notifying him that he is in violation of his parole and will be automatically imprisoned for life if he commits one more criminal offense. Zepp pockets the letter and, after lying that he has several weeks to report for duty, asks to stay onboard the boat. Joe, undaunted by Dorothy's opposition, returns to the War Relief office to enlist as a recruit and Dorothy puts him to work knitting. The next day, Joe wins Dorothy's admiration when he uses a trick coin to get McDougal, a purveyor of used blankets, into donating his merchandise to the war effort. When Dorothy asks Joe why he is so interested in aiding her organization, he sees some newspaper headlines announcing the Nazi invasion of the Varda Valley and tells her that his family lives there and he just wants to do his part. Feeling guilty, Dorothy invites Joe to accompany her to the docks, where Comstock, a supplier, has refused to unload a shipment of supplies without payment. At the docks, Joe follows Comstock into his office and strongarms him into releasing the supplies. In the struggle, Comstock tears Joe's jacket and Dorothy insists on bringing him home to repair it. On the drive home, Joe teaches Dorothy a form of rhyming slang in which the words "my darling" would be transposed as "briny marlin." Joe thinks that Dorothy invited him home for romantic reasons, and when she denies this, he offers to settle their differences by playing the same coin game he used on McDougal. When Dorothy incorrectly assumes that he plans to trick her, Joe, insulted, coldly informs her that his motto is "never give a sucker an even break, but don't cheat a friend." Joe's words shame Dorothy into offering him the gambling concession, and a triumphant Joe returns to the ship and informs his gang that they will soon sail to Havana with the ball proceeds. Joe requires $6,000 to start the games rolling, and consequently, when Dorothy writes a personal check in the same amount as a deposit on a freighter, Joe offers to deliver the check to Hargraves, the shipping commissioner. At the commissioner's office, Joe watches as Hargraves endorses the check and then convinces him that it is unpatriotic to demand a down payment. Chagrined, Hargraves returns the check and Joe pretends to tear it up. When Joe cashes the check, Dorothy's grandfather, Mr. Bryant, notifies the police, who then visit the War Relief office to arrest Joe Bascopolous for parole violations. After the police appear at the office, Dorothy pretends that Joe is the water man and arranges to meet him later that afternoon. Picking him up in her car, Dorothy, who hates Joe's loud ties, presents him with a new tie and drives him to her country house in Maryland. When they arrive, she tells him about the police and calls her grandfather and threatens to marry Joe unless he calls off the police. Resenting Dorothy's threat, Joe accuses her of feeling superior to him, but she denies this and kisses him. They then drive back to New York, and after dropping Dorothy at her house, Joe speeds away, confused. Later, Joe appears at Dorothy's door, and after asking her to reknot his tie, he kisses her. That evening, before the ball, Joe asks Swede about Bascopolous, and Swede shows him a letter, written in Greek, addressed to the dead sailor. Taking the letter to a Greek priest for translation, Joe learns that the letter is from Bascopolous' mother, notifying him that his two brothers have died while defending their village from the Nazis. After the priest comforts him with a prayer, Joe goes to the ball, puts $6,000 in an envelope addressed to Hargraves, and then declares that

all the proceeds will go to War Relief, Inc. Zepp overhears Joe's announcement and tells the gang that he is planning to double-cross them. Later that evening, when Mr. Bryant arrives with the police to confront Joe about Hargraves' check and to demand a stop to the gambling, Joe hands him the envelope addressed to Hargraves and orders the proceeds totalled. In the cashier's cage, Joe is confronted by Zepp and the others, who threaten to expose him as a draft dodger unless he remains silent about the false bottoms in the cash boxes. After the War Relief workers leave the office with a paltry $812 retrieved from the boxes, Zepp unloads the bottoms, rolling the money in a newspaper. Aware that she has been cheated, Dorothy returns to the cage and demands the money. Joe, knowing that Zepp has a gun in his pocket pointed at her, slaps Dorothy unconscious and then slugs Zepp, who shoots Joe. Before the crowd can return, the wounded Joe kicks Zepp in the head, gathers the money and escapes. The next day, at the Bryant house, a distraught Dorothy is about to make a statement to the press when Swede arrives to deliver the bundle of money. Although Swede refuses to tell Dorothy where Joe is hiding, she tracks him down when she hears that the *Fortuna* has been turned into a medical ship and renamed the *Briny Marlin*. Racing to the docks, Dorothy arrives just in time to see Joe sail away. Although she begs him to let her join him, he refuses. Swede concludes his story by telling the watchman that after delivering the medical supplies, the ship was sunk and he and Joe enlisted in the Merchant Marine and are now home on leave. When Joe joins Swede at the docks, the watchman orders them to move their dinghy, which is tied up to the pier on which Dorothy is standing. The watchman suggests that they flip a coin to decide who will move it, and employing a two-headed coin, he tricks Joe into losing. As Joe begins to walk toward the boat, Dorothy sees him and the two embrace. Confidence men. Gamblers. Military service, Compulsory. Moral reformation. Patriotism. Romance. World War II. Charity balls. Checks. Class distinction. Coins. Gambling ships. Grandfathers. Greek Americans. Impersonation and imposture. Letters. Maryland. New York City. Priests. Robbery. Sea captains. Socialites. War relief organizations.

Note: The working titles of this film were *Bundles for Freedom* and *From Here to Victory.* According to a Mar 1942 news item in *HR*, RKO bought Milton Holmes's story "Bundles for Freedom" at the request of Cary Grant, who wanted to star in it. The studio purchased the story for $30,000 prior to its publication in *Cosmopolitan.* Materials contained in the RKO Archives Script Files at the UCLA Arts Library-Special Collections reveal that the character of "Joe" dies at the end of Holmes's original story. In a 1969 *HR* news item, Holmes claimed that his story was inspired by Edward G. Neales, the owner of the Clover Club on the Sunset Strip. In 1936, Neale rigged a one-night gambling benefit at the Beverly Hills Hotel to raise $40,000 for a church. According to other materials contained in the Script Files, in Jun and Jul 1942, Charles Bracket worked with Holmes on a treatment and adaptation of his story. Although not credited onscreen, Dudley Nichols wrote a final script for *From Here to Victory,* dated 23 Oct 1942, just five days prior to the start of the film's production. The CBCS also credits Nichols with screenplay. According to materials contained in the RKO Archives Production Files, Kenneth Earl, M. M. Musselman and Edmund Joseph also worked on continuities for the film. The exact nature of the contribution of these writers to the completed film has not been confirmed, however.

According to other materials contained in the production files, Ruth Warrick tested for the part of "Dorothy." A news item in *HR* adds that Anna Lee was also considered for a leading role. This picture marked Alan Carney's screen debut. Laraine Day was borrowed from M-G-M to co-star with Grant and photographer George Barnes was borrowed from David O. Selznick's company to film the production. In 1959-60, CBS broadcast a television series based on Holmes's story. That series, titled *Mr. Lucky,* was created by Blake Edwards and starred John Vivyan. According to news items in *LAEx* and *LAT,* in 1956, RKO approached Frank Sinatra and Dean Martin about starring in a musical version of the film. Cary Grant and Laraine Day reprised their roles in a 18 Oct 1943 *Lux Radio Theatre* broadcast of the story.

Box 8 May 1943. DV 4 May 1943, p. 3, 7. FD 11 May 1943, p. 6. HR 11 Mar 1942, p. 1. HR 14 Oct 1942, p. 4. HR 19 Oct 1942, p. 2. HR 30 Oct 1942, p. 3. HR 4 May 1943, p. 4. HR 26 Jul 1943, p. 8. HR 7 May 1969. LAEx 7 Mar 1956. LAT 10 Nov 1956. MPH 8 May 1943. MPHPD 8 May 1943, pp. 1301-02. NYT 23 Jul 1943, p. 21. Var 5 May 1943, p. 16.

MR. MOTO AT THE RINGSIDE see MR. MOTO'S GAMBLE

MR. MOTO IN DANGER ISLAND (Japanese Americans)
Twentieth Century-Fox Film Corp. *Dist* Twentieth Century-Fox Film Corp. 7 Apr **1939**; New York opening: week of 20 Mar 1939; Prod: late Nov—late Dec 1938 [©Twentieth Century-Fox Film Corp.; 7 Apr 1939; LP9023]. Sd (Western Electric Mirrophonic Recording); b&w. 7 reels, 6,230 ft. 63 min. PCA cert no. 4939.
Series: Mr. Moto.
Assoc prod John Stone. *Dir* Herbert I. Leeds. [*Asst dir* Charles Hall and Bill Forsyth]. *Scr* Peter Milne. *Based on story ideas by* John

Reinhardt and George Bricker. [*Additional scenes* Jack Jungmeyer, Jr. and Edith Skouras]. [*Contr wrt* John Reinhardt and George Bricker]. *Photog* Lucien Andriot. [*Cam op* Eddie Fitzgerald]. [*Asst cam* Roger Sherman]. [*Head of camera dept.* Dan Clark]. *Art dir* Richard Day and Chester Gore. *Film ed* Harry Reynolds. [*Cutter* Harry Reynolds]. *Set dec* Thomas Little. [*Set dresser* Walter Scott and Al Orenbach]. *Cost* Herschel. [*Ward man* Clinton Sandeen]. *Mus dir* Samuel Kaylin. *Sd rec* Bernard Freericks and William H. Anderson. [*Recorder* W. P. Mathewson]. [*Boom man* Jim Burnett]. [*Hair* Hazel Rogers]. [*Makeup* Newton Jones]. [*Prod mgr* Wm. Koenig]. [*Unit mgr* Ben Wurtzel]. [*Scr clerk* Helen Parker]. [*Grip* Hank Gersen]. [*Props* Don Greenwood]. [*Gaffer* Jack McAvoy]. [*Best boy* Ken McDonald]. [*Casting* Phillip Moore]. [*Cableman* Carl Daniels]. [*Still photog* Anthony Ugrin].

Source: Based on the character created by John P. Marquand and the novel *Murder in Trinidad* by John W. Vandercook (New York, 1933).

Cast: PETER LORRE (*Mr. Moto*), Jean Hersholt (*Sutter*), Amanda Duff (*Joan Castle*), Warren Hymer (*Twister McGurk*), Richard Lane (*Commissioner Gordon*), Leon Ames (*Commissioner Madero*), Douglas Dumbrille (*La Costa*), Charles D. Brown (*Major Thomas Castle*), Paul Harvey (*Col. John Bentley*), Robert Lowery (*Lieut. George Bentley*), Eddie Marr (*Capt. Dahlen*), Harry Woods (*Grant*), [Neely Edwards (*Moore*)], [Harry Strang (*Henchman*)], [George Magrill (*Officer*)], [Grace Hayle (*Mrs. Brown*)], [Tony Martelli, Louis Mercier (*Servants*)], [Gloria Roy (*Nurse*)], [Edwin Stanley (*Doctor*)], Jack Stoney], Lee Shumway (*Guards*)], [Jimmie Dundee (*Driver*)], [Al Kikume (*Sergeant*)], [Ralph Dunn (*Policeman*)], [Lester Dorr (*Ambulance attache*)], [Ray Walker (*Ambulance attache*)], [Don Douglas (*Petty officer*)], [Max Wagner (*First member of crew*)], [Oscar G. Hendrian (*Second member of crew*)], [Ward Bond (*Wrestler*)], [Juan Duval (*Carlos*)], [Renie Riano (*Librarian*)], [W. R. Deming (*Drunk*)], [Edward Keane (*Washington official*)], [Willie Best (*Pilot*)].

Detective. [*Print viewed*]. Mr. Moto, accompanied by Twister McGuirk, a wrestler who has apprenticed himself to the famous detective in order to learn his jiu jitsu tricks, arrives in Puerto Rico on the trail of a diamond smuggling ring. After the murder of a secret agent, Moto follows a trail of clues that leads him to a sinister swamp, a reputed haunting grounds for ghosts. When the governor of the island is slain in the same manner as the agent, Moto and Twister return to the swamp, where they are captured by the smugglers, who have appropriated the pond as their hideout. While a prisoner, Moto discovers that the diamonds are being smuggled inside of coconuts, and after accumulating enough evidence to indict the smugglers, the detective and his apprentice escape to the mainland. Moto returns to the smugglers' hideout, accompanied by the police and Sutter, the head of the diamond dealers, but they arrive just in time to see the head of the ring speed away in his boat. Sutter takes aim and shoots the criminal, and the wounded man is taken to the hospital. That night, an attempt is made on the man's life, but Moto emerges from the shadows just in time to unmask the murderer as Sutter, the real head of the smugglers. After explaining that Sutter had planned to prevent the wounded man from exposing the diamond dealer as the real criminal, Moto reveals that Sutter's bullet had really killed the smuggler in his attempted escape from the swamp, and that the sly detective had used the dead man's corpse to bait a trap for the real crime boss. Detectives. Impersonation and imposture. Murder. Puerto Rico. Smuggling. Wrestlers and wrestling. Boats. Diamonds. Escapes. Ghosts. Hideouts. Hospitals. Japanese Americans. Jiu-jitsu. Police. Secret agents. Swamps. Traps.

Note: The working titles of this film were *Mr. Moto in Puerto Rico* and *Mr. Moto in Trinidad.* It was also reviewed as *Danger Island.* According to the Twentieth Century-Fox Produced Scripts Collection at the UCLA Theater Arts Library, the film was originally to have been a Charlie Chan picture. The first treatment written by John Reinhardt in 1938 was entitled *Chan in Trinidad.* In Sep 1938, George Bricker wrote another treatment titled *Mr. Moto in Trinidad.* According to materials contained in the Twentieth Century-Fox Records of the Legal Department at the UCLA Theater Arts Library, Antonio Moreno was originally to have played the role of "La Costa." Fox produced a film in 1934 based on the same source entitled *Murder in Trinidad* (see *AFI Catalog of Feature Films, 1931-40;* F3.2997). Twentieth Century-Fox produced *The Caribbean Mystery* in 1945 based on the same source which starred James Dunn and was directed by Robert Webb. For additional information about the series, consult the Series Index and see below for *Think Fast Mr. Moto* (1937).

DV 10 Mar 1939, p. 3. FD 29 Mar 1939, p. 8. HR 11 Mar 1939, p. 3. MPD 17 Mar 1939, p. 9. MPH 4 Mar 1939, p. 53. MPH 18 Mar 1939, p. 49. NYT 20 Mar 1939, p. 13. Var 22 Mar 1939, p. 20.

MR. MOTO IN EGYPT *see* MR. MOTO'S LAST WARNING

MR. MOTO IN PUERTO RICO *see* MR. MOTO IN DANGER ISLAND

MR. MOTO IN TRINIDAD *see* MR. MOTO IN DANGER ISLAND

MR. MOTO TAKES A CHANCE (Japanese Americans)

Twentieth Century-Fox Film Corp. *Dist* Twentieth Century-Fox Film Corp. 24 Jun **1938**; New York opening: 11 Jun 1938; Prod: 19 Jul–mid-Aug 1937 [©Twentieth Century-Fox Film Corp.; 24 Jun 1938; LP8380]. Sd (Western Electric Mirrophonic Recording); b&w. 7 reels, 5,736 ft. 57 or 63 min. PCA cert no. 3642.

Series: Mr. Moto.

Exec prod Sol M. Wurtzel. *Dir* Norman Foster. [*Asst dir* William Eckhardt and Tom Dudley]. *Scr* Lou Breslow and John Patrick. *Orig story* Willis Cooper and Norman Foster. *Photog* Virgil Miller. [*Cam op* Irving Rosenberg]. [*Asst cam* Charles Bohny and Ed Garvin]. [*Gaffer* Fred Hall]. *Art dir* Albert Hogsett. *Film ed* Nick DeMaggio. *Cost* Herschel. [*Ward man* Ernest Rotchy]. [*Ward girl* Viola Richards]. *Mus dir* Samuel Kaylin. *Sd* Bernard Freericks and Harry M. Leonard. [*Asst sd* L. B. Dix]. [*Boom man* Paul Gilbert]. [*Cableman* P. Kelly]. [*Hair* Marie Livingston]. [*Makeup* Bill Cooley]. [*Prod mgr* Ed. Ebele]. [*Scr clerk* Jack Vernon]. [*Grip* Roger Murphy]. *Props* Joe Behm. [*Asst prop* Ancil Whitlow and Elmer Poggi]. [*Best boy* John Grady and Frank Gilroy]. [*Still photog* Steve McNulty]. [*Stand in* Emily Baldwin, Rollo Dix and Delmar Costello].

Source: Based on the character created by John P. Marquand.

Cast: PETER LORRE (*Mr. [K.] Moto*), Rochelle Hudson (*Victoria Mason*), Robert Kent (*Marty Weston*), J. Edward Bromberg (*Rajah Ali*), Chick Chandler (*Chick Davis*), George Regas (*Bokor*), Frederick Vogeding (*Zimmerman*), [Gloria Roy (*Wife*)], [Al Kikume (*Yao*)].

Espionage, **Detective**. [*Print viewed*]. When aviatrix Victoria Mason, who is flying around the world, reaches the small kingdom of Tong Moi, above Siam, she throws a flare into the rear of her plane and parachutes to safety before the plane crashes in flames. The crash is seen by Mr. Moto, leading an archaeological dig, and by American newsreel cameramen Marty Weston and Chick Davis. After Moto helps Vicky, he sends a note about her arrival via carrier pigeon. Vicky is presented to ruler Rajah Ali, who insists above the objections of his high priest Bokor that she stay as his guest. As Marty and Chick shoot footage of them, Bokor objects that this displeases the gods. However, the ruler states that the cinema is not dangerous, and filming proceeds until Keema, his favorite wife, falls dead. While Marty and Chick are taken by Bokor to a hidden temple for a trial before the gods, Moto discovers that a poison dart from a blowgun killed Keema. Deemed guilty, Marty and Chick are about to be thrown into a well, when a fire erupts and an old guru, on a pilgrimage from the Himalayas, emerges from the temple. After he proves his powers to Bokor, he orders the men freed. The next day, in the cave of the temple, the guru discovers cans of explosives in a secret room below. After he subdues one of Bokor's men, the guru removes his mask and reveals himself to be Moto. He then sends a message by pigeon, stating that he has located the munitions base and that Bokor is the leader of the revolt. However, Rajah Ali shoots down the pigeon and, at a celebration that night, serves it to Moto. When Vicky graciously agrees to become the rajah's next wife in his harem, Marty, who is attracted to her, prepares to leave. After Vicky finds information that Moto is a spy and locates his map of the temple, she heads there followed by Bokor. Convinced by Chick that she is in danger, Marty hastens there also, but he is captured along with Vicky. After Zimmerman, the munitions dealer, arrives and captures Chick, Bokor has Zimmerman killed. He then proclaims that his revolt has begun and will not end until every foreigner is driven from Asia. Moto, who has emerged again as the guru, attempts to deflect Bokor's bloodlust, but when Chick is about to be executed, Vicky reveals Moto's identity and, in the confusion that follows, a fight breaks out. With the munitions, Moto and Vicky, who is working for British Intelligence, fight alongside Marty and Chick to stave off Bokor's men. As they run out of ammunition, Rajah Ali arrives with troops and captures Bokor and his followers. When he says that he will execute Moto, Vicky, Marty and Chick, Moto threatens to blow them all up by dropping a torch into the room with the explosives. Marty throws a gun at Rajah Ali, who falls into the room. Moto then lights a fuse of film that he rigged up leading to the explosives, and after they escape, the temple

explodes. On a sailboat, Vicky and Marty banter affectionately, as Moto scares Chick with tales of their next adventure together. *Asia, Southeastern. Imaginary lands. Impersonation and imposture. Japanese Americans. Spies. Undercover agents. Uprisings. Women air pilots. Archaeologists. Blowguns. Executions. Explosives. False accusations. Fights. Great Britain. Intelligence Service. Gurus. Harems. Maps. Munitions. Murder. Newsreel cameramen. Pigeons. Poison. Priests. Skydivers. Temples. Tribal chiefs.*

Note: The working title of this film was *Look Out, Mr. Moto*. Although this was the second film to be produced in the "Mr. Moto" series and was reviewed in Oct 1937 under the early title, it was not released until Jun 1938, when it was the fourth in the series. A 5 Aug 1937 *HR* news item, during the shooting of this film, indicated that the next Mr. Moto picture, which was then ready for production, would be held up temporarily while the studio watches the developments of the Sino-Japanese War. The news item noted that because the "leading character is a Japanese...the script may have to be overhauled to avoid injured feelings." While this news item pertains to the next film in the series, presumably *Thank You, Mr. Moto*, which went into production in Oct 1937 (see below), it is possible that the release of *Mr. Moto Takes a Chance* was held up because of the war. According to the pressbook for the film, director Norman Foster insisted that the characters speak real Cambodian, and to insure accuracy in the language, the studio hired Louis Vincenot, who was born in Cambodia, to teach the language to the extras. The pressbook also indicates that Rochelle Hudson wore Cambodian gowns and jewelry in the film, that the temple set was designed using Khymer architecture and that Peter Lorre studied jiu-jitsu, which he used in the film. For more information about the Mr. Moto series, please see the entry above for *Think Fast, Mr. Moto* and consult the Series Index.

Box 6 Nov 1937. *DV* 23 Oct 1937, p. 3. *FD* 16 Jun 1938, p. 6. *HR* 19 Jul 1937, p. 15. *HR* 5 Aug 1937, p. 16. *HR* 9 Aug 1937, p. 15. *HR* 23 Oct 1937, p. 2. *MPD* 26 Oct 1937, p. 3. *MPH* 11 Sep 1937, p. 34. *MPH* 30 Oct 1937, p. 50. *NYT* 13 Jun 1938, p. 15. *Var* 15 Jun 1938, p. 14.

MR. MOTO TAKES A VACATION (Japanese Americans)

Twentieth Century-Fox Film Corp. *Dist* Twentieth Century-Fox Film Corp. 7 Jul **1939**; New York opening: week of 19 Jun 1939; Prod: late Aug–late Sep 1938 [©Twentieth Century-Fox Film Corp.; 7 Jul 1939; LP8966]. Sd (Western Electric Mirrophonic Recording); b&w. 6 reels, 5,632 ft. 65 min. PCA cert no. 4649.

Series: Mr. Moto.

[*Prod* Sol M. Wurtzel]. *Dir* Norman Foster. [*Asst dir* Jasper Blystone and David Hall]. *Orig scr* Philip MacDonald and Norman Foster. *Photog* Charles Clarke. *Art dir* Bernard Herzbrun and Haldane Douglas. *Film ed* Norman Colbert. *Set dec* Thomas Little. *Mus dir* Samuel Kaylin. *Sd* Alfred Bruzlin and William H. Anderson. [*Prod mgr* V. L. McFadden].

Source: Based on the character created by John P. Marquand.

Cast: PETER LORRE (*Mr. Moto*), Joseph Schildkraut (*Hendrik Manderson*), Lionel Atwill (*Professor Hildebrand*), Virginia Field (*Eleanor Kirke*), John King (*Howard Stevens*), Iva Stewart (*Susan French*), George P. Huntley, Jr. (*Archie Featherstone*), Victor Varconi (*Paul Borodoff*), John Bleifer (*Wendling*), Honorable Wu (*Wong*), Morgan Wallace (*David Perez*), Anthony Warde (*Joe Rubla*), Harry Strang (*O'Hara*), John Davidson (*Prince Suleid*), [Willie Best (*Driver*)], [Stanley Blystone (*Ship's officer*)], [Robert Winckler (*Boy*)], [Tom O'Grady (*Husband*)], [Isabelle La Mal (*Matronly woman*)], [Bobby Hale (*Steward*)], [Leyland Hodgson (*Waiter*)], [George Chandler (*Cameraman*)], [Ralph Dunn, Lee Phelps, Pat O'Malley (*Policemen*)], [William Gould (*Police captain*)], [Chick Collins (*Driver of armored car*)], [Lester Dorr (*Reporter*)], [Jack Clifford (*Sergeant on motorcycle*)], [Brooks Benedict (*Gangster*)], [Jimmy Aubrey (*Bum*)], [Victor Wong (*Proprietor*)], [Chan Suey (*Musician*)], [Mae Leung (*Singer*)], [Jadine Wong (*Dancer*)], [Iris Wong (*Waitress*)], [Sam Hayes (*Announcer*)], [Major Sam Harris (*Professor*)], [Eddie Abdo (*Arabian officer*)], [Hank Mann].

Detective. [*Print viewed*]. Hoping to unmask the psychotic jewel thief known as Metaxa, detective Mr. Moto follows archaeologist Howard Stevens, who has just discovered the crown of the Queen of Sheba, on his voyage home from Egypt to San Francisco. Moto's cover as a Japanese tourist is blown when he meets his old friend, amateur detective Archie Featherstone, whom he introduces to the Stevens and fellow passenger, Eleanor Kirke. Meanwhile, in San Francisco, jewel thieves Joe Rubla and David Perez make plans to steal the crown, but decide that they must also eliminate Moto. Upon docking in San Francisco, Stevens is met by Hendrik Manderson, the philanthropist who has financed the expedition, and Fremont museum curator Professor Hildebrand and his secretary, Susan French. As Wendling, a

member of Perez' gang, follows Moto in a cab, Joe tries to steal the armored car in which the jewels are housed, but he is foiled by the police and Archie, then escapes. The next day, the crowd reconvenes at the museum for the unveiling of the crown. Archie, who has witnessed the armored car robbery, is trailed by Perez, who deliberately breaks Archie's camera in order to lure him into a death trap later that night. Back at his hotel, Moto receives an urgent call from Manderson's servant Wong, who asks the detective to meet him at a Chinatown restaurant called the Laughing Buddha. When Moto arrives at the restaurant, however, he discovers that Wong has been murdered. Archie, who is also in Chinatown, tells Moto of his plan to meet Perez later that night, but Moto, recognizing the meeting as a set-up, convinces him not to go. Instead, the pair drive to the museum, where they find Hildebrand and Manderson playing chess and the phone and alarm dead. Paul Borodoff, the insurance company investigator, then appears and tries to steal the crown for himself, but he is stopped by Mr. Moto who announces that Metaxa is in the room. Just after Moto accuses Hildebrand of being Metaxa, Rubla tries to steal the jewels, but he is arrested by the police. Moto then unmasks Manderson as the real Metaxa when he attempts to steal the crown.
Detectives. Impersonation and imposture. Jewel thieves. San Francisco (CA)–Chinatown. Archaeologists. Chess. Expeditions. Hotels. Insurance–Investigators. Japanese Americans. Murder. Museums. Ocean liners. Philanthropists. Police. Professors. Secretaries. Servants. Tourists. Traps.

Note: *DV* credits David Hall as assistant director, but his name does not appear in other sources, and the onscreen credits list Jasper Blystone in that capacity. For additional information about the series, consult the Series Index and see entry below for *Think Fast, Mr. Moto.*

DV 11 Nov 1938, p. 3. *FD* 25 Jul 1939, p. 8. *HR* 27 Aug 1938, pp. 10-11. *HR* 11 Nov 1938, p. 3. *MPD* 18 Nov 1938, p. 6. *MPH* 19 Nov, 1938, p. 44. *NYT* 19 Jun 1939, p. 12. *Var* 16 Nov 1938, p. 15.

MR. MOTO'S GAMBLE (Japanese Americans)
Twentieth Century-Fox Film Corp. *Dist* Twentieth Century-Fox Film Corp. 25 Mar **1938**; Prod: 10 Jan–mid-Feb 1938 [©Twentieth Century-Fox Film Corp.; 25 Mar 1938; LP8170]. Sd (Western Electric Mirrophonic Recording); b&w. 8 reels, 6,565 ft. 71 min. PCA cert no. 4053.
Series: Mr. Moto.
[*Prod* Sol M. Wurtzel]. *Assoc prod* John Stone. *Dir* James Tinling. [*Dial dir* Harvey G. Parry, Arthur Berthelet and Lionel Bevans]. [*Asst dir* Jasper Blystone and Charles Faye]. *Orig scr* Charles Belden and Jerry Cady. *Photog* Lucien Andriot. [*Cam op* Edward Fitzgerald]. [*1st asst cam* Roger Sherman]. [*2d asst cam* Edward Collins]. [*Gaffer* Jack McAvoy]. *Art dir* Bernard Herzbrun and Haldane Douglas. *Film ed* Nick De Maggio. [*Asst cutter* Jack Lebowitz]. *Cost* Helen A. Myron. [*Ward girl* Gladys Isaacson]. [*Ward man* Jack Adams]. *Mus dir* Samuel Kaylin. *Sd* Bernard A. Freericks and William H. Anderson. [*Asst sd* Joe Mazzoletti]. [*Boom man* Harry Roberts]. [*Cableman* Fred Casey]. [*Makeup* Webster Phillips]. [*Prod mgr* Ed. Ebele]. [*Unit mgr* Ben Wurtzel]. [*Scr clerk* Stanley Scheuer]. [*Grip* Hank Gersen]. [*Asst grip* Jimmie Reemer]. [*Props* Don Greenwood]. [*Asst prop* Stanley Detlie and Aaron Wolf]. [*Best boy* Kenneth McDonald]. [*Still photog* John Jenkins].
Source: Based on the character created by John P. Marquand.
Cast: PETER LORRE (*Mr. Moto*), Keye Luke (*Lee Chan*), Dick Baldwin (*Bill Steele*), Lynn Bari (*Penny Kendall*), Douglas Fowley (*Nick Crowder*), Jayne Regan (*Linda Benton*), Harold Huber (*Lieutenant Riggs*), Maxie Rosenbloom ([*Horace "Knockout"*] *Wellington*), John Hamilton (*Philip Benton*), George E. Stone ([*Jerry*] *Connors*), Bernard Nedell (*Clipper McCoy*), Charles Williams (*Gabby Marden*), Ward Bond (*Biff Moran*), Cliff Clark (*McGuire*), Edward Marr (*Sammy*), Lon Chaney, Jr. (*Joey*), Russ Clark (*Frankie Stanton*), Pierre Watkin (*District attorney*), Charles D. Brown (*Editor*), [Paul Fix (*Gangster*)], [Dick Dickinson (*Knockdown timer*)], [Fred Kelsey (*Mahoney*)], [Ralph Dunn, David Newell, Frank McGlynn, Jr. (*Detectives*)], [George Magrill, Bob Ryan, Eddie Hart, James Blaine, Harry Strang, Stanley Blystone, Lee Shumway, Dick Rush, Adrian Morris, Max Wagner (*Policemen*)], [Jack Stoney (*Kid Grant*)], [Edwin Stanley, Landers Stevens (*Doctors*)], [Frank Fanning (*Turnkey*)], [Allen Mathews (*Handler*)], [Lester Dorr, Allen Fox, Franklin Parker, Dick French (*Reporters*)], [Emmett Vogan (*Fingerprint man*)], [Edward Earle (*Medical examiner*)], [Gladden James (*Cashier*)], [Sherry Hall (*Ticket taker*)], [Matty Roubert (*Elevator boy*)], [William E. Coe (*Timekeeper*)], [Bob Perry, George

Blake, Larry McGrath (*Referees*)], [Gary Breckner (*Announcer*)], [Dan Toby (*Fight announcer*)], [Joe Gray, Tommy Herman, Pete De Grasse (*Fighters*)], [Stanley Mack, Jack Gargan (*Ushers*)], [Syd Saylor (*Hotel clerk*)], [Don Brodie (*Ticket seller*)], [Arthur Gardner (*Elevator boy*)], [Irving Bacon (*Sheriff*)], [Olin Howland (*Deputy sheriff*)], [Matty Fain, Harrison Greene, Wilbur Mack, Dick Elliott (*Gamblers*)], [George Chandler (*Man in fight crowd*)], [Gloria Roy], [Chester Clute].
Boxing, Detective. [*Print viewed*]. At the end of one of detective Mr. Moto's classes in criminology, student Lee Chan, the son of the famous Honolulu detective Charlie Chan, notices that his watch has been stolen. Horace "Knockout" Wellington, another student, confesses that he is the culprit and reveals, to the mirth of all, that he cannot help taking things that attract his eye and later cannot remember where he purloined the objects. Moto invites Lee to accompany him and Lieutenant Riggs to a boxing match between Bill Steele and Frankie Stanton to decide who will fight world champion Biff Moran eight weeks later. Before the fight, gambler Nick Crowder bets $10,000 with bookie Clipper McCoy that Stanton will not last until the fifth round. Because he has already taken similar bets from gamblers in six other cities, Clipper warns Stanton's manager, Jerry Connors, that Stanton better not throw the fight. Riggs, Moto and Lee sit with Philip Benton, whose company owns the arena, and Benton's snooty daughter Linda, who is interested in Bill even though he likes sports reporter Penny Kendall. After Stanton's eye is cut, the referee threatens to stop the fight. Connors applies collodion to close the wound, and in the next round, Bill knocks Stanton out. When the doctor pronounces Stanton dead, Moto recovers a dried bit of collodion. Connors, who threw the bottle he used out a window, gives Moto another bottle to examine. Benton, who earlier told Riggs that he never bets, calls Clipper, who has lost $130,000 on the fight, to say that he will send a check for $10,000 to cover his bet. The poison that killed Stanton is found on Bill's gloves, and he is charged with manslaughter and suspended by the boxing commission. Although Penny convinces her editor to put up the bond money, she finds Bill leaving jail with Linda, who has already paid with a check from her father. When Moto proves to his class that the poison was shot onto Bill's glove from someone outside the ring, Lee and Wellington leave to investigate. Moto finds that Wellington has taken his overcoat and left one he earlier took from the arena, which has a stain on the inside that matches the stain found on Bill's glove. Meanwhile, at Moran's training camp, Benton and press agent Gabby Marden overhear Clipper accuse Nick of placing bets in other cities to keep the odds up at the fight. As Gabby goes to call Riggs with the information, someone takes a shot at him. After Riggs and Moto find that the owner of the overcoat, John Howard, has died from the same poison that killed Stanton, Moto, believing that Howard was a fall guy, convinces the boxing commission to lift his suspension of Bill and promises to have the murderer arrested at ringside the night of Bill's fight with Moran. In his room, Moto is confronted with an armed man, but Moto's cat Lena knocks over a vase, which allows Moto to grab the gun before the intruder escapes. At the vacant arena, a mysterious figure places a gun attached to a clock under the ring, and aims it at Moto's seat. Before the fight, Penny kisses Bill and wishes him well and then berates Linda for only caring for a winner. With the gun pointed at him, Moto surveys his suspects as the fight proceeds. He then invites Linda to sit in his seat, and after Bill knocks out Moran, Moto announces that he will shortly produce Stanton's murderer. When he insists, despite Benton's attempt to get his daughter away, that Linda remain in the seat, Benton rushes to the ring and disconnects the gun before it fires. Moto explains that he investigated the arena before the fight, because he knew that the murderer would try to kill him to keep him from revealing his identity, and he took the bullets out of the gun. As Penny hugs Linda, Benton dashes to his office, where Clipper shoots and kills him for arranging the bets on Stanton from the other cities. The police then capture Clipper as Lee and Wellington arrive, having discovered the murder weapon, a water gun filled with poison. Back in his classroom, Moto explains why he suspected Benton and, as he goes to leave, discovers his timepiece missing. Wellington returns it, and Moto reveals that he now has Wellington's wallet, which, it turns out, Wellington stole from Lee.
Boxing. Criminologists. Detectives. Gambling. Japanese Americans. Murder. Bookies. Cats. Chinese Americans. Coats. False arrests. Kleptomania. Poison. Police. Romantic rivalry. Women reporters.

Note: The working title of this film was *Mr. Moto at the Ringside*. MPD reviewed this film under the title *Mr. Moto's Diary*. According to news items and information in the Twentieth Century-Fox Records of the Legal Department at the UCLA Theater Arts Library, this film was developed after production on *Charlie Chan at the Ringside* was halted. The studio began production of the latter film on 10 Jan 1938 with Warner Oland starring as Chan. Production was halted on 17 Jan 1938 after $93,820.59 was spent, due to a disagreement between Oland and the studio. At that time, news items speculated about a successor to Oland in the role. On 24 Jan 1938, production began again as part of the "Mr. Moto" series, with all but two of the original cast: Oland, who was replaced by Lorre as Moto, and Paul Hurst, who was replaced by Harold Huber. According to correspondence from producer Sol Wurtzel, $46,341.10 was salvaged by converting the story to the "Mr. Moto" series. Wurtzel suggested that the bill for the remainder, $39,979.49, should be sent to Oland. No information has been located to determine whether this was done. Oland subsequently died before another "Charlie Chan" film was produced. Chick Chandler was originally scheduled to be in *Charlie Chan at the Ringside*, and John Carradine was listed in *HR* production charts for both films, but neither appeared in the final film. For further information on the "Mr. Moto" series, please see the entry below for *Think Fast, Mr. Moto* and consult the Series Index.

Box 19 Mar 1938. *DV* 12 Mar 1938, p. 3. *FD* 11 Apr 1938, p. 6. *HR* 10 Jan 1938, p. 3, 19. *HR* 22 Jan 1938, p. 1. *HR* 24 Jan 1938, p. 5, 11. *HR* 7 Feb 1938, p. 11. *LAT* 21 Jan 1938. *MPD* 23 Mar 1938, p. 7. *MPH* 12 Mar 1938, p. 35. *MPH* 19 Mar 1938, p. 46. *NYT* 8 Apr 1938, p. 17. *Var* 13 Apr 1938, p. 15.

MR. MOTO'S LAST WARNING (Japanese Americans)

Twentieth Century-Fox Film Corp. *Dist* Twentieth Century-Fox Film Corp. 20 Jan **1939**; Prod: 6 Jun—29 Jun 1938. Sd (Western Electric Mirrophonic Recording); b&w. 7 reels, 6,376 ft. 71 min. PCA cert no. 4445.

Series: Mr. Moto.

Exec prod Sol M. Wurtzel. *Dir* Norman Foster. [*Asst dir* Jasper Blystone and Charles Faye]. *Orig scr* Philip MacDonald and Norman Foster. *Photog* Virgil Miller. [*Cam op* William Whitley]. [*Asst cam* Jack Warren]. [*Gaffer* L. V. Johnson]. *Art dir* Bernard Herzbrun, Lewis Creber and [Freddie Stoos]. *Film ed* Norman Colbert. [*Asst cutter* Doug Biggs]. *Set dec* Thomas Little. [*Set dresser* Walter Scott]. [*Asst prop* Larry Haddock and Walter Poggi]. *Cost* Helen A. Myron. [*Ward man* Sandy Sandeen]. *Mus dir* Samuel Kaylin. *Sd* E. Clayton Ward and William H. Anderson. [*Asst sound* Emmet O'Brien]. [*Boom man* Harry Roberts]. [*Hair* Jean Thomas]. [*Makeup* Fred Phillips]. [*Prod mgr* V. L. McFadden]. [*Unit mgr* Sam Schneider]. [*Scr clerk* Helen Torres]. [*Grip* Roger Murphy]. [*Asst grip* Dan Wurtzel]. [*Props* George Peckham]. [*Casting* Phillip Moore]. [*Best boy* F. Mime]. [*Cable man* M. Braggins]. [*Still photog* Tad Gillum].

Source: Based on the character created by John P. Marquand.

Cast: PETER LORRE (*Mr. Moto*), Ricardo Cortez (*Fabian*), Virginia Field (*Connie [Porter]*), John Carradine (*Danforth [also known as Burke]*), George Sanders (*Eric Norvel*), Joan Carol (*Mary Delacour*), Robert Coote (*Rollo*), Margaret Irving (*Madame Delacour*), Leyland Hodgson (*Hawkins*), John Davidson (*Hakim*), [Teru Shimada (*Fake Mr. Moto*)], [Georges Renavent (*Admiral Delacour*)], [E. E. Clive (*Commandant*)], [Holmes Herbert (*Bentham*)], [C. Montague Shaw (*First Lord of admiralty*)], [George Humbert (*Stage manager*)], [Jacques Lory (*Juggler*)], [Denis d'Auburn (*Deck officer*)], [Eric Wilton (*Deck steward*)], [Jimmy Aubrey (*Waiter*)], [Lal Chand Mehra (*Customs officer*)], [Victor Metzetti (*Cab driver*)], [Bert Roach (*Hotel clerk*)], [Jack Perry (*Mug*)], [A. R. Bogard (*Hoist man*)], [Wayne Rivers (*Cable man*)], [Daniel Boone, Al Wesslen (*Deep sea divers*)], [H. W. Stroele, Robert F. Owens (*Tenders*)], [Neil Fitzgerald (*English sergeant*)].

Espionage, Detective. [*Print viewed*]. Fabian, the leader of a spy ring, plots to disrupt the peaceful relations between England and France by blowing up the French fleet as it steams through Port Said in the Suez Canal. Although Fabian is posing as a ventriloquist to hide his sinister activities, British agent Burke has infiltrated the ring under the alias of Danforth, and has warned the French of imminent danger. Consequently, the arrival of the fleet has been delayed. Meanwhile, Mr. Moto, an agent of the International Police who is masquerading as an antique dealer, is also trying to uncover Fabian's plot. After ordering Eric Norvel, one of his men, to trick the admiral's wife, Madame Delacour, into revealing the arrival date of the fleet, Fabian discovers that Danforth is a British agent and cleverly disposes of him by drowning him at the site of the explosives, thus making it seem as if the British are responsible for the sabotage. Becoming suspicious of the antique dealer, Fabian orders his girl friend, Connie Porter, to follow him. Connie's report confirms Fabian's suspicions that the antique dealer is Mr. Moto, and Fabian orders that he be killed, but

Moto cleverly escapes. As the fleet steams into port, Fabian readies to give Norvel the signal to detonate the explosives, but Moto intercepts Norvel and sets off the explosives before the fleet can reach port. Fabian then tries to kill Moto himself, but his attempt is cut short when Connie, who has discovered his treachery, shoots him. *Foreign agents. Impersonation and imposture. Japanese Americans. Sabotage. Spies. Antique dealers. Attempted murder. Drowning. Escapes. Explosives. France. Great Britain. Navy. Suez Canal (Egypt). Ventriloquists and ventriloquism.*

Note: The working titles of this film were *Mr. Moto No. 6, Winter Garden* and *Mr. Moto in Egypt*. A *HR* production chart adds Virginia Bruce to the cast, but she was not in the released film. According to materials contained in the Twentieth Century-Fox Records of the Legal Department at the UCLA Theater Arts Library, Miles Mander was originally cast as Danforth. This film was the last in the "Mr. Moto" series. For additional information about the series, see *Think Fast, Mr. Moto* (below) and consult the Series Index.

FD 31 Jan 1939, p. 8. *HR* 6 Jun 1938, p. 11. *HR* 20 Jun 1938, pp. 12-13. *HR* 22 Jul 1938, p. 3. *MPH* 24 Dec 1938, p. 36. *NYT* 27 Jan 1939, p. 17. *Var* 25 Jan 1939, p. 11.

MR. SKEFFINGTON (Jewish Americans)

Warner Bros. Pictures, Inc.; A Warner Bros.—First National Picture. *Dist* Warner Bros. Pictures, Inc. 12 Aug **1944**; New York opening: 25 May 1944; Prod: 11 Oct 1943–late Jan 1944 [©Warner Bros. Pictures, Inc.; 12 Aug 1944; LP12774]. Sd (RCA Sound System); b&w. 11,457 ft. 146 min.

Exec prod JACK L. WARNER. *Prod* Julius J. Epstein and Philip G. Epstein. *Dir* Vincent Sherman. *Scr* Julius J. Epstein and Philip G. Epstein. *Dir of photog* Ernest Haller. *Mont* James Leicester. *Art dir* Robert Haas. *Film ed* Ralph Dawson. *Set dec* Fred M. MacLean. *Gowns* Orry-Kelly. *Orch arr* Leonid Raab. *Mus dir* Leo F. Forbstein. *Mus* Franz Waxman. *Sd* Robert B. Lee. *Makeup artist* Perc Westmore.

Source: Based on the novel *Mr. Skeffington* by Mary Annette Beauchamp, Countess Russell (New York, 1940).

Cast: BETTE DAVIS [(*Fanny Trellis Skeffington*)], Claude Rains [(*Job Skeffington*)], Walter Abel [(*George Trellis*)], George Coulouris [(*Dr. Byles*)], Richard Waring [(*Trippy Trellis*)], Marjorie Riordan [(*Fanny Junior*)], Robert Shayne [(*MacMahon*)], John Alexander [(*Jim Conderley*)], Jerome Cowan [(*Ed Morrison*)], Johnny Mitchell [(*Johnny Mitchell*)], Dorothy Peterson [(*Manby*)], Peter Whitney [(*Chester Forbish*)], Bill Kennedy [(*Thatcher*)], [Tom Stevenson (*Reverend Hyslup*)], [Halliwell Hobbes (*Soames*)], [Walter Kingsford (*Dr. Melton*)], [William Forrest (*Clinton*)], [Harry Bradley (*The rector*)], [Creighton Hale (*Employee*)], [John Vosper (*Artist*)], [Lottie Williams (*Housekeeper*)], [Vera Lewis (*Justice's wife*)], [Edward Fielding (*Justice of the peace*)], [Kit Carson (*Young man*)], [Lucille Lamarr (*Young girl*)], [Joe Devlin (*Attendant on ferry*)], [Charles Jordan (*Projectionist*)], [Erskine Sanford (*Dr. Fawcette*)], [Joan Winfield (*Nurse*)], [Ann Doran (*Nursemaid*)], [Ghislaine Perreau (*Fanny, two years old*)], [Dick Erdman (*Western Union boy*)], [Bunny Sunshine (*Fanny, five years old*)], [Charles Marsh (*Tailor*)], [Cyril Ring (*Perry Lanks*)], [Chef Milani (*Speakeasy doorman*)], [Dolores Gray (*Singer*)], [Crane Whitley ("*Louie*")], [Hans Herbert (*Waiter*)], [Molly Lamont (*Miss Norris*)], [Saul Gorss (*Plainclothesman*)], [Sylvia Arslan (*Fanny, ten years old*)], [Ann Codee (*French modiste*)], [Antonio Filauri (*Modiste*)], [Bruce Warren (*Handsome man in cafe*)], [Minerva Urecal (*Woman in beauty shop*)], [Doria Caron (*Beauty operator*)], [Jack George (*Henri*)], [Angela Greene (*Hairdresser*)], [Georgia King (*Dr. Eyles' nurse*)], [Georgia Caine (*Mrs. Newton*)], [Lelah Tyler (*Mrs. Forbish*)], [Mary Field (*Mrs. Hyslup*)], [Regina Wallace (*Mrs. Conderly*)], [Bess Flowers (*Mrs. Thatcher*)], [Frances Sage (*Skeffington's first secretary*)], [Janet Barrett, Tom Wilson (*Witnesses*)], [Wallis Clark, Richard Kipling (*Men's club men*)], [Matt McHugh, Will Stanton (*Drunks*)], [Tom Quinn, Ronnie Rondell, Danny Dowling, Patrick Michael Cunning, Ray Cooper (*Playboys*)], [Helen Eby-Rock, Isabelle LaMal (*Women in cafe*)], [Dagmar Oakland].

Melodrama. [*Print viewed*]. In 1914, beautiful Fanny Trellis is courted by many men including Jim Conderley, Ed Morrison and Thatcher. One evening, while her suitors wait downstairs, Fanny's cousin, George Trellis, returns home after several years away. George learns that contrary to their extravagant lifestyle, Fanny and her brother Trippy have no money. Trippy, however, now has a job working on Wall Street for Jewish Job Skeffington. Later that evening, Job calls unexpectedly for Trippy, who angrily refuses to see him. At George's instigation, he and Fanny speak to Job instead. Job has fired Trippy for embezzling and has come to ask him to repay the stolen

money. He is stunned when Fanny explains their financial situation. The next day, Trippy threatens to commit suicide. Determined to save her brother, Fanny sets her cap for Job and soon marries him, even though Job fully realizes that Fanny does not love him. Her ploy backfires, however, when an angry Trippy leaves for Europe, and that night, Fanny locks Job out of her room. Fanny's suitors are unfazed by her marriage and continue to pursue her. Job endures their presence because, although Fanny enjoys their attentions, she always sends them away. On the night of the Skeffingtons' first anniversary, they learn that Trippy has joined the Lafayette Esquadrille and that Fanny is pregnant. Although Job is delighted by the coming child, Fanny sees it as a sign that she is growing old and insists on leaving for California until the baby is born and she is once again beautiful. Shortly after Fanny Junior is born, the U.S. enters the war. When Trippy is killed, Fanny blames Job for his death, and Job finally realizes that Fanny will never love him. After the war ends, Job devotes himself to his daughter, while Fanny occupies herself with a series of lovers. During prohibition, Fanny attracts a bootlegger named MacMahon, who is determined to marry her. To convince her to divorce Job, he demonstrates that Job has had several mistresses during their marriage. Although Fanny's rejection of her husband can be seen as partly responsible for his behavior, Job agrees to a divorce. Not wanting to be bothered by a child, Fanny suggests that Job take custody of their daughter. Job is reluctant because of the difference in their religions and also because he plans to live in Europe, where the Fascists are coming to power. Fanny Junior's distress at losing her father, however, convinces Job to take her with him. Several years later, a middle-aged Fanny becomes involved with the much younger Johnny Mitchell, and Fanny Junior returns to the U.S. from Berlin. After sailing in stormy weather with Johnny, Fanny falls seriously ill with diphtheria. She recovers, but the illness ages her greatly, and she begins to hallucinate, imagining that she sees Job everywhere. A psychiatrist tells her the hallucinations are a subconscious manifestation of a need to see her former husband because, now that she is fifty, her romantic life is over. Determined to prove him wrong, Fanny throws a dinner party for her old suitors, only to discover that they are all appalled by her aged appearance. Only Edward still seems smitten, but Fanny quickly realizes that he is only interested in her money. When Fanny Junior later announces that she and Johnny are getting married and moving to Seattle, Fanny is left totally alone. The next morning, George tells Fanny that he has seen Job, now a broken man after his stay in a concentration camp. George begs Fanny to care for Job in return for his generous care of her, but she refuses, believing that her lack of beauty will drive Job away as it did all the others. When she realizes that Job is blind, however, she knows that here is one man who will always remember her as beautiful and welcomes him home. *Beauty, Personal. Brothers and sisters. Flirts. Jews. Marriage. Blindness. Bootleggers. Cousins. Dinners and dining. Diphtheria. Divorce. Embezzlement. Fathers and daughters. Hallucinations. Infidelity. Mothers and daughters. Neglected husbands. New York City. Pregnancy. Psychiatrists. Weddings. World War I. World War II.*

Note: A 12 Apr 1940 *HR* news item notes that Selznick-International was bidding for the screen rights to Countess Russell's novel. After Warner Bros. bought the book, a *LAEx* news item dated 28 Oct 1941 notes that Tallulah Bankhead, Gloria Swanson and Norma Shearer were all considered to play the role of "Fanny Skeffington." At the time, M-G-M was rumored to be interested in the film as a vehicle for one of that studio's many actresses. Other *HR* news items add the following information about the production: Warner Bros. considered Irene Dunne as a possible star for the film. Before his death in 1940, James Stephenson was cast as "Job Skeffington." Later, Paul Henreid was announced for the role opposite Bette Davis. Richard Waring was also tested for the lead, and Faye Emerson and Jean Sullivan were tested for the role of "Fanny Junior." Waring was eventually cast as "Trippy." Charles Drake was scheduled for a part but was drafted, although *HR, Var* and *NYT* erroneously credit him with the part of "Johnny Mitchell." Instead, actor Johnny Mitchell, who was formerly known as Douglass Drake, made his screen debut in the part. According to studio memos reproduced in a modern source, in 1940, when Bette Davis was initially offered the role of "Fanny Skeffington," she turned it down, believing that as a thirty-two year old woman she could not convincingly play a woman of fifty.

The Office of War Information objected to one version of the script because of its portrayal of American anti-semitism and because American financiers were characterized as "shady." In a letter to Warner Bros., the OWI stated: "This is just the kind of picture of America which the Fascists would like to see. They have deluged the world with propaganda about the money-mad Americans, and today are using this line to create a breach between us and our allies. Is this the picture we want to give other peoples as representative of America and the

American way?.." The finished picture still contained the sections the OWI found objectionable.

Modern sources add the following information about the picture: Bette Davis requested Vincent Sherman as her director. Color tests were made, but the studio ultimately decided to make the film in black and white. Shortly after completing Davis' wardrobe of around forty costumes, forty-one-year-old Orry-Kelly was drafted into the army. Bette Davis was nominated for an Oscar for Best Actress and Claude Rains was nominated for Best Supporting Actor. Bette Davis reprised her role in a *Lux Radio Theatre* broadcast on 1 Oct 1945, co-starring Paul Henreid.

Box 27 May 1944. *DV* 26 May 1944, pp. 3-4. *FD* 31 May 1944, p. 10. *HR* 12 Apr 1940. *HR* 4 Nov 1940, p. 6. *HR* 26 Jun 1941, p. 1. *HR* 14 Jul 1941, p. 1. *HR* 13 Aug 1943, p. 4. *HR* 21 Sep 1943, p. 7. *HR* 22 Sep 1943, p. 6. *HR* 12 Oct 1943, p. 4. *HR* 5 Nov 1943, p. 14. *HR* 24 Nov 1943, p. 9. *HR* 26 May 1944, p. 3. *HR* 29 May 1944, p. 10. *HR* 14 Sep 1944, p. 2. *LAEx* 28 Oct 1941. *MPHPD* 4 Dec 1943, p. 1654. *MPHPD* 27 May 1944, p. 1909. *NYT* 26 May 1944, p. 23. *Var* 31 May 1944, p. 20.

MR. WASHINGTON GOES TO TOWN (African Americans)
Dixie National Pictures, Inc. *Dist* Dixie National Pictures, Inc.; Consolidated Film Exchange. **1940?**; Los Angeles preview: 11 Apr 1940; New York opening: week of 13 Jun 1941. Sd; b&w. 4,956 ft. 55 or 64-65 min. PCA cert no. 6217.

Prod Jed Buell and James K. Friedrich. *Assoc prod* Maceo B. Sheffield. *Dir* Jed Buell. *Scr* Walter Weems and Lex Neal. *Story* Walter Weems. *Photog* Jack Greenhalgh. *Art dir* Fred Prebble. *Film ed* William Faris. *Mus dir* Harvey Brooks. *Sd eng* Hans Weeren. *Sd eff* Treg Brown. *Prod mgr* Bert Sternbach. *Asst prod mgr* Charlie Wayne.

Cast: F. E. Miller (*Wallingford*), Mantan Moreland (*Schenectady*), Maceo B. Sheffield (*Brutus Blake*), Arthur Ray (*Blackstone*), Margaret Whitten (*Lady Queenie*), Clarence Morehouse (*Gorilla*), Monte Hawley (*Stiletto*), Zerita Steptean (*Mrs. Brutus*), Florence O'Brien (*Chambermaid*), Vernon McCalla (*Invisible man*), John Lester Johnson (*Headless man—long*), DeForrest Covan (*Headless man—short*), Edward Boyd (*Lonesome ranger*), Clarence Hargrave (*Man with gorilla*), Johnnie Taylor (*Magician*), Walter Knox (*Man on crutches*), Geraldine Whitfield (*Beautiful girl*), Sam Warren (*Barber*), Cleo Desmond (*Old maid*), Charlie Hawkins (*Goldberg*), Nathan Curry (*Policeman*), Slick Garrison (*Man in barber chair*), Henry Hastings (*Uncle Utica*).

African American, Fantasy, Comedy. [*Not viewed*]. When prison inmate Schenectady learns that his uncle has died and left him the Hotel Ethiopia, he falls asleep and dreams of the hotel: He goes to work as a bellhop and elevator operator and makes his prison buddy Wallingford his assistant. Next, a maid comments that nothing ever happens at the hotel, and Schenectady notices that the hotel is a strange place. Among the visitors is a man in white tails with a gorilla, a headless man carrying his head, a stiletto thrower and a reappearing invisible man. A magician frightens Schenectady by producing a goldfish bowl around his head, and a "lonesome ranger" enters riding a goat. Brutus Blake, who holds some of the many mortgages on the hotel, wants to get the money to buy the establishment, and contests Schenectady's claim. Later, Brutus tears up the floors and walls searching for hidden gold. After scaring the chambermaid, Brutus is chased by the gorilla and by his wife, who has arrived unexpectedly. He meets the hotel's attractive beautician, Lady Queenie, on whom he uses all his romantic charm. Just as things begin to get wild, Schenectady is awakened by the jailer, and his dream ends. Wallingford suggests that they go to the hotel when they are released from prison, but Schenectady says that he has just been there and wants nothing more to do with it. *African Americans. Dreams. Hotels. Inheritance. Prisoners. Bellboys. Cowboys. Gorillas. Jails. Magicians. Maids. Mortgages. Treasure. Uncles.*

Note: A working title for this film was *Mr. Jones Goes to Town.* The film was the first picture to be produced by Dixie National Pictures, Inc., a company formed in Mar 1940 by Jed Buell, who earlier produced *Harlem on the Prairie* (see entry above). James K. Friedrich, a minister who made the religious film *The Great Commandment* (see *AFI Catalog of Feature Films, 1931-40*; F3.1707) was Dixie's biggest investor. Modern sources note that Ted Toddy helped form the company. Although contemporary sources indicate that the film was previewed at the Lincoln Theater in Los Angeles in Apr 1940, it may not have been released until Jun 1941 when, according to the *Var* review, it opened in Harlem. As noted in *Time*, there are no characters in the film named "Washington." The picture, which the press preview program called the "first all negro feature comedy ever made," was written, produced and directed by white men, and was made in six days at a reported cost of $15,000. According to *FD*, many of the actors playing the hotel's "guests" were vaudeville performers.

DV 12 Apr 1940, p. 3. *Exh* 1 May 1940, p. 519. *FD* 19 Apr 1940, p. 9. *HR* 12 Apr 1940, p. 4. *MPD* 18 Apr 1940, p. 4. *MPH* 20 Apr 1940, p. 35. *Time* 29 Apr 1940. *Var* 18 Jun 1941, p. 18. *Var* 25 Jun 1941.

MISTER WEST POINT *see* **THE LONG GRAY LINE**

MR. WHISKERS *see* **GAMBLING HOUSE**

MR. WONG AT HEADQUARTERS *see* **THE FATAL HOUR**

MR. WONG, DETECTIVE (Chinese Americans)

Monogram Pictures Corp.; Scott R. Dunlap in charge of production. *Dist* Monogram Pictures Corp. **1938**; Prod: began 24 Aug 1938 [©Monogram Pictures Corp.; 5 Oct 1938; LP8334]. Sd (Western Electric Sound System); b&w. 8 reels, 6,301 ft. 67-70 min. PCA cert no. 4690.

Series: Mr. Wong.

Assoc prod William Lackey. *Dir* William Nigh. *Asst dir* W. B. Eason. *Scr* Houston Branch. *Dir of photog* Harry Neumann. *Film ed* Russell Schoengarth. [*Mus dir* Abe Meyer]. *Rec eng* Karl Zint. *Tech dir* E. R. Hickson. *Prod mgr* C. J. Bigelow.

Source: Based on characters created by Hugh Wiley in the "James Lee Wong" short stories in *Collier's*.

Cast: BORIS KARLOFF [(*Mr. James Lee Wong*)], Grant Withers [(*Captain Sam Street*)], Maxine Jennings [(*Myra Ross*)], Evelyn Brent [(*Olga, also known as Countess Dubois*)], George Lloyd [(*Devlin*)], Lucien Prival [(*Anton Mohl, also known as the Baron*)], John St. Polis [(*Carl Roemer*)], William Gould [(*Theodore Meisle*)], Hooper Atchley [(*Christian Wilk*)], John Hamilton [(*Simon Dayton*)], Wilbur Mack [(*Russell*)], Lee Tong Foo [(*Tchin*)], [Lynton Brent], [Grace Wood], [Frank Bruno].

Mystery. [*Print viewed*]. Soon after San Francisco businessman Simon Dayton asks for help from famous detective James Lee Wong to prevent his murder, Dayton is found dead in his office. The logical suspect is Carl Roemer, an inventor who had just threatened Dayton with a gun for stealing his formula. Because the police had been summoned after the threat, Captain Sam Street is on hand to arrest the scientist, but Wong is not convinced of Roemer's guilt. He finds thin particles of glass in Dayton's office, which lab experts tell him were originally shaped like a sphere and were made of extremely brittle Bavarian glass. Dayton's autopsy also reveals that he died from poison gas. Later Wong discovers that a duplicate he has made of the sphere shatters when certain sounds are emitted. As Street tries to build his case, his girl friend, Myra Ross, who was also Dayton's secretary, helps Wong because she is certain Roemer is innocent. When one of Dayton's partners, Christian Wilk, is also found murdered in a locked room beside the glass particles, Wong's suspicions turn to a baron and his companion, Olga, also known as the Countess Dubois. Next, Devlin, Roemer's other partner, is found murdered the same way. Because Roemer was in jail at the time, he is released and is invited by Wong to come to his home. The mystery is unfolded through a trap when Wong reveals that the glass sphere cracked at the sound of a police siren and that the sphere contained poison gas, which was to be sold to a foreign power through the agents, Olga and the Baron. Dayton's company was used to smuggle the poison out of the country. As a siren is heard in the background, Roemer jumps up and tries to flee, but Wong has used an empty sphere as a decoy. It is finally revealed that Roemer killed all of the men by planting the sphere, then much later, arranged for situations in which the police had to be summoned, thus causing the sphere to break. *Chinese Americans. Detectives. Murder. Police. Scientists. Spies. Gases, Asphyxiating and poisonous. Glass. Nobility. Partnership. San Francisco (CA). Secretaries. Servants. Smuggling.*

Note: Some reviews incorrectly list actor Lee Tong Foo as Tchin, the name of the character he played. This was the first film in Monogram's "Mr. Wong" series. Five additional films were made in 1939 and 1940, ending with *Phantom of Chinatown* in 1940. The first five films, all directed by William Nigh, starred Karloff as "Mr. James Lee Wong," and Grant Withers as "Street," whose first name and rank changed from film to film. Three of the films co-starred Marjorie Reynolds as "Street's" girl friend. The last film starred Keye Luke as "Jimmy Lee Wong," a college student studying criminology. For additional titles in the series, consult the Series Index. The 1947 Monogram film, *Docks of New Orleans* (see above), directed by Derwin Abrahams and starring Roland Winters, was a partial remake of *Mr. Wong, Detective*, substituting the fictional detective "Charlie Chan" for "Mr. Wong" and moving the action to New Orleans.

Box 8 Oct 1938. *DV* 27 Sep 1938, p. 3. *FD* 3 Oct 1938, p. 8. *HR* 24 Aug 1938, p. 4. *HR* 27 Sep 1938, p. 3. *MPD* 3 Oct 1938, p. 6. *MPH* 17 Sep 1938, p. 44. *MPH* 1 Oct 1938, p. 39. *NYT* 21 Nov 1938, p. 14. *Var* 23 Nov 1938, p. 14.

MR. WONG IN CHINATOWN (Chinese Americans)

Monogram Pictures Corp.; Scott R. Dunlap in charge of production. *Dist* Monogram Pictures Corp. 1 Aug **1939**; Prod: 9 Jun 1939 [©Monogram Pictures Corp.; 18 Jul 1939; LP8991]. Sd (Western Electric Sound System); b&w. 8 reels. 70 min. PCA cert no. 5515.

Series: Mr. Wong.

Assoc prod William T. Lackey. *Dir* William Nigh. *Asst dir* W. B. Eason. *Scr* Scott Darling. *Photog* Harry Neumann. *Film ed* Russell Schoengarth. *Ward* Louis Brown. *Mus dir* Edward Kay. *Sd* Karl Zint. *Tech dir* E. R. Hickson. *Prod mgr* Charles J. Bigelow.

Source: Based on characters created by Hugh Wiley in the "James Lee Wong" short stories in *Collier's*.

Cast: Boris Karloff (*James Lee Wong*), Grant Withers (*Inspector Street*), Marjorie Reynolds (*Bobby Logan*), Peter George Lynn (*Captain Guy Jackson*), William Royle (*Captain Jalme*), Huntley Gordon (*Mr. Davidson*), James Flavin (*Sergeant Jerry*), Lotus Long (*Princess Lin Hwa*), Richard Loo (*Aged Chinese*), Bessie Loo (*Lilly May*), Lee Tong Foo (*Willie*), Little Angelo (*Dwarf*), Guy Usher (*Commissioner*), [Ernie Stanton].

Detective. [*Print viewed*]. When Chinese Princess Lin Hwa is murdered in the home of eminent detective James Lee Wong, the only clue to her killer is her hastily scribbled note reading "Captain J." Inspector Street is summoned to the scene of the crime and is followed by reporter Bobby Logan, who identifies the victim as a Chinese princess. Wong turns to the Tong for information and discovers that the princess was on a mission to buy arms for her brother's army. The princess brought with her a letter of credit for one million dollars, and Wong soon discovers that the money has been withdrawn from the bank through forged checks. As the princess' servants are murdered, suspicion points to Captain Guy Jackson, a phony airplane manufacturer; Captain Jalme, the skipper of the princess' boat; and Mr. Davidson, the bank president. After Wong and Davidson are captured by Jackson and Jalme, Inspector Street traces the two captains to Davidson and comes to the rescue of Wong and the bank president. Wong then unmasks Davidson as the forger and murderer of the princess and her servants. *Chinatowns. Chinese Americans. Detectives. Murder. Princesses. Tongs (Secret societies). Bank presidents. Forgers and forgery. Police. Reporters. Rescues. Sea captains.*

Note: For additional information about the series, consult the Series Index and see entry above for *Mr. Wong, Detective*.

DV 14 Jul 1939, p. 3. *FD* 19 Jul 1939, p. 19. *HR* 8 Jun 1939, p. 6. *HR* 17 Jun 1939, pp. 6-7. *HR* 14 Jul 1939, p. 3. *MPD* 18 Jul 1939, p. 4 *MPH* 22 Jul 1939, p. 50. *Var* 2 Aug 1939, p. 18.

MR. WU (*foreign version*) *see* **WU LI CHANG**

MR. YANCEY OF VIRGINA *see* **THE VANISHING VIRGINIAN**

MIXED BLOOD (Latino, Irish Americans)

Universal Film Mfg. Co.; Red Feather Photoplays. *Dist* Universal Film Mfg. Co. 18 Dec **1916** [©Universal Film Mfg. Co.; 7 Dec 1916; LP9678]. Si; b&w. 5 reels.

Dir Charles Swickard. *Scen* J. Grubb Alexander. *Story* Willard Mack. *Cam* Harry Maguire.

Cast: Claire McDowell (*Nita Valyez*), George Beranger (*Carlos*), Roy Stewart (*Big Jim*), Wilbur Higby (*Joe Nagle*), Jessie Arnold (*Lottie Nagle*), Harry Archer (*Blootch White*), Mrs. Emmons (*Mrs. Valyez*), Doc Crane.

Western. For Nita Valyez, who is half-Spanish and half-Irish, Carlos represents potential violence and danger, two things to which she is both attracted and repelled. In contrast, she has only a passing interest in Big Jim, the town's honest, good-hearted sheriff. Then, after Carlos kills a faro dealer, he forces Nita to make an escape with him. Jim follows them, and finally catches up to them in a small border town where the plague has broken out, and where Nita is taking care of a dying Carlos. Although impressed by her devotion to Carlos, Jim brings Nita back with him in order to save her from the plague, and also to try to convince her to love him. *Fidelity. Plague. Sheriffs. Faro (GAME). Irish. Spaniards.*

ETR 16 Dec 1916, p. 137. *MPN* 23 Dec 1916, p. 4023, 4044, 4047. *MPW* 23 Dec 1916, p. 1814. *MPW* 30 Dec 1916, p. 2006. *Wid's* 4 Jan 1917, p. 6.

MIZREKH UN MAYREV *see* **MAZEL TOV**

MOBILIZING OF JOHANNA *see* **JOHANNA ENLISTS**

MOBY DICK (*foreign version*) *see* **DÄMON DES MEERES**

A MODERN CAIN (Africa Americans)
   Fife Production Co. *Dist* Comet Film Co. 1921; Chicago opening: 22 Nov 1921. Si; b&w. 6 reels.
   Dir J. W. Fife. *Wrt* J. W. Fife.
   Cast: Norman Ward (*William Moore*), Theodore Williams (*Paul Moore*), Fred Williams (*Everett Moore*), Z. Y. Young (*James Hagan*), Vivian Quarles (*Leonore Blackwell*), Harriet Harris (*Mrs. Blackwell*), Hugh Mason (*Samuel Egan*), Munzall Everett (*Mrs. Egan*).
   Melodrama, **African American**. John and Paul, African-American twin brothers, are orphaned at an early age and left in the care of an uncle. Grown to manhood, John invests his inheritance in a business, while Paul squanders his share. They fall in love with the same girl. Avaricious and inflamed with jealousy, Paul pushes John off a cliff and reports him as missing. John, who is not killed, becomes a half-wit and wanders around in an amnesic fog until he is cured by a doctor. John returns home and finds that Paul has died from dope addiction. He marries his sweetheart, and thus all ends well. *African Americans. Amnesia. Attempted murder. Brothers. Drug addicts. Drugs. Fratricide. Greed. Missing persons, assumed dead. Orphans. Physicians. Twins. Falls from heights.*
   Note: The Fife Production Co. was located in Chicago. According to information in the George P. Johnson Collection at the UCLA Special Collections Library, J. W. Fife worked earlier at the Unique Film Co. of Chicago and may have produced at the Selig Polyscope Co.
   ChiDef 19 Nov 1921, p. 7.

MOHAWK (Native Americans, Iroquois, Mohawk, Tuscarora)
   National Pictures Corp. *Dist* Twentieth Century-Fox Film Corp. Apr **1956**; Prod: Aug 1955 [©National Pictures Corp.; 15 Apr 1955; LP5829]. Sd; col (Pathé). 9 reels, 7,146 pr 7,110 ft. 79 min. PCA cert no. 17730.
   Pres by EDWARD L. ALPERSON. *Assoc prod* Charles B. Fitzsimons. *Dir* Kurt Neumann. *Asst dir* Lee Wm. Lukather. *Scr and story* Maurice Geraghty and Milton Krims. *Photog* Karl Struss. *Prod des* Ernst Fegté. *Film ed* Wm. B. Murphy. *Set dec* Darrell Silvera. *Ward des* Norma. *Mus* Edward L. Alperson, Jr. *Mus cond* Raoul Kraushaar. *Sd* Richard Tyler. *Makeup* Louis Hippe. *Hair* Lillian Lashin. *Prod mgr* Herbert Mendelson. *Tech adv* D. R. O. Hatswell. *Dial supv* Herold Goodwin. *Exec asst* Richard Einfeld.
   Song(s): "Mohawk" and "Love Plays the Strings of My Banjo," music by Edward L. Alperson, Jr., lyrics by Paul Herrick.
   Cast: Scott Brady (*Jonathan [Adams]*), Rita Gam (*Onida*), Neville Brand (*Rokhawah*), Lori Nelson (*Cynthia [Stanhope]*), Allison Hayes (*Greta*), John Hoyt (*Butler*), Vera Vague (*Aunt Agatha*), Rhys Williams (*Clem Jones*), Tommy Cook (*Keoga*), John Hudson (*Captain Langley*), Ted De Corsia (*Kowanen*), Mae Clarke (*Minikah*), Michael Granger [(*Priest*)], James Lilburn [(*Sergeant*)], Chabon Jadi [(*Dancer*)], Clegg Hoyt [(*Driver*)], Kenneth B. Harp [(*Militiaman*)], [Harry O. Tyler, John Bennes, Robert Carson, Sid Clute, Lyle Latell, Paul Lukather, Troy Melton, James Nusser, Jack Rutherford (*Settlers*)].
   Historical, **Drama**. [*Print viewed*]. In eighteenth-century New York, early Mohawk Valley settler Butler, who wants to keep the valley for himself, is alarmed when a new group of settlers arrives and warns Mohawk Chief Kowanen that the settlers have brought a shipment of arms with them. Kowanen refuses to declare war on the white man, explaining that there is enough land for all. When Rokhawah, a Tuscarora brave, warns that the white man took his own tribe's land, however, Kowanen's son Keoga organizes a raiding party to steal the muskets from the fort. Meanwhile, artist Jonathan Adams, commissioned by the Massachusetts Society to paint landscapes of the valley, is torn between his attentions to local barmaid Greta and his visiting fiancé, a proper Boston society woman named Cynthia Stanhope. That night, Keoga and his beautiful sister Onida secretly lead the raiding party into the fort. As they are stealing the arms, however, a guard spots them and shooting erupts. All of the braves escape or are shot, leaving Onida trapped inside the fort. Jonathan finds her hiding in his cabin and, struck by her beauty, smuggles her out of the fort the next morning. Realizing that Jonathan bears no ill will against Indians, Onida asks him to observe the ways of her people and then explain to the white man that the Mohawk want to live in

peace. Jonathan eagerly agrees, and while he is visiting the village, he falls in love with Onida. At the fort, Greta and Cynthia fear Jonathan has been attacked by the Mohawk and urge Captain Langley to take action. Eager to be rid of both the Mohawk and the settlers, Butler warns that the Indians will slaughter all the settlers if their village is not destroyed first. Langley, who respects the Mohawk, visits the village and urges Jonathan to return home in order to quiet the alarmed populace. As the artist heads back to the fort with Keoga, however, Butler, hiding behind a tree, shoots the young brave. Jonathan brings Keoga's body back to the village, but when Rokhawah convinces the tribe to declare war because of the killing, Jonathan becomes their prisoner. Onida helps him to escape, and he returns to the fort to warn the settlers. Jonathan surmises that Butler killed Keoga, whereupon Butler is ejected from the fort and killed by the approaching warriors. The battle has already begun, however, and before reinforcements arrive to save the fort at the last moment, many are killed. Although he is now a prisoner, Kowanen declares that all of the Iroquois, including the Mohawk and the Tuscarora, will drive the white man out of the valley. Upon learning that Butler caused all the trouble, however, he relents and makes peace with Langley. Cynthia returns to Boston with Jonathan's paintings, while the artist goes to live with Onida and the Mohawk tribe. *Greed. Indians of North America. Iroquois Indians. Settlers. Artists. Aunts. Barmaids. Battles. Bostonians. Escapes. Forts. Jealousy. Mohawk Valley (NY). New York (State). Revenge. Romance. Tribal chiefs. Tribal life. United States–History–19th century.*
   Note: Working titles for the film included *Mohawk Massacre* and *Mohawk: A Legend of the Iroquis*. The released film contained the phrase "A legend of the Iroquis..." above the opening title. According to news items, Peter Lawford was initially cast in the leading role and Twentieth Century-Fox acquired distribution rights to the film in mid-December 1955, after the picture was completed. Information in the file on the film in the MPAA/PCA Collection at the AMPAS Library indicates that much of the film was shot on location in Utah.
   Box 24 Mar 1956. *DV* 13 Dec 1955. *DV* 21 Mar 1956, p. 3. *FD* 2 Apr 1956, p. 6. *HR* 5 May 1955. *HR* 12 Aug 1955, p. 13. *HR* 26 Aug 1955, p. 9. *HR* 21 Mar 1956, p. 3. *LAT* 21 Mar 1956. *MPD* 21 Mar 1946. *MPHPD* 24 Mar 1956, p. 833. *Var* 21 Mar 1956, p. 6.

THE MOHICAN'S DAUGHTER (Native Americans, Mohegan)
   P. T. B., Inc. *Dist* American Releasing Corp. 7 May **1922** [©P. T. B., Inc.; 7 May 1922; LP18109]. Si; b&w. 5 reels, 4,697 ft.
   Dir S. E. V. Taylor. *Scen* S. E. V. Taylor. *Photog* Oliver Marsh and Lester Lang. *Art dir* Charles Cadwallader.
   Source: Based on the short story "The Story of Jees Uck" by Jack London in *Faith of Men and Other Stories* (New York, 1904).
   Cast: Nancy Deaver (*Jees Uck*), Hazel Washburn (*Kitty Shannon*), Sazon Kling (*Neil Bonner*), William Thompson (*Amos Pentley*), Jack Newton (*Jack Hollis*), Paul Panzer (*Father La Claire*), Nick Thompson (*Chatanna*), Mortimer Snow (*Nashinta*), John Webb Dillon (*A half-breed*), Myrtle Morse (*Inigo, his wife*), Rita Abrams (*Their child*).
   Romance. Jees Uck, a half-breed maiden desired by Chatanna, chief of the tribe with which she lives, defies tribal law by getting medicine from the trading post for the sick child of her friend, Inigo. Nashinta, the medicine man, defends her against the chief. Chatanna kills Nashinta and puts the blame on Jees Uck, who flees into the arms of Neil Bonner, trading post manager, who loves her. The post is attacked, but Jees Uck surrenders to save her white friends. Neil finds evidence against the chief, delivers him to the authorities, and marries Jees Uck. *Indians of North America–Mixed blood. Medicine. Medicine men. Mohegan Indians. Trading posts.*
   ETR 23 Sep 1922, p. 1140. *Var* 22 Sep 1922, p. 42.

MOKEY (African Americans)
   Metro-Goldwyn-Mayer Corp.; controlled by Loew's Inc. *Dist* Loew's Inc. Apr **1942**; Prod: 21 Dec 1941–31 Jan 1942 [©Loew's Inc.; 24 Mar 1942; LP11251]. Sd (Western Electric Sound System); b&w. 9 reels, 7,915 ft. 87-88 min. Passed by the National Board of Review. PCA cert no. 8115.
   Prod J. Walter Ruben. *Dir* Wells Root. [*Asst dir* Hugh Boswell]. *Scr* Wells Root and Jan Fortune. *Dir of photog* Charles Rosher. *Art dir* Cedric Gibbons. *Assoc* Wade B. Rubottom. *Film ed* Frank Sullivan. *Set dec* Edwin B. Willis. *Rec dir* Douglas Shearer. [*Prod mgr* Jay Marchant].
   Source: Based on the novel *Mokey* by Jennie Harris Oliver (New York, 1936).
   Cast: Dan Dailey, Jr. (*Herbert Delano*), Donna Reed (*Anthea Delano*), Bobby Blake (*Mokey Delano*), Cordell Hickman (*Booker T.*

Cumby), William "Buckwheat" Thomas (*Brother Cumby*), Etta McDaniel (*Cindy Molishus*), Marcella Moreland (*Begonia Cumby*), George Lloyd (*Pat Esel*), Matt Moore (*Mr. Pennington*), Cleo Desmond (*Aunt Deedy*), Cliff Clark (*Mr. Graham*), Mary Field (*Mrs. Graham*), Bobby Stebbins (*Brickley Autry*), Sam McDaniel (*Uncle Ben*), [Addison Richards (*Judge*)], [Walter Soderling (*Mr. Pukuliar*)], [Frank Ward (*Tony*)], [Shirley Coates (*Tina Lundstrum*)], [Marga Ann Deighton (*Mrs. Lundstrum*)], [Milton Parsons (*Mr. Larkspur*)], [Harry Tyler, Pat West (*Hoboes*)], [Alonzo Price (*Mr. Autry*)], [Rose Langdon (*Mrs. Autry*)], [Mme. Sul-te-wan (*Old black woman*)], [Vincent Graeff, Paul Graeff (*Boys*)], [Frank Faylen (*Desk sergeant*)], [Jules Cowles (*Man on street*)], [Margaret Bert (*Woman on street*)], [Howard Mitchell, Tom Murray (*Men in searching party*)], [Billy Engle (*Janitor*)], [Edward Hearn (*Policeman*)], [Bob Lawson (*Hotel clerk*)].

Domestic, Youth, Drama. [*Print viewed*]. Eight-year-old Mokey Delano misses the warmth and affection of a mother and so is very excited when his widowed father Herbert remarries. Mokey immediately takes to the young woman, Anthea, but she has not had experience with children and does not know how to respond to Mokey's open affection. Herbert frequently travels on business and must leave Anthea alone with Mokey in the small town in which they live. Though not a bad child, Mokey frequently gets into mischief and Herbert tells Anthea that she must be firm with the boy, whose friends include the wild Brickley Autry and neighboring black children Booker T., Brother and Begonia Cumby. One day, Mokey accidentally ruins a new pair of curtains made by Anthea, who confines him to his room while she goes to church to play the organ. Soon after she has gone, Mokey decides to walk through the woods. When he learns from the Cumby children that Brick has stolen from Pennington's grocery and will be arrested, Mokey tries to warn him. Brick, who has been chronically beaten by his alcoholic parents, tries to hop a freight train with some hoboes, but they plan to take his goods and leave without him. Mokey interrupts them just as the local policeman, Pat Esel, arrives. He catches the boys and arrests them both, even though Brick tells him that Mokey was not involved in the robbery. At their trial, Brick is ordered to go to the nearby reform school, Rocky Run, but Mokey, who, at eight, can legally be sent there as well, is given a year's probation. After eight months, Mokey's sentence is reduced for good behavior, but Anthea has still not warmed to him. No matter how Mokey tries to show his affection for Anthea, who is soon to have her own baby, nothing seems to please her until he decides to try out for a job at Pennington's. She gives him money for new overalls, but by the time he arrives at the store, Pennington informs him that his wife has already given the job to another boy. Too embarrassed to admit he has failed, Mokey tells Anthea that he got the job and pretends to go to work every afternoon. One evening, when Mokey returns home late, Anthea is concerned. When he boasts that Pennington has such confidence in him that he lets him make the store's deposits at the bank, Anthea angrily phones Pennington to complain that Mokey is too young for such a responsibility. After Pennington tells her that Mokey does not even work for him, she is humiliated and tells Mokey she never wants anything to do with him again. Mokey is so hurt that he runs away and asks the Cumbys to take him home and say that he is their "Cousin Julius." To fool their guardian, Aunt Deedy, the children blacken Mokey's skin and put him into dirty, torn clothing. The kindly, nearsighted Aunt Deedy gladly takes the boy in, and Mokey realizes how much he still misses a mother's affection. After three weeks, Herbert fears that Mokey will never be found, and Anthea, who has given birth to the new baby, feels guilty that Mokey left because of her. At Aunt Deedy's house, meanwhile, Cindy Molishus, who has worked as a housekeeper for the Delanos, stops by and tells Aunt Deedy about the baby. A short time later, Pat and Herbert drive to Aunt Deedy's to ask the children if they have seen Mokey, whose clothing was found in the woods. When they say no, Herbert breaks down. Realizing that his father loves him, Mokey reveals himself, after which his father warmly embraces, then spanks him. At home, while Herbert again tells Anthea to take a firm hand with Mokey while he is away, Mokey goes to see the baby and immediately loves her, but accidentally knocks her out of her cradle. Even though the baby is not injured, Anthea explodes with anger and threatens to leave Herbert if Mokey is not sent to boarding school immediately. Herbert chastises her, then leaves for his business trip. Mokey feels so badly that he writes a sweet goodbye note to Anthea,

telling her that he is going "to California." He tries to hop a freight, but is interrupted by Pat. Mokey then eludes Pat by stealing the town doctor's car and driving to a nearby farm. There the kindly farmer and his wife, whose own son had recently died, take him in when he says that he is an orphan. Soon Pat tracks him down, however, and returns him to town. The doctor presses charges and after a night in the jailhouse, Mokey goes to court. The judge says that he has no choice but to send Mokey to Rocky Run, but because Mokey has learned that Brick died there, he begins to cry and begs the judge to reconsider. Touched by Mokey's sincere tears, Anthea also cries and pleads with the judge to give her another chance at being a mother, because it is really she who is at fault. The judge agrees and Mokey goes home, where Anthea hugs and kisses him goodnight. *African Americans. Children. Fathers and sons. Stepmothers. Accidental death. Alcoholics. Automobile theft. Battered children. Bigotry. Curtains. Deception. Escapes. Farmers. Jails. Judges. Juvenile delinquents. Organists. Police. Probation. Racial impersonation. Robbery. Small town life. Spanking. Trains. Trials. Wards and guardians. Widowers.*

Note: The film was at one time called *Mokey Delano*. Jennie Harris Oliver's novel was a compilation of several "Mokey" short stories that had previously been published in magazines. An *HR* news item noted that Laraine Day was originally to be the female lead of the film. According to other *HR* news items, Mantan Moreland, Ruby Elsey and Pat McVeigh were in the film. Moreland was not in the viewed print, however, and the appearances of Elsey and McVeigh have not been confirmed.

Box 28 Mar 1942. *DV* 9 Jan 1942. *DV* 25 Mar 1942, p. 3. *FD* 25 Mar 1942, p. 6. *HR* 27 Nov 1941, p. 3. *HR* 2 Dec 1941, p. 1. *HR* 26 Dec 1941, p. 10. *HR* 29 Dec 1941, p. 6. *HR* 23 Jan 1942, p. 10. *HR* 2 Feb 1942, p. 2, 4. *HR* 25 Mar 1942, p. 4. *MPHPD* 28 Mar 1942, p. 574. *Var* 25 Mar 1942, p. 8.

MOLLY (Jewish Americans)

Paramount Pictures, Inc. *Dist* Paramount Pictures, Inc. Apr **1951**; Limited run: Nov 1950; Philadelphia, PA premiere: 23 Dec 1950 [©Paramount Pictures, Inc.; 23 Jan 1951; LP786]. Sd (Western Electric Recording); b&w. 9 reels, 7,429 ft. 83 min. Passed by the National Board of Review.

Prod Mel Epstein. *Dir* Walter Hart. [*Asst dir* Oscar Rudolph]. *Scr* Gertrude Berg and N. Richard Nash. *Dir of photog* John F. Seitz. [*Cam op* Otto Pierce]. [*Stills* Bud Fraker]. *Art dir* Hal Pereira and Henry Bumstead. *Ed* Ellsworth Hoagland. *Set dec* Sam Comer and Bertram Granger. *Mus score* Van Cleave. *Sd rec* Harry Lindgren and Gene Garvin. *Makeup supv* Wally Westmore. [*Makeup artist* Carl Silvera]. [*Hair* Gertrude Reade]. [*Prod mgr* Roy Burns]. [*Scr supv* Marvin Weldon]. [*Grip* Fred True]. [*Gaffer* Walter Taylor].

Source: Based on the radio series *The Rise of the Goldbergs* created by Gertrude Berg (20 Nov 1929—1945).

Cast: Gertrude Berg (*Molly Goldberg*), Philip Loeb (*Jake Goldberg*), Eli Mintz (*Uncle David*), Eduard Franz (*Alexander [Abie]*), Larry Robinson (*Sammy [Goldberg]*), Arlene McQuade (*Rosalie [Goldberg]*), Betty Walker (*Mrs. Kramer*), Sara Krohner (*Tante Elka*), David Opatoshu (*Mr. Dutton*), Barbara Rush (*Debby*), Peter Hanson (*Ted [Gordon]*), Helen Brown (*Mrs. Morris*), Edit Angold (*Mrs. Schiller*), Josephine Whittell (*Mrs. Van Nest*), Shari Robinson (*Nomi*), Erno Verebes (*Mr. Mendell*), [Gary Jackson (*William*)], [Nellie Casman (*Mrs. Kramer's mother*)], [Morris Strassberg (*Hazelkorn*)], [Frances Driver (*Louise*)], [Douglas Spencer (*Superintendent*)], [Charles Wagenheim (*Painter*)], [Marvin Paige (*Hymie*)], [Phyllis Kennedy (*Woman in classroom*)], [Mary George], [Mary Benoit], [Ethel Greenwood], [Sylvia Simms].

Domestic, Comedy-drama. [*Print viewed*]. Jewish mother Molly Goldberg looks after her neighbors in her Bronx, New York, tenement as if they were family, and still has plenty of love and energy for her stern and reserved husband Jake, her uncle David, a tailor, her college-age son Sammy, and her daughter Rosalie. When Molly's former flame, Alexander Abel, comes to town, Jake insists on inviting him as a dinner guest, and tries to impress the department store owner by hiring a maid and boasting that he is sending his son to college and Rosalie to summer camp. The Goldbergs are surprised when Alexander introduces his twenty-three-year-old fiancée Debby, but nevertheless welcome her warmly and invite her to stay with them while she shops for her trousseau. In order to further impress Alexander, Jake hires additional seamstresses to work at his factory for a day, even though his partner, Mendell, insists that they cannot afford it. When Alexander announces that he is opening a series of chain stores and wants to purchase clothing from Jake and Mendell, both men nervously take out loans and sell their life insurance policies to

lease a larger factory. Debby, meanwhile, has unintentionally fallen in love with Ted Gordon, who teaches Molly's music appreciation class. As Molly believes that Debby is not right for Alexander, she encourages a friendship between Alexander and her attractive, widowed neighbor, Mrs. Morris, whose son has grown fond of him. Although Debby finally rejects Ted because of her commitment to Alexander, Ted shows up unexpectedly at a dinner where Molly's neighbor, Mrs. Van Nest, unwittingly gossips about Molly's plans and Debby's near infidelity. As a result, Alexander angrily breaks off his engagement, and ends his friendship with Molly. Jake then blames Molly for losing the chain store accounts and ruining his business, after Alexander decides to sell his business. Molly goes to see Alexander and, speaking from her heart, tells him that a marriage to Debby would be inappropriate, not because of her age, but because she is immature, as Alexander himself is immature. Alexander soon sees the wisdom of Molly's words and attends a Parent-Teacher Association dance in order to propose to Mrs. Morris. When Mrs. Morris accepts, Molly seeks to ward off Debby's guilty conscience by steering her into Ted's class, where she and Ted reunite. Meanwhile, Sammy, who at first refused to attend college, decides to go after all, and Alexander arranges for Jake to meet the new chain store owner. With the situation resolved, Molly convinces her worried husband that he has achieved the success he dreamed of by becoming a manufacturer, and reassures him that "we don't want to conquer the world, we only want to live in it." *Engagements. Family relationships. Jews. Neighbors. New York City–Bronx. Clothing industry. Dances. Department store owners. Dinners and dining. Factory owners. Maids. Music teachers. Rivalry. Romance–Age difference. Tenement-houses. Widows.*

Note: Gertrude Berg was the creator, writer and star of the radio series *The Rise of the Goldbergs*, which ran from 20 Nov 1929 through 1945. At the time this film was made, the show was being broadcast on the CBS network; however, it originated on NBC. Actor Eli Mintz recreated his role from the radio series for the film. Although Berg grew up in Harlem, her show was inspired by New York Jewish immigrants living on the Lower East Side. The radio show led to a 1948 Broadway play titled *Molly and Me*, and a television series entitled *The Goldbergs*, which ran from 1949-1954.
Paramount released the film for a test-run in Nov 1950 as *The Goldbergs*. According to contemporary reviews, the title was changed to *Molly* after public response to the film was not as favorable as hoped; it was then released in 1951. *Var* noted that, "it was feared that the Jewish connotation of the title might hurt the chances of what otherwise was considered an entertaining picture, and the test shots apparently bore out the theory." Although the *HR* review wrote that "at best the appeal [of the film] is a limited one that will appear almost esoteric to most audiences," many reviews, like the film itself, did not overtly refer to the "Goldbergs" as a Jewish family, and instead identified them merely as being from the Bronx. Other reviews, however, such as the *IFJ*, noted that "the dialects, English-Jewish idiomatic expressions and Jewish characteristics are presented without stooping to degrading stereotypes. The Goldbergs and their acquaintances are people to laugh with, not to laugh at." *Time* magazine commented that the film captured the "authentic flavors of Jewish family life in The Bronx," while the *LAT* reviewer noted that "non-Jews should find it as recognizably human as the Gaelic characteristics of, say, *Going My Way*.".
Box 2 Dec 1950. FD 24 Nov 1950, p. 8. HR 24 Nov 1950, p. 3. IFJ 2 Dec 1950. LAT 2 Mar 1951. MPHPD 2 Dec 1950, p. 597. NYT 8 Mar 1951, p. 37. Time 29 Jan 1951. Var 22 Nov 1950, p. 8. Var 13 Dec 1950. Var 10 Jan 1951.

MOMENTO LOCO see MI ÚLTIMO AMOR

MONERÍAS (Spanish language)
Hal Roach Studios, Inc.; Metro-Goldwyn-Mayer Corp.; controlled by Loew's, Inc. *Dist* Metro-Goldwyn-Mayer Distributing Corp. 1931; Mexico City opening: 8 Apr 1931; San Juan, Puerto Rico opening: 18 Jul 1931. Sd; b&w. 4 reels. Spanish language.
Prod Hal Roach. *Dir* James Parrott. *Orig dial by* H. M. Walker. *Photog* Art Lloyd. *Film ed* Richard Currier. *Sd* Elmer Raguse.
Song(s): by Luis Llaneza.
Cast: Charley Chase (*Carlos*), Angelita Benítez (*Antoinette*), Enrique Acosta (*El capitán*), Manuel Granado (*El teniente*), Julio Abadía, Luis Llaneza.
Military, Sea, Comedy. [*Not viewed*]. World War I is over, and the troops embark for the voyage home. Carlos' pet monkey comes along, and Carlos smuggles his French girl friend on board the troop ship. At sea, a lieutenant discovers the girl and threatens to reveal her presence. However, the captain intervenes and agrees to marry Carlos and the girl. *Americans in foreign countries. Romance. Ships. Soldiers. Stowaways. French. Monkeys. Officers (Military). Threats. Weddings. World War I.*
Note: This was an expanded Spanish-language version of the three-reel, 1931

English-language film *Rough Seas*, which was directed by James Parrott and starred Charley Chase, Thelma Todd, Carlton Griffin and Frank Brownlee. It is probable that some of the actors in the English-language version were also in the Spanish version, but the complete composition of the Spanish cast has not been ascertained. Luis Llaneza wrote at least one of the songs in the film.

THE MONEY MANIAC (Immigrants)
Pathé Exchange, Inc. *Dist* Pathé Exchange, Inc. Jul 1921 [©Pathé Exchange, Inc.; 2 Jul 1921; LU16722]. Si; b&w. 5 reels, 5,000 ft.
Dir Léonce Perret. *Scr* Léonce Perret. *Photog* Jacques Monteran.
Source: Based on the novel *La Divine* by Louis Letang (Paris, 1914) and his novel *Rolande Immolée* (Paris, 1914).
Cast: Robert Elliott (*Didier Bouchard*), Henry G. Sell (*Milo d'Espail*), Marcya Capri (*Roland Garros*), Lucy Fox (*Thírise Garros*), Ivo Dawson (*Joe Hoggart*), Eugene Breon (*Bill Shopps*).
Melodrama. En route to America, Joe Hoggart persuades several other immigrants to pool their money to buy a tract of land, which years later proves to be rich in oil. Hoggart, with the assistance of Shopps, seeks to control the other members' certificates. In Spain, he finds that Garros has died, and he kidnaps Garros' daughter Rolande and announces her death. Bouchard, another member of the group, who has become wealthy, gathers all its members and the heirs together. Hoggart lures them into a building where, ostensibly, the sale is to take place, and imprisons them, but they escape in time to be present at the sale. Bouchard marries Thírise, another Garros daughter, and d'Espail, learning that Rolande is still alive, rescues her from Hoggart. *England. France. Immigrants. Kidnapping. Oil. Spain. Speculation.*
Note: This picture was filmed on location in the United States, Spain, France, and England.
ETR 30 Jul 1921, p. 606. *FD* 24 Jul 1921.

MONSIEUR LE FOX (Spanish language)
Metro-Goldwyn-Mayer Corp.; controlled by Loew's Inc. *Dist* Metro-Goldwyn-Mayer Distributing Corp. Dec **1930**; Barcelona, Spain, opening: 12 Dec 1930; Los Angeles opening: 16 Jan 1931. Sd (Western Electric Sound System); b&w. 8 reels, 6,055 ft. 66 min. Passed by the National Board of Review. Spanish language.
[*Supv* George Kann]. *Dirigida por* [*Dir*] Hal Roach. [*Dial dir* Roberto E. Guzman]. *Diálogo y arreglo cinematográfico por* [*Dial and scr*] Richard Schayer. *Argumento de* [*Story*] Willard Mack. *Adaptación cinematográfico en español por* [*Spanish version adpt*] Roberto E. Guzman. *Fotografiada por* [*Photog*] Ray Binger. *Director artístico* [*Art dir*] Cedric Gibbons. *Editada por* [*Ed*] Eugenio De Rue. *Director de bailes* [*Dance dir*] Sammy Lee. *Acústica* [*Sd*] Douglas Shearer.
Cast: Gilbert Roland (*Luis* [*Le Bay*]), Rosita Ballesteros (*Nedra*), Pablo Alvarez (*El Papá*), Ralph Navarro (*El sargento Mooney*), Francisco Madrid (*El cabo Smith*), Lillian Savin (*Woolie-Woolie*), [Federico Godoy (*Charlie*)], [María Calvo (*Minnie*)], [Manuel Conesa (*Buck Simms*)], [Raúl Lechuga (*Father Vircombe*)], [Arturo Turich (*Tendero*)], [Vicente Padula], [Roberto Saa Silva].
Adventure, Melodrama. [*Not viewed*]. Luis Le Bay, a French Canadian trapper, is in love with Nedra, the daughter of a mine owner, but is accused of robbing several of the mine's gold shipments and flees. While being chased by a Mounted Police patrol, Luis saves the life of a sergeant and rescues Nedra and her father from a snow avalanche. At his trial, Luis is found innocent after testimony from the local priest resolves the mystery of the stolen gold. *False accusations. French Canadians. Gold miners. Robbery. Trappers. Trials. Avalanches. Canadian Northwest. Chases. Fathers and daughters. North West Mounted Police. Priests. Rescues. Romance. Snow.*
Note: M-G-M made four foreign-language versions of *Men of the North* (see *AFI Catalog of Feature Films, 1921-30*; F2.3558), a 1930 film that starred Gilbert Roland and was directed by Hal Roach. Roach also directed the simultaneously shot Spanish, Italian, French and German versions. While the Spanish and Italian versions were approved for exhibition in New York State in 1931, no information regarding U.S. showings of the French and German versions has been located. The onscreen credits were taken from studio cutting continuities. No credit was given for the German adaptation. While the continuities give the titles of the Italian and German versions as *Monsieur la Volpe* and *Monsieur le Fox* respectively, Italian and German sources list the release titles as *Luigi la volpe* and *Das Land Ohne Gesetz*. The Spanish version was shown in San Juan, Puerto Rico under the title *El zorro*. Actress Cora Montes was cast in the Spanish version, but her role was elimated before the film's release.

Other language version(s):
Monsieur la Volpe (Italian language)

1930; Sd (Western Electric Sound System); b&w. 8 reels, 6,721 ft. 74 min. Italian language.

Direzione [Dir] Hal Roach. *Storia [Story]* Willard Mack. *Dialogo [Dial]* Richard Schayer. *Versione italiana [Italian version]* Marino Bello and Francesco Maran. *Fotografia [Photog]* Ray Binger. *Direttore artistico [Art dir]* Cedric Gibbons. *Editore del film [Film ed]* Eugenio De Rue. *Sincronizzazione [Sd]* Douglas Shearer. *Direzione coreografica [Dance dir]* Sammy Lee.

Italian-language cast: Franco Corsaro (*Louis*), Barbara Leonard (*Nedra*), Paolo Porcasi (*John Ruskin*), Marino Bello (*Sergeant Mooney*), Giorgio Davis (*Caporale Smith*), Lillian Savin (*Woolie-Woolie*). [*Italian version not viewed*].

Cinl Nov 1930, p. 30. *CM* Jan 1931, p. 22.

MONTICELLO, HERE WE COME! (Jewish Americans, Yiddish language)

Cinema Service Corp. *Dist* Cinema Service Corp. **1950** [©Cinema Service Corp.; 13 Oct 1950; LP2977]. Sd; b&w. 6,206 ft. 74 or 77 min. Yiddish, English and Hebrew language.

Prod Joseph Seiden. [*Dir* Joseph Seiden].

Song(s): "Oy Doctor," "You're Lovely in My Eyes," "Forty Years Ago," "Everything Comes from Upstairs" and "I Want a Divorce," composers undetermined; "Kol Nidre," traditional Jewish hymn.

Cast: Menashe Skulnick, Joseph Buloff, Leo Fuchs, Michel Rosenberg, Max Wilner, Michel Michalesko, Seymour Rechtzeit, Yetta Zwerling, Larry Daniels, Esta Salzman, Burton Sisters, Favish Finkel, [Cantor Leibele Waldman], [Mary Forest].

Variety, Yiddish. [*Print viewed*]. At a Monticello, New York establishment, host Larry Daniels tells stories and introduces a number of performers, including the Burton Sisters singing "You're Lovely in My Eyes"; comedian Menashe Skulnick performing the song-skit "Oy Doctor"; Seymour Rechtzeit singing a love song with Esta Salzman; Cantor Leibele Waldman singing the Hebrew prayer "Kol Nidre" in a synagogue; comedian Max Wilner; female cantor Mary Forest; Joseph Buloff portraying a Russian shoemaker in a skit entitled "The Shoemaker's Romance"; comedian Favish Finkel performing the song-skit "I Want a Divorce;" Michel Rosenberg; song and dance team Leo Fuchs and Yetta Zwerling; and actor Michel Michalesko performing a song and a scene. *Jews. Monticello (NY). Musical revues. Cantors, Jewish. Comedians. Impersonations (Comic). Singers.*

Note: The opening credits read, "'*Monticello, Here We Come!*' A Borscht Circuit Revue." Portions of the film consisted of shorts made in 1930 by Judea Film, a company owned by director Joseph Seiden. "Oy Doctor" was taken from a two-reel film of the same name, and "The Shoemaker's Romance," from the two-reel film *Shuster Libe*; both of these sequences were also included in the 1933 film *Live and Laugh* and in the 1941 film *Mazel Tov Yidden* (see entry above). According to modern sources, in 1950, Seiden also released *Borsht Belt Follies*, which either was this film under a different title, or another picture incorporating some of this film's material.

Exb 31 Jan 1951, p. 3022.

MOON OVER HARLEM (African Americans)

Meteor Productions, Inc.; Edgar G. Ulmer's Production. *Dist* Meteor Productions, Inc. **1939**; New York opening: 31 Oct 1939; Prod: at Meteor Studios [©Meteor Productions, Inc.; 26 Jun 1939; LP8950]. Sd (Variray Blue Seal Recording); b&w. 8 reels.

Assoc prod Peter E. Kassler. *Dir* Edgar G. Ulmer. *Asst dir* Fred Kassler and Gustav Heinz. *Scr* Sherle Castle. *Orig story and dial* Mathew Mathews. *Photog* J. Burgi Contner and Edward Hyland. *Settings* Eugene. *Film ed* Jack Kemp. *Mus score and numbers comp* by Donald Heywood. *Score arr* by Lorenzo Calduel and Kenneth Macomber. *Orch and choir cond* by Donald Heywood. *Sd* Edwin Schabbeha and Edward Fenton. [*Prod mgr* Gustav H. Heimo]. [*Scr supv* Shirley Ulmer].

Song(s): "One River to Cross," music and lyrics by Uncle Dave Macon; "Teach Me How to Sing Again," music and lyrics by Donald Heywood.

Cast: Bud Harris (*Dollar Bill [Richards]*), Nora Green (*Minnie*), Izinetta Wilcox (*Sue*), Earl Gough (*Bob*), Zerita Steptean (*Jackie*), Petrina Moore (*Alice*), Daphne Ray (*Pat*), Mercedes Gilbert (*Jackie's mother*), Frances Harrod (*Ma*), Alec Lovejoy (*Faron*), Walter Richardson (*Brother Horns*), Jim Thompson (*Long-G*), Freddie Robinson (*Half Pint*), John Bunn (*Walter Street*), Marieluise Bechet (*Nina Mae Brown*), Archie Cross, William Woodward (*The boys*

from Newark), John Fortune (*Jamal*), Audrey Talbird (*Connie*), Marie Young (*Jeff*), Christopher Columbus, and his Swing Crew, Sidney Bechet and his Clarinet.

African American, Crime, Melodrama. [*Print viewed*]. After ardent wooing, Dollar Bill Richards finally marries widow Minnie, a maid and an excellent cook. The wedding reception is a disaster, however, when Dollar's uncouth friends act disdainfully toward Minnie's family. When a picture of Minnie's first husband is thrown to the ground, their daughter Sue picks it up. Sue is adored by Bob, a handsome young political organizer who loves Harlem and is planning to clean up the city's graft. When Sue and Bob announce their engagement, Dollar accuses Bob of paying for his education by living off women, and the two men fight. Dollar pulls a gun, and to save Bob, Sue promises never to see him again. Sue then finds work at Broadway Slick's Plantation nightclub, where Minnie works. Later, a man known as Wall Street demands that Dollar, who is chasing a young girl named Connie and giving her money, increase the take at the club, instead of squandering Minnie's life insurance money at the races. Although Minnie is warned of Dollar's true ways, she believes that he is an honest grocer. When Sue needs sixty-nine dollars to pay her college tuition, Minnie persuades her to take the money from her hated stepfather. While Bob speaks to a ladies' group, urging them to help clean up the rackets in Harlem, Dollar is ordered to assert his gang's authority by killing someone. Dollar makes a pass at Sue, but Minnie blames her daughter rather than her husband, and demands that Sue leave home. Sue goes to the home of Jackie and Alice, two of her schoolmates, and decides to leave school for a career on Broadway with the help of Slick. Meanwhile, Faron, a man from Detroit, has moved in on the Harlem rackets. When Dollar sends his men to get money from a Jamaican, they beat up his wife instead. Faron, who knows that Dollar spends more than he makes, demands $15,000 from him and then shoots Minnie. Despite the tragedy, Sue performs that night, and when she arrives home, hymns are being sung because her mother has died. Dollar soon announces his intentions to marry another woman, but when Wall Street arrives, a shootout ensues and both men are killed. To everyone's relief, the gangs are then broken. Bob and Sue are now free to resume their romance and appreciate the moon over Harlem. *African Americans. Mothers and daughters. New York City–Harlem. Nightclubs. Racketeers. Stepfathers. Choirs (Music). Cooks. Deception. Education. Fights. Funerals. Gambling. Infidelity. Life insurance. Murder. Politicians. Romance. Singers. Weddings. Widows.*

Note: Screenplay writer Sherle Castle was the wife of producer and director Edgar G. Ulmer, and was also known as Shirley Ulmer. Unidentified contemporary news items in the George Johnson Collection at UCLA indicate that the picture was produced by Benjamin F. Resnick, manager of the Brooklyn Regent Theater, which also exhibited the film. According to modern sources, the running time is 67 minutes. Modern sources also indicate that Frank Wilson authored the story; that the cast included Patrina Waples; and that the film featured a chorus of twenty girls, a four-voice choir and a mixed sixty-piece symphony orchestra. According to a modern interview with Ulmer, the film was shot in four days—two days in a studio in New Jersey, and two days at actual locations in New York. The file for the film in the MPAA/PCA Collection at the AMPAS Library contains a letter, dated 1 Jun 1939 and addressed to Mercury Film Laboratories, in which the PCA stated that it could not approve the picture because the film's two murderers are "left unpunished."

Exb 26 Jul 1939, p. 355.

MOONRISE (African Americans)

Chas. K. Feldman Group Productions; Marshall Grant Pictures. *Dist* Republic Pictures Corp. 1 Oct **1948**; Prod: late Dec 1947—late Jan 1948 [©Chas. K. Feldman Group Productions; 9 Sep 1948; LP1852]. Sd (RCA Sound System); b&w. 8,123 ft. 90 min. Passed by the National Board of Review. PCA cert no. 13064.

Prod Charles Haas. [*Exec prod* Marshall Grant]. *Dir* FRANK BORZAGE. [*Asst dir* Lee Lukather]. *Scr* Charles Haas. *Dir of photog* John L. Russell. [*Cam op* Jack Warren]. [*Stills* Don Keyes]. *Spec eff* Howard Lydecker and Theodore Lydecker. *Optical eff* Consolidated Film Industries. *Prod des* Lionel Banks. *Film ed* Harry Keller. *Set dec* John McCarthy, Jr. and George Sawley. *Cost des* Adele Palmer. *Mus* William Lava. *Sd* Earl Crain, Sr. and Howard Wilson. *Makeup supv* Bob Mark. *Hair stylist* Peggy Gray. [*Prod mgr* Virgil Hart]. [*Scr supv* Dorothy Yutzi]. [*Grip* Ben Bishop].

Song(s): "The Moonrise Song (It Just Dawned on Me)," music by William Lava, lyrics by Harry Tobias; "Lonesome," music and lyrics by Theodore Strauss and William Lava; "Work, For the Night Is Coming," music and lyrics by Al Coghill and Lowell Mason.

Source: Based on the novel *Moonrise* by Theodore Strauss (New York, 1946).

Cast: Dane Clark [(*Danny Hawkins*)], Gail Russell [(*Gilly Johnson, schoolteacher*)], Ethel Barrymore [(*Grandma*)], Allyn Joslyn [(*Clem Otis*)], Rex Ingram [(*Mose Johnson*)], Henry Morgan [(*Billy Scripture*)], David Street [(*Ken Williams*)], Selena Royle [(*Aunt Jessie*)], Harry Carey, Jr. [(*Jimmy Biff*)], Irving Bacon [(*Judd Jenkins*)], Lloyd Bridges [(*Jerry Sykes*)], Houseley Stevenson [(*Uncle Joe Jingle*)], Phil Brown [(*Elmer*)], Harry V. Cheshire [(*J. B. Sykes*)], Lila Leeds [(*Julie*)], [Virginia Mullen (*Miss Simpkins*)], [Oliver Blake (*Ed Conlon*)], [Tom Fadden (*Homer Blackstone*)], [Charles Lane (*Man in black*)], [Clem Bevans (*Jake*)], [Helen Wallace (*Martha Otis*)], [John Harmon (*Baseball attendant*)], [Michael Branden, Bill Borzage, Tiny Jimmie Kelly, Ed Rees, Casey MacGregor (*Barkers*)], [Monte Lowell (*Father*)], [Timmie Hawkins (*Alfie*)], [Steven Peck (*Danny, age 7*)], [Tommy Ivo (*Jerry, age 7*)], [Johnny Calkins (*Danny, age 13*)], [Michael Dill (*Jerry, age 13*)], [Bob Hoffman, Joel McGinnis (*Boys in dance hall*)], [Linda Lombard, Stelita Ravel (*Dancers*)], [Renee Donatt (*Ticket seller*)], [George Backus, Monte Montague (*Hunters*)], [Jimmie Hawkins, Gary Armstrong, Buzzy Henry, Jimmy Crane (*Boys*)], [Doreen McCann, Candy Toxton (*Girls*)], [Harry Lauter].

Rural, Film noir. [*Print viewed*]. When his wife becomes ill, Virginian Jeb Hawkins phones a doctor, but the doctor refuses to visit her, saying that her condition is not serious. Shortly thereafter, she dies, causing Jeb to lose control and kill the doctor. One evening, many years after Jeb has been hanged for murder, his son Danny decides to visit a dance hall near a swamp called Brother's Pond. When another young man, Jerry Sykes, a banker's son, teases Danny for being a murderer's son, Danny grabs a rock and smashes his skull. Realizing that he has killed Jerry, Danny quickly departs the scene, leaving an important clue, his pocketknife, behind. When Danny remembers that he stuck his knife in a tree before killing Jerry, he decides to return to the scene with his only friend, a mentally handicapped deaf-mute named Billy Scripture. Unable to find the knife, Danny goes to the dance hall to dance with Jerry's unsuspecting sweetheart, schoolteacher Gilly Johnson. Danny convinces her to come for a drive with another couple, but nearly crashes when he thinks he sees Jerry's corpse in the road. Danny later confesses his love to Gilly, and she apologizes for misleading him, saying that she is engaged to Jerry. Later, Danny visits his black friend, Mose Johnson, at his home, a shack near Brother's Pond. As he watches Mose's bloodhounds chase and kill a raccoon, Danny begins to fear his own capture. Later, Gilly tells Danny that she is worried because Jerry has not phoned her since the dance. After Mose finds Jerry's decomposing body, Sheriff Clem Otis decides to question Danny about his feelings for Gilly. From the shop across the street, Danny fondles a knife similar to the one he left in Brother's Pond while watching Jerry's corpse being carried into the coroner's office. After a bank examiner tells J. B. Sykes that his son Jerry stole $2,000 from his cash box, Clem learns that Jerry owed some money to Ken Williams, the drummer for the dance hall band. Later, Clem asks Danny if he saw Ken leave the bandstand during the dance on the night that Jerry was killed, and he says no. The next day, Clem and his wife Martha see Danny and Gilly at the county fair. Gilly tells Danny that after his missing knife was found by Billy, Clem came to ask her some questions. As Danny boards the ferris wheel with Gilly, he notices Clem and his wife also boarding the ride. After Danny panics and falls from his seat, he limps to Brother's Pond on a badly injured leg. Inside Mose's shack, Danny sees Billy resting peacefully and, in a fit of desperation, nearly strangles him. When Clem and his deputies arrive at the swamp, Danny limps to the home of his grandmother, who lives nearby. There, Danny takes up his father's rifle, but after a reflective moment at his mother's and father's graves, decides to turn himself in. When Clem sees that Danny is willing to cooperate, he forgoes the handcuffs and allows him to walk to jail "like a man." *Family relationships. Guilt. Hereditary tendencies. Investigations. Murder. Schoolteachers. African Americans. Bank examiners. Coroners. Dance halls. Deaf-mutes. Dogs. Engagements. Fairs. Falls from heights. Ferris wheels. Hanging. Knives. Mentally handicapped persons. Musicians. Physicians. Raccoons. Sheriffs. Strangling. Swamps. Thieves.*

Note: According to information contained in the file for the film at the MPAA/PCA Collection at the AMPAS Library, as of 17 Dec 1945, Theodore Strauss's story had not yet been published in novel form, but was being prepared for serialization in *Collier's*. According to a 3 Dec 1945 *LAT* news item, Paramount

Pictures originally purchased Strauss's story in hope of casting "one of the younger men emerging from the service" in the male lead and hired Strauss to write the screenplay. On 6 Nov 1946, *LAT* reported that Garson Kanin had intended to purchase the story as a vehicle for John Garfield, but that he had been out-bid by John Farrow, who wanted to produce it as a vehicle for Alan Ladd. According to a 9 Feb 1947 *NYT* news item, Marshall Grant Pictures then acquired the property and hired Vladimir Pozner to write a treatment. This news item also notes that Burt Lancaster was being considered for the male lead. The contribution of Pozner to the completed film has not been confirmed. On 24 Feb 1947, *LAT* reported that Grant had assigned William Wellman to direct the film and was seeking James Stewart for the lead. *Var* noted on the same day that Stewart, if signed to star, would cast and direct the film as well. On 15 Oct 1947, *HR* reported that the film had been sold to Charles K. Feldman, who planned to produce it with Frank Borzage for Republic Studios. Lillian Gish was announced as one of the film's stars in Jan 1948, but she did not appear in the final film. According to copyright information, "The Moonrise Song" was popularized by radio star David Street. According to memos in the file on the film in the MPAA/PCA Collection at the AMPAS Library, the PCA objected to a scene in which a group of children tar-and-feather another child. This scene was excluded from the final print. Republic's sound department, headed by Daniel J. Bloomberg, was nominated for an Academy Award for Best Sound Recording. *HR* production charts include Art Smith in the cast, but his participation in the released film has not been confirmed.

Box 18 Sep 1948. *DV* 9 Sep 1948, p. 3. *FD* 10 Sep 1948, p. 5. *HR* 25 Aug 1947. *HR* 15 Oct 1947. *HR* 26 Dec 1947, p. 12. *HR* 30 Jan 1948, p. 21. *HR* 9 Sep 1948, p. 3, 10. *LAEx* 29 Oct 1946. *LAEx* 1 Feb 1947. *LAT* 3 Dec 1945. *LAT* 24 Feb 1947. *LAT* 18 Jan 1948. *MPD* 24 Sep 1948. *MPHPD* 26 Jun 1948, p. 4219. *MPHPD* 18 Sep 1948, p. 4317. *NYT* 7 Mar 1949, p. 17. *Var* 15 Sep 1948, p. 20.

THE MORALS OF HILDA (Immigrants)

Universal Film Mfg. Co.; Red Feather Photoplays. *Dist* Universal Film Mfg. Co. 11 Dec **1916** [©Universal Film Mfg. Co.; 6 Dec 1916; LP9670]. Si; b&w. 5 reels.

Dir Lloyd B. Carleton. *Scen* A. W. Coldeway. *Story* H. C. Warnack. *Cam* Roy H. Klaffki.

Cast: Frank Whitson (*August*), Gretchen Lederer (*Hilda*), Richard Morris (*Harris Grail*), Adele Farrington (*Esther Grail*), Lois Wilson (*Marion*), Emory Johnson (*Stephen*).

Drama. Recent immigrants August and Hilda cannot understand the American emphasis on weddings, because in their country, couples never get married. Fearing that he will be arrested for living with a woman who is not his wife, August stows away on a ship and dies in a wreck at sea. Afterward, Hilda tries to commit suicide, but the wealthy Esther Grail saves her, and then adopts her infant son Stephen. Years later, Esther tells him the circumstances of his birth, and so Stephen goes on a crusade for the rights of illegitimate children. He is soon elected governor, but during his inaugural speech, a fanatic tries to shoot him. Hilda, however, not having seen Stephen for years but deciding to come hear him speak out for the underprivileged, sees the madman and, jumping in front of her son before the bullet hits him, dies in his place. *Assassination. Cultural conflict. Governors. Illegitimacy. Immigrants. Marriage. Self-sacrifice. Adoption. Attempted suicide. Fanatics. Insanity. Mothers and sons. Shipwrecks. Stowaways.*

ETR 16 Dec 1916, p. 136. *MPW* 16 Dec 1916, p. 1692. *Wid's* 21 Dec 1916, p. 1185.

MORDPROZESS MARY DUGAN see EL PROCESO DE MARY DUGAN

MOTEL THE OPERATOR (Yiddish language)

Cinema Service Corp. *Dist* Cinema Service Corp. **1939**; Brooklyn opening: Dec 1939. Sd; b&w. 8 reels, 7,659 or 7,851 ft. 88 min. Yiddish language with English subtitles.

[*Prod* Joseph Seiden]. *Dir* Joseph Seiden. *Asst dir* H. Rosen. *Photog* Don Malkames and Charles Levine. *Settings* F. Allstadt. *Mus* Sholem Secunda. *With* Cantor Leibele Waldman and Joel Feigs [sic] Famous Choir. *Sd* M. Dichter and P. Jacobs.

Source: Based on the play *Motel the Operator* by Chaim Tauber (New York, 1936).

Cast: Chaim Tauber (*Motel [Friedman]*), Malvina Rappel (*Esther, his wife*), Maurice Kroner (*Benjamin Rosenwald*), Bertha Hart (*Rebecca Rosenwald*), Seymour Rechtzeit (*Jack Rosenwald*), Jacob Zanger ([*Yosel*] *Joseph Frumkin*), Yetta Zwerling (*Chane Beile [Annabella] Frumkin*), Gertrude Krause (*Ruth Frumkin*), Herman Rosen (*The doctor*), Izidor Frankel (*The boss*), [Joseph Schoengold].

Yiddish, Domestic, Social, Melodrama, with songs. [*Print viewed*]. In New York's Lower East Side, Motel Friedman works twelve hours a day sewing in a sweatshop. He has gained the nickname "Motel the Operator" because of the machine he operates. After Motel and other workers, including Yosel, a presser, go on strike,

Motel's wife Esther cannot pay the doctor for her ill son Jackie's medicine or buy needed food for the boy. To get rid of the strikers, the boss hires a gangster, who hits Motel over the head as he pickets. Motel is taken to Bellevue Hospital, where the doctor reports that his head is fractured and that he will never be the same if he lives. When Esther is threatened with eviction, Yosel's wife Chane talks to William H. Benson, the head of an adoption agency, about Jackie. Wealthy Benjamin Rosenwald comes to the agency offering $500 to the parents and $1,000 to the agency to secretly adopt a poor child. Although Esther rebukes Benson when he tells her that wealthy, decent people want to adopt Jackie, when the doctor warns that the child is starving, she signs Jackie away. Benson only gives her $50. Esther then turns on the gas in her apartment and asphyxiates herself. Three years later, Motel leaves the hospital to go home, but he finds that his apartment building has been demolished. Motel wanders twenty years, from 1920 until 1940, and becomes a bearded flower seller. Meanwhile, at the Rosenwald home, Jack has become a full-fledged lawyer. He is engaged to marry Ruth, the daughter of Yosel and Chane, who, now that Yosel is a successful pants manufacturer, call themselves Josef and Annabella. As a wedding gift, Rosenwald gives Jack a lease on a Fifth Avenue office and a chance to become his partner in business. Because Benson has lost money in Wall Street and needs $5,000, he tries to blackmail Rosenwald by threatening to tell Jack that Rosenwald is not his real father. Rosenwald refuses and Benson vows to find Jack's father. Seeing Motel selling flowers, Benson offers him money to impersonate Motel the Operator. When he hears this, Motel faints. Benson introduces Motel to the Rosenwald family as an old friend, and Motel again faints when he meets Jack. When Motel is alone with Benson and Rosenwald, Benson claims that Motel is Jack's real father. Rosenwald gets a gun, which Motel takes away, then offers money if they'll go away. Seeing that the Rosenwalds are a good family, Motel threatens to kill Benson if he doesn't leave, and in a struggle for the gun, Benson is shot and killed. Feeling that it is his duty to defend the unfortunate, Jack takes Motel's case. After Motel ascertains that Jack loves his "parents," Motel says that Benson promised him money to say that he was Jack's real father. Motel then converses with a vision of Esther, who tries to convince him that he has a right to his son and to happiness, but Motel says that it is too late and that he will soon be with her. After Jack appeals to the humane feelings of the jury and proports the idea that Motel was a messenger from God sent to execute a judgment on Benson, the jury brings in a not guilty verdict. Following the wedding, Yosel recognizes Motel, who does not want anyone to know his real identity. Motel tells Rosenwald that he will keep quiet and only asks that he be allowed to visit sometimes. Rosenwald, however, insists that Motel remain with them always. *Fathers and sons. Impersonation and imposture. Jews. Long-lost relatives. New York City–East Side. Poverty. Self-sacrifice. Adoption. Blackmail. Employer-employee relations. Flower vendors. Gangsters. Lawyers. Recognition. Shootings. Strikes and lockouts. Suicide. Sweatshops. Trials.*

Note: Chaim Tauber, a radio personality known as "The Singing Poet," also played the lead role in the stage production. Although the film includes songs, no information concerning their identity has been located.

FD 24 Jan 1940, p. 7. *MPD* 22 Jan 1940, p. 3. *NYT* 16 Jan 1940, p. 19.

MOTHER LOVE see **THE GREATEST LOVE**

MOTHER MACHREE (Irish Americans)

Fox Film Corp. *Dist* Fox Film Corp. Mar **1928**; Premiere: 22 Jan 1928 [©Fox Film Corp.; 12 Jun 1927; LP24071]. Si; b&w. 7 reels, 6,807 ft. [Also mus score & sd eff (Movietone); released 21 Oct 1928.].

Pres William Fox. *Dir* John Ford. *Asst dir* Edward O'Fearna. *Scen* Gertrude Orr. *Titles* Katherine Hilliker and H. H. Caldwell. *Photog* Chester Lyons. *Film ed* Katherine Hilliker and H. H. Caldwell.

Source: Based on the short story "The Story of Mother Machree" by Rida Johnson Young in *Munsey's Magazine* (Feb 1924).

Cast: Belle Bennett (*Ellen McHugh*), Neil Hamilton (*Brian McHugh*), Philippe De Lacy (*Brian, as a child*), Pat Somerset (*Robert De Puyster*), Victor McLaglen (*Terrence O'Dowd*), Ted McNamara (*Harpist of Wexford*), John MacSweeney (*Irish priest*), Eulalie Jensen (*Rachel Van Studdiford*), Constance Howard (*Edith Cutting*), Ethel Clayton (*Mrs. Cutting*), William Platt (*Pips*), Jacques Rollens (*Signor Bellini*), Rodney Hildebrand (*Brian McHugh, Sr.*), Joyce Wirard (*Edith Cutting, as a child*), Robert Parrish (*Child*).

Society, Melodrama. In an Irish village in 1899, Ellen McHugh's husband is killed in a storm. Convinced that America holds the best future for her son, Brian, she immigrates, only to face discouragement until Terrence O'Dowd induces her to join a sideshow, posing as a "half-woman." Brian is placed in a fashionable school, but when his mother's profession is discovered, the principal forces Ellen to surrender the boy legally into his care. She becomes a housekeeper in the Fifth Avenue home of the Cuttings and rears her employer's daughter, Edith. Years later, Edith and Brian meet and fall in love, on the eve of war; eventually the boy and his mother are reunited, and all ends happily. *Boarding schools. Housekeepers. Immigrants. Ireland. Irish. Irish Americans. Motherhood. New York City–Fifth Avenue. Sideshows. Widows.*

FD 22 Jan 1928. *NYT* 6 Mar 1928, p. 20. *Var* 27 Mar 1928, p. 23.

MOTHER'S BOY (Irish Americans)

Pathé Exchange, Inc. *Dist* Pathé Exchange, Inc. 12 May **1929** [©Pathé Exchange, Inc.; 19 May 1929; LP395]. Sd (Photophone); b&w. 8 reels, 7,423 ft.

Prod Robert T. Kane. *Dir* Bradley Barker. *Dial supv* James Seymour. *Story, scen and dial* Gene Markey. *Photog* Harry Stradling, Walter Strenge and Philip Tannura. *Film ed* Edward Pfitzenmeier. *Set des* Clark Robinson. *Rec eng* V. S. Ashdown and J. A. Delaney.

Song(s): "There'll Be You and I," words and music by Bud Green and Sam H. Stept; "Come to Me," words and music by Bud Green, Sam H. Stept and Will Collins; "The World Is Yours and Mine," words and music by Bud Green, Sam H. Stept and James F. Hanley.

Cast: Morton Downey (*Tommy O'Day*), Beryl Mercer (*Mrs. O'Day*), John T. Doyle (*Mr. O'Day*), Brian Donlevy (*Harry O'Day*), Helen Chandler (*Rose Lyndon*), Osgood Perkins (*Jake Sturmberg*), Lorin Raker (*Joe Bush*), Barbara Bennett (*Beatrix Townleigh*), Jennie Moskowitz (*Mrs. Apfelbaum*), Jacob Frank (*Mr. Apfelbaum*), Louis Sorin (*Mr. Bumble*), Robert Gleckler (*Gus Le Grand*), Tyrrell Davis (*Duke of Pomplum*), Allen Vincent (*Dinslow*), Leslie Stowe (*Evangelist*).

Musical. Tommy O'Day, an Irish lad with a golden voice who lives on the Lower East Side of New York, is unjustly accused by his father of stealing the family savings. Tommy leaves home and meets up with Joe Bush, a press agent who gets him a job singing in a cabaret. Tommy is a success and soon obtains a leading part in a Broadway revue. As the curtain is about to rise on opening night, however, Tommy receives word from his sweetheart, Rose Lyndon, that his mother, whom he has not seen since leaving home, is apparently dying. Tommy deserts the show and goes to her bedside, bringing her back to life and health with a beautiful song. Tommy's mother completely recovers, and he is excused by the revue manager. Tommy becomes a star. *Cabarets. Family life. Family relationships. Irish Americans. Musical revues. New York City–Broadway. New York City–Lower East Side. Press agents. Robbery. Singers.*

FD 12 May 1929. *NYT* 8 May 1929, p. 34.

MOTHERS OF TODAY (Yiddish language)

Lynn Productions, Inc. *Dist* Apex Productions, Inc. 27 Feb **1939**; Prod: at the Biograph Studios, Bronx, New York. Sd; b&w. 9 reels, 8,734 ft. 92 or 95 min. Yiddish language with English subtitles.

Prod Henry Lynn. *Dir* Henry Lynn. *Scr* Henry Lynn. *Story* Simon Wolf.

Cast: Esther Field (*Esther Waldman*), Max Rosenblatt (*Solomon Waldman*), Simon Wolf (*Getzel Boxer*), Paula Lubelska (*Breindel Boxer*), Arthur Winters, Leon Seidenberg, Vera Lubow, Gertrude Krause, Jack Shargel, Louis Goldstein.

Yiddish, Domestic, Melodrama. [*Not viewed*]. After Esther Waldman, a widowed Jewish immigrant living in New York who owns a small store, lights candles on Sabbath eve, her daughter Annie excitedly exhibits a diamond ring, which the new neighbor boy, Hymie Boxer, gave her, but Esther urges her daughter to return it. Hymie's father Getzel, a bungler, comes to the Waldmans' apartment, and impressed with the traditional Sabbath atmosphere, he laments that his own wife Breindel is a "mother of today," who cares more about card games than the Sabbath. After Esther's son Solomon, a cantor, arrives, Hymie comes in out-of-breath, followed by a jewelry store owner and a police officer, who say they pursued a thief to the building. Hymie puts stolen jewelry into Solomon's pocket and escapes through a window. Although Solomon is arrested, Hymie's criminal cohorts are afraid that Solomon can prove he was in the

synagogue during the robbery, so Hymie, following their orders, shoots Solomon when he is released on bail. As Solomon recovers in the hospital, he tells the newspapers that he thinks Hymie was involved. Hymie then implores his sister Evelyn to make Solomon fall in love with her so that he will not testify against him. Evelyn visits Solomon in the hospital, and a few days later they have fallen in love with each other. Esther gives a small party to celebrate Solomon's return, but when Annie brings Hymie, Esther orders him to leave. Solomon asks her not to chase his guests away, and Esther leaves in anger. Hymie, who has been threatened by his gang for bungling the attempted murder, convinces Annie to elope with him so that he can get out of town. When Esther learns of this, she says that though the heart may break, one mustn't cry. As Solomon practices his singing before *Yom Kippur*, the Day of Atonement, Evelyn convinces him that if he wants to marry her, he must quit as a cantor and attempt a career singing in concerts and over the radio. Esther then faces another blow when Solomon tells her that he will no longer be a cantor. Four weeks after Annie and Hymie have eloped, Esther receives a telegram from a lawyer in Buffalo, who says that Annie was arrested when Hymie attempted a holdup of a store and a watchman was killed. Esther visits Annie in jail and vows to sell her store to get cash to pay for Annie's legal expenses, but before she returns, Evelyn convinces Solomon to sell the store for money so that they can elope. Esther sees Solomon just before he is to leave and urges him not to marry Evelyn, but he refuses to listen and throws her down when she tries to block his path. Esther loses her sight in the accident, and Getzel takes care of her. Annie is freed because she did not know about the robbery, while Hymie is sentenced to death in the electric chair. During his confession to a rabbi, he says that parents should not let their children be independent when they are too young, because that is the path to crime. When Breindel visits, Hymie tells her that because she neglected him to play cards and go to parties, he was induced to find acquaintances from the street, and he started to steal. Both Annie and Solomon, who is very contrite, visit Esther, and she says that a mother cannot stay angry with her children. Solomon says that doctors have told him that her blindness may only be temporary, and Evelyn asks Esther's forgiveness. Breindel confesses that she has paid the price for her sins, and Esther convinces Getzel to forgive her. Solomon says that he will become a cantor again, and he sings the prayer for *Yom Kippur*. Family relationships. Jews. Motherhood. Attempted murder. Blindness. Brothers and sisters. Buffalo (NY). Cantors, Jewish. Confession. Diamonds. Dismissal (Employment). Electric chair. Elopement. Frame-ups. Gangs. Neglected children. Neglected husbands. New York City. Parties. Prayer. Rabbis. Rites and ceremonies. Seduction. Storekeepers. Thieves. Yom Kippur.

Note: The plot summary was based on a dialogue continuity at NYSA. The Yiddish title of this film is *Hayntige Mames.* Esther Field was billed as "The Yiddishe Mama."

Detroit Jewish Chronicle 9 Jun 1939. *FD* 14 Mar 1939, p. 6. *MPH* 11 Mar 1939, p. 42. *NYT* 2 Mar 1939, p. 19.

THE MOUNTAIN DEVIL *see* **THE BOTTLE IMP**

MUD ON THE STARS *see* **WILD RIVER**

MUJER *see* **YO, TÚ Y ELLA**

LA MUJER DEL OTRO *see* **EL IMPOSTOR**

LA MUJER X (Spanish language)
Metro-Goldwyn-Mayer Corp.; controlled by Loew's, Inc. *Dist* Culver Export, Inc. **1931**; San Juan, Puerto Rico opening: 28 Mar 1931; New York opening: 3 Apr 1931; Prod: Dec 1930—Jan 1931. Sd (Western Electric Sound System); b&w. 8 reels, 7,116 ft. 79 min. Passed by the National Board of Review. Spanish language.
[*Supv* Frank Davis]. *Dirigida por* [*Dir*] Carlos Borcosque. [*Dial dir* Eduardo Ugarte]. *Diálogo por* [*Dial*] Willard Mack. *Versión española de* [*Spanish version*] Eduardo Ugarte and José López Rubio. *Fotografiada por* [*Photog*] Leonard Smith. *Director artístico* [*Art dir*] Cedric Gibbons. *Editada por* [*Ed*] Richard Kilpatrick. *Acústica por* [*Sd*] Douglas Shearer.
Source: Based on the play *La femme X...* by Alexandre Bisson (Paris, 15 Dec 1908).
Cast: MARÍA LADRÓN DE GUEVARA (*Jaquelina*), JOSÉ CRESPO (*Raimundo*), RAFAEL RIVELLES ([*Luis*] *Floriot*), Juan Martínez Plá (*Noêl*), Carmen Rodríguez (*Rosa*), Luis Llaneza (*Doctor*), Alfredo del Diestro (*Col. Hamby*), Fred Malatesta (*La Roque*), Manuel Arbó

(*Merrival*), José Peña ["Pepet"] (*Perissard*), Julio Peña (*Darrell*), Lucio Villegas (*Valmorin*), Antonio Vidal (*Juez*), [Tetsu Komai], [Julián Rivero].
Melodrama. [*Not viewed*]. [The following plot summary is based on the English-language version of this film, *Madame X*; character names refer to that version. For further information regarding the English-language version, please see the note below and the entry for *Madame X* in the *AFI Catalog of Feature Films, 1921-30.*] Jacqueline leaves her husband for another man, and when she returns to take care of her sick son, her husband flatly rejects her. She leaves without seeing the boy; and beginning her path on the downgrade, she meets and helps a cardsharp named Laroque. When they return to France, her home, Laroque decides that because of her name he can squeeze out a goodly sum from her. At the threat of blackmail, Jacqueline, in a rage, shoots him and is subsequently defended in court by her son, who does not know her true identity. In the final court scene, Jacqueline confesses, without using names, that she shot Laroque so as not to allow her son to discover her degrading life. *Blackmail. Cardsharping. Desertion (Marital). France. Motherhood. Murder. Public defenders. Trials.*

Note: This was a Spanish-language version of M-G-M's 1929 film, *Madame X,* which was directed by Lionel Barrymore and starred Ruth Chatterton and Lewis Stone. Please see *AFI Catalog of Feature Films, 1921-30*; F2.3328. The onscreen Spanish credits were taken from a studio cutting continuity. Some sources include Henry Armetta, Agostino Borgato, Carlos Ramos, Otto Lang, Rosita Granada, Manuel Rea, José Fernández and Manuel Santigosa in the cast, but their participation in the released film has not been confirmed. For information on other film adaptations of Alexandre Bisson's play, please consult the entry for M-G-M's 1937 film, *Madame X* in *AFI Catalog of Feature Films, 1931-40*; F3.2649.

CM Jun 1931, p. 469. *HF* 10 Jan 1931, p. 24.

THE MUMMY'S CURSE (Cajuns)
Universal Pictures Co., Inc. *Dist* Universal Pictures Co., Inc. 16 Feb **1945**; Prod: 26 Jul—early Aug 1944 [©Universal Pictures Co., Inc.; 20 Nov 1944; LP12973]. Sd (Western Electric Recording); b&w. 5,413 ft. 60 min. PCA cert no. 10432.
Series: The Mummy.
[*Exec prod* Ben Pivar]. *Assoc prod* Oliver Drake. *Dir* Leslie Goodwins. [*Asst dir* Mack Wright]. *Scr* Bernard Schubert. *Orig story and adpt* Leon Abrams and Dwight V. Babcock. *Dir of photog* Virgil Miller. *Spec photog* John P. Fulton. *Art dir* John B. Goodman and Martin Obzina. *Film ed* Fred R. Feitshans, Jr. *Set dec* Russell A. Gausman and Victor A. Gangelin. *Mus dir* Paul Sawtell. *Dir of sd* Bernard B. Brown. [*Sd*] *tech* Robert Pritchard.
Song(s): "Hey, You," music by Oliver Drake, lyrics by Frank Orth.
Cast: LON CHANEY (*Mummy* [*Kharis*]), Peter Coe ([*Dr.*] *Ilzor* [*Zandaab*]), Virginia Christine (*Princess Ananka*), Kay Harding (*Betty* [*Walsh*]), Dennis Moore ([*Dr. James*] *Halsey*), Martin Kosleck (*Ragheb*), Kurt Katch (*Cajun Joe*), Addison Richards (*Pat Walsh*), Holmes Herbert (*Dr. Cooper*), Charles Stevens (*Achilles*), William Farnum (*Sacristan*), Napoleon Simpson (*Goobie*), [Herbert Heywood (*Hill*)], [Ann Codee (*Tante Berthe*)], [Nina Bara (*Cajun girl*)], [Eddie Abdo (*Pierre*)], [Tony Santoro (*Ulysses*)], [Al Ferguson], [Heenan Elliott], [Budd Buster].
Horror, Drama. [*Print viewed*]. A group of Cajuns are worried about the government clearing of a local swamp, as they believe the marsh lands are haunted by the mummy Kharis, who carried the reincarnation of his ancient love, Princess Ananka, into its depths twenty-five years earlier. Pat Walsh, the superintendent in charge of the swamp clearing, is met by two representatives of the Scripps Museum, archaeologists Dr. James Halsey and Dr. Ilzor Zandaab, who ask for his help in excavating the remains of Kharis and Ananka. Soon thereafter, the murdered body of one of Pat's workmen is discovered in the swamps, and Halsey finds what seems to be Kharis' empty grave nearby. Unknown to Halsey, Zandaab, a high priest in the ancient religion of Amon-Ra, has unearthed Kharis with the help of Ragheb, a local workman, and now plans to re-animate the mummy with tanna leaves so that Kharis can recover Ananka's body and they both can be returned to their ancient tombs in Egypt. After Kharis is re-animated by Zandaab inside an abandoned monastery, the mummy kills Michael, the self-appointed caretaker of the chapel. Later, in the midst of the swamp's excavation, an old and withered Ananka emerges from the marshes, but is transformed into a beautiful, youthful woman upon the touch of the sun's rays. She is then discovered by Cajun Joe, a foreman, and he takes the amnesiac woman

to Tante Berthe's café. Ragheb, however, hears Ananka calling Kharis' name and rushes to inform Zandaab. Kharis is then sent to the café to reclaim his love, but Ananka does not recognize him and runs away. She faints near the roadway, where she is found by Halsey and Betty Walsh, Pat's secretary and niece. Meanwhile, Tante is discovered strangled to death, with ancient mold around her neck. Later, Ananka becomes Halsey's assistant, and the archaeologist is amazed by her unexplained expertise in ancient Egypt. Upon seeing Zandaab, however, Ananka goes into a trance and begins calling for Kharis, but the trance is quickly broken when she is shaken by Halsey. That night, Kharis once again tries to reclaim Ananka, but when she makes his escape, the mummy kills Dr. Cooper, the local physician. Seeing Ananka as the common link in the string of murders, Halsey and the workmen search the swamps for the missing woman. During the search, Cajun Joe is strangled by Kharis. Afterward, Ananka returns to the worker's camp, where she seeks refuge in Betty's tent. This time, Kharis manages to capture his love and goes back to the deserted monastery, where Zandaab feeds Ananka the sacred tanna leaves. Betty and the lustful Ragheb then arrive, but when Zandaab insists on killing the innocent Betty to preserve the secret of Kharis and Ananka, Ragheb stabs the high priest to death. Halsey then arrives at the monastery, where he and Ragheb fight over Betty. As Ragheb is about to kill Halsey, Kharis enters and, enraged by the death of Zandaab, tears down a wing of the monastery in an attempt to get at the murderous Ragheb. Both Kharis and Ragheb are buried in the rubble, and Ananka's mummified body is later found by Halsey and Pat. Halsey then makes plans to unearth Kharis and return both mummies to the Scripps Museum, and publicly announces his romantic intentions toward Betty. *Archaeologists. Egyptians. Love. Mummies. Murder. Revivification. African Americans. Amnesia. Cafés. Cajuns. Chases. Escapes. Fights. Louisiana. Monasteries. Museums. Nieces. Physicians. Priests. Rescues. Searches. Secretaries. Singers. Strangling. Swamps. Uncles.*

Note: The working title of this film was *The Mummy's Return*. According to a Dec 1943 *HR* news item, Ted Richmond was orginally set to produce the film. The film contains footage from two earlier Universal films, *The Mummy* and *The Mummy's Hand* (see *AFI Catalog of Feature Films, 1931-40*; F3.2980 and F3.2982). Although it is consistent with the plot of Universal's previous "Kharis" film, *The Mummy's Ghost*, in that "Kharis" and "Ananka" disappear into the swamps at the end of *The Mummy's Ghost*, *The Mummy's Curse* should have been set in the late 1960s. This was the fourth and final film at Universal featuring Kharis, the Mummy. For additional information on this series, consult the Series Index. Modern sources add the following names to the crew credits: *Contr wrt* Ted Richmond; *Cam op* William Dodds; *Prop* Ernie Smith and Eddie Case; *Makeup* Jack P. Pierce; *Gowns* Vera West; *Lon Chaney's doubles* Eddie Parker and Bob Pepper; and *Stunts* Carey Loftin and Teddy Mangean.

Box 20 Jan 1945. *DV* 20 Dec 1944, p. 4. *FD* 20 Dec 1944, p. 4. *HR* 27 Dec 1943, p. 1. *HR* 21 Jul 1944, p. 1. *HR* 10 Aug 1944, p. 3. *HR* 20 Dec 1944, p. 4. *MPHPD* 23 Dec 1944, pp. 2238-39. *NYT* 31 Mar 1945, p. 16. *Var* 20 Dec 1944, p. 17.

MURAGLIE see **PARDON US**

MURDER AT HARVARD see **MYSTERY STREET**

MURDER BY ALPHABET see **SHANGHAI CHEST**

MURDER CHAMBER see **BLACK MAGIC**

MURDER IN HARLEM see **LEM HAWKINS' CONFESSION**

MURDER IN THE AIR see **THE SKY DRAGON**

MURDER IN THE FUNHOUSE see **THE CHINESE CAT**

MURDER IN VILLA CAPRI (Italian Americans)
Burton Picture Productions. *Dist* Screen Guild Productions. 1955. Sd; b&w. 68 min. PCA cert no. 17460.

Prod Paul Burton-Mercur. *Dir* Otto Simetti. *Scr* Paul Burton-Mercur. *Dir of photog* Ira Cavrel. *Set des* Char. *Mus* Roger Rogers.
Song(s): "Down in Villa Capri," music and lyrics by Florence Mercur.
Cast: John Heath (*Lt. Roberti*), Neil Hamilton (*Capt. Brady*), Linda Blodgett (*Jeany*), Denise Griffin (*Lola Roberti*), Joe Wippler (*Frankie*), Anstide Sigismondi (*Don Luigi*), Esther Miniciotti (*Mama Flumeri*), Robert Argent (*Angelo*), Bern Hoffman (*Tony*), Florence Mercur.

Crime, Drama. [*Not viewed*]. Assigned to eradicate a lottery racket operating among the members of the Italian-American community, Lt. Roberti is warned by the racketeers to drop his investigation. Despite

the pleas of his wife Lola, who fears for his safety, the lieutenant ignores the gang's threats. One day, at the Villa Capri restaurant, the gang murders one of their members who has been double-crossing them. Lt. Roberti shoots at the fleeing killers, but instead hits and kills his friend when he accidentally steps into his line of fire. After their daughter is then killed by the ruthless underworld barons, Lola leaves her husband. Driven by a sense of duty and feeling of guilt for having killed his friend, Lt. Roberti relentlessly pursues the racketeers. After finally bringing them to justice, he reconciles with Lola. *Murder. Police. Racketeers. Fathers and daughters. Guilt. Gun accidents. Italian Americans. Restaurants. Separation (Marital).*

Note: According to the *Exb* review, much of the film's dialogue is spoken in Italian. The review adds that the story was allegedly based on a true crime story. According to materials contained in the MPAA/PCA files at the AMPAS Library, this picture was shot in New Jersey. This film was re-released in 1956 as *Code of the Underworld*.

Exb 15 Jun 1955, p. 3981. *Exb* 18 Apr 1956, p. 4137.

MURDER ON LENOX AVENUE (African Americans)
Colonnade Pictures Corp.; An Arthur Dreifuss Production. *Dist* International Roadshows. Dec 1941. Sd; b&w. 6,620 ft. 71 min.

Dir Arthur Dreifuss. *Asst dir* Charles Wasserman. *Orig story* Frank Wilson. *Scr adpt* Vincent Valentini and Bryna Ivens. *Cine* George Webber. *Art dir* William Salter. *Ed* Robert Crandall. *Cost* Al Stevens. *Orch arr* Ken Macomber. *Sd* Ed Fenton. *Unit mgr* Irving C. Miller.
Song(s): "Trying to Forget," "I'll Get Even with You" and "What You Know About That," music and lyrics by Donald Heywood.
Cast: Alberta Perkins (*Mercedes*), Sidney Easton (*Speed Simmons*), Alex Lovejoy (*Flivver Johnson*), Dene Larry (*Ola Wilkins*), Gus Smith (*Pa Wilkins*), Ernie Ransom (*Jim Branton*), Earl Sydnor (*Gregory*), Norman Astwood (*Marshall*), Herman Green (*Lomax*), George Williams (*Montoute*), Mamie Smith (*Hattie*), Cristola Williams (*Rosalia*), Emily Santos (*Emily*), Flo Lee (*Flo*), Wahneta San (*Wahneta*), [Edna Mae Harris (*Cabaret singer*)].

African American, Comedy-drama, with songs. [*Print viewed*]. Moments after shots ring out in the foyer of a crowded and noisy Harlem apartment building, the police break up a fight between Lomax, a notorious, hunchbacked thug, and Montoute, a young black immigrant hoping to become an American citizen. To protect Montoute, Pa Wilkins, a civic-minded reformer, hides Montoute's gun from the police. Later, at the Wilkinses, Pa's daughter Ola plans to elope with her boyfriend Gregory, a schoolteacher. Pa disapproves of Greg and prefers that she marry Jim Branton, the son of his old Army buddy, but Ola is not interested in Jim. Although Jim has been involved with Rosalia, a woman who lives in the same apartment building as the Wilkinses, he wants to marry Ola to obtain a trust fund that has been set aside for her future husband. At a community meeting, pie-seller Mercedes suggests that promoter Marshall, the head of the Business League, be forced to resign because he told her to buy useless equipment for her pie shop. After others at the meeting speak up in anger against Marshall, he steps down, but not without vowing revenge. Pa is then nominated to replace him. Hoping that Greg will make friends with Pa, Ola invites him to a surprise birthday party for her father. Her plans backfire, however, when Pa orders Greg to leave and tells him that Ola will marry Jim. This news stuns Rosalia, who hurriedly leaves the party. Later, at a cabaret, Greg tries to persuade Ola to marry him and then head to the South to work for racial equality. Jim walks in on their conversation, and when he repeats his intention to marry Ola himself, Greg punches him. Later, Ola elopes with Greg to the South. Pa is devastated by the news, but Hattie, Rosalia's mother, tells him that although her daughter is pregnant and will not tell her who the father is, she will not abandon her. She then counsels Pa to stand by his daughter. In Pa's first speech as head of the business association, he makes an appeal for racial unity. Marshall, however, decides to exploit Jim's anger at Ola and enlists his help in getting "certain people out of the way." Now that Ola is married, Rosalia believes that Jim will marry her and looks for him at the cabaret. When she overhears him making love to another woman, however, she returns home and, distraught, leaps to her death. Meanwhile, Ola reads in the newspaper that a bomb intended for her father was found in the community meeting hall and, worried about his safety, returns to New York. She and Greg find a note that Rosalia left for Jim and hurry to the meeting hall, where Pa is about to give another speech. Before they arrive, Pa announces that Montoute has become a citizen. Ola hands the note to Jim and then

tells Pa what has happened. Because Marshall's attempt to kill Pa with a bomb was foiled, he now instructs Lomax, his henchman, to shoot Pa. The plan nearly succeeds, but Jim, who is ashamed of his behavior, jumps in front of the bullet intended for Pa. Before he dies, Jim begs Pa's forgiveness. Greg and Ola decide to stay in New York and help Pa fight to save the future of their community. *African Americans. Businessmen. Fathers and daughters. New York City–Harlem. Reformers.* Attempted murder. Band leaders. Bombs. Elopement. Fistfights. Gunfights. Hunchbacks. Immigrants. Jazz music. Jealousy. Marriage–Arranged. Nightclubs. Police. Revenge. Self-sacrifice. Singers. Suicide. Teachers. Vamps.

Note: Although onscreen credits include a copyright statement, it was not registered for copyright.

Exb 31 Dec 1941.

MURDER OVER NEW YORK (Chinese Americans)

Twentieth Century-Fox Film Corp. *Dist* Twentieth Century-Fox Film Corp. 13 Dec **1940**; Prod: began mid-Jul 1940 [©Twentieth Century-Fox Film Corp.; 13 Dec 1940; LP10207]. Sd (RCA Sound System); b&w. 65 min. PCA cert no. 6517.

Series: Charlie Chan.

Exec prod Sol M. Wurtzel. *Dir* Harry Lachman. [*Asst dir* William Eckhardt]. *Orig scr* Lester Ziffren. *Dir of photog* Virgil Miller. *Art dir* Richard Day and Lewis Creber. *Film ed* Louis Loeffler. *Set dec* Thomas Little. *Cost* Herschel. *Mus dir* Emil Newman. *Sd* Joseph E. Aiken and Harry M. Leonard.

Source: Based on the character "Charlie Chan" created by Earl Derr Biggers.

Cast: Sidney Toler (*Charlie Chan*), Marjorie Weaver (*Patricia Shaw*), Robert Lowery (*David Elliott*), Ricardo Cortez (*George Kirby*), Donald MacBride (*Inspector Vance*), Melville Cooper (*Herbert Fenton*), Joan Valerie (*June Preston*), Kane Richmond (*Ralph Percy*), Sen Yung (*Jimmy Chan*), Leyland Hodgson (*Boggs*), Clarence Muse (*Butler*), Frederick Worlock (*Hugh Drake*), [John Sutton (*Richard Jeffrey*)], [Lal Chand Mehra (*Rumullah*)], [Dorothy Dearing (*Mrs. Percy*)], [Catherine Craig (*Stewardess*)], [Lee Phelps (*First policeman*)], [Stanley Blystone (*Fingerprint expert*)], [Ralph Dunn (*Second policeman*)], [Shirley Warde (*Mrs. Felton*)], [George Walcott (*First mechanic*)], [Paul Kruger (*Guard*)], [Alan Davis (*Pilot*)], [Carl Faulkner, Jimmie Dundee, Eddy Chandler, Frank Fanning (*Policemen*)], [Shemp Howard (*Canarsie kid*)], [Trevor Bardette (*Hindu businessman*)], [Frank Coghlan, Jr. (*Gilroy*)], [Bud Geary (*Second mechanic*)].

Detective. [*Print viewed*]. En route to a police convention in New York, Charlie Chan meets his old friend, Hugh Drake, a British intelligence officer who is on the trail of Paul Narvo, the spy who has been sabotaging U.S. built bombers bound for England. At the airport in New York, Drake is met by his host, aircraft tycoon George Kirby, who invites Chan to a party he is giving for Drake. Later that night, Chan arrives at Kirby's party to find Drake murdered by a poison gas pellet. Aided by police inspector Vance, Chan interrogates the assembled guests: Herbert Fenton, Drake's old school friend; actress June Preston; stockbroker Richard Jeffrey; Ralph Percy, an aircraft designer; and Kirby's butler, Boggs. Learning little from the guests, Chan tracks down Narvo's ex-wife, Patricia Shaw, who explains that she fled from her husband and his sinister servant, Rumullah, upon learning that he was a spy. Chan also questions David Elliott, a chemist who visited Drake on the night of his death. After Chan's search for Rumullah ends in the servant's death and Kirby is found poisoned, Chan assembles all the suspects on the test flight of a bomber that is to be sabotaged by poison gas pellets. As the bomber descends to the level that will trigger the gas, Fenton grabs the hidden pellets, revealing himself to be involved in the plot. As the plane lands safely, however, Chan announces that Fenton is too old to be Narvo, and then cleverly tricks the real Narvo, Dick Elliott, into exposing himself as the spy. *Chinese Americans. Detectives. Espionage. Impersonation and imposture. Murder. Sabotage.* Actors and actresses. Aircraft industry. Airplane accidents. Airplanes. Butlers. Chemists. Ex-spouses. Fathers and sons. Gases, Asphyxiating and poisonous. New York City. Spies. Stockbrokers.

Note: The working title of this film was *Charlie Chan in New York*. According to Fox publicity material contained in the AMPAS Library files, the studio changed the title in order to prevent the public from confusing this film with other Chan features. For additional information about the series, consult the Series Index and see *Charlie Chan Carries On* (above).

DV 2 Dec 1940, p. 3. *FD* 6 Dec 1940, p. 11. *HR* 12 Jul 1940, pp. 8-9. *HR* 2 Dec 1940, p. 3. *MPD* 4 Dec 1940, p. 5. *MPH* 7 Dec 1940, p. 44. *Var* 4 Dec 1940, p. 12.

MURDER WITH MUSIC *see* MISTAKEN IDENTITY

MURIETTA *see* ROBIN HOOD OF EL DORADO

MUSIC FOR MADAME (Italian Americans)

RKO Radio Pictures, Inc.; Jesse L. Lasky Productions. *Dist* RKO Radio Pictures, Inc. 8 Oct **1937**; Prod: 10 Jun–29 Jul 1937 [©RKO Radio Pictures, Inc.; 1 Oct 1937; LP7450]. Sd (RCA Victor System); b&w. 8 reels. 77 min. PCA cert no. 3500.

[*Exec prod* Samuel J. Briskin]. *Dir* John Blystone. *Scr* Gertrude Purcell and Robert Harari. *Orig story* Robert Harari. [*Contr to scr const* Hans Kraly, Lynn Starling and F. Hugh Herbert]. *Photog* Joseph H. August. *Spec eff* Vernon L. Walker. *Art dir* Van Nest Polglase. *Art dir assoc* Perry Ferguson. *Ed* Desmond Marquette. *Set dresser* Darrell Silvera. *Gowns* Edward Stevenson. *Mus dir* Nathaniel Shilkret. *Rec* George D. Ellis.

Song(s): "I Want the World to Know" and "Bambina," music by Rudolf Friml, lyrics by Gus Kahn; "Music for Madame," music and lyrics by Herbert Magidson and Allie Wrubel; "King of the Road," music and lyrics by Nathaniel Shilkret and Eddie Cherkose; "Vesti la giubba" from the opera *I pagliacci* by Ruggiero Leoncavallo.

Cast: NINO MARTINI (*Nino [Maretti]*), Joan Fontaine (*Jean [Clemens]*), Alan Mowbray ([*Leon] Rodowsky*), Billy Gilbert (*Krause*), Alan Hale ([*Detective] Flugelman*), Grant Mitchell (*Robinson, District Attorney*), Erik Rhodes ([*Spaghetti] Nadzio*), Lee Patrick (*Nora*), Romo Vincent (*Truck driver*), Frank Conroy ([*Morton] Harding*), Bradley Page (*Rollins*), George Shelley (*Barret*), Jack Carson (*Assistant director*), [Ward Bond (*Violets*)], [Barbara Pepper (*Blonde on bus*)], [Edward H. Robins (*William Goodwin*)], [Alan Bruce (*Groom*)], [Ada Leonard (*Miss Goodwin*)], [Grace Hayle (*Fat woman*)], [Milburn Stone (*Detective*)], [Jack Mulhall (*Guest*)], [Myra McKinney (*Admirer*)].

Comedy-drama, Musical. [*Print viewed*]. When jewel thieves Morton Harding and Rollins hear Italian immigrant Nino Maretti singing on a Hollywood-bound bus, they plot to use him as part of their scheme to rob motion picture director William Goodwin. By pretending to be talent scouts, Harding and Rollins convince Nino to perform unannounced at the wedding reception of Goodwin's daughter, where a valuable pearl necklace is on display. During Nino's stunning solo, which draws the opera-loving Detective Flugelman away from his watch, Harding and Rollins steal the necklace then, with Nino in tow, flee. After the theft is reported, District Attorney Robinson questions Jean Clemens, an aspiring operetta composer who had "crashed" the Goodwin wedding to meet famous conductor Leon Rodowsky. At the same time, Nino, who has been warned to keep quiet by the crooks, shows up at the police station, but is scared off when he realizes that he is the police's only suspect. As he leaves the station, Nino meets Jean and tells her that he is a music promoter whose most valuable possession has been stolen. After enjoying a romantic evening with Nino, Jean finds him a job as an extra for a movie musical that is being directed by Rodowsky. Because Rodowsky has been called on repeatedly by Robinson to identify the mystery tenor's voice, Nino, fearing for his life, remains mute. Later, however, Jean hears Nino singing one of her songs and, hurt by his apparent deception, angrily rejects him. As an apology, Nino turns himself in to collect Goodwin's $25,000 reward, which he tells Jean's roommate Nora to use to finance Jean's operetta. Before he claims the reward, Flugelman shows up with Spaghetti Nadzio, a cabaret tenor whom the detective is sure is Nino. To prove Nadzio's identity, Flugelman and Robinson arrange a radio broadcast in which the two tenors are to sing the same aria. When Rodowsky hears Nino singing, he immediately recognizes his voice but, in order to protect his brilliant "discovery," tells the police that Nino is innocent. Rodowsky then offers Nino a chance to sing at the Hollywood Bowl. Just before the performance, however, the jewel thieves send two of their henchmen to "silence" Nino, but the thugs mistake Nadzio for Nino and are later apprehended by Flugelman. Cleared of all suspicion, Nino tops off his sensational debut by singing one of Jean's compositions, which makes him a hit with both the audience and Jean. *Composers. Frame-ups. Italian Americans. Jewel thieves. Opera singers. Romance.* Buses. Cabaret performers. Conductors (Music). District Attorneys. The Hollywood Bowl (Los Angeles, CA). Immigrants. Impersonation and imposture. Los Angeles (CA). Motion picture actors

and actresses. Motion picture directors. Pearls. Police detectives. Radio broadcasting. Recognition. Rewards. Roommates. Ruffians. Talent agents. Weddings.

Note: RKO borrowed Romo Vincent from Paramount for this production, which was the first that Jesse Lasky made for the studio. According to *HR* production charts, Frank M. Thomas and Fred Santley were cast members. *HR* news items state that Timothy Ward, an "oldtime monologist," and Lionel Pape were also cast. The participation of these actors in the final film has not been confirmed. Several reviewers made note of Alan Mowbray's obvious caricature of well-known orchestra conductor Leopold Stokowski in the picture. According to a *HR* news item, newsreel company March of Time selected this film as "most representative of the current pictures in production for use in a sequence titled 'Hollywood Influences the World.'" Modern sources state that the film lost $375,000 at the box office. According to modern sources, the cast included the following additional actors: Ben Hall (*Bus passenger*), Larry Steers, Harold Miller and Ralph Brooks (*Guests*), George Meeker (*Orchestra leader*), Stanley Blystone and Pat O'Malley (*Policemen*), Robert Homans (*Desk sergeant*), Harry Tenbrook (*Electrician*), James Donlan (*Suspect with cold*), Russ Powell (*"Asleep in the Deep" singer*), Sam Hayes (*KAFF announcer*), Jac George (*Violinist*), and Ralph Lewis, Mary Carr, Ben Hendricks and William Corson. In addition, modern sources complete the onscreen character list: Grant Mitchell (*District Attorney Ernest Robinson*), Lee Patrick (*Nora Burns*) and Alan Bruce (*The groom [The director]*).

DV 9 Sep 1937, p. 3. *FD* 15 Sep 1937, p. 8. *HR* 11 Jun 1937, p. 4. *HR* 12 Jun 1937, p. 2. *HR* 14 Jun 1937, pp. 16-17. *HR* 28 Jun 1937, p. 22. *HR* 6 Jul 1937, p. 8. *HR* 8 Jul 1937, p. 8. *HR* 21 Jul 1937, p. 15. *HR* 23 Jul 1937, p. 6. *HR* 30 Jul 1937, p. 2. *HR* 10 Sep 1937, p. 3. *MPD* 13 Sep 1937, p. 14. *MPH* 17 Jul 1937, p. 69. *MPH* 18 Sep 1937, p. 42, 44. *NYT* 23 Oct 1937, p. 14. *Var* 15 Sep 1937, p. 13.

MUSIC IN MY HEART (Immigrants)

Columbia Pictures Corp. *Dist* Columbia Pictures Corp. 10 Jan 1940; New York opening: week of 4 Jan 1940; Prod: began late Oct 1939 [©Columbia Pictures Corp.; 26 Dec 1939; LP9306]. Sd; b&w. 8 reels. 70 min. PCA cert no. 5877.

Prod Irving Starr. *Dir* Joseph Santley. *Dial dir* William Castle. *Asst dir* Eugene Anderson. *Story and scr* James Edward Grant. *Photog* John Stumar. *Art dir* Lionel Banks. *Film ed* Otto Meyer. *Gowns* Kalloch. *Mus dir* M. W. Stoloff. *Vocal arr* Charles Henderson. *Sd* George Cooper.

Song(s): "Oh What a Lovely Dream," "Punchinello," "I've Got Music in My Heart," "It's a Blue World," "No Other Love" and "Hearts in the Sky," music and lyrics by Bob Wright and Chet Forrest.

Cast: TONY MARTIN (*Robert Gregory*), Rita Hayworth (*Patricia O'Malley*), Edith Fellows (*Mary*), Alan Mowbray (*Charles Gardner*), Eric Blore (*Griggs*), George Tobias (*Sascha*), Joseph Crehan (*Mark C. Gilman*), George Humbert (*Luigi*), Joey Ray (*Miller*), Don Brodie (*Taxi driver*), Julietta Novis (*Leading lady*), Eddie Kane (*Blake*), Phil Tead (*Marshall*), Marten Lamont (*Barrett*), Andre Kostelanetz, and his band.

Comedy, with songs. [*Print viewed*]. Englishman Robert Gregory, an understudy in a Broadway musical, gets an opportunity to play the leading role on the eve of his deportation from the country. En route to the boat, his taxi collides with another cab that is carrying Patricia O'Malley, who is also headed to the boat to marry Charles Gardner, an eccentric millionaire she doesn't love. It is a case of love at first sight, and they are very much relieved when they discover that they have missed the boat. Meanwhile, aboard the boat, Pat's tardiness prompts Charles to believe that he has been jilted, and accompanied by his butler, Griggs, he disembarks before it sails, while Bob's absence prompts the immigration authorities to issue a warrant for his arrest. Learning of Bob's jeopardy, Pat insists that he spend the night at her Uncle Luigi's, where he immediately wins the favor of Pat's kid sister Mary. The next day, Charles begins a campaign to win Pat back, and sends Griggs to Sascha's restaurant as an ambassador. To disrupt the peace talks, Bob pretends to be a waiter, and Griggs finds his face vaguely familiar. After Griggs departs, Bob proposes to Pat and she accepts. That night at dinner, Pat tells Charles of her decision, and Briggs, finally recognizing Bob as the fugitive whose picture appeared in the paper, suggests that they turn him into the police. When Charles, always the gentleman, refuses, Griggs plants a story in the paper about the wife and three children that Bob has left behind, causing Pat to return to Charles. Meanwhile, Bob, dejected, learns that Sascha is threatened with eviction and offers to turn himself in while performing on Andre Kostelanetz's new radio program. As Pat despondently listens to the sound of Bob's voice over the radio, Charles realizes that she still loves him and, upon learning of Griggs' scheme, reconciles the lovers and adopts Bob to make him a citizen. *Deportation. Eccentrics. English. Fortune hunters. Fugitives. Singers.* Butlers. Disguise. Duplicity. Engagements. New York City–Broadway. Newspapers. Radio broadcasting. Sisters. Taxicabs. Uncles.

Note: The working title of this film was *Passport to Happiness*.

DV 9 Jan 1940, p. 3. *FD* 5 Jan 1940, p. 5. *HR* 21 Oct 1939, pp. 3-4. *HR* 9 Jan 1940, p. 3. *MPD* 11 Jan 1940, p. 7. *MPH* 25 Nov 1939, p. 35. *MPH* 13 Jan 1940, p. 40. *NYT* 4 Jan 1940, p. 19. *Var* 10 Jan 1940, p. 16.

THE MUSIC MAKER *see* TONIGHT WE SING

MUSIC MAN (Italian Americans)

Monogram Pictures Corp. *Dist* Monogram Pictures Corp. 5 Sep 1948; Los Angeles opening: 16 Jul 1948; Prod: early May—mid-May 1948 [©Monogram Pictures Corp.; 5 Sep 1948; LP1878]. Sd (Western Electric Recording); b&w. 5,960 ft. 66 min. PCA cert no. 13232.

Prod Will Jason. *Assoc prod* Maurice Duke. *Dir* Will Jason. *Asst dir* Melville Shyer. *Orig scr* Sam Mintz. *Dir of photog* Jackson Rose. [*Cam op* Bill Margolies]. [*Stills* Al St. Hilaire]. *Supv film ed* Otho Lovering. *Film ed* William Austin. *Set dec* Raymond Boltz, Jr. *Mus dir* Edward J. Kay. *Sd* L. J. Myers. [*Hair stylist* Lela Chambers]. *Prod mgr* Allen K. Wood. *Dial coach* Jameson Brewer. *Tech dir* Dave Milton. [*Scr supv* Bobbie Sierkes]. [*Grip* George Booker].

Music: "The Frog," composer undetermined.

Song(s): "Shy Ann," music and lyrics by Freddie Stewart and Arnold Ross; "Comm'e bella 'a Stagione (When I Hold You In My Arms)," music by R. Falvo, Italian lyrics by G. Pisano, English lyrics by George Brown; "Bella, Bella, Marie," music and lyrics by Erhard Winkler, Don Pelosi and Leo Towers; "I Could Swear It Was You," music and lyrics by Phil Brito, Larry Stock and Allan Flynn; "Little Man You've Had a Busy Day," music and lyrics by Mable Wayne, Maurice Sigler and Al Hoffman.

Cast: Freddie Stewart [(*Freddie Russo*)], Phil Brito [(*Phil Russo*)], Jimmy Dorsey [(*Himself*)], Alan Hale, Jr. [(*Joe*)], June Preisser [(*June Larkin*)], Noel Neill [(*Kitty*)], Grazia Narciso [(*Mrs. Russo*)], Chick Chandler [(*Sanders*)], Norman Leavitt [(*Sam*)], Jimmy Dorsey's Orchestra, [Helen Woodford (*Secretary*)], [Gertrude Astor (*Mrs. Larkin*)], [William Norton Bailey (*Mr. Larkin*)], [Herman Cantor (*Pianist*)], [Roy Aversa, Paul Bradley (*Italians at party*)], [Eddie Rio (*Valdeti*)], [Renata Vanni, Rosa Barbato (*Italian women*)], [Lester Dorr (*Mailman*)], [Sven Hugo Borg (*Janitor*)], [Sid Kane (*Process server*)], [Edward J. Kay (*Conductor*)], Ernie Felice.

Show business, Drama, with songs. [*Print viewed*]. In New York City, Italian American songwriting brothers Phil and Freddie Russo turn out one successful song after another for their publisher, Sanders. One day, Freddie and Phil accept an invitation from attractive June Larkin to sing at a benefit that her parents are hosting. Kitty, the brothers' secretary, is secretly in love with Phil, but Phil is smitten with June. Following the benefit party, Kitty visits Phil and Freddie's mother, who lives alone in an East Side tenement, and asks her to help stop the bickering between her sons. Mrs. Russo tells Kitty that she has refused to play favorite with either son, and that she has turned down separate invitations from Phil and Freddie to live with them. Joe, a milkman and an aspiring songwriter who adores Mrs. Russo, drives Kitty home and, en route, recites the lyrics of one of his new songs. Later, Mrs. Russo throws a party to bring her sons together, and they sing a song written especially for her. Mrs. Russo eventually consents to live with her two sons in a large apartment, but the arrangement soon sours when the two brothers become embroiled in a jealous rivalry over June. The dispute results in Freddie moving into his own apartment. Although Freddie refuses to speak with Phil, the brothers manage to continue writing songs together. However, when the feud begins to take its toll on the quality of the brothers' songs, Sanders tells Freddie that he will no longer publish their work. Frustrated by his inability to find a new publisher, Freddie decides to start his own publishing business. The company makes little money, and goes bankrupt soon after, but Freddie refuses to accept financial help from band leader Jimmy Dorsey. Later, Kitty enlists Joe's help to force a reconciliation between the estranged brothers. As part of Kitty's plan, Joe poses first as a lyricist and then as a composer, tricking the brothers into collaborating on a musical comedy without the other's knowledge. The show appears destined for success until the brothers discover the ruse and threaten to stop the show with an injunction. When Mrs. Russo tells her sons that she has invested heavily in their show, however, they call off their injunctions and allow the show to go on. The show is a hit, and the two sons are finally reconciled. *Brothers. Feuds. Italian Americans. Romantic rivalry. Songwriters.* Bands (Music). Bankruptcy. Hoaxes. Impersonation and imposture. Investors. Milkmen. Mothers and sons. Music publishers and publishing. Musicians. New York City. New York City–East Side. Nightclubs. Reconciliation. Secretaries. Singers.

Note: This film's working title was *Manhattan Folksong*. According to a *HR* production chart, Norman Leavitt appears to have replaced the previously cast George Beatty in the role of "Sam."

Box 24 Jul 1948. *DV* 15 Jul 1948, p. 3. *HR* 7 May 1948, p. 12. *HR* 15 Jul 1948, p. 3. *MPD* 20 Jul 1948. *MPHPD* 24 Jul 1948, p. 4251.

THE MUSIC MASTER see **TONIGHT WE SING**

MUSS 'EM UP (African Americans, Italian Americans)

RKO Radio Pictures, Inc.; A Pandro S. Berman Production. *Dist* RKO Radio Pictures, Inc. 14 Feb **1936**; New York opening: week of 1 Feb 1936; Prod: 5 Nov—7 Dec 1935 [©RKO Radio Pictures, Inc.; 14 Feb 1936; LP6151]. Sd (RCA Victor System); b&w. 8 reels. 68.5 or 70 min. PCA cert no. 1800.

Dir Charles Vidor. [*Asst dir* Doran Cox]. *Scr* Erwin Gelsey. *Photog* J. Roy Hunt and Joseph August. *Art dir* Van Nest Polglase. *Art dir assoc* Perry Ferguson. *Ed* Jack Hively. *Mus dir* Roy Webb. *Rec* Denzil A. Cutler and [Clem Portman].

Source: Based on the novel *The Green Shadow* by James Edward Grant (New York, 1935).

Cast: Preston Foster [(*Tippecanoe "Tip" O'Neil*)], Margaret Callahan [(*Amy Hutchins*)], Alan Mowbray [(*Paul Harding*)], Ralph Morgan [(*Jim Glenray*)], Big Boy Williams [(*"Red" Cable*)], Maxie Rosenbloom [(*"Snake"*)], Molly Lamont [(*Nancy Harding*)], John Carroll [(*Gene Leland*)], Florine McKinney [(*Corinne*)], Robert Middlemass [(*Inspector Brock*)], Noel Madison [(*Tony Spivali*)], Maxine Jennings [(*Cleo*)], Harold Huber [(*Maratti*)], Clarence Muse [(*William*)], Paul Porcasi [(*Luigi Tersiniani*)], Ward Bond, John Adair [(*Gangsters*)], [Willie Best (*Janitor*)].

Detective. [*Print viewed*]. In response to a telegram, New York private detective Tippecanoe "Tip" O'Neil travels to see Paul Harding, an old friend and employer, at his Lakeside estate. Although Paul, a gun enthusiast, protests that he did not send the telegram, he confides in Tip that his dog was shot and that someone has sent him letters demanding $200,000. After concluding that the dog killer had used one of Paul's rifles, Tip questions Amy Hutchins, Paul's attractive, gun-toting secretary, who confesses that she sent the telegram. That night, after Tip observes Paul's brother-in-law, Jim Glenray, slip out of the house, Corinne, Paul's ward, is kidnapped by two thugs. Paul insists that Tip, who enjoys a reputation as a tough, "no-holds-barred" detective, handle the kidnapping, but when the son of William, the black chauffeur, is found dead near the estate, Inspector Brock drops by for questioning. The next morning, the kidnappers contact Paul and demand a ransom of $200,000. While Paul delivers the money, "Red" Cable, a bodyguard whom Paul had hired to watch his daughter Nancy, finds thug Maratti on the grounds. With Amy behind the wheel, Red and Tip push Maratti into a car at gunpoint and force him to admit that he was after Jim because he was having an affair with his sister Cleo. After Paul returns from his rendezvous without Corinne, however, Gene Leland, her anxious fiancé, informs Tip that another gangster, Tony Spivali, once had contacted Paul. Armed with this clue, Tip finds Tony at his gambling house and demands information. When Tony refuses to divulge his secret for less than $5,000, Tip seeks the help of Luigi Tersiniani, a Mafia godfather, who intimidates Tony into revealing that Jim had gambling debts with him and was using William, his chauffeur, as a go-between. Tony then states that William had approached him with a proposition involving two hired thugs. Before Tip is able to extract a confession out of William, however, the chauffeur is shot in Harding's study with Amy's gun. Now a suspect, Amy takes Tip to her apartment, where she is attacked by an unseen assailant. After knocking out an over-zealous Gene, Tip then delivers an additional $50,000 to the thugs, unaware that Corinne is an accomplice in her own kidnapping. Corinne, who is then double-crossed by her co-conspirators, returns home and is observed by Tip in an intimate embrace with Paul. When Tony then identifies Paul, not Jim, as the gambler, Tip deduces that Paul and Corinne planned the kidnapping in order to get $200,000, which Nancy had donated from her trust fund. Tip also learns that the thugs accidentally killed William's son, that Paul killed William, and that Paul had attacked Amy because she had a carbon of a list of phony currency serial numbers that Paul had given the police. Thus cornered, Paul attempts to escape with Corinne, but crashes in his automobile and dies. *Conspiracy. Kidnapping. Murder. Private detectives. Thieves. African Americans. Automobile accidents. Bodyguards. Brothers and sisters. Chauffeurs. Confession (Law). Escapes. Firearms. Gamblers. Love affairs. Mafia. Money. Police inspectors. Secretaries. Telegrams. Wards and guardians.*

Note: The working title of this film was *The Green Shadow*. *HR* production charts add Nicholas Soussanin, Pat Flaherty and Jerry Larkin to the cast list, but their participation in the final film has not been confirmed. One *HR* production charts lists Clem Portman, not Denzil A. Cutler, as the sound recorder. According to modern sources, New York police commissioner Lewis J. Valentine used a slang expression similar to "muss 'em up" when describing how his officers should handle criminals during police roundups, and from thus the film's title was born.

DV 5 Nov 1935, p. 2. *DV* 7 Dec 1935, p. 2. *DV* 16 Jan 1936, p. 3. *FD* 21 Jan 1936, p. 8. *HR* 11 Nov 1935, p. 11. *HR* 2 Dec 1935, pp. 6-7. *MPD* 17 Jan 1936, p. 3. *MPH* 14 Dec 1935, p. 51. *MPH* 25 Jan 1936, p. 38. *NYT* 3 Feb 1936, p. 21. *Var* 5 Feb 1936, p. 12.

MUTINY IN THE ARCTIC (Native Americans, Native Alaskans)

Universal Pictures Co., Inc. *Dist* Universal Pictures Co., Inc. 18 Apr **1941**; Prod: 7 Mar—mid-Mar 1941 [©Universal Pictures Co., Inc.; 21 Apr 1941; LP10419]. Sd (Western Electric Mirrophonic Recording); b&w. 5,509 ft. 60-61 min. PCA cert no. 7239.

Assoc prod Ben Pivar. *Dir* John Rawlins. [*Asst dir* Edwin Tyler]. *Dial dir* Maurice Wright. *Scr* Maurice Tombragel and Victor McLeod. *Orig story* Paul Huston. *Dir of photog* John W. Boyle. *Art dir* Jack Otterson. *Assoc* Ralph M. DeLacy. *Film ed* Ed Curtiss. *Set dec* R. A. Gausman. *Gowns* Vera West. *Mus dir* H. J. Salter. *Sd supv* Bernard B. Brown. [*Sd*] *tech* Robert Pritchard.

Cast: RICHARD ARLEN (*Dick* [*Barclay*]), ANDY DEVINE (*Andy* [*Adams*]), Anne Nagel (*Gloria* [*Adams*]), Addison Richards (*Ferguson*), Don Terry (*Cole*), Oscar O'Shea (*Captain Morrissey*), Harry Cording (*Harmon*), Jeff Corey (*Cook*), Harry Strang (*Helmsman*), John Rogers (*Mess boy*), [Dave Wengren, Gibson Gowland, Charles Sullivan, Jack Roper (*Sailors*)], [John Bagni (*Lamo*)], [William Moore, Eddie Dew (*Radio operators*)], [Stanley Blystone (*Bosum*)], [Sam Adams (*Svenson*)], [David Sharpe (*Lookout*)], [Leo Abbey (*Eskimo*)].

Adventure, Drama. [*Print viewed*]. Engaged explorers Dick Barclay and Gloria Adams return from an Arctic expedition with valuable aerial maps. They are met in San Francisco by Gloria's brother Andy, who, much to the chagrin of Dick, prefers to do his exploring in books. Dick discovers that they have photographed a radium deposit near an old mine owned by Gloria and Andy's father. Upon the advice of promoter Ferguson, the trio charters the vessel *Astoria* from Captain Morrissey, whom they offer a twenty percent partnership in the radium mine. Morrissey, however, refuses to sail with Gloria aboard, saying that women are bad luck, so she is forced to remain behind in San Francisco. Unknown to the new partners, Ferguson has hired one of the crew members, first mate Cole, to sabotage the voyage. Along the way, Cole sends crew member Harmon to search for the map to the radium mine, and he knocks Andy out when he is nearly discovered in the explorer's cabin. Later, Cole discovers Morrissey with the map and steals it from the captain's desk. Fog sets in, so Morrissey orders the ship to drop anchor. A mess boy, having seen Cole steal the map, goes to Ferguson, who stops him from reporting it to the captain. Harmon then kills the mess boy and tosses his body overboard. The murderer later tricks Morrissey into going down to the engine room, then kills him as well. Cole takes over the ship and falsely accuses Dick, Andy and Ferguson of mutiny. Cole orders the ship ahead, threatening to kill any crew member who refuses to follow his orders. When the ship rams into an iceberg, Cole orders the ship abandoned. While Cole and his crew escape on a lifeboat, Dick, Andy and Ferguson break out of their locked cabin, and, along with the ship's cook and dog, climb aboard the iceberg as the ship sinks. Gloria learns of the ship's distress signal in San Francisco and leaves to attempt an air rescue. The stranded men then hop aboard an ice floe in hopes of finding land. After being forced aboard another iceberg, they take shelter in a cave. Gloria begins her aerial search of the region, but upon her arrival at the Eskimo village near her father's mine, she finds only Cole and his crew. As the ice around them begins to break, Ferguson confesses all. Back at the village, Gloria leaves to continue her search, unaware of Cole's treachery. When Gloria's plane flies overhead, Dick and the others send her a distress signal by setting their tent afire. She attempts to land her plane, only to crash into another iceberg. Meanwhile, Cole and Harmon plan their expedition to the mine, despite warnings from the Eskimo chief about the dangers of the winter thaw. A desperate Ferguson attempts to kill a polar bear for food, but is killed himself by a second bear. When Andy tells Dick that they have drifted within four miles of the Eskimo village, he takes it upon himself to go for help. With the help of the Eskimos and their canoes, Dick manages to

save Andy and the others just as their iceberg falls apart. Cole returns to the village, and after he attempts to kill Dick in his sleep, the explorer captures the crooked sailor with the help of the Eskimo chief. Returning to San Francisco, Andy is proclaimed a hero for his navigational expertise, and Dick and Gloria make plans to settle down, along with the ship's dog and its litter of new puppies. *Arctic regions. Brothers and sisters. Explorers. Mutiny. Rescues. Sea captains. Ships. Women explorers. Airplane accidents. Cooks. Correspondence schools and courses. Deception. Dogs. Fights. Icebergs. Murder. Native Alaskans. Polar bears. Promoters. San Francisco (CA). Seaplanes. Women air pilots.*

Note: The working title of this film was *Northern Lights.* According to the *HR* review, this film made extensive use of stock footage of the arctic regions, including icebergs and Eskimo villages, compiled from the 1933 Universal film *White Hell of Pitz Palu* (see AFI Catalog of Feature Films, 1931-40; F3.5456) and the 1929 German silent film *S.O.S. Iceberg.*

Box 17 May 1941. *DV* 25 Apr 1941. *FD* 8 May 1941, p. 6. *HR* 26 Feb 1941, p. 4. *HR* 7 Mar 1941, p. 17. *HR* 10 Mar 1941, p. 3. *HR* 25 Apr 1941, p. 4. *MPHPD* 19 Apr 1941, p. 111. *NYT* 3 May 1941, p. 20. *Var* 1 Jan 1941. *Var* 7 May 1941, p. 12.

MY AMERICAN WIFE (Immigrants)

Paramount Productions, Inc. *Dist* Paramount Productions, Inc. 7 Aug **1936** [©Paramount Productions, Inc.; 7 Aug 1936; LP6532]. Sd (Western Electric Noiseless Recording); b&w. 8 reels. 65, 70 or 75 min. Passed by the National Board of Review. PCA cert no. 2389.

[*Exec prod* William LeBaron]. *Dir* Harold Young. [*Asst dir* Richard Harlan]. *Scr* Virginia Van Upp. [*Contr to trmt* William Slavens McNutt]. *Photog* Harry Fischbeck. *Art dir* Hans Dreier and Robert Odell. *Ed* Paul Weatherwax. *Int dec* A. E. Freudeman. *Cost* Travis Banton. [*Orig score and mus dir* Boris Morros]. *Sd rec* Earl Hayman and Louis Mesenkop. [*Makeup* Newt Johns]. [*Props* Charles Mason].

Source: Based on the short story "Old Timer" by Elmer Davis in *The Saturday Evening Post* (20 Apr 1935).

Cast: FRANCIS LEDERER (*Count Ferdinand* ['*Ferdie*'] *von und zu Reidenach*), ANN SOTHERN (*Mary Cantillon*), Fred Stone (*Lafe Cantillon*), Billie Burke (*Mrs. Robert Cantillon*), Ernest Cossart (*Adolph*), Grant Mitchell (*Robert Cantillon*), Hal K. Dawson (*Stephen Cantillon*), Helene Millard (*Mrs. Vincent Cantillon*), Adrian Morris (*Vincent Cantillon*), Dora Clemant (*Mrs. Stephen Cantillon*), Montague Shaw (*Butler*), [William Wagner (*Footman*)], [Janet Elsie Clark (*Helena*)], [Buck Connors (*Old Timer*)], [Dale Armstrong (*Announcer*)], [Noble Johnson (*Indian Chief*)], [Henry Roquemore (*Fat committee man*)], [Eddie Dunn, Jimmy Vandiveer, Frank Marlowe, Don Brodie (*Reporters*)], [Art Rowlands (*Cameraman*)], [Jim Toney (*Section hand*)], [Ernie Adams (*Second cameraman*)], [Isabelle LaMore, Nina Borget, Nenette Lafayette (*French maids*)], [Florence Wix (*Mrs. Van Dusen*)], [Phillips Smalley (*Mr. Van Dusen*)], [Billy Gilbert (*French chef*)], [Margaret Brayton (*Secretary*)], [Heinie Conklin (*Baggageman*)], [Doodles Weaver (*Cowhand*)], [Leonard Trainor (*Chuck*)], [George Guhl (*Policeman*)], [Spencer Charters (*Engineer*)], [Dorothy Tennant], [Edwin Stanley], [Sarah Edwards].

Comedy-drama. [*Print viewed*]. Count Ferdinand von und zu Reidenach arrives in Smelter City, Arizona, with his American bride, Mary Cantillon. Mary's grandfather, Lafe Cantillon, founded the town and disapproves of Mary's marriage to a foreigner. Mary and her mother, however, are thrilled with the fact that Mary is now a countess, and they make the most of it via various social occasions. "Ferdie," however, is tired of high society and has dreams of becoming a "real" American by running his own ranch. He has a difficult time fitting in with the Cantillon family, who grudgingly give him a position at their bank, but provide him with no work to do. Ferdie's determination eventually wins Lafe over, and the two men become buddies, much to the disgust of the rest of the family, who find Lafe's rough, earthy manners intolerable. The final blow comes when Ferdie informs Mary he has begun building a ranch house for the two of them, and she refuses to live there. At a family meeting Ferdie announces that he is surrendering trusteeship of Mary's inheritance and is dissolving their marriage because he wants to be an American, but she only wants what her mother wants. Before Mary heads for Reno, she realizes she loves Ferdie, and that he protected her inheritance out of love for her, while the rest of the family lost their money in a bad stock investment. When she hears that a redhead named Helena is moving in with Ferdie, she becomes infuriated and drives out to the ranch, where she discovers that Helena is the valet Adolph's homely daughter. By this time, however, Mary has decided

to "grow up" and return to her husband, who happily embraces her. *Family relationships. Immigrants. Snobs and snobbishness. Social climbers. The West. Arizona. Bankers. Bigotry. Covered wagons. Fistfights. Grandfathers. Inheritance. Jealousy. Maturation. Mothers and daughters. Newlyweds. Nobility. Ranches. Separation (Marital). Valets.*

Note: The working titles of the film were *The Old-Timer* and *The Count of Arizona.* Copyright records, CBCS, and *HR* production charts indicate Edith Fitzgerald contributed to the screenplay, however, she is not credited elsewhere, nor does her name appear in the Paramount story files at the AMPAS library. Cast credited in pre-release sources includes Terry Ray, Jeanne Perkins, Gail Sheridan, Ann Evers, Irene Bennett, Louise Stanley, Fred Parent and Marvin Jones. According to the pressbook and an article in *DV*, some scenes were filmed on location in Bel Air, Beverly Hills, Palmdale, Pasadena and Victorville, CA.

DV 18 Jul 1936, p. 3. *FD* 21 Jul 1936, p. 11. *HR* 18 Jul 1936, p. 3. *MPD* 20 Jul 1936, p. 8. *MPH* 18 Jul 1936, p. 60. *MPH* 25 Jul 1936, p. 66. *NYT* 21 Aug 1936, p. 12. *Var* 26 Aug 1936, p. 20.

MY BOY (Immigrants)

Jackie Coogan Productions. *Dist* Associated First National Pictures. 2 Jan **1922**; New York, Los Angeles, and Washington premieres: ca25 Dec 1921 [©Sol Lesser; 27 Dec 1921; LP17446]. Si; b&w. 5 reels, 4,967 ft.

Pres Sol Lesser. *Supv* Jack Coogan, Sr. *Dir* Victor Heerman and Albert Austin. *Titles* Shirley Vance Martin and Max Abramson. *Photog* Glen MacWilliams and Robert Martin. *Film ed* Irene Morra.

Cast: Jackie Coogan (*Jackie Blair*), Claude Gillingwater (*Captain Bill*), Mathilde Brundage (*Mrs. Blair*), Patsy Marks (*Little Girl*).

Comedy-drama. Jackie Blair arrives in the United States as a steerage passenger and faces deportation because his mother has died during the voyage. Captain Bill, a retired skipper, tries his best to amuse Jackie while arrangements are being made for his return trip, but Jackie escapes and follows the captain to his shanty home. Although the captain loves the boy, his poverty and age preclude his keeping him. Meanwhile, a wealthy matron who is Jackie's grandmother, missing Jackie at Ellis Island, begins a search for him. When the captain is taken ill, Jackie earns money by dancing in the streets and buys medicine for his patron, and at the settlement house where he attends a party given by the rich matron Jackie steals some grapes. Tracked by the police to the captain's shanty, Jackie is taken into custody and learns that he is Mrs. Blair's grandson; he and the captain then find a happy home with his wealthy relative. *Grandmothers. Immigrants. New York City–Ellis Island. Orphans. Sea captains.*

ETR 7 Jan 1922. *FD* 1 Jan 1922. *MPW* 7 Jan 1922, p. 112. *MPW* 14 Jan 1922, p. 202. *Var* 6 Jan 1922, p. 43.

MY COUNTRY 'TIS OF THEE see IT'S A BIG COUNTRY: AN AMERICAN ANTHOLOGY

MY COUSIN (Italian Americans)

Famous Players-Lasky Corp. *Dist* Famous Players-Lasky Corp.; Artcraft Pictures. 17 Nov **1918** [©Famous Players-Lasky Corp.; 28 Sep 1918; LP12918]. Si; b&w. 5 reels, 4,710 ft.

Pres Adolph Zukor. *Dir* Edward José. *Story and scen* Margaret Turnbull. *Cam* Hal Young.

Cast: Enrico Caruso (*Mario Nanni/Cesare Carulli*), Henry Leone (*Robert Bombardi*), Carolina White (*Rosa Ventura*), Joseph Ricciardi (*Pietro Ventura*), A. G. Corbelle (*Luigi Veddi*), Bruno Zirato (*Secretary*), William Bray (*Ludovico*).

Comedy-drama. Mario Nanni, a poor but proud artist living in New York's Little Italy, boasts that he is the cousin of the great tenor, Cesare Carulli, in order to impress Rosa Ventura, the girl he passionately loves. Although Rosa returns Mario's affections, her father wishes her to marry Robert Bombardi, the proprietor of a fruit and vegetable stand. After attending Carulli's performance of *I Pagliacci*, Mario and Rosa visit a café, where Carulli fails to recognize his cousin. Later the sculptor tries to give Carulli a bust, but the tenor's secretary mistakes him for an aspiring singer and turns him away. Mario's status in Little Italy has plummeted, and even Rosa is ready to abandon him when Carulli, having learned of Mario's troubles, visits the artist's studio and loudly commissions a bronze bust from his cousin. *Cousins. Italian Americans. Opera singers. Recognition. Sculptors. Cafés. Grocers. New York City–Little Italy. Statues.*

Note: This film was originally scheduled for release 20 Oct 1918 but was delayed because of the influenza epidemic. In some reviews, the Mario Nanni character is called Tomaso Longo. Reviewers note this as Caruso's first film.

Carolina White was the operatic soprano of the Metropolitan. The film includes scenes showing the interior and exterior of the Metropolitan Opera House in New York, Caruso's dressing room there, and his home.

ETR 23 Nov 1918, pp. 1987-89. *MPN* 7 Dec 1918, p. 3423. *MPW* 19 Oct 1918, p. 450. *MPW* 7 Dec 1918, p. 1119. *NYDM* 7 Dec 1918, p. 846. *NYT* 25 Nov 1918, p. 11. *Photo-Play World* Feb 1919, p. 33. *Var* 29 Nov 1918, p. 41. *Wid's* 1 Dec 1918, p. 18.

MY FIGHTING GENTLEMAN (African Americans)

American Film Co.; Mutual Star Productions. *Dist* Mutual Film Corp. 12 Mar **1917**. Si; b&w. 5 reels.

Dir Edward Sloman. *Scen* Doris Schroeder. *Story* Nell Shipman.

Cast: William Russell (*Frank Carlisle*), Francelia Billington (*Virginia Leighton*), Charles Newton (*Colonel Carlisle*), Jack Vosburgh (*Huntly Thornton*), Clarence Burton (*Isaiah Gore*), Harry Von Meter (*Judge Pembroke*), William Carroll (*Jubilee*), Sid Algier (*Jim*), Lucille Ward.

Historical, Drama. With the Civil War over, Frank Carlisle, the son of a Southern colonel, returns home to his ravaged Virginia plantation to be ostracized by his neighbors and sweetheart Virginia Leighton, because of his allegiance to the North. Although Frank, like the other whites, expresses concern over the blacks' newfound freedom, he is further disdained when he works alongside his former slave Jubilee, an action that is an outrage to the Southern sense of gentlemanly pride. Virginia forsakes Frank for Huntly Thornton, a dissolute Southern aristocrat who has formed an alliance with carpetbagger Isaiah Gore. When Frank opposes Thornton for a seat in the Senate, Thornton and Gore scheme to discredit him. They plan to drug a young African-American boy and terrorize him with "voodoo" spells so that he will be induced to rape Frank's mother. Thornton and Gore believe Frank, in a rage, will then kill the boy. Their plan backfires, however, when the boy attacks Virginia instead. Thornton shoots the boy and carries Virginia away, while Frank is led to believe that Jubilee has killed the boy while protecting Mrs. Carlisle. To shield his mother, Frank claims that he killed the boy, and Gore organizes a mob to lynch him. Frank, however, obtains a confession from Thornton, unmasks Gore and wins Virginia. *African Americans. Elections. Frame-ups. Murder. Political alliances. Self-sacrifice. Southerners. United States–History–Reconstruction, 1865-1898. United States–South. Carpetbaggers. Confession (Law). Lynching. Mobs. Ostracism. Plantations. Virginia.*

Note: This film was also known as *A Son of Battle*. *MPW* commented, "The incidents of the story in an indirect way touch on what we believe to be authentic facts in the history of the South."

Motog 17 Mar 1917, p. 589. *MPN* 10 Mar 1917, p. 1574. *MPW* 3 Mar 1917, p. 1407. *MPW* 10 Mar 1917, p. 1589. *MPW* 17 Mar 1917, p. 1714 (ad insert), 1822.

MY GIRL GODFREY see HIS BUTLER'S SISTER

MY GIRL TISA (Immigrants)

United States Pictures, Inc.; A Warner Bros.—First National Picture. *Dist* Warner Bros. Pictures, Inc. 7 Feb **1948**; Prod: late May—mid-Aug 1947 [©United States Pictures, Inc.; 7 Feb 1948; LP1461]. Sd (RCA Sound System); b&w. 94 or 97-98 min.

Prod Milton Sperling. *Dir* Elliott Nugent. [*Asst dir* Art Lueker]. [*2d asst dir* Russ Llewellyn]. *Scr* Allen Boretz. *Dir of photog* Ernest Haller. [*Asst cam* Larry Cairns and Bob Hoffman]. [*Cam op* George Nogel]. *Stills* Pat Clark]. [*Gaffer* James Goldenhaur]. *Spec eff dir* Harry Barndollar. *Spec eff* H. F. Koenekamp. *Art dir* Robert Haas. *Film ed* Christian Nyby. *Set des* Fred M. MacLean. [*Props* John More]. [*Asst props* Walter Douglas]. *Ward* Leah Rhodes, [Vick Vallejo and Helen Goodman]. *Mus dir* Leo F. Forbstein. *Mus* Max Steiner. *Sd* Oliver S. Garretson. *Makeup artist* Perc Westmore. [*Makeup* Eddie Voight]. [*Hair* Marsha Masa]. [*Unit mgr* Chuck Hansen]. [*Scr supv* Bill Hole]. [*Best boy* Paul Butner]. [*Grip* Stanley Young].

Song(s): "Every Little Movement Has a Meaning All Its Own," words by Otto Harbach, music by Karl Hoschna.

Source: Based on the play *Ever the Beginning* by Lucille S. Prumbs and Sara B. Smith (production date undetermined).

Cast: LILLI PALMER (*Tisa Kepes*), SAM WANAMAKER (*Mark Denek*), Akim Tamiroff (*Mr. Grumbach*), Alan Hale ([*Thomas*] *Dugan*), Hugo Haas (*Tescu*), Gale Robbins (*Jenny Kepes*), Stella Adler (*Mrs. Faludi*), Benny Baker (*Herman*), Sumner Getchell (*Georgie*), Sid Tomack (*Binka*), John Qualen (*Swenson*), Tom Dillon (*Riley*), Sidney Blackmer (*Theodore Roosevelt*), Fritz Feld (*Prof. Tabor*), John Banner (*Otto*), [Gabriel Canzano (*Organ grinder*)], [Rudy Wissler (*Patrucci*)], [Charles Jordan, George Sherwood (*Immigration officers*)], [Frank Conlan (*Emil Faludi*)],

[Olga Fabian, Max Barwyn (*Boarders*)], [Bunty Cutler (*Mother*)], [David Newell (*Father*)], [Ralph Peters (*Customer*)], [Doria Caron (*Hilda*)], [Dorothy Lotta (*Lilly*)], [Anitra Sparrow (*Mary*)], [Harry Seymour (*M.C.*)], [Gene Collins, Fred Chapman, Ray Dolciame, Billy Scallon, Donald Olsen, Vincent Graeff, Jerry Wissler (*Children at picnic*)], [Maxine Gates (*Mrs. O'Hooliban*)], [Juggling Normans (*Themselves*)], [Hobart Cavanaugh (*Sigmund*)], [John Wesley (*Voorhes*)], [Oliver Crawford (*Henchman*)], [Jack Mower (*Postman*)], [Martin Berliner (*Felix*)], [Ralph Dunn (*Attendant*)], [Charles Middleton (*Examiner*)], [Harry Shannon (*Judge*)], [James Flavin, Ian MacDonald (*Guards*)], [Ivan Simpson (*Old man*)], [Ed Deering (*Jailer*)], [Frederick Ledebur (*Igor*)], [Garry Owen (*Policeman*)], [Richard Kipling (*Admiral*)], [Ben Hall, Elliott Nugent (*Men on boat*)], [Phyllis Godfrey (*Woman on boat*)], [Edward Clark], [Francis Morris].

Historical, Drama. [*Print viewed*]. In New York City, in 1905, immigrant Tisa Kepes works in a garment factory run by Mr. Grumbach, who is studying to become an American citizen. Tisa and her cousin Jenny live in Mrs. Faludi's boardinghouse. Fellow boarder Mark Denek, who is employed by alderman Thomas Dugan, dreams of becoming a lawyer and adviser to his idol, President Teddy Roosevelt. Learning that Tisa needs extra money because she is saving to bring her father to America, Mark brags that he will help her get a job. Mark eventually persuades ice cream store owner Swenson to hire Tisa to work in the evenings after she finishes her work at Grumbach's, but later quarrels with Swenson over Roosevelt and causes Tisa to lose her job. Despite this, Mark and Tisa fall in love, although their lack of money prevents them from expressing these feelings to each other. After Mark's ambitious self-promotion causes Dugan to fire him, he asks Grumbach for the money to finish his correspondence course in law. When Grumbach refuses, Tisa asks Tescu, the shipping agent to whom she is paying her father's passage, to give her $100 from the money she has saved. Tescu gives Tisa the money, and informs her that her father could come to America immediately if he agreed to work off his passage after his arrival. Tisa consents to this arrangement, but when Mark learns what has happened, he explains that her father will be working off his passage in a distant state for many years. When Tisa confronts Tescu, he offers to return the contract in exchange for sexual favors. After she refuses, Tescu tells Mark that he has sold her father's contract to someone else. Mark asks Grumbach for a loan to buy back the contract, and again, Grumbach refuses to part with his money. A vengeful Tescu then lies to immigration officials in an effort to get Tisa deported. Mark offers to marry her so that, as his wife, she will become a citizen, but before they can be married, Tisa is arrested. Due to a misunderstanding, the judge believes that Tisa paid Mark to marry her, orders her deported and sends Mark to jail. Happy that he has finally passed his citizenship exam, Grumbach bails Mark out of jail, but Tisa is sent to Ellis Island to await deportation. While waiting, Tisa sees her father's ship dock. Mark visits Tisa to say that he loves her and is determined to become a lawyer and change the laws so that she will be able to return. As Mark leaves, he learns that Teddy Roosevelt is at the dock to meet a head of state. Mark convinces Roosevelt to intervene on Tisa's behalf, and she is able to meet her father's ship. *Immigrants. New York City. Romance. Seamstresses. Boardinghouses. Citizenship. Cousins. Deportation. Ice cream parlors. Indentured servants. New York City–Ellis Island. Politicians. Theodore Roosevelt. Sexual harassment. Trials.*

Note: The film's working titles were *Tisa* and *Ever the Beginning*. This film marked Sam Wanamaker's screen debut.

Box 24 Jan 1948. *DV* 20 Jan 1948, p. 3, 6. *FD* 20 Jan 1948, p. 7. *HR* 29 May 1947, p. 19. *HR* 15 Aug 1947, p. 14. *HR* 20 Jan 1948, p. 3, 15. *HR* 26 Feb 1948, p. 6. *MPHPD* 10 Jan 1948, p. 4010. *MPHPD* 24 Jan 1948, p. 4029. *NYT* 21 Feb 1948, p. 9. *Var* 21 Jan 1948, p. 8.

MY LIFE IS YOURS see NATION AFLAME

MY LUCKY STAR (Norwegian Americans)

Twentieth Century-Fox Film Corp.; Darryl F. Zanuck in charge of production. *Dist* Twentieth Century-Fox Film Corp. 2 Sep **1938**; Prod: 25 Apr—1 Jul 1938 [©Twentieth Century-Fox Film Corp.; 2 Sep 1938; LP8520]. Sd (Western Electric Mirrophonic Recording); b&w with sepia seq. 10 reels, 7,574 ft. 81 or 84 min. PCA cert no. 4279.

Assoc prod Harry Joe Brown. *Dir* Roy Del Ruth. [*Asst dir* Booth McCracken]. *Scr* Harry Tugend and Jack Yellen. *Story* Karl Tunberg and Don Ettlinger. *Photog* John Mescall. *Art dir* Bernard Herzbrun and Mark-Lee Kirk. *Film ed* Allen McNeil. *Set dec* Thomas Little. *Cost*

Royer. *Mus dir* Louis Silvers. *Skating ensembles staged by* Harry Losee. *Sd* Eugene Grossman and Roger Heman.

Song(s): "By a Wishing Well," "Could You Pass in Love," "This May Be the Night," "I've Got a Date with a Dream," "Classy Clothes Chris," "Plymouth Rock," "Marching Along," "Plymouth Farewell Song," music and lyrics by Mack Gordon and Harry Revel.

Cast: SONJA HENIE (*Kristina Nielson*), RICHARD GREENE (*Larry Taylor*), Joan Davis (*Mary Dwight*), Cesar Romero (*George Cabot, Jr.*), Buddy Ebsen (*Buddy*), Arthur Treacher (*Whipple*), George Barbier (*George Cabot, Sr.*), Louise Hovick (*Marcelle [La Verne]*), Billy Gilbert (*Nick*), Patricia Wilder (*Dorothy*), Paul Hurst (*Louie*), Elisha Cook, Jr. (*Waldo*), Robert Kellard (*Pennell*), Brewster Twins (*June and Jean*), Kay Griffith (*Ethel*), Charles Tannen (*Saier*), Paul Stanton (*Dean Reed*), Ed Le Saint (*Executive*), Frederick Burton (*Pilsbury*), Frank Jaquet (*Burton*), [Sumner Getchell (*Fat freshman*)], [John Dilson (*Department head*)], [Cully Richards (*Photographer*)], [Matt McHugh (*Cab driver*)], [Dora Clemant, June Gale (*Secretaries*)], [Arthur Rankin, Harold Goodwin (*Cameramen*)], [Fred Kelsey (*Detective*)], [Eddy Conrad (*Gypsy*)], [Arthur Jarrett, Jr.], [*Alice in Wonderland* ballet: Bert Clark (*White Rabbit*)], [Jack Heasley, Bob Heasley (*Tweedledee & Tweedledum*)].

College, Musical comedy. [*Print viewed*]. When George Cabot, Sr., owner of Cabots Fifth Avenue department store, learns that his son, George, Jr., has eloped with cabaret performer Marcelle La Verne, and that Marcelle's lawyer wants a cash settlement to end the marriage, he threatens to have bodyguards take his son to his Oklahoma ranch. George escapes down the department store's fire escape and sees through a window Kristina Nielson, an employee, ice-skating on the store's rink. After George slips on the ice, Kristina helps him to his apartment, where Marcelle sees them and endeavors to get Kristina's name as a co-respondent. A fortune-teller then suggests that George get Kristina to leave New York, and he convinces his father and the board of directors to send Kristina to Plymouth University as a student with a multitude of winter outfits to encourage the girls to shop at Cabots. Kristina agrees, but at the college, she makes an enemy of Dorothy, one of her roommates, because of the interest Kristina shows in Larry Taylor, Dorothy's beau. Dorothy then borrows Kristina's clothes and has the boys wear them during a tryout for the winter ice carnival, during which they sing an insulting song about Kristina. After Larry convinces Kristina not to leave, she ice-skates and wins the students' respect and affection. Her talent is the subject of a *Life* magazine cover story, which Marcelle sees. After Marcelle names Kristina in the divorce suit, the college dean suspends her. Larry and Kristina find Marcelle in New York, and sympathizing with Kristina, whom she is convinced is innocent, Marcelle says that if George will pay her $50,000 in cash, she will tell the newspapers that Kristina is innocent. George cannot pay, but when Larry suggests that he combine the ice carnival with a fashion show at the department store, George, whose father is in Havana, arranges it. The carnival is a great success, Cabot, Sr. returns and gives his son a bonus to pay Marcelle, and Kristina returns with Larry to P.U. *Clothes. College life. Courtship. Department stores. Divorce. Fashion shows. Ice skaters and ice skating. Cabaret performers. Department store owners. Fathers and sons. Fortune-tellers. Jealousy. Life (Magazine). Norwegian Americans. Roommates.*

Note: The working title of this film was *They Met in College*. This was Norwegian ice-skating Olympic champion Sonja Henie's fourth film. In 1938, she was ranked third biggest money-making star in an *MPH* poll of exhibitors. The film was 90 minutes at its preview in Westwood on 26 Aug 1938. *Var* noted that the closing "Alice in Wonderland" number was "done in sepia and very effective." The name of the character played by Joan Davis was "Mary Dwight" in the film, but "Mary Boop" in trade advertising billing sheets and reviews. Davis suffered a sprain of her back muscles while trying to lift Buddy Ebsen during a rehearsal and was hospitalized for three weeks, according to publicity for the film. To follow Sonja Henie as she skated in the rink, an apparatus was built containing a camera platform with metal sled runners attached to a metal stake driven into the center of the rink, which measured 100 by 145 feet, and had been used in all of Henie's films. During the production, the brace supporting the platform, which held two cameras, crews, three large lights and electricians, snapped, and Henie barely escaped being hit by skating out of the way, according to publicity. Louise Hovick was also known as the burlesque star Gypsy Rose Lee. According to a *HR* news item in Jan 1938, Don Ameche was expected to be in this film. The Twentieth Century-Fox Produced Scripts Collection at the UCLA Theater Arts Library contains in the file for this film a treatment by Sam Hellman from a play by Sheridan Gibney and Victor Wittgenstein, but this does not seem to have been used for this film. The film's end credit contains the statement, "This is one of the movie quiz $250,000 contest pictures." No information has been located concerning this contest.

Box 3 Sep 1938. *DV* 27 Aug 1938, p. 3. *FD* 12 Sep 1938, p. 8. *HR* 14 Jan 1938, p. 1. *HR* 25 Apr 1938, p. 9, 11. *HR* 27 Jun 1938, p. 7. *HR* 27 Aug 1938, p. 3. *MPD* 30 Aug 1938, p. 4. *MPH* 16 Jul 1938, p. 63. *MPH* 3 Sep 1938, pp. 38-39. *NYT* 12 Jun 1938. *NYT* 10 Sep 1938, p. 20. *Var* 14 Sep 1938, p. 15.

MY MAN AND I (Latino)

Metro-Goldwyn-Mayer Corp.; controlled by Loew's Inc. *Dist* Loew's Inc. 26 Sep 1952; New York opening: 5 Sep 1952; Prod: late Mar—late Apr 1952 [©Loew's Inc.; 14 Aug 1952; LP1915]. Sd (Western Electric Sound System); b&w. 10 reels, 8,916 ft. 99 min. Passed by the National Board of Review. PCA cert no. 15974.

Prod Stephen Ames. *Dir* William A. Wellman. *Asst dir* George Rhein. *Wrt* John Fante and Jack Leonard. [*Contr wrt* Marguerite Roberts and Millard Kaufman]. *Dir of photog* William Mellor. *Spec eff* Warren Newcombe. *Montage seq by* Peter Ballbusch. *Art dir* Cedric Gibbons and James Basevi. *Film ed* John Dunning. *Set dec* Edwin B. Willis and Fred MacLean. *Mus* David Buttolph. *Rec supv* Douglas Shearer. [*Sd* Conrad Kahn]. *Makeup* William Tuttle. *Hair styles by* Sydney Guilaroff.

Song(s): "Stormy Weather," words by Ted Koehler, music by Harold Arlen; "Noche de ronda," words and music by Maria Teresa Lara.

Cast: Shelley Winters (*Nancy*), Ricardo Montalban (*Chu Chu Ramirez*), Wendell Corey (*Ansel Ames*), Claire Trevor (*Mrs. Ansel Ames*), Robert Burton (*Sheriff*), José Torvay (*Manuel Ramirez*), Jack Elam (*Celestino Garcia*), Pascual Garcia Pena (*Willie Chung*), George Chandler (*Frankie*), Juan Torena (*Vincente Aguilar*), Carlos Conde (*Joe Mendacio*), [John Indrisano (*Foreman*)], [Jay Adler (*Bartender*)], [Jack Daly (*Bank teller*)], [Lillian Molieri (*Bride*)], [Joe Mell (*Labor board commissioner*)], [Tom Greenway, John McKee (*Patrolmen*)], [Edward Hearn (*Deputy*)], [Martha Wentworth (*Landlady*)], [Dennis Fraser (*Sailor*)], [Lee Phelps, Fred Coby (*Plainclothesmen*)], [Dabbs Greer (*Court clerk*)], [Earl Lee (*Judge Wells*)], [Jim Hayward (*Jury foreman*)], [Tyler McVey], [Alan Dreeben], [Peter Leeds], [George Lynn], [Cliff Clark].

Romance, Drama. [*Print viewed*]. Chu Chu Ramirez, an itinerant farm laborer from Mexico who has recently become an American citizen, treasures a letter he has received from the President in response to one Chu Chu wrote to him. Chu Chu's cousin Manuel Ramirez and friends, Celestino Garcia and Willie Chung, spend their last pay from the California grape season on gambling and women, but Chu Chu buys clothes and an encyclopedia, as he is determined to improve his situation. An employment agency arranges an interview for him with farmer Ansel Ames and his wife Elena. Although Mrs. Ames regards Chu Chu as "another foreigner," Ames gives him a month's work clearing land. After a week, Mrs. Ames, who no longer loves her husband, shows interest in the virile, young Chu Chu. She apologizes to him for her remark but adds that she does not like having "a dirty rag head or a chink around." Chu Chu adds, "or a greaser like Chu Chu Ramirez." Mrs. Ames states that she did not mean to imply a dislike for him but tells him that he has one thing in common with all Mexicans, "he sure can look mean." One night, all dressed up, Chu Chu goes to a bar in town and meets Nancy, who has come north from Sacramento looking for a job. Chu Chu helps get her car started and drives her back to Sacramento, where he puts up his letter from the President as collateral for some cash which he then gives to Nancy. One night, just before Chu Chu is due to finish his job, Mrs. Ames tries to seduce him but he sends her away. Later, in Sacramento, when Chu Chu goes to cash his pay check, the bank refuses payment. Chu Chu again encounters Nancy, who, intoxicated, tells of her marriage to a test pilot who was killed in a crash. He takes her back to the cheap motel she is living in, on the road to Stockton, and although she tells him he should not waste his time on a "wino," he wants her to be his girl. When Chu Chu tells Ames that his check is no good, Ames accuses him of trespassing and threatens him with a shotgun. Chu Chu brings Ames before a labor conciliation board and is promised his pay within sixty days. Nancy tells Chu Chu that she is leaving Sacramento for Los Angeles, but he says he will follow, bring her back and marry her. Two months later, when Chu Chu visits Ames to be paid, Ames tries to attack him, but Chu Chu knocks him down. After Chu Chu leaves, Mrs. Ames tells her husband that Chu Chu is worth ten of him. Ames beats her up, but when he pushes her against a shotgun rack, one gun falls and shoots him in the shoulder. When Chu Chu learns that Nancy is sick in Los Angeles, he prepares to go to her, but is arrested for shooting Ames. After Manuel visits Chu Chu in jail and tells him that Nancy has attempted suicide by gassing

herself, Chu Chu escapes, and although handcuffed, jumps on a freight train and breaks the handcuffs on one of the train's wheels. He finds Nancy quite ill, working in a dance hall, but he is arrested by plainclothesmen who have staked out the hall. At his trial, both Mr. and Mrs. Ames give false testimony while Chu Chu's friends speak on his behalf. The jury finds that Chu Chu did assault Ames with a deadly weapon, but requests a light sentence due to the provocation he had to endure. Before he is sentenced, Chu Chu asks to read from a letter he has written to the President of the United States in which he states that as a convict, he will no longer be a citizen, which is worse than death to him. However, Chu Chu is sentenced to a year and a day. Chu Chu's friends begin to haunt the Ames farm in an attempt to pressure them into confessing the truth. After Nancy, still very ill, collapses at the farm after accusing Ames of destroying Chu Chu, Manuel and the others take her to a hospital. Mrs. Ames tries to reconcile with her husband and says that they should get Chu Chu out of jail even though they will be charged with perjury. They embrace and by their confession, Chu Chu is freed. Chu Chu visits Nancy in the hospital, but she still wants him to forget her. He refuses to ever leave her and tells her she must get well for him, and finally, she agrees. *Alcoholics. Bigotry. Citizenship. Farm hands. Mexican Americans. Mexicans. Romance.* Attempted suicide. Banks. Bars. Battered women. Cats. Confession (Law). Conscience. Cousins. Dance halls. Dogs. False arrests. Farmers. Firearms. Gunshot wounds. Handcuffs. Hats. Hospitals. Jailbreaks. Landladies. Letters. Los Angeles (CA). Marriage. Moral reformation. Motels. Neglected wives. Perjury. Police. Rifles. Sacramento (CA). Sailors. Seduction. Strikes and lockouts. Trains. Trials. Vending machines. Weddings. Widows.

Note: This film's working titles were *Shameless* and *Letter from the President.* M-G-M purchased the John Fante/Jack Leonard original late in 1950. Fante, from an immigrant Italian family, wrote four novels about the life of a fictional Italian American, Arturo Bandini. Another Fante novel, *Full of Life,* also about an Italian American, was made into the film of the same name by Columbia (see above).

According to documents in the MPAA/PCA Collection at the AMPAS Library, producer Stephen Ames asked if it would be possible to present the principal character as being addicted to marijuana but was told that the PCA would not approve any stories that dealt with drug addiction. Studio documents list actors Tristram Coffin and Philip Van Zandt as appearing in the film but their roles were eliminated before the film's release. The participation of James H. Harrison, Billie Bird, Rhea Mitchell and Ralph Moody in very minor roles has not been confirmed. The film's title is derived from the lyrics of the song "Stormy Weather," which is sung during the opening titles.

DV 15 Aug 1952. *HR* 15 Aug 1952. *LAT* 25 Sep 1951. *MPD* 19 Aug 1952. *MPH* 23 Aug 1952. *NYT* 6 Sep 1952. *Var* 22 Aug 1952.

MY PAL WOLF (Norwegian Americans)

RKO Radio Pictures, Inc. *Dist* RKO Radio Pictures, Inc. **1944**; New York opening: week of 8 Oct 1944; Prod: 16 May—mid-Jun 1944 [©RKO Radio Pictures, Inc.; 4 Oct 1944; LP12911]. Sd (RCA Sound System); b&w. 6,729 ft. 74 min. PCA cert no. 10193.

Prod Adrian Scott. [*Exec prod* Sid Rogell]. *Dir* Alfred Werker. *Asst dir* Fred A. Fleck. *Scr* Lillie Hayward, Leonard Praskins and John Paxton. *Orig story* Frederick Hazlitt Brennan. *Dir of photog* Jack MacKenzie. *Spec eff* Vernon L. Walker. *Art dir* Albert S. D'Agostino and Carroll Clark. *Ed* Harry Marker. *Set dec* Darrell Silvera and Al Fields. *Gowns* Renie. *Mus dir* C. Bakaleinikoff. *Mus* Werner R. Heymann. *Rec* Phillip N. Mitchell. *Re-rec* Terry Kellum.

Cast: Sharyn Moffett [(*Gretchen Anstey*)], Jill Esmond [(*Miss Elizabeth Munn*)], Una O'Connor [(*Mrs. Blevin*)], George Cleveland [(*Wilson*)], Charles Arnt [(*Papa Eisdaar*)], Claire Carleton [(*Ruby*)], Leona Maricle [(*Mrs. Priscilla Anstey*)], Bruce Edwards [(*Mr. Paul Anstey*)], Edward Fielding [(*Secretary of War*)], Olga Fabian [(*Mama Eisdaar*)], Grey Shadow ("*Wolf*" [*the dog*]), [Larry Olsen (*Fred Eisdaar*)], [Jerry Michelson (*Alf Eisdaar*)], [Bobby Larson (*Karl Eisdaar*)], [Marc Cramer (*Sergeant Blake*)], [Victor Cutler, Carl Kent (*Wolf's trainers*)], [Bryant Washburn (*Commanding officer*)], [J. Louis Johnson (*Butler*)], [Tom Burton (*Reporter*)], [Bert Moorhouse (*Police officer*)], [Alan Ward (*Truck driver*)], [Chris Drake].

Animal, Youth, Drama. [*Print viewed*]. Priscilla Anstey, the owner of a cosmetics factory in Washington, D. C., shows more concern for her business than for her daughter Gretchen. To supervise the little girl's upbringing, Mrs. Anstey hires Miss Elizabeth Munn, a stern disciplinarian. Upon arriving at the Anstey farm in Virginia, Miss Munn alienates Wilson, the handyman, and Mrs. Blevin, the housekeeper, when she proclaims that the waiflike Gretchen is undisciplined and demands order. Except for Wilson and Mrs. Blevin,

Gretchen's only friends are the neighboring Eisdaar family, and when Miss Munn forbids her to join the family on a picnic, Gretchen breaks into tears. At bedtime that night, Gretchen tells Miss Munn about her pal, "Wolf," causing the governess to scold her for having an overactive imagination. Later that night, Gretchen slips out of the house to feed Wolf, a dog that she found trapped in a dried-up old well. Upon returning to her room, Gretchen is confronted by Miss Munn, who asks where she has been. Refusing to believe Gretchen's story of the trapped dog, the governess orders her to bed. The next morning, Gretchen is lowering herself into the well to offer Wolf some water when the rope snaps. At Gretchen's command, the dog leaps to freedom and runs to the Eisdaar house for help. After Gretchen is rescued, Wilson finds the dog's identification collar and puts it in the little girl's room. When Gretchen begs for permission to keep Wolf, Miss Munn summons Mrs. Anstey to the farm and announces that she is resigning as Gretchen's governess. Mr. Anstey, a busy aircraft executive, also comes to visit his daughter and persuades Miss Munn to stay by putting her in charge of the staff. Noticing that Wolf's neck has been rubbed by a collar, Miss Munn questions Gretchen, who denies that the dog was wearing a collar. Doubting Gretchen's word, Miss Munn searches her room and finds the collar with the identification "U.S. Army 82" written on it. Insisting that Gretchen must face reality and return the dog, Miss Munn notifies the Army about Wolf, and the next day two soldiers come to claim him. Heartbroken by the loss of Wolf, Gretchen and the Eisdaar children visit the army compound and offer to buy Wolf. The sergeant informs them that Wolf, a combat trained dog, has been assigned to active duty and that only a directive from the Secretary of War could release him from duty. As the children leave camp, Wolf sees them and escapes from the compound to follow them into the woods. Rather than give up her beloved Wolf, Gretchen decides to travel to Washington to petition the Secretary of War to give her the dog. Two of the Eisdaar children join her while little Fred Eisdaar returns home to mow the lawn. While the children hitchhike to Washington, the story of their trek receives newspaper coverage, and their parents anxiously gather at the Anstey house for news. When Miss Munn accuses Gretchen of lying about the collar, Wilson admits he put it in the little girl's room, and Mr. Anstey fires the governess. That night, the children arrive in Washington. To gain admittance to the house of the Secretary of War, Gretchen tells the butler that she is the Secretary's niece. After she is ushered into the surprised Secretary's office, Gretchen begs him to let her keep Wolf. Remembering the story in the paper, the Secretary calls Gretchen's parents. As the Ansteys and Papa Eisdaar drive to Washington, he patiently explains to the little girl that Wolf has been trained to deliver messages in battle and therefore has a special duty to serve his country. Gretchen accepts his explanation, and after she tearfully bids Wolf goodbye, the parents arrive to take their children home. All ends happily when Mrs. Anstey foresakes her job to come to Virginia and care for her daughter, and Gretchen receives a cuddly puppy as a gift from the Secretary of State. *Dogs, War use of. Governesses. Neglected children.* Butlers. Cabinet officers. Children. Duty. Government officials. Handymen. Housekeepers. Parenthood. Washington (D.C.). Wells.

Note: The working title of this film was *The Pumpkin Shell.* Although a *HR* production chart credits Walter Daniels as art director, the extent of his contribution to the released film has not been determined. This picture marked the screen debut of child actress Sharyn Moffett. Moffett and writer Lillie Hayward, who later became a producer, worked on two other RKO pictures together. Adrian Scott made his producing debut with this picture.

Box 23 Sep 1944. *DV* 19 Sep 1944, p. 3. *FD* 25 Sep 1944, p. 10. *HR* 17 May 1944, p. 9. *HR* 19 May 1944, p. 15. *HR* 16 Jun 1944, p. 13. *HR* 19 Sep 1944, p. 3. *MPHPD* 5 Aug 1944, p. 2032. *MPHPD* 23 Sep 1944, p. 2110. *NYT* 9 Oct 1944, p. 17. *Var* 20 Sep 1944, p. 10.

MY PAST see AMOR IN MONTAGNA

MY SON (Portuguese Americans)

First National Pictures, Inc. *Dist* First National Pictures, Inc. 19 Apr **1925** [©First National Pictures, Inc.; 1 Apr 1925; LP21291]. Si; b&w. 7 reels, 6,552 ft.

Pres Edwin Carewe. *Dir* Edwin Carewe. *Asst dir* Wallace Fox. *Scen* Finis Fox. *Photog* L. W. O'Connell. *Art dir* John D. Schulze. *Film ed* Laurence Croutz.

Source: Based on the play *My Son* by Martha M. Stanley (New York, 17 Sep 1924).

Cast: Nazimova (*Ana Silva*), Jack Pickford (*Tony, her son*), Hobart Bosworth (*Ellery Parker, the sheriff*), Ian Keith (*Felipe Vargas, a fisherman*), Mary Akin (*Rosa Pina*), Charles Murray (*Capt. Joe Bamby*), Constance Bennett (*Betty Smith*), Dot Farley (*Hattie Smith*).

Domestic, Drama. In a small New England fishing village populated largely by Portuguese, Ana Silva keeps the general store in order to provide for her adored son, Tony. When a wealthy woman named Hattie Smith arrives in the village for a summer vacation, her daughter, Betty, flirts with Tony and upsets his relationship with his sweetheart, Rosa Pina. Tony falls in love with the irresponsible flapper and steals Mrs. Smith's diamond bracelet in order to finance a trip to New York with Betty. Ana discovers the theft and confronts Tony with the evidence; he attempts to run away, and his mother hits him over the head with a shovel, knocking him unconscious. She then arranges with Captain Bamby for Tony to be taken away on a boat in order to save him from arrest by Sheriff Parker, who has discovered Tony's misdeed. Rosa sails away with Tony on Bamby's boat, and Ana gives her heart to Felipe. *Fishing villages. Flappers. General stores. Motherhood. New England. Portuguese Americans. Robbery.*

FD 12 Apr 1925. *MPW* 18 Apr 1925. *Var* 22 May 1925, p. 34.

MY SON (1932) *see* CUORE D'EMIGRANTE

MY SON (Yiddish language)

Jewish Talking Picture Co. *Dist* Cinema Service Corp. **1939**; New York opening: May 1939 [©Jewish Talking Picture Co.; 2 Jun 1939; LU8879]. Sd; b&w. 9 reels, 8,175 or 8,240 ft. 90 min. Yiddish language with English subtitles.

Dir Joseph Seiden. *Asst dir* Herman Rosen. [*Author* Chiam Touber and Joseph Seiden]. *Photog* Burgi Contner and Edward Hyland. *Settings* John Alstadt and Maurice McDermott. *Mus dir* Alexander Olshanetzky. *Sd* Murry Dichter and Paul Jacobs. *Make-up artist* Ira Senz.

Song(s): by Max Schwartz and Philip Kanapoff.

Source: Based on the play *My Sonny* by Sholem Secunda (production undetermined).

Cast: Fania Rubina [(*Freda Berger*)], Gustave Berger [(*Muni Berger*)], Jerry Rosenberg [(*Benny Berger*)], Herman Rosen [(*Mr. Salkin*)], Harry Feld [(*Chiam Green*)], Jacob Zanger [(*Lebke*)], Jenny Cashier [(*Malka Berger*)], Ida Divorkin [(*Sarah Berger*)], Rose Schwartzberg.

Yiddish, Domestic, Melodrama, with songs. [*Print viewed*]. Muni Berger, a celebrated Jewish singer in New York, is devoted to his son Benny. Muni is upset that his wife Freda, an actress, is so preoccupied with rehearsals before the opening of her new play, *Mother Love*, that she has not seen Benny for a week. When she comes home at three in the morning and later misses a party for Muni's thirty-five-year-old sister Malka and her lazy fiancée Lebke, Muni demands that she choose between the play and her family. Freda decides to leave for Chicago even though Benny has a slight cold, and Muni vows she will never see Benny again. While Freda is gone, the doctor tells Muni that Benny needs dry air and recommends California. Muni calls Freda's theater in Chicago, but the manager doesn't let him speak with her. Muni then gives up his own career and takes the boy to California. Four weeks later, at the end of the play's run, Freda discovers that the manager has been holding her telegrams and leaves immediately for New York, where she finds Muni and Benny gone. Although she hires a detective, Freda cannot locate them. Ten years later, Muni's mother Sarah is blind and in a home for the aged, Malka has three children, Benny, who thinks that his mother has died, sings as he sells newspapers, and Muni, who is broke, spends his money on liquor. Freda, meanwhile, has made money and become a success while she has searched Europe, South America and Africa for her child. In New York, Freda protests to her manager that she doesn't want to play a scene involving a baby lying dead in a crib. In the midst of their discussion, Benny delivers a telegram from the detective agency, and Freda, taking a liking to him, gives him two tickets to her play. Meanwhile, Muni sings drunkenly in a Roumanian cellar, and Chiam Green, a singing celebrity, whom Muni helped at the beginning of his career, sees him. When Freda sings "Give Me Back My Child" at a concert at the home for the aged, Sarah interrupts and blames her for ruining her son's life and for her blindness. Freda gets Muni's address from Sarah and visits as Chiam offers Muni a job on radio. Embittered, Muni tells Freda that it is too late for her to get

Benny back. Hoping to save Benny from Muni's squalid surroundings, Freda offers him a violin, bicycle and finally, anything he wants, if he will live with her, but he refuses, saying that Muni will have nothing if he goes. Muni, who overhears, promises Benny that he won't drink again and that he will find them a new apartment. When the landlady accuses Benny of stealing $350, Benny confesses that he took the money because Muni needs a doctor. Horrified that his son might grow up to be a liar, thief and loafer, Muni tells Benny that he doesn't love him, so that he will go with Freda. Benny moves in with his mother, who asks the manager to tell Muni that she never saw his telegrams. Chiam then tells her that Muni is extremely sick and that he may die. Benny, meanwhile, has left Freda a note saying that he doesn't want to live without both her and Muni. He tells Muni, who has since learned about the telegrams, that he wants a papa and a mama. Encouraged by Chiam to forgive and understand, Muni proposes a comeback of the husband and wife team, The Great Bergers. Freda refuses, and says she now has a new career as Muni's wife and Benny's mother. *Actors and actresses. Family life. Jews. Marriage. Self-sacrifice. Singers. Vocational obsession. Alcoholics. Blindness. Chicago (IL). Detectives. Mothers-in-law. New York City. Physicians. Plays. Retirement homes. Sisters. Telegrams. Theatrical managers.*

Note: The Yiddish title of this film is *Mayn Zundele*. The names of Fania Rubina and Gustave Berger were missing from the credits of the print viewed. According to a summary of the film, this was the first screen appearance of Rubina and Berger in America. A modern source notes that Rubina, a Polish soprano, was paid $150 to appear in the film. According to records at NCJF, the Ohio censorship board demanded that a scene be eliminated in which the character "Lebke" says, "I should work, for whom? For Morgan, for Rockefeller, for Henry Ford. If the capitalists will go to work then I will work. They don't have to work, they have plenty of money." According to NYSA records, an affidavit was submitted to the New York censors in 1950 to have the title changed to *The Living Orphan*. Upon its re-release the film was also known under the Yiddish title of *Der Lebediker Yusem*.

Jewish Independent 19 Jan 1940. *NYT* 10 May 1939, p. 28.

MY SONS *see* LIFE GOES ON

MY TWO LOVES *see* MIS DOS AMORES

MY WILD IRISH ROSE (Irish Americans)

Warner Bros. Pictures, Inc.; A Warner Bros.—First National Picture. *Dist* Warner Bros. Pictures, Inc. 27 Dec **1947**; New York opening: 24 Dec 1947; Prod: late Sep 1946—early Feb 1947 [©Warner Bros. Pictures, Inc.; 27 Dec 1947; LP1364]. Sd (RCA Sound System); b&w. 98-99 min.

Exec prod JACK L. WARNER. *Prod* William Jacobs. *Dir* David Butler. *Dial dir* Charles Vance. *Scr* Peter Milne. [*Addl dial* Edwin Gilbert and Sidney Fields]. *Dir of photog* Arthur Edeson. *Mont* James Leicester. *Spec eff dir* Harry Barndollar. *Spec eff* Robert Burks. *Technicolor col dir* Natalie Kalmus. *Technicolor col assoc* Mitchell Kovaleski. *Art dir* Ed Carrero. *Film ed* Irene Morra. *Set dec* Lyle Reifsnider. *Ward* Travilla. *Addl mus comp and adapt by* Max Steiner. *Orch arr* Murray Cutter. *Vocal arr* Dudley Chambers. *Mus dir* Leo F. Forbstein. *Mus numbers orch and cond by* Ray Heindorf. *Mus numbers created and dir by* LeRoy Prinz. *Sd* Stanley Jones and David Forrest. *Makeup artist* Perc Westmore.

Song(s): "Wee Rose of Killarny," "The Natchez and the Robert E. Lee," "Miss Lindy Lou," "There's Room in My Heart for Them All," words by Ted Koehler, music by M. K. Jerome; "Come On Ma Evenin' Star," words by Robert B. Smith, music by John Stromberg; "My Wild Irish Rose," words and music by Chauncey Olcott; "A Little Bit of Heaven, Sure They Call It Ireland," words by J. Keirn Brennan, music by Ernest R. Ball; "Mother Machree," words by Rida Johnson Young, music by Chauncey Olcott and Ernest R. Ball; "Wait Till the Sun Shines, Nelly," words by Andrew B. Sterling, music by Harry Von Tilzer; "You Tell Me Your Dream," words by Gus Kahn, music by Charles Neil Daniels; "Will You Love Me in December as You Do in May?" words by James J. Walker, music by Ernest R. Ball; "By the Light of the Silvery Moon," words by Edward Madden, music by Gus Edwards; "Dear Old Donegal," words and music by Steve Graham; "One Little Sweet Little Girl," words and music by Dan Sullivan; "My Nelly's Blue Eyes," words and music by William J. Scanlan; "In the Evening By the Moonlight," words by James A. Bland; "When Irish Eyes Are Smiling," words by Chauncey Olcott and George Graff, Jr., music by Ernest R. Ball.

Source: Based on the book *Song in His Heart* by Rita Olcott (New York, 1939).

Cast: DENNIS MORGAN (*Chauncey Olcott*), Arlene Dahl (*Rose Donovan*), Andrea King (*Lillian Russell*), Alan Hale (*John Donovan*), George Tobias (*Nick Popolis*), George O'Brien (*Duke Muldoon*), Sara Allgood (*Mrs. Brennan*), Ben Blue (*Hopper*), William Frawley (*William Scanlon*), Don McGuire (*Terry O'Rourke*), Charles Irwin (*Foote*), Phil Stanton (*Augustus Pitou*), George Cleveland (*Captain Brennan*), Clifton Young (*Joe Brennan*), Oscar O'Brien (*Pat Daly*), Ruby Dandridge (*Vella*), Grady Sutton (*Brown*), Three tycoons: William Davidson (*Brewster*), Douglas Wood (*Rawson*), and Charles Marsh (*Stone*), Igor Dega, Pierre Andre, The Three Dunhills, Lou Wills, Jr. (*Dance specialties*), [Andrew Tombes, Monte Blue (*Barmen*)], [Charles Williams (*Husband*)], [Faith Kruger (*Wife*)], [Kernan Cripps, Johnny Morris, Donald Kerr (*Hecklers*)], [Rodney Bell (*Lame-brain*)], [Robert Lowell (*Tenor*)], [Philo McCullough (*Theater manager*)], [Gino Corrado (*Maitre'd*)], [Joe Bernard (*Bus driver*)], [Eddie Parker (*Bruiser*)], [George Anderson, Jack Mower (*Policemen*)], [Ross Ford (*Office boy*)], [Eddie Kane (*Webb*)], [Tom Stevenson (*Lee*)], [George Campeau, Herbert Anderson (*Reporters*)], [Joe Devlin, Brooks Benedict (*Irishmen*)], [Peggy Knudsen (*Leading lady*)], [Cy Shindell (*Gallery god*)], [Susanne Rosser (*Tall, sexy girl*)], [Wally Ruth (*Drummer*)], [Emmett Vogan (*Doctor*)], [Edward Clark (*Justice of the peace*)], [William Gould (*Mr. O'Rourke*)], [Brandon Hurst (*Gardner*)], [Forbes Murray (*Chauncey Olcott's stage father*)], [Winifred Harris (*Chauncey Olcott's stage mother*)], [Sylvia Andrew, Lillian Castle (*Cleaning women*)], [Billy Green (*River boat captain*)].

Biography, with songs. [*Print viewed*]. During the late 1800s, Chauncey Olcott, a tugboat operator with show business aspirations, talks his way into a dinner party for star Lillian Russell. After he sings, Lillian speaks approvingly of his voice, and with that to bolster him, Chauncey tells his mother, Mrs. Brennan, that he intends to leave home to pursue a singing career. Mrs. Brennan gives Chauncey a watch that belonged to his father, and asks him not to use his father's name until he can honor it with success. Chauncey pawns the watch to buy a banjo and, using the stage name Jack Chancellor, travels around the country singing by the roadside. One day, he trades his carriage and some money to a singing waiter for the lease on a bar in the country. Later, he stops a runaway horse carrying beautiful Rose Donovan and immediately falls in love with her. Chauncey's plans are stymied when he learns the real owner of the bar is Nick Popolis, who demotes Chauncey to janitor, and to make matters worse, Rose is engaged to a man named Terry O'Rourke. Vowing to love Rose from afar, Chauncey joins a minstrel show. Rose brings Popolis, Terry and her father John to New York to hear Chauncey sing in the minstrel show. There, Terry discovers Chauncey's feelings for Rose and sends some of his friends to beat up the singer. After Chauncey wins the fight with the help of his friends, Rose suggests that he meet her and her father at church the next day, but before he gets there, Chauncey is arrested on a warrant sworn out by Terry's friends. Several days later, Duke Muldoon, another member of the minstrel show, pays Chauncey's bail, but by this time, he has lost his job. Searching for a new job, Chauncey again encounters Lillian Russell, and she hires him to sing in her show. Publicity rumors of a romance between Lillian and Chauncey so disturb Rose that she travels to New York to discover the truth. Although Chauncey tries to explain, Rose misunderstands, and hurt, returns home. When Lillian's show closes, Popolis, who manages the Irish singer William Scanlon, hires Chauncey to sing in the show. For the first time, Chauncey performs using his own name. On St. Patrick's Day, Scanlon is unable to sing, and Chauncey takes his place. Although the crowd is furious at first, Chauncey's voice enchants them, and Scanlon dubs Chauncey his successor by giving him a watch he received from the Prince of Wales. Chauncey's mother is so moved by his singing that she apologizes for not being more supportive. Because Donovan, an alderman, only saw Chauncey perform in minstrel makeup and under a pseudonym, he does not recognize him and asks him to sing at a political rally. Chauncey agrees, then asks Rose to elope with him. Duke is delegated to bring Donovan to Greenwich, Connecticut after the ceremony. At first Donovan is furious, but when Chauncey promises to marry Rose again in church, Donovan gives the couple his blessing. *Irish Americans. Chauncey Olcott. Singers.* Elopement. Fathers and

daughters. Letters. Minstrel shows. Mothers and sons. New York City. Politicians. Lillian Russell. William Scanlon. Watches.

Note: Chauncey Olcott was born in Buffalo, New York in 1860. He began his professional career in 1876 with the Thatcher, Primrose & West minstrel shows and became a well-known soloist before studying singing in London in 1890. In the United States, Olcott starred in Irish musical plays such as *The Minstrel of Clare* and *The Heart of Paddy Whack*, and popularized such songs as "My Wild Irish Rose" and "Mother Machree." He divorced his first wife, Cora, and then married Margaret O'Donovan. Olcott died on 18 Mar 1932. *HR* news items add the following information about the production: The property, including all of Olcott's songs, was purchased from Charles R. Rogers Productions. Alexis Smith was to play a leading role. Nelson Eddy and Lee Sullivan were considered for the role of "Chauncey Olcott." According to a news item in *HR*, Dennis Morgan's nine-year-old daughter made her screen debut in the film, but she is not listed in the film's credits. Ray Heindorf and Max Steiner received an Oscar nomination for their musical score.

FD 11 Dec 1947, p. 6. *HR* 15 Feb 1946, p. 1. *HR* 17 Jul 1946, p. 7. *HR* 13 Sep 1946, p. 6. *HR* 27 Sep 1946, p. 19. *HR* 31 Jan 1947, p. 19. *HR* 9 Dec 1947, p. 3. *IFJ* 4 Jan 1947, p. 35. *MPHPD* 13 Dec 1947. *NYT* 25 Dec 1947, p. 32. *Var* 10 Dec 1947, p. 12.

MY YIDDISHE MAMA (Jewish Americans, Yiddish language)

Judea Films. **1930**; New York State license: 29 May 1930 [©Joseph Seiden; 4 Oct 1930; LU1641]. Sd; b&w. 5 or 6 reels, 4,400 or 5,250 ft. Yiddish language.

Prod Joseph Seiden. **Dir** Sidney M. Goldin. **Author** Isadore Lillian.

Cast: Mae Simon.

Domestic, Drama. A prologue referring to Abraham and Isaac stresses the desirability of honoring one's parents, especially mothers, who sacrifice their lives for their children. The story opens with a surprise birthday party for Eddie Rabinowitz given by his parents, David and Mae (played by Mae Simon), his brother, Seymour, and his sister, Helen, all of whom obviously are fond of one other. When David is killed, however, Mae must go to work, and the children cause her no end of anguish: Eddie Stein leads Helen astray, and Seymour spends his mother's money. Years later, Seymour, now a prominent lawyer, hears of a woman abandoned by her children, agrees to force them to support her, and is introduced to his own mother. Mae forgives him, and the family is reunited. *Abraham (Biblical character). Family relationships. Isaac (Biblical character). Jews. Lawyers. Motherhood. Widows.*

Note: This film may also have been known as *The Yiddish Mama*.

THE MYSTERIOUS DESPERADO (Latino)

RKO Radio Pictures, Inc. **Dist** RKO Radio Pictures, Inc. 10 Sep **1949**; Prod: 29 Mar—mid-Apr 1949 [©RKO Radio Pictures, Inc.; 25 Aug 1949; LP2525]. Sd (RCA Sound System); b&w. 5,461 ft. 60-61 min. PCA cert no. 13763.

Prod Herman Schlom. **Dir** Lesley Selander. [**Asst dir** John Pommer]. **Wrt** Norman Houston. **Dir of photog** Nicholas Musuraca. [**Cam op** Fred Bentley and Willard Barth]. [**Gaffer** Charles Beckett]. [**Stills** Gaston Longet]. **Art dir** Albert S. D'Agostino and Feild Gray. **Film ed** Les Millbrook. **Set dec** Darrell Silvera and Jack Mills. **Mus dir** C. Bakaleinikoff. **Mus** Paul Sawtell. **Sd** Phil Brigandi and Clem Portman. [**Makeup** Jack Barron]. [**Hair stylist** Hazel Rogers]. [**Scr supv** Dan Ullman]. [**Grip** Tom Clement].

Cast: TIM HOLT [(*Tim Holt*)], Richard Martin [(*Chito Rafferty*)], Edward Norris [(*Ramon Bustamante*)], Movita Castaneda [(*Luisa*)], Frank Wilcox [(*"Honest" John Jordan*)], William Tannen [(*Elias P. Stevens*)], Robert Livingston [(*Bart Barton*)], Robert B. Williams [(*Barton*)], Kenneth MacDonald [(*Sheriff Anders*)], Frank Lackteen [(*Pedro*)], Leander DeCordova [(*Padre*)].

Western. [*Print viewed*]. When Arizona cowboy Chito Rafferty receives word that his uncle, rancher Manuel Bustamante, has died without leaving a will, he and his best friend, Tim Holt, leave for California to help settle the estate. Upon arriving in the bustling town of Santo Domingo, the cowboys go to see Elias P. Stevens, the local land administrator who is handling the Bustamante property, but are told by his clerk, Whittaker, that Stevens is not available. Later, while dining in the town's saloon, Tim and Chito are accosted by "Honest" John Jordan and his partner, Bart Barton, land sharks who have been sent by Whittaker to "take care of" Chito. Although Jordan and Barton try to kill Chito during the ensuing brawl, Tim gets the better of both of them. Tim and Chito then ride to the abandoned Bustamante ranch, where Chito is attacked from behind by a man who turns out to be Chito's cousin, Ramon Bustamante. After Tim subdues Ramon, who is Manuel's son, Ramon accuses his cousin of trying to steal his inheritance. Stevens and Sheriff Anders then ride up and demand custody of Ramon, who they claim murdered his father, but Ramon

escapes. That night at the ranch, Tim and Chito are visited by Ramon's devoted sweetheart Luisa, who explains that Ramon and his father argued bitterly about their romance because she was not of "pure blood," but insists that Ramon did not kill Manuel. Just then, an unseen gunman fires shots at the house, and Tim concludes that Tim was the intended target. At the land office the next morning, Stevens explains to Tim and Chito that, because Ramon is a wanted felon, he cannot inherit the sprawling Bustamante ranch. Consequently, as the only other living Bustamante, Chito will inherit the property as soon as he produces proof of his identity. After leaving town, Tim and Chito are followed by Jordan and Barton, who, acting on Stevens' orders, shoot at Chito. Chito is hit in the leg, but Tim shoots at Barton, seriously wounding him. Tim delivers Chito to a mission, where Luisa and a priest tend to his leg. Suspecting that Ramon is responsible for the attack, Tim then asks Luisa to set up a meeting with the fugitive, promising that if Ramon proves his innocence, he will not turn him in for Manuel's killing. Luisa's secret signals to the hidden Ramon are detected by a sheriff's informant, and during Tim's meeting with Ramon, a posse surrounds the ranch and captures Ramon. After he accuses Tim of betraying him, Ramon is taken to town, where Stevens has formed a citizens' committee to assure his quick execution. Stevens also orders Jordan to hide the wounded Barton at his ranch to prevent him from confessing in his weakened state. Later, as Tim and the recuperated Chito are leaving the mission, they spot Jordan riding by and follow him to his ranch. There, the gun-wielding Tim and Chito surprise the outlaws, but Jordan manages to escape on his horse. While Chito takes Barton to the Bustamante ranch, Tim tracks Jordan to town and sees him with Stevens. Tim then prevents Ramon's hanging and delivers his cousin to his ranch, where Chito forces Barton to reveal Stevens' guilt in Manuel's murder and his plans to take over the Bustamante ranch. At that moment, the ranch is surrounded by Stevens and his men, and a gunfight ensues. After Tim manages to flee on his horse, he directs the sheriff and his posse to the ranch. There Tim knocks out Stevens as he tries to escape, and the posse overwhelms the remaining outlaws. Later, after witnessing Ramon and Luisa's wedding, Chito and Tim return to their Arizona home. *Attempted murder. Cousins. False accusations. Inheritance. Mexican Americans. Ranches. Arizona. California. Clerks. Confession (Law). Fights. Hanging. Land claims. Land developers. Missions. Posses. Priests. Saloons. Sheriffs.*

Note: The working titles of this film were *Renegade of the Rancho* and *In Old Capistrano*. Although *HR* news items list Dick Simmons in the cast, his participation in the final film has not been confirmed. Some scenes were shot in Lone Pine, CA, according to *HR*. Modern sources add Kermit Maynard to the cast.

Box 27 Aug 1949. *DV* 15 Aug 1949, p. 3. *FD* 18 Aug 1949, p. 8. *HR* 24 Mar 1949, p. 8, 9. *HR* 29 Mar 1949, p. 4. *HR* 15 Aug 1949, p. 3-4. *MPHPD* 27 Aug 1949, p. 4731. *Var* 17 Aug 1949, p. 22.

THE MYSTERIOUS MR. WU CHUNG FOO (Chinese Americans)
Feature Photoplay Co. Jul **1914**?. Si; b&w. Length undetermined.

Drama. After a game of cards at the Astor Club, Lord Lister, a detective, notices an inscription on a dollar bill which reads, "We are held prisoners by a Chinese gang at Cosia, near Sacramento. Send help!" Lister and his friend, Charles Brand, determined to unravel this mystery, travel to Cosia where they encounter the mysterious Chinese merchant Wu Chung Foo. Wu Chung tells Lister and Brand about the unexplained disappearances of many men on his grounds. At Wu Chung's home, his adopted daughter Hattie's attraction to Brand angers the merchant into having him secretly taken to his underground prison where men are worked to death. Lister's suspicions about Brand's disappearance force Wu Chung to have the detective taken there as well. Hattie discovers the secret and gets help from some soldiers who capture Wu Chung and release Brand and the others. *Chinese Americans. Detectives. English. Imprisonment. Merchants. Nobility. Sacramento (CA). Cards. Clubs. Foster parents. Gangs. Slaves. Soldiers.*

Note: This film possibly was of foreign origin. Based on plot information, feature length is assumed.

MPW 18 Jul 1914, p. 482.

MYSTERY IN SWING (African Americans)
Goldport Productions; Aetna Film Corp. *Dist* International Road Shows, Inc. **1940**; Prod: began 24 Jan 1940. Sd; b&w. 6,890 ft. 75-76 min. PCA cert no. 6060.

Prod Arthur Dreifuss. *Assoc prod* Rudolph Brent. *Dir* Arthur Dreifuss. *Dial dir* William Werckenthien. *Scr* Arthur Hoerl. *Addl dial* F. E. Miller and William Werckenthien. *Dir of photog* Mack Stengler. *Spec eff* Ray Mercer. *Montage Effects Courtesy* "The California Eagle" *Settings* Louis Diage. *Ed* Robert Crandall. *Furs* Stearns. *Mus dir* Ross Di Maggio. *The Entire Score Played by* Ceepee Johnson, and His Orchestra. *Sd* Glen Glenn. *Coiffures* Ruth.

Song(s): "Jump, the Water's Fine" and "Let's Go to a Party," words and music by The Four Toppers; "You Can't Fool Yourself About Love," "Beat My Blues Away" and "Swinging Sweet and Lightly," words and music by Ceepee Johnson.

Cast: Monte Hawley (*Biff Boyd*), Marguerite Whitten (*Linda Carroll*), Tommie Moore (*Mae Carroll*), Edward Thompson (*Captain Hall*), Buck Woods (*Buck Bedford*), Jess Lee Brooks (*John Carroll*), Josephine Edwards (*Maxine Ray*), Sybil Lewis (*Cleo Ellis*), Robert Webb (*Prince Ellis*), Alfred Grant (*Chet Wallace*), Thomas Southern (*Sgt. Phipps*), Halley Harding (*Editor Bailey*), Leonard Christmas (*Lawyer Jones*), Earl Morris (*Reporter Wayburn*), John Lester Johnson (*Himself*), F. E. Miller (*Sgt. Slim*), The Four Toppers, Ceepee Johnson, and His Orchestra, [Charles Andrews (*Turnkey*)].

African American, Show business, Mystery. [*Print viewed*]. When Prince Ellis, a noted trumpet player, signs a Hollywood contract, reporter Biff Boyd is assigned to interview him at the Penguin Club. Biff's girl friend, Linda Carroll, a newspaper secretary, joins him. Linda's younger sister Mae is in love with Prince, and their father, John Carroll, writes music for him. Although John and Linda advise Mae that Prince is a lothario who is not worthy of her, she refuses to believe them. While Mae adores her autographed photo of Prince, Prince's wife Cleo smashes hers. At the Penguin, Biff and Linda notice that Prince is giving Maxine Ray the runaround. Maxine was hired as a lead singer at the club by Chet Wallace, whom she spurned in favor of Prince. Instead of getting the interview, Biff and Linda ask Prince and Maxine to join them as they get drunk, and Biff and Prince get into a fight. The next day, Prince is visited by Mae, for whom he promises to send as soon as his divorce comes through; Cleo, who demands her alimony; and John, who warns Prince that he will kill him if he continues to see Mae. When Maxine arrives, Prince puts his trumpet to his mouth to play, but suddenly collapses and dies. A knife then passes before Maxine's face with a note attached, which warns her not to reveal the killer. Biff and Linda arrive at the apartment in time to find the body and see Maxine leaving. She is picked up for questioning after Biff telephones Captain Hall. It is soon determined that Prince died from poison placed on the mouthpiece of his trumpet. Biff gathers all the suspects at the Penguin, where Maxine collapses at the end of a song from a knife wound and dies. Biff discovers a clue when he learns that the sister of Buck Bedford, Prince's servant, killed herself following a love affair with Prince. Biff finds Buck unconscious in his apartment, but Buck escapes when the foolish Sergeant Slim, who was supposed to guard him, falls asleep during a card game. When Biff, Linda and the police enter Prince's apartment, they are shot at, and the culprit escapes, leaving a song sheet signed that day by John. Hall is ready to charge John, but Biff, who does not believe that John is the murderer, is given forty-eight hours to prove his innocence. After learning that Prince left no will, Biff assembles the suspects once again and has Lawyer Jones read a fake will in which one possession is left to each of his friends. Chet, who inherits Prince's trumpet, gives himself away as the murderer when he refuses to play it because of the poison. Chet then admits that he killed Maxine too because she threatened to expose him. The mystery solved, Biff and Linda plan to marry. *African Americans. Jealousy. Murder. Musicians. Philanderers. Reporters. Sisters. Apartments. Cards. Drunkenness. Editors. False accusations. Fathers and daughters. Fistfights. Jazz music. Marriage. Nightclubs. Photographs. Poisoning. Police. Romance. Secretaries. Servants. Singers. Threats. Traps. Trumpets. Wills.*

Note: Onscreen credits indicate the picture was copyrighted by Aetna Film Corp. in 1940, but no registration has been found. Some contemporary sources erroneously list the name of "Prince Ellis'" wife as "Maxine" and spell the actress' last name as "Lewis" rather than "Louis." Some contemporary sources also list Josephine Edwards as Joan Edwards, and indicate that the picture was roadshown in 900 theaters on a state rights basis.

DV 19 Feb 1940, p. 3. *Exh* 21 Aug 1940, p. 588. *FD* 28 Feb 1940, p. 7. *HR* 23 Jan 1940. *HR* 20 Feb 1940, p. 3. *MPD* 26 Feb 1940, p. 5. *MPH* 2 Mar 1940, p. 34.

MYSTERY MANSION see **THE JADE MASK**

THE MYSTERY OF MR. WONG (Chinese Americans, Russian
Americans)

Monogram Pictures Corp. *Dist* Monogram Pictures Corp. 8 Mar
1939; Prod: began early Feb 1939 [©Monogram Pictures Corp.; 1 Mar
1939; LP8686]. Sd (Western Electric Sound System); b&w. 8 reels. 67
min. PCA cert no. 5128.

Series: Mr. Wong.

Assoc prod William Lackey. *In charge of production* Scott R.
Dunlap. *Dir* William Nigh. *Asst dir* W. B. Eason. *Scr* Scott Darling. *Dir
of photog* Harry Neumann. *Film ed* Russell Schoengarth. *Ward* Louis
Brown. *Mus dir* Edward Kay. *Rec eng* Karl Zint. *Tech dir* E. R.
Hickson. *Prod mgr* Chas. J. Bigelow.

Source: Based on characters created by Hugh Wiley in the "James
Lee Wong" short stories in *Collier's*.

Cast: BORIS KARLOFF [(*Mr. Wong*)], Grant Withers [(*Detective-
Sergeant Street*)], Dorothy Tree [(*Valerie Edwards*)], Craig Reynolds
[(*Peter Harrison*)], Ivan Lebedeff [(*Strongonoff/also known as
Petrovich*)], Holmes Herbert [(*Professor Ed Janney*)], Morgan
Wallace [(*Brandon Edwards*)], Lotus Long [(*Drina*)], Chester Gan
[(*Sing*)], Hooper Atchley [(*Carslake*)], Bruce Wong, Jack Kennedy,
Joe Devlin, Lee Tong Foo [(*Willie*)], Wilbur Mack, Dick Morehead.

Mystery. [*Print viewed*]. Brandon Edwards, a heartless collector of
ancient Chinese treasures, smuggles the precious jewel "Eye of the
Daughter of the Moon" out of China. A day before he obtained it,
however, he received a note warning him that the possessor of the
jewel faces death. Later, during a charade skit at a party at the
Edwards' San Francisco home, Edwards is shot. Among the suspects is
Edwards' secretary, Peter Harrison, who is in love with Edwards' wife
Valerie and was holding a gun filled with blanks that was to be used
in a mystery sketch when Edwards was killed. Detective Wong, who
attended the party with his criminologist friend, Professor Ed Janney,
investigates the murder with Detective-Sergeant Street of the San
Francisco police. Peter is arrested until a ballistics report confirms
that the fatal bullet was fired from the balcony. Before he died,
Edwards wrote the name of a suspect on a piece of paper and told
Wong it would be in his safe. Wong learns that Valerie is the patron
of a Russian singer, Strongonoff, who lives with the Edwards.
Strongonoff's sweetheart is a Chinese woman, Drina, who took a job
as the Edwards' maid so she and Strongonoff could procure the jewel.
Drina had hoped Strongonoff would marry her when they got to
America, but realizes now he is in love with Valerie. Drina steals
Edward's note from the safe, but discovers that the jewel is already
missing. Wong then learns from Edwards' lawyer, Carslake, that
Edwards had cut Valerie from his will, leaving a majority of his estate
to his faithful Chinese butler, Sing. While Wong and Janney are
staying in the Edwards house in order to pick up clues, they discover
both the jewel and the letter missing. Drina accuses Strongonoff of
stealing the jewel and backing out on his promise to marry her, then
threatens to send Wong the note. She is killed by a poisoned cigarette
before she is able to do so, however. Sing contacts Wong regarding
the note and is knocked on the back of the head before he can tell
Wong where it is. On the day Wong expects to receive the note in the
mail from Sing, all the suspects converge at his office. Methodically,
Wong rules out every suspect but one. It was obvious to all that Peter
and Valerie loved each other and had a motive for the murder, but
both were standing next to Edwards when he was shot. Wong knows
Strongonoff is really a thief named Petrovich, but is not the killer.
Carslake, who quarreled with Edwards when he cut Valerie out of the
will, had an alibi for the night of the murder. The real murderer,
Wong tells his audience of suspects, is Janney, who hated Edwards for
driving Janney's sister, Edwards' first wife, to suicide. When Janney
saw Edwards emotionally torturing Valerie the way he had his sister,
he decided to kill him. Janney admits his guilt and shakes Wong's
hand goodbye, slipping him the jewel. With the case solved, Wong
sends his valet to China to return the jewel to the Chinese people.
*Art-Collectors and collecting. Chinese Americans. Detectives. Jewel
thieves. Murder. Revenge.* Butlers. False accusations. Lawyers. Maids.
Marriage. Parties. Police detectives. Romantic rivalry. Russians. San
Francisco (CA)–Chinatown. Secretaries. Singers. Wills.

Note: This picture was the second film in the "Mr. Wong" series. For
additional information, consult the Series Index and see entry above for *Mr.
Wong, Detective (above)*.

DV 11 Mar 1939, p. 3. *FD* 20 Mar 1939, p. 10. *HR* 11 Feb 1939, pp. 5-6. *HR* 11 Mar 1939,
p. 4. *MPH* 18 Mar 1939, p. 49. *Var* 12 Apr 1939, p. 13.

THE MYSTERY OF THE GOLDEN EYE see **THE GOLDEN EYE**

MYSTERY RANCH (Native Americans, Apache)

Fox Film Corp. *Dist* Fox Film Corp. 12 Jun 1932; Prod: 1 Apr—mid-
May 1932 [©Fox Film Corp.; 24 May 1932; LP3068]. Sd (Western
Electric System); b&w. 6 reels, 4,900 ft. 55-56 or 65 min. Passed by
the National Board of Review.

Dir David Howard. [*Asst dir* Walter Mayo]. *Scr* Al Cohn. *Photog*
Joseph August and George Schneiderman. [*Cam op* C. Curtis Fetters
and Irving Rosenberg]. [*Asst cam* Harry Webb, Jack Epstein, Lou
Kunkle and James Gordon]. *Art dir* Joseph Wright. [*Ed* Paul
Weatherwax]. *Ward* David Cox. *Mus dir* George Lipschultz. *Sd rec*
Albert Protzman. [*Still photog* Bert Lynch].

Source: Based on the short story "The Killer" by Stewart Edward
White in his collection *The Killer* (New York, 1919).

Cast: George O'Brien [(*Bob Sanborn*)], Cecilia Parker [(*Jane
Emory*)], Charles Middleton [(*Henry Steele*)], Charles Stevens
[(*Tonto*)], Forrester Harvey [(*Artie Brower*)], Noble Johnson
[(*Mudo*)], Roy Stewart [(*Buck Johnson*)], Betty Francisco [(*Appetite
Mae*)], Russ Powell [(*Sheriff Bill Burnap*)].

Western. [*Print viewed*]. In the hills outside the Arizona ranch of
the tyrannical Henry Steele, a deputy sheriff is killed by Mudo, a
renegade Apache in Steele's service. Mudo, according to Steele, had
his tongue cut out because he was a liar in his youth. Sometime later,
Bob Sanborn, a ranger sent to apprehend Steele, rescues a man shot by
one of Steele's Apaches. The man tells Bob that Steele is trying to run
the homesteaders out of the valley. At the nearby town of Paraiso, Bob
is warned by his friend, Buck Johnson, that Steele will not
countenance anyone who will not bow down to him. On his approach
to the ranch, Bob sees a woman fall from her horse while trying to
flee. Bob carries her to the ranch, where Steele, who introduces the
woman as his niece, Jane Emory, invites Bob to stay. That evening, as
Steele perversely plays a wedding march on his piano, Jane hides a
note for Bob asking for help. After Bob retrieves the note, Steele
demands it, but Bob denies any knowledge of it. Later, Bob visits Jane
and learns that Steele is not her uncle, but that he was her deceased
father's business partner; after her father's death, Steele sent for her,
but has not as yet transferred her father's share to her as he had
agreed. The next day, after Steele spies them speaking together, he
escorts Bob to the end of his ranch and warns him never to return. Bob
responds that he will return when he is ready and leaves, narrowly
escaping bullets shot by Mudo and Tonto, another Apache working for
Steele. When Steele tells Jane that he has made plans to marry her the
next day, Artie Brower, Steele's British servant who was devoted to
Jane's father, overhears and rides to Paraiso where he alerts Bob and
Buck. After Bob wires for more rangers, he finds that Tonto and Mudo
have abducted Artie. Bob hurries back in time to rescue Artie who, at
Steele's command, has been strapped to a runaway, unbroken horse.
At night, Bob climbs into the ranch house and struggles with Steele,
before a large group of Indians subdue him. Artie sneaks in and unties
Bob, who then rescues Jane just as Steele, who has entered her room,
is coming toward her. Bob and Jane ride to an old Apache stronghold
in the hills, while Artie dies trying to stop the pursuing Apaches.
While attacking from behind, Mudo loses his balance after hitting Bob
and falls to his death. As Bob and Jane embrace, Steele threatens to
shoot them both if Jane doesn't stand aside. She refuses, but Buck,
leading the rangers, shoots Steele's pistol from his hand. Before Bob
can serve Steele a warrant for murder, he tells Jane that the ranch is
hers, and says to Bob, "Young man, if you want to serve that on me,
you'll have to do it in Hell!" Steele then jumps to his death. As the
Indians are rounded up, Jane asks Bob to be manager of her ranch, and
he agrees as they kiss and embrace. *Megalomania. Ranchers. Rangers.
Rescues.* Apache Indians. Arizona. Chases. English. Falls from heights.
Homesteaders. Jumps from heights. Land rights. Marriage-Forced.
Murder. Mutes. Pianists. Renegades. Servants. Sheriffs. Suicide. Wild
horses.

Note: While the screen credits say that this film was from the novel *The
Killer* by Stewart Edward White, the work was actually a short story collected
in a book with the same title. The Fox trade paper advertising billing sheet calls
the film *Death Valley*, but no evidence has been located to indicate that the
film was ever released under this title. According to reviews, when the film
showed at the Winter Garden theater in New York, it was billed on the marquee
as *The Killer*, the name of the story on which it was based and the film's working
title, while the actual print shown in the theater was titled *Mystery Ranch*. The

Var reviewer surmised that because Westerns did not go over big on Broadway while gangster pictures did, the former title was used. While Virginia Herdman is listed as a cast member playing "Homesteader's wife" in the Fox trade paper advertising billing sheet and in all of the reviews, she does not appear in the print viewed and her role is not in the dialogue continuity taken from the screen in the copyright descriptions for the film; it is possible that her scenes were cut before the final release. The *NYT* reviewer noted that the film "has some of the most beautiful glimpses that have ever been seen on the screen. The photography is so good that it seems almost stereoscopic." Benjamin B. Hampton Productions made a film based on the same source, entitled *The Killer*, which was released by Pathé in 1921; it was directed by Howard Hickman and starred Jack Conway and Claire Adams (see *AFI Catalog of Feature Films, 1921-30*; F2.2869).

FD 1 Jul 1932, p. 6. *HF* 7 May 1932, p. 8. *IP* Jul 1932, p. 31. *MPH* 25 Jun 1932, p. 28. *NYT* 30 Jun 1932, p. 26. *Var* 5 Jul 1932, p. 14.

MYSTERY SHIP (Immigrants)

Columbia Pictures Corp. *Dist* Columbia Pictures Corp. 4 Sep **1941**; Prod: 15 May—28 May 1941 [©Columbia Pictures Corp.; 4 Sep 1941; LP10761]. Sd; b&w. 5,855 ft. 65 min.

Prod Jack Fier. *Exec prod* Irving Briskin. *Dir* Lew Landers. *Asst dir* Seymour Friedman. *Scr* David Silverstein and Houston Branch. *Story* Alex Gottlieb. *Dir of photog* L. W. O'Connell and Benjamin Kline. *Art dir* Lionel Banks and Robert Peterson. *Film ed* James Sweeney. *Sd eng* Karl Zint.

Cast: Paul Kelly (*Allan Harper*), Lola Lane (*Patricia Marshall*), Larry Parks (*Tommy Baker*), Trevor Bardette (*Ernst Madek*), Cy Kendall (*Condor*), Roger Imhoff (*Captain Randall*), Eddie Laughton (*Turillo*), John Tyrrell (*Sam*), Byron Foulger (*Wasserman*), Dick Curtis (*Van Brock*), Dwight Frye (*Rader*), Kenneth MacDonald (*Gorman*), Bob Perry, Walter Sande (*Sailors*), Wade Boteler (*O'Shea*), Earle Dewey, Eddie Earle (*Magistrates*), Chuck Hamilton, Joe McGuinn, Harry Anderson, John Merton, Budd Fine (*Guards*), Hector Sarno (*Chef*), Bill Lally (*Inspector*), Jack O'Malley (*Sparks*), John Dilson (*Warden*), Richard Merski (*Secretary*), Vinegar Roan, Tommy Coats, Art Dillard, Bob Woodward, Earl Bunn, Dick Jensen, Joe Palma, Al Rhein, Al Seymour, Herman Marks (*Prisoners*), George Magrill, Harry Tenbrook (*Mugs*), Stanley Blystone, Walter Shumway (*Government men*), Ernie Adams (*Taxi driver*), Harry Bradley (*Clerk*), Cy Ring (*Clark's assistant*), Herbert Rawlinson (*Inspector Clark*).

Espionage, Prison, Sea, Drama. [*Not viewed*]. Patricia Marshall, ace reporter, greets her wedding day with trepidation because during her twelve previous attempts to get married, her fiancé, government agent Allan Harper, has been called from the altar at the last minute. History repeats itself when just before the wedding, Allan is summoned to a meeting with his boss, Inspector Clark. At headquarters, Allan and his co-worker, Tommy Baker, are handed an envelope containing sealed orders and told to sail at four o'clock in the morning. When Pat learns that her wedding is to be postponed again, she realizes that there must be a sensational story in Allan's emergency call. Trailing him in a taxi to the docks, Pat watches Allan leave his cab with Tom handcuffed as his prisoner while armed guards swarm around the pier entrance. Although Pat flashes her press card, the guards refuse her entrance, but with the help of a police sergeant, she hides in an ambulance that is about to be loaded onto the waiting ship. The ship's cargo consists of malevolent convicts and spies culled from state and federal penitentiaries around the country and designated by the United States government for deportation. Tom is herded in with the other prisoners and penned in a brig lined with solid steel. It soon becomes obvious to Tom that a man named Condor has assumed leadership of the convicts, although his authority is being challenged by Ernst Madek, another prisoner. Meanwhile, in the captain's cabin, Allan and Captain Randall open their sealed orders and are instructed to proceed to a point six hours and thirty-two minutes west of Lisbon. After the ship's radio operator picks up strange signals emanating from the ambulance, Pat is discovered hiding inside the vehicle and the captain forbids her to go below decks. When a fight breaks out among the prisoners, Wasserman, one of them, is injured and taken to the captain's cabin for first aid. In reality, Wasserman is conspiring with Condor to escape from their confinement. Because there is no doctor on board, Allan sends for Madek, who was once a practicing physician. Madek uses the opportunity to steal some drugs from the ship's medicine cabinet and gives them to Rader, another prisoner, who combines them with mercury from a thermometer and sulphur from some matches to produce a bomb. After blasting open the bulkhead door with the

bomb, Rader and the others imprison the guards and take Allan and the captain to the boiler room, where they are forced to shovel coal. When Allan decides that their only salvation is to reach the ambulance housing Pat's radio to send a message for help, the captain puts a boiler out of commission, thus allowing Allan to escape through its smokestack. Upon reaching the deck, Allan arms himself and heads for the ambulance. Meanwhile, Madek overthrows Condor and orders Pat to send a message to his comrades. After decoding the reply, Pat instructs Madek to meet a convoy "six hours and thirty-two minutes west of Lisbon." When the ship reaches this point, it is met by a convoy of American destroyers, which, having been alerted by Allan, seize control of the ship from the prisoners. Allan then sends Pat home on a destroyer and continues his mission. When Allan returns to New York, a determined Pat is waiting for him with a tattered marriage license, a preacher and two roughnecks from the circulation department of her paper. *Foreign agents. Government agents. Prisoners. Reporters. Ships. Ambulances. Bombs. Deportation. Impersonation and imposture. Sea captains. Stowaways. Weddings.*

Note: A *HR* production chart lists Benjamin Kline as photographer and Robert Peterson as art director, although L. W. O'Connell and Lionel Banks are credited onscreen in those positions. This picture marked the screen debut of Larry Parks.

Box 9 Aug 1941. *DV* 29 Jul 1941. *FD* 18 Aug 1941, p. 7. *HR* 23 May 1941, p. 8. *HR* 29 Jul 1941, p. 18. *MPH* 2 Aug 1941. *MPHPD* 26 Jul 1941, p. 194. *MPHPD* 6 Sep 1941, p. 248. *NYT* 16 Aug 1941, p. 18. *Var* 6 Aug 1941, p. 8.

MYSTERY STREET (Latino)

Metro-Goldwyn-Mayer Corp.; controlled by Loew's Inc. *Dist* Loew's Inc. 28 Jul **1950**; Prod: late Oct—mid-Dec 1949 [©Loew's Inc.; 16 May 1950; LP111]. Sd (Western Electric Sound System); b&w. 8,341 ft. 92-94 min. Passed by the National Board of Review. PCA cert no. 14285.

Prod Frank E. Taylor. *Dir* John Sturges. [*Asst dir* Sid Sidman]. *Scr* Sydney Boehm and Richard Brooks. *Story* Leonard Spigelgass. *Dir of photog* John Alton. *Art dir* Cedric Gibbons and Gabriel Scognamillo. *Film ed* Ferris Webster. *Set dec* Edwin B. Willis. *Assoc* Ralph S. Hurst. *Mus* Rudolph G. Kopp. *Rec supv* Douglas Shearer. *Hair styles des* by Sydney Guilaroff. *Makeup created by* Jack Dawn. [*Unit prod mgr* Charles Hunt].

Cast: Ricardo Montalban (*Peter Moralas*), Sally Forrest (*Grace Shanway*), Bruce Bennett (*Dr. McAdoo*), Elsa Lanchester (*Mrs. Smerrling*), Marshall Thompson (*Henry Shanway*), Jan Sterling (*Vivian Heldon*), Edmon Ryan (*James Joshua Harkley*), Betsy Blair (*Jackie Elcott*), Wally Maher (*Tim Sharkey*), Ralph Dumke (*A tattooist*), Willard Waterman (*A mortician*), Walter Burke (*An ornithologist*), Don Shelton (*A district attorney*), [Brad Hatton (*A bartender*)], [Douglas Carter (*Counterman*)], [William F. Leicester (*Doctor*)], [Arthur Loew, Jr. (*Sailor*)], [Sherry Hall, Charles Wagenheim (*Clerks*)], [James Hayward (*Constable Fischer*)], [Eula Guy (*Mrs. Fischer*)], [Virginia Mullen (*Neighbor*)], [King Donovan, Ralph Brooks, George Cooper, George Sherwood, John Crawford (*Reporters*)], [Fred E. Sherman, Allen O'Locklin (*Photographers*)], [Melvin H. Moore (*Oyster shucker*)], [Ned Glass (*Dr. Levy*)], [Matt Moore (*Dr. Rockton*)], [Maurice Samuels (*Tailor*)], [John Maxwell (*Kilrain*)], [Robert Foulk (*O'Hara*)], [Louise Lorimer (*Mrs. Shanway*)], [Napoleon Whiting (*Red Cap*)], [Jack Shea, Robert Strong (*Policemen*)], [Mary Jane Smith, Juanita Quigley (*Daughters*)], [Lucile Curtis (*Mrs. Harkley*)], [David McMahon (*Garrity*)], [Michael Patrick Donovan (*Porter*)], [Frank Overton (*Guard*)], [Bert Davidson (*Dr. Thorpe*)], [May McAvoy (*Nurse*)], [Mack Chandler (*Doorman*)], [Elsie Baker (*Elderly lady*)], [Ralph Montgomery (*Waiter*)], [Jim Frasher (*High school boy*)], [Ernesto Morelli (*Portuguese fisherman*)], [George Brand (*Man in bedroom*)], [Fred Santley (*Pawnbroker*)], [Perry Ivins (*Alienist*)], [Peter Thompson (*Law student*)].

Crime, Suspense, Drama. [*Print viewed*]. Vivian Heldon, a "B-girl" at the Grass Skirt café in Boston, lives in a boardinghouse operated by Mrs. Smerrling. Desperate for rent money, Vivian telephones James Joshua Harkley, a married man with whom she had an affair, and demands that he meet her at the Grass Skirt. While waiting for Harkley, Vivian meets Henry Shanway, a drunk and despondent young man whose wife has just lost their baby in childbirth. When Harkley fails to show up, Vivian offers to drive Henry home and steals his car. She then arranges a meeting with Harkley at Lakeman's Hollow, on Cape Cod. When Vivian demands money from Harkley, he shoots her and tries to cover up the murder

by sending her car into a pond. Three months later, the skeletal remains of Vivian's body are found on a Cape Cod beach. Police Lieutenant Peter Moralas and his associate, Detective Tim Sharkey, begin an investigation into the murder by visiting the Department of Legal Medicine at Harvard University. There they meet forensics expert Dr. McAdoo, who determines that the victim was a female in her mid-twenties who died sometime in late May. While searching through photographs of all the missing persons in the area, Peter and Tim discover Vivian's photograph, and realize that her facial features match the contours of the victim's skull. To learn more about Vivian's disappearance, Peter visits Mrs. Smerrling's boardinghouse, where they find items in Vivian's suitcase that clearly establish her as the murder victim. When Mrs. Smerrling learns that Vivian was murdered near Hyannis, she tracks down Harkley through a Hyannis telephone number scrawled on the wall near the hallway telephone. Mrs. Smerrling then visits Harkley and makes an unsuccessful attempt to extort money from him in exchange for her silence. Before leaving, however, Mrs. Smerrling manages to secretly steal Harkley's gun. Meanwhile, Peter visits a number of Vivian's former associates, including a bartender, a mortician and a physician. Peter later visits Henry when it is determined that he owned the car in which Vivian was last seen. Henry denies any association with Vivian, but a tattoo artist friend of Vivian's later identifies Henry as the man who escorted Vivian home from the Grass Skirt on the night she was killed. Peter charges Henry with the strangulation murder of Vivian, but complications arise in the case when McAdoo determines that Vivian died of a gunshot wound. Realizing that his case against Henry can only proceed if the pistol used to kill Vivian is found, Peter begins questioning other people who may have associated with Vivian. A check of the boardinghouse telephone bill leads Peter to Harkley, who denies having known Vivian and watches nervously as Peter searches his office. Later, Harkley visits Mrs. Smerrling, accuses her of stealing his pistol and offers her $500 in exchange for the gun. When Mrs. Smerrling demands $20,000, Harkley forces her to tell him where it is hidden and then knocks her unconscious with a candlestick. Moments later, Peter arrives at the boardinghouse and sees a man fleeing, but he is unable to catch him. A breakthrough in the case comes when Peter finds a train station baggage check receipt hidden in Mrs. Smerrling's bird cage. Peter and Tim race to the train station, and arrive in time to catch Harkley trying to flee with Mrs. Smerrling's suitcase. Harkley is then arrested and charged with Vivian's murder, and Henry is cleared of any wrongdoing. *Boardinghouse mistresses. False arrests. Forensic pathology. Investigations. Murder. Police detectives.* Automobile theft. Blackmail. Boston (MA). Cafés. Cape Cod (MA). Chases. Drunkenness. Grief. Harvard University. Latino. Hyannis (MA). Jails. Mistresses. Ornithologists. Pistols. Reporters. Roommates. Shipbuilders. Skeletons. Train stations. Undertakers and undertaking. Waitresses.

Note: The working title of this film was *Murder at Harvard.* The following written acknowledgement appears in the onscreen credits: "Metro-Goldwyn-Mayer wishes to thank the president and fellows of Harvard College for their generous cooperation in the making of this motion picture." The film marked the initial production effort of Frank Taylor, a former literary editor at Random House. An Aug 1949 *HR* news item announced that Joseph Losey was originally set to direct the film. A 4 Oct 1949 *DV* news item notes that Harold Kress was to direct the picture. Some filming took place in Boston, MA, and at the Harvard University campus in Cambridge, MA. Although an Oct 1949 *DV* news item notes that Johnny Indrisano was to appear, his participation in the released film has not been confirmed. The film was nominated for an Academy Award for Best Motion Picture Story.

Box 20 May 1950. *DV* 4 Oct 1949, p. 4. *DV* 19 Oct 1949, p. 11. *DV* 4 Nov 1949, p. 2. *DV* 17 May 1950, p. 3. *FD* 1 Jun 1950, p. 6. *HR* 26 Jan 1949, p. 3. *HR* 3 Aug 1949, p. 1. *HR* 28 Oct 1949, p. 14. *HR* 9 Dec 1949, p. 9. *HR* 17 May 1950, p. 3. *MPHPD* 20 May 1950, p. 302. *NYT* 28 Jul 1950, p. 12. *Var* 17 May 1950, p. 6.

MYSTERY SUBMARINE (German Americans)

Universal-International Pictures Co., Inc. *Dist* Universal Pictures Co., Inc. Dec **1950**; Prod: mid-Jul—early Sep 1950 [©Universal Pictures Co., Inc.; 16 Nov 1950; LP536]. Sd (Western Electric Recording); b&w. 7,021 ft. 78-79 min. PCA cert no. 14916.

Prod Ralph Dietrich. *Dir* Douglas Sirk. *2d unit dir* Frank Shaw, Jr. [*Asst dir* Milton Carter]. *Story and scr* George W. George and George F. Slavin. *Suggested by a story by* Ralph Dietrich. *Dir of photog* Clifford Stine. *Spec photog* David S. Horsley. *Art dir* Bernard Herzbrun and Robert Boyle. *Film ed* Virgil Vogel, [Russell Schoengarth and Ralph Dawson]. *Set dec* Russell A. Gausman and Otto Siegel. *Gowns* Bill Thomas. *Mus dir* Joseph Gershenson. *Sd* Leslie I.

Carey and Joe Lapis. *Hair stylist* Joan St. Oegger. *Makeup* Bud Westmore. *Tech adv* Comdr. B. R. Van Buskirk, U.S.N.

Cast: Macdonald Carey ([*Dr.*] *Brett Young*), Marta Toren (*Madeline Brenner*), Robert Douglas (*Commander [Eric] Von Molter*), Carl Esmond ([*Lieut.*] *Heldman*), Ludwig Donath (*Dr. Adolph Guernitz*), Jacqueline Dalya Hilliard (*Carla*), Fred Nurney (*Bruno*), Katharine Warren (*Mrs. Weber*), Howard Negley (*Captain Elliott*), Bruce Morgan (*Kramer*), Ralph Brooke (*Stefan*), Paul Hoffman (*Hartwig*), Peter Michael, Larry Winter, Frank Rawls, Peter Similuk (*Crew members*), [Damian O'Flynn (*Commandant*)], [James Hayward (*Yacht captain*)], [Lester Sharpe (*"North Star" captain*)], [George Spaulding (*Admiral Fletcher*)], [Keith Richards (*Jenkins*)], [Orlando Beltram (*Native intern*)], [Judd Holdren (*Wireless operator*)], [Richard Mayer (*Navy lieutenant*)].

Espionage, Drama. [*Print viewed*]. German Madeline Brenner, a naturalized U.S. citizen, is brought before the United States Attorney for the District of New York under the charge of treason. Madeline tells him how she met Eric Von Molter, a renegade German submarine commander, along the beach in Cape Cod, Massachusetts: Von Molter tells her that her husband, whom she thought was killed during World War II, is actually alive and well. She is then told that she must help with the abduction of German scientist, Dr. Adolph Guernitz, if she wishes to be reunited with her husband. After abducting Guernitz and torpedoing the yacht that the scientist had been traveling on, Von Molter then tells Madeline that her husband had indeed died five years earlier, as she had previously believed. Later, Dr. Brett Young testifies that he was assigned by U.S. Naval Intelligence to find the renegade German submarine and rescue Guernitz. Pretending to be an escaped German prisoner-of-war, Brett finds Von Molter's base along the eastern coastline of Mexico and is soon accepted into their group. As a physician, Brett is then given the task of caring for the seriously ill Guernitz. In the meantime, Von Molter declares his romantic interests in Madeline, while planning for the transfer of Guernitz to an unnamed foreign power. Later, Von Molter catches Brett attempting to use the submarine's radio, but does nothing, as he needs Brett to continue taking care of Guernitz. With Guernitz growing weaker, Von Molter decides to take to sea immediately for a planned rendezvous with the Panamanian tanker *Citadel*. Brett tries to leave a message for U.S. Naval Intelligence when Von Molter raids a port hospital, seeking medication for the ill scientist, but the German submarine commander discovers his note and places Brett under arrest. With Guernitz seemingly lost, the German submarine is spotted by a U.S. Navy search plane. After Madeline releases a flare, the submarine is soon set upon by three passing U.S. Navy destroyers. Von Molter, however, tricks the ships into thinking that the submarine has been sunk by setting off an oil slick, releasing floatables and diving deep. Brett secretly writes the exact location of the submarine's planned rendezvous with the *Citadel* on one of the released life preservers, and Von Molter is captured after boarding the *Citadel*. Von Molter informs his captors that the submarine will torpedo the tanker if he is not immediately released. A squadron of U.S. Navy planes arrives, however, and destroys the German submarine before it can fire on the tanker. Based on her cooperation and Brett's testimony, all charges against Madeline are then dropped. *German Americans. Immigrants. Kidnapping. Scientists. Soldiers of fortune. Submarine boats. Undercover agents.* Beaches. Brothers. Cape Cod (MA). Deception. Dogs. False accusations. Germans. Hospitals. Impersonation and imposture. Lawyers. Mexicans. Mexico. Murder. Physicians. Sailors. Torpedoes. Treason. United States. Navy. Widows. Yachts and yachting.

Note: The working title of this film was *Phantom Submarine.* The film begins with the following written statement: "In the making of this picture, the cooperation of the Department of Defense and the United States Navy is gratefully acknowledged." This was the first Universal film directed by Douglas Sirk, a German immigrant who became best known for his work at that studio on such melodramas as *Magnificent Obsession* (1954), *Written on the Wind* (1956) and *Imitation of Life* (1959). Although Russell Schoengarth and Ralph Dawson are listed as the film's editors by *HR* production charts, Virgil Vogel is credited in the position by contemporary reviews and the film's onscreen credits.

Box 9 Dec 1950. *DV* 22 Nov 1950, p. 3. *FD* 24 Nov 1950, p. 8. *HR* 21 Jul 1950, p. 11. *HR* 28 Jul 1950, p. 13. *HR* 4 Aug 1950, p. 9. *HR* 21 Aug 1950. *HR* 8 Sep 1950, p. 11. *HR* 22 Nov 1950, p. 3. *MPHPD* 25 Nov 1950, p. 590. *NYT* 2 Feb 1951, p. 19. *Var* 22 Nov 1950, p. 8.

MYSTIC FACES (Chinese Americans)

Triangle Film Corp. *Dist* Triangle Distributing Corp. 8 Sep **1918**. Si; b&w. 5 reels.

Dir E. Mason Hopper. *Story and scen* E. Magnus Ingleton. *Cam* Clyde R. Cook.

Cast: Jack Abbe (*Yano*), Martha Taka (*Tama*), Larry Steers (*Frank Maxwell*), Clara Morris (*Letty Stanford*), Liu Chung (*Mao Li*), M. Seke (*Goro*), W. H. Bainbridge (*Letty's father*).

Espionage, World War I, Comedy-drama. Yano, a romantic young man who is in love with the pretty Tama, delivers packages for his uncle Goro, the proprietor of a San Francisco Chinatown antique shop. Yano befriends Letty Stanford, a World War I Red Cross worker, and later Letty and her fiancé, Frank Maxwell, rescue Yano's beloved dog from the dogcatcher. One evening, Yano finds that he is locked out of his uncle's house and is forced to spend the night in the street. He enters a gambling den but escapes the police raid, after which he learns that Letty has been abducted by German spies. With the aid of a disguise, Yano helps Letty to escape and the spies are arrested. Letty's father rewards Yano so handsomely that he finally is able to build a cottage for himself, his dog and Tama. *Abduction. Delivery boys. Rescues. Rewards. San Francisco (CA)–Chinatown. Spies. Disguise. Dogs. Gambling houses. Germans. Police raids. Uncles. World War I.*

ETR 7 Sep 1918, p. 1173. MPN 14 Sep 1918, p. 1760. MPW 14 Sep 1918, p. 1614. MPW 21 Sep 1918, p. 1771. NYDM 19 Oct 1918, p. 590. Var 13 Sep 1918, p. 41. Wid's 8 Sep 1918, p. 9-10.

DIE NACHTE WAHRHEIT see **LA PURA VERDAD**

NADA MÁS QUE UNA MUJER (Spanish language)

Fox Film Corp. *Dist* Fox Film Corp. **1934**; New York opening: 23 Nov 1934; *Prod*: late Jul—mid-Aug 1934. Sd (Western Electric Noiseless Recording); b&w. 9 reels, 7,621 ft. 85 min. Spanish language.

[*Prod* John Stone]. *Dirección de* [*Dir*] Harry Lachman. *Adaptación cinematográfica de* [*Scr*] Raymond Van Sickle and John Reinhardt. *Versión española de* [*Spanish version*] Miguel de Zárraga. [*Spanish version* Enrique Jardiel Poncela]. [*Photog* Rudolph Maté]. [*Gowns* Royer]. [*Mus dir* Samuel Kaylin].

Song(s): Poems: "La rumba," by José Z. Tallet; "Pregones de Buenos Aires," by Alberto Vacarezza; "Hombres necios," by Sor Juana Inés de la Cruz; "Canción de los que buscan olvidar," by Gabriela Mistral.

Source: Based on the short story "The Painted Lady by Larry Evans in *The Saturday Evening Post* (30 Nov 1912).

Cast: BERTA SINGERMAN (*Mona Estrada*), Alfredo del Diestro (*Julio Franchoni*), Juan Torena (*David Landeen*), Luana Alcañiz (*Gilda*), Lucio Villegas (*Doctor Steiner*), Carmen Rodríguez (*Madame Lascar*), Julián Rivero (*Hansen*), [Fraser Acosta (*Ali*)], [Juan Ola, Jimmie Dime (*Natives*)].

Island, Drama. [*Print viewed*]. [The following plot summary is based on the English-language version of this film, *Pursued*; character names refer to that version. For further information regarding the English-language version, please see the note below and the entry for *Pursued* in the *AFI Catalog of Feature Films, 1931-40*.] David Landeen of San Francisco arrives at the port of Ropangi, British North Borneo, in order to take over his deceased uncle's plantation on the neighboring island of Tilo. Beauregard, who owns the next plantation and who has taken control of the Landeen property, sends a group of island natives to beat David up and take his papers. The natives leave David for dead, and Mona, who sings at a casino, rescues him. She calls Dr. Otto Steiner, who reports that David has been temporarily blinded and that he must convalesce in Mona's room, despite Mona's protestations, because the tropical sun might cause permanent damage to his eyes. At the casino that night, Beauregard asks Mona to live with him on his island, and he tries to give her a pearl. She refuses both offers, and her friend Gilda chides her for not taking advantage of Beauregard's bounty. Beauregard follows Mona home and after forcing his way into her room, sees a figure in bed, whom he does not recognize as David. When Beauregard grabs Mona, she slashes his arm with a knife. Ashamed of her circumstances, Mona tells David, whose eyes are still bandaged, that her apartment is actually a wing of a large plantation house owned by her rich father. When David declares to Mona that he loves her, he prematurely pulls the bandages from his eyes, extolls her beauty, and then asks her to marry him. She agrees, but Gilda later insists that David will leave her when he discovers that

she is not a rich man's daughter but only a cabaret singer. Mona seeks the advice of her friend, Dr. Steiner, and he recommends that she go to San Francisco, where he will arrange for her a job as a student nurse. Mona decides to take his advice and, in a note she leaves for David, says she is going away to become the girl that he believes her to be. At the boat dock, Beauregard lures Mona on board a schooner by offering her a ride to Sandican, where, he says, she can pick up the boat bound for the States. Beauregard, however, takes her to his plantation on Tilo and keeps her there by force, hoping that eventually she will want him. When he discovers that Mona has left, David tells Dr. Steiner that her past does not matter to him, but the doctor convinces him to give her a chance to remake her life. A week later, David, now recovered, arrives in Tilo to take over the Landern plantation. He is shocked to see Mona at Beauregard's house, and when she acts as if their romance was not serious, David leaves in disgust for his own house. Beauregard then instructs his cohort Hansen to kill David, but Hansen refuses, and Beauregard knocks him out. Mona, who has overheard their quarrel, gets a gun, but Beauregard takes it away. After she pleads for David's life and relates how she came to know him, Beauregard slugs her and goes off to David's with his gun. Mona follows and then struggles with Beauregard as he is about to shoot David. As Beauregard and David fight, David gets the gun. While Mona explains to David that she did not willingly leave Ropangi with Beauregard, Beauregard grabs the gun, and the two men struggle once again. As Hansen arrives, Beauregard knocks David out. Mona gets the gun, and as Beauregard is about to kill David with his machete, Mona shoots Beauregard three times. Hansen then tells the natives that Beauregard died accidentally. While David is unconscious, Mona goes to the boat to leave. David awakens, however, and stops her from going, despite her pleas, by telling her that he needs her. She falls to her knees and they embrace. *Americans in foreign countries. Blindness–Temporary. Borneo. Cabaret performers. Duplicity. Moral reformation. Nursing back to health. Romance. South Sea islands. Abduction. Ambushes. Casinos. Fights. Knife fighting. Physicians. Plantations. Proposals (Marital). Shootings.*

Note: The working titles of this Spanish-language version were *La llama blanca* and *La venda en los ojos*. According to information in the Twentieth Century-Fox Records of the Legal Department at the UCLA Theater Arts Library, although Miguel de Zárraga received screen credit for writing the Spanish version, Enrique Jardiel Poncela was the actual author. The studio substituted de Zárraga's name because they were concerned that the public, upon seeing Poncela's name, might consider the film to be a comedy, as Poncela had a reputation as a writer of comedies. The plot of the Spanish version differs somewhat from the English version. In the Spanish version, Mona performs poetry rather than songs at the cabaret, and her recitations mesmerize the predominantly male audience. Also, at the end, as David and Mona's abductor, who is called "Franchoni" in this version, fight, a fire starts. David knocks Franchoni through a wall and rescues Mona, and then, as Franchoni is about to shoot David, Hansen shoots Franchoni. Later, Mona and David find that they are on the same boat, and they declare their love for each other. According to *NYT*, the Spanish-language version marked "the introduction to American screen audiences of Berta Singerman, an Argentine diseuse well known and popular in Ibero-America." *NYT* went on to praise Singerman and noted that "her presentation of 'Pregones de Buenos Aires' is so realistic that the spectator only has to close his eyes to imagine himself listening to the varied and strangely alluring calls in the streets of the Argentine metropolis." Fox earlier produced two films based on the same source: the 1917, *When a Man Sees Red*, directed by Frank Lloyd and starring William Farnum and Jewel Carmen (see *AFI Catalog of Feature Films, 1911-20*; F1.4876); and the 1924, *The Painted Lady*, directed by Chester Bennett and starring George O'Brien and Dorothy Mackaill (see *AFI Catalog of Feature Films, 1921-30*; F2.4110). For information on the English-language version, *Pursued*, which was directed by Louis King and starred Rosemary Ames, Victor Jory and Russell Hardie, please see the entry for that film in the *AFI Catalog of Feature Films, 1931-40*; F3.3572.

CM Dec 1934, p. 680. FD 27 Nov 1934, p. 7. MPH 24 Nov 1934, p. 39. NYT 26 Nov 1934, p. 12. Var 27 Nov 1934, p. 63.

NAKED IN THE SUN (Native Americans, Seminole)

Empire Studios, Inc. *Dist* Allied Artists Pictures Corp. 29 Sep **1957**; Los Angeles opening: 17 Sep 1957 [©Allied Artists Pictures Corp.; 6 Oct 1957; LP9250]. Sd (RCA Sound System); col (Eastman Color); 1.85. 7,967 or 7,169 ft. 72 or 78-79 or 82 min. Passed by the National Board of Review. PCA cert no. 18671.

Prod R. John Hugh. *Dir* R. John Hugh. *Asst dir* Gayle S. De Camp. *Orig story and scr* Frank G. Slaughter. *Addl dial* R. John Hugh. *Dir of photog* Charles O'Rork. *Cam* Glenn Kirkpatrick, Jr. *Spec eff* Henderson Gus Bockway. *Art dir* Larry D. Lossing. *Ed supv* William A. Slade. *Props* Ray T. Kline, Jr. Waldo B. and Waldo B. Moon. *Ward* Lois McGee. *Mus comp and cond* Laurence Rosenthal. *Sd rec* H. R. Hathaway, Jr. *Makeup artist* Rudolph G. Liszt. *Hair dressing* Irene

Aparicio. *Unit mgr* Chester L. Seymour, Jr. *Prod mgr* Robert H. Threadgill. *Script* Oneida Hathaway.

Source: Based on the novel *The Warrior* by Frank G. Slaughter (Garden City, NY, 1956).

Cast: JAMES CRAIG [(*Osceola*)], LITA MILAN [(*Chechotah*)], BARTON MACLANE [(*Wilson*)], Introducing Dennis Cross [(*Coacoochee*)], Robert Wark [(*Maj. Francis Dade*)], Jim Boles [(*Arthur Gillis*)], Douglas Wilson [(*Capt. Pace*)], Peter Dearing [(*Gen. Finch*)], Don Eagle, Tony Morris [(*Micanopah*)], Mike Grecco [(*Amathla*)], Tony Hunter [(*Captain in Dade's column*)], Kurt Bryant, Bill Armstrong [(*Lieutenant in Dade's column*)], Eddie Butler.

Historical, Drama. [*Print viewed*]. In 1835, in the dense greenery of the Florida Everglades, a Seminole woman named Chechotah is awakened by the sound of men approaching on horseback. Led by a brutal Georgia slave trader named Wilson, the raiders burn the woman's village to the ground and capture some of the Seminoles, including Chechotah. The next morning, Wilson visits Arthur Gillis, the Indian agent for the Florida Territory, at Fort King and complains that a number of the ''slaves'' he had taken from the village were stolen from his camp during the night. Gillis informs Wilson that it was probably Osceola, a chief highly respected among the Seminoles and often called Rising Sun, who freed the captives. He also reminds Wilson that even though the slave trader has permission to take escaped black slaves from the Seminole villages, where slaves had been harbored for years, he is not to capture black people born and reared there. Wilson scoffs at this, and later, he drunkenly confronts Osceola. Maj. Francis Dade, who grew up among the Seminoles in Florida, intervenes in the conflict, remarking that it is the slave traders who are causing the U.S. government's problems with the Indians. Dade later visits Osceola and his new wife, Chechotah, and asks him to persuade the Seminole chiefs to accept the terms of the new treaty and retreat to the safety of the reservation in Oklahoma. Osceola, who has himself lived among white people and who has known and trusted Dade for years, shakes his head and replies, ''If war comes, it comes.'' Chechotah is distressed by the conversation but later declares proudly that legends will be told about Osceola. As Osceola and his pretty wife frolic among the trees, Wilson and his men appear. Wilson, who lusts after Chechotah, claims that she is an escaped slave, and after beating the Seminole chief, takes her away. Osceola angrily orders Gillis to secure her return, exclaiming, ''My wife is a Seminole, not a slave!'' Drunk, Gillis refuses, whereupon Osceola threatens him with a knife. Gillis imprisons the chief, releasing him only after he has summoned the other Seminole chiefs to sign the Treaty of Payne's Landing. At the signing, Osceola hears that Chechotah has been killed, and he is filled with rage. Meanwhile, Micanopah, chief of all the Seminoles, states that because the U.S. considers all Seminoles of African-American descent to be escaped slaves, a fact earlier hidden from the Seminoles, he will not sign the treaty. Gen. Finch proclaims that the U.S. no longer considers the chiefs to have any authority, whereupon Osceola nearly plunges his knife through Finch's hand. Finch swears to avenge this indignity, and both sides of the dispute prepare for war. Micanopah declares Osceola warrior chief of the Seminoles. After shooting a chief who agreed to take his band to the reservation, Osceola orders his warriors into battle and proceeds to attack and destroy Fort King. Meanwhile, a trusted chief named Alligator ambushes an approaching column of soldiers led by Maj. Dade. Osceola arrives just after Alligator's men have killed almost every soldier in the column, including Dade. Deeply saddened, Osceola buries his ''white brother,'' but new troops are sent, and the fighting continues for many months. Exhausted and hungry, many of the Seminole bands surrender, but Osceola hopes to take his people to a safe and peaceful land to the south. When he, too, arrives at the fort to sign the treaty, he learns that Wilson, who had become the territory's Indian agent after Gillis was killed at Fort King, has lied to the Indians about the safety of the escaped slaves. Secretly, Wilson plans to deliver all slaves and Seminole villagers of black ancestry to Georgia slave traders. As Osceola hurries to organize his warriors, he sees Chechotah, who tells her husband that she is dead to him because Wilson has shamed her. Overjoyed, Osceola embraces Chechotah and then finds Wilson in his room and kills him. He then returns to his people, but later, his friend Wildcat, just released from a white prison, tells the chief that Gen. Finch will imprison any Seminole he finds until Osceola signs the

peace treaty. After Micanopah and Chechotah, calling him ''the spirit of this nation,'' bid Osceola farewell, the chief arrives at the fort, only to be told that he must turn over all escaped slaves. When he and Wildcat protest, they are imprisoned, to the delight of revenge-crazed Gen. Finch. The general is relieved of duty for having captured Indians who arrived under a flag of truce, but Osceola realizes that if he returns to his people, the war will continue. Too many have been killed because of hatred and revenge. He tells Wildcat as the latter slips through the bars of their cell. Promising to care for Chechotah and lead Osceola's people to a peaceful existence in the south, Wildcat escapes from the fort, saying, ''I take your spirit with me. The Rising Sun shall never set.'' *Osceola, Seminole chief, 1804–1838. Revenge. Seminole Indians. Seminole War, 2d, 1835-1842. Slave traders. African Americans. Battles. Dade's Battle, 1835. Duplicity. Everglades (FL). Florida. Forts. Friendship. Hate. Indian agents. Indians of North America. Kidnapping. Marriage. Obsession. Officers (Military). Racism. Rape. Slavery. Treaties. Tribal chiefs. United States. Army.*

Note: The working title of this film was *Osceola.* Author Frank G. Slaughter's name appears above the title in the film's opening credits. An onscreen, narrative introduction to the story states that this ''true story,'' which took place long ago in the Florida Everglades, ''begins with the love of a man for a woman, and ends in a war never won.'' Modern historians describe the actual events portrayed in the film as follows: Following the First Seminole War, 1817-1818, which began when U.S. troops crossed into Florida in pursuit of runaway slaves harbored by the Seminoles, the U.S. purchased the Florida territory from Spain. As white settlers advanced into the new lands, the government instituted the Removal Act, whereby all Eastern Indians were to be relocated to Indian Territory (present-day Oklahoma). In 1832, upon the signing of the Treaty of Payne's Landing, the Seminoles were required to relocate and classified with African-Americans as runaway slaves. Osceola, along with Wildcat and Halek, resisted the treaty, periodically raiding U.S. troops and then disappearing into the Florida swamp country. Osceola's warriors killed Gen. Wiley Thompson at Fort King, on the same day in 1835 as three hundred Seminoles under chiefs Micanopah, Alligator and Jumper massacred Maj. Francis Dade's column of one hundred soldiers. In 1837, Osceola attended peace talks under a flag of truce, but Gen. Thomas Jesup captured the elusive chief. Osceola died in a South Carolina prison cell in 1838. Only about three hundred of the four thousand Seminoles inhabiting Florida at the time remained on reservations near Lake Okeechobee, but those who did, unlike the Seminoles who were removed to Oklahoma, retained some of their Indian identity and traditional ways.

According to information in the MPAA/PCA files at the AMPAS Library, *Naked in the Sun* was rejected by the PCA in Jun 1956 because the film, as shot, included a ''pre-marital affair'' between Osceola and Chechotah, as well as ''bathing scene nudity.'' The PCA did not grant approval to the picture until Aug 1957. Contemporary sources note that the film was shot on location in Florida. Sources conflict as to the length of the film, listing running times between 72 and 82 minutes. It is possible that footage was added after early screenings of the film. According to modern sources, an 88 minute version was also circulated. R. John Hugh's company was also listed as Everglades Studios, Inc. in some contemporary sources.

Daily Cinema 30 Jul 1958. *Exb* 11 Dec 1957, p. 4413. *HR* 6 May 1957. *MPHPD* 30 Nov 1957, p. 626.

NANOOK OF THE NORTH (Native Americans, Native Alaskans)

Revillon Freres. *Dist* Pathé Exchange, Inc. 11 Jun **1922** [©Pathé Exchange, Inc.; 17 May 1922; LU17888]. Si; b&w. 6 reels.

Dir Robert Flaherty. *Scen and titles* Robert Flaherty. *Titles* Carl Stearns Clancy. *Photog* Robert Flaherty. *Asst film ed* Charles Gelb.

Cast: Personages:, Nanook, Nyla, Allee, Cunayou, Comock.

Educational/Cultural, Documentary. Nanook and his family typify Eskimo life in the Arctic. Their continuous search for food necessitates their nomadic life. In the summer they journey to the river to fish for salmon and hunt walrus. In the winter they often approach starvation before any food is found. At night the entire family assists in building an igloo, then crawl under fur robes to sleep, using their clothes for pillows. In the morning the quest continues. *Arctic regions. Fishing. Native Alaskans. Nomads.*

Note: This film was re-issued in 1948 with a newly written narration by Ralph Schoolman, which was spoken by Berry Kroger. An original score for the picture, written in Jan 1945 by famed conductor Rudolf R. A. Schramm, was included on re-issue prints.

ETR 24 Jun 1922, p. 241. *FD* 18 Jun 1922. *MPW* 24 Jun 1922, p. 735. *NYT* 12 Jun 1922, p. 16. *Var* 16 Jun 1922, p. 40. *Var* 1 Sep 1948, p. 14.

NÄR ROSORNA SLÅ UT *see* **UN HOMBRE DE SUERTE**

NATALKA POLTAVKA (Ukrainian language)

Avramenko Film Productions, Inc. *Dist* Kinotrade, Inc. **1937**; New York opening: 13 Feb 1937; *Prod*: began 15 Sep 1936 at Biograph Studios, New York [©Avramenko Film Productions, Inc.; 3 Dec 1936; LP6747]. Sd; b&w. 10 reels, 8,673 ft. 86 min. Ukrainian language with English subtitles.

Dir Vasile Avramenko, Edgar G. Ulmer and M. J. Gann. *Scr* V. Avramenko and M. J. Gann. *Mus score and arr* C. N. Shvedoff. *Scr supv* Shirley Ulmer.

Song(s): melodies by Mykola Lysenko.

Source: Based on the operetta *Natalka Poltavka* by Iwan Kotlyarevsky (1818).

Cast: Thalia Sabanieeva (*Natalka*), Dimitri Creona (*Petro*), Olena Dibrova (*Terpylykha*), Michael Shvetz (*Vyborny*), Mathew Vodiany (*Vozny*), Theodore Swystun (*Mykola*), Vladimir Zelitsky (*Palamar*), Lydia Berezovska (*Mariyka*), Mykola Novak (*Landlord*), Michael Skorobohach (*Office clerk*), Fedir Braznick (*Peasant*), Maria Lavryk (*His wife*), Peter Kushabsky (*Terpylo*), Andrew Stanislavsky (*Lirnyk*).

Rural, Romance, with songs. [*Not viewed*]. In a Ukrainian village, the young maiden Natalka greets her fellow villagers as she carries a yoke with two buckets to the well. At the well, she begins to cry and remembers a sad moment in her life: During a dance in the square of the village of her birth, Poltava, she teasingly runs from her sweetheart Petro, an orphan who had been given a home by her parents. As the assemblage kneel in prayer, the two lovers slip away hand-in-hand. Later, Natalka's father orders Petro to leave the village, and he complies so as not to destroy the family. He and Natalka vow to belong to each other forever, even though they are separated. He wanders by a votiv cross, and Natalka envisions Petro's face and the cross. Back in the present, Natalka addresses Petro's image in the well, wondering where he is, and the image dissolves as water pours from her bucket. A peasant couple pass Natalka on their way to the house of Vozny, a high-hatted money baron. After Vozny wheedles a bribe from the couple, whose cow has been arrested, he learns that the widow Diachonicha is waiting for him to come to her house. His lustful desires aroused, Vozny starts out with his new hat and cane. On his way to the widow's, Vozny sees Natalka in the distance hanging up laundry. Struck by her beauty, he greets her and, to her outrage, says he loves her and asks her to marry him. Natalka protests that they are not equals, but he responds that love makes everyone equal and admits that he has loved her since she moved there. As he continues his plea, Natalka squirts him in the face as she wrings out a piece of clothing before running to the house. Meanwhile, in a field near another town, Petro pitches hay and sings, still longing for Natalka. Mariyka, the landowner's daughter, rides by in her carriage and stops to question him. She learns that he is an orphan and that he has been working for her for two years. Attracted to him, she invites him to work at her home. When Natalka's mother, whose husband has since died, begs Natalka to marry to relieve their poverty, Natalka grudgingly agrees to marry the first man who wants her. Vozny's drunken pal Vyborny then arrives to make his case for Vozny, and although Natalka contends that one should marry to live in happiness and harmony and fears that if she marries a society man, he will always look down on her and that her life will be worse than a servant's, she agrees to the marriage, but asks that she not be rushed. After a year has passed, Mariyka, seeing that Petro is always sad, confesses that she loves him. He says he is not her equal, but she throws her arms around him and kisses him. At night, Petro prays by the water for help to get Natalka back. When Mariyka comes by, he reveals that he loves another, whereupon she says he should go to her, and proudly walks off. Mariyka's father gives Petro money, and Marikya sadly watches him leave. Meanwhile, Natalka goes through a ritual of tying a scarf around Vozny's arm, which means that she has voluntarily consented to marry him. At a creek outside of town, Petro, on his way to find Natalka, meets Mykola, another orphan, who is grazing cattle, and they become friends. As Petro and Mykola walk to town, they meet Vozny and Vyborny coming from Natalka's house, and from their conversation, Petro suspects that Vozny's fiancée is Natalka. During the dances before the wedding, Mykola questions Natalka, and she tells him that her only choice besides marriage was to drown herself. He then reveals that Petro is waiting by the water. As she and Vozny kneel, and her mother blesses their union, she imagines Petro beside her. When she then sees Vozny instead, she flees the gathering. A mob led by Vozny follows, and they find Petro and Natalka embracing by the river. Vozny commands Petro to leave, and Vyborny threatens to have Natalka imprisoned for breech of promise. When Mykola raises his sickle against the mob, Petro consents to go and urges Natalka to learn to love Vosni. He gives her his bag of money so that Vozny will not be able to say he married a penniless girl and says goodbye.

Mykola, however, huddles with Vozny and Vyborny, and Vozny then stops Petro from leaving. He says that Petro's noble action has changed his mind and relates that since his birth, he has had the feeling that he must do a good deed, but that until now, he has not done anything of worth. He then blesses the couple and gives Natalka her freedom. After her mother blesses the union, Mykola takes the scarf from Vozny's arm and puts it on Petro's, and Natalka asks Vozny to be the guest of honor at the wedding party, to which she invites the mob. They march to the town in song and leave Petro and Natalka to embrace as the sun sets. *Class distinction. Love. Marriage–Forced by circumstances. Mothers and daughters. Orphans. Peasantry. Pledges. Poverty. Ukraine. Village life. Breach of promise. Dances. Drunkenness. Engagements. Fathers and daughters. Friendship. Inns. Land rights. Matchmakers. Mobs. Prayer. Proposals (Marital). Rites and ceremonies. Scarves. Transformation. Unrequited love. Weddings. Wells.*

Note: Reviews translated the title into English as "The Girl from Poltava." *Var* stated that the songs from the operetta *Natalka Poltavka* "are said to be the source for many of Tchaikovsky's best compositions," and *DW* noted that Moussorgsky also was "said to have found Kotlyarevsky's songs an infinite source of inspiration" for many of his compositions. In a document in director Edgar G. Ulmer's file at the AMPAS Library, Joseph Steiner stated that he was instrumental in bringing Ulmer to New York from Hollywood to direct the film. However, in a modern interview, Ulmer stated that he was hired to be the associate producer and that Leo Bulgakov, an actor from the Moscow Art Theatre who had directed a few films in Hollywood, was the original director. Ulmer worked on the script with eight others, he related, and began to direct on the third day of shooting, after the Ukrainian backers were unhappy with the footage directed by Bulgakov. Sources disagree concerning the director. While the copyright records lists only Vasile Avramenko, *Var* lists Ulmer and M. J. Gann as directors, and Avramenko as "Ukrainian director."

According to a *FD* news item, the film went into rehearsal in Jul 1936. News items and reviews noted that this was to be the first in a series of up to six films to be made by the newly-formed Avramenko Film Productions and based on works by well-known Ukrainian authors. The company, however, made only one additional film, *Cossacks in Exile* (see above). Ulmer, in the modern interview, related that the company was formed by a nationalist Ukrainian movement made up of members of the Union of Window Washers in New York, who raised $18,000 for the production costs by selling advance tickets to the film to chapter houses throughout the U.S. and Canada. Sets were built on a Ukrainian farm in Flemington, N.J. by the window washers' Ukrainian friends in the Finnish Carpenter Union in New York and a Ukrainian who knew how to cut thatched roofs. Ulmer also recounted that children from all over the country arrived on the set with their own costumes for the dance numbers. Modern sources state that Vasile Avramenko introduced Ukrainian dancing to the U.S. Thalia Sabanieeva, who played the lead role, was a soloist with the Metropolitan Opera Company, according to *Var*, which commented that she was "perhaps a little overweight for the character she plays" and that "the camera is far from flattering in some close-ups." According to a *HR* news item, after the film's premiere, Sabanieeva was signed by Avramenko to star in two additional films; however, she did not appear in their other production of *Cossacks in Exile*. According to reviews, this film was shown in New York approximately two months after a Soviet-made film based on the same source and with the same title had its New York premiere. (Modern sources state that the American film had a preview on Broadway on 24 Dec 1936, the same day as the Soviet film opened.) The Soviet film was directed by E. Kavaleridze and starred M. Litvinenko Volmut and E. Patorzinski. Reviews praised the American-made version above the Soviet-made film. *NYT* remarked, "the made-in-America product is more enjoyable than the imported article. This is due to the fact that it contains more funny incidents and is photographed much better."

DW 27 Dec 1936. *FD* 8 Jul 1936, p. 3. *FD* 18 Feb 1937, p. 8. *HR* 14 Sep 1936, p. 8. *HR* 24 Feb 1937, p. 7. *NYT* 13 Feb 1937, p. 9. *Var* 17 Feb 1937, p. 23.

NATION AFLAME (Italian Americans)
Treasure Pictures Corp.; A Victor and Edward Halperin Production. *Dist* Television Pictures; Treasure Pictures Corp. 16 Oct **1937**; Prod: 16 Nov—early Dec 1936. Sd; b&w. 8 reels, 6,945 ft. 73-74 or 76 min. PCA cert no. 2964.

Prod Edward Halperin. *Dir* Victor Halperin. *Dial dir* Charles Gerson. *Asst dir* Paul Hughes. *Scr* Oliver Drake. *Story* Thomas Dixon, Oliver Drake, Leon D'Usseau and Rex Hale. *Addl dial* William Lively. *Photog* Arthur Martinelli. *Operating cameraman* H. C. Ramsay. *Art dir* Leigh Smith. *Film ed* Holbrook Todd and Frank Bayes. *Mus dir* Dr. Edward Kilenyi. *Rec eng* J. S. Westmoreland. *Production* F. Herrick Herrick.

Cast: Noel Madison [(*Frank Sandino, later known as Sands*)], Norma Trelvar [(*Wynne Adams*)], Lila Lee [(*Mona Burtis*)], Douglas Walton [(*Tommy Franklin*)], Harry Holman [(*Roland Adams*)], Arthur Singley [(*Bob Sherman*)], Snub Pollard [(*Wolfe*)], Earl Hodgins [(*Wilson*)], Si Wills [(*Walker*)], Roger Williams [(*Dave Burtis*)], Alan Cavan [(*Harry Warren*)], Dorothy Kildaire [(*Toots*)], Elaine Deane, Lee Phelps, Carl Stockdale, C. Montague Shaw [(*President of the U.S.*)], [Lee Shumway (*Campbell*)].

Political, **Drama**. [*Print viewed*]. Roland Adams, a crooked former mayor, and his fellow conmen, Frank Sandino, Wolfe, Wilson and Walker, are run out of a town by a mob upset at their phony land selling racket. After thinking about the mob, Sandino, the fast-talking hawker of the group, gets an idea to form a secret lodge, the Avenging Angels, based on intolerance of religion and prejudice against "foreigners." They hope to attract thousands of people they think of as "suckers," who are suffering from the Depression. Adams visits his daughter Wynne in Middleton, hoping that she will support them financially until they get members. During a party for Bob Sherman, the district attorney, Sandino, now calling himself "Sands," expounds on the way to save the country's youth through reverence to the flag and the constitution, protection of American unemployed, the security of the home and an absolute boycott against foreigners. Although Bob fears that Sands's inflamatory ideas will only lead to mob violence, Wynne, fascinated with Sands, gives money for the Angels. Soon many Middleton citizens have paid twenty-five dollars for the initiation fee, and in black cloaks and hoods, they swear allegiance to their superiors. Following an outbreak of violence, ruination of property and strikes, Bob argues with Wynne, who often dates Sands, and she walks out. In the next two years, Sands has Adams elected governor, and they infiltrate every public office with Avenging Angels. On the eve of Adams's re-election campaign, Sands calls upon his followers to eradicate newspaper publisher Harry Warren, who has published Bob's accusations that the leaders operate for personal gain. Sands has unemployed lodge member Dave Burtis, who is a friend of Warren's, bring Warren to a car filled with Angels. They drive Warren to a clearing in a wood and, in a ceremony, kill him. After Bob matches the type on an anonymous note to that of a job application, which Dave's wife Mona typed for him, Dave is arrested for murder. Mona pleads with Sands to save him, but Sands tries to kiss her. To protect herself, she pulls out a pistol, and in their struggle, she is killed. Dave, freed for lack of evidence, finds her, and her death is ruled a suicide. When hundreds of hungry men and women wait outside the governor's mansion for Adams to sign a relief bill, which Sands orders him to refuse, Adams, angry that Sands wants to marry Wynne, tells the crowd from his balcony that he will sign the bill. Dave, acting on Sands's orders, shoots Adams, and he is in turn killed by police. Wynne then offers to infiltrate the lodge. She forms a women's auxiliary, and with its success, Sands is encouraged to form a national movement. After she disrupts a meeting by coming out of Sands's bedroom in a robe, rumors spread about them. When Tommy Franklin, the head of the youth division, questions Wynne about the rumors, she does not deny them, and Tommy tells the other youth leaders that Bob's charges are true. Angel-bolters help Bob, who is running for governor against Wilson. To further ruin Sands, Wynne entices him to an evening of drinking. Early in the morning, they return to her home and continue drinking. When Sands sees the press arrive for a conference that Wynne earlier scheduled, he realizes it is a frame-up and pulls a gun. Police shoot Sands, and Bob, putting on an act, indignantly rebukes Wynne. The Avengers then burn effigies of Wynne and Sands. Bob proposes to Wynne, but she says that because the people have to believe in him, they can't reveal the frame-up. She tells him, however, that sometime they will be together. As the President of the United States rides with Bob, now governor, in his inaugural parade, he acknowledges that the nation owes Wynne a debt of gratitude that it can never publicly repay, and Wynne, in a veil, watches from the side. The president tips his hat to her, and he lifts her veil. Bob then removes his hat, and Wynne, teary-eyed, blows him a kiss, then moves back into the crowd as she breaks down and cries. Confidence men. District attorneys. Lodges. Mobs. Secret societies. Undercover operations. Xenophobia. Assassination. The Depression, 1929. Drunkenness. Elections. Fathers and daughters. Governors. Italian Americans. Newspapers. Patriotism. Publishers and publishing. Rites and ceremonies. Scandal. Unemployment. United States. Presidents.

Note: Some of the credits were missing from the print viewed. The working titles of this film were *Avenging Angels* and *My Life Is Yours*. Sources disagree concerning the source of this film. Reviews state that the film was based on a story by Thomas Dixon, while a *HR* news item dated 29 Jun 1936 says that the story was an original written by Leon D'Usseau. Writing credits were missing from the print viewed. Ethel Jackson is listed as a cast member in *HR* production charts, but her participation in the final film has not been confirmed. Reviews noted that the film was based in part on the activities of the Black Legion and the Ku Klux Klan. For information about the Black Legion, please see the entry above for *The Black Legion*.

FD 21 Nov 1936, p. 8. *FD* 20 Oct 1937, p. 6. *HR* 29 Jun 1936, p. 2. *HR* 16 Nov 1936, p. 15. *HR* 30 Nov 1936, p. 19. *HR* 13 Oct 1937, p. 3. *MPD* 22 Oct 1937, p. 8. *MPH* 23 Oct 1937, p. 54. *Var* 7 Apr 1937, p. 15.

NATIVE SON (African Americans)

Argentina Sono Film S.A.C.I., Buenos Aires. *Dist* Classic Pictures, Inc. Jun **1951** [©Walter Gould; 8 Mar 1951; LP1023]. Sd (RCA Sound System); b&w. 11 reels. 90-91 min. *Country of origin* Argentina.
Pres WALTER GOULD. *Prod* James Prades. *Dir* Pierre Chenal. *Scr* Pierre Chenal and Richard Wright. *Dial* Richard Wright. *Dir of photog* A. U. Merayo. *Location seq* R. A. Hollahan. *Ed* George Garate. *Sets* Gori Munoz. *Mus* John Elhert. *Vocal Quintette* Katherine Dunham Company. *Sd rec* Mario Fezia and Chas. Marin.
Song(s): "The Dreaming Kind," words and music by Lillian Walker Charles; "Leanin' (On the Ever Lastin' Lord)," traditional.
Source: Based on the novel *Native Son* by Richard Wright (New York, 1940).
Cast: Jean Wallace (*Mary Dalton*), Richard Wright (*Bigger Thomas*), Nicholas Joy (*Mr. Dalton*), Gloria Madison (*Bessie Mears*), Charles Cane (*Britten*), George Rigaud (*Farley*), George Green (*Panama*), Willa Pearl Curtiss (*Hannah*), Gene Michael (*Jan Erlone*), Don Dean (*Max*), Ned Campbell (*Buckley*), Ruth Roberts (*Mrs. Dalton*), George Nathanson (*Joe*), George Roos (*Scoop*), Lewis MacKenzie (*Stanley*), Cecile Lezard (*Peggy*), Charles Simmonds (*Ernie*), Leslie Straugh (*Buddy*), Lidia Alves (*Vera*).
African American, **Social**, **Crime**, **Psychological**, **Drama**. [*Print viewed*]. In Chicago's "black belt," where nearly half a million African Americans are crowded in, Hannah Thomas lives in a small kitchenette with three children, Vera, Buddy and her oldest, twenty-five-year-old Bigger, having left the South twelve years earlier following the lynching of her husband. When a rat, whom the family has nicknamed "old man Dalton," after their landlord, scampers across the floor, Bigger kills it. After a relief agency worker offers Bigger a job as a chauffeur for the Dalton family, Bigger, who is somewhat reluctant to take the job, goes to see his girl friend, Bessie Mears, a waitress in a South Side club. Bessie is excited that the owner of the club, Ernie, is going to give her a chance to sing the following evening. Bigger warns Ernie not to pursue her, then plans a robbery with some cohorts. When Ernie interrupts them and threatens to call the police, Bigger breaks his phone. The robbery does not come off, so Bigger goes with his friend Panama to the all-night movies. He decides to take the Dalton job, and despite Bigger's police record, Henry Dalton gives him the job, which includes a room in the tower of his large house. Bigger takes Bessie for a drive in the Dalton car, and when she expresses suspicion of his interest in Dalton's daughter Mary, he says he would not swap Bessie for all the blondes in Chicago. When he picks up Mary later that night, supposedly to take her to the university library, she has him pick up her friend, Jan Erlone, a labor radical. They insist on going to Ernie's club and invite Bigger to sit with them, and Bessie becomes upset when she sees Bigger with Mary. Mary and Jan make patronizing remarks about blacks, and Mary mollifies Bessie's jealousy by giving her an orchid. When Bigger drives Mary and Jan home at two in the morning, they are very drunk. As Bigger leaves Jan off, Jan gives him some radical books to read. At the Dalton home, Mary asks Bigger to carry her to her bedroom, and he nervously puts her to bed. When he hears her blind mother come in, his fear of being found with Mary prompts him to put a pillow over her face to stifle her sounds. After her mother leaves, Bigger tries to awaken Mary, but is shocked to find that he has killed her. He then carries her body to the furnace in the cellar. The next morning, when Bigger is questioned about Mary's disappearance, he says that Jan carried her in. Dalton calls Britten, a racist police detective, who finds Jan's books in Bigger's room and surmises that labor radicals have planted Bigger in the house, but Dalton stops him and vouches for Bigger. Britten then interrogates Jan and arrests him after he lies. Bigger returns home, and as he sees his mother scrubbing floors, he questions the way they live, compared to the way the Daltons live. He then finds Bessie and tells her of his plan to get $10,000 ransom money by saying that they have kidnapped Mary. Although Bessie is uneasy with the idea, she agrees to help. After Bigger leaves a ransom note, Dalton, believing that Jan and the radicals are behind the kidnapping, tells reporters who have gathered at the house that he has asked that Jan be released from jail and that he is paying the ransom. Jan refuses to leave jail, however, and plans to sue Dalton for false arrest. Ralph

Farley, one of the reporters, suggests to Bigger, as the furnace begins to smoke, that maybe Mary was murdered and the perpetrator has burned her body in the furnace. Although Farley and the other reporters are joking, when they find a human bone and Mary's ring and earring in ashes that the gardener shovels out of the furnace, Bigger runs from the house, and the reporters assume that he assaulted and murdered Mary. As the police search for Bigger, he and Bessie race to an abandoned building where the ransom money was to be left. Bigger confesses killing Mary to Bessie, but he explains that he tried to smother her cries when Mrs. Dalton came in because he had heard all his life of black men being killed for being with white girls. Bessie suggests that he give himself up, but he refuses to listen and pushes her away. He then sends her to the drugstore across the street to get a bottle of whisky. While at the drugstore, Bessie hears a radio bulletin about a $10,000 reward for Bigger, who, they say, raped and beheaded Mary. Snippy, who hangs out at Ernie's, passes by the drugstore and after hearing about the reward, sees Bessie go to the apartment building. He stops a police car and tells where they are hiding. When the police bust in, Bigger climbs to a roof and shoots at them, then climbs up a water tank and continues firing. The police knock him down with water from a fire hose and he is captured. The Thomases visit Bigger in jail and Hannah asks her son to pray. Jan confesses that when he first learned that Bigger killed Mary, he wanted to kill him, like the mob that has gathered outside the jail, but he realized that would not solve anything. Meanwhile, Farley, with help from Panama, finds Bessie's body in an elevator shaft. Bigger admits that he killed Bessie and tells his lawyer Max about a dream he had while Bessie went to buy the whisky, in which she betrayed him. When he woke up and saw Snippy looking at the building, he thought she really had betrayed him and threw her down the elevator shaft. Farley relates that Snippy said Bessie never even suspected that he had located them. Bigger says he hopes what happened to him does not happen to another black boy and that he is thankful to have gotten to know Max. He asks Max to tell Jan hello as he prepares himself for death in the electric chair. *Accidental death. African Americans. Chicago (IL). Murder. Racism.* Amusement parks. Blindness. Boxers. Chases. Chauffeurs. Dreams. Drugstores. Drunkenness. Elevators. Family life. Frame-ups. Jealousy. Landlords. Lawyers. Motion picture theaters. Nightclub owners. Orchids. Police detectives. Poverty. Radicalism. Ransom. Rats. Religiosity. Reporters. Shootouts. Singers.

Note: Richard Wright's novel was produced as a play by Orson Welles and John Houseman. The play, which was directed by Welles, written by Wright and Paul Green, starred Canada Lee, opened on Broadway on 24 Mar 1941. According to a *LADN* article about the film, when producer James Prades, a Uruguayan, and French director Pierre Chenal, who had left Paris for South America during the Nazi occupation, initially spoke to Wright about making the film, he worried about the changes that would come in transferring it to the screen. Prades and Chenal assured him they wanted to remain faithful to the novel and suggested he write the screenplay. Later, they also asked him to play the lead role in the film. Wright, in a *NYT* article, stated that he believed a Hollywood company would water down the story and that a company from a country that relies on American aid would not risk offending the U.S. Argentina, however, seemed not to care about that consideration. Although the *NYT* article reported that Wright received no compensation for the rights, a *HR* news item stated that he was to get $6,000 and one-sixth of the film's profits.

The film was originally to be made in English, Spanish and French-language versions, according to a Jan 1951 *Ebony* article. It is not known if the French and Spanish versions were ever produced. News items stated that the film was aimed at the U.S. market and was the first English-language film made in an Argentinean studio and the first made in Argentina with a U.S. setting. Argentina Sono Film, the producer, hoped the film would focus attention on Argentinean productions. Background shooting began in Chicago. Wright noted on his return to the city that conditions seemed to be worse for South Side blacks than when he published the novel in 1940. In Chicago, the filmmakers found Gloria Madison, a graduate student in archaeology, through a theatrical agency, and offered her the part of "Bessie Mears." Willa Pearl Curtiss, who played "Hannah Thomas," came from Hollywood, as did Jean Wallace. Other roles were filled by English-speaking people living in Argentina. Gene Michael, on a visit from California, did a screen test for the role of a policeman and so impressed the filmmakers that they offered him the role of "Jan Erlone."

The film was rejected at first by the New York State censors and was approved only after extensive editing took place. According to information in the MPAA/PCA Collection at the AMPAS Library, scenes deleted or changed by the censors include Mary caressing Bigger's hair as he puts her to bed, and Bigger bending over her; lines that identify Jan as a labor leader; indications that Bigger was accused of raping Mary; and the words "white" and "nigger" in a number of instances. In addition, the censors noted that the following scenes, to which they had objected in the script, did not appear in the print submitted: the killing of the rat at the beginning; lines from Mary and Jan's initial conversation with Bigger expressing their understanding and solidarity with the plight of blacks; and lines about lynching in the South. In Ohio, the film was rejected as

harmful because it "contributes to racial misunderstanding, presenting situations undesirable to the mutual interests of both races. [It is] against public interest in undermining confidence that justice can be carried out. [It] presents racial frictions at a time when all groups should be united against everything that is subversive." In Pennsylvania, the film was passed with some deletions and with the warning that "if this film causes real distress at any place or for any people in the state, we reserve the privilege to revoke the license."

Reviews for the film were mixed, with several reviewers comparing the film unfavorably with the novel. *NYT* commented, "The script is so clumsily constructed and it is so amateurishly played by Mr. Wright and a cast of virtual unknowns...that it loses all of the strange terror and authenticity of the original." *LADN*, in calling the film a "great disappointment," related a theme of the book that they felt was missing from the film: "[the novel] eloquently indicted society as the neglectful criminal—not Bigger Thomas....Society has set up the rules and the conditions and thus had made the murder the logical end to a sequence of events. The movie almost entirely disregards this thought-provoking premise and instead sinks to the level of a low-grade, uninteresting chase." Other reviewers, however, praised the film for the way it gave audiences the opportunity to judge the situations portrayed. *SatRev* lauded the film's "unwillingness to compromise with standard entertainment patterns" and stated that Wright "leaves it to the audience to search out the social implications of Bigger's tragedy." *LAEx* noted, "the sociological message, which is more a plea for better understanding between Negroes and whites than it is an indictment against any racial group, gets over with subtle implication rather than attempting to pound a message home."

Cue 16 Jun 1951. *DV* 3 May 1951. *DV* 28 Jan 1953. *Ebony* Jan 1951, pp. 82-86. *Exh* 4 Jul 1951, p. 3104. *FD* 29 Jun 1951, p. 6. *HR* 3 Oct 1949. *HR* 27 Feb 1951. *HR* 2 Mar 1951. *HR* 4 Apr 1951. *LADN* 21 Mar 1951. *LADN* 13 Aug 1951. *LAEx* 13 Aug 1951. *LAT* 13 Aug 1951. *MPHPD* 23 Jun 1951, p. 906. *Newsweek* 9 Jul 1951. *NYT* 16 Oct 1949. *NYT* 18 Jun 1951, p. 19. *NYT* 24 Jun 1951. *SatRev* 7 Jul 1951. *Var* 15 Nov 1950. *Var* 25 Apr 1951, p. 14. *Var* 20 Jun 1951.

NAUGHTY MARIETTA (French Americans)

Metro-Goldwyn-Mayer Corp.; controlled by Loew's Inc. *Dist* Loew's Inc. 29 Mar **1935**; World premiere in Washington, D.C.: 8 Mar 1935; New York opening: 22 Mar 1935; Prod: 4 Dec 1934—7 Feb 1935 [©Metro-Goldwyn-Mayer Corp.; 6 Mar 1935; LP5468]. Sd (Western Electric Sound System); b&w. 11 reels. 105-106 min. Passed by the National Board of Review. PCA cert no. 622.

Prod Hunt Stromberg. *Dir* W. S. Van Dyke. [*Asst dir* Edward Woehler]. *Scr* John Lee Mahin, Frances Goodrich and Albert Hackett. *Photog* William Daniels. [*2d cam* Bill Riley and Al Lane]. [*Gaffer* Floyd Porter]. *Art dir* Cedric Gibbons. *Art dir assoc* Arnold Gillespie and Edwin B. Willis. *Film ed* Blanche Sewell. [*Cost* Adrian]. *Mus adpt* Herbert Stothart. [*Orch* Paul Marquardt, Jack Virgil, Charles Maxwell, Leonid Raab and Wayne Allen]. *Rec dir* Douglas Shearer. [*Elec* Bill Allen]. [*Grip* Arnold Webster and Pop Arnold]. [*Props* Harry Albiez]. [*Still photog* Frank Tanner]. [*Press agent* Howard Dietz].

Song(s): "Chansonette," "Antoinette and Anatole," "Tramp, Tramp, Tramp Along the Highway," "Owl and the Pole-cat," " 'Neath the Southern Moon," "Italian Street Song," "Dance of the Marionettes," "Ship Ahoy," "I'm Falling in Love with Someone" and "Ah, Sweet Mystery of Life," music by Victor Herbert, lyrics by Rida Johnson Young, additional lyrics by Gus Kahn.

Source: Based on the operetta *Naughty Marietta*, music by Victor Herbert, book and lyrics by Rida Johnson Young (London, 24 Oct 1910).

Cast: JEANETTE MacDONALD (*Marietta [Franini, assumed name of Princess Marie de Namours de la Bonfain]*), NELSON EDDY ([*Richard*] *Warrington*), Frank Morgan (*Governor d'Annard*), Elsa Lanchester (*Madame d'Annard*), Douglas Dumbrille (*Uncle*), Joseph Cawthorne (*Herr Schuman*), Cecilia Parker (*Julie*), Walter Kingsford (*Don Carlos [de Braganza]*), Greta Meyer (*Frau Schuman*), Akim Tamiroff (*Rudolpho*), Harold Huber (*Abe [Abraham]*), Edward Brophy (*Zeke [Ezekial Cramer]*), [Cora Sue Collins (*Felice*)], [Mary Doran, Marjorie Main, Jean Chatburn, Pat Farley, Jane Barnes, Jane Mercer, Linda Parker, Kay English (*Casquette girls*)], [Dr. Edouard Lippe (*Landlord*)], [Harry Cording (*Pirate*)], [William Burress (*Bouget, pet-shopkeeper*)], [Helen Shipman (*Marietta Franini*)], [Catherine Griffith (*Prunella, Marie's maid*)], [Billy Dooley (*Drunk, Marietta's "brother"*)], [Guy Usher (*Ship's captain*)], [Henry Roquemore, Richard Powell (*Heralds*)], [James C. Morton (*Barber*)], [Louis Mercier (*Dueler*)], [Robert McKenzie (*Town crier*)], [J. Delos Jewkes (*Priest on dock*)], [William Moore (*Jacques, suitor*)], [Harry Tyler (*Suitor*)], [Ben Hall (*Mama's boy*)], [Edward Keane (*Major Cornell*)], [Roger Gray (*Sergeant*)], [Edward Norris (*Marie's suitor*)].

Historical, Musical, Drama. [*Print viewed*]. In 18th century France, French princess Marie de Namours de la Bonfain, an orphan who lives with her uncle, Prince de la Bonfain, refuses to marry

Spanish grandee Don Carlos de Braganza. Although the marriage has been sanctioned by King Louis XV, Marie tells her confidant, Herr Schuman, that she prefers to marry a man who will be "tall and strong in the wind." She calls Don Carlos, who has come from Madrid to take her to Spain with him, an "odious" man. Marie disregards her uncle's warning about the dire consequences that will befall her if she refuses to obey the king's wishes, and decides to escape from France when she learns that her maid, Marietta Franini, is departing for Louisiana. After Marietta tells Marie that she is leaving for the colonies because she is too poor to stay in Paris and marry her sweetheart Giovanni, Marie offers her money in exchange for permission to take her place aboard the ship. Marietta accepts the offer, and Marie, disguised as Marietta, boards the ship in her stead. Soon after the princess' departure, a public notice is posted proclaiming that she is a fugitive, and a reward of 550 Louis D'ors is offered for information on her whereabouts. On the ship, the princess takes her place among the many *casquette* girls, who are sailing to Louisiana to fulfill their contract with the king and marry colonists in New Orleans, and tells Julie, one of the girls, that she will not do what is expected of her upon their arrival. Following an attack on the ship by pirates, and the massacre of its sailors, the ship is commandeered and taken ashore somewhere in the colonies. As soon as the *casquette* girls disembark from the ship, a bloody battle between the pirates and Yankee Scouts ensues. Once the pirates are defeated, the handsome leader of the Scouts, Richard Warrington, becomes enamoured of the princess. The girls are then taken to New Orleans, where they are greeted by the Governor and a lively group of prospective husbands. While the girls are being led to the convent, the princess tries to disqualify herself from marriage by telling the Governor that she is an immoral woman. As a result, Marie is assigned to work at a nearby marionette show, where Richard, who is still in love with her, finds her. No sooner are the two reunited than Richard hears the news about a reward for a missing French princess and, realizing his sweetheart is a fugitive, attempts to hide her. The princess, however, is soon captured and is arrested at the Governor's orders. When Julie visits the princess, she tells her that the Governor has banished Richard and will force her to return to France with Don Carlos and her uncle, who have come to fetch her. While Marie's uncle advises her to mend her relationship with Don Carlos by telling him that she left him on a whim only to intrigue him, Julie finds Richard and informs him that the Governor intends to harm him if Marie refuses to comply with France's orders. Before their departure, Marie, her uncle and the others attend the Governor's farewell ball, where Richard shows up unexpectedly. Marie reaffirms her love for him in a song, and he persuades her to elope with him into the wilderness, where he promises her that they will never again be disturbed by her family or the French government. *France–History–19th century. Fugitives. Impersonation and imposture. Marriage–Arranged. New Orleans (LA). Princesses. Soldiers. Balls (Parties). Colonies. Elopement. Governors. Louis XV, King of France, 1710-1774. Maids. Musicians. Orphans. Pirates. Puppets. Rewards. Ships. Spaniards. Uncles.*

Note: *Naughty Marietta* marked the first of eight Jeanette MacDonald-Nelson Eddy M-G-M musicals, and was originally purchased by M-G-M as a Marion Davies vehicle. The film also provided Eddy with his first starring role. The title card in the onscreen credits reads: "Victor Herbert's Naughty Marrietta." Modern sources note that at the film's initial press showing on 2 Mar 1935, the running time was approximately eighty minutes. Between 2 Mar and 29 Mar, however, additional footage was added and the running time of the picture was boosted to 106 minutes. Although a *HR* pre-production news item announced that Chester Hale was assigned to direct the dances in the picture, his participation in the released film has not been confirmed. *HR* pre-production news items also note that Robert Z. Leonard, who was first assigned to direct this film, was relieved of the assignment after a day of shooting at his own request. An Apr 1934 *DV* news item noted that New York playwright Lawrence Eyre was set to "handle the script," but his participation in the production has not been confirmed.

HR pre-release news items note that, despite his protests, Frank Morgan was required to shave his moustache for the film—something he reportedly had not done for seventeen years. *HR* pre-release news items list actors Robert Graves, Rober Gray, Beatrice Roberts, Vessie Farrell, Richard Hemingway, Olin Howland, Judith Voselli, Pat Flaherty, Milton Douglas, Elena Ulana and Charles Bruins in the cast, but their appearance in the released film has not been confirmed. Actors Lawrence Grant, Crauford Kent, Georgia Caine, Kit Guard, Margaret Bloodgood, Jean Chatburn, Mary Loos, Walter Long and William Desmond were listed in *HR* production charts, but their appearance in the released film has also not been confirmed. Modern sources, however, confirm Desmond and Long's appearance and list their characters as "Havre gendarme chief" and "Pirate captain" respectively. Modern sources indicate that the following players appeared in the film: Arthur Belasco, Tex Driscoll, Edward

Hearn, Edmund Cobb, Charles Dunbar and Ed Brady (*Mercenary Scouts*); Olive Carey (*Madame Renavent*); Frank Hagney and Constantine Romanoff (*Pirates*); Mary Foy (*Duenna*); Zaruhi Elmassian (*Voice of Suzette*); Harry Tenbrook (*Suitor*); Ralph Brooks (*Marie's suitor*); Wilfred Lucas (*Herald at ball*); and Jack Mower (*Nobleman*). In addition, modern sources note the following about the film: Edouard Lippe was Nelson Eddy's vocal coach; and five songs from the original stage production of *Naughty Marietta* were featured in the film, with new lyrics added by Gus Kahn for songs "Tramp, Tramp, Tramp" and " 'Neath the Southern Moon." Some controversy reportedly arose over the inclusion of the song "Ah, Sweet Mystery of Life" in the film because it was known by many to be the theme song of Forest Lawn Cemetery.

According to a *NYT* news item, Woody Allen's 1971 comedy film, *Bananas*, features a scene in which a character is tortured by being forced to listen to the continuous playing of the record of *Naughty Marietta*.

Naughty Marietta was nominated for an Academy Award for Best Picture of 1935, and sound engineer Douglas Shearer won an Academy Award for his work on the film. The picture was also named by the *FD* critics poll as one of the ten best pictures of 1935, and won the *Photoplay* Gold Medal Award for best picture. A television adaptation of *Naughty Marietta*, directed and produced by Max Liebman, and starring Patrice Munsel and Alfred Drake, aired on the NBC television network on 15 Jan 1955.

DV 17 Apr 1934, p. 4. *DV* 18 Feb 1935, p. 3. *FD* 20 Feb 1935, p. 9. *HR* 13 Oct 1934, p. 3. *HR* 26 Oct 1934, p. 1. *HR* 5 Dec 1934, p. 3. *HR* 10 Dec 1934, p. 5. *HR* 13 Dec 1934, p. 1. *HR* 14 Dec 1934, p. 8. *HR* 15 Dec 1934, p. 4. *HR* 18 Dec 1934, p. 4. *HR* 20 Dec 1934, p. 7. *HR* 22 Dec 1934, p. 7. *HR* 26 Dec 1934, p. 6. *HR* 7 Jan 1935, p. 8, 10. *HR* 8 Jan 1935, p. 4. *HR* 12 Jan 1935, p. 4. *HR* 14 Jan 1935, p. 6. *HR* 16 Jan 1935, p. 2. *HR* 26 Jan 1935, p. 4. *HR* 11 Feb 1935, p. 8. *HR* 18 Feb 1935, p. 3. *HR* 26 Mar 1935, p. 2. *MPD* 19 Feb 1935, p. 4. *MPH* 23 Feb 1935, p. 66. *MPH* 2 Mar 1935, p. 54. *MPSI* Apr 1935, p. 11, 48. *NYT* 23 Mar 1935, p. 11. *Var* 27 Mar 1935, p. 15.

EL NAVAJO (Native Americans, Navajo)
Santa Fe Railway, Film Bureau, Chicago. **1945.** Sd; col. 45 min.

Educational/Cultural. [*Not viewed*]. The Navajo Reservation, as photographed by the Santa Fe Railway, is shown. Also included are glimpses of work at Ganado Mission. *Indians of North America-Reservations. Missions. Navajo Indians.*

Note: This film was listed in an educational film catalog. No additional information about the film's release has been found.

NAVAJO (Native Americans, Navajo, Ute)
Bartlett-Foster Productions, Inc. *Dist* Lippert Pictures, Inc. Feb **1952**; New York premiere: 20 Feb 1952; Prod: 9 Oct—17 Dec 1950 [©B-F Productions; 7 Dec 1951; LP1494]. Sd (Western Electric Recording); b&w. 8 reels, 6,349 or 6,279 ft. 70-71 min. PCA cert no. 15360.

Prod Hall Bartlett. *Dir* Norman Foster. *Wrt* Norman Foster. *Dir of photog* Virgil E. Miller. *Cam op* Ernest Smith. *Asst cam* Craig Smith. *Ed* Lloyd Nosler. *Mus* Leith Stevens. [*Narr spoken by* Sammy Ogg]. [*Interpreter* Keeyah Deshine].

Cast: [Francis Key Teller (*Son of the Hunter*)], [John Mitchell (*Grey Singer*)], [Mrs. Kee Teller (*Good Weaver*)], [Billy Draper (*Billy, Ute guide*)], [Hall Bartlett (*Indian school counsellor*)], [Virgil E. Miller (*Trader*)], [Cozy McSparron (*Himself, trading post owner*)], [Eloise Teller], [Linda Teller].

Youth, Western. [*Print viewed*]. In 1940, on the Navajo Indian Reservation, Son of the Hunter, a seven-year-old boy, runs a race every morning as he tends his sheep and goats so that the sun, his true father, will see him and know that he wants a horse. After hearing an owl hoot three times in daylight, Son of the Hunter tells Grey Singer, a former medicine man whom the boy's mother, Good Weaver, has let stay with them because he has no family of his own. Grey Singer, whom the boy calls his grandfather, realizes that the owl's presence means they must now move. As Son of the Hunter's father has been away for a long time working for the railroad, Grey Singer, who teaches the boy about their people's traditions, takes him to look for pasture land and to get piñon nuts above the Great Rock Canyon, known to the white man as Canyon de Chelly. During their long travel they come to a pile of stones, which Grey Singer says has been there for one hundred years. As directed by the older man, the boy throws a rock on the pile along with a juniper stick and makes a wish that they will find many piñon nuts and that he will not have to wait too long for a horse. At the Great Rock Canyon, which has been a stronghold for the Navajo, Grey Singer points out ruins of their ancestors and tells Son of the Hunter that their people gathered there for protection during their war with white soldiers; they would not have been found, but their enemies, the Ute, betrayed them to the soldiers. Most of the Navajos were starved into surrendering, then taken far away, the older man relates. Grey Singer's mother, however, escaped from the soldiers and lived in a secret cave for three years.

Son of the Hunter is proud that the survivors killed white soldiers with rocks, and as he picks piñon nuts, the boy tells Grey Singer of his hatred for all whites. Grey Singer warns that evil thoughts lead only into darkness and advises that the boy think of beauty and follow the path of light. At night, as evil spirits lead the boy to think of his starving ancestors, the voice of the wind awakens him and he sees a rattlesnake approach. He is about to kill it with a rock, when Grey Singer takes the rock away and says that they do not kill their brothers, the animals and snakes. He then sings a chant so that the snake will not be offended. At the Chinlee Valley Store, Son of the Hunter overhears people say that the white chief in Washington has determined that all Indian children between the ages of six and twelve must go to school. Son of the Hunter does not want to go. At night, they camp at Rock Standing Up, where Grey Singer talks to the stars to find a place with water and pasture for the sheep. They return to their hogan and leave with Good Weaver and the boy's sisters. After traveling many days, they find land with a big water hole and peach trees, which they decide will be their new home. Grey Singer leaves to find Good Weaver's husband, as she believes that he will return once he learns about the new home. Son of the Hunter explores the area alone and in the rocks finds a coyote trap, old pictures drawn on a wall and human bones. Grey Singer returns with food and news that Good Weaver's husband has taken another wife, who is half-white, and that he is in jail. Son of the Hunter's hatred of whites increases with this news, while his mother stoically urges them to forget about her husband and get to work on their new land. Grey Singer soon realizes that he is dying as a result of the trip and following tradition, asks the family to take him, with food and water to last four days, to a place where he can die alone. He gives Son of the Hunter his horse and tells the boy that his body, which has been lent to him, will go back to the earth and his spirit to the land of peace from whence it came. He urges the boy to always follow the path of light and to never let evil thoughts grow. By dawn of his second day alone, Grey Singer has died. Son of the Hunter is sent to the trading post by his mother, and while in town, he is apprehended by police and taken to a school. He refuses to give his name, because he thinks the whites would then have power over him, and views the other Indian boys as traitors to their race for learning the white man's tongue. The white counsellor, trying to establish a friendship, offers Son of the Hunter his pocketknife, and the boy grabs it and runs off. The counsellor goes with a Ute guide, Billy, whom Son of the Hunter despises, to a Franciscan mission to find the boy, and they learn that Good Weaver and one of her daughters have died from sickness, and that the boy's other sister is now being taken care of by nuns. Son of the Hunter finds his hogan burned and cooking utensils broken. With evil thoughts, he goes off to hide. The boy's description is sent to traders and the Navajo police. He returns to Rock Standing Up, where he remembers the comforting thought from Grey Singer that nothing really dies and that he will be together with his family again some day. The next day, faced with hunger, he goes to the Chinlee Valley Store and attempts to trade the pocketknife for food. When he is recognized from the circulated descriptions, he runs off. The school is notified, and soon the counsellor and Billy trail the boy to the canyon. Seeing his pursuers, the boy covers his tracks, then climbs up the Canyon of Death. As dusk sets in, the counsellor and Billy set up camp hoping the boy will come down when he sees their fire. Despite being frightened by human bones and a skull, the boy remains all night, and the next day, Billy hears him pounding the wall to make a coyote trap. Billy climbs and is injured by falling rocks set for the trap. While the counsellor climbs to help Billy, Son of the Hunter goes to their camp to get their food. The counsellor yells to the boy to get help for Billy, but he runs off. At night, he tries to forget his pursuers, but the wind of the cold night seems to him like the voice of Grey Singer telling him to put aside evil thoughts. The boy then realizes that the men are not his enemies, but friends, and he runs to the valley store for help with the good thought that in everything there is beauty. *Indians of North America–Social life and customs. Navajo Indians. Rites and ceremonies. Escapes. Grand Canyon (AZ). Guides. Horses. Medicine men. Missions. Mothers and sons. School superintendents and principals. Trading posts. Ute Indians.*

Note: The opening credits of this film contain the following statement: "This motion picture was filmed entirely on the Navajo Indian Reservation." The working title of this film was *The Voice of the Wind*. This was Hall Bartlett's first film as a producer. According to news stories, Bartlett began his career in Hollywood as an actor and wrote four treatments that did not sell before Stanley

Kramer, who had become a close friend, advised him to give up acting and become a producer. Bartlett raised $25,000 for this film in Los Angeles and from family and friends in his hometown of Kansas City. Director Norman Foster, a friend of Bartlett, agreed to work without pay and share the revenues with Bartlett. At the Navajo Indian Reservation in northeastern Arizona, Bartlett received the approval of the tribal council for members of the tribe to act in the film. Most of the film was shot at Canyon de Chelly, Death Canyon and the trading post of Chinle. The company selected as their star seven-year-old Francis Key Teller, who did not speak English and had never seen a film. John Mitchell, who played the role of "Grey Singer," was an elderly medicine man. News stories state that he was paid a bale of hay and a sheep before shooting every day.

According to *Var*, the score by Leith Stevens was an adaptation of original Indian music. Veteran cinematographer Virgil E. Miller came out of semi-retirement to work on the film. Miller, who, in his forty-year career, had shot over 250 features and 55 Fitzpatrick travelogues and headed Paramount's camera department, had recently taken a part-time job repairing cameras. He shot the film with only a camera, tripod and four reflectors, using a crew of three. Miller, who played a small role in the film, stated in a *LAT* article following production, "I have made up my mind that in my future pictures I again will try to achieve simple, natural setups, as far as possible, and to avoid any of the customary so-called box-office cliches and standards." Miller's black-and-white cinematography in this film was nominated for an Academy Award. Production of the film cost $24,220 and a total of $51,000 was spent by the end of post-production. Lippert Pictures acquired the distribution rights, planning to release the film on the art house circuit. *Var* noted that Lippert's usual releases were "straight commercial, exploitation pictures."

In *Screen*, Dr. Harry Tschopik, who had lived among the Navajo, stated, "The film makes no pretense at documenting Navajo culture in its entirety, although details of Navajo belief, custom, and history are introduced in a casual, realistic manner whenever they are pertinent to the plot. Instead, the story focuses upon the dilemma of a small boy caught between two very different, and traditionally antagonistic, ways of life." Reviews were favorable concerning the film. *Var* called it "an offbeat film that ranks right along with, if not topping, most of the foreign art imports that have previously impressed cosmopolitan critics." The film was nominated for an Academy Award for best feature documentary, although *Newsweek* commented, "Documentary is a dull word for this moving and unusual film." It won the top award at the Edinburgh Film Festival and won twenty-six national awards, many of which were given by national magazines. According to *HCN*, in Jan 1953, Robert Bice, an actor and writer, filed a $100,000 plagiarism suit charging that *Navajo* "embodied the 'dramatic core'" of a story he wrote in 1948, entitled "Little Moji." Bice contended that he showed the story in 1949 to director of photography Virgil Miller and that he told Miller of "distinctive production features which would save $50,000." Bice charged that his production idea was used "in shaping *Navajo*." No information concerning the disputation of the suit has been located.

AmCin May 1952, pp. 202-03, 216-20. *Box* 9 Feb 1952. *Christian Science Monitor* 26 Feb 1952. *Cleveland Plain Dealer* 27 Mar 1952, p. 13. *Cue* 23 Feb 1952. *DV* 28 Jan 1952, p. 3. *Exb* 13 Feb 1952, p. 3237. *Har* 16 Feb 1952, p. 27. *HCN* 26 Jan 1952. *HCN* 20 Jun 1952. *HCN* 21 Jun 1952. *HCN* 8 Jan 1953. *HR* 19 Sep 1951. *HR* 28 Jan 1952, p. 3 *HR* 29 Feb 1952. *HR* 3 Mar 1954. *LADN* 17 Jan 1952. *LADN* 26 Jan 1952. *LAEx* 26 Jan 1952. *LAT* 29 Jul 1951. *LAT* 2 Dec 1951. *LAT* 26 Jan 1952. *LAT* 21 Jun 1952. *MPD* 11 Feb 1951. *MPHPD* 9 Feb 1952, p. 1230. *Newsweek* 18 Feb 1952, pp. 102-03. *New Yorker* 8 Mar 1952. *NYT* 11 Feb 1951. *NYT* 21 Feb 1952, p. 24. *Screen* Apr 1952, p. 191. *SatRev* 15 Mar 1952. *Time* 17 Mar 1952. *Var* 19 Sep 1951. *Var* 30 Jan 1952, p. 6. *Var* 15 Feb 1952.

THE NAVAJO TRAIL (Native Americans, Navajo)

Great Western Productions, Inc. *Dist* Monogram Pictures Corp. 5 Jan **1945**; Prod: began 9 Oct 1944 [©Monogram Pictures Corp.; 26 Dec 1944; LP13097]. Sd; b&w. 5,035 ft. 56 min.

Supv by Charles J. Bigelow. *Dir* Howard Bretherton. *Asst dir* Bobby Ray. *Scr* Frank H. Young. *Orig story* Jess Bowers. *Photog* Marcel LePicard. *Art dir* E. R. Hickson. *Film ed* Arthur H. Bell. *Set dresser* Vin Taylor. *Sd* Glen Glenn.

Cast: Johnny Mack Brown (*Nevada*), Raymond Hatton (*Sandy*), Jennifer Holt (*Mary Trevor*), Riley Hill (*Paul*), Jim Hood (*Rusty*), Jasper L. Palmer (*Sergeant Trevor*), Edmund Cobb (*Farr*), Bud Osborne (*Brad*), Earl Crawford (*Joe*), Charles King (*Red*), Ray Bennett (*Slim Ramsey*), Tom Quinn (*Tober*), Josh Carpenter (*Steve*), Mary MacLaren (*Stella Ramsey*).

Western. [*Not viewed*]. Sandy, an undercover agent for the U.S. Marshal's Office, is waiting at his ranch for a visit from his old friend Nevada, a fellow undercover agent, when he is met by Sergeant Trevor of the Texas Rangers. Just as Trevor tells Sandy that he is tracking an escaping outlaw named Slim Ramsey, he is shot in the back by Ramsey, who then escapes on Sandy's horse. Nevada arrives at the ranch, and learning what has happened, tracks Ramsey to a nearby cabin, where the outlaw mistakes him for another hunted man. Nevada continues the deception, and when he brags about his efficiency at selling stolen horses, Ramsey takes him to his boss, Farr, who makes Nevada part of the gang. After Tober, another outlaw, is shot by Farr for failing to meet his boss's expectations, Nevada takes him to the cabin of Sergeant Trevor's daughter Mary, where Paul, a

Texas Ranger, waits to question him once he is nursed back to health. Meanwhile, Sandy arrives in town with a herd of horses, which he claims to have stolen from the Indians, and offers to sell them to Farr. The outlaw leader, however, learns of Sandy's true identity as a U.S. Marshal. Soon thereafter, another member of the gang discovers Tober at Mary's cabin, and after overhearing his confession to Paul, he summons the gang. Paul, in turn, rides off to find Nevada and Sandy. Farr and his men attack the cabin, but Mary and Tober are able to hold them off long enough for Nevada, Sandy, and Paul to arrive and capture the outlaws. *Horse thieves. Undercover agents. United States. Marshals.* Confession (Law). Friendship. Gunshot wounds. Murder. Navajo Indians. Nursing back to health. Ranches. Rescues. Texas. Texas Rangers.

Note: The working title of this film was *The Texas Terror.* The film was also reviewed under the title *Navajo Trails.* According to *HR* news items, Raphael Bennett, Henry Carr, Sam Appel and Boone Hazlett were cast, but their participation in the released film has not been determined. Modern sources include Edward Cassidy in the cast.

DV 2 Mar 1945, p. 3. *Exb* 7 Mar 1945, p. 1674. *HR* 6 Oct 1944, p. 11. *HR* 9 Oct 1944, p. 9. *HR* 24 Oct 1944, p. 13. *HR* 2 Mar 1945, p. 3. *HR* 22 Mar 1946, p. 3. *MPHPD* 10 Mar 1945, p. 2349.

THE NAVY COMES THROUGH (Latino, Austrian Americans)
RKO Radio Pictures, Inc. *Dist* RKO Radio Pictures, Inc. 30 Oct 1942; World premiere at Treasure Island Naval Base, San Francisco, CA: 27 Oct 1942; *Prod:* 2 Jun—late Jul 1942 [©RKO Radio Pictures, Inc.; 6 Oct 1942; LP11717]. Sd (RCA Sound System); b&w. 7,357 ft. 80-82 min. PCA cert no. 8509.

Prod Islin Auster. *Dir* A. Edward Sutherland. *Asst dir* Edward Killy. *Scr* Roy Chanslor and Aeneas MacKenzie. *Adpt* Earl Baldwin and John Twist. *Dir of photog* Nicholas Musuraca. *Spec eff* Vernon L. Walker. *Art dir* Albert D'Agostino and Carroll Clark. *Ed* Samuel E. Beetley. *Set dec* Darrell Silvera and Harley Miller. *Gowns* Renie. *Mus dir* C. Bakaleinikoff. *Mus score* Roy Webb. *Rec* Bailey Fesler. *Tech adv* Capt. James A. Randall.

Source: Based on the short story "Pay to Learn" by Borden Chase in *The Saturday Evening Post* (14 Jan 1939).

Cast: Pat O'Brien [(*Michael Mallory*)], George Murphy [(*Lieutenant Thomas L. Sands*)], Jane Wyatt [(*Myra Mallory*)], Jackie Cooper [(*Joe "Babe" Dudson*)], Carl Esmond [(*Richard "Dutch" Kroner*)], Max Baer [(*Berringer*)], Desi Arnaz [(*Tarriba*)], Ray Collins [(*Captain McCall*)], Lee Bonnell [(*Kovac*)], Frank Jenks [(*Sampier*)], John Maguire [(*James Bayliss*)], Frank Fenton [(*Hodum*)], Joey Ray [(*Dennis*)], Marten Lamont [(*Navy doctor*)], [Cyril Ring (*Officer*)], [Edgar Dearing (*C.P.O.*)], [Monte Montague (*Third mate*)], [Bud Geary (*Quartermaster*)], [Malcolm Waite (*Top lookout*)], [William Haade (*Marine sergeant*)], [Mary Young (*Mrs. Duttson*)], [Joe Cunningham (*Mr. Duttson*)], [Ralph Dunn (*Police officer*)], [Lyle Latell (*Oiler*)], [Max Waizman (*German agent*)], [Stanley Andrews (*Judge advocate*)], [Joe Girard (*Naval captain*)], [Bob Stevenson (*First officer of Odin*)], [William Vaughn (*Captain of Odin*)], [Helmut Dantine (*Young German seaman*)], [Egon Brecher (*German sub commander*)], [Sigurd Tor (*German first officer*)], [Howard Lane, Fred Sweeney (*Lookouts*)], [Hans Schumm, Hans von Twardowski, George Blagoi (*Captains of sub*)], [Nick Vehr, Jack Martin, Sven Borg (*First officers of sub*)], [George Melford (*Chief engineer*)], [Russell Hoyt].

Sea, World War II, Drama. [*Print viewed*]. At a Navy court of inquiry in Washington, D.C., Chief Gunnersmate Michael Mallory testifies that the negligence of Lieutenant Thomas L. Sands caused a lethal explosion aboard their ship. Protesting his innocence but unable to clear his name, Tom resigns his commission and renounces his sweetheart, nurse Myra Mallory, who happens to be Mike's sister. When war is declared after the bombing of Pearl Harbor, Myra enlists as a Navy nurse, while her brother is given command of a gunnery crew assigned to protect a Merchant Marine ship on its voyage across the Atlantic to Belfast. Tom, who has rejoined the Navy as an enlisted man, is assigned to Mike's crew. Other crew members include Joe "Babe" Dudson, an eager young seaman; Tarriba, a Cuban who feels a debt to the U.S. for liberating his country; Richard "Dutch" Kroner, an Austrian violin virtuoso who is wanted by the Germans; and Berringer, a former boxer. Once they are settled in their quarters, the men begin to gossip about Tom's dubious past. Soon after leaving port, the ship is attacked by a German submarine, and James Bayliss, one of the recruits, is wounded. Because the ship has no medical facilities, the captain signals for a medic from the hospital convoy,

and Myra accompanies the doctor on board. As a thick fog spreads, the ship receives a report of a German battleship in nearby waters. With danger imminent, Myra insists upon seeing Tom. Mike delivers her message, but warns Tom that Myra will never be happy until she forgets him. Consequently, when Myra tells Tom that she still loves him, he makes up a story about being in love with someone else. The next day, as Dutch plays a waltz on his violin, German dive bombers attack the ship and Myra is knocked unconscious by some falling debris. Tom leaves his post to carry Myra to safety, but when Berringer, the only man who can attest to Tom's motivation, is killed in the attack, the others accuse him of cowardice and abandoning his post. Soon after the attack, Babe, an amateur shortwave radio operator, unscrambles a German radio message from a submarine on its way to rendezvous with a German supply ship. Mike convinces the captain to intercept the ship, and after the Americans fire a shot across the ship's bow, the Germans surrender. Mike and his crew then board the German ship, but Tom, suspicious of the ease with which the Germans surrendered, cautions Mike to hold the crew on board as insurance. This frightens one of the Germans into confessing that a torpedo has been set to explode. After disarming the torpedo, Mike asks Tom to navigate the ship to Belfast. As an alternative, Mike suggests arming the torpedoes and delivering them to the German subs to detonate. Donning German uniforms, the Americans sink several subs until their ruse is discovered. Attacked by two submarines at once, the American gunners sink one of the boats when the ship's magazine catches fire. After Tom risks his life to pull Mike from the flames, the Merchant Marine ship comes to the rescue and sinks the other submarine. Tom's courage forces Mike to realize that he has misjudged him, and Tom is reinstated as an officer when the ship reaches land. After he and Myra reconcile, Tom says goodbye at the Naval base, and then marches off with Mike on a new mission. *Courage. False accusations. Patriotism. United States. Navy. World War II.* Austrians. Brothers and sisters. Cubans. Fog. Germany. Navy. Gun accidents. Merchant Marine. Nurses. Radio. Short wave. Reconciliation. Rescues. Ships. Submarine boats. Trials. Violinists.

Note: The working titles of this film were *Pay to Learn* and *Battle Stations.* The opening credits feature a foreword that reads: "The Navy comes through has been such an established fact that it is now taken for granted. As a result, we do not realize that the backbone of the Navy is not ships, planes and submarines—BUT MEN." According to the *DV* review, Borden Chase's short story "Pay to Learn" was the only story ever to be published twice by *SEP*. A *HR* news item notes that this production marked the studio's first use of a new radio signal trademark that spelled out the word "victory." Prior to this, the studio's radio signal trademark spelled out "RKO."

According to pre-production news items in *HR*, Eddie Albert was slated for the role of "Thomas Sands" until a scheduling conflict prevented his appearance. The role was then assigned to Randolph Scott, who was later replaced by George Murphy. Another pre-production news item in *HR* credits Robert Stevenson as director. This picture marked Islin Auster's debut as a RKO producer and Lee Bonnell's last appearance before joining the Coast Guard. News items in *HR* note that art director Carroll Clark and Albert D'Agostino developed a special sky and horizon machine for this film that created the effect of water motion against the horizon. The *HCN* adds that the sea shots were filmed on land using rocking arc lamps that projected waves upon an acre of muslin. The guns in the film were built from junkyard materials, according to *HCN*. The film's world premiere was held on Navy Day at the Treasure Island Naval Base in San Francisco, CA. This picture received an Academy Award nomination for Best Special Effects. In Jan 1943, the story was dramatized on "Anchors Away," a government-sponsored radio program broadcast over the Mutual Network. Henry Fonda, who was in the Navy at the time, played the part of Thomas Sands in that production. Pat O'Brien and George Murphy reprised their roles in a *Lux Radio Theatre* broadcast on 3 May 1943. Another version was presented on 29 Nov 1943.

Box 17 Oct 1942, p. 3. *DV* 14 Oct 1942, p. 3. *FD* 15 Oct 1942, p. 6. *HCN* 27 Jun 1942. *HR* 13 Jan 1942, p. 3. *HR* 27 Mar 1942, p. 2. *HR* 31 Mar 1942, p. 2. *HR* 1 Jun 1942, p. 6. *HR* 24 Jul 1942, p. 7. *HR* 27 Aug 1942, p. 1. *HR* 5 Oct 1942, p. 7. *HR* 14 Oct 1942, p. 3. *HR* 20 Oct 1942, p. 1. *MPHPD* 17 Oct 1942, p. 957. *NYT* 12 Nov 1942, p. 30. *Var* 14 Oct 1942, p. 8.

NAZI AGENT (German Americans)
Metro-Goldwyn-Mayer Corp.; controlled by Loew's Inc. *Dist* Loew's Inc. Mar 1942; *Prod:* early Nov—16 Dec 1941 [©Loew's Inc.; 20 Jan 1942; LP11350]. Sd (Western Electric Sound System); b&w. 8 reels, 7,517 ft. 82-83 min. Passed by the National Board of Review. PCA cert no. 8025.

Prod Irving Asher. *Dir* Jules Dassin. [*Asst dir* Tom Andre]. *Scr* Paul Gangelin and John Meehan, Jr. *Based on an idea by* Lothar Mendes. *Dir of photog* Harry Stradling. *Art dir* Cedric Gibbons. *Assoc* Stan Rogers. *Film ed* Frank E. Hull. *Set dec* Edwin B. Willis. [*Assoc* Richard Pefferle]. *Gowns* Shoup. *Mus score* Lennie Hayton. *Rec dir* Douglas

Shearer. *Hair styles for Miss Ayars by* Sydney Guilaroff. *Makeup created by* Jack Dawn.

Cast: Conrad Veidt (*Otto Becker/Baron Hugo Von Detner*), Ann Ayars (*Kaaren De Relle*), Frank Reicher (*Fritz*), Dorothy Tree (*Miss Harper*), Ivan Simpson (*Professor [Jim] Sterling*), William Tannen (*Ludwig*), Martin Kosleck (*Kurt Richten*), Marc Lawrence (*Joe Aiello*), Sidney Blackmer (*Arnold Milbar [also known as Frederick Williams]*), Moroni Olsen (*Brenner*), Pierre Watkin (*Grover Blaine McHenry*), [Margaret Bert (*Mrs. Dennis*)], [Mark Daniels, Robert Davis (*Taxi drivers*)], [Harry B. Stafford (*Elderly man*)], [Roger Moore (*Messenger*)], [Stuart Crawford (*Radio commentator's voice*)], [Hal Cooke (*Clerk*)], [George Noisom (*Bellboy*)], [Roland Varno (*Bauer*)], [William Norton Bailey (*Cigar clerk*)], [Tim Ryan (*Officer*)], [Tom Stevenson (*Headwaiter*)], [Christian Rub (*Mohr*)], [Hermine Sterler (*Mrs. Mohr*)], [Jeff York (*Keeler*)], [Jessie Arnold (*Landlady*)], [Cliff Danielson (*Youth*)], [James Millican (*Operator*)], [Philip Van Zandt, George Magrill (*Thugs*)], [Brick Sullivan (*Radio operator*)], [Joe Yule (*Barney*)], [Bernadene Hayes (*Rosie*)], [Art Belasco, Charles Sherlock (*Detectives*)], [William Post, Jr. (*Harry's voice*)], [Clyde Courtright (*Doorman*)], [Polly Bailey (*Overweight woman*)], [Joe Gilbert (*Sub-radio person*)], [Walter Byron (*Officer*)], [Edward Hearn, Jack Daley, Drew Demerest, Wilbur Mack (*Reporters*)], [Baldy Cooke (*Waiter*)], [Frank Marlowe, Ernie Alexander, Duke York (*Sailors*)], [Ray Teal (*Officer Graves*)], [Russell Simpson, Robert Homans (*Captains*)], [Roy Barcroft (*Chief Petty Officer*)], [Barbara Bedford].

Espionage, Drama. [*Print viewed*]. Kindly German-American bookstore owner and stamp collector Otto Becker is rejoicing in a recent acquisition given to him by his friend, Prof. Jim Sterling, when his twin brother, German consul Baron Hugo von Detner pays him a visit. The brothers have not seen each other since Otto fled Nazi Germany over eight years before. Although Otto tells Hugo that he has happily become an American citizen, Hugo suggests that the bookshop would make an excellent message exchange site for German agents. Otto angrily refuses Hugo's suggestion, but when Hugo reminds Otto that he entered the country illegally, then reveals that Otto's long-time assistant, Miss Harper, is a Nazi operative, Otto knows that he has no choice. Some time later, when Otto hears a radio news report about a bombed ship and realizes that his shop was used to relay information to the saboteurs, he determines to inform the police. He tries to give a secret letter to Jim, but Miss Harper observes him and that night Hugo announces that Jim has had an "accident." Hugo draws a gun on Otto, but in an ensuing struggle, Hugo is killed. Because there are several Nazi agents waiting outside, Otto decides to shave his beard, exchange clothes with Hugo and assume his identity. Otto then goes to Hugo's apartment, where he meets dress designer Kaaren De Relle, who apparently is one of Hugo's operatives. The next morning, Fritz, Hugo's butler and an old family servant, recognizes a scar on Otto's shoulder, but says nothing. Meanwhile, Otto orders Ludwig, the consulate chauffeur, to stop the car at a cigar store and there uses a public telephone to anonymously tip the police about the two agents responsible for the sabotage. Otto then goes to Hugo's luncheon appointment and encounters Arnold Milbar, a Nazi posing as an American businessman named Frederick Williams. During lunch, Kaaren arrives and makes a point of snubbing "Hugo" when someone offers to introduce them. That evening, Otto goes to see Brenner, the head of the local Gestapo, and learns of the arrest of the two agents. Brenner and Milbar suspect a turncoat and suggest that it is Kaaren, whom Hugo had previously labeled "reluctant." Later, at the apartment, Fritz confronts Otto and explains that he hated Hugo's politics and wants to help Otto. Kaaren then arrives with information that is supposed to be passed on to Brenner, the name of a ship, the S.S. *Farrington*. While she is still in the apartment, Otto calls Brenner to tell him the name of the ship and say that Kaaren is absolutely reliable. Kaaren is startled that Hugo would help her and begins to soften toward him. The next evening, while Nazi agents plant explosives on the *Farrington*, Fritz, who knows that Kaaren is being forced to work for the Nazis to save her family, arranges for her to dine with Otto. Without revealing himself, Otto tells Kaaren that he will help her, but says that first he has a job to finish. The two then take a moonlit drive, listen to the radio and enjoy the music of Felix Mendelssohn, a Jewish composer banned by the Nazis. A few days later, Joe Aiello, who is one of Brenner's hired thugs, and trying to extort more money, inadvertently reveals to Otto that the *Farrington*

has been rigged to explode as it passes through the Panama Canal. Otto then sends Kurt Richten, Hugo's assistant, to Brenner to report Aiello and mails papers containing the names of all Nazi agents, except Kaaren, to the FBI. He also secretly calls the police to have them stop the *Farrington* and arrest Aiello. Brenner and Milbar find Aiello first, but in a gunfight, Brenner and Milbar are killed, and Aiello is wounded just as the police arrive. When Miss Harper and Richten learn about Aiello's arrest, they wait for "Hugo" at Otto's shop. Because Otto's canary happily sings when he arrives, Miss Harper suspects him, so Richten goes to the consulate to investigate. There he discovers that the information on the agents is missing and telephones Miss Harper to confirm her suspicions, but the police have already come to arrest her. The next day, the other agents are apprehended and the consulate is closed. Richten then goes to Otto, threatening to expose Kaaren to the police. Nothing will dissuade Richten until Otto offers to accompany him back to Germany as a hostage to ensure Kaaren and her family's safety. After Otto makes Fritz promise to look after Kaaren but not reveal his secret, he boards a ship bound for Germany, and is humiliated by jeers from the people at the dock. As he catches his last glimpse of America, Otto is despondent, but gains strength as the ship passes the Statue of Liberty. Consuls. Fratricide. German Americans. Impersonation and imposture. Nazis. Sabotage. Spies. Twins. Apartments. Beards. Booksellers and bookselling. Businessmen. Butlers. Canaries. Chauffeurs. Citizenship. Couturiers. Extortion. Gestapo. Gunfights. Hostages. Letters. Felix Mendelssohn. Nobility. Panama Canal (Panama). Police. Postage-stamps–Collectors and collecting. Professors. Radio programs. Restaurants. Romance. Scars. Secret documents. Ships. Statue of Liberty National Monument (New York City). Telephone. United States. Federal Bureau of Investigation.

Note: Working titles for the film included *House of Spies* and *Out of the Past*. The picture was reviewed in *Salute to Courage* by *Var* and some other sources. According to a *HR* news item, Ludwig Stossel was cast in the production, but he was not in the released film. Another news item includes Pat O'Malley in the cast, but his appearance in the released film has not been confirmed. *Nazi Agent* was the first feature film directed by Jules Dassin, who had previously directed short subjects at M-G-M. After leaving M-G-M in 1947, Dassin directed two well-received films for Universal, *Brute Force* and *The Naked City*. Dassin was blacklisted in the late 1940s and moved to Europe, where he directed a number of critically regarded pictures over the next thirty years. Dassin, who was married to Greek actress Melina Mercouri, star of his 1959 film *Never on Sunday*, died in 1995.

Box 24 Jan 1942. *DV* 21 Jan 1942, p. 3. *FD* 21 Jan 1942. *HR* 14 Nov 1941, p. 8. *HR* 27 Nov 1941, p. 4. *HR* 12 Dec 1941, p. 8. *HR* 16 Dec 1941, p. 4. *HR* 17 Dec 1941, p. 7. *HR* 21 Jan 1942, p. 3. *MPHPD* 24 Jan 1942, p. 474. *NYT* 13 Jun 1942, p. 11. *Var* 10 Jun 1942, p. 8.

NAZI TERROR *see* **THE WANDERING JEW**

'NEATH THE ARIZONA SKIES (Native Americans)
Lone Star Productions; Monogram Pictures Corp.; A Paul Malvern Production. *Dist* Monogram Pictures Corp. 5 Dec 1934 [©Monogram Pictures Corp.; 15 Jan 1935; LP5249]. Sd (Balsley & Phillips Recording System); b&w. 6 reels. 52, 54 or 56-57 min.
   Dir Harry Fraser. *Story and scr* Burl Tuttle. *Photog* Archie Stout. *Art dir* E. R. Hickson. *Film ed* Charles Hunt and [Carl Pierson]. *Rec* Ralph Shugart.
   Cast: JOHN WAYNE [(*Chris Morrell*)], Sheila Terry [(*Clara Moore*)], Shirley Jean Rickert [(*Nina Morrell*)], Jack Rockwell [(*Vic Byrd*)], Yakima Canutt [(*Sam Black*)], Weston Edwards, Buffalo Bill, Jr. [(*Jim Moore*)], Phil Keefer [(*Jameson Hodges*)], [Frank Hall Crane (*Express agent*)], [George Hayes (*Matt Downing*)], [Earl Dwire].
   Western. [*Print viewed*]. As cowboy Chris Morrell and Nina, his adopted half-Indian daughter, prepare to leave town to find Nina's long-lost father, whom they need to sign papers that will entitle Nina to a $50,000 Indian oil claim, they are accosted by Sam Black and his gang. After an exhausting chase, Chris tells Nina to take their horse and ride to a ranch owned by friend Bud Moore, while he stalks the gang on foot. In a grove, Chris lures the men off their horses, then causes the animals to stampede. Although Chris manages to take one horse for himself, he is injured while escaping and eventually falls off the horse, unconscious. While on the ground, Chris is approached by a man who has just robbed an express office. The man, believing Chris is still unconscious, switches clothes with him and leaves him to be discovered by Clara Moore, Bud's sister. After Chris introduces himself, Clara tells him that Bud was killed in a range war and that Vic Byrd has since taken over their ranch. Clara then takes Chris to her homestead and introduces him to her brother Jim, whom Chris

recognizes as the robber. While Chris tells Clara about Nina and Sam Black, Jim and Vic Byrd, who is holding Nina at his ranch, eavesdrop through an open window. On the range, Byrd and Jim locate Black and his still stranded gang and offer to exchange Nina for $10,000 and Chris's scalp. Then, Chris, who has met up with Matt Downing, an old friend who works as a cook at Byrd's ranch, sees Byrd kill Jim and flee with the stolen express money. Byrd returns to his ranch to fetch Nina but is killed by Tom, one of his hands, who is also Nina's real father. As Black and his men arrive at Byrd's ranch with Clara as hostage, Chris and Tom confront the gang with gunshot. Once the showdown stalemates, Chris offers to exchange himself for Clara but, with Tom's help, tricks the outlaws and storms the house where Nina is hiding. During the ensuing scuffle, Tom is fatally shot and Byrd escapes with Nina on horseback. Chris eventually overtakes Byrd, who falls into a river with Nina, and drowns him during a fierce fight. Happily reunited with Nina, Chris returns to Clara's loving arms. *Cowboys. Foster children. Inheritance. Outlaws. Betrayal. Brothers and sisters. Chases. Cooks. Falls from heights. Fights. Gunshot wounds. Horses. Hostages. Indian agents. Indians of North America–Mixed blood. Murder. Oil. Parentage. Rescues. Rivers. Robbery. Romance.*

Note: Burl Tuttle's screen story was titled "Gun Glory." Although Charles Hunt is credited on the film, Carl Pierson is listed as the film's editor by press material and other contemporary sources. Tuttle's story and script were first used in a 1933 Superior Pictures' production called *Circle Canyon* (see entry above). Some aspects of the story, including the outlaws' motivation for pursuing "Nina," were either clarified or changed for this production. Modern sources add Artie Ortego (*Shorty*) and Tex Phelps, Herman Hack and Eddie Parker (*Henchmen*) to the cast, and list Earl Dwire's character name as "Tom, Nina's father."

Box 22 Dec 1934. p. *FD* 11 Dec 1934, p. 6. *MPH* 15 Dec 1934, p. 44. *Var* 20 Mar 1935, p. 31.

THE NEBRASKAN (Native Americans, Dakota)

Columbia Pictures Corp. *Dist* Columbia Pictures Corp. Dec **1953**; Prod: 16 Jun—29 Jun 1953 [©Columbia Pictures Corp.; 1 Dec 1953; LP3081]. Sd; col (Technicolor); 3-D. 7 reels, 5,998 ft. 68 min. PCA cert no. 16626.

Prod Wallace MacDonald. *Dir* Fred F. Sears. *Asst dir* Jack Corrick and Milton Feldman. *Scr* David Lang and Martin Berkeley. *Story* David Lang. *Dir of photog* Henry Freulich. *Technicolor col consultant* Francis Cugat. *Art dir* Robert Peterson. *Film ed* Al Clark and James Sweeney. *Set dec* Louis Diage. *Mus dir* Ross DiMaggio. *Sd eng* Frank Goodwin.

Cast: Phil Carey (*Wade Harper*), Roberta Haynes (*Paris*), Wallace Ford (*McBride*), Richard Webb (*Ace Eliot*), Lee Van Cleef (*Reno*), Maurice Jara (*Wingfoot*), Regis Toomey (*Col. Markham*), Jay Silverheels (*Spotted Bear*), Pat Hogan (*Yellow Knife*), Dennis Weaver (*Capt. DeWitt*), Boyd "Red" Morgan (*Sgt. Phillips*), Nick Thompson (*Medicine man*), Robert B. Williams, Glenn Thompson (*Troopers*), Frank Fenton (*Captain*), J. P. Catching (*Anderson*), Guy Teague (*Sergeant*), Bernie Gozier (*Warrior*).

Western. [*Not viewed*]. Wade Harper, an Army scout, and Wingfoot, his Indian aide, reach Fort Kearney, Nebraska, with a horde of Sioux Indians in hot pursuit. Led by Spotted Bear and his son, Yellow Knife, the Indians demand that Wingfoot be turned over to them for the murder of a tribal chieftain. Col. Markham, the commanding officer of the fort, refuses their demand, explaining that under the laws of the new state of Nebraska, Wingfoot is entitled to a fair trial. Rejecting the colonel's edict, the Indians threaten war. Wingfoot is jailed along with Reno, a renegade soldier, and forced to accompany him when he escapes that night. Harper, Capt. DeWitt and two other soldiers go after them. Despite Wingfoot's protests, Reno shoots at their pursuers, killing the three soldiers and wounding Wade. Posing as Army scouts, the two fugitives then join a group of cavalrymen from a distant fort. While riding with the platoon, Reno and Wingfoot help rescue a stagecoach under attack by Indians. Inside the coach are Ace Eliot, a gambler, and Paris, a beautiful young dance hall girl, bound for Omaha. Reno and Wingfoot volunteer to accompany the couple to McBride's way station. As soon as the cavalrymen are out of sight, Reno holds up the couple and forces Wingfoot to help him. Unexpectedly, Wade reappears and disarms the two men with the help of Ace. McBride, an ex-cavalryman who knows and welcomes Wade, gives the party lodging in his deserted way station. Having been informed by their scouts of Wingfoot's presence at McBride's, the Indians, led by Spotted Bear, come for him. Ace urges Wade to turn over Wingfoot, but Wade refuses to give in to the Sioux demands.

Though surrounded, the garrison fights off repeated attacks. When Ace shows his cowardice, Paris denounces him and joins Wade, with whom she had once been in love. After the Indians blast a gaping hole in the corner of McBride's building, Ace, frightened, attempts to kill Wade, but Wingfoot proves his allegiance by saving Wade's life and killing Ace. Led by Yellow Knife, a band of Sioux break into the building, kill Reno and abduct Paris. During the attack, Yellow Knife is knocked unconscious. Realizing that Paris is being held hostage, Wingfoot asks Spotted Bear to free the whites if he gives himself up. Spotted Bear agrees, but goes back on his word once Wingfoot surrenders. Meanwhile, Yellow Knife lies unconscious in a building engulfed in flames. After Wade risks his life to save the Indian lad, Yellow Knife repays him by admitting to the tribe that his father, not Wingfoot, killed the tribal chieftan. When Spotted Bear orders the medicine man to brand Wade with a red hot iron, Yellow Knife locks in mortal combat with his father, who is killed. With Spotted Bear's death, Paris, Wade, Wingfoot and McBride are freed by Yellow Knife, who, appointed chief by his tribe, promises peace. As the group starts back for Fort Kearney, Wade and Paris embrace. *Dakota Indians. False accusations. Fugitives. Jailbreaks. Renegades. Scouts (Frontier). Dance hall girls. Fathers and sons. Forts. Gamblers. Impersonation and imposture. Murder. Nebraska. Romance. United States. Army. Cavalry.*

Note: According to the film's pressbook, Pat Hogan, who plays "Dark Thunder," was the son of a full-blooded Oneida Indian.

Box 7 Nov 1953. *DV* 6 Nov 1953, p. 3. *Exh* 4 Nov 1953, p. 3634. *FD* 3 Dec 1953, p. 6. *Har* 7 Nov 1953, p. 179. *HR* 19 Jun 1953, p. 14. *HR* 6 Nov 1953, p. 3. *MPHPD* 7 Nov 1953, p. 2062. *Var* 4 Nov 1953, p. 6.

NEEDLE IN A HAYSTACK see TOP O' THE MORNING

NEGRO ARTISTS AT WORK see A STUDY OF NEGRO ARTISTS

THE NEGRO OF TODAY (African Americans)

C. B. Campbell Co. of N.Y. **1921**. Si; b&w. Length undetermined. [Feature length assumed.].

African American, Documentary. [No information about the precise nature of this film has been found.]. *African Americans.*

Note: According to information in the George P. Johnson Collection at the UCLA Special Collections Library, E. L. Cummings Distributing Co. of Pensacola, FL distributed the film in twelve southern states.

THE NEGRO SOLDIER (African Americans)

United States. War Department. Special Service Division. Army Service Forces; with the cooperation of The Signal Corps; Project 6022; Orientation Film #51. *Dist* War Activities Committee. Feb **1944**. Sd; b&w. 5 reels, 3,631 ft. 40, 42, or 46 min.

[*Supv* Col. Frank Capra]. [*Dir* Capt. Stuart Heisler]. [*Asst dir* Lt. Lee Katz, Lt. Holly Morse, George Blair and Ralph Donaldson]. [*Wrt* Carleton Moss]. [*Aide in script preparation* Jo Swerling]. [*Cam* Lt. Paul C. Vogel]. [*2d cam* Capt. Horace Woodward and C.P.O. Alan Thompson]. [*Asst cam* Sgt. William Birch, Sgt. Jack Hageny, Sgt. Lloyd Fromm and Sgt. Dean]. [*Spec eff* Consolidated Laboratories, Ray Mercer, Albert Schmidt, Gordon Jennings, Farciot Edouart and Paul Lerpae]. [*Film cutter* Sgt. Jack Ogilvie]. [*Asst film cutter* Sgt. Hugh Fowler]. [*Anim* Walt Disney Productions]. [*Church set des by* Haldane Douglas]. [*Mus dir* Dimitri Tiomkin]. [*Mus comp* Howard Jackson, Al Glasser, Maj. Paul Horgan, Maj. Meredith Willson and Earl Robinson]. *Mus* Army Air Forces Orchestra. [*Cond* Maj. Eddie Dunstedter]. [*Choir under the dir of* Jester Hairston]. [*Mr. Tiomkin's staff* William Grant Still, Earl Robinson, Al Glasser, Howard Jackson, Phil Moore, Calvin Jackson, Jester Hairston and Cpl. Dave Tamkin]. [*Orch* P. A. Marquardt, Leo Arnaud, E. G. Still and John C. Jackson]. [*Mus cutter* Jimmy Graham]. [*Asst mus cutter* Sgt. Ed. Hare]. [*Sd cutter* Cpl. Tom McAdoo]. [*Chief of sd* Lt. William Montague]. [*Sd crew* Sgt. Harold Lee, Cpl. William Hamilton and Pvt. Cyril Harper]. [*Prod mgr* Ralph Nelson]. [*2d asst dir* Capt. Mort Lewis]. [*Consultant* Maj. Charles Dollard]. [*Liaison officer* Capt. Maurice Monette]. [*Narr* Carleton Moss]. [*Tech adv* Carleton Moss]. [*Chief elec* Sgt. Howard Roberts]. [*Grip* Sgt. Cecil Axemear and Sgt. Ed Comport].

Cast: [Men and women of the Armed Forces of the United States], [Pvt. Robert Brooks], [Capt. Colin Kelly], [Sgt. Meyer Levin], [Sgt. Dorie Miller], [Sgt. Clyde Turner (*Church soloist*)], [Carleton Moss (*Minister*)], [William Broadus (*Jim*)], [Bertha Wolford (*Mrs. Bronson*)], [Lt. Norman Ford (*Robert Bronson*)], [Clarence Brooks (*Chaplain*)], [Joe Louis].

War documentary, Educational/cultural works. [*Print viewed*]. Inspired by the singing of one of his parishioners, an Army

sergeant, a minister of a black church addresses his congregation about the role of black soldiers in contemporary America. To emphasize the importance of America's resistance to Nazism, the minister reads passages from Hitler's book *Mein Kampf*, in which Hitler decries progress for blacks and calls for the extermination of all who oppose him. Using the 1932 championship bout between Joe Louis and Max Schmeling as a metaphor for the conflict between the United States and Germany, the minister details the participation of blacks in various struggles throughout American history, including the Revolutionary War, the War of 1812, the Civil War, the Spanish American War and World War I. Specific heroes of those wars—Peter Salem of the Revolutionary War, Thomas Wilson of the War of 1812 and Samuel Washington of World War I—are cited by the minister, as are various black military units, such as the 371st Infantry, which distinguished itself in combat during World War I. After mentioning many prominent blacks of the past and present, including Booker T. Washington and George Washington Carver, and citing the achievements of black academic institutions, such as Howard University and Tuskegee Institute, the minister recalls the 1936 Berlin Olympics in which black athletes such as Jesse Owens and Ben Johnson defeated their German opponents. As the minister reminds his congregation of the attack on Pearl Harbor and of German atrocities, a woman interrupts and starts to read from a letter written by her son Bob, a recently promoted army officer. In his letter, Bob describes his army training, from his induction to his intensive drilling and preparation for battle. The minister then describes the range of jobs for black men and women in the military, from fighter pilot, to quartermaster, to tank destroyer, to infantryman, to road builder, to anti-aircraft gunner. In a final prayer, the minister enjoins his congregation to participate in America's continuing fight for liberty and justice for all. *African Americans. United States. Army. World War II. Aerial combat. George Washington Carver. Churches. Combat. Germany. Army. Adolf Hitler. Japan. Army. Ben Johnson. Letters. Joe Louis. Mein Kampf (Book). Military posts. Military service, Voluntary. Ministers. Jesse Owens. Pearl Harbor (HI), attack on, 1941. Prayer. Max Schmeling. Tuskegee Institute. United States—History—Civil War, 1861-1865. United States—History—Revolutionary War, 1776-1783. United States—History—War of 1812. United States. Women's Army Corps. Booker T. Washington. Samuel Washington. Thomas Wilson. World War I.*

Note: The film opens with the following written statement: "In the film you are about to see free use has been made of motion pictures with historical backgrounds. Also, a few authentic incidents have been recreated. All other film comes from official War Department films, newsreels, United Nations sources and captured enemy material." The working title of the film was *The Negro Soldier in World War II*. According to government documents at NARS, work began on the scenario on 15 Jun 1942, and the first answer print was submitted for approval on 9 Jul 1943. The approximate cost of production was $78,254.01. In addition to film shot especially for the production, footage was used from American newsreels, U.S. government sources, Japanese newsreels, and a number of feature films including *Mr. Smith Goes to Washington*, *America*, *Triumph of the Will*, *The River*, *Yankee Doodle Goes to Town* and *Flying Tigers*, and the war documentaries *The Battle of Midway* and *December 7*. In addition to original music composed for the film, the score included a number of popular tunes and spirituals including "Since Jesus Came into My Heart," "Our Boys Will Shine," "This Is the Army, Mr. Jones," "Yankee Doodle Girl," "Sleepy Lagoon" and "Holy, Holy."

According to Capra's autobiography, the project began with Undersecretary of War Robert Patterson, whose adviser, Truman Gibson, showed alarming examples of discrimination against black troops in the South. According to modern sources, the Army's Information and Education Division conducted research on what kind of film could end racial confrontations as a test of social engineering. Capra asked his Research Branch to draw up a code for the depiction of blacks in their films, urging the avoidance of stereotypes and potentially divisive depictions for blacks and whites, by emphasizing the middle class. An early script for *The Negro Soldier* written by Marc Connelly, author of *The Green Pastures*, was deemed too dramatic, while a second draft by Ben Hecht and Jo Swerling was regarded as insufficiently factual. Originally the film was to be directed by William Wyler, who did research in Alabama with Moss and Connelly before his transfer to the Air Force, but direction was finally given to Stuart Heisler, who earlier directed *The Biscuit Eater*, which was filmed in the South and had a black child as one of its protagonists. According to *Var*, production of *The Negro Soldier* lasted over two years, requiring fourteen U.S. Army technicians and the services of black author Carleton Moss, who wrote the script, did research, technical advice, and played the pastor. Modern sources state that the Army rejected his first draft, entitled *Men of Color to Arms*, and Capra, according to his autobiography, ordered rewrites to take the anger out of Moss's scripts. Unable to mention segregation, Moss, in his script, showed black soldiers as comrades-in-arms while not violating the army's own segregation policy.

According to modern sources, shooting began in Jan 1943, with Heisler,

Moss, researcher Charles Dollard and a crew travelling to between nineteen and thirty Army camps, virtually every facility where black troops were trained. Modern sources also credit William Hornbeck as editor, and noted that the cast also included jazz pioneer W. C. Handy. According to modern sources, *The Negro Soldier* was approved for exhibition in Jan 1944 after an answer print was taken to the Pentagon by Anatole Litvak and examined by five of the top War Dept. officials, who suggested certain changes regarding racial sensibilities. These included the deletion of scenes of black officers, as well as a sequence of a black soldier in the hospital with a white nurse, the addition of shots showing World War I blacks in roles other than at the front lines, and the modification of the portrayal of combat experience of blacks in the current conflict. According to a government document dated 17 Jan 1944, Capra requested that two unrevised prints of the film be destroyed. A commercial release was undertaken at the urging of Moss and several groups to spread the film's message. The picture was approved by Elmer Davis of the Office of War Information for exhibition in all theaters except such southern centers as Atlanta, and the War Activities Committee planned national distribution. The Army Pictorial Service did not distribute it until it opened in commercial houses. According to modern sources, *The Negro Soldier* made even less than the meager returns for other government war documentaries, partly because its running time required a change in the length of average programs. Although not receiving as broad a commerical run as the *Why We Fight* films, *The Negro Soldier* became popular in nontheatrical circuits. According to government documents, a two-reel shortened version of the film was released in Jul 1944.

DV 15 Feb 1944. *DV* 24 Apr 1944, p. 7. *DV* 10 May 1944. *Film News* Apr 1944, p. 8. *HCN* 15 Feb 1944. *HCN* 14 Apr 1944. *HR* 15 Feb 1944, p. 3. *HR* 24 Apr 1944. *HR* 5 May 1944. *HR* 10 May 1944. *HR* 22 Jun 1944. *The Independent* 5 Aug 1944. *LADN* 15 Feb 1944. *LADN* 7 Apr 1944. *LAEx* 7 Apr 1944. *LASent* 30 Mar 1944. *LASent* 6 Apr 1944. *Nation* 11 Mar 1944, p. 316. *Newsweek* 27 Mar 1944, pp. 94, 96. *NYP* 22 Apr 1944. *New Yorker* 6 May 1944. *NYT* 22 Apr 1944, p. 8. *PM* 23 Apr 1944. *People's World (San Francisco)* 8 Apr 1944. *SatRev* 18 Mar 1944, p. 28. *Theatre Arts* Jun 1944, pp. 346-347. *Time* 27 Mar 1944, pp. 94, 96. *Var* 23 Feb 1944, p. 10.

NEVER LOVE A STRANGER (Jewish Americans)

M & A Alexander Productions; Allied Artists Pictures Corp.; A Harold Robbins Production; A Caryn Production. *Dist* Allied Artists Pictures Corp. 4 May 1958; Prod: 9 Sep—mid-Oct 1957 at Gold Medal Studios, NY [©Allied Artists Pictures Corp.; 17 Jun 1958; LP10835]. Sd; b&w; 1.85. 8,210 ft. 90-91 min. PCA cert no. 18906.

Prod Harold Robbins and Richard Day. *Assoc prod* Peter Gettinger. *Dir* Robert Stevens. *Asst dir* Chas. J. Maguire, Jr. and William Gerrity. *Scr* Harold Robbins and Richard Day. *Dir of photog* Lee Garmes. *Art dir* Leo Kerz. *Film ed* Sidney Katz. *Cost* Ruth Morley. *Furs* Reiss and Fabrizzio. *Mus* Raymond Scott. *Asst mus supv* Lawrence Elow. *Orch cond* Jack Shaindlin. *Orch* Nathan Van Cleave. *Sd rec* Ernest Zatorsky. *Prod mgr* Charles J. Maguire. *Casting* Selma Lynch.

Song(s): "Never Love a Stranger" and "Oh, Baby!" music by Raymond Scott, lyrics by Lawrence Elow. Main title vocal by Dorothy Collins.

Source: Based on the novel *Never Love a Stranger* by Harold Robbins (New York, 1948).

Cast: John Drew Barrymore [(*Frank Kane*)], Lita Milan [(*Julie*)], Robert Bray [(*"Silk" Fennelli*)], Steve McQueen [(*Martin Cabell*)], Salem Ludwig [(*Moishe Moscowitz*)], R. G. Armstrong [(*Flix*)], Douglas Rodgers [(*Brother Bernard*)], Felice Orlandi [(*Bert*)], Augusta Merighi [(*Mrs. Cozzolina*)], Vince Barbi, Abe Simon [(*"Fats" Crown*)], Dolores Vitina [(*Frances Kane*)], [Joseph Leberman (*Price*)], [Dort Clark (*Madigan*)], [Robert O'Connell (*Kelly*)], [Michael O'Dowd (*Piggy*)], [John Dalz (*Father Quinn*)], [Mike Enserro (*Tony, the bartender*)], [Gino Ardito (*Willy*)], [Joseph Costa (*Joe*)], [Walter Burke (*Keough*)].

Crime, Drama. [*Print viewed*]. Frank Kane is shot in a New York City 12th Avenue garage, but manages to drive away before dying behind the wheel and crashing into a cement wall. Years earlier, in 1912, before Frank was born, Frances Kane, his pregnant mother, struggles to a boardinghouse run by Italian Mrs. Cozzolina: Mrs. Cozzolina puts her suitcase in a closet, but it accidentally falls behind a shelf and is forgotten after Frank's mother dies in childbirth. The baby is named Francis, after his mother and is sent to the Orphanage of St. Therese. In the spring of 1928, Frank works as a shoeshine boy and gets a big tip from ganster "Silk" Fennelli, who runs a protection and numbers racket in the local speakeasies. One day Frank, who still lives at the orphanage, encounters some neighborhood friends beating up Martin Cabell because he is Jewish. Frank comes to Marty's defense and Marty invites him over to his house to teach him how to fight. Frank falls in love with Marty's housekeeper, Julie, and becomes a "ratboy," collecting money for Silk's numbers racket. One day, Mrs. Cozzolina arrives at the Orphanage of St. Therese, and gives Brother Bernard the suitcase belonging to Frances Kane, which she discovered in the closet. Inside the suitcase is a Jewish Bible, and the church

board votes to send Frank to a Jewish school because of a law that states orphans must be placed among people with the same religious beliefs. Frank, meanwhile, is with Silk when he is shot by a rival gang, and Silk asks him to keep the $500 he has collected until he gets medical treatment. When Bernard, who has been like a father to Frank, informs Frank that the orphanage is sending him away because they have discovered he is Jewish, Frank feels betrayed, and refuses to accept his heritage. Frank goes to Julie and asks her to return the money to Silk, and leaves a marker for twenty dollars. He then runs away and hops a freight train. Silk takes an interest in Julie and pays for her singing lessons. In time, she becomes a nightclub performer, while Marty goes to college and earns his degree as a lawyer. However, Frank becomes an itinerant worker, and years of hard-living turn his hair gray. After working on many ships and docks, Frank returns to New York, taking hand-outs from soup kitchens, and working one day a week for the W.P.A. In 1935, Frank is accidentally hit by a truck while he is working, and Marty discovers him at the hospital. Frank bitterly asks Marty to forget that he ever saw him, but accepts twenty dollars, which he uses to pay his old marker to Silk. Silk immediately hires Frank, who is stunned to discover that Julie is the racketeer's lover. That day, Silk's rival, "Fats" Crown, tries to take over his racket, but Frank takes him and his thugs unaware and kills Fats. Over the course of the next two years, Frank and Silk engage in territorial battles with rival gangsters, until Frank suggests a way of ending the war. Silk calls a meeting of all the heavyweights, but to his surprise, Frank takes control of the meeting and appoints himself "commissioner" of the gangs. Frank insists that the gangsters form a peaceful network among themselves so they do not drive themselves out of business. Silk is the only person to protest, and Frank quiets him with a fist. Frank operates his gambling racket in New Jersey until the governor publicly declares war against him. Marty, as special prosecutor for the district attorney, is appointed to bring him to justice. One night, Marty and Frank meet alone in a roadside tavern, where Marty asks Frank to give himself up. Frank refuses and returns the twenty dollars he borrowed years earlier. Frank is unafraid of the threat of arrest, but Silk organizes the other gangsters against him because he is afraid Frank's cavalier attitude will also bring them down. Julie and Frank reunite and hide from Silk, who calls the police after Frank shows up at Julie's nightclub. One day, Frank's racketeer friend Moishe Moscowitz seeks his help in retiring. When he asks Frank if he is Jewish, Frank replies only that "some people say so," and urges Moishe to leave town quietly before the other racketeers learn of his retirement plans. Bernard comes to see Frank and brings him his mother's Bible, which he refused to accept years earlier. Bernard urges Frank to accept his heritage and reject his criminal life, but Frank refuses to heed him. Silk kidnaps Moishe, and hires a professional killer named Flix, who takes Frank and Julie hostage. Flix forces Frank to send for Marty, planning to frame Frank for Marty's murder, then kill them. When Marty arrives, however, Frank attacks Flix, and Marty reluctantly allows his prey to leave so he can rescue Moishe. Frank kills Silk after the gangster shoots him in the back, then struggles to his car intending to go to Julie, but dies before he reaches her. Later, Bernard receives a letter from Julie in which she tells him that she has given birth to Frank's illegitimate son, and now asks Bernard to provide the boy with the fatherly love that Frank never knew. *Jews. Moral corruption. Orphans. Racketeers. Adolescents. Bigotry. Boardinghouse mistresses. Boxing. Bullies. Catholics. Clergy. Debt. Fistfights. Friendship. Gunfights. Hired killers. Italian Americans. Kidnapping. Lawyers. Loyalty. Murder. Orphanages. Rivalry. Romance. Singers. Vagabonds.*

Note: This film was shot on location in New York City. The *HR* review made the following comments about the film: "A baby brought into a Catholic orphanage would in all likelihood be baptised a Catholic and, since the Catholic church has no racial nor national qualifications for membership, he would be as much a Catholic as any other. And no law would be violated unless he was deprived of a free exercise of his will in choosing his religion. The picture never says this....Having led you to expect an interesting conflict between Catholic and Jewish tradition the script makes no use of either. His people seem unimportant to the hero until a Jewish gangster is about to be put on the spot when he wants to retire. At this point Barrymore sacrifices his life protecting him."

Box 7 Jul 1958. *DV* 27 Jun 1958, p. 3. *Exh* 9 Jul 1958, p. 4485. *FD* 9 Jul 1958, p. 5. *FilmFacts* 3 Dec 1958, pp. 204-05. *Har* 5 Jul 1958, p. 106. *HR* 6 Sep 1957, p. 14. *HR* 18 Oct 1957, p. 10. *HR* 27 Jun 1958, p. 3. *MPHPD* 16 Aug 1958, p. 944. *NYT* 27 Nov 1958, p. 27. *STR* 14 Sep 1957. *Var* 25 May 1960, p. 7.

NEW BORDERTOWN see **BORDERTOWN**

THE NEW GOVERNOR see **THE NIGGER**

NEW MEXICO (Native Americans, Acoma)
Irving Allen Productions, Inc. *Dist* United Artists Corp. 24 Aug 1951; *Prod:* mid-Apr—early Jun 1950 [©Irving Allen Enterprises, Inc.; 18 May 1951; LP924]. Sd (RCA recording); col (Ansco Color). 9 reels, 7,066 or 7,072 ft. 78 or 84 min. PCA cert no. 14699.
    Pres JOSEPH JUSTMAN. *Prod* Irving Allen. *Dir* Irving Reis. [*2d unit dir* Irving Allen]. *Asst dir* Robert Aldrich and William Calihan. *Orig scr* Max Trell. *Dir of photog* William Snyder. *Addl photog* Jack Greenhalgh and Lester White. *Spec eff* Harry Redmond, Jr. and Ray Mercer. *Art dir* George Van Marter. *Film ed* Louis H. Sackin. [*Asst ed* John Sheets]. *Set dec* Edward Ray Robinson. [*Men's ward* Wesley Jefferies]. [*Women's ward* Evelyn Cornwell]. *Mus* Lucien Moraweck and René Garriguenc. *Cond* Paul Sawtell. *Mus supv* Lud Gluskin. *Sd rec* Leon Becker, Mac Dalgleish and [Art Smith]. *Makeup* Kiva Hoffman and [Terry Miles]. [*Hairdresser* Gertrude Wheeler]. *Prod mgr* Glenn Cook. *Tech adv* Richard Van Opel. [*Prod asst* Oscar Demejo]. [*Scr supv* Mary Gibson]. [*Props* Arden Cripe and Abe Solk].
    Song(s): "Soldier, Soldier Won't You Marry Me," traditional.
    Cast: LEW AYRES [(*Lt. Hunt, later Capt.*)], Marilyn Maxwell [(*Cherry*)], Andy Devine [(*Sgt. Garrity*)], Robert Hutton [(*Lt. Vermont*)], Donald Buka [(*Pvt. Van Vechten*)], Ted De Corsia [(*Acoma*)], Lloyd Corrigan [(*Judge Verne Wilcox*)], John Hoyt [(*Sgt. Harriton*)], Jeff Corey [(*Coyote*)], Raymond Burr [(*Pvt. Anderson*)], Verna Felton [(*Feathers Fenway*)], Ian MacDonald [(*Pvt. Daniels*)], Peter Price [(*Chia-Kong, "Charlie"*)], Walter N. Greaza [(*Col. McComb*)], [Robert Osterloh (*Pvt. Parsons*)], [William Tannen (*Pvt. Cheever*)], [Arthur Loew, Jr. (*Pvt. Finnegan*)], [Bob Duncan (*Cpl. Mack*)], [Jack Kelly (*Pvt. Clifton*)], [Allen Mathews (*Pvt. Vale*)], [Jack Briggs (*Pvt. Lindley*)], [Hans Conried (*Abraham Lincoln*)], [Ralph Volkie (*First rider*)], [Bud Rae (*Stage driver*)].
    Western. [*Print viewed*]. After receiving a report by Lt. Hunt on the Indian situation in the New Mexico territories, President Abraham Lincoln travels there to meet Acoma, chief of the Indian nations of the territories. They avow their friendship and shake hands to symbolically link their peoples in peace. Lincoln expresses the view that the land contains many people, but only one nation, and presents Acoma with an inscribed cane. After Lincoln's assassination, Judge Verne Wilcox, the Bureau of Indian Affairs commissioner, inaugurates a campaign against the Indians, resulting in discrimination, evictions and foreclosures. When three Indians are arrested for stealing rations at Fort Union, Hunt, now a captain, protests to the fort's commander, Colonel McComb, that the rations had been held from the Indians illegally and warns him to release the men or face trouble. The bigoted, autocratic colonel then tells Acoma, who has come for his braves, to get out. When Acoma reminds the colonel that Lincoln gave him the authority to judge his own people, McComb knocks the cane from Acoma's hands and orders him and the three braves accompanying him arrested. The three ride off and McComb orders his men to shoot, killing two. Acoma steps on the cane and vows revenge against McComb and Wilcox before he is taken to the jail house. McComb then arrests Hunt for attempting to countermand his orders. That night, a number of Indians sneak into the fort and kill the jail guard with a hatchet to his back. They release Acoma, who then kills McComb and warns Hunt not to follow. Hunt takes command of the fort and suspends travel west by civilians. This upsets dance hall entertainer Cherry, who is on her way to Las Vegas, but she convinces Judge Wilcox to take her west in a stagecoach. Hunt leads a small party to go after Acoma, hoping to avert a war. After five days of tiresome travel through the desert, the men grow increasingly critical of Hunt, especially when he will not allow them to fight Indians who fire on them. Hunt sees in the distance a pueblo on top of a plateau and learns from his scout Coyote that the place, called "Rock with Wings," is sacred to the Indians. Hundreds of years earlier, during a siege, the Indians held off the Spanish army with only bows and arrows and rocks; the Spanish built a church after they prevailed, but an earthquake later destroyed the only trail leading to the top. Coyote leads the men on a treacherous climb, but they find the pueblo deserted. As they are about to leave, a church bell rings, and they discover two young sons of Acoma. Anderson, the most disgruntled of the soldiers, shoots the older boy as they try to run away and kills him. The younger boy, Chia-Kong, whom the men call "Charlie," vows

revenge. As the soldiers drive off Indians attacking the stage, Hunt rescues Cherry. Acoma then proposes a truce, but Hunt wants the chief to return to the fort to face punishment for the attack, which cost the lives of four soldiers. Acoma refuses and warns that the soldiers have very little ammunition, food or water left. When he learns of his son's death, Acoma demands to have his younger son and the killer of his eldest, but Hunt says the boy is safer with the soldiers and that the killer will be punished. Judge Wilcox urges Hunt to accept the truce, until Acoma says he wants the judge also. Hunt refuses and Acoma rides off. Hunt then orders everyone to the top of the plateau. At night, Hunt rescues Cherry from a drunken soldier, but he calls her a "parasite," and she breaks down in tears. Charlie comforts her and takes her to a secret underground spring, where guns and ammunition are hidden, but he is distressed when she says she must tell the others to avert further fighting. The judge, to save himself, convinces Charlie to lead him to Acoma, but the Indians bury the judge in sand up to his shoulders and then trample him with their horses. During the ensuing battle, Coyote is shot by other Indians, Anderson and other soldiers are killed, and Hunt is shot. Cherry carries him to the pueblo, where he sets up a fuse leading to the ammunition, which he knows Acoma plans to use for a rebellion. When he swoons, she carries him out, and he tenderly thanks her and expresses regret that he didn't see before what she was really like. Acoma stops his people from shooting Hunt and Cherry, then goes with his son to the room with the ammunition. As a dying soldier is about to shoot the chief and the boy, Hunt warns them, and the chief takes a bullet that otherwise would have hit his son. Hunt urges Cherry to take the boy and go, and she kisses Hunt before leaving. Acoma then grabs Hunt's hand, and Hunt smiles. The pueblo explodes and burns, but Cherry and Charlie survive and comfort each other. *Acoma. Acoma Indians. Cultural conflict. Indians of North America. Murder. Officers (Military). Pueblos. Racism. Revenge. Tribal chiefs. Battles. Churches. Dance hall girls. Deserts. Explosions. Fathers and sons. Forts. Indian agents. Judges. Abraham Lincoln. Reconciliation. Rescues. Self-sacrifice. Springs. Stagecoaches. Thirst. Treaties. United States. Bureau of Indian Affairs.*

Note: Material in the film's pressbook states that producer Irving Allen "hopes that the picture will raise a chorus of popular voices demanding that something be done for the Indian—just as such films as *Home of the Brave*, *Gentleman's Agreement*, *Pinky* and *Lost Boundaries* clamored for a square deal for their minorities." (See below for entries on the above films.) The pressbook also comments that "the film suggests strongly that Lincoln, had he lived long enough, would next have turned to the Indian in his role of great emancipator." *IP* called the film "the newest in a film cycle to interest itself in minority problems." They stated, "It seriously and conclusively points up the American Indian's unfortunate plight by leveling a penetrating lens at the unscrupulous, merciless and ruthless forces which brought about his decline."
   The film was originally listed in reviews and release charts as having a 18 May 1951 national release, but was subsequently pushed back to 24 Aug 1951. According to news items, the original story by Max Trell was purchased by Irving Allen in Oct 1946; Allen originally planned to star Eddie Albert in the film. According to a *LAT* news item in Dec 1949, Lew Ayres planned to co-direct, in addition to starring in the film. News items and material in the pressbook state that the film was shot for three weeks on location in New Mexico at Gallop and the Paguate pueblo at Acoma Rock, and information in the MPAA/PCA Collection at the AMPAS Library states that some filming was done at a ranch in the Santa Susana Pass in California. Over 300 members of the Navajo, Zuni and Laguna tribes appeared in the film, and the Zuni and Navajo tribes were paid $25,000, according to the pressbook. Interiors were shot at Motion Picture Center in Hollywood, according to reviews. According to *NYT*, the film cost $635,000 to make. Peter Price, who played "Charlie," was the grandson of blackface comedian George Moran. According to *NYT*, the film was the first feature issued on a new Ansco print stock. Reviews were critical of the color process. *Har* noted that the color "is atrocious, with the exception of some exterior scenes; the faces and hands of the players are ceramic—that is, in terra cotta." *NYT* commented, "the whole thing has been pretentiously smeared in Ansco color which makes the cast, Indians included, look lobster-red."

Box 12 May 1951. *Cue* 21 Jul 1951. *DV* 21 Oct 1946. *DV* 2 May 1951. *DV* 14 May 1951, p. 3. *Exb* 9 May 1951, p. 3071. *FD* 4 May 1951, p. 6. *Har* 5 May 1951, p. 70. *HR* 21 Apr 1950. *HR* 2 May 1951, p. 3. *IP* Jul 1950, p. 10, 12. *LADN* 28 Sep 1951. *LAEx* 3 Jun 1950. *LAEx* 28 Sep 1951. *LAT* 19 Oct 1946. *LAT* 12 Dec 1949. *LAT* 28 Sep 1951. *MPD* 3 May 1951. *MPHPD* 12 May 1951, p. 845. *New Yorker* 21 Jul 1951. *NYT* 28 May 1950. *NYT* 14 Jul 1951, p. 7. *Var* 2 May 1951, p. 6.

NEW MOON (French Americans)

Metro-Goldwyn-Mayer Corp.; controlled by Loew's Inc. *Dist* Loew's Inc. 28 Jun **1940**; Prod: early Nov 1939—early Jan 1940 [©Loew's Inc.; 17 Jun 1940; LP9721]. Sd (Western Electric Sound System); b&w. 105 min. PCA cert no. 6046.

Prod Robert Z. Leonard. *Dir* Robert Z. Leonard and [W. S. Van Dyke]. [*Asst dir* Marvin Stuart and Hugh Boswell]. *Scr* Jacques Deval and Robert Arthur. *Dir of photog* William Daniels and Oliver Marsh]. [*Steamboat scenes photog* by Clyde de Vinna]. *Art dir* Cedric Gibbons. *Art dir assoc* Eddie Imazu. *Film ed* Harold F. Kress. *Set dec* Edwin B. Willis. *Gowns* Adrian. *Men's cost* Gile Steele. *Mus dir* Herbert Stothart. *Dances* Val Raset. *Rec dir* Douglas Shearer. *Makeup* Jack Dawn. [*Vocal Stand-in for Jeanette MacDonald* Lorraine Bridges].

Song(s): "One Kiss," "Wanting You," "Lover Come Back to Me," "Stouthearted Men," "Softly as in a Morning Sunrise," "Marianne," "Tavern Scene (Take a Flower)" "Gorgeous Alexander" and "Funny Little Sailor Men," music by Sigmund Romberg, lyrics by Oscar Hammerstein II; "Bayou Voices," music and lyrics by Herbert Stothart; "La Marseillaises," music and lyrics by Claude Joseph Rouget de Lisle; "Soon I Will Be Done," composer unknown.

Source: Based on the operetta *New Moon*, book and lyrics by Oscar Hammerstein II, Frank Mandel and Laurence Schwab, music by Sigmund Romberg (New York, 19 Sep 1928).

Cast: JEANETTE MacDONALD (*Marianne de Beaumanoir*), NELSON EDDY (*Charles [Michon "also known as" Duke de Vidier]*), Mary Boland (*Valerie de Rossac*), George Zucco (*Vicomte Ribaud*), H. B. Warner (*Father Michel*), Grant Mitchell (*Governor of New Orleans*), Richard Purcell (*Alexander*), John Miljan (*Pierre Brugnon*), Ivan Simpson (*Guizot*), William Tannen (*Pierre*), Bunty Cutler (*Julie*), Claude King (*Monsieur Dubois*), Cecil Cunningham (*Governor's wife*), Joe Yule (*Maurice*), George Irving (*Ship's captain*), Edwin Maxwell (*Captain de Jean*), Paul E. Burns (*Guard on ship*), Rafael Storm (*Monsieur de Piron*), Winifred Harris (*Lady*), [Stanley Fields (*Tambour*)], [Robert Warwick (*Commissar*)], [Ray Walker (*Coco*)], [Trevor Bardette (*Foulette*)], [LeRoy Mason (*Grant*)], [George Lloyd (*Quartermaster*)], [Gayne Whitman, Warren Rock (*Mates*)], [George Magrill (*Guard*)], [Ed O'Neill (*Lookout*)], [Sarah Edwards (*Marquise*)], [Max Marx, Jack Perrin (*Officers*)], [Alden Chase (*Citizen*)], [Claire Rochelle (*Drunk girl*)], [Frank Elliott, Kenneth Gibson, Victor Kendall, Gerald Fielding, Bea Nigro, Florence Shirley, Hillary Brooke (*Guests*)], [Nat Pendleton, Buster Keaton, Christian J. Frank, Arthur Belasco, Edward Hearn, Nick Copeland, Gino Corrado, Ralph Dunn, Harry Strang, Ray Teal, Ted Oliver, Fred Graham (*Bondsmen*)], [Dorothy Granger (*Fat bridesmaid*)], [June Gittelson (*Madeline*)], [David Alison (*Troubadour*)], [Forbes Murray (*Commandant*)], [Abe Dinovitch, Sally Mueller, Austin Grant (*Solo bits "Stouthearted Men"*)], [Jean Fenwick], [Frank Remsden], [Jewel Jordan].

Historical, Musical, Comedy-drama. [*Print viewed*]. In 1789, the Duke de Vidier, a young French aristocrat, renounces his claim of nobility to further the cause of the revolution by freeing the bond servants in New Orleans. Then while posing as a deported servant named Charles Michon, the duke sails on a ship bound for New Orleans, where he meets the spoiled Marianne de Beaumanoir, who mistakes him for a ship's officer. At the family plantation in New Orleans, Marianne is shocked when she discovers that Charles is her new footman. The town gossips are enthralled by the charming and sophisticated footman, who claims he worked for a dashing duke, and Marianne falls in love with him. Consequently, when the Vicomte Ribaud appears at the plantation to arrest the duke, who he claims is impersonating a servant, Marianne orders Charles to leave. Learning that his plot has been uncovered, Charles rallies the bond servants to seize a ship named the *New Moon*, and they sail off to freedom. A lonely Marianne decides to sail back to France on the next available ship, and hence, she and her aunt board the *Fleur de Lys*, a vessel bearing a cargo of brides bound for Martinique. At sea, the *New Moon* attacks the *Fleur de Lys*, and in the ensuing battle, the *New Moon* is sunk and her men take command of the *Fleur de Lys* and her cargo. During a severe storm, the ship is thrown off course and wrecked on the reef of an unchartered island. After settling on the island, Charles announces that the men and women should pair off to establish a new society based on liberty and equality. This presents problems for Marianne, who is pursued by a pack of suitors, and out of desperation, she reluctantly agrees to marry Charles, who she has decided is an incorrigible womanizer. On their wedding night, the roar of cannons draw the men to shore in defense of their new home, and a terrified Marianne realizes that she really loves Charles. When Charles returns with the news that the French fleet has arrived with

news that France is free, he and Marianne declare their love for each other. *France–History–Revolution, 1789-1799. French. Impersonation and imposture. Nobility. Revolutionaries. Servants. Aunts. Islands. Mistaken identity. New Orleans (LA). Newlyweds. Plantations. Ships. Shipwrecks. Storms. Weddings.*

Note: The working title of this picture was *Lover Come Back*, and it was broadcast on television as *Parisian Belle*. *HR* news items in late Nov 1939 note that director W. S. Van Dyke worked on this film for about two weeks, but was reassigned to direct *I Take This Woman*, leaving producer Robert Z. Leonard to take his place. An item in *HR* comments that Nat Pendleton was to have appeared in this picture. Pendleton can be seen very briefly early in the picture as a bondsman standing next to Nelson Eddy. It is possible that his part was intended to be longer but was cut prior to the film's preview. In the same scene, silent star Buster Keaton is seen on the opposite side of Eddy, however, he is also unbilled in contemporary sources. According to *HR*, the steamboat scenes were filmed by Clyde de Vinna at Santa Catalina Island, CA. Reviews commented on the similarity between this film and M-G-M's 1935 film *Naughty Marietta*, which also starred Eddy and Jeanette MacDonald. In 1931, M-G-M filmed another version of *New Moon* starring Grace Moore and Lawrence Tibbett (see *AFI Catalog of Feature Films, 1931-40*; F3.3107).

DV 12 Jun 1940, p. 3. *FD* 18 Jun 1940, p. 5. *HR* 11 Nov 1939, pp. 6-7. *HR* 25 Nov 1939, p. 4, 6-7. *HR* 9 Dec 1939, pp. 5-6. *HR* 11 Dec 1939, p. 9. *HR* 13 Jun 1940, p. 3. *MPD* 18 Jun 1940, p. 4. *MPH* 27 Jan 1940, p. 61. *MPH* 22 Jun 1940, pp. 50-51. *NYT* 19 Jul 1940, p. 22. *Var* 19 Jun 1940, p. 14.

NEW ORLEANS (African Americans)
Majestic Productions, Inc. *Dist* United Artists Corp. 18 Apr 1947; *Prod*: mid-Sep—early Nov 1946 [©Majestic Productions, Inc.; 18 Apr 1947; LP999]. Sd (Western Electric Recording); b&w. 10 reels, 8,010 ft. 89 min. PCA cert no. 12164.

Pres JULES LEVEY. *Prod* Jules Levey. *Assoc prod* Herbert J. Biberman. *Dir* Arthur Lubin. *Asst dir* Maurie Suess. *Scr* Elliot Paul and Dick Irving Hyland. *Orig story* Elliot Paul and Herbert J. Biberman. *Dir of photog* Lucien Andriot. [*Spec eff* Nick Carmona]. *Art dir* Rudi Feld. *Ed supv* Bernard W. Burton. *Women's cost des* Teddy Barri. *Ward* Elmer Ellsworth. *Mus dir* Nat W. Finston. *Mus ed* Leon Klatzkin. *Sd rec* Roy Meadows and [Roy Raguse]. *Makeup* Karl Herlinger. [*Hairdresser* Peggy Shannon]. *Prod mgr* Joseph H. Nadel. [*Singing voice for Dorothy Patrick* Theodora Lynch]. [*Pianist for Richard Hageman* Artie Schutt].

Song(s): "New Orleans," "The Blues Are Brewin'" and "Endie," music by Louis Alter, lyrics by Eddie Delange; "Where the Blues Were Born in New Orleans," music by Bob Carleton, words by Cliff Dixon; "Farewell to Storyville," music and lyrics by Spencer Williams.

Cast: Arturo De Cordova [(*Nick Duquesne*)], Dorothy Patrick [(*Miralee Smith*)], Marjorie Lord [(*Grace Voiselle*)], Irene Rich [(*Mrs. Rutledge Smith*)], John Alexander [(*Colonel McArdle*)], Richard Hageman [(*Henry Ferber*)], Jack Lambert [(*Biff Lewis*)], Bert Conway [(*Tommy Lake*)], Joan Blair [(*Constance Vigil*)], John Canady, Louis Armstrong and his band, and Billie Holiday [(*Endie*)], Woody Herman and his orchestra, Original New Orleans Ragtime Band:, Zutty Singleton [(*Drummer*)], Barney Bigard [(*Clarinet player*)], Kid Ory [(*Trombonist*)], Bud Scott [(*Guitarist*)], Red Callender [(*Bass player*)], and Charlie Beal [(*Piano player*)], Meade Lux Lewis [(*Piano man*)], Papa Mutt Carey, Lucky Thompson.

Historical, Musical. [*Print viewed*]. In 1917, in the Storyville district of New Orleans, Louisiana, Louis "Satchmo" Armstrong plays ragtime music with his band in the basement of the Orpheum cabaret. The cabaret, which also operates as a casino, is owned by Nick Duquesne, the "King of Basin Street." One of Nick's patrons, a wealthy widow named Mrs. Rutledge Smith, from Baltimore, Maryland, is joined in New Orleans by her daughter Miralee, a classically trained singer. Miralee's black maid, Endie, who is Satchmo's girl friend, introduces Miralee to the blues, and takes her to a "jam" session featuring Satchmo and his band. Nick discourages Miralee's love of ragtime because high society considers it immoral, and orders Grace Voiselle, a debutante, who is in love with Nick, to take her home. Jealous of Nick's attention toward Miralee, Grace calls Mrs. Smith and warns her to keep Miralee away from Nick. Mrs. Smith, who earlier had lost ten thousand dollars at the Orpheum, wins it back in roulette and offers it to Nick on the condition that he discourage Miralee's involvement with him. After a month of successfully keeping Miralee out of Basin Street, Nick determines to show her its sordid side to teach her a lesson. At dawn, assuring Nick she has no illusions about him, Miralee kisses him, and they are seen by her mother. Mrs. Smith appeals to her friend, Colonel McArdle, and he has an article printed about the dangers facing unchaperoned debutantes visiting Storyville. He also suggests to the Public Safety

Commissioner that he condemn the district. One night, Nick orders Grace, who is drunk, to leave the club, and she is hit by a car and killed. The incident causes a grand jury to order that Storyville be evacuated by the United States Navy. Satchmo and his friends pack up and leave, and Nick makes plans to move to Chicago. Miralee begs Nick to take her with him, and in order to spare her feelings, he accepts an expensive bracelet from Mrs. Smith to make it look as if he never loved Miralee. He returns the bracelet to Henry Ferber, Miralee's music teacher, to give to Mrs. Smith, but she does not tell Miralee. Determined to give up the gambling business in favor of spreading jazz music across the nation, Nick opens the Club Orleans in Chicago, with Satchmo and piano player Meade Lux Lewis as performers of Chicago style blues. Meanwhile, Miralee becomes a famous opera singer in Europe. Eventually, Satchmo and Endie are married, and he and his band tour Europe. In Paris, Satchmo sees Miralee and tells her that Nick returned the bracelet and has been heartbroken ever since. He also tells her that Nick gave up gambling, has a new job as a music agent, and has been busy trying to introduce New York to the blues. Finally, at a concert in Symphony Hall, Miralee surprises Nick by including Woody Herman and his band and Satchmo and his band in the program. For an encore, Miralee sings Endie's old favorite, "New Orleans," for Nick. *African Americans. Band leaders. Class distinction. Jazz music. New Orleans (LA)–Storyville. Opera singers. Romance. Singers. Automobile accidents. Chicago (IL). Debutantes. Drunkenness. Gambling houses. Impresarios. Maids. Mothers and daughters. Musicians. New York City. Nightclub owners. Opera singers.*

Note: Louis Armstrong is listed twice in the opening credits, once as "Louis Armstrong and his band" and once as a member of the New Orleans Ragtime Band. The opening credits include a "grateful acknowledgement" to the National Jazz Foundation based in New Orleans for its assistance in the production of the picture. *New Orleans* marked the first and only feature film appearance by renowned blues and jazz singer Billie Holiday. The *Var* review commented about musician Louis Armstrong's acting: "…'Satchmo' Armstrong is the star of the film, proving as solid in a generous dramatic role as he is on the trumpet." Portions of the film were shot on location in New Orleans, LA, including the front steps of the city hall building, which, as reported in the *NYT*, had remained unchanged since 1917. According to a *HR* news item, musical director Nat Finston organized a group called the Ensemble Symphonique to record the music for the film.

A soundtrack album of the film was released in 1983 and included complete versions of the songs performed in the film, as well as numbers that were omitted from the final release. Among the many numbers found on the album are "Tiger Rag" by the Original Dixieland Jazz Band; "Milenberg Joys" by Leon Rappolo, Paul Mares and "Jelly Roll" Morton; "King Porter Stomp" by "Jelly Roll" Morton; "Shim-Me-Sha-Wabble" by Spencer Williams; "Basin Street Blues," music and lyrics by Spencer Williams; "Beale Street Blues," music by Chris Smith, lyrics by Jim Burris; and "Dipper Mouth Blues," music by Joe "King" Oliver, lyrics by Walter Melrose.

Box 3 May 1947. *DV* 25 Apr 1947, p. 3. *Down Beat* 21 May '47, p. 7. *FD* 25 Apr 1947, p. 11. *HR* 30 Jul 1946, p. 7. *HR* 20 Sep 1946, p. 19. *HR* 1 Nov 1946, p. 17. *HR* 25 Apr 1947, p. 3. *HR* 24 Jun 1947. *IFJ* 28 Sep 1946, p. 43. *The Mississippi Rag* Feb 1984, p. 12. *MPHPD* 3 May 1947. *NYT* 3 Nov 1946. *NYT* 20 Jun 1947, p. 25. *Var* 30 Apr 1947, p. 10.

NEW ORLEANS ADVENTURE *see* **ADVENTURES OF CAPTAIN FABIAN**

THE NEW REFUGEE *see* **JOURNEY TO FREEDOM**

THE NEW SOUTH *see* **BROKEN CHAINS**

NEW YORK TOWN (Polish Americans, Refugees)
Paramount Pictures, Inc. *Dist* Paramount Pictures, Inc. 31 Oct **1941**; Prod: early Nov—late Dec 1940 [©Paramount Pictures, Inc.; 31 Oct 1941; LP10811]. Sd (Western Electric Mirrophonic Recording); b&w. 8 reels, 8,384 ft. 75 min. Passed by the National Board of Review.

[*Exec prod* William LeBaron]. *Prod* Anthony Veiller. *Dir* Charles Vidor. [*Asst dir* Stanley Goldsmith and Holly Morse]. *Scr* Lewis Meltzer. *Story* Jo Swerling. *Dir of photog* Charles Schoenbaum. *Art dir* Hans Dreier and William Pereira. *Ed* Doane Harrison. *Cost* Edith Head. *Mus dir* Sigmund Krumgold. *Mus score* Leo Shuken. *Sd rec* Hugo Grenzbach and Gene Garvin.

Song(s): "Yip-I-Addy-I-Ay!" music by J. H. Flynn, lyrics by Will D. Cobb, arranged by Jule Styne.

Cast: FRED MacMURRAY (*Victor Ballard*), MARY MARTIN (*Alexandra Curtis*), ROBERT PRESTON (*Paul Bryson, Jr.*), Akim Tamiroff (*Stefan Janowski*), Lynne Overman (*Sam*), Eric Blore (*Vyvian*), Fuzzy Knight (*Gus Nelson*), Cecil Kellaway (*Shipboard host*), Oliver Prickett (*Bender*), Ken Carpenter (*Master of ceremonies*), Edward McNamara (*Brody*), Sam McDaniel (*Henry*),

[Iris Adrian (*Toots O'Day*)], [Margaret Hayes (*Lola Martin*)], [Regis Toomey (*Jim Martin*)], [Laura Hope Crews (*Apple Annie*)], [Charles Lane (*Census taker*)], [Monte Blue (*McAuliffe*)], [Jimmy Conlin (*Burt the newsman*)], [Cliff Nazarro (*Burt's companion*)], [James Flavin (*Recruiting sergeant*)], [Marshall Ruth (*Spectator in broadcasting station*)], [Grace Hayle (*Mrs. Bixby*)], [Chester Clute (*Mr. Cobbler*)], [Nell Craig (*Mrs. Gus Nelson*)], [Linda Gage, Frances Morris, Alice Keating (*Nurses*)], [Marjorie Deane (*Girl with Oliver*)], [Jack Rice (*Oliver*)], [Lilyan Irene (*Yvonne*)], [George Davis (*Waiter in French pavilion*)], [John Bagni (*The Dip*)], [Maynard Holmes (*Scion on boat*)], [Paul Fierro, Paul McVey, Jack Arnold (*Gentlemen on boat*)], [Ted Barnick (*Officer at gangplank*)], [Kenneth Hunter (*Elderly gentleman*)], [Philip Van Zandt (*Peddler*)], [Wallace Rairden (*Pedestrian*)], [Kate Lawson (*Landlady*)], [Ann Doran (*Demonstrator in department store*)], [Nicholas Bela (*Hungarian father*)], [Delmar Watson (*Hungarian boy*)], [Milton Kibbee (*Postman*)], [Tommy Bond (*Willie*)], [Gus Reed (*Businessman*)], [Jack Gardner (*Clerk*)], [Ray Flynn (*Passerby*)], [Patricia Knox (*Telephone operator*)], [Pauline Wagner (*Switchboard operator*)], [John H. Dilson (*Doctor*)], [Jack Carr, Herbert Vigran, Sidney Melton, Lee Prather (*Barkers*)], [Ralph Peters (*Box office man*)], [Keith Richards (*Young man*)], [Gloria Williams], [Ethel Clayton], [Wanda McKay], [Jean Phillips], [Olivia Steele], [Ella Neal], [Eva Gabor].

Comedy-drama. [*Print viewed*]. Victor Ballard, a happy-go-lucky albeit impoverished sidewalk photographer, shares a New York City studio apartment with Polish immigrant painter Stefan Janowski. The big city doles out joy and misery indiscriminately: In the apartment below Victor and Steve, Gus Nelson learns that his wife has given birth to quintuplets, while the lonely tenant in the apartment below Gus has given up on life and committed suicide. One day while hawking his work on Fifth Avenue, Victor snaps a picture of recently impoverished Alexandra Curtis, and intuits that she is desperate and naïve. Victor befriends Alexandra and shares with her his tricks for survival, such as getting meals by eating free food samples in a market, and "crashing" shipboard parties before the ship leaves. Victor brings Alexandra home as a third roommate, and proposes that she become a salesman for his photo "business," which involves taking a photo of a passerby on the street, getting his name and address, then going to the pedestrian's home and selling him either an enlarged photo for five dollars, or an oil painting of the photo by Steve for fifty dollars. In order to get Alexandra's belongings out of hock, Victor and Steve take her to a radio broadcast of a quiz show that gives cash prizes. Alexandra becomes a contestant after the first contestant faints, and she wins sixty-four dollars with a little coaching from Victor. Victor and Steve's friend Sam, meanwhile, a legless veteran who sells pencils on the street, uses his military pension to hire Bender, a lawyer, to get Steve citizenship. Bender's advice, however, is that Steve get a position at a university. Alexandra becomes depressed when she is unable to sell any paintings, and in order to cheer her up, Victor takes her out for a night of fun, during which they crash a private party on a cruise ship before it sails for Rio de Janeiro. Victor decides that Alexandra's best "career" would be marriage, and the next day, he insists that she try to sell a painting to his most wealthy client, Paul Bryson. Alexandra resents Victor's practical suggestion, as she wants to marry for love, but she goes to Bryson's Park Avenue home anyway. Alexandra is delighted when she meets Bryson's handsome son, also named Paul, and learns that Bryson, Sr., is on his honeymoon. Alexandra and Paul hit it off, and to his own surprise, Victor becomes jealous. Victor's pride is then hurt when Paul gets Steve an interview with the dean of a university, and Steve is hired. When Paul casually proposes to Alexandra as they plan a vacation together, she admits that she is a gold digger, but Paul is undisturbed. Victor, meanwhile, gets drunk while celebrating Steve's good fortune, and then goes to Paul's house. After telling him that Alexandra has been living with him, Victor hits Paul. A fistfight ensues, but on the way home, Alexandra and Victor admit their love for each other and kiss. Artists. Immigrants. New York City. Photographers. Poverty. Romance. Apartments. Butlers. Citizenship. Contests. Dogs. Drunkenness. Fistfights. Handicapped. Jealousy. Lawyers. Parties. Polish Americans. Proposals (Marital). Quintuplets. Radio programs. Roommates. Ships. Suicide. Veterans.

Note: Jo Swerling's original screen story was called "Night Time." Mitchell Leisen was originally slated to direct this film, but, according to *HR*, was replaced by Charles Vidor after Leisen was assigned to direct *I Wanted Wings*. Vidor was borrowed from Columbia Pictures. A *LAT* news item announced that

Betty Brewer was cast in the film, but her appearance in the final film has not been confirmed. Some background scenes were shot on location in New York City. Ken Carpenter was a radio announcer for the *Edgar Bergen and Charlie McCarthy* show, and for the *Kraft Music Hall* radio show. The quiz show in this film was modeled after *Take It or Leave It*, also known as *The Sixty-Four Dollar Question*, a 1940s radio contest in which participants could win up to sixty-four dollars by answering a battery of questions. According to a *NYT* article, the film's ending originally contained a scene showing a Bund parade, but was re-shot, as Paramount executives felt that the pro-Nazi German faction of the Bunds would soon disband.

Box 2 Aug 1941. *DV* 30 Jul 1941. *FD* 30 Jul 1941, p. 4. *HR* 2 Aug 1940, p. 3. *HR* 10 Sep 1940, p. 4. *HR* 23 Sep 1940, p. 4. *HR* 25 Oct 1940, p. 6. *HR* 8 Nov 1940, p. 8. *HR* 27 Dec 1940, p. 10. *HR* 30 Jul 1941, p. 3. *LAT* 18 Oct 1940. *MPH* 2 Aug 1941. *MPHPD* 9 Aug 1941, p. 207. *MPHPD* 6 Sep 1941, p. 248. *NYT* 16 Mar 1941. *NYT* 13 Nov 1941, p. 35. *Var* 30 Jul 1941, p. 8.

NG LOG SHEN PING *see* **YU LUH SHEN PING**

THE NIGGER (African Americans)
Fox Film Corp. *Dist* Fox Film Corp. 29 Mar **1915** [©William Fox; 5 Apr 1915; LP5235]. Si; b&w. 5 reels.
Pres William Fox. *Dir* Edgar Lewis. *Asst dir* George De Carlton. *Scen* Edgar Lewis.
Source: Based on the play *The Nigger* by Edward Brewster Sheldon (New York, 4 Dec 1909).
Cast: Philip Morrow (*William Farnum*), Claire Whitney (*Georgiana Bird*), George De Carlton.
Drama. Philip Morrow, raised in aristocratic Southern society, is persuaded to run for governor by whiskey distiller and political boss Cliff Noyes. After winning the election, Governor Morrow decides to sign a prohibition bill that would ruin Noyes's liquor business. Furious, Noyes confronts Morrow with proof that the governor is of Negro ancestry and threatens to expose him in the newspaper. Realizing that he faces political ruin as well as the loss of his sweetheart, Georgiana Byrd, Governor Morrow bravely signs the bill and resigns his office. Georgiana begs to stay with him, but Morrow departs alone for a new life in the North, where he hopes to improve the plight of blacks in America. Governors. Political corruption. Racism. Reformers. United States–South. African Americans–Mixed blood. Blackmail. Distillers. Elections. Parentage. Political bosses. Prohibition. Self-sacrifice. Upper classes.

Note: This film was also released under the title *The New Governor*. Location scenes were filmed in Augusta, GA. According to the 1921 *MPSD*, Carey Lee was the author of this film. As Edgar Lewis is credited as scenarist in reviews, and the film was based on a play by Edward Brewster Sheldon, Lee's role is unclear. According to information in the NAACP Collection at the Library of Congress, the film was censored and passed by the National Board of Censorship on 20 Mar 1915, subject to the following changes and eliminations: the name of the film was changed to read "*The New Governor*, based on Sheldon's *The Nigger*"; a subtitle following the title card, which stated that an impossible gulf exists between the white and black races, was to be eliminated; a scene in which a drunken black man meets a little girl in the woods and attacks her was to be altered substantially; the scene of her brothers finding her was to be cut substantially; the subtitle "The Man Hunt" was to be cut; a close view of the black man being pulled from his horse and struggling with his captors was to be cut; the subtitle "Reaping the Penalty" was to be cut; and a scene in which the black man is shown tied to a tree with fire burning around him was to be cut substantially.

Motog 27 Mar 1915, p. 509. *MPN* 6 Feb 1915, p. 32. *MPN* 13 Mar 1915, pp. 10-11. *MPN* 20 Mar 1915, p. 39, 51. *MPN* 3 Apr 1915, pp. 36-37. *MPN* 17 Apr 1915, p. 5. *MPW* 24 Jul 1915, p. 734.

A NIGHT AT THE OPERA (Italian Americans)
Metro-Goldwyn-Mayer Corp.; controlled by Loew's Inc. *Dist* Loew's Inc. 15 Nov **1935**; New York premiere: 8 Nov 1935; Prod: 14 Jun—13 Aug 1935; retakes began 19 Aug 1935 [©Metro-Goldwyn-Mayer Corp.; 22 Oct 1935; LP5926]. Sd (Western Electric Sound System); b&w. 10 reels. 90 min. Passed by the National Board of Review. PCA cert no. 1613.
[*Exec prod* Irving Thalberg]. *Dir* Sam Wood. [*Asst dir* Lesley Selander]. *Scr* George S. Kaufman and Morrie Ryskind. *Story* James Kevin McGuinness. [*Addl dial* Al Boasberg]. *Photog* Merritt B. Gerstad. *Art dir* Cedric Gibbons. *Art dir assoc* Ben Carre and Edwin B. Willis. *Film ed* William LeVanway. *Ward* Dolly Tree. *Mus score* Herbert Stothart. [*Vocal coach* Paul Lamkoff]. [*Vocal coach for chorus* Paul Taylor]. *Dances by* Chester Hale. *Rec dir* Douglas Shearer. [*Whistling double for Harpo Marx* Enrico Ricardi].
Song(s): "Alone," music by Nacio Herb Brown, lyrics by Arthur Freed; "Così-Cosà," music by Bronislaw Kaper and Walter Jurmann, lyrics by Ned Washington; "Take Me Out to the Ball Game," music by Albert von Tilzer, lyrics by Jack Norworth; selections from the operas

Il trovatore, music by Giuseppe Verdi, libretto by Salvatore Cammarano and *I pagliacci*, music and libretto by Ruggiero Leoncavallo.

Cast: GROUCHO MARX (*Otis B. Driftwood*), CHICO MARX (*Fiorello*), HARPO MARX (*Tomasso*), Kitty Carlisle (*Rosa*), Allan Jones (*Ricardo [Barone]*), Walter King ([*Rudolfo*] *Lassparri*), Siegfried Rumann ([*Herman*] *Gottlieb*), Margaret Dumont (*Mrs. Claypool*), Edward Keane (*Captain*), Robert Emmet O'Connor (*Henderson*), Lorraine Bridges [(*Louisa*)], [Claude Payton (*Police captain*)], [Rita and Rubin (*Dancers*)], [Luther Hoobvner (*Ruiz*)], [Rodolfo Hoyos (*Count di Luna*)], [Olga Dane (*Azucena in Il Trovatore*)], [Jonathan Hale (*Stage manager*)], [Otto Fries (*Elevator man*)], [William Gould (*Captain of police*)], [Leo White, Jay Eaton, Rolfe Sedan (*Aviators*)], [William "Billy" Gilbert (*Orchestra leader*)], [Wilbur Mack, Phillips Smalley, Selmer Jackson, George Irving (*Committee*)], [George Guhl (*Policeman*)], [Harry Tyler (*Sign painter*)], [Fred Malatesta (*Stage hand*)], [Gennaro Curci, Harry Allen (*Doormen*)], [Edna Bonnett, Ines Palange (*Maids*)], [Harry "Zoop" Welsh (*Steward*)], [Alan Bridge (*Immigration inspector*)], [James Wolfe, Rodolfo Hoyos (*Soloist in Il Trovatore*)], [Ludovico Tomarchio, Henry Avila, Roone Carrere, Enrico Martinelli, Antonio Filauri, A. Capreoli, Manuel Emanuel, Ettore Campana, Nina Campana, J. Artizoni, Alexander Giglio (*Bits in Pagliacci*)], [Tandy McKenzie (*Tenor in "Questa o quella"*)], [Fanchon and Marco (*Dance team*)], [Stanley Blystone], [Earl Seaman].

Comedy. [*Print viewed*]. In Milan, wealthy Mrs. Claypool has hired Otis B. Driftwood to help her enter society, but he merely helps himself to her money. He does introduce her to opera impresario Herman Gottlieb, however, who convinces her to hire tenor Rudolfo Lassparri for his New York opera company. Lassparri is a cad who beats his dresser Tomasso, and tries to captivate Rosa, a soprano who only loves chorus singer Ricardo Barone. Rosa also has an offer to go to America and is sad to leave Ricardo, until she learns that he is stowing away with Tomasso and his old friend Fiorello, who has a mutilated contract with Driftwood for Ricardo's services. They stay in Driftwood's room, which is crowded with one occupant, but bulges to overflowing as the stowaways, assorted maids, waiters, repairmen, and a woman looking for her Aunt Minnie, wander in. When they dock in New York, the stowaways unsuccessfully pose as a trio of bearded aviators, then hide in Driftwood's hotel to avoid deportation. Meanwhile, although Rosa and Lassparri are set to perform *Il Trovatore*, Lassparri refuses to sing with her because she rejects his amorous advances. Driftwood, Tomasso and Fiorello have a plan, though, and turn the performance into chaos. Tomasso crosses bows with the conductor, the music to "Take Me Out to the Ball Game" is substituted for the opera's score, and Driftwood sells peanuts in the aisles. When Detective Henderson arrives with the police looking for the stowaways, the stage is a shambles, but the day is saved when Lassparri refuses to perform any longer and Ricardo takes his place, with Rosa by his side. *Fortune hunters. New York City. Opera singers. Romance. Stowaways. Air pilots. Cads. Deportation. Italian Americans. Maids. Milan (Italy). I Pagliacci (Opera). Ships. Staterooms. Il Trovatore (Opera).*

Note: The opening title card for the film reads, "Metro-Goldwyn-Mayer presents the Marx Bros. Groucho Chico Harpo." As the Marx Bros. names are introduced, music from the Ruggerio Leoncavallo opera *I Pagliacci* (The Clowns) is heard on the soundtrack. This was the first film that the Marx Bros. made without brother Zeppo, who last appeared in the 1933 Paramount film *Duck Soup* (see *AFI Catalog of Feature Films, 1931-40*, F3.1141). Some reviews erroneously credit the assistant direction to "George" Selander, instead of Lesley Selander. An *HR* news items noted that at one time the Marx Bros. insisted that Selander be fired because they objected to his disciplinary actions on the set. The same news item indicates that considerable reshooting was being required because a change in the picture's make-up men resulted in the "wrong" set of beards being used by the Marx. Bros. (in the sequence in which they impersonate aviators). Other news items include Robert Graves, Purnell Pratt and George Brent in the cast, however, they were not in the released film. Ann Demetrio, Egon Breecher and Kay English are also included in the cast in production news items, but their appearance in the released film cannot be confirmed.

According to a 9 Jul 1935 news item, New York's Metropolitan Opera House chorus was to be recorded for selections from *Pagliacci* and the Giuseppe Verdi opera *Il Trovatore*. This was the first of the Marx Bros. films made at M-G-M. According to modern sources, M-G-M production head Irving Thalberg personally signed the brothers when their contract with Paramount was completed. Modern sources note that many of the "gags" in the film were used by the brothers in earlier acts, and the *MPH* review notes that some of the material was "tried out in tours up and down the 'Coast' first." A *HR* news item

also mentions the tryouts of material and notes that the Marx Bros. frequently tested sketches and gags before reworking them for their films. The film's presskit notes that this film marked the first time that Harpo did not wear his characteristic red wig on screen. According to other press information, M-G-M sponsored a Marx Bros. "Look-Alike" contest simultaneous to the film's release. In its review of the film, the *NYT* called the picture "The Marxist assault on grand opera." The song "Alone" was one of the most popular songs of the year, toping sales charts for several weeks after its release. The 1992 film *Brain Donars* credited *A Night at the Opera* as its source, but many of the situations and most of the dialogue of the in the earlier film was not included in the latter.

DV 14 Oct 1935, p. 3. *FD* 17 Oct 1935, p. 4 *HR* 12 Jun 1935, p. 6. *HR* 14 Jun 1935, p. 1. *HR* 21 Jun 1935, p. 6. *HR* 24 Jun 1935, p. 2. *HR* 28 Jun 1935, p. 2. *HR* 9 Jul 1935, p. 1. *HR* 12 Jul 1935, p. 7. *HR* 20 Jul 1935, p. 5. *HR* 2 Aug 1935, p. 1. *HR* 17 Aug 1935, p. 4. *HR* 19 Aug 1935, p. 3. *HR* 14 Oct 1935, p. 3. *HR* 28 Oct 1935, p. 5. *MPD* 15 Oct 1935, p. 8, 10. *MPH* 26 Oct 1935, p. 72. *MPH* 28 Oct 1935, p. 345. *NYT* 7 Dec 1935, p. 22 *Var* 11 Dec 1935, p. 19.

A NIGHT AT THE RITZ (Hungarian Americans)

Warner Bros. Pictures, Inc. *Dist* Warner Bros. Pictures, Inc.; The Vitaphone Corp. 23 Mar **1935**; Prod: began 20 Dec 1934 [©Warner Bros. Pictures, Inc.; 1 Apr 1935; LP5439]. Sd; b&w. 60 or 62-63 min. PCA cert no. 609.

[*Prod* Sam Bischoff]. [*Exec prod* Jack L. Warner and Hal B. Wallis]. *Dir* William McGann. *Dial dir* Frank McDonald. *Story and scr* Albert J. Cohen and Robert T. Shannon. *Addl dial* Manuel Seff. *Photog* James Van Trees. *Art dir* Esdras Hartley. *Ed* Jack Killifer. *Mus dir* Leo F. Forbstein.

Cast: William Gargan (*Duke Regan*), Patricia Ellis (*Marcia [Jaynos]*), Allen Jenkins (*Gyp [Beagle]*), Dorothy Tree (*Kiki [Lorraine]*), Erik Rhodes (*Leopold [Jaynos]*), Berton Churchill (*Mr. Vincent*), Gordon Westcott (*Scurvin*), Bodil Rosing [(*Mama Jaynos*)], Arthur Hoyt [(*Mr. Hassler*)], Paul Porcasi [(*Henri*)], William Davidson [(*Connolly*)], Mary Treen [(*Isabelle*)], Mary Russell [(*Miss Barry*)], [Lillian Castle (*Newswoman*)], [Cliff Saum (*Truck driver*)], [William Jeffrey (*Sales manager*)], [Tom Wilson (*Patron*)], [Russ Powell (*Cook*)], [Olive Jones (*Laundry girl*)], [Fred "Snowflake" Toones (*Porter*)], [David Newell (*Clerk*)], [William Arnold (*Waiter*)], [Louis Natheaux (*Nick*)], [Sam Rice (*Spectator*)], [Harrison Greene (*Garage owner*)], [Donald Downen (*Bell boy*)], [Leo White (*Salesman*)], [Gordon Elliott (*Vincent's assistant*)], [Dick Winslow (*Messenger*)], [Douglas Wood (*Chairman*)], [John H. Elliott, John Hale, Edward LeSaint (*Directors*)], [Louise Seidel (*Cashier*)], [Jack Wise (*Bus boy*)], [Edwin Stanley (*Doctor*)], [Joseph E. Bernard (*Captain of waiters*)], [Maude Turner Gordon, Leila McIntyre (*Elderly women*)], [Edwin Mordant, William Worthington (*Bankers*)], [Samuel T. Godfrey (*Thin man*)], [Sam Flint (*Toastmaster*)], [Louise Bates], [Georgia Cooper].

Comedy. [*Print viewed*]. Press agent Duke Regan is in love with Marcia Jaynos, although she does not return his affection. Refusing to take no for an answer, Duke invites himself to Marcia's home for dinner, and he is greatly impressed with the delicious meal he believes was cooked by Leopold, Marcia's brother. In reality, although Leopold is convinced he is a great chef, he can't cook at all; it was Marcia's Hungarian mother who cooked the splendid dinner. Duke, however, believes he has made a great discovery, and by creating a mystique around Leopold, he manages to convince Mr. Vincent, the head of the Ritz hotel, to hire Leopold as head chef for an enormous salary. When Marcia learns that Leopold is set to cook dinner for a convention of bankers, she tells Duke that Leopold cannot cook at all. At first he doesn't believe her but when his friend Gyp Beagle eats one of Leopold's creations, he is so sick he has to go to bed for two days. Out of jealousy, Kiki, Duke's former girlfriend, brings reporter Scurvin to the hotel, hoping to break the news and ruin Duke. Gyp shuts Scurvin in a closet to keep the secret and Duke tries to prevent Leopold from cooking, but to no avail. Imagining a roomful of people with severe indigestion, Duke is surprised to see everyone at the convention enjoying their food. When he visits the kitchen, he realizes that Marcia has brought her mother to cook the meal. The delighted Vincent places her under contract and Duke is rewarded with Marcia. *Cooks. Eccentrics. Motherhood. Press agents. Cleveland (OH). Confidence men. Conventions (Gatherings). Hotels. Hungarian Americans. Indigestion. Jealousy. Kidnapping. Manicurists. Reporters. Singers. Taxicab drivers.*

Note: The working title of the film was *King of the Ritz*. According to news items in *DV*, Paul Lukas was to replace William Gargan in the film but negotiations with M-G-M fell through when the studio decided it would be too costly to loan him.

DV 22 Mar 1935, p. 3. *DV* 8 Aug 1934, p. 3. *DV* 18 Dec 1934, p. 4. *DV* 20 Dec 1934, p. 3. *FD* 16 May 1935, p. 10. *HR* 22 Mar 1935, p. 3. *MPD* 25 Mar 1935, p. 6, 9. *MPH* 26 Jan 1935, p. 54. *MPH* 25 May 1935, pp. 54-55. *NYT* 16 May 1935, p. 20. *Var* 22 May 1935, p. 16.

A NIGHT AT TONY PASTOR'S *see* **THE DAUGHTER OF ROSIE O'GRADY**

THE NIGHT BIRD (Italian Americans)
Universal Pictures Corp. 16 Sep 1928 [©Universal Pictures Corp.; 15 Aug 1928; LP25539]. Si; b&w. 7 reels, 6,702 ft.
Dir Fred Newmeyer. *Scen and adpt* Earle Snell. *Adpt* Nick Barrows. *Story* Frederick Hatton and Fanny Hatton. *Titles* Albert De Mond. *Photog* Arthur Todd. *Film ed* Maurice Pivar.
Cast: Reginald Denny (*Kid Davis*), Betsy Lee (*Madelena*), Sam Hardy (*Gleason*), Harvey Clark (*Silsburg*), Corliss Palmer (*Blonde*), Jocelyn Lee (*Redhead*), Alphonse Martel (*Pete*), George Bookasta (*Joe*), Michael Visaroff (*Mario*).
Comedy. Kid Davis, girl-shy contender for the light heavyweight championship, bolts a party and starts home across Central Park, meeting on the way Madelena, a young Italian girl who has run away from home rather than marry a man she does not love. She insists on going home with The Kid and spends the night chastely in his apartment. The two fall in love, but Gleason, The Kid's manager, convinces Madelena that a match with The Kid is impossible. She sadly returns home, and The Kid goes into the ring, disheartened and unprepared. He is taking a bad beating when Madelena's brother comes to ringside and tells him that he must come and save Madelena from marriage to another man. The Kid then knocks out his opponent in nothing flat, goes to Madelena's home, stops the ceremony, and insists that it cannot continue unless he is the groom. It does, and he is. *Boxers. Boxing managers. Brothers and sisters. Italian Americans.*
FD 7 Oct 1928. *NYT* 2 Oct 1928, p. 23. *Var* 3 Oct 1928, p. 23.

NIGHT CLUB GIRL *see* **ONE DARK NIGHT**

THE NIGHT HAWK (Latino)
Stellar Productions, Inc. *Dist* W. W. Hodkinson Corp. 17 Feb 1924. Si; b&w. 6 reels, 5,100-5,200 ft.
Pres Hunt Stromberg. *Dir* Stuart Paton. *Adpt* Joseph Poland. *Story* Carlysle Graham Raht.
Cast: Harry Carey (*"The Hawk"*), Claire Adams (*Clia Milton*), Joseph Girard (*Sheriff Milton*), Fred Malatesta (*José Valdez*), Nicholas De Ruiz (*Manuel Valdez*).
Western. New York City police are chasing "Night Hawk," a crook, when José Valdez, a Mexican American, helps him escape in exchange for Night Hawk's promise to kill a certain sheriff. Night Hawk agrees to do the job, but, arriving in the West, he falls in love with the sheriff's daughter and is unable to complete his mission. He joins the sheriff's posse when José's father, a cattle rustler, illegally makes himself sheriff; then, singlehanded, Night Hawk rescues the girl from José's brigands. *Criminals–Rehabilitation. Gangs. Mexican Americans. New York City. Sheriffs. Rustlers.*
Var 16 Apr 1924.

A NIGHT IN NEW ARABIA (Jewish Americans)
Broadway Star Features Co.; O. Henry Series. *Dist* General Film Co. Nov 1917 [©Broadway Star Features Co., Inc.; 22 Oct 1917; LP11623]. Si; b&w. 4 reels.
Dir Thomas R. Mills. *Scen* F. R. Buckley.
Source: Based on the short story "A Night in New Arabia" by O. Henry in *Strictly Business* (New York, 1910).
Cast: J. Frank Glendon (*Tom McLeod*), Patsey De Forest (*Celia Spraggins*), Horace Vinton (*Jacob Spraggins*), Hattie Delaro (*Henrietta*), Hazlan Drouart (*Annette McCorkle*).
Drama. Jacob Spraggins, a Jewish self-made multi-millionaire, donates to charities to relieve his troubled conscience. When these institutions treat him coldly and continually ask for more, Jacob hires a detective to find the heir of the man he long ago swindled out of property worth ten thousand dollars, so that he can right the wrong. Meanwhile, Jacob's daughter Celia, whose passion for whistling has not been appreciated in her father's financial class, falls in love with the whistling grocery delivery boy, Thomas McLeod, who is the grandson of the man Jacob wronged. Clothed in her housemaid's cap and apron, Celia courts Thomas and wins his love. After Jacob's detective locates Thomas, Jacob, admiring Thomas' independence, gives him ten thousand dollars and hints that he might want to marry

his daughter. Thomas refuses to meet her, but takes the money and elopes with Celia. When Jacob learns this, he pursues them to give his blessing. A year later, Jacob cancels his contributions to charity and raises the price of vinegar three cents per gallon so that his grandson will have all the money he wants. *Conscience. Fathers and daughters. Guilt. Impersonation and imposture. Millionaires. Charities. Delivery boys. Detectives. Elopement. Grandsons. Jews.*
Note: Sources conflict concerning the name of the actress portraying the character "Annette McCorkle." One review lists Hazlan Dorouart, while another lists Hazlan Delaro, and a third credits Hazlan Drouart.
MPN 17 Nov 1917, p. 3485. *MPW* 3 Nov 1917, p. 719, 751. *MPW* 17 Nov 1917, pp. 1032-33. *NYDM* 10 Nov 1917, p. 25.

NIGHT OF THE QUARTER MOON (African Americans)
Albert Zugsmith Productions, Inc. *Dist* Loew's Inc. Feb 1959; Prod: late Aug—late Sep 1958 [©Loew's Inc. & Albert Zugsmith Productions, Inc.; 2 Feb 1959; LP13010]. Sd (Westrex Recording System); b&w; CinemaScope; Process lenses by Panavision. 10 reels, 8,628 ft. 96 min. PCA cert no. 19161.
Dir Hugo Haas. *Asst dir* Ridgeway Callow. *Wrt* Frank Davis and Franklin Coen. *Dir of photog* Ellis Carter. *Art dir* William A. Horning and Malcolm Brown. *Film ed* Ben Lewis. *Set dec* Henry Grace and Jack Mills. *Women's cost* Kitty Mager. *Mus supv and cond by* Albert Glasser. *Rec supv* Franklin Milton. *Makeup* William Tuttle. [*Stunt nurse* Carl Saxe and Al Wyatt].
Song(s): "The Night of the Quarter Moon," lyrics by Sammy Cahn, music by James Van Heusen; "To Whom It May Concern," lyrics by Charlotte Hawkins, music by Nat King Cole; "Blue Moon," lyrics by Lorenz Hart, music by Richard Rodgers.
Cast: *Starring:* Julie London (*Ginny Nelson*), John Drew Barrymore (*Roderic "Chuck" Nelson*), Anna Kashfi (*Maria Robbin*), Dean Jones (*Lexington Nelson*), Agnes Moorehead (*Cornelia Nelson*), *and* Nat King Cole (*Cy Robbin*), *Guest Stars:* Ray Anthony [(*The hotel manager*)], Jackie Coogan [(*Sergeant Bragan*)], Charles Chaplin, Jr. [(*The neighbor*)], Billy Daniels [(*The headwaiter*)], *And Introducing:* Cathy Crosby [(*The singer*)], *With:* James Edwards [(*Asa Tully*)], Arthur Shields [(*Capt. Tom O'Sullivan*)], Edward Andrews [(*Clinton Page*)], Robert Warwick [(*The judge*)], Marguerite Belafonte [(*The hostess*)], Bobi Byrnes [(*The girl in the woods*)], [Joseph Cordovan (*The boy in the woods*)], [Jack Kosslyn (*Dr. Parkson*)], [Katharine Scott (*Amanda*)], [Frank Gorshin (*Bib boy*)], [John Day, Fred Schwieller (*Officers*)], [Boots Wade, Barbara Walden (*Dancers*)], [Ken Patterson, George E. Stone, Burt Douglas, Nicky Blair (*Detectives*)], [William Vaughn, Ivan Bonar (*Photographers*)], [Bill Layne (*Cameraman*)], [Hamil Petroff (*Choreographer*)], [Buck Young, Mark Lowell, Jerry Murray, Carl Christian (*Reporters*)], [Lee Belser (*Woman reporter*)], [Irwin Berke (*Realtor*)], [Charles Horvath (*Carter*)], [Peter G. Vaiches (*Sid Joss*)], [Norman Grabowski (*Tough kid*)], [Glenn Jacobson (*Second boy*)], [Gene Walker (*Patrolman*)], [Helene Marshall (*Miss Kirby*)], [Arthur Marshall (*Stranger*)], [Phyllis Douglas, Kay Windsor (*Teenage girls*)], [Joe Green (*Bailiff*)], [John Harding (*Major Arnold Folsey*)], [Pat Cawley (*Miss Murphy*)], [Patricia Lloyd (*Police matron*)], [Ike Jones (*Cab driver*)], [Joe Bardot (*Man at shipyard*)].
Social, Legal, Psychological, Drama, with songs. [*Print viewed*]. As newlywed Ginny Nelson, wearing a revealing robe, hangs paintings in her new home, four smirking teenagers throw rocks through her window, and she is cut on the forehead from flying glass. Terrified, she calls her husband Roderic, who is known as Chuck, and he races home. He fights with one of the boys, then slugs a police officer and is arrested. After the father of one of the arrested boys tells police that Ginny came to the window half undressed, she is also arrested. Harassed during her interrogation, Ginny thinks back to her life in the village in Mexico where she met Chuck: Recently discharged from the service after spending two years in a Korean prison camp, Chuck, on a fishing vacation with his brother Lexington, keeps to himself. One day he comes across Ginny, whose father owns the fishing resort, swimming in the nude. Later, they chat and she asks about the prison camp. He angrily describes the ordeal, then apologizes for his outburst. At night, unable to sleep, Chuck views Ginny from a distance as she again swims in the nude. When the brothers are called home by their mother Cornelia because of a tax problem in Washington, Chuck decides to remain, and later that day, he swims with Ginny, and they kiss and embrace. When she reveals that her grandmother on her mother's side was Portuguese Angolan

and that she is one-quarter black, he says he does not care. Nervous about their involvement, Ginny attempts to leave for Mexico City, but Chuck catches her at the bus station. She agrees to marry him, and they go to San Francisco, where his wealthy family lives. Ginny's cousin, Maria Robbin, invites her to the nightclub she and her husband Cy own in the city. Chuck is introduced to Cy, a dark-skinned African American, and photos are taken of the four, which appear in the newspaper captioned, "Social Leader's Bride Revealed as Quadroon." Chuck and Ginny are then told they must leave the hotel in which they are honeymooning. They buy a new home with cash and move in immediately. Three neighbors come to their door and say they do not want their area turned into a "colored neighborhood" because their real estate values will be lowered, and attest that the restriction clause in their deed forbids anyone but Caucasians from living there. After recalling being taunted by the neighborhood kids, Ginny's thoughts return to the present interrogation at the police station. When Chuck falls in another room, a doctor gives him a shot, and in his stupor, Chuck imagines that his interrogators are Korean officers. Ginny is let go after Chuck is released to his mother's custody. When Ginny comes to his family's home, Bay End, Cornelia warns her never to see her son again if she wants him to get well. As private police escort Ginny to her car, she yells Chuck's name. Dazed, Chuck asks about Ginny's voice, and he is given more sedatives. Marie visits Ginny and suggests she get as much money from the Nelsons as she can, then return to Mexico. Ginny cries, saying she loves Chuck, and Maria expresses her bitterness about whites and warns Ginny not to try to marry into their families. Just then, Chuck calls and says he cannot think straight, but that he loves her, before Lex hangs up the phone. Ginny resolves to get a lawyer, and Maria has her talk to Cy. He tests her to see if she will try to exploit race to get money from the Nelsons, and when he sees she is sincere, he has Maria take her to meet Asa Tully, a black attorney who is playing guitar at a jazz club to make money. Asa, who has had limited employment opportunities as a lawyer because of discrimination, calls Cornelia and threatens to get a court order to allow Ginny to see Chuck. She invites them to Bay End, where a process server gives Ginny a summons to appear at an annulment hearing. At the widely publicized trial, the Nelsons' attorney, Clinton Page, presents an affadavit signed by Chuck stating he did not know of Ginny's African heritage at the time of their marriage, and a statement by the family's physician that Chuck is not well enough to attend. When Asa asks for a postponement, Ginny urges him to proceed as quickly as possible because she is concerned about Chuck's health. Page attempts to prove that Chuck was emotionally withdrawn and thus susceptible to lies and deceit, and that Ginny knew the family was wealthy and swam naked to entice him. Asa questions her father, Captain O'Sullivan, who says that while he never concealed Ginny's heritage from Chuck, he also never bragged about the fact that she is descended from an African princess. After Asa proves that the police interrogation took over two hours, the judge grants his request for a court-appointed doctor to examine Chuck to see if he is able to appear. Chuck escapes from the sanitarium where he is being held, however, upon learning that Cornelia used the power of attorney he gave her when he left for Korea to file the annulment suit. He goes to Cy and Maria's club and finds that Ginny is staying with Maria. Opposed to their reuniting, Maria relates that there is a "black curtain" dividing the races and convinces Chuck to make Ginny hate him for her own good. In court, Chuck falsely testifies that he did not know of Ginny's African blood when he married her. Ginny, in tears, relates that Chuck saw her without a bathing suit and thus knew she was dark all over, and not just tan. To settle the issue, Asa asks her to disrobe, and the judge agrees, stating that the case rests on the color of her skin, then clears the courtroom. When Ginny hesitates, Asa rips the back of her dress, and Chuck yells at him to stop, then covers her with his coat and hugs her. He tells the judge he thought he was doing what was right for his wife by going along with the annulment, but knows now he was wrong. He leads Ginny out of the courtroom and tells the press that he feels like a human being again. After they leave by cab, Asa, alone, walks from the courtroom. *African Americans–Mixed blood. Class distinction. Duplicity. Marriage–Mixed. Racism. Trials. African Americans. Brothers. Cousins. Discrimination in housing. Drugging. Family relationships. Fishing villages. Honeymoons. Interrogation. Irish. Jazz music. Lawyers. Marriage–Annulment. Mental illness. Mexico. Nightclubs. Nudity. Physicians. San Francisco (CA). Swimming. Veterans. Youth.*

Note: This film was re-released in 1961 under the title *Flesh and Flame* by Cinema Associates, according to *HR*, and in 1966 under the title *The Color of Her Skin*, according to *Filmfacts*. In Aug 1958, prior to production, M-G-M considered using two titles for this film, planning to use an "exploitation" title, either *I Crossed the Color Line* or *Quadroon*, and a "prestige" title, *Night of the Quarter Moon*, according to a *DV* news item. The studio planned to let exhibitors choose to play either one, but realized that the exploitation titles "will not play in the South." No further information has been located concerning the exhibition of the film under the exploitation titles.

According to information in the MPAA/PCA Collection at the AMPAS Library, PCA officials, upon reading the script for this film, warned the producers about showing "Ginny" in the nude, urged them to use restraint in the vandalization scene, and asked them to review the police interrogation scene, complaining that the third degree methods "constitute a very bad portrayal of our police." In addition, the PCA objected to the climax of the film in which "Ginny" is instructed to disrobe in the courtroom: "The business of a woman being allowed to expose her intimate parts in the presence of a judge and other principles, in order to prove that the color of her skin is the same all over, is in our judgment an unacceptable portrayal of our Courts of Law. The thought comes to mind that any judge in maintaining the dignity of the Court would in a situation of this kind appoint a female doctor to make this examination privately and report her findings." According to *LAMirror-News*, Anna Kashfi, who portrayed "Maria," protested this scene as it was filmed and ran from the stage "in hysterics." Kashfi stated, "It's humiliating. I am not a Negro but what they are doing is exploiting the race." Kashfi, according to the article, was forced to return, and though she expressed the wish to leave the project, director Hugo Haas said that would be impossible.

Many reviews were critical of the courtroom scene. *BHCN* complained that the film "ends on a note of the preposterous" and "descends to mere cheap sensationalism." *Monthly Film Bulletin* called the film "vulgar, sensational and humanly false." The film was refused a permit by the Atlanta Censor Board in 1959. Reviews praised James Edwards' performance. *MPD* called his the film's best, while *HR* wrote his character was "brilliantly enacted." *HR* also praised Nat King Cole's performance as an "off-beat and interesting characterization of a self-made, successful colored man who is sick of racial issues." Cole sang the song "To Whom It May Concern" in the film, while Cathy Crosby, the daughter of Bob Crosby, made her film debut singing "Blue Moon" in a nightclub scene. Anna Kashfi, in her book about her life with Marlon Brando, to whom she was married at the time of this film, stated that originally her character was to have been the daughter of a character played by Louis Armstrong, but when Nat King Cole got the role instead, her role was changed to his wife. Kashfi also states that she won the best supporting actress award for this film at the 1961 Cartagena Film Festival.

BHCN 2 Apr 1959. *Box* 16 Feb 1959 *Cue* 7 Mar 1959. *DV* 4 Sep 1957. *DV* 8 Aug 1958. *DV* 12 Aug 1958. *DV* 6 Feb 1959, p. 3. *Exh* 11 Feb 1959, p. 4558. *FD* 6 Feb 1959, p. 6. *Filmfacts* 1966, p. 388. *Har* 14 Feb 1959, p. 27. *HR* 29 Aug 1958, p. 8. *HR* 26 Sep 1958, p. 10. *HR* 6 Feb 1959, p. 3. *HR* 6 Jul 1961. *LAEx* 2 Apr 1959, sec. 3, p. 2. *LAT* 3 Apr 1959, pt. II, p. 10. *Monthly Film Bulletin* 1959, p. 73. *LAMirror-News* 11 Sep 1958. *LAMirror-News* 2 Apr 1959. *MPD* 6 Feb 1959. *MPHPD* 21 Feb 1959, p. 165. *New Yorker* 14 Mar 1959. *NYT* 5 Mar 1959, p. 35. *Var* 11 Feb 1959, p. 6.

NIGHT WIND (German Americans)

Twentieth Century-Fox Film Corp.; Sol M. Wurtzel Productions, Inc. *Dist* Twentieth Century-Fox Film Corp. Oct **1948**; Los Angeles opening: 8 Oct 1948; Prod: early—late Apr 1948 at Motion Picture Center Studio [©Twentieth Century-Fox Film Corp.; 25 Aug 1948; LP2060]. Sd (Western Electric Recording); b&w. 7 reels, 6,130 ft. 68 min. PCA cert no. 13169.

Pres SOL M. WURTZEL. *Dir* James Tinling. *Asst dir* Paul Wurtzel. *Orig story* Robert G. North. *Scr* Arnold Belgard and Robert G. North. *Dir of photog* Benjamin Kline. [*Cam op* Perry Finerman]. [*Stills* Buddy Longworth]. *Art dir* George Van Marter. *Supv film ed* William F. Claxton. *Film ed* Roy V. Livingston. *Set dec* Fay Babcock. *Mus supv* David Chudnow. *Mus score* Ralph Stanley. *Sd tech* Earl Sitar. *Makeup artist* Ray Lopez. *Hair stylist* Elaine Ramsey. *Prod asst* Cliff R. Gans. [*Scr supv* Sascha Laurence]. [*Grip* C. O. Morris].

Cast: Charles Russell [(*Ralph Benson*)], Virginia Christine [(*Jean Benson*)], Gary Gray [(*Johnny Benson*)], John Ridgely [(*Walters*)], James Burke [(*Sheriff Hamilton*)], Konstantin Shayne [(*Dr. Ulding*)], William Stelling [(*Barlow*)], Guy Kingsford [(*Dick Wilson*)], Charles Lang [(*John Steele*)], Deanna Woodruff [(*Margie Benson*)], Flame [(*Big Dan*)], [William Bakewell (*Captain Kingston*)], [Harry Cheshire (*Judge Thorgeson*)], [William Benedict (*Irv Bennett*)], [Michael Chapin (*Vinnie Jardine*)], [Harlan Warde (*Colonel*)].

Animal, Domestic, Adventure. [*Not viewed*]. Young Johnny Benson lives in California with his mother Jean, stepfather Ralph, half sister Margie and German shepherd dog Big Dan. Big Dan and Johnny's real father, John Steele, saved an infantry company during World War II, and Johnny's father was killed while on a mission. Johnny is having difficulty accepting Ralph, a rocket scientist, as his new father. Ralph works with exiled German scientist Dr. Ulding, who lodges with the Bensons. One night, on their way home, Ralph and Ulding give a ride to three hunters, Dick Wilson, Walters and Sheriff Hamilton. Walters

leaves his trench coat in the car and, when Ulding goes to return it, Big Dan follows him. After Walters gives the coat, which has the smell of duck blood on it, to Wilson to hang in a shed, Big Dan attacks Wilson and breaks his neck. The sheriff assumes that the killer is a wild wolf-dog and organizes a hunt to track it down. Ralph does not permit Johnny to go along on the hunt but takes Big Dan. During the hunt, Walters attempts to shoot the sheriff but is knocked down by Big Dan and then claims the shooting was an accident. Later, Walters suggests to the sheriff that Big Dan might be the killer. When Ulding keeps a dinner appointment with Walters and his associate, Barlow, he asks to see the trench coat. Barlow goes to get it, but is attacked by Big Dan, who takes off as soon as Walters and Ulding run up. Ulding finds an I.D. tag in the coat for a Capt. C. J. Calvin. Meanwhile, Big Dan sits beside the grave of Johnny's father and remembers an incident during the war when they both were parachuted into a war zone to keep a rendezvous with a Captain Calvin: Unknown to them, the real Captain Calvin has been killed and his identity assumed by a German soldier, Walters—who shoots and kills Steele. Big Dan attacks Walters and rips open his leg but is knocked out by a blow from a shot gun. In the present, the sheriff comes to the Benson home to tell them that Barlow has been killed and that Big Dan's collar was found, clutched in his hand. Ralph has to explain to Johnny that Big Dan may not have been sufficiently detrained by the army and could still be a killer. As the sheriff takes Big Dan away, Walters tries to shoot the dog but is grabbed by Ralph. Later, Ulding tells Ralph that he has sent a telegram to the FBI in an effort to discover why Walters is in possession of a dead army officer's trench coat. Ralph recognizes Calvin's name from Johnny's father's last mission and phones Counter Intelligence. Meanwhile, Johnny packs a bag, goes to the sheriff's station and takes Big Dan from the yard. Before Johnny and Big Dan get far, however, they encounter Ralph, who persuades Johnny to let the law prove Big Dan innocent. Johnny agrees and, in Judge Thorgeson's office, the case is discussed. with all concerned parties present. Walters makes his statement, then asks to be excused as he has a plane to catch. Big Dan sees Walters leave and tries to go after him. Johnny pleads with the judge not to have Big Dan destroyed, and Ralph asks him to delay his decision. Big Dan manages to escape and chases after Walters. Meanwhile, Kingston, a Counter Intelligence officer, arrives at Walters' house and begins to interrogate him but Walters knocks him out with his cane. The sheriff, Ralph and Johnny arrive to warn Walters that Big Dan is loose and probably headed his way. As they are about to leave, Big Dan arrives and attacks Walters but Johnny calls him off. The sheriff tells Johnny that he will have to shoot the dog and Johnny bids Big Dan a tearful farewell. However, Kingston recovers and Johnny sees him and calls Ralph. After Kingston explains who he is, Ralph grabs Walters and sends Johnny to stop the sheriff from shooting Big Dan. Johnny now regards his stepfather as a hero, and he and Big Dan are free to play together once again. *Children. German shepherd dogs. Germans. Stepfathers. Animal traps. Coats. Dogs, war use of. Hunters. Judges. Military intelligence. Parachuting. Scientists. Sheriffs. War heroes. World War II.*

Note: The film's working title was *Big Dan*, and it was reviewed by *HR* under the title *Night Watch*. Although the film was was not viewed, the credits and summary were taken from a cutting continuity in the Twentieth Century-Fox Produced Scripts Collection at the UCLA Arts–Special Collections Library. According to a *HR* news item, location shooting was done in the Santa Monica Mountains.

Box 11 Sep 1948. *DV* 11 Oct 1948, p. 3. *FD* 1 Sep 1948, p. 7. *HR* 9 Apr 1948, p. 14. *HR* 11 Oct 1948, p. 4. *MPHPD* 4 Sep 1948, p. 4302. *Var* 25 Aug 1948, p. 8.

THE NIGHTINGALE (Italian Americans)

All Star Feature Corp. *Dist* Alco Film Corp. 5 Oct **1914**. Si; b&w. 5 reels.

Scen Augustus Thomas.

Cast: Ethel Barrymore (*Isola Franti, "The Nightingale"*), William Courtleigh, Jr. (*Tony Franti*), Frank Andrews (*Andrea Franti*), Conway Tearle (*Charles Marden*), Charles A. Stevenson (*Nathan Marden*), Irving Brooks (*"Red" Galvin*), Mario Majeroni (*David Mantz*), Philip Hahn (*Jean de Resni*), Ida Darling (*Mrs. Belmore*), Bobby Stewart (*Nathan Marden, II*), Henri Antiznat (*Prefect of police*), Frank Dudley (*Frank*), M. Monet (*Gazzi Catassi*), Caroline French (*Maid*), Mrs. Cooper (*Nola*), Claude Cooper (*Madonni*), Ed West (*Police sergeant*).

Drama. Widowed Italian organ grinder Tony Franti lives in a New York ghetto with his daughter Isola, a street singer, and son Andrea, a member of the Black Hand. When Tony is killed by a bomb planted by the Black Hand, Isola begins voice instructions, unaware that the lessons are financed by Charles Marden, the son of wealthy banker Nathan Marden. On the evening of her triumphant debut in *Aida* at the Paris Opera, Charles drunkenly tries to seduce her, telling her of her obligation to him. She flees, but later becomes a star at the Metropolitan Opera in New York. A remorseful Charles proposes to Isola and they are married, over his father's initial objections. Some time later, Andrea robs Nathan's house and kills him. Isola tends to Andrea's wounds, unaware of his involvement in Nathan's death, but when she discovers the truth, she confronts him. Because she has been away from home so much, Charles thinks that Isola has been unfaithful and believes Andrea to be her lover. She leaves Charles and takes their small son, but when Andrea dies and Charles discovers that he was Isola's brother, he quickly goes to her and begs for forgiveness. *Black Hand (United States). Family relationships. Italian Americans. Murder. Nursing back to health. Opera singers. Seduction. Bankers. Bombs. Drunkenness. Metropolitan Opera (New York City). Organ grinders. Paris (France). Robbery.*

Note: This film marked the motion picture debut of Ethel Barrymore and according to contemporary sources was written especially for her by Augustus Thomas. It was also the first film distributed by Alco Film Corp.

Motog 18 Jul 1914, p. 98. *Motog* 10 Oct 1914, p. 509. *MPN* 10 Oct 1914, p. 47. *MPW* 3 Oct 1914, p. 76. *MPW* 10 Oct 1914, p. 192. *MPW* 24 Oct 1914, p. 560. *NYDM* 30 Sep 1914, p. 32. *Var* 3 Oct 1914, p. 21.

1937 PIGSKIN PARADE *see* **LIFE BEGINS IN COLLEGE**

NO DEJES LA PUERTA ABIERTA (Spanish language)

Fox Film Corp. *Dist* Fox Film Corp. **1933**; New York opening: 3 Nov 1933; Prod: May—Jun 1933. Sd (Western Electric Noiseless Recording); b&w. 8 reels. Passed by the National Board of Review. Spanish language.

Dirección de [*Dir*] Lou Seiler. [*Dial dir* Miguel de Zárraga]. [*Asst dir* Sam Schneider]. *Adaptación cinematográfica de* [*Scr*] Paul Perez and José López Rubio. [*Photog* L. William O'Connell]. *Dirección musical de* [*Mus dir*] Samuel Kaylin. [*Sd* E. Clayton Ward].

Song(s): "It's Our Anniversary Day (Hace un año que me casé)," "Spend an Evening at Home (Esta noche en casa los dos)," "Sing a Song of Sin (Beber para olvidar)" and "Cupid in the Moonlight (Luna turbadora)," music by Desider Josef Vecsei, English lyrics by L. Wolfe Gilbert and Spanish translations by José López Rubio and Raúl Roulien.

Source: Based on the play *Pleasure Cruise* by Austen Allen (London, 26 Apr 1932).

Cast: Raúl Roulien (*Raúl*), Rosita Moreno (*Rosa*), Mona Maris (*Sra. [Lucrecia] Delfi*), Jorge Lewis (*Darmant*), Romualdo Tirado (*Tom*), Ralph Navarro (*Murchison*), Rosita Granada (*Janet*), Alfredo Sabato (*Sr. Delfi*), Martín Garralaga (*Entrenador*), Manuel Noriega (*Barbero*), Frances Drake (*Modelo*), [José Peña "Pepet" (*Steward*)], [Fred Martens (*Page boy*)], [Carlos Villarías (*Purser*)], [Blanca Vischer].

Comedy. [*Print viewed*]. [The following plot summary is based on the English-language version of this film, *Pleasure Cruise*; character names refer to that version. For further information regarding the English-language version, please see the note below and the entry for *Pleasure Cruise* in the *AFI Catalog of Feature Films, 1931-40*.] After he loses his fortune, English gentleman Andrew Poole is delighted to discover that his fiancée Shirley still wishes to marry him. Shirley works in an office, while Andrew tends the house and writes a novel. By their first wedding anniversary, Andrew has become consumed with jealousy over the men Shirley meets at work. Fed up with Andrew's incessant nagging, Shirley decides that she needs a "marriage holiday" and books passage for herself on the ocean liner *Nebula*. Andrew says that he is going fishing but instead gets a job in the *Nebula*'s barber shop. He spies on Shirley as she makes friends with other passengers and scares off one of her potential suitors, Murchison, by intimating that Shirley and her husband, who is secretly on the boat, run a scam to blackmail her admirers. Andrew then frightens off another male passenger, Rollins, by telling him that Shirley's jealous husband killed the last man he caught in her boudoir. Meanwhile, Mrs. Signus, a flirtatious older woman, develops a liking for Andrew, whom she mistakenly thinks is a prince in hiding. One morning, Andrew is spying on Shirley from Mrs. Signus' cabin when Mrs. Signus suddenly appears and catches him. She then hides him in the closet when Shirley arrives for a chat. Shirley confides that her husband is the only man who has ever kissed her and that she

would like to have more experience. Andrew sneezes in the closet, and Shirley assumes that the hidden man is Mrs. Signus' lover. She thanks Mrs. Signus for her example and prepares to attend a gala costume ball that evening. Shirley is accompanied by English playboy Richard Taversham, who is dressed as "Romeo." Andrew, disguised as "Neptune," overhears as Richard romances Shirley and begs her to leave her cabin door open that night so that he may visit her. While Richard is in his cabin preparing for the tryst, Andrew steals some of his "Stolen Love" cologne, then ties his cabin door shut. Meanwhile, Shirley has become tipsy on the champagne sent by Richard and imagines that Andrew's photograph indicates for her to lock her door. Deciding to be faithful, Shirley locks the door but does not notice as the bolt does not catch. Andrew enters after Shirley has turned out the lights and makes love to her without saying a word. When he leaves, he takes the monogrammed cigarette case that he gave to her before they were married. The next morning, Richard apologizes to Shirley for not coming to her cabin, and Shirley realizes in horror that she does not know the identity of her lover. She disembarks early and goes home, where her friend, Judy Mills, advises her not to tell Andrew of her "infidelity." Just then, Richard arrives and Shirley is confused by his claim that the barber shop attendant gave him her address and said that she wanted him to visit her. Andrew arrives home a short time later, and Richard is shocked to recognize him as the attendant. As Andrew escorts Richard to the door, he shows him the cigarette case, and the relieved Richard nods that he understands Andrew's subterfuge. Shirley sees the interchange in a mirror and figures out the deception her husband has practiced. She confesses that she spent the night with another man, but states that she is not ashamed, for she is proud to have appealed to "such a lover." Shirley then tells Andrew that her lover is in the bedroom, and as he looks at himself in the mirror, she informs him that she knew all along that he was on the boat. She then tells him to knock the next time he wants to make love to a lady, and closes the bedroom door. Andrew smiles and knocks, then goes into the bedroom. *English. Impersonation and imposture. Jealousy. Marriage. Ocean liners. Working wives. Auctions. Barbers and barbershops. Cigarette cases. Drunkenness. Masked balls. Novelists. Photographs. Playboys. Ship crews. Wedding anniversaries.*

Note: The English working title of this Spanish version was *Trip to Nowhere*, and the Spanish working titles were *Viaje de placer* and *¿Dónde has pasado la noche?* Andrés de Segurola was originally in the cast, but his role was cut from the final film. Contemporary sources include Juan Torena and Tom Patricola in the cast of the Spanish version, but their participation in the completed film has not been confirmed. For information on the English-language version, *Pleasure Cruise*, which was directed by Frank Tuttle and starred Genevieve Tobin and Roland Young, please see the entry for that film in the *AFI Catalog of Feature Films, 1931-40*; F3.3478.

FD 13 Nov 1933, p. 8. *NYT* 6 Nov 1933, p. 24.

NO GREATER LOVE (Irish Americans, Jewish Americans)
Columbia Pictures Corp. *Dist* Columbia Pictures Corp. 4 Jun 1932; New York opening: week of 13 May 1932 [©Columbia Pictures Corp.; 16 May 1932; LP3030]. Sd; b&w. 6 reels, 5,531 ft. 59-60 min.
Supv Benjamin Stoloff. *Dir* Lewis Seiler. *Story and dial* Isadore Bernstein. *Cont* Lou Breslow. *Photog* William Thompson.
Cast: Dickie Moore (*Tommy Burns*), Alexander Carr (*Sidney Cohen*), Richard Bennett (*Surgeon*), Beryl Mercer (*Mrs. Burns*), Hobart Bosworth (*Doctor*), Betty Jane Graham (*Mildred Flannigan*), Alec Francis (*Priest*), Mischa Auer (*Rabbi*), Helen Jerome Eddy (*Superintendent*), Martha Mattox (*Investigator*), Tom McGuire (*Policeman*).
Melodrama. [*Not viewed*]. Sidney Cohen, the Jewish owner of a delicatessen located in the tenement district, is a warm-hearted old bachelor who cares for everyone, especially Mildred Flannigan, a wheelchair-bound Irish Catholic child who lives upstairs. When Mildred's mother passes away, Sidney happily adopts the girl and soon fills her life with an abundance of love, Yiddish ballads and a determination to walk. Sidney's dearest hope is that someday Mildred's legs will be strong enough for her to walk, and she repays "Uncle" Sidney's devotion by worshipping him. Their lives are made complete by Tommy Burns, Mildred's young playmate, and his grandmother, who cooks their meals in exchange for desperately needed money. After learning that a great European surgeon who is about to visit the country is the only one who can assist Mildred, Sidney sells his deli for a fraction of its value to obtain the money for the doctor's fees. He returns to his former occupation as a street peddler in order to provide for Mildred, whose operation proves to

be a failure. They remain hopeful, however, and for Sidney's sake Mildred continues her painful exercises. More misfortune strikes when a group of stern charity workers decide that Mildred would be better off in an orphanage. Despite the pleas of two of Sidney's friends, a priest and a rabbi, Mildred is taken to the institution, where she is desperately unhappy. Sidney also cannot bear the separation, and in order to see Mildred one last time, promises to make her hate him so that she will be content to stay at the orphanage. Sidney tells the child that he no longer loves her, and her pathetic tears break his heart. He then wanders in the street during a rainstorm and catches pneumonia. Without Mildred, Sidney feels he has no reason to live, and the priest, realizing that he is near death, retrieves the child from the orphanage. Mildred and Sidney experience a near miracle, as her presence gives him the will to recover, and her reborn faith and love for him allow her to walk. Mildred again comes to live with Sidney, and as she gradually improves, he builds business in a new deli. *Adoption. Handicapped. Jews. Love. Orphans. Catholic Church. Charity workers. Delicatessens. Grandmothers. Irish Americans. Operations, Surgical. Orphanages. Peddlers and peddling. Physicians. Pneumonia. Priests. Rabbis. Songs. Tenement-houses.*

Note: According to *FD*, the audience at a screening at the Roxy Theatre wept throughout the movie. The *MPH* review noted that an onscreen foreword espoused the cause of handicapped orphans. Columbia remade the picture as *City Streets* in 1938 (see above).
FD 15 May 1932, p. 10. *MPH* 21 May 1932, p. 103. *NYT* 14 May 1932, p. 11. *Var* 17 May 1932, p. 14.

NO GREATER LOVE (1938) *see* **CITY STREETS**

NO MATARÁS (Spanish language)
Hispano International Film Corp. of Hollywood. *Dist* Modern Film Sales. **1935**; New York opening: 8 Nov 1935; Prod: Aug—Sep 1935 at Talisman Studios. Sd; b&w. 92 min. Spanish language.
Prod Miguel Contreras Torres. *Dir* Miguel Contreras Torres. *Asst dir* Bartlett Carré and Miguel de Zárraga, Jr. *Scr* Miguel Contreras Torres. *Photog* Arthur Martinelli. *Ed* Earl Turner. *Mus* Ernesto González Jiménez and Carlos Gianotti. *Sd* Cliff Ruberg.
Cast: Ramón Pereda (*Antonio*), Adriana Lamar (*Amapola*), Alberto O'Farrill, Estela Segarra, Paul Ellis, José Luis Tortosa, Francisco Marán, José Peña "Pepet", Lucio Villegas, Vernon Steele, Rita Luna, Miguel de Zárraga, Juan Duval, José Rocco, Elisa Muriel, Cuarteto México, Carlos y Greta, Los de Lima (*Dancers*), Fernando Luis Leal (*Master of ceremonies*).
Gangster, Comedy-drama. [*Not viewed*]. During the last months of Prohibition, Antonio, a handsome young Spaniard of good family, is driven by misfortune to become a gangster involved with New York bootleggers. However, because of his courageous, noble brother, and the love of a cabaret singer, Antonio is finally redeemed. *Bootleggers. Criminals–Rehabilitation. New York City. Nightclubs. Romance. Singers. Spanish Americans. Brothers.*

Note: The working title for this film was *Mi hermano es un gangster*. The *NYT* translated the title as *Thou Shalt Not Kill*. According to *NYT*, the film was shot in New York and assembled in Hollywood.
FD 12 Nov 1935, p. 7. *NYT* 11 Nov 1935, p. 20.

NO OTHER WOMAN *see* **BUCCANEER'S GIRL**

NO PLACE TO DIE *see* **GUN BATTLE AT MONTEREY**

¡NO TE CASES! *see* **DOS MÁS UNO, DOS**

NO WAY OUT (African Americans)
Twentieth Century-Fox Film Corp. *Dist* Twentieth Century-Fox Film Corp. Oct **1950**; New York opening: 17 Aug 1950; Prod: 28 Oct—20 Dec 1949; addl scenes started 14 Feb 1950 [©Twentieth Century-Fox Film Corp.; 16 Aug 1950; LP518]. Sd (Western Electric Recording); b&w. 12 reels, 9,590 ft. 106 min. PCA cert no. 14257.
Pres DARRYL F. ZANUCK. *Prod* Darryl F. Zanuck. *Dir* Joseph L. Mankiewicz. [*Asst dir* William Eckhardt]. *Wrt* Joseph L. Mankiewicz and Lesser Samuels. [*Contr wrt* Philip Yordan]. *Dir of photog* Milton Krasner. [*Cam op* Paul Lockwood]. [*Stills* Anthony Ugrin]. *Spec photog eff* Fred Sersen. *Art dir* Lyle Wheeler and George W. Davis. *Film ed* Barbara McLean. *Set dec* Thomas Little and Stuart Reiss. *Ward dir* Charles Le Maire. *Cost des* Travilla. [*Ward* Josephine Brown]. *Mus* Alfred Newman. *Orch* Edward Powell. *Sd* Bernard Freericks and Roger Heman. *Makeup artist* Ben Nye. [*Hair stylist* Irene Brooks and Gladys Witten]. [*Prod mgr* Sidney Bowen]. [*Scr supv* Wesley Jones]. [*Tech adv* Valentine A. Becker and Dr. Ben Sacks]. [*Casting dir* William Gorder]. [*Assoc casting dir* W. H. Maybery].

Cast: RICHARD WIDMARK [(*Ray Biddle*)], LINDA DARNELL [(*Edie Johnson*)], STEPHEN McNALLY [(*Dr. Daniel Wharton*)], Sidney Poitier [(*Dr. Luther Brooks*)], Mildred Joanne Smith [(*Cora Brooks*)], Harry Bellaver [(*George Biddle*)], Stanley Ridges [(*Dr. Sam Moreland*)], Dots Johnson [(*Lefty Jones*)], [Amanda Randolph (*Gladys*)], [Bill Walker (*Alderman Mathew Tompkins*)], [Ruby Dee (*Connie*)], [Ossie Davis (*John*)], [Ken Christy (*Edward Kowalski*)], [Frank Richards (*Mac*)], [George Tyne (*Whitey*)], [Robert Adler (*Assistant deputy*)], [Bert Freed (*Rocky*)], [Jim Toney (*Deputy sheriff*)], [Maude Simmons (*Luther's mother*)], [Ray Teal (*Day deputy*)], [Will Wright (*Dr. Cheney*)], [Harry Lauter, Harry Carter, Don Kohler, Ray Hyke (*Orderlies*)], [Wade Dumas (*Jonah*)], [Fred Graham (*Ambulance driver*)], [William Pullen (*Ambulance doctor*)], [Jasper Weldon (*Henry*)], [Ruben Wendorff (*Polish husband*)], [Laiola Wendorff (*Polish wife*)], [Ernest Anderson (*Schoolteacher*)], [Victor Kilian, Sr. (*Father*)], [Mack Williams (*Husband*)], [Dick Paxton (*Johnny Biddle*)], [Eleanor Audley, Doris Kemper (*Wives*)], [Stan Johnson, Frank Overton (*Interns*)], [Kitty O'Neil (*Landlady*)], [Phil Tully (*Sergeant*)], [J. Louis Johnson (*Elderly black man*)], [Ian Wolfe (*Watkins*)], [Emmett Smith (*Joe*)], [Ralph Dunn (*Sam*)], [Ruth Warren (*Sam's wife*)], [Robert Davis (*Hoodlum*)], [Ann Morrison, Eda Reis Merin, Ann Tyrrell (*Nurses*)], [Kathryn Sheldon (*Mother*)], [Ralph Hodges (*Terry*)], [Thomas Ingersoll (*Priest*)], [Herbert Lytton, Gil Herman, Don Hicks, Jerry Sheldon, Charles Conrad, Joe Hartman, Art Thompson, William R. Klein (*Doctors*)], [Charles J. Flynn (*Deputy*)], [Howard Mitchell (*Bailiff*)], [John Whitney (*Assistant*)], [Charles McAvoy (*Riley*)], [Eileen Boyle, Johnnie Jallings, Gertrude Tighe, Betsy Blair, Frances Ruth, Marie Lampe (*Telephone operators*)], [Frank Jaquet (*Reilly*)], [Elzie Emanuel, William Washington, Sam Marlowe, Jr., Edwin Sneed (*Students*)], [Bernice Dalton (*Secretary*)], [Genie Hershon (*Girl*)], [Al Murphy (*Cab driver*)], [Duke Watson (*Gas station attendant*)], [Butch Bradbeck (*Boy*)], [Jessie Arnold], [Polly Bailey], [Katharine Marlowe], [Maudie Prickett], [John Butler], [Jack Daley], [Alice Goering], [Barbara Pepper], [Daniel Meyers], [Florence Allen].

Medical, Social, Drama. [*Print viewed*]. Dr. Luther Brooks, an intern who has just passed the state board examination to qualify for his license to practice, is the first African-American doctor at the urban county hospital at which he trained. Because he lacks self-confidence, Luther requests to work as a junior resident at the hospital for another year. Johnny and Ray Biddle, brothers who were both shot in the leg by a policeman as they attempted a robbery, are brought to the hospital's prison ward. As Luther tends to the disoriented Johnny, he is bombarded with racist slurs by Ray, who grew up in Beaver Canal, the white working class section of the city. Believing that Johnny has a brain tumor, Luther administers a spinal tap, but Johnny dies during the procedure. Wondering if Ray's antagonism may have caused him to be careless, Luther consults his mentor, chief medical resident Dr. Daniel Wharton, and Wharton concedes that a brain tumor was only one possibility. Feeling that he must prove the accuracy of his diagnosis, Luther requests an autopsy, but Wharton informs him that according to state law, they cannot proceed without the permission of the deceased's family. When Ray refuses, as he does not want his brother's body to be cut up, Wharton confers with the head of the hospital, Dr. Sam Moreland, about requisitioning an autopsy. Moreland, aware that a scandal over the black doctor's actions could endanger funding, denies the request in the hope that the incident will be forgotten. Upon learning from police records that Johnny was married, Wharton and Luther visit his widow, Edie Johnson, who tells the doctors that she divorced Johnny a year and a half before, and that she hates his whole family. Although she does not reveal it to Wharton, his sympathetic attitude persuades her to visit Ray to ask about the autopsy. Ray tells her, however, that Johnny would be alive if he had had a white doctor, and that Wharton wants to have the autopsy to cover up the truth about Luther's actions. Edie's racist feelings are revived by Ray, with whom she had committed adultery, and he convinces her that Wharton played her for a "chump," and that she can make up for her past infidelity to Johnny by contacting Beaver Canal club owner Rocky Miller and telling him about Johnny's death. Accompanied by Ray's other brother George, who is a deaf-mute, Edie goes to the club, where Rocky and his pals lay plans to attack the black section of town, which they call "Niggertown." Although Edie desperately wishes to leave, Rocky forces her to stay. Meanwhile, Luther arrives at the hospital and learns

about the upcoming attack from Lefty Jones, a black elevator operator. Luther tries to dissuade Lefty from organizing a counterattack, but Lefty reminds him of a race riot that occurred while Luther was away at school, during which Lefty and his sister were beaten. Luther then contacts Alderman Tompkins to try to avert the riot, while Lefty and a large group of blacks, including Luther's brother-in-law John, meet and plan their strategy. Edie watches in disgust as the whites prepare their weapons, but leaves before the blacks surprise the whites by attacking first. As victims of the riots are brought in to the hospital, Wharton is called in from home. Before he departs, however, a drunken and disheartened Edie arrives at his house, and Wharton leaves her in the care of his black maid, Gladys. Although Edie fears that Gladys will harm her because of her connection to the riot, Gladys tenderly cares for her when she collapses. At the hospital, Luther tends to the victims until a white woman orders him to take his "black hands" off her son. Stunned, Luther walks out, and the next morning, after Wharton returns home to find Edie chatting with Gladys, Luther's wife Cora arrives and announces that Luther has given himself up to the police for the murder of Johnny Biddle. Cora relates that after he left the hospital, Luther realized that the coronor would be forced to conduct an autopsy if he were charged with murder. Wharton assures Cora that he will stand by Luther, and after he leaves with Edie, Cora's stoic demeanor in front of the whites crumbles and she cries in Gladys' arms. Following the autopsy, the coroner confirms that Johnny died of a brain tumor and that Luther was justified in performing the spinal tap. Wharton, Cora and Edie are pleased that Luther has been exonerated, but Ray insists that the doctors are conspiring to bury the truth. Luther leaves with Cora, following by Edie, who denounces Ray before she departs. After overhearing Wharton tell the coroner that he is leaving town for a much-needed rest, Ray and George overpower the police guard and escape. When Edie returns to her apartment, she finds Ray and George waiting, and Ray, whose leg is bleeding profusely, beats Edie to make her call Luther and tell him to meet Wharton at his house. Drunk and in shock, Ray raves that he is going to kill Luther, then leaves Edie with George. By turning up the volume on her radio, which George does not notice, Edie cause her neighbors to break down her door, then escapes and calls the hospital prison ward for help. Meanwhile, when Luther enters Wharton's house, Ray holds a gun on him, beats hi and shouts racist slurs. Edie arrives and tries to stop Ray from killing Luther, but Ray's physical pain and obsessive hatred have pushed him beyond reason. Edie turns out the lights as Ray shoots at Luther, and although Luther is wounded in the shoulder, he retrieves Ray's gun as he collapses in pain. Edie coldly tells Luther to let Ray's leg bleed, but Luther asserts that he cannot kill Ray simply because of his racism, then uses the gun and Edie's scarf to fashion a tourniquet. As a siren announces the arrival of the police, Luther tells the hysterical Ray, "Don't cry, white boy, you're gonna live." *African Americans. False accusations. Physicians. Psycopaths. Racism.* Apartments. Attempted murder. Autopsy. Brothers. Coroners. Deaf-mutes. Drunkenness. Elevator operators. Escapes. Family life. Gunshot wounds. Hospitals. Maids. Marriage. Police. Riots. Self-confidence.

Note: According to various news items and information in the Twentieth Century-Fox Records of the Legal Department at the UCLA Arts—Special Collections Library, Twentieth Century-Fox purchased the motion picture rights to Lester Samuels' original story in Jan 1949 and signed him to a ten-week contract to write the screenplay. Paramount, Universal, Warner Bros. and Columbia also had bid for the rights. Samuels, in a *NYT* article dated 30 Jul 1950, stated that he originally wanted to write about "the cancerous results of hatred," but did not intend to focus on an African-American doctor until he learned from colleagues of his daughter's fiancé, a doctor, about the problems faced by African-Americans doctors. According to correspondence in the Twentieth Century-Fox Produced Scripts Collection, a number of Fox producers who examined the story before the purchase were enthusiastic about it and wanted to produce it, including Otto Preminger, Sol Siegel and Nunnally Johnson. Johnson called the story, "the most reasonable approach to the racial question in a dramatic form that I have seen. It argues for professional fairness and equality, not for social reasons but for purely practical purposes." According to a 29 Dec 1948 memo, Fox public relations counsel Jason Joy was concerned about "the violence which this story contains and the fear that might be raised in some quarters that it might touch off violence in their sections of the country." After the purchase of Samuels' story, writer Philip Yordan made a number of suggestions that were incorporated into the final film. He advised going "into Luther's home. We will see real Negroes and how they live, as human beings. He will have a real brother, a real sister, a real father and mother—all human beings." In a later memo, studio production head Darryl Zanuck stated that the film was to "conscientiously avoid propaganda, but at

the same time the final result of our efforts should be a picture which is actually powerful propaganda against intolerance." Zanuck, like Joy, worried about the violence in the story and warned, "even in certain so-called white cities, such as Detroit, Omaha, St. Louis and Philadelphia, we are apt to have the picture banned totally by the Police Commission. We already know that we will lose about 3,000 accounts in the South who will not play the picture under any circumstances. But it would be a terrible thing if we have something in the picture which would give the so-called white cities a chance to turn us down because then the picture will be a fatal financial disaster." Although, in Feb 1949, Zanuck liked the ending of the current script, in which "Luther" was killed, he changed his mind by Apr 1949 and wrote in a conference note that the ending left a "feeling of utter futility. Luther, a wonderful character, is hideously slaughtered. If his death resulted in *something*, if something were accomplished either characterwise or otherwise, it would be different and I would accept it." Joseph Mankiewicz prepared a preliminary script in Jun 1949, with a new story line and new characterizations, which Zanuck approved in Aug 1949.

A 17 Oct 1949 *DN* article asserted that the picture, which was about to start shooting, "will differ from its predecessors in that it will consider Negroes as everyday citizens in a big American city. Previous pictures have dealt with less representative phases of Negro life." In the article, Mankiewicz stated, "we are dealing with the absolute blood and guts, the bread and potatoes, so to speak, of Negro hating. Darryl Zanuck decided to produce this picture because, as he said, 'We want to tell a story of the Negro in a white man's everyday world, rather than the Negro in the Negro's everyday world.' We are going to show the kind of hate the Negro runs up against in his daily life, how he is afraid to walk on certain streets." Studio press material noted that the studio delayed the film so that it would be released a year after *Pinky* (see below) in order to achieve "a gradual build-up to audience receptivity."

No Way Out marked the feature film debut of Sidney Poitier, who, according to studio publicity, had earlier appeared in three Signal Corps short films. The picture also marked the screen debut of Ossie Davis, and was the first film in which Davis appeared with his wife, Ruby Dee. Stephen McNally was borrowed from Universal for the production, for which technical director Valentine A. Becker, a California State Rehabilitation Officer for the Deaf, taught sign language to Linda Darnell, Richard Widmark and Harry Bellaver. "Alderman Mathew Tompkins," the character portrayed by Bill Walker, is referred to twice in the film, but was not seen in the print viewed.

According to a 23 Aug 1950 *DV* news item, the National League of Decency condemned the film. In Chicago, on 22 Aug 1950, police captain Harry Fullmer held up a permit for exhibition of the film in the city and recommended banning the film to police commissioner John Prendergast because it "might cause more racial unrest than we have now," according to a 24 Aug 1950 *HCN* article. On the day of Fullmer's action, Walter White, Executive Secretary of the NAACP, sent a telegram to Chicago Mayor Martin D. Kennelly objecting to the ban, according to information in the NAACP Papers at the Library of Congress. White wrote, "This picture is the most forthright and courageous picturization of the evil of race prejudice which has yet been made....*No Way Out* exposes the evil nature of [racial prejudice] and instead of inciting to riot as police censor claims [it] will do enormous good in the exactly opposite direction." After Commissioner Prendergast approved the ban, the *Chicago Sun-Times* published an editorial on 28 Aug 1950 sharply criticizing the censors. Mankiewicz, who called the ban "absurd," was quoted by *Life* as saying, "I find it highly commendable for the city fathers to be keeping Chicago, with its high cultural standards, isolated from any violence." The mayor convened a special committee of the Cook County Crime Prevention Bureau, and after a screening on 30 Aug, they recommended to the mayor that the ban be rescinded, according to news items. Mayor Kennelly lifted the ban after three to four minutes of the film were cut, including scenes of blacks and whites preparing for a riot.

In Maryland, Ohio, Pennsylvania and Virginia, the film was shown in a cut version, and the film was prohibited from being shown on Sundays in Massachusetts. At the time of the Chicago ban, an official of Fox's sales department stated that no attempt had been made to release the film in the South. After the Maryland State Board of Motion Picture Censors deleted scenes of blacks preparing to defend themselves before the riot and a subsequent scene showing the victory of the blacks, the NAACP branches in Baltimore and Maryland complained that the film's "original message is hopelessly lost." Walter White and officers of the local branches wrote to the board urging that the film be restored to its uncut state, or, barring that, for the board to delete scenes of racial epithets, but the board refused to change its decision. In explaining the refusal to White, board chairman Sidney Traub noted that the board and local police departments found the actions of the blacks during the riot scenes to be "highly provocative and crime inciting."

According to information in the MPAA/PCA Collection at the AMPAS Library, at a meeting in mid-Oct 1950, the board of directors of the Negro Newspaper Publishers Association adopted a resolution to protest "the use of epithets in all motion pictures and particularly the excessive employment of these epithets in the motion picture, *No Way Out....* Its authors err in their belief that in order to make the villain thoroughly contemptible, he and others, on thirty-five different occasions utter indecent epithets applied to the colored race. Some of these terms of opprobrium have never been heard or used by millions of Americans of both races. Their employment in the motion picture screens throughout the country builds up a vocabulary of undesirable expressions which should not be spoken in decent society." The resolution was sent to the PCA, which responded, "The company which produced it has stated, quite frankly, that they deliberately sought to be as forceful and dramatic as possible for the sake of the Negro, having no thought to hurt him, but, rather, to help him."

Reviews were mixed concerning the film. *MPH* commented, "The screen has

tackled the problem of race prejudice in various ways ever since Hollywood acquired a social conscience, but rarely has it come to grips with the whole tragic question quite so dramatically and forcefully as in this picture." The reviewer stated that the film "makes its point without flinching and with little regard for the feelings of the white audience." *DV*, however called it "tedious with words" and *Fortnight* was critical of the film's "lack of genuine feeling and insight into the motives of the very people it pretends to champion." *SatRev* reviewer Hollis Alpert's comment that "at some points this movie made me uncomfortable," provoked an angry letter from Walter White, who questioned, "I wonder what would have happened to [Alpert's] stomach had he been with me when I investigated a lynching in Georgia some years ago of an eight-months-pregnant Negro mother who had committed the crime of crying out in her grief that her recently lynched husband was innocent? Or if he had been with me in Detroit as policemen directed Negroes into the hands of mobs who slew their victims with incredible bestiality?" Alpert responded that he and White stood for the same things, but that Hollywood is "ducking its responsibility when it insists upon casting its problem films in sheerly melodramatic terms."

The film received an Academy Award nomination for Best Writing (Story and Screenplay: Mankiewicz and Samuels). New York foreign language press film critics gave Zanuck a special award for "great timeliness and unusual entertainment value which makes a major contribution to the advancement of improved race relations in the United States."

Afro-American (Baltimore) 14 Oct 1950. *Box* 5 Aug 1950. *DN* 17 Oct 1949. *DV* 13 Apr 1949. *DV* 2 Aug 1950, p. 3. *DV* 23 Aug 1950. *FD* 2 Aug 1950, p. 6. *Fortnight* 13 Oct 1950. *HCN* 24 Aug 1950. *HCN* 14 Oct 1950. *HR* 5 Jan 1949. *HR* 28 Aug 1949, p. 15. *HR* 2 Aug 1950, p. 3. *HR* 31 Aug 1950. *IFJ* 12 Aug 1950. *LAT* 5 Jan 1949. *LAT* 13 Oct 1949. *LAT* 6 Aug 1950, p. 1, 3. *LAT* 14 Oct 1950. *Life* 4 Sep 1950. *Life* 25 Sep 1950. *Look* 12 Sep 1950. *MPD* 2 Aug 1950. *MPH* 2 Sep 1950. *MPHPD* 5 Aug 1950, p. 413. *New Yorker* 26 Aug 1950. *NYT* 1 Jan 1949. *NYT* 9 Jan 1949. *NYT* 6 Nov 1949. *NYT* 30 Jul 1950. *NYT* 6 Aug 1950. *NYT* 17 Aug 1950, p. 23. *NYT* 24 Sep 1950. *SatRev* 2 Sep 1950, pp. 28-29. *SatRev* 14 Oct 1950. *Time* 21 Aug 1950. *Var* 2 Aug 1950, p. 16. *Var* 23 Aug 1950. *Var* 30 Aug 1950.

NO WOMAN KNOWS (Jewish Americans)
Universal Film Manufacturing Co.; A Tod Browning Production. *Dist* Universal-Jewel. 19 Sep **1921**; New York opening: 4 Sep 1921 [©Universal Film Manufacturing Co.; 17 Sep 1921; LP16969]. Si; b&w. 7 reels, 7,031 ft.

Pres Carl Laemmle. *Dir* Tod Browning. [*Asst dir* Leo McCarey]. *Scen* Tod Browning and George Yohalem. *Photog* William Fildew.

Source: Based on the novel *Fanny Herself* by Edna Ferber (New York, 1917).

Cast: *In order of appearance*: Max Davidson (*Ferdinand Brandeis*), Snitz Edwards (*Herr Bauer*), Grace Marvin (*Molly Brandeis*), Bernice Radom (*Little Fanny Brandeis*), Danny Hoy (*Aloysius*), E. A. Warren (*Rabbi Thalman*), Raymond Lee (*Little Theodore Brandeis*), Joseph Swickard (*The Great Schabelitz*), Richard Cummings (*Father Fitzpatrick*), Joseph Sterns (*Little Clarence Hyle*), Mabel Julienne Scott (*Fanny Brandeis*), John Davidson (*Theodore Brandeis*), Earl Schenck (*Clarence Hyle*), Stuart Holmes (*Michael Fenger*).

Drama. [*Viewed print incomplete*]. In Winnebago, Wisconsin, a Jewish family comprising Molly and Ferdinand Brandeis and their two children, Fanny and Theodore, run a modest dry goods store. Theodore is studying violin and auditions for a famous violinist, The Great Schabelitz, who is giving a local concert. Schabelitz is impressed by the boy's talent and recommends that he plan to study in Dresden, Germany. After Ferdinand dies, the family makes many sacrifices to enable Theodore to study in Dresden, where he eventually marries a worthless chorus girl and causes his mother's death from a broken heart. Although she continues to contribute to Theodore's support, Fanny decides to live her own life and moves to Chicago. There she becomes a highly efficient businesswoman in a department store, spurred on by her colleague and admirer Michael Fenger, who is trapped in a loveless marriage. A former school friend, Clarence Hyle, also attempts to woo Fanny. Later, Theodore, who has been deserted by his wife, returns from Europe with his baby daughter and comes to live with Fanny. When he eventually becomes a successful performer, he leaves Fanny a message saying that he is returning to his wife. After so much self-sacrifice, Fanny decides to live only for herself and is about to sail to Honolulu with Fenger when Clarence makes her realize that her true happiness lies with him. Brothers and sisters. Chicago (IL). Family relationships. Jews. Self-sacrifice. Violinists. Winnebago (WI). Women in business. Chorus girls. Department stores. Dresden (Germany). Mothers and sons. Priests. Rabbis. Romance. Small town life. Winter.

Note: The viewed print was missing two reels. The missing section presumably contained the events surrounding the death of the father.

Wid's 4 Sep 1921.

NOB HILL (Irish Americans)

Twentieth Century-Fox Film Corp. *Dist* Twentieth Century-Fox Film Corp. Jul **1945**; San Francisco opening: 13 Jun 1944; Los Angeles opening: 13 Jul 1945; Prod: 31 Jul—late Sep 1944; retakes 22 Dec—27 Dec 1944 [©Twentieth Century-Fox Film Corp.; 13 Jun 1945; LP13449]. Sd (Western Electric Recording); col (Technicolor). 11 reels, 8,922 ft. 95 min.

Prod Andre Daven. *Dir* Henry Hathaway. [*Asst dir* Henry Weinberger and Gerald Graun]. *Scr* Wanda Tuchock and Norman Reilly Raine. *From a story by* Eleanore Griffin. [*Chinese translations* Benson Fong]. *Dir of photog* Edward Cronjager. [*2d cam* Henry Cronjager]. *Spec photog eff* Fred Sersen. *Technicolor dir* Natalie Kalmus. *Assoc* Richard Mueller. *Art dir* Lyle Wheeler and Russell Spencer. *Film ed* Harmon Jones. *Set dec* Thomas Little. *Assoc* Walter M. Scott. *Mus settings des by* Joseph C. Wright. *Cost* Rene Hubert. *Mus dir* Emil Newman and Charles Henderson. *Incidental mus* David Buttolph. *Orch arr* Gene Rose. [*Mus coordinator* Callie Holden]. *Dances staged by* Nick Castle. *Sd* W. D. Flick and Roger Heman. [*Mus mixer* Murray Spivak and Vinton Vernon]. *Makeup artist* Ben Nye. [*Prod mgr* R. A. Klune]. [*Tech adv* Frank Tang]. [*Research dir* Frances C. Richardson]. [*Research asst* Maude Clague].

Song(s): "I Walked In (With My Eyes Wide Open)," "I Don't Care Who Knows It" and "Touring San Francisco," music by Jimmy McHugh, lyrics by Harold Adamson; "Holy God, We Praise Thy Name," music and lyrics by Peter Ritter; "San Francisco," music by Bronislaw Kaper and Walter Jurmann, lyrics by Gus Kahn; "On San Francisco Bay," music by Gertrude Hoffman, lyrics by Vincent Bryan; "Hello Frisco (I Called Up to Say Hello)," music by Louis A. Hirsch, lyrics by Gene Buck; "When You Wore a Tulip and I Wore a Big Red Rose," music by Percy Wenrich, lyrics by Jack Mahoney; "When Irish Eyes Are Smiling," music by Ernest R. Ball, lyrics by Chauncey Olcott and George Graff, Jr.; "Too-ra-loo-ra-loo-ral, That's an Irish Lullaby," music and lyrics by J. R. Shannon; "Happy Birthday to You," music by Mildred J. Hill, lyrics by Patty Smith Hill; "Hello! Ma Baby," music and lyrics by Joseph E. Howard and Ida Emerson; "San Francisco, the Paris of the U.S.A.," music and lyrics by Hirshel Hendler; "What Do You Want to Make Those Eyes at Me For," music and lyrics by Joe McCarthy, Howard Johnson and James V. Monaco; "For He's a Jolly Good Fellow," traditional.

Cast: GEORGE RAFT [(*Tony Angelo*)], JOAN BENNETT [(*Harriet Carruthers*)], VIVIAN BLAINE [(*Sally Templeton*)], PEGGY ANN GARNER [(*Katie Flanagan*)], Alan Reed [(*Dapper Jack Harrigan*)], B. S. Pully [(*Joe the bartender*)], Emil Coleman At the Piano, Edgar Barrier [(*Lash Carruthers*)], Joe Smith, Charles Dale [(*Singing waiters*)], [George Anderson (*Rafferty*)], [Don Costello (*Fighting bartender*)], [Joseph J. Greene (*Headwaiter*)], [J. Farrell MacDonald (*Cabby*)], [The Three Swifts], [William Haade (*Big Tim*)], [Beal Wong (*High*)], [George T. Lee (*Low*)], [Frank McCown (*Jose*)], [Robert Greig (*Patton, butler*)], [Charles Cane (*Chips Conlon*)], [Helen O'Hara, Dorothy Ford (*Showgirls*)], [Nestor Paiva (*Luigi*)], [Anita Bolster (*Housekeeper*)], [Jane Jones (*Ruby*)], [Otto Reichow, Sven Hugo Borg, George Blagoi (*Swedish sailors*)], [Mike Mazurki (*Rafferty's fighter*)], [Arthur Loft (*Turner*)], [Chick Chandler (*Guide*)], [Harry Shannon, Tom P. Dillon, Ralph Peters, Brooks Hunt, Harry Strang (*Policemen*)], [Edna Mae Jones (*Dance hall girl*)], [Virginia Walker, Carol Andrews, Susan Scott, Harrison Greene (*Slummers*)], [Bill "Red" Murphy (*Sailor*)], [Chief Thundercloud (*Indian chief*)], [Ralph Sanford, Arthur Thalasso, Edward Keane, George Lloyd, Sam Flint, Eddie Hart (*Politicians*)], [George Leigh (*Mr. Van Buren*)], [Grandon Rhodes (*Mr. Devereaux*)], [Barbara Sears (*Mrs. Devereaux*)], [Merian Margie Davis (*Mrs. Van Buren*)], [Susanne Rosser, Jacqueline Huber (*Girls*)], [Forbes Murray (*Mayor*)], [Byron Foulger (*Usher*)], [Lillian Salvaneschi, Mario Salvaneschi (*Specialty dance team*)], [Robert Filmer, Fred Graham, Louis Bacigalupi, William Hunter, John Kelly (*Bouncers*)], [Vincent Graeff, Paul Graeff, Freddie Chapman, Irving Gump, Danny Hood, Danny Shaw, Gerald Mackey, Hugh Maguire, Eddie Nichols, Robert Ferrero (*Newsboys*)], [Joe Bernard (*Printer*)], [Paul Hurst (*Stage doorman*)], [George Reed (*Black man*)], [Earle Hodgins (*Barker*)], [Benson Fong (*Chinese boy*)], [Doria Caron (*Madeleine, French maid*)], [Larry Williams (*Candidate*)], [Olive Blakeney (*Housekeeper*)], [Bruce Wong, Eddie Lee (*Chinese men*)], [Marvin Davis, Mickey Mascari, David Polonsky, Ray Dolciame, Ronnie Pattison, Rudy Wissler (*Boys*)], [Claire Emery, Darleen Garner, Marie King, Vicki Lang, Virginia Lynden, Darlene Ottum, Naomi Keene, Mabel Boehlke, Bonnadene Wolfe, Evelyn Dewey, Charlotte Dewey, Ben Jade (*Acrobatic specialty dancers*)], [Priscilla White (*Aerial acrobatic specialty*)], [Tiny Kline (*Aerial stunt performer*)], [Sam Ash, Freeman High (*Specialty singers*)], [Teri Toy, Jean Wong (*Chinese showgirls*)], [Frank Orth], [Lester Dorr], [Harry Harvey, Sr.], [Julius Tannen], [Will Stanton], [Syd Saylor], [Marshall Ruth], [Alphonse Martell], [Almira Sessions], [Polly Bailey], [Leila McIntyre], [Peter Micheal], [Gwen Donovan], [Antonio Filauri], [Jean De Briac], [Lorraine Collier], [Jane Hazard], [Claire Rochelle], [Mary Zavian].

Musical, **Comedy-drama**. [*Print viewed*]. In turn of the century San Francisco, Tony Angelo runs the Barbary Coast's most successful saloon, which features his sweetheart, singer Sally Templeton. One night, Tony is enjoying his duties as host when a young girl named Katie Flanagan arrives and asks for her uncle Pete. Katie, who has just gotten off a boat from Ireland, is devastated when Sally and Tony inform her that her uncle is dead, and becomes even more despondent when Tony decides to send her back to Ireland on the next boat. Upon hearing that Katie has no family left, Sally insists that she at least be allowed to stay the night. Tony acquiesces, and soon after, Katie's earnest charm wins his affections and convinces him to allow her to stay for a few months while the boat first journeys to Seattle. Katie happily settles into life at the Gold Coast, Tony's saloon, although she insists that Tony take her to church. Knowing that Katie is expecting a proper Catholic church, Sally instructs Tony to take her to the fancy church on Nob Hill. Although Katie is awed with its magnificent houses, Tony tries to explain to her that the snobbish Nob Hill residents do not mix with their kind. His words are disproven, however, by the friendliness of Harriet Carruthers, the beautiful socialite who made Katie's acquaintance on the boat. When Harriet brings her brother Lash, who is running for district attorney, to the Gold Coast, Sally grows uneasy about Harriet's attentions to Tony. Sally's fears deepen after Tony and Katie dine at Harriet's mansion and Katie tells Sally that Tony kissed Harriet. Tony brushes aside Sally's jealousy and announces that he is backing Lash in his election bid, despite the worries of his fellow saloon owners, who fear that Lash will close them down. Although Katie loves Sally, she approves of Tony's growing infatuation with Harriet, for she wants to live on Nob Hill. Harriet's overt flirtations drive Sally to work in another saloon, and Tony conceals the truth about her disappearance from Katie. Tony campaigns hard for Lash, and on the night Lash is elected, goes to the Carruthers mansion to celebrate. Tony's hopes for a life with Harriet are crushed, however, when Lash offers him a large sum of money for his help and Harriet states that while she is fond of him, their worlds will never mix. Dejected, Tony returns to the Gold Coast, where his former friends tell him that they will organize a boycott against him for his part in Lash's election. Tony sinks into a drunken despair and the saloon is soon closed. Katie tries to reach Sally, who refuses to listen to her, and in desperation, the child alerts Harriet about Tony's woes. Harriet then tells Sally that Tony needs her and warns her that if Sally does not return, she will forget her Nob Hill pride and stand by him herself. While Katie is gone, Tony's friends return and tell him that Lash has publicly acknowledged his help and vowed to close down only the corrupt parts of the Barbary Coast. Sally also returns and celebrates with Tony, but when the reunited couple goes up to Katie's bedroom to thank her for her interference, they discover that she has run away. Tony alerts the police, who begin a search that forces Katie into a scary adventure in Chinatown. When it seems that Katie has disappeared completely, Tony realizes that she must be at the vacant lot next to Harriet's house. He goes there with Sally, and they promise the overjoyed Katie that they will be a family forever. *Children. Class distinction. Irish. Romance. San Francisco (CA)–Barbary Coast. San Francisco (CA)–Nob Hill. Chinese Americans. Churches. Disillusionment. Dogs. Drunkenness. Elections. Fights. Immigrants. Jealousy. Mummies. Saloons. San Francisco (CA)–Chinatown. Servants. Shamrocks. Singers.*

Note: Eleanore Griffin's original story, which was titled "Crocus Hill," was purchased by Harry Sherman in 1943 for a United Artists release, according to a *FD* news item. Sherman sold the rights to Twentieth Century-Fox in Sep 1943. *HR* news items reveal the following about the production: Actors considered for the role of "Tony Angelo" included Brian Donlevy, Michael O'Shea, James Cagney and Fred MacMurray, and actresses considered for a leading role included Merle Oberon and Lynn Bari. Gregory Ratoff was originally set to direct the picture, and in late Apr 1944, he was scheduled to travel to New York to test theater actress Nancy Nugent for a part. *HR* news items and studio press releases include the following actors and dancers in the film, although their

participation in the completed picture has not been confirmed: Chester Conklin, Neil Hart, Jack Richardson, John Ince, Pat McGee, Elinor Troy, Carol K. Hartsock, Bess Flowers, John Merkyle, Dorothy Costello, Ruth Costello, Fred Steele, Red Shellac, Valerie Traxler, Evelyn Eager, and The Troupers, a dance group consisting of Jimmy Cross, Les Clark, Merrill Long and Jack Barnett. According to information in the Twentieth Century-Fox Produced Scripts Collection and Records of the Legal Department, both located at the UCLA Arts–Special Collections Library, Henry Morgan was signed to play a character named "Goofy Gus," but that role does not appear in the completed film. Studio records and other contemporary sources also note that famed comedy team Joe Smith and Charlie Dale were scheduled to perform their well-known "Dr. Cronkhite" skit, with Veda Ann Borg performing as a nurse. Although Smith and Dale are in the picture, neither the skit nor Borg appears in the released film. Another skit, the "Hungarian Rhapsody," which was to feature the team and actors George E. Stone and George McKay, also was eliminated. Studio records reveal that the film's opening, during which singers and saloons on a Barbary Coast street are shown, is the same footage used to open the 1943 Twentieth Century-Fox film *Hello Frisco, Hello*. The legal files also note that William Rankin, the ex-husband of writer Eleanore Griffin, filed suit claiming that Griffin had plagiarized "Crocus Hill" from a story written by him. Rankin's attempt to obtain an injunction to prevent Twentieth Century-Fox from making the film was unsuccessful, although the disposition of his suit against Griffin and Harry Sherman is not known.

Box 2 Jun 1945. *DV* 29 May 1943, p. 3. *FD* 15 Mar 1943, p. 7. *FD* 29 May 1945, p. 8. *HR* 6 Oct 1943, p. 1. *HR* 11 Nov 1943, p. 4. *HR* 26 Nov 1943, p. 1. *HR* 24 Apr 1944, p. 1, 15. *HR* 4 May 1944, p. 3. *HR* 10 May 1944, p. 3. *HR* 7 Jun 1944, p. 3. *HR* 28 Jul 1944, p. 15. *HR* 1 Aug 1944, p. 5. *HR* 8 Aug 1944, p. 4. *HR* 9 Aug 1944, p. 12. *HR* 19 Sep 1944, p. 12. *HR* 6 Oct 1944, p. 12. *HR* 22 Dec 1944, p. 12. *HR* 27 Dec 1944, p. 4. *HR* 29 May 1945, p. 3. *HR* 8 Jun 1945, p. 12. *HR* 11 Jul 1945, p. 8. *LAEx* 14 Jul 1945. *MPD* 29 May 1945. *MPHPD* 7 Oct 1944, p. 2131. *MPHPD* 2 Jun 1945, p. 2477. *NYT* 4 Jul 1945, p. 10. *Var* 30 May 1945, p. 16.

NOBODY'S CHILDREN *see* **OUR CHRISTIANITY AND NOBODY'S CHILD**

NOCHE DE DUENDES (Spanish language)

Hal Roach Studios, Inc.; Metro-Goldwyn-Mayer Corp.; controlled by Loew's, Inc. *Dist* Metro-Goldwyn-Mayer Distributing Corp. **1931**; San Juan (Puerto Rico) opening: 16 Oct 1930; Los Angeles opening: 16 Jan 1931; Madrid opening: 23 Jan 1931. Sd (Sistema Western Electric [Western Electric System]); b&w. 5 reels. 51 min. Passed by the National Board of Review. Spanish language.

Pres HAL ROACH. *Dirección* [*Dir*] James Parrott. *Diálogo* [*Dial*] H. M. Walker. *Fotografía* [*Photog*] George Stevens. *Editor de película* [*Film Ed*] Richard Currier. *Fonografía* [*Rec*] Elmer Raguse.

Cast: STAN LAUREL [(*Stan Laurel*)], OLIVER HARDY [(*Oliver Hardy*)], [Alfonso Pedroza (*Chief detective*)], [Robert O'Connor (*Train conductor*)], [Stanley Sandford (*Policeman*)], [Dell Henderson (*Murderer*)], [Dorothy Granger (*Angry woman*)], [Frank Austin (*Butler*)], [Charlie Hall, Clara Guiol (*Train passengers*)], [Lon Poff (*Old man*)], [Stanley Blystone (*Detective*)].

Comedy. [*Print viewed*]. While enjoying a quiet day of fishing from a pier, Oliver Hardy reads a notice in a newspaper requesting that relatives of a deceased millionaire, Mr. Laurel, attend the reading of his will. Presuming that the millionaire was an uncle of Ollie's friend, Stan Laurel, Ollie takes Stan on a train to Chicago, where they hope to complete the necessary proceedings to achieve riches the fast way. Upon entering the deceased's gloomy mansion, they are informed by a detective that Laurel was murdered and that no one is allowed to leave the mansion until the case is closed. During the night, Stan and Ollie experience a variety of terrors associated with haunted houses: sliding panels, floating bed sheets and bats disturb their attempts to sleep as the murderer rapidly reduces the number of heirs. Just as Ollie is about to be stabbed to death by a sinister hand, he wakes up in fright on the edge of the pier. His nightmare begins to fade, but the inheritance also vanishes. *Bumblers. Dreams. Inheritance. Investigations.* Bats. Detectives. Fishing. Haunted houses. Millionaires. Trains.

Note: This film, which was also released under the title *Deudos y duendes*, was an expanded version of a 1930 short made by Stan Laurel and Oliver Hardy entitled *The Laurel-Hardy Murder Case*. It also included reworked scenes from their 1929 short *Berth Marks*. The German version of the feature, entitled *Der Spuk um Mitternacht*, included Otto Fries as the conductor, and the French version, *Feu mon oncle*, featured Jean de Briac as the detective. Some modern sources list *La maison de la peur* as the title of the French version. No U.S. screenings of the German or French versions have been located. For more information about Laurel and Hardy's career together and their foreign language films, please see entry below for *Pardon Us*.

NOCHES HABANERAS *see* **SOMBRAS HABANERAS**

NONE SO BLIND (Jewish Americans)

State Pictures. *Dist* Arrow Film Corp. 1 May **1923**; New Jersey premiere: 19 Feb 1923 [©Arrow Film Corp.; 12 Feb 1923; LP18662]. Si; b&w. 6 reels.

Dir Burton King. *Story* Leota Morgan and Kathleen Kerrigan. *Photog* Alfred Ortlieb.

Cast: Dore Davidson (*Aaron Abrams*), Zena Keefe (*Rachel Abrams Mortimer/Ruth*), Anders Randolf (*Roger Mortimer*), Edward Earle (*Sheldon Sherman*), Sonia Nodell (*Rebecca*), Bernard Siegel (*Saul Cohen*), Robert Bentley (*Louis Cohen*), Maurice Costello (*Russell Mortimer*), Gene Burnell (*Hazel Mortimer*).

Drama. Rachel Abrams, daughter of struggling ghetto pawnbroker Aaron Abrams, elopes with Russell Mortimer, a wealthy young member of society. Russell's father quickly offers $10,000 to terminate the match. Aaron accepts over Rachel's objections, hoping to use the money for revenge. Rachel dies in giving birth to a daughter, Ruth; Aaron becomes a ruthless moneylender on Wall Street; and love develops between Ruth and Sheldon Sherman, protégé of Russell Mortimer, and between Hazel Mortimer, Russell's daughter, and Saul Cohen, son of an old friend of Aaron Abrams. Under a pseudonym, Aaron puts the squeeze on Russell and insists that Ruth marry Saul. There are complications of love and finance; Abrams sends Ruth away for giving her love to a gentile; but the old man finally relents, and all are reconciled. *Grandfathers. Jews. Moneylenders.* New York City–Wall Street. Pawnbrokers.

Note: The working title of this film was *Shylock of Wall Street*. *FD* 25 Feb 1923.

NORTH OF ARIZONA (Native Americans)

Reliable Pictures Corp. *Dist* State Rights. **1935**; Prod: at California Sound Studios, Inc.. Sd; b&w. 5,340 ft. 60 min. PCA cert no. 924.

Assoc prod Harry S. Webb. *Dir* B. B. Ray. *Orig scr* Carl Krusada. *Photog* Henry Kruse.

Cast: Jack Perrin, Blanche Mehaffey, Al Bridge, Lane Chandler, Murdock MacQuarrie, Artie Ortego, George Chesebro.

Western. [*Not viewed*]. In a saloon, honest cowboy Jack Loomis comes to the defense of some Indians when a group of patrons attempt to get them drunk in order to cheat them out of their gold. Jack is subsequently approached by George Tully, who offers him a job as his ranch foreman. Unknown to Jack, however, Tully is the head of a gang of thieves and has only hired Jack, whom he considers gullible, as a blind. Later, Jack catches Dick, one of Tully's men, in the act of stealing gold from two Indians, Red Cloud and Grey Wolf, and after Jack intervenes, the Indians reveal that all of Tully's men are crooks and promise to help Jack if he ever needs them. At the local general store, Jack meets pretty Madge Herron, the daughter of the owner, Elmer Herron, and asks to take her out. Their flirtation is interrupted by the arrival of one of Madge's suitors, express agent Ray Keeler, who becomes jealous of Jack and picks a fight with him. Jack knocks him out and a humiliated Keeler then vows to get revenge. That evening, on the way to meet Madge, Jack happens on a robbery in progress at the express office, but the two burglars escape. Herron, who is also the town marshal, arrives to investigate and finds Keeler tied up near the empty safe. When his gag is removed, Keeler points to Jack as the thief, and due to circumstantial evidence against him, Jack is arrested. Jack then makes a daring getaway and goes to the Indians for protection, while Herron puts out a reward of $1,000 for his capture. Tully tracks Jack down and offers to protect him from the law if Jack will participate in the gang's upcoming robbery of a gold shipment. Jack carries out the robbery with Dick, but at the last minute turns the tables on him with the aid of Red Cloud and Grey Wolf. After sending the Indians into town to alert Herron and his posse, Jack heads over to Tully's ranch to stall for time, claiming that the robbery has come off without a hitch. Once there, Jack discovers that Keeler is a member of Tully's gang, and when the men move to attack him, Jack single-handedly fights them, ties them up and forces them to sign confessions. Herron and Madge arrive, and Herron makes Jack the new town marshal after which Jack and Madge embrace. *Gangs. Impersonation and imposture. Indians of North America. Thieves.* Confession (Law). Escapes. False accusations. False arrests. General stores. Gold. Jealousy. Rewards. Robbery. Saloons.

Note: The plot synopsis is based on a dialogue continuity deposited in the NYSA on 5 Jul 1935. Although no exact release date was found, the film was reviewed by *Exh* on 15 Oct 1935. Modern sources add the following credits: Rose Gordon, *Continuity*; Carl Hartman, *Dial*; William Nolte, *Asst dir*; William

Austin, *Ed*; J. S. Westmoreland, *Sd*; and Jerry Kumler, *Art tech*. Cast members credited in modern sources include: Jack Perrin (*Jack Loomis*); Blanche Mehaffey (*Madge Harron*); Lane Chandler (*Ray Keeler*); Al Bridge (*George Tully*); Murdock McQuarrie (*Marshal Elmer Harron*); George Chesebro (*Dick Smith*); Artie Ortego (*Red Cloud*); Budd Buster (*Grey Wolf*); Frank Ellis (*Joe Borga*); Blackie Whiteford, Hank Bell, Ray Henderson (*Barflies*); Steve Clark (*Bartender Steve*); George Morrell (*Dancer in bar*); Oscar Gahan (*Fiddler*); Barney Beasley (*Barney*); and the horse Starlight.

Exh 15 Oct 1935, p. 34. *HR* 6 May 1935, p. 7.

NORTH OF NEVADA (Native Americans)

Monogram Pictures Corp. *Dist* Film Booking Offices of America. 24 Feb **1924** [©Monogram Pictures Corp.; 7 Feb 1924; LP19907]. Si; b&w. 5 reels, 4,929 ft.

Prod Harry J. Brown. *Dir* Albert Rogell. *Story and scen* Marion Jackson. *Photog* Ross Fisher.

Cast: Fred Thomson (*Tom Taylor*), Hazel Keener (*Marion Ridgeway*), Josef Swickard (*Mark Ridgeway*), Joe Butterworth (*Red O'Shay*), Chester Conklin (*Lem Williams*), Taylor Graves (*Reginald Ridgeway*), George Magrill (*Joe Deerfoot*), Wilfred Lucas (*C. Hanaford*), Silver King (*Himself, a horse*).

Western. Mark Ridgeway, the owner of a large ranch in Nevada, intends to leave the property to his foreman, Tom Taylor, but when he dies intestate the ranch goes to his niece and nephew, Marion and Reggie Ridgeway. These two easterners arrive at the ranch, and Tom falls in love with Marion. Joe Deerfoot, an evil, college-educated Indian, offers Reggie $10,000 for the ranch, aware that the water rights on the property are worth a fortune. Reggie, a stupid, effeminate boy, agrees to the deal and signs the contract. Joe kidnaps Marion to force her also to sign it, but Tom, having overheard the plans, rides Silver King to Joe's lair in the mountains. There, with the horse's help, he overcomes Joe and rescues Marion. *Effeminacy. Indians of North America. Inheritance. Nevada. Ranch foremen. Ranches. Water-rights.*

FD 2 Mar 1924. *MPW* 15 Mar 1924. *Var* 2 Apr 1924, p. 23.

NORTH OF THE GREAT DIVIDE (Native Americans)

Republic Pictures Corp. *Dist* Republic Pictures Corp. 15 Nov **1950**; Prod: late Apr—mid-May 1950 [©Republic Pictures Corp.; 21 Dec 1950; LP562]. Sd (RCA Sound System); col (Trucolor). 5,995 ft. 67 min. Passed by the National Board of Review. PCA cert no. 14650.

Assoc prod Edward J. White. *Dir* William Witney. [*Asst dir* Jack Lacey]. *Wrt* Eric Taylor. *Dir of photog* Jack Marta. [*Cam op* Joe Novak]. [*Stills* Mickey Marigold]. *Spec eff* Howard Lydecker and Theodore Lydecker. *Optical eff* Consolidated Film Industries. *Art dir* Frank Hotaling. *Film ed* Tony Martinelli. *Set dec* John McCarthy, Jr. and George Milo. *Cost supv* Adele Palmer. *Mus* R. Dale Butts. *Sd* Dick Tyler. *Makeup supv* Bob Mark. [*Hair stylist* Louise Landmeir]. [*Makeup* Steve Drumm]. [*Scr supv* Marie Messinger]. [*Grip* Gary Lambert]. [*Gaffer* Ossie Herrick].

Song(s): "By the Laughing Spring," "Just Keep a' Movin'" and "North of the Great Divide," music and lyrics by Jack Elliott.

Cast: Roy Rogers [(*Roy Rogers*)], Trigger The Smartest Horse in the Movies, Penny Edwards [(*Ann Keith*)], Gordon Jones [(*Splinters*)], Roy Barcroft [(*Banning*)], Jack Lambert [(*Lt. Stagg*)], Douglas Evans [(*Sgt. Douglas*)], Keith Richards [(*Dacona*)], Noble Johnson [(*Chief Nogura*)], Foy Willing, and The Riders of the Purple Sage, [Stephen Chase (*Sheriff Bradley*)], [Bruce Carruthers (*Mountie*)], [Frank Lacteen, Iron Eyes Cody (*Indians*)], [Mel Archer (*Proprietor*)], [Alan Bridge (*Henry Gates*)], [Rose Higgins (*Indian woman*)], [Petra Silva (*Mexican woman*)], [Holly Bane (*Deputy Sheriff Bill Hartley*)].

Western, with songs. [*Print viewed*]. Near the Canadian-American border, Indian agent Roy Rogers joins the Oseka Indians in celebrating the return of the salmon to spawn. As part of the festivities, Roy competes against several Royal Canadian Mounted Policemen in the tribe's annual horseback race. Later, a fish cannery owner named Banning and his foreman, Stagg, visit Oseka Chief Nogura to explain their plans to build a new cannery on the river. Nogura tries to reason with them, saying that his people have barely enough to eat as it is, without the added competition of another cannery. Later, a field nurse named Ann Keith tells Roy that the entire Oseka tribe is in danger of starving if their situation does not improve. When Roy meets with American government official Henry Gates, he learns that the government is considering forcing the tribe onto a reservation. Later, Nogura's son Dacona jumps onto the back of Banning's cannery wagon and begins knocking crates off onto the

road. Stagg then grabs Dacona, ties him to the back of the wagon and drags him. When Roy witnesses this, he jumps aboard and begins punching Stagg in the face. Later, Banning agrees to let more fish reach the Indians if they, in turn, will promise to quit sabotaging the cannery. Later, Nogura tells Roy that his fishermen found a dead Mountie in the river some time ago. A mark on his neck seemed to indicate that the Mountie had been strangled before being dumped into the river. As he was running from the river, Nogura explains, he dropped his rifle and now fears being accused of the crime. Soon, Mounties arrive to search the Indian village for Nogura, while the real culprit, Stagg, who had killed the Mountie while trying to burn down the competing Canadian cannery, is free from suspicion. Later, when Deputy Bill Hartley captures Nogura, he is turned over to Roy's custody. On Roy's urging, Nogura returns to his village, where he is promptly arrested by Sheriff Bradley. When Roy meets Mountie Sgt. Douglas, he urges him to work toward a salmon fishing agreement which all parties must honor. While the Indian braves clamor for war, Roy goes to the jail to visit Nogura and realizes that he has been kidnapped. Guessing that Banning is responsible, Roy and his friend Splinters break into his office. After the gang arrives and Roy rescues Nogura, he determines that the mark left on Nogura's neck by Stagg's whip is identical to the one found on the dead Mountie. When Roy learns that the gang has set several burning rafts drifting toward the Canadian cannery, he rushes to extinguish the flames. Roy then captures Stagg, using his own whip to lasso him from his horse. After Roy delivers Stagg and Banning to the Mounties, the Indians once again celebrate the river's teeming salmon population. *Canneries. Indian agents. Indians of North America. Arrests. Arson. Canadian-American border region. Deputies. Fathers and sons. Firearms. Foremen. Government officials. Horseracing. Indians of North America–Reservations. Kidnapping. Murder. North West Mounted Police. Nurses. Officers (Military). Rafts. Sabotage. Salmon. Sheriffs. Starvation. Torture. Whips and whippings.*

Note: The working title of the film was *Song of the Bandit*.

Box 25 Nov 1950. *DV* 15 Nov 1950, p. 5. *FD* 21 Nov 1950, p. 6. *HR* 5 May 1950, p. 13. *HR* 19 May 1950, p. 10. *HR* 15 Nov 1950, p. 4. *MPHPD* 2 Dec 1950, p. 598. *Var* 22 Nov 1950, p. 18.

NORTH OF THE KLONDIKE *see* **NORTH TO THE KLONDIKE**

NORTH OF THE RIO GRANDE *see* **COLORADO TERRITORY**

NORTH OF 36 (Native Americans, Comanche)

Famous Players-Lasky Corp. *Dist* Paramount Pictures. 22 Dec **1924** [©Famous Players-Lasky Corp.; 10 Dec 1924; LP20843]. Si; b&w. 8 reels, 7,908 ft.

Pres Adolph Zukor and Jesse L. Lasky. *Dir* Irvin Willat. *Scr* James Shelley Hamilton. *Photog* Alfred Gilks.

Source: Based on the novel *North of 36* by Emerson Hough (New York, 1923).

Cast: Jack Holt (*Dan McMasters*), Ernest Torrence (*Jim Nabours*), Lois Wilson (*Taisie Lockheart*), Noah Beery (*Sim Rudabaugh*), David Dunbar (*Dell Williams*), Stephen Carr (*Cinquo Centavos*), Guy Oliver (*Major McCoyne*), William Carroll (*Sánchez*), Clarence Geldert (*Colonel Griswold*), George Irving (*Pattison*), Ella Miller (*Milly*).

Western. In order to find a market for her cattle, Taisie Lockheart, owner of a large Texas ranch, decides to drive a herd across the thousand miles of Indian territory between the Lone Star State and the new railhead at Abilene. Sim Rudabaugh, the state treasurer, who is amassing a fortune by the accumulation of land scrip, plots to steal the scrip for Taisie's ranch but is foiled by Dan McMasters, who is in love with her. When suspicion unjustly falls on Dan, he is fired by Taisie; he then joins up with Rudabaugh so as to discover Rudabaugh's plans and forestall them. On the trail, Rudabaugh's men stampede Taisie's herd at night, and only the skill of her ranch hands prevents the loss of the cattle. Rudabaugh then kills two Comanche squaws, and the Indians go on the warpath but are fought off by the Lockheart men, led by the foreman, Jim Nabours. After a gala arrival in Abilene, Taisie sells her cattle at $20 a head and Dan overpowers Rudabaugh in a fight, handing him over to the Comanche chief. Taisie and Dan are reconciled and soon get married. *Abilene (KS). Cattle. Comanche Indians. Government officials. Land barons. Ranch foremen. Ranchers. Secret documents. Texas.*

FD 7 Dec 1924. *MPW* 13 Dec 1924. *NYT* 8 1924, p. 13. *Var* 10 Dec 1924, p. 35.

NORTH TO THE KLONDIKE (Chinese Americans)

Universal Pictures Co., Inc. *Dist* Universal Pictures Co., Inc. 23 Jan 1942; Prod: late Sep—15 Oct 1941 [©Universal Pictures Co., Inc.; 21 Jan 1942; LP11347]. Sd (Western Electric Mirrophonic Recording); b&w. 5,256 ft. 58 min. PCA cert no. 7924.

Assoc prod Paul Malvern. *Dir* Erle C. Kenton. [*Asst dir* Charles Gould]. *Scr* Clarence Upson Young, Lou Sarecky and George Bricker. *Based on a story by* William Castle. *Dir of photog* Charles Van Enger. *Art dir* Jack Otterson. *Assoc* Ralph M. DeLacy. *Film ed* Ted Kent. *Set dec* R. A. Gausman. *Gowns* Vera West. *Mus dir* H. J. Salter. *Sd dir* Bernard B. Brown. [*Sd*] *tech* Robert Pritchard. [*Unit pub wrt* Alanson Edwards].

Cast: Broderick Crawford (*John Thorn*), Evelyn Ankers (*Mary Sloan*), Andy Devine (*Klondike*), Lon Chaney, Jr. (*Nate Carson*), Lloyd Corrigan (*Doctor Curtis*), Willie Fung (*Waterlily*), Keye Luke ([*K.*] *Wellington Wong*), Stanley Andrews (*Jim* [*Tom*] *Allen*), Dorothy Granger (*Mayme Cassidy*), Monte Blue (*Burke*), Roy Harris (*Ben Sloan*), Paul Dubov (*Piety Smith*), Fred Cordova ([*Indian*] *Joe*), Jeff Corey (*Lafe Jordon*), [Armand Cortes (*Pete*)], [Tony Paton (*Bart*)], [Robert Homans (*Officer of the river boat*)], [Lee Phelps (*Pilot of the river boat*)], [William Ruhl (*Captain*)].

Northwest, Drama. [*Print viewed*]. Old engineer Klondike reminisces with a river boat captain about the adventures he and mining engineer Johnny Thorn enjoyed in Haven, Alaska thirty years earlier: Klondike and Johnny travel to Haven by tugboat. When the boat's whistle scares the horse of Waterlily, Johnny jumps into the river to save the drowning Chinese man. Upon arriving in Haven, Johnny is met by Nate Carson, a gold miner who has just lost the mineral rights of a prime gold prospecting area to the new settlers. Unable to work his mine and afraid the settlers may uncover its value, Carson tries to pay Johnny to leave the area, but the engineer refuses. Later, settler Mary Sloan enlists the aid of Johnny and Klondike to drag drunken physician, Dr. Curtis, from a poker game in Carson's saloon in order to deliver a baby. After the baby is born, settler Mayme Cassidy tries to bring Johnny and Mary together, but meets with little success, as Mary's brother Ben has already had a brief run-in with Johnny. Johnny then learns from Curtis that anyone associated with Carson is immediately disliked by most of the settlers. Johnny sets up a camp, only to have Waterlily arrive with his Harvard educated son, K. Wellington Wong, who explains that his "eccentric" father believes that Johnny is now indebted to him because the engineer stopped him from "joining his ancestors." That night, Carson's men successfully set the tugboat afire, destroying the settlers' supplies in hopes that they will be forced to leave Haven and abandon their land rights. Knowing that they will need new supplies before the first snow, settler Tom Allen agrees to go alone to fetch them, while encouraging the settlers to build their cabins in preparation for the hard winter ahead. After Johnny and Klondike find Allen murdered, they interrupt Mary's surprise birthday party to tell her the news. They later find Ben murdered by his cabin, as he had earlier refused to sell his land to Carson. Unknown to anyone else, Johnny and Klondike send Curtis for the supplies, and the physician and Indian Joe shoot the rapids. Meanwhile, Johnny and his people go to work building Mary's cabin. A shootout with Carson's men soon ensues, during which Piety Smith, Carson's chief henchman, is killed. Johnny delivers the dead man's body to Carson, and warns the miner not to interfere again with the construction of Mary's cabin. Carson then breaks the news of Allen's death to the settlement, but when Mary tells them that she has sent the unreliable Curtis in his place, the settlers decide to give up and raft back up the river. Back at Mary's cabin, Waterlily discovers Carson's mine inside a waterfall, and Johnny once again saves his life, this time from the hands of Carson's men. Johnny then leads the settlers to Carson's post, where the two men fight. After Johnny defeats the crooked miner, Curtis arrives with the supplies and a marshal. Back in the present, the old Klondike tells the river boat captain that the gold mine was actually empty, and Johnny was "ruined," as he married Mary and became a "dirt farmer." *Alaska. Engineers. Gold miners. Mines and mineral resources. Settlers. Brothers and sisters. Canoes and canoeing. Chinese Americans. Drunkenness. Fathers and sons. Fistfights. Murder. Parties. Physicians. Rapids. Saloons. Waterfalls.*

Note: Although the film's opening credits read "Jack London's *North to the Klondike*" and state that the picture was suggested by London's short story "Gold Hunters of the North," no publication information on the story has been found. It is probable that the filmmakers only used London's name. The

working title of this film was *North of the Klondike*. The opening credits read "Jack London's *North to the Klondike*." No information a Actor Lon Chaney, Jr. is listed without the "Jr." in the opening credits, although it is included in the end credits. Actor Stanley Andrews' character is listed in the film's credits as "Jim Allen," though he is clearly called "Tom Allen" in the film. According to a Universal memo to the AMPAS, the "based on a story by" credit for writer William Castle was agreed upon by a Writers Guild of America arbitration ruling. Universal press materials state that the film was shot on location in Big Bear, CA for one week.

According to *DV*, the film was originally planned as a "low-budget picture shot in 12 days," but Universal executives were so impressed by the fight sequence between actors Broderick Crawford and Lon Chaney, Jr. that they ordered "new scenes and fresh material" to upgrade the picture. Universal publicity materials also state that while actors Willie Fung and Keye Luke played father and son in this film, Fung spoke Cantonese and Luke spoke Manchu Chinese; therefore, in their scenes together, when they are speaking "Chinese," they are actually speaking in two, completely different languages. Modern sources include Spade Cooley in the cast.

Box 17 Jan 1942. *DV* 25 Nov 1941. *DV* 14 Jan 1942, p. 4. *FD* 22 Jan 1942, p. 8. *HR* 29 Aug 1941, p. 10. *HR* 23 Sep 1941, p. 2. *HR* 3 Oct 1941, p. 9. *HR* 16 Oct 1941, p. 3. *HR* 14 Jan 1942, p. 3. *MPHPD* 24 Jan 1942, p. 475. *NYT* 12 Mar 1942, p. 24. *Var* 21 Jan 1942, p. 18.

THE NORTH WIND'S MALICE (Jewish Americans)

Eminent Authors Pictures, Inc. *Dist* Goldwyn Distributing Corp. Aug **1920** [©Rex Beach; 7 Aug 1920; LP15434]. Si; b&w. 7 reels, 6,275 ft.

Pres Samuel Goldwyn and Rex Beach. *Mgr of prod* Robert B. McIntyre. *Dir* Carl Harbaugh and Paul Bern. *Story* Rex Beach. *Cam* Lucien Tainguy, Oliver Marsh, George Peters and Roy Vaughan.

Source: Based on the short story "The North Wind's Malice" by Rex Beach in *Laughing Bill Hyde and Other Stories* (New York, 1917).

Cast: Tom Santschi (*Roger*), Jane Thomas (*Lois*), Joe King (*Carter*), Henry West (*Harkness*), William H. Strauss (*Abe Guth*), Walter Abel (*Tom*), Vera Gordon (*Rachel Guth*), Edna Murphy (*Dorothy*), Dorothy Wheeler (*Malice*), Julia Stewart (*Mrs. Carter*).

Drama. When Lois Folsom's continual complaints about her husband Roger's sloppiness finally drive him out of the house, Lois seeks solace in the company of their friend, Henry Carter. Roger's brother Tom, angry at Lois because of her interference in his courtship of Dorothy Halstead, the ward of Jewish storekeeper Abe Guth, informs his brother that Lois has kissed Carter. This knowledge propels him to accept Jack Harkness' invitation to join in a gold mining expedition of Arctic City in Alaska. Unaware that his wife is pregnant, Roger leaves, and Lois, who is now desperate, accepts Carter's care. In the meantime, the Guth's store is destroyed by fire and Tom sustains the family by stealing food, but is jailed for his efforts. After Lois' baby is born, Carter ventures North to inform Roger. After an initial confrontation between the two men, Roger returns to his wife and frees Tom from jail. Tom, realizing the damage that his lies have caused, confesses his deceit and wins Dorothy's heart. *Alaska. Brothers-in-law. Marriage. Pregnancy. Separation (Marital). Fires. Jews. Prisons. Prospectors. Revenge. Robbery. Storekeepers.*

Note: Some scenes in this film were shot at Port Henry, NY, on the shore of Lake Champlain, and in Pittsburgh, PA. Two Curtiss airplanes, piloted by Charles Tatem and William Kelly, were used at Port Henry to blow the snow used in the blizzard scenes. One contemporary source lists Roy Vaughan as Edward Vaughan. The film had its premiere in Detroit the week of 8 Aug 1920. Reviewers praised the performances of Vera Gordon and William H. Strauss as the Jewish storekeeper and his wife. *Wid's* stated, "they practically walk away with the picture and the audience is uneasy until they appear again." *NYMT* noted, "In this merry theatrical and cinema year there is no surer fire ammunition than the introduction of a couple of Jewish characters—sympathetically and humanly presented. Vera Gordon and William H. Strauss give the outstanding performances in *The North Wind's Malice*. A touch of our own New York throws into obscurity all the virile, red-blooded heroes of the North." According to some reviews, the Jewish couple also go to Alaska and find gold, but their claim is disputed by Harkness. At the end, however, their rights are secured. The mine turns out to be worth a fortune, and Roger is saved from starvation, along with his wife and daughter, because of the mine.

ETR 30 Oct 1920, p. 2279. *MPN* 20 Mar 1920, p. 2728. *MPN* 28 Aug 1920, p. 1704. *MPN* 9 Oct 1920, p. 2762. *MPN* 30 Oct 1920, p. 3445. *MPW* 21 Aug 1920, p. 1068. *NYMT* 21 Oct 1920. *NYR* 23 Oct 1920. *NYT* 18 Oct 1920, p. 13. *Wid's* 24 Oct 1920, p. 15.

NORTHERN LIGHTS (Native Americans)

Life Photo Film Corp. *Dist* State Rights. Aug **1914**. Si; b&w. 5 reels. *Dir* Edgar Lewis.

Source: Based on the play *Northern Lights* by Edwin Barbour and James W. Harkins, Jr. (New York, 23 Dec 1895).

Cast: William H. Tooker (*Dr. Sherwood*), Harry Knowles (*Colonel Gray*), Harry Springler (*Wallace Gray*), George De Carlton (*Lieutenant Charlie*), William F. Sorrell (*Swiftwind*), Iva Shepard

(*Florence Dunbar*), Anna Laughlin (*Dorothy Dunbar*), Katherine La Salle (*Helen Dare Sherwood*), David Wall (*Horton*).

Drama. Following the shocking news that her husband, a U.S. Army colonel, has been wounded, Mrs. Gray gives birth to Wallace, a boy who bears the mark of his father's injury on his forehead and is cowardly by nature. In college he is ridiculed for his timidity, but is befriended by Swiftwind, an Indian boy who is studying medicine. Upon their graduation, Swiftwind is given a post as an army surgeon at Fort Terry where Colonel Gray is also stationed. Wallace meanwhile escorts his father's wards, Florence and Dorothy Dunbar, to the fort, but when they are menaced by marauding Indians, he flees. Despite his behavior, neither sister is injured, but Wallace cannot face Florence, whom he loves. Hoping to erase the memory of the incident, Wallace enlists in another regiment, but again retreats from danger. Colonel Gray, unaware that the coward is his son, sentences the deserter to death. Later, however, following many complications, Wallace is able to redeem himself by saving the fort from an Indian attack about which he was warned by Swiftwind. *Childbirth. Cowardice. Desertion, Military. Friendship. Hereditary tendencies. Indians of North America. Physicians. Birthmarks. Forts. United States. Army. Cavalry.*

Motog 22 Aug 1914, p. 271. *MPN* 22 Aug 1914, p. 47. *MPW* 22 Aug 1914, p. 1146. *MPW* 29 Aug 1914, p. 1250. *MPW* 12 Sep 1914, p. 1560. *MPW* 3 Oct 1914, p. 16. *MPW* 12 Aug 1914, p. 28.

NORTHERN LIGHTS (1941) *see* **MUTINY IN THE ARCTIC**

NORTHWEST OUTPOST (Russian Americans)
Republic Pictures Corp. *Dist* Republic Pictures Corp. 25 Jun **1947**; Prod: late Oct—mid-Dec 1946 [©Republic Pictures Corp.; 18 Jun 1947; LP1111]. Sd (RCA Sound System); b&w. 90-91 or 95 min. Passed by the National Board of Review. PCA cert no. 12216.
[*Assoc prod* Allan Dwan]. *Dir* Allan Dwan. [*Asst dir* Johnny Grubbs]. *2nd unit dir* Yakima Canutt. *Scr* Elizabeth Meehan and Richard Sale. *Orig story* Angela Stuart. *Adpt* Laird Doyle. *Dir of photog* Reggie Lanning. *Spec eff* Howard Lydecker and Theodore Lydecker. *Art dir* Hilyard Brown. *Assoc art dir* Frank Hotaling. *Film ed* Fred Ritter. *Set dec* John McCarthy, Jr. and James Redd. *Cost supv* Adele Palmer. *Orig mus score comp* Rudolf Friml. *Mus dir* Robert Armbruster. *Orch* Ned Freeman. *Sd* Earl Crain, Sr. and Howard Wilson. *Makeup supv* Bob Mark. *Hair stylist* Peggy Gray. *Tech adv* Alexis Davidoff.
Music: Traditional Russian church music: "Slava" (Praise) and "Paskha Nova" (New Easter).
Song(s): "Weary," "Nearer and Dearer," "Love Is the Time," "Tell Me with Your Eyes," "Raindrops on a Drum" and "One More Mile to Go," music by Rudolf Friml, lyrics by Edward Heyman.
Cast: Nelson Eddy [(*Capt. Jim Laurence*)], Ilona Massey [(*Natalie Alanova*)], Joseph Schildkraut [(*Count Igor Savin*)], Elsa Lanchester [(*Princess Tanya*)], Hugo Haas [(*Prince Nickolai Balinin*)], Lenore Ulric [(*Baroness Kruposny*)], Peter Whitney [(*Volkoff*)], Tamara Shayne [(*Olga*)], Erno Verebes [(*Kyril*)], George Sorel [(*Baron Kruposny*)], Rick Vallin [(*Dovkin*)], and The American G.I. Chorus [(*Prisoners*)], [Countess Rosanska, Dina Smirnova, Antonina Barnett, Lola DeTolly, Myra Sokolskaya (*Noble ladies*)], [George Blagoi, Sam Savitsky, Igor Dolgoruki, Nestor Bristoff (*Noble gentlemen*)], [Michael Visaroff (*Captain Tikhonoff*)], [Muni Seroff (*Sentry*)], [Max Willenz, Nicco Romoff, Henry Kulky (*Peasants*)], [Nina Hansen (*Princess Tanya's maid*)], [Eugene Sigaloff (*Priest*)], [Henry Brandon (*Chinese junk captain*)], [Michael Mark (*Small convict*)], [Dick Alexander (*Large convict*)], [George Paris (*Ship's officer*)], [Ray Teal (*Wounded trapper*)], [John Bleifer (*Groom*)], [Molio Sheron (*Naval officer*)], [Gene Gary (*Second sentry*)], [John Peters (*Officer*)], [Jay Silverheels (*Indian scout*)], [Constantine Romanoff (*Convict*)], [Peter Gurs (*Trumpeter*)], [Marvin Press (*Younger man*)], [Abe Dinovitch (*Rough man*)], [Nicholas Kobliansky (*Deacon*)], [Zoia Karabanova], [Gregory Golubeff], [Inna Gest], [Peter Seal].
Historical, Musical. [*Print viewed*]. In the 1830s, at their home at Fort Ross, a Russian colony near California's Russian River, Prince Nickolai Balinin and his wife, Princess Tanya, welcome Natalie Alanova, a young woman who has just arrived from Russia. Although Natalie claims to have come for her health, the princess suspects otherwise. That evening, Natalie and her maid Olga hear a gang of singing convicts and anxiously scan the group for Natalie's husband, Count Igor Savin, whom Natalie was forced to marry for political reasons. In the garden of his home, the prince tells Natalie that Jim Laurence, an ex-American army captain who now works for the

prince, will need to validate her emigration papers, explaining that the fort will soon come under Laurence's command. When Laurence arrives, he examines Natalie's papers, but refuses to sign them when he realizes that the Russian signature has been forged. Later, the warden of the chain gang, Volkoff, whips a prisoner until Laurence confiscates the whip and throws it into the bushes. The whip startles Natalie's horse, which bolts, but Laurence rescues her. She then asks him why he has not turned her over to the authorities and explains that she had to forge the signature on her papers because of her father's political enemies. Several hours later, Natalie and Laurence see a convict ship arrive and Laurence asks if she knows Savin, who is on board, but she claims that she does not. Later an alarm is sounded and Laurence leaves to fight the Indians. Natalie goes to see Savin, who threatens to have Natalie's father killed by turning him in to the czar if she will not use her influence with Laurence to help him escape. As the Russians prepare for Easter celebrations, Lawrence returns, angry that Natalie has not yet returned home. Natalie sends Laurence a note asking him to meet her at the Easter feast, where he gives her the cross of St. George which the czar awarded him. She decides not to ask him for help and instead gives Savin all her jewels, including Savin's own cross of St. George, so that he can bribe Volkoff. Natalie tries to tell Laurence the truth about her relationship to Savin when word of his escape arrives, but before she can speak, Laurence and his men leave to search for Savin and Volkoff. As they escape, Volkoff shoots Laurence, who falls and hits his head on a rock and is knocked unconscious. Laurence's scout recovers the jewels and Laurence mistakes Savin's cross for his own. The next day, Laurence arranges for Natalie and Olga to leave on the next cargo ship bound for the Orient. When the two board, they discover Savin and Volkoff hiding out in their cabin, and when a Russian soldier sees Savin on board, he reports back to the prince. When the prince and princess arrive with Laurence, Savin pulls a gun, but Laurence kills Savin and Volkoff, and they all return to Fort Ross. *California–History. Expatriates. Fort Ross (CA). Forts. Officers (Military). Princes. Princesses. Russians. Bribery. Chain gangs. Forgers and forgery. Indians of North America. Jewelry. Political prisoners. Ships.*
Note: A written onscreen foreword to the film explains that the American G.I. Chorus "was organized by Major Herbert Wall and is composed entirely of Ex-G.I.s who served on every battlefield of the world during World War II. These men are the proud bearers of 152 decorations awarded by the various branches of the Armed Forces in which they served." This film was the last of three films in which Ilona Massey and Nelson Eddy co-starred. It was also Eddy's last appearance in a feature film. Actor Jay Silverheels who portrayed "Tonto" in *The Lone Ranger* television series in the 1950s, made his motion picture debut in this film. Working titles of the film included "End of the Rainbow" and "Will Tomorrow Ever Come."

Box 17 May 1947. *DV* 8 May 1947, p. 3. *FD* 22 May 1947, p. 5. *HR* 8 May 1947, p. 3. *HR* 6 Nov 1947, p. 3. *MPHPD* 17 May 1947. *NYT* 8 Aug 1947, p. 10. *Var* 14 May 1947, p. 15.

NORTHWEST PASSAGE (BOOK I—ROGERS' RANGERS) (Native Americans)
Metro-Goldwyn-Mayer Corp.; controlled by Loew's Inc.; A King Vidor Production. *Dist* Loew's Inc. 23 Feb **1940**; Boise, ID premiere: 20 Feb 1940; Prod: 1 Jul 1939—13 Sep 1939; retakes and additional scenes mid-Nov—29 Dec 1939 [©Loew's Inc.; 27 Feb 1940; LP9597]. Sd (Western Electric Sound System); col (Technicolor). 14 reels. 125 min. Passed by the National Board of Review. PCA cert no. 5725.
Prod Hunt Stromberg. *Dir* King Vidor. [*Dir of addl scenes* Jack Conway]. [*2nd unit dir* Norman Foster]. [*Asst dir* Robert Golden and Bert Sperling]. [*2nd asst dir* Bill Lewis]. *Scr* Laurence Stallings and Talbot Jennings. [*Contr wrt* Robert E. Sherwood, Frances Marion, Jules Furthman, Conrad Richter, Noel Langley, Bruno Frank, Jack Singer, Sidney Howard, Richard Schayer, Jane Murfin, King Vidor and Elizabeth Hill]. *Dir of photog* Sidney Wagner and William V. Skall. [*Asst cam* Raoul Bassette]. [*Photog 1938 loc scenes* Leonard Smith and Ray Rennahan]. *Technicolor col dir* Natalie Kalmus. *Assoc* Henri Jaffa. *Art dir* Cedric Gibbons. *Art dir assoc* Malcolm Brown. *Film ed* Conrad A. Nervig. *Set dec* Edwin B. Willis. *Mus score* Herbert Stothart. [*Addl mus* Daniele Amfitheatrof and Dr. William Axt]. [*Orch* Paul Marquardt, Charles Maxwell, Leonid Raab and Murray Cutter]. *Rec dir* Douglas Shearer. *Makeup created by* Jack Dawn. [*Head of makeup staff* Lyle Dawn, Jr.]. [*Makeup staff* Jack Young, Charles Gorman, Bert Lindley, Don Robertson, Lois Stanfield, Rae Foreman and Lelia Chambers]. [*Unit mgr* Jay Marchand, Joe Cooke and Frank Messenger]. [*Caterers* Brittingham's].

Source: Based on the novel *Northwest Passage: Book One, Rogers' Rangers* by Kenneth Roberts (New York, 1937).

Cast: Spencer Tracy (*Major [Robert] Rogers*), Robert Young (*Langdon Towne*), Walter Brennan (*"Hunk" Marriner*), Ruth Hussey (*Elizabeth Browne*), Nat Pendleton (*"Cap" Huff*), Louis Hector (*Reverend Browne*), Robert Barrat (*Humphrey Towne*), Lumsden Hare (*Lord Amherst*), Donald McBride (*Sergeant McNott*), Isabel Jewell (*Jennie Coit*), Douglas Walton (*Lieutenant Avery*), Addison Richards (*Lieutenant Crofton*), Hugh Sothern (*Jesse Beacham*), Regis Toomey (*Webster*), Montagu Love (*Wiseman Clagett*), Lester Matthews (*Sam Livermore*), Truman Bradley (*Captain Ogden*), [Andrew Pena (*Konkapot*)], [Don Castle (*Richard Towne*)], [Rand Brooks (*Eben Towne*)], [Kent Rogers (*Odiorne Towne*)], [Verna Felton (*Mrs. Towne*)], [Richard Cramer (*Sheriff Packer*)], [Ray Teal (*Bradley McNeil*)], [Edward Gargan (*Captain Butterfield*)], [John Merton (*Lieutenant Dunbar*)], [Gibson Gowland (*MacPherson*)], [Frank Hagney (*Capt. Grant*)], [Gwendolen Logan (*Mrs. Brown*)], [Addie McPhail (*Jane Brown*)], [Helen MacKellar (*Sarah Hadden*)], [Arthur Aylesworth (*Flint, innkeeper*)], [Ted Oliver (*Farrington*)], [Lawrence Porter (*Billy, Indian boy*)], [Tony Guerrero (*Captain Jacobs*)], [Ferdinand Munier (*Stoodley*)], [George Eldredge (*McMullen*)], [Robert St. Angelo (*Solomon*)], [Denis Green (*Capt. Williams*)], [Peter George Lynn (*Turner*)], [Frederick Worlock (*Sir William Johnson*)], [Hank Worden, Tom London, Eddie Parker, C. E. Anderson, Captain (*Rangers*)].

Adventure. [*Print viewed*]. After his expulsion from Harvard for making an insulting sketch of the president of the college, young Langdon Towne returns to his home in Portsmouth, New Hampshire in 1759 and announces to his sweetheart, Elizabeth Browne, that he is going to be a great artist. Forced to flee from the wealthy and powerful rogue Wiseman Clagett, whom he has also insulted, Langdon and his friend "Hunk" Marriner meet Major Robert Rogers. Rogers, who is about to undertake a dangerous mission to annihilate a tribe of warring Indians, wants Langdon to join his rangers as mapmaker, but is only able to sign up him and Hunk by getting them drunk on his favorite drink, hot-buttered rum. Stealthily launching their boats on the smooth surface of Lake Champlain, the rangers begin their punitive mission to the Indian village at St. Francis along the St. Lawrence River, moving carefully through the rough terrain and trying to avoid the hostile Indians who have aligned themselves with the French in their war against the British. When they discover French ships at the mouth of the river, the rangers are forced to portage their boats by foot and then trudge through swamps, bogs and rapids until they finally reach their destination. At St. Francis, the rangers swoop down upon the Indians, who have been massacring the white settlers, and in the bloody battle, Langdon is seriously wounded. The Indians defeated, the rangers begin the long and grueling trip to Fort Wentworth with the wounded Lagndon hobbling behind, aided by an Indian boy and an embittered white woman, Jennie Coit, who had been adopted by the Indians and hates the English. For days they march with only handfuls of dried corn to keep them alive, until the starving men vote to break up into hunting parties and meet at Eagle Mountain. With little success in their attempts to fish and capture game, when the men reconvene, their ranks have dwindled from one hundred and fifty to fifty. Despite their discouragement, the men bravely continue on, encouraged by Rogers, who promises them that there will be ample food at Fort Wentworth. As they approach the fort, Rogers runs ahead and discovers that the soldiers have gone, leaving nothing behind. Though at the point of desperation himself, Rogers tries to rally his men by telling them how much better off they are than some biblical figures who fasted for even longer than they. As the men start to rally, the British arrive, carrying ample food and supplies. Their mission completed and their stomachs filled, Rogers and his rangers march on in search of the Northwest Passage to the Pacific Ocean, while Langdon remains behind with Elizabeth, who plans to go with him to London while he trains to be a great artist. As Rogers marches away, Langdon tells Elizabeth that the world will remember Rogers through his paintings. *Artists. English in foreign countries. Explorers. Indians of North America. Massacres. Rescues. Major Robert Rogers. United States–History– French and Indian War, 1755-1763. Artists. Drunkenness. Engagements. Forts. Friendship. Hotels. Insanity. St. Lawrence River. Maps. Portsmouth (NH). Rivers. Starvation. Torture.*

Note: The working title of the film was *Northwest Passage*, and most reviews and modern sources refer to the film under that title. Part of Kenneth Roberts' novel was serialized in *The Saturday Evening Post*, under the title *Rogers' Rangers* (26 Dec 1936–6 Feb 1937). The following information has been obtained from news items, production charts and the film's pressbook, unless otherwise noted: *Northwest Passage* was first considered for purchase in Nov 1936, when William Fadiman, M-G-M's New York story editor, read galley pages of its *SEP* serialization. M-G-M purchased the rights in Sep 1937 and planned the film as its first three-strip Technicolor feature. In Mar 1938, W. S. Van Dyke, who initially was to direct the picture, had a two-week hiatus from his work on *Marie Antoinette* (see *AFI Catalog of Feature Films, 1931-40*; F3.2750), and went to British Columbia to scout locations. In late Mar 1938, a *HR* news item announced that John Arnold, head of the M-G-M camera department, had assigned cameraman Leonard Smith to take a month's training at the Technicolor plant to prepare for filming. That same week, color tests were made of Spencer Tracy, who was, according to the pressbook, the studio's "immediate choice for Major Robert Rogers." In Apr 1938, Wallace Beery was announced for the role of "Sergeant McNatt" (portrayed by Donald McBride in the film), and later Robert Taylor was announced for the role of "Langdon Towne" (portrayed by Robert Young). At that time, a news item in *HR* announced that the production was budgeted at $1,500,000. M-G-M attempted to borrow RKO star Anne Shirley for the film in late Jun 1938, probably for the role of "Elizabeth Browne" (portrayed by Ruth Hussey), but possibly for the role of "Ann" (portrayed by Laraine Day, but cut from the completed film).

In Jun 1938, delays in preparations led to the decision of M-G-M executives to postpone principal photography on *Northwest Passage*. At that time, the first few days of black-and-white footage shot on the musical *Sweethearts* (see *AFI Catalog of Feature Films, 1931-40*; F3.2190) was scrapped, and that film became the first M-G-M Technicolor production. In Aug, Robert Z. Leonard was assigned to finish direction of the final number of *Sweethearts* so that Van Dyke, who had been directing the musical, could devote more time to preparations for *Northwest Passage*. Additional background locations were scouted by Van Dyke and others during 1938 throughout the Western United States. During Jul and Aug, M-G-M unit manager Frank Messenger headed a crew of sixty-eight persons who shot 60,000 feet of backgrounds for the picture in the vicinity of McCall, Idaho. In Aug, Van Dyke was supposed to go to Idaho himself, but the trip was canceled after the decision was made to postpone the project until Spring 1939. Inclement weather, which M-G-M felt could cause an increase of $500,000 to the budget of the picture was cited as the reason for the delay. Beery and Taylor were cast in the Western *Stand Up and Fight* in the interim (see below).

In late Feb 1939, Van Dyke was taken off the picture because of a scheduling conflict with *It's a Wonderful World* (see *AFI Catalog of Feature Films, 1931-40*; F3.2190) were considered as replacements. Vidor was the final choice, although Conway directed some additional scenes for the picture in Nov 1939. In Mar 1939, exteriors were shot at Payette Lake, Idaho and, while additional pre-production location work was done at McCall and Payette throughout Apr, May and Jun 1939, principal photography did not commence until 6 Jul. At that time, a cast and crew of approximately two thousand people were based in McCall, which had its own telecommunications system and diesel power plant, and catering was provided by Brittingham's of Hollywood. Smaller groups would travel from McCall to Payette Lake, and Glacier National Park for various sequences. By the time principal photography began, McBride had replaced Beery, and Young had replaced Taylor. Modern sources indicate that by the time filming began, M-G-M had decided not to make the picture an "all-star" production to keep escalating costs down.

In addition to credited scenarists Laurence Stallings and Talbot Jennings, the following writers worked on the project at various stages: Conrad Richter, Robert E. Sherwood, Frances Marion, Jules Furthman, Noel Langley, Bruno Frank, Jack Singer, Sidney Howard, Richard Schayer, Jane Murfin, Elizabeth Hill and director King Vidor. According to modern sources, Conrad Richter was the first writer assigned to the project, followed by M-G-M contract writers Marion, Furthman, Langley, Frank and Singer. Sherwood was brought onto the production in Feb 1938, and Howard was asked to work on revisions of Sherwood's work in Apr 1938. Schayer was assigned additional revisions in Nov 1939. Stallings came onto the project in Mar 1939, and Jennings in Jun. According to modern sources, Vidor and his then wife Elizabeth Hill also contributed significantly to the final screenplay.

At the start of principal photography, cameramen Sidney Wagner and William V. Skall replaced Leonard Smith and Technicolor photographer Ray Rennahan. According to a *HR* news item, Norman Foster was brought in to act as "associate director," a position which the item states was not an assistantship or unit director position, but which other sources call the second unit director. Over three hundred Indians from the Nez Perce reservation and, according to a *HR* news item, "the entire Blackfoot tribe" participated in filming at Glacier National Park. The McCall company started to disband in early Aug, and by 16 Aug most of the principals had returned to Southern California. Filming at the M-G-M studio began a few days later, although a second unit remained in McCall and an additional location trip to Glacier National Park was considered for Sep. According to modern sources, the "human chain" sequence of the film was started at Payette Lake, but had to be completed at the M-G-M backlot exterior "tank" due to the treacherous conditions at the Lake. The studio tank was made to match closely the appearance of Payette Lake so that shots of the real location could be edited into the studio footage. Water in the tank was artificially churned by huge motors to create a "current." The last production chart for the film appears on 9 Sep 1939, but news items in mid-Nov 1939 indicate that retakes, including a new ending for the story, were shot at that time by director Jack Conway. According to the pressbook, filming was completed on 29 Dec after seventy days of shooting. Modern sources have noted that between late Sep and early Nov 1939, producer Hunt Stromberg and M-G-M executives pondered

the question of whether to film the entire Roberts novel as one book or to divide it into two parts, as originally planned. It was eventually decided to complete the film in late Dec and in late Jan 1940, M-G-M studio head Louis B. Mayer announced that the film would be released as a single film, with the possibility of a sequel later. No sequel was filmed, and the released picture ends at approximately the mid-point of Roberts' novel.

According to information in the Howard Strickling Collection at the AMPAS Library, the final cost of the picture was $2,677,672. Modern sources have speculated that several hundred thousand dollars of the final cost was the result of the ultimately useless location trips in 1938, various delays and large fees for the book and screenplay. Sidney Wagner and William V. Skall were nominated for an Academy Award for Best Cinematography (Color), but lost to Georges Perinal for *The Thief of Bagdad*. The picture was one of the top twenty films at the box office in 1940, but, according to modern sources, lost money because of the high cost of production. M-G-M made a short film about the making of *Northwest Passage*, entitled *Northward, Ho!*. A television series, inspired by the Roberts novel, was broadcast on the NBC television network from Sep 1958 to Jul 1959. The series starred Keith Larsen as "Rogers," Buddy Ebsen as "'Hunk' Mariner" and Don Burnett as "Langdon Towne." Modern sources add the following additional credits: *Tech consultant* George Greene; *2nd unit photog* Jack Smith; *Addl photog* Charles Boyle; *Cam op and asst* Fred Mayer, William T. Cline, A. J. "Duke" Callahan, Roger Mace, Kyme Meade, Paul Uhl, Joe Noecker, Nady McIntyre, Richard Mueller and James Stone.

AmCin Mar 1940, P. 100, 110. *DV* 7 Feb 1940, p. 3. *FD* 12 Feb 1940, p. 5. *HR* 17 Mar 1938, p. 2. *HR* 28 Mar 1938, p. 7. *HR* 2 Apr 1938, p. 1. *HR* 12 Apr 1938, p. 1. *HR* 20 Jun 1938, p. 12. *HR* 22 Jun 1938, p. 2. *HR* 2 Jul 1938, p. 1. *HR* 22 Jul 1938, p. 2. *HR* 18 Aug 1938, p. 2. *HR* 19 Aug 1938, p. 3. *HR* 7 Nov 1938, p. 1. *HR* 20 Feb 1939, p. 1. *HR* 2 Mar 1939, p. 13, 18. *HR* 20 Apr 1939, p. 4. *HR* 8 May 1939, p. 21. *HR* 16 May 1939, p. 2, 4. *HR* 17 May 1939, p. 8. *HR* 6 Jun 1939, p. 8. *HR* 10 Jun 1939, p. 4. *HR* 28 Jun 1939, p. 1. *HR* 29 Jun 1939, p. 15, 16. *HR* 1 Jul 1939, p. 1. *HR* 5 Jul 1939, p. 1. *HR* 8 Jul 1939, p. 1. *HR* 17 Jul 1939, p. 6. *HR* 20 Jul 1939, p. 2. *HR* 3 Aug 1939, p. 7. *HR* 8 Aug 1939, p. 5. *HR* 9 Aug 1939, p. 3. *HR* 15 Aug 1939, p. 7. *HR* 19 Aug 1939, p. 3. *HR* 21 Aug 1939, p. 3. *HR* 9 Sep 1939, p. 6. *HR* 16 Nov 1939, p. 6. *HR* 16 Jan 1940, p. 2. *MPD* 13 Feb 1940, pp. 1-5. *MPH* 14 Oct 1940, p. 37. *MPH* 17 Feb 1940, p. NYT 8 Mar 1940, p. 25. *Var* 14 Feb 1940, p. 18.

NOT AS A STRANGER (Swedish Americans, Jewish Americans)
Stanley Kramer Pictures Corp. *Dist* United Artists Corp. Jun **1955**; New York premiere: 28 Jun 1955; Prod: mid-Sep—mid-Dec 1954 at Kling Studio [©Stanley Kramer Pictures Corp.; 29 Jun 1955; LP4949]. Sd (RCA Sound Recording); b&w. 12,248 ft. 136 min. PCA cert no. 17281.

Prod Stanley Kramer. *Dir* Stanley Kramer. *Asst dir* Carter DeHaven, Jr. *Dial dir* Anne Kramer. *Written for the screen by* Edna Anhalt and Edward Anhalt. *Photog* Franz Planer. *Cam op* Bud Mautino. *Prod des* Rudolph Sternad. *Art dir* Howard Richmond. *Film ed* Fred Knudtson. *Set dec* Victor Gangelin. *Cost supv* Joe King. *Gowns* Don Loper. *Mus* George Antheil. *Mus cond* Paul Sawtell. *Sd eng* Earl Snyder. *Makeup* Bill Wood. *Hair styles* Esperanza Corona. *Prod mgr* John E. Burch. *Scr supv* John Franco. *Prod asst* Sally Hamilton. *Company grip* Morris Rosen. *Tech adv* Morton Maxwell, M.D. *Asst tech adv* Josh Fields, M.D. and Marjorie Lefevre, R.N. [*Dialect consultant* Virginia Christine].

Song(s): "Not As a Stranger," music by James Van Heusen, lyrics by Buddy Kaye.

Source: Based on the novel *Not As a Stranger* by Morton Thompson (New York, 1954).

Cast: Olivia de Havilland (*Kristina [Hedvigson]*), Robert Mitchum (*Lucas [Marsh]*), Frank Sinatra (*Alfred [Boone]*), Gloria Grahame (*Harriet [Lang]*), Broderick Crawford (*Dr. Aarons*), Charles Bickford (*Dr. [David W.] Runkleman*), Myron McCormick (*Dr. [Clem] Snider*), Lon Chaney (*Job [Marsh]*), Jesse White ([*Ben*] *Cosgrove*), Harry Morgan (*Oley*), Lee Marvin (*Brundage*), Virginia Christine (*Bruni*), Whit Bissell (*Dr. Dietrich*), Jack Raine (*Dr. Lettering*), Mae Clarke (*Miss Odell*), William Vedder ([*Carl*] *Emmons*), John Dierkes (*Bursar*), [Jerry Paris (*Student*)], [Will Wright, Carl "Alfalfa" Switzer, Frank Orth, Harry Shannon, Frank Jenks (*Patients*)], Peggy Maley, Patti Brill, Eve McVeagh, Paul Guilfoyle.

Drama, Medical. [*Print viewed*]. Lucas Marsh, a very ambitious medical student, who desperately needs money for his tuition, goes to see his alcoholic father Job, who has squandered money that Luke's mother had saved for him. Job tells him that he will never be a doctor because something was left out of him, leaving him with no emotion or empathy. Although Alfred Boone, a fellow student, lends Luke some money and pathologist Dr. Aarons gives him a lab job, it is not enough. Aarons advises him to quit school, work for a year then come back, but Luke is unwilling to lose the time. Aarons tells Luke that he has too much self-pity and that he, Aarons, had experienced equal difficulties and, being Jewish, was one of the five percent admitted to the school only because the authorities were ashamed to entirely exclude Jews. With a check received from Aarons, Luke is able to make a partial payment to the school's bursar, but is informed that, unless he pays the balance within thirty days, he will not be allowed to attend classes. After Luke and Al witness an operation, shy spinster Kristina Hedvigson, the head operating room nurse, invites them to a smorgasbord the following weekend at the home of Swedish-American friends. There her friend Bruni off-handedly reveals that Kris is thrifty and has saved a considerable amount of money. The comment is not lost on Luke, who invites Kris to dinner and a movie and romances her to the extent that she tells Bruni that she is in love with him. When Luke asks Kris to marry him, he tells her that he is about to have to leave the school and she offers him money. He pretends to be proud and refuses the help, but then relents. Al accuses him of exploiting a woman who is afraid of becoming an old maid and is allowing himself to be kept, but still agrees to be his best man. After Luke and Kris are married, he continues his studies. While observing an operation, Luke criticizes the surgeon, Dr. Dietrich, for failing to use a new, proven technique. Aarons is outraged by Luke's behavior and, although he admits that the surgeon was wrong, tells Luke that he will not be allowed to intern at the hospital unless he apologizes to Dietrich. Luke refuses to apologize and implies to Kris that she is too stupid to understand his dogmatic view that when a doctor does something wrong, he must be stopped. The following day, however, Luke reluctantly apologizes to Dietrich. Time passes and Luke and Al become interns and are on duty one night when an ambulance brings in the dead body of a man who fell under a bus and it turns out to be Job. Showing emotion for the first time, Luke cries for his father. Some time later, when Luke discovers that Al has removed a patient's mole which Luke had earlier recognized as a melanoma and refused to touch, he threatens to report it but Al does so himself. When Kris criticizes Luke for his treatment of Al, Al admits that Luke was correct in behaving the way he did. After completing his internship, Luke takes a position in Greenville, a farm community, as assistant to general practitioner Dr. David W. Runkleman. As Kris believes their marriage has stabilized, she would like to start a family but Luke is uninterested. He has recently met a young widow, Harriet Lang, a horse breeder. One day, while testing a new stethoscope on Runkleman, Luke discovers what Runkleman has known for some time, that he has a serious heart condition. Luke advises him to retire, but he refuses. When they are performing an operation, Dr. Clem Snider, director of the local hospital who also serves as an anaesthetist, almost causes the death of their patient. Later, at a night spot, Runkleman tells Luke and Kris that Snider is a political appointee and nothing can be done about him. During dinner they meet Harriet and her lawyer Ben Cosgrove. Luke gets into a argument with Cosgrove, and later, at home Luke argues with Kris because she drank too much and was annoyed by his dancing with Harriet. Although Luke apologizes, Kris realizes that their marriage is crumbling and asks him again about starting a family, but Luke tells her that he does not want to have children. Some time later, after Harriet tells Luke that she cannot afford to fall in love with him, they start an affair. When Kris goes to see Al to confirm that she is twelve weeks pregnant, she reveals that she has not told Luke and Al advises her to do so. Later, at the hospital, Luke discovers that Mr. Carl Emmons, an elderly patient Snider has diagnosed as dying, has typhoid but can be saved. After Luke puts Emmons in isolation and threatens to kill Snider, he asks Kris to help him and, together, they save Emmons. Genuinely admiring Kris's nursing abilities, Luke tells her that she should return to work and that a family is not for her. When Al comes to visit, Runkleman and Luke are busy innoculating the townspeople against typhoid. Al advises Kris again that she must tell Luke about the baby. Meanwhile, Luke visits Harriet and tells her that he feels guilty and must end their relationship. When he returns home, Al is waiting outside and tells him that Kris is pregnant. Stunned, Luke apologizes to Kris and asks for another chance, but she rejects him angrily, realizing that he has always used her, and tells him to leave. Later, Runkleman collapses due to his heart condition and Luke decides to operate immediately, ordering Snider to assist. They manage to save Runkleman, but while Luke attempts an added procedure to give him an extra chance, he makes a miscalculation which causes the aorta to rupture and Runkleman dies despite their valiant efforts. As Luke leaves the operating room, Snider says, "God help him, he made a mistake." Distraught, Luke walks through town and at last realizing his own humanity, returns home to Kris, who welcomes him with open arms and comforts him. *Ambition. Idealism.*

Marriage of convenience. Opportunists. Physicians. Surgeons. Alcoholics. Fathers and sons. Femmes fatales. Financial crisis. Horse owners. Hospitals. Jews. Lawyers. Medical colleges. Medical students. Nurses. Operations, surgical. Pathologists. Pregnancy. Small town life. Swedish Americans. Typhoid fever. Widows.

Note: The main title reads: Morton Thompson's Not As a Stranger. Thompson died a few weeks before the publication of his novel. A *Var* news item of 3 Feb 1954 reveals that producer Stanley Kramer made a pre-publication deal to purchase the screen rights in early Dec 1953 for $75,000. The novel subsequently became a bestseller. *Not As a Stranger* was Kramer's first film as a director. Buildings on the UCLA campus served as exteriors for the medical school. Although James Van Heusen and Buddy Kaye are credited onscreen with the song "Not As a Stranger," and it was recorded by Frank Sintra, only the instrumental version was heard in the film. *Not As a Stranger* received an Academy Award nomination for Best Sound Recording.

AmCin Jul 1955, pp. 396-97, 433, 435. *Box* 18 Jun 1955. *DV* 15 Jun 1955, p. 3. *Exb* 29 Jun 1955, p. 3988. *FD* 15 Jun 1955, p. 6. *Har* 18 Jun 1955, p. 100. *HR* 15 Jun 1955, p. 3. *Life* 27 Jun 1955, pp. 77-80. *LAT* 30 Jun 1955. *Look* 31 May 1955, pp. 87-88. *MPHPD* 18 Jun 1955, p. 481. *NYT* 29 Jun 1955, p. 24. *Var* 3 Feb 1954. *Var* 15 Jun 1955, p. 6.

NOTHING BUT THE TRUTH *(foreignversion) see* **LA PURA VERDAD**

NOTORIOUS (German Americans)

RKO Radio Pictures, Inc.; By Arrangement with David O. Selznick. *Dist* RKO Radio Pictures, Inc. 6 Sep **1946**; New York opening: 15 Aug 1946; Los Angeles opening: 22 Aug 1946; Prod: 10 Oct 1945—17 Jan 1946; retakes and addl scenes 18 Jan—25 Jan 1946, 4 Apr—5 Apr 1946 [©RKO Radio Pictures, Inc.; 15 Aug 1946; LP557]. Sd (RCA Sound System); b&w. 9,130 ft. 101 or 103 min. PCA cert no. 11261.

Prod ALFRED HITCHCOCK. *Dir* Alfred Hitchcock. *Asst dir* William Dorfman. [*Dial dir* Ruth Roberts]. *Wrt* Ben Hecht. *Dir of photog* Ted Tetzlaff. *Spec eff* Vernon L. Walker and Paul Eagler. *Art dir* Albert S. D'Agostino and Carroll Clark. *Ed* Theron Warth. *Set dec* Darrell Silvera and Claude Carpenter. *Miss Ingrid Bergman's gowns by* Edith Head. *Mus dir* C. Bakaleinikoff. *Mus* Roy Webb. *Orch arr* Gil Grau. *Sd* John E. Tribby and Terry Kellum. *Prod asst* Barbara Keon. [*Pub wrt* Bill Porter]. [*Stand-in for Ingrid Bergman* Betty Brooks]. [*Stand-in for Cary Grant* Dan Cassell]. [*Stand-in* Leo Snell, J. Dodds, D. Barton and Sam Lufkin].

Cast: CARY GRANT ([*T. R.*] *Devlin*), INGRID BERGMAN (*Alicia Huberman*), Claude Rains (*Alexander Sebastian*), Louis Calhern (*Paul Prescott*), Madame Konstantin (*Mme. [Anna] Sebastian*), Reinhold Schunzel (*Dr. Anderson [previously known as Otto Rensler]*), Moroni Olsen (*Walter Beardsley*), Ivan Triesault (*Eric Mathis*), Alex Minotis (*Joseph*), Wally Brown (*Mr. Hopkins*), Sir Charles Mendl (*Commodore*), Ricardo Costa (*Dr. [Julio] Barbosa*), Eberhard Krumschmidt ([*Emil*] *Hupka*), Fay Baker (*Ethel*), [Gavin Gordon (*Ernest Weylin*)], [Antonio Moreno (*Senor Ortiza*)], [Frederick Ledebur (*Knerr*)], [William Gordon (*Adams*)], [Charles D. Brown (*Judge*)], [Peter Von Zerneck (*Rossner*)], [Fred Nurney (*John Huberman*)], [Herbert Wyndham (*Mr. Cook*)], [Aileen Carlyle (*Woman at party*)], [Harry Hayden (*Defense council*)], [Dink Trout (*Court clerk*)], [John Vosper, Eddie Bruce, Don Kerr, Ben Erway, Emmett Vogan, Paul Bryan, Alan Ward, James Logan (*Reporters*)], [Howard Negley, Frank Marlowe, George Lynn (*Photographers*)], [Warren Jackson (*District attorney*)], [Howard Mitchell (*Bailiff*)], [Tom Coleman (*Court stenographer*)], [Garry Owen, Lester Dorr (*Motorcycle officers*)], [Patricia Smart (*Mrs. Jackson*)], [Candido Bonsato, Ted Kelly (*Waiters*)], [Tina Menard (*Maid*)], [Alfredo De Sa (*Ribero*)], [Frank Wilcox (*F.B.I. man*)], [Bee Benadaret, Virginia Gregg, Bernice Barrett (*File clerks*)], [Alfred Hitchcock (*Party goer*)], [Sandra Morgan], [Lillian West], [Beulah Christian], [Alameda Fowler], [Richard Clark], [Francis McDonald], [Leota Lorraine], [Luis Serrano], [Ramon Nomar].

Espionage, Romance. [*Print viewed*]. After her Nazi father is convicted of treason by a Miami, Florida jury, German-born Alicia Huberman tries to forget her pain by throwing a loud party and flirting with uninvited guest T. R. Devlin. Late that evening, an intoxicated Alicia takes Devlin on a drive and is stopped for speeding by a motorcycle officer. When Devlin flashes his official credentials, however, the officer allows Alicia to go without a ticket. Alicia, who has been hounded by reporters and police, is infuriated at Devlin and denounces him as a double-crossing "cop." Although Devlin disapproves of Alicia's self-destructive, promiscuous life style, he is confident of her patriotic feelings toward America, having heard secretly recorded comments she has made, and offers her a job

infiltrating a Nazi industrial combine in Brazil. The embittered Alicia at first rejects Devlin's offer, but eventually agrees to accompany him to Rio de Janeiro. While waiting for her assignment, Alicia enjoys a romantic, carefree week in Rio and proudly tells Devlin she is a changed woman. Devlin is skeptical about her reformation, but nonetheless finds himself falling in love with her. The couple's newfound bliss is shortlived, however, as Devlin's boss, Paul Prescott, informs him that Alicia's assignment is to woo her former suitor, German-born Alexander Sebastian, and determine what his war machine combine is manufacturing. Although Alicia is conflicted, Devlin refuses to tell her what to do, and believing that he doesn't truly love her, she accepts the assignment. Devlin, in turn, views Alicia's acceptance as proof of her fickleness. As pre-arranged, Alicia encounters Alex while riding in a park and encourages him to pursue her. At a dinner party at Alex's home, Alicia notices one of the guests, Emil Hupka, gesture nervously at a wine bottle sitting on a mantle. Later, Alex and his other male guests discuss Hupka's improper dinner behavior and agree that he must be eliminated, a job the sinister Eric Mathis eagerly assumes. Soon after, Alicia reports to Devlin, who is posing as a public relations representative, at a Rio racetrack and tells him with sarcasm that the lovestruck Alex is her new "playmate." Devlin reacts to the remark with disgust, but easily plays the part of Alicia's rejected lover in front of Alex. When a jealous Alex then questions Alicia about Devlin, she reassures him that the handsome American "means nothing" to her. A short time later, Alicia pays an unexpected call on Prescott and Devlin and informs them that Alex has proposed to her. Although stunned by the news, Devlin once again refuses to interfere, and a heartbroken Alicia agrees to the marriage. After a brief honeymoon, the newlyweds return to Alex's house, where his domineering mother Anna views her new daughter-in-law with jealous disdain. Alicia immediately inspects the layout of the house and learns from butler Joseph that only Alex has the key to the house's large wine cellar. Some days later, Devlin instructs Alicia to throw a party and secure the key long enough for him to investigate the wine cellar. Before the party, Alicia sneaks the wine cellar key off Alex's key ring and later passes it to Devlin. Alicia then slips away from Alex's watchful eye and accompanies Devlin to the cellar, where they discover that one of the bottles contains not wine, but a mineral substance. When Devlin accidentally drops the bottle, Alicia quickly drains a similar bottle and helps him pour the spilled contents into it. As they are leaving the cellar, Alex approaches with Joseph, and Devlin kisses Alicia to distract him. Although Alex falls for the ruse at first, he soon notices that his cellar key is missing. Early the next morning, after he finds the key back on his ring and discovers that the bottle has been tampered with, he deduces Alicia's true mission and informs his mother. The quick thinking Anna declares that to keep Alex's slip from their ruthless group, they must slowly poison Alicia. Over the next few weeks, Alicia grows sicker from Anna's poison, which is placed in Alicia's coffee. At their next meeting, Prescott informs Alicia that the mineral substance is uranium and asks her to find out where the group is mining it. He also tells Alicia that Devlin has requested a transfer, a fact Devlin denies when he next meets with her. Instead, Devlin questions Alicia about her obvious illness and believes her when she claims she has a hangover. Later, however, when she fails to show up for their next meeting, Devlin realizes that Alicia was really ill. Alicia, in turn, deduces what Alex and Anna are doing to her, as well as the location of the mine, but is now too weak to escape. With Prescott's backing, Devlin goes to Alex's house to rescue Alicia, confident that the Nazi will not try to stop him in front of the group. Although sedated, Alicia is overjoyed to see Devlin, and they confess their love for each other. As Devlin carries Alicia to his car, a helpless Alex announces to his suspicious comrades that he is taking Alicia to the hospital. When Devlin calmly refuses to allow Alex in the car, however, the Nazi's blunder is revealed, and his fate, sealed. *Government agents. Nazis. Regeneration. Rio de Janeiro (Brazil). Romance. Spies. Butlers. Drunkenness. Fathers and daughters. Germans. Jealousy. Keys. Marriage. Miami (FL). Mothers and sons. Parties. Patriotism. Poisoning. Police. Promiscuity. Surveillance devices. Treason. Uranium. Wine cellars.*

Note: Before RKO became involved, independent producer David O. Selznick controlled this film. Although an Oct 1944 *HR* news item listed Lois Anderson as the film's story writer, no other source credits her. Modern sources provide the following information about the film's inception: The inspiration for *Notorious* came from a 1921 *Saturday Evening Post* short story by John Taintor Foote entitled "The Song of the Dragon." In Foote's story, as in

Notorious, a woman sacrifices herself sexually in order to gather information from her enemies, and undergoes a transformation as a result of her efforts. Ben Hecht, who had worked with director Alfred Hitchcock and Selznick on the very successful 1944 film *Spellbound*, was signed to write the screenplay in late 1944 at a salary of $5,000 per week, with a fifteen-week guarantee. Working together in New York, Hecht and Hitchcock produced a fifty-page treatment in three weeks and then returned to Los Angeles to write additional treatments.

In Apr 1945, months before the atomic bomb was tested for the first time in New Mexico, the uranium plot element was added to the story. In a modern interview, Hitchcock recalled that a writer friend had told him about a secret scientific project "some place in New Mexico," and that he, himself, was aware that the Germans were conducting heavy water tests in Norway. According to the modern interview, Hecht and Hitchcock consulted Dr. Robert Millikan, a Nobel Prize winner credited with the discovery of cosmic rays, on how to make an atomic bomb. Millikan reportedly refused to answer the question directly, but confirmed the writers' contention that the crucial bomb ingredient (uranium) could fit into a wine bottle. As a result of the uranium device, Hitchcock was put under surveillance by the FBI for several weeks.

Before the script was completed, modern sources continue, Selznick, who was struggling to finish *Duel in the Sun* (see above entry), approached independent producer Hal Wallis to take over the production. Wallis, who questioned the credibility of the uranium device, soon abandoned the project, however, and in mid-Jul 1945, RKO entered into a deal with Selznick. According to the terms of the contract, RKO bought Selznick's "package"—Hecht, Hitchcock, Cary Grant and Ingrid Bergman—for $800,000 and fifty percent of the net profits. Although Hitchcock received no money from the sale, he was designated as the film's producer and was given free creative reign at the studio. *Notorious* was the first American film on which Hitchcock worked as both producer and director.

RKO script files contained in the UCLA Arts Library—Special Collections add the following information about the production: Although not credited on screen, Hitchcock co-wrote the screenplay with Hecht. In addition to Hecht and Hitchcock, Clifford Odets, who is listed on one draft as A. B. Clifford, worked on the script, although the extent of his contribution to the completed film has not been determined. (Modern sources claim that Odets was hired to write dialogue for the love scenes.) An early draft of the screenplay included two "happy" endings. In both, "Alicia" and "Devlin" are seen either already married or getting married. In early drafts of the treatment, according to modern sources, Devlin, who was called "Wallie Fancher," dies while fighting with "Sebastian."

MPAA/PCA files contained at the AMPAS Library add the following information about the production: Responding to an early draft of the screenplay, PCA director Joseph I. Breen stated in a 25 May 1945 letter to Selznick that *Notorious* was "definitely" unacceptable as far as the Code was concerned, because the heroine is a "grossly immoral woman, whose immorality is accepted in stride." Breen suggested changing Alicia from a prostitute to a gold digger whose "total loss of faith in her father" leads her to "get what she can out of life." Although Alicia's sexual habits were toned down in later drafts, Breen continued to object to her character and was especially distressed by an early scene in which an illicit relationship between Alicia and "Ernest" was implied. That scene was eventually altered to appease Breen. In the 25 May 1945 letter, Breen also advised Selznick to take "counsel" with the FBI, noting that the "industry has had a kind of 'gentleman's agreement' with Mr. J. Edgar Hoover, wherein we have practically obligated ourselves to submit to him, for his consideration and approval, stories which importantly involve the activities" of the FBI. (Modern sources note that Hoover did, in fact, object to the story, both in terms of its sexual content, and its depiction of agent Devlin.) Breen also recommended that Selznick consult with the Brazilian government concerning the film's depiction of that country. In order to obtain the necessary U.S. government clearances, modern sources state, Selznick arranged for Hitchcock and a company representative to meet with Assistant Secretary of State Archibald MacLeish in Washington, D.C.

According to modern sources, Selznick, hoping to capitalize on the bombing of Hiroshima and Nagasaki on 6 Aug and 9 Aug 1945, tried unsuccessfully to convince RKO to replace Grant, who was tied up until Oct 1945, with Joseph Cotten and rush the film into production. Modern sources state that Selznick originally wanted Clifton Webb to play Sebastian, while Hitchcock considered George Sanders and opera star Ezio Pinza for the role. Hitchcock approached Ethel Barrymore to play "Madame Sebastian," but she turned down the part, according to modern sources. Madame Leopoldine Konstantin, who eventually played the role, made her first and only American screen appearance in *Notorious*. *HR* noted that Hitchcock went to New York to cast the film, and a *NYT* article commented that he had "set something of a precedent" by signing four New York stage actors to play small roles in the film. According to a *HR* news item, Hitchcock tested Don Douglas for a "top role" in the production. (Douglas was not cast, however, and died on 31 Dec 1945 of appendicitis.) The CBCS lists both Luis Serrano and Ramon Nomar in the role of "Dr. Silva." It is not known which actor played the part, or if both actors appeared in the final film in different roles. *HR* production charts include Lenore Ulric in the cast, but her participation in the final film has not been confirmed. In late Dec 1945, Bergman's five-year, $2,000-per-week contract with Selznick expired, and, according to a *NYT* article, *Notorious* was the last film she made as a Selznick star.

In a modern interview, Hitchcock recalled that, because of the height difference between Claude Rains and Bergman, he had Rains stand on a box during his close-up shots with the actress. In another shot, Hitchcock had a graduated plank constructed, which enabled him to film Rains and Bergman walking toward the camera in a single shot while maintaining the height illusion. A *HCN* news item revealed that cinematographer Ted Tetzlaff created his famous "upside down shot" point-of-view shot of Grant, seen early in the film, with the use of mirrors. According to a Nov 1946 *NYT* article, Hitchcock originally wanted to make his customary onscreen appearance playing a "deaf-mute walking inconspicuously through a street scene 'talking' in sign language to his woman companion." As the couple passes in front of the camera, the woman was to slap Hitchcock's face. When word of the proposed bit got out, Hitchcock received scores of protest letters from deaf-mutes and dropped the idea. In the final film, Hitchcock appears drinking a glass of champagne at Alicia's party.

According to modern sources, in the spring of 1945, Selznick hired Gregg Toland to film rear-projection footage of South America. According to *HR*, background shots were filmed in Miami, FL. Production files indicate that other scenes were taken in Baldwin Park in Los Angeles, Beverly Hills and at the Santa Anita Racetrack near Los Angeles. RKO borrowed Edith Head from Paramount for the production. According to modern sources, the film cost two million dollars to make, but made eight million dollars in profits. Claude Rains was nominated for an Academy Award as Best Supporting Actor and Hecht was nominated in the Best Writing (Original Screenplay) category. Ingrid Bergman reprised her role in a *Lux Radio Theatre* broadcast on 26 Jan 1948, co-starring Joseph Cotten. *Notorious* was remade in 1992 by Hamster-ABC Productions. Colin Bucksey directed and Jenny Robertson and John Shea starred in the television version, which was first broadcast on the Lifetime cable television network on 28 Jan 1992.

Box 27 Jul 1946. DV 24 Jul 1946, pp. 3, 11. FD 25 Jul 1946, p. 7. HCN 6 Sep 1946, p. 5. HR 17 Oct 1944, p. 3. HR 23 Aug 1945, p. 14. HR 27 Aug 1945, p. 5. HR 30 Aug 1945, p. 2. HR 16 Oct 1945, p. 5. HR 15 Nov 1945, p. 11. HR 21 Nov 1945, p. 8. HR 28 Dec 1945, p. 14. HR 24 Jul 1946, p. 6. HR 20 Aug 1946, p. 12. MPHPD 2 Mar 1946, p. 2870. MPHPD 27 Jul 1946, p. 3113. NYT 28 Oct 1945. NYT 16 Dec 1945. NYT 16 Aug 1946, p. 19. NYT 3 Nov 1946. Var 24 Jul 1946, p. 14.

THE NOTORIOUS ELINOR LEE (African Americans)

Micheaux Pictures Corp. *Dist* Sack Amusement Enterprises, Inc. 1940; Harlem premiere: mid-Jan 1940. Sd; b&w. 10 reels, 9,579 ft.

Pres ALFRED N. SACK. [*Assoc prod* Hubert Fauntleroy Julian]. *Dir* Oscar Micheaux. *Dial dir* Jack Kollin. *Wrt* Oscar Micheaux. *Photog* Lester Lang. *Ed* Leonard Weiss. *Mus score* Jack Shilkret. *Rec dir* Nelson Minnerly.

Cast: Gladys Williams (*Elinor Lee*), Carman Newsome ([*Norman*] *Haywood*), Robert Earl Jones (*Benny Blue*), Edna Mae Harris (*Fredi*), Vera Burrelle (*Sherry*), Eddie Lemons (*Brownlee*), Columbus Jackson (*"Crocker" Johnson*), Laura Bowman (*Benny's mother*), Madeline Donegan (*"Mary"*), Amanda Randolph (*Mary's mother*), Robert Paquin (*Reporter*), O. W. Polk (*Blakely*), Charles Latorre (*Farbacker*), Don De Leo (*Feretti*), Abe Simon (*Hererra*), Sandy McDonald (*Bradley*), Harry Kadison (*Hans Wagner*), Lew Hearn (*Joe Grim*), Jack Effrat (*Chief reporter*), Harry Ballou (*Announcer*), Sam Taub (*Commentator*), Lou Goldberg (*Referee*), Juano Hernandez (*John Arthur*), Fred Palmer's Orchestra, "Rubberneck" Holmes, Ralph Brown (*Dancers*), Sally Gooding, Ella Mae Waters.

African American, Boxing, Drama, with songs. [*Print viewed*]. While visiting sports bosses Farbacker and Feretti, gangster moll Elinor Lee tells them that she has a fighter named Benny Blue under contract for ten years. Confident that the chances of a black man becoming boxing champion are remote, they plan to make $500,000 by building him up and then forcing him to take a dive and throw a fight. Lee soon enlists boxing managers Norman Haywood and "Crocker" Johnson to engage Fredi, an old friend of Benny's, to become his sweetheart. Benny fights an Italian and beats him in the sixth round by a knockout. Although he no longer writes to her, Benny later asks his mother about Mary, a girl who she believes would look out for him. Benny's mother is worried about her son, for she knew Lee when she lived in St. Louis, where she was charged with murder and acquitted under suspicious circumstances. After winning his next fight, Benny goes to a nightclub and celebrates with Fredi all night. The next day, Benny, in poor shape, loses his bout with a German, Hans Wagner, who refuses a rematch. Benny is soon reduced to fighting anyone, but when he begins to win his bouts, Wagner agrees to a rematch. Fredi, meanwhile, has been bribed and threatened by Lee into urging him to throw the rematch, but when Benny convinces Fredi that his affection for her can overcome her troubles, she confesses to him that she is an escaped convict and that she is afraid of Lee. Two years after his first match against Wagner, Benny again faces the German, who suspects that his opponent will be using the same poor tactics he used in their last fight. Benny, however, has changed, and as reporters bet on "Blue dynamite vs. Arayan mentality," Benny scores a quick knockout, and Lee and her backers are ruined. *African Americans. Boxing. Frame-ups. Gangsters. Romance.* Blackmail. Boxing managers. Cabarets. Confession. Ex-convicts. Germans. Mothers and sons. Nightclubs. Promoters. Racism. Threats.

Note: According to modern sources, the producers were Hubert Julian, the "Black Eagle," and Oscar Micheaux. A Jan 1940 *Time* article noted that the picture was filmed in an old Biograph studio in the Bronx, NY. Although contemporary sources indicate that the film had its premiere in Jan 1940, the exact release date of the picture has not been found. Song titles for this film have not been found.

Time 29 Jan 1940, pp. 67-68.

NOW IT CAN BE TOLD *see* THE HOUSE ON 92ND ST.

NUIT D'ESPAGNE (French language)

RKO Radio Pictures, Inc.; Herbert Brenon's Production. *Dist* RKO Radio Pictures, Inc. 1931. Sd; b&w. Length undetermined. French language.

Dir Henri de la Falaise. *Scr* Jean Daumery and Elizabeth Meehan.

Source: Based on the novel *The Next Corner* by Kate Jordan (Boston, 1921).

Cast: Jeanne Helbling (*Elsie Maury*), Rose Dione (*Paula Vrain*), Geymond Vital (*Le marquis de Lupa*), Jean Delmour (*Robert Maury*), Marcelle Corday, Adrienne d'Ambricourt.

Domestic, Melodrama. [*Not viewed*]. [The following plot summary is based on the English-language version of this film, *Transgression*; character names refer to that version. For further information regarding the English-language version, please see the note below and the entry for *Transgression* in the *AFI Catalog of Feature Films, 1931-40*.] When a job assignment forces him to relocate in India, English businessman Robert Maury ignores the admonitions of his spinster sister Honora and sends his young country wife Elsie to live in Paris for a year. After a short time in Paris, Elsie loses her social naïveté and becomes a sophisticated woman-about-town, attracting the attention of Don Arturo de Borgus, a handsome Spanish bachelor. Out of fear that her attachment to Arturo will lead her to adultery, Elsie informs the Spaniard that their year-long platonic affair must end. On the same day, Elsie receives word that Robert will be arriving from India that night, thus strengthening her resolve to terminate her relationship with Arturo. The ever persistent Arturo, however, begs Paula Vrain, a friend of Elsie, to invite Elsie to a party at a viscountess' home that afternoon. At the party, Arturo romances Elsie and, after a slow tango, convinces her to join him for a few days at his estate in Spain. To Elsie's surprise, Robert, having arrived early in Paris, shows up at the party and is stunned by the changes he perceives in his wife. Elsie, too, finds Robert transformed—colder and more distant—and her discomfort encourages her to postpone her departure for London and slip away to Arturo's remote estate. There, Arturo and his servant Serafin plot to seduce Elsie, who soon succumbs to the don's kisses. Before she will make love to him, however, Elsie insists on writing a letter to Robert in which she declares her love for the nobleman. As Elsie is about to give in to Arturo, Carlos, a local peasant, enters and reveals that the don had seduced his teenaged daughter, who then died in childbirth. Elsie watches horrified as Juan kills Arturo, then remembers the damning letter that has already been mailed to Robert. Unable to intercept the letter in Spain, Elsie rushes home to England and waits day after day for the letter to arrive. Her interest in the mail arouses the suspicions of Honora, who finds a newspaper clipping in which Arturo's murder is discussed in connection with a mysterious "dark lady." Sure that Elsie is the "dark lady," Honora accuses her of adultery in front of a disbelieving Robert, then announces her intention to move. Later, Serafin shows up at the house, posing as a businessman, and threatens to show Robert the letter, which he had never mailed, if Elsie refuses to help him defraud her husband in a business deal. Robert, having overheard Serafin's threats, grabs the envelope and reveals that it contains only blank paper. Thus unarmed, Serafin is forced to depart, while Elsie, who realizes that Arturo had substituted her letter for blank paper, tries to confess to Robert. The devoted Robert, however, refuses to listen and embraces his repentant wife. *English in foreign countries. Infidelity. Innocents. Marriage. Seduction. Transformation. Blackmail. Brothers and sisters. Businessmen. Confession. England. Fraud. Letters. Murder. Nobility. Paris (France). Parties. Peasantry. Revenge. Servants. Spain. Spinsters. Tango (Dance). Womanizers.*

Note: A *FD* news item states that A. Le Bailley was hired by the studio to do the adaptation and dialogue of this French-language version; other sources, however, credit Jean Daumery with the script. In 1924, Sam Wood directed Conway Tearle, Lon Chaney and Dorothy Mackaill in a silent Paramount version of this story called *The Next Corner* (see *AFI Catalog of Feature Films, 1921-30*; F2.3821). For information on the English-language version,

Transgression, which was directed by Herbert Brenon and starred Kay Francis and Paul Cavanagh, please see the entry for that film in the *AFI Catalog of Feature Films, 1931-40*; F3.4747.

O FESTINO O LA LEGGE (Italian Americans, Italian language)

Sandrino Giglio. *Dist* Sandrino Giglio. 1932; Brooklyn, NY showing: 16 Oct 1932; Prod: at Metropolitan Studios, Fort Lee, NJ. Sd; b&w. 6 reels, 5,400 ft. 60 min. Italian language.

Prod Clemente Giglio. *Dir* Bud Pollard.

Cast: Oreste Sandrino.

Drama?, with songs. [*Not viewed*]. [No information concerning this film's plot has been located, except for material submitted to the New York State censors. This material consist of lyrics to a number of songs, dialogue to three short scenes, and "omissions" apparently not in the final film. A description of each part of this material follows.] *First Song, "By the Sea":* The singers relate making love on a ferry to the battery in New York and acknowledge that it isn't the bay of Naples, and that in the place of Vesuvius stand skyscrapers. They bid goodbye to brothers leaving for home and sing Italian songs on the foreign sea of their new home, America. *Second Song, "Magic Isle":* A song of longing for the "magic isle" of a thousand colors, the "luring sea" and "land of homes kissed by the sea," where mothers knit and smile to their sons at sea, fishermen "sing to the beat of the waves," realizing the sea is beautiful, but treacherous, as they pull in their nets. *Third Song, "The Feast":* As a wedding goes on in a happy town, Tore, the scorned lover of the bride Carmela, who married his best friend, drinks wine to drown his misery, then vows to kill her with his knife before she betrays him; the next day, when the people ask who killed her, he plans to shout "It was I, Tore, her first lover!" *Third Song, "The Law":* Following the murder, Tore, unremorseful, asks to be taken to prison. He wonders how his love could have been so beautiful, yet so vile. He asserts that in the eyes of God, he killed in self-defense, because she wanted his life. *Third Song, The Judge's Sentence:* Tore is condemned to a sentence of thirty years imprisonment; he will suffer and may not live until the end. The judge warns against passions that are insane. *Fourth Song, "Oh, Marie!":* The singer implores Marie to love him, complaining of the sleep he loses over her. *Spoken dialogue between Rose and Armando:* Rose surprises Armando by coming to his home to ask forgiveness, as she is tortured by remorse. She promises to be an affectionate and loyal wife. Armando, however, refuses her entreaties, saying she should pray to God. He refuses to betray the memory of a dead friend and tells her goodbye. *Song sung over the radio:* The singer's dream of finding "the purest flower" has been shattered; he compared his love to a rose, and find that she had thorns. He knows now that women, though they may be beautiful, are not sincere. *Second spoken dialogue between Armando and Rose:* While taking his neighbor's child to school, Armando runs into Rose and is shocked to discover that she has become a nun. She tells him that she followed his advice and gave herself to God. They are happy that they did not suffer the fate of Tore and Carmela in the film *O festino o la legge (Thou Shalt Not Kill)*. He now wants only to dedicate his life to "the one person in the world who is most deserving—my mother!" As they say goodbye, Rose wishes he will be an example to all sons who neglect their mothers. *Song to Mother:* The singer wonders why men struggle after love from women who aren't faithful when they have their loyal mothers, whose love never falters, and whose only request is for the voice that calls her "Mother." *Title Song:* The singer attests to his mother that her love is the only love divine, and that a mother's love lasts for eternity. *Last song sung on the radio:* "The woman lives, who will love you forever, Your mother dear, will leave you never!" *Omissions:* In a dialogue between mother and son at a table, the mother asks if he still thinks of a certain woman, and he says no, she has become a nun. A mother prays before the Virgin for her son to be cured and returned to her. A worker in a factory warns someone to be careful, he may hurt someone else. *Betrayal. Italian Americans. Mothers and sons. Murder. Revenge. Drunkenness. Ferryboats. Forgiveness. Homesickness. Immigrants. Judges. New York City. Nuns. Trials. Weddings.*

Note: *FD* lists the English-language title of the film as *Thou Shalt Not Kill*. Information within the dialogue continuity deposited in the NYSA, suggests that *O festino o la legge* may have been a reissue of a silent film with a number of dialogue scenes and songs added, a practice was also used for a number of Yiddish-language releases of the early 1930s put together in New York. No reviews for this film have been located. *FD* news items note that an English version was also recorded and that this was the first in a series of Italian films

planned by producer and impresario Clemente Giglio. The film marked Italian-American actor Oreste Sandrino's feature film debut.

FD 11 May 1932, p. 2. *FD* 6 Jun 1932, p. 2. *FD* 27 Jul 1932, p. 2. *FD* 14 Oct 1932, p. 8.

OBEY THE LAW (Italian Americans)
Foy Productions, Ltd. *Dist* Columbia Pictures Corp. 20 Jan **1933**; Prod: 8 Nov–22 Nov 1932 [©Columbia Pictures Corp.; 5 Jan 1933; LP3527]. Sd; b&w. 7 reels. 64-65 or 69 min.

Prod Bryan Foy. *Dir* Benjamin Stoloff. *Asst dir* Sam Katzman and Lester Neilson. *Scr* Arthur Caesar. *Story* Harry Sauber. *Photog* Joseph Valentine. *Sd eng* Dean Daly.

Cast: Leo Carrillo (*Tony Pasqual*), Dickie Moore (*Dickie Chester*), Lois Wilson (*Grace Chester*), Henry Clive (*"Big Joe" Rierdon*), Eddie Garr (*Bob Richards*), Gino Corrado (*Giovanni*), Ward Bond (*Kid Paris*).

Drama. [*Not viewed*]. Tony Pasqual is an Italian immigrant making a living as a barber on New York's East Side. He is deeply patriotic and his greatest day is when he receives American citizenship. That same day, Bob Richards robs Tony of his last five dollars, but instead of reporting Bob to the local policeman, Tony takes Bob home and feeds him, his sister, Grace Chester, and her son, Dickie. After learning that Bob is a decorated World War I veteran who is deeply cynical about the government Tony so loves, Tony lands Bob work at a local café. One day Bob is killed during a fight at the neighborhood gambling house while trying to take a young boy out at his mother's request. Tony, who has fallen in love with Grace, takes over the support of her and Dickie. Despite threats to his life, Tony testifies about Bob's murder. He is shot and wounded while leaving the courtroom, but this does not prevent him from naming Kid Paris as Bob's murderer from his hospital bed. "Big Joe" Rierdon, the local crime boss who also controls the neighborhood assemblyman, gives free shoes to the neighborhood, hoping his charity will blind Tony to his activities, since Tony has become an unofficial spokesman for the tenement neighbors. Tony discovers that Rierdon owns the gambling establishment, however, and even after Rierdon tries to keep him quiet by bombing his shop, Tony makes a public radio broadcast to expose Rierdon. Rierdon's arrest leaves Tony and Grace free to marry. *Barbers and barbershops. Children. Good Samaritans. Italian Americans. New York City–East Side. Patriotism. Political bosses. Citizenship. Family relationships. Gambling houses. Gunshot wounds. Immigrants. Mothers and sons. Murder. Radio broadcasting. Reformers. Robbery. Self-sacrifice. Trials.*

Note: The working title of this film was *East of Fifth Avenue*.

FD 11 Mar 1933, p. 4. *HR* 14 Nov 1932, p. 6. *MPH* 18 Mar 1933, p. 36. *NYT* 13 Mar 1933, p. 18. *Var* 14 Mar 1933, p. 15.

OBSESSION *see* **WILD IS THE WIND**

ODDS AGAINST TOMORROW (African Americans, Italian Americans)
HarBel Productions, Inc. *Dist* United Artists Corp. **1959**; New York opening: 15 Oct 1959; Prod: late Feb—late Apr 1959 at Gold Medal Studios, the Bronx, New York [©HarBel Productions, Inc.; 13 Oct 1959; LP15186]. Sd (RCA Sound System); b&w. 8,621 or 9,022 ft. 95-96 min. PCA cert no. 19371.

Prod Robert Wise. *Assoc prod* Phil Stein. *Dir* Robert Wise. *Asst dir* Charles Maguire. *Scr* John O. Killens and Nelson Gidding. *Photog* Joseph Brun. *Cam op* Sol Midwall. *Settings* Leo Kerz. *Film ed* Dede Allen. *Set dec* Fred Ballmeyer. *Cost* Anna Hill Johnstone. *Mus comp and cond* John Lewis. *Sd* Edward Johnstone and Richard Voriseck. *Makeup* Robert Jiras. *Mgr of prod* Forrest E. Johnston. *Scr supv* Marguerite James.

Song(s): "All Men Are Evil" and "My Baby's Not Around," words and music by Milton Okun and Harry Belafonte.

Source: Based on the novel *Odds Against Tomorrow* by William P. McGivern (New York, 1957).

Cast: HARRY BELAFONTE ([*Johnny*] *Ingram*), ROBERT RYAN ([*Earl*] *Slater*), SHELLEY WINTERS (*Lorry*), Ed Begley ([*David*] *Burke*), Gloria Grahame (*Helen*), Will Kuluva (*Bacco*), Kim Hamilton (*Ruth*), Mae Barnes (*Annie*), Richard Bright (*Coco*), Carmen De Lavallade (*Kitty*), Lou Gallo (*Moriarity*), Lois Thorne (*Eadie* [*Ingram*]), Wayne Rogers (*Soldier in bar*), Zohra Lampert (*Girl in bar*), Allen Nourse (*Police chief* [*Melton*]), [Fred J. Scollay (*Cannoy*)], [William Zuckert (*Bartender*)], [Burtt Harris (*George*)], [Clint Young (*Policeman in park*)], [Ed Preble (*Hotel clerk*)], [Mil Stewart (*Elevator operator*)], [Ronnie Stewart (*Man with dog*)],

[Marc May (*Ambulance attendant*)], [Paul Hoffman (*Garry*)], [Cicely Tyson (*Fra*)], [Lou Martini (*Captain of waiters*)], [Robert Jones (*Guard at door*)], [Floyd Ennis (*Solly*)], [William Adams (*Bank guard*)], [Fred Herrick (*Bank manager*)], [Mary Boylan (*Bank secretary*)], [John Garden (*Clerk*)].

Social, Drama. [*Print viewed*]. In New York City, David Burke, a former policeman who once served a prison sentence, asks bigoted Southern tough guy Earl Slater to rob a bank with him, promising him $50,000 in small bills if the robbery is successful. Earl is reluctant to accept Burke's proposal but feels he needs the money to support his live-in girlfriend Lorry. Burke also tries to recruit Johnny Ingram, a nightclub entertainer who is hopelessly addicted to gambling, but Johnny turns him down. Undaunted, Burke visits Bacco, an Italian mobster to whom Johnny is deeply in debt. Shortly thereafter, Bacco stops by Johnny's club and threatens to kill not only the singer but also his ex-wife and daughter unless the debt is paid by the next day. The next day, Johnny takes his daughter Eadie to Central Park, and when he realizes that two of Bacco's men are following him, he calls Burke and agrees to help with the robbery. Meanwhile, Earl accompanies Burke to Melton, a small town along the Hudson River. Burke shows Earl the bank and explains that because pay day is on Friday, the bank is full of cash on Thursday evenings. Burke adds that a black waiter brings sandwiches to the small staff at the same time each week, and only an aging guard stands watch. Earl refuses the job when he learns that Johnny, a "colored boy," is to take part in it, however. Lorry assures Earl that money is unimportant to her, but he remains gloomy, ashamed that she supports them both. Finally, he decides to meet with Burke, but before he goes, he makes love to Helen, an upstairs neighbor who is fascinated with him because he once killed a man. When Johnny's ex-wife comes by to pick up Eadie, Johnny declares that he still loves her. She seems to love him, too, but complains that his gambling makes him an unfit father. Angry, Johnny replies that by trying to fit into a white world by, for example, serving on a mostly white PTA committee, she is only fooling herself. Late that night, the three men meet at Burke's, and when Earl calls Johnny "boy," Burke reminds him that they are equal partners in the venture. The next day, each man travels to Melton separately, meeting near the river to discuss the details of the crime. Earl continues to insult Johnny, and Burke tries to keep the two from fighting. While waiting for nightfall, Earl shoots a rabbit, and Johnny worriedly flings stones into the river. At six o'clock, Burke arrives at the restaurant near the bank. He tries to knock into the waiter who usually carries the food order to the bank, but some small boys bump the waiter instead, spilling the coffee and food into the street. Disgruntled, the waiter returns to the restaurant, whereupon Johnny, dressed in waiter clothes, knocks on the side door of the bank. When the guard opens the door, the three robbers rush inside. While Johnny and Burke stuff money into bags, Earl needlessly hits several of the frightened employees. Then, ignoring previously discussed plans, Earl gives Burke the car keys, unwilling to trust Johnny with driving the getaway car. As Burke leaves the bank, he is seen by two policemen, and when the burglar alarm sounds, the shooting begins. Burke is shot, and because he now has the car keys, Earl and Johnny, crouching behind the corner, are unable to escape. Burke calls, "Run, Johnny, I'm sorry," and dies, whereupon Earl remarks that at least the old man won't be able to confess their identity to the police. Enraged, Johnny begins shooting at Earl, who manages to escape to a nearby oil refinery. Johnny pursues Earl to the top of an oil tank, and when the two fire on each other, the refinery bursts into flame. Later, as officials are viewing the charred bodies, one of them asks, "Which is which?" "Take your pick," replies the other. *African Americans. Bank robberies. Gamblers. Racism. Explosions. Family relationships. Fear. Flirtation. Gangsters. Greed. Homosexuality. Infidelity. Italian Americans. Manhood. Manslaughter. New York (State). New York City. Nightclub entertainers. Police corruption. Ruffians. Threats.*

Note: HarBel Productions, Inc. was Harry Belafonte's independent production company. Except for one sequence, the entire film was shot in New York City. Howard Fortune, Edward Knott and Kenn Collins appear in the onscreen credits, but because they were difficult to read in the viewed print, their exact credits are undetermined. According to modern sources, John Lewis' score was performed by a large orchestra that included Milt Jackson on vibes, Percy Heath on bass, Connie Kay on drums, Bill Evans on piano, and Jim Hall on guitar. Harry Belafonte performs vocals on one of the songs. The *Var* reviewer commented on the presence of the word "ofay," a derogatory term for whites, in the film and also noted that the picture presents "a unique view (for films) of a normal, middle-class Negro home." This film marked Wayne Rogers'

film debut. Although not a crucial element in the plot, one of the characters, a henchman of the mobster "Bacco," is portrayed as a homosexual who flirts with Belafonte's character, "Johnny Ingram."

AmCin Aug 1959, pp. 478-79, 510. *Box* 12 Oct 1959. *DV* 2 Oct 1959, p. 3. *FD* 5 Oct 1959, p. 15. *HR* 27 Feb 1949. *HR* 24 Apr 1959, p. 19. *HR* 2 Oct 1959, p. 3. *MPHPD* 3 Oct 1959, p. 436. *NYT* 16 Oct 1959, p. 27. *Var* 7 Oct 1959, p. 6.

AN ODYSSEY OF THE NORTH (Native Americans, Native Alaskans)

Bosworth, Inc. *Dist* Paramount Pictures Corp. 3 Sep **1914** [©Bosworth, Inc.; 5 Aug 1914; LU3131]. Si; b&w. 6 reels.

Dir Hobart Bosworth. *Scen* Hettie Gray Baker. *Cam* Gus C. Peterson.

Source: Based on the short story "An Odyssey of the North" in *The Son of the Wolf* by Jack London (New York, 1900).

Cast: Hobart Bosworth (*Naass*), Rhea Haines (*Unga*), Gordon Sackville (*Axel Gunderson*).

Adventure. Naass, the sole survivor of an Alaskan sailing family, tells Klondike miner Cal Galbraith his life story: On the day of his wedding to Unga, the last member of a native tribe, she is abducted by Axel Gunderson. Naass follows Gunderson's ship to the seal hunting grounds, but there he is captured by Russians and sent to Siberia. After a period of forced labor, Naass is released, after which he resumes his search, only to discover that Unga and Gunderson are now happily married. Because Unga does not even recognize her former intended, Naass plans a cruel revenge. Using a map to the gold mines of Alaska as his lure, Naass convinces Unga and Gunderson to enter the Alaskan interior, where he steals their food and kills their dogs. He watches with pleasure as Gunderson starves to death then he reveals himself to Unga. To his surprise, Unga chastises Naass and refuses to leave the body of her husband. Naass then returns alone to civilization where he confides his odyssey to Cal. *Abduction. Alaska. Native Alaskans. Revenge. Traps. Dogs. Hunters. Imprisonment. Maps. Miners. Russians. Sailors. Ships. Siberia. Starvation. Weddings.*

Note: According to papers in the Jack London collection scenes from the film were shot in Truckee, CA and in Seattle, WA, disputing the claim in some contemporary news items that scenes were shot in Alaska. Myrtle Stedman is credited with the female lead in some contemporary sources, but this is not supported by reviews. One modern source credits Joe Ray as a mountie in the film.

Lousiville Post 9 Sep 1914. *MPN* 26 Sep 1914, p. 54. *MPW* 21 Feb 1914, p. 966. *MPW* 13 Jun 1914, p. 1525. *MPW* 29 Aug 1914, p. 1193. *MPW* 5 Sep 1914, p. 1387. *MPW* 19 Sep 1914, p. 1694. *NYDM* 18 Feb 1914, p. 32. *NYDM* 23 Sep 1914, p. 28. *Newark News* 29 Aug 1914. *Var* 19 Sep 1914, p. 19.

OF ONE BLOOD (African Americans)

Sack Amusement Enterprises. *Dist* Sack Attractions. **1945.** Sd (RCA Recording); b&w. 7 reels, 5,779 ft. 64 min.

Prod H. W. Kier. *Dir* Spencer Williams, Jr. *Wrt* Spencer Williams, Jr.

Cast: J. W. Hemmings, Spencer Williams, Jr. [(*Wesley Hill*)], Geraldine Maynard [(*Zelma Jordan*)], Edwin T. Henry, Hugo Martin, L. K. Smith, "Jackie" Thomas, Elroy Easley, [Robert Orr (*Dancer*)].

African American, Crime, Social, Drama. [*Print viewed*]. In the Hall of Human Records, in heaven, the Keeper of Books, a white-bearded old man in a white robe, records the dates of births and deaths of all humankind. A page is devoted to the family of Zeke and Zenobia Ellis, a Southern black couple with two children, Zebedee and Zachariah. In 1915, a new addition is recorded with the birth of Zion. When Zeke expresses a slight regret that he has another son, because, as he says, "boys seem to have a hard time in this country, especially colored boys," elderly midwife Granny Lee reassures him that a rooster crowed three times just before the birth, a sign that Zion will have good luck. Eight years later, when the river near the Ellises' property floods its banks, the local inhabitants are instructed to move to higher ground. Zeke is forced to pull the family's cart beside his mule Jupiter because his other mule has run off, but general store owner Jim Potter, a generous white man, sends Zebedee and Zachariah to catch two of his best mules to give to Zeke. Despite his brother's warning that one of the mules is strange, Zachariah tries to ride it and is thrown. Potter advises the family to take the injured boy, who now cannot speak, to a doctor in Baylor Junction, and in his desperation, Zeke disregards a sign warning against travel on the road there because of the flood. When a thunderstorm erupts, a levee breaks, causing more flooding. Zeke and Zenobia are killed, while Zebedee and Zion swim safely to shore. The Keeper of Books is about to write in the death date for Zachariah, but hesitates, then closes the book as the boy reaches shore in a daze. Later, at a Red Cross

emergency station, Zebedee and Zion meet Wesley Hill, an older black child from the North. Wesley tells the brothers that their parents have died, and after warning that they will be sent to an orphan home, he advises them to clear out, as he has experienced life in one himself. The three boys jump a train, and when it stops, Wesley gets off to bring Zion some water, but is unable to get back on before the train pulls out. Years later, in a large Northern city, Zebedee works as a bootblack in order to put Zion through school. In the evenings, Zion, who wishes to become a lawyer, shares his learning with his brother, while Zebedee, hoping to be a policeman, tells Zion about his daily experiences. By 1938, Zebedee has reached his goal. Zion attends a law college, where he has become engaged to fellow student Zelma Jordan, the daughter of a black newspaper publisher. Zebedee tries to dissuade his brother from marrying before he has established himself, but Zion vows to find any work he can so that they can marry. In 1941, Zelma's father and policeman Zebedee undertake to rid their city of a bootlegging gang. Jordan explains to his daughter that he is getting involved in the campaign because all "colored people" are related and "of one blood." After the police capture one of the gang's members, the leader, Jones, is reluctant to trust anyone new, but finally hires a deaf-and-dumb man to help in their operation. Jordan, meanwhile, discusses the gang problem during a civic meeting attended by various members of the black community, as well as Zion, now a lawyer, and Zelma. Jordan cautions that the younger generation will face the fires of racial retribution unless blacks can get together as a people to confront the problem. He then reminds the crowd that recently thirty-six people, twenty-five of whom were black, lost their lives in a race riot, and that seventeen blacks in their city died from drinking poisoned liquor. Because of recent miscarriages of justice, the group decides that the district attorney's office needs a black representative, and Zion is soon made a deputy district attorney. Concerned about Zion, Jones tells his cohorts not to make deliveries until things "cool off." One day, Zelma goes horseback riding near the gang's hideout and suffers a fall. The deaf-and-dumb man sees the accident and carries Zelma inside, where he revives her and writes on a piece of paper for her to remain silent. Meanwhile, Carlos, one of Jones's subordinates, suggests that the gang kidnap Zelma so that Jordan's newspaper will leave the gang alone. Carlos and his cohorts, Sam and Joe, capture Zelma as she is telephoning for help. Zebedee traces the call and arrives at the hideout with the police. Jones is about to shoot Zebedee when the deaf-and-dumb man hits Jones over the head with a bottle, and the gang is captured. Just before Jones dies, he speaks incoherently about riding a mule and reveals himself to be Zachariah. The supposedly deaf-and-dumb man then speaks and reveals that he is Wesley Hill and is now an FBI agent. Back in the Hall of Human Records, Zachariah's death in 1943 is recorded by the Keeper, and it is said that God made all nations of men, "of one blood." *African Americans. Bootleggers. Brothers. Lawyers. Missing persons, Assumed dead. Police. Religion. Accidental death. Bootblacks. Deaf-mutes. Drowning. Engagements. Family life. Floods. General stores. Generosity. Heaven. Hideouts. Kidnapping. Meetings. Midwives. Mules. Newspaper publishers. Red Cross. Riding accidents. Self-sacrifice. Trains. Undercover agents. United States–South. United States. Federal Bureau of Investigation.*

Note: According to NYSA records, this film was approved for showing in New York in 1945, but modern sources list it as a 1944 release.

OH SAY CAN YOU SING see SLIGHTLY SCANDALOUS

OH! SUSANNA (Native Americans, Dakota)

Republic Pictures Corp. *Dist* Republic Pictures Corp. 28 Mar **1951**; Prod: late May–late Jun 1950 [©Republic Pictures Corp.; 23 Mar 1951; LP829]. Sd (RCA Sound System); col (Trucolor). 10 reels, 8,104 ft. 90 min. Passed by the National Board of Review. PCA cert no. 14734.

Pres HERBERT J. YATES. *Assoc prod* Joseph Kane. *Dir* Joseph Kane. [*Asst dir* Nate Barrager]. *Wrt* Charles Marquis Warren. *Dir of photog* Jack Marta. *Spec eff* Howard Lydecker and Theodore Lydecker. *Optical eff* Consolidated Film Industries. *Art dir* Frank Arrigo. *Film ed* Arthur Roberts. *Set dec* John McCarthy, Jr. and George Milo. *Cost des* Adele Palmer. *Mus* R. Dale Butts. *Sd* T. A. Carman and Howard Wilson. *Makeup supv* Bob Mark. *Hair stylist* Peggy Gray. *Tech adv* Jack Pennick.

Song(s): "The Regular Army, Oh," by Ed Harrigan; "Is Someone Lonely," by Jack Elliott; "Oh! Susanna," by Stephen Foster.

Cast: Rod Cameron [(*Capt. Web Calhoun*)], Adrian Booth [(*Lia Wilson*)], Forrest Tucker [(*Lt. Col. Lloyd Unger*)], Chill Wills [(*Sgt. Barbydt*)], William Ching [(*Corp. Donlin*)], Jim Davis [(*Ira Jordan*)], Wally Cassell [(*Trooper Muro*)], James Lydon [(*Trumpeter Benton*)], Douglas Kennedy [(*Trooper Emers*)], William Haade [(*Trooper Riorty*)], John Compton [(*Lt. Cutter*)], James Flavin [(*Capt. Worth*)], Charles Stevens [(*Charlie Grass*)], Alan Bridge [(*Jave Ledbetter*)], Marion Randolph [(*Mrs. Worth*)], Marshall Reed [(*Trooper Murray*)], John Pickard [(*Rennie*)], Ruth Brennan [(*Young wife*)], Louise Kane [(*Mary Bannon*)], [Edwin Rand (*Crane*)], [Sarah Padden (*Mrs. Ledbetter*)], [Isabel Randolph (*Mrs. Blankenship*)], [Carol Forman (*Blonde*)], [Dorothy Christy, Sarah Spencer, Almira Sessions (*Officers' wives*)], [Doris Patton (*Piano player*)], [Sam Sebby (*Sergeant*)], [Francis McDonald (*Fisher*)], [Rory Mallinson (*Vern Davis*)], [Ray Teal (*Corporal*)], [Mary Newton (*Woman in cafe*)], [Daniel White (*Clerk*)], [Barbara Billingsley (*Mrs. Lark*)], [Pedro de Cordoba (*Pactola*)], [Eugene Roth (*Mac*)], [Tex Terry (*Bartender*)], [Hal Landon (*Ken Ledbetter*)], [Merrill McCormick (*Rusher*)], [Monte Montague (*Rusher driver*)], [Anne Warren (*Jesse Bannon*)], [Al Murphy (*Band leader*)], [William Bakewell (*Lieutenant*)], [George Chesebro (*Drunk*)], [Duke York], [Crane Whitley].

Western, with songs. [*Print viewed*]. In 1875, in the Black Hills of the Dakota Territory, which has been ceded by a treaty to its original owners, the Sioux Nation, the discovery of gold brings "rushers," who develop a hatred for the U.S. Cavalry soldiers assigned to enforce the treaty and keep them off Sioux land. After a company of misfits commanded by Capt. Web Calhoun comes across a dead dog with an arrow through its throat, they chase a family of rushers, the Ledbetters, in a wagon nearby. After telling them that Indians killed their dog as a warning, Calhoun orders them to leave. At the town of Dawson, frustrated rushers taunt the cavalry with calls of "Indian lover." Calhoun finds his ex-sweetheart, Lia Wilson, in the company of his commanding officer, Col. Lloyd Unger. Disdainful of Calhoun's West Point training, Unger kisses Lia in front of him. Angered by their rivalry, Lia, who works as a "hostess" for saloon owner Ira Jordan, says she is no one's personal property. Lia followed Calhoun from the South to the frontier after he volunteered for duty there so he wouldn't have to fight his own people in the Civil War. Unger, Calhoun believes, received his commission as commander of the fort because he did favors for politicians who are against the treaty, believing it stops the "progress" of the nation on its way to acquire all the land to the Pacific Ocean. At the saloon, Calhoun finds that Jordan has a cache of Henry repeating rifles and warns him that some have gotten to the Sioux. Jordan admits that he would like to see an Indian war, because after the Sioux are defeated, his business will increase with more rushers swarming into the area. The next day, Sergeant Barhydt finds the body of ex-scout Charlie Grass, who was three-fourths Indian, hanging upside-down in a tree. The alcoholic Grass, who criticized Calhoun's policy of protecting Sioux lands, was killed, Barhydt surmises, because he betrayed his own people. When Unger learns about the murder, he orders a combat patrol to be readied. Calhoun, however, contends that the Sioux have not violated the treaty because Grass had resigned the previous night, so was no longer working for the government, and Unger angrily rescinds his order. Men whom Calhoun believes to be connected with Jordan pursue and shoot at his troop in the hills. In town, he accuses Jordan of attempted murder, but has no proof. At a dance for newly arrived Lt. Cutter, Jordan tells Unger that the Sioux have begun to attack isolated ranchers east of the boundary line, claiming that Pactola, the Sioux chief, is retaliating for settlers coming into the hills. He suggests, though, that Unger wait before attacking the Sioux. When the women at the dance begin to leave, offended by Lia's presence, Unger takes her back to her tent, where she slaps him when he suggests they have a drink together, saying he can have the drink with her only at Jordan's. After he leaves, she finds Calhoun in the tent, and although they kiss, he tells her he doesn't want to see her again. When the patrol finds a ranch burned down and Unger learns that the rancher's family was massacred, he vows to track down the "Redsticks" responsible. Calhoun says that smoke signals he has seen indicate that the Sioux are gathering inside the hills, not outside, and believes the attack is a decoy devised by Jordan. Unger, however, orders Calhoun to guard the fort while he attacks the Sioux. After the

cavalry leave, Lia tells Calhoun that a wagon train loaded with supplies and repeating rifles was sent out by Jordan, who is trying to provoke a war. When Lia promises to be there for him if he is court-martialled for disobeying orders, Calhoun leaves the fort and rides off with his troop for the hills. They hear the sound of repeating rifles and chase down the Ledbetters, who admit that they fired on the Indians first. Meanwhile, Unger and Cutter find that an "Indian" wounded by the Ledbetters is really a white man sent by Jordan, and Unger realizes that Calhoun was right. Back at the fort, as the Sioux battle those left inside, Calhoun and his men charge through and enter. He castigates Jordan and has Lia lead the women and children to the magazine where the gunpowder is kept. When the women refuse to follow her, she convinces them by saying that whatever she has been through will seem "delicate" compared to their treatment if they are captured by "savages." When the Indians are about to break through the gates, Calhoun gives orders to blast the magazine, but the Sioux stop, and he rides out to meet with Pactola, who recognizes him as the one white who hasn't forgotten the treaty. Pactola allows the persons in the fort to leave for the East. The Indians take over the fort, while Calhoun leads the people past the scene of the massacre of Unger and his men. Unger, barely alive, tells Calhoun to keep fighting "your way" before he dies. Subsequently, Calhoun becomes a colonel, fighting at Powder River, Warbonnet, Wounded Knee and White Clay Creek. If he had been listened to, however, the deaths of one thousand men would have been prevented. *Bigotry. Black Hills (SD and WY). Dakota Indians. Deception. Gold rushes. Officers (Military). Treaties. United States–History–Indian campaigns. United States. Army. Cavalry. Alcoholics. Arson. Class distinction. Dances. Dogs. Hostesses. Impersonation and imposture. Indians of North America–Mixed blood. Massacres. Prostitution. Ranchers. Rifles. Romantic rivalry. Saloon keepers. Sieges. Southerners.*

Note: The working titles of this film were *The Black Hills* and *The Golden Tide*. *NYT*, in their review, noted "the mystery of the title [*Oh! Susanna*] is never explained."

Box 17 Mar 1951. *DV* 9 Mar 1951, p. 3. *Exh* 14 Mar 1951, p. 3038. *FD* 12 Mar 1951, p. 6. *Har* 17 Mar 1951, p. 42. *HR* 18 Jan 1950. *HR* 2 Jun 1950, p. 15. *HR* 9 Jun 1950. *HR* 23 Jun 1950, p. 11. *HR* 9 Mar 1951. *LADN* 4 Apr 1951. *LAT* 4 Apr 1951. *MPD* 12 Mar 1951. *MPHPD* 17 Mar 1951, p. 758. *NYT* 30 Mar 1951, p. 28. *Var* 14 Mar 1951, p. 6.

O'HENRY'S ROMANTIC BAD MAN THE CISCO KID *see* THE CISCO KID

¡OJO, SOLTEROS! *see* DOS MÁS UNO, DOS

OKLAHOMA JIM (Native Americans)

Monogram Pictures Corp. *Dist* Monogram Pictures Corp. 10 Oct **1931**. Sd; b&w. 53 or 60-61 min.

Prod Trem Carr. *Dir* Harry Fraser. *Scr* Harry Fraser. *Adpt* G. A. Durham. *Photog* Archie Stout.

Cast: Bill Cody (*Oklahoma Jim Kirby*), Marion Burns (*Betty Rankin*), Andy Shuford (*Jerry*), William Desmond (*Lacy*), Si Jenks (*Driver*), Franklyn Farnum (*Captain*), John Elliott (*Agent*), Ed Brady (*Cash Riley*).

Western. [*Not viewed*]. Oklahoma Jim Kirby, a gambler, and Lacy, the owner of a saloon, happen upon a wedding ceremony between Natoma, a chief's daughter, and War Eagle. The wedding is interrupted when it is revealed that Natoma had been tricked into a false marriage with a white man. She will not name him, however, and commits suicide out of shame. Later, Lacy claims rights in his deceased partner's business, the Indian Range trading post. Jim had planned to run the gambling games for Lacy and is surprised to learn that he plans to sell the successful business to Cash Riley. Before the transaction can be completed, however, Betty Rankin, the previous owner's niece, arrives from the East. Meanwhile, the Indians have taken to the warpath to avenge Natoma's honor. In order to prevent war, an Indian agent agrees to help them find the man who dishonored her. Betty is repelled by the roughness of the country and the people in the West and decides to return to Boston. She then befriends Jerry, a young white boy who has been reared by the Indians. Jerry tries to stop Lacy from selling alcohol to the Indians, and Jim rescues him from Lacy's subsequent wrath. Jim then suggests that he and Jerry set up a home together. Jim learns from Jerry that Betty plans to sell the trading post to Riley and return home, and he becomes outraged when he hears how little she was offered. When Lacy demands his share of the money from Riley so that he can leave town, Riley, angry because Lacy earlier tried to sell him something that he did not really own, refuses. Riley is killed, but before he dies,

names Lacy as his killer. Jerry shows Betty the trading post books, and she realizes that Lacy was trying to cheat her. When the agent arrests Jim and Lacy as suspects in Natoma's suicide, Betty tells Jim that she will be waiting for him if he comes through the Indian trial. The two men are asked by the Indians to drink a poison that will make the guilty man faint. Jim drinks it and when Lacy refuses, the Indians proclaim his guilt. His name cleared, Jim asks Betty to marry him. He will run the gambling tables at the trading post, and the couple will adopt Jerry. *Frame-ups. Indians of North America. Nieces. Revenge. Seduction. Adoption. Deception. Easterners. Escapes. Gamblers. Liquor. Marriage–Fake. Miscegenation. Saloon keepers. Suicide. Trading posts. Trials. Weddings.*

Note: Modern sources include G. D. Wood, Earl Dwire, Iron Eyes Cody, Ann Ross and Artie Ortego in the cast.

FD 27 Dec 1931, p. 10. *MPH* 23 Jan 1932, p. 48. *Var* 29 Dec 1931, p. 169.

OKLAHOMA TERRITORY (Native Americans, Cherokee)

Premium Pictures, Inc. *Dist* United Artists Corp. 22 Aug 1960; Prod: began 15 Jul 1959 at Paramount-Sunset Studios [©Premium Pictures, Inc.; 17 Dec 1958; LP15664]. Sd (Ryder Sound Service); b&w; 1.85. 6,007 ft. 66-67 min. PCA cert no. 19441.

Prod Robert E. Kent. *Dir* Edward L. Cahn. *Asst dir* Herbert S. Greene. *Wrt* Orville H. Hampton. *Dir of photog* Walter Strenge. *Art dir* Bill Glasgow. *Supv ed* Grant Whytock. *Film ed* Michael Minth. *Eff ed* Henry Adams. *Mus ed* Edna Bullock. *Set dec* Robert Bradfield. *Prop master* Victor Petrotta. *Ward man* Einar Bourman. *Ward woman* Sabine Manela. *Mus dir* Albert Glasser. *Sd* John Kean. *Makeup artist* Gene Hibbs. *Hair stylist* Frances Sperry. *Prod mgr* Joseph Small. *Casting dir* Betty Pagel. *Scr supv* John Franco. *Chief tech* Buzz Gibson.

Cast: Bill Williams (*Temple Houston*), Gloria Talbott (*Ruth Red Hawk*), Ted de Corsia (*Buffalo Horn*), Grant Richards (*Bigelow*), Walter Sande (*Marshal [Pete] Rosslyn*), X Brands (*Running Cloud*), Walter Baldwin (*Ward Harlan*), Grandon Rhodes ([*George*] *Blackwell*), [John Cliff (*Larkin*)].

Western. [*Print viewed*]. In 1872, the Oklahoma territory is simmering with tensions between the Indians and the white people. While out riding one day, Temple Houston, the district attorney of Fort Smith and the son of Sam Houston, sees a band of white riders attack a group of Indians. When Temple intervenes, one of the white assailants claims that he and his posse have been deputized to arrest Buffalo Horn, the chief of the Cherokees, for the murder of Indian Commissioner Allen Barbee. Although Temple is Buffalo Horn's friend, he has no choice but to uphold the law and arrest the chief. In the town of Fort Smith, meanwhile, Bigelow, an agent for the railroad, instructs Larkin, the gunfighter he hired to murder Barbee and frame Buffalo Horn, to arrange for the chief's death. Upon delivering Buffalo Horn to Marshal Pete Rosslyn's jail, Temple is beseeched by Ruth Red Hawk, the chief's daughter and Temple's sweetheart, to release her father. When Temple refuses, Ruth warns of an impending war with the Indians. Soon after, a lynch mob led by Larkin storms the jail, but Rosslyn and Temple disperse the crowd with gunfire. A review of the evidence against Buffalo Horn reveals an airtight case: Barbee was killed with the chief's knife and an eyewitness, Tom Badger, has sworn that he saw Buffalo Horn stab Barbee. Although he admits to having argued with Barbee over the commissioner's plan to disperse jointly held tribal lands to individual Indians, Buffalo Horn swears that he never harmed Barbee and that he spent the night of the murder with a family of white settlers named Lindstrom. When Rosslyn counters that the settlers have denied Buffalo Horn's alibi, Temple rides to Barbee's house to conduct his own investigation. There, he finds Barbee's journal and discovers that the commissioner had made plans to travel to Washington, D.C., to present his proposal, thus strengthening Buffalo Horn's motive for murder. Next, Temple rides to the Cherokee reservation to confer with Sparrow Hawk, Buffalo Horn's hot-tempered son. Sparrow Hawk, spoiling for war, orders Temple beaten and dumped on the marshal's doorstep. Although Buffalo Horn continues to protest his innocence, Temple refuses to believe his old friend. As the date of the trial approaches, George Blackwell, a political power in the territory, comes to town, summoned by Bigelow. Hoping to influence Temple, Bigelow proposes that Blackwell offer the district attorney the position of governor if he wins a conviction, but Temple postpones his decision until after the trial. At the trial, Temple exhibits the overwhelming evidence against Buffalo Horn. When Ward Harlan, the

editor of the local paper, overhears Blackwell's plan for using a guilty verdict to propel Temple to the governor's office, he pens an editorial against political corruption. After Buffalo Horn is found guilty and sentenced to hang, Ruth breaks off her relationship with Temple, gallops out of town and dispatches three braves to search for the Lindstrom family. Harlan, meanwhile, informs Temple that under an 1867 treaty, the Cherokees must forfeit their lands to the railroad if they go to war. Sensing a link between Bigelow and the chain of pat evidence against Buffalo Horn, Temple decides to reopen his investigation. When Ruth reports that the Lindstrom family has been found and will testify in her father's defense, Temple tricks Badger, the eyewitness, into revealing that his eyesight is failing. Before Badger can be deposed, however, Larkin shoots him. Upon discovering that Baily, the man who refuted Buffalo Horn's testimony about spending the night with the Lindstroms, had been bribed by Badger, Temple decides to reopen the trial. Bigelow, however, learns that the Lindstroms have been located and arranges for Buffalo Horn's execution to be moved up before the Lindstroms can reach town. To save his friend's life, Temple breaks him out of jail. At the new hearing, Temple then announces that he is now acting as Buffalo Horn's attorney and calls the Lindstroms to the stand. After the Lindstroms confirm the chief's alibi, Temple is about to denounce Larkin and Bigelow when Larkin stands and fires at Temple, who ducks and shoots Larkin. After Rosslyn arrests Bigelow, Buffalo Horn is exonerated of all charges, and Temple and Ruth reconcile. *Cherokee Indians. District attorneys. Frame-ups. Oklahoma. Political corruption. Railroad agents. Trials. Diaries. Editors. Evidence. Fathers and daughters. Fathers and sons. Gunfighters. Indian agents. Indians of North America–Reservations. Marshals. Murder.*

Note: According to a Jul 1959 *HR* production chart, Adele Mara was originally to play the role of "Ruth Red Hawk," but had to withdraw due to a scheduling conflict.

Box 22 Feb 1960. *DV* 10 Feb 1960, p. 3. *Exh* 17 Feb 1960, p. 4678. *FD* 17 Feb 1960, p. 45. *Har* 13 Feb 1960, p. 26. *HR* 10 Feb 1960, p. 3. *HR* 15 Jul 1959, p. 2. *MPHPD* 27 Feb 1960, p. 603. *Var* 10 Feb 1960, p. 6.

THE OKLAHOMAN (Native Americans)

Allied Artists Pictures Corp. *Dist* Allied Artists Pictures Corp. 19 May 1957; New York opening: 14 May 1957; Prod: mid-May to early Jun 1956 [©Allied Artists Pictures Corp.; 30 Apr 1957; LP8213]. Sd (Western Electric); col (DeLuxe); CinemaScope. 7,198 ft. 80 min.

Prod Walter Mirisch. *Assoc prod* Richard Heermance. *Dir* Francis D. Lyon. *Asst dir* Austen Jewell. *Wrt* Daniel B. Ullman. *Dir of photog* Carl Guthrie. *Art dir* Dave Milton. *Film ed* George White. *Set dec* Joseph Kish. *Set cont* Richard M. Chaffee. *Set des* Jimmy West. *Props* Sam Gordon. *Ward* Bert Henrikson. *Mus ed* Harry Eisen. *Mus comp and cond by* Hans Salter. *Sd ed* Charles Schelling. *Rec eng* Ralph Butler. *Makeup artist* Emile LaVigne. *Hair styles* Alice Monte. *Prod mgr* Allen K. Wood.

Cast: Joel McCrea (*John [Brighton]*), Barbara Hale (*Anne [Barnes]*), Brad Dexter ([*Cass*] *Dobie*), Gloria Talbott (*Maria [Smith]*), Michael Pate (*Charlie [Smith]*), Verna Felton (*Mrs. Waynebrook*), Douglas Dick (*Mel [Dobie]*), Anthony Caruso ([*Jim*] *Hawk*), Esther Dale (*Mrs. Fitzgerald*), Adam Williams ([*Bob*] *Randall*), Ray Teal (*Stableman*), Peter Votrian (*Little Charlie [Smith]*), John Pickard (*Marshal*), Mimi Gibson (*Louise [Brighton]*), I. Stanford Jolley (*Storekeeper*), [Diane Brewster (*Eliza*)], [Sheb Wooley (*Cowboy*)], [Harry Lauter (*Grant*)], [Robert Hinkle (*Driver*)], [Wheaton Chambers (*Lounger*)], [Earle Hodgins (*Bartender*)], [Watson Downs, Leslie Kimmell (*Farmers*)], [Rankin Mansfield (*Doctor*)], [Don Marlowe, Lennie Geer (*Riders*)], [Laurie Mitchell, Jenny Lea (*Girls*)], [Tod Farrell (*Tommy*)], [Scotty Beckett (*Young man*)], [Al Kramer (*Wild Line*)], [Doris Kemper], [Dorothy Neumann], [Gertrude Astor].

Western. [*Print viewed*]. In 1870, after his wife Louise dies in childbirth on the way to California, Dr. John Brighton decides to remain in the nearby town of Cherokee Wells in the Oklahoma Territory with his newly born daughter, whom he names after her mother. Five years later, the Brightons are settled at the home of elderly widow Mrs. Fitzgerald, who is helping to rear Louise. Cherokee Wells is generally a peaceful town, but wealthy rancher Cass Dobie and his brother Mel will stop at nothing to get their own way. One day, John is visited by Charlie Smith, an Indian, whose son Little Charlie developed a stomach ache after drinking some swamp water. Noticing that Charlie's eighteen-year-old daughter Maria is

good with children, Mrs. Fitzgerald hires her to care for the energetic Louise. Afterward, John visits the ranch of widow Anne Barnes and her mother, Mrs. Waynebrook, who invites John, Mrs. Fitzgerald, Louise and Maria to attend her sixtieth birthday party. Later, Mrs. Fitzgerald dies after suffering a stroke and, when Maria stays on to care for Louise, the townspeople begin to gossip about the relationship between John and Maria. Dobie, meanwhile, has secretly discovered oil on Charlie's land and offers to buy the land. When Charlie refuses, Dobie threatens him. During Mrs. Waynebrook's party, Mel sneaks onto Charlie's land to get a sample of the oil. Charlie discovers him, and when Mel shoots at him, he kills him in self-defense. Dobie's men interrupt the party to announce that Charlie has given himself up to the sheriff, pleading self-defense. Anne begs John not to get involved in the quarrel, but believing that Charlie will not get a fair trial, John comes to his defense. Because of John's intervention, Charlie is allowed to return home, and his fellow Indians set up a guard on his property. That evening, to John's surprise, Maria announces that she is in love with him. The following day, John defends her against Dobie, thus making an enemy of the rancher. Then, on his way to Oklahoma City to fetch an Indian agent to attend the inquest, John's horse is killed by Dobie. John walks to Anne's ranch and together, they check on Charlie. John begins to suspect that Dobie did not intend to kill him, but rather wanted to stop him from reaching the Indian agent. When Little Charlie shows John the jar of water Mel was collecting from the swamp, he realizes that the swamp is full of petroleum. The next morning, John, Anne and Charlie ride into town for the inquest. John tells the marshal and the townspeople about the oil. The marshal reports that Mel's gun had been fired, confirming Charlie's claims of self-defense. Dobie then calls John a liar and in the ensuing gunfight, Dobie is killed and John is wounded. Realizing that Anne and John are in love, Maria tells Anne that she will return to her father. When he recovers, John proposes to Anne, to the delight of her mother. *Indians of North America. Oil. Oklahoma. Physicians. Racism. Ranchers. Birthdays. Brothers. False accusations. Fathers and daughters. Fathers and sons. Gossip. Gunfights. Marshals. Mothers and daughters. Parties. Proposals (Marital). Romance. Self-defense. Swamps. Unrequited love. Widowers. Widows.*

Box 27 Apr 1957. DV 19 Apr 1957, p. 3. Exh 26 Jun 1957, p. 4341. FD 25 Apr 1957, p. 6. Har 20 Apr 1957, p. 63. HR 18 May 1956, p. 16. HR 8 Jun 1956, p. 12. HR 19 Apr 1957, p. 3. MPHPD 27 Apr 1957, p. 354. NYT 15 May 1957, p. 39. Var 1 May 1957, p. 7.

OLD CLOTHES (Jewish Americans, Irish Americans)

Jackie Coogan Productions. *Dist* Metro-Goldwyn Distributing Corp. 22 Nov **1925**; New York premiere: 8 Nov 1925 [©Metro-Goldwyn-Mayer Corp.; 1 Dec 1925; LP22057]. Si; b&w. 6 reels, 5,915 ft.

Prod under pers supv of Jack Coogan, Sr. *Dir* Edward Cline. *Wrt* Willard Mack. *Titles* Robert Hopkins. *Photog* Frank B. Good and Harry Davis.

Cast: Max Davidson (*Max Ginsberg*), Joan Crawford (*Mary Riley*), Allan Forrest (*Nathan Burke*), Lillian Elliott (*Mrs. Burke*), James Mason (*Dapper Dan*), Stanton Heck (*The Adjuster*), Dynamite (*Himself, a horse*), Jackie Coogan (*Tim Kelly*).

Comedy. Max Ginsberg, an elderly Jew, and his little Irish partner, Tim Kelly, have made their fortune in rags but lose it by investing in Vista Copper and return to the junk business. They take in Mary Riley, an impoverished young girl, as a boarder and later as a partner. Mary falls in love with Nathan Burke, the son of wealthy parents. Nathan's mother, however, disapproves of Mary. The Burke family fortune suffers a setback, but Tim saves the day with the Vista Copper stock, and all ends well for Mary and Nathan. *Horses. Irish Americans. Jews. Junk trade. Speculation. Upper classes. Wealth.*

FD 15 Nov 1925. NYT 9 Nov 1925, p. 25. Var 11 Nov 1925, p. 43.

OLD JUDGE PRIEST see JUDGE PRIEST

OLD LOS ANGELES (Latino)

Republic Pictures Corp. *Dist* Republic Pictures Corp. 25 Apr **1948**; Prod: Oct 1947 [©Republic Pictures Corp.; 31 Mar 1948; LP1594]. Sd (RCA Sound System); b&w. 82 or 87 min. Passed by the National Board of Review. PCA cert no. 12817.

Assoc prod Joe Kane. *Dir* Joe Kane. [*Asst dir* Dick Moder]. *Scr* Gerald Adams and Clements Ripley. *Orig story* Clements Ripley. *Dir of photog* William Bradford. [*Cam op* Herb Kirkpatrick]. [*Stills* Don Keyes]. *Spec eff* Howard Lydecker and Theodore Lydecker. *Art dir* James Sullivan. *Film ed* Richard L. Van Enger. *Set dec* John McCarthy, Jr. and Charles Thompson. *Cost des* Adele Palmer. *Mus score* Nathan Scott and Ernest Gold. *Mus dir* Morton Scott. *Sd* Fred Stahl and Howard Wilson. *Makeup supv* Bob Mark. [*Hair stylist* Peggy Gray]. [*Prod mgr* Kenny Holmes]. [*Scr supv* Dorothy Yutzi]. [*Grip* Ben Bishop].

Song(s): "Eres tan fina," music and lyrics by Aaron Gonzales and Nathan Scott; "On the Boulevard" (Jesusita en Chihuahua), music and lyrics by Quirino F. Mendoza y Cortés and Jack Elliott; "Jarabe tapatio," "Ever Faithful" and "Tus ojos," traditional.

Cast: William Elliott [(*Bill Stockton*)], John Carroll [(*Johnny Morrell*)], Catherine McLeod [(*Marie Marlowe*)], Joseph Schildkraut [(*Luis Savarin*)], Andy Devine [(*Sam Bowie*)], Estelita Rodriguez [(*Estelita Del Rey*)], Virginia Brissac [(*Senora Del Rey*)], Grant Withers [(*Marshal Luckner*)], Tito Renaldo [(*Tonio Del Rey*)], Roy Barcroft [(*Clyborne*)], Henry Brandon [(*Larry Stockton*)], Julian Rivero [(*Diego*)], Earle Hodgins [(*Horatius P. Gassoway*)], Augie Gomez [(*Miguel*)], [Chris-Pin Martin (*Waiter*)], [Lucio Villegas (*Don Alvarado*)], [Alex Montoya (*Mexican guard*)], [Rosa Turich (*Mercedes*)], [Sam Flint (*Martin*)], Robert Peters, Lynn Farr (*Henchmen*)], [Hank Bell (*Driver*)], [Tex Terry (*Bartender*)], [Ethyl May Halls (*Woman in livery stable*)], [Franklyn Farnum].

Western, with songs. [*Print viewed*]. In Los Angeles, during the California gold rush, prospector Larry Stockton and his friend, Miguel, are attacked by a gang of outlaws, and Larry is forced to sign over his gold claim. The two are then shot, and soon the U.S. Army assigns Larry's brother Bill, an ex-Missouri marshal, to find their killer. After Bill and his partner, Sam, question one of the suspects, saloon owner Luis Savarin, they are attacked by outlaws. When Bill and Sam shoot one of the outlaws, killing him, Marshal Luckner threatens to arrest them for murder. Hoping to win favor with Bill and Sam, Savarin steps in on their behalf. Later, they are introduced to one of the outlaws, Johnny Morrell, Savarin's fiancée, Marie Marlowe, and Estelita Del Rey, a rancher's daughter. When Estelita's brother Tonio tries to force her to return home, Bill punches him. Bill advises her to go, and later, kisses Marie at Las Flores Canyon. When Diego, who has been hired to guard the mine, sees them nearby, he draws his gun and orders them to leave the area. Back in town, Marie tells Savarin that Bill has invited them to visit his ranch. Johnny returns to the saloon, where Estelita's mother, Señora Del Rey, learns that Las Flores Canyon Dam is under threat of attack. As Tonio prepares to leave, Don Alvarado and Señor Martin enter with news that cattle rustlers have invaded the Marando Rancho. When the townspeople gather to repair the dam, which has been destroyed by the gang, they are suddenly ambushed. Although Estelita vouches for him, Johnny is arrested for trying to detonate the dam. When Luckner threatens to report his arrest to Savarin, Johnny shoots him. Later, Marie tells Bill that she is marrying Savarin for his money. That evening, Estelita ignores Tonio's wishes and sneaks out to meet Johnny. Bill and Sam follow her, and when Bill begins fighting with Johnny, Estelita slaps him in the face. Later, Bill tells Marie that there are valuable gold deposits at the dam site. After Johnny steals Diego's clothes and goes to the mine, which he has been guarding, he finds a rich vein of gold underneath a 1,500 pound rock. When Bill, Sam and Tonio see Johnny lurking around the mine, they grab him. Meanwhile, Bill is kidnapped by Luckner and tells Savarin that Johnny has been captured. After Marie reveals that she is the gang's leader, she leaves on the Sacramento stage. Johnny grabs Luckner's gun, kills him and escapes. When he finds Savarin, Johnny kills him as well. Bill catches up to the stage, and Marie admits that she knew Savarin was not the owner of the land for which he was selling deeds. At the ranch, Señora Del Rey reports that the outlaws have escaped with the gold, so Bill follows them to Big Tujunga. After he shoots Savarin's henchman, Clyborne, Johnny escapes and rides into town. When Estelita rushes to embrace Johnny, she is accidentally shot and killed by Bill. After Estelita is buried, Marie prays for peace to return to Los Angeles. *Dams. Gold mines. Land claims. Rustlers. Accidental death. Alibi. Arrests. Big Tujunga Creek (Los Angeles, CA). Brothers. California–History. Deeds. Engagements. Escapes. Firearms. Gangs. Kidnapping. Kisses. Las Flores Canyon (Los Angeles, CA). Marshals. Murder. Partnership. Ranches. Saloons. Stagecoaches. Threats. United States. Army.*

Note: A pre-production news item in *HR* indicated that Ilona Massey was scheduled to appear in the cast. According to a notation in the MPAA/PCA Collection at the AMPAS Library, this film was re-edited and re-released in 1953 under the title *California Outpost*. Modern sources include House Peters, Jr. in the cast.

Box 17 Apr 1948. *DV* 6 Apr 1948, p. 3. *FD* 13 Apr 1948, p. 7. *HR* 26 Aug 1947, p. 2. *HR* 3 Oct 1947, p. 14. *HR* 24 Oct 1947, p. 16. *HR* 6 Apr 1948, p. 3. *MPHPD* 17 Apr 1948, p. 4127. *MPHPD* 10 Jul 1948, p. 4283, 4285. *NYT* 12 Jul 1948, p. 11. *Var* 7 Apr 1948, p. 10.

OLD LOUISIANA (Latino)

Crescent Pictures Corp. *Dist* Crescent Pictures Corp. 1 Mar **1937**; Prod: began 3 Feb 1937 at Hollywood Studios. Sd; b&w. 7 reels, 5,798 ft. 63-64 min. PCA cert no. 3142.

Prod E. B. Derr. *Assoc prod* Bernard A. Moriarty. *Prod supv* Frank Melford. *Dir* I. V. Willat. *Asst dir* Raoul Pagel. *Scr* Mary Ireland. *Orig story* John T. Neville. *Photog* Arthur Martinelli and [Paul Ivano]. *Art dir* Edward C. Jewell. *Film ed* Donald Barratt. *Mus dir* Abe Meyer. *Rec* Karl Zint.

Cast: Tom Keene [(*John Colfax*)], Rita Cansino [([*Dona*] *Angela Gonzalez*)], Will Morgan [(*Steve*)], Robert Fiske [(*Luke E. Gilmore*)], Raphael Bennett [(*Flint*)], Bud Buster [(*Kentuck*)], Carlos DeValdez [(*Don Jose Gonzalez*)], Ramsay Hill [(*Spanish official*)], Allan Cavan [(*President Thomas Jefferson*)], Wally Albright (*Davey*).

Historical, **Drama**. [*Print viewed*]. On October 16, 1803, the Spanish governor of Louisiana, alarmed at the growing American trade on the Mississippi, imposes a tax on all American goods shipped through New Orleans. Luke E. Gilmore, factor of the Louisiana Fur Company, sends his henchman Flint to stir up a rebellion among the American settlers so that Gilmore can become head of the territory. However, respected leader John Colfax persuades the Americans to hold off any action until he lays their grievances before President Thomas Jefferson, whom John once saved. After Flint, sent to kill John, fails, John convinces Jefferson of Gilmore's plot. Jefferson, who wants to acquire the territory peacefully, signs a note stating that the settlers should follow John's leadership. On the ferry back across the Mississippi, John meets Dona Angela Gonzalez, the daughter of the district governor of Upper Louisiana. After John and his scout Kentuck throw a bale of tobacco, containing hidden guns for Gilmore, into the river, they fight Gilmore's men. John escapes with Angela and takes her to her home in St. Louis, where her father insists that according to Spanish custom, John and Angela must marry because they spent the night together in the woods. When John argues against it, Angela is insulted. Her father arrests John because Gilmore and Flint accuse him of smuggling the guns, and they find Jefferson's letter. Angela gets a message to Kentuck and John's friends, who break him out of jail, after which he confesses his love to Angela. Meanwhile, Gilmore and Flint organize men to attack Gonzalez' soldiers and then try to convince Gonzalez to declare Louisiana an independent republic. When he refuses, they threaten to kill him and Angela if he doesn't sign a resignation note, but John and the settlers arrive and rescue them. Kentuck kills Flint and Gilmore is arrested for treason. John, hugging Angela, agrees willingly to remain until confirmation is received concerning the Louisiana Purchase, and now happily consents to Gonzalez' request that he observe the Spanish custom still in force regarding marriage. *False accusations. Fur traders. Louisiana Purchase. Settlers. Spaniards. Treason. Cultural conflict. Fathers and daughters. Ferryboats. Fights. Governors. Gunrunners. Thomas Jefferson. James Madison. Mississippi River. Rescues. St. Louis (MO). United States–History–19th century.*

Note: The first working title of the film was *Drums of Destiny*, which was the title of John T. Neville's original story. Crescent subsequently released another Tom Keene film using this title (see above). The working title of this film was later changed to *The Louisiana Purchase*. John Auer was originally scheduled to direct this film, according to a *DV* news item. Reviews noted that this was part of a series of American history action films produced by E. B. Derr and starring Tom Keene. According to a news item in *HR*, Keene and cameraman Paul Ivano planned to leave on 3 Jan 1937 for St. Louis to shoot river backgrounds. Studio production did not begin until 3 Feb 1937, however, according to a *HR* news item. Although a contemporary review credits Ramsay Hill with the role of a Spanish official, modern sources state that he played Secretary of State James Madison. According to NYSA, the title of this film was changed in 1943 to *Louisiana Gal*, which was the title of the print viewed. Rita Hayworth's name is above the title in this version; however, all reviews of the 1937 release list her as Rita Cansino and list Tom Keene above her in the credits. The film was possibly re-released at that time to capitalize on Hayworth's fame. It is possible that Keene's name was above the titles in the original version. Modern sources credit Lou Brown as costume supervisor and Steve Corso as makeup supervisor.

Box 27 Mar 1937. *DV* 9 Mar 1937, p. 3. *FD* 12 Mar 1937, p. 6. *HR* 22 Dec 1936, p. 3. *HR* 31 Dec 1936, p. 12. *HR* 6 Jan 1937, p. 4. *HR* 19 Jan 1937, p. 6. *HR* 21 Jan 1937, p. 2. *HR* 3 Feb 1937, p. 14. *HR* 5 Feb 1937, p. 2. *HR* 8 Feb 1937, p. 11. *HR* 9 Mar 1937, p. 3. *MPD* 24 Mar 1937, p. 8. *MPH* 20 Mar 1937, p. 49. *Var* 13 Jul 1938, p. 17.

OLD MAN MURPHY see HIS FAMILY TREE

OLD NEW MEXICO see IN OLD NEW MEXICO

OLD OVERLAND TRAIL (Native Americans, Apache)

Republic Pictures Corp. *Dist* Republic Pictures Corp. 25 Feb **1953**; Prod: Sep 1952 [©Republic Pictures Corp.; 28 Jan 1953; LP2528]. Sd (RCA Sound System); b&w. 5,401 ft. 60 min. PCA cert no. 16166.

Assoc prod Edward J. White. *Dir* William Witney. *Asst dir* Robert Shannon. *Wrt* Milton Raison. *Dir of photog* John MacBurnie. *Spec eff* Howard Lydecker and Theodore Lydecker. *Opt eff* Consolidated Film Industries. *Art dir* Frank Arrigo. *Film ed* Harold Minter. *Set dec* John McCarthy, Jr. and George Milo. *Mus* R. Dale Butts. *Sd* T. A. Carman. *Makeup supv* Bob Mack.

Song(s): "Cowboy's Dream of Heaven," words and music by Jack Elliott; "Work for the Night Is Coming," words and music by Annie L. Coghill, Lowell Mason and Darol Rice; "Just a Wanderin' Buckaroo," traditional.

Cast: Rex Allen The Arizona Cowboy [(*Rex Allen*)], Koko The Miracle Horse of the Movies, Slim Pickens [(*Slim Pickens*)], Roy Barcroft [(*John Anchor*)], Virginia Hall [(*Mary Peterson*)], Gil Herman [(*Jim Allen*)], Wade Crosby [(*Draftsman*)], Leonard Nimoy [(*Chief Black Hawk*)], Zon Murray [(*Mack*)], Harry Harvey [(*Proprietor*)], The Republic Rhythm Riders, [Billy Dix (*Joe*)], [Lee Shumway (*Roger Peterson*)], [Joe Yrigoyen (*Pete*)], [Marshall Reed (*Sergeant*)].

Western, **with songs**. [*Print viewed*]. Rex Allen, who is working for the Bureau of Indian Affairs, and his partner, Slim Pickens, are sent west to investigate some Apache uprisings near the construction site of a new railroad spur line. Near the town of Red Creek, Rex and Slim encounter a couple of drunken Indians and subdue them. Moments later, Chief Black Hawk rides up, and Rex warns him to stay on the reservation. After Rex and Slim leave, however, Black Hawk meets with some white men, who give him rifles. In town, Rex and Slim arrive at the headquarters of Anchor Construction, where Rex's older brother Jim is working. Co-owner John Anchor tells Rex that Jim is leading a wagon train of settlers from the drought-stricken Midwest and expresses his fears that the Indian troubles will interfere with the company's work on the spur line. Rex and Slim decide to meet the wagon train, and while camped, they hear gunfire and discover that the wagon train is under attack. To Rex's surprise, however, the Indians ride off after destroying the contents of a few wagons. Afterward, Rex rides to the reservation, and Jim reports to Anchor. Jim accuses Anchor of fomenting the attack, charges that Anchor denies. Anchor then tells Jim that he will employ the settlers for low wages, which will increase the company's profits. At the reservation, Rex accuses Black Hawk of leading the attack, and the angry chief challenges him to a fight. Rex wins the fight, but stops short of killing the Indian. Meanwhile, the settlers begin work on the railroad, but do not receive even their meager wages when the stagecoach carrying the funds is reported robbed. Unknown to the settlers, the stagecoach drivers are in league with Anchor. When the settlers complain that they must buy supplies, Anchor offers to pay them with script, which he promises will be redeemable in the town store. Later, when the storekeeper redeems the script for only twenty-five cents on the dollar, Rex accuses Jim of participating in a swindle. The two brothers fight fiercely. When the fight is over, Rex and Slim hold up the stage before the stagecoach driver hands the money to Anchor. Jim, meanwhile, tells Anchor that he wants to end their partnership, so Anchor kills him, then blames his death on Rex. When Rex returns with the payroll money, Mary Peterson, one of the settlers, warns Rex that he is wanted for Jim's murder, and he and Slim hide out in the hills. Anchor secretly offers Black Hawk enough guns for the entire tribe if he will capture Rex and Slim. When Black Hawk finds them, he admits that Anchor is behind all the trouble. Unknown to Anchor, Rex has managed to send a telegram to Washington, D.C., apprising his superiors of the situation, and when Anchor learns that there will be an investigation, he decides to steal the final payroll and leave town. However, because the payroll is being sent by train, Anchor needs Black Hawk's help. When Anchor arrives at the reservation without the promised guns, Black Hawk angrily refuses to help him, and Anchor shoots him. Anchor then convinces the other Indians to help him destroy the railroad. After they leave, the wounded Black Hawk cuts Rex free in return for Rex sparing his life earlier. Rex and Slim hurriedly rouse the settlers, and they head for the spur line.

During the ensuing fight, Anchor escapes, followed by Rex. Anchor tries to ambush Rex, but Black Hawk kills him, and then dies himself. With the troublemakers all dead, the settlers and Indians work together to develop the area. *Apache Indians. Brothers. Greed. Railroads. United States. Bureau of Indian Affairs. Ambushes. Drunkenness. False accusations. Firearms. Fistfights. Gunshot wounds. Knife fighting. Murder. Railroad workers. Stagecoach robberies. Swindlers and swindling. Wagon trains.*

Note: The film's working titles were *Overland Trail Riders* and *Song of the Overland Trail.*

Box 28 Feb 1953. *DV* 20 Feb 1953, p. 3. *Exb* 11 Mar 1953, p. 3480. *HR* 15 Aug 1952, p. 11. *HR* 19 Sep 1952, p. 15. *HR* 26 Sep 1952, p. 10. *HR* 20 Feb 1953, p. 3. *MPHPD* 28 Feb 1953, p. 1742. *Var* 25 Feb 1953, p. 6.

OLD SAN FRANCISCO (Chinese Americans)
Warner Bros. Pictures, Inc. *Dist* Warner Bros. Pictures, Inc. 4 Sep 1927; New York premiere: 21 Jun 1927 [©Warner Bros. Pictures, Inc.; 10 May 1927; LP23957]. Si; b&w. 8 reels, 7,961 ft.

Dir Alan Crosland. *Scen* Anthony Coldewey. *Story* Darryl Francis Zanuck. *Titles* Jack Jarmuth. *Photog* Hal Mohr. *Vitaphone score* Hugo Riesenfeld.

Cast: Dolores Costello (*Dolores Vasquez*), Warner Oland (*Chris Buckwell*), Charles Emmett Mack (*Terrence O'Shaughnessy*), Josef Swickard (*Don Hernández Vásquez*), John Miljan (*Don Luis*), Anders Randolf (*Michael Brandon*), Sojin (*Lu Fong*), Angelo Rossitto (*Dwarf*), Anna May Wong (*Chinese girl*).

Melodrama. Chris Buckwell, cruel and greedy czar of San Francisco's tenderloin, is heartless in his persecution of the Chinese, though he himself is secretly a half-caste. Buckwell, eager to possess the land of Don Hernández Vásquez, sends Michael Brandon, an unscrupulous attorney, to make an offer. Brandon's nephew, Terrence, meets the grandee's beautiful daughter, Dolores, while Vásquez refuses the offer. Terry tries to save the Vásquez land grants, but when Chris causes the grandee's death, Dolores takes an oath to avenge her father. Learning that Chris is a half-caste, Dolores induces his feeble-minded dwarf brother to denounce him; he captures her and Terry, but they are saved from torture and death by the great earthquake of 1906 that kills the villain. *Brothers. Chinese Americans. Dwarfs. Half-castes. Intellect. Land rights. Lawyers. Politicians. Revenge. San Francisco (CA). San Francisco earthquake, 1906. Spaniards.*

FD 3 Jul 1927. *MPW* 25 Jun 1927. *NYT* 23 Jun 1927, p. 23. *Var* 29 Jun 1927, p. 18.

THE OLD 69TH see **THE FIGHTING 69TH**

AN OLD SPANISH CUSTOM see **THE FABULOUS SENORITA**

OLD SPANISH TRAIL see **SADDLEMATES**

THE OLD-TIMER see **MY AMERICAN WIFE**

OLIMPIA (Spanish language)
Metro-Goldwyn-Mayer Corp.; controlled by Loew's Inc. *Dist* Metro-Goldwyn-Mayer Distributing Corp. Oct **1930**; Los Angeles opening: 10 Oct 1930. Sd (Western Electric Sound System); b&w. 10 reels, 8,170 ft. 91 min. Passed by the National Board of Review. Spanish language.

[*Supv* Frank Davis]. *Diálogo dirigido por* [*Dial dir*] Juan de Homs. [*Scr* Willard Mack]. *Versión española por* [*Spanish version*] Miguel de Zárraga. *Fotografiada por* [*Photog*] Henry Sharp. *Director artístico* [*Art dir*] Cedric Gibbons. *Editada por* [*Ed*] Peggy O'Day. *Vestuario por* [*Ward*] Adrian. *Acústica* [*Sd*] Douglas Shearer.

Source: Based on the play *Olympia* by Ferenc Molnár (Budapest, Mar 1928).

Cast: José Crespo (*Kovacs*), María Alba (*Princesa Olimpia*), Elvira Morla (*Princesa Ettingen*), Carmen Rodríguez (*Condesa Lina*), Juan de Homs (*Conde Alberto*), Juan Aristi Eulate (*General Príncipe Ettingen*), Luis Llaneza (*Coronel Krebl*), Gabriel Rivas (*Burgomaestre*), Mario Diminici (*Embajador de Francia*).

Romance, Drama. [*Not viewed*]. Princess Olimpia, a recently named lady-in-waiting to the heiress to the Austrian throne, is in love with cavalry captain Kovacs, a man as famous for his skill with horses as his success with women. Although the couple try to keep their romance secret, Olimpia's mother finds out and advises her to end the affair, as she cannot possibly marry a commoner. Although Olimpia obeys her mother's wishes, Kovacs spreads a rumor that he is a notorious swindler and compromises Olimpia's family by arranging to spend a night with her in his quarters, where the couple reconcile.

Austria. Class distinction. Mothers and daughters. Officers (Military). Princesses. Romance. Royalty. Rumors. Ruses.

Note: The 1929 film *His Glorious Night*, which was directed by Lionel Barrymore and starred John Gilbert and Catherine Dale Owen (see *AFI Catalog of Feature Films, 1921-30;* F2.2513), was remade in Spanish, French and German versions. The onscreen cast and crew credits for all three versions were taken from studio cutting continuities. The Spanish version's working title was *Si el emperador lo supiera.* Some contemporary sources wrongly list dialogue director Juan de Homs as director, while others suggest that producer Frank Davis or Tom Kilpatrick may have directed. Modern sources attribute the direction to Chester M. Franklin. Some sources include Ernesto Piedra, José Fernández and Adolfo Viñas in the cast of the Spanish version, but their participation in the film has not been confirmed. All three foreign-language versions were passed by the censor board for exhibition in New York state. Ferenc Molnár's play was also used as the basis of the 1960 film *A Breath of Scandal.* That version was directed by Michael Curtiz and starred Sophia Loren and John Gavin.

Other language version(s):
Si l'empereur savait ça! (French language)
1930; Une Production de Jacques Feyder. Paris opening: early Nov 1930; New York opening: 20 Feb 1931. Sd (Western Electric Sound System); b&w. 10 reels, 7,776 ft. 86 or 90 min. French language.

Réalisation de [*Dir*] Jacques Feyder. [*Scr* Willard Mack]. *Adaptation française* [*French adpt*] Yves Mirande. *Découpage* [*Shooting script*] Anne Mauclair. *Photographie* [*Photog*] William Daniels. *Décorateur* [*Art dir*] Cedric Gibbons. *Editeur* [*Ed*] Gunther Fritsch. *Costumes* [*Cost*] Adrian. *Ingénieur du son* [*Sd eng*] Douglas Shearer.

French-language cast: Tania Fédor (*Renata*), André Luguet (*Kovacz*), Françoise Rosay (*La Princesse Ettingen*), André Berley (*Krebl*), Marcel André (*Albert*), Georges Mauloy (*Le Général Prince Ettingen*), Suzanne Delvá (*Lina*). [*French version not viewed*]

Olympia (German language)
1930; Eine Jacques Feyder Produktion. Berlin opening: 7 Nov 1930. Sd (Western Electric Sound System); b&w. 11 reels, 8.975 ft. 84 or 100 min. German language.

Regie [*Dir*] Jacques Feyder. [*Scr* Willard Mack]. *Original manuskript* [*Scr*] Yves Mirande. *Manuskript* [*German adpt*] Leo Birinski and Heinrich Fraenkel. *Photographie* [*Photog*] William Daniels. *Bauten* [*Art dir*] Cedric Gibbons. *Filmschnitt* [*Film ed*] Finn Ulback. *Kostüm* [*Cost*] Adrian. *Tontechniker* [*Sound tech*] Douglas Shearer.

German-language cast: Nora Gregor (*Olympia*), Theo Shall (*Kovacz*), Julia Serda (*Prinzessin Ettingen*), Karl Etlinger (*Krebl*), Arnold Korff (*General Prinz Ettingen*), Hans Junkermann (*Albert*), Annemarie Frey (*Lina*). [*German version not viewed*]

Cinl Nov 1930, p. 30. *CM* Dec 1930, p. 1,200. *NYT* 7 Dec 1930. *NYT* 23 Feb 1931. *Var* 22 Oct 1930. *Var* 19 Nov 1930. *Var* 26 Nov 1930.

OLSEN'S BIG MOMENT (Swedish Americans)
Fox Film Corp. *Dist* Fox Film Corp. 17 Nov **1933**; Prod: began 18 Sep 1933 [©Fox Film Corp.; 19 Oct 1933; LP4210]. Sd (Western Electric Noiseless Recording); b&w. 7 reels, 6,000 ft. 66 or 70 min. Passed by the National Board of Review. PCA cert no. 1841-R [4 Dec 1935].

Dir Malcolm St. Clair. *Scr* Henry Johnson and James Tynan. *Story* George Marshall. *Photog* L. W. O'Connell. *Settings* Lewis Creber. *Gowns* Royer. *Mus dir* Samuel Kaylin. *Sd* Pat Costello. [*Double for Walter Catlett* Buddy Mason].

Cast: El Brendel (*Knute Olsen*), Walter Catlett (*Robert Brewster III*), Barbara Weeks (*Jane Van Allen*), Susan Fleming (*Virginia West*), John Arledge (*Harry Smith*), Maidel Turner (*Mrs. Van Allen*), Edward Pawley (*Joe "Monk" West*), Joseph Sauers ([*"Dapper"*] *Danny Reynolds*), [Harvey Clark (*Jenkins*)], [O. G. Hendrian, James P. Burtis (*Detectives*)].

Comedy. [*Print viewed*]. At the Cromwell Arms, janitor Knute Olsen tries to enjoy his night off but is harassed by telephone calls from demanding tenants and an unsympathetic manager, Jenkins. Tenants Mrs. Van Allen and her daughter Jane plan Jane's wedding to the rich Robert Brewster III, whose mother owns the building, although Jane loves another man, Harry Smith. Brewster arrives at the Van Allen apartment and Jane is disgusted by his drunken, nonsensical behavior. After Olsen helps Harry arrange a secret rendezvous with Jane, Jane gets angry when Harry insists that only her mother impedes their union and says she never wants to see him again. Mrs. Van Allen then orders Olsen to see Brewster to a cab, but Brewster instead drags Olsen with him to a speakeasy. Brewster approaches Virginia West, and when her protective brother, notorious gangster Joe "Monk"

West, arrives, he erroneously assumes that Brewster is Virginia's secret lover, "Dapper" Danny Reynolds. Although he is disgusted that Virginia would be in love with an upper class playboy, Monk orders Brewster to marry her the next day and threatens to kill Olsen if he does not bring Brewster to City Hall at four o'clock. The next day at the West home, Virginia introduces Monk to her new husband, Danny. Happy that Virginia is married to Danny, who is also a criminal, Monk schemes with his brother-in-law to rob guests at Brewster and Jane's wedding, the announcement of which Monk read in the newspaper that morning. They send their henchmen, Al and Elbows, to impersonate policemen and pretend to watch the presents. As the wedding guests arrive, the intoxicated Brewster realizes that he cannot marry both Virginia and Jane and offers to commit suicide to save Olsen from Monk's wrath when they fail to appear at City Hall. Olsen relates his predicament to Al and Elbows when they arrive, and they offer their protection. Brewster makes desultory attempts at suicide throughout the pre-nuptial proceedings, and a now grief-deranged Harry tells Olsen that he will kill Jane, Brewster, Olsen and himself if Olsen cannot prevent the wedding. While Olsen saves Brewster, who is about to jump from the building's roof, Monk and Danny arrive for the robbery. When Harry threatens to kill Brewster, Brewster turns the gun on himself, saying that he cannot marry Jane because of the scandal surrounding his potential bigamy. Meanwhile, Olsen locks Danny and Monk in another room and relates his actions to Al and Elbows, who proceed to hold up the guests. A fight ensues between the guests and the thieves with Olsen stealing a gun and saving the day before detectives arrive and take the crooks away. Jane is unperturbed and sits on Harry's lap in her bedroom during the entire fiasco. Brewster stays contentedly drunk, while his mother fires Jenkins and makes the capable Olsen the apartment manager. *Alcoholics. Apartments. Gangsters. Janitors. Marriage–Forced by circumstances. Swedish Americans. Attempted suicide. Brothers and sisters. Dismissal (Employment). Dogs. Engagements. Extortion. Fights. Fortune hunters. Impersonation and imposture. Mistaken identity. Molls. Mothers and daughters. Romance. Speakeasies. Telephone. Weddings.*

Note: The working titles of this film were *I Come from Hell* and *Olsen's Night Out*. According to the Twentieth Century-Fox Records of the Legal Department at the UCLA Theater Arts Library, Andrew Bennison worked with George Marshall as a gag writer on an original story for El Brendel entitled *I Come from Hell*. Although *I Come from Hell* bears little, if any, resemblance to *Olsen's Big Moment*, a letter in the legal records notes that Marshall "contended that the story upon which [Henry] Johnson and [James] Tynan had worked incorporated his original ideas," and he was therefore given story credit on the final film. Bennison was removed from the project before the story was completed, however, and his contribution to the finished film is undetermined. The film was reviewed in *Var* under the title *Olsen's Night Out*. According to a *FD* news item, Dixie Nelson Pantages Martin, who had previously worked as Sally Eilers' stand-in, was scheduled to appear in the film. Her participation in the finished film has not been verified, however.

FD 18 Sep 1933, p. 8. *FD* 21 Sep 1933, p. 8. *FD* 9 Jan 1934, p. 7. *LAEx* 6 Jul 1933. *MPH* 28 Oct 1933, p. 58. *Var* 9 Jan 1934, p. 17.

OLYMPIA *see* OLIMPIA

ON THE BORDER (Chinese Americans, Latino)

Warner Bros. Pictures, Inc. *Dist* Warner Bros. Pictures, Inc. 15 Mar **1930** [©Warner Bros. Pictures, Inc.; 18 Feb 1930; LP1085]. Sd (Vitaphone); b&w. 5 reels, 4,452 ft. [Also possibly si.].

Dir William McGann. *Story, scen and dial* Lillie Hayward. *Photog* William Rees. *Rec eng* Dolph Thomas.

Cast: Rin-Tin-Tin (*Rinty*), Armida (*Pepita*), John B. Litel (*Dave*), Philo McCullough (*Farrell*), Bruce Covington (*Don José*), Walter Miller (*Border Patrol Commander*), William Irving (*Dusty*).

Animal, Adventure. At the impoverished hacienda of Don José, near the Mexican border, five men, headed by Farrell, stop with truckloads of vegetables, but the rancher's dog, Rinty, detects the presence of the Chinese the men are smuggling. Farrell, who covets Pepita, the rancher's daughter, plans to buy the ranch for smuggling operations; meanwhile, Dave and Dusty, two apparent tramps who are border agents, discover the smugglers' ruse, and Pepita and Rinty take an interest in Dave. Don José innocently falls in with the plans of Farrell's men. Following a series of complications, Dave is captured by the smugglers but is saved in a last-minute rescue by Rinty. The border patrol subdues the gang at the ranch, and Rinty overpowers Farrell as he flees in an automobile. *Border patrols. Chinese Americans. Dogs. Mexican Americans. Mexican-American border region. Ranchers. Smuggling. Tramps.*

FD 9 Feb 1930. *NYT* 3 Feb 1930, p. 17. *Var* 5 Feb 1930, p. 31.

ON THE OLD SPANISH TRAIL (Gypsies)

Republic Pictures Corp. *Dist* Republic Pictures Corp. 15 Oct **1947**; Prod: late Apr–late May 1947 [©Republic Pictures Corp.; 12 Nov 1947; LP1296]. Sd (RCA Sound System); col (Trucolor). 72 or 75 min. Passed by the National Board of Review. PCA cert no. 12493.

Assoc prod Edward J. White. *Dir* William Witney. [*Asst dir* Jack Lacey]. *Scr* Sloan Nibley. *Orig story* Gerald Geraghty. *Dir of photog* Jack Marta. *Spec eff* Howard Lydecker and Theodore Lydecker. *Art dir* Frank Hotaling. *Film ed* Tony Martinelli. *Set dec* John McCarthy, Jr. and Helen Hansard. *Cost supv* Adele Palmer. *Mus dir* Morton Scott. *Sd* Earl Crain, Sr. *Makeup supv* Bob Mark.

Song(s): "I'll Never Love Again," based on "La borrachita," music and Spanish lyrics by Ignacio Fernandez Esperon, English lyrics by Al Stewart; "Guadalajara," music and lyrics by Pepe Guizar; "My Adobe Hacienda," music and lyrics by Louise Massey and Lee Penny; "On the Old Spanish Trail," music and lyrics by Jimmy Kennedy and Kenneth L. Smith; "Una furtiva lagrima" ("A Furtive Tear") from the opera *L'elisir d'amore*, music by Gaetano Donizetti, libretto by Felice Romani; "Here Is My Helpin' Hand," music and lyrics by Bob Nolan; "Bolero," music and lyrics by M. H. Sturgis and W. P. Blake.

Cast: Roy Rogers [(*Roy Rogers*)], Trigger The Smartest Horse in the Movies, Tito Guizar [(*Ricco Perado*)], Jane Frazee [(*Candy Martin*)], Andy Devine [(*"Cookie" Bullfincher*)], Estelita Rodriguez [(*Lola Gitana*)], Charles McGraw [(*Harry Blaisdell*)], Fred Graham [(*Marcos the Great*)], Steve Darrell [(*Al*)], Marshall Reed [(*Gus*)], Wheaton Chambers [(*Silas MacIntyre*)], Bob Nolan and the Sons of the Pioneers, [Edward Keane (*Burnett*)], [Bill Murphy (*Hotel clerk*)], [George "Shug" Fisher (*Spectator*)], [Edward Cassidy (*Sheriff*)], [Billy Mitchell (*Porter*)].

Show business, Western, with songs. [*Print viewed*]. When the sheriff arrives at the Great Southwestern Tent Show camped near Sioux City, Iowa, he tells performers The Sons of the Pioneers that a man named Burnett is coming to collect on their $10,000 loan, which was countersigned by local rancher and fellow entertainer, Roy Rogers. Burnett warns them that he will be forced to confiscate their show equipment if they cannot pay, but agrees to give them a few weeks in which to raise the money. Later, on a road outside of town, a suitcase falls from the top of a car driven by Candy Martin, a performer joining the show, and Roy soon comes across it. Candy returns to claim the case, just as Roy discovers a love poem from a gypsy named Ricco Perado and some photographs of Candy among the spilled contents. When she is not looking, Roy slips one of the photographs inside his shirt, but it is later stolen by Ricco. At the wagon where he lives, Ricco adds the photograph to the many already covering the walls, much to the annoyance of his sweetheart, Lola Gitana. She asks Ricco to leave town with her, showing him a Wanted poster with his description on it, but he refuses. Roy's sidekick, Cookie Bullfincher, then tells Roy about a $10,000 reward for the capture of a gypsy who has been robbing oil companies of their payroll funds. After Roy discovers that the Great Southwestern Tent Show was in the vicinity during each of the robberies, he decides to visit the show, hoping to capture the gypsy so that he can pay off the loan with the reward money. At the show, the real culprit in the oil company robberies, Harry Blaisdell, introduces Roy to Candy, who apologizes for being rude to him on the road. Later in Candy's dressing tent, Lola demands that Candy stay away from Ricco, but Candy explains she has never met the gypsy. When Candy later deduces that Ricco is the gypsy on the Wanted posters, she informs Roy, who chases him. Ricco dives into a river and swims away, followed by Roy. At a gypsy camp, Ricco is professing his innocence to his peers when shots are fired at him from the adjacent trees. Meanwhile, Lola kidnaps Candy and brings her to the camp as well. Harry and his men, who are themselves responsible for the oil company robberies, arrive at the camp and draw their guns. Although Ricco lassos one of Harry's men as he tries to escape, he is the one arrested by Cookie. Later, Harry and his men decide to free Ricco from jail while simultaneously committing another robbery, hoping that Roy and Cookie will then be convinced of Ricco's guilt. After Roy discovers Ricco missing from his cell and Candy tied up in his place, Ricco returns to explain what has happened. Convinced that he is an escaped prisoner, however, Roy takes him into custody. Later, Harry suggests that Roy and his men perform a mock holdup in town to promote the show. Just as the "holdup" is about to begin, Candy

realizes that Harry is the leader of the outlaws, and Ricco tries to stop him from robbing the Inter-City Oil Company. The robbery is foiled and Cookie escapes with the cash boxes, as Roy leaps from his horse Trigger onto a moving carriage in an effort to catch the thieves. After Harry and his men are arrested, Candy opens the cash boxes and is shocked to find them empty. Meanwhile, Ricco returns to Lola with the stolen money, and the tent show moves on to its next venue. *Cowboys. Debt. Entertainers. Frame-ups. Gypsies. Robbery. Show business. Automobiles. Constables. Firearms. Fugitives. Hotel owners. Hotels. Iowa. Jails. Jealousy. Kidnapping. Mexicans. Oil companies. Photographs. Poetry. Rivers. Sheriffs. Suitcases.*

Note: The film's working titles were *Heart of Mexico* and *Outlaws of Sioux City*; the latter title was also a working title for Republic's *Rustlers of Devil's Canyon* (see below). Modern sources include Jack O'Shea in the cast.

Box 1 Nov 1947. *DV* 22 Oct 1947. *FD* 22 Oct 1947. *HR* 25 Apr 1947, p. 16. *HR* 29 May 1947, p. 18. *HR* 22 Oct 1947, p. 3. *IEJ* 7 Jun 1947, p. 39. *Var* 22 Oct 1947, p. 13.

ON WITH THE DANCE (Russian Americans)
Famous Players-Lasky Corp.; Paramount-Artcraft Pictures. *Dist* Famous Players-Lasky Corp. 15 Feb **1920** [©Famous Players-Lasky Corp.; 16 Jan 1920; LP14660]. Si; b&w. 7 reels, 6,483 ft.
Pres Adolph Zukor. *Dir* George Fitzmaurice. *Scen* Ouida Bergère. *Cam* Arthur Miller and Georges Benoit.
Source: Based on the play *On With The Dance* by Michael Morton (New York, 29 Oct 1917).
Cast: Mae Murray (*Sonia Varinoff*), David Powell (*Peter Derwynt*), Alma Tell (*Lady Jeane Tremelyn*), John Miltern (*Schuyler Van Vechtan*), Robert Schable (*Jimmie Sutherland*), Ida Waterman (*Countess of Raystone*), Zola Talma (*Fay Desmond*), James A. Furey.
Drama. Sonia Varinoff, a Russian peasant girl, Peter Derwynt, a Southern architect, Lady Jeane Tremelyn, a member of the British aristocracy, and Jimmie Sutherland, an uncultivated parvenu, are all thrown together by chance in New York City. Derwynt and Lady Jeane, both with high ideals and cultivated tastes, are mutually attracted, but Sonia throws herself at Derwynt, offending Lady Jeane so greatly that she marries Sutherland, thus allowing Sonia to catch Derwynt on the rebound. After discovering that her husband's income cannot support her spendthrift ways, Sonia accepts Sutherland's offer to dance in his cabaret, and be billed as the "masked dancer." Upon uncovering his wife's exhibitionism, Derwynt angrily confronts Sutherland, and in the ensuing fight Derwynt shoots his wife's lover. To save her husband's life, Sonia testifies that the shooting was justified by her misconduct. Derwynt is acquitted and marries Lady Jeane while Sonia marries Van Vechtan, an old friend of her husband. *Cabaret performers. Dancers. Infidelity. Marriage. Russian Americans. Architects. Disguise. English. Fights. Murder. New York City. Nobility. Peasantry. Southerners. Spendthrifts. Trials.*

ETR 7 Feb 1920, p. 1001. *MPW* 10 Jan 1020, p. 174. *MPW* 17 Jan 1920, p. 326. *MPW* 21 Feb 1920, p. 1279. *MPW* 28 Feb 1920, p. 1525. *NYT* 16 Feb 1920, p. 8. *Var* 20 Feb 1920, p. 40. *Wid's* 15 Feb 1920, p. 13.

ON YOUR BACK (*foreign version*) *see* **ESCLAVAS DE LA MODA**

ONE ANGRY DAY *see* **LAST TRAIN FROM GUN HILL**

ONE DARK NIGHT (African Americans)
Million Dollar Productions, Inc. *Dist* Sack Amusement Enterprises, Inc. **1939**; New York opening: week of 24 Nov 1939. Sd; b&w. 8 reels, 7,440 ft. 80-81 min. PCA cert no. 5657.
Prod Harry M. Popkin. *Dir* Leo C. Popkin. *Story* Billy Myers.
Song(s): "West of Harlem," "Shake It and Break It," "Sharpest Man in Town" and "Alone Again," music and lyrics by Lew Porter and Johnny Lange.
Cast: Mantan Moreland (*Brown*), Betty Treadville (*Mrs. Brown*), Josephine Pearson (*Brown's daughter*), John Thomas (*Brown's daughter's boyfriend*), Arthur Ray (*Brown's father-in-law*), Jessie Grayson (*Brown's mother-in-law*), Bobby Simmons (*Brown's son*), Lawrence Criner (*The nightclub owner*), Ruby Logan (*The singer*), Alfred Grant, Guernsey Morrow, Herbert Skinner, Monte Hawley, The Four Tones.
African American, Domestic, Comedy-drama, with songs.
[*Not viewed*]. While waiting twenty-three years for a business deal to come through, Brown lets his wife and two children support him. Living with them are his in-laws, who insult him often. Ashamed, Brown leaves, and it is believed he is dead. The family continues to live as before, but an old suitor begins to court Brown's wife again. Wandering in the desert, Brown finds a deposit of radium and strikes

it rich. When he returns home, he buys a nightclub owned by a man who has been making advances to his daughter, a dancer, who already has a boyfriend. Brown frightens the suitor away, and now that he has money, he buys new clothes for his forgiving family. *African Americans. Desertion (Marital). Family life. Fatherhood. In-laws. Laziness. Missing persons, Assumed dead. Clothes. Dancers. Deserts. Nightclubs. Nouveaux riches. Radium.*

Note: According to information contained in the New York State Archives censorship material, the title of the film was changed to *Night Club Girl* soon after it was submitted to the agency for review. The *Var* review indicates that the picture was billed as the first installment in what was to be the Brown Family series, Million Dollar Productions' "colored counterpart of the Hardy's, Joneses and other film family groups." No further Brown Family films were made.

Exh 13 Dec 1939, p. 434. *FD* 1 Dec 1939, p. 8. *MPD* 30 Nov 1939, p. 10. *Var* 3 May 1939, p. 16.

ONE EIGHTH APACHE (Native Americans, Apache)
Berwilla Film Corp. *Dist* Arrow Film Corp. 15 Jul **1922** [©Arrow Film Corp.; 8 Aug 1922; LP18122]. Si; b&w. 6 reels, 5,634 ft.
Dir Ben Wilson. *Scen* J. Grubb Alexander.
Source: Based on a short story by Peter Bernard Kyne (publication undetermined).
Cast: Roy Stewart (*Brant Murdock*), Kathleen Kirkham (*Norma Biddle*), Wilbur McGaugh (*Charlie Longdeer*), George M. Daniel (*Tyler Burgess*), Dick La Reno (*Joseph Murdock*).
Western. When Tyler Burgess goes west to make his fortune, a marriage is arranged between Norma, his society sweetheart, and Brant, the son of a cattle and oil baron. With the aid of a renegade Indian, Burgess breaks up their wedding by casting aspersions on Brant's birth and killing Brant's father. Burgess then marries Norma, but they are unhappy. Brant exposes the frameup, the Indian kills Burgess, and Brant and Norma are reunited. *Apache Indians. Marriage. Murder. Ranchers. Socialites.*

ETR 23 Sep 1922, p. 1110.

ONE HOUR WITH YOU (*foreign version*) *see* **UNE HEURE PRÈS DE TOI**

ONE LAW FOR BOTH (Russian Americans)
Ivan Film Productions, Inc. *Dist* State Rights. 19 May **1917** [©Ivan Film Productions, Inc.; 18 Jun 1917; LU11038]. Si; b&w. 8 reels.
Dir Ivan Abramson. *Asst dir* William Abramson. *Scen* Ivan Abramson. *Cam* Marcel A. LePicard.
Cast: Rita Jolivet (*Elga Pulaski*), James Morrison (*Ossip Pulaski*), Leah Baird (*Helen*), Vincent Serrano (*Hutchinson*), Paul Capellani (*Slezak*), Helen Arnold (*Magda*), Pedro de Cordoba (*Count de Fernac*), Margaret Greene (*Renee*), Anders Randolf (*The governor*), Hassan Mussalli (*Feodor Wolski*), Walter Gould (*Henri*).
Social, Drama. Elga Pulaski and her brother Ossip leave Russia, where they have been persecuted, for America where Elga finds happiness as the wife of Norman Hutchinson. There is a cloud over their relationship, however, because in Russia, Elga had slept with the governor who held her brother's life in his hands. When Norman discovers his wife's past, he orders her to leave the house, acting contrary to what he had argued against in the case of his sister who had married a man who later proved to be the father of an illegitimate son. The sister then asks him to practice the principle that he advocated for her, and at last Norman sees things in the proper perspective and asks Elga to forgive him and remain his wife. *Brothers and sisters. Marriage. Reputation. Russian Americans. Self-sacrifice. Political corruption. Russia.*

ETR 12 May 1917, p. 1609. *Motog* 12 May 1917, p. 1015. *MPN* 19 May 1917, p. 3163. *MPW* 19 May 1917, p. 1137, 1179. *NYDM* 12 May 1917, p. 28. *Var* 4 May 1917, p. 26. *Wid's* 10 May 1917, pp. 296-97.

ONE MAD KISS (*foreign version*) *see* **EL PRECIO DE UN BESO**

THE ONE MAN *see* **CRASHIN' THRU**

ONE MAN IN A MILLION (Immigrants, Italian Americans)
Sol Lesser. *Dist* Robertson-Cole Distributing Corp. 13 Feb **1921** [©Robertson-Cole Distributing Corp.; 13 Feb 1921; LP16201]. Si; b&w. 6 reels.
Dir George Beban. *Scen* Dorothy Yost. *Story* George Beban. *Photog* Ross Fisher.
Cast: George Beban (*Lupino Delchini*), Helen Jerome Eddy (*Flora Valenzi*), Irene Rich (*Madame Maureveau*), Lloyd Whitlock (*Clyde Hartley*), George B. Williams (*Gustave Koppel*), Jennie Lee (*Mrs. Koppel*), Wade Boteler (*Immigration inspector*), George Beban, Jr.

(*The Belgian Waif*), Bo-Bo (*Himself, a parrot*), Toddles (*Himself, a dog*).

Drama. Lupino Delchini, a waiter in a little restaurant, is discharged for giving food to a penniless beggar; and Hartley, a detective, rewards the Italian by getting him an appointment as poundmaster. Flora is attracted to Lupino by his kindness, but when he adopts a small Belgian boy he falls in love with Madame Maureveau, whom he believes to be the boy's mother. Madame Maureveau accepts his marriage offer only to avoid being deported; actually, she is in love with Hartley, who traces her real son to another family. Renouncing his engagement, Delchini finds happiness with the boy and Flora. *Adoption. Belgians. Dog-catchers. Dogs. Immigrants. Italian Americans. Parrots. Waifs.*

ETR 22 Jan 1921, p. 757. *FD* 16 Jan 1921.

ONE MILE FROM HEAVEN (African Americans)

Twentieth Century-Fox Film Corp. *Dist* Twentieth Century-Fox Film Corp. 13 Aug **1937**; Prod: 15 Mar—early Apr 1937 [©Twentieth Century-Fox Film Corp.; 13 Aug 1937; LP7681]. Sd (Western Electric Mirrophonic Recording); b&w. 7 reels, 6,144 ft. 68 min. PCA cert no. 3224.

Exec prod Sol M. Wurtzel. *Dir* Allan Dwan. *Asst dir* Samuel Schneider. *Scr* Lou Breslow and John Patrick. *Orig story* Judge Ben B. Lindsey, Robin Harris and Alfred Golden. *Photog* Sidney Wagner. *Art dir* Bernard Herzbrun. *Film ed* Fred Allen. *Cost* Herschel. *Mus dir* Samuel Kaylin. *Sd* George Leverett and Harry M. Leonard.

Source: Based on "The Koudenhoffen Case" by Judge Ben B. Lindsey and Wainwright Evans in their book *The Revolt of Modern Youth* (New York, 1925).

Cast: Claire Trevor (*Lucy "Tex" Warren*), Sally Blane (*Barbara Harrison*), Douglas Fowley (*Jim Tabor*), Fredi Washington (*Flora Jackson*), Joan Carol (*Sunny*), Ralf Harolde (*Moxie McGrath*), John Eldredge (*Jerry Harrison*), Paul McVey (*Johnny*), Ray Walker (*Mortimer Atlas*), Russell Hopton (*Peter Brindell*), Chick Chandler (*Charlie Milford*), Eddie Anderson (*Henry Bangs*), Howard Hickman (*Judge Clarke*), Bill Robinson (*Officer Joe [Dudley]*), [Charles Wilson (*Fletcher*)], [George Sparks (*Desmond Bangs*)], [Lon Chaney, Jr., John Lester Johnson, Fred Kelsey, Russ Clark (*Policemen*)], [Robert Murphy (*Master of ceremonies*)], [Eddie Dunn (*Detective*)], [Billy McClain (*Gus*)], [George Chandler (*Herman*)], [Tom McGuire (*Court attaché*)], [Charles Lane (*Webb*)], [Frank Fanning (*Jailer*)], [George Reed (*Photographer*)], [Hal K. Dawson (*Information clerk*)], [Eric Wilton (*Butler*)], [Raymond Brown (*Alderman*)], [Harry McKee (*Gas station attendant*)], [Ralph Dunn (*Doorman*)], [Ivan Miller (*Warden*)], [Lew Harvey (*Prisoner*)], [Floyd Criswell, Lee Phelps (*Radio cops*)], [Homer Dickinson], [Bruce Warren].

Newspaper, Social, Drama. [*Print viewed*]. After she beats three male reporters from rival papers in a poker game, Lucy "Tex" Warren is tricked by them into going to a junk shop in a black neighborhood in search of a bogus murder story. While she watches with admiration as Officer Joe Dudley tap-dances with some children, Tex notices a little white girl named Sunny, whom Flora Jackson, a black seamstress, claims is her daughter. When Tex reports the incident, her editor arranges for a juvenile court hearing, and the judge postpones judgment until an investigation can be conducted. Tex offers to help Flora if she will answer her questions, but the three rival reporters invade Flora's house, and one steals a photo of Flora with Sunny as an infant. The reporters locate the photographer and then the hospital where Flora gave birth to her child. After they examine the hospital's records, their papers publish stories with the picture and state that the child really is Flora's. In prison, convict Jim Tabor notices the picture in a newspaper and tells his cellmate, Moxie McGrath, who is to be released the next day, that Sunny is the child of his deceased pal, Cliff Lucas. Tabor convinces Moxie that they can make a lot of money if Moxie can get a gun to him. After he gets out, Moxie sends Tabor a gun, but he also informs the warden of Tabor's planned escape, and Tabor is gunned down as he makes his escape attempt. Moxie then drives to Flora's home with his cohort Johnny and says that they came from the juvenile court to take the child. Tex also arrives, and after Joe tells the men that they must have a court order to take the child, Tex gets their license plate number as they leave. Tex follows them to a hotel, where she overhears Moxie call Lucas' former wife Barbara, who is celebrating her first anniversary to oilman Jerry Harrison. Moxie tells Barbara that her child, whom she thought was dead, is alive and that she can have her back if she brings $15,000

to a meeting place in a park. Tex goes to the park and sees Barbara get into a car with Moxie and Johnny. Barbara tells them that she could not get the money in time and instead offers jewels. When Johnny notices that Tex is following, Moxie pushes Barbara out of the car. Tex then calls the police and reports that her car has been stolen, giving the license plate number of Moxie's car. After the crooks' car is spotted, Moxie shoots at the police pursuing them. One of the officers shoots the tire of Moxie's car, and it crashes over a bridge, killing Moxie and Johnny. At the hearing, Barbara explains that after she secretly married Lucas, she learned that he was a criminal and tried to run away with her baby, but Lucas followed. Barbara's car crashed into a lake, and she was told that her daughter drowned. In reality, Lucas rescued the baby and had Flora, who worked at his boardinghouse, take care of her. When Lucas was killed by police, Flora did not want the baby to go to an orphanage, so she reared her as her own. Seeing Flora's strong attachment to Sunny, Barbara asks Flora to live with them as a nurse. The judge forbids Tex to publish her story, feeling that the notoriety would negatively affect Sunny. When the other reporters lock Tex into their room and demand her story, she types out a false story and then, as if she is not satisfied with her prose, throws the paper away. The reporters retrieve the paper, and their newspapers print a story that claims Sunny's real parents were a diva and a count who drowned in a car accident. The reporters are jailed for libel, and Tex visits them to say that she is returning to Waco, Texas to be the society editor of the *Cattleman's Daily Bugle*. She then attends a party at the Harrison estate attended by Sunny's friends from Maple Heights. Flora plans to marry Joe, who, due to Jerry's intervention, has been transferred to their area of town. *African Americans. Child custody. Deception. Missing persons, Assumed dead. Mothers and daughters. Wards and guardians. Women reporters.* Automobile accidents. Editors. Ex-convicts. Falls from heights. Judges. Libel and slander. Photographs. Police. Prison escapes. Prison wardens. Rivalry. Ruses. Seamstresses.

Note: According to modern sources, in 1899, Judge Benjamin B. Lindsey, who the story on which this film is based, wrote the statute that established, in Denver, the first juvenile court in the United States. As presiding judge of the Denver juvenile court from 1900 until 1927, Lindsey instituted many reforms for the treatment of juveniles. The Twentieth Century-Fox Produced Scripts Collection at the UCLA Theater Arts Library contains Lindsey's original story, which appears to be based on fact. According to his story, Lindsey was informed that a black woman in Denver was rearing a blonde six-year-old, who claimed to be the woman's daughter. Through his investigations, Lindsey learned that the woman worked for a midwife, and that one of her responsibilities was to burn in a furnace the bodies of babies born dead. The child in question was born to a society debutante from Chicago, and the midwife, thinking that the baby was dead, gave it to her assistant. The black woman noticed that the baby was still alive, and she nursed it to health and reared it as her own. After the story appeared in the newspapers, the real mother claimed her child and agreed to have the black woman live with them. Commenting on possible reaction to controversial aspects of the film, *Box* noted, "Although the greatest care and judgment must be exercised in exploiting this film to prevent any friction from developing over the highly detonous phases in which it cautiously touches on what appears to be racial inter-marriage, there is no reason it cannot be good boxoffice, for it carries a tremendous appeal to all women."

Box 31 Jul 1937. *DV* 15 Jul 1937, p. 3. *FD* 20 Jul 1937, p. 10. *HR* 4 Mar 1937, p. 4. *HR* 22 Mar 1937, p. 11. *HR* 5 Apr 1937, p. 7. *HR* 15 Jul 1937, p. 3. *MPD* 17 Jul 1937, p. 3. *MPH* 17 Apr 1937, p. 41. *MPH* 24 Jul 1937, p. 47, 50. *NYT* 19 Aug 1937, p. 23. *Var* 21 Jul 1937.

ONE MORE AMERICAN (Italian Americans)

Jesse L. Lasky Feature Play Co.; Famous Players-Lasky Corp. *Dist* Famous Players-Lasky Corp.; Paramount Pictures. 25 Feb **1918** [©Jesse L. Lasky Feature Play Co.; 15 Feb 1918; LP12069]. Si; b&w. 5 reels.

Pres Jesse L. Lasky. *Dir* William C. de Mille. *Asst dir* John Brown. *Scen* Olga Printzlau. *Cam* Charles Rosher. *Art dir* Wilfred Buckland.

Source: Based on the play *The Land of the Free* by William C. de Mille (New York, 2 Oct 1917).

Cast: George Beban (*Luigi Riccardo*), Camille Ankewich (*Maria Riccardo*), May Giraci (*Tessa Riccardo*), Helen Jerome Eddy (*Lucia*), Raymond Hatton (*Bump Rundle*), Jack Holt (*Sam Potts*), Horace B. Carpenter (*Mike Regan*), Hector Dion (*Dr. Ross*), May Palmer (*Mrs. Ross*), Ernest Joy (*Mr. Fearing, Immigration Commissioner*), Signor Buzzi (*Piano player*).

Drama. Luigi Riccardo, the proprietor of a marionette theater in New York's Little Italy, eagerly anticipates the arrival of his wife Maria and daughter Tessa, whom he has not seen in five years. Luigi dreams of becoming an American citizen, but because he refuses to make graft payments to Regan, the ward boss, he is informed that he will not receive his naturalization papers. When Regan orders Dr. Ross, an

Ellis Island physician, to classify Maria and Tessa as unfit to enter the country, Luigi becomes wild with grief. Newspaper reporter Sam Potts learns of the Italian's misfortune and, through local prizefighter Bump Rundle, offers Regan a phony bribe in exchange for Luigi's papers. Regan accepts and Sam exposes him publicly, enabling Luigi to welcome his wife and daughter as American citizens. *Citizenship. Immigrants. Italian Americans. New York City–Little Italy. Political bosses. Political corruption. Puppets. Boxers. Bribery. Graft. Hoaxes. New York City–Ellis Island. Physicians. Reporters.*

Note: Actress Camille Ankewich changed her name to Marcia Manon in 1918. Sources conflict concerning the name she used for this film.

ETR 2 Mar 1918, p. 1066. *MPN* 2 Mar 1918, p. 1319. *MPN* 23 Mar 1918, p. 1721. *MPW* 2 Mar 1918, p. 1269, 1275. *NYDM* 26 Jan 1918, p. 26. *NYDM* 2 Mar 1918, p. 18. *NYDM* 9 Mar 1918, p. 26. *Wid's* 7 Mar 1918, pp. 986-87.

ONE OF THE BRAVEST (Jewish Americans)

Gotham Productions. *Dist* Lumas Film Corp. Oct **1925** [©Lumas Film Corp.; 19 Oct 1925; LP21923]. Si; b&w. 6 reels, 5,679 ft.

Pres Samuel Sax. *Supv* Renaud Hoffman. *Dir* Frank O'Connor. *Asst dir* Glenn Belt. *Story* James J. Tynan. *Cont* Henry McCarty. *Photog* Ray June. *Film ed* Irene Morra.

Cast: Ralph Lewis (*John Kelly*), Edward Hearn (*Dan Kelly*), Sidney Franklin (*Morris Levin*), Pat Somerset (*"Satin" Sanderson*), Claire McDowell (*Mrs. Kelly*), Marion Mack (*Sarah Levin*).

Melodrama. Though Dan Kelly is brave enough to save tailor Morris Levin and his daughter Sarah from three thugs, he has a deadly fear of fires. After receiving his assignment as fireman, Dan disgraces himself in the eyes of his father—John Kelly, captain of Engine 95 and one of the bravest firefighters in the department. Mrs. Kelly is persuaded by con man "Satin" Sanderson to invest the money entrusted to her husband for the fireman's ball in a phony stock. John finds the money missing and blames Dan. Sarah gets her father to give Dan enough money to replace the missing funds. When a three-alarm fire breaks out, Dan sees a chance to redeem himself and rushes to the scene. He spots Sanderson in the burning building, mounts a scaling ladder, beats up the swindler, saves his father, and with Sanderson jumps to safety into a net. The Irish and Jewish families become reconciled, and Dan and Sarah are betrothed. *Confidence men. Firemen. Irish. Jews. Phobias. Tailors.*

FD 22 Nov 1925. *Var* 3 Mar 1926, p. 38.

THE ONLY ROAD (Latino)

Metro Pictures Corp. *Dist* Metro Pictures Corp. 3 Jun **1918** [©Metro Pictures Corp.; 31 May 1918; LP12479]. Si; b&w. 5 reels.

Dir Frank Reicher. *Scen* George D. Baker. *Story and scen* Albert Shelby Le Vino. *Cam* John Arnold.

Cast: Viola Dana (*Nita*), Casson Ferguson (*Bob Armstrong*), Edythe Chapman (*Clara Hawkins*), Fred Huntley (*Ramon Lupo*), Monte Blue (*Pedro Lupo*), Paul Weigel (*Manuel Lopez*), Marie Van Tassell (*Rosa Lopez*), Gertrude Short (*Bianca*).

Western. Nita, a tomboy who sells vegetables in a sleepy California town, believes herself to be the daughter of poor ranch workers Manuel and Rosa Lopez. Traveling into town, she is attacked by Pedro Lupo, the son of lawyer Ramon Lupo, but Bob Armstrong, an Easterner visiting his father's wealthy friend, Clara Hawkins, defends her. When Pedro learns that she is actually Clara's daughter, stolen at birth and long presumed dead, he insists that she marry him, but she refuses. Bob rescues Nita from the room in which she has been imprisoned, and the Lupos, furious at his interference, tell the sheriff that he has compromised the girl. Bob marries Nita at the sheriff's gunpoint and then places her in a convent, from which she later escapes. Nita flees to the Hawkins ranch, and after Ramon reveals her identity to Clara, she is happily reunited with her mother and her new husband. *Long-lost relatives. Marriage–Forced. Mexican Americans. Parentage. Ranches. Rescues. Tomboys. Attempted rape. California. Convents. Escapes. False accusations. Rescues. Sheriffs. Small town life.*

Note: One reviewer stated that George D. Baker directed. The release date is also listed as 10 Jun, 13 Jun, and 20 Jun 1918.

ETR 15 Jun 1918, p. 128. *MPN* 22 Jun 1918, p. 3690. *MPW* 15 Jun 1918, p. 1623. *MPW* 22 Jun 1918, p. 1755. *NYDM* 22 Jun 1918, p. 886. *NYDM* 6 Jul 1918, p. 965. *Wid's* 16 Jun 1918, pp. 19-20.

ONLY THE VALIANT (Native Americans, Apache)

Cagney Productions, Inc.; A William Cagney Production. *Dist* Warner Bros. Pictures, Inc. 21 Apr **1951**; New York opening: 13 Apr 1951; Prod: late Jul—early Sep 1950 [©Cagney Productions, Inc.; 30 Mar 1951; LP818]. Sd (RCA Sound System); b&w. 9,423 ft. 104 or 107 min.

Dir Gordon Douglas. *Asst dir* William Kissel. *Scr* Edmund H. North and Harry Brown. *Dir of photog* Lionel Lindon. *Prod des* Wiard Ihnen. *Film ed* Walter Hannemann and Robert S. Seiter. *Set dec* Armor B. Marlowe. *Ward* Leah Rhodes. *Mus* Franz Waxman. *Orch* Leonid Raab. *Sd* Leslie G. Hewitt. [*Interpreter* Howard Wilson].

Source: Based on the novel *Only the Valiant* by Charles Marquis Warren (New York, 1943).

Cast: GREGORY PECK [(*Capt. Richard Lance*)], Barbara Payton [(*Cathy Eversham*)], Ward Bond [(*Corp. Timothy Gilchrist*)], Gig Young [(*Lt. Bill Holloway*)], Lon Chaney [(*Kebussyan*)], Neville Brand [(*Sgt. Ben Murdock*)], Jeff Corey [(*Joe Harmony*)], Warner Anderson [(*Rutledge*)], Steve Brodie (*Onstot*), Dan Riss [(*Lt. Jerry Winters*)], Terry Kilburn [(*Saxton*)], Herbert Heyes [(*Col. Drumm*)], Art Baker [(*Capt. Jennings*)], Hugh Sanders [(*Capt. Eversham*)], Michael Ansara [(*Tucsos*)], Nana Bryant [(*Mrs. Drumm*)], [Harvey Udell (*Capt. Conrahan*)], [Claire James (*Jenny*)], [Clark Howat (*Lt. Underwood*)], [Harlan Howe (*Junior sergeant*)], [John Halloran (*Sentry*)], [David Clarke (*Guard*)], [William Newell (*Corporal of the guard*)], [John Doucette (*Sergeant*)], [William Phillips (*Medical assistant*)].

Western. [*Print viewed*]. In New Mexico after the Civil War, a detachment of soldiers, including Capt. Richard Lance and scout Joe Harmony, arrive at Ft. Invincible, near a narrow pass frequently used by hostile Apache Indians. The fort has been burned to the ground and its soldiers killed. Although most of the Apaches have left the area, Lance manages to capture Tucsos, the chief. Harmony wants to kill Tucsos, but Lance, who is known for his rigid adherence to military rules, insists that they take their prisoner back to Ft. Winston. After they arrive at Ft. Winston, commanding officer Col. Drumm tells Lance that he, too, wishes Tucsos had been killed because the undermanned fort will not be able to fight off an Apache rescue effort. He then orders Lance to choose an officer to head a detail that will convey Tucsos to the better defended Ft. Grant. Knowing that the detail may never get through, Lance decides to lead it himself. He then visits Cathy Eversham, a captain's daughter, with whom he is in love. When he arrives, Cathy's other admirer, Lt. Bill Holloway, is already there. After Lance tells Cathy goodbye, Holloway proposes, but she refuses him because she is in love with Lance. Holloway affectionately kisses Cathy, and Lance, who is passing by, sees the kiss. When Drumm, who is very ill, learns that Lance intends to lead the detail, he orders him to send Holloway instead because Lance is the only officer he trusts to run the fort if he becomes too sick to do it himself. After Lance delivers the new orders to Holloway, Cathy is convinced that he changed the orders to eliminate his rival. Several days later, the detail returns with Holloway's body. When Harmony reports that Holloway was tortured by the Apaches before he died, the entire fort turns against Lance, and Kebussyan, one of the survivors, tries to kill him. Harmony believes that Tucsos, who knows the fort is vulnerable, will attack soon, before reinforcements can arrive. To buy time, Lance convinces Drumm to allow him to lead a patrol to Ft. Invincible and try to hold the pass until an expected relief column of 400 soldiers arrives. For the patrol, Lance purposely picks misfits and those who hate him the most: Lt. Jerry Winters, who is dying of tuberculosis; Corp. Timothy Gilchrist, a drunk; Sgt. Ben Murdock, who hates Lance for blocking his promotion; Onstot, a deserter from the Confederate Army; Kebussyan; Harmony; Rutledge, who is motivated by revenge; and Saxton, a coward. At Ft. Invincible, Winters discovers that the cistern is dry, which means the men will have to survive on the water they carried with them. That night, the men mine the pass with dynamite. Over the next few days, several attempts are made on Lance's life. Then a mortally wounded Harmony returns to warn Lance that Tucsos has learned that there are only thirty-one men in the relief column, not the 400 who were expected. After Harmony dies, Lance tells the men that he picked them because he believed they were the most expendable and, at their request, details his reasons. When he has finished, Gilchrist responds that Lance must be there because he is responsible for Holloway's death. While on sentry duty, Onstot and Murdock are captured, and Tucsos' men attack the fort. After the Apaches retreat, Lance sends Winters to intercept the relief column and redirect them to Ft. Invincible. As he leaves, Winters is wounded, but is able to continue. Lance then requests a meeting with Tucsos, and orders Gilchrist to set off the dynamite at his signal. Gilchrist is unable to comply because the fuse has been removed, and they lose the chance to destroy Tucsos. At the fort,

Rutledge admits that he removed the fuse, hoping to kill Lance. That night, during another assault, Rutledge is killed, and Kebussyan is wounded. The next morning, Lance and Kebussyan attempt to set a new fuse. Meanwhile, Tucsos, realizing how much Murdock and Onstot hate each other, decides to let them kill each other. When the Apaches discover Lance and Kebussyan in the pass, they attack them. Before he dies, Kebussyan holds off the Indians until Lance sets off the dynamite, blocking the pass almost completely. Only Lance, Gilchrist and Saxton are left alive, and they have no water. Once again, the Indians storm the fort. The situation appears to be hopeless, but just then the relief column of thirty-one soldiers arrives. The Indians turn their attack toward the new soldiers, who fire on them with a Gatling gun, which fires 350 rounds per minute. Faced with this new weapon, the Indians surrender. Tucsos manages to reach the fort, and after a struggle, Lance kills him with his own knife. When he returns to Ft. Winston, Lance learns that he has been made acting commander, as Drumm has left his post because of ill health. Later, Lance is reunited with Cathy, who now knows that he was not responsible for Holloway's death. *Apache Indians. False accusations. Rescues. Soldiers. United States. Army. Cavalry. Attempted murder. Cowardice. Disease. Drunkenness. Explosions. Forts. Knife fighting. Machine-guns. New Mexico. Officers (Military). Proposals (Marital). Romantic rivalry. Self-sacrifice. Tuberculosis. Water. Wounds and injuries.*

Note: On 29 Aug 1947, *LAEx* reported that James Cagney would reunite for this film with the entire cast of the 1948 picture *Time of Your Life*, which included William Bendix, Wayne Morris, Broderick Crawford and Jeanne Cagney, and was also produced by William Cagney. Ward Bond was the only actor from *Time of Your Life* who was cast in *Only the Valiant*. Portions of the film were shot on location in Gallup, N. M.

Box 10 Mar 1951, p. 3. *DV* 6 Mar 1951, p. 3. *FD* 7 Mar 1951, p. 4. *HR* 28 Jul 1950, p. 13. *HR* 1 Sep 1950, p. 11. *HR* 6 Mar 1951, p. 3. *LAEx* 29 Aug 1947. *MPHPD* 10 Mar 1951, p. 749. *NYT* 14 Apr 1951, p. 9. *Var* 7 Mar 1951, p. 6.

OPEN RANGE (Native Americans)

Paramount Famous Lasky Corp. 5 Nov **1927** [©Paramount Famous Lasky Corp.; 5 Nov 1927; LP24630]. Si; b&w. 6 reels, 5,599 ft.

Pres Adolph Zukor and Jesse L. Lasky. *Dir* Clifford S. Smith. *Scr* John Stone and J. Walter Ruben. *Titles* Roy Briant. *Photog* Hal Rosson.

Source: Based on the short story "Open Range" by Zane Grey (publication undetermined).

Cast: Betty Bronson (*Lucy Blake*), Lane Chandler (*Tex Smith*), Fred Kohler (*Sam Hardman*), Bernard Siegel (*Brave Bear*), Guy Oliver (*Jim Blake*), Jim Corey (*Red*), George Connors (*Sheriff Daley*), Flash (*The Wonder Horse*).

Western. Cowpuncher Tex Smith is intrigued by a poster portrait of Lucy Blake, who lives in the cattle settlement of Marco. Meanwhile, Brave Bear, an Indian chief, bitter at the encroachments of whites, conspires with Sam Hardman to steal the town's cattle during a rodeo, and Tex is mistakenly identified as one of the rustlers. At the rodeo, he tries to impress Lucy by riding a bronco; when she loses control of her team in the buggy race, he rescues her, but he evades the sheriff's men. Red and Hardman plan to get Tex before the sheriff gets him, but Lucy, convinced of his innocence, hides him at her ranch. Tex discovers the gang's hideout and forces a confession from Hardman, who warns Brave Bear. When the Indians attack the town, Tex and his men stampede the cattle ahead of them, and Tex saves Lucy and her father from their burning shelter. Hardman falls on his own knife and dies. *Cowboys. Indians of North America. Racing. Rodeos. Rustlers. Stampedes.*

Var 21 Mar 1928, p. 26.

THE OPEN ROAD *see* THE SLEEPING LION

OPEN SECRET (Jewish Americans)

Marathon Pictures Corp.; A Harry Brandt Production. *Dist* Eagle-Lion Films, Inc.; controlled by Pathe Industries, Inc. 14 Feb **1948**; New York opening: 31 Jan 1948; Prod: mid-Aug—late Aug 1947 at Motion Picture Center Studios [©Pathe Industries, Inc.; 5 May 1948; LP1681]. Sd (RCA Sound System); b&w. 8 reels, 6,239 ft. 69 min. Passed by the National Board of Review. PCA cert no. 12757.

Prod Frank Satenstein. *Assoc prod* Robert L. Joseph. *Asst to the prod* Leo Rose. *Dir* John Reinhardt. *Asst dir* Ralph Slosser and [Leon Chooluck]. *Asst to the dir* Peter A. Mayer. *Dial dir* Willard Holland. *Scr* Henry Blankfort and Max Wilk. [*Addl dial* John Bright]. *Orig story* Max Wilk and Ted Murkland. *Dir of photog* George Robinson. *Art dir* George Van Marter. *Ed supv* Jason H. Bernie. *Film ed* Stanley Frazen. *Set dec* Earl Wooden. [*Props* George Bahr]. *Mus comp and cond* Herschel Gilbert. *Mus supv* David Chudnow. *Sd eng* Hugh

McDowell. *Makeup artist* Ted Larsen. *Prod mgr* George Moskov.

Cast: John Ireland [(*Paul Lester*)], Jane Randolph [(*Nancy Lester*)], Roman Bohnen [(*Roy Locke*)], Sheldon Leonard [(*Sergeant Mike Frontelli*)], George Tyne [(*Harry Strauss*)], Morgan Farley [(*Larry Mitchell, also known as Phillips*)], Ellen Lowe [(*Mrs. Locke*)], Anne O'Neal [(*Mrs. Tristram*)], Arthur O'Connell [(*Carter*)], John Alvin [(*Ralph*)], Bert Conway [(*Mace*)], Rory Mallinson [(*Hill*)], Helena Dare [(*Mrs. Hill*)], Charles Waldron, Jr. [(*Ed Stevens*)], Leo Kaye [(*Bartender*)], [King Donovan (*Fawnes*)], [Tom Noonan (*Bob*)].

Social, Drama. [*Print viewed*]. When newly-weds Paul and Nancy Lester arrive in the city, they phone Paul's army buddy Ed Stevens, who checks with his landlady, Mrs. Tristram, and invites them to stay him him. Ed receives another phone call and, before he goes out to meet the caller, conceals a roll of film in a drawer. Paul and Nancy show up that night but, by the next morning, Ed has not returned. The couple goes out to take some photographs in the neighborhood and, when they return to Ed's, they discover that the apartment has been burgled. After Nancy finds some racist pamphlets among Ed's belongings, they receive a phone message from someone saying that Ed wants to meet them at a nearby intersection. Paul decides to go alone and, as he leaves, meets Larry Mitchell from "Snap Magazine," who tells him that Ed has some important information for him. Mitchell and Paul both wait for Ed who does not show up. At the apartment, meanwhile, a man enters but runs off when Nancy screams. Later, Paul reports the sequence of events to police sergeant Mike Frontelli. As they talk, a large rock is thrown through a window of the house across the street where a Mrs. Fisher, whose husband was killed the week before by a hit-and-run driver, lives. When Paul takes his film to Harry Strauss's camera shop for developing, he accidentally mixes Ed's roll in with his. As he leaves the shop, Paul discovers that some kids have slashed a tire on Strauss's car. Strauss tells Paul and Nancy that his car has been vandalized three times as part of a neighborhood antisemitic campaign. After Paul helps him to change the tire, the newlyweds meet a Mrs. Hill who asks them why they patronize Strauss's shop. She states that Strauss should "move elsewhere, with his own sort." Later, Sgt. Frontelli summons Paul to the morgue, where he indentifies Ed's body. Frontelli tells him that, although Ed was run over by a truck, he had already been murdered. When Fisher's body was found, Frontelli explains, he was holding on to the torn sleeve of a striped shirt, the same shirt Ed was wearing. After Ed's funeral, Paul and Nancy tell Mrs. Tristram that they will be leaving the next day. Paul tells Nancy that he saw a torn shirt in one of Ed's drawers and that, after the break-in, the shirt was missing and Ed was found wearing it. This causes Paul to think that Ed may have been framed. While pretending to be one of the group, Ed had photographed them with a concealed camera in order to expose their activities. Believing he might obtain some information there, Paul goes to a neighborhood bar frequented by Ed. The bartender complains about Ed's death, blaming it on "foreigners," while Locke, another patron, slaps his wife when she tries to get him to stop drinking and return home. Nancy goes to the camera shop to pick up Paul's photos but, after Harry's assistant, Ralph, sees a shot of two people painting "Jew" on the window of the store among the photos, he tells her they are not ready yet. However, Harry finds them and gives them to Nancy. Ralph goes to the apartment to retrieve the photos, but Paul opens the envelope and finds his own photos and will not return them. After Ralph leaves, however, Paul finds the incriminating pictures Ed has taken of the group's racist activities. Paul recognizes Locke in one of the photos and goes to see Mrs. Locke, who tells him, despairingly, that her husband is perpetually drunk and blames all his problems on "kikes and wops." She also tells Paul that he and and a friend named Mace were trying to get Ed to help them run Jews out of the neighborhood and she states that she saw Ed, Locke and Mace run down Fisher with Mace's car. Ed got out and tried to help Fisher, but the others slugged him. After Paul promises Mrs. Locke that he will protect her, Locke enters, gun drawn. Paul offers him a deal and shows him an incriminating photo Ed took of him setting a fire. While Locke examines the photo, Paul hits him with a vase. They struggle but Paul is overpowered by Mace, who has been watching through a window. Meantime, Nancy shows Harry the photos and he suggests that she hide them until they can be handed over to Mitchell. Harry thinks Paul may be at the bar and goes there to check while Nancy phones Frontelli. Mace and Carter, one of the group's leaders, realize that Nancy must have the photos, and when

Harry is taken into the bar's backroom, he finds Paul being held by Ralph and the others. Harry tells Carter that Nancy gave him the prints and negatives for safekeeping at his shop, so Harry is forced to return there. The group then decides to kill Paul, even though he tells them that Frontelli knows they killed Fisher and Ed. At the shop, Harry tricks Hill, his captor, and they have a fistfight. The others tie Paul's hands behind his back and stop by the shop, where Ralph tries to go to Harry's aid. Frontelli arrives and arrests the entire group, who blame their activities on Phillips, a ward heeler. Meantime, Mitchell calls on Nancy to pick up the photos to use in his magazine's exposé. However, Mitchell is really Phillips, the ring leader, and Nancy become suspicious of him. Paul and Frontelli arrive as Nancy and Mitchell are struggling for possession of the photos. Mitchell jumps through a window and runs up an alley but is shot by Frontelli. Frontelli phones the police station and calm returns to the neighborhood. *Antisemitism. Murder. Neighbors. Photographs. Alcoholics. Bars. Cameras. Clothes. Fascism. Fights. Landladies. Newlyweds. Police. Racism.*

Note: This film was produced by Marathon Pictures Corp. under the Producers Releasing Corp. banner, but was eventually released by Eagle-Lion when that company took over P.R.C. In a pre-production news item, Peter Maher was announced as the film's director. According to documents in the PCA file on the film in the AMPAS Library, the PCA tried to persuade producer Frank Satenstein to reduce the number of racial epithets used in the film. In an Aug 1947 letter to Satenstein, Joseph I. Breen wrote: "We feel that the sheer repetition of these offensive epithets, even in a story of this kind, will probably give rise to resentment on the part of large numbers of the moving picture audience." The print viewed appears to be from a 1955 reissue and is approximately two minutes shorter than the original. A comparison with film's original cutting continuity, filed with the copyright application, reveals that a number of racial epithets were removed from the print viewed. The character portrayed by Tom Noonan is in a scene cut from the version viewed.
The film was very poorly received when it opened in New York. Bosley Crowther of *NYT* wrote, "It is cheap, amateurish, tactless and incredibly poorly played." Archer Winsten, critic for the *NYPost*, stated, "The film makers and the performers work hard and earnestly. It's not enough. This is thin ice, the point of a needle. It can make you feel actually uncomfortable as you realize that this is the big tragedy, this is the feeling that killed millions of living persons, and it's being attacked here in a manner worthy of the battle to prove that crime does not pay or never bet on fights."
Box 24 Jan 1948. *Exb* 15 Jun 1955. *FD* 15 Jan 1948, p. 7. *HR* 1 Aug 1947, p. 10. *HR* 13 Jan 1948, p. 3. *HR* 5 Feb 1948, p. 6. *MPD* 16 Jan 1948. *MPHPD* 17 Jan 1948, p. 4018. *NYT* 2 Feb 1948, p. 15. *Var* 14 Jan 1948, p. 10.

OPERATOR 13 (African Americans)

Metro-Goldwyn-Mayer Corp.; controlled by Loew's Inc.; A Cosmopolitan Production. *Dist* Loew's Inc. 8 Jun **1934**; Prod: 19 Feb—26 Apr 1934 [©Metro-Goldwyn-Mayer Corp.; 11 Jun 1934; LP4782]. Sd (Western Electric Sound System); b&w. 9 reels. 85-86 min. Passed by the National Board of Review.

[*Prod* Lucien Hubbard]. *Dir* Richard Boleslavsky. [*Asst dir* Red Golden]. *Scr* Harvey Thew, Zelda Sears and Eve Greene. *Photog* George Folsey. *Art dir* Cedric Gibbons. *Art dir assoc* Arnold Gillespie and Edwin B. Willis. *Film ed* Frank Sullivan. *Gowns* Adrian. *Synchronization* Dr. William Axt. [*Orch* Paul Marquardt, Jack Virgil, Charles Maxwell, Maurice de Packh and Wayne Allen]. *Rec dir* Douglas Shearer. [*Sd* Stan Lambert].

Song(s): "The Colonel, Major and the Captain," "Once in a Lifetime" and "Sleepy Head," words and music by Walter Donaldson and Gus Kahn; "Jungle Fever," words and music by Walter Donaldson and Howard Dietz.

Source: Based on the novel *Secret Service Operator* by Robert W. Chambers (New York, 1934).

Cast: Marion Davies (*Gail Loveless [also known as Lucille, Operator 13 and Anne Claybourne]*), Gary Cooper (*Captain Jack Gailliard*), Jean Parker (*Eleanor [Shackleford]*), Katharine Alexander (*Pauline [Cushman, also known as Mrs. Vale and Operator 27]*), Ted Healy ([*Captain] Doctor Hitchcock*), Russell Hardie (*Littledale*), Henry Wadsworth (*John Pelham*), Douglas Dumbrille (*General Stewart*), Willard Robertson (*Captain [Cornelius] Channing*), Fuzzy Knight (*Sweeney*), Sidney Toler (*Major Allen [Pinkerton]*), Robert McWade (*Colonel Sharpe*), Marjorie Gateson (*Mrs. Shackleford*), Wade Boteler (*Gaston*), Walter Long (*Operator 55*), The Four Mills Brothers, [Sterling Holloway (*Wounded Union soldier*)], [Samuel S. Hinds (*Union officer*)], [Sam McDaniel (*Rufus*)], [Hattie McDaniel (*Annie*)], [Francis McDonald (*Denton*)], [William Griffith (*Mac*)], [Marjorie Gateson (*Mrs. Shackleford*)], [James Marcus (*Staff colonel*)], [Buddy Roosevelt (*Civilian*)], [Si Jenks (*White trash*)], [Frank McGlynn, Jr., Wheeler Oakman (*Scouts*)], [Don

Douglas, Frank Marlowe (*Confederate officers*)], [Reginald Barlow (*Colonel Storm*)], [Jim Marcus (*Staff officer*)], [Ernie Alexander, Richard Powell (*Confederate sentries*)], [Belle Daube (*Mrs. Dandridge*)], [Wilfred Lucas (*Judge*)], [Bob Stevenson (*Guard*)], [Martin Turner (*Hickman*)], [Frank Burt (*Confederate lieutenant*)], [Wally Howe (*Clergyman*)], [William Henry (*Young lieutenant*)], [Richard Tucker (*Execution officer*)], [Arthur Grant (*Chaplin*)], [Sherry Tansey (*Officer*)], [Lia Lance (*Witch woman*)], [Charles Lloyd (*Union private*)], [De Witt C. Jennings (*Artillery man*)], [Sam Ash (*Lieutenant*)], [Ernie Adams (*Orderly*)], [Clarence Hummel Wilson (*Claybourne*)], [Franklin Parker (*John Hay*)], [Claudia Coleman (*Nurse*)], [Sherry Hall (*Army officer*)], [Douglas Fowley (*Union officer*)], [Fred Warren (*Grant*)], [John Elliott (*Lee*)], [Frank Leighton (*Union major*)], [James C. Morton (*Secret service man*)], [John Larkin].

Historical, **Drama**, **with songs**. [*Print viewed*]. Early in the Civil War, the Second Battle of Bull Run is a disaster for the North. At a camp show for Union soldiers, performer Gail Loveless is recruited to become a spy by her friend, Pauline Cushman, who is herself a spy known as "Operator 27." Working for agent Major Allen Pinkerton, Gail agrees to become a spy known by the code name "Operator 13." She then goes South with Pauline to the headquarters of Confederate General "Jeb" Stuart. Posing as Pauline's black maid, Gail encounters Captain Jack Gailliard, a Confederate officer, when he rides by her washing and ruins it. Jack is a spy for the South, and when Pauline asks too many questions about him at a ball that evening, he and Captain Cornelius Channing become suspicious and have her room searched. Meanwhile, a traveling medicine show run by Doctor Hitchcock, who is secretly a captain in the Northern army, arrives looking for Operators 27 and 13. Gail is able to transfer information about Confederate troop movements to Hitchcock just as Pauline is being arrested. Gail is also suspected of being a spy, but when she is brought to testify at Pauline's trial, she divulges Pauline's real identity and says that her mistress "turned Yankee." Pauline is then sentenced to death, but Gail and Hitchcock help her to escape. Back in Washington, Pinkerton knows that Pauline can no longer operate across enemy lines, so he entrusts Gail with the mission to learn more about the activities of Jack, whom Pinkerton suspects is working with "Copperheads," Southern sympathizers, who live in the North. To make herself believable, Gail, using the name "Anne Claybourne," openly jeers at marching Union soldiers. She and a man posing as her father are then "arrested." When the incident is reported in Southern newspapers, "Anne" becomes a heroine and is deported to Richmond, where she becomes the guest of Mrs. Shackleford and her daughter Eleanor. Gail also re-encounters Jack, who is attracted to her, but suspects that he has seen her before. While at the Shackleford's, Gail is able to pass on information to the North that results in an important victory, but which causes the death of Eleanor's fiancé, John Pelham, just a few hours before their wedding. Feeling guilty over her part in John's death, Gail goes into the garden to cry and is met by Jack, who tells her that he loves her. Because she has also fallen in love with him, she moves him out of the aim of one of her operatives who is spying on them from the bushes. Soon, however, she gets away from Jack and, dressed in a Confederate soldier's uniform, heads North after the operative tells her that the Confederates now know she is a spy. As Jack and Channing chase her into the woods, they split up and Jack finds Gail asleep in a spring house. He then angrily calls her a a traitor and vows to take her back for a court-martial. He handcuffs Gail, but as they leave the house, they see Union soldiers execute Channing. Gail's operative then rushes toward the soldiers, but because of his rebel uniform, he is shot. The Union soldiers then decide to search the house, but leave after finding no one. Gail and Jack, who had hidden in the spring, now escape together and, after a blacksmith files their handcuffs off, Jack heads South, while Gail tearfully goes North. A few years later, the war is finally over and Gail and Jack reunite and pledge their love to each other. *Actors and actresses. Escapes. Romance. Spies. United States–History–Civil War, 1861-1865. United States. Army. Bull Run, Battle of, 1862. Courts-martial and courts of inquiry. Executions. Medicine shows. Racial impersonation. Slavery. Soldiers. Southerners. Springs.*

Note: Robert W. Chambers' novel was serialized in *Hearst's International-Cosmopolitan*, and the film credits the source as "the stories of Robert W. Chambers," rather than the novel. According to a news item in *HR* in Aug 1933, Fred Niblo, Jr. and C. Gardner Sullivan were collaborating on a

screenplay for *Operator 13*, but the extent of their participation in the completed film has not been determined. According to various news items in *DV* and *HR*, production began on 1 Feb 1934 under Walter Wanger's supervision and Raoul Walsh's direction, with Al Shenberg working as the assistant director. On 12 Feb 1934, production was stopped on orders from William Randolph Hearst, the head of Cosmopolitan Pictures. A *DV* news item notes that all of the film shot was scrapped and a new story was written. At that time, Wanger was replaced by Lucien Hubbard, who was originally intended to produce the picture. Because Walsh protested against the new script, he was also taken off the film. The picture resumed production on 19 Feb 1934, under Hubbard's supervision, with Richard Boleslavsky the new director and Red Golden the new assistant director. Although the CBSC lists Jay Lloyd as "Gaston," Wade Boteler is credited with that role on the film. *Var* commented, "Miss Davies is particularly effective as a colored wench, a disguise she simulates in one major chapter as the maid to Katherine Alexander. Her dialect and mannerisms are decidedly effective."

DV 1 Feb 1934, p. 3. *DV* 13 Feb 1934, p. 1. *DV* 17 Feb 1934, p. 1. *DV* 26 Apr 1934, p. 6. *FD* 2 Jun 1934, p. 4. *HF* 3 Feb 1934, p. 8. *HF* 10 Mar 1934, p. 12. *HR* 28 Apr 1934, p. 4. *HR* 23 Aug 1934, p. 3. *MPD* 4 Jun 1934, p. 5. *MPH* 19 May 1934, p. 61. *MPH* 16 Jun 1934, p. 78. *NYT* 23 Jun 1934, p. 16. *Var* 26 Jun 1934, p. 16.

THE ORDEAL OF ROSETTA (Italian Americans)

Select Pictures Corp. *Dist* Select Pictures Corp. May **1918** [©Select Pictures Corp.; 27 May 1918; LP12456]. Si; b&w. 5 reels, 4,865 ft.

Dir Emile Chautard. *Scen* Paul West. *Story* Edmund Goulding. *Cam* Jacques Bizeul.

Cast: Alice Brady (*Lola Gelardi/Rosetta Gelardi*), Crauford Kent (*Aubrey Hapgood*), Ormi Hawley (*Ruth Hapgood*), Henri Leone (*Prof. Gelardi*), Maude Turner Gordon (*Mrs. Hapgood*), Hazel Washburn (*Mildred Sanders*), Ed Burns (*Dick*), George Henry (*Theatrical agent*).

Drama. Twin sisters Rosetta and Lola Gelardi live happily with their aging father, Professor Gelardi, until their Sicilian village is destroyed by an earthquake. Unable to find Lola, the professor and Rosetta move to New York, where she obtains employment as a stenographer to author Aubrey Hapgood. Rosetta captivates Aubrey and his friends, but Mildred Sanders, who had hoped to win Aubrey for herself, tries to ruin Rosetta's reputation. On a drive with Aubrey, Rosetta relates her life story, whereupon Aubrey, claiming he loves her, takes her to an inn. Although he promises to marry her, she later reads of his engagement to Mildred. Rosetta shoots herself, after which Lola appears to avenge her death by causing the ruin of Aubrey's sister. Aubrey fires on Lola, but Rosetta awakens in his car and realizes that it was all a dream. While the chauffeur repairs the car, she and Aubrey walk into town to find a preacher. Authors. Dreams. Immigrants. Italian Americans. Long-lost relatives. Revenge. Secretaries. Sisters. Suicide. Twins. Chauffeurs. Earthquakes. Inns. New York City. Pledges. Professors. Rivalry. Seduction. Sicily.

Note: The working title of the film was *The Phantom Feud*.

ETR 1 Jun 1918, p. 2031. *MPN* 8 Jun 1918, p. 3343. *MPW* 8 Jun 1918, p. 1479. *NYDM* 29 Jun 1918, p. 927. *Var* 19 Jul 1918, p. 36. *Wid's* 21 Jul 1918, pp. 25-26.

ORDERS FROM TOKYO see SAMURAI

OREGON PASSAGE (Native Americans, Shoshoni)

Lindsley Parsons Productions, Inc. *Dist* Allied Artists Pictures Corp. Jan **1958**; Prod: late Jul—early Aug 1957 [©Allied Artists Pictures Corp.; 7 Jan 1958; LP9556]. Sd; col (DeLuxe); CinemaScope. 7,191 or 7,372 ft. 80-82 min. PCA cert no. 18729.

Prod Lindsley Parsons. *Assoc prod* John H. Burrows. *Dir* Paul Landres. *Asst dir* Lindsley Parsons, Jr. *Scr* Jack DeWitt. *Dir of photog* Ellis Carter. *Film ed* Maury Wright. *Set dec* Jerry Welch. *Ward man* Henry West. *Ward woman* Vou Lee Giokaris. *Mus comp and cond* Paul Dunlap. *Sd eff ed* John Blunk. *Rec* Tom Lambert. *Makeup* Willard Colee. *Hairdresser* Eve Newing. *Prop master* Elmer Stock. *Set cont* Bobbie Sierks. *Chief set elec* Lloyd L. Garnell.

Source: Based on the novel *Rio Bravo* by Gordon D. Shirreffs (New York, 1956).

Cast: John Ericson [(*Lieut. Niles Ord*)], Lola Albright [(*Sylvia Dane*)], Toni Gerry [(*Little Deer*)], Edward Platt [(*Maj. Roland Dane*)], Judith Ames [(*Marion*)], H. M. Wynant [(*Black Eagle*)], Jon Shepodd [(*Lieut. Baird Dolby*)], Walter Barnes [(*Sgt. Jed Ershick*)], Paul Fierro [(*Nato*)], Harvey Stephens [(*Capt. Boyson*)].

Western. [*Print viewed*]. In the rugged Oregon Cascade country of 1871, the U.S. Cavalry searches for the elusive Black Eagle, a Shoshoni warrior who has inflamed the otherwise peaceful local Indians to make frequent attacks on the fort. Determined to subdue Black Eagle, Lieut. Niles Ord, who has spent his life among tribal peoples, raids a ceremonial village, but instead of capturing the rebellious brave, he

takes a more willing prisoner: Little Deer, who had been captured from another tribe to be Black Eagle's bride. Upon returning to the fort, Niles meets his new commander, Maj. Roland Dane, an arrogant man who mistakenly assumes that the Shoshone are similar to the Plains Indians he fought in the Midwest. Dane, insanely jealous of even the smallest attentions shown his pretty but flirtatious wife Sylvia, is already suspicious of Niles, who had a brief romance with Sylvia two years before she met her husband. Bored and resentful at having been brought to a frontier outpost, Sylvia begs Niles to run away with her. Meanwhile, Little Deer tries to convince Niles that she is the woman destined to be his wife. Niles is amused by these attentions, but he is worried about Capt. Boyson, the former commander of the fort, who, because he lapsed into alcoholism after suffering torture at the hands of the Indians, faces a court-martial. Determined to be rid of Boyson, Dane sends him to another fort to face charges, accompanied by only a few soldiers. Soon afterward, Black Eagle returns Boyson, his belly slit open, to Dane's fort on horseback. Niles and his Indian scout Nato try to convince Dane that Black Eagle wants to lure small groups of soldiers from the fort, thereby gradually depleting it of manpower. Dane scoffs at these assertions, however, and orders a detail to find the braves who killed Boyson. Leading the patrol himself, Dane is unaware that the men are being led into a trap. When Black Eagle attacks, all but Dane and one other soldier are killed. Back at the fort, Dane sends Nato to Fort Rock to request reinforcements, but the scout returns with distressing orders: Dane must send troops to Fort Rock to help battle the Modocs. Realizing that few men are left to protect the fort, Niles decides that he must find and kill Black Eagle, who, the drums say, is in a holy place preparing himself for the big attack on the fort. Because Little Deer knows the location of the holy site, she volunteers to lead Niles to the spot, and Niles, impressed with her bravery, finally accepts her love. Niles and Little Deer find Black Eagle, but the warrior escapes. Shortly afterward, Sylvia is captured while taking her daily ride outside the fort. Dane tracks the raiding party to Black Eagle's camp, where, rather than see his wife touched by Indians, he shoots her. They, in turn, kill him, and then ride out to launch the big attack. Back at the fort, the remaining soldiers prepare for the approaching war party by hiding in the cemetery outside the gates, a strategy designed by Niles. As the attacking braves draw near, the troopers surprise them with gunfire, throwing them into complete disarray. Niles pursues Black Eagle and the two men engage in a knife fight. Niles pins Black Eagle to the ground, finally suffocating him in the dirt. As the Cavalry returns to the fort, Little Deer runs out to greet her beloved Niles. *Indians of North America–Social life and customs. Jealousy. Oregon. United States. Army. Cavalry. Abduction. Alcoholics. Battles. Courage. Forts. Indians of North America–Mixed blood. Infidelity. Insubordination. Officers (Military). Romance. Traps. Tribal chiefs. United States–History–Indian campaigns.*

Note: The picture was filmed on location in Oregon's Deschutes National Forest with, as noted in the credits, "the co-operation of the Forest Service, U.S.D.A., and the Bend, Oregon, Chamber of Commerce." *Var* incorrectly lists the name of Jon Sheppod's character as Lieut. Baird Dobson.

DV 23 Jan 1958, p. 3. *FD* 29 Jan 1958, p. 6. *HR* 26 Jul 1957, p. 12. *HR* 9 Aug 1957, p. 12. *HR* 23 Jan 1958, p. 3. *MPHPD* 22 Feb 1958, p. 725. *Var* 29 Jan 1958, p. 6.

THE OREGON TRAIL (Native Americans, Arapaho)

Twentieth Century-Fox Film Corp. *Dist* Twentieth Centery-Fox Film Corp. 13 Aug **1959**; World premiere in Portland, OR: 12 Aug 1959; Prod: late May—early Jun 1959 [©Twentieth Century-Fox Film Corp.; 12 Aug 1959; LP14426]. Sd (RCA Sound System); col (DeLuxe); CinemaScope; CinemaScope lenses by Bausch & Lomb. 7,737 ft. 82 or 86 min. PCA cert no. 19390.

Prod Richard Einfeld. *Dir* Gene Fowler, Jr. *Asst dir* Ralph J. Slosser. *Scr* Louis Vittes and Gene Fowler, Jr. *Story* Louis Vittes. *Dir of photog* Kay Norton. *Art dir* Lyle R. Wheeler and John Mainsbridge. *Supv film ed* Betty Steinberg. *Set dec* Walter M. Scott and Joseph Kish. *Mus comp and cond by* Paul Dunlap. *Makeup* Del Aceredo. *Prod mgr* Harold E. Knox. *Scr supv* Mary Gibson. *Indian tech adv* Iron Eyes Cody.

Song(s): "Ballad of the Oregon Trail," music by Paul Dunlap, lyrics by Charles Devlan; "Never Alone," music and lyrics by Will Miller.

Cast: Fred MacMurray [(*Neal Harris*)], William Bishop [(*Capt. George Wayne*)], Nina Shipman [(*Prudence Cooper*)], Gloria Talbot [(*Shona Hastings*)], Henry Hull [(*Seton*)], John Carradine

[(*Zachariah Garrison*)], John Dierkes [(*Gabe Hastings*)], Roxene Wells [(*Flossie Shoemaker*)], Elizabeth Patterson [(*Maria Cooper*)], Gene N. Fowler [(*Richard Cooper*)], James Bell [(*Jeremiah Cooper*)], John Slosser [(*Johnny*)], Ralph Sanford [(*Mr. Decker*)], Sherry Spalding [(*Lucy*)], Tex Terry [(*Brizzard*)], Ollie O'Toole [(*James G. Bennett*)], Arvo Ojala [(*Ellis*)], Ed Wright [(*Jesse*)].

Western, with songs. [*Print viewed*]. In 1846, the United States, under President James K. Polk, plans to extend the country's borders to the edge of the Oregon territory, despite conflicting claims by the British. Facing possible war, Polk orders soldiers disguised as civilians into the territory. Newspaper publisher James G. Bennett hears rumors of this and dispatches reporter Neal Harris to investigate. Harris joins a wagon train headed by Seton. Also in the train are Capt. George Wayne and soldiers Brizzard and Ellis, all in civilian disguise; beautiful Prudence Cooper, her father Richard, grandmother Maria and brother Jeremiah; and Zachariah Garrison, who is transporting apple trees to Oregon. Along the trail, the wagon train discovers the remains of other settlers, who were attacked by Indians. Seton reveals that he had been married to a Sioux woman who was killed by Arapahos, and the same Indians cut out the tongue of Seton's assistant, Jesse. As the journey continues, Harris begins to suspect that Wayne, Ellis and sadistic drunk Brizzard are soldiers. The settlers' water supplies run low, and just as it starts to rain, ailing Maria dies. Prudence and Wayne fall in love. When Harris interrogates Wayne, the soldier evades his questions, stating that it is dangerous to ask them. Later, they find an Arapaho warning signal and shortly after, Seton is killed. Jesse shoots the Indian who killed Seton, and Wayne takes over as leader of the wagon train. When Harris announces that he is going to notify his paper that soldiers are being sent to the Oregon territory, Wayne assigns Brizzard to guard him. That night, however, Brizzard gets drunk, and Harris steals his horse and leaves the train. Wayne then sends Brizzard to follow him. Harris reaches Fort Laramie and learns that the soldiers have abandoned it. Trapper Gabe Hastings then arrives with his half-Indian daughter Shona, and Harris defends the woman when her father brutally attacks her. Harris sees the wagons approaching and offers to pay Hastings to send his dispatch to the newspaper. Hastings takes his money and then offers to hide Harris in Shona's village. At the fort, Wayne learns that the Oregon boundary dispute has been settled and that the United States is now at war with Mexico. Before he leaves for Mexico, Prudence promises to wait for him. Meanwhile, Harris, Shona and Hastings arrive in the Indian village and see Brizzard tied in the sun. On Hastings' orders, Harris is also taken prisoner. Hastings denounces the settlers for driving the Indians off their land and threatening the livelihood of trappers like him. That night, the Indians hold a war dance, and in the morning, they take Brizzard away. After they leave, Shona, who has fallen in love with Harris, kills his guard and cuts him free. Together they warn the fort that Indians will be attacking. The soldiers, who have not yet left, supply the settlers with guns. As Indians surround the fort, Brizzard appears in a wagon, and Wayne orders the gates open, not knowing that the wagon is filled with Indians. After an intense battle, during which many settlers, including Cooper and Garrison, are killed, the Indians are driven off. Shona renounces her people and continues to Oregon with Harris, who has quit his job on the newspaper. In their wagon is the last of Garrison's apple trees. *Disguise. Indians of North America. Oregon Trail. Reporters. Soldiers. Wagon trains.* Arapaho Indians. Battles. Boundaries. Fathers and daughters. Fort Laramie (WY). Grandmothers. Indians of North America–Mixed blood. Newspaper publishers. James K. Polk. Romance. Ruses. Trading posts. Trappers. Trees.

Note: On 18 May 1959, the *LAT* reported that *Oregon Trail* would have its premiere on the 100th anniversary of Oregon's admission to the Union. Several historical inaccuracies in the film were described in the *HR* review, including the use of Colt revolvers, which were not part of Army equipment until a year later than portrayed in the film, and the fact that the troops marching to the Mexican war were wearing Spanish-American war uniforms. The *Var* reviewer noted that the low-budget film used footage from other pictures and called scenes shot with a painted backdrop "embarrassingly phony." The same reviewer complimented Del Acerdo's Indian makeup, however.

Box 24 Aug 1959. *DV* 13 Aug 1959, p. 3. *Exb* 26 Aug 1959, p. 4618. *FD* 13 Aug 1959, p. 6. *Har* 22 Aug 1959, p. 135. *HR* 29 May 1959, p. 15. *HR* 5 Jun 1959, p. 11. *HR* 13 Aug 1959, p. 3. *LAT* 18 May 1959. *MPHPD* 22 Aug 1959, p. 381. *NYT* 10 Dec 1959, p. 51.

OREGON TRAIL SCOUTS (Native Americans)
Republic Pictures Corp. *Dist* Republic Pictures Corp. 20 May **1947** [©Republic Pictures Corp.; 7 May 1947; LP1112]. Sd (RCA Sound System); b&w. 58 min. Passed by the National Board of Review. PCA cert no. 11957.

Series: Red Ryder.

Assoc prod Sidney Picker. *Dir* R. G. Springsteen. [*Asst dir* Dick Moder and Joe Kramer]. *Orig scr* Earle Snell. *Dir of photog* Alfred Keller. *Spec eff* Howard Lydecker and Theodore Lydecker. *Art dir* Paul Youngblood. *Film ed* Harold R. Minter. *Set dec* John McCarthy, Jr. and George Milo. *Mus dir* Mort Glickman. *Sd* William E. Clark. *Makeup supv* Bob Mark.

Source: Based on the comic strip "Red Ryder" by Fred Harman (1938—1964), by special arrangement with Stephen Slesinger.

Cast: ALLAN LANE (*Red Ryder*), Bobby Blake [(*Little Beaver*)], Martha Wentworth [(*The Duchess*)], Roy Barcroft [(*Bill Hunter*)], Emmett Lynn [(*Bear Trap*)], Edmund Cobb [(*Jack*)], Earle Hodgins [(*Judge*)], Edward Cassidy [(*Bliss*)], Frank Lackteen [(*Running Fox*)], Billy Cummings [(*Barking Squirrel*)], Jack Kirk [(*Stagedriver*)], [Forrest Burns, Ted Elliott, Jack Sparks, Ernest "Tex" Young (*Henchmen*)].

Western. [*Print viewed*]. Near the western town of Wild Horse, fur trapper Red Ryder and his men return from an expedition along the Snake River, and Red meets with Bliss, the agent representing the Indians who control the local trapping rights. Later, an underhanded fur trapper named Bill Hunter tries to persuade the tribe's chief, Running Fox, to allow him to trap beaver in the river. The chief, however, delays his decision, saying he will first need to confer with Bliss. When Red and his Indian friend, Bear Trap, later visit the agent's cabin, they find a note warning them to leave immediately. Red ignores the note and promptly enters the cabin, where he is fired upon by Hunter and his men. A gang of Indian braves comes to Red's aid, and Red escapes. Red decides not to report the incident to the sheriff, knowing that it would worry his aunt, The Duchess. Later, at the Indian village, Red and his pal, Little Beaver, meet with Running Fox, who grants Red unlimited and exclusive rights to trap along the river. In town, Hunter, meanwhile, learns that a confidence man who had interferred with the gang's plot to hold the chief's infant grandson for ransom some years previously, has returned to Wild Horse. Aware that the confidence man is now posing as an apothecary, Hunter finds his medicine wagon and demands to know what he did with the infant. The confidence man refuses to answer, so Hunter kills him and stuffs his body inside the wagon. Moments later, Red begins fighting with Hunter, and the struggle causes the confidence man's corpse to slip from the wagon. Hunter escapes, and Red and Bliss notice later that Little Beaver is missing from the Indian camp. Red then leaves with the confidence man's wagon full of supplies, unaware that The Duchess and Little Beaver have stowed away inside it. Meanwhile, Hunter devises a plot to attack the shipment. That evening, after Red stops to pitch camp, he discovers Little Beaver and The Duchess. After scolding The Duchess for not showing more responsibility, Red leaves the camp to return Little Beaver to town. Along the way, they pass by Hunter's cabin, where his henchmen grab their guns. Red is dragged inside, but escapes after Little Beaver shoots Hunter with an arrow. Red and Little Beaver rush back to the camp to check on The Duchess, then discover that she has been kidnapped. When Little Beaver tells the Indian braves what has happened, they race to Red's aid once again. The braves stop the gang from escaping, and when Hunter grabs Little Beaver, The Duchess hits him over the head with a frying pan. Later, Red and Running Fox realize that Little Beaver is the infant who was kidnapped by the gang. They tell the chief the news, and he explains that Little Beaver's mother died some time ago. When the chief laments that he is too old to care for the boy, Red decides to adopt Little Beaver as his companion. *Adoption. Fur trappers. Indians of North America. Kidnapping. Outlaws.* Aunts. Cabins. Confidence men. Corpses. Escapes. Fights. Grandsons. Hideouts. Indian agents. Medicine shows. Orphans. Sheriffs. Snake River (NW United States). Stowaways.

Note: Modern sources include Jack O'Shea and Chief Yowlachie in the cast. Although this film was a late entry in the "Red Ryder" series, the events depicted predate the first entry, and reveal how "Little Beaver" became Red Ryder's "moppet sidekick." For more information on the "Red Ryder" series, please consult the Series Index and see the entry below for *Tucson Raiders*.

Box 24 May 1947. *DV* 19 May 1947, p. 3. *FD* 20 May 1947, p. 5. *HR* 19 May 1947, p. 3. *MPHPD* 24 May 1947. *Var* 21 May 1947, p. 15.

ORO DE CALIFORNIA see **LA CRUZ Y LA ESPADA**

ORPHAN OF THE SAGE (Native Americans)

FBO Pictures. 23 Dec **1928** [©F.B.O. Productions, Inc.; 23 Dec 1928; LP25972]. Si; b&w. 6 reels, 4,923 ft.

Dir Louis King. *Asst dir* Ken Marr. *Story and cont* Oliver Drake. *Titles* Helen Gregg. *Photog* Nick Musuraca. *Film ed* Jack Kitchen and Della King.

Cast: Buzz Barton (*David [Red] Hepner*), Frank Rice (*Hank Robbins*), Tom Lingham (*Jeff Perkins*), Annabelle Magnus (*Mary Jane Perkins*), Bill Patton (*Nevada Naldene*).

Western. When Red Hepner and his pal, Hank, an old Army scout, join a wagon train headed for Oregon, Nevada Naldene, another old fighter, quickly comes to resent their presence. Hank beats Naldene in a fight, and Naldene frames him for a robbery; Red and Hank are then asked to leave the wagon train. Red discovers Naldene talking to a band of hostile Indians, and rides to warn the wagon train. There is a bitter fight between the settlers and the Indians, and Red rides to Fort Hall for aid. The soldiers rout the Indians, and Red and Hank drift along. *Frame-ups. Indians of North America. Oregon. Scouts (Frontier). Settlers. United States. Army. Cavalry. Wagon trains.*

ORPHANS OF THE GHETTO see **SHOULD A BABY DIE?**

ORPHANS OF THE NORTH see **TAKU**

ORPHEUS see **A LOVE SUBLIME**

OSCAR HAMMERSTEIN'S CARMEN JONES see **CARMEN JONES**

OSCEOLA see **NAKED IN THE SUN**

OST UND WEST see **MAZEL TOV**

TEN OSTATNI (Polish language)

Polonaise Film Productions. **1941**; World premiere in Chicago: 26 Apr 1941. Sd; b&w with some color scenes. Length undetermined. Polish language.

Dir Stefan Zieliński.

Historical, World War II, Documentary, Drama, with songs. [*Not viewed*]. The Nazi invasion of Poland in Sep 1939 is shown, along with the defense efforts of the people of Warsaw, led by their mayor, Stefan Starzynski. Documentary footage includes scenes of German airplanes bombing Poland and citizens falling; destroyed villages and cities; citizens finding shelter from German bombs in basements; and the survival of King Sigismund's Column from the bombing. In the countryside, Janka and Marysi are married in a traditional wedding. Later, they bid each other farewell, moments before the invasion begins. Marysi is wounded during the bombing and dies a few days later in a Warsaw underground shelter. *Invasions. Nazis. Poland–History. Poles. War victims. Warsaw (Poland). World War II. Bombing, Aerial. Mayors. Stefan Starzynski. Village life. Weddings.*

Note: The English language translation of the film's title is *The Last.* Newspaper articles and announcements appearing in Chicago Polish-language newspapers call this the first Polish film made in Hollywood and state that it "was made due to the efforts of Poles to show how Warsaw and the whole country defended itself against the German invasion in September 1939." An announcement states that the film "depicts the whole truth about defending the Polish capital; the gigantic struggle of the Polish people, their suffering, terror, devastation, [and] the resistance of the citizens of Warsaw led by the brave president of Warsaw, Stefan Starzynski."

The characters of "Janka" and "Marysi" are fictional, as is the story of the wedding. Some of the scenes were shot in color, and the film included some Polish songs. An announcement in a Polish-language newspaper for the premiere at the Holy Trinity Auditorium in Chicago on 26 Apr 1941 stated "we must support what is ours."

Polonaise Film Productions had studios in Topanga Canyon, CA. Director Stefan J. Zieliński was a Chicago-based actor, theater director and radio announcer, who was born in Poland and came to the U.S. as a child. Zieliński also founded and directed theaters in Polish communities in large American cities other than Chicago. Another Polish-language film dealing with the Nazi invasion of Poland, also produced in Hollywood and shown in Chicago in May 1941, was *Z Dymem Pożarów* (see below).

Dziennik Chicagoski 5 Apr 1941, p. 3. *Dziennik Chicagoski* 14 Apr 1941, p. 5. *Dziennik Chicagoski* 24 Apr 1941, p. 3. *Dziennik Chicagoski* 25 Apr 1941, p. 8. *Dziennik Chicagoski* 26 Apr 1941, p. 3. *Dziennik Chicagoski* 16 May 1941, p. 11. *Dziennik Chicagoski* 17 May 1941. *Dziennik Związkowy (Zgoda)* 22 Feb 1941. *Dziennik Związkowy (Zgoda)* 3 Apr 1941. *Dziennik Związkowy (Zgoda)* 9 Apr 1941. *Dziennik Związkowy (Zgoda)* 24 Apr 1941. *Dziennik Związkowy (Zgoda)* 26 Apr 1941.

OTHELLO IN HARLEM see **PARADISE IN HARLEM**

THE OTHER MAN see **THEY KNEW WHAT THEY WANTED**

THE OTHER MAN'S WIFE (Jewish Americans)

A Carl Harbaugh Production. *Dist* Frank G Hall through Film Clearing House, Inc. and Independent Sales Corp. 29 Jun **1919** [©British-American Pictures Finance Corp.; 17 May 1919; LP13733]. Si; b&w. 6 reels.

Pres Frank G. Hall. *Dir* Carl Harbaugh. *Story and scen* Mary Murillo. *Cam* William Crowley.

Cast: Ellen Cassidy (*Mrs. Fred Hartley*), Stuart Holmes (*J. Douglas Kerr*), Ned Hay (*Fred Hartley*), Olive Trevor (*Elsie Drummond*), Halbert Brown (*Bruce Drummond*), Mrs. Garrison (*Mrs. Bruce Drummond*), Lesley Casey (*Wilbur Drummond*), Danny Sullivan (*Jimmy Moore*), Regina Quinn (*Betty Moore*), Laura Newman (*Mrs. Moore*), Georgie Jessel (*Davy Simon*), Evelyn Brent (*Becky Simon*).

Society, Drama. Three New York families are introduced: wealthy Fred Hartley and his wife, who, feeling neglected, encourages the attentions of debonair J. Douglas Kerr; the middle-class Moore family, consisting of mother, daughter, and son Jimmie who supports them; and the Simons, an East Side Jewish family. When America enters the war, Hartley, Jimmie, and Davy Simon enlist. When Jimmy says goodbye to his sweetheart Becky, one of Davy's three sisters, her father refuses to consider him as a future son-in-law. Kerr sends Mrs. Hartley a cablegram reporting Hartley's death in the war. She puts off responding to Kerr's proposal, and after the armistice, Hartley finds her trying to break free from Kerr's embrace. When Kerr hastily exits, an irate butler grabs his trousers. Mr. Simon accepts Jimmie as Becky's fiancé, and Kerr is last seen squatting so that his overcoat covers his backside. *Class distinction. Family life. Marriage–Mixed. Military service, Voluntary. Missing persons, Assumed dead. World War I. Butlers. Cads. Jews. Neglected wives. New York City.*

Note: The film opened in New York on 8 Jun 1919. *Wid's* credits William Crowley as the cameraman for this film, but the name is probably a misspelling of William S. Crolly, who shot numerous other films. The film was dedicated to women who proved during World War I that they were equal to men.

ETR 21 Jun 1919, p. 221. *MPN* 21 Jun 1919, p. 4215. *MPW* 7 Jun 1919, p. 1434 (ad insert). *MPW* 21 Jun 1919, p. 1827. *NYT* 9 Jun 1919, p. 16. *Var* 13 Jun 1919, p. 50. *Wid's* 15 Jun 1919, p. 11.

EL OTRO SOY YO (Spanish language)

Darío Productions, Inc. *Dist* Paramount Pictures, Inc. **1939**; San Juan, Puerto Rico opening: 27 Oct 1939; Los Angeles opening: 27 Aug 1940; Prod: Feb 1939 at Grand National Studios. Sd; b&w. Length undetermined. PCA cert no. 5211. Spanish language.

Prod Darío Faralla. *Dir* Richard Harlan. *Dial dir* Gabriel Navarro. *Orig story* Dana Wilma. *English scr* Mortimer Braus. *Spanish dial* Enrique Uhthoff. *Photog* Jerry Ash. *Mus dir* Lud Gluskin. *Prod mgr* Irving Applebaum.

Song(s): "Tal vez mañana," "Capricho gitano," "Matarili-ri-li-ron" and "El vagabundo," words and music by Tito Guízar.

Cast: Tito Guízar (*Pepe Nuñez/Tomás Nuñez*), Renée Torres (*María Ramírez*), Pilar Arcos (*Tía Crescencia*), Martín Garralaga (*Francisco Jerez*), Amanda Varela, Tana, Robina Duarte, Carlos Villarías, José Luis Tortosa, José Peña "Pepet", María Nieves, Carlos Montalbán, José Perez, King Wallace, "Arroyito", Raúl Lechuga.

Romantic comedy, with songs. [*Not viewed*]. Handsome young Pepe Nuñez prefers to roam the world as a vagabond singer and fisherman, while his staid identical twin brother Tomás manages the family shoe factory. While visiting his brother in San Francisco, Tomás tells Pepe that he is needed in Panama for an important business deal and asks Pepe to impersonate him while he is gone so that his competitors, the Bermejillos, will not know that he has left town. Happy-go-lucky Pepe agrees to pose as Tomás, president of the Nuñez Shoe Company, and his first act is to appoint his sidekick, Paco Jerez, as an efficiency expert. In the role of Tomás, Pepe revolutionizes office routines at the factory. He introduces streamlined shoes, entertains the employees with his singing and promotes the pretty blonde information clerk to the position of Paco's secretary. He also presents Rita Castro, Tomás' cabaret-singer girlfriend, with a $10,000 bracelet and falls in love with his Aunt Crescencia's niece, Eva Collado. When Paula Bermejillo, the pretty business representative from the rival firm, suggests a merger, Pepe, who finds her attractive, proposes that they discuss it over dinner. After visiting the night

spots, a very drunk Pepe blunders into the nightclub where Rita is performing and causes a jealous scene. In the morning, Pepe learns that while drunk, he signed a contract prohibiting the Nuñez Shoe Company from making rubber galoshes. When Pepe learns that Tomás has sent a fleet carrying raw rubber from Panama, he decides to manufacture rubber tires, and promotes the new product on a radio broadcast featuring himself as a mystery singer. Although the radio program is a great success, Tomás wires Pepe to discontinue it. When Eva discovers that Pepe is only posing as president, she condemns him, and Pepe, believing that he has lost her love, disappears with Paco. Soon after, Tomás returns and realizes that Pepe's radio tire project is a sensation and he and Eva, now contrite for their condemnation of Pepe, begin to search for him. They find him at the docks, aboard a tramp steamer, singing for the tire company by remote control. Pepe is delighted when he discovers that he has redeemed himself in Tomás' eyes, especially when Eva comes aboard and suggests a honeymoon cruise for two. *Impersonation and imposture. Shoe manufacturers. Twins. Vagabonds. Aunts. Business competition. Contracts. Cousins. Drunkenness. Jealousy. Radio broadcasting. Rubber. Secretaries. Singers. Tires. Rubber.*

Note: The summary of this film was based on materials contained in the Paramount Script Files at the AMPAS Library. The working title of the picture was *La vuelta del hijo pródigo* (*The Prodigal Returns*), and it was released in Chile on 5 Mar 1940 under the title *El vagabundo.*

CM Jun 1939, p. 250. *DV* 30 Mar 1939. *HR* 31 Mar 1939, p. 3.

OUR CHRISTIANITY AND NOBODY'S CHILD (African Americans)
Maurice Film Co. *Dist* Maurice Film Co. Jul—Sep 1920. Si; b&w. 5-6 reels, 5,500 ft.

Cast: Richard Maurice, Jacques Farmer, Alex Griffin, Joe Green, Max Johnson, Vivian Maurice, Howard Nelson.

African American, Drama. A motherless brother and sister are persecuted by their evil stepfather, who kidnaps the girl and imprisons her in a dive. A fistfight between the boy and the stepfather leads to the death of the latter, and the boy is arrested and sentenced to death. The boy's cellmate, a former drug addict, helps him escape from prison, and the boy is finally exonerated, pardoned, and reunited with his sister. *African Americans. Brothers and sisters. Executions. Orphans. Stepfathers. Drug addicts. Fistfights. Kidnapping. Prison escapes.*

Note: First exhibited in the fall of 1920 under the titles *Our Christianity and Nobody's Child* and *Our Christianity and Nobody's Children,* this black production was renamed *Nobody's Children* and was first exhibited under that title on 22 Dec 1920. Contemporary sources alternately refer to one of the cast members as Jacques Farmer and Jacque Farmer. Modern sources state that in order to free his sister, the protagonist kills the stepfather's gangster crony as well as the stepfather, and is arrested for both killings.

ChiDef 24 Jul 1920. *ChiDef* 11 Dec 1920, p. 4. *ChiDef* 25 Dec 1920, p. 4. *ChiDef* 8 Jan 1921, p. 5.

OUR DAILY BREAD (Italian Americans, Jewish Americans, Swedish Americans)
Viking Productions, Inc. *Dist* United Artists Corp. 28 Sep 1934; Prod: 2 Apr—early May 1934 at United Artists Studios [©Viking Productions, Inc.; 28 Sep 1934; LP5019]. Sd (Western Electric Sound System); b&w. 80 min. PCA cert no. 59.

Dir King Vidor. [*Dial dir* Mortimer Offner]. [*Asst dir* Ralph Slosser]. *Story* King Vidor. *Scenario* Elizabeth Hill. *Dial* Joseph Mankiewicz. *Photog* Robert Planck. [*2d cam* Reggie Lanning]. *Film ed* Lloyd Nosler. *Rec* Vinton Vernon. [*Sd eng* Russell Hanson]. [*Tech dir* Lloyd Brierly]. [*Prod mgr* Vernon Keays]. [*Casting* Ray Hanson]. [*Agricultural adv* Otho Wilhite]. [*Still photog* Madison Lacey].

Cast: Karen Morley (*Mary Sims*), Tom Keene (*John Sims*), Barbara Pepper (*Sally*), Addison Richards (*Louie* [*Fuente, alias of Harry J. Parkman*]), John Qualen (*Chris* [*Larsen*]), Lloyd Ingraham [(*Uncle Anthony*)], Sidney Bracey [(*Rent collector*)], Henry Hall [(*Carpenter*)], Nellie V. Nichols [(*Cohen's wife*)], Frank Minor [(*Plumber*)], Bud Rae [(*Stone mason*)], Harry Brown [(*Little man*)], [Madame Bonita (*Mother*)], [Harold Berquist (*Father*)], [Marion Ballou (*Old lady*)], [Alma Ferns (*Mrs. Larsen*)], [Three Milsfield children (*Larsen children*)], [Lionel Backus (*Barber*)], [Harris Gordon (*Cigar salesman*)], [Bill Engle (*A. Cohen*)], [Frank Hammond (*Undertaker*)], [Lynton Brant (*Bully*)], [Harry Bradley (*Professor*)], [C. E. Anderson, Captain (*Blacksmith*)], [Harrison Greene (*Sheriff*)], [Cy Clegg (*Lawyer*)], [Ray Spiker (*Tough guy*)], [Eddie Baker (*Deputy sheriff*)], [Harry Barnard (*Chief*)], [Doris Kemper (*First gossiping woman*)], [Florence Enright (*Second gossiping woman*)], [Harry

Semels (*Italian shoemaker*)], [Sidney Miller (*Jewish boy*)], [Alex Schumberg (*Violinist*)], [Bob Reeves (*George Hannibal*)], [Edward Peil, Sr. (*Powerhouse man*)], [Jack Baldwin (*Motorcyclist*)], [Mary Gordon (*Woman in cottage*)], [Clarence Geldert].

Social, Drama. [*Print viewed*]. Overwhelmed by bill collectors, Mary Sims and her unemployed husband John eagerly accept the proposal of Mary's uncle Anthony to move from the city and farm a tract of fallow land on which Anthony has been paying mortgage. Soon after the young New Yorkers arrive at the ramshackled farm, however, they realize that, their enthusiasm not withstanding, they are ill-equipped to restore the barren land. Consequently, when Chris Larsen, a dispossessed, Swedish farmer from Minnesota, is stopped alongside the Sims's field with a flat tire, John suggests that, in exchange for his farming expertise, he and his family live on his land and share in the farm's output. After Chris accepts the offer, John is seized with an idea that other unemployed but skilled men could benefit the farm effort and, the next day, puts signs along the highway advertising work for ten men with trades. To his surprise, the signs bring in dozens of men and their families, all of whom beg John for a chance to work hard. Although only some of the men have labor skills, John accepts every one into the group, and after all the families agree to pool their meager resources, the group, which includes a Jewish and an Italian family, elects John "boss" of the operation. Working together as a collective, the men till the land and plant corn seeds, while the women make homes out of hand-built shacks. Eventually, corn seedlings sprout, and a baby boy is born to the Jewish family. However, the joy of the collective is soon tempered by the realization that, because no mortgage payments have been made on the land, the farm is to be auctioned by the county sheriff. At the auction, the potential buyers are intimidated into silence by the group, and the sheriff is forced to sell the farm for $1.85 to a member of the collective. Soon after, Sally, a tough-talking platinum blonde, drives up to the farm during a rainstorm and, when she learns that her drunken male companion has just died, accepts Mary's offer to stay. As Mary grapples with the growing food shortage, Sally begins to flirt with John and ignores the warnings of the taciturn but loyal Louie Fuente to leave John alone. When the food shortage nears the crisis point, Louie goes to Chris and, after showing him a poster that identifies him as a fugitive, offers to turn himself in for the $500 reward. Although Chris refuses to help Louie, Sally agrees to pose as Mary in town and collect the reward money. After Sally returns to the farm with the money, John arranges for the group lawyer to plead Louie's case in court. Assured that Louie will serve a minimum sentence, the group spends the reward money, and the hunger crisis passes. Soon, however, the corn is plagued by drought, and total crop failure appears imminent. As the dry days drag on, the community falls into despair, and John is filled with self-doubt. When Mary hears John talk scathingly about the farm, she suspects Sally is behind his unhappiness and confronts her rival directly. Sally confesses to loving John and threatens to leave the farm with him in tow. Unable to resist Sally's seductive pull, John sneaks away with her the next night, but is soon stopped on the road by a vision of Louie. With Louie's disapproving face still lingering in his mind, John notices that the local power plant has resumed operation and has filled a nearby stream with water run-off. Inspired with an idea, John dumps Sally and rushes back to the farm. After gathering the disillusioned group together, John proposes that, if they work day and night, they can build a trench from the stream and divert enough water to save the corn. Although skeptical at first, the group pledges to make the effort, and after two backbreaking days, the trench is built and the crops are salvaged. As water rushes into the parched corn field, a reunited John and Mary embrace. *Agriculture, Cooperative. Farms. Infidelity. Self-sacrifice. Unemployment. Auctions. Childbirth. Corn. Droughts. Food. Fugitives. Hunger. Italian Americans. Jews. Lawyers. Mortgages. Rainstorms. Rewards. Rivers. Sheriffs. Swedish Americans. Visions.*

Note: The title frame of the viewed print included the qualifier: "Inspired by the Headlines of Today." Director King Vidor describes the genesis of the picture in his autobiography: "I wanted to take my two protagonists out of *The Crowd* [a 1928 silent film directed by Vidor] and follow them through the struggles of a typical young American couple in this most difficult period [the Depression]. I started by clipping every article relating to the subject from the local newspapers. Then I read a short article by a college professor in *Reader's Digest.* It proposed the organization of co-operatives as a solution to the unemployment problem." (According to a publicity item included in the copyright records, the article was titled "The Agricultural Army.") Not under contract to any studio, Vidor first took his idea to Irving G. Thalberg at M-G-M,

according to Vidor's autobiography, and although Thalberg was enthusiastic about the concept, he was unable to sell it to his studio and told Vidor that it was not "an appropriate subject for M-G-M." Vidor says: "The fact that my characters were unemployed and down to their last few pennies seemed to scare the studios. They seemed intrigued by the story...but all the major companies were afraid to make a film without glamor, even though admitting that the struggle depicted was a heroic one."

Modern sources and Vidor's autobiography describe how the production progressed: In the summer of 1933, Vidor took his idea to Merian C. Cooper at RKO Radio Pictures and offered to forego his directorial salary in exchange for a production deal. Cooper was more than agreeable and instructed RKO's legal department to draw up a one-picture contract in which Vidor would receive $25,000 in advance against a 50% equity in the gross receipts after double negative costs. In exchange, Vidor was expected to post a $50,000 bond for the any production cost over the studio's $250,000 budget. While his contract was being written, Vidor and his wife, screenwriter Elizabeth Hill, began working on a script based on the articles. RKO hired various writers, including John Bright, a Chicago journalist and screenwriter, to assist them. Bright contributed the character of "Sally" to the story. In addition, Vidor's good friend, Charlie Chaplin, offered story suggestions. (According to *NYT* review, Vidor got the idea for the character of "Louie" from Chaplin.) By the end of Nov 1933, however, RKO's New York legal department concluded that because the terms of Vidor's contract could result in the director earning more profits than the studio, the deal was untenable. For the next few months, Cooper fought the decision of the New York office but got nowhere. Finally, after being turned down by all the major studios, Vidor decided to finance the picture himself and formed Viking Productions on 9 Feb 1934, with himself as president and sole stockholder.

Before any banks would lend him production money, however, Vidor had to find a distributor. He appealed to Chaplin, one of the owners of United Artists, for support. Although with Chaplin's help, Vidor secured a tentative releasing agreement with United Artists, he still was unable to get a bank loan because "when a banker reads a script in which a bank forces a sheriff to make a foreclosure sale which a disreputable-looking group of neighbors won't permit, he doesn't feel kindly toward your venture."

Despite his lack of financial backing, Vidor started production work in mid-Mar 1934 and advanced $89,628 of his own money to the effort. According to a mid-Mar 1934 *HR* news item, Vidor moved his cast and crew from General Studios, where he had preparing for two months, to United Artists' Studios. To save money on location shooting, Vidor rented part of an abandonded golf course in Tarzana, near Los Angeles, and erected tents to house the cast and crew. According to copyright materials, some of the farm scenes in the film were shot at Edgar Rice Burrough's 160-acre ranch, "Tarzana." Several weeks into filming, Vidor finally received a $125,000 loan from Bank of America, with the proviso that he mortgage his remaining assets.

Because he saw the picture as a continuation of *The Crowd*, Vidor's first impulse was to cast James Murray, the star of *The Crowd*, in the lead. However, when he discovered that Murray had slipped deeply into alcoholism, he gave up on the idea and cast Tom Keene, an actor he thought resembled Murray. In addition to choosing a Murray look-alike, Vidor also gave Keene's and Karen Morley's characters the same first names as their equivalents in *The Crowd*. According to a Feb 1934 *HR* news item, Arline Judge was under consideration for a role in the film. Modern sources claim that Adele Thomas also was tested for a role. *HR* production charts include Henry Burroughs in the cast, but his participation in the final film has not been confirmed. Although Harry Holman is credited in several contemporary and modern sources as playing the part of "Uncle Anthony," Lloyd Ingraham actually appeared in the role.

In his autobiography, Vidor describes his technique for shooting the final ditch digging sequence: "We dispensed with all sound-recording equipment and used instead a metronome and a bass drum. The picks came down on the counts of one and three, the shovels scooped dirt on count two and tossed it on four. Each scene was enacted in strict 4/4 time with the metronome's speed gradually increasing on each cut. When the increased speed of the metronome resounding through the bass drum had driven the diggers to their most feverish pitch, we then resorted to decreasing the camera speed gradually, which in turn further increased the tempo of the workers." This sequence took ten days to stage and photograph. When the production ran over schedule, somes scenes were changed to cut costs. The total cost of filming was a modest $102,811, and the negative cost was $150,339. Vidor recalls that he eventually recouped his initial investment but never made significant money on the picture. A late May 1934 *HR* news item claimed that Vidor hired a 35-person "synchronizing and editing staff" and spread them over a 24-hour work schedule in order to ready the film for its release.

A 1 Aug 1934 *FD* news item notes that the picture had its premiere in Chicago at the "Century of Progress" exhibition. The opening was attended by 15,000 people, including international celebrities, area civic and industrial leaders, newspapermen and the governors of Illinois, Massachusetts, Mississippi, Rhode Island, Vermont and South Carolina. In early Oct 1934, the picture had a special White House screening, which President Roosevelt attended, according to *FD*. The *DV* running time of ninety minutes suggests that the film was cut by at least ten minutes before its general release. It is possible that some of the above-listed supporting actors were cut from the final film.

According to Vidor's autobiography, the film won second prize in the annual film exhibition in Moscow, and also won a League of Nations award "for its contribution to humanity." In 1935, the film was distributed under the title *The Miracle of Life*, according to AMPAS records. Although United Artists distributed the film in its initial release, Astor Pictures Corp., which was credited on the viewed film, eventually took over distribution. Modern sources note that Astor sold the picture as an exploitation film and retitled it *Hell's Crossroads*.

DV 2 Apr 1934, p. 4. *DV* 2 Jul 1934, p. 3. *FD* 1 Aug 1934, p. 2. *FD* 8 Aug 1934, p. 7. *FD* 2 Oct 1934, p. 8. *HR* 24 Feb 1934, p. 3. *HR* 13 Mar 1934, p. 2. *HR* 19 Mar 1934, p. *HR* 2 May 1934, p. 3. *HR* 24 May 1934, p. 3. *HR* 2 Jul 1934, p. 3. *IP* May 1934, p. 16. *MPD* 3 Jul 1934, p. 7. *MPH* 19 May 1934, p. 61. *MPH* 18 Aug 1934, p. 38. *NYT* 3 Oct 1934, p. 25. *Var* 9 Oct 1934, p. 18.

OUR VINES HAVE TENDER GRAPES (Norwegian Americans)
Metro-Goldwyn-Mayer Corp.; controlled by Loew's Inc. *Dist* Loew's Inc. Sep **1945**; New York opening: 6 Sep 1945; Prod: 16 Oct—27 Dec 1944; added scenes began 9 Apr 1945 [©Loew's Inc.; 1 Sep 1945; LP13461]. Sd (Western Electric Sound System); b&w. 9,491 ft. 105 min. Passed by the National Board of Review. PCA cert no. 10713.

Prod Robert Sisk. *Dir* Roy Rowland. [*Asst dir* Horace Hough]. *Scr* Dalton Trumbo. *Dir of photog* Robert Surtees. [*2d cam* A. Lindsley Lane]. *Spec eff* A. Arnold Gillespie and Danny Hall. [*Matte paintings* Warren Newcombe]. [*Matte paintings, cam* Mark Davis]. *Art dir* Cedric Gibbons and Edward Carfagno. *Film ed* Ralph E. Winters. *Set dec* Edwin B. Willis. *Assoc* Hugh Hunt. *Cost supv* Irene. *Assoc* Kay Carter. *Mus score* Bronislau Kaper. *Rec dir* Douglas Shearer. [*Unit mixer* Frank B. MacKenzie]. [*Re-rec and eff mixer* Standish J. Lambert, Robert W. Shirley, Newell Sparks, William Steinkamp, Michael Steinore and John A. Williams]. [*Mus mixer* Edward Baravalle and M. J. McLaughlin]. *Makeup created by* Jack Dawn. [*Unit mgr* Keith Weeks].

Source: Based on the novel *For Our Vines Have Tender Grapes* by George Victor Martin (New York, 1940).

Cast: EDWARD G. ROBINSON (*Martinius Jacobson*), MARGARET O'BRIEN (*Selma Jacobson*), James Craig (*Nels Halverson*), Frances Gifford (*Viola Johnson*), Agnes Moorehead (*Bruna Jacobson*), Morris Carnovsky (*Bjorn Bjornson*), Jackie "Butch" Jenkins (*Arnold Hanson*), Sara Haden (*Mrs. Bjornson*), Greta Granstedt (*Mrs. Faraassen*), Dorothy Morris (*Ingeborg Jensen*), Arthur Space (*Pete Hanson*), Elizabeth Russell (*Kola Hanson*), Louis Jean Heydt (*Mr. Faraassen*), Charles Middleton (*Kurt Jensen*), Francis Pierlot (*Minister*), Johnnie Berkes (*Circus driver*), [Arthur Hohl (*Dvar Svenson*)], [Tommye Adams (*Girl*)], [Rhoda Williams (*Marguerite Larson*)].

Rural, Drama. [*Print viewed*]. While walking down a road in Fuller Junction, Wisconsin, a town settled by Norwegian immigrants, seven-year-old Selma Jacobson tries to impress her five-year-old cousin, Arnold Hanson, by throwing a rock at a squirrel. Much to Selma's dismay, the rock hits the squirrel and kills it. While Selma tearfully mourns the death of the squirrel, Ingeborg Jensen, a young, emotionally frail Norwegian woman, approaches Selma and Arnold and offers them her friendship. Ingeborg's visit is interrupted, however, by her strict father Kurt, who demands that she return to her chores. Later, while driving Arnold and Selma home, Nels Halverson, the editor of the local newspaper, stops to greet Viola Johnson, the new schoolteacher, who has just arrived from Milwaukee. Viola accepts a ride from Nels, and when asked about her impression of Fuller Junction, she complains that the town is too small for her. She also tells Nels that she is working on her doctorate in education, and that she was sent to Fuller Junction because she is of Norwegian descent and speaks Norwegian. Determined to change her impression of Fuller Junction, Nels offers to show Viola some of the town's hidden charms. When Selma returns home, she reports the squirrel incident to her devoted father Martinius, who tries to help his daughter forget about it by giving her a new calf. Viola, meanwhile, befriends Ingeborg and encourages her to enroll in school. Her efforts are thwarted, however, when Kurt refuses to allow Ingeborg to leave the farm. One day, Martinius punishes Selma for selfishly refusing to share her rollerskates with Arnold, and sends her to bed without dinner. Later that night, Martinius, feeling guilty about punishing Selma, takes her to see a circus troupe that is passing through town. A short time later, Ingeborg dies unexpectedly, and her death saddens Viola, the only person in town who made an effort to understand her. A romance eventually develops between Nels and Viola, but Viola resists further intimacy because she plans to return to Milwaukee. On Christmas Day, at her church, Selma gives a moving recitation of the story of the Nativity, and afterward presents her father with a brand new knife. Months later, when springtime floodwaters engulf the town, Selma and Arnold play in an old bathtub, which they use as a makeshift rowboat. The two quickly lose control of the tub, however, and are carried away by a raging current. The near tragedy ends happily, however, when Arnold and Selma are rescued by some of the townspeople. One night, during a thunderstorm, Bjorn Bjornson's

barn catches fire and is destroyed. At a church service, Nels solicits donations to help the Bjornsons rebuild their barn. The townspeople drop only a few coins into collection box until Selma shames everyone by generously donating her calf. Her donation inspires the townspeople to give more money, and prompts Viola to reconsider her harsh judgment of the town. Realizing that she has fallen in love with both the town and Nels, Viola decides to stay in Fuller Junction. *Children. Family life. Norwegian Americans. Rural life.* Barns. Battered Children. Charity. Christmas. Circuses. City-country contrast. Cousins. Editors. Elephants. Farmers. Farms. Fathers and daughters. Fires. Floods. Grief. Mental illness. Mothers and daughters. Proposals (Marital). Rescues. Roller-skating. Romance. Schoolteachers. Wisconsin.

Note: Some *HR* production charts list Connie Gilchrist in the cast, but she did not appear in the final film. Portions of the film were shot at the Rowland V. Lee ranch in the San Fernando Valley. In Jul 1946, according to a *HR* news item, Mrs. Selma Martin, the estranged wife of author George Victor Martin, and Arnold Hansen, a Tacoma, WA, salesman, filed a $25,000 lawsuit against M-G-M, claiming that the film was based on their lives, and that the picture caused them to suffer "undue public attention, mental anguish and humiliation." The outcome of the suit is not known. Margaret O'Brien and Frances Gifford recreated their roles for a *Lux Radio Theatre* version of the story, which was broadcast on 2 Sep 1946.

Box 21 Jul 1945. *DV* 20 Jul 1945, p. 3. *FD* 20 Jul 1945. *HR* 6 Oct 1944, p. 11. *HR* 17 Oct 1944, p. 8. *HR* 24 Nov 1944, p. 16. *HR* 22 Dec 1944, p. 14. *HR* 27 Dec 1944, p. 1. *HR* 10 Apr 1945, p. 9. *HR* 19 Jul 1945, p. 3. *HR* 10 Sep 1945, p. 8. *HR* 29 Jul 1946, p. 3. *MPHPD* 16 Dec 1944, p. 2230. *MPHPD* 21 Jul 1945, p. 2553. *NYT* 7 Sep 1945, p. 21. *Var* 18 Jul 1945, p. 34.

OUT OF A CLEAR SKY (Belgian Americans)

Famous Players-Lasky Corp. *Dist* Famous Players-Lasky Corp.; Paramount Pictures. 15 Sep **1918**. Si; b&w. 5 reels.

Pres Adolph Zukor. *Dir* Marshall Neilan. *Scen* Charles Maigne. *Cam* Walter Stradling.

Source: Based on the novel *Out of a Clear Sky* by Maria Thompson Daviess (New York, 1917).

Cast: Marguerite Clark (*Countess Celeste de Berseck et Krymn*), Thomas Meighan (*Robert Lawrence*), E. J. Radcliffe (*Uncle Dyreck*), Bobby Connelly (*Bill*), Raymond Bloomer (*Crown prince*), Robert Dudley (*Father*), Walter P. Lewis (*Steve*), Maggie H. Fisher (*Granny White*), Helene Montrose (*Jane Forsythe*), Robert Vivian (*Valet*), Nell Clark Keller (*Mamie*).

Drama. During World War I, the Countess Celeste de Berseck et Krymn flees her native Belgium in order to escape forced marriage with a German prince. Furious, Celeste's traitorous Uncle Dyreck pursues her to the United States, and when she realizes that he is on her train, she departs at the nearest station, Greenwood, Tennessee, and runs straight into the arms of the wealthy Robert Lawrence. Promising to protect her, Robert takes the countess to Steve Budd's cabin and then goes in search of Uncle Dyreck. Celeste befriends a young boy named Bill, who asks her to accompany him to Granny White's house, where his mother is having a baby, and as the two are leaving, the Budd cabin is hit and completely destroyed by lightning. Upon his return, Robert assumes the worst, and Uncle Dyreck, believing his niece to be dead, returns to Belgium. Robert is overjoyed to find Celeste and Bill at Granny White's, and after the countess discovers that Robert loves her, she happily bids farewell to her title and prepares to become an American housewife. *Belgian Americans. Immigrants. Nobility. Tennessee. Wealth.* Childbirth. Lightning. Marriage–Forced. Trains. Traitors. Uncles. World War I.

ETR 5 Oct 1918, p. 1527. *MPN* 5 Oct 1918, p. 2249. *MPW* 28 Sep 1918, p. 1926. *MPW* 5 Oct 1918, p. 120. *NYT* 23 Sep 1918, p. 7. *Var* 27 Sep 1918, p. 42. *Wid's* 29 Sep 1918, p. 2.

OUT OF THE CRIMSON FOG (African Americans)

Paragon Pictures. *Dist* State Rights. **1932**; Prod: late Mar—mid Apr 1932. Sd; b&w. Length undetermined.

Dir Charles White. *Cam* George Coudert.

Cast: Thomas Moseley, Inez Clough, Fay Miller, Lawrence Chenault.

African American, Drama. [*Not viewed*]. [No information concerning the plot of this film has been located.]. *African Americans.*

Note: The only contemporary information located concerning this film are two 1932 *FD* news items: A 21 Mar news item calls the film *Hell Valley* and states that it was "scheduled for immediate production" with an "all Negro cast." On 17 Apr, *FD* noted that production on *Out of the Crimson Fog* had been completed. Paragon Pictures was located in New York City. No additional information concerning the film's release has been located. Although *FD* calls the film a "feature," its exact length has not been determined. Modern sources refer to both a 1931 film, *Hell's Alley*, and a 1932 film, *The Crimson Fog*, as

having been produced by Paragon with Thomas Moseley and Fay Miller in the cast. As no contemporary information has been located concerning either *Hell's Alley* or *The Crimson Fog*, it is likely that both are the same as *Out of the Crimson Fog*. Modern sources include Jean Webb in the cast of *Hell's Alley*, and list Hattie Watkins and Jean Webster as the writers. Additional cast members, listed in modern sources, for *The Crimson Fog* include Vera Temple, Billy Andrews, Kitty Arblanche, Billy Sheppard and Alvin Childress. Modern sources also indicate that *The Crimson Fog* was a silent film.

FD 1 Mar 1932, p. 2. *FD* 17 Apr 1932, p. 4.

OUT OF THE FOG *see* ESCAPE IN THE FOG

OUT OF THE PAST *see* NAZI AGENT

OUTBREAK *see* PANIC IN THE STREETS

THE OUTLANDER *see* UNTAMED FURY

THE OUTLAW (Native Americans)

Hughes Productions. *Dist* United Artists Corp.; RKO Radio Pictures, Inc. **1943**; Feb **1946**; Jan **1950**; World premiere in San Francisco: 5 Feb 1943; Prod: mid-Nov 1940—early Feb 1941 at General Service Studios and Samuel Goldwyn Studios; addl shooting began late Mar 1941 [©Hughes Productions; 15 Feb 1941; LP177]. Sd; b&w. 121 or 123 min. PCA cert no. 7440.

Pres HOWARD HUGHES. *Prod* Howard Hughes. *Dir* Howard Hughes and [Howard Hawks]. *Asst dir* Sam Nelson and [Art Black]. [2d unit dir Arthur Rosson]. [Fill-in dir Jules Furthman]. *Scr* Jules Furthman. *Photog* Gregg Toland and [Lucien Ballard]. *Photog eff* Roy Davidson. *Supv film ed* Otho Lovering. *Film ed* Wallace Grissell. *Settings* Perry Ferguson. *Mus dir* Victor Young. *Sd* Frank Maher. *Prod mgr* Cliff Broughton.

Cast: Jack Beutel [(*William Bonney, also known as Billy the Kid*)], Thomas Mitchell [(*Pat Garrett*)], Jane Russell [(*Rio McDonald*)], Walter Huston [(*Doc Holliday*)], [Mimi Aguglia (*Guadalupe*)], [Joe Sawyer (*Charley Woodruff*)], [Gene Rizzi (*Stranger*)], [Emory Parnell (*Dolan*)], [Martin Garralaga (*Waiter*)], [Julian Rivero (*Pablo*)], [Bobby Callahan (*Boy*)], [Arthur Loft (*Swanson*)], [Ethan Laidlaw (*Deputy*)].

Western. [*Print viewed*]. Shortly after he disembarks at the Lincoln, New Mexico train depot, gunslinging gambler Doc Holliday reunites with his old friend and former partner-in-crime, Pat Garrett. When Pat, who is now the town's sheriff, hears that the penniless Doc is searching for his horse Red, who has been stolen, he directs his friend to the local dentist's office. There Doc finds Red tied up outside and confronts the young man who comes to claim the horse. Although the youth, William Bonney, an infamous gunslinger known as Billy the Kid, maintains that he bought Red from a stranger, Doc insists that he stole him. Despite their disagreement, Doc takes Billy's side when Pat tries to arrest him for theft. Annoyed, Pat orders Doc and the smooth-talking, quick-fisted Billy to leave town by sundown. Doc and Billy, however, ignore Pat's command and play cards together in the cantina. Doc wins hand after hand from Billy and is unruffled when his rival accuses him of cheating. After Doc announces he is giving Red to Billy as a gift, however, he tries to sneak the horse out of the barn, but is caught in the act by a watchful Billy. Moments later, as Billy is about to settle down next to Red, he is shot at by an unseen assailant. In the darkness of the barn, Billy overpowers his attacker, who turns out to be a beautiful woman named Rio McDonald. While struggling to free herself, Rio condemns Billy for murdering her brother and vows to kill him. Billy admits to shooting Rio's brother in a fight over a woman, but insists that the match was fair and gives Rio a passionate kiss. The next morning, in the cantina, Billy is approached by a stranger who identifies himself only as an enemy of Pat. The stranger enlists Billy's help in confronting Pat and suggests they stage a mock fight as practice. Suddenly sensing a set-up, Billy draws his guns one second before the stranger does and kills him. After they learn that the stranger was actually a friend of Pat, Doc advises Billy to flee, but Billy insists on facing the sheriff. Maintaining that he was pushed into the gunfight, Billy refuses to give himself up to Pat and his deputies, and is shot by Pat. Before Pat can fire his rifle again, Doc shoots the gun out of his hand and downs two of his deputies. As Doc and a wounded Billy are about to leave the cantina, Pat angrily declares his friendship with Doc "finished." Doc takes Billy to recuperate at Rio's house, unaware that Rio, his girl friend, had previously tried to kill Billy. After Doc leaves, Rio contemplates stabbing the unconscious Billy, but is unable to do the deed. Instead, Rio and her aunt Guadalupe nurse Billy through fever and chills until,

one month later, he is recovered. Rio admits to Billy that she is Doc's "girl," but gives in to his seductive charm and kisses him. Soon after, Doc returns and learns that Rio married Billy during one of his delirious periods but has not told him about their new relationship. Although Doc is angered by Rio's change of heart, he is more infuriated by Billy's continued insistence that Red is his horse. To resolve the matter, Billy offers Doc a choice between Red and Rio. Doc quickly picks Red over Rio, and the two men ride off toward the desert together. When they see Pat approaching in the distance, they deduce that Rio revealed their route and then discover that she filled their canteens with sand. After a thirsty night, Doc wakes to find Billy gone and Pat at his side. Pat arrests Doc, while Billy sneaks into Rio's house and takes her by surprise. Later, on the trail, Doc and Pat find Rio tied between two rocks, abandonded with no water. Confident that Billy will return to free Rio, Doc and Pat lie in wait for him. As predicted, Billy shows up the next morning and is apprehended. While Doc and Billy argue about whether Billy is in love with Rio, a hostile Indian group sends smoke signals announcing the white men's presence. Pat, Billy and Doc jump on their horses and head for nearby Fort Sumner, but are soon overtaken by the Indians. Reluctantly, Pat gives Billy and Doc guns, and the three men charge madly for the fort, chased closely by the Indians. By dragging cacti behind them, the men create a moving dust storm, which causes the Indians to give up their pursuit. While the men stop at a house to rest, Pat gives owner Pablo a note to deliver to the Fort Sumner marshal. Overhearing Pat and Pablo's conversation, Doc is about to flee on Red when he is stopped by Billy, who insists once more that the horse belongs to him. Billy challenges Doc to a duel over Red, and although Billy outdraws Doc, he is unable to shoot him. Annoyed by Billy's sudden passivity, Doc shoots the youth's hand and then his earlobes. Stating that Doc is the only partner he has ever had, Billy refuses to fight back, however, and the two men finally reconcile. Humiliated by Doc's obvious preference for Billy, Pat explodes with anger and shoots Doc. The next morning, after a remorseful Pat and Billy bury their friend, Pat allows Billy to leave. As he is about to ride off, Billy invites Rio to join him, and Rio happily accepts. *Billy the Kid. Friendship. Fugitives. Pat Garrett. Doc Holliday. Rivalry. Romance. Sheriffs.* Aunts. Burial. Chases. Deserts. Duels. False accusations. Gunfights. Gunshot wounds. Horses. Indians of North America. Kisses. Marriage–Secret. Mexican Americans. New Mexico. Nursing back to health. Poker (Game). Reputation. Revenge. Thirst.

Note: The film's title card reads: "Howard Hughes presents his production of *The Outlaw*." The film includes a written epilogue, which states that the truth about Billy the Kid "lies hidden forever among the secrets of the Old West." Unlike the character in the film, the real Pat Garrett, a New Mexico sheriff, tracked down and shot Billy the Kid in 1881. Before becoming a lawman, Garrett had been a buffalo hunter, a cowboy and a Texas Ranger. In 1882, Garrett wrote a book called *The Authentic Life of Billy the Kid*. While working as a rancher in 1902, he was shot and killed by an unidentified gunman. Many films have featured Pat Garrett, including the 1930 M-G-M film *Billy the Kid* (see *AFI Catalog of Feature Films, 1921-30*; F2.0419), directed by King Vidor and starring Wallace Beery as Garrett; the 1950 film *I Shot Billy the Kid*; and the 1973 film *Pat Garrett and Billy the Kid*, in which James Coburn played Garrett. Although Doc Holliday was a gambler and gunman, as depicted in the film, he is not known to have tangled with Billy the Kid or Pat Garrett. Best known for his association with Wyatt Earp and Bat Masterson, Holliday died of tuberculosis and alcoholism in 1887. Other films featuring Doc Holliday include the 1946 John Ford picture *My Darling Clementine*, in which Victor Mature played the character, and the 1994 Warner Bros. Western *Wyatt Earp*, directed by Lawrence Kasdan and starring Dennis Quaid as Holliday.

Contemporary news items add the following information about the film's production: Howard Hawks, who had worked with Hughes on the 1932 film *Scarface*, was the film's initial director, and Twentieth Century-Fox was its initial distributor. When production began, Hughes and Fox were in competition with M-G-M, which was readying to shoot *Billy the Kid*, and a spring 1941 release date was set. In mid-Nov 1940, Hawks and his crew left for location shooting in Arizona and New Mexico. Some scenes were filmed in Moencopi, near Tuba City, AZ, and second unit shooting was done in Socorro, NM. On 10 Dec 1940, after two weeks of shooting, Hawks quit the project. According to a 15 Dec 1940 *NYT* article, Hughes, who had the dailies flown back to Los Angeles every day, accused Hawks of economizing too much and not "taking enough time" with filming. Hawks reportedly argued that, as his salary consisted of a percentage of the film's profits, it was in his best interest to keep production costs down. In a modern interview, however, Hawks claimed that he left the production so that he could shoot *Sergeant York* with Gary Cooper and happily turned the reins over to Hughes.

Hughes took over direction of the film on the Samuel Goldwyn lot in late Dec 1940. Hawks's director of photography, Lucien Ballard, was replaced by Gregg Toland at that time, and Hughes announced that the entire picture would be reshot. It has not been determined if any of Hawks and Ballard's material was used in the released film. (In her autobiography, Jane Russell noted that Hawks did not direct any of her scenes.) Pat West, Billy Newell and Nena Quartero were announced as cast members, but their participation in the final film has not been confirmed. According to an internal memo contained in the MPAA/PCA files at the AMPAS Library, screenwriter Jules Furthman filled in for Hughes as director on 31 Dec 1940, after Hughes became "indisposed." Modern sources state that Furthman filled in as director for many days.

Although the film was completed and copyrighted in Feb 1941, it was not shown theatrically until Feb 1943. The delay was due, in part, to censorship problems with the PCA. Materials in the MPAA/PCA files at the AMPAS Library provide the following information about the picture's censorship battle: In a late Dec 1940 letter to Hughes, PCA director Joseph I. Breen complained that the film's final script depicted Billy the Kid as a "major criminal who goes unpunished." He also objected to the suggestion of "illicit sex between Billy and Rio," the "trick marriage," and the "undue brutality and unnecessary killings." Furthman conferred with PCA official Geoffrey Shurlock and agreed to change the objectionable elements of the script, in part by showing that Billy was innocent of the crime for which he was being hunted. Modern sources add that, during filming, Furthman repeatedly alerted Shurlock and others at the PCA about possible problem scenes in the production. In Mar 1941, Hughes also notified Shurlock about a new scene he was adding—a "bed" scene in which Rio nurses Billy by warming him with her body—which Shurlock approved. The 1941 retakes and added scenes, including the bed scene, cost Hughes $127,000, according to a *NYT* article.

After the film itself was screened in late Mar 1941, however, Breen wrote to Hughes that the picture was in violation of the Code and would not be issued a certificate. In addition to objections regarding the "illicit relationship between Doc and Rio," which was epitomized by the bed scene, Breen condemned the "countless shots of Rio in which her breasts" were not "fully covered." In a Mar 1941 interoffice memo, Breen said about *The Outlaw*: "...in my more than ten years of critical examination of motion pictures, I have never seen anything quite so unacceptable as the shots of the breasts of the character of Rio....Throughout almost half the picture the girl's breasts, which are quite large and prominent, are shockingly emphasized..." Breen acknowledged in the same memo, however, that, because of the way in which the scenes were filmed, most of the "breast" shots could not be easily eliminated. After Breen refused to issue a certificate for *The Outlaw*, Hughes requested an appeal hearing from the MPPDA in New York. The MPPDA board of directors screened the picture in early Apr 1941 and ruled in mid-May to uphold the MPAA/PCA decision. Both Breen and MPPDA representatives conferred with Hughes about eliminations, and a long list of specific cuts involving Russell's breasts was drawn up. Hughes made the requested changes, and by late May 1941, Breen agreed to approve the film, with a "footnote" stating that "approval is based upon the understanding and agreement that all prints put into general release are to conform exactly to the changes agreed upon." In all, approximately forty feet of film was actually cut.

In mid-Aug 1941, after Breen had left the PCA to be production chief at RKO, a PCA memo reported that Hughes had submitted an unedited version of the picture to various state censor boards, hoping to bypass the PCA in those areas. According to the memo, Hughes discovered that some state censors wanted many more cuts than the PCA had demanded. At the same time, Fox, which would have been subject to a $25,000 MPPDA fine for releasing an unapproved picture, backed out of its distribution deal. Hughes continued to battle the state censors until the end of 1941, then shelved the picture for over a year. (Modern sources note that after America's entrance into World War II, Hughes focused all of his attention on his airplane manufacturing company and all but abandoned his filmmaking ventures.)

According to modern sources, by late 1942, his film company had spent months trying to find and acquire the best theater in which to open the picture. The picture, running at 115 minutes, finally opened in San Francisco's Geary Theater on 5 Feb 1943 and caused an immediate furor. MPAA/PCA files indicate that The Legion of Decency condemned the picture and questioned the PCA's wisdom in approving it. In addition, a new controversy erupted over the film's advertising, which had been engineered by Hughes's publicist, Russell Birdwell. Birdwell, who had spent much of 1942 promoting Russell as Hollywood's newest star, ordered billboards to be posted around the city, with a still of the actress in a provocative pose, captioned by phrases such as "How would you like to tussle with Russell?" The Motion Picture Council of San Francisco wrote to the PCA to object to the "very disgusting portrayal of the feminine star...on large billboards." After public protests by the Council, the police ordered the billboards removed. In its review of the San Francisco opening, *Var* called Birdwell's ad campaign "bosom art" and speculated that the film would profit at the box office because of it. As predicted, *The Outlaw* did well in San Francisco, grossing $10,000 in its first week. Russell and co-star Jack Beutel performed a live twenty-minute scene that had been cut from the film's script following each screening of the six-week San Francisco run. Comedian Frank McHugh was added to the stage show on 15 Feb 1943.

In Mar 1943, MPPDA official Francis S. Harmon screened a print of *The Outlaw* in Hollywood in anticipation of the film's New York run and noted that it contained footage that had not been previously approved. Hughes maintained that he was merely re-editing the picture because of complaints by critics that it was too long, but in Jul 1943, Harmon revealed in an interoffice memo that seven prints of the film were in existence and only one print, Print 3, contained the PCA approved edits. Harmon advised Hughes to use Print 3 in New York to appease its censor board, which had already condemned the film. In the same memo, Harmon expressed fears that the picture might inspire juveniles to commit crimes and that Hughes and Hollywood would be blamed. Still preoccupied with the war, Hughes instead withdrew *The Outlaw* after its San Francisco run and put it back on the shelf until early 1945.

At that time, *HR* announced that United Artists, which was not a signatory

with the MPPDA, would release the film in early 1946 as part of its new distribution deal with Hughes and his then filmmaking partner, Preston Sturges. Although Harmon assured the president of United Artists in a Jan 1946 letter that the picture "Hughes intends to release is the same as the picture approved in 1941," problems regarding the film's advertising delayed the film's re-issue. In a 9 Apr 1946 letter to Hughes, the secretary of the MPAA in New York noted that the unapproved advertising and exploitation of the picture constituted "grounds for...suspension or expulsion from [MPAA] membership" as they violated Article XIV of the organization's by-laws. According to the secretary, the by-laws specified that "standards of fair representation and good taste in the advertising of motion pictures" must be honored and that all advertising must be submitted in advance to the Advertising Code Administration for approval.

On 24 Apr 1946, the day after the film re-opened in San Francisco, Al Dunn, the manager of the United Artists theater, was arrested for exhibiting a film "offensive to decency," and prints of the film were seized. (Dunn was later cleared of all charges.) On 26 Apr 1946, Hughes, anticipating the revocation of the film's Production Code seal, announced his resignation from the MPAA and filed a $1,000,000 lawsuit against the organization in New York, with a request for triple damages. Hughes, under his corporate name, Hughes Tool Co., motioned for a stay of judgment empowering the MPAA to revoke its seal. A temporary injunction restraining the MPAA from interfering with the distribution of prints or advertising accessories was issued at that time by Judge Vincent L. Leibell, pending a later hearing. Through Russell Birdwell, Hughes argued that the Hays Office was "violating the First Amendment of the Constitution of the United States" and was in violation of anti-trust laws. In court, Hughes's lawyers argued that, through implied monetary penalties, which would result if the MPAA refused to issue a certificate to a given film, the MPAA used coersive tactics to force its members to comply with its demands. In an amended complaint, dated 18 Mar 1947, Hughes's lawyers added that Hughes's company had lost an estimated 7.5 million dollars in revenue as a result of the revocation.

On 14 Jun 1946, Judge John Bright vacated Judge Leibell's restraining order and ruled against Hughes, maintaining that the MPAA had not breached their contract and that Hughes Tool Co. "cannot have its cake and eat it too." Hughes immediately appealed Bright's ruling, and the MPAA agreed that it would take no action against the film pending the appeal. On 6 Sep 1946, however, Breen announced that *The Outlaw's* certificate was being revoked because of Hughes's continued refusal to submit for approval "all advertising and publicity material" connected to the film. The MPAA then filed a counter-claim against Hughes, asking the court to order Hughes to remove the Production Code seal from all prints of *The Outlaw*. Hughes eventually lost his appeal.

Despite the various legal battles, United Artists continued to roadshow *The Outlaw* in 1946 and 1947. An elaborate countrywide promotional tour, complete with skywriting and a blimp, set off in Jun 1946. The film, however, generated protests and bans throughout the country. Archbishop John J. Cantwell, writing in the Catholic publication *The Tidings*, stated that no Catholic could see *The Outlaw* "with a free conscience." In Minneapolis, *The Outlaw* was pulled in May 1946 and replaced by *The Postman Always Rings Twice*, a picture that also encountered censorship difficulties. The Interstate Circuit in Texas refused to show the film in Jun 1946 because of complaints from clergymen. In Sep 1946, municipal Judge E. Paul Mason upheld an exhibition ban in Maryland, commenting that Russell's "breasts hung like a thunderstorm over a summer landscape." A Kansas censor complained to the PCA that Hughes's office had hired lawyers to try to force the Kansas censor board into passing the picture without eliminations. After Hughes refused to make some requested cuts, the Ohio censors banned the film in mid-Dec 1946. In Indianapolis, however, the mayor refused to ban the picture, calling it "just a western." *HR* reported that many projectionists had practiced "inadvertent" censorship of the film, clipping out the "hot" scenes for their own private collections. A version dubbed in Spanish was completed in mid-Nov 1946 at the Eastern Service Studios in Astoria, New York.

An uncensored version of the film opened in London on 29 Nov 1946. Although the film itself received poor reviews, the British press praised Hughes for battling the MPAA. London journalist Sunderland Echo was quoted as saying, "This long-delayed attack on American censorship is welcome, for if Hughes wins his case it will open the way to more wholehearted sincerity in American films and will provide a better market for British films." A huge advertising banner of Russell generated a "nudity complaint" from the London County Council, however.

New York's censor board banned the picture in Nov 1946, an action that was publicly denounced by the National Board of Review of Motion Pictures. In mid-Dec 1946, after an appellate division upheld the board's decision, United Artists asked the New York Supreme Court to rule on the state's decision. In late Dec 1946, New York City's licensing commissioner tried to have the film's license revoked, but when the State Board of Regents discovered that it did not have the authority to revoke the film's license, it asked the state legislature in late Jan 1947 to give the Department of Education the authority to revoke film licenses on grounds of suggestive advertising. Hughes's lawyers then filed an appeal with the New York Supreme Court, requesting that the License Commission's claims be dismissed. In early Apr 1947, Hughes's appeal was dismissed, and after some consideration, Hughes chose not to pursue the matter any further. In mid-Sep 1947, the New York licensing commissioner finally lifted the ban on the film, saying that the objectionable material had been adequately altered. *The Outlaw* opened in New York on 11 Sep 1947 and was screened on a twenty-four-hour-a-day schedule, with "cleaned-up" advertising. In Nov 1947, General Bennett Meyers stated at a Congressional hearing investigating Howard Hughes's wartime business dealings that Hughes had authorized him to offer $150,000 to the Legion of Decency in exchange for the lifting of the New York ban. Hughes reportedly denied the charge, saying that it would not have been worth it for him to buy off the Legion.

In Aug 1948, Hughes forced Howard Hawks to recut a "gun-draw" scene from his 1948 United Artist release *Red River* because, he claimed, it was plagiarized from *The Outlaw*. Hughes argued that he had paid Hawks $150,000 for the story rights to *The Outlaw*, as well as for his services as director. Borden Chase, the credited writer on *Red River*, stated in affidavits that he resigned from the project in protest when Hawks asked him to write the disputed scene. In mid-Aug 1948, Hughes filed a motion for an injuction against *Red River* before its opening in Texas, and a hearing to consider the motion was scheduled for 19 Aug 1948 in Dallas. Anxious to avoid a lawsuit, United Artists executive Edward Small agreed to allow Hughes to cut the scene himself, and Hughes subsequently removed the entire scene from the film. However, in the end, only 30 seconds were cut from *Red River*. (For more information on the dispute, see entry below for *Red River*.)

Despite the complaints and the bans, *The Outlaw* broke box office records everywhere it was shown. A late Feb 1947 *HR* news item speculated that, in cities where it had played, the film had been seen by about sixty-five percent of the total population. In late Aug 1948, after Hughes had become production head at RKO, the film was acquired for distribution by RKO, but because it lacked a PCA certificate, the studio did not immediately release it. In late Oct 1949, however, the PCA reinstated the film's certificate and the Legion of Decency, in reaction to certain changes made by Hughes, removed the picture from its "C" classification. By that time, the picture, which was made for approximately $1,200,000, had already made $4,500,000. Hughes sued United Artists in Nov 1950, claiming that the company had short-changed him $133,000 in receipts. The disposition of that suit is not known. By Apr 1952, the picture had grossed $2,600,000 for RKO. In Jun 1968, *HR* reported that *The Outlaw* had made over $20 million at the box office.

As noted above, Russell made her screen debut in *The Outlaw*. Jack Beutel also made his official screen debut in the picture. According to modern sources, Beutel was compelled by Hughes to change the spelling of his name to "Buetel," and although his name appears as "Beutel" in the onscreen credits, advertisements and some reviews list it as "Buetel." *HR* reported that Russell was tested by 20th Century-Fox in mid-1940, but was subsequently dropped by the studio. According to an unidentified contemporary source, Hughes picked the nineteen-year-old Russell, a doctor's receptionist, during a search for new talent. The same source noted that for the scene in which Rio writhes while tied between two stakes, Hughes designed a special brassiere for the actress to wear. In her autobiography, Russell stated that Hughes wanted a seamless look for the shot, but as his bra was extremely uncomfortable, she created the desired effect with her own bra by covering the seams with tissue and pulling the straps off her shoulders. The *NYT* review said of Russell's performance in the picture: "This was the first picture in which the beauteous Jane Russell appeared and, while she is undeniably decorative in low-cut blouses, she is hopelessly inept as an actress." In her autobiography, Russell herself described her performance as "terrible."

In addition to Russell's performance, the film itself was soundly criticized. The *Time* reviewer described the picture as a "strong candidate for the flopperoo of all time." The *NYT* reviewer pronounced *The Outlaw* "strictly second-rate," noting that it was "long and tedious and crudely acted for the most part." In May 1948, the Library of Congress, however, publicly acclaimed the film as a "picture that truly reflected the modes and morals of the times in which the action takes place." For their compliment, Hughes gave the Library two prints of the film. Modern sources add the following actors to the cast: Frank Darien, Carl Stockdale, Dickie Jones, Ed Brady, William Steele, Wallace Reid, Jr., Ed Peil, Sr., Lee "Lasses" White, Ted Mapes, Lee Shumway, Dick Elliott, John Sheehan, Frank Ward and Cecil Kellogg.

Box 13 Feb 1943. *DV* 3 Dec 1940. *DV* 8 Feb 1943, p. 3. *DV* 9 Sep 1946. *DV* 10 Sep 1946. *DV* 25 Oct 1949. *FD* 15 Feb 1943, p. 7. *HR* 8 Nov 1940, p. 3. *HR* 18 Nov 1940, p. 2. *HR* 29 Nov 1940, p. 10. *HR* 10 Dec 1940, back cover. *HR* 12 Dec 1940, p. 3. *HR* 13 Dec 1940, p. 3. *HR* 21 Jan 1941, p. 3. *HR* 31 Jan 1941, p. 11. *HR* 16 May 1941, p. 1. *HR* 9 Dec 1941, p. 7. *HR* 8 Feb 1943, p. 3. *HR* 20 Feb 1945, p. 2. *HR* 25 Apr 1946, p. 1. *HR* 6 May 1946, p. 2. *HR* 8 May 1946, p. 16. *HR* 9 May 1946, p. 1. *HR* 22 May 1946, p. 15. *HR* 27 May 1946, p. 2. *HR* 7 Jun 1946, p. 1. *HR* 17 Jun 1946, p. 20. *HR* 24 Jun 1946, p. 2. *HR* 28 Jun 1946, p. 2. *HR* 2 Jul 1946, p. 3. *HR* 28 Aug 1946, p. 4. *HR* 10 Sep 1946, p. 1. *HR* 12 Sep 1946, p. 1, 9. *HR* 2 Oct 1946, p. 4. *HR* 4 Nov 1946, p. 1. *HR* 12 Nov 1946, p. 3. *HR* 27 Nov 1946, p. 14. *HR* 2 Dec 1946, p. 4, 16. *HR* 11 Dec 1946, p. 1. *HR* 16 Dec 1946, p. 3. *HR* 14 Jan 1947, p. 23. *HR* 20 Jan 1947, p. 11. *HR* 24 Jan 1947, p. 1. *HR* 24 Feb 1947, p. 13. *HR* 4 Apr 1947, p. 1. *HR* 25 Apr 1947, p. 1. *HR* 5 Sep 1947, p. 3. *HR* 12 Sep 1947, p. 2. *HR* 17 Sep 1947, p. 1. *HR* 13 Nov 1947, p. 6. *HR* 11 Feb 1948, p. 4. *HR* 18 May 1948, p. 10. *HR* 16 Aug 1948, p. 1, 5. *HR* 19 Aug 1948, p. 1. *HR* 20 Aug 1948, p. 1, 4. *HR* 27 Aug 1948, p. 1. *HR* 30 Sep 1948, p. 1. *HR* 10 Oct 1949, p. 1, 4. *HR* 3 Jan 1950, p. 1, 4. *HR* 17 Jan 1950, p. 2. *HR* 2 Nov 1950, p. 1, 8. *HR* 26 Jun 1968. *LAEx* 21 Oct 1940. *LAHE* 20 Sep 1947. *LAT* 10 Oct 1949. *MPH* 13 Apr 1946. *MPH* 27 Apr 1946, p. 15. *MPHPD* 13 Feb 1943, p. 1157. *MPHPD* 23 Mar 1946, p. 2905. *MPHPD* 31 Dec 1949, p. 138. *NYT* 15 Dec 1940. *NYT* 30 Mar 1941. *NYT* 11 May 1941. *NYT* 25 May 1941. *NYT* 6 Sep 1942. *NYT* 6 May 1945. *NYT* 6 Jan 1946. *NYT* 12 Sep 1947, p. 18. *NYT* 11 Nov 1947. *SF Chron* 5 Feb 1943. *SF Chron* 8 Feb 1943. *SF Chron* 28 Mar 1943. *Var* 10 Feb 1943. *Var* 23 Apr 1952.

OUTLAW EXPRESS (Latino)

Universal Pictures Co., Inc. *Dist* Universal Pictures Co., Inc. 17 Jun **1938**; Prod: began early May 1938 [©Universal Pictures Co.; 17 Jun 1938; LP8092]. Sd (Western Electric Mirrophonic Recording); b&w. 6 reels. 56 min. PCA cert no. 4300.

[*Prod* Trem Carr]. [*Assoc prod* Paul Malvern]. *Dir* George Waggner. *Asst dir* Glenn Cook. *Orig story and scr* Norton S. Parker. *Cine* Harry Neumann. *Art dir* Charles Clague. *Film ed* Charles Craft. *Set dresser* Albert Greenwood. *Mus dir and arr* Frank Sanucci. *Sd tech* Charles Carrol and Edwin Wetzel. [*Publicity unit wrt* Wallace X. Rawles].

Song(s): "Amigo Mio," "Down the Trail with the Pony Express," "Out to California," "Outlaw Express," "Shot" and "Then You'll Be My Loreta," words and music by Fleming Allan.

Cast: BOB BAKER (*Bob* [*Bradley*]), Cecilia Callejo (*Lorita* [*Ricardo*]), Don Barclay (*Andy* [*Sharpe*]), Leroy Mason (*Sommers*), Nina Campana (*Lupe*), Martin Garralaga (*Don Ricardo*), Forrest Taylor (*Ferguson*), Carlyle Moore (*Bill Cody*), Julian Rivero (*Don Diego*), Jack Kirk (*Phelps*), Carleton Young (*Ramon*), Apache (*Apache*), [Arthur Van Slyke (*Postmaster*)], [Ed Cassidy (*Officer*)].

Historical, Western, with songs. [*Print viewed*]. In 1860, Captain Bob Bradley of the United States Cavalry, is sent on an undercover assignment with his sidekick, Andy Sharpe, to find out why Pony Express riders on the California/Nevada route are being killed but not robbed. In Placita, California, at the United States Land Office, Spanish land grants are being recorded and then the applications are sent via Pony Express to Washington, D.C. After being hired to pose as Pony Express riders, Andy and Bob head out to the Ricardo ranch to purchase more horses for the Express. While there, Bob falls in love with Don Ricardo's beautiful and spirited daughter Lorita. When Ricardo's neighbor and friend, Don Diego, is killed after filing a grant, and outlaw ranchers then claim his land as their own by presenting a signed land grant application, Bob realizes a connection exists between the Express killings and the Spanish land grants. Andy overhears the outlaws plot to take over all of the ranching area by killing Express riders and stealing the land grants. Andy forewarns Don Ricardo, the outlaws' next intended victim, and as predicted, finds Bob on the trail with the dead body of the Express agent. This time, however, it is clear that Don Ricardo's land grant has been stolen. Realizing that Don Ricardo is in danger, Bob forms a posse from the Express riders and rides to the Ricardo ranch, which is under siege. Although many are killed, the posse arrives in time to save Ricardo and his daughter, and eradicate the thieving outlaws. With the murderers caught, the Pony Express and Don Ricardo's ranch are restored to peace, and Bob and Andy decide to quit the cavalry so they can live the California ranch lifestyle. *Bandits. California–History–1846-1850. Latino. Land rights. Murder. Pony express. Undercover operations. Indians of North America. Ranchers. United States. Army. Cavalry.*

Note: The working title of this film was *Pony Express Days*. This film marks Cecelia Callejo's American film debut. Although her first name is listed as "Cecelia" on this film, she is listed as "Cecilia" in later films. Modern sources include Jack Ingram, Tex Palmer, Chief Many Treaties, Ray Jones, Joe Dominguez and William McCauley in the cast.

FD 20 Jul 1938, p. 6. *HR* 9 Mar 1938, pp. 14-15. *MPH* 28 May 1938, p. 58. *Var* 20 Jul 1938, p. 12.

OUTLAW TRAIL (Native Americans)

Monogram Pictures Corp. *Dist* Monogram Pictures Corp. 29 Apr **1944**; Prod: early Dec 1943 [©Monogram Pictures Corp.; 16 Mar 1944; LP12534]. Sd; b&w. 4,804 ft. 53 min.

Series: The Trail Blazers.

Prod Robert Tansey. *Dir* Robert Tansey. *Asst dir* Art Hammond. *Orig story* Alvin Neitz. *Scr* Frances Kavanaugh. *Cine* Edward Kull. *Film ed* John C. Fuller. *Mus dir* Frank Sanucci. *Sd eng* Glen Glenn. *Prod mgr* Fred Hoose.

Cast: HOOT GIBSON [(*Hoot Gibson*)], BOB STEELE [(*Bob Steele*)], CHIEF THUNDERCLOUD [(*Chief Thundercloud*)], Rocky Camron [(*Sheriff Rocky Camron*)], Jenifer [sic] Holt [(*Alice Thornton*)], Cy Kendall [("*Honest John*" *Travers*)], Geo. Eldridge [(*Carl Beldon*)], Warner Richmond, Chas. King [(*Chuck Walters*)], Bud Osborn [(*Blackie*)], Jim Thorp [sic] [(*Spike*)], John Bridges [(*Ed Knowles*)], Hal Price [(*H. A. Fraser*)], Chas. Murray, Jr.

Western. [*Print viewed*]. Banker "Honest John" Travers controls Johnstown by issuing his own scrip to the ranchers and then forcing them to comply with his terms or go bankrupt. Travers' dominion is threatened when Carl Beldon, a representative of the Midwest Packing Company, arrives in town with $20,000 in cash to buy cattle from the local ranchers. When Beldon disappears soon after, his employer suspects foul play and notifies the U. S. Marshal's office. Marshals Hoot Gibson, Bob Steele and Chief Thundercloud, known as "The Trail Blazers," eagerly accept the case after they receive a letter from their dying friend, Bob Thornton, the owner of the Flying T ranch in Johnstown. In his letter, Thornton, who has been mortally wounded by a gang of renegades, appeals to his friends to manage the ranch for his daughter Alice. Upon arriving in town, Bob goes to the saloon, posing as the new foreman of the Flying T, while Hoot visits

their old friend, Sheriff Rocky Camron, to enlist his help in ending the lawlessness that pervades the territory. At the saloon, Bob antagonizes Blackie and Spike, two of Travers' henchmen, and Hoot and the Chief come to his aid. The Blazers then ride to the Flying T, but find that it is deserted. Blackie, who has followed them there, listens at the window as the marshals discuss Alice's impending arrival on the next stage. The Blazers then ride into town to meet Alice, but when the stage arrives, they learn that a man in a wagon has already picked her up just outside of town. Alice, meanwhile, has discovered that Blackie, the man who came to greet her, really intends to kidnap her. Soon after, the marshals gallop to her rescue and apprehend Blackie. Travers' gang observes the proceedings and dispatches Bud, a deputy in Travers' employ, to take Blackie into custody. After riding away with Blackie, Bud releases him and Blackie rides to town to notify Travers that Alice has arrived. Meanwhile, the Blazers accompany Alice to the Flying T, where Hoot discovers a scrap of burnt paper with Beldon's name written on it. Soon after, Rocky comes to the ranch and Hoot shows him the paper. When Rocky proposes that either Bud or Chuck Walters, Travers' right-hand man, could explain the meaning of the paper, Hoot suggests investigating Travers but Rocky objects, claiming that Travers has been like a father to him. Soon after, the marshals learn that Travers is forcing the ranchers to include their herds in his cattle drive, and Bob rides to Jud Hanson's ranch to investigate. Arriving just as one of Travers' thugs is ordering Hanson to add his cattle to the drive, Bob intervenes and thrashes the thug. Bob then solicits Hanson's cooperation in destroying Travers and asks him to assemble the ranchers so that they can stop the drive. In town, meanwhile, Travers has learned of Bob's interference and instructs Rocky to arrest him for attempted murder. Rocky refuses, however, and tells Travers that Bob is a U.S. Marshal. That night, Rocky rides to the Flying T to notifiy the marshals that Travers has started the drive early and that all the supply wagons have left except one. When Rocky mentions that he saw the wagon parked alongside the bank, the marshals become suspicious. While Bob and Hoot ride to town to investigate, the Chief waits at the ranch for Hanson and the others. By the time Bob and Hoot arrive at the bank, the wagon is gone. When Bob opens the safe, he discovers Travers' dead body inside and all the cash missing. Surmising that Walters shot Travers and then stole the money, Bob and Hoot follow the wagon tracks. Walters, meanwhile, has hidden the cash in an abandoned mine, and consequently, when Hoot and Bob find the wagon, it is empty. Returning to the ranch, Hoot and Bob are met by Hanson, who tells them that the ranchers have gone to halt the drive. Soon after, the Chief returns to the ranch and tells Bob that he has found the cash stashed in the mine. Rocky and the Blazers then ride back to town to confront Walters and his gang. When Walters sees them, he realizes that something has gone amiss and sends Bud to the sheriff's office to discover what is happening. As Bud enters the office, Rocky pulls a gun on him and forces him to confess that Walters killed Travers and Beldon. While Bob confronts Walters at the saloon, Hoot and the Chief face Blackie and the others in the street. After apprehending Walters and his gang, the Blazers return the cash to the ranchers, then leave Alice and the Flying T in Rocky's care and ride off to their next assignment. *Bankers. Murder. Outlaws. Ranchers. United States. Marshals. Cattle drives. Confession (Law). Deputies. Fathers and daughters. Indians of North America. Kidnapping. Letters. Rescues. Robbery. Saloons. Sheriffs. Undercover operations.*

Note: Although a *HR* production chart places Henry Hall in the cast, his participation in the released film has not been confirmed. Modern sources add Frank Ellis, Al Ferguson, Tex Palmer, Lee Roberts and Denver Dixon to the cast. For additional information on the "Trail Blazers" series, please consult the Series Index.

Box 3 Jun 1944. *DV* 24 Mar 1944, p. 6. *HR* 3 Dec 1943, p. 8. *HR* 24 Mar 1944, p. 3. *MPHPD* 4 Mar 1944, p. 1786. *MPHPD* 1 Apr 1944, p. 1826. *Var* 10 May 1944, p. 10.

OUTLAW VALLEY see RUSTLERS

OUTLAWS OF SIOUX CITY see RUSTLERS OF DEVIL'S CANYON

OUTLAWS OF SIOUX CITY see ON THE OLD SPANISH TRAIL

OUTRAGE see THE LAWLESS

OUTSIDE OF PARADISE (Irish Americans)

Republic Pictures Corp. *Dist* Republic Pictures Corp. 7 Feb **1938**; Prod: 19 Nov—mid-Dec 1937 [©Republic Pictures Corp.; 7 Feb 1938; LP7802]. Sd (RCA "High Fidelity" Sound System); b&w. 8 reels,

5,995 ft. 66 or 68 min. Passed by the National Board of Review. PCA cert no. 3979.

Assoc prod Harry Sauber. *Dir* John H. Auer. *Asst dir* Phil Ford. *Orig scr* Harry Sauber. *Photog* Jack Marta. *Art dir* John Victor Mackay. *Film ed* Ernest Nims. *Supv ed* Murray Seldeen. *Cost* Irene Saltern, Marjorie Montgomery and Patricia Perkins. *Mus dir* Alberto Colombo. "Shenanigan" number staged by Larry Ceballos. *Prod mgr* Al Wilson.

Song(s): "Outside of Paradise," words and music by Jack Lawrence and Peter Tinturin; "Sweet Irish Sweetheart of Mine," "Shenanigans," "I Was the Power Behind the Throne," "All for One and One for All" and "A Little Bit of Everything," words and music by Jack Lawrence.

Cast: PHIL REGAN [(*Daniel "Danny" Francis O'Toole*)], PENNY SINGLETON [(*Colleen Kerrigan*)], C01, The Mad Russian Bert Gordon [(*Mischa*)], Leonid Kinskey [(*Ivan Petrovitch*)], Ruth Coleman [(*Dorothy Stonewall*)], Mary Forbes [(*Mrs. Stonewall*)], Lionel Pape [(*Mr. Stonewall*)], Ralph Remley [(*Timothy*)], Renie Riano [(*Ellen*)], Lind Hayes [(*Lind*)], Joe E. Marks [(*Bass*)], David Kerman [(*Felix*)], Billy Young [(*Johnny*)], Cliff Nazarro [(*Cliff*)], Harry Allen [(*Old man*)], [Robert Homans (*Uncle Terence*)].

Musical, Romantic comedy. [*Print viewed*]. When Daniel "Danny" Francis O'Toole, a singer in a New York Russian café, learns that he has inherited an Irish estate, the members of his band decide to incorporate to pay his way to Ireland to collect the money from his inheritance. There he discovers that his estate is an ancestral castle, half of which belongs to Colleen Kerrigan, descendent of a clan which has feuded with the O'Tooles for centuries. Although attracted to each other, Colleen and Danny don't get along any better than their ancestors did and fight constantly. Because she must approve the sale of the property, Danny begs her to do so, but she refuses. With relations strained, she even insists that Danny make his own meals in the great hall. One night, when Danny is making himself an American style hamburger with onions, English travelers Mr. and Mrs. Stonewall and their daughter Dorothy take refuge in the castle during a bad storm. Impressed with the hamburgers, Mr. Stonewall gives Danny the idea to open a restaurant in the castle. At first Colleen is against the idea, but soon approves as she and Danny start to fall in love. After "Hamburger Dan's" starts to become a success, the band, which is thrown out of work when the café closes, comes from New York, financed by their former boss, Ivan Petrovitch. Ivan thinks he can make a successful nightclub out of the castle, so the band members ask Dorothy to give them financial backing, which she does, because she is attracted to Danny. When Colleen finds out that it is Dorothy and not Ivan who financed the club, she becomes jealous and decides to sell the castle, not realizing that Danny also assumed that Ivan used his own money. To prevent the sale of the castle, the band works on a plan in which one of the musicians, Lind, imitates Danny's voice telling Dorothy that he loves Colleen as Colleen listens, but the plan backfires when Colleen sees Danny and Dorothy together a few moments later. When Colleen tearfully tells her uncle Terence how much she "hates" Danny, he spreads a rumor that the O'Tooles are taking advantage of a Kerriagn. As the rumor becomes more and more exaggerated, dozens of Kerrigans show up at the castle on Saturday night. Just after a big musical number in the club, Colleen's relatives start a huge brawl, during which Ivan confesses everything to Colleen. As Colleen and Danny start to make up, a ghost in armor comes toward them and Danny tells her that the ancient feud can only be stopped if she agrees to marry an O'Toole. She agrees, even though the "ghost" turns out to be band member Mischa. *Americans in foreign countries. Feuds. Inheritance. Ireland. Irish Americans. Restaurants. Romance. Singers. Ballerinas. Bands (Music). Castles. Dancers. English. Hamburgers. Impersonation and imposture. Jealousy. Lawyers. New York City. Nightclubs. Rainstorms. Rumors. Russians. Socialites.*

Note: According to *SAB*, the film's title was *Love on Approval* at one time, although all other pre-release information and reviews refer to it as *Outside of Paradise*. Some pre-production news items refer to Penny Singleton as Dorothy McNulty, her former stage name. According to information in the film's press pack, Arthur Murray offered courses valued at one hundred dollars each at his chain of dance studios, as prizes in a promotional tie-in contest for the film. Prizes were available in every city with a population of over one hundred thousand.

Box 19 Feb 1938. *DV* 12 Feb 1938, p. 3. *FD* 11 Feb 1938, p. 15. *HR* 19 Nov 1937, p. 8. *HR* 22 Nov 1937, p. 6. *HR* 12 Feb 1938, p. 2. *MPD* 14 Feb 1938, p. 3. *MPH* 19 Feb 1938, pp. 46-47. *Var* 16 Feb 1938, p. 17.

OUTSIDE THE LAW (Chinese Americans)

Universal Film Mfg. Co.; A Universal-Jewel Production De Luxe. *Dist* Universal Film Mfg. Co. 26 Dec **1920** [©Universal Film Mfg. Co.; 25 Jan 1921; LP16049]. Si; b&w. 8 reels, 7,754 ft.

Pres Carl Laemmle. *Prod* Tod Browning. *Dir* Tod Browning. *Asst dir* Leo McCarey. *Story and scen* Tod Browning. *Scen* Lucien Hubbard. *Subtitle ed* Gardner Bradford. *Cam* William Fildew. *Art dir* E. E. Sheeley. *Art titles* Lewis Lipton and Fred Archer.

Cast: Priscilla Dean (*Molly Madden, known as Silky Moll*), Wheeler Oakman (*Dapper Bill Ballard*), Lon Chaney (*Black Mike Sylva/Ah Wing*), Ralph Lewis (*Silent Madden*), E. A. Warren (*Chang Low*), Stanley Goethals ("*That Kid Across the Hall*"), Melbourne MacDowell (*Morgan Spencer*), Wilton Taylor (*Inspector*).

Crime, Drama. [*Not viewed*]. Silent Madden and his daughter Molly, both criminals, are persuaded to reform by Confucian Chang Low, but a frame-up by gang leader Black Mike sends Madden to prison. Unaware of Black Mike's role in the frame-up, an embittered Molly joins his gang and agrees to aid in a jewel robbery, but learning that she likewise is to be framed, she and Dapper Bill Ballard abscond with the jewels and hide out in a tiny apartment. Molly resists Dapper Bill's declarations of love, but the affection of a young boy from the neighboring apartment eventually changes her poor opinion of love and motherhood. The gang finally discovers Bill and Molly's hideout, and a battle ensues that leaves Black Mike dead and Bill and Molly in the hands of the police. Chang Low intervenes, however, and with the return of the jewels, Bill and Molly are freed. *Children. Confucianism. Criminals–Rehabilitation. Fights. Frame-ups. Fugitives. Gangsters. Apartments. Chinese Americans. Fathers and daughters. Jewelry. Robbery.*

Note: The film opened in Los Angeles on 26 Dec 1920, but its general release was in Jan 1921. It was re-cut and re-released in mid-1926, and Universal and Browning remade the story in 1930. (See *AFI Catalog of Feature Films, 1921-30;* F2.4085.) Contemporary reviewers credited the scenario to Hubbard alone, but the copyright records credit both Hubbard and Browning. Pre-production charts in trade journals listed "Harris" as the film's cinematographer, but Fildew replaced Harris in the charts at the beginning of production. Tom Gubbins worked on the film as a consultant on the authenticity of the Chinese characterizations. Exteriors for the film were shot in San Francisco in Chinatown, on Nob Hill, and in the waterfront area.

Camera 12 Jun 1920. *Camera* 28 Aug 1920, p. 18. *MPN* 21 Aug 1920, p. 1549. *MPN* 25 Dec 1920, pp. 10-11. *MPN* 22 Jan 1921, p. 915. *MPW* 22 Jan 1921, p. 465. *MPW* 15 May 1926, p. 249. *NYT* 12 May 1926, p. 31. *Var* 21 Jan 1921, p. 40. *Wid's* 9 Jan 1921, p. 2.

OVERLAND PACIFIC (Native Americans, Comanche)

World Films. *Dist* United Artists Corp. Feb **1954**; Prod: late Aug—early Sep 1953 at Samuel Goldwyn Studios [©Superior Pictures, Inc.; 17 Mar 1954; LP3518]. Sd (Western Electric Recording); col (Color Corp. of America). 73-74 min. PCA cert no. 16749.

[*Prod* Edward Small]. *Dir* Fred F. Sears. *Asst dir* William McGarry and Harry Anderson. *Scr* J. Robert Bren, Gladys Atwater and Martin Goldsmith. *Story* Frederic Louis Fox. *Dir of photog* Lester White. *Spec eff* David Koehler. *Art dir* Frank Sylos. *Film ed* Buddy Small. *Set dec* Edward G. Boyle. *Ward* Charles Keehne. *Mus* Irving Gertz. *Sd* Fred Lau. [*Prod mgr* Doc Merman]. [*Casting dir* Jack Baur].

Cast: Jock Mahoney [(*Ross Granger*)], Peggie Castle [(*Ann Dennison*)], Adele Jergens [(*Jessie Lorraine*)], William Bishop [(*Del Stewart*)], Chubby Johnson [(*Sheriff Blaney*)], Walter Sande [(*Mr. Dennison*)], Pat Hogan [(*Dark Thunder*)], Chris Alcaide [(*Jason*)], Fred Graham [(*Phil Chambers* (*Weeks*)], [George Eldredge (*Broden*)], [Dick Rich (*Saber*)], [House Peters, Jr. (*Perkins*)].

Western. [*Print viewed*]. Ross Granger, a Civil War veteran, poses as a telegraph operator in order to investigate acts of sabotage that have been plaguing the building of the Overland Pacific. As he travels by stage to Oaktown, where he is to work as the new telegraph operator, he sees a corpse pierced by Indian arrows swinging from the telegraph wires. Once in Oaktown, Ann Dennison, the daughter of the man responsible for bringing the railroad to the region, identifies the dead man as a railroad worker. Granger is surprised to encounter his old wartime buddy, Del Stewart, who has become the owner of the town's saloon, the Silver Dollar, and is engaged to marry Ann, despite her father's disapproval. Granger also befriends Jessie Lorraine, a dance hall girl, who is also in love with Stewart. The next day, as Dennison and Ann show Granger the territory, the railroad camp is attacked by Comanches, who resent the railroad being built in their territory. Dennison believes that someone besides the Comanches is behind the attacks and his suspicions are confirmed when the men report that the Indians had repeating rifles. Granger telegraphs the

central office with the news, and later, Stewart and a rich cattleman, Broden, discuss their plan to sell guns to the Indians, whose attacks will then force the railroad company to reroute the tracks through Oaktown, where they both own land. Later, after Stewart tries to bribe Dennison into changing the railroad path, Dennison accuses him of masterminding the Indian raid. Just then, Broden's henchman, Jason, shoots Dennison dead. Stewart brings Dennison's body back to the railroad camp and announces that Indians shot him, but later, Granger shows Stewart and the dishonest Sheriff Blaney, who is also in on the scheme, the slug from Dennison's body, which he claims came from a white man's gun. Later, Stewart accidentally meets Dark Thunder, the Comanche chief, who is angry that the whites have not moved the railroad out of his territory, and Stewart offers him more guns to continue his raids. Meanwhile, Sheriff Blaney admits his involvement in the gun-running scheme, telling Granger that the guns were smuggled in Stewart's whiskey barrels. As Blaney takes Granger to see where the rifles are hidden, Jason, hidden in the rocks, shoots and hits Granger in the shoulder, and in the ensuing fight, Jason is killed. When Granger gets back to town, Jessie and Ann tend to his wounds, and Granger demands that Stewart show him his whiskey barrels, much to Jessie and Ann's shock. Although Ann and Granger do not discover any rifles in the warehouse, they do find Blaney, who has committed suicide. As Ann, who broke off her engagement to Stewart after her father's death, addresses the railroad workers and tells them that she plans to continue her father's dream for the future, Perkins, the new construction boss, arrives and announces that the railroad will be rerouted through Oaktown. Back at the saloon, Stewart has reunited with an overjoyed Jessie, but when Perkins reveals that he is involved in the sabotage scheme with Stewart, she angrily informs Stewart that she plans to turn him in. Stewart shoots Jessie, but before she dies, she tells the piano player to tell Granger that the new construction boss is a fake. After Stewart goes to see Dark Thunder to tell him that the railroad will be rerouted out of Comanche territory, he, Perkins and Broden are taken hostage while Dark Thunder attacks the railroad camp. Ann, Granger and the men successfully fight off the attack and Granger kills Stewart. Their troubles over, Ann and Granger walk away arm-in-arm. *Comanche Indians. Firearms. Overland Pacific Railroad. Railroad agents. Sabotage. Undercover operations. Civil War veterans. Gunfights. Murder. Railroad workers. Romantic rivalry. Saloons. Stagecoaches. Suicide. Telegraph.*

Note: This film's working title was *The Silver Dollar*. The following written prologue appears after the onscreen credits: "Soon after the devastating war between the States, America's prosperity depended on a linking of its widely separated boundaries. As a result, several railroad lines commenced to push west-ward, plagued every foot of the way by hostile Indians. But what has been forgotten today is that there were also hostile Whites, and considerable blood was shed in disputes over the projected routes. This is an account of one such incident." The film's pressbook reported that exterior sequences were shot in Chatsworth, CA. In addition to World Films, which is listed onscreen, contemporary sources also credit Reliance Productions and Edward Small Productions as the film's production company. A review of this film in the journal *Filmindia* states that "Indians should learn from America's tragic experience in crime and the censors should ban pictures like these to protect Indian homes from being flooded with criminal and violent ideas."

Box 13 Feb 1954. *DV* 8 Feb 1954, p. 3. *Exb* 10 Feb 1954, pp. 3696-97. *FD* 23 Feb 1954, p. 6. *Filmindia* Jun 1954. *HR* 28 Aug 1953, p. 11. *HR* 4 Sep 1953, p. 15. *Har* 13 Feb 1954, p. 27. *HR* 8 Feb 1954, p. 3. *MPD* Feb 9, 1954. *MPHPD* 13 Feb 1954, p. 2182. *Var* 10 Feb 1954, p. 6.

THE OVERLAND STAGE (Native Americans, Dakota)

Charles R. Rogers Productions, Inc. *Dist* First National Pictures, Inc. 31 Jan **1927** [©First National Pictures, Inc.; 14 Dec 1926; LP23435]. Si; b&w. 7 reels, 6,392 ft.

Pres Charles R. Rogers. *Dir* Albert Rogell. *Story and scen* Marion Jackson. *Photog* Sol Polito. *Prod mgr* Harry J. Brown.

Cast: Ken Maynard (*Jack Jessup*), Kathleen Collins (*Barbara Marshall*), Tom Santschi (*Hawk Lespard*), Sheldon Lewis (*Jules*), Dot Farley (*Aunt Viney*), Florence Turner (*Alice Gregg*), Jay Hunt (*John Gregg*), William Malan (*John Marshall*), Paul Hurst (*Hell A-Poppin' Casey*), Fred Burns (*Butterfield*).

Western. At a trading post in the Northern Dakotas, Hawk Lespard, an unscrupulous trader, is opposed by Jack Jessup, posing as a gambler but actually a scout for the Overland Stage Co., and Kunga-Sunga, a wizard with the lariat. John Gregg comes to town as storekeeper with his niece, Barbara Marshall, and Jessup falls in love with her. Meanwhile, Lespard's men disguise themselves as Indians, giving the post a bad name for whites and inciting the Sioux chiefs

against the white man. In a fight, Jessup is disclosed as Kunga-Sunga, and the superstitious Indians, aroused by Lespard, force him into hiding. Lespard leads a renegade band against a wagon train of new settlers, but Jack, in disguise, informs the chief of the trader's treachery, and the settlers defeat their attackers. The Indians are reconciled when Lespard reveals his true intentions, and Barbara and Jack are married. *Dakota Indians. Dakota Territory. Disguise. Gamblers. Overland Stage Co.. Scouts (Frontier). Settlers. Traders. Wagon trains.*

FD 6 Feb 1927.

THE OVERLAND TELEGRAPH (Native Americans)

Metro-Goldwyn-Mayer Corp.; controlled by Loew's Inc. *Dist* Metro-Goldwyn-Mayer Distributing Corp. 2 Mar **1929** [©Metro-Goldwyn-Mayer Distributing Corp.; 12 Mar 1929; LP204]. Si; b&w. 6 reels, 4,815 ft.

Dir John Waters. *Scen* George C. Hull. *Adpt* Edward Meagher. *Story* Ward Wing. *Titles* Harry Sinclair Drago. *Photog* Arthur Reed. *Film ed* William Le Vanway. *Ward* Lucia Coulter.

Cast: Tim McCoy (*Captain Allen*), Dorothy Janis (*Dorothy*), Frank Rice (*Easy*), Lawford Davidson (*Briggs*), Clarence Geldert (*Major Hammond*), Chief Big Tree (*Medicine man*).

Historical, Drama. "Young army captain tries his luck against marauding Indians, and incidentally wins the hand of the prettiest girl at the post. Action takes place at outbreak of Civil War." (*MPNBG* 15 Apr 1920, p. 97.). *Glacier Bay National Park and Preserve (AK). Indians of North America. Telegraph. United States–History–Civil War, 1861-1865.*

Note: Filmed on location in Glacier National Park.

FD 24 Mar 1929.

OVERLAND TRAIL RIDERS *see* **OLD OVERLAND TRAIL**

OVERTURE TO GLORY (Yiddish language)

Elite Productions, Inc. *Dist* G & L Motion Picture Corp. **1940**; New York opening: 9 Feb 1940 [©G. & L. Motion Picture Corp.; 1 Mar 1940; LP9474]. Sd; b&w. 9 reels, 7,714 ft. 85 min. Yiddish language with English subtitles.

Exec prod Ludwig Landy and Ira Greene. *Dir* Max Nosseck. *Asst dir* Ben Parker. *Scr* Max Nosseck and Ossip Dymow. *Story* Ossip Dymow. *Titles* Julian Leigh. *Dial* Jacob Gladstone. *Photog* Larry Williams and Don Malkames. *Art dir* Maurice McDermott. *Art advisor* Irving Scharf. *Film ed* Leslie Vidor. *Mus dir and orig mus* Alexander Olshanetsky. *Sd tech* Nelson Minnerly and Edward Fenton. *Makeup* Ira Senz. *Tech adv* Morris Strassberg. *Production supv* George Moskov. *First asst* Julian Zimet. *Second asst* Henry Landon.

Cast: MOISHE OYSHER (*Yoel Duvid Strashunsky*), Helen Beverley (*Countess Wanda Mirova*), Florence Weiss (*Chana, Yoel's wife*), Lazar Freed (*Rabbi*), Jack Mylong Munz ([*Stanislawa*] *Manyushko* [*i.e. Moniuszko*]), Leonard Elliott (*Tilchinski—Conductor*), Erika Zaranova (*Prima donna*), Maurice Krohner (*Reb Aaron, Chana's father*), Baby Winkler (*Peretz, their son*), Omus Hirshbein (*Peretz's friend*), Benjamin Fishbein (*Nute, the shames*), Ivan Busatt (*Director of opera*), Luba Wesoly (*Countess*), Werner Bass (*Pianist*), Ossip Dymow (*Count Parnofsky*), Max Willenz (*Little shames*), Herman Blass (*Tailor*), Manfried Lewandowski (*Cantor*).

Yiddish, Show business, Melodrama, with songs. [*Print viewed*]. On *Rosh Hashanah*, the Jewish New Year, the famous Polish composer Manyushko visits the synagogue in Vilna to listen to cantor Yoel Duvid Strashunsky sing. Very impressed, Manyushko invites Yoel to his home to cultivate his voice. Yoel says that he learned from his deceased father that singing with feeling is most important for Jewish prayers. This is what Yoel teaches his son Peretz, yet he is intrigued with the music of Beethoven and Chopin, which he hears at Manyushko's home, and he learns to read notes as he secretly visits every night. Nute, the *shames*, or sexton of the synagogue, follows Manyushko one evening on orders from Yoel's father-in-law, Reb Aaron, who has taken care of Yoel since he was thirteen and made him the cantor of the Vilna synagogue. Reb Aaron demands that Yoel vow to never set foot in Manyushko's house again, and the rabbi reminds Yoel of the necessity for a cantor to keep his heart and thoughts clean so that his prayers for the congregation will be pure. Yoel agrees not to return to Manyushko's, but one evening, when he is out with his wife Chana, he hears strains of Manyushko's new opera. Seeing that he longs to visit, Chana encourages him to go in. Manyushko tells Yoel that he is leaving for Warsaw in a few days to prepare for the opening of the opera, *Halka*, and invites him to be the leading singer. The

rabbi is crushed when Yoel announces that he wants to go to Warsaw, and Reb Aaron says that a *dybbuk*, or evil spirit, has taken hold of him. Yoel argues that if he sings in Polish, those who hate the Jews will be able to understand their suffering and what goes on in the Jewish heart. The rabbi counters that the world has been deaf to the Jews for thousands of years and warns Yoel that if he leaves, he'll live between two worlds, and, in fact, be nowhere. Before he leaves for Warsaw, Yoel sings Peretz to sleep, then visits the deserted synagogue, where he is disturbed as he imagines voices in song, but he regains his determination. Yoel is a great success at his first exhibition in Warsaw. As he leaves the theater, he finds Countess Wanda Mirova, the twenty-two-year-old student of Manyushko, waiting in his carriage to take him to Manyushko's banquet. Wanda flatters him and gives him a flower as a present, whereupon he says she is as beautiful as a flower. Although Yoel writes asking Chana and Peretz to come, Reb Aaron forbids them to go to Warsaw. Soon Yoel is plagued with longing for Vilna and dark thoughts about his choice to leave. He tells Wanda that he feels like a stranger in Warsaw and that he has lost the world where his soul resides. Although Wanda tells him that she feels she is growing closer to him, Yoel longs to sing in a synagogue again, and an assistant at the opera arranges for him to sing prayers at a Passover service. Afterward, Yoel realizes that he must go back to Vilna, and when he tells this to Manyushko a week before the opening of the opera, Manyushko and the director become greatly agitated. However, Wanda pleads with Yoel to stay, and he remains in Warsaw. Meanwhile in Vilna, Peretz becomes very ill. Before he dies, Chana sings to him the same song that Yoel sang before he left. Backstage midway through the opera, Yoel excitedly thanks Wanda for giving him the courage to continue, and when Reb Aaron arrives to tell Yoel the news about Peretz, it is obvious to him that Yoel and Wanda are deeply affected by each other. Reb Aaron says that Peretz's death is God's punishment to Yoel, and when Yoel returns to the stage, he attempts to sing the lullaby he once sang to Peretz and then collapses. A doctor diagnoses a nervous breakdown and says that Yoel has lost his voice. Yoel then disappears and wanders through the countryside. On the eve of *Yom Kippur*, the Day of Atonement, Yoel arrives at the Vilna synagogue and sings the *Kol Nidre*, a prayer to absolve the congregation from any vows taken. He then dies at the altar, and the rabbi says that through the generations it will be remembered that Yoel, "our Vilna *balabessel*," or beloved citizen, sang for "them" and prayed for "us." *Cantors, Jewish. Cultural conflict. Fathers and sons. Homesickness. Infatuation. Jews. Opera singers. The Vilna Balabessel (historical person). Vilnius (Lithuania). Composers. Fathers-in-law. Marriage. Stanislaw Moniuszko. Music teachers. Mutes. Nervous breakdown. Nobility. Poles. Prayer. Rabbis. Rosh Hashanah. Synagogues. Wanderers. Warsaw (Poland). Yom Kippur.*

Note: The Yiddish title of this film was *Der Vilner Shtot Khazn*. According to the screen credits, the film was based on the legend of "The Vilna *Balabessel*," the most famous cantor of the 19th century. An essay in the copyright descriptions relates the following information: The *Balabessel* was born Joel David Levenstein to the cantor of Vilna. His father began his education after he showed talent at age six, and at age eleven, the boy prayed at the altar in the main synagogue. The wife of one of the leading Jewish citizens decided then that he would marry her daughter, and Joel was married at age thirteen. The next year, he became the chief cantor after his father died. His singing powers were so inspirational that they attracted not only Jews to the synagogue, but Christians also. The famous Polish composer Stanislaw Moniuszko induced Joel to leave Vilna, and he went to Warsaw with a retinue of religious Jews. He caused a sensation at a concert in Warsaw when the daughter of a count kissed him in front of thousands. According to the legend, the two had met earlier when he passed her home and overheard her playing the piano, and to spite those who gossiped about them, she kissed him in public. The cantor's visits to the daughter of the count ceased, and in the midst of his success, he returned to Vilna. He was overwhelmed by the sudden deaths of two children, and he divorced his wife, to whom he was never well-suited. He then developed severe melancholia, and to help him, some townsfolk traveled with him to a foreign country, but he developed consumption and died in Warsaw at age 34. This was European director Max Nosseck's first film in the U.S. Modern sources state that the film was based on Mark Arnshteyn's play *Der Vilner Balabesl*, which was based on the legend and first produced in Polish in Lodz, Poland in 1902 under the title *Piesniarze*. Although the film includes songs, no information concerning their identity has been located.

Box 24 Feb 1940. *Cue* 15 Dec 1951. *Exh* 21 Feb 1940. *FD* 14 Jan 1940, p. 7. *LAT* 29 Aug 1945, pt. I, p. 9. *NYHT* 12 Feb 1940. *NYT* 21 Feb 1940, p. 14. *Var* 14 Feb 1940, p. 28.

THE OX-BOW INCIDENT (African Americans, Latino)

Twentieth Century-Fox Film Corp. *Dist* Twentieth Century-Fox Film Corp. 21 May **1943**; New York opening: 8 May 1943; Prod: late Jun—early Aug 1942; addl seq and retakes mid-Aug—late Aug 1942

[©Twentieth Century-Fox Film Corp.; 19 Nov 1943; LP12907]. Sd (Western Electric Recording); b&w. 8 reels, 6,776 ft. 75 min. PCA cert no. 8590.

[*Exec prod* William Goetz]. *Prod* Lamar Trotti. *Dir* William A. Wellman. [*2d unit dir* James Tinling]. [*Asst dir* Ad Schaumer]. *Wrt for the scr by* Lamar Trotti. *Dir of photog* Arthur Miller. *Art dir* Richard Day and James Basevi. *Film ed* Allen McNeil. *Set dec* Thomas Little and Frank E. Hughes. *Cost* Earl Luick. *Mus* Cyril J. Mockridge. *Sd* Alfred Bruzlin and Roger Heman.

Music: "Red River Valley," traditional.

Song(s): "You Got to Go Through the Lonesome Valley" and "We Will All Stand Together on That Day," music and lyrics by Leigh Whipper.

Source: Based on the novel *The Ox-Bow Incident* by Walter Van Tilburg Clark (New York, 1940).

Cast: Henry Fonda [(*Gil Carter*)], Dana Andrews [(*Donald Martin*)], Mary Beth Hughes [(*Rose Mapen*)], Anthony Quinn [(*Francisco Morez*)], William Eythe [(*Gerald Tetley*)], Henry Morgan [(*Art Croft*)], Jane Darwell [(*Jenny "Ma" Grier*)], Matt Briggs [(*Judge Daniel Tyler*)], Harry Davenport [(*Arthur Davies*)], Frank Conroy [(*Major Tetley*)], Marc Lawrence [(*Jeff Farnley*)], Paul Hurst [(*Monty Smith*)], Victor Kilian [(*Darby*)], Chris-Pin Martin [(*Poncho*)], Willard Robertson [(*Sheriff Risley*)], Ted North [(*Joyce*)], [George Meeker (*Mr. Swanson*)], [Almira Sessions (*Miss Swanson*)], [Margaret Hamilton (*Mrs. Larch*)], [Dick Rich (*Butch Mapes*)], [Francis Ford (*Alva "Dad" Hardwick*)], [Stanley Andrews (*Bartlett*)], [Billy Benedict (*Greene*)], [Rondo Hatton (*Gabe Hart*)], [Paul Burns (*Winder*)], [Leigh Whipper (*Sparks*)], [George Lloyd (*Moore*)], [George Chandler (*Jimmy Carnes*)], [Hank Bell (*Red*)], [Forrest Dillon (*Mark*)], [George Plues (*Alec Small*)], [Tom London (*Deputy*)], [Donald House, Dan Dix, Ben Watson, Walter Robbins, Frank McGrath, Ed Richard, Cap Anderson, Tex Cooper, Clint Sharp, Larry Dodds, Tex Driscoll (*Posse*)].

Western, **with songs.** [*Print viewed*]. In 1885, cattlemen Gil Carter and Art Croft travel from their small ranch to the nearby town of Bridger's Wells, Nevada, after the winter round-up. Gil is hoping to meet his sweetheart, Rose Mapen, and is infuriated when Darby, the bartender, informs him that she left town to be married. Gil's temper worsens when rancher Jeff Farnley insinuates that he and Art, as the only strangers present, may be responsible for the recent cattle rustling that has hit every rancher in the area. Gil and Farnley engage in a fistfight, which ends when Darby shatters a bottle over Gil's head. As Gil and Art are standing outside afterward, a rider rushes into the saloon. Gil and Art rejoin the crowd, which has just learned that Larry Kincaid, a well-respected local rancher, has been murdered, presumably by the rustlers. Farnley, Kincaid's best friend, is easily whipped into a frenzy by the town drunk, Monty Smith, and other bored men who insist that the perpetrators should be lynched. Storekeeper Arthur Davies tries to persuade the men to wait for Sheriff Risley and Judge Daniel Tyler, but when they persist in forming a posse, Davies sends Gil and townsman Joyce to get Tyler. Davies asks Gil to avoid involving Butch Mapes, the brutish deputy sheriff, but Mapes is at Tyler's house, and when he learns of the excitement, he joins the gathering crowd. Tyler tries to dissuade the men from pursuing the alleged criminals, but Smith, Farnley and the others insist that Tyler's justice moves too slowly. Smith caustically suggests that black preacher Sparks should come, and even though he knows Smith is kidding him, Sparks decides to go in case prayer is needed. The mob is joined by Jennie "Ma" Grier, a tough woman who also insists that they find Kincaid's killers. Tyler and Davies have almost persuaded the crowd to desist, however, when Major Tetley, a former Confederate soldier who now fancies himself a town leader, arrives and announces that three men were seen on Bridger's Pass, and that they had forty head of cattle bearing Kincaid's brand. Despite Tyler's protests that only Risley can appoint new deputies, Mapes swears in the posse members and they set off for the pass. Gil and Art reluctantly go along, for they fear that suspicion will fall on them if they do not participate. Gil's uneasiness about the situation increases when Sparks remarks that he still has nightmares about seeing his brother lynched many years previously. Night falls as the posse travels, and everyone begins to suffer from the cold. As they stop on the mountain road to rest, a stagecoach passes by and the driver mistakenly assumes that the crowd are robbers. Art is shot in the shoulder during the ensuing confusion, and while his wound is being

cleaned, Gil discovers that the passengers are Rose, her new husband, Swanson, and his sister. After the wealthy Swanson vaguely warns Gil to stay away from Rose, the stage departs. Art is determined to stick with the posse, which continues on to the Ox-Bow Valley. There they find three sleeping men and the cattle bearing Kincaid's brand. After surrounding them, the mob awakens the three men, who are led by young rancher Donald Martin. Martin's companions are Alva Hardwick, an addled old man whom Martin calls "Dad," and a Mexican named Francisco Morez, who does not appear to speak English. Martin is amazed by Tetley's accusations and immediately protests their innocence. Martin insists that he moved to nearby Pike's Hole three days earlier and purchased the cattle from Kincaid, who was too busy to provide him with a bill of sale. Gil tries to persuade the others to bring the trio back to the judge, but Art reminds him that they may get lynched as well if they interfere. Davies also pleads for the men's lives, and finally, Tetley agrees to give them until dawn to prepare themselves. Martin writes a letter to his wife and two young children, while Dad sits in a daze and Morez hungrily consumes a meal prepared by Ma. While Davies tries to get Tetley to read Martin's moving letter, Morez attempts to escape. He is shot in the leg and brought back, and Kincaid's gun is found on him. Morez, who now reveals that he does speak English, asserts that he found the gun along the road, but the presence of the weapon seals his fate. Davies again protests the lynching, and this time, Sparks, Gil, Art, Tetley's cowardly son Gerald and two other men stand by him. They are outnumbered, however, and the condemned men are put on horseback. Tetley tries to force Gerald to whip the horse from underneath Martin, and when he cannot, Tetley knocks him unconscious. Martin, Dad and Morez are hanged, after which the now somber crowd leaves. Before they have journeyed far, though, they are joined by the sheriff, who tells them that not only is Kincaid alive, but his attackers have been caught. Risley promises that those responsible for the lynching will pay dearly, and the group rides back to town. There, Gerald castigates his father for his cruelty, and the distraught major commits suicide. Meanwhile, in the crowded saloon, a collection is taken up for Martin's wife. Gil and Art contribute, and Gil tries to get Art to read Martin's letter. Art cannot read, however, so Gil reads the letter aloud, and the men are ashamed to hear Martin's stirring words about the nature of justice and conscience. Gil and Art then leave Bridger's Wells on their way to deliver the letter and look after Martin's wife and children. *Conscience. False accusations. Injustice. Lynching. Mobs.* African Americans. Bartenders. Bullies. Cattlemen. Circumstantial evidence. Cowardice. Deputies. Fathers and sons. Fistfights. Judges. Letters. Mexicans. Nevada. Prayer. Rustlers. Saloons. Storekeepers. Suicide. Women ranchers.

Note: Lamar Trotti's onscreen credit reads "Produced and written for the screen by Lamar Trotti." According to contemporary news items, the rights to Walter Van Tilburg Clark's book were originally acquired in 1941 by Harold Hurley, a former Paramount producer who tried unsuccessfully to make a distribution deal with United Artists. Modern sources note that director William Wellman bought the rights from Hurley and then interested Twentieth Century-Fox production chief Darryl F. Zanuck in producing the story. Zanuck agreed on the condition that Wellman direct two other films for the studio, *Thunderbirds* and *Buffalo Bill.* A 18 May 1942 studio press release indicated that Preston Foster was to be cast in a "key role," and *HR* news items note that Sara Allgood was originally cast in the role of "Jennie 'Ma' Grier," but was replaced by Florence Bates. Bates was then injured in a horseback riding scene, necessitating her replacement by Jane Darwell, who appears in the finished film.

A 23 Apr 1942 *HR* item reported that due to "defense regulations hindering exterior shooting in the Hollywood area," the film would be shot in Nevada, but later items indicate a limited amount of location shooting was instead done at the Iverson Ranch in Chatsworth and in Lone Pine, CA. On 10 Aug 1942, *HR* announced that production on the film would be shut down for a week or ten days "due to the $5,000-per-film limit on new construction materials." During the shutdown, already used sets were torn down so that their material could be re-used to build the mountain pass set. Studio publicity noted that the Ox-Bow Valley setting was "the largest set ever constructed" by Fox, and that it covered 26,703 feet.

According to information in the MPAA/PCA file for the film at the AMPAS Library, the PCA initially was reluctant to approve the script because of its suggestion that the sheriff condoned the lynchings. The treatment of the lynchings and the characterization of those participating were discussed by the PCA and the studio at great length, and in a 9 Jun 1942 letter, PCA director Joseph Breen advised studio public relations head Jason S. Joy that the script would be approved if: "Major Tetley's" suicide is retained, "thus constituting a punishment for the ring-leader of the lynching party;" there is an indication that the whole gang will be arrested; the character of "Gil" is rewritten to make him less callous and more active in trying to stop the lynchings; and "Davies'" denunciation of the killings is retained. A 17 Sep 1942 *HR* news item

commented on how unusual it was for the Hays Office to approve a film containing a lynching, and stated that "the early period [1885] was partly responsible for the exception."

A 20 Jul 1942 studio publicity synopsis indicates that early versions of the script included the suicide of "Gerald Tetley" and that the film was to end with the reappearance of "Rose Mapen" and her husband in the saloon rather than with "Gil" and "Art" leaving to take the letter to "Martin's" wife. A modern source notes that the contents of Martin's letter are not revealed in the book, but Wellman thought that it was important to make them explicit and had Trotti compose the letter. In the letter, Martin tells his wife: "Law is a lot more than words you put in a book, or judges or lawyers or sheriffs you hire to carry it out. It's everything people have ever found out about justice and what's right and wrong. It's the very conscience of humanity. There can't be any such thing as civilization unless people have a conscience, because if people touch God anywhere, where is it except through their conscience?"

According to a 4 Sep 1942 *HR* news item, Henry Fonda was to do a special trailer for the film in which he would speak about Clark's novel. The *Ox-Bow Incident,* which marked the screen debut of stage actor William Eythe, was selected as the best drama film of the year by the National Board of Review. It also received an Academy Award nomination for Best Picture, but lost to *Casablanca.* Although the picture generally received positive reviews, commentators did note that it might not do well financially. The *NYT* reviewer praised the "all-round excellent cast [which] played the film brilliantly," but noted that "it is hard to imagine a picture with less promise commercially." The *Life* reviewer commented that the film was "an unusual Hollywood product, lofty in its purpose, stark in its realism and slashing in its savagery. But it is likely that these very distinctions will make it unpopular." The *MPH* reviewer also stated that the picture was "a well produced and well acted film which may present a rather special selling problem." According to Wellman's autobiography, the picture did not return a profit to the studio until after it was well-received abroad and then re-released in the United States.

Box 15 May 1943. *DV* 6 May 1943, p. 3. *FD* 16 Feb 1942. *FD* 10 May 1943, p. 6. *HR* 12 Feb 1942, p. 1. *HR* 23 Apr 1942, p. 8. *HR* 15 Jun 1942, p. 8. *HR* 26 Jun 1942, p. 11. *HR* 13 Jul 1942, p. 2. *HR* 29 Jul 1942, p. 7. *HR* 7 Aug 1942, p. 9. *HR* 10 Aug 1942, p. 3. *HR* 20 Aug 1942, p. 3. *HR* 4 Sep 1492, p. 7. *HR* 17 Sep 1942, p. 2. *HR* 27 Nov 1942, p. 2. *HR* 6 May 1943, p. 3, 12. *HR* 17 May 1943, p. 13. *HR* 24 Dec 1943, p. 1, 6. *Life* 24 May 1942, pp. 41-42, 44. *MPD* 6 May 1943. *MPHPD* 29 Aug 1942, p. 872. *MPHPD* 8 May 1943, p. 1302. *MPHPD* 28 Aug 1943, p. 1507. *NYT* 10 May 1943, p. 15. *NYT* 16 May 1943. *Var* 12 May 1943, p. 8.

OY DI SHVIGER! *see* **WHAT A MOTHER-IN-LAW!**

PACHUCO *see* **THE RING**

PADDY O'DAY (Irish Americans, Russian Americans)
Twentieth Century-Fox Film Corp. *Dist* Twentieth Century-Fox Film Corp. 17 Jan **1936**; Prod: Sep 1936 [©Twentieth Century-Fox Film Corp.; 17 Jan 1936; LP6047]. Sd (Western Electric Noiseless Recording); b&w. 8 reels, 6,800 ft. 75-76 min. PCA cert no. 1665.

Exec prod Sol M. Wurtzel. *Dir* Lewis Seiler. [*Asst dir* Aaron Rosenberg and Sam Schneider]. *Scr* Lou Breslow and Edward Eliscu. *Photog* Arthur Miller. *Art dir* Duncan Cramer and Lewis Creber. *Film ed* Al De Gaetano. *Cost* Helen Myron. *Mus dir* Samuel Kaylin. *Dances staged by* Fanchon. *Sd* Alfred Bruzlin.

Song(s): "Keep That Twinkle in Your Eye" and "I Like a Balalaika," words by Edward Eliscu and Sidney Clare, music by Harry Akst; "Changing My Ambitions," words and music by Pinky Tomlin and Coy Poe; "Which Is Which," words by Sidney Clare, music by Troy Sanders; "Sleep My Baby (Bauishka Bain)," Russian lullaby.

Cast: Jane Withers (*Paddy O'Day*), Pinky Tomlin (*Ray [i.e. Roy] Ford*), Rita Cansino (*Tamara Petrovitch*), Jane Darwell (*Dora*), George Givot (*Mischa*), Francis Ford (*Immigration officer [Tom] McGuire*), Vera Lewis (*Aunt Flora Ford*), Louise Carter (*Aunt Jane Ford*), Russell Simpson (*Benton*), Michael Visaroff (*Popushka Petrovitch*), Nina Visaroff (*Momushka Petrovitch*), [Pat O'Malley (*Wilson*)], [Robert Dudley (*Chauffeur*)], [Selmer Jackson, Ruth Clifford, Larry Steers (*First class passengers*)], [Harvey Clark (*Ship's doctor*)], [Jessie Pringle, Evelyn Selbie (*Immigrant women*)], [Myra Marsh (*Matron*)], [Jane Keckley (*Maid*)], [Tommy Bupp, Sherwood Bailey, Harry Watson (*Street boys*)], [Russ Clark (*New York traffic policeman*)], [Larry Fisher (*Truck driver*)], [Hal K. Dawson (*Motorist*)], [Egon Brecher, Leonid Snegoff, Demetrios Alexis (*Russian musicians*)], [Clarence H. Wilson (*Brewster*)], [Richard Powell (*Taxi driver*)], [Aaron Rosenberg].

Youth, Social, Comedy-drama, with songs. [*Print viewed*]. Paddy O'Day, an eight-year-old Irish girl, travels with her dog Tim to New York to live with her mother, a cook working for the wealthy Ford family. At Ellis Island, after the Fords' servant Benton informs immigration officer Tom McGuire that Paddy's mother died a few days earlier, McGuire tells Paddy that her mother is sick and could not come, and although he is pained by the situation, he arranges for Paddy to be sent back to Ireland. Tamara Petrovitch, an immigrant

from Russia, with whom Paddy made friends on the boat, learns that Paddy's mother has died and offers to take care of her because she has no family in Ireland, but McGuire refuses. To escape the island and visit her mother, Paddy hides in a large milk container on a dairy truck and makes her way to Manhattan. After she gets into a fight with a street tough who makes fun of her Irish brogue, a sympathetic Irish cop orders a driver whom he has stopped for speeding to take Paddy to the Ford home in Southampton, where Roy Ford, a recluse whose only pleasures come from songwriting and his collection of stuffed birds, lives with his two domineering, spinster aunts, Flora and Jane. When Paddy arrives, Dora, the Fords' maid, reveals that her mother has died and convinces Benton and the other servants to hide Paddy in the house. As the two aunts pack to leave on a trip, Tim corners the Fords' cat Mathilda on top of a grandfather clock, and their subsequent chase is heard by the aunts. Paddy retrieves Tim and hides in Roy's room, where Tim goes after a prized stuffed bird. When Paddy gets the bird without allowing Tim to mangle it, Roy is greatly relieved. He hides Paddy when his aunts come to his door, and they leave after commanding him to remain on his vegetable diet and to keep his feet warm. Tamara and her brother Mischa, who runs the Café Petrovitch, come looking for Paddy, and Tamara convinces Roy to let Paddy live with her, because, she believes, the immigration officers would never think to look for her there. Mischa also induces Roy, who is attracted to Tamara, to put up $10,000 and become his partner in remodeling the café to put on a big stage show. Although Tamara warns Roy that Mischa's imagination often gets the best of him, Roy nonetheless is enthusiastic. Soon Roy's home is filled with live birds in cages rather than stuffed ones, and he sports a mustache and Russian outfit and drinks vodka. When his aunts return and protest, he says that his new friends are teaching him how to live, whereupon Flora and Jane faint. The day before the opening of the show, which contains songs written by Roy, his aunts learn that Tamara has been harboring Paddy. They plan to have both Paddy and Tamara deported and to commit Roy to a sanitarium until he gets over his infatuation. After the successful performance, McGuire, notified by the aunts, comes to the club to take Paddy and Tamara. Roy offers to adopt Paddy and then confesses to his aunts that he and Tamara were secretly married the day before. The aunts faint again, while Mischa talks to McGuire about investing in the club. Finally, the aunts are won over. Roy cannot kiss Tamara because the air-filled suit that he wears for the act gets in the way, so Paddy punches the air out of it. *Adolescents. Aliens, Illegal. Immigrants. Irish Americans. Recluses. Rejuvenation.* Aunts. Birds. Brothers and sisters. Cafés. Cats. Chases. Dogs. Escapes. New York City–Ellis Island. Partnership. Police. Romance. Russian Americans. Servants. Songwriters. Spinsters. Vegetarians.

Note: The working titles of this film were *The Immigrant, Immigrants* and *The Little Immigrant.* According to a *Var* news item, dated 31 Jun 1935, this film was to be a remake of Fox's 1931 production *Delicious* (see above). While the plot of this film has similarities to that of *Delicious,* the writers of the earlier film, Guy Bolton and Sonya Levien, were not given story credit for this film. According to a *HR* news item, Aaron Rosenberg, a former U.S.C. football star who became an assistant director, also appears in the film. While Pinky Tomlin's character is called "Roy Ford" throughout the film, the screen credits list the character name as "Ray Ford."

DV 26 Oct 1935, p. 3. *FD* 29 Oct 1935, p. 6. *HR* 24 Aug 1935, p. 2. *HR* 4 Sep 1935, p. 2. *HR* 17 Sep 1935, p. 6. *HR* 21 Sep 1935, p. 4. *HR* 26 Oct 1935, p. 3. *MPD* 28 Oct 1935, p. 9. *MPH* 2 Nov 1935, p. 57. *NYT* 8 Feb 1936, p. 19. *Var* 31 Jun 1935. *Var* 12 Feb 1936, p. 18.

THE PADRE *see* **GOING MY WAY**

PAGAN LOVE (Chinese Americans, Irish Americans, Jewish Americans)

Hugo Ballin Productions, Inc. *Dist* W. W. Hodkinson Corp., through Pathé Exchange, Inc. Dec **1920** [©Hugo Ballin Productions, Inc.; 7 Dec 1920; LP15912]. Si; b&w. 6 reels.

Pres Hugo Ballin. *Dir* Hugo Ballin. *Scen* Hugo Ballin, George S. Hellman and Achmed Abdullah. *Cam* J. Roy Hunt and H. Farrell.

Source: Based on the short story "The Honourable Gentleman" by Achmed Abdullah in *The Pictorial Review* (30 Sep 1919).

Cast: Togo Yamamoto (*Tsing Yu-Ch'ing*), Mabel Ballin (*Kathleen Levinsky*), Rockcliffe Fellowes (*Dr. Hardwick*), Charlie Fang (*The Hatchetman*), Nellie Fillmore (*Mrs. O'Grady*).

Drama. Tsing Yu-Ch'ing, a young Chinese, is sent to America from his native land to study Western civilization and carry on work for the Chinese republic. After attending an American university, Tsing starts

a Chinese newspaper in New York where he falls in love with a pretty blind girl, Kathleen Levinsky, the daughter of a Jew and an Irish woman. The girl, whose life is barren of love, accepts his attentions gladly. When Dr. Hardwick, a classmate from college, calls on Tsing and meets Kathleen, he offers to operate upon her eyes. The surgery is a success, but with the return of her sight, Kathleen flees in fear from Tsing. The latter returns to China, carrying his wounded love and desirous of nothing but the love eternal he believes he will find with Kathleen in the hereafter. He dies by his own hand while Kathleen, in America, finds herself attracted to Dr. Hardwick. *Blindness. Chinese. Cures. Miscegenation. Physicians. Racism. Suicide.* Afterlife. China. Irish. Jews. New York City. Newspapers. Operations, Surgical. Students.

Note: The working title for this film was *The Honourable Gentlemen.* This picture was Hugo Ballin's first independent production.

MPN 16 Oct 1920, p. 3028. *MPN* 4 Dec 1920, p. 4351. *MPN* 18 Dec 1920, p. 4551. *MPW* 4 Dec 1920, p. 640. *Wid's* 26 Dec 1920, p. 9.

THE PAGEANT OF SAN FRANCISCO (Latino)

California Motion Picture Corp.; Pageant Film Co.; An Alliance Special. *Dist* Alliance Films Corp. 15 Mar **1915** [©Pageant Film Co.; 8 Dec 1914; MU250]. Si; b&w. 5 reels.

Prod Herbert Payne. *Dir* Earl Emlay. *Story* A. Mackay Sutherland. *Cam* H. E. Butler and A. Powelson. *Scenic artist* W. T. Berry.

Historical, Drama. Don Gasper Portola leaves the Spanish settlement of San Diego with a band of adventurers and discovers the Golden Gate leading to a beautiful bay. He hurries back to San Diego and tells the Royal Viceroy, who sends a group of settlers led by Juan Baptista Anza and Padre Junipero Serra, a monk, on a hazardous journey to establish a Spanish colony there. The banners of the church and of Spain are raised, and the settlement is named in honor of St. Francis. Many years later, the first Yankee arrives. After the Mexican war, California becomes a territory of the United States. The gold rush of 1849 brings thousands to the area, and within a year, California is granted statehood. In the following decade, San Francisco is beset by lawless politicians, but eventually the law-abiding citizens prevail. After the devastating earthquake and fire of 1906, the city is rebuilt, and in 1914, the Panama-Pacific Exposition opens. *California–History. San Francisco (CA).* Colonies. Earthquakes. Explorers. Fires. Gold rushes. Panama-Pacific International Exposition. Political corruption. San Diego (CA). Settlers. Spaniards.

Note: This film was produced to promote the Panama-Pacific International Exposition held in San Francisco in 1915. The spellings of names of historical personages in the plot synopsis of this film reflect the way the names appear in contemporary reviews. However, the correct spellings, according to modern authorities, are as follows: Gaspar de Portolá, Juan Bautista de Anza and Junípero Serra.

Motog 13 Mar 1915, p. 400. *Motog* 27 Mar 1915, p. 508. *MPN* 13 Mar 1915, p. 70-71. *MPN* 20 Mar 1915, p. 71. *MPN* 10 Apr 1915, p. 64. *MPW* 20 Mar 1915, p. 1788. *MPW* 27 Mar 1915, p. 2004. *MPW* 10 Apr 1915, p. 244.

PAGLIACCI (Italian language)

Audio Cinema, Inc. *Dist* Leo Brecher. **1931**; New York premiere: 20 Feb 1931. Sd (Western Electric Sound System); b&w. 80 min. Italian language.

Prod Fortune Gallo. *Opera supv* Fortune Gallo. *Dir* Joe W. Coffman. *Dir of photog* Al Wilson. *Art dir* Alex Hall. *Ed* Joe W. Coffman. *Mus dir* Carlo Peroni. *Ballet mus* Carlo Peroni. *Ballet dir* Leon Leonidoff. *Rec dir* Nelson Minnerly.

Song(s): Libretto and music by Ruggiero Leoncavallo.

Source: Based on the opera *I pagliacci,* music and libretto by Ruggiero Leoncavallo (Milan, 21 May 1892).

Cast: THE SAN CARLO GRAND OPERA COMPANY, Fernando Bertini (*Canio, in the play Pagliaccio, Master of a troupe of strolling players*), Alba Novella (*Nedda, in the play Columbine, Wife of Canio*), Mario Valle (*Tonio, in the play Taddeo, the clown*), Francesco Curci (*Beppe, in the play Arlecchino,*), Guiseppe Interranti (*Silvio, a villager*), [San Carlo Symphony Orchestra].

Musical, Drama. [*Print viewed*]. The San Carlo Symphony Orchestra is conducted during the opera's prologue. Tonio then appears from behind a curtain and sings about the story. During the 1860s in Montalto, Italy, as the residents are celebrating the Feast of the Assumption, a troupe of traveling players arrives dressed in the costume of the characters in the play they are to perform. The local citizens stage a folk dance and others join in the singing. Canio tells the crowd of the troupe's play concerning Pagliaccio and his unfaithful wife. Alone in front of the stage, Nedda sings of her fears

that Canio will discover her infidelity with a villager, calming herself with thoughts of singing birds and her childhood. When Tonio approaches and tries to force himself upon her, she mockingly refuses his advances and repulses him with a whip. Departing, he threatens revenge. Nedda's lover, Silvio, enters and assures her that they are alone. As they embrace and plan their post-performance elopement, Tonio overhears them. He retrieves Canio from a nearby tavern in time for him to hear Nedda proclaim to Silvio, "Tonight, love, and forever I am yours." Canio chases the man, but he escapes. Canio then demands the name of her lover from Nedda, but she refuses to reveal his identity. Beppe restrains Canio as he tries to stab Nedda, then Tonio tells the husband that his wife's lover will surely betray himself by some action at the performance that night. As the troupe readies itself for the performance, Tonio collects admissions. The curtain opens and eight women, four each dressed as Columbines and Arlecchinos, perform a short minuet. Next, Nedda, as Columbine, sets a table in the room. She invites her lover, Arlecchino, played by Beppe, who has been serenading her with a lyre, to join her. Taddeo, portrayed by Tonio, enters and makes exaggerated love to her, but Arlecchino enters through a back window and mimics Taddeo, who departs. Silvio makes his way into the audience watching the play, while Arlecchino and Columbine dance and play with a trick chicken. Arlecchino has brought a bottle of wine and some sleep-inducing formula to facilitate his elopement with Columbine later. Taddeo returns and informs the lovers that Columbine's drunken husband Pagliaccio, played by Canio, is approaching. Taddeo hides in a closet and Arlecchino makes a quick escape out the window as Columbine recites, "Tonight, love, and forever I am yours," the same words used earlier with Silvio. Taddeo is retrieved from the closet by Columbine; he half-heartedly insists that Columbine has not deceived her husband. Canio, no longer acting, demands, "his name!" from Nedda, who vainly tries to maintain a theatrical facade. The audience is absorbed in the acting and applauds when Canio throws Nedda to the ground. Taking a knife, Canio, again refused the name of the lover by Nedda, stabs and kills her. When the audience restrains the obviously moved Silvio, Canio plunges the dagger into him, and he falls dead at Nedda's feet. *Actors and actresses. Infidelity. Escapes. Italy. Murder. Revenge.*

Note: Screen credits note that this was the "world's first sound picture grand opera." It was made in Italian, although it was shot on Long Island, according to *MPH*, which also notes that the San Carlo Opera Company had 150 members and the Symphony Orchestra had 75 members. Mayor Jimmy Walker attended the New York premiere at the Central Park Theater, where top admission was $5.50.

FD 1 Feb 1931, p. 10. *FD* 19 Feb 1931, p. 3. *MPH* 7 Mar 1931, p. 60. *Var* 25 Feb 1931, p. 22.

THE PALEFACE (Native Americans)
Paramount Pictures, Inc. *Dist* Paramount Pictures, Inc. 24 Dec **1948**; Prod: 28 Jul—1 Oct 1947; addl scenes: 10 Oct 1947 and 22 Jan 1948 (©Paramount Pictures, Inc.; 24 Dec 1948; LP2183]. Sd (Western Electric Recording); col (Technicolor). 10 reels. 89 or 91 min. Passed by the National Board of Review. PCA cert no. 12786.
Prod Robert L. Welch. *Dir* Norman Z. McLeod. *Asst dir* Alvin Ganzer. [*2d asst dir* Danny McCauley and Mickey Moore]. [*Dir, 2d unit* Gordon Jennings]. [*Asst dir, 2d unit* Richard McWhorter and Ralph Axness]. *Orig scr* Edmund Hartmann and Frank Tashlin. *Addl dial* Jack Rose. [*Contr on spec seq* Monte Brice and Barney Dean]. [*Contr wrt* Melville Shavelson]. *Dir of photog* Ray Rennahan. [*Cam op* Archie Dalzell]. [*Stills* Ed Henderson]. [*Cam, 2d unit* D. Jennings and Wallace Kelley]. [*Cam asst* Charles Leahy]. *Spec photog eff* Gordon Jennings. *Process photog* Farciot Edouart. [*Transparencies cam* Wallace Kelley]. *Technicolor color dir* Natalie Kalmus. *Assoc* Monroe W. Burbank. [*Technicolor cam* Paul Hill and Harry Marsh]. *Art dir* Hans Dreier and Earl Hedrick. [*Art dir asst* Al Roelofs]. *Ed* Ellsworth Hoagland. [*Asst cutter* Floyd Knudtson]. *Set dec* Sam Comer and Bertram Granger. [*Props* Art Camp]. [*Props, 2d unit* J. Thompson]. [*Props asst* Charles Mason]. *Cost* Mary Kay Dodson. *Men's ward* Gile Steele. [*Ward* Ed Fitzharris, A. Levine and Grace Harris]. *Mus score* Victor Young. *Dances staged by* Billy Daniels. [*Dance dir* Josephine Earl]. *Sd rec* Gene Merritt and John Cope. [*Rec* George Hamer]. *Makeup supv* Wally Westmore. [*Makeup artist* Charles Berner, Bill Woods and F. Thayer]. [*Hair* LaVaughn Speer, Gertrude Reade and Dean Cole]. [*Tech adv* Joe DeYong]. [*Prod mgr* R. L. Johnston and Charles Woolstenhulme]. [*Asst prod mgr, 2d unit* Andy Durkus and Stanley Goldsmith]. [*Dial coach* John Maxwell and Len Hendry].

[*Casting* Joe Egli]. [*Casting, 2d unit* Al Mann and Eddie Morse]. [*Pub* Al Jermy]. [*Scr supv* Claire Behnke]. [*Scr clerk, 2d unit* Marvin Weldon]. [*Grip* Darrell Turnmire]. [*Stage eng* Paul Franz]. [*Cableman* Tony Denocenzo]. [*Grip* Darrell Turnmire]. [*Mike grip* John Smirch]. [*Grip, 2d unit* E. Newmeyer]. [*Gaffer* Howard Kelly]. [*Elec* Joe Schuster]. [*Livestock* Bill Hurley]. [*Stunts* Don House, Buster Wiles, G. Bruggman, B. St. Angelo, R. Morales, L. Greenhill and P. Moore]. [*Double for Bob Hope* H. Wills]. [*Double for Jane Russell* W. Willingham].

Song(s): "Buttons and Bows" and "Meetcha 'Round the Corner," music and lyrics by Jay Livingston and Ray Evans; "Get a Man," music and lyrics by Joseph J. Lilley.

Cast: Bob Hope (*"Painless" Peter Potter*), Jane Russell (*Calamity Jane*), Robert Armstrong (*Terris*), Iris Adrian (*Pepper*), Robert Watson (*Toby Preston*), Jack Searl (*Jasper Martin*), Joseph Vitale (*Indian scout*), Charles Trowbridge (*Governor Johnson*), Clem Bevans (*Hank Billings*), Jeff York (*Joe*), Stanley Andrews (*Commissioner Emerson*), Wade Crosby (*Jeb*), Chief Yowlachie (*Chief Yellow Feather*), Iron Eyes Cody (*Chief Iron Eyes*), John Maxwell (*Village gossip*), Tom Kennedy (*Bartender*), Henry Brandon (*Wapato, Medicine Man*), Francis J. McDonald (*Lance*), Frank Hagney (*Greg*), Skelton Knaggs (*Pete*), Olin Howland (*Undertaker*), George Chandler (*First patient*), Nestor Paiva (*Second patient*), [Earl Hodgins (*Clem*)], [Arthur Space (*Zach*)], [Edgar Dearing (*Sheriff*)], [Dorothy Grainger (*Bath house attendant*)], [Charles Cooley (*Mr. "X"*)], [Eric Alden (*Bob*)], [Babe London (*Woman on wagon train*)], [Loyal Underwood (*Bearded character*)], [Billy Engle, Al M. Hill, Houseley Stevenson (*Pioneers*)], [Margaret Field, Laura Corbay (*Guests*)], [Patsy O'Byrne (*Charwoman, in bathhouse*)], [Lorna Jordan (*Girl in bathhouse*)], [Jody Gilbert (*Woman in bathhouse*)], [Harry Harvey, Paul E. Burns (*Justices of the peace*)], [Hall Bartlett (*Handsome cowboy*)], [Stanley Blystone, Bob Kortman (*Onlookers*)], [Oliver Blake (*Western character*)], [Lane Chandler (*Tough looking galoot*)], [Syd Saylor (*Cowboy*)], [Walden Boyle (*Hotel clerk*)], [John "Skins" Miller (*Bellhop*)], [Len Hendry (*A westerner*)], [Duke York, Ethan Laidlaw (*Henchmen*)], [Rolando Barrera, Rudolph Valentino (*Indians*)], [Dick Elliott (*The mayor*)], [Sharon McManus (*Child*)], [Carl Andre, Ted Mapes, Trevor Bardette, Kermit Maynard (*Horsemen*)], [Paul Dunn], [Jerry Hunter], [Eugene Persson], [Billy Andrews], [Marlyn Gladstone], [June Glory], [Maria J. Tavares], [Betty Hannon], [Dee La Nore], [Charmienne Harker], [Jerry James], [William Meader], [Dorothy Abbott], [Lee Blanchard], [Kuka Tuima], [Ralph Gomez], [Milton Frieburn], [Sonny Chorre], [Ralph Willingham], [Titus Spencer], [LeRoy Johnson], [Tim Nelson], [Chick Hannon], [Ethel Bryant], [Dick Farnsworth].

Comedy, Western, with songs. [*Print viewed*]. Sharpshooter and outlaw Calamity Jane is released from prison in order to catch renegades who have been smuggling guns to the Indians. She is ordered to Fort Deerfield, where she plans to join up with lawyer Jim Hunter and pose with him as a pioneer couple traveling West. Hunter is killed before Jane reaches him, but has left word for her to contact a friend of his named Hank Billings in the small town of Buffalo Flats. Jane is followed there, and makes a narrow escape with "Painless" Peter Potter, a timid, quack correspondence school dentist, whom she marries for the wagon train trip. Painless, completely oblivious to Jane's ulterior motives for marrying him, attempts to make love to her, but is met with a sharp thud on the back of his head every time he tries to kiss her. During an Indian attack on a pioneer camp, Jane deftly kills nearly a dozen Indians singlehandedly, but lets everyone, including Painless, believe he did the killing, hoping that the renegades will believe he is a federal agent. Meanwhile, in Buffalo Flats, Toby Preston, the renegades' leader, receives word that a new federal agent is about to arrive with the wagon train. When the wagon train pulls into town, Jane learns from Hank that two loads of dynamite came with them. Believing him to be the agent, Preston's men immediately attempt to get rid of Painless by ordering a saloon girl named Pepper to seduce him, thereby inciting the lethal jealousy of her boyfriend Joe. Painless talks tough and gives Joe until sundown to get out of town, and Jane decides to let him be killed in order to get rid of him. At the last minute, as Painless walks out into the street to meet Joe for a duel, Jane decides to save Painless in order to use him as bait, and shoots for him from a window, killing Joe. Hank later enters Jane and Painless' room with an arrow in his back and tells her that the dynamite is in the undertaker's parlor. Jane sends Painless

after the dynamite, and he bravely holds up the renegades, but then is abducted by an Indian. He and Jane are then taken hostage at an Indian camp, where she confesses that she married him to aid her in catching the outlaws, but now loves him. Also at the camp is the white turncoat, Jasper Martin, whom Jane recognizes as one of the governor's aides. As Jane is tied to a stake and prepared for burning, Painless, transformed by Jane's love, rigs the dynamite to blow, and they escape. Later, as Jane and Painless leave for their honeymoon, she is pulled from the wagon by one of the horses and dragged off into the distance. *Calamity Jane. Impersonation and imposture. Marriage—Forced by circumstances. Outlaws. Renegades. Sharpshooters. Dentists. Duels. Duplicity. Dynamite. Explosions. Forts. Governors. Hostages. Indians of North America. Jealousy. Quacks and quackery. Rescues. Saloons. Singers. Timidity. Transformation. Wagon trains.*

Note: In the film's closing scene, after Jane Russell is dragged off, Bob Hope says to the camera, "What do you want, a happy ending?" According to a *ParNews* item, Paramount negotiated with representatives of Howard Hughes, who at the time of production had Russell under personal contract, to obtain the actress for this film. Information in the Paramount Collection at the AMPAS Library reveals the following information about the production: The filmmakers originally considered Barbara Stanwyck for the part of "Calamity Jane." The wagon chase scene was shot on location in Chatsworth, and other scenes were shot at China Flats, Iverson Ranch, and the Conejo Airport in CA. *HR* news items include the following actors in the cast, however, their appearances in the final film have not been confirmed: Clint Dorrington, Speed Hansen, Ethel Greenwood, Marian Grey, Victor Travers, Al Stewart, Harry Ansel, Elmo Lincoln, Jack Ford, Tex Driscoll, The Cirillo Brothers, Robert Espinosa, James Archuletta, Richard Numena, Hilda Dozal and Chief Skyeagle.

Songwriters Jay Livingston and Ray Evans won an Academy Award for Music for their song "Buttons and Bows." Although *ParNews* reported in Oct 1947 that the Robert Mitchell Boychoir had been signed to sing "Buttons and Bows" in *Paleface*, the song was performed in the film as a solo by Bob Hope. A recording of the song was released prior to the film's opening, and several reviews mention that it became a hit without the aid of the film. A reported three million copies of the record and 700,000 copies of the sheet music were sold as of 1949, when orchestra leader and songwriter Freddie Rich filed a plagiarism suit over the song. Paramount, Jay Livingston and Ray Evans, Decca, Famous Music, RCA Victor, Columbia Records and Capital Records were named as defendants in the half-million-dollar suit. After "Buttons and Bows" was used in the film's 1952 sequel, *Son of Paleface*, Rich, who claimed portions of the song were taken from his score for Paramount's 1942 film *Wildcat*, added $250,000 to his estimate of damages. According to various sources, twenty-two to thirty-two bars of "Buttons and Bows" were in question. A jury turned in a verdict in favor of Paramount, and Rich lost a later appeal in Feb 1955.

As noted above, in 1952, Hope and Russell starred in a sequel to *The Paleface* called *Son of Paleface*, directed by Frank Tashlin. In 1968, *The Paleface* was remade into *The Shakiest Gun in the West*, with Alan Rafkin directing and Don Knotts and Barbara Rhoades starring. Among the many other films featuring Martha Jane Canary, popularly known as "Calamity Jane," are: the 1923 Famous Players-Lasky film *Wild Bill Hickock*, directed by Clifford S. Smith and starring Ethel Grey Terry and William S. Hart (see *AFI Catalog of Feature Films, 1921-30*; F2.6360); the 1936 Cecil B. DeMille film *The Plainsman*, starring Gary Cooper and Jean Arthur (see below); the 1949 film *Calamity Jane and Sam Bass*, directed by George Sherman, and starring Yvonne de Carlo and Howard Duff; and the 1995 United Artists film *Wild Bill*, directed by Walter Hill, and starring Ellen Barkin and Jeff Bridges.

Box 23 Oct 1948. *DV* 20 Oct 1948, p. 3, 9. *DV* 22 Feb 1955. *FD* 20 Oct 1948, p. 8. *Har* 23 Oct 1948. *HCN* 1 Jul 1953. *HR* 1 Aug 1947, p. 14. *HR* 8 Aug 1947, p. 13. *HR* 11 Aug 1947, p. 13. *HR* 17 Sep 1947, p. 12. *HR* 22 Sep 1947, p. 11. *HR* 24 Sep 1947, p. 11. *HR* 26 Sep 1947, p. 13, 16. *HR* 29 Sep 1947, p. 9. *HR* 20 Oct 1948, p. 4. *HR* 20 Dec 1948, p. 3. *HR* 17 Jun 1953. *HR* 1 Jul 1953. *HR* 2 Jul 1953. *HR* 14 Jul 1953. *HR* 14 Jul 1953. *LAT* 19 Dec 1948. *MPHPD* 30 Oct 1948, p. 4366. *NYT* 16 Dec 1948, p. 41. *Var* 20 Oct 1948, p. 11.

THE PALISER CASE (Portuguese Americans)

Goldwyn Pictures Corp. *Dist* Goldwyn Distributing Corp. Feb **1920** [©Goldwyn Picture Corp.; 31 Dec 1919; LP14692]. Si; b&w. 5 reels.

Pres Samuel Goldwyn. *Dir* William Parke. *Scen* Edfrid Bingham. *Story* Edgar Saltus. *Cam* Edward Gheller.

Cast: Pauline Frederick (*Cassy Cara*), Albert Roscoe (*Lennox*), James Neil (*Cara*), Hazel Brennan (*Margaret Austen*), Kate Lester (*Mrs. Austen*), Carrie Lee Ward (*Tambourina*), Warburton Gamble (*Monty Paliser*), Alec Francis (*Paliser, Sr.*), Eddie Sutherland (*Jack Menzies*), Tom Ricketts (*Maj. Archie Phipps*), Virginia Foltz (*Mrs. Colquhoun*).

Mystery. Cassy Cara, a struggling young singer and daughter of an old, crippled Portuguese violinist, is in love with Keith Lennox, an upstanding young man who is engaged to socialite Margaret Austen. Margaret's mother wishes her to wed the wealthy but unscrupulous Monty Paliser and succeeds in breaking her daughter's engagement by reporting that she had witnessed Cassy emerging from Lennox's apartment. However, Paliser admires Cassy, who, to relieve her father's financial distress, agrees to marry the scoundrel. The victim of a mock ceremony, Cassy discovers Paliser's treachery too late and

leaves him in a rage, going directly to Lennox with her story. She plans to kill Paliser that night at the opera, while, unknown to her, Lennox has formulated a similar plan to which he alludes at his club. That night, Paliser is stabbed to death, and Lennox arrested for the crime. To shield him, Cassy confesses to the crime, but Lennox denies her statement. Before either can be prosecuted, Cassy's father admits that he stabbed Paliser and then dies of a heart attack, thus clearing both lovers. *Cads. Marriage—Fake. Murder. Self-sacrifice. Clubs. Confession (Law). Duplicity. Fathers and daughters. Handicapped. Heart disease. Opera. Portuguese Americans. Singers. Socialites. Violinists.*

Note: Carrie Lee Ward may actually be Carrie Clark Ward.

ETR 28 Feb 1920, 1323. *MPN* 10 Jan 1920, p. 751. *MPN* 7 Feb 1920, p. 1533. *MPW* 10 Jan 1920, p. 191. *MPW* 14 Feb 1920, p. 1115. *NYT* 16 Feb 1920, p. 8. *Var* 20 Feb 1920, p. 40. *Wid's* 22 Feb 1920, p. 14.

THE PALOMINO (Latino)

Columbia Pictures Corp. *Dist* Columbia Pictures Corp. Mar **1950**; Prod: 13 Jul—28 Jul 1949 [©Columbia Pictures Corp.; 14 Mar 1950; LP2902]. Sd; col (Technicolor). 6,557 ft. 72 or 75 min.

Prod Robert Cohn. *Dir* Ray Nazarro. *Asst dir* Carter De Haven, Jr. *Scr* Tom Kilpatrick. *Dir of photog* Vincent Farrar. *Technicolor color dir* Morgan Padelford. *Art dir* Perry Smith. *Film ed* Aaron Stell. *Set des* James Crowe. *Mus dir* Mischa Bakaleinikoff. *Sd* George Cooper.

Cast: Jerome Courtland (*Steve Norris*), Beverly Tyler (*Maria Guevara*), Joseph Calleia (*Miguel Gonzales*), Roy Roberts (*Ben Lane*), Gordon Jones (*Bill*), Robert Osterloh (*Sam*), Tom Trout (*Williams*), Harry Garcia (*Johnny*), Trevor Bardette (*Brown*), Juan Duval (*Manuel*), Sam Flint (*Veterinarian*).

Animal, Drama. [*Viewed print incomplete*]. Determined to prove that he can be an asset to his father's meatpacking firm, Steve Norris persuades Brown, a cattle buyer, to let him try to convince the ranchers in the Santa Ynez Valley to sell their cattle to Norris rather than his competitor, Bannister. Along the road, Steve stops to ask directions from Miguel Gonzales, who explains that the palomino colt with him is The Duke, grandson of the famous palomino stallion, El Rey. Steve explains his mission, and Miguel suggests that he talk to Maria Guevara, whose family has been in the valley for two hundred years. When Steve arrives at the ranch, Maria whispers that a new foal is about to be born and, because of a superstition that a stranger can change a foal's color, asks him to stay away from the barn. Steve readily agrees, but later, accidentally walks by the barn, and when the foal is born black, Maria blames him and orders him away. Steve is forced to remain at the ranch, however, when his car has a flat tire, and as a result, he and Maria become friends. Maria reveals that she hopes to return to raising the palominos that made the ranch famous when her father was alive. Palominos are more valuable than ordinary horses, she explains, but because they are a color, not a breed, there is no way to ensure that a horse will be born a palomino. El Rey, the palomino stallion who sired many palomino colts, disappeared five years earlier after her father's death. Although Miguel believes that El Rey is still alive on El Monte, the nearby mountain, Maria is sure that their only hope for the future is The Duke. Later, Maria suggests that Steve approach Ben Lane who, as one of the newest ranchers in the valley, might be more willing to sell his cattle to Norris. Lane quickly agrees to sell Steve his cattle, but when Steve offers to hunt down some troublesome wild animals on El Monte, Lane suddenly changes his mind and sends Steve out of town. Lane, who has befriended Maria, actually stole El Rey and hid him on El Monte and has been selling his foals in the East. During a roundup on Maria's ranch, one of Lane's colts gets loose, and Maria mistakes him for The Duke. In an effort to help, Steve ropes the horse and inadvertently breaks its neck. Maria believes that he has killed The Duke, and Lane, who is lurking nearby, decides to take advantage of her mistake to kidnap The Duke. Later, Miguel, who had charge of The Duke, gets drunk with Steve, and Steve discovers that the colt was killed before Miguel lost The Duke. The two men then decide to search for the missing colt and bring along some mares to attract El Rey. During the night, Lane and his men spot Miguel and Steve and free the mares. Later, Miguel notices that the hobble he put on one of the mares has been cut and correctly assumes that someone moved the mares so that they would not attract El Rey. Steve and Miguel then return to El Monte, where they find the missing stallion. After Steve sends Miguel to fetch Maria, Lane plots an "accident" for him, but the trap catches one of Lane's men instead. Finally, Miguel persuades a skeptical Maria to come with him to El Monte, but when Steve tells Maria that Lane tried to kill him,

she refuses to believe him. Anxious to avoid discovery, Lane decides to ship all his horses East that night. Maria and Steve see the herd, but she is still not convinced that Lane is stealing the horses. Later, Lane tries to kill El Rey when the stallion attacks him, but is stopped by Steve. Maria is finally assured of Lane's guilt when she identifies Lane's brand on the mares. After Lane is arrested, Maria decides to leave El Rey in the mountains and bring her mares to him. Now that the future of her ranch is assured, Maria proposes to Steve, pointing out that everyone in the valley will gladly sell cattle to her husband. *Cattlemen. Horse owners. Horse thieves. Palomino horses. Women ranchers. Attempted murder. Cattle. Drunkenness. Mexican Americans. Mexicans. Mountains. Romance. Superstition. Traps.*

Note: The viewed print was less than half the length of the released film. Some plot information was obtained from reviews.

AmCin Feb 1950, p. 48, 62. *Box* 28 Jan 1950. *FD* 6 Feb 1950, p. 7. *HR* 2 Feb 1950, p. 3. *MPHPD* 4 Feb 1950, p. 178. *Var* 1 Feb 1950, p. 20.

PALS IN PARADISE (Jewish Americans)

Metropolitan Pictures Corp. of California. *Dist* Producers Distributing Corp. 22 Nov 1926 [©Metropolitan Pictures Corp. of California; 1 Nov 1926; LP23281]. Si; b&w. 7 reels, 6,696 ft.

Pres John C. Flinn. *Supv* Will M. Ritchey. *Dir* George B. Seitz. *Asst dir* Ed Bernoudy. *Adpt* Albert Kenyon and Will M. Ritchey. *Photog* Georges Benoit. *Art dir* Charles Cadwallader. *Prod mgr* Bert Gilroy.

Source: Based on the short story "Pals in Paradise" by Peter Bernard Kyne (publication undetermined).

Cast: Marguerite De La Motte (*Geraldine Howard*), John Bowers (*Bill Harvey*), Rudolph Schildkraut (*Abraham Lezinsky*), May Robson (*Esther Lezinsky*), Alan Brooks (*John Kenton*), Ernie Adams (*Butterfly Kid*), Bruce Gordon (*Gentleman Phil*).

Melodrama. Bill Harvey, a young prospector who has taken over a mining claim belonging to the now-deceased John Howard, strikes gold and precipitates a rush to the California site. With Esther and Abraham Lezinsky, he establishes a town known as Paradise. Geraldine, Howard's daughter, arrives with a claim to her father's mine. Kenton, who has a police record, convinces Jerry that she should fight him and speaks disparagingly of Bill. Jerry accuses Bill of stealing her claim papers, then discovers that he is innocent; however, when he tells her Kenton is a crook, she indignantly declares herself engaged to him. Kenton and his henchmen stage a raid on the express office, and Bill arrests him—winning the confidence and finally the love of Jerry. *California. Courtship. Jews. Mining claims. Prospectors.*

FD 12 Dec 1926. *MPW* 29 Nov 1926. *NYT* 24 Nov 1926, p. 26. *Var* 24 Nov 1926, p. 15.

PALS OF THE WEST (Chinese Americans)

Film Art Productions. *Dist* Clark-Cornelius Corp. 3 Oct 1922. Si; b&w. 5 reels, 4,021-4,083 ft.

Cast: R. Lee Hill (*Paul Preston*), William A. Lowery (*Dan Hallet*), M. McWade (*Lee Wong*), Esther Ralston (*Nina*), Jack Patterson (*"Black Bill"*).

Western. "Dan Hallet and Paul Preston, inseparable pals, rescue Nina, white girl, from bondage of Lee Wong. Nina, later, still under Wong's influence, contrives to get him job as cook with Hallet and Preston at their mining camp. Wong, with help of Black Bill, tries to make bad feeling between the pals, trying to make it seem that Paul is about to rob Dan and take the girl. The Oriental's scheme fails and events prove that Nina is really the daughter of Dan. Romantic finish between Paul and Nina." (*MPNBG* 4 Apr 1923, p. 68.) According to *Var* the half-caste Wong's grudge against Dan stems from the fact that long ago he deserted Wong's half sister, who was white and the mother of Nina, upon learning of the Oriental blood in the family. *Bigotry. Chinese Americans. Desertion (Marital). Friendship. Half-castes. Mining towns.*

Note: This film was also known as *Her Half Brother*.

PANIC IN THE STREETS (Immigrants)

Twentieth Century-Fox Film Corp. *Dist* Twentieth Century-Fox Film Corp. 15 Sep 1950; Prod: 19 Dec 1949—9 Feb 1950 [©Twentieth Century-Fox Film Corp.; 3 Jul 1950; LP417]. Sd (Western Electric Recording); b&w. 10 reels, 8,642 ft. 93 or 96 min. PCA cert no. 14313.

Prod Sol C. Siegel. *Dir* Elia Kazan. [*Asst dir* Johnny Johnston]. [*Dial dir* Michael Audley]. *Scr* Richard Murphy. *Adpt* Daniel Fuchs. *From a story by* Edna Anhalt and Edward Anhalt. [*Contr wrt* John Lee Mahin and Philip Yordan]. *Dir of photog* Joe MacDonald. *Spec photog eff*

Fred Sersen. *Art dir* Lyle Wheeler and Maurice Ransford. *Film ed* Harmon Jones. *Set dec* Thomas Little and Fred J. Rode. *Ward dir* Charles Le Maire. *Cost des* Travilla. *Mus* Alfred Newman. *Orch* Edward Powell, Herbert Spencer, [Benny Carter, Bernard Mayers, Red Nichols and Ernie Felice]. *Sd* W. D. Flick and Roger Heman. *Makeup artist* Ben Nye. [*Unit mgr* F. E. Johnston].

Song(s): "No Good Man (Blues)," words by Paul Vandervoort, II, music by Benny Carter; "The Old Master Painter," words by Haven Gillespie, music by Beasley Smith.

Cast: RICHARD WIDMARK [(*Dr. Clinton Reed*)], PAUL DOUGLAS [(*Police Captain Warren*)], BARBARA BEL GEDDES [(*Nancy Reed*)], Walter Jack Palance [(*Blackie*)], Zero Mostel [(*Fitch*)], Dan Riss [(*Neff*)], Tommy Cook [(*Vince*)], [Alexis Minotis (*John Mefaris*)], [Guy Thomajan (*Poldi*)], [Edward Kennedy (*Jordan*)], [H. T. Tsiang (*Cook*)], [Lewis Charles (*Kochak*)], [Raymond Muller (*Dubin*)], [Tommy Rettig (*Tommy Reed*)], [Lenka Peterson (*Jeanette*)], [Pat Walshe (*Pat*)], [Paul Hostetler (*Dr. Gafney*)], [George Ehmig (*Kleber*)], [John Schilleci (*Lee*)], [Waldo Pitkin (*Ben*)], [Leo Zinser (*Sergeant Phelps*)], [Beverly Brown (*Dr. Mackey*)], [William Dean (*Cortelyou*)], [H. Waller Fowler, Jr. (*Mayor Murray*)], [Rex Moad (*Wynant*)], [Irving Vidacovich (*Johnston*)], [Val Winter (*Commissioner Quinn*)], [Wilson Bourg, Jr. (*Charlie*)], [Mary Liswood (*Mrs. Fitch*)], [Aline Stevens (*Rita*)], [Ruth Moore Mathews (*Mrs. Dubin*)], [Stanley J. Reyes (*Redfield*)], [Darwin Greenfield (*Violet*)], [Emile Meyer (*Captain Beauclyde*)], [Herman Cottman (*Scott*)], [Al Theriot (*Al*)], [Juan Villasana (*Hotel proprietor*)], [Robert Dorsen (*Coast Guard Lieutenant*)], [Henry Mamet (*Anson*)], [Tiger Joe Marsh (*Bosun*)], [Arthur Tong (*Lascar boy*)], [Edward Alana (*Attendant*)], [Mildred Fossier (*Woman in morgue*)], [Robert Smith, Preston Rowe (*Photographers*)], [Hunter Waites (*Willie*)], [Julius Alford (*Mayor's assistant*)], [H. C. "Dutch" Ohme (*Tout*)], [Henry Otnott, Philip Bourgeos (*Policemen*)], [Louis Lockhart, Edgar J. Curole, Jr., William Kiesel, Clifford Le Blanc (*Interrogators*)], [Joyce Hiatt, Lillian Rodriguez (*Hustlers*)], [John E. Dillon, Gean Greathouse, Vivian Scanlon, George Walker, John R. Jacobs, John E. Lewis, Charles Sanborn, Mary Skinner, Lillian Walker, Margaret Parmenter (*Suspects*)], [John H. Coffey (*Mulcahy*)], [Manuel Estrada (*Master at arms*)], [Leo Hebert (*Announcer*)], [John McDougall (*Big man*)], [Bremond White (*Assistant dispatcher*)], [Alberto Flores (*Black seaman*)], [Peter Mulder, Mack McCarthy, Milton Schmidt, Edward L. Thompson, John Walorz (*Seamen*)], [George Beninato (*Tom*)], [William Essaris (*George*)], [William Walker, Sr. (*Police lieutenant*)], [Ernest Simoneaux (*Police sergeant*)], [Guy Forrest (*Watchman*)], [Louis Sambola (*Police announcer*)], [Edward Manzey (*Deckhand*)], [Young Gee (*Chinese cook*)], [Edward "Skipper" McNally, Eddie Manuel, Allen Mitchell, Ira Blalock, Richard Morales, Dwain Lattimer, Pascal Newman (*Sailors*)], [Eugene Sonfield (*Watchman*)], [Abe Berenson (*Captain James*)], [Robert H. Kirby (*Harbor Patrol*)], [Charles Kennedy (*Doc Robbins*)], [Miriam Scott (*Nurse*)], [Elizabeth Dombourajian (*Grandmother*)], [John David (*Fruit salesman*)], [G. S. Cambias (*Catholic priest*)], [Robert Jourdan, Francis Jeansonne (*Boys*)], [Jewel King (*Black singer*)], [Edward Dillon].

Disaster, Drama. [*Print viewed*]. After brawling over a card game in the wharf area of New Orleans, a man named Kochak, suffering visibly from a flu-like illness, is killed by gangster Blackie and his two flunkies, Kochak's cousin Poldi and a man named Fitch. They leave the body on the docks, and later when the dead man, who carries no identification, is brought to the morgue, the coroner grows suspicious about the virus present in his blood and calls his superior, Dr. Clinton Reed, a uniformed doctor working for the U.S. Public Health Service. Reed is enjoying a rare day off with his wife Nancy and their son Tommy, but decides to inspect the body. After careful examination, he determines that Kochak had "pneumonic plague," the pulmonary version of bubonic plague. Reed springs into action, insisting that everyone who came into contact with the body be inoculated. He also orders that the dead man's identity be determined, as well as his comings and goings during the previous few days. Reed meets with people from the mayor's office, the police commissioner and other city officials, but they are skeptical of his claims. Eventually, however, his impassioned pleas convince them that they have forty-eight hours to save New Orleans from the plague. Reed must also convince police captain Warren and the others that the press must not be notified, because report of a plague would

spread mass panic. Warren and his men begin to interview Slavic immigrants, as it has been determined that the body may be of Armenian, Czech or mixed blood. Burdened by the knowledge that the massive investigation has little chance of success, Reed accuses Warren of not taking the threat seriously enough. In turn, Warren admits that he thinks Reed is ambitious and trying to use the situation to further his career. Reed, angry, decides to take matters into his own hands and, acting on a hunch that the man may have entered the city's port illegally, goes to the National Maritime Union hiring hall and passes out copies of the dead man's picture. Although the workers tell Reed that seamen never talk, he goes to a café next door hoping that someone will meet him with a tip. Eventually a young woman shows up and takes Reed to see her friend Charlie, who reluctantly admits that he worked aboard the ship, the *Nile Queen*, upon which the already ill man was smuggled. Meanwhile, Fitch, who was questioned by Warren but claimed to know nothing, goes to Blackie and warns him about the investigation. Blackie plans to get out of town, but begins to suspect that his sidekick Poldi received expensive smuggled goods from Kochak, explaining the police's intense investigation of the man's murder. Reed and Warren, who is now convinced of Reed's integrity, go to the *Nile Queen* and convince the crew to talk by telling them that they will die if the sick man was indeed on their ship. After carrying up a sick cook from the hold, the seamen then permit Reed and Warren to inoculate and question them, revealing in the process that Kochak boarded at Oran and was fond of shish-kebob. With this lead, Reed and Warren canvas the city's Greek restaurants, and just after they leave one such establishment, Blackie arrives to meet Poldi, who is very ill. A short time later, Reed receives word that a woman, Rita, has died of the fever and realizes that she was the wife of the Greek restaurant proprietor who had earlier lied about having served Kochak. Reed returns to headquarters to discover that a reporter is threatening to break the story that a virus is endangering the city. Reed is impressed when the deeply committed yet unorthodox Warren throws the reporter into jail to keep him quiet. Late in the evening, a beleaguered Reed returns home for a few hours of sleep, and his wife announces that she is pregnant. She then tries to restore her husband's flagging self-confidence. A few hours later, Reed and Warren learn that the mayor is angry about the treatment of the reporter. The reporter, who has been released, announces that the story will appear in the morning paper in four hours, giving Reed and Warren little time to find their man. Meanwhile, Blackie goes to Poldi's room and tries to force him to reveal information about some smuggled goods, but the dying Poldi is delirious and only rants nonsensically. Blackie then brings in his own doctor and tells Poldi's grandmother that they will take care of him. Just then, Reed, having been tipped off by the Greek restaurant owner, arrives, and Blackie and Fitch, who are carrying Poldi down the stairs, pitch the man over the side and flee. Reed chases the two to the docks, where he tries to explain to them about the plague. The men run desperately through depots, docks and a warehouse, and at one point, Warren shoots and injures Blackie, preventing him from shooting Reed. Blackie accidentally shoots Fitch and then tries to struggle onto a ship but, exhausted, falls into the water. His work finally done, Reed heads for home, and on the way, Warren offers to give him some of the smuggled perfume that Poldi had indeed received from Kochak. As the radio announces the resolution of the crisis, a proud Nancy greets her husband. *Epidemics. Health officials. New Orleans (LA). Plague. Waterfronts. Aliens, Illegal. Armenian Americans. Chases. Coroners. Corpses. Family relationships. Greek Americans. Immigrants. Marriage. Mayors. Police chiefs. Reporters. Restaurateurs. Sailors. Ships. Slavic Americans. Smuggling. Urban life. Warehouses.*

Note: The working titles of this film were *Port of Entry* and *Outbreak*, and the original motion picture story by Edna and Edward Anhalt was titled "Quarantine." The screen story was partially based on a short story by Edward Anhalt, titled "Some Like It Cold," which was published under his pseudonym, Andrew Holt, in *Dime Detective Magazine*, Feb 1949. In his autobiography, director Elia Kazan writes that Twentieth Century-Fox's sales department, which was worried about the film's potential for "popular appeal," chose the title *Panic in the Streets*. Kazan also claims that he collaborated closely with writer Richard Murphy on the script, stating, "we rewrote every scene every day."

Panic in the Streets was shot on location in New Orleans, and featured many local residents in small roles and as extras. Production notes for the film claim that only twelve of the 112 actors with speaking parts were brought in from Hollywood and New York. The same source states that H. Walter Fowler, Jr., who plays "Mayor Murray," was a New Orleans stockbroker, and that Emile Meyer, who plays "Captain Beauclyde," was a cab driver. *Panic in the Streets*

marked the first screen appearance of Jack Palance (billed onscreen as Walter Jack Palance). Many critics praised his performance, including the *LAT* reviewer, who described the actor as a "hulking giant with a catlike grace and a caressing voice." According to a 21 Feb 1949 *NYHT* news item, Dana Andrews and Linda Darnell were originally cast in the film.

In the Anhalts' original motion picture story, the first man to die of the disease is named "Ramon Sanchez," not "Kochak," as in the film. Although characters "Poldi" and "Kochak" speak some Armenian in the picture, material in the MPAA/PCA Collection at the AMPAS Library contains the following note: "It is suggested in the script and studio synopsis that Charles Thomajian [sic], and Thomajian's [sic] mother are Armenian. However, this is not specifically stated in the film. The restaurant owner and his wife are possibly Greek, possibly Hungarian—no specific nationality is stated." On 5 Mar 1951, *Lux Radio Theatre* broadcast a version of the story with Richard Widmark, Paul Douglas and Joyce MacKenzie. In his autobiography, Kazan claims that by casting Zero Mostel in the film, he "rescued" him from the Hollywood blacklist of communist sympathizers, and in so doing, gained much admiration from Hollywood's left. Kazan's later "friendly" testimony during the HUAC hearings cost him that admiration, however.

Box 24 Jun 1950. *DV* 14 Jun 1950, p. 3, 7. *FD* 21 Jun 1950, p. 7. *HR* 6 Jan 1950, p. 11. *HR* 10 Feb 1950, p. 21. *HR* 14 Jun 1950, p. 3. *LAT* 16 Sep 1950. *MPD* 14 Jun 1950. *MPHPD* 17 Jun 1950, p. 345. *NYHT* 21 Feb 1949. *NYT* 5 Aug 1950, p. 9. *Var* 14 Jun 1950, p. 8.

PAPÁ SOLTERO (Spanish language)

Darío Productions, Inc. *Dist* Paramount Pictures, Inc. **1939**; Santiago, Chile opening: 9 May 1939; San Juan, Puerto Rico opening: 25 May 1939; Los Angeles opening: 10 Oct 1939; Prod: Dec 1938 at Grand National Studios. Sd; b&w. 9 reels, 7,806 ft. 87 min. PCA cert no. 5016. Spanish language.

Prod Darío Faralla. *Dir* Richard Harlan. *Dial dir* Gabriel Navarro. *Asst dir* Ruby Rosenberg. *Scr* Dana Wilma and Arthur Vernon Jones. *Orig story* Dana Wilma. *Spanish version* Enrique Uhthoff and Gabriel Navarro. *Photog* Jerry Ash. *Art dir* Ralph Berger. *Set dec* Glenn P. Thompson. *Mus dir* Lud Gluskin. *Mus arr* Lucien Moraweck. *Mus supv* Abe Meyer. *Chorus master* Harry Simeone. *Sd rec* Hal Baumbaugh. *Makeup* Max Factor. *Prod mgr* Irving Applebaum.

Song(s): "Yo ya me voy," "Chichén-Itzá," El amor que florece" and "Es un pecado querer," words and music by Tito Guízar and Nenette Noriega; "Perdí mi amor" and "Pececitos" words and music by Tana; "Canción de cuna," words by Ralph Freed, music by Frederick Hollander, Spanish lyrics by Tana; "Pardonnez-moi, Madame," words and music by Alec Templeton, Neville Fleeson and Tana.

Cast: Tito Guízar (*Carlos del Rio*), Amanda Varela (*Marta Cortez/Teresa*), Tana (*Tana*), Paul Ellis (*Cruz Ramos*), Sarita Wooton (*Lolita*), Paco Moreno (*Cándido*), Martín Garralaga (*Pérez*), Barry Norton (*Ricardo*), Arroyito (*Chicho*), Raúl Lechuga (*Tomás*), Rosa Turich (*Romualda*), Carlos Villarías (*Buenrosto*), King Wallace (*Police sergeant*), Lucio Villegas (*Don Pedro*), José Peña "Pepet" (*"El sordo"*), Carlos Ruffino (*Crespo*), Carlos Montalbán (*Esteban*), Daniel F. Rea (*Agustín*), Antonio Vidal (*Juez*).

Drama, with songs. [*Not viewed*]. Carlos del Rio, a handsome young singer, works as a laborer on a road construction project near the Rio Grande in Texas. One night, a touring car and truck collide outside the camp and Carlos goes to their rescue. He finds the driver of the car, Pedro Medina, an elderly man who is taking his young granddaughter Lolita to Los Angeles to live with her older sister Teresa, seriously injured. When Pedro dies, Carlos, who has been notified that the will of his late uncle is being probated in Los Angeles, decides to take Lolita with him to California. There, Carlos rents a room in a boarding house and learns from his uncle's lawyer, Martinez, that, other than a cash settlement to Cruz Ramos, the owner of a gambling casino, Carlos has inherited the bulk of his uncle's estate. Martinez suggests that Carlos meet with Ramos, who has been named executor. At Ramos's apartment, Carlos meets Marta Cortez, a young singer who works as a cigarette girl at Ramos's gambling casino. Although Ramos informs Carlos that his uncle's estate consists of a retreat in the country that he has leased for $100 a month, in reality, Ramos has rented the property to a gambling syndicate for a huge amount of money. Through Tana, an actress in his boarding house, Carlos wins an audition at the casino where he again meets Marta, and the pair fall in love. When Ramos returns from a brief vacation, he becomes enraged upon learning that the proceeds from the gaming room and roulette wheel have declined. Meanwhile, through Marta and Tana, Carlos learns that Ramos has been cheating him out of his inheritance. In protest, they all quit Ramos' employ, and later discover that Marta is Lolita's long-lost sister Teresa. Soon after, the police raid the casino, and Ramos directs them to Carlos,

who is arrested for owning an illegal gambling hall. Martinez testifies in Carlos's behalf, and Ramos is arrested and brought to justice. Carlos then reopens the casino on a legitimate basis and all ends happily. *Casino owners. Inheritance. Long-lost relatives. Automobile accidents. Casinos. Executors. False arrests. Lawyers. Police raids. Singers. Sisters. Wards and guardians. Wills.*

Note: The English working title of this film was *Bachelor Father.* This was the second Spanish language film, starring Tito Guízar, produced by Darío Faralla in Hollywood for Paramount release. Materials contained in the MPAA/PCA Collection at the AMPAS Library note that in late 1939, Paramount sold the United States distribution rights to Victoria Films. Assistant director Ruby Rosenberg is listed as Ruby Rosen in a *HR* production chart. He may have been known by both names.
DV 2 Feb 1939, p. 3. *HR* 4 Nov 1938, p. 5. *HR* 17 Dec 1938, p. 7. *HR* 24 Dec 1938, p. 7. *HR* 3 Feb 1939, p. 4. *NYT* 6 Nov 1939, p. 20.

PAPAGO WELLS *see* APACHE TERRITORY

PARADISE IN HARLEM (African Americans)

Jubilee Pictures Corp. *Dist* International Road Shows, Inc. **1940.** Sd; b&w. 9 reels, 7,846 ft. 87 min. PCA cert no. 01050.

Prod supv Jack Goldberg. *Dir* Joseph Seiden. *Orig story* Frank Wilson. *Scr adpt* Vincent Valentini. *Cine* Don Malkames and Charles Levine. *Sd rec* Murray Dichter and Paul Jacobs. *Unit mgr* Irvin G. Miller.

Song(s): "I Gotta Put You Down," music and lyrics by Lucky Millinder; "Harlem Blues," music and lyrics by Perry Bradford; "Why Am I So Blue?" music and lyrics by Joe Thomas; "Harlem Serenade," music and lyrics by Vincent Valentini.

Cast: Frank Wilson (*Lem Anderson*), Mamie Smith (*Madame Mamie [Smith]*), Norman Astwood (*Rough Jackson*), Edna Mae Harris (*Doll Davis*), Merritt Smith (*Ned Avery*), Francine Everett (*Desdemona [Jones]*), Sydney Easton (*Sneeze Ancrum*), Babe Matthews (*Laura Lou*), Lionel Monogas (*Milt Gilson*), Madeline Belt (*Acme Delight*), Herman Green (*Ganaway*), Percy Verwayne (*Spanish*), George Williams (*Runt*), Alec Lovejoy (*Misery*), Lucky Millinder, and His Orchestra, Juanita Hall Singers, The Alphabetical Four.

African American, Crime, Drama. [*Print viewed*]. Backstage at Harlem's Standard Cabaret, Lem Anderson, long typecast as a comedian, yearns to be a dramatic actor and play Shakespeare's *Othello.* After Lem witnesses the gangland killing of Slim Jewett, he is warned not to talk, and two of the gang, Ganaway and Spanish, follow him home, where his wife Emma is gravely ill. Hearing the strangers, Emma climbs out of her bed and dies. When the criminals warn Lem that his beloved nephew, Ned Avery, will be hurt unless he leaves town, Lem goes south, where he becomes a drunkard and loses his acting job. In Tennessee, singer Sneeze Ancrum and his partner find Lem asleep in a bar and offer him a part in a play, which Lem refuses because he does not want to play "Uncle Tom" anymore. When Sneeze telegraphs Ned, Ned sends for his uncle and arranges to cast him in a local church production of *Othello.* Meanwhile, the gang, angered by Lem's return, sends Ganaway to knock Ned unconscious as a warning to Lem. Later, the gang leader orders a reluctant Doll Davis to tempt Lem into a drunken escapade and disgrace him. Not realizing that Doll is widely known as a "bad" cabaret girl, Lem hires her for the play, and she entices him to her apartment. As Ganaway shoots Lem, the repentant Doll jumps in front of Lem, taking the bullet, but she escapes a fatal injury. Back at the Standard, Lem enters drunk and attacks Rough Jackson as a warning to the gang that he will not leave. The police arrest Lem and only release him long enough to do the play. At the hospital, Mamie urges Doll to confess, which she does in the presence of the police. At first, *Othello* is heckled, but when it becomes a musical production, the audience joins in and dances. Outside, in an alley, the gang leader and Milt face off in a shootout and both are killed. Lem is soon cleared of suspicion, and the play, a hit, is headed for Broadway. *Actors and actresses. African Americans. Entertainers. Gangsters. Plays. Alcoholics. Cabarets. Comedians. Confession (Law). Hospitals. Murder. Musicians. Nephews. New York City–Harlem. Orchestras. Othello (Play). Police. Seduction. Self-sacrifice. William Shakespeare. Shootings. Singers. Tennessee. Threats. United States–South. Witnesses.*

Note: This film began production under the title *Othello in Harlem.* According to a *NYT* article, *Paradise in Harlem* was filmed in Fort Lee, NJ. Modern sources list actors Perry Bradford and Joe Thomas in the cast and Dave Goldberg as the co-producer. Modern sources also put the running time at 83 or 85 minutes. Although the onscreen credits claim that the picture was

copyrighted in 1940 by Jubilee Pictures Corp., no copyright registration has been found. Jubilee Pictures Corp. was formed in 1940 by Jack Goldberg, and this film was the company's first release. Several songs performed in the picture were not acknowledged in the onscreen credits.
Exb 10 Jul 1940, p. 563. *NYT* 3 Aug 1941.

PARAMOUNT ON PARADE (*foreign version*) *see* GALAS DE LA PARAMOUNT

PARDON US (Racial impersonation)

Hal Roach Studios, Inc.; Metro-Goldwyn-Mayer Corp.; controlled by Loew's Inc. *Dist* Metro-Goldwyn-Mayer Distributing Corp. 15 Aug **1931;** Prod: began 24 Jun 1930 [©Metro-Goldwyn-Mayer Distributing Corp.; 10 Sep 1931; LP2460]. Sd (Western Electric System); b&w. 6 reels. 55 min. Passed by the National Board of Review.

Pres HAL ROACH. *Dir* James Parrott. *Dial* H. M. Walker. *Photog* Jack Stevens. *Ed* Richard Currier. [*Prison set des* Frank Durloff]. *Rec eng* Elmer Raguse. [*Purchasing agent* L. A. French].

Song(s): "Lazy Moon," music by J. Rosamond Johnson, lyrics by Bob Cole; "I Want to Go Back to Michigan," music and lyrics by Irving Berlin; "Swing Along, Chillun," by Will Marion Cook; "Hand Me Down My Silver Trumpet, Lord" and "Dar's a Jubilee" composers undetermined.

Cast: STAN LAUREL [(*Stan Laurel*)], OLIVER HARDY [(*Oliver Hardy*)], June Marlowe [(*The warden's daughter*)], Wilfred Lucas [(*The warden*)], James Finlayson [(*Instructor*)], Walter Long [(*Tiger*)], Stanley J. Sandford [(*Officer LeRoy Shields*)].

Prison, Comedy. [*Print viewed*]. Bootleggers Stan Laurel and Oliver Hardy are arrested and sent to prison after Stan sells a bottle of beer to a police officer. Stan is afflicted with a loose tooth that makes a buzzing "raspberry" sound every time he speaks, much to the chagrin of their tough cellmate, Tiger, and the prison warden, who suspect that Stan is making fun of them. Stan and Ollie go to the prison school but are sent for a stint in solitary after Ollie shoots an ink ball at Tiger and hits the teacher instead. Later, after they rejoin the others in the yard, Tiger and his tough pals plan an escape, and although they are caught, Stan and Ollie make it to freedom. The warden sends bloodhounds to track them, but the boys charm the dogs into becoming their pets. Sometime later, the boys have disguised themselves with blackface and are happy members of a group of cotton pickers. Stan has even devised a way of using chewing gum to stop his tooth from buzzing. One day, the warden and his daughter are driving by the field where Stan and Ollie are working when their car breaks down. The warden requests the boys's help, which they give even though they recognize him. The warden does not recognize them, however, until Stan removes his chewing gum and his tooth buzzes as he bids them farewell. Back at the prison, Stan's buzz annoys yet another guard, who sends him to the prison dentist. Terrified, Stan brings Ollie in with him, and the dentist mistakes Ollie for his patient and takes out one of his teeth before Ollie can explain. The dentist then sets to work on Stan, but extracts the wrong tooth, so, still buzzing, Stan goes back with Ollie to their cell, where Tiger is planning yet another escape. Later, in the mess hall, the prisoners pass out guns and bullets, and when Stan and Ollie accidentally fire their guns, a riot begins. Tiger and the others capture the warden and the guards, but Stan and Ollie's inept handling of their guns again causes chaos, this time keeping the other prisoners at bay until police troops arrive to save the day. The warden gives pardons to the boys in gratitude for their bravery, but when he offers to help them go straight, Stan asks him if he wants to buy a couple cases of beer, after which the warden chases them out of his office. *Bootleggers. Bumblers. Pardons. Prison escapes. Prison life.* Chewing gum. Cotton. Dentists. Dogs. Firearms. Mistaken identity. Prison wardens. Racial impersonation. Riots. Teachers.

Note: The working titles of this film were *The Rap* and *Their First Mistake*, which was also the release title of a 1932 short made by Stan Laurel and Oliver Hardy. A 9 Aug 1930 *EHW* review noted that a preview of *The Rap* (as the picture was then called) ran for 70 min. According to modern sources, after the film's Aug preview, retakes and foreign language versions were shot from mid-Sep—1 Dec 1930. A 15 Nov 1930 *EHW* news item reported that "In an effort to make *Their First Mistake*, originally titled *The Rap*...louder and funnier, Hal Roach is adding sequences to it before it is finally released for the entertainment of the millions of Laurel and Hardy fans." According to company records located at the USC Cinema-Television Library, the prison set was designed from photographs of San Quentin and Sing Sing. Although the onscreen credits and contemporary sources list Jack Stevens as the photographer, modern sources often credit Jack's brother, George Stevens.

This was the first feature-length film in which Laurel and Hardy starred.

Between 1929 and 1951, they appeared in twenty-seven feature-length, English-language films, four of which featured the comedians in guest appearances rather than starring roles. The first picture in which Laurel and Hardy appeared together was the 1921 Reelcraft short entitled *The Lucky Dog*. Many modern sources note that, while Laurel and Hardy worked at Roach, Laurel was actively involved in all facets of production, including writing, directing and editing, although he did not receive onscreen credit for these contributions. Modern sources also state that "the boys," as Laurel and Hardy were known, occasionally reworked gags and story lines from their shorts into their features. Among the actors who often appeared in Laurel and Hardy shorts and features were James Finlayson, Stanley J. "Tiny" Sandford, Charlie Hall, Sam Lufkin, Baldwin Cooke, and Mae Busch. Among their frequent directors and writers, both on the shorts and features, were James Horne, James Parrott, Leo McCarey and Charley Rogers.

In addition to a Spanish-language version, French, German and Italian language versions, entitled *Sous les verrous*, *Hinter Schloss und Riegel* and *Muraglie*, respectively, were also produced. No information concerning the release of these versions in the U.S. has been located. Boris Karloff may have appeared in the French version (some modern sources state that he played "Tiger," but another modern source asserts that Walter Lang and June Marlowe played "Tiger" and the warden's daughter in all five versions.) Lucien Prival was in the German version and Guido Trento was in the Italian version. According to the company records, the production crew listed above also worked on the foreign-language versions, which were shot simultaneously after the English version was completed. Laurel and Hardy were taught their foreign language lines phonetically, and dialogue scenes were shot using each of the languages. They used this procedure for the foreign releases of several shorts, and for some shorts that were combined into feature-length films, while for other films, they shot the foreign versions at the same time as the English-language version. The pressbooks for the foreign versions of this film, contained in the company records, reveal that the plot was slightly different: During the riot caused by Stan and Ollie's inept handling of a weapon passed to them in the mess hall, a fire starts in the warden's home. Stan and Ollie rescue the warden's daughter, and thus win their parole. According to modern sources, the fire and rescue scenes were filmed for the English version but were deleted. *De bote en bote*, which was viewed, utilizes the fire/rescue sequence and includes two more songs, but dispenses with the schoolroom sequence. Modern sources note that S. C. Baden was the sound mixer for all of the foreign versions. Modern sources credit John Whitaker with assisting Elmer Raguse in mixing the sound of the English version, and John Harrison and Ralph Butler with the location sound recording.

Modern sources also include the following actors in the cast of the English version: Charlie Hall (*Dental assistant/deliveryman*); Sam Lufkin, Silas D. Wilcox and George Miller (*Prison guards*); Frank Holliday (*Officer in classroom*); Harry Bernard (*Warren, the desk sergeant*); Robert Burns (*Prone dental patient*); Frank Austin (*Dental patient in waiting room*); Otto Fries (*Dentist*); Robert Kortman and Leo Willis (*Tiger's pals*); Jerry Mandy (*Convict who can't add*); Bobby Dunn, Eddie Dunn, Baldwin Cooke, Charles Dorety, Dick Gilbert, Will Stanton, Jack Herrick, Jack Hill, Gene Morgan, Charles A. Bachman, Blackie Whiteford and Charley Rogers (*Insurgent convicts*); Gordon Douglas (*Typist at desk*); James Parrott (*Prisoner marching in formation next to Hardy, right after the boys's recapture*); Hal Roach (*Prisoner marching in front of Hardy*); Eddie Baker (*Plantation overseer on horseback*); The Etude Ethiopian Chorus (*Cotton pickers*); and Belle (*Bloodhound*). Modern sources also note that Bobby Mallon and Buddy MacDonald, playing boys fishing by a stream, were cut from the final release print, and that the incidental music scoring was by LeRoy Shield, Edward Kilenyi, Arthur J. Lamb, H. W. Petrie, Will Marion Cook, Irving Berlin, Abe Olman, M. Ewing, Frederic Van Norman, L. E. de Francesco, J. S. Zamecnik, Frieta Shaw and Marvin Hatley.

Other language version(s):

De bote en bote (Spanish language)

1931; San José, Costa Rica opening: 8 Mar 1931; San Juan, Puerto Rico opening: 15 Apr 1931. Sd (Western Electric System); b&w. 7 reels. 63 min. Spanish language.

Prod Hal Roach. *Dir* James Parrott. *Dial* H. M. Walker. *Photog* Jack Stevens. *Ed* Richard Currier. *Sd* Elmer Raguse and S. C. Baden.

Song(s): "Lazy Moon," music by J. Rosamond Johnson, lyrics by Bob Cole; "I Want to Go Back to Michigan," music and lyrics by Irving Berlin, translator of Spanish lyrics undetermined; "Swing Along, Chillun," by Will Marion Cook; "The Savior is a-Comin' Bye and Bye," "Dar's a Jubilee" and "All Aboard for Birmingham," composers undetermined.

Spanish-language cast: Stan Laurel (*Stan Laurel*), Oliver Hardy (*Oliver Hardy*), [Walter Long (*Tiger*)], [Enrique Acosta (*The warden*)], [June Marlowe (*The warden's daughter*)], [Tiny Sandford (*Gutiérrez*)], [Alfonso Pedroza (*Dentist*)]. [*Spanish version viewed*].

EHW 9 Aug 1930, p. 34. EHW 15 Nov 1930, p. 45. FD 23 Aug 1931, p. 18. MPH 29 Aug 1931, p. 36. NYT 22 Aug 1931, p. 7. Var 25 Aug 1931, p. 14.

PARIGI AFFASCINA; OVVERO, MALAVITA (Italian language)

Excelsior TalkFilms Productions. *Dist* Claudia Film Co. **1932**; Prod: at Sight and Sound Studios, New York. Sd; b&w. 6 reels, 5,850 ft. Italian language.

Supv T. R. Milana. *Adpt* T. R. Milana. *Photog* Larry Williams and Joe Sedita. *Mus composition* Salvatore Virzi' *Sight & Sound Studio* Henry "Buck" Jones.

Song(s): "Paris Fascinates," words by T. R. Milana, music by Salvatore Virzi', sung by Arturo Gervasi (tenor); "I Am Jealous" and "Blue Eyes," words by T. R. Milana, music by Salvatore Virzi', sung by Tecla Rolandi (soprano).

Cast: Adriana Dori, Gina Pozzi, Alberto Roberti, Renato de Mila', Muriel Kingston, Ada Pardee, Jack Halliday, Lee Timmons.

Comedy, with songs. [*Not viewed*]. Jack Merrill, a young American in Paris, tells the girl he loves, Dolores, about a dream he had about her the night before: When a canoe in which she and his rival, the Count de Moyon, were sitting, capsized, Jack jumped in the water and swam to her rescue. He woke up, though, soaking wet and realized he had tipped over the fish bowl in his sleep. When Dolores' mother, of noble birth, arrives with the count and others, Dolores says that Jack has invited them to join him that night at the Black Cat in Montmartre. The count makes his apologies to Dolores and says he will be unable to join them, then plots against Jack with his friend Fifi and Julot, a bartender, and promises to give them money for helping him. After Dolores' mother scolds Jack for wanting to take Dolores to a club like the Black Cat, Jack and Dolores meet in the garden, and Jack urges her to forget the count and return to America to be with him. Dolores, however, suggests that they wait. Later, Dolores telephones Jack and blames him for the count's disappearance. Soon after, Dolores and the count are reunited and kissing, when Jack arrives and Dolores' parrot Polly makes an embarrassing sound. The count, thinking Jack has insulted him, challenges him to a duel. The count then informs a business associate, Perille, that he cannot fly with him for a planned publicity visit to New York, but he agrees to send an impostor in his place. Dolores, her mother and Jack eat dinner in the ship's dining room on their way to New York. Jack insists that a particular waiter serve them, as he realizes this is the count in disguise. Dolores, horrified when she sees the count dressed as a waiter, marries Jack. *Americans in foreign countries. Mothers and daughters. Paris (France). Romantic rivalry. Bartenders. Canoes and canoeing. Dreams. Duels. Impersonation and imposture. Nightclubs. Nobility. Ocean liners. Parrots. Rescues. Waiters.*

Note: *FD* lists the film's English title as *Paris Fascinates*. The plot summary was based on an incomplete translation of a dialogue continuity deposited with the NYSA. The film appears to be an Italian-language version of the 1928 film *The Masked Lover*, produced by Golden Stars Film Productions. Three of the actors credited for the Italian film, Jack Halliday, Muriel Kingston and Lee Timmons, are listed in the credits for *The Masked Lover*. (See *AFI Catalog of Feature Films, 1921-30*; F2.3513).

FD 21 Feb 1932, p. 5.

PARISIAN BELLE *see* **NEW MOON**

THE PARISIAN WIFE *see* **HIS PARISIAN WIFE**

PARLOR, BEDROOM AND BATH (*foreign version*) *see* **BUSTER SE MARIE**

EL PASADO ACUSA (Spanish language)

Columbia Pictures Corp. *Dist* Columbia Pictures Corp. **1931**; Panama opening: 20 Aug 1931; Los Angeles opening: 21 Aug 1931; Prod: May—Jun 1931. Sd; b&w. 8 reels, 6,490 ft. 72 min. Spanish language.

Dir David Selman. *Dial dir* Julio Villarreal. *Scr* Jo Swerling. *Spanish version* René Borgia.

Source: Based on the novel *The Good Bad Girl* by Winifred Van Duzer (New York, 1926).

Cast: Luana Alcañiz (*Eva Miller/Eva Stanton*), Barry Norton (*Roberto Robinson*), Carlos Villarías (*Carlos Morán*), Rosita Granada (*Matilde Barnes*), Paul Porcasi (*Tony Pagano*), Paul Ellis (*Sanders*), Alfredo del Diestro (*Detective Palmer*), María Calvo (*Señora Robinson*), Julio Villarreal (*Señor Robinson*), George Berliner (*Numan*), Amelia Suso, Max Barón.

Gangster, Melodrama. [*Not viewed*]. [The following plot summary is based on the English-language version of this film, *The Good Bad Girl*; character names refer to that version. For further information regarding the English-language version, please see the note below and the entry for *The Good Bad Girl* in the *AFI Catalog of Feature Films, 1931-40*.] Marcia Cameron, the mistress of gang leader Dan Tyler, desires to end their relationship after she falls in love with Bob Henderson, an honest banker's son who does not wish to know about

her past. Tyler refuses to let Marcia go, however, and threatens to kill her if she attempts to flee. Marcia confides in her friend Trixie, the mistress of nightclub proprietor Pagano, that she wants to marry Bob and raise a family. That night, Tyler murders fellow gangster Moreland when he does not make good on a $30,000 gambling debt. Tyler pressures Marcia to provide him with an alibi, but when she refuses, he is forced to go to Philadelphia to hide. Trixie sardonically observes that "nobody goes to Philadelphia unless they have to." Marcia marries Bob, whose parents, also knowing nothing about her past, welcome her into the family. When she goes to Trixie and Pagano to tell them about her marriage, she is followed by Detective Donovan. To protect Marcia, Trixie hides her and informs Donovan about Tyler's whereabouts. After Tyler is arrested, his thugs forcibly take Marcia to the prison, where he once again orders her to testify on his behalf. He threatens to kill Bob if she does not comply, but she counters by stating that she will tell the police that the murder was premeditated if he does not leave Bob alone. As she leaves, photographers take her picture, and she is identified in the newspapers as the "gunman's girl." Horrified by this revelation, the Hendersons demand that Bob and Marcia separate. Despite her love for Bob and her knowledge that she is pregnant with his child, Marcia agrees that this is for the best. Bob reluctantly acquiesces and goes to Paris to secure a divorce. Tyler receives a life sentence, while Marcia goes to live with Trixie and Pagano and has her baby. Tyler escapes from prison and goes to find Marcia, whom he believes tipped off the police to his whereabouts. Just as Tyler is about to kill Marcia, Donovan and his men arrive and shoot him. Before Tyler dies, however, he tells Marcia that his men will kill her and her baby. The terrified Marcia goes to Mrs. Henderson, whose help she had previously refused, and gives her the baby for safekeeping. Marcia then returns to the nightclub to pack, and as she leaves, she is followed by Tyler's men. Bob, having returned from Paris, finds her just as Tyler's men are overtaking her. He saves her from the gangsters, and the reunited couple embrace as he reveals that he did not obtain a divorce. Bob makes Marcia promise never to leave him again, and the couple return to his home. *Gangsters. Marriage. Mistresses. Murder.* Alibi. Bankers. Detectives. Friendship. In-laws. Infants. Informers. Italian Americans. Nightclub owners. Philadelphia (PA). Photographs. Police. Prison escapes. Rejuvenation. Reporters. Reputation. Revenge. Wealth.

Note: For information on the English-language version of this film, *The Good Bad Girl*, which was directed by R. William Neill and starred Mae Clarke, please see the entry for that film in the *AFI Catalog of Feature Films, 1931-40*; F3.1675.

CM Oct 1931, p. 750.

¡PASO AL MARINO! *see* EN CADA PUERTO UN AMOR

PASQUALE (Italian Americans)
Oliver Morosco Photoplay Co. *Dist* Paramount Pictures Corp. 18 May **1916** [©Oliver Morosco Photoplay Co.; 26 Apr 1916; LP8189]. Si; b&w. 5 reels.

Dir William D. Taylor. *Story in collaboration with Lawrence McCloskey* George Beban. *Story* Lawrence McCloskey. *Cam* Homer Scott.

Cast: George Beban (*Pasquale*), Helen Jerome Eddy (*Margarita*), Page Peters (*Bob Fulton*), Jack Nelson (*Charlie Larkin*), Myrtle Stedman (*Mrs. Martinelli*), Nigel de Brullier (*Mario Martinelli*).

Drama. Pasquale, an Italian immigrant grocer, finally earns enough money to propose to Margarita, but tired of waiting, she marries Charlie Larkin instead. Then Pasquale is drafted into the Italian army, and before leaving for the front, he gives his business to Charlie so that he can support his new wife. After being wounded, Pasquale is discharged, and he returns to America to find that Charlie has become an alcoholic, has ruined the business and frequently has beaten Margarita. Finally, however, Charlie dies in a car crash while blackmailing Mrs. Martinelli, after which a sadder but wiser Margarita quickly accepts Pasquale's marriage proposal. *Battered women. Grocers. Immigrants. Italian Americans. Marriage.* Alcoholics. Automobile accidents. Blackmail. Grocery stores. Italy. Army. Military service. Compulsory. War injuries.

Motog 27 May 1916, p. 1221. *MPN* 27 May 1916, p. 3268. *MPW* 27 May 1916, p. 1532. *MPW* 3 Jun 1916, p. 1713. *NYDM* 20 May 1916, p. 26. *NYT* 22 May 1916, p. 20. *Var* 26 May 1916, p. 20. *Wid's* 18 May 1916, p. 579.

PASSAGE WEST *see* ESCAPE TO GLORY

THE PASSAIC TEXTILE STRIKE (Polish Americans)
S. B. Russack. *Dist* International Workers Aid. **1926**; Premiere in Passaic, New Jersey: Oct 1926. Si; b&w. 7 reels.

Documentary. [*Print viewed*]. A prologue tells the following story: In 1907, in the growing textile city of Passaic, New Jersey, Stefan Breznac, a Polish immigrant worker, gets a fifty cent a week raise and writes to his sweetheart Kada in the Polish farmlands to come share his new prosperity. When she sees the Statue of Liberty from the deck of her crowded boat, Kada thinks she has reached the land of liberty and riches at last. As the years go by and their family increases, they find the courage to face their growing problems. When Stefan gets another wage cut, he suggests that their fourteen-year-old daughter Vera go to work to make up for the cut. Although Kada would like Vera to stay in school, Vera boasts she is strong and tells her not to worry. When Mulius, the "big boss," sees Vera, he invites her to his office, and soon she gets a raise. One day, he offers to drive her home and then takes her for a ride. They stop after awhile, and the chauffeur says they are out of gas. Mulius sends him to get some, and as the chauffeur smokes a cigarette by a tree, Mulius attacks Vera. Two months later, Vera learns that Mulius is married. When she questions him about it, Mulius sends a foreman with a note saying she is fired. Stefan increases his hours to sixty-six a week and plans to try seventy-two despite Kada's warning and the concern of fellow workers that he'll kill himself. Breaking under the strain, he is reduced from a weaver to a transporter at less pay. As he pushes a bin, he falters, and though a foreman tells him to get back to work, another worker brings him home. Although a doctor prescribes that he rest for at least two weeks, Stefan goes back to work the next morning. When his friend sees him struggling, the friend suggests to other workers that they form a union. Two days later, Kada tries to wake Stefan for breakfast, but she finds her husband dead. With no time to mourn, she gets a mill job working the night shift, and at home sits in despair.

In the film's main section, entitled *The Strike*, the Passaic Strike of 1926 is described as "part of the great undertaking of American Labor to organize the unorganized, to set up a 'United Front of the Workers Against the United Front of the Bosses.'" It is stated that only four million out of twenty-nine million workers in the U.S. are organized into unions. The meager wages of textile mill workers only allow the workers to live in dark, crowded areas. Lint and dust of the mills harm the health of the workers. The death rate from tuberculosis is 100% above normal. The mansions of the owners are shown to contrast with the shacks of the workers. Talk begins of forming a union following the wage-cut of October 1925. When a worker confronts his boss to get the cut revoked, he is fired, and others decide that the only way to talk to bosses is with a union. Albert Weisbord begins to quietly organize workers. When Mulius sees Gus Deak meeting with other workers, he offers him a better job, but Deak tears up the new contract rather than take the bribe. On January 24, 1926, Weisbord tells a meeting of delegates that they will present the boss with their demands on the following day. Although there is a risk of a strike, the group decides to go ahead. On the next day, those who demand a withdrawal of the wage-cut are fired. The strike begins, and the union assembles masses of workers to picket. Police allow mill workers to cross the lines, as a man on the picket lines exhorts those crossing to join the picket. Within three days, the mill is tied up. Pickets spread to the mills of neighboring Clifton, Garfield and Lodi, and soon workers from eight mills present new demands, including an increase in wages of 10% above the rate prior to the latest wage-cut; payment of money that workers did not get due to the wage-cut; time and one-half for overtime; a forty-four hour work week; decent and sanitary work conditions; no discrimination against union workers; and recognition of the union. Under the leadership of Weisbord, a small group of organizers set up an office for the United Front Committee of Textile Workers of Passaic and Vicinity, and 12,000 strikers join. They send the "Textile Strike Bulletin" to the American Labor Movement. The workers, coming from many countries and ethnic groups, include Hungarians, Russians, Ukrainians, Lithuanians, Germans, Czechoslovakians, Jews, Spanish, Polish, Italians, African Americans, Mexicans, Bohemians and English. Forty-seven church organizations parade to demonstrate their support. Police, responding to the owners, arrest 560 strikers, but they are bailed out immediately and get back to the lines. Police soon begin to club the strikers, and bandaged, beaten men and women are shown. Throngs

fill the street where the casket of a martyred striker, Frank Dido, is moved from a house to a hearse. Though police smash movie cameras, shots taken from a roof show police clubbing strikers. Gas bombs are used to disperse crowds, but strikers learn to wear gas masks. Alfred Wagenknecht, director of working class relief campaigns, opens an office for relief work, and 125 strikers are assigned to it. An appeal goes out to the labor movement, and a picture book about the strike is sent out. The strikers receive contributions from the American Labor Movement, and caravans of trucks bring relief supplies. Relief stores distribute food and supplies to strikers with food cards. In union meetings, the goal of joining the A.F. of L. is announced, so that with a union, the workers can fix their own hours and wages. Visiting representatives of unions speak to the workers. After the sheriff of Bergen County illegally establishes martial law, issuing a proclamation that orders those assembled to disperse, a representative of the American Civil Liberties Union is thrown in jail for questioning its legality. The strikers' halls are closed and meetings are forbidden. A.C.L.U. attorneys get an injunction against the sheriff, and the halls are reopened and daily meetings resumed. Weisbord is arrested on charges of sedition and inciting to riot, but other leaders step forward to take his place. *Employer-employee relations. Immigrants. Labor leaders. Passaic (NJ). Polish Americans. Strikes and lockouts. Textile mills. Trade unions.* American Civil Liberties Union. American Federation of Labor. Arrests. Chauffeurs. Dismissal (Employment). Family relationships. Gas masks. Gases, Asphyxiating and poisonous. Martial law. Newsreel cameramen. Police brutality. Seduction. Statue of Liberty National Monument (New York City).

Note: The opening credits read: "*The Passaic Textile Strike*. The Battle for Life of the Workers who make the cloth that clothes you. Begun: January 25, 1926. To End: When Victory is Won. An International Workers Aid Picture. This is the story of 16,000 unorganized workers who went on strike against merciless wage cuts—and found their strength in the Union they built to carry them on to Victory." The Prologue is introduced with the following statements: "To show the life they live, the Passaic strikers have played for you this simple story of the Breznac Family [which is any family of textile workers], who came to America, the Land of Promise, only to find industrial oppression and bitter struggle. The players lay no claim to art, except as art is compounded of simple truth. The incidents are just the common facts of the textile workers' lives, empty perhaps of those flaming passions seen so often on the screen, but full of the actual tragedy of deadening labor and despairing struggle."

International Workers Aid was associated with the Communist organization Workers' International Relief, which organized the relief effort during the strike. Labor leaders and other personages who appear in the film include, Albert Weisbord, Gustav Deak, Clarence Miller, Leona Smith, George Ashkenudse, Elizabeth Gurley Flynn, Alfred Wagenknecht, John J. Ballam, J. O. Bentall, Mother Bloor, P. P. Cosgrove, Leo Krzycki, Ellen Wilkinson, Robert Dunn, Norman Thomas, Jack Rubinstein, Thomas DeFazio, Joseph Magliacano, Lena Chernenko, and Martin Winkler.

According to an interview with Gustav Deak, who plays himself in the film, the film's first director (whose name has not been determined) was hired from an independent film company by the Relief Committee, headed by Alfred Wagenknecht, who also appears in the film. This director did not sympathize with the strike and eventually was fired. Cameraman Sam Brody states that Sam Russak, a professional still photographer who had done some work with motion pictures, finished the direction, and that Brody and Lester Balog, both of whom later founded the Film and Photo League, shot the film. (NYSA records list the manufacturer's name as S. B. Russack.) A third director may have worked on the film before Russak. Subtitles were written by Margaret Larkin. The film was shown during the strike and was used to raise money for relief efforts. It had its first showings to strikers in Sep 1926 at Belmont Park, NJ, and was shown to the public beginning in Oct 1926 at Passaic.

The film toured the country accompanied by Communist activist speaker Ella Reeve "Mother" Bloor, who appears in it. The strike ended in Feb 1927, with the strikers failing to get the wage-cut withdrawn, but winning the right to affiliate with the American Federation of Labor and a promise of no discrimination against strikers seeking reemployment. Existing prints are missing two reels of the seven that were originally shown in 1926. [According to NYSA records, in 1926, the film was 6,263 ft. in length following eliminations ordered by the New York State censors.] In a book about the strike, Albert Weisbord, one of the strike's organizers, noted that the mills in the Passaic area were owned for the most part by Germans, who hired immigrants from numerous nationalities to avoid worker solidarity.

PASSION (Latino)

Filmcrest Productions, Inc. *Dist* RKO Radio Pictures, Inc. 6 Oct 1954; *Prod:* mid-Apr—mid-May 1954 [©RKO Radio Pictures, Inc.; 30 Oct 1954; LP4197]. *Sd* (RCA Sound System); col (Technicolor); SuperScope. 8 reels, 7,584 ft. 84 min. PCA cert no. 17043.

Pres BENEDICT BOGEAUS. *Prod* Benedict Bogeaus. *Dir* Allan Dwan. *Asst dir* Nathan Barrager. *Scr* Beatrice A. Dresher and Josef Leytes. *Adpt* Howard Estabrook. *Based upon a story by* Beatrice A. Dresher, Miguel Padilla and Josef Leytes. *Dir of photog* John Alton. *Art dir* Van

Nest Polglase. *Supv ed* James Leicester. *Film ed* Carl Lodato. *Set dec* John Sturtevant. *Ward des* Gwen Wakeling. *Mus score* Louis Forbes. *Sd* Francis N. Sarver. *Prod supv* Lee Lukather. [*Dog trainer* Rudd Weatherwax].

Cast: CORNEL WILDE [(*Juan Obreon*)], YVONNE DE CARLO [(*Tonya Melo/Rosa Melo*)], Raymond Burr [(*Capt. Rodriguez*)], Lon Chaney [(*Castro*)], Rodolfo Acosta [(*Salvador Sandro*)], John Qualen [(*Gaspar Melo*)], Anthony Caruso [(*Muñoz*)], Frank de Kova [(*Martinez*)], [Peter Coe (*Colfre*)], [John Dierkes (*Escobar*)], [Richard Hale (*Don Domingo*)], [Rozene Kemper (*Grandmother Melo*)], [Belle Mitchell (*Señora Carrisa*)], [Alex Montoya (*Manuel Felipe*)], [Zon Murray (*Marca*)], [Rosa Turich (*Maraquita*)], [Stuart Whitman (*Bernal*)], [James Kirkwood (*Don Rosendo*)], [Robert Warwick (*Padre*)], [Pal, a dog], [Cocaine, a horse].

Western. [*Print viewed*]. In old California, a cattle rancher named Juan Obreon drives his herd to the grazing lands he plans to lease from his old friend, Gaspar Melo. Upon arriving near the town of Granada, Juan learns that Gaspar's granddaughter Rosa has recently given birth to his baby. Overjoyed, Juan proposes marriage, and Rosa accepts. Later, Juan rides into town to make arrangements for the wedding, while Salvador Sandro, overseer for wealthy landowner Don Domingo, leads a group of men to Gaspar's hacienda. The land on which the hacienda sits had been given to the Melo family, but because the gift was never transacted legally, Gaspar has no deed to prove his ownership. Sent by Don Domingo to reclaim the land, Sandro orders Gaspar and his family to leave immediately, but the old man refuses, so Sandro's man Castro begins shooting. Rosa's sister Tonya escapes on horseback, but Rosa and her grandparents are killed. Just before Sandro shoots her, Rosa hides her baby inside a hollow wall of the hacienda, which is set on fire. A passing couple hears the baby's cries and rescues the child. Tonya and Juan are certain that Sandro and his men are guilty of the killings, but having no proof, they are unable to convince Capt. Rodriguez to arrest the murderers. After Juan defeats him in a knife fight, Castro gives Juan the names of the men working for Sandro. When Castro pulls a hidden knife from his boot and tries to stab Juan, however, the rancher is forced to kill his only witness in self-defense. Rodriguez, one of Juan's closest friends, threatens to arrest Juan for murder but quietly allows him and Tonya to escape. Taking the law into his own hands, Juan then begins to kill Sandro's henchmen, offering each the chance to defend himself with a knife. Convinced that Juan has become a cold-blooded killer, Rodriguez vows to capture his old friend. Juan rides into Granada in search of Sandro, the last of the killers, despite Tonya's warnings that he is now wanted. Almost caught by Don Domingo, Juan hides in the house of a friend and overhears Sandro making plans to escape to the border. While pursuing Sandro across the territory, Juan and Tonya stop at the Sierra Nevada hacienda of his old friend Don Rosendo, who offers to hide Tonya. Rodriguez and his deputy arrive just as Juan is leaving, and when the captain sees Tonya, he realizes Juan must be nearby. After Rodriguez departs, Manuel Felipe, a hired hand, confesses that he and his wife took Juan's son, whom they believed had been orphaned, after which he and Tonya rush to tell Juan that his son is alive. As a deadly storm approaches, Juan, who has been given warm clothing for the journey, catches sight of the ill-equipped Sandro climbing a steep glacier. When Sandro falls, Juan forces him to walk until, in the snow and wind, he loses consciousness. Arriving at a mountain shelter, Juan examines Sandro and realizes he is near death. Just then, Rodriguez arrives, shoots Juan in the arm, and orders him from the shelter. When Tonya and Manuel arrive, Tonya rushes into the cabin to tell Juan about his son. When Rodriguez enters, Sandro confesses his guilt, whereupon the captain promises to testify on Juan's behalf. Realizing that Tonya cares for him, Juan promises her that he will recover from his wound because he has much to live for. *California–History–To 1846. Justice. Land claims. Mexicans. Murder. Revenge.* Abduction. Arson. Cattlemen. Confession (Law). Glaciers. Gunfights. Haciendas. Hired hands. Infants. Knife fighting. Mountains. Police. Priests. Sierra Nevada Mountains (CA and NV). Snow storms.

Note: The working title of this film was *Where the Wind Dies*. Opening credits include the following written statement: "Early California...under Mexican rule...the timeless mountains and eternal snows looking down on the everlasting struggle of man against man." According to a 9 Mar 1954 *LAT* news item, Harmon Jones was originally scheduled to direct the film.

Box 9 Oct 1954. *DV* 6 Oct 1954, p. 3. *FD* 22 Oct 1954, p. 14. *HR* 16 Apr 1954. *HR* 7 May 1954. *HR* 6 Oct 1954, p. 3. *LADN* 2 Oct 1954. *LAEx* 28 Oct 1954. *LAT* 9 Mar 1954. *MPHPD* 16 Oct 1954, p. 178. *Newsweek* 18 Oct 1954. *NYT* 11 Dec 1954, p. 11. *Var* 6 Oct 1954, p. 6.

THE PASSIONATE PLUMBER (*foreign version*) *see* **LE PLOMBIER AMOUREUX**

PASSPORT HUSBAND (Latino)

Twentieth Century-Fox Film Corp. *Dist* Twentieth Century-Fox Film Corp. 15 Jul **1938**; Prod: 9 May—late May 1938 [©Twentieth Century-Fox Film Corp.; 15 Jul 1938; LP8429]. Sd; b&w. 7 reels, 6,200 ft. 67 min. PCA cert no. 4363.

Exec prod Sol M. Wurtzel. *Dir* James Tinling. *Scr* Karen De Wolf and Robert Chapin. *Orig story* Hilda Stone. *Contr to trmt* Robin Harris and Lester Ziffren. *Photog* Edward Snyder. *Art dir* Bernard Herzbrun and Haldane Douglas. *Film ed* Nick De Maggio. *Set dec* Thomas Little. *Cost* Herschel. *Mus dir* Samuel Kaylin. *Sd* E. Clayton Ward and William H. Anderson.

Cast: Stuart Erwin (*Henry Cabot*), Pauline Moore (*Mary Jane Clayton*), Douglas Fowley (*Tiger Martin*), Joan Woodbury (*Conchita Montez*), Robert Lowery (*Ted Markson*), Harold Huber (*Blackie Bennet*), Edward S. Brophy (*Spike*), Paul McVey (*H. C. Walton*), Lon Chaney, Jr. (*Bull*), Joseph Sawyer (*Duke Selton*), Max Wagner (*Henchman*), Regis Toomey, Alan Davis, Lane Chandler (*G-men*), Allen Fox (*Busboy*), Charles Judels (*Captain of busboys*), George Davis (*Waiter*), Theresa Harris (*Maid*), Paul Kruger, Phillip Morris,ʼ Eddie Hart (*Firemen*), Victor Mike Kilian, Robert Dalton (*Gangsters*), Romaine Callender (*Judge*), Wade Boteler (*Police sergeant*), James Blaine (*Battalion chief*), Lee Shumway, Stanley Blystone, George Magrill (*Policemen*), Billy Wayne (*Chauffeur*), Don Marion (*Messenger*), Frank Moran, Syd Saylor, Murray Alper, Heinie Conklin (*Baggagemen*), Ruth Warren (*Apartment house manager*), Harrison Greene (*Customer*), Irving Bacon (*Counter man*).

Crime, Comedy. [*Not viewed*]. At the Club Habana, Henry Cabot, a bumbling busboy, is infatuated with the club's dancer, Conchita Montez. As Tiger Martin, the leader of a gang of thieves, gives Conchita a diamond bracelet, he is arrested. After Tiger is deported, Duke Selton, of Tiger's gang, pays a visit to Conchita and tells her he believes that Blackie Bennet, the leader of a rival gang, is responsible for tipping off the police about Tiger's citizenship. With hopes of winning her for himself, Blackie offers Conchita a better diamond bracelet and calls Tiger a "cheap ape." Insulted, Conchita throws the bracelet out the window, and it lands on Henry's head. Henry, who has been fired from his job for breaking dishes, returns the bracelet to Conchita, who promises to get his job back for him. When Blackie informs Conchita that she will also be deported unless she marries an American, she tells Henry that she is wanted in her own country for political crimes. Henry then accepts her proposal, and they are married right away. Jealous, Blackie wants Henry killed, but his attorney, H. C. Walton, reminds him that Henry must remain alive for their scheme to work. Just then, Duke receives a telegram from Tiger, who, having heard about Conchita's marriage, instructs Duke to kill Henry. When Henry learns the real reason that Conchita married him, he tells her he is going to file for an annulment. Blackie and Walton decide that the only way to stop the annulment is to convince Conchita to move in with Henry. As she is moving her belongings into Henry's apartment, Henry arrives and tells her to go. Blackie and Walton are satisfied, however, as they believe that the annulment will now be denied because Conchita attempted the move. As Conchita is leaving, the landlady, who has intercepted a telegram for Henry, informs her that he has inherited a million dollars from his Uncle Charlie, who invented the pinball machine. Henry's friend, Mary Jane Clayton, then arrives, and when the landlady tells her that Conchita is moving in again, Mary Jane sends a second telegram, which voids the first. She then goes to the apartment and tells Henry that he should make Conchita prove her love by cleaning the entire apartment. As Conchita finishes the cleaning, Mary Jane's telegram arrives, and Conchita leaves humiliated. Having heard about Henry's possession of his uncle's pinball machine business, both gangs attempt to extort distribution rights out of him. The gangs gather at Blackie's apartment, but Henry siphons smoke in to make the crooks think there is a fire. After accepting Henry's proposal of marriage, Mary Jane locks Conchita in the revolving door of the building. One by one, the crooks jump out the window into a fire net, where the authorities are waiting to take them away. After ushering the last crook out the window, Henry is so happy that he too falls out the window. *Bumblers. Busboys. Dancers. Deception. Gangsters. Latino. Infatuation. Innocents. Marriage-Forced by circumstances. Apartments.*

Deportation. Diamonds. Dismissal (Employment). Fires. Landladies. Lawyers. Marriage–Annulment. Nightclubs. Pinball machines. Rivalry. Telegrams.

Note: The plot summary was based on a screen continuity in the Twentieth Century-Fox Produced Scripts Collection at the UCLA Theater Arts Library. This marked the first screen credit for story writer Hilda Stone, the wife of Twentieth Century-Fox producer John Stone. The Produced Scripts Collection contains an undated 1937 article from the *LAEx Magazine*, entitled " 'Arabian Nights' Adventure of the Poor Theatre Usher," which was the basis of Stone's story. According to the article, a Russian showgirl asked a nineteen-year-old theater usher in New York to marry her, without telling him that, as an illegal immigrant, she feared she would have trouble returning to the U.S. after a planned trip to England. After their marriage, the dancer left, vowing to divorce the usher, and because the usher heard nothing further from her, he retained the hope that she would return. A couple of years later, during the trial of racketeer "Lucky" Luciano, the usher read in the newspapers that his wife was one of Luciano's "sweethearts" and realized that she married him so that she could travel freely anytime the gangster sent for her. The usher then had the marriage annuled. The Produced Scripts Collection contains a treatment entitled "Meet the Countess," based on Stone's story, by Charles Belden and Jerry Cady, but it is not known if any of this material was included in the final film.

Box 2 Jul 1938. *DV* 24 Jun 1938, p. 3. *FD* 26 Jul 1938, p. 7. *HR* 9 May 1938, p. 15. *HR* 23 May 1938, p. 11. *HR* 24 Jun 1938, p. 4. *MPD* 11 Jul 1938, p. 6. *MPH* 11 Jun 1938, pp. 48-50. *MPH* 2 Jul 1938, p. 42. *NYT* 5 Aug 1938, p. 11. *Var* 23 Jul 1937. *Var* 27 Jul 1938, p. 17.

PASSPORT TO HAPPINESS *see* **MUSIC IN MY HEART**

PASSPORT TO LOVE *see* **SUN VALLEY SERENADE**

THE PATHFINDER (French Americans, Native Americans, Mohegan, Mingo, Tuscarora)

Esskay Pictures Co. *Dist* Columbia Pictures Corp. Apr **1953**; Prod: 1 Apr—11 Apr 1952 [©Columbia Pictures Corp.; 5 Dec 1952; LP2127]. Sd (RCA Sound System); col (Technicolor). 10 reels, 7,011 ft. 78 min. PCA cert no. 15963.

Prod Sam Katzman. *Dir* Sidney Salkow. *Asst dir* Paul Donnelly. *Scr* Robert E. Kent. *Dir of photog* Henry Freulich. *Spec eff* Jack Erickson. *Technicolor color consultant* Francis Cugat. *Art dir* Paul Palmentola. *Film ed* Jerome Thoms. *Set dec* Sidney Clifford. *Mus dir* Mischa Bakaleinikoff. *Sd eng* Josh Westmoreland. *Unit mgr* Herbert Leonard. [*Dir of pub* George Lait].

Source: Based on the novel *The Pathfinder; or, The Inland Sea* by James Fenimore Cooper (Philadelphia, 1840).

Cast: George Montgomery [(*Pathfinder*)], Helena Carter [(*Welcome Alison, also known as Paulette*)], Jay Silverheels [(*Chingachgook*)], Walter Kingsford [(*Col. Duncannon*)], Rodd Redwing [(*Chief Arrowhead*)], Stephen Bekassy [(*Col. Brasseau*)], Elena Verdugo [(*Lokawa*)], Bruce Lester [(*Capt. Clint Bradford*)], Chief Yowlachie [(*Eagle Feather*)], [Ed Coch, Jr. (*Uncas*)], [Russ Conklin (*Togamak*)], [Vi Ingraham (*Ka-letan*)], [Adele St. Maur (*Matron*)].

Historical, Drama. [*Print viewed*]. In 1754, the British and the French vie for control of the territory surrounding the Great Lakes. Forced to take sides, the peaceful Mohican tribe forms an alliance with the English, while the warlike Mingo people join with the French. On the day on which war is declared, the Mingos attack and destroy a Mohican village, leaving alive only a small boy and a brave named Chingachgook. Chingachgook's friend, the Pathfinder, a white man reared by the Indians, is loath to assist either the British or the French because both countries are guilty of taking land from the Indians. When he realizes, however, that the Mingos and the French, enemies of the Mohicans, vastly outnumber the British, he agrees to become a spy for British Col. Duncannon. The colonel tells Pathfinder to pose as a scout for the French and assigns Welcome Alison, an attractive young Englishwoman, to serve as his interpreter. The two take an immediate dislike to each other and bicker all the way to the French fort at San Vincent, a key post through which all of the supplies to the surrounding French forts are carried. At San Vincent, Col. Brasseau, who for some time has tried to persuade the renowned Pathfinder to serve as a scout for the French, welcomes Pathfinder amiably, even though Arrowhead, the Mingo chief, still considers him a Mohican enemy. Welcome is introduced as Paulette, the sole survivor of a Delaware Indian attack. Later that day, Pathfinder challenges Arrowhead to a fight in order to win the respect of the Mingo tribe. He fights bravely and wins, but Arrowhead still distrusts him. During a *soirée* held in her honor, Welcome charms a French officer and learns enough about the route of the expected supply

train to enable Pathfinder to intercept it. When she reports this information to Pathfinder late that night, both finally admit their feelings for each other and embrace. The next day, Pathfinder makes the French believe that the Delawares are about to attack San Vincent, and in the resulting confusion, he steals two kegs of gunpowder. He and Chingachgook then blow up the road to San Vincent, making it impossible for the supply train to deliver its goods to the fort. Later, Capt. Clint Bradford, a renegade British officer who earlier had abandoned Welcome for Lokawa, the daughter of a Tuscarora chief, arrives at San Vincent to negotiate an alliance between the Tuscarora and the French. Bradford visits Welcome during the night and offers to accompany her back to London with the gold the French will give him for negotiating the alliance. When Welcome repulses his advances, he angrily threatens to reveal her identity. Welcome later tells Lokawa about Bradford's plans, but Bradford appears and slaps his wife, calling her a "red pig." Pathfinder and Chingachgook set off explosions at the Mingo camp, and while Brasseau is away from his quarters, they sneak in and steal the French territorial defense plans. Bradford sees them, however, and although Chingachgook escapes with the plans, Pathfinder and Welcome are arrested as spies. The two are about to be executed when the British launch a surprise attack on the fort. As the troops engage in battle, Bradford tries to take control of a ship loaded with women and children. Pathfinder shoots Bradford and rescues Welcome, however, and after Brasseau surrenders to the British, the two lovers share a passionate kiss. *English in foreign countries. Espionage. French. Friendship. Mingo Indians. Mohegan Indians. Romance. United States–History–French and Indian War, 1755-1763. Balls (Parties). Battles. Explosions. Firing squads. Forts. Great Lakes. Knife fighting. Marriage–Mixed. Massacres. Officers (Military). Political alliances. Racism. Renegades. Rescues. Sabotage. Scouts (Frontier). Spies. Threats. Translators. Tuscarora Indians.*

Note: According to the film's pressbook, some scenes in this film were shot near Van Nuys and Camarillo and in the Malibu Mountains in the greater Los Angeles area. According to information in the MPAA/PCA Collection at the AMPAS Library, the PCA issued its certificate for this film only on the understanding that a scene containing an open-mouthed kiss would be deleted. The film was banned in Egypt because it showed British troops victorious over the French. Several modern sources state that the film was based not only on James Fenimore Cooper's novel, *The Pathfinder*, but on a variety of novels in the author's *Leatherstocking Tales.*

Box 20 Dec 1952. *DV* 10 Dec 1952, p. 3. *Exb* 31 Dec 1952, p. 3437. *FD* 18 Dec 1952, p. 6. *Har* 20 Dec 1952, p. 202. *HR* 10 Dec 1952, p. 3. *LAT* 11 Dec 1952. *MPD* 22 Dec 1952. *MPHPD* 20 Dec 1952, p. 1646. *Var* 17 Dec 1952, p. 6.

PAWN TICKET 210 (Jewish Americans)

Fox Film Corp. *Dist* Fox Film Corp. 24 Dec **1922** [©William Fox; 31 Dec 1922; LP19086]. Si; b&w. 5 reels, 4,871 ft.

Pres William Fox. *Dir* Scott Dunlap. *Scen* Jules Furthman. *Photog* George Schneiderman.

Source: Based on the play "Pawn Ticket No. 210" by David Belasco and Clay M. Greene (production undetermined).

Cast: Shirley Mason (*Meg*), Robert Agnew (*Chick Saxe*), Irene Hunt (*Ruth Sternhold*), Jacob Abrams (*Abe Levi*), Dorothy Manners (*Mrs. Levi*), Fred Warren (*Harris Levi*).

Melodrama. Harris Levi brings up Meg, who was left in his father's pawnshop by her mother, Ruth Sternhold. Anxious that she have a good environment, Harris takes her to live with his friend Robert Strong. When Ruth returns to claim Meg, Strong is revealed to be both Meg's father and the man with whom Harris' wife eloped. Meg is happily reunited with her parents and her sweetheart, Chick Saxe. *Jews. Parentage. Pawnbrokers. Waifs.*

ETR 20 Jan 1923, p. 422. *FD* 18 Jan 1923. *Var* 25 Jan 1923, p. 41.

PAWNEE (Native Americans, Pawnee)

Hilber Corp.; Gross-Krasne, Inc. *Dist* Republic Pictures Corp. 7 Sep **1957**; Prod: early Sep—early Oct 1956 at California Studios [©Republic Pictures Corp.; 13 Jun 1957; LP9772]. Sd (Roderick Sound, Inc.); col (Trucolor by Consolidated Film Industries); 1.85. 8 reels, 7,085 ft. 79-80 min. PCA cert no. 18475.

Prod Jack J. Gross and Philip N. Krasne. *Assoc prod* Sol Dolgin. *Dir* George Waggner. *Asst dir* Hal Klein. *Wrt* George Waggner, Louis Vittes and Endre Bohem. *Dir of photog* Hal McAlpin. *Spec eff* Jess Davison. *Optical eff* Consolidated Film Industries. *Art dir* Nicolai Remisoff. *Film ed* Kenneth G. Crane. *Sd eff ed* Marshall Pollack. *Set dec* G. W. Berntsen. *Ward* Byron Munson. *Mus comp and cond* Paul Sawtell. *Mus supv* Alec Compinsky. *Sd* Herman Lewis. *Makeup* Kiva Hoffman and Hazel Kraft. *Scr cont* Helen Gailey. *Property master* Artie Friedrich.

Cast: GEORGE MONTGOMERY [(*Pale Arrow, also known as Paul Fletcher*)], Bill Williams [(*Matt Delaney*)], Lola Albright [(*Meg Alden*)], Francis J. McDonald [(*Uncle Tip Alden*)], Robert E. Griffin [(*Doc Morgan*)], Dabbs Greer [(*John Brewster*)], Kathleen Freeman [(*Mrs. Carter*)], Charlotte Austin [(*Dancing Fawn*)], Ralph Moody [(*Wise Eagle*)], Anne Barton [(*Martha Brewster*)], Raymond Hatton [(*Obie Dilks*)], Charles Horvath [(*Crazy Fox*)], Robert Nash [(*Carter*)], [Pat O'Moore].

Western. [*Print viewed*]. As Meg Alden and her Uncle Tip attempt to catch up to the wagon train led by boss Matt Delaney, their wagon is set on fire by Pawnee Indian braves led by Crazy Fox, a fierce warrior who wants to fight the whites rather than make peace with them. Tip is shot with an arrow as he and Meg attempt to cross a river, and the Indians make off with their horses and cattle. Pale Arrow, a white man who was reared by Pawnee chief White Eagle following the death of his parents in the desert, sees the attack and rides to help Tip. As he tries to remove the arrow, Meg goes for her rifle. Pale Arrow struggles with her and takes the rifle away, then strips off her shirt sleeve and uses it to stop the blood from Tip's wound. He leads them close to the wagon train, then rides off before Matt and the others find Tip and Meg. At the Pawnee camp, Pale Arrow and Crazy Fox taunt each other. White Eagle, who believes that the future of his people lies in living peacefully with the white man, sees that Pale Arrow has become disturbed by his contact with his own people and advises him to go to them and find answers to what is troubling him, and then to return to the tribe. White Eagle plans, upon his own death, for Pale Arrow and Crazy Fox to rule together so that each will complement the other's strengths and weaknesses. Although Pale Arrow is to marry White Eagle's daughter, Dancing Fawn, at the next moon, he joins up with the wagon train. Wearing white man's clothes and using the name "Paul Fletcher," he becomes their scout. Crazy Fox follows the wagon train, and after Paul humiliates him, Matt is about to shoot at the departing Indian, but Paul stops him, saying that Crazy Fox brought a message and that the wagon train is under the protection of White Eagle. At the Pawnee camp, Crazy Fox tries to win Dancing Fawn for himself by discrediting his rival, but she refuses him saying she belongs completely to Pale Arrow. Although Paul tries to keep aloof from the rest of the wagon party, Meg finds him bathing and recognizes him as the one who rescued Tip. He confesses that he has come because he wanted to hold her again, and Meg, whom Matt wants to marry, is happy that Paul really is whom she suspected. She gladly kisses him when he awkwardly says he has heard of a custom the whites have that does away with words. Their kiss is interrupted by an arrow shot into the tree at which they stand, and he identifies the arrow as a message for him to return to the Pawnee camp. Before going, he tells Meg that the wagon train should continue on their course south, around Pawnee territory. Meg relates Paul's true identity to the group, but because one of the women, Martha Brewster, is to give birth soon, they vote to go west through Pawnee country, hoping to reach Fort Baxter in three days. At the Pawnee camp, Paul finds that White Eagle has died. Dancing Fawn, who shot the arrow, wants Paul to remain as chief despite seeing him kiss Meg, so that he can lead her people in peace; however, Paul says that he no longer belongs with them. Crazy Fox leads the Pawnees in an attack, which takes the lives of fifteen settlers, including Martha, who dies giving birth to a son. Matt and Martha's grief-stricken husband John blame Paul, suspecting that he planned to trap them. When Paul appears at Martha's funeral, Tip stops the others from hanging him, but tells Paul now that he has repaid him for saving his life, he will kill him if he sees him again. Paul goes back to the Pawnee camp and berates the braves for following Crazy Fox, but after a scout brings news of a war council to wipe out the whites forever, Crazy Fox encourages his people to strike now or forever be the white man's slaves. Paul is tied to a post, and after the braves leave, he is beaten by squaws and children. Before he is to suffer "squaw torture," Dancing Fawn releases him and he rides off to Fort Baxter. By identifying himself as Pale Arrow, he convinces the colonel that the Pawnee plan to join six northern tribes and that they must be surprised on open ground, otherwise the fort will be overrun and all the whites killed. Meanwhile, Tip locates a cave from which the wagon party can view the whole valley, and leaving their wagons and cattle in the valley, the party holes up in the fortress. After they see the Indians approach, they are heartened to see Paul arrive with the first group of soldiers. Matt joins Paul as he fires at the Indians from

a rocky vantage point. The rest of the cavalry arrive and rout the Indians, while Paul chases down Crazy Fox and drowns him. As a wedding present, Matt gives Paul and Meg his wagon and goes off to California. Meg then reminds Paul of the kissing custom, and they kiss as they ride off with the rest of the wagon train. *Pawnee Indians. Racism. Romance. Scouts (Frontier). Wagon trains. Caves. Death in childbirth. Debt. Engagements. False accusations. Forts. Kisses. Massacres. Recognition. Rescues. Romantic rivalry. Torture. Tribal chiefs. Uncles. United States. Army. Cavalry.*

Note: The film's national release date was originally scheduled for 21 Jun 1957. *Har* made the following comments about the film's plot: "As in most stories of this type, the trouble between a wagon train of settlers and the redskins stems from the hot-tempered actions of one Indian who resents the invasion of the white man." They also noted the extensive use of stock shots in the battle scenes.
Box 27 Jul 1957, p. 3. *DV* 10 Jul 1957, p. 3. *Exb* 7 Aug 1957, pp. 4361-62. *FD* 18 Jul 1957, p. 6. *Har* 13 Jul 1957, p. 110. *HR* 14 Sep 1956, p. 13. *HR* 5 Oct 1956, p. 16. *HR* 10 Jul 1957, p. 3. *MPD* 22 Jul 1957. *MPHPD* 20 Jul 1957, p. 458. *Var* 17 Jul 1957, p. 6.

PAY OR DIE (Italian Americans)

Allied Artists Pictures Corp. *Dist* Allied Artists Pictures Corp. May 1960; New York opening: 26 May 1960; Prod: early Nov—mid-Dec 1959 [©Allied Artists Pictures Corp.; 3 May 1960; LP16060]. Sd; b&w; 1.85. 10,089 ft. 110-111 min. Passed by the National Board of Review. PCA cert no. 19525.

Prod Richard Wilson. *Asst to prod* Joseph Sargent. *Dir* Richard Wilson. *Asst dir* Clark L. Paylow. *Wrt* Richard Collins and Bertram Millhauser. *Dir of photog* Lucien Ballard. *Spec eff* Milt Olsen. *Mont ed* Neil Brunnenkant. *Prod des* Fernando Carrere. *Film ed* Walter Hannemann. *Set dec* Darrel [sic] Silvera. *Prop master* Sam Gordon. [*Props* Allen Gordon]. *Ward supv* Roger J. Weinberg. [*Ward* Sol Rous, Marty King, Norah Sharpe and Marie Osborne]. *Mus* David Raksin. *Mus ed* Harry Eisen. *Sd eng* Ralph Butler. *Sd ed* Marty Greco. [*Sd rec* Paul Schmutz, Sr.]. *Makeup* Lou La Cava and Bob Mark. *Hairdresser* Fritzy La Bar. *Prod mgr* Edward Morey, Jr. *Unit mgr* Jim Henderling. [*Scr supv* Virginia Barth]. [*Gaffer* George Satterfield]. [*Sculptor of St. Rosalia statue* Katherine Stubergh].

Song(s): Selections from the opera *Lucia di Lammermoor*, music by Gaetano Donizetti, libretto by Salvatore Cammarano.

Cast: ERNEST BORGNINE [(*Lt. Joseph Petrosino*)], Zohra Lampert [(*Adelina Saulino*)], Alan Austin [(*Johnny Viscardi*)], Renata Vanni [(*Mama Saulino*)], Bruno Della Santina [(*Papa Saulino*)], Franco Corsaro [(*Vito Zarillo*)], Robert F. Simon [(*Police commissioner*)], Robert Ellenstein [(*Luigi Di Sarno*)], Howard Caine [(*Enrico Caruso*)], John Duke [(*Lupo Miano*)], John Marley [(*Caputo*)], Mario Siletti [(*Loria*)], Mimi Doyle [(*Sister Theresa*)], Mary Carver [(*Mrs. Rossi*)], Paul Birch [(*Mayor George B. McClellan*)], Vito Scotti [(*Simonetti*)], Nick Pawl [(*Palumbo*)], Vince Barbi [(*Fabraka*)], Sherry Alberoni [(*Giulia Di Sarno*)], Leslie Glenn [(*Girl at bombing*)], Sal Armetta [(*Botti*)], David Poleri (*The Voice of Caruso*), [Carlo Tricoli (*Don Cesare*)], [Bart Bradley (*Nicolo*)], [Marian Collier (*Phyllis, girl from opera*)], [Joseph D. Sargent (*Sorgente*)], [Sam Capuano (*Rossi*)], [Judy Stranges (*Marisa Rossi*)], [Robert Christopher (*Digilio*)], [Larry Chance (*Buzzuffi*)], [Don Kennedy (*Patrolman Sullivan*)], [John Lomma (*Malliotti*)], [Robert Ruggiero (*Angelo*)], [Ralph Gary (*Dondera*)], [Lester Fletcher (*Charles*)], [Lidia Vana, Theresa Testa (*Crones*)], [Jerry Martin (*Costa*)], [George Chirello (*Antonio*)], [Elvira Curci (*Mrs. Viscardi*)], [Charles La Torre (*Bartolatta*)], [Delia Salvi (*Secretary*)], [David Fresco (*Triscola*)], [Jim Bacon (*Guard*)], [Chuck Fox (*Rocco*)], [Jerado (*Brigante*)], [Francisco Villalobos (*Priest*)], [Lew Brown (*Steward*)], [Paul McGuire (*Proctor*)], [Ida Smeraldo (*Mother*)], [Norman Nazarr (*Man with rifle*)], [Saverio Lo Medico (*Newspaperman*)], [Vance Skarstedt (*Driver*)], [Les Green (*Intern*)], [Margarita Cordova (*Lupo's girl*)], [Ernest Molinari, Manuel Alda (*Customers*)], [John Close, Tony Dante (*Policemen*)], [Joseph La Cava, Charles Cirillo, Michael Tellegen (*Businessmen*)], [Doug Williams (*Wagon driver*)], [Margaret Bacon (*Nun*)], [Leonard Graves (*Opera singer*)], [Anna Stein (*Crying woman*)], [Oreste Seragnoli (*Doctor*)], [Hart Sprager (*Officer*)], [Louise Colombet (*Female customer*)], [Gloria Ruggiero (*Angel*)], [Emily La Rue].

Crime, Drama. [*Print viewed*]. In Manhattan's Little Italy in 1909, a criminal causes a small girl to be seriously injured during a crowded Sicilian-American religious festival. The child's distressed mother accuses her husband of foolishly placing their daughter in danger, but when Lt. Joseph Petrosino, an Italian-American police officer,

questions the father about the perpetrator, the frightened man refuses to speak. Joe has been trying to persuade the local victims of a group of extortionists known as La Mano Nera, or the Black Hand, to testify against the thugs, but the business owners who receive written warnings to "pay or die" are too distrustful of the police to cooperate. One day a baker known as Papa Saulino receives one of the dreaded warnings, which are identified by a drawing of a black hand dripping in blood, but his daughter Adelina's urgings that he report the incident fall on deaf ears. The extortionists, angered by Saulino's refusal to pay, destroy the bakery and lock him in the oven, and after he emerges from the hospital, the baker finally tells Joe about the note. Because Adelina is brutally attacked by two Black Hand men, however, Saulino soon withdraws the charges. During a visit with Adelina, Joe reveals his desire to become the first Italian captain on the New York police force and engages the pretty young woman to tutor him in preparation for the required literacy test. Next, Joe asks the New York police commissioner to give him an "Italian squad" of five or six plainclothesmen to patrol the city's Little Italy neighborhood. The commissioner balks at first, remarking that Italians don't seem to "catch on to our ways," but Joe assures him that if his people are freed from their fear of petty criminals, they will work hard to become Americans. Impressed, the commissioner quietly grants Joe's request. With Joe's detectives posing as members of the community, the squad is able to identify and convict a number of Black Hand criminals. One day, beloved Italian opera singer Enrique Caruso asks for protection, revealing that he, too, has received a Black Hand warning. Following Caruso's performance at the Metropolitan Opera that evening, Joe saves the singer from becoming the victim of a car bomb, but the city's wealthiest Italian-American citizens are convinced that Joe is too poorly educated to lead the squad, and nonetheless demand his removal. The police commissioner defends Joe, who, despite Adelina's tutoring, fails his sixth academic test for the position of captain. Despondent, Joe ends his visits to Adelina, assuming she will marry her more successful student, the handsome young Johnny Viscardi. Following an attempt on Joe's life, however, Adelina proposes to Joe, and the two are wed. Later, after Joe persuades a jeweler to ignore a Black Hand demand for money, the jewelry shop is bombed, and the child of Black Hand lawyer Luigi Di Sarno is killed while gazing at trinkets through the window. Di Sarno hangs himself, but Joe and Johnny are able to locate the bomber, who reveals that the crime was commissioned by respected citizen Vito Zarillo. On hearing the word "Mafia" in connection with Zarillo, Joe begins to believe what he had earlier considered nonsense: that the Black Hand might be linked to the powerful Sicilian crime organization. He bids an emotional farewell to Adelina and Johnny and travels to Sicily to investigate. In Palermo, Joe learns by searching police records that many of New York's Black Handers, including Zarillo, are wanted for crimes in Italy. This information he sends home, but Joe decides to trust only himself with some shocking evidence that, as he writes to Johnny, confirms his worst fears about the Mafia's presence in the United States. On the night before he is to return home, Joe encounters Don Cesare, the leader of the Mafia, but before he can escape, one of Cesare's henchmen kills him. At Joe's funeral, Adelina sadly tells Johnny that although Joe thought he was ugly, "he was beautiful to me." Johnny hides when Zarillo enters and spits on Joe's body. He then arrests the criminal, whispering, "Joe, we got him." *Black Hand (United States). Extortion. Heroism. Italian Americans. Mafia. New York City–Little Italy. Joseph Petrosino. Assimilation (Sociology). Attempted murder. Bakers and bakeries. Bombings. Enrico Caruso. Examinations, Academic. Fear. Festivals. Immigrants. Literacy. Metropolitan Opera (New York City). Murder. Opera. Palermo (Sicily). Police commissioners. Police detectives. Romantic rivalry. Suicide. Threats. Tutors and tutoring. Undercover operations.*

Note: According to a statement in the opening credits, the film is "based on the life of an authentic American hero, Lieut. Joseph Petrosino, New York Police Force. Events of 1906-1909." The Black Hand was a group of petty extortionists who victimized primarily lower-class Italians in a number of American cities during the early twentieth century. Although Petrosino, who emigrated to the United States from Salerno at age thirteen, never believed that the thugs who extorted money from poor immigrants in Little Italy, a practice common among many urban-based ethnic groups at that time, were tied to the Mafia, the film suggests that he gradually discovered the existence of a powerful crime syndicate that was largely controlled by Mafia dons in Palermo. Petrosino's murder in Palermo in 1909 deeply affected the Italian-American community. Although the *SAB* indicates that this film is based on Burnett

Hershey's short story "Pay Off in Sicily," other information found at the AMPAS Library indicates that the screenplay was not based on "previously published material." The *NYT* review commented that "all the Italo-American faces and dialects in the cast...authentically flavor [the] production." According to information in the MPAA/PCA Collection at the AMPAS Library, Murvyn Vye was initially cast to play "Mayor George B. McClellan." Although *HR* production charts include Robert Shannon in the cast, his participation in the completed film has not been confirmed. The street festival depicted in the opening scenes honors Santa Rosalia, a Catholic saint who was believed to have saved Palermo from pestilence. In 1912, Feature Photoplay Co. also released a film about Petrosino and his investigation of The Black Hand. See the entry above for *The Adventures of Lieutenant Petrosino*.

Box 2 May 1960. *DV* 26 Apr 1960, p. 3. *Exh* 11 May 1960, p. 4701. *FD* 27 Apr 1960, p. 6. *Har* 14 May 1960, p. 79. *HR* 6 Nov 1959, p. 14. *HR* 18 Dec 1959, p. 19. *HR* 26 Apr 1960, p. 3. *MPHPD* 30 Apr 1960, p. 675. *NYT* 27 May 1960, p. 22. *Var* 27 Apr 1960, p. 6.

PAY THE DEVIL *see* **MAN IN THE SHADOW**

PAY TO LEARN *see* **THE NAVY COMES THROUGH**

PEACOCK ALLEY (French Americans)

Tiffany Productions, Inc. *Dist* Metro Pictures Corp. 23 Jan **1922** Si; b&w. 8 reels, 7,500 ft.

Supv Robert Z. Leonard. *Dir* Robert Z. Leonard. *Scen* Edmund Goulding. *Story* Ouida Bergere. *Titles* Frederic Hatton and Fanny Hatton. *Photog* Oliver Marsh. *Art sets* Charles Cadwallader.

Cast: Mae Murray (*Cleo of Paris*), Monte Blue (*Elmer Harmon*), Edmund Lowe (*Phil Garrison*), W. J. Ferguson (*Alex Smith*), Anders Randolph (*Hugo Fenton*), William Tooker (*Joseph Carleton*), Howard Lang (*Abner Harmon*), William Frederic (*Mayor of Harmontown*), M. Durant (*Monsieur Dubois*), Jeffrys Lewis (*Toto*), Napoleon (*Himself, a dog*).

Drama. When Elmer Harmon goes to Paris to sign a contract with the French government, he meets Cleo, a dancer with whom he falls in love and who is instrumental in acquiring the contract for him. They are married, and Elmer takes his bride back to his home town in Pennsylvania where the natives are shocked by Cleo's manners and her Parisian attire. In New York, Elmer exhausts his finances, forges his uncle's name to a check, and is arrested. Cleo, in an effort to raise money for her husband's bail, accepts a theatrical engagement, but Elmer misunderstands her association with an old friend and denounces her, returning to Harmontown. Later, he learns the truth and returns to ask her forgiveness. *Dancers. Dogs. Forgers and forgery. French Americans. Marriage. New York City. Paris (France). Pennsylvania. Xenophobia.*

THE PEACOCK FAN (Chinese Americans)

Chesterfield Motion Picture Corp. 1 Aug **1929**. Si; b&w. 6 reels, 5,387 ft.

Pres George R. Batcheller. *Prod* Lon Young. *Dir* Phil Rosen. *Scen* Arthur Hoerl. *Story* Adeline Leitzbach. *Titles* Lee Authmar. *Photog* M. A. Anderson. *Film ed* James Sweeney.

Cast: Prologue: Lotus Long (*Feliti*), Fujii Kishii (*Okuri*), Wong Foo (*Men Ching*), **Cast—Story:** Lucien Prival (*Dr. Chang Dorfman*), Dorothy Dwan (*Peggy Kendall*), Tom O'Brien (*Sergeant O'Brien*), Rosemary Theby (*Mrs. Rossmore*), Carlton King (*Mr. Rossmore*), Gladden James (*Bertram Leslie*), David Findlay (*Jerry Carlyle*), James Wilcox (*Bob Kendall*), Fred Malatesta (*Thomas Elton*), Alice True (*Lily*), Spencer Bell (*Arthur*), John Fowler (*Dr. Whalen*).

Mystery. A prologue shows the tragic history of a peacock fan, which figured in a jealous Chinese husband's murder of his wife and her lover. In the story, the fan comes into the possession of a wealthy American curio collector, who is mysteriously murdered. Dr. Chang Dorfman enters the scene to unravel the mystery, implicates a dozen people, and finally establishes the guilt of the collector's wife and her lover. *Chinese Americans. Collectors and collecting. Infidelity. Legends. Murder.*

FD 17 Mar 1929. *Var* 22 May 1929, p. 27

THE PEANUT MAN (African Americans)

Nola Productions. *Dist* Consolidated Pictures. **1947**. Sd; col. 3,639 ft. 40 or 45 min. PCA cert no. 12275.

Prod Tony Paton. *Dir* Tony Paton. *Asst dir* Howard Joslin. *Scr* Tony Paton. *Cam* Harry Hallenberger. *Film ed* Frank Bracht. *Set const expert* Juan Lipari. *Choir dir* Jester Hairston. *Sd* Glen Glenn. *Makeup supv* Charley Huber. *Prod mgr* Frank Parmenter.

Song(s): "When the Saints Go Marching In," music by James M. Black, lyrics by Katharine E. Purvis; "Brighten the Corner Where You Are," music by Charles H. Gabriel, lyrics by Ina Duley Ogdon; "Now the Day is Over," music by Joseph Barnby, lyrics by Sabine Baring-Gould; "Swing Low, Sweet Chariot," arranged by Henry Thacker Burleigh, music and lyrics based on a traditional black spiritual.

Cast: Clarence Muse (*Dr. George Washington Carver*), Ernest Anderson (*Robert*), Maidie Norman (*Lucretia*), Shelby Bacon (*Augustus*), Wade Crosby (*Jeffries*), Ray Teal (*Dr. Miller*), Bernard Gorcey (*Murphy*), Pom Pom, the dog (*Junior*), Gloria Jeter, Virginia Grant, Maudice Giles, Marguerite McGuin, Jessie Patterson, Hall Johnson Choir, Tony Paton.

African American. [*Not viewed*]. At the offices of Consolidated Producers Corporation, producer Tony Paton is determined to make a film about the great African American chemist, George Washington Carver. His backer, Murphy, is skeptical about the marketability of such a project, but Paton convinces him that it is time to depict the truth about races, creeds, and religions and trust that ticket buyers will make their own decisions about the merits of such an unusual film. The story begins in Alabama, at the great Negro university, the Tuskegee Institute: Carver, who teaches as well as does research at the institute, chats on his front porch with two children. One of the children, a boy named Augustus, tells Carver that he wants to be just like him when he grows up, and then asks if the scientist, who has demonstrated the many uses of the peanut, can even make the homely crop sing. A bemused Carver then asks the children to sing a Sunday school song, as the music gives him inspiration to continue his labors. Later, in his laboratory, Carver assists his young apprentice, Robert, in perfecting a "chemurgy" process which will make the earth's soil more productive. One day, Mr. Jeffries, an entrepreneur, arrives with a business proposition for Carver. Jeffries suggests that they manufacture soap, butter, flour and axle grease, all to be made using Carver's formulas. Carver rejects the proposition, however, as he wants no profits from his work, and sends the disappointed Jeffries away. Lucretia, Augustus's mother and Robert's fiancée, next knocks on the lab door to tell the men that her son is very sick. Carver is at first annoyed at having his work again interrupted, but when he sees the note that the boy's physician, Dr. Miller, has written, he discovers to his shock that the boy has poliomyelitis. Carver tells Lucretia to go to her sister's house and pray, imploring her to maintain a "mustard seed of faith." With his own mustard seed of faith, Carver determines to find a cure for the damaging effects of the polio virus. Carver goes to visit Augustus and, looking at a picture of the boy's father, tells Robert that the man was one of Tuskegee's best students, but died as a medic in the war. Carver then says he hopes that Augustus, who will surely pursue his father's career, will not be a wheelchair-bound scientist. Carver tries an experimental treatment on Augustus, which includes massage, to promote circulation and re-establish the connection of the brain to the atrophied muscles. Time passes, and Augustus makes great progress. Years later, Robert and Lucretia, now married, and Augustus, go to visit Carver. Lucretia says that they will take Carver home with them to dine upon his favorite dish. Carver replies that he has a hunch that he should not go. Sensing that his death is near, Carver tells the men to learn more about the polio virus, and then tells Lucretia to make herself useful by sewing dresses for a few more little girls. He finishes his speech by telling Augustus never to forget the benefits of education as well as the peanut and all its uses. Carver says he must complete his final experiment in eternity, and his figure is seen passing through a closed door upon which a flower is painted. *African Americans. George Washington Carver. Chemists. Children. Peanuts. Poliomyelitis. Tuskegee Institute. Agriculture. Chemistry. Cures. Engagements. Entrepreneurs. Faith. Motion picture producers. Prayer. Widows.*

Note: Although a print of this film was not viewed, the above credits and plot summary were taken from a cutting continuity deposited with the NYSA. The following foreward appears in the opening credits: "Because each of you, individually, is a part of the melting pot that is America, yours is the serious and supreme task—even obligation—of the hour: to understand, to appreciate and to work harmoniously with one another, and to be tolerant. The environments into which you were born and reared had much to do with the shaping of your lives, but many of you have progressed far beyond those environments, despite sometimes seemingly impassable barriers of color, race and creed. This is the story of one such man who, born in slavery and ignorance..." The foreward also introduces George Washington Carver's story and contributions. The opening credits, as written in the continuity, are presented in an unusual introductory sequence in which director Tony Paton, playing himself, tries to convince his backer Murphy, played by Bernard Gorcey, to finance the film. Paton tells "Murphy" that Hollywood is afraid to produce films which represent "the truth about races and religions." Paton then reads the cast and credit names in a

conversational manner and introduces the story proper by flipping the switch of a projector. Song titles listed above are included in the continuity. Other songs were also performed in the film, but their titles and composers have not been determined.

According to a Jul 1947 feature article on the film in *Ebony* magazine, the film cost $50,000 to produce and was made by Paton after an experience he had while on an airplane. According to the article, Paton was on a flight from New Orleans to Los Angeles, saw actor Clarence Muse sitting in the front of the plane and decided to sit with him. At that point a stewardess told Paton that only "Negroes" could sit in the front seats until the plane past Dallas. After the plane flew past Dallas, the two men sat together and "concluded arrangement to film a story of Carver."

George Washington Carver (1864-1943), a former slave, was a graduate of Iowa State College of Agriculture. He became a faculty member at Iowa, where he specialized in bacteriology, after which he moved to the Tuskegee Normal and Industrial Institute (now the Tuskegee Institute). He experimented with peanuts and discovered hundred of uses for the crop. He additionally developed uses for sweet potatoes and soybeans and helped to increase the efficiency of farming techniques. He was honored both during and after his lifetime for his efforts to advance the stature of African Americans and helping the economy of the Southern farmer.

Ebony Jul 1947, pp. 48-49.

PECK O' PICKLES (German Americans)
American Film Co.; A Mutual Star Production. *Dist* Mutual Film Corp. 13 Nov **1916**. Si; b&w. 5 reels.
Dir T. N. Heffron. *Story* Frank Stammers.
Cast: C. William Kolb (*Rudolph Schlitz*), May Cloy (*Louise, his daughter*), Max M. Dill (*Adolph Busch*), Frank Thompson (*Sergeant Todd*), Marie Van Tassell (*Caroline Pickett*), Josephine Clark (*Lutie, Busch's daughter*), Burdell Jacobs (*Jed, the town sheriff*), Alan Forrest (*Bobbie Bennett*).
Comedy. Rudolph Schlitz, a cobbler, finds a lottery ticket in a shoe he is repairing and, determined to make some money from it, he sells an interest in the ticket to his friend, Adolph Busch. Then, fed up with the way temperance leader Caroline Pickett rails against the evils of alcohol, Bobbie Bennett spikes the cider at Caroline's picnic. All of the villagers in attendance get drunk, including Rudolph and Adolph, who then dream that they have arrived in Washington to claim their lottery winnings. Besides being transported to the nation's capital, however, they also have been transported through time back to the Civil War and barely escape from the fighting alive. Rudolph and Adolph then wake up from their shared nightmare, and remembering the link between gambling and Gettysburg, they swear off lotteries and other games of chance forever. *Dreams. Drunkenness. German Americans. Lotteries. Picnicking. Combat. Gambling. Gettysburg, Battle of, 1863. Shoemakers. Shoes. Temperance. United States–History–Civil War, 1861-1865. Washington (D.C.).*
Note: *MPN* calls the film *A Peck o' Pickles.*
Motog 25 Nov 1916, p. 1196. *MPN* 11 Nov 1916, p. 3022. *MPW* 25 Nov 1916, p. 1223.

THE PEDDLER (Jewish Americans)
US Amusement Corp. *Dist* Art Dramas, Inc. 25 Jul **1917**. Si; b&w. 5 reels.
Dir Herbert Blaché. *Scen* Frederic Chapin. *Cam* John G. Haas.
Source: Based on the play *The Peddler* by Hal Reid (New York, 15 Dec 1902).
Cast: Joe Welch (*Abraham Jacobs*), Sidney Mason (*Sammy*), Catherine Calvert (*Sarah*), Kittens Reichert (*Mary*), Sally Crute (*Mrs. Morgan*).
Drama. Abraham Jacobs, an itinerant Jewish country peddler, saves his pennies until he can afford to open a small second-hand clothing store. Unfortunately, Abraham's son Sonny has not inherited his father's decent, hard working instincts, and when his mistress, Mrs. Morgan, is in need of money, Sammy robs Abraham's safe and then disappears. Time passes, and oil is discovered on a tract of land left to Abraham by his late wife. Although he can now afford to live in comfort with his adopted daughter Mary, Abraham still strongly feels the loss of his son. His life is finally made complete when Sammy returns repentant to marry Abraham's housekeeper Sarah, and the old peddler, his struggles now over, is able to spend the rest of his days surrounded by his family. *Clothing industry. Fathers and sons. Jews. Moral reformation. Robbery. Foster children. Housekeepers. Inheritance. Oil. Peddlers and peddling.*
Note: Yiddish comedian Joe Welch reprised his stage role for this film. *MPW* commented, "Joe Welch's voice is missed. But the titles in his dialect, which are inserted so often for their own sake, not to make the situations more intelligible, may well have been spared."

MPN 28 Jul 1917, p. 628. *MPW* 28 Jul 1917, p. 656. *MPW* 4 Aug 1917, p. 850. *NYDM* 11 Aug 1917, p. 16. *Wid's* 16 Aug 1917, p. 525.

THE PELL STREET MYSTERY (Chinese Americans)
Robert J. Horner Productions. *Dist* Rayart Pictures. 1 Nov **1924**. Si; b&w. 5 reels, 4,776 ft.
Dir Joseph Franz.
Cast: George Larkin, Carl Silvera.
Melodrama. "... centering about a newspaper reporter who is running down clews to murderer of wealthy man in Chinatown. He takes up with a notorious gang and when they learn who he is they set upon him. The timely interference of the police saves him, and he wins a girl and a scoop for his paper as well." (*MPNBG* 8 Apr 1925, p. 63.). *Chinatowns. Chinese Americans. Murder. Police. Reporters.*
Var 21 Jan 1925, p. 36.

THE PENITENTES (Latino, Native Americans)
Fine Arts Film Co. *Dist* Triangle Film Corp. 26 Dec **1915** [©Triangle Film Corp.; 20 Dec 1915; LP7977]. Si; b&w. 5 reels.
Supv D. W. Griffith. *Dir* John Conway. *Scen* Mary H. O'Connor. *Mus accompaniment comp* Joseph Carl Breil.
Source: Based on the novel *The Penitentes* by R. Ellis Wales (publication undetermined).
Cast: Orrin Johnson (*Manuel*), Seena Owen (*Dolores*), Paul Gilmore (*Col. Juan Banca*), Irene Hunt (*Senorita Carmelia*), Josephine Crowell (*Her mother*), F. A. Turner (*Father Rossi*), Charles Clary (*Father David*), A. D. Sears (*The Chief Brother*), Dark Cloud (*Indian chief*).
Historical, Drama. In a seventeenth century New Mexico village, after Indians attack and kill everyone except two monks and a baby named Manuel, the neighboring Penitentes, a violent, fanatical Catholic sect, lay claim to all property, including the estate belonging to Manuel's family. Years later, during a regional fiesta, Father David, the local religious leader, notices the striking Manuel, now grown, and questions the Penitentes' chief about his background. Fearing exposure, the chief induces his followers to choose Manuel as their annual sacrificial victim, to be crucified on the upcoming Good Friday. Dolores, Manuel's sweetheart, attempts to sway him from the group, but he insists on participating in the ceremony. At the urging of Father David, Colonel Banca orders his troops to stop the ceremony, and Manuel narrowly escapes crucifixion. Later, the confession of one of the old monks reveals the true identity and heritage of Manuel. *Cults. Human sacrifice. Indians of Central America. New Mexico. Parentage. Catholic Church. Confession. Crucifixion. Good Friday. Massacres. Monks. United States. Army. Cavalry.*
Note: One pre-production article lists Harry Hann, Joseph Henabery and Edward Warren as cast members. According to one pre-release article, Charles F. Lummis, an historian and author, was hired to assist with details of staging in this film. A period Mexican village was recreated in Chatsworth Park, north of Los Angeles. Working titles for this film include *The Penitent* and *The Penitents.*
Motog 11 Dec 1915, pp. 1241-42. *MPN* 11 Sep 1915, pp. 67-68. *MPN* 2 Oct 1915, p. 68. *MPN* 13 Nov 1915, p. 35. *MPN* 27 Nov 1915, p. 77. *MPN* 4 Dec 1915, p. 86. *MPW* 25 Dec 1915, p. 2450. *NYDM* 27 Nov 1915, p. 32. *NYT* 22 Nov 1915, p. 12. *Var* 3 Dec 1915, p. 21.

PENNSYLVANIA UPRISING *see* ALLEGHENY UPRISING

A PENNY'S WORTH OF LOVE *see* THE CITY OF TEARS

PERCHÉ NO? *see* DOÑA MENTIRAS

LE PÈRE CÉLIBATAIRE (French language)
Metro-Goldwyn-Mayer Corp.; controlled by Loew's, Inc.; A Robert Z. Leonard Production; A Marion Davies Production. *Dist* Metro-Goldwyn-Mayer Distributing Corp. **1931**; Prod: began early Feb 1931. Sd (Western Electric Sound System); b&w. 10 reels. 88 min. Passed by the National Board of Review. French language.
Réalisation de [*Dir*] Chester Franklin. [*Asst dir* Al Shenberg]. *Scenario de* [*Scr*] Laurence E. Johnson. *Adaptation française de* [*French adpt*] Jacques Deval. [*French dial* Yves Mirande]. *Photographie de* [*Photog*] André Barlatier. *Décorateur* [*Art dir*] Cedric Gibbons. *Montage de* [*Ed*] Helene Warne. *Costumes de* [*Cost*] Adrian. *Ingénieur du son* [*Sd eng*] Douglas Shearer.
Source: Based on the play *The Bachelor Father* by Edward Childs Carpenter (New York, 13 Feb 1928).
Cast: LILY DAMITA [(*Vivette Mouffard*)], André Luguet [(*John Ashley*)], George Mauloy [(*Sir Gerald Winterton*)], André Burgère [(*George Trent*)], Vital, Marcel André, André Berley [(*Larkin*)], Jeanne Helbling [(*Mrs. Webb*)].

Domestic, Comedy-drama. [*Not viewed*]. [The following plot summary is based on the English-language version of this film, *The Bachelor Father*; character names refer to that version. For further information regarding the English-language version, please see the note below and the entry for *The Bachelor Father* in the *AFI Catalog of Feature Films, 1931-40*.] Sir Basil Winterton, once a dashing young ladies' man, now lives alone at Rooksfold, his enormous Surrey, England estate, with only his servants as company. Occasionally, the temperamental old English aristocrat is visited by his friend, Doctor Frank MacDonald, who tells Basil that what he needs is the love and warmth of a family. To that end, the doctor suggests that Basil look up the addresses of his three illegitimate children, who are now adults and are living in different parts of the world, and then takes charge of bringing them to live at the manor. One of Basil's daughters, the vivacious Tony Flagg, is a dancer who has been living modestly in New York with her guardian, Mrs. Berney, and Mrs. Berney's son Dick. Tony and Mrs. Berney are shocked when Frank offers to take Tony away to live with her estranged father, but Mrs. Berney agrees because she realizes that Basil will be able to provide a better life for her. Though she knows that Basil's real daughter died twenty years ago, Mrs. Berney, believing that she is acting in Tony's best interest, suppresses the information and allows the girl to go. At Rooksfold, Tony meets her two siblings, Maria Credaro, a singer from Florence, Italy, and Geoffrey Trent. To Basil's dismay, his three children immediately engage in wild merriment. Appalled by their behavior, Basil calls them swine and regrets having invited them to stay. In response to Basil's hostile behavior, the three form a protective union and vow to stick together. When Basil tells Tony that she is not behaving in a manner befitting a woman in his social circle, Tony calls Basil hardboiled. The two bicker until Basil learns that Tony's mother is no longer living, whereupon he apologizes for his behavior and they make up. Eventually, Basil takes a liking to his offspring and allows them to stay. However, the three playfully suggest a probation period of one month before they decide if they want to stay. After meeting Basil's friend, John Ashley, Tony immediately falls in love with him and a romance ensues. Meanwhile, back in New York, Mrs. Berney is interrogated by Mr. Creswell, a lawyer intent on proving that Tony Flagg is not Basil's real daughter. When Dick, an aviator, flies his airplane to Surrey to visit Tony, he delivers a note from home that reveals the truth about her relationship to Basil. Tony, who has just accepted an engagement ring from John, is devastated by the news. She prepares to tell Basil the truth about herself, but Mr. Creswell beats her to it, thus making Tony look like an impostor. Embarrassed by the situation, Tony returns John's ring and explains to Basil that she did not tell him about the news right away because she did not want to ruin their lovely relationship. Tony then insists on flying out of England with her brother on a risky transatlantic flight, but when Dick and Basil find out about her plans, Dick is sent to stop her. Dick arrives too late, and while listening to the radio coverage of the aerial event, Basil hears the news that the airplane has crashed. Miraculously, though, Tony escapes with only minor injuries and is taken back to Rooksfold, where Basil and John argue over who will have the privilege of keeping her. Tony settles the matter by suggesting that she be Basil's daughter by day and John's wife by night. *England. Family life. Fathers and daughters. Loneliness. Millionaires. Parentage. Air pilots. Airplane accidents. Dancers. Engagements. Family relationships. Guilt. Italians. Lawyers. Manors. New York City. Physicians. Radio broadcasting. Wards and guardians.*

Note: The onscreen credits for this French-language version of *The Bachelor Father* were taken from a studio cutting continuity. *Some sources credit Arthur Robison with direction of the French version. The file for* The Bachelor Father *in the MPAA/PCA Collection at the AMPAS Library contains a series of letters sent between mid-Jun 1929 and Feb 1931, which indicate that the Hays Office initially objected to the production of any film based on Edward Childs Carpenter's play, due to the fact that the story concerned illegitimate children. The Hays Office called the play "unsuitable for production in motion pictures," but also stated that it might be all right for filming if "some irresponsible company does not get a hold of it." In addition, the Hays Office insisted that the title of the story be changed and called for the removal of any hint that the children in the story are illegitimate. The Hays Office went on to insist that no connection be made between the film and the play in its publicity or advertising. In Feb 1931, the foreign manager of the Hays Office noted that while all the English versions of the film had been released with an added scene that was designed to make it clear that the children were legitimate, the French version was released without the scene. He went on to state, however, that "for continental distribution, it is allright without any reference to the marriage status of Sir Basil. In fact, it makes it more spicy of course not to have this...I'm*

not so sure about England. The picture is so full of broad remarks which I imagine the English speaking world will censor." When Will H. Hays learned of the difference between the two versions, he called it a "very serious matter...to have one version for America and one version for the continent." He also raised an objection to the scene in which "Sir Basil's" lawyer implies that his client made payments to the women from his past. Following its release, *The Bachelor Father* underwent dialogue deletions by censors in New Zealand, Australia, Alberta, Milwaukee, Massachusetts and Virginia, and was banned in Ireland. Most of the eliminations related to the subject of illegitimate children. For further information on the English-language version, which was directed by Robert Z. Leonard and starred Marion Davies, please see the entry for that film in the *AFI Catalog of Feature Films, 1931-40*; F3.0203.

THE PERFECT DREAMER (African Americans)
Young Producers Filming Co. **1922.** Si; b&w. Length undetermined. [Feature length assumed.].

Melodrama (?), African American. No information about the precise nature of this film has been found. *African Americans.*

PERFIDIA (Spanish language)
Filmica Internacional. *Dist* RKO Radio Pictures, Inc. Feb **1940** [©RKO Radio Pictures, Inc.; 27 Apr 1939; LP8802]. Sd; b&w. 11 reels. 110 min. *Country of origin* Mexico. Spanish language.
Prod William Rowland. *Dir* William Rowland. *Scr* René Borgia, Josep Carner Ribalta, Ernesto Cortazar and Rafael A. Saavedra. *Orig story* William Rowland. *Photog* Alex Phillips. *Art dir assoc* Jorge Fernandez. *Ed* H. E. Mandl. *Mus dir* Rafael de Paz. *Dance dir* Larry Ceballos. *Sd* B. J. Kroger. *Tech adv* Carlos J. Pani. *Prod mgr* Antonia Guerrero Tello.
Song(s): "Bola de nieve," music by Rafael Herández, lyrics by Ernesto Cortazar; "Arriba la conga," music and lyrics by Rafael Hernandez; "Cancion del abanico," music by Manuel Esperon, lyrics by Ernest Cortazar; "Cajita de musica," music by Miguel Prado, lyrics by Ernesto Cortazar; "Perfidia," music and lyrics by Alberto Dominguez; "Tu no comprendes," music and lyrics by Rafael Hernández; "Cancion de benito," music by Miguel Prado, lyrics by Ernesto Cortazar; "Finale," music by Manuel Esperon, lyrics by Ernesto Cortaza.
Cast: María Teresa Montoya (*Adela Baroni*), Marina Tamayo (*Virginia, her daughter*), Domingo Soler (*Benito, the cook*), Magda Haller (*Dolores, the chorus girl*), Ramón Vallarino (*Roberto [Ramos], the producer*), Gaby Macías (*Lucia, the jealous girl*), Carlos López Moctezuma (*Armando, the millionaire backer*), Eduardo Arozamena (*Ernesto, Baroni's old friend*), Alberto Marti (*Frappe, cabaret owner*), Felipe Montoya (*Alfredo, a poet*), María Calvo (*Socorro, housekeeper*), Amparo Arozamena (*Murial, a golddigger*), Manuel Sanchez Navarro (*Montel, a go-between*), Raul Guerrero (*Muchadio, delivery boy*), Armando Velasco (*Cobrador, light collector*).
Drama, with songs. [*Not viewed*]. In Paris Adela Baroni, a retired singer and actress of considerable fame, has converted her home into an actors' hostelry where thespians thrive, although a good many neglect to pay their bills. Living there is Dolores, an ambitious young actress who works in a cabaret owned by Monsieur Frappe, who is in love with her; and Anita, Lucia and Rosa, girls who also work at Frappe's nightclub. Roberto Ramos, a young writer and friend of Baroni's, is a frequent visitor to the house, where he tries to induce Baroni to return to the stage in a play that he has written. One day, he is reading the lines of a love passage when Virginia, Baroni's daughter, who has just returned from college, overhears him. They meet and fall in love, causing Lucia, who is also in love with Roberto, to become jealous. Frappe and Montel, friends of Roberto, are trying to convince the wealthy playboy Armando Conti to back Roberto's play, and to accomplish this, Montel shows Armando some photos of Dolores, which prompt him to offer half the required capital if Dolores appears in the play. When Dolores comes to Armando's apartment for an audition, he falls in love with her. Meanwhile, Lucia, in jealous despair, goes to Madame Baroni and tells her that Roberto has ruined the reputation of many girls. Extremely upset, Baroni orders Virginia to return to college, but she refuses and insists on entering the theater. To persuade her daughter to give up her theatrical aspirations, Baroni reveals her own sad story of an actress married to a writer. When Virginia persists in her ambitions, Baroni collapses and is rushed to the hospital for a blood tranfusion. All the girls volunteer their blood, but only Lucia's is acceptable, prompting the guilty Lucia to admit that she lied about Roberto. After leaving Baroni's bedside, the doctor tells Dolores that her blood test indicated that she is

pregnant, and she rushes to Armando's apartment, where she finds him making love to another woman. A violent scene follows in which Dolores accidently fractures her arm. The accident prevents Dolores from appearing in the show, and Don Ernesto, who has been giving Virginia acting lessons, suggests that Virginia play Dolores' role. Baroni reacts to the news by disappearing from the hospital and soon after, Armando repents and begs for Dolores' forgiveness. Back at the theater, Don Ernesto finds Baroni in Virginia's dressing room where she realizes that she was unfair to Virginia and Roberto and agrees to play the part offered to her by Roberto, thus contributing to the success of the show. *Actors and actresses. False accusations. False accusations. Mothers and daughters. Blood–Transfusion. Infidelity. Paris (France). Playboys. Playwrights. Theatrical backers. Theatrical troupes.*

Note: Although a print of this film was not viewed, the above credits and plot summary were taken from a cutting continuity contained in copyright records. In the *HR* review, Ernesto Cortaza and Rafael Saavedra were credited with the screenplay, but their names were crossed off the copyright records. According to an unidentified contemporary source contained in the AFI library, this picture, made in Mexico City at the Clasa Studio, was the second Spanish language film made for RKO release.

FD 21 Apr 1939, p. 10. *HR* 5 Feb 1940, p. 3. *NYT* 17 Feb 1940, p. 9.

THE PERIOD OF THE JEW (Jewish Americans)

Boris Thomashefsky Film Co. *Dist* Boris Thomashefsky. **1915**?. Si; b&w. Length undetermined.

Dir Sidney M. Golden.

Source: Based on a Yiddish play (production undetermined).

Cast: Boris Thomashefsky.

Drama?. [No information about the plot of this film has been located.]. *Jews.*

Note: An ad for this film called it *The Period of Jew*. The Boris Thomashefsky Film Co. was located in New York City and made films based on Yiddish plays. According to a news item, Thomashefsky, who was called "perhaps the best known Yiddish actor in the world," opened the first Yiddish theater in America some thirty years earlier. Although the news item stated that this film had been made, no information has been located concerning its exact release or length.

MPW 30 Jan 1915, p. 757. *MPW* 6 Feb 1915, p. 809.

PERSONAL MAID (Irish Americans)

Paramount Publix Corp. *Dist* Paramount Publix Corp. 12 Sep **1931**; Prod: at Paramount-Publix New York Studios (Astoria, Long Island) [©Paramount Publix Corp.; 12 Sep 1931; LP2472]. Sd (Western Electric Noiseless Recording); b&w. 8 reels. 70, 74 or 77 min. Passed by the National Board of Review.

Dir Monta Bell. [*Fill-in dir* Lothar Mendes]. [*Asst dir* George Hippard]. *Scr* Adelaide Heilbron. *Photog* Karl Freund. [*2d cam* George Webber and George Hinners]. [*Art dir* Charles Kirk]. [*Ed* Arthur Ellis]. [*Mus adv* Frank Tours]. [*Sd rec* C. A. Tuthill]. [*Chief elec* Arthur Maher]. [*Still photog* Herman Zerrenner].

Source: Based on the novel *Personal Maid* by Grace Perkins (New York, 1931).

Cast: NANCY CARROLL (*Nora Ryan*), Pat O'Brien (*Peter Shea*), Gene Raymond (*Dick Gary*), Mary Boland (*Mrs. Otis Gary*), George Fawcett (*Gary Gary*), Hugh O'Connell (*Kipp*), [Ernest Lawford (*Barrows*)], [Charlotte Wynters (*Gwen Gary*)], [Jessie Busley (*Ma Ryan*)], [Donald Meek (*Pa Ryan*)], [Clara Langsner (*Mrs. Wurtz*)], [Terry Carroll (*Anna Ryan*)], [Ronnee Madson (*Personal maid*)].

Comedy-drama. [*Print viewed*]. Nora Ryan, who comes from a poor Irish family in the East side of New York, is fed up with their uncouth ways. Deciding to change her life, she becomes a personal maid to wealthy women, because she believes that the wealthy have superior morals and manners, in addition to a finer standard of living. After a few years training, Nora obtains a position as personal maid to Mrs. Otis Gary and her family. The family are extremely pampered and live in fear of aged grandsire Gary Gary, copper magnate, who occupies the top floor and controls the money. Mrs. Gary finds out her son Dick has been expelled from college. Fearing an outburst from old G. G., she pays Nora an exorbitant sum to meet Dick at the train station and escort him to an aunt's home in Virginia. Dick is a flirtatious rascal, and after meeting him, Nora is both appalled by his spoiled behavior and charmed by his flattery. Despite his entreaties, Dick is unable to con Nora out of any of her money, even after he offers her an engagement ring left over from another romance. Nora awakens in her sleeper car in the morning to find the ring and a promissory note in place of her money. Nora returns to New York and reports to G. G. who, despite his dotage, is aware of the situation. He confesses that Dick is his favorite grandson, and discovers that Nora

is in love with him despite herself. Through Nora's influence he decides not to have Dick arrested when he writes a $500 check from his father's account and reportedly sets sail for Havana. G. G. buys back the ring from Nora and she secretly covers Dick's check with the money. In the course of their conversation, G. G. calls Nora a "common servant girl." Indignant, Nora assumes an alias and uses the rest of her money and vacation time to live "like a real lady" in a fine hotel. She runs into Peter Shea, G. G.'s business manager who does not seem to recognize her as the Garys' maid. On a date with him, she finds out that Dick is in New York. G. G. recognizes her at the hotel and humiliates her in front of Peter by demanding she return to the house. Later, G. G. has a meeting with her and tells her he is impressed with her behavior and would like her to marry Dick. Now disillusioned with the wealthy, Nora declares she hates the entire Gary family. Downstairs, she runs into Peter, who confesses he always knew who she was, and if she is interested, he will get her what he thinks she wants. Nora is repelled by his intimation, especially after Dick returns. G. G. dies that day, and Dick leaves to work in another country, believing Nora is in love with Peter. With the help of the chauffeur Kipp, who has been her ally all along, Nora follows Dick and surprises him on the train, where he proposes for real with the engagement ring, and she accepts. *Class distinction. Family relationships. Grandfathers. Lure of riches. Maids. Playboys. Chauffeurs. Disillusionment. Drunkenness. Engagements. Expulsion. Hotels. Irish Americans. Poverty. Romance. Thieves. Trains.*

Note: According to reviews in *NYT* and *Var*, Lothar Mendes took over direction toward the end of the production. Terry Carroll is Nancy Carroll's sister. Although she also plays her sister in the film, *Var* notes that she appears only in silhouette.

FD 14 May 1931, p. 64. *FD* 17 May 1931, p. 9. *FD* 30 Aug 1931, p. 10. *MPH* 12 Sep 1931, p. 26. *MPH* 26 Sep 1931, p. 27. *NYT* 5 Sep 1931, p. 7. *Var* 8 Sep 1931, p. 15.

THE PERSONAL TOUCH *see* DARK DELUSION

PETER PAN (Native Americans)

Famous Players-Lasky Corp. *Dist* Paramount Pictures. 29 Dec **1924** [©Famous Players-Lasky Corp.; 23 Dec 1924; LP20980]. Si; b&w. 10 reels, 9,593 ft.

Pres Adolph Zukor and Jesse L. Lasky. *Dir* Herbert Brenon. *Scr and adpt* Willis Goldbeck. *Photog* James Howe. *Spec eff* Roy Pomeroy.

Source: Based on the novel *Peter Pan, or the Boy Who Wouldn't Grow Up* by James Matthew Barrie (1904).

Cast: Betty Bronson (*Peter Pan*), Ernest Torrence (*Captain Hook*), Cyril Chadwick (*Mr. Darling*), Virginia Brown Faire (*Tinker Bell*), Anna May Wong (*Tiger Lily*), Esther Ralston (*Mrs. Darling*), George Ali (*Nana, the dog*), Mary Brian (*Wendy*), Philippe De Lacey (*Michael*), Jack Murphy (*John*).

Fantasy. Peter Pan, the boy who never grew up, is looking for his shadow in the Darling nursery when he awakens the Darling children—Wendy, John, and Michael. Peter tells the children of Never-Never Land, teaches them to fly, and guides them to his forest home, where he is the king of the Little Lost Boys. Tinker Bell, a fairy, becomes jealous of Wendy and persuades one of the boys to shoot her with an arrow. Wendy recovers and is adopted by the boys as their mother. Captain Hook, a notorious pirate whose hand Peter once cut off, kidnaps the children after a fierce fight with Indians who are the children's friends and guardians. Peter, discovering that the children are missing, goes to the pirate ship and frees them. The children fight the pirates and subdue them. Captain Hook is forced to walk the plank. Peter then returns with the Darling children to their nursery. Wendy asks him to stay, but Peter refuses and returns to his home in the woods. *Children. Family life. Indians of North America. Jealousy. Kidnapping. Pirates.*

FD 11 Jan 1925. *NYT* 29 Dec 1924, p. 11. *Var* 31 Dec 1924, p. 26.

LE PETIT CAFÉ (French language)

Paramount Publix Corp. *Dist* Paramount Publix Corp. **1931**; San Francisco opening: 15 Jan 1931. Sd; b&w. 7,839 ft. 83 min. French language.

Dir Ludwig Berger. *Adpt* Vincent Lawrence and Jacques Bataille-Henri. *Dial* Jacques Bataille-Henri.

Song(s): music by Richard Whiting and Newell Chase, lyrics by Jacques Bataille-Henri.

Source: Based on the play *Le petit café* by Tristan Bernard (Paris, 12 Oct 1911).

Cast: Maurice Chevalier (*Albert Loriflan*), Yvonne Vallée (*Yvonne Philibert*), Tania Fédor (*Mlle. Bérangère*), André Berley (*Pierre Bourdin*), Emile Chautard (*Philibert*), Françoise Rosay (*Mlle. Edwige*), George Davis (*Paul Michel*), Jacques Jou-Jerville (*M. Cadaeux*), André Baugé (*Cook*), Sonia Sebor.

Musical comedy. [*Not viewed*]. [The following plot summary is based on the English-language version of this film, *Playboy of Paris*; character names refer to that version. For further information regarding the English-language version, please see the note below and the entry for *Playboy of Paris* in the *AFI Catalog of Feature Films, 1921-30*.] Yvonne, daughter of Philibert, a Paris café owner, is in love with dreamy, blundering Albert, a waiter, though he pays little attention to her. Philibert plans to marry his daughter to a wealthy Parisian, but upon learning that Albert is to come into a large inheritance, he conspires to place him under a longterm contract, confident that he willingly will pay a forfeit to break it. Albert, however, elects to remain a waiter by day and devote his nights to a gay social life with Mlle. Bérengère, a gold digger; he drops dishes and insults patrons, but Philibert will not discharge him. Angrily, Yvonne follows him to a rendezvous with Bérengère at a restaurant and denounces him as a waiter, precipitating a fight between the two girls. Albert defends Yvonne against another gentleman and is challenged to a duel—but the man refuses to fight a waiter. Insulted, Albert slaps him, but Yvonne faints from fright, and all ends happily as Albert realizes his love for her. *Courtship. Duels. Gold diggers. Inheritance. Paris (France). Restaurateurs. Waiters.*

Note: While *Var* lists the running time as 64 minutes, this is probably incorrect, as *FD* lists 83 minutes and the running time calculated from footage given in NYSA records is 87 minutes. This is the French-language version of the 1930 Paramount film *Playboy of Paris*, which was directed by Ludwig Berger and starred Maurice Chevalier and Frances Dee. Both versions were produced at the Paramount studios in Hollywood. The French version did not open in Paris until 8 May 1931. *Var* commented about the French version, "It is so much better than the original English version and Chevalier's work in it is so much superior to that in any of his American films in English....He is more at ease in his own language, acts with more abandon, does the same Chevalier tricks with a more Chevalierish air. His best American appearances result as imitations of the real Maurice." *Var* noted that the French version contained several songs that were not in the English-language version. Chevalier, who attended the New York premiere, and actress Yvonne Vallée were married at the time of this film. According to modern sources, this was the only film Vallée made in the U.S. In 1919, a comedy based on the same source was made in France starring Max Linder and directed by Raymond Bernard, the son of the playwright. According to modern sources, Chevalier, desiring to remake the Linder film, encouraged Paramount to purchase the property.

FD 25 Jan 1931, p. 11. *NYT* 25 Jan 1931, sect. VIII, p. 5. *Var* 28 Jan 1931, p. 40. *Var* 27 May 1931, p. 57.

PETTICOAT BRIGADE *see* **THE GUNS OF FORT PETTICOAT**

THE PHANTOM FEUD *see* **THE ORDEAL OF ROSETTA**

PHANTOM HOOFS *see* **THE AVENGER**

PHANTOM OF CHINATOWN (Chinese Americans)

Monogram Pictures Corp. *Dist* Monogram Pictures Corp. 18 Nov 1940 [©Monogram Pictures Corp.; 18 Nov 1940; LP10160]. Sd (Western Electric Mirrophonic Recording); b&w. 6 reels. 62 min. PCA cert no. 6779.

Series: Mr. Wong.

Prod Paul Malvern. *Dir* Phil Rosen. [*Asst dir* Mack Wright]. *Scr* Joseph West. *Orig story* Ralph Bettinson. *Dir of photog* Fred Jackman. *Spec eff* Jackman Process Corp. *Art dir* Charles Clague. *Film ed* Jack Ogilvie. *Int dec* David Milton. *Mus score* Edward Kay. *Sd dir* William Fox.

Source: Based on characters created by Hugh Wiley in the "James Lee Wong" short stories in *Collier's*.

Cast: KEYE LUKE [(*Jimmy Lee Wong*)], Grant Withers [(*Captain Street*)], Lotus Long [(*Win Len*)], Charles Miller [(*Dr. John Benton*)], Huntley Gordon [(*Wilkes*)], Virginia Carpenter [(*Louise Benton*)], John H. Dilson [(*Charles Fraser*)], Paul McVey [(*Grady*)], John Holland [(*Mason*)], Dick Terry [(*Toreno*)], Robert Kellard [(*Tommy Dean*)], William Castello [(*Jonas*)], Lee Tung Foo, [Victor Wong (*Charley One*)].

Detective. [*Print viewed*]. Dr. John Benton, in San Francisco following an archaeological expedition in the Mongolian desert, gives a film presentation for his colleagues. The film shows his discovery of the precious ancient tomb of a Ming emperor, for which archaeologists have been searching for centuries. The tomb contains a scroll that tells the secret of the Temple of Eternal Fire, which is of great financial importance to China as it could reveal an enormous untapped reserve of oil. The film of the trip shows a violent windstorm that erupted when the tomb was opened, in keeping with an ancient curse. Mason, the co-pilot on the trip, was lost during the storm, and the expedition party was forced to continue on without him. During the presentation, as Benton is about to reveal the exact contents of the scroll, he chokes and dies. Captain Street of Chinatown Homicide tells Benton's daughter Louise, who was also on the expedition, that her father was poisoned. Win Len, Benton's secretary, who works for the Chinese government, denies any knowledge of the contents of the scroll, which is missing from Benton's safe. Meanwhile, James Lee Wong, a student of Benton's, investigates the case himself and finds the glass cup and pitcher that contained the poison, and Street identifies it as an oriental vegetable poison. While Jimmy and Street view a film of Benton's lecture, Charles Fraser, the expedition's cameraman, receives an anonymous call that lures him away from Benton's house. Win then arrives to search the house, but on a hunch, Fraser returns and is attacked. When Jimmy and Street arrive, they find Win locked in a closet and Fraser injured. Jonas, Benton's butler, is scheming with Mason, who faked his death and now possesses the sacred sarchophagus of the emperor. Street then traces Fraser's phone call to a Chinese restaurant on the waterfront that has a secret room in which Jonas and Mason hide. Mason escapes through a trap door, but Street and Wong find a trinket that Win reveals is a statuette of the "God of Vengeance" and is from the same district as the tomb. Street and Jimmy then find Jonas dead in a coffin, knifed in the chest, but actually killed by poison. Jimmy has headlines printed that claim Jonas lies in St. Christopher's Hospital suffering from tropical fever in order to lure the killer to Mason. Jimmy, wearing a hidden microphone, poses as Mason as the police stake out the hospital. Mason eventually cuts the microphone's wires and enters the room through the window and finds Frazier, who tried to double-cross Mason and broke into Benton's home to find the scroll. Jimmy fights Mason as Street enters with policeman Grady. It is then revealed that Frazier edited out the part of the expedition film that showed the scroll and killed Benton in order to possess the secret of the oil himself. Frazier then killed Jonas because he and Mason were also after the scroll. Although Frazier destroyed the original scroll, Street finds Frazier's photograph of it and returns it to Win so that she may restore it to the Chinese people. *Archaeologists. Chinese Americans. Detectives. Murder. Oil. San Francisco (CA)–Chinatown. Secret documents. Air pilots. Butlers. Curses. Expeditions. Hideouts. Hospitals. Lectures. Missing persons, Assumed dead. Motion picture cameramen. Poisoning. Police. Thieves. Tombs. Traps. Wind storms.*

Note: This was the first and only of the Wong pictures in which Keye Luke replaced Boris Karloff in the role of Wong, and was the first feature in which Luke had the leading role. This picture was the last in the Wong series. For more information on the series, see the entry for *Mr. Wong, Detective* above and consult the Series Index.

DV 15 Nov 1940, p. 3. *Exb* 27 Nov 1940, p. 644. *HR* 15 Nov 1940, p. 3. *MPD* 19 Nov 1940, p. 3. *MPH* 23 Nov 1940, p. 49. *Var* 1 Jan 1941, p. 14.

THE PHANTOM OF PARIS (*foreign version*) *see* **CHERI-BIBI**

THE PHANTOM OF SANTA FE (Latino)

Burroughs-Tarzan Pictures, Inc.; An Ashton Dearholt Production. *Dist* Dearholt—Stout—Cohen. 21 Dec 1936 [©Burroughs-Tarzan Pictures, Inc.; 21 Dec 1936; LP7160]. Sd (Sd equipment by Balsley & Phillips); col (Cinecolor). 6 reels, 5,249 ft. 55 min. PCA cert no. 2231.

Dir Jacques Jaccard. *Dial dir* Frederick H. Shields. *Adpt and dial* Chas. Royal. *Cine* Otto Himm. *Spec eff* Frank Williams. *Film ed* Walter Thompson. *Sd rec* Dave Stoner. *Sd ed* Thos. Neff.

Cast: Nena Quartaro [(*Teresa Valarde*)], Carmelita Geraghty [(*Lola*)], Norman Kerry [(*Miguel Morago, also known as "The Phantom of Santa Fe," alias "The Hawk"*)], Frank Mayo [(*Steve Gant*)], Tom O'Brien [(*Kilbaine*)], Jack Mower [(*Captain Rubio*)], [Fernando Valdez (*Ramirez*)].

Western. [*Print viewed*]. In the early nineteenth century, the Mission Guadalupe in Santa Fe is attacked by a band of unknown renegades and robbed of priceless treasures used during the morning ceremonial pageant. Some colonists vow revenge on The Hawk and his men, whom they claim to be the robbers. Because no one has been able to identify The Hawk, he has been called "The Phantom of Santa Fe." At a cantina near the mission, Steve Gant, an American, rebukes

his gunman Kilbaine for letting The Hawk get away. After Gant announces that whoever delivers The Hawk to him dead or alive can name their reward, Miguel Morago enters, and Kilbaine swears that he is The Hawk. Gant just laughs, unable to believe that Miguel is the notorious outlaw, and vouches that Miguel was at the hacienda of Don Carlos Valarde, the wealthiest of the Spanish settlers, all day. Lola, a cantina girl, entices Miguel into her room and tells him she wants the reward more than anything because then she would demand that Gant marry her. As a wagon train belonging to Gant makes its way along the mesa, The Hawk, who actually is Miguel, and his men attack. After finding nothing they want in the wagons, they take two prisoners for questions and then, seeing Captain Rubio with soldiers approaching, spread out in retreat. At the Valarde rancho, Don Carlos expresses his delight to Gant that he will marry his daughter Teresa the next day, but their conversation is interrupted when they overhear Teresa say that she is in love with Miguel, whom Don Carlos thinks is a loafer, and will never marry Gant. When Captain Rubio arrives and reports the attack to Gant, Miguel sneaks up to the balcony and exchanges clothes with his servant Chico, who, disguised as Miguel, has been pretending to be sleeping on the balcony. Don Carlos gives Teresa orders not to have intimate conversations with Miguel, so they confess their love for one another through a drain pipe. Teresa reponds to Miguel's vow that she will never marry Gant by saying that if Miguel were a man like The Hawk, he would carry her off on his horse to the hills. At the cantina, Gant makes plans to move the mission treasure across the border in a wagon train the next day during his wedding. Captain Rubio brings in Chico, whom he says is The Hawk, but when they see that he wears a false mustache, Gant thinks that Miguel may actually be The Hawk. In the hills, Miguel and his followers question their prisoners about the stolen treasure, which they believe Gant has hidden, but even under threat of death from being tied to wild horses, the prisoners refuse to talk. Admiring their loyalty, Miguel has them freed. The next day, as the wedding is about to begin, Miguel gives himself up to Lola and arranges for Gant and a padre to come to her room. When she demands that Gant now marry her as her reward for the capture of The Hawk, Gant refuses, so she reveals that the treasures are in one of the wagons heading for the border. Gant pulls a gun and tries to leave, but the padre says, "In the name of the Lord, stop," and a crucifix falls, knocking the gun from Gant's hand. Miguel struggles with him, and when Gant retrieves his gun, Miguel's follower Ramirez shoots Gant. Kilbaine, hearing Gant's warning call, races off with the wagons, but Miguel leads his men in pursuit. They torch the wagons and find the treasure, which Miguel gives to the padre. He then takes Teresa onto his horse and rides into the hills, where he reminds her of her wish. *False accusations. Impersonation and imposture. Outlaws. Santa Fe (NM). Thieves.* Americans in foreign countries. Cantinas. Chases. Crucifixes. Fires. Haciendas. Marriage–Forced. Missions. Priests. Rewards. Rites and ceremonies. Romance. Servants. Shootings. Soldiers. Wagon trains. Weddings.

Note: According to modern sources, this film was originally produced in 1931 under the title *The Hawk,* but was not released until 1936 in a re-scored, re-edited version. According to a *FD* news item in Jun 1936, Burroughs-Tarzan Pictures had just signed a contract with Cinecolor which allowed them to use the process in any color films they released. Modern sources list the following additional cast members: Monte Montague, Frank Ellis and Merrill McCormack.
DV 25 Jan 1937, p. 3. *Exh* 1 Aug 1936. *FD* 4 Jun 1936, p. 11.

PHANTOM OF THE PLAINS (Native Americans)

Republic Pictures Corp. *Dist* Republic Pictures Corp. 7 Sep **1945;** Prod: began late Jan 1945 [©Republic Pictures Corp.; 16 Aug 1945; LP13494]. Sd (RCA Sound System); b&w. 6 reels, 4,979 ft. 56 or 58 min. Passed by the National Board of Review. PCA cert no. 10769.

Series: Red Ryder.

[*Exec prod* William J. O'Sullivan]. *Assoc prod* R. G. Springsteen. *Dir* Lesley Selander. [*Asst dir* Don Verk]. *Orig scr* Earle Snell and Charles Kenyon. *Photog* William Bradford. [*2d cam* Joseph Novak]. [*Miniatures and spec photog eff* Howard Lydecker and Theodore Lydecker]. [*Transparency projection shots* Gordon C. Schaefer]. *Art dir* Hilyard Brown. *Film ed* Charles Craft. *Set dec* Charles Thompson. *Mus dir* Richard Cherwin. *Sd* Ed Borschell. [*Re-rec and eff mixer* Thomas A. Carman and John Stransky, Jr.]. [*Re-rec, eff and mus mixer* Howard Wilson]. *Makeup supv* Bob Mark.

Source: Based on the comic strip "Red Ryder" by Fred Harmon (1938–1964), by special arrangement with Stephen Slesinger.

Cast: WILD BILL ELLIOTT (*Red Ryder*), Bobby Blake [(*Little Beaver*)], Alice Fleming [(*The Duchess*)], Ian Keith [(*Fancy Charlie, also known as Talbot Wilberforce Champneys*)], William Haade [(*Ace Hanlon*)], Virginia Christine [(*Celeste*)], Bud Geary [(*Pete Burdett*)], Henry Hall [(*Banker*)], Fred Graham [(*Chuck*)], Jack Kirk [(*Sheriff*)], Jack Rockwell [(*Stage driver*)], [Earle Hodgins, Tom London (*Ranchers*)].

Western. [*Print viewed*]. In 1895, confidence man Fancy Charlie, who has married and murdered many wealthy women, comes to the town of Blue Springs, where he assumes an English accent and the name Talbot Wilberforce Champneys in order to romance the Duchess, a prosperous rancher and businesswoman. The Duchess' other suitors are disgruntled when her engagement to Charlie is announced, and the announcement also shocks her nephew, Red Ryder, and his Indian ward, Little Beaver, who are returning to town after a trip. While Red is in town discussing the situation with friends, Charlie is at the ranch with the Duchess and his confederate Celeste, who is posing as a couturier. Charlie is upset when outlaws Ace Hanlon and Pete Burdett appear at the ranch, for Burdett was once Charlie's cellmate and threatens to expose his scheme if he does not cut him in for a share of the Duchess' money. Charlie refuses, and as Burdett is beating him, Red arrives and captures Burdett, although Hanlon escapes. Red is suspicious of Charlie's claim that Burdett is merely an acquaintence who cheated him in a poker game, but lets Burdett go when Charlie insists. The Duchess is eager for Red to approve of Charlie, but Red is worried that she has been swayed by the promise of an aristocratic lifestyle in England, and knows little about her fiancé. Red's suspicions grow when Charlie beats a horse that afternoon, for as Red points out, the English are well known for their kind treatment of animals. In town, Red wires the British consul for information about "Champneys." Afraid that Red will ruin his plans, Charlie offers Hanlon and Burdett a fifty-percent share of his profits if they "take care" of Red and Little Beaver. Charlie then tells the Duchess that he has to return to England immediately, and she agrees to go with him and be married on the way, despite Red's strenuous objections. After Celeste overhears Red and Little Beaver discussing plans to pick up the reply from the British consul, Hanlon and Burdett ambush them at the telegraph office. Red and Little Beaver are held prisoner over night, and the next morning, Charlie taunts them by congratulating Red on seeing through his act and assuring him that the Duchess will soon be dead. To prevent Charlie from double-crossing them, Hanlon and Burdett intend to keep Red alive until after Duchess has been killed, but Red and Little Beaver succeed in escaping. They chase after the stage carrying the Duchess, Charlie and Celeste, and reach it just as Hanlon is about to kill Charlie for trying to double-cross him. During the ensuing fray, Red shoots Burdett and bests Hanlon in a fight, and the Duchess has the satisfaction of hitting Charlie in the face with their wedding cake. *Confidence men. Cowboys. Engagements. Outlaws. Women ranchers.* Aliases. Aunts. Betrayal. Cake. Chases. Cruelty to animals. English. Fistfights. Indians of North America. Wards and guardians.

Note: The working titles of this film were *Texas Manhunt* and *Desperadoes of Dakota.* The character "Ace Hanlon" also appears in another "Red Ryder" film, *The San Antonio Kid,* although he is played by Glenn Strange in that picture (see below). Modern sources include Rose Plummer in the cast. For more information on the "Red Ryder" series, please consult the Series Index and see the entry below for *Tucson Raiders.*
DV 5 Oct 1945, p. 4, 13. *HR* 26 Jan 1945, p. 10. *HR* 11 Jul 1945, p. 9. *HR* 5 Oct 1945, p. 8. *MPHPD* 26 May 1945, p. 2467. *MPHPD* 13 Oct 1945, p. 2677, 2679.

PHANTOM SUBMARINE *see* **MYSTERY SUBMARINE**

PHILIP YORDAN'S ANNA LUCASTA *see* **ANNA LUCASTA**

PIER 13 *see* **ME AND MY GAL**

PIERNAS DE SEDA (Spanish language)

Fox Film Corp. *Dist* Twentieth Century-Fox Film Corp. **1935;** New York opening: 4 Oct 1935; Prod: 7 May–1 Jun 1935 [©Twentieth Century-Fox Film Corp.; 11 Sep 1935; LP5777]. Sd (Western Electric Noiseless Recording); b&w. 8 reels, 7,199 ft. 80 min. Passed by the National Board of Review. PCA cert no. 960. Spanish language.

[*Prod* John Stone]. *Dirección de* [*Dir*] John J. Boland. [*Asst dir* Sam Schneider]. [*Dial dir* Enrique de Rosas and Miguel de Zárraga, Jr.]. [*Story* Frederica Sagor]. *Adaptación cinematográfica* [*Scr*] Paul Perez. *Versión española* [*Spanish version*] José López Rubio. [*Photog* Harry Jackson]. *Dirección musical* [*Mus dir*] Samuel Kaylin. [*Dance dir* Sammy Lee].

Song(s): "You've Got Me That Way," "Penitentiary Blues" and, in the stocking show sequence, "Stocking Show Opening," "Pantalette," "Rhythmic Dialog," "Modern Girl" and "Futuristic Lady," music by William Kernell, lyrics by Raúl Roulien.

Cast): ROSITA MORENO [(*Lolita Baxter, also known as Mary Smith*)], RAÚL ROULIEN [(*Frank Alton*)], Enrique de Rosas [(*John Baxter*)], Paco Moreno (*Conroy*), Romualdo Tirado (*Fishback*), Manuel Peluffo (*Enrique*), Rodolfo Hoyos (*Lloyd*), Manuel París (*Morán*), Antonio Vidal (*Brown*), Rosita Granada (*Secretaria*), [Martín Garralaga (*Evans*)], [Jose Peña "Pepet"], [Hoit Porter], [Donald Brown], [Dixie Dean, Philippa Hilbere, Anita Thompson, Dorothy Dearing, Florence Dickson, Lucille Miller, Esther Brodelet, Rita Cansino (*Bailarinas*)].

Romantic comedy, with songs. [*Not viewed*]. When singer Frank Alton is late for work at a radio station in New York, Conroy, the manager, fires him. Without Frank on the program, Ninón Silk Stockings, the show's sponsor, begins to lose sales. The president of the company, John Baxter, and his bored daughter Lolita, are then dismayed to learn that Frank has begun to work for their competitor, Bon Soir Stockings. After learning that Frank is stealing their customers, Lolita convinces her father and his associates, who do not believe that women can do "men's" work, to let her sell stockings. Using the name of Mary Smith, Lolita makes an appointment with Mr. Morán, one of Frank's customers, and then sells him 150 gross of stockings. Discovering that he is being undermined, Frank determines to win his next sale with a man named Fishback, whom he meets for dinner. At the restaurant, Fishback confesses that women are his weakness and eyes "Mary" from across the room. Not realizing that she is the salesperson who stole his customer, Frank enlists her help. When Fishback places his order for 300 gross, Lolita uses the Ninón order form without Frank's knowledge. After this second failure, Frank travels to Pottsville, where his customer, Mr. Brown, meets him at the station to tell him that he's already signed an order for Ninón stockings. At an inn in Pottsville, Frank meets Lolita, still in the guise of Mary, and having caught on to the fact that she is stealing his trade, gives her a list of the customers he's planning to see and challenges her to steal them away. The next morning on the train, Frank dresses up like the porter and tricks Lolita into getting off at the wrong stop. When Frank jokingly tells the conductor about the ruse, the conductor places him under arrest. Lolita gets Frank out of jail and tells him that the customer he has come to see, Mr. Evans, is out of town. They decide to declare a truce, and Lolita suggests that they take the rest of the afternoon off. They drive to an isolated spot for a picnic, and when Frank makes a pass at Lolita, she breaks their agreement by returning to the city and leaving him stranded. At Ninón headquarters, Baxter slights Conroy as they plan for the upcoming Annual Stocking Show. At the show, Frank flaunts his new advertising slogan, "Follow me—I won't run," which he has printed on buttons. In the Ninón dressing room, Conroy, to sabotage Lolita, takes one of Frank's buttons and rips holes in the Ninón stockings. When the models appear in ripped hose, the audience is aghast. Next, Frank sings a song for Bon Soir Stockings and sends his models out into the audience for orders. Lolita stops Fishback as he is about to place an order and, after telling the customers that the runs in Ninón's hosiery were the work of a diabolical competitor, demonstrates their resilience. After the customers flock to buy from Lolita, Frank's boss, who believes that he sabotaged the Ninón show, fires him. Frank then visits Lolita at her home and still unaware of her true identity, mistakenly thinks that Baxter, her father, is making sexual advances toward her. Frank hits Baxter in the face, and after the misunderstanding is cleared up, Frank explains that Conroy ruined the show. Baxter then agrees to rehire Frank, while he and Lolita plan their wedding. *Business competition. Hosiery. Impersonation and imposture. Romance. Ruses. Salesmen. Saleswomen. Singers. Advertising. Buttons. Dismissal (Employment). Fathers and daughters. Picnicking. Porters. Radio broadcasting. Restaurants. Revenge. Sabotage. Train conductors.*

Note: The plot summary was based on a screen continuity in the Twentieth Century-Fox Produced Scripts Collection, and the onscreen credits were taken from a screen credits sheet, both of which are located at the UCLA Theater Arts Library. The working title of this film was *Free and Easy*. The running time listed above was calculated from footage given in NYSA records. In 1927, Fox produced a version of this film entitled *Silk Legs*, which was directed by Arthur Rosson and starred Madge Bellamy and James Hall (see *AFI Catalog of Feature Films, 1921-30*; F2.5068).

CM Sep 1935, p. 544. *DV* 8 May 1935, p. 4. *HR* 6 May 1935, p. 2. *HR* 3 Jun 1935, p. 2.

PIGSKIN PARADE OF 1937 *see* **LIFE BEGINS IN COLLEGE**

PIGSKIN PARADE OF 1938 *see* **LIFE BEGINS IN COLLEGE**

PILLARS OF THE SKY (Native Americans, Coeur d'Alene, Palouse, Spokane, Skitswish)

Universal-International Pictures Co., Inc.; *Dist* Universal Pictures Co., Inc. Oct 1956; *New York opening:* 12 Oct 1956; *Prod:* mid-Aug–late Sep 1955 [©Universal Pictures Co.; 20 Aug 1956; LP7234]. Sd (Western Electric Recording); col (Technicolor). 8,525 ft. 94-95 min. PCA cert no. 17682.

Prod Robert Arthur. *Dir* George Marshall. *Asst dir* Marshall Green, [Terry Nelson and Ray DeCamp]. [*Dial dir* George Marshall, Jr.]. *Scr* Sam Rolfe. *Dir of photog* Harold Lipstein. *Technicolor color consultant* William Fritzsche. *Art dir* Alexander Golitzen and Bill Newberry. *Film ed* Milton Carruth. *Set dec* Russell A. Gausman and Oliver Emert. *Cost* Rosemary Odell. *Mus supv* Joseph Gershenson. *Sd* Leslie Carey and Frank H. Wilkinson. *Hair stylist* Joan St. Oegger. *Makeup* Bud Westmore. [*Unit prod mgr* Tom Shaw].

Song(s): "Down in the Valley," traditional.

Source: Based on the novel *To Follow a Flag* by Will Henry (New York, 1953).

Cast: JEFF CHANDLER (*First Sergeant Emmett Bell*), DOROTHY MALONE (*Calla Gaxton*), Ward Bond (*Dr. Joseph Holden*), Keith Andes (*Captain Tom Gaxton*), Lee Marvin (*Sergeant Lloyd Carracart*), Sydney Chaplin (*Timothy*), Willis Bouchey (*Colonel Edson Stedlow*), Michael Ansara (*Kamiakin*), Olive Carey (*Mrs. Anne Avery*), Charles Horvath (*Sergeant Dutch Williams*), Orlando Rodriguez (*Malachi*), Glen Kramer (*Lieutenant Winston*), Floyd Simmons (*Lieutenant Hammond*), Pat Hogan (*Jacob*), Felix Noriego (*Lucas*), Paul Smith (*Morgan*), Martin Milner (*Waco*), Robert Ellis (*Albie*), Ralph J. Votrian (*Music*), Walter Coy (*Major Donahue*), Alberto Morin (*Sgt. Major Frenchy Desmonde*), Richard Hale (*Isaiah*), Frank de Kova (*Zachariah*), Terry Wilson (*Captain Fanning*), Philip Kieffer (*Major Randall*), Gilbert Conner (*Elijah*), [Dan Borzage (*Soldier*)], [Maureen Hingert (*Indian woman*)], [Bryson G. Liberty (*Warrior at the mission*)], [Bob Herron].

Western. [*Print viewed*]. In Oregon country, in 1868, First Sgt. Emmett Bell, chief of the Cavalry's Indian police force, rides into the mission of his friend, Dr. Joseph Holden, accompanied by several of the Nez Perce scouts who serve under him. Several of the region's chiefs, whom Dr. Holden has baptized as Christians, inform him that Kamiakin, the warlike chief of the Palouse Indians, has summoned them to council to discuss the movement of Army troops and cannons into their lands. Deeply concerned, Emmett heads for the encampment of the U.S. Cavalry, bursts into the office of the new commanding officer, Col. Edson Stedlow, and barks, "What's the idea?" Also present is Capt. Tom Gaxton, whose wife Calla fell in love with Emmett when both men fought together during the Civil War. Stedlow explains that because a clause in the treaty allows the Army to build a road through the reservation, his command of young soldiers has been ordered to do so. Stedlow informs an outraged Emmett that he will serve only as a scout on the building expedition, then has the sergeant arrested for drinking on duty. The colonel remarks to Stedlow that although Emmett is rowdy and insubordinate, he is valuable to the Army because there is a deep mutual respect between him and the Indians. Later, Emmett's scout Timothy, a Nez Perce, reports that Kamiakin, enraged that the Army has constructed a bridge over the Snake River into Indian lands, has called for total annihilation of the troops. Emmett leads Stedlow to the mission, where they meet with chiefs Elijah of the Spokane, Isaiah of the Coeur d'Alene, Simon of the Umatilla, Isaac of the Wallawalla, and Kamiakin of the Palouse. After the colonel refuses to remove his troops, Kamiakin urges the chiefs to fight. Timothy argues that the Indians, having become too bound up with the white man, must learn to live with him in peace, but Kamiakin replies scornfully that his tribe will not be "swallowed up in the belly of a different people." While both sides prepare for war, Emmett and his scouts steal into Kamiakin's camp and rescue two women who were earlier captured by Kamiakin: Calla Gaxton and Mrs. Anne Avery, whose husband and son were killed during an ambush. Calla declares her love for Emmett, and although he resists her at first, he soon succumbs to her charms. Emmett's party encounters Stedlow and his troops, who have crossed into the reservation and are now surrounded. The colonel boasts that

into the reservation and are now surrounded. The colonel boasts that his column will defeat any attack, but as Indian snipers begin to pick off the men, and soldiers are found hacked to pieces, he finally realizes the hopelessness of their situation. Emmett and Holden try to secure safe passage for the women, but chief Zachariah responds violently to this request, and soon the column is attacked by a huge force of Indians. Many warriors are killed, but Stedlow's troops are decimated, and only a small group of white survivors reaches the top of the hill. The colonel is stunned and sorry, but Emmett declares that, considering his orders, he did the best he could. As they await a nighttime attack, Emmett drinks whiskey with his friend, Sgt. Lloyd Carracart, whose serious injury has not dampened his devil-may-care Irish temperament. Tom and Calla each accept the blame for their unhappy marriage, but when Calla goes to Emmett, she realizes that it is her husband, not Emmett, who truly loves her. Holden determines that Kamiakin's forces are massing at the foot of the hill, thereby leaving a section of the surrounding land unguarded. While the party quietly makes its way down the hill in an attempt to escape to Holden's mission, Carracart, who expects to die soon, remains behind to tend the fires. The party does reach the mission, but Tom is injured, and Calla rushes to his side. Kamiakin's warriors arrive at daybreak, and the mission is set on fire. Realizing that the situation is desperate, Holden rides out to the Indians' position and raises his arm in peace. Kamiakin kills him just before Emmett and Timothy arrive. Enraged, Emmett accuses the chiefs and their followers of being little better than animals. Kamiakin aims his gun at Emmett, but Isaiah, deeply ashamed at Kamiakin's cowardly actions, shoots the Palouse chief down. Everyone walks slowly back to the mission, where the Christian chiefs ask Emmett to take Holden's place. Emmett opens the Bible and prays that they might all be comforted. *Coeur d'Alene War, 1858. Kamiakin. Missionaries. Officers (Military). Palouse Indians. Romantic rivalry. Scouts (Frontier). Tribal chiefs. Assimilation (Sociology). Battles. Bible. Christianity. Conversion (Religious). Drunkenness. Escapes. Friendship. Heroism. Indians of North America. Infidelity. Massacres. Missions. Political alliances. Rescues. Self-sacrifice. Skitswish Indians. Spokan Indians. Treaties. United States. Army. Cavalry. Wounds and injuries.*

Note: Although, according to onscreen credits, the film *Pillars of the Sky* was based on the novel *Frontier Fury* by Will Henry, the actual source novel was *To Follow a Flag*, which was reprinted in 1956 under the title *Pillars of the Sky.* An *HR* news item refers to "Frontier Fury" as a magazine story, but as far as can be determined, Henry did not publish a novel or short story with this title. The picture was filmed in Eastern Oregon. News items in *DV* noted that Patrick Ford, the son of director John Ford, and Borden Chase were assigned at various times to write the script, but the extent of their contributions to the final film is undetermined. Reviewers generally praised the film's cast, and the *NYT* reviewer added: "*Pillars in the Sky* with a nice, surprising mixture of compassion and cynicism, keeps insisting that...all [the characters] matter, red and white." The Paloos Indians are also known as the Palouse Indians, and the Skitswish Indians are also known as the Coeur d'Alene Indians. During the 1850s, Chief Kamiakin of the Yakimas urged these tribes, along with the Spokane Indians, to unite against the U.S. Army. In 1858, the Indians defeated a column of 164 troops that had crossed the Snake River under the command of Maj. Edward Steptoe. Later that year, however, the Indians suffered two crushing defeats at Spokane Plain and the Battle of Four Lakes, and several of Kamiakin's relatives were executed. Although wounded at Spokane Plain, Kamiakin escaped into Canada, returning three years later to lead a quiet life on the Spokane reservation. He died in 1877.

Box 11 Aug 1956. *DV* 18 Oct 1953. *DV* 5 Feb 1954. *DV* 7 Aug 1956, p. 3. *Exh* 8 Aug 1956, p. 4199. *FD* 8 Aug 1956, p. 6. *Har* 4 Aug 1956, p. 126. *HR* 19 Jul 1955, p. 15. *HR* 30 Sep 1955, p. 15. *HR* 7 Aug 1956, p. 3. *MPHPD* 11 Aug 1956, p. 25. *NYT* 13 Oct 1956, p. 15. *Var* 8 Aug 1956, p. 6.

PINKY (African Americans)

Twentieth Century-Fox Film Corp. *Dist* Twentieth Century-Fox Film Corp. Nov **1949**; New York premiere: 29 Sep 1949; Prod: early Mar—23 May 1949 [©Twentieth Century-Fox Film Corp.; 29 Sep 1949; LP2671]. Sd (Western Electric Recording); b&w. 11 reels, 9,148 ft. 101-02 min. PCA cert no. 13731.

Pres DARRYL F. ZANUCK. *Prod* Darryl F. Zanuck. *Dir* Elia Kazan. [*Asst dir* Wingate Smith]. *Scr* Philip Dunne and Dudley Nichols. [*Contr to scr* Jane White and Elia Kazan]. *Dir of photog* Joe MacDonald. [*Cam op* Til Gabanni]. [*Gaffer* Les Everson]. [*Stills* Anthony Ugrin]. *Spec photog eff* Fred Sersen. *Art dir* Lyle Wheeler and J. Russell Spencer. *Film ed* Harmon Jones. *Set dec* Thomas Little and Walter M. Scott. *Ward dir* Charles LeMaire. *Mus* Alfred Newman. *Orch* Edward Powell. *Sd* Eugene Grossman and Roger Heman. *Makeup artist* Ben Nye. [*Makeup* Frank Prehoda]. [*Hair stylist* Lillian Hokom and Addie Baker]. [*Prod mgr* Joe Behm]. [*Scr supv* Rose Steinberg]. [*Grip* Frank Corey].

Source: Based on the novel *Quality* by Cid Ricketts Sumner (Indianapolis, 1946).

Cast: JEANNE CRAIN [(*Patricia "Pinky" Johnson*)], ETHEL BARRYMORE [(*Miss Em*)], ETHEL WATERS [(*Dicey Johnson*)], WILLIAM LUNDIGAN [(*Dr. Thomas Adams*)], Basil Ruysdael [(*Judge Walker*)], Kenny Washington [(*Dr. Canady*)], Nina Mae McKinney [(*Rozelia*)], Griff Barnett [(*Doc Joe*)], Frederick O'Neal [(*Jake Waters*)], Evelyn Varden [(*Melba Wooley*)], Raymond Greenleaf [(*Judge Shoreham*)], [Dan Riss (*Stanley*)], [William Hansen (*Mr. Goolby*)], [Arthur Hunnicutt (*Police chief*)], [Robert Osterloh (*Police officer*)], [Jean Inness (*Saleslady*)], [Shelby Bacon (*African-American boy*)], [Everett Glass (*Mr. Wooley*)], [Bert Conway, Reed Killgore (*Loafers*)], [Renee Beard (*Teejoe*)], [Tonya Overstreet, Juanita Moore, Margaret Brayton, Bobby Dugan, Mildred Boyd (*Nurses*)], [Preston Braxton, Wilfred Jackson (*Boys*)], [Frank Jaquet (*Bailiff*)], [Tiger Joe Marsh (*Deputy sheriff*)], [Paul Brinegar (*Western Union clerk*)], [Ruth Rickaby (*Matron*)], [George Spaulding (*Medical director*)], [Jim Toney (*Baggage man*)], [Warren Mace (*Intern*)], [Edgar Washington], [Pat Kane], [Betty Beard], [Katherine Sparks], [Bessie Wade], [Major Philip Kieffer], [Noble "Kid" Chissell], [Mike Jeffers], [Pat Walshe], [Harry Tenbrook], [Dick Dickinson], [Eve Conrad], [Beverly Jordan], [Patsy Boniface], [Geraldine Jordan], [Josette Deegan], [Jasper Weldon].

Social, Drama. [*Print viewed*]. Patricia "Pinky" Johnson, a light-skinned African-American woman, returns by train to her childhood home in a small Southern town. Her grandmother Dicey, a hard-working, religious washerwoman, is happy that Pinky has come back from the northern school to which Dicey sent her when she was very young. Pinkie is now a fully qualified nurse, and Dicey hopes that she will use her knowledge to help their community. Dicey suspects that Pinky has passed for white up North, and when Pinky confesses that she has, her grandmother, ashamed that Pinky has denied her own racial identity, makes her pray for forgiveness. Pinky is haunted, however, by thoughts of her fiancé, Thomas Adams, a white Boston doctor to whom she wants to return. When Pinky learns that neighbor Jake Waters has kept money that the illiterate Dicey gave him to mail to her, she confronts Jake at his shack. Jake, a conniving lay-about, gives her fifteen dollars belonging to his wife Rozelia and promises to return the rest soon, but Rozelia sees Pinky leave with the money and threatens her. Two police officers see the confrontation and, believing Pinky to be white, begin to slap Rozelia. When Rozelia reveals that Pinky also is black, the police arrest them and shove them all into their car. At the courthouse, Judge Walker, who is fond of Dicey, releases Pinky with a warning to keep out of trouble. Later, after the distressed Pinky goes out walking, Jake visits Dicey and finds a letter addressed to Pinky that Dicey had been keeping from her. Dicey snatches it back and burns it, but Jake warns that the white doctor whose return address is on the envelope will surely come looking for Pinky and offers to send a telegram to stop him. While walking alone, Pinky is accosted by two intoxicated white men, and after she escapes their lecherous grasp, she returns home and begins to pack. Dicey stops her, however, and tells her that she has volunteered her as a nurse for Miss Em, a sickly white woman living in a nearby, decaying mansion. When Pinky refuses, saying that Miss Em treated her as an inferior in the past, Dicey berates Pinky for her hardened heart and relates that when she had pneumonia, Miss Em slept in her shack, fed and washed her, and even emptied her "slops" until Dicey recovered. Pinky then agrees to nurse Miss Em for Dicey's sake. Although she is humiliated by the domineering old woman, Pinky realizes that Miss Em will die soon, after which she will be able to leave. When Miss Em castigates Pinky for pretending to be what she is not, Pinky disparages the racial rules set by white society. One day, Pinky is met by Tom, who has located her after receiving the telegram sent by Jake. Pinky reveals that she is black, and Tom tenders his belief that no race is superior to another and his hope that he has no hidden racist feelings. He asks her to return North with him and live as a white, but she insists she must continue with her case and not join him after she is finished. When Melba Wooley, the wife of Miss Em's cousin, visits Miss Em, not wanting a long visit from the busybody, has Pinky remain in the room. Mrs. Wooley, obvlivious to Miss Em's sarcastic attempts to get rid of her, reveals that her maid, Rozelia, has been spreading gossip that Pinky is a thief. Although Mrs. Wooley does not want Miss Em to make a will, after she leaves, Miss Em sends Pinky away and writes one. She collapses as Pinky is returning, and

when Miss Em revives, she has Doc Joe, her physician, witness the will without Pinky's knowledge. Pinky has grown fond of the old woman, who has never been afraid to speak her mind, and is saddened when Miss Em dies. When Mrs. Wooley sees Pinky at the dry goods store soon after, she castigates the owner for allowing his saleslady, who is unaware that Pinky is black, to sell to "nigras" before whites. She then implies that Pinky, who is there to purchase a mourning veil, is using money stolen from Miss Em. After the funeral, Pinky and Dicey learn from Doc Joe that Miss Em left Pinky her home and land as an expression of regard and confidence that she would put the property to good use. Outraged, Mrs. Wooley decides to contest the will, and rumors spread among the whites in town that Pinky drugged Miss Em and forced her to make the will. Jake warns Pinky that she and the other blacks in town will face severe repercussions if she accepts the bequest, but Pinky, touched by Miss Em's faith in her, decides not to return North until the matter is settled. Although Judge Walker believes that Miss Em acted unadvisedly, Pinky prevails upon his lifelong friendship with Miss Em and he agrees to represent her. Unable to obtain nursing work and needing money for the court expenses, Pinky does washing for Dicey, who is ill now herself. When Tom visits, he tries to convince Pinky to drop the case, but she is adamant that she does not want to let down Miss Em, herself or her people. She states that if the whites are going to get the house and land by cheating, she wants it out in the open for all to see, and Tom pledges his support. During the trial, Mrs. Wooley's lawyer tries to prove that Pinky exerted undue influence over Miss Em, but the presiding judge rules that the will is a binding legal document. Afterwards, Judge Walker expressed to Pinky his doubts that winning the case has served any interests of the community other than justice. When Tom tells Pinky that he plans to join a clinic in Denver because too many people in Boston have read about the trial, Pinky realizes that Miss Em gave her the house so that she would stay in the South and be herself. She tells Tom that she cannot deny she is a Negro and that she does not want to be anything else, then asks him to go. Using the house and land, Pinky establishes "Miss Em's Clinic and Nursery School" for the black community and operates it with Dr. Canady, a black physician, Doc Joe and Dicey. *African Americans. Grandmothers. Miscegenation. Nurses. Racism. Transformation. United States–South.* Attempted rape. Cousins. Friendship. Gossip. Judges. Laundresses. Literacy. Ne'er-do-wells. Physicians. Police brutality. Racial impersonation. Storekeepers. Trials. Wills.

Note: The working titles of this film were *Quality* and *Crossover*. The novel was originally published in an abridged form in the Dec 1945 issue of *Ladies' Home Journal*. At the time of the *Ladies' Home Journal* publication, the NAACP, in an internal memo dated 27 Dec 1945, written by Annette Peyser, included in the NAACP Papers at the Library of Congress, noted that the publication marked "the first time in any popular national magazine a short novel in which the protagonist was a Negro... dealt with apparent sympathy and realism with Negro problems in white society." The NAACP, criticized the story, however, stating that it was "propaganda of the most insidious sort" because "each social or political problem presented is resolved most frequently through an advocacy of the status quo" rather than through "positive legal or social action." According to information in the Twentieth Century-Fox Records of the Legal Department at the UCLA Arts—Special Collections Library, author Cid Ricketts Sumner also wrote a play based on the book.

Motion picture rights to the novel were originally optioned in Feb 1948 by Nathan Dyches, a Twentieth Century-Fox publicist, according to news items and information in the legal records. Dyches acquired the rights to the story in Apr 1948 and formed Pomeroy Enterprises, Inc., with Harry Brand (the head of Fox publicity) and Nicholas Nayfuck to make the film, then hired Richard Hubler to write a screenplay. Fox production chief Darryl F. Zanuck became interested in producing the film, and Jason Joy, Fox's liaison with the PCA, sent the office a synopsis for their approval. According to information in the MPAA/PCA Collection at the AMPAS Library, the PCA was concerned that a film based on the story might lead to distribution and exhibition problems in the South. A PCA official worried that should the film be made the industry might be accused of siding with President Truman's civil rights program; that new local or state censor boards might be established, which could cause difficulties for the industry; and that its release might lead to a rise in Ku Klux Klan activity. The PCA chose not to issue a policy decision regarding the proposed film, however, or films dealing with similar subject matter, though they did point out their concerns to studio officials.

A year later, in Feb 1949, as Fox was about to put the film into production, PCA Director Joseph I. Breen urged the studio to "avoid physical contact between Negroes and whites, throughout this picture" in order to avoid offending audiences "in a number of sections of this country." In his response to Breen, Joy pointed out that the role of "Pinky" would be played by a white actress, and stated, "It is our intention... to have many instances of physical contact between Dr. Chester [who became Dr. Thomas Adams in the final film] and Pinky. We believe these contacts to be absolutely necessary to the power

of the story as it relates to these two unhappy people." PCA official Francis Harmon, a white Southerner, suggested to the studio "that Pinky should be shown to be the daughter of one of 'Miss Em's' male relatives. I know case after case where just such situations arose. There is a constant conflict in Southern life and thought around this point: that Southern white people condone or tolerate 'social equality' on the level of vice while shouting to high heaven their opposition to 'social equality' on the level of virtue. Those responsible for producing and directing this picture will miss a great opportunity if the picture fails to drive home the point that the very people who attack social equality on the level of virtue continue to accept illicit sex relations, of which Pinky and her kind are innocent and tragic victims." Zanuck, in replying to Harmon, noted, "we have consulted the Negro representatives of many different Negro point of views, and without exception they have objected to the suggestion of miscegenation."

Fox purchased the rights from Dyches after he and Brand realized that they could not produce the film independently. A letter dated 3 May 1948 in the Fox legal records notes that "because of the peculiar nature of the story [Zanuck] does not want any publicity given to it at this time as he would like to be the first in the field with this type of story." In Aug 1948, *Var* reported, "Highly publicized production of 'message' pictures has been virtually abandoned by studios, with no attendant fanfare. Twentieth-Fox's *Quality* planned as a followup to *Gentleman's Agreement* (see above) has been placed on the shelf." A 30 Jan 1949 *NYT* news item stated that Zanuck's personal project for 1949 was to be *Pinky*, based on a "free adaptation" of *Quality* by Dudley Nichols. They stated that the studio "is officially describing it as an original story by Nichols" and was not admitting its connection with *Quality*. At that time, John Ford was scheduled to direct the picture.

Zanuck sent a copy of the 7 Jul 1948 script by Dudley Nichols to the NAACP for their comments, and NAACP Executive Secretary Walter White gave copies to Arthur B. Spingarn, president of the NAACP; Poppy Cannon, a writer with whom White had collaborated; Roy Wilkins, editor of *The Crisis*, a journal published by the NAACP; and his daughter, Jane White, for their reactions. White and his associates reacted negatively to the script, which Cannon called "a bid for complete submission on the part of colored people." Cannon further stated, "Pinky, the heroine, is a silly sentimental little fool....[Granny] is a female Uncle Tom but she hasn't half the brains or courage of the original Uncle Tom. Among the other Negro characters there is not one decent or believable person." Jane White noted, "The point of view which this script holds is that any kind of action taken by Negroes to secure their rights is rebellion and inspired by 'Northern agitators.'" (The original novel and early scripts included the character of "Arch Naughton," a black newspaperman from New York and an activist, who tries to get Pinky to join him and give up being a nurse; in subsequent versions of the screenplay, that character was dropped, and some of his ideas were incorporated into Pinky's dialogue.) Walter White stated, "Had the story been written around the turn of the century, it would have been novel and even revolutionary. Today it is dated, inaccurate both as to the thinking of Negroes and intelligent Southern whites, and even dangerous in its advocacy of acceptance of the status quo." White suggested that Zanuck scrap the story and get another source for a new film dealing with African Americans.

In Zanuck's response to White, he expressed his "utter disagreement with the judgments rendered in your letter and those of your associates." He warned that in the current social and political climate, "A motion picture which deals with the Negro minority in the United States must be above all things non-propagandist. All it can hope to do, at its boldest, is to make the white majority experience emotionally the injustice and daily hurts suffered by colored people." Zanuck noted that the picture would have to be less confrontational so that it would appeal to and affect people with prejudices, and that "if the picture is not shown and seen in those regions where injustice and racial prejudice are strongest, no good can be accomplished."

Although Zanuck criticized the comments of White and the others, he praised Jane White for her "constructive criticism" (although he disagreed with many of her points) and suggested that she help in revising the script. She subsequently was hired by the studio and suggested changes and additions to the 12 Jan 1949 script by Philip Dunne. (Dunne was hired to replace Nichols in Nov 1948. In a May 1949 *NYT* article, Dunne stated that Nichols "had to drop the job half finished because of a prior commitment elsewhere.") According to an *Ebony* article of Sep 1949, Jane White recommended "drastic changes" but they were not made. Her suggestions, according to a list in the Produced Scripts Collection, included adding a "dark-skinned Southern Negro character to manifest the forthright militance that Arch [who had been eliminated from the 12 Jan 1949 script] possessed." She wrote, "I would like to be made aware that here is a man who has lived all his life in the South, under its proscription, who has not been defeated or blunted, or made to shrink from his responsibilities as a Negro and a citizen." The character was not added, although a number of her other suggestions were accepted.

John Ford began directing *Pinky* in Mar 1949, but worked on it only about a week before he left because of illness, according to news items. In a *DN* article before he was replaced, Ford stated, "We are not attacking any section of the country or any group of people... but we are attacking a bigotry that should have been uprooted from the American scene a long time ago." Elia Kazan replaced Ford, and according to a 29 May 1949 *NYT* article, "Kazan said that, despite his admiration for Ford, he had redone the material shot by his colleague because he could not attempt to match the Ford style." The *NYT* article stated that "scouting rumors to the contrary, Kazan confirmed the official studio explanation that the substitution was made because Ford was seriously ill." In his autobiography, Kazan states that Ford had a case of shingles, but also relates that Ford left the picture because of conflicts with actress Ethel Waters.

The finished film was accepted for showing in Atlanta, where it made its

Southern debut. The Atlanta censor stated, "I know this picture is going to be painful to a great many Southerners. It will make them squirm, but at the same time it will make them realize how unlovely their attitudes are." The Roxy Theatre, where the Atlanta debut took place, opened its entire balcony to African Americans. (Previous policy was to limit blacks to just a few gallery seats.) After the first-day showing broke a box-office record, the film was booked for additional southern showings. In the East Texas town of Marshall, prior to a scheduled showing in Feb 1950, a censorship board was formed when theater owner W. L. Gelling refused to cancel the booking even though individuals and the Kiwanis Club complained. The board rejected the film for exhibition in the town, but Gelling presented it anyway, and he was arrested and fined. He appealed, backed by the PCA, who wanted to make the incident a test case of censorship, hoping that the Supreme Court would revoke their 1915 decision that motion pictures could not claim the same rights as the press. After the Texas Court of Criminal Appeals upheld the lower court ruling, the Supreme Court, in Jun 1952, struck down the censor's decision, citing their decision from the previous week regarding the Italian film *The Miracle*. The issue of applying freedom of the press rights to motion pictures, however, was not decided at that time.

The film received three Academy Award nominations: Jeanne Crain for Best Actress and both Ethel Barrymore and Ethel Waters for Best Supporting Actress. It was highly praised by reviewers. *HR* called the film a "brilliantly compelling presentation" and stated, "Its power is drawn from purely creative forces rather than the realism of documentation or the crutch of psychiatric exploration. *Pinky* is the kind of story the screen does best, a pictorial novel with a factual basis and with which there is that all-important element of self-identification. Neither white man nor Negro can appraise *Pinky* without thinking earnestly: 'What would I do under the same circumstances?' " *NYT*, while appreciating that the film did not "skirt around the edges, intellectual or geographical, of racial discrimination," criticized it for coming "perilously close to denying the very equality it seems to espouse by accepting paternalism as the easiest and the happiest way out." On 18 Sep 1950, the *Lux Radio Theatre* presented a radio broadcast of Pinky starring Jeanne Crain, William Lundigan and Ethel Barrymore.

Box 8 Oct 1949. *Dallas Morning News* 3 Nov 1950, p. 1, 8. *DN* 23 Mar 1949. *DV* 2 May 1949. *DV* 30 Sep 1949, p. 3. *DV* 17 Nov 1949. *DV* 21 Nov 1949. *DV* 2 Dec 1949. *DV* 31 Jan 1952. *DV* 11 Mar 1952. *Ebony* Sep 1949, p. 2725. *FD* 30 Sep 1949, p. 3. *Har* 1 Oct 1949, p. 159. *HCN* 12 Dec 1949. *HR* 19 Jan 1949. *HR* 11 Mar 1949, p. 11. *HR* 30 Sep 1949, p. 3. *HR* 17 Nov 1949. *HR* 18 Nov 1949. *HR* 14 Mar 1952. *LAEx* 22 Oct 1949. *LAT* 22 Oct 1949. *LAT* 3 Jun 1952. *MPD* 30 Sep 1949. *MPH* 2 Feb 1952. *MPH* 22 Mar 1952. *MPH* 7 Jun 1952. *MPHPD* 1 Oct 1949, p. 33. *NYT* 23 May 1948. *NYT* 30 Jan 1949. *NYT* 6 Mar 1949. *NYT* 1 May 1949. *NYT* 29 May 1949. *NYT* 30 Sep 1949, p. 28. *NYT* 9 Oct 1949. *NYT* 29 Oct 1949. *NYT* 6 Nov 1949. *NYT* 12 Feb 1950. *NYT* 31 Jan 1952. *Time and Tide* 3 Dec 1949. *Var* 18 Aug 1948. *Var* 5 Oct 1949, p. 8. *Var* 16 Apr 1952. *Var* 4 Jun 1952.

PINTO RUSTLERS (Latino)

Reliable Pictures Corp. *Dist* Reliable Pictures Corp. 14 May **1936**; Prod: began late Mar 1936. Sd; b&w. 56 or 60 min. PCA cert no. 2277.

Prod Bernard B. Ray. *Assoc prod* Harry S. Webb. *Dir* Henri Samuels. *Asst dir* R. G. Springsteen. *Orig story and cont* Robert Tansey. *Photog* William Hyer. *Ed* Fred Bain. *Sd* Johnnie Eilers. *Prod mgr* Ira S. Webb.

Cast: TOM TYLER (*Tom Dawson*), George Walsh (*Nick Furnicky*), Al St. John (*Mack*), Catherine Cotter (*Ann Walton*), Earl Dwire (*Bud Walton*), William Gould (*Inspector*), George Chesebro (*Spade*), Roger Williams (*Lugo*), Bud Osborne (*Buck*), Murdock McQuarrie (*Dad Walton*), Charles Whittaker (*Sheriff*), [Sherry Tansey (*Outlaw*)].

Western. [*Print viewed*]. A gang of thieves called the "Pinto Rustlers," led by Mexican bandit Nick Furnicky, have been raiding Evans Valley. When "Pop" Evans is killed during a raid, his son, Tom Dawson, becomes a deputy to avenge his father's murder. By printing a "Wanted" poster bearing a picture of himself, Tom convinces Furnicky he is an outlaw and is recruited in the gang. With rustler Bud Walton's help, the gang raids the Walton ranch and takes Bud's brother, Dad Walton, hostage, hoping to crack his safe. Tom then gets hired by Ann Walton as a ranch hand. At Furnicky's orders, Tom meets safecracker Lugo, but Tom ties him up and has his partner Mack pose as Lugo. Tom then warns the Waltons with an anonymous note that the rustlers are planning a raid at sunrise. At dawn, Tom and Mack crack the safe and hide the money, then are chased off the ranch by the Waltons. Still hoping to locate Dad Walton, they return to the gang with the excuse that they were caught before cracking the safe. When Tom reports for work later, Ann dismisses him for being absent during the raid. Meanwhile, Lugo, who has escaped, catches up with the gang and reveals Tom and Mack's duplicity. Furnicky then ties them up, but, to their surprise, Lugo releases them before leaving with Furnicky and his men to crack the safe. Tom then intimidates a young gang member into confessing it was Furnicky who murdered Pop. At the Waltons', Lugo holds up Furnicky and is wounded. Lugo is really the sheriff's deputy Ed, who has been impersonating Lugo, whom the sheriff arrested after his escape. Tom and Mack, with the help of the

sheriff and the Waltons, fight the gang from outside the house. When all of Furnicky's men, including Bud, have been shot, Furnicky offers Ed to the sheriff in exchange for Tom. When Tom enters, he tells Furnicky he knows Furnicky killed his father, then beats him up and has him arrested. Tom then turns in his badge, and he and Ann ride off together. *Deputies. Impersonation and imposture. Murder. Revenge. Rustlers. Brothers. Duplicity. False accusations. Gunfights. Horses. Hostages. Mexicans. Safecrackers. Sheriffs.*

Note: It is unclear from the viewed print what happens to "Dad Walton" after he is kidnapped, but presumably, he is rescued. *Var* incorrectly calls George Chesebro's character "Spud." Modern sources add Charles King, Milburn Morante, Bob Burns, Wally West and Dick Cramer to the cast.

HR 20 Mar 1936, p. 6. *HR* 30 Mar 1936, p. 7. *Var* 27 Jan 1937, p. 24.

THE PIONEERS (Native Americans)

Monogram Pictures Corp.; An Edward Finney Production. *Dist* Monogram Pictures Corp. 10 May **1941**; Prod: began early Apr 1941 [©Monogram Pictures Corp.; 10 May 1941; LP10468]. Sd; b&w. 6 reels, 5,346 ft. 61 min.

Dir Al Herman. *Asst dir* Al Alt. *Scr* Charles Anderson. *Dir of photog* Marcel A. LePicard. *Tech dir* E. R. Hickson. *Film ed* Fred Bain. *Mus score and dir* Frank Sanucci. *Sd* Glen Glenn. *Prod aide* Samuel R. Wallis.

Song(s): "Rollin' Along" and "Song of the Trail," music and lyrics by Betty Laidlaw and Robert Lively; "Wild Galoot from Tuzigoot," music and lyrics by Jack Smith; "Smokey Joe," music and lyrics by Johnny Lange and Lew Porter; "Hi Yo, Hi Yi, Ki Yo," music and lyrics by Red Foley and Lee Penny.

Source: Inspired by the novel *The Pioneers; Or the Sources of the Susquehanna* by James Fenimore Cooper (Philadelphia, 1823).

Cast: TEX RITTER (*Tex* [*Ritter*]), with His Horse "WHITE FLASH", Arkansas "Slim" Andrews (*Slim*), Red Foley and His Saddle Pals, Star of NBC's Station WLS *National Barn Dance* (Chicago) (*Red Foley*), Doye O'Dell, Star of NBC's Station WTIC (Hartford, Conn.) (*Doye O'Dell*), Wanda McKay (*Suzanna* [*Ames*]), Del Lawrence (*Ames*), George Chesebro (*Wilson*), Karl Hackett ([*J. W.*] *Carson*), Lynton Brent (*Jingo*), Gene Alsace (*Sheriff*), Chief Many Treaties (*Warcloud*), Chief Soldani (*Lonedeer*), [Post Park (*Benton*)], [Chick Hannan (*Pete*)], [Jack C. Smith (*Judge Potts*)].

Western, with songs. [*Print viewed*]. Wagon train guide Tex Ritter and his men save a wagon train from an Indian attack, much to the dismay of land office owner J. W. Carson. Along with his henchmen, Wilson and Jingo, Carson orchestrated the attack so that he could get the settlers' intended land, a rich parcel in Beaver Creek. Settler Ames, unaware of Carson's treachery, introduces him to his daughter Suzanna, whom Carson plans on courting. That night, while Carson and Tex vie for Suzanna's attention at a celebration, Jingo searches Ames's trunk for the maps to the settlers' land. Ames discovers Jingo and is killed during the ensuing struggle. Tex happens along just before Ames's body is found and is blamed for the murder. Tex is arrested, while Carson and his housekeeper promise to care for Suzanna until the wagon train leader, Red Foley, sends for her. Carson plots with Wilson and Jingo to stop the wagon train, and Tex enlists his friend Slim's aid in escaping from the "necktie party" to which he has been invited. Tex reaches the wagon train as Foley is trying to convince Chief Warcloud to let them pass. Tex and Warcloud are old friends, and Tex promises to respect the Indians' land if they allow the settlers to pass through. The wagon train moves on, and Tex, Slim and one of their pals scout ahead for a camp for the night. Meanwhile, Wilson tries to convine Warcloud to attack the settlers, but he refuses to break his promise of safe passage to Tex. Carson then orders Wilson to have their men attack the settlers, and frame the Indians by leaving their weapons at the massacre site. The attack begins and everyone is killed except Foley, who crawls to safety after being wounded. Hearing that the Indians are on the warpath, the sheriff and his posse arrest a surprised Warcloud, who maintains that his people are innocent. Tex arrives on the scene and points out to the sheriff the distinctive hoofprints signifying that the attackers' horses had shoes, thereby clearing the Indians of guilt as their horses are never shod. When Jingo, who is with the posse, makes a hasty exit after Foley is found, Tex realizes that Jingo, Wilson and Carson must be behind the murderous affair. Jingo races to Carson's cabin, where he confronts Carson and demands to be paid his share of their stolen money. Suzanna overhears Jingo mention the murder of her father and the other settlers, and sees Carson kill Jingo. Tex and the posse arrive as

Wilson and Carson attempt to flee, and the two killers are captured. Suzanna tells the sheriff what she has heard, and all ends well as she joins Tex, who is leading a new wagon train to Beaver Creek. *Duplicity. Frame-ups. Indians of North America. Scouts (Frontier). Wagon trains. Evidence. Housekeepers. Land rights. Maps. Murder. Rescues. Sheriffs.*

Note: James Fenimore Cooper's novel was also published as the first of five novels in his 1853 compilation known as *The Leatherstocking Tales.* The film's onscreen credits note that the picture was "inspired by" Cooper's novel of the same name and *The Leatherstocking Tales.* According to a 4 May 1939 *LAEx* news item, Monogram first considered Jack Randall for the leading role. Modern sources include Art Dillard, Sherry Tansey and Tex Palmer in the cast and note that portions of the "Indian attack" footage were taken from the 1933 Mascot serial *Fighting with Kit Carson.*

Box 10 May 1941. *DV* 29 Apr 1941. *FD* 24 Jun 1941, p. 7. *HR* 6 Feb 1941, p. 2. *HR* 28 Mar 1941, p. 13. *HR* 29 Apr 1941, p. 3. *LAEx* 4 May 1939. *MPH* 3 May 1941. *Var* 25 Jun 1941, p. 20.

PIRATES OF MONTEREY (Latino)

Universal-International Pictures Co., Inc. *Dist* Universal Pictures Co., Inc. Dec **1947**; New York Opening: 16 Dec 1947; *Prod:* late Apr—mid-Jun 1946. Sd (Western Electric Recording); col (Technicolor). 75 or 77-78 min. PCA cert no. 11877.

Exec prod Joe Gershenson. *Prod* Paul Malvern. *Dir* Alfred Werker. *Asst dir* William Holland. *Scr* Sam Hellman and Margaret Buell Wilder. *Orig story* Edward T. Lowe and Bradford Ropes. *Dir of photog* Hal Mohr, W. Howard Greene and Harry Hallenberger. *Technicolor color dir* Natalie Kalmus. *Assoc* William Fritzsche. *Art dir* Jack Otterson and Richard H. Riedel. *Film ed* Russell Schoengarth. *Set dec* Russell A. Gausman and Leigh Smith. *Cost for Maria Montez* Travis Banton. *Gown supv* Vera West. *Mus* Milton Rosen. *Dir of sd* Bernard B. Brown. *[Sd] tech* Charles Carroll. *Dir of makeup* Jack P. Pierce. *Hair stylist* Carmen Dirigo.

Cast: MARIA MONTEZ [(*Marguerita Novarro*)], ROD CAMERON [(*Phillip Kent*)], Mikhail Rasumny [(*Pio*)], Philip Reed [(*Lt. Carlos Ortega*)], Gilbert Roland [(*Major De Roja*)], Gale Sondergaard [(*Señorita de Sola*)], Tamara Shayne [(*Filomena*)], Robert Warwick [(*Governor de Sola*)], Michael Raffetto [(*Sergeant Gomora*)], Neyle Morrow [(*Manuel De Roja*)], Victor Varconi [(*Captain Cordova*)], Charles Wagenheim [(*Juan*)], [George J. Lewis, George Magrill (*Pirates*)], [Joe Bernard (*Doctor*)], [George Navarro (*Lieutenant*)], [Victor Romito, Don Driggers (*Thugs*)], [Lucio Villegas (*Padre*)], [Chris-Pin Martin (*Caretta man*)], [Julia Andre (*Young woman*)], [Lilo Yarson, Fred Cordova (*Sentries*)], [Dick Dickinson (*Jailor*)].

Historical, Adventure, Romance. [*Print viewed*]. In 1840, American soldier of fortune Phillip Kent is hired by the Mexican government to take a shipment of rifles from Mexico City to California. Upon the caravan's arrival on the outskirts of Los Angeles, Phillip and Pio, his Mexican associate, rescue aristocrat Marguerita Novarro and Filomena, her maid, from a runaway carriage. Later that night, Phillip orders the caravan to leave immediately for the north after their camp is infiltrated by two Spanish royalists. He is unaware, however, that Marguerita and Filomena have stowed away among their cargo, having missed the northbound stagecoach to Santa Barbara. The caravan arrives in Santa Barbara with its extra cargo during the Fiesta of the Harvest, but rather than accepting payment for safely transporting the wealthy Marguerita, Phillip merely asks for the honor of the first dance with her during the festival. The two quickly fall in love, but when Phillip goes to call upon Marguerita the next morning, he discovers that she has already left town. The caravan then resumes its trek northward, but is ambushed along the way by Spanish royalists. They escape the trap, however, and arrive safely at the Mexican army post in Monterey, where Phillip is delighted to be reunited with his best friend, Lt. Carlos Ortega. Later, Phillip's delight turns to shock, as he learns that Carlos is engaged to Marguerita. In order to protect his friend, Phillip pretends not to know Marguerita, and she agrees to go along with his ruse. That night, Carlos is attacked and wounded by royalists attempting to steal the new rifles. Manuel De Roja, one of the royalists, is captured by Phillip, who then turns the prisoner over to Major De Roja, the post's commandant. Unknown to Phillip and the others, however, is the fact that De Roja is Manuel's brother and a royalist. De Roja later arranges for his brother to be killed while trying to escape in order to protect his true allegiance. With the injured Carlos confined to bed, Phillip is asked to act as Marguerita's escort at numerous engagement parties. Marguerita soon confesses her love to Phillip, so he attempts to leave Monterey, only to be followed by Marguerita. She convinces him to return to Monterey and tell Carlos all, but the two are instead captured and taken to De Roja's royalist hideout. There, De Roja tells Phillip that he plans to take over the army post with the help of royalists pirates, led by Captain Cordova. Pio, having discovered his friend missing, returns to the army post and uncovers the royalist plot by torturing De Roja's associate, Sergeant Gomora. Meanwhile, a jealous Carlos goes in search of Phillip and Marguerita, and he too is captured by the royalists. Phillip and Carlos escape, however, and Phillip kills De Roja in a sword fight. At the same time, the pirates, without the element of surprise, are routed by the Mexican soldiers as they attempt to land at the beach front. Phillip and Marguerita are later married, with Carlos' full blessings. *Americans in foreign countries. California–History–To 1846. Friendship. Mexicans. Romantic rivalry. Soldiers of fortune. Brothers. Dancing. Engagements. Escapes. Festivals. Fires. Gunrunners. Gunshot wounds. Mexico. Army. Murder. Officers (Military). Parties. Pirates. Riding. Spaniards. Stowaways. Sword fights. Torture. Traitors. Traps.*

Note: The film begins with the following written foreword: "Throughout history men have struggled for possession of new instruments of destruction, for they have often meant the difference between extinction and survival...So it was in the early part of the last century, when the young republic of Mexico fought valiantly against ravaging hordes of royalists pirates to safeguard her richest jewel—California." Although the opening credits indicate that Universal Pictures Co., Inc. copyrighted the film in 1946, the film is not included in the *Catalog of Copyright Entries.*

Box 22 Nov 1947. *FD* 13 Nov 1947, p. 6. *HR* 26 Apr 1946, p. 19. *HR* 12 Nov 1947, p. 3. *IFJ* 25 May 1946, p. 41. *MPHPD* 3 Aug 1946, p. 3127. *MPHPD* 22 Nov 1947. *NYT* 17 Dec 1947, p. 41. *Var* 12 Nov 1947, p. 8.

LA PISTE DES GÉANTS see LA GRAN JORNADA

THE PLAINSMAN (Native Americans, Cheyenne, Dakota)

Paramount Pictures, Inc.; A Cecil B. DeMille Production. *Dist* Paramount Pictures, Inc. 1 Jan **1937**; *Prod:* began mid-Jul 1936 [©Paramount Pictures, Inc.; 1 Jan 1937; LP6847]. Sd (Western Electric Mirrophonic Recording); b&w. 12 reels, 10,154 ft. 112-113 or 115 min. Passed by the National Board of Review. PCA cert no. 2597.

Pres ADOLPH ZUKOR. *Prod* Cecil B. DeMille. [*Exec prod* William LeBaron.] *Dir* Cecil B. DeMille. [*Assoc dir* Arthur Rosson]. [*Asst dir* Richard Harlan]. *Scr* Waldemar Young, Harold Lamb and Lynn Riggs. *Material comp* Jeanie MacPherson. *Dial supv* Edwin Maxwell. [*Contr to scr const* Grover Jones]. *Photog* Victor Milner and [George Robinson]. *Spec photog eff* Farciot Edouart, Dewey Wrigley and [Gordon Jennings]. *Art dir* Hans Dreier and Roland Anderson. *Ed* Anne Bauchens. *Int dec* A. E. Freudeman. *Cost des* VISART, Dwight Franklin and Joe DeYong. *Mus dir* Boris Morros. *Orig mus by* George Antheil. *Sd rec* Harry Lindgren and Louis Mesenkop. [*Stunt doubles* John Eckert, Lloyd Sanders, Al Burk, Slim Hightower and Jimmy Phillips].

Source: Based on stories by Courtney Ryley Cooper and the novel *Wild Bill Hickok, the Prince of the Pistoleers* by Frank J. Wilstach (Garden City, NY, 1934).

Cast: GARY COOPER (*Wild Bill Hickok*), JEAN ARTHUR (*Calamity Jane*), James Ellison (*Buffalo Bill Cody*), Charles Bickford (*John Lattimer*), Helen Burgess (*Louisa Cody*), Porter Hall (*Jack McCall*), Paul Harvey (*Yellow Hand*), Victor Varconi (*Painted Horse*), John Miljan (*General George A. Custer*), Frank McGlynn, Sr. (*Abraham Lincoln*), Granville Bates (*Van Ellyn*), Frank Albertson (*A young trooper*), Purnell Pratt (*Captain Wood*), Fred Kohler (*Jake, a teamster*), Pat Moriarty (*Sergeant McGinnis*), Charles Judels (*Tony, the barber*), Harry Woods (*Quartermaster sergeant*), Anthony Quinn (*A Cheyenne indian*), Francis McDonald (*A river gambler*), George Ernest (*A boy*), George MacQuarrie (*General Merritt*), George Hayes (*Breezy*), [Fuzzy Knight (*Dave*)], [Irene Bennett, Louise Stuart, Gail Sheridan (*Girls*)], [George Sparks (*Boy*)], [Curtis Nero (*Roustabout*)], [Billy McClain (*Old servant*)], [Arthur Singley (*First man*)], [Bud Flanagan (*Second man*)], [Ralph Malone (*Third man*)], [E. W. Borman (*Bartender*)], [Walter McGrail (*First gambler*)], [Wilbur Mack (*Second gambler*)], [Max Davidson (*Third gambler/Banker*)], [Buck Connors (*Old timer*)], [Oscar Rudolph (*Younger man*)], [Philo McCullough (*Stagecoach guard*)], [Jack Clifford (*Orderly*)], [Frank Layton (*Adjutant*)], [Noble Johnson (*First Indian with painted horse*)], [Sonny Chorre (*Second Indian*)], [Richard Robles (*Third Indian*)], [Greg Whitespear (*Fourth Indian*)], [Chief Thundercloud (*Fifth Indian*)], [Clay Deroy (*Sixth Indian*)], [Wesley Giraud (*Young bugler*)], [Chuck Hamilton, Hank Bell, Lane Chandler, Myron Geiger, Bob Burns, Duke Lee, Jack

Walters, Frank Watson, Kenneth Gibson, Ben F. Hendricks, James Baker, Kenny Cooper, Cecil Kellogg, Whitey Severn, Ervey Collins, Frank Cordell, John Eckert, Lloyd Saunders, Al Burk, Slim Hightower, Jimmy Phillips (*Troopers*)], [Captain William H. Royal (*Corporal Brannigan*)], [Ted Oliver (*First teamster*)], [James Mason (*Second teamster*)], [Richard Alexander (*Third teamster*)], [David Clyde (*Second miner*)], [Hooper Atchley (*Captain*)], [Robert Wilber (*First cavalry private*)], [Bud Osborne (*Second cavalry private*)], [Francis Sayles, Franklyn Farnum, Don Rowan (*Men on Deadwood Street*)], [Earl Askam (*Tim*)], [Stanley Andrews], [Sherwood Bailey], [Edgar Deering], [Edwin Maxwell], [Bruce Warren], [Mark Strong], [P. E. "Tiny" Newland], [Sidney D'Albrook], [Ed Schaefer], [Bob Ellsworth], [Nelson McDowell], [Marty Joyce], [Blackjack Ward], [Jess Caven], [Jane Keckley], [Cora Shumway], [Everett Brown], [Louis Natheaux], [Colin Chase], [Jack Fife], [Bud Fine], [Blue Washington].

Biography, Historical, Western. [*Viewed print incomplete*]. At the close of the Civil War, President Abraham Lincoln is assassinated in the East while General George Custer fights the Indians in the West. As John Lattimer arrives in Leavenworth, Missouri, to sell seven-shot rifles to the Indians, Buffalo Bill Cody and his new wife Louisa are reunited with Wild Bill Hickok and Calamity Jane. Following the massacre of half the garrison at Fort Piney by thousands of Sioux Indians, General Custer orders Cody to take ammunition to the fort, while Hickok goes after their chief, Yellow Hand. As Louisa confesses her pregnancy to Jane, Cheyenne Indians attack the Cody home and Jane is taken to the Cheyenne camp, where the Indians threaten to kill Hickok unless she tells them Cody's whereabouts. Jane, in love with Hickok, saves his life, but sacrifices Cody's men, who are ambushed by Cheyenne using Lattimer's rifles. As Hickok makes his way to the front, he sends Jane to alert Custer. Cody and Hickok, along with what is left of the men at Fort Piney, defend themselves against the Indians. As the fort's bugler dies, Custer's bugle is heard in the distance and the Indians retreat. Back in town, Hickok challenges John Lattimer to a draw, but is forced to kill three of Lattimer's men, former soldiers, instead. After Hickok follows Lattimer into the Black Hills, Custer orders Cody to bring him Hickok dead or alive for murdering soldiers. Weeks later, as Cody tracks Hickok, a lone Cheyenne Indian, carrying the U.S. 7th Cavalry's flag, tells of Custer's defeat. Meanwhile, Yellow Hand and Sitting Bull plot to extinguish the white man using Lattimer's rifles as Hickok and Cody meet in Deadwood to the stop Lattimer's shipment. There Hickok shoots Lattimer dead in self-defense and rounds up his co-conspirators in the Bella Union saloon, where they play poker. As Hickok plays his hand of black aces and eights, Jack McCall, who had earlier warned Lattimer about Hickok, shoots him in the back, killing him. McCall is then arrested by Merritt and Cody's troopers, and Merritt exonerates Cody. Calamity kisses Cody, saying, "That's one kiss you won't wipe off." Hickok and Custer and his troops later ride off to battle. *Calamity Jane. Cheyenne Indians. Buffalo Bill Cody. General George Armstrong Custer. Dakota Indians. Friendship. Wild Bill Hickok. Little Big Horn, Battle of the, 1876. Murder. Scouts (Frontier). Sitting Bull. United States–History–Civil War, 1861-1865. Black Hills (SD and WY). Deadwood (SD). Abraham Lincoln. Newlyweds. Poker (Game). Pregnancy. Rifles. St. Louis (MO). United States. Army. Cavalry. Chief Yellow Hand.*

Note: The ending of the film following the poker game was missing from the viewed print. The conclusion of the plot summary was taken from the release dialogue script found in the Paramount Script Collection at the AMPAS Library. The film's opening narration states, "Among the men who thrust forward America's frontier were Wild Bill Hickok and Buffalo Bill Cody. The story that follows compresses many years, many lives, and widely separated events into one narrative—in an attempt to do justice to the courage of the plainsman of the West." The closing narration states: "It shall be as it was in the past.../Not with dreams,/but with strength and with courage/Shall a nation be molded to last." Wild Bill Hickok's well-deserved reputation as a gunfighter was established in an interview with Colonel George Ward Nichols published in *Harper's New Monthly Magazine* in 1867. Hickok was a good shot and probably killed at least seven men. He was a scout in the Union Army during the Civil War and after the war, he became a marshal in Hays City, KS, and then in Abilene, KS. He appeared in a play with Buffalo Bill Cody in 1873, and in 1876, Hickok was shot in the back by Jack McCall during a poker game in Deadwood, Dakota Territory. For more biographical information about Buffalo Bill Cody, please see then entry above for *Buffalo Bill*, and for additional information on General George Armstrong Custer, please consult the entry below for *They Died With Their Boots On*.

As reported in *DV* and *HR*, shooting on a three-acre set of Deadwood City in 1865 built by Paramount began on 21 Jul 1936. While DeMille directed interiors, he gave instructions to second unit director Arthur Rosson, who was on location, via telephone. DeMille had with him a ten-foot model of Rosson's

location scenes, as well as charts marked with every camera set-up. The cavalry sequences were shot with the Wyoming National Guard at Pole Mountain, Wyoming, twenty-one miles east of Laramie. On 17 Jul 1936, *HR* reported that two guardsmen has been badly hurt the previous day while Rosson was shooting a charge scene. The scene of Custer's massacre was shot on the Cheyenne Indian Reservation at Lame Deer, Montana, where two thousand Indian actors were used as extras. Additional scenes were also shot in Birney, Montana. While location work continued in Montana, one production unit went on location at the Paramount ranch outside Los Angeles on 24 Jul 1936. According to a *HR* news item on 16 Jul 1936, DeMille engaged actor Edwin Maxwell to serve temporarily as dialogue director. According to modern sources, Paramount studio executives wanted "Wild Bill" to survive the card game shoot-out at the end of the film, but DeMille resisted. Modern sources list the following character names: Edgar Dearing (*A courier from Custer*), Edwin Maxwell (*Stanton, Secretary of War*) and Bruce Warren (*Purser of the "Lizzie Gill"*). Modern sources also add the following names to the cast: Francis Ford, Irving Bacon, John Hyams, Charles Stevens, Arthur Aylesworth, Douglas Wood, George Cleveland, Lona Andre, Leila McIntyre, Harry Stubbs, Davison Clark, Charles W. Hertzinger, William Humphries, Sidney Jarvis, Wadsworth Harris, Tex Driscoll, and Stanhope Wheatcroft.

FD 24 Nov 1936, p. 7. *DV* 7 Jul 1936, p. 3. *DV* 22 Jul 1936, p. 2. *DV* 24 Jul 1936, p. 8. *HR* 1 Jul 1936, p. 6. *HR* 16 Jul 1936, p. 2. *HR* 17 Jul 1936, p. 10. *HR* 20 Jul 1936, p. 4. *HR* 22 Jul 1936, p. 4. *HR* 21 Nov 1936, p. 3. *MPD* 23 Nov 1936, p. 6. *MPH* 28 Nov 1936, p. 66. *NYT* 14 Jan 1937, p. 16. *Var* 20 Jan 1937, p. 14.

PLAYBOY OF PARIS (*foreign version*) see **LE PETIT CAFÉ**

PLAYMATES (Latino)

RKO Radio Pictures, Inc. *Dist* RKO Radio Pictures, Inc. 26 Dec 1941; *Prod:* 22 Jul—early Sep 1941 [©RKO Radio Pictures, Inc.; 6 Nov 1941; LP10850]. Sd (RCA Sound System); b&w. 11 reels, 8,642 ft. 96 min. PCA cert no. 7570.

Prod David Butler. *Dir* David Butler. *Asst dir* Fred A. Fleck. [*Dial dir* Herbert Farjeon]. *Scr* James V. Kern. *Story* James V. Kern and M. M. Musselman. *Addl dial* Arthur Phillips. *Dir of photog* Frank Redman. *Spec eff* Vernon L. Walker. *Mont* Douglas Travers. *Art dir* Albert D'Agostino and Carroll Clark. *Ed* Irene Morra. *Set dec* Darrell Silvera. *Gowns* Edward Stevenson. *Mus dir* Roy Webb. *Mus arr* George Duning. *Dances staged by* Jack Crosby. *Rec* Earl A. Wolcott.

Song(s): "Humpty Dumpty Heart," "How Long Did I Dream?" "Thank Your Lucky Stars and Stripes," "Romeo Smith and Juliet Jones" and "Que chica," music by James Van Heusen, lyrics by Johnny Burke.

Cast: Kay Kyser [(*Himself*)], John Barrymore [(*Himself*)], Lupe Velez [(*Carmen del Toro*)], Ginny Simms [(*Ginny*)], May Robson [(*Grandma Kyser*)], Patsy Kelly [(*Lulu Monahan*)], Peter Lind Hayes [(*Peter Lindsey*)], Kay Kyser's Band, featuring Harry Babbitt, Ish Kabibble, Sully Mason, [George Cleveland (*Mr. Pennypacker*)], [Alice Fleming (*Mrs. Penelope Pennypacker*)], [Joe Bernard (*Thomas*)], [Ray Cooke (*Bellhop*)], [Hobart Cavanaugh (*Tremble*)], [Jacques Vanaire (*Alphonse*)], [Sally Cairns (*Manicurist*)], [Fred Trowbridge (*Hotel clerk*)], [Dorothy Babb (*Autograph girl*)], [Leon Belasco (*Prince Maharoobu*)], [Grace Lenard (*Madeline*)], [Sally Payne (*Gloria*)], [Jack Arnold (*Commentator*)], [William Halligan (*Mr. Loomis*)], [Jack Carr (*Pee Wee*)], [Bill Cartledge (*Page boy*)], [George McKay (*Taxi driver*)], [Bill Chaney (*Call boy*)], [Dave Willock (*Tom, cameraman*)], [William Emile (*Fencing instructor*)], [Marshall Ruth, Wally Walker (*Members bull comedy team*)], [Rube Schaffer (*Masseur*)], The Guardsmen.

Comedy, with songs. [*Print viewed*]. Lulu Monahan, press agent to actor John Barrymore, is trying to sell her client's services to Mr. Pennypacker, the sponsor of a local radio show. When Pennypacker rejects Barrymore because he is no longer in the public eye, Lulu devises a stunt to generate publicity for Barrymore. Teaming up with Peter Lindsey, press agent to band leader Kay Kyser, Lulu concocts a publicity stunt in which Barrymore will teach Shakespeare to Kay. Barrymore is reluctant to work with the "Dixieland MacBeth" until the Internal Revenue Service demands payment of his back taxes and Lulu assures him that the alliance will result in a lucrative radio contract with Pennypacker. When Lulu embellishes the stunt by promising a summer festival of Shakespearean plays starring Kay and Barrymore, Pennypacker's social-climbing wife is so impressed by the concept that she offers their Long Island estate for the festival. Barrymore then begins to tutor Kay, who recites Shakespeare with his Carolina twang. Although Barrymore fails to win the admiration of his pupil, he charms Kay's grandmother and Ginny, Kay's lead singer. When female bullfighter and former girl friend Carmen del Toro bursts upon the scene and demands Barrymore's attentions, the thespian devises a scheme to eliminate Kay by incinerating him with

Carmen's fiery charms. Rather than exhausting Kay, however, Carmen's rumbas and congas energize him, thwarting Barrymore's plan. Four days before the performance, Kay is recording his speech when he leaves the room to speak to Grandma. The recorder is still running when Barrymore and Lulu enter the room and Barrymore relates a new scheme to eliminate Kay. When Kay replays the recording, he hears Barrymore's plans and decides to reciprocate. After arranging for Barrymore's guru, Prince Maharoohu, to summon the actor to meet the Grand Lama, Kay masquerades as the Grand Lama and tricks Barrymore into revealing his scheme to spray Kay's throat with an elixir that will render him speechless. When Ginny, who has accompanied Barrymore, insists on seeing the Grand Lama, Kay foretells two futures for her: one with an aging actor, the other with a nice young band leader. On the day of the festival, Kay pours the elixir into Barrymore's champagne glass and refills the atomizer with a harmless liquid. After drinking a toast to success, Barrymore takes command of the stage and is beginning to welcome the audience when he loses his ability to speak and is hooted off the stage. Kay and his band then take his place to present their swing version of Shakespeare, "Romeo Smith and Juliet Jones." Pennypacker is so impressed by the performance that he presents Barrymore with a radio contract, after which Ginny, taking the guru's advice, awards Kay with an embrace. *Actors and actresses. Band leaders. Bands (Music). Publicity stunts. Bullfighters and bullfighting. Contracts. Dancers. Gurus. Press agents. Radio sponsors. Recordings. Romantic rivalry. William Shakespeare. Singers. Social climbers.*

Note: According to a pre-production news item in *HR*, Dennis O'Keefe was initially slated for a male romantic lead in this picture. In the CBCS, the character played by Peter Lind Hayes was originally named "Chuck Deems" and Lupe Velez's character was named "Conchita." Singer Ginny Simms made her last screen appearance with the Kay Kyser band in this picture before embarking upon her solo career as an actress. This was John Barrymore's last screen appearance; he died on 29 May 1942. The picture also marked the third Kay Kyser-David Butler collaboration produced by RKO.

Box 15 Nov 1941. *DV* 6 Nov 1941. *FD* 10 Nov 1941. *HR* 11 Jun 1941, p. 9. *HR* 22 Jul 1941, p. 6. *HR* 5 Sep 1941, p. 10. *HR* 7 Nov 1941, p. 3. *MPHPD* 8 Nov 1941, pp. 349-50. *NYT* 26 Dec 1941, p. 21. *Var* 12 Nov 1941, p. 9.

PLEASURE BEFORE BUSINESS (Jewish Americans)

Columbia Pictures Corp.; Columbia Pictures Corp. 20 Apr **1927** [©Columbia Pictures Corp.; 30 Apr 1927; LP23896]. Si; b&w. 6 reels, 5,569 ft.

Prod Harry Cohn. *Dir* Frank Strayer. *Scr* William Branch. *Photog* J. O. Taylor.

Cast: Pat O'Malley (*Dr. Burke*), Virginia Brown Faire (*Ruth Weinberg*), Max Davidson (*Sam Weinberg*), Rosa Rosanova (*Sarah Weinberg*), Lester Bernard (*Morris Fishbein*), Tom McGuire (*Scotchman*), Jack Raymond (*Louie*), Henri Menjou (*Captain*).

Comedy. Sam Weinberg, an industrious cigar manufacturer, falls into bad health, and his daughter, Ruth, an assistant to Dr. Burke, uses her dowry to promote his leisure, pretending that it is a legacy from her Uncle Max. Sam embarks on an orgy of spending and betting on golf games and horse races. Then Max unexpectedly arrives from Australia, and Morris, who has been promised to Ruth, retrieves his engagement ring. Realizing he has spent the dowry money, Sam regrets having bet a large sum on a racehorse. The horse refuses to budge until the jockey speaks to her in Yiddish; she then wins the prize money for Sam. Morris tries to repair the engagement, but Ruth is happily united with the Irish doctor. *Cigars. Dowry. Golf. Horseracing. Horses. Invalids. Irish. Jews. Physicians. Wagers. Wealth.*

FD 8 May 1927. *MPW* 14 May 1927. *Var* 4 May 1927, p. 22.

PLEASURE CRUISE (*foreign version*) see NO DEJES LA PUERTA ABIERTA

LE PLOMBIER AMOUREUX (Frenc language)

Metro-Goldwyn-Mayer Corp.; controlled by Loew's, Inc.; A Buster Keaton Production. *Dist* Metro-Goldwyn-Mayer Distributing Corp. **1932.** Sd; b&w. Length undetermined. French language.

Prod Buster Keaton. *Dir* Claude Autant-Lara. *Scr* Laurence E. Johnson.

Source: Based on the play *Her Cardboard Lover* by Valerie Wyngate and P. G. Wodehouse (New York, 21 Mar 1927).

Cast: Buster Keaton, Jimmy Durante, Jeannette Ferney, Polly Moran, Barbara Léonard, Irene Purcell, Maude Eburne, Jean Del Val, George Davis, Fred Perry.

Comedy. [*Not viewed*]. [The following plot summary is based on the English-language version of this film, *The Passionate Plumber*; character names refer to that version. For further information regarding the English-language version, please see the note below and the entry for *The Passionate Plumber* in the *AFI Catalog of Feature Films, 1931-40*.] Elmer E. Tuttle, a Parisian plumber, is summoned by socialite Patricia Jardine's chauffeur, Julius J. McCracken, to fix her shower. Patricia is in love with Tony Lagorce, whom she met in Monte Carlo, but is trying to avoid him because Tony has told her he is married to Nina Estrados, who will not give him a divorce. Tony is not really married, however, and tells Nina that he can't marry her because he is married to Patricia and she will not give him a divorce. When Tony, who has just arrived in Paris, breaks into Patricia's room, he sees Elmer come out of the shower and assumes that he is her lover. He then challenges Elmer to a duel, which neither wins. At a fancy dress party, Elmer, helped by Julius, tries to show famous French general Bouschay the new pistol he has invented, but when he does, the general thinks that Elmer is an assasin and runs away. Because Elmer has fallen in love with Patricia, he is desperate to sell his invention so he can court her, and crashes the party once more. When Tony sees Elmer, he again thinks that Elmer is Patricia's lover, and she encourages his misconception when she takes Elmer to the baccarat table. There Elmer again encounters the general, who is as frightened of the gun as he was the first time, and pandemonium erupts. Later that night, Julius drags Elmer back to Patricia's house and she asks him to act as her lover to keep her away from Tony. Because she fears that her resolve may weaken, she tells Elmer to use force, if necessary, to keep her and Tony apart. When Tony arrives and asks Patricia to go away with him, she succombs to his charms, but then Elmer enters the bedroom and starts to kiss her, inciting a jealous Tony to leave. Elmer stays outside Patricia's bedroom door until morning, angering Patricia, who asks her maid Albine to think of a way to get rid of him. but nothing works. During one of her attempts to oust Elmer from the house, Patricia's Aunt Charlotte comes for a visit and suspects that Patricia is entertaining a man in her room. To save Patricia's reputation, Elmer then pretends that he is a doctor. When he briefly leaves the room, Patricia sneaks away in her aunt's clothes and goes to Tony, after which Elmer calls him and tells him to come to Patricia's house. Soon a furious Nina arrives at Patricia's house, followed by Patricia, who has just returned from Tony's. When the two women start to exchange information, they suddenly realize that Tony has been deceiving them both. When Tony arrives, they hide and listen as Tony explains his technique with women to Elmer. Infuriated, the women then appear and start throwing most of Patricia's furnishings at the incredulous Tony. After the mêlée, Tony leaves, followed by Nina, who decides that he really is the man for her. Then Patricia goes to Elmer, suddenly realizing that she loves him, and Julius goes to Albine, who is his perfect woman. *Impersonation and imposture. Jealousy. Paris (France). Plumbers. Socialites. Aunts. Chauffeurs. Fights. Firearms. Generals. Parties. Physicians.*

Note: The play *Her Cardboard Lover* was adapted from the French play *Dans sa candeur naïve* by Jacques Deval (Paris, 13 Jan 1926). The Broadway version of the play starred Jeanne Eagels and Leslie Howard. According to a modern source, this French version of *The Passionate Plumber* had only a few, unimportant changes from the English-language original. M-G-M made another film adaptation of the play in 1942 under the title *Her Cardboard Lover*. That film was directed by George Cukor and starred Norma Shearer and Robert Taylor. For information on the English-language version, which was directed by Edward Sedgwick and also starred Buster Keaton and Jimmy Durante, please see the entry for that film in the *AFI Catalog of Feature Films, 1931-40*; F3.3395.

THE PLOW WOMAN (Native Americans, Scottish Americans)

Universal Film Mfg. Co.; A Butterfly Picture. *Dist* Universal Film Mfg. Co. 2 Jul 1917 [©Universal Film Mfg. Co.; 23 Jun 1917; LP10983]. Si; b&w. 5 reels.

Dir Charles Swickard. *Scen* J. Grubb Alexander. *Cam* Harry Maguire.

Source: Based on the novel *The Plow Woman* by Eleanor Gates (New York, 1906).

Cast: Mary MacLaren (*Mary MacTavish*), H. C. De More (*Andy MacTavish*), Marie Hazelton (*Ruth MacTavish*), L. C. Shumway (*Lieut. Jack Fraser*), Kingsley Benedict (*Surgeon Fraser*), Hector V. Sarno (*Buck Mathews*), Clara Horton (*Mary, as a child*), Eddie Polo (*Bill Mathews*), George Hupp (*Jack, as a child*), Tommy Burns (*Trooper*).

Melodrama, Western. After her mother's death, Mary not only becomes the household slave of her overbearing father, Scottish American Andy MacTavish, but also becomes a mother to her little sister Ruth at their home on the Dakota plains. Years later, Jack Fraser, the son of a surgeon at the nearby fort and a steady visitor at the MacTavish home, secretly marries Ruth although he is deeply loved by Mary. Sometime later, a baby is born to Ruth, and Mary, doubting her sister's assertion that she is married to Fraser, takes the child to the fort to find out the truth from Fraser himself. Andy, believing the baby to be Mary's, orders her from the house. In the meantime, the Indians go on the warpath and Mary is surrounded. Buck Mathews, a half-breed who has lusted after Mary, sees her with the child, and pitying the helplessness of the girl, leaves the Indians to protect Mary. Fraser arrives just as Buck is fatally wounded, rescues Mary, who forgives Buck before he dies. Fraser now acknowledges that he is the husband of Ruth. *Indians of North America. Indians of North America–Mixed blood. Marriage–Secret. Sieges. Sisters.* Drudges. Fathers and daughters. Forts. Infants. Physicians. Rescues. Scottish Americans. Self-sacrifice.

Note: *ETR* commented, "This is a picture that will particularly interest all the Scots. It would be well to specially circularize all Scottish societies, clubs and organizations telling them just why they will like this picture and a bit of the story. The name of Mary MacLaren should be featured.... The house staff could be dressed in kilts and a man sent around town to distribute advertising matter, costumed the same way." In a synopsis of the film appearing in *MPW*, the decision of the half-breed Buck to turn against the Indians about to kill Mary and to rescue her occurs because when he sees the child she is carrying, "his white blood [is] aroused."

ETR 7 Jul 1917, p. 344. *Motog* 14 Jul 1917, p. 104. *MPN* 14 Jul 1917, p. 280. *MPN* 21 Jul 1917, p. 457. *MPW* 14 Jul 1917, p. 256. *MPW* 28 Jul 1917, p. 690. *Wid's* 5 Jul 1917, pp. 421-22.

THE PLUNDERERS (Latino)

Allied Artists Pictures Corp.; August Productions. *Dist* Allied Artists Pictures Corp. Nov **1960**; *Prod:* early May—mid-Jun 1960 [©Allied Artists Pictures Corp. & August Productions; 7 Nov 1960; LP17374]. Sd (Todd-AO Sound); b&w. 8,440 ft. 94 min. PCA cert no. 19732.

Exec prod Scott R. Dunlap. *Prod* Joseph Pevney. *Assoc prod* Jess Rand. *Dir* Joseph Pevney. *Asst dir* Robert Saunders. *Wrt* Bob Barbash. *Dir of photog* Eugene Polito. *Spec eff* Milt Olsen. *Art dir* David Milton. *Film ed* Tom McAdoo. *Mus ed* Richard C. Harris. *Sd ed* Charles Schelling. *Set dec* Joe Kish. *Props* Ted Mossman. *Ward* Roger J. Weinberg and Norah Sharpe. *Mus comp and cond* Leonard Rosenman. *Sd* Ralph Butler. *Makeup artist* Emile Lavigne. *Prod mgr* Edward Morey, Jr. *Set contin* Ellya Jacobus. *Constr supv* James West.

Cast: JEFF CHANDLER [(*Sam Christie*)], JOHN SAXON [(*Rondo*)], DOLORES HART [(*Ellie Walters*)], Marsha Hunt [(*Kate Miller*)], Jay C. Flippen [(*Sheriff Tom McCauley*)], Ray Stricklyn [(*Jeb Lucas Tyler*)], James Westerfield [(*Mike Baron*)], Dee Pollock [(*Davy*)], Roger Torrey [(*Mule, also known as William Thompson*)], Vaughn Taylor [(*Jess Walters*)], Harvey Stephens [(*Doc Fuller*)], Joseph Hamilton [(*Abilene*)], [Ken Patterson, William Challee (*Citizens*)], Ray Ferrell [(*Billy Miller*)], [Ella Ethridge (*Mrs. Phelps*)].

Western. [*Viewed print incomplete*]. Four young cowboys, Rondo, Jeb, Mule and Davy, ride into the small town of Trail City. The cowboys are unable to pay for their drinks at Mike Baron's saloon, so Sheriff Tom McCauley jails them for the night after they state that they will be moving on the next morning. The next day, rancher Sam Christie, a Civil War veteran with a paralyzed right arm, is buying supplies in Jess Walters' general store when the young men come in and ask Jess's daughter Ellie to serve them. Once again, they refuse to pay for their purchases, but Sam chooses not to get involved. The youngsters continue their bullying tactics by taking two rooms at Kate Miller's hotel without paying. When Baron, Walters and Miller ask Sam to join them in insisting that McCauley act against the intruders, he refuses, saying that he has to return to his ranch. McCauley's attempt to force the men to leave fails, and Kate goes to see Sam to appeal again for his help as they have been long-time friends. Kate asks him to stand up to the young men, but he has had his fill of fighting and, when he refuses, she accuses him of being afraid. Meanwhile, the cowboys have returned to Baron's saloon and are intimidating him and his customers. When Baron tells them to leave, Mule, the biggest of the gang, beats him up. Later, Rondo, a Mexican, tells Ellie that he had nothing to do with the beating and kisses her, but she does not respond. Sam comes into town as Dr. Fuller is treating Baron's wounds. When McCauley decides to face the

hoodlums, Jeb shoots and kills him although Davy is disturbed by this turn of events. Sam informs Fuller, Baron and the others that he is going back to his ranch for his gun, and asks Doc to round up volunteers. However, Abilene, the town drunk, tips off the gang and they are waiting for Sam at his ranch. After Mule badly beats Sam, they take his horses and wagon and return to town. Ellie rides out to Sam's, helps him clean himself up and tells him that there is some response to his appeal for volunteers. Sam, however, feels that only a few will want to follow him, "half a man." Ellie kisses and embraces him, prompting him to return to the fray. Meanwhile, Davy tells Rondo that he wants to leave and asks him to go with him. In a stable, Sam tells the assembled volunteers that Rondo is the most dangerous of the group. When Davy comes to collect his horse, he draws his gun on Sam and the volunteers, saying that he does not want to kill any of them, then drops the gun and weeps. Rondo then surprises Ellie at her home and attacks her, but she claws him and escapes. When Sam captures Rondo, the other citizens want to hang him but Sam dissuades them. Ellie sees Rondo pull out a knife and head toward Sam's back, and shoots and kills him. After Jeb and Mule retreat to the saloon, Sam challenges Mule to come out and faces him armed with Rondo's knife. They fight and Mule dies when he falls on the knife. Jeb, panicked, tries to escape but Sam shoots and kills him. Sam tells Davy to get his horse and leave, then he and Ellie reunite. *Bullies. Civil War veterans. Cowboys. Handicapped. Pacifism and pacifists.* Alcoholics. Fathers and daughters. Gunfights. Hotels. Knives. Mexicans. Paralysis. Physicians. Ranches. Saloon keepers. Saloons. Sheriffs. Stables. Storekeepers.

Note: The print viewed was missing thirteen minutes, some of which included events surrounding the killing of "McCauley." August Productions was a company set up by Jeff Chandler, Jess Rand and Bob Barbash and *The Plunderers* may have been its first and only film.

Box 14 Nov 1960 *DV* 4 Nov 1960, p. 3. *Exh* 9 Nov 1960, p. 4765. *FD* 4 Nov 1960, p. 6. *Har* 13 May 1961, p. 74. *HR* 13 May 1960, p. 14. *HR* 17 Jun 1960, p. 10. *HR* 4 Nov 1960, p. 3. *LAT* 6 Apr 1961. *MPD* 10 Oct 1960. *MPHPD* 12 Nov 1960, p. 917 *Var* 9 Nov 1960, p. 19.

PLUNDERERS OF ELDORADO see **GUNFIRE AT INDIAN GAP**

POCOMANIA see **THE DEVIL'S DAUGHTER**

POLICY MAN (African Americans)

Dist Sack Amusement Enterprises, Inc. 1 Jul **1938**. Sd; b&w. 61 min. **African American, Drama.** [*Not viewed*]. [No information concerning the plot of this film has been found.]. *African Americans.*

Note: No contemporary reviews of *Policy Man* have been located; however, *MPH* release charts lists this film as having been released by Sack Amusement Enterprises on 1 Jul 1938 with a running time of 61 minutes. According to modern sources, this was a Creative Cinema Corp. production, with a cast including Ann Harleman, Henri Wessell, Jimmy Baskette, Ethel Moses, Count Basie and his Orchestra, and The Plantation Club Chorus.

POLITIQUERÍAS (Spanish language)

Hal Roach Studios, Inc.; Metro-Goldwyn-Mayer Corp.; controlled by Loew's, Inc. *Dist* Metro-Goldwyn-Mayer Distributing Corp. **1931**; San José, Costa Rica opening: 1 May 1931; Buenos Aires, Argentina opening: 11 Jun 1931; San Juan, Puerto Rico opening: 24 Jun 1931. Sd (Sistema Western Electric [Western Electric System]); b&w. 6 reels. 56 min. Passed by the National Board of Review. Spanish language.

Pres HAL ROACH. *Dirección* [*Dir*] James W. Horne. *Diálogo por* [*Dial*] H. M. Walker. *Fotografía* [*Photog*] Jack Stevens. [*Photog* Art Lloyd]. *Editor de película* [*Film ed*] Richard Currier. *Fonografía* [*Record*] Elmer Raguse.

Cast: STAN LAUREL [(*Stan Laurel*)], OLIVER HARDY [(*Oliver Hardy*)], [Rina de Liguoro (*Antigua amiga de Oliver Hardy*)], [James Finlayson (*Criado*)], [Linda Loredo (*Señora Hardy*)], [Carmen Granada (*Señora Laurel*)], [Enrique Acosta (*El juez*)], [María Calvo (*La esposa del juez*)], [Nelly Fernández (*Amiga de la Sra. Laurel*)], [Charlie Hall (*Ascensorista*)], [A. J. Cantú (*Magician*)], [Hadji Ali (*Regurgitator*)].

Comedy. [*Print viewed*]. Stan Laurel and Oliver Hardy are successful businessmen, and Ollie is a candidate for mayor. Unfortunately, a former lady friend shows up in Ollie's office one day and threatens to expose their relationship unless he gives her some money. Ollie arranges to meet her that evening to straighten everything out. Soon after, Ollie's wife arrives to tell him that she has planned a dinner party for that evening and has invited guests who are important to his electoral campaign. Stan is drafted to go to the "old flame's" apartment and stall her until Ollie can get there. The lady

thinks she is being tricked, however, and so she calls Ollie and threatens to go to his house unless he comes to her apartment immediately. While Ollie tries to sneak out, Stan attempts to keep the lady occupied. She eventually gets out, however, and during their struggle, Stan is spotted by a busy-body friend of his wife's. Stan and the ex-girl friend arrive at Ollie's house, where they are introduced as husband and wife. After the other guests leave, Ollie threatens the lady and she faints. The boys are endeavoring to remove her from the house when the real Mrs. Laurel shows up with a hatchet. *Blackmail. Bumblers. Gold diggers. Wives. Deception. Parties. Political candidates.*

Note: This film is an expanded version of a 1931 English language three-reel short entitled *Chickens Come Home*, which starred Stan Laurel and Oliver Hardy. Some sources state that Pedro Regas (whom modern sources credit as playing an office worker), Arturo Turich, Arturo Turich jr., Panchita Acosta, Elena Durán, Mary Emery, Al Flores and Rafael Valverde appeared in the picture in secondary roles, but their participation in the film has not been confirmed. Although Jack Stevens is credited on screen as the photographer, Art Lloyd is credited as the photographer in publicity. Some reviews erroneously interchange the roles of Carmen Granada and Rina de Liguoro. Modern sources add the following actors to the cast: Ellinor Van Der Veer, Vera Zouroff and Benito Fernandez (*Dinner party guests*). For more information about Laurel and Hardy's career together and their foreign language films, see entry above for *Pardon Us.*

PONY EXPRESS DAYS see OUTLAW EXPRESS

POOR HEART see ALMA DE GAUCHO

POOR LITTLE PEPPINA (Italian Americans)

Famous Players-Mary Pickford Co. *Dist* Paramount Pictures Corp. 20 Feb **1916.** Si; b&w. 7 reels.

Dir Sidney Olcott. *Story* Kate Jordan.

Cast: Mary Pickford (*Peppina*), Eugene O'Brien (*Hugh Carroll*), Antonio Maiori (*Soldo*), Ernesto Torti (*Pietro*), Edwin Mordant (*Robert Torrens*), Jack Pickford (*Beppo*), Edith Shayne (*Mrs. Torrens*), Cesare Gravina (*Villato*), W. T. Carleton (*The detective chief*), N. Cervi (*Dominica*), Mrs. A. Maiori (*Bianca*), Francesca Guerra (*The stoker*).

Drama. Holding a grudge against Robert Torrens and his wife, who live in Italy, a member of the Mafia kidnaps their infant daughter Lois. Fifteen years later, after having been raised by Italian peasants, Lois, now called Peppina, dresses as a boy and stows away on a ship to America in order to avoid a marriage to a particularly loathsome count. While aboard ship she befriends Hugh Carroll, an assistant district attorney, who arranges first-class transportation for the "boy." In New York, she once again meets her kidnapper, who fled to America after the crime. He forces Peppina to maintain the masculine disguise and to pass counterfeit bills for him, for which she is arrested. Peppina gladly exposes the kidnapper's operation to the authorities, one of whom, Hugh, recognizes her as the "boy" he met on the ship. Then, once the kidnapper has been apprehended, Peppina is reunited with her parents, after which she and Hugh, who has finally discovered that she is female, get married. *Counterfeiters and counterfeiting. District attorneys. Italians. Italy. Kidnapping. Mafia. Male impersonation. Peasantry. Infants. New York City. Nobility. Revenge. Stowaways.*

Note: This film was the first production of the Famous Players-Mary Pickford Co., the productions of which the actress retained one-half interest. The film began a special release in several large cities on 20 Feb 1916, and then went into general release on 2 Mar 1916. *MPW* reports that the film was to be cut from seven reels to five for its general release. The film was also called *Little Peppina.*

Motog 4 Mar 1916, p. 531. *MPN* 12 Feb 1916, p. 826. *MPN* 4 Mar 1916, p. 1317. *MPW* 4 Mar 1916, p. 1491. *NYDM* 5 Feb 1916, p. 23. *NYDM* 26 Feb 1916, p. 24. *NYDM* 4 Mar 1916, p. 28. *NYT* 21 Feb 1916, p. 9. *Var* 25 Feb 1916, p. 22.

PORGY AND BESS (African Americans)

Samuel Goldwyn Productions. *Dist* Columbia Pictures Corp. 24 Jun **1959;** World premiere in New York: 24 Jun 1959; Prod: 22 Sep—10 Dec 1958 [©Samuel Goldwyn Productions; 24 Jun 1959; LP14519]. Sd (Westrex Recording System); col (Technicolor); Todd-AO. 35 and 70mm. 14 reels, 15,335 ft. 146 min. Passed by the National Board of Review. PCA cert no. 19297.

Pres SAMUEL GOLDWYN. *Prod* Samuel Goldwyn. *Dir* Otto Preminger. *Asst dir* Paul Helmick. *Scr* N. Richard Nash. *Dir of photog* Leon Shamroy. *Prod des* Oliver Smith. *Art dir* Serge Krizman and Joseph Wright. *Film ed* Daniel Mandell. *Mus ed* Richard Carruth. *Sd ed* Don Hall, Jr. *Set dec* Howard Bristol. *Cost des* Irene Sharaff. *Mus supv and cond* Andre Previn. *Assoc* Ken Darby. *Orch* Alexander

Courage, Conrad Salinger, Robert Franklyn and Al Woodbury. [*Instrumentals* Felix Slatkin, Victor Arno, Israel Baker, Milton Thomas, David Frisini, Louis Kaufman, Lloyd Ulyate, Pete Candoni, Shelley Manne, Benny Carter, Bud Shank, Bill Holman, Dave Tell and Frank Capp]. *Choreography* Hermes Pan. *Sd rec supv* Fred Hynes. *Mus rec* Murray Spivack and Vinton Vernon. *Makeup* Frank McCoy and Layne Britton. *Hair styles* Joan St. Oegger. *Prod mgr* Doc Merman. *Dial coach* Max Slater. *Todd-AO consultant* Schuyler A. Sanford. [*Elec asst* Bert Challacombe]. [*Singing double for Sidney Poitier* Robert McFerrin]. [*Singing double for Dorothy Dandridge* Adele Addison]. [*Singing double for Diahann Carroll* Loulie Jean Norman]. [*Singing double for Ruth Attaway* Inez Matthews].

Song(s): "Summertime," "A Woman Is a Sometime Thing," "Honey Man's Call," "They Passby Singing," "Oh Little Stars," "Gone, Gone, Gone," "Fill Up De Saucer," "My Man's Gone Now," "The Train Is at the Station," "Oh, I Got Plenty O' Nuttin'," "Bess, You Is My Woman Now," "Oh, I Can't Sit Down," "I Ain' Got No Shame," "It Ain't Necessarily So," "What You Want Wid Bess," "It Take a Long Pull to Get There," "Strawberry Woman's Call," "Crab Man's Call," "I Loves You, Porgy," "Oh, De Lawd Shake De Heaven," "Dere's Somebody Knockin' at De Do'," "A Red Headed Woman," "Clara, Don't You Be Downhearted," "There's a Boat Dat's Leavin' Soon for New York," "Good Mornin' Sistuh," "Bess, Oh Where's My Bess" and "Oh, Lawd, I'm on My Way," music by George Gershwin, lyrics by DuBose Heyward and Ira Gershwin.

Source: Based on the play *Porgy* by DuBose and Dorothy Heyward, originally produced for the stage by the Theatre Guild (Oct 1927).

Cast: Sidney Poitier (*Porgy*), Dorothy Dandridge (*Bess*), Sammy Davis, Jr. (*Sportin' Life*), Pearl Bailey (*Maria*), Brock Peters (*Crown*), Leslie Scott (*Jake*), Diahann Carroll (*Clara*), Ruth Attaway (*Serena*), Claude Akins (*Detective*), Clarence Muse (*Peter*), Everdinne Wilson (*Annie*), Joel Fluellen (*Robbins*), Earl Jackson (*Mingo*), Moses La Marr (*Nelson*), Margaret Hairston (*Lily*), Ivan Dixon (*Jim*), Antoine Durousseau (*Scipio*), Helen Thigpen (*Strawberry woman*), Vince Townsend, Jr. (*Elderly man*), William Walker (*Undertaker*), Roy Glenn, Sr. (*Frazier*), Maurice Manson (*Coroner*), [Scatman Crothers (*Crabman*)].

African American, Musical. [*Print viewed*]. At Catfish Row, the courtyard home to a southern, African-American fishing community, the men shoot dice one evening while the women gossip about Bess, who for five years has lived with Crown, a local bully. The women declare that Porgy, a cripple who gets around on a cart pulled by a goat, is "soft on her," but Porgy denies that he is and laments that the life of a cripple is meant to be lonesome. When Crown and Bess come to the courtyard and Crown joins the dice game, Sportin' Life, a slick drug pusher, sells Crown some "happy dust," or cocaine, against Bess's wishes, and Crown snorts it. Robbins, whose religious wife Serena stakes him because she fears that otherwise Bess might, wins his point, and the angry Crown fights with him until he kills Robbins with a blow. Bess sends Crown away to protect him from the police, then asks Sportin' Life for some happy dust. Sportin' Life suggests that they leave for New York together, but Bess turns him down in disgust. When the police arrive, Bess tries to hide, but no one lets her in. Desperate, Bess knocks at Porgy's door, and he agrees to let her stay. Serena tries to collect from her neighbors for Robbins' burial, and although she does not want to accept Bess's contribution, Porgy encourages the neighbors to give more and Bess collects from them. When a white detective accuses old "honey man" Peter of the murder and threatens him, Peter reveals that he saw Crown kill Robbins. Peter is then locked up as a material witness until Crown is caught. The detective warns Serena that if Robbins is not buried by the next day, the board of health will turn the body over to medical students. Serena pleads with the undertaker to accept the fifteen dollars she has collected and let her pay the rest when she earns it, and he acquiesces. Bess continues to live with Porgy, and the neighbors soon comment that he is happier. Lawyer Frazier comes to give Bess a divorce from Crown so she can marry Porgy, for which Porgy pays him a dollar, but when Frazier learns that Bess never married Crown, he demands an extra half-dollar. When they balk, Frazier accuses them of living in sin, and Porgy reluctantly pays the rest. On the day of a church picnic, Sportin' Life again tempts Bess to go to New York and offers her happy dust, but Porgy threatens to break his neck if he does not stay away. Porgy then tells Bess that she is now his woman and she agrees to stay with him. After the picnic, Crown, who is hiding in the woods,

confronts Bess when she is alone. She struggles, but when Crown kisses her, she embraces him and lets him carry her off. Bess returns to Catfish Row two days later and remains in a delirious state for more than a week as Porgy tends to her. Peter returns from jail and recommends that Porgy take Bess to the county hospital, but he refuses and instead asks Serena to pray. She does and says that Bess will be well when the church bell strikes six times. The next morning, when the bell chimes, Bess comes out of her delirium and calls for Porgy. She cries, realizing she betrayed him with Crown, but Porgy says he understands. Although she confesses that she loses control when Crown touches her, she tells Porgy she loves him and asks him not to let Crown take her. He assures her that he will take care of Crown and that she has a man now. When a hurricane hits after some of the men have gone out in their fishing boats, the people congregate at Serena's home, where Clara, a new mother, worries about her husband Jake. Crown enters and taunts Porgy about his relationship with Bess, then laughs at those who are afraid of the storm. Clara runs out in search of Jake, after giving Bess her baby, and Crown also leaves, saying that he will be back for Bess. Following the storm, the community mourns for the lost men and Clara. When Serena tries to get Bess to give up Clara's baby, saying it needs a proper Christian raising, Porgy implores Serena to let Bess alone, as she wants to keep the baby, and Serena agrees. Later, Crown sneaks into the courtyard and goes to Porgy's window, and when Porgy awakens, they fight. Crown draws his knife, but Porgy throws him down and Crown is killed. As the people repair their buildings from the storm damage, the detective returns with a coroner to find a witness to Crown's killing. Suspecting Serena killed Crown for revenge, the detective questions her, but she has an alibi. The detective then orders Porgy to come to the jail to identify the body. Porgy refuses, not wanting to look at Crown, and Sportin' Life says that if he looks at Crown's face, his wounds will begin to bleed, giving Porgy away. The detective then carries Porgy into the police wagon as he is screaming that he will not look at Crown's face. Sportin' Life finds Bess crying and tells her that Porgy will give himself away and end up dying in jail. He offers her some happy dust, and after she accepts, Sportin' Life's talk of New York and a life in a mansion appeals to her in her drugged state. Sometime later, the police bring Porgy back to the courtyard. He tells his friends that the wounds did not bleed when he looked at them and brings gifts he bought with money he won from shooting craps in jail. When he asks for Bess, however, the people scatter. He then sees Serena with Clara's baby and demands to know where Bess is. He finally learns that she went to New York with Sportin' Life after he convinced her that Porgy would not return from jail. Porgy states that he cannot go on without her and starts off for New York in his goat cart with the good wishes of his friends. *African Americans. Drug dealers. Handicapped. Murder. Poverty. Romance. Romantic rivalry. Accidental death. Bullies. Burial. Cocaine. Coroners. Craps (Game). Drug addicts. Fights. Fishing villages. Goats. Hurricanes. Infants. Islands. Lawyers. Nursing back to health. Picnicking. Police detectives. Prayer. Religiosity. Rural life. Undertakers and undertaking. United States–South. Witnesses.*

Note: According to a 5 Apr 1959 *LAT* article by Bennett Cerf, DuBose Heyward came up with the idea to write the original play while working as a cotton checker in Charleston, SC, and becoming intrigued with the life and culture of the Gullah, or "Low Country" Negroes who worked under him. A "Study Guide" to the film states that Heyward based "Porgy" on Sammy Smalls, a crippled beggar, after reading in a newspaper account in Aug 1924 that Smalls, in a fit of jealous rage, shot the woman of whom he was enamored. Cerf, however wrote that Smalls attempted to shoot his own grandfather. Both sources state that Smalls traveled by means of a goat cart. After Heyward wrote the novel *Porgy*, his wife Dorothy wrote a play based on the novel, also entitled *Porgy*, which opened in 1927 as a Theatre Guild production. The play was directed by Rouben Mamoulian, who later directed the 1935 production of the opera, *Porgy and Bess*, and was originally hired to direct this film. In 1928, Heyward wrote the following dedication: "To Smalls, I make acknowledgment of my obligation. From contemplation of his real, and deeply moving tragedy, sprang Porgy, a creature of my imagination... upon whom, being my own creation, I could impose my own... conception of a summer of aspiration, devotion and heartbreak across the color wall."

Composer George Gershwin, who wanted to write an American opera, read Heyward's book in 1926 and wrote to Heyward suggesting that they collaborate on the project. Gershwin then visited Charleston and James Island, where he heard traditional singing at Gullah revival meetings. Although by 1933, Oscar Hammerstein II and Jerome Kern discussed basing a musical on the book and play for Al Jolson, Gershwin went to work on it in the fall of 1933 and collaborated with Heyward by mail. Gershwin moved to Folly Island near Charleston in the summer of 1934 and composed the music between Jun 1934

and Apr 1935. The opera, with lyrics by Heyward and Ira Gershwin, previewed in Boston on 30 Sep 1935 and opened in New York in Oct. Gershwin stated concerning the work: "I have been asked why it is a folk opera. *Porgy and Bess* is a folktale. When I first began work on the music I decided against the use of original folk material because I wanted the music to be all of one piece. Therefore I wrote my own spirituals and folk songs. But they are still folk music—and, being operatic in form, *Porgy and Bess* becomes a folk opera." After some twenty-five to thirty-five minutes were cut from the three-hour Boston opening, the opera played in New York for 124 performances and toured for three months, during which it received some negative reviews. *Var*, reviewing the Boston opening, commented, "Gershwin's version of spirituals is an inadequate substitute for the originals."

In 1942, *Porgy and Bess* was revived in a version produced by Cheryl Crawford, in which the lengthy recitatives of the 1935 original were eliminated or replaced with dialogue scenes. This version, which was no longer called an opera, was a success, playing in New York for eight months and 286 performances before it went on a twenty-six city tour. The musical was revived again in 1952, and it toured the U.S. before playing in New York for 305 performances and in twenty-eight foreign countries. In Nov 1953, *NYHT* reported that independent producer Berman Swartz was negotiating with the estates of DuBose Heyward and George Gershwin to make a film using the touring cast. The estates withheld their permission, however, as the executors first wanted to see if Swartz's current project, a film of the musical *New Faces* with the Broadway cast, would be successful.

In May 1957, it was announced that Samuel Goldwyn had acquired the rights to the play, which he would film using a widescreen process, for 10% of the world-wide gross, with a down payment of $650,000. It was also announced that Robert Breen, the producer and director of the 1953 revival, would be "associated" with Goldwyn in the project. Both Louis B. Mayer, acting independently following his retirement from M-G-M, and Columbia Pictures had offered $1,000,000 against a percentage of the gross for the rights. In addition, George Seaton and William Perlberg, with Paramount financial backing, had made an offer to make the film in Germany. According to news items, Goldwyn, who had been negotiating to acquire the rights for a decade, was chosen by the estates because of his reputation. Breen was quoted as saying that other interested parties proposed unacceptable changes, including one producer who wanted to make the film with a white cast starring Fred Astaire and Rita Hayworth. Ira Gershwin stated in *LAT* in Apr 1958 that over ninety producers had approached him to acquire the screen rights, and that Al Jolson wanted to play the role of "Porgy" in blackface, with an otherwise all-black cast. Gershwin noted that the Heyward estate presented legal technicalities making it difficult for the film rights to be acquired, but that Goldwyn persisted through seven months of negotiations. The deal was formalized on 8 Oct 1957, and Goldwyn planned at that time to handle the initial distribution through his own company, to be followed by a subsequent release handled by an established distributor.

According to *NYT*, in Oct, Goldwyn hired New York playwright N. Richard Nash to write the screenplay. (Modern sources state that Goldwyn approached a number of other writers, including Langston Hughes, Paul Osborn, Frances Goodrich and Albert Hackett, Sidney Kingsley, Jerome Lawrence and Robert E. Lee, and Clifford Odets.) Nash decided to accept only if he could work in New York and not have to give Goldwyn the drafts page by page. Goldwyn, who was used to working closely with writers, agreed reluctantly. Early in Nov it was announced that Rouben Mamoulian, who had directed both the 1927 play and the 1935 opera, was signed as director for the film. (Modern sources state that Goldwyn first considered hiring Elia Kazan, Frank Capra or King Vidor.) In a *NYT* article, Mamoulian stated that he had "every intention of respecting the spirit and concept of the folk opera.... It will have to be a stylized version, set in 1910 and not the turn of the century as on stage, to capture the truth, reality and emotions of the characters. It will be a challenge to enlarge and expand it to fit the vast scope and unique nature of the camera. And, the songs may have to be cut or condensed."

In a 2 Dec 1957 *Time* article, Goldwyn stated that he had experienced a "quiet boycott" among leading African-American actors and entertainers, who refused to appear in the film. Harry Belafonte, who turned down the leading role, was quoted in a interview, reprinted in a modern biography, as saying, "in this period of our social development, I doubt that it is healthy to expose certain images of the Negro. In a period of calm, perhaps this picture could be viewed historically. But skins are still too thin and emotions still too sensitive for a lot of Uncle Toms in *Porgy and Bess* to be shown now." Goldwyn characterized the "boycott" as "an underground movement by radicals." Previous complaints by some African Americans about the play and musical had also worried other potential filmmakers before Goldwyn was selected to make the film. In a statement to *Time*, dated 22 Nov 1957, Roy Wilkins of the NAACP commented on black reaction to the show: "Among Negro Americans there is a divergence of opinion as to the value of this play. Some regard it as a folk opera, an artistic creation. Others feel that it misrepresents Negro life in America. The fear of these latter is that the public may regard Catfish Row as a typical picture of Negro American life rather than as a period piece depicting merely a segment. Officially, the NAACP has taken no position on *Porgy and Bess*."

On 4 Nov 1957, Goldwyn announced that Sidney Poitier had been signed for the lead. On 11 Nov, however, *Var* reported that Poitier had "vacated" the spot over the weekend. Goldwyn explained Poitier's refusal to play the role by stating that he had demanded script approval, a condition Goldwyn had never given before. On 11 Dec, in a press conference, Poitier's subsequent acceptance of the role was announced. The following story of the turnabout was circulated in the press at the time: Poitier explained that his agents had committed him to the role prematurely. After he examined recordings the

company sent him about the play, which he had neither read nor seen, he did not have "sufficient creative enthusiasm for the part" and also feared that "if improperly handled *Porgy and Bess* could conceivably be to my mind injurious to Negroes." *HR* and *DV* reported that Poitier, who had been working in the British Virgin Islands at the time of the deal, had phoned Goldwyn about his lack of interest. Poitier later felt, according to *HR*, that he was being unfair in assuming that Goldwyn "might mistreat the property" and that Goldwyn deserved a more thorough explanation about Poitier's "feelings as a Negro," so he came to California to discuss the situation. After meeting with Goldwyn and Mamoulian, Poitier's reservations were "washed away." At the press conference, when African-American reporters asked Goldwyn what guarantees he could make that the film would not portray blacks in a bad light, Goldwyn stated, "I stand on my record," and predicted that the film "will be the greatest propaganda the Negro can have." Goldwyn then invited African-American author Langston Hughes to go over the script with him in order to change any offensive elements.

In his autobiography, Poitier gives a different account of the reasons he accepted the role. He states that the press release about his decision to do the picture "was all to Goldwyn's advantage. I got screwed again and there were reverberations in the black community." Poitier relates that an unnamed female agent associated with Martin Baum, his own agent, told Goldwyn that she would get Poitier for the role, not knowing that Poitier "had a considerable aversion to *Porgy and Bess* because of its inherent racial attitudes." When Poitier learned of the offer, he called Baum and said he was not interested. Upon Poitier's return from the Virgin Islands, and after his refusal of the role was reported in the press, Baum convinced him to go to California because of the misrepresentation to Goldwyn. Poitier met with Goldwyn, who failed to convince him to accept, but nonetheless persuaded him to give the matter more thought. Wishing to give priority to *The Defiant Ones* (see above), Poitier communicated to Goldwyn that he was not interested in *Porgy and Bess*, but Goldwyn announced that he would hold Poitier to the original promise made by the female agent. Warned by his agents that Goldwyn he could "blackball" him, Poitier realized he was going to "get burned a little," and he agreed to do *Porgy and Bess* if Goldwyn would not let him out of the deal.

In Apr 1958, Goldwyn announced that after six months of

According to news stories, in the early morning of 2 Jul 1958, a studio guard discovered a fire in a sound stage at the Goldwyn Studios, where tests were to begin a few hours later with the main cast members of the film. The Charleston waterfront set was completely destroyed, along with all the costumes and the original sketches for them, $200,000 worth of rented electrical equipment, props that the studio accumulated in the previous thirty years, and the only acetate recordings of all the Goldwyn sound films. No one was injured, but damage was estimated to be between two and five million dollars. An arson squad sergeant doubted that the cause of the fire would ever be determined because of the extent of the damage. Although reports circulated that minority groups unhappy with the production might have set the fire, studio officials rejected that possibility. Goldwyn denied that protests had been received by organizations objecting to the depiction of blacks, as had been reported by several Hollywood columnists, and stated that the NAACP had approved Nash's script. The chairman of the West Coast legal committee of the NAACP, Loren Miller, called the implications of the press reports "ridiculous" and noted that the NAACP was "looking forward to Mr. Goldwyn's production." Goldwyn announced that production would be halted until mid-Sep, but that the same cast would be in the film.

On 27 Jul 1958, the press was informed that Mamoulian had been replaced as director by Otto Preminger. In a press release, Goldwyn stated, "I have the greatest respect for Rouben Mamoulian, but he and I could not see eye to eye on various matters." Later press reports stated that Goldwyn was unhappy with recent publicity given to Mamoulian and with Mamoulian's public statements concerning a number of matters over which he and Goldwyn disagreed. Two hours after the issuance of Goldwyn's press release, according to *HR*, Mamoulian issued a statement charging, "In the eight months that I have been working on *Porgy and Bess* for the screen...there has not been one iota of dissention [sic] between me and Mr. Goldwyn concerning *Porgy and Bess*. There have been, however, other dissensions on his part unrelated to the production which were trespasses upon my private and professional life." Mamoulian's complaints included Goldwyn's insistence that he fire his public relations counselor, Russell Birdwell, and work without compensation during the ten-week layoff period following the fire. Mamoulian claimed that Goldwyn wanted "to be identified publicity-wise as the sole creator" of the film. According to Mamoulian's agent, Irving Lazar, Mamoulian said he would not agree to a settlement, but would force Goldwyn to honor his contract. Lazar stated that the contract did not prevent Goldwyn from getting another director, and only required that Mamoulian be paid the entire amount due to him. This figure was quoted in the press as $75,000 plus 2 1/2% of the film's profits, and Mamoulian was paid the total amount owed to him as specified in his contract.

Preminger, who himself came close to buying the rights to *Porgy and Bess* twice, according to *LAMirror-News*, had earlier directed the all-black cast musical *Carmen Jones* (see below). Following Preminger's acceptance, Mamoulian complained to the Screen Directors Guild, which held a special meeting on 28 Jul 1958 to hear Mamoulian's complaints. They voted to invite Goldwyn to appear before the Guild board of directors and give his side of the dispute, but Goldwyn rejected the invitation. The Guild board reportedly was "profoundly disturbed" by Goldwyn's refusal to meet with them. On 2 Aug, Preminger walked out of a Guild meeting, and the Guild subsequently ruled that none of their members, which included directors and assistant directors, could work for Goldwyn until he became a signator to an interim agreement between the Association of Motion Picture Producers and the Guild, which he had not signed in Apr 1958, when the previous contract lapsed. At the time, a new "and hotly contested basic work contract" was in the process of being worked out.

On 6 Aug 1958, the president of the Negro Actors Guild of America, Leigh Whipper, an African-American actor who had previously worked with Mamoulian and was to appear in the film as "Crabman," gave a press conference with Russell Birdwell in which he announced that he was withdrawing from the film. Whipper charged that with Preminger directing, the film was now "in hands unsympathetic to my people." Whipper stated, "*Porgy and Bess* has always been a theatrical property which, in unknowing or unsympathetic hands could be made and has been made an unfortunate slur upon my people. *Porgy* and *Porgy and Bess* have achieved the heights of human dignity and spiritual content when they have originally been directed by Mr. Rouben Mamoulian." Whipper also claimed to have "first hand information concerning the new director which brands him, to me, as a man who has no respect for my people." Whipper refused to divulge the source of his information, but claimed that it pertained to an incident that occurred ten years earlier involving a female African-American star. Whipper stated that in addition to being cast as "Crabman," he had worked with Mamoulian as a script counselor "deleting words he felt would be detrimental to the Negro race," according to *DV*. (The role of "Crabman" was subsequently performed by Scatman Crowthers.)

In response to Whipper's comments, Loren Miller of the NAACP stated, "I think that an attempt to make a racial issue out of the choice of directors on this picture is ill advised." Noble Sissle, co-founder and past president of the Negro Actors Guild of America, sent a telegram to Goldwyn stating, "Whatever Mr. Whipper's feelings were, whether right or wrong, we feel it was very unfair and unethical for him to express them as recently elected president of the Negro Actors Guild when he knows it is strictly against the life-long policy of the Guild to enter into such a damaging controversial affair involving accusations of racial discrimination." Many of the leading African-American cast members issued statements in support of Preminger and Goldwyn following Whipper's press conference. Pearl Bailey, who had appeared in *Carmen Jones*, told *HR*, "Introduction of the racial issue into the controversy is the most vicious thing I ever heard of. I've worked with Mr. Preminger, and if he's anti-Negro I never saw nor heard it." Poitier called Whipper's statement "ridiculous," according to *Var*.

On 7 Aug, after an exchange of letters with Goldwyn regarding the interim work agreement, the Screen Directors Guild granted waivers to Preminger and the assistant directors on the film to work for Goldwyn until a proposed meeting with Goldwyn on 13 Aug. In addition, the Guild agreed to "take under consideration" a charge by Preminger that he had been "defamed" by Mamoulian and Birdwell. *Var* speculated that the Guild's move in support of Goldwyn and Preminger came as a backlash to Whipper's attack. In one of the board meetings, Preminger stated "I'm Jewish. I ran away from Hitler. How can they say I'm anti-Negro?" At the last minute, the Guild canceled its planned meeting with Goldwyn for 13 Aug. According to *NYT*, the Guild was criticized for basing their decision to have members boycott Goldwyn on Goldwyn's refusal to sign the interim agreement. *NYT* also noted that Mamoulian's contract with Goldwyn was not negotiated through the Guild and specifically did allow for his dismissal. Although Mamoulian appealed to the Guild to have his name appear on the film, due to the preparation work he did, the Guild's board of directors ruled unanimously in Feb 1959 that Preminger was to receive sole credit as director.

In Sep 1958, Goldwyn made a number of staff changes, including substituting director of photography Leon Shamroy for Ellsworth Fredericks, who had been offered another film during the layoff period. In addition, actor Thaddeus Jones, who was cast as "Peter," was replaced by Clarence Muse (who played "Porgy" in the original West Coast production), and Everdinne Wilson was given a different role than originally planned. Assistant director Art Black left to work for Frank Capra, and production manager Gus Schroder was replaced by "Doc" Merman. Filming began on 22 Sep 1958 on Venice Island in the San Joaquin River near Stockton, CA. The picnic and fish fry scenes were shot across the river at Tule Island. After ten days of location work, shooting moved to a Goldwyn sound stage, which Goldwyn closed to visitors, citing the dangerous work conditions with the large quantity of lights necessary for the Todd-AO process.

Songs performed by four of the character roles were dubbed by singers other than the onscreen actors. In a *Life* magazine article, Robert McFerrin detailed the working process he and Poitier went through to create their role. McFerrin stated, "We had to get to know Porgy as a man. It could not be Poitier the actor or McFerrin the singer. It had to be Porgy, a blend of both." First Poitier read the lines, then acted them for McFerrin. Poitier then listened to recordings of McFerrin singing the songs and sang to the recordings while studying his appearance in a mirror. Dorothy Dandridge's singing was not used because her soprano voice did not match McFerrin's baritone, in the opinion of the filmmakers. Although Goldwyn originally wanted all of the off-screen singers to be black, Diahann Carroll's voice was thought not to be right for the film, and after scouts failed to find an available African American whose voice was judged to be satisfactory, so Loulie Jean Norman, a French-English white singer, was selected to perform "Summertime."

The film's production cost was over seven million dollars, according to *Time*. In Sep 1959, Goldwyn announced in the *BHCN*, "No financial benefits can come to me, because every dollar of my profits are earmarked for charity through the Samuel Goldwyn Foundation." He estimated that he would need fifteen or sixteen million dollars to break even. On 1 Mar 1961, *Var* reported that Goldwyn was withdrawing the film from circulation in the South because of racial tension there. In Chapel Hill, NC, pickets protested the exclusion of blacks from a theater where the film had been shown. Critical reaction to the film was mixed. *NYT* called it a "fine film version," while *DV* stated it was "a

sometime thing." *DV* noted, "The racial stereotype dangers have mostly been sterilized and faded to innocuousness." In comparing the film with the stage productions, *DV* "This is not the gruesome Negro ghetto-underworld of the old Theatre Guild productions, though dope is still peddled. It would appear that in designing the set... and in costuming the natives ... there was a conscious intention to show the environment and the garb as dirt-poor but never dirty." Other reviewers criticized the visual style as "cinematic monotony" (*Time*) and "a photographed stage production rather than a movie in the usual sense of the word" (*BHCN*). A number of reviews commented on Sammy Davis, Jr.'s portrayal of "Sportin' Life." Bosley Crowther of *NYT* wrote, "In previous stage production of this folk opera, Sportin' Life has come through as a sort of droll and impious rascal with the bright, lively quality of a minstrel man.... But there's nothing charming or sympathetic about the fellow that Mr. Davis plays. He's a comprehension of evil on an almost repulsive scale."

Porgy and Bess was Goldwyn's last film. It won Academy Awards for Best Scoring (Andre Previn and Ken Darby), Best Costume Design (Irene Sharaff) and Best Sound Recording (Gordon Sawyer). The American Society of Recording Artists awarded the film a Grammy for best soundtrack of the year in any motion picture.

In Apr 1959, Robert Breen, executive producer of the 1952 revival, sued Goldwyn and others associated with him, and demanded $5 million in damages, claiming he had been eased out of the film version and that Goldwyn took the film rights by "false and fraudulent promises." In 1963, the amount of the suit had changed to $2,350,000, and Breen claimed that he had been hired as associate producer for $750 a week and 5% of the profits, but that he left after five weeks because Goldwyn had not given him "joint artistic control." In Mar 1963, a jury decided in Goldwyn's favor.

In a 19 Jan 1993 *LAT* article, Michael Strunsky, who was the sole trustee and executor of Ira Gershwin's estate, and the nephew of Gershwin's wife Leonore, stated that his uncle and aunt were critical of the film: "My aunt didn't want it distributed. She and my uncle felt it was a Hollywoodization of the piece. We [the estate] now acquire any prints we find and destroy them. We are often approached for permission to show the film, which we consistently deny." A subsequent letter published on 27 Nov 1994 in *LAT* stated that "the safety negative was secure in the Goldwyn vaults."

AmCin Aug 1959, pp. 476-77, 496, 498-99. *BHCN* 16 Jul 1959, p. 5. *BHCN* 15 Sep 1959, p. 5. *BHCN* 15 Feb 1960. *Box* 29 Jun 1959. *Box* 6 Jul 1959. *Box* 15 Oct 1962. *Cue* 20 Jun 1959. *Cue* 4 Jul 1959. *DV* 14 Feb 1954. *DV* 9 May 1957, p. 1, 4. *DV* 19 Nov 1957. *DV* 12 Dec 1957, p. 1, 13. *DV* 20 Mar 1958. *DV* 12 May 1958. *DV* 5 Jun 1958. *DV* 3 Jul 1958. *DV* 9 Jul 1958. *DV* 28 Jul 1958, p. 1, 5. *DV* 5 Aug 1958. *DV* 7 Aug 1958, p. 1. *DV* 11 Aug 1958. *DV* 12 Aug 1958. *DV* 25 Aug 1958, p. 1. *DV* 10 Sep 1958. *DV* 21 Oct 1958. *DV* 21 Nov 1958. *DV* 11 Feb 1959, p. 1. *DV* 25 Jun 1959, p. 3. *DV* 11 Jan 1960. *DV* 1 Feb 1963, p. 1, 4. *DV* 22 Mar 1963. *DV* 26 Mar 1963. *Exh* 1 Jul 1959, p. 4602 *FD* 25 Jun 1959, p. 1, 5-19, 25. *Har* 27 Jun 1959, pp. 102-03. *HCN* 16 Jul 1959. *HR* 23 Jan 1942. *HR* 7 Apr 1942. *HR* 16 Aug 1943. *HR* 10 Mar 1953. *HR* 11 Mar 1955. *HR* 31 Jan 1956, p. 1, 19. *HR* 2 Feb 1956. *HR* 12 Dec 1957. *HR* 24 Mar 1958. *HR* 2 Jul 1958. *HR* 28 Jul 1958, p. 1, 3. *HR* 31 Jul 1958, p. 1, 7. *HR* 6 Aug 1958. *HR* 7 Aug 1958, p. 1. *HR* 8 Aug 1958. *HR* 12 Aug 1958. *HR* 13 Aug 1958. *HR* 14 Aug 1958. *HR* 25 Aug 1958, pp. 6-7. *HR* 4 Sep 1958. *HR* 19 Feb 1959. *HR* 22 Feb 1959. *HR* 24 Jun 1959, p. 3. *HR* 20 Apr 1961. *HR* 14 Sep 1962. *HR* 11 Mar 1963. *HR* 26 Mar 1963. *LAEx* 5 Jan 1955. *LAEx* 8 Apr 1958. *LAEx* 23 Apr 1958. *LAEx* 22 Sep 1958. *LAEx* 14 Dec 1958, pp. 10-11. *LAEx* 11 Apr 1959. *LAT* 10 May 1957. *LAT* 7 Mar 1958. *LAT* 8 Apr 1958. *LAT* 3 Jul 1958. *LAT* 28 Jul 1958. *LAT* 5 Aug 1958. *LAT* 19 Oct 1958. *LAT* 2 Mar 1959. *LAT* 5 Apr 1959. *LAT* 11 Apr 1959. *LAT* 5 Jul 1959. *LAT* 16 Jul 1959, p. 2, 29. *LAT* 19 Jan 1993, p. F1, F5. *LAT* 23 Jan 1993. *LAT* 3 Oct 1993. *LAT* 27 Nov 1994. *LATribune* 15 Aug 1958. *Life* 16 Feb 1959, p. 103. *Life* 15 Jun 1959. *LAMirror-News* 2 Jul 1958, p. 1, 10. *LAMirror-News* 31 Jul 1958. *LAMirror-News* 10 Dec 1958. *LAMirror-News* 11 Jul 1959, p. 3. *LAMirror-News* 16 Jul 1959. *MPD* 25 Jun 1959. *MPH* 27 Jun 1959, p. 22. *MPHPD* 11 Jul 1959, p. 333. *New Theatre* Dec 1935, pp. 5-6. *Newsweek* 6 Jul 1959. *NYHT* 19 Nov 1953. *New Yorker* 4 Jul 1959. *New Yorker* 14 Apr 1962. *NYT* 14 Sep 1943. *NYT* 12 May 1957. *NYT* 3 Nov 1957. *NYT* 15 Dec 1957. *NYT* 22 Jun 1958. *NYT* 3 Jul 1958. *NYT* 28 Jul 1958. *NYT* 4 Aug 1958. *NYT* 7 Aug 1958. *NYT* 9 Aug 1958. *NYT* 10 Aug 1958. *NYT* 17 Aug 1958. *NYT* 2 Nov 1958. *NYT* 11 Feb 1959. *NYT* 21 Jun 1959. *NYT* 25 Jun 1959, p. 20. *NYT* 28 Jun 1959. *NYT* 2 Aug 1959. *NYT Magazine* 19 Oct 1958, pp. 34-35. *Redbook* Jul 1959, p. 10. *SatRev* 4 Jul 1959. *Time* 22 Nov 1957. *Time* 2 Dec 1957. *Time* 6 Jul 1959. *Var* 2 Oct 1935. *Var* 25 Nov 1953. *Var* 7 Mar 1956. *Var* 15 May 1957. *Var* 9 Oct 1957. *Var* 6 Nov 1957, p. 1, 8. *Var* 11 Nov 1957. *Var* 13 Aug 1958. *Var* 1 Jul 1959, p. 6. *Var* 27 May 1959. *Var* 2 Aug 1959. *Var* 30 Sep 1959. *Var* 2 Dec 1959. *Var* 1 Mar 1961.

PORO COLLEGE IN MOVING PICTURES (African Americans)

1927; Prod: Pittsburgh, PA showing: 14 Dec 1927. Si; b&w. 7 reels.

African American, Documentary. [*Not viewed*]. The history and activities of Poro College in St. Louis, Missouri are shown, including depictions of the college's beginnings in a cabin in Lovejoy, Illinois and its current palatial home in St. Louis. *African Americans. Poro College (St. Louis, MO).*

Note: Poro College was founded in 1900 by Annie M. Malone, according to an ad for this film. Mrs. Malone was scheduled to speak at a Pittsburgh church showing in connection with graduating exercises. The ad stated that the film depicted "commercial and cultural progress."

PittsC 17 Dec 1927, pt. I, p. 7, pt. II, p. 2.

PORT OF ENTRY see PANIC IN THE STREETS

PORT OF MISSING MEN see HARBOR OF MISSING MEN

LA PORTA DEL DESTINO (Italian language)

1931?; Prod: began mid-Sep 1931 at the Metropolitan Studios in Fort Lee, NJ.. Sd; b&w. Length undetermined. Italian language.

Dir Lewis Maisell. *Photog* Frank Zucker. *Asst cam* Buddy Harris. **Drama?**. [*Not viewed*]. [No information on the plot has been found.]. *Italians.*

Note: Although *FD* notes that the film began production, no information confirming the film's completion and release has been located.

FD 16 Sep 1931, p. 4.

PORTRAIT OF JENNIE (Irish Americans)

Vanguard Film, Inc. *Dist* Selznick Releasing Organization. 22 Apr **1949**; World premiere in Los Angeles: 25 Dec 1948; New York opening: 22 Mar 1949; Prod: late Mar—mid-Apr 1947; mid-Jun—early Oct 1947 at RKO Pathe Studios, NYT [©Vanguard Film, Inc.; 29 Mar 1949; LP2188]. Sd (Western Electric Recording); b&w with Technicolor and sepia seq. 82 or 86 min. PCA cert no. 12700.

[*Exec prod* Cecil Barker]. *Prod* David O. Selznick. *Assoc prod* David Hempstead. *Dir* William Dieterle. [*Asst dir* Arthur Fellows and Sal Scappa, Jr.]. *Scr* Paul Osborn and Peter Berneis. *Adpt* Leonardo Bercovici. *Photog* Joseph August. *Spec eff* Clarence Slifer and [Russell Shearman]. [*Eff ed* Charles Freeman]. [*Process and miniature photog* Paul Eagler]. *Prod des* J. McMillan Johnson. *Assoc* Joseph B. Platt. [*Film ed* Gerard Wilson and Noel Coppleman]. *Prod des* J. McMillan Johnson. *Set dec* Claude Carpenter. *Cost* Lucinda Ballard. *Asst* Anna Hill Johnstone. *Mus score wrt and cond* Dimitri Tiomkin. [*Mus ed* Aubrey Lind]. [*Sd* Don McKay]. *Staff exec* [*Prod mgr*] Argyle Nelson. *Staff exec* [*Tech supv*] James G. Stewart. *Staff exec* [*Film ed*] William Morgan. *Staff exec* Don McKay. *Staff exec* [*Hair stylist*] Larry Germain. *Staff exec* [*Scen asst*] Lydia Schiller. *Staff exec* [*Asst dir*] Arthur Fellows. *Staff exec* [*Unit mgr*] Clem Beauchamp. *Staff exec* Gerard Wilson. *Staff exec* [*Makeup*] Mel Berns. [*Prod mgr* Dewey Starkey]. [*Portrait painted* by Robert Brackman].

Music: Musical score based on "The Maid With the Flaxen Hair" and other themes by Claude Debussy.

Source: Based on the novel *Portrait of Jennie* by Robert Nathan (New York, 1940).

Cast: Jennifer Jones [(*Jennie Appleton*)], Joseph Cotten [(*Eben Adams*)], Ethel Barrymore [(*Miss Spinney*)], Lillian Gish [(*Mother Mary of Mercy*)], Cecil Kellaway [(*Mr. Matthews*)], David Wayne [(*Gus O'Toole, taxi driver*)], Albert Sharpe [(*Mr. Moore, saloon keeper*)], Henry Hull [(*Eke*)], Florence Bates [(*Mrs. Jekes, the landlady*)], Felix Bressart [(*The old doorman*)], Clem Bevans [(*Capt. Catch Cobb*)], Maude Simmons [(*Clara Morgan*)], Esther Somers [(*Mrs. Bunce*)], John Farrell [(*The policeman*)], Robert Dudley [(*An old mariner*)].

Fantasy. [*Print viewed*]. In the winter of 1934, artist Eben Adam's work is rejected by art dealers Matthews and Spinney. Depressed, Eben goes to Central Park, where he sits down on a bench next to an object wrapped in newspaper. When he begins to open it, Eben hears a young girl named Jennie Appleton call out that it is hers. Jennie, who is dressed in turn-of-the-century clothes, claims that her parents are actors at a vaudeville house called Hammerstein's Victoria, but Eben says that theater was torn down decades earlier. She begins examining his paintings and becomes frightened by one depicting a lighthouse on a rocky point off Cape Cod. Jennie tells Eben that she must leave, so he turns to get her package for her. When he turns back a moment later, however, Jennie is gone. Inside his room at a boardinghouse, Eben opens the package, which contains Jennie's silk scarf. Eben then begins his portrait of Jennie, and the next day, while dining at a restaurant, tells his taxi driver friend, Gus O'Toole, about her. Eben takes out the scarf to show Gus and notices an advertisement for Jennie's parents' act on the newspaper, which is dated 1910. Later, Gus introduces Eben to restaurant's Irish American owner, Mr. Moore, and convinces him to hire Eben to paint a mural of Irish politician "Mic" Collins above the bar, which Gus insists will attract patriotic Irish customers. Days later, Eben again encounters Jennie in the park and is surprised to see that she is already a teenager. When Eben asks to meet her parents, Jennie agrees to return to the park with them, but does not. Eben decides to look for her in Times Square. There, he finds the place where Hammerstein's had been, and the guard at the new building, Pete, who had also worked for Hammerstein's, tells Eben to see a black woman named Clara Morgan. Clara, who knew the Appletons well, shows him photographs of Jennie and tells him that Jennie's parents were killed one night when their high-wire broke during a performance. Afterward, Jennie was sent to live at a convent. That evening, Eben goes back to the park where a sobbing Jennie tells him about her parents' death, which she

maintains occurred earlier in the evening. Later, Moore holds a big party to celebrate the unveiling of the Collins mural. When Jennie returns again, she has matured into a beautiful college student. Soon after Eben finishes the portrait, Jennie leaves, but tells him that they will meet again. After she is gone, Eben goes to the convent where she lived and learns that Jennie drowned years ago after her boat was lost in a tidal wave off Cape Cod. Hoping to rescue her across time, Eben rents a boat and rows out to the spot near the lighthouse where Jennie drowned. Suddenly a storm erupts, and Eben's boat is smashed against the rocks below the lighthouse. After calling out Jennie's name, Eben sees her boat tossing in the waves and rushes to help her onto the rocks. The tide is too strong though, and she is swept away. *Ghosts. Love. Painters (Of paintings). Paintings. Adolescents. Advertisements. African Americans. Art dealers. Bars. Boardinghouses. Boats. Cape Cod (MA). Convents. Drowning. Guards. Irish Americans. Lighthouses. New York City–Central Park. Newspapers. Parties. Photographs. Scarves. Tidal waves. Winter.*

Note: The working title of this film was *Tidal Wave.* The opening credits include a written acknowledgement to Bernard Herrmann, Robert Brackman and the Metropolitan Museum of Art. The picture opens with an offscreen narrator (uncredited), who introduces the story. The narration is then taken over by Joseph Cotten as "Eben Adams," who periodically provides a voiceover that bridges the various appearances of "Jennie." A number of scenes open with shots which resemble a tapestry, an effect which was achieved through optical printing. Among the themes heard in the film are some from Debussy's "Afternoon of a Faun." The picture was shot on location in New York City, parts of New England and Boston's Graves End Lighthouse. News items reported that *Portrait of Jennie* was the first feature to be shot at RKO's newly constructed New York studios. According to a 9 Mar 1949 *HR* news item, New York and Los Angeles screenings of the film featured a "Cycloramic screen together with Multi-sound" during the storm sequences. *DV* commented that the screen "opens up to thrice normal size for a magnificently lensed hurricane; a spellbinding score by Dimitri Tiomkin; four tints for various sequences—black-and-white during early footage, green for the storm, sepiatone for the lull that follows, and a Technicolor finale." The film's special effects crew received an Academy Award for their efforts on the film, and Joseph August, who died during the film's production, was nominated for Best Cinematographer (b&w). Lee Garmes photographed the few remaining scenes. Joseph Cotten was awarded the Venice Film Festival Best Actor of the Year Award for his portrayal of "Eben Adams."

Modern sources add the following production credits: *Ed asst* Barbara Keon; *2d asst dir* Harry Anderson; *Scr clerk* Charlsie Bryant; *Research* Ann Harris; *Cast dir* Ruth Burch; *Cam op* Curt Fetters; *Stills* John Miehle; *Ward supv* Frank Beetson; *Asst* Ann Peck; *Const supv* Harold Fenton; *Chief elec* Ed Harman; *Head grip* Morris Rosen; *Props* Arden Cripe; *Draperies* Harry Apperson; *Eff projection* Robert Hansard; *Spec eff cam* Harry Wolf; *Asst cam* Joe Kelly; *Skating supv* Skippy Baxter; *Stills* John Miehle. As indicated by *HR* production charts, filming on *Portrait of Jennie* was halted in mid-Apr 1947. Modern sources attribute the five-week delay in production to David O. Selznick's dissatisfaction with "the script, the cost, the location sites and the way Jennifer Jones photographed." He then hired a new writer to rework the script while production was shut down. A radio adaptation of the film was broadcast on *Lux Radio Theatre* on 31 Oct 1949 and featured Joseph Cotten and Anne Baxter in the title role. According to a *Var* news item, the film was acquired for redistribution in Dec 1973. Nat King Cole's 1949 hit, "Portrait of Jennie," music by J. Russell Robinson and lyrics by Gordon Burdge, was not heard in the film. According to modern sources, Gregory Peck and Laurence Olivier were considered for the role of Eben Adams.

Box 1 Jan 1949. *DV* 24 Dec 1948, p. 3. *FD* 30 Dec 1948, p. 6. *HR* 24 Dec 1948, p. 3, 9. *HR* 9 Mar 1949, p. 4. *HR* 29 Mar 1949, p. 8. *HR* 7 Sep 1949, p. 9. *MPHPD* 24 Apr 1948, p. 4139. *MPHPD* 1 Jan 1949, p. 4441. *NYT* 30 Mar 1949, p. 31. *Var* 29 Dec 1948, p. 6. *Var* 12 Dec 1973. *Var* 10 Apr 1974.

POTASH AND PERLMUTTER (Jewish Americans)
Goldwyn Pictures Corp. *Dist* Associated First National Pictures. 16 Sep **1923** [©Samuel Goldwyn; 19 Sep 1923; LP19413]. Si; b&w. 8 reels, 7,636 ft.

Pres Samuel Goldwyn. *Dir* Clarence Badger. *Scen* Frances Marion. *Photog* Rudolph Berquist. *Art dir* William B. Ihnen. *Art titles* Oscar C. Buchheister. *Cost* Madame Frances, Madame Stein, Madame Blaine and Evelyn McHorter. *Prod mgr* Charles J. Hunt.

Source: Based on the play *Potash and Perlmutter* by Montague Glass and Charles Klein (New York, 16 Aug 1913).

Cast: Alexander Carr (*Morris Perlmutter*), Barney Bernard (*Abe Potash*), Vera Gordon (*Rosie Potash*), Martha Mansfield (*The Head Model*), Ben Lyon (*Boris Andrieff*), Edward Durand (*Feldman*), Hope Sutherland (*Irma Potash*), De Sacia Mooers (*Ruth Goldman*), Jerry Devine (*The Office Boy*), Lee Kohlmar (*Pasinsky*), Leo Donnelly (*The Wide-Awake Salesman*), Tiller Girls (*Cabaret dancers*).

Comedy. Two Jewish Americans, Abe Potash and Morris Perlmutter, become partners in the clothing business. They hire Andrieff, a poor

Russian violinist, as a fitter. Andrieff falls in love with Irma Potash, to the disappointment of Abe, who had hoped to have his daughter marry Feldman, a wealthy lawyer. Andrieff is arrested following the shooting on the premises of a labor agitator, but the man recovers and Andrieff is vindicated. He marries Irma with parental blessing. *Clothing industry. Jews. Labor agitators. Lawyers. Partnership. Violinists.*
FD 16 Sep 1923. *MPW* 22 Sep 1923. *NYT* 24 Sep 1923, p. 5. *Var* 13 Sep 1923, p. 28.

POVERO CUORE *see* **ALMA DE GAUCHO**

THE POWER OF LIFE (Yiddish language)
Lynn Productions, Inc. *Dist* Lynn Productions, Inc. **1938.** Sd (Variray Blue Seal Recording); b&w. 9 reels, 8,422 ft. 92 min. Yiddish language with English subtitles.

Prod Henry Lynn. *Dir* Henry Lynn. *Scr* Henry Stuart. *Photog* J. Burgi Contner and Charles Levine. *Art dir* Morris Strassberg. *Ed* Jack Kemp. *Mus dir* Jack Stillman. *Sd eng* Nelson Minnesly [sic]. *Make-up artist* Ira Senz. *Laboratory supv* Paul A. Guffanti.

Song(s): lyrics by Wm. Mercur.

Source: Based on the play *The Power of Life* by Isidore Zolotarefsky (production undetermined).

Cast: MICHAL MICHALESKO [(*Nathan Rabinowitz*)], Morris Strassberg [(*Sam Schindler*)], Charlotte Goldstein [(*Leah Rabinowitz*)], Abraham Lax [(*Kuzlik*)], Bertha Hart [(*Grandma*)], Sam Josephson, Frank Schechtman [(*Nathan's sons*)], Saul Josephson, Mike Wilensky, M. B. Samuylow.

Yiddish, Domestic, Melodrama, with songs. [*Print viewed*]. Nathan Rabinowitz, a bookkeeper for Feinberg Dress Company, devotes his spare time to his inventions. Nathan is offered $3,000 for an invention, and he promises to give an answer by the next day. When he learns that Sam Schindler, his daughter Leah's fiancé, needs $500 to avoid going to jail for embezzling money from the bank where he works, Nathan visits Sam's father, who refuses to loan Sam the money. Nathan argues that the power of life comes through finding happiness in one's children's lives and that parents must not forget their obligations to their children; however, Schindler replies that Sam stole from his account and that few children love their parents. He contends, in fact, that children are the enemies of their parents. Later that night, Feinberg gives Nathan $2,000 in cash and a $3,000 check to deposit because he must leave town to be with his dying father. Nathan then learns that his son Julius has decided to give up his law studies and leave town. After the prospective buyer of the invention calls and promises to close the deal the next day, Nathan hears a scream and finds Leah, who has tried to poison herself, struggling with her grandmother. Nathan gets $1,000 of the company's money, which he tells his family the buyer left as an option, and gives up $500 to Leah for Sam, $300 to Julius for tuition, and $200 so that his young son Maxie, who is sick, could be taken to the country. Two years later, a new bookkeeper has found out about the stolen $1,000. At Leah's wedding, when Feinberg confronts Nathan, Nathan explains that because the invention was never sold, he has not been able to pay back the money. Feinberg, who is interested in Leah, tells Nathan that she can save him, but Nathan, who values her happiness more than his own freedom, accepts the fact that he will go to prison. Nathan is released three years later, but Sam, now a partner in his father's firm, does not want Nathan to live with him and Leah. Nathan now agrees with Schindler's view of children. Julius, who is a lawyer, is loathe to accept Nathan because his wife is sick. Nathan cannot find work, and when Maxie, who coughs up blood, needs money for medicine, Nathan gets it from an old friend. Five years later, Maxie has died and Nathan has disappeared. Grandma invites the family to meet a Mr. Guderman from Los Angeles, who has word of Nathan. Sam, who now is considerate, offers to put up Nathan when his father tells him that Guderman said that Nathan, destitute and sick, has been staying in old men's homes. Julius argues that he wants Nathan to stay with him, and Schindler points out that they at last appreciate the value of parents. Nathan himself then appears well-dressed, having become wealthy from his invention, and Julius and Leah are ashamed. Sam asks Nathan's forgiveness, and Nathan explains that this is the power of life—no matter how much he has suffered, he is ready to forgive his children and forget. *Bookkeepers. Family life. Fathers and daughters. Inventors. Jews. Moral reformation. Attempted suicide. Dressmakers. Embezzlement. Ex-convicts. Lawyers. Prisons. Weddings.*

Note: The Yiddish title of this film was *Di Kraft fun Lebn.* According to *FD,* most of the cast was from the Yiddish Art Theater Group. Sound engineer Nelson Minnerly's name is spelled incorrectly in the onscreen credits. Although no release date has been located, the film was approved for showing in New York State on 19 Apr 1938 and was reviewed by *FD* on 9 May 1938. This film was re-released by Cinema Service Corp.

FD 9 May 1938, p. 24.

THE POWER OF LOVE (Latino)
Perfect Pictures. **1922**; Los Angeles premiere: 27 Sep 1922. Si; b&w. 5 reels, 4,600 ft.
Dir Nat Deverich. *Photog* Harry Fairall.
Cast: Elliott Sparling (*Terry O'Neil*), Barbara Bedford (*Maria Almeda*), Noah Beery (*Don Almeda*), Aileen Manning (*Ysabel Almeda*), Albert Prisco (*Don Alvarez*), John Herdman (*The Old Padre*).
Melodrama. "Because of financial reverses Don Almeda offers his daughter, Maria, to Don Alvarez, though she does not love him. Terry O'Neill arrives at the Southern California settlement in which the Almedas live, and is slightly wounded when Alvarez's henchmen seek to rob him. He is found by Maria, to whom he loses his heart. Just before the wedding, O'Neill waylays Alvarez ... and takes his place at a fiesta. Alvarez appears and denounces him. Later, Alvarez ... slays the padre with O'Neill's knife. Denouncing O'Neill as the murderer, Alvarez tries to shoot him, but wounds Maria, who throws herself in front of him. Later, she succeeds in proving that Alvarez is the thief and murderer, and everything ends happily for Maria and O'Neill." (*MPW* 21 Oct 1922, p. 704.). *California. Clergy. Finance–Personal. Latino. Murder. Robbery.*
Note: Employs the Fairall process of producing stereoscopic effects.
MPW 21 Oct 1922.

THE PRAIRIE (Jewish Americans, Native Americans, Dakota)
Zenith Pictures, Inc.; An Edward F. Finney Production. *Dist* Screen Guild Productions, Inc. 10 Nov **1949**; New York opening: 17 Aug 1948; Los Angeles opening: 11 Oct 1949; Prod: Aug 1947 at Motion Picture Center Studios [©Zenith Pictures, Inc.; 29 May 1948; LP1715]. Sd (RCA Sound System); b&w. 5,957 ft. 65-67 min. PCA cert no. 12686.
Exec prod Edward F. Finney. *Prod* George Moskov. *Dir* Frank Wisbar. *Asst dir* Ben Kadish. *Scr* Arthur St. Claire. *Dir of photog* James S. Brown. [*Cam op* Harvey Gould]. [*Stills* M. B. Paul]. *Photog eff* Ray Mercer. *Spec eff* Robert L. Clark. *Prod des* F. Paul Sylos. *Art dir* Perry Smith. *Film ed* Douglas Bagier. *Set landscaping* Louis Honig. *Set dec* Earl B. Wooden. *Master of props* George Bahr. *Mus dir and score* Alexander Steinert. *Sd* Ferol M. Redd. *Makeup artist* Robert M. Cowan. [*Hair stylist* Merle Reeves]. *Lighting tech* William D. King. *Dir of publicity* Peter O'Crotty. *Asst to prod* Sidney Smith. [*Prod mgr* Leon Chooluck]. [*Scr supv* Tessie Wise]. [*Grip* Fred Russell].
Source: Based on the novel *The Prairie; A Tale* by James Fenimore Cooper (New York, 1827).
Cast: Lenore Aubert [(*Ellen Wade*)], Alan Baxter [(*Paul Hover*)], Russ Vincent [(*Abiram White*)], Jack Mitchum [(*Asa Bush*)], Charles Evans [(*Ishmael Bush*)], Edna Holland [(*Esther Bush*)], Chief Thundercloud [(*Eagle Feather*)], Fred Coby [(*Abner Bush*)], Bill Murphy [(*Jess Bush*)], David Gerber [(*Gabe Bush*)], Don Lynch [(*Enoch Bush*)], George Morrell [(*Luke*)], Chief Yowlachie [(*Matoreeh*)], Jay Silverheels [(*Running Deer*)], Beth Taylor [(*Annie Morris*)], [Frank Hemingway (*Narrator*)].
Rural, Drama. [*Print viewed*]. In 1803, Ishmael Bush, his wife Esther, her brother Abiram White and the couple's sons, Asa, Abner, Gabe, Jess and Enoch, join a group of homesteaders for the journey into an unsettled area of the Louisiana Purchase. After traveling some distance, the group stops for the evening. In the middle of the night, the homesteaders are awakened by the sound of thundering hooves, after which a herd of buffalo stampedes through their small camp, trampling to death the entire family of pretty Ellen Wade. Later, a tribe of Sioux Indians tries to kidnap Ellen, but Abiram and Asa frighten them away. Dazzled by Ellen's charms, Abiram persuades Ishmael to accept her as part of the family for the remainder of the journey. Later, Asa, who is also attracted to Ellen, threatens to tell her about Abiram's fugitive status. The next morning, the family meets a cartographer named Paul Hover, who tells them about a nearby creek. Paul leads them to the creek, where the family stops to rest. Later, Abiram is chosen to guard the wagons, while the others are asleep. Abiram becomes distracted, however, and the Indians creep up on the

family, steal their horses and livestock, and kidnap Paul and Ellen. After Paul and Ellen escape from the Indians, they return to the camp, where the family agrees to follow Paul to a defensible knoll about six miles away. With no animals to pull their wagons, the family must haul them, inch by inch, themselves. Days later they reach the knoll, where Paul loads his musket. Despite Ellen's pleas that he take her away from the Bushes, Paul leaves to meet his friend, a Pawnee Indian named Eagle Feather. Later, Eagle Feather suggests that if Paul loves Ellen, he should return for her. When he returns to the knoll, however, Paul is fired upon by the jealous Asa and Abiram, who have realized that Ellen loves Paul. Later, Asa proposes marriage to Ellen, and she reminds him that Ishmael, who resents having to care for her, would never agree. Later, Abiram tries to force himself on Ellen and inadvertently knocks her over. The next morning, the family finds Asa's corpse, which has been shot in the back, lying on the ground next to the surveyor scale that Asa had earlier stolen from Paul. Ishmael accuses Paul of the murder, so he leaves, but later returns to rescue Ellen. Suddenly, several Sioux braves kidnap them and take them to their village. Abiram, who witnessed the attack, tells Ishmael about it, and the Bush men attack the Indians at their village. After they free Paul and Ellen, the Bushes takes them back to the knoll so that they can hang Paul themselves. There, as Ishmael drapes a noose from a tree, a conscience-stricken Abiram confesses to his nephew's murder. Despite Abiram's pleas for mercy, Ishmael orders him to remain on the knoll until the rest of the family has left the area. Now alone, a terrified Abiram hallucinates that Esther and Ishmael have returned to curse and condemn him, after which he staggers into the noose and hangs himself. *Cartographers. Family relationships. Homesteaders. Jews. Louisiana Purchase. Romantic rivalry. Bison, American. Brothers. Camps. Cattle. Corpses. Dakota Indians. False accusations. Firearms. Fugitives. Guilt. Gunshot wounds. Hallucinations. Horses. Kidnapping. Lynching. Pawnee Indians. Rivers. United States–History–19th century. Unrequited love. Villages. Wagon trains.*
Note: The film opens with spoken, offscreen narration. A news item in *LAEx* dated 4 May 1949 indicated that *The Prairie* was scheduled to be produced by Monogram Studios. According to a 31 Jul 1947 *HR* news item, George Spelvin was to appear in the cast. The same publication noted on 5 Aug 1947 that Arthur St. Claire received permission to drive a herd of 30 buffalo, shipped from Alberta, Canada, from the freight yards near Burbank to Motion Picture Center, where the film was shot. *The Prairie* was the first production of Zenith Pictures, Inc.
Box 29 Oct 1949. *DV* 12 Oct 1949, p. 3. *Exh* 1 Sep 1948. *HR* 22 Jul 1947, p. 4. *HR* 31 Jul 1947, p. 9. *HR* 1 Aug 1947, p. 15. *HR* 5 Aug 1947, p. 3. *HR* 15 Aug 1947, p. 13. *HR* 12 Oct 1949, p. 3. *LAEx* 4 May 1949. *Var* 25 Aug 1948, p. 8.

PRAIRIE PIONEERS (Latino)
Republic Pictures Corp. *Dist* Republic Pictures Corp. 16 Feb **1941**; Prod: began 2 Jan 1941 [©Republic Pictures, Inc.; 16 Feb 1941; LP10304]. Sd (RCA Sound System); b&w. 6 reels, 5,122 ft. 58 min. Passed by the National Board of Review. PCA cert no. 7028.
Series: The Three Mesquiteers.
Assoc prod Louis Gray. *Dir* Lester Orlebeck. [*Asst dir* Harry Knight]. *Scr* Barry Shipman. *Orig idea* Karl Brown. *Photog* Ernest Miller. *Film ed* Ray Snyder. *Mus score* Cy Feuer. Al Wilson.
Song(s): "La cucaracha," Mexican folk song; "Chiapanecas" and "Jarabe (Hat Dance)," traditional.
Cast: Robert Livingston (*"Stony" Brooke*), Bob Steele (*"Tucson" Smith*), Rufe Davis (*"Lullaby" Joslin*), Esther Estrella [(*Dolores Ortega*)], Robert Kellard [(*Roberto Ortega*)], Guy D'Ennery [(*Don Miguel Ortega*)], Davison Clark [(*Carlos Montoya*)], Jack Ingram [(*Wade*)], Ken McDonald [(*Fields*)], Lee Shumway [(*Nelson*)], Mary MacLaren [(*Martha Nelson*)], Yakima Canutt [(*Morrison*)], Jack Kirk [(*Al*)].
Western, with songs. [*Print viewed*]. Soon after the Mexican-American War and California's admission to the United States, "Stony" Brooke, "Tucson" Smith and "Lullaby" Joslin, friends known as The Three Mesquiteers, lead a group of settlers to Provedencia Valley in California. Meanwhile, Don Miguel Ortega and his children, Roberto and Dolores, discuss with their friend, Carlos Montoya, the problems arising from the "Americanos" invading Spanish-owned ranches. Telling Don Miguel that he will be forced out by the settlers, Montoya tries to persuade him to sell his large ranch, but Don Miguel refuses. Unknown to the Ortegas, Montoya is working with hydraulic gold mine owner Fields, who wants to strip-mine their land. Upon hearing that some Americans have entered the valley, Roberto and his vaqueros investigate and become embroiled in an argument with the

four settlers, who refuse to believe that they are encroaching on the Ortega ranch. As the argument turns violent, it is broken up by the Mesquiteers, who are riding by. Stony blames the vaqueros, but Tucson, who has been friends with Roberto since childhood, believes his side of the story. While Don Miquel is inviting everyone to put aside their differences and come to a fiesta at the hacienda the next evening, Carlos plots with disgruntled setters Morrison and Wade to fuel the fire between the Spaniards and the setters and thereby obtain the Ortegas' land. Just before the fiesta, Roberto receives a note, allegedly from Tucson, asking him to come to the settlers' camp. When Roberto goes to the camp, he is ambushed by Morrison and Wade. The gang then puts on Spanish outfits and attacks two sentries while destroying the settlers' camp. Wade goes to the hacienda and tells the others of the attack, and when they rush to the site, they find Roberto in a daze. Wade shoots Nelson, one of Roberto's pursuers, and the crime is blamed on Roberto, but Tucson, believing his claims about the note and ambush, helps him escape from the mob. Soon after, Wade stirs up the settlers into attacking Don Miguel, but Stony saves the old man, who suffers a nervous collapse. Stony convinces Dolores to tell him Roberto's hiding place so that he can be brought back to comfort their father, but when Montoya learns what Dolores has done, he sends word to Army Captain Blake to follow Stony. Roberto is arrested and he, Tucson and Dolores mistakenly blame Stony for his capture. After Roberto is tried and convicted, Stony and Tucson become suspicious of Montoya and soon uncover his schemes with Fields. The two friends patch up their differences, and with Lullaby's help, set out to find the necessary evidence to prove Roberto's innocence before he is shot by a firing squad and Don Miguel sells his land to Montoya. The Mesquiteers find the disguises used by Wade and the others at the mine headquarters, and after a shootout with the gang, Stony and Tucson take Wade to town just as Roberto is about to be executed. Wade confesses that he killed Nelson and implicates Montoya and Fields in the affair. Lullaby and Tucson round up the two men, after which the Mesquiteers receive the Ortegas' thanks. Cowboys. Frame-ups. Land rights. Settlers. Spaniards. California–History–1850-1950. Dancers. Disguise. Escapes. Family relationships. Fiestas. Gunfights. Hydraulic mining. Murder.

Note: The opening title card to the film reads "Republic Pictures presents The Three Mesquiteers in Prairie Pioneers," followed by pictures of Robert Livingston, Bob Steele and Rufe Davis with their names and character names superimposed. According to a HR news item, Eddie Cherkose was signed to write "special material and lyrics for Rufe Davis." His contribution to the completed film has not been confirmed, however. Modern sources include the following actors in the cast: Wheaton Chambers, Carleton Young, Frank Ellis, Cactus Mack, Curley Dresden, Frank McCarroll, Ray Henderson, Tom Smith, Bob Burns, Chuck Baldra, Dan White, Pascale Perry and Jim Corey. For additional information about the series, consult the Series Index and see the entry for The Three Mesquiteers in AFI Catalog of Feature Films, 1931-40, F3.4617.

Box 1 Mar 1941. FD 24 Feb 1941, p. 5. HR 2 Jan 1941, p. 2. HR 3 Jan 1941, pp. 17-18. HR 10 Jan 1941, p. 7. MPH 1 Mar 1941, p. 41. MPHPD 25 Jan 1941, p. 47. Var 26 Feb 1941, p. 18.

PRAIRIE SCHOONERS (Native Americans, Dakota)

Columbia Pictures Corp. Dist Columbia Pictures Corp. 30 Sep **1940**; Prod: 26 Jul–2 Aug 1940 [©Columbia Pictures Corp.; 11 Oct 1940; LP9966]. Sd; b&w. 6 reels. 58 min. PCA cert no. 6659.

Series: Wild Bill Hickok.

[Prod Leon Barsha]. [Exec prod Irving Briskin]. Dir Sam Nelson. [Asst dir Thomas Flood]. Orig scr Robert Lee Johnson and Fred Myton. Dir of photog George Meehan. Film ed Al Clark.

Source: Based on the short story "Into the Crimson West" by George Cory Franklin in Western Story Magazine (13 Sep 1930).

Cast: Bill Elliott (Wild Bill Hickok), Evelyn Young (Virginia Benton), Dub Taylor (Cannonball), Kenneth Harlan (Dalton Stull), Ray Teal (Wolf Tanner), Bob Burns (Jim Gibbs), Netta Packer (Cora Gibbs), Richard Fiske (Adams), Edmund Cobb (Rusty), Jim Thorpe (Chief Sanche), [Sammy Stein (Dude Getter)], [Ned Glass (Skinny Hutch)], [Lucien Maxell (Indian boy)].

Western. Virginia Benton and her foreman, Cannonball, are attempting to stop a group of farmers from lynching Dalton Stull, who is taking advantage of a drought in Kansas to foreclose on loans, when their old friend, Wild Bill Hickok, drifts by. Bill agrees to represent them in peaceful negotiations, but when he fails to affect Stull's position, he suggests that the farmers pay off their debt on their equipment and livestock and move to Colorado. Virginia shares her savings and joins the wagon train. Stull and his partner, Wolf Tanner, believe that the group's destination may jeopardize their lucrative fur

business, so they ride ahead, taking guns to the Sioux. They attack the settlers, and Stull takes Virginia hostage. At the Indian camp, Bill pleads in vain for the farmers' rights, but Cannonball recognizes Tanner and exposes him as the man who led the Sioux against the people. Chief Sanche realizes that Stull and Tanner are their enemies, and the Indians allow the farmers to cross peacefully to Colorado. Although Bill says that he is considering a homestead, Virginia knows he will not give up his wanderlust. Dakota Indians. Farmers. Fur traders. Wagon trains. Colorado. Debt. Droughts. Wild Bill Hickok. Hostages. Kansas. Lynching. Tribal chiefs.

Note: The working title of this film was Into the Crimson West. Bill Elliott first appeared as Hickok in the 1938 Columbia serial The Great Adventures of Wild Bill Hickok, from which he adopted the sobriquet "Wild Bill." In 1940, Columbia inaugurated a feature-length series of Wild Bill Hickok pictures, beginning with Prairie Schooners. The series, which does not accurately portray the historical facts of Hickok's life, consisted of eight films and ended with the 1942 picture Prairie Gunsmoke. All films in the series starred Elliott as Hickok and were produced by Leon Barhsa. In the first films, Dub Taylor played Hickok's sidekick, "Cannonball." Taylor was replaced by Frank Mitchell in the 1942 films Prairie Gunsmoke and The Devil's Trail. In the 1941 picture King of Dodge City, Tex Ritter joined the ensemble. Modern sources add Merrill McCormack and George Morrell to the cast. For more information about the real Hickok, please see the entry above for The Plainsman.

FD 11 Nov 1940, p. 5. HR 26 Jul 1940, pp. 8-9. Var 13 Nov 1940, p. 16.

PRAIRIE THUNDER (Native Americans, Kiowa)

Warner Bros. Pictures, Inc.; A First National Picture. Dist Warner Bros. Pictures, Inc. 11 Sep **1937** [©Warner Bros. Pictues, Inc.; 28 Jul 1937; LP7379]. Sd; b&w. 6 reels. 54 min. PCA cert no. 3535.

[Prod Bryan Foy]. [Exec prod Jack L. Warner and Hal B. Wallis]. [Assoc prod Gordon Hollingshead]. Dir B. Reeves Eason. [Asst dir William Kissell]. Orig scr Ed. Earl Repp. Photog Ted McCord. Art dir Ted Smith. Film ed Harold McLernon. Sd Dolph Thomas.

Song(s): "Sunset on the Rainbow Trail," "Over the Trail Again," "Give Me a Song" and "The Prairie Is My Home," composer unknown.

Cast: Dick Foran (Rod Farrell), Ellen Clancy (Joan Temple), Smoke the Wonder Horse, Frank Orth (Wichita), Wilfred Lucas (Nate Temple), Albert J. Smith ([Keo] Lynch), Yakima Canutt ([Chief] High Wolf), George Chesebro (Matson), Slim Whitaker [(Blacky)], J. P. McGowan [(Colonel Stanton)], John Harron [(Lieutenant Adams)], Jack Mower [(Foreman)], Henry Otho [(Chris)], Paul Panzer [(Jed)].

Western, with songs. [Print viewed]. United States Army scout Rod Farrell and his sidekick Wichita are sent to investigate Kiowa Indians who are interfering with the building of a telegraph line in the West. On the way to the Indian camp, Rod discovers horse shoe tracks, indicating a white man's horse. Rod questions Chief High Wolf, who explains his tribe is against the telegraph and the railroad because they will bring soldiers and frighten the buffalo. Trader Keo Lynch encourages this belief because without the railroad, he has a monopoly on trade goods brought into the area. Lynch has been supplying the Indians with guns and ammunition, and Rod follows him from the camp, capturing the gang. Rod brings the gang into town to hold them until the cavalry arrives in town to escort them back to the stockade. One of Lynch's men sees the arrest and summons the Indians to their rescue. They release Lynch's gang and capture Rod and his girl friend, Joan Temple. Wichita witnesses the capture and, when Lynch sends the Indians to break the telegraph line, helps Rod escape from the Indian camp. The cavalry finally returns to their base, arriving just in time to rescue the telegraph workers from an Indian attack. Rod notices Lynch escape and captures him personally. When the railroad comes to town, Rod gets a Congressional medal and is made a colonel. Duplicity. Kiowa Indians. Traders. United States. Army. Cavalry. Disguise. Escapes. Firearms. Gunfights. Jailbreaks. Railroads. Rescues. Telegraph.

MPD 3 Dec 1937, p. 7. Var 1 Dec 1937, p. 29.

THE PRAIRIE WIFE (Swedish Americans)

Eastern Productions, Inc. Dist Metro-Goldwyn Distributing Corp. 23 Feb **1925** [©Eastern Productions, Inc.; 9 Mar 1925; LP21217]. Si; b&w. 7 reels, 6,487 ft.

Dir Hugo Ballin. Asst dir James Chapin. Story Arthur Stringer. Cont Hugo Ballin. Titles Katherine Hilliker and H. H. Caldwell. Photog James Diamond. Film ed Katherine Hilliker and H. H. Caldwell.

Cast: Dorothy Devore (Chaddie Green), Herbert Rawlinson (Duncan MacKail), Gibson Gowland (Ollie), Leslie Stuart (Percy), Frances Prim (Olga), Boris Karloff (Diego), Erich von Ritzau (Doctor), Rupert Franklin (Rufus Green).

Western. While in Europe, Chaddie Green, a society girl, discovers that she has been left penniless. She returns to the United States and meets Duncan MacKail, who is equally broke though he owns grainland in the West. Duncan and Chaddie are married and go west to homestead. Duncan hires Ollie, a Swedish caretaker, who frightens Chaddie. When business takes Duncan away, Chaddie goes to take care of Percy Woodhouse, an Englishman who has become ill at his place fifteen miles away. Her horse runs away, and she is forced to spend the night there. She sleeps under a wagon, but Duncan is nevertheless angry and jealous. Chaddie moves Percy to her house in order to nurse him back to health and to use his presence to restrain the violent Ollie. Duncan leaves in a fit of jealousy, but he soon returns with Olga, a servant, as a peace offering. Percy and Olga fall in love. Ollie hangs himself, leaving a note confessing to murderous instincts. Chaddie has a baby, and she and Duncan find happiness and prosperity in their prairie home. *Caretakers. English. Homesteaders. Jealousy. Suicide. Swedish Americans.*

FD 10 May 1925. *MPW* 16 May 1925.

EL PRECIO DE UN BESO (Spanish language)

Fox Film Corp. *Dist* Fox Film Corp. Jul **1930**; San Antonio, TX opening: 26 Jul 1930; Prod: Apr 1930. Sd (Western Electric System); b&w. 8 or 9 reels. 71 min. Passed by the National Board of Review. Spanish language.

Presenta [*Pres*] William Fox. *Bajo la supervisión editorial de* [*Supv*] John Stone. *Dirección* [*Dir*] James Tinling. *Adaptación cinematográfica* [*Scr*] Dudley Nichols. *Argumento de* [*Story*] Adolph Paul. *Versión española de* [*Spanish version*] Francisco Moré de la Torre. *Fotografía de* [*Photog*] Ross Fisher. *Escenografía* [*Art dir*] Stephen Goosson. *Editor de la película* [*Film ed*] Louis Loeffler. *Vestuario de* [*Ward*] Sophie Wachner. *Sonido* [*Sd*] A. C. Ward.

Song(s): "¿En dónde estás?" music by Troy Sanders, lyrics by José Mojica; "Florero español," music by Troy Sanders and José Mojica, lyrics by José Mojica; "Un beso loco," music by José Mojica, lyrics by José Mojica and Troy Sanders; "Fiesta," music and lyrics by Troy Sanders and José Mojica; "Mono en el cordel," music by James Hanley, lyrics by Joseph McCarthy, Spanish lyrics by José Mojica; "Solo tú para mi," music by Dave Stamper, lyrics by Clare Kummer, Spanish lyrics by José Mojica; "In My Arms" and "I Am Free," music and lyrics by William Kernell, Spanish lyrics by José Mojica; "Once in a While," music by Cecil Arnold and Dave Stamper, lyrics by Clare Kummer, Spanish lyrics by José Mojica.

Source: Based on the play *Lola Montez, the Spanish Dancer* by Adolf Paul (Germany, 1917).

Cast: José Mojica [(*José Savedra*)], Mona Maris [(*Rosario Montes*)], Antonio Moreno [(*Estrada*)], Tomas Patricola [(*Paco*)], [Fred Malatesta], [Juan Torena], [Carlos Villarías], [Enrique Acosta], [Martín Garralaga], [Eumenio Blanco].

Romance, Musical. [*Not viewed*]. Estrada, the chief government official of the region, has put a price on the head of José Savedra for causing the local people to rebel against his tax collectors. Dancer Rosario Montes also thinks that the tax levied against her "Fandango Café" is excessive and is not inclined to pay. With typical bravura, José posts notices all over the town that, on his next visit to the café, he will kiss Rosario on the lips. With Estrada and the local police present, the intrepid joker, disguised as a waiter, fulfills his boast. Realizing that there is a relationship between José and Rosario, Estrada writes a note to José in Rosario's name, arranging a rendezvous at her house, and arrests him when he keeps the appointment. When Rosario discovers Estrada's trick, she pretends to dislike José and obtains permission from Estrada to repay the affront of José's kiss with her own traitor's kiss. However, Rosario takes advantage of her visit to José's cell to pass him a pistol, which he uses to secure his freedom. As Rosario and José escape on horseback, the governor of the territory arrests Estrada, charging him with abuse of power. *Dancers. Outlaws. Political corruption. Taxation. Cafés. Jails. Kisses. Romance. Ruses. Territorial governors. Waiters.*

Note: This was a Spanish version of the 1930 film *One Mad Kiss* (see *AFI Catalog of Feature Films, 1921-30*; F2.4002), which was filmed in late 1929 and directed by Marcel Silver. According to documents in the Twentieth Century-Fox Records of the Legal Department and the Twentieth Century-Fox Produced Scripts Collection at the UCLA Arts—Special Collections Library, the studio was apparently unhappy with Silver's version and assigned James Tinling to reshoot several sequences, in addition to preparing a version in Spanish. A private preview of *El precio de un beso* was held at the Los Angeles Fox-Criterion on 31 May 1930. The film opened in San Antonio, Texas, under the

title *Un beso apasionado*, in New York as *Un beso de pasión* and in Los Angeles as *El precio de un beso*. Some sources include Soledad Jiménez and Alexander Kahble in the cast, but their participation in the released film has not been confirmed. Tom Patricola's voice was dubbed by either Rafael Valverde, Vicente Padula or Romualdo Tirado.

Cinl Aug 1930, p. 32. *CM* Oct 1930, p. 976. *FD* 1 Aug 1933. *MPH* 26 Apr 1930, p. 54. *NYT* 25 Jul 1933.

PREJUDICE (Jewish Americans, Swedish Americans)

Protestant Film Commission; Edmund L. Dorfmann Productions. *Dist* The Religious Film Association; Motion Picture Sales Corp. Feb **1949**; New York opening: 17 Oct 1949; Prod: began 9 Aug 1948 at Nassour Studios. Sd (RCA Sound System); b&w. 5,130 ft. 57 min.

Pres THE PROTESTANT FILM COMMISSION and THE ANTI-DEFAMATION LEAGUE. *Exec prod* Paul F. Heard. *Dir* Edward L. Cahn. *Asst dir* Bert Glazer. *Orig story and scr* Jarvis Couillard. *Scr* Ivan Goff and Ben Roberts. *Cam* Jackson Rose. *Process* Mario Castegnaro. *Art dir* Lewis H. Creber. *Film ed* Phil Cahn. *Set dec* Harry Reif. *Ward* Albert Conti. *Mus* Irving Gertz. *Sd* Garry Harris. *Unit mgr* Elbert Spurlin.

Cast: David Bruce (*Joe Hanson*), Mary Marshall (*Beth Hanson*), Tommy Ivo (*Joey Hanson*), Bruce Edwards (*Al Green*), Barbara Billingsley (*Doris Green*), James Seay (*Minister*), Joe Crehan (*Mr. [J. P.] Baker*), Billy Kimbley (*Eddie*), Jimmy Conlin (*Young Joe*), Sharon McManus (*Ellen Green*), Anne Nagle, Frank Cady, Mira McKinney, Grace Field, Ruth Clifford, Kay Christopher, John Dehner, Buddy Swan, Margaret Bert, Belle Mitchell, Clarence Hennecke.

Social, Religious, Drama. [*Print viewed*]. Joe Hanson arrives in the town of Springville with his wife Beth and son Joey to take a new job his company has offered. They are pleased with the look of the community, and little Joey quickly makes friends with the little girl next door, Ellen Green. At the factory, Joe begins work as production manager, a position he feels is his first chance to do the kind of work he wants. His boss, J. P. Baker, praises him, saying he was picked because he knows how to handle machines and people. Ellen's father Al, who had temporarily filled in as production manager before Joe arrived, now becomes his assistant. The two men drive home together, and when a black man's stalled car blocks the way, they hear an irate white man complain, "These niggers shouldn't be allowed to drive cars." Joe tells Al he "doesn't go for that sort of thing," after which Al reveals that he is Jewish and often faces prejudice himself. Joe confides that he is a Scandinavian Protestant, and Al's religion makes no difference to him. At home, Joe reveals to Beth that the Greens are Jewish and cautions her not to make any "slips." When Joey asks, "What's wrong with Jews?" Joe replies they are exactly like other people. At the Green home, Al tells his wife Doris about the incident and says that the Hansons look like nice people. Doris chidingly asks, "Even though they are Gentiles?" and they laugh. After pamphlets are distributed in town condemning Jews, blacks and foreigners as menaces to America, the minister at the Hansons' church delivers a sermon about prejudice, calling it a disease, and asks his congregation to search their hearts so that they can face their feelings of prejudice and replace them with brotherhood and love. Following the service, the minister is troubled when Beth and Joe say that Joey must be careful about what he says around others. Although Joe and Al seemingly work well together, Joe begins to get suspicious that Al may be trying for his job when Al fills in for him at a meeting because he is late. One evening, as the minister is visiting, Joey comes home after having been in a fight and complains about the "dirty wops" on their block. Embarrassed, Joe tells the minister that his son must have picked up his feelings of hate from other children, but the minister questions Joe about his own bigotry. Joe remembers incidents from his childhood: Although he became friends with children named "Ike," "Mike" and "Ole," whose last names he could not pronounce, his parents complained about "queer" foreigners crowding in and competing for jobs, and stated that the "white man" is better. Soon he stopped playing with those other children. He also remembers one of his mother's friends asserting, "I don't call any nigger 'Mrs.'" Joe recalls asking the teacher in a religious class if Jesus loves Negroes, and though his teacher said Jesus loves everyone, he felt she was holding something back. He next remembers that when he wanted a bicycle one summer and planned to get a job at a Jewish shopkeeper's store to earn enough money, the shopkeeper ultimately gave the job to a Jewish boy. Joe then remembers the first time he felt prejudice: During a football game after school, Joe fumbles the ball following a tackle. When another boy says that a "dirty Jew" unfairly tackled him,

Joe agrees, pleased that the fumble was not his fault at all. The minister now explains that the basis for all prejudice is scapegoating, which stems from insecurity. At work, Joe soon suspects that Al is aggressively courting the boss's favor and says nothing when a colleague comments, "They're all alike; give them an inch and they take a mile." When Baker asks Joe about Al's performance, as his trial period is coming to an end, Joe, under great stress from overwork because he refuses to let Al help him, praises Al, but confides that some people do not like to work with a Jew. Worried that such conflicts can ruin an organization, Baker transfers Al to another office. Al is downcast about the situation, but tells Joe that if everyone were as straight as he has been, this would not have happened. At home, however, Al angrily tells Doris that "they" make it a crime to be born Jewish and expresses his exasperation over having to move again because someone complained. When Doris conveys the hope that Ellen will not have to face the same prejudices, Al cynically says that things will never be different. Meanwhile, Baker, suspecting that Joe is afraid to have good men working under him, tells the curious minister that Joe lacks confidence. On Sunday, the minister gives another sermon about prejudice, reaffirming that fearful and insecure people attempt to alleviate their suffering through blaming others for their misfortunes. He concludes that people who are prejudiced have no faith in God or themselves and that the key to eradicating prejudice is the acceptance of God's love and grace, which brings dignity, security and strength. The next day, when Joe drives Ellen and Joey to school, the children say in unison, "Ellen is a Jew." She cries, then runs off, and Joey, who earlier had been called a "dumb Swede" by some of the children, follows. Joe drives past the church, remembering the minister's promise that confidence and dignity will be gained if one accepts God, then goes to the factory to meet with Baker. *Antisemitism. Bigotry. Children. Christianity. Factory management. Family relationships. Jews. Ministers. Neighbors. Small town life. Swedish Americans. African Americans. Bicycles. Churches. Employer-employee relations. Football. Racism. Scapegoats. Schools. Self-confidence. Sermons.*

Note: According to *Look*, the Protestant Film Commission, which represented nineteen major denominations and thirteen interdenominational agencies, was formed in the mid-1940s "as part of the Churches' effort to use mass media of communication to promote Christian living." Prints of the film, which was the Protestant Film Commission's first to be exhibited theatrically, were sold outright. The film also had a non-theatrical release, opening in 100 churches in the U.S. and Canada on 18 Oct 1949, according to *HR*. The film showed at Town Hall in New York and in London. The Protestant Film Commission planned twelve pictures for the next two years dealing with Japan's internal struggle, alcoholism, mental health, marital incompatibility and adjusting to bereavement, according to *Look*. Although *Var* notes that New World Films and producer Edmund L. Dorfmann were connected to the film, and the 1950 *FDYB* lists the film as a New World release, the company was most likely involved only in the state rights distribution of the film.

Var criticized this film, stating it "suffers from punching too hard, too directly and too repetitiously. The story elements are developed without plausibility, serving only as an obvious peg for several long sermons which are used as a substitute for dramatic situations. General production values also suffer paradoxically from a slickness which lessens the impression of sincerity." *DV* predicted that the film "will prove acceptable fare in churches, clubs, schools, etc. When it comes to selling it to theatres, however, distributors will likely bump into the answer 'another film which tries to capitalize on intolerance.'"

Box 12 Mar 1949. *DV* 17 Feb 1949, p. 3. *Exh* 2 Mar 1949, p. 2573. *FD* 29 Mar 1949, p. 4. *Har* 5 Mar 1949, p. 38. *HR* 17 Feb 1949, p. 3. *MPHPD* 5 Mar 1949, p. 4522. *SF Chron* 12 Oct 1949, p. 36. *Var* 23 Feb 1949, p. 11.

THE PRESCOTT KID (Latino)

Columbia Pictures Corp. *Dist* Columbia Pictures Corp. 8 Nov **1934**; Prod: 12 Sep—22 Sep 1934 [©Columbia Pictures Corp.; 12 Nov 1934; LP5094]. Sd (Western Electric Noiseless Recording); b&w. 6 reels. 55-56 or 58 min. PCA cert no. 332.

Dir David Selman. [*Asst dir* Wilbur McGaugh]. *Scr* Ford Beebe. *Photog* Benjamin Kline. *Film ed* Ray Snyder and [Richard Cahoon]. [*Sd eng* Edward Bernds]. [*Riding double for Sheila Mannors* Nellie Walker]. [*Stand-in and double for Tim McCoy* Bert Dillard]. [*Stand-in for Sheila Mannors* Betty Taylor].

Source: Based on the short story "Wolves of Catclaw" by Claude Rister in *Rangeland Love Magazine* (Nov 1933).

Cast: TIM McCOY (*Tim Hamlin*), Sheila Mannors (*Dolores [Ortega]*), Joseph Sauers ([*Captain*] *Willoughby*), Alden Chase ([*Ed*] *Walton*), Hooper Atchley (*Bonner*), Albert J. Smith (*Frazier*), Harry Todd (*Dr. Haley*), Walter Brennan (*Stage driver*), Carlos De Valdez ([*Don Rafael*] *Ortega*), Ernie Adams (*Red Larson*), Steve Clark

(*Crocker*), [Tom London (*Slim, benchman*)], [Charles King (*J. Bones*)], [Eddie Cobb (*Buck*)], [Jack Curtis (*Bartender*)], [Bud Osborne (*Ames*)], [Charles Brinley (*Manuel*)], [Dick Botiller (*Isadoro*)], [Joe Delacruz (*Antonio*)], [Slim Whittaker, Artie Ortego, Jack Rockwell (*Cowboys*)], [Julia Bejarano (*Juanita*)], [Enrique Acosta (*Servant*)], [Joseph Rickson (*Bystander*)].

Western. [*Print viewed*]. In the town of San Lorenzo, Ed Walton reports twelve more of his cattle stolen, while another rancher, Don Rafael Ortega, sends a message to Prescott, Arizona, that San Lorenzo needs a marshal. On the stagecoach, Red Larson is brought in wounded after being shot by a stranger on a white horse. When a stranger, Tim Hamlin, arrives in town, the saloon keeper, Bonner, assumes Tim is responsible for Red's injury and warns him that Red has many friends. Tim shoots Bonner's gun from his hand and backs out of the saloon. Ed comes to Tim's aid and Tim explains that he is not Captain Willoughby, the new marshal, but a cowpoke looking for a job as a foreman. Ed suggests Tim try the Ortega ranch, and after Tim meets Rafael's daughter Dolores, he agrees to help the rancher out. Bonner holds a note on the Ortega ranch, which Rafael cannot pay because his cattle are being stolen. Tim is slightly hurt when he stops a raid, and Ed, Bonner's secret leader, is surprised to find Tim alive when he arrives to propose to Dolores. Meanwhile, Dr. Haley warns Tim that Ed is not the man he seems. A vigilante group forms and takes Tim prisoner, but he escapes in time to see the stagecoach arrive, carrying a wounded Rafael. Tim is suspected of the crime when his horse is found sweaty from a hard ride, and escapes a crowd ready to lynch him by pulling a gun. Meanwhile, Ed tells Rafael that he will buy the note from Bonner if Dolores will agree to marry him, and she does. The new marshal, Willoughby, arrests Tim and leaves him in Bonner's care, but Tim escapes and forces Bonner to open the safe, which holds Rafael's money. The men fight, and hearing the scuffle, Ed's men come to Bonner's rescue. With all the crooks in one place, Willoughby places them all under arrest and tells Tim that his incarceration was a trick to capture the rustlers. Then Willoughby announces that the law is in San Lorenzo to stay, and Tim is united with Dolores. *Duplicity. Mexican Americans. Mistaken identity. Rustlers. Sheriffs. Arizona. Debt. False arrests. Fistfights. Gunshot wounds. Horses. Law and order. Lynching. Marriage–Forced by circumstances. Physicians. Ranch foremen. Ranchers. Rustlers. Saloons. Stagecoach robberies. Strangers. Vigilantes.*

Note: The working titles for this film were *Fighting Back* and *Wolves of Catclaw*. Although a 5 Jan 1935 *MPH* release chart gives a release date of 8 Nov 1934 for this film, it was not screened in New York until 16 Oct 1936, at which time it was reviewed by *FD* and *Var*. According to modern sources, the cast also included Art Mix, Lew Meehan, Fred Burns, Al Haskell and Bob Card.

DV 12 Jul 1934, p. 5. *DV* 12 Sep 1934, p. 11. *DV* 25 Sep 1934, p. 8. *FD* 17 Oct 1936, p. 3. *Var* 21 Oct 1936, p. 17.

EL PRESIDIO (Spanish language)

Metro-Goldwyn-Mayer Corp.; controlled by Loew's Inc.; Cosmopolitan Productions; Una Producción Cosmopolitan. *Dist* Metro-Goldwyn-Mayer Distributing Corp. Nov **1930**; Los Angeles opening: 14 Nov 1930; Prod: Aug—Sep 1930. Sd (Western Electric Sound System); b&w. 10 reels, 8,054 ft. 89 min. Passed by the National Board of Review. Spanish language.

[*Supv* Frank Davis]. *Dirigida por* [*Dir*] Ward Wing. [*Asst to dir and dial dir* Edgar Neville]. *Argumento* [*Story*] Frances Marion. *Diálogo adicional* [*Addl dial*] Joe Farnham and Martin Flavin. *Versión española y diálogo por* [*Spanish version and dial*] Edgar Neville. *Fotografiada por* [*Photog*] Leonard Smith and Max Fabian. *Director artístico* [*Art dir*] Cedric Gibbons. *Editada por* [*Ed*] Peggy O'Day. *Acústica por* [*Sd*] Douglas Shearer. [*Sd* J. Russell Franks].

Cast: José Crespo (*Morgan*), Juan de Landa (*Butch*), Tito Davison (*Kent Marlowe*), Luana Alcañiz (*Ana Marlowe*), Giovanni Martino (*Wallace*), Luis Llaneza (*Pop*), Juan de Homs (*Director*), José Soriano Viosca (*Detective Donlin*), Romualdo Tirado (*Putnam*), César Vanoni ("*El Lobo*"), Carlos Cea (*Dopey*), Vicente Padula (*Dunn*), Gabry Rivas (*Joe*), Roberto Saa Silva (*Sandy*), Alma Real (*Sra. Marlowe*), Antonio Vidal (*Sr. Marlowe*), Julián Rivero (*Oliver*).

Prison, Melodrama. [*Not viewed*]. Sentenced to prison for vehicular manslaughter, Kent Marlowe shares a cell with Morgan and Butch, who are serving time for forgery and murder, respectively. The resourceful Morgan manages to escape and seeks shelter with Kent's sister Ana, who runs a bookshop, and they fall in love. Morgan is soon recaptured, but influenced by his feelings for Ana, decides to serve the rest of his time on good behavior, but never to the extent of

becoming an informer. The weakling Kent, on the other hand, collaborates with the warden to quell a mutiny, led by Butch, against the terrible conditions in the prison. The prisoners who rebelled suspect Morgan of having been the informer and demand an accounting between him and Butch. Unwillingly, the two old comrades face each other in a gunfight and both are seriously wounded. Morgan recovers, but Butch dies, convinced of his friend's loyalty. Kent dies riddled with bullets in another battle. Morgan's intervention in smothering another dangerous situation gains him his freedom. *Convicts. Criminals–Rehabilitation. Informers. Prison escapees. Prison guards. Prison reform. Prison wardens.* Booksellers and bookselling. Brothers and sisters. Gunfights. Manslaughter. Romance.

Note: *El presidio* was a Spanish-language version of M-G-M's 1930 film, *The Big House,* which was directed by George Hill and starred Chester Morris and Wallace Beery (see *AFI Catalog of Feature Films, 1921-30;* F2.0398). Early in 1931, French and German versions were also made in Culver City, but no record of their exhibition in the U.S. has been located. According to studio records, the French film was titled *Big House,* but was also known as *Révolte dans le prison.* The German version was entitled *Menschen hinter Gittern.* A version in Italian, *Carcere,* was a dubbed version of *El presidio.* Although all the cast and crew credits were derived from studio cutting continuities, a modern German source states that E. W. Brandes, Walter Hasenclever and Ernst Toller worked on the screenplay of the German version, and that Harold Wenstrom photographed it.

Cinl Dec 1930, p. 30.

THE PRETENDERS (English Americans)
Rolfe Photoplays, Inc. *Dist* Metro Pictures Corp. 21 Aug **1916** [©Metro Pictures Corp.; 22 Aug 1916; LP8973]. Si; b&w. 5 reels.

Dir George D. Baker and Charles J. Hundt. *Scen* George D. Baker. *Story* Channing Pollock and Rennold Wolf. *Cam* William Wagner.

Cast: Emmy Wehlen (*Helen Pettingill*), Paul Gordon (*Hubert Stanwood*), Charles Eldridge (*Silas T. Pettingill*), Kate Blancke (*Maria Pettingill*), Edwin Holt (*Inspector Burke*), William Davidson (*Macklin Thurston*), Howard Truesdell (*John Stafford*), Jerome Wilson (*Joseph Bailey*), Ilean Hume (*Rita*), Hugh Jeffrey (*Andrews*), Harry Neville (*Dugan*), George Stevens.

Comedy-drama. After oil is discovered on the family farm, Silas T. Pettingill, his wife Maria, and their daughter Helen abandon the country for Fifth Avenue, but the New York social elite fail to acknowledge their presence. One night, coming home from a drinking binge, Silas brings British cab driver Hubert Stanwood with him, and the next morning, to satisfy Maria's status-consciousness, he introduces the guest as a count. Maria is delighted with her visitor until, outranking the count, the Earl of Bradford arrives. This nobleman, however, is really Macklin Thurston, a crook hoping to steal the Pettingill fortune. The family soon discovers the masquerade and has Macklin thrown in jail, after which the Pettingills learn that Hubert is the real Earl of Bradford. Then, the former farmers themselves become a part of the royal family, as Hubert marries Helen. *English. Impersonation and imposture. New York City. Nobility. Social climbers. Taxicab drivers.* Drunkenness. Farms. Oil. Thieves.

Motog 2 Sep 1916, p. 557. *MPW* 26 Aug 1916, p. 1451. *MPW* 2 Sep 1916, p. 1532. *NYDM* 26 Aug 1916, p. 26. *Var* 25 Aug 1916, p. 23. *Wid's* 31 Aug 1916, p. 829.

THE PRICE OF APPLAUSE (German Americans)
Triangle Film Corp. *Dist* Triangle Distributing Corp. 4 Aug **1918**. Si; b&w. 5 reels.

Dir Thomas N. Heffron. *Scen* Doris Schroeder. *Cam* C. H. Wales.

Source: Based on the short story "The Price of Applause" by Nina Wilcox Putnam and Norman Jacobsen in *The Saturday Evening Post* (publication date undetermined).

Cast: Jack Livingston (*Karl le Barron*), Claire Anderson (*Amy*), Joe King (*Marcarson*), Walt Whitman (*Profesor Arnold*).

World War I, Drama. Karl le Barron, a Greenwich Village poet of German heritage who craves attention, declares himself a German sympathizer at the outbreak of the war merely to gain notoriety. With the sinking of the *Lusitania,* however, his position becomes untenable, and he is soon a patriotic American, claiming that he will fight for the U.S. in France. A coward at heart, Karl is horrified to find himself on the battlefield, and to save himself, he exchanges uniforms with the corpse of a German soldier and later is reported dead himself. Karl is taken prisoner in a British camp, where he learns that his poems, published as the work of a hero killed in a battle, have become immensely popular. Eager to claim his glory, Karl escapes and returns home, only to find that his friends do not recognize him and that his wife Amy has remarried. In the end, Karl lives up to his

own heroic reputation by sacrificing his life to thwart a group of German spies. *Cowardice. German Americans. Heroism. Hoaxes. Missing persons, Assumed dead. Moral reformation. Poets. Self-sacrifice. Soldiers. World War I.* Corpses. Escapes. France. Germans. S.S. *Lusitania.* New York City–Greenwich Village. Prisoners of war. Spies.

Note: One source credits the photography to George McDaniel.

ETR 3 Aug 1918, p. 747. *ETR* 10 Aug 1918, p. 841. *MPN* 17 Aug 1918, p. 1119. *MPW* 10 Aug 1918, p. 885. *MPW* 17 Aug 1918, p. 1016. *Var* 9 Aug 1918, p. 32. *Wid's* 4 Aug 1918, pp. 15-16.

THE PRIDE OF PALOMAR (Latino, Japanese Americans)
Cosmopolitan Corp. *Dist* Paramount Pictures. 26 Nov **1922** [©William Randolph Hearst; 15 Nov 1922; LP18459]. Si; b&w. 8 reels, 7,494 ft.

Dir Frank Borzage. *Scen* Grant Carpenter and John Lynch. *Photog* Chester A. Lyons.

Source: Based on the novel *The Pride of Palomar* by Peter Bernard Kyne (New York, 1921).

Cast: Forrest Stanley (*Don Mike Farrell*), Marjorie Daw (*Kay Parker*), Tote Du Crow (*Pablo*), James Barrows (*Father Dominic*), Joseph Dowling (*Don Miguel*), Alfred Allen (*John Parker*), George Nichols (*Conway*), Warner Oland (*Okada*), Mrs. Jessie Hebbard (*Mrs. Parker*), Percy Williams (*Butler*), Mrs. George Hernandez (*Caroline*), Edward Brady (*Lostolet*), Carmen Arselle (*Mrs. Supaldio*), Eagle Eye (*Nogi*), Most Mattoe (*Alexandria*).

Melodrama. Mike Farrell, the son of a Spanish don, comes home from his army service in Siberia to discover that his father is dead and his ranch, Palomar, is in the hands of John Parker. While Parker is maneuvering to turn Palomar over to Okada, a Japanese potato baron who desires the land for a colonization scheme, Mike falls in love with Kay Parker. After Mike is attacked and seriously wounded by Okada, Kay nurses him to health and their love grows. By a clever ruse and with a good horse, Mike regains the ranch. *California. Colonies. Latino. Japanese Americans. Land barons. Veterans.*

Note: The novel was originally serialized in *Cosmopolitan* magazine. According to publicity for the film, Rancho Guajome, where the story is set, was leased for shooting by Cosmopolitan. The rancho had formerly been part of the San Luis Rey Mission, founded by Fra Junipero Serra in 1769. Helen Hunt Jackson had lived there and gathered information for her novel *Ramona.*

ETR 2 Dec 1922, p. 51. *FD* 16 Nov 1922. *MPW* 2 Dec 1922. *NYT* 20 Nov 1922, p. 21. *Var* 24 Nov 1922, p. 34.

PRIDE OF THE MARINES (Jewish Americans, Latino)
Warner Bros. Pictures, Inc.; A Warner Bros.—First National Picture. *Dist* Warner Bros. Pictures, Inc. 1 Sep **1945**; New York opening: week of 24 Aug 1945; Prod: mid-Nov 1944—mid-Feb 1945 [©Warner Bros. Pictures, Inc.; 1 Sep 1945; LP13451]. Sd (RCA Sound System); b&w. 10,757 ft. 119-120 min. PCA cert no. 10661.

Exec prod JACK L. WARNER. *Prod* Jerry Wald. *Dir* Delmer Daves. [*Asst dir* Arthur Lueker]. *Scr* Albert Maltz. *Adpt* Marvin Borowsky. *Dir of photog* Peverell Marley. [*Fill-in photog* Sol Polito]. [2d cam James Bell]. *Spec eff* L. Robert Burks and Edwin Du Par. [*Spec photog eff* William McGann]. *Art dir* Leo Kuter. [*Supv art dir* Max Parker]. *Film ed* Owen Marks. *Set dec* Walter F. Tilford. *Ward* Milo Anderson. *Orch arr* Leonid Raab. *Mus dir* Leo F. Forbstein. *Mus* Franz Waxman. *Sd* Stanley Jones. [*Re-rec and eff mix* Gordon M. Davis and E. Kenneth Martin]. [*Mus mix* Charles David Forrest]. *Makeup artist* Perc Westmore. *Tech adv* Major Louis Aronson, United States Marine Corps and Major Gordon Warner, United States Marine Corps.

Source: Based on the book *Al Schmid, Marine* by Roger Butterfield (New York, 1944).

Cast: John Garfield [(*Al Schmid*)], Eleanor Parker [(*Ruth Hartley*)], Dane Clark [(*Lee Diamond*)], John Ridgely [(*Jim Merchant*)], Rosemary DeCamp [(*Virginia Pfeiffer*)], Ann Doran [(*Ella May Merchant*)], Ann Todd [(*Lucy Merchant*)], Warren Douglas [(*Kebabian*)], Don McGuire [(*Irish*)], Tom D'Andrea [(*Tom*)], Rory Mallinson [(*Doctor*)], Stephen Richards [(*Ainslee*)], Anthony Caruso [(*Johnny Rivers*)], Moroni Olsen [(*Captain Burroughs*)], [Dave Willock (*Red*)], [John Sheridan (*Marine*)], [John Miles (*Lieutenant*)], [John Compton (*Corporal*)], [Lennie Bremen (*Lenny*)], [Michael Browne (*Corpsman*)].

Biography, World War II, Drama. [*Print viewed*]. In Philadelphia, in 1941, confirmed bachelor Al Schmid, a welder, lives with his friends, Jim and Ella May Merchant, and their young daughter Lucy. The happily married Ella continually introduces Al to eligible women. To discourage her, Al is very rude to Ruth Hartley, whom Ella

has invited to dinner, and is shocked when, at the end of the evening, Ruth chides him for his boorish behavior. Chastened, Al asks for another chance, and he and Ruth grow to love each other. After the Japanese bomb Pearl Harbor, Hawaii, Al enlists in the Marines. Before he leaves, he advises Ruth to forget him, but she disregards his advice, and early the next morning, sees him off at the train station. There, Al finally admits that he loves her and asks her to wait for him. Al is sent to Guadalcanal in the South Pacific, where he and other Marines defend the island from a Japanese attack. After killing almost 200 Japanese soldiers, Al is blinded by a grenade. At the naval hospital in San Diego, Red Cross nurse Virginia Pfeiffer encourages Al to tell Ruth about his eyes, but Al is convinced that his blindness is only temporary. When an operation fails to restore his sight, Al is bitter and refuses to learn how to function as a blind man. Not wanting Ruth to be tied to a helpless man, Al dictates a letter to Virginia breaking off their engagement. When a broken-hearted Ruth calls Al, he will not speak to her, but Virginia secretly tells Ruth about Al's blindness and advises her to keep writing to him. Al learns that he is not alone in his fears for the future. While some of the injured veterans look forward to attending college on the G.I. Bill, others remember the way their fathers were treated after World War 1 and doubt that they will fare any better. When Al is notified that he and his friend, Lee Diamond, will be awarded the Navy Cross in Philadelphia, he does not want any of his old friends to see him. On the train, Lee accuses Al of cowardice and points out that he himself has faced discrimination because of anti-semitism. Despite Al's wishes, Ruth is waiting at the station, and through a ruse, takes him home without his knowing who she is. Although it is Christmas Eve, Al does not want to go inside, but the Merchants rush out to welcome him. They do their best to encourage Al to stay with them, and Ruth tells him he has been promised his old job if he takes a training course for the blind. When the Merchants leave Al alone with Ruth, however, he insists that she take him to the hospital. Ruth is furious and finally convinces Al that she loves him and wants him, whether or not he is blind. The next day, when Al is awarded his Navy Cross, Ruth and the Merchants are there to applaud. As they leave the ceremony, Al realizes that he is able to distinguish bright colors and is hopeful that he may regain some sight. *Blindness. Handicapped. Romance. Al Schmid. War heroes. World War II. Awards. Bowling and bowling alleys. Christmas Eve. Engagements. Guadalcanal Island (Solomon Islands), Battle of, 1942-1943. Japan. Army. Jews. Loyalty. Nurses. Philadelphia (PA). Trains. Uncles. United States. Marine Corps. War injuries. Welders.*

Note: The film's working title was *This Love of Ours*. As depicted in the film, Al Schmid was a welder who won fame during the battle of Guadacanal when he killed 200 Japanese soldiers during a night attack. Schmid was blinded by a grenade early in the morning, but refused to relinquish his position and continued to fight by having a wounded soldier tell him where to point his gun. A 3 Sep 1945 article in *Time* notes that at that time Schmid was living in Philadelphia with his wife and one-year-old son. According to the article, Schmid spent his time typing letters to his friends, listening to Bing Crosby recordings and fishing. His eyesight was limited to the perception of bright colors and moving objects. News items in *HR* add the following information about the production: Some scenes were shot on location in Philadelphia and at the San Diego Naval Hospital. Ann Doran was borrowed from Paramount for the picture. Cinematographer Sol Polito substituted for Peverell Marley while the latter was out with the flu. In an article in 12 Jan 1946 issue of *SEP*, actor John Garfield cited "Al Schmid" as his favorite movie role. The writer Albert Maltz, who was nominated for an Academy Award for the screenplay of *Pride of the Marines*, was later blacklisted. John Garfield and Eleanor Parker reprised their roles in a *Lux Radio Theatre* broadcast on 31 Dec 1945.

Box 11 Aug 1945. *DV* 7 Aug 1945, p. 3. *FD* 7 Aug 1945, p. 5. *HR* 26 Oct 1944, p. 3. *HR* 17 Nov 1944, p. 15. *HR* 12 Dec 1944, p. 3. *HR* 19 Dec 1944, p. 4. *HR* 9 Jan 1945, p. 3. *HR* 17 Jan 1945, p. 7. *HR* 16 Feb 1945, p. 15. *HR* 7 Aug 1945, p. 8. *HR* 4 Sep 1945, p. 8. *MPHPD* 30 Dec 1944, p. 2250. *MPHPD* 11 Aug 1945, p. 2589. *NYT* 25 Aug 1945, p. 7. *SEP* 12 Jan 1946. *Time* 3 Sep 1945. *Var* 8 Aug 1945, p. 22.

PRIMAVERA EN OTOÑO (Spanish language)

Fox Film Corp. *Dist* Fox Film Corp. **1933**; Barcelona opening: 21 Mar 1933; New York opening: May 1933; Prod: Nov—Dec 1932. Sd; b&w. 8 reels. 75 min. Passed by the National Board of Review. Spanish language.

[*Prod* John Stone]. *Supervisión de* [*Supv*] Gregorio Martínez Sierra. *Dirección de* [*Dir*] Eugene J. Forde. *Adaptación cinematográfica de* [*Scr*] José López Rubio and John Reinhardt. [*Photog* Robert Planck].

Song(s): Selections from the opera *Tristan und Isolde*, music and libretto by Richard Wagner; "Flamenco," traditional Andalusian dance rhythm, lyrics by Gregorio Martínez Sierra.

Source: Based on the play *Primavera en otoño* by Gregorio Martínez Sierra (Madrid, 3 Mar 1911).

Cast: CATALINA BÁRCENA (*Elena* [*Montero*]), Antonio Moreno (*Enrique*), Mimi Aguglia (*Rosina*), Luana Alcañiz (*Agustina*), Julio Peña (*Manolo* [*Fresneda*]), María Calvo (*Ama Justa*), Agostino Borgato (*Empresario*), Hilda Moreno (*Nena* [*Torres*]), *y* Raúl Roulien (*Juan Manuel* [*Valladares*]), [Romualdo Tirado (*Antonio, guarda rural*)], [Adrienne D'Ambricourt (*Montrésor*)], [Juan Martínez Plá (*Monti*)], [Ada Lozano (*Eva*)], [Primo Brunetti (*Paoletti*)], [Rudolph Amendt (*Tristán*)], [Enrique Jardiel Poncela], [José López Rubio].

Romantic comedy. [*Not viewed*]. Not having seen her mother Elena Montero in over eight years, Agustina arrives backstage at the opera house where her mother is performing. The next day, after attending mass, Agustina's conservative boyfriend, Manolo Fresneda, arrives, and they argue about her new appearance, which has been dictated by Elena. Agustina's father Enrique arrives to cajole Elena into coming back to live with him so that Manolo's parents will give their approval to Manolo and Agustina's marriage; however, Elena will have nothing to do with the plan because she does not like Manolo, so Enrique leaves Agustina in Madrid while he returns to his ranch. Enrique and Elena are married but live apart so that she may pursue her own career and he may continue ranching. When he is gone, Agustina expresses sadness at her mother's decision, and Elena guiltily agrees to go through with the plan only to show Agustina the ludicrousness of it. Agustina and Elena arrive at Enrique's home with a large group of Elena's friends in tow, who too readily make themselves at home. The next morning, Enrique shows Elena around, and she wistfully takes note of the growth and change that have occurred in her absence. Her friends interrupt, and she and Agustina, dressed in bathing suits, join them in exercise. Manolo is infuriated by Agustina's flamboyant costume, and he tries to convince her to return to her old self. They argue and Agustina leaves, followed by Juan Manuel Valladares, Elena's friend, who is the attaché of the Brazilian Embassy. They are caught in a rain storm and seek shelter in the home of the farm's keeper. The old keeper serves them brandy, and Juan remarks that the same situation in Japan would have merited a glass of rice wine. Agustina is intrigued, and the keeper expresses his preference of Juan over Manolo to Agustina. That evening, having watched Elena's friends make a mess of his home, Enrique orders them to leave, which causes Elena to pack her bags as well. As Elena prepares to leave, Juan comes in and confesses his love for Agustina. His ensuing embrace with Elena is seen by Enrique, who assumes that it is one of romantic affection and orders Juan to leave. Juan returns in the morning and invites Agustina to travel to Tokyo with him as his wife. Enrique is informed of the upcoming marriage by Elena, and embarrassed by his previous fit of jealousy, he tells the moving men to stop loading Elena's trunks. Angry because he did not speak his wish for her to stay to her, Elena leaves to board a ship. As she stands at the gangplank, Enrique arrives and they flip a coin to decide if she will stay with him or if he will go with her. The coin lands in the water, and they decide to split their time equally between Madrid and the farm. They walk arm-in-arm aboard the ship as the gangplank is pulled away. *Mothers and daughters. Spaniards. Brazilians. Diplomats. Jealousy. Madrid (Spain). Opera singers. Rainstorms. Ranches.*

Note: The plot summary was based on a screen continuity in the Twentieth Century-Fox Produced Scripts Collection, and the onscreen credits were taken from a screen billing sheet in the Twentieth Century-Fox Records of the Legal Department, both of which are at the UCLA Theater Arts Library.

CM May 1933, p. 260. *NYT* 18 May 1933, p. 17.

THE PRIMITIVE CALL (Native Americans)

Fox Film Corp. *Dist* Fox Film Corp. 22 Jan 1917 [©William Fox; 21 Jan 1917; LP10035]. Si; b&w. 5 reels.

Dir Bertram Bracken. *Scen* Bertram Bracken. *Cam* Rial B. Schellinger.

Cast: Gladys Coburn (*Betty Malcolm*), Fritz Leiber (*Brain Elkhorn*), John Webb Dillion (*Bart Jennings*), George Alan Larkin (*Percy Malcolm*), Lewis Sealy (*John Malcolm*), Velma Whitman (*Elsie Jennings*), Kittens Reichert (*Buttons Jennings*).

Western. After the Eastern-educated Indian Brain Elkhorn prevents capitalist Percy Malcolm from cheating his tribe of their land, Malcolm's daughter Betty decides to use her feminine wiles to gain possession of the land. Betty bewitches Elkhorn and presents a deed of sale to him when he proposes marriage. As soon as he signs, Betty repulses him and, penitent, Elkhorn confesses his treachery to the

tribe, who ostracize him. Vengeful, Elkhorn throws off the veneer of civilization and carries Betty off to his lonely wigwam on a mountain top where he lives in exile from his people. Here she realizes that her former contempt for him has turned to love, but his heart has turned to an Indian maiden, and the society girl returns to her frivolous environment, sadder but wiser. *Duplicity. Indians of North America. Land rights. Racism. Socialites. Abduction. Businessmen. Deeds. Ostracism. Tribal life.*

ETR 3 Feb 1917, p. 632. *Motog* 10 Feb 1917, p. 315. *MPN* 3 Feb 1917, p. 761. *MPW* 3 Feb 1917, p. 705, 743. *NYDM* 27 Jan 1917, p. 50. *Wid's* 25 Jan 1917, p. 49.

PRIMITIVE LOVE (Native Americans, Native Alaskans)
1927; New York showing: ca 28 May 1927. Si; b&w. 6 reels, 5,400 ft.

Dir Frank E. Kleinschmidt. *Photog* Frank E. Kleinschmidt.

Cast: Ok-Ba-Ok (*Modern Caveman*), Sloca Bruna (*His Wife*), Wenga (*Flapper Daughter*).

Documentary. A portrayal of the Eskimo way of life, which focuses on a family consisting of father, mother, and two grown daughters and on several small boys and two young trappers. There is an effort to give some continuity to the sequences with the courtship of a daughter by rival trappers, but the emphasis is on the daily struggle for existence in the Arctic wastes—including scenes of hunting a polar bear on ice floes, 'hand-to-hand' combat with the bear, and a walrus hunt. *Alaska. Arctic regions. Native Alaskans. Polar bears. Trappers. Walruses.*

FD 12 Jun 1927. *NYT* 30 May 1927, p. 9. *Var* 1 Jun 1927, p. 21.

THE PRINCE AND THE PAUPER see YISKOR

A PRINCE OF HIS RACE (African Americans)
Colored Players Film Corp. **1926**; New York opening: 4 Dec 1926. Si; b&w. 8 reels.

Dir Roy Calnek. *Wrt* Roy Calnek.

Cast: Harry Henderson (*Tom Bueford*), William A. Clayton, Jr. (*Jim Stillman*), Lawrence Chenault (*Mr. Arnold*), Arline Mickey (*The Arnolds' maid*), Ethel Smith (*Miss Arnold*), Shingzie Howard.

Melodrama, African American. "Tom Bueford, a member of good family, has fallen into disgrace through unscrupulous associates and is found in jail serving the last 6 months of a 5 year term for manslaughter. His sweetheart's appeal to the Governor results in a 24 hour leave of absence so that he can solace his dying mother. A nerve-wracking, death-defying drive over the State highway brings him to her bedside in time to see her breathe her last. En route home, the auto in which Tom is riding is seen by the man whose testimony sent Tom to jail. After Tom's release from jail, he is thwarted in his attempt to see his sweetheart by the same man who sent him to jail. This rival advises Tom to leave town and, during Tom's absence, succeeds in gaining the consent of the young woman through her father, and everything is arranged for the wedding. Just as the wedding is about to be performed, Tom returns and there is an unexpected climax." (*New York Age* 4 Dec 1926). *African Americans. Family relationships. Jails. Manslaughter. Weddings.*

Note: This film was manufactured during April and May of 1926. Colored Players Film Corp. was located in Philadelphia. African-American comedian Sherman H. Dudley was the company's president. This was their first production. According to *ChiDef*, the cost of the production was conservatively put as $14,000, a costly figure for black-cast films of the time.

ChiDef 27 Nov 1926, p. 7. *New York Age* 4 Dec 1926, p. 6.

PRINCESS AND THE PAUPER see ELSA MAXWELL'S PUBLIC DEB NO. 1

THE PRINCESS FROM HOBOKEN (Russian Americans)
Tiffany Productions, Inc. 1 Mar 1927 [©Tiffany Productions, Inc.; 16 Apr 1927; LP23870]. Si; b&w. 6 reels, 5,419 ft.

Dir Allan Dale. *Story and scen* Sonya Levien. *Photog* Robert Martin and Joseph Dubray. *Art dir* Edwin B. Willis. *Film ed* James C. McKay.

Cast: Edmund Burns (*Terence O'Brien*), Blanche Mehaffey (*Sheila O'Toole*), Ethel Clayton (*Mrs. O'Brien*), Lou Tellegen (*Prince Anton Balakrieff*), Babe London (*Princess Sonia Alexandernova Karpoff*), Will R. Walling (*Mr. O'Brien*), Charles McHugh (*Pa O'Toole*), Aggie Herring (*Ma O'Toole*), Charles Crockett (*Whiskers*), Robert Homans (*McCoy*), Harry Bailey (*Cohen*), Sidney D'Albrook (*Tony*), Broderick O'Farrell (*Immigration officer*), Boris Karloff (*Pavel*).

Comedy. To enliven their business, the O'Tooles, restaurant owners in Hoboken, New Jersey, transform their restaurant into the

Russian Inn when they hear that a famous Russian princess is stranded in Chicago. Sheila, the daughter, is persuaded to impersonate the princess, who unfortunately arrives at the restaurant on opening night. Among the patrons are Terry O'Brien, who begs an introduction, and Prince Anton, an unscrupulous Russian who has been living in luxury on funds for Russian refugees. In a series of amusing complications, the prince is unmasked after he threatens to reveal Sheila's imposture. Sheila at last finds happiness with O'Brien. *Hoboken (NJ). Impersonation and imposture. Restaurateurs. Royalty. Russian Americans. Russians.*

FD 22 May 1927. *Var* 25 May 1927, p. 20.

EL PRÍNCIPE DEL DÓLAR (Spanish language)
Hal Roach Studios, Inc.; Metro-Goldwyn-Mayer Corp.; controlled by Loew's, Inc. *Dist* Metro-Goldwyn-Mayer Distributing Corp. **1930**; Havana, Cuba opening: 15 Dec 1930; San Juan, Puerto Rico opening: 25 Jul 1931; Prod: Jul 1930. Sd; b&w. 5 reels, 4,011 ft. 45 min. Spanish language.

Prod Hal Roach. *Dir* James W. Horne. *Orig dial* H. M. Walker. *Photog* Art Lloyd. *Film ed* Richard Currier. *Sd* Elmer Raguse.

Song(s): "A una ola," by María Grever.

Cast: CHARLEY CHASE (*Carlos*), Rita Rey (*La millonaria*), James Finlayson (*Detective del hotel*).

Comedy. [*Not viewed*]. Carlos inherits two million dollars from his uncle who lived in Australia. His lawyer advises him to go to some remote area far from the clutches of gold diggers. A young millionairess, with a similar problem, arrives at the same hotel and asks for her regular room, which has been assigned to Carlos. The coincidence results in mutual suspicion, and both feel that the meeting is not by chance and could be related to their respective fortunes. When they become convinced that these suspicions are groundless, they forget their prejudice and fall in love. *Hotels. Inheritance. Mistaken identity. Romance. Wealth. Fortune hunters. Gold diggers.*

Note: The Spanish and French-language films were expanded versions of a three-reel, 1930 English-language film entitled *Dollar Dizzy*, which was directed by James W. Horne and starred Charley Chase, Thelma Todd, Edgar Kennedy and James Finlayson. It is probable that other actors who were in the English-language version were also in the foreign versions, but the composition of the foreign casts has not been ascertained. A modern source suggests that Rita Rey may be a pseudonym for Nancy Torres.

Other language version(s):
Les chercheuses d'or (French language)
1931. Sd; b&w. 5 reels. 41 min. French language.

Prod Hal Roach. *Dir* James W. Horne. *Film ed* Richard Currier. *Photog* George Stevens. *Scr* H. M. Walker. *Sd* Elmer Raguse.

Charley Chase, Georgette Rhodes, James Finlayson. [*French version not viewed*].

Arte y Cinematografía Jan 1932.

EL PRÍNCIPE GONDOLERO (Spanish language)
Paramount Publix Corp. *Dist* Paramount Publix Corp. **1931**; Los Angeles opening: 10 Jul 1931; Prod: Feb 1931. Sd (Western Electric System); b&w. 8 reels, 7,095 ft. 79 min. Spanish language.

Supv Geoffrey Shurlock. *Dir* E. D. Venturini. *Scr* Henry Myers. *Spanish version written by* Josep Carner Ribalta. *Photog* Gilbert Warrenton. *Mus* María Grever and Karl Hajos.

Song(s): "Barcarola coreada," "Veneciana," "La mujer ha de dominar" and "Vals," composers undetermined.

Source: Based on the short story "Honeymoon Hate" by Alice Muriel Williamson in *The Saturday Evening Post* (9 Jul—16 Jul 1927).

Cast: Roberto Rey (*El príncipe Pietro Dantarini*), Rosita Moreno (*Miss Adela Grant*), Andrés de Segurola (*El príncipe Dantarini*), Manuel Arbó (*Mr. John Grant*), José Peña "Pepet" (*Salustiano Green*), Juan de Homs (*El abogado*), "Don Catarino" (*Beppo*), Elena Landeros (*Muchacha veneciana*), Luis Llaneza (*Manager*).

Musical comedy. [*Not viewed*]. In Venice, the irascible, bearded nobleman Dantarini lives with his handsome grandson, Prince Pietro Dantarini, in a palace. Over the entrance hangs a coat-of-arms bearing the motto, "By persuasion or by force," words that have been defended in war and love for generations. Elderly American hammer manufacturer John Grant and his beautiful, spoiled granddaughter Adela arrive in Venice determined to procure the plaque bearing the coat-of-arms as a trademark for their company. When Adela mistakes the singing Pietro for a gondolier, he pretends to be one and escorts

her via the canals to his palace. Later, Adela and Pietro see Dantarini, who is outraged by Grant's audacity at naming a price for the shield, brandishing a war axe over Grant's head. Pietro rescues Grant by wisking him away in a gondola. That night, during a masked ball in the palace, Grant dons a costume that is a replica of Dantarini's and, with the help of Salustiano Green, Adela's suitor, tries to remove the plaque. To make Pietro jealous, Adela lures Salustiano into the torture chambers, and when he gets caught in an ancient set of manacles, she abandons him. Dantarini's relatives attack Grant, but in the scuffle, mistake Dantarini for Grant, and he escapes. Later Dantarini is enraged to learn that Pietro has married Adela, and he challenges Grant to a duel in which each will command a gondola. The first to "ungondola" the other will win. Scorning her new husband, Adela goes to Salustiano in the dungeon. Pietro follows, however, and releases him, then scares him off by sharpening a knife, after which he embraces Adela. The duel ends in a tie when both men are thrown into the canal, and all then embrace. *Americans in foreign countries. Gondolas and Gondoliers. Heraldry. Impersonation and imposture. Nobility. Carnivals. Duels. Factory owners. Family honor. Granddaughters. Grandsons. Millionaires. Palaces. Romantic rivalry. Torture. Venice (Italy).*

Note: The running time listed above was calculated from footage given in NYSA records. Some sources include María Calvo, Soledad Jiménez, Rodolfo Hoyos, Renée Torres, Hipólito Mora, Marujita Pirrín and María Valdealde in the cast; however, their participation in the completed film has not been determined. In 1927, Paramount produced an English-language version of Alice Muriel Williamson's story entitled *Honeymoon Hate*, directed by Luther Reed, and starring Florence Vidor and Tullio Carminati (see *AFI Catalog of Feature Films, 1921-30*; F2.2573).

FD 13 Sep 1933, p. 10. *NYT* 11 Sep 1933, p. 20.

EL PRINCIPE Y LA ALDEANA *see* **RESURRECCIÓN**

PRISON BAIT *see* **REFORM SCHOOL**

PRISONER OF JAPAN (Japanese Americans)
Atlantis Pictures Corporation; Producers Releasing Corp.; An Arthur Ripley production; Leon Fromkess in charge of production. *Dist* Producers Releasing Corp. 22 Jul **1942**; *Prod:* Mid-Apr—mid-Jun 1942 [©Producers Releasing Corp.; 3 Jul 1942; LP11480]. Sd (RCA Sound System); b&w. 7 reels, 5,980 ft. 54 or 64 min. PCA cert no. 8427.

Prod Seymour Nebenzal. *Asst to prod* Andre Dumonceau. *Dir* Arthur Ripley. *Asst dir* Herman Pett. *Story* Edgar G. Ulmer. *Orig scr* Robert Chapman [sic] and Arthur Ripley. *Dir of photog* Jack Greenhalgh. *Film ed* Holbrook N. Todd. *Mus score* Leon Erdody. *Sd eng* Percy Townsend. *Makeup* H. Ross.

Cast: ALAN BAXTER (*David Bowman*), GERTRUDE MICHAEL (*Toni Chase*), introducing Ernest Dorian (*Matsuru*), Corinna Mura (*Loti [Bowman]*), Tommy Seidel (*Ensign Bailey*), Billy Moya (*Maui*), Ray Bennett (*Lieutenant Morgan*), Dave O'Brien (*U.S. Marine*), Ann Staunton (*Edie*), Beal Wong (*Japanese radio operator*), Gilbert Frye (*U.S. radio operator*), Kent Thurber (*Commander McDonald*).

Espionage, War, Drama. [*Print viewed*]. On the South Pacific island of Nukuloa, American naval officers Lieutenant Morgan and Ensign Bailey, are treated during shore leave to the hospitality of Loti Bowman, a Japanese-American woman who serves them food and plays guitar for them. During their visit, a radio call comes in for David Bowman, who is introduced as the hostess' American husband. Although David receives coded information over the radio suggesting that he is running a busy trading post, actually, he is being held prisoner on the island by the sadistic Japanese spy Matsuru. Later, while David shows Morgan his telescope, Mrs. Bowman, who is employed by Matsuru, manages to coax Bailey into telling her about his unit's secret mission. The mission, Bailey tells her, is to comb the island to search for directional shortwave transmitters that have been sending undetectable signals to the Japanese about the exact location of American ships in the region. Bailey immediately realizes his error in having told Mrs. Bowden this secret, but feels secure with her promise to keep the information secret. Some time later, Toni Chase, an American civilian living on the island, pays a visit to David in the hope that he will help her get off the island, and is perplexed by his casual reaction to news of an imminent threat to an American fleet off the island's coast. She soon realizes the reason for his bizarre behavior when she tries to place a warning call to the Americans and Matsuru prevents her from doing so by shooting the transmitter. Bailey's ship is destroyed in a Japanese bomber attack, and soon after he washes

ashore as the sole survivor, Matsuru orders his execution. That night, Maui, a young Japanese boy who gave David directions on how to escape the island, is found murdered. Back at the Bowman house, Toni becomes hysterical when she discovers the extent of Matsuru's operation, and Matsuru silences her by striking her. When Matsuru confesses that he killed the young boy, David pounces on him and, with the help of Loti, who has changed her loyalties, overpowers Matsuru and holds him at gunpoint. While David enters the secret communications center under the house and shoots the radio operators, Matsuru orders one of his guards to execute Loti. David tries unsuccessfully to get a radio response from the American ship convoy and realizes that they must think he is setting a trap for them. In a race against time, David and Toni realize that in order to warn the fleet before the Japanese bombers learn the convoy's location, they must sacrifice their lives and order the American ships to bomb the communications center. Time is crucial, as Matsuru and his radiomen are trying to drill their way into the room. Right after David professes his love for Toni, a bomb lands on the compound and they are killed. *Abduction. Japan. Army. Self-sacrifice. Spies. World War II. Americans in foreign countries. Astronomers. Japanese Americans. Murder. Radio operators. Radio, Short wave. Romance. Soldiers. South Sea islands. United States. Navy.*

Note: Working titles for this film were *Isle of Forgotten Sins* and *Island of Forgotten Sins. Isle of Forgotten Sins* was used by Producers Releasing Corp. as the release title for a 1943 film that was also written by Edgar G. Ulmer. Screenplay writer Robert Chapin's name is misspelled in the onscreen credits as "Chapman." The *Var* review credits Lee Kahler with the musical score, but this conflicts with the onscreen credits, which list Leon Erdody in that capacity. The extent of Kahler's contribution to the final film has not been determined. In a 1974 interview, Ulmer stated that he was hired to replace the original writer, Emil Ludwig, who wrote an unusable draft of the script. Ulmer further stated that he collaborated on the screenplay with his wife Shirley and writer Peretz Hirshbein, and that he directed the last two days of the picture's six-day shoot.

Box 11 Jul 1942. *DV* 10 Jul 1942, p. 3. *FD* 30 Jun 1942, p. 7. *HR* 17 Apr 1942. *HR* 16 Jun 1942, p. 7. *HR* 10 Jul 1942, p. 3. *MPHPD* 4 Jul 1942, p. 750. *Var* 25 Nov 1942, p. 16.

THE PRISONER OF SHARK ISLAND (African Americans)
Twentieth Century-Fox Film Corp.; A Darryl F. Zanuck Twentieth Century Production. *Dist* Twentieth Century-Fox Film Corp. 28 Feb **1936**; New York opening: 12 Feb 1936; *Prod:* 12 Nov 1935—early Jan 1936 [©Twentieth Century-Fox Film Corp.; 21 Feb 1936; LP6233]. Sd (Western Electric Noiseless Recording); b&w. 10 reels, 8,666 ft. 95 min. PCA cert no. 1907.

Pres JOSEPH M. SCHENCK. *Assoc prod* Nunnally Johnson. *Dir* John Ford. *Asst dir* Ed O'Fearna. *Scr* Nunnally Johnson. *Photog* Bert Glennon. *Art dir* William Darling. *Settings* Thomas Little. *Film ed* Jack Murray. [*Ed asst* Harvey Manger and Thomas Vincent]. *Cost* Gwen Wakeling. *Mus dir* Louis Silvers. *Sd* W. D. Flick and Roger Heman.

Cast: Warner Baxter (*Dr. Samuel Alexander Mudd*), Gloria Stuart (*Mrs. Peggy Mudd*), Claude Gillingwater (*Colonel Dyer*), Arthur Byron (*Mr. Erickson*), O. P. Heggie (*Doctor MacIntyre*), Harry Carey (*Commandant*), Francis Ford (*Corporal O'Toole*), John McGuire (*Lieutenant Lovell*), Francis McDonald (*John Wilkes Booth*), Douglas Wood (*General Ewing*), John Carradine (*Sergeant Rankin*), Joyce Kay (*Martha Mudd*), Fred Kohler, Jr. (*Sergeant Cooper*), Ernest Whitman (*Buck*), Paul Fix (*David Herold*), Frank Shannon (*Mr. Holt*), Frank McGlynn, Sr. (*Abraham Lincoln*), Leila McIntyre (*Mrs. Abraham Lincoln*), Etta McDaniel (*Aunt Rosabelle*), J. M. Kerrigan (*Judge Maiben*), Arthur Loft (*Carpet bagger*), Paul McVey (*General Hunter*), Maurice Murphy (*Orderly*), [Paul Stanton (*Orator*)], [Ronald J. Pennick (*Signal man*)], [Raymond Turner, John Lester Johnson, Paul Kruger, Vester Pegg (*Soldiers*)], [Merrill McCormick (*Commandant's aide*)], [James Marcus (*Blacksmith*)], [Gus Reed (*Black man*)], [Earl Eby (*Usher*)], [Jan Duggan (*Actress*)], [Lloyd Whitlock (*Major Rathbone*)], [Dick Elliott (*Actor*)], [Murdock MacQuarrie (*Spangler*)], [Duke Lee, Bud Geary, Robert E. Homans (*Sergeants*)], [Robert Dudley (*Druggist*)], [Wilfred Lucas (*Colonel*)], [Cecil Weston (*Mrs. Surratt*)], [Cyril Thornton (*Maurice O'Laughlin*)], [Beulah Hall Jones (*Blanche*)], [Charles Haefeli (*Prisoner*)], [Paul McAllister (*Doctor*)], [J. P. McGowan (*Ship's captain*)], [Harry Strang (*Mate*)], [Arthur Millett], [Stanley Blystone], [Henry Washington].

Historical, Prison, Medical, Drama. [*Print viewed*]. On the night of April 9, 1865, the day of General Robert E. Lee's surrender, revelers parade to the White House, where President Abraham Lincoln appears on the balcony. His request for the band to play "Dixie" is

greeted by exuberant cheers. On April 14, while the president watches Laura Keene in *Our American Cousin* at Ford's Theatre, popular actor John Wilkes Booth assassinates Lincoln and breaks his own leg jumping to the stage. During a raging storm, Booth and his comrade, David Herold, ride to a Maryland cabin where they ask for a doctor. A black man directs them to the home of Dr. Samuel Mudd, who, not knowing Booth's identity, sets the leg. The next day, while Dr. Mudd is away delivering the baby of his former slaves, Buck and Aunt Rosabelle, soldiers invade his home searching for Booth, and when one discovers Dr. Mudd's young daughter Martha playing with Booth's boot, Dr. Mudd is arrested for conspiracy in the assassination. Although Booth is killed in Virginia, eight persons are tried as conspirators by a military court because the assassination has brought the country to the verge of hysteria. After Assistant Secretary of War Erickson instructs the members of the court-martial not to let their judgment be troubled by "pedantic" regard for the customary rules of evidence or by the notion of reasonable doubt, the hooded prisoners are tried and three are publicly hanged. Dr. Mudd is sentenced to life imprisonment at the military prison at Ft. Jefferson in Dry Tortugas, an island in the Gulf of Mexico near the Florida Keys, which is surrounded by a moat filled with sharks. Shunned by the prison doctor, Dr. MacIntyre, and sadistically threatened by Sergeant Rankin, Dr. Mudd is cheered to find Buck, now in the regiment of black guards, with news from his wife Peggy that a judge, who has stated that Dr. Mudd's conviction would not hold up in a civil court, has agreed to reopen the case if Dr. Mudd can get to Key West. Dr. Mudd plans a breakout with Buck, but during the attempt, Rankin has Buck arrested and orders his men to bring back Dr. Mudd dead. The soldiers shoot at Dr. Mudd on the prison's ledge, and when he falls into the moat, the sharks are driven away by the gunfire. Dr. Mudd reaches Peggy's boat, but Rankin, who has been ordered by his commandant to bring him back alive, boards the boat with soldiers, who fight and kill Peggy's elderly father, Colonel Dyer. Rankin retrieves Dr. Mudd and throws him and Buck into a pit below the prison. When a yellow fever epidemic spreads and Dr. MacIntyre is striken, the commandant asks Dr. Mudd to help without the hope of a reward. The doctor convinces the black soldiers, who have barricaded themselves in the mess hall, to help, but he gets the disease himself. When boats offshore with doctors and medicine refuse to come nearer, Dr. Mudd, brandishing a pistol, orders the black gun crew to shoot their cannon at them, whereupon the ships head in. After the epidemic is controlled and Dr. Mudd is out of danger, Rankin, whom the doctor cared for, is the first to sign a letter to the President urging executive clemency. The doctor returns home to Peggy and Martha with Buck, who is overjoyed to greet Rosabelle and their twelve children. *Dry Tortugas (FL). False arrests. Islands. Dr. Samuel Mudd. Ostracism. Physicians. Prisons. United States–History–Reconstruction, 1865-1898. African Americans. Assassination. John Wilkes Booth. Epidemics. Ford's Theatre (Washington, DC). David Herold. Judges. Laura Keene. Abraham Lincoln. Maryland. Moats. Parades. Prison escapes. Rainstorms. Sadism. Sharks. Shoes. Soldiers. Mary Suratt. Washington (D.C.). Yellow fever.*

Note: The working title of this film was *Shark Island*. After the opening credits, a quotation by George L. Radcliffe, U.S. Senator from Maryland, is presented: "The years have at last removed the shadow which rested upon the name of Dr. Samuel A. Mudd of Maryland, and the nation which once condemned him now acknowledges the unjustice it visited on one of the most unselfish and courageous men in American history." According to a news item, Congress cleared Dr. Mudd's name shortly before the film's release. Mudd died in 1883. A *NYT* news story from Jan 1992 states that the Mudd family had lobbied Congress for seven decades since the pardon by President Andrew Johnson to have the charges dropped entirely. The latest attempt, as stated in the article, occurred at a hearing before a panel of the Army Board of Correction of Military Records on 23 Jan 1992.

According to news items, in Feb 1935, Twentieth Century Pictures, before they merged with Fox, purchased the rights to the film *The Life of Dr. Mudd* by Nettie Mudd Monroe, the doctor's daughter. The film's credits, however, make no reference to Monroe or her book. Modern sources state that Darryl Zanuck, Twentieth Century's vice-president in charge of production, got the idea to make the film after he read an article in *Time* magazine about the prison camp for political prisoners on the Dry Tortugas island.

When the planned film was first publicized in Feb 1935, Fredric March was announced to play the lead, but in Oct 1935, Warner Baxter was assigned the lead instead, as March was scheduled to be loaned to Warner Bros. In Aug 1935, Henry King was announced as director, and in Oct 1935, a news item stated that the studio wanted Jack Holt for the prison commandant. Harry Carey later played that role. The screen credits erroneously spell sound recordist Roger Heman's name "Hemen." The Twentieth Century-Fox trade paper advertising

billing sheet lists the release date as 10 Apr 1936, while release charts in *MPH* list it as 28 Feb 1936. The trade paper billing sheet also states that the film was "personally produced by Darryl F. Zanuck" and that it had "a cast of one thousand." According to *DV*, for the preview at Grauman's Chinese Theater in Hollywood on 11 Feb 1936, the film ran 105 minutes. Frank McGlynn, Sr. was known for his impersonation of Abraham Lincoln. E. C. Ward was listed for sound, and William Stelling was listed as a cast member in *HR* production charts, but their participation in the final film have not been confirmed.

According to news items in *NYT*, director John Ford stated about the film that "it has some of the qualities of *The Informer*, but it's more Hollywood." A *NYT* news item states that Ford was outraged that the film was edited by studio head Zanuck without his participation and was reported to have declared that he would never go to the Twentieth Century-Fox lot again. Ford, in fact, directed a number of subsequent films for the studio. This was screenwriter Nunnally Johnson's first film as an associate producer. Modern sources report a story related by Johnson that Zanuck, after he viewed early rushes, told him to have Ford do something about Baxter's "phony" Southern accent. When Zanuck subsequently viewed more rushes with Baxter using the same accent, he confronted Ford on the set, whereupon Ford threatened to quit. After Zanuck yelled that nobody threatens him, Ford walked over to Baxter and talked to him about the accent. Modern sources list Whitney Bourne and Robert Parrish as additional cast members. In 1958, the Westinghouse Desilu Playhouse presented *The Case for Dr. Mudd* over the CBS television network, which was produced by Jerry Stagg, directed by Allen Miner and starred Lew Ayres.

Box 28 Feb 1936. *DV* 12 Feb 1936, p. 3. *FD* 13 Feb 1936, p. 7. *HR* 11 Feb 1935, p. 1. *HR* 29 Jul 1935, p. 8. *HR* 12 Aug 1935, p. 1. *HR* 23 Oct 1935, p. 4. *HR* 24 Oct 1935, p. 2. *HR* 13 Nov 1935, p. 1. *HR* 18 Nov 1935, p. 1. *HR* 30 Dec 1935, p. 11. *HR* 12 Feb 1936, p. 2. *HR* 17 Oct 1936, sect. II, p. 69. *MPD* 13 Feb 1936, p. 10. *MPH* 1 Feb 1936, pp. 44-45. *MPH* 22 Feb 1936, p. 59. *NYT* 13 Feb 1936, p. 25. *NYT* 24 Jan 1992, p. A7. *Var* 22 Feb 1935. *Var* 19 Feb 1936, p. 12.

PRIVATE IZZY MURPHY (Jewish Americans)

Warner Bros. Pictures, Inc. *Dist* Warner Bros. Pictures, Inc. 30 Oct **1926** [©Warner Bros. Pictures, Inc.; 20 Oct 1926; LP23177]. Si; b&w. 8 reels, 7,889 ft.

Dir Lloyd Bacon. *Asst dir* Sandy Roth. *Adpt* Philip Lonergan. *Story* Raymond L. Schrock and Edward Clark. *Cam* Virgil Miller. *Asst cam* Walter Robinson.

Cast: George Jessel (*Izzy Murphy*), Patsy Ruth Miller (*Eileen Cohannigan*), Vera Gordon (*Sara Goldberg*), Nat Carr (*The Shadchen, Moe Ginsburg*), William Strauss (*Jacob Goldberg*), Spec O'Donnell (*The Monohan Kid*), Gustav von Seyffertitz (*Cohannigan*), Douglas Gerrard (*Robert O'Malley*), Tom Murray (*The Attorney*).

Comedy-drama. Isadore Goldberg, an enterprising Russian Jew, comes to the United States and establishes himself in the delicatessen business so that he can one day send for his parents. Forced to vacate his store, Izzy relocates in an Irish neighborhood; there, after he changes his surname to "Murphy," his business prospers. While waiting for a subway train, Izzy recovers a girl's handkerchief; later, he meets her in his store and learns that she is Eileen Cohannigan, from whose father he buys foodstuffs. After the arrival of Izzy's parents, he embarks for France with an all-Irish regiment and inspires his comrades to deeds of valor. He is welcomed home by Cohannigan, but when Cohannigan learns that he is Jewish, he denounces his daughter for loving him. With the aid of his service buddies, however, Izzy and Eileen head for City Hall to be married. *Bigotry. Courtship. Delicatessens. Immigrants. Irish. Jews. New York City. Russians. World War I.*

FD 14 Nov 1926. *MPW* 30 Oct 1926. *NYT* 10 Nov 1926, p. 25. *Var* 10 Nov 1926, p. 14.

PRIVATE LINE TO BERCHTESGADEN *see* THE HOUSE ON 92ND ST.

EL PROCESO DE MARY DUGAN (Spanish language)

Metro-Goldwyn-Mayer Corp.; controlled by Loew's, Inc. *Dist* Culver Export, Inc. **1931**; New York opening: 26 Jun 1931; *Prod:* Feb—Mar 1931. Sd (Western Electric Sound System); b&w. 9 reels, 7,963 ft. 88 min. Passed by the National Board of Review. Spanish language.

Director Marcel De Sano. [*Asst dir* Harold S. Bucquet]. [*Dial dir* Gregorio Martínez Sierra]. *Versión cinematográfica de* [*Scr*] Becky Gardiner. *Diálogo de* [*Dial*] Eduardo Ugarte and José López Rubio. *Fotografía de* [*Photog*] Gordon Avil. *Director artístico* [*Art dir*] Cedric Gibbons. *Editada por* [*Ed*] Richard Kilpatrick. *Vestuario de* [*Cost*] René Hubert. *Ingeniero de sonido* [*Sd eng*] Douglas Shearer.

Source: Based on the play *The Trial of Mary Dugan* by Bayard Veiller (New York, 19 Sep 1927).

Cast: María Ladrón de Guevara (*Mary Dugan*), José Crespo (*Jimmy Dugan*), Ramón Pereda ([*Edward*] *West*), Rafael Rivelles (*Fiscal*), Elvira Morla (*Sra. Rice*), Adrienne D'Ambricourt (*Marie Ducrot*),

Celia Montalván (*May Harris*), Delia Magaña (*Dagmar Lorne*), Juan de Landa (*Inspector Hunt*), Soriano Viosca (*Juez*), Julio Villarreal (*Dr. Welcome*), Lucio Villegas (*Capitán Price*), Manuel París (*Henry Plaisted*), Romualdo Tirado (*James Madison*), [Paco Moreno (*Secretario*)].

Melodrama. [*Not viewed*]. [The following plot summary is based on the English-language version of this film, *The Trial of Mary Dugan*; character names refer to that version. For further information regarding the English-language version, please see the note below and the entry for *The Trial of Mary Dugan* in the *AFI Catalog of Feature Films, 1921-30*.] Pretty Mary Dugan is placed on trial for the murder of her sugardaddy, who was found shot to death in the apartment he kept for her. Edward West, Mary's attorney, deliberately restrains himself in his cross-examination of the witnesses for the prosecution, and Mary's brother, Jimmy, who is a fledgling lawyer, strongly protests. West withdraws from the case, and Jimmy takes over his sister's defense. Jimmy puts Mary on the stand, and her subsequent testimony reveals that she had been the mistress of four successive men in order to earn enough money to put Jimmy through law school. Jimmy brings about Mary's acquittal by proving that Edward West was the man who murdered Mary's benefactor. *Brothers and sisters. District attorneys. Finance–Personal. Lawyers. Mistresses. Murder. Trials.*

Note: M-G-M remade the 1929 English-language film *The Trial of Mary Dugan*, which was written and directed bu Bayard Veiller and starred Norma Shearer and Lewis Stone, in Spanish, French and German versions. The onscreen credits were taken from studio cutting continuities. Some sources include actor Juan Duval in the credits of the Spanish version, but his participation in the released film has not been confirmed.

Other language version(s):
Le procès de Mary Dugan (French language)
1931; Prod: late Jan—early Feb 1931. Sd (Western Electric Sound System); b&w. 11 reels. 100 min. Passed by the National Board of Review. French language.
Réalisation de [*Dir*] Marcel De Sano. *Scénario de* [*Scr*] Becky Gardiner. *Adaptée en français par* [*French adpt*] Henry Torrès and H. [Honoré] de Carbuccia. *Dialogue de* [*Dial*] Jacques Deval and Jean Blanchon. *Photographie de* [*Photog*] Gordon Avil. *Décorateur* [*Art dir*] Cedric Gibbons. *Montage de* [*Ed*] Conrad A. Nervig. *Costumes de* [*Cost*] René Hubert. *Ingénieur du son* [*Sd eng*] Douglas Shearer.
French-language cast: Huguette ex-Duflos (*Mary Dugan*), Charles Boyer (*Le procureur*), André Burgère (*Jimmy Dugan*), Marcel André (*West*), Françoise Rosay (*Mme. Rice*), Adrienne d'Ambricourt (*Jeanne Ducrot*), Rolla Norman (*Inspecteur Hunt*), George Mauloy (*Le juge*), Emil Chautard (*Dr. Welcome*), Jean Perry (*Capitaine Price*), Jacques Jou-Jerville (*Henry Plaisted*), Jeanne Helbling (*Dagmar Lorne*), Mireille (*May Harris*), George Davis (*James Madison*). [*French version not viewed*]
Mordprozess Mary Dugan (German. language)
Dist Culver Export, Inc. **1931**. New York opening: 13 Jan 1931; Berlin opening: 2 Feb 1931; Sd (Western Electric Sound System); b&w. 12 reels, 115 min. German. language.
Regie [*Dir*] Arthur Robison. *Drehbuch* [*Scr*] Becky Gardiner. *Deutscher dialog* [*German dial*] Arthur Robison. *Photographie* [*Photog*] Henry Sharp. *Bauten* [*Art dir*] Cedric Gibbons. *Filmschnitt* [*Ed*] Anson Stevenson. *Kostueme* [*Cost*] René Hubert. *Tontechniker* [*Sd tech*] Douglas Shearer.
German-language cast: Nora Gregor ([*Mary Dugan*]), Egon von Jordan ([*Jimmy Dugan*]), Lucy Doraine ([*Ilona*]), Arnold Korff ([*Prosecutor*]), Julia Serda ([*Marie*]), Hedwiga Reicher ([*Frau Rice*]), Margaret Knapp, Peter Erkelenz ([*West*]), Reginald Pasch, Leo White, Hermann Bing. [*German. version not viewed*].
HF 31 Jan 1931, p. 24. *Var* 4 Mar 1931, p. 22.

THE PRODIGAL RETURNS see EL OTRO SOY YO

PROFESSOR CREEPS (African Americans)
Dixie National. *Dist* Consolidated National Film Exchanges. **1942**; Los Angeles opening: week of 28 Feb 1942. Sd; b&w. 5,960 ft. 63 min. PCA cert no. 8138.
Prod Jed Buell. *Assoc prod* Dick L'Estrange and Maceo B. Sheffield. *Dir* William Beaudine. *Scr* William X. Crowley, Roy Clements, Jed Buell and Robert Edmunds. *Orig story* Robert Edmunds. *Cine* Arthur Martinelli. *Film ed* Dan Milner. *Sd eng* Ben Winkler.
Cast: F. E. Miller (*Jefferson*), Mantan Moreland (*Washington*), Arthur Ray (*Professor Whackingham Creeps*), Florence O'Brien (*Daffodil Dixon*), Maceo B. Sheffield (*Landlord*), Margaret Whitten

(*Mrs. Green*), Shelton Brooks (*Jackson*), Jessie Cryer (*Mr. Green*), Billy Mitchell (*Schenectady*), Zack Williams (*Phone man*), Charles Hawkins (*Pawnbroker*), Clarence Hargrave (*Alexander*), John Lester Johnson (*Keeper*), Nappie Whiting (*Taxi driver*).

African American, Detective, Comedy. [*Not viewed*]. Washington and Jefferson, a pair of bumbling private investigators who run a nearly bankrupt agency called "Bloodhound Ink," elude with clever disguises the various bill collectors and the landlord who come to demand their payments. Later that day, Washington dreams that the alluring Daffodil Dixon, or "Daffy," a Harlem debutante, visits the private investigators for help in locating her boyfriend, Alexander, who has mysteriously disappeared. The detectives soon discover that Alexander is not the first boyfriend to vanish and that every time a suitor is on the verge of proposing to Daffy, he vanishes without a trace. To solve the case, Washington and Jefferson go to the scene of the mysterious events, the house belonging to Daffy's uncle, Professor Whackingham Creeps, and when they decide to recreate the events of Alexander's disappearance, they fight over who gets to play the lucky suitor. Jefferson wins and then disappears like the others. The professor then arrives, and Jefferson reappears. The professor demonstrates how he can defy gravity and turn people into animals with a squirt from his special gun. From behind a door, the detectives suddenly hear Alexander's voice, telling them that he was squirted because if Daffy marries she will receive an inheritance that the professor covets. Alexander adds that the cellar is full of Daffy's former suitors, who now boast horns and other deformities, as well as a Japanese man who was squirted in retaliation for Pearl Harbor. When the boys try to get the professor's squirt gun, he turns Jefferson into a gorilla, and Jefferson retaliates by turning the professor into a duck. Meanwhile, a real gorilla, Lulu, has escaped from the local circus, and in the confusion to find the squirt gun and give Jefferson back his human form, Washington and Lulu's keepers confuse Jefferson with the gorilla. Finally, Washington wakes up, relieved that the events at the home of Professor Creeps were only a dream. *African Americans. Dreams. Mad scientists. Missing persons. Private detectives. Transmutation. Bill collectors. Circuses. Disguise. Gorillas. Heiresses. Inheritance. Japanese.*

Note: The film's original title was *Goodbye Mr. Creeps*. In the file on the film contained in the MPAA/PCA Collection at the AMPAS Library, a 21 Jan 1942 telegram sent to PCA official Geoffrey Shurlock, PCA official Carl Milliken expressed concern over the film's title, stating that travesties on "important titles" must be approved by the producer concerned, in this case M-G-M, which made the film *Goodbye Mr. Chips*. Shurlock responded that because the film was an "all-Negro" production destined only for Negro theaters, it seemed unlikely that it would conflict with the M-G-M film. No additional correspondence was found, and although the film was indeed released under another title, it is not clear whether the conflict with *Goodbye Mr. Chips* was responsible for the change. Despite Shurlock's prediction, *Professor Creeps* was previewed to a racially mixed audience at Los Angeles' Lincoln Theatre, located on Central Avenue, according to a *NYT* item. The *HR* reviewer commented that the Hollywood reviewers who attended the preview on Central Avenue "in the heart of the colored district were treated to a new experience when they sat in a yelling, screaming audience that unrestrainedly relished every moment of the film." The critic for the *PittsC* stated, "even the heretofore...'Anti' all-Negro picture critics, including your correspondent, who came to slash and lambast the 'Professor,' were lost in the...mirth of the youngsters." Contemporary reviews praised the film's "medicine show" and "minstrel show era" humor, a type of entertainment that, according to *FD*, the film's producers were trying to introduce "to the screens of formerly restricted theaters." Reviewers almost unanimously proclaimed the film's marketability to white as well as African American audiences, and urged exhibitors to take a chance with the film at their white-patronage theaters. Contemporary reviewers also compared stars F. E. Miller and Mantan Moreland to Abbott and Costello, with *MPD* terming them the "sepia Abbott and Costello."

Box 14 Mar 1942. *FD* 26 Feb 1942, p. 6. *HR* 20 Feb 1942, p. 3. *MPHPD* 28 Feb 1942, p. 526. *NYT* 1 Mar 1942. *PittsC* 5 Mar 1942.

PROUD HEART see HIS PEOPLE

THE PRUSSIAN CUR (German Americans)
Fox Film Corp. *Dist* Fox Film Corp. 1 Sep **1918** [©William Fox; 1 Sep 1918; LP12795]. Si; b&w. 8 reels.
Pres William Fox. *Dir* R. A. Walsh. *Story and scen* R. A. Walsh. *Cam* Roy Overbaugh.
Cast: Miriam Cooper (*Rosie O'Grady*), Sidney Mason (*Dick Gregory*), Capt. Horst von der Goltz (*Otto Goltz*), Leonora Stewart (*Lillian O'Grady*), James Marcus (*Patrick O'Grady*), Patrick O'Malley (*Jimmie O'Grady*), Walter McEwen (*Count Johann von Bernstorff*), William W. Black (*Wolff von Eidel*), Ralph Faulkner (*Woodrow Wilson*), Walter M. Lawrence (*Emperor William II*),

Charles Reynolds (*Emperor William I*), William Harrison (*Crown Prince Frederick*), James Hathaway (*Field Marshal von Hindenburg*), P. C. Hartigan (*Admiral von Tirpitz*), John E. Franklin (*James W. Gerard*), John W. Harbon (*U.S. Congressman*).

Espionage, **World War I**, **Drama**. Before diplomatic relations between the United States and Germany have been severed during World War I, Count Johann von Bernstorff establishes an intricate spy network in America, headed by the treacherous Otto Goltz and his ally, Wolff von Eidel. Their activities result in labor strikes, factory explosions, and transportation disasters. Headquartered in a major U.S. industrial center, Otto marries Lillian O'Grady and treats her so brutally that she eventually dies. Lillian's death is avenged by a young American soldier named Dick Gregory, who is in love with her sister Rosie. Following Otto's death, von Eidel is arrested, but when a group of German sympathizers tries to rescue him, a patriotic vigilante group attacks the jail, shooting the spy and imprisoning the disloyal Americans. In the end, as American forces storm France, Kaiser Wilhelm grows desperate. *German Americans. Germans. Revenge. Sabotage. Spies. Vigilantes. World War I. Battered women. Explosions. Jails. Marriage. Murder. Nobility. Soldiers. Strikes and lockouts. Traitors. Wilhelm II, German Emperor, 1859-1941. Woodrow Wilson.*

Note: Capt. Horst von der Goltz was an actual German spy operating in the United States, Mexico and Canada. Ralph Faulkner was known for his resemblance to President Woodrow Wilson. According to one reviewer, about two-thirds of the film was made up of weekly news footage. The scenario included in the copyright descriptions was entitled "The Invisible Embassy."

ETR 17 Aug 1918, p. 862. *ETR* 31 Aug 1918, p. 1091. *MPN* 7 Sep 1918, p. 1592. *MPW* 7 Sep 1918, p. 1455. *MPW* 5 Oct 1918, pp. 125-26. *Wid's* 25 Aug 1918, pp. 19-20.

THE PUBLIC BE DAMNED see **ELSA MAXWELL'S PUBLIC DEB NO. 1**

PUBLIC DEB NO. 1 see **ELSA MAXWELL'S PUBLIC DEB NO. 1**

PUBLIC RELATIONS see **ELSA MAXWELL'S PUBLIC DEB NO. 1**

PUDD'NHEAD WILSON (African Americans)

Jesse L. Lasky Feature Play Co. *Dist* Paramount Pictures Corp. 31 Jan 1916 [©The Mark Twain Co.; 5 Feb 1916; LU7572]. Si; b&w. 5 reels.

Dir Frank Reicher. *Asst dir* Frank Lidell. *Scen* Margaret Turnbull. *Cam* Walter Stradling. *Art dir* Wilfred Buckland.

Source: Based on the novel *Pudd'nhead Wilson* by Mark Twain (Hartford, 1894).

Cast: Theodore Roberts (*Pudd'nhead Wilson*), Alan Hale (*Tom Driscoll*), Thomas Meighan (*Chambers*), Florence Dagmar (*Rowena Cooper*), Jane Wolff (*Roxy*), Ernest Joy (*Judge Driscoll*), Gertrude Kellar (*Mrs. Driscoll*).

Comedy-drama. In the pre-Civil War South, lawyer Pudd'nhead Wilson suffers the mockery of the community because of his obsession with fingerprints. Two of his samples are the infant prints of Tom Driscoll, the son of a white woman, and Chambers, whose mother is a mulatto nurse. Both boys have the same father, however, and both are about the same age, and after their birth, Roxy, angry at the Driscolls, switches them, so that quadroon valet. Then, the false Tom murders his uncle and tries to blame his valet for the crime. Pudd'nhead defends the accused, and while comparing new fingerprint samples against the old, discovers the switch that was made years before. He then convinces an initially skeptical jury to accept the infallibility of fingerprint evidence, after which the real Tom is restored as the Driscoll heir and the false one goes to jail. *Criminologists. False arrests. Half brothers. Lawyers. Murder. Trials. United States–South. Valets. African Americans-Mixed blood. Heirs. Juries.*

Note: A theatrical version of the novel by Frank Mayo opened in New York on 15 Apr 1895. The novel was originally published as a serial in *The Century Magazine* from Dec 1893 to Jun 1894. Although the *Var* review of this film mentions Cecil B. DeMille as the "producer," it seems unlikely that he had any direct association with the picture. As DeMille was the Director-General of the company at that time, *Var* may have been referring to this position rather than the actual producer or director credit. According to a news item in *NYDM* this film was to be the first in a series of Mark Twain stories to be adapted for the screen by the Lasky Co., but the series did not continue after *Pudd'nhead Wilson*. The film was remade in 1984 and shown on the American Playhouse television series, with Ken Howard starring and Alan Bridges directing.

MPN 12 Feb 1916, p. 866. *MPW* 12 Feb 1916, p. 1030. *MPW* 26 Feb 1916, p. 1311. *NYDM* 22 Jan 1916, p. 31. *NYDM* 26 Feb 1916, p. 32. *Var* 4 Feb 1916, p. 24.

THE PULSE OF LIFE (Italian Americans)

Bluebird Photoplays, Inc. *Dist* Bluebird Photoplays, Inc. 2 Apr **1917** [©Bluebird Photoplays, Inc.; 9 Mar 1917; LP10342]. Si; b&w. 5 reels.

Dir Rex Ingram. *Scen* Rex Ingram. *Story* E. Magnus Ingleton. *Cam* Duke Hayward.

Cast: Gypsy Harte (*Lisetta*), Wedgewood Nowell (*Guido Serrani*), Dorothy Barrett (*Buckety Sue*), Molly Malone (*Molly Capels*), Nicholas Dunaew (*Domenic*), Millard K. Wilson (*Standford Graham*), Albert MacQuarrie (*"Dago" Joe*), Edward Brown (*Luigi Maseto*), Seymour Hastings (*Hasting Capels*), William Dyer (*Fish merchant*).

Drama. Lisetta, the daughter of a fisherman, lives with her father and brother on the island of Capri. When Serrani, an Italian who has grown wealthy in New York, visits the island, he induces Lisetta to accompany him to America. There he abandons her and she becomes a dancer in an underworld café owned by "Dago" Joe, where she meets the artist Stanford Graham, who employs her as a model. Meanwhile Lisetta's brother Domenic comes to New York to avenge his sister's dishonor. As he arrives, Graham's fiancée's father asks Serrani to use his influence with the artist to separate Graham and Lisetta, and Serrani visits the studio, where he is denounced by Lisetta and threatened by Graham. Later Domenic visits Serrani and stabs him with an ornamental dagger owned by Graham. Circumstantial evidence convicts the artist, who is about to die in the electric chair when Domenic confesses. Realizing that she is not a fit wife for Graham, Lisetta then refuses to marry him and returns to her island home. *Capri (Italy). Family honor. Italian Americans. Italians. Murder. New York City. Artists. Brothers and sisters. Cafés. Circumstantial evidence. Confession (Law). Dancers. Desertion (Marital). Fishermen. Models.*

Note: The synopsis included in the copyright descriptions was originally entitled "Humanity." Some character names in this synopsis differ from those included in reviews.

ETR 24 Mar 1917, p. 1107. *Motog* 21 Apr 1917, p. 847. *MPN* 31 Mar 1917, p. 2029. *MPW* 31 Mar 1917, pp. 2119-20. *MPW* 14 Apr 1917, p. 325. *NYDM* 24 Mar 1917, p. 26. *Var* 23 Mar 1917, p. 25. *Wid's* 22 Mar 1917, p. 183.

THE PUMPKIN SHELL see **MY PAL WOLF**

PUPPETS (Italian Americans)

Al Rockett Productions. *Dist* First National Pictures, Inc. 11 Jul **1926**; New York premiere: 20 Jun 1926 [©First National Pictures, Inc.; 21 Jun 1926; LP22831]. Si; b&w. 8 reels, 7,468 or 7,486 ft.

Dir George Archainbaud. *Asst dir* Al Lena. *Scen* John F. Goodrich. *Photog* Charles Van Enger. *Art dir* Milton Menasco. *Film ed* Arthur Tavares. *Prod mgr* Al Rockett.

Source: Based on the play *Puppets* by Frances Lightner (production date undetermined).

Cast: Milton Sills (*Nicki*), Gertrude Olmstead (*Angela*), Francis McDonald (*Bruno*), Mathilde Comont (*Rosa*), Lucien Prival (*Frank*), William Ricciardi (*Sandro*), Nick Thompson (*Joe*).

Melodrama. Nicola Riccobini, a puppet master in New York's Italian quarter, is an energetic and domineering man in the family, in contrast to his dreamy, poetic cousin Bruno. Rosa (the wardrobe mistress), Sandro (the veteran handyman who worships Nicki), and Frank (a sinister betrayer of girls who plays the piano for puppet performances) constitute the group. Nicki falls in love with Angela, a wistful runaway, but is summoned to war before they can be married; he instructs Bruno to protect her from Frank while he is gone. When Nicki is reported dead, Bruno and Angela fall in love, though she is desired also by Frank. Nicki returns unexpectedly, deaf from shell shock, and the lovers plot in his presence to run away. Frank conspires to have Angela abducted, but Nicki intervenes; the shock of the experience cures his deafness. When Bruno struggles with Nicki, the theater catches on fire. Bruno's cowardice is revealed, and Angela is reunited with Nicki. *Fires. Italian Americans. New York City–Little Italy. Puppets. Shell shock. Theater. Veterans. World War I.*

FD 25 Jul 1926. *MPW* 3 Jul 1926. *NYT* 21 Jun 1926, p. 17. *Var* 23 Jun 1926, p. 14.

PUPPETS OF FATE (Italian Americans)

Metro Pictures Corp. *Dist* Metro Pictures Corp. 28 Mar **1921** . [©Metro Pictures Corp.; 29 Mar 1921; LP16340]. Si; b&w. 6 reels.

Dir Dallas M. Fitzgerald. *Scen* Ruth Ann Baldwin and Molly Parro. *Story* Brian Oswald Donn-Byrne. *Photog* John Arnold. *Art dir* Sidney Ullman.

Cast: Viola Dana (*Sorrentina Palombra*), Francis McDonald (*Gabriel Palombra*), Jackie Saunders (*"Babe" Reynolds*), Fred Kelsey (*Bobs*), Thomas Ricketts (*Father Francesco*), Edward Kennedy (*Mike Reynolds*).

Melodrama. Gabriel Palombra, who operates a Punchinello street show in Venice, decides to fulfill his ambition of going to America. He leaves behind his wife, Sorrentina, promising to send for her. In the United States, disillusioned, he takes a job as porter in a barbershop, but when he is rewarded for returning a lost pocketbook, manicurist "Babe" Reynolds persuades him to bet on a winning horse. Under her influence he rises to wealth. Meanwhile, Sorrentina arrives in New York and takes work as a flower vendor. Having married Gabriel, "Babe" brings charges of bigamy against him, but the judge, perceiving her game, sentences Gabriel, then paroles him to Sorrentina for life. *Barbers and barbershops. Bigamy. Flower vendors. Immigrants. Italian Americans. Manicurists. Porters. Puppets. Venice (Italy).*

ETR 16 Apr 1921, p. 1797.

LA PURA VERDAD (Spanish language)
Films Paramount; controlled by Paramount Publix Corp. *Dist* Paramount Publix Corp. **1931**; Buenos Aires, Argentina opening: 4 Dec 1931; San Juan, Puerto Rico opening: 12 Dec 1931; Barcelona, Spain opening: 24 Dec 1931; Los Angeles opening: 22 Jan 1932; Prod: Jun—Jul 1931 at Paramount studios in Joinville, France. Sd; b&w. 8,045 ft. 89 min. *Country of origin* France. Spanish language.
Dir Manuel Romero. *Dial dir* Florián Rey. *Scr* John McGowan. *Adpt and Spanish dial* Pedro Muñoz Seca.
Song(s): By Alvaro Cubas.
Source: Based on the play *Nothing but the Truth* by James H. Montgomery (New York, 14 Sep 1916).
Cast: José Isbert (*Señor Lamberti*), Enriqueta Serrano (*Emilia Lamberti*), Manuel Russell (*Roberto*), María Brú (*Señora Lamberti*), Goyita Herrero (*Sabel*), Amalia de Isaura (*Presidenta*), José Soria (*Ricardo*), Manuel Vico (*Apolodoro*), Pedro Valdivieso (*Reverendo Doran*), Pilar Casteig (*Mabel*), Pedro González (*Silvan*), Antoñita Colomé (*Esther*), María González (*Secretaria*), Leda Ginelli (*Marta*), Gaby Morelle (*Enfermera*), Freddy Castel (*Cubano*), Joaquín Carrasco (*Doctor*), Pelayo Corgo (*Banquero*), Ramón Portavella (*Jardinero*), Francisco Alarcón (*Chófer*), José Sierra de Luna (*Director del cabaret*).
Comedy. [*Not viewed*]. The Association for Social Action Against Nudity is holding a charity ball. Present at the event are the banker Lamberti, his wife, and daughter Emilia, the treasurer of the association. Emilia has a check for 250,000 francs and, in order not to lose it, entrusts it to a businessman. The next day the newspaper announces the latest financial scandal: the businessman has fled. Emilia asks her boyfriend Roberto for help, but as he doesn't have enough money, he consults the girl's father. The banker doesn't want to get involved but suggests that Roberto take charge of selling some worthless stocks by tricking the buyer. Before this proposition, Roberto had made a bet not to lie for an entire day. He now becomes the center of attraction for all interested in learning the truth about any delicate matter. A dancer has confessed to the banker's jealous wife that she has been the banker's lover ever since he seduced her as a young girl. Roberto, although still involved in the bet, denies to Emilia that the story about her father is true. The friends say that with this reply Roberto has lost the bet, but he proves to them that a day has in fact elapsed and that the bet is over. *Bankers. Fathers and daughters. Wagers. Balls (Parties). Businessmen. Confession. Dancers. Infidelity. Jealousy. Marriage. Nudism. Scandal. Stocks.*

Note: James Montgomery's play was based on the novel *Nothing But the Truth* by Frederic Stewart Isham. In 1929, Paramount released *Nothing but the Truth*, which was based on Montgomery's play. That film was directed by Victor Schertzinger and starred Richard Dix and Helen Kane (see *AFI Catalog of Feature Films, 1921-30;* F2.3896). Paramount's Joinville studio produced foreign-language versions of this film in French, Spanish and German in 1931, and the New York State censors approved the Spanish and German versions for exhibition in 1932, but no information has been located to suggest that the French version was ever shown in the U.S. No reviews were located for the Spanish or German versions. The running times were calculated from footage given in NYSA records. *Rien que la verité*, the French-language version, which opened in Paris on 11 Sep 1931, was directed by René Guissart and starred Meg Lemonnier and Saint-Granier. In 1939, a Swedish film entitled *Rena rama sanningen*, based on the play, was produced by Fribergs Filmbyrå. It was directed by Weyler Hildebrand and starred Erik "Bullen" Berglund and Tollie Zellman.

Other language version(s):
Die nackte Wahrheit (German language)
1932; Berlin opening: 12 Jan 1932; Prod: at Paramount studios in Joinville, France. Sd; b&w. 6,845 ft. 76 min. German language.
Dir Karl Anton. *Wrt* Paul Schiller. *Photog* René Dantan. *Art dir* Henry Ménessier.
German-language cast: Otto Wernicke, Trude Hesterberg, Jenny Jugo, Oskar Karlweis, Tibor von Halmay, Hans Adalbert Schlettow, Alexander Kökert, Harry Hardt, Marita Angeles, Jaro Fürth, Harry Nestor. [*German version not viewed*].
Var 29 Sep 1931, p. 31.

DER PURIMSPIELER *see* **THE JESTER (DER PURIMSPIELER)**

THE PURPLE CIPHER (Chinese Americans)
Vitagraph Co. of America. *Dist* Vitagraph Co. of America. 11 Oct **1920** [©The Vitagraph Co. of America; 14 Aug 1920; LP15432]. Si; b&w. 5 reels.
Pres Albert E. Smith. *Dir* Chester Bennett. *Scen* J. Grubb Alexander.
Source: Based on the short story "The Purple Hieroglyph" by Will F. Jenkins in *Snappy Stories* (1 Mar 1920).
Cast: Earle Williams (*Leonard Staunton*), Vola Vale (*Jeanne Baldwin*), Ernest Shields (*Jack Baldwin*), Allen Forrest (*Alan Fitzhugh*), Henry A. Barrows (*Frank Condon*), Goro Kino (*Hop Lee*), Frank Seki (*Wang Foo*).
Mystery. Jeanne Baldwin, Leonard Staunton, Alan Fitzhugh and Jack Baldwin are guided on a tour of underground dens in Chinatown by Hop Lee. During their trip, Wang Foo abducts Jeanne, and she and her companions are rescued through the intervention of private detective Frank Condon. Three months later, Fitzhugh is missing, supposedly murdered by the Chinese. Jack Baldwin is threatened, poisoned and his body disappears. Next, a threat against Jeanne is received by Staunton. To save her life, he is to meet the blackmailers at a bay in the harbor. Enlisting the aid of a submarine, Staunton captures the three conspirators, who turn out to be the missing victims in the case, led by Condon. The three had planned the escapade to extort money from Staunton. The mystery thus resolved, Staunton and Jeanne are married. *Conspiracy. Detectives. Extortion. Missing persons, Assumed dead. Chinese Americans. Guides. Kidnapping. Poisoning. Rescues. San Francisco (CA)–Chinatown. Submarine boats.*

Note: The working title of this film was *The Purple Hieroglyph*. Some scenes in this film were shot in the shipyards of San Francisco and at the naval station at San Diego, CA. First National Pictures made a film based on the same story in 1930 entitled *Murder Will Out*, which was directed by Clarence Badger and starred Jack Mulhall. (See *AFI Catalog of Feature Films, 1921-30;* F2.3730.).
ETR 23 Oct 1920, p. 2184. MPN 18 Sep 1920, p. 2256. MPN 19 Jun 1920, p. 4974. MPW 5 Jun 1920, p. 1351. MPW 16 Oct 1920, p. 995.

PURPLE DAWN (Chinese Americans)
Dist Aywon Film Corp. **1923**; New York showing: ca10 May 1923. Si; b&w. 5 reels, 4,850 ft.
Pres Nathan Hirsh. *Dir* Charles R. Seeling. *Story and scr* Charles R. Seeling. *Photog* Raymond Walker and Vernon Walker.
Cast: Bert Sprotte (*Red Carson, sea captain*), William E. Aldrich (*Bob*), James B. Leong (*Quan Foo*), Edward Piel (*Wong Chang, Tong leader*), Bessie Love (*Mui Far*), William Horne (*Mr. Ketchell*), Priscilla Bonner (*Ruth Ketchell, Bob's sweetheart*).
Melodrama. Bob, a young sailor, unwittingly becomes involved in drug smuggling activities in San Francisco when he is sent to deliver a package of opium to Wong Chang, a Tong leader. A rival gang waylays him, steals the drugs, and drops him off in the country. In his wandering, he gets a job in a country store and falls in love with local girl Ruth Ketchell, forgetting the Chinese girl, left behind in the city, who loves him. Wong Chang finds him and returns him to the ship's captain, who beats Bob for allegedly stealing the drugs. The Tong kidnap Ruth and threaten to kill Bob, but the Chinese girl, who happens to be Wong Chang's daughter, saves the two. The last hundred feet of the film are tinted a light purple (hence the film's title), showing the Chinese girl, aware of the futility of her love, walking off in the early morning light after having united the loving couple. It is not clear whether she commits suicide or returns to her Chinese fiancé. *Chinese Americans. Drugs. Gangs. Sailors. San Francisco (CA). Sea captains. Smuggling. Tongs (Secret societies).*

Note: There is some doubt about the credit to Vernon Walker for photography.
FD 15 Apr 1923. Var 17 May 1923, p. 26.

THE PURPLE HIEROGLYPH *see* **THE PURPLE CIPHER**

PURSUED *(foreign version) see* **NADA MÁS QUE UNA MUJER**

THE PUSHER (Latino)

M. K. R. Films, Inc. *Dist* United Artists Corp. Jan **1960**; Prod: Jan 1958 [©United Artists Corp.; 25 Nov 1959; LP16076]. Sd; b&w. 10 reels, 7,300 ft. 81-82 min. Passed by the National Board of Review. PCA cert no. 19051.

Prod Gene Milford and Sidney Katz. *Assoc prod* Bernard Storper. *Prod exec* Ralph Rosenblum. *Dir* Gene Milford. *Asst dir* Tony LaMarca and Jack Berk. *Scr* Harold Robbins. *Dir of photog* Arthur J. Ornitz. *Art dir* Sam Leve. *Ed* Sidney Katz. *Mus dir* Raymond Scott. *Orch* Van Clave. *Orch cond* Jack Shaindlin. *Asst mus dir* Lawrence Elow. *Sd rec* Edward Fenton. *Makeup* Clay Lambert. *Hairdresser* Ian Forrest. *Prod mgr* Donn Huffsmith. *Casting dir* Selma Lynch. *Script* Sascha Laurance. [*Tech adv* William L. Rowe].

Song(s): "Where Have You Been Billie Boy," music by Raymond Scott, lyrics by Lawrence Elow.

Source: Based on the novel *The Pusher* by Ed McBain (New York, 1956).

Cast: Introducing Kathy Carlyle [(*Laura Byrne*)], Douglas F. Rodgers [(*Lt. Peter Byrne*)], Felice Orlandi [(*Gonzo, the pusher, also known as Doug*)], Robert Lansing [(*Steve Carella*)], Sara Aman [(*Maria Hernandez*)], Sloan Simpson [(*Harriet Byrne*)], Beatrice Pons [(*Mrs. Hernandez*)], Jim Boles [(*Newspaper vendor*)], Ernesto Gonzales [(*Ernesto*)], John Fostini [(*Harry*)], [David Ford (*Detective Kling*)], [William Doerner (*Patrolman Genero*)], [Antonio Obregon (*Shoeshine boy*)], [Jeno Mate (*Bartender*)], [Lee Jones (*Young man*)], [Donna Maran (*Gert*)], [Joanna Merlin (*Shoeshine boy's mother*)].

Social, Melodrama. [*Print viewed*]. In the Puerto Rican tenements of New York's Spanish Harlem, a loud radio attracts a policeman to the basement rooms of the Green Tigers gang. There he finds the body of a teenaged boy named Anibal Hernandez, and near it, a hypodermic needle. Lt. Peter Byrne and his partner, Steve Carella, attribute the death to suicide, believing that the youth hanged himself. Anibal's mother, however, describes her son as a happy boy who would never kill himself. Admitting that Anibal was a drug addict, Mrs. Hernandez adds that he learned his habit from his sister Maria, who had not taken drugs until she immigrated to the United States. Mrs. Hernandez then begs Lt. Byrne to find her son's murderer, even "though we are Puerto Rican." Meanwhile, Byrne's daughter Laura, who is engaged to Steve, visits her pusher and informs him of Anibal's death. Remarking that "spic punks" are unpredictable, the pusher denies involvement with the murder and offers Laura a fix. While swearing that she is not addicted, Laura accepts the heroin, but slips from the pusher's grasp when he tries to kiss her. Angry, the pusher reminds her that her fingerprints were on the hypodermic case that was found near Anibal's body. Byrne and Steve, meanwhile, interrogate the Green Tigers and incarcerate the four who have needle marks on their arms. At Byrne's home, Laura's mother Harriet notices that she is unusually jumpy but attributes this to her daughter's impending marriage. Later, Laura tells the pusher that the police now regard Anibal as a murder victim and that she is becoming frightened. Unconcerned, he conducts business as usual on the street. At the Baby Doll Club, a Puerto Rican night spot where the pusher meets many of his contacts, Steve asks Anibal's sister Maria, a dancer, if a pusher might have murdered her brother. Maria warns Steve that the club is dangerous and offers to meet him at her apartment the following day. Unknown to these two, the pusher overhears the conversation from a nearby table, and that night, after claiming that he loves Maria, he stabs her to death. Before she dies, Steve enters and hears her murmur, "Gonzo." The next day, Laura admits to Steve that she is "sick" but then rushes away. Steve follows her and sees the pusher, whose name he hears as "Gonzo," give Laura a packet of heroin. After she leaves, Steve confronts Gonzo, who explains that he gets young women hooked by giving them "powders" to calm their nerves. He then takes Steve into the bushes and shoots him. Because Steve had managed to inform Byrne of his whereabouts, the lieutenant finds his wounded partner and takes him to the hospital. At police headquarters, the gang members are beginning to experience withdrawal symptoms, and the leader mentions the name Gonzo. Later, Byrne receives a note from "G" informing him that the prints on the hypodermic case belong to his daughter. Horrified, Byrne returns home to find Laura preparing

to shoot heroin into her arm. The two argue, and Byrne locks her into her room, thereby forcing her to endure a "cold turkey" withdrawal. Tormented by her screams, moans and ominous silences, Laura's parents sit by her door for many hours. At one point, Laura accuses Byrne of trying merely to protect his "cushy" job, but the next morning, she emerges from her room and apologizes. She then gives Byrne an address and tells him that the pusher's name is Doug, although the neighborhood's Puerto Ricans call him Gonzo. At the pusher's apartment, a disgruntled drug runner directs Byrne to Gonzo's hideout. Byrne finds Gonzo there, but he escapes. The lieutenant later surprises the pusher at his apartment and, after nearly killing him in a rage, turns him over to another officer. Later, at the hospital, Steve awakens from a coma and in response to Laura's tearful plea for forgiveness, assures her that "what we have to do, we'll do together." *Drug addicts. Drug dealers. Fathers and daughters. Heroin. Murder. Police. Assimilation (Sociology). Bars. Chases. Dancers. Engagements. Gangs. Latino. Immigrants. Investigations. Motherhood. New York City–Spanish Harlem. Nightclubs. Puerto Ricans. Shootings. Stabbings.*

Note: Although the onscreen copyright notice lists 1958 as the year of copyright, the official registration date was 1959. News items and other pre-release sources list the production company as Miro Productions and note that *The Pusher* was to be the first in a series of films shot in New York, under the aegis of producers Harold Robbins and Raymond Scott. That company name is not included in the onscreen credits, however, nor any other post-production reference source. Gene Milford, a former Oscar-winning editor, made his directorial debut with this film. Technical adviser William L. Rowe was the former Deputy Police Commissioner of New York. Contemporary sources note that the picture was filmed entirely in Manhattan.

Box 25 Jan 1960. *DV* 13 Jan 1960, p. 3. *Exb* 6 Jan 1960, p. 4666. *FD* 12 Jan 1960, p. 10. *Har* 16 Jan 1960, pp. 10-11. *HR* 17 Jan 1958, p. 13. *HR* 24 Jan 1958, p. 17. *HR* 13 Jan 1960, p. 3. *MPHPD* 6 Feb 1960, p. 581. *Var* 20 Jan 1960, p. 6.

PUZZLE MAN *see* **RENDEZVOUS**

QING HOI YIN HONE *see* **CHIN HAI IN SIONG**

QUALITY *see* **PINKY**

QUAND ON EST BELLE (French language)

Metro-Goldwyn-Mayer Corp.; controlled by Loew's, Inc. *Dist* Metro-Goldwyn-Mayer Distributing Corp. **1931**; Prod: began mid-Jan 1931. Sd (Western Electric Sound System); b&w. 9 reels. 85 min. Passed by the National Board of Review. French language.

Réalisation de [*Dir*] Arthur Robison. *Adaptation de* [*Adpt*] Edith Ellis. *Dialogue français de* [*French dial*] Roger Ferdinand. *Photographie de* [*Photog*] Peverell Marley. *Décorateur* [*Art dir*] Cedric Gibbons. *Montage de* [*Ed*] Helene Warne. *Costumes de* [*Cost*] Adrian. *Ingénieur du son* [*Sd eng*] Douglas Shearer.

Source: Based on the play *The Easiest Way* by Eugene Walter (New York, 19 Dec 1909).

Cast: LILY DAMITA (*Laura* [*Murdock*]), André Luguet (*Brockton*), André Burgère (*Jack Madison*), Françoise Rosay (*Elfie* [*Brown*]), Mona Goya (*Peg*), Rolla Norman (*Nick*), André Berley (*Ben Murdock*), Adrienne d'Ambricourt (*Mme. Murdock*), Jacques Jou-Jerville (*Bud Williams*), Renée Damonde (*Mme. Williams*), Jean Del Val (*Gensler*), Frank O'Neill (*Chris*), George Savidan (*Bob*), Willy Savidan (*Andy*), Georgette Rhodes (*Tillie*).

Drama. [*Not viewed*]. [The following plot summary is based on the English-language version of this film, *The Easiest Way*; character names refer to that version. For further information regarding the English-language version, please see the note below and the entry for *The Easiest Way* in the *AFI Catalog of Feature Films, 1931-40.*] Laura Murdock and her siblings live in poverty and work hard to support their indolent father Ben, an out-of-work longshoreman who would rather live off his children than find another job. Although Ben and his wife Agnes are eager to see their daughter Peg marry Nick, because he makes a decent income, Laura tells them that she would rather marry for love. One day, while working at her department store job, Laura is approached by a man from the Brockton Advertising Agency, who offers her a modelling job at his fashionable agency. Laura accepts the offer and on her first visit to the agency befriends Elfie, a veteran model, who gives her some learned advice about the profession. Soon after starting at the agency, Laura is called in to meet Willard Brockton, the head of the agency, who, upon learning that Laura has no boyfriend, convinces her to join him for a drive through the park. Laura quickly becomes successful at modelling and finds an elegant city apartment. No sooner does Laura find success, however,

than her mother refuses to see her because she is convinced that her daughter has changed for the worse. Brockton continues to woo Laura by inviting her to move into his luxury apartment and showering her with gifts. When Laura visits her sister Peg, who is now married to Nick and has a child, her showy wealth meets with resentment from Nick, who asks her to leave. While vacationing with Brockton in Colorado, Laura meets newspaper reporter Jack Madison, and they soon fall in love. When Jack takes a long overseas assignment, Laura, who promised to leave Brockton and wait for him to return, tells her boss that their relationship is through. Brockton responds by requesting the return of his gifts and then sticking Laura with the room bill. Destitute, Laura takes a job at Macy's department store and asks Elfie to loan her some money, but Elfie refuses. Later, Ben visits Laura with news that her mother is gravely ill and in need of money for a stomach specialist. He also tells her that she is still disgusted with her lifestyle and does not want to see her. Following her mother's death, the desperate Laura calls Brockton, and though he refuses to loan her money, he takes her back on the condition that she write Jack and inform him that their relationship is finished. Soon after she returns to Brockton, Jack returns from South America and calls Laura. Brockton eavesdrops on the telephone conversation and later threatens to tell Jack about their relationship himself. Laura, however, promises to tell Jack as soon as he shows up. When Elfie drops in on Laura, broke, widowed and wanting to borrow money, Laura gives her a piece of jewelry. Elfie then advises Laura to marry Jack right away and leave Brockton. Laura's plan to elope with Jack crumbles when Brockton returns home unexpectedly, sees her packed bags and informs Jack about her life with him. Though Laura tries to explain the situation, Jack is angered and leaves her. The devastated Laura then leaves Brockton and goes to Peg's on Christmas Eve. Outside their house, Laura stands in the street and sadly watches her family enjoying the holiday. Nick, upon discovering Laura in such a ruined state, has a change of heart and tries to comfort her with a prediction that Jack will come looking for her someday. *Blackmail. Employer-employee relations. Gold diggers. Millionaires. Mistresses. Models. Ostracism. Poverty. Snobs and snobbishness. Advertising. Billiards and billiard parlors. Christmas. Colorado. Department stores. Family life. Fathers and daughters. Reporters. Romance. Saleswomen.*

Note: This French-language version of *The Easiest Way* was formerly called *La bonne vie.* The onscreen credits for the French version were taken from a studio cutting continuity. The file for *The Easiest Way* in the MPAA/PCA Collection at the AMPAS Library indicates that between 1927 and 1931 the Hays Office received letters from various film producers who were interested in filming a picture based on the Eugene Walter play. First National appears to have been the first studio to plan a film based on the play. A telegram dated 30 Sep 1927 indicates that the studio had set David Fink as the producer, Henry King as the director, and Belle Bennett and Conrad Veidt as the stars. At the time, Jason S. Joy of the AMPP wrote that he personally thought that if the story was "not already on the 'list' [of unacceptable material] it ought to be." Joy also noted that in his conversation with Fink, the producer told him that if *Sadie Thompson* (1928) could be produced, he could not see why his film could not be produced. Fink eventually abandoned the project, perhaps as a result of the Hays Office's warning that the story would likely run into censorship problems.

In Mar 1928, after the story was considered and then dropped by producers David O. Selznick and Joseph M. Schenck and by Universal, it was offered to one of the DeMilles, who, after discussing the matter with MPPDA President Will H. Hays, also decided to drop the picture. On 28 Oct 1928, a telegram sent from a Hays Office official to Joy noted that producer Pat Powers had purchased the story from Universal and was planning to film it. The official also told Hays that he ought to warn Powers not to "undertake a thing which other responsible companies have already decided would not be good for the industry." A similar warning went out to Fox producer Sam E. Rork in 1929 when he considered making the film. A memo in the Hays Office file indicates that the Hays Office was trying to play down its role in discouraging producers from making the film, but in Jan 1930, when Pathé inquired about the property, the office persuaded the studio not to film it because "if they bought it and then got into trouble with having it barred in various localities it would probably cost them money."

Finally, M-G-M purchased the story, but not until Columbia had rejected it following the Hays Office's insistence that the studio use a different title and make changes to bring the story into conformity with the Production Code. By Nov 1930, producer Irving Thalberg owned the rights to the play, and the Hays Office, after reviewing the M-G-M screen adaptation, informed him that "the trouble with the adaptation is that it builds up audience sympathy for Laura Murdock and supplies her with the means of securing sympathetic excuses for, if not actual approval of, her weakness of character." The Hays Office also called the adaptation "much more dangerous than the original play, which for a long time has itself been considered dangerous motion picture material," and complained that the story did not go "far enough in building up the idea that Laura is being punished." As a solution to this problem, the Hays Office

suggested that the end of film "show Laura in successive steps on her way to the gutter." In accordance with the suggestion, producer Hunt Stromberg informed the Hays Office that he would insert a scene in which Laura "makes it plain that the life she has been leading has been hideous, destructive, shameful and unhappy."

Following the English-language version's release in Feb 1931, Columbia sent a letter to the Hays Office, accusing it of unfairly preventing the studio from making the film, while allowing M-G-M to produce it. The letter describes Columbia producer Harry Cohn as being "incensed because he had his heart set at the time on making *The Easiest Way.*"

Walter's play was first filmed in 1917 as *The Easiest Way,* a silent produced by Clara Kimball Young, who also starred in the picture, and directed by Albert Capellani (see *AFI Catalog of Feature Films, 1911-20*; F1.1136). For information on the English-language version, which was directed by Jack Conway and starred Constance Bennett, Adolphe Menjou and Robert Montgomery, please see the entry for that film in the *AFI Catalog of Feature Films, 1931-40*; F3.1164.

Var 12 Apr 1932, p. 29.

QUEEN FOR A DAY (Polish Americans)

Robert Stillman Productions, Inc. *Dist* United Artists Corp. 13 Apr **1951**; Prod: 22 Sep—late Oct 1950 at Motion Picture Center [©Robert Stillman Productions, Inc.; 14 Jun 1951; LP1062]. Sd (Western Electric Recording); b&w. 11 reels, 9,647 or 9,646 ft. 107 min. PCA cert no. 15052.

Prod Robert Stillman. *Assoc prod* Seton I. Miller. *Dir* Arthur Lubin. *Asst dir* Ivan Volkman. *Dial dir* Jus Addiss. *Scr* Seton I. Miller. *Dir of photog* Guy Roe. *Prod des* Perry Ferguson. *Film ed* George Amy. *Set dec* Edward G. Boyle. *Ward* Joseph King and Ann Peck. *Mus* Hugo Friedhofer. *Mus dir* Emil Newman. *Sd* Jean Speak. *Makeup artist* Louis Phillippi. *Hair stylist* Louise Miehle. *Prod mgr* Charles Kerr. *Props* Irving Sindler. *Casting dir* Russell Trost. *Prod asst* John Stillman, Jr. *Tech* Charles Rose and Morris Rosen. [*Stunts* Sol Solomon].

Source: Based on the short stories "The Gossamer World" by Faith Baldwin in *Woman's Home Companion* (Aug 1948); "High Diver" by John Ashworth in *Harper's Magazine* (May 1948); and "Horsie" by Dorothy Parker in *Harper's Bazaar* (Dec 1932).

Cast: Faith Baldwin's "The Gossamer World": Phyllis Avery (*Marjorie [Watkins]*), Darren McGavin (*Dan [Watkins]*), Rudy Lee (*Pete [Watkins]*), Frances E. Williams (*Anna*), Joan Winfield (*Laura*), Lonny Burr (*Charles*), Tristram Coffin (*Doctor*), [Jiggs Wood (*Mr. Beck*)], [Casey Folks (*Jim*)], [George Sherwood (*Mr. Garmes*)], John Ashworth's "High Diver": Adam Williams (*Chunk [Pete Nalawak]*), Kasia Orzazewski (*Mrs. Nalawak*), Albert Ben-Astar (*Mr. Nalawak*), Tracey Roberts (*Peggy*), Larry Johns (*Deacon McAllister*), Bernard Szold (*Daredevil Rinaldi*), Joan Sudlow (*Mrs. McAllister*), Grace Lenard (*Mrs. Rinaldi*), Leonard Nimoy (*Chief*), Danny Davenport (*Satchelbutt*), [Madge Blake (*Mrs. Kimpel*)], Dorothy Parker's "Horsie": Edith Meiser (*Miss [Ella] Wilmarth*), Dan Tobin (*Owen Cruger*), Jessie Cavitt (*Camilla Cruger*), Douglas Evans (*Freddy Forster*), Don Shelton (*Jack Minot*), Louise Curry (*Secretary*), Sheila Watson (*Mary*), [Minna Phillips (*Cook*)], [Byron Keith (*Chauffeur*)], In the Broadcast Studio: Jack Bailey, Jim Morgan, Fort Pearson (*By themselves*), Melanie York (*First contestant*), Cynthia Corley (*Second contestant*), Kay Wiley (*Third contestant*), [Helen Mowery (*Jan*)], [Diane Fauntelle (*Helena*)], [Gertrude Astor, Leah Baird, Kathleen Key (*Audience members*)].

Social, Comedy-drama. [*Print viewed*]. For thirty minutes everyday, five million women listen to the radio show *Queen for a Day*. On each show, five candidates, representing a cross-section of everyday people, tell their dreams to host Jack Bailey. The audience, with their applause, chooses one winner, who is crowned and awarded prizes. Following one show, producer Jim Morgan reads to Bailey a thank-you letter from Marjorie Watkins, a contestant who did not win, telling how happy they have made her boy Pete by sending the toy engine she requested. In the letter, she tells their story: Pete's rampant imagination leads him to think of himself in a variety of adult roles. One day he is a farmer, the next an engineer, the following a plumber. Marjorie expresses concern to her easy-going husband Dan that there are no other children living nearby. When Pete's cousin Charles visits, Pete imagines himself a big game hunter, then hits Charles with a rock when Charles says Pete is too little to be a hunter. Sometime later, Pete, imagining himself to be an oil driller, introduces his imaginary friend "Shun," short for "distinction," to his parents and blames Shun for his own accidents. While Dan laughs, Marjorie worries that Pete will grow up to be a "buck passer." Dan

speaks with Pete, who promises that Shun will behave. When the train from the *Queen for a Day* show arrives, both Pete and Dan become engrossed playing with it. On his first day of school, Pete takes Shun with him as he boards the school bus. Anna, the family's black maid whose own child has gone off to war, empathizes with Marjorie, saying it is always the mothers who see their children going off or coming home. Pete returns from school with a new friend, Jim, and admits that Shun was just a silly game. At dinner, Pete complains of a stiff neck and sore back, explaining that he and Jim had been drilling water wells. Marjorie has Dan call the doctor. After examining Pete, the doctor tells Marjorie and Dan that Pete may have polio and urges them to drive him to the hospital that night. Marjorie cries and remembers Anna's words. She ends the letter saying that during Pete's five days in the hospital, the train meant everything to him, and that now it means more, because when he is the engineer, he can travel the world. The train will be the only way he can get around until he walks again someday.

Back at the studio, the audience, mostly women, file through lines to watch the show. One contestant, Mrs. Marisa Nalawak, who was born in Warsaw, Poland and now lives in Torrance, California, says that she wants to win for her son Frank, who is called "Chunk" by his friends, a scholarship to go to an engineering school in Chicago. He worked for two years at the mill where his father works, but left home the previous night to find work to pay for school. That night, while waiting for the next eastbound bus, Chunk wanders over to a traveling circus and learns that it will be near Chicago in two weeks. At the high dive, Daredevil Rinaldi, who is supposed to do a backward somersault dive from 110 feet into 4 feet of water, keels over drunk to the boos of the crowd. When Chunk offers to do the dive, Deacon McAllister, who runs the circus with his wife, agrees to let him try tomorrow. That night, Chunk remembers the argument he had with his father, who did not want him to quit the mill job. In his remembrance, Chunk contends that every American has the right to make something of himself. His father boasts that in Poland, men are proud of working with their hands, but Chunk disparages his father's experience and says he wants to use technology to make it work for him. His father ends the argument by demanding that he work to bring home money if he wants to remain in the house. The next day, Chunk, whose only past experience diving was at a quarry, impresses Peggy, a "vestal virgin" at one of the sideshows. When Rinaldi learns that McAllister plans to hire Chunk, he raves, calling McAllister a "murderer," and warns Chunk of dangers, then gives him some pointers. With the advance that McAllister gives him, Chunk invites two of his mill football teammates, Chief and Satchelbutt, to dinner. Word soon spreads that Chunk is planning to make the dive. When Marisa comes home from the show and tells her husband Jan that she was made "Queen" and won the scholarship, he tells her about the carnival. Before the jump, Peggy kisses Chunk good luck, and as he climbs to the top, his parents arrive. He realizes he left his rabbit's foot behind and at the top, almost slips. When a man taunts him, Peggy slaps the man. Remembering Rinaldi's advice, and repeating to himself "I can do it," Chunk completes the dive, but does not come to the surface until a number of suspenseful seconds have gone by. His parents hug him and his father asks him to come home. As the family walks off, Peggy watches in disappointment.

After a television broadcast of *Queen for a Day*, an unattractive woman who had been in the audience, Ella Wilmarth, returns to her apartment and receives a call offering her a job. Ella, who works as a nurse to newborn infants, agrees to spend three weeks at the luxurious home of Owen and Camilla Cruger to take care of Camilla and her newborn daughter Jessica. Cruger is stunned by Ella's appearance and compares her face to that of a horse. Since nurses are not to be treated as servants, Ella dines every night with Cruger, as Camilla cannot leave the bedroom. At the office, Cruger draws doodles of horses, and at home, begins referring to Ella as "Horsie" behind her back. When he learns that she likes *Queen for a Day*, he offers to get her tickets, hoping she will go the next night and leave them alone, but she says she cannot leave her patient. Soon Cruger takes to drink. He invites his colleagues, Jack Minot and Freddie Forster, to dinner, and while they are in his wife's bedroom, he tells them, "Wait 'til you see our Seabiscuit," not realizing the door to Ella's adjoining room is slightly open; however, he finds that she did not hear, and she joins them at the table in an extremely awkward gown. At the office, on the last day of Ella's stay, Cruger is ecstatic as

he sings, "The Old Gray Mare." He races home to find that the florist must have mixed up his order of orchids, his wife's favorite flower, as gardenias instead have arrived. He gives Ella the flowers, and she nearly breaks down in tears. Cruger gives her tickets to the show for tomorrow night, and as she rides away, she cries and tells the driver it is the first time a man has given her flowers. The next night, Cruger and his wife turn on television and find that "Horsie" has been chosen as a contestant. She explains to Jack Bailey that she has been an infant nurse for thirty years and just finished with her 311th baby. She says she wants an electric razor to give to Cruger, and when she calls him the nicest and kindest man she ever worked for, Cruger is speechless. At the end of the show, Ella is crowned Queen. With her crimson velvet and ermine robe and crown, she is led to a throne and presented with a silver scepter and four dozen red roses. She is given the razor, and also a trip to Honolulu, with new luggage and wardrobe, and a one-year's lease on a new apartment with all new furnishings. Ella is in tears, and the Crugers smile. *Beauty, Personal. Children. Circus performers. Divers and diving. Family relationships. Impersonation and imposture. Nurses. Poliomyelitis. Polish Americans. Television programs. African Americans. Circus owners. Cousins. Flowers. Horses. Infants. Letters. Maids. Sideshows. Torrance (CA). Toy trains.*

Note: The opening credits on the viewed print begin, "Robert Stillman Productions present three American stories." The actual title *Queen for a Day* does not appear on this print, although all the reviews, news items, PCA and copyright material concerning the film have that title. The radio program *Queen for a Day* was created by the Raymond R. Morgan agency. It began on 29 Apr 1945 on the Mutual Broadcasting Network and became a top-rated daytime show. It made its television debut on 5 Jan 1950. According to news items, rights to produce a film using the show, with host Jack Bailey appearing, were purchased in 1947 by Seymour Nebenzal. In Mar 1949, Jesse Lasky and Walter MacEwan closed a deal with Morgan to make the film on a participation basis with the agency. In Dec 1949, the rights were sold by Morgan to Robert Stillman, who the next month acquired the O. Henry Memorial Award-winning story "High Diver" by John Ashworth, a Columbia University professor, planning at that time to make a separate film based on that story after *Queen for a Day*. "The Gossamer World" by Faith Baldwin was purchased for use in the film by Stillman in Feb 1950. According to a *LAT* news item, he wanted to cast five-year-old Mickey Rooney, Jr. in the role of the boy, but his father refused to allow it. The story "Horsie" by Dorothy Parker was purchased in Jun 1950.

Charlotte Greenwood was originally considered for the role of "Ella Wilmarth," according to *LAT*. *Var* noted that the film was the "first of a bevy of American films due this year comprising series of short stories linked by a unifying theme" and explained the trend by referring to the recent success of the British films *Quartet* and *Trio*, and the European trilogy *Ways of Love*. (The 1952 release *It's a Big Country* was one of these films; see entry above.) According to *Var*, the film was plugged on the show for a year previous to its release, and the show held a "Queen City" contest to select a city for the premiere. According to *DV*, the film did not do well at the box office after several test openings, and on 7 Jul 1951, United Artists released it under the title, *Horsie* with a new ad campaign to link director Arthur Lubin with his previous successful "Frances" pictures. The episode "The Gossamer World" was filmed at a house in Reseda. The company rented the carnival show of the Pan-American Amusement Corp. and set it up at a vacant lot at the corner of Beverly and La Cienaga in Los Angeles, for scenes in the episode "High Diver." The high dive from 110 feet into 6 feet of water, was accomplished by Sol Solomon, who insisted on 6 feet, rather than the 4 feet called for in the script. The broadcast studio scenes were shot at the Mutual Broadcasting Station. This was Adam Williams' first film. According to news items, Stillman discovered him working at a Los Angeles Thrifty Drug Store as a soda jerk. Edith Meiser, a Broadway actress, was having her teeth "bucked" to prepare for her role in the "Horsie" segment, according to *LAEx*. According to *IP*, a number of silent stars played audience members at the "Queen for a Day" studio, including Gertrude Astor, Leah Baird and Kathleen Key.

Reviews were critical of the film and its concept. *Cue* commented, "Each story fatuously, unctuously and smugly relates how the big-hearted sponsors of this program play God." *Var* stated that the direction and script "are attempts at telling the stories broadly, on a lowest-common-denominator basis, rather than playing for sharp, incisive wittiness or delicate character portrayals of both Miss Parker and Ashworth in their original yarns." They called the "Gossamer World" episode, "a vignette of the slick-mag version of family life, with mama, papa and junior ever so happy in their pleasant slice of suburbia." *HR* thought that the original Parker story (which they praised as a "miniature work of art") "never should have left the pages of her collections. On the screen its subtleties and ironies are totally lost." Concerning the film's concept, they complained, "Taken separately, [the stories] are representative art pieces—fine for a limited audience interested in short story screen technique, camera work, and performances by unknowns.... But why wrap it up as *Queen for a Day*!"

Box 24 Mar 1951. *DV* 21 Mar 1951, p. 4. *Exb* 28 Mar 1951, p. 3050. *FD* 26 Jan 1950. *FD* 21 Mar 1951, p. 6. *Har* 24 Mar 1951, p. 48. *HR* 12 Jan 1950. *HR* 26 Jan 1950. *HR* 22 Sep 1950, p. 9. *HR* 20 Oct 1950, p. 15. *HR* 21 Mar 1951, p. 4. *LAEx* 15 Sep 1950. *LAT* 7 Feb 1950. *LAT* 17 Jun 1950. *LAT* 10 Aug 1950. *LAT* 19 Sep 1950. *MPHPD* 24 Mar 1951, p. 766. *Var* 21 Mar 1951, p. 6.

THE QUEEN OF SPARTA see LA REGINA DI SPARTA

QUEEN X (Chinese Americans)

Mutual Film Corp.; A Mutual Star Production; Edna Goodrich Series; "Big Stars Only" Series. *Dist* Mutual Film Corp. 1 Oct 1917 [©Mutual Film Corp.; 1 Oct 1917; LP11988]. Si; b&w. 5 reels.

Dir John B. O'Brien. *Story* Edwin M. Stanton.

Cast: Edna Goodrich (*Janice Waltham, Queen X*), Hugh Thompson (*George Evans*), Lucille Taft (*Miriam Evans*), Dora Adams (*Mrs. Evans*), William Wolcott (*Arnold Somers*), Jack Hopkins (*Nippo*), P. Tamato (*Togo*).

Social, Drama. In New York's notorious Pell Street district, U.S. District Attorney Arnold Somers' men capture Queen X, known to drug smugglers as "The Queen of Chinatown," a woman with a cross-shaped birthmark on her wrist. Summers recognizes her as Janice Waltham, formerly a prominent society woman. After becoming an addict and dealer, Janice was imprisoned in underground dens filled with opium fumes to prevent her from recovering and betraying her suppliers. She refuses to name her associates despite third degree questioning. As Janice is about to be sentenced to a long prison term, Miriam Evans, whose brother George is the assistant district attorney, recognizes Janice as the former schoolmate who rescued her in a convent fire. Somers allows Miriam to take Janice home and advises George to court her to get the names of the gang leaders. With George's help, Janice develops enough will power to kick her drug habit, while George, according to their pact, stops smoking cigarettes and drinking coffee. After George secures the names, Janice, threatened by a Chinese cohort, learns about George's deal, but George, now in love, confesses this and they marry. *Drug addicts. Drug dealers. New York City–Chinatown. Pledges. Regeneration. Birthmarks. Chinese Americans. District attorneys. Opium. Smuggling.*

Note: The author of this story, Edwin M. Stanton, was the Assistant U.S. District Attorney for New York who conducted the government's fight against Chinese drug smugglers. Modern sources credit Sol Polito as cameraman.

ETR 20 Oct 1917, pp. 1592-93. *MPN* 6 Oct 1917, p. 2345. *MPW* 6 Oct 1917, p. 43, 99, 126. *MPW* 8 Dec 1917, p. 1480. *Wid's* 11 Oct 1917, p. 656.

QUICKER'N LIGHTNIN' (Native Americans)

Action Pictures, Inc. *Dist* Weiss Brothers Artclass Pictures. **1925**; New York State license: 21 Aug 1925. Si; b&w. 5 reels, 4,222 ft.

Pres Lester F. Scott, Jr. *Dir* Richard Thorpe. *Scen* Betty Burbridge. *Story* Reginald C. Barker.

Cast: Buffalo Bill Jr. (*Quicker'n Lightnin'*), B. F. Blinn (*John Harlow*), Dorothy Dorr (*Helen Harlow*), Harry Todd (*Al McNutt*), J. Gordon Russell (*Mowii*), Raye Hampton (*Squaw*), Lucille Young (*Morella*), Charles Roberts (*Truxillo*).

Western. Indians murder John Harlow and abduct his daughter, Helen. Quicker'n Lightnin' rescues Helen before Mowii's squaw can sacrifice her to the sun god. *Abduction. Human sacrifice. Indians of North America. Murder. Religion.*

MPW 6 Jun 1925.

THE QUIET MAN (Irish Americans)

Argosy Pictures Corp.; John Ford and Merian C. Cooper's Argosy Production. *Dist* Republic Pictures Corp. 14 Sep **1952**; Prod: early Jun—late Aug 1951 in Ireland [©Republic Pictures Corp.; 31 Jan 1952; LP2030]. Sd (RCA Sound System); col (Technicolor). 11,631 ft. 129 min. PCA cert no. 15529.

Pres Herbert J. Yates. [*Prod* Merian C. Cooper]. *Dir* John Ford. [*Asst dir* Wingate Smith]. *Scr* Frank S. Nugent. *Dir of photog* Winton C. Hoch. *2nd unit photog* Archie Stout. *Technicolor color consultant* Francis Cugat. *Art dir* Frank Hotaling. *Film ed* Jack Murray. *Set dec* John McCarthy, Jr. and Charles Thompson. *Cost* Adele Palmer. *Mus* Victor Young. *Sd* T. A. Carman and Howard Wilson.

Song(s): "The Isle of Innisfree," words and music by Richard Farrelly; "Galway Bay," words and music by Dr. Arthur Colahan; "The Humour Is on Me Now," words and music by Richard Hayward; "The Young Man Moon," words and music by Thomas Moore; "The Wild Colonial Boy" and "Mush-Mush-Mush tural-i-addy," words and music by Sean O'Casey and Dennis O'Casey.

Source: Based on the novel *The Quiet Man* by Maurice Walsh in his *Green Rushes* (Philadelphia, 1935).

Cast: John Wayne [(*Sean Thornton*)], Maureen O'Hara [(*Mary Kate Danaher*)], Barry Fitzgerald [(*Michaeleen Flynn*)], Ward Bond [(*Father Lonergan*)], Victor McLaglen [(*"Red" Will Danaher*)], Mildred Natwick [(*Mrs. Tillane*)], Francis Ford [(*Tobin*)], Irish

players: Eileen Crowe [(*Mrs. Playfair*)], May Craig [(*The woman*)], Arthur Shields [(*Rev. Playfair*)], Charles Fitzsimmons [(*Forbes*)], James Lilburn [(*Father Paul*)], Sean McClory [(*Owen Glynn*)], Jack McGowran [(*Feeney*)], Joseph O'Dea [(*Guard*)], Eric Gorman [(*Engine driver*)], Kevin Lawless [(*Fireman*)], Paddy O'Donnell [(*Porter*)], [Web Overlander (*Station master*)], [Don Hatswell (*Guppy*)], [Harry Tyler (*Coban*)], [Ken Curtis (*Dermot Fahy*)], [Harry Tenbrook (*Sgt. Hanan*)], [David H. Hughes (*Constable*)], [Billy Jones (*Bugler*)], [Ruth Clifford (*Mother*)], [Jack Roper (*Boxer*)], [Freddie Ridgeway (*Boy*)], [Darla Ridgeway (*Girl*)], [Al Murphy (*Referee*)], [Douglas Evans (*Doctor*)], [Tiny Jones (*Maid*)], [Hank Worden (*Trainer in flashback*)], [Pat O'Malley], [Ken Kurtis], [Mae Marsh].

Romantic comedy. [*Print viewed*]. After fatally knocking out his opponent in the boxing ring, Irish-American boxer Sean Thornton returns to the place of his birth, Inisfree, Ireland. Seeking a life of quiet and rest, Sean plans to buy "White O'Mornin," his family's old cottage, and keep his boxing identity of "Trooper Thorn" a secret. En route to Inisfree, Sean catches sight of Mary Kate Danaher and is captivated by her beauty. In Inisfree, Sean's meeting with the wealthy widow Tillane, who owns White O'Mornin, is interrupted by the arrival of Mary Kate's brother "Red" Will Danaher, an ill-mannered bully who wants to buy the property himself. Although Will, a neighbor of Tillane's, claims to have been the first to place a bid on the land, the widow sells the property to Sean after Will's presumptuousness annoys her. Later, at the Inisfree pub, Sean's American ways are met with general disapproval, but the parish priest, Father Peter Lonergan, the Anglican Reverend Cyril Playfair and matchmaker Michaeleen Flynn welcome him home. As one of the few protestants in a community of Roman Catholics, Playfair identifies with Sean's difference from the locals and forms a special bond with him. Their friendship is further cemented when Playfair, a boxing enthusiast, recognizes Sean as Trooper Thorn, but agrees to keep his secret. On his first visit to White O'Mornin, Sean is surprised to find Mary Kate, who has been cleaning the cottage. As the silent Mary Kate tries to flee into the windy night, Sean grabs and passionately kisses her. She returns his feelings, but quickly leaves because Irish custom demands a proper courtship. Although he does not understand the custom, Sean allows Michaeleen to become his matchmaker and Mary Kate happily agrees to a courtship. Because Will is still bitter over the property, he refuses to give his permission, making both Sean and Mary Kate miserable, as she will not breach custom by going against her brother's wishes. Some time later, on the day of the Inisfree horse race, some of the locals decide to help the unhappy couple by tricking Will into giving his blessing to their courtship. They "secretly" tell Will that the widow Tillane, whom he has long admired, would gladly marry him but is reluctant because she does not want to come into a house in which another woman is living. Will soon relents and a courtship between Sean and Mary Kate begins. Although a long courtship is traditional, Sean and Mary Kate's passion, and the fact that they are no longer young, shorten the time and they are soon married. At their wedding reception, after a drunken Will shows the guests the £230 in gold coins that are part of Mary Kate's dowry, he boasts of his own impending nuptials to the widow Tillane, but she is so insulted by his brash proposal that she leaves. Enraged at the trick that has been played on him, Will throws a punch at Sean, who falls to the ground and, in a daze, momentarily recalls the tragic moment when he killed his boxing opponent. Because he has resolved never again to fight, Sean grabs Mary Kate's hand and leaves, refusing to allow her to pick up the coins that have fallen to the floor. They spend their wedding night at Sean's cottage, but Mary Kate remains so concerned about her lost money and furniture that they argue and Sean spends the night alone in a sleeping bag. The next morning, some of their friends arrive with her things, but say that Will still refuses to relinquish the money. Sean and Mary Kate still do not understand each other's ways and, in a moment of truce, decide to go to town together. After Sean refuses to ask Will for the money, Mary Kate goes to Father Lonergan and Sean goes to the Reverend Playfair. Although Sean feels that Mary Kate is only interested in the money, reminding him that greed led him to be such a fierce boxer, Playfair makes him realize that in Ireland it is the custom that is important and subtly convinces Sean to fight Will to show his mettle. That night, Mary Kate and Sean tenderly reunite at the cottage and consummate their marriage. The next morning, however, when Sean awakens, Michaeleen is waiting outside the

cottage to tell him that Mary Kate has left for the Dublin train. Now enraged, Sean rides his horse to the station. Now resolved that he must show her and everyone that he follows the Irish ways, he summarily grabs Mary Kate off the train and drags her to the Danaher farm, followed by a rapidly swelling crowd, shouting their approval. When they arrive at the farm, Sean throws Mary Kate towards Will and demands the dowery. Cornered, Will gives Sean the money, after which a happy Mary Kate assists Sean in burning it. Now proud of Sean, Mary Kate goes to their cottage, leaving Sean and Will to resolve their animosity in a fight. As the brawling ensues, the entire village watches and wagers among themselves. Soon even neighboring villages enter into the spirit of the contest, taking sides and cheering the men on. The fight lasts so long that Will and Sean must take a break at the local pub, after which they fight again and finally stop when both are too exhausted to continue. After the fight, Sean and Will get drunk together and become friends and Mary Kate welcomes them at the cottage. The next day, as Michaeleen takes the happy Will and Tillane on a courtship outing, the entire village, including Father Lonergan, gather to cheer a visiting Anglican bishop, hoping to impress him with the size of the Reverend Playfair's congregation. *Americans in foreign countries. Boxers. Brothers and sisters. Clergy. Ireland. Irish Americans. Marriage. Romance. Courtship. Desertion (Marital). Dowry. Drunkenness. Fistfights. Greed. Honeymoons. Horseracing. Ireland. Jealousy. Matchmakers. Priests. Proposals (Marital). Pubs. Revenge. Train stations. Village life. Wagers. Weddings. Widows.*

Note: According to news items in *HR* and *FD* in May 1937, *The Quiet Man* was to be the first John Ford production of Renowned Artists, for release by United Artists. The production was never realized at that time; then, in May 1947, according to a *LADN* news item, it was set to begin filming in Ireland sometime in 1948. In Apr 1948, a *HR* news item noted that the film was to be produced with "frozen funds" that were part of the "Anglo-American film agreement." A 1950 *HR* news item indicated that half the film was to be shot in Ireland and half in Italy, but no additional references to Italian location filming have been found. Reviews and contemporary news items note that filming took place near Galway, Ireland, in Connemara. Actor Charles Fitzsimmons was actress Maureen O'Hara's younger brother, and actor Ken Curtis was director John Ford's son-in-law.

Modern sources note that four of John Wayne's children appeared in the film, Patrick, Antonia, Melinda and Michael, who were children watching the horse rase. Modern sources also credit John Wayne and Patrick Ford, the director's son, as second unit directors. Actors Bob Perry and Frank Baker are also included in the cast in modern sources. In various interviews, John Ford stated that he wrote "bits" of the script for *The Quiet Man* and used his own parish priest as a technical adviser on the film. The film received Academy Awards for Best Cinematography and Best Direction, and was nominated for awards in the following categories: Best Picture, Best Screenplay, Best Sound Recording, Best Art Direction and Best Supporting actor (Victor McLaglen). The film was also voted best picture of 1952 by the General Federation of Women's Clubs. According to the AMPAS Library file for the film, a restored version of *The Quiet Man* was shown at the Galway Film Festival in Galway, Ireland in Jul 1991.

Box 17 May 1952. *DV* 12 May 1952, p. 3. *FD* 29 May 1937, p. 2. *FD* 12 May 1952, p. 6. *HR* 28 May 1937, p. 2. *HR* 13 Apr 1948. *HR* 17 Nov 1950. *HR* 8 Jun 1951, p. 10. *HR* 24 Aug 1951, p. 10. *HR* 12 May 1952, p. 3. *HR* 12 Jan 1953. *HR* 2 Sep 1953. *LADN* 29 May 1947. *MPHPD* 17 May 1952, p. 1365. *NYT* 22 Aug 1952, p. 13. *Var* 14 May 1952, p. 6. *Var* 2 Sep 1953.

THE QUIET ONE (African Americans)

Film Documents, Inc. *Dist* Mayer-Burstyn Inc. **1949**; New York opening: 12 Feb 1949. Sd; b&w. 16mm. 67 min. Passed by the National Board of Review.

Prod Janice Loeb. *Assoc prod* William Levitt. *Dir* Sidney Meyers. *Wrt* Helen Levitt, Janice Loeb and Sidney Meyers. *Commentary and dial wrt* James Agee. *Photog* Richard Bagley. *Doc photog* Helen Levitt and Janice Loeb. *Ed* Helen Levitt, Janice Loeb and Sidney Meyers. *Mus* Ulysses Kay. *Sd eff ed* Stanley Katis. *Spec sd eff* Richard Bagley and Jack Kling. *Psychiatric consultant* Viola Bernard, M.D. *Tech asst* Robert L. Cooper and Nathan Stillman.

Cast: Gary Merrill (*Narrator*), Donald Thompson (*Donald Peters*), Clarence Cooper (*The counselor* [*Clarence*]), Sadie Stockton (*The grandmother*), Estelle Evans (*The mother*), Paul Baucum (*The stepfather*), The staff and the boys of Wiltwyck School, [Sidney Meyers (*Psychiatrist*)].

Documentary, Drama. [*Print viewed*]. Ten-year-old Donald Peters, who is black, is one of the boys attending the Wiltwyck School for Boys at Esopus, New York. For months Donald makes no friends, does not smile and barely talks. Donald, whose father abandoned his family, and whose mother became involved with another man and rejected him in favor of her new family, receives no letters and cannot read. Donald's life before coming to Wiltwyck was hard: After his

mother leaves him, Donald stays with his grandmother, who resents his presence and frequently beats him. Donald has a hard time in school, and the teachers are too busy to help him. Donald often wanders alone through the city, and his anger at his situation often erupts in destructive behavior. This background has brought him to Wiltwyck. Eventually, Donald shyly makes friends with Clarence, one of the counselors. Mrs. Johnson, one of the teachers, helps the children work out their problems by making various objects. One day, while working with clay, Donald remembers a day at the beach with his family and, for the rest of the afternoon, is deeply disturbed. Clarence helps comfort him and through that connection, Donald starts to change. Donald learns to read and begins to interact with the other boys. When Donald wishes to give his mother a bowl he has made, the psychiatrist sadly tells him that his mother has disappeared. After some thought, Donald puts a plant in the bowl and gives it to Clarence, a sign of healing. Donald is not healthy enough yet to understand that he must share Clarence's attention with the other boys, however, and jealously takes back his gift and then tears apart the dorm room. The teachers allow Donald to work out his problems for himself. After stealing Clarence's cigarette lighter, Donald runs away, but eventually begins to accept his life and returns to school. He returns the lighter to the sympathetic Clarence and begins to make friends with other boys his age. Although he has not overcome all his pain, Donald has started on the road to recovery. *African Americans. Family relationships. Neglected children. Wiltwyck School for Boys. Art objects. Fistfights. Jealousy. New York City. Psychiatrists. Teachers.*

Note: Helen Levitt, Janice Loeb and Sidney Meyers' credit reads: "Written and edited by." The film begins with the following written foreword: "This film was made in New York City and at the Wiltwyck School at Esopus, New York. Wiltwyck is a school for boys of New York City who have reacted with grave disturbance of personality to neglect in their homes and in their community, and who, for various reasons of age, religion, race or special maladjustments are not cared for by other agencies." According to reviews, the story was based on case histories at Wiltwyck.

Production notes add the following information about the film: This was the first production of Film Documents, Inc., which had been organized two years earlier. Donald Thompson was not a professional actor. Because his father would not allow him to miss school to make the film, the picture was shot after school and on the weekends. Filming took place during the summer, when Thompson lived at Wiltwyck with the other boys. Clarence Cooper was an actual counselor at Wiltwyck, and Paul Baucum was a musician. Estelle Evans and Sadie Stockton were the only professional actors in the film. Levitt and Loeb had previously made a short film in East Harlem, and according to the *Var* review, some scenes in this film were also shot in Harlem. The review also notes that "while Thompson is a Negro, the film makes no explicit comments on any racial problems, developing a story that could have happened to any kid." A 12 Nov 1948 *HR* news item notes that the 16mm film was made for $30,000. It received Academy Award nominations for Best Documentary Feature and for Best Writing.

Box 23 Apr 1949. *DV* 31 Mar 1949, p. 3. *FD* 7 Apr 1949, p. 7. *HR* 12 Nov 1948. *HR* 17 Feb 1949, p. 6. *HR* 1 Apr 1949, p. 4. *NYT* 14 Feb 1949, p. 15. *Var* 16 Feb 1949, p. 13.

QUINCANNON, FRONTIER SCOUT (Native Americans, Arapaho)

Bel-Air Productions. *Dist* United Artists Corp. 5 Oct **1956**; *Prod*: Aug 1955 [©Northridge Productions, Inc.; 6 Apr 1956; LP6432]. Sd; col (De Luxe); 1.85. 7,577 ft. 83 min.

Exec prod Aubrey Schenck. *Prod* Howard W. Koch. *Dir* Lesley Selander. *Asst dir* Bud Andrews. *Scr* John C. Higgins and Don Martin. *Photog* Joseph F. Biroc. *Ed* John F. Schreyer. *Mus* Les Baxter.

Song(s): "Quincannon, Frontier Scout," music by Hal Borne, lyrics by Sammy Cahn.

Source: Based on the novel *Frontier Feud* by Will Cook (publication undetermined).

Cast: TONY MARTIN [(*Linus Quincannon*)], Peggie Castle [(*Maylene Mason*)], John Bromfield [(*Lt. Burke*)], John Smith [(*Lt. Hostedder*)], Ron Randell [(*Capt. Bell*)], John Doucette [(*Sgt. Calvin*)], Peter Mamakos [(*Blackfoot Sam*)], Edmund Hashim [(*Iron Wolf*)], [Morris Ankrum (*Col. Harry Conover*)].

Western. [*Print viewed*]. Dressed as civilians, Lt. Burke and Sgt. Calvin search for Linus Quincannon, a soldier who quit the Army in protest over a brutal Indian massacre and now makes his living as a scout. They have been ordered to bring Quincannon to an Army fort to speak with his former commanding officer, Col. Harry Conover. When Quincannon refuses to go with them, the soldiers arrest him. At the fort, Conover tells Quincannon that a shipment of repeating rifles was stolen from a train during a violent raid by hostile Arapaho Indians, led by Iron Wolf. Because Quincannon has lived among the Indians, Conover wants him to hunt for the missing guns. Quincannon turns him down, but as he is leaving, attractive Maylene

Mason arrives. She requests an escort to take her to Fort Smith, where she plans to ransom her brother from the Arapaho, who, she believes, captured him during the rifle robbery. Conover denies her request because he is convinced that the reports listing her brother as dead are correct. Knowing that the Indians have no use for money, Quincannon's suspicions are roused by Maylene's story, and he suddenly changes his mind about the scouting assignment. He is sure that something unlawful is going on at Fort Smith and hopes that Maylene will help him uncover it. He requests that Burke and Calvin, whose persistence he admires, accompany them. As the party advances into Indian country, Quincannon spots a small band of Indians. He and Burke investigate, and when an Indian shoots an arrow at Quincannon, he kills him with a knife. He identifies the dead Indian as an Arapaho and cuts off his braids. Quincannon then helps the others disguise themselves as Indians, and they safely cross through Sioux, Arapaho and Cheyenne territories. At Fort Smith, the party is warmly welcomed by Capt. Bell, who verifies the death of Maylene's brother, adding that Lt. Hostedder was the only survivor of the raid. Quincannon questions Hostedder, whose story seems dubious to him. Later, after conferring with Maylene, Quincannon hides in the barn to see who comes for the ransom that she is supposed to leave there. After capturing Hostedder, Quincannon searches his room and finds $2,000 in gold hidden in an Arapaho bag. He speculates that the money is from a train robbery and was used by the Arapaho to buy information about the gun shipment. Later, Bell kills Hostedder to prevent him from exposing his part in the theft of the guns, but accidentally reveals to Quincannon knowledge of the rifles, which proves that he was involved. Determined to bring Bell to justice, Quincannon, Burke and Calvin set out to find Iron Wolf, the only remaining witness to Bell's betrayal. They first buy whiskey from Blackfoot Sam, a whiskey trader, and learn that a big powwow is being held nearby. Later, on Bell's orders, the three are ambushed leaving camp. After killing all but one of Blackfoot Sam's men, they proceed to the powwow location. Secretly, they observe Iron Wolf's demonstration of the repeating rifles and from his speech, learn the location of the rifles. When they reach the hiding place, Quincannon and Burke get the Indians in the camp drunk on whiskey. Meanwhile, Calvin locates the rifles and uses gunpowder to blow them up. Just then, Iron Wolf appears with a band of Indians and chases the white men. After several gunfights, Quincannon captures Iron Wolf and keeps him prisoner until Bell arrives to arrest Quincannon for the murder of Blackfoot Sam. After Iron Wolf identifies Bell as the man who told him about the rifle shipment, however, Quincannon arrests Bell. Later, Quincannon proposes to Maylene and is reinstated into the Army. *Arapaho Indians. Scouts (Frontier). Soldiers. United States. Army. Cavalry. Ambushes. Disguise. Drunkenness. Explosions. Forts. Gunfights. Gunshot wounds. Liquor. Money. Murder. Officers (Military). Ransom. Rifles. Romance. Salesmen.*

Note: The viewed print was titled *Frontier Scout*, which was also the working title of the film. The *Var* review notes that scenes were shot near Kanab, UT. The *HR* review commented that "The color, by De Luxe, seems to have a slightly bluish-green tinge to it but this actually helps the mood at times."

Box 21 Apr 1956. *DV* 16 Dec 1955. *DV* 17 Apr 1956, p. 4. *Exh* 2 May 1956, p. 4151. *FD* 10 May 1956, p. 10. *Har* 21 Apr 1956, p. 64. *HR* 12 Aug 1955, p. 13. *HR* 26 Aug 1955, p. 9. *HR* 17 Apr 1956, p. 3. *MPHPD* 21 Apr 1956, p. 866. *Var* 18 Apr 1956, p. 7.

QUISO SER MADRE *see* **MIRACLE ON MAIN STREET**

QUOTA GIRL *see* **WINTERTIME**

THE RABBI'S POWER (Yiddish language)
High Art Pictures Corp. *Dist* High Art Pictures Corp. **1934**; Prod: by Meteor in Poland in 1924; new scenes added in U.S. in 1934. Sd (R.S.A. System); b&w. 6 reels, 5,921 ft. 62 min. *Country of origin* Poland. Yiddish language.
[*Prod of 1924 film* Henryk Bojm and Leo Forbert]. *Dir* George Roland. [*Dir of 1924 film* Zygmunt Turkow]. *Text written by* Jacob Mestel. [*Screenplay of 1924 film* Henryk Bojm]. *Photog* Chas. Hanley. [*Photog of 1924 film* Seweryn Steinwurcel]. *Art dir* Joseph Crain.
Cast: *With the celebrated Jewish star* Joseph Buloff (*as the narrator*), *Supported by the Russian Jewish Art Players* Ida Kaminska [(*Rachel Kronberg*)], Siegmund Turkoff [(*Elijah, the Prophet*)], Jacob Mestel [(*1st traveller*)], L. Kodison [(*2d traveller*)], B. Fishbein [(*Tavern keeper*)], Ben Basenko [(*3d traveller*)], [Lev Mogilov (*Schmuhl Levine*)], [Simchah Balanoff (*Playboy, Jacob Mandel*)], [Adam Domb (*Chaym Kronberg*)], [Moshe Litman (*Boruch Mandel*)], [Ester-Rokhl Kaminska (*Mrs. Kronberg*)].

Yiddish, Drama. [*Print viewed***].** In a tavern, three Jewish men, traveling to see a rabbi, hear the following tale, which was told to the teller by the Vilna Rabbi: Elijah the Prophet, when it is necessary, assumes guises of ordinary persons to see to it that people keep their vows. After wandering through villages and cities, Elijah reaches Vilna, "the Jerusalem of Lithuania," and assuming the role of a wanderer, witnesses two *Talmud* students, Chaym Kronberg and Boruch Mandel, vow before a rabbi that their children shall marry each other. Twenty years later, Boruch has moved with his wife and son Jacob to a small town to manage his family's forests, while Chaym has remained in Vilna with his wife and daughter Rachel. During World War I, a German entrusts Chaym with a jewel box for safekeeping. The jewels are hidden, and a receipt is given the soldier, with a copy kept in the box. Days later, upon reading a telegram that his son has died in the war, Chaym himself falls dead. After the war, the German tries to claim the jewels, but Rachel does not know where they are, so she is forced to sell the house to repay the man, and she and her mother become poor. Meanwhile, Elijah, in the guise of a teacher, visits Boruch and suggests he send Jacob to Vilna, where his good friend, Schmuhl Levine, who has bought the Mandels' house, will take care of him. At Schmuhl's home, Jacob sees Rachel through a window. As Jacob, a religious student, prepares to begin his prayers, Elijah, in a beggar's guise, appears in the courtyard, and Jacob watches as Rachel rushes down to give him alms. Jacob throws down a coin, and as he and Rachel see each other, the beggar disappears. Later, Rachel and her mother sell fruit at the *yeshive*, or religious school. Seeing that the students are poor, Jacob buys apples and distributes them to the others. Afterward, he cannot concentrate on his studies, as he thinks of Rachel. He imagines her as Rachel in the Bible and himself as the biblical Jacob. He also has a vision of two students personifying Good and Evil, and he follows the evil one, but Elijah comes and saves him. Schmuhl, while praying, accidentally bashes a hole in a wall and finds the box of jewels with the note. He plans to keep the treasure for himself, and when Rachel comes to visit Jacob, who is sick, Schmuhl attempts to flirt with her. Realizing that Jacob is his rival, Schmuhl writes to Jacob's father and tells him that Jacob, who has begun to associate with Schmuhl's assimilated son, is following the wrong path. Boruch travels to Vilna and, after seeing Jacob taking dancing lessons, brings him home. When Boruch insists that Jacob become engaged, Elijah, in disguise, warns him that bad luck that will befall him. Soon Boruch has to sell the family's forests. Elijah, now in the guise of a woodsman, breathes life into a bird that is killed and says, "So may the souls of Jacob and Rachel be free." Boruch then has a vision of Chaym and a forest fire, and realizes that the vow must be kept. When Rachel, who has become betrothed to Schmuhl, learns that Jacob is to be married, she faints. By her father's grave, she dreams that the dead rise from graves to dance at her wedding. She sees herself and Jacob, and when he turns into Schmuhl, she awakens and, embracing her mother, says she will never marry Schmuhl. When Jacob learns about Rachel's impending marriage, he travels to Vilna. At the wedding, Elijah, now in the guise of a wealthy citizen, pours a drink on his clothes, and from this sign, the rabbi understands his identity. When Boruch interrupts the wedding, Elijah convinces the gathering to let him speak. Boruch relates the promise he and Chaym made. Jacob says that Rachel is his and kisses her. Later, through Elijah's insistence, the box of jewels is returned to Chaym's widow. Elijah then disappears to fulfill other assignments. Back at the tavern, the moral of the story is stated: What the Lord ordains, no one on earth can change. A song about Elijah is then sung, which expresses the hope that he will come speedily "in our days" with the Messiah. *Biblical characters. Family relationships. Impersonation and imposture. Jews. Pledges. Romance. Strangers. Students. Vilnius (Lithuania). Beggars. Dancing. Deception. Dreams. Engagements. Forest fires. Germans. Graves. Hotels. Jewelry. Matchmakers. Parties. Rabbis. Religiosity. Revivification. Romantic rivalry. Schoolteachers. Visions. Wanderers. Weddings. World War I.*

Note: The Yiddish title of this film was *Dem Rebns Koyekh*. This was a re-release, with a sound narration and added sequences, of a 1924 Polish film entitled *Tkies Kaf*. The added sequences, comprising the tavern scenes in the prologue, epilogue and a few scenes in the middle, were filmed in New York. According to modern sources, actor and director Zygmunt Turkow, who is credited in the cast as Siegmund Turkoff, was the leader of the Warsaw Jewish Art Theater (Varshiver Yidisher Kunst Teater, or VYKT). He was married to actress Ida Kaminska, who was the daughter of Ester-Rokhl Kaminska, known as the "mother of Yiddish theater" and the "Jewish Duse." The Polish film, which had its premiere in Warsaw in May 1924, was called by a Polish critic the best

Polish film made up to that time. The film was re-released in 1949 under the title *A Vilna Legend*, with English language titles by Charles Clement. A Polish remake was produced in 1937, which also starred Turkow.

FD 2 Jun 1934, p. 4. *NYT* 26 Sep 1949, p. 17. *Var* 28 Sep 1949, p. 6.

RACETRACK (Italian Americans)

James Cruze Productions, Inc.; Tiffany Productions, Inc. *Dist* World Wide Pictures, Inc.; Fox Film Corp. 25 Feb **1933**; Prod: 1931 [©World Wide Pictures, Inc.; 25 Feb 1933; LP3683]. Sd (R.C.A. Photophone); b&w. 9 reels, 7,037 ft. 78-79 or 83 min.

Prod Samuel Zierler. *Dir* James Cruze. *Dir of racing scenes* B. Reeves Eason. *Asst to James Cruze* Gaston Glass. *Story* J. Walter Ruben and Wells Root. *Adpt* Walter Lang. *Adpt and dial* Douglas Doty. *Dial* Gaston Glass, Claire Carvalho and Ernest Pagano. *Photog* Charles Schoenbaum. *Ed* Rose Loewinger. *Rec eng* W. C. Smith and Frederick Lau.

Cast: Leo Carrillo (*Joe Tomasso*), Junior Coghlan (*Jackie [Curtis]*), Kay Hammond (*Myra Curtis*), Lee Moran (*"Horseface"*), Huntley Gordon (*Attorney*), Wilfrid Lucas (*Mr. Ryan*), Joseph Girard (*Judge*).

Horse race, Drama. [*Not viewed*]. When Joe Tomasso, an Italian American bookie, loses $60,000 on a horse race, he is no longer able to afford eating at expensive restaurants, and must now get his meals at cheap lunchrooms. One day, while eating at a lunchroom, Joe witnesses a young boy stealing a roll, after which the owner hauls him off to jail. After getting the boy, Jackie, released from jail, Joe learns that he is a homeless orphan and decides to adopt him. Soon Jackie tells Joe that he wants to be a jockey, and Joe consents to it on the condition that he ride straight. Two years pass, and Jackie, now an apprentice jockey, is located by his mother Myra Curtis, who left him when he was a boy, but now tries to get him back. When Jackie asks Joe's permission to ride Joe's prize horse, "Warrior," in an upcoming race, Joe refuses. Upset, Jackie throws a pebble at a horse, which causes it to rear and unseat its rider, Kent, who receives an injury from the fall. Myra witnesses her son's bad behavior and tells Joe that the track has corrupted the boy. Joe, realizing that the Jackie's place is with his mother, devises a plan to get him away from the tracks forever. After instructing Jackie to throw the next race, Joe tells the judges about the boy's action and he is disqualified for riding for good. Joe then lies to Jackie, telling him that the only reason he adopted him was to use him to ride crooked. Jackie leaves the track with Myra, but Joe, sad that he lost the boy, knows that Jackie will forever be an honest bookie. *Bookies. Horseracing. Horses. Italian Americans. Long-lost relatives. Mothers and sons. Orphans. Adoption. Corruption. Jails. Lawyers. Self-sacrifice. Thieves.*

Note: Although a Sep 1931 *FD* news item noted that Robert Warwick and Frank Mayo were cast in the film, their appearance in the released picture has not been confirmed. This film was reviewed in *Har* in Nov 1931, but was not listed as being released nationally until Feb 1933. According to contemporary sources, the racetrack scenes were filmed at Agua Caliente, Mexico.

FD 13 Sep 1931, p. 5. *FD* 7 Mar 1933, p. 2. *Har* 14 Nov 1931, p. 182. *MPH* 11 Mar 1933, p. 24. *NYT* 6 Mar 1933, p. 16. *Var* 7 Mar 1933, p. 54.

RACING BLOOD *see* **SPEED TO BURN**

RACING LUCK (Italian Americans)

Grand-Asher Distributing Corp. *Dist* Associated Exhibitors, Inc. 11 May **1924** [©Associated Exhibitors, Inc.; 18 Apr 1924; LU20088]. Si; b&w. 6 reels, 5,516 ft.

Dir Herman C. Raymaker. *Story* Jean Havez and Lex Neal. *Photog* Ray June.

Cast: Monty Banks (*The Boy [Mario]*), Helen Ferguson (*The Girl [Rosina]*), Martha Franklin (*The Mother [Mrs. Bianchi]*), D. J. Mitsoras (*The Father [Bianchi]*), Lionel Belmore (*The Uncle*), Francis McDonald (*Tony Mora*), William Blaisdell (*Cafe proprietor*), Al Martin, Al Thompson, Ed Carlie, Scaduto (*Members of Tony's gang*).

Comedy. Mario Bianchi comes to the United States and moves in with his uncle, who runs a restaurant in New York City. Mario falls in love with his uncle's adopted daughter, Rosina, and gets into trouble with gangster Tony Mora, knocking Tony down for forcing his attentions on the girl. Tony forces Mario's uncle to fire him and sees to it that Mario cannot keep a job. Mario, mistaken for a famous racing driver, signs with a car manufacturer to drive in an important race. Tony sabotages the car, but Mario wins anyway, receiving a substantial amount of prize money. Mario and Rosina are married. *Automobile racing. Gangsters. Italian Americans. Mistaken identity. New York City. Restaurateurs. Uncles.*

MPW 26 Jul 1924.

THE RACKET MAN (Italian Americans)

Columbia Pictures Corp. *Dist* Columbia Pictures Corp. 18 Jan **1944**; Prod: 18 Oct–2 Nov 1943 [©Columbia Pictures Corp.; 23 Mar 1944; LP12555]. Sd (Western Electric Mirrophonic Recording); b&w. 5,714 ft. 67 min. PCA cert no. 9789.

Prod Wallace MacDonald and [John Stone]. *Dir* D. Ross Lederman. [*Asst dir* Louis Germonprez and Ben Kadish]. *Scr* Paul Yawitz and Howard J. Green. *Based on a story by* Casey Robinson. *Dir of photog* James Van Trees. *Art dir* Lionel Banks. *Assoc* Walter Holscher. *Film ed* Paul Borofsky. *Set dec* George Montgomery. *Mus dir* M. W. Stoloff. [*Sd eng* William Randall].

Cast: Tom Neal [(*Matt Benson*)], Hugh Beaumont [(*"Irish" Duffy*)], Jeanne Bates [(*Phyllis Lake*)], Larry Parks [(*Larry Lake*)], Douglas Fowley [(*Toby Sykes*)], [Lewis Wilson (*Capt. Anderson*)], [Clarence Muse (*George*)], [Mary Gordon (*Ma Duffy*)], [Anthony Caruso (*Tony Ciccardi*)], [Warren Ashe (*Burton*)], [Pauline Drake (*Maimie*)], [John Tyrrell (*Pinky*)], [Eddie Laughton (*Chuck*)], [Charles D. Brown (*Clark*)], [Ted Mapes (*Sgt. Mowbray*)], [Joseph Palma (*Bud*)], [George Magrill (*George*)], [Robert Williams (*Sergeant*)], [Kenneth MacDonald (*Captain*)], [Mel Schubert (*Lieutenant*)], [Charles Hamilton (*Sgt. Johnson*)], [Buddy Yarus, Edwin Mills, Robert Lowell (*Soldiers*)], [Dick Jensen, Ray Flynn (*Police officers*)], [Edwin Stanley (*Doctor*)], [Brian O'Hara (*Ratson*)], [Paul Kingsley (*Franklin*)], [Pat O'Malley (*Postman*)], [George Eldredge (*Jerry*)], [Marilyn Johnson].

Gangster, Homefront, Drama. [*Print viewed*]. On the day that Matt Benson is found not guilty of racketeering, his best friend, policeman "Irish" Duffy, gruffly congratulates him and hands him something that he hopes will reform Matt: his draft notice. Irish receives his draft notice also, and that night, they eat dinner with their other childhood pal, Phyllis Lake, for whom they are now friendly romantic rivals, and her brother, cub reporter Larry Lake. Matt, who loves easy money, assures his friends that he will fit into the Army easily, as he can find an "angle" in any situation, but Irish and Phyllis warn him that the Army needs team players. The next day, Matt turns over his racketeering business to ambitious Toby Sykes, who agrees to watch over the business in exchange for a full partnership upon Matt's return. Matt then reports to the induction center with Irish, who is declared 4-F due to his flat feet. Matt laughingly tells Irish that he will take care of the Army, but soon after his induction, Matt has become sick of the rules and regulations. Matt is lectured by Italian-born Tony Ciccardi, who tells him that the United States needs him, and that being in the military means being a part of something bigger than himself. Matt jeers at Tony's patriotism but is soon forced to take orders from him when Tony is promoted to sergeant. Later, Matt gets into a fight with two soldiers who razz him about being a big shot, and Tony tries to stop them. Matt hits Tony, who refuses to strike him back because of his lower rank. Tony castigates Matt for being ungrateful and not taking advantage of the opportunities being given to him, but does not report the fistfight in order to keep Matt out of trouble. Tony is demoted for not reporting the incident, after which he requests a transfer to the front lines. Tony sends his sergeant's stripes to Matt, who is stunned by Tony's sacrifice. Thereafter, Matt becomes a model soldier and grows to like the discipline and patriotism of Army life. Irish and Phyllis are gratified by the change in Matt, who requests a transfer overseas. Camp commander Captain Anderson states that Mr. Burton, a special government agent, has another job for him, which Matt at first refuses, because he wishes to find Tony and return his stripes. When Anderson informs Matt that Tony was recently killed in action, Matt agrees to work for Burton, who wants him to go undercover in his former racketeering outfit to find the black market dealers of such rationed goods as meat, rubber and gasoline. Burton admonishes Matt that he can tell no one about his work, and so Matt allows Irish, Phyllis, Sykes and others to believe that he was discharged from the Army for not fitting in. Phyllis and Irish are then devastated to see Matt apparently slipping into his former lifestyle. Matt gathers information that enables Burton to recover black market goods being sold by other racketeers and by Sykes, who has double-crossed Matt and gone into business for himself. The criminals are mystified by the police raids and believe that Larry, who has been investigating black market organizations, is the source of the leaks to the federal government. Matt attempts to protect Larry and warns him to stay away from the story. Matt proposes

to Phyllis, but she tearfully tells him that she will have him only if he changes his life. Soon after, another raid convinces Sykes to take action, and he has Larry brought to his warehouse for questioning. When Larry does not show up for work, Matt becomes suspicious and goes to Sykes's warehouse, where he succeeds in freeing the young reporter. During the ensuing gunfight, however, Irish hears the shots and sees Matt shoot one of his pursuers, although it looks like murder to the late-arriving Irish. When Matt returns home, he discovers that Larry has been killed and leaves to take his revenge on Sykes. While Matt tangles with Sykes, Irish enters and demands that Matt give himself up. Sykes shoots Matt in the back while he is distracted, and Irish kills Sykes. As Matt lays dying, Burton informs Phyllis and Irish of Matt's dedicated service, and they comfort their friend with words of praise for his heroic actions. *Black market. Moral reformation. Racketeers. Romantic rivalry. Undercover operations. 4-F. African Americans. Brothers and sisters. Fights. Freezers. Government agents. Irish Americans. Italian Americans. Military life. Military service, Compulsory. Murder. Patriotism. Reporters. Revenge. Self-sacrifice. Shamrocks. World War II.*

Note: Although a *HR* production chart places Cliff Clark, Janis Carter and Shelley Winters in the cast, their appearance in the released film has not been confirmed. This picture marked director D. Ross Lederman's return to Columbia after working for three years at Warner Bros. According to materials contained in the National Archives in Washington, D.C., this film was disapproved for export by the Los Angeles Board of Review of the Office of Censorship because of its depiction of "an organized gang of racketeers operating a black market." According to a *NYT* news item, the MPAA adopted more stringent new guidelines in 1947, and deemed this picture "unsuitable for re-release or reissue." The 1931 Columbia film *The Last Parade*, starring Jack Holt and Tim Moore and directed by Erle C. Kenton, was also based on the Casey Robinson story (see *AFI Catalog of Feature Films, 1931-40*; F3.2390).

DV 14 Feb 1944, p. 3. *HR* 22 Oct 1943, p. 10. *HR* 14 Feb 1944, p. 3. *MPHPD* 8 Jan 1944, p. 1706. *NYT* 4 Dec 1947.

RADIO TROUBADOUR *see* **EL TROVADOR DE LA RADIO**

RAFTER ROMANCE (Jewish Americans)

RKO Radio Pictures, Inc. *Dist* RKO Radio Pictures, Inc. 1 Sep 1933; Prod: began mid-Jun 1933 [©RKO-Radio Pictures, Inc.; 14 Sep 1933; LP4120]. Sd; b&w. 8 reels. 70 min. Passed by the National Board of Review. PCA cert no. 1512-R [11 Sep 1935].

Assoc prod Kenneth Macgowan. *Dir* William Seiter. [*Asst dir* Doran Cox]. *Scr* H. W. Hanemann and Sam Mintz. *Adpt* Glenn Tryon. *Photog* David Abel. [*Cam op* Joe Biroc]. [*Asst cam* Charles Bohny]. *Settings* Van Nest Polglase and John J. Hughes. *Ed* James B. Morley. [*Asst ed* Henry Berman]. *Mus dir* Max Steiner. *Rec* Hugh McDowell, Jr. [*Asst rec* Victor Appel and Harold Stine]. [*Chief elec* Frank Uecker]. [*Chief grip* Whitey Holcomb]. [*Props* Kenny Holmes]. [*Still photog* Alex Kahle].

Source: Based on the novel *Rafter Romance* by John Wells (New York, 1932).

Cast: Ginger Rogers (*Mary [Carroll]*), Norman Foster (*Jack [Bacon]*), George Sidney (*Eckbaum*), Robert Benchley ([*H. Harrington*] *Hubbell*), Laura Hope Crews (*Elise [Peabody Worthington Smythe]*), Guinn Williams (*Fritzie*), Sidney Miller (*Julius [Eckbaum]*), [Ferike Boros (*Rosie Eckbaum*)].

Romantic comedy. [*Print viewed*]. At "Ye Eckbaum Arms," a Greenwich Village tenement, Eckbaum, the Jewish landlord, has an idea as to how two of his tenants, Jack Bacon and Mary Carroll, who each owe him three months rent, can continue to reside there: they can both rent the fourth floor attic, as artist Jack, who works as a nightwatchman, only requires the room during the day, which would allow unemployed Mary to occupy the room during the night. Jack and Mary, who have not met each other, object strenuously to the plan. Even though Mary soon gets a job with the Icy Refrigerator Company as a telephone solicitor, she returns home after her first day of work to find that Eckbaum has moved her things to the attic. She calls the arrangement vile and horrible, but as Eckbaum has already rented her old room, she is agrees to use the attic only between 8 p.m. and 8 a.m. While waiting to occupy the room that evening, Mary sits outside a nearby delicatessen practicing her sales pitch and is spotted by Jack. Impressed by her looks, Jack flirts with her, unaware of her identity, then returns to his room, where he sees his new roommate's possessions. He berates Eckbaum and insults Mary, characterizing her as a small town spinster who came to Greenwich Village looking for romance. Mary overhears him outside the door and cries to Eckbaum's wife Rosie, then after Jack leaves, writes him a note asking him not to

leave his pajamas all over the place. This begins an exchange of written insults and innuendos. At work, Mary's boss, H. Harrington Hubbell, tries to ask her to dinner, but she succeeds in slipping out. Later, she sits at the deli waiting to go up to the apartment when Jack comes by again. Anxious to impress her, he says his aunt owns a housing development and will probably buy at least six refrigerators. After they enjoy a romantic walk in the park, Jack gives Mary his telephone number at work, and they plan to meet the next evening at 6:30. The next day, when Hubbell asks Mary to go to dinner, she gives him an excuse and rushes home in the rain. She makes sure Jack is not in, then gets in the makeshift shower, which Jack, via an insulting note, claims to have fixed. The pail with holes that serves as a shower, however, falls on her head. In retaliation, she hangs his only suit in the shower, and later, after Jack comes in to dress, he turns on the shower and ruins his suit. Jack angrily puts on his overcoat over his shirt and underwear and goes to the tailor's across the street but finds it locked with a "back in 15 minutes" sign on the door. As Jack waits, Mary is getting soaked at the park from the storm. She goes to wait in front of the deli as he runs to the park, then leaves the deli right before he arrives there. The next day, he calls her at work, and she hangs up on him. When Hubbell invites her to see the Ziegfeld Follies that night, she accepts. Learning that Hubbell is her boss, Eckbaum lets her have her old room back to impress him, but when she says she does not live there and a drunk in the hall goes into the room after they leave, Hubbell gets the idea that she is the man's mistress. While Mary is busy deflecting Hubbell's romantic advances with help from taxi driver Fritzie, Jack saws through part of his bed to make it collapse on his roommate. Elise Peabody Worthington Smythe, an alcoholic older woman who is infatuated with him, comes to visit, and when she learns that a woman also lives there, she refuses to leave until she sees her. Jack leaves and runs into Mary, who tries to walk away. He convinces her to have dinner with him, and they reconcile over a Chinese meal. When Mary returns happily to her room, she is shocked to find Elise there, passed out. Mary sees Elise out, then flops on the bed and cries when it collapses on her. Later, Jack accompanies Mary to an office picnic. After they kiss in a rowboat, they hear the horn of the company bus and rush to try to get on before it leaves. Jack falls and sprains his ankle, forcing them to take a taxi into the city. Mary is surprised when they stop in front of her building, but helps Jack upstairs. Upon entering her own apartment, Mary realizes that Jack is the roommate she has grown to hate. When Eckbaum finds them together and berates them for being there at the same time, Jack realizes who Mary is, and they argue with each other about past events. Elise arrives hoping to take Jack away and gets into a name calling match with Mary. Hubbell then arrives just as Mary tears out. She cries outside and complains to Fritzie, who happens to be there with his taxi, about the "filthy, horrible, dispicable" man in her apartment. Having just seen Hubbell go in, Fritzie rushes upstairs and punches him. While Jack finds Mary again in the cab and apologizes, Elise helps Hubbell. Fritzie then comes outside after Jack, but Mary protects him, and Fritzie, seeing them kiss, drives them to the park. Watching them from his window, Eckbaum expresses pride on arranging their soon-to-be marriage. *New York City–Greenwich Village. Romance. Roommates. Tenement-houses. Alcoholics. Artists. Delicatessens. Fights. Infatuation. Jews. Picnicking. Practical jokes. Rainstorms. Restaurants. Rowboats. Saleswomen. Sexual harassment. Taxicab drivers.*

Note: According to a Feb 1933 *FD* news item, Joel McCrea and Dorothy Jordan were first slated to star in this picture. In Jun 1933, *HR* announced that Lew Ayres was to co-star with Ginger Rogers, and that Ben Hendricks, Jr. had been added to the cast. The participation of Hendricks, Jr. in the final film has not been confirmed. Modern sources credit Bernard Newman as costumer, Mel Berns as make-up artist, and John Miehle as still photographer. In 1937, RKO made a second version of John Wells's story called *Living on Love* (see *AFI Catalog of Feature Films, 1931-1940*; F3.2542). Although modern sources claim that three other films, the 1932 German production *Ich bei Tag und du bei Nacht*, the 1932 French production *A Moi le jour, à toi nuit* and the 1933 British production *Early to Bed* are also based on the Wells novel, these pictures are actually based on a screenplay by Robert Liebmann and Hans Székely. Their general plot lines are similar to the Wells novel, however.

FD 21 Feb 1933, p. 7. *FD* 9 Jan 1934, p. 7. *HF* 17 Jun 1933, p. 8. *HR* 1 Jun 1933, p. 3. *HR* 24 Jun 1933, p. 3. *IP* Jul 1933, p. 38. *MPD* 5 Jan 1934, p. 10. *MPH* 5 Aug 1933, p. 38. *Var* 16 Jan 1934, p. 15.

THE RAGE OF PARIS (French Americans)

Universal Pictures Co., Inc.; Charles R. Rogers in charge of production. *Dist* Universal Pictures Co., Inc. 1 Jul **1938**; *Prod*: 21 Mar—mid-May 1938 [©Universal Pictures Co.; 29 Jun 1938; LP8112]. Sd; b&w. 9 reels. 75 or 78 min. PCA cert no. 4204.

Prod B. G. DeSylva and [Henry Koster]. *Dir* Henry Koster. *Asst dir* Frank Shaw. *Orig story and scr* Bruce Manning and Felix Jackson. *Dir of photog* Joseph Valentine. *Art dir* Jack Otterson. *Art dir assoc* Richard H. Riedel. *Film ed* Bernard Burton. *Set dec* R. A. Causman. *Gowns* Vera West. *Mus dir* Charles Previn. *Sd* Bernard B. Brown and William Hedgcock.

Cast: Danielle Darrieux (*Nicole* [*de Cortillon*]), Douglas Fairbanks, Jr. (*Jim Trevor*), Mischa Auer (*Mike*), Louis Hayward (*Bill* [*Jerome* Duncan*]), Helen Broderick (*Gloria* [*Patterson*]), Charles Coleman (*Rigley*), Samuel S. Hinds (*Mr. Duncan*), Nella Walker (*Mrs. Duncan*), Harry Davenport (*Caretaker*), [Lionel Pape (*Uncle Josephus*)], [Frances Robinson (*Outside secretary*)], [Mary Forbes (*Woman in opera box*)], [Howard Hickman (*Man in opera box*)], [Leonard Mudie (*Uncle Eric*)], [Edwin Maxwell (*Hotel manager*)], [Wade Boteler (*Manager*)], [Arthur Hoyt (*Assistant manager*)], [Corbet Morris (*Secretary*)], [Tempe Pigott (*Landlady*)], [Edward Earle (*Waiter*)], [Charles Sherlock (*Elevator boy*)], [Sidney Bracy (*Attendant*)], [Edwin August (*Receptionist*)], [William E. "Babe" Lawrence (*Steward/Doorman*)], [Alfred P. James (*Old man*)], [Jenifer Gray (*Telephone operator*)], [Beryl Wallace (*Model*)], [Hugh Huntley (*Hotel clerk*)], [David Oliver, Jason Robards, Charles D. Lane, Phil MacKenzie, Matt McHugh (*Department heads*)], [Edward Gargan, Dewey Robinson (*Truck drivers*)].

Romantic comedy. [*Print viewed*]. At the Tower Modeling Agency in New York City, unemployed Nicole de Cortillon, a former Parisian, lies her way into the office of the boss, Mr. Wright. She leaves angrily, however, when he offers her a job posing in the nude for an artist. Moments later, Nicole thinks better of the paying position and grabs what she believes is the job's address from Wright's desk. After arriving at the office of advertising executive Jim Trevor, she starts to undress. Jim suspects her of trying to set him up for a blackmail scheme and when Nicole realizes that he is not the photographer, she flees. Nicole then learns that her landlady has locked her out for being behind in the rent. Another lodger, Gloria, takes in Nicole and introduces her to Mike, a friend and waiter at the Savoy Grand Hotel. Mike has saved $3,000 to buy a restaurant of his own, but still needs another $2,000. Gloria believes that the only job for a woman is marriage and persuades Mike to invest his savings to establish the beautiful Nicole as a rich, eligible girl in the hope that she will capture and marry a wealthy man. With Gloria impersonating Nicole's aunt and chaperone, Mike arranges for her to take a room in the Savoy across from multi-millionaire William Jerome Duncan. Nicole pretends to mistake Bill for a childhood friend, kissing him, then withdraws in shame as the "error" is realized. Bill is enchanted by the beautiful woman and takes Nicole and Gloria to the opera. There, he encounters his old friend, Jim, who recognizes Nicole. At a celebration afterward, Jim threatens to tell Bill how he met her, but she lies to explain the situation and make Bill jealous. Jim, believing Nicole only wants to marry and divorce Bill to receive alimony, locks her in his apartment, but she outsmarts his butler, Rigley, and escapes. As Bill celebrates his engagement to Nicole by introducing her to his enormous family, Jim enters, and the two men quarrel. When Nicole follows Jim to his car, he abducts her and takes her to his cottage in the country, where the caretaker mistakes the couple for newlyweds. Finally, Nicole tells Jim the true scheme and says that she has fallen in love with him, but he still believes the worst of her. Nicole takes the milk truck back to the city. Bill, fearing a breach of promise suit, agrees with Mike's plan to send Nicole back to Paris, for which Mike receives $5,000. After Bill brags that he has escaped cheaply, Jim tells him he is going to marry Nicole. Jim meets Nicole on a ship and arranges for a wedding at sea. *French. Friendship. Gold diggers. Hotels. Millionaires. Romantic rivalry. Waiters. Abduction. Aunts. Breach of promise. Butlers. Caretakers. Clothes. Hotels. Impersonation and imposture. Investments. Jealousy. Landladies. Models. New York City. Opera. Poverty. Restaurateurs. Ships. Socialites.*

Note: The Call Bureau Cast Service lists the name of Danielle Darrieux's character as Michele although she is called Nicole in the film. This was Darrieux's first American film. After her highly touted performance in the 1936 French film *Mayerling*, critics predicted stardom for her. *The Rage of Paris* had a premiere-style preview at the Pantages Theater in Hollywood on 9 Jun 1938,

according to *MPH*. Later, the film won an Acting Prize at the 1938 Venice Film Festival. According to modern sources Broadway musical comedy star Mary Martin made her motion picture debut in a "bit" in this film. Contemporary sources confirm that Martin worked as a singing double for Margaret Sullavan in the M-G-M film *The Shopworn Angel*, which was made at about the same time as *The Rage of Paris*, and that film may have marked her first work in motion pictures.

DV 9 Jun 1938, p. 3. *FD* 14 Jun 1938, p. 5. *HR* 21 Mar 1938, p. 2, 18-19. *HR* 9 May 1938, pp. 14-15. *HR* 9 Jun 1938, p. 3. *MPD* 13 Jun 1938, p. 2. *MPH* 28 May 1938, p. 60. *MPH* 18 Jun 1938, p. 39. *MPH* 17 Sep 1938, p. 64. *NYT* 2 Jul 1938, p. 10. *Var* 15 Jun 1938, p. 14.

THE RAGING MEN *see* SHAKE HANDS WITH THE DEVIL

THE RAGING TIDE (Swedish Americans)

Universal-International Pictures Co., Inc. *Dist* Universal Pictures Co., Inc. Nov **1951**; *Prod*: late Feb—late Mar 1951 [©Universal Pictures Co.; 25 Sep 1951; LP1192]. Sd (Western Electric Recording); b&w. 8,339 ft. 92-93 min. PCA cert no. 15302.

Prod Aaron Rosenberg. *Assoc prod* John W. Rogers. *Dir* George Sherman. [*Asst dir* Frank Shaw]. *Scr* Ernest K. Gann. *Dir of photog* Russell Metty. *Spec photog* David S. Horsley. *Art dir* Bernard Herzbrun and Hilyard Brown. *Film ed* Ted J. Kent. *Set des* Russell A. Gausman and Oliver Emert. *Gowns* Bill Thomas. *Mus* Frank Skinner. *Sd* Lesley I. Carey and Corson Jowett. *Hair stylist* Joan St. Oegger. *Makeup* Bud Westmore. *Tech adv* Harvey McDowell.

Source: Based on the novel *Fiddler's Green* by Ernest K. Gann (New York, 1950).

Cast: SHELLEY WINTERS [(*Connie Thatcher*)], RICHARD CONTE [(*Bruno Felkin*)], STEPHEN McNALLY [(*Lt. Kelsey*)], CHARLES BICKFORD [(*Hamil Linder*)], ALEX NICOL [(*Carl Linder*)], John McIntire [(*Corky Mullins*)], Tito Vuolo [(*Barney Schriona*)], Chubby Johnson [(*General Ball*)], Minerva Urecal [(*Jonnie Mae Swanson*)], [Syd Saylor (*Proprietor*)], [John "Skins" Miller (*Hooligan*)], [Pepito Perez (*Mr. Fancy*)], [Robert O'Neil (*Spade Face*)], [Ray Walker (*Neil*)], [Irvin Berwick (*Gas man*)].

Crime, Sea, Drama. [*Print viewed*]. In San Francisco, racketeer Bruno Felkin murders his rival Marty Prince, calls the police to report the death, then escapes into the night. Bruno first goes to his girl friend Connie Thatcher's apartment, believing she will provide him with an alibi, but when he discovers she is not home, hides in a boat at the wharf which sails out at four the next morning. In the meantime, police detective Kelsey has already pegged Bruno as a likely suspect, and questions Connie. Connie, a tough hat check girl whom Bruno treats like a princess, is shocked to learn that Bruno may be a murderer and defends him, although she allows Kelsey to remain in her apartment to see if Bruno returns. When the boat *Taage* reaches the open sea, Bruno overhears the Swedish captain, Hamil Linder, arguing with his grown son Carl, who hates his father's "old world" ways as much as he hates working as a fisherman. Carl is surprised when he sees Bruno through the window, and Hamil, a judicious and compassionate man, allows Bruno to stay aboard after he explains that he fell asleep in the boat because he was drunk and lost his job. Later, Bruno offers Carl a job collecting money from resistant customers so that Bruno can maintain his business while he hides, and Carl leaps at the chance. Bruno stays aboard the boat and learns the fishing trade while Carl runs his collection business on land. Bruno comes to appreciate the beauty of the sea, Hamil's kindness and philosophical nature, and the honest hard work. Carl, meanwhile, befriends Connie when he brings money from Bruno to pay for her education. As time passes, Kelsey hangs around the docks and has Connie followed. Bruno learns that an elderly seaman, Corky Mullins, saw him running to the pier on the night of the murder, so Bruno gives Corky enough money to fix his unreliable boat and put out to sea. One day Hamil berates Carl for his sloppy work on the boat, and Carl knocks his father off the deck onto the pier. Bruno becomes enraged, as he has already warned Carl that he should treat his father with respect, and attacks Carl. After Bruno beats Carl in the fistfight, Hamil tends to his son's injuries, and thanks Bruno for standing up for him. One day, Kelsey tells Connie, who has fallen in love with Carl despite her loyalty to Bruno, that he knows about her "new boyfriend," and that Carl purchased a new car in Corky's name because he is on probation for auto theft. Connie denies that Carl is her boyfriend, but later confronts him. Carl admits the truth, and she worries that Kelsey will find Bruno through Carl. On the next fishing trip, Carl apologizes to his father for pushing him, marking his first step toward an emotional reconciliation. One day, the fishermen realize that Corky is dead after finding a piece of his boat floating in the water. Bruno secretly meets

with Connie and after reaffirming their love, he asks her to obtain letterhead from Marty Prince's company. When they meet the next night, Bruno tells Connie that he plans to sail for South America and wants her to accompany him, but she must first call Kelsey and identify Carl as Marty's killer. Connie tries to protest, but Bruno quiets her with a kiss and leaves. That night, Carl tells Bruno that he has decided to quit working for him and return to fishing to help his father, so that he can marry Connie. Carl also demands that Bruno leave the boat after they return to the dock. Bruno receives the news quietly, having already hidden the murder weapon among Carl's clothes. Connie reluctantly tells Kelsey the truth about Bruno's whereabouts. That night, the *Taage* is caught in a violent storm, and Hamil, who has become a father figure to Bruno, tells Bruno that he is grateful for steering Carl back to him, and thinks of him as a son. Bruno feels guilty for trying to frame Carl and removes the gun. As the storm worsens, Bruno and Carl struggle to keep the boat afloat. Carl is washed overboard by a giant wave, and, knowing that he cannot swim, Bruno dives into the ocean to rescue him. Although he gets Carl safely aboard, Bruno is drowned by a massive wave. Later, Kelsey gently delivers the news of Bruno's death to Connie. Hamil retires from fishing and turns his business over to Carl, who has plans to marry Connie. *Fathers and sons. Fishermen. Fugitives. Moral reformation. Murder. Police detectives. Swedish Americans. Aged men. Business competition. Confession (Law). Drowning. Drunkenness. Fistfights. Frame-ups. Hat check girls. Loyalty. Prayer. Probation. Racketeers. Rescues. Romantic rivalry. San Francisco (CA). Storms. Wharfs.*

Note: The working title of this film was *Fiddler's Green*.

Box 20 Oct 1951. *DV* 11 Oct 1951, p. 3. *Exb* 24 Oct 1951, pp. 3175-76. *FD* 15 Oct 1951, p. 6. *Har* 13 Oct 1951, p. 164. *HR* 23 Feb 1951, p. 13. *HR* 2 Mar 1951, p. 13. *HR* 30 Mar 1951, p. 17. *HR* 11 Oct 1951, p. 3. *MPHPD* 13 Oct 1951, p. 1057. *Var* 17 Oct 1951, p. 6.

THE RAIDERS (Latino)
Universal-International Pictures Co., Inc. *Dist* Universal Pictures Co., Inc. Nov 1952; Los Angeles opening: 20 Nov 1952; *Prod:* early Mar—early Apr 1952 [©Universal Pictures Co.; 2 Nov 1952; LP2048]. Sd (Western Electric Recording); col (Technicolor). 7,202 ft. 80 min. PCA cert no. 15956.

Prod William Alland. *Dir* Lesley Selander. *Asst dir* Fred Frank and [George Lollier]. [*Dial dir* Leon Charles]. *Scr* Polly James and Lillie Hayward. *Story* Lyn Crost Kennedy. *Dir of photog* Carl Guthrie. *Technicolor color consultant* William Fritzsche. *Art dir* Bernard Herzbrun and Richard Riedel. *Film ed* Paul Weatherwax. *Set dec* Russell A. Gausman and John Austin. *Cost* Bill Thomas. *Mus dir* Joseph Gershenson. *Sd* Leslie I. Carey and Glenn E. Anderson. *Makeup* Bud Westmore. *Hair stylist* Joan St. Oegger. [*Unit prod mgr* Percy Ikerd].

Cast: RICHARD CONTE [(*Jan Morrell*)], VIVECA LINDFORS [(*Elena de Ortega*)], Barbara Britton [(*Elizabeth Ainsworth*)], William Bishop [(*Marshal Bill Henderson*)], Hugh O'Brian [(*Hank Purvis*)], Morris Ankrum [(*Thomas Ainsworth*)], Margaret Field [(*Mary Morrell*)], Richard Martin [(*Felipe de Ortega*)], William Reynolds [(*Frank Morrell*)], Palmer Lee [(*Marty Smith*)], John Kellogg [(*Jack Welch*)], Frank Wilcox [(*Sam Sterling*)], Carlos Rivero [(*Ramon*)], I. Stanford Jolley [(*Mountain Jim Ferris*)], Neyle Morrow [(*Juan*)], Francis McDonald [(*Mr. John Cummings*)], George Lewis [(*Vicente*)], [Terry Frost (*Clerk*)], [Clayton Moore (*Boone Logan*)], [Lane Bradford (*Pete Robbins*)], [Riley Hill (*Clarke Leftus*)], [Rush Williams (*Henderson's scout*)], [Dennis Weaver (*Dick Logan*)], [Miguel Fernandez (*Dancer*)], [Virginia Mullen (*Mrs. Abby Cummings*)], [Sydney Mason (*Governor*)], [Leo Curley (*Prosecutor*)], [Edward Earle (*Judge*)], [Paul Newlan (*Bartender*)], [Dennis Ross (*Sam Cummings*)], [Monte Montague (*Gunsmith*)], [Enrique Valdez (*José*)], [Larry Hudson (*Gate guard*)], [Edwin Parker (*Boiler tender*)], [Lee Morgan (*Clerk*)], [Marvin Press (*Salesman*)], [Edmund Cobb (*Jailer*)], [Ethan Laidlaw (*Miner*)], [Clem Fuller (*Stagecoach driver*)], [Paul Kruger, Philo McCollough, Buddy Roosevelt (*Bystanders*)], [Bill Fawcett], [Max Wagner], [Leo McMahon], [Bob Burrows], [Jim Van Horn], [Henry Wills], [Frank Ellis], [F. Patrick Henry], [Boyd Stockman], [Forrest Burns], [Frank O'Connor], [Boyd Morgan], [Stanley Blystone].

Western. [*Print viewed*]. In 1849, after the discovery of gold in California, thousands trek there seeking their fortunes. Prospector Jan Morell receives a letter from his uncle advising him that he has located good farming land in the Napa Valley. Jan hopes that if he continues to find gold, he will be able to buy a farm and move there

with his wife Mary. While Jan helps his brother Frank, prospecting in a nearby river bed, a gang of thugs led by Jack Welch and Hank Purvis kill Mary and take Jan's gold. Purvis also takes a cameo necklace Jan gave to Mary. Frank sees the gang ride off and Jan swears vengeance. After looking for the gang at a saloon, Frank is shot and killed and Jan wounded. Mexican Felipe de Ortega takes Jan to his home where his sister Elena nurses him back to health. Later, Elena shows Jan all the land that once belonged to the Rancho de Ortega and which mayor Thomas Ainsworth, operating as the Sierra Land Co., stole from their father. She hopes that when California becomes a state, the courts will protect the family from further losses. Felipe tells Jan that Ainsworth's men killed Mary and Frank, as Ainsworth wanted to take over Jan's claim because the area is rumored to contain the mother lode. Meantime, Ainsworth instructs Welch and Purvis to continue taking over claims, but to use less violence, as the governor is sending a marshal to the area. Ainsworth also learns that the governor is planning a constitutional convention in Monterey with delegates attending from all over the state. Most are in favor of statehood, but Ainsworth stands to benefit most if California becomes an independent republic. After Jan confirms that Ainsworth has stolen his claim, Felipe introduces him to several local men, including cousins Juan and Ramon, who all have a score to settle with Ainsworth. They band together and begin their campaign against Ainsworth by rustling a large herd of his horses and killing two of his men. When they return from selling the horses, they find posters, signed by U.S. Marshal William Henderson, announcing a $5,000 reward for their capture. Elena, who is romantically interested in Jan, asks him to abandon their outlaw tactics. Although Jan and Felipe open the Sunset Land Co. in San Andreas to compete against Ainsworth, they continue to clandestinely attack his interests. When they hold up a stagecoach carrying Ainsworth's daughter Elizabeth to Monterey, Jan notices that Purvis, who is along as an extra guard, is wearing a fob made from Mary's cameo necklace, but although he states that he bought it, Jan and Felipe take him prisoner. Later, Elizabeth, who is unaware of her father's criminal activities, tells him that the holdup's masked leader accused Purvis of killing a woman and was demanding the names of three accomplices. At his hideout, Jan beats Purvis and prepares to hang him, but Purvis finally gives him the names and tells him of Ainsworth's involvement. Purvis then breaks loose but is killed while escaping. Jan, looking for the other killers, goes to see Ainsworth and meets Elizabeth, who does not recognize him from their previous encounter. She tells him that Welch can be found at one of her father's mines. At the mine, Jan and Welch fight while the rest of the gang make off with a wagon full of gold. Welch is killed in error by his own men, and Felipe is also fatally wounded. As he dies at the home of the widow Cummings, whose husband was murdered by Welch and Purvis, Felipe asks Jan to promise to make Ainsworth give back his land and to take care of Elena. Later, Jan apologizes to Elena for Felipe's death and promises to take her away once he has dealt with Ainsworth, but she prepares to leave. Marshal Henderson begins to have doubts about Ainsworth's honesty and persuades him to go to the Sunset Land Co. to request a loan. The clerk takes Ainsworth's application to Jan's hideout and the marshal follows him. Jan plans to trick Ainsworth into mortgaging all his land, just as he did to others. When Henderson and Ainsworth attack Jan and the others as they leave the hideout, Jan escapes but Ainsworth recovers a satchel containing gold the gang earlier stole and sends it to Monterey, where the gold is to be used to bribe delegates. Jan goes to Ainsworth's house and forces him to prepare a written confession of everything. However, when Ainsworth draws a gun, Jan has to shoot and kills him. Henderson arrests Jan but arranges to represent him, as he is also a member of the bar and is now convinced of Ainsworth's guilt. However, the jury finds Jan guilty and he is sentenced to be hanged. In jail, Jan learns that California has joined the Union and the governor, under a general amnesty, pardons him. Henderson frees Jan and he finds Elena waiting for him. *California–History–1846-1850. Gangs. Land barons. Land claims. Mexicans. Murder. Prospectors. Revenge. Brothers and sisters. Fathers and daughters. Friendship. Gold. Gold mines. Land companies. Necklaces. Outlaws. Pardons. Rewards. Romance. Rustlers. Saloons. Settlers. Stagecoach robberies. Statehood (American politics). Trials. United States. Marshals. Widows.*

Note: This film's working title was *The Riding Kid*. The print viewed was, apparently, prepared for television distribution. The main title reads: "*Riders of Vengeance*—released theatrically as *The Raiders*."

Box 18 Oct 1952. *DV* 8 Oct 1952, p. 4. *Exb* 22 Oct 1952, pp. 3399-3400. *FD* 14 Oct 1952, p. 6. *Har* 11 Oct 1952, pp. 162-63. *HR* 7 Mar 1952, p. 14. *HR* 8 Oct 1952, p. 19. *LAEx* 21 Nov 1952. *LAT* 21 Nov 1952. *MPD* 9 Oct 1952. *MPHPD* 11 Oct 1952, p. 1558. *NYT* 13 Dec 1952, p. 19. *Var* 8 Oct 1952, p. 12.

RAIDERS OF OLD CALIFORNIA (Latino)

Gavel Inc.; An Albert C. Gannaway Production. *Dist* Republic Pictures Corp. 1 Nov **1957**; Prod: late Jun—late Jul 1956. Sd (Glen Glenn Sound); b&w; Widescreen. 6,532 ft. 72 min. PCA cert no. 18556.

Prod Albert C. Gannaway. *Assoc prod* Sam Roeca and Thomas G. Hubbard. *Dir* Albert C. Gannaway. *Asst dir* Les Guthrie. *Wrt* Sam Roeca and Thomas G. Hubbard. *Photog* Charles Straumer. *Optical eff* Consolidated Film Industries. [*Art dir* Steve Gusson]. *Supv ed* Carl Pingitore. [*Film ed* Warren Adams]. *Ward* Bob Richards. *Sd mixer* Leon M. Leon. *Makeup* Carlie Taylor. *Tech adv* Bill Ward. *Scr supv* Mai Dietrich. *Prod asst* Richard La Croix.

Cast: Jim Davis [(*Angus Clyde McKane*)], Arleen Whelan [(*Julie Johnson*)], Faron Young [(*Marshal Faron Young*)], Marty Robbins [(*Timothy Voyle*)], Lee Van Cleef [(*Pardee*)], Louis Jean Heydt [(*Judge Ward*)], Harry Lauter [(*Scott Johnson*)], Douglas Fowley [(*Sheriff*)], Larry Dobkin [(*Don Miguel Sebastian*)], Bill Coontz [(*Turk*)], Don Diamond [(*Pepe*)], Ric Vallin [(*Burt*)], Tom Hubbard [(*Emmet*)], [Edward Colmans].

Western. [*Print viewed*]. In 1847, during the war with Mexico, before news reaches Mexican Captain Don Miguel Sebastian in Old California that General Santa Anna has withdrawn his forces in defeat, United States soldiers led by Angus Clyde McKane attack Sebastian's hacienda. A battle ensues resulting in the death of all other the Mexican soldiers. When Pardee, one of McKane's men, takes down the Mexican flag, Sebastian knocks him off his horse. McKane has to restrain Pardee from killing the Mexican captain. A courier then brings word to Sebastian that the war is over. Three years later, the Mexicans who once had farms on Sebastian's land are poverty-stricken and homeless, having been uprooted by McKane and his men. As Pardee beats a Mexican, Scott Johnson, another of McKane's men, stops him from killing the man. Pardee fights Scott and is about to kill him when McKane stops them. Scott then leaves the gang and is warned not to cross paths with them again. Meanwhile, Judge Ward and his son, U.S. Marshal Faron Young, arrive in McKaneville to investigate some property disputes. Pardee explains that McKane needs the disputed land for the cattle trail to Santa Fe and that McKane gave the farmers fair notice and paid them, but the judge says McKane can't force them to sell their land. Diego, a farmer, tells the judge that McKane tricked Sebastian. McKane contends that Sebastian sold the deed while drunk and in debt. McKane now sends Pardee to Scott to force him, through intimidation of his attractive wife Julie, to tell the judge the same story. Scott agrees, provided McKane give the land back to the people. Later, as Scott talks with the judge and the marshal, McKane and his men ride up and a gun battle ensues. Faron shoots some of them and knocks Pardee out by the river, but Scott is shot. Thinking he is about to die, Scott reveals that Sebastian, assumed to be dead, was seen recently by Diego. Pardee, now recovered, overhears. The doctor examines Scott and says he will recover. A group of McKane's men promise Diego the title to his land if he reveals Sebastian's location. He refuses at first, but gives in when they threaten him. Pardee then shoots him so he won't tell anyone else. Faron finds Diego's wife, whom Diego had hidden from McKane's men, crying over him, and she tells him to go to Los Cresta in Mexico to find Sebastian. McKane's three men take a short cut through Comanche territory. Seeing Faron approach from a hill, they are about to fire on him, when they see Indians chase him and leave it to them to kill Faron. He survives, however, killing three Indians in battle. When the horse of one of McKane's men pulls up lame, Pardee wants to leave the man stranded, but the other pulls his gun on Pardee, and Pardee tells them to ride double, then goes on ahead. Faron catches up to the two and kills one in a gun battle, while wounding the other. Faron takes the wounded man with him to Los Cresta. Pardee, after killing a man in the town, finds Sebastian, now the town's padre, and is about to kill him when Faron shoots and kills Pardee. When McKane learns that Sebastian is now on his way to testify in court, he sends his boys to kill him and Faron. McKane's men ambush them, but Faron bests them in a gunfight. Two die and two return to McKane, who makes plans to stampede cattle to disrupt the trial if he loses, then

shoot everyone in the courtroom. McKane first tries to get the townsfolk on his side by promising them land and the opportunity to make their own laws, asserting that the country is his. Sebastian testifies that after Santa Anna's surrender, he was glad to see the war end, and he wanted to make amends for his life. In Sebastian's recollection, McKane, at Sebastian's hacienda, threatens to execute him as a traitor. McKane offers to swap his land for his life. Sebastian agrees to sign over the land granted to his ancestors by King Philip of Spain stretching from West Pecos to the Rio Grande, and from Chihuahua to Santa Fe. When Scott objects that McKane is using his uniform to extort and that he is collaborating with the enemy, McKane orders Scott to sign the deed or be listed as a casualty of battle. McKane assures Sebastian that the farmers living on the land will be treated fairly. Happy to be given a chance at another life, Sebastian rides off, but McKane sends Pardee to kill him. Pardee kills the courier accompanying Sebastian, but runs out of bullets. He makes Sebastian fall down a hill and leaves him for dead. Sebastian testifies that God's will kept him alive. Judge Ward now dismisses the jury saying the transfer of the title was legal; however, he rules that because no U.S. soldier can bargain with the enemy during wartime, the title still belongs to Sebastian. He remands McKane to the custody of Faron to stand trial under military court-martial for collaboration and high treason. The cattle now stampede and McKane smiles as everyone panics, but he himself is trampled in the street with other townsfolk. With McKane dead, his men disperse. Sebastian says that the land now belongs to the people living on it and gives Scott and Julie the land on which they are living to own legally. *California–History–1846-1850. Land grants. Land rights. Megalomania. Mexican Americans. Mexicans. Priests. Alcoholics. Battles. Cattle. Chases. Comanche Indians. Death by animals. Deeds. Extortion. Farmers. Gunfights. Haciendas. Judges. Mexico. Murder. Officers (Military). Sadism. Saloons. Stampedes. Subpoena. Threats. Treason. Trials. United States–History–War with Mexico, 1845-1848. United States. Marshals.*

Note: The working titles of this film were *The Gun and the Gavel*, *Six Guns and a Gavel* and *The Violent Land*. Although *HR* production charts indicate that the film was scheduled to be shot in color, it was shot in black and white in Kanab, UT. While the screen credits state that the film was copyrighted by Gavel Inc., no copyright registration for the film has been located.

Box 7 Dec 1957. *Exb* 11 Dec 1957, p. 4413. *FD* 18 Dec 1957, p. 6. *Har* 7 Dec 1957, p. 194. *HR* 22 Jun 1956, p. 9. *HR* 27 Jul 1956, p. 13. *HR* 24 Jul 1957. *HR* 27 Jul 1957. *MPHPD* 30 Nov 1957, p. 626.

RAIDERS OF TOMAHAWK CREEK (Native Americans)

Columbia Pictures Corp. *Dist* Columbia Pictures Corp. **1950**; Prod: 6 Jun—13 Jun 1950 [©Columbia Pictures Corp.; 17 Oct 1950; LP403]. Sd; b&w. 4,984 ft. 55-56 min. PCA cert no. 14713.

Series: The Durango Kid.

Prod Colbert Clark. *Dir* Fred F. Sears. *Asst dir* Gilbert Kay. *Scr* Barry Shipman. *Story* Robert Schaefer and Eric Freiwald. *Photog* Fayte Browne. *Art dir* Charles Clague. *Film ed* Paul Borofsky. *Mus dir* Mischa Bakaleinikoff. *Sd* Russell Malmgren.

Song(s): "I'm Too Smart for That" and "The Grasshopper Polka," words and music by Smiley Burnette.

Cast: Charles Starrett (*The Durango Kid, also known as Steve Blake*), Smiley Burnette (*Smiley Burnette*), Edgar Dearing (*Randolph Dike*), Kay Buckley (*Janet Clayton*), Billy Kimbley (*Billy Calhoun*), Paul Marion (*Chief Flying Arrow*), Paul McGuire (*Sheriff*), Bill Hale (*Jeff Calhoun*), Lee Morgan (*Saunders*).

Western, with songs. [*Not viewed*]. While out riding on their ranch, young Billy Calhoun and his brother Jeff become alert when they spot a group of Indians, but relax when they notice that Randolph Dike, the Indian agent, is with them. Dike tells the brothers that he has been fired from his job for excessive drinking and then introduces them to the new agent, Steve Blake, who also masquerades as the masked avenger The Durango Kid. Steve mentions that Jeff's ranch is partly on Indian territory, but Jeff indignantly proclaims his intention to remain where he is. Then Chief Flying Arrow calls attention to Jeff's ring, which he calls an "evil-way" ring. Making peace, Steve offers to find Jeff a comparable piece of land on the other side of Tomahawk Creek. Later, Jeff is murdered with a medicine man's tomahawk, and Steve, who is called to investigate, notices that Jeff's distinctive ring is missing. Dike brings the bereft Billy to stay with Steve's friend, Smiley Burnette. Later, the sheriff tells Steve that two weeks earlier, a rancher named Holt Clayton was also killed with a tomahawk. He suspects that Indians are responsible for the murders,

but Steve is not convinced. Then Smiley, who has just completed a course in detective work, offers his services to Steve. Steve decides to question Janet Clayton, the murdered man's daughter, but on his way out to the ranch, he is stopped by a rancher named Saunders, who warns him to keep the Indians out of the area. At the ranch, Janet reveals that her father also had a silver ring like Jeff's, which was given to him by an old prospector named Pete Barker. She adds that both her father and Jeff had helped Pete at different times. Steve shows her the silver ring that he wears, which Pete sent to him in Texas in return for certain favors. Later, Smiley and Billy spy on the Indians, who chase them away. They are rescued from the Indians by Steve, disguised as The Durango Kid. Steve later questions Chief Flying Arrow about the rings, but Flying Arrow insists that Indians are not responsible for the murders. He reveals that after the tribe's medicine man made five rings for Pete, he was tortured to death and that is why the rings are "evil." Flying Arrow suggests that Dike may know more about the rings. When Steve questions him, however, Dike claims to know nothing. Later, Smiley remembers that Luke Alker was wearing a similar ring and asks Dike to convey that information to Steve. Instead, Dike orders Saunders to kill Alker and steal his ring. Later, pointing to the ring that Steve wears, Dike convinces the sheriff that Steve is the killer, and he is arrested. The next day, while the sheriff is holding a hearing, Saunders tries to steal Steve's ring, but finds the box in which it is stored empty, because Smiley, determined to solve the mystery, had previously stolen it. Later, Billy and Smiley are caught spying on Dike and his henchmen. Saunders notices that Smiley is wearing Steve's ring, but while he tries to remove it, Billy escapes and summons The Durango Kid. After a shoot out, Steve, dressed as The Durango Kid, shows Flying Arrow the five rings and learns that when put together, they give directions to a silver mine on Indian land. *Indian agents. Indians of North America. Murder. Rings.* Amateur detectives. Brothers. Disguise. False accusations. Fistfights. Mines. Sheriffs. Shootouts.

Note: For additional information on "The Durango Kid" series, consult the Series Index.

Box 4 Nov 1950. *DV* 1 Nov 1950, p. 3. *FD* 8 Nov 1950, p. 6. *HR* 1 Nov 1950, p. 3. *MPHPD* 4 Nov 1950, p. 554. *Var* 8 Nov 1950, p. 18.

RAINBOW ON THE RIVER (African Americans)
Principal Productions, Inc.; Bobby Breen Productions, Inc. *Dist* RKO Radio Pictures, Inc. 25 Dec **1936**; New York opening: week of 17 Dec 1936; Prod: mid-Sep—mid-Oct 1936 at RKO Pathé Studios. Sd; b&w. 85, 88 or 91 min. PCA cert no. 2836.

Prod Sol Lesser. [*Assoc prod* Edward Gross]. *Dir* Kurt Neumann. *Asst dir* George Sherman. *Scr* Harry Chandlee, Earle Snell and William Hurlbut. *Addl dial* Clarence Marks. *Photog* Charles Schoenbaum. *Art dir* Harry Oliver. *Art dir assoc* Lewis J. Rachmil and Earl Wooden. *Film ed* Robert Crandall. *Cost supv* Albert Diano. *Mus setting conceived and dir by* Hugo Riesenfeld. [*Mus*] *assoc* Abe Meyer. *Sd eng* Hal Bumbaugh. [*Unit mgr* Ray Heinz].

Song(s): "Rainbow on the River," words and music by Paul Webster and Louis Alter; "Flower Song," words and music by Hugo Riesenfeld and Selma Hautzik; "Waitin' for the Sun," words and music by Karl Hajos and Arthur Swanstrom; "Old Folks at Home," "Ring, Ring de Banjo" and "De Camptown Races," words and music by Stephen Foster; "Ave Maria," words traditional, music by Charles Gounod, adapted from the First Prelude in *The Well-Tempered Clavichord* by Johann Sebastian Bach; "Holy, Holy, Holy! Lord Almighty," based on "Nicaea," words by Reginald Heber, music by John Bacchus Dykes.

Source: Based on the novel *Toinette's Philip* by Mrs. C. V. Jamison (New York, 1894).

Cast: Bobby Breen (*Philip* [*Ainsworth*]), May Robeson [sic] (*Mrs.* [*Harriet*] *Ainsworth*), Chas. Butterworth (*Barrett*), Alan Mowbray (*Ralph Layton*), Benita Hume (*Julia Layton*), Henry O'Neil (*Father Josef*), Louise Beavers (*Toinette*), Marilyn Knowlden (*Lucille Layton*), Hall Johnson Choir, [Lillian Yarbo (*Seline*)], [Stymie Beard (*Abraham Lincoln Stonewall Jackson George Washington Lilybell Jones*)], [Eddie Anderson (*Doctor*)], [Betty Blythe (*Flower buyer*)], [Theresa Maxwell Conover (*Mrs. Logan*)], [Clarence H. Wilson (*Pedestrian*)], [Lew Kelly (*Cabman*)], [Lillian Harmer (*Superintendent*)], [St. Luke's Choristers].

Historical, Melodrama, Musical. [*Print viewed*]. In 1873, Philip, whose Northern-born father was a casualty of the Civil War and whose Southern mother was a victim of fire, is reared and sheltered in New

Orleans by former slave Toinette. Touched by Toinette's devotion to Philip, a gifted singer and banjo player, kindhearted Father Josef traces the boy's surviving family to New York and determines that Mrs. Harriet Ainsworth, a wealthy widow, is his grandmother. Josef writes to Mrs. Ainsworth explaining the situation, but because she hates Southerners and still resents her son for marrying one, Mrs. Ainsworth views Josef's claims with great skepticism. Mrs. Ainsworth's niece, the fortune-hunting Julia Layton, also views Josef's letter with loathing, fearing that with a grandson, Mrs. Ainsworth will cut her and her daughter Lucille out of her will. Despite her reservations, however, Mrs. Ainsworth sends Julia's henpecked husband Ralph to New Orleans to investigate Philip's parentage. Although no documentation of Philip's birth survived the war, Ralph takes a liking to the talented boy and agrees to take him back to New York. Urged by Father Josef to unite Philip with his natural family, Toinette reluctantly parts with her charge, comforted only by the thought that he will have better opportunities in the North. Once in New York, Philip is ignored by Mrs. Ainsworth, who detests Southerners and still harbors doubts about Philip's parentage, while Julia and the bratty Lucille plot to have him adopted into another family. Comforted only by his dancing pet mice and by Barrett, Mrs. Ainsworth's gentle butler, Philip leads a lonely existence at his grandmother's and yearns for the warmth of Toinette. Gradually, however, Philip's natural charm and cheeriness warm the heart of his stern grandmother, and a genuine friendship is formed. Philip's budding relationship with Mrs. Ainsworth does not curtail the Laytons' cruelty, however. At her birthday party, Lucille becomes jealous of the attention that Philip's singing and banjo playing attracts and orders another boy to release his mice into a crowd of children. After the ensuing ruckus, Lucille informs Philip that they are sending him to an orphanage the next day and have drowned his mice. Alerted by Barrett, Mrs. Ainsworth finally sees through Julia and Ralph's scheming and stops Philip from running away to New Orleans. Mrs. Ainsworth then takes Philip back to Toinette, who has been pining for her lost child and has become physically debilitated with grief. Moved by Toinette and Philip's intense reunion, Mrs. Ainsworth finally embraces Philip as own her flesh and blood. *Foster parents. Grandmothers. Northerners. Orphans. Parentage. Southerners. United States–History–Reconstruction, 1865-1898.* African Americans. Aunts. Banjos. Birthdays. Brats. Butlers. Class distinction. Cousins. Fortune hunters. Henpecked husbands. Mice. New Orleans (LA). New York City. Parties. Priests. Singers. Uncles. Widows.

Note: The working title of the film was *Toinette's Philip*. According to a *HR* news item, Principal borrowed Herman Mankiewicz from M-G-M to write dialogue for this film. Mankiewicz, however, did not receive screen credit nor was he credited as a contributing writer by *SAB*. According to a letter to Mankiewicz from Principal, his credit was omitted because, in the judgment of Principal executives, only a "minimum part, if any" of the work contributed by him was used in the final script. In Aug 1936, *HR* announced that Principal had offered Edward Everett Horton the comic lead in the picture, but that actor did not appear in the film. Principal borrowed Harry O'Neill from Warner Bros. for this production. Although *HR* announced that RKO was borrowing Edith Fellows from Columbia for the production, her participation in the final film has not been confirmed. Lee Prather was announced as both a cast member and a dialogue director, but his participation in the final film has not been confirmed. *HR* production charts and news items add Jack Luden, Frank McGlynn, Sr., Robert Strange, Monte Montague, Jesse Clarke and Billy Watson to the cast. Their participation in the final film has not been confirmed. Spencer Charters is also included in *HR* production charts, but his participation in the final film is doubtful. Scenes for this film were shot at the Universal Studios "river" lot and in Bakersfield, CA, according to *HR* news items. In addition, *HR* noted that "recording" of the film began on 10 Sep 1936 at St. Paul's Cathedral in Los Angeles, where Breen performed with the St. Luke's Choristers.

DV 2 Dec 1936, p. 3. *FD* 5 Dec 1936, p. 7. *HR* 27 Jul 1936, p. 4. *HR* 22 Aug 1936, p. 4. *HR* 11 Sep 1936, p. 7. *HR* 16 Sep 1936, p. 10. *HR* 18 Sep 1936, p. 2. *HR* 25 Sep 1936, p. 4. *HR* 26 Sep 1936, p. 4. *HR* 28 Sep 1936, p. 3, 14. *HR* 9 Oct 1936, p. 15. *HR* 12 Oct 1936, p. 6. *HR* 2 Dec 1936, p. 3. *HR* 23 Dec 1936, pp. 5-13. *MPD* 3 Dec 1936, p. 4. *MPH* 21 Nov 1936, p. 36. *MPH* 12 Dec 1936, p. 52. *NYT* 18 Dec 1936, p. 31. *Var* 23 Dec 1936, p. 18.

THE RAINBOW TRAIL (Native Americans)
Fox Film Corp. *Dist* Fox Film Corp. 5 Jan **1932**; Prod: 5 Oct—early Nov 1931 [©Fox Film Corp.; 3 Dec 1931; LP2698]. Sd; b&w. 6 reels, 5,420 ft. 60 or 62 min. Passed by the National Board of Review. PCA cert no. 1639-R [8 Oct 1935].

[*Assoc prod* Edmund Grainger]. *Dir* David Howard. [*Asst dir* P. A. Ikerd]. *Adpt and dial* Philip Klein and Barry Conners. *Photog* Daniel Clark. [*2d cam* Curtis Fetters]. [*Asst cam* Bud Mautino and Lou Kunkel]. *Art dir* William Darling. [*Ed* Al De Gaetano]. *Cost* Guy Duty. *Sd rec* Albert Protzman. [*Unit mgr* R. E. Goux]. [*Casting dir* J. E.

Gardner]. [*Still photog* Alexander Kahle]. [*Stunt double for George O'Brien* Cliff Lyons]. [*Riding double for Cecilia Parker* Aline Goodwin]. [*Stunt double* Frank McGrath].

Song(s): "My Wife Does Fancy Work," words by Barry Conners, music by Frank Tresselt and Hugo Friedhofer.

Source: Based on the novel *The Rainbow Trail* by Zane Grey (New York, 1915).

Cast: George O'Brien [(*Shefford*)], Cecilia Parker [(*Fay Larkin*)], Minna Gombell [(*Ruth*)], Roscoe Ates [(*Ike Wilkins*)], J. M. Kerrigan [(*Paddy Harrigan*)], James Kirkwood [(*Venters*)], W. L. Thorne [(*Dyer*)], Robert Frazer [(*Lone Eagle*)], Ruth Donnelly [(*Abigail*)], Niles Welch [(*Willets*)], Landers Stevens [(*Presby*)], Laska Winter [(*Singing Cloud*)], [Edward Hearn (*Jim Lassiter*)], [Alice Ward (*Jane Withersteen*)], [George Burton (*Elliott*)], [Dick Hunter, Herman Nowlin, Clint Sharp, Vinegar Roan (*Horsemen*)], [Edward Burns, Cy Clegg (*Cowboys*)], [Iron Eyes Cody, George Metz, Little Pine (*Indians*)], [Frank McGrath], [Cliff Lyons].

Western. [*Not viewed*]. In Arizona, in 1885, Shefford takes a job on a pack train in order to discover the whereabouts of a secluded gold-filled gorge, "Surprise Valley," where a group of travelers were trapped fifteen years earlier while trying to elude Dyer, an infamous outlaw. The pack train arrives at its destination, a settlement where Dyer and his men keep their "women folk," and Shefford meets a young woman who, unknown to him, is Fay Larkin, one of the Surprise Valley dwellers who has been brought against her will to Dyer's quasi-brothel. Shefford tells her about Surprise Valley and his desire to find and help the people trapped there. Fearing for the safety of the couple who adopted her, Jane Withersteen and Jim Lassiter, Fay tells Shefford that "Fay" is dead and urges him to leave the area. Shefford later saves an Indian girl from the clutches of Willets, one of Dyer's outlaws, and he asks the girl's appreciative brother, Lone Eagle, if he knows about Surprise Valley. When Shefford returns to camp, Willets recognizes him and orders him to be tied up and led to a cliff's edge, but Lone Eagle arrives and threatens that the Navajos will declare war on Dyer's settlement if Shefford is not set free. After Lone Eagle tells Shefford that the young woman whom he met is really Fay Larkin, Shefford promises her that he will rescue Jane and Lassiter. Fay tells him that the valley is marked by a red stone shaped like a rainbow. Shefford goes to the valley, sees Lassiter below and throws him a note stating his promise to return the next day to rescue them. Shefford then returns to the settlement to discover Dyer stabbed. Wearing Dyer's mask and coat, Shefford escapes the area with Fay. Lone Eagle helps Shefford throw ropes down to Jane and Lassiter, as Dyer's men pursue them. Once Jane and Lassiter have been pulled out of the valley, the group heads toward the river in order to escape Dyer's men. They cross a narrow chasm over a fallen tree before disengaging it from the hillside, and thus elude their pursuers. Lone Eagle confesses that he killed Dyer and says that by protecting Fay from Dyer's advances, he was paying Shefford back for saving the woman that he loves. Fay and Shefford embrace. *Heroism. Indians of North America. Kidnapping. Outlaws. Rescues. Attempted rape. Brothers and sisters. Chases. Impersonation and imposture. Rivers. Threats.*

Note: The credits were taken from a screen credits sheet in the Twentieth Century-Fox Records of the Legal Department, and the plot summary was based on a screen continuity in the Twentieth Century-Fox Produced Scripts Collection, both of which are at the UCLA Theater Arts Library. The title card of this film reads "Zane Grey's *The Rainbow Trail*." The novel originally appeared in serial form under the title *The Desert Crucible* in *Argosy Magazine*, May-Sep 1915. This film was a sequel to the 1931 Fox film *Riders of the Purple Sage*, which was also based on a Zane Grey novel, and which starred George O'Brien in the role of "Lassiter" (see *AFI Catalog of Feature Films, 1931-40*; F3.3749). Reviews praise the picture's views of the Grand Canyon, where some scenes were shot. *NYT* notes that at the film's New York showing at the Roxy Theatre, it was shown on an enlarged screen. *HR* erroneously states that this was David Howard's first film as a director; while it was his first feature-length English-language film as a director, he had in the previous year directed a number of Spanish-language films for Fox, most of which were also made in English-language versions by other directors. Fox made films based on the same source in 1918 and 1925; the 1918 film was directed by Frank Lloyd and starred William Farnum (see *AFI Catalog of Feature Films, 1911-20*; F1.3634), while the 1925 film was directed by Lynn Reynolds and starred Tom Mix (see *AFI Catalog of Feature Films, 1921-30*; F2.4438). *Var* commented concerning the three versions and their stars, "In the lead role O'Brien probably resembles Farnum more than Mix. The latter made *Rainbow Trail* a fast-moving chase film. O'Brien is more suggestive of power than action. He's the best built guy in Hollywood and his thin jersey shirt always shows it."

FD 31 Jan 1932, p. 10. *HF* 31 Oct 1931, p. 12. *HR* 19 Nov 1931, p. 3. *HR* 4 Feb 1932, p. 2. *IP* Jan 1932, p. 36. *MPH* 5 Dec 1931, p. 55. *NYT* 30 Jan 1932, p. 13. *Var* 2 Feb 1932, p. 15.

RAINTREE COUNTY (African Americans)

Metro-Goldwyn-Mayer Corp.; controlled by Loew's Inc. *Dist* Loew's Inc. Oct **1957**; World premiere in Louisville, KY: 2 Oct 1957; Prod: early Apr—13 May; 23 Jul—16 Oct 1956 [©Loew's Inc.; 31 Dec 1957; LP9771]. Sd (Westrex Recording System); col (Technicolor); Camera 65; Photographic lenses by Panavision. 22 reels, 16,537 ft. 182, 185, or 187 min. PCA cert no. 18351.

Prod David Lewis. *Assoc prod* Millard Kaufman. *Dir* Edward Dmytryk. *Asst dir* Ridgeway Callow. *Scr* Millard Kaufman. *Dir of photog* Robert Surtees. *Spec eff* Warren Newcombe. *Color consultant* Charles K. Hagedon. *Art dir* William A. Horning and Urie McCleary. *Film ed* John Dunning. *Set dec* Edwin B. Willis and Hugh Hunt. *Cost* Walter Plunkett. *Mus* Johnny Green. *Rec supv* Dr. Wesley C. Miller. *Makeup created by* William Tuttle. *Hairstyles* Sydney Guilaroff.

Song(s): "The Song of Raintree County," music by Johnny Green, lyrics by Paul Francis Webster, sung by Nat "King" Cole.

Source: Based on the novel *Raintree County* by Ross Lockridge, Jr. (Boston, 1948).

Cast: MONTGOMERY CLIFT [(*John Wickliff Shawnessy*)], ELIZABETH TAYLOR [(*Susanna Drake Shawnessy*)], EVA MARIE SAINT [(*Nell Gaither*)], NIGEL PATRICK [(*Prof. Jerusalem Webster Stiles*)], Lee Marvin [(*Orville "Flash" Perkins*)], Rod Taylor [(*Garwood B. Jones*)], Agnes Moorehead [(*Ellen Shawnessy*)], Walter Abel [(*T. D. Shawnessy*)], Jarma Lewis [(*Barbara Drake*)], Tom Drake [(*Bobby Drake*)], Rhys Williams [(*Ezra Gray*)], Russell Collins [(*Niles Foster*)], DeForest Kelley [(*Southern officer*)], [Myrna Hansen (*Lydia Gray*)], [Oliver Blake (*Jake the bartender*)], [John Eldredge (*Cousin Sam*)], [Isabelle Cooley (*Soona*)], [Ruth Attaway (*Parthenia*)], [Eileene Stevens (*Miss Roman*)], [Rosalind Hayes (*Bessie*)], [Don Burnett (*Tom Conway*)], [Michael Dugan (*Nat Franklin*)], [Ralph Vitti (*Jesse Gardner*)], [William Challee, Frank Kreig, Joe Brown, Nesdon Booth, Robert Forrest (*Spectators*)], [Phil Chambers (*Starter*)], [James Griffith (*Bourbon voice*)], [Burt Mustin (*Grandpa Peters*)], [Dorothy Granger (*Madam Gobert*)], [Owen McGiveney (*Blind man*)], [Charles Watts (*Fat man*)], [Heinie Brock, Jack Daly (*Photographers*)], [Stacy S. Harris (*Lieutenant*)], [Donald Losby (*Jim Shawnessy, age 2*)], [Mickey Maga (*Jim Shawnessy, age 4*)], [Robert Foulk (*Pantomimist*)], [Bill Walker (*Old black man*)], [Janet Lake], [Luana Lee], [Judi Jordan], [Phyllis Douglas], [Sue George], [Mil Patrick], [Josephine Cummins].

Social, Drama. [*Print viewed*]. In the town of Freehaven in Raintree County, Indiana, the high school class of 1859 poses for a photograph. Everyone expects great things of valedictorian John Wickliff Shawnessy, in particular his sweetheart, Nell Gaither, who admires Johnny for his idealism, poetry and respect for truth and justice. Before graduation, Prof. Jerusalem Webster Stiles, who smilingly describes himself as "pitiful and harmless," relates to his students a local legend: Raintree County is named for a golden raintree, which was planted somewhere in the region by Johnny Appleseed. Find it, declares the professor in an unusually pensive mood, and you will learn the secret of life itself. Johnny immediately sets out to locate the tree, but as he wanders through a swamp, he nearly drowns. Back in town, Orville "Flash" Perkins boasts that, in addition to being "half horse, half alligator," he is the area's top runner. Johnny challenges him to a race, and on the Fourth of July, the two competitors meet in the street. Before the race, the men engage in a drinking contest, and although Johnny, who has never before drunk whiskey, is rendered nearly senseless, he nonetheless wins the race. Later that day, Johnny goes to the river for a picnic with the professor, an attractive married woman named Lydia Gray, and a beautiful visitor from the South named Susanna Drake. Johnny and Susanna go swimming, and then, in a moment of passion, make love. The next day, Susanna returns to New Orleans, and Johnny returns to Nell. When Stiles tries to run away with Lydia, her outraged husband Ezra tries to shoot him, but after Stiles swears that he never touched Lydia, Johnny helps the professor to leave town. The same train that carries Stiles to safety, however, brings Susanna back to Freehaven with a desperate message for Johnny: She is pregnant. Johnny announces their marriage, whereupon his father, T. D. Shawnessy, a gentle and educated minister, somewhat sadly wishes the young man

happiness. Nell also wishes him well but tearfully confesses that she still loves him. On the boat trip to New Orleans, Susanna is shocked to discover that Johnny is an abolitionist and nervously proclaims that nothing is worse than having a drop of Negro blood in one's veins. The couple visits the ruins of a family plantation that burned when Susanna was a child. Acting strangely, Susanna sorrowfully declares that she dearly loved her former nanny, a black Cuban named Henrietta Courtney, who perished with the girl's parents in the conflagration. Johnny questions Susanna's cousin and learns that after her parents were married, her mother went slowly insane. Her father met Henrietta and brought her home to care for little Susanna. When the bodies were taken from the fire, it appeared that the child's father and Henrietta had been shot, but no one was able to prove this. Johnny brings Susanna back to Raintree County, where he becomes a teacher. Susanna admits that she was never really pregnant, but Johnny assures her of his love nonetheless. When Lincoln wins the presidential election, Susanna announces that to please her husband, she has freed her two slaves and now pays them wages. This prompts several of their guests to laugh, and Susanna, believing she has again displeased her husband, becomes hysterical. Johnny calms her, but later, after giving birth to a son on the very day that Civil War is declared, Susanna informs him that two babies were born, and that "they" threw the dark one away. Several years later, Nell returns to Freehaven after living for a time in Indianapolis, and it is clear that she still loves Johnny. Susanna's nightmares and wild-eyed outbursts have become more frequent, and one evening, Johnny persuades her to tell him about the fire: Jealous of Susanna's love for Henrietta, the child's mother had flown into a rage, thereby angering the little girl. When Susanna realized that her father also loved Henrietta, she vengefully revealed this in an anonymous note to her mother. That night, she heard a crackling sound in Henrietta's room, and soon afterward, the fire consumed the house. Believing her mother had killed the lovers because of her note, Susanna had always felt responsible for the tragedy. Johnny tries to comfort Susanna, but one day, he arrives home to find that she has taken their son Jim and fled to Georgia. With his wife gone, Johnny joins the Union Army, and as his train departs, Nell confesses that she has never stopped loving him. Johnny joins an Indiana brigade that includes not only Flash, but his old friend Stiles, who is now a war correspondent. The men participate in a number of hellish battles, and in November 1864, find themselves in Atlanta. Wary of rebel snipers, Johnny and Flash approach an old cabin that once belonged to Henrietta. Inside are little Jimmy and two Drake slaves. One of them explains that although Susanna was not Henrietta's child, she always believed that she was. Consumed by madness, Susanna had been taken to an asylum some time earlier. Johnny carries little Jim toward the Union camp, but as they run through the woods, Flash is shot by rebel soldiers and dies. After the war, Johnny finds Susanna in a wretched asylum and takes her home. He returns to teaching, but his friends believe he should run for Congress. Susanna realizes that it is she who holds him back, and that Nell still deeply loves him. That night, Susanna, telling Jimmy that she hopes to find the golden raintree for Johnny, says goodbye and runs toward the swamp. Alarmed, Jimmy follows her, and soon afterward, a search party is organized. In the morning, Stiles, who has returned to Raintree County to marry the widowed Lydia Gray, discovers that Susanna has drowned. In agony, Johnny continues to search for his son. The weeping boy hears his father's voice, and with great relief, Johnny, Nell and Jimmy head out of the swamp, unaware of the tall tree gleaming golden in the sunlight. *Idealists. Indiana. Insanity. Legends. Romantic rivalry. United States–History–Civil War, 1861-1865. Abolitionists. African Americans. Atlanta (GA). Battles. Children. Drowning. Fourth of July. Friendship. Guilt. Infidelity. Loyalty. Marriage–Forced by circumstances. New Orleans (LA). Premarital sex. Racing. Searches. Slavery–Emancipation. Small town life. Teachers.*

Note: Onscreen credits acknowledge the cooperation of "the Baltimore and Ohio Railroad Company, the Tennessee State Game & Fish Commission at Reelfoot Lake and the people of the Commonwealth of Kentucky." The picture opens with a five-minute musical overture. Following "Johnny's" departure to fight in the Civil War, there is an intermission and brief musical interlude. Act Two begins as Johnny joins his brigade. The *NYT* review lists a running time of 168 minutes. Apparently, fifteen minutes of the film were cut after its premiere.

The picture was, as the *Var* reviewer notes, "one of the biggest and costliest (estimated at $5,000,000) productions from Metro since its release of David O. Selznick's *Gone With the Wind*." It took M-G-M six years to turn the novel into a screenplay. According to modern sources, shortly after the novel's publication, M-G-M purchased the film rights from author Ross Lockridge, Jr. for $150,000, but did not produce the film until 1956 because of script problems. Modern sources also note that *Raintree County* was Lockridge's only novel, and that he committed suicide in 1948.

Filming was halted after Montgomery Clift's automobile accident on 13 May 1956 and did not resume until 23 Jul 1956. In the accident, which occurred after Clift had been to a dinner party at Elizabeth Taylor's house, the actor's face was severely injured. Modern sources note that numerous facial lacerations and broken bones altered the structure of Clift's face so much that filming of his scenes after his return to the production was difficult. Modern sources also note that audiences frequently went to the film to make comparisons of "before" and "after" shots of Clift.

Raintree County was the first picture to be filmed using Panavision's "Camera 65" process. Most release prints, however, were issued as 35mm anamorphic prints. Most of the film was shot on location near Danville, KY. *Var* reported that the swamp scenes were filmed at Reelfoot Lake, Tiptonville, TN, and that mansions were photographed in Natchez and Port Gibson, MS. The film received Academy Award nominations for Best Actress (Taylor), Best Art Direction, Best Score and Best Costume Design.

AmCin Apr 1956, p. 194. *Box* 12 Oct 1957, p. 30. *Box* 19 Oct 1957. *DV* 4 Oct 1957, p. 3. *Exh* 16 Oct 1957, pp. 4389-90. *FD* 4 Oct 1957, p. 10. *Har* 12 Oct 1957, p. 162. *HR* 6 Apr 1956, p. 12. *HR* 12 Oct 1956, p. 16. *HR* 17 Oct 1956, p. 1. *HR* 28 Aug 1957, p. 13. *HR* 4 Oct 1957, p. 3. *MPHPD* 12 Oct 1957, p. 562. *NYT* 21 Dec 1957, p. 22. *Var* 9 Oct 1957, p. 6.

RAMONA (Native Americans, Latino, Scottish Americans)
Clune Film Producing Co. *Dist* State Rights. Feb **1916** [©W. H. Clune; 3 Apr 1916; LU7994]. Si; b&w. 10-14 reels.
Supv Lloyd Brown. *Prod* W. H. Clune. *Dir* Donald Crisp. *Cam* Enrico Vallejo and Bert Glennon. *Art dir* John K. Holden. *Mus accompaniment comp* Lloyd Brown and Emil Bierman.
Source: Based on the novel *Ramona* by Helen Hunt Jackson (Boston, 1884).
Cast: Adda Gleason (*Ramona*), Mabel Van Buren (*Ramona, in the prologue*), Anna Lehr (*Ramona, as a child*), Monroe Salisbury (*Alessandro Assis*), N. de Brullier (*Felipe Moreno*), Richard Sterling (*Angus Phail*), Princess Red Wing (*His wife*), Lurline Lyons (*Senora Moreno*), Alice Morton Otten (*Starlight*), James Needham (*Jim Farrar*), Mrs. H. Davenport (*Marda*), E. Valencia (*Juan Canito*), H. M. Best (*Father Salvierderra*), Arthur Tavares (*Lieut. Francis Ortegna*), Victor Vallejo, Beatrice Burnham, Mrs. Gordon, J. Wesley Warner, Chief Standing Bear, Inez Gomez, Rosa Dray, J. L. Franck, Hubert Whitehead.
Historical, Drama. During the nineteenth century, while white settlers in Southern California cruelly mistreat the Mission Indians, Alessandro, a full-blooded Indian, marries Ramona, who is half-Scot and half-Indian. Hounded by the prejudiced townspeople, the couple moves from community to community until one of the settlers murders Alessandro. *California–History. Frontier and pioneer life. Indians of North America. Indians of North America–Mixed blood. Racism. Murder. Scots.*
Note: Many of the scenes were shot at authentic period locations in California. *Ramona* was released in varying lengths. The director, Donald Crisp, appearing in the film as Jim Farrar, chose the pseudonym "James Needham." The film had its premiere at Clune's Auditorium in Los Angeles on 7 Feb 1916. In the Los Angeles showings, and possibly at other cities, the presentation included two stage settings showing a mission where men and women received the blessings of one of the Padres, and an Indian campfire scene in a valley in the mountains. Neither scene contained dialogue. The film opened in New York on 5 Apr 1916. *Ramona* was the first film of the Clune Film Producing Co., formed by W. H. Clune after the success of *The Birth of a Nation*, which had its premiere in Clune's Auditorium, convinced Clune and his general manager Lloyd Brown that the demand for big productions had not been met by the supply of these films. For information on other versions of *Ramona*, see entry below for the 1936 Twentieth Century-Fox film directed by Henry King and starring Loretta Young.
Motog 22 Apr 1916, p. 937. *MPN* 9 Oct 1915, p. 74. *MPN* 1 Apr 1916, p. 1882. *MPN* 30 Dec 1916, p. 4151, 4216. *MPW* 11 Sep 1915, p. 1816. *MPW* 22 Apr 1916, p. 640. *NYDM* 19 Feb 1916, p. 26. *NYDM* 15 Apr 1916, p. 28. *NYT* 6 Apr 1916, p. 11. *Var* 25 Feb 1916, p. 23. *Var* 7 Apr 1916, p. 21. *Wid's* 13 Apr 1916, p. 499.

RAMONA (Native Americans)
Inspiration Pictures, Inc. *Dist* United Artists Corp. May **1928** [©Inspiration Pictures, Inc.; 6 Mar 1928; LP25048]. Si; b&w. 8 reels, 7,650 ft.
Dir Edwin Carewe. *Asst dir* Leander De Cordova and Richard Easton. *Scen and titles* Finis Fox. *Cinematog* Robert B. Kurrle. *Asst cam* Al M. Greene. *Art dir* Al D'Agostino. *Film ed* Jeanne Spencer. *Settings* Tec-Art Studios.
Song(s): "Ramona," music by Mabel Wayne, lyrics by L. Wolfe Gilbert.

Source: Based on the novel *Ramona* by Helen Hunt Jackson (Boston, 1884).

Cast: Dolores Del Rio (*Ramona*), Warner Baxter (*Alessandro*), Roland Drew (*Felipe*), Vera Lewis (*Señora Moreno*), Michael Visaroff (*Juan Canito*), John T. Prince (*Father Salvierderra*), Mathilde Comont (*Marda*), Carlos Amor (*Sheepherder*), Jess Cavin (*Bandit leader*), Jean (*Himself, a dog*), Rita Carewe (*Baby*).

Historical, Drama. Ramona, a half-breed, is adopted by Señora Moreno, a wealthy Spanish sheep rancher, and reared under cruel restraints. Her only consolation is Felipe, the woman's son. At sheep-shearing time, Ramona discovers her ancestry and defies her guardian by eloping with Alessandro, a young Indian chieftain. Their pastoral happiness is marred by the death of their daughter after an outlaw attack; they retreat to the mountains, where Alessandro, accused of horse thievery, is murdered by a settler. Ramona suffers a nervous collapse and becomes a wandering outcast; Felipe finds her and tries to restore her memory. His efforts are fruitless until a childhood song reminds Ramona of her youthful abandon and returns her to the present. *Amnesia. Dogs. Indians of North America. Indians of North America–Mixed blood. Murder. Spaniards.*

Note: For the 1916 and 1928 film adaptation of Helen Hunt Jackson's novel, see entries above and below.

FD 20 May 1928. *NYT* 15 May 1928, p. 17. *Var* 16 May 1928, p. 13.

RAMONA (Native Americans, Latino)

Twentieth Century-Fox Film Corp.; Darryl F. Zanuck in Charge of Production. *Dist* Twentieth Century-Fox Film Corp. 25 Sep 1936; Prod: 11 May—29 Jun 1936 [©Twentieth Century-Fox Film Corp.; 25 Sep 1936; LP6957]. Sd (Western Electric Noiseless Recording); col (Technicolor). 9 reels, 7,536 ft. 84 min. PCA cert no. 2413.

Exec prod Sol M. Wurtzel. *Assoc prod* John Stone. *Dir* Henry King. *Asst dir* Robert Webb. *Scr* Lamar Trotti. [*Contr wrt* Stuart Anthony, Sonya Levien, Lillian Wurtzel and Paul Hervey Fox]. *Assoc cine* Chester Lyons. *Technicolor photog* William V. Skall. *Technicolor color dir* Natalie Kalmus. *Art dir* Duncan Cramer. *Film ed* Al De Gaetano. *Cost* Gwen Wakeling. *Mus score* Alfred Newman. [*Dance dir* Jose Fernandez]. *Sd* Joseph Aiken and Harry M. Leonard. [*Makeup* Ern Westmore]. [*Tech adv* Tito A. Davison]. [*Location mgr* R. C. Moore].

Song(s): "Señorita," "Sunrise Hymn," "La Fiesta," "How the Rabbit Lost His Tail" and "Under the Redwood Tree," words and music by William Kernell; "Ramona," words and music by L. Wolfe Gilbert and Mabel Wayne.

Source: Based on the novel *Ramona* by Helen Hunt Jackson (Boston, 1884).

Cast: Loretta Young [(*Ramona*)], Don Ameche [(*Alessandro*)], Kent Taylor [(*Felipe Moreno*)], Pauline Frederick [(*Señora Moreno*)], Jane Darwell [(*Aunt Ri Hyar*)], Katherine de Mille [(*Margarita*)], Victor Kilian [(*Father Gaspara*)], John Carradine [(*Jim Farrar*)], J. Carroll Naish [(*Juan Can*)], Pedro de Cordoba [(*Father Salvierderra*)], Charles Waldron [(*Dr. Weaver*)], Claire Du Brey [(*Marda*)], Russell Simpson [(*Scroggs*)], William Benedict [(*Joseph Hyar*)], Robert Spindola [(*Paquito*)], Chief Thunder Cloud [(*Pablo*)], [Erville Alderson (*Doctor at hacienda*)], [Martin Faust (*Luigi*)], [Del Campo (*Señor Valez*)], [Donald Reed, Enrico Ricardi, A. Van Nostrand (*Vaqueros*)], [Dillon Ober (*Comedy singer*)], [Cecil Weston (*Pablo's wife*)], [Evelyn Selbie (*Indian woman*)], [Kathryn Sheldon (*Mrs. Scroggs*)], [Helen Sky Eagle (*Mrs. Farrar*)], [Charles Middleton, Tom London (*American settlers*)], [Ethan Laidlaw (*Bill*)], [Lee Kohlmar (*Woodcarver Lang*)], [D'Arcy Corrigan (*Jeff*)], [Beverly Firestine (*Baby*)], [Edna Lawrence, Velma McCandless, Anita Camargo, Delores Reyes, Carmen La Roux, Colleen Traxler, Maria Morales, Maria Iturbi, Lita Cortez, Laura Puente, Frances Norton, Elena Durán, Janet Barrett, Muriel Barrett, Maclovia Ruiz, Jose Bottolo, George Mendoza, Paul Loredo, Alfonso de Larios, Miguel Fernandez, Jess Escobar, Rudolfo Mendina, Guy Scarpitta, George Travell, Ramon Ros, David Robel, Tito Renaldo, Cesar Tapia, Fred Velasco, Lewis Orozco (*Dancers*)], [Charles Harrison, Rafael Sino, Edward Mestas, Charles Tosi, Bahe Denetdeel, Big Eagle Penna, Adolf Ruiz, James Lono, I. R. Swift Eagle, Elmo Red Fox, John Isaac, Roy Bellas, Harold Morongo, Tom Humphrey, Sonny Chorre, Clarence Morrow, Delmar Costello (*Indians*)], [Richard Botiller, Frank Leyva, Paul Lopez, Dave Kashner, Joe de la Cruz, Sam Appel, Lillian Nicholson, Gertrude Chorre, Mary Lopez, Shilia Fritz, Lucille Porcett, Soledad Gonzales, Marie Chorre, Anita Ray, Carmen Bailey (*Servants*)], [Lucille Miller, Christine

Gossett, Dorothy Jones, Delores Young, Emilie Cabanne, Gertrude Pedlar, Rubi Gutierrez, Julia Bejarano, Myrta Bonillas, Beulah Parkington, Elsie Bishop, Margaret Morgan, Enrique Acosta, James Cooley, Henry Orozco, Fred Godoy, Manuel Lopez, Valentine Martin, Guillermo Arcos, Louis Aldez, Captain Fernando Garcia, Howard Davies (*Guests*)].

Historical, Romance, Drama. [*Print viewed*]. In 1870 California, at the hacienda of Señora Moreno, everyone prepares for a fiesta and the arrival of Father Salvierderra, who will celebrate Mass for the ranch inhabitants and the Indians who are making their yearly appearance to shear the sheep. The Señora welcomes her handsome son Felipe and sends him to find Ramona, the Señora's lovely ward, who has gone to meet Salvierderra. After they all arrive back at the hacienda, Felipe also welcomes Alessandro, the Indian leader. That night, at the fiesta, Felipe tells Ramona how beautiful she is, and while Ramona feels a sisterly affection for him, it is obvious that she does not share his passion. Alessandro sees her dancing and finds out who she is, while elsewhere, the Señora complains to Salvierderra about Felipe's interest in Ramona. The next morning, as everyone goes to Mass, Ramona, charmed by Alessandro's singing, questions Felipe about him. That afternoon, Felipe falls from his horse and is seriously injured during a race with Alessandro. Weeks later, after Felipe's recovery, Alessandro is about to leave when Ramona declares her love for him, and he asks her to marry him. The Señora, alerted by the jealous servant Margarita, who loves Alessandro herself, sends Alessandro away, and tells Ramona that she will have to go to a convent. The Señora then informs Ramona that her mother was an Indian, and her father a former suitor of the Señora's sister, who adopted Ramona as a baby and then appointed the Señora her guardian when she herself died. Ramona is pleased by the scandalous news, and feels that, as an Indian, she belongs with Alessandro. Later that night, Felipe helps her sneak out of her room and meet Alesssandro. The lovers are married and, years later, have a baby girl and a prosperous farm until white settlers are given title to the Indian lands by the government. A bitter Alessandro packs up his family and they are forced by a rainstorm to stop at the cabin of kindly Aunt Ri, whose distrust of Indians is put aside upon finding out that they are Christians. They are still there two days later, unable to leave due to the baby's fever. Alessandro rides to town for Dr. Weaver, who cannot leave because many others are also ill. On the way back, his horse becomes lame, so Alessandro goes to Jim Farrar's house, where he takes a horse after not finding Farrar, who returns in time to see Alessandro leaving. When Alessandro reaches home, he comforts Ramona with a lie that the doctor will come soon. Farrar arrives, and Ramona mistakes him for the doctor as he goes to find Alessandro, whom he shoots on sight. After Alessandro's funeral, Aunt Ri tells Ramona to be grateful for the baby, and as they walk to the cabin, Ramona sees Felipe, who has come to help her. Ramona holds her baby and smiles through her tears, glad that she has some part of Alessandro still with her. *California–History–1846-1850. Indians of North America. Indians of North America–Mixed blood. Racism. Romance. Christianity. Dances. Funerals. Horse thieves. Horseracing. Jealousy. Land rights. Marriage. Mexican Americans. Murder. Physicians. Priests. Servants. Settlers. Wards and guardians.*

Note: A 18 Sep 1934 *Var* news item announcing Fox's purchase of the rights to *Ramona* from Edwin Carewe, who had produced an earlier version of Helen Hunt Jackson's novel, noted that a Spanish version was also likely to be filmed, however, none was made. A 30 Jan 1935 *HR* news item noted that Philip Klein and Robert Yost had been signed to work on the adaptation, but their contribution to the completed picture has not been confirmed. Pre-production work on this film began before Twentieth Century and Fox merged in the summer of 1935, while actual shooting was done after the merger. A 18 Mar 1935 *HR* news item states that John Ford was scheduled to direct the film, while the Twentieth Century-Fox Records of the Legal Department at the UCLA Theater Arts Library add that Eugene Forde was originally signed as the director before Henry King. *HR* news items also noted that Lew Pollack and Paul Francis Webster had been assigned to write the music for the picture. Among the actors considered for the part of "Alessandro" were Pietro Gentili, Phillip Reed, Gilbert Roland (who was also considered for the part of "Felipe") and John Boles (who was released from the role when he ended his contract with the studio). A 24 Aug 1935 *HR* news item reported that Charles Sellon, who was cast as "Juan Can," was forced to drop out of the film due to illness, and the legal records confirm that O. P. Heggie, who was contracted to play "Father Salvierderra," went instead into Twentieth Century-Fox's 1936 production, *The Prisoner of Shark Island* (see below). According to *HR* news items, Frances Dee was considered for the part of "Ramona," which was first assigned to Rita Hayworth (then known as Rita Cansino,) and then to Loretta Young after Darryl F. Zanuck, Twentieth Century-Fox's vice-president in charge of production,

announced that "the story is in the special class and deserves more elaborate treatment than formerly called for." Production was delayed from late Jul, and Twentieth Century-Fox considered removing Kent Taylor, who had been borrowed from Paramount for the role of "Felipe," to replace him with "a more important name," however, Taylor did play the part. The film was again postponed in late Aug 1935 by Young's illness. When she was still not ready to begin by mid-Oct 1935, she was replaced by Rochelle Hudson. In late Oct, Zanuck announced that the picture was to be shot in Technicolor, which, because the film would be "80 percent exteriors," required another postponement to avoid the rainy season. By the time shooting began on 11 May 1936, Young had been reinstated in the part of "Ramona."

The film was shot on location at Warner Hot Springs and the Mesa Grande Indian Reservation, both in San Diego County, CA. According to a modern source, the Indian extras from the reservation were descendents of the Indians about whom Jackson wrote her novel. A 17 Jun 1936 LAT news item reported that Young saved two-year-old Raymond Lugo, with whom she was performing a scene, from a fire that started on the set in Mesa Grande. HR production charts list the following cast members, whose participation in the completed film has not been confirmed: Paul Stanton, Martin Faust and Fritz Leiber. According to a HR news item, the picture's release was delayed because Technicolor could not supply enough prints in time to meet the deadline. Although a 9 Sep 1936 HR news item noted that Ramona was to have its world premiere simultaneously in Pittsburgh and Bar Harbor, ME, the date of the premiere has not been confirmed. This was the first Twentieth Century-Fox film shot in Technicolor. The NYT reviewer praised the color, commenting: "Chromatically, the picture is superior to anything we have seen in the color line," and the Var reviewer noted: "...the fact that the color angle becomes less noticeable as the picture unwinds, and never interferes with the telling or reception of the story, is evidence that color has finally found its place in film production." According to a 15 Sep 1935 NYT article, the film was estimated to cost in excess of $750,000 to produce, but in a modern source, King stated that it was produced for a little under $600,000. Jackson's novel was previously filmed three times, all of which were titled Ramona. The first version, a 1910 Biograph film, was directed by D. W. Griffith and starred Mary Pickford and Henry B. Walthall (see Film Beginnings, 1893-1910; A.12778). Donald Crisp directed Adda Gleason and Monroe Salisbury in the 1916 Clune Film Producing Co. version (see above) and Edwin Carewe directed Dolores Del Rio and Warner Baxter in the 1928 Inspiration Pictures production (see above). From 1922 to the early 1940s, a "Ramona Pageant" was held every spring in a natural outdoor amphitheatre near Hemmet, CA. The pageant, which was resumed after World War II, recreated incidents from Jackson's book. In the 1936 pageant, John Carradine played "Jim Farrar," which was also his role in the film. According to modern sources, the producers of the picture viewed the pageant in the early 1930s for ideas.

Box 20 Jun 1936. Box 19 Sep 1936. DV 12 Sep 1936, p. 3. FD 11 May 1936, p. 8. FD 30 Jun 1936, p. 15. FD 16 Sep 1936, p. 25. HR 30 Jan 1935, p. 1. HR 18 Mar 1935, p. 4. HR 6 Apr 1935, p. 1. HR 11 May 1935, p. 4. HR 4 Jun 1935, p. 2. HR 13 Jun 1935, p. 2. HR 19 Jun 1935, p. 10. HR 9 Jul 1935, p. 2. HR 11 Jul 1935, p. 3. HR 27 Jul 1935, p. 4. HR 29 Jul 1935, p. 3. HR 31 Jul 1935, p. 10. HR 24 Aug 1935, p. 5. HR 26 Aug 1935, p. 2. HR 27 Aug 1935, p. 7. HR 28 Aug 1935, p. 4. HR 3 Oct 1935, p. 10. HR 15 Oct 1935, p. 4. HR 23 Oct 1935, p. 3. HR 2 May 1936, p. 3. HR 11 May 1936, p. 13. HR 1 Jun 1936, p. 13. HR 19 Jun 1936, p. 4. HR 20 Jun 1936, p. 3. HR 22 Jun 1936, p. 9. HR 30 Jun 1936, p. 2. HR 13 Aug 1936, p. 2. HR 9 Sep 1936, p. 1. HR 12 Sep 1936, p. 3. HR 26 Sep 1936, pp. 5-10. LAT 7 Apr 1936. LAT 17 Jun 1936. MPD 14 Sep 1936, p. 6. MPH 25 Apr 1936, p. 45. MPH 4 Jul 1936, pp. 16-17. MPH 19 Sep 1936, p. 45. MPH 19 Nov 1936, p. 45. NYT 16 Dec 1934. NYT 15 Sep 1935. NYT 7 Oct 1936, p. 32. Var 18 Sep 1934. Var 14 Oct 1936, p. 15.

THE RAMPARTS WE WATCH (Austrian Americans, German Americans)

The March of Time. Dist RKO Radio Pictures, Inc. 16 Aug **1940** Sd; b&w. 7,828 ft. 85 or 87 min.

Prod Louis de Rochemont. Assoc prod Thomas Orchard. Dir Louis de Rochemont. Assoc dir Thomas Orchard, James L. Shute, Shepard Traube, George Black and Beverly Jones. Scr Robert L. Richards and Cedric R. Worth. Photog Charles E. Gilson and John A. Geisel. Film ed Lothar Wolff. Cost David Pardoll and Marguerite Brown. Mus dir Louis De Francesco. Mus score Louis De Francesco, Jacques Dallin and Peter Brunelli. Rec eng David Y. Bradshaw and Kenneth Hawk. Tech adv Captain Reed M. Fawell. Comm Westbrook Van Voorhis. Prod mgr James L. Wolcott. Historical research Samuel W. Bryant, Jr. Prod representative from Time and Life Roy E. Larsen and William D. Geer. Tech staff Arthur Jones, William Sikes, Frank Calabria, George Dangerfield and William Gerrity.

Song(s): "I Didn't Raise My Boy to Be a Soldier," music by Al Piantadosi, lyrics by Alfred Bryan.

Cast: John Adair (Dan Meredith), John Sommers (Joe Kovacs), Julia Kent (Mrs. Joe Kovacs), Ellen Prescott (Anna Kovacs), Andrew Brummer (John Slavetz), Myrtle Paseler (Mrs. Slavetz), Alfredo U. Wyss (Professor Gustav Bensinger), Marguerite Brown (Dora Bensinger), Georgette McKee (Hilda Bensinger), Robert Rapelye (Fred Bensinger), Frank McCabe (Edward Averill), Myra Archibald (Mrs. Averill), Edward Wragge (Walter Averill), Harry C. Stopher (Stuart Gilchrist), Jane Stuart (Mrs. Gilchrist), Elliott Reid (Ralph Gilchrist), C. W. Stowell (Hon. John Lawton), Ethel Hudson (Mrs.

John Lawton), Augusta Durgeon (Mrs. Dora Smith), Albert Gattiker (Eddie Reed), H. G. Brady (Capt. John Kellogg), Thomas S. Bernie, Jr. (Tommy), Roberta Maaski (Mrs. Barbara Davis), W. W. Pinkerton (Chief of police), Richard McCracken (Hal Fisher), David Dean (Montana), Lila Lyman (Lila Bishop), George Jackson (Karl Von Schleich), H. G. Wescott (George Wescott), Lorenzo Gallant (Rathskeller singer), A. A. Nourie, E. C. Lucey (Telegraph operators), Gordon Hall (Gordon Hall, Captain of Marines), Reginald Reynolds (Stump speaker), Harry Feltcorn (Postman), Reverend Byron Ulric Hatfield (Himself), Andrew Bizub (Y.M.C.A secretary), Benjamin Semaskay (Brakeman), W. J. Londregan (Baggageman), Thomas McElarney (Barber), Gabriel Kerekes (Austrian consular official), Louis de Rochemont, Jr. (Liberty gardener).

War, Documentary, Drama. [Print viewed]. In the summer of 1914, when over 100,000 soldiers are serving in the U.S. Army, and while aircraft are being tested for military purposes, the "Hesitation Canter," a dance similar to the "Turkey Trot," is gaining popularity on America's dance floors. Although Americans learned in June that Austria had declared war on Serbia, and that country after country since then has been mobilizing for war, most of the nation does not appear to be bothered by the news. Some foreign-born Americans are directly affected by the war in Europe, however. Joe Kovacs, who lives in a small town, receives a letter from Austria requesting that he return to his fatherland to fight in the war. Joe bids farewell to his wife and his daughter Anna and quickly leaves for Austria. Following the German invasion of Belgium, a partisan argument erupts in the town, and a Belgian relief rally is organized. Meanwhile, Anna, unable to pay for her education, drops out of school. Suspicion of foreign-born nationals soon runs rampant in the town, and the Bensingers, a German American family, are believed to be German sympathizers. In 1915, following the German Zeppelin bombing of London and the sinking of the Lusitania, Americans march against the German Kaiser and meet with their Congressmen to discuss the developments in Europe and their implications. While a debate over American neutrality takes place, an elite military corps made up of young volunteers, called the Lafayette Escadrille, attracts many Americans who want to get involved in the war, including Edward Averill's son Walter. When Dora Bensinger and her daughter Hilda are suspected of being a spy family, they are asked to leave the ladies' bandage packing circle. In 1916, President Woodrow Wilson is seen marching at the head of a war preparedness parade. That same year, Anna, now working at the hat check desk at a local dance hall, receives news of her father's death. Tensions mount in the country as news reaches Americans that a number of munitions plants in New Jersey have been exploded in apparent acts of sabotage. On 2 Apr 1917, President Wilson declares war and gives a speech dilineating his reasons for entering the war. Months after the Bensingers are told that their son will not be permitted to go overseas because of his father's nationality, the Germans concede defeat and an armistice is signed. The film concludes with a commentary on the need to remind Americans that a similar threat is brewing in the year 1940, this time with the menacing Adolph Hitler leading the German nation to war. Austrian Americans. German Americans. Newsreels. Small town life. War preparedness. World War I. Belgium. Congressmen. Dancing. Gossip. Adolf Hitler. Herbert Hoover. London (England). S.S. Lusitania. Military service, Compulsory. Military service, Voluntary. Nationalism. Newspapers. Ostracism. Paranoia. Rallies. Sabotage. Woodrow Wilson. World War II.

Note: No credits appeared in the viewed print of the film, except for the following: "The editors of Time and Life present a saga of modern America produced by the staff of The March of Time." This was the first feature-length film produced by The March of Time, a subsidiary of Time, Inc., that was primarily known for its short newsreel films. RKO originally copyrighted the film on 16 Aug 1940, but because the studio revised the ending of the picture, a second copyright registration was requested. Although a Jul 1940 HR news item noted that the premiere of the film was to be held in Washington, D.C. during the last week of that month, the copyright files contain a letter from RKO to a copyrighting agency, dated 22 Oct 1940, which states that the revised, and presumably final, version of the film had its first public showing on 30 Aug 1940. The copyright records also indicate that the second version was twelve minutes (or 1,101 feet) shorter than the first version. The title of the film was taken from a book published in 1938 entitled The Ramparts We Watch: A Study of the Problems of American Defense by Major George Fielding Eliot. Studio publicity material indicates that producer Louis de Rochemont "hired no movie actors" for the picture, but instead "picked businessmen, housewives, college students who simply played themselves before the

camera." Many of those who appeared in the picture were residents of New London, CT, where the picture was filmed. According to a *Time* article, New London was chosen as the location because it had not changed in appearance since the late 1910s. Studio publicity material also notes that the film was made over an eighteen month period at a cost of $400,000.

According to contemporary news items in *NYT* and *HR*, scenes from the 1939 German-produced Nazi propaganda film *Baptism of Fire* were used in the film. The inclusion of footage from the German film reportedly resulted in UFA, Inc., a German film distribution company, accusing Time, Inc. of pirating the film. Producer Louis de Rochemont responded to the accusation by asserting that the German film was confiscated by the British contraband control in Bermuda and obtained legally through the Canadian government. The German government warned RKO that if it used footage from *Baptism of Fire*, it should expect "reprisals" and legal action. According to a *NYT* news item, the Pennsylvania Board of Censors, fearing its "terrifying effect on the masses," cut the footage taken from *Baptism of Fire*. An Oct 1940 *HR* news item notes that RKO and The March of Time took the Pennsylvania censors to court over the deleted footage, arguing that because the material was news, it was not subject to censorship. Information as to the outcome of the trial has not been located.

DV 24 Jul 1940, p. 3. *FD* 24 Jul 1940, p. 5. *HR* 8 Sep 1939, p. 3. *HR* 22 Sep 1939, p. 4. *HR* 1 Jun 1940, p. 5. *HR* 3 Jul 1940, p. 6. *HR* 24 Jul 1940, p. 3, 6. *HR* 5 Aug 1940, p. 4. *HR* 13 Aug 1940, p. 8. *HR* 2 Oct 1940, p. 1, 4. *MPH* 27 Jul 1940, pp. 34-35. *NYT* 8 Sep 1940. *NYT* 19 Sep 1940. *NYT* 20 Sep 1940, p. 27. *Time* 29 Jul 1940, p. 44. *Var* 24 Jul 1940, p. 14.

EL RANCHO DEL PINAR *see* **CUANDO CANTA LA LEY**

RANGE WAR *see* **STORM OVER WYOMING**

RANGE WARFARE (Native Americans)
Willis Kent Productions. *Dist* State Rights. **1935**; Prod: mid-Mar 1935 at California Sound Studios, Inc.. Sd; b&w. 4,995 ft. 60 min.
Dir S. Roy Luby. *Photog* James Diamond. *Ed* Roy Claire.
Source: Based on the short story "The Death Whistler" by E. B. Mann (publication undetermined).
Cast: Reb Russell (*Reb*), Lucille Lund (*Little Feather*), Wally Wales, Roger Williams, Charles Whittaker, Lafe McKee, Edward Boland, Dick Botiller, Ed Porter, Gene Alsace, Chief Black Hawk, "Rebel" the horse.
Western. [*Not viewed*]. Reb sees Brady being cruel to Little Feather, an Indian who occasionally works for Callahan. Callahan later tells Reb that Little Feather is rarely let off the Indian Reservation and that De Kalb, the corrupt official in charge of the Reservation, is cheating the Indians by charging them exorbitant prices for food. Reb goes to the reservation to investigate and, posing as a rustler, gets De Kalb to reveal that he is buying cattle stolen by Sheriff Turner and his gang. Reb arrests DeKalb and takes him back to Callahan's ranch in order to sign a statement implicating the members of the rustling operation and clearing Tommy of any involvement. Then, Monroe sends Reb a message supposedly from Slade challenging Reb to a duel at a local saloon. Reb soon realizes that Slade did not send the message, but the surly Slade nevertheless initiates a gun battle and Reb kills him. In the meantime, Sue is kidnapped by Turner and Monroe, and Reb, Callahan and Little Feather go to the rescue. Reb succeeds in capturing Turner and Monroe and they are turned over to federal authorities. Tommy, his name now cleared, is given a job on a neighboring ranch, and a grateful Callahan and Sue bid farewell as Reb rides off to new adventures. *False accusations. Government agents. Indians of North America. Ranchers. Rustlers. Sheriffs. Gunfights. Horses. Indians of North America–Reservations. Ranch foremen. Saloons.*
Note: The plot synopsis is based on a dialogue continuity deposited in the NYSA on 25 Apr 1935. Some credits were obtained from a fragment of a re-release version of the film titled *Vengeance*. Although an exact release date has not been found, the film was reviewed by *Exh* on 1 Jun 1935. According to modern sources, the cast included Bart Carre.
Exh 1 Jun 1935, p. 48. *HR* 11 Mar 1935, p. 15.

THE RANGER (German Americans)
W. H. Clifford Photoplay Co.; Shorty Hamilton Series. *Dist* State Rights; Ernest Shipman. Jun **1918**. Si; b&w. 5 reels.
Dir Bob Gray. *Story* W. H. Clifford.
Cast: Shorty Hamilton (*Jim Slater*), Charles Arling ("*Red*" *Haggerty*), William Colvin (*Carl Werner*), Mattie Connolly (*Belle Werner*), Kenneth Nordyke (*Office boy*).
World War I, Western. Jim Slater, a Texas Ranger, learns that German propaganda is being distributed across the Mexican border and traces the anti-American materials to Carl Werner, the editor of the *Silver City News* and secretly a German spy. Posing as a reporter for the *News*, Jim falls in love with Carl's daughter Belle, who, although opposed to her father's activities, informs him that Jim

works for the U.S. government. Carl then assigns Jim the job of interviewing "Red" Haggerty, a criminal who bears Carl a bitter grudge. Red learns that Jim is the son he left in the East years before and consequently refrains from harming him, whereupon Carl, realizing that he is beaten, poisons himself. Accused of Carl's murder, Red gives himself up to Jim upon discovering that there is a large reward for his capture. Jim arrives at the jail too late to save Red from the vigilance committee, but Red's letter reveals their relationship and asks Jim to send his wife the reward. All danger removed, Jim and Belle are united. *Criminals–Rehabilitation. Family relationships. German Americans. Long-lost relatives. Newspapers. Parentage. Self-sacrifice. Spies. Texas Rangers. Editors. False accusations. Impersonation and imposture. Informers. Jails. Letters. Mexico. Poisoning. Propaganda. Reporters. Rewards. Suicide. Vigilantes.*
Note: The picture was re-issued on a state rights basis in Jul 1919 by Victor Kremer. *Var* calls Shorty Hamilton's character "Scotty." The film's pre-release title was *The Texas Ranger*.
ETR 15 Jun 1918, p. 125. *MPN* 15 Jun 1918, p. 3548. *NYDM* 15 Dec 1917, back cover. *NYDM* 15 Jun 1918, p. 851. *Var* 31 May 1918, p. 31.

RANGER CODE *see* **THE RENEGADE RANGER**

RANGER OF CHEROKEE STRIP (Native Americans, Cherokee)
Republic Pictures Corp. *Dist* Republic Pictures Corp. 4 Nov **1949**; Prod: began late Jul 1949 [©Republic Pictures Corp.; 28 Oct 1949; LP2603]. Sd (RCA Sound System); b&w. 60 min. Passed by the National Board of Review. PCA cert no. 14072.
Assoc prod Melville Tucker. *Dir* Philip Ford. [*Asst dir* Herb Mendelson]. *Scr* Bob Williams. *Story* Earle Snell. *Dir of photog* Ellis W. Carter. [*Cam op* Jud Curtis]. [*Stills* Frank Bjerring]. *Optical eff* Consolidated Film Industries. *Art dir* Frank Hotaling. *Film ed* Irving M. Schoenberg. *Set dec* John McCarthy, Jr. and James Redd. *Mus* Stanley Wilson. *Sd* Earl Crain, Sr. *Makeup supv* Bob Mark. [*Makeup* Howard Smit]. [*Grip* Glen Kizer]. [*Scr supv* Emilie Ehrlich]. [*Gaffer* Hap Hodges].
Song(s): "Hangman, Slack Your Rope," traditional.
Cast: Monte Hale [(*Steve Howard*)], Paul Hurst [(*Jug Mason*)], Alice Talton [(*Mary Bluebird*)], Roy Barcroft [(*Mark Sanders*)], Douglas Kennedy [(*Joe Bearclaws*)], George Meeker [(*Eric Parsons, also known as "The Mad Hatter"*)], Frank Fenton [(*Randolph McKinnon*)], Monte Blue [(*Chief Charles Hunter*)], Neyle Morrow [(*Tokata*)], Arthur Walsh [(*Will Rogers*)], [George Chesebro (*Horseman*)], [Tommy Coats (*Stan*)], [Dale Van Sickel (*Homesteader*)], [Michael Royal (*Farmer*)].
Western. [*Print viewed*]. In Kansas in the 1890s, a Cherokee convict named Joe Bearclaws escapes from the state penitentiary and decides to return to see his wife Mary Bluebird. Unaware that he is being followed by ranger Steve Howard, Joe steals a horse from a fellow traveler. After some distance, Steve finally catches up to Joe and takes out his rope to tie him up. Before his hands have been secured, however, Joe grabs the rope and ties Steve up instead. Joe then goes to the town of Buckskill, where he tells Sheriff Jug Mason that he was attacked by a stranger, whom he left tied up on the trail. Jug accompanies Joe to the place where Joe claims to have left Steve, but Steve, who has untied himself, hides in the bushes nearby when they approach. Jug and Joe decide to cross the border into Cherokee territory, and Steve follows closely behind. When he sees a sniper take aim at Jug and Joe, Steve knocks the gun from his hand and convinces Joe to continue with him to Eagle Junction and go to the Sequoian Saloon. There, patron Will Rogers tells Joe and Steve that Chief Charles Hunter is upstairs meeting with the "boss," Randolph McKinnon. McKinnon sees Joe waiting downstairs, and quickly scribbles a note, tossing it to his henchmen outside the window. When Joe leaves the saloon and is attacked by McKinnon's gang, Steve comes to his aid. Later, Steve and Joe advise the chief not to lease his land to McKinnon and his men. Meanwhile, McKinnon's henchman, Mark Sanders, persuades a hat salesman, Eric Parsons, who is also known as "The Mad Hatter," to disguise himself as Joe. After Mark and Parsons, dressed as Joe, stab the chief, they forge Joe's signature on some documents and claim that he is involved with the gang. When they see Mark leave later, Steve and Jug follow him to Mary's house, where they find Joe being held hostage. They free Joe, who then races to town and begins fighting with Mark. After Joe and Steve escape from the gang, Steve places Joe in jail for his own protection. Steve learns that Parsons is wanted for forgery and grand theft, and Jug takes him to the gallows and threatens to hang him unless he reveals Mark's

involvement with the gang. Later, Steve and Joe return to the saloon, where Tokata, an Indian servant, tells them that Mark is planning to drive some cattle across the border the following day. When McKinnon overhears Jug pretending to beat Mark, he rushes in with a gun. Meanwhile, Mark sets off a loud explosion, which causes the herd to stampede. Thinking quickly, Steve ignites some dry brush to scare the cattle into retreating. After Steve captures Mark and the gang, Jug delivers Joe to Mary's custody. *Outlaws. Prison escapees. Rangers. Boundaries. Cattle. Cherokee Indians. Explosions. Fires. Fugitives. Horse thieves. Hostages. Impersonation and imposture. Jails. Kansas. Prisoners. Salesmen. Saloons. Schools. Servants. Sheriffs. Snipers. Stabbings. Stampedes. Threats. Tribal chiefs.*

Note: Modern sources include Lane Bradford in the cast.

Box 12 Nov 1949. *DV* 4 Nov 1949. *FD* 7 Nov 1949, p. 8. *HR* 29 Jul 1949, p. 11. *HR* 4 Nov 1949, p. 3. *MPHPD* 12 Nov 1949, p. 81. *Var* 9 Nov 1949, p. 16.

RANGERS OF THE NORTH *see* **DANGEROUS MISSION**

RANSOM (Chinese Americans)

Columbia Pictures Corp.; Columbia Pictures Corp. 30 Jun **1928** [©Columbia Pictures Corp.; 21 Jul 1928; LP25516]. Si; b&w. 6 reels, 5,484 ft.

Prod Harry Cohn. *Dir* George B. Seitz. *Asst dir* Joe Nadel. *Adpt* Elmer Harris. *Story* George B. Seitz. *Cont* Dorothy Howell. *Titles* Mort Blumenstock. *Photog* Joseph Walker. *Art dir* Joseph Wright.

Cast: Lois Wilson (*Lois Brewster*), Edmund Burns (*Burton Meredith*), William V. Mong (*Wu Fang*), Blue Washington (*Oliver*), James B. Leong (*Scarface*), Jackie Coombs (*Bobby*).

Melodrama. Burton Meredith, a chemist working for the government, discovers the formula for a deadly gas, and Wu Fang, the leader of the Chinese underworld, sets out to rob him of the discovery. He kidnaps Bobby Brewster, the son of Burton's fiancée, Lois, and promises to return the boy unharmed if Lois can obtain the poison gas for him. Lois goes to Burton's laboratory and begs him for the formula; he refuses, and, in a frenzy, she steals a vial of gas and, before Burton can stop her, takes it to Wu Fang. The bottle does not contain the nerve gas, however, and Wu Fang prepares to torture her. Burton discovers the location of the Chinese hideout and rescues Bobby and Lois from death. The police arrive and arrest the gang, and Lois and Burton decide to get hitched. *Chemists. Chinese Americans. Gangs. Gases, Asphyxiating and poisonous. Kidnapping. Torture. Widows.*

FD 26 Aug 1928. *Var* 15 Aug 1928, p. 17.

THE RAP *see* **PARDON US**

RASCALS (Gypsies)

Twentieth Century-Fox Film Corp. *Dist* Twentieth Century-Fox Film Corp. 20 May **1938**; Prod: mid-Dec 1937—late Jan 1938 [©Twentieth Century-Fox Film Corp.; 20 May 1938; LP8288]. Sd (Western Electric Mirrophonic Recording); b&w. 8 reels, 6,900 ft. 77 min. PCA cert no. 3993.

Assoc prod John Stone and [John Reinhardt]. [*Asst prod* Louis F. Moore]. *Dir* H. Bruce Humberstone. [*Dial dir* Arthur Berthelet and George Wright]. [*Asst dir* Gordon Cooper and Hal Herman]. *Orig scr* Robert Ellis and Helen Logan. *Photog* Edward Cronjager. [*Cam op* William Whitley]. [*Asst cam* Henry Cronjager and Roy Ivey]. [*Gaffer* Ray Jones]. *Art dir* Bernard Herzbrun and Haldane Douglas. *Film ed* Jack Murray. [*Asst cutter* Harvey Manger]. [*Music cutter* Cliff Ransom]. *Cost* Helen A. Myron. [*Ward man* John Hassett]. [*Ward girl* Viola Richards]. *Mus dir* Samuel Kaylin. *Sd* E. Clayton Ward and William H. Anderson. [*Asst sd* L. B. Dix]. [*Boom man* Art Wright]. [*Hair* Wilma Ryan]. [*Hair (Jane Withers)* Marie Livingston]. [*Makeup* Bud Westmore]. [*Prod mgr* Ed. Ebele]. [*Unit mgr* Duke Goux]. [*Scr clerk* Rose Steinberg]. [*Grip* George Schwietzer]. [*Asst grip* Bruce Hunsaker]. [*Props* Mac Elliot]. [*Cable man* Roy Martin]. [*Best boy* James Witherspoon]. [*Asst prop* Bill Fremdling and Monroe Liebgold]. [*Casting* Phillip Moore]. [*Jane Withers' teacher* Lola Figland]. [*Doorman* Jack Breth]. [*Still photog* Ray Nolan]. [*Publicity dir* Harry Brand].

Song(s): "Take a Tip from a Gypsy," "Song of the Gypsy Band" and "Blue Is the Evening," music by Harry Akst, words by Sidney Clare; "Carnival Song (Czardas)," music by D. J. Vecsei, lyrics (entitled "What a Gay Occasion") by Sidney Clare and Harry Akst.

Cast: JANE WITHERS (*Gypsy*), Rochelle Hudson (*Margaret Adams* [*also known as "Rawnie"*]), Robert Wilcox (*Tony*), Borrah

Minevitch (*Gino*), Minevitch Gang (*Themselves*), Steffi Duna (*Stella*), Katharine Alexander (*Mrs. Adams*), Chester Clute (*Mr. Adams*), Jose Crespo (*Baron Von Brun*), Paul Stanton (*Dr. Carter*), Frank Reicher (*Dr. Garvey*), Edward Cooper (*Butler*), Kathleen Burke, Myra Marsh (*Nurses*), Frank Puglia (*Florist*), Robert Gleckler (*Police lieutenant*), Eddie Dunn (*Dugan*), Howard Hickman (*Judge*), [Phil Smalley, Mary Treen, Tom Herbert, George Chandler, Billy Bletcher (*Patients*)], [Marcelle Corday (*Sit down gag woman*)], [Billy Wayne (*Elevator starter*)], [Gloria Roy (*Gypsy*)], [Jack Baxley (*Storekeeper*)], [Edward Gargan, Ivan Miller (*Officers*)], [Gino Corrado (*Gypsy singer in cap*)], [Wilfred Lucas (*Storekeeper*)], [Si Jenks (*Bashful trainer*)], [Phillis Coghlan (*Maid*)], [Jerry Mandy (*Electrician*)], [Charles Middleton], [Bert Roach], [John Sheehan].

Youth, Road, Comedy-drama, with songs. [*Print viewed*]. After a gypsy caravan is chased out of a town, they pitch camp on the road and prepare "Mulligan stew" with the vegetables that were thrown at them as they left. When Gypsy, a rambunctious adolescent, whines that she wants meat, Gino, her thieving pal, and his gang capture a goose. During the meal, Tony, an ex-Yale football player, who has traveled with the gypsies since his marriage broke up because of his wife's unfaithfulness, rebuffs the flirtations of Stella, the fortune-teller. Just then, a woman in a fur coat at the top of a hill faints and falls. When the police arrive and order the gypsies off private property, Tony hides the woman in his wagon. As they travel on, the woman revives and says that she cannot remember anything except that she was running away. Although Tony is skeptical of her story and cynical of her "type," Gypsy welcomes the woman, whom she calls her "Rawnie," which means "lady" in the Gypsy language, and teaches her how to tell fortunes. Meanwhile, Mr. and Mrs. Adams, a wealthy couple, learn that police have found the wrecked car belonging to their daughter, who vanished just before her wedding was to take place. The police think that the daughter ran away to avoid marrying fortune-hunting Baron Von Brun. After Gypsy introduces Rawnie to patrons as the world's greatest gypsy fortune-teller, Stella, jealous, starts a fight. When Tony pulls Rawnie off Stella, she bites him. That night, when Rawnie goes to Tony's tent to apologize, Gypsy encourages the others to play romantic music. Tony insults Rawnie and she slaps him. He pushes her out of the tent; however, when he sees Stella throw a knife at her, he rushes to Rawnie and kisses her passionately. After the gypsy camp is put into quarantine because of an outbreak of mumps, Gypsy and Rawnie sneak out to make money in town to buy food. When a man accuses Rawnie of taking his tie pin and calls the police, Gypsy and Rawnie run, and Rawnie is hit by a laundry truck. After the doctor suggests that a previous blow at the back of her head may have been the cause of her amnesia, Tony finally believes that Rawnie has been telling the truth and has not just been using them to avoid another situation. The doctor states that an operation might restore Rawnie's memory, but that afterward, she might have no memory of the period during her amnesia. Despite Gypsy's plea that they not risk it, Tony makes plans to raise the money. After Gypsy convinces a specialist to do the operation, Rawnie at first does not want it because she has been happy with the gypsies and knows that there must have been something frightening in her past from which she ran away. Tony convinces her; however, when Gypsy goes to see her after the operation, she does not recognize her. Soon Tony reads in the newspaper that Rawnie, identified as Margaret Adams, is going to marry Baron Von Brun. Although Gypsy tries to encourage Tony to steal her away, he refuses. Gypsy then goes to the Adams house and tells Mrs. Adams that her daughter has a gypsy husband, who is irate and skilled at throwing knives. Gypsy is then locked into a room, as is Gino, who has tried to impersonate the husband. They send a pigeon back to their camp with a message, and Tony leads the gypsies to the house, where they disrupt the wedding. Gypsy has Gino play romantic gypsy music, and Margaret, recognizing Tony, says his name and kisses him. Gypsy then arranges for them to be married. *Adolescents. Amnesia. Cynics. Gypsies. Romance. Caravans. Fights. Fortune hunters. Fortune-tellers. Mumps. Nobility. Physicians. Pigeons. Police. Quarantine. Weddings.*

Note: The working titles of this film were *Gypsy, Little Gypsy* and *Little Dynamite*.

Box 9 Apr 1938. *DV* 2 Apr 1938, p. 3. *FD* 7 Apr 1938, p. 7. *HR* 20 Dec 1937, p. 15. *HR* 17 Jan 1938, p. 39. *MPD* 5 Apr 1938, p. 2. *MPH* 29 Jan 1938, p. 37. *MPH* 9 Apr 1938, p. 40. *NYT* 27 May 1938, p. 12. *Var* 25 May 1938, p. 13.

RAVISHED ARMENIA see **AUCTION OF SOULS**

RAW EDGE (Native Americans, Yakima)

Universal-International Pictures Co., Inc. *Dist* Universal Pictures Co., Inc. Jul **1956**; New York opening: 27 Jul 1956; Prod: late Oct—Mid Nov 1955 [©Universal Pictures Co.; 6 Jul 1956; LP6822]. Sd (Western Electric Recording); col (Print by Technicolor). 6,859 ft. 76 min. PCA cert no. 17853.

Prod Albert Zugsmith. *Dir* John Sherwood. [*Asst dir* Joseph E. Kenny, George Lollier and Ray DeCamp]. [*Dial dir* Harold Goodwin]. *Scr* Harry Essex and Robert Hill. *Story* William Kozlenko and James Benson Nablo. *Dir of photog* Maury Gertsman. *Spec photog* Clifford Stine. *Technicolor color consultant* William Fritzsche. *Art dir* Alexander Golitzen and Alfred Sweeney. *Film ed* Russell Schoengarth. *Set dec* Russell A. Gausman and Ruby R. Levitt. *Cost* Bill Thomas. *Mus supv* Joseph Gershenson. *Sd* Leslie I. Carey, Frank H. Wilkinson and [John Kemp]. *Makeup* Bud Westmore. *Hair stylist* Joan St. Oegger. [*Prod mgr* Norman Deming].

Song(s): "Raw Edge," words, music and vocal by Terry Gilkyson.

Cast: RORY CALHOUN (*Tex Kirby*), YVONNE DE CARLO (*Hannah Montgomery*), MARA CORDAY (*Paca*), Neville Brand (*Tarp Penny*), Rex Reason (*John Randolph*), Emile Meyer (*Pop Penny*), Herbert Rudley (*Gerald Montgomery*), Robert J. Wilke (*Sile Doty*), John Gilmore (*Dan Kirby*), Gregg Barton (*McKay*), Ed Fury (*Whitey*), William Schallert (*Missionary*), Francis McDonald (*Chief Kiyuva*), [Robert Hoy (*Five Crows*)], [Julia Montoya (*Indian*)], [Paul Fierro (*Frenchie, bartender*)], [Richard James (*Clerk*)].

Western. [*Print viewed*]. In 1842 in Oregon, a territory claimed by both the United States and Great Britain, there is no law, save that of Gerald Montgomery, who dominates an area like a feudal baron and has decreed that an unmarried woman is owned by the first man to claim her. Montgomery's wife Hannah is attacked in a dark barn by an assailant she does not see but manages to bite him before she passes out. Pop and Tarp Penny, Montgomery's henchmen, tell him that they suspect trapper Dan Kirby, who is involved in a land dispute with Montgomery, of the attack, and a mark, which Kirby received in an earlier fight with Tarp, is found on his arm. Paca, Dan's Indian wife, seeks Hannah's help, and she admits that her attacker was a heavier man than Dan. However, Hannah and Paca return too late to prevent Montgomery from hanging Dan. When Paca attempts to return to her people, the Yakima, she is pursued by Montgomery's men. Indian brave Five Crows tries to defend her but is killed, and Paca is claimed by Sile Doty as his wife. Later, after Montgomery leaves his stockade to do a land survey, Hannah discovers that her Indian maids are deserting her. At a saloon in town, a stranger, after having located the Kirby ranch and found Dan's body, meets gambler John Randolph and is advised to see Doty if he wants work on Montgomery's land. At Doty's place, the stranger, Dan's brother Tex, is suprised to find Paca, whom he knew as Dan's wife, but she explains Montgomery's law to him. Later, Doty pressures Paca into revealing that Tex is Dan's brother, and Randolph informs him that Tex has quite a reputation as a gunfighter. The Pennys set out to warn Montgomery at his mountain camp, but Randolph tips off Tex that an ambush is being prepared for him. Pop Penny, however, intends to let Montgomery be killed and, thereafter, claim his land and widow. At the stockade, Randolph also warns Hannah that Tex is gunning for her husband. When the Indians go on the warpath as a result of Five Crows' death, the Pennys return to the safety of the stockade, where Hannah accuses them of abandoning her husband. Later, Tex enters the stockade to await Montgomery's return, and the Pennys agree to let Tex continue his mission. The next day, Doty and Paca ride into Montgomery's camp, but they are trapped by the Indian uprising. Montgomery asks Paca for help, warning that she will hang if she refuses, and she goes to speak with Chief Kiyuva. At the stockade, Hannah confesses to Tex that she no longer loves Montgomery because of what he has become. Pop and Tarp Penny start drinking and feuding over who is going to get Hannah. Randolph involves them in a card game to determine who will own Hannah, and as they begin to brawl, Hannah escapes. Tarp finds her and offers to take her to her husband but, on the way, attacks her, and she realizes that it was he, not Dan Kirby, who previously assaulted her. Tex catches up with them and sends Tarp on his way. Although Hannah still thinks that Tex intends to kill her husband, they move on, followed by Tarp who shoots Hannah in the shoulder. Due to a growing affection for Hannah, Tex decides to return with her to the stockade. Paca reports to Montgomery that Chief Kiyuva will

allow him and his men to leave if he helps find the killer of Five Crows. Montgomery intends to hand over Tex as the killer, but when Paca takes him to meet Chief Kiyuva, Montgomery himself is indentified as the man the Indians want. He pleads for Paca's help as he is dragged away, but the next day, his body is delivered to the stockade, and Paca rides off with her people. Tarp then returns and Pop draws a gun on Tex and Randolph. After Tarp deliberately shoots his own father, Tex enters the house where Tarp is holed up and a gunfight ensues. When their ammunition runs out, they continue in a brawl until Tarp impales himself on the horns of a fallen steer's head. Tex plans to leave for San Antone, and Hannah accepts his invitation to accompany him. *Dictators. Gunfighters. Marriage—Forced. Oregon. Revenge. Attempted rape. Brothers. False accusations. Fathers and sons. Fistfights. Gamblers. Gunfights. Gunshot wounds. Indians of North America. Land barons. Lynching. Miscegenation. Parricide. Ranches. Revenge. Saloons. Trappers. Tribal chiefs. United States-History. Widows. Yakima Indians.*

Box 4 Aug 1956. *DV* 24 Jul 1956, p. 3. *FD* 24 Jul 1956, p. 8. *HR* 28 Oct 1955, p. 8. *HR* 11 Nov 1955, p. 12. *HR* 24 Jul 1956, p. 3. *LAT* 2 Aug 1956. *MPD* 24 Jul 1956. *MPHPD* 18 Aug 1956, p. 34 *NYT* 28 Jul 1956, p. 10. *Var* 25 Jul 1956, p. 18.

RAWHIDE see **THE ARIZONA RANGER**

THE RAWHIDE BREED see **THE RAWHIDE TRAIL**

THE RAWHIDE KID (Jewish Americans)

Universal Pictures Corp.; Universal-Jewel. 29 Jan 1928 [©Universal Pictures Corp.; 28 Oct 1927; LP24595]. Si; b&w. 6 reels, 5,383 ft.

Pres Carl Laemmle. *Dir* Del Andrews. *Adpt* Isadore Bernstein. *Story* Peter B. Kyne. *Cont* Arthur Statter. *Titles* Tom Reed. *Photog* Harry Neumann. *Art dir* David S. Garber. *Film ed* Rodney Hickok.

Cast: Hoot Gibson (*Dennis O'Hara*), Georgia Hale (*Jessica Silverberg*), Frank Hagney (*J. Francis Jackson*), William H. Strauss (*Simon Silverberg*), Harry Todd (*Comic*), Tom Lingham (*Deputy*).

Western. Dennis O'Hara, a spirited young Irishman who is a constant source of annoyance to J. Francis Jackson, the town's leading citizen, beats Jackson each year in the annual horse race until Jackson acquires the winning horse in a gambling game. Simon Silverberg and his daughter, Jessica, arrive in town and try to sell clothing, but the men, led by Jackson, drive them from town. Dennis intervenes on their behalf and takes them to his cabin. When Dennis earns the money to buy back his horse and Jackson refuses to sell it, Dennis steals the horse; later, Dennis returns to find Jackson virtually in control of the town and wagering his fortune against Simon that he will win the annual race. Jackson conspires to prevent Dennis from winning, and after much difficulty with the other riders, Dennis beats Jackson's rider and then whips Jackson. Dennis and Jessica are united. *Gambling. Horseracing. Irish. Jews. Peddlers and peddling. Small town life.*

FD 25 Dec 1927. *Var* 18 Jan 1928.

THE RAWHIDE TRAIL (Native Americans, Comanche)

Allied Artists Pictures Corp.; Terry & Lyon Productions. *Dist* Allied Artists Pictures Corp. 26 Jan 1958; Prod: early Oct—mid-Oct 1957 at the Autry Ranch [©Allied Artists Pictures Corp.; 11 Feb 1958; LP9915]. Sd; b&w. 6,062 ft. 67 min. PCA cert no. 18878.

Exec prod J. William Hayes. *Prod* Earle Lyon. *Assoc prod* James Terry. *Dir* Robert Gordon. *Asst dir* Kenny Kessler. *Dial dir* Pat Dorian. *Wrt* Alexander J. Wells. *Photog* Karl Struss. *Cam op* Joe Dorris. *Spec eff* George Olah. *Art dir* David Milton. *Film ed* Paul Borofsky. *Sd ed* Del Harris. *Mus ed* Carl Sands. *Set dec* Joseph Kish. *Men's ward* Elmer Elsworth. *Women's ward* Irene Caine. *Mus comp and cond* Andre S. Brummer. *Orch* Dave Strech. *Sd rec* Clarence Peterson and Russ Ashley. *Makeup artist* Jack Pierce. *Hair stylist* Eve Newing. *Prod mgr* K. M. Kessler. *Scr supv* Dick Walton. *Prop master* Ted Mossman. *Constr supv* James West. *Chief elec* Ding Woodhouse.

Song(s): "The Rawhide Trail" music by Andre S. Brummer, lyrics by Jack Lloyd, sung by The Guardsmen.

Cast: Rex Reason (*Jess Brady*), Nancy Gates (*Marsha Collins*), Richard Erdman (*Rupe Pardee*), Ann Doran (*Mrs. Cartwright*), Rusty Lane (*Captain*), Jana Davi (*Keetah*), Sam Buffington (*James Willard*), Robert Knapp (*Farly Durand*), Frank Chase (*Corporal*), William Murphy (*Elbe Rotter*), Richard Warren (*Collier*), John Dierkes (*Hangman*), Richard Geary, Red Schryver (*Soldiers*), Chet Sampson (*Telegrapher*), Al Wyatt (*Stagecoach driver*), Vance

Howard (*Sergeant*), Bru Danger (*Jailer*), Cecil Elliott (*Dowager*), Joseph H. Hamilton (*Elderly man*).

Western. [*Not viewed*]. Jess Brady and Rupe Pardee have been wrongfully accused of leading a wagon train into a Comanche ambush and are waiting to be hanged in a Gunsight, Texas, jail. Their claim that the Comanches want to kill them appears to be justified when the Indians attack the jail in an attempt to capture them. After the Comanches are defeated by soldiers, the garrison's captain decides to move Jess, Rupe and Rupe's Indian wife, Keetah, who has been wounded in the attack, to another location. The Comanches follow, however, and the soldiers and their prisoners take shelter at a stagecoach line's way station. A stagecoach arrives carrying Marsha Collins, her fiancé, Farly Durand, a government supply officer, and James Willard, a newspaper reporter. All are trapped overnight in the station, and the captain is wounded during one of the Comanche attacks. The situation becomes more tense when Jess and Durand, who had served together during the Civil War, become involved in a personal dispute. The captain agrees to allow Jess to try to lead them to safety, and Jess divides the party into groups in an attempt to decoy the Comanches. Rupe and his group become trapped and he discovers that Durand is the person responsible for the attack on the wagon train. Rupe and Keetah manage to escape and are able to arrange the rescue of Jess and Marsha, who join them as they head for Mexico. *Comanche Indians. False accusations. Government agents. Soldiers. Traitors. Engagements. Escapes. Jails. Reporters. Sieges. Stagecoach lines. Texas. Wounds and injuries.*

Note: This film's working title was *The Rawhide Breed*.

Exb 30 Apr 1958, p. 4457. *HR* 18 Oct 1957. *LAT* 6 Oct 1957. *MPHPD* 7 Jun 1958, p. 857.

REACH FOR THE STARS see THE STARS ARE SINGING

REACHING FROM HEAVEN (Immigrants)
Roland Reed Production. *Dist* Visual Education Service, The Lutheran Church—Missouri Synod. Feb **1948**; Prod: 1947 at Enterprise Studios. Sd (RCA Sound System); b&w. 81 min.

Pres The Lutheran Church, Missouri Synod. *Dir* Frank Strayer. *Wrt* Charles Palmer. *Orig idea* The Reverend Henry Rische. *Theological collaborator* The Reverend H. W. Gockel. *Dir of photog* Walter Strenge. [*Stills* James Doolittle]. *Film ed* Roy Luby. *Mus dir* Al Colombo. *Sd eng* Ferol Redd. *Prod supv* Guy V. Thayer, Jr. *Tech adv* T. G. Eggers. *Consultant* The Rev. Paul Koenig and The Rev. L. Meyer, D.D.

Cast: Hugh Beaumont (*Bill Starling*), Cheryl Walker (*Madeline Bradley*), John Qualen (*The Stranger*), Regis Toomey (*Pastor*), Chas. Evans (*Walter Graves*), Margaret Hamilton (*Sophia [Manley]*), Addison Richards (*Max Bradley*), Nana Bryant (*Mrs. [Kay] Bradley*), Mae Clarke (*Dorothy Gram*), Jack Lambert (*Buck Huggins*), Ann Lee Doran (*Martha Kestner*), Geo. Chandler (*Bert Kestner*), [Gene Roth (*Kestners' neighbor*)], [George Eldredge].

Religious, Drama. [*Print viewed*]. In a small American town, a lonely, humble immigrant receives a telegram advising him that his wife has died in Europe just as she and their young daughter were about to embark on a ship to join him. In need of someone to talk with about his troubles, "The Stranger" approaches several people, but they will not listen to him. He stops in front of a Lutheran Church, but is unable to speak with the pastor, who is busy greeting his congregation after a service. The stranger walks away and is hit by a car driven by Madeline Bradley, who is on her way to play golf, and is criticized by church member Bill Starling as the stranger is taken off to a hospital. Later, the pastor tells his wife that he has doubts about the effectiveness of his sermons on the theme of "Each one, reach one" and the need for people to become responsible for each other's welfare. Meanwhile, when Madeline contritely tells her parents about the accident, her father, Max, assures her that his insurance will pay for the stranger's hospital bills and that a quick settlement will be made to avoid a lawsuit. Madeline's mother points out that if the family had all been in church, where they belonged, the accident would not have happened. Max, however, who as a child was forced to practice religion, feels that his child does not need that. Assuming responsibility for her actions, Madeline decides to visit the stranger in the hospital and firmly rejects her father's offer to fix everything with money. At the hospital, after donating blood to help the stranger, Bill encounters Madeline again and she convinces him of her genuine concern for the stranger. Bill works as a construction foreman for contractor Walter Graves, a competitor and old friend of Madeline's

father, whom she regards as an "uncle." Madeline, who wants to earn money of her own and not be dependent upon her father, asks Walt for a job and is hired to work in the office with Walt's secretary, Sophia Manley. After the pastor visits the stranger in the hospital and reads another telegram stating that the man's young daughter will be arriving shortly, he tells members of the congregation that he has discovered that the stranger was separated from his family by the war and that his wife and daughter Anna were on their way to join him when the wife died. The pastor then decides to find the stranger work and a home and church members volunteer to fix up an unused apartment for him. When Bill invites Madeline to go to church with him, she declines, as she feels that she does not need the church. Later, when Madeline's father and Walt are bidding on a construction project, her father asks her to get him details of Walt's bid. As the stranger recovers in the hospital, he tells the pastor that he has repented for his life of lies and theft, and would like to join the church. After Bill and Madeline work on getting the job bid finalized, he shows her the apartment the congregation is fixing up and tries to convince her to accept Jesus Christ as her savior. She is not totally convinced, although she is falling in love with Bill. At a tunnel construction site which Bill and Madeline visit, foreman Buck Huggins, who has been teasing Bill about his church-going, sets off an unapproved dynamite blast and becomes trapped. Bill goes to his rescue, and although both are injured in the explosion, they recover and Buck tells his crew that they will be attending church the next Sunday morning. When the bids are announced, it is revealed that Walt's was not received because the love-struck Madeline had forgotten to mail it. Sophia accuses Madeline of deliberately sabotaging the bid, causing Walt to now face bankruptcy. When the contract is awarded to Madeline's father, he assumes that she sold Walt out and promises her a new car as a reward. Madeline is very upset about letting Walt down and faces the prospect of losing Bill. She decides to leave town, but before doing so visits the stranger, who tells her that he has found solace and help in the Bible and in God and that she, too, can experience this. Later, Bill and the stranger meet Anna at the railroad station and Bill drives them to their new home where they are surprised and overcome by the congregation's welcome. In the meantime, Madeline's parents discover that she has gone but has left for them the bid envelope she forgot to mail. They realize that they have been wrong and although they have made a fortune, they have lost everything that matters. They then decide to make a new start and pray for guidance. At the welcoming party, the pastor announces that the stranger will become the church's custodian. Madeline's father finds her at the party and returns the envelope, after which Madeline explains to the group that she simply forgot to mail the bid. Sophia and Walt forgive her and her father announces that he has signed over the contract to Walt, seeks forgiveness and will be in church the following Sunday. Madeline and Bill are reunited and she indicates that she will be attending church with him for a long, long time. *Christian ethics. Fathers and daughters. Good Samaritans. Immigrants. Lutheran Church. Religion. Romance. Accidents. Boardinghouses. Business ethics. Business rivals. Clergy. Contractors. Explosions. Foremen. Forgiveness. Housewarmings. Prayer. Secretaries.*

Note: Although this film bears a copyright statement in the onscreen credits, it was not registered for copyright. "Sophia," the character played by Margaret Hamilton, is also called "Sophie" in the film.

Exb 6 May 1953, p. 3518. *HR* 24 May 1950, p. 7.

READY MONEY see RIDING HIGH

REAL FOLKS (Irish Americans)
Triangle Film Corp. *Dist* Triangle Distributing Corp. 10 Feb **1918**. Si; b&w. 5 reels, 4,620 ft.

Dir Walter Edwards. *Scen* Jack Cunningham. *Story* Kate Corbaley. *Cam* C. G. Peterson.

Cast: Francis McDonald (*Jimmie Dugan*), Alberta Lee (*Mrs. Dugan*), J. Barney Sherry (*Pat Dugan*), Fritzi Ridgeway (*Joyce Clifton*), Marion Skinner (*Lady Blessington*), Betty Pearce (*Margaret Van Arsden*), George Pearce (*Van Arsden*), T. D. Crittenden.

Comedy-drama. Suspecting that his California farmland is rich in oil, transplanted Irishman Pat Dugan spends his last penny on prospecting and is richly rewarded when his oil shaft finally gushes. Although Pat's son Jimmie is happy on their modest farm, the elder Dugan insists that his newly wealthy family assume its place in society

and sends Jimmie to an exclusive Eastern college. On his first day, Jimmie gets involved in a fight and departs for Long Island, where he opens a flower shop with an Italian named Garbaldi. When Jimmie delivers some shrubs to Lady Blessington's estate, he meets and falls in love with her pretty but poor goddaughter, Joyce Clifton. He also meets his parents, who, hoping to find their son, have come East and rented the adjoining estate. When Pat threatens to disinherit Jimmie unless he marries into society, the young man ignores him and quietly marries Joyce. She soon earns a place in the stubborn old Irishman's heart, however, which greatly pleases his equally stubborn son. *Fathers and sons. Florists. Irish Americans. Nouveaux riches. Social climbers. California. College students. Disinheritance. Farms. Fights. Godparents. Long Island (NY). Oil. Prospectors.*

ETR 16 Feb 1918, pp. 912-13. *MPN* 16 Feb 1918, p. 1017, 1036-37. *MPW* 9 Feb 1918, p. 873. *MPW* 16 Feb 1918, p. 1004. *NYDM* 16 Feb 1918, p. 18. *Var* 8 feb 1918, p. 40. *Wid's* 14 Feb 1918, pp. 945-46.

THE REBEL GENERATION *see* **ALL THE FINE YOUNG CANNIBALS**

REBELLION (Latino)

Crescent Pictures Corp. *Dist* Crescent Pictures Corp. 27 Oct **1936**; Prod: 27 Aug—late Sep 1936 at Talisman Studios. Sd; b&w. 60 or 62 min. PCA cert no. 2679.

Prod E. B. Derr. *Assoc prod* Bernard A. Moriarty. *Supv* Frank Melford. *Dir* Lynn Shores. *Asst dir* Fred Spencer. *Story and scr* John T. Neville. *Photog* Arthur Martinelli. *Art dir* Edward C. Jewell. *Film ed* Donald M. Barratt. *Mus dir* Abe Meyer. *Rec* J. S. Westmoreland.

Cast: Tom Keene (*Captain John Carroll*), Rita Cansino (*Paula Castillo*), Duncan Renaldo (*Ricardo Castillo*), William Royle (*Harris*), Gino Corrado (*Pablo*), Roger Gray (*Honeycutt*), Robert McKenzie (*Judge Moore*), Allen Cavan (*President Zachary Taylor*), Jack Ingram (*Hank*), Lita Cortez (*Marquita*), Theodore Lorch (*General Vallejo*), Merrill McCormick (*Dr. Semple*).

Historical, Western. [*Not viewed*]. In 1850, in California after the signing of the Guadelupe-Hidalgo treaty with the United States, which ended the Mexican War, Mexicans fight for land guaranteed to them by the treaty. President Zachary Taylor sends Cavalry officer Captain John Carroll, his personal aide, to insure the rights of Mexican citizens after Paula Castillo recounts to him the atrocities committed by American land-grabbers, including the murder of her father. Paula and Carroll quickly fall in love, and he befriends her brother Ricardo, who, as leader of a band of Mexican guerillas, has been outlawed by the terrorists. At first the Mexicans are suspicious of Carroll, until he fends off the raiders and their leader, Harris, when they invade the Castillo hacienda during a fiesta. Ricardo and his guerillas agree to lay down their arms in favor of Carroll's plan of non-violent resistance. Harris, who controls the crooked and weak officials, has Carroll jailed on a trumped up charge, and Ricardo dies in a skirmish with the raiders while helping Carroll to escape. Carroll then decides to have the Mexicans take up their arms and leads a series of night attacks, which drive the Americans off the land they usurped. Paula, meanwhile, is kidnapped by the brigands and her hacienda is jeopardized during a gun siege, but Carroll saves Paula and her home by fighting Harris hand-to-hand. The Mexicans celebrate the restoration of their land at a large fiesta, and Carroll wins Paula's hand and the governorship of California. *California–History–1846-1850. Land rights. Mexican Americans. Usurpers. Festivals. Fistfights. Gunfights. Kidnapping. Murder. Officers (Military). Prison escapes. Romance. Self-sacrifice. State governments. Zachary Taylor. Thieves. Treaties. United States–History–War with Mexico, 1845-1848. United States. Presidents.*

Note: The working title for this film was *31st Star.* According to a news item in *FD*, this was the second in a series of Tom Keene films made by E. B. Derr (see entry for *The Glory Trail* above). A 1938 *Var* review claims that Robert McKenzie played the part of President Taylor, and Allen Cavan, who is credited on the screen as Taylor, a part called Kito. The same review lists Roger Gray's character as Halsing, and Jack Ingram is erroneously listed as Jack Cortez playing Halde, while Lita Cortez is credited as playing Lolita. The 1938 review suggests the film was either re-released in 1938 or was not released in New York until then. There is no evidence that the names of the characters were changed or that the film was re-made. According to a modern source, this film was re-issued in 1946 as *Lady from Frisco.*

DV 30 Jul 1936, p. 5. *DV* 6 Oct 1936, p. 3. *FD* 22 Sep 1936, p. 4. *FD* 10 Oct 1936, p. 7. *HR* 26 Aug 1936, p. 11. *HR* 6 Oct 1936, p. 3. *MPD* 9 Oct 1936, p. 13. *MPH* 17 Oct 1936, p. 47, 50. *Var* 4 May 1938, p. 15.

RECKLESS MONEY (African Americans)

1926. Si; b&w. Length undetermined. [Feature length assumed.].

Dir Sherman H. Dudley, Jr. *Photog* Watkins.

Cast: Sherman H. Dudley, Jr., John La Rue.

Comedy, African American. No information about the precise nature of this film has been found. *African Americans.*

Note: According to an unidentified news item in the George P. Johnson Collection at the UCLA Special Collections Library, this film was produced in Durham, NC.

THE RECKONING DAY (German Americans)

Triangle Film Corp. *Dist* Triangle Distributing Corp. 20 Oct **1918.** Si; b&w. 5 reels, 4,650 ft.

Dir Harry Clements. *Story and scen* Bob Hill. *Cam* R. E. Irish.

Cast: Belle Bennett (*Jane Whiting*), Jack Richardson (*Frederick Kube*), J. Barney Sherry (*Senator Wheeler*), Tom Buckingham (*Frank Wheeler*), Lenore Fair (*Lola Schram*), Louise Lester (*Mrs. Schram*), Lee Phelps (*Jimmy Ware*), Lucille Desmond (*Tilly Ware*), Sidney De Grey (*District attorney*), Joe Bennett.

World War I, Drama. During World War I, Jane Whiting, a bright young lawyer who is engaged to Senator Wheeler, is assigned by the district attorney to expose a gang of spies who are collecting money for the German government through the operation of a fraudulent charity organization. Wheeler's son Frank has fallen in love with Lola Schram, whose pro-German mother is forcing the girl to work for Frederick Kube, the head of the spy ring, but when Kube learns of the romance, he orders Mrs. Schram to break it off. When Lola finally confesses her activities to Frank, Kube kills her and then frames Frank for the murder. Meanwhile, Jane, through the help of Jimmy and Tilly Ware, has discovered Kube's headquarters and *modus operandi.* By means of a carefully set trap, she finally succeeds in clearing Frank's name and bringing Kube and his gang to justice. *Family relationships. Frame-ups. German Americans. Germans. Murder. Spies. Traitors. Traps. Women lawyers. Charities. Confession. District attorneys. Engagements. Fraud. United States. Congress. Senate. World War I.*

Note: *MPW* lists the release date as 17 Nov 1918. *Wid's* credits Roy Clements as director, while other reviews cite Harry Pollard. Modern sources cite Sol Polito as cameraman.

ETR 26 Oct 1918, p. 1774. *MPN* 2 Nov 1918, p. 2803. *MPW* 26 Oct 1918, p. 544. *MPW* 7 Dec 1918, p. 1123. *NYDM* 9 Nov 1918, p. 698. *Var* 18 Oct 1918, p. 38. *Wid's* 27 Oct 1918, p. 8.

RED BALL EXPRESS (African Americans)

Universal-International Pictures, Inc. *Dist* Universal Pictures Co., Inc. May **1952;** New York opening: 29 May 1952; Prod: early Nov—mid-Dec 1951 [©Universal Pictures Co.; 8 Apr 1952; LP1668]. Sd (Western Electric Recording); b&w. 7,501 ft. 80 or 83 min.

Prod Aaron Rosenberg. *Dir* Budd Boetticher. [*Asst dir* John Sherwood]. *Scr* John Michael Hayes. *Suggested by a story by* Marcel Klauber and Billy Brady, Jr. *Dir of photog* Maury Gertsman. *Art dir* Bernard Herzbrun and Richard H. Riedel. *Film ed* Edward Curtiss. *Set des* Russell A. Gausman and Oliver Emert. *Mus dir* Joseph Gershenson. *Sd* Leslie I. Carey and Joe Lapis. *Hair stylist* Joan St. Oegger. *Makeup* Bud Westmore. *Tech adv* Major Frank S. Ross, U.S. Army, Retired.

Cast: Jeff Chandler (*Lt. [Chick] Campbell*), Alex Nicol (*Sgt. [Red] Kallek*), Charles Drake ([*Pvt. Ronald*] *Partridge*), Judith Braun (*Joyce [McClellan]*), Sidney Poitier ([*Corp. Andrew*] *Robertson*), Jacqueline Duval (*Antoinette [Dubois]*), Bubber Johnson ([*Pvt.*] *Taffy [Smith]*), Robert Davis ([*Pvt. Dave*] *McCord*), Hugh O'Brian ([*Pvt.*] *Wilson*), Frank Chase ([*Pvt.*] *Higgins*), Cindy Garner (*Kitty [Walsh]*), Palmer Lee (*Tank lieutenant*), John Hudson (*Tank sergeant*), Jack Kelly ([*Pvt. John*] *Jeyman*), Howard Petrie (*General Gordon*), [Syl Lamont (*Jones*)], [Howard Negley (*Major general*)], [Thomas B. Henry, Arthur Space (*Colonels*)], [Walter Reed (*Major*)], [Robert Karnes (*Engineer captain*)], [Ted Ryan (*Sgt. Gorio*)], [Douglas Evans (*Brigadier general*)], [Eugene Borden (*French peasant father*)], [Yola D'Avril (*Barmaid*)], [Sid Clute, Clark Howat (*M.P. captains*)], [Emmett Smith (*M.P.*)], [Tommy Long, Robert Dane (*Guards*)], [Nan Boardman (*French peasant mother*)], [Don Hicks (*Soldier in bistro*)], [Harry Lauter (*Lt. Michaelson*)], [Harold Dyrenforth (*German sergeant*)], [Peter Michael (*German corporal*)], [George Dee (*French waiter*)], [James McLaughlin (*First sergeant*)], [Roger McGee (*Sergeant*)], [Douglas Banks, Mike Dale (*Mechanics*)], [Jack Hyde (*M.P. lieutenant*)], [Murray Olshansky (*Tank private*)], [Richard F. Gaston (*Tank corporal*)], [William

Martin (*First lieutenant*)], Leonard Schneider (*Phone corporal*), [Gordon Walsh, Joe Freiden (*Tankers*)], [Forrest Burns].

World War II, Drama. [*Print viewed*]. In July 1944, the United States Army launches a massive invasion to break through German lines into France. At the forefront of the assault, General George Patton's swift moving combat forces outrun Allied supply lines, forcing the Transportation Corps to devise a new method to supply Patton's tanks. Dubbed the "Red Ball Express," a new outfit is formed to truck gasoline and ammunition to the front. When Lt. Chick Campbell is put in charge of the outfit, his subordinate, Sgt. Red Kallek, seethes with resentment because he holds a personal grudge against Campbell. As the men climb into their trucks, Kallek confides to his driving partner that Campbell killed his brother. Campbell teams up with Andrew Robertson, a young black corporal, but when Robertson tries to strike up a conversation, Campbell rebuffs him. As the convoy races to reach Paris, Kallek declares that the company is comprised of misfits and challenges Campbell's authority. After driving for two solid days, the men reach their objective and are ordered to unload the trucks, prompting them to complain about performing manual labor. Without any sleep, the convoy heads back, and one driver, suffering exhaustion, crashes his truck into a tree, forcing the outfit to stop. While they are waiting, Antoinette Dubois, a French girl, peddles her bike along the roadside, and after Private Ronald Partridge greets her, she invites him home to meet her family. Upon discovering that the Dubois have been subsisting on meager crusts of bread and watery soup, Partridge promises to bring them some food. Before Partridge can return, however, his partner, Taffy Smith, a black soldier, is ordered to join the convoy, leaving Partridge behind. Peddling furiously on Antoinette's bike, Partridge finally rejoins Smith. The outfit then continues on to a relief camp. There, Pvt. Wilson calls Robertson a "black boy," sparking racial tensions that result in a fistfight. After Campbell stops the fight, Robertson visits him in his tent and requests a transfer. Declaring that he has not been schooled in race relations, Campbell denies his request. Upon returning to his tent, Robertson complains to his black tentmates, Smith and Pvt. Dave McCord, that Robertson is a racist, but McCord defends the lieutenant. Continuing their mission, the trucks approach a heavily mined area, and although aware of the danger, McCord forges ahead into certain death. After McCord's truck is blown up, Campbell stops to conduct a funeral service for the slain soldier, thus earning the respect of his men. Soon after, the convoy meets a company of armored tanks, and when the tank sergeant derides the truckers as the "Foul Ball Express," the company of misfits finally coalesces to defend their honor. Later, the returning convoy passes Antoinette's house, and Partridge returns her bike and delivers a package of food. When the company pulls out without him again, Partridge is once again forced to peddle his way back. Upon reaching their base, the truckers unload their supplies and Campbell informs Robertson that he has approved his transfer. Robertson, who has developed respect for Campbell, replies that he wants to stay. At the base canteen, Kallek tells Joyce McClellan, a Red Cross worker, that Campbell killed his brother Al. Kallek claims that Campbell and Al were driving a rig through the Rockies when the truck jackknifed, trapping Al in the cab. Finding Campbell standing next to him at the bar, Kallek disparages Campbell's story that he was knocked unconscious and therefore unable to help Al. When Kallek challenges Campbell, the lieutenant orders his arrest. Soon after, the convoy is dispatched on a dangerous mission through German lines and Campbell orders Kallek's release. Along the road, they are pinned down by a German tank and Partridge sacrifices himself by crashing his truck into the tank. Upon discovering that the only road to their objective, a convoy of stranded tanks, runs through a city engulfed in flames, Campbell orders Kalleck to drive the lead truck into the inferno. Losing control of his truck, Kallek crashes his vehicle into a building. Risking his own life, Campbell stops to pull Kalleck from the flames, finally earning his esteem. As the convoy reaches the tanks, it is greeted with cheers. Its mission completed, the convoy begins its trek back to the base. As they near the Dubois house, Smith braces to give Antoinette the sad news about Partridge when he sees Partridge standing along the roadside with Antoinette. After being warmly greeted by his friends, Partridge explains that he was only knocked unconscious in the crash and was to peddle his way back to Antoinette. *African Americans. Heroism. Tank warfare. Truck drivers. United States. Army. World War II. Americans in foreign countries.*

Bicycles. False accusations. Feuds. Fistfights. France. Officers (Military). Racism. Rescues. Self-sacrifice.

Note: The film opens with a voice-over narration delivered by "Pvt. Partridge," outlining the 1944 Allied invasion to free Europe. The title credit does not appear until Partridge's narration is completed, about fifteen minutes into the film. The onscreen production and cast credits are withheld until the end of the film. The picture closes with the following written acknowledgement: "We gratefully acknowledge the cooperation of the Department of Defense, the Transportation Corps of the Army and the Virginia National Guard in the making of this motion picture." As depicted in the film, the Red Ball Express, formally known as the 371st Quartermaster Truck Company of the Army Transportation Corps, was a division of 6,000 trucks formed by Major General Frank Ross, the film's technical adviser, to rush ammunition, gasoline and other supplies through enemy held territory to General George Patton's tanks. The division included many African American soldiers. According to the *HR* review, location scenes for this picture were shot at Fort Eustis, VA, the headquarters of the Army Transportation Corps. Although a *HR* production chart places Susan Cabot and Richard Garland in the cast, their participation in the released film has not been confirmed.

Box 3 May 1952. DV 30 Apr 1952, p. 3. Exb 7 May 1952, p. 3291. FD 30 Apr 1952, p. 6. Har 3 May 1952. p. 70. HR 2 Nov 1951, p. 15. HR 14 Dec 1951, p. 15. HR 30 Apr 1952, p. 3. MPHPD 3 May 1952, p. 1349. NYT 30 May 1952, p. 11. Var 30 Apr 1952, p. 6.

RED CLAY (Native Americans)
Universal Pictures Corp.; Blue Streak Western. 17 Apr **1927** [©Universal Pictures Corp.; 28 Apr 1925; LP21418]. Si; b&w. 5 reels, 4,626 ft.
　　Pres Carl Laemmle. *Dir* Ernst Laemmle. *Scen* Charles Logue and Frank L. Inghram. *Story* Sarah Saddoris. *Titles* Ruth Todd. *Photog* Ben Kline. *Art dir* David S. Garber.
　　Cast: William Desmond (*Chief John Nisheto*), Marceline Day (*Agnes Burr*), Albert J. Smith (*Jack Burr*), Byron Douglas (*Senator Burr*), Billy Sullivan (*Bob Lee*), Lola Todd (*Betty Morgan*), Noble Johnson (*Chief Bear Paw*), Felix Whitefeather (*Indian chief*), Ynez Seabury (*Minnie Bear Paw*).
　　Melodrama. During World War I, Chief John Nisheto is drafted. While fighting in France, he saves the life of Jack Burr, the son of a congressman sympathetic to the Indians. After the war, John returns home and begins to go out with Jack's sister, Agnes. Although John is both a scholar and a star football player, Jack objects, not knowing that John is the man who once saved his life. John is later mortally wounded and dies in Jack's arms, revealing at last his own heroism in the trenches. Jack repents of his prejudice and does his best to comfort his sister. *Football. France. Indians of North America. Racism. United States. Congress. War heroes. World War I.*

FD 17 Apr 1927. Var 20 Apr 1927, p. 25.

THE RED DRAGON (Chinese Americans, African Americans)
Monogram Pictures Corp. *Dist* Monogram Pictures Corp. 2 Feb **1946**; Prod: early—late Sep 1945 [©Monogram Pictures Corp.; 22 Dec 1945; LP74]. Sd (Western Electric Mirrophonic Recording); b&w. 64 min. PCA cert no. 11289.
　　Series: Charlie Chan.
　　Prod James S. Burkett. *Dir* Phil Rosen. *Asst dir* Eddie Davis. *Orig scr* George Callahan. *Dir of photog* Vincent Farrar. *Spec eff* Robert Clark. *Tech dir* Dave Milton. *Ed* Ace Herman. *Mus dir* Edward J. Kay. *Sd rec* Tom Lambert. *Prod mgr* Glenn Cook.
　　Song(s): "My Heart Is Yours," composer undetermined.
　　Source: Based on characters created by Earl Derr Biggers.
　　Cast: Sidney Toler [(*Charlie Chan*)], Fortunio Bonanova [(*Luis Caverro*)], Benson Fong [(*Tommy Chan*)], Robert E. Keane [(*Alfred Wyans*)], Willie Best [(*Chattanooga Brown*)], Carol Hughes [(*Marguerite Fontan*)], Marjorie Hoschelle [(*Countess Irena*)], Barton Yarborough [(*Joseph Bradish*)], George Meeker [(*Edmund Slade*)], Don Costello [(*Charles Masack*)], Charles Trowbridge [(*Prentiss*)], Mildred Boyd [(*Josephine*)], Jean Wong [(*Iris Ling*)], Donald Dexter Taylor [(*Dorn*)], [Lucio Villegas (*Chemist*)], Toni Raimondo [(*Woman in powder room*)], Richard Lopez [(*Bellboy*)], Augie Gomez [(*Cab driver*)].
　　Detective, Comedy-drama. [*Print viewed*]. In Mexico City, when an attempt is made to steal the papers of the mysterious Alfred Wyans, his secretary, Dorn, who is working undercover with the United States government, begs Mexican police inspector Luis Caverro to send for Charlie Chan. The next day, Dorn is shot during a luncheon party at Wyans' house, but before he dies, he manages to type a few cryptic letters on his typewriter. After Chan, an old friend of Luis', arrives, accompanied by his third son Tommy and his assistant, Chattanooga Brown, Luis tells him that no gun was found at the scene of the

murder and that, although the guests only heard one shot, two bullet holes were discovered. To Luis, Chan explains that Wyans' papers reveal the discovery of a new element that could be used in a bomb many times more powerful than the atomic bomb. Chan suspects one of the party guests, who include Marguerite Fontan, with whom Luis is in love; Edmund Slade, a former gunrunner; Joseph Bradish, an international smuggler; the Countess Irena, a singer; and Charles Masack, a Nazi propagandist. After he questions the guests, Chan accompanies Luis to the police lab and learns that the bullet that killed Dorn has no firing marks, indicating that it was not fired from a gun. Wyans complains to the police that his typewriter has been stolen, and Chan warns him to protect his papers. Later, Chan discloses that Marguerite has connections in Czechoslovakia, where the papers were stolen from the Allies by Wyans. While all the suspects are at dinner, Chan and Luis search Wyans' baggage, but are interrupted by the others, who all have the same idea. After the suspects leave, Chan and Luis discover the missing typewriter. Then Wyans tells them that he knows how Dorn was killed, but before he can reveal the answer, he is shot in the same manner as Dorn. At the nightclub where Irena sings, Chan reveals that she is not nobility, but is married to Charles Masack, who spies for several countries. Irena starts to reveal the secret, but she too is killed. After an attempt is made on Chan's life in a similar manner, Chan tries to discover why a bottle of indelible Chinese Red ink was found on Dorn's desk. Luis locates Chinese artist Iris Ling, who visited Wyans' hotel before Dorn's death. Iris tells Chan that she sold Wyans the ink to use on his "bandarillas." Chan surmises that the "bandarillas" were actually his typewriter ribbons. They examine the ribbon that Dorn removed from the typewriter before he was killed and discover on it the secret information written in indelible ink. Chan clears Marguerite from suspicion when he discloses that her uncle had discovered the secret element. He then explains that Bradish committed the murders to acquire the information, using a remote control device disguised as a thermostat that exploded the bullet that he had earlier slipped into his victims' pockets or purses. *Chinese Americans. Detectives. Mexico City (Mexico). Murder. Police. Secret formulas. Typewriters. African Americans. Artists. Bombs. Fathers and sons. Forensics. Nazis. Propaganda. Secretaries. Singers. Smuggling. Spies. Undercover agents.*

Note: The film's working title was *Charlie Chan in Mexico.* The title card reads "Charlie Chan in *The Red Dragon.*" For more information on the Charlie Chan series, consult the Series Index and see the entry above for *Charlie Chan Carries On.*

Box 29 Dec 1945. *DV* 20 Feb 1946, p. 3. *FD* 18 Dec 1945, p. 10. *HR* 7 Sep 1945, p. 16. *HR* 21 Sep 1945, p. 8. *HR* 14 Dec 1945, p. 6. *MPHPD* 22 Dec 1945, p. 2765. *Var* 2 Jan 1946, p. 16.

RED HEADED SAVAGE see **CALL HER SAVAGE**

THE RED HORNET see **THE CHINESE RING**

RED LOVE (Native Americans, Dakota)
Lowell Film Productions. *Dist* Davis Distributing Division. May 1925 [©Davis Distributing Division, Inc.; 4 Dec 1925; LP22076]. Si; b&w. 6 reels, 6,300 ft.
Dir Edgar Lewis. *Story* L. Case Russell.
Cast: John Lowell (*Thunder Cloud*), Evangeline Russell (*Starlight*), F. Serrano Keating (*James Logan, Little Antelope*), William Calhoun (*Sheriff La Verne*), Ann Brody (*Mrs. La Verne*), William Cavanaugh (*Dr. George Lester*), Wallace Jones (*Bill Mosher*), Charles W. Kinney (*Sam Gibbons*), Frank Montgomery (*Two Crows*), Dexter McReynolds (*Scar-Face*), "Chick" Chandler (*Tom Livingston*).
Western. Thunder Cloud, a Sioux and a graduate of Carlisle, becomes an outcast when he believes he has slain the villainous Bill Mosher, a white man. He steals horses and cattle but always leaves money or a promissory note for what he takes. He falls in love with Starlight, the half-breed daughter of Sheriff La Verne, and eventually abducts her during the Indian Fair and takes her to his hideout. They are followed by Little Antelope, also in love with Starlight. The adopted son of white parents, he is now a member of the Indian Police. Thunder Cloud recognizes Little Antelope as his younger brother, but nevertheless is arrested. At the trial, it is revealed that Mosher was not slain and that the allegation was only a plot against Thunder Cloud. Starlight gives up her job as teacher to marry Thunder Cloud. *Brothers. Carlisle (PA). United States Indian School. Dakota*

Indians. Fairs. Indians of North America–Mixed blood. Police. Schoolteachers.
FD 12 Jul 1925. *MPW* 23 May 1925.

THE RED MENACE (Italian Americans, Jewish Americans, African Americans)
Republic Pictures Corp. *Dist* Republic Pictures Corp. 1 Aug **1949**; World premiere in Los Angeles: week of 9 Jun 1949; New York opening: 26 Jun 1949; Prod: Mar 1949 [©Republic Pictures Corp.; 1 Aug 1949; LP2448]. Sd (RCA Sound System); b&w. 7,904 ft. 81 or 87 min. Passed by the National Board of Review. PCA cert no. 13766.
Exec prod Herbert J. Yates. *Dir* R. G. Springsteen. [*Asst dir* Art Vitarelli]. *Scr* Albert DeMond. *Story* Albert DeMond. *Scr* Gerald Geraghty. *Dir of photog* John MacBurnie. [*Cam op* Joe Novak]. [*Stills* Ira Hoke]. *Spec eff* Howard Lydecker and Theodore Lydecker. *Optical eff* Consolidated Film Industries. *Art dir* Frank Arrigo. *Film ed* Harry Keller. *Set dec* John McCarthy, Jr. and James Redd. *Cost supv* Adele Palmer. *Mus* Nathan Scott. *Sd* T. C. Carman. *Makeup supv* Bob Mark. [*Makeup* Howard Smit]. [*Hair* Lyn Burke]. [*Grip* C. B. Lawrence]. [*Gaffer* Wilbur Kinnett]. [*Scr supv* Joan Eremin].
Cast: Robert Rockwell (*Bill Jones*), Hanne Axman (*Nina Petrovka*), Betty Lou Gerson (*Yvonne Kraus [previously known as Greta Bloch]*), Barbra Fuller (*Mollie O'Flaherty*), Shepard Menken (*Henry Solomon*), Lester Luther (*Earl Partridge*), William J. Lally (*Jack Tyler*), Norman Budd (*Reachi*), Leo Cleary [(*Father O'Leary*)], William Martel [(*Riggs*)], Duke Williams [(*Sam Wright*)], Robert Purcell [(*Sheriff*)], Gregg Martell [(*Schultz*)], Kay Riehl [(*Mrs. O'Flaherty*)], James Harrington [(*Martin Vejac*)], Napoleon Simpson [(*Tom Wright*)], Royal Raymond [(*Benson*)], Jimmie Hawkins [(*Boy*)], Lloyd G. Davies Member of City Council, Los Angeles, California (*Narrator/Inspector O'Toole*), [Marshall Bradford (*Mr. Chandler*)], [John Pimley (*Riley*)], [Jim Hayward (*Carnival man*)], [George Taylor (*Gas station owner*)], [Marilyn Criss Kraft (*Girl in classroom*)], [Bill Free, Gail Bonney (*People in real estate office*)], [Theodore T. Sackett, Ralph Loretz, Joe Wallace (*People in classroom*)], [Arthur Millan (*Policeman*)], [William Hitch (*Officer*)], [Oscar Weidhaas, Mary DeGolyer (*Proprietors*)], [Bernie Marcus (*Office manager*)], [Jean Leighton], [Harry Scher], [Joe Duval], [Bill Hudson].
Drama. [*Print viewed*]. While driving through Arizona, Bill Jones and Nina Petrovka speak fearfully of the people they left behind in California. They then think back to their escape: After returning from the war, GI Bill Jones and his fiancée try to buy a house, but are cheated out of their savings by an unlicensed real estate broker. Bill complains to officials at the Veteran's Service Center, but when they ignore him, he leaves. A man named Jack Tyler, who has overheard Bill's complaint, follows him and offers to buy him a drink. At a local bar, Bill meets Jack's friends, Yvonne Kraus, Irish-American Mollie O'Flaherty, and a Jewish-American poet named Henry Solomon, and receives words of sympathy when he explains that his fiancée left him after they were cheated. Later, Jack visits his friend, black writer Sam Wright at a newspaper office headed by Communist party leader Earl Partridge, where a reporter has been fired for speaking about the Communist party. Knowing that the reporter will be deported, and thus become a martyr, the party informs the Immigration and Naturalization Service about his Communist activities. Later, while speaking to Bill, Mollie praises the party for its efforts to help Jews and Negroes. The next day, Jack attends a violent protest meeting for disgruntled GIs at the corrupt Hillside Realty Co., accompanied by lovely Russian party leader, Nina Petrovka. When party members incite a riot, Bill and Nina flee to an amusement park across the street. While riding the Ferris wheel, Nina explains that she teaches Marxism at the party's headquarters. Some time later, after an Italian-American student named Reachi questions Yvonne's statements, she calls him a "Mussolini-spawned dago," and he is beaten up and humiliated. When party members kill him, Nina begins to question her role in the party. She decides to phone Earl to say that she is ill and will be unable to attend that evening's meeting. Later, when Yvonne sees Bill and Nina leave together, she reports to Partridge. At the same time, parish priest Father O'Leary, who is aware of Mollie's communist involvement, visits the young woman to praise the United States, the world's "melting pot." At a party meeting, Henry reads a poem he has written suggesting that rather than being completely original in his theories, Marx actually built upon the ideas of other great thinkers. The party leaders are distressed by Henry's statements, and when he

refuses to retract them, they force him out of the party. Henry criticizes party officials, who claim to fight racial discrimination, while repeatedly reminding other members of their ethnicity. Even after he has left the party, Henry is repeatedly fired from low paying jobs because the party keeps telling his employers about his Communist activities. Some time later, at the newspaper office, Henry gives Sam a letter to deliver to Mollie in the event of his death. Later, when he tries to stop Partridge from disciplining Mollie for speaking with him, Henry jumps to his death from his high-rise office window. After Sam learns about this, he delivers the note, which begs Mollie to return to church and her mother, and she does. Later, Bill, who has already told Nina that he disagrees with party methods, tells her that they are issuing a card to him the following day, and they decide to escape together. Meanwhile, officers from the Immigration and Naturalization Service interrogate Yvonne until she admits that she is actually a dissident named Greta Bloch, who took Yvonne's place after she was murdered by party officials. Yvonne then becomes hysterical and is taken away. Later, Sam receives a visit from his father, who tells him that their church deacon says that more slaves exist in Communist countries than anyplace else and urges him to come home. Before leaving with his father, Sam writes a brief epitaph praising Henry as a hero. When an official reads his words later, he curses the "African ingrate." Believing that the party is trying to capture them, Bill and Nina flee by car, and after many hours on the road, decide to stop at a police station in Texas. They explain their predicament to the sheriff, who calmly reminds them that they live in a free country and have no reason to run. On their way out, Bill and Nina meet a little boy, who tells them that townsfolk have nicknamed the kindly sheriff "Uncle Sam." *Communism. Political corruption. Veterans. Amusement parks. Arizona. Bars. Churches. Deportation. Eavesdropping. Engagements. Escapes. Forgers and forgery. Fraud. Gas stations. Meetings. Mothers and daughters. Murder. Newspapers. Poets. Police. Prayer. Priests. Real estate agents. Reporters. Riots. Russians. Sexual harassment. Sheriffs. Teachers. Texas.*

Note: The film's working title was *Fathoms Deep*. According to a *NYT* news item dated 6 May 1949, Republic chose this title to disguise the nature of the film's subject matter. The item added that "the producer of the picture will never be officially identified...because his family is vulnerable to 'reprisals.'" While Republic president Herbert J. Yates is credited onscreen as executive producer, no producer credit is listed. *The Red Menace* was originally planned by Irving Allen and James S. Burkett as an independent production, according to a notation in the film's file in the MPAA/PCA Collection at the AMPAS Library. A *LAT* item claimed that "fully 500 persons were interviewed for the nine leading parts in the film and its 10 supporting players." Republic purposely chose unknowns for the cast, according to *Var*, and many cast members made their screen debuts in the picture. According to a *MPH* article, the picture was filmed on a closed set, and when word about the story's content was leaked to the press, the communist paper *People's World* issued a scathing attack against the film, quoting verbatim from its script. In a 15 May 1949 *NYT* article, writer Albert DeMond was quoted as saying, "There are Communists working at the studio, I know....That's how they got the scenario."

A *HR* news item noted that to advertise the picture, Republic Studios launched its most extensive promotional campaign to date, calling it "the most impressive exploitation campaign in...the history of the motion picture business." An unidentified, undated news item found in the AMPAS Library stated that because of "disappointing grosses," Republic withdrew *The Red Menace* from release several months after its opening, and planned to re-edit it significantly and re-issue it under the title *Underground Spy*. Ads for the film, dated Nov 1953, indicate that the picture was, in fact, re-released as *Underground Spy*. According to a 28 May 1949 *MPH* news item, after the film's release, Yates was given a special commendation by the Senate Fact-Finding Committee on Un-American Activities, which stated "in recognition of the great contribution that has been made by Republic Studios in the fight against those forces who seek to deprive the American people of the freedoms we all cherish so dearly, the Senate Committee does commend Republic Studios and those persons who have so courageously assisted in this production." Shortly after this film's release, RKO released its own anti-Communist film, *The Woman on Pier 13*, which like *The Red Menace*, was a box-office flop.

Arts Jul 1949 *Box* 4 Jun 1949. *DV* 25 May 1949, p. 3. *FD* 26 May 1949, p. 6. *HR* 4 Mar 1949, p. 13. *HR* 18 Mar 1949, p. 11. *HR* 25 May 1949, p. 3. *LAT* 6 May 1949. *MPD* 7 Jun 1949. *MPH* 28 May 1949. *MPHPD* 4 Jun 1949, p. 4634. *NYT* 15 May 1949. *NYT* 27 Jun 1949, p. 18. *Var* 25 May 1949, p. 8.

THE RED RAIDERS (Native Americans, Dakota)

Charles R. Rogers Productions, Inc. *Dist* First National Pictures, Inc. 4 Sep 1927 [©First National Pictures, Inc.; 6 Sep 1927; LP24349]. Si; b&w. 7 reels, 6,214 or 7,050 ft.

Pres Charles R. Rogers. *Supv* Harry J. Brown. *Dir* Albert Rogell. *Story and scen* Marion Jackson. *Titles* Don Ryan. *Photog* Ross Fisher.

Cast: Ken Maynard (*Lieut. John Scott*), Ann Drew (*Jane Logan*), Paul Hurst (*Sergeant Murphy*), J. P. McGowan (*Captain Ortwell*),

Chief Yowlache (*Scar Face Charlie*), Harry Shutan (*Private Izzy*), Tom Day (*Earl Logan*), Hal Salter (*Spike Dargan*).

Western. Lieut. John Scott, an adventurous young United States Army officer, is assigned to a frontier military post in the heart of Sioux territory. Encountering a band of Indians attacking a stagecoach, John thwarts the raid and wins the admiration of Jane Logan, en route to join her brother at a nearby ranch. He establishes himself with his men by subduing an outlaw horse turned over to him as a prank, but he is rebuked by Captain Ortwell when he objects to engaging the services of Scar Face Charlie, a treacherous Indian who is spying at the post. In spite of attempts to declare peace, Charlie incites the Sioux to war. Scott arouses their superstitious dread by disguising himself as a medicine man, but is unsuccessful. The troops are then induced to leave the fort by a message from Charlie. Lieutenant Scott, however, leads the men back to the fort, and the Sioux attack is repulsed. *Dakota Indians. Frontier and pioneer life. United States. Army. Cavalry.*

FD 2 Oct 1927. *MPW* 15 Oct 1927. *Var* 12 Oct 1927, p. 24.

THE RED, RED HEART (Native Americans)

Bluebird Photoplays, Inc. *Dist* Bluebird Photoplays, Inc. 8 Apr **1918** [©Bluebird Photoplays, Inc.; 15 Mar 1918; LP12187]. Si; b&w. 5 reels.

Dir Wilfred Lucas. *Adpt* Bess Meredyth. *Cam* Dal Clawson and Allan Siegler.

Source: Based on the novel *The Heart of the Desert (Kut-le of the Desert)* by Honore McCue Willsie Morrow (New York, 1913).

Cast: Monroe Salisbury (*Kut-le*), Ruth Clifford (*Rhoda Tuttle*), Val Paul (*Jack Newman*), Gretchen Lederer (*Katherine Newman*), Allan Sears (*John DeWitt*), Monte Blue (*Billy Porter*), Princess Neola (*Molly*).

Western. Concerned about the failing health of Rhoda Tuttle, his fiancée, John DeWitt takes her to the lavish Arizona home of his friends, Jack and Katherine Newman. Although the Newmans try to cheer Rhoda, who has lost her parents in a train wreck, she remains listless and melancholy. While walking in the desert, Rhoda is bitten by a tarantula but is saved by Kut-le, a Yale-educated Indian employed as a superintendent on Newman's irrigation project. Because of his strong belief in the curative effects of life in the desert, Kut-le kidnaps Rhoda and forces her to live in a manner far removed from the comforts and confinements of civilization. Outraged, John and Kut-le's enemy, Billy Porter, search for Rhoda, but after they finally defeat the Indian in a fierce fight, she declares that she prefers to remain with the man who helped her to regain the joy of living. *Abduction. Arizona. Deserts. Indians of North America. Miscegenation. Nursing back to health. Convalescence. Fights. Irrigation. Tarantulas.*

Note: The film's working title was *The Heart of the Desert*.

ETR 26 Jan 1918, p. 663. *ETR* 6 Apr 1918, p. 1467. *MPN* 9 Mar 1918, p. 1453. *MPN* 13 Apr 1918, p. 2206, 2257. *MPW* 13 Apr 1918, p. 281, 285-86. *NYDM* 6 Apr 1918, p. 24. *Var* 29 Mar 1918, p. 46. *Wid's* 18 Apr 1918, p. 1086.

THE RED RIDER (Native Americans)

Universal Pictures Corp.; Blue Streak Western. 2 Aug **1925** [©Universal Pictures Corp.; 3 Jul 1925; LP21633]. Si; b&w. 5 reels.

Dir Clifford S. Smith. *Story* Isadore Bernstein. *Photog* Harry Neumann. *Addl photog* Robert Kurrle.

Cast: Jack Hoxie (*White Elk*), Mary McAllister (*Lucille Cavanagh*), Jack Pratt (*Black Panther*), Natalie Warfield (*Natauka*), Marin Sais (*Silver Waters*), William McCall (*John Cavanagh*), Francis Ford (*Brown Bear*), George Connors (*Tom Fleming*), Frank Lanning (*Medicine Man*), Clark Comstock, Duke R. Lee, Chief Big Tree (*Indian chiefs*), William Welsh (*Ben Hanfer*), Virginia True Boardman (*Polly Fleming*).

Western. White Elk, a light-skinned Indian chief, incurs the enmity of Chief Black Panther when he prevents him from looting a westbound wagon train. White Elk, who is betrothed to an Indian princess, is torn from her by his love for a white girl from the East. When he is tricked into signing away the lands of his tribe, White Elk is condemned to be burned alive by Black Panther. He is saved from certain death by a cloudburst and makes his escape. He is later told that he is really a white man, who as a child was saved from death and brought up as an Indian. The white girl with whom he has fallen in love is captured by the Indians and strapped in a canoe that is set adrift above a waterfall. White Elk saves the girl, and the Indian princess takes her place in the canoe, offering herself as a sacrifice. White Elk discovers that his father is the old scout who leads the

wagon train, and he and the white girl make plans to be united. *Human sacrifice. Indians of North America. Land claims. Scouts (Frontier). Treaties. Wagon trains. Waterfalls.*

Note: Known also as *The Open Trail.*
FD 3 May 1925.

RED RIVER (Native Americans, Apache, Comanche, Latino)
Monterey Productions. *Dist* United Artists Corp. 17 Sep **1948**; World premiere: 26 Aug 1948; Prod: 5 Sep—late Dec 1946 at Samuel Goldwyn Studios; addl scenes began 29 Apr 1947 [©Monterey Productions; 17 Sep 1948; LP1809]. Sd (Western Electric Recording); b&w. 13 reels, 11,363 ft. 126 min. PCA cert no. 12398.

[*Exec prod* Charles K. Feldman]. *Prod* HOWARD HAWKS. *Dir* Howard Hawks. *Co-dir* Arthur Rosson. *Asst dir* William McGarry. *Scr* Borden Chase and Charles Schnee. *Photog* Russell Harlan. *Spec eff* Donald Steward. *Spec photog eff* Allan Thompson. *Art dir* John Datu Arensma. *Film ed* Christian Nyby. *Mus comp and dir* Dimitri Tiomkin. *Sd* Richard DeWeese. *Mus rec* Vinton Vernon. *Makeup* Lee Greenway. *Prod mgr* Norman Cook. [*Scr clerk* Bobby Sierkes]. [*Grip* Thomas Thompson]. [*Stunt double for John Wayne* Riley R. Waters].

Song(s): "Settle Down," words and music by Dimitri Tiomkin.

Source: Based on the serial novel *The Chisholm Trail* by Borden Chase in *The Saturday Evening Post* (7 Dec 1946—11 Jan 1947).

Cast: John Wayne [(*Thomas Dunson*)], Montgomery Clift [(*Matthew Garth*)], Joanne Dru [(*Tess Millay*)], Walter Brennan [(*Groot Nadine*)], Colleen Gray [(*Fen*)], Harry Carey, Sr. [(*Melville*)], John Ireland [(*Cherry Valance*)], Noah Beery, Jr. [(*Buster Magee*)], Harry Carey, Jr. [(*Dan Latimer*)], Chief Yowlachie [(*Quo*)], Paul Fix [(*Teeler Yacey*)], Hank Worden [(*Sims*)], Mickey Kuhn [(*Garth as a boy*)], Ray Hyke [(*Walt Jurgens*)], Hal Taliaferro [(*Old leather*)], [Paul Fierro (*Fernandez*)], [Bill Self (*Wounded cowboy*)], [Lane Chandler (*Meeker*)], [Glenn Strange (*Naylor*)], [Ivan Parry (*Bunk Kenneally*)], [Shelley Winters (*Girl with wagon train*)], [Dan White (*Laredo*)], [Tom Tyler].

Western. [*Print viewed*]. In 1851, Thomas Dunson and his friend, Groot Nadine, leave St. Louis and join a wagon train headed for California. When they reach the northern border of Texas, they decide to remain there and establish a cattle ranch. Fen, Tom's sweetheart, wants to stay with him, but he tells her that he will send for her later and gives her his mother's bracelet. Soon after Tom and Groot take their wagon and bull and head south to the Red River, they look back and see that the wagon train has been attacked and burned by Comanche Indians. That night, several Indians attack Tom and Groot's camp, and Tom is horrified to discover the bracelet he gave to Fen on the wrist of an Indian he killed in the struggle. The next day as Tom and Groot break camp, a young boy, Matthew Garth, who has escaped the wagon train massacre, wanders toward them with his cow. Tom and Groot take the dazed boy with them, cross the Red River and head farther south until, near the Rio Grande, Tom finds an area he likes. The land legally belongs, by land grant, to a Mexican, but after Tom kills one of the owner's gunmen and drives off another, he claims it for himself. Tom's bull and Matt's cow then become the beginning of a great herd sporting the Red River-D brand. Fifteen years later, the ranch boasts thousands of cattle, but Tom faces ruin unless he can move them from the impoverished, post-Civil War market. He decides to take ten thousand head a thousand miles to Missouri, where the railroads serve the North and East, and Matt, now grown to manhood and like a son to Tom, helps to plan the drive. Tom also agrees to take several head belonging to a neighboring rancher, and one of the neighbor's ranch hands, Cherry Valance, joins the drive. Both Cherry and Matt are expert gunmen and enjoy a friendly, if intense, rivalry. After a few days on the trail, the men reach the Brazos. Hills and rocks impede their progress and the cowboys become tired and unhappy. One night, when the cattle are restless, cowboy Bunk Kenneally, takes some sugar from Groot's chuckwagon and accidentally knocks over pots and pans, spooking the cattle and causing a stampede. Cowboy Dan Latimer is killed in the stampede, and although Bunk admits his mistake, he refuses to allow Tom to whip him and draws his gun. However, Matt shoots Bunk before he can shoot Tom. Forty days into the drive, the men are forced to endure heavy rains and short rations, as a grub wagon was lost in the stampede. Tom becomes very demanding and faces dissension among the cowboys. Some days later, a wounded wrangler from another drive rides into camp and explains that his group was attacked by a large gang of outlaws after they crossed the Red River. He also tells

them about a trail blazed by an Indian trader, Jesse Chisholm, to a railroad terminus in Abilene, Kansas. When three of Tom's men state that they should be heading to Abilene instead of Missouri and threaten to quit, Tom kills them. More men desert with supplies and Tom sends Cherry after them. When the herd reaches the Red River, Tom decides to cross immediately despite the men's exhaustion. That night, Groot suggests to Tom, who has not been sleeping and has started drinking, that he tell the men that they did well, but he refuses. The next day, when Cherry returns with two of the deserters, Tom says he is going to hang them but Matt intervenes. As Tom goes to draw his gun on Matt, Cherry shoots him in the hand. Matt then assumes command of the drive, and they head to Abilene, leaving Tom behind. Tom swears that one day he will catch up with Matt and kill him. On the drive, Matt and the others encounter a wagon train being attacked by Apache Indians whom they help to drive off. Matt meets Tess Millay, one of the wagon train's settlers, and before he resumes the drive, they have fallen in love. Tom and some new men he has hired to pursue the train catch up with it, and when Tess tells Tom that she had wanted to go with Matt, Tom remembers leaving Fen. Tess then tries to persuade Tom not to kill his "son," and Tom offers her half of everything he owns if she will bear him a son. Tess agrees on condition he abandons his mission to kill Matt, but Tom declines. On 14 Aug 1865, Matt's team reaches Abilene and becomes the first cattle drive to cross over the Chisholm Trail. They receive a great welcome from the townspeople, and Melville, a representative of an Illinois trading company, makes Matt a very good offer for the herd and gives him a check payable to Tom. That night, Matt finds Tess waiting for him at his hotel. She warns him that Tom will be coming into town just after dawn to kill him. The next day, as Matt prepares to face Tom, Cherry challenges Tom, who shoots him but is injured by his return fire. Matt refuses to draw his gun against Tom, but when Tom attacks him with his fists, Matt fights back. Their brawl is interrupted by Tess, who fires a gun and angrily reminds them that they both love each other. After Tom tells Matt that he should marry Tess, he and Matt are finally reconciled. Tom then tells Matt that, as he had promised years before, he will create a new branding iron to include Matt's name, as he has earned it. *Cattle drives. Chisholm Trail. Rivalry. Texas. Vocational obsession. Abilene (KS). Apache Indians. Bracelets. Branding. Comanche Indians. Cooks. Cowboys. Fistfights. Friendship. Grief. Gunfights. Land claims. Mexicans. Obsession. Railroads. Ranches. Rivers. Romance. Stampedes. United States–History–Reconstruction, 1865-1898. Wagon trains.*

Note: The summary was based on a viewing of a modern "Restored Director's Cut" of the film. In a letter contained in the AMPAS Library file on the film, the attorney for Monterey Productions stated that the company bought the original story from Borden Chase, and after certain changes had been made, the story was published in *The Saturday Evening Post*. Exterior photography was done around Elgin, AZ, south of Tucson, and interiors were filmed on the Samuel Goldwyn lot. *Red River* was the first film Montgomery Clift made, although his second, *The Search*, was released first. According to an interview with Howard Hawks in a modern source, Joanne Dru was a last-minute substitute for Margaret Sheridan, who had to be replaced when she was discovered to be pregnant. A 1 Feb 1948 *NYT* news item noted that the film's original budget was $1,800,000 and that an organization of private capitalists known as Motion Picture Investors provided a bond guaranteeing the film's completion at an eventual cost of $2,700,000. In Dec 1948, *DV* reported that the film's final cost was $4,100,000 and that the domestic gross was "being figured all the way from $4,000,000 to $5,500,000," with an additional $2,000,000 in foreign revenues.

Immediately prior to the film's premiere on 26 Aug 1948 in theaters in Texas, Oklahoma and Kansas, millionaire producer Howard Hughes filed an injunction against the film's openings in Texas, contending that the climactic gunfight sequence between "Tom" and "Matt" paralleled that in Hughes's *The Outlaw*, a production on which Hawks had briefly worked in 1940. To placate Hughes, Hawks cut approximately 28 seconds from the scene. A *DV* news item reported that Consolidated and Pathé laboratories worked through the weekend prior to the film's premiere to produce prints of the revised sequence and that editor Mel Thorsen was sent to film exchanges in Dallas, Kansas City and New York to supervise the changes. For more information on the controversy, see entry above for *The Outlaw*.

The "Director's Cut" of *Red River*, which was issued in 1987, is approximately seven minutes longer than the original release print and reinstates the footage excised due to the Hughes injunction. The 1948 version includes a spoken narration by Walter Brennan's "Groot Nadine" character, whereas the later version eliminates the narration and uses handwritten text from the *Early Tales of Texas* "diary." Other minor differences include additional shots before the stampede and the saving of the wagon train sequences, as well as a brief conversation between "Matt" and "Melville" as the cattle enter Abilene.

Modern sources add Pierce Lyden, Lee Phelps, George Lloyd, John Merton and

Richard Farnsworth to the cast. A radio adaptation of the film, starring Wayne and Dru, was broadcast on *Lux Radio Theatre* on 7 Mar 1949. *Red River* received Oscar nominations in the Motion Picture Story and Film Editing categories. On 10 Apr 1988, the CBS network broadcast a remake of Chase's story, starring James Arness and Bruce Boxleitner, and directed by Richard Michaels.

Box 17 Jul 1948. *DV* 12 Jul 1948, p. 3, 6. *DV* 23 Aug 1948. *DV* 7 Dec 1948. *FD* 14 Jul 1948, p. 4. *HR* 5 Sep 1946, p. 1. *HR* 6 Nov 1946, p. 3. *HR* 29 Apr 1947, p. 10. *HR* 12 Jul 1948, p. 3. *HR* 16 Aug 1948. *HR* 18 Oct 1948, p. 7. *LAT* 20 Aug 1948. *MPHPD* 17 Jul 1948, p. 4241. *NYT* 1 Feb 1948. *NYT* 1 Oct 1948, p. 31. *Var* 14 Jul 1948, p. 12. *Var* 21 Oct 1987.

RED SNOW (Native Americans, Native Alaskans)

All American Film Corp. *Dist* Columbia Pictures Corp. Jul **1952**; Los Angeles opening: 21 Jun 1952. *Prod:* early Nov 1950—late Jan 1951 at the Hal Roach Studios [©Columbia Pictures Corp.; 25 Feb 1952; LP1506]. Sd (Western Electric Recording); b&w. 6,711 ft. 74-75 min. PCA cert no. 15235.

Prod Boris L. Petroff. *Assoc prod* G. William Perkins. *Dir* Boris L. Petroff and Harry S. Franklin. *Alaskan unit dir* Ewing Scott. *Asst dir* Leonard J. Shapiro. *Dial dir* Lawrence Moore. *Scr* Tom Hubbard and Orville Hampton. *Based on a story by* Robert Peters. *Dir of photog* Paul Ivano. *Art dir* Daniel Hall. *Ed* Merrill White. *Assoc ed* Albert Shaff. *Mus dir* Michael Terr. *Mus score* Alex Alexander and June Starr. *Sd ed* Bruce Schoengarth. *Sd* Earl J. Snyder. *Makeup* Harry Thomas. *Tech dir* Bernard Stanley.

Cast: Guy Madison (*Lieut. Johnson*), Ray Mala (*Sgt. Koovuk*), Carole Mathews (*Lieut. Jane*), Gloria Saunders (*Alak*), Robert Peyton (*Major Bennett*), John Bryant (*Alex*), Richard Vath (*Elia*), Phillip Ahn (*Tuglu*), Tony Benroy (*Cpl. Savick*), Gordon Barnes (*Capt. MacLoflin*), John Bleifer (*Commissar Volgan*), Gene Roth (*Major Duboff*), Muriel Maddox (*Ruth*), Robert Bice (*Chief Nanu*), Renny McEvoy (*Sgt. Koops*), Bert Arnold (*Riggs*), Richard Emory (*Stone*), Richard Pinner (*Long*), George Pembroke (*Major Slavin*), Robert Carson (*General*), William Fletcher (*Krasnick*), Richard Barron (*Russian officer*), William Shaw (*Narr*).

Military, Drama. [*Print viewed*]. In the icy wilderness of northern Alaska, soldiers stationed at a U.S. Air Force base and local Eskimos see mysterious lights flashing in the sky over Siberia, only a few miles away. Soon after, Major Bennett arrives from Washington to investigate the government's suspicion that the Russians are testing a new bomb. Three Eskimo soldiers, including Sgt. Koovuk, are assigned to return to their villages on the Bering Strait in order to report back any unusual activities, while Lt. Johnson, a pilot, is ordered to tail an unmarked black plane sighted near the border. That night, strange lights shoot into the sky from the Alaskan side of the border and the troops begin to panic. However, Bennett calms them with the news that the U.S. government is testing its own nuclear weapons in the area. After a long journey by dogsled, Koovuk reaches his village on Little Diomedes Island and is warmly greeted by Chief Nanu, who introduces him to a new villager named Tuglu. Tuglu, a Siberian Eskimo from Big Diomedes Island, claims to have escaped the Russians, but when he begins to ask Koovuk questions about his work in the Air Force, Koovuk suspects he is spying for the Soviet Union. Koovuk then goes off to find his sweetheart Alak and asks her to be his wife. Later, Koovuk learns that the tribe is on the verge of starvation. Hunting parties have ventured over the border into Siberia in their desperate search for game, but only Tuglu has returned. After praying to the God of the Hunt, Koovuk forms a hunting party and crosses into Siberia. The Russian pilots flying the mysterious black plane are signaled by Tuglu, who lets them know that Koovuk's hunting party has entered Siberia. The Russians then send a coded message to their base command and Russian soldiers prepare to capture Koovuk and his men. Johnson, however, picks up the message on his radio, and the Air Force is able to crack the code in time to warn Koovuk. Safely back in U.S. waters, the hunting party encounters a large school of walrus and brings home enough meat to ensure the tribe's survival. After much feasting and dancing, Alak presents Koovuk with ceremonial wedding pants symbolizing his authority in their union, and the two are pronounced man and wife. That night, an American Eskimo who has escaped captivity in Siberia is brought into the village, and, when everyone is asleep, Tuglu tries to kill him. Tuglu is taken prisoner, but Koovuk decides that the tribe is no longer safe in the area, so preparations are made to travel south to the mainland. In the meantime, the Russians have readied their bomb for its final test, and pilots Alex and Elia are assigned to deploy it in the border zone through which Koovuk's tribe is traveling. Once in the air, Alex reveals to Elia that he has learned that their flight is a suicide mission and therefore he has sabotaged the test so that he can defect to the U.S. with the new weapon technology. However, Elia, a fanatical supporter of the Communist regime, grabs the controls of the plane, causing it to crash. Both men die in the crash, but Koovuk retrieves the intact bomb. As Koovuk's tribe continues its journey, the treacherous ice floes begin to break apart, creating deadly avalanches. Johnson locates the tribe and the Air Force succeeds in rescuing them by helicopter. Back at the base, Koovuk turns the Russian weapon over to the Air Force General and is given a promotion, while Johnson is cited for his bravery in rescuing Koovuk's tribe. *Arctic regions. Native Alaskans. Russians. United States. Air Force. Wilderness areas. Air pilots. Airplanes. Alaska. Avalanches. Bombs. Boundaries. Codes. Communists. Defectors. Dogs. Ice floes. Igloos. Nuclear weapons. Rescues. Rites and ceremonies. Russians. Sabotage. Siberia. Tribal life. Weddings. Wild animals.*

Note: The working title for this film was *S.O.S. Alaska.* Opening credits include a written dedication to the Alaskan Air Rescue Service and to the American Eskimo, "whose skill and courage have long been unheralded." A large portion of *Red Snow* consists of footage shot in Alaska twenty years earlier for the 1932 documentary *Igloo* (see above). *Igloo* was directed by Ewing Scott, who receives a credit as Alaskan unit director on this film. The documentary footage is linked to the contemporary scenes through the character played by Ray Mala, who had a starring role in *Igloo*, appearing under his tribal name of "Chee-ak." Mala, under the name Ray Wise, is also credited with camerawork on *Igloo*. In addition, voice-over narration by William Shaw in the role of "Sgt. Koovuk" serves to connect scenes depicting Eskimo tribal life to the film's Cold War storyline. An unidentified news item dated 28 Jan 1951 reported that producer Boris Petroff was also planning to include footage from his 1949 film *Arctic Fury* (see above) in *Red Snow. Arctic Fury* made liberal use of scenes from *Tundra,* a 1936 Burroughs-Tarzan film (see below). It has not been determined, however, if this additional footage was actually incorporated into *Red Snow.*

News items in *HR* dated 3 Nov 1950 and 9 Sep 1951 billed *Red Snow* as "the first film based on the possibility of a Russian attack upon the United States." Correspondence dated 26 Jan 1951 and contained in the file on this film in the MPAA/PCA Collection at the AMPAS Library indicates that Production Code officials were concerned about a story "involv[ing] the Russian military without naming them" and advised Petroff to seek clearance with the U.S. State Department.

Box 21 Jun 1952. *DV* 20 Jun 1952, p. 3. *Exb* 2 Jul 1952, p. 3321. *FD* 7 Apr 1952, p. 4. *Har* 21 Jun 1952, p. 98. *HR* 3 Nov 1950. *HR* 10 Sep 1951. *HR* 20 Jun 1952, p. 4. *LAT* 23 Jun 1952. *MPD* 20 Jun 1952. *MPH* 21 Jun 1952. *MPHPD* 21 Jun 1952, p. 1418. *Var* 25 Jun 1952, p. 6.

THE RED VIPER (Russian Americans)

Tyrad Pictures, Inc. *Dist* Tyrad Pictures, Inc.; State Rights. 7 Sep **1919** [©Tyrad Pictures, Inc.; 4 Oct 1919; LU14294]. Si; b&w. 6-7 reels.

Prod Jacques Tyrol. *Dir* Jacques Tyrol. *Story and scen* Winifred Dunn. *Cam* Edward Wynard.

Cast: Gareth Hughes (*David Belkov*), Ruth Stonehouse (*Mary Hogan*), Jack Gilbert (*Dick Grant*), Irma Harrison (*Yolanda Kosloff*), R. H. Fitzsimmons (*"Charles Smith"*), Alberta Lee (*Mrs. Hogan*), Alfred Hollingsworth (*Pat Hogan*).

Social, Drama. David Belkov, a newsboy born of foreign parents who live in "New York's crucible," the East Side, admires the late Theodore Roosevelt, but when he sees a poor family being evicted, he joins the Hogan Street anarchist group, of which his father's friends and his sweetheart Yolanda Kosloff, are members. The group plans to assassinate Judge Norton, who earlier condemned one of their comrades to the electric chair. After David witnesses the bravery of twelve-year-old Mary Hogan, who sings patriotic ditties to drown out the soap box orations of the anarchists, he prints leaflets to combat the anarchist views. Mary is killed trying to thwart the anarchists' plot, and David is caught and badly beaten. After government agents, thought to be converts, break up the gang, David arrives just in time to stop Yolanda, who is dancing at a celebration at Norton's home, from dropping a bomb. David is shot by the anarchist leader, but Yolanda, realizing her error, nurses him to health. *Anarchists. Assassination. Courage. New York City–East Side. Patriotism. Poverty. Russian Americans. Eviction. Government agents. Gunshot wounds. Judges. Nursing back to health.*

ETR 6 Sep 1919, p. 1177. *MPN* 6 Sep 1919, p. 2057. *MPW* 6 Sep 1919, pp. 1531-32. *Wid's* 31 Aug 1919, p. 21.

RED WOMAN (1934) *see* BEHOLD MY WIFE!

THE RED WOMAN (Native Americans)
World Film Corp. *Dist* World Film Corp. 12 Feb **1917** [©World Film Corp.; 31 Jan 1917; LU10165]. Si; b&w. 5 reels.

Pres William A. Brady. *Scen* H. R. Durant.

Cast: Gail Kane (*Maria Temosach*), Mahlon Hamilton (*Morton Deal*), Ed F. Roseman (*Sancho*), June Elvidge (*Dora Wendell*), Charlotte Granville (*Her mother*), Gladys Earlcott (*Chica*).

Western. Morton Dean, the spendthrift son of a millionaire mine owner, is asked by his father to develop some properties in New Mexico. Morton refuses to go, using as an excuse his impending marriage to socialite Dora Wendell. This angers his father, who changes his will so that Morton will inherit only a few thousand dollars and deeds to the mine. Upon his father's death, Morton discovers that Dora loves only the money that he was expected to inherit. Spurning her, Morton goes to New Mexico. Meanwhile, Maria Temosach, an Indian maiden, graduates with honors from an Eastern school, but she is not accepted socially. She gladly returns to her home in New Mexico, where she repulses the advances of Sancho, a cattle thief. When Maria shows an interest in Morton, the jealous Sancho wounds him in an attack, but he is rescued by Maria and taken to her cabin. They fall in love, and she destroys the idol she has worshipped, declaring that Morton now will be "her god." One night, Maria walks in her sleep to Morton's bed. When Sancho, with Dora, comes looking for Morton, Maria paints him as the idol and places him on the idol's pedestal. Although Sancho and Dora do not find Morton, when Maria learns from Dora that Morton's father has left another will giving him the entire estate, she convinces him to go back with Dora. Later, Maria becomes pregnant, and Sancho claims that he is the father; however, when the baby is born with blonde hair and white skin, Maria realizes that it is Morton's. Although Dora has tried to win Morton back, he returns to New Mexico to the love of his Indian maiden. *Disillusionment. Gold diggers. Indians of North America. Mine owners. Miscegenation. New Mexico. Wills. Americans in foreign countries. Bandits. Fathers and sons. Millionaires. Pregnancy. Socialites. Spendthrifts.*

Note: This film was also known as *Her God*. *MPN* commented, "*The Red Woman* shatters precedent and ends with a white man and an Indian woman in one another's arms with a priest disappearing over the brow of a hill." *MPW*, in describing the Indian character, stated, "her eastern education must have made radical changes in her nature; she has all the characteristics of a white woman when she returns to New Mexico, and exhibits the grace, mental alertness and volubility of the race."

ETR 10 Feb 1917, p. 704. *Motog* 17 Feb 1917, p. 371. *MPN* 17 Feb 1917, p. 1091-92. *MPW* 17 Feb 1917, p. 1034, 1081. *NYDM* 10 Feb 1917, p. 26. *Wid's* 1 Feb 1917, pp. 71-72.

THE REDEMPTION OF DAVID CORSON (Gypsies)
Famous Players Film Co. *Dist* State Rights. 10 Apr **1914**. Si; b&w. 4 reels.

Pres Daniel Frohman.

Source: Based on the novel *The Redemption of David Corson* by Charles Frederick Goss (New York, 1900).

Cast: William Farnum (*David Corson*), Robert Broderick (*Dr. Parcelsus*), Constance Mollineaux (*Pepeeta, the gypsy girl*), Hal Clarendon (*Andy MacFarlane*), Helen Aubrey (*David's mother*), William Cowper (*Elder Sprague*), Leonard Grover (*Justice of the peace*), William Vaughn (*The gypsy chief*).

Drama. Quaker minister David Corson is so fascinated with the gypsy girl Pepeeta that he leaves his home to join her "owner" Dr. Parcelsus' traveling medicine show. When David discovers that Parcelsus and Pepeeta are married, he bribes a minister to tell her that the ceremony was illegal, and the two lovers run away. Parcelsus follows them and blinds David in a fight, after which he becomes a pathetic drunk. He is helped by Andy MacFarlane, a kindly lumberjack who had once been inspired by David's religious fervor. Eventually Paracelsus dies and David and Pepeeta are able to return home as lawful man and wife. *Clergy. Gypsies. Infatuation. Marriage. Quakers. Rivalry. Blindness. Bribery. Charity. Drunkenness. Elopement. Friendship. Lumberjacks. Medicine shows.*

Motog 2 May 1914, pp. 295-96. *MPW* 25 Apr 1914, p. 518, 538, 582. *NYDM* 18 Mar 1914, p. 32. *NYDM* 1 Apr 1914, p. 38.

REDHEAD FROM MANHATTAN (Latino)
Columbia Pictures Corp. *Dist* Columbia Pictures Corp. 6 May **1943**; Prod: 18 Jan–8 Feb 1943 [©Columbia Pictures Corp.; 30 Apr 1943; LP12013]. Sd (Western Electric Mirrophonic Recording); b&w. 5,795 ft. 63-64 min. PCA cert no. 9196.

Prod Wallace MacDonald. [*Exec prod* Irving Briskin]. *Dir* Lew Landers. [*Asst dir* William O'Connor]. *Scr* Joseph Hoffman. *Story* Rex Taylor. *Dir of photog* Philip Tannura. *Art dir* Lionel Banks. *Assoc* Perry Smith. *Film ed* James Sweeney. *Set dec* George Montgomery. *Gowns* Travilla. *Mus dir* M. W. Stoloff. [*Dance dir* Eddie Prinz]. [*Sd eng* Jack Haynes].

Song(s): "An Ounce of Bounce," "The Fiestigo," "I'm Undecided (Can't Make Up My Mind)" and "Let's Fall in Line," music and lyrics by Walter Samuels and Saul Chaplin.

Cast: Lupe Velez [(*Rita de Silva/ Maria de Silva, also known as Elaine Manners*)], Michael Duane [(*Jimmy Randall*)], Tim Ryan [(*Mike Glendon*)], Gerald Mohr [(*Chick Andrews*)], Lillian Yarbo [(*Polly*)], Arthur Loft [(*Sig Hammersmith*)], Lewis Wilson [(*Paul*)], Douglas Leavitt [(*Joe*)], Clancy Cooper [(*Policeman*)], Douglass Drake [(*Marty Britt*)], [Ben Carter (*Black boy*)], [Al Herman (*Bartender*)], [Shirley Patterson, Alma Carroll (*Telephone operators*)], [Ben Gerien, Peter Dunne (*Henchmen*)], [Jack Gardner (*Booker*)], [Stanley Brown (*Clarinet player*)], [Lynton Brent (*Musician*)], [Roger Gray, Frank Richards, Richard Talmadge (*Fishermen*)], [Dewey Robinson (*Truck driver*)], [Pat O'Malley (*Policeman*)], [Adele Mara (*Check girl*)], [Larry Parks (*Flirt*)], [Robert Hill (*Counterman*)], [Eddie Kane (*Orchestra leader*)], [Edythe Elliott (*Nurse*)], [Jerry Franks], [Margaret Savage], [Gertrude Messinger], [John Estes], [Mickey Rentschler], [Donald Kerr].

Comedy. [*Print viewed*]. When their ship is torpedoed off the Atlantic coast, American saxophone player Jimmy Randall and Latin American stowaway Rita de Silva, the only two survivors, take refuge on a small raft, in the hopes that they will be rescued and taken to New York. The raft eventually makes landfall on a remote American beach, where Rita and Jimmy find a cache of thousand-dollar bills and dynamite belonging to Nazi saboteurs. Soon afterward, some local fishermen discover Rita and Jimmy holding a Nazi flag, and accuse them of being saboteurs. A struggle ensues between the shipwrecked couple and the fisherman, but Rita manages to subdue the fishermen by hitting them with Jimmy's saxophone. Though they manage to escape on the back of truck, Rita and Jimmy soon realize that they will be the subjects of a nationwide manhunt when the fishermen report their discovery to the police. Fearing that they will arouse unwanted suspicion if they use any of the thousand-dollar bills, Jimmy and Rita decide to entertain at a roadhouse to make enough money to buy bus tickets to New York. When Jimmy and Rita arrive in New York, Rita makes an unsuccessful attempt to contact her cousin, Maria de Silva, whom she hoped would help them sort out their troubles. In the bus station, Jimmy is provoked into a fistfight with a stranger, after which he and Rita flee in haste. As they run out of the station, Jimmy suggests that they split up and meet later. Rita eventually finds Maria, her look-alike, performing on Broadway under the name "Elaine Manners." Maria, who is married to Paul, an F.B.I. agent, is pregnant, and has kept her marriage a secret from tough nightclub owner Chick Andrews, who wants to marry her himself. Things look bad for both Maria and Rita until Mike Glendon, Maria's manager, suggests that Rita replace and impersonate Maria while Maria leaves the show to have her baby. As a result, Rita misses her rendezvous with Jimmy, and believes she will never see him again. One day, Jimmy, substituting for a member of the orchestra in Rita's show, sees Rita on stage, but when he tries to get her attention, he is thrown out of the theater. After the show, Chick, unaware that Rita is impersonating Maria, demands that Rita respond to his marriage proposal. When Rita rejects Chick and tells him that she loves Jimmy, Chick and a few of his men find Jimmy and rough him up. Chaos ensues when Chick and Jimmy go to Maria's apartment and discover Rita, Maria, an infant child, and Paul. Rita explains everything to Chick and Jimmy, after which Jimmy tells her that they are no longer being pursued. Rita then consents to marry Jimmy, and looks forward to becoming an American citizen. *Cousins. Fugitives. Impersonation and imposture. Latin Americans. Romance. Singers. African Americans. Assimilation (Sociology). Doubles. Dynamite. Explosions. False accusations. Fishermen. Marriage–Secret. Musicians. New York City–Broadway. Nightclubs. Police. Pregnancy. Proposals (Marital). Racial impersonation. Rafts. Roadhouses. Saxophones. Shipwrecks. Theatrical managers.*

Note: The working title of this film was *Redhead from Rio*. Although a *HR* production chart places Frank Sully in the cast, his participation in the released film has not been confirmed. The picture contains a scene in which Lupe Velez appears in blackface, speaking Southern jive talk.

Box 22 May 1943. *DV* 21 May 1943, p. 3. *HR* 29 Dec 1942, p. 1. *HR* 4 Jan 1943, p. 3. *HR* 29 Jan 1943, p. 6. *HR* 21 May 1943, p. 3. *MPH* 29 May 1943. *MPHPD* 3 Apr 1943, p. 1241. *MPHPD* 29 May 1943, p. 1338. *Var* 16 Jun 1943, p. 16.

REDHEAD FROM RIO *see* **REDHEAD FROM MANHATTAN**

REDSKIN (Native Americans, Navajo)

Paramount Famous Lasky Corp. 23 Feb **1929** [©Paramount Famous Lasky Corp.; 23 Feb 1929; LP161]. Mus score and sd eff (Movietone); b&w with col sequences (Technicolor). 9 reels, 7,643 ft. [Also si; 7,402 ft.].

Dir Victor Schertzinger. *Story and scen* Elizabeth Pickett. *Titles* Julian Johnson. *Photog* Edward Cronjager. *Technicolor seq* Ray Rennahan and Edward Estabrook. *Film ed* Otto Lovering. *Mus score* J. S. Zamecnik.

Song(s): "Redskin," music by J. S. Zamecnik, lyrics by Harry D. Kerr.

Cast: Richard Dix (*Wing Foot*), Gladys Belmont (*Corn Blossom*), Jane Novak (*Judy*), Larry Steers (*John Walton*), Tully Marshall (*Navajo Jim*), Bernard Siegel (*Chahi*), George Rigas (*Chief Notani*), Augustina Lopez (*Yina*), Noble Johnson (*Peublo Jim*), Joseph W. Girard (*Commissioner*), Jack Duane (*Barrett*), Andrew J. Callaghan (*Anderson*), Myra Kinch (*Laughing Singer*), Philip Anderson (*Wing Foot, age 9*), Lorraine Rivero (*Corn Blossom, age 6*), George Walker (*Pueblo Jim, age 15*), Paul Panzer.

Western. After attending preparatory school and college in the East, Wing Foot returns to his Navajo tribe and renounces their customs and beliefs, becoming an outcast among his own people. Wing Foot later secretly visits the village of a rival tribe in order to see Corn Blossom, his sweetheart, who has also been to school in the East. Her people discover his presence, and he is forced to flee into the desert, where he discovers oil. White prospectors also find the oil, and Wing Foot races them to the claim office, filing his claim first. Faced with marriage to a man she does not love, Corn Blossom takes refuge in the Navajo village. Her people come to take her back, and a pitched battle between the tribes is averted only when Wing Foot arrives and tells both tribes of the new good fortune of the Indian nations. He then claims Corn Blossom as his own. *Canyon de Chelly (AZ). Deserts. Navajo Indians. Oil. Prospectors.*

Note: The final 6 minutes of this film were projected in Magnascope. Filmed on location in Canyon de Chelly.

FD 3 Feb 1929. *Var* 30 Jan 1929, p. 34.

REET, PETITE AND GONE (African Americans)

Astor Pictures Corp. *Dist* State Rights. **1947.** Sd (RCA Sound System); b&w. 6,408 ft. 69 min.

Pres R. M. SAVINI and BERLE ADAMS. *Prod* William Forest Crouch. *Dir* William Forest Crouch. *Orig story* William Forest. *Scr* Irwin Winehouse. *Dir of photog* Don Malkames. *Film ed* Leonard Anderson. *Settings* Frank Namczy. *Rec eng* Nelson Minnerly.

Song(s): "Texas and Pacific," words and music by Jack Wolf Fine and Joseph E. Hirsch; "Tonight Be Tender to Me," words and music by William Forest Crouch, Gloria Parker and Barney Young; "The Green Grass Grows All Around," words and music by J. Mayo Williams and "Stovepipe" Johnson; "I Know What You're Puttin' Down," words and music by Louis Jordan and Bud Allen; "Let The Good Times Roll," words and music by Sam Theard and Fleecie Moore; "Reet, Petite and Gone," words and music by Spencer Lee and Louis Jordan; "That Chick's Too Young to Fry," words and music by Tommy Edwards and Jimmy Hilliard; "Ain't That Just Like a Woman," words and music by Claude Demitrius and Fleecie Moore; "If It's Love You Want," words and music by Sid Robin; "All for the Love of Lil," "The Blues Ain't Nothin'," "I've Changed Completely," "Wham Sam (Dig Those Gams)" and "You Got Me Where You Want Me," composers undetermined.

Cast: Louis Jordan and his Tympany Five (*Schyler Jarvis [Jr.]/Louis Jarvis*), June Richmond (*June*), Milton Woods (*Sam Adams*), Bea Griffith (*Honey Carter/Lovey Linn*), David Bethea (*Dolph*), Lorenzo Tucker ([*Henry*] *Talbot*), Vanita Smythe (*Rusty*), Mabel Lee (*Mabel*), Dots Johnson (*Michaels*), Pat Rainey (*Pat Rains*), Rudy Toombs (*Hal*), J. Lewis Johnson (*Schyler Jarvis, Sr.*), Joe Lillard (*Lt. Jerome*).

African American, Show business, Romance, with songs. [*Print viewed*]. While performing in a radio studio with his band, singer Louis Jarvis receives the urgent message that his father, Schyler Jarvis, is on his deathbed. Meanwhile, the beautiful Honey Carter travels to New York City by plane with her best friend, June. Honey had been contacted by Schyler, who wanted to see her before his death as he was once in love with her late mother, singer Lovey Linn. In response to June's queries, Honey relates how, many years ago, the young Schyler met her mother in New Orleans and invited her to New York to become his singing partner. Lovey and Schyler wanted to marry, but Lovey's mother refused her consent and forced Lovey to marry a wealthier man. Honey's father, who died when she was a child, subsequently lost his money in the Great Depression, and Lovey never forgot Schyler, her first love, who went on to become famous and wealthy. Before the arrival of Honey and Louis, Schyler confers a sealed letter to his trusty valet, asking that it not be opened until four weeks after his death. Worried that Louis will never meet his true love, Schyler cryptically declares that his will has been designed to help Louis in his quest. After sending for his lawyer, Henry Talbot, Schyler dictates the terms of his will as Talbot's secretary, Rusty, types the document. The will states that Louis must marry a young woman of a very specific physical description or risk losing his father's sizeable estate. Immediately after signing the will, Schyler dies. Before heading off to the airport to send Honey back home, the greedy Talbot instructs Rusty to change the will to suit her physical description and to add the clause that the estate goes to Talbot if Louis does not comply with the terms of the will. At the airport, Talbot gives Honey and June plane fare home, but they decide to use the money to stay in New York. After Honey reveals that she met Schyler and Louis at her mother's funeral, June urges Honey to approach Louis for a job, but Honey demurs. She changes her mind when Louis' press agent, Sam Adams, announces on the radio that an open audition will be held for the female lead of Louis' next Broadway show. The only catch is that, in addition to singing and dancing, the lucky girl must have the specific physical dimensions required for the job and must wear a bathing suit at the audition so that she can be measured. At the audition, Sam checks each contestant's height and measures a seemingly endless series of busts, waists, hips and thighs, but none of the young women has the qualifications specified in Schyler's will. Honey shows up late and shyly disrobes down to a bathing suit, but her measurements don't meet the requirements either. Nevertheless, Louis is smitten, and when he learns that Honey is Lovey Linn's daughter, he asks her out on a dinner date. Learning of Honey's dire financial situation, Louis promises her a job in the show and also hires June after hearing her sing at the following day's rehearsal. Much to their dismay, Louis and Sam learn that their primary backer, Mr. Baxter, is pulling out of the show. Later, at Talbot's office, Louis realizes that Talbot has bribed Baxter in an attempt to trick Louis into marrying Rusty out of desperation for his father's money, as she is the only woman who matches the description in Schyler's will. Even though it means closing his show, Louis refuses because he has fallen in love with Honey. The angry conversation is interrupted when Schyler's valet phones, asking Louis and Talbot to meet him for the unsealing of the secret letter Schyler entrusted to him. The letter reveals the true description of the girl Louis is to marry, and explicitly states Schyler's desire that Honey and Louis find each other. Talbot is unmasked as a fraud, and he and Rusty are taken away by the police. Louis' show then goes on as scheduled and, at its finale, he croons a love song to Honey, his future wife. *Fraud. Jazz music. Marriage–Arranged. Romance. Singers. Wills. Auditions. Death and dying. Fathers and sons. Lawyers. Letters. Mothers and daughters. New York City. Radio stations. Secretaries. Theatrical producers. Valets.*

Note: The title of this film was taken from a musical number made famous by Louis Jordan. "Reet, Petite and Gone" is a slang term for an attractive woman. Although the opening credits indicate that Astor Pictures Corp. copyrighted the film in 1947, the film is not included in the *Catalog of Copyright Entries*. The above release year is based on correspondence contained in the MPAA/PCA Collection at the AMPAS Library, which indicates that regional censors ordered the elimination of a number of suggestive songs and dance sequences featuring "indecent" abdominal movements. *Reet, Petite and Gone* marked the final appearance in a feature film of Lorenzo Tucker, who was widely known as the "black Valentino."

Exh 12 Nov 1947, p. 2280.

REFORM SCHOOL (African Americans)

Million Dollar Productions, Inc. *Dist* Million Dollar Productions, Inc. 27 Apr **1939**. Sd; b&w. 8 reels, 6,849 ft. 76, 80 or 82 min. PCA cert no. 5286.

Exec prod Harry M. Popkin. *Assoc prod* Sara Francis. *Dir* Leo C. Popkin. *Asst dir* V. O. Smith. *Scr* Zella Young. *Orig story* Joe O'Donnell and Hazel Barnes Jamieson. *Photog* William Hyer. *Ed* Bart Rauw. *Mus settings* Lou Frohman. *Sd* Glen Glenn.

Cast: Louise Beavers (*Mother Barton*), Reginald Fenderson (*Freddie Gordon*), Monte Hawley (*Jackson*), Eugene Jackson (*Pete*), Freddie Jackson (*Eddie*), Eddie Lynn (*Joe*), DeForrest Covan (*Bill*), Bobby Simmons (*Johnny*), Maceo Sheffield (*Mr. Stone*), Edward Thompson, Vernon McCalla (*Reform school officials*), Alfred Grant (*Jones, Guard*), Milton Hall (*Jackie Rogers*), Clifford Holland (*Slim*), Edward Patrick (*Mr. Gordon*), Charles Andrews (*Gas station attendant*), Harold Garrison (*Guard*), Edward Tony (*Tony*).

African American, Social, Drama. [*Not viewed*]. In Harlem, parole violator Freddie Gordon, who is unsuccessful at finding a job because of his reform school record, turns instead to crime. After robbing a gas station, Freddie is caught by the police and sent back to reform school, where he becomes a victim of the brutal superintendent, Mr. Stone, and his corrupt guard, Jackson. The cruel treatment Freddie suffers at the school leads him on the road to becoming a hardened criminal, until his case is brought to the attention of Mother Barton, a probation officer. Seeing the abhorrent conditions at the school, Barton forces Stone's removal and begins a crusade to teach the boys honor and respect for the law, while putting them on the honor system. At first, the boys are less than cooperative with the new humane approach, and they take advantage of Barton. However, when Freddie and his pals feign illness one day, Barton fixes things with her castor oil remedy. Barton's efforts are almost ruined when Jackson robs the school safe and plants the deposit box under Freddie's mattress, which puts Freddie under suspicion and casts doubt on the effectiveness of Barton's policies. The boys rally behind Freddie and Barton, however, and, after escaping from the reformatory, go after Jackson and spend the night in town. When Barton is informed of the escape, she finds the boys at Jackson's rooming house, where Jackson confesses and makes an attempt to flee. He is soon caught, however, and taken into custody by the police. With her vindication, a new order is instituted at all the state's reform schools, and the boys look forward to getting good jobs when they are released. *African Americans. Honor. Juvenile delinquents. Probation. Reformatories. Schools. Confession. Escapes. Fathers and sons. Frame-ups. Guards. Law and order. New York City–Harlem. Parole. School superintendents and principals. Thieves. Unemployment.*

Note: According to the *MPH* review, the picture was previewed at the Million Dollar theater in Los Angeles. Although New York state censorship records list Leo C. Popkin Dist. Co. as the film's distributor, no further information on the company or its role in distributing this film has been found. Eugene Jackson, DeForrest Covan, Eddie Lyon, and Bob Simmons were billed as the comedic "Harlem Tuff Kids." *Reform School* was retitled *Prison Bait* for re-release in 1944.

DV 28 Apr 1939, p. 3. *Exb* 28 Jun 1939, p. 338. *FD* 12 May 1939, p. 12. *MPD* 4 May 1939, p. 4. *MPH* 6 May 1939, p. 38. *Var* 3 May 1939, p. 16.

REFORMATION (African Americans)

Loyalty Film Co. *Dist* State Rights; Loyalty Film Co. 10 Aug **1920?**. Si; b&w. 5 reels.

Dir Capt. Leslie T. Peacocke. *Scen* Capt. Leslie T. Peacocke. *Story* Sidney P. Dones.

Cast: Sidney P. Dones (*Carter Spencer*), Geraldine Steele (*Clarice Penlow*), Webb King, Vera Lavassor, Yvonne Dumont, Bert Haily, Fred Scott, Vernol Moore.

African American, Drama. Carter Spencer, the son of a devout mother and a member of a fashionable tennis club, has a taste for flirtation, gambling and drinking. He falls in love with choir singer Clarice Penlow, who loves him but disapproves of his wild ways. At the onset of prohibition, Clarice urges Carter to become a Secret Service agent to enforce the new law, and he complies out of love. [No other information about the plot has been discovered.]. *African Americans. Prohibition. Secret Service. Socialites. Flirts. Gambling. Religion. Singers.*

Note: The Loyalty Film Co, formerly the Democracy Film Co., included both whites and blacks in its management and produced films with black casts. It is unclear whether this film, its second production, was ever completed or released.

THE REFUGEE see THREE FACES WEST

REGENERACIÓN (Fox Film Corp., 1931) *see* **DEL INFIERNO AL CIELO**

REGENERACIÓN (Spanish language)

Guillermo Calles. *Dist* J. H. Hoffberg Co. **1931**; Mexico City opening: 2 Apr 1931; New York opening: 17 Jul 1931; Prod: 1930. Sd; b&w. 5 reels, 4,605 ft. 51 min. Spanish language.

Dir Guillermo Calles.

Cast: Dorita Ceprano (*Julieta*), Enrique Areu (*Roberto*), José Areu (*Carlos*), Roberto Areu (*Don Felipe*), Oscar Guisado (*Luisito*), Juan Aristi Eulate, Ramón Muñoz, Angelita Calles.

Melodrama. [*Not viewed*]. The lead tenor in a small theatrical company quits after a disappointing love affair with Julieta, the company's leading lady, who has not wanted to marry him. Due to this unexpected setback, the manager, Julieta's father, must, to save the show, engage the only professional available, Roberto, who has a good singing voice, but has had the misfortune of having spent some time in a psychiatric hospital. Having fallen in love at their first meeting, Julieta and Roberto become a new team on stage and eventually get married. The spurned suitor finds out about Roberto's secret illness and bribes the maid to put a bottle of alcohol in his rival's dressing room, knowing that a drink will have disastrous consequences. The singer goes on stage drunk and insults everyone, and the scandal puts an end to his theatrical career. However, he later has success as a composer and once again regains the trust of his family. *Actors and actresses. Alcoholics. Marriage. Singers. Theatrical troupes. Bribery. Composers. Fathers and daughters. Jealousy. Maids. Mental illness. Revenge. Scandal. Theatrical managers. Unrequited love.*

Note: *Regeneración* was previewed in Los Angeles on 23 Dec 1930. Contemporary sources list dancers "La Jana," Amanda Cárdenas, Carmen Coronel, Consuelo López, Rosalina Meléndez and the "Pizarro" orchestra as possible cast members, but their participation in the completed film has not been confirmed.

FD 26 Jul 1931, p. 10.

REGENERATION (African Americans)

Norman Film Mfg. Co. 25 Dec **1923**; Jacksonville, FL opening: 24 Dec 1923. Si; b&w. 5-6 reels, 4,820 ft.

Cast: Stella Mayo, M. C. Maxwell, Alfred Norcrum, Charlie Gaines, Clarence Rucker, Dr. R. L. Brown, Steve Reynolds.

African American, Sea, Island, Drama. [*Not viewed*]. After her father, a widowed sea captain, perishes, Violet Daniels is left a map detailing the location of buried treasure on an unknown South Seas island. She leaves to find the treasure with Jack Roper, who is in love with her, on his fishing schooner, the "Anna Bell." During the voyage, the ship's mate, "Knife" Hurley attempts to gain possession of the map, and there is a fight involving the crew he has recruited among the nefarious elements of the waterfront. The ship is set on fire, and Knife escapes overboard with the map and his crew, leaving Violet and Jack to die on the burning boat. They survive on a raft they build, however, and after days of drifting, hungry and thirsty, they arrive at an uninhabited island. They name it "Regeneration" and begin life anew. Sometime later, Knife and his crew land on Regeneration, which turns out to be the island on which the treasure is buried. [No additional information concerning the conclusion of the plot has been located]. *African Americans. Buried treasure. Islands. Regeneration. Romance. South Sea islands. Fights. Fires. Fishing boats. Maps. Orphans. Sea captains. Shipwrecks.*

Note: An ad for this film calls it "A Super Feature with an all star Colored Cast."

LA REGINA DI SPARTA (Italian language)

Itala Film Co. *Dist* State Rights. **1931**. Si with synchronized sd; b&w. 9 reels. 80 min. Italian language.

Dir Manfred S. Noa. *Scr* Casare Origo and Guito Redaelli.

Cast: Antonio Moray, Viola Larosa, Franco Faris, Bernardo Camilli, Guisseppi Laroy, Carlo Borelli, Putro Costo.

Historical, War, Drama. [*Not viewed*]. After the kidnapping of Elena, Queen of Sparta, Priamo, the King of Troy, is informed that she must return to her kingdom or war between the Spartans and the Trojans will ensue. While Paride, Prince of Troy, begs his father not to return his beloved, Elena insists on averting warfare by returning to her home. When Priamo hears that the Spartans have begun to revolt, he insists on fighting, but Elena begs Paride to stay with her rather than risk his life on the battlefield. Priamo's consort, the queen, asks Elena to beg Ettore, Paride's brother, not to fight.

However, Ettore insists on going to battle and takes leave of his wife Andromacke and his son despite the former's pleading and her accusations against Elena that Ettore is in love with her. Priamo enlists Paride to lead the troops against Menelave, Elena's husband. Meanwhile, at the Spartan camp, a messenger announces the Trojans' approach. When Achilles' request to have the honor of killing Paride and Ettore is refused by Menelave, who desires to do the job himself, Achilles refuses to fight. Paride loses the duel with Menelave, and Elena, fearing for Paride, orders a chariot and begs Menelave to throw down his arms, which he does. But Acamendole, another Spartan, convinces Menelave to continue the fight and to avenge the kidnapping of Elena. On the Trojan side, Ettore gives the command to fight and many Spartans are killed. A messenger announces the Trojans' rapid progress toward the Spartan camp, and in his fury, Achilles strangles the messenger and then tries to distract himself from the urge to do battle by watching acrobats and dancers perform. Back in Troy, Spartan prisoners arrive and Elena begs Priamo to spare them, reminding him that she too is a Spartan. Priamo menaces Elena, and Paride in turn menaces Priamo, who then orders his son taken away. Protoclo, a Spartan, begs to take Achilles' place as high commander in order to save Sparta. Achilles agrees, calls the men to arms, and then sends Protoclo out, the latter eventually being killed when he engages in combat with Ettore. When Protoclo's body is brought back to the camp, Achilles vows to avenge his fallen friend and takes up arms, although the Trojans have already declared victory. Achilles fights with Ettore in front of the walls of Troy, but Andromacke takes her son to the scene and begs her husband not to fight. As Ettore tries to run to his family, Achilles pierces his throat with a sword. Achilles takes the body and announces that Protoclo is avenged. The Trojan women denounce Elena, and a prophet from Athens foretells the death of Paride and Ettore and the fall of Troy. Priamo has the prophet burned to death. Next, Priamo, the queen, and Andromacke go to Achilles and beg that Ettore's body be returned for a proper burial. Achilles says he will only give the body up if Elena relinquishes her crown and has it placed on Protoclo's tomb. Priamo agrees but secretly plans to avenge Ettore's death by asking Paride to thrust a poisoned arrow into Achilles' heel. He refuses until Priamo threatens to send Elena to do the job. Elena tries to stop Paride, but is too late. He kills Achilles and, ashamed at his father's treachery, tries to attack Priamo with the poisoned arrow. Priamo has him seized and orders that he be put to death. Acamendole decides on a plan to destroy Troy: he will declare peace, then send a huge horse filled with Spartan soldiers as a friendship offering. Paride, in prison, is visited by Elena and his mother, the queen. He says he will kill himself if Elena leaves him. As the Trojans rejoice in their victory, the horse is brought in. Elena and Paride are sentenced to death and the queen tries to help them to escape, although the brave Elena wishes to stay and die by Paride's side. They see Menelave emerge from the horse, and then the Spartan king kills Elena's lover. Priamo tries to poison Elena, but when he sees the Spartans, he drinks the poison himself. Menelave enters and Elena tells him to kill her. He tells her to commit suicide, but then changes his mind and invites her to return with him to Sparta. Greece–History. Helen of Troy. Trojan War. Turkey–History.

Note: The English-language title of the film is *The Queen of Sparta*. The plot summary was based on a dialogue continuity deposited at the NYSA. According to *FD*, this film was produced in Hollywood.

FD 8 Mar 1931, p. 11.

THE RENAISSANCE AT CHARLEROI (French Americans)
Broadway Star Features Co. *Dist* General Film Co. 10 Nov **1917** [©Broadway Star Features Co., Inc.; 5 Nov 1917; LP11687]. Si; b&w. 4 reels.

Dir Thomas R. Mills. *Scen* Katherine Reed.
Source: Based on the short story "The Renaissance at Charleroi" by O. Henry in *Roads of Destiny* (New York, 1903).
Cast: J. Frank Glendon (*Grandemont Charles*), Eleanor Lawson (*His mother*), Agnes Ayres (*Adele Fauquier*), Webster Campbell (*Victor Fauquier*), Marguerite Forrest (*The octoroon*), Ethel Northrup (*Adele's friend*).
Drama. When Grandemont Charles, a descendant of one of the South's most aristocratic French families, discovers that Victor Fauquier, the brother of his fiancée Adele, is entangled with an octoroon, he pays for the woman to go North. An infuriated Victor disappears, and Adele, blaming Grandemont, refuses to marry him

until her brother is found. Grandemont spends his entire fortune in a futile search for Victor. Years later, his only income now derived from his job as clerk, Grandemont saves six hundred dollars with which to restore the former glory of the family estate at Charleroi for one night. He rents the mansion, sends out invitations to a grand banquet and eagerly awaits his guests. His only visitor, however, is a tramp, who is made the honored guest. At dinner's end, Grandemont discovers that the tramp is none other than Victor, who had been held prisoner in Mexico. With the return of her brother, Adele agrees to marry Grandemont and a reconciliation is effected. *Aristocrats. Brothers and sisters. Family honor. French Americans. Missing persons. United States–South. African Americans–Mixed blood. Bribery. Clerks. Mansions. Miscegenation. Reunions. Tramps.*
MPN 17 Nov 1917, p. 3445. *MPW* 24 Nov 1917, p. 1222. *MPW* 1 Dec 1917, p. 1335.

RENDEZVOUS (German Americans)
Metro-Goldwyn-Mayer Corp.; controlled by Loew's Inc. *Dist* Loew's Inc. 25 Oct **1935**; Prod: 24 Jun–29 Jul 1935; and 6 Sep–26 Sep 1935. [©Metro-Goldwyn-Mayer Corp.; 23 Oct 1935; LP5915]. Sd (Western Electric Sound System); b&w. 10 reels. 91 or 94-96 min. Passed by the National Board of Review. PCA cert no. 1656.
Prod Lawrence Weingarten. *Dir* William K. Howard and [Sam Wood]. [*Asst dir* Dolph Zimmer]. *Scr* P. J. Wolfson and George Oppenheimer. *Adpt* Bella Spewack and Samuel Spewack. [*Contr wrt* E. A. Dupont, Horace McCoy, Herman Mankiewicz and Howard Emmett Rogers]. *Photog* William Daniels and James Wong Howe]. *Art dir* Cedric Gibbons. *Art dir assoc* Joseph Wright and Edwin B. Willis. *Film ed* Hugh Wynn. *Ward* Dolly Tree. *Mus score* Dr. William Axt. *Rec dir* Douglas Shearer.
Source: Based on the book *The American Black Chamber* by Major Herbert O. Yardley (Indianapolis, 1939).
Cast: WILLIAM POWELL ([*Lieutenant*] *Bill Gordon*), Rosalind Russell (*Joel* [*Carter*]), Binnie Barnes (*Olivia*), Lionel Atwill ([*Major*] *William Brennan*), Cesar Romero ([*Colonel*] *Nieterstein*), Samuel S. Hinds (*[John] Carter*), Henry Stephenson (*Ambassador*), Frank Reicher (*Dr.* [*R. A.*] *Jackson*), Charley Grapewin (*Martin*), Leonard Mudie (*Roberts*), Howard Hickman (*G-man*), Charles Trowbridge (*Secretary of War* [*Baker*]), Murray Kinnell (*de Segroff*), [Sterling Holloway (*Taxi driver*)], [Mickey Rooney (*Country boy*)], [Charles Wilson (*Editor*)], [Melville Cooper (*Doorman*)], [Bert Morehouse (*2nd Lieutenant*)], [Blair Davies (*Sentry*)], [Cyril Ring, Rollo Dix (*Orderlies*)], [Earl Eby, Bob Perry (*G Men*)], [Henry Mowbray (*Diplomat*)], [Mary Forbes (*Lady Cavendish*)], [Lowden Adams (*Butler*)], [Eric Wilton (*Kesterman*)], [Winter Hall (*Chaplain*)], [Sherry Hall (*Private Dean*)], [John Arthur (*Wizened man*)], [Leonid Snegoff (*Kaieneff*)], [Jack Hatfield (*Drug store clerk*)], [William Stack (*Head waiter*)], [Richard Powell (*Taxi driver*)], [Samuel R. McDaniel (*Porter*)], [James P. Burtis (*Private*)], [James Flavin (*Military police*)], [Arno Frey (*Army officer*)], [Al Bridge (*Sergeant*)], [Jeanie Roberts (*Secretary to Burns*)], [Bernadene Hayes (*Bobbie Burns*)], [Harry "Zoop" Welsh (*Barber*)], [Morgan Wallace (*Gardner*)], [Monty Vandegrift (*Sailor*)], [Rudolph Amendt (*Radio operator*)], [Sam Ash (*Mexican*)], [Sidney Bracy (*Doctor's assistant*)], [Frank Lackteen (*Customs officer*)], [Charles Coleman (*Doorman*)], [Wally Maher (*Reporter*)], [Harry C. Bradley (*Cashier*)], [Lee Kohlmar (*Tailor*)], [Tom Dugan (*Recruiting officer*)], [Guy Usher (*Ship's captain*)].
Espionage, Drama. [*Print viewed*]. The sinking of a United States warship in the Atlantic in 1914 by a German submarine prompts Washington to take special measures to insure that the Germans are kept ignorant of the exact location of Navy vessels sailing the Atlantic. A high-level military meeting results in an agreement to create a convoy system, whereby British destroyers will meet U. S. troop ships at a secret rendezvous location in the Atlantic and escort them safely to the French coast. The plan hinges on a new strategy in which the exact location of the rendezvous will be transmitted at the very last moment to the ships by a wireless code. Major William Brennan, a military cryptologist with three years' experience on the European front, provides the War Department with the new code, which is to be tested on a munitions ship rendezvous before it is used for a troop ship. Meanwhile, at the nearby Park Hotel, the German intelligence headquarters buzzes with espionage activity. Bill Gordon, a former newspaperman and author of an invaluable book on military codes, is about to leave for Europe, where he plans to serve his country on the battlefront, when he becomes romantically involved with socialite Joel Carter. The meddling Joel falls in love with the

lieutenant and, upon discovery of his expertise in cryptology, arranges to have him transferred to a desk job at the War Department through her uncle, John Carter, who is the Assistant Secretary of War. For Bill, Joel throws over suitor Colonel Nieterstein, who, unknown to her, is loyal to his German fatherland and reads top secret military information over the phone to Dr. R. A. Jackson, a contact in San Diego. One such message alerts the spies as to the exact bearings of a mid-sea Navy rendezvous scheduled for the next day. Aware of the War Department's trial run, Nieterstein advises the Germans not to pursue the munitions-carrying *S. S. Dependable*, but to wait instead for a bigger pay-off, a troop ship. Bill protests his reassignment to a desk job, but quickly proves his worth when he cracks the German code and learns that the enemy has decoded the Americans' new code and knows about the *S. S. Dependable*. The military has three days in which to either find the code thieves and retrieve the code, or intercept all future German spy communications. When Brennan suspects that his mistress, Olivia, is an undercover enemy agent, he sets a trap for her, and she falls for it. Fearing for her safety, Olivia kills Brennan but, after reporting the incident to her superiors, is told to sacrifice herself to Army investigators to prevent trouble for Germany. Olivia complies with the order and is captured by Bill, who calls her bluff at a restaurant with a phony deciphered message he says he found in her mailbox. Olivia is about to confess when Joel and Nieterstein show up at their table and interrupt her. Having been slipped a message by another German agent, which says that Nieterstien is to be sacrificed to the U. S. Army in order to give the false impression that it is once again safe to send their ships coded messages, Olivia provides Bill with evidence of Nieterstein's complicity in the espionage ring. Upon his arrest, Nieterstien commits suicide. Bill and Olivia go to the Park Hotel and are followed by the jealous Joel, who is taken hostage by members of the German intelligence network. The agents use Joel as a bargaining tool to force Bill, who has also been captured, to decode the latest rendezvous location. Bill translates the code and is then granted a private meeting with Joel, which is interrupted by a spray of bullets from a machine gun. Bill and Joel manage to escape death and overpower their would-be assassins just as Department of Justice agents arrive. The authorities, having been tipped off by Bill's encoded message, arrest the spies and send orders to arrest Dr. Jackson in San Diego. As promised by Carter, Bill is granted permission to fight in Europe, but just as his train is about to leave, his reassignment to a local desk job arrives. Espionage. German Americans. Secret codes. Secret Service. United States. War Department. World War I. Blackmail. Fistfights. Jealousy. Mexico. Mistresses. Murder. Patriotism. Reporters. Romance. San Diego (CA). Socialites. Suicide. Women's suffrage.

Note: Working titles for this film were *Blonde Countess, White Bird, Puzzle Man* and *The Black Chamber*. According to contemporary sources, Herbert O. Yardley, the author of the book on which the film was based, was head of the United States Secret Service during World War I. *Rendezvous* marked Rosalind Russell's first star billing in a film. *HR* pre-production news items indicate that the picture was originally intended as a William Powell—Myrna Loy vehicle, and that A. E. Dupont, who aided producer Lawrence Weingarten on the script, was named as a possible director. The extent of Dupont's participation on the film has not been determined. While *HR* production charts and pre-release news items list actors Alan Cavan, Lee Phelps, Zita Johann, Hedwiga Reicher (actor Frank Reicher's sister), Belle Mitchell, Jerry Mandy, Haila Stoddard and Walter King (formerly known on Broadway as Walter Woolf) in the cast, their appearance in the released film has not been confirmed. Jul and Aug 1935 *HR* news items note that production on the film was suspended due to actress Binnie Barnes' bout with apendicitis. A day after it erroneously reported that M-G-M had decided to re-write and re-shoot the entire picture, *HR*, on 24 Aug 1935, clarified the matter by printing a letter written by director William K. Howard, who denied the implication that the studio was dissatisfied with Barnes's work. He wrote that M-G-M is trying to decide on a very effective last act for the picture...which will exploit the talents of Miss Rosalind Russell." The director conceded that from the start the production "never had a satisfactory ending," and that they were awaiting the results of preview audience reactions to a better ending. Howard also wrote that he was leaving the production because he had taken an assignment on a Walter Wanger film. Sam Wood then took over the direction of the film and Herman Mankiewicz and Howard Emmett Rogers were assigned to the script. James Wong Howe replaced William Daniels as the photographer. *HR* also noted that George Kaufman was to sit in on some of the story meetings, and that some seventeen new sets would be constructed for the second round of filming.
   Although onscreen credits list Lionel Atwill's character as "William Brennan," his spoken name in the film is "Charles." Also, while most contemporary sources list Cesar Romero's character as "Nickolajeff," the film credits and dialogue refer to him as "Nieterstein." The *Var* review erroneously refers to actor Cesar Romero as Hugh Romero. The released film was cut from its preview length of 106 minutes. Modern sources indicate that the casting of

Rosalind Russell as William Powell's co-star, instead of his usual teaming with star Myrna Loy, was due in part to Loy's absence from M-G-M during her strike for better pay. *Rendezous* was remade by M-G-M in 1942 as *Pacific Rendezvous*, directed by George Sidney and starring Jean Rogers and Mona Harris.
   DV 23 Oct 1935, p. 3. *FD* 23 Oct 1935, p. 4. *HR* 27 Mar 1935, p. 3. *HR* 30 Mar 1935, p. 4. *HR* 17 May 1935, p. 4. *HR* 5 Jun 1935, p. 2. *HR* 18 Jun 1935, p. 2. *HR* 19 Jun 1935, p. 11. *HR* 22 Jun 1935, p. 4. *HR* 24 Jun 1935, p. 2. *HR* 26 Jun 1935, p. 6. *HR* 2 Jul 1935, p. 22. *HR* 25 Jul 1935, p. 4. *HR* 30 Jul 1935, p. 8. *HR* 7 Aug 1935, p. 2. *HR* 23 Aug 1935, p. 1, 6. *HR* 24 Aug 1935, p. 5. *HR* 7 Sep 1935, p. 3. *HR* 9 Sep 1935, p. 6. *HR* 23 Sep 1935, p. 14. *HR* 25 Sep 1935, p. 10. *HR* 23 Oct 1935, p. 3. *MPD* 26 Oct 1935, p. 3. *MPH* 19 Oct 1935, p. 90. *MPH* 9 Nov 1935, p. 64. *NYT* 26 Oct 1935, p. 12. *Var* 30 Oct 1935, p. 14.

RENDEZVOUS 24 (German Americans, Refugees)
   Twentieth Century-Fox Film Corp.; Sol M. Wurtzel Productions, Inc.; A Sol M. Wurtzel Production. *Dist* Twentieth Century-Fox Film Corp. May **1946**; Los Angeles opening: 25 Jun 1946; *Prod:* mid-Jan–late Jan 1946 at California Studios [©Twentieth Century-Fox Film Corp.; 21 May 1946; LP394]. *Sd* (Western Electric Mirrophonic Recording); b&w. 8 reels, 6,625 ft. 74 min. PCA cert no. 11458.
   Dir James Tinling. *Asst dir* Rex Bailey. *Orig story and scr* Aubrey Wisberg. *Dir of photog* Benjamin Kline. *Art dir* Jerome Pycha. *Film ed* William F. Claxton. *Set dec* Syd Moore. *Mus dir* Emil Newman. *Sd tech* John Carter. *Prod mgr* Sherman A. Harris. [*Asst to prod* Winifred Shank].
   Cast: William Gargan [(*Larry Cameron*)], Maria Palmer [(*Greta Holvig*)], Pat O'Moore [(*George Timothy*)], Herman Bing [(*Herr Schmidt*)], Kay Connors [(*Kay*)], Kurt Katch [(*Heligmann*)], David Leonard [(*Gustave Heinrich Kleinheldt*)], John Bleifer [(*Becker*)], Henry Rowland [(*Otto Kurt Mannfred*)], George Sorel [(*Zarek*)], Eilene Janssen [(*Anchaka*)], [Ilka Gruning (*Frau Schmidt*)], [Boyd Irwin (*Carstairs*)], [Evan Thomas (*Sinclair*)], [Paul Kruger (*Leopold*)], [Leslie Denison (*Clark*)], [Douglas Fowley (*Hanover*)], [Jon Gilbreath (*Lindsey*)], [Art Gilmore (*Thompson*)], [Drew Allen (*Redding*)], [Leyland Hodgson (*Benson*)], [Marin Sais (*Rina*)], [John Banner (*Ernst*)], [Otto Reichow (*Sigmund*)], [Arno Frey (*Kutner*)], [Claude Wisberg (*English radio operator*)], [Betty Fairfax (*Cashier*)], [Bert Roach (*Herr Kompenik*)], [Frieda Stoll (*Frau Kompenik*)], [Charles Knight (*Customs inspector*)], [Clifford Moore (*Chubby man*)], [Jimmy Aubrey (*Conductor*)], [John Dehner (*Harris*)], [Charles Miller (*Dr. Upton*)], [George Carleton (*Milford*)], [Ferris Taylor (*Senator Bradley*)], [Emmett Vogan (*Griswold*)], [Bernard Berg (*Hans Zeidler*)], [Hans Tanzler (*Herr Zinderhoff*)], [Angela DeWitt (*Frau Zinderhoff*)], [Frederick Brunn (*German radio operator*)], [Ann Harper, Gary Gray, Castle McCall (*Radio voices*)], [Arthur Gilmore (*Narrator*)].
   Espionage, Drama. [*Not viewed*]. Although atom bombs have been dropped on Hiroshima and Nagasaki, a group of German scientists still labors, deep in the Harz mountains of Thuringia, Germany, to fulfill Hitler's dream of supremacy. They intend to explode their own atom bombs, via remote radio detonation, in major cities throughout the world. In New York, German-born Professor Gustave Heinrich Kleinheldt, who is a member of the U.S. atomic team but is secretly working for the Nazis, tells Larry Cameron, the Secret Service agent assigned to guard him, that he is leaving on a fishing trip with his driver Mannfred. Larry decides to follow them and sees their car go off a mountain road. When Larry pulls Kleinheldt from the wreckage, Mannfred shoots Kleinheldt, who as he dies, tells Larry to get to "Kyffhauser." Larry learns that Kleinheldt became a naturalized citizen five years earlier and that Mannfred, who was also naturalized, had worked for him for fifteen years. While Mannfred is being interrogated by the FBI, he takes a poison capsule and dies without revealing anything significant. However, by examining fingerprints taken from Kleinheldt's body, Larry establishes that it was not the real Kleinheldt in the car but a double. When it is discovered that the genuine Kleinheldt has flown to Germany, Larry is assigned to follow him. In the Harz Mountains, Larry meets Greta Holvig, a reporter for the Scandinavian Press Syndicate, who tells him that she has read about his involvement in the Kleinheldt case. Using the password "Rendezvous 24," Larry meets up with George Timothy, a British agent, who is working undercover as a waiter at the inn where Larry and Greta are staying. Greta is actually a German agent sent to kill Larry, but her initial attempt on his life is thwarted. While Larry and George try to decipher a possible clue to the location of the scientists, Greta reports to her contact, Dr. Heligmann, who sends agents Becker and Ernst to trap them. Larry and George trace a radio signal, which has been interfering with their radio communication with London, to

a remote cabin, which Becker and Ernst have booby-trapped. However, Larry spots the wires, and discovers through another clue that Kyffhauser is in Russian occupied territory. Later, Larry is caught by one of Heligmann's men and a false message is sent to George asking him to join Larry at Heligmann's farmhouse. London intelligence advises George that Greta is a German agent so that when she brings the phony message, George knows that it is a trap. Heligmann learns from scientist Zarek that Kleinheldt has perfected the remote, radio-controlled explosion of an atomic bomb and proceeds with plans to explode one in Paris that evening. As George and Greta reach the farmhouse, George draws a gun on Greta and tells her that the body of the real Greta Holvig was found two days earlier. George pushes her into the room where Larry is being held prisoner and, in the ensuing confusion, Larry grabs one of his guard's guns. A gunfight errupts and Greta is hit. As George and Larry chase Heligmann and Zarek into a tunnel beneath the farmhouse, Larry shoots Zarek and takes Heligmann prisoner. A small electric car carries Larry, George and Heligmann directly into a laboratory in the Kyffhauser mountain, where Kleinheldt is preparing to detonate the bomb. With only seconds to spare, Larry shoots Kleinheldt and Paris is saved. *Atomic bomb. Espionage. Germany. Scientists. Secret Service. Americans in foreign countries. Automobile accidents. Automobiles. Electric. Cabins. Chauffeurs. Doubles. Farms. Fingerprints. German Americans. Gunfights. Impersonation and imposture. Innkeepers. Inns. Traps. Tunnels. Undercover operations. United States. Federal Bureau of Investigation. Waiters.*

Note: Although this film was not viewed, the credits and summary were taken from a cutting continuity in the Twentieth Century-Fox Produced Scripts Collection at the UCLA Arts—Special Collections Library. This was the first independent film made by long-time Twentieth Century-Fox producer Sol M. Wurtzel. A final shooting script includes a scene in which Jack Norton and Lorraine Miller were listed as cast members, but that scene does not appear in the cutting continuity.

Box 4 May 1946. *DV* 2 May 1946, p. 3. *FD* 7 May 1946, p. 6. *HR* 11 Jan 1946, p. 15. *HR* 2 May 1946, p. 3. *MPHPD* 20 Apr 1946, p. 2951. *MPHPD* 4 May 1946, p. 2974. *Var* 1 May 1946, p. 8.

RENEGADE GIRL (Native Americans)
Affiliated Productions, Inc. *Dist* Screen Guild Productions, Inc. 25 Dec 1946; Prod: mid-Sep 1946 [©Screen Guild Productions, Inc.; 15 Nov 1946; LP779]. Sd (Western Electric Mirrophonic Recording); b&w. 5,871 ft. 65 min.

Pres ROBERT L. LIPPERT. *Prod* William Berke. *Assoc prod* Samuel K. Decker. *Dir* William Berke. *Orig scr* Edwin V. Westrate. *Dir of photog* James Brown, Jr. *Supv ed* Arthur A. Brooks. *Mus dir* David Chudnow. *Mus score* Darrell Calker. *Sd rec* Max Hutchinson. *Prod mgr* Carl Hittleman.

Cast: Alan Curtis (*Captain Fred Raymond*), Ann Savage (*Jean Shelby [also known as Marie Carroll]*), Edward Brophy (*Bob Crandall*), Russell Wade (*Jerry Long*), Jack Holt (*Major Barker*), Ray Corrigan (*Bill Quantrill*), Claudia Drake (*Mary Manson*), John King (*Corporal Brown*), Chief Thunder Cloud (*Chief White Cloud*), Edmund Cobb (*Sergeant James*), Richard Curtis (*Joe Barnes*), Nick Thompson (*Tom Starr*), James Martin (*Bob Shelby*).

Historical, Drama. [*Print viewed*]. In Missouri, in 1864, Jean Shelby encounters a Union cavalry unit. Together with her brother Bob, Jean is suspected of aiding the notorious Rebel guerrillas led by Bill Quantrill, and so the soldiers escort her to their headquarters. Before they arrive, Chief White Cloud tells Major Barker that a wounded Bob is hiding at his parents' home. Chief White Cloud has vowed to kill the entire Shelby family because he was banished by the Cherokees after he tried to kidnap Mrs. Shelby. At headquarters, Jean overhears the soldiers' plans to capture Bob and, through a ruse, escapes. Jean arrives home before the soldiers, and she and Bob head for Quantrill's hideout. Bob is too weak to complete the journey, however, and Jean leaves him behind while she goes for help. White Cloud finds Bob where he is resting and kills him. In the meantime, Jean has captured Captain Fred Raymond. Soon after Jean discovers Bob's body, Quantrill and his men arrive and vow to avenge Bob. They decide to hang Fred, but Jean, who has fallen in love with him, intervenes. After Quantrill's men leave, Fred insists on accompanying Jean when she brings Bob's body home. They arrive at the Shelby home in the midst of an attack by White Cloud. Jean is badly wounded and both of her parents are killed. Fred leaves Jean with the Manson family and departs on his army mission. Months later, Jean recovers and, disillusioned because Fred has not contacted her, goes after

White Cloud. Learning that Quantrill is dead and that his men have become outlaws now that the war is over, Jean agrees to join them if they will help her kill White Cloud. Shortly after Jean leaves the Mansons', Fred arrives in search of her. Unaware of this, Jean, who is using the pseudonym Marie Carroll, promises to marry the man who helps her to avenge her brother. Her promise causes trouble among the men, especially Jerry Long, who thinks of Jean as his girl. Just as they get close to capturing White Cloud, a fight breaks out among the outlaws, and all the men except Jerry are killed. Soldiers find the distraught Jean and bring her to their headquarters, which are now administered by Fred. Not knowing of Jean's recent activities, Fred is overjoyed to see her and explains that he could not contact her because he had been captured by Quantrill's men. He adds that he gave Jerry several letters to smuggle to her. Fred asks Jean to marry him, but when she learns that he is looking for Marie Carroll, she pretends to be staying with friends and sneaks off to finish her mission to kill White Cloud. When Fred learns where Jean has gone from a captured Jerry, he hurries after her, but by the time he arrives, Jean has killed the Indian and has been severely wounded. After telling Fred that she loves him, Jean dies in his arms. *Brothers and sisters. Missouri. Revenge. Romance. United States–History–Civil War, 1861-1865. Escapes. Gunfights. Indians of North America. Outlaws. Romantic rivalry. United States. Army.*

Note: The film begins with the following written foreword: "Far from the main battle fronts in the latter days of the Civil War, Missouri was torn by violent partisan and guerrilla warfare. So vicious and widespread was this conflict that it paved the way directly for the wave of outlawry which scourged the Border Region throughout the Reconstruction Days and for years thereafter. And one of the most ominous in the changes of events which brought this about began when a lone rider appeared on this lonely road on a late summer afternoon in 1864." The character of "Bill Quantrill" was loosely based on William Clark Quantrill, who organized a band of guerrillas, which harried Union soldiers and anti-slavery civilians. Quantrill's Raiders were eventually made part of the regular Confederate army. Quantrill was fatally wounded in May 1965. Among the men who fought with Quantrill were the James brothers and the Youngers.

HR 20 Sep 1946, p. 19. *MPHPD* 14 Dec 1946, p. 3363

RENEGADE OF THE RANCHO *see* **THE MYSTERIOUS DESPERADO**

THE RENEGADE RANGER (Latino)
RKO Radio Pictures, Inc. *Dist* RKO Radio Pictures, Inc. 16 Sep 1938; Prod: late Jul—early Aug 1938 [©RKO Radio Pictures, Inc.; 16 Sep 1938; LP8327]. Sd (RCA Victor System); b&w. 6 reels, 5,311 ft. 59 min. PCA cert no. 4521.

Prod Bert Gilroy. *Dir* David Howard. [*Asst dir* Sam Ruman]. *Scr* Oliver Drake. *Story* Bennett Cohen. *Photog* Harry Wild. *Art dir* Van Nest Polglase. *Art dir assoc* Lucius Croxton. *Ed* Frederic Knudtson. *Mus dir* Roy Webb. *Rec* Hugh McDowell, Jr.

Song(s): "Move Slow, Little Doggie," words and music by Willie Phelps; "Señorita," words and music by Albert Hay Malotte.

Cast: GEORGE O'BRIEN [(*Captain Jack Steele*)], Rita Hayworth [(*Judith Alvarez*)], Tim Holt [(*Larry Corwin*)], Ray Whitley [(*Happy*)], Lucio Villegas [(*Don Juan Campielo*)], William Royle [(*Ben Sanderson*)], Cecilia Callejo [(*Tonia Campielo*)], Neal Hart [(*Sheriff Joe Rawling*)], Monte Montague [(*Monty*)], Robert Kortman [(*Idaho*)], Charles Stevens [(*Manuel*)], James Mason [(*Hank*)], Tom London [(*Red*)], [Guy Usher (*Major Jameson*)], [Chris Pin Martin (*Filipe*)], [Frank M. Thomas (*Carsen*)].

Western, with songs. [*Print viewed*]. While Captain Jack Steele of the Texas Rangers is assigned by Major Jameson to bring in renegade leader Judith Alvarez, the suspected murderer of rancher Sam Dunning, his friend, Larry Corwin, is dismissed from the Rangers for brawling in a saloon. Sure that Jack betrayed him to the major, Larry angrily rejects his friend, who then leaves with Happy, another Ranger, to find Judith. In Pecos City, Jack and Happy pose as cowboys and inquire about Ben Sanderson, an influential rancher and political boss who has posted a large reward for Judith's capture. After witnessing a tense scene between Sanderson and another rancher, who is worried that he, like Judith, will lose his ranch because he is unable to pay his back taxes, which Sanderson is responsible for levying, Jack sees Judith and her armed men storm into Sanderson's office. During the robbery by Judith, a fight breaks out, and Judith and her men are pursued by Sanderson's men. Jack saves Judith from sure death and is wounded in the process. Grateful, Judith takes Jack to her mountain hideout to recuperate, and there Jack discovers that Larry

has become part of Judith's gang. Unmoved by Jack's arguments, Larry, who is in love with the daughter of another disenfranchised rancher, threatens to reveal Jack's cover if he tries to arrest Judith. Soon after, Judith, having heard a promising report about Sanderson's cattle, organizes a scouting mission with Jack and Larry, unaware that Hank, one of her men, is a spy for Sanderson and is relaying the news to him. Before they depart, Larry alerts Don Juan Campielo, Judith's lead man, of Jack's identity, and Jack is told that he will soon meet with an "accident." On the way to Sanderson's range, Sanderson's gang, lead by Monty, ambush Judith's group. Before Sanderson's gang claims Judith, however, Jack reveals his identity and arrests her. After Sanderson's men, posing as Judith's men, execute a phony jailbreak and take Judith hostage, Jack and her gang ride to Sanderson's ranch to retrieve her. While circling the ranch house, Jack overhears Monty confess to killing Dunning on Sanderson's orders. Before Sanderson sends Judith to her death, Jack and her men break in and, following an intense gunfight, rescue her. Sanderson is arrested for murder, while Judith, who has forgiven Jack, is restored to her land and Larry is re-instated as a Ranger. *Frame-ups. Graft. Mexican Americans. Murder. Ranchers. Renegades. Texas Rangers.* Betrayal. Confession (Law). Cowboys. Dismissal (Employment). Fistfights. Friendship. Gunfights. Impersonation and imposture. Jailbreaks. Pardons. Political bosses. Rescues. Romance. Saloons. Taxation. Undercover operations.

Note: The working title of this film was *Ranger Code.* According to the opening frame in the copyright cutting continuity, the picture was one of the "$250,000 movie quiz contest pictures." No additional information about this contest has been found. RKO borrowed Rita Hayworth from Columbia Pictures for this production. According to *HR,* scenes for the production were shot in Chatsworth, CA. Modern sources add Tom Steele (*Outlaw*) and Ken Card and The Phelps Brothers (*Musicians*) to the cast. RKO made its first filmed version of Bennett Cohen's screen story in 1932 as *Come On Danger!* (see *AFI Catalog of Feature Films, 1931-40;* F3.0778). In 1942, Edward Killy directed Tim Holt and Frances Neal in another RKO remake of Cohen's story, also called *Come On Danger!*

DV 9 Sep 1938, p. 3. *FD* 21 Feb 1939, p. 8. *HR* 23 Jul 1938, p. 8. *HR* 29 Jul 1938, p. 4. *HR* 30 Jul 1938, p. 10. *HR* 9 Sep 1938, p. 2. *MPH* 20 Aug 1938, p. 54. *MPH* 25 Feb 1939, p. 42. *NYT* 17 Feb 1939, p. 17. *Var* 5 Oct 1938, p. 21.

RENEGADE ROUNDUP *see* **APACHE AMBUSH**

RENEGADES OF SONORA (Native Americans)
Republic Pictures Corp. *Dist* Republic Pictures Corp. 24 Nov 1948; Prod: mid—late Sep 1948 [©Republic Pictures Corp.; 24 Nov 1948; LP2040]. Sd (RCA Sound System); b&w. 60 min. Passed by the National Board of Review. PCA cert no. 13466.

Assoc prod Gordon Kay. *Dir* R. G. Springsteen. [*Asst dir* Johnny Grubbs]. *Wrt by* M. Coates Webster. [*Scr supv* Joan Eremin]. *Dir of photog* John MacBurnie. [*Cam op* Enzo Martinelli]. [*Stills* Don Keyes]. [*Optical eff* Consolidated Film Industries]. *Art dir* Frank Arrigo. *Film ed* Tony Martinelli. *Set dec* John McCarthy, Jr. and George Milo. *Mus* Stanley Wilson. *Sd* T. A. Carman. *Makeup supv* Bob Mark. [*Makeup* Howard Smit]. [*Grip* C. B. Lawrence]. [*Gaffer* Austin P. Heric]. *Scr supv* Joan Eremin.

Cast: Allan "Rocky" Lane [(*Allan "Rocky" Lane*)], and his stallion Black Jack, Eddy Waller [(*Nugget Clark*)], Roy Barcroft [(*George Keeler*)], Frank Fenton [(*Sheriff Jim Crawford*)], Mauritz Hugo [(*Pete Lasker*)], George J. Lewis [(*Chief Eagle Cloud*)], Holly Bane [(*Jeff*)], Dale Van Sickel [(*Brad*)], Marshall Reed [(*Deputy*)], House Peters, Jr. [(*Hank, the courier*)].

Western. [*Print viewed*]. On a Western trail, a courier named Hank ambushes two Indians and steals their sacred belt. During the attack, Chief Blue Feather is killed, which sends his tribe on the warpath. Meanwhile, in a nearby town, at the stage and freight depot that he operates, George Keeler informs townsman Nugget Clark about the war, saying that Sheriff Jim Crawford will attempt to negotiate peace with the Indians. Later, when Hank delivers the belt to George, he learns about the war and decides to return the belt, which is not particularly valuable. On his way to deliver the belt to an Indian agent in Sonora, California, Hank is followed by three men who shoot at him. Rocky Lane, who is on his way to buy a ranch in Wyoming, hears the shots and tries to save Hank, but is too severely wounded. As he dies, Hank makes Rocky promise to deliver the belt to the agent. Rocky finds the agent and explains that Hank has been killed. The agent then assures Rocky that the murder will be reported to the sheriff. Later, when the agent is found dead, Nugget tells the sheriff that he saw Rocky leaving the agent's office earlier, and Rocky is arrested. They then question Rocky, who explains that the man found

dead was not the person who had taken the belt from him. With Rocky in jail, the sheriff's deputies look for the agent's body, but George informs the sheriff that the agent has returned safely. Later, as the Indians prepare to attack, Eagle Cloud visits the sheriff demanding to know why his "brother," the Indian agent, was killed and says that he will attack at sunrise unless the belt is returned. Meanwhile, at the depot, Pete Lasker, who has been posing as the dead agent, gives George the belt. They prepare to evacuate with the prospector's gold after the Indians have destroyed the town, and return as heroes with the belt. When Rocky sees Pete leaving the depot, he breaks out of the jail cell across the street and follows him. When Nugget catches Rocky, he explains that he has seen the man who impersonated the agent, and they decide to follow Pete together. Pete attempts to escape, but gets his neck caught on a hanging vine and strangles to death. Now suspicious of George, Rocky and Nugget go to the depot that evening, where they see George's men loading wagons for the evacuation. Pretending to be one of the men, Rocky rides his horse Black Jack into the depot and tells Nugget to go get the sheriff. When George's men discover Nugget and Black Jack outside the depot, they bind and gag both of them. After Keeler's gang has left for Bedrock Pass, Black Jack uses his teeth to untie their ropes. Rocky and Nugget travel to the Indian camp to recruit the Indians' help in retrieving the belt. The Indians force Keeler's wagon train into a circle, and as Rocky fights with him, George is accidentally stabbed with his own knife. After the belt is returned to the Indians and the town made safe from attack, Rocky says farewell to Nugget and the townspeople. *Belts. Cowboys. Indians of North America.* Ambushes. Arrests. Brothers. Couriers. Escapes. Evacuations. Gold. Impersonation and imposture. Indian agents. Jailbreaks. Pledges. Sheriffs. Shootings. Sonora (CA). Stabbings. Thieves. Tribal chiefs. Wagons.

Note: Modern sources include the following in the cast: William Henry, Douglas Fowley and Art Dillard.

DV 7 Jan 1949, p. 3. *HR* 24 Sep 1948, p. 15. *HR* 7 Jan 1949, p. 3. *MPHPD* 4 Dec 1948, p. 4410. *MPHPD* 8 Jan 1949, p. 4450.

REPRISAL! (Native Americans)
Romson Productions, Inc.; Columbia Pictures Corp. *Dist* Columbia Pictures Corp. Nov 1956; Los Angeles opening: 24 Oct 1956; Prod: 21 Mar—10 Apr 1956 [©Columbia Pictures Corp.; 30 Nov 1956; LP7274]. Sd (Westrex Recording System); col (Technicolor); 1.85. 8 reels, 6,672 ft. 74 min. PCA cert no. 17768.

Prod Lewis J. Rachmil. *Assoc prod* Helen Ainsworth. *Dir* George Sherman. *Asst dir* Sam Nelson. *Scr* David P. Harmon, Raphael Hayes and David Dortort. *Scr story* David P. Harmon. *Dir of photog* Henry Freulich. *Art dir* Walter Holscher. *Film ed* Jerome Thoms. *Set dec* William Kiernan and Robert Priestly. *Mus cond* Mischa Bakaleinikoff. *Sd* Lambert Day. *Rec supv* John Livadary. *Sd* Lambert Day. *Technicolor color consultant* Henri Jaffa.

Source: Based on the novel *Reprisal* by Arthur Gordon (New York, 1950).

Cast: Guy Madison (*Frank Madden*), Felicia Farr (*Catherine Cantrell*), Kathryn Grant (*Taini*), Michael Pate (*Bert Shipley*), Edward Platt (*Neil Shipley*), Otto Hulett (*Sheriff Jim Dixon*), Wayne Mallory (*Tom Shipley*), Robert Burton (*Jeb Cantrell*), Ralph Moody (*Matara*), Frank de Kova (*Charlie Washackie*), Paul McGuire (*Whitey*), Don Rhodes (*Buck*), Philip Breedlove (*Takola*), Malcolm Atterbury (*Luther Creel*), Eve McVeagh (*Nora Shipley*), Victor Zamudio (*Kileni*), Pete Kellett (*Foreman*), Jack Lomas (*Bartender*), Addison Richards (*Judge*), John Zaremba (*Mister Willard*), Roger L. Perry (*Chief's son*), Arthur Lovejoy (*Prosecutor*), Patrick R. Brown, Luther E. Ogletree, Ike Thomason, Fred Aldrich, Eddie Parker, Ken Terrell, Ken Worthen, John Marshall, Bill Hale, Steve Raines, Dirk Thane, Bruce Cameron, Fred Krone.

Western. [*Not viewed*]. Frank Madden arrives in the prairie town of Kendall, Oklahoma, to take possession of a ranch he has purchased. In the saloon, which has been temporarily converted into a courthouse, three brothers, Neil, Bert and Tom Shipley, are on trial for murder, having lynched an Indian man and woman. Ignoring the judge's instruction to disregard the race of the victims, the all-white jury promptly acquits the brothers. Later, sheriff Jim Dixon directs Frank to the land agent, Jeb Cantrell, whose daughter Catherine is distraught over the unfair verdict. Frank is unwilling to express an opinion on the issue. He tells Catherine that he prefers not to take sides, but in truth Frank is part Indian himself. Catherine accompanies Frank to his property, which is bordered by the Shipley

brothers' land. Frank angers the brothers when he fences his land to keep their cattle from grazing on it, and he is beaten up when he defends an Indian boy who has been injured by Bert. The Shipley brothers now look for opportunities to provoke Frank into a fight, and the hostility between them grows when Frank comes to the rescue of an Indian girl, Taini, who has been the object of Bert's unwanted attentions. Taini falls in love with Frank, but he is in love with Catherine, although he will not admit this to her because of his Indian blood. Soon, Frank's grandfather, Matara, shows up at the ranch hoping to convince Frank to come back to his own people. When Frank refuses, Matara stays on at the ranch in the guise of a servant. Meanwhile, the young Indians in the town are beginning to rebel against their persecution. Takola, the husband of the woman lynched by the Shipley brothers, comes back for revenge, and he ambushes and kills Tom. Neil immediately blames Frank, and he and Bert are about to shoot Frank when the sheriff puts Frank in jail for his own safety. Neil and Bert organize a mob and abduct Frank from the jail, and are about to lynch him when Taini comes forth and announces that Frank could not have killed Tom because he had spent the night with her. Frank is released, but Catherine is hurt and outraged that Frank would have an affair with an Indian girl. He tries to explain that Taini was only lying to save him, but Catherine refuses to listen to him. Bert also believes the lie, and he jealously sets out to kill Frank and Taini. He comes across them one day as Frank and Matara stop to talk with Taini on their way back to the ranch. Bert opens fire, killing Matara and Taini and wounding Frank, who shoots and kills both Bert and Neil. Frank tells the townspeople that he is an Indian, bitterly denouncing his own attempts to pass for white. Later, as Frank is burying his grandfather, the sheriff tries to persuade him to stay in town. Frank refuses, choosing instead to start over in a new place, this time living as an Indian. As he rides out of town, Catherine, who now knows that Frank was telling the truth about Taini, joins him. *Indians of North America. Indians of North America–Mixed blood. Racism. Revenge. Abduction. Ambushes. Cattle. False accusations. Grandfathers. Gunfights. Jails. Jealousy. Judges. Juries. Lynching. Oklahoma. Racial impersonation. Sheriffs. Trials.*

Note: According to a *HR* news item, Columbia's sales and promotions executives decided to add an exclamation point to the end of the novel's title. The novel on which this film was based was actually set in Georgia at a later period and was about the lynching of an African American, according to the *Newsweek* review. An Oct 1955 *DV* news item states that Gil Orlowitz was polishing the script, but his contribution to the final film has not been confirmed.

Box 6 Oct 1956. *DV* 6 Oct 1955. *DV* 3 Oct 1956, p. 3. *Exb* 3 Oct 1956, p.4230. *FD* 8 Oct 1956, p. 8. *Har* 6 Oct 1956, p. 160. *HR* 13 Jun 1956. *HR* 3 Oct 1956, p. 3. *MPHPD* 6 Oct 1956, p. 97. *Newsweek* 19 Nov 1956. *Var* 3 Oct 1956, p. 6.

LA REPÚBLICA NO PELIGRA *see* **DOS NOCHES**

RESCUE SQUAD (Indo-Americans)
Mayfair Productions, Inc. *Dist* State Rights; Empire Film Distributors, Inc. 7 Mar **1935** [©Empire Film Distributors, Inc.; 28 Mar 1935; LP5445]. Sd; b&w. 7 reels. 61 min. PCA cert no. 512.
Dir Spencer Gordon Bennet. *Story* Charlotte Arthur and Margel Gluck. *Dial* Betty Burbridge. *Cont* George Morgan. *Photog* Gilbert Warrenton. *Rec eng* Corson Jowett. *Prod mgr* Lester F. Scott, Jr.
Cast: Ralph Forbes (*De Witt Porter*), Verna Hillie (*Norma Britt*), Kate Pentzer (*Molly Borden, an artist*), Sheila Terry (*Rose, a model*), Beth Hartman (*Daisy, a model*), Frank Leigh (*Akoor*), Catherine Cotter (*Jennie [Akoor]*), Jimmy Aubrey (*Henry*), Leon Waycoff (*Lester Vaughn, a philanderer*), Catherine Stoker (*An artist*).
Romance. [*Not viewed*]. Heiress Norma Britt decides to marry philandering Lester Vaughn, despite of the misgivings of her artist friend Molly Borden. Vaughn has been having an affair with Molly's model, Rose, who becomes upset when she learns of Vaughn's plans to marry Norma. DeWitt Porter, a wealthy and cultured collector of antiques, lives in the studio next to Molly. She invites Porter to a party, hoping he will make Norma forget about Vaughn. At Akoor's curio shop, Jennie, the shop owner's daughter, stops Porter from buying a rare Buddha, explaining that it is cursed. She adds that her little brother is crippled, a fact that she attributes to the god's anger at Akoor for marrying a white woman. Speeding to Molly's party, Norma crashes into Porter's car and wrecks it. Porter and Norma quarrel over the accident and Norma becomes so angry that she drives away. When Porter arrives at the party, Molly is amazed to learn that he and Norma have already met. Later Akoor informs Porter that he

will sell the Buddha, despite his fear that such an action will bring a curse on his house, as he needs the money to pay for his son's operation. Akoor then prepares poisoned wine for Porter as he plans to keep the Buddha, thereby avoiding its curse, while still obtaining the money he needs to save his son. In the meantime, Vaughn persuades Norma to sail with him to Europe and be married at sea. At the same time that Norma leaves Molly's studio for the ship, Porter departs for Akoor's shop, and they meet in the apartment elevator. The elevator then becomes trapped between floors. Several hours later Rose finds them and Porter asks her to call Vaughn and the rescue squad. When the building superintendent discovers the stuck elevator, he mistakenly pulls a switch that causes a short circuit and sets fire to the elevator shaft. After the fire department rescues the pair, Jennie warns Porter of her father's plan. Porter drives Norma to the docks, but the ship carrying Vaughn has already departed. On board the vessel, Vaughn learns to his dismay that his stateroom is shared, not by Norma, but by Rose. Back on shore, Porter and Norma realize that they both are glad that she missed the boat. *Artists. Curses. East Indians. Heiresses. Antique dealers. Automobile accidents. Elevators. Elopement. Fires. Handicapped. Idle rich. Love affairs. Miscegenation. Models. Parties. Philanderers. Rescues. Ships.*

FD 3 Apr 1935, p. 10. *HR* 16 Dec 1935, p. 3.

THE REST CURE (*foreign version*, Metropolitan Pictures Corp., 1935) *see* **DE LA SARTÉN AL FUEGO**

REST CURE (Fox Film Corp. 1935) *see* **TE QUIERO CON LOCURA**

RESURRECCIÓN (Spanish language)
Universal Pictures Corp. *Dist* Universal Pictures Corp. **1931**; New York opening: 6 Mar 1931; Prod: Dec 1930. Sd; b&w. 10 reels, 7,647 ft. 85 min. Spanish language.
Prod supv Paul Kohner. *Dir* Edwin Carewe. *Dial dir* Eduardo Arozamena. *Scr* Finis Fox. *Spanish version* Baltasar Fernández Cué. *Photog* Robert B. Kurrle.
Source: Based on the novel *Voskraeseniye (Resurrection)* by Leo Tolstoy (Moscow, 1899).
Cast: Lupe Vélez (*Katusha Maslowa*), Gilbert Roland (*Príncipe Dimitri*), Miguel Faust Rocha (*Capitán Shenbok*), Soledad Jiménez (*María*), Amelia Senisterra (*Sofía*), Eduardo Arozamena, Blanca de Castejón.
Drama. [*Not viewed*]. [The following plot summary is based on the English-language version of this film, *Resurrection*; character names refer to that version. For further information regarding the English-language version, please see the note below and the entry for *Resurrection* in the *AFI Catalog of Feature Films, 1931-40*.] Russian Prince Dmitri Ivanovitch Nekhludof falls in love with his aunts' ward, Katusha Maslova, while visiting their farm in the Ural Mountains. Katusha returns his love, but he is called to St. Petersburg to join the army, and becomes a changed man. On his way to fight in the war against Turkey, Dmitri's regiment stops over at his aunts' farm. Military life has roughened Dmitri's temperament, and that night he rapes Katusha. Katusha becomes pregnant and is thrown out of the household because of her "indiscretion." Her child is stillborn, and out of desperation, Katusha turns to prostitution to survive. One year later, Katusha is accused of murder, and Dmitri serves on the jury at her trial. He is shocked to see her dissipation, but his plea on her behalf fails to sway his fellow jurors, and Katusha is exiled to Siberia. Dmitri visits her in prison, but she is drunk and solicits him. Dmitri is so horrified that his actions have so denigrated the woman he once loved that he sells everything he owns and follows the train carrying convicts into Siberia. After the train journey ends, the prisoners continue on foot across the frozen land, and although Katusha tells Dmitri to return to civilization, he stays with her. Dmitri finally gets a pardon for Katusha at a Siberian station and proposes to her. She does not respond immediately, but tells him if she stays at the station in the morning, she will marry him. In the morning, Katusha clearly rejects his proposal as she joins the other prisoners on their march to their destiny. *Dissipation. Exiles. Moral corruption. Rape. Russia. Aunts. Drunkenness. Pregnancy. Prisons. Prostitution. Romance. Siberia. Soldiers. Trials. Unmarried mothers. Wards and guardians.*

Note: This was a Spanish-language version of the 1931 film *Resurrection*, which was directed by Edwin Carewe and starred John Boles and Lupe Vélez, please see the entry for that film in the *AFI Catalog of Feature Films, 1931-40*; F3.3699. When exhibited in San Juan, Puerto Rico, the Spanish version was entitled *El principe y la aldeana*. Edwin Carewe also directed a 1927 film

based on Tolstoy's novel for United Artists, starring Rod La Rocque and Dolores Del Rio (see *AFI Catalog of Feature Films, 1921-30*; F2.4553). Among other film versions of Tolstoy's novel are a 1909 one-reel film produced by Biograph Co., titled *Resurrection*, directed by D. W. Griffith and starring Florence Lawrence; a 1915 Fox film entitled *A Woman's Resurrection*, directed by J. Gordon Edwards and starring Betty Nansen and a 1918 Famous Players-Lasky film entitled *Resurrection* (see *AFI Catalog of Feature Films, 1911-20*; F1.3693 and F1.5115); a 1934 film entitled *We Live Again* (see below); and a two-part Mosfilm production, entitled *Voskresenie*, directed by Mikhail Chveitser, starring Tamara Skomina, which was released in Europe in 1960 and 1962, and in the United States (as *Resurrection*) in 1963 (see *AFI Catalog of Feature Films, 1961-70*; F6.4076).

Cinl Apr 1931, p. 32.

RESURRECTION (*foreign version*) see **RESURRECCIÓN**

RETURN OF BUFFALO BILL see **BUFFALO BILL RIDES AGAIN**

RETURN OF CUSTER see **7TH CAVALRY**

RETURN OF MANDY'S HUSBAND (African Americans)
Lucky Star Production. *Dist* Toddy Pictures Co. **1947**?. Sd; b&w. 4,405 ft. 49 min.
[*Exec prod* Ted Toddy].
Cast: Mantan Moreland (*Mantan* [*also known as Prince Alabastar Amsterdam*]), Flournoy E. Miller (*Alex*), John D. Lee, Jr., E. Hensley, McKinley Reeves, Terry Knight.
African American, Comedy. [*Not viewed*]. In order to make some cash, buddies Mantan and Alex found the "Ghost Association," which will hold mock séances for the local residents. After studying the details of the locals' various deceased relatives, Alex insists that the reluctant Mantan, who is afraid of ghosts, play "Prince Alabastar Amsterdam" and fool people into thinking that he is in communication with their dead loved ones. Meanwhile, Henry Coffee, local resident Mandy's husband, has staged his own disappearance because he can no longer tolerate his wife's nagging. He takes refuge at Morgan's place, an old barn, where he encounters a band of thugs who take him hostage. Soon after, Alex and Mantan, who have chosen the Morgan place for their first Ghost Association séance, show up at the old barn where the gangsters are planning their getaway. Inside, the timorous Mantan, who senses the presence of the gangsters, believes that the barn is haunted, especially after one of the gangsters knocks Alex out and hides him, leaving Mantan alone. Eventually the police come, have a shoot-out, and then haul the gangsters away, giving Alex, who says that Prince Alabastar heroically caught the gangsters, a good publicity story for his enterprise. Later, Mandy and her friend, Miss Sarah, discuss with Mantan and Alex the upcoming séance, and, because he realizes that he knows nothing about Miss Sarah's late husband, Mantan warns her that the man may have changed since his death. At the old barn, the audience arrives and Alex tells Mantan, who will impersonate the voices of the dearly departed, to hide in a stall. Mantan is terrified, however, because he thinks he hears a real ghost, unaware that Henry Coffee, who is still hiding in the barn's loft. When Mandy asks "Alabastar" to conjure her husband Henry, the latter overhears and believes he's been discovered, but when a distraught Mandy, hearing her husband's voice, says she would never mistreat him again if he came back, he cries "You won, Honey." The weak floor-boards of the loft then break and Henry crashes down from the heavens to reunite with his wife. *Disguise. Get-rich-quick schemes. Mediums. Séances. Swindlers and swindling. Deception. Gangsters. Ghosts. Henpecked husbands. Hideouts. Police. Shootouts.*
Note: Although the film was not registered for copyright, there is a copyright statement on the dialogue continuity for the film, dated 1947 for Toddy Pictures. The plot summary was taken from a dialogue continuity deposited with the NYSA, and the credits were obtained from an advertisement for this film. No release date or reviews have been located for the film, which was received on 13 May 1947 by the New York State censor board.

THE RETURN OF RIN TIN TIN (Refugees)
Romay Pictures, Inc. *Dist* Eagle-Lion Films, Inc. 1 Nov **1947**; Prod: began early Sep 1946 [©Romay Pictures, Inc.; 15 Nov 1947; LP1304]. Sd (Western Electric Wide Range System); col (Vitacolor; Cinecolor). 6,061 ft. 64-65 or 67.5 min. PCA cert no. 12192.
Prod William Stephens. *Dir* Max Nosseck. *Asst dir* Harold Knox. *Scr* Jack DeWitt. *Orig idea* William Stephens. *Photog* Carl Berger. *Art dir* F. Paul Sylos. *Film ed* Michael Luciano and Elmo J. Veron. *Set dresser* Ken Swartz. *Ward* Wanda Armstrong and Emanuel Barton. *Mus* Endody. *Sd* Frank McWhorter and B. J. Remington. *Makeup dir* Leo

White. *Unit mgr* George Yohalem. *Tech adv* Father Celestine Quinlan. *Owner-trainer of Rin Tin Tin* Lee Duncan.
Cast: Rin Tin Tin III, Donald Woods [(*Father Matthew*)], Bobby Blake [(*Paul, the refugee lad*)], Gaylord Pendleton [(*Melrose*)], Claudia Drake [(*Mrs. Graham*)], [Earle Hodgins].
Animal, Youth, Drama. [*Print viewed*]. Paul, a European war orphan who is the ward of his mother's childhood friend, Mrs. Graham, whose husband was also killed in the war, has difficulty adjusting to his new life in a rural area of the U.S. Haunted by the air raid death of his parents and brother, Paul remains aloof at school, insecure about his language skills and his ability to fit in with the other children. Afraid that Paul will be taken away by the authorities if they are not happy together, Mrs. Graham sends him to spend the summer with Father Matthew at the Santa Ynez Mission in California, hoping the priest will help him. Paul quickly adjusts to his job as caretaker of the mission's animals and even uses newly acquired American slang in his conversations with the animals. When a stray German Shepherd named Rin Tin Tin arrives at the mission, Paul grows to love him. He confides in the dog about his loss of faith because of the destruction of his family and village. After a few weeks, Rin Tin Tin's stern owner, Mr. Melrose, retrieves the dog, and Paul is heartbroken because he is convinced that he loses everything he loves. While Rin Tin Tin repeatedly attempts to escape and return to the mission, Father Matthew encourages Paul to have faith, assuring him that no one in America wants to hurt him, but that they want to be his friend. One night, when Melrose arrives to retrieve Rin Tin Tin, Paul hides him in the barn loft. When the hay in the loft catches fire, Rin Tin Tin adroitly douses a rag with water and puts out the fire before being rescued. Melrose then gives Paul a stern warning that he must shun Rin Tin Tin if he comes back or he will beat the dog to teach him a lesson. As Rin Tin Tin makes his next escape attempt, Melrose beats him with a club, inciting the dog to bite him and flee again to the mission. This time, with Melrose's threat ringing in his ears, Paul sadly shuns the dog, who lopes off to the nearby woods. That night, Paul prays to God that Rin Tin Tin will return. Melrose arrives at the mission in a rage and demands that Father Matthew put down Rin Tin Tin because he is rabid. While searching for the dog in the dark woods, Melrose is attacked by a wild dog and is saved by Rin Tin Tin, who then leads Father Matthew and Paul into the woods to rescue him. Later, Melrose gives Rin Tin Tin to Paul, and no longer afraid of people, Paul attends Mass at the mission for the first time. *Cruelty to animals. Dogs. Faith. Missions. Orphans. Priests. War refugees. Assimilation (Sociology). Faith. Forests. Post-war life. Rescues. Santa Ynez Mission (CA). Slang. Transformation. Widows.*
Note: The opening credits on the viewed print stated "Photographed in gorgeous natural color at the Santa Ynez Mission." As noted in the *Var* review, the film was shot in Vitacolor and processed in Cinecolor. According to records of the U.S. War Department, Bureau of Public Relations, footage for the film's opening dream sequence, in which "Paul" dreams of his family's death in the bombing of a European city, was taken from John Huston's 1944 documentary *San Pietro*.
Box 8 Nov 1947. *DV* 3 Nov 1947. *Exh* 12 Nov 1947, p. 2275. *FD* 11 Nov 1947, p. 7. *Har* 8 Nov 1947, p. 179. *HR* 6 Sep 1946, p. 15. *HR* 13 Sep 1946, p. 17. *HR* 3 Nov 1947, p. 3. *MPHPD* 8 Nov 1947. *Var* 5 Nov 1947, p. 8.

THE RETURN OF THE CISCO KID (Latino)
Twentieth Century-Fox Film Corp.; Darryl F. Zanuck in charge of production. *Dist* Twentieth Century-Fox Film Corp. 28 Apr **1939**; Prod: 22 Feb—27 Mar 1939 [©Twentieth Century-Fox Film Corp.; 28 Apr 1939; LP9104]. Sd (Western Electric Mirrophonic Recording); b&w. 6,378 ft. 70-71 min. PCA cert no. 5182.
Series: The Cisco Kid.
Assoc prod Kenneth Macgowan. *Dir* Herbert I. Leeds. [*Asst dir* Sidney Bowen]. *Scr* Milton Sperling. [*Contr wrt* Al Cohn, Marion Jackson and Rich James]. *Photog* Charles Clarke. *Art dir* Richard Day and Wiard B. Ihnen. *Film ed* James B. Clark. *Set dresser* Thomas Little. *Cost* Gwen Wakeling. *Mus dir* Cyril J. Mockridge. *Sd* Arthur von Kirbach and Roger Heman. [*Tech adv* Ernesto A. Romero].
Source: Based on the character created by O. Henry.
Cast: WARNER BAXTER [(*The Cisco Kid, also known as Señor Gonzales Sebastian Rodrigo Don Juan Chicquello*)], Lynn Bari [(*Ann Carver*)], Cesar Romero [(*Lopez*)], Henry Hull [(*Colonel Jonathan Bixby*)], Kane Richmond [(*Alan Davis*)], C. Henry Gordon [(*Mexican captain*)], Robert Barrat [(*Sheriff McNally*)], [Chris Pin Martin (*Gordito*)], [Adrian Morris (*Deputy Johnson*)], [Soledad Jimenez (*Mama Soledad*)], [Victor Kilian (*Bartender*)], [Harry Strang

(*Deputy*)], [Arthur Aylsworth (*Stagecoach driver*)], [Paul Burns (*Hotel clerk*)], [Eddy Waller, Ralph Dunn (*Guards*)], [Ruth Gillette (*Frowsy blonde*)], [Ward Bond (*Tough guy*)], [Gino Corrado (*Waiter*)], [Herbert Heywood (*Proprietor*)], [Charles Tannen (*Teller*)], [Ethan Laidlaw], [Max Wagner], [Lee Shumway], [Harry Depp].

Western. [*Viewed print incomplete*]. In 1900, in Northern Mexico near the Arizona border, the Cisco Kid, the famous bandit known as Señor Gonzales Sebastian Rodrigo Don Juan Chicquello, faces a firing squad. That night, he arises from his grave with the help of his two friends, Lopez and Gordito, who had placed blanks in the soldiers' guns the previous night. The three head for Arizona where Cisco makes the acquaintance of Colonel Jonathan Bixby and his granddaughter, Ann Carver, who are traveling to the ranch in which they invested all their money. Cisco joins them and foils an attempted robbery of their stagecoach. In town, Bixby and Ann discover that Sheriff McNally, the local land baron, holds the deed to their ranch and has thrown their partner's son, Alan Davis, in jail to keep it. When Bixby and Ann demand his release, McNally, both sheriff and judge, puts them in jail as well. Learning of their arrest, Cisco sets the local store on fire, using the confusion to break the group out of jail. Alan is shot in the escape, but Cisco lances his bullet wound. He takes the trio to the home of Mama Soledad, where they are cared for. Back in town, Cisco meets with McNally, telling him he is a cattleman interested in buying Bixby's ranch. McNally refuses to sell, however, claiming the land is a gold mine. When Cisco offers him $100,000, McNally finally agrees, but Cisco robs McNally's bank for the money. While his friends want to keep the money, Cisco insists it is for Ann, his new love. Unknown to Cisco, Ann and Alan are in love. McNally, realizing he has been double-crossed, prepares a trap for Cisco, but Cisco is too smart for him and gets the deed to the ranch. When Cisco learns of Ann's engagement to Alan, he feels betrayed and orders his friends to find Alan and send him through a pass that the Mexican army has been told the Cisco Kid will be using. However, when Cisco learns from Ann that she never loved him or meant to mislead him, Cisco rides off to save Alan. As McNally and the Mexican soldiers wait at the pass, Cisco sneaks behind them and captures the group. Cisco agrees to stay away from McNally if he will leave Alan and Ann alone, and McNally consents. As Cisco, Lopez and Gordito then ride back into Mexico, Cisco decides to go see an old girl friend. *Arizona. Bandits. Bank robberies. Deeds. Land rights. Mexicans. Southerners. Arson. Escapes. Firing squads. Gunshot wounds. Jailbreaks. Jealousy. Mexican-American border region. Mexico. Army. Ranches. Rescues. Sheriffs. Stagecoach robberies. Traps.*

Note: The summary and onscreen credits for this film were based on a viewing of an incomplete print and on a dialogue continuity in the copyright descriptions. According to a *HR* production chart, Harold Huber was to have appeared in this film. *HR* stated that former Mexican vice-counsul Ernesto A. Romero worked on the film as a technical director, dialogue coach and writer. According to a Twentieth Century-Fox press release, much of the film was shot on location in Arizona, with the company working out of Tucson. While the dialogue continuity deposited for copyright states that the film is "A Cosmopolitan Production," this statement is not included in the opening credits of the print viewed. For more information on the Cisco Kid series, see the entry above for *The Cisco Kid.*

Box 29 Apr 1940. *DV* 18 Apr 1939, p. 3. *FD* 24 Apr 1939, p. 5. *HR* 11 Jan 1939, p. 2. *HR* 21 Feb 1939, p. 2. *HR* 23 Feb 1939, p. 4. *HR* 28 Feb 1939, p. 8. *HR* 27 Mar 1939, p. 2. *HR* 19 Apr 1939, p. 3. *MPH* 22 Apr 1939, p. 38. *NYT* 29 Apr 1939, p. 13. *Var* 26 Apr 1939, p. 12.

REVENGE! *see* **GUN FEVER**

REVENGE AT MONTE CARLO (*foreign version*) *see* **DOS NOCHES**

REVISTA HISPANO-AMERICANA (Spanis language)
Hispano América Movitonal Films. Jan **1930**; New York opening: 1 Jan 1930; Prod: late 1929. Sd; b&w. Length undetermined.
Prod Juan J. Pablo.
Cast: Reva Reyes, José Moriche, Li Ho Chang, Carmen Rodríguez, Rodolfo Hoyos, Alberto de Lima, Tomasita Núñez, Olivia Zenor, Nilo Menéndez, Orquesta Puertorriqueña Sanabria, Plaza Hotel (N.Y.) Jazz Orquesta.

Variety. [*Not viewed*]. This film is a collection of musical performances, magic and comedy sketches. *Entertainers. Magicians. Musicians. Singers.*

Note: This film was produced by Juan J. Pablo for his New York City-based company, Hispano América Movitonal Films. Pablo, who was better known as

the magician Li Ho Chang, also performed in the film, which was released in Mexico City early in Jan 1930. It is possible that the film's title was only used as an "umbrella" for a package of short films.

REVISTA MUSICAL CUGAT *see* **CHARROS, GAUCHOS Y MANOLAS**

REVOLT AT FORT LARAMIE (Native Americans, Dakota)
Bel-Air Productions. *Dist* United Artists Corp. Mar **1957**; Prod: mid-May—late May 1956 [©Prospect Productions, Inc.; 6 Mar 1957; LP8145]. Sd (Western Electric Sound System); col (DeLuxe). 72-73 min. PCA cert no. 18161.
Exec prod Aubrey Schenck. *Prod* Howard W. Koch. *Dir* Lesley Selander. *Asst dir* Paul Wurtzel. *Wrt* Robert C. Dennis. *Photog* William Margulies. *Op cam* Ben Colman. *Photog eff* Jack Rabin and Louis DeWitt. *Prod des* Jack T. Collis. *Ed* John F. Schreyer. *Set dec* Clarence Steenson. *Prop master* Arden Cripe. *Ward* Wesley V. Jeffries and Angela Alexander. *Mus* Les Baxter. *Mus ed* Sam Waxman. *Sd mixer* Joe Edmondson. *Sd ed* Mike Pozen. *Re-rec* Charles Cooper. *Makeup artist* Ted Coodley. *Hair styles* Mary Westmoreland. *Key grip* Herschel Brown. *Lighting tech* Robert J. Campbell.
Cast: John Dehner [(*Major Seth Bradner*)], Gregg Palmer [(*Captain James Tenslip*)], Frances Helm [(*Melissa Bradner*)], Don Gordon [(*Jean Salignac*)], Robert Keys [(*Sergeant Darrach*)], Wm. "Bill" Phillips [(*Serrell*)], Cain Mason [(*Ezra*)], Robert Knapp [(*Lieutenant Waller*)], Frederick Ford, Eddie Little [(*Red Cloud*)], [Dean Stanton (*Rinty*)], [Bill Barker (*Hendrey*)], [Clay Randolph (*Caswell*)], [Kenne Duncan (*Captain Foley*)].

Western. [*Print viewed*]. Although they have been promised a shipment of gold in exchange for their acceptance of a peace treaty, Sioux warriors in the Wyoming territory attack a supply wagon heading for Fort Laramie. The fort's soldiers, led by Captain James Tenslip, successfully defend the wagon. Back at the fort, Tenslip and Major Seth Bradner, the commander, determine that the Sioux have been attempting to steal gold from the supply wagons as a means of enriching their tribe without having to sign the treaty. Bradner sends his scout, the Frenchman Jean Salignac, who is part Sioux, to negotiate with Red Cloud, the Sioux chief. After Bradner, a Virginian, receives a message that the Confederacy has elected Jefferson Davis as its president, a violent brawl breaks out between the fort's Northern and Southern soldiers. Melissa Bradner, the major's niece and the object of Tenslip's affections, greatly fears the growing conflict and begs Tenslip, who is from the North, to marry her before the situation worsens. Bradner gives Tenslip permission to marry his niece and promises to announce the engagement at that evening's dance. However, a Pony Express messenger interrupts the festivities, and when Bradner addresses the crowd, he announces not the engagement, but the Confederacy's attack on Fort Sumter and President Lincoln's subsequent call for military action against the rebels. A group of soldiers from the South then plot to take over the fort and steal the next gold shipment in order to bring war funds to the nearest Confederate fort in Texas. They approach Bradner for his support, but Bradner angrily denounces the plot as an act of treason. Hendrey, a Southerner, informs Tenslip of the plot, and, to the tune of "Dixie," is savagely murdered and scalped as a traitor by the Southern soldiers. Later, Tenslip reveals his mistaken belief that the major is a participant in the Southerners' plot, and both the major and Melissa are greatly angered by the accusation. Salignac then returns from his mission to report that Red Cloud has refused to come to Fort Laramie and has demanded that the signing of the treaty and the turning over of the gold take place on neutral ground. After Bradner receives an order from his superiors calling for the release of all soldiers whose loyalty to the Union is in doubt, he turns the command of the fort over to Tenslip, renewing the younger man's admiration for the dignified commander. The following day, Bradner and his men, joined by Salignac, bid goodbye to the fort and head for the nearest Conderate outpost in Texas, confident that the Sioux will not attack as they are no longer soldiers. In the meantime, Melissa, still angry at Tenslip, makes plans to return home to Viriginia. Riding through Sioux territory, Bradner and his men are soon confronted by Indians, and Bradner has Salignac explain that the Sioux will receive the promised gold from Tenslip once their convoy has made its way safely out of the area. However, Red Cloud, fearing a trick, attacks the small group of men and demands Bradner as a hostage. Although Bradner is willing to serve as hostage, his men refuse to surrender him, fearing that the Yankee Tenslip will not pay his ransom. Salignac manages to sneak

through enemy lines in order to get help from Fort Laramie, and although Tenslip greatly dislikes and mistrusts Salignac, his conscience dictates that he make certain his former commander is safe. Grateful that Tenslip is willing to help her uncle, Melissa finally forgives him for his misguided accusations and she and Tenslip redeclare their love for each other. Tenslip and his men reach the small band of battle-weary Southerners and, during a protracted battle with the Sioux, the soldiers lay aside their hostilities to fight alongside each other. United, the soldiers finally manage to prevail against the Sioux, but Bradner is killed. Tenslip offers the Southerners a chance to stay with him, but although they are grateful for the Northerners' help and have a newfound respect for Tenslip, they decide to ride on to the Confederate fort. Salignac, now redeemed, joins Tenslip and his men, and together they return to Fort Laramie, above which the Union's Stars and Stripes blows in the wind. *Dakota Indians. Fort Laramie (WY). Political alliances. United States–History–Civil War, 1861-1865. United States. Army. Cavalry. False accusations. French Americans. Gold. Indians of North America–Mixed blood. Loyalty. Messengers. Pony Express. Proposals (Marital). Scouts (Frontier). Soldiers. Southerners. Treaties. Tribal chiefs.*

Note: The working title of this film was *Fort Laramie.* Aubrey Schenck's and Howard Koch's production company was called both Bel-Air Productions and Prospect Productions. *Revolt at Fort Laramie* was shot on location in Kanab, Utah.

Box 16 Feb 1957. *DV* 11 Mar 1957, p. 3. *Exb* 20 Mar 1957, p. 4303. *FD* 11 Mar 1957, p. 12. *Har* 23 Mar 1957, p. 48. *HR* 11 May 1956, p. 21. *HR* 25 May 1956, p. 11. *HR* 11 Mar 1957, p. 3. *MPD* 5 March 1957. *MPHPD* 16 Mar 1957, p. 298. *Var* 27 Mar 1957, p. 6.

REX BEACH'S THE BARRIER *see* **THE BARRIER**

REX, KING OF THE WILD HORSES *see* **KING OF THE WILD HORSES**

EL REY DE LOS GITANOS (Spanish language)
Fox Film Corp. *Dist* Fox Film Corp. **1933**; Barcelona, Spain opening: 23 May 1933; Los Angeles opening: 26 May 1933; Prod: 16 Dec 1932–6 Jan 1933. Sd; b&w. 8 reels, 7,344 ft. 82 min. Passed by the National Board of Review. Spanish language.

[*Prod* John Stone]. *Dirección de* [*Directed by*] Frank Strayer. *Adaptación cinematográfica de* [*Screenplay by*] Llewellyn Hughes and Paul Perez. *Versión española de* [*Spanish version by*] José López Rubio. [*Contr wrt* Dwight Cummings, Robert M. Low, Anthony Veiller and Enrique Jardiel Poncela]. [*Photog* Robert Planck]. [*Cam op* William Dietz and Paul Garnett]. [*Asst cam* Roger Sherman and Frank McDonald].

Song(s): "Cuando el amor llama (Love Calls)," "Zíngaro vagabundo (Song of the Romany Band)," "Mansión sin amor (Without Love in a Palace of Dreams)" and "Serenata bufa (Serenade)," words by L. Wolfe Gilbert, music by Desider Josef Vecsei, translated into Spanish by José Mojica; "Canción del carnaval (Carnival Song)" and "Canción de la buenaventura (Fortune Telling Song)," words by L. Wolfe Gilbert, music by D. J. Vecsei, translated into Spanish by José López Rubio.

Cast: JOSÉ MOJICA (*Karol*), Rosita Moreno ([*Princess*] *María Luisa*), Julio Villareal (*El Gran Duque Alejandro*), Romualdo Tirado (*Remetz*), Ada Lozano (*Renée*), Antonio Vidal (*Primer ministro*), Martín Garralaga (*Gregor*), Paco Moreno (*Cabo*).

Musical, Romance, Comedy-drama. [*Not viewed*]. Princess María Louisa, bored with the stuffy and morose atmosphere of the court palace, dresses like a peasant girl and goes to the village fair with her maid, Renée, where she meets Karol, the King of the Gypsies. The Grand Duke Alejandro, her fiancé, who is more interested in affairs of the state than of the heart, pursues her and finds her kissing Karol, whom she then threatens to have imprisoned for his transgression. María Louisa loses her brooch, and Alejandro insists that Karol stole it. The coach driver finds the brooch and returns it to Alejandro; however, he continues to insist on Karol's guilt. Karol believes that he has been arrested for kissing the princess and so confesses to the crime. While serving his sentence of seven days of hard labor, he works in the royal kitchen, where he makes a "love salad" which María Louisa adores. When she discovers that he is the salad's creator, however, she retracts her praise. Renée reveals to the princess that she saw the coachman give the brooch to Alejandro, and María Louisa goes to apologize. She discovers Karol and Alejandro fighting, and Karol then escapes the palace, taking María Louisa captive. At the gypsy camp, María Louisa insists on working like the others. Remetz,

also taken to the gypsy camp by force, escapes and alerts Alejandro, who arrives at the camp with an army. Karol and Alejandro duel in the woods, and after Alejandro shoots a hole in Karol's hat, he flees in fear of Karol's better aim. Karol orders that the gypsies break camp and tells María Louisa that their paths crossed happily but that he must move on. María Louisa sadly watches his caravan recede in the distance. *Class distinction. Gypsies. Imaginary lands. Princesses. Abduction. Duels. Engagements. Fairs. False arrests. Fights. Jewelry. Kisses. Maids. Palaces. Salads.*

Note: The plot summary was based on a screen continuity in the Twentieth Century-Fox Produced Scripts Collection, and the onscreen credits were taken from a screen billing sheet in the Twentieth Century-Fox Records of the Legal Department, both of which are at the UCLA Theater Arts Library. The film's working title was *El zíngaro vagabundo.* Reviews translated the title as "The King of the Gypsies." The running time listed above was calculated from footage given in NYSA records.

CM Jun 1933, p. 320. *FD* 31 May 1933, p. 7. *IP* Jan 1933, p. 21. *NYT* 29 May 1933, p. 22.

EL REY DEL JAZZ *see* **KING OF JAZZ**

RHAPSODY IN BLUE (Jewish Americans)
Warner Bros. Pictures, Inc.; A Warner Bros.—First National Picture. *Dist* Warner Bros. Pictures, Inc. 22 Sep **1945**; New York opening: 26 Jun 1945; Prod: 19 Jul—12 Oct 1943 [©Warner Bros. Pictures, Inc.; 22 Sep 1945; LP13486]. Sd (RCA Sound System); b&w. 12,522 ft. 130 min.

Prod Jesse L. Lasky. *Exec prod* JACK L. WARNER. *Dir* Irving Rapper. *Dial dir* Felix Jacoves. [*Asst dir* Bob Vreeland]. [*2d asst dir* Clarence Ernest]. *Orig story* Sonya Levien. *Scr* Howard Koch and Elliott Paul. [*Contr wrt* Harry Chandlee, Clifford Odets and Robert Rossen]. *Dir of photog* Sol Polito. *Addl mus numbers photog* Merritt Gerstad and Ernest Haller. [*Cam op* Al Green]. [*Asst cam* Frank Evans]. [*Stills* Bill Wallace and Micky Marigold]. [*Gaffer* Charles O'Bannon]. *Dir spec eff* Roy Davidson. *Spec eff* Willard Van Enger. *Mont* James Leicester. *Art dir* John Hughes and Anton Grot. *Film ed* Folmer Blangsted. *Set dec* Fred M. MacLean. *Gowns* Milo Anderson. [*Ward* Ted Shultz, Einar Bourman, Roy Dumont, Katherine Garabedian and Jeanette Stork]. *Mus dir* Leo F. Forbstein. *Mus adpt* Max Steiner. *Orch arr* Ray Heindorf. *Orch arr of "Rhapsody in Blue"* Ferde Grofe. *Vocal arr* Dudley Chambers. *"Rhapsody in Blue" orch cond* Paul Whiteman. *"Rhapsody in Blue" and "Concerto in F" piano solo* Oscar Levant. *Addl piano solo rec* Ray Turner. [*Clarinet solos* Al Gallodoro]. *Dance numbers created and dir by* LeRoy Prinz. *Sd* David Forrest and Stanley Jones. *Makeup artist* Perc Westmore. [*Makeup* Joe Stinton]. [*Hair* Tillie Starrett and Geraldine Cole]. [*Best boy* Jim Peters]. [*Props* Maurice Goldman]. [*Unit mgr* Louis Baum]. [*Scr clerk* Meta Carpenter]. [*Grip* Harold Noyes]. [*Voice double for Joan Leslie* Sally Sweetland].

Music: *Concerto in F, Cuban Overture, An American in Paris* and *Rhapsody in Blue,* by George Gershwin.

Song(s): "Smiles," words by J. Will Callahan, music by Lee G. Roberts; "Blue Monday," "Delishious" "Embraceable You," "Fascinating Rhythm," "I Got Rhythm," "(I'm) Biding My Time," "It Ain't Necessarily So," "Oh, Lady Be Good," "Love Walke In," "The Man I Love," "Somebody Loves Me," "Someone to Watch Over Me," "Stairway to Paradise," "Summertime," " 'S Wonderful," "You Are Mine" and "Liza," words by Ira Gershwin, music by George Gershwin; "Has Anyone Seen My Joe," "135th Street Blues" and "Do It Again," words by B. G. DeSylva, music by George Gershwin; "Swanee," words by Irving Caesar, music by George Gershwin; "The Yankee Doodle Blues," words by Irving Caesar and B. G. DeSylva, music by George Gershwin.

Cast: Robert Alda (*George Gershwin*), Joan Leslie (*Julie Adams*), Alexis Smith (*Christine Gilbert*), Charles Coburn (*Max Dreyfus*), Julie Bishop (*Lee Gershwin*), Albert Basserman (*Professor Frank*), Morris Carnovsky (*Poppa [Morris] Gershwin*), Rosemary DeCamp (*Momma [Rose] Gershwin*), Oscar Levant, Paul Whiteman, Al Jolson, George White, Hazel Scott, Anne Brown (*Themselves*), Herbert Rudley (*Ira Gershwin*), John B. Hughes (*Himself*), Mickey Roth (*George Gershwin, as a boy*), Darryl Hickman (*Ira Gershwin, as a boy*), Charles Halton (*Mr. Kast*), Andrew Tombes (*Mr. Million*), Gregory Golubeff (*Mr. Katzman*), Walter Soderling (*Mr. Muscatel*), Eddie Marr (*Buddy DeSylva*), Theodore Von Eltz (*Foley*), Bill Kennedy (*Herbert Stone*), Oscar Loraine ([*Maurice*] *Ravel*), Johnny Downs (*Dancer*), Ernest Golm (*Otto Kahn*), Martin Noble (*Jascha Heifetz*), Hugo Kirchhoffer (*Walter Damrosch*), Will Wright

(*Rachmaninoff*), [Tom Patricola (*Singer*)], [Robert Sayne (*Christine's escort*)], [George Riley (*Comic*)], [Virginia Sale (*Cashier*)], [Tom Stevenson (*Ragged bum*)], [Yola D'Avril (*Prima donna*)], [Claire DuBrey (*Receptionist*)], [Christian Rub (*Swedish janitor*)], [Esther Michelson (*Housewife*)], [Robert Wilbur (*Piano mover*)], [Ivan Lebedeff (*Nightclub guest*)], [Odette Myrtil (*Madame DeBreteuil*)], [Jay Novello (*Orchestra leader*)], [LeRoy Antoine (*Bootblack*)], [Jack Chefe (*Headwaiter*)], [Charles Waldron (*Doctor*)], [Lillian Bronson (*Telephone operator*)], [John Henry Morton (*Newsboy*)], [Sam Savitsky (*Masseur*)], [Broderick O'Farrell (*Butler*)], [Robert Johnson (*Sport*)], [William Gillespie (*Porgy*)], [Ernie Adams (*Customer in bakery*)], [John Dilson (*Music critic*)], [Armand Cortez (*Hotel clerk*)], [Jacques Lory (*Taxi driver*)], [Edward Harvey (*Theater manager*)], [Ben Moroz (*Tall man*)], [Jesse Graves (*Coachman*)], [Oliver Prickett, Carl Neubert (*Painters*)], [Clay Womack, Frank Pharr (*Men in Turkish bath*)], [Kate Harrington, Walter White (*Music teachers*)], [Bernard DeRoux, Fred Dosh (*Porters*)], [Harry Seymour, Joe Sullivan, Clarence Badger, Jr. (*Song pluggers*)], [Frank Reicher, Georges Renavent, Lynne Baggett, Elsa Basserman (*Guests*)], Constance Purdy, Caroline Burke, Milton Mack, Joan Winfield, Ralph McColm (*Party guests*)], [Nellie Nichols (*Other woman*)], [Al Gallodoro (*Clarinetist*)].

Biography, Musical. [*Print viewed*]. When young brothers George and Ira Gershwin are growing up on New York City's Lower East Side, their mother Rose saves enough money to buy a piano, so that Ira, the eldest, can take lessons. George becomes the student, however, when he demonstrates his natural musical abilities. Under the instruction of Professor Frank, George becomes progressively better at the piano. He first obtains a job as a pianist in a vaudeville theater and then in a music store, but his dream is to become a composer. One day singer Julie Adams comes into the store looking for music to use in an audition. George plays "Swanee," one of his own compositions, for her, but when his boss hears him, he loses his job. Later, George is offered a two-year contract at Harms, another music publisher, and Max Dreyfus, the company head, sells "Swanee" to Al Jolson, who makes it a hit. Despite Frank's warning against squandering his talents on popular music, George takes a job writing songs for the Broadway show *Half Past Eight*, starring Julie, but the show fails. After the success of *George White's Scandals of 1921*, for which George writes the music, his career takes off, and together with Ira, who now writes lyrics, George composes a series of hit shows. After George writes "Blue Monday Blues," a song derived from Negro spirituals, which is not well received, conductor Paul Whiteman asks him to compose a serious piece based on the blues for a jazz concert he is planning, The result is *Rhapsody in Blue*, and upon hearing his prize pupil's composition being performed for a radio broadcast, Professor Frank dies. Later, when Walter Damrosch of the New York Symphony commissions a concerto from him, George goes to Paris to begin a serious study of music. There he meets wealthy painter Christine Gilbert, who introduces him to Maurice Ravel and other composers. The slightly older Christine and George return to the United States, causing a jealous Julie a great deal of pain. Realizing that George is more in love with his music than with her, Christine leaves George and, after composing another Broadway show, George returns to Paris and completes his concerto. George's father dies of leukemia after advising his son that he was wrong to separate from Julie. While living in Los Angeles, George begins to compose frantically. He wins a Pulitzer prize for the musical *Of Thee I Sing* and writes *Porgy and Bess*, an opera featuring black performers. Later, George experiences numbness and headaches. After he collapses during a rehearsal, Julie plans to come to California immediately. In New York, George's friend, Oscar Levant, then performs George's *Concerto in F* to great acclaim, but the occasion is saddened by the announcement of the composer's untimely death. *Brothers. Composers. George Gershwin. Ira Gershwin. Actors and actresses. African Americans. Dancers. Dogs. Family relationships. The Hollywood Bowl (Los Angeles, CA). Jews. Leukemia. Los Angeles (CA). Music publishers and publishing. Music teachers. New York City–Broadway. Painters (Of paintings). Paris (France). Pianists. Maurice Ravel. Romance. Singers. Vaudeville.*

Note: George Gershwin was born in Brooklyn, New York on 26 Sep 1898. As depicted in the film, he began his musical career selling songs for the Remick publishing company when he was sixteen years old. Later he worked as a rehearsal pianist. When he was twenty, he was commissioned to write the score for *La La Lucille* and then wrote the music for five of George White's *Scandals*. He attracted the attention of serious composers with *Rhapsody in Blue*, which

was first played by Paul Whiteman at the Aeolian Hall on 12 Feb 1924. His opera *Porgy and Bess* was the first to use an all-black cast. Although Gershwin had many romantic attachments, there was no counterpart in his life to the character of "Julie." He died of a brain tumor at age 38 on 11 Jul 1937.

This film marked the motion picture debuts of Broadway actors Robert Alda and Herbert Rudley. Although *DV* lists the preview running time as 143 minutes, the *Var* review gives a running time of 130 minutes. In the film, Al Jolson sings "Swanee," the song he made famous, and Anne Brown, the original "Bess," sings "Summertime" from the opera *Porgy and Bess*. According to *Var*, the unbilled Tom Patricola "reprises 'Somebody Loves Me' as he did in 'Scandals.'" Paul Whiteman also re-creates some of his real-life numbers. Press releases included in the file on the film at the AMPAS Library add the following information about the production: Clifford Odets wrote an early version of the screenplay and Robert Rossen was at one time assigned to work on the script from an outline prepared by Ira Gershwin and Kathryn Scola. (Although Odets and Rossen are mentioned in production files for the film, Scola is not.) Five original paintings from George Gershwin's personal art collection were loaned to Warner Bros. for use in the film. These included "Army Doctor" by Amedeo Modigliani; "Abstraction" by Antoine Masson; Georges Roualt's "Three Clowns;" and Maurice de Vlaminck's "Near Paris." Another press release notes that John Garfield was tested for the lead. An 8 Jul 1945 *NYT* reports that Oscar Levant wanted the filmmakers to include a scene in which he quarrels with George Gershwin—as he frequently did—but the studio thought that an argument would put too much strain on the relationship between the two men as depicted in the film. *HR* news items add the following information about the production: Cary Grant was considered for the role of "George Gershwin." Kay Swift worked with Ira Gershwin on the musical arrangements. Oscar Levant dubbed Robert Alda's piano playing. Several theaters, including The Apollo, the Aeolian Hall, Times Square Theater, The Music Box, Carnegie Hall, Lewisohn Stadium, the Los Angeles Philharmonic Auditorium and His Majesty's Theatre in London, were recreated for the film. Nathan Levinson's sound recording was nominated for an Oscar as was Ray Heindorf and Max Steiner's score. Gershwin's *Var* obituary notes that the rights to most of his music were controlled by the Warner Bros. publishing group. In 1946, *HR* reported that Chico Marx sued Warner Bros for $200,000 for damages and "payment owed for services rendered." Marx alleged that the filmmakers used his name "many times" in the film. Studio officials admitted that Marx's name had been used in the film, but were unclear about what services the comedian had rendered. The diposition of the suit is not known. According to modern sources, Joan Leslie's singing voice was dubbed by Louanne Hogan, but contemporary sources credit Sally Sweetland.

Box 30 Jun 1945. *Box* 15 Sep 1945. *DV* 27 Jun 1945, p. 3. *Down Beat* 1 Jul 1945, p. 7. *Down Beat* 15 Aug 1943, p. 6. *FD* 27 Jun 1945, p. 7. *HR* 14 Jul 1937, p. 1. *HR* 30 Jan 1942, p. 1. *HR* 20 Feb 1942, p. 4. *HR* 1 May 1942, p. 1. *HR* 13 Aug 1942, p. 23. *HR* 16 Jul 1943, p. 7. *HR* 23 Jul 1943, p. 6. *HR* 28 Jul 1943, p. 10. *HR* 8 Oct 1943, p. 3. *HR* 16 Dec 1943, p. 3. *HR* 27 Jun 1945, p. 3. *HR* 2 Jul 1945, p. 16. *HR* 4 Mar 1946, p. 1, 11. *MPHPD* 30 Jun 1945, p. 2521. *NYT* 28 Jun 1945, p. 22. *NYT* 8 Jul 1945. *Var* 27 Jun 1945, p. 16.

RHYTHM OF THE RIO GRANDE (Latino)
Boots and Saddles Pictures, Inc. *Dist* Monogram Pictures Corp. 2 Mar **1940**; Prod: began mid-Jan 1940 [©Monogram Pictures Corp.; 1 Mar 1940; LP9472]. Sd; b&w. 6 reels. 53 or 57 min. PCA cert no. 6025.

Prod Edward Finney. *Supv* Robert Tansey. *Dir* Al Herman. *Asst dir* Arthur Hammond. *Scr* Robert Emmett. *Photog* Marcel A. LePicard. *Mus dir and score* Frank Sanucci. *Sd rec* Glen Glenn. *Tech dir* E. R. Hickson.

Song(s): "Mexicali Moon" and "Rhythm of the Rio Grande," music and lyrics by Frank Harford; "Pablo, the Mexican Bandit," music and lyrics by Johnny Lange and Lew Porter.

Cast: Tex Ritter (*Tex*), Suzan Dale (*Ruth Crane*), Warner Richmond (*Buck*), Martin Garralaga (*Pablo*), Frank Mitchell (*Shorty*), Mike J. Rodriguez (*Lopez*), Juan Duval (*Rego*), Tristam Coffin (*Banister*), Chick Hannon (*Pete*), Earl Douglas (*Blackie*), Forrest Taylor (*Crane*), Glenn Strange (*Hayes*), James McNally (*Ransom*), Slim Andrews, Wally West, White Flash.

Western, with songs. [*Not viewed*]. Seeking to avenge the murder of a friend, Tex and his sidekick Shorty ride into the gold rich Cinco Valley, arriving in the midst of a raid on the Crane house, which is allegedly being led by Mexican bandit Pablo. After Tex drives the bandits away, Ruth Crane informs him that the settlers of the valley are victims of a campaign of robbery and pillaging perpetrated by the Mexican marauder and his men, but Tex has recognized one of the raiders as Blackie, one of rancher Banister's men. At the Banister ranch, Tex finds an emblem similar to ones found after every raid, and becoming suspicious, he tracks down Pablo's gang and discovers that Pablo is innocent. Suspecting that Banister has been staging the raids in order to drive the settlers from the valley and thus acquire their mining property for pennies, Tex convinces Pablo to help him set a trap for Banister. Before they can spring the trap, however, Tex is arrested for being in league with the bandits, and seeing Tex with the sheriff, Pablo believes that he has been double-crossed. Determined to bring Banister to justice, Tex escapes from jail and races to Pablo's

hideout just in time to save him from the barrel of Banister's gun. As the posse arrives in pursuit of Tex, Tex proves that Banister is responsible for the raids, thus exonerating Pablo. *Bandits. Cowboys. Frame-ups. Land developers. Mexicans. Ranchers.* False accusations. Gold mines. Jailbreaks. Mexican-American border region. Murder. Revenge. Robbery. Sheriffs.

Note: According to an unidentified contemporary source contained in the AMPAS Library production files, this film was shot on location at Palmdale, CA.

DV 18 Apr 1940, p. 3. *FD* 26 Apr 1940, p. 8. *HR* 13 Jan 1940, pp. 6-7. *HR* 18 Apr 1940, p. 4. *MPD* 24 Apr 1940, p. 4. *MPH* 10 Feb 1940, p. 49. *MPH* 27 Apr 1940, p. 54. *Var* 13 Mar 1940, p. 18.

RHYTHM ON PARADE *see* **SLIGHTLY TERRIFIC**

RICH GIRL—POOR GIRL *see* **CASTLES FOR TWO**

THE RICHEST MAN IN THE WORLD *see* **SINS OF THE CHILDREN**

IL RICHIAMO DEL CUORE *see* **TODA UNA VIDA**

RIDDLE RANCH (Latino)

Black King Productions, Inc. *Dist* Beaumont Pictures, Inc. 16 Dec **1935**; Prod: Sep 1935 at International Film Studios. Sd; b&w. 56 or 59 min. PCA cert no. 1701.

Prod Mitchell Leichter. *Dir* Charles Hutchison. *Asst dir* Roy Rice. *Scr* L. V. Jefferson and [E. J. Thornton]. *Cam* Bob Doran. *Art dir* Jeanette. *Ed* George Halligan. *Sd* T. T. Triplett. *Rec eng* Ralph Like.

Cast: Black King, David Worth (*Bob Horton*), Julian Rivero ([*Don*] *Carlos*), Fred "Snowflake" Toones (*Snowflake*), June Marlowe (*Helen*), Baby Charline Barry (*Betty*), Rychard Cramer (*Jim Riddle*), Arturo Feliz (*Pedro*), Henry Sylvester (*Sheriff*), Ray Gallagher (*Deputy sheriff*), Budd Buster (*Antonio*).

Western. [*Print viewed*]. Cowboy Bob Horton is in love with Helen, the niece of his employer, Jim Riddle. Riddle refuses to agree to their marriage, however, because he does not want Helen to marry a cowboy. Don Carlos, a Mexican bandit, wants Black King, a wild horse in Riddle's stables, but Riddle will not sell him. Carlos then goads Riddle into a race pitting Black King against Carlos' best horse. To ensure that he wins, Carlos twists a wire around one of Black King's legs. Riddle reluctantly accepts Bob as Black King's rider, as he is the only person who can handle the horse. During the race, Black King stumbles and loses, and Riddle believes that Bob betrayed him. Rather than give the horse to Carlos, however, Riddle lets the animal escape. Later, Carlos kills Dan, the card dealer at the saloon, because he believes that Dan cheated during a card game. Although the dying Dan tells Riddle that Carlos killed him, the sheriff believes that Bob is guilty because Carlos used Bob's gun for the murder. Riddle does not reveal the truth in order to keep Bob away from Helen. When he learns that he is suspected of murder, Bob hides out in the desert. He finds Black King and discovers the wire that made him lame. Bob seeks refuge in Carlos' cabin, but one of Carlos' henchmen reveals his whereabouts to the sheriff. Helen warns Bob of Carlos' betrayal, but he is captured and found guilty. When he realizes that Bob will be executed, Riddle finally names Carlos as Dan's murderer and agrees to Bob and Helen's marriage. *Fixed horse races. Horses. Mexican Americans. Uncles.* African Americans. Betrayal. Deserts. Ranches. Rewards. Romance.

Note: According to *FD*, interiors were shot at International Studios and location shooting took place at Highland Springs, CA and in Arizona near the Mexican border. *Riddle Ranch* was later released on television as *Western Show Down.* The only credit that appeared on the viewed print was David Worth; other credits come from contemporary sources. Black King was billed as "The horse with the human brain." Although press materials credit L. V. Jefferson as the author, a *FD* review credits E. J. Thornton with the screenplay. Modern sources include Ace Bain in the cast.

FD 30 Sep 1935, p. 2. *FD* 25 Oct 1935, p. 12. *FD* 3 Dec 1935, p. 8.

THE RIDDLE: WOMAN (Danish Americans)

Associated Exhibitors, Inc. *Dist* Pathé Exchange, Inc. 3 Oct **1920** [©Pathé Exchange, Inc.; 28 Aug 1920; LU15466]. Si; b&w. 6 reels, 5,785 ft.

Dir Edward José. *Scen* John B. Clymer. *Cam* Max Schneider. *Titles and spec eff photog* Stewart B. Moss.

Source: Based on the play *The Riddle: Woman* by Carl Jacobi, adapted by Charlotte E. Wells and Dorothy Donnelly (New York, 23 Oct 1918).

Cast: Geraldine Farrar (*Lilla Gravert*), Montague Love (*Larz Olrik*), Adele Blood (*Kristine*), William P. Carleton (*Eric Helsingor*), Frank Losee (*Sigurd Gravert*), Madge Bellamy (*Marie Meyer*), Louis Stern (*Isaac Meyer*).

Drama. After her attempted suicide over an unhappy love affair is thwarted by Larz Olrik, Lilla Gravert leaves Denmark for New York and marries her savior. At their fifth wedding anniversary celebration Lilla meets Eric Helsingor, the man who betrayed her. Helsingor now demands money in return for his silence and Lilla complies. When Lilla and Larz adopt a baby boy referred to them by their lifelong friend Kristine, Lilla discovers that the child is actually Kristine and Helsingor's. Larz suspects that Helsingor is blackmailing Kristine, but when the latter is injured in a fight, Larz takes him home to recover. There Helsingor meets Marie Meyer, the daughter of an old mentor of Lilla, and attempts to convince the girl to elope with him. Becoming enraged at Helsingor's repeated offenses, Lilla attacks him and they struggle until Kristine shoots Helsingor and then herself. Lilla insists that Larz read the blackmailer's letters, but he throws them into the fire instead, eliminating all barriers between husband and wife. *Adoption. Blackmail. Danish Americans. Immigrants. Infants. Marriage.* Attempted suicide. Denmark. Fights. Letters. Murder. New York City. Parentage. Suicide. Wedding anniversaries.

Note: The play was originally written in Danish. Some exterior scenes were shot at Marblehead, MA. Interiors were filmed in the old Thanhouser studio at New Rochelle, NY. An early news item indicated that the film began with a prologue showing Leonardo da Vinci finishing the *Mona Lisa* and then dropping on a sofa baffled by his own creation. As no review mentioned this scene, it has not been determined whether it was included in the released film.

ETR 16 Oct 1920, p. 2094. *MPN* 31 Jul 1920, p. 961. *MPN* 28 Aug 1920, p. 1694. *MPN* 23 Oct 1920, p. 3174. *MPN* 13 Nov 1920, p. 3734. *MPN* 27 Nov 1920, p. 4023. *MPW* 16 Oct 1920, p. 921. *NYT* 8 Nov 1920, p. 20.

RIDE A CROOKED TRAIL (Creoles)

Universal-International Pictures Co., Inc. *Dist* Universal Pictures Co., Inc. Sep **1958**; Prod: late Aug—early Oct 1957 [©Universal Pictures Co.; 20 Jul 1958; LP12610]. Sd; col (Eastman Color by Pathe); CinemaScope. 87-88 min. PCA cert no. 18831.

Prod Howard Pine. *Dir* Jesse Hibbs. *Asst dir* William Holland. [*Dial dir* Harold Goodwin]. [*Asst dir* Ray DeCamp]. *Scr* Borden Chase. *Story* George Bruce. *Dir of photog* Harold Lipstein. *Art dir* Alexander Golitzen and Bill Newberry. *Film ed* Edward Curtiss. *Set dec* Russell A. Gausman and Ray Jeffers. *Cost* Bill Thomas. *Mus supv* Joseph Gershenson. *Sd* Leslie I. Carey and Donald McKay. *Makeup* Bud Westmore. [*Hair stylist* Virginia Jones]. [*Unit mgr* Gene Anderson]. [*Unit prod mgr* Lou Leary].

Cast: AUDIE MURPHY [(*Joe Maybe, also known as U.S. Marshal Tom Noonan*)], GIA SCALA [(*Tessa Milotte*)], Walter Matthau [(*Judge Kyle*)], Henry Silva [(*Sam Teeler*)], Joanna Moore [(*Little Brandy*)], Eddie Little [(*Jimmy*)], Mary Field [(*Mrs. Curtis*)], Leo Gordon [(*Sam Mason*)], Mort Mills [(*Pecos*)], Frank Chase [(*Ben, the deputy*)], Bill Walker [(*Jackson*)], Ned Wever [(*Attorney Clark*)], Richard H. Cutting [(*Mr. Curtis*)].

Western. [*Print viewed*]. Judge Kyle of Webb City, a tough river town, deals out the law with a personal touch by checking the identity of every newcomer who enters his town. When he gets a tip that a criminal, Joe Maybe, who has unsuccessfully held up a bank in Wascovia, is heading toward Webb City, he identifies his man on sight. However, Maybe was earlier being chased by U.S. Marshal Jim Noonan and when Noonan fell to his death over a canyon, Maybe snatched the marshal's badge, a star with one missing point. As the judge's men check Maybe, he shoots, injuring the judge. At that moment, however, the judge, seeing the famous four-point star, identifies Maybe as Noonan and offers to buy the man a drink, as the badge has belonged to many a marshal renowned for his bravery. The judge eventually persuades Maybe to remain in Webb City as his marshal, even though Maybe, uncomfortable with his assumed identity, is anxious to get away. That day, the riverboat arrives carrying Tessa Milotte, a Creole woman from New Orleans, who knows Maybe and calls him by name. Maybe, quickly covering up, claims to the judge that she said "Baby" and that she is his wife. Maybe tries to convince the judge that his wife has met him so that they can be on their way, but the judge insists that she stay, too, and leads the couple to their new home. Once alone, Tessa says that she has been in business with Sam Teeler, one of Maybe's criminal rivals, and that she has arrived before Teeler to investigate the town's bank, which Teeler plans to rob. Later, at a ceremony commemorating the opening of the railroad into Webb City, the judge asks Maybe to speak, and at that moment, Teeler and his gang ride into town. Following his speech, Maybe goes to see the gang in the saloon, where Teeler reveals that he plans to rob the railway payroll the next day.

Maybe suggests that they wait for the big money that will soon come with the cattle drive that is scheduled to pass through Webb City. When the judge appears, a shootout ensues, and Teeler and the gang leave. Teeler later expresses his willingness to go along with Maybe, but half of Teeler's gang decide to rob the bank the next day by themselves. Jimmy, an orphan boy who lived with the judge until the town's women encouraged him to move in with Maybe and Tessa, tells Maybe that the gang is back and that they are robbing the bank. Maybe rushes to the scene and, after a gunfight, chases off the outlaws. Later, a distraught Jimmy runs away from Maybe and Tessa's house, and Maybe finds him doing his homework at the judge's shanty boat. The two talk, and Maybe tells Jimmy about his own troubled childhood. Jimmy decides to return to his "family," and then accompanies Maybe to help bring in the trail herd. When they arrive at the cattle trail, they see Teeler and his men, who are posing as cowboys in preparation for the big robbery. During a stampede, Jimmy is injured but is saved from sure death by Maybe. While Maybe goes for a doctor, Jimmy warns Tessa that the judge is suspicious of Maybe. Teeler then shows up at Tessa's and, after trying to kiss her, tells her that he is going to rob the bank and frame Maybe. That night, Tessa entertains Maybe and the judge, insisting that they keep drinking and then takes them to the saloon for a dance, so that Maybe will have an alibi. Just then, they hear dynamite, and realize that Teeler is robbing the bank. Maybe blames Tessa, and the judge challenges Maybe to a quick draw, without revealing that he has another man covering him. From the window at Tessa and Maybe's neighboring house, Jimmy shoots out a chandelier so that Maybe can get away, and then informs Maybe that Teeler fled on the cattle trail. Maybe finds Teeler, and the two men fight it out. The next morning, Tessa prepares to leave on the river boat, and the judge rides back into town not having found Maybe. Just then Maybe arrives with Teeler tied up and returns the stolen money. The couple prepare to board the boat, but before they can depart, the judge pins the marshal badge for real on Maybe's shirt. The judge then demands that the couple arrive in his chambers the next morning at nine o'clock so that he can make their union legal. *Bank robberies. Duplicity. Impersonation and imposture. Law and order. Moral reformation. Outlaws.* Cattle drives. Creoles. Dance hall girls. Drunkenness. Gunfights. Orphans. Payrolls. Railroads. River boats. Romantic rivalry. Saloons. United States. Marshals.

Note: The film's working title was *Middle of the Street.* Although the ethnicity of Gia Scala's character "Tessa Milotte" is not stated in the film, it is implied that she is Creole. The *HR* review notes that the story "Joe Maybe," which tells about the title character's rough childhood in which he was raised by a dancer in a saloon, was inspired by the actual childhood of Billy the Kid. *HR* adds that the river town setting of *Ride a Crooked Trail* is historically accurate as most "trail drives" prior to the Civil War headed for New Orleans, Shreveport and St. Louis, but that most Westerns tend to forget this fact. The reviewer speculates that the unnamed river is probably the Mississippi or Red River. *HR* production charts add Morgan Woodward to the cast, but his participation in the final film has not been confirmed.

Box 28 Jul 1958. *DV* 18 Jul 1958, p. 3. *Exb* 23 Jul 1958, p. 4494. *FD* 23 Jul 1958, p. 8. *Har* 19 Jul 1958, p. 114. *HR* 30 Aug 1957, p. 12. *HR* 4 Oct 1957, p. 13. *HR* 27 Nov 1957. *HR* 18 Jul 1958, p. 3. *LAT* 9 Sep 1957. *LAT* 19 Sep 1958. *MPHPD* 26 Jul 1958, p. 920. *Var* 23 Jul 1958, p. 6.

THE RIDE BACK (Latino, Native Americans, Apache)

Associates & Aldrich Co., Inc. *Dist* United Artists Corp. Apr 1957; New York opening: 29 Apr 1957; Prod: mid-Sep—mid-Oct 1956 [©Associates & Aldrich Co., Inc.; 29 Apr 1957; LP8707]. Sd (Glenn Glenn Sound Recording); sepia (Sepiatone). 7,180 ft. 79 min. PCA cert no. 18386.

Prod William Conrad. *Assoc prod* Walter R. Blake. *Dir* Allen H. Miner. *Asst dir* Robert Justman. *Wrt* Antony Ellis. *Photog* Joseph Biroc. *Spec eff* Lee Zavitz. *Art dir* William Glasgow. *Film ed* Michael Luciano. *Set dec* Glen Daniel. *Prop master* Max Frankel. *Ward* Oscar Rodriguez. *Mus comp and cond by* Frank de Vol. *Sd* Joe L. Edmondson. *Makeup* William Phillips. *Casting coordinator* Jack Murton. *Scr supv* M. E. M. Gibsone. *Prod supv* Jack R. Berne.

Song(s): "The Ride Back," words and music by Frank de Vol, sung by Eddie Albert.

Cast: ANTHONY QUINN [(*Roberto Kallen*)], William Conrad [(*Chris Hamish*)], Lita Milan [(*Elena*)], Victor Millan [(*Father Ignacio*)], George Trevino [(*Guard*)], Ellen Hope Monroe [(*Child*)], Joe Dominguez [(*Luis*)], [Louis Towers (*Boy*)].

Western. [*Print viewed*]. On a quest to bring fugitive Roberto Kallen to trial for murder, Chris Hamish, the deputy sheriff of Scottsville, Texas, crosses the border into Mexico where Kallen, a Mexican-American, has sought refuge. When Hamish questions Father Ignacio, the village priest, about the fugitive, the priest tells him that Kallen has defiled his young cousin Elena and offers to lead him to Kallen. The wily Kallen cordially welcomes the two to his cabin, but when Kallen pulls his gun, the priest steps in front of the weapon and disarms him. After Hamish arrests him, Kallen, sensing the deputy's fear and weakness, assures Elena that he will soon return. As they begin the long ride back to Texas, the self-assured Kallen challenges Hamish's abilities. After they set up camp for the evening, Elena, who has followed them, appears, and Kallen orders her to return home the next morning. When Elena stubbornly dogs them to the border, Kallen asks the border guard to restrain her from crossing. Upon crossing the border, Hamish and Kallen encounter a band of drunken Apaches, and later, Kallen asserts that he killed in self-defense. The next morning, Kallen and Hamish see a ranch in the distance. Upon entering the house, they discover the family has been slaughtered by the Indians. Moved, Kallen tenderly embraces the lifeless body of a small girl and then proceeds to bury the family, placing a rag doll on the little girl's grave. Fired upon by the marauding Apaches, Kallen and Hamish seek refuge in the cabin, their horses having been frightened off by the gunfire. As night falls, Kallen taunts Hamish about his cowardice and his incompetence in handling a gun. When Kallen's horse returns, Kallen pulls the animal into the cabin and then jumps Hamish. After recovering his gun, Hamish vows to bring Kallen back for trial. The next morning, Kallen spots a little girl running for her life. After catching her, he discovers that she is the twin of the dead girl and realizing that she has been rendered mute from fear, gently tries to reassure her. After hitching the horse to a buckboard, Kallen and Hamish put the girl in the back and then gallop off, dodging Indian bullets. While Kallen soothingly coaxes the girl to eat, Hamish treats her with impatience. When the horse begins to limp, they are forced to abandon the wagon and proceed on foot. While camped around the fire that night, Hamish promises Kallen a fair trial and Kallen then confides his dreams of settling down with Elena. When Kallen asks Hamish why he is so determined to bring him back, Hamish confesses that he has been a failure his entire life and that bringing Kallen to trial is his only chance at redemption. After Hamish falls asleep, Kallen instructs the girl to steal his gun. Awakening suddenly, Hamish gruffly slaps the little girl and snatches back his gun. The next day, Hamish insists upon taking a shortcut through the open countryside. When a roving band of Apaches fires on them and wounds Hamish, the lawman is forced to turn his gun over to Kallen for protection. Scaling the hills, Kallen shoots two of the Indians and drives off the others. Seizing the opportunity to flee back to Mexico, Kallen mounts his horse and rides away, the little girl gazing forlornly after him. She then gingerly approaches the wounded lawman, touches his hand and begins to cry. A short time later, Kallen returns, helps Hamish climb onto his horse and leads him and the girl to town. *Deputies. Fugitives. Mexican Americans. Mutes. Orphans. Self-confidence. Vocational obsession.* Apache Indians. Mexican-American border region. Mexico. Priests. Raids. Texas. Twins.

Note: The film opens with a pre-title sequence in which gunshots are heard, followed by shots of "Kallen" running from the saloon, mounting his horse and galloping out of town. "Hamish" is then seen as he paces in his office, walks over to a map and begins to mark on it. The sequence contains no dialogue; the song "The Ride Back" is heard over the images. An Apr 1956 *HR* news item stated that this was to be a co-production between Associates & Aldrich and producer/actor William Conrad, director Allan Miner and writer Antony Ellis. Although *HR* production charts include Ellen and Hope Schwartz in the cast, these may be the same child actors billed as Ellen Hope Monroe, who is listed in the onscreen credits and is credited in reviews as playing the orphan. Although the *Var* review noted that the film was released in Sepiatone, the print viewed was in black and white. According to a Jan 1958 *HR* news item, the story was originally conceived as a "Gunsmoke" radio episode. At the time, Conrad was the voice of "Marshal Matt Dillon" on "Gunsmoke."

Box 18 May 1957. *DV* 17 Apr 1957, p. 3. *Exb* 1 May 1957, p. 4319. *FD* 26 Apr 1957, p. 10. *Har* 20 Apr 1957, p. 63. *HR* 9 Apr 1956. *HR* 10 May 1956. *HR* 21 Sep 1956, p. 17. *HR* 5 Oct 1956, p. 17. *HR* 17 Apr 1957, p. 3. *HR* 4 Jan 1958. *MPHPD* 27 Apr 1957, p. 354. *NYT* 30 Apr 1957, p. 24. *Var* 1 May 1957, p. 7.

RIDE ON VAQUERO (Latino)

Twentieth Century-Fox Film Corp. *Dist* Twentieth Century-Fox Film Corp. 18 Apr 1941; Prod: mid-Dec 1940—mid-Jan 1941 [©Twentieth Century-Fox Film Corp.; 18 Apr 1941; LP10466]. Sd (Western Electric Mirrophonic Recording); b&w. 7 reels, 5,744 ft. 64 min. PCA cert no. 6980.

Series: The Cisco Kid.

Exec prod Sol M. Wurtzel. *Dir* Herbert I. Leeds. [*Asst dir* Sam Schneider and Charles Hall]. *Orig scr* Samuel G. Engel. *Dir of photog* Lucien Andriot. *Art dir* Richard Day and Chester Gore. *Film ed* Louis Loeffler. *Set dec* Thomas Little. *Cost* Herschel. *Mus dir* Emil Newman. [*Dance seqs supv by* Edouardo Cansino]. *Sd* George Leverett and Harry M. Leonard.

Source: Based on the character created by O. Henry.

Cast: Cesar Romero ([*The*] *Cisco Kid* [*also known as Don Juan*]), Mary Beth Hughes (*Sally* [*Slocum*]), Lynne Roberts (*Marguerita* [*Martinez*]), Chris-Pin Martin (*Gordito*), Robert Lowery (*Carlos* [*Martinez*]), Ben Carter (*Watchman* [*Bullfinch*]), William Demarest (*Barney*), Robert Shaw (*Cavalry officer*), Edwin Maxwell ([*Dan* Clark*), Paul Sutton (*Sleepy*), Don Costello (*Redge*), Arthur Hohl (*Sheriff* [*Johnny Burns*]), Irving Bacon (*Baldy*), Dick Rich (*Curly*), Paul Harvey (*Colonel* [*Warren*]), Joan Woodbury (*Dolores*), [Hector V. Sarno (*Miguel*)], [Frank Orth (*Murphy*)], [Paco Moreno (*Gypsy*)], [Joe Whitehead (*Joe*)], [Paul Kruger (*Hank*)], [Alec Craig (*Limey*)], [Victor Potel (*Ole*)], [Max Wagner (*Partner*)], [Edgar Edwards (*Sergeant*)], [James Flavin (*Officer*)], [Eva Puig (*Maria*)], [Herbert Ashley], [Jack Norton], [Lee Shumway].

Western. [*Print viewed*]. U.S. Cavalry troops in the Arizona territory are baffled by a series of kidnappings allegedly committed by a notorious but charming bandit known as "The Cisco Kid." Cisco and his sidekick Gordito are betrayed to the troopers by Cisco's girl friend Dolores, who wants the reward offered for his capture. The post commander, Colonel Warren, knows that Cisco would not stoop to kidnapping, however, and offers to let him escape if he will find the real culprits. Cisco at first refuses, but when Warren reveals that the kidnappers recently killed Don Pedro Martinez while abducting his son Carlos, Cisco changes his mind. When Cisco emigrated to America from Portugal, the Martinez family were his closest friends, and Cisco is determined to avenge Don Pedro's death and free Carlos. Cisco travels with Gordito to the Martinez ranch and learns from Carlos' wife Marguerita that she has obtained a $50,000 mortgage on the ranch from banker Dan Clark in order to pay the ransom. Cisco assures Marguerita, who knows him only as Don Juan, that he will find Carlos, then goes with Gordito to the town saloon, which is run by Redge and his henchman Sleepy. Clark, Redge and the corrupt town sheriff, Johnny Burns, are the ringleaders of the kidnapping gang, and have been acquiring the land of local ranchers after they are forced to mortgage their ranches to Clark in order to pay the ransoms. At the saloon, Cisco runs into dancer Sally Slocum, who is still bitter about their brief romance that ended years earlier. Cisco promises Sally that he is there to help the Martinez family, and she agrees not to turn him in. After Marguerita receives a message about where to leave the ransom, Cisco drops off the money and recognizes Redge and Burns as the couriers. He then trails them to Clark's office, where he realizes that they are all part of the gang. Later that evening, Cisco and Gordito find Carlos, ill but alive, in a deserted cabin, but are apprehended by Burns and his posse. Upon learning Cisco's true identity, Marguerita refuses to believe his story that Clark, Burns and Redge are the culprits, and he and Gordito are jailed. Cisco thinks that Sally turned him in, but actually he was identified by a Mexican blacksmith and his family. Cisco tries to contact Warren, but the colonel is killed in an Indian raid on the post. Sally engineers Cisco and Gordito's escape from jail, after which they succeed in capturing Clark. With the help of Bullfinch, the bank's night watchman, Cisco tricks Clark, Redge and Burns into signing confessions. Sally then holds the criminals at bay while Cisco and Gordito escape before the soldiers arrive. *Bandits. Bankers. False arrests. Kidnapping. Outlaws. Portuguese Americans. African Americans. Arizona. Dancers. Duplicity. Escapes. Mexicans. Ranchers. Ransom. Saloon keepers. Sheriffs. Watchmen.*

Note: *Ride on, Vaquero* was the last entry in Twentieth Century-Fox's "Cisco Kid" series. According to a 15 May 1942 *HR* news item, the studio did plan to make another picture in the series, to be titled *The Cisco Kid Rides Again*, with Ralph Dietrich acting as producer and Cesar Romero and Chris-Pin Martin reprising their roles. A 14 Aug 1942 *HR* news item noted that the picture was "shelved," however, because after consulting with Addison Durland, the Latin-American Adviser of the MPAA, studio officials "feared unfavorable reaction from Mexican nationals." The news item further reported that "future Cisco Kid stories will be produced only after stories [are] approved by Motion Picture Society for the Americas." In 1945, Monogram released *The Cisco Kid Returns*, the first of a five-film "Cisco Kid" series starring Duncan Renaldo (see above). Renaldo also played the character in *The Cisco Kid* television series, which ran from 1951 to 1955. In Feb 1994, TNT released a made-for-cable film

entitled *The Cisco Kid*, which was directed by Luis Valdez and starred Jimmy Smits as "Cisco" and Cheech Marin as his friend "Pancho." For additional information on the series, please consult the Series Index and the above entry for *The Cisco Kid*.

Box 5 Apr 1941. *DV* 28 Mar 1941. *FD* 21 Apr 1941, p. 6. *HR* 20 Dec 1940, p. 11. *HR* 10 Jan 1941, p. 8. *HR* 28 Mar 1941, p. 4. *HR* 15 May 1942, p. 3. *HR* 14 Aug 1942, p. 1. *MPH* 5 Apr 1941. *MPHPD* 22 Feb 1941, p. 64. *NYT* 19 Apr 1941, p. 20. *Var* 2 Apr 1941, p. 16.

RIDE OUT FOR REVENGE (Native Americans, Cheyenne)

Bryna Productions, Inc. *Dist* United Artists Corp. Nov **1957**; *Prod:* late Mar—early Apr 1957 [©Bryna Productions, Inc.; 6 Feb 1958; LP10311]. Sd (Westrex Recording System); b&w; 1.85. 6,972 ft. 78–79 min. PCA cert no. 18567.

Prod Norman Retchin. *Assoc prod* Victor Orsatti. *Dir* Bernard Girard. *Asst dir* Ralph Black. *Wrt* Norman Retchin. *Dir of photog* Floyd Crosby. *Art dir* McClure Capps. *Film ed* Leon Barsha. *Set dec* Rudy Butler. *Ward supv* Elmer Ellsworth. [*Ward* Bernice Pontrelli]. *Mus comp and cond* Leith Stevens. *Sd* Jack Goodrich. *Makeup* Lee Greenway. *Prod mgr* Barney Briskin.

Cast: RORY CALHOUN [(*Marshal Tate*)], GLORIA GRAHAME [(*Amy Porter*)], LLOYD BRIDGES [(*Capt. George*)], JOANNE GILBERT [(*Pretty Willow*)], Vince Edwards [(*Little Wolf*)], Richard Shannon [(*Garvin*)], Frank De Kova [(*Chief Yellow Wolf*)], Michael Winkelman [(*Billy*)], Cyril Delevanti [(*Preacher*)], [John Merrick (*Lieutenant*)].

Western. [*Print viewed*]. In the Dakotas around 1868, Cheyenne Chief Yellow Wolf and his son Little Wolf travel on foot from their destitute village to the town of Sand Creek because their tribe has so few horses. The townspeople stare at them coldly as they approach the office of Capt. George, a cowardly, heavy-drinking U.S. Cavalry officer. Yellow Wolf explains that with winter approaching, his people need warm clothing, but George dismisses his concerns, stating that he cares only about what "his people need." George then reveals that he has been given orders to send the Cheyenne to a reservation in Oklahoma. Yellow Wolf replies that the Black Hills region is home to the Cheyenne, and that he is prepared to trade recently discovered gold for assurances that his people will be left in peace. George reluctantly agrees to the trade, but after the two Indians leave, he sends his man Garvin to shoot Yellow Wolf in the street. Marshal Tate, who loves Yellow Wolf's daughter Pretty Willow and believes that the Cheyenne should be allowed to remain on their lands, tries to caution George that Little Wolf may send warriors to avenge the chief's death. The captain and the rest of the townspeople dismiss this warning, demanding that Tate turn in his star. Disgusted, Tate complies and informs his nephew Billy, who has lived with him since the Indians killed his parents, that they soon will leave Sand Creek. Billy protests the move, and Amy Porter, a widow who looks after Billy and runs the local boardinghouse, declares that she would be a better wife for Tate than Pretty Willow, a "dirty, uncivilized" savage. Tate's gentle attempt to persuade Amy that her hatred stems from the loneliness of widowhood ends in an argument, and he storms out of the house. Determined to run away from Tate during the night, Billy climbs out his window just as the Cheyenne start to raid Cavalry headquarters for guns and horses. While trying to escape, the boy is shot and killed. After Billy's funeral, George approaches Tate in a panic. Having stolen most of the town's horses and weapons, the Cheyenne, he fears, will massacre everyone. Tate remarks sadly that to save the townspeople, he must kill Little Wolf, but when he follows the Indian to a deserted location, he finds he is unable to pull the trigger. Little Wolf places some gold near a tree, and after he leaves, Tate carries it back to the boardinghouse. Angry at Tate for refusing her love, Amy brings the gold straight to George, who suspects that Tate has made a deal with the Cheyenne. At George's prompting, Garvin tells Little Wolf that Tate is planning to kill him. In exchange for this information, the Cavalry, he lies, wants to accept Yellow Wolf's proposal to trade gold for Cheyenne lands. Having learned during one of her secret meetings with Tate that he had planned to kill her brother, Pretty Willow confirms Garvin's accusation. Little Wolf tells Garvin that he will meet George after settling his score with Tate, not realizing that George plans to ambush both men at their dueling place. The next morning, Pretty Willow and Little Wolf meet Tate at the appointed spot near the river. As Tate and Little Wolf battle each other with knives, Captain George and his men surround the area and begin shooting. Tate falls in the river, apparently dead, and Little Wolf is shot while attacking Garvin. Back in town, Amy looks after the grief-stricken Pretty Willow, an

experience which dissolves her hatred and fills her with remorse. With the arrival of Cavalry reinforcements, George proceeds with his plan to place the Cheyenne on an Oklahoma reservation, but first he orders Pretty Willow to show him where the tribe's gold is hidden. When she takes him there, Tate appears and kills George in a gun battle. The Cheyenne are nonetheless forced to leave their homes, and as Pretty Willow, now reunited with Tate, watches them go, she wonders aloud what white men would do if some new race tried to take their lands. Would they fight like the Cheyenne, she asks? Just like the Cheyenne, Tate replies. *Cheyenne Indians. Little Wolf (Cheyenne Indian). Marshals. Racism. Treachery. United States. Army. Cavalry. Alcoholics. Black Hills (SD and WY). Boardinghouse mistresses. Brothers and sisters. Cowardice. Gold. Grief. Gunfights. Jealousy. Knife fighting. Miscegenation. Murder. Nephews. Officers (Military). Raids. Revenge. Romance. Saloons. Transformation. Tribal chiefs.*

Note: Norman Retchin's onscreen credit reads: "Produced and written by Norman Retchin." Bryna Production, Inc. was owned by actor Kirk Douglas. Although reviewers generally did not praise the film, they did comment positively on its "contemporary" depiction of Native Americans. In 1864, at Sand Creek, CO, volunteers slaughtered some two hundred Cheyenne Indians, most of them women and children, who thought they were under military protection. In 1879, over two hundred northern Cheyenne Indians under Chiefs Dull Knife, Wild Hog and Little Wolf surrendered to government forces and were sent to Fort Reno, OK, as prisoners. Nearly half of this group were killed in escape attempts. It is possible that *Ride Out for Revenge* was based, in part, on these historical events.
Box 23 Nov 1957. *Cue* 21 Jun 1958. *DV* 17 Oct 1957, p. 3. *Exh* 30 Oct 1956, p. 4397. *FD* 14 Nov 1957, p. 12. *Har* 26 Oct 1957, p. 171. *HR* 22 Mar 1957, p. 17. *HR* 5 Apr 1957, p. 12. *HR* 17 Oct 1957, p. 3. *MPD* 22 Oct 1957. *MPHPD* 26 Oct 1957, p. 578. *Var* 23 Oct 1957, p. 6.

RIDE, RANGER, RIDE (Native Americans)

Republic Pictures Corp. *Dist* Republic Pictures Corp. 30 Sep **1936** [©Republic Pictures Corp.; 30 Sep 1936; LP6637]. Sd; b&w. 6 reels. 59 or 63 min. PCA cert no. 2555.

Prod Nat Levine. *Assoc prod* Armand Schaefer. *Dir* Joseph Kane. *Scr* Dorrell McGowan and Stuart McGowan. *Orig story* Bernard McConville and Karen DeWolf. *Photog* William Nobles. *Film ed* Lester Orlebeck. *Supv ed* Murray Seldeen. *Mus supv* Harry Grey. *Sd eng* Terry Kellum.

Song(s): "Ride, Ranger, Ride" and "Song of the Pioneers," words and music by Vern (Tim) Spencer; "On the Sunset Trail," words by Sidney D. Mitchell, music by Sam H. Stept; "Goin' Down the Road," words and music by The Tennessee Ramblers; "The Bugle Song," words and music by Smiley Burnette; "Yellow Rose of Texas," traditional.

Cast: GENE AUTRY [(*Gene Autry*)], Smiley Burnette [(*Frog Jones*)], Kay Hughes [(*Dixie Summerall*)], Monte Blue [(*Duval, also known as "Tavibo"*)], George Lewis [(*Lieutenant Bob Cameron*)], Max Terhune [(*Rufe*)], Robert E. Homans [(*Colonel Summerall*)], Lloyd Whitlock [(*Major Crosby*)], Chief Thundercloud [(*Little Wolf*)], The Tennessee Ramblers [(*Ranger musicians*)], Champion, the horse (*Himself*).

Western, with songs. [*Print viewed*]. At Fort Adobe, Texas, scout Gene Autry and cavalry lieutenant Bob Cameron are competing for the attentions of Colonel Summerall's daughter Dixie, when an Indian war party calls them to duty. A peace treaty is signed with the help of Duval, the Fort's interpreter, but Gene and his buddies, Rufe and Frog Jones, suspect Duval may be working with the Indians and go to his canteen to investigate. There, Duval's attempt to kill Gene results in a barroom brawl, after which, Gene and his friends are court-martialed. Gene tries to warn Colonel Summerall and Major Crosby about the interpreter, but is arrested for the murder of a Comanche brave. Gene's arrest leaves Duval, whom the Indians know as "Tavibo," free to continue his plot to re-route a supply train so that the Comanches can attack and capture the cavalry's ammunition. Gene escapes jail and joins the bloody fight between the cavalry and the Comanches. Frog arrives with the Rangers to win the battle, during which Duval is killed and his true identity is revealed. Finally, after peace is restored, Colonel Summerall apologizes to Gene, and Gene wins Dixie as his bride. *Duplicity. False arrests. Indians of North America. Secret plans. Texas Rangers. United States. Army. Cavalry. Ammunition. Attempted murder. Courts-martial and courts of inquiry. Jailbreaks. Marriage. Officers (Military). Romantic rivalry. Translators.*

Note: Modern sources list Louis Germonprez as assistant director, and add the following cast members: Frankie Marvin, Iron Eyes Cody, Sonny Chorre, Bud Pope, Nelson McDowell, Shooting Star, Arthur Singley, Greg Whitespear and Robert C. Thomas.

Var 21 Apr 1937, p. 15.

RIDE, RYDER, RIDE! (Native Americans)

Equity Pictures, Inc. *Dist* Eagle Lion Films, Inc. 23 Feb **1949**; Prod: late Sep—mid-Oct 1948 [©Pathe Industries, Inc.; 23 Feb 1949; LP2140]. Sd (RCA Sound System); col (Cinecolor). 7 reels, 5,215 ft. 57-59 min. PCA cert no. 13506.

Series: Red Ryder.

Prod Jerry Thomas. *Dir* Lewis D. Collins. *Asst dir* Ralph Slosser. *Dial dir* Marshall Edson. *Orig scr* Paul Franklin. *Dir of photog* Gilbert Warrenton. [*Cam op* Joe Novak]. [*Gaffer* Frank Jenkins]. [*Stills* Bert Lynch]. *Spec eff* Ray Mercer. *Cinecolor consultant* Henry J. Staudigl. *Tech dir* Fred W. Kline. *Film ed* Joseph Gluck. *Set dec* Vin Taylor. *Ward dir* Vern Murdock. *Mus comp and cond* Darrell Calker. *Mus supv* David Chudnow. *Sd eng* Victor Appel. *Makeup dir* Herbert Offord. *Prod mgr* Bartlett Carré. [*Scr supv* Dorothy Hughes]. [*Grip* Al Bollinger].

Source: Based on the comic strip "Red Ryder" by Fred Harman (1938—1964), by special arrangement with Stephen Slesinger.

Cast: Jim Bannon (*Red Ryder*), Little Brown Jug (*Little Beaver*), Emmett Lynn (*Buckskin* [*Blodgett*]), Marin Sais (*Duchess*), Edwin Max [(*Frenchy Beaumont*)], Peggy Stewart [(*Libby Brooks*)], Steve Pendleton [(*Gerry Brooks*)], Enya Doyle [(*Marge*)], Jack O'Shea [(*Blackjack*)], Fred Coby [(*Henry W. Iverson*)], William Fawcett [(*Judge*)], Steve Clark [(*Tom*)], Billy Hammond [(*Pinto*)].

Western. [*Print viewed*]. On their way into the town of Devil's Hole, cowboy Red Ryder and his friends, Buckskin and Little Beaver, see a gang of bandits chasing a stagecoach. After frightening the bandits away, Red stops the stagecoach, on which newspaper editor Libby Brooks and her brother Gerry are riding. Gerry tells Red that he suspects that the leader of the gang, which has been terrorizing the townspeople for some time, is Frenchy Beaumont, the owner of the Parisian Hotel. Later, at the newspaper office in Devil's Hole, Gerry tells Tom, the typesetter, that he wants to print an article implicating Beaumont in the attempted holdup. When Beaumont reads the article, he instructs his henchman, Blackjack, to go to the newspaper office and provoke a fight so that he will be able to shoot Gerry and claim that he was defending himself. Blackjack follows Beaumont's orders, but when he draws his gun, Red arrives suddenly and shoots it out of his hand. Later, Red, Little Beaver and Buckskin visit Libby, who is at home with a cold. Meanwhile, Beaumont encounters Gerry in the street and demands that he meet him at dawn for a duel at Hangman's Oak. Later, Gerry's fiancée Marge senses his distraction, but he refuses to tell her about the duel. The next morning, Libby learns about the duel and tells Red about it. Red, Buckskin and Little Beaver rush to Hangman's Oak, arriving just in time to see Beaumont shoot and kill Gerry. Later, Red tells Libby about his plan to try to arrest Beaumont and put him in jail so that reluctant witnesses will be encouraged to come forward with their claims against him. Following Red's instructions, Libby arranges for the printing of a special edition of the paper, which contains another condemnation of Beaumont. When Beaumont and Blackjack learn of these latest accusations, they go to the newspaper office and demand to see the edition. Buckskin hands them the bogus copy, and when they read Libby's charges, Blackjack punches him in the mouth. Beaumont then takes the paper to his lawyer, Henry W. Iverson, who advises him that it is a clear cut case of criminal libel. Iverson rushes the case to trial, and Red, who is serving as Libby's counsel, explains that the edition that Beaumont saw was never distributed. Red then charges Beaumont with battery, and after he dismisses the libel charge, the judge sentences Blackjack to three years in prison. His plan foiled, Red goes to the hotel and issues a challenge to meet Beaumont at Hangman's Oak. The next morning during the duel, Beaumont's bullet grazes Red's temple, then lodges in a tree behind him. Later on that day, Red returns to the spot, retrieves the bullet and determines that the barrels of Beaumont's dueling pistols are not properly aligned. At the hotel, Red accuses Beaumont of rigging his pistols. When Beaumont punches him, Red arrests him and takes him to jail. The next morning, the paper reports that Beaumont has been indicted for manslaughter. *Bandits. Cowboys. Hotel owners. Newspapers. Arrests. Duels. Engagements. Family relationships. Firearms. French Americans. Head colds. Indians of North America. Judges. Lawyers. Manslaughter. Set-ups. Shootings. Stagecoaches. Trials.*

Note: All reviews and press information credit Jean Budinger with the role of "Marge," but the onscreen credits list Enya Doyle in the part. It is possible that

Enya Doyle was a stage name assumed by Jean Budinger. *Ride, Ryder, Ride!* was the first of four "Red Ryder" films produced by Equity Pictures and starring Jim Bannon. Previously, the series was produced by Republic Pictures Corp. and featured a different cast. For additional information on the "Red Ryder" series, please consult the Series Index and see the entry below for *Tucson Raiders*.

Box 12 Mar 1949. *DV* 2 Mar 1949, p. 3. *FD* 22 Mar 1949, p. 6. *HR* 1 Oct 1948, p. 12. *HR* 8 Oct 1948, p. 14. *HR* 2 Mar 1949, p. 3. *MPHPD* 5 Mar 1949, p. 4522. *Var* 2 Mar 1949, p. 20.

RIDE THE PINK HORSE (Latino)

Universal-International Pictures Co., Inc. *Dist* Universal Pictures Co., Inc. 12 Sep **1947**; Prod: early May—early Jul 1947 [©Universal Pictures Co., Inc.; 31 Oct 1947; LP1338]. Sd (Western Electric Recording); b&w. 100-101 min.

Prod Joan Harrison. *Dir* Robert Montgomery. *Asst dir* John F. Sherwood. *Scr* Ben Hecht and Charles Lederer. *Dir of photog* Russell Metty and [Maury Gertsman]. *Art dir* Bernard Herzbrun and Robert Boyle. *Film ed* Ralph Dawson. *Set dec* Russell A. Gausman and Oliver Emert. *Gowns* Yvonne Wood. *Mus* Frank Skinner. *Orch* David Tamkin. *Sd* Leslie I. Carey and Jack A. Bolger, Jr. *Hair stylist* Carmen Dirigo. *Makeup* Bud Westmore.

Source: Based on the novel *Ride the Pink Horse* by Dorothy B. Hughes (New York, 1946).

Cast: in order of appearance ROBERT MONTGOMERY (*Lucky Gagin*), Thomas Gomez (*Pancho*), Rita Conde (*Carla*), Iris Flores (*Maria*), Wanda Hendrix (*Pila*), Grandon Rhodes (*Mrs. Edison*), Tito Renaldo (*Bellboy*), Richard Gaines (*Jonathan*), Andrea King (*Marjorie*), Art Smith (*Bill Retz*), Martin Garralaga (*Bar keeper*), Edward Earle (*Locke*), Harold Goodwin (*Red*), Maria Cortez (*Elevator girl*), Fred Clark ([*Frank*] *Hugo*), [Paul Maxey (*Portly man*)], [Howard Negley, Jimmy Ames, John Doucette, Jack Worth (*Thugs*)], [Leon Lenoir (*Mexican workman*)], [Beatrice Roberts (*Manageress*)], [Julian Rivero, Jerry De Castro (*Mexican men*)], [Paul Bryan, Lyle Latell (*State troopers*)], [Harry J. Vejar (*Barber*)], [Charles Stevens (*Drunken Mexican*)], [William Ruhl (*Mr. Blane*)], [Ernest Hilliard (*Elderly man*)], [Virginia Ware (*Waitress*)], [Ralph Montgomery (*Waiter*)], [Amadita Garcia, Connie Asins, Rose Marie Lopez, Martha Brenes, Olga Perez, Carmen Pallais (*Mexican girls*)], [Miguel Tapia, Roque Ybarra, Jr., José Alvarado, Robert Espinosa, Harry Garcia (*Mexican boys*)], [Enrique Valadez, Robert Cabal (*Muchachos*)], [Donald Kerr (*Head waiter*)], [Margarita Savilla (*Spanish girl*)], [Kenneth Ross-MacKenzie].

Crime, Drama, Film noir. [*Print viewed*]. Veteran Lucky Gagin arrives in the New Mexico town of San Pablo, where he hopes to blackmail Frank Hugo, a former war profiteer who murdered his friend, Shorty Thompson. After hiding a canceled check inside a bus terminal locker, Lucky meets Pila, a young Mexican American girl, who gives him a good luck charm. Lucky then goes to Hugo's hotel room, where he has a run-in with Hugo's secretary, Jonathan. There, he also meets Marjorie, Hugo's gold-digging girl friend. Upon leaving Hugo's room, Lucky is invited to lunch by Bill Retz, a government agent, who warns Lucky against avenging Shorty's death. With all the town's hotel rooms filled because of an upcoming fiesta, Lucky goes to the Cantina de las tres violetas, where he meets Pancho, a carousel operator. After a evening of drinking, the drunken Lucky and Pancho spend the night at the Mexican's outdoor domicile. They are soon joined by the homeless Pila, who falls asleep on Pancho's merry-go-round. Later, Retz arrives and warns Lucky that Locke, Hugo's partner, has hired two thugs to kill him. The next morning, Lucky meets with Hugo, who is deaf, and he admits to having killed the blackmailing Shorty. Lucky then tells Hugo that he has a canceled check for $100,000 which Hugo used to bribe a high government official, and demands $30,000 for its return. Hugo concedes to Lucky's demands, and they agree to meet that night at the Tip Top Café. Marjorie then offers to join forces with Lucky, hoping to blackmail Hugo for even more money, but Lucky refuses. That night at the café, Marjorie lures Lucky outside, where he is attacked and stabbed by two of Hugo's men. Lucky defeats the mobsters, killing one, and escapes into the woods. Pila finds him, the she and Pancho tend to his wounds and hide him from Hugo's thugs. Lucky and Pila later go back to the cantina, where he gives her the canceled check. Red, one of Hugo's goons, arrives at the cantina, but he is knocked unconscious by Pila, who then places the semi-conscious Lucky inside a bus. As she tries to find the ticket master, however, Lucky wanders back into town. Before Pila can stop him, Lucky arrives at Hugo's room, and they are both beaten up by Hugo's men because the injured Lucky cannot

remember where the check is. They are saved by Retz, and after Hugo offers him $300,000 for the check, Lucky defiantly gives the check to the government agent. A few days later, Lucky frets about how he is going to leave town without breaking Pila's heart, but it is she who says goodbye to him, making her the envy of all her friends. *Blackmail. Gangsters. Mexican Americans. Revenge. Romance. United States. Federal Bureau of Investigation. Veterans. Bellboys. Cafés. Cantinas. Checks. Deafness. Drunkenness. Escapes. Fiestas. Hotels. Merry-go-rounds. Murder. New Mexico. Parades. Profiteering. Secretaries. Stabbings.*

Note: According to Universal press materials, portions of *Ride the Pink Horse* were filmed on location in Santa Fe, NM. Universal press materials also state that the fictional town of "San Pablo" was a composite of the Hispanic areas of Santa Fe, Albuquerque and Taos, NM. According to *LAT*, Universal paid the city of Taos $2,000 to ship "Tio Vivo," its 1882 carousel, to California for use on this film.

According to information contained in the file on the film in the MPAA/PCA Collection at the AMPAS Library, the original script for *Ride the Pink Horse* was approved by the PCA, though the Breen Office did harbor reservations about the drunkenness present in the story. In a 23 Oct 1947 letter to the Breen Office, independent producer Sol Wurtzel complained about the excessive drinking in *Ride the Pink Horse*, and asked "If there is a different rule in the association for 'A' pictures and a different one for so-called 'B' pictures?" In 1948, *NYT* reported that Ben Hecht's name was omitted from the screen credits of *Ride the Pink Horse* in England because of the writer's critical remarks about the British military presence in Palestine. Thomas Gomez was nominated for an Academy Award as Best Supporting Actor for his performance in *Ride the Pink Horse*, but lost to Edmund Gwenn for his work in the Twentieth Century-Fox film, *Miracle on 34th Street*. Robert Montgomery, Wanda Hendrix and Thomas Gomez reprised their roles in a *Lux Radio Theatre* version of *Ride the Pink Horse* on 8 Dec 1947. The Dorothy B. Hughes novel was filmed again for television in 1964 under the title *The Hanged Man*. The NBC network production starred Edmond O'Brien and Robert Culp, and was directed by Don Siegel.

Box 20 Sep 1947. *FD* 12 Sep 1947, p. 10 *HR* 9 May 1947, p. 21. *HR* 10 Sep 1947, p. 3. *IFJ* 24 May 1947, p. 51. *LAT* 1 Jun 1947. *MPHPD* 20 Sep 1947, p. 3841. *NYT* 9 Oct 1947, p. 32. *NYT* 14 Oct 1948. *Var* 17 Sep 1947, p. 16.

RIDE, VAQUERO! (Latino)

Metro-Goldwyn-Mayer Corp.; controlled by Loew's Inc. *Dist* Loew's Inc. 17 Jul **1953**; Prod: late Jul—early Sep 1952 [©Loew's Inc.; 17 Jun 1953; LP2682]. Sd (Western Electric Sound System); col (Ansco color); Prints by Technicolor. 11 reels, 8115 ft. 90-91 min. PCA cert no. 16157.

Prod Stephen Ames. *Dir* John Farrow. *Asst dir* Jerry Thorpe. *Scr* Frank Fenton. *Dir of photog* Robert Surtees. *Col consultant* Alvord Eiseman. *Art dir* Cedric Gibbons and Arthur Lonergan. *Film ed* Harold F. Kress. *Set dec* Edwin B. Willis and Fred MacLean. *Cost des* Walter Plunkett. *Mus* Bronislau Kaper. *Rec supv* Douglas Shearer. [*Sd* Stan Lambert]. *Hair styles* Sydney Guilaroff. *Makeup created by* William Tuttle. *Sp eff* A. Arnold Gillespie.

Cast: ROBERT TAYLOR (*Rio*), AVA GARDNER (*Cordelia Cameron*), HOWARD KEEL (*King Cameron*), Anthony Quinn (*Jose Esqueda*), Kurt Kasznar (*Father Antonio*), Ted de Corsia (*Sheriff Parker*), Charlita (*Singer*), Jack Elam (*Barton*), Walter Baldwin (*Adam Smith*), Joe Dominguez (*Vincente*), Frank McGrath (*Pete*), Charles Stevens (*Vaquero*), Rex Lease, Tom Greenway (*Deputies*), [Paul Fierro (*Valero*)], [Percy Helton, Jimmie Fox (*Storekeepers*)], [Norman Leavitt (*Dentist*)], [Movita Castaneda (*Hussy*)], [Robert L. Diamond (*Boy with circular*)], [John Call, Jim Hayward (*Clerks*)], [Monte Blue, Frank Hagney (*Bartenders*)], [Philip Van Zandt (*Dealer*)], [Stanley Andrews (*General Sheridan*)], [Pedro Regas (*Comrade*)], [Terry Wilson, Henry Wills, Archie Butler (*Stunt actors*)], [Capt. George Watkins (*Seaman*)], [Harry Brown (*Pianist*)], [Joey Ray (*Croupier*)], [Italia De Nubila (*Specialty dancer*)], [Wilson Wood (*Orderly*)], [Manuel Alda (*Manuel*)], [Kay English (*Woman in park*)], [James H. Harrison], [Robert Stephenson], [Emmet Vogan], [Stuart Holmes], [Almira Sessions].

Western. [*Print viewed*]. Following the end of the Civil War, rough-hewn Mexican bandit leader Jose Esqueda warns the people in his South Texas village that they are in danger of losing their land to the homesteading "Americanos," who are descending upon the Brownsville area. While the villagers cheer Esqueda when he vows to burn down the settlers' homes, Rio, an American who was reared by Esqueda's mother and regards him as a brother, shows little support for the plan. The first hacienda the bandits set on fire is the new home built by rancher King Cameron for his wife Cordelia. Risking his life to do what he believes is right, Cameron organizes a meeting at the local church to put a stop to Esqueda's raids. Esqueda and Rio are among those attending the meeting, and when Cameron calls Esqueda

a "murderer, a thief and a coward," the bandit laughs openly at his accusations. The meeting ends abruptly after Cameron vows to fight Esqueda. No sooner does Cameron rebuild his house, than Esqueda sends Rio and his men to burn it down again. Father Antonio, the respected village priest, warns Cameron that Esqueda is planning an attack on his property and, while praying for the couple's safety, helps them ward off the gang. The gun battle is cut short with the arrival of the rangers, and Rio is captured by Cameron. Instead of turning Rio over to the soldiers, Cameron offers him a partnership, and insists that the bandit help him bring over some horses from Mexico. Though Cordelia disapproves of the plan, believing that Rio should not be trusted, the two men quickly depart for Mexico. Along the way, Rio proves his trustworthiness when he saves Cameron from drowning in a river. Soon after Cameron and Rio return from Mexico, Esqueda discovers their partnership, but forgives his foster brother's apparent desertion as he believes that Rio joined Cameron because he is in love with Cordelia. Cordelia eventually comes to trust Rio, and when he takes her to Esqueda, she pleads with him to end his raids. Angered by Esqueda's rude dismissal of her request, Cordelia grabs his gun and threatens to kill him. She decides not to shoot, however, when Esqueda tells her that Rio would be killed by his gang as a consequence of her action. Later, Cordelia, now in love with Rio, steals a kiss from him, but he strikes her for the impropriety. When Esqueda learns that Rio has been spurned by Cordelia, he believes that Rio will now remain loyal to him and will not interfere with a raid on the "gringo" town of Brownsville. Esqueda and his gang then shoot their way into Brownsville, kill the sheriff and rob the bank. In a drunken rage, Esqueda decides to kill Rio, Cordelia and Cameron, and sends one of his men to find them. Meanwhile, word of the siege of Brownsville reaches the Cavalry commander, who immediately sets out to regain control of the town. Esqueda's men flee when they see the approaching Cavalry, but the bandit leader stays behind to kill Cameron. After wounding Cameron with two gunshots, Esqueda is about to kill him, when Rio arrives and points his gun at him. The two face off in a gun draw and are killed simultaneously. Cameron survives his gunshot wounds, and returns to the arms of Cordelia, whom he forgives for her feelings for Rio. *Bandits. Brownsville (TX). Foster children. Homesteaders. Mexicans. Texas–History. Arson. Bank robberies. Casinos. Chases. Drowning. Drunkenness. Gunfights. Infidelity. Outlaws. Priests. Rescues. Sheriffs. Sieges. United States. Army. Cavalry.*

Note: The working title for this film was *Vaquero*. The picture marked John Farrow's first film for M-G-M. According to studio publicity material, the picture was filmed in Kanab, Utah.

Box 20 Jun 1953. *DV* 19 Jun 1953, p. 3. *Exb* 1 Jul 1953, p. 3546. *FD* 1 Jul 1953, p. 6. *Har* 20 Jun 1953, p. 98. *HR* 14 Mar 1952. *HR* 1 Aug 1952, p. 10. *HR* 5 Sep 1952, p. 10. *HR* 19 Jun 1953, p. 3. *MPHPD* 20 Jun 1953, p. 1879. *NYT* 16 Jul 1953, p. 17. *Var* 14 Mar 1952. *Var* 24 Jun 1953, p. 6.

RIDERS OF THE DESERT (Native Americans, Apache)

Trem Carr Pictures, Ltd. *Dist* Sono Art-World Wide Pictures, Inc. 24 Apr 1932 [©Sono Art-World Wide Pictures, Inc.; 4 Apr 1932; LP3025]. Sd (RCA Photophone System); b&w. 6 reels, 5,338 ft. 57 or 59 min. Passed by the National Board of Review.

Dir Robert N. Bradbury. *Story and adpt* Wellyn Totman. *Photog* Archie Stout. *Ed* Carl Pierson. *Rec* John Stransky. *Tech dir* Ernest R. Hickson. *Prod mgr* Paul Malvern. *Lighting* Edward Cox.

Cast: BOB STEELE [(*Bob Houston*)], Gertie Messenger [(*Barbara Reynolds*)], Al St. John [(*Slim*)], George Hayes [(*Hashknife Brooks*)], John Elliott [(*Houston*)], H. B. Carpenter [(*Capt. Jim Reynolds*)], José Domínguez [(*Gomez*)], Greg Whitespear [(*Apache Joe*)], Louise Carver [(*Buck Lawlor*)], Tex O'Neil [(*Cochimo*)].

Western. [*Print viewed*]. Bob Houston on vacation from school visiting his father in Apache Gulch, and discovers that the Arizona Rangers, of which is father is a member, has been officially disbanded. The Rangers decide to go on one last mission, and they capture the notorious Hashknife Brooks, guilty of stagecoach robbery and murder. Although they arrest Hashknife, the rest of his gang remains at large, and their cache of gold is never found. Bob returns home after finishing school to rekindle his romance with Barbara Reynolds, daughter of Ben Reynolds, the former captain of the Rangers. Ben has been killed and Bob and his father suspect Brooks, who recently escaped from prison. The Rangers join together again to capture Brooks. When Ranger Buck Lawlor trails after Gomez, a suspect, Apache Joe shoots him in the back. Bob seizes the Indian, who refuses to confess. At the ranch, Brooks and Gomez kidnap Bob's father and

Barbara. Under duress, the Indian promises to lead the Rangers to the gang hideout. Bob and Slim, another Ranger who barely escaped from his domineering wife in order to rejoin his pals, find his father and Barbara at a different location. Houston rides to warn the Rangers of an ambush before they reach their destination, while after tying up Brooks, Bob rides to his friends, the Apache Indians, to call on their help, and Slim takes Barbara to the ranch. After their wagon crashes, Brooks, who has been released by Gomez, kidnaps Barbara. Houston reaches the Rangers just as they are ambushed, but they win the battle with the help of the Apaches, and Apache Joe is killed. After Bob struggles with Brooks, Slim shoots Brooks and helps Bob rescue Barbara from quicksand, where Brooks left her to die. *Arizona. Murder. Outlaws. Prison escapes. Rangers. Apache Indians. Indians of North America. Kidnapping. Quicksand. Rescues.*

Note: Actor Greg Whitespear was an Apache Indian who worked to get other Apaches to appear in this film. José Domínguez was a noted *vaquero*. The Arizona Rangers discontinued their service in 1910. A modern source includes Earl Dwire in the cast.

FD 22 May 1932, p. 10. *MPH* 28 May 1932, p. 89. *Var* 12 Jul 1932, p. 17.

RIDERS OF THE PONY EXPRESS (Native Americans)

Kayson Productions, Inc. *Dist* Screencraft Pictures, Inc. **1950** [©Kayson Productions, Inc.; 15 May 1949; LP2304]. Sd; col. 61 min.

Prod Richard Kay and D. A. Anderson. *Dir* Michael Salle. *Asst dir* Nat Merman. *Wrt* Michael Salle. *Photog* Howard A. Anderson, Jr. *Spec eff* Larry Chapman. *Film ed* Ray Snyder. *Props* Gene Stone. *Mus dir* Raoul Kraushaar. *Set dec* Leo Lotito. *Unit prod mgr* Richard Kay.

Cast: Ken Curtis [(*Tom Blake, also known as Tom Bledsoe*)], Shug Fisher ("*Doc*" *Baker*), Cathy Douglas (*Judy Blair*), Billy Benedict (*Eddie Lund*), Billy Hammond ("*Tex*" *Jarvis*), Eddie McLean (*Mac Duncan*), Truman Van Dyke (*Steven Blair*), John Dehner (*John Dakin*), Lou Marcelle (*Dan Cutter*), Rod Redwing (*Bearclaw*), Flicka, a horse, Zane, a horse.

Western, with songs. [*Not viewed*]. Looking for a night of fun, ranch hand Tom Blake rides into a western town, and after joining a card game, accuses a cowboy named Custic of cheating. After Tom is later ambushed by Custic and his friends, he shoots Custic, then escapes. Believing Custic to be dead, Tom goes to see veterinarian "Doc" Baker and borrows a fresh horse to continue his escape from Custic's friends. In the desert, Tom's horse becomes lame, so he decides to turn it loose. He begins walking and encounters passing rider John Dakin, who refuses to help him. Tom perseveres, eventually arriving at a watering hole, where he captures a wild horse. While he is training his new horse, Tom encounters three cowboys, Eddie Lund, Tex Jarvis and Mac Duncan, who are on their way to join the newly formed Pony Express, and decides to join them. At the district headquarters of the Express, Tom, who has taken the alias Tom Bledsoe, meets Doc, who has also been hired to ride for the Express. Awaiting their first assignment, the new riders gather in the corral to sing some songs. Suddenly, Dakin and his henchman arrive and, when they try to confiscate the group's guitar, a fight ensues. Then, Dakin identifies himself as the Express's district supervisor, and orders Tom and his new friends, who include local express manager Steven Blair and his niece Judy, to the dangerous Desert Station. Unknown to the others, Dakin is a half-breed Indian, who secretly heads a band of renegade braves bent on stopping the progress of the Express. When the Indians, led by another half-breed named Dan Cutter, try to kill the group heading for Desert Station, Tom bravely holds the braves at bay until the party can pass to safety. Eventually, the party arrives at the station and begins practicing their mounts to speed the mail's delivery. The result of their experiments is the spectacular "Pony Express Mount," in which the driver mounts an already moving horse. Meanwhile, Cutter waylays an Express agent who is bringing supplies to Desert Station and assumes his identity. After he picks a fight with Tom, Cutter shows Blair a wanted poster with Tom's likeness on it, and Tom is removed from the group. On the evening before the new riders' first run, however, Tom catches Cutter trying to poison their horses, and is later permitted to deliver the mail. On his first run, the Indians attack Desert Station, and although the mail gets through, the Blairs are captured. Then, Tom and his fellow riders follow the braves back to their hideout, where they free Judy and Steven, kill Cutter and arrest Dakin. Back at Desert Station, a letter arrives asking that the wanted posters on Tom be withdrawn as his victim, Custic, has been found alive. Just then, the relay rider enters the station and passes the mail bags to Tom, who mounts his

moving horse to carry the mail across the forbidding desert. *Cowboys. Pony Express. Postal workers. Renegades. Aliases. Animal trainers. Cards. Deserts. Escapes. False accusations. Fights. Fugitives. Guitars. Hideouts. Horses. Indians of North America–Mixed blood. Letters. Nieces. Shootings. Singers. Veterinarians. Water.*

Note: According to the *Exb* review, several "traditional western songs" are performed in the picture, but their titles and composers have not been identified.

Exb 21 Jun 1950.

RIDERS OF THE RANGE (Latino)

RKO Radio Pictures, Inc. *Dist* RKO Radio Pictures, Inc. 11 Feb **1949**; Prod: 15 Jun—late Jun 1949 [©RKO Radio Pictures, Inc.; 19 Oct 1949; LP2676]. Sd (RCA Sound System); b&w. 5,444 ft. 60 min. PCA cert no. 13941.

Prod Herman Schlom. *Dir* Lesley Selander. [*Asst dir* John E. Pommer]. *Wrt* Norman Houston. *Dir of photog* J. Roy Hunt. [*Cam op* Richard Davol and Emmett Bergholz]. [*Gaffer* Orville Beckett]. [*Stills* Oliver Sigurdson]. *Art dir* Albert S. D'Agostino and Feild Gray. *Film ed* Robert Swink. *Set dec* Darrell Silvera and Jack Mills. *Mus dir* C. Bakaleinikoff. *Mus* Paul Sawtell. *Sd* John Cass and Clem Portman. [*Makeup* Jack Barron]. [*Hair stylist* Josephine Sweeney]. [*Scr supv* Charles Martin]. [*Grip* Henry Burton].

Cast: TIM HOLT [(*Kansas Jones*)], Richard Martin [(*Chito Rafferty*)], Jacqueline White [(*Drusilla "Dusty" Willis*)], Reed Hadley [(*Clint Burrows*)], Robert Barrat [(*Sheriff Cole*)], Robert Clarke [(*Harry Willis*)], Tom Tyler [(*Ringo Kid*)], William Tannen [(*Trump Dixon*)], [Holly Bane (*Guard*)].

Western. [*Print viewed*]. Upon arriving in Arizona, out-of-work cowboys Kansas Jones and Chito Rafferty head for the nearest saloon to see if there are any jobs in the area. There they become embroiled in a fight between saloon owner Clint Burrows and Drusilla "Dusty" Willis. Dusty, a rancher, is furious at Burrows for allowing her weak-willed brother Harry to gamble in his saloon and strikes him with her riding crop. When Burrows begins to hit back, Kansas and Chito intercede on Dusty's behalf, and out of gratitude, Dusty offers the cowboys work on her ranch. Burrows, meanwhile, confronts Harry about his $3,000 gambling debt, demanding that he pay up with Dusty's cattle by the next morning. Although Dusty has ordered Kansas and Chito to help her brother in the south flat, Harry abandons the cowhands so that he can round up cattle for Burrows, who has arranged for Ringo Kid, a notorious rustler, and Trump Dixon, his own henchman, to take the herd. As Ringo, Trump and their men descend on the cattle, however, Kansas and Chito ride up and drive off the rustlers. Harry pretends to join in the fight against the rustlers and then feigns an injury, but when Dusty arrives on the scene, she detects his ruse and chastises him. In town, meanwhile, Ringo accuses Burrows of setting him up and demands his payment. When Burrows refuses to pay, Ringo robs his safe at gunpoint and takes a billfold full of money. Angry that he has been double-crossed, Burrows goes to confront Harry, who has decided to leave the ranch for good, and is about to shoot him when Chito and Kansas interrupt. After forcing Burrows off the ranch, Kansas convinces Harry to "come clean" with Dusty and return to the ranch. Impressed by Harry's honesty, Dusty offers to pay his gambling debt and then entrusts Chito and Kansas with the money. On the road to town, the cowboys spot Ringo on his horse and, recognizing him as a rustler, chase him. Chito finally corners Ringo among some rocks, but the rustler knocks him out and flees. Later, Kansas finds Burrows' billfold in the dirt and takes it with him to town. At the saloon, Kansas and Chito buy up Harry's IOUs, an exchange witnessed by Ringo. After the cowboys leave, Ringo sneaks into Burrows' office, steals the money again and kills Burrows. Kansas and Chito are accused of the crime, but when Sheriff Cole and his posse are about to arrest them, they escape. While Chito distracts the pursuing posse, Kansas rides to town to find Trump. At gunpoint, Kansas forces Trump to take him to Ringo's remote hideout, and there Kansas engages the rustlers in a gunfight. Chito, meanwhile, has been caught by the sheriff, but the trusting Dusty connives to free him. With Chito's help, Kansas defeats the rustlers and lassos Ringo. Kansas then shows the sheriff that Ringo was carrying the stolen money and thereby vindicates himself and Chito. Although Kansas and Chito then head for Prescott to testify against Ringo, Dusty is confident that they will return soon, as Kansas has deliberately left Chito's beloved "lucky peso" with Harry. *Brothers and sisters. Cowboys. False accusations. Ranchers. Robbery. Rustlers.*

Arizona. *Debt. Fights. Gambling. Gunfights. Mexican Americans. Money. Posses. Saloon keepers. Saloons. Sheriffs.*

Note: The working title of the film was *Arizona Ambush*. The *Var* review incorrectly lists Tom Tyler's character name as "Kid Ringo." According to modern sources, the picture lost $50,000 at the box office.

Box 29 Oct 1949. *DV* 19 Oct 1949, p. 3. *FD* 24 Oct 1949, p. 7. *HR* 24 Jun 1949, p. 13. *HR* 19 Oct 1949, p. 3. *MPHPD* 29 Oct 1949, p. 66. *Var* 26 Oct 1949, p. 8.

RIDERS OF THE RIO (Latino)

Round-Up Pictures. *Dist* State Rights. 31 Dec **1931**. Sd (National Electric Recording System); b&w. Length undetermined.

Dir John Tansey. *Scr* R. E. Barringer. *Photog* Amos Stillman.

Cast: Lane Chandler (*Bob Lane*), Karla Cowan (*Nieta*), Benny Corbett ("*One Shot*"), Sheldon Lewis (*Tony*), Fred Parker (*Dad Lane*), Jack Kirk ("*Tim," Bob Lane's pal*), Sherry Tansey ("*Buck*"), Bud Duncan (*The peddler*), Mary Thompson (*Mrs. Lane*), Bob Card (*Travis*), H. B. Carpenter (*Sheriff*), Amleio Mio (*Captain Fernandez*), Lorena Carr (*Doris Hart*), Owen McLean (*The wrangler*), Betty Lou Gay.

Western. [*Not viewed*]. Beautiful Nieta is the main attraction in her father's Sonoma cantina. Planning to manage his father's ranch, Bob Lane arrives in town after attending school in the East. Travis, another rancher, is the Lanes's main competitor and is suspected of being a rustler. When Bob and Travis meet at the cantina, they quarrel over Nieta. Bob's family wants him to marry Doris Hart, a woman of his own class, and to give up the idea of running the ranch. Doris begs Nieta to send Bob back to her, and Nieta responds that it is Doris' job to take him back. Some time later, Travis poisons one of Bob's watering holes, and when Bob confronts him, Travis' men overpower him and frame him for the poisoning. Nieta warns Bob that the sheriff, who is in league with Travis, is on his way to arrest Bob, and he escapes over the Mexican border. There he finds Travis' daughter, who is suffering from a broken leg. Bob returns the little girl and Nieta fools Travis by pretending to shoot Bob. Nieta and Bob leave the Mexican government to deal with Travis and then embrace and ride away together. *Mexican Americans. Ranchers. Romantic rivalry. Rustlers. Accidents. Cantinas. Cattle. Children. Family relationships. Frame-ups. Mexico. Poison. Sheriffs.*

Note: According to a news item in *FD*, the film was re-released by Sack Amusement Enterprises in 1932. Modern sources list Robert and John Tansey as producers.

FD 18 Apr 1932, p. 1, 4.

THE RIDERS OF THE WHISTLING SKULL (Native Americans)

Republic Pictures Corp. *Dist* Republic Pictures Corp. 4 Jan **1937**; Prod: late Oct—mid-Nov 1936 [©Republic Pictures Corp.; 4 Jan 1937; LP6829]. Sd (RCA Victor "High Fidelity" Sound System); b&w. 6 reels, 5,009 ft. 55-56 min. Passed by the National Board of Review. PCA cert no. 2859.

Series: The Three Mesquiteers.

Prod Nat Levine. *Assoc prod* Sol C. Siegel. *Dir* Mack V. Wright. [*Asst dir* Louis Germonprez]. *Scr* Olive [sic] Drake and John Rathmell. *Orig story* Bernard McConville and Oliver Drake. *Photog* Jack Marta. *Film ed* Tony Martinelli. *Supv ed* Murray Seldeen. *Mus supv* Harry Grey. [*Sd* John Stransky]. *Sd eng* Harry Jones.

Source: Based on the novel *Riders of the Whistling Skull* by William Colt MacDonald (New York, 1934).

Cast: ROBERT LIVINGSTON (*Stony Brooke*), RAY CORRIGAN (*Tucson Smith*), MAX TERHUNE (*Lullaby Joslin*), Mary Russell [(*Betty Marsh*)], Roger Williams [(*Rutledge*)], Fern Emmett [(*Henrietta McCoy*)], C. Montague Shaw [(*Faxon*)], Yakima Canutt [(*Otah*)], John Ward [(*Brewster*)], George Godfrey [(*Professor Fronc*)], Earle Ross [(*Professor Cleary*)], Frank Ellis [(*Coggins*)], Chief Thunder Cloud [(*High priest*)], John Van Pelt [(*Professor Marsh*)].

Western, Mystery. [*Print viewed*]. Betty Marsh, along with her friend, Henrietta McCoy, and archaeologists Cleary, Fronc, Brewster and Coggins, attempts to hire a guide at Rutledge's trading post so that they can find Betty's father, who disappeared three months earlier while searching for the lost Indian city of Luckachakai. The Three Mesquiteers—Stony Brooke, Tucson Smith and Lullaby Joslin—arrive at the trading post with Professor Faxon, Marsh's companion, whom they found wandering in the desert. Faxon rambles incoherently about a whistling skull and the city of gold, and warns Betty that she must rescue her father before he is tortured by his captors. Faxon is stabbed before he can reveal more about the

mystery, and as the sheriff does not have sufficient evidence to hold them, Betty, her companions, the Mesquiteers and Rutledge and his Indian guide Otah set off in search of Marsh. They argue over who will keep Marsh's notebook, which contains a map to the whistling skull, and although only Betty can read the Indian hieroglyphics her father wrote in, Tucson suggests splitting the map up among all of them. Soon after they leave, Cleary is killed by a mysterious arrow inscribed with the same writing that was on the knife that killed Faxon. The Mesquiteers then discover that Cleary's piece of the map is missing. The discouraged group makes camp for the night, and when they set off in the morning, they find Fronc wandering in the desert after he has been branded by the members of an Indian cult, the Sons of Anatazia. Fronc's piece of the map is gone, and while Rutledge, Brewster and Coggins wish to turn back, Betty insists on going forward. After they begin again, the mysterious Indians spook some of the horses, who run wild. Tucson and Stony retrieve the horses, but Betty is kidnapped by the Indians in the confusion. The Mesquiteers follow the trail left by the kidnappers and soon rescue Betty, after which, the group presses onward. While following Otah and Rutledge, Stony and Tucson find water and then the whistling skull rock formation. The group takes refuge in the cave of the skull when the Indians, led by the half-breed Rutledge, attack them. They then find Marsh, who tells them that Rutledge has kept him prisoner for not revealing the location of the treasure of Luckachakai. The Mesquiteers leave the cave to get help, but Stony is captured and held hostage. Before Stony can be sacrificed, however, Tucson finds the sheriff, who has been following them with a posse in case they needed help, and they rescue Stony. Rutledge and his men are buried in an avalanche, and later, Tucson happily reads his detective magazine, while Henrietta admires Lullaby's new suit, and Stony romances Betty. *Archaeologists. Cowboys. Cults. Indians of North America. Murder. Rescues. Avalanches. Branding. Caves. Deserts. Fathers and daughters. Guides. Human sacrifice. Indians of North America–Mixed blood. Kidnapping. Maps. Sheriffs. Stabbings. Torture. Trading posts. Treasure.*

Note: According to a modern source, this film was an original story based partly on William Colt MacDonald's *Riders of the Whistling Skull*, in addition to his *The Singing Scorpion* (New York, 1934). Modern sources add the following additional cast members: Edward Piel (*Sheriff*), Jack Kirk (*Deputy*), Iron Eyes Cody (*Indian*), Tracy Layne (*Henchman*), Tom Steele, Wally West, Eddie Boland and Ken Cooper. The film was remade by Monogram and released in 1949 as a Charlie Chan picture entitled *The Feathered Serpent* (see above). Although MacDonald is not credited in reviews of the later film, Oliver Drake is credited with original screenplay. It was directed by William Beaudine and starred Roland Winters as Chan and Robert Livingston as the villain. For more information on the Three Mesquiteers series, please consult the Series Index and see entry for *The Three Mesquiteers* in *AFI Catalog of Feature Films, 1931-40*; F3.4618.

FD 3 Jun 1937, p. 8. *HR* 2 Nov 1936, p. 15. *HR* 9 Nov 1936, p. 7. *MPD* 5 Jun 1937, p. 3. *MPSI* Jan 1937, p. 30. *Var* 21 Apr 1937, p. 15.

RIDERS OF VENGEANCE *see* **THE RAIDERS**

RIDING HIGH (African Americans)
Paramount Pictures Inc. *Dist* Paramount Pictures Inc. **1943**; New York opening: 22 Dec 1943; Prod: 16 Jan—late Feb 1943 [©Paramount Pictures, Inc.; 10 Nov 1943; LP12430]. Sd (Western Electric Mirrophonic Recording); col (Technicolor). 10 reels, 7,964 ft. 88-89 min. Passed by the National Board of Review. PCA cert no. 9093.

[*Exec prod* B. G. DeSylva]. *Assoc prod* Fred Kohlmar. *Dir* George Marshall. [*Asst dir* Art Black]. *Scr* Walter DeLeon, Arthur Phillips and Art Arthur. [*Contr to trt* Joseph Schrank]. *Dir of photog* Karl Struss and Harry Hallenberger. *Process photog* Farciot Edouart. *Technicolor color dir* Natalie Kalmus. *Assoc* Morgan Padelford. *Art dir* Hans Dreier and Ernst Fegté. [*Scenic backdrop paintings of AZ* P. T. Blackburn]. *Ed* LeRoy Stone. *Set dec* Stephen Seymour. *Cost* Edith Head. *Mus dir* Victor Young. *Mus adv* Troy Sanders. *Vocal arr* Joseph J. Lilley. *Dances staged by* Danny Dare. *Sd rec* Gene Merritt, Joel Moss and [Loren Ryder]. *Makeup artist* Wally Westmore.

Song(s): "You're the Rainbow," "Whistling in the Light" and "Get Your Man," music by Ralph Rainger, lyrics by Leo Robin; "Injun Gal Heap Hep," music by Ralph Rainger, lyrics by Leo Robin and Joseph J. Lilley; "Willie the Wolf of the West," music and lyrics by Joseph J. Lilley and Leo Robin; "I'm the Secretary to the Sultan," music and lyrics by Leo Robin; "He Loved Me Till the All-Clear Came," music and lyrics by Harold Arlen and Johnny Mercer.

Source: Based on the play *Ready Money* by James Montgomery (New York, 19 Aug 1912).

Cast: DOROTHY LAMOUR [(*Ann Castle*)], DICK POWELL [(*Steve Baird*)], VICTOR MOORE [(*Mortimer J. Slocum*)], Gil Lamb [(*Bob "Foggy" Day*)], Cass Daley [(*Tess Connors*)], Bill Goodwin [(*Chuck Stuart*)], Rod Cameron [(*Sam Welch*)], Glen Langan [(*Jack Holbrook*)], Milt Britton and Band, [George Carleton (*Dad Castle*)], [Andrew Tombes (*P. D. Smith*)], [Douglas Fowley (*Brown*)], [Tim Ryan (*Jones*)], [Pierre Watkin (*Masters*)], [James Burke (*Pete Brown*)], [Roscoe Karns (*Shorty*)], [Patricia Mace (*Jean Holbrook*)], [Gwen Kenyon (*Ginger*)], [Lorraine Miller (*Blanche*)], [Stanley Andrews (*Reynolds*)], [Wade Boteler (*Mailman*)], [Fred Kelsey (*Honest John Kelsey*)], [Russell Simpson (*Frenchy McGuire*)], [Matt McHugh (*Murphy*)], [Tom Kennedy (*Wilson*)], [Stanley Price, James Flavin (*Train conductors*)], [Dwight Butcher, Lane Chandler, William Edwards (*Cowboys*)], [Bruce Cameron (*Head of Cameron Troupe*)], [Leonard St. Leo, Ray Spiker, Walter Pietila, Bonnadene Wolfe, Flash Gordon, Paula Unger, Ramon Schaller, Richard Gottlieb (*Members of Cameron Troupe*)], [Charles R. Moore (*Porter*)], [Hal K. Dawson (*Master of ceremonies*)], [Snub Pollard (*Waiter*)], [Charles Soldani (*Indian chief*)], [James Millican (*Photographer*)], [Napoleon Whiting (*Red Cap*)], [Marcella Phillips, Roberta Jonay, Marjorie Deanne (*Dancers*)], [John Hiestand (*Commentator*)].

Musical, **Romantic comedy**. [*Print viewed*]. When her burlesque show *Strip, Strip, Hooray!* closes, dancer Ann Castle returns home to her father's Grenada Silver Mine in the Arizona desert, and learns his new partner, Steve Baird, has not yet paid him the $1,000 for the partnership. Steve has been trying to interest his friends in becoming investors in the mine, but to no avail. Ann is hired as a featured performer at Tess Connors' Bubbling Well guest ranch, and angrily fends off Steve's advances because she believes he is a cheat. Counterfeiter Mortimer J. Slocum becomes interested in Steve's situation and, after befriending him, gives him $20,000 in counterfeit $1,000 bills, in an effort to become a partner in the mine. Before Steve realizes that the money is counterfeit, he flashes the bills in front of friends, who believe that the mine has a mother lode and give Steve the $1,000 he has been seeking. Steve tries to return the money to Slocum after he realizes it is fake, but circumstances intervene to prevent him from unloading it. Ann then expresses new interest in Steve now that he can pay Dad, and after she performs in the ranch's show that night, Steve romances her by the lake, unaware that Tess is also romancing Slocum. The next day, dim-witted sheriff Bob "Foggy" Day and his deputy make an earnest effort to capture Slocum spending the counterfeit bills, and insist on searching Slocum, his room and Steve. Despite some close calls, Steve and Slocum outwit Foggy by slipping the envelope of money into Ann's purse. Ann attempts to mail the envelope, believing it is a letter to her aunt, but it is returned for insufficient postage. At dinner, Foggy reveals Slocum and Steve's subterfuge, and Steve's friends demand their checks back, even after Dad appears and reports that he has hit a mother lode of copper. Slocum then bets the counterfeit $20,000 that Tess's chuckwagon can beat rancher Frenchy McGuire's wagon in the annual chuckwagon race. Following orders, Frenchy's hired hand Shorty switches the racing order sign on her wagon. The next day, Tess angrily demands that the sign be corrected, and Shorty blames the sabotage on Slocum. In the ensuing mêlée, Foggy's gun accidentally discharges, and the horses pulling Tess's wagon take off with Ann and Slocum aboard. Neither Ann nor Slocum know how to guide the horses, and much to Slocum's dismay, half of the wagon drops off as he sawed it the previous night, thinking that it was McGuire's wagon. Steve races on horseback to catch up with the wagon, and all the other wagons join the premature race. When Tess's wagon begins to lose with Steve at the reins, Slocum throws counterfeit bills behind them. The competing wagons slow to catch the money, and Tess's wagon comes in first, earning Steve the $1,000 prize. Now that he has proof of his counterfeiting, Foggy arrests Slocum, and Steve refuses to accept McGuire's $20,000 check because Slocum cheated. McGuire nevertheless insists on giving Steve the money as an investment in the mine. As he is being hauled away, Slocum advises Tess to marry Foggy, and Steve then revives a fainted Ann in a manner characteristic of their loving relationship: with a splash of cold water. *Counterfeiters and counterfeiting. Dude ranches. Miners. Musical revues. Romance. Arizona. Burlesque. Fathers and daughters. Investors. Partnership. Racing. Wagers. Wagons.*

Note: The working titles of this film were *Calgary Stampede*, *Canadian Capers* and *Ready Money*. *HR* news items reveal the following information about the production: When titled *Calgary Stampede* and *Canadian Capers*, the film was to have a Canadian background. In Aug 1942, second unit director Hal Walker was preparing to take a crew to Calgary to shoot the chuckwagon sequence and other exteriors. However, due to transportation difficulties, the trip was canceled and the story's locale was changed to Arizona. It is not known if Walker worked on the completed film. Paramount planned to use producer Harry Sherman as a technical adviser for the chuckwagon sequences, but his participation in the final film has not been confirmed. Some scenes were filmed on location in Chatsworth, CA.

According to information in the MPAA/PCA Files at the AMPAS Library, the song "He Loved Me Till the All-Clear Came," by Harold Arlen and Johnny Mercer, was originally written for Cass Daley to perform in Paramount's 1943 film *Star Spangled Rhythm*. Although the song was recorded in 1943, it was not included in that film. In addition, the file reveals that the PCA insisted that certain "sex suggestive" lyrics in the songs "You're the Rainbow," "Get Your Man" and "I'm the Secretary to the Sultan" be re-written. This film was nominated for an Academy Award in the category of Sound Recording (Loren Ryder). In 1914, Paramount released *Ready Money*, which was also based on James Montgomery's play, directed by Oscar C. Apfel and starred Edward Abeles and Monroe Salisbury (see *AFI Catalog of Feature Films, 1911-20*, F1.3644). Fred MacMurray starred with Rhonda Fleming in a 12 May 1952 *Lux Radio Theatre* broadcast of the story.

Box 13 Nov 1943. *DV* 22 Jan 1943. *DV* 5 Nov 1943, p. 4. *FD* 10 Nov 1943, p. 43. *HR* 31 Jul 1942, p. 2. *HR* 11 Aug 1942, p. 2. *HR* 10 Nov 1942, p. 7. *HR* 19 Nov 1942, p. 1. *HR* 15 Jan 1943, p. 2. *HR* 4 Feb 1943, p. 7. *HR* 12 Feb 1943, p. 4. *HR* 26 Feb 1943, p. 8, 10. *HR* 5 Nov 1943, p. 8. *HR* 27 Dec 1943, p. 7. *MPH* 6 Nov 1943. *MPHPD* 17 Jul 1943, p. 1431. *MPHPD* 6 Nov 1943, p. 1613. *NYHT* 19 Dec 1942. *NYT* 12 Dec 1943. *NYT* 23 Dec 1943, p. 26. *Paramount News* 16 Dec 1943. *Var* 10 Nov 1943, p. 34.

THE RIDING KID *see* **THE RAIDERS**

THE RIDING RENEGADE (Native Americans)
FBO Pictures. 19 Feb **1928** [©F.B.O. Productions, Inc.; 4 Feb 1928; LP24948]. Si; b&w. 5 reels, 4,729 ft.
Dir Wallace W. Fox. *Asst dir* Frederick Fleck. *Story and cont* Frank Howard Clark. *Titles* Randolph Bartlett. *Photog* Charles Boyle. *Film ed* Della M. King.
Cast: Bob Steele (*Bob Taylor*), Dorothy Kitchen (*Janet Reynolds*), Lafe McKee (*Sheriff Jim Taylor*), Bob Fleming (*Ed Stacey*), Ethan Laidlaw (*Pete Hobart*), Nick Thompson (*White Cloud, Indian Chief*), Pedro Riga (*Little Wolf*).
Western. Bob Taylor, son of a sheriff, becomes a wanderer and is adopted by an Indian tribe when he saves the life of Little Wolf, son of Chief White Cloud. He and Little Wolf prevent Pete Hobart and Ed Stacey from robbing the stagecoach, by riding away with the strongbox and passenger Janet Reynolds; Bob's father, however, arrests him for robbery, and Pete Hobart escapes with the box after wounding Little Wolf. Eventually Sheriff Taylor perceives that his son has behaved properly, and he forgives him before pursuing Stacey and Hobart. The two bandits overpower Sheriff Taylor, but Bob and the Indians rescue him. *Bandits. Family relationships. Indians of North America. Sheriffs. Stagecoach robberies. Wanderers.*

RIDING SPEED (Chinese Americans)
Dist State Rights; Superior Talking Pictures, Inc. **1934.** Sd; b&w. 5 reels.
Cast: Buffalo Bill, Jr. (*Steve Funney*).
Western. [*Not viewed*]. Steve Funney of the border patrol is sent to investigate a band of outlaws who are smuggling Chinese across the Mexican border. While riding in the border area, Steve comes to the aid of a spunky young woman after her car runs off the road. Unaware of his identity, the woman teases Steve, and while he helps her with her car, he dryly dubs her "Miss Funny." Later, Steve rides to the ranch of John Vale and, after showing him a letter from his boss, asks to be hired as a hand so that he can investigate the smugglers in secret. Vale agrees to the plan and, without mentioning Steve's last name, introduces him to his daughter Gypsy, who turns out to be "Miss Funny." As soon as Vale informs his foreman, Bill Dirky, of Steve's hiring, Dirky, who is the head of the smuggling gang, becomes suspicious. When Steve attempts to follow other members of the gang, who are on their way to the border with a group of Chinese, they shoot at him and presume him dead. Vale, meanwhile, discovers Dirky's part in the gang and confronts him. Dirky knocks Vale over the head and leaves him for dead, then rides off to rejoin his gang. At the same time, Gypsy falls into a hole while riding and is found by Steve. Steve attempts to rescue Gypsy, but ends up falling into the hole himself. While Steve and Gypsy exchange loving quips in the hole, Dirky orders his men to rush to the border with the Chinese, while he disposes of Vale's body by burning down his ranch house. On his way

back to the ranch, however, Dirky stops and rescues Gypsy, whom he desires, but leaves Steve in the hole. Dirky and Gypsy are met by one of Vale's loyal hands, who has been sent by a revived Vale to warn Steve of Dirky's duplicity. Although beaten up by Dirky, the hand manages to rescue Steve, who then rounds up the gang and saves Gypsy and her father. Having proven himself a true hero, Steve reveals his identity to Gypsy and proposes that she change her name from "Miss Funny" to "Mrs. Funney." *Border patrols. Mexican-American border region. Ranchers. Romance. Smuggling. Undercover operations. Automobile accidents. Chinese. Fights. Proposals (Marital). Ranch foremen. Rescues.*

Note: No contemporary reviews or news items were found for this film. The above plot summary was taken from a dialogue continuity submitted to the New York State Censor Board in Apr 1934. According to the records of the Board, the picture was approved "with eliminations" on 11 Apr 1934 and was listed as 4,820 feet at that time. Modern sources credit Jay Wilsey (Buffalo Bill, Jr.) as director, Ella May Cook as story writer, and Delores Booth as screenwriter on the production. In addition, modern sources add the following actors to the cast: Joile Benet (*Gypsy Vale*), Bud Osborne (*Bill Dirky*), Lafe McKee (*John Vale*), Clyde McClary (*Joe*), Allen Holbrook (*Roberts*), Ernest Scott and Denver Dixon. Modern sources refer to the film as a "Victor Adamson (Denver Dixon)" production

RIDING THE CALIFORNIA TRAIL (Latino)
Monogram Pictures Corp. *Dist* Monogram Pictures Corp. 11 Jan **1947**; *Prod:* late Sep—early Oct 1946 [©Monogram Pictures Corp.; 27 Jan 1947; LP813]. Sd; b&w. 59 min. PCA cert no. 12102.
Series: The Cisco Kid.
Prod Scott R. Dunlap. *Dir* William Nigh. *Asst dir* Eddie Davis. *Orig story and scr* Clarence Young. *Photog* Harry Neumann. *Spec eff* Augie Lohman. *Film ed* Fred Maguire. *Set dresser* Vin Taylor. *Sd tech* Tom Lambert. *Rec* John Kean. *Prod mgr* William Calihan.
Song(s): "Mi amor ya volvia," words and music by Gladys Flores and Edward Kay.
Source: Based on the character created by O. Henry.
Cast: Gilbert Roland (*The Cisco Kid* [*also known as Don Luis Salazar*]), Martin Garralaga (*Don José Ramirez*), Frank Yaconelli (*Baby*), Teala Loring (*Raquel*), Inez Cooper (*Dolores* [*Ramirez*]), Ted Hecht (*Raoul*), Marcelle Grandville (*Duenna*), [Eve Whitney (*Maria*)], [Frank Marlo (*Police captain*)], [Alex Montoya (*Police lieutenant*)], [Gerald Echeverria (*Footman*)], [Rosa Turich (*Señorita*)], [Julia Kent (*Flower woman*)].
Western. [*Print viewed*]. The Cisco Kid, an elusive gentleman bandit who is wanted by the California police, arrives in the town of San Lorenzo with his partner, Baby, and meets a Spanish dancer named Raquel in a saloon. Later, in her dressing room, Cisco hides while Raquel gets rid of her boyfriend, Raoul. Raquel explains to Cisco that Raoul is about to marry beautiful heiress Dolores Ramirez, who is called the "Angel of San Lorenzo" because of her charity work, and has promised to share Dolores' inheritance with Raquel after the wedding. When Raoul catches Cisco and Raquel embracing, he starts a brawl, and Cisco is chased out of town. The next day, Cisco and Baby hijack a carriage and pay a visit to the Ramirez hacienda. Cisco introduces himself to Dolores' uncle, Don José, as famous California adventurer Don Luis Salazar. He then learns that Dolores plans to give all of her inheritance to the poor. When Cisco asks her if she loves Raoul, she admits only that she dearly loved her departed father, who arranged the marriage. Raoul soon arrives at the hacienda and, accusing Cisco of being an impostor, engages him in a sword fight, which Cisco wins. As the police approach, Dolores' duenna tells Cisco that she knows he is not who he says he is, and begs for his help in stopping the marriage, which her father arranged out of greed. In town, after Cisco tricks Raquel into confessing that Raoul and Don José had a written agreement regarding the Ramirez inheritance, Cisco holds up Raoul and finds a note for $500,000 pesos from Don José to Raoul. Cisco returns to the Ramirez hacienda with the note, finds a forged will in Don José's strongbox, and confronts Don José in front of Dolores. When Raoul arrives and holds up Cisco, Baby shoots the gun out of Raoul's hand. Cisco then starts a sword fight with Raoul, which is interrupted by the approach of the police. Dolores hides Cisco and kisses him before he escapes and rides out of town. *Bandits. California. Duplicity. Inheritance. Marriage–Arranged. Spanish Americans. Vigilantes. Chaperons. Dance hall girls. Disguise. Duplicity. Ex-convicts. Forgers and forgery. Greed. Haciendas. Impersonation and imposture. Philanthropists. Romantic rivalry. Sword fights. Uncles. Wills.*
Note: The film's working title was *Cisco and the Angel*. The title card on the

viewed print reads: "The Cisco Kid in *Riding the California Trail.*" Some of the above credits were missing from the viewed print and were taken from a studio production sheet. For more information on "The Cisco Kid" series, consult the Series Index and see the entry above for *The Cisco Kid.*

Box 11 Jan 1947. *DV* 2 May 1947. *HR* 20 Sep 1946, p. 18. *HR* 4 Oct 1946, p. 18. *HR* 7 Nov 1946, p. 15. *HR* 2 May 1947, p. 4.

RIDING WEST (Native Americans)

Columbia Pictures Corp. *Dist* Columbia Pictures Corp. 18 May 1944; Prod: 30 Nov–8 Dec 1942 [©Columbia Pictures Corp.; 18 May 1944; LP12784]. Sd; b&w. 5,213 ft. 60-61 min. PCA cert no. 9059.

Prod Jack Fier. *Exec prod* Irving Briskin. *Dir* William Berke. *Asst dir* William O'Connor. *Story and scr* Luci Ward. *Dir of photog* Benjamin Kline. *Art dir* Lionel Bank. *Assoc* Arthur Royce. *Film ed* Jerome Thoms. *Int dec* Robert Priestley. *Sd eng* Tom Lambert.

Cast: Charles Starrett (*Steve Jordan*), Arthur Hunnicutt (*Professor Arkansas Higgins*), Shirley Patterson (*Alice Morton*), Ernest Tubb and His Singing Cowboys (*Ernie Tubbs*), Steve Clark (*Alexander Morton*), Wheeler Oakman (*Capt. Amos Karnes*), J. P. "Blackie" Whiteford (*Sgt. Dobbs*), Clancy Cooper (*Blackburn/Johnson*), Bill Wilkerson (*Red Eagle*), Johnny Bond (*Red*), Cal Shrum (*Curly*), Wes Tuttle (*Mose*), Art Wenzel (*Mike*), Stanley Brown (*Tommy*), Lloyd Bridges (*Larry*), Tom London (*Gubbins*), Ted Mapes (*Keller*), [Frosty Royce, George Fiske (*Pony boys*)].

Western, with songs. [*Not viewed*]. When he is chased out of Texas for killing the leader of a band of desperadoes, Steve Jordan seeks refuge in a shack owned by his old friend and teacher Professor Arkansas Higgins. After Steve explains that he was unjustly charged with murder for shooting the man in self-defense, the professor helps him elude his pursuers and escape. Along the trail Steve spies a riderless horse. When he approaches the animal, however, he notices a man with a broken leg lying alongside the road. Steve sets the broken leg, and in gratitude, the man, Alexander Morton, gives Steve his horse. Continuing down the trail, Steve meets his old friend Ernie Tubbs, who persuades him to accompany him to St. Joe, where he plans to seek employment with the Pony Express. In St. Joe, Steve discovers that Morton is the owner of the Express. Morton hires Steve and his friend, but when Capt. Amos Karnes, a strict military disciplinarian, is put in charge of the operation, the men rebel. Alice, Morton's daughter, convinces the men not to quit, however, and they are assigned to a deserted Pony Express outpost. After renegade Indians capture their supply wagon and kill Blackburn, the man assigned to guard it, Johnson, the white leader of the renegades, assumes Blackburn's identity. Upon returning to the post, Blackburn approaches Morton and tells him that a group of gamblers is willing to pay him $10,000 if the Express fails. When Morton refuses his offer, Blackburn signals the Indians to kill him. Concerned about Morton's prolonged absence, Steve goes to look for him and discovers his body. When he questions Blackburn about Morton's death, Blackburn repeats his offer to Steve, and Steve accuses him of murder and orders his arrest. Blackburn escapes, however, and launches a series of Indian raids on Express outposts. Dedicating himself to saving the Express, Steve does the work of three riders, but when he returns to the outpost, Karnes arrests him for the Texas murder. When the Indians kidnap Karnes and hold him for ransom, Steve convinces the captain's aide that Blackburn is involved in a plot to defeat the Pony Express and persuades the aide to release him. Organizing a raid on the Indian village, Steve and his men free Karnes, and the Indians, feeling betrayed, kill Blackburn. Upon returning to the outpost, Steve is exonerated of all murder charges when it is discovered that the man he allegedly killed is alive and serving a jail term for embezzlement. In recognition of Steve's efforts to help build the Pony Express, Karnes rewards Steve with a lifetime job. *False accusations. Impersonation and imposture. Murder. Pony Express. Bounty hunters. Bribery. Fathers and daughters. Gamblers. Indians of North America. Professors.*

Note: Although reviews note that several songs were performed in this film, neither their titles nor composers have been identified.

Box 28 Oct 1944. *DV* 26 May 1944, p. 4. *FD* 25 Sep 1944, p. 10. *HR* 26 May 1944, p. 4. *MPHPD* 8 Apr 1944, p. 1835. *MPHPD* 23 Sep 1944, p. 2111. *Var* 20 Sep 1944, p. 10.

RIGHT CROSS (Latino, Irish Americans)

Metro-Goldwyn-Mayer Corp.; controlled by Loew's Inc. *Dist* Loew's Inc. 6 Oct 1950; Prod: 25 Jan–early Mar 1950 [©Loew's Inc.; 13 Jul 1950; LP270]. Sd (Western Electric Sound System); b&w. 8,064 ft. 89-90 min. Passed by the National Board of Review. PCA cert no. 14481.

Prod Armand Deutsch. *Dir* John Sturges. [*Asst dir* Dolph Zimmer]. *Wrt* Charles Schnee. *Dir of photog* Norbert Brodine. [*Cam op* Curtis Fetters]. [*Stills* Robert Quirk]. *Art dir* Cedric Gibbons and Gabriel Scognamillo. *Set dec* Edwin B. Willis. *Film ed* James E. Newcom. *Assoc* Alfred E. Spencer. *Women's cost* Helen Rose. *Mus* David Raksin. *Rec supv* Douglas Shearer. [*Sd* Robert Lee]. *Hair styles des by* Sydney Guilaroff. [*Hair stylist* Ethel Neejus]. *Makeup created by* Jack Dawn. [*Makeup* Kiva Hoffman]. *Tech adv* John Indrisano. [*Prod mgr* Al Shenberg]. [*Scr supv* John Banse]. [*Grip* Phil Emery]. [*Gaffer* Bob Worl].

Song(s): "Allá En El Rancho Grande," music and lyrics traditional.

Cast: JUNE ALLYSON (*Pat O'Malley*), DICK POWELL (*Rick Gavery*), RICARDO MONTALBAN (*Johnny Monterez*), Lionel Barrymore (*Sean O'Malley*), Teresa Celli (*Marina Monterez*), Barry Kelley (*Allan Goff*), Tom Powers (*Tom Balford*), Mimi Aguglia (*Mom Monterez*), Marianne Stewart (*Audrey*), John Gallaudet (*Phil Tripp*), [Wally Maher, Larry Keating, Ken Tobey (*Third reporter*), Bert Davidson (*Fourth reporter*), [David Fresco (*Gump*)], [Eddie Simms (*Marty Lynn*)], [Smoki Whitfield (*Nassau*)], [John Maxwell (*Walker*)], [Harry Shannon (*Haggerty*)], [Frank Ferguson (*Dr. George Esmond*)], [Courtland Shepard (*Al Heldon*)], [David Wolfe (*Totem*)], King Donovan, John Mitchum, George Sherwood (*Reporters*)], [Joe La Cava, Lynton Brent, John Crawford, Sig Froelich (*Photographers*)], [Tom Garland (*Heldon's sparring partner*)], [Dewey Robinson (*Hanger-on*)], [Jim Hayward (*Sergeant*)], [Jack Daley (*Turnkey*)], [June Whitley, Harry Stanton (*Nurses*)], [Robert Stephenson, Harry Cody, Jack Barnett, Mack Chandler (*Patrons*)], [William Cabanne (*Dynamite Nelson*)], [James O'Gatty (*Gateman*)], [Teddy Pavelec (*Sparring partner*)], [James Holbrook (*Attendant*)], [Margaret Bert (*Maid*)], [John Hamilton (*Horse owner*)], [Jim Pierce (*Moe*)], [Bert Moorhouse (*Customer at steam bath*)], [Robert Board (*Bob*)], [Juan Duval (*Waiter*)], [Ed Dearing (*Ring announcer*)], [Al Hill (*Heldon handler*)], [Russ Clark (*Referee*)], [Tom Hanlon (*Sports announcer*)], [Bob E. Perry (*Timekeeper*)], [Marilyn Monroe (*Dusky La Dieu*)].

Boxing, Drama. [*Print viewed*]. Sean O'Malley, a wheelchair-bound fight promoter who was once known as the best in his business, has lost his professional stature and is now suffering from poor health. Sean's daughter Pat has taken over many of her father's responsibilities, and is romantically involved with Sean's best fighter, Johnny Monterez. Though Sean had hoped that Johnny would help to revive his flagging career, he dislikes the fact that Johnny is ashamed of his Mexican heritage. When Sean tells Pat that promoter Allan Goff is trying to steal Johnny from him, Pat decides to visit Johnny at his training camp. Pat arrives in time to watch Johnny fight a practice match, but the match ends abruptly when fighter Marty Lynn injures Johnny's hand. While Johnny's hand is being examined at the hospital, Pat looks for her friend, Rick Gavery, a hard-drinking sports reporter who has been following Johnny's career. Pat eventually finds Rick in jail, where she has found him on many previous occasions. When Johnny's physician, Dr. George Esmond, tells him that his hand is now vulnerable to permanent injury, Johnny asks the doctor to keep his condition a secret. After telling Pat and some reporters that his hand is merely bruised, Johnny returns to his training camp. A short time later, Johnny receives word that his trouble-prone cousin, Luis, is in jail again and needs two hundred dollars for bail. The news reminds Johnny that Luis, who is also a Mexican immigrant, has not had the same opportunities that he has had to lift himself out of poverty. Believing that his hand injury may end his boxing career at any moment, Johnny decides to sign a lucrative contract with Goff, who has promised to provide him with a guaranteed income from promotional sales after his retirement. Johnny takes Rick to visit his mother, but soon after they arrive, Johnny tells his sister Marina that she must stop dating her boyfriend, Bob, because he is a "gringo." Johnny also tells Marina that Bob is interested in her only because she is the sister of a famous fighter. When Rick accuses Johnny of harboring a prejudice against whites, Johnny sends him away with an insult. Later, Pat, expecting a marriage proposal from Johnny, is disappointed when Johnny tells her that he has decided to sign with Goff. Sean dies a short time later, and Pat accuses Johnny of killing her father with his act of betrayal. Realizing that he has nearly lost Pat's love and Rick's friendship as a result of his actions, Johnny decides to get out of boxing forever by purposely losing the upcoming title match against Al Heldon. Though he loses the match, Johnny does not

cause permanent injury to his hand until he punches Rick for being honest with him. With help from Rick, Pat and Johnny reconcile and look forward to a happy future together. *Boxers. Fathers and daughters. Mexican Americans. Promoters. Romance. Sports reporters. Assimilation (Sociology). Bigotry. Boxing trainers. Brothers and Sisters. Business rivals. Contracts. Drunkenness. Handicapped. Immigrants. Irish Americans. Lawyers. Miscegenation. Models. Physicians. Playboys. Retirement. Secrets.*

Note: A Mar 1949 *HR* news item indicates that actress Gloria De Haven was originally cast in the role played by June Allyson. A Nov 1949 *DV* news item adds that Ava Gardner was to play the feminine lead. Although a Feb 1950 *DV* news item lists Polly Bailey in the cast, her participation in the released film has not been confirmed. Marilyn Monroe appears in the film briefly as a model named "Dusky La Dieu."

AmCin May 1950, p. 161, 177. *Box* 26 Aug 1950. *DV* 8 Nov 1949, p. 1. *DV* 27 Jan 1950, p. 11. *DV* 1 Feb 1950, p. 11. *DV* 16 Aug 1950, p. 3. *FD* 22 Aug 1950, p. 5. *HR* 10 Mar 1949, p. 2. *HR* 16 Aug 1950, p. 3. *MPHPD* 19 Aug 1950, pp. 441-42. *NYT* 16 Nov 1950, p. 39. *Var* 16 Aug 1950, p. 11.

RIGHT GUY *see* **GOOD LUCK, MR. YATES**

THE RIGHT TO HAPPINESS (Jewish Americans)

Universal Film Mfg. Co.; Jewel Productions, Inc. *Dist* Universal Film Mfg. Co. 30 Aug 1919 [©Universal Film Mfg. Co.; 2 Sep 1919; LP14145]. Si; b&w. 8 reels.

Dir Allen Holubar. *Asst dir* Reeves Eason. *Story and scen* Allen Holubar. *Scen* Olga Linek Scholl. *Cam* Harry Harris, Al Lathem and Norman Dawn.

Cast: Dorothy Phillips (*Sonia/Vivian*), William Stowell (*Tom Hardy*), Robert Anderson (*Paul*), Henry Barrows (*Hardcastle*), Winter Hall (*Forrester*), Margaret Mann (*Mother Hardy*), Stanhope Wheatcroft (*Monte*), Alma Bennett (*Lilly*), Hector Sarno (*Sergius*), Maxine Elliott Hicks.

Drama. In 1898, wealthy American businessman Andrew Hardcastle lives in Russia with his twin daughters, Vivian and Dorothea. When the drunken Cossacks stage a pogrom against Jews and prominent persons, Hardcastle escapes to America with Vivian, believing Dorothea to be dead. Dorothea actually is adopted by a poor Jewish family, renamed Sonia, and at the age of nineteen, sent to America with her adopted brother Paul and also Sergius, to gain support for the revolutionary cause. Sonia and her comrades find Hardcastle's factory, with its blatant oppression of the workers, a ripe center for converts. Vivian, meanwhile, has grown up in wealth and luxury, and has fallen in love with her father's honest foreman, Tom Hardy. Sonia leads the enraged workers against Hardcastle from his factory to his mansion. At the steps of his home, however, Sonia denounces mob violence and sacrifices her own life for the life of Vivian, as she learns that she is really Vivian's sister. *Americans in foreign countries. Jews. Labor violence. Long-lost relatives. Revolutionaries. Russia. Self-sacrifice. Twins. Adoption. Cossacks. Factories. Fathers and daughters. Foremen. Mansions. Mobs. Pogroms.*

Note: This film had its New York premiere on 31 Aug 1919. The Ohio censors recalled the film twice when it played in Cleveland and demanded that objectionable subtitles be removed from the print.

ETR 13 Sep 1919, p. 1285. *MPN* 30 Aug 1919, p. 1869. *MPW* 5 Jul 1919, p. 116. *MPW* 23 Aug 1919, pp. 1175-76. *NYT* 1 Sep 1919, p. 5. *Var* 5 Sep 1919, p. 61. *Wid's* 24 Aug 1919, p. 23.

RILEY THE COP (Irish Americans)

Fox Film Corp. *Dist* Fox Film Corp. 25 Nov 1928 [©Fox Film Corp.; 19 Dec 1928; LP25842]. Sd eff and mus score (Movietone); b&w. 6 reels, 6,132 ft. [Also si; 5,993 ft.].

Pres William Fox. *Dir* John Ford. *Asst dir* Phil Ford. *Story and cont* Fred Stanley and James Gruen. *Photog* Charles Clarke. *Film ed* Alex Troffey.

Cast: Farrell MacDonald (*James Riley*), Louise Fazenda (*Lena Krausmeyer*), Nancy Drexel (*Mary Coronelli*), David Rollins (*Joe Smith*), Harry Schultz (*Hans Krausmeyer*), Mildred Boyd (*Caroline*), Ferdinand Schumann-Heink (*Julius Kuchendorf*), Del Henderson (*Judge Coronelli*), Mike Donlin (*Crook*), Russell Powell (*Mr. Kuchendorf*), Tom Wilson (*Sergeant*), Billy Bevan (*Paris cabman*), Otto Fries (*Munich cabman*).

Comedy-drama. Joe Smith, an ordinary lad who works at the town bakery, becomes engaged to wealthy Mary Coronelli, and her snobbish aunt takes her to Europe to break up the affair. Using his own hard-earned savings, Joe goes after her, and is unjustly accused of embezzlement when the bakery funds are discovered missing. Riley the cop, a lifelong flatfoot well-liked by all, goes in pursuit of

Joe; while in Europe, Riley falls in love with a German flapper in a beer garden, only to discover that she is the sister of Krausmeyer, the adjoining beat cop and Riley's nemesis. Riley brings Joe back to the United States, and he is proven innocent. All ends well. *Aunts. Bakers and bakeries. Embezzlement. Flappers. German Americans. Germans. Germany. Injustice. Irish Americans. Munich (Germany). Paris (France). Police. Snobs and snobbishness.*

FD 9 Dec 1928. *NYT* 4 Dec 1928, p. 29. *Var* 5 Dec 1928, p. 19.

THE RING (Latino)

King Bros. Productions, Inc. *Dist* United Artists Corp. 26 Sep **1952**; Prod: began mid-Jan 1952 at Goldwyn Studios [©King Bros. Productions, Inc.; 26 Sep 1952; LP1960]. Sd (Western Electric Recording); b&w. 9 reels, 6,328 or 7,115 ft. 70 or 78-79 min. PCA cert no. 15849.

Prod Maurice King and Frank King. *Dir* Kurt Neumann. *Dial dir* Clarence Marks. *Scr* Irving Shulman. *Dir of photog* Russell Harlan. *Art dir* Theobold Holsopple. *Supv ed* Merrill White. *Film ed* Bruce B. Pierce. *Set dec* Ray Boltz. *Mus comp and dir* Herschel Burke Gilbert. *Sd eng* John R. Carter. *Re-rec ed* George Emick. *Makeup artist* Don Cash. *Asst to the prod* Ben Kadish. *Exec talent dir* Fred H. Messenger. *Set cont by* Jack Herzberg. *Prop master* John Orlando. *Chief set elec* William Neff. *Tech adv* Frankie Van.

Song(s): "A Cheep, A Cheep," music by Herschel Burke Gilbert, lyrics by Lenny Adelson.

Source: Based on the novel *The Square Trap* by Irving Shulman (Boston, 1953).

Cast: Gerald Mohr [(*Pete Genusia*)], Rita Moreno [(*Lucy Gomez*)], Lalo Rios [(*Tomas Cantanios, also known as Tommy Kansas*)], Robert Arthur [(*Billy Smith*)], Robert Osterloh [(*Freddy Jack*)], Martin Garralaga [(*Vidal Cantanios*)], Art Aragon [(*Himself*)], Jack Elam [(*Harry Jackson*)], Peter Brocco [(*Barney Williams*)], Robert Shayne [(*Police officer*)], Julia Montoya [(*Rosa*)], Lillian Molieri [(*Helen Cantanios*)], Pepe Hern [(*Rick*)], Victor Millan [(*Pablo*)], Tony Martinez [(*Go-Go*)], Ernie Chavez [(*Joe*)], Edward Sieg [(*Benny*)], and introducing Robert Altuna (*Pepe [Cantanios]*), [Frankie Van (*Himself, referee*)].

Boxing, Youth, Social, Drama. [*Print viewed*]. In Los Angeles, on Olvera Street, where the pueblo that grew into the city was originally established by Mexican families, "Anglo" tourists buy traditional Mexican articles and make disparaging remarks about "the lazy Mexican." Vidal Cantanios, who has just been laid off from his job, refuses a job offer of pretending to sleep for the tourists because the job is undignified. At home, Vidal, who dreams of owning his own stand on Olvera Street, argues with his son Tomas, who then visits his club, where two police officers harass him and his friends by calling them "pachucos." Later that evening, Tommy tries to enter a skating rink with his girl friend, Lucy Gomez, but they are refused entrance and told that "Mexicana" night is the next night. Embittered, Tommy takes Lucy to a bar, where two "Anglos" whistle at her and insult her. After putting Lucy on a bus to go home, Tommy fights the two men, then runs when he hears a police whistle. Pete Genusia, a boxing manager, sees the incident and picks Tommy up in his car. Pete, a more assimilated Mexican American than Tommy, urges the boy to become a prizefighter, telling him that if he is successful, he will make a lot of money and people will look up to him. Impressed with Pete's easy manner with women, and their attention toward him, Tommy agrees to try. Using the name "Tommy Kansas," he wins his first fight, a preliminary match, but in so doing, goes against the instructions of Pete and his trainer, Freddie Jack, who advise him not to slug it out with his opponent. When Tommy gives the money he has earned to his family, Vidal berates him, calling fighters brutes who have no dignity. Tommy argues that he is trying to make enough money to move the family into a better area of town and to put his father in a business on Olvera Street, Vidal is moved, but he refuses to allow his son to fight and orders him to leave the house. Tommy's mother, however, tells her husband that Tommy can stay as long as he wants. Lucy also is upset when Tommy tells her about fighting because she feels it is dangerous. His friends at the club, however, are impressed and root for him during his next bouts. After his eighth bout, Tommy, who still does not heed the instructions of Pete and Freddie, refuses to fight anymore preliminaries, and Pete reluctantly matches him in a semi-final against a more experienced fighter, Chocolate Ganz, who beats him badly. Tommy, however, believes the decision is close. His fights continue badly, and after he loses in

Pomona on a technical knockout, he realizes it is time to quit. That night, he joins his friends on a drive to the beach and insists, despite their protests, that they stop along the way at a café in Beverly Hills. The group is stared at by the clientele and given the "water treatment" by a hostile waitress, who purposely spills glasses of water on their table. After the manager puts out a sign stating that they reserve the right to refuse service to anyone, a police officer recognizes Tommy and orders the waitress to serve them. The boys realize that they were served because Tommy is "somebody," and Tommy decides to continue fighting. He vows to Pete and Freddie to obey their instructions and to train like he never trained before. He is scheduled for a semi-final in San Diego, but when a fighter set for the main event withdraws because of illness, Harry Jackson, the arena promoter, tries to get Tommy to fight in his place. Pete, aware that Tommy is not ready, refuses although Tommy wants to fight. When the promoter reveals that the "ill" fighter was seen earlier that day with his manager, Barney Williams, in a bar, he threatens to call off the fight and ruin the fighter and Williams. Pete then agrees to let Tommy fight if the opponent, Art Aragon, doesn't hurt him and demands $450 from Williams. Tommy is aghast until Pete gives him the money for his father's stand. Although Aragon, also a Mexican American, agrees to let Tommy look flashy for the first four rounds and then let him lose gracefully, Tommy refuses to throw the fight. Although he battles furiously in the first round, Aragon knocks him unconscious with ease in the second. At home, when Tommy finds his young adoring brother Pepe shadow boxing with his gloves, he burns the gloves and the boxing robe that Pete gave him. On Olvera Street, Lucy convinces Tommy that he should go on fighting for things he believe are right. When he sees his father, now happily selling items on the street, Tommy agrees that maybe there are other things he could do. *Bigotry. Boxers. Fathers and sons. Los Angeles (CA)–Olvera Street. Mexican Americans. Racism. Youth. Assimilation (Sociology). Bars. Beverly Hills (CA). Boxing managers. Boxing trainers. Brothers. Fixed fights. Parties. Police. Pomona (CA). Restaurants. San Diego (CA). Waitresses.*

Note: The working title of this film was *Pachuco,* a usually derisive term applied to Mexican-American young men living in East Los Angeles, who often wore "flashy" clothes and were members of local gangs. According to Aug 1949 news items in *LAT,* it was originally to have been made by Ida Lupino and her husband Collier Young's company, Filmakers, Inc. and was to star Leo Penn. According to information in the MPAA/PCA Collection at the AMPAS Library, the screenplay that King Bros. Production submitted to the PCA in Nov 1951 was entitled "The Ring Is a Trap." After reading the script, PCA officials suggested various changes in the dialogue, commenting, "We feel it would not be good to infer that the police discriminate against these boys because of their nationality."

Reviews were mixed concerning the film's subject matter and manner of treatment. *DV* stated, "the film has a worthy aim but an indecisive presentation that lessens its significance....The writing is inconclusive and often illogical in dealing with a subject that needs more intelligent handling if it is to be used as screen material." *HR* panned the film, calling it "a depressing, rather pointless harangue on American discrimination against its Mexican minority group" and speculating the film would only be of interest to "East Los Angeles, the Mexican-American population and those who love films depicting minorities as abused in America." They criticized the film as presenting "such a bleak outlook for the Mexican-American that it emerges only as the type that does this country definite disservice abroad" and as intending "to show that if a Mexican can't make good in the ring, or in some other exhibitional profession, there isn't much hope for him in this 'land of bigotry.'" According to *HR,* boxer Art Aragon, who played himself in the film, had a large following in Los Angeles.

Box 30 Aug 1952. *DV* 5 Dec 1951. *DV* 20 Aug 1952, pp. 3-4. *Exb* 27 Aug 1952, p. 3355. *FD* 28 Aug 1952, p. 6. *Har* 23 Aug 1952, p. 134. *HCN* 17 Sep 1952. *HR* 18 Jan 1952. *HR* 20 Aug 1952, p. 3. *LADN* 18 Sep 1952. *LAEx* 18 Sep 1952. *LAT* 15 Aug 1949. *LAT* 25 Aug 1949. *LAT* 18 Sep 1952. *MPHPD* 30 Aug 1952, p. 1510. *Time* 8 Sep 1952. *Var* 20 Aug 1952, p. 6.

RIO BRAVO *see* RIO GRANDE (1950)

RIO GRANDE (Latino)

Edwin Carewe Productions, Inc. *Dist* Pathé Exchange, Inc. 25 Apr **1920** [©Pathé Exchange, Inc.; 6 Apr 1920; LU14964]. Si; b&w. 7 reels.

Dir Edwin Carewe. *Scen* Madge Tyrone and Edwin Carewe. *Cam* Robert Kurrle.

Source: Based on the play *Rio Grande* by Augustus Thomas (New York, 4 Apr 1916).

Cast: Rosemary Theby (*Maria Inez*), George Stone (*Danny O'Neil*), Allan Sears (*Danny O'Neil at 8 years*), Peaches Jackson (*Maria Inez at 6 years*), Hector V. Sarno (*Felipe Lopez*), Adele Farrington (*Alice Lopez*), Arthur Carew (*Don Jose Alvarado*), Harry S. Duffield (*Father O'Brien*).

Western. Felipe Lopez hates all gringos even though his wife Alice is an American. One day he takes his young daughter Maria and crosses the Mexican border, leaving Alice and their adopted son, Danny O'Neil, behind. Years later Maria is now a rebel fighting with her father against the Mexican government while Danny has become a member of the Texas Rangers. One day, while fleeing across the river from her father's enemies, Maria meets Danny and, failing to recognize her adopted brother, invites him to a dance at her father's hacienda. Danny braves many dangers to attend the ball, where he is captured but escapes with Maria's help. Later, believing that Danny is to blame for the capture of her father, Maria leads an attack on the American town in which the Mexicans are beaten and Maria is made captive. Felipe recognizes Alice, and on his deathbed informs Maria that Danny's foster mother is in fact her own mother. Realizing the folly of her ways and her love for Danny, Maria returns to Mexico to teach the schoolchildren to love their American neighbors. Her penitence thus accomplished, Maria accepts Danny's love. *Brothers and sisters. Fathers and daughters. Foster children. Mexican-American border region. Mexicans. Mexico. Racism. Revolutionaries. Texas Rangers. Balls (parties). Parentage. Prisoners of war. Schoolteachers.*

Note: This was the first Edwin Carewe production to be released through Pathé.

ETR 24 Apr 1920, p. 2415. *MPN* 24 Apr 1920, p. 3742. *MPW* 24 Apr 1920, p. 600. *Var* 7 May 1920, p. 34. *Wid's* 18 Apr 1920, p. 17.

RIO GRANDE (Native Americans, Apache)

Argosy Pictures Corp. *Dist* Republic Pictures Corp. 15 Nov **1950;** Prod: mid-Jun—late Jul 1950 [©Republic Pictures Corp.; 30 Nov 1950; LP565]. Sd (RCA Sound System); b&w. 9,439 ft. 105 min. Passed by the National Board of Review. PCA cert no. 14822.

Prod John Ford and Merian C. Cooper. *Pres* Herbert J. Yates. *Dir* John Ford. *Asst dir* Wingate Smith. *2d unit dir* Cliff Lyons. *Scr* James Kevin McGuinness. *Photog* Bert Glennon. *2nd unit photog* Archie Stout. [*Stills* Ira Hoke]. *Spec eff* Howard Lydecker and Theodore Lydecker. *Opt eff* Consolidated Film Industries. *Art dir* Frank Hotaling. *Film ed* Jack Murray. *Set dec* John McCarthy, Jr. and Charles Thompson. *Props* R. Dudley Holmes. *Cost des* Adele Palmer. *Uniforms* D. R. Overall Hatswell. *Mus score* Victor Young. *Sd* Earl Crain, Sr. and Howard Wilson. *Makeup supv* Bob Mark. *Hair stylist* Peggy Gray. *Tech adv* Maj. Philip J. Kieffer, USA.

Song(s): "My Gal is Purple," "Footsore Cavalry" and "Yellow Stripes," words and music by Stan Jones; "Aha, San Antone," words and music by Dale Evans; "Cattle Call," words and music by Tex Owens; "I'll Take You Home Again Kathleen," words and music by T. P. Westendorf; "Down By the Glen Side," music and lyrics by Peader Kearney and P. J. Ryan; "You're in the Army Now," words by Tell Taylor and Ole Olson and music by Isham Jones; "Erie Canal," traditional.

Source: Based on the short story "Mission with No Record" by James Warner Bellah in *The Saturday Evening Post* (27 Sep 1947).

Cast: Starring John Wayne [(*Col. Kirby Yorke*)], Maureen O'Hara [(*Mrs. Kathleen Yorke*)], Co-starring Ben Johnson [(*Trooper Tyree*)], Claude Jarman, Jr. [(*Trooper Jefferson "Red" Yorke*)], Harry Carey, Jr. [(*Trooper Boone*)], Chill Wills [(*Dr. Wilkins*)], J. Carrol Naish [(*Gen. Sheridan*)], Victor McLaglen [(*Sgt. Maj. Tim Quincannon*)], Grant Withers [(*Deputy Marshal*)], Sons of the Pioneers: Ken Curtis, Hugh Farr, Karl Farr, Lloyd Perryman, Shug Fisher, Tommy Doss, Peter Ortiz [(*Capt. St. Jacques*)], Steve Pendleton [(*Capt. Prescott*)], Karolyn Grimes [(*Margaret Mary*)], Alberto Morin [(*Lieutenant*)], Stan Jones [(*Sergeant*)], Fred Kennedy [(*Heinze*)], Eve March [(*School teacher*)], Chuck Roberson [(*Indian*)], Jack Pennick, Patrick Wayne, Cliff Lyons.

Western, with songs. [*Print viewed*]. Some time after the Civil War, at a cavalry fort near the Rio Grande River, anxious women and children await the return of their men from battle with Apache Indians, who have been leading attacks on the U.S. side of the border and then crossing into Mexico, where the cavalry has been forbidden to go. Later, when Col. Kirby Yorke returns with his men, he learns that Jefferson, his son whom he has not seen for fifteen years, has dropped out of West Point after failing mathematics. When Yorke, a no-nonsense career soldier, learns that "Red," as his son is known, is among the new recruits at the fort, he warns him not to expect any special treatment because of their kinship. The next day, while the recruits are having a riding lesson, when a U.S. deputy marshal arrives and asks to speak with one of the men, southerner Travis Tyree, who

is suspected of murdering his sweetheart's brother. Later, Red overhears another soldier, Heinze, insult Yorke and call Yorke's old friend Sgt. Maj. Tim Quincannon a "chowder-headed Mick Sergeant." After Red punches him in the face, Quincannon arrives and stops the fight. When he learns the reason for their dispute, Quincannon instructs them to return that evening to settle their disagreement. They meet later and resume fighting, but are again interrupted, this time by Yorke. Yorke demands an explanation for the fight, but Heinze says nothing, for which Red is grateful. Later, Yorke's estranged wife Kathleen arrives at the fort and tries to buy her son's discharge from the cavalry for $100, but Yorke refuses her offer. A short time later, the Indians attack the fort, tearing a large hole in one wall. After Yorke orders Capt. St. Jacques to mobilize Troop "A," the deputy marshal arrests Trooper Tyree and holds him temporarily inside the infirmary. Later, Quincannon tells the infirmary's Dr. Wilkins that, during the Civil War, Gen. Sheridan ordered Yorke to burn down the plantation operated by Kathleen's family and that is why she left him and kept Red from seeing him. At the infirmary, Tyree admits to having had a violent dispute with his sweetheart's brother, but insists he did not kill him. When Yorke receives the order for Tyree's arrest, he instructs Quincannon to help him escape. Despite their standing orders, Gen. Sheridan, who is still Yorke's commanding officer, instructs Yorke to lead his men across the Rio Grande. The next day, when he learns that the Indians are preparing to attack, Yorke orders Red to evacuate the women and children to neighboring Fort Bliss. Just then, the Apaches attack a wagon train filled with evacuating civilians. They kidnap the children and take them back to their village, where they are held hostage inside a small church. After Tyree catches up to the regiment, Yorke orders him to organize a militia to rescue the children. Yorke leads the militia into the village, where he is shot in the chest with an arrow. Red removes the arrow and helps Yorke onto his horse for the ride back to the fort. Later, Red receives a commendation for his bravery, while Tyree escapes from the deputy marshal by riding away on Gen. Sheridan's horse. *Fathers and sons. Forts. Officers (Military). United States. Army. Cavalry. Bow and arrow. Churches. Escapes. Evacuations. Fistfights. Fugitives. Gratitude. Navajo Indians. Physicians. Riding. Rio Grande. Saloons. General Philip Henry Sheridan. United States Military Academy. United States–History–Reconstruction, 1865-1898. Wagon trains.*

Note: The working titles of this film were *Rio Bravo* and *Rio Grande Command*. The film was the last of John Ford's cavalry trilogy, which also included *Fort Apache* (see above) and *She Wore a Yellow Ribbon* (see below). It was shot on location in Moab, Monument Valley and Mexican Hat, UT. According to a modern source, *Rio Grande* was made as part of a deal to secure financing for Ford's *The Quiet Man* (see above), which Herbert Yates agreed to back on the condition that Ford, Wayne, O'Hara, Victor McLaglen and Barry Fitzgerald first make a western for him. In a 17 Dec 1995 *LAT* article, O'Hara discussed the arrangement: "Yates read the script and said: 'This is a silly, little Irish story and it will never make a penny, but if the same director and the same producer [Merian C. Cooper] make me a film with the same actors—a western to make up the money you are going to lose on this story—I will finance it.'" According to a modern source, while on location in Moab, the crew "brought fifty Navajo up from the reservation to play Apache in the film, accompanied by Lee Bradley, who again served as translator. Billy Yellow, one of the Indians selected for closeups, stated forty years later that the Navajo weren't told that they were portraying Apache." Modern sources add the following names to the crew credits: *Asst ed* Barbara Ford; *2d unit dir* Cliff Lyons.

Box 11 Nov 1950. *DV* 2 Nov 1950, p. 3. *FD* 2 Nov 1950, p. 6. *HR* 16 Jun 1950, p. 11. *HR* 21 Jul 1950, p. 11. *HR* 2 Nov 1950, p. 3. *MPH* 4 Nov 1950. *MPHPD* 11 Nov 1950, p. 562. *NYT* 20 Nov 1950, p. 21. *Var* 8 Nov 1950, p. 6.

RIO GRANDE COMMAND *see* **RIO GRANDE** (1950)

RIO GRANDE PATROL (Latino)

RKO Radio Pictures, Inc. *Dist* RKO Radio Pictures, Inc. **1950**; Prod: 17 May—late May 1950 [©RKO Radio Pictures, Inc.; 2 Nov 1950; LP499]. Sd (RCA Sound System); b&w. 5,386 ft. 60 min. PCA cert no. 14594.

Prod Herman Schlom. *Dir* Lesley Selander. [*Asst dir* John E. Pommer]. *Wrt* Norman Houston. *Dir of photog* J. Roy Hunt. [*Cam op* Richard Du Valle]. [*Gaffer* Leo Crabtree]. [*Stills* Ollie Sigurdson]. [*Spec eff* Walter Costello]. *Art dir* Albert S. D'Agostino and Feild Gray. *Film ed* Desmond Marquette. *Set dec* Darrell Silvera and Jack Mills. *Mus dir* C. Bakaleinikoff. *Mus* Paul Sawtell. *Sd* John Cass and Clem Portman. [*Hair stylist* Annabelle Levy]. [*Makeup* Irving Burns]. [*Scr supv* Jerry Wright]. [*Grip* Jim Kirly].

Song(s): "You May Not Remember," words by George Jessel, music by Ben Oakland; "De Camptown Races," words and music by Stephen Foster.

Cast: TIM HOLT [(*Kansas*)], Jane Nigh [(*Sherry Bliss*)], Douglas Fowley [(*Bragg Orcutt*)], Cleo Moore [(*Peppie*)], Rick Vallin [(*Captain Trevino*)], John Holland [(*Fowler*)], Tom Tyler [(*Chet Yance*)], Larry Johns [(*Dr. Reynolds*)], Harry Harvey [(*Stationmaster*)], Richard Martin (*Chito Rafferty*).

Western, with songs. [*Print viewed*]. After he inadvertently allows two gold-rich American crooks to cross the Mexican border into Arizona, border patrolman Chito Rafferty is informed by his partner Kansas that they are both to report to a Captain Trevino in Laredo. There Kansas and Chito happily reunite with their old friend Trevino, who has been sent by the Mexican government to investigate a possible smuggling operation. From Trevino, Chito and Kansas learn that one of the men whom Chito stopped earlier is notorious smuggler Bragg Orcutt. Orcutt, meanwhile, meets with Laredo's crooked saloon owner, Fowler, who offers to sell Orcutt a shipment of machine guns, which he is smuggling in the luggage of some chorus girls he is bringing in from the East. Although Fowler at first demands $5,000 apiece for the newly invented firearms, he lowers his price after he is questioned by Trevino. Trevino has been alerted to Fowler's suspicious behavior by saloon singer Sherry Bliss, who is engaged to the captain. The next day, the train bringing the chorus girls pulls into town, and Trevino, Kansas and Chito are there to meet it. Before the lawmen can inspect the women's luggage, however, Orcutt shoots Trevino and tricks Kansas and Chito into pursuing him, while Fowler unloads the machine guns and hides them in the saloon. Later, when Chito and Kansas try to search the saloon, Fowler demands to see a search warrant and turns them away. Fowler then rides to Orcutt's hideout and tells him that he cannot make delivery on the guns until Chito and Kansas have been killed. For a price, Orcutt's sharpshooting henchman Chet Yance offers to murder Chito and Kansas that night while they are watching Sherry's new saloon act. Just as Yance is about to shoot Chito, however, Sherry spots his gun and warns the patrolman. During the ensuing gunfight, Yance manages to escape and races back to Orcutt's hideout. The next morning, Fowler informs Sherry and the chorus girls that they are moving the show to Monterey, Mexico. Before leaving Laredo, Sherry says goodbye to the recuperating Trevino and tells Chito and Kansas that Fowler may be hiding the guns in their luggage wagons. Determined to find the contraband, Kansas accompanies Fowler's wagon to the border, but is captured by Orcutt and Yance and taken to their hideout. Kansas' horse Lightning escapes, however, and eventually leads Chito and Trevino to the hideout. While Trevino tries to keep an agitated Lightning quiet, Chito sneaks up on the hideout and takes Yance by surprise. Yance gets away, but Chito and Kansas are able to return to Laredo in time to stop the wagons carrying the guns and apprehend Orcutt and his men. Later, Trevino and Sherry marry, and confirmed bachelor Chito is scared out of town by Peppie, a marriage-hungry chorus girl. *Attempted murder. Border patrols. Gunrunners. Mexican-American border region. Saloon keepers. Arizona. Chorus girls. Engagements. Gunfights. Gunshot wounds. Hideouts. Horses. Machine-guns. Mexican Americans. Mexicans. Singers.*

Note: According to *HR*, exteriors for the film were shot in Little Rock, in California's Mojave Desert. Modern sources add Forrest Burns to the cast.

Box 18 Nov 1950. *DV* 7 Nov 1950, p. 3. *FD* 1 Dec 1950, p. 7. *HR* 18 May 1950, p. 4. *HR* 19 May 1950, p. 10. *HR* 26 May 1950, p. 8. *HR* 6 Nov 1950, p. 3. *MPHPD* 9 Dec 1950, p. 606. *Var* 8 Nov 1950, p. 18.

RIO RITA (Latino)

Metro-Goldwyn-Mayer Corp.; controlled by Loew's Inc. *Dist* Loew's Inc. Apr **1942**; Prod: early Nov 1941—14 Jan 1942 [©Loew's Inc.; 24 Mar 1942; LP11252]. Sd (Western Electric Sound System); b&w. 9 reels, 8,179 ft. 90-91 min. Passed by the National Board of Review. PCA cert no. 8091.

Prod Pandro S. Berman. *Dir* S. Sylvan Simon. [*Asst dir* William Ryan]. *Scr* Richard Connell and Gladys Lehman. *Spec material for Abbott and Costello by* John Grant. *Dir of photog* George Folsey. [*Loc dir of photog* Clyde DeVinna and Harold Lipstein]. *Spec eff* Warren Newcombe. *Art dir* Cedric Gibbons. *Assoc* Eddie Imazu. *Film ed* Ben Lewis. *Set dec* Edwin B. Willis. [*Assoc* Buford Robert]. *Gowns* Kalloch. *Men's ward* Gile Steele. *Mus dir* Herbert Stothart. *Vocals and orch* Murray Cutter, Leo Arnaud and Paul Marquardt. [*Dance dir* David Robel]. *Rec dir* Douglas Shearer. [*Vocal stand-in for Kathryn Grayson* Lorraine Bridges].

Music: "Tico Tico" by Zequinha Abreu.

Song(s): "Rio Rita" and "The Ranger's Song," music by Harry Tierney, lyrics by Joseph McCarthy; "Long Before You Came Along," music by Harold Arlen, lyrics by E. Y. Harburg; "The Shadow Song" from the opera *Dinorah, ou le pardon de Ploërmel*, music by Giacomo Meyerbeer, libretto by Jules Barbier and Michel Carré.

Cast: BUD ABBOTT (*"Doc"*), LOU COSTELLO (*"Wishy"* [*Dunn*]), Kathryn Grayson (*Rita Winslow*), John Carroll (*Ricardo Montera*), Patricia Dane (*Lucette Brunswick*), Tom Conway (*Maurice Craindall*), Peter Whitney (*Jake*), Barry Nelson (*Harry Gantley*), Arthur Space (*Trask*), Dick Rich (*Gus*), Eva Puig (*Marianna*), Joan Valerie (*Dotty*), Mitchell Lewis (*Julio*), Eros Volusia, [William Tannen (*Pet store owner*)], [David Oliver (*Golfer*)], [Julian Rivero (*Mexican gent*)], [Douglass Newland (*Control man*)], [Lee Murray (*Little Mexican*)], [Inez Cooper (*Pulque*)], [Jenny Mac, Vangie Beilby, Ruth Cherrington (*Club women*)], [Frank Penny (*Chef*)], [Robert Bradford (*Whistling solo*)], [J. Delos Jewkes, Nacho Galindo, Alfredo Garmo (*Soloists in "The Ranger's Song"*)], [Mercedes Ruffino], [Morton Scott], [Tudor Williams], [The Guadalajara Trio], [Flores Brothers].

Comedy, with songs. [*Print viewed*]. Stranded New Yorkers "Wishy" Dunn and "Doc," who have been fired from their pet store jobs in Texas, hide in the trunk of a car with a New York license plate, hoping to get back home. Unfortunately, the car belongs to radio singing star Ricardo Montera, who is on his way home to Vista Del Rio for the first time in ten years. Rita Winslow, the young owner of the town's resort hotel, is Ricardo's childhood sweetheart, and hopes that stardom has not changed him. Unknown to Rita, the hotel's manager, Maurice Craindall, is a Nazi agent who is going to use Ricardo's planned national radio broadcast to send a coded sabotage message. At the hotel, while Doc and Wishy find their way out of the trunk, Ricardo rides out into the desert and hears one of his recordings being accompanied by Rita. She pretends that she is not impressed by him, but when they return to the hotel, she becomes jealous of Lucette Brunswick, one of Craindall's cohorts, who has been told to make a play for Ricardo. A few minutes later, two of Craindall's men, who also work for the hotel, find the starving Doc and Wishy stealing food. When the kind-hearted Rita realizes what is happening, she says that she gave them the food, then gives them jobs as house detectives. In return for her kindness, Doc and Wishy decide to help her and Ricardo get together. That night, Ricardo sings to Rita at the hotel's nightclub, but she refuses to listen because she thinks he has turned into a playboy. Later, Doc and Wishy find Lucette in Craindall's office, and, with money they have found, try to bribe her to stay away from Ricardo. After she leaves, they find some flammable liquid and a code book, which they decide to keep. Harry Gantley, who is also working at the hotel, sneaks in through a window a moment later and tells Doc and Wishy that he is a member of the Secret Service. He starts to tell them what to do if he is killed, but is shot dead before he can finish. Just after the frightened Doc and Wishy flee the office, Craindall and his cohorts enter, along with Ricardo and some other guests. Trask, Craindall's right-hand man, feigns surprise at finding the body and says that there must have been a robbery. Later Lucette confronts Ricardo in the garden and lies that she is Gantley's partner and is trying to capture some Nazi spies. When Rita, who has decided to give Ricardo another chance, happens by, Lucette pretends to make love to him. Ricardo then goes to Wishy and Doc and they tell him about the code book. Later, Ricardo tells Rita that he has always loved her and tries to tell her about Craindall, but she will not listen. That same night, Lucette goes to Wishy's room to find the book, but is unsuccessful. Later, Ricardo tells Wishy that he hid the book and will try to get it to Washington. Doc and Wishy then go through a series of escapes and captures by Craindall's men, while at the same time, Ricardo is prevented from leaving and he and Rita are forced at gunpoint to proceed with the broadcast. Just as Craindall's code is about to be broadcast, he hears animal hooves and men singing "The Ranger's Song" and thinks that the Texas Rangers have arrived to arrest them. This is all thanks to Wishy's use of some donkeys and his request that the local radio station play "The Ranger's Song." After the spies escape in waiting taxicabs, a huge explosion is heard, and Wishy says "Goodnight, folks." *House detectives. Mexican Americans. Resorts. Romance. Singers. Spies.* Automobiles. Bribery. Cactus. Codes. Deserts. Dogs. Donkeys. Escapes. Explosions. Food. Garages. Jealousy. Laundries. Murder. Nazis. Pet shops. Radio programs. Recordings. Sabotage. Starvation. Taxicabs. Texas. Texas Rangers. Undercover operations.

Note: Several Bud Abbott and Lou Costello sight and language gags and burlesque sketches are used throughout the film. One long sequence involves their attempts to get out of the car's trunk after discovering that it has been elevated on a garage lift. Another prominent gag involves their escape through a laundry chute and Costello's attempts to get out of the hotel laundry's huge automatic washing machine.

According to a 19 Oct 1938 *HR* news item, M-G-M was about to purchase from RKO the rights to *Rio Rita*, a 1927 Broadway musical produced by Florenz Ziegfeld, written by Guy Bolton and Fred Thompson, with songs by Harry Tierney and Joseph McCarthy. At that time, M-G-M planned to make a musical version of the play as a vehicle for their popular singing team Jeanette MacDonald and Nelson Eddy. A Jan 1941 *HR* news item noted that RKO wanted to sell the picture rights to M-G-M and that, according to RKO president George J. Schaefer, a year previously M-G-M had agreed to a sale price of $85,000 plus the loan of Robert Young, Robert Montgomery or James Stewart, but that the deal "may now turn sour." The agreement was apparently completed by early Jun 1941, but additional details of the terms between the two studios have not been found. Although two songs from the Broadway musical were retained for the M-G-M film, the title song and "The Ranger's Song," the film's story line bears no resemblance to the play and the film's screenplay was credited as an "original" by the SAB. Two additional songs were written for the film, according to *HR* news items, "Unusual Weather" and "Whippoorwill," but they were not in the released picture and may not have been filmed.

Pre-production news items indicate that M-G-M originally wanted to borrow Arthur Lubin from Universal to produce the picture and that opera singers Marta Eggerth and Risë Stevens were both considered for the female lead. Although Bud Abbott and Lou Costello were under contract to Universal, terms of their contract enabled them to make one picture a year away from their home studio. Location shooting was completed near Palm Springs, CA. *HR* news items indicate that Clyde DeVinna shot exteriors and locations for the film, while George Folsey shot the studio scenes. One news item indicated that Harold Lipstein shot some exteriors near Hemet, CA. Brazilian dancer Eros Volusia made her screen debut in the film. Actors who were mentioned in news items, but whose appearances in the released film cannot be confirmed include Diane Brook, Grace Ritchie, Janet Barrett, Dorothy Ward, Mina Harragut, Dorothy Gilmore, Marjorie Raymond, Eleanore Kallejian, Anita Maisnik and Mary Manners. In addition to the Luther Reed-directed RKO production of *Rio Rita*, which was produced in 1929, starring Bebe Daniels and John Boles (see *AFI Catalog of Feature Films, 1921-30*; F2. 4625), an NBC television version of the musical play was produced in 1950.

Box 14 Mar 1942. *DV* 16 Mar 1942, p. 3. *FD* 11 Mar 1942, p. 7. *HR* 19 Oct 1938, p. 2. *HR* 24 Jan 1941, p. 4. *HR* 5 Jun 1941, p. 1. *HR* 12 Aug 1941, p. 1. *HR* 14 Oct 1941, p. 1. *HR* 31 Oct 1941, p. 21. *HR* 4 Nov 1941, p. 4. *HR* 16 Nov 1941, p. 12. *HR* 10 Nov 1941, p. 2. *HR* 11 Nov 1941, p. 7. *HR* 12 Nov 1941, p. 7. *HR* 13 Nov 1941, p. 6. *HR* 24 Nov 1941, p. 1, 7. *HR* 3 Dec 1941, p. 8. *HR* 17 Dec 1941, p. 7. *HR* 18 Dec 1941, p. 4. *HR* 6 Jan 1942, p. 10. *HR* 15 Jan 1942, p. 3. *HR* 16 Mar 1942, p. 3. *MPHPD* 14 Mar 1942, p. 549. *NYT* 8 May 1942, p. 27. *Var* 18 Mar 1942, p. 8.

LA RIVA DEI BRUTI *see* **TROPENNÄCHTE**

ROAD AGENT (Latino)

Universal Pictures Co., Inc. *Dist* Universal Pictures Co., Inc. 19 Dec **1941**; Prod: mid-Oct—late Oct 1941 [©Universal Pictures Co., Inc.; 8 Dec 1941; LP10884]. Sd (Western Electric Mirrophonic Recording); b&w. 5,507 ft. 60 min. PCA cert no. 7909.

Assoc prod Ben Pivar. *Dir* Charles Lamont. [*Asst dir* Howard Christie]. *Scr* Morgan Cox, Arthur Strawn and Maurice Tombragel. *Orig story* Sherman Lowe and Arthur St. Claire. *Dir of photog* Jerome Ash. *Art dir* Jack Otterson. *Assoc* Ralph M. DeLacy. *Film ed* Frank Gross. *Set dec* R. A. Gausman. *Gowns* Vera West. *Mus dir* H. J. Salter. *Sd dir* Bernard B. Brown. [*Sd*] *tech* Robert Pritchard. [*Unit pub wrt* Alanson Edwards].

Song(s): "Cielito lindo," traditional; "Ridin' Home," music by Jimmy McHugh, lyrics by Harold Adamson.

Cast: DICK FORAN (*Duke* [*Masters, also known as "Douglas"*]), LEO CARRILLO (*Pancho*), ANDY DEVINE, Anne Gwynne (*Patricia* [*Leavitt*]), Samuel S. Hinds ([*Sam*] *Leavitt*), Richard Davies ([*Tom*] *Martin*), Anne Nagel (*Lola*), Morris Ankrum (*Big John* [*Morgan*]), John Gallaudet (*Steve*), Reed Hadley (*Shayne*), Eddy Waller (*Lewis*), Ernie Adams (*Jake*), Lew Kelly (*Luke*), [Chuck Morrison (*Bart*)], [Jack Rockwell (*Frank*)], [George Lewis (*Lace*)], [Emmett Lynn (*Teller*)], [William Ruhl, Al Bridge, Harry Strang (*Ranchers*)], [Luana Walters (*Teresa*)], [Leyland Hodgson (*Jackson*)].

Western, with songs. [*Print viewed*]. After a stagecoach robbery, cowboys Duke Masters, Pancho and Andy steal the strongbox from the bandits. In Calliope, the local ranchers complain to banker president Sam Leavitt about the recent rash of holdups and threaten to take their money to another town. The robbed stagecoach then arrives, with the town's murdered sheriff and deputies aboard. Later, Duke and his men return the strongbox, less their "ten percent commission," to the bank, and the townspeople accuse them of the murder. After saloon singer Lola stands up for Duke, he visits her and learns that she is now married to Steve, whom Duke recognizes as one of the real

bandits. Under the alias "Douglas," Duke pretends to be an out-of-town rancher and opens a large account in Leavitt's bank, where he meets the banker's lovely daughter Patricia. At Leavitt's party, Duke's true identity is discovered, and despite Patricia's warning, Duke, Pancho and Andy are captured. The townspeople plan to hang the accused murderers the next morning, but Lola's testimony, backed by her husband, convinces all of their innocence. After a speech by Tom Martin, Duke is made sheriff, and Pancho and Andy, his deputies. Duke's first official action is to ban firearms in town, and when saloon owner Shayne refuses to abide, Duke and his men are forced into a fight. Using a cannon, they force Steve and the other outlaws to leave town. Later, Patricia learns that outlaw leader Big John Morgan is coming to town, so she tries to convince Duke to leave. Instead, Duke meets with Morgan, who agrees to follow all of the town's new laws. Morgan then meets with his secret partner, Leavitt, who tries unsuccessfully to convince the outlaw to go straight. An election is held for mayor, with Tom the leading candidate. At the same time, Lola is tricked into telling Duke that Morgan plans to kidnap Patricia and ransom her for the bank's holdings. Duke and his men then rob the bank, much to the chagrin of Morgan, who had the same idea. Duke takes the money to the Leavitt ranch, where he shoots it out with Morgan and his gang. The townspeople, rallied by Tom, then arrive at the ranch and capture Morgan and his men. Despite Tom's efforts, Duke, Pancho and Andy make their escape, leaving behind the bank's money and a note to Leavitt, telling him that Duke is actually a special agent for Wells Fargo Express and that he can now run his bank honestly. *Cowboys. Deputies. False accusations. Murder. Outlaws. Sheriffs. Undercover agents.* Aliases. Bankers. Cemeteries. Elections. Fathers and daughters. Fights. Gunfights. Jails. Mexican Americans. Parties. Posses. Saloon keepers. Saloons. Stagecoach robberies. Wells Fargo & Co.

Note: *Var* mistakenly gives the running time of this film as sixty-nine minutes. *HR* notes that actor Richard Davies was optioned by Universal to appear in this film after his supporting performance in that studio's *Unfinished Business.* According to modern sources, the film was re-released under the title *Texas Road Agent.*

Box 13 Dec 1941. *DV* 4 Dec 1941, p. 3. *FD* 17 Dec 1941, p. 6. *HR* 17 Oct 1941, p. 17. *HR* 22 Oct 1941, p. 7. *HR* 5 Dec 1941, p. 4. *MPHPD* 13 Dec 1941, p. 407. *Var* 10 Dec 1941, p. 18.

ROAD DEMON (Italian Americans)
Twentieth Century-Fox Film Corp. *Dist* Twentieth Century-Fox Film Corp. 2 Dec **1938**; Prod: 27 Jun—late Jul 1938 [©Twentieth Century-Fox Film Corp.; 2 Dec 1938; LP8735]. Sd (Western Electric Mirrophonic Recording); b&w. 7 reels, 6,350 ft. 70 min. PCA cert no. 4501.

Series: Sports Series.

Assoc prod Jerry Hoffman. *Dir* Otto Brower. [*Asst dir* Henry Weinberger]. *Orig scr* Robert Ellis and Helen Logan. *Photog* Edward Snyder. [*Background photog* Barney McGill and J. O. Taylor]. *Art dir* Bernard Herzbrun and Boris Leven. *Film ed* Jack Murray. *Set dec* Thomas Little. *Cost* Herschel. *Mus dir* Samuel Kaylin. *Sd* Bernard Freericks and William H. Anderson. [*Tech adv* Jim Thorne]. [*Unit mgr* Ben Wurtzel].

Cast: Henry Arthur (*Jimmy Blake*), Joan Valerie (*Jean Rogers*), Henry Armetta (*Papa Gambini*), Tom Beck (*Ted Rogers*), Bill Robinson (*Zepher*), Jonathan Hale (*Anderson*), Murray Alper (*Hap Flynn*), Edward Marr (*Skid Miller*), Lon Chaney, Jr. (*Bud Casey*), Inez Palange (*Mama Gambini*), Johnny Pironne, Jr. (*Tony Gambini*), Eleanor Virzie (*Rosa Gambini*), Betty Greco (*Maria Gambini*), [Gennaro Curci (*Rocco*)], [Eddy Conrad (*Satorri*)], [Alex Palasthy (*Sculptor*)], [Arthur Rankin, Charles Haefeli (*Mechanics*)], [Harry Strang, Marty Faust, George Magrill (*Guards*)], [Ben Hendricks (*Truck driver*)], [Jane Keckley (*Mrs. Givney*)], [Edward Gargan (*Beefy*)], [Joseph Crehan (*Douglas*)], [Eddie Acuff (*Smitty*)], [Stanley Andrews (*Chairman*)], [Ed. Stanley (*Doctor*)], [Hooper Atchley (*Official*)], [Gary Breckner (*Announcer*)].

Automobile racing, Drama. [*Print viewed*]. Tony Gambini, whose father runs a delicatessan, joins his friend, truck driver Jimmy Blake, for his morning produce pick-up. Jimmy, a champion "dirt track" driver, whom Tony idolizes, hopes to win the five dollar prize that goes to the first truck to arrive at the market each morning. On a curvy, mountain road, Jimmy passes a driver who earlier picked up two champion racecar drivers, Skid Miller and Hap Flynn, whose car had stalled. Skid takes the wheel and passes Jimmy. Jimmy gives chase, but when a truck comes the other way, he is forced off the road

and into a tree. With the spindle damaged and axle bent, Jimmy surmises that he will be fired, so he and Tony go to the speedway to watch time tryouts. One of the drivers is Ted Rogers, whose father died a year earlier due to scheme perpetrated by Anderson, an owner of racecars. Anderson's drivers, Skid, Hap and Bud Casey, got Ted's father drunk the night before a race and then interfered with him during the race. The subsequent accident that caused Rogers' death was blamed on him because of alcohol found in his blood. While testing a stabilizer for his boss Douglas, Ted takes a spill, which greatly upsets his sister Jean, with whom Jimmy has unsuccessfully tried to flirt. Later, Jimmy, now working as a delivery driver for Papa Gambini, almost hits Jean in Papa's new truck. They have lunch together, and Jimmy makes a date with her for that evening. Skid, who is troubled by Ted's resemblance to his father, and his cohorts get Ted drunk that night. Jimmy tries to sober him up for the test the next day and breaks the date with Jean. The next day, when Ted is not ready, Jimmy tells Douglas that Ted is sick and offers to test the car himself. Ted and Jean arrive, and when Jimmy crashes against the wall, Jean screams. After Jimmy is declared alright at the hospital, Douglas says that he is through with racing because of the danger. Jean then berates Jimmy because she thinks that he lied about Ted so that he could get the chance to drive himself; however, Ted later reveals to Jean that Jimmy protected his reputation. Jimmy convinces Papa to buy the wreck of the Douglas car with Jimmy's money, so that they can build it up and race it. He then convinces Papa to put up money for new tires and the entry fee, and to hire Ted as the driver, without letting anyone know that he is behind it. To raise the money, Mama Gambini goes to various relatives and sells percentages in the car, but Papa discovers that she has sold 120% and figures that if the car wins, he will be in debt. On the day of the race, Anderson tells the racing official of Ted's drinking, and Ted is suspended. When Jean learns that Jimmy is driving instead, she thinks he is double-crossing her brother. After Jimmy takes the lead and goes two laps in front of the field, the three drivers working for Anderson try to block him, but he gets through. When Hap's wheels lock, forcing him out of the race, Jimmy hits the wall and hurts his arm. In the hospital, Hap confesses to Jimmy that he and his cohorts spiked Ted's father's drink. Jimmy then convinces the official to reinstate Ted as a driver. Meanwhile, the Gambini relatives have learned that their car is out of the race, and Mama is able to buy back their shares for 10% of what they paid. During the race, Casey is flagged out when he tries to force Ted to the wall. Casey then tells Anderson that he is through and slugs him. With three laps to go, Skid looks at Ted and remembering Ted's father, loses control and crashes over the wall. Ted wins and sets a new speed record. Jean kisses Jimmy and Mama hugs Papa, after assuring him that they won't have to go to the poorhouse. *Automobile accidents. Brothers and sisters. False accusations. Race car drivers. Romance.* Confession. Conscience. Delicatessens. Drunkenness. Fathers and sons. Italian Americans. Truck drivers.

Note: The opening credits read, "Twentieth Century-Fox presents *Road Demon* A Sports Adventure." This was the second in Twentieth Century-Fox's "Sports Series." For information regarding the series, please see the entry below for *Speed to Burn.* According to *HR*, a unit consisting of director Otto Brower, cameramen Barney McGill and J. L. Taylor, and unit manager Ben Wurtzel went to Indianapolis to film the Memorial Day Speedway Classic for this film. *Var* noted that the film included footage of famous Indianapolis speedway accidents. *Box* commented that the film boasted "the best race sequences ever captured on film."

Box 27 Aug 1938. *DV* 18 Aug 1938, p. 3. *FD* 23 Aug 1938, p. 7. *HR* 26 May 1938, p. 5. *HR* 27 Jun 1938, p. 7. *HR* 28 Jun 1938, p. 2. *HR* 23 Jul 1938, p. 8. *HR* 18 Aug 1938, p. 4. *MPD* 1 Sep 1938, p. 15. *MPH* 27 Aug 1938, pp. 53-54. *Var* 14 Dec 1938, p. 15.

ROAD TO ELDORADO *see* IN OLD CALIENTE

A ROADSIDE IMPRESARIO (Italian Americans)
Pallas Pictures. *Dist* Paramount Pictures Corp. 18 Jun **1917** [©J. C. Ivers; 28 May 1917; LP10874]. Si; b&w. 5 reels.

Dir Donald Crisp. *Story* George Beban. *Cam* Faxon M. Dean.

Cast: George Beban (*Giuseppe Franchini*), Jose Melville (*Francesca Franchini*), Julia Faye (*Adelaide Vandergrift*), Harry De Vere (*J. Stewart Vandergrift*), Harrison Ford (*Craig Winton*), Fred Huntley (*John Slade*), W. A. Carroll (*Gibbs, the butler*), Adele Farrington (*Lizzie Cosgrove*), Bruno the bear (*Himself*).

Drama. Giuseppe Franchini lives with his little daughter Francesca and pet bear Bruno on the Italian coast. One day, Giuseppe sees a shipwrecked man offshore and swims to his rescue, but in doing so, he is carried out to sea. Upon his return, he finds that his wife has died

of shock at the news of his drowning, and the stranger has taken away the little girl. Years later, Giuseppe travels to America with Bruno where they are arrested for invading an apiary on the Vandergrift estate. Giuseppe is befriended by Vandergrift's daughter Adelaide, but Bruno is sent to jail for his crimes. To pay Bruno's fine, Giuseppe takes a job in a roadhouse owned by John Slade. Here, he learns of Slade's plans to smear Adelaide's fiancé, Craig Winton, the reform candidate for mayor. Giuseppe presents proof of Slade's corruption to Adelaide, who turns it over to her father. When Giuseppe meets Vandergrift, he recognizes him as the man he rescued, but, realizing that Adelaide is happy in her life, he leaves town without letting her know that he is her real father. *Adoption. Bears. Immigrants. Italian Americans. Missing persons, assumed dead. Reformers. Upper classes. Death by shock. Imprisonment. Italy. Political corruption. Recognition. Rescues. Roadhouses. Self-sacrifice.*

Note: *NYDM* erroneously credits George Beban with direction. The copyright entry lists J. C. Ivers as author. As Ivers was the head of Pallas Pictures, this listing may have been given only for copyright purposes and not to indicate that she wrote the story or scenario.

ETR 16 Jun 1917, p. 122. *Motog* 23 Jun 1917, p. 1339. *MPN* 23 Jun 1917, p. 3948. *MPW* 23 Jun 1917, p. 1949, 1994. *NYDM* 16 Jun 1917, p. 29. *Var* 22 Jun 1917, p. 23. *Wid's* 28 Jun 1917, p. 413.

ROAR OF THE NATION see MIN JOK JAY HUNG SING

ROARIN' BRONCS (Chinese Americans)

Action Pictures, Inc. *Dist* Pathé Exchange, Inc. 27 Nov **1927** [©Pathé Exchange, Inc.; 18 Nov 1927; LU24677]. Si; b&w. 5 reels, 4,375 ft.

Pres Lester F. Scott, Jr. *Dir* Richard Thorpe. *Scen* Frank L. Inghram. *Story* Norton S. Parker. *Photog* Ray Ries.

Cast: Buffalo Bill Jr. (*Bill Morris*), Ann McKay (*Rose Tracy*), Harry Todd, Lafe McKee, George Magrill (*Henry Ball*).

Western. Bill Morris, a member of the U. S. Border Patrol assigned to investigate the smuggling of Chinese across the border, gets work at the Tracy and Ball Ranch, suspected to be the smugglers' headquarters. Unable to operate a motorcycle with sidecar, two ranch hands are helped by Bill, who chases Rose Tracy's frightened horse. Henry Ball, the ranch partner's son and leader of the smugglers, fancies Rose, but Bill fails to obtain evidence against him until he overhears his plans at a party given for Rose. Bill gives chase on the motorcycle but is overwhelmed by the smugglers, who take cover in an abandoned shack. Although bound, Bill manages to operate a tractor to rout the gang and take them prisoner. *Border patrols. Chinese Americans. Cowboys. Mexican-American border region. Motorcycles. Smuggling.*

FD 11 Dec 1927.

THE ROARING WEST see SONORA STAGECOACH

ROBBERS' ROOST (English Americans)

Fox Film Corp. *Dist* Fox Film Corp. 1 Jan **1933**; 13 Sep—early Nov 1932 [©Fox Film Corp.; 23 Nov 1932; LP3476]. Sd; b&w. 7 reels, 5,715 ft. 64 min. Passed by the National Board of Review. PCA cert no. 1642-R [8 Oct 1935].

Dir Louis King. [*Asst dir* Booth McCracken]. *Scr* Dudley Nichols. [*Contr wrt* Al Cohn and Garnett Weston]. *Photog* George Schneiderman. [*Cam op* Charles Fetters]. [*Asst cam* James Gordon and Lou Kunkel]. *Art dir* Joseph Wright. *Ward* David Cox. *Mus dir* George Lipschultz. *Sd rec* Bernard Freericks. [*Still photog* Bert Lynch]. [*Double for George O'Brien* Cliff Lyons]. [*Double for Maureen O'Sullivan* Opal Ernie].

Song(s): "Listen to the Lambs" and "Shout All Over Heaven," spirituals; "Cowboy's Heaven" and "I Adore You (Yo te adoro)," words and music by Val Burton and Will Jason.

Source: Based on the novel *Robbers' Roost* by Zane Grey (New York, 1932).

Cast: George O'Brien [(*Jim Wall*)], Maureen O'Sullivan [(*Helen Herrick*)], Walter McGrail [(*Brad*)], Maude Eburne [(*Aunt Ellen*)], Reginald Owen [(*Cecil Herrick*)], William Pawley [(*Hank Hays*)], Clifford Stanley [(*Happy Jack*)], Robert Greig [(*Tulliver*)], [Doris Lloyd (*Prossie*)], [Gilbert Holmes (*Briggs*)], [Frank Rice (*Daniels*)], [William Nestell (*Mac*)], [Vinegar Roan (*Smoky Slocum*)], [Ted Oliver (*Latimer*)], [Fred "Snowflake" Toones (*Ferryboat driver*)], [Frank McGrath (*Mexican*)], [Dick Hunter, Frank Cordell, Clint Sharp (*Horsemen*)].

Western. [*Print viewed*]. In Arizona, when a shootout erupts during a card game, Texan Jim Wall, now and then a cowboy, crashes a chair into a window and escapes. At a river, he demands that the ferryboat driver take him across even though the man has instructions to wait for Hank Hays, foreman of the Star Ranch. Hays arrives and provokes a fight with Jim, who knocks him into the water. Upon seeing Jim's shooting ability, Hays realizes that he would be a good man for his cattle rustling scheme and hires him as a hand on the ranch, which is owned by Englishman Cecil Herrick, who takes a liking to Jim. Hays and his cohorts plan to rustle the cattle in a month. When Herrick's sister Helen, who owns half the ranch, arrives by train, Jim, to his displeasure, is sent to meet her. During their encounters with one another, Helen tries to taunt Jim, but ends up being humiliated. While riding one day, Helen taunts Jim to jump a cliff and get a white flower on the other side. Jim retrieves the flower and, seeing that she is terrified because of the chance he took, kisses her and rides off. That night, Jim tells Hays he is quitting, but Hays warns him to see the deal through. Helen sees Jim preparing to leave and calls him a quitter. She then asks him to return something he took and passionately kisses him back. The next day, when Jim tells Helen that he has decided to stay because of the kiss, he acts flippant and says that she has kissed many men and that it doesn't mean anything. Jim goes with the ranch hands to round up the cattle in preparation to rustle them that night, but when a stampede occurs and he sees, from the other side of a gorge, Helen racing on her horse just ahead of the cattle, he jumps with his horse into the water, swims across and then rides toward her. When she is thrown, Jim wrestles a bull and blocks her with it to keep her from being trampled. At night, Jim tells the one cowhand he likes, Happy Jack, that he can't go through with the theft and convinces Happy to ride to the sheriff. Brad, one of the rustlers, overhears them and kills Happy on his way to town. Meanwhile, Jim goes to tell the Herricks, but Helen, thinking that he has come to propose, is embarrassed that he intends to speak in front of her brother, who has warned her that she and Jim are not of the same class. She calls Jim crude and says she would not marry him if he were the last man on earth. Hays and his men converge on Jim when he rides off and take his gun, as he sees Happy's horse dragging his body. Helen rides to find Jim, and she is captured by Hays and his men, who take her to Robbers' Roost, a hideout in the mountains once used by the Dalton gang. At night, they spot Herrick and other riders below in pursuit. Jim sneaks away and climbs down the mountain to alert Herrick. As Hays, who has tried to seduce Helen, starts to get rough with her, Brad interrupts and announces that Jim is gone. As Jim climbs back up, Brad cuts his rope. Jim manages to grab hold of the cliff and climb back up. He stops Hays as he is grabbing Helen and after a struggle, escapes from the cabin with her. During a shootout, Herrick and the others arrive, and Herrick shoots Hays as he tries to flee. As Helen hugs her brother, Jim rides off, but she pursues him and asks for another proposal. He says that he did not propose the first time, and after asking first for something she took from him, he kisses her. *Cowboys. Ranchers. Romance. Rustlers. Arizona. Attempted rape. Battle of the sexes. Brothers and sisters. Cards. Cattle. Class distinction. English. Ferryboats. Fistfights. Hideouts. Kisses. Mountains. Murder. Proposals (Marital). Ranch foremen. Rescues. Shootouts. Stampedes.*

Note: The novel was originally published serially in *Collier's Magazine* (11 Oct—27 Dec 1930). According to *FD*, the novel ranked among current fiction's best-sellers. According to a *FD* news item, some scenes were shot in Sonora, California. According to information in the Twentieth Century-Fox Records of the Legal Department at the UCLA Theater Arts Library, Stanley Blystone was originally cast as "Mac." In 1955, United Artists released a film based on the same source, produced by Robert Goldstein, directed by Sidney Salkow and starring George Montgomery.

FD 8 Sep 1932, p. 6. *FD* 9 Nov 1932, p. 6. *FD* 18 Mar 1933, p. 4. *HF* 15 Oct 1932, p. 16. *IP* Jan 1933, p. 33. *MPD* 1 Apr 1933, p. 24. *Var* 21 Mar 1933, p. 27. *VarB* 2 Dec 1932.

EL ROBIN HOOD DE MÉXICO (Spanish language)

1928; Hollywood opening: 12 Jul 1928. Si, with Spanish and English titles; b&w. 5 reels. Spanish language.

Prod Antonio Fernández. *Dir* Antonio Fernández. *English titles* Jésus Urueta.

Cast: Pedro Valenzuela (*Pancho Villa*), Chano Urueta (*Pancho Villa as a boy*), Carmen La Roux, Carmen Castillo, Antonia Barrias.

Biography, Drama. [*Not viewed*]. [The film portrays the life of Mexican bandit and revolutionary leader Francisco "Pancho" Villa.]. *Francisco "Pancho" Villa.*

Note: This film, which was also called *El Robin Hood Mexicano*, was previewed in Hollywood to Mexican journalists on 30 Jun 1928. According to a news story in the Spanish-language newspaper *La Opinión*, the film was to be the first of a series of films on the life of Villa. The article also noted that exteriors were shot in Chihuahua, Mexico, while interiors were shot in Hollywood. For information on a 1916 documentary about Villa, please see the entry above for *Following the Flag in Mexico*.

La Opinión 1 Jul 1928. *La Opinión* 8 Jul 1928.

EL ROBIN HOOD MEXICANO *see* EL ROBIN HOOD DE MÉXICO

ROBIN HOOD OF EL DORADO (Latino)

Metro-Goldwyn-Mayer Corp.; controlled by Loew's Inc. *Dist* Loew's Inc. 17 Apr **1936**; New York opening: week of 13 Mar 1936; Prod: 11 Jul—late Aug 1935; retakes filmed intermittently until 22 Dec 1935 [©Metro-Goldwyn-Mayer Corp.; 4 Mar 1936; LP6214]. Sd (Western Electric Sound System); b&w. 9 reels. 84, 86 or 88 min. Passed by the National Board of Review. PCA cert no. 1707.

Prod John W. Considine, Jr. *Dir* William A. Wellman. [*Asst dir* Tom Andre]. *Scr* William A. Wellman, Joseph Calleia and Melvin Levy. [*Contr to dial* Peter B. Kyne, Howard Emmett Rogers and Dan Totheroh]. [*Special seq wrt* James Kevin McGuinness]. [*Contr wrt* C. Gardner Sullivan and Lynn Starling]. [*Contr to trmt* Rowland Brown]. [*Contr to scr const* John Thomas Neville]. *Photog* Chester Lyons. *Art dir* David Townsend and Gabriel Scognamillo. *Film ed* Robert J. Kern. *Ward* Dolly Tree. *Mus score* Herbert Stothart. [*Dance dir of bandit number* Chester Hale]. *Rec dir* Douglas Shearer. [*Tech adv* H. O. Bombacher]. [*Warner Baxter's Spanish accent coach* Allan Garcia].

Source: Based on the book *The Robin Hood of El Dorado* by Walter Noble Burns (New York, 1932).

Cast: WARNER BAXTER (*Joaquin Murrieta*), Ann Loring (*Juanita de la Cuesta*), Bruce Cabot (*Bill Warren*), Margo (*Rosita*), J. Carrol Naish (*Three Fingered Jack*), Soledad Jimenez (*Madre Murrieta*), Carlos de Valdez (*Jose Murrieta*), Eric Linden (*Johnnie Warren*), Edgar Kennedy (*Sheriff Judd*), Charles Trowbridge (*Ramon de la Cuesta*), Harvey Stephens (*Captain Osborne*), Ralph Remley (*Judge Perkins*), George Regas (*Tomas*), Francis McDonald (*Pedro, the spy*), Kay Hughes (*Louise*), Paul Hurst (*Wilson*), Boothe Howard (*Tabbard*), Harry Woods (*Pete*), [G. Pat Collins (*Doc*)], [Harold Goodwin (*Slocum*)], [Ivan "Dusty" Miller (*Marshal*)], [Tom Moore (*Sheriff Hannan*)], [Rychard Cramer (*Bartender*)], [Carlotta Monti, Perez (*Dancers*)], [Charles Stevens (*Bandit*)], [J. P. McGowan (*Danglong*)], [Nick De Ruiz (*Mexican peon*)], [Lew Harvey (*Bill Young*)], [Ben Taggart (*Rancher*)], [Cully Richards (*Juan*)], [Jason Robards (*Pancho*)], [Duke Green (*Guerrera*)], [Marc Lawrence (*Manuel*)], [Frank Campeau (*Steve*)], [Robert Perry (*Miner at grave*)], [Frank Yaconelli (*Peon*)], [Lee Shumway (*Deputy*)], [Frank Hagney (*Phil*)], [Lee Phelps (*Hank*)], [George MacQuarrie (*Smithers*)], [Sam Ash (*Arriga*)], [Inez Palange (*Nurse*)], [Nigel De Brulier (*Padre*)], [Mathilde Comont (*Señorita Martinez*)], [Lou Yaconelli (*Julio Anton*)].

Biography, Historical, Drama. [*Print viewed*]. In 1848, California is thought by many to be "El Dorado," the mythical land of overflowing riches. It is there that Mexican farmer Joaquin Murrieta lives. He is engaged to Juanita de la Cuesta, daughter of Ramon de la Cuesta, who owns the rancho on which he lives. When Captain Osborne, the governor's inspector, visits the spanish-speaking village, many of the residents distrust the Americano's motives. After an arrow is fired in Osborne's direction, narrowly missing him, Roman is angered by the deed and demands that the man who shot the arrow step forward. Joaquin bravely accepts the blame for the fired arrow when no one else will. As a result, Joaquin is banished from the village and forced to flee into the country. When gold is discovered at Sutter's Mill, the ensuing gold rush brings in many ruthless fortune hunters. One of the prospectors, Bill Warren, shoots a man named Tomas, who is immediately taken to Joaquin's mother for treatment. Following an attack on Joaquin by the white settlers, who want to force him off his land, Rosita is killed and Joaquin swears revenge upon the men who killed her. When Joaquin and his brother Jose kill one of the Americanos, a one thousand dollar reward is posted for Joaquin's capture. Meanwhile, Pete, an unscrupulous prospector, harasses Joaquin and falsely accuses Joaquin of riding a horse that belongs to him, and a fight ensues. Later, Joaquin kills Pete and tells his men to bear arms and join Three Fingered Jack's band of bandits. Joaquin's camp is set up at Hidden Valley, where a meeting is held to discuss the Americanos' take-over

of California. In response to the Americanos' threat, Mexicans under Three Fingered Jack's leadership loot the Americanos and the rich Mexican "hacendados." Joaquin takes part in the raids, and during one such operation, is reuntied with Juanita, the hacienda señorita from de la Cuesta's rancho. Juanita, now a rich Mexican socialite, forgives Joaquin's banditry and joins him in fight against the plundering "gringos." When two Americanos are killed by Mexicans, a posse is organized to punish the Mexicans. Following a bungled stagecoach robbery by the bandits, in which the coach driver and a young bride-to-be are unintentionally murdered, Johnnie Warren, the young girl's fiancé, organizes a posse and goes to Hidden Valley to kill Joaquin. Meanwhile, at Joaquin's camp, Joaquin delivers an emotional speech in which he says that he can no longer be the bandits' leader in the wake of his complicity in the young girl's accidental death. Joaquin then bids the bandits farewell, but before he can flee to Mexico, the posse arrives and a shootout ensues. Three Fingered Jack is killed in the attack, and Joaquin, while attempting to escape, is shot and killed at Rosita's grave. Bandits. California–History–1846-1850. Engagements. Exiles. False accusations. Land claims. Mexicans. Murder. Self-sacrifice. Vigilantes. Accidental death. Attempted murder. Class distinction. Fathers and daughters. Fortune hunters. Gold rushes. Government agents. Mothers and sons. Posses. Prospectors. Revenge. Romance. Sutter's Mill (CA).

Note: Working titles for this film were *Born to Die, I Am Joaquin, In Old California* and *Murietta*. The film is loosely based on the life of legendary Mexican bandit Joaquin Murieta. For more information on Murieta, see the entry above for *The Avenger*, which was also about him. A Jan 1936 *HR* news item noted that although this picture was nearly completed in late Aug 1935, M-G-M held up its release in order to "get the full effect of the serialization of the story." The novelization of the film was written by Peter B. Kyne and appeared serially in 130 newspapers throughout the country. The studio set an Apr 1936 release date; however, a Mar 1936 *HR* article stated that M-G-M decided to rush the release of the picture due to a temporary shortage of M-G-M pictures ready for release in the New York area. The article also indicates that the studio planned to "roadshow" the film in Boston and Miami Beach one week after the New York showing. The Miami Beach booking was reportedly designed to "grab off business" before the end of the Florida tourist season. According to an Apr 1936 *HR* news item, the release of the picture in England was held up due to objections raised by the British censor board to three aspects of the film: scenes showing horses falling; the depiction of a man being shot to death following a fighting scene; and references to the slicing off a Chinese man's ears. The British release was postponed until M-G-M completed protection shots for those scenes.

A *HR* pre-production news item stated that actor Leo Carrillo was to star in this film, and that Raoul Walsh was sought to direct. Subsequent *HR* news items noted that Joseph Calliea, who was originally signed to play "Three Fingered Jack," was moved to the starring role. Calliea was later pulled from the lead because the studio decided he was too old to play the part of a man who died at the age of twenty-three. Ironically, his replacement, Warner Baxter, was forty-four at the time of the production, six years older than Calliea. *HR* pre-production news items also noted that actress Margo replaced Jean Parker as "Juanita," and was later shifted to the role of "Rosita" after a young Brooklyn College student named Anita Kurtin won a Hollywood screen test and the starring role in the film. Following Kurtin's assignment to the part, her name was changed to Ann Loring. In addition, *HR* notes that William Henry was originally set to play "Johnny Warren," and Bradley Page was set for the part of "Slocum." *HR* news items list actors Lucio Villegas, Elizabeth Wilbur, George Chandler and Gayne Whitman in the cast, but their appearance in the released film has not been confirmed. According to *HR*, one month prior to the start of production, M-G-M sent a troupe of twenty-seven carpenters, painters and art directors to Sonoma County, California, to reconstruct several old mining camps, including the local landmarks Angels Camp and Sawmill Flats. *HR* news items also relate the following information: Chester Hale prepared the bandit dance number, featuring Carlotta Monti and Perez. (Perez's first name has not been determined.) H. O. Bombacher, one of the oldest residents of the ghost town of Springfield, California, was hired as a technical adviser on the picture. Director William Wellman planned to use three hundred cowboys in the film. Warner Baxter suffered from a "nervous strain" which was attributed to having to wear a noisy pair of forged iron spurs for twelve weeks. The actor was advised by his physician to recover in the quiet of his home.

DV 12 Mar 1936, p. 3. *FD* 13 Mar 1936, p. 6. *HR* 16 Jan 1935, p. 3. *HR* 2 Feb 1935, p. 3. *HR* 1 Mar 1935, p. 3. *HR* 7 Mar 1935, p. 3. *HR* 8 Mar 1935, p. 1. *HR* 10 Apr 1935, p. 3. *HR* 15 May 1935, p. 1. *HR* 24 May 1935, p. 1. *HR* 31 May 1935, p. 6. *HR* 17 Jun 1935, p. 9. *HR* 19 Jun 1935, p. 10. *HR* 28 Jun 1935, p. 4. *HR* 2 Jul 1935, p. 22. *HR* 5 Jul 1935, p. 11. *HR* 6 Jul 1935, p. 3. *HR* 8 Jul 1935, p. 1, 4, 18. *HR* 13 Jul 1935, p. 4. *HR* 24 Jul 1935, p. 4. *HR* 14 Sep 1935, p. 1. *HR* 25 Sep 1935, p. 3. *HR* 27 Sep 1935, p. 6. *HR* 30 Sep 1935, p. 2. *HR* 9 Oct 1935, p. 11. *HR* 29 Oct 1935, p. 1. *HR* 27 Nov 1935, p. 2. *HR* 30 Jan 1936, p. 5. *HR* 10 Mar 1936, p. 3. *HR* 12 Mar 1936, p. 3. *HR* 7 Apr 1936, p. 2. *MPD* 9 Mar 1936, pp. 10-11. *MPH* 7 Mar 1936, p. 69. *NYT* 14 Mar 1936, p. 10. *Var* 18 Mar 1936, p. 17.

ROBIN HOOD OF MONTEREY (Latino)

Monogram Pictures Corp. *Dist* Monogram Pictures Corp. 6 Sep **1947**; Los Angeles opening: 6 Aug 1947; Prod: 24 Apr—early May 1947 [©Monogram Pictures Corp.; 11 Aug 1947; LP1143]. Sd (Western Electric Recording); b&w. 51 or 56-57 min.

Series: The Cisco Kid.

Prod Jeffrey Bernerd. *Dir* Christy Cabanne. *Asst dir* Eddie Davis. *Orig story and scr* Bennett R. Cohen. *Addl dial* Gilbert Roland. *Dir of photog* William Sickner. [*Spec eff* Augie Lohman]. *Tech dir* Ernest Hickson. *Film ed* Roy Livingston. *Set dec* Vin Taylor. *Mus dir* Edward J. Kay. *Rec eng* Earl Sitar. [*Rec* John Kean]. *Makeup* Harry Ross. *Prod supv* Glenn Cook.

Source: Based on the character created by O. Henry.

Cast: Gilbert Roland (*The Cisco Kid*), Chris Pin Martin (*"Pancho"*), Evelyn Brent [(*Maria Sanchez Belmonte*)], Jack La Rue [(*Don Ricardo Gonzales*)], Pedro DeCordoba [(*Don Carlos Belmonte*)], Donna DeMario [(*Lolita*)], Travis Kent [(*Eduardo Belmonte*)], Thornton Edwards [(*El Capitan*)], Nestor Paiva [(*Alcalde*)], Ernie Adams [(*Pablo*)], [Julian Rivero (*Dr. Martinez*)], [Felipe Turich (*Guard*)], [Alex Montoya (*Juan*)], [Fred Cordova (*Manuel*)], [George Navarro (*Player*)].

Western. [*Print viewed*]. While riding the range in Monterey, California, notorious fugitives The Cisco Kid and his faithful companion Pancho, come to the rescue of Eduardo Belmonte, the son of Cisco's friend, Don Carlos, who is being chased and shot at by three men. To save the wounded Eduardo from being killed, Cisco knocks the young man unconscious, then tells his pursuers that he is dead. After the men leave, Eduardo explains that the men were pursuing him because Don Carlos has been murdered and he has been falsely accused of committing the crime. Eduardo then describes how he came to be a fugitive: During a party at the Belmonte hacienda, Eduardo overhears his attractive stepmother Maria pledging her love to Don Ricardo Gonzales, a man whom she has claimed is her cousin. Eduardo confronts Maria and, hoping to spare his father from heartbreak, offers her money to leave the ranch. Seeing Don Carlos enter the room, Maria suddenly accuses Eduardo of making unwanted advances, and enraged with jealousy, Don Carlos threatens his son with a pistol. The two men struggle, and a few moments later, the party guests hear a gunshot. After Don Carlos is found and declared dead, Maria denounces Eduardo as his killer, and Eduardo flees the hacienda. At Cisco's hideout, Eduardo concludes his story and agrees to "stay dead" while a trusting Cisco and Pancho go to investigate. Cisco and Pancho trick their way into the Belmonte hacienda, and Cisco finds Maria, whom he recognizes as former cantina singer Maria Sanchez. Reminding her that she is still wanted for killing the cantina owner, Cisco coaxes Maria into a pact of silence, while sneaking a bullet from her derringer. As soon as Cisco leaves, however, Maria orders Don Ricardo to report Cisco's presence to the alcalde in nearby San Blas. Cisco and Pancho also go to San Blas, where the doctor who examined Don Carlos' body confirms that the fatal bullet looked exactly like the one from Maria's gun. Later, at the local saloon, Cisco is spotted by Don Ricardo, who has just met with the alcalde. The blustering alcalde arrests Cisco, but with Pancho's help, Cisco escapes and rides out of town. While fleeing the alcalde's soldiers, Cisco and Pancho come across Lolita, Eduardo's fiancée, who has been forced to work as a servant at the Belmonte hacienda. Lolita begs Cisco to take her away from Belmonte, and while he and Pancho are listening to her pleas, the soldiers catch up and arrest them. Cisco is put before a firing squad and as, Maria, Don Ricardo, and a teary, imprisoned Pancho watch, is shot. After the crowd disperses, however, an unharmed Cisco frees Pancho, explaining that he bribed one of the guards to load the rifles with blanks and allow him to escape. At their hideout, Cisco and Pancho learn that Eduardo, fearing for Lolita's safety, has gone to the hacienda. There, Eduardo and Lolita overhear the alcalde informing Maria and Don Ricardo about Cisco's "resurrection," then Eduardo is caught by Maria's guards. Unknown to them, Cisco is on the grounds and sees Eduardo being carried off. On the road to town, Cisco lays in wait for the alcalde and, after jumping into his open carriage from a tree, orders him at gunpoint to feign illness and send his men ahead with Eduardo. Once alone, Cisco shows the alcalde the bullet taken from Don Carlos' body and points out that Eduardo only carries pistols. Cisco makes an agreement with the alcalde to give himself up in exchange for the alcalde's help in proving Eduardo's innocence. Cisco and Pancho then sneak back into the hacienda and confront Maria with the bullet. She admits that she killed Don Carlos and offers Cisco money for his silence. When Cisco refuses her bribe, Maria pulls a gun on him, but before she can fire it, the alcalde, having overheard her confession, appears and arrests her. Later, after the now-vindicated Eduardo reunites with Lolita,

Cisco turns himself in to the alcalde, who out of respect for his honesty, lets him and Pancho go. *California. Frame-ups. Fugitives. Mexican Americans. Murder. Stepmothers. Bribery. Bullets. Confession (Law). Engagements. Escapes. False accusations. Fathers and sons. Firearms. Firing squads. Gunshot wounds. Hideouts. Impersonation and imposture. Jealousy. Mayors. Monterey (CA). Parties. Physicians. Pledges. Ranches. Saloons. Soldiers.*

Note: The film's opening title card reads: "Monogram Pictures Corporation Present The Cisco Kid in *Robin Hood of Monterey*." Although Ray Jones and Jack Hendricks are listed in a *HR* news item as cast members, their participation in the final film has not been confirmed. An Apr 1947 *LAEx* news item noted that actor Jack La Rue agreed to appear in the picture after losing a bid for a Los Angeles city councilmen's seat. Although modern sources credit Gilbert Roland with additional dialogue on a previous "Cisco Kid" film, *Robin Hood of Monterey* marked the first time that he received an onscreen writing credit. For additional information on "The Cisco Kid" series, see the entry above for *The Cisco Kid* and consult the Series Index.

DV 7 Aug 1947. HR 24 Apr 1947, p. 2. HR 25 Apr 1947, p. 12, 16. HR 9 May 1947, p. 20. HR 7 Aug 1947, p. 3. IFJ 10 May 1947, p. 44. LAEx 19 Apr 1947. MPHPD 13 Sep 1947.

ROBOT MURDER see **THE SCARLET CLUE**

ROCK ISLAND TRAIL (Native Americans)

Republic Picture Corp. *Dist* Republic Pictures Corp. 19 May **1950**; World premiere in Rock Island, Moline, East Moline, IL, and Davenport, IA: 20 Apr 1949.; Prod: early Sep—mid-Oct 1949 [©Republic Pictures Corp.; 9 May 1950; LP108]. Sd (RCA Sound System); col (Trucolor). 8,082 ft. 90 min. Passed by the National Board of Review. PCA cert no. 14223.

Pres HERBERT J. YATES. *Assoc prod* Paul Malvern. *Dir* Joseph Kane. [*Asst dir* Richard Moder]. *Scr* James Edward Grant. *Dir of photog* Jack Marta. *Spec eff* Howard Lydecker and Theodore Lydecker. *Optical eff* Consolidated Film Industries. *Art dir* Frank Arrigo. *Film ed* Arthur Roberts. *Set dec* John McCarthy, Jr. and George Milo. *Cost des* Adele Palmer. *Mus dir* R. Dale Butts. *Sd* T. A. Carman and Howard Wilson. *Makeup supv* Bob Mark. *Hair stylist* Peggy Gray. *Asst to assoc prod* Harvey Harry. [*Tech adv* William B. Hayes].

Song(s): "Rock Island Trail," music and lyrics by William Roy.

Source: Based on the novel *A Yankee Dared: A Romance of Our Railroads* by Frank J. Nevins (Chicago, 1933).

Cast: [Forrest Tucker (*Reed Loomis*)], [Adele Mara (*Constance Strong*)], [Adrian Booth (*Aleeta*)], [Bruce Cabot (*Kirby Morrow*)], [Chill Wills (*Hogger*)], [Barbra Fuller (*Annabelle Marsh*)], [Grant Withers (*David Strong*)], [Jeff Corey (*Abe Lincoln*)], [Roy Barcroft (*Barnes*)], [Pierre Watkin (*Major*)], [Valentine Perkins (*Annette*)], [Jimmy Hunt (*Stinky*)], [Olin Howlin (*Saloon keeper*)], [Sam Flint (*Mayor*)], [John Holland (*Major Porter*)], [Kate Drain Lawson (*Mrs. McCoy*)], [Dick Elliott (*Conductor*)], [Emory Parnell (*Senator Wells*)], [Billy Wilkerson (*Lakin*)], [Tex Terry (*McIntyre*)], [Larry Steers (*Colonel Cavenport*)], [Billy Mitchell (*Carriage driver*)], [Clarence Brooks (*Butler*)], [George Taylor (*Employee*)], [Frank Jaquet (*Mr. Smith*)], [Dick Curtis (*Barton*)], [Ralph Moody (*Keokuk*)], [Alex Gerry (*Masters*)], [Charles J. Conrad (*Bailiff*)], [Everett Glass (*Judge*)], [Kathryn Sheldon (*Old lady*)], [Edward Clark (*Old gentleman*)], [Dick Alexander, William Haade (*Henchmen*)], [Steve Darrell (*Stagecoach driver*)], [Noble Johnson (*Bent Creek*)], [Jerry Miley (*Surveyor*)], [I. Stanford Jolley, James Flavin (*Card players*)], [Don Summers (*Mail carrier*)], [John Compton (*Trooper*)], [Jack Pennick (*Sergeant*)], [Sam Flint (*Lieutenant*)], [Monte Montague (*Yard boss*)], [Emil Sitka, George Barton (*Firemen*)], [Norman Rainey (*Minister*)], [Frank McFarland (*Gentleman*)], [Charles Morton (*McCarthy*)], [Stanley Andrews], [Harmon Stevens], [Marshall Reed], [Emmett Lynn].

Historical, Drama. [*Print viewed*]. While riding onboard a stagecoach in Illinois, two young women, Constance Strong and Annabelle Marsh, discuss an upcoming race in which a stage line, a steamboat line and a rail line will compete for a lucrative mail contract. When they arrive at their destination, the town of Rock Island, Constance and Annabelle are greeted by Reed Loomis, chief engineer of the Chicago and Rock Island Rail Lines. Although Constance is engaged to the owner of the steamboat line, Kirby Morrow, she agrees to meet Reed for a walk in the moonlight. Later, Reed's mechanic reports that two of Morrow's men tried to bribe him to sabotage the train's engine so that they would lose the race. Reed then rushes to Morrow's estate, where a party is in progress, and accuses him of attempted bribery. Eager to protect his reputation, Morrow challenges Reed to a duel, and when one of Morrow's guests

reminds them that dueling is illegal in Illinois, Morrow invites Reed to take one of his boats up the Mississippi River to a state where dueling is still legal. Once they arrive, Reed and Morrow decide to enjoy a drink at the saloon. Morrow then asks Reed to select a weapon for the duel, and he grabs a couple of mops from a nearby bucket. They begin slapping each other with the wet mops, but are forced to declare a draw when their weapons are reduced to splintered mop handles. They return home, and early the next day, the race begins. The rail line wins by a wide margin, after which Constance's father David hosts a party at his estate. At the party, Constance first breaks her engagement to Morrow and then hints to Reed that she intends to marry him someday. Although he appears to be in love with her, Reed responds teasingly, saying that he would never marry a wealthy woman because they henpeck their husbands. Later, onboard a train traveling to the end of the track, where workers are continuously laying new track, Constance meets a passenger named Aleeta. The elegant, French-educated Aleeta explains that she is the granddaughter of the Indian peacemaker Keokuk. When the train arrives at "end-of-track," Aleeta, who has changed into her native dress, is escorted home by a band of Indian braves. Later, Morrow ignites one of Reed's boats, which is carrying a load of explosives, and sets it drifting toward a nearby bridge, where it explodes. Morrow is convicted of arson, and sometime later, Reed and Aleeta meet in the wilderness. She offers to send her braves to help his workers at end-of-track and then boldly tries to seduce him. Although he rebuffs her advances, Aleeta keeps her promise to send her braves the next morning. Later, Aleeta sees Morrow chasing Reed on horseback and decides to follow them. When Morrow shoots Reed's horse, Aleeta gives him one of her coach horses so that he can escape. Later, Aleeta sees Morrow's men attacking the workers at end-of-track, and after summoning her braves to help them, is fatally shot. Later, with peace and order restored, the smitten Reed capitulates and marries his beloved Constance. *Indians of North America. Railroad companies. Railroad engineers. Romantic rivalry. Arson. Bridges. Chases. Chicago and Rock Island Railroad. Clothes. Construction workers. Contracts. Convicts. Duels. Engagements. Estates. Explosions. Fathers and daughters. Honor. Illinois. Mechanics. Parties. Pledges. Racing. Rescues. Saloons. Stagecoaches. Steamboats. Traveling companions. United States–History–Social life and customs.*

Note: The following written prologue appears in the onscreen credits: "The period trains and equipment seen in this picture are used by courtesy of the Rock Island Lines and were loaned by the Baltimore and Ohio Railroads, and the Railroad and Locomotive Historical Society, Inc." The opening credits also include a dedication to "the men and women who devoted their lives to developing and perfecting the railroads of our country and to those carrying on that vast public service." According to *HR*, this film was made on location in McAllister, OK, where Republic Studios was granted the right to use an abandoned stretch of track belonging to the Rock Island Rail Lines. This same publication reported on 12 Apr 1950 that a special section of the Rock Island's Golden State Limited would be used to commemorate the film's premiere. Modern sources add Jack Pennick to the cast.

Box 6 May 1950. *DV* 28 Apr 1950, p. 3. *FD* 28 Apr 1950, p. 16. *HR* 2 Aug 1949, p. 4. *HR* 2 Sep 1949, p. 11. *HR* 7 Oct 1949, p. 11. *HR* 28 Apr 1950, p. 3-4. *MPHPD* 6 May 1950, p. 286-7. *NYT* 5 Jun 1950, p. 19. *Var* 3 May 1950, p. 6.

A ROCKET AND FOUR STARS *see* **I AIM AT THE STARS; THE WERNHER VON BRAUN STORY**

ROCKIN' THE BLUES (African Americans)
Austin Productions; Fritz Pollard Associates. *Dist* Jewel Productions, Inc. **1956**; World premiere in Harlem: Nov 1956. Sd (Western Electric Recording); b&w. 7 reels, 5,870 ft. 66, 68 or 70 min.

Entire prod staged by Irvin C. Miller. [*Exec prod* Fritz Pollard]. *Dir* Arthur Rosenblum. *Photog* Jack Etra. *Mus supv* Andy Kirk. *Arr* Teacho Wiltshire. *Sd* Irving Korman. *Prod mgr* Henry Van Kirk. *Prod asst* Joan Hardy.

Song(s): "Oozing Down," "Having a Ball," "Go! Go! Go!" "First, Last and Only Girl," "You May Not Know," "Army Life," "Lazy," "Fast Moving Mama," "TV's the Thing," "They Raided the Joint," "Owee Baby," "Mambo Boogie," "Rock 'n' Roll is the Latest Fad," "Walking and Talking," "High Flying Baby" and other songs, composers undetermined.

Cast: Mantan Moreland, F. E. Miller, Connie Carroll, Harptones, Linda Hopkins, Wanderers, Pearl Woods, Hurricanes, Miller Sisters, Reese La Rue, Marilyn Bennett, Elyce Roberts, Lee Lynn, The Cuban Dancers, introduced by Hal Jackson, [Billy Washington], [Toni Harris], [Anita Turner], [Teacho Wiltshire Hot Band].

African American, Variety, Musical. [*Print viewed*]. Two black women are attracted by a theater marquee that announces, "Now playing, Rock 'n' Roll Revue." They enter the theater, and soon afterward, the show begins. New York disc jockey Hal Jackson first introduces Connie Carroll, then "the singing, swinging Wanderers," a male vocal quartet. Outside the theater, meanwhile, two men push their vegetable cart up to the building, where they, too, are attracted by the marquee. As Jackson introduces the five Miller Sisters inside, the vegetable peddlers, who, although penniless, are intent upon seeing beautiful showgirls, try to enter the theater but are immediately thrown out. The more persistent of the two sits by a theater window, his leg tucked underneath him, hoping to catch a glimpse of the girls inside. After the next number, a well-dressed woman walks past the building. Seeing the peddler, she assumes he has lost his leg and gives him some coins. Surprised and pleased, the man mumbles, "This is a great hustle!" and continues to elicit sympathy and money from passersby. The show continues with vocalist Linda Hopkins, followed by the Wanderers. In front of the theater, the two men discuss their lack of money, which leads to an argument about numbers. While one of the men has trouble distinguishing one number from another, the other peddler tries to prove that seven goes into twenty-eight thirteen times. Next, Jackson introduces the Hurricanes, a male vocal quartet, and during their performance, one of the peddlers sneaks backstage and tells a pretty dancer that he recognizes her from the film *Anna Lucasta*. In turn, she identifies him as "Birmingham" from the "Charlie Chan" pictures. Soon, a policeman enters and begins looking for the intruder. On stage, Pearl Woods performs, and just before Connie Carroll is re-introduced, the peddler excitedly tells her how much he admires her. After a female dancer performs to an instrumental tune, the peddler is ejected from the theater, but immediately starts thinking of a way to use his book on jiu-jitsu to get back in. While the Harptones sing their number inside, the peddler tries his missing leg routine again. After the second peddler indignantly sends him away with the exclamation, "You're robbing people!" he tries the routine himself. Linda Hopkins performs a number and then introduces The Cuban Dancers. Police chase the peddlers away from the theater as the Harptones, the final act of the show, sing their rock 'n roll numbers. *African Americans. Musical revues. Peddlers and peddling. Blues music. Confidence men. Dancing. Disc jockeys. New York City. Police. Show girls. Theaters.*

Note: Although the statement "Copyright Austin Productions" appears on the film, no copyright registration was made. Although the picture was not listed in release charts, it was reviewed in the *Amsterdam News (New York)* in Sep 1956. According to modern sources, however, the film was first released in 1955. Fritz Pollard Associates was a public relations firm. The *Exh* review noted that the film would "probably be best appreciated in theatres catering to the Negro."

Amsterdam News (New York) 29 Sep 1956. *Exh* 3 Apr 1957, p. 4310. *LATribune* 21 Nov 1956. *Var* 3 Oct 1956, p. 26.

ROCKY (Scottish Americans)
Norwalk Productions; A Lindsley Parsons Production. *Dist* Monogram Pictures Corp. 7 Mar **1948**; Los Angeles opening: 23 Apr 1948; Prod: late Jul–late Aug 1947 [©Monogram Pictures Corp.; 21 Feb 1948; LP1558]. Sd (Western Electric Recording); b&w. 6,897 ft. 76 min. PCA cert no. 12699.

Assoc prod Roddy McDowall and Ace Herman. *Dir* Phil Karlson. *Asst dir* Wesley Barry. *Scr* Jack DeWitt. *Orig story* George Wallace Sayre. *Addl dial* Tim Ryan and W. Scott Darling. *Photog* William Sickner. [*Cam op* John Martin]. [*Stills* Talmadge Morrison]. *Spec eff* Ray Mercer. *Art dir* Dave Milton. *Ed* Robert Warwick, Jr. *Mus dir* Edward J. Kay. *Rec* Tom Lambert. *Makeup* Harry Ross. *Stylist* Lorraine MacLean. [Ilona Vas]. [*Grip* George Booker].

Cast: RODDY McDOWALL [(*Chris Hammond*)], Gale Sherwood [(*Ellen Forrester*)], Nita Hunter [(*Kathy Forrester*)], Edgar Barrier [(*John Hammond*)], Jonathan Hale [(*Forrester*)], Irving Bacon [(*Bert Hillman*)], William Ruhl [(*Drew*)], Claire Whitney [(*Hortense*)], John Alvin [(*Jack*)], [Rags, as *Rocky*)].

Animal, Teenage, Drama. [*Print viewed*]. While fishing, Scottish-American house painter John Hammond and his teenaged son Chris encounter Bert Hillman, a ranch foreman hunting for a wild dog that killed one of his sheep. When Hillman and his ranch hand find the dog, they kill it and one of its puppies. Seeing that one of the dog's puppies was left untouched, Chris and his father adopt it and name it Rocky. Though John believes that dogs born to sheep-killers will

become sheep-killers, he gives his son a chance to raise the dog and prove otherwise. Chris spends his days training Rocky until the dog is full-grown and domesticated. One day, Rocky accidentally knocks clothes belonging to Chris' neighbor, Kathy Forrester, into a lake. When Kathy finds Chris holding her wet clothes, she thinks he stole them as a prank and pushes him into the water. Kathy eventually realizes that it was the dog who was responsible and apologizes to Chris. Kathy falls in love with Chris and invites him to dinner, but Ellen, her older sister, soon vies for his attention. Ellen becomes especially enamored of Chris when Kathy tells her that his father is a painter. Kathy, however, does nothing to correct Ellen's assumption that Chris's father is an artist. When Chris arrives at the Forresters', he is overwhelmed by Ellen's beauty as she descends the staircase in an alluring dress. Ellen and her father, who are both interested in art, are impressed with Chris's "artist" father, but Chris believes they are making fun of him and leaves. Humiliated, Chris asks his father to take him back to their ancestral home in Edinburgh, Scotland. Meanwhile, local ranchers, suspecting that Rocky is responsible for a recent rash of sheep killings, begin to organize a search for him. Chris overhears Hillman tell John about the ranchers' concerns, and worries that Rocky will fall victim to their vengeance. Kathy later apologizes to Chris in a letter, and the two meet at the lake, where Chris tells her, on an oath of secrecy, that Rocky's mother was a sheep killer. When Ellen steals Chris away from Kathy as her date for an upcoming picnic, Kathy sends an urgent telegram to Ellen's former sweetheart, Jack Arnold, who lives in Arizona, instructing him to return to Ellen at once. Kathy's plan succeeds, and she ends up taking Chris to the picnic. During the picnic, Rocky attacks the dog responsible for the sheep killings, and returns to Chris covered with blood. Chris sadly concludes that the blood is evidence that Rocky is the sheep killer, and decides to turn him over to Hillman. Things look bad for Rocky until the real sheep-killer, a dog that resembles him and that came from the same litter, is found. Hillman apologizes to Chris for mistaking his dog for the killer, and Rocky returns to the arms of his loving owner. *Adolescents. Dogs. Fathers and sons. House painters. Romantic rivalry. Sisters. Cooks. Domesticity. Fishing. Hunters. Jealousy. Lakes. Picnicking. Ranchers. Rescues. Scottish Americans. Secrets. Sheep. Shepherds.*

Note: Exteriors were shot at Bridgeport (CA.) The *HR* review noted that this was the "first film on which Roddy McDowall is credited with a co-associate producer chore."

Box 14 Aug 1948. *DV* 26 Apr 1948, p. 3. *HR* 26 Apr 1948, p. 3 *MPHPD* 5 Jun 1948, p. 4189.

ROCKY MOUNTAIN (Native Americans)

Warner Bros. Pictures, Inc.; A Warner Bros.—First National Picture. *Dist* Warner Bros. Pictures, Inc. 11 Nov **1950** [©Warner Bros. Pictures, Inc.; 13 Oct 1950; LP404]. Sd (RCA Sound System); b&w. 7,458 ft. 83 min.

Prod William Jacobs. *Dir* William Keighley. [*Asst dir* Frank Mattison]. *Scr* Winston Miller and Alan LeMay. *Story* Alan LeMay. *Dir of photog* Ted McCord. *Art dir* Stanley Fleischer. *Film ed* Rudi Fehr. [*Set des* L. S. Edwards]. *Ward* Marjorie Best. *Orch* Murray Cutter. *Mus* Max Steiner. *Sd* Stanley Jones.

Cast: ERROL FLYNN [(*Lafe Barstow*)], Patrice Wymore [(*Johanna Carter*)], Scott Forbes [(*Lt. Rickey*)], Guinn Williams [(*Pap Dennison*)], Dick Jones [(*Jimmy Wheat*)], Howard Petrie [(*Cole Smith*)], Slim Pickens [(*Plank*)], Chubby Johnson [(*Gil Craigie*)], Buzz Henry [(*Kip Waterston*)], Sheb Wooley [(*Kay Rawlins*)], Peter Coe [(*Pierre Duchesne*)], Rush Williams [(*Jonas Weatherby*)], [Steve Dunhill (*Asb*)], [Alex Sharpe (*Barnes*)], [Yakima Canutt (*Ryan*)], [Nakai Snez (*Mandog*)].

Western. [*Print viewed*]. On 26 Mar 1865, a detachment of Confederate cavalry, led by Captain Lafe Barstow, crosses the state line into California. The soldiers are under secret orders from General Robert E. Lee to meet with outlaw Cole Smith, who allegedly commands 500 men, in order to persuade him to bring them into the war on the side of the South. The rendezvous point is Rocky Mountain, also known as Ghost Mountain. When Barstow and his seven men—Kip Waterston, Pierre Duchesne, Pap Dennison, Kay Rawlins, Jimmy Wheat, Jonas Weatherby and Plank—arrive, Smith is waiting for them. From their vantage point on the mountain, the men see a war party of Indians attack a stagecoach. Barstow's men ride to the rescue and return with Gil Craigie, the driver, and his passenger, Johanna Carter, who is on the way to join her fiancé, Union soldier Lt.

Rickey. That night, the Indians burn the stage, and the following morning, a detachment of four Union soldiers and three Shoshone scouts examine the ashes. Barstow and his men capture the soldiers, who include Rickey. From them, Barstow learns that the Union knows about their presence in California. Smith now leaves to round up his men, planning to return in two days. In the meantime, Craigie learns that the scouts are really a chief and his two sons. He tells Barstow his belief that they will escape and return with their tribe. That night, while Jimmy is on watch, the Indians escape. The soldiers kill two of them, but the chief evades their bullets. In the morning, Rickey suggests that he take Johanna to a nearby garrison before the Indians arrive. Barstow, however, hopes that Smith's men will come before the Indians do and rejects the suggestion. That night, Rickey escapes, leaving Johanna behind. The following morning, the men find Smith's riderless horse and realize that he has been killed. Now that the men know no help is coming, they decide to engage the Indians in battle to distract them while Johanna and Craigie escape. Billy leaves his small dog Spot with Johanna, but shortly after the men ride away, Spot wriggles free and runs after his friend. A fierce battle ensues between the Indians and the greatly outnumbered soldiers. During the fight, the Union cavalry reaches Johanna's hiding place, and she tells Rickey what has happened. The cavalry rides to the rescue, but they are too late; all the men have been killed. In their honor, Rickey raises the rebel flag on top of Rocky Mountain and the troops salute it. *Confederate States of America. Army. Indians of North America. United States–History–Civil War, 1861-1865. United States. Army. California. Dogs. Outlaws. Rescues. Romance. Self-sacrifice. Stagecoach drivers.*

Note: The film's working title was *Ghost Mountain*. *HR* news items add the following information about the production: Ronald Reagan was considered for the lead, and Lauren Bacall was suspended for the sixth time in six years when she refused to work in this film. Shortly after filming, Patrice Wyman became Errol Flynn's fourth wife. This was the first Warner Bros. film since the war to be entirely shot on location. It was filmed in Gallup, New Mexico.

Box 7 Oct 1950. *DV* 3 Oct 1950, p. 3. *FD* 4 Oct 1950, p. 4. *HR* 4 Nov 1948, p. 3. *HR* 10 May 1950, p. 3. *HR* 12 May 1950, p. 2. *HR* 3 Oct 1950, p. 3. *MPHPD* 7 Oct 1950, p. 509. *NYT* 4 Nov 1950, p. 13. *Var* 4 Oct 1950, p. 6.

ROGUE OF THE RIO GRANDE see LUCKY CISCO KID

LE ROI S'ENNUIE see ECHEC AU ROI

ROLL THUNDER ROLL! (Latino, Native Americans)

Equity Pictures, Inc. *Dist* Eagle Lion Films, Inc.; controlled by Pathe Industries, Inc. 7 Apr **1949**; Prod: late Oct—early Nov 1948 at Motion Picture Center [©Pathe Industries, Inc.; 23 Mar 1949; LP2433]. Sd (Glenn Glen Sound Recording); col (Cinecolor). 6 reels, 5,256 ft. 57-60 min. PCA cert no. 13564.

Series: Red Ryder.

Prod Jerry Thomas. *Assoc prod* Lincoln A. Widder. *Dir* Lewis D. Collins. *Asst dir* Ralph Slosser. *Dial dir* Gloria Welsch. *Orig scr* Paul Franklin. *Dir of photog* Gilbert Warrenton. *Cinecolor consultant* Henry J. Staudigl. *Film ed* Frank Baldridge. *Set dec* Vin Taylor. *Dir of ward* Don Wakeling. *Mus comp and dir* Ralph Stanley. *Mus supv* David Chudnow. *Sd eng* Earl Snyder. *Dir of makeup* Vern Murdock. *Tech dir* Fred W. Kline.

Source: Based on the comic strip "Red Ryder" by Fred Harman (1938—1964), by special arrangement with Stephen Slesinger.

Cast: Jim Bannon (*Red Ryder*), Little Brown Jug (*Little Beaver*), Emmett Lynn (*Buckskin*), Marin Sais (*Duchess*), I. Stanford Jolley [(*El Conejo*)], Nancy Gates [(*Carol Loomis*)], Glenn Strange [(*Ace Hanlon*)], Lee Morgan [("*Happy*" *Loomis*)], Lane Bradford [(*Wolf*)], Steve Pendleton [(*Marshal Bill Faugh*)], Charles Stevens [(*Josh Culvert*)], William Fawcett [(*Felipe*)], Dorothy Latta [(*Dorothy Culvert*)], Joe Green [(*Pat*)], [Rocky Shahan (*Red's double*)], [Carol Henry (*Henchman*)], [George Chesebro (*Ben Garson*)], [Jack O'Shea (*Bartender*)].

Western. [*Print viewed*]. Cowboy Red Ryder rides into a Texas town, where he is greeted by his Indian sidekick, Little Beaver, his aunt, The Duchess, and his friend, Buckskin. Red then finds his friend, Carol Loomis, at her office and tells her that Josh Culvert's ranch has just been raided. Carol tells him that he can find Marshal Bill Faugh, her fiancé, at a barbershop operated by her uncle Happy. At the barbershop, Red shows Bill a pair of round buckles called conchas, which he found at Josh's ranch, as well as at the sites of nine previous raids. Red says that the conchas are the trademark of El Conejo, a bandit from California, who has never been known to operate in Texas. At his Silver Dollar Bar, meanwhile, outlaw leader Ace Hanlon

shares a drink with his henchman, Wolf. Just then, El Conejo enters the bar with his partner, Felipe, and threatens to kill Ace, whose gang has been framing him for the raids. Suddenly, Red enters and arrests El Conejo and Felipe. Red, Buckskin and Little Beaver take the prisoners to the jail, but along the way, Buckskin develops a cramp in his back and is forced to stop. Red tells Little Beaver to wait with Buckskin, while he continues on with El Conejo and Felipe. A short distance away, however, El Conejo calls to his men, who suddenly appear and disarm Red. After Felipe and the men leave, El Conejo takes Red to a nearby cabin to shoot him. Inside, El Conejo tells Red that he can prove his innocence, so Red persuades him to turn himself in so that they can catch the real culprits. When Ace and Happy see Red taking El Conejo to jail, they decide to break him out so that they can continue to frame him for their raids. Later, Ace's men don masks and attack Buckskin, who has been assigned to guard El Conejo, knocking him unconscious. When Red and Bill discover the jailbreak, they round up a posse. Carol, who does not realize that her uncle is secretly involved with the gang, tells him that Red plans to transfer El Conejo to the county jail. Later, Red and The Duchess dress Buckskin up to look like El Conejo and take him to the jail. After Happy tells Ace about Red's plan to move El Conejo, the gang chases Buckskin, believing that he is El Conejo. Later, Happy catches Red searching through the desk drawers inside his shop, but Red claims that he came in for a shave. While Happy is shaving him, Red reveals that he found the conchas inside his drawer. After Red pulls his gun, Ace enters and begins fighting with him. Happy then draws his own gun, but Buckskin enters and shoots it out of his hand, while Red knocks Ace unconscious. After the gang is arrested, Bill and Carol are able to turn their attention toward their marriage plans. *Barbers and barbershops. Frame-ups. Marshals. Outlaws. Robbery. Aunts. Bars. Cabins. Chases. Engagements. False arrests. Impersonation and imposture. Indians of North America. Jailbreaks. Kidnapping. Mexican Americans. Nieces. Posses. Ranches. Texas. Threats.*

Note: The working title of this film was *Counselor at Gun-Law.* For additional information on the "Red Ryder" series, please consult the Series Index and see the entry below for *Tucson Raiders.*

Box 16 Jul 1949. *DV* 11 Dec 1950, p. 4. *FD* 16 May 1949, p. 6. *HR* 29 Oct 1948, p. 14. *HR* 11 Dec 1950, p. 4. *MPHPD* 14 May 1949, p. 4610. *Var* 11 May 1949, p. 6.

ROMANCE DE CALIFORNIA *see* **LA CRUZ Y LA ESPADA**

ROMANCE FOR ROMA *see* **SET FREE**

ROMANCE IN CHICAGO *see* **VIVA CISCO KID**

ROMANCE IN MANHATTAN (Czech Americans)
RKO Radio Pictures, Inc.; A Pandro S. Berman Production. *Dist* RKO Radio Pictures, Inc. 11 Jan **1935**; Prod: 14 Sep—19 Oct 1934 [©RKO Radio Pictures, Inc.; 11 Jan 1935; LP5255]. Sd (RCA Photophone System); b&w. 8 reels. 75 or 78 min. PCA cert no. 389.

Dir Stephen Roberts. [*Asst dir* Dewey Starkey]. *Scr* Jane Murfin and Edward Kaufman. *Story* Norman Krasna and Don Hartman. [*Contr to scr* Norman Krasna]. *Photog* Nick Musuraca. *Photog eff* Vernon Walker. *Art dir* Van Nest Polglase and Charles Kirk. *Ed* Jack Hively. *Mus dir* Al Colombo. *Rec* John Tribby. [*Research* Elizabeth McGaffey].

Cast: FRANCIS LEDERER [(*Karel Novak*)], GINGER ROGERS [(*Sylvia Dennis*)], Arthur Hohl [(*Halsey J. Pander*)], Jimmy Butler [(*Frank Dennis*)], J. Farrell MacDonald [(*Officer Murphy*)], Helen Ware [(*Miss Anthrop*)], Eily Malyon [(*Miss Evans*)], Lillian Harmer [(*Landlady*)], Donald Meek [(*The minister*)], Sidney Toler [(*Police sergeant*)], Oscar Apfel [(*The judge*)], Reginald Barlow [(*Chief customs inspector*)], [Guinn Williams], [Harold Goodwin], [Spencer Charters].

Comedy-drama. [*Print viewed*]. When Czechoslovakian immigrant and would-be farmer Karel Novak arrives at Ellis Island, he discovers that the entrance fee has been raised to $200, $142 more than he has in his wallet. Hauled back to the steamship for deportation, Karel jumps overboard and swims ashore but loses his money on the dock. Penniless, he wanders the Manhattan streets until he meets Sylvia Dennis, a pretty nineteen-year-old chorus girl who catches him stealing doughnuts from the rehearsal hall. Sylvia takes Karel to her apartment and introduces him to her young brother Frank, whom she cares for and supports. After selling newspapers with Frank, Karel, who sleeps on Sylvia's rooftop each night, gets a job as a cab driver and dreams of becoming a millionaire so that he can marry Sylvia. When Frank is caught for truancy, the presiding judge orders him to live at the Benton Institution until the now

unemployed Sylvia gets married. Desperate to help Sylvia but worried about his illegal alien status, Karel contacts Halsey J. Pander, a crooked lawyer who secretly reports him to the authorities for money. On the day that Frank is taken away, Karel is picked up and sent to the police station with Sylvia. Although Pander insists that Karel be deported, Murphy, a sympathetic policeman, rallies his fellow officers to thwart the shyster and make Karel a citizen and Sylvia's husband before the morning deadline. *Chorus girls. Citizenship. Czechoslovakian Americans. Immigrants. New York City. Poverty. Brothers and sisters. Finance–Personal. Judges. Lawyers. Marriage. News vendors. Orphans. Police. Steamboats.*

Note: According to the *SAB,* the script of this film was developed from an original idea "proposed" by Don Hartman and a "screen story" by Norman Krasna. A plot synopsis in *MPH's* "In the Cutting Room" differs considerably from the actual screen story. In the pre-release synopsis, the Francis Lederer character is a young Balkan shepherd who, after being fleeced of his money by a crook selling sheep in Central Park, becomes a star singing waiter, marries a girl from the country, loses her, then gets her back the American way, through divorce. According to a *HR* news item, director Stephen Roberts replaced Sidney Lanfield, who had been replaced on the 1933 RKO film *Melody Cruise* by Mark Sandrich, who was originally slated to direct this production. The *NYT* review mentions the use of the Dunning process of rear projection in this film. Modern sources credit Mel Berns with makeup and John Miehle as still photographer and add the following additional cast members: Christian Rub (*Immigrant*), Frank Sheridan (*Customs inspector*), Irving Bacon (*Counterman*), Andy Clyde (*Scottish liquor store owner*).

DV 13 Sep 1934, p. 1. *DV* 19 Oct 1934, p. 3. *DV* 5 Nov 1934, p. 3. *FD* 21 Nov 1934, p. 11. *HF* 22 Sep 1934, p. 8. *HR* 1 Jun 1933, p. 1. *HR* 20 Jul 1933, p. 4. *HR* 5 Nov 1934, p. 3. *MPH* 13 Oct 1934, pp. 45-46. *MPH* 1 Dec 1934, pp. 38-39. *NYT* 18 Jan 1935, p. 29. *Var* 22 Jan 1935, p. 14.

ROMANCE IN NEW YORK *see* **VIVA CISCO KID**

ROMANCE OF THE RIO GRANDE (Latino)
Fox Film Corp. *Dist* Fox Film Corp. 17 Nov **1929**; New York premiere: 8 Nov 1929 [©Fox Film Corp.; 11 Nov 1929; LP845]. Sd (Movietone); b&w. 10 reels, 8,460 ft. 94 min. [Also Si; 7,757].

Pres William Fox. *Dir* Alfred Santell. *Asst to the dir* Marty Santell. *Scen* Marion Orth. *Photog* Arthur Edeson. *Film ed* Paul Weatherwax. *Set des* Joseph Wright. *Sd* Frank Pierce.

Song(s): "You'll Find Your Answer in My Eyes," "Ride On Vaquero" and "When My Toreador Starts To Snore," music by Abel Baer, lyrics by L. Wolfe Gilbert.

Source: Based on the novel *Conquistador* by Katharine Fullerton Gerould (New York, 1923).

Cast: Warner Baxter (*Pablo Wharton Cameron*), Mona Maris (*Manuelita*), Mary Duncan (*Carlotta*), Antonio Moreno (*Juan*), Robert Edeson (*Don Fernando*), Agostino Borgato (*Vincente*), Albert Roccardi (*Padre Miguel*), Solidad Jiminez (*Catalina*), Majel Coleman (*Dorry Wayne*), Charles Byer (*Dick Rivers*), Merrill McCormick (*Luca*).

Western. Pablo, the son of a Mexican mother and an American father, hates his grandfather, Don Fernando, for disowning his mother. As the supervisor of a railroad construction gang, he is injured in an attack by bandits and brought to the ranch of his grandfather. Following his recovery, Pablo plans to leave, though he has fallen in love with Manuelita. Then, a clash develops between Pablo and Juan, who has designs on becoming the family heir. Finally, touched by Don Fernando's remorse at his treatment of his daughter, Pablo is reconciled to him and finds happiness with the girl. *Family relationships. Grandfathers. Mexican Americans. Mexico. Railroads. Ranchers.*

ROMANCE OF THE RIO GRANDE (Latino)
Twentieth Century-Fox Film Corp. *Dist* Twentieth Century-Fox Film Corp. 17 Jan **1941**; New York opening: 24 Dec 1940; Prod: early Sep—2 Oct 1940 [©Twentieth Century-Fox Film Corp.; 17 Jan 1941; LP10398]. Sd (RCA Sound System); b&w. 6,555 ft. 72-73 min. PCA cert no. 6712.

Series: The Cisco Kid.

Exec prod Sol M. Wurtzel. *Dir* Herbert I. Leeds. [*Asst dir* Charles Hall]. *Scr* Harold Buchman and Samuel G. Engel. *Dir of photog* Charles Clarke. *Art dir* Richard Day and Chester Gore. *Film ed* Fred Allen. *Set dec* Thomas Little. *Cost* Herschel. *Mus dir* Emil Newman. *Sd* George Leverett and Harry M. Leonard. [*Prod mgr* William Koenig].

Song(s): "You'll Find Your Answer in My Eyes" and "Ride on Vaquero," music by Abel Baer, words by L. Wolfe Gilbert.

Source: Based on the novel *Conquistador* by Katherine Fullerton Gerould (New York, 1923), and suggested by the character "The Cisco Kid" created by O. Henry.

Cast: Cesar Romero (*Cisco Kid/[Carlos Hernandez]*), Patricia Morison (*Rosita*), Lynne Roberts (*Maria*), Ricardo Cortez (*Ricardo*), Chris-Pin Martin (*Gordito*), Aldrich Bowker (*Padre [Martinez]*), Joseph McDonald (*Carlos Hernandez*), Pedro de Cordoba (*Don Fernando [de Vega]*), Inez Palange (*Mama Lopez*), Raphael Bennett (*Carver*), Trevor Bardette (*Manuel*), Tom London (*Marshal*), Eva Puig (*Marta*), [Francis Ford (*Stage driver*)].

Western. [*Print viewed*]. Don Fernando de Vega, the proud and elderly owner of Rancho Santa Margarita, the oldest and wealthiest Spanish-owned ranch in Arizona, realizes he may die soon. Don Fernando knows his nephew Ricardo is hungry to gain control of the ranch, but does not trust him, so he sends to Granada, Spain, for his grandson, Carlos Hernandez, whose mother Don Fernando exiled for marrying against his will. Carlos' stagecoach is attacked near the ranch, and both the driver and Carlos are shot. After the assailants depart, "The Cisco Kid," an infamous bandit, and his companion Gordito, search the carriage for valuables. They discover that Carlos is an exact double for Cisco, and as he is still alive, they take him to Mama Lopez, who removes the bullet. Upon finding the letter from Don Fernando, which promises the ranch to Carlos, Cisco decides to impersonate Carlos and rob the de Vega family of their heirlooms while Carlos convalesces. When Cisco, as Carlos, arrives at the de Vega ranch, Ricardo and Rosita are shocked to see "Carlos" alive, as they hired cowboy Carver to assassinate him in order to gain control of the ranch. Cisco is warmly received by Don Fernando, and is enamored of both Maria, Don Fernando's youthful goddaughter, and the spirited and beautiful Rosita. In the evening, Cisco tries to romance Maria, but she rebuffs him because she feels he should be more concerned about the cattle raids that Ricardo says are led by The Cisco Kid. He later overhears Ricardo and Carver in conversation and realizes that Ricardo hired Carver to kill Carlos, and that he will probably try again. Cisco grows fond of Don Fernando, and when Don Fernando states that he is pleased his grandson will someday own the ranch, Cisco promises that he will. One night an unseen assailant tries to kill Cisco, but misses, and when Don Fernando emerges from his room, he is bludgeoned by the escaping assailant. On his deathbed, Don Fernando states his desire that Carlos run the ranch and marry Rosita. Cisco is deeply moved by Don Fernando's death and, abandoning his plans of robbery, decides to bring the real Carlos home, but Carlos is still too ill to be moved. Cisco assures Maria that she still has a place in the ranch because he may prefer to marry her, although Rosita has told her she will become a servant if Rosita marries Carlos. At that moment, they overhear Ricardo telling Rosita that by the next day, he will be the owner of the ranch. The next day, Cisco and Gordito accompany Ricardo on the range to inspect the herd, but Cisco is prepared for the worst and insists Ricardo lead them into a canyon. As arranged by Ricardo, the first two men are fired upon by Carver and his men. Ricardo escapes unharmed, while Cisco and Gordito fend off the gunmen. Ricardo and Carver stop at Mama Lopez' for food, where they discover Carlos, who has recovered from his wound. Ricardo pretends to be a friend of Carlos' and tells him that he will arrange for a carriage to bring him to the ranch. Mama Lopez slips out unnoticed to warn Cisco and Gordito, while Ricardo leaves Carver to murder Carlos after he goes for the sheriff. Ricardo and the sheriff identify Cisco, and Ricardo brings a posse home with him. With the help of Mama Lopez, Cisco and Gordito escape, take the posse hostage and leave them without horses miles from town. Cisco goes to Mama Lopez' house and, after saving Carlos from death at the hands of Carver, takes Carver hostage. Cisco introduces himself to Carlos, who is grateful to Cisco, and Cisco informs him that he intends to keep his promise to Don Fernando. Cisco returns to the ranch as Carlos and, by pretending to be still ill, convinces Ricardo and Rosita that he is the true Carlos. He tells them that Cisco was arrested and Carver was shot at Mama Lopez' by the posse. When they are alone, Maria, believing she is talking to Carlos, reveals that she loves Cisco. Cisco kisses her and tells her that the kiss was sent by the bandit. Later, Cisco overhears Rosita and Ricardo arguing. When he knocks at the door, Ricardo hides on the balcony. Cisco tells Rosita that he wishes to marry her the next day, and Rosita happily consents. After he leaves, Ricardo, consumed by jealous anger, threatens Rosita and she shoots him. As he lays dying, Ricardo grabs the gun and shoots

Rosita to death. Cisco smiles when he hears the gunshots, and in the morning, his job done, he and Carlos bid farewell. Cisco and Gordito ride into the desert, while Carlos and Maria pick up where Cisco left off. *Bandits. Doubles. Latino. Impersonation and imposture. Moral reformation. Ranchers. Romance. Arizona. Gunshot wounds. Jealousy. Murder. Priests. Romantic rivalry. Stagecoach drivers. Wards and guardians.*

Note: Although this film was not officially released until Jan 1941, it had a public preview at the Palace Theater in New York on 24 Dec 1940. According to studio publicity contained in the Production Files at the AMPAS Library, Cesar Romero had just recovered from a bout of paratyphoid when he filmed this picture. Nevertheless, he performed all his own riding and stunt work for the film. Fox borrowed Patricia Morison from Paramount for the role of Rosita. The picture was filmed on location at Vasquez Rocks in the Angeles National Forest, and at Chatsworth, CA. Fox also filmed the Katherine Fullerton Gerould novel in 1929 under the same title, starring Warner Baxter and directed by Alfred Santell (see *AFI Catalog of Feature Films, 1921-30*; F2.4677). The 1929 film contained the same two songs as this film. For additional information about the series, consult the Series Index and see entry above for *The Cisco Kid*.

DV 31 Dec 1940, p. 3. *DV* 2 Jan 1941, p. 3. *FD* 3 Jan 1941, p. 7. *HR* 5 Sep 1940, pp. 14-15. *HR* 10 Sep 1940, p. 2. *HR* 3 Oct 1940, p. 2. *HR* 2 Jan 1941, p. 9. *MPH* 21 Jan 1941. *NYT* 25 Dec 1940, p. 33. *Var* 1 Jan 1941, p. 14.

ROMANCE OF THE WEST (Native Americans)

PRC Pictures, Inc. *Dist* Producers Releasing Corp. 20 Mar **1946** [©Producers Releasing Corp.; 10 Feb 1946; LP98]. Sd (Western Electric Mirrophonic Sound); col (Cinecolor). 58 or 60 min. PCA cert no. 11147.

Prod Robert Emmett. *Dir* Robert Emmett. *Asst dir* William L. Nolte and [Harold Knox]. *Orig scr* Frances Kavanaugh. *Dir of photog* Marcel le Picard. *Col supv* W. T. Crespinel. *Art dir* Edward C. Jewell. *Film ed* Hugh Winn. *Set dec* George Montgomery. *Mus dir* Carl Hoefle. *Sd eng* Frank W. Webster. *Dir of makeup* Bud Westmore. *Prod mgr* Raoul Pagel.

Song(s): "Indian Dawn," music and lyrics by J. S. Zamecnik; "Ridin' the Trail to Dreamland," music and lyrics by Sam Franklin; "Love Song of the Waterfall," music and lyrics by Bob Nolan, Bernard Barnes and Carl Winge.

Cast: EDDIE DEAN [(*Eddie Dean*)], Emmett Lynn [(*Ezra*)], Joan Barton [(*Melodie*)], Forrest Taylor [(*Father Sullivan*)], Robert McKenzie [(*Matthews*)], Jerry Jerome [(*Marks*)], Stanley Price [(*Rockwood*)], Chief Thundercloud [(*Chief Eagle Feather*)], Don Reynolds [(*Little Brown Jug*)], Lottie Harrison [(*Miss Twitchell*)], [Rocky Camron (*Chico*)], [Lee Roberts (*Hadley*)], [Don Williams (*Brent*)], [Jack Richardson (*Smithers*)], [Matty Roubert (*Wildhorse*)], [Forbes Murray (*Comm. Wright*)], [Jack O'Shea (*Marshall*)].

Western, with songs. [*Print viewed*]. As some Indians believe that it brings bad luck to leave their ancestral lands, a tribe headed by Chief Eagle Feather is pleased when Eddie Dean, the local Indian agent, and his friend Ezra tell them that the U.S. government has agreed that they can live on their land as long as they keep the peace. Eddie is especially happy to deliver the good news because, as an orphan, he was reared by them. In a nearby town, however, corrupt selectmen Matthews, Marks and Rockwood hire a man named Chico to run the Indians off the land, so that they can mine its silver deposits. Chico in turn hires some renegade Indians, who kill two members of the tribe, leaving a child orphaned. Eddie takes the boy to the mission to be cared for by Father Sullivan and names him Little Brown Jug. Later, Eddie asks Captain Hadley at the nearby fort to protect the Indians, but Hadley refuses without orders from the government, and Eddie is disappointed by the captain's lack of sympathy. When Father Sullivan asks the selectmen to post a reward for the killers, they angrily send him away. Meanwhile, Chico distributes guns to the renegade Indians, and they attack a stagecoach. Eddie, Ezra and Father Sullivan, who are returning from town, rescue the passengers. Despite the passengers' demands, Eddie refuses to let the stage continue its journey until he knows what happened. Eagle Feather suspects that Wildhorse, who was banished from the tribe, is behind the attack. When the selectmen complain to Hadley, he offers to talk to Eagle Feather and help capture Wildhorse if he is persuaded that Eagle Feather is telling the truth. Back at the mission, Melodie, one of the passengers, makes friends with Little Brown Jug. Determined to get rid of Eddie, the selectmen now complain to Eddie's boss, Commissioner Wright, who fires him. Despite this, Eddie vows to have Eagle Feather tell his side of the story. Meanwhile the selectmen plot with Chico to prevent Eagle Feather from talking. As Eddie and Eagle Feather ride to town, the renegade Indians attack

them. Eddie and Eagle Feather evade the attackers, but during the ensuing shootout at the mission, Little Brown Jug is shot and killed. Father Sullivan recognizes Chico among the attackers, and Eddie pursues him. After he captures Chico, Eddie allows him to escape and then follows him to Marks's place. There, he discovers the claims on the Indian land that were filed by the selectmen. During a shootout, Eddie and Ezra are rescued by the arrival of Eagle Feather and his men. Now that it is safe, the stagecoach continues its journey, but Melodie, having fallen in love with Eddie, remains behind to teach school at the mission. *Indian agents. Indians of North America. Orphans. Political corruption. Priests. Missions. Murder. Shootouts. Silver. Stagecoaches. United States. Army.*

Box 16 Feb 1946. *DV* 5 Feb 1946, p. 3. *DV* 6 Sep 1946, p. 4. *FD* 19 Feb 1946, p. *HR* 5 Feb 1946, p. 3. *MPHPD* 5 Jan 1946, p. 2792. *MPHPD* 9 Feb 1946, p. 2838. *Var* 13 Feb 1946, p. 10.

THE ROMANTIC JOURNEY (East Indian Americans)

Astra Film Corp.; GOld Rooster Plays. *Dist* Pathé Exchange, Inc. 24 Dec 1916 [©Pathé Exchange, Inc.; 18 Dec 1916; LU9751]. Si; b&w. 5 reels.

Dir George Fitzmaurice. *Scen* Ouida Bergère. *Cam* Harold Louis Miller.

Cast: William Courtenay (*Peter*), Macey Harlan (*Ratoor*), Alice Dovey (*Cynthia*), Norman Thorpe (*Broadhurst*).

Drama. Ratoor, an East Indian antique dealer, has put Cynthia under his hypnotic control and plans to engineer a marriage between her and the millionaire Broadhurst in order to get his hands on Broadhurst's fortune. While visiting Ratoor's shop, Peter discovers that Cynthia is being held there against her will. He starts to investigate and soon falls in love with Cynthia but keeps his distance, even as the hypnotized bride sleepwalks through her wedding. After the ceremony, Ratoor kills Broadhurst and compels Cynthia to sign over her claim to her late husband's estate. Then, when Ratoor makes plans to bury Cynthia alive, Peter decides that it is time to step in. He rescues Cynthia from Ratoor and, after breaking the East Indian's spell, begins a romance with her. *Antique dealers. East Indians. Hypnotism. Hypnotists. Marriage–Forced. Live burial. Murder.*

Note: A reviewer commented, "A story dealing with the pitting of wits of an American against the cunning of a foreigner, especially of a Hindoo, has a natural appeal to the patriotism of an audience." They advised exhibitors, "Keep well before your patrons that...it is American wits against Oriental cunning."

ETR 16 Dec 1916, p. 134. *Motog* 16 Dec 1916, p. 1348. *MPN* 16 Dec 1916, p. 3862, 3951. *MPN* 23 Dec 1916, p. 4013. *NYDM* 9 Dec 1916, p. 26. *Wid's* 21 Dec 1916, p. 1189.

ROSA DE FRANCIA (Spanish language)

Fox Film Corp. *Dist* Twentieth Century-Fox Film Corp. **1935**; New York opening: 25 Oct 1935; Prod: 4 Jun–20 Jun 1935 [©20th Century Fox Film Corp.; 12 Oct 1935; LP5844]. Sd (Western Electric Noiseless Recording); b&w. 8 reels, 7,191 ft. 80 min. Passed by the National Board of Review. PCA cert no. 1077. Spanish language.

[*Prod* John Stone]. *Dirigida por* [*Dir*] Gordon Wiles. [*Asst dir* Sam Schneider and Charles Faye]. *Supervisión y dirección de diálogo* [*Supv and dial dir*] José López Rubio. *Adaptación cinematográfica de* [*Scr*] José López Rubio. [*Cont* Helen Logan]. *Fotografía* [*Photog*] Joseph MacDonald. [*Art dir* Duncan Cramer and Lewis Creber]. *Trajes* [*Cost*] Alberto Luza. *Dirección musical* [*Mus dir*] Samuel Kaylin. [*Sd* E. Clayton Ward].

Source: Based on the play *Rosa de Francia* by Eduardo Marquina and Luis Fernández Ardavín (Madrid, 31 Mar 1923).

Cast: ROSITA DÍAZ (*Luisa Isabel de Orleans*), Julio Peña (*Luis I*), Antonio Moreno (*Felipe V*), Consuelo Frank (*Isabel de Farnesio*), Don Alvarado (*El marqués de Magny*), Enrique de Rosas (*El mariscal de Tesse*), María Calvo (*La condesa de Altamira*), Martín Garralaga (*El marqués de Grimaldo*), Rubí Gutiérrez (*Rosalba*), Jinx Falkenberg (*Algarina*), María Luisa Sierra (*Clarisa*), Carlos Montalbán (*Andrés*), Chito Alonso (*Cirilo*), Tito Davison (*Simón*), Antonio Vidal (*El duque de Pópoli*), Hector Briceño (*El marqués de Santa Cruz*), Lucio Villegas (*El arzobispo de Toledo*), D'Arcy Corrigan (*El inquisidor general*), Manuel París (*El padre Laubrussel*), José Peña Pepet (*Valouse*), [Rosa Rey (*Laura, la doncella*)], [Julio Abadía (*El heraldo*)], [Aura de Silva (*Condesa de Montellano*)], Germaine de Néel (*Madame Corinne*)], [Paul Portanova (*Guardia*)], [Joyce Kay (*Princesa joven*)], [Jack LaVern Cosby, Varick Steel (*Infantes*)], [Antonio Manfredi].

Historical, Drama. [*Not viewed*]. Luisa Isabel de Orleans, the "Rose of France," betrothed to Luis, the prince of Asturias, arrives at the palace of the Spanish royal family. Luisa, a charming and fun-loving girl, shocks King Felipe, Queen Isabel de Farnesio, and her husband-to-be with her irreverence and indecorous behavior. The two wed in great solemnity nonetheless, and Luisa gaily arranges her wedding suite. Farnesio and her husband decide, however, that the marriage cannot be consummated as the French princess has not proven herself trustworthy. Luis leaves Luisa alone on their wedding night, and Farnesio continues to prevent a real marital union between the young couple, though Felipe urges otherwise. When Felipe receives the news that his nephew, King Louis XV of France, is deathly ill, Farnesio tells him to abdicate so that he can take his place as the rightful heir of the French crown, which would thus leave the Spanish throne to Luisa and Luis. Realizing that he would then be the *de facto* ruler of Spain, in addition to being king of France, Philip agrees. Tesse, a nobleman and royal attendant, realizes that the royal couple must consummate their union so that Spain will have a strong monarchy. He calls on the marquis of Magny to flirt with Luisa to incite the jealousy of Luis. Luisa refuses to attend a Sunday church service with the royal family and instead has a picnic with her friends, including Magny. When Magny's flirtations become too serious, Luisa reacts with embarrassment. As the Royal family arrives, however, Magny carries Luisa from a tree where she has been concealing herself in a game of hide-and-seek. Shocked at her conduct, Luis orders her to leave the country estate for Madrid where she will be granted her liberty, but he is sorry to see her go. Hearing that Luis is fond of dressing up like a commoner for midnight adventures through the city, Luisa dresses like a common woman, veils herself and seeks out her husband. In a city park, Luis sees the disguised Luisa and falls in love, confessing that the "queen," Luisa, does not care for him. Felipe then arrives at the garden to find his son disturbing the peace. He scolds Luis for fraternizing with an unescorted lady and then orders her arrest. Luisa laughs at this, and Luis immediately recognizes her charming giggle. He takes her back to his home, and when Felipe and Farnesio arrive to tell him of Luisa's absence from the palace, the now happily married couple hide behind the curtains of his bed. *Fathers-in-law. French. Marriage–Arranged. Mothers-in-law. Royalty. Spain. Disguise. Flirtation. Mistaken identity. Nobility. Parks. Picnicking. Weddings.*

Note: The plot was based on a dialogue continuity in the Twentieth Century-Fox Produced Scripts Collection, and the onscreen credits were taken from a screen credit sheet in the Twentieth Century-Fox Records of the Legal Department, both of which are at the UCLA Theater Arts Library. The English translation of the title given in reviews is "Rose of France." According to *HR*, this was art director Gordon Wiles's first film as a director and, as the last of Fox's Spanish language films, was budgeted at double the amount usually spent on their other Spanish language films.

FD 29 Oct 1935, p. 6. *HR* 5 Jun 1935, p. 6. *HR* 10 Jun 1935, p. 14. *HR* 20 Jun 1935, p. 4. *NYT* 28 Oct 1935, p. 16. *Var* 26 Feb 1936, p. 37.

LA ROSA DE FUEGO (Spanish language)

Tom White Productions. **1930**; World premiere in Los Angeles: 29 Mar 1930. Sd; b&w. 7 reels. Spanish language.

Prod Tom White. *Dir* W. L. Griffith.

Source: Based on a story by Eustace Hale Ball.

Cast: Don Alvarado, Renée Torres, Raúl Lechuga, Rafael Blanco, George Rigas, Miguel Silva, Julieta Mora, Rafaela Quintero, Emanuel Martínez, José de Rayas.

Melodrama. [*Not viewed*]. Only the following summary, from publicity materials, has been found for this film: "Upon his return from university, Alvarado finds his family's ranch in the hands of villains.... Alvarado throws out the people depriving his parents of their wealth and also wins the hand of a young lady." *Family relationships. Land claims. Ranches. Romance. Students.*

Note: *La rosa de fuego* received a very negative review in *La Opinión*, the Los Angeles Spanish-language newspaper. The reviewer complained about the lack of a sense of time or place in the story, the distinctly amateurish direction, poor photography, sound and synchronization, the fact that, at one point, Don Alvarado appeared to be reading his lines off "cue cards" and, additionally, that Renée Torres forgot one of her lines and began again from the preceding paragraph. This film may have been reissued in a similar or revised version in 1936 under the title *Amor que vuelve* (see above).

La Opinión 1 Apr 1930.

THE ROSARY (Irish Americans)

Selig Polyscope Co.; A Red Seal Play. *Dist* V-L-S-E, Inc. 28 Jun **1915** [©Selig Polyscope Co.; 16 Jun 1915; LP5584]. Si; b&w. 7 reels.

Dir Colin Campbell. *Scen* Lanier Bartlett. *Cam* Dal Clawson and Harry W. Gerstad.

Source: Based on the play *The Rosary* by Edward E. Rose (New York, 24 Oct 1910).

Cast: Kathlyn Williams (*Vera Wallace*), Charles Clary (*Father Brian Kelly*), Wheeler Oakman (*Bruce Wilton*), Gertrude Ryan (*Alice Wallace*), Eugenie Besserer (*Widow Kelly*), Harry Lonsdale (*Kenward Wright*), Roland Sharp (*Young Brian Kelly*), Frank Clark (*Father Ryan*), Sidney Smith (*Skeeters Martin*), Fred Huntly (*Evarts*), Utahna La Reno (*Young Madge Callahan*), Adda Gleason (*Madge Callahan*), Roy Clark (*Young Bruce*), George Hernandez (*Barrister*), Robert Landers (*Tim*), Edwin Green (*American consul*), Jack McDonald (*Doctor*), Anna Dodge (*Bridget*).

Drama. In a small Irish village, Brian Kelly gives up his sweetheart, Madge Callahan, to enter the priesthood. Father Kelly settles in Ohio and later New York, where, responding to the dying request of Edward Wilton, the priest promises to look after young Bruce Wilton, whom he later learns is Madge's son. Father Kelly sends Bruce to college, and the young man becomes a successful stockbroker. On a trip to the West, Bruce marries Vera Wallace, not knowing that his friend, Kenward Wright, also loves her. After Bruce builds Father Kelly a cathedral, the vengeful Kenward visits the married couple, but Vera's sister Alice, whom Kenward betrayed, also appears, promising to reveal Bruce's financial secrets if he will marry her. Kenward then ruins Bruce on Wall Street, after which Bruce, believing that Vera betrayed him, becomes an alcoholic. On the steps of Father Kelly's church, Kenward clears Vera's name, whereupon Bruce takes her hand and enters the cathedral. *Betrayal. Irish Americans. Jealousy. New York City—Wall Street. Priests. Regeneration. Alcoholics. Churches. Confession. Ireland. Sisters. Stockbrokers. Wards and guardians.*

Note: Although publicity for this film noted that it was "written by Edward E. Rose from his wonderful stage drama," Lanier Bartlett is credited as the scenarist in Selig Collection information.

Motog 3 Jul 1915, pp. 26-27, 47. *MPN* 17 Apr 1915, p. 97. *MPN* 26 Jun 1915, p. 12, 68. *MPN* 3 Jul 1915, p. 69. *MPW* 19 Jun 1915, p. 2014. *MPW* 26 Jun 1915, p. 2105. *NYDM* 30 Jun 1915, p. 28.

THE ROSE AND THE FLAME *see* KISS OF FIRE

ROSE OF CIMARRON (Cherokee, Comanche, Native Americans)

Alco Pictures Corp.; An Edward L. Alperson Production. *Dist* Twentieth Century-Fox Film Corp. Jan **1952**; Los Angeles opening: 28 Jan 1952; *Prod:* mid-Jul—mid-Aug 1951 [©Twentieth Century-Fox Film Corp.; 15 Mar 1952; LP1703]. Sd (RCA Sound System); col (Cinecolor). 8 reels, 6,577 ft. 74 min. PCA cert no. 15476.

Pres EDWARD L. ALPERSON. *Assoc prod* Edward L. Alperson, Jr. *Dir* Harry Keller. *Asst dir* Ben Chapman. *2d asst dir* Gordon McLean and [Herb Mendelson]. *Wrt* Maurice Geraghty. *Dir of photog* Karl Struss. [*Spec eff* Norman Skeete]. [*Col consultant* Wilton R. Holm and Clifford Shank]. *Prod des* Boris Leven. *Film ed* Arthur Roberts. *Ward des* Norma. *Women's ward* Fay Moore. *Men's ward* S. Kring. *Mus* Raoul Kraushaar and Edward L. Alperson, Jr. *Sd* Earl Crane, Sr. *Makeup* Gene Hibbs. *Hair stylist* Hazel Keithley. *Exec asst* Al Zimbalist. *Scr supv* John Erimen. [*Stunt double* Polly Burson and Tom Steele]. [*Stand-in for Mala Powers* Pat Marlowe]. [*Utility stand-in* Ernest Baldwin].

Cast: Jack Buetel [(*Marshal Hollister*)], Mala Powers [(*Rose of Cimarron*)], Bill Williams [(*George Newcomb*)], Jim Davis [(*Willie Whitewater*)], Art Smith [(*Deacon*)], Bob Steele [(*Rio*)], Lillian Bronson [(*Emmy Anders*)], William Phipps [(*Jeb Dawley*)], Irving Bacon [(*Sheriff*)], Dick Curtis [(*Clem Dawley*)], Alex Gerry [(*Judge Kirby*)], Monte Blue [(*Lone Eagle*)], Tom Monroe [(*Mike Finch*)], Polly Burson, George Chandler [(*Deputy*)], Tom Steele, John Doucette [(*Drunk*)], Tommy Cook [(*Young Willie*)], William Schallert [(*Express clerk*)], Wade Crosby [(*Hostler*)], Kenneth MacDonald [(*Sheriff Lewis*)], Byron Foulger [(*Coroner*)], Argentina Brunetti [(*Red Fawn*)], [Tony Layng (*Express messenger*)], [Esther Howard (*Ma Bruce*)], [William Fawcett (*Store clerk*)], [Tex Terry (*Rancher*)], [Charles Stevens (*Painted Shields*)], [Hank Patterson (*Hunter*)], [Frank Scannell (*Sharper*)], [Martha Mitrovich (*Mother*)], [Edythe Elliott], [Mira McKinney], [Marjorie Eaton], [Ellanora Reeves], [Claire Du Brey], [Caleen Calder].

Western. [*Print viewed*]. After an ambush by Comanche Indians on a wagon train traveling through Oklahoma, a young Cherokee named Willie Whitewater surveys the remains of the devastated train and finds a fair-skinned baby girl hidden in a trunk. He takes the infant to his parents, who name her "Rose of Cimarron" and rear her as they would their own Indian child. Years later, Rose's foster parents are murdered while trying to stop outlaws George Newcomb, Clem Dawley and Mike Finch from stealing their horses. When Rose discovers this, she vows revenge and goes in search of the three missing horses—a skewbald, a palomino and a sorrel. Rose's search takes her to Dodge City, where she seeks the aid of Marshal Hollister, known as one of the best lawmen in the West. Despite Hollister's attempt to persuade Rose that she must abide by the white man's law, which requires a fair trial before punishment can be meted out, she demands that the three outlaws be hanged immediately upon capture. Hollister and Rose soon fall in love, and Hollister promises repeatedly that he will bring the outlaws to justice. However, when Rose finds Dawley and Finch, she takes matters into her own hands and kills them in a gun battle. Hollister imprisons Rose and places her in a jail cell adjacent to Deacon, one of Newcomb's men. Later, Deacon and Rose, with the help of Rio, another Newcomb outlaw, make a jailbreak. Realizing that his only hope of tracking down the outlaws is through Rose, Hollister attempts to lure her back by placing Willie under arrest on trumped-up charges. When Rose returns to Dodge City, she discovers that a $1,000 bounty has been placed on her head, and that Hollister is planning to transport Willie to a federal prison on the same eastbound train that the Newcomb gang is planning to rob. As the train speeds along, nearing the stretch of track that has been destroyed by the Newcomb gang, Rose, on horseback, manages to overtake it and climb on board. Once on the train, Rose pulls the emergency cord, thus preventing a train wreck. No sooner does the train come to a halt, however, than the outlaws begin looting the train's gold cargo. A blistering gun battle ensues, during which Hollister is wounded by Newcomb, and Rose and Willie escape. Later, Deacon is wounded by a Newcomb bullet during a dispute over the gold. Hollister eventually tracks down Rose, Newcomb and Deacon, and discovers, through Deacon's deathbed confession, that Newcomb is one of the men who killed her Indian foster parents. Newcomb makes an attempt to flee, but Rose and Hollister catch up with him, and Hollister kills him. Satisfied with the demise of the Newcomb gang, Rose and Hollister ride off together to begin life anew. *Cherokee Indians. Foundlings. Marshals. Murder. Outlaws. Revenge. Train robberies. Bounty hunters. Comanche Indians. Confession. Fistfights. Foster parents. Gunfights. Horse thieves. Horses. Jails. Oklahoma. Romance. Sabotage. Saloons.*

Note: Although most sources list this film's production company as Edward L. Alperson Productions, Inc., the copyright registration gives it as Alco Pictures Corp., another Alperson-owned company. *HR* production charts list Lane Bradford in the cast, but his appearance in the released film has not been confirmed. Production charts also indicate that exteriors were shot in Topanga Canyon, near Los Angeles. Contemporary reviews noted the film's use of Cinecolor's "Natural Color," which was a three-color, single-negative process. Modern sources add Frank Ferguson to the cast.

Box 29 Mar 1952, p. 3. *DV* 6 Mar 1952, p. 3. *FD* 6 Mar 1952, p. 12. *HR* 20 Jul 1951, p. 13. *HR* 10 Aug 1951, p. 11. *HR* 6 Mar 1952, p. 3. *MPHPD* 8 Mar 1952, p. 1262. *Var* 12 Mar 1952, p. 16.

ROSE OF THE GOLDEN WEST (Latino)

First National Pictures, Inc. *Dist* First National Pictures, Inc. 2 Oct **1927**; New York premiere: 25 Sep 1927 [©First National Pictures, Inc.; 3 Oct 1927; LP24462]. Si; b&w. 7 reels, 6,477 ft.

Pres Richard A. Rowland. *Dir* George Fitzmaurice. *Scen and adpt* Bess Meredyth and Philip Bartholomae. *Titles* Mort Blumenstock. *Photog* Lee Garmes. *Cost* Max Ree.

Source: Based on the short story "Rose of the Golden West" by Minna Caroline Smith and Eugenie Woodward (publication undetermined).

Cast: Mary Astor (*Elena*), Gilbert Roland (*Juan*), Gustav von Seyffertitz (*Gómez*), Montagu Love (*General Vallero*), Flora Finch (*Señora Comba*), Harvey Clark (*Thomas Larkin*), Roel Muriel (*Mother Superior*), André Cheron (*Russian prince*), Romaine Fielding (*Secretary*), Thur Fairfax (*Orderly*), William Conklin (*Commander Sloat*), Christina Montt (*Señorita González*), Cullen Tate.

Romance. In 1846, California patriots join forces to avert a suspected plan of dictator General Vallero to sell out to Russia. Juan,

a handsome youth, is selected to crush the plot, preventing his plan to elope with Elena, a convent novice. General Vallero, actually Elena's father, visits the convent, tells her he is a friend of her dead father, and takes her to Monterey; en route, Juan stops Vallero's runaway team, winning the general's profuse thanks. Both men remain unaware of each other's identity. Believing he has been tricked, Juan is about to fulfill his mission during a fiesta when he is seized by soldiers; later he returns to Vallero's home and is recaptured and sentenced to be shot. Elena manages, however, to summon marines from a warship in the bay; Juan is saved from death, and he and Elena are reunited. *California–History–To 1846. Conspiracy. Dictators. Fatherhood. Monterey (CA). Nuns. Russia. United States. Marine Corps.*

MPW 8 Oct 1927. NYT 26 Sep 1927, p. 27. Var 28 Sep 1927, p. 25.

ROSE OF THE RANCHO (Latino)

Jesse L. Lasky Feature Play Co. *Dist* Paramount Pictures Corp. 30 Nov **1914** [©Jesse L. Lasky Feature Play Co.; 28 Oct 1914; LU3618]. Si; b&w. 5 reels.

Pres David Belasco. *Dir* Cecil B. DeMille and Wilfred Buckland.

Source: Based on the play *Rose of the Rancho* by Richard Walton Tully and David Belasco (New York, 27 Nov 1906).

Cast: Bessie Barriscale (*Juanita*), Jane Darwell (*Señora Castro-Kenton*), Dick La Reno (*Ezra Kincaid, land jumper*), J. W. Johnston (*Kearney of the U.S. Gov't*), Monroe Salisbury (*Don Luis del Torre*), James Neill (*Padre Antonio*), Sydney Deane (*Espinoza*), William Elmer (*Half-breed*), Jeanie McPherson (*Isabelita, Espinoza's daughter*), Padre Francisca de la Vinna (*Priest at wedding ceremony*).

Western. In 1850 the Federal Government sends secret agent Kearney to investigate land fraud in California among the Spanish owned rancheros. Ezra Kincaid, a land jumper, goes to Señor Espinoza's ranch to seize the property, and in the raid Espinoza and his daughter Isabella die. Meanwhile, Kearney sees Juanita, the "Rose" of the Castro rancho, and they become mutually attracted, although Juanita is engaged to Don Luis del Torre. When Kearney discovers that Kincaid plans to seize the Castro ranch, he warns Juanita and her mother, but Señora Castro-Kenton does not believe "The Gringo," and refuses to register her ranch. At Juanita's betrothal dance, Kearney is able to coerce Kincaid into delaying his raid, and the federal troops arrive just in time. In the end, the ranch is saved, and Kearney and Juanita are married. *California. Claim jumpers. Fraud. Latino. Land rights. Ranches. Secret agents. Balls (Parties). Weddings.*

Note: *MPW* mentions in a news item that this was the first Lasky-Belasco feature. A photograph of the San Fernando mission in Southern California, which was used as a location site for the film, appears in *NYDM* 14 Oct 1914, p. 28. Modern sources list Wilfred Buckland as the film's art director. Richard Walton Tully assisted in the production. *Rose of the Rancho* was remade in 1936 by Paramount by Marion Gering and starred John Boles (see below).

Motog 12 Dec 1914, p. 829. MPN 28 Nov 1914, p. 41. MPW 21 Nov 1914, p. 1078. MPW 28 Nov 1914, p. 1294. MPW 12 Dec 1914, p. 1531. NYDM 25 Nov 1914, p. 32. Var 20 Nov 1914, p. 27.

ROSE OF THE RANCHO (Latino)

Paramount Pictures, Inc. *Dist* Paramount Pictures, Inc. 10 Jan **1936**; New York opening: week of 7 Jan 1936; Prod: began 27 Jun 1935; retakes shot late Oct—early Nov 1935 [©Paramount Pictures, Inc.; 20 Jan 1936; LP6071]. Sd (Western Electric Noiseless Recording); b&w. 9 reels. 85 min. Passed by the National Board of Review. PCA cert no. 1463.

Pres ADOLPH ZUKOR. *Prod* William LeBaron. *Dir* Marion Gering. [*Dir of retakes* Robert Florey]. *Scr* Frank Partos, Charles Brackett, Arthur Sheekman and Nat Perrin. *Adpt* Harlan Thompson and Brian Hooker. *Photog* Leo Tover. *Art dir* Hans Dreier and Ernst Fegte. *Ed* Hugh Bennett. *Miss Swarthout's cost des by* Travis Banton. *Dance ensembles staged by* LeRoy Prinz. *Sd rec* Martin M. Paggi, Louis H. Mesenkop and Frank Goodwin.

Song(s): "If I Should Lose You," "Thunder Over Paradise," "Little Rose of the Rancho," "Got a Girl in Cal-i-for-ni-ay," "There's Gold in Monterey," "Where Is My Love" and "The Padre and the Bride," music and lyrics by Ralph Rainger and Leo Robin.

Source: Based on the play *Rose of the Rancho* by Richard Walton Tully and David Belasco (New York, 27 Nov 1906).

Cast: John Boles (*Jim Kearney*), Gladys Swarthout (*Rosita Castro [also known as] Don Carlos*), Charles Bickford (*Joe Kincaid*), Grace Bradley (*Flossie*), Willie Howard (*Pancho Spiegelglass*), Herb

Williams (*Phineas P. Jones*), H. B. Warner (*Don Pasqual Castro*), Charlotte Granville (*Dona Petrona*), Don Alvarado (*Don Louis [Espinosa]*), Minor Watson (*Jonathan Hill*), Louise Carter (*Guadalupe*), Pedro de Cordoba (*Gomez [also known as] Cortez*), Paul Harvey (*Boss Martin*), Arthur Aylesworth (*Sheriff James*), Harry Woods (*Bull Bangle*), Russell Hopton (*Stranger, Frisco*), [Benny Baker (*Hill-Billy boy*)], [James Marcus (*Very old Spaniard*)], [Robert Kortman, Ted Oliver, Merrill McCormick (*Kincaid henchmen*)], [Evelyn Selbie (*Old woman*)], [George Bookasta (*Bellows boy*)], [Harry Semels (*Blacksmith*)], [Lalo Encinas (*Overseer*)], [Eleanor Virzie (*Small girl*)], [Ernest S. Adams (*Bus boy*)], [Robert E. Homans (*Passenger*)], [Lew Kelly (*Coach driver*)], [Ed Dearing (*Stranger*)], [Russell Powell (*Bartender*)], [Jack Norton (*Croupier*)], [Eddie Dunn (*Waiter*)], [Sam Blum (*Master of ceremonies, Tecolaro*)], [Nelson McDowell (*Decrepit old man*)], [Eddie Borden (*Barfly*)], [Redmond Flood (*Drunk at table*)], [Lester Sharpe (*Bystander in saloon*)], [S. S. Simon (*Man at pancho's table*)], [Olin Francis (*Bouncer*)], [Paul Sotoff, Ivan Christy, Sam Lufkin, Edwin J. Brady (*Bystanders*)], [Lillian Pearl (*Comedy dancer*)], [Charles Stevens, Frank Lackteen (*Peon spies*)], [Charles Middleton (*Horse doctor*)], [Charles Morris (*Old Spaniard*)], [Jules Cowles, Sam Appel, Jack Perry, Harry Lamont, Nick Thompson, John Nasborough (*Vigilantes*)].

Historical, Musical, Western. [*Print viewed*]. In Monterey, in 1852, shortly after California is made a state, the peaceful Spanish region lies helpless against the plundering of ruthless land grabbers. To protect families and property from murderous attacks, the ranchers band together as vigilantes and are led by the mysterious, masked Don Carlos. Although elderly Don Pasqual Castro urges the alcalde to use his influence to stop the vigilantes, the alcalde will do nothing to thwart the predatory raids of Joe Kincaid and his men. Kincaid files claims on local ranches that were given to various families generations before by the king of Spain, violently expelling the occupants as squatters when they are unable to provide deeds to the land. Pasqual's daughter Rosita is engaged to Don Louis Espinosa, who does not believe in taking action to thwart Kincaid, but Rosita listens to Dona Petrona, who urges taking the law into one's own hands. Rosita is, in fact, the masked Don Carlos. Juan, the bartender in the Golden Nugget, which Kincaid's men frequent, regularly sends word to Rosita of Kincaid's upcoming attacks, and Rosita sings to alert her men to assemble. From the stagecoach, Jim Kearney sees Kincaid about to be lynched by the vigilantes and saves him, believing that executions should be the government's business. That very evening Rosita transforms herself from Don Carlos to the queen of the fiesta and meets Kearney on the way to the celebration. There, she makes Kearney aware of her interest in him by dancing on his sombrero during a song. Rosita and Kearney begin to meet regularly until Pasqual makes her pledge, as a woman engaged since birth, to see him no more. Kearney, meanwhile, has become a friend of Kincaid, who is sincerely grateful to him for saving his life. Rosita learns of their fellowship and suspects Kearney is an outlaw, but is more concerned that Kearney might meet another woman. Rosita summons the vigilantes to a meeting, and when Kearney interrupts her as she is changing her dress, he assumes she is Don Carlos' mistress. Upon arriving at the rendezvous, the vigilantes take Kearney prisoner, and when Rosita releases him, they disband, assuming she has betrayed them. Frisco, a recently released convict, informs Kincaid that Kearney is a federal agent. Rosita is warned by Juan that Kincaid is planning a final raid, and as Kearney finally realizes that Rosita is Don Carlos, he joins the vigilantes in the defense of the Pasqual ranch and kills Kincaid and defeats his forces. *California–History–1846-1850. Land rights. Male impersonation. Outlaws. Raids. Ranches. Vigilantes. Bartenders. Dancing. Disguise. Engagements. Ex-convicts. Fathers and daughters. Government agents. Hats. Holidays. Law and order. Lynching. Mayors. Romance. Salesmen. Saloons. Singers. Songs.*

Note: According to the *HR* review, the film, which was in production for nearly five months, cost over $1,000,000. According to a news item in *DV* on 25 Oct 1935, Robert Florey directed ten days of retakes for this film after director Marion Gering left the production to work on another film. According to a modern source, Florey directed retakes of the opening scenes of the film at the Paramount ranch. The pressbook noted that the film was the first to use the "so-called 'reverberation track,'" which used two non-directional microphones, and had just been developed by Electrical Research Products Corp. The microphones enabled photographers to shoot nearly a 360 degree circle around actors Gladys Swarthout and John Boles during the singing of "Rose of the Rancho." This film marked the screen debut of Swarthout, a Metropolitan Opera star. This was the first film in which Willie Howard acted.

He also appeared in the 1935 Paramount film *Millions in the Air*, which was released first, but was shot later. A news item in *HR* on 28 Dec 1935 stated that Ralph Rainger was a guest artist on the Shell radio broadcast, where he played the score he wrote for this film. *Rose of the Rancho* was first filmed in 1914 by Paramount. Cecil B. DeMille and Wilfred Buckland directed and Bessie Barriscale starred in this silent version (see above).

DV 2 Aug 1935, p. 2. *DV* 25 Oct 1935, p. 5. *DV* 26 Dec 1936, p. 1. *DV* 7 Jan 1936, p. 3. *FD* 4 Jan 1936, p. 3. *HR* 26 Jun 1935, p. 6. *HR* 28 Dec 1935, p. 5. *HR* 7 Jan 1936, p. 4. *MPD* 4 Jan 1936, p. 4. *MPH* 17 Aug 1935, pp. 41-42. *MPH* 11 Jan 1936, p. 52. *NYT* 9 Jan 1936, p. 25. *Var* 15 Jan 1936, p. 18.

ROSE OF THE TENEMENTS (Italian Americans, Jewish Americans)
R-C Pictures Corp. *Dist* Film Booking Offices of America. 5 Dec 1926 [©R-C Pictures Corp.; 22 Nov 1926; LP23353]. Si; b&w. 7 reels, 6,678 ft.

Pres Joseph P. Kennedy. *Dir* Phil Rosen. *Asst dir* Jimmy Dugan. *Adpt and cont* J. Grubb Alexander. *Photog* Lyman Broening.

Source: Based on the novel *The Stumbling Herd* by John A. Moroso (New York, 1923).

Cast: Shirley Mason (*Rosie [Rose] Rossetti*), Johnny Harron (*Danny Lewis*), Evelyn Selbie (*Sara Kaminsky*), Sidney Franklin (*Abraham Kaminsky*), James Gordon (*Tim Galligan*), Frank McGlynn, Jr. (*Mickey Galligan*), Scott McKee (*Paddy Flynn*), Jess Devorska (*Izzie Kohn*), Mathilde Comont (*Mrs. Kohn*), Valentina Zimina (*Emma Goldstein*), Kalla Pasha (*Willofsky*).

Melodrama. Rose Rossetti, the orphaned daughter of a New York gangster, and Danny Lewis, also an orphan, are reared by the Kaminskys, an elderly Jewish couple who operate an artificial flower factory on the East Side. The Kaminskys die, telling Rose of her parentage, and leave the shop to Danny and Rose. Danny drifts into the clutches of Willofsky, a Bolshevik agitator, and Emma Goldstein, his coworker, to whom Danny is attracted. While agitating against the war with Germany, Willofsky and Emma are attacked by a crowd; Danny, after assaulting a policeman, prevents Emma from throwing a bomb. Through Galligan, a ward leader, he is exonerated by the police and allowed to enlist, to Rose's joy. After the war, Danny returns and finds that he is in love with Rose. *Bolshevists and Bolshevism. Flowers. Italian Americans. Jews. New York City–East Side. Orphans. Protest marches. World War I.*

FD 19 Dec 1926. *Var* 13 Apr 1927, p. 22.

ROSE OF THE YUKON (Native Alaskans, Native Americans)
Republic Pictures Corp. *Dist* Republic Pictures Corp. 5 Jan **1949**; Prod: began early Aug 1948 [©Republic Pictures Corp.; 10 Jan 1949; LP2090]. Sd (RCA Sound System); b&w. 5,350 ft. 59 min. Passed by the National Board of Review. PCA cert no. 13368.

Assoc prod Stephen Auer. *Dir* George Blair. [*Asst dir* Herb Mendelson]. *Orig scr* Norman S. Hall. *Dir of photog* John MacBurnie. [*Cam op* Enzo Martinelli]. [*Stills* Bert Anderson]. *Optical eff* Consolidated Film Industries. *Art dir* Frank Hotaling. *Film ed* Harry Keller. *Set dec* John McCarthy, Jr. and James Redd. *Mus supv* Adele Palmer. *Mus score* Stanley Wilson. [*Mus dir* Morton Scott]. *Sd* Dick Tyler. *Makeup supv* Bob Mark. [*Makeup* Sam Kaufman]. [*Scr supv* Bob Walker]. [*Grip* Ben Bishop]. [*Gaffer* Bab Stafford].

Song(s): "It's Not the First Love," music and lyrics by Eddie Maxwell and Nathan Scott.

Cast: Steve Brodie [(*Maj. Geoffrey Barnett*)], Myrna Dell [(*Rose Flambeau*)], William Wright [(*Capt. Tom Clark*)], Emory Parnell [(*Tim MacNab*)], Jonathan Hale [(*Brig. Gen. Craig Butler*)], Benny Baker [(*Jack Wells*)], Gene Gary [(*Frenchy Frenay*)], Dick Elliott [(*Doc Read*)], Francis McDonald [(*Alaskan*)], Lotus Long [(*Eskimo girl*)], Eugene Sigaloff [(*Capt. Rossoff*)], Wade Crosby [(*Alaskan*)], [Rex Lease, Stanley Blystone (*Workmen*)], [Charles Soldani (*Eskimo man*)], [House Peters, Jr.], [Charles Griffin (*Brandon Beach*)].

Detective, Drama. [*Print viewed*]. Every spring, the residents of a small Alaskan outpost called Nenana participate in a contest in which the person who most accurately predicts when the first crack in the ice will occur is declared the winner of $85,000. Inside the Klondike saloon, Capt. Tom Clark promises everyone a bottle of "Jack" if he wins and promises his companion, Rose Flambeau, a mink-lined parka. The ice breaks at 3:46, and Tom is pronounced the winner. When a photographer suddenly takes his picture, however, Tom punches him and departs abruptly. Later, Doc Read explains what he knows about Tom to reporter Jack Wells, but is unable to say why Tom would assault his photographer. At the office of Brig. Gen. Craig Butler of Military Intelligence, Maj. Geoffrey Barnett reads a newspaper item announcing Tom's win. Barnett tells the general that

during the war, Tom, a sergeant, an interpreter and two soldiers were assigned to take Japanese headquarters on Attu Island. After all except one of soldiers were reported dead, they assumed Tom had perished. Barnett orders Tom's casket to be exhumed, and the remains are determined to be that of one of the soldiers. Later, Barnett goes to the Klondike, where he asks Rose about Tom. Noticing Barnett's West Point class ring, Rose lies, saying Tom is away, but will return in a few days. Early the next morning, Rose leaves Nenana to return to her cabin in an Eskimo village. After dog trainer Frenchy Frenay agrees to sell Barnett a dog sled and team, Barnett goes to the village. When Barnett tells Rose that Tom is wanted for desertion and is suspected of killing the other members of his mission with a grenade, Rose explains that no one knows the location of Tom's gold mine, where she suspects Tom is hiding. Later, two baby bears, "Pete" and "Mike," break into Tom's cabin, and Barnett who is searching in the area, enters to chase them out. Inside, he discovers a Japanese Assay Report and some maps, which prove that Tom has betrayed his country. In the middle of the night, Tom returns and admits to Rose that he is guilty. He explains that upon reaching Japanese headquarters, he had discovered maps revealing the discovery of rich deposits of pitchblende, an ore containing both gold and uranium, in northern Alaska. Tom realized that the United States did not know of these deposits and quickly purchased the land with plans to sell the ore to a "foreign" government. Tom returns to his mine, and the next morning, Rose, who lost two brothers during the war, informs Barnett about his past. Barnett rushes to the mine and tries to arrest Tom, but after shooting Rose in the shoulder, Tom escapes on a dog sled. Barnett captures Tom, locks him inside a cabin and boards up the windows. After Barnett leaves, Frenchy lets Tom out of his temporary prison. Frenchy gives a gun to Tom, who thanks him and then stabs him to death. Barnett, however, shoots Tom, killing him, and after he receives a promotion, the major proposes to Rose. *Alaska. Desertion. Military. Traitors. Uranium mines. Bears. Brothers and sisters. Cabins. Confession. Dogsledding. Engagements. Escapes. Firearms. Fistfights. Fur coats. Gold mines. Grenades. Gunshot wounds. Investigations. Jewelry. Maps. Photographers. Physicians. Reporters. Soldiers. Stabbings. Sweepstakes. United States Military Academy. World War II.*

Box 29 Jan 1949. *DV* 21 Jan 1949, p. 3. *FD* 27 Jan 1949, p. 7. *HR* 6 Aug 1948, p. 13. *HR* 21 Jan 1949, p. 4. *MPHPD* 29 Jan 1949, p. 4479. *Var* 26 Jan 1949, p. 11.

THE ROSE TATTOO (Italian Americans)
Paramount Pictures, Inc. *Dist* Paramount Pictures, Inc. Dec **1955**; New York opening: 12 Dec 1955; Prod: 3 Nov–31 Dec 1954 [©Paramount Pictures Corp., Hal B. Wallis & Joseph H. Hazen; 14 Dec 1955; LP5859]. Sd (Western Electric Recording); b&w; VistaVision Motion Picture High Fidelity. 13 reels, 10,489 ft. 116-117 min. PCA cert no. 17395.

Pres HAL B. WALLIS. *Prod* Hal B. Wallis. *Dir* Daniel Mann. *Asst dir* Richard McWhorter. *Scr* Tennessee Williams. *Adpt* Hal Kanter. *Dir of photog* James Wong Howe. *Spec photog eff* John P. Fulton. *Process photog* Farciot Edouart. *Art dir* Hal Pereira and Tambi Larsen. *Ed supv* Warren Low. *Set dec* Sam Comer and Arthur Krams. *Cost* Edith Head. *Mus score* Alex North. *Sd rec* Harold Lewis and Gene Garvin. *Makeup supv* Wally Westmore. [*Interpreter for Anna Magnani* Mrs. Natalie Murray].

Music: "The Sheik of Araby," by Ted Snyder.

Song(s): "Come le rose," music and lyrics by Adolfo Genise and Gaetano Lama.

Source: Based on the play *The Rose Tattoo* by Tennessee Williams, as produced by Cheryl Crawford (New York, 3 Feb 1951).

Cast: ANNA MAGNANI [(*Serafina Delle Rose*)], BURT LANCASTER [(*Alvaro Mangiacavallo*)], Marisa Pavan [(*Rosa Delle Rose*)], Ben Cooper [(*Jack Hunter*)], Virginia Grey [(*Estelle Hohengarten*)], Jo Van Fleet [(*Bessie*)], Sandro Giglio [(*Father De Leo*)], Mimi Aguglia [(*Assunta*)], Florence Sundstrom [(*Flora*)], [Dorrit Kelton (*Schoolteacher*)], [Rossana San Marco (*Italian woman, Peppina*)], [Augusta Merighi (*Italian woman, Giuseppina*)], [Rosa Rey (*Italian woman, Mariella*)], [Georgia Simmons (*The strega*)], [Zolya Talma (*Miss Mangiacavallo*)], [George Humbert (*Pop Mangiacavallo*)], [Margherita Pasquero (*Grandma Mangiacavallo*)], [May Lee (*Mamma Shigura, tattoo artist*)], [Lewis Charles, Virgil Osborne (*Taxi drivers*)], [Larry Chance (*Rosario Delle Rose*)], [Jean Hart (*Violetta*)], [Roger Gunderson (*Doctor*)], [Roland Vildo (*Salvatore*)], [Fred Taylor (*Cashier*)], [Natalia Murray (*Townswoman*)], [Albert Atkins (*Mario*)], [Joe Roque], [Norman Markwell].

Domestic, Psychological, Drama. [*Print viewed*]. Serafina Delle Rose, a seamstress living in an Italian-American community on the Gulf of Mexico, idolizes her husband Rosario, unaware that the truck driver has been having a long-term affair with Estelle Hohengarten, a blonde blackjack dealer. Serafina, who is pregnant with her second child, is also ignorant of Rosario's smuggling activities and is completely possessed by grief when he is killed in a highway explosion while attempting to escape from the police in his truck. After suffering a miscarriage, Serafina devotes herself to mourning, even cremating Rosario's body against the dictates of the Church, so that she may keep his ashes in the house. Three years later, Serafina's pretty eighteen-year-old daughter Rosa meets a sailor named Jack Hunter at her graduation dance and falls deeply in love. Rosa introduces Jack to her mother, but Serafina, having heard that morning about Rosario's affair with Estelle, is so preoccupied with her anger and suspicion that she hardly notices them at first. While gazing at the happy young couple, Serafina's bitterness overcomes her, and she accuses the young man of wanting to violate her daughter's innocence. After Jack vows by the Blessed Virgin that he will respect Rosa, Serafina claims that she is satisfied and lets the young people go out together. Later that day, Serafina meets Alvaro Mangiacavallo, a simple-minded Sicilian-born truck driver, whose strong body reminds her of her husband and reawakens her passion. Eager to impress Serafina, Alvaro has a rose tattooed on his chest, just as Rosario had done. Alvaro's romantic overtures anger Serafina, but when she learns that he is acquainted with Estelle, she forces him to take her to the woman. When confronted by Serafina, Estelle defiantly admits that she loved Rosario and publicly displays the tattoo imprinted on her own chest. Horrified, Serafina rushes home and smashes the urn containing her husband's ashes. Later, after loudly saying goodbye to Alvaro, Serafina asks him to return secretly and spend the night. In the meantime, Alvaro gets drunk and passes out shortly after he arrives at the house. In the morning, a groggy Alvaro sees Rosa asleep on the couch and stares longingly at her face. Rosa awakes and runs screaming into Serafina's room. Thinking that Alvaro attacked Rosa, Serafina drives him out. Rosa, weary of her mother's vigilance and hypocrisy, angrily informs Serafina that she plans to elope with Jack, but when he arrives, Serafina surprises the couple by giving them her blessing. Alvaro then clumsily declares his love for Serafina, whereupon, at the urging of the neighboring women, she happily invites him into the house. *Courtship. Grief. Infidelity. Italian Americans. Loyalty. Mothers and daughters. Widows. Accidental death. Adolescents. Catholic Church. Loneliness. Neighbors. Priests. Sailors. Seamstresses. Smuggling. Tattoos. Truck drivers.*

Note: This film marked Anna Magnani's first Hollywood picture and her first English-speaking role. According to the *NYT* reviewer, Tennessee Williams wrote his play with Magnani in mind. When the play opened in New York City, however, she was not available to take the part. On 10 Aug 1952, *NYT* reported that Vittorio De Sica might direct the film version of the play, and an 11 Apr 1954 *NYT* article reported that Pier Angeli would play the part of "Rosa." (Marisa Pavan, who ultimately played "Rosa," was Angeli's twin sister.) According to a Jul 1954 *NYT* item, Jan Merlin tested for the role of "Jack." Information in the MPAA/PCA collection at the AMPAS Library reveals that PCA officials initially rejected Williams' play, stating that the story was absorbed with "lust and gross sex" and confused religion with superstition. According to the Jul 1954 *NYT* article, producer Hal Wallis suggested that Williams temper the play's sexual aspects and make a clear distinction between Roman Catholic beliefs and "Serafina's" superstitions. The completed script was then accepted by the PCA. Some scenes were shot on location in Key West, FL, according to contemporary sources. Magnani won an Academy Award for Best Actress; James Wong Howe won the Oscar for Best Black and White Cinematography; Hal Pereira and Tambi Larsen won for Black and White Art Direction; and Sam Comer and Arthur Krams won for Best Black and White Set Decoration. The film received a nomination for Best Picture and Pavan was nominated for Best Supporting Actress. In addition, the film was nominated in the following categories, Best Costume Design, Editing and Music. Magnani won a Golden Globe award for Best Actress in a drama, and Marisa Pavan won a Golden Globe Best Supporting Actress award. Director Daniel Mann also directed the Broadway play, and Dorrit Kelton, Rossana San Marco and Augusta Merighi appeared in both the film and the stage play.

Box 12 Nov 1955. *DV* 1 Nov 1955, p. 3. *FD* 1 Nov 1955, p. 6. *HR* 1 Nov 1955, p. 3. *MPHPD* 5 Nov 1955, p. 657. *MPW* 10 Aug 1952. *NYT* 11 Apr 1954. *NYT* 4 Jul 1954. *NYT* 13 Dec 1955, p. 55. *Var* 2 Nov 1955, p. 6.

ROSEMARY CLIMBS THE HEIGHTS (Dutch Americans)
American Film Co. *Dist* Pathé Exchange, Inc. Nov **1918?** [©American Film Co.; 11 Oct 1918; LP12966]. Si; b&w. 5 reels.
Dir Lloyd Ingraham. *Scen* Daniel F. Whitcomb. *Story* Bernard McConville.

Cast: Mary Miles Minter (*Rosemary Van Voort*), Allan Forrest (*Ricardo Fitzmaurice*), Margaret Shelby (*Wanda Held*), Charlotte Mineau (*Mme. Thamar Fedoreska*), George Periolat (*Godfrey Van Voort*), Nanine Wright (*Hilda Van Voort*), Jack Farrell (*Jacob Lowenstein*), Carl Stockdale (*Andrieff*), Lewis King (*Cornelius Simpson*), Rosita Marstini (*Mrs. Preston-Carr*).

Crime, Drama. Rosemary Van Voort, who lives in the country with her elderly Dutch parents, develops a genius for carving wooden dolls. She so impresses a group of artists who are picnicing in the area, including aspiring opera singer Ricardo Fitzmaurice, that they convince her to move to New York's Bohemia to develop her talent. With the help of Ricardo and Wanda Held, Rosemary soon becomes the most successful artist in the colony. She is completely happy in her new station until Madame Thamar Fedoreska, whose jealousy of Ricardo's attentions to Rosemary has driven her insane, threatens to kill her. Still carrying Rosemary's revolver, Mme. Fedoreska returns to her room, where she is shocked to find the husband and son she deserted in Russia waiting for her. The angry husband shoots his wife and then, taking the boy, disappears, leaving Rosemary to face a murder charge. Because Ricardo is in Chicago for the debut of his opera, Rosemary is deprived of her only alibi, and things appear hopeless until the boy, whose father has died, confesses to the police. Unburdened of their woes, Rosemary and Ricardo face a bright future. *Artists. Bohemians and Bohemianism. Country girls. Dutch Americans. False arrests. Lure of the city. Murder. Opera singers. Woodworkers. Children. Confession (Law). Desertion (Marital). Dolls. Firearms. Jealousy. New York City. Russian Americans.*

ETR 19 Oct 1918, p. 1719. *ETR* 26 Oct 1918, p. 1761. *MPN* 19 Oct 1918, p. 2607. *MPN* 26 Oct 1918, p. 2709. *MPW* 26 Oct 1918, p. 542. *MPW* 30 Nov 1918, p. 989. *NYDM* 9 Nov 1918, p. 698. *Var* 1 Nov 1918, p. 38. *Wid's* 28 Oct 1918, p. 4.

ROSIE O'GRADY (Irish Americans)
Apollo Pictures. *Dist* Art Dramas, Inc. 1 Feb **1917** [©Thomas A. Edison, Inc.; 20 Mar 1916; LP7868]. Si; b&w. 5 reels.
Dir John H. Collins. *Scen* John H. Collins. *Cam* John Arnold.
Cast: Viola Dana (*Rosie O'Grady*), Thomas F. Blake ("*Chimmie*"), James Harris ("*Cyclone*" *Johnny Allen*).
Drama. Rosie O'Grady, a little "newsy" of the East side, idolizes champion prizefighter "Cyclone" Johnny Allen. When Rosie is insulted by a masher, her brother Chimmie gives the man a thrashing, but during the scuffle, Chimmie is badly hurt. While taking care of the newsstand for her brother, Rosie meets Johnny Allen who, after several dates, suggests that Rosie accompany him to Europe. Taking advantage of her innocence, Johnny has a mock marriage performed and then casts Rosie aside once they reach Europe. With the aid of the ambassador, Rosie returns to America where she learns that her brother has killed Johnny to avenge her and has just been brought to trial. He is sentenced to death, but just when things seem darkest, Rosie wakes up to find that it has all been a dream. *Boxers. Dreams. Idolatry. Ingenues. Marriage–Fake. Americans in foreign countries. Brothers and sisters. Desertion (Marital). Fights. Irish Americans. Lechery. New York City–East Side. News vendors. Revenge. Trials. United States. Diplomatic and Consular Service.*

Note: The working title of this film was *His Sister's Champion*, under which it was copyrighted.

ETR 10 Feb 1917, p. 704. *MPN* 17 Feb 1917, p. 1090. *MPW* 17 Feb 1917, p. 1034. *NYDM* 10 Feb 1917, p. 26. *Wid's* 8 Feb 1917, p. 85.

ROUGH SEAS (*foreign version*) see MONERÍAS

ROUGH SKETCH see WE ERE STRANGERS

ROULETTE see WHEEL OF CHANCE

THE ROYAL BED (*foreign version*) see ECHEC AU ROI

THE ROYAL BOX see DIE KNIGSLOGE

RUBBER RACKETEERS (Chinese Americans)
K-B Productions. *Dist* Monogram Pictures Corp. 26 Jun **1942**; *Prod:* 15 May—late May 1942 [©Monogram Pictures Corp.; 26 Jun 1942; LP11487]. Sd; b&w. 7 reels, 5,876 ft. 65-67 min. PCA cert no. 8340.
Prod Maurice King. *Assoc prod* Franklin King. *Dir* Harold Young. *Asst dir* Arthur Gardner and Herman King. *Orig scr* Henry Blankfort. *Photog* L. Wm. O'Connell. *Art dir* Frank Dexter, Sr. *Film ed* Jack Dennis. *Mus dir* David Chudnow. *Sd eng* Glen Glenn. *Prod mgr* Mack V. Wright.

Cast: Ricardo Cortez (*Gilin*), Rochelle Hudson (*Nikki*), Bill Henry (*Bill Barry*), Barbara Read (*Mary Dale*), John Abbott (*Dumbo*), Dick Rich (*Mule*), Dewey Robinson (*Larkin*), Sam Edwards (*Freddy Dale*), Kam Tong (*Tom*), Milburn Stone (*Angel*), Pat Gleason (*Curley*), Alex Callam (*Butch*), Alan Hale, Jr. (*Red*), Dick Hogan (*Bert*), Marjorie Manners (*Lila*).

Crime, Drama. [*Not viewed*]. One night while driving home, ex-convict Gilin collides with defense workers Bill Barry and Mary Dale. Bill's tires are destroyed, and when the insurance company is unable to replace them, Gilin's girl friend Nikki convinces him to exchange Bill's car for the car of Gilin's Chinese servant Tom, who has enlisted in the Army. With government restrictions on rubber in place due to the war, Gilin goes into business stealing and re-selling good tires, then sells tires retreaded with cheap synthetic rubber to used-car lots. When one of Gilin's retreads blows out and causes the death of Mary's brother, Bill and his co-workers are outraged and become determined to find the culprit behind the shoddy tires. Gilin worries that his scheme will be discovered after Bill traces a tire to his lot. Nikki is pressured by Gilin to accept a date with Bill, but pretends not to be able to reach him, then secretly warns Mary of Gilin's murderous intentions. However, Bill goes to see Nikki, intending to ask her about the tire, and falls right into Gilin's trap. Gilin knocks Bill out and plans to kill him with Tom's help, but Tom refuses to participate when he learns that Gilin has been short-changing the war effort for his own gain. Gilin shoots Tom and escapes with Nikki to his warehouse. With his last breath, Tom awakens Bill and tells him to follow Gilin. Bill calls his co-workers and the police, and they raid the warehouse en masse. During the mêlée, Gilin is shot by one of his own thugs, who is appalled that Gilin would kill Tom, a soldier. *Defense plant workers. Ex-convicts. Murder. Racketeers. Rubber. Accidental death. Automobile accidents. Brothers and sisters. Chinese Americans. Police. Rationing in wartime. Servants. Warehouses.*

Note: The working titles of this film were *Tire Gangster* and *Hot Rubber*. According to a *HR* news item, both Monogram and 20th Century-Fox initially registered the title *Hot Rubber*, and both stories dealt with tire racketeers. The Fox film was never made, however.

Box 4 Jul 1942. *DV* 20 Mar 1942. *DV* 28 May 1942. *DV* 24 Jun 1942, p. 3. *FD* 30 Jun 1942, p. 7. *HR* 6 Apr 1942. *HR* 24 Jun 1942, p. 4. *MPHPD* 27 Jun 1942, p. 751. *Var* 1 Jul 1942, p. 8.

RUBY *see* **LAZY RIVER**

RUGGLES OF RED GAP (English Americans)
Essanay Film Mfg Co.; Perfection Pictures; A George K Spoor Ultra Feature. *Dist* George Kleine System. 25 Feb **1918** [©Essanay Film Mfg. Co.; 14 Feb 1918; LP12094]. Si; b&w. 7 reels.
Dir Lawrence C. Windom. *Adpt* Charles J. McGuirk. *Cam* Arthur E. Reeves.
Source: Based on the novel *Ruggles of Red Gap* by Harry Leon Wilson (New York, 1915).
Cast: Taylor Holmes (*Marmaduke Ruggles*), Frederick Burton (*Cousin Egbert Floud*), Lawrence D'Orsay (*Hon. George Vane-Basingwell*), Virginia Valli (*Widow Judson*), Edna Phillips (*"Klondike" Kate Kenner*), Lillian Drew (*Mrs. Effie Floud*), Rose Mayo (*Ma Pettingill*), Charles Lane (*Earl of Brinstead*), Rod La Rocque (*Belknap Jackson*), Frances Conrad (*Mrs. Belknap Jackson*), James F. Fulton (*Jeff Tuttle*), Ferdinand Munier (*Sen. Floud*).
Western, Comedy. After the Hon. George Vane-Basingwell loses his valet, Marmaduke Ruggles, to U.S. Senator Floud and his wife Effie in a Paris poker game, the impeccably groomed and well-mannered valet finds himself en route to Red Gap, Arizona. Hoping to improve her gruff cousin Egbert's uncouth manners and appearance, Mrs. Effie places Ruggles in Egbert's care, and the Westerner, quite taken with the valet, introduces him to the townspeople as "Col. Ruggles of England." Mistaking him for an aristocrat, Red Gap gives Ruggles a royal welcome, and later, he opens the town's most elegant restaurant. On a visit to Arizona, the Hon. George falls in love with "Klondike" Kate Kenner, which so disturbs Ruggles that he wires George's brother, the Earl of Brinstead, to come to Red Gap immediately. The earl, however, falls for Kate even harder and finally marries her, while Ruggles, having filed for American citizenship, proposes to the charming widow Judson. *Arizona. English. Mistaken identity. Nobility. Restaurants. Valets. Brothers. Citizenship. Cousins. Etiquette. Paris (France). Poker (Game). Proposals (Marital). United States. Congress. Senate. Widows.*

Note: *Ruggles of Red Gap* was also produced as a play in New York, opening 25 Dec 1915, and ran as a serial in *The Saturday Evening Post*. Some of the exterior scenes were filmed in the Grand Canyon, AZ. Taylor Holmes and Edna Phillips were married at the time of the film. For other film adaptations of Harry Leon Wilson's play, see entry below for the 1935 *Ruggles of Red Gap*.
ETR 2 Mar 1918, p. 1068. *MPN* 16 Mar 1918, p. 1608. *MPW* 2 Mar 1918, p. 1275. *MPW* 9 Mar 1918, pp. 1408-09. *NYDM* 16 Mar 1918, p. 22. *Var* 15 Mar 1918, p. 43. *Wid's* 14 Mar 1918, pp. 1066-67.

RUGGLES OF RED GAP (English Americans)
Famous Players-Lasky Corp. *Dist* Paramount Pictures. 7 Oct **1923**; New York premiere: 9 Sep 1923 [©Famous Players-Lasky Corp.; 12 Sep 1923; LP19404]. Si; b&w. 8 reels, 7,590 ft.
Pres Jesse L. Lasky. *Dir* James Cruze. *Scen* Walter Woods and Anthony Coldeway. *Photog* Karl Brown.
Source: Based on the play *Ruggles of Red Gap* by Harry Leon Wilson (New York, 25 Dec 1915).
Cast: Edward Horton (*Ruggles*), Ernest Torrence (*Cousin Egbert Floud*), Lois Wilson (*Kate Kenner*), Fritzi Ridgeway (*Emily Judson*), Charles Ogle (*Jeff Tuttle*), Louise Dresser (*Mrs. Effie Floud*), Anna Lehr (*Mrs. Belknap-Jackson*), William Austin (*Mr. Belknap-Jackson*), Lillian Leighton (*Ma Pettingill*), Thomas Holding (*Earl of Brinstead*), Frank Elliott (*Honorable George*), Kalla Pasha (*Herr Schwitz*), Sidney Bracey (*Sam Henshaw*), Milt Brown (*Senator Pettingill*), Guy Oliver (*Judge Ballard*), Mister Barker (*Himself, a dog*).
Western, Comedy. Newly rich, uncouth Cousin Egbert Floud wins Ruggles, the valet of a British gentleman, in a poker game during a sojourn in Europe with his wife, Effie, and, to his family's chagrin, introduces Ruggles to Red Gap as a colonel. The people of Red Gap treat "Colonel" Ruggles as an honored guest. Ruggles' former employer visits them and falls in love with Kate Kenner, from the other side of the tracks. The chap's brother is summoned to break up the match: he does so by marrying Kate. Meanwhile Ruggles has opened a successful restaurant and married Emily Judson, charming protegée of Kate Kenner. *Dogs. English in foreign countries. Nouveaux riches. Poker (Game). Restaurants. Valets.*
Note: For other filmed adaptations of Harry Leon Wilson's play, see entry below for the 1935 *Ruggles of Red Gap*.
MPW 22 Sep 1923. *NYT* 10 Sep 1923, p. 15.

RUGGLES OF RED GAP (English Americans)
Paramount Productions, Inc. *Dist* Paramount Productions, Inc. 8 Mar **1935**; *Prod:* began 6 Nov 1934 [©Paramount Productions, Inc.; 19 Feb 1935; LP5344]. Sd (Western Electric Noiseless Recording); b&w. 10 reels, 8,106 ft. 90 min. Passed by the National Board of Review. PCA cert no. 537.
Pres ADOLPH ZUKOR. *Prod* Arthur Hornblow, Jr. [*Exec prod* Emanuel Cohen]. *Dir* Leo McCarey. [*Asst dir* A. F. Erickson]. *Scr* Walter DeLeon and Harlan Thompson. *Adpt* Humphrey Pearson. [*Contr to adpt* Jack Cunningham and William Slavens McNutt]. [*Contr on special seq* Arthur Macrae]. [*Contr to trmt* Garnett Weston]. *Photog* Alfred Gilks. [*Art dir* Hans Dreier and Robert Odell]. [*Film ed* Edward Dmytryk]. [*Cost* Travis Banton]. [*Sd* Phil G. Wisdom]. [*Press agent* Robert M. Gillham].
Music: "The Maple Leaf Rag" by Scott Joplin.
Song(s): "Pretty Baby," music and lyrics by Gus Kahn; other songs, music by Ralph Rainger, lyrics by Sam Coslow.
Source: Based on the novel *Ruggles of Red Gap* by Harry Leon Wilson (New York, 1915).
Cast: CHARLES LAUGHTON ([*Colonel Marmaduke "Bill"*] *Ruggles*), MARY BOLAND (*Effie Floud*), CHARLIE RUGGLES (*Egbert* [*"Sourdough"*] *Floud*), ZASU PITTS (*Mrs. [Prunella] Judson*), ROLAND YOUNG (*Earl of Burnstead* [*also known as Hon. George Vane Bassingwell*]), LEILA HYAMS (*Nell Kenner*), Maude Eburne (*"Ma" Pettingill*), Lucien Littlefield (*Charles Belknap-Jackson*), Leota Lorraine (*Mrs. Belknap-Jackson*), James Burke (*Jeff Tuttle*), Dell Henderson (*Sam*), Clarence Wilson (*Jake Henshaw*), [Ricard Cezon (*Baby Judson*)], [Augusta Anderson (*Mrs. Wallaby*)], [Brenda Fowler (*Mrs. Judy Ballard*)], [Sarah Edwards (*Mrs. Myron Carey*)], [Alice Ardell (*Lisette*)], [George Burton (*Hank*)], [Frank Rice (*Buck*)], [William Welsh (*Eddie*)], [Genaro Spagnoli (*Frank*)], [Willie Fung (*Willie*)], [Victor Potel, Harry Bernard (*Cowboys*)], [Lee Kohlmar (*Red Gap jailer*)], [Rolfe Sedan (*Barber*)], [Jack Norton (*Barfly*)], [James Welch (*Man in saloon*)], [Libby Taylor (*Black servant*)], [Armand Kaliz (*Clothing salesman*)], [Rafael Storm (*Second clothing salesman*)], [Harry Bowen (*Photographer*)], [Henry Roquemore, J. W.

Johnston, Heinie Conklin, Scott Seaton, Edward Le Saint (*Men at wedding*)], [Charles Fallon (*Paris cafe waiter*)], [Albert Petit (*Waiter at carousel*)], [Carrie Daumery, Isabelle La Mal (*Effie's guests in Paris*)], [Alex Chivra (*First chef*)], [C. L. Sherwood (*Second chef*)], [Ernest S. Adams (*Dishwasher*)], [Patsy O'Byrne, Jane Kerr, Jane Keckley (*Cooks*)], [Frank O'Connor (*Station agent*)].

Comedy, Social, Western. [*Print viewed*]. In Paris in the spring of 1908, the Earl of Burnstead regretfully informs his manservant, Marmaduke Ruggles, that he has lost Ruggles in a poker game to the genial, but roughhewn millionaire Egbert "Sourdough" Floud, who, on the insistence of his dominating, society-conscious wife Effie, intends to take Ruggles to their home in Red Gap, Washington. Before they leave Paris, however, Ruggles, who is assigned to oversee his new master's cultural education, begins to fall under Egbert's egalitarian influence, getting drunk and abandoning many of his professional traditions. In Red Gap, Egbert continues to treat Ruggles as an equal. He playfully introduces Ruggles as a colonel and generates a false newspaper article that obliges Effie and her snobbish brother-in-law, Charles Belknap-Jackson, to pretend that Ruggles is an honored guest instead of a servant. When Belknap-Jackson dismisses Ruggles, he sadly packs his bags and, while waiting for the train, enters the Silver Dollar Saloon. There, Egbert and his wealthy, down-to-earth mother-in-law, "Ma" Pettingill, are outraged to learn that Belknap-Jackson fired Ruggles without their consent. A discussion of egalitarianism ensues, and when no one in the bar can remember President Abraham Lincoln's address at Gettysburg, Ruggles recites the speech in full from memory to the astonishment of the crowd. He then decides to become the first Ruggles in generations to quit being a manservant and go into business for himself. With the help of widow Prunella Judson, a local woman with whom he is smitten, and a business loan from Egbert and Ma, Ruggles begins work on his restaurant. When Effie informs Ruggles of the impending visit of the Earl of Burnstead, who wants him to return to his service, Ruggles' loyalty to the earl and to his profession causes him to hesitate. When the earl arrives and Ruggles is found missing, Prunella fears he may have jumped in the river, but his Americanization has gone too far; he shows up and declares his independence to the earl, who congratulates him. The night Ruggles' Anglo-American Grill opens, Effie, Belnap-Jackson and their society friends are among the guests. When the earl arrives with his bride, Nell Kenner, a dancer and native of Red Gap, Belnap-Jackson insults the earl for marrying beneath his class, and Ruggles throws him out. Returning to the kitchen, Ruggles fears the incident has caused his ruin, but the earl gives a speech in Ruggles' honor. The crowd then breaks into a chorus of "For He's a Jolly Good Fellow," and Ruggles is overjoyed to realize they are singing, not for the earl, but for him. *Class distinction. English in foreign countries. In-laws. Nouveaux riches.* Social climbers. Valets. The West. Americans in foreign countries. City-country contrast. Cowboys. Drunkenness. Friendship. *The Gettysburg Address.* Henpecked husbands. Millionaires. Mistaken identity. Newspapers. Nobility. Paris (France). Poker (Game). Restaurateurs. Saloons. Washington (State). Widows.

Note: Harry Leon Wilson's novel was serialized in *SEP* and was adapted for the stage by Harrison Rhodes (New York, 25 Dec 1915). A production still for the film shows actress Georgia Caine in one scene, but her appearance in the released film has not been confirmed. On 3 Aug 1934, *DV* announced that Charlie Ruggles had been replaced by Sidney Toler because Ruggles was working on *The Pursuit of Happiness*. By 24 Aug, however, Ruggles was back in the cast so that Paramount could capitalize on the "team build-up" of Ruggles and Mary Boland. Their first film in which they played husband and wife was *The Night of June 13* (see *AFI Catalog of Feature Films, 1931-40*; F3.3137). In an early script, dated 3 Nov 1934—three days before production began—Baby LeRoy is listed for the role of "Baby Judson," but was later replaced by Ricard Cezon. According to *HR* news items, shooting on this film was delayed because Charles Laughton was returned to Paramount from M-G-M with a shaved head, after playing the part of Micawber in M-G-M's *David Copperfield* for two days. M-G-M dismissed Laughton and replaced him with W. C. Fields (for more information, see the entry on *David Copperfield* in *AFI Catalog of Feature Films, 1931-40*; F3.0971) Paramount reportedly asked M-G-M to pay the studio for the delay.
Ruggles of Red Gap was nominated for an Academy Award for Best Picture of 1935, as were two other Laughton films: *Les Miserables* and *Mutiny on the Bounty*, which won the award (see *AFI Catalog of Feature Films, 1931-40*; F3.2900 and F3.3020). The New York Film Critics Circle, in their first annual award, selected Laughton as Best Actor of 1935 for his performance as Ruggles and his portrayal of Captain Bligh, for which he was nominated for an Academy Award for Best Actor. *Ruggles of Red Gap* was one of *FD*'s "Ten Best Pictures of 1935" and was listed in the 1935-36 *MPA* as a Mar 1935 "Box Office

Champion." Although Ralph Rainger and Sam Coslow are credited with having written songs for this film, no titles were found. According to the autobiography of Elsa Lanchester, Laughton's wife, Paramount bought the story and appointed McCarey as director at Laughton's request. Before the film began shooting, Lanchester states, Laughton worked with McCarey and the film's writers on the script, and hired an old friend, Arthur MacRae, who later became a playwright in England, to add the "necessary Englishness" of Ruggles.
Reviews praised Laughton highly for his performance in this film. *DV* reported that "for the first time in pictures, he has not been cast as a psychopathic subject." *Var* remarked that "it's not satire; it's not a pathological character study. Just plain comedy, and he's splendid, especially when he uses that dead pan." *NYT* stated that "Laughton gives us a pudgy, droll and quite irresistible Ruggles who reveals only the briefest taint of the Laughton pathology." Laughton specifically was praised for his serious delivery of Lincoln's "Gettysburg Address" to a silenced audience of barflies and cowboys in a saloon. *Var* called McCarey's insertion of the speech "dangerous" and "audacious." *DV* reported that the sequence brought "sustained applause from the audience, due to Laughton's delivery." In an article in *SEP* in 1949, Laughton wrote that Ruggles became his favorite role. He referred to his reading of the "Gettysburg Address" in the film as "one of the most moving things that ever happened to me." According to a modern source, Laughton recited the address to the cast and crew of *Mutiny on the Bounty* on the last day of shooting on Catalina Island and again on the set of *The Hunchback of Notre Dame*. According to a modern source, Nazi Germany banned the release of any German-dubbed version of this film because of the Gettysburg Address speech.
A modern source also reports that Laughton wanted Ruth Gordon to play the role of Mrs. Judson. According to Lanchester's biography, while rehearsing for *Ruggles of Red Gap*, Laughton was hospitalized for several weeks for a rectal abscess. According to *DV*, following the box office success of this film, M-G-M optioned all of the Harry Leon Wilson "Ma Pettingill" stories, and Wilson joined the M-G-M writing staff on 15 Apr 1935. Paramount re-issued *Ruggles of Red Gap* in late Aug 1937. Wilson's story was the source of a 1918 Essanay film directed by Lawrence C. Windom, starring Taylor Holmes; a 1923 Famous Players-Lasky film directed by James Cruze and starring Edward Everett Horton (see above entries); and the 1950 Paramount film, *Fancy Pants*, starring Bob Hope and Lucille Ball.

DV 3 Aug 1934, p. 1. *DV* 6 Nov 1934, p. 3. *DV* 2 Feb 1935, p. 3. *DV* 13 Apr 1935, p. 1. *FD* 19 Feb 1935, p. 6. *HR* 29 Oct 1934, p. 2. *HR* 2 Feb 1935, p. 3. *HR* 14 Mar 1935, p. 2. *HR* 28 Aug 1937, p. 4. *MPD* 4 Feb 1935, p. 9. *MPH* 17 Nov 1934, p. 45. *MPH* 16 Feb 1935, p. 47. *NYT* 7 Mar 1935, p. 26. *SEP* 28 May 1949. *Var* 13 Mar 1935, p. 15. *Var* 20 Mar 1935, p. 15.

RUN OF THE ARROW (Native Americans, Dakota)
Globe Enterprises, Inc.; RKO Teleradio Pictures, Inc. *Dist* Universal Pictures Co., Inc. Sep **1957**; New York opening: 2 Aug 1957; Prod: mid-Jun—mid-Jul 1956 [©RKO Teleradio Pictures, Inc.; 21 Apr 1957; LP8675]. Sd (RCA Sound System); col; RKO-Scope. 7,712 ft. 85-86 min. PCA cert no. 18169.

Prod Samuel Fuller. *Dir* Samuel Fuller. *Asst dir* Ben Chapman. *Wrt* Samuel Fuller. *Dir of photog* Joseph Biroc. *Art 'dir* Albert S. D'Agostino and Jack Okey. *Film ed* Gene Fowler, Jr. *Mus ed* Audray Granville. *Set dec* Bert Granger. *Mus* Victor Young. *Sd* Virgil Smith and Terry Kellum. *Sd eff ed* Bert Schoenfeld. *Makeup supv* Harry Maret, Jr. *Hair stylist* Larry Germain. *Unit mgr* Gene Bryant.

Cast: Rod Steiger [(*O'Meara*)], Sarita Montiel [(*Yellow Moccasin*)], Brian Keith [(*Capt. Clark*)], Ralph Meeker [(*Lt. Driscoll*)], Jay C. Flippen [(*Walking Coyote*)], Charles Bronson [(*Blue Buffalo*)], Olive Carey [(*Mrs. O'Meara*)], H. M. Wynant [(*Crazy Wolf*)], Neyle Morrow [(*Lt. Stockwell*)], Frank de Kova [(*Red Cloud*)], Col. Tim McCoy [(*Gen. Allen*)], Stuart Randall [(*Col. Taylor*)], Frank Warner [(*Ballad singer*)], Billy Miller [(*Silent Tongue*)], Chuck Hayward [(*Corporal*)], Chuck Roberson [(*Sergeant*)], [Don Orlando (*Pvt. Vinci*)], [Bill White, Jr. (*Sgt. Moore*)], [Tex Holden (*Peg leg man*)], [Frank Baker (*Gen. Robert E. Lee*)], [Emile Avery (*Gen. Ulysses S. Grant*)], [Roscoe Ates (*Man on pier*)], [Frank O'Connor (*Man on dock*)], [Ray Stevens (*Man in boat*)], [Carleton Young (*Surgeon*)], [George Ross (*Archer*)].

Western. [*Print viewed*]. On 9 April 1865, the final day of the Civil War, O'Meara, an Irish American serving in the Virginia Infantry, shoots a Union officer and carries his wounded body back to the Confederate field hospital at Appomattox. While there, he watches as General Robert E. Lee, having just surrendered to General Ulysses S. Grant, dejectedly leaves Appomattox Courthouse. The doctor removes the bullet, the last one fired during the war, from his patient and gives it to O'Meara's friends. O'Meara returns home, where he receives the bullet as a war trophy, but is bitter nonetheless. Even his mother is unable to persuade him to accept defeat at the hands of the North, and filled with hatred, he leaves Virginia. Aware that the Sioux Indians are engaged in a war against the United States government, O'Meara guides his horse toward Sioux territory in the West. On the way he meets an old Oglala scout named Walking Coyote, who claims

that he is going home to die. Amused by O'Meara's fascination with the Sioux, Walking Coyote agrees to instruct him in Sioux customs and language. As they near Walking Coyote's tribal homeland, however, the two are captured by a group of rowdy warriors. Led by Crazy Wolf, the Indians are about to execute the men when Walking Coyote requests the "run of the arrow," a ritual in which the pursuers allow the prisoners a head start in a race for their lives. Explaining that no one has ever survived a run, Walking Coyote encourages O'Meara to exert himself, but shortly after the chase begins, the older man's heart gives out and he dies. O'Meara runs until he, too, collapses in exhaustion, but a group of Sioux women hides him from his pursuers. The next day, O'Meara presents himself to the local chief, Blue Buffalo, claiming that he has survived the run of the arrow. Crazy Wolf is baffled by the white man's escape but accepts Blue Buffalo's pronouncement that no Sioux may kill one who has survived the run. Yellow Moccasin, who hid O'Meara in her tent on that first night, nurses him back to health, and the two fall in love. Blue Buffalo agrees to accept O'Meara as a full member of the Sioux nation, allowing him both to retain his Christian religion and to marry Yellow Moccasin. The couple adopts Silent Tongue, Yellow Moccasin's mute and orphaned young companion, and the family lives happily for a time. When Sioux chief Red Cloud and Cavalry general Allen agree on terms by which the U.S. government may build a stronghold named Fort Lincoln, Red Cloud asks O'Meara to accompany the builders to the approved site. During the journey, a Yankee soldier sacrifices his life to save Silent Tongue from a pool of quicksand. Moved, O'Meara listens when the leader of the expedition, Captain Clark, remarks that Lee's surrender, rather than marking the South's demise, was "the birth of the United States." The group arrives at the appointed site, but as they begin construction, Crazy Wolf and his band of renegades attack, killing Clark. Realizing that Crazy Wolf is trying to start a war, O'Meara disarms him and gives him the opportunity to run for his life. Lieutenant Driscoll, the Indian-hating Yankee whom O'Meara had shot near Appomattox, interferes in the ritual, wounding Crazy Wolf with a bullet. O'Meara takes Crazy Wolf back to Blue Buffalo, while Driscoll, now in charge of the construction party, orders his men to build the fort in a more strategic site. Yellow Moccasin returns to the village to warn Blue Buffalo that construction is occurring outside of the agreed-upon corridor, whereupon the tribe prepares for war. Under a flag of truce, O'Meara orders the builders to return to the original site or lose their scalps. Driscoll injures O'Meara and orders his men to hang him for treason. At that moment, Blue Buffalo signals a large force to attack the expedition, and in the fierce battle that follows, most of the soldiers are killed. The Indians capture Driscoll, and as Crazy Wolf is skinning him alive for having violated the run of the arrow, O'Meara, unable to endure Driscoll's screams, kills him with the same bullet he used at Appomattox. Yellow Moccasin convinces O'Meara of his own allegiance to the U.S. flag, and together they accompany the surviving soldiers back to Fort Laramie. *Dakota Indians. Disillusionment. Racism. Rites and ceremonies. Transformation.* Adoption. Ambushes. Appomattox Campaign, 1865. Civil War veterans. Euthanasia. Fort Abraham Lincoln (ND). Indians of North America. Irish Americans. Marriage–Mixed. Massacres. Mutes. Racing. Rescues. Rites and ceremonies. Scouts (Frontier). Self-sacrifice. Soldiers. Torture. Tribal chiefs. United States–History–Civil War, 1861-1865. United States. Army. Cavalry.

Note: Samuel Fuller's onscreen credit reads: "Written, produced-directed by Samuel Fuller." The film includes the following written prologue: "Palm Sunday, April 9, 1865, Appomattox, Virginia. The last day of the war between the states." It closes with the following statement: "The end of this story can only be written by you." According to production notes contained in the AMPAS Production Library, the military outpost set was built in the desert outside of St. George, UT. The set was completely razed by fire during the Indian attack sequence. The production files add that 150 Navajo Indians were brought from Arizona to work as extras on the production. Frank M. Warner, a leading interpreter of American folk music, made his screen debut in the film. Modern sources note that Angie Dickinson dubbed the voice of Sarita Montiel. According to a modern source, this production was completed at the time of RKO Radio Pictures demise as a producing and releasing organization, and consequently, the domestic distribution of the film was taken over by Universal-International.

Box 15 Jun 1957. *DV* 28 May 1957, p. 4. *Exb* 12 Jun 1957, p. 4338. *FD* 6 Jun 1957, p. 6. *Har* 1 Jun 1957, p. 87. *HR* 15 Jun 1956, p. 10. *HR* 25 Jul 1956, p. 10. *HR* 28 May 1957, p. 3. *MPHPD* 1 Jun 1957, p. 402. *NYT* 3 Aug 1957, p. 8. *Var* 29 May 1957, p. 6.

RUNAWAY *see* **SO YOUNG, SO BAD**

RUNAWAY ROMANY (Gypsies)

Ardsley Art Film Corp.; A Pathé Special. *Dist* Pathé Exchange, Inc. 23 Dec **1917** [©Pathé Exchange, Inc.; 22 May 1918; LU12440]. Si; b&w. 5 reels.

Dir George W. Lederer. *Story and scen* Marion Davies. *Cam* H. J. Butler.

Cast: Marion Davies (*Romany*), Joseph Kilgour (*Theodore True*), Matt Moore (*Bud Haskell*), Ormi Hawley (*Anitra St. Clair*), Gladden James ("*Inky*" *Ames*), Boyce Combe (*Hobart*), W. W. Bittner (*Zelaya*), Pedro de Cordoba (*Zinga*).

Drama. Press agent "Inky" Ames, in a quandary to publicize showgirl Anitra St. Clair, convinces her to paint a birthmark on her shoulder and pose as millionaire mine owner Theodore True's long-lost daughter. The impersonation works, and Anitra accompanies True to inspect a Western mine. Bud Haskell, True's Western representative and schoolmaster to a gypsy tribe, introduces the beautiful gypsy Romany, who ran away to escape marrying the chief's son Zinga, to True, who takes Romany back East with them. When Anitra begins cavorting with True's willing nephew Hobart, Inky confesses the ruse to True. Meanwhile, Romany, back from boarding school, happily receives Bud at her first party. After Romany catches Hobart robbing his uncle's strong box, Zinga tracks her down and she leaves True's home. Romany is suspected of the theft, but after True turns Anitra out, Hobart confesses. Zinga lures Romany aboard a ship, but Bud arrives to rescue her after fighting Zinga, who reveals that Romany really is True's daughter. Romany and Bud now plan to marry. *Gypsies. Impersonation and imposture. Mine owners. Schoolteachers. Show girls.* Birthmarks. Confession (Law). Long-lost relatives. Mines. Nephews. Parentage. Press agents. Publicity. Rescues. Robbery. Ships.

Note: This was Marion Davies' first film. Director George W. Lederer earlier was married to Davies' sister Reine. According to a modern source, newspaperman Paul Block, who earlier had been romantically involved with Davies, financed the film. Block had been a colleague of William Randolph Hearst, who had a long-term romantic liaison with Davies. Newspaper reporter Clarence Lindner came up with the story idea, and Davies' mother Rosa Dourdas suggested the film's title.

ETR 22 Dec 1917, p. 295. *Motog* 21 Jul 1917, p. 146. *MPN* 29 Dec 1917, pp. 4585-86. *MPW* 8 Sep 1917, p. 1514. *MPW* 22 Dec 1917, p. 1734 (ad insert), 1813. *MPW* 29 Dec 1917, p. 1954, 2001. *MPW* 12 Jan 1918, p. 274. *NYDM* 22 Dec 1917, p. 28. *Wid's* 20 Dec 1917, p. 811.

RUSSELL JANNEY'S THE MIRACLE OF THE BELLS *see* **THE MIRACLE OF THE BELLS**

RUSTLERS (Latino)

RKO Radio Pictures, Inc. *Dist* RKO Radio Pictures, Inc. 14 May **1949**; Prod: early Jun—mid-Jun 1948 [©RKO Radio Pictures, Inc.; 10 Apr 1949; LP2279]. Sd (RCA Sound System); b&w. 5,467 ft. 61 min. PCA cert no. 13215.

Prod Herman Schlom. *Dir* Lesley Selander. [*Asst dir* John Pommer]. *Orig scr* Jack Natteford and Luci Ward. *Dir of photog* J. Roy Hunt. [*Cam op* Edwin Pyle and James Daly]. [*Gaffer* Frank Uecker]. [*Stills* Ollie Sigurdson]. *Art dir* Albert S. D'Agostino and Feild Gray. *Film ed* Frank Doyle. *Set dec* Darrell Silvera and James Altwies. *Mus dir* C. Bakaleinikoff. *Mus* Paul Sawtell. *Sd* John Tribby and Terry Kellum. [*Makeup* Gordon Bau and Jack Barron]. [*Hair stylist* Hazel Rogers and Kay Shea]. [*Scr supv* Mercy Weireter]. [*Grip* Frank Williams].

Song(s): "Annabella's Bustle," words by Harry Harris, music by Lew Pollack; "Darling Nellie Gray," words and music by Benjamin Russell Hanby.

Cast: TIM HOLT [(*Dick McBride*)], Richard Martin [(*Chito Rafferty*)], Martha Hyer [(*Ruth Abbott*)], Steve Brodie [(*Wheeler*)], Lois Andrews [(*Trixie Fontaine*)], Harry Shannon [(*Sheriff Harmon*)], Addison Richards [(*Frank Abbott*)], Frank Fenton [(*Brad Carew*)], Robert Bray [(*Hank*)], Don Haggerty [(*Drake*)], Monte Montague [(*Hawkins*)], Stanley Blystone [(*Cook*)], [Herman Nowlin (*Peter*)], [Francis McDonald (*Pierre*)], [Bert Howard (*The Professor*)].

Western, with songs. [*Print viewed*]. Soon after out-of-work cowhands Dick McBride and Chito Rafferty arrive in the town of Trail Cross, they are confronted by Wheeler, a rustler. Wheeler objects to the attention that saloon singer Trixie Fontaine pays to Chito, her wandering beau, and picks a fight with him. Saloon owner Brad Carew, who is part of Wheeler's Salt River gang, breaks up the ensuing brawl, then orders Wheeler to go to the Bar One ranch. There, as

rancher Frank Abbott discusses with his neighbors the gang's recent cattle thefts, Wheeler delivers a ransom note written by Carew. The gang demands $2,000 for the return of Frank's stolen cattle, but the beleaguered rancher refuses to pay and declares his intention to sell the Bar One. Frank's feisty daughter Ruth, however, is determined to thwart the gang and suggests that they can identify the rustlers by paying the ransom with marked money. Agreeing to Ruth's plan, the ranchers pool their cash, which Ruth then marks by cutting off the corners of the bills. Dick and Chito, meanwhile, ride toward the Bar One, having seen a "help wanted" notice for the ranch. Along the way, the cowboys are shot at by Ruth, who assumes they are rustlers. Dick soon disarms Ruth and, after spanking her, playfully chastises her for being unfeminine. Later, at the ranch house, Dick and Chito speak with Frank, who tells them that he is probably selling the ranch and therefore is not hiring. Frank then delivers the ransom to a masked Wheeler, who refuses to reveal the cattle's whereabouts until later. While Wheeler hands the marked money over to Carew, Chito goes to the saloon to say goodbye to Trixie. During his farewells, Chito accidentally drops a coin on a roulette wheel number and inadvertently wins a bet. Feeling lucky, he plays the number again and wins $6,000. When Chito and Dick go to Carew's office to collect, however, Carew pulls a gun on them. Dick disarms Carew, and while he holds the saloon keeper at gunpoint, Chito removes $6,000 from the office safe. The cowboys then escape with their winnings and ride to the Bar One. There Frank agrees to sell Dick and Chito one quarter of his ranch for $5,000, but when he and Ruth see the marked ransom money in Dick's cash, they immediately draw their guns. Frank and Ruth turn Dick and Chito over to Sheriff Harmon and demand that Carew, who has accused the cowboys of stealing his money, be arrested as well. The sheriff, who is the gang's silent leader, then tells Carew to leave town and reveals his intention to kill Dick and Chito during a staged jailbreak. Before Harmon can execute his plan, however, Trixie slips Dick and Chito a cake with a gun planted inside. After Dick and Chito escape, they catch Carew outside of town and force him to go to the Bar One. There they extract a confession out of Carew and are about to learn the name of the gang's leader when Wheeler shoots the saloon keeper through a window. After Wheeler eludes the pursuing Dick and rides to town, Trixie tells Dick that Wheeler and Harmon are in Carew's office. Deducing that Harmon is the gang's leader, Dick confronts the two men at gunpoint. Soon Dick is involved in a gunfight with the gang, who trap him in a stable and set the building on fire. While Dick tries to shoot his way out, Trixie rides to the Bar One to tell Frank and Ruth, who are holding Chito, about the sheriff. Finally convinced of the cowboys' innocence, Frank releases Chito and helps rescue Dick, who then lassos the fleeing sheriff. Later, an apologetic Ruth, adorned in a frilly dress, begs Dick to stay, and he happily reveals that he and Chito have bought a share of the Bar One. Hearing the news, Trixie then suggests to Chito that they "get hitched," but the confirmed ladies' man takes off on his horse in a panic. *Cowboys. Frame-ups. Ranchers. Rustlers. Sheriffs. Chases. Confession (Law). Fathers and daughters. Fights. Fires. Gunfights. Jailbreaks. Mexican Americans. Money. Murder. Ransom. Romance. Roulette (Game). Saloon keepers. Singers. Spanking. Wagers.*

Note: The working title of this film was *Outlaw Valley*. Modern sources add Pat Patterson, George Ross, Mike Jeffers, Tom Lloyd, Art Souvern and Bob Robinson to the cast. According to modern sources, some scenes in the film were shot at the Jack Garner ranch in Idyllwild, CA.

Box 26 Mar 1949. *DV* 23 Mar 1949, p. 3. *FD* 29 Mar 1949, p. 4. *HR* 4 Jun 1948, p. 15. *HR* 23 Mar 1949, p. 3. *MPHPD* 26 Mar 1949, p. 4550. *Var* 23 Mar 1949, p. 20.

RUSTLERS OF DEVIL'S CANYON (Native Americans)

Republic Pictures Corp. *Dist* Republic Pictures Corp. 1 Jul **1947**; Prod: late Sep—mid-Oct 1946 [©Republic Pictures Corp.; 15 Jul 1947; LP1167]. Sd (RCA Sound System); b&w. 58 min. Passed by the National Board of Review. PCA cert no. 12071.

Series: Red Ryder.

Assoc prod Sidney Picker. *Dir* R. G. Springsteen. [*Asst dir* Eddie Stein]. *Orig scr* Earle Snell. *Dir of photog* William Bradford. *Spec eff* Howard Lydecker and Theodore Lydecker. *Art dir* Frank Arrigo. *Film ed* Harry Keller and [Harold Minter]. *Set dec* John McCarthy, Jr. and Otto Siegel. *Mus dir* Mort Glickman. *Sd* Victor B. Appel. *Makeup supv* Bob Mark.

Source: Based on the comic strip "Red Ryder" by Fred Harman (1938—1964), by special arrangement with Stephen Slesinger.

Cast: ALLAN LANE (*Red Ryder*), Bobby Blake [(*Little Beaver*)], Martha Wentworth [(*The Duchess*)], Peggy Stewart [(*Bess*)], Arthur Space [(*Dr. Cole*)], Emmett Lynn [(*Blizzard*)], Roy Barcroft [(*Clark*)], Tom London [(*Sheriff*)], Harry Carr [(*Tad*)], Pierce Lyden [(*Matt*)], Forrest Taylor [(*Dr. Glover*)], [Frank O'Connor (*Stableman*)].

Western. [*Print viewed*]. After the Spanish-American War, American soldier Red Ryder returns to Sioux City, Wyoming, where he is processed by an Army Discharge Center. Later, in town, Red meets Dr. Cole, a physician working for the center, who reports that Red's friend, Blizzard, has become ill. He also states that rustlers have been devastating the cattle herds owned by homesteaders who have established ranches in the area. Days later, after Blizzard has recovered, he and Red go scouting for clues in Lava Basin, where the rustlers were last seen. When they meet Red's faithful companion, Little Beaver, he reports that he has seen a posse chasing the rustlers. Rustlers Matt and Frank ambush the posse, however, shooting a few of the men and causing the herd to stampede. Later, on the trail, the sheriff informs Red about the ambush, and they continue the chase, while Little Beaver returns to town. There Cole, who is in cahoots with the rustlers, suggests that the homesteaders pool their cattle and bait the rustlers with one large cattle drive. Further east, at Sherwin's Veterans Hospital, Dr. Glover tries to recruit men for homesteading, and the veterans agree to allow Glover's assistant, Mr. Clark, to lead them to Sioux City. When homesteader Bess and her brother Tad learn that Red has called a cattlemen's meeting, they gather with the rest of the homesteaders to discuss the rustling problem. At the meeting, Red recognizes Clark as the man who tried to cheat a previous group of homesteaders. As the two fight, the rustlers decide to ambush the group, and Tad is shot. After the outlaws shoot Clark, Red rides into town, where he asks Cole to examine Tad's wounded arm. The next morning, Cole surreptitiously visits the rustlers' hideout to tend to their wounds. Later, a rock is thrown through the window at The Duchess' ranch, with a threatening note signed by the homesteaders attached. The homesteaders drive the cattle as planned, but when a fire breaks out in the Duchess' barn, Red and Blizzard are forced to leave the herd unattended in order to fight the blaze. Once the fire is extinguished, Blizzard discovers the empty oil can used to set it. At The Duchess' ranch, the sheriff questions Tad and Bess. Pretending to be homesteaders, the rustlers attack the sheriff, then tie up Tad and drag him by a horse. Tad blames Red, who escapes when the sheriff tries to arrest him and is chased by a posse. Little Beaver decides to go to the rustlers' hideout and asks Cole to come to the cave where Red is hiding. Bess discovers the cave just as Cole is giving Red some sleeping pills. He grabs her gun and locks her in a tool shed, but she quickly escapes. Matt and Cole return to the cave and fight with Red. When Blizzard and Little Beaver rush in with the sheriff, Bess faints in Red's arms, and Little Beaver becomes jealous. *Homesteaders. Physicians. Ranchers. Rustlers. Ambushes. Arson. Cattle. Caves. Fainting. Fires. Gunshot wounds. Hideouts. Horses. Hospitals. Meetings. Posses. Rocks. Sheriffs. Sleeping potions. Stampedes. Veterans.*

Note: The working title for the film was *Outlaws of Sioux City*. Modern sources include Bob Burns and Yakima Canutt in the cast. For more information on the "Red Ryder" series, please consult the Series Index and see the entry below for *Tucson Raiders*.

Box 12 Jul 1947. *DV* 7 Jul 1947. *FD* 10 Jul 1947, p. 7. *HR* 4 Oct 1946, p. 19. *HR* 11 Oct 1946, p. 11. *HR* 7 Jul 1947, p. 3. *MPHPD* 19 Jul 1947. *Var* 9 Jul 1947, p. 17.

LA RUTA DEL MARINO *see* **EN CADA PUERTO UN AMOR**

SS 111 *see* **CRASH DIVE**

THE SABLE LORCHA (Chinese Americans)

Fine Arts Film Co. *Dist* Triangle Film Corp. 17 Oct **1915** [©Triangle Film Corp.; 22 Nov 1915; LP7886]. Si; b&w. 5 reels.

Supv D. W. Griffith. *Dir* Lloyd Ingraham. *Asst dir* Henry Kotani. *Scen* Chester B. Clapp. *Cam* Hugh C. McClung. *Asst cam* Henry Kotani. *Mus accompaniment comp* J. A. Raynes.

Source: Based on the novel *The Sable Lorcha* by Horace Hazeltine (Chicago, 1912).

Cast: Tully Marshall (*Soy*), Thomas Jefferson (*Robert Cameron/ Donald Cameron*), Charles Lee (*Yup Sing*), Elmer Clifton (*Clyde*), Loretta Blake (*Evelyn*), George Pearce (*Murphy*), Hal Wilson (*The detective*), Raymond Wells (*Central office man*), Earle Raymond.

Crime. Retired businessman Robert Cameron receives three mysterious threats at his Connecticut home, the last of which warns him of his impending death. Accompanied by Phillip Clyde, his

future son-in-law, Robert sails out to sea on his yacht where he picks up a Chinese man, Soy, whom he believes to be a castaway fisherman. Soy drugs Robert and Phillip, rendering them both unconscious, and after releasing Phillip on shore, kidnaps Robert. While holding him captive in a box, Soy reveals his desire to kill the old man for causing the death of dozens of his countrymen many years before during a disastrous smuggling attempt. Unknown to Soy, Robert has a twin brother Donald, who made his money bringing in illegal aliens on a Chinese junk, or sable lorcha, and was the actual perpetrator of the crime. Leaving Robert to endure a slow, torturous death, Soy returns to shore where Phillip tracks him down to Chinatown. The twin brother shows up outside Robert's mansion and is badly beaten by two of Soy's confederates. On a tip from Phillip, the police follow one of the attackers and rescue Robert from Soy's deadly trap. *Chinese Americans. Kidnapping. Mistaken identity. Revenge. Twins. Businessmen. Connecticut. Drugs. Imprisonment. Junks. New York City–Chinatown. Police. Smuggling. Torture. Yachts and yachting.*
   Motog 17 Jul 1915, p. 100. *Motog* 6 Nov 1915, p. 972. *Motog* 4 Dec 1915, p. 1211. *MPN* 10 Jul 1915, p. 62. *MPN* 4 Sep 1915, p. 50, 61. *MPN* 30 Oct 1915, p. 86. *MPN* 27 Nov 1915, p. 114.

THE SABRE AND THE ARROW *see* **LAST OF THE COMANCHES**

SACAJAWEA OF THE SHOSHONES *see* **THE FAR HORIZONS**

THE SACRED FLAME *(foreign version) see* **LA LLAMA SAGRADA**

SADDLEMATES (Native Americans)
   Republic Pictures Corp. *Dist* Republic Pictures Corp. 26 May **1941**; Prod: 14 Apr–23 Apr 1941 [©Republic Pictures Corp.; 26 May 1941; LP10537]. Sd (RCA Sound System); b&w. 6 reels, 5028 ft. 55-56 min. Passed by the National Board of Review. PCA cert no. 7321.
   Series: The Three Mesquiteers.
   Assoc prod Louis Gray. *Dir* Les Orlebeck. *Scr* Albert DeMond and Herbert Dalmas. *Orig story* Bernard McConville and Karen DeWolf. *Photog* William Nobles and [Bud Thackeray]. *Film ed* Tony Martinelli. *Mus score* Cy Feuer. *Prod mgr* Al Wilson.
   Song(s): "Just Imagine That," words and music by Smiley Burnette.
   Source: Based on characters created by William Colt MacDonald.
   Cast: Robert Livingston (*"Stony" Brooke*), Bob Steele (*"Tucson" Smith*), Rufe Davis (*"Lullaby" Joslin*), Gale Storm [(*Susan Langley*)], Forbes Murray [(*Colonel Langley*)], Cornelius Keefe [(*Lieutenant Bob Manning*)], Peter George Lynn [(*LeRoque, also known as Wanechee*)], Marin Sais [(*Mrs. Langley*)], Marty Faust [(*Thunder Bird*)], Glenn Strange [(*Little Bear*)], Ellen Lowe [(*Aunt Amanda*)], Iron Eyes Cody [(*Black Eagle*)], [Jack Kirk (*Han*)].
   Western. [*Print viewed*]. When Congress changes a boundary between Mexico and Texas, the rangers of the Red River headquarters leave their station, and a U.S. Cavalry unit, headed by Colonel Langley, takes over and prepares to deal with the hostile Indians. Ranger Captain Miller warns Langley that the warmongering Wanechee will be difficult to apprehend, and that his own best men, "Stony" Brooke, "Tucson" Smith and "Lullaby" Joslin, who are known as "The Three Mesquiteers," are searching for him. When the Mesquiteers return to the post, they learn that Langley wants them to stay on as scouts. The Mesquiteers want nothing to do with the cavalry, but change their minds after meeting Langley's pretty daughter Susan. After they sign on, the Mesquiteers tell Langley that he is wrong to initiate peace talks with the Indians, but he insists that the fighting must end. He sends Stony, Tucson and two troopers to follow the post's half-breed interpreter, LeRoque, on a mission to propose a peaceful meeting with Wanechee and the other chiefs. LeRoque, who is actually Wanechee, plans an ambush, but Tucson spots the trap. Although Tucson and Stony escape, one of the troopers is killed, and Langley, thinking that the Mesquiteers are to blame, arrests them. Susan, who believes that they should be given another chance, talks Langley into releasing them, but after they are involved in a saloon brawl, Stony is discharged from the cavalry and Susan turns against him. Determined to investigate LeRoque, of whom they have become suspicious, Tucson and Lullaby also get discharged. While exploring the hills, the Mesquiteers are captured by Wanechee, whom they do not recognize as LeRoque, while he is preparing a trap for a wagon train. The Mesquiteers escape with two Indians as prisoners, and while they question them at their hideout, LeRoque tells Langley that there will be no peace while the Mesquiteers keep their prisoners. Langley sends Lieutenant Bob Manning to get the

Mesquiteers, but while they are talking to the troopers, LeRoque's henchman beats the prisoners to death to prevent them from talking. After the Mesquiteers are arrested for murder, LeRoque convinces peaceful Chief Thunder Bird that the Indians must attack the wagon train, which carries rifles as well as Langley's wife and son. As Manning is returning the Mesquiteers to the post, LeRoque sends word to Langley that the wagon train has been delayed until the next day, and that he should meet the chiefs for a peace treaty. Langley and his men are captured by LeRoque, and after the Indians put on their uniforms, they meet the wagon train. Meanwhile, the Mesquiteers reach the post, and Susan pleads with Bob to let them go. He refuses, but the Mesquiteers escape from the guardhouse, and while Lullaby and Stony ride to find the colonel, Tucson goes to aid the wagon train. Stony and Lullaby arrive with Langley as the settlers are about to be overwhelmed, and soon LeRoque is exposed as Wanechee. Later, the Langleys express their thanks to the Mesquiteers, who then leave to begin peace talks with Thunder Bird. *Duplicity. Indians of North America. Indians–Mixed blood. Texas Rangers. United States. Army. Cavalry. Ambushes. Aunts. Fistfights. Impersonation and imposture. Murder. Officers (Military). Wagers. Wagon trains.*
   Note: The working title of this film was *Old Spanish Trail.* A 18 Apr 1941 *HR* production chart lists Bud Thackeray as the photographer, although the onscreen credits list William Nobles. Modern sources include Chief Yowlachie, Henry Wills, Bill Hazlett and Major Bill Keefer in the cast. For additional information on the series, consult the Series Index and see entry for *The Three Mesquiteers* in *AFI Catalog of Feature Films, 1931-40;* F3.4617.
   Box 21 Jun 1941. *FD* 11 Jun 1941, p. 4. *HR* 10 Apr 1941, p. 4. *HR* 18 Apr 1941, p. 10. *HR* 24 Apr 1941, p. 7. *MPH* 14 Jun 1941, p. 36. *Var* 18 Jun 1941.

SAILOR IZZY MURPHY (Jewish Americans)
   Warner Bros. Pictures, Inc. *Dist* Warner Bros. Pictures, Inc. 8 Oct **1927** [©Warner Bros. Pictures, Inc.; 28 Sep 1927; LP24456]. Si; b&w. 7 reels, 6,020 ft.
   Dir Henry Lehrman. *Asst dir* Frank Shaw. *Story and scen* E. T. Lowe, Jr. *Cam* Frank Kesson.
   Cast: George Jessel (*Izzy Goldberg*), Audrey Ferris (*Marie*), Warner Oland (*Monsieur Jules de Gondelaurier*), John Miljan (*Orchid Joe*), Otto Lederer (*Jake*), Theodore Lorch (*First mate*), Clara Horton (*Cecile*).
   Comedy-drama. Izzy, a perfume vendor, is urged by Jake, his partner, to sell Monsieur Jules, a millionaire perfume merchant, their special formula, but the merchant is incensed to see his daughter's picture on Izzy's perfume bottles and gives him the bum's rush. Aboard Jules's palatial yacht, he receives from Orchid Joe notes threatening his life. Joe is a lunatic who hates people who destroy flowers, and he plans to kill Jules with the help of a crew of maniacs on the yacht. Izzy gets aboard by announcing himself as "Muscle-Bound Murphy," along with Jake, and they promise to help the millionaire and his daughter, Marie. When Izzy is assigned to kill Jules, he feigns great joy and induces Jake to stand in for the assassination, but they are captured by the crew. Through his cleverness, Izzy outsmarts the maniacs and attracts a rescue party, thus closing the sale and winning the love of Marie. *Jews. Lunatics. Millionaires. Partnership. Perfume. Yachts and yachting.*

THE SAILOR TAKES A WIFE (Romanian Americans, African
      Americans)
   Metro-Goldwyn-Mayer Corp.; controlled by Loew's Inc. *Dist* Loew's Inc. Jan–Feb **1946**; Prod: mid-Mar–late May 1945 [©Loew's Inc.; 12 Dec 1945; LP4]. Sd (Western Electric Sound System); b&w. 91-92 min. Passed by the National Board of Review. PCA cert no. 10949.
   Prod Edwin H. Knopf. *Dir* Richard Whorf. [*Asst dir* Jack Greenwood]. *Scr* Chester Erskine, Anne Morrison Chapin and Whitfield Cook. *Dir of photog* Sidney Wagner. [*2d cam* John Schmitz]. *Spec eff* Warren Newcombe. [*Matte paintings, cam* Mark Davis]. [*Transparency projection shots* A. Arnold Gillespie]. *Art dir* Cedric Gibbons and Edward Carfagno. *Film ed* Irvine Warburton. *Set dec* Edwin B. Willis. *Cost supv* Irene. *Assoc* Kay Carter. *Mus score* Johnny Green. *Rec dir* Douglas Shearer. [*Unit mixer* Charles J. Burbridge]. [*Re-rec and eff mixer* Standish J. Lambert, Ralph A. Pender, Robert W. Shirley, Newell Sparks, William Steinkamp, Michael Steinore and John A. Williams]. [*Mus mixer* M. J. McLaughlin and Herbert Stahlberg]. [*Unit mgr* Bill Kaplan]. [*Research dir* George Richelavie]. [*Research asst* Leo Linder].
   Source: Based on a play by Chester Erskine (production date undetermined).

Cast: ROBERT WALKER (*John [Hill]*), JUNE ALLYSON (*Mary [Breckenridge]*), Hume Cronyn (*Freddie [Potts]*), Audrey Totter (*Lisa [Borescu]*), Eddie "Rochester" Anderson (*Harry*), Reginald Owen (*Mr. Amboy*), Gerald Oliver Smith (*Butler*), [Franklin Pangborn (*Salesman*)], [Fortunio Bonanova (*Telephone man*)], [Roland Dupree (*Delivery boy*)], [Henry Hall (*Justice*)], [Anna Q. Nilsson (*Clerk*)], [Sara Berner (*Elevator girl*)], [Mary Lord (*Office worker*)], [Marek Windheim (*Headwaiter*)], [Shimen Ruskin (*Busboy*)], [Moyna Macgill (*Irate woman*)], [Chester Clute (*Lone diner*)], [Joe DeRita (*Waiter*)], [Betsy Stoddard (*Mrs. Schlesinger*)], [Harry Tyler (*Painter*)], [Eileen Morris (*Model in window*)], [Harry Hayden (*Auction attendant*)], [Katharine Booth (*Pretty woman*)], [Jack Luden (*Naval officer*)], [Johnny Lane (*Soldier*)], [John Carlyle (*Young soldier*)], [Nelson Leigh (*Canadian officer*)], [George Sorel (*French officer*)], [Martin Garralaga (*Brazilian officer*)], [Phillip Pine (*Aide*)], [Marie Harmon, Mary Bovard (*W.A.C.s*)], [Eugene Sigaloff (*Mr. Kabochnick*)], [Mary Jane French (*Carla*)], [Lillian Yarbo (*Black cook*)], [Jane Green].

Domestic, Romantic comedy. [*Print viewed*]. In New York City, on an October night in 1944, John Hill, a sailor from California, shares a carriage ride and a kiss with Mary Breckenridge, a young stenographer he met only six hours earlier. John and Mary are married later the same night, and immediately begin planning the honeymoon they hope to take when John returns from his military base. The following day, Mary tells her boss, Freddie Potts, a pot manufacturer, that she has married a sailor. Although Freddie himself had hoped to marry her, he helps Mary find a new apartment. John returns to the city two days earlier than expected, and tells Mary that he received a medical discharge from the Navy because of a childhood back injury. As the newlyweds settle into their new apartment, they become embroiled in a series of minor disputes, including one angry quarrel that begins when John ridicules Mary's pajamas. One day, John becomes trapped in his apartment building elevator with Lisa Borescu, a beautiful Romanian shop owner. While Harry, the apartment janitor, tries to free the two stranded tenants, John and Lisa become fast friends. Later that afternoon, Lisa tries to help John find an advertising job at a company owned by her wealthy friend, Mr. Amboy. In the hope of impressing John's future boss, Mary invites Mr. Amboy to a home-cooked meal. Freddie and Lisa are also invited to the dinner, and Freddie arrives bearing a gift of pots for the newlyweds. When Mr. Amboy, a plastic pot manufacturer, presents Mary with his company's pots as a gift, Freddie is angered and becomes argumentative with Mr. Amboy. The evening ends in disaster when John trips and accidentally spills the dinner on Freddie and Mr. Amboy. Freddie leaves the dinner party in a rage, and while Mr. Amboy leaves to change his clothes, Lisa tricks John into visiting her in her apartment. There, Lisa flirts with John, gets him drunk and sends him home with lipstick stains on his face. Believing that John is having an affair with Lisa, Mary becomes upset and locks herself in the bedroom. The next day, on Mary's birthday, John tries to make amends with his wife by cooking her dinner and buying her a black lace nightgown. The plan nearly works until a lavish gift sent by Freddie arrives, and John becomes jealous. A quarrel ensues, and Mary goes to Freddie's seeking comfort. John follows Mary to Freddie's, where he threatens to harm Freddie if he continues to meddle in their marriage. All ends happily, though, when Lisa helps John and Mary reconcile, and the couple agrees to put aside their petty quarreling. *Jealousy. Marriage. Newlyweds. Romance.* Accidents. Advertising. African Americans. Birthdays. Canteens (War-time, emergency, etc.). Cooks. Drunkenness. Elevators. Employer-employee relations. Janitors. Military discharge. Romanian Americans. Romantic rivalry. Sailors. Stenographers.

Note: Working titles for this film were *John and Mary* and *For Better, For Worse*.

Box 5 Jan 1946. *DV* 28 Dec 1945, p. 3. *FD* 28 Dec 1945, p. 16. *HR* 23 Mar 1945, p. 8. *HR* 18 May 1945, p. 18. *HR* 28 Dec 1945, p. 3. *HR* 4 Mar 1946, p. 6. *MPHPD* 21 Jul 1945, p. 2555. *MPHPD* 5 Jan 1946, p. 2787. *NYT* 1 Mar 1946, p. 17. *Var* 2 Jan 1946, p. 8.

ST. LOUIS BLUES (African Americans)

Paramount Pictures Corp. *Dist* Paramount Pictures Corp. Apr 1958; World premiere in St. Louis, MO: 10 Apr 1958; New York opening: 11 Apr 1958; Los Angeles opening: 23 Apr 1958; Prod: 7 Oct–1 Nov 1957 [©Paramount Pictures Corp.; 5 Apr 1958; LP10305]. Sd (Westrex Recording System); b&w; VistaVision Motion Picture High Fidelity. 8,429 ft. 94 min. PCA cert no. 18815.

Prod Robert Smith. *Dir* Allen Reisner. *Asst dir* Richard Caffey. *Wrt* Robert Smith and Ted Sherdeman. *Dir of photog* Haskell Boggs. *Spec photog eff* John P. Fulton. *Art dir* Hal Pereira and Roland Anderson. *Ed* Eda Warren. *Set dec* Sam Comer and Robert Benton. *Cost* Edith Head. *Mus arr and cond* Nelson Riddle. *Sd rec* Gene Merritt and Charles Grenzbach. *Makeup supv* Wally Westmore. *Hair style supv* Nellie Manley.

Song(s): "Yellow Dog Blues," "St. Louis Blues," "Chantez les Bas," "Steal Away to Jesus," "Beale Street Blues," "Goin' to See My Sarah," "Got No More Home Dan a Dawg," "Hist the Window, Noah," "Harlem Blues" and "They That Sow in Tears," music and lyrics by W. C. Handy; "Sheriff Honest John Baile" and "Morning Star," music by W. C. Handy, new lyrics by Mack David; "Careless Love," music by W. C. Handy, additional lyrics by Martha Koenig and Spencer Williams; "Friendless Blues," music by W. C. Handy, lyrics by Mercedes Gilbert.

Cast: Nat "King" Cole [(*William "W. C." Handy*)], Eartha Kitt [(*Gogo Germaine*)], Cab Calloway [(*Blade*)], Ella Fitzgerald [(*Herself*)], Mahalia Jackson [(*Bessie May*)], Ruby Dee [(*Elizabeth*)], Juano Hernandez [(*Rev. Charles Handy*)], Teddy Buckner, Barney Bigard, George "Red" Callender, Lee Young, George Washington [(*Musicians*)], Billy Preston [(*W. C. as a boy*)], and Pearl Bailey (*Aunt Hagar*), [Constantin Bakaleinikoff (*New York Symphony conductor*)], [Bill Green (*Musician*)], [Roy Edwin Glenn, Sr. (*Bullneck*)], [Ralph Sanford (*McInerny*)], [Bill Baldwin (*Mawson*)], [Charles Arthur Space (*Duckett*)], [Jay Loft-Lynn (*Janitor*)], [Hal Taggart (*Ticket seller*)], [Samuel R. McDaniel, Nick Stewart (*Drunks*)], [Morgan Roberts, Buck Woods (*Crap shooters*)], [Bobby Johnson (*Gambler*)], [Milas Clark (*Boy*)], [Fay Fifer].

Biography, Musical. [*Print viewed*]. In Memphis, around the turn of the century, the young William C. Handy accompanies some men on his cornet as they sing a work song. Distressed that they will once again be late for church, the boy's aunt Hagar hides the instrument and rushes him into the Methodist Episcopal Church, where his father, Charles Handy, is minister. Will plays the organ as the choir sings a hymn, but the bluesy feel of Hagar's singing angers Rev. Handy, and he cuts the song short. Bellowing from the pulpit, Rev. Handy proclaims, "There are only two kinds of music in this world: the devil's and the Lord's." After church, the minister tells his son that he would rather see him dead than making music for the devil. Years pass, and Will returns home from his studies. His sweetheart Elizabeth, whom he plans to marry, is distressed when he confesses that he played with bands and minstrel shows during school vacations. Not wishing to see Will anger his father, Elizabeth encourages him to apply for a teaching position. Will agrees to this plan, but soon afterward, he enters a friend's bar and begins to play the piano. When a white man offers him money to play for a political rally, Will enthusiastically writes a song for the candidate, "Sheriff Honest John Baile." He quickly assembles a band, which, along with the song, is so successful that nightclub singer Gogo Germaine invites him to play at the club of her boyfriend Blade. The combination of Gogo's singing and Will's songs is an instant hit, but the young musician keeps this news from his father. One day a lawyer appears and buys the rights to Will's song "Yellow Dog Blues" for an unnamed client. Will's next song is "Careless Love," and as he rehearses it with Gogo, she realizes that he is attracted to her but cautions him not to let his feelings interfere with their music. Bessie May, a choir member who cleans up at the Big Rooster Club, is horrified to see Will at the piano and tells his father everything. Will tries to explain that the music he plays is the music of their people, and when Rev. Handy forces his son to choose between him and the club, Will reluctantly rents a room on Beale Street. Will writes "St. Louis Blues" and "Chantez les Bas," but he misses Elizabeth and his family. One day a publisher offers him six hundred dollars for the recording rights to "Yellow Dog Blues," but Will learns that because Blade had earlier bought full rights to the song for only fifty dollars, he no longer owns it. Furious, Will fights with Blade, but Gogo reminds him that there will be other songs. When royalty checks do begin to appear, Will, remembering his deceased mother's wish for a piano, buys a beautiful instrument for his father, playing "Morning Star" on its keys. Rev. Handy is unmoved, however. Gogo announces that she and Will have been offered work in New York, but after she leaves, Will buries his head in his hands and tells Elizabeth that he has gone blind. Believing that the affliction is God's punishment for his evil music, Will moves

home and begins to write hymns for the church. As Bessie May sings one of them, "Steal Away to Jesus," his sight suddenly returns, and "Prof. W. C. Handy" begins to offer piano lessons. Dissatisfied with this profession, Will restlessly takes a walk one day. Passing a club, he hears Ella Fitzgerald and the Memphis Jazz Quartet perform his "Beale Street Blues." At home, Aunt Hagar sings his "St. Louis Blues," but when he imagines his father's anger at the song, he runs from the house. After praying for guidance, Will leaves town and is soon performing throughout the Midwest as the leader of the W. C. Handy Trio. Anxious to inform Will that the New York Symphony plans to perform "St. Louis Blues" in Aeolian Hall, Gogo returns to Memphis, and when Elizabeth admits that she is unaware of Will's whereabouts, she angrily accuses both Elizabeth and Rev. Handy of trying to destroy him. Elizabeth is moved by the singer's speech, and on the day of the concert, she arrives at the opulent hall with Aunt Hagar and Rev. Handy. The minister is astonished when the Symphony's conductor praises his son as the man most responsible for the emergence of America's only pure art form. Will is equally shocked to find his father, his aunt and his onetime sweetheart backstage. Father and son embrace, and Will performs his song with the orchestra. *African Americans. Blues music. Fathers and sons. Ministers. Songwriters. W. C. Handy. Aunts. Bands (Music). Beale Street (Memphis, TN). Blindness–Temporary. Choirs (Music). Churches. Cornets. Fame. Hymns. Jealousy. Love. Loyalty. Memphis (TN). Musicians. Nightclub entertainers. Nightclub owners. Nightclubs. Orchestras. Organs. Pianos. Psychosomatic illness. Rallies. Reconciliation. Romance. Singers. Swindlers and swindling.*

Note: As noted in the opening credits, this film is based on the life and music of noted blues composer and musician W. C. Handy. Born on 16 Nov 1873 in Florence, AL, William Christopher Handy was educated in public schools and by his father and paternal grandfather, both of whom were clergymen. He left home at age fifteen to begin a career as a cornet player with a traveling minstrel show. In 1893, Handy formed a quartet which performed at the World's Columbian Exposition in Chicago. After working as a music teacher at the Agricultural and Mechanical College in Huntsville, AL, Handy turned to composing in 1907, and his first published song was "Memphis Blues", which was based on a campaign song he had written for Edward "The Boss" Crup, the mayor of Memphis, TN. Most notable among his sixty-plus compositions are "St. Louis Blues" (1914), "Beale St. Blues" (1917) and "Loveless Love" (1921). Although he lost his eyesight in 1903, Handy continued to conduct his own orchestra until 1921. His eyesight was partially restored for a time, but then was completely lost again after a fall from a New York City subway platform in 1943. Handy died in New York on 29 Mar 1958, just a few days before the film's premiere. During a Hollywood dinner given in his honor in Nov 1957, however, Handy proclaimed Nat King Cole's depiction of him as "forever a monument to my race," according to an Apr 1958 *DV* news item.
According to *NYT* and *LAT* news items, because producer Robert Smith was unable to obtain copyright clearance for Handy's "Memphis Blues," a later Handy composition, "Yellow Dog Blues," is presented as the song which launched the musician's career. Billy Preston, who played Handy as a child in the film, went on to have a successful career in music as a singer and keyboard player. Constantin Bakaleinikoff, who plays the symphony conductor in the film, was the music director at Paramount at the time of the production. The *DV* reviewer noted: "A real and successful effort has been made to avoid any possible charge of 'Uncle Tom' in the characters. But for this reason or others, the result is such a genteel portrayal of life in Memphis in the early years of this century that you might wonder why the Negroes ever sang the blues."
Box 14 Apr 1958. *DV* 2 Apr 1958. *DV* 8 Apr 1958, p. 3. *Exh* 16 Apr 1958, pp. 444-45. *FD* 15 Apr 1958, p. 8. *Har* 12 Apr 1958, p. 59. *HR* 8 Apr 1958, p. 3. *LAT* 7 Mar 1958. *MPH* 12 Apr 1958, p. 792. *MPHPD* 12 Apr 1958, p. 792. *NYT* 20 Oct 1957. *NYT* 12 Apr 1958, p. 13. *Var* 9 Apr 1958, p. 6.

THE SAINTLY SHOW GIRL see **SPOTLIGHT SADIE**

¡SALGA DE LA COCINA! see **CHÉRIE**

SALLY IN OUR ALLEY (Jewish Americans, Italian Americans)
Columbia Pictures Corp.; Columbia Pictures Corp. 3 Sep **1927** [©Columbia Pictures Corp.; 29 Sep 1927; LP24461]. Si; b&w. 6 reels, 5,892 ft.
Prod Harry Cohn. *Dir* Walter Lang. *Asst dir* Bert Siebel. *Story* Edward Clark. *Cont* Dorothy Howell. *Photog* J. O. Taylor. *Art dir* Robert E. Lee.
Cast: Shirley Mason (*Sally Williams*), Richard Arlen (*Jimmie Adams*), Alec B. Francis (*Sandy Mack*), Paul Panzer (*Tony Garibaldi*), William H. Strauss (*Abraham Lapidowitz*), Kathlyn Williams (*Mrs. Gordon Mansfield*), Florence Turner (*Mrs. Williams*), Harry Crocker (*Chester Drake*).
Romantic comedy. Sally, a girl of the tenements, is adopted by neighbors Sandy Mack, Abraham Lapidowitz, and Tony Garibaldi after her mother's death, and subsequently leads a happy home life with

her foster fathers. Jimmie Adams, a young plumber who loves Sally, visits the house frequently. The group is broken up when Mrs. Mansfield, Sally's wealthy aunt, takes the girl away to her luxurious home to give her the advantages of social position; she also introduces Sally to Chester Drake, a very wealthy young man. When Sally invites her foster fathers and Jimmie to her eighteenth birthday party, she is embarrassed by their table manners. Mrs. Mansfield tells of Sally's interest in Adams, causing Jimmie to leave her, but Sally learns of her aunt's social snobbery and is reunited with him before he sets sail on a ship. *Aunts. Etiquette. Foster parents. Italian Americans. Jews. Orphans. Plumbers. Scots. Snobs and snobbishness. Tenement-houses. Upper classes.*
FD 6 Nov 1927. *Var* 2 Nov 1927, p. 21.

SALOME OF THE TENEMENTS (Jewish Americans)
Famous Players-Lasky Corp. *Dist* Paramount Pictures. 23 Feb **1925** [©Famous Players-Lasky Corp.; 3 Mar 1925; LP21209]. Si; b&w. 7 reels, 7,017 ft.
Pres Adolph Zukor and Jesse L. Lasky. *Dir* Sidney Olcott. *Scen* Sonya Levien. *Photog* Al Ligouri and David W. Gobbett. *Prod mgr* John Lynch.
Source: Based on the novel *Salome of the Tenements* by Anzia Yezierska (New York, c1923).
Cast: Jetta Goudal (*Sonya Mendel*), Godfrey Tearle (*John Manning*), José Ruben (*Jakey Solomon*), Lazar Freed (*Jacob Lipkin*), Irma Lerna (*Gittel Stein*), Sonia Nodell (*Mrs. Peltz*), Elihu Tenenholtz (*Banker Ben*), Mrs. Weintraub (*Mrs. Solomon*), Nettie Tobias (*Widow*).
Drama. Sonya Mendel makes her way through life with a combination of good looks and a wit sharpened to the gutterstone of the East Side. As a reporter for an ethnic newspaper, she is assigned to interview philanthropist John Manning, who is attracted to her and invites her to dinner. She persuades Jakey Solomon, a former sweatshop stitcher who operates a fashionable shop on Fifth Avenue, to provide her with an attractive dress for the evening, and she borrows $1,500 from Banker Ben, a usurer, with the written promise to repay it after she has married Manning. Manning hires her as his secretary and later marries her. Knowing nothing of Sonya's dealings with Banker Ben, Manning attempts to secure an indictment against him. Ben, anticipating that Sonya will try to get back her note, slyly gives her the chance to steal it from his safe, apprehends her, and threatens her with arrest. He then proposes to Manning that he not press charges against Sonya if Manning will refrain from prosecuting him for usury. Manning instead threatens to have Ben jailed for blackmail, forces him into accepting payment on the note, and is reconciled with Sonya. *Blackmail. Couturiers. Jews. New York City. Newspapers. Philanthropists. Reporters. Secretaries. Usury.*
FD 8 Mar 1925. *NYT* 24 Feb 1925, p. 17. *Var* 25 Feb 1925, p. 31.

SALOME, WHERE SHE DANCED (Austrian Americans, Russian Americans)
Universal Pictures Co., Inc. *Dist* Universal Pictures Co., Inc. 27 Apr **1945**; Prod: mid-Sep—early Dec 1944 [©Universal Pictures Co., Inc.; 3 Apr 1945; LP13195]. Sd (Western Electric Recording); col (Technicolor). 8,148 ft. 90 or 93 min.
Pres WALTER WANGER. *Assoc prod* Alexander Golitzen. *Dir* Charles Lamont. *Asst dir* Fred Frank. *Dial dir* Ernest Truex. *Scr* Laurence Stallings. *From an orig story by* Michael J. Phillips. *Dir of photog* Hal Mohr and W. Howard Greene. *Technicolor col consultant* Natalie Kalmus. *Assoc* William Fritzsche. *Art dir* John B. Goodman and Alexander Golitzen. *Film ed* Russell Schoengarth. *Set dec* Russell A. Gausman and Victor A. Gangelin. *Gowns* Vera West. *Mus score and dir* Edward Ward. *Dance dir* Lester Horton. *Chase seq* Breezy Eason. *Dir of sd* Bernard B. Brown. *[Sd] tech* William Hedgcock. *Makeup dir* Jack Pierce.
Song(s): "The Blue Danube," music by Johann Strauss, special lyrics by Everett Carter; "Tannenbaum, O Tannenbaum," German folk song; selections from the opera *The Bohemian Girl*, music by Michael William Balfe, libretto by Alfred Bunn.
Cast: Yvonne DeCarlo [(*Salome, also known as Anna Maria*)], Rod Cameron [(*Jim Steed*)], David Bruce [("*Stagecoach" Cleve Blunt*)], Walter Slezak [(*Colonel Ivan Dimitrioff*)], Albert Dekker [(*Count Erik Von Bohlen*)], Marjorie Rambeau [(*Madam Europe*)], J. Edward Bromberg [(*Professor Max*)], Abner Biberman [(*Dr. Ling*)], John Litel [(*General Robert E. Lee*)], [Kurt Katch (*Otto Eduard Leopold von Bismarck*)], [Arthur Hohl (*Bartender*)], [Nestor Paiva (*Panatela*)],

[Gavin Muir (*Colonel Henderson*)], [Will Wright (*Sheriff*)], [Joseph Haworth (*Henry*)], [Matt McHugh (*Lafe*)], [Poni Adams, Barbara Bates, Daun Kennedy, Kathleen O'Malley, Karen Randle, Jean Trent, Kerry Vaughn], [Jan Williams, Doreen Tryden, Bert Dole, Emmett Casey (*Specialties*)], [Eddie Dunn (*Lineman*)], [Charles Wagenheim (*Telegrapher*)], [Gene Garrick (*German sergeant*)], [Eric Feldary (*Uhlan sergeant*)], [Sylvia Field (*Maid*)], [Richard Ryen (*Theater manager*)], [Colin Campbell (*Mate*)], [George Sherwood (*Bartender*)], [Charles McAvoy (*Policeman*)], [Al Ferguson (*Deputy*)], [Alan Edwards (*Bret Harte*)], [George Leigh (*Bayard Taylor*)], [Ina Ownbey (*Girl*)], [Eddie Cobb (*Stage driver*)], [Jack Clifford (*Messenger*)], [Peter Seal (*Russian chasseur*)], [Bud Osborne (*Gambler*)], [George Morrell, George Chesebro (*Miners*)], [Hank Bell, Jasper Palmer (*Cowhands*)], [Budd Buster (*Desert rat*)], [Dick Alexander (*Shotgun*)], [Cecilia Callejo (*Bar girl*)], [Jimmy Lang (*Chinese guard*)].

Historical, Melodrama, with songs. [*Print viewed*]. On 9 April 1865, Jim Steed, a celebrated war correspondent, telegraphs his story, announcing the surrender of General Robert E. Lee and the end of the American Civil War, to his newspaper, *Leslie's Weekly*. Later, Jim travels to Berlin, where he is invited to a ball hosted by the Prussian leader, Count Otto Eduard Leopold von Bismarck. Jim quickly runs afoul of Bismarck's close adviser, Count Erik Von Bohlen, and tells Anna Maria, better known as Salome, the noted Austrian ballerina, that Von Bohlen is interested in her. Using that information, Salome agrees to entertain Von Bohlen in order to uncover Bismarck's plans for the anticipated Prussian invasion of Austria. On the first day of the Austrian-Prussian war, Jim witnesses the death of an Austrian prince who was romantically involved with Salome. Von Bohlen then arrives and threatens to have Jim executed for looting, but Jim informs him that he has found papers on the dead prince which prove that Von Bohlen divulged military secrets to Salome. Upon his release, Jim then helps Salome and her music teacher, Professor Max, escape from Berlin to America. After traveling cross-country for twenty-eight days, the three arrive in the western desert town of Drinkman's Wells, where they are taken in by Madame Europe, a hotel proprietor. In order to raise enough money to travel to San Francisco, they put on a show, and the beautiful Salome is an immediate hit with the local miners. Her performance is interrupted, however, by "Stagecoach" Cleve Blunt, an ex-Confederate soldier turned bandit, who steals the show's receipts. Despite a recent marital proposal by Jim, Salome is immediately attracted to and becomes involved with Cleve, as he is a double for her deceased Hapsburg prince. At Salome's urgings, Cleve returns all his stolen loot, and in gratitude, the townspeople rename Drinkman's Wells "Salome, Where She Danced." Salome, Jim and Max then travel to San Francisco, with Cleve and Madame Europe joining their theatrical troupe. Unable to find sponsorship for their show, Jim suggests that Salome become acquainted with Colonel Ivan Dimitrioff, a wealthy Russian diplomat. Cleve soon becomes jealous of Salome's involvement with Dimitrioff, who has gone so far as to give the ballerina a painting by Rembrandt. Upon the suggestion of his adviser, Dr. Ling, a Scottish-trained Chinese physician, Dimitrioff arranges a position for the newly pardoned Cleve with a stagecoach line, in hopes that distance will remove his romantic rival from Salome's heart. Instead, Cleve joins up with his old outlaw gang, only to be convinced once more into going straight by Ling and Salome. As a parting gift, Salome gives Cleve the locket with her picture inside that her Hapsburg prince once owned. On the night of her San Francisco opening, Von Bohlen arrives in town with a diplomatic warrant for Salome's arrest. Cleve comes to Salome's defense, however, and kills the Prussian count in a sword fight. Though she offers to return to Virginia with him, Cleve rejects Salome and announces his plans to return to his life as a highwayman. Despite Dimitrioff's threats, Salome refuses to dance that night and retires from the stage. With Jim and Ling's help, Cleve escapes with Salome aboard the Russian's private carriage. Though Dimitrioff is aware of their plot, he allows the couple to leave with his blessings. *Austrians. Ballerinas. Bandits. Reporters. Romantic rivalry.* Americans in foreign countries. Balls (Parties). Berlin (Germany). Otto Eduard Leopold von Bismarck. Chases. Chinese Americans. Criminals–Rehabilitation. Dancing. Escapes. Espionage. Hapsburg Family. Jealousy. Robert E. Lee. Lockets. Miners. Music teachers. Officers (Military). Paintings. Physicians. Proposals (Marital). Prussians. Royalty. Russians. Saloons. San Francisco (CA). Stagecoaches. Sword fights. Traps. United States–History–Civil War, 1861-1865.

Note: According to *HCN* in May 1944, Jean Moseman, a twenty-one-year-old secretary at Universal, was selected by producer Walter Wanger to play the lead in *Salome, Where She Danced*. In Jun 1944, however, *HR* announced that Wanger was conducting a nationwide search for a new female star to play the lead. Photographers were asked to submit pictures of the most beautiful young women they had ever photographed, while dancing and singing schools, theaters, drama classes, magazines and newspapers were also invited to participate in the search. *HR* later reported that Wanger was receiving approximately 500 letters a week in connection to this talent hunt. In Aug 1944, Wanger announced that he had selected eight finalists, including Mary Lou Campbell, Kerry Vaughn and Barbara Bates, all of whom were given screen tests for the role of "Salome." Yvonne De Carlo, however, was finally selected, having beaten out over 20,000 submissions. Vaughn and Bates were cast in small roles as "Salome girls." According to *NYT*, De Carlo, formerly Peggy Yvonne Middleton of Vancouver, B.C., was under contract to RKO at the time.

According to information in the file on the film in the MPPDA/PCA Collection at the AMPAS Library, the first submitted script for *Salome, Where She Danced* was rejected on 31 Aug 1944 on two main grounds: first, the character of "Stagecoach Cleve Blunt" was an outlaw who went unpunished for his illegal acts; and second, unacceptable references to the biblical story of Herod Antipas and Salome during a planned dance sequence were to be included. Universal submitted a revised script on 14 Sep 1944, which was passed by the PCA with minor objections.

Erle C. Kenton was originally set to direct *Salome, Where She Danced*, but he was replaced by Charles Lamont due to conflicting production schedules, according to *HR* news items. An Aug 1944 *HR* news item announced that Dean Harens had been cast as one of the male leads in the film, but he did not appear in the released film. *HR* news items also state that locations were scouted in San Francisco, Monterey, Carmel and Santa Cruz, CA, but it has not been determined if any of these locals were actually used. According to *NYT*, this film was shot at a cost of 1.2 million dollars. *HR* news items include Paul Stanton and Harold Goodwin in the cast, but their appearance in the released film could not be confirmed.

Box 21 Apr 1945. *DV* 11 Apr 1945, p. 3. *FD* 17 Apr 1945, p. 6. *HCN* 19 May 1944. *HR* 9 Jun 1944, p. 6. *HR* 2 Aug 1944, p. 1. *HR* 4 Aug 1944, p. 1. *HR* 17 Aug 1944, p. 21. *HR* 28 Aug 1944, p. 11. *HR* 30 Aug 1944, p. 11. *HR* 8 Sep 1944, p. 1. *HR* 18 Sep 1944, p. 4. *HR* 22 Sep 1944, p. 15. *HR* 25 Oct 1944, p. 11. *HR* 2 Nov 1944, p. 10. *HR* 11 Apr 1945, p. 3. *HR* 7 May 1945, p. 20, 23. *MPHPD* 16 Dec 1944, p. 2230. *MPHPD* 14 Apr 1945, p. 2402. *NYT* 17 Dec 1944. *NYT* 3 May 1945, p. 27. *Var* 11 Apr 1945, p. 14.

SALT OF THE EARTH (Latino)
The International Union of Mine, Mill and Smelter Workers; Independent Productions Corp. *Dist* Independent Productions Corp.; IPC Distributors, Inc. **1954**; World premiere in New York and Yorkville, NY: 14 Mar 1954; Prod: 20 Jan—6 Mar 1953 [©Independent Productions Corp.; 8 Mar 1954; LP3558]. Sd; b&w. 8,320 ft. 94 min.

Prod Paul Jarrico. *Dir* Herbert J. Biberman. [*Wrt*] *by* Michael Wilson. *Mus* Sol Kaplan. *Staff exec* Sonja Dahl and Adolfo Barela.

Cast: The Professional Cast: Will Geer [(*Sheriff*)], David Wolfe [(*Barton*)], David Sarvis [(*Hartwell*)], Mervin Williams [(*Alexander*)], Rosaura Revueltas [(*Esperanza Quintero*)], The Non-Professional Cast: E. A. Rockwell [(*Vance*)], William Rockwell [(*Kimbrough*)], Juan Chacón [(*Ramón Quintero*)], Henrietta Williams [(*Teresa Vidal*)], Angela Sanchez [(*Consuela Ruiz*)], Clorinda Alderette [(*Luz Morales*)], Virginia Jencks [(*Ruth Barnes*)], Clinton Jencks [(*Frank Barnes*)], Joe T. Morales [(*Sal Ruiz*)], Ernest Velasquez [(*Charlie Vidal*)], Charles Coleman [(*Antonio Morales*)], Victor Torres [(*Sebastian Prieto*)], Frank Talevera [(*Luis Quintero*)], Mary Lou Castillo [(*Estella Quintero*)], Floyd Bostick [(*Jenkins*)], E. S. Conerly [(*Kalinsky*)], Adolfo Barela [(*Alfredo*)], Albert Muñoz [(*Vicente*)], And other brothers and sisters of Mine-Mill Local 890, [Alford Roos (*District attorney*)].

Social, Drama. [*Print viewed*]. Thirty-four-year-old Esperanza Quintero, who is pregnant with her third child, lives in Zinc Town, New Mexico, a mining town owned by Delaware Zinc. Esperanza's husband Ramón, a miner, narrowly escapes a catastrophe when he lights dynamite that has a defective fuse. When Ramón later objects to the dangerous working conditions, company man Barton replies that Ramón can easily be replaced by "an American." That night, Esperanza complains to Ramón that she must chop wood for hot water five times a day, while the Anglo miners' homes have hot running water. Ramón, however, insists that safety at the mine is their most important concern. One day, a group of women decides to picket at the mine for better sanitary conditions. As they try to convince Esperanza, who is reluctant to get involved, to join them, an alarm sounds at the mine. Ramón tells superintendent Alexander that the accident would not have happened if conditions were better. Barton accuses Ramón of lying, and when Alexander orders the men back to work, they strike. That night, a few of the women, including Esperanza, attend the union meeting, and one suggests that the

strikers also demand sanitation and plumbing for their houses. The men, however, table the discussion. As the men begin picketing outside the mine entrance, out-of-town strikebreakers are recruited, but they turn back when they see the size of the picket lines. After his son Luís and a friend spy some "scabs" at the mine, Ramón chases them, and when he discovers that one of them is a Mexican American whom he knows, he spits on the man and is arrested. As Ramón is beaten by bigoted police, Esperanza goes into labor. Despite the sheriff's refusal to send for a doctor, she delivers a healthy boy. Esperanza waits to christen the baby until Ramón returns from jail. That night, while all the strikers celebrate at the Quintero home, Ramón is criticized for his distrust of whites, but takes the union leader, an Anglo named Frank Barnes, to task for not having learned about Mexican culture. Barnes admits he was at fault, but criticizes Ramón's paternalistic view of women, until his wife Ruth points out his own deficiencies. By the seventh month of the strike, money and food are running low, and some families leave, but soon aid arrives from workers around the country. When the sheriff delivers a Taft-Hartley injunction ordering the striking workers to stop picketing, Barnes explains that if the men obey the order, the strike is lost, as scabs will move in as soon as the picket line is gone. If they defy the order, however, they will be arrested and the strike will be broken. As the men argue, one of the wives suggests that the women take over the picketing since the order applies only to striking miners. The idea is greeted with laughter and then debate. Esperanza insists that the women be allowed to vote along with the men, and the motion narrowly passes. Women from all around the area join the wives of the strikers, while the men watch from the side, but Ramón forbids Esperanza to participate. When a fight breaks out between the deputies and the women, Esperanza passes the baby to Ramón and with a shoe, knocks a gun from an officer's hands. Temporarily defeated, Barton calls off his men. Esperanza now joins the picket line, taking the children with her. After further efforts by the police fail to dislodge the women, Hartwell, a company official from New York, asks the sheriff to arrest them. The Mexican-American scab points out the leaders and includes Esperanza, who brings her baby and little girl to jail with her. When the baby refuses the milk the sheriff provides, the women start to chant. Ramón and Luís retrieve the children. Seeing the determination of the women, Ramón begins to do the housework and realizes the validity of the women's complaints. After four days, Esperanza and the other women are released from jail. Ramón insists that the women have no chance of winning, but Esperanza contends that they can outlast the company and criticizes him for treating her as the bosses treat him. On a hunting trip, Ramón thinks about Esperanza's words. Later, the company obtains an eviction order against the striking miners, and begin their efforts with Ramón and Esperanza. As the women gather outside the Quintero home, the sheriff and his men remove their belongings. The men return from a hunting trip and join the women, and as word spreads, workers and women gather outside the Quintero house. When Ramón understands that the company has resorted to the evictions because, as Esperanza predicted, they cannot fight the picket line, he suggests that Esperanza take her belongings back inside. The other women follow her, and the sheriff, who does not want the women in his jail again, leaves with his men. After Alexander and Hartwell decide to settle the strike, Ramón thanks the "sisters and brothers" and publicly praises Esperanza for her dignity and determination. She now knows that they have won something the bosses cannot take away, which they can leave to their children, the "salt of the earth." *Mexican Americans. Miners. Picketing. Sexual equality. Strikes and lockouts. Trade unions. Childbirth. Family relationships. Jails. Marriage. Mine accidents. New Mexico. Parties. Police. Sheriffs. Strikebreakers.*

Note: Independent Productions Corp. was incorporated in 1951 by Simon Lazarus, Herbert J. Biberman and Paul Jarrico to employ blacklisted filmmakers. Writer Michael Wilson based the film's story on a 1951-52 strike by the International Union of Mine, Mill and Smelter Workers against Empire Zinc, a subsidiary of New Jersey Zinc, in which Juan Chacón and Clinton Jencks participated. Chacón, who played "Ramón," was president of Local 890 of the UMMSW and worked for Kennecott Copper Corp. at the time of filming. Jencks, who performed the role of "Frank Barnes," was an international representative of the union. Many of the other characters were also played by miners and their families. In an article, Chacón wrote about the unequal treatment of Mexican American miners: "The companies built houses for the Anglos while we were given shacks....the miners who spoke Spanish would be put to work as 'helpers' to the 'skilled' Anglos—doing the same work for which the Anglo was paid twice

as much....separate pay windows, separate washrooms, the separation even in the movies." According to Biberman's book about the making of the film, the role of "Esperanza" was intended for his wife, Gale Sondergaard, and the part of "Ramón" was also to be played by a non-Hispanic actor, but the filmmakers changed their minds when they realized that they subconsciously believed Hispanics were incapable of portraying leads.

Contemporary news items add the following information about the production: In Feb 1953, during filming, California Republican Representative Donald Jackson, a member of the House Committee on Un-American Activities from California, declared that the picture was "deliberately designed to inflame racial hatreds," and was "a new weapon for Russia." Jackson claimed that "in one sequence, two deputy sheriffs...proceed to pistol whip the miner's very young son." Wilson countered that "there is not one shred of truth in [Jackson's] description of the subject." He called the film "pro-American in the deepest sense. It...depicts honest working men and women of our country in a light most Hollywood films have ignored....It stresses brotherhood and unity." Jackson named investors in the film and portrayed them as having ties to the Communist party. He singled out Biberman, Sondergaard, Jarrico, Wilson and actor Will Geer, who had all been hostile witnesses before HUAC. Lazarus was called to testify before Jackson's committee in 1953. A UMMSW representative denied that the picture was being made "under Communist auspices," and added that Sondergaard was not connected with the film. He also noted that no "violence against any young Mexican-American boy" is depicted in the film, as Jackson claimed. After Jackson's denunciation, Roy M. Brewer, head of the American Federation of Labor Film Council and the international representative of IATSE, told reporters that he and other union officials, including Walter Pidgeon, president of the Screen Actors Guild, had been trying to halt production of the film for over a year. Later, Jackson submitted a request to the Secretary of State, the Secretary of Commerce and the Attorney-General to find legal means to ban the export of the "propaganda film."

On 25 Feb 1953, Mexican actress Rosaura Revueltas, who played "Esperanza," was arrested and held without bail because her passport had not been stamped at the border. In response, Jorge Negreta, president of the National Association of Actors of Mexico City, threatened to bar Hollywood actors from Mexico unless Revueltas was permitted to finish the film. SAG then stated that the actress was working for "a non-union company not signatory to our contract." Biberman and Jarrico countered that every member of the crew carried a union card (although not from IATSE unions for the most part) and that they had hired people who had been effectively blacklisted by IATSE, including four African Americans, the assistant to the director, an assistant cameraman and two technicians, excluded under IATSE's Jim Crow policies. On 6 Mar 1953, Revueltas returned to Mexico, and her last scene was filmed near Mexico City. Her voice-over narration, modern sources note, was also taped there.

On 2 Mar 1953, the film's cast and crew were met by a citizen's committee in Central, NM, and ordered to leave town. The following day, in Silver City, NM, the company was warned to "get out of town...or go out in black boxes." Jencks was beaten and shots were fired at his car while it was parked outside his home. When the company did not capitulate to the demands, there was a "citizens' parade" led by a sound car blaring, "We don't want communism; respect the law; no violence, but let's show them we don't like it." The UMMSW, which had been expelled from the Congress of Industrial Organizations for alleged pro-communist leanings, responded that "we have the right to make and complete our movie." Then on 8 Mar 1953, the union hall in Bayard, NM, was set on fire, and the union hall in nearby Carlsbad was burned to the ground, according to Biberman's book. Biberman also notes that cast member Floyd Bostick's home was destroyed by fire. A 15 Mar 1954 *LAT* article notes that the majority of the film was shot on a New Mexico ranch owned by Alford Roos, who also appeared in the picture.

In his book, Biberman states that before filming began, Lazarus asked Brewer to supply a union crew for the film. Brewer refused, stating that he would not allow union members to work for blacklisted filmmakers. Afterward, according to Biberman, Pathé Laboratories in Hollywood refused to process their exposed film. Consequently, the filmmakers were unable to view the rushes. Soon other technical companies followed suit. According to a modern source, Howard Hughes of RKO stated, "If the motion picture industry—not only in Hollywood, but throughout the United States—will refuse these skills [processing, dubbing, editing, etc.]...the picture cannot be completed in this country."

In Jul 1953, Brewer asked Film Council members and other studio workers not to work on the film, calling it "one of the most anti-American documentaries ever attempted." Before a preview screening in New York, IATSE projectionists refused to run the film, provoking *Var* to comment that "IATSE like any other organization is entitled to its opinions and prejudices, but in this instance...the precedent is a bad one." The editorial added that IATSE opposition would make the picture seem more important and powerful than it was. Finally, on 14 Mar 1954, *Salt of the Earth* had its premiere at an independent theater in Yorkville, NY, and at the Grande Theatre in New York, also a non-IATSE house. Although an extra detail of police was assigned to the neighborhood in Yorkville, no trouble was reported. A 15 Mar 1954 *DV* article noted that both the *New York Mirror* and *The Journal-American*, owned by William Randolph Hearst, ignored the film's opening. (According to modern sources, the film had its premiere at the Sky-Vue Drive In near Silver City and played there for three weeks.) Chicago screenings were canceled in early Jun 1954, according to *MPH*, after protesting projectionists failed to show up for work. The picture was never generally released in the U.S., modern sources state, although it appeared occasionally in theaters in New York, Los Angeles, Berkeley and San Francisco.

Salt of the Earth was received favorably overseas and won the grand prize at the Prague Film Festival. Revueltas also won an award for her portrayal of

"Esperanza." She was blacklisted by the Mexican film industry after her work in the picture, modern sources note, but continued to act in theater in East Berlin and Havana. On 24 May 1959, *NYT* reported that the United States Information Agency had provided Congress with a list of eighty-two movies that the agency refused to show overseas. Among them was *Salt of the Earth*. In the article, Republican Representative Frank T. Bow of Ohio stated that such films created a false picture of the United States. The film was re-released in 1965.

In a 1953 anti-trust suit, Independent Productions Corp. and I.P.C. Distributors Inc. charged Brewer, Jackson, Hughes, RKO and Pathé Laboratories, among others, with an "illegal conspiracy" to prevent production, distribution and exhibition of the film. The suit was appealed several times. Finally, in Nov 1964, a Federal Court jury found in favor of the defendants, now reduced to twenty-five. A documentary titled *A Crime to Fit the Punishment*, about the making of the film, was released in 1984 and was directed by Barbara Moss and Stephen Mack.

Box 17 Apr 1954. *Box* 23 Nov 1964. *DV* 25 Feb 1953. *DV* 3 Mar 1953. *DV* 21 Jul 1953. *DV* 8 Mar 1954. *DV* 12 Mar 1954. *DV* 15 Mar 1954, p. 1, 3. *DV* 3 Jun 1958. *DV* 28 Sep 1959. *DV* 4 Apr 1960. *DV* 4 Nov 1960. *Exb* 24 Mar 1954, p. 3720. *FD* 13 Nov 1964. *Har* 12 Jun 1954, p. 96. *HCN* 24 Feb 1953. *HCN* 5 Mar 1953. *HCN* 7 Mar 1953. *HCN* 21 Jul 1953. *HCN* 15 Mar 1954. *HR* 27 Feb 1953. *HR* 2 Mar 1953. *HR* 29 Jul 1953. *HR* 22 May 1959. *LADN* 25 Feb 1953. *LADN* 26 Feb 1953. *LADN* 27 Feb 1953. *LADN* 3 Mar 1953. *LADN* 21 Jul 1953. *LAEx* 14 Feb 1953. *LAEx* 25 Feb 1953. *LAEx* 1 Mar 1953. *LAEx* 5 Mar 1953. *LAEx* 9 Mar 1953. *LAEx* 15 Feb 1953. *LAT* 25 Feb 1953. *LAT* 2 Mar 1953. *LAT* 3 Mar 1953. *LAT* 4 Mar 1953. *LAT* 15 Mar 1954. *MPH* 20 Mar 1954, p. 28. *MPH* 5 Jun 1954, p. 26. *NYT* 11 Mar 1953. *NYT* 15 Mar 1954, p. 20. *Time* 16 Mar 1953. *Var* 25 Feb 1953. *Var* 29 Jul 1953. *Var* 17 Feb 1954. *Var* 3 Mar 1954. *Var* 17 Mar 1954. *Var* 3 Jun 1958. *Var* 6 Apr 1960. *Var* 18 Nov 1964.

SALT TO THE DEVIL *see* **GIVE US THIS DAY**

SALUTE TO COURAGE *see* **NAZI AGENT**

SAM DAVIS, THE HERO OF TENNESSEE (African Americans)
The Connor Producing Co. **1915?** [©The Connor Producing Co.; 12 Jul 1915; LU5793]. Si; b&w. Length undetermined.

Scen Lillian Nicholson Shearon.

Historical, Drama. At the start of the Civil War, Sam Davis leaves his plantation family to enlist in the Confederate Army. Two years later, returning to battle after a brief furlough, Sam meets Polly Dover in Pulaski, Tennessee and falls in love. Posing as a Union herb doctor, Captain H. B. Shaw infiltrates the Union camp and passes military secrets to his Confederate peers. Betty English, another spy, tricks a Union captain into drawing a diagram of an upcoming maneuver, then with the help of her black slave, delivers the paper to Shaw, who entrusts Sam to take it to the front. After kissing Polly goodbye, Sam rides off with the document, followed closely by Union soldiers. Sam gives them a good chase but is finally caught. Despite numerous questionings and a trial, Sam refuses to reveal the identity of his fellow spies and is sentenced to hang. Surrounded by crying, admiring onlookers, Sam dies, a hero. *Couriers. Espionage. Tennessee. United States–History–Civil War, 1861-1865. War heroes. African Americans. Chases. Executions. Impersonation and imposture. Physicians. Plantations. Pulaski (TN). Secret documents. Soldiers. Spies. Trials.*

Note: Although no precise information on the length of this film is available, the copyright scenario suggests a story of feature-length complexity. This film may be the same as another 1915 film, *The Life of Sam Davis: A Confederate Hero of the Sixties*, copyrighted in May, but as they were both based on actual persons and events whose own fiftieth anniversary was being celebrated at that time, it is possible that more than one film on the subject was made.

SAMUEL FULLER'S THE BARON OF ARIZONA *see* **THE BARON OF ARIZONA**

SAMURAI (Japanese Americans)
Cavalcade Pictures Co. *Dist* Cavalcade Pictures Co. **1945**; New York opening: 24 Aug 1945; Prod: early 1944. Sd; b&w. 5,812 ft. 62 min. PCA cert no. 9923.

Prod Ben Mindenburg. *Assoc prod* Frank Wong. *Dir* Raymond Cannon. *Orig story* Ben Mindenburg and Frederick C. Bond. *Scr* Raymond Cannon. *Narr by* Frederick C. Bond. *Cine* Marcel Le Picard. *Montage eff* Ray Mercer. *Ed* Adrian Weiss and [George Merrick]. *Mus* Lee Zahler. *Sd eng* Glen Glenn. *Prod mgr* Dick L'Estrange. *Tech adv* Prof. David Chow.

Cast: Paul Fung (*Dr. Ken [Kenikitchi] Morrey*), Luke Chan (*Priest*), David Chow (*Secret Service man*), Barbara Wooddell (*Mrs. Morrey*), Fred C. Bond (*Mr. [John] Morrey*), Larry Moore (*Frank Morrey*), Ronald Siu (*Young Ken*), Beal Wong (*Engineer*), Joseph Kim (*Secret Service man*), Sung Lee (*General [Sujiyama]*), Frances Chan (*Chinese prisoner*), Mary Ellen Butler (*White prisoner*).

Espionage, Drama. [*Print viewed*]. After the 1923 Tokyo earthquake, which kills over 300,000 persons, American evangelists Mr. and Mrs. John Morrey adopt a Japanese orphan, Kenikitchi, and bring him to their home in San Francisco. As he grows up, Ken becomes Americanized. One day while he is still a boy, he is painting by the seaside, when he is approached by a Japanese priest, who educates him about the doctrine of Bushido, a religion which follows the traditions of Japanese samurai warriors. Unknown to his parents, Ken becomes indoctrinated as a samurai. As a young adult, Ken travels to Europe, where he receives advanced degrees in medicine and art. However, he continues to lead a double life, and never writes his parents about his secret associations with the samurai worldwide. When Ken returns home, he is a changed man, and believes that the Japanese are destined to conquer the world. Ken meets with the priest and informs him of the political turmoil in Europe, and that he believes the Germans will ally themselves with the Japanese. At one of Ken's art exhibitions, he shows the priest how he has concealed maps of vital points in California in his artwork. The priest arranges for Ken to become the curator of a Japanese art exhibition for the Golden Gate Exposition. Ken is sent to Japan to buy artwork, but instead spreads the doctrine of Bushido. In Tokyo, Ken meets with military intelligence chief Namakura, and demonstrates his secret painting method. Ken's activities are watched closely by the Black Dragon Society of Japan, which distrusts anyone with close ties to the United States. In Shanghai, where the Japanese have begun to oppress the Chinese, Ken takes photographs of the populace, and later doctors the photographs so that Chinese missionaries and nurses are seen to be wearing emblems of the Rising Sun, thereby leading the viewer to believe that the Japanese are kind to the Chinese. In 1939, a member of the Black Dragons informs Ken that his former school chum, an English reporter, is printing stories about the Japanese atrocities against the Chinese. Ken murders the reporter, and then meets with Japanese General Sujiyama in Peking, who heads the invading Japanese army. After testing Ken's allegiance by forcing European and Chinese women prisoners to entertain him, Sujiyama commissions Ken to be the next governor of California. Ken is ordered to organize a military force of Japanese residents to prepare for a Japanese invasion of the state, after which he returns home and informs the priest of their orders. When his younger adopted brother Frank discovers Ken's secret while he is away, he takes their parents to Ken's studio and tells them that Ken is a spy. The Morreys are shocked and dismayed, but see the proof in Ken's paintings. While Frank goes to the police, Ken returns to the studio and convinces his parents that he is a double agent working for their country, then stabs his parents to death. Now wanted for murder, Ken goes to the temple after receiving word that the "zero hour" has been set for the invasion of California. Ken becomes hysterical and power hungry with the thought of the invasion, but is subdued after learning that most of his comrades have been arrested. As the samurai doctrine states that a man who fails his mission must take his own life, the priest prepares to commit suicide, and demands that Ken watch so that he will be prepared if he should ever meet the same fate. As the priest dies, police attack the temple, and Paul escapes to the beach. There, he is shot and killed by the police. *Bushido. Espionage. Japanese Americans. Priests. Treachery. Adoption. Americans in foreign countries. Assimilation (Sociology). Attempted rape. China. Earthquakes. Family relationships. Hara-kiri. Japan. Japan. Army. Loyalty. Missionaries. Murder. Paintings. Police. Political prisoners. Samurai. San Francisco (CA). Secret societies. Sino-Japanese conflict, 1937-1945. World War II.*

Note: The working title of this film was *Orders from Tokyo.* Although fictional, the film is narrated and presented in the style of a documentary. Onscreen credits include a 1944 copyright statement, but the film is not listed in copyright records. Information in the MPAA/PCA Collection at the AMPAS Library provides the following information about the production: After reading an initial script, the PCA wrote to producer Ben Mindenburg on 10 Nov 1943 that the sequence in which "General [Sujiyama] and Ken indulge in sadism with the Chinese and White girl" was unacceptable, and that it was "imperative that it be omitted or changed....Furthermore, we recommend that you consult the War Department as to a recent directive they have issued prohibiting any scenes of Japanese atrocities and brutality." According to a plot synopsis in the file, the phone call "Ken" receives informing him of the "zero hour," just before he kills his parents, is a decoy by the "Secret Service" to trick Ken into action. This is not clear in the film, however. The synopsis also includes a scene after "Ken" murders his parents in which "Frank" returns to the studio, and "Ken innocently tells Frank that the folks left for home. Frank does not believe Ken...finds both dead. There is a fight between Ken and Frank, with Ken being the victor, as he tries to choke Frank...[who] is left for dead." This scene was not included in the viewed print.

On 12 Jun 1944, the PCA wrote the following to Mindenburg after viewing an eight-reel rough cut of the film: "The principal objections to the material received by us were...[a] scene suggesting the rape of a White girl by the leading Japanese villain. It was explained to Mr. Mindenburg that this scene was

completely unacceptable....There were numerous scenes, from newsreels, dealing with the bombing of Shanghai, etc., which contained unacceptably gruesome scenes of dead bodies. It was pointed out to Mr. Mindenburg that these should be deleted when the film is reedited." The PCA also viewed "a two-reel Technicolor film of the San Francisco Exposition, with Japanese narration, parts of which [Mindenburg] intends to cut into the picture." While a contemporary credits sheet lists the film's footage as 6,760 ft., the PCA listed the film's length as 5,812 ft., and included the following addendum: "[I]ssued with the understanding that the dialogue in connection with the prison scene, the scene and sounds of attempted rape, and also the scene of actual Hara Kiri, are eliminated from all release prints."

This film includes what appears to be newsreel footage of the 1 Sep 1923 earthquake in Tokyo. The *Exh* reviewer commented that *Samurai* is "a very poor, dated film," but suggested using ad lines such as "The True Secret About Jap Fraternization with White Women" and "At Last! The True Story of Jap Activities in America" to promote the film.

Exh 5 Sep 1945, p. 1786. *NYT* 24 Aug 1945. *NYT* 25 Aug 1945.

SAN ANTONE (Latino)

Republic Pictures Corp. *Dist* Republic Pictures Corp. 15 Feb **1953**; Prod: mid-Oct—late Oct 1952 [©Republic Pictures Corp.; 15 Jan 1953; LP2377]. Sd (RCA Sound System); b&w. 8,106 ft. 90 min. PCA cert no. 15750.

Assoc prod Joseph Kane. *Dir* Joseph Kane. *Asst dir* Herb Mendelson. *Scr* Steve Fisher. *Photog* Bud Thackery. *Spec eff* Howard Lydecker and Theodore Lydecker. *Opt eff* Consolidated Film Industries. *Art dir* Frank Arrigo. *Film ed* Tony Martinelli. *Set dec* John McCarthy, Jr. and Charles Thompson. *Cost des* Adele Palmer. *Mus* R. Dale Butts. *Sd* Earl Crain, Sr. *Makeup supv* Bob Mark. *Hair stylist* Peggy Gray.

Song(s): "The Cowboy's Lament," traditional; "South of the San Antone" and "10,000 Cattle," composers undetermined.

Source: Based on the novel *The Golden Herd* by Curt Carroll (New York, 1950).

Cast: Rod Cameron [(*Carl Miller*)], Arleen Whelan [(*Julia Allerby*)], Forrest Tucker [(*Lt. Brian Culver*)], Katy Jurado [(*Mistania Figueroa*)], Rodolfo Acosta (*Chino Figueroa*), Roy Roberts [(*John Chisum*)], Bob Steele [(*Bob*)], Harry Carey, Jr. [(*Dobe*)], James Lilburn [(*Jim*)], Andrew Brennan [(*Ike*)], Richard Hale [(*Abraham Lincoln*)], Martin Garralaga [(*Mexican*)], Argentina Brunetti [(*Mexican woman*)], Douglas Kennedy [(*Capt. Garfield*)], Paul Fierro [(*Bandit leader*)], George Cleveland [(*Col. Allerby*)], [Joseph Crehan (*Gen. Grant*)], [Francis McDonald (*Middle-aged man*)], [William Haade (*Soldier*)], [Robert Keys, Jack Shea (*Young officers*)], [Peter Ortiz (*Rider*)], [James Craven (*Union officer*)], [Pepe Hern, Alex Montoya, Charles Stevens (*Mexicans*)], [James Harrison (*Hank*)], [Chuck Hayward (*Willie*)], [Steve Darrell (*Gen. Shelby*)], [Lee Shumway (*Gen. Lee*)], [John Halloran (*Sergeant*)], [Charles Cane (*Bartender*)], [Chris-Pin Martin (*Ramon*)], [Karolee Kelly (*Girl*)], [Tom Monroe], [Marshall Reed], [Scott Lee].

Historical, Drama. [*Print viewed*]. In 1861, Lt. Brian Culver, newly commissioned in the Confederate army, rides to the Allerby plantation near San Antonio, Texas, to propose marriage to Julia Allerby. Julia accepts, but when she spots Chino Figueroa approaching, runs off to meet him secretly. Chino, whose family once owned the land surrounding the plantation, but now work for the Allerbys, informs Julia that he and his family are leaving for Mexico to fight with Benito Juarez. Determined to keep the Figueroas as her servants, Julia seductively provokes Chino to kiss her and then claims that he attacked her. A lynch mob forms rapidly, despite the efforts of Col. Allerby, Julia's father, to intervene. Before the lynching can be carried out, however, wealthy cattleman Carl Miller stops the mob at gunpoint. Carl, who is Chino's best friend, left the area three years earlier as a poor man and has returned to deliver orders to Culver. Although Carl does not believe in the war, he has agreed to carry out a cattle drive on behalf of the Confederacy. Anxious for battle, Culver is outraged to learn that he has been assigned to lead a squadron in support of the drive. To make matters worse, Carl, although a civilian, will be the man in charge. Later, when Carl criticizes Julia for her actions toward Chino, she tries to seduce him and he slaps her. She then vows to have Culver kill him. Carl pays a visit to the Figueroas before they leave for Mexico, and he and Chino's sister Mistania affirm their love for each other. Afterward, Carl learns that his father, a German immigrant, will be in Germantown for the duration of the war. From the beginning of the cattle drive, Culver and Carl are in conflict with each other because Culver resents the fact that he is not in the midst of a battle. Three weeks after the beginning of the drive,

Carl leads the men and the cattle through a pass. Expecting the pass to be ambushed by Union soldiers, he directs the men to travel at night, and as soon as the men come under gunfire, Culver deserts. Outmanned, Carl's troops are captured by Union soldiers, and because he is leading them, Carl is taken prisoner, even though he is a civilian. After the war ends, a group of former Confederate soldiers under the leadership of Gen. Shelby, decide to offer their services to the French in their fight against Juarez. When Carl returns to San Antonio, he meets Bob, Dobe and Jim, three of the men who accompanied him on the cattle drive, and they sign on with John Chisum to round up wild cattle and deliver them to market. Carl then sets out to look for his father, and at his father's cabin, finds Mistania waiting for him. She informs him that Chino has captured a group of marauders led by Culver and is holding them for ransom. Later, Carl learns from Julia that Culver killed his father during a raid on Germantown. Determined that Culver will pay for his father's murder, Carl decides to ransom the men whom Chino is holding. Julia begs Carl to take her with him, but he refuses, knowing how much Chino hates her. Along with Bob, Dobe, Jim and Mistania, Carl rounds up the cattle necessary to ransom the Americans and heads into Mexico. Julia manages to cross the border, and when Carl and Mistania encounter her in a cantina, Carl agrees to take her only as far as Monterrey, where she may be able to find an escort back to the States. His plans change, however, when he learns that Monterrey has fallen to the French. To bypass the city, the herd must go through hostile Apache territory. Hoping to avoid contact with the Indians, Mistania leads the group through waterless territory. Julia continues to behave seductively with Carl, and although her wiles have no effect on him, she rouses Mistania's jealousy. When they finally reach the waterhole, they discover that it has been poisoned and head farther into Apache territory. That night, they successfully fight off a raiding party. Knowing that the Apaches will return, Julia professes her love for Carl and suggests that they desert the others and save themselves. Again rejecting Julia, Carl prepares for battle. In the morning a war party arrives and a fierce battle ensues. The group is saved by the arrival of some of Chino's men, who have discovered the cattle. At Chino's encampment, Carl fights Culver, but decides not to kill him. Learning that the French have refused Shelby's offer of military help, he sends Culver back across the border with Julia, sure that the two will punish each other. Finally free to be together, Carl and Mistania embrace. Cattlemen. Mexican Americans. Revenge. Texans. Apache Indians. Brothers and sisters. Class distinction. Fathers and daughters. Fathers and sons. Fistfights. Jealousy. Knife fighting. Mexican-American border region. Mexico–History. Prisoners of war. Ransom. Romance. Servants. Soldiers. Southern belles. United States–History–Civil War, 1861-1865.

Note: The film's working titles were *South of San Antone* and *Women of Destiny*. Joseph Kane's onscreen credit reads "Associate Producer—Director." The tune "Oh Shenandoah" was used as the music for the song "South of San Antone"

Box 7 Mar 1953. *DV* 25 Feb 1953, p. 3. *Exb* 11 Mar 1953, p. 3480. *FD* 26 Mar 1953, p. 6. *Har* 28 Feb 1953, p. 35. *HR* 17 Oct 1953, pp. 12-13 *HR* 22 Oct 1952. *HR* 31 Oct 1952, p. 12. *HR* 25 Feb 1953, p. 3. *MPHPD* 7 Mar 1953, p. 1751. *Var* 4 Mar 1953, p. 18.

SAN ANTONIO DE BEXAR *see* THE LAST COMMAND

THE SAN ANTONIO KID (Native Americans)

Republic Pictures Corp. *Dist* Republic Pictures Corp. 16 Aug **1944**; Los Angeles release: 27 Jul 1944; Prod: early May—17 May 1944 [©Republic Pictures Corp.; 18 Jul 1944; LP12778]. Sd (RCA Sound System); b&w. 6 reels, 4,972 ft. 59 min. Passed by the National Board of Review. PCA cert no. 10199.

Series: Red Ryder

[*Exec prod* William J. O'Sullivan]. *Assoc prod* Stephen Auer. *Dir* Howard Bretherton. *2d unit dir* Yakima Canutt. [*Asst dir* Allen Wood]. *Orig scr* Norman S. Hall. *Photog* William Bradford. *Art dir* Gano Chittenden. *Film ed* Tony Martinelli. *Set dec* Charles Thompson. *Mus score* Joseph Dubin. *Sd* Earl Crain, Sr.

Source: Based on the comic strip "Red Ryder" by Fred Harmon (1938–1964), by special arrangement with Stephen Slesinger.

Cast: WILD BILL ELLIOTT (*Red Ryder*), Bobby Blake [(*Little Beaver*)], Alice Fleming [(*The Duchess*)], Linda Stirling [(*Ann Taylor*)], Earle Hodgins [(*Happy Jack*)], Glenn Strange [(*Ace Hanlon*)], LeRoy Mason [(*Walter Garfield*)], Duncan Renaldo [(*Johnny Bennett, also known as The San Antonio Kid*)], Tom London [(*Lon*)], Jack Kirk [(*Ben Taylor*)], Bob Wilke [(*Bailey*)], Cliff

Parkinson [(*Ed*)], Jack O'Shea [(*Bartender*)], [Joe Garcia, Billy Vincent (*Cowboys*)], [Bud Geary (*Mason*)].

Western. [*Print viewed*]. Just before the turn of the century, Metropolitan Oil Company scout Walter Garfield comes to the town of Maverick, where he discovers a huge oil deposit under the caves on land owned by Ben Taylor. Believing that the deposit extends to the surrounding ranches as well, Garfield wires his company that oil may be present, then, along with saloon owner Ace Hanlon and his gang, instigates a wave of terror against the ranchers. Garfield hopes to drive the ranchers away, buy their land cheaply and then make a fortune selling it to Metropolitan. After the gang succeeds in driving off three ranchers, they raid Taylor's house, and during a shootout with Taylor and his daughter Ann, they kill Taylor. Taylor's closest neighbors, the Duchess, her nephew, Red Ryder, and his Indian ward, Little Beaver, look after Ann and wonder who is behind the attacks, which Red does not believe are the work of ordinary rustlers. Fearing that Hanlon's men will strike the Duchess' ranch next, Red and foreman Happy Jack confront Hanlon. After Red trounces Hanlon in a fistfight, Hanlon decides to have Red killed and sends for Johnny Bennett, an old friend who is known as The San Antonio Kid. Although Johnny is not a killer, Hanlon thinks he can pressure him into accepting the assignment because of his gambling debts. Meanwhile, Red, Happy Jack and Little Beaver find oil seeping through the ground of Taylor's cave, and Red realizes why Hanlon purchased the ranches. Red swears the others to secrecy, then, to protect Ann from the raiders, buys her ranch with the assurance that she can purchase it back at the same price if she changes her mind. Desperate to get the Taylor ranch before his company orders him to move on, Garfield offers Ann twice what Red paid for it, and when Red refuses to sell, Ann accuses him of swindling her. After Garfield leaves, however, Red tells Ann and the Duchess about the oil and Ann apologizes. Soon after, Johnny is traveling to Maverick when his horse is spooked and tosses him off a cliff. Johnny, holding onto a branch, is about to fall to his death when Red passes by and saves him. Red takes him to the ranch, where Johnny takes an immediate liking to the family atmosphere. Although she is shocked that Johnny is a gambler, the Duchess offers him a job when he professes a desire to go straight. After Johnny agrees to start work once he finishes a job for a friend who lent him money, he goes to the saloon, where Hanlon tells him that to clear his debt, he must kill Red. Johnny refuses until Hanlon asserts that he will have Red killed anyway. Johnny informs Red of the situation, and the two plan to trap Hanlon. Later, Johnny distracts Garfield and Hanlon with a poker game while Red searches Hanlon's office. There he finds proof of the oil discovery and Hanlon's partnership with Garfield. Red arranges for a confrontation with Hanlon the next day, and when Johnny does not kill Red as ordered, one of Hanlon's men shoots him. Johnny is only wounded, however, and helps Red, Happy Jack and Little Beaver as they engage in a shootout with the gang. Red chases Garfield and Hanlon to the caves, where a fight breaks out and one of the oil pools is set on fire. Garfield is felled by the blaze, and the gang is rounded up. Later, Red, Little Beaver and Happy Jack ride off in search of another adventure, and Johnny promises to look after the Duchess and Ann. *Cowboys. Duplicity. Oil. Outlaws. Saloon keepers. Women ranchers. Aunts. Caves. Debt. Fires. Fistfights. Friendship. Latino. Indians of North America. Land sales. Poker (Game). Ranch foremen. Rescues. Shootouts. Wards and guardians.*

Note: The character "Ace Hanlon" also appears in another "Red Ryder" film, *Phantom of the Plains*, although he is played by William Haade in that film (see above). Modern sources add the following actors to the cast: Tex Terry, Bob Woodward, Herman Hack, Henry Wills, Tom Steele and Pascale Perry. For more information on the "Red Ryder" series, please consult the Series Index and see the entry below for *Tucson Raiders*.

DV 28 Jul 1944, p. 3. *HR* 12 May 1944, p. 23. *HR* 15 May 1944, p. 14. *HR* 28 Jul 1944, p. 4. *MPHPD* 5 Aug 1944, p. 2030.

SANDS OF IWO JIMA (Italian Americans, Greek Americans, Irish Americans, Jewish Americans, Polish Americans)

Republic Pictures Corp. *Dist* Republic Pictures Corp. 1 Mar **1950**; World premiere in San Francisco, CA: 14 Dec 1949; Los Angeles, CA: 28 Dec 1949; *Prod:* early Jul—late Aug 1949 [©Republic Pictures Corp.; 16 Dec 1949; LP2757]. Sd (RCA Sound System); b&w. 9,845 ft. 109-110 min. Passed by the National Board of Review. PCA cert no. 14111.

Pres HERBERT J. YATES. *Assoc prod* Edmund Grainger. *Dir* Allan Dwan. [*Asst dir* Nate Barrager]. *Scr* Harry Brown and James Edward Grant. *Story* Harry Brown. *Dir of photog* Reggie Lanning. [*Cam op* Herb Kirkpatrick]. [*Gaffer* Syd Swaney, Jr.]. [*Stills* Don Keyes]. *Spec eff* Howard Lydecker and Theodore Lydecker. *Optical eff* Consolidated Film Industries. [*Spec eff* Jack Coffee]. *Art dir* James Sullivan. *Film ed* Richard L. Van Enger. *Set dec* John McCarthy, Jr. and Otto Siegel. *Cost supv* Adele Palmer. *Mus* Victor Young. *Sd* T. A. Carman and Howard Wilson. *Makeup supv* Bob Mark. [*Makeup* Vern Murdock]. *Hair* Peggy Gray. [*Prod mgr* Lee Lukather]. [*Scr supv* Robert Walker]. [*Grip* Nelson Mathias]. [*Tech adv* Capt. Leonard Fribourg].

Song(s): "The Marine's Hymn," words anonymous, music based on a theme from the opera *Geneviève de Brabant* by Jacques Offenbach.

Cast: John Wayne [(*Sgt. Strykker*)], John Agar by arrangement with David O. Selznick [(*Pfc. Peter Conway*)], Adele Mara [(*Allison Bromley*)], Forrest Tucker [(*Corp. Al Thomas*)], Wally Cassell [(*Pfc. Benny Ragazzi*)], James Brown [(*Pfc. Charlie Bass*)], Richard Webb [(*Pfc. Dan Shipley*)], Arthur Franz [(*Corp. Robert Dunne*)], Julie Bishop [(*Mary*)], James Holden [(*Pfc. Soames*)], Peter Coe [(*Pfc. George Hellenopolis*)], Richard Jaeckel [(*Pfc. F. Flynn*)], Bill Murphy [(*Pfc. E. Flynn*)], George Tyne [(*Pfc. Harris*)], Hal Fieberling [(*Pvt. "Ski" Choynski*)], John McGuire [(*Capt. Joyce*)], Martin Milner [(*Pvt. Mike McHugh*)], Leonard Gumley [(*Pvt. Sid Stein*)], William Self [(*Pvt. L. D. Fowler, Jr.*)], Col. D. M. Shoup, U.S.M.C., Lt. Col. H. P. Crowe, U.S.M.C., Capt. Harold G. Schrier, U.S.M.C., And the three living survivors of the historic flag raising on Mount Suribachi: Pfc. Rene A. Gagnon, Pfc. Ira H. Hayes, PM 3/c John H. Bradley, [Lt. Gen. Holland M. Smith, Ret.], [Dick Wessel (*Tough Marine Sergeant*)], [I. Stanford Jolley (*Forrestal*)], [David Clarke (*Wounded Marine*)], [Gil Herman (*Lt. Baker*)], [Dick Jones, Conrad Binyon, Billy Lechner, Glen Vernon, Steve Wayne, Bill Hudson, Mickey McCardle, Bruce Edwards, Fred Datig, Jr. (*Marines*)], [Don Haggerty (*Colonel*)], [Frank O'Connor (*Waiter*)], [Al Murphy (*Bartender*)], [Dorothy Ford (*Tall woman*)], [Judy Sochor, Joy Windsor, Carole Gallagher, Margot Powers (*USO women*)], [John Whitney (*Lt. Thompson*)], [Roger McGee (*Sailor*)].

World War II, Drama. [*Print viewed*]. In 1943, speaking to a group of Marines at a World War II base in New Zealand, Corp. Robert Dunne recounts his first tour of duty: Before Dunne and his friends, Italian-American Benny Regazzi, Greek-American George Hellenopolis, Polish-American "Ski" Choynski, Jewish-American Sid Stein, two Irish-American brothers named Flynn, Dan Shipley and Charlie Bass, met their battle-hardened commander, Sgt. Strykker, they had heard rumors that he had been demoted for striking a fellow officer. One morning, Strykker learns that Peter Conway, the son of his former commanding officer, Col. Sam Conway, has joined his unit. When the mail arrives later, Strykker is saddened to find no letter from his own son back home. Later, the unit receives some leave time, and Strykker's men decide to visit a dance hall, where Pete meets and falls in love with Allison Bromley. Later, Strykker urges Pete not to become too attached, but Pete marries Allison right away. A few days later, the unit is sent to an atoll called Tarawa, which is currently occupied by Japanese forces. After Strykker's unit lands, he orders two of his men to cross a dangerous minefield and place a charge inside a bunker where the Japanese have hidden some explosives. Strykker watches as both men are shot down, then rushes forward to grab the charge and completes the mission single-handedly. Once the bunker is detonated, the Marines advance and take shelter inside foxholes. Soon, the gunfire subsides, and after a few days, the unit begins to relax. Later, Corp. Al Thomas decides to take a coffee break in the mortar men's foxhole, while leaving his subordinates, Bass and Hellenopolis, alone in theirs. While he is gone, the foxhole is overrun by Japanese soldiers, and Bass and Hellenopolis are bayoneted. The unit, which is forced backward some distance, then takes refuge in a trench. There, Strykker is ordered to "hold the line," and despite the pleas of his men to rescue the wounded Bass and Hellenopolis, Strykker refuses to violate his orders. All night long, the unit is forced to listen to Bass's plaintive cries from the trench. The next morning, Bass is rescued, while Hellenopolis dies of his wounds. Later, the unit arrives in Hawaii, where Bass tells Strykker that Thomas was absent from his post during the attack. When Thomas enters a few moments later, Strykker punches him in the face. After a major is called to break up the fight, he demands to know who started it. Thomas, who realizes that another demotion could end Strykker's career, decides to say nothing. While on leave in Honolulu, Strykker convinces Pete to

name his son "Sam" after his father. Ten days later, the unit is ordered to complete a difficult landing on the rocky, island cliffs of Iwo Jima. After three weeks of intense fighting, the unit finally gains the top of Mount Suribachi. Strykker instructs his men to hoist the American flag, then sits down for a moment, and is killed when a random bullet ricochets toward him. Pete drops to his knees to embrace Strykker's corpse and finds a letter that he had been writing to his son. With fond remembrance of his brave commander, Pete finishes the letter. *Combat. Islands. Iwo Jima (Japan). Officers (Military). United States. Marine Corps. War heroes. Bayonets. Camp Paekakariki (New Zealand). Corpses. Dance halls. Explosives. Fathers and sons. Fistfights. Flags. Greek Americans. Honolulu (HI). Irish Americans. Italian Americans. Japan. Army. Jews. Letters. Military bases. Military leave. Mount Suribachi (Iwo Jima, Japan). New Zealand. Polish Americans. Rescues. Rumors. Tarawa (Kiribati). World War II. Wounds and injuries.*

Note: The onscreen credits include a dedication to the U.S. Marine Corps and a historical note which states that "The first American flag was raised on Mount Suribachi by the late Sgt. Ernest I. Thomas, Jr., U.S.M.C. on the morning of February 23, 1945." According to a *NYT* news item, the United States Marine Corps approved the film's scenario. Appearing in the picture as themselves are Lt. Gen. Holland M. Smith (Ret.), wartime commander of the Fifth Amphibious Corps; Capt. Harold Schrier, who led the platoon of marines up the slopes of Suribachi; Col. Irving Crowe, a batallion commander on Tarawa; and Col. David Shoup, who was awarded the Congressional Medal of Honor. A *DN* news item notes that nearly 2000 Marines were used as extras in the making of the picture. According to a *LAT* news item, for the shots depicting the flag raising, Maj. Andrew Greer loaned Republic the original flag, which was housed at the Marine Museum at Quantico, Virginia. The sequence is based on newsreel footage taken of the actual flag raising, as well as Joe Rosenthal's photograph, which appeared in the 26 Mar 1945 edition of *Life*. For his Pulitzer Prize-winning photograph, Rosenthal asked that the participants re-enact the actual flag raising, which had occured some hours previous. Furthermore, this image is represented at the Marine Corps Memorial in Arlington, VA.

The review in *Var* noted that many of the film's battle sequences were made up of "footage taken at the actual fighting at Tarawa and Iwo Jima." *NYT* notes indicated that filming took place at Camp Pendleton, Camp Del Mar and El Toro Marine Air Station in Southern California. A modern source notes that Wayne's foot and handprints were placed at Grauman's Chinese Theatre in conjunction with the opening of the film there. The source went on to say that two 100-lb. bags of sand had been brought from Iwo Jima for the occasion. Wayne received his first Academy Award nomination for Best Actor for this film. Other nominations included Richard L. Van Enger for film editing, Harry Brown for writing and Republic Studios' Sound Department for sound recording. According to a 5 Feb 1950 *NYT* news item, Republic was planning a sequel to this film, called *Devil Birds*, which was to have starred Wayne, but no record of the film has been found.

Box 24 Dec 1949. *DN* 3 Aug 1949. *DV* 14 Dec 1949, p. 3. *FD* 14 Dec 1949, p. 7. *HR* 8 Jul 1949, p. 19. *HR* 19 Aug 1949, p. 23. *HR* 14 Dec 1949, p. 3. *LADN* 3 Aug 1949. *LADN* 28 Dec 1949. *LAEx* 29 Dec 1949. *LAT* 29 Dec 1949. *MPHPD* 17 Dec 1949, p. 121. *NYT* 7 Aug 1949, p. 1. *NYT* 31 Dec 1949, p. 9. *NYT* 5 Feb 1950. *Var* 14 Dec 1949, p. 8.

SANDY (Scottish Americans, Irish Americans)

Famous Players-Lasky Corp. *Dist* Famous Players-Lasky Corp.; Paramount Pictures. 1 Jul **1918** [©Famous Players-Lasky Corp.; 22 Jun 1918; LP12588]. Si; b&w. 5 reels.

Pres Jesse L. Lasky. *Dir* George H. Melford. *Asst dir* Claude Mitchell. *Scen* Edith M. Kennedy. *Cam* Paul Perry. *Set des* Wilfred Buckland.

Source: Based on the novel *Sandy* by Alice Caldwell (Hegan) Rice (New York, 1905).

Cast: Jack Pickford (*Sandy Kilday*), Louise Huff (*Ruth Nelson*), James Neill (*Judge Hollis*), Edythe Chapman (*Mrs. Hollis*), Julia Faye (*Annette Fenton*), George A. Beranger (*Carter Nelson*), Raymond Hatton (*Ricks Wilson*), Clarence Geldart (*Dr. Fenton*), Louise Hutchinson (*Aunt Nelson*), Jennie Lee (*Aunt Melvy*), J. Parks Jones (*Jimmy Reed*), Don Lykes (*Sid Gray*).

Drama. Sandy Kilday, a poor but hopeful Scottish-Irishman who has boarded a ship bound for New York, is discovered as a stowaway, but a fellow passenger, pretty Ruth Nelson, persuades her aunt to pay the lad's fare. In New York, Sandy joins forces with ex-jockey Ricks Wilson, and the two work their way toward Kentucky, where Ricks plans to ride in the Derby. Judge and Mrs. Hollis adopt Sandy, who meets Ruth again at a country fair. Ruth's alcoholic brother Carter bribes Ricks to foul another jockey, but the rider is seriously hurt, and Ricks is arrested. That same day, Sandy prevents Carter from eloping with Annette Fenton, but they return to find that the judge has been shot and Ricks accused. The crowd attacks Sandy when he tries to defend the innocent Ricks, but Carter's dying confession saves him. The judge recovers in time to witness the marriage of Sandy and Ruth. *Attempted murder. Bribery. Immigrants. Jockeys. Kentucky Derby.*

Adoption. Alcoholics. Aunts. Confession (Law). Elopement. False accusations. Fixed horse races. Judges. Kentucky. New York City. Ships. Stowaways.

Note: According to publicity for the film, Jack Pickford joined the U.S. Naval Reserve immediately after filming was completed.

ETR 6 Jul 1918, p. 401. *MPN* 6 Jul 1918, p. 65, 117-18. *MPW* 13 Jul 1918, p. 247, 255. *NYDM* 6 Jul 1918, p. 964. *NYT* 15 Jul 1918, p. 9. *Var* 19 Jul 1918, p. 37. *Wid's* 30 Jun 1918, pp. 9-10.

SANGAREE (African Americans, Latino)

Paramount Pictures Corp. *Dist* Paramount Pictures Corp. May **1953**; *Prod:* mid-Jan—early Mar 1953 [©Paramount Pictures Corp.; 27 May 1953; LP2632]. Sd (Western Electric Recording); col (Technicolor); 3 Dimension. 8,540 ft. 94-95 min. PCA cert no. 16414.

Prod William H. Pine and William C. Thomas. *Dir* Edward Ludwig. *Asst dir* Herbert Coleman. *Wrt for the scr by* David Duncan. *Adpt for the scr by* Frank Moss. *Dir of photog* Lionel Lindon. *2d unit photog* Wallace Kelley. *Process photog* Farciot Edouart. *Spec photog eff* John P. Fulton and Paul Lerpae. *Technicolor color consultant* Richard Mueller. *Art dir* Hal Pereira and Earl Hendrick. *Ed* Howard Smith. *Set dec* Sam Comer and Ross Dowd. *Cost* Edith Head. *Mus score* Lucien Cailliet. *Sd rec* Harold Lewis and John Cope. *Makeup supv* Wally Westmore.

Source: Based on the novel *Sangaree* by Frank G. Slaughter (Garden City, NY, 1948).

Cast: FERNANDO LAMAS [(*Dr. Carlos Morales*)], ARLENE DAHL [(*Nancy Darby*)], PATRICIA MEDINA [(*Martha Darby*)], Francis L. Sullivan [(*Dr. Bristol*)], Charles Korvin [(*Felix Pagnol*)], Tom Drake [(*Dr. Roy Darby*)], John Sutton [(*Harvey Bristol*)], Willard Parker [(*Gabriel Thatch*)], Charles Evans [(*Judge Armstrong*)], Lester Mathews [(*Gen. Darby*)], Roy Gordon [(*Dr. Tyrus*)], Lewis L. Russell [(*Captain Bronson*)], Russell Gaige [(*McIntosh*)], William Walker [(*Priam*)], [Felix Nelson (*Billy*)], [Voltaire Perkins (*Crowther*)].

Historical, Drama. [*Print viewed*]. In Georgia, at the end of the Revolutionary War, the wealthy Gen. Darby, lying on his deathbed, asks his friend, Dr. Carlos Morales, to take over Sangaree, his estate, and establish an experimental program designed to give slaves and indentured servants their freedom. Carlos, the son of indentured servants, is grateful to Darby for providing him with an education, and accepts the responsibility, which calls for the creation of free clinics and schools for the children of slaves. Though Carlos proudly accepts the charge, Roy Darby, the general's son and a friend of Carlos, knows that his sister Nancy will contest the terms of the will and fight to gain control of the estate. Roy's prediction proves accurate, but before Nancy begins to wage her battle, she disguises herself as a country girl and boards the boat taking Carlos to Savannah to get a look at him. Introducing herself as "Dolly Lake," Nancy asks Carlos about his plans, and when he tells her that he intends to take over the plantation the following day, she warns him that "Miss Darby" and her fiancé, the attorney Harvey Bristol, will fight him. By the time he and Nancy reach Savannah, Carlos sees through Nancy's ruse, but plays along with her and steals a kiss before she leaves. In Savannah, Carlos attends an elegant party hosted by his former sweetheart, Martha Darby, who, although she is now married to Roy, still carries a torch for him. During the festivities, Martha tells Carlos that she intends to expose Nancy as an accomplice to Felix Pagnol, a French pirate who has been harassing ships off the coast of Savannah. Carlos urges Martha to suppress the information when he realizes that she intends to use it to blackmail Nancy into dropping her legal challenge to Carlos' inheritance. When Roy arrives with news of a plague outbreak, Dr. Bristol rudely dismisses the announcement as nonsense, and concurs with his son's belief that Carlos and Roy are merely using the threat of plague to generate interest in Darby's free clinic. During the trial to contest her father's will, Nancy renounces her fiancé when he tries to prove that her father was "insane." As a result, the judge rules in Carlos' favor, and the provisions of the will remain intact. Later, at a tavern, Bristol challenges Carlos to a fight, but Carlos trounces both Bristol and his henchman. Having broken off her engagement to Bristol, Nancy begins pursuing Carlos in earnest. After overhearing two pirates discussing plans to intercept a Darby ship, Carlos accuses Nancy of betraying her own company, but she denies the accusation. Carlos and his friend, Gabriel Thatch, later explode the pirate ship on its way to menace the Darby cargo. Later, as Carlos prepares to fight as Gabriel's second in his duel with Pagnol, Pagnol tells him that Bristol is behind the piracy. Carlos finds the stolen

Darby cargo in the Bristol warehouse, and when he also discovers that the warehouse is the source of the plague, he orders it burned. Martha contracts the plague, but before dying, she confesses to have been Bristol's accomplice after she shoots Bristol and tells Carlos that she joined the pirates to get at the Darby fortunes. Free to resume their romance, Nancy and Carlos look forward to running Sangaree as husband and wife. *Georgia. Indentured servants. Plantations. Romance. United States–History–18th century. Wills.* African Americans. Benefactors. Blackmail. Death and dying. Duels. Engagements. Explosions. Fistfights. Foster children. French. Impersonation and imposture. Inheritance. Jealousy. Maids. Marriage–Arranged. Murder. Physicians. Pirates. Plague. Savannah (GA). Slavery–Emancipation.

Note: The working title of this film was *Savannah.* The film marked Paramount's first three-dimensional, wide-screen Technicolor picture. A May 1953 *NYT* article noted that some of the picture was originally shot in 2-D. According to the article, the decision to reshoot the film in 3-D was made at the urging of Paramount board chairman Adolph Zukor, who wanted to "tackle the challenge of our time in show business." According to a Feb 1952 *HR* news item, the film was originally slated as a starring vehicle for Clark Gable and Lana Turner. The same article noted that director Edward Ludwig was to collaborate on the script, but his contribution to the final screenplay has not been confirmed.

Box 30 May 1953. *DV* 27 May 1953, p. 3. *FD* 27 May 1953, p. 6. *HR* 25 Feb 1952. *HR* 19 Dec 1952. *HR* 19 Jan 1953, p. 14. *HR* 27 Feb 1953, p. 12. *HR* 27 May 1953, p. 3. *MPHPD* 30 May 1953, p. 1853. *NYT* 31 May 1953. *NYT* 5 Jun 1953, p. 19. *Var* 27 May 1953, p. 6.

SANTA FE BOUND *see* **DRIFTING WESTWARD**

SANTA FE PASSAGE (Native Americans, Kiowa)

Republic Pictures Corp. *Dist* Republic Pictures Corp. 12 May **1955**; Prod: ended late Oct 1954 [©Republic Pictures Corp.; 24 Feb 1955; LP5152]. Sd (RCA Sound Recording); col (Trucolor by Consolidated); 1.66-1. 10 reels, 8,098 ft. 90-91 min. PCA cert no. 17304.

Pres HERBERT J. YATES. *Assoc prod* Sidney Picker. *Dir* William Witney. *Asst dir* A. J. Vitarelli. *Scr* Lillie Hayward. *Dir of photog* Bud Thackery. *Spec eff* Howard Lydecker and Theodore Lydecker. *Optical eff* Consolidated Film Industries. *Art dir* Frank Arrigo. *Film ed* Tony Martinelli. *Set dec* John McCarthy, Jr. and Glenn P. Thompson. *Cost des* Adele Palmer. *Mus* R. Dale Butts. *Sd* Roy Meadows and Howard Wilson. *Makeup supv* Bob Mark.

Source: Based on the short story "Santa Fe Passage" by Clay Fisher in *Esquire* (Apr 1952).

Cast: John Payne [(*Kirby Randolph*)], Faith Domergue [(*Aurelie St. Clair*)], Rod Cameron [(*Jess Griswold*)], Slim Pickens [(*Sam Beekman*)], Irene Tedrow [(*Ptewaquin*)], George Keymas [(*Satank*)], Leo Gordon [(*Tuss McLawery*)], Anthony Caruso [(*Chavez*)], [Tyler McVey (*Laughton*)], [Edward Colmans (*Padre*)], [John Patrick (*Marony*)], [Howard J. Negley (*Big man*)], [Tom Monroe (*Blacksmith*)], [Earl Robie (*Boy*)], [Hal Smith (*Bartender*)].

Western. [*Print viewed*]. When his pal, Sam Beekman, captures an Indian sneaking near their wagon train, scout Kirby Randolph, realizing the brave is a follower of Satank, the fierce Kiowa chief, lets him go then devises a plan to get through the treacherous Cottonwood Draw. He sends the wagons through the night to Laird's Way Station, on the other end of the pass, and goes with Sam to meet Satank and trade some old useless guns for a promise that Satank will not attack the wagons. Kirby is suspicious that Satank has such a small party of Indians with him, and when he and Sam reach Laird's Way Station, they are horrified to learn that the main force of Satank's braves attacked the wagon train and killed all the settlers. Kirby and Sam are accused of collaborating with the Indians for money and ostracized when they try to get work in another town. Sam learns of an express freight outfit heading for Santa Fe looking for a scout. The owner, Jess Griswold, says that every man is entitled to one mistake and hires Kirby and Sam. Kirby, a self-avowed Indian hater, slugs wagon boss Tuss McLawery, whose mother was a Dakota Sioux, when McLawery taunts him about the massacre. When Kirby finds Ptewaquin, an old Indian woman, driving the wagon of Aurelie St. Clair from New Orleans, he orders the woman off, but Aurelie adamantly states that Ptewaquin goes wherever she goes. Learning that Aurelie has made a deal with Jess to transport rifles to sell to the Mexican army, Kirby warns that Satank will try to capture them. Seeing the tension between Kirby and Aurelie, Jess informs Kirby that he intends to marry her. Along the trail, Kirby's quick thinking saves the wagons from a herd of stampeding horses. During the encounter, Aurelie's dress catches fire, and Kirby rolls her in the dirt and pats her down to put it out. At night, Aurelie tells Kirby about being ostracized

growing up because of her no-good father and that she feels this is her one chance to make enough money to be somebody. Ptewaquin soon detects that Aurelie is falling in love with Kirby and warns that he would hate her if he learned that her mother was a squaw. One night, as Kirby is on guard duty, Aurelie playfully approaches him with a knife to his back. He wrestles her into his tent and angrily tell her never to sneak up on a man like a "dirty, thieving Indian." As they lie in each other's arms, she tries to tell him her secret, but they end up kissing passionately instead. While they continue their lovemaking, Tuss hears a Kiowa bird call and runs off into the woods. Jess sees Tuss run off, and he sends his assistant Chavez to follow. Jess then sees Kirby and Aurelie exit the tent from opposite sides. The next day, Jess announces that there is a traitor in camp. He shoots and kills Tuss after giving him the chance to shoot first and reveals that Chavez overheard Tuss make an arrangement for Satank to steal the rifles as they cross the river. Kirby devises a counterplan, and during the subsequent battle, Kirby partially scalps Satank before he is shot in the shoulder with an arrow. Kirby gets drunk to blunt the pain as Ptewaquin cuts the arrow from his shoulder. Afterward, in front of Jess, he kisses Aurelie, but later, Jess tells him that she is a "breed," whose mother was the daughter of a Kiowa chief. Jess taunts him by relating Kiowa customs he will have to follow if they marry. As they travel, Kirby avoids Aurelie. When Aurelie gives Kirby a good luck charm she made from the arrowhead he stopped and a knot of Satank's hair, he says he does not want to marry a half-breed and throws the charm in the fire. Jess comforts her, and when he proposes, she says she will let him know her decision before they get to Santa Fe. Chavez convinces Jess that Aurelie will never marry him while Kirby is alive, so they plan to make a deal with Satank for Kirby's scalp in return for safe passage. Jess sends Kirby ahead to scout for water, and he is captured by Satank, who then decides he also wants the rifles and Aurelie. Meanwhile, Jess leaves Sam in charge of the wagons while he takes the pack animals, Aurelie and Ptewaquin through a pass in the mountains, planning to send water back. While Satank goes after the wagons, Kirby escapes and warns Jess. Jess is about to shoot Kirby, but Aurelie stops him. They fight rolling down a hill, and Jess breaks his leg. Kirby, Aurelie and Ptewaquin carry Jess to the horses, but Jess maneuvers away from them, grabs a rifle, and orders them to leave him, saying they will never make it with him along. After they ride off, the Indians attack and kill Jess. As the whites outmaneuver the Indians by splitting trails, Kirby reconciles with Aurelie. Satank approaches with his braves from the rocks above, but Sam, who has learned about Satank's attack, appears in the distance. Kirby, Aurelie and Ptewaquin lead the Kiowa into a trap, and they are routed by Sam and the others. As Satank is about to kill Sam, Kirby rescues him. Satank then tries to stab Kirby, but Ptewaquin stabs and kills the Kiowa chief. Ptewaquin is shot in the back with an arrow, and she dies in Aurelie's arms. Looking at Kirby, she speaks words in the Kiowa language, and after she dies, Aurelie tells Kirby that she said he shall be her daughter's husband. She then reveals that Ptewaquin was her mother. Later in Mexico, Sam sees that Kirby has tied his pony in front of Aurelie's tepee. According to the Kiowa custom, as soon as she finishes feeding the pony, she and Kirby will be married. As the lovers are about to go into the tepee, Sam asks them to make the marriage legal and brings a padre. As the ceremony is about to begin, Kirby and Aurelie kiss. *Bigotry. Gunrunners. Indians of North America–Mixed blood. Kiowa Indians. Personality change. Romance. Santa Fe Trail. Satank. Scouts (Frontier). Secrets. Wagon trains.* Drunkenness. Escapes. Fights. Fires. Horses. Jealousy. Massacres. Mexican Americans. Mothers and daughters. Priests. Proposals (Marital). Romantic rivalry. Santa Fe (Mexico). Self-sacrifice. Social customs. Stampedes. Traitors.

Note: Location shooting for this film was done in Utah.

Box 14 May 1955. *DV* 5 May 1955, p. 3. *Exh* 18 May 1955, pp. 3962-63. *FD* 13 May 1955, p. 24. *Har* 14 May 1955, p. 79. *HR* 5 May 1955, p. 3. *MPHPD* 21 May 1955, p. 442. *Var* 11 May 1955, p. 9.

SANTA FE TRAIL (African Americans)

Warner Bros. Pictures, Inc.; A Warner Bros.—First National Picture; Jack L. Warner in charge of production. *Dist* Warner Bros. Pictures, Inc. 28 Dec **1940**; World premiere in Santa Fe: 13 Dec 1940; Prod: mid-Jul–mid-Sep 1940 [©Warner Bros. Pictures, Inc.; 28 Dec 1940; LP10140]. Sd (RCA); b&w. 12 reels. 110 min. PCA cert no. 6559.

Exec prod Hal B. Wallis. *Assoc prod* Robert Fellows. *Dir* Michael Curtiz. *Dial dir* Jo Graham. [*Asst dir* Jack Sullivan]. *Orig scr* Robert Buckner. *Photog* Sol Polito. *Spec eff* Byron Haskin and H. F.

Koenekamp. *Art dir* John Hughes. *Film ed* George Amy. *Cost* Milo Anderson. *Mus dir* Leo F. Forbstein. *Mus score* Max Steiner. *Orch arr* Hugo Friedhofer. *Sd* Robert B. Lee. *Makeup* Perc Westmore. [*Unit mgr* Frank Mattison].

Cast: ERROL FLYNN (*Jeb Stuart*), OLIVIA DE HAVILLAND (*Kit Carson Halliday*), Raymond Massey (*John Brown*), Ronald Reagan (*George [Armstrong] Custer*), Alan Hale (*Tex Bell*), William Lundigan (*Bob Halliday*), Van Heflin ([*Carl*] *Rader*), Gene Reynolds (*Jason Brown*), Henry O'Neill (*Cyrus Halliday*), Guinn "Big Boy" Williams (*Windy Brody*), Alan Baxter (*Oliver Brown*), John Litel (*Martin*), Moroni Olsen (*Robert E. Lee*), David Bruce (*Phil Sheridan*), Hobart Cavanaugh (*Barber Doyle*), Charles D. Brown (*Major Sumner*), Joe Sawyer (*Kitzmiller*), Frank Wilcox (*James Longstreet*), Ward Bond (*Townley*), Russell Simpson (*Shubel Morgan*), Charles Middleton (*Gentry*), Erville Alderson (*Jefferson Davis*), Spencer Charters (*Conductor*), Suzanne Carnahan (*Charlotte*), William Marshall (*George Pickett*), George Haywood (*John Hood*), [Wilfred Lucas (*Weiner*)], [Russell Hicks (*J. Boyce Russell*)], [Napoleon Simpson (*Samson*)], [Cliff Clark (*Instructor*)], [Harry Strang (*Sergeant*)], [Emmett Vogan (*Lieutenant*)], [Selmer Jackson, Joseph Crehan, De Wolfe Hopper (*Officers*)], [Clinton Rosemond, Ernest Whitman (*Black men*)], [Bernice Pilot, Mildred Gover, Libby Taylor (*Black women*)], [Roy Barcroft, Frank Mayo (*Engineers*)], [Louis Jean Heydt (*Farmer*)], [Grace Stafford (*Farmer's wife*)], [Lane Chandler (*Adjutant*)], [Richard Kipling (*Army doctor*)], [Jack Mower (*Surveyor*)], [Trevor Bardette, Nestor Paiva (*Agitators*)], [Georgia Caine (*Officer's wife*)], [Arthur Aylsworth, Walter Soderling, Henry Hall (*Abolitionists*)], [Theresa Harris (*Black maid*)], [Jess Lee Brooks (*Black doorman*)], [Maris Wrixon, Lucia Carroll, Mildred Coles (*Girls*)], [Eddy Chandler, Ed Cobb, Ed Peil, Edward Hearn (*Guards*)], [Victor Kilian (*Dispatch rider*)], [Creighton Hale (*Telegraph operator*)], [Addison Richards (*Sheriff*)], [Lafe McKee (*Minister*)], [Reverend Neal Dodd (*Preacher*)], [Alec Proper (*Townsman*)], [John Meyer (*Workman*)], [Harry Cording], [Mira McKinney], [James Farley], [Alan Bridge], [Eddy Waller].

Historical, Drama. [*Print viewed*]. At the West Point Academy in 1854, cadet Carl Rader, a disciple of the fanatic John Brown, is dishonorably discharged for conspiracy. His classmates, Jeb Stuart and George Custer, graduate and are assigned to duty at Fort Leavenworth, Kansas, the most dangerous post in the army. On the way to Kansas, Custer and Stuart meet Cyrus Halliday, the man in charge of building the railroad to Santa Fe, and his daughter Kit Carson, with whom both soldiers fall in love. Arriving at the fort, they find the state bloodstained and war-torn, a victim of John Brown's relentless crusade against slavery. Meanwhile, Rader has enlisted as a mercenary in Brown's army, which has been terrorizing the countryside with their bloody raids. During Brown's raid on a freight wagon under the protection of the U.S. Army, Stuart and Custer capture Brown's injured son Jason, and before dying, the troubled boy informs them about his father's hideout at Shubel Morgan's ranch in Palmyra. In disguise, Stuart rides into Palmyra, the center of the underground slave railroad, but is recognized by Rader, who takes him at gunpoint to Brown. While trying to escape, Stuart is trapped in a burning barn but is saved as Custer leads the troops to the rescue and drives Brown into seclusion. Believing that Brown's force has been broken, Stuart and Custer are sent back to Washington, where Stuart proposes to Kit. However, far from being a broken man, Brown is planning to ignite war by raiding the arsenal at Harper's Ferry. When Brown refuses to pay Rader for his services, Rader rides to Washington to inform Stuart of Brown's plans, and the troops arrive just in time to crush the rebellion and hang Brown. *John Brown. General George Armstrong Custer. Officers (Military). Slavery. Jeb Stuart. United States–History. Disguise. Expulsion. Fathers and sons. Fort Leavenworth (KS). Harper's Ferry (WV). Hideouts. Proposals (Marital). Railroads. Rescues. Romantic rivalry. United States Military Academy. Washington (D.C.).*

Note: The working title of this film was *Diary of the Santa Fe*. According to a news item in *HR*, it was planned as a follow-up to the success of *Dodge City* which also starred Errol Flynn and Olivia de Havilland. Other news items in *HR* note that this picture was part of a trend towards big-budget big-name Westerns. The trend was spurred by the success of Fox's 1939 film *Jesse James* and the Warner Bros. 1939 film *Dodge City* and their 1940 film *Virginia City*. A news item in *HR* adds that the film was shot on location around Santa Fe, NM.

DV 16 Dec 1940, p. 3. *FD* 16 Dec 1940, p. 7. *HR* 14 Apr 1939, p. 8. *HR* 21 Jun 1940, p. 1, 4. *HR* 2 Jul 1940, p. 1. *HR* 12 Jul 1940, pp. 8-9. *HR* 13 Sep 1940, p. 7. *HR* 6 Nov 1940, p. 3. *HR* 16 Dec 1940, p. 3. *MPD* 16 Dec 1940, p. 1, 4. *NYT* 21 Dec 1940, p. 21. *Var* 18 Dec 1940, p. 16.

SANTA FE UPRISING (Native Americans)

Republic Pictures Corp. *Dist* Republic Pictures Corp. 15 Nov **1946**; Prod: 28 Feb–early Mar 1946 [©Republic Pictures Corp.; 24 Sep 1946; LP622]. Sd (RCA Sound System); b&w. 56-58 min. Passed by the National Board of Review. PCA cert no. 11588.

Series: Red Ryder.

Assoc prod Sidney Picker. *Dir* R. G. Springsteen. *2d unit dir* Yakima Canutt. [*Asst dir* Don Verk]. *Orig scr* Earle Snell. *Photog* Bud Thackery. [*2d cam* Enzo Martinelli]. *Spec eff* Howard Lydecker and Theodore Lydecker. [*Matte paintings* Lewis Physioc]. [*Transparency projections shots* Gordon Schaefer]. *Art dir* Fred A. Ritter. *Film ed* Wm. P. Thompson. *Set dec* John McCarthy, Jr. and Earl Wooden. *Mus dir* Mort Glickman. *Sd* Victor Appel. [*Re-rec and eff mixer* Thomas A. Carman and Howard Wilson]. [*Mus mixer* John Stransky, Jr.]. *Makeup supv* Bob Mark.

Source: Based on the comic strip "Red Ryder" by Fred Harman (1938–1964), by special arrangement with Stephen Slesinger.

Cast: ALLAN LANE (*Red Ryder*), Bobby Blake [(*Little Beaver*)], Martha Wentworth [(*The Duchess*)], Barton MacLane [(*Crawford*)], Jack La Rue [(*Bruce Jackson*)], Tom London [(*Lafe Dibble*)], Dick Curtis [(*Luke Case*)], Forrest Taylor [(*Moore*)], Emmett Lynn [(*Hank*)], Hank Patterson [(*Jake*)], Pat Michaels [(*Sonny Dibble*)], Edmund Cobb [(*Madison Pike*)], Kenne Duncan [(*Henchman*)], Edythe Elliott [(*Mrs. Dibble*)], [George Chesebro (*Stableman*)], [Britt Wood (*Charlie, the bartender*)].

Western. [*Print viewed*]. The ranchers of Bitter Springs, in the New Mexico territory, are outraged when yet another marshal is killed trying to protect goods being transported along the free government road to Santa Fe. At a town meeting, Lafe Dibble bitterly proclaims that the only person not affected by the series of attacks is Madison Pike, who charges exorbitant amounts on his private toll road. Unknown to the townspeople, the secret leader of the rustlers and thieves is newspaper publisher Crawford, who is in league with Pike. Their henchmen, Bruce Jackson and Luke Case, run the gang that attacks the government road, then act as "protection" for Pike's toll road. Lafe declares that he is driving his cattle over the government road, and his eager son Sonny accompanies him. Jackson and his men lie in wait, and during their night raid on the camp, both Lafe and Pike are mortally wounded. Crawford fails to get Pike's signature on the toll road deed before he dies, and the road must be put up for auction. In another city, rancher The Duchess reads about Pike's death, which has been declared accidental. She shows the article to her nephew, Red Ryder, and comments that as Pike's fourth cousin, she is his only surviving relative. Red sends a telegram to Bitter Springs announcing that the Duchess is Pike's legal heir and then sends her ahead while he finishes the cattle roundup. Anxious to keep the Duchess from interfering with their plans, Crawford and Jackson order Luke to dispose of her. He attempts to do so by wildly driving the stage in which she is riding, but Red and his Indian ward, Little Beaver, arrive in time to rescue her. After Red wins a fierce fistfight with Luke, the townsfolk decide that he should be their new marshal, and he sends for the Duchess' ranch hands, including old Hank, to act as his deputies. Crawford asks the Duchess to sell him the road, but she after refuses, he and Jackson concoct a scheme to ruin her. Saying that he wishes to drive a small herd to Santa Fe, Jackson pays to use the toll road, and the Duchess' men act as guards. Red is suspicious, however, and by following one of Jackson's henchmen, discovers that the gang is preparing an ambush. Red sends the herd to the government road, but they are spotted by Sonny, who recognizes the cattle as his own even though Jackson has altered the Dibble brand. The impetuous young man shoots at the deputies, and in the confusion, Jackson attempts to shoot Red. When Hank stops him, Jackson kills the old man. Red captures Sonny, who explains that the cattle are really his. Red is forced to arrest Sonny until he can prove his claim, however, and when they return to town, circumstantial evidence points to Sonny as Hank's killer. Jackson and Crawford attempt to stir up a lynch mob so that Sonny will not be alive to prove that Jackson's cattle are his, but Red disperses them. Jackson then kidnaps Little Beaver, and after a distraught Red spends frantic days searching for him, the gang sends a note that the boy will be freed if Sonny is turned over to them. Wishing to print his answer in the newspaper, Red goes to Crawford's office, and there sees that the note came from Crawford's writing tablet. Needing more evidence, Red pretends to fall out with his men and then enlists Crawford's help to go to the gang's cave hideout. Not

knowing that Red has filled his gun with blanks, Crawford shoots Red, who falls as if hit. Crawford soon discovers Red's ruse when he tries to kill Little Beaver. With the help of his men, Red rescues Little Beaver and defeats the gang. Later, the Duchess decides to turn the toll road over to the citizens of Bitter Springs, and Sonny thanks Red for his help. *Kidnapping. Marshals. Murder. Newspaper publishers. Rustlers. Aunts. Cats. Cattle. Caves. Deputies. Evidence. Fathers and sons. Fistfights. Indians of North America. Inheritance. Mobs. New Mexico. Searches. Wards and guardians.*

Note: *Santa Fe Uprising* marked Allan Lane's debut as "Red Ryder" and was also the first in the series featuring Martha Wentworth as "The Duchess." According to a 31 Jan 1946 *HR* news item, Republic substituted this film for another, less expensive entry in the series in order to make "Lane's debut in the former Wild Bill Elliott role more impressive." Lane went on to star in six more pictures in Republic's series, as well as in the television series, which began in 1956. Modern sources include Frank Ellis, Art Dillard, Lee Reynolds and Forrest Burns in the cast. For more information about the "Red Ryder" series, please consult the Series Index and see the entry below for *Tucson Raiders.*

DV 28 Mar 1947, p. 4. *HR* 31 Jan 1946, p. 13. *HR* 26 Feb 1946, p. 6. *HR* 1 Mar 1946, p. 10. *HR* 8 Mar 1946, p. 46. *HR* 28 Mar 1947, p. 3. *LAT* 2 Mar 1946. *MPHPD* 23 Nov 1946, p. 3322.

SANTA LUCIA LUNTANA *see* **CUORE D'EMIGRANTE**

SARAH AND SON *(foreign version) see* **TODA UNA VIDA**

SARATOGA TRUNK (Creoles, rench Americans)
Warner Bros. Pictures, Inc.; A Hal B. Wallis Production; A Warner Bros.—First National Picture. *Dist* Warner Bros. Pictures, Inc. 30 Mar **1946**; Prod: 23 Feb–25 Jun 1943 [©Warner Bros. Pictures, Inc.; 30 Mar 1946; LP188]. Sd (RCA Sound System); b&w. 135 min. PCA cert no. 9279.

Exec prod JACK L. WARNER. *Dir* Sam Wood. [*Asst dir* Phil Quinnd]. *Scr* Casey Robinson. *Dir of photog* Ernest Haller. [*Fill-in photog* Bert Glennon]. *Spec eff* Lawrence Butler. *Mont* Don Siegel. *Prod des* Joseph St. Armand. *Art dir* Carl Jules Weyl. *Film ed* Ralph Dawson. *Set dec* Fred MacLean. *Gowns* Leah Rhodes. *Mus dir* Leo F. Forbstein. *Orch arr* Bernard Kaun. *Mus* Max Steiner. *Sd* Robert B. Lee. *Makeup artist* Perc Westmore. *Tech adv* Dalton S. Reymond. [*Unit mgr* Eric Stacey]. [*Stand-in for Ingrid Bergman* Betty Brooks]. [*Stand-in for Gary Cooper* Ted Mapes]. [*Stand-in for Flora Robson* Joleen King]. [*Stand-in for Jerry Austin* Harry Monty].

Song(s): "Dansez Codaine," composers undetermined.

Source: Based on the novel *Saratoga Trunk* by Edna Ferber (New York, 1941).

Cast: GARY COOPER [(*Clint Maroon*)], INGRID BERGMAN [(*Clio Dulaine*)], Flora Robson [(*Angelique*)], Jerry Austin [(*Cupidon*)], John Warburton [(*Bartholomew Van Steed*)], Florence Bates [(*Mrs. Coventry Bellop*)], Curt Bois [(*Augustin*)], John Abbott [(*Roscoe Bean*)], Ethel Griffies [(*Madame Clarissa Van Steed*)], Minor Watson (*J.P. Reynolds*), Louis Payne (*Raymond Soule*), Fred Essler (*Monsieur Begue*), Adrienne D'Ambricourt (*Grandmother Dulaine*), Helen Freeman (*Madame Dulaine*), Sophie Huxley (*Charlotte Dulaine*), [Jacqueline Dewitt (*Guilia Forosini*)], [J. Lewis Johnson, Libby Taylor, Lillian Yarbo (*Servants*)], [Geneva Williams (*Blackberry woman*)], [Ruby Dandridge (*Black woman with turban*)], [Paul Bryant, Shelby Bacon (*Urchins*)], [Peter Cusanelli (*Coffee proprietor*)], [George Humbert (*Jambalaya proprietor*)], [Bertha Woolford (*Flower woman*)], [George Reed (*Carriage driver*)], [Amelia Liggett (*Mme. Begue*)], [George Beranger (*Leon, the headwaiter*)], [John Sylvester (*Young man escort*)], [Edmund Breon (*McIntyre*)], [William B. Davidson (*Mr. Stone*)], [Edward Fielding (*Mr. Bowers*)], [Thurston Hall (*Mr. Pound*)], [Sarah Edwards (*Miss Diggs*)], [Alice Fleming (*Woman on piazza*)], [Ralph Dunn (*Engineer*)], [Lane Chandler (*Joe*)], [Dick Elliott (*Politician*)], [Glenn Strange (*Man in foreground*)], [Frank Hagney (*Leader of Soule's gang*)], [Chester Clute (*Hotel clerk*)], [Theodor Von Eltz (*Hotel manager*)], [Alan Bridge (*Engineer of Soule's gang*)], [Monte Blue (*Fireman on train*)], [Boyd Davis (*Poker player*)], [Georges Renavent (*Captain of ship*)], [Robert Barron (*Officer*)], [Louis Mercier (*First mate*)], [Frances Carson].

Historical, Romance. [*Print viewed*]. In 1875, Clio Dulaine, the illegitimate daughter of an aristocratic New Orleans Creole man and a French woman, returns from Paris to her birthplace in Rampart Street to avenge her mother's mistreatment at the hands of her father's family, the Dulaines. Years ago Clio's mother accidentally killed Dulaine when he tried to prevent her from committing suicide, and

the scandalized Dulaines then exiled Clio and her mother to Paris. Clio is accompanied by her mulatto maid, Angelique, and her dwarf manservant, Cupidon. After fixing up the rundown house in Rampart Street, Clio ventures out, hoping to encounter the Dulaines. At the French marketplace, Clio stops for a bowl of jambalaya and is immediately attracted to Clint Maroon, a tall Texan in a white hat, who is eating at the counter. The attraction is mutual, and Clint offers to drive Clio to the cathedral in his carriage, but a disapproving Angelique interferes, and Clio leaves without him. After the service, Clio, Angelique and Cupidon breakfast at the restaurant patronized by the Dulaines every Sunday. Announcing to the maitre d' that she is a relative, Clio sits at the table reserved for the Dulaines, but when the Dulaines arrive, they recognize her by her resemblance to her mother and leave without a confrontation. Clint and Clio meet again at the restaurant, and afterward, he drives her home. Eventually, Clint moves into Clio's house. Although Clio and Clint are in love with each other, Clio, who is obsessed with her plans for revenge, intends to marry a rich and powerful man to prove that she is as good as her father's family. Clint, a gambler, who never intends to marry, is out for revenge on the railroaders who ruined his father in Texas. While Clio continues to embarrass the Dulaines at every opportunity, planning, if necessary, to interrupt the debut of her half-sister Charlotte, Clint, exasperated by Clio's unrelenting machinations, leaves for Saratoga. As the result of Clio's scheming, the Dulaines pay her $10,000, agree to destroy the Rampart Street house and bury her mother in a New Orleans cemetery. Later, Clio joins Clint in Saratoga, where she plots to marry wealthy railroad heir Bartholomew Van Steed. Clio's arrival with Angelique and Cupidon causes quite a stir, and because the hotel is completely booked, Clint, who is now calling himself Colonel Maroon, offers Clio two of the rooms in his suite. Privately, he explains that Bart owns a railroad, the Saratoga Trunk, which is suddenly worth millions of dollars because it connects the coal country with New York. Railroader Raymond Soule, the same man who ruined Clint's father, is trying to steal the railroad from Bart. Clio poses as the widow of a French count, a claim that many doubt until she is unexpectedly backed up by socialite Mrs. Coventry Bellop, who intensely dislikes Van Steed's mother. Clio's beauty and melodramatic posturing quickly capture Bart's attentions. In the meantime, Clint offers to save the Saratoga Trunk from Soule in exchange for shares in the railroad. When Clio learns that Bart is paying Clint to do his dirty work, she hysterically accuses him of cowardice and sends him away. This excites Bart, who explains that he knows about her background, but wants to marry her anyway. The costume ball that evening is interrupted by the arrival of Clint and Cupidon, who were seriously wounded during a pitched battle with Soule's men. Clio realizes that she loves Clint too much to marry another man and nurses him back to health. Clint then tells Clio that, having saved the Saratoga Trunk from Soule, his railroad shares have made him a very rich man. *Gamblers. Revenge. Romance. African Americans–Mixed blood. Blackmail. Churches. Dwarfs. Fistfights. Illegitimacy. Maids. Mothers and daughters. Mothers and sons. New Orleans (LA). Opera. Poker (Game). Railroads. Restaurants. Saratoga (NY). Texans. Train wrecks. Upper classes.*

Note: According to a 25 Mar 1941 *HR* news item, Warner Bros paid $175,000 for the rights to the novel. A 1941 press release states that the film was to be made in Technicolor. *Saratoga Trunk* was completed in 1943 and not released until 1946. It was exhibited to the armed forces overseas, but held back in the United States in deference to more timely war-themed and patriotic films. The film ends with a plea to buy war bonds. News items in *HR* note that Richard Travis tested for the role of "Clint Maroon," and Errol Flynn was also considered for the part. Ann Sheridan and Olivia De Havilland tested for the role of "Clio Dulaine." According to information in the file on the film at the USC Cinema-Television Library Eleanor Parker and Tamara Toumanova also tested for the part of Clio. An early 1941 press release states that Vivian Leigh was also considered for the role. An undated press release reports that Nina Foch was to make her film debut, but she does not appear in the picture. Flora Robson, who portrays "Angelique," was a white, British actress who wore darkened makeup to appear black in the film.

HR news items add the following information about the production: Some background footage was shot at the actual location of the Saratoga trunk line. *Saratoga Trunk* was one of the last productions to film at Busch Gardens in Pasadena, CA before it was auctioned off in early Apr 1943. Over 150 stunt men were used in the scenes of the battle for possession of the railroad trunk line. Warner Bros. purchased the complete wardrobe of Susan Dreer Volkmar, which comprised thirty dresses dating from 1880-1910, some made in Paris, including a complete mourning outfit; a cream colored wedding gown of princess lace; a hostess gown of black satin; a white broadcloth suit; a navy blue suit; and a Chantilly lace parasol. It is not known if these costumes appeared in the film.

The filmmakers studied actual footage of the 1909 arrival of the Mississippi steamer *Bald Eagle* for technical information. Ingrid Bergman's singing coach was technical adviser Dalton S. Reymond, former dean of the College of Music at Louisiana State University. Sophie Huxley, who played the role of "Charlotte Dulaine," was the niece of writer Aldous Huxley. Memos at the USC Cinema-Television Library, indicate that montage director Don Siegel shot the fight scenes after the two trains collided. Because of differences between director Sam Wood and producer Hal B. Wallis, Siegel's unit continued to shoot for 19 days. Only one day had been budgeted for the entire scene. Cinematographer Bert Glennon filled in for Ernest Haller while the latter was ill. Flora Robson was nominated for a Best Supporting Actress Oscar but lost to Anne Baxter. Ida Lupino and Zachary Scott starred in a 24 Nov 1947 *Lux Radio Theatre* broadcast of the story.

Box 24 Nov 1945. *DV* 21 Nov 1945, p. 3. *FD* 23 Nov 1945. *HR* 25 Mar 1941, p. 1. *HR* 21 Jan 1942, p. 3. *HR* 23 Mar 1942, p. 1. *HR* 27 Nov 1942, p. 6. *HR* 8 Feb 1943, p. 2. *HR* 16 Feb 1943, p. 8. *HR* 23 Feb 1943, p. 2. *HR* 24 Feb 1943, p. 7. *HR* 22 Mar 1943, p. 2. *HR* 30 Mar 1943, p. 7. *HR* 31 Mar 1943, p. 3. *HR* 13 May 1943, p. 13. *HR* 21 Nov 1945, p. 3. *HR* 26 Nov 1945, p. 6. *MPHPD* 24 Nov 1945, p. 2725. *NYT* 22 Nov 1945, p. 39. *Var* 21 Nov 1945, p. 10.

SASKATCHEWAN (Native Americans, Cree, Dakota)

Universal-International Pictures Co., Inc. *Dist* Universal Pictures Co., Inc. Mar **1954**; New York opening: 10 Mar 1954; Prod: early Aug—mid-Sep 1953 [©Universal Pictures Co.; 29 Mar 1954; LP3256]. Sd (Western Electric Recording); col (Technicolor). 9 reels, 7,832 ft. 87 min. PCA cert no. 16782.

Prod Aaron Rosenberg. *Dir* Raoul Walsh. *Asst dir* Frank Shaw, [Marshall Green and Jimmy Welch]. *Story and scr* Gil Doud. *Dir of photog* John Seitz. *Technicolor color consultant* Willam Fritzsche. *Art dir* Bernard Herzbrun and Richard H. Riedel. *Film ed* Frank Gross. *Set dec* Russell A. Gausman and John Austin. *Cost* Bill Thomas. *Mus dir* Joseph Gershenson. *Sd* Leslie I. Carey and Joe Lapis. *Makeup* Bud Westmore. *Hair stylist* Joan St. Oegger. [*Unit mgr* Tommy Thompson]. *Tech adv* Inspector R. E. Mercer, R.C.M.P. Ret.

Cast: ALAN LADD ([*Thomas*] *O'Rourke*), SHELLEY WINTERS (*Grace* [*Markey*]), Robert Douglas (*Benton*), J. Carroll Naish (*Batoche*), Hugh O'Brian ([*Carl*] *Smith*), Richard Long (*Abbott* [*Patrick J. Scanlon*]), Jay Silverheels (*Cajou*), Antonio Moreno (*Chief Dark Cloud*), George J. Lewis (*Lawson*), Lowell Gilmore (*Banks*), Anthony Caruso (*Spotted Eagle*), Frank Chase (*Keller*), Henry Wills (*Merrill*), Robert D. Herron (*Brill*), [Russ Saunders (*Burkhart*)], [John Cason (*Cook*)], [Dick Taylor].

Adventure. [*Print viewed*]. In Canada's Saskatchewan River country, in the spring of 1877, North West Mounted Police officer Thomas O'Rourke and Cajou, his Cree Indian friend, are returning from outpost duty to headquarters when they encounter a burned-out wagon train and a sole survivor, Grace Markey, who tells them that the train was attacked by Indians whose tribe she cannot identify. Although she wants to continue to another destination, O'Rourke decides to take her to the Mountie fort in Saskatchewan. En route, Grace steals a horse and rides off, only to be chased by four Indians. O'Rourke and Cajou rescue her and shoot two of the Indians, whom they identify as American Sioux, a group not seen in the area for many years. When they reach the fort, O'Rourke is greeted by Batoche, a French Canadian scout, who tells him that some of Chief Crazy Horse's Sioux have crossed the border into Canada after massacring General Custer at the Little Bighorn. Benton, the fort's new commander, who is recently arrived from England, is highly critical of O'Rourke's brotherly friendship with Cajou. Benton has confiscated all the Cree's guns and powder, which they need to hunt their food, and as a result, talk of an alliance between the Cree and the Sioux erupts. When O'Rourke visits Cree Chief Dark Cloud, an old friend, Cajou decides to rejoin his people in their struggle and breaks his friendship with O'Rourke. Later, U.S. Marshal Carl Smith arrives at the fort looking for Grace, who is wanted in Montana for killing his brother, and O'Rourke turns Grace over to him. When Benton receives orders to close the fort and transfer all troops to reinforce Fort Walsh on the Canadian-American border, Smith chooses to accompany them. On the journey they encounter a Cree hunting party, and when an Indian takes Smith's rifle in order to hunt for food, Smith shoots him. This angers O'Rourke and he and Smith fight. Later, O'Rourke tells Grace that he was orphaned as a boy and reared by Cajou's father. Smith then intimates to Grace that he could be "persuaded" not to take her back to Montana, but she declines his offer. As the troops cross the Saskatchewan River, they are attacked by Sioux and, to keep their ammunition from falling into Indian hands, they explode it all. Later, when O'Rourke refuses to proceed by the route Benton has chosen, Benton orders him arrested. The others side

with O'Rourke, however, and Benton promises that they will all be court-martialed and hanged. O'Rourke then organizes the journey by a safer, though slightly longer, route. From a distance, they see a large number of Cree, led by Dark Cloud and Cajou, and Sioux going to a powwow. After O'Rourke and Smith have a dispute about a wounded officer slowing them down, O'Rourke threatens to take Smith prisoner. Grace tells O'Rourke that she is innocent of the murder charge. The troops eventually reach a trapper's cabin, where they expected to acquire boats to finish the last part of the journey, only to find that the Sioux have burned the cabin, killed the trapper and destroyed the boats. O'Rourke and Batoche spy on the Sioux camp on the lake shore and discover Sitting Bull and Crazy Horse preparing for a powwow. At night the Mounties steal some of the Indians' canoes and resume their journey. Smith offers Grace her freedom if she will go away with him and, after O'Rourke breaks up a struggle between them, Smith admits that he killed his own brother. Smith draws a gun on the unarmed O'Rourke, but Benton shoots first and kills him. However, the gunshot alerts the Indians and they pursue the whites, but O'Rourke prepares an ambush, during which most of the Indians are killed. After sending the others on, O'Rourke goes to talk with Dark Cloud, not as a Mountie, but as a friend. Dark Cloud informs him that the Sioux have told him that, unless the Cree join forces with them, they will make war on them. O'Rourke offers to negotiate with superintendent Banks at Fort Walsh for the return of their guns. However, Banks and Benton have O'Rourke arrested and imprisoned with the other men. After Banks and Benton leave with a large contingent to meet with the Sioux, Cajou sneaks into the fort to warn O'Rourke that the Sioux plan to attack the fort, then wage war on the Cree. Cajou and Grace, who is in love with O'Rourke, free him and the others, and they leave the fort with wagons full of guns and ammunition for the Cree. Meanwhile, Banks, Benton and the troops come under attack by the Sioux and are outnumbered, but after O'Rourke, his men and the Cree ride to their rescue, the Sioux retreat. Later, Dark Cloud thanks Banks and Benton for saving his people and for bringing peace. Benton apologizes to O'Rourke, withdrawing his charges against him and his men, then orders him to escort Grace to Montana and help her to establish her innocence. *Canadians. Cree Indians. Dakota Indians. Mutiny. North West Mounted Police. Saskatchewan (Canada).* Bigotry. Canadian-American border region. Canoes and canoeing. Chases. Chief Crazy Horse. English. False accusations. Forts. Fratricide. French Canadians. Fugitives. Lakes. Lechery. Orphans. Rescues. Rivers. Romance. Scouts (Frontier). Sitting Bull. United States. Marshals.

Note: The opening credits include the following written statement: "The motion picture you are about to see was photographed in the locales where the actual events upon which it is based occurred...events that gravely threatened the peaceful development of Western Canada." Although the character portrayed by Richard Long is listed in the onscreen cast list as "Abbott," in the film he is called "Patrick J. Scanlon." Additionally J. Carrol Naish's character is listed as "Batoche," although other characters call him "Batouche."

Box 27 Feb 1954. *DV* 24 Feb 1954, p. 3. *Exb* 24 Feb 1954, pp. 3703-04. *FD* 25 Feb 1954, p. 10. *Har* 27 Feb 1954, p. 34. *HR* 24 Feb 1954, p. 3. *LAT* 18 Mar 1954. *MPHPD* 27 Feb 1954, p. 2197. *NYT* 11 Mar 1954, p. 26 *Var* 24 Feb 1954, p. 6.

SATAN'S CRADLE (Latino)

Inter-American Productions, Inc. *Dist* United Artists Corp. 7 Oct **1949**; Prod: late Jul 1949 [©Inter-American Productions, Inc.; 7 Oct 1949; LP2772]. Sd (RCA Sound System); b&w. 6 reels, 5,404 ft. 60 or 63 min. PCA cert no. 14077.

Series: The Cisco Kid.

Pres PHILIP N. KRASNE. *Prod* Philip N. Krasne. *Assoc prod* Duncan Renaldo. *Dir* Ford Beebe. *Asst dir* Louis Germonprez. *Orig scr* Jack Benton. *Dir of photog* Jack Greenhalgh. [*Cam op* Ernest Smith]. [*Stills* Milton Gold]. [*Gaffer* George Breslow]. *Art dir* Frank Sylos. *Film ed* Marty Cohn. *Set dec* Helen Hansard. *Property master* Gene Stone. *Ward* Sidney Dunnam. *Mus comp and cond* Albert Glasser. *Sd* Ben Winkler. *Makeup artist* Arthur Dupuis. *Asst to prod* Mel Mark. [*Scr supv* Don Weis]. [*Grip* Charles Turner].

Source: Based on the character created by O. Henry.

Cast: Duncan Renaldo ([*The*] *Cisco* [*Kid*]), Leo Carrillo (*Pancho*), Ann Savage [(*Lil*)], Douglas Fowley [(*Steve Gentry*)], Byron Foulger [(*Henry Lane*)], Claire Carleton [(*Belle*)], Buck Bailey [(*Rocky*)], George De Normand [(*Idaho*)], Wes Hudman [(*Peters*)].

Western. [*Print viewed*]. In the streets of Silver City, New Mexico, itinerant preacher Henry Lane decries the sinful influence of the town's newest inhabitant, a woman named Lil, who runs the Silver

Lode Saloon. Suddenly, Rocky and Idaho, two henchmen working for Lil's lawyer, Steve Gentry, interrupt Henry's sermon and drag him away. On their way into Silver City, wandering Mexican American cowboy Cisco tells his sidekick Pancho that they are going to see Lil, whose beauty is widely praised. When they come across Henry lying bruised on the ground, he tells them how trouble came to Silver City: After town founder Jim Mason, who owned the saloon and nearby San Miguel mine, was killed during a mine cave-in, Lil arrived in town with a twenty-year-old marriage certificate dated the 15th of June establishing her as Jim's wife. After she claimed Mason's property, Lil put Steve in charge of the mine. Back at the saloon, Lil's maid Belle objects to Steve's violent treatment of a preacher, which, she points out, is not part of their scheme. A short time later, Cisco, Pancho and Henry enter the saloon, and Cisco fires his weapon into the air to attract the attention of the saloon patrons, who listen to Henry's announcement that services will be held on Sunday as usual. Cisco, Pancho and Henry leave the saloon and go down the street to begin converting a vacant building into the town's new church. When Idaho follows, shooting at Cisco, he is forced to kill him in self-defense. Realizing that Henry is in danger, Cisco and Pancho take him to a spot in the mountains called Satan's Cradle, where they pitch camp. There, Henry tells Cisco that because of a fire at the court house in Callaway, Oklahoma, Lil's marriage cannot be verified. Cisco then tells Henry to stay at the camp while he returns to the saloon. There, he catches Lil in a lie when he asks her why she would get married on the unlucky 13th, and she fails to correct him on the date. Later, Henry gives Cisco and Pancho directions to the mine, where they find the caved-in section. After finding a portion of burnt fuse, indicating Mason's death was murder, Cisco guesses that a second entrance was used by the escaping killer. Outside, meanwhile, Steve and Rocky dynamite the main entrance, then return to the saloon. When Steve tells Lil what they have done, she instructs Belle to pack her things so that they can leave on the next stage. A short time later, Cisco climbs through Lil's balcony window, while Steve's henchman Lucky, who saw Cisco sneak in, reports to his boss. Steve quickly climbs up to the balcony and eavesdrops on Cisco and Lil's conversation. He hears Cisco ask Lil to tell the sheriff what she knows, but Lil draws her gun and says she is leaving town. When she begins to implicate Steve in the plot, Steve fires through the window at her. Steve misses, and he and Rocky are later captured and taken to jail. When he learns that Lil has decided to speak to the sheriff, Cisco is satisfied that justice has finally been served. Cisco and Pancho then leave for California to search for the most beautiful woman in San Lorenzo. *Fraud. Mexican Americans. Preachers. Saloon keepers. Arrests. Balconies. Camps. Churches. Conspiracy. Cowboys. Dynamite. Eavesdropping. Forgers and forgery. Hideouts. Lawyers. Mines. Mountains. Self-defense. Shootouts. Superstition. Widows.*

Note: The film's opening title card reads: "The Cisco Kid in Satan's Cradle." For additional information on the series, please consult the Series Index and see the above entry for *The Cisco Kid.*

Box 19 Nov 1949. *FD* 7 Nov 1949, p. 8. *HR* 29 Jul 1949, p. 11. *HR* 25 Nov 1949, p. 3. *MPHPD* 12 Nov 1949, p. 82. *Var* 9 Nov 1949, p. 6.

SATCHMO THE GREAT (African Americans)

Columbia Broadcasting System, Inc. *Dist* United Artists Corp. Sep 1957; Prod: filmed in 1955 [©Columbia Broadcasting System, Inc.; 13 Sep 1957; LP9400]. Sd; b&w. 5,755 ft. 63 min.

Prod Edward R. Murrow and Fred W. Friendly. *Cam* Charles Mack. *Drawings* Ben Shahn. *Ed* Aram Avakian. *Sd* Robert Huttenloch.

Song(s): "What Did I Do to Be So Black and Blue," music by Thomas "Fats" Waller and Harry Brooks, lyrics by Andy Razaf; "St. Louis Blues," music and lyrics by W. C. Handy; "Mack the Knife," music by Kurt Weill, German lyrics by Bertolt Brecht, English lyrics by Marc Blitzstein; " My Bucket's Got a Hole in It," music and lyrics by Clarence Williams; "Basin Street Blues," music and lyrics by Spencer Williams; "Memphis Blues," music by W. C. Handy, lyrics by George A. Norton; "Indiana," music by James F. Hanley, lyrics by Ballard Macdonald; "C'est Si Bon," music by Henri Betti and André Hornez, French lyrics by André Hornez, English lyrics by Jerry Seelen.

Source: Based on the television documentary "Two American Originals" on *See It Now* (CBS, 13 Dec 1955).

Cast: Louis Armstrong, Edward R. Murrow (*Narrator and interviewer*), Edmund Hall (*Clarinet*), Trummy Young (*Trombone*), Barrett Deems (*Drums*), Billy Kyle (*Piano*), Arvell Shaw (*String bass*), Jack Lesberg (*String bass*), Velma Middleton (*Vocalist*), Lucille Armstrong, Leonard Bernstein.

Biography, Musical, Documentary. [*Not viewed*]. Louis "Satchmo" Armstrong, the great jazz trumpeter and singer, flies over the North Sea with his entourage to begin a tour of Europe and Equatorial Africa. With his All-Stars, Armstrong plays in Stockholm, Paris, Zurich, Geneva, London and other cities in Europe. He and the band also play on planes and trains on the way to engagements. In Paris, early one morning, following a jam session with the Claude Luter Dixieland Combo, narrator Edward R. Murrow interviews Armstrong about the nature and appeal of jazz, and its varieties and significance. Asked to define jazz, Armstrong responds that it is music "you can pat your foot to." After Europe, Armstrong travels to the Gold Coast in Africa, home to his ancestors. Hailed as a national hero, Armstrong is greeted by tribal chieftains. He listens to the music of the people and plays for them, as they dance in native costume. Velma Middleton, vocalist for the band, and Armstrong's wife Lucille join the dancers. The prime minister of the country attends one of the evening concerts, during which Armstrong sings and plays the song "What Did I Do to Be So Black and Blue," which deals with racial discrimination. At a school in the Gold Coast, Armstrong tells a class of boys about his own struggles. Armstrong next returns to New York for a concert at Lewisohn Stadium, accompanied by the New York Philharmonic Orchestra, which is conducted by Leonard Bernstein. During Armstrong's solo of "St. Louis Blues," a visibly moved W. C. Handy, who composed the song, is seen in the audience. Bernstein praises Armstrong, calling him a "dedicated artist." *Africa. African Americans. Ghana. Jazz music. Europe. New York City. Racism. Schools. Tribal chiefs.*

Note: This film was an expansion of half of a one-hour segment of Edward R. Murrow's *See It Now*, which aired on 13 Dec 1955 on the CBS television network. Entitled "Two American Originals," the show also profiled the painter Grandma Moses. The broadcast did not include scenes in the film taking place in Africa or the New York concert. *DV* suggested that the distributor should "remove the CBS-TV credits if contractually possible; there may be some audience annoyance at the prospect of paying for a product that has already been shown free in the homes." *Var* noted that "Large line drawings by Ben Shahn, in a jazzy artistic style, illustrate some of Armstrong's early days in New Orleans." Reviewers praised the film, *Exh* commenting, "The personality of Louis Armstrong is as potent as his music, and a brilliant film editing job and narration makes the most of this highly entertaining subject." *Var* stated, "this is a valuable documentary record of a standout performer and his extraordinary impact on jazz buffs here and abroad."

Box 21 Sep 1957. *DV* 11 Sep 1957, p. 3. *Exh* 18 Sep 1957, p. 4378. *FD* 13 Sep 1957, p. 4. *Har* 14 Sep 1957, p. 148. *HR* 11 Sep 1957, p. 3. *MPD* 12 Sep 1957. *MPHPD* 21 Sep 1957, .p. 538. *NYT* 1 Mar 1958, p. 12.

SATURDAY NIGHT (Irish Americans)

Famous Players-Lasky Corp. *Dist* Paramount Pictures. 5 Feb **1922**; New York premiere: ca22 Jan 1922 [©Famous Players-Lasky Corp.; 21 Jan 1922; LP17496]. Si; b&w. 9 reels, 8,443 ft.

Pres Jesse L. Lasky. *Dir* Cecil B. De Mille. *Story and scen* Jeanie Macpherson. *Photog* Alvin Wyckoff and Karl Struss.

Cast: Leatrice Joy (*Iris Van Suydam, a society girl*), Conrad Nagel (*Richard Wynbrook Prentiss, her fiancé*), Edith Roberts (*Shamrock O'Day, a laundress*), Jack Mower (*Tom McGuire, a chauffeur*), Julia Faye (*Elsie, Richard's sister*), Edythe Chapman (*Mrs. Prentiss*), Theodore Roberts (*Van Suydan*), John Davidson (*The Count Demitry Scardoff*), James Neill (*Tompkins, butler*), Winter Hall (*The Professor*), Sylvia Ashton (*Mrs. O'Day, a washerwoman*), Lillian Leighton (*Mrs. Ferguson*).

Society, Melodrama. Iris Van Suydam and Richard Wynbrook Prentiss, a wealthy society couple, are engaged. Iris, however, is attracted to her chauffeur, Tom McGuire, who is in love with her; and Richard meets Shamrock O'Day, beautiful daughter of a washerwoman, and falls in love with her. Consequently, they cancel their engagement, and each marries the partner of his choice. Too late, they discover their inability to adjust to another social set: Tom has difficulty in the world of opera, fashionable cabarets, and concerts of Iris; while Shamrock is ill at ease at a formal dinner party and becomes intoxicated. One night, after a party, Tom and Shamrock sneak off to Coney Island where they become stranded on a Ferris wheel; returning home, they find Richard and Iris awaiting them. Tom declares his love for Shamrock, and a fight between Tom and Dick is interrupted by a fire. Following Iris' rescue by Dick, divorces are obtained; Tom marries Shamrock; and Richard, Iris. *Chauffeurs. Class distinction. Divorce. Ferris wheels. Irish Americans. Laundresses. Marriage. New York City–Coney Island. Socialites.*

ETR 4 Feb 1922, p. 715. *FD* 29 Jan 1922. *MPW* 4 Feb 1922, p. 550. *MPW* 11 Feb 1922, p. 656. *Var* 27 Jan 1922, p. 39.

SATURDAY'S HERO (Polish Americans)

Sidney Buchman Enterprises, Inc.; Columbia Pictures Corp. *Dist* Columbia Pictures Corp. Sep **1951**; Prod: 12 Jun–9 Sep 1950 [©Columbia Pictures Corp.; 14 Jun 1951; LP970]. Sd (Western Electric Recording); b&w. 12 reels, 9,920 ft. 111 min. PCA cert no. 14623.

Prod Buddy Adler. *Dir* David Miller. *Asst dir* Jack Corrick and [Joe Boyle]. *Wrt for the scr by* Millard Lampell and Sidney Buchman. *Dir of photog* Lee Garmes. [*Cam op* Frank "Kit" Carson]. [*Asst cam* Val O'Malley and Edward Garvin]. *Art dir* Robert Peterson. *Film ed* William Lyon. *Set dec* James Crowe. [*Gowns* Jean Louis]. *Mus dir* Morris Stoloff. *Mus score* Elmer Bernstein. *Sd eng* Lambert Day. *Re-rec* Richard Olson. [*Sd* Frank Goodwin]. *Makeup* Clay Campbell. *Hair styles by* Helen Hunt. [*Dir of pub* Lou Smith]. [*Football trainer* Mickey McCardle and Paul Cleary].

Song(s): "Loyal Sons of Psi Gamma," by Sammy Cahn and Saul Chaplin; "The Canteen Song" and "Jackson Fight Song," by Paul Mertz and Morris Stoloff; "Hail Jackson U," by Paul Mertz; "Pije Kuba" (Polish drinking song); "Lulujze Jezuniu" (Polish Christmas Carol).

Source: Based on the novel *The Hero* by Millard Lampell (New York, 1949).

Cast: John Derek [(*Steve Novak*)], Donna Reed [(*Melissa*)], Sidney Blackmer [(*T. C. McCabe*)], Alexander Knox [(*Professor Megroth*)], Elliott Lewis [(*Eddie Abrams*)], Otto Hulett [(*Coach Preacher Tennant*)], Howard St. John [(*Belfrage*)], Aldo DaRe [(*Gene Hausler*)], Alvin Baldock [(*Francis Clayborne*)], Wilbur Robertson [(*Bob Whittier*)], Charles Mercer Barnes [(*Moose Wagner*)], Bill Martin [(*Joe Mestrovic*)], Mickey Knox [(*Joey Novak*)], Sandro Giglio [(*Jan Novak*)], Tito Vuolo [(*Manuel*)], Don Gibson [(*Red Evans*)], [Peter Virgo (*Vlatko*)], [Don Garner (*Jamieson*)], [Robert Foulk (*Butler*)], [John W. Baer (*Turner Wylie*)], [Mervin Williams (*Dr. Comstock*)], [Peter Thompson (*John Fitzbugh*)], [Noel Reyburn (*Toby Peterson*)], [Steven Clark (*Ted Bricker*)], [Mickey McCardle, Glenn Souers, Hal Braly, Breck Stroschein, Darrel Riggs, Volney Peters, Al Cantor, Newell Oestreich, Frederick Maumetz, Robert "Bob" DeLauer, Edward Saenz, Robert Simpson, Tom Colley, John "Jack" Zilly, Ralph Pucci, Harold Hatfield, William W. Armstrong, Jack Finlay, Floyd Collier, Hubie Kerns, Don R. Clark, Ray Pourchot, Leon C. McLaughlin, Rod Scott Craig, Howard Hansen, Tony Linehan, George Murphy, Boyd "Red" Morgan, Albert R. Carmichael, John Nikcevich (*Football players*)], [Paul Cleary (*Dobbs*)], [Sunny Vickers (*Girl*)], [Fred F. Sears, Don Kohler, Barry Brooks, Clark Howat (*Reporters*)], [Ann Duncan (*High school girl*)], [James Pierce, Oscar Dutch Hendrian (*Assistant coaches*)], [Glenn Thompson (*Deke Roberts*)], [Charles Horvath (*Baldy*)], [Tom Fears (*Lineman*)], [Ted Stanhope, Sam Flint (*Alumni*)], [Thomas Kingston (*Equipment manager*)], [Tom Daly, Dick Cogan (*Voices*)], [Thomas Brown Henry (*Keppler*)], [Candy McDowell (*The girl*)], [Frank Eldredge (*Alumni chairman*)], [Lewis Ward (*Gamma boy*)], [Sammy McKim (*Student*)], [Frances Chaney (*Nurse*)], [Luther Crockett (*Principal*)], [Harry S. Anderson], [Tom Herman], [William Scully], [Richard Mickelsen], [James McGregor], [Warren Mace], [Frank Baker], [Nubar Arthur Astor], [Walter Clinton].

Football, Social, Drama. [*Print viewed*]. On a Saturday afternoon in autumn in a small mill town in New Jersey, halfback Steve Novak leads his high school football team to a 21-0 victory. Following the game, Steve, his father Jan, a Polish immigrant, and his older brother Joey, a wounded, unemployed war veteran, sing together in Polish outside the neighborhood bar. Steve wants to go to college at Jackson in Virginia, considered one of the best schools in the world, but local newspaperman Eddie Abrams discourages him, saying that the school does not pay its players and that his chances for becoming an All-American there would be slim because Jackson is not a top football school. After graduation, a representative from Jackson, which is trying to build a good team, invites Steve to enroll, saying that occasionally certain alumni benefactors will "adopt" a boy and pay for his tuition. While Eddie accuses Steve of desiring to become "Joe College," a rich snob in his eyes, Jan proudly sends Steve off with a saying in Polish. Joey, drunk and feeling sorry for himself, snidely suggests that Steve may want to change his name from "Novak" to "Nelson." Steve becomes the top scorer in the freshman circuit as Jackson wins its games by large margins. His teammates include a number of working-class youths, who contrast greatly with the rest of the student body. Gene Hausler, from a mining town, brags to Steve that he is getting money under the table for playing and encourages him to do the same. When Hausler calls the school a "racket," Bob Whittier, a local rich boy, is insulted, as his father is an alumnus. Steve soon encounters Melissa, the niece and ward of his benefactor, millionaire entrepreneur T. C. McCabe, when she flirts with him at a fraternity party. In his sophomore year, at a party following the varsity's eighth straight victory, Melissa taunts Steve, calling him "T. C.'s latest toy," but before he leaves to go home for Christmas, she kisses his cheek and says he is very sweet. At home, Steve finds that Joey has a new job. During the family's Christmas celebration, Melissa phones and says she is nearby. Steve meets her and they kiss passionately, but she slaps him when he tries to go further. She then relates that after her own mother, who was poor, died, she went to live with T. C. and his wife. She warns that she is now the only thing left in T. C.'s life and that he will try to hold onto her. At Jackson, Steve's adviser, Professor Megroth, a stuffy but devoted academic, instructs Steve that the ability to honestly examine oneself is a sign of growing up. When another school offers Steve a lot of money to switch schools, Steve refuses to listen. Hausler, whose recent injury has increased his cynicism, is about to accept until Eddie, now the head of public relations for athletics at Jackson, convinces T. C. to increase the amount paid to the top players. Melissa, whom McCabe sent to Mexico to get her away from Steve, returns against his orders and tells Steve she realizes that this is the first time anyone has ever mattered to her. Steve's school work suffers, as a publicity campaign instigated by T. C. keeps him on the road, but his professors give him passing grades. As Steve's junior year begins, he and Melissa declare their love for each other, and Steve learns in a letter from Joey that their father has been ill. During a tough game, Steve's arm is injured from a number of hard tackles. At halftime, the coach has the doctor shoot him with novocaine, and Steve remains in the game. In the second half, he does not get up following a hard tackle by three opponents, one of whom later apologizes, saying that $150 was offered if he put Steve out of the game. Steve is disheartened when Whittier refuses to intercede to help a fellow teammate, Francis Clayhorne, also from a working-class family, who is about to be expelled. The doctor diagnoses a shoulder separation and warns Steve he will risk having a bad shoulder for the rest of his life if he continues to play. T. C. tells Steve that he'll have a chance to become All-American in his senior year if he plays. Knowing that now he can't compete academically, Steve continues to play despite suffering hard tackles, until he becomes dazed. He is taken to a hospital, where he confides to Professor Megroth that he now has really looked at himself, and that rather than stay at Jackson and be a "charity case," he wants to leave. As Steve packs, Eddie brings a telegram from Joey saying that Jan died of a heart attack. Melissa wants to go back with Steve and marry him, and he admits that until now he has been ashamed to tell her about his home in the mill town, or his immigrant father. When Melissa tells McCabe that she is going to marry Steve, McCabe, who says Steve has nothing to offer her, threatens him with his cane. Melissa separates them and tells Steve to go, but promises to follow tomorrow. At home, after Joey berates Steve for never making time for their father, Steve knocks his trophies off their shelf and admits to his brother that he quit school and took a beating. He asks Joey for help to get a job so that he can go to night school. Joey puts his hand on Steve's shoulder and proudly calls his brother an "educated man." The phone then rings with news from Melissa that she plans to arrive in the morning. *Ambition. Assimilation (Sociology). Benefactors. Class distinction. College sports. Corruption. Football players. Manhood. Polish Americans. Romance. Brothers. Christmas. Entrepreneurs. Fathers and sons. Football coaches. Honor. Immigrants. Laborers. Millionaires. New Jersey. Physicians. Professors. Reporters. Uncles. Virginia. Wards and guardians. Wounds and injuries.*

Note: The working title of this film was *The Hero*. The title was changed, according to *Var*, so that patrons would not think they were going to see a war film. According to news items, Columbia bought the film rights to the novel, Millard Lampell's first, in Nov 1948 before publication for budding star John Derek, who had recently appeared in *Knock on Any Door*. Plans were set for production to begin in the spring of 1949; however, in Aug 1949, writer-producer Sidney Buchman, who had been the executive assistant to Columbia studio's chief, Harry Cohn, acquired the rights to produce the film for Columbia. A *NYT* news item stated that the film was to be Buchman's first directorial effort. Buchman, in a Jun 1950 *NYT* article, stated that his purpose

in making the film was to expose "the great American hypocrisy of football" in a manner similar to the way the recent films *Champion, Body and Soul* and *The Set-Up* treated boxing. Buchman hired as technical advisers former University of Southern California star players Mickey McCardle and Paul Cleary, who sympathized with his aims.

According to information in the MPAA/PCA Collection at the AMPAS Library, when PCA officials read a draft of the proposed film dated 21 Feb 1950, they viewed the film as subversive. One official, E. G. Dougherty, wrote to Cohn on 3 Mar 1950 that the story "is one of shame-faced class distinction—one that milks and exploits that theme to its fullest extent. The story is thoroughly un-American—in fact, anti-American. This is a vicious kind of story, particularly because it is very well written." Dougherty backed up the charge by quoting dialogue from the script spoken by the character of "Professor Megroth" in which he calls the U.S. "a country that makes it a humiliation to be Polish or poor or Italian or Jewish—to have a father who speaks with an accent, a mother who came over from the old country. The story means "in an insulting manner" and for suggestions that the word "Polack" was used "in an insulting manner" and for suggestions that the relationship between "McCabe" and "Melissa" might involve an "abnormal attraction." According to a memo of 19 Feb 1951, after the film was shot, Buchman agreed to cut out elements that the PCA still felt might be suggestive of an incestuous relationship. Dougherty wrote at that time, "There is, still... a very peculiar quality not generally found in normal family relationships, but we believe this can be interpreted merely as the attitude of an overly possessive man who has shown an attitude similar to this towards other characters in the story."

Football sequences were shot at Pomona College, the Pasadena Rose Bowl and the Los Angeles Coliseum with over 100 college and professional football players, according to an article in the *Christian Science Monitor*. Twenty players were from the USC and UCLA teams, according to *DV*. Those schools reached an agreement with Columbia that the studio would issue no publicity concerning the players' names because of the fear that fans might think their appearance in the film would compromise their amateur status. This marked the film debut of Aldo Ray, who at the time used his original name of Aldo DaRe. *Var* noted that previous to the film, he had been an elected constable in Crockett, CA. *Time* called Ray the "film's most natural performer."

The film was shot a few months before a West Point athletics "cribbing scandal" was uncovered. According to *NYT*, Senator William Fulbright of Arkansas, author of a Congressional resolution to overhaul the educational system at West Point, appeared in a trailer endorsing the film, which also was made before the scandal at West Point made the news. Fulbright, in the trailer, says, "many who see this picture may not believe that such things exist. Unfortunately, there is too much evidence to the contrary." Controversy concerning the film occurred when pickets in Los Angeles charged that Buchman, Lampell and actor Alexander Knox were Communists. According to news stories, Buchman admitted in a 1951 House Un-American Activities Committee hearing that he once had been a Communist. Columbia issued a statement that at the time the film was made, none of those mentioned were members of the Communist Party, and Harry Cohn threatened legal action against the group picketing after Knox stated that he had never been a member. Buchman was found guilty of contempt of Congress in 1953 when he refused to name Communists or former Communists. He received a suspended sentence and was fined $150, according to *NYT*. Both Buchman and Lampell were blacklisted by the industry.

Box 8 Sep 1951. *Christian Science Monitor* 4 Nov 1950. *Cue* 15 Sep 1951. *DV* 20 Mar 1950. *DV* 2 Aug 1950. *DV* 22 Aug 1951, p. 3. *DV* 19 Oct 1951. *DV* 22 Oct 1951. *DV* 24 Oct 1951. *Exb* 29 Aug 1951, p. 3133. *FD* 23 Aug 1951, p. 6. *Har* 25 Aug 1951, p. 134. *HCN* 19 Oct 1951. *HR* 23 Nov 1948. *HR* 25 Jan 1949. *HR* 9 Jun 1950, p. 12. *HR* 1 Sep 1950, p. 10. *HR* 22 Aug 1951, p. 3. *IP* Oct 1951, p. 4, 16-17. *LADN* 19 Oct 1951. *LAEx* 8 Feb 1949. *LAT* 21 Dec 1948. *LAT* 19 Oct 1951. *Look* 25 Sep 1951. *MPD* 23 Aug 1951. *MPHPD* 25 Aug 1951, p. 989. *Newsweek* 10 Sep 1951. *NYT* 7 Aug 1949. *NYT* 11 Jun 1950. *NYT* 26 Aug 1951. *NYT* 12 Sep 1951, p. 37. *NYT* 9 Feb 1960. *NYT* 12 May 1960. *Time* 15 Oct 1951. *Var* 22 Aug 1951, p. 10. *Var* 10 Oct 1951. *Var* 17 Oct 1951.

THE SAVAGE (Native Americans, Dakota)

Paramount Pictures Corp. *Dist* Paramount Pictures Corp. Nov **1952**; Los Angeles opening: 26 Nov 1952; Prod: mid-Jun—late Jul 1951 [©Paramount Pictures Corp.; 1 Nov 1952; LP2108]. Sd (Western Electric Recording); col (Technicolor). 11 reels, 8,814 ft. 94-95 min. PCA cert no. 15444.

Prod Mel Epstein. *Dir* George Marshall. [*Asst dir* Oscar Rudolph]. *Scr* Sydney Boehm. *Dir of photog* John F. Seitz. *Spec photog eff* Gordon Jennings. *Technicolor color consultant* Robert Brower. *Art dir* Hal Pereira and William Flannery. *Ed* Arthur Schmidt. *Set des* Sam Comer. *Set dec* Ray Moyer. *Cost* Edith Head. *Mus score* Paul Sawtell. *Sd rec* Harold Lewis and Walter Oberst. *Makeup supv* Wally Westmore. *Indian tech adv* David H. Miller.

Source: Based on the novel *The Renegade* by L. L. Foreman (New York, 1942).

Cast: Charlton Heston [(*James Aherne, Jr., also known as Warbonnet*)], Susan Morrow [(*Tally Hathersall*)], Peter Hanson [(*Lt. Weston Hathersall*)], Joan Taylor [(*Luta*)], Richard Rober [(*Capt. Arnold Vaugant*)], Donald Porter [(*Running Dog*)], Ted de Corsia [(*Iron Breast*)], Ian MacDonald [(*Chief Yellow Eagle*)], Milburn Stone [(*Corp. Martin*)], Angela Clarke [(*Pehangi*)], Orley Lindgren [(*Jim "Whopper" Aherne, Jr., as a boy*)], Michael Tolan [(*Long Mane*)],

Howard J. Negley [(*Col. Robert Ellis*)], Frank Richards [(*Sgt. Norris*)], [John S. Peters (*Sgt. Dolin*)], [David Miller (*Lt. Eric Stanley*)], [Frank Cordell, James Van Horn, Willard Willingham (*Cavalrymen*)], [Roger Creed (*Holmes*)], [Henry Wills (*Firth*)], [Ben Black Elk (*Crow chief*)], [Kirk Alyn (*Orderly*)], [Jim Hayward (*Doctor*)], [John Miljan (*White Thunder*)], [Jimmie Dundee (*Dark Hawk*)], [Marion Gray (*Mrs. Ellis*)], [Iron Eyes Cody (*Warrior*)], [Ben American Horse], [John Sitting Bull].

Western. [*Print viewed*]. His Virginia home having been devastated during the Civil War, schoolmaster James Aherne accompanies his eleven-year-old son, James, Jr., toward a new life in the West. As the party traverses South Dakota's Black Hills, which they have been informed can be safely crossed if they observe the rules set down by the Sioux nation, they are attacked without warning by a group of Crow Indians. Although everyone else in the party is killed, young Jim is saved by the arrival of Chief Yellow Eagle and his Miniconjou Sioux warriors, who have been trying to rid the territory of Crow raiders. Because of his bravery during the attack, Yellow Eagle names the boy Warbonnet and rears him as a Sioux. Warbonnet reaches manhood as tensions between whites, who are after newly discovered gold in the Black Hills, and the Sioux, who expect their sovereignty of the territory to be respected, as stated in the treaty signed years earlier, reach their peak. Running Dog, who has always hated Warbonnet, believes that the chief's adopted son would be unable to fight his own people in the event of war, but at a council of Sioux chiefs, Warbonnet asserts his loyalty to the tribe and his love of Yellow Eagle, his mother Pehangi, and his sister Luta. When Warbonnet nevertheless urges that the decision to go to war be made with caution, his father sends him to Fort Duane to determine whether the U.S government actually intends to break the treaty. On his way, Warbonnet is instrumental in saving a party of soldiers, led by Lt. Weston Hathersall, from attacking Crow Indians. As a result, Warbonnet is commended for bravery and treated warmly by Fort Duane's Col. Robert Ellis. Wes's sister Tally is attracted to Warbonnet, and both she and her brother are surprised when the newcomer, who dresses and acts like an Indian, recites an Omar Khayyam poem from memory. He is distrusted, however, by Capt. Arnold Vaugant, an Indian-hater who calls him a "savage." As the days pass, Luta wonders why he has not yet returned home, while Long Mane, Warbonnet's closest friend, suspects that he may have found "new friends." Warbonnet leaves the fort immediately upon learning through smoke signals that Luta has been captured by soldiers. He soon encounters Long Mane and Running Dog, who inform him that a party of Crow had killed the soldiers and captured Luta. Warbonnet leads a party of five Sioux to the Crow camp, where he bravely rescues his "little sister." While returning to their village, however, they are attacked by Vaugant's men, and Luta is killed. After denouncing his white heritage, Warbonnet challenges and kills Running Dog for having abandoned him at the Crow camp. Convinced that the whites intend to kill his people, he then agrees to lead the soldiers at Fort Duane into a Miniconjou ambush. Back at the fort, Ellis reads the new orders from Washington, instructing him to move all the Indians to reservations, using force if necessary. Acting as their scout, Warbonnet leads Vaugant's men to the Crow encampment, which they soon destroy with cannon fire. Vaugant then moves into the woods to fight the rest of the Crow, even though Warbonnet warns him that his plan will only get the soldiers killed. Warbonnet and Corp. Martin, acting independently, use explosives to flush the Indians out of the woods, where Wes's men are waiting to subdue them. Furious, Vaugant tries to shoot Warbonnet, but Martin grabs his arm, and Vaugant dies instead. That night, Warbonnet meets secretly with Yellow Eagle and his warriors, and plans to ambush the column are finalized. When Yellow Eagle directs his men to take no prisoners, however, Warbonnet begins to doubt the wisdom of the attack. The next morning, a wagon train carrying women and children joins Wes's column for protection. As they pull out, Martin remarks that whites and Indians should be able to share the land, but that simple arithmetic insures a U.S. victory if the Indians insist on fighting. Realizing that Martin is right, Warbonnet helps the wagon train to escape the planned ambush, but he is hit in the shoulder with an arrow. That night, a feverish Warbonnet sneaks away from Fort Duane and attempts to persuade Yellow Eagle that continuing the war will only lead to their deaths, and that many of the whites he has met are good at heart. In observance of Miniconjou law, Yellow Eagle flings

a lance into his adopted son and wounds him for betraying him earlier that day. He assures Pehangi that he had no intention of killing her son, but she is deeply distressed and declares that Warbonnet spoke the truth. In the morning, the Miniconjou take Warbonnet back to the gates of Fort Duane, and Yellow Eagle asks him to make a place for his people among the whites. After promising to return to them, Warbonnet greets Tally and Martin and explains that the Miniconjou have decided to give the whites "a little elbow room." *Dakota Indians. Fathers and sons. Forts. Loyalty. Miniconjou Indians. Revenge. United States. Army. Cavalry. Adoption. Ambushes. Battles. Betrayal. Black Hills (SD and WY). Crow Indians. Dances. Family relationships. Friendship. Indians of North America. Massacres. Officers (Military). Oglala Indians. Rescues. Rites and ceremonies. Romantic rivalry. Scouts (Frontier). Teton Indians. Treaties. Tribal chiefs.*

Note: The working title of this film was *Warbonnet*. According to onscreen credits, the picture was photographed in the Black Hills of South Dakota. Studio publicity material adds that twenty-five separate South Dakota locations were used, including several in Custer State Park. Actor Michael Tolan is listed as Lawrence Tolan in most contemporary reviews and news items. *The Savage* may have been Tolan's first onscreen credit. According to MPAA/PCA records, contained at the AMPAS Library, Don Martin wrote a draft of the film's screenplay. Martin's contribution to the final film has not been confirmed, however. According to studio publicity, over 200 Sioux Indians, including Sitting Bull's 91-year-old son John Sitting Bull, were cast in the picture. The *Var* reviewer remarked that "the core of the [racial] matter, while suggested throughout, has been bypassed for a standard round-up of reactionaries and liberals, both red and white....But in a few cryptic scenes between the hero and a grizzled, plain-talking sergeant...this Hollywood semi-sermon has its best moments and hits the nail squarely on the head."

Box 20 Sep 1952. *DV* 18 Sep 1952, p. 3. *Exh* 24 Sep 1952, p. 3382. *FD* 25 Sep 1952, p. 10. *Har* 20 Sep 1952, p. 150. *HR* 8 Jun 1951, p. 10. *HR* 15 Jun 1951, p. 8. *HR* 27 Jul 1951, p. 10. *HR* 18 Sep 1952, p. 3. *MPHPD* 20 Sep 1952, p. 1534. *NYT* 2 Jan 1953, p. 11. *Var* 14 Jan 1953, p. 6.

SAVANNAH *see* SANGAREE

SAY THAT YOU LOVE ME *see* DI QUE ME QUIERES

SCANDAL (African Americans)

Lincoln Pictures, Inc. *Dist* State Rights. **1933?**. Sd; b&w. 7 reels, 6,300 ft.

Cast: Lucky Millinder, and his orchestra.

African American, Show business, Drama. [*Not viewed*]. At a rehearsal of the Attucks Theater Company, Eva Clarke has left to get married, leaving the show without a star on the night before it is scheduled to open. Mr. Jenkins, the show's manager, decides to change the billing to amateur night and hold a contest, offering the winner a job with the company. They choose a young woman named Connie Jackson and begin rehearsals immediately. Putney, the piano player, teaches Connie how to sing the blues and, during lay-over on the tour, Connie tells Putney how much she likes performing. Later, Putney gets drunk with his buddies and makes a pass at a chorus girl named Frankie Parsons. The boss, Jim Evans, finds out that Putney was drunk again during a performance and fires him. When Connie hears of this, she is heart-broken and quits the show. Putney is replaced in the show by Lucky Millinder, while Connie is replaced by Clara Thompson. Lucky, who is comfortable with the show's routine, helps the novice Clara get settled by arranging for her lodging at Mrs. Havlin's boarding house, where he is also staying. On the eve of her first performance, Clara overhears Frankie, who is jealous at being passed over for the lead part in the show, complaining to the other chorus girls. After an exceptional first show, Lucky takes Clara out for dinner to celebrate. When Jim Evans, the richest man in black show business, comes to town, he asks to meet with Clara. When she hesitates, Clara's costume lady tells her that Evans can make her famous, so she goes to meet him. Later, before that evening's performance, Lucky asks Clara to marry him and she says she will as soon as he has made a name for himself in music. Knowing that Evans is in the audience and will be impressed by Lucky's playing, she asks him to give the best performance he can. After the show, Evans asks Lucky to work for him in the Lazy Levee night club in Harlem. As he is leaving to return to New York that evening, Evans asks Connie to see him off at the station. Frankie, who has also been asked to work for Evans, tells Lucky that they will be able to have fun together in New York. When he protests that he is devoted to Clara, Frankie tells him that Clara has been seeing Evans behind his back. Lucky becomes jealous and allows Frankie to talk him into leaving with out saying good-bye to Clara. Later, Clara is nursing a broken heart when Evans visits and tells her that Lucky is a great hit in New York, but that he

has spent all his money on Frankie, who has since left him. Then he tells her that he is risking his job by drinking during performances. Eventually, Lucky is fired and Evans asks Clara to come to New York to help Lucky get back on track. She rescues him and they star in a show together in Harlem. *Theatrical managers. Theatrical troupes. Boardinghouses. Chorus girls. Drunkenness. Jealousy. New York City–Harlem. Proposals (Marital).*

Note: The plot summary of this film is based on a dialogue continuity, dated 28 Apr 1933, that was deposited at NYSA. In one place in the continuity, the lead female character is called "Connie Jackson," and in another, "Connie Freeman." No other information has been located concerning the film. For more information on Lincoln Pictures, see entry below for *Harlem Is Heaven*.

THE SCAR (Latino)

World Film Corp. *Dist* World Film Corp. 14 Apr **1919** [©World Film Corp.; 14 Apr 1919; LU13621]. Si; b&w. 5 reels.

Dir Frank Crane. *Scen* Hamilton Smith. *Cam* Lucien Tainguy.

Cast: Kitty Gordon (*Cora*), Irving Cummings (*George Reynolds*), Jennie Ellison (*Mrs. Reynolds*), Eric Mayne (*Hastings*), Charles Dungan (*Cavanaugh*), Frank Farrington (*Thaddeus Tabor*), Ruth Findlay (*Frances Tabor*), Paul Doucet (*Valdez*), David Herblin (*Caryl Haskill*), Herbert Bradshaw (*Willard*), Amelia Barleon (*Cora's maid*).

Drama. American George Reynolds duels with Spaniard Valdez over Cora, a Spanish adventuress living in South America. Valdez is wounded and Reynolds takes Cora to America and establishes her in a cottage where he visits her frequently. Cora becomes involved with Reynolds' friend Caryl Haskill. Reynolds struggles with Cora and the revolver accidentally discharges, wounding her, as a result of which Reynolds is sent to prison for five years. Cora visits the prison gang at road work details in order to taunt Reynolds, then years later she runs a New York gambling house. Caryl loses his fortune there and then drowns himself. After being released on parole, Reynolds marries Frances Tabor, but Cora still seeks revenge. She attempts to break up Reynolds' marriage and have him arrested, but is unsuccessful. Cora loses her sanity and is confined to an asylum. *Adventuresses. Gambling houses. Revenge. Spaniards. Americans in foreign countries. Drowning. Duels. Gun accidents. Insanity. Marriage. Parole. Prison life. South America.*

Note: The copyright entry states that this film was "adapted from an old play," but no information on a possible literary source has been found.

ETR 12 Apr 1919, p. 1441. *MPW* 12 Apr 1919, p. 270. *Var* 4 Apr 1919, p. 68. *Wid's* 6 Apr 1919, p. 19.

THE SCAR *see* SCARFACE (1932)

SCAR OF SHAME *see* BROKEN HEARTS (1920)

THE SCAR OF SHAME (African Americans)

Colored Players Film Corp. **1927**. Si; b&w. 8 reels, 8,023 ft.

Dir Frank Perugini. *Story* David Starkman. *Photog* Al Ligouri.

Cast: Harry Henderson (*Alvin Hillyard*), Norman Johnstone (*Eddie Blake*), Ann Kennedy (*Lucretia Green*), Lucia Lynn Moses (*Louise Howard*), William E. Pettus (*Spike Howard*), Lawrence Chenault (*Ralph Hathaway*), Pearl McCormick (*Alice Hathaway*).

African American, Melodrama. One afternoon at Mrs. Lucretia Green's high class boardinghouse, Alvin Hillyard, a struggling young composer, witnesses a drunken man abusing a young woman in the tenement yard next door. He climbs out the window and saves the girl, Louise Howard, then carries her to the boardinghouse, where Mrs. Green comforts her. Mrs. Green offers Louise a room in exchange for helping around the house, hoping to keep her safe from her violent, drunkard stepfather Spike. Meanwhile, Eddie Blake, a saloon owner and another one of Mrs. Green's boarders, encourages Spike to drink and then tries to drag Louise back to her father as he wants to hire the girl, to whom he is attracted, as an entertainer in his seedy club. Alvin once again intervenes, and Mrs. Green tells Eddie to pack his bags while Alvin vows to teach the lout how to have respect for "our" women. Later, at a saloon, Spike and Eddie discuss Louise, and Spike tells the ruffian to leave the girl alone, blaming his own violence on the alcohol that Eddie has given him. Eddie proceeds to push alcohol on the susceptible Spike, and after he has become thoroughly inebriated, he goes to Louise's room and tries to grab her. Alvin rescues Louise once again and then decides that he will marry her so that she will finally be safe. Three months later, Spike, in a state of alcohol withdrawal, begs Eddie for a drink, and Eddie says he will serve him only if he helps kidnap Louise and set up a cabaret in

another town, where with her looks and his brains they will make a killing. The pair devises a scheme which involves sending a fake telegram calling Alvin away to his sick mother's bedside. As Alvin packs to leave, Louise offers to accompany him, but Alvin confesses that he has never told his class-conscious mother about their marriage. Alvin leaves as Spike watches the house, and Louise, distraught, ruins a photo of Alvin's mother and then discovers and tears up letters in which the matron mentions her hopes that Alvin will marry a young woman of their own class. Her final acts of defiance are to remove her wedding ring and tear up her marriage license. Although Spike has tried to dissuade him, Eddie enters Louise's room and then tells her to join him in a business deal in another town, a proposition to which Louise agrees, provided their relationship remains strictly business. Alvin discovers the trick played upon him once he arrives at his mother's home and, having dropped his house key, breaks into his and Louise's room through a window and pulls a gun on the pair. The two men fire their guns, and when the police arrive, they find Louise unconscious and wounded. Alvin is convicted of assault based on Louise's testimony, and the girl is left with a disfiguring scar on her neck. Later, Alvin escapes from prison and becomes a successful music teacher under the name "Arthur Jones" in the same city where Louise and Eddie have set up a chic gambling club, the Club Lido. Alvin begins to fall in love with his star music pupil, Alice Hathaway, but cannot declare his feelings because of his past. One day, her father, Ralph Hathaway, a wealthy lawyer, receives a call from Louise inviting him to come to a "whoopie" party at the club, of which Hathaway is the sponsor and protector. When a letter is left for Hathaway, Alice, now engaged to Alvin, asks her fiancé to bring it down to the club, where much to his shock, he is introduced to Louise. Louise blackmails Alvin into dancing with her in front of Hathaway, and then later into coming to visit her at her home. When he arrives, she tries to seduce him, then confesses that she has always loved him. He throws her down and leaves, and, distraught and hopeless, Louise writes a letter and asks her maid to deliver it to Hathaway. She begs God's forgiveness and drinks poison, and when her maid tries to revive her, she begs her to simply deliver the letter. The maid calls Hathaway to come to Louise's side, and before he arrives, Eddie enters the room and finds a letter informing him that she finally plans to clear Alvin's good name. Hathaway arrives, reads his letter, and exclaims in sorrow that his people have much to learn. In the meantime, Alvin, having confessed all to Alice, tries to comfort her, but Hathaway arrives bearing the truth conveyed in Louise's letter: that Eddie had actually shot Louise, who is now dead, and that Alvin is innocent. Alice and her future husband, now exonerated, embrace. *African Americans. Music teachers. Romance. Singers. Suicide.* Alcoholics. Attempted rape. Battered children. Boardinghouses. Class conflict. Composers. Fathers and daughters. Gamblers. Gunshot wounds. Innocence. Lawyers. Lechery. Marriage. Nightclubs. Parties. Police. Prison escapees. Saloons. Stepfathers.

Note: According to a modern source, this film was produced in Philadelphia. The same source states that the production team on the film, including the writer and director, were white, and that Sherman Dudley acted as the African-American front for white financing. The onscreen credits include a foreword describing the importance of environment in the shaping of a life. It includes the following lines: "If early in life some knowing, loving hand lights the lamp of knowledge and with tender care keeps it burning, then our course will run true 'til the end of our useful time on this earth, but if that lamp should fail through lack of loving hands to tend its hungry flame—then will come sorrow and SHAME!"

SCAR ON A NATION *see* **SCARFACE**

SCARFACE (Italian Americans)

The Caddo Co. *Dist* United Artists Corp. 9 Apr **1932** Sd (Western Electric Sound System); b&w. 10 reels. 90, 95 or 99 min.

Pres HOWARD HUGHES. [*Supv* E. B. Derr]. *Dir* Howard Hawks. *Co-dir* Richard Rosson. *Screen story* Ben Hecht. *Cont and dial* Seton I. Miller, John Lee Mahin and W. R. Burnett. [*Adpt* Fred Pasley]. *Photog* Lee Garmes and L. W. O'Connell. [*Cam op* Warren Lynch and Roy Clark]. [*Asst cam* Warner Cruze and Charles Bohny]. [*Process photog* Howard Anderson]. *Settings* Harry Oliver. *Film ed* Edward Curtiss. *Ed adv* Douglass Biggs. [*Ed for alternate versions* Lewis Milestone]. *Mus dir* Adolph Tandler and Gus Arnheim. *Sd eng* William Snyder. *Prod mgr* Charles Stallings. [*Still photog* Eugene Kornman]. [*Gen press representative* Lincoln Quarberg].

Source: Based on the novel *Scarface* by Armitage Trail (New York, 1930).

Cast: Paul Muni (*Tony [Camonte]*), Ann Dvorak (*Cesca [Camonte]*), Karen Morley (*Poppy*), Osgood Perkins ([*Johnny] Lovo*), C. Henry Gordon (*Guarino*), George Raft ([*Guino] Rinaldo*), Vince Barnett (*Angelo*), Boris Karloff (*Gaffney*), Purnell Pratt (*Publisher*), Tully Marshall (*Managing editor*), Inez Palange (*Tony's mother*), Edwin Maxwell (*Detective chief*), [Harry J. Vejar (*Big Louie Costillo*)], [Henry Armetta (*Pietro*)], [Bert Starkey (*Epstein*)], [Gus Arnheim, and his Cocoanut Grove orchestra], [Maurice Black].

Gangster, Drama. [*Print viewed*]. Italian mob leader Big Louie Costillo is killed by Tony Camonte, setting off gang wars over the control of Chicago's bootlegging business. Under orders from their boss Johnny Lovo, Tony and Guino Rinaldo terrorize South side bars to maintain it as Lovo's territory. Afterward, they go on a several month long shooting spree, killing innocent bystanders as well as intended victims. When Tony kills O'Hara, the North side boss, Lovo becomes scared. Poppy, Lovo's mistress, visits Tony, and he shows her the neon Cook's Tours sign outside his window that has become his slogan: "The World Is Yours." Tony takes over the North side, and goes on another shooting spree. On St. Valentine's Day, seven gangsters are lined up in a garage and shot execution style. After Tony kills the last of the big gang leaders, he goes to the Paradise Club, where he sees his sister Cesca dancing with a man. In a jealous rage, Tony takes her home and beats her. Then, when he leaves, he is chased by unknown gangsters. Both cars go over the side of the road, but Tony survives. When he finds out that Lovo set him up, Tony and Guino kill him, then Tony and Poppy hide out in Florida for a month. While they are gone, Guino and Cesca fall in love and marry. Tony returns to find Guino in Cesca's apartment and kills him before she can explain that they were married. A short time later, the police surround Tony's apartment, and he and Cesca fight them off until she dies of a gunshot wound. Finally, Tony surrenders after his room is inundated with tear gas and he cannot stand to be alone. At the last minute, he makes a dash for freedom, but is gunned down by the police and dies under the Cook's Tours sign. *Bootleggers. Chicago (IL). Gangsters. Italian Americans. Murder. Police.* Barbers and barbershops. Brothers and sisters. Cowardice. Gunfights. Gunshot wounds. Hired killers. Jealousy. Love affairs. Loyalty. Marriage. Molls. Mothers and daughters. Mothers and sons. Nightclubs. Reporters. St. Valentine's Day Massacre, 1929.

Note: [The plot summary was based on a viewed print, which contains material from the various versions of *Scarface* as described below.] *Scarface* was produced in 1931 at a time when the question of censoring films was receiving great focus by local organizations. *FD* reports on various bills being introduced to specifically prohibit the release of gangster pictures in areas such as New York City, Salem, Oregon and Atlantic City, New Jersey. Although most of the bills introduced were defeated, the issue remained controversial. According to information in the MPAA/PCA Collection at the AMPAS Library, the MPPDA first heard of Howard Hughes's proposed production of a film based on the life of gangster Al Capone in Jan 1931 and expressed their doubts about the feasibility of bringing a film of this nature to screen. Caddo Co. (Hughes's production corporation) correspondence in the Howard Hawks Collection at Brigham Young University reveals that the creators of the film drew their characters and situations from real life criminals, and additional sources reveal that they were working with Fred Pasley, Al Capone's biographer. Among the incidents from criminal history that influenced the screenplay were the 1920 murder of gang leader James "Big Jim" Colosimo in his Chicago restaurant by Johnny Torrio, under orders of Al Capone; the 1924 Torrio-ordered murder of crime boss Dion O'Bannion in his flower shop; a murder by Jack "Legs" Diamond; the 1929 "St. Valentine's Day Massacre" in Chicago, reportedly ordered by Capone; and the 1931 "Siege of West 90th Street," a gun battle in which hoodlum Francis "Two Gun" Crowley fought off scores of police from his apartment in New York, while a crowd of spectators looked on. In an oral history, Howard Hawks stated that he and Ben Hecht interviewed many gangsters and also compiled information on them from Chicago reporters. Hawks and Hecht based their main characters on Al Capone and the powerful Renaissance Italian family, the Borgias. News items in *FD* and *NYT* confirm that Hawks himself met with Capone, who took a personal interest in the film.

Howard Hughes, supervisor E. B. Derr and Howard Hawks met regularly with the AMPP in Los Angeles to consult on the script. On 26 May 1931, Derr sent a copy of the script to Colonel Jason Joy, AMPP director of the Studio Relations Committee, advising him that the film was "cast and ready to shoot," and that, in the script, "where we mention specific names, we proposed to change those names if they refer to any real person; likewise we will not definitely refer to Chicago but rather will always substitute the word 'city.'" Joy responded on 3 Jun 1931 highlighting his recommendations for changes to the script. His biggest remaining concern was in the depiction of "Tony Camonte," and he noted that the film "unquestionably tends to glorify [the] gangster" and in addition to this, that the depiction of "Camonte" as a "home loving man" makes it "all...more dangerous because of [his] resemblance to [a] well-known gangster who so far has succeeded in defeating the law...." Joy urged that,

886

among other things, "in [the] final scenes 'Camonte' should be shown as [a] cringing coward." By 19 Jun 1931, PCA files reveal that Hughes, who was at first reluctant to "weaken" the story, seemed to relent somewhat and agreed to some of the recommended changes. Nonetheless, Jul 1931 memos in the file continue to reveal the AMPP's concern over the subject matter: "inasmuch as they have everything in the story, including the inferences of incest, the picture is beginning to look worse and worse to us, from a censorship point of view." In a 23 Jul 1931 memo from Joy to Will H. Hays, president of the MPPDA, Joy notes that "there are only three things I've asked that they [Hawks and Derr] have not agreed to try to do. I think they will do these three before we are finished. One is a suitable 'foreword'—second is a strong speech by a suitable character along the lines of Carleton Simon's suggestion—and the third is the finish in which I wish 'Scarface' to turn 'yellow.'" (Dr. Carleton Simon, a psychologist consulted by the Hays Office, read the scenario in Jun 1931 and recommended the following: that the mother of "Camonte" explain to her son that he is bringing shame to the Italian race; that the character of a Jewish lawyer named "Epstein," apparently in the initial scenario, "should not be so pronouncedly Jewish...as it will react at least racially against the picture"; that "Guino" and "Cesca" should be secretly married rather than just live together so that the "moral effect" on the audience would improve; that "in the final scene, the nemesis of 'Scarface', the detective, should not be killed, but he should 'get his man'"; and that the character of "Camonte," who in the end is "endowed with humane kindly qualities especially as applied to the welfare of his sister," should be altered, "otherwise it crowns the criminal with a halo.") A rough cut of the completed film, referred to in the correspondence files as Version A, was viewed by the AMPP on 8 Sep 1931, at which time the AMPP told Hughes that the ending must be altered in order to negate the heroism of "Camonte."

Although Hughes initially rejected the AMPP's suggestion that he "weaken the story by characterizing 'Scarface' in the final sequences as a weakling and a coward," by 21 Sep 1931, as Joy noted in a memo in the file, "we have come to a final and definite decision concerning the remaining retakes....This involves an entire new ending which will take four days to shoot and an expenditure of $25,000. Mr. Hughes has officially informed us that he will go through with this plan." Joy's memo also noted that M-G-M's powerful producer Irving G. Thalberg viewed the film on 21 Sep and called it one of the "strongest pictures" he had ever seen.

The Hays Office further urged Hawks and Hughes to add an anti-gun statement to the film. Their suggestion was inspired by the contemporary national focus on implementing legislation that would restrict the sale of firearms, with the intention of keeping the weapons out of the hands of gangsters. In New York, then Governor Franklin Delano Roosevelt and Police Commissioner Edward P. Mulrooney supported a law which would prevent a civilian from purchasing a machine gun; Pennsylvania instituted the Witkins Firearms Act; and a national summit was called to discuss uniform state laws to govern the sale of firearms. By 30 Sep 1931, Joy had viewed the virtually complete film (Version A) "twenty times," and in a letter noted, "and still it has the power to move me." He further described that "the theme [of anti-gun policy] strikes directly at the current thought of the country....What Hawks has done is to insert in about ten places in the picture scenes and dialogue pointing up the idea that "Scarface" is a killer as long as he has his guns....These new sequences, together with a strong, forceful foreword...do much to change the aspect of the picture and make it worthwhile propaganda as well." Joy noted in a later memo to Hays that the insertion of these elements met with Hughes's "personal consent and apparently his entire approval."

Although Derr and Hawks initially opposed the idea to add a foreword, they worked closely on it with Lamar Trotti, Joy's assistant at the AMPP. The lengthy and strongly-worded foreword authored by Derr and Trotti was submitted to Joy on 2 Oct 1931 and was subsequently condensed by the MPPDA. Trotti noted in his accompanying letter to Joy that "all it now needs is for the Bronxville High School to walk on singing America, or perhaps George Cohan with two flags." A portion of this first submitted foreword reads as follows: "Take from this coward the weapon with which he indiscriminately shoots down men, women and children, deprive him of the boasted protection that is found in his trigger finger, and what remains will be the sniveling coward and yellow bully so easily held in check by the police before the advent of this shooting, killing beast....This cancer can never be removed while its evil power continually increases proportionately with the weapons surreptitiously furnished the gangster to carry on his bloody work....[T]he responsibility will be borne to every man and woman that it is his or her duty to uphold every department of law enforcement, demand the enaction of statutes throughout the country which will take from this foul parasite the opportunity of machine gunning his way to power and end his civil war against righteousness and decency." The foreword was then reduced to approximately four sentences. This greatly revised version appears on the film: "This picture is an indictment of gang rule in America and of the callous indifference of the government to this constantly increasing menace to our safety and liberty. Every incident in this picture is the reproduction of an actual occurrence, and the purpose of this picture is to demand of the government: What are you going to do about it? The government is your government. What are you going to do about it?" Correspondence in the Lincoln Quarberg files at the AMPAS Library indicates that Caddo Co. publicist Quarberg also wrote a foreword, but that it was rejected by the Hays Office. The version with the foreword and revised ending was referred to as Version B.

Hays enlisted the assistance of New York Police Commissioner Mulrooney for an endorsement. A 28 Oct 1931 telegram from Trotti to Joy reveals that they planned to open the film with a segment of Mulrooney speaking the foreword. In a 29 Oct 1931 inter-office memo, Hays related that Mulrooney declined to endorse the film, and noted that Mulrooney stated that he "could not be mixed up with it at all" because he felt strongly that the film "glorified the gangster

up to the very last minute." Alternately, according to a press release, West Coast police officials representing the California Crime Commission and various Los Angeles police commissioners praised the film. (Hays also reveals in the memo that several psychologists were consulted to find out the possible influence the film might have on audiences.)

FD notes that editor Edward Curtiss was scheduled to confer with the censor boards of various states in Oct 1931, and a memorandum in the MPAA/PCA Collection notes that in the same month, New York censors refused to approve the film. Because of the film's subject matter, a print (Version B) was sent to New York early in Oct 1931 for consideration by the Board of Directors of the MPPDA, which recommended further changes. In response to the Board's recommendations, a new ending was shot. A 26 Oct 1931 telegram from Trotti to Joy notes that "new ending Scarface will arrive New York Tuesday night stop Have just seen retakes stop He is completely executed." In the new ending, "Camonte" is captured, tried and hanged for his crimes. Scenes of the hanging were completed without Paul Muni, as he had already returned to New York to appear in a play, and a double was used in his place.

In a 16 Nov 1931 memo, Hays outlined the crucial things that in his opinion would still be required to make the film acceptable to the MPPDA: "First, all sympathy for the heavy must be eliminated; Second, a very much stronger presentation of the anti-easy purchase of guns propaganda must be developed; Third, and very important, is the change of the title." Hays met with strong resistance from Hughes against the change of title from Scarface. In a telegram to Hays, United Artists representative Al Lichtman strenuously objected that "major value [in] this picture is in its title...any change will result in great losses to its owner." Hays remained unmoved on this point, however, and a 9 Dec 1931 telegram reveals that three titles were considered by Lichtman: The Shame of the Nation, Yellow and Man Is Still Savage. News items in FD document further considerations, including Scar on a Nation and The Scar, and correspondence in the Quarberg files note that the title The Menace was also considered. The Shame of the Nation was chosen and registered by United Artists on 4 Dec 1931.

By that month, over two months since the picture had initially been completed, Hughes and Hawks had responded to drastic changes called for by the MPPDA in order to make the film acceptable under the Production Code. Joy noted in an inter-office memo to Hays that by agreeing to the changes, "Hughes made an honest effort to save [the film's] value and at the same time the reputation of the industry." Further recommendations were made on how to lessen the MPPDA's difficulties with the picture, including deleting the entire "series of lap dissolves known as the reign of terror...with the exception of the St. Valentine's day massacre"; and shortening the closing sequence when "Camonte" is captured. More revisions were also made on the foreword by the MPPDA. According to a modern source, some of the deletions included a scene in which "Camonte" embraces his sister "Cesca" after he has slapped her; a scene on "Camonte's" yacht; and a scene in which "Camonte" purchases a gift for his mother. An outline in the MPAA/PCA Collection of some of the overall changes made to the film are as follows: "...such touches as saluting the sign 'The world is yours,' were removed"; "the police speeches were built up to develop the prestige of law and order"; a scene in which "Camonte" knocks down policeman "Guarino" when he is first arrested was deleted; and "the relationship between 'Scarface' and his sister was changed to minimize the protective brother-sister situation and to imply a situation in which Scarface was planning to use her for ulterior purposes." (Although modern film criticism apparently did not comment on the incest motif in Scarface until the late 1960s, the Hays Office was aware of the connotations of the relationship between "Camonte" and his sister in Jul 1931, as noted above. Indeed, Hawks and Hecht's use of the Borgia family as an historical basis for this story signifies their awareness of the modern belief that Lucrezia and Alexander Borgia, brother and sister, had an illegitimate son together. However, no other mention of the issue of incest was made by the Hays Office in their correspondence.) Upon the completion by 24 Dec 1931 of the revisions noted above, the film was referred to as Version C.

The MPAA/PCA file for Hughes's production of Cock of the Air (see AFI Catalog of Feature Films, 1931-40; F3.0749) includes a 22 Dec 1931 telegram from Joy to Hays in which he stated the following: "...understand Hughes has print of quote Scarface unquote with him enroute New York stop Have not seen this in final version while desiring to help this man am certain steps should be taken to keep him from breaking down the machinery." The "machinery" referred to the MPPDA and AMPP offices. However, reportedly, Joy personally brought Version C from Hollywood to New York, where it was approved by Mulrooney. This version was sent to New York censors in Feb 1932, where it was viewed and rejected by chairman Dr. James Wingate. Incensed that the film continued to be rejected despite the enactment of changes required by censors, Hughes reassembled his film in its original version (Version A) and previewed it for an audience of critics on 2 Mar 1932 at Grauman's Chinese Theatre in Hollywood. Hughes then telegrammed UA president Joseph Schenck, who had assured Hays that only Version C would be released, that the critics were "apprais[ing the film] to the skies and almost all stating they could see nothing censorable, objectionable, and nothing which should be withheld from public." Hughes further requested that the film be released in its original form, Version A, in all territories that did not have censor boards. In a 10 Mar 1932 transcription of a telephone conversation between Hays and Hughes, Hughes states, "I have had this picture on the shelf for eight months and nothing has happened....If we called it Shame of the Nation nobody would have gone. We were supposed to call it Scar and Warner Brothers had a title registered Scar and would not give it up....I gave up Queer People to cooperate [a film Hughes intended to produce prior to Scarface but which he abandoned due to Hays Office objections] and I cut up The Cock of the Air until it wasn't any good in order to cooperate....What I want to do is to...use the last version...if I can use

the last two hundred feet.'' Throughout the conversation, Hughes remained adamant that he be allowed to use the original title of the film, and Hays explained the MPPDA's position that it was crucial not to release the original version in states that did not have censor boards, but that he would review the film again. Memoranda in the MPAA/PCA Collection indicate that because the film failed to get approval from the New York censors, Schenck authorized, and the MPPDA approved, director Lewis Milestone to make cuts in *Scarface* for censor-governed states. Milestone had previously cut approximately 1,800 feet of film from Hughes's *Cock of the Air* at the request of the MPPDA.

Hughes gathered endorsements from various authorities, including Los Angeles district attorney Buron Fitts and the California Crime Commission. By the end of Mar 1932, Version C with the Version B ending, which, according to an MPPDA inter-office memo dated 23 Mar, seemed ''satisfactory'' to the Hays Office, was premiered in New Orleans and had been released in various states, but New York censors continued to refuse its approval for exhibition. According to publicity, Hughes prepared to wage a legal war against the New York censorship board, and, according to an Apr 1932 *FD* news item, invited attorneys Clarence Darrow, Samuel Untermeyer, Arthur Garfield Hays and Morris L. Ernst to join him. A late Apr 1932 Los Angeles advertisement released by Quarberg stated that *Scarface* was ''the picture that powerful interests have tried to suppress.'' This brought cries of protest and ''misrepresentation'' from the MPPDA to Schenck, who agreed that it was adverse publicity for them. Hughes instructed his Los Angeles attorneys, Roger Marchetti and Neil S. McCarthy, to prepare to file suit in New York. In an Apr 1932 press release in the Quarberg files, written by Ronald Wagoner, United Press correspondent, Hughes stated, ''This court action, if successful, will relieve the entire film industry of the evils of unfair and unjust censorship. I am sure Mr. Hays will support this action with enthusiasm, because in many of his public utterances Hays has declared that 'censorship is un-American.' And certainly if censorship in general is unpatriotic, the politically-inspired censorship of *Scarface* is un-Americanism of the worst type.'' In early May, *FD* published the following statement by Hughes: ''I intend to show *Scarface* in its original, unaltered version in every state in the United States, including New York, where the opposition to the film is most persistent.'' The lawsuit never came to fruition. According to a 12 May 1932 telegram from Hughes to Hays, New York censors rescinded their original judgment. By 25 Jun 1932, the film was released in New York with the title *Scarface, the Shame of a Nation*. The New York and Pennsylvania releases, and possibly those of other states, included the hanging of ''Camonte'' at the end.

In Jun 1932, *FD* reported that the Massachusetts Grand Council of the Order of the Sons of Italy in America was proposing that Massachusetts city mayors ban the showing of the film because ''it reflects discredit on their race.'' In a letter in the MPAA/PCA Collection from Colonel F. L. Herron, the MPPDA foreign liaison, to Joy, Herron notes that he was having difficulty with the Italian government regarding this film; however, he also noted that Fascist Italian dictator Benito Mussolini had requested to see the film. By Jul, the only territories reluctant to pass the film were Kansas and Cook County, IL. Controversy continued, however, as reflected by an Oct *FD* news item which noted that the *Giornale d'Italia* in Rome ''urged the film be banned'' due to the ''offensive allusions to Italy'' contained therein. In addition, the Italian American Women's Club, Inc. requested that all Italian names be deleted from the film, according to a Jul 1932 telegram, and in Aug 1932, as reported by the *Oregonian*, Colonel G. T. Woodlaw, president of the Circle Theater in Portland, Oregon, was arrested for exhibiting *Scarface* after the local censor board had banned it on the basis of protests by the local Italian community.

The film was voted one of the ten best pictures of 1932 by the *FD* Nation Wide Poll, and the National Board of Review nominated it as one of the best American films of 1932. In the film, ''Camonte'' and his thugs attend the play *Rain* by John Colton and Clemence Randolph (New York, 7 Nov 1932). Modern sources note that the original script took eleven days to complete in Jan 1931. According to modern sources, Harold Lloyd's brother Gaylord lost one eye from a gunshot while on the set during production. Although Hughes reportedly withdrew the film from circulation a few years after its release, MPAA/PCA files show that in 1935 Atlantic Pictures Corp. applied to the PCA for a certificate of approval in order to re-issue the film, but the request was denied by Joseph I. Breen, then director of the PCA. The file also reveals that the film was shown in various parts of the country in 1935, 1937, 1940, 1942 and 1947-49—possibly without the approval of the PCA. After the death of Howard Hughes, the Summa Corporation, which handled his estate, sold the rights to the film to Universal in 1979. Modern sources state that the prints in circulation since the 1979 sale, while containing material from various of the versions prepared in 1931 and 1932, correspond most closely to Version B, although they do include material used only in the version on which Milestone worked. In 1983, Universal released another version of *Scarface* based on the 1932 film. Brian DePalma directed, Oliver Stone wrote the screenplay, and Al Pacino, Steven Bauer, Michelle Pfeiffer and Mary Elizabeth Mastrantonio starred. For information about other films inspired by Al Capone, see entry above for *Al Capone*.

FD 23 Jun 1931, p. 7. *FD* 1 Jul 1931, p. 10. *FD* 8 Jul 1931, p. 4. *FD* 29 Jul 1931, p. 8. *FD* 16 Aug 1931, p. 5. *FD* 31 Aug 1931, p. 1. *FD* 1 Sep 1931, p. 1. *FD* 3 Sep 1931, p. 1. *FD* 6 Sep 1931, p. 1. *FD* 13 Sep 1931, p. 1, 2. *FD* 15 Sep 1931, p. 4. *FD* 14 Oct 1931, p. 7. *FD* 15 Oct 1931, p. 6. *FD* 2 Feb 1932, p. 2. *FD* 12 Feb 1932, p. 2. *FD* 25 Mar 1932, p. 1, 12. *FD* 4 Apr 1932, p. 2. *FD* 17 Apr 1932, p. 10. *FD* 26 Apr 1932, p. 1. *FD* 2 May 1932, p. 1. *FD* 11 May 1932, p. 6. *FD* 12 May 1932, p. 1. *FD* 13 May 1932, p. 1. *FD* 20 May 1932, p. 1. *FD* 15 Jun 1932, p. 2. *FD* 13 Jul 1932, p. 1. *FD* 4 Oct 1932, p. 1. *FD* 5 Oct 1932, p. 12. *Har* 23 Apr 1932, p. 66. *HR* 24 Oct 1931, p. 3. *HR* 4 Feb 1932, p. 2. *HR* 10 Feb 1932, p. 7. *HR* 26 Feb 1932, p. 2. *HR* 3 Mar 1932, p. 3. *HR* 8 Jun 1932, p. 3. *HR* 6 Oct 1932, p. 7. *IP* Apr 1932, p. 28. *MPH* 17 Oct 1931, p. 25. *MPH* 12 Mar 1932, p. 55. *MPH* 28 May 1932, p. 17. *NYT* 13 Mar 1932. *NYT* 20 May 1932, p. 22. *Oregonian* 23 Aug 1932. *Oregonian* 25 Aug 1932. *Var* 24 May 1932, p. 29.

THE SCARLET CLUE (Chinese Americans, African Americans)
Monogram Pictures Corp. *Dist* Monogram Pictures Corp. 11 May **1945**; New York opening: week of 10 May 1945; Prod: Jan 1945 [©Monogram Pictures Corp.; 1 Apr 1945; LP13234]. Sd (Western Electric Recording); b&w. 5,808 ft. 65 min. PCA cert no. 10732.
    Series: Charlie Chan.
    Prod James S. Burkett. *Dir* Phil Rosen. [*Asst dir* Eddie Davis]. *Orig scr* George Callahan. *Dir of photog* William Sickner. *Ed* Richard Currier. *Mus dir* Edward J. Kay. *Sd rec* Tom Lambert. *Tech dir* Dave Milton. *Prod mgr* Wm. Strohbach.
    Source: Based on characters created by Earl Derr Biggers.
    Cast: Sidney Toler [(*Charlie Chan*)], Mantan Moreland [(*Birmingham Brown*)], Ben Carter [(*Ben Carter*)], Benson Fong [(*Tommy Chan*)], Virginia Brissac [(*Mrs. Marsh*)], Robert E. Homans [(*Capt. Flynn*)], Jack Norton [(*Willie Rand*)], Janet Shaw [(*Gloria Bayne*)], Helen Devereaux [(*Diane Hall*)], Victoria Faust [(*Hulda Swenson*)], [Milt Kibbee (*Herbert Sinclair*)], [I. Stanford Jolley (*Ralph Brett*)], [Reid Kilpatrick (*Wilbur Chester*)], [Charles Sherlock (*Sgt. McGraw*)], Leonard Mudie [(*Horace Carlos*)].
    Detective, Drama. [*Print viewed*]. On the trail of a spy ring intent on stealing government radar plans, world-famous Chinese-American detective Charlie Chan, now working as a federal agent, enlists the aid of Captain Flynn of the New York City police. Unfortunately, Flynn follows Chan's one lead to the spies, a scientist named Rausch, too closely, and Rausch is murdered by his mysterious, unnamed boss. Discovering that the murderer escaped in the stolen car of Diane Hall, a radio performer, Chan's and his two assistants—his son Tommy and his chauffeur, Birmingham Brown—go to the Cosmo Radio Center, where they find a footprint identical to one left at the murder scene. Meanwhile, Ralph Brett, the studio manager, telephones the spy ring leader, who uses the Western Union telegram service to warn Brett to be more careful or meet the same fate as Rausch. Later, Chan goes to the Hamilton Laboratory, which is located in the same building as the radio center, and is told of numerous, unsuccessful attempts to break in and steal the radar plans from the laboratory's safe. Chan then places phony radar plans in the safe in case the spies are more successful in the future. After actress Gloria Bayne attempts to blackmail Brett, having found his matches in Diane's recovered car, she is killed by an unidentified poison. Realizing that Chan is onto him, Brett asks his boss for help in escaping, but the spy instead kills him using a trap door in the service elevator. Upon finding the murdered studio manager, Chan has a voice impersonator call the spy leader, who, thinking that Brett is still alive, orders him to use the service elevator once more. After escaping the trap, Chan questions the people who worked with Brett and Gloria. Later, Willie Rand, an actor, is killed while taping a television show after telling Chan that he may have uncovered some information. The detective soon discovers that both Gloria and Willie were killed by a poisonous gas which was activated by cigarette smoke. After searching the building and finding the spy leader's office, the leader is chased through the radio studio by Chan, Tommy, Birmingham and the police, only to be killed by the elevator's trap door. In the basement of the building, they discover the dead body of Mrs. Marsh, the ruthless radio sponsor, and Chan declares the case solved. Actors and actresses. African Americans. Chauffeurs. Chinese Americans. Fathers and sons. Government agents. Murder. Spies. Cigarettes. Docks. Elevators. Gases, Asphyxiating and poisonous. Impersonation and imposture. Laboratories. Police. Radar. Radio performers. Radio programs. Radio sponsors. Rehearsals. Scientists. Television programs. Traps.
    Note: The working title of this film was *Robot Murder*. The title card on the viewed print reads: ''Charlie Chan in *The Scarlet Clue*.'' *HR* production charts include Harry Bradley and William Gould in the cast, but their participation in the released film has not been confirmed. *HR* production charts also note that director of photography William Sickner was borrowed by Monogram from Universal for his work on this film. The minor role of actor ''Horace Carlos'' is obviously based on noted horror film actor Boris Karloff, while the film's killer wears a mask modeled on actor Rondo Hatton. Modern sources add the following actors to the cast: Charles Jordan (*Nelson*) and Kernan Cripps (*Detective*). For additional information about this series, consult the Series Index and see the entry above for *Charlie Chan Carries On*.

Box 28 Apr 1945. *DV* 19 Apr 1945, p. 3. *FD* 24 Apr 1945, p. 8. *HR* 19 Jan 1945, p. 14. *HR* 19 Apr 1945, p. 3. *MPHPD* 10 Mar 1945, p. 2354. *MPHPD* 7 Apr 1945, pp. 2425-26. *Var* 16 May 1945, p. 8.

SCARLET DAYS (Latino)

D. W. Griffith. *Dist* Famous Players-Lasky Corp.; Paramount-Artcraft Pictures. 30 Nov **1919** [©D. W. Griffith; 24 Oct 1919; LP14367]. Si; b&w. 7 reels, 6,916 ft.

Pres D. W. Griffith. *Dir* D. W. Griffith. *Story and scen* S. E. V. Taylor. *Cam* G. W. Bitzer.

Cast: Richard Barthelmess (*Alvarez*), Clarine Seymour (*Chiquita*), Eugenie Besserer (*Rosie Nell*), Carol Dempster (*Lady Fair, her daughter*), Ralph Graves (*John Randolph*), Walter Long (*King Bagley*), George Fawcett (*The sheriff*), Kate Bruce (*The aunt*), Rhea Haines (*Spasm Sal*), Adolph Lestina (*Randolph's partner*), Herbert Sutch (*The marshal*), J. Wesley Warner (*Alvarez's man*).

Western. In the days of '49, Rosie Nell, a dance hall girl, saves gold from her prospecting customers to enable her to join her daughter in Boston. After another dance hall girl, trying to rob Nell, dies of a heart attack, Nell's hanging is stopped when word comes that her daughter, Lady Fair, has arrived. The Mexican bandit Alvarez and John Randolph, a Virginian miner, both attracted to Lady Fair, persuade the sheriff to allow Nell three days with her, which are the happiest of Nell's life, although the daughter is nearly driven insane when she learns the source of her boarding school funding. When King Bagley, the dance hall proprietor, decides to make Lady Fair his star attraction, Alvarez and Randolph protect the women in Randolph's cabin, from Bagley's men. The sheriff and a posse arrive after Alvarez offers to give himself up, and although Nell dies, the gang is dispersed. After Chiquita, whom Alvarez spurned, persuades the sheriff to allow Alvarez to escape with her, Lady Fair marries Randolph. *Bandits. California–History–1846-1850. Dance hall girls. False arrests. Mexicans. Mothers and daughters. Self-sacrifice. Dance hall owners. Heart disease. Posses. Prospectors. Sheriffs.*

Note: The character of Alvarez was suggested by the exploits of the bandit Joachin Murrieta. The film opened in New York on 9 Nov 1919. According to modern sources, James Smith was the film editor.

ETR 22 Nov 1919, p. 2143. *MPC* Jan 1920, pp. 56-57. *MPN* 22 Nov 1919, p. 3792. *MPW* 22 Nov 1919, p. 453. *NYMT* 16 Nov 1919. *NYT* 10 Nov 1919, p. 18. *Var* 14 Nov 1919, p. 58. *Wid's* 23 Nov 1919, p. 3.

THE SCARLET DRAGON (Chinese Americans)

Park-Whiteside Productions. *Dist* State Rights; Photoplay Libraries; Pioneer Film Corp. **1920?** Si; b&w. 6 reels.

Dir Frank Reicher. *Scen* J. Clarkson Miller. *Story* Willard King Bradley. *Cam* George Benoit. *Art dir* A. Béla Viragh-Flower.

Cast: Gail Kane (*Gloria Travers*), Thurston Hall (*Henry Livingston*), J. Herbert Frank (*Adolph Pym*), William Bechtel (*Commissioner Deering*), Nellie Burt (*Marjorie Travers*), Norbert Wicki (*Mock Lee*), Paul Lane (*Robert Deering*), Mlle. Dazie (*Dancer*), Ted Lewis and his band, May Kitson, Rene Gerard.

Crime, Drama. The Travers sisters move to New York in search of a stage career. Shortly after their arrival, Gloria's younger sister Marjorie disappears during a visit to Chinatown. After their mother dies of shock, Gloria appeals to the mayor for help. He then consults the commissioner on vice, but he secretly runs the underworld and proceeds to block all of the mayor's efforts to find the girl. After many misadventures involving the commissioner's son, who is an opium fiend, Marjorie is rescued unharmed. The mayor's interest in Gloria has since developed into love, and he asks her to be his wife. *Crime. Gangsters. Mayors. Missing persons. New York City. Political corruption. Sisters. Drug addicts. New York City–Chinatown. Opium.*

Note: The film was at least partly shot by Mar 1920, but it is unlikely that it was released that year. It was released in May-Jun 1921 as *Idle Hands.* Photoplay Libraries was the distributor as late as Mar 1920, but Pioneer Film Corp. distributed the film when it was released in 1921. Rene Gerard is listed as a cast member only in pre-release trade articles. May Kitson probably played the role of Mrs. Travers, mother to Gloria and Marjorie.

MPN 13 Mar 1920, p. 2541. *MPN* 27 Mar 1920, p. 2920, 2946, 2956. *MPW* 13 Mar 1920, p. 1784. *MPW* 14 May 1921, p. 210. *Var* 10 Jun 1921, p. 35.

THE SCARLET OATH (Russian Americans)

World Film Corp.; Peerless. *Dist* World Film Corp. 23 Oct **1916** [©World Film Corp.; 12 Oct 1916; LU9349]. Si; b&w. 5 reels.

Pres William A. Brady. *Dir* Frank Powell and Travers Vale. *Scen* Gardner Hunting. *Story* Frederic Kulz. *Cam* A. Barlatier.

Cast: Gail Kane (*Olga Pavloff/Nina Pavloff*), Philip Hahn (*Ivan Pavloff*), Carleton Macey (*Victor Karenin*), Lillian Paige (*Mrs. Victor Karenin*), Alan Hale (*John Huntington*), Montagu Love (*Nicholas Savaroff*), Boris Korlin (*Caganov*).

Drama. Exiled from Russia, nihilist Ivan Pavloff sails with his infant twin daughters, Nina and Olga, to the United States. On the steamers, a wealthy Russian couple offers a large amount of money to adopt Nina, and the impoverished Ivan finally consents. Years later, Ivan and Olga return to Russian territory to kill Nicholas Savaroff, who murdered Ivan's wife. The plan succeeds only partially, however, as Nicholas' men kill Ivan, after which Olga murders Nicholas. During her escape, Olga meets John Huntington, Nina's fiancé, and pretends to be her sister so she can accompany him safely out of the country. Upon her arrival in the United States, however, Russian spies kill Olga, and John, still unaware of the masquerade, is despondent until Nina appears to welcome him home. *Doubles. Impersonation and imposture. Murder. Nihilists. Russia. Russian Americans. Russians. Twins. Adoption. Exiles. Fathers and daughters. Sisters. Spies. Steamboats.*

Motog 11 Nov 1916, p. 1093. *MPN* 28 Oct 1916, p. 2711. *MPW* 28 Oct 1916, p. 534. *MPW* 4 Nov 1916, p. 754. *NYDM* 21 Oct 1916, p. 26. *Var* 13 Oct 1916, p. 25. *Wid's* 19 Oct 1916, p. 1043.

SCARLET SAINT (French Americans)

First National Pictures, Inc. *Dist* First National Pictures, Inc. 8 Nov **1925** [©First National Pictures, Inc.; 29 Oct 1925; LP21951]. Si; b&w. 7 reels, 6,784 ft.

Prod under the supv of Earl Hudson. *Dir* George Archainbaud. *Scen* Eugene Clifford and Jack Jungmeyer. *Titles* John Krafft. *Photog* George Folsey. *Art dir* Milton Menasco. *Film ed* Arthur Tavares.

Source: Based on the short story "The Lady Who Played Fidele" by Gerald Beaumont in *Red Book* (Feb 1925).

Cast: Mary Astor (*Fidele Tridon*), Lloyd Hughes (*Philip Collett*), Frank Morgan (*Baron Badeau*), Jed Prouty (*Mr. Tridon*), Jack Raymond (*Josef*), George Neville (*Trainer*), Frances Grant (*Cynthia*), J. Wesley Jenkins (*Butler*).

Melodrama. Betrothed as a child to Baron Badeau, Fidele Tridon, daughter of a wealthy New Orleans importer, finds herself in love with Philip Collett on the day the baron comes to claim her as his bride. The baron refuses to release her, and she plans to elope with Philip. The baron tricks Philip into a duel; Philip wounds him in the arm and is sent to jail. Fidele marries the baron to free Philip but flees to her lover after the ceremony. Finding her gone, the baron is stricken with paralysis, and Fidele returns to nurse her husband. The baron recovers after a year, but conceals this fact from his wife lest he lose her. On the night of the Mardi Gras ball he dresses as a jester and is mistaken by Fidele for Philip. She reveals to him that she is aware that her husband is faking; and when the baron's valet enters disguised as his master, she offers the valet a choice of two glasses of water, one of which contains poison. The baron, realizing that he has lost Fidele, gives her her freedom, and Fidele comes into her rightful love. *Antenuptial contracts. Disguise. Duels. French Americans. Handicapped. Infidelity. Mardi Gras. New Orleans (LA). Nobility. Paralysis.*

FD 15 Nov 1925.

THE SCARLET WEST (Native Americans)

Frank J. Carroll Productions. *Dist* First National Pictures, Inc. 26 Jul **1925** [©First National Pictures, Inc.; 2 Jul 1925; LP21625]. Si; b&w. 9 reels, 8,390 ft.

Pres Frank J. Carroll. *Dir* John G. Adolfi. *Scen* Anthony Paul Kelly. *Photog* George Benoit, Benjamin Kline, Victor Shuler and F. L. Hoefler.

Source: Based on the short story "The Scarlet West" by A. B. Heath (publication undetermined).

Cast: Robert Frazer (*Cardelanche*), Clara Bow (*Miriam*), Robert Edeson (*General Kinnard*), Johnny Walker (*Lieutenant Parkman*), Walter McGrail (*Lieutenant Harper*), Gaston Glass (*Captain Howard*), Helen Ferguson (*Nestina*), Ruth Stonehouse (*Mrs. Custer*), Martha Francis (*Harriett Kinnard*), Florence Crawford (*Mrs. Harper*).

Western. Cardelanche, the son of an Indian chief, has been educated in the East, and he returns to his reservation and encounters the hostility of his people, who believe that he has turned his back on his own race. When Cardelanche saves a detachment of cavalry from a gang of renegade Indians, he is made a captain in the United States Army. He falls in love with Miriam, the daughter of the commandant of Fort Remington, further cutting himself off from his own people. Lieutenant Parkman, who is also in love with Miriam, is demoted to the ranks when he gets into a fight over the girl. Cardelanche's tribe

goes on the warpath and slaughters the troops of General Custer. Cardelanche then decides that his true allegiance lies with his own people, and he gives up both Miriam and his commission, returning to the hills where his ancestors once lived and fought. *General George Armstrong Custer. Indians of North America. United States. Army. Cavalry.*

FD 27 Sep 1925. Var 16 Sep 1925, p. 41.

SCARS OF JEALOUSY (Cajuns)

Thomas H. Ince Corp. *Dist* Associated First National Pictures. 5 Mar **1923** [©Thomas H. Ince Corp.; 19 Mar 1923; LP18790]. Si; b&w. 7 reels, 6,246 ft.

Pres Thomas H. Ince. *Pers supv* Thomas H. Ince. *Dir* Lambert Hillyer. *Adpt* Lambert Hillyer. *Story* Anthony H. Rudd. *Photog* J. O. Taylor.

Cast: Frank Keenan (*Colonel Newland*), Edward Burns (*Jeff Newland*), Lloyd Hughes (*Coddy Jakes*), Marguerite De La Motte (*Helen Meanix*), James Neill (*Colonel Meanix*), Walter Lynch (*Pere Jakes*), James Mason (*Zeke Jakes*), Mattie Peters (*Mandy*), George Reed (*Mose*).

Drama. After years of waywardness Jeff Newland is disinherited by his father, Colonel Newland, who goes into the hills to seek a new heir from among the Cajuns. He returns with Coddy Jakes, introduces him to Helen Meanix, and educates him. Coddy is suspected of murder, however, and he disappears into the hills, where he encounters Jeff Newland and succeeds in making a man of him. When Coddy is captured and about to be lynched, Helen effects his escape, and they find love together after they are rescued by Jeff and the colonel from a forest fire. *Alabama. Cajuns. Family relationships. Forest fires. Lynching.*

FD 11 Mar 1923. MPW 17 Mar 1923. MPW 7 Apr 1923. NYT 7 May 1923, p. 19. Var 10 May 1923, p. 22.

THE SCHEMERS (African Americans)

Reol Productions Corp. **1922** [©Reol Productions Corp.; 19 Aug 1922; LU18157]. Si; b&w. Length undetermined. [Feature length assumed.].

Story Wallace Johnson.

Cast: Edna Morton, G. Edward Brown, Lawrence Chenault, Walter Thomas, Bob Slater, Orma Crosby.

Melodrama, African American. Paul Jackson, a black research chemist with a drug company, is close to success in his attempt to develop a chemical substitute for gasoline. Juan Bronson, who is the private secretary of John Davidson, the president of the company, conspires with Miguel Anderson to steal Paul's formula. Believing Paul to be carrying the formula, Bronson and Anderson kidnap him, but the papers are not on his person. Paul manages to call Isobel Benton, his sweetheart, and instructs her to go to his laboratory for the papers. Anderson overhears the conversation and also goes there, but Isobel outwits him and gets away with the formula. Anderson then frames Paul for the theft of some other important formulas, and Paul gives his formula back to Isobel for safekeeping. Anderson abducts Isobel, and Paul rescues her with the help of Davidson and a detective. Isobel proves Paul's innocence, and the detective tells Davidson that Bronson and Anderson are notorious criminals, wanted by a South American government. *African Americans. Chemists. Detectives. Drugs. Gasoline. Kidnapping. Laboratories. Secret formulas. Secretaries.*

SCHOOL BELLS see HEARTS OF MEN

SCHOOL FOR SABOTEURS see THEY CAME TO BLOW UP AMERICA

SCOTLAND YARD (foreign version) see EL IMPOSTOR

THE SCRAPPER (Swedish Ameicans)

Universal Film Mfg. Co.; Universal Special. 6 Feb **1922** [©Universal Film Mfg. Co.; 23 Jan 1922; LP17492]. Si; b&w. 5 reels, 4,491 ft.

Pres Carl Laemmle. *Dir* Hobart Henley. *Scen* E. T. Lowe, Jr. *Photog* Virgil Miller.

Source: Based on the short story "Malloy Campeador" by Ralph G. Kirk in *The Saturday Evening Post* (17 Sep 1921).

Cast: Herbert Rawlinson (*Malloy*), Gertrude Olmstead (*Eileen McCarthy*), William Welsh (*Dan McCarthy*), Frankie Lee (*The Kid*), Hal Craig (*Speed cop*), George McDaniels (*McGuirk*), Fred Kohler (*Oleson*), Edward Jobson (*Riley*), Al MacQuarrie (*Simms*), Walter Perry (*Rapport*).

Romance. Malloy, a young Irish construction engineer just out of college, is assigned to a project and immediately falls in love with the contractor's daughter, Eileen. The contractor's secretary, who also loves the girl, hires Oleson, a Swede, to work with Malloy and delay the building sufficiently to arouse the ire of the contractor. Under these conditions, however, Malloy works all the harder, never looking gloomy or restraining his Irish humor until the Swede comes to blows with him over a strike. After thus proving himself, he takes Eileen to the priest, and her resistance is overcome. *Contractors. Engineers– Civil. Irish. Secretaries. Swedish Americans.*

ETR 28 Jan 1922, p. 643. FD 22 Jan 1922. MPW 28 Jan 1922, p. 431. MPW 18 Feb 1922, p. 748.

THE SEA GOD (foreign version) see EL DIOS DEL MAR

SEA SPOILERS (Native Amricans, Native Alaskans)

Universal Productions, Inc. *Dist* Universal Productions, Inc. 28 Sep **1936**; Prod: began early Jul 1936 [©Universal Productions, Inc.; 21 Sep 1936; LP6606]. Sd (RCA Photophone Recording); b&w. 7 reels. 62-63 min. PCA cert no. 2474.

[*Prod* Trem Carr]. *Assoc prod* Paul Malvern. *Dir* Frank Strayer. *Asst dir* Glen Cook. *Scr* George Waggoner. *Orig story* Dorrell McGowan and Stuart E. McGowan. *Cine* A. J. Stout and Edward Snyder. *Art dir* E. R. Hickson. *Film ed* Hanson Fritch and Ray Lockert. *Mus dir* Herman Heller. *Sd tech* Joe Lapis. *Tech adv* Commander R. L. Jack, USCG.

Cast: JOHN WAYNE (*Bob Randall*), Nan Grey (*Connie Dawson*), William Bakewell (*Lieutenant Mays*), Fuzzy Knight (*Hogan*), Russell Hicks (*Phil Morgan*), George Irving (*Commander Mays*), Lotus Long (*Marie*), Harry Worth (*Nick Austin*), Ernest Hilliard (*Reggie*), George Humbert (*Hop Scotch*), Ethan Laidlaw (*Louie*), Chester Gann (*Oil*), Cy Kendall (*Detective*), Harrison Green (*Fats*).

Sea, Crime, Drama. [*Print viewed*]. Bob Randall is in temporary command of the Coast Guard ship *Niobe* when his commander's son, Lieutenant Mays, replaces him at the helm, and he is made first mate. When Bob's girl friend, Connie Dawson, is kidnapped by seal poachers who murder a wealthy yacht owner who protested their use of his yacht, Commander Mays orders the *Niobe* to search every vessel with which they come in contact. Lieutenant Mays searches a fishing boat owned by Hop Scotch, but believes the captain when he tells him his wife is sick in a bunk; in reality, Hop Scotch is working with the poachers and the "sick wife" is Connie lying under a blanket. An Eskimo nicknamed "Oil" signals the *Niobe* to come ashore because he has information for them regarding the poachers. Mays panics on the raft in rough water, a result of a childhood experience when he witnessed his mother's drowning, and he founders the raft. Bob rescues him, and when they return to the base, Mays resigns from his post and takes up flying for the Coast Guard because he is more comfortable in the air. At Bob's request, Commander Mays assigns him and fellow Coast Guard seaman Hogan to undercover work to locate the poachers. Hogan and Bob go in disguise as fishermen and search every local Alaskan island. One day, Mays notifies them by radio that he is landing due to engine trouble, and both man and plane disappear. On a nearby island, known to the Coast Guard as "pie a la mode," Bob contacts the poachers, but they imprison both him and Hogan with Mays, whom they had picked up earlier. Knowing the Coast Guard will soon find them, the head poacher, Phil Morgan, beats up both Hogan and Mays, who refuse to radio a false location to the base. After Morgan threatens to harm Connie if Bob does not comply, Bob sends a radio message in secret code to the base, informing them of the true location. The poachers arm themselves when the see the Coast Guard arriving, and are about to set off explosions in the mined harbor. A native girl friend of one of the poachers releases the hostages because she is resentful of the poachers, and Bob manages to throw a grenade into the cabin where the mine control is, killing Morgan. A fierce fight between the poachers and the Coast Guard ensues, and although Bob and Hogan are both injured, the Coast Guard is victorious. With the poachers eradicated, Hogan is promoted to bosun mate, and Bob is promoted and reunited with Connie. *Kidnapping. Poachers. Rivalry. United States. Coast Guard. Air pilots. Alaska. Fishermen. Islands. Mines. Military. Murder. Native Alaskans. Phobias. Radio broadcasting. Sea rescues. Seals (Animals). Secret codes. Undercover operations.*

Note: The working title of the film was *Casey of the Coast Guard.*

DV 25 Sep 1936, p. 3. *FD* 24 Oct 1936, p. 7. *HR* 13 Jul 1936, p. 9. *HR* 25 Oct 1936, p. 3. *MPD* 12 Oct 1936, p. 3. *MPH* 28 Nov 1936, p. 68. *Var* 28 Oct 1936, p. 15.

SEALED VALLEY (Native Americans)

Metro Pictures Corp.; A Metro DeLuxe Feature. *Dist* Metro Pictures Corp. 2 Aug **1915** [©Metro Pictures Corp.; 2 Aug 1915; LP6468]. Si; b&w. 5 reels.

Dir Lawrence B. McGill. *Cam* W. C. Thompson.

Source: Based on the novel *The Sealed Valley* by Hulbert Footner (New York, 1914).

Cast: Dorothy Donnelly (*Nahnya Crossfox*), J. W. Johnson (*Doctor Cowdray*), Rene Ditline (*Kitty Sholto*).

Western. Nahnya Crossfox leaves her Indian settlement in the Sealed Valley, an area encrusted with virgin gold, to find a doctor for her ailing mother. Upon seeing the gold Nahnya offers him in pre-payment, Doctor Cowdray of Fort Edward agrees to make the dangerous seven-day journey to the settlement. During the trip, Cowdray falls in love with Nahnya, but she refuses his proposal, fearing the consequences of a mixed blood marriage. After stumbling on a secret, gold-laden cavern, Cowdray returns to Fort Edward but, lovesick, decides to make the trip back to the valley. Cowdray is thrown into river rapids by two gold-hungry thieves but is rescued from drowning by Kitty Sholto, a miner's daughter. The thieves try to penetrate the valley but are repelled by a group of Indians led by Nahnya. Sacrificing her love for Cowdray, Nahnya encourages the doctor to marry Kitty and returns to her tribe alone. *Gold. Indians of North America. Racism. Self-sacrifice.* Caves. Miners. Physicians. Rescues. Rivers.

Note: According to publicity articles, this film was the first produced by Metro at their new studios in New York. Some reviews called this film *The Sealed Valley*.

Motog 31 Jul 1915, p. 200. *MPN* 31 Jul 1915, p. 7, 56. *MPN* 7 Aug 1915, p. 11. *MPW* 14 Aug 1915, p. 1232. *Var* 6 Aug 1915, p. 17.

THE SEARCHERS (Comanche, Native Americans, Swedish Americans)

C. V. Whitney Pictures, Inc.; The C. V. Whitney Picture. *Dist* Warner Bros. Pictures, Inc. 26 May **1956**; Prod: mid-Jun—mid-Aug 1955 [©C. V. Whitney Pictures, Inc.; 26 May 1956; LP8335]. Sd (RCA Sound Recording); col (Technicolor); VistaVision. 10,681 ft. 119 min. Passed by the National Board of Review. PCA cert no. 17787.

Exec prod Merian C. Cooper. *Assoc prod* Patrick Ford. *Dir* John Ford. *Asst dir* Wingate Smith. *Scr* Frank S. Nugent. *Photog* Winton C. Hoch. *2d unit photog* Alfred Gilks. *Spec eff* George Brown. *Technicolor color consultant* James Gooch. *Art dir* Frank Hotaling and James Basevi. *Film ed* Jack Murray. *Set dec* Victor Gangelin. *Props* Dudley Holmes. *Men's ward* Frank Beetson. *Women's ward* Ann Peck. *Mus* Max Steiner. *Orch* Murray Cutter. *Sd* Hugh McDowell and Howard Wilson. *Makeup* Web Overlander. *Hair dresser* Fae Smith. *Prod supv* Lowell J. Farrell. *Scr supv* Robert Gary. [*Stunts* Billy Cartledge, Chuck Hayward, Slim Hightower, Fred Kennedy, Frank McGrath, Chuck Roberson, Dale Van Sickle, Henry Wills and Terry Wilson].

Song(s): "The Searchers," music and lyrics by Stan Jones; "Skip to My Lou" and "Shall We Gather at the River," traditional.

Source: Based on the novel *The Searchers* by Alan Le May (New York, 1954).

Cast: JOHN WAYNE [(*Ethan Edwards*)], Jeffrey Hunter [(*Martin Pawley*)], Vera Miles [(*Laurie Jorgensen*)], Ward Bond [(*Capt. Rev. Samuel Johnson Clayton*)], Natalie Wood [(*Debbie Edwards*)], John Qualen [(*Lars Jorgensen*)], Olive Carey [(*Mrs. Jorgensen*)], Henry Brandon [(*Chief Scar*)], Ken Curtis [(*Charlie McCorry*)], Harry Carey, Jr. [(*Brad Jorgensen*)], Antonio Moreno [(*Emilio Figueroa*)], Hank Worden [(*Mose Harper*)], Beulah Archuletta [(*Look*)], Walter Coy [(*Aaron Edwards*)], Dorothy Jordan [(*Martha Edwards*)], Pippa Scott [(*Lucy Edwards*)], Pat Wayne [(*Lt. Greenhill*)], Lana Wood [(*Debbie Edwards as a child*)], [Robert Lyden (*Ben Edwards*)], [Bill Steele (*Ed Nesby*)], [Cliff Lyons (*Col. Greenhill*)], [Away Luna, Billy Yellow, Bob Many Mules, Exactly Sonnie Betsuie, Feather Hat, Jr., Harry Black Horse, Jack Tin Horn, Many Mules Son, Percy Shooting Star, Pete Gray Eyes, Pipe Line Begishe, Smile White Sheep (*Comanche*)].

Western. [*Print viewed*]. Martha Edwards opens the door of her cabin to the arid Texas landscape outside just as her brother-in-law, Ethan Edwards, approaches on horseback. Although it is 1868, Martha, her husband Aaron, their children Debbie, Lucy and Ben, and their adopted son, Martin Pawley, have not seen Ethan since he left them to fight for the Confederacy during the Civil War. Because Martin, an earnest but friendly young man, is part Cherokee, Ethan treats him coldly, even though it was he who rescued the lad when his parents were massacred in an Indian raid years earlier. Soon after Ethan's arrival, Rev. Samuel Johnson Clayton, a captain in the Texas Rangers as well as an old family friend, announces that the cattle of local rancher Lars Jorgensen have been stolen. Although Ethan is somewhat contemptuous of Sam, he joins Martin and a posse in pursuit of the thieves. When they find that the bulls have been killed with Comanche lances, Ethan declares that what the Indians really wanted was to lure the men away from home, thereby leaving their ranches open to attack. The men head back, but it is too late, for upon their arrival at the Edwards home, they discover that everyone has been brutally murdered except for Lucy and Debbie, who have been taken by the Comanche. The posse then sets out to find the girls. On finding a fresh Comanche grave, the men unearth the body but are shocked when Ethan shoots out its eyes. According to Comanche belief, Ethan explains, this will prevent the dead man's spirit from entering the spirit lands and force him to wander forever. The next day, the Comanche raiding party, led by Chief Scar, surrounds and attacks the posse, but the rangers drive them off. When Sam refuses to pursue the Comanche, explaining that they should be allowed to bury their dead in peace, Ethan explodes, and storms away from the men, intending to continue the search on his own. Both Martin, who endures Ethan's insults for the sake of his missing sisters, and young Brad Jorgensen, who loves Lucy, insist on joining him. One day, Brad returns from a scouting mission and joyfully announces that he has seen Lucy's blue dress at a nearby Indian encampment. Ethan reveals that he found Lucy's body and covered it, then angrily warns Brad never to ask him to reveal more. Wild with grief, Brad rides into the Indian camp and is shot to death while Ethan and Martin look on in horror. One year later, Ethan and Martin visit the Jorgensen ranch, and Ethan admits to Lars that they have lost the war party's trail. Lars replies that a Texas merchant named Futterman claims to have knowledge of Debbie's whereabouts. Meanwhile, Martin confides in Lars's daughter Laurie, who is in love with the young man, his fears that Ethan may kill Debbie because of her long association with the Comanche. To Laurie's dismay, Martin then leaves to follow Ethan, who has departed without a word. The two give Futterman money in exchange for the news that Debbie is held captive by Scar. That night, Futterman tries to shoot Martin and Ethan, but Ethan kills him and his henchmen, then retrieves his money. Time passes, and Laurie, who is now being courted by the bumbling Charlie McCorry, receives her only letter from Martin. In it, he confesses that he inadvertently "bought" a squaw he named Look, who trembled when he asked her about Scar, but left him an arrow fashioned of rocks before leaving him during the night. Later, Martin and Ethan discover that Look joined the Comanche but was killed when the band was raided by the U.S. Cavalry. Ethan and Martin examine the prisoners taken during the raid, but do not find Debbie among the several white women found living with the Indians. His voice tinged with loathing, Ethan watches the women and remarks, "They ain't white anymore. They're Comanche." In a New Mexico cantina, the two searchers meet Mose Harper, a dull-witted but loyal old friend who, in exchange for the promise of a comfortable rocking chair, introduces them to Mexican Emilio Figueroa, who claims to know Scar. Emilio takes them to Scar's village, where they finally meet their elusive enemy, who explains that because his two sons were killed by white men, he has taken many white scalps in revenge. One of his wives, a young white woman, then displays some of the scalps on a pole. Later that day, Ethan and Martin are visited by the woman, who, although admitting she is Debbie, begs them to leave and states that the Comanche are now her people. Disgusted that Debbie has been "living with a buck," Ethan aims his gun at her, but Martin steps between them. At that moment, Scar attacks, and while Debbie runs back to the Indians, Ethan and Martin escape. Ethan eventually recovers from a gunshot wound received during the encounter, and the two return to the Jorgensen ranch, just as Laurie and Charlie are about to exchange marriage vows. Laurie is thrilled at the return of the man she really loves, but Charlie is angry and challenges Martin to a fight. The altercation ends amicably, and Charlie calls off the wedding. Clayton, who was planning to marry the couple, assumes his role as the local lawman and arrests Martin and Ethan for the apparent murder of Futterman. Just then, cavalry lieutenant Greenhill arrives with orders

from Col. Greenhill, the flustered young officer's father. The rangers are to join the colonel in the field for a "joint punitive action" against the Comanche. Greenhill brings in Mose, who has been held captive by Scar. Injured and shaken, Mose reveals Scar's location, whereupon the men immediately prepare for a surprise attack. Worried that Debbie will be killed in the coming battle, Martin sneaks into Scar's camp to rescue her, even after Ethan reveals that one of the scalps on Scar's pole belonged to Martin's mother. When Martin enters Debbie's tent, she screams but admits that she wants to leave. When Scar appears, Martin shoots him, and Sam and the rangers attack the camp. Ethan finds Scar's lifeless body and scalps it, after which he begins to chase the frantic Debbie. As the battle rages around them, Martin tries to stop Ethan, but Ethan catches Debbie and, instead of killing her, suddenly lifts her into the air, tenderly cradles her in his arms and says, "Let's go home, Debbie." Sam and his rangers win the battle, after which everyone returns home. Ethan delivers Debbie to Mrs. Jorgensen's tearful embrace, and Laurie joyfully greets Martin, while Mose, looking on from his rocking chair, smiles. Ethan surveys the scene from the door of the house, turns around and slowly walks away. *Comanche Indians. Family honor. Family relationships. Kidnapping. Obsession. Racism. Revenge. Searches.* Attempted murder. Battles. Corpses. Fistfights. Indians of North America–Mixed blood. Letters. Long-lost relatives. Massacres. Mexican Americans. Ministers. Miscegenation. Ranchers. Rape. Reconciliation. Rescues. Swedish Americans. Texas. Texas Rangers. United States. Army. Cavalry. Weddings.

Note: Alan LeMay's best-selling novel, on which the film was based, was also serialized in *The Saturday Evening Post*. The *HR* review gives the film's running time as 110 min. According to a 1 Apr 1955 *HR* news item, some scenes were shot on location in Canada and Colorado. *HR* production charts noted that the majority of location shooting was done in Monument Valley, Utah, while studio sequences were shot at RKO-Pathé.

The Searchers was the first film produced by C. V. Whitney Pictures. Whitney, a well-known sportsman and millionaire, had previously been a partner with David O. Selznick in Pioneer Pictures and other ventures, including the production of *Gone With the Wind* and the formation of the Technicolor company. Whitney also had a long association with producer Merian C. Cooper, one of director John Ford's partners in Argosy Pictures.

Ford's son Patrick acted as the associate producer and his son-in-law, Ken Curtis, played "Charlie McCorry"; John Wayne's son Pat played "Lt. Greenhill"; and Lana Wood, who played "Debbie" as a young girl, was actress Natalie Wood's sister. Olive Carey and Harry Carey, Jr. were the widow and son of the late western actor Harry Carey, who was a long-time friend of and major influence on both Ford and Wayne. Many modern sources note that at the end of *The Searchers*, Wayne paid tribute to Carey by grasping his right elbow with his left hand, a gesture which Carey often made in his pictures.

The film received mostly positive reviews, although some reviewers commented negatively on the complexity of the "Ethan Edwards" character and the lack of explanation of his actions. According to an early plot synopsis contained in the film's file in the MPAA/PCA Collection at the AMPAS Library, Ethan's rescue of "Debbie" at the film's end was to be explained by his statement that she resembled her late mother, with whom Ethan was in love. Although many modern critics have noted an implied romantic relationship between Ethan and "Martha," it is only vaguely hinted at in the film.

The Searchers was a financial success, but it did not receive any Academy Award nominations. In 1972, however, a *Sight and Sound* poll of international film critics included it on a list of the twenty best films of all time, and a number of modern directors have cited the picture as an influence on their work. Modern sources include the following actors in the cast: Jack Pennick (*Private*); Peter Mamakos (*Futterman*); Ruth Clifford, Mae Marsh and Dan Borzage. In his autobiography, *Iron Eyes Cody* states that he also was in the cast. In 1991, Warner Bros. released a thirty-fifth anniversary video edition of the film, which included documentary footage of the making of *The Searchers*. The footage was broadcast on several segments of the 1956 *Warner Brothers Presents* television program.

Box 17 Mar 1956. *Box* 24 Mar 1956. *DV* 13 Mar 1956, p. 3, 9. *Exh* 21 Mar 1956, p. 4124. *FD* 13 Mar 1956, p. 6. *FIR* Jun–Jul 1956, pp. 284-285. *Har* 17 Mar 1956, p. 43. *HCN* 12 Nov 1954. *HR* 1 Apr 1955, p. 3. *HR* 17 Jun 1955, p. 11. *HR* 15 Jul 1955, p. 15. *HR* 12 Aug 1955, p. 13. *HR* 13 Mar 1956, p. 3, 11. *MPHPD* 31 Mar 1956, p. 843. *NYT* 31 May 1956, p. 21. *Var* 14 Mar 1956, p. 6.

SECOND FIDDLE *see* **MEN ARE SUCH FOOLS**

SECOND HAND ROSE (Jewish Americans)
. Universal Film Mfg. Co.; Universal-Special. 8 May **1922** [©Universal Film Mfg. Co.; 1 May 1922; LP17809]. Si; b&w. 5 reels, 4,433 ft.
Pres Carl Laemmle. *Dir* Lloyd Ingraham. *Story and scen* A. P. Younger. *Photog* Bert Cann.
Source: Suggested by the song "Second Hand Rose" by Grant Clarke and James F. Hanley (New York, 5 Jul 1921).
Cast: Gladys Walton (*Rose O'Grady*), George B. Williams (*Isaac Rosenstein*), Eddie Sutherland (*Nat Rosenstein*), Wade Boteler

(*Frankie "Bull" Thompson*), Max Davidson (*Abe Rosenstein*), Virginia Adair (*Rebecca Rosenstein*), Alice Belcher (*Rachel Rosenstein*), Jack Dougherty (*Terry O'Brien*), Walter Perry (*Tim McCarthy*), Bennett Southard (*Hawkins*), Camilla Clark (*Little Rosie*), Marion Faducha (*Little Nat*).
Romance. Rose, the adopted Irish daughter of the Rosensteins, Second Avenue pawnshop owners, is much sought after by Tim McCarthy, a wealthy Irish contractor many years her senior. Her adopted brother, Nat, is accused of stealing from his firm and is arrested and put in jail; Rosenstein, heartbroken, becomes seriously ill. McCarthy offers to pay Nat's bail provided that Rose will marry him; and although she is in love with Terry O'Brien, Rose consents to the marriage. Shortly afterward, Nat is released and proves his innocence; and McCarthy, realizing that Rose is unhappy with a "second-hand" husband, releases her so that she may marry young O'Brien. *Contractors. Courtship. Irish. Jews. New York City–East Side. Pawnbrokers.*
FD 7 May 1922. *MPW* 13 May 1922, p. 199. *MPW* 3 Jun 1922, p. 487. *Var* 10 Feb 1922, p. 35.

LE SECRET DU DOCTEUR *see* **EL SECRETO DEL DOCTOR**

SECRET ENEMIES (German Americans)
Warner Bros. Pictures, Inc.; A Warner Bros.–First National Picture. *Dist* Warner Bros. Pictures, Inc. 17 Oct **1942** [©Warner Bros. Pictures, Inc.; 7 Nov 1942; LP11675]. Sd (RCA Sound System); b&w. 5,167 ft. 56 or 58-59 min. PCA cert no. 8439.
Dir Ben Stoloff. *Dial dir* Harry Seymour. [*Asst dir* Don Page]. *Scr* Raymond L. Schrock. *Dir of photog* James Van Trees. *Spec eff* Edwin A. DuPar. *Art dir* Hugh Reticker. *Film ed* Doug Gould. *Set dec* Casey Roberts. *Gowns* Milo Anderson. *Sd* Oliver S. Garretson. *Makeup artist* Perc Westmore.
Cast: Craig Stevens (*Carl Becker*), Faye Emerson (*Paula Fengler*), John Ridgely (*John Trent*), Charles Lang (*Jim Jackson*), Robert Warwick (*Dr. Woodford* [*pseudonym of Otto Zimmer*]), Frank Reicher (*Henry Bremmer*), Rex Williams (*Hans*), Frank Wilcox (*Counter-espionage man*), George Meeker (*Rudolph*), Roland Drew (*Fred* [*the chauffeur*]), Addison Richards (*Travers*), Cliff Clark (*Capt. Jarrett*), Monte Blue (*Hugo*), [Fred Kelsey (*Malone*)], [Stacy Keach, Lee Powell, Lane Chandler, Victor Zimmerman (*Counter-espionage men*)], [Stuart Holmes (*Adolph*)], [Ray Teal (*Motor cop*)], [Ruth Ford (*Miss Charlton*)], [Sol Gorss (*Joe*)], [Leah Baird (*Maid*)], [Jack Mower (*Medical examiner*)], [Frank Mayo (*Patrolman's voice*)], [Marian Hall (*Secretary*)], [Ernst Hausman (*Bellhop*)], [Rudolf Steinbeck, Robert Stevenson (*Spies*)], [Rolf Lindau (*Spy radio operator*)], [Harry Lewis (*Radio operator*)], [Bill Hopper (*Ensign*)].
Espionage, World War II, Drama. [*Print viewed*]. On 8 December 1941, the day after the Japanese attack on Pearl Harbor, New York City hotel owner Henry Bremmer, anticipating that the Germans will declare war on the United States, begs his lawyer and friend, Carl Becker, to use his influence to get Henry's wife out of Germany. While Carl travels to Washington, D.C. on Henry's behalf, Fred, Henry's chauffeur, introduces Henry to Dr. Woodford, a Nazi spy. Woodford offers to help Henry if he will agree to work for the Nazis. At first, Henry refuses, but when Carl is unable to help him, Henry gives in to Woodford's demands. When Jim Jackson, a secret service agent on Woodford's trail and Carl's friend, arrives in New York, Carl suggests that he stay in Henry's hotel. Jim is recognized by other employees working with the Germans, however, and is murdered with poisoned gas. After Jim's body is discovered by his fellow agent, John Trent, the death is ruled a suicide, but Trent and Carl are both convinced that Jim was murdered. In order to avenge Jim's death, Carl joins the secret service. Trent is impressed by Carl's dedication and when the opportunity arises to go after Woodford, Trent and Carl head the investigation. Carl tells both Henry and Paula Fengler, the singer who is his fiancée, that he intends to find the men responsible for Jim's death. The Germans then order Henry to leave for his hunting lodge in the Adirondacks so that he cannot warn Carl. Later, the spies try to kill Carl. He pretends to be dead and, with Trent's help, overcomes the killers. Not realizing that Paula is also an enemy agent, Carl tells her that the arrested men are on a train heading for Washington, D.C., and she arranges for their escape. Thanks to a clue left behind by Henry, Carl realizes that the escaped men are hiding at the lodge. The secret service surround the lodge and a gunfight ensues. During the shooting, Henry sneaks into the

radio room and is killed when he signals the location of a German U-boat. Woodford escapes again and is followed by Carl to Paula's apartment. Carl kills Woodford and Paula pretends that she was forced into hiding him, but Carl reveals that he knows Paula was married to Woodford, whose real name is Otto Zimmer. When Carl and Trent learn that a U-boat was destroyed because of Henry's message, they realize that he has always been loyal to the United States. *Hotel owners. Lawyers. Nazis. Spies.* Adirondack Mountains. Engagements. Extortion. Gases, Asphyxiating and poisonous. Government agents. Hotels. Impersonation and imposture. Marriage–Secret. New York City. Singers. Submarine boats.

Box 22 Aug 1942. *DV* 17 Aug 1942, p. 3. *FD* 18 Aug 1942, p. 6. *HR* 17 Aug 1942, p. 7. *MPHPD* 22 Aug 1942, p. 854. *NYT* 1 Jan 1943, p. 27. *Var* 19 Aug 1942, p. 8.

THE SECRET GAME (German Americans)

Jesse L. Lasky Feature Play Co. *Dist* Paramount Pictures Corp. 3 Dec **1917** [©Jesse L. Lasky Feature Play Co.; 24 Nov 1917; LP11743]. Si; b&w. 5 reels.

Dir William C. de Mille. *Asst dir* Harry Haskin. *Story and scen* Marion Fairfax. *Cam* Charles Rosher.

Cast: Sessue Hayakawa (*Nara-Nara*), Jack Holt (*Major John Northfield*), Florence Vidor (*Kitty Little*), Mayme Kelso (*Miss Loring*), Raymond Hatton (*"Mrs. Harris"*), Charles Ogle (*Dr. Ebell Smith*).

Espionage, Drama. In the office of Major Northfield, the quartermaster of the Pacific Coast, a leak has been discovered which may endanger the safety of American transports that are secretly carrying troops across the Pacific. Nara-Nara, a Japanese detective, is assigned to the case because his country has guaranteed safety to these transport ships. Nara-Nara believes that Northfield is guilty, although in reality it is Northfield's secretary Kitty Little, a girl of German ancestry, who is passing information to Dr. Ebell Smith, a German agent. Nara-Nara falls in love with Kitty, but soon after discovers that she is the leak in the quartermaster's office. Kitty, who is in love with Northfield, is beginning to have doubts about her mission, but nevertheless, delivers a message to Smith's house. Nara-Nara follows, kills Smith, and then commits suicide rather than turn Kitty over to the police. Kitty, finally realizing that she had betrayed her country as well as her love for Northfield, forsakes her career as a spy and marries the vindicated Northfield. *Detectives. Espionage. German Americans. Japanese. Officers (Military). Secretaries. Spies. Suicide. Treason. United States. Army.* Foreign agents. Germans. Moral reformation. Pacific Ocean. Ships.

ETR 8 Dec 1917, p. 60. *MPN* 15 Dec 1917, p. 4223. *MPW* 15 Dec 1917, p. 1643. *MPW* 29 Dec 1917, p. 1684. *NYDM* 17 Nov 1917, p. 25. *NYDM* 8 Dec 1917, p. 18. *Var* 7 Dec 1917, p. 50. *Wid's* 6 Dec 1917, p. 775.

THE SECRET GIFT (Dutch Americans)

Universal Film Mfg. Co. *Dist* Universal Film Mfg. Co. 20 Sep 1920 [©Universal Film Mfg. Co.; 14 Sep 1920; LP15553]. Si; b&w. 5 reels, 4,890 ft.

Dir Harry L. Franklin. *Story and scen* George C. Hull. *Cam* Harold Janes.

Cast: Lee Kohlmar (*Jan*), Rudolph Christians (*Peter*), Doris Baker (*Bertha*), Gladys Walton (*Winnie*), Carl Gerrard (*Sydney Ullman*), Fred Gamble (*Benjamin Ullman*), Carl Ullman (*Larry*), Jennie Lee (*Aunt Sophie*), Verne Winters (*Timmy*).

Drama. Jan Saxe and Peter Harlingen, two young men from Holland, arrive in America with little orphan Bertha Kruger whom they have befriended during the trip and whom they both love. Bertha has come to live with her blind Aunt Sophie, and when Jan secretly raises $500 for an operation to restore her aunt's sight, Bertha marries Peter, believing that he was the donor of the "secret gift." Twenty years elapse, Bertha dies and Peter prospers as a businessman, while Jan attains contentment as a watchmaker. Peter's daughter Winnie frequently visits her Uncle Jan's shop where she meets and falls in love with Larry, a young man whom Jan has helped since boyhood. Winnie's father wishes her to marry Sidney Ullman, the son of a wealthy business associate. Jan disapproves of Peter's plan and, after much arguing, Peter finally realizes from his past experience that his daughter should marry for love rather than money. *Businessmen. Clock and watch makers. Dutch Americans. Fathers and daughters. Gifts. Immigrants. Orphans.* Aunts. Blindness. Cures. Operations, Surgical.

ETR 11 Sep 1920, p. 1616. *MPN* 18 Sep 1920, p. 2319. *MPW* 11 Sep 1920, p. 250. *NYMT* 5 Sep 1920. *Wid's* 5 Sep 1920, p. 25.

THE SECRET HOUR (Italian Americans)

Paramount Famous Lasky Corp. 4 Feb 1928 [©Paramount Famous Lasky Corp.; 4 Feb 1928; LP24988]. Si; b&w. 8 reels, 7,194 ft.

Pres Adolph Zukor and Jesse L. Lasky. *Dir* Rowland V. Lee. *Scen* Rowland V. Lee. *Titles* Julian Johnson. *Photog* Harry Fischbeck. *Film ed* Robert Bassler.

Source: Based on the play *They Knew What They Wanted* by Sidney Howard (New York, 24 Nov 1924).

Cast: Pola Negri (*Amy*), Jean Hersholt (*Tony*), Kenneth Thomson (*Joe*), Christian J. Frank (*Sam*), George Kuwa (*Ah Gee*), George Periolat (*Doctor*).

Romance, Drama. Tiring of bachelorhood, Tony, an elderly fruit grower, sends a photograph of Joe, his foreman, to capture the heart of an attractive waitress named Amy. She falls in love with the photograph, and Tony is left out in the cold when an automobile accident prevents him from meeting her train and he sends Joe instead. Joe and Amy abandon themselves to their magnetism for each other and secretly marry, regretting their action the next morning. Three months later, able to walk again, Tony is planning to marry Amy. They tell him their secret. Furious at first, Tony orders them from the house; later he relents and forgives them, seeing that it was his fault for substituting Joe's photograph. *Automobile accidents. Bachelors. Italian Americans. Marriage. Mistaken identity. Waitresses.*

Note: In 1930, M-G-M produced a film based on the same source, entitled *A Lady to Love* (see above), directed by Victor Seastrom and starring Vilma Banky and Edward G. Robinson, and in 1940, RKO produced *They Knew What They Wanted* (see below), directed by Garson Kanin and starring Carole Lombard and Charles Laughton.

Var 14 Mar 1928, p. 25.

THE SECRET OF EVE (Gypsies)

Popular Plays and Players, Inc. *Dist* Metro Pictures Corp. 26 Feb **1917** [©Popular Plays and Players, Inc.; 24 Feb 1917; LP10254]. Si; b&w. 5 reels.

Dir Perry Vekroff. *Scen* Wallace C. Clifton. *Story* Aaron Hoffman. *Cam* Neil Bergman.

Cast: Madame Olga Petrova (*Eve, in the Garden of Eden/Hagar, the gypsy woman/Eve, the Quakeress/Eve, the wife of Brandon*), Arthur Hoops (*Arthur Brandon*), William L. Hinckley (*Robert Blair*), Edward Roseman (*Fothergill*), Laurie Mackin (*Deborah, wife of Fothergill*), Florence Moore (*Rosa*), George Morrell (*Beppo*).

Drama. Hagar, a gypsy woman, is determined that her child Eve shall have a good chance in life, so she leaves her on the doorstep of the Fothergills, a Quaker family who raise her as their own daughter. Grown to womanhood, Eve longs for a more exciting life and so falls easy prey to Arthur Brandon, an extravagant man of the world. Eve marries Brandon then discovers too late that her husband is a drunkard who abuses the workers in his factory. She is moved by the nobility of Richard Blair, a young philanthropist who is investigating the conditions of Brandon's factory and who fights for the rights of a little girl who is blinded while working in the factory. Beppo, the girl's father, assaults Brandon for his daughter's injuries and is arrested. Brandon, misunderstanding his wife's friendship with Blair, accuses her of infidelity, thus driving her from the house. Eve then enlists in the cause of charity to combat her husband's abuses. After Beppo's release he seeks out and kills Brandon, thus removing all obstacles between Blair and Eve. *Employer-employee relations. Reformers. Alcoholics. Blindness. Children. False accusations. Fights. Foster parents. Gypsies. Murder. Philanthropists. Quakers.*

ETR 10 Mar 1917, p. 975. *MPN* 10 Mar 1917, p. 1575. *MPN* 3 Mar 1917, p. 1589. *MPN* 10 Mar 1917, p. 1410. *NYDM* 3 Mar 1917, p. 27. *Wid's* 8 Mar 1917, pp. 159-60.

THE SECRET OF THE DEATH see COSÌ È LA VITA

THE SECRET OF THE PUEBLO (Native Americans, Pueblo)

William Steiner Productions, Inc. 15 Feb **1923** [©William Steiner Productions, Inc.; 5 Jan 1923; LU18556]. Si; b&w. 5 reels, 4,670 ft.

Dir Neal Hart. *Story* Alvin J. Neitz. *Photog* Jake Badaracco and William Steiner, Jr.

Cast: Neal Hart (*Bob Benson*), Hazel Deane (*Ruth Bryson*), Tom Grimes (*Pueblo Charlie*), Monte Montague.

Western. "Scenes are laid in Arizona. Story deals with the mystic and weird cliff-dwelling Pueblo Indians. Bob Benson, a young knight of the plains, locates the secret entrance to the Indians' memorial altar room where the heroine is held captive. He rescues her from the hands of the Pueblos. Action of picture embraces hard-riding

cowboys, fights and escapes, with a romance running throughout." (*MPNBG* 4 Apr 1923, p. 90.). *Arizona. Cowboys. Pueblo Indians.*
  MPNBG 4 Apr 1923, p. 90.

SECRET OF THE WASTELANDS (Chinese Americans)
  Paramount Pictures, Inc. *Dist* Paramount Pictures, Inc. **1941**; Prod: early May—mid-May 1941 [©Paramount Pictures, Inc.; 1 Nov 1941; LP10813]. Sd (Western Electric Wide Range System); b&w. 7 reels, 5,913 ft. 66 min.
  Series: Hopalong Cassidy.
  Prod Harry Sherman. *Assoc prod* Lewis J. Rachmil. *Dir* Derwin Abrahams. *Asst dir* John Sherwood. *Scr* Gerald Geraghty. *Photog* Russell Harlan. *Art dir* Ralph Berger. *Supv ed* Sherman A. Rose. *Ed* Fred Feitshans, Jr. *Set dec* Emile Kuri. *Ward* Earl Moser. *Mus dir* Irvin Talbot. *Mus score* John Leipold. *Sd* Chas. Althouse. *Sd rec* General Service Studios.
  Song(s): "I Can't Play My Banjo with Susannah on My Knee," composer undetermined.
  Source: Based on characters created by Clarence E. Mulford and the novel *Secret of the Wastelands* by Bliss Lomax (New York, 1940).
  Cast: William Boyd (*Hopalong Cassidy*), Andy Clyde (*California Carlson*), Brad King (*Johnny Nelson*), Soo Yong (*Moy Soong*), Barbara Britton (*Jennifer Kendall*), Douglas Fowley (*Slade Salters*), Keith Richards (*Clay Elliott*), Richard Loo (*Quan*), Lee Tung Foo (*Doy Kee*), Gordon Hart (*Dr. Birdsall*), Earl Gunn (*Clanton*), Ian McDonald [sic] (*Hollister*), John Rawlings (*Williams*), Roland Got (*Ying*), Hal Price (*Prof. Waldo Stubbs*), Jack Rockwell (*Sheriff Mulhall*).
  Western. [*Print viewed*]. In a western town, Hopalong Cassidy and his ranch hands, Johnny Nelson and California Carlson, meet a stagecoach carrying archaeologist Dr. Birdsall, his niece, Jennifer Kendall, Professor Stubbs and Clay Elliott of the U.S. Mint. Birdsall has hired Hoppy and his friends to lead his expedition to the ancient desert ruins of Pueblo Grande. Before their departure, Jennifer hires Doy Kee, a Chinese cook, to accompany them. Unknown to Hoppy, the expedition is being watched both by Moy Soong, owner of a Chinese trading company, and lawyer Slade Salters, who claims to represent the Chinese community. Salters sends three cohorts to follow the expedition, and Hoppy starts to worry when a knife thrown by a Chinese man narrowly misses him. While en route to Pueblo Grande, Elliott explains to Hoppy that he has come into possession of some gold nuggets whose source he cannot identify. Elliott suspects that the Chinese community is involved because similar nuggets have been sold through Chinese shopkeepers. Later that night, someone knocks out California and causes the horses to stampede through camp, but Hoppy awakens in time to alert everyone. The next day, a wheel falls off Doy Kee's wagon and Hoppy finds evidence of sabotage. However, Birdsall refuses to abandon the project and the expedition finally reaches Pueblo Grande. While digging in the ruins, Stubbs finds a relatively new statue of Buddha buried next to some ancient remains. Hoppy warns everyone not to stray from camp, but Jennifer disobeys his order, and is surprised when Doy Kee threatens her with a gun so she will not climb above the ridge. The second time Jennifer slips away, however, she disappears behind a secret wall in the ruins. After failing to find her, Hoppy discovers that their water supply has been depleted, and that Doy Kee has been murdered and a charm left on his body. Hoppy insists that the group go to the town of Piute to get water, and when Salters learns about the expedition's activities, he plots to take over the dig for his own profit while the expedition is in town. Hoppy, meanwhile, earns Johnny's anger after he refuses to go to the sheriff about Jennifer's disappearance. Instead, Hoppy goes to the Chinese mercantile and meets with Moy Soong, who agrees to return Jennifer in exchange for Hoppy's silence. Hoppy is followed into the desert by the sheriff and his posse, who have been alerted by Johnny, and by Salters and his gang. When the posse rides up, the Chinese believe that Hoppy has broken his word, but he helps them escape to the ruins. A gunfight erupts among the ruins until the Chinese take Hoppy and his friends behind the secret wall and into a long corridor, which leads to a secret valley. Hoppy is surprised by the appearance of the lush valley, and learns that the Chinese have cultivated it for years, and have supported it with the gold they have mined adjacent to the ruins. After seeing that Jennifer is unharmed, Hoppy meets with Moy Soong, and the valley's elder, Soo Chen, who seek his advice on how to buy the property. As they are all native Californians, Hoppy explains that they simply need to stake a claim

on the mine, and that the land is in the public domain. Elliott, whose only thought is of the gold, attempts to flee, but Hoppy knocks him out. The sheriff and his men then infiltrate the valley, and Moy Soong sends Hoppy to Piute to file the claim for her. Elliott again tries to escape, but is shot. Hoppy races to Piute, reaching town at the same time as Salters. After knocking Salters out in a fistfight, Hoppy files a claim on behalf of the Chinese Americans. Later, Moy Soong expresses her gratitude to Hoppy on behalf of her people, and Birdsall continues his archaeological dig. *Archaeologists. Chinese Americans. Expeditions. Land claims. Lawyers. Ranchers. Aged men. Claim jumpers. Cooks. Deserts. Gold. Mines. Missing persons. Murder. Posses. Ruins. Sabotage. Secret societies. Sheriffs. Stampedes. Traders.*
  Note: The working title of this film was *Ghosts of Rimrock*. Actor Ian MacDonald's surname is misspelled "McDonald" in the opening credits. The picture marked the feature film debut of Brad King, and the introduction of his character "Johnny Nelson" to the Hopalong Cassidy series. "Johnny" replaced the character "Lucky Nelson," played by Jimmy Ellison and Russell Hayden. For additional information on the series, consult the Series Index, and see the entry for *Hop-Along Cassidy* in *AFI Catalog of Feature Films, 1931-40*; F3.1990.
    Box 27 Sep 1941. *DV* 23 Sep 1941. *FD* 29 Sep 1941, p. 11. *HR* 19 Mar 1941, p. 2. *HR* 2 May 1941, p. 14. *HR* 9 May 1941, p. 24. *HR* 16 May 1941, p. 6. *HR* 23 Sep 1941, p. 3. *MPHPD* 27 Sep 1941, p. 287.

SECRET OF TREASURE MOUNTAIN (Native Americans, Apache)
  Columbia Pictures Corp. *Dist* Columbia Pictures Corp. Jun **1956**; Prod: 3 Dec—14 Dec 1955 [©Columbia Pictures Corp.; 26 Jun 1956; LP6613]. Sd (Westrex Recording System); b&w; 1.85. 9 reels, 6,094 ft. 66-68 min. PCA cert no. 17755.
  Prod Wallace MacDonald. *Dir* Seymour Friedman. *Asst dir* Eddy Saeta. *Story and scr* David Lang. *Cam* Benjamin H. Kline. *Art dir* Carl Anderson. *Film ed* Edwin Bryant. *Set dec* Charles Vassar. *Mus cond* Mischa Bakaleinikoff. *Sd* Edward Levinson.
  Cast: Valerie French (*Audrey Lancaster*), Raymond Burr (*Cash Larsen*), William Prince (*Robert Kendall*), Lance Fuller (*Juan Alvarado*), Susan Cummings (*Tawana*), Pat Hogan (*Vahoe*), Reginald Sheffield (*Edward Lancaster*), Rodolfo Hoyos (*Francisco Martinez*), Paul McGuire (*Sheriff*), Tom Hubbard (*Sam*), Boyd Stockman (*Stub McCurdy*).
  Western. [*Not viewed*]. While being pursued by a posse for damage he caused during a minor saloon brawl, adventurer Robert Kendall accidentally crosses paths with two bank robbers, Francisco Martinez and Cash Larsen, and escapes with them into an isolated mountain fortress. There they discover two cabins set in a clearing on a rocky plateau. One is inhabited by Edward Lancaster, a British gold prospector, and his daughter Audrey, who welcome the strangers. The owner of the other cabin is Juan Alvarado, a halfbreed student of Indian lore, who shuns the newcomers. Other members of Juan's household are Tawana, his Apache housekeeper, and Vahoe, his Apache aide, who secretly envies Juan because Tawana harbors an unrequited love for him. That night, Kendall tells Audrey about his companions and reassures her that he is a harmless adventurer. When Larsen notices a unique gold cross hidden in a drawer in Juan's house, Lancaster tells him that according to Indian legend, a fortune in gold was buried in the hills by the Spaniards 200 years earlier, and explains that the cross may be one of the keys to locating the treasure. After Larsen makes improper advances to Tawana, Vahoe confronts him outside the cabin. As Larsen is about to draw his gun, Kendall jumps him, sending the two men tumbling down an embankment. Their fall loosens some rocks, allowing Kendall to uncover another cross, which he hides in his shirt. Thrown out because of Larsen's crude behavior, Larsen and Martinez leave at daybreak. Later, while exploring the countryside, Audrey and Kendall find some unusual rock formations, and in a rock archway, Kendall notices that his body throws a shadow across the area of Juan's cabin. Vahoe, who has been secretly following Audrey and Kendall, informs Juan that they have discovered the key to the secret mountain and insists that they be eliminated. When Juan balks, Vahoe tells him that he has been sent by the Apache chiefs to insure that Juan keep his sacred oath to prevent white men from finding the hidden treasure. To stop Vahoe and Tawana from exposing his failure, Juan kills them both. Meanwhile, Kendall and Lancaster are preparing to dynamite the mountain when Larsen returns. After admitting that he killed Martinez, Larsen demands his share of the treasure. Having fallen in love with Audrey, Juan tells her of the treasure and offers to share it with her if she will marry him. Audrey, who is in love with Kendall, hurries to warn him and her father. As soon as she departs, Larsen captures Juan and starts

to torture him into revealing the location of the gold. Just then, Kendall arrives and during the ensuing struggle, he sends Larsen careening to his death in the rocks below. When Kendall promises Juan that he will no longer seek the gold, Juan, seemingly in gratitude, invites Kendall, Lancaster and Audrey to his cabin and opens a secret panel that reveals the treasure vaults in a cave below. Once in the cave, Juan pulls out a gun and says that the secret of the gold must die with them. After Juan lights a dynamite fuse, Kendall knocks him off balance and escapes with Audrey and her father. A series of dynamite blasts then seals Juan and the gold in the cave for eternity. *Adventurers. Apache Indians. Buried treasure. Fugitives. Indians of North America–Mixed blood. Legends. Murder. Thieves.* Caves. English. Explosions. Fathers and daughters. Housekeepers. Jealousy. Murder. Prospectors. Unrequited love.

Note: The *Var* review commented that the plot of this film resembles that of the 1949 Columbia picture *Lust for Gold*, and speculated that some of the stock footage included in this film was taken from the earlier picture.

Box 26 May 1956. *DV* 16 May 1956, p. 7. *Exb* 30 May 1956, pp. 4165-66. *FD* 24 May 1956, p. 14. *Har* 19 May 1956, p. 79. *HR* 16 May 1956, p. 3. *MPHPD* 19 May 1956, p. 898. *Var* 30 May 1956, p. 18.

THE SECRET SIN (Chinese Americans)

Jesse L. Lasky Feature Play Co. *Dist* Paramount Pictures Corp. 21 Oct **1915** [©Jesse L. Lasky Feature Play Co.; 12 Oct 1915; LU6619]. Si; b&w. 5 reels.

Dir Frank Reicher. *Asst dir* Frank Lidel. *Story and scen* Margaret Turnbull. *Cam* Walter Stradling. *Art dir* Wilfred Buckland.

Cast: Blanche Sweet (*Edith Martin/Grace Martin*), Hal Clements (*Dan Martin*), Alice Knowland (*Mrs. Martin*), Sessue Hayakawa (*Lin Foo*), Thomas Meighan (*Jack Herron*).

Drama. Edith Martin and her twin sister Grace work as seamstresses to help their unemployed father make ends meet. An invalid, Grace falls prey to the temptations of Chinatown opium and becomes an addict, a condition worsened by a misguided physician who prescribes morphine to ease her pain. After Mr. Martin strikes oil, the family enjoys a new prosperity and the sisters meet the eligible Jack Herron, a fellow oil prospector. To Grace's dismay, Jack falls in love with Edith and in her jealousy, Grace tells Jack that Edith, not she, has a drug problem. Hinting that her sister will soon need more morphine, Grace arranges for a dinner in Chinatown with the couple. While her sister and Jack dance, Grace slips away to an opium den. Edith follows her, but ends up in the wrong den and is arrested in an ensuing drug raid. After he bails her out of jail, Edith takes an angry Jack to search for Grace and stumbles across her half-conscious body lying in the street. The truth about the sisters is revealed, and after sending Grace to a sanitarium in the country, Jack and Edith happily wed. *Chinatowns. Drug addicts. Jealousy. Sisters. Twins.* Drugs. False accusations. Oilmen. Opium dens. Physicians. Police raids. Seamstresses.

Note: A Paramount publicity release credits Loyola O'Connor, not Alice Knowland, in the role of Mrs. Martin.

Motog 13 Nov 1915, p. 1050. *MPN* 4 Sep 1915, p. 60. *MPN* 11 Sep 1915, p. 72. *MPN* 25 Sep 1915, p. 11, 144. *MPN* 6 Nov 1915, p. 88. *MPW* 30 Oct 1915, p. 983, 1034. *NYDM* 13 Nov 1915, p. 32.

THE SECRET SORROW (African Americans)

Reol Productions Corp. 1 Oct **1921**. Si; b&w. 6 reels, 5,544 ft.

Story J. C. Brown.

Cast: George Edward Brown, Percy Verwayen, Edna Morton, Lawrence Chenault, Inez Clough, Ida Anderson.

African American, Drama. [*Not viewed*]. Anne Morgan, a poverty-stricken black woman, decides to give up one of her two sons and finds a prominent black doctor willing to adopt him. The doctor treats the child, whom he names Arthur, as his own son and sends him to law school, after which he becomes the assistant district attorney of New York. Meanwhile, the other brother, Joe, a boxer and gangster, has joined the city's criminal underworld and works for crooked politician Sam Dungan. When a murder takes place in one of the dives that Dungan owns, Joe is charged with the crime, and Arthur is assigned to the case as the prosecuting attorney. During the trial, Arthur calls Anne to the stand, not realizing that she is his own mother, and accuses her of moral degeneracy as she tries to paint an evil portrait of Joe. Dungan's daughter Grace, who is Arthur's sweetheart, discovers the truth about the brothers, and after finding the real murderer, sees that the mother and the two boys are reunited. She then joins the happy family as Arthur's bride. *Adoption. African*

Americans. Boxers. Brothers. District attorneys. Gangsters. Long-lost relatives. Murder. Political corruption. Politicians. Poverty. Widows. New York City. Physicians. Romance. Trials.

Note: This film was also known as *Secret Sorrow*. An ad in the George P. Johnson Collection at the UCLA Special Collections Library referred to J. C. Brown as a "celebrated race author." According to modern sources, the cast also included J. H. Woodson and Henry Pleasant.

EL SECRETO DEL DOCTOR (Spanish language)

Cinéstudio Continental; controlled by Paramount Publix Corp. *Dist* Paramount Publix Corp. Nov **1930**; Los Angeles opening: 8 Nov 1930; *Prod:* Jun 1930 at Paramount studios in Joinville, France. Sd (Western Electric); b&w. 6,132 ft. 68 min. *Country of origin* France. Spanish language.

Dir Adelqui Millar. *Scr* William C. de Mille. *Span dial* Camilo Aldao.

Source: Based on the play *Half an Hour* by James Matthew Barrie (London, 29 Sep 1913).

Cast: Eugenia Zúffoli (*Lillian Garson*), Félix de Pomés (*Richard Garson*), Tony D'Algy (*Hugo Colman*), Manuel Soto (*Dr. Brody*), Mercedes Servet (*Sra. Redding*), José Bódalo (*Sr. Redding*), Carmelita Fernández García (*Suzy*).

Melodrama. [*Not viewed*]. Lillian Garson, a woman of noble English ancestry who is married to a commoner, has written a letter to her husband, ending their marriage. She intends to take a trip to Egypt with her lover, Hugo Colman, who is from the same social class as she. However, just as they are about to leave, Colman is killed in an automobile accident. On the advice of a doctor friend, Lillian hurries to recover the letter to her husband. After destroying the evidence of her unfaithfulness, Lillian continues her life as if nothing has happened. *Class distinction. Infidelity. Letters. Marriage. Physicians.* Automobile accidents.

Note: This film is a Spanish-language version of the 1929 Paramount film *The Doctor's Secret* (see *AFI Catalog of Feature Films, 1921-30*; F2.1378), which was directed by William C. de Mille and starred Ruth Chatterton and H. B. Warner. The original film was shot in the U.S., but in 1930, Paramount made seven foreign-language versions at their Joinville studio near Paris, France. Of the seven versions, only the Spanish, Italian, French and Hungarian versions appear to have been released in the U.S., according to NYSA records. The working title of the Spanish-language version was *Media hora*. Some sources indicate that writer Josep Carner Ribalta wrote a Spanish version for production in Hollywood, but it has not been determined if any of that screenplay was used in the version produced in France. A Swedish version, *Doktorns Hemlighet*, was directed by John W. Brunius and starred Ivan Hedqvist and Pauline Brunius. A Czech version, *Tajemstvi lékarovo*, was directed by Julius Lébl and starred Anna Sedláčková and Václav Vydra, while a Polish adaptation, *Tajemnica lekarza*, was directed by Ryszard Ordyński and starred Maria Gorczyńska and Paweł Owerłło.

Other language version(s):

Il segreto del dottore (Italian language)

1930. San Francisco (CA) opening: 1 Jan 1931; Sd (Western Electric); b&w. 6,498 ft. 72 min.; Country of origin: France. Italian language.

Dir Jack Salvatori.

Italian-language cast: Soava Gallone, Alfredo Robert, Lamberto Picasso, Antonio Niccodemi. [*Italian version not viewed*]

Le secret du docteur (French language)

1930. Paris (France) opening: early Oct 1930; Sd (Western Electric); b&w. 6,613 ft. 73 or 77 min.; Country of origin: France. French language.

Dir Charles de Rochefort. *Adpt and French dial* Denys Amiel. *Photog* Ted Pahle. *Film ed* Roger Capellani, Jacques de Casembroot and Jacques Mirande.

French-language cast: Marcelle Chantal (*Liliane Garner*), Max Maxudian (*Dr. Brady*), Léon Bary (*Richard Garner*), Jean Bradin (*Jean Colman*), Hubert Daix (*Mr. Reading*), Alice Tissot (*Mrs. Reading*), Odette Joyeux (*Suzy, the maid*). [*French version not viewed*]

Az orvos titka (Hungarian language)

1930. Sd (Western Electric); b&w. 6,972 ft. 77 min.; Country of origin: France. Hungarian language.

Dir Tibor Hegedüs. *Adpt* Zsolt Harsányi.

Hungarian-language cast: Arthur Somlay, Gizi Bajor, Dezső Kertész, Blanke [?] Szombathelyi, Sándor Góth, Gusztáv Pártos, Vilma Gömöry, Eva Horváth, Odón Bárdi. [*Hungarian version not viewed*].

Var 29 Oct 1930.

THE SECRETS OF WU SIN (Chinese Americans)

Invincible Pictures Corp.; A George R. Batcheller Production. *Dist* Chesterfield Motion Pictures Corp. 15 Dec **1932**; Prod: at Universal City. Sd (RCA Photophone); b&w. 65 min. Passed by the National Board of Review.

Pres MAURY M. COHEN. *Dir* Richard Thorpe. *Asst dir* Melville Shyer. *Story* Basil Dickey. *Adpt and cont* William J. McGrath. *Dial* Betty Burbridge. *Photog* M. A. Anderson. *Ed* Vera Wade. [*Sd* Pete Clark]. *Sd rec* Richard Tyler.

Cast: Lois Wilson (*Mona Gould*), Grant Withers (*James Manning*), Dorothy Revier (*Margaret King*), Robert Warwick (*Roger King*), Tetsu Komai (*Wu Sin*), Toshia Mori (*Miao Lin*), Richard Loo (*Charlie San*), Luke Chan (*Luke*), [James] Wang [(*Pete*)], [Eddie Boland].

Detective, Newspaper, Drama. [*Print viewed*]. Managing editor James Manning saves Mona Gould from attempted suicide, and after discovering that she is a destitute writer, he hires her to write for the *Tribune*. He assigns reporter Eddie Morgan to investigate Chinese immigrants entering San Francisco illegally. Having previously lived near Chinatown, Mona secretly follows Eddie. She is familiar with many of the locals, including Miao Lin, whose guardian, Wu Sin, will not allow her to marry Charlie San, a young bank employee. Always one step ahead of Eddie, Mona discovers that the smugglers bring people in on the ship *Hirondella* and transfer them to a private truck. Mona hires a detective who finds out that the *Hirondella* is owned by millionaire Roger King, whose daughter Margaret is engaged to James. Mona goes to Margaret to warn her of her father's illegal dealings, but Margaret refuses to believe her. Margaret informs her father, who asks Wu Sin for protection. Wu Sin, head of the Tongs, manages the entry of the illegal immigrants. He calls a meeting of the Tongs, who choose Charlie San to kill James. Charlie is horrified by his assignment, but he agrees to do it when Wu Sin says his reward will be marriage to Miao Lin. A newspaperman through and through, James agrees to print the story about Margaret's father even though it means losing his engagement to Margaret. Miao Lin confesses to Mona about Charlie's assignment, and when Mona and James go to Mona's apartment one night, he is shot by Charlie. He receives only a flesh wound, however, and because Mona knows Charlie's story, they understand his motives. Police discover Wu Sin dead in his home. Roger King and Margaret leave on the *Hirondella*. After Charlie San is granted probation, he and Miao Lin marry, while at the same time, James and Mona marry, after having finally acknowledged their love for each other. *Aliens, Illegal. Chinese Americans. Editors. Reporters. Smuggling. Tongs (Secret societies). Attempted suicide. Detectives. Engagements. Fathers and daughters. Gunshot wounds. Hired killers. Millionaires. Poverty. San Francisco (CA)–Chinatown. Wards and guardians.*

Note: According to modern sources, Wu Sin commits suicide, however, this scene was not included in the viewed print. Modern sources add the following credits: *Art dir*, Edward C. Jewell; *Film ed*, Roland Reed; *Mus dir*, Abe Meyer; *Cast*: Lafe McKee (*Minister*) and Henry Hall (*Informant*).

FD 3 Feb 1933, p. 6. *Var* 28 Feb 1933, p. 39.

SEE HOW THEY RUN *see* **BRIGHT ROAD**

SEGREGATION AND THE SOUTH (African Americans)

Fund for the Republic. *Dist* Contemporary. **1957**. Sd; b&w. 52 min. *Prod* George M. Martin, Jr.

Educational/Cultural. [*Not viewed*]. The effects of the Supreme Court's 1954 ruling against the segregation of schools and subsequent integration orders are examined. *African Americans. Education. Segregation. United States–South. United States. Supreme Court.*

Note: This film was listed in an educational film catalog. No additional information about its release has been located.

IL SEGRETO DEL DOTTORE *see* **EL SECRETO DEL DOCTOR**

IL SEGRETO DI UNA MORTA *see* **COSÌ È LA VITA**

DIE SEHNSUCHT JEDER FRAU *see* **A LADY TO LOVE**

SEI TU L'AMORE (Italian language)

Italotone. *Dist* Capital Film Exchange. Nov **1930**; New York opening: 14 Nov 1930. Sd; b&w. 7,800 ft. 75 min. Italian language. *Dir* Dr. Alfredo Sabato. *Mus dir* Maestro Cabarra.

Song(s): "Is It You, Love?," and other songs, composers undetermined.

Source: Based on a play by P. A. Mazzolotti (production undetermined).

Cast: Luisa Caselotti (*Giorgina*), Alberto Rabagliati (*Mario, the painter*), Enrico Armetta (*The exporter*), Mario De Domenicis (*The philosopher*), Augusto Galli (*Roger, the engineer*), Ines Palange (*The modiste*), Luigi Colombo (*James, the butler*).

Comedy-drama, Musical comedy. [*Not viewed*]. As Roger, Raffaele and Claude, three wealthy Italian men, play cards with their girlfriends, James, the butler, and his wife Placida inform them that the girl from the top floor, Giorgina, has attempted suicide. Giorgina is an orphan who works for a dressmaker, and upon waking she tells the group her sorrowful story: She dreamed that she shot and killed an unfaithful lover and his new girlfriend. In her dream she ran away across the rooftops and then grabbed an electric wire. Upon awakening, she discovered that the wire was actually a gas pipe and that she was gassing herself. The women are a little disappointed at the story, but the men are intrigued. They leave Giorgina some clothes and four-hundred lire, but the sweet girl only takes fifty, leaving the rest for James and Placida. Dressed up in the clothes left for her, Giorgina looks like a "coquette" when she answers the door and meets Mario, a handsome young painter who has come to the house to pick up the plans which Roger, a successful engineer, has left for him. Mario is nervous about talking to Giorgina because he believes that she must be Roger's mistress, but then discovers that she is the girl from the top floor who almost killed herself. One day, Giorgina leaves the dress shop early for a date with Mario. The young man declares his love, but Giorgina says that she will never again trust any man. Later, Claude, Roger, and Raffaele go to the dress shop where they purchase dresses, hats and other accessories for Giorgina, although she believes that they are for another woman. Giorgiana's shop friends, Rita and Juccia, think that Giorgiana has landed a rich lover, and when the girl realizes that the men have bought the items for her, she insists that men never offer anything to a woman for free. The trio reply that they want nothing in return except Giorgina's promise not to betray "the triumvirate," as they term their group. Later, at a masked party thrown for Giorgina, Claude, Roger, and Raffaele all try to get the young girl's attentions, but she informs them that they must find a more moral solution to the problem of their foursome. Everyone at the party, including Mario, who earlier proposed to Giorgina and was accepted, believes that she is a coquette and will choose one of the three men as her protector. Mario becomes angry, but Giorgina swears that she is innocent, despite appearances. Giorgina's plan all along has been to go into business with the rich men by having them buy her the dress shop. She meets them at the shop to examine the books and tells them that Giorgina and Co. must be reorganized financially and morally, but that the world may continue to believe that she is a coquette, as that is her biggest asset. Mario arrives and apologizes, and Raffaele, Claude and Roger go off to find another attempted suicide to save. *Attempted suicide. Charity. Idle rich. Italy. Women in business. Dreams. Dressmakers. Engineers. Masked balls. Orphans. Proposals (Marital). Romantic rivalry. Rumors.*

Note: This film was reviewed in *FD* under the title *Is This Love?* Although the film included several songs in addition to the title song, none of the titles or composers could be verified. The plot summary is based on a dialogue continuity deposited with the NYSA. Contemporary reviews state that the film was shot in Hollywood, and the *Var* review states that the film was the first Italian dialogue film to be made in that city. The *Var* review also states that the film cost $150,000 and that the lead actress, Luisa Caselotti, was from the Columbia Opera Co.

FD 16 Nov 1930. *NYT* 18 Nov 1930, p. 28. *Var* 19 Nov 1930.

SEINE FREUNDIN ANNETTE *see* **DOÑA MENTIRAS**

SEMINOLE (Native Americans, Seminole)

Universal-International Pictures Co., Inc. *Dist* Universal Pictures Co., Inc. Mar **1953**; Los Angeles opening: 20 Mar 1953; Prod: late Jun—late Jul 1952 [©Universal Pictures Co.; 2 Feb 1953; LP2248]. Sd (Western Electric Recording); col (Technicolor). 7,804 ft. 86 or 89 min. PCA cert no. 16154.

Prod Howard Christie. *Dir* Budd Boetticher. *Asst dir* Tom Shaw and [Gordon McLean]. [*Dial dir* Jack Daniels]. *Story and scr* Charles K. Peck, Jr. *Dir of photog* Russell Metty. *Technicolor color consultant* William Fritzsche. *Art dir* Alexander Golitzen and Emrich Nicholson. *Film ed* Virgil Vogel. *Set dec* Russell A. Gausman and Joseph Kish. *Cost* Rosemary Odell. *Mus dir* Joseph Gershenson. *Sd* Leslie I. Carey

and Glenn E. Anderson. *Hair stylist* Joan St. Oegger. *Makeup* Bud Westmore. *Military tech adv* Col. Paul R. Davison, U.S.A., Rtd. *Unit prod mgr* Dewey Starkey.

Cast: ROCK HUDSON (*Lance Caldwell*), BARBARA HALE (*Revere [Muldoon]*), ANTHONY QUINN (*Osceola [previously known as John Powell]*), RICHARD CARLSON (*Major [Harlan] Degan*), Hugh O'Brian (*Kajeck*), Russell Johnson (*Lt. Hamilton*), Lee Marvin (*Sgt. Magruder*), Ralph Moody (*Kulak*), Fay Roope (*Zachary Taylor*), James Best (*Corp. Gerad*), John Day (*Scott*), [Don Gibson (*Capt. Streller*)], [Howard Erskine (*Corp. Smiley*)], [Frank Chase, Scott Lee, Earl Spainard (*Troopers*)], [Duane Thorsen (*Hendricks*)], [Walter Reed (*Farmer*)], [Robert Karnes (*Corporal*)], [Robert Dane (*Trader Taft*)], [John Phillips (*Major Lawrence*)], [Soledad Jiménez (*Mattie Sue Thomas*)], [Don Garrett, Alex Sharp (*Officers*)], [Robert Bray (*Captain Sibley*)], [Peter Cranwell (*Sentry*)], [Jack Finlay, Jody Hutchinson (*Guards*)], [William Janssen].

Historical, Western. [*Print viewed*]. In 1835, at Fort King, the U.S. Army headquarters for the Florida territory, Col. Zachary Taylor is presiding over the court-martial of Second Lieutenant Lance Caldwell, who faces a death sentence for disobeying orders, insubordination and murder. Lance pleads his innocence, and tells his version of the story, beginning at the time when he first rode into the Florida Territory as a graduate from West Point: Soon after arriving at Fort King, Lance is told by Major Degan, his strict commanding officer, of plans to move the "savage" Seminole Indians to reservations in the West to make room for agricultural development. Degan also tells Lance that Chief Osceola, the leader of the Seminoles, is standing in the way of their plans by refusing to let his people be driven from Florida. Lance's suggestion that the Army open a dialogue with the Seminoles is met with the swift reproach of Degan, who believes that "flushing out" the Indians by force is the only way to remove them. Later that evening, Lance visits his childhood sweetheart, Revere Muldoon, whom he has not seen since he left for West Point five years earlier. The two reminisce about their half-Indian friend, John Powell, who, Revere says, has disappeared. Revere evades further questions about John, as he is actually Osceola, her sweetheart. Later, Osceola tells Revere that he would like to meet with Lance to discuss peace, and sends her back to the camp with an invitation. Meanwhile, Lance and his detail, scouting the everglade region, encounter Seminoles, and one of Lance's men shoots a retreating Indian chief in the back. The dead chief is Kulac, whose son, Kajeck, is eager to wage a battle with the whites. Back at the fort, Degan reprimands Lance for stalling the offensive against the Seminoles, and for dressing down the soldier who shot at the "hostiles." Degan then dismisses Lance's warning against an immediate attack on the Seminoles and forms a small detachment to move against Osceola. The detachment is almost completely wiped out by Seminole warriors. Lance is wounded in the battle, but is taken to safety by Osceola, who recognizes Lance as his old friend. Only Degan and one of his officers make it back to the fort, where the colonel, driven to distraction by the defeat, makes a desperate attempt to cover up his misguided "expedition." He calls in Revere, and after accusing her and Lance of consorting with the enemy, gives her an opportunity to prove her innocence by arranging a powwow with Osceola. Degan's guarantee of a truce proves false, however, when, during the powwow, Degan has Osceola beaten nearly to death and thrown in a pit. When Lance angrily accuses Degan of deception, Degan strikes Lance across the face and vows to court-martial him. Later that night, Kajeck sneaks into the fort, kills a guard and tries to knife Osceola for "failing" his people. Lance makes an unsuccessful attempt to save Osceola from the attack, but when Kajeck flees, Lance is accused of murdering the sentry. Lance concludes his testimony before the court-martial by swearing on oath that his version of the story is true. The court finds Lance guilty of murdering the sentry, and he is sentenced to death. Moments before Lance's scheduled execution, Revere arrives with Kajeck, who confesses his guilt. Lance is exonerated and Degan is disgraced. *Florida. Officers (Military). Osceola, Seminole chief, 1804–1838. Seminole Indians. Tribal chiefs. United States–History–Indian campaigns.* Confession (Law). Courts-martial and courts of inquiry. Deception. Duplicity. Everglades (FL). Fathers and sons. Forts. Friendship. Indians of North America–Mixed blood. Indians of North America–Reservations. Jealousy. Murder. Quicksand. Rescues. Romance. Zachary Taylor. Treaties. United States. Army.

Note: According to a written onscreen foreword, the film's story was "taken from the pages of history." While many of the historical and biographical details presented in the film were factual, some of the names in the film, including Major Francis Dade, were changed. Modern sources add Dan Poore to the cast. For information about Chief Osceola and the Seminole Wars, see above entry for *Naked in the Sun.*

Box 21 Feb 1953. *DV* 19 Feb 1953, p. 3. *FD* 4 Mar 1953, p. 10. *HR* 27 Jun 1952, p. 11. *HR* 25 Jul 1952, p. 10. *HR* 19 Feb 1953, p. 3. *MPHPD* 21 Feb 1952, p. 1733. *Var* 25 Feb 1953, p. 6.

SEMINOLE UPRISING (Native Americans, Seminole)
Clover Productions, Inc. *Dist* Columbia Pictures Corp. May **1955**; Prod: 21 Jul–28 Jul 1954 [©Columbia Pictures Corp.; 8 Apr 1955; LP4593]. Sd (Western Electric Recording); col (Technicolor); 1.85. 8 reels, 6,444 ft. 71 or 74 min. PCA cert no. 17208.
Prod Sam Katzman. *Dir* Earl Bellamy. *Asst dir* Jack Corrick. *Scr* Robert E. Kent. *Dir of photog* Henry Freulich. *Spec eff* Jack Erickson. *Technicolor color consultant* Francis Cugat. *Art dir* Paul Palmentola. *Film ed* Jerome Thoms. *Set dec* Sidney Clifford. *Mus cond* Mischa Bakaleinikoff. *Rec supv* John Livadary. *Sd* Josh Westmoreland. *Unit mgr* Leon Chooluck. [*Dir of pub* George Lait].
Source: Based on the novel *Bugle's Wake* by Curt Brandon (New York, 1952).
Cast: George Montgomery [(*Lt. Cam Elliott*)], Karin Booth [(*Susan Hannah*)], William Fawcett [(*Cubby Crouch*)], Steve Ritch [(*Black Cat*)], Ed Hinton [(*Capt. Phillip Dudley*)], John Pickard [(*Sgt. Chris Zanoba*)], Jim Moloney [(*Tony Zanoba*)], Rory Mallinson [(*Toby Wilson*)], Howard Wright [(*Col. Hannah*)], Russ Conklin [(*High Cloud*)], Jonni Paris [(*Malawa*)], Joanne Rio [(*Tasson Li*)], Richard Cutting (*Col. Robert E. Lee*), [Paul McGuire (*Spence*)], [Kenneth MacDonald (*Denker*)], [Rube Schaffer (*Wood*)], [Edward Coch (*Marsh*)].

Western. [*Print viewed*]. In 1855, Black Cat, a chief of mixed Seminole and Caucasian descent, escapes from a Florida reservation, heads for Texas, and leads a series of attacks on settlers there. Robert E. Lee sends for Lt. Cam Elliott, who, half Indian himself, had known Black Cat as a boy, and orders him to Fort Clark to assist Col. Hannah in subduing the troublesome Seminole. Cam accompanies his scout, Cubby Crouch, to Fort Clark, where he encounters Hannah's daughter Susan, who had once allowed Cam to make love to her. Cam assumed Susan had rejected him because of his Indian blood, but Susan now claims she bears no ill will against Indians and that she hopes Cam will court her again. Cam still loves Susan, but when he learns that Fort Clark's Capt. Phillip Dudley plans to marry her as soon as he settles his debts, he decides to avoid her. Cam plans to lead his own unit into battle with Black Cat, while a small detachment of cavalrymen, led by Dudley, takes several Seminole women and children as hostages. In exchange for the hostages, Cam hopes Black Cat will surrender two prisoners, the wife and son of a local settler named Toby Wilson. As Dudley is capturing Black Cat's wife and son, Wilson unexpectedly arrives on the scene. Learning that the Indians have killed his wife and son, Wilson quietly promises to relieve Dudley of all his debts in exchange for Black Cat's family. Dudley agrees, and Wilson later kills both the woman and the boy. Assuming that Hannah is responsible, Black Cat asks to meet Cam in private, greeting him as his brother Grey Eagle. The Seminole explains that Wilson's wife and son were killed because they tried to stab a Seminole woman, but that his own family was innocent of any wrongdoing. After threatening revenge, Black Cat rides away. When Cam and his men return to the fort, they find that Susan has been taken captive and the fort set on fire. Cam pursues the Seminoles across the desert, and Hannah orders Dudley to position a fresh water supply on the lieutenant's return route. Meanwhile, Susan, upon learning that Black Cat plans to trade her for guns, asks the chief if his sons will forgive him for having prevented them from becoming civilized. Cam defeats Black Cat's braves in a surprise attack from the hills, whereupon the chief agrees to send his people back to the reservation and to stand trial himself at Fort Clark. Dudley secretly empties the water barrels meant for Cam's men, and when young soldier Tony Zanoba discovers his treachery, he kills the captain. Black Cat, who feels Cam and Susan can help his people, shows them how to find water hidden under the sand just as Susan is about to die of thirst. She revives and declares her love for Cam, and the party returns to the fort with Black Cat, who reveals to Cam that in reality he is not a half-breed, as both of Cam's parents were white, and Cam was found in a wagon by the Seminoles. In the end, Cubby explains,

Black Cat realized that Texas had to be tamed sooner or later. *Indians of North America–Mixed blood. Miscegenation. Officers (Military). Seminole Indians. Seminole War, 3d, 1855-1858. Texas. United States. Army. Cavalry. Battles. Desert survival. Escapes. Fathers and daughters. Fires. Forts. Hostages. Robert E. Lee. Murder. Racism. Revenge. Romance. Romantic rivalry. Scouts (Frontier). Settlers. Thirst. Treachery. United States–History–Indian campaigns.*

Note: The working title of this film was *Bugle's Wake.* The film opens with the voice-over narration spoken by William Fawcett as "Cubby Crouch" explaining how, in 1855, the Indian chief "Black Cat" incited the Indians to attack the settlers in Texas. Although the first two Seminole Wars took place in Florida, the third war, from 1855-1858, was fought in Texas. In its review, *HR* commented, "one wonders why [screenwriter Robert E.] Kent decided to call these horse Indians, operating on the Texas plains, Seminoles. The Seminoles were canoe Indians native to the Florida swamps. Sometimes one wonders if some secret rule of the [PCA] Johnston office stipulates that there must be one major inaccuracy in every Indian picture." Reviewers also noted that the film included stock shots in the battle scenes.

Box 30 Apr 1955. *DV* 22 Apr 1955, p. 3. *Exb* 4 May 1955, p. 3957. *FD* 2 May 1955, p. 6. *Har* 23 Apr 1955, pp. 66-67. *HR* 22 Apr 1955, p. 3. *MPHPD* 23 Apr 1955, p. 409. *Var* 27 Apr 1955, p. 6.

SENG FUNG KEO FUNG *see* SHUANG FENG CHEO HUANG

SEÑOR AMERICANO (Latino)

Ken Maynard Productions. *Dist* Universal Pictures Corp. 10 Nov **1929** [©Universal Pictures Corp.; 30 Oct 1929; LP813]. Sd (Movietone); b&w. 6 reels, 6,662 ft. [Also si; 5,418 ft.].

Pres Carl Laemmle. *Dir* Harry J. Brown. *Scen* Bennett Cohen. *Story* Helmer Bergman and Henry McCarthy. *Dial and titles* Lesley Mason. *Cam* Ted McCord. *Film ed* Fred Allen.

Cast: Ken Maynard (*Michael Banning*), Kathryn Crawford (*Carmelita*), Gino Corrado (*Ramirez*), J. P. McGowan (*Maddux*), Frank Yaconelli (*Mañana*), Frank Beal (*Don Manuel*), Tarzan (*The horse*).

Western. Michael Banning, a U.S. Army lieutenant sent to Southern California to investigate lawless land-grabbing, wins a golden bridle in a riding contest sponsored by Carmelita, daughter of Spanish grandee Don Manuel. He thus incurs the enmity of Ramírez, who is in love with her; the Mexican attempts to steal the bridle, but Banning subdues him. Maddux, leader of a gang that plans to steal Don Manuel's land, sends a spy to follow Banning, who returns from San José with the news that California has been admitted to the Union; Maddux then has him jailed. When Maddux tries to force Don Manuel into surrendering his grants, Ramírez turns against him. Banning, freed by his servant, arrives with a rescue party, and peace is restored. *California. Investigations. Land rights. Mexicans. Spaniards.*

FD 12 Jan 1930. *Var* 1 Jan 1930, p. 28.

SEÑORA CASADA NECESITA MARIDO (Spanish language)

Fox Film Corp. *Dist* Fox Film Corp. **1935**; New York opening: 8 Feb 1935; Prod: 10 Sep—29 Sep 1934 [©Fox Film Corp.; 12 Nov 1934; LP5162]. Sd; b&w. 8 reels, 6,449 ft. PCA cert no. 347. Spanish language.

Supervisión Gregorio Martínez Sierra. *Dirección [Directed by]* James Tinling. *Adaptación cinematográfica [Screenplay by]* José López Rubio. [*Contr wrt* Dudley Nichols and Eunice Chapin]. [*Photog* Daniel Clark]. [*Mus dir* Samuel Kaylin].

Song(s): "¿Qué sabes tú?" music by María Grever, Spanish lyrics by Enrique Jardiel Poncela; "A Guy What Takes His Time," music by Ralph Rainger, Spanish lyrics by Enrique Jardiel Poncela.

Source: Based on the novel *Az Én Második Feleségem* by Eugene Heltai (1907) and his play *Édes Teher*, which is adapted from the novel (production undetermined).

Cast: CATALINA BÁRCENA (*Irma Karen*), Antonio Moreno (*Tomás Karen*), José Crespo (*Alejandro Koltai*), Valentín Parera (*Antoñito Orbok*), Barbara Leonard (*Betty Morgan*), Romualdo Tirado (*Tío Max*), Mimi Aguglia (*Juana Blomberg*), Tito Coral (*Cantante*), José Peña Pepet (*Julio*), Mawita Castañeda (*Doncella*), Carlos Villarias (*Cliente*), [José López Rubio (*Secretario*)].

Domestic, Comedy. [*Print viewed*]. In Budapest, attorney Tomás Karen and his wife Irma, who have been married for five years and fighting the last two, have a series of arguments at dinner which culminates when Irma demands a divorce. When Tomás then changes her mind and threatens not to get a divorce unless Tomás finds her a new husband, Tomás, completely fed up, agrees. After she provokes his jealousy by showing a feigned interest in wealthy playboy and gambler Antoñito Orbok, Tomas demands a family council to settle

their problem. Juana Blomberg, Irma's mother, suggests that she place an ad for a husband, but their lecherous Uncle Max answers it, not knowing that Irma placed the ad. To then prove to a mocking Tomás that she can attract men, Irma walks seductively down a busy street, but when a man does attempt to flirt with her, Tomás breaks it up. Exasperated, Irma decides to leave Budapest and gets on the next train without even knowing its destination. On the train Irma meets famous playwright Alejandro Koltai, who is traveling with English dance hall girl Betty Morgan, whom he is unsuccessfully trying to teach to act. After Alejandro invites Irma to join them in Zurich, she wires Tomás and says that she is a new woman, which causes him to leave immediately for Zurich. At their hotel, Alejandro has organized a grand benefit fete at which all the guests are taking part. Irma does an imitation of Mae West and provokes Tomás' jealousy by saying that she will marry Alejandro after the divorce. After Tomás, whom Irma introduces as her attorney, enlists Betty's help and gets Irma intensely jealous of Betty's supposed affection for him, Alejandro learns that Betty has left with a man for Monte Carlo, and he and Irma follow. Irma embarrassingly, but relievedly, finds Antoñito, who has followed Irma to Zurich, in Betty's bathroom, but Tomás, who has trailed his wife and Alejandro, accuses her of betraying him. When Irma demands that Alejandro marry her because of the scandal, he half-heartedly agrees to "sacrifice himself," and they board a train for Budapest. After Antoñito leaves Betty on the train to return to the roulette wheels of Monte Carlo, Alejandro quarrels with Irma, who is upset at his sudden lack of interest in her, and he is comforted by Betty. Irma finds Tomás outside her door and they reconcile. When Tomás suggests that they vow not to quarrel, Irma complains that she so loved to, so they agree to quarrel only every Thursday from three to five. They then sneak off the train hoping to avoid Alejandro, while he and Betty also sneak off hoping to avoid Irma. They meet rounding a corner of the station, the women congratulate each other, and after a laugh, the couples get into a horse-drawn coach together. *Divorce. Hungarians. Jealousy. Marriage. Separation (Marital). Shrews. Advertisements. Budapest (Hungary). Dance hall girls. False accusations. Hotels. Lawyers. Mistaken identity. Monte Carlo (Monaco). Mothers and daughters. Playboys. Playwrights. Roulette (Game). Scandal. Trains. Uncles. Zurich (Switzerland).*

Note: The working title of this film was *Mi segunda mujer (My Second Wife)*, and its translated title was given in Fox records and reviews variously as "Married Woman Needs Husband," "Married Lady Needs Husband" and "A Married Woman Needs a Husband." In 1937, Twentieth Century-Fox produced a film based on the same source entitled *The Lady Escapes*, directed by Eugene Forde and starring Gloria Stuart and Michael Whalen (see *AFI Catalog of Feature Films, 1931-40*; F3.2344).

CM Jan 1935, p. 6. *DV* 8 Sep 1934, p. 3. *DV* 29 Sep 1934, p. 3. *FD* 12 Feb 1935, p. 8. *NYT* 11 Feb 1935, p. 14.

SENZA MAMMA E'NNAMURATO (Italian Americans, Italian language)

Cinema Productions, Inc. *Dist* Cinema Productions, Inc. **1932**; Prod: began 30 Aug 1932 at RCA Sound Studios. Sd; b&w. 7 reels, 6,029 ft. 67 min. Italian language.

Prod Angelo De Vito. *Dir* Harold Godsoe. *Cont and dial* Alberto Campobasso. *Mus score* Giuseppe De Luca. *Casting dir* S. V. Casolaro.

Cast: Rosina De Stefano (*Matalena*), Catherine Campagnone (*Maria*).

Musical, Drama. [*Not viewed*]. In the early morning, Pasquale, the owner of an Italian restaurant who has made a good deal of money in the thirty years he has worked hard in America, prepares for a large party. His fish dealer, Biasiello, arrives and as they chat, he repeats the popular dictum that men chase after Pasquale's daughter Annarella because of the restaurant owner's money. Pasquale castigates some of his staff for their tardiness, and soon Ciccillo, who is to get married, arrives with two carloads of friends and family. As his bride-to-be, Maria, has not yet arrived, the guests wait. A boat then pulls up with the rest of the party, Maria, her mother Matalena, and Rafiluccio, a friend of Ciccillo's, who rows. A number of the guests sing songs, including Rafiluccio, who sings in the Neapolitan style. As he sings, Maria comments that Ciccillo looks strange and sad. Rafiluccio teases Maria, convincing her to sing, and then insists she drink some wine. Unable to control his anger, Ciccillo accuses Rafi of flirting and calls Maria shameless. Rafi castigates Ciccillo, insisting that he loves Maria as a sister, as they have been brought up together. Ciccillo yells at Matalena to take her daughter home, adding that the brazen girl is

more at home in Rafi's arms than in his own. Annarella is quietly pleased at the emotional scene, as she loves Ciccillo. After the gathering breaks up, Annarella and Ciccillo take a romantic boat ride together. At home, as Maria sobs, Matalena insists that Ciccillo accused her of loving Rafi so that he could break his promise to marry her and throw himself into Annarella's arms. Although Matalena believes that someone else will come along for her daughter, she faints when she learns from the stricken girl that she is no longer a virgin. Maria collapses in moans. Sometime later, while Matalena is still ill from the shock, Maria arrives home from her factory job and announces that she's been dismissed as there is no more work. At night, Maria comes home late and drops on her bed in sobs, then refuses to answer her mother's inquiries. During the wedding of Ciccillo and Annarella, Maria listens to the festivities from her window in anger and sadness. Matalena dies in Maria's arms while the dancing and the music at the wedding continue. Sometime after Maria prays beside her mother's tomb, a headline in *Il Progresso Italo-Americano* announces Maria's pitiful suicide. *Deception. Engagements. False accusations. Italian Americans. Mothers and daughters. Dismissal (Employment). Factory workers. Fathers and daughters. Fishmongers. Parties. Premarital sex. Restaurateurs. Rowboats. Songs. Suicide. Weddings.*

Note: The plot summary was based on a dialogue continuity deposited at NYSA. Although no initial release information was found, the film was approved for exhibition in New York State in Oct 1932. The film was originally registered under both the Italian title and the English title of *Love's Tragedy;* however, the English title was corrected to *Without a Mother and Sweetheart* in Jan 1933. According to correspondence in the NYSA records, the film played in a New York theater in May 1944. According to *FD* news items, Rosina De Stefano was an opera singer, and Catherine Campagnone, an Italian American, was the recent winner of the 1932 Miss Italy contest.

FD 6 Jul 1932, p. 7. *FD* 13 Aug 1932, p. 9. *FD* 31 Aug 1932, p. 8.

SEPIA CINDERELLA (African Americans)

Herald Pictures, Inc. *Dist* Screen Guild Productions, Inc. 18 Oct 1947; World premiere in New York: 25 Jul 1947; Prod: mid-Dec—late Dec 1946 at Filmcraft Studios, NY [©Herald Pictures, Inc.; 6 Jul 1947; LP193]. Sd (RCA); b&w. 6,387 ft. 70 min. Passed by the National Board of Review.

Prod Jack Goldberg and Arthur Leonard. *Dir* Arthur Leonard. *Story and scr* Vincent Valentini. *Dir of photog* George Webber. *Art dir* Frank Namczy. *Film ed* Jack Kemp. *Cost* Ann Blazier. *Mus dir* John Gluskin. *Sd eng* Nelson Minnerly. *Makeup artist* Edward Scanlon. *Casting dir* Billy Shaw. *Tech adv* Jacob M. Lehrfeld.

Song(s): "Long Legged Lizzie," words and music by Herman Fairbanks and Deek Watson; "Is It Right?" words and music by Deek Watson and Willie Best; "Cinderella" and "Ring Around My Rosie," words and music by Walter Fuller; "Can't Find a Thing to Say," words and music by Milt Shaw; "(Oh Ho) It's a Lovely Day," words and music by Eric Miller, Ruble Blakey and Rudy Toombs.

Cast: Sheila Guyse (*Barbara*), Billy Daniels (*Bob [Jordan]*), Tondaleyo (*Vivian [Marston]*), Hilda Offley Thompson (*Mama Keyes*), Ruble Blakey (*Barney [Ray]*), Emory Richardson (*Great Joseph*), Jack Carter (*Ralph [Williams]*), Percy Verwayen (["*Mac'*] *MacMillan*), Dusty Freeman (*Mooney*), George Williams (*Sonny*), Fred Gordon (*Press agent [Lester]*), Al Young (*Chinaman*), Specialties: Deek Watson and Brown Dots, John Kirby's Band, Leonardo & Zola, Apus & Estrellita, Walter Fuller's Orchestra, Guest star: Freddie Bartholomew, [Harold Norton (*M. C.*)], [Lora Pierre (*Evelyn*)], [Gertrude Saunders (*Mrs. Dryden*)], [Jimmy Fuller (*Collins*)], [Big Sid Catlett].

African American, Show business, Musical. [*Print viewed*]. When band leader and fledgling songwriter Bob Jordan encounters difficulty finishing his first song, "Cinderella," Barbara, the adopted daughter of Bob's landlady, Mama Keyes, encourages him to put love into his words. Bob confesses that he has never been in love, and Barbara, who has fallen for him, helps him complete the song. Barbara, whose deceased parents were "troopers," wants to go into show business, feeling it is in her blood. Mama Keyes, however, disapproves of Barbara's ambitions and looks down on the activities of another tenant, the Great Joseph, a soothsayer who attempts to read the future in his crystal ball. After Bob's song becomes a hit, he is introduced at a society party to Vivian Marston, the largest stockholder at the swank Swan Club, the city's top nightclub. Although she is engaged to Ralph Williams, a down-to-earth man who hopes to end her capricious ways, Vivian flirts with Bob and offers

him a booking at the club, even though Bob does not want to shove the current band leader, Barney Ray, out. When Bob comes home late after the party, he tells a suspicious Barbara about the job at the Swan Club and offers her a share of his royalty check, saying it takes a woman to write "heart interest stuff." Vivian arranges with the manager of the club, MacMillan, for Barney to change the club's name to the "Cinderella Club" in honor of Bob's song. At Bob's debut, which is attended by Barbara, Mama Keyes and the Great Joseph, Bob is a hit, but complains about muffing the last line of "Cinderella." Barbara suggests he hold a "Cinderella slipper" during the song with the lyrics written inside, but is unable to give him hers, as she has dancing plates on them. Later, Barney complains to Lester, the press agent, that Vivian, who now flirts with Bob, had him removed because he refused to play up to her. Soon news of Vivian and Bob's romance appears in the gossip columns. Bob rarely comes home to the boardinghouse, and Barbara, stoically accepting her apparent defeat, gets a job singing at the Hang Out Club. Ralph is angered by Vivian's claim that the gossip about her and Bob is false and insists that they are indeed lovers. After Vivian slaps him, he threatens to inform the newspapers that he is finished with her, but she begs him not to break their engagement. Later, when Bob, who never knew about the engagement, arrives at the club, Vivian tells him that he is just a friend to her. Knowing that Vivian will now offer no resistance, Mac, who is angered at the fact that Bob never shows up for rehearsals, fires him. Meanwhile, at the Hang Out Club, Barney, who is impressed with Barbara's singing, asks her to join his band, but when he insults Bob, she slaps him. Sometime later, Bob visits the Hang Out Club and apologizes to Barney, saying that the job of replacing him was too big. Lester finds them together and says that Mac has been looking for both of them because business has fallen off since Bob left the club. Lester then comes up with the idea to have Bob be the vocalist for Barney's band. Lester presents the idea to Mac, then suggests they have a contest in which all the women will bring a slipper, and Bob will pick one. The owner will receive a cash prize plus a week's engagement at the club if she is a singer. When Bob returns to the club, Vivian explains that she had to agree to let him go because her reputation was at stake. She tries to rekindle their romance, but Bob walks away from her. On the night of the contest, Bob, remembering Barbara's early words, picks a slipper with a tap dancing plate attached. She kisses him and they both sing "Cinderella." After she announces that she is not going to let him get away this time, Lester arranges for them to marry in the club. As Bob and Barbara marry, Vivian sits with Ralph. *African Americans. Band leaders. Cinderella (Fictional character). Romance. Singers. Songwriters. Theatrical backers. Contests. Engagements. Flirtation. Fortune-tellers. Landladies. Nightclub owners. Nightclubs. Parties. Press agents. Rivalry. Shoes. Songs. Weddings.*

Box 9 Aug 1947. *Exb* 6 Aug 1947, p. 2211. *FD* 18 Jul 1947. *HR* 13 Aug 1947, p. 4. *MPHPD* Aug 1947. *Var* 30 Jul 1947, p. 27.

SERENADE (Italian Americans)

Warner Bros. Pictures, Inc.; A Warner Bros-First National Picture. *Dist* Warner Bros. Pictures, Inc. 21 Apr 1956; Prod: early Sep—early Dec 1955 [©Warner Bros. Pictures, Inc.; 21 Apr 1956; LP8170]. Sd (RCA Sound Recording); col (Warner Color); 1.85. 121-122 min. PCA cert no. 17795.

Prod Henry Blanke. *Dir* Anthony Mann. *Asst dir* Charles Hansen, Dick Moder and [Al Alleborn]. *Scr* Ivan Goff, Ben Roberts and John Twist. *Dir of photog* J. Peverell Marley. *Art dir* Edward Carrero. *Film ed* William Ziegler. *Set dec* William Wallace. *Cost des* Howard Shoup. [*Mus adv* Jakob Gimbel.] *Sd* Robert B. Lee, Dolph Thomas and Charles Lang. *Makeup supv* Gordon Bau. *Operatic adv* Walter Ducloux. *Operatic coach* Giacomo Spadoni.

Song(s): "Serenade" and "My Destiny," music by Nicholas Brodszky, lyrics by Sammy Cahn; "Ave Maria," music by Charles Gounod, lyrics traditional; "Lamenti di Frederico" from the opera *L'Arlesiana,* music by Francesco Cilea, libretto by Leopoldo Marenco; the prayer from Act 3, Part 4, and "Dio Ti Giocondi" from the opera *Otello,* music by Guiseppi Verdi, libretto by Arrigo Boito; "Di Quella Pira" from the opera *Il Trovatore,* music by Guiseppi Verdi, libretto by Salvadore Cammarano and Bardare; the tenor aria from the opera *Der Rosenkavalier,* music by Richard Strauss, libretto by Hugo von Hofmannsthal; "Torna a Surriento" words and music by Ernesto De Curtis; "O Paradiso" from the opera *L'Africaine,* music by Giacomo Meyerbeer, libretto by Eugène Scribe; "Nessun Dorma" from the opera *Turandot,* music by Giacomo Puccini, libretto by Giuseppe

Adami and Renato Simoni; "O Soave Fanciulla" from the opera *La Boheme*, music by Giacomo Puccini, libretto by Giuseppe Giacosa and Luigi Illica; "Amor Ti Vieta" from the opera *Fedora*, music by Umberto Giordano, libretto by Arturo Colautti; "Il Mio Tesoro" from the opera *Don Giovanni*, music by Wolfgang Amadeus Mozart, libretto by Lorenzo Da Ponte.

Source: Based on the novel *Serenade* by James M. Cain (New York, 1937).

Cast: MARIO LANZA [(*Damon Vicenti*)], JOAN FONTAINE [(*Kendall Hale*)], Sarita Montiel [(*Juana Montes*)], Vincent Price [(*Charles Winthrop*)], Joseph Calleia [(*Maestro Marcatello*)], Harry Bellaver [(*Tonio*)], Vince Edwards [(*Marco Roselli*)], Silvio Minciotti [(*Lardelli*)], Frank Puglia [(*Manuel*)], Edward Platt [(*Carter*)], Licia Albanese [(*Desdemona*)], Jean Fenn [(*Soprano*)], [Frank Yaconelli (*Giuseppe*)], [Maria Serrano (*Rosa*)], [Eduardo Noriega (*Felipe*)], [Joseph Vitale (*Baritone*)], [Victor Romito (*Bass*)], [Jose Govea (*Paco*)], [Antonio Triana (*Man in the bull*)], [Leo Mostovoy (*Chef*)], [Nick Moro (*Luigi, waiter*)], [Joe DeAngelo, William Fox, Jack Santoro (*Busboys*)], [Mario Siletti (*Sanroma*)], [Mickey Golden (*Cab driver*)], [Elizabeth Flournoy (*Elevator operator*)], [Johnstone White (*Hughes, butler*)], [Stephen Bekassy (*Russell Hanson*)], [Creighton Hale (*Assistant store manager*)], [Martin Garralaga (*Romero*)], [Vincent Padula (*Pagnil*)], [Martha Acker (*American woman*)], [Jose Torvay (*Mariachi leader*)], [Billy McLean (*Gerald*)], [Perk Lazelle, April Stride, Diane Gump (*Party guests*)], [Ralph Volkie (*Policeman*)], [Autumn Russell, Helene Hawley, Abdullah Abbas (*Accident witnesses*)], Don Turner (*Bus driver*)], [Norma Zimmer (*Mimi in La Boheme*)], [Francis Barnes (*Iago in Othello*)], [Lillian Molieri (*Tosca in Tosca*)], [Laura Mason (*Fedora in Fedora*)], [Richard Cable (*Shepherd boy in L'Arlesiana*)], [Richard Lert (*Conductor in L'Ariesiana*)].

Melodrama, Musical. [*Print viewed*]. Damon Vincenti, an Italian American with a beautiful operatic singing voice, leaves his job picking grapes at a California vineyard when he gets an audition at Lardelli's, a San Francisco opera restaurant where several great tenors have gotten their starts. One night, Charles Winthrop, a famous concert promoter, visits Lardelli's with Kendall Hale, a beautiful heiress whom Damon had met one day when she and prizefighter Marco Roselli were lost in the wine country. After the show, Winthrop invites Damon to join him and Kendall at the Mark Hopkins hotel for dinner, and when he arrives, she introduces him to Maestro Marcatello, a famous opera coach. Damon explains that as a child he received singing lessons only when the harvest was good, and that after his parents died, he worked making wine and had little time for artistic instruction. Marcatello asks Damon to sing, and the young man shows so much potential that the maestro offers to train him. As the group discusses Damon's talents, Roselli arrives and screams at Kendall for not having attended his championship fight that night, and storms out. After Kendall declares to the group that she never told Roselli that she loved him, she asks Damon to stay once the others have left. He declines, and in the cab on the way home, Winthrop tells him that Kendall is a dangerous woman. Later, at Lardelli's, Damon's cousin Tonio makes elaborate plans for the tenor, but Damon, who is falling in love with Kendall and fighting against it, is worried that his life is changing too quickly. Finally having given in to Kendall's seductions, Damon invites her and Winthrop to go on tour with him. In New York, however, he is forced to cancel a date with Kendall in order to rehearse for his debut at the Met, where he is to sing Othello. After the rehearsal, Damon finds Kendall with a young sculptor, Russell Hanson, who is sculpting a bust of the icy blonde, and grows jealous. While he sings the part of Othello on stage at the Met, Damon looks anxiously around the hall for Kendall, who never shows up. In the middle of a duet with a soprano, he shocks everyone by storming offstage. He rushes to Kendall's home and learns that she has left on a trip with Russell. Enraged, Damon leaves and heads for Mexico City, where he is scheduled to sing at the National Theatre. During a rehearsal, he loses his voice and breaks down. After the directors replace him, Damon goes to the small town of San Miguel de Allende, where, during a fiesta, he falls ill with a malaria-like disease. Juana Montes, a Mexican girl, tends to him and then brings him to recuperate at the Montes farm, where she lives with her aunt and uncle, Manuel and Rosa. Damon offers to work in the fields to pay back the money that Juana has spent on his hotel and doctor's fees. One day, Damon picks up a guitar and discovers that he still cannot

sing. When Juana suggests that he return to singing after the harvest is over, Damon bitterly replies that his voice is gone for good. Juana insists that it is the fault of the "Americana," and that he must find his voice again. At a fiesta commemorating the death of Juana's father, a bullfighter who died in the ring, Juana dresses up as a toreador and re-enacts the bullfight. Felipe, a young man who is in love with Juana and jealous of Damon, calls Juana's father a coward, prompting Juana to threaten him with her drawn sword. When Damon goes to comfort her, she explains to him that when her mother ran away with another man, her father lost his will to live and became easy prey to a charging bull. Juana goes to church to ask for forgiveness, and Damon follows her. When he hears her pray for him, he begins to sing "Ave Maria," and then cries tears of joy. Damon announces that he will return to the U.S. to sing in the opera and asks Juana to accompany him, but she refuses. As she drives him to the airport at Mazatlan, however, a storm breaks out and the pair is stranded in the mud. Juana tries to resist Damon's advances, but finally gives in and they kiss. Back in San Francisco, Damon shows up at Lardelli's with Juana as his bride. Later, after Damon is reunited with cousin Tonio, Winthrop arrives at the restaurant and offers Damon a chance to regain his celebrity by singing "La Luciana" with the San Francisco Opera. Kendall attends the performance with the intent of winning Damon back, and jealous Juana encourages Damon to take a job in New York, even though Kendall will be nearby. Kendall invites the couple to a cocktail party, and when they arrive, she takes Juana aside, ostensibly to show her the Mexican treasures she bought when she was looking for Damon south-of-the-border. When she gets Juana alone, she warns the girl that she will take Damon away from her and make him a big star. While still in the bedroom, Juana finds a bullfighter's sword and performs her toreador reenactment for the guests, brandishing the sword at Kendall's throat. After Damon calls Juana from her trance, she runs away, whereupon Damon tells Kendall with confidence that he no longer has feelings for her. Out in the street, Juana is hit by a bus, and when Damon finds her, she tells him that he must go to his performance and not worry about her. At the concert, Damon sings the song "Serenade" in dedication to his beloved, and begins to cry when Tonio tells him from backstage that Juana will recover. *Fame. Italian Americans. Jealousy. Mexico. Opera singers. Romance. Agriculture. Auditions. Boxers. Bullfighters and bullfighting. California. Churches. Cousins. Disease. Fiestas. Mark Hopkins Hotel (San Francisco, CA). Marriage. Metropolitan Opera (New York City). Mexico City (Mexico). Othello (Opera). Psychosomatic illness. Restaurants. San Francisco (CA). Sculptors. Seduction. Vineyards. Vocal instructors. Wounds and injuries.*

Note: According to the file on the film in the MPAA/PCA Collection at the AMPAS Library, the Breen Office spent nearly twenty years working with different studios to arrive at an acceptable adaptation of James M. Cain's novel. In the novel, a washed-up opera singer named Sharp wanders down to Mexico, where he meets and falls in love with a prostitute, Juana. Returning to Los Angeles with Juana and strengthened by her love, he becomes a famous singing star. Later, he goes to New York to perform at the Metropolitan Opera House and has a homosexual love affair with an opera impressario named Warfield. In the novel's climactic scene, Juana murders Warfield by dressing up as a toreador and performing a mock bullfight. According to an inter-office memo, PCA director Joseph I. Breen objected to many aspects of the first screen treatment of Cain's story, which he received in Dec 1937, including the unacceptable depiction of "illicit sex," prostitution, and homosexuality. He also wrote that the treatment of Mexicans "will probably be found objectionable to the authorities of that country."

Correspondence from early 1944 indicates that RKO was interested in turning the novel into a film, as was M-G-M. Between Jun and Nov 1944, the Breen Office and M-G-M worked out solutions to the problematic content of Cain's original story. The homosexual was changed to a rich, powerful older woman, whom the main character marries, Juana was no longer be a prostitute, and a sex scene in a church was eliminated. Also, the "squalor, poverty, etc," of Juana and the main character's life together was not to be shown. Finally, according to Al Block of M-G-M, "what would emerge, then,...seems...to be a good honest story, with no trace of the homosexuality which figured in the book, or indeed anything objectionable, that I can see." The file on the film contains no other correspondence regarding the M-G-M production of *Serenade*, however, and it appears that the project was dropped at this stage.

Warner Bros. was the next studio to take an interest in the project, as evidenced by a 22 Jan 1945 letter from studio executive James. J. Geller to the Breen Office. Geller asked for Breen's opinion on a five-page treatment written by Jerry Wald. Although Geller asserted that the studio's decision as to whether it would buy the rights to Cain's novel would depend on Breen's opinion, Breen responded that the treatment is too "general and nebulous" to warrant a definite statement. Wald's treatment eliminated the homosexuality and suggested making the main character a doctor. Wald insisted that the most important point about the character Juana is that she is "Indian—a simple,

beautiful girl with direct emotion." According to Wald, the theme of the film—a "conflict between a cheap, somewhat degrading love and a deep simple one"—would resemble the theme of Somerset Maugham's *Of Human Bondage*.

The studio and the Breen Office continued to argue about the film's content, especially about what the Breen Office termed an "inescapable flavor of sexual perversion suggested by the present relationship of Warfield and Sharp." Throughout the project, the Breen Office expressed concern that the Mexicans in the film be represented in the most favorable light possible. In particular, Breen requested that all "pidgin English" spoken by the Mexican characters be eliminated. This planned production of *Serenade*, which according to a press release was to co-star Ann Sheridan and Dennis Morgan, was shelved in Aug 1946. It was picked up again in May 1948. The revised project was to star Jane Wyman and be directed by Michael Curtiz. In a 10 Mar 1949 news item, however, Curtiz remarked on the difficulty he had been experiencing casting the film, and by 1951, according to a 22 Dec 1954 *DV* item, Robert Sisk was in as director. In Aug 1955, after years of discussion and rewriting, the script finally was deemed acceptable by the PCA.

The film was shot on location in San Miguel d'Allende and includes scenes shot at the Palace of Fine Arts in Mexico City. Onscreen credits include the following acknowledgement: "Palace of Fine Arts Photographed Through Courtesy of the National Art Institute, Mexico." According to a 3 May 1956 *LAEx* review, Mario Lanza had not performed for three years prior to appearing in *Serenade*. The *HR* review noted that a pudgy Lanza had thinned down for the role of the tormented Damon Vicenti. In 1958, Jakob Gimbel filed suit against Warner Bros. and RCA Victor, claiming that he agreed to act as the film's musical adviser and offscreen pianist on the strict proviso that his name would not be listed in connection with the picture. Although Gimbel did not receive credit onscreen or in reviews, his name did appear on the soundtrack album. The final disposition of the suit is not known.

Box 17 Mar 1956. *DV* 22 Dec 1954. *DV* 13 Mar 1956, p. 3. *Exb* 21 Mar 1956, pp. 4123-24. *FD* 13 Mar 1956, p. 6. *Har* 17 Mar 1956, p. 42. *HR* 16 Sep 1955, p. 11. *HR* 9 Dec 1955, p. 17. *HR* 13 Mar 1956, p. 3, 11. *HR* 6 Aug 1958. *LAEx* 3 May 1956. *LAT* 25 Jun 1948. *MPD* 13 Mar 1956, p. 1, 4. *MPHPD* 17 Mar 1956, p. 817. *NYT* 13 Nov 1955. *NYT* 23 Mar 1956, p. 21. *Var* 14 Mar 1956, p. 6.

SERENADE TO SUZETTE *see* **THE TOAST OF NEW ORLEANS**

SERGEANT HOUCK *see* **TROOPER HOOK**

SERGEANT RUTLEDGE (African Americans)

Warner Bros. Pictures, Inc.; John Ford's Production. *Dist* Warner Bros. Pictures, Inc. 28 May **1960**. New York opening: 25 May 1960; Prod: late Jul–early Sep 1959 [©Warner Bros. Pictures, Inc.; 28 May 1960; LP20182]. Sd (RCA Sound Recording); col (Technicolor). 11 reels. 111 min. PCA cert no. 19413.

Prod Willis Goldbeck and Patrick Ford. *Dir* John Ford. *Asst dir* Russ Saunders and Wingate Smith. *Wrt* James Warner Bellah and Willis Goldbeck. *Dir of photog* Bert Glennon. *Art dir* Eddie Imazu. *Film ed* Jack Murray. *Set dec* Frank M. Miller. *Cost des* Marjorie Best. *Mus* Howard Jackson. *Sd* M. A. Merrick. *Makeup supv* Gordon Bau.

Song(s): "Captain Buffalo," words by Mack David, music by Jerry Livingston.

Cast: Jeffrey Hunter [(*Lt. Tom Cantrell*)], Constance Towers [(*Mary Beecher*)], Billie Burke [(*Cordelia Fosgate*)], Woody Strode [(*Sergeant Braxton Rutledge*)], Juano Hernandez [(*Sgt. Matthew Luke Skidmore*)], Willis Bouchey [(*Col. Otis Thornton Fosgate*)], Carleton Young [(*Capt. Shattuck*)], Judson Pratt [(*Lt. Mulqueen*)], [Bill Henry (*Capt. Dwyer*)], [Walter Reed (*Capt. MacAfee*)], [Fred Libby (*Chandler Hubble*)], [Toby Richards (*Lucy Dabney*)], [Charles Seel (*Dr. Eckner*)], [Chuck Hayward (*Capt. Dickinson*)], [Mae Marsh (*Nellie*)], [Cliff Lyons (*Sam Beecher*)], [Jan Stine (*Chris Hubble*)], [Chuck Roberson (*Capt. Dannemuller*)], [Jack Pennick (*Court sergeant*)], [George Shug Fisher (*Owen*)], [Hank Worden (*Laredo*)], [Bobby Johnson (*Newcomb*)], [Rafer Johnson, James Johnson, Marvin Luster, Louis Byrd, David Washington, Bobby Lee Smith, Walter Torrence, Trusse R. Norris, Clifton Brandon, Eugene Gaines, Lloyd Winston, Naaman Brown (*Troopers*)], [Ruth Clifford, Eva Novak (*Officers' wives*)], [Bill Wellman, Jr., Phillip Adams (*Court guards*)], [Mario Arteaga (*Mexican*)], [Clarence Straight (*White Hand*)], [Edward Sweeny (*Sentry*)], [Estelle Winwood (*Woman in courtroom*)].

Legal, Drama. [*Print viewed*]. In the summer of 1881, a young woman named Lucy Dabney and her father, Maj. Dabney, are found dead in their quarters at Fort Linton in the Arizona Territory. Lt. Tom Cantrell arrives at the U.S. Army's southwestern headquarters to defend the accused, a black sergeant named Braxton Rutledge, who served bravely under Cantrell in the all-black Ninth Cavalry for over six years. Because Lucy was raped and beaten before her brutal strangulation, the case attracts a group of spectators, who harass Rutledge as he is led into the courtroom. Presiding over the court-martial is Col. Otis Thornton Fosgate. After Fosgate ejects the onlookers from the room, angering his fluttery wife Cordelia, prosecutor Capt. Shattuck questions a series of witnesses, who describe the events that occurred on the day of the murders. Mary Beecher relates how she returned to Arizona on that day after an absence of twelve years. Because her father failed to meet her at the train station, she found herself alone. Upon discovering the station master's lifeless body, she became utterly terrified. Rutledge then suddenly appeared and defended her from two attacking Indians who, along with a larger group of Mescaleros, had broken out of the San Rosario Reservation earlier in the day. Cordelia then tells the court that she saw Rutledge tumble from Dabney's quarters after hearing two shots fired. Earlier in the day, Cordelia had told Lucy that even though Rutledge had been the girl's friend and riding instructor for years, it was unseemly for her to speak with him. As the fort doctor and then Tom himself take the witness stand, the court learns that Rutledge, arriving at Dabney's to warn the major of the Apache breakout, found Lucy's body, but was forced to shoot the major in self-defense when Dabney, entering the room, wildly fired on him. Convinced that no one would believe a black man's story, Rutledge then fled in a panic to the train station, where he aided Mary. Tom, leading a detachment of Ninth Cavalry soldiers, followed and arrested Rutledge, then proceeded toward the Beecher ranch in pursuit of the Apaches. On the way, they discovered the body of young Chris Hubble, who had been killed by an Apache lance. During a subsequent skirmish with the Apaches, Rutledge escaped, but as he approached the Beecher ranch, he realized that the patrol was riding into an Apache ambush. After warning the soldiers, he commanded them during the battle, only to be taken back into custody afterward. Following Rutledge's testimony, Shattuck declares that the sergeant's heroic actions were intended merely to earn him the court's mercy, whereupon Rutledge protests that the Ninth Cavalry is his home and the source of his self-respect. Next, Mary testifies that after the battle, Tom found young Lucy's gold cross as well as a jacket marked "CH" on the body of a dead Apache. Tom presents these items as evidence that Chris was the murderer. Shattuck angrily accuses Tom of attempting to pin the crime on a dead white boy merely to salvage the life of a black. Chandler Hubble, Chris's father, then admits under oath that his deceased son committed the crimes. Realizing that the jacket was too large for young Chris, Tom accuses the elder Hubble of the murders, whereupon Hubble confesses. Following Rutledge's acquittal, Mary and Tom are united, and the sergeant again leads his proud soldiers. *African Americans. Courts-martial and courts of inquiry. False arrests. Heroism. Murder. Officers (Military). Racism. United States. Army. Cavalry. Acquittals. Apache Indians. Arizona. Battles. Circumstantial evidence. Duty. Escapes. Gratitude. Lawyers. Loyalty. Raids. Rape. Rescues. Self-respect. Soldiers. Train stations.*

Note: The film's working titles were *Captain Buffalo* and *The Trial of Sergeant Rutledge*. Portions of the film were shot in Monument Valley, along the Arizona-Utah border. The CBCS mistakenly credits Edward Shaw in the role of "Chris Hubble." After the Civil War, four all-black units, the 9th and 10th Cavalry and the 24th and 25th Infantry, played a major role in developing the Western frontier. The Native Americans who faced these men in battle called them "buffalo" soldiers, in honor of their fighting spirit, as well as the buffalo coats and hats they wore. After seeing combat in World War II, the 9th and 10th Cavalry were deactivated in 1944. At that time, the 25th Infantry was also scattered, although the 24th Infantry survived to do battle in Korea. All trace of these all-black units was lost when the Army desegregated in the early 1950s.

In interviews published by modern sources, producer/writer Willis Goldbeck credited director John Ford with much of the screenplay's construction, including the film's courtroom setting. Modern sources also state that Ford was paid $300,000 for his work on the film. Numerous film scholars have stated that *Sergeant Rutledge* marked an important step in the evolution of racial consciousness in Ford's films, as it is his only film to feature an African-American protagonist.

Box 18 Apr 1960. *DV* 22 Jun 1959. *DV* 8 Apr 1960, p. 3. *Exb* 13 Apr 1960, pp. 4694-95. *Har* 16 Apr 1960, p. 64. *HR* 17 Jul 1959, p. 20. *HR* 4 Sep 1959, p. 10. *HR* 8 Mar 1960. *HR* 8 Apr 1960, p. 3. *LAT* 24 Apr 1960. *MPHPD* 9 Apr 1960, p. 652. *NYT* 26 May 1960, p. 37. *Var* 13 Apr 1960, p. 6.

SET FREE (Gypsies)

Bluebird Photoplays, Inc. *Dist* Bluebird Photoplays, Inc. 9 Dec **1918** [©Bluebird Photoplays, Inc.; 2 Dec 1918; LP13093]. Si; b&w. 5 reels.

Dir Tod Browning. *Scen* Rex Taylor and Tod Browning. *Story* Joseph Franklin Poland. *Cam* Alfred G. Gosden.

Cast: Edith Roberts (*Roma Wycliffe*), Harry Hilliard (*John Roberts*), Harold Goodwin (*Ronald Blair*), Molly McConnell (*Mrs. Roberts*), Blanche Gray (*Aunt Henrietta*).

Comedy-drama. Roma Wycliffe, a high-spirited girl bored with the lavender-and-old-lace atmosphere of her Aunt Henrietta's estate, discovers that her grandmother was a gypsy and decides to become one herself. Wearing gypsy clothing, she runs away to New York, where she is arrested on the suspicion that she is Gypsy Nan, a thief. Mrs. Roberts, whose poodle had attracted Roma's attention, intercedes for the girl and, promising to care for her, takes her to her lavish home. Young John Roberts falls in love with Roma, but the "gypsy" imagines him too stodgy. To win her love, John declares himself the leader of a band of gypsy thieves and then hires a gang of ruffians to prove his claim. When the thugs actually rob a bank, John has them arrested, and Roma, realizing the darker side of gypsy life, marries John. *Gypsies. Impersonation and imposture. Upper classes. Aunts. Bank robberies. Criminals. False arrests. Mistaken identity. New York City.*

Note: The pre-release titles of this film were *Double Crossed* and *Romance for Roma*. Some sources erroneously list the story credit as James P. or James F. Poland. Copyright records and Universal studio records state that Browning alone was responsible for the scenario, while reviews credit only Rex Taylor.
ETR 14 Dec 1918, p. 147. *MPN* 19 Oct 1918, p. 2607. *MPN* 16 Nov 1918, p. 2985. *MPW* 14 Dec 1918, p. 1249. *MPW* 21 Dec 1918, p. 1386. *NYDM* 28 Dec 1918, p. 998. *Var* 6 Dec 1918, p. 37. *Wid's* 8 Dec 1918, pp. 5-6.

SEVEN ANGRY MEN (African Americans)
Allied Artists Pictures Corp. *Dist* Allied Artists Pictures Corp. 27 Mar **1955**; Prod: mid-Sep—mid Oct 1954 [©Allied Artists Pictures Corp.; 7 Mar 1955; LP4450]. Sd (Western Electric Recording); b&w; 1.85. 8,261 ft. 90-91 min.
Prod Vincent M. Fennelly. [*Exec prod* Walter Mirisch]. *Dir* Charles Marquis Warren. *Asst dir* Edward Morey, Jr. *Story and scr* Daniel B. Ullman. *Dir of photog* Ellsworth Fredericks. *Spec eff* Milt Rice. *Photog eff* Ray Mercer. *Art dir* David Milton. *Supv film ed* Lester A. Sansom. *Film ed* Richard C. Meyer. *Set dec* Joseph Kish. *Construction supv* James West. *Props* Sam Gordon. *Ward* Bert Henrikson. *Mus comp and cond by* Carl Brandt. *Rec eng* Ralph Butler. *Sd ed* Delmore Harris. *Makeup artist* Eddie Polo. *Hair styles* Mary Smith. *Prod mgr* Allen K. Wood. *Set cont* Mary Chaffee.
Cast: Raymond Massey [(*John Brown*)], Debra Paget [(*Elizabeth Clark*)], Jeffrey Hunter [(*Owen Brown*)], Larry Pennell [(*Oliver Brown*)], Leo Gordon [(*Rev. White*)], John Smith [(*Frederick Brown*)], James Best [(*Jason Brown*)], Dennis Weaver [(*John Brown, Jr.*)], Guy Williams [(*Salmon Brown*)], Tom Irish [(*Watson Brown*)], James Anderson [(*Thompson*)], James Edwards [(*Ned Green*)], John Pickard [(*Wilson*)], Smoki Whitfield [(*Newby*)], Jack Lomas [(*Doyle*)], Robert Simon [(*Col. Lewis Washington*)], Dabbs Greer [(*Doctor*)], Ann Tyrell [(*Mrs. Mary Brown*)], [Rayford Barnes (*William Doyle*)], [Dick Paxton (*Drury Doyle*)], Robert Osterloh [(*Lt. Col. Robert E. Lee*)], [Richard Emory (*Stevens*)], [John Lupton (*Lt. Stuart*)], [I. Stanford Jolley (*Druger*)], [William Newell (*Farmer*)], [Barbara Woodell (*Mrs. Doyle*)], [Gregg Barton (*O'Neil*)], [Al Wyatt (*Overseer*)], [Leighton Noble (*Merchant*)], [Selmer Jackson (*Emerson*)], [Mickey Simpson (*Blacksmith*)], [Lester Dorr (*Thoreau*)], [Kenneth McDonald (*Clark*)], [Don Kennedy (*Militia guard*)], [Joel Fluellen (*Heyward*)], [David Wolfson (*Drummer*)], [Richard Cutting (*Mayor Beckham*)], [Gayle Kellogg (*Determined young man*)], [Paul Bryar (*Train fireman*)], [Lane Bradford, Don C. Harvey (*Ruffians*)], [Donald Murphy (*Hoyt*)], [Carleton Young (*Judge*)], [William Hamel].
Historical, Drama. [*Print viewed*]. In 1856, settlers in the Kansas Territory face an election to determine if Kansas will join the Union as a slave or a free state. To help ensure its entry as a free state, abolitionist John Brown has come from Ohio with his sons, John, Jr., Frederick, Salmon and Jason. Later, Brown's sons Owen and Oliver travel to join the others. On the train to Kansas, Owen meets Elizabeth Clark, who expresses her belief that his notorious father is a dangerous man. Some time later, Rev. White, the leader of opposition forces known as the Border Ruffians, approaches Brown's settlement and orders the black and white settlers to leave the territory in forty-eight hours. During a raid by the Ruffians on the town of Lawrence, Elizabeth's father, along with four others, is killed. Proclaiming that "the war has begun," Brown marshals his men. After kidnapping some of the men who have been identified as participating in the raid, Brown summarily executes five of them, citing the biblical command to exact "an eye for an eye." His actions sicken John, Jr., and fearing for his sanity, Jason decides to turn himself and his brother over to the Union army. Later Frederick, horrified by the morning's events, also

decides to leave. Owen, however, remains despite Elizabeth's accusation that he has become a murderer like his father. Frederick is later killed at his campsite, and the Ruffians attack and burn the settlement. After Owen is seriously wounded during the attack, Elizabeth overcomes Brown's disapproval to nurse him back to health. In the meantime, Brown orders the discouraged settlers to rebuild the settlement, so that they will be able to vote in the statehood election. When Owen recovers, he tells Elizabeth that he loves her, and she admits that she returns his affection, although she still dislikes his values. Brown's other two sons return to Ohio, leaving only Owen to support his father. On the day the voting takes place, Elizabeth speculates bitterly that even if the vote goes his way, Brown will not be satisfied but will continue his fight elsewhere. Owen does not believe her, but promises that no matter what, he will return to Ohio to continue farming. Elizabeth then accepts his marriage proposal. Elizabeth proves to be prophetic, however, and after the family is reunited in Ohio, Brown announces that his work is not finished. Only Oliver and Brown's youngest son Watson are willing to follow him, but then, despite his promise to Elizabeth, Owen vows to join his father. In 1858, Brown raises money from Boston intellectuals, including Henry David Thoreau and Ralph Waldo Emerson. With the money, he buys guns and ships them to Harpers Ferry in Virginia, where he expects slaves to escape and join him in a revolt. While Owen and two other men wait in a nearby schoolhouse for the escaping slaves, Brown leads the rest of the men in an attack on the federal arsenal at Harpers Ferry. When Brown tells the black guard that he has come to free the slaves, the man responds that he has been free for eight years and does not step aside. After he has secured some hostages, Brown, who intends to exchange them for the freedom of the slaves, sends a soldier to inform the army of his actions. To Brown's mortification, the expected revolt does not take place, and Watson and Oliver are killed in the ensuing fight with the Army, led by Lt. Col. Robert E. Lee. At the schoolhouse, Ned Green, a freed slave, prevents Owen from joining Brown, pointing out that his father's efforts have failed. Later, Brown is found guilty of treason and sentenced to death by hanging. Owen attempts to gain his father's release, but Brown states his belief that it is his duty to be martyred. In 1859, Brown is hanged. *Abolitionists. John Brown. Fanatics. Fathers and sons. Kansas. Slavery. African Americans. Hanging. Harpers Ferry (WV). Hostages. Mental illness. Murder. Nursing back to health. Racism. Revenge. Romance. Treason. United States. Army.*

Note: The film's working titles were *John Brown's Raiders*, *God's Angry Men* and *God's Angry Man*. According to an unidentified Feb 1953 news item, Arthur Orloff was originally hired to write the film's story. Orloff's contribution to the final film has not been determined. John Brown, a *Mayflower* descendent, was violently opposed to slavery. During the 1820s and 1830s, his home was a station on the underground railroad, which helped runaway slaves, and he organized an armed group of blacks. When Kansas was opened for settlement in 1854, Brown and five sons moved to the new territory to fight for a free Kansas. He organized a guerrilla band, whose most notorious act was the Pottawatomie massacre on 24 May 1856, when five pro-slavery men were killed.
On 16 October 1859, Brown led a group of twenty-one men, including five blacks and his sons Oliver and Watson, in an attack on the federal arsenal at Harpers Ferry, which was then a part of Virginia. With the arms, he planned to equip slaves whom he believed would join him eagerly. Local slaves did not join the revolt, and after two days, during which his two sons were killed, and he was wounded, Brown surrendered to Col. Robert E. Lee. Contrary to Brown's hopes, the raid aided Southern extremists in their fight for secession from the United States. Immediately after he was hanged on 2 December 1859, Brown became a folk hero. The folk song "John Brown's Body," which used the same melody as "The Battle Hymn of the Republic," became one of the Civil War's marching songs, and Stephen Vincent Benet wrote an epic poem of the same name in 1929. Some scholars have speculated that Brown was insane, but this has not been proven. Raymond Massey also played John Brown in the 1941 Warner Bros. picture, *Santa Fe Trail*. In 1954, Massey, Anne Baxter and Tyrone Power toured with a stage show depicting the incident at Harpers Ferry.
Box 12 Mar 1955. *DV* 9 Jul 1954. *DV* 3 Feb 1955. *DV* 7 Mar 1955, p. 3. *Exh* 23 Mar 1955, p. 3937. *FD* 8 Mar 1955, p. 6. *Har* 12 Mar 1955, p. 42. *HR* 7 Mar 1955, p. 3. *HR* 9 Mar 1955. *MPHPD* 19 Mar 1955, p. 361. *NYT* 2 Apr 1955, p. 15. *Var* 9 Mar 1955, p. 6.

SEVEN CITIES OF GOLD (Latino, Native Americans, Diegueño)
Twentieth Century-Fox Film Corp. *Dist* Twentieth Century-Fox Film Corp. Sep **1955**; World premiere in San Diego, CA: 8 Sep 1955; Los Angeles opening: 21 Sep 1955; Prod: began 22 Mar 1955 [©Twentieth Century-Fox Film Corp.; 8 Sep 1955; LP5558]. Sd (Western Electric Recording); col (De Luxe); CinemaScope; Cinemascope lenses by Bausch & Lomb. 12 reels, 9,243 ft. 103 min. PCA cert no. 17451.

[*Exec prod* Darryl F. Zanuck]. *Prod* Robert D. Webb and Barbara McLean. *Dir* Robert D. Webb. *Asst dir* Eli Dunn. [*Dial dir* Ben Wright]. [*Asst dir* Sanchez Tello and Jaime Contreras]. *Scr* Richard L. Breen and John C. Higgins. *Addl dial* Joseph Petracca. [*Contr wrt* Frank Fenton]. *Dir of photog* Lucien Ballard. [*Cam op* Kenny Williams]. *Spec photog eff* Ray Kellogg. [*Spec eff* Ray Deter]. *Color consultant* Leonard Doss. *Art dir* Lyle R. Wheeler and Jack Martin Smith. *Film ed* Hugh S. Fowler. *Set dec* Walter M. Scott. *Ward dir* Charles LeMaire. *Cost des* Adele Balkan. [*Ward* Norman Martien]. *Mus* Hugo Friedhofer. *Orch* Edward B. Powell. *Vocal supv* Ken Darby. *Cond* Lionel Newman. *Sd* W. D. Flick and Harry M. Leonard. *Makeup* Ben Nye. *Hair styling by* Helen Turpin. [*Hairdresser* Linda Cross]. [*Tech adv* Father Maynard Geiger]. [*Scr supv* Dolores Rubin]. [*Props* Max Goldman]. [*Asst props* Bob McLaughlin]. [*Transportation capt* Frank McGarry]. [*Livestock* Kenny Lee and Post Parks]. [*Greensman* Charles Hixon]. [*Stunts* David A. DaLie].

Song(s): "Señorita Carmelita," words and music by Ken Darby; "El capotin" (The Rain Song) and "El trobador," composers undetermined, adapted by Ken Darby.

Source: Based on the novel *The Nine Days of Father Serra* by Isabelle Gibson Ziegler (New York, 1951).

Cast: RICHARD EGAN [(*Lt. José Mendoza*)], ANTHONY QUINN [(*Don Gaspar de Portola*)], MICHAEL RENNIE [(*Father Junípero Serra*)], JEFFREY HUNTER [(*Matuwir*)], RITA MORENO [(*Ula*)], Eduardo Noriega [(*Sergeant*)], Leslie Bradley [(*José de Gálvez*)], John Doucette [(*Juan Coronel*)], Victor Juncos [(*Lt. Fages*)], Julio Villareal [sic] [(*Pilot Vila*)], [Miguel Inclán (*Schrichak*)], [Carlos Múzquiz (*Dr. Pratt*)], [Pedro Galván (*Father Vizcaíno*)], [Angelo De Stiffney (*Capt. Rivera*)], Ricardo Adalid Black (*Pilot Pérez*), [Fernando Wagner (*Blacksmith*)], [Guillermo Calles (*Miscomi*)], [Eduardo González Pliego (*Axajui*)], [Yerye Beirute (*Atanuk*)], [Anna María Gómez (*Kukura*)], [Jaime González Quiñones (*Indian boy*)], [Luciel Nieto (*Rano*)], [Olga Gutiérrez (*Dira*)], [Juan José Hurtado (*Guitar player*)], [Jack Mower (*Father*)], [Kathleen Crowley (*Mother*)], [Gilda Fontana (*Spanish girl*)], [Daniel Nuñez (*Spanish soldier*)], [John Gusick, José Vasques Silva, Fernando Chehuan, Jorge Treviño (*Soldiers*)].

Historical, Drama, with songs. [*Print viewed*]. In 1769, Don Gaspar de Portola and his friend José Mendoza, a lieutenant, travel by carriage to Mexico City, New Spain. At their insistence, the carriage travels so fast that it hits an old woman and kills her. Padre Junípero Serra gives the woman last rites and then chastises the soldiers for their carelessness. Upon arriving at their destination, the soldiers are given orders to occupy California, which, although discovered by the Spanish in 1536, has not yet been conquered. The soldiers also hope to discover the legendary Seven Cities of Gold. Two parties are dispatched by sea, and an advance group takes an overland route to San Diego Bay. The main expedition, commanded by Portola, is ordered to meet the other three parties at San Diego and then proceed northward to Monterey Bay. Padre Serra, who hopes to found a string of missions in California, is named spiritual director of the expedition. As he blesses the departing soldiers, however, Serra startles the men with an accusation. Serra denounces the Spanish military's plans to enslave the "childlike" Indians and plunder their Seven Cities and, pressing a burning torch to his breast, urges the men to behave like "children of God." Before they depart, José complains that Serra carries too many religious "trinkets," but after the expedition is surrounded by armed Indians, the priest prevents an attack by giving the curious visitors strings of colorful beads. When a soldier is killed by an arrow in camp that night, however, José argues that Serra's method of handling Indians is ineffective. Determined to be rid of Serra, Portola feigns concern about an abscess on the priest's leg and orders him back to Mexico City. Serra becomes even more determined to found his missions, however, and that night, submits to a painful procedure that cures his leg. Later, Serra and José become separated from the column and lose their way in a fierce desert windstorm. Out of nowhere, a shack appears, and they receive food and water from the man, woman and child who live inside. Serra believes they have been miraculously rescued by the Holy Family, but José, an earthy unbeliever, is skeptical. The Portola expedition finally arrives at San Diego Bay, only to discover that Rivera's advance party has been decimated by disease. Portola sends the *San Antonio* back to Mexico City for supplies, places José in charge of the San Diego camp and proceeds northward to Monterey. That night, the Diegueño

Indians attack the camp, and Matuwir, grandson of Diegueño chief Miscomi, is wounded. Serra nurses Matuwir back to health and then releases him, thereby infuriating José. Serra soon befriends the villagers, however, and although none of them agrees to be baptized, they begin to visit the Serra's Mission San Diego de Alcala regularly. When Miscomi dies, Matuwir is named chief of the Dieguenos. Unknown to him and Serra, José pursues and finally makes love to Matuwir's sister Ula. Months later, exhausted and starving, Portola and his men appear, reporting that they were unable to find anything but parched lands and "savages too useless to fight." Because the supply ship has not yet returned from Mexico City, Portola decides to abort the entire California expedition, but Serra persuades him to remain in camp until Saint Joseph's Day. Ula receives Matuwir's permission to accompany José to Mexico City as his wife, but José advises her to remain with her own people. Deeply distressed, Ula runs from José and falls from a cliff to her death. Portola refuses to have José punished "for the benefit of Indians," and Serra refuses to turn him over to the vengeful Matuwir. War drums sound for several days, and the Diegueños sabotage Portola's remaining supply of fresh water. Finally, aware that they will be destroyed by the more numerous Indians, Portola orders his men to attack. As Serra blesses them, José confesses his sins and slowly walks out of the camp toward Matuwir's warriors. Serra weeps when José's body, with its heart cut out, is returned to the camp. Because Saint Joseph's Day has dawned without the supply ship having arrived, the expedition abandons the mission and sets out for Mexico City. Shortly after their departure, however, the *San Antonio* sails into the bay, and the exuberant party returns. As the sailors unload bells meant for the mission at Monterey, Serra rings out a loud, clear tone, "one my Indians will love. I can hear them coming!" *Diegueño Indians. Military occupation. Mission San Diego de Alcala. Missions. Accidental death. Battles. Betrayal. California–History–To 1846. Catholic Church. Deserts. Disease. Expeditions. Faith. Falls from heights. Greed. Indians of North America. Miracles. Missionaries. Moral reformation. Officers (Military). Racism. Religious articles. Revenge. San Diego (CA). Sandstorms. Seduction. Self-sacrifice. Ships. Spaniards. Starvation.*

Note: The working title of this film was *The Gun and the Cross*. In a spoken foreword, the film announces that only "one language" would be used in the dialogue, despite the varying ethnic backgrounds of the characters. In the onscreen credits, actor Julio Villarreal's surname is incorrectly spelled "Villareal." *Seven Cities of Gold* was filmed in Mexico, in and around the west coast town of Manzanillo and the deserts of Guadalajara. An Indian village was built as a set in the hills near Manzanillo, and a reproduction of the original San Diego mission was constructed on the beach. Although studio publicity material credits Mexican director/producer Rene Cardona as Robert Webb's co-director, and Mexican director of photography Jorge Stahl as Lucien Ballard's camera operator, it is likely that they were hired only to fulfill union requirements and did not actually work on the production. As depicted in the film, in 1769, Padre Junípero Serra accompanied the expedition of José de Galvez to Upper California and founded the Mission San Diego de Alcala. It was the first of twenty-one Franciscan missions established in California. The *MPH* reviewer remarked that *Seven Cities of Gold* was the "first important film dealing with this subject," while the *HR* review commented that it was "the first film to pay attention to the important contributions of culture and humanity made by the Spanish to the development of more than half of the new world." Director/producer Webb and producer Barbara McLean were married at the time of this production.

Box 17 Sep 1955. *DV* 9 Sep 1955, p. 3. *Exb* 21 Sep 1955, p. 4034. *FD* 9 Sep 1955, p. 8. *Har* 17 Sep 1955, p. 151. *HR* 9 Sep 1955, p. 3. *LAT* 9 Sep 1955. *MPHPD* 17 Sep 1955, p. 593. *NYT* 8 Oct 1955, p. 13. *Var* 14 Sep 1955, p. 6.

SEVEN HILLS OF ROME (Italian Americans)

Le Cloud Productions; Titanus S.p.a.; Metro-Goldwyn-Mayer Presents. *Dist* Loew's Inc. Jan **1958**; *Prod*: late May—late Aug 1957 at Titanus Studios in Rome [©St. Cloud Productions, Inc. & Gregor Productions, Inc. & Loew's Inc.; 31 Dec 1957; LP10091]. Sd (Perspecta Sound); col (Technicolor); Technirama. 12 reels, 9,282 or 9,291 ft. 102-103 min. PCA cert no. 18717.

Prod Lester Welch. *Dir* Roy Rowland. *Asst dir* Mario Russo. *Scr Art* Cohn and Giorgio Prosperi. *Story* Giuseppe Amato. *Dir of photog* Tonino delli Colli. [*Photog* Giuseppe Rotunno]. *Art dir* Piero Filippone. *Film ed* Gene Ruggiero. *Set dec* Luigi Gervasi. *Cost des* Maria Barony. *Mus coordinator* Irving Aaronson. *Mus supv and cond* George Stoll. *Choreographer* Paul Steffen. *Sd rec* Mario Messina. *Makeup* Otello Fava. *Hairdressing* Tina Cosetti. *Titanus chief of prod* Silvio Clementelli.

Music: "Don't Play That Riff Too Stiff," music by George Stoll.

Song(s): "The Seven Hills of Rome," music by Victor Young, lyrics by Harold Adamson; "Arrivederci, Roma," music by Renato Rascel, lyrics by P. Garinei and S. Giovannini, English lyrics by Carl Sigman; "Calypso Italiano," music and lyrics by George Stoll; "Come Dance with Me," music by Dick Leibert, lyrics by George Blake; "Lolita," music and lyrics by A. Buzzi-Peccia; "Questa o quella," from the opera *Rigoletto*, music by Giuseppe Verdi, lyrics by Francesco Maria Piave; "All the Things You Are," music by Jerome Kern, lyrics by Oscar Hammerstein II; "Ay! Ay! Ay!," music and lyrics by Osman Perez Freire; "The Loveliest Night of the Year," music by Juventino Rosas, adapted by Irving Aaronson, lyrics by Paul Francis Webster; "M'appari tutt amor," from the opera *Martha*, music by Friedrich von Flotow, libretto by Friedrich Wilhelm Riese; "Temptation," music by Nacio Herb Brown, lyrics by Arthur Freed; "Jezebel," music and lyrics by Wayne Shanklin; "Memories Are Made of This," music and lyrics by Terry Gilkyson, Richard Dehr and Frank Miller; "I Love You Oh So Very Much (Ti voglio bene, tanto, tanto)" music by Renato Rascel, lyrics by Robert Mellin; "Goodbye My Friends, Goodbye," " 'Na canzone pe' fa'amore," "Venticello di Roma," "E' Arrivato la bufera" and "Ostricaro innamorato," music and lyrics by Renato Rascel. "When the Saints Go Marching In," traditional.

Cast: MARIO LANZA [(*Marc Revere*)], Renato Rascel [(*Pepe Bonelli*)], Marisa Allasio [(*Raffaella Marini*)], Peggy Castle [(*Carol Ralston*)], Clelia Matania [(*Beatrice*)], Carlo Rizzo [(*Director Ulpia Club*)], Rossella Como [(*Anita*)], Guido Celano [(*Luiggi*)], [Amos Ravoli (*Carlo*)], [Marco Aulli (*Romoletto*)], [Giorgio Gandos (*Commissario Rugarello*)], [Carlo Giuffre (*Franco Cellis*)], [Adriana Hart (*Landlady*)], [Patrick Crean (*Mr. Fante*)], [Pennachi (*Helicopter pilot*)], [April Hannessy (*Mrs. Stone*)], [Stuart Hart (*Miller*)], [Luisa DiMeo (*Street singer*)].

Musical. [*Print viewed*]. As he sings during a television broadcast, famous Italian-American tenor Marc Revere sees his fiancée, wealthy socialite Carol Ralston, with another man. After the song, Marc storms into the booth and berates Carol. Just as he is called to sing again, she says she is going to Europe tomorrow. Then, before Marc sings, he twists the nose of her companion. Marc travels to Europe to pursue Carol and is on a train in Italy from Monte Carlo, when an attractive young Italian woman from Savona, Raffaella Marini, slips in the rain and loses her purse as she boards the moving train. When Marc overhears the conductor threaten to throw her off at the next stop, he offers to pay her way to Rome, her destination. She says she plans to get a job in Rome and stay with her uncle, and tells Marc that she learned English during and after the war, when Americans expected everyone to speak it. In Rome, when they find that her uncle has gone to Argentina, Marc insists that she come with him to his cousin, Pepe Bonelli, a jovial pianist who lives in a bohemian garret. That night, they have a party, during which Raffaella, falling in love with Marc, is disappointed when he asks another woman to dance. As the party ends the next day, one of the guests takes Marc, Pepe and Raffaella on a helicopter ride over Rome and its surrounding sights. The next day, Pepe and Marc awaken to find that Raffaella has shoplifted food for them, although she keeps notes in order to repay. When the landlady demands 40,000 lire in back rent by the next day, Marc decides to get a booking in one of Rome's best nightclubs, and Raffaella says she will get a job doing anything that's respectable. Pepe invites her to come to Signora Beatrice's, where he is playing for a fashion show, and offers to speak with Beatrice about a job for her. Raffaella kisses him on the cheek and says he is a kind man, which affects him. At the fashion show, Beatrice, aware of Marc's celebrity, mentions that Carol had been there three weeks ago and that she is in Capri but plans to return. Raffaella, who is jealous when she hears about Carol, is hired as an assistant. Marc is turned down for a job at the "Ulpia," where the owner does not know him. At the next club, the "Tivoli," he is told by an American owner that Italy exports, not imports, singers, as tenors are one of its greatest resources. At night, he and Raffaella meet Pepe at a cinema in Trastevere, where Pepe plays for "amateur nights." Pushed onto the stage, Marc wins the competition and is signed to sing nightly at 4,000 lire a night, or a bit more than five dollars. Following a performance, Marc brings a friend and two American women back to Pepe's room. He unconsciously treats Raffaella like a servant, then leaves with his guests without eating the meal she has prepared. When Pepe rebukes him for hurting her, Marc is surprised to learn of her romantic feelings for him. Later, as Pepe is about to propose to Raffaella, Marc interrupts with news that he has

just got a good offer from the Ulpia and wants Pepe as his accompanist. As Marc rehearses an aria with Pepe, he is drowned out by rock-and-roll coming from a party outside. When the group at the party learn he is an American, Marc, to their enjoyment, imitates Italian-American singers Perry Como, Frankie Laine and Dean Martin, and then Louis Armstrong, who, he says, doesn't need to be Italian. On the afternoon before the opening, Marc runs into Carol. They both apologize for the scene in New York, and she invites him to a yacht party, assuring him they could get back before the Ulpia opening; however, because of engine problems, they do not return until the next morning. Raffaella berates Marc for his selfishness and for treating her like a child. Pepe, who has lost the Ulpia job because of Marc, overhears her say that Marc is not good enough to be Pepe's accompanist. After Marc leaves, Raffaella cries on a bed, and Pepe comforts her, but refrains from embracing her. Raffaella decides to leave Rome and go home. As she puts away some dresses at work, she finds a diamond bracelet and locks it in a cabinet. That night, Marc arrives ten minutes late for a date with Carol and finds that she has gone to the Ulpia Club. When he finds her there dancing with an Italian man, Marc twists this man's nose also, which begins a large brawl that ends in damages totaling over one million lire, or about $1,600. Pepe pleads with Beatrice for a loan, but she refuses, saying she doesn't like tenors, having fallen in love with one once. Just then, an American woman, Mrs. Stone, comes looking for the diamond bracelet she has lost, and Raffaella says she has not seen it. Carol apologizes to Marc and offers to write a check for the damages, but he refuses. Raffaella then brings Marc the bracelet, saying she now can repay him for helping her. He demands to know where she got it, causing her to cry, and Pepe, seeing him yell, slaps Marc. Pepe realizes that the bracelet belongs to Mrs. Stone and says Raffaella will return it. Marc goes to the Ulpia Club and agrees to work for two weeks at half-price to pay the damages, if they will pay Pepe full scale. He then asks Raffaella to convince Pepe to take it. Although Marc and Pepe avoid looking at each other as they dress before the show, after they catch each other's eye, they embrace. At the opening, Raffaella sees Marc kiss Carol and tells Pepe that she is now leaving Rome. When Pepe lets Marc know, he says he was saying good-bye to Carol, as they realize their affair will never work. Pepe reveals that Raffaella has always loved him, and Marc runs after her. As they embrace, Pepe sees them from the balcony of the club. They wave at Pepe then walk together toward the ruins of Rome. *Italian Americans. Italians. Romance. Rome (Italy). Singers. Bohemians and bohemianism. Bracelets. Cousins. Dismissal (Employment). Dressmakers. Engagements. Fashion shows. Fights. Helicopters. Jealousy. Nightclubs. Parties. Pianists. Shoplifting. Socialites. Television programs. Trains. Unrequited love. Yachts and yachting.*

Note: According to *Var*, an Italian-language version of this film was also made. Le Cloud Productions was owned by star Mario Lanza and producer Lester Welch. According to reviews, this was Lanza's first film in two years and his first made abroad. According to the *New York World Telegram*, in a highly publicized incident similar to a scene in the film, Lanza failed to perform at the last minute at a club in Las Vegas because of "turbulent personal difficulties." Renato Rascel, who played "Pepe" and wrote the song "Arrivederci, Roma," among others, was a top Italian singer and comedian. *LAT* stated that the song "The Seven Hills of Rome" was reportedly the last that Victor Young wrote before he died.

HR production charts note that Giuseppe Rotunno was replaced as the film's directory or photography by Tonino delli Colli. Charts also include Charles Fawcett in the cast, but his appearance in the released film has not been confirmed. Reviews praised the travelogue aspects of the film, while denigrating the story. *Var* stated, "*Three Coins in the Fountain* started the easy-chair, cinematic Cook's Tour of Rome in Technicolorful celluloid and Mario Lanza's *The Seven Hills of Rome* completes it." About the helicopter scene, *NYT* commented, "The views of St. Peter's Square, Ponte Palatino and various other famed Roman ruins such as the Colosseum, have never, if memory serves, looked lovelier than they do in this airborne view." About the film as a whole, however, they wrote, "a solid story might have helped all concerned considerably." About Lanza, *Cue* stated, "Mario has lost weight. He is broad-shouldered, lantern-jawed, lean and unhappily hard—in body and in voice. His golden tenor has turned brassy, the brilliant notes that once shattered champagne glasses at 20 paces now strike hard and thin upon the sound track." Of Marisa Allasio, *Var* wrote, "She has the physical attributes of such other famed Italo beauts as Gina [Lollobrigida] and Sophia [Loren] but is a fresher and younger personality." According to modern sources, music supervisor George Stoll conducted the Italian National Radio Symphony, and the prerecordings were done at the Vatican's Auditorium Angelico.

Box 13 Jan 1958. *Box* 20 Jan 1958. *Cue* 1 Feb 1958. *DV* 8 Jan 1958, p. 3. *Exb* 8 Jan 1958, p. 4422. *FD* 13 Jan 1958, p. 6. *Har* 18 Jan 1958, p. 10. *HCN* 6 Feb 1958. *HR* 31 May 1957, p. 11. *HR* 30 Aug 1957, p. 13. *HR* 10 Jan 1958, p. 3. *LAEx* 6 Feb 1958. *LAMirror-News* 8

Feb 1958. *LAT* 26 Jan 1958. *LAT* 6 Feb 1958. *MPD* 8 Jan 1958. *MPHPD* 18 Jan 1958, p. 682. *Newsweek* 27 Jan 1958. *NYP* 31 Jan 1958. *New Yorker* 8 Feb 1958. *NYT* 31 Jan 1958, p.24. *Var* 8 Jan 1958.

SEVEN SWEETHEARTS (Dutch Americans)

Metro-Goldwyn-Mayer Corp.; controlled by Loew's Inc.; A Frank Borzage Production. *Dist* Loew's Inc. Sep–Nov 1942; New York opening: week of 13 Nov 1942; Prod: 23 Mar–11 May 1942 [©Loew's Inc.; 11 Aug 1942; LP11525]. Sd (Western Electric Sound System); b&w. 11 reels, 8,792 ft. 98-99 min. Passed by the National Board of Review. PCA cert no. 8530.

Prod Joseph Pasternak. *Dir* Frank Borzage. [*Asst dir* Lew Borzage]. *Orig scr* Walter Reisch and Leo Townsend. *Dir of photog* George Folsey and [Leonard Smith]. *Art dir* Cedric Gibbons. *Assoc* Paul Groesse. *Film ed* Blanche Sewell. *Set dec* Edwin B. Willis. *Assoc* Jack Moore. *Gowns* Shoup. *Mus score* Franz Waxman. *Dance dir* Ernst Matray. *Rec dir* Douglas Shearer. *Hair styles* Sydney Guilaroff. *Make-up created by* Jack Dawn.

Song(s): "Little Tingle Tangle Toes," "You and the Waltz and I," music by Walter Jurmann, lyrics by Paul Francis Webster; "Tulip Time," music and lyrics by Burton Lane and Ralph Freed.

Cast: *The Seven Sweethearts:* Kathryn Grayson [(*Billie Van Maaster*)], Marsha Hunt [(*Regina Van Maaster*)], Cecilia Parker [(*Victor Van Maaster*)], Peggy Moran [(*Albert Van Maaster*)], Dorothy Morris [(*Peter Van Maaster*)], Frances Rafferty [(*George Van Maaster*)], Frances Raeburn [(*Cornelius Van Maaster*)], *The Seven Sweethearts' Boy Friend:* Van Heflin [(*Henry Taggart*)], *The Seven Sweethearts' Other Boy Friends:* Carl Esmond [(*Jan Randall*)], Michael Butler [(*Bernard Groton*)], Cliff Danielson [(*Martin Leyden*)], William Roberts [(*Anthony Vreeland*)], James Warren [(*Theodore Vaney*)], Dick Simmons [(*Paul Brandt*)], *The Seven Sweethearts' Father:* S. Z. Sakall [(*Mr. Van Maaster*)], Diana Lewis [(*Mrs. Nugent*)], Lewis Howard [(*Mr. Nugent*)], Isobel Elsom [(*Miss Robbins*)], Donald Meek [(*Minister*)], Louise Beavers [(*Petunia*)], [Cecil Stewart (*Organist*)], [John Maxwell (*City editor*)], [Gladys Blake (*Telephone operator*)], [Lorraine Bridges, Terry Koechig, Faith Kruger (*Specialty bits in "Tingle Tangle Toes" number*)].

Musical, Romance. [*Print viewed*]. Reporter Henry Taggart arrives in the quaint town of Little Delft, Michigan, to cover the hamlet's annual tulip festival, and meets Papa Van Maaster, the local hotel proprietor, who strongly believes that the town's easy-going, old-fashioned ways are the best. Papa has seven daughters, all beautiful, and all but the oldest, spoiled Regina, have boys names and work at the hotel. New Yorker Henry is at first befuddled by the casual ambiance at the hotel, but soon brightens when he meets Papa's youngest and feistiest daughter, Billie. Although it is early May, constant rain prevents Henry from taking photographs for his article and forces him to extend his stay, during which he learns more about Delft's way of life. One evening, he meets vain and lazy Regina, who is determined to be an actress. Because Regina is unmarried, family tradition dictates that her younger sisters cannot marry, even though all but Billie are secretly engaged. The family encourages Henry to take a drive with Regina and he tries to impress her with talk about his "Broadway" friends. He still prefers Billie, who tells him that Regina is Papa's favorite and asks him not to encourage her to go to New York. He asks Billie to be the "Dutch" girl in his pictures, and the next evening, all of the sisters except self-centered Regina, who has a cold, notice the blossoming romance. During a ride in the rain, Henry confesses to Billie how much he likes her, and tries to kiss her, but she says that she does not want to be familiar with a guest. The next day, after church, Miss Robbins, a long-standing guest at the hotel, tells Henry that Billie is in love with him, and he admits that he wants to marry her. At the festival, the townspeople are all dressed in traditional Dutch costumes and go through various rituals, including the washing of the street and buildings. Papa is in the marching band and the girls perform a wooden shoe dance, during which Henry grabs Billie away and proposes. She loves him, but tells him that she could not leave their home because, like flowers, she would die if transplanted. She also tells him about the eldest daughter tradition. Not dissuaded, Henry plans to ask Papa for Billie's hand, but when he and Billie arrive back at the hotel, Regina is angry that he is no longer interested in her. Jan Randall, a Viennese musician who has lived at the hotel for several years, has secretly had a crush on Billie, but, on Henry's suggestion, decides to pursue Regina, whom he had thought unobtainable. Henry then goes to Papa, who guesses that he is asking for his daughter's hand, but thinks that Regina is the one. When Papa ecstatically fetches Regina, Henry is so flustered that he cannot explain what is wrong. Regina knows the truth, but secretly tells Henry that she wants him to take her to New York right away and threatens to tell Papa if he tries to talk his way out of it. In his panic, Henry asks the sisters and Miss Robbins to help him elope with Billie, but she refuses because of the tradition. She and the other sisters then try to talk Regina out of going to New York and hurting Papa. When Regina callously says she doesn't care what Papa wants, Billie slaps her. A few moments later, Papa tells Billie to go to sing her song at the festival. When she cannot continue singing and leaves the stage, Papa runs after her to see what is wrong. Henry follows them and tells Papa that he loves Billie and wants to take her to New York. Papa sadly tells them to go immediately, but after he leaves, Billie tells Henry that she could never hurt Papa by leaving and kisses him goodbye. Some time later, when Henry is in New York and completing his article on the festival, he gets a call from Regina, who is also in New York and wants to see him and meet his producer friends. As she waits for Henry at her hotel, Papa arrives and tells her that he will not stand in her way and plans to send her to the best acting schools. He also reveals that he has brought Miss Robbins and Randall with him to be her guardians. When Henry arrives, Papa reveals his plans for Regina and then "proposes" that he and Billie should marry. Papa is happy at Henry's eager acceptance because he now has a son—Henry the Eighth. Finally, at a large wedding ceremony in Delft, all of the sisters marry their fiancés, including Regina, who returns home, happily in love with Randall. *Dutch Americans. Fathers and daughters. Hotels. Reporters. Romance. Singers. Sisters. Churches. Elevators. Engagements. Festivals. Head colds. Honeymoons. Magazines. Maids. Michigan. Musicians. New York City. Rainstorms. Small town life. Tulips. War refugees. Widowers. Windmills.*

Note: Working titles of the film were *The House of the Seven Tulips, Seven Tulips, Seven Sisters* and *Tulip Time*. The film opens with the following written prologue: "To this great land the Dutch once came to plant their tulips...They grit their teeth, pulled in their belts, produced New York and the Roosevelts...Enriched this best of melting pots with their traditions, towns and tots...BEHOLD! in Michigan today there's still a Holland, U.S.A...A town that flaunts the windmill touch, to prove you just can't beat the Dutch." According to a *HR* news item, Frank Morgan was originally cast in the role of Mr. Van Maaster. One *HR* news item indicated that Van Johnson was set to play the lead, but this was probably a typographical error for Van Heflin. News items also note that Ann Rutherford, Philip Van Zandt and Douglas MacPhail were to be in the cast, but they were not in the released film. Frances Raeburn, who portrayed "Cornelius Van Maaster," was lead actress Kathryn Grayson's real-life sister. According to a 30 Apr 1942 news item, cameraman Leonard Smith shot exteriors for the film in Playa Del Rey, CA.

Although the onscreen credits and the SAB credit Walter Reisch and Leo Townsend with writing an original screenplay, in 1949, a \$200,000 lawsuit was filed against them, M-G-M and producer Joseph Pasternak by Hungarian playwright Ferenc Herczeg, claiming that they took the idea for the film from his 1903 play *Seven Sweethearts*. According to news items in *HR* and *Var* in Mar 1954, the case, which was presided over by Los Angeles Superior Court Judge Philip H. Richard, was settled out-of-court for a "substantial" amount. The articles also related that Herczeg, who was represented by attorney Jacques Leslie, had been confined in a Nazi concentration camp when the film was released in 1942 and did not become aware of it until 1948.

Seven Sweethearts was the first M-G-M film produced by Joseph Pasternak. Pasternak, who had been at Universal for many years and had produced young singing star Deanna Durban's highly successful films, remained at M-G-M for more than a decade. Most of his films at M-G-M were big-budget, commercially successful musicals such as *Anchors Away* and *In the Good Old Summertime*. Many featured the operatic talents of singers such as Kathryn Grayson and Mario Lanza.

Box 15 Aug 1942. *DV* 12 Aug 1942, p. 3. *FD* 12 Aug 1942, p. 6. *HR* 3 Mar 1942, p. 2. *HR* 4 Mar 1942, p. 2. *HR* 12 Mar 1942, p. 1. *HR* 16 Mar 1942, p. 1. *HR* 19 Mar 1942, p. 4. *HR* 24 Mar 1942, p. 3. *HR* 27 Mar 1942, p. 6. *HR* 31 Mar 1942, p. 6. *HR* 17 Apr 1942, p. *HR* 30 Apr 1942, p. 10. *HR* 8 May 1942, p. *HR* 12 May 1942, p. 7. *HR* 12 Aug 1942, p. 3. *HR* 2 Mar 1954. *MPHPD* 15 Aug 1942, p. 839. *NYT* 13 Nov 1942, p. 28. *Var* 12 Aug 1942, p. 8. *Var* 3 Mar 1954.

SEVEN TULIPS *see* SEVEN SWEETHEARTS

7TH CAVALRY (Native Americans, Dakota)

Producers-Actors Corp.; A Scott-Brown Production. *Dist* Columbia Pictures Corp. Dec 1956; Prod: 12 Jan–3 Feb 1956 [©Producers-Actors Corp.; 1 Dec 1956; LP7330]. Sd (RCA Sound System); col (Technicolor). 6,856 ft. 76 min.

Prod Harry Joe Brown. *Assoc prod* Randolph Scott. *Asst to prod* David Breen. *Dir* Joseph H. Lewis and [Raphael J. Sevilla]. *Asst dir* Abner E. Singer and [Jesús Marín]. *Scr* Peter Packer. *Dir of photog* Ray Rennahan. *Techicolor col consultant* Henri Jaffa. *Art dir* George

Brooks and [Jesús Bracho]. *Film ed* Gene Havlick. *Set dec* Frank Tuttle. *Mus cond by* Mischa Bakaleinikoff. [*Sd* Gene Valentino]. [*In charge of production* Antonio Guerrero Tello].

Source: Based on the short story "A Horse for Mrs. Custer" by Glendon E. Swarthout in *New World Writing 5* (New York, 1954).

Cast: RANDOLPH SCOTT [(*Captain Tom Benson*)], Barbara Hale [(*Martha Kellogg*)], Jay C. Flippen [(*Sergeant Bates*)], Frank Faylen [(*Kruger*)], Jeanette Nolan [(*Mrs. Charlotte Reynolds*)], Leo Gordon [(*Vogel*)], Denver Pyle [(*Dixon*)], Harry Carey, Jr. [(*Corporal Morrison*)], Michael Pate [(*Captain Benteen*)], Donald Curtis [(*Lieutenant Bob Fitch*)], Frank Wilcox [(*Major Reno*)], Pat Hogan [(*Young Hawk*)], [Russell Hicks (*Colonel Kellogg*)], [Peter Ortiz (*Pollock*)], [William Leslie (*Lieutenant Murray*)], [Jack Parker, Al Wyatt (*Officers*)], [Edward F. Stidder (*Orderly*)].

Western. [*Print viewed*]. In 1876, together with his fiancée, Martha Kellogg, Captain Tom Benson returns to his command under General George Custer. As they approach the fort, Tom notices that the garrison flag is not flying. Leaving Martha behind, Tom investigates and discovers that the fort is largely deserted. From Charlotte Reynolds, a distraught soldier's wife, Tom learns that most of the soldiers were massacred during a battle with the Sioux at Little Big Horn. Charlotte accuses Tom of deliberately avoiding the battle when he left the fort to fetch Martha. Although Tom insists that Custer gave him permission to leave, and that he did not know the battle was to take place so soon, the surviving soldiers are not convinced. Tom, who was Custer's right-hand man, is shocked to hear the other soldiers blame Custer's incompetence and ego for the defeat. Despite the bad feeling toward Tom, Martha remains supportive, but he decides to send her away so that she will not be affected by his blackened reputation. His plans are interrupted by the arrival of Martha's father, Colonel Kellogg, who has been charged with investigating the massacre. During the inquiry, Major Reno reveals that Custer made several serious mistakes, among them dividing his force into three battalions, which contributed to his defeat. Another soldier states that Custer began the attack against the advice of his scouts. When Tom tries to defend Custer, Kellogg orders him confined to quarters. Later, when asked why he left the fort on personal business so close to the time of the coming assault, Tom replies that Custer gave him direct orders, but because the orders were verbal, he has no proof. Determined to clear himself of charges of cowardice, Tom volunteers to lead a burial detail that has been ordered by President Ulysses S. Grant to remove the bodies of the officers from Little Big Horn. Tom "persuades" the soldiers who did not fight in the battle because they were in the stockade to volunteer along with him. As the detail travels toward Little Big Horn, Tom must contend with hostile soldiers as well as the threat of Indian attack. Near Little Big Horn, the soldiers encounter a warning indicating that Sitting Bull has made the site a sacred place for the Sioux, and the men become certain that they are riding into an ambush. Meanwhile, at the fort, Corporal Morrison returns and informs Martha that he heard Custer order Tom to leave. Then mounted on Dandy, a double for Vic, the horse that died with Custer, Morrison hurries to deliver the news to Tom. At Little Big Horn, the soldiers remove the officers' bodies and load them in wagons to be carried back to the fort. While they are working, the Sioux surround them. Young Hawk, a Sioux who was educated by whites, tells Tom that the soldiers are defiling sacred ground. He explains that the Sioux believe that the spirits of the dead men and horses live on in the Indians who defeated them in battle. When Tom dismisses his concerns as superstition, Young Hawk adds that if Custer's body is removed, his spirit would go with him and the fruits of their victory would be lost to the Sioux. When Tom still refuses to leave without Custer's body, the men rebel. Rather than further defile the sacred ground by shedding more blood, the Sioux surround the soldiers, planning to wait until they die. Meanwhile, Morrison approaches Little Big Horn. After he is killed by a lookout, the riderless horse continues to Little Big Horn. The Sioux recognize the horse as Custer's and, believing him to be the spirit of the dead Vic, disperse. Tom takes advantage of Dandy's appearance to bring his men home. Kellogg apologizes and gives his blessing to Martha and Tom's marriage. *Cowardice. Dakota Indians. Little Big Horn, Battle of the, 1876. Religion. Reputation. Soldiers. United States. Army. Cavalry. Burial. General George Armstrong Custer. Engagements. False accusations. Fathers and daughters. Forts. Horses. Rites and ceremonies.*

Note: The film's working title was *The Return of Custer*. For more information about the life of General George Armstrong Custer and the Battle of Little Big Horn, please see the entry below for *They Died With Their Boots On*.

Box 27 Oct 1956. *DV* 19 Oct 1956, p. 3. *Exb* 31 Oct 1956, pp. 4241-42. *FD* 2 Jul 1956, p. 12. *Har* 27 Oct 1956, p. 170. *HR* 19 Oct 1956, p. 3. *MPHPD* 3 Nov 1956, p. 130. *Var* 24 Oct 1956, p. 6.

SEVILLA DE MIS AMORES (Spanish language)
Metro-Goldwyn-Mayer Corp.; controlled by Loew's Inc. *Dist* Metro-Goldwyn-Mayer Distributing Corp. Dec **1930**; Los Angeles opening: 5 Dec 1930; Prod: Aug—Sep 1930. Sd (Western Electric Sound System); b&w. 12 reels, 9,120 ft. 101 min. Passed by the National Board of Review. Spanish language.

[*Supv* B. P. Fineman]. *Dirigida por* [*Dir*] Ramón Novarro. *Asistente director* [*Asst dir*] Carlos F. Borcosque. *Argumento de* [*Story*] Dorothy Farnum. *Diálogo por* [*Dial*] John Colton. *Versión española de* [*Spanish version by*] Ramón Guerrero. *Fotografiada por* [*Photog*] Merritt B. Gerstad. *Director artístico* [*Art dir*] Cedric Gibbons. *Editada por* [*Ed*] Thomas Held. *Música de* [*Mus*] Herbert Stothart and Ramón Novarro. *Acústica por* [*Sd*] Douglas Shearer. [*Sd* Antonio Samaniego].

Song(s): "Eres poco para mi," "Añoranzas" and "¡Hoy nada más!" words by Ramón Novarro, music by Herbert Stothart.

Cast: Ramón Novarro (*Juan de Dios*), Conchita Montenegro (*María Consuelo*), José Soriano Viosca (*Tío Esteban*), Sra. L. G. de Samaniego (*Madre superiora*), Rosita Ballesteros (*Lola*), Martín Garralaga (*Enrique Vargas*), Sra. María Calvo (*Lulú Laponco*), Michael Vavitch (*Empresario*), [Ramón Guerrero (*Sacerdote*)].

Romance, Drama. [*Not viewed*]. María Consuelo, a young novice nun, admires the voice of café singer Juan de Dios and builds a romantic fantasy around him, eventually forcing her to leave her convent to be with him. Juan, who aspires to a career in opera, responds to María with affection and would like to adopt and protect her, but falls in love with her and they become engaged. However, Lola, who was Juan's former partner and is in love with him, encourages María's brother Enrique to separate the couple, and María eventually returns to her convent. Although Juan goes on to a successful career in opera in Madrid, he becomes profoundly depressed by the loss of María. When her mother superior learns about María's situation, she frees her from the obligation of taking her final vows. María finds Juan and they promise never to be apart again. *Courtship. Nuns. Opera. Singers. Brothers and sisters. Cafés. Convents. Madrid (Spain). Priests. Religion. Seville (Spain). Vocal instructors.*

Note: *Sevilla de mis amores* is a Spanish-language version of the 1930 M-G-M film *Call of the Flesh*, starring Ramón Novarro and Dorothy Jordan and directed by Charles Brabin (see *AFI Catalog of Feature Films, 1921-30*; F2.0737). The onscreen credits for this version were taken from a studio cutting continuity. Some contemporary sources include Christina Montt, José Peña "Pepet", Gabry Rivas, Marina Ortiz and Alfonso Azaf in the cast, but their participation in the released film has not been confirmed. There was also a French-language version of the film, entitled *Le chanteur de Seville*, also directed by Ramon Novarro, that starred Novarro and Suzy Vernon, but no record of any U.S. exhibition of that version has been found.

Cinl Feb 1931, p. 32. *CM* Dec 1930, p. 1,199.

THE SHADOW (African Americans)
Micheaux Pictures. Oct **1921**. Si; b&w. 7 reels.

Melodrama (?), African American. No information about the specific nature of this film has been found. *African Americans.*

THE SHADOW OF THEIR WINGS *see* **WINGS FOR THE EAGLE**

SHADOWS (1919) *see* **A HEART IN PAWN**

SHADOWS (Chinese Americans)
Preferred Pictures, Inc. *Dist* Al Lichtman Corp. 10 Nov **1922** [©Preferred Pictures, Inc.; 7 Oct 1922; LP18347]. Si; b&w. 7 reels, 7,040 ft.

Pres B. P. Schulberg. *Dir* Tom Forman. *Scen* Eve Unsell and Hope Loring. *Photog* Harry Perry.

Source: Based on the short story "Ching, Ching, Chinaman" by Wilbur Daniel Steele in *Pictorial Review* (Jun 1917).

Cast: Lon Chaney (*Yen Sin, "The Heathen"*), Marguerite De La Motte (*Sympathy Gibbs*), Harrison Ford (*John Malden*), John Sainpolis (*Nate Snow*), Walter Long (*Daniel Gibbs*), Buddy Messenger (*"Mister Bad Boy"*), Priscilla Bonner (*Mary Brent*), Frances Raymond (*Emsy Nickerson*).

Melodrama. After Daniel Gibbs is lost at sea, his wife, Sympathy, marries Rev. John Malden. They are supremely happy until John receives a blackmail note falsely indicating that Gibbs is alive. John's dilemma is solved when the Maldens' dying friend, Yen Sin, agrees to become a Christian in exchange for the revelation that Nate Snow sent the note. *Blackmail. Chinese Americans. Clergy. Religious conversion.*
ETR 11 Nov 1922, p. 1517. *FD* 5 Nov 1922. *MPW* 11 Nov 1922. *Var* 3 Nov 1922, p. 42.

SHADOWS OF CHINATOWN (Chinese Americans)

Bud Barsky Corp. 1 Mar 1926. Si; b&w. 5 reels.
Dir Paul Hurst.

Cast: Kenneth McDonald (*Jimmy King*), Velma Edele (*Velma*), Elmer Dewey (*The Ace*), Ben Corbett (*The Weasel*), Lee Chung (*Wing Lee*), Frank Chew (*Wo Hop*).

Crime, Drama. "Crooks cloak their operations in Chinatown. Navy Lieutenant is assigned task of exterminating gang. Is aided by friendly Chinese but captured by crooks and faces death with young woman agent disguised as Chinese. They are saved by Police." (*MPNBG* 11 Oct 1926, p. 47.). *Chinatowns. Chinese Americans. Gangs. Impersonation and imposture. United States. Navy.*

SHADOWS OF THE ORIENT (Chinese Americans)

Larry Darmour Productions; Monogram Pictures Corp. *Dist* Monogram Pictures Corp.; Empire Film Distributors, Inc. 18 Aug 1937; *Prod:* began late Dec 1935 [©Monogram Pictures Corp.; 23 Aug 1937; LP7444]. Sd; b&w. 7 reels. 65 or 69-70 min. Passed by the National Board of Review. PCA cert no. 1928.
Prod Larry Darmour. *Dir* Burt Lynwood. *Asst dir* Harry Knight. *Orig story* L. E. Heifetz. *Scr and adpt* Charles Francis Royal. *Photog* James S. Brown, Jr. *Settings* Paul Palmentola. *Ed* Dwight Caldwell. *Mus dir* Lee Zahler. *Sd rec* Tom Lambert.

Cast: Esther Ralston [(*Viola Avery*)], Regis Toomey [(*Baxter, also known as Keeler and "Tricky" Thomas*)], J. Farrell MacDonald [(*Sullivan*)], Oscar Apfel [(*Judge Avery*)], Sidney Blackmer [(*King Moss*)], Eddie Featherstone [(*James "Flash" Dawson*)], Matty Fain [(*Gangster*)], Kit Guard [(*Spud Nolan*)], James Leong [(*Chin Chu*)].

Social, Crime, Drama. [*Print viewed*]. Suspended airman James Dawson, called "Flash," works for a gang of smugglers who move Chinese across the Mexican border for a high price. When the pilot of plane "X-26" is unable to land because of police patrolling the airfield, the shipment of Chinese isn't delivered to smuggling chief Chin Chu, and he refuses to pay Flash and accuses him of murdering his countrymen. In revenge, Flash informs on the smugglers, tipping off veteran police inspector Sullivan to raid a gambling house called the Canton House, where Chin Chu and his gang meet. While he is on the phone, Flash is shot to death by one of Chin Chu's men, causing Sullivan and Morgan, his partner in the Immigration Service to race to the Canton House with backup policemen. Among those being corralled into paddy wagons is Viola Avery, daughter of Judge Avery, who has been up all night playing fan-tan. When a mysterious curio collector rescues her from Sullivan, insisting she is the judge's daughter, Viola is grateful and agrees to attend his cocktail party the next day. Meanwhile, police chief Graves breaks up the ineffectual team of Morgan and Sullivan and pairs Sullivan with rookie investigator Baxter to solve the informer's murder. Suspicious of the woman who claimed to be Viola Avery, Baxter calls her, and when she comes to retrieve her purse, he drives her home and questions her about the strange man. At the Avery home, Viola and Baxter are met by a throng of reporters, but Baxter staves off a scandal by informing the press that Viola's implication in the raid was a case of mistaken identity. Baxter then tells her father that she was with him the previous night and promises to meet her at the curio collector's cocktail party. Later, Baxter deduces that the informer was a grounded pilot who recently began flying again, and orders Sullivan to identify him. Using the name Keeler, Baxter poses as an aficionado of Oriental law and gets himself invited to the strange man's party whose name he learns is King Moss. During the party, Moss is visited by one of his henchmen, Spud Nolan, who informs him they are short a pilot for the next run of Chinese. At the party, Viola tells Moss and Baxter that her father locked up her plane and revoked her license and that she would love to fly with Moss. Meanwhile, Sullivan has identified the corpse as Flash, and he and Baxter go to Flash's apartment, where they find a hole in the newspaper want-ads. Tracing the paper, they discover that Flash answered an ad for an aviator who is "fearless and ready to take a chance." They also learn that the day after Flash's

death, the same ad appeared in all the papers around town. Hoping to identify the smugglers, Baxter goes undercover as gangster pilot Tricky Thomas and meets the smugglers at an Acme Trucking Company warehouse. Spud gets suspicious when one of his men tells him that the real Tricky is in jail and calls in a gangster named Steve to identify Baxter. When Spud tells Moss their new flier might be a phony, he asks Viola to make a secret flight with him to his "ranch," warning her she might have to fly the plane back alone. Meanwhile, Baxter tries to escape by knocking out Rod, one of the guards, but a thug named Tiger enters and helps Rod tie up Baxter. Across the border, Chinese liaison Yung Yow insists Moss leave a hostage to ensure a safe passage for his countrymen, and Moss agrees to leave Viola. When Viola realizes she is a hostage, she escapes and takes off in the plane filled with Chinese, which Moss pursues. Meanwhile, at the warehouse, Steve exposes Baxter as a fake and Sullivan calls for backup and raids the warehouse, saving Baxter just as Rod is about to shoot him. Sullivan and Baxter then go to Mercer Field to meet the shipment and arrest Spud. Baxter goes up in a plane and orders plane X-26 to land. When Baxter discovers Chinese in the plane, he tells Viola he will have to arrest her, but she insists she was a hostage. Baxter then goes up in his plane to bring down Moss and shoots down his plane and arrests him. Baxter confiscates half of a letter written in Chinese from Moss, and Sullivan matches it with the one he found on one of the Chinese. With their evidence intact, Sullivan prepares to resign, but Baxter handcuffs Viola to him and tells him to report to Graves that he eloped with the secret agent who helped him solve the case. *Air pilots. Chinese Americans. G-men. Smuggling. Actors and actresses. Advertisements. Airplane accidents. Chinatowns. Collectors and collecting. Elopement. Escapes. Gambling houses. Gangsters. Hostages. Immigrants. Impersonation and imposture. Informers. Judges. Mexican-American border region. Murder. Partnership. Police chiefs. Police raids. Rescues. Scandal. Warehouses. Women air pilots.*

Note: An onscreen foreword states, "Since the passing of the Oriental exclusion act the smuggling of aliens has been constant. Although the smuggling is less than a few years ago, when Chinese were brought into the United States from Mexico in carlots, the traffic has by no means ceased, according to immigration officials. The length of the frontier and sparsely settled regions makes patrolling impossible. These smugglers have no regard for human life and resort to any means to accomplish their selfish ends. The boss of the ring, at the time, is receiving fifteen hundred dollars per head on safe delivery." The film was completed in Jan 1936 and was reviewed by *HR*, *MPD* and *MPH* in early Feb 1936; however, *MPH* release charts give a release date of 18 Aug 1937, and it was not reviewed by *FD*, *NYT* or *Var* until the second week of Oct 1937. As announced in a news item in *HR* on 29 Oct 1935, Empire Film Distributors of New York struck a deal with Larry Darmour Productions to handle the sales of this, and five other, Darmour films scheduled for the 1935-36 season. The 1937 *FDYB* lists this film under Monogram Pictures Corp.'s production line-up for the 1937-38 season. *MPH* release charts list the film under Empire in the 1936 charts, and under Monogram in the 1937-38 charts. It may have been released in 1936 by Empire and in 1937 by Monogram.
Box 22 Feb 1936. *FD* 13 Oct 1937, p. 8. *HR* 29 Oct 1935, p. 2. *HR* 30 Dec 1935, p. 11. *HR* 5 Feb 1936, p. 4. *MPD* 8 Feb 1936, p. 4. *MPH* 1 Jan 1938, p. 65. *MPH* 15 Feb 1936, p. 44, 48. *MPH* 3 Jul 1937, p. 75. *NYT* 11 Oct 1937, p. 26. *Var* 13 Oct 1937, p. 16.

SHADOWS OF THE WEST (Japanese Americans)

Cinema Craft; Motion Picture Producing Co. of America. *Dist* National Exchanges. Aug 1921. Si; b&w. 8 & 5 reels.
Supv Charles Hickman. *Dir* Paul Hurst. *Scen* James Dayton. *Story* Seymour Zeliff.

Cast: Lt. Pat O'Brien (*Jim Kern*), Hedda Nova (*Mary*), Virginia Dale (*Lucy Norton*), Seymour Zeliff (*Frank Akuri*), Benjamin Corbett (*Jim's pal*).

Western. California cowpuncher Jim Kern and his pal enlist in the war against Germany and, shortly thereafter, meet Frank Akuri, who has pledged to colonize the United States for his homeland, Japan. While Jim and other white males are fighting in France, Akuri forces Jim's sweetheart Mary to sell her ranch, as she is not able to run it because the only men left, the Japanese, have pledged not to work for the whites. With the ranch, Akuri begins his colony. Mary counters by organizing her society women friends to appeal to Congress against the "yellow menace." When it seems that his plans will be thwarted, Akuri issues orders for the death of Mary and her friends, but Jim and his pal return and rescue them. Akuri then kidnaps Mary and takes her to his apartment, but with the help of Akuri's wronged Japanese lover, Jim learns her whereabouts. He organizes a posse of American Legion locals and rescues Mary just as Akuri is about to murder her. Akuri's group is routed out. *California. Colonies. Cowboys. Japanese Americans. Racism. Ranchers. Xenophobia. American Legion. Kidnapping. Rescues. Soldiers. United States. Congress. World War I.*

Note: Reviews in late 1920, from which the synopsis is taken, label this film as 8 reels in length, produced by Cinema Craft, highly propagandistic, and anti-Japanese. *MPW* described the film at length and expressed doubts concerning whether a film of this sort should, in fact, be exhibited: "A propaganda picture pure and simple, based on the presence of thousands of Japanese in California is *Shadows of the West*.... It attacks the Japanese in a way that, should it attain wide circulation, will increase the difficulties between this country and the island empire. The sons of Nippon are shown as profiteers, wife-beaters and would-be murderers. They are shown dumping fish into the sea in order to maintain high prices (which idea is not wholly Japanese), and are accused of violations of various laws. The direct accusation is made that they menace this country's integrity. They are held up to public view in the worst light, in a way that is calculated to make them nationally hated. In fact, the evident purpose of the picture is to bring about such an overwhelming sentiment against them, and such pressure to bear on Congress, that the legislators will take some action against the Japanese to permanently keep them away from American life. The newspapers advise us that relations between the United States and Japan are delicate and if this be so the circulation of a picture damning the Japanese might well be questioned. A sub-title quotes the principal female character as saying to a mob: 'As a representative of the women voters, I request you to allow the senate to handle this vital question.' This gives a suggestion. The situation, serious without question, could properly be handled by the government and without the necessity for a picture which inflames the minds of the people against the Japanese." Apparently the Motion Picture Producing Co. of America reduced the film to 5 reels, played down the "yellow peril" menace, and emphasized the western aspects.

ETR 27 Nov 1920, p. 2733. *MPNBG* Dec 1921. *MPW* 27 Nov 1920, p. 513.

SHADOWS OVER CHINATOWN (1940) *see* DOOMED TO DIE

SHADOWS OVER CHINATOWN (Chinese Americans)

Monogram Pictures Corp. *Dist* Monogram Pictures Corp. 27 Jul **1946**; Prod: mid—late Mar 1946 [©Monogram Pictures Corp.; 5 Jul 1946; LP420]. Sd (Western Electric Mirrophonic Recording); b&w. 64 min.

Series: Charlie Chan.

Prod James S. Burkett. *Dir* Terry Morse. *Asst dir* Wm. Callahan, Jr. *Orig scr* Raymond Schrock. *Photog* William Sickner. *Tech dir* Dave Milton. *Supv film ed* Richard Currier. *Ed* Ralph Dixon. *Mus dir* Edward J. Kay. *Rec* Tom Lambert. *Makeup* Harry Ross. *Prod mgr* Glenn Cook.

Source: Based on characters created by Earl Derr Biggers.

Cast: Sidney Toler [(*Charlie Chan*)], Mantan Moreland [(*Birmingham*)], Victor Sen Young [(*Jimmy Chan*)], Tanis Chandler [(*Mary Conover*)], John Gallaudet [(*Jeff Hay*)], Paul Bryar [(*Mike Rogan*)], Bruce Kellogg [(*Jack Tilford, also known as John Thompson*)], Alan Bridge [(*Captain Allen*)], Mary Gordon [(*Mrs. Conover*)], Dorothy Granger [(*Joan Mercer*)], Jack Norton [(*Cosgrove*)], George Eldredge [(*Lannigan*)], Tyra Vaughn [(*Miss Chalmers*)], Lyle Latell [(*Police clerk*)], Myra McKinney [(*Kate Johnson*)], Gladys Blake [(*Myrtle*)], [George Chan, James B. Leong (*Chinese Americans*)], [Jack Mower (*Hobart*)], [John Hamilton (*Pronnet*)], [Harry Depp (*Dr. Denby*)], [Charlie Jordan (*Jenkins*)], [Louise Franklin (*Maid*)], [Frank Mayo (*Police lieutenant*)], [Kit Carson (*Hotel clerk*)], [Doris Fulton (*Angie*)], [Jimmy Dugan (*Police driver*)].

Detective, Comedy-drama. [*Print viewed*]. Famous detective Charlie Chan, his son Jimmy and his chauffeur Birmingham are all on a bus traveling to San Francisco to investigate a murder case involving an armless, legless, headless torso. A short time later, when the bus breaks down, several passengers notice that they have been robbed. After they are joined by a U.S. Marine, who calls himself Jack Tilford, Chan speaks privately to another passenger, Cosgrove, suggesting that if he returns the stolen items, his crime will not be revealed. Grateful, the pickpocket promises to return the favor in the future. Back on the bus, Chan learns that Mrs. Conover is traveling to San Francisco to search for her missing granddaughter Mary. In San Francisco, Chan, Jimmy and Birmingham visit the Bureau of Missing Persons, where Chan reveals to Captain Allen that he has two purposes. The first, on behalf of an insurance company, is to discover the identity of the torso; the second is to learn the whereabouts of Mary Conover. Chan suspects that the torso belongs to a former showgirl named Grace Gortner, whose wealthy husband, Homer B. Pendleton, died after taking out a large insurance policy. On Allen's desk, Chan spots a photograph of A.W.O.L. Marine Corporal John Thompson and realizes that he is the same man who called himself "Tilford." Chan returns to the hotel where Mrs. Conover is staying with her friend, Kate Johnson. After reassuring Mrs. Conover that the body, which has an appendectomy scar, cannot be Mary's, he and Jimmy lunch in the

hotel restaurant. There Chan recognizes their waitress as Mary with dyed blonde hair. Before Chan can bring her grandmother to confirm her identity, however, Mary is recognized by her former employer, Mike Rogan, and flees the hotel. Jimmy and Birmingham follow, but when Chan later meets them at Mary's apartment, they are joined by private detective Jeff Hay, who tells Chan he has followed their bus driver, who is actually Mike Rogan, to this location. Inside the apartment they discover Kate's body, and Chan suspects that the killer mistook her for Mary. Chan returns to the Bureau of Missing Persons and learns that Grace had been in love with a man named Craig Winfield before her marriage. Then John is picked up by the police and explains that he went A.W.O.L. to find Mary, with whom he was in love. He adds that Mary worked at an escort bureau and was frightened of her employer, Rogan. When Chan returns to his hotel, Hay is waiting with the information that he has found Rogan in Chinatown, but when they arrive there, Rogan is dead. Then Mary is picked up and explains that Rogan discovered that John's father was wealthy and suggested that she marry John, take out a large insurance policy and become a wealthy widow. After reuniting Mary and her grandmother, Chan asks Mary to help him set a trap for the owner of the escort bureau. At the escort bureau, Mary is waylaid by Hay, but when he learns that she is part of a police trap, he kidnaps her, intending to kill her. In the meantime, a photograph has come over the bureau's wire service that identifies Hay as Winfield. Following a hunch, Chan finds Hay and Mary in Chinatown. Although Hay tries to shoot Chan, Cosgrove has removed the bullets from his gun. Chan then explains that Hay killed Kate, mistaking her for Mary, and also killed Rogan, in order to blame him for the other deaths. *Chinese Americans. Missing persons. Murder. Private detectives. San Francisco (CA). African Americans. Buses. Fathers and sons. Grandmothers. Hotels. Impersonation and imposture. Life insurance. Pickpockets. United States. Marine Corps.*

Note: The film's working titles were *Corpus Delicti* and *The Mandarin's Secret*. For more information on the Charlie Chan series, consult the Series Index and see the entry above for *Charlie Chan Carries On.*

HR 15 Mar 1946, p. 18. *HR* 22 Mar 1946, p. 12. *HR* 16 Apr 1946, p. 18. *MPHPD* 27 Apr 1946, p. 2963. *Var* 18 Sep 1946, p. 22.

SHAKE HANDS WITH THE DEVIL (Irish Americans)

Troy Films, Ltd.; Pennebaker, Inc. *Dist* United Artists Corp. Jun **1959**; World premiere in Dublin, Ireland: 21 May 1959; Los Angeles opening: 3 Jun 1959; Prod: 8 Sep—mid-Nov 1958 at the Ardmore Studios (Bray, Ireland) [©Troy Films, Ltd.; 22 May 1959; LP13960]. Sd (Westrex Recording System); b&w. 110 min. PCA cert no. 19203.

Exec prod George Glass and Walter Seltzer. *Prod* Michael Anderson. *Prod supv* Bill Kirby. *Dir* Michael Anderson. *Asst dir* Chris Sutton. *Scr* Ivan Goff and Ben Roberts. *Adpt* Marian Thompson. *Dir of photog* Erwin Hillier. *Cam op* Roy Sturgess. *2d unit photog* Eric Besche. *Spec eff* Cliff Richardson and Roy Whybrow. *Prod des and art dir* Tom Morahan. *Ed supv* Gordon Pilkington. *Set dec* Josie MacAvin. [*Props* Steve Grogan]. *Ward supv* John McCorry. *Ladies' cost des* Irene Gilbert. *Mus comp* William Alwyn. *Played by* Sinfonia of London. *Mus cond* Muir Mathieson. *Dubbing ed* Rusty Coppleman. *Sd rec* L. B. Bulkeley and J. B. Smith. *Makeup* Tony Szforzini. *Hairdressing* Joan White. *Continuity* Angela Martelli. *Spec military adv* Lt. Col. William O'Kelly, Irish Defense Force. *Cast dir* Robert Lennard.

Source: Based on the novel *Shake Hands with the Devil* by Rearden Conner (London, 1933).

Cast: JAMES CAGNEY (*Sean Lenihan*), DON MURRAY (*Kerry O'Shea*), DANA WYNTER (*Jennifer Curtis*), GLYNIS JOHNS (*Kitty Brady*), Michael Redgrave (*The general*), Sybil Thorndike (*Lady Fitzhugh*), Cyril Cusack (*Chris Noonan*), and introducing Marianne Benet (*Mary Madigan*), John Breslin (*McGrath*), Harry Brogan (*Cassidy*), Robert Brown (*1st Sgt., Black & Tans*), Lewis Casson (*The judge*), Christopher Casson (*Brigadier*), John Cairney (*Mike O'Callaghan*), Harry Corbett (*Clancy*), Eileen Crowe (*Mrs. Madigan*), Alan Cuthbertson (*Captain*), Donal Donnelly (*Willie Lafferty*), Wilfred Downing (*Tommy Connor*), Eithne Dunne (*Eileen O'Leary*), Paul Farrell (*Doyle*), Richard Harris (*Terence O'Brien*), William Hartnell (*Sgt. Jenkins*), John Le Mesurier (*British general*), Niall MacGinnis (*Michael O'Leary*), Patrick McAlinney (*Donovan*), Ray McAnally (*Paddy Nolan*), Clive Morton (*Sir Arnold Fielding*), Noel Purcell (*Liam O'Sullivan*), Peter Reynolds (*Captain, Black & Tans*), Christopher Rhodes (*Col. Smithson*), Ronald Walsh (*Sgt., Black & Tans*), Alan White (*Capt. Fleming*).

Political, **Drama**. [*Print viewed*]. In 1921, young American medical student Kerry O'Shea, whose Irish father was killed in an uprising against the British, comes to Dublin, and soon helps weapons smuggler Eileen O'Leary hide from the "Black and Tans." Kerry tells her that although his heart is with the cause, he does not believe that "violence ever solved anything," and later he remarks to his nationalistic roommate, Paddy Nolan, that the rebellion is "your war." As the two friends leave a pub one evening, Kerry tries to help a terrorist who has been shot by a Black and Tan soldier. While dragging Kerry out of danger, Paddy is also shot, whereupon Kerry takes him to the home of a rebel sympathizer. There he learns that one of his professors, respected surgeon Sean Lenihan, is "the Commandant," the second-in-command of the rebel army. Despite Lenihan's best efforts, Paddy dies, and Kerry, having dropped a textbook inscribed with his name at the scene of the shootout, finds himself a wanted man. Lenihan takes him to "headquarters," where he meets "the General," who knew his father. Kerry is then taken to a small farm overlooking the ocean, to await the boat that will take him out of the country. There Kerry is introduced to Chris Noonan, a gentle poet who writes in Gaelic; Kitty Brady, a feisty barmaid who offers her own brand of comfort to the men, despite Lenihan's orders that she stay away; and Terence O'Brien, a swaggering thug who accuses Kerry of cowardice for not committing himself to the Irish cause. He also briefly meets the charming Lady Fitzhugh, an elderly rebel sympathizer who plans to smuggle an injured Irish terrorist named Liam O'Sullivan to safety. The plan goes awry, and Lady Fitzhugh is arrested just outside a pub near rebel headquarters. When O'Brien's gun falls to the floor, the Black and Tans assume it belongs to Kerry, and he is dragged from the pub and imprisoned. Kerry is tortured by the Black and Tans, and by the time Lenihan and the others rescue him, he is ready to join the rebellion. During his recovery, Kerry deepens his friendship with Noonan and romances Kitty, who willingly accepts his attentions. When it is learned that Lady Fitzhugh has been on a hunger strike since her arrest, Lenihan suggests that they take a hostage who may be used to effect an exchange. Kerry assists in the kidnapping of Jennifer Curtis, the widowed daughter of military adviser Sir Arnold Fielding, but soon after her imprisonment in a nearby lighthouse, he finds himself falling in love with her. Lenihan reminds Kerry that there is no room for pity and mercy in their war, whereupon Kerry replies that no war is worth winning if those human qualities are forgotten. The discovery by the British of Lenihan's involvement in the kidnapping forces the Commandant underground, and when he meets with the General, he learns that British officials are considering a treaty that would guarantee dominion status for Ireland. Horrified that the General would approve of such a compromise, Lenihan swears to fight until all of Ireland is declared a fully independent republic. Later, Lenihan and the other men meet at the lighthouse to discuss their plan to go to Dublin, where they can ambush and kill Col. Smithson of the Black and Tans. Kitty's presence infuriates Lenihan, and he orders her into the back room with Jennifer. Later, Kitty sneaks out to the beach for a swim in the nude, and when she realizes Lenihan has been watching her, she dares him to touch her. Burning with hatred, Lenihan orders her to leave. Back at her pub, when she discovers that the Black and Tans are looking for her, Donovan, her employer, gives her enough money to book passage to England. Meanwhile, Kerry, aware that the coming morning's ambush is fraught with danger, bids farewell to Jennifer, who by now returns his love. At dawn, the men take their places on the dock, ready to attack Col. Smithson's approaching vehicle. Meanwhile, as Kitty is about to board a vessel to Liverpool, she is detained by Black and Tans. Because of her surprise at seeing O'Brien on the dock, the guards become suspicious and chase him. A gun battle begins, during which Lenihan, assuming Kitty has betrayed them, ignores her pleas and shoots her repeatedly. Seeing this, Kerry is horrified at Lenihan's brutality. Kerry then goes to the Dublin headquarters and hears the General announce that the proposed treaty has been approved, and that he is on his way to London. Following his departure, however, the remaining rebels learn that Lady Fitzhugh has starved to death. When Lenihan returns to the lighthouse, he hands Jennifer a bible and leads her to the shore, where he plans to carry out an execution of revenge. Kerry pursues them, reminding Lenihan of the treaty and shouting that the Commandant now kills solely for the sake of killing. As Lenihan aims at Jennifer, Kerry cries, "I'm not going to fight your war!" and shoots

him. Following Lenihan's death, Kerry looks with pain at his gun and flings it into the sea. *Americans in foreign countries. Ireland. Loyalty. Obsession. Revolutionaries. Terrorism. Uprisings. Ambushes. Barmaids. Dublin (Ireland). Executions. Explosions. Fathers and sons. Grenades. Hideouts. Hostages. Hunger strikes. Irish Americans. Kidnapping. Medical students. Misogyny. Poets. Prison escapes. Pubs. Revenge. Romance. Roommates. Surgeons. Torture. Treaties.*

Note: The working title of this film was *The Raging Men*. Although most contemporary sources list the film's running time as 110 minutes, the *DV* and *Var* reviews list the running time as 104 minutes at a preview showing, and the *HR* review gives a running time of 101 minutes. Several reviewers noted that the title was taken from an Irish proverb: "Those who shake hands with the devil often find they have trouble getting their hands back." According to an 18 Apr 1958 *LAT* news item, Anthony Perkins was originally set to co-star in the film. The picture was filmed at the Ardmore Studios in Bray, Ireland, and, as stated in the credits, "on actual Irish locations," including the streets of Dublin. Although some contemporary sources state that *Shake Hands with the Devil* was the first American picture to be filmed entirely in Ireland, *The Quiet Man* was shot on location in Ireland in 1951. *Shake Hands with the Devil* was the first American film shot at Ardmore Studios, however, and was the first production of both Troy Films, which was Michael Anderson's production company, and Pennebaker Productions, which was founded by Marlon Brando and his father, Marlon Brando, Sr., in 1955. Producers George Glass and Walter Seltzer, who were also partners in Pennebaker, were former press agents who made their producing debut with this picture.

According to studio publicity, the film marked the screen debut of actress Marianne Benet. Don Murray and Dana Wynter were borrowed from Twentieth Century-Fox for the production. The onscreen credits note that Michael Redgrave and Sybil Thorndike appear "by special arrangement." According to a *NYT* article, Lt. Col. William O'Kelly, the picture's special military adviser, was formerly a member of the Irish Republican Army. The film depicts a period of the Irish "troubles," during which the "Black and Tans," consisting of former soldiers recruited by the British government, attempted to quell the Irish nationalist rebellion in 1920. Feared for their brutal methods, the Black and Tans were disbanded with the creation of the Irish Free State by the treaty of 6 Dec 1921. Although the film does not specify what part of Ireland was subject to the treaty, only the Southern counties gained dominion status and became the country of Eire. Northern Ireland remains British territory. According to an 8 Jul 1959 *HR* news item, *Shake Hands with the Devil* was banned from exhibition in Northern Ireland, where officials feared that the film would incite riots due to its subject matter. The ban was lifted in late Aug 1959, however, according to a *HR* news item.

Box 18 May 1959. *DV* 8 May 1959, p. 3. *Exh* 20 May 1959, pp. 4586-87. *FD* 8 May 1959, p. 6. *Har* 9 May 1959, p. 75. *HR* 21 Apr 1958. *HR* 11 Jun 1958, p. 3. *HR* 5 Sep 1958, p. 7, 9. *HR* 14 Nov 1958, p. 10. *HR* 8 May 1959, p. 3, 30. *HR* 21 May 1959. *HR* 8 Jul 1959. *HR* 28 Aug 1959. *LAT* 18 Apr 1958. *MPD* 8 May 1959. *MPHPD* 9 May 1959, p. 252. *Newsweek* 3 Nov 1958. *NYT* 2 Nov 1958. *NYT* 25 Jun 1959, p. 20. *Var* 13 May 1959, p. 6. *Var* 26 Aug 1959.

SHALL I TELL 'EM? *see* **LET'S HAVE FUN**

SHAME (Chinese Americans)

Fox Film Corp. *Dist* Fox Film Corp. 16 Oct **1921**; New York premiere: 31 Jul 1921 [©William Fox; 18 Sep 1921; LP17116]. Si; b&w. 8-9 reels, 8,322 ft.

Pres William Fox. *Dir* Emmett J. Flynn. *Scen and adpt* Emmett J. Flynn and Bernard McConville. *Photog* Lucien Andriot.

Source: Based on the short story "Clung" by Max Brand in *All Story Weekly* (10 Apr—15 May 1920).

Cast: John Gilbert (*William Fielding/David Fielding, his son*), Mickey Moore (*David, at 5*), Frankie Lee (*David, at 10*), George Siegmann (*Foo Chang*), William V. Mong (*Li Clung*), George Nichols (*Jonathan Fielding*), Anna May Wong (*The Lotus Blossom*), Rosemary Theby (*The Weaver of Dreams*), Doris Pawn (*Winifred Wellington*), "Red" Kirby (*"Once-over" Jake*).

Melodrama. William Fielding, who lives in Shanghai with his young son David, is close friends with his secretary, Li Clung, after the death of his wife. Foo Chang, a trader, loves the young woman who cares for young David and kills Fielding when he assumes that she is the boy's mother. Li Clung takes the child to his grandfather in San Francisco, where he grows up and inherits the Fielding estate. Following David's marriage, Foo Chang tries to bribe David to help him bring a cargo of opium into the city, informing him that he is a half-caste. Without warning to learn the truth from Li Clung, David takes his infant son and goes to Alaska. He is followed by his wife and his faithful servant Li Clung, who kills Foo Chang and explains that David's mother was not Chinese. Brought to his senses, David returns with them to San Francisco. *Alaska. Chinese. Chinese Americans. Grandfathers. Half-castes. Opium. San Francisco (CA). Secretaries. Shanghai (China).*

ETR 13 Aug 1921, p. 757. *FD* 7 Aug 1921. *NYT* 1 Aug 1921, p. 6 or 8. *Var* 5 Aug 1921, p. 25.

SHAMELESS *see* MY MAN AND I

THE SHAMROCK AND THE ROSE (Jewish Americans)

Chadwick Pictures Corp. 15 Apr **1927**. Si; b&w. 6-7 reels, 6,700 ft.

Dir Jack Nelson. *Scen* Isadore Bernstein. *Story* James Madison. *Photog* Ernest Miller.

Source: Based on the play *The Shamrock and the Rose* by Owen Davis (publication undetermined).

Cast: Mack Swain (*Mr. Kelly*), Olive Hasbrouck (*Rosie Cohen*), Edmund Burns (*Tom Kelly*), Maurice Costello (*Father O'Brien*), William Strauss (*Mr. Cohen*), Dot Farley (*Mrs. Kelly*), Rosa Rosanova (*Mrs. Cohen*), Leon Holmes (*Sammy Cohen*), Otto Lederer (*Rabbi Naser*), Coy Watson, Jr. (*Mickey Kelly*).

Comedy-drama. A feud between the "Ice Cream Cohens" (according to their business card) and the Kellys, who have a hot dog stand, cannot prevent the Cohen girl, Rosie, and the Kelly boy, Tom, from falling in love. There are sorrows, miniature warfare, and laughs until the two families are finally reconciled by their children's marriage. *Feuds. Ice cream. Irish. Jews. Street vendors.*

FD 7 Oct 1927. *Var* 6 Jul 1927, p. 23.

SHAMROCK HILL (Irish Americans)

Equity Pictures, Inc.; A Vinson Production. *Dist* Eagle Lion Films, Inc. Feb **1949**; Prod: early Dec—mid-Dec 1948 at Motion Picture Center [©Pathe Industries, Inc.; 15 May 1949; LP2387]. Sd (RCA Sound System); b&w. 8 reels, 6,897 ft. 70-71 or 76-77 min. PCA cert no. 13574.

Exec prod Joseph Levinson. *Prod* Arthur Dreifuss. *Assoc prod* Lincoln A. Widder. *Dir* Arthur Dreifuss. *Asst dir* Nate Levinson and [Arthur Alexander]. *Scr and orig story* Arthur Hoerl. *Scr* McElbert Moore. *Dir of photog* Philip Tannura. [*Cam op* Al Myers]. [*Gaffer* George Neff]. [*Stills* M. B. Paul]. *Spec eff* Ray Mercer. *Art dir* Danny Hall. *Supv ed* Arthur A. Brooks. *Set dec* Murray Waite. *Ward* Barbara Brier. *Mus dir* Herschel Gilbert. *Dance dir* Nick Castle. *Sd eng* Victor B. Appel. *Makeup* Kiva Hoffman. *Dream seq des* Neill E. McGuire. [*Scr supv* Violet Neufeld]. [*Grip* Charles Morris].

Song(s): "A Fine, Fine Day," "Don't Take Your Troubles to Bed," "Do You Believe?" and "The Leprechaun Song," words and music by Robert Bilder; "Madcap Mood," words by George O. Walbridge, music by Robert Bilder.

Cast: PEGGY RYAN (*Eileen Rogan*), Ray McDonald (*Larry Hadden*), Featuring Trudy Marshall (*Carol Judson*), Rick Vallin (*Oliver Mathews*), John Litel (*Ralph Judson*), Mary Gordon (*Grandma Rogan*), Tim Ryan (*Uncle Dan*), James Burke (*Michael Rogan*), Lanny Simpson (*Joey Rogan*), Douglas Wood (*Judge Mayer*), Patsy Bolton (*Patsy*), Barbara Brier (*Doris*), Tim Graham (*Officer Merrick*).

Fantasy, with songs. [*Print viewed*]. Atop Shamrock Hill, in the front garden of an abandoned mansion, a group of children gather to listen to their friend, Eileen Rogan, telling fanciful fairy stories. When a police officer approaches, the children scatter, but Eileen refuses to leave the hill, which she considers her second home. Eileen is arrested for trespassing, and some time later, she is summoned to court. After the judge hears all the evidence, including Eileen's testimony that she has seen and spoken to leprechauns on Shamrock Hill, he decides to dismiss the charge. The plaintiff, Ralph Judson, who plans to build a television station on Shamrock Hill, instructs his lawyer, Oliver Mathews, to do what he can to keep Eileen off his property. Later, Oliver takes his sweetheart, Judson's daughter Carol, up to the hill, where Eileen is amusing the children with another story. As they listen, Carol sees an enchanted look on Oliver's face and becomes jealous. Later, Oliver decides that he cannot in good conscience remove Eileen from the hill and gives Judson his resignation. Later, Oliver goes to Eileen's home to have dinner with her father and grandmother. Then, Eileen's old friend and invited guest, electronics engineer Larry Hadden, arrives, but Eileen tells him to go away. The next day, Larry tells Eileen that Carol promised him a job working at the new television station. Eileen becomes angry and returns home, where her grandmother advises her to ask the leprechauns what she can do to save Shamrock Hill. Eileen returns to the hill, where her spirits are lifted by the leprechauns' encouragement. Later, she goes to Judson's office to plead her case and tells him that his television station would displace the leprechauns. Judson responds by jokingly issuing a challenge: If Eileen can persuade the leprechauns to perform a miracle, he will

gladly select another site for his station. Eileen leaves feeling confident and happy, and some time later, returns to the hill. There, she is amazed that all the withered potted bushes and trees have been transformed into full bloom. Thrilled, Eileen rushes to Judson's office with the news of the miracle. When Judson, Carol and Larry scoff at her claim, she convinces them to come and witness it for themselves. They all go to the hill, and Judson is initially impressed. Moments later, however, he discovers a receipt for the sale of the plants lying on the ground. Hoping to preserve Eileen's faith in the leprechauns, Carol asks her father to forget about the receipt, and Oliver affectionately kisses her. Judson then tells Eileen that he has decided upon another site for his television station, and she thanks him. After Judson and Carol leave, a worker from the nursery arrives and begins speaking with Larry. Eileen then realizes that her "miracle" was actually a gift from Larry, for which she warmly embraces him. *Children. Gardens. Lawyers. Leprechauns. Storytellers. Dinners and dining. Employer-employee relations. Engineers. Family relationships. Gifts. Irish Americans. Jealousy. Judges. Mansions. Police. Subpoena. Television. Trees. Trials. Tycoons.*

Note: The working titles of this film were *Enchanted* and *Enchanted Dream*. According to a 9 Dec 1948 *HR* news item, Gwen O'Connor, performer Donald O'Connor's wife, was scheduled to make her screen debut in the film, but her appearance in the final film has not been confirmed.

Box 14 May 1949. *DV* 15 Apr 1949, p. 3. *FD* 18 May 1949, p. 6. *HR* 3 Dec 1948, p. 18. *HR* 9 Dec 1948, p. 11. *HR* 10 Dec 1948, p. 14. *HR* 15 Apr 1949, p. 3. *MPHPD* 30 Apr 1949, p. 4590. *NYT* 30 Nov 1948. *Var* 20 Apr 1949, p. 11.

THE SHAMROCK TOUCH *see* THE LUCK OF THE IRISH

SHANGHAI CHEST (Chinese Americans)

Monogram Pictures Corp. *Dist* Monogram Pictures Corp. 11 Jul **1948**; Prod: early Feb—mid-Feb 1948 [©Monogram Pictures Corp.; 11 Jul 1948; LP1879]. Sd (Western Electric Recording); b&w. 5,872 ft. 65 min. PCA cert no. 13021.

Series: Charlie Chan.

Prod James S. Burkett. *Dir* William Beaudine. *Asst dir* Wesley Barry. *Scr* W. Scott Darling and Sam Newman. *Orig story* Sam Newman. *Addl dial* Tim Ryan. *Photog* William Sickner. [*Cam op* William Margulies]. [*Stills* James Fullerton]. *Art dir* David Milton. *Ed* Ace Herman. *Supv film ed* Otho Lovering. [*Set dec* Raymond Boltz, Jr.]. *Mus dir* Edward J. Kay. *Rec* Frank McWhorter. [*Hair stylist* Lela Chambers]. *Prod supv* Glenn Cook. [*Scr supv* Jules Levy]. [*Grip* Harry Lewis].

Source: Based on characters created by Earl Derr Biggers.

Cast: Roland Winters [(*Charlie Chan*)], Mantan Moreland [(*Birmingham*)], Tim Ryan [(*Lt. Mike Ruark*)], Victor Sen Young [(*Tommy Chan*)], Deannie Best [(*Phyllis Powers*)], Tristram Coffin [(*Ed Seward*)], John Alvin [(*Victor Armstrong*)], Russell Hicks [(*District Attorney Frank Bronson*)], Pierre Watkins [(*Judge Wesley Armstrong*)], Philip Van Zandt [(*Joseph Pindello*)], Milton Parsons [(*Mr. Grail*)], Olaf Hytten [(*Bates*)], Erville Alderson [(*Walter Somervale*)], George Eldredge [(*Pat Finley*)], [Charlie Sullivan (*Officer Murphy*)], [Eddie Coke (*Thomas Cartwright*)], [William Ruhl (*Jailer*)], [Lois Austin (*Landlady*)], [Chabing (*Receptionist*)], [John Shay (*Stacey*)], [Paul Scardon (*Cemetery custodian*)], [Willie Best].

Detective, Drama. [*Print viewed*]. In San Francisco, Judge Wesley Armstrong is stabbed to death in his study by an intruder, and Victor Armstrong, the judge's nephew, who has come to see him, is slugged by the same assailant. Police lieutenant Mike Ruark is alerted by the judge's secretary, Phyllis Powers, and discovers Victor recovering consciousness with a knife in his hand. Meanwhile, Tommy Chan, the second son of renowned private detective Charlie Chan, and Birmingham, Chan's chauffeur, are walking home from a movie when they spot an apparent burglar entering a house by a window. When it turns out that the "burglar" was the house's owner, district attorney Frank Bronson, however, they both end up spending the night in jail. Later, Bates, the judge's butler, tells Bronson that the judge had denied Vic entrance to the house, and Vic had sneaked in through a window. Phyllis then admits to Bronson that she overheard Vic, her boyfriend, and the judge arguing about an unwise stock deal in which Vic had invested $30,000 of his assets. The judge called his lawyer, Ed Seward, and arranged to meet him the following morning to draw up a new will which would exclude Vic, then his sole heir. Bronson assumes that if the judge had not been killed the night before, Vic would have been totally disinherited, thus making it appear that he had every motivation to kill his uncle. When Chan comes to see

Bronson to apologize about Tommy and Birmingham, Bronson and Ruark are notified that two sets of fingerprints were found on the knife—Vic's and Tony Pindello's. Aware that Pindello was executed in the San Quentin gas chamber six months before, having been sentenced by Judge Armstrong, Ruark asks for Chan's help with the case. Later, someone shoots and kills Bronson, then removes papers he was examining related to the Pindello case. Ruark tells Chan about Bronson's murder and that Pindello's fingerprints were found on Bronson's desk. At Judge Armstrong's office, Chan and Ruark discover Walter Somervale, the judge's clerk of court, going through papers in a filing cabinet. While Chan and Ruark examine the judge's papers, Seward shows up and tells them that, before he became the judge's personal attorney, he defended Pindello in his murder trial. In the judge's safe, the detectives find papers regarding a commission investigating racketeering in the insurance business, on which Seward is also serving. They also find a letter addressed to Vic, to be opened only in the event of the judge's death. In the letter, the judge states that he had uncovered evidence suggesting that Pindello may have been innocent and that he intended to inform Bronson of such. After Chan learns that Pindello was buried in a local cemetery, they go there and discover that the coffin has been removed. Chan requests that all members of the Pindello jury be placed under police protection as he fears for their safety. However, Ruark fails to locate one juror, Thomas Cartwright. Chan tells Ruark that he thinks that there may be a connection between the Pindello case and the insurance swindle. Pat Finlay, Ruark's assistant, locates Cartwright's new address but, before he can reach him, someone enters Cartwright's room and slugs him. When Finlay arrives, he finds Cartwright dead by hanging and, once again, Pindello's fingerprints are found at the crime scene. After Chan discovers that it is possible to forge fingerprints, he asks Ruark to arrange a meeting with Phyllis, Vic and Seward at the judge's home. While they are in the study, the lights go out and a masked gunman locks them in a closet, then leaves. They manage to break out and find that all the papers related to the Pindello case are gone. Later, Chan discovers that the director of a funeral parlor has recently reburied a sealed coffin and obtains the address of the man who arranged for the burial. Chan breaks into the man's room but is surprised by Joseph Pindello, Tony's brother. Later, Ruark assembles all the principals in the case and Chan explains that Pindello had a brother Joseph, who was in jail when Tony wrote to him telling him that he was about to be executed for a crime he had not committed. According to Chan, when Joseph got out of jail, he dug up his brother's body and intended to kill everyone associated with his execution. As Chan explains this, Joseph enters, holds everyone at gunpoint and says that he simply intended to give his brother a proper burial. Before he can continue, Joseph is tackled from behind by Tommy and is taken prisoner. However, Chan tells the group that Joseph is not the murderer of Armstrong, Bronson or Cartwright, but that Seward is. Although Seward denies it, Chan states that he was involved with Tony Pindello in an insurance swindle. Seward wanted all the money, however, and framed Tony for murder. Fearing that Armstrong and Bronson were about to discover this, Seward murdered them and added Cartwright to make it look like a series of killings. Seward grabs Joseph's gun and explains how he used copies of Tony's fingerprints to divert attention from himself. Chan then reveals that Joseph was part of the set-up they have just gone through and that the gun is not loaded. As Seward tries to leave, he collides with Birmingham and is captured. *Chinese Americans. Frame-ups. Judges. Murder. Private detectives.* African Americans. Brothers. Burglars. Butlers. Cemeteries. Chauffeurs. District attorneys. Fathers and sons. Fingerprints. Firearms. Investigations. Jails. Landladies. Lawyers. Letters. Nephews. Police detectives. Receptionists. San Francisco (CA). San Francisco (CA)-Chinatown. Secret documents. Secretaries. Undertakers and undertaking.

Note: This film's working title was *Murder by Alphabet.* Louis Mason is listed in CBCS in the role of the cemetery custodian, but that part was actually played by Paul Scardon. For additional information on the "Charlie Chan" series, please consult the Series Index and see the above entry for *Charlie Chan Carries On.*

DV 7 Sep 1948, p. 3. *HR* 6 Feb 1948, p. 15. *HR* 9 Sep 1948, p. 6. *MPHPD* 3 Jul 1948, p. 4226. *Var* 8 Sep 1948, p. 18.

THE SHANGHAI COBRA (Chinese Americans)

Monogram Pictures Corp. *Dist* Monogram Pictures Corp. 29 Sep 1945; Prod: late May–mid-Jun 1945 [©Monogram Pictures Corp.; 5 Aug 1945; LP56]. Sd (Western Electric Recording); b&w. 5,797 ft. 63-64 min.

Series: Charlie Chan.

Prod James S. Burkett. *Dir* Phil Karlson. [*Asst dir* Eddie Davis]. *Scr* George Callahan and George Wallace Sayre. *Orig story* George Callahan. *Dir of photog* Vincent Farrar. [*Art dir* Vin Taylor and Dave Milton]. *Ed* Ace Herman. *Mus dir* Edward J. Kay. *Rec* Tom Lambert. *Prod mgr* Glenn Cook. [*Tech dir* Ormand McGill].

Source: Based on characters created by Earl Derr Biggers.

Cast: Sidney Toler [(*Charlie Chan*)], Mantan Moreland [(*Birmingham Brown*)], Benson Fong [(*Tommy Chan*)], James Cardwell [(*Ned Stewart*)], Joan Barclay [(*Paula Webb, also known as Pauline Webster and Paula Van Horn*)], Addison Richards [(*John Adams also known as Jan Van Horn*)], Arthur Loft [(*Bradford Harris also known as Hume*)], Janet Warren [(*Lorraine*)], Gene Stutenroth [(*Morgan*)], Joe Devlin [(*Taylor*)], James Flavin [(*H. R. Jarvis*)], Roy Gordon [(*Walter Fletcher*)], Walter Fenner [(*Inspector Harry Davis*)], [George Chandler (*Joe Nelson*)], [Mary Moore (*Rita*)], [Cyril Delevanti (*Larkin*)], [Stephan Gregory (*Samuel Black*)], [Bob Blair (*Corning*)], [Bill Ruhl (*Gregory*)], [John Goldsworthy (*Mainwaring*)], [Tiny Newlan (*Guard*)], [Andy Andrews (*Policeman*)], [Karon Knight (*Telephone supervisor*)], [Diane Quillan (*Telephone operator*)], [Jack Richardson (*Postman*)].

Detective, Drama. [*Print viewed*]. After Samuel Black is killed by a cobra bite, Inspector Harry Davis of the New York City homicide squad telegrams his old friend, Charlie Chan, the famous Chinese-American private detective, for help. Davis knows that Chan had captured Jan Van Horn, an accused murderer, in Shanghai, China, eight years earlier, and the disfigured Van Horn, an escaped felon, was accused of using cobra bites on his victims. Chan, now working as a government agent, arrives in New York and quickly learns that Black and two similar victims were employed by the Sixth National Bank, whose vault holds millions of dollars worth of the government's radium. With the help of his son Tommy and his chauffeur, Birmingham Brown, Chan learns that Ned Stewart, a novice private detective, had been seen with Black on the night of his death. After Stewart tells Chan that he had been hired by an unknown man to watch Paula Webb, the bank president's secretary, Chan checks with Paula, who corroborates his story. Meanwhile, Larkin, a police undercover agent working at Sixth National, disappears after calling Davis for help. Soon thereafter, Davis learns that gangsters Morgan and Taylor were seen in the office of bank president Walter Fletcher, and Tommy and Birmingham follow the hoodlums into a nearby laundry. Discovering a secret passageway from the laundry into the sewers, Tommy and Birmingham uncover Larkin's murdered body. An autopsy concludes that Larkin was also killed by cobra venom, so Chan reasons that there must also be a secret passageway into the bank. Back in the sewers, Chan, Ned and Davis discover a secret entrance into Paula's office. The investigators then go to a nearby coffee shop, whose proprietor, Joe Nelson, tells them that he purchased his video jukebox from Van Horn. Recognizing the jukebox operator's voice from the bank, Chan and Davis search the office of chemical engineer H. R. Jarvis, where they find Lorraine operating the jukebox from a secret room. Chan quickly discovers that Black and the other victims were poisoned by cobra venom when they requested change from the jukebox. Chan then lies to the local newspapers that the government plans to remove its radium the next day, hoping it will force the gangsters to act. While Chan checks the bank's vault, Tommy and Birmingham follow Morgan into the laundry, and become caught in the sewer after the gangsters attempt to blow open the bank's vault. Along with Chan, the two become trapped when their section of the sewer caves in, but Chan uses the telephone lines to send a message in Morse code to David. The police arrive at the bank in time to capture the gangsters and rescue Chan, Tommy and Birmingham. Later, Chan concludes that John Adams, a bank guard, is actually Van Horn, and Paula is his daughter. Van Horn tells how he followed Jarvis to America, believing that he was one of the men who framed him for murder in Shanghai. Chan then recognizes bank officer Bradford Harris as Special Agent Hume of the Shanghai police, and he is arrested as the real killer and leader of the gang. With the case solved, Chan learns that he has been issued a ticket by the New York City police for making an illegal turn. African Americans. Chauffeurs. *Chinese Americans.* Fathers and sons. Government agents. Murder. Aliases. Bank presidents. Banks. Chases. Coffee shops. Escapes. False arrests. Fathers and daughters. Gangsters. Jukeboxes. Laundries. Morse code. New York City. Poisoning. Police inspectors. Private

detectives. Radium. Rainstorms. Rescues. Secret passageways. Secretaries. Sewers. Vaults.

Note: The title card on the viewed print reads: "Charlie Chan in *The Shanghai Cobra.*" For additional information about this series, consult the Series Index and see the entry above for *Charlie Chan Carries On.*

Box 11 Aug 1945. *DV* 3 Aug 1945, p. 3. *FD* 7 Aug 1945, p. 5. *HR* 25 May 1945, p. 18. *HR* 3 Aug 1945, p. 3. *MPHPD* 18 Aug 1945, p. 2598. *Var* 8 Aug 1945, p. 22.

SHARK ISLAND *see* THE PRISONER OF SHARK ISLAND

SHE DEVIL *see* DRUMS O' VOODOO

SHE GOT WHAT SHE WANTED (Russian Americans)

James Cruze Productions, Inc. *Dist* Tiffany Productions. 18 Dec **1930** [©James Cruze Productions, Inc.; 19 Dec 1930; LP1844]. Sd (Photophone); b&w. 9 reels.

Prod Samuel Zierler. *Dir* James Cruze. *Story and dial* George Rosener. *Photog* C. Edgar Schoenbaum.

Cast: Betty Compson (*Mahyna*), Lee Tracy (*Eddie*), Alan Hale (*Dave*), Gaston Glass (*Boris*), Dorothy Christy (*Olga*), Fred Kelsey (*Dugan*).

Society, Comedy. Mahyna, a dissatisfied Russian peasant girl, marries Boris and comes to New York in search of "the soul of love," only to become a drudge in their cheap flat. Meanwhile, Boris, a bookshop keeper, dreams of a prosperous future from the book he is writing. Their boarder, Dave, a partner in a gambling establishment, makes a play for Mahyna; she is tempted to leave with him when Eddie, a former admirer, arrives on the scene, and the two get into constant arguments over her. A year later, she is married to Dave, and it is agreed that Boris will live with them. Boris becomes well-to-do with the sale of his book and begins an affair with Olga, the Happiness Girl on radio. A series of complications ensue, as the unreliable Eddie returns to renew his suit and Dave is involved in a murder case. Ditched by both men, Mahyna at last finds that Boris is indeed her only true love. *Ambition. Authors. Booksellers and bookselling. Gamblers. Marriage. Murder. New York City. Radio performers. Russian Americans.*

FD 9 Nov 1930. *NYT* 29 Dec 1930, p. 18.

SHE WAS A LADY (English Americans)

Fox Film Corp. *Dist* Fox Film Corp. 20 Jul **1934**; Prod: Late May—late Jun 1934 [©Fox Film Corp.; 15 Jul 1934; LP4834]. Sd (Western Electric Noiseless Recording); b&w. 8 reels, 7,033 ft. 68-69 or 77 min. Passed by the National Board of Review. PCA cert no. 6.

Prod Al Rockett. [*Exec prod* Winfield R. Sheehan]. *Dir* Hamilton MacFadden. [*Asst dir* George Blair]. *Scr* Gertrude Purcell. *Photog* Bert Glennon. [*Cam op* Joseph MacDonald]. [*Asst cam* Lou Kunkle and Harry Webb]. *Settings* Max Parker. [*Film ed* Dorothy Spencer]. *Gowns* William Lambert. *Mus dir* Louis De Francesco. *Sd* W. D. Flick. [*Still photog* Emmett Schoenbaum].

Song(s): "Moonlight Bay," words and music by Percy Wenrich and Edward Madden.

Source: Based on the novel *She Was a Lady* by Elisabeth Cobb (Indianapolis, 1934).

Cast: Helen Twelvetrees (*Sheila Vane*), Donald Woods (*Tommy Traill*), Ralph Morgan (*Stanley Vane*), Monroe Owsley (*Jerry Couzins*), Irving Pichel (*Marco*), Doris Lloyd (*Alice Vane*), Kitty Kelly (*Daisy*), Halliwell Hobbes (*George Vane*), Mary Forbes (*Lady Diana Vane*), Jackie Searl (*Herbie Vane*), Barbara Weeks (*Moira*), Karol Kay (*Sheila, the child*), Paul Harvey (*Jeff Dyer*), Harold Goodwin (*Yank*), Anne Howard (*Iris Vane*), [Dora Clement (*Lady Vane, for portrait only*)], [Sidney Jarvis, Otto Fries (*Bartenders*)], [Samuel S. Hinds (*Mr. Traill*)], [Ara Haswell (*Secretary*)], [Carlton E. Griffin (*Clerk*)], [Charles Bimbo (*Joey*), [Tut Mace (*Amy*)], [Edward Gargan (*Bull*)], [Frank Dawson (*Huggins*)], [Douglas Gordon (*Chauffeur*)], [Paul Stanton], [Edward Earle].

Melodrama. [*Print viewed*]. Sheila Vane, daughter of Stanley, an English aristocrat, and Alice, a former maid of the Vane family, has displayed the traits of her aristocratic heritage since childhood. While living in Acoola, Montana, where the couple settled after Stanley's family shunned him for his marriage to a woman not of his class, Stanley persuades his daughter to return someday to England and reclaim her rightful place in the Vane home. Sheila takes a job as a riding instructor at a dude ranch in order to fulfill her father's wishes, and there meets Tommy Traill, a young and reckless Eastern playboy, who immediately falls in love with her charming combination of Western ruggedness and English good breeding. Sheila befriends

Tommy, but when he proposes to her, she chides him for his tendency toward drink and tomfoolery. Sheila urges Tommy to go to South America, where his father, who owns fruit plantations, has promised him a chance to make a success of himself. Stanley, meanwhile, is killed while trying to save a horse during a barn fire, leaving Alice penniless. Sheila gives her mother the $600 her father had saved for her trip to England, then leaves home. Sheila takes a job as a trick rider at a circus, where she meets Jerry Couzins, a confidence man who is working as the circus publicist. Before she finallly embarks for England, Shelia meets Tommy in New York and promises to come back to him. In England, Sheila arrives at Vane Manor and is received coldly by her Aunt Diana and Uncle George. As their daughter will be presented at court soon, they feel that news that Shelia's maternal grandfather is still the family butler and her mother their former maid must not resurface. Sheila leaves despondent, and back in New York, Tommy takes her to the Traill house to meet his father. Mr. Traill rejects Sheila as a potential marriage partner for his son because of her class. In a passionate speech, Sheila reveals her background and states her own ideas about class, that honesty and decency are more important than station. Sheila then refuses to marry Tommy until Mr. Traill asks her, as not to suffer the same fate as her parents. The couple breaks up, and two weeks later, Sheila meets Jerry at her hotel and accepts his offer of a job enducing rich men to gamble at the nightclub he runs. Two months later, Tommy enters the club drunk and accuses Sheila of seeing Jerry throughout their own romance. Angered by Tommy's appearance, Sheila lies that she intends to marry Jerry, but after Jerry and Tommy fight, Sheila brings an unconscious Tommy home to his father, who finally asks her to marry his son. She refuses at first, telling the elder Traill what she has now become, but he informs her that it doesn't matter anymore. The reunited couple embraces and decides to marry the next day. *Class distinction. English. Fathers and daughters. Ostracism. Playboys. Proposals (Marital). Aristocrats. Circuses. Confidence men. Drunkenness. Dude ranches. England. Fathers and sons. Fights. Fires. Gambling houses. Hotels. Manors. Montana. New York City. Nightclubs. Publicists. Ranches. Riding. Romance. Scandal.*

Note: The Twentieth Century-Fox Produced Scripts Collection at the UCLA Theater Arts Library contains a screenplay by Josephine Lovett and Ainsworth Morgan. It is not known whether any material from this source was used in the final film. According to a pre-production news item, eight-year-old Edith Fellows was signed to be in the film. No information to verify her participation has been located.

Box 4 Sep 1934. *DV* 25 Jul 1934, p. 3. *FD* 22 Aug 1934, p. 4. *HR* 19 Apr 1934, p. 7. *HR* 28 May 1934, p. 10. *IP* Jun 1934, p. 21. *MPD* 22 Aug 1934, p. 7. *MPH* 1 Sep 1934, p. 36. *NYT* 22 Aug 1934, p. 21. *Var* 28 Aug 1934, p. 15.

THE SHE WOLF (Chinese Americans)

Frohman Amusement Corp. *Dist* State Rights. 23 Jun **1919**. Si; b&w. 5 reels.

Pres William L. Sherrill. *Dir* Cliff Smith. *Scen* Raymond L. Schrock. *Titles* Harvey Thew. *Story* John Colton. *Cam* Steve Rounds.

Cast: Texas Guinan (*The She Wolf*), George Chesboro (*The stranger*), Ah Wing (*Mui Fing*), Charles Robertson (*Dud Bigby*), Anna Wild (*Sallie Bigby*), Jack Richardson (*Sheriff of Mad Dog*), Josie Sedgwick (*Belle of the dance hall*).

Western. The She Wolf, a man-hater, lives alone near Mad Dog, a mining camp, whose sheriff secretly leads an outlaw band. Saloon keeper Mui Fing, desiring the drunkard Dud Bigby's virginal daughter Sallie, who secretly is engaged to the absent miner John Williams, gets Dud's promise of her hand. The She Wolf, entering the saloon, sees the Stranger, who once befriended her, being cheated in a poker game, and rescues him, although he is wounded in the ensuing gunfight. She nurses him in her cabin and drives off the sheriff who tries to arrest him. After kidnapping a minister from a stagecoach, who was to perform Mui Fing's marriage to Sallie, the She Wolf sees the sheriff about to marry them in the saloon. Riding through the window on her horse with two guns blazing, she shoots Mui Fing and the sheriff, and rescues Sallie. Sallie and Williams then marry, as do the She Wolf and the Stranger. *Chinese Americans. Gunfighters. Manhaters. Mining towns. Recluses. Rescues. Saloon keepers. Strangers. Abduction. Alcoholics. Clergy. Engagements. Gunfights. Nursing back to health. Poker (Game). Virginity.*

Note: This was to be the first of thirteen two reel productions starring night club entertainer Texas Guinan in a role modeled after that of William S. Hart. Since it turned out to be five reels, it was released to the exchanges at the charge agreed upon for the two reel attractions. Reviewers consistently

commented on Guinan's attempt to be the "female William S. Hart," although they disagreed about her success at it.

ETR 14 Jun 1919, p. 137. *MPN* 21 Jun 1919, p. 4222. *MPW* 21 Jun 1919, pp. 1823-25. *NYMT* 8 Jun 1919. *Var* 11 Jul 1919, p. 60.

SHE WORE A YELLOW RIBBON (Native Americans, Arapaho, Cheyenne)

Argosy Pictures Corp. *Dist* RKO Radio Pictures, Inc. 22 Oct **1949**; Kansas City, KS premiere: 26 Jul 1949; Prod: late Oct—late Nov 1948 [©Argosy Pictures Corp.; 26 Jul 1949; LP2493]. Sd (RCA Sound System); col (Technicolor). 9,316 ft. 103-104 min. PCA cert no. 13509.

Pres JOHN FORD and MERIAN C. COOPER. *Assoc prod* Lowell Farrell. *Dir* John Ford. *Asst dir* Wingate Smith and Edward O'Fearna. *Scr* Frank Nugent and Laurence Stallings. *Dir of photog* Winton Hoch. *2d unit photog* Charles Boyle. *Cam op* Harvey Gould. [*Gaffer* Robert Campbell]. [*Stills* Alex Kahle]. *Spec eff* Jack Caffee. *Sd eff* Patrick Kelley. *Technicolor color dir* Natalie Kalmus. *Assoc* Morgan Padelford. *Art dir* James Basevi. *Film ed* Jack Murray. *Set dec* Joe Kish. *Props* Jack Golconda. *Men's ward* Michael Meyers. *Women's ward* Ann Peck. *Mus score* Richard Hageman. *Mus arr* Lucien Cailliet. *Mus cond* C. Bakaleinikoff. *Sd* Frank Webster and Clem Portman. *Makeup* Don Cash. *Hairdresser* Anna Malin. *Cost res* D. R. O. Hatswell. *Tech adv* Major Philip Kieffer, U.S.A., Retd. and Cliff Lyons. [*Scr supv* Meta Sterne]. [*Grip* Tom Clement].

Song(s): "She Wore a Yellow Ribbon," by M. Ottner, additional lyrics by Leroy Parker.

Source: Based on the short story "The Big Hunt" by James Warner Bellah in *The Saturday Evening Post* (6 Dec 1947) and his short story "War Party" in *The Saturday Evening Post* (19 Jun 1948).

Cast: John Wayne [(*Capt. Nathan Brittles*)], Joanne Dru [(*Olivia Dandridge*)], John Agar [(*Lt. Clint Cohill*)], Ben Johnson [(*Sgt. Tyree*)], Harry Carey, Jr. [(*Lt. Ross Pennell*)], Victor McLaglen [(*Sgt. Quincannon*)], Mildred Natwick [(*Abby Allshard*)], George O'Brien [(*Major "Mac" Allshard*)], Arthur Shields [(*Dr. O'Laughlin*)], Michael Dugan [(*Hochbauer*)], Chief John Big Tree [(*Pony-That-Walks*)], Fred Graham [(*Hench*)], Chief Sky Eagle, Tom Tyler [(*Corp. Mike Quayne*)], Noble Johnson [(*Red Shirt*)], [Harry Woods (*Karl Rynders*)], [Cliff Lyons (*Trooper Cliff*)], [Mickey Simpson (*Wagner*)], [Frank McGrath (*Bugler*)], [Fred Libby (*Col Krumrin*)], [Jack Pennick (*Sergeant major*)], [Billy Jones (*Courier*)], [Bill Goettinger, Post Park (*NCOs*)], [Fred Kennedy (*Badger*)], [Rudy Bowman (*Pvt. John Smith*)], [Ray Hyke (*McCarthy*)], [Lee Bradley (*Interpreter*)], [Francis Ford (*Bartender*)].

Historical, Western. [*Print viewed*]. In 1876, immediately after the death of General George Armstrong Custer at Little Big Horn, a government stagecoach crossing the remote southwest desert is robbed of its payroll and its driver is killed. Capt. Nathan Brittles, who oversees the Seventh Cavalry at nearby Fort Stark, is disturbed to learn that the attackers were southern Cheyenne Indians, as he knows that the Cheyenne rarely venture so far south. Later, while thinking aloud by his wife Mary's grave, Nathan, who is retiring from the army in six days, realizes that his last mission will be to drive the Cheyenne back north. The next day, however, Nathan's commander, Major "Mac" Allshard, orders him to take his wife Abby and genteel niece, Olivia Dandridge, along with the Indian patrol and deliver them to Sudros Wells, where they are to catch a stagecoach East. After registering a formal protest with Allshard, Nathan leads the large patrol from the fort, with Olivia and Abby in tow. Upon seeing the pretty Olivia with a yellow ribbon in her hair, rival suitors Lt. Clint Cohill and Lt. Ross Pennell each wonder if she is wearing the symbolic ribbon in their honor, but she refuses to reveal her preference. Soon after leaving the fort, Nathan hears from his scout, the southern Sgt. Tyree, that two white men have been spotted riding toward Sudros Wells. Tyree later reports that a large group of Arapaho Indians are also traveling toward Sudros Wells. Concerned for the women's safety, Nathan orders his patrol to take a different, slightly longer route to the depot, fully aware that the detour may mean missing the stage. Along the new route, the patrol is surprised to see a large herd of grazing buffalo. Tyree and Nathan speculate that an inter-tribal council meeting is being planned, at which the white men, Indian agent Karl Rynders and his interpreter, will be selling guns, and Red Shirt, an ambitious, radical Arapaho chief, will be claiming responsibility for the return of the buffalo. In order to protect the depot residents, Nathan orders Tyree to go to Paradise

River and bring the small unit he commands there to Sudros Wells. Before Tyree reaches Paradise River, however, Tyree's unit is attacked by Indians, who are then chased off by Nathan's men. As a storm breaks over the desert, the patrol rides on and wounded Paradise River Corp. Mike Quayne is operated on by Dr. O'Laughlin. By the time the patrol reaches Sudros Wells, the outpost has been decimated by the Indians, and the patrol is forced to turn back for Fort Stark. That night, Clint, who has been quarreling with Ross over Olivia during the entire trip, spies on the council meeting with Nathan and Tyree and watches as Rynders and the interpreter are brutally murdered by the Indians. When the patrol reaches Paradise River the next day, Nathan orders Clint and three squadrons of men to stay behind and cover their crossing. After Nathan promises to return the next day to relieve Clint, Olivia kisses the lieutenant goodbye, finally indicating her romantic choice. Back at Fort Stark, Nathan declares the mission a failure and, despite his imminent retirement, asks permission to return to Paradise River. Allshard, however, insists that Ross, who will soon be second in charge under Clint, lead the men back to the river. Although Nathan agrees with Allshard that the lieutenants' mettle should be tested and proudly accepts a silver retirement watch from his troops, he later joins the patrol at the river. Noting that he is technically still in charge, Nathan orders Clint and the troops to remain at the river, while he and Tyree try to negotiate peace with the Indians. Despite a warm reception from Pony-That-Walks, an elderly chief, Nathan is unable to alter the Indians' drive toward war. Consequently, he orders his men to attack the Indian camp at midnight and scatter their horses. With no deaths or casualties, the raid is a success, and the Indians are forced to return to their reservations on foot. Just as Nathan is about to ride off for California, Tyree presents him with a letter from the War Department, promoting him to chief of scouts at a new post. The newly-assigned lieutenant colonel accepts the congratulations of his fellow cavalrymen at Fort Stark, where a dance is in progress and, after blessing Clint and Olivia's engagement, leaves the party to share his good news with Mary. *Indians of North America. Romantic rivalry. Soldiers. United States–History–Reconstruction, 1865-1898. United States–Southwest. United States. Army. Cavalry. Arapaho Indians. Bison, American. Cheyenne Indians. Dance parties. Deserts. Forts. Graves. Indian agents. Nieces. Physicians. Retirement. Rivers. Southerners. Stagecoaches. Storms. Translators. Tribal chiefs. Wives. Wounds and injuries.*

Note: An offscreen narrator provides commentary intermittently throughout the film. In addition to "She Wore a Yellow Ribbon," the traditional song "The Girl I Left Behind Me" is also heard in part in the film. *She Wore a Yellow Ribbon* was the second film in John Ford's "cavalry" trilogy, and the only one to be shot in color. *HR* news items add the following information about the production: In Aug 1948, Argosy Pictures was negotiating for Charles Bickford to play the film's lead. As with Ford's previous cavalry film, *Fort Apache*, most of the picture was shot in Monument Valley in southern Utah and northeastern Arizona. Harold von Schmidt, an illustrator for *The Saturday Evening Post*, was hired to do "special advertising" illustrations for the picture. Modern sources add the following information about the film: James Warner Bellah worked on the original screen adaptation of his short stories. After Bellah, Laurence Stallings was brought in to improve the script's pacing, structure and dialogue. In addition to expanding certain moments from the short stories, Stallings developed the romantic sub-plot between "Olivia" and the two lieutenants. Frank Nugent was then hired to polish the script.

The film was budgeted at $1,851,290, $40,000 less than *Fort Apache*, and because of Ford's familiarity with the Monument Valley area, it was completed after only thirty-one days of shooting and was brought in almost $500,000 under budget. In a modern interview, Ford notes that he and photographer Winton Hoch attempted to duplicate the style of Frederic Remington's western paintings in their screen images. During production, Hoch filed a formal protest with the American Society of Cinematographers, complaining that a scene that Ford ordered him to shoot during a desert storm was not acceptable to him. Hoch won an Academy Award for Best Cinematography (Color) for his work on this film, and despite his differences with Ford during the production, went on to shoot other notable pictures for him, including *The Quiet Man* and *The Searchers*. Modern sources credit Barbara Ford (Ford's daughter) as assistant editor and add Paul Fix and Dan White to the cast. For more information on Ford's cavalry trilogy, see above entry for *Fort Apache*. John Wayne reprised his role in a 12 Mar 1951 *Lux Radio Theatre* broadcast, co-starring Mel Ferrer.

Box 30 Jul 1949. *DV* 27 Jul 1949, p. 3, 5. *FD* 28 Jul 1949, p. 7. *HR* 19 Aug 1948, p. 3. *HR* 17 Sep 1948, p. 1. *HR* 29 Oct 1948, p. 14. *HR* 26 Nov 1948, p. 14. *HR* 23 Jun 1949, p. 14. *HR* 27 Jul 1949, pp. 3-5. *MPHPD* 30 Jul 1949, p. 4697. *NYT* 18 Nov 1949, p. 35. *Var* 27 Jul 1949, p. 12.

SHEP COMES HOME (Latino)

Lippert Productions, Inc.; A Robert L. Lippert Production. *Dist* Screen Guild Productions, Inc. 3 Oct **1948**; Prod: late Sep 1948 [©Lippert Productions, Inc.; 5 Dec 1948; LP2084]. Sd (Glen Glenn Sound System); b&w. 7 reels, 5,582 ft. 62 min. PCA cert no. 13479.

Prod Ron Ormond. *Assoc prod* Ira Webb and June Carr. *Dir* Ford Beebe. [*Asst dir* Austin Jewell]. *Dial* [*dir*] Gloria Welsch. *Story wrt* Ford Beebe. *Story idea* Carl Hittleman. *Dir of photog* Ernest Miller. [*Cam op* Archie Dalzell]. [*Stills* James Doolittle]. *Spec eff* Ray Mercer. *Art dir* Fred Preble. *Film ed* Hugh Winn. *Set dec* Theo Offenbecker. *Ward* Don Wakeling. *Mus* Walter Greene. *Sd eng* Glen Glenn and Earl Snyder. [*Makeup* Ted Larson]. Moree Herring. Noble Craig.

Cast: Robert Lowery [(*Mark Folger*)], Billy Kimbley [(*Larry Havens*)], Martin Garralaga [(*Manuel Ortiz*)], Margia Dean [(*Martha Langley*)], Sheldon Leonard [("*Swifty*" *Lewis*)], Michael Whalen [("*Chance*" *Martin*)], J. Farrell MacDonald [(*Cap Weatherby*)], Lyle Talbot [(*Doctor*)], Frank Jenks [(*Iceman*)], Edna Holland [(*Mrs. Fleming*)], Matt Willis [(*George*)], Ben Erway [(*Mr. Gardner*)], Howard Gould, Flame—the dog [(*Shep*)].

Animal, Drama, Youth. [*Print viewed*]. In St. Louis, nine-year-old Larry Havens is told by two welfare workers that, as his mother has just died and his father lost his life in the Italian campaign, he will be sent to an orphanage. Larry's dog, Shep, will not be allowed to go with him. The workers want to put Shep in a pound, even though the dog won a Purple Heart medal when he saved Larry's dad's life at Anzio. Larry and Shep run away and end up in rural California where they hitch a ride with an itinerant Mexican, Manuel "Mike" Ortiz, to the small town of Los Mochis. While Manuel gasses his truck, Larry goes to a restaurant run by Martha Langley and asks for work in exchange for food. There the boy meets Martha's boy friend, Mark Folger, who works for the immigration service and has been alerted by the sheriff about several missing Mexican nationals who jumped the fence at a labor camp. Another of Martha's customers, Sheriff Weatherby, admires Shep but spots the St. Louis license and asks Larry not to leave town until he can check on him with St. Louis authorities. Because Larry doesn't want to do that, the sheriff takes him and Shep to the jailhouse. There they are shortly joined by Manuel, who has been unable to find his passport which Mike had requested to examine. A short time later, criminals "Swifty" Lewis and "Chance" Martin who killed a cashier in a bank robbery, are on the run and stop at Los Mochis for gas. The sheriff is suspicious of their car's Kansas plates and is shot by Swifty. Meanwhile, Shep has helped Larry and Manuel to escape by bringing them the cell keys, and they leave town in Manuel's truck. While Martha tends to the wounded sheriff, Mark deputizes a posse to hunt for Larry and Manuel, whom he suspects have shot the sheriff. By now firm "compadres", Larry and Manuel take a wrong turn and find themselves in a ghost town where they decide to spend the night. There Manuel finds his passport inside his coffee pot. When their car runs out of gas, Swifty and Chance come to the same town and seek hospitality from Larry and Manuel. The bank robbers are about to leave in Manuel's truck when Mark and four posse members arrive and spot the vehicle. Swifty orders Manuel to give himself up and reveal nothing about the others while he holds Larry and Shep as hostages. Mike then arrests Manuel for shooting the sheriff. While Swifty leaves to get gas for their car, Chance is left to guard Larry and Shep, but Shep attacks him and Larry ties him up. While Mark is concerned that some of the townspeople might try to lynch Manuel, Swifty drives into town as Larry and Shep's prisoner. Larry then returns the stolen money and tells Mark where he can find Chance. For his capture of the bank robbers Larry gets a $5,000 reward which he wants to share with Manuel. The sheriff recovers and Martha, who had spurned Mark's previous marriage proposals as she felt he would be away from home too much, relents and agrees to marry him when he gives up his job and returns to ranching. The couple then adopt Larry and Shep and hire Manuel to work with Mark on the ranch, allowing the "compadres" to remain together. *Dogs, War use of. Friendship. Immigrants. Mexicans. Orphans. Small town life. Bank robberies. Mexican-American border region. Posses. Restaurants. Sheriffs. Trucks. United States. Border Patrol. Vigilantes. World War II.*

Note: Ford Beebe's onscreen credit reads, "Story written and directed by". The credits also noted that exteriors were filmed at Jack Ingram's ranch, located in Topanga Canyon, CA. According to the file on the film in the MPAA/PCA Collection at the AMPAS Library, the Code Administration not only disallowed use of the expression "Nuts to you!" but also forbad "Nogales to you, señor!" The producer was also cautioned to "...make certain...that there will be nothing likely to give offense to the sensibilities of our Latin American neighbors."

Box 8 Jan 1949. *DV* 30 Dec 1948, p. 3. *FD* 3 Jan 1949, p. 25. *HR* 24 Sep 1948, p. 14. *HR* 30 Dec 1948, p. 3. *MPHPD* 4 Dec 1948, p. 4410. *MPHPD* 8 Jan 1949, p. *Var* 12 Jan 1949, p. 8.

THE SHERIFF OF FRACTURED JAW (English Americans, Native Americans)

Twentieth Century-Fox Film Corp. *Dist* Twentieth Century-Fox Film Corp. Jan 19**59**; London opening: 28 Oct 1958; Prod: began 26 Apr 1958; interiors shot at Pinewood Studios [©Twentieth Century-Fox Film Corp.; 29 Dec 1958; LP12858]. Sd; col (DeLuxe); CinemaScope; Lenses by Bausch & Lomb. 9,254 ft. 100 or 102-103 min. PCA cert no. 19147.

Pres DANIEL M. ANGEL. *Prod* Daniel M. Angel. *Dir* Raoul Walsh. *Asst dir* Jack Causey. *Scr* Arthur Dales. *Dir of photog* Otto Heller. *Cam op* Harold Haysom. *2d unit cam* Lionel Baines. *Art dir* Bernard Robinson. *Ed* John Shirley. *Cost des* Julie Harris. *Mus comp* Robert Farnon. *Played by* Sinfonia of London. *Cond* Muir Mathieson. *Choreographer* George Carden. *Recordist* Dudley Messenger. *Sd ed* Winston Ryder. *Makeup* George Partleton. *Hairdressing* Iris Tilley. *Prod supv* Edward Joseph. *Loc mgr* Basil Somner. *Cont* Shirley Barnes.

Song(s): "In the Valley of Love," "Strollin' Down the Lane with Bill," and "If the San Francisco Hills Could Only Talk," music and lyrics by Harry Harris; "In the Valley of Love" sung by Connie Francis.

Source: Based on the short story "The Sheriff of Fractured Jaw" by Jacob Hay in *MacLean's Magazine* (Apr 1954).

Cast: KENNETH MORE (*Jonathan Tibbs*), JAYNE MANSFIELD (*Kate*), Henry Hull ([*Doc*] *Masters*), Bruce Cabot (*Jack*), Ronald Squire (*Toynbee*), William Campbell (*Keeno*), Sidney James (*The drunk*), Reed de Rouen (*Clayborne*), Charles Irwin (*Luke*), Donald Stewart (*The drummer*), Clancy Cooper (*A barber*), Gordon Tanner ([*Bud*] *Wilkins*), Robert Morley (*Uncle Lucius* [*Tibbs*]), David Horne (*James, his butler*), Eynon Evans (*Mason, Manager, Jonathan Tibbs & Co.*), Tucker McGuire (*Luke's wife*), Nick Brady (*Slim*), Larry Taylor (*The gun guard*), Jack Lester (*The coach driver*), Nicholas Stuart (*Feeney*), Sheldon Lawrence (*Johnny*), Susan Denny (*Cora*), Charles Farrell (*Bartender*), Chief Jonas Applegarth (*Running Deer*), Deputy Chief Joe Buffalo (*Red Wolf*).

Western, Comedy, with songs. [*Print viewed*]. At his manor house in the English countryside, the wealthy Lucius Tibbs consults his solicitor, Mr. Toynbee, as to the whereabouts of his ne'er-do-well nephew Jonathan. Jonathan is soon located in the coach house working on his latest invention, a horseless carriage. When Jonathan's invention fails miserably, he decides to enter the family firm, the venerable Tibbs and Company, purveyors of guns and hunting rifles since 1605. Jonathan quickly realizes that the company, stuck in archaic ways of doing business, is turning only a small profit, so he sets off for America to sell Tibbs firearms in the "Wild West." While traveling by stagecoach, the bemused Tibbs finds himself in the company of a drunk and a hair tonic salesman. The stagecoach is attacked by Indians, but Tibbs, blissfully unaware of the danger and excited about the prospect of meeting a real Indian, jumps off the stage and walks up to a brave about to launch a tomahawk. Tibbs rescues the stage by restraining the Indian with his walking stick, then forces the confused warrior to shake his hand as a gentlemanly gesture of peace. The stagecoach enters the town of Fractured Jaw where the locals praise Tibbs for his bravery. Soon, however, the town's bad element, mercenaries involved in a feud over water rights between the Box N and Lazy S ranches, challenge Tibbs to a gunfight, but quickly disperse when he draws his gun with lightning speed. Tibbs checks into the local hotel and meets its proprietess, a buxom blonde named Miss Kate, who warns him that Fractured Jaw is a lawless town which has been without a sheriff for six months. Late that night, Tibbs is awakened by noise emanating from the hotel's rowdy barroom, where Miss Kate sings and dances, but when he goes downstairs to complain, Kate and the patrons make fun of his sense of decorum. Tibbs is lured into a drinking contest by the malevolent Keeno, a Box N mercenary who mistakenly believes that Tibbs is working undercover for the Lazy S. A brawl ensues in which Keeno is shot dead, but the barroom quickly returns to normal after Miss Kate casually orders the body removed and drinks for everyone. Seeing Tibbs's shock at the bar patrons' cavalier response, the mayor, Doc Masters, explains that the townspeople's cynicism is the result of their inability to retain a live sheriff. Before he knows it, an inebriated Tibbs has been tricked into accepting the position. The next morning, Tibbs attempts to relinquish the badge, but the mayor refuses to accept it, especially after Tibbs skillfully disarms Bud Wilkins, one of the Lazy S henchmen, with his quick draw. Impressed, Kate flirts with

Tibbs, but soon learns that Tibbs's lightning draw is the result of a special spring device he keeps up his sleeve. Kate, who finds Tibbs's Old World manners charming, advises him to keep his inability to shoot a secret and offers to give him lessons. During target practice, Kate and Tibbs declare their attraction to each other and Tibbs proposes marriage. Kate accepts on the condition that Tibbs give up his sheriff's badge, but Tibbs refuses because he now feels an obligation to clean up Fractured Jaw. The town undertaker begins shadowing Tibbs, certain that he will soon be adding him to the collection of sheriffs in Boot Hill Cemetery. Later, while attempting to sell guns to a local farmer, Tibbs succeeds in stopping a gun battle between representatives of the feuding ranchers, both of whom swear revenge on the new sheriff. Riding back to town, Tibbs is kidnapped by Indians and strung up for target practice, but Running Deer, the Indian whom Tibbs met on the way into Fractured Jaw, praises Tibbs's bravery and the tribe ends up making him an honorary member. Given the choice between becoming a "dead Englishman or a live Indian," Tibbs drinks the blood of a wild buffalo and smokes the peace pipe, but stops short of accepting the chief's offer of an Indian bride. Meanwhile, in town, the war between the ranchers escalates, but both sides decide to temporarily stop fighting while they concentrate on getting rid of the annoying Sheriff Tibbs. After Tibbs attempts to reason with the men and they respond by taking a potshot, Tibbs calls on the Indians for assistance. The Indians succeed in routing the ranchers, who are then taken to jail, after which the undertaker finally leaves, realizing that Tibbs is there to stay. Tibbs appoints Running Deer to the position of deputy and then begins the task of civilizing his Indian blood brother, first by teaching him how to make a proper cup of English tea. Having finally won the respect of the feuding ranchers, Tibbs elicits a promise that they will peacefully share the local watering hole with one another and with the Indians. As bells chime, an exuberant Sheriff Tibbs changes into formal wear and heads over to the chapel to wed Miss Kate, who is given away by Tibbs's adoptive father, Chief Red Wolf. *Cultural conflict. English in foreign countries. Firearms. Range wars. Sheriffs. Blood brotherhood. Dance hall girls. Drunkenness. Gunfights. Hotelkeepers. Indians of North America. Mayors. Proposals (Marital). Saloons. Stagecoaches. Traveling salesmen. Undertakers and undertaking. Weddings.*

Note: Connie Francis sings "In the Valley of Love" over the opening credits, but she does not appear in the film. The film's opening scenes, which take place in England, were shot at London's Pinewood Studios, but most of the film was shot in various locations in Spain's Andalusia province. A *HR* news item, dated 2 Apr 1958, stated that Twentieth Century-Fox was shooting the film in Spain in order to "defreeze some... frozen funds" tied up in Europe. *The Sheriff of Fractured Jaw* opened in London in late Oct 1958, approximately two months prior to its U.S. release. Although most of the critics present at the London opening viewed the film as a novel and entertaining spoof of the Western genre, the *NYT* critic dismissed *The Sheriff of Fractured Jaw* as a "pathetically tired attempt at a Western comedy."

Box 1 Dec 1958. *DV* 3 Nov 1958, p. 3. *FD* 18 Nov 1958, p. 8. *Exh* 26 Nov 1958, p. 4535. *Har* 22 Nov 1958, p. 187. *HR* 4 Apr 1958. *HR* 12 Jan 1959, p. 3. *MPD* 18 Nov, 1958. *MPHPD* 22 Nov 1958, p. 61. *NYT* 14 Mar 1959, p. 27. *Var* 5 Nov 1958, p. 6.

SHERIFF OF LAS VEGAS (Native Americans)

Republic Pictures Corp. *Dist* Republic Pictures Corp. 31 Dec **1944**; Los Angeles opening: 28 Dec 1944; Prod: completed late Jul 1944 [©Republic Pictures Corp.; 12 Dec 1944; LP13068]. Sd (RCA Sound System); b&w. 6 reels, 4,917 ft. 56 min. Passed by the National Board of Review. PCA cert no. 10333.

Series: Red Ryder.

[*Exec prod* William J. O'Sullivan]. *Assoc prod* Stephen Auer. *Dir* Lesley Selander. [*Asst dir* Harry Knight]. *Orig scr* Norman S. Hall. *Photog* Bud Thackery. [*2d cam* Enzo Martinelli]. [*Transparency projection shots* Gordon C. Schaefer]. *Art dir* Fred A. Ritter. *Film ed* Charles Craft. *Set dec* Earl Wooden. *Mus dir* Richard Cherwin. *Sd* Ed Borschell. [*Re-rec and eff mixer* John Stransky, Jr.]. [*Re-rec, mus and eff mixer* Howard Wilson].

Source: Based on the comic strip "Red Ryder" by Fred Harman (1938—1964), by special arrangement with Stephen Slesinger.

Cast: WILD BILL ELLIOTT (*Red Ryder*), Bobby Blake [(*Little Beaver*)], Alice Fleming [(*The Duchess*)], Peggy Stewart [(*Ann Carter*)], Selmer Jackson [(*Arthur Stanton*)], Wm. Haade [(*Dan Sedley*)], Jay Kirby [(*Tom Blackwell*)], John Hamilton [(*Judge Homer T. Blackwell*)], Kenne Duncan [(*Whitey*)], Bud Geary [(*Nick*)], Jack Kirk [(*Buck*)], Dickie Dillon [(*Oliver Blake*)], [Freddie Chapman (*Ulysses Botts*)], [Frank McCarroll (*Sheriff Lonergan*)], [Bob Wilke].

Western. [*Print viewed*]. Cowboy Red Ryder, who lives with his Indian ward, Little Beaver, and aunt, The Duchess, in Las Vegas, Nevada, promises to help schoolteacher Ann Carter, who wants him to speak to her wild sweetheart, Tom Blackwell. Red finds Tom drunk in the saloon owned by Dan Sedley, cautions him to grow up and warns him that he is disappointing his father, territorial judge Homer T. Blackwell. Red's lecture is interrupted, however, by an attempted bank robbery. Red foils the robbery and retrieves the money bags, which he returns to bank president Arthur Stanton. Unknown to Red, Stanton has embezzled $40,000 from his bank and, in order to hide the shortage, asked Sedley to stage the robbery. Later, Stanton sees another opportunity to protect himself when Blackwell announces that he is going to cut Tom out of his will. The Duchess and Ann overhear Blackwell make his proclamation, and despite Ann's pleas to give Tom another chance, Blackwell refuses and asks Stanton to bring a list of his securities to his office that night. Soon after, Stanton and Sedley urge Tom to visit his father that night and reconcile with him. Tom agrees, but when he attempts to talk to Blackwell, the judge angers him and Tom storms out. Tom quickly regrets his harsh words, however, and tells Sedley that he will make it up with Blackwell in the morning. Sedley then sneaks into the judge's office and kills him with a derringer, and Red, who has been appointed sheriff, is forced to arrest Tom due to the circumstantial evidence against him. Tom goes along quietly, but when Red has a newspaper story printed stating that he has new evidence of Tom's innocence, the worried Stanton orders Sedley to stir up a lynch mob to take care of Tom. Stanton's goal is to eliminate Tom as Blackwell's heir and then use the judge's large estate to cover the embezzled funds. In order to protect Tom from the mob, Red releases him to the Duchess, then tells Stanton that he is hiding in Ann's schoolhouse. Red's suspicions of Stanton are confirmed when Stanton then sends Sedley to the schoolhouse to kill Tom. Sedley is mortally wounded by the waiting Red, but he confesses to the judge's murder before dying. Still needing evidence of Stanton's complicity, Red sends Tom to his office, as if for help. Stanton draws a gun on Tom, but Red is captures him before he shoots. Soon after, Stanton is convicted, and the reformed Tom is ready to settle down with Ann. When Tom vows to use some of his inheritance to elect Red to the office of territorial governor, however, Red runs off with Little Beaver. *Cowboys. Fathers and sons. Frame-ups. Moral reformation. Murder. Sheriffs. Aunts. Bank presidents. Bank robberies. Circumstantial evidence. Confession (Law). Disinheritance. Firearms. Handcuffs. Indians of North America. Judges. Las Vegas (NV). Mobs. Saloon keepers. Schoolteachers. Wards and guardians.*

Note: Although the *DV* review lists the film's running time as 56 minutes, *MPH* gives the running time as 66 minutes. For more information about the "Red Ryder" series, consult the Series Index and see the entry below for *Tucson Raiders.*

DV 29 Dec 1944, p. 3. *HR* 14 Jul 1944, p. 15. *HR* 21 Jul 1944, p. 9. *HR* 29 Dec 1944, p. 3. *MPHPD* 14 Oct 1944, p. 2142. *MPHPD* 6 Jan 1945, p. 2257.

SHERIFF OF REDWOOD VALLEY (Native Americans)

Republic Pictures Corp. *Dist* Republic Pictures Corp. 29 Mar **1946**; Prod: Jul 1945 [©Republic Pictures Corp.; 29 Mar 1946; LP311]. Sd (RCA Sound System); b&w. 54 or 56-57 min. Passed by the National Board of Review. PCA cert no. 11073.

Series: Red Ryder.

Assoc prod Sidney Picker. *Dir* R. G. Springsteen. [*Asst dir* Don Verk]. *Orig scr* Earle Snell. *Photog* Reggie Lanning. [*2d cam* Herbert Kirkpatrick]. [*Matte paintings* Lewis Physioc]. [*Miniatures and special opt eff* Howard Lydecker]. [*Special opt eff* Theodore Lydecker]. [*Transparency projection shots* Gordon Schaefer]. *Art dir* Fred A. Ritter. *Film ed* Ralph Dixon. *Set dec* John McCarthy, Jr. and Allan Alperin. *Mus dir* Richard Cherwin. *Sd* Fred Stahl. [*Re-rec and eff mixer* Thomas A. Carman and Howard Wilson]. [*Mus mixer* John Stransky, Jr.]. *Makeup supv* Bob Mark.

Source: Based on the comic strip "Red Ryder" by Fred Harman (1938—1964), by special arrangement with Stephen Slesinger.

Cast: WILD BILL ELLIOTT (*Red Ryder*), Bobby Blake [(*Little Beaver*)], Bob Steele [(*The Reno Kid*)], Alice Fleming [(*Martha "The Duchess" Wentworth*)], Peggy Stewart [(*Molly*)], Arthur Loft [(*Harvey Martin*)], James Craven [(*Bidwell*)], Tom London [(*Sheriff*)], Kenne Duncan [(*Jackson*)], Bud Geary [(*Strong*)], John Wayne Wright [(*Johnny*)], Tom Chatterton [(*Doc Ellis*)], Budd Buster [(*Crump*)], Frank McCarroll [(*Pete*)], [Frank Linn (*Dog man*)], [Jack Kirk (*Stagecoach driver*)].

Western. [*Print viewed*]. In 1895, stagecoach robber The Reno Kid escapes from San Quentin and begins his journey home to Redwood Valley. The news troubles the citizens of the valley, who are feuding with their neighbors in nearby Indian Gap over a proposed railroad spur line. If they can send the railroad enough money to tunnel through Whitehorse Mountain, the valley residents will get the line, but they are worried that Reno will rob the stage of the outgoing shipment. At a town meeting, prominent citizen Bidwell suggests using the stage as a decoy while the money is carried by the sheriff aboard a wagon. Unknown to the townspeople, Bidwell and crooked lawyer Harvey Martin are the leaders of a gang bent on bringing the railroad to Indian Gap and obtaining a huge profit by selling illegally gotten land rights to the railroad company. The next day, Bidwell drives the sheriff's wagon, while rancher Red Ryder and his Indian ward, Little Beaver, guard the stage. Two of Bidwell's henchmen, Jackson and Strong, attack the wagon and are given the money by Bidwell after they wound the sheriff. Bidwell then tells Red that a man answering Reno's description attacked them, and the sheriff appoints Red as his successor. During his pursuit of Jackson and Strong, Red is injured, but his horse Thunder and Little Beaver succeed in taking him to an isolated shack for help. At the shack is Reno, who has just returned home to his wife Molly and their young son Johnny. Molly wants to send them away, but Reno insists on helping the injured Red. Red deduces Reno's identity but sympathizes with him when Reno describes how the "real" Reno was innocent of any crime but was so badly misrepresented by Martin that he was convicted. Reno had signed over the deed of his ranch to Martin as payment for his services, and consequently, Molly and Johnny now live in poverty. Little Beaver brings the Duchess, Red's aunt, to the shack to tend to Red's wound, and she declares that the little family must come to her ranch, where the worn-out Molly and ailing Johnny can recuperate. As the others travel to the ranch, Red and Little Beaver double back to look for Reno, who he suspects is searching for the loot he supposedly still possesses. At the same time, Jackson, Strong and Pete, another henchman, are looking for Reno on orders from Martin, who fears that Reno is gunning for him. As Red and Little Beaver reach the shack, the outlaws attack Reno, but he escapes and goes to Indian Gap, where he orders Martin to sign over the deed to his old ranch to Molly. Jackson and the others arrive, however, and Reno is trying to escape when Red catches him. Martin tries to claim Reno, but Red states that he has prior jurisdiction for the shooting of the sheriff. Red allows Reno to go to the Duchess' ranch to say goodbye to Molly and Johnny, and then escorts him to jail. Bidwell identifies Reno as the robber who wounded the recovering sheriff, but the suspicious Red decides to investigate Martin. When Bidwell learns of Red's plans, he arranges for Reno to break out of jail with the intention of killing him. Reno escapes, however, and rides to Indian Gap. There, Red is interrogating Martin, who admits that Reno's ranch was the key piece of land in his scheme. As Martin and Red struggle for a gun, a masked man enters. Believing that it is Reno, Martin shoots him, but it turns out to be Bidwell, who wanted to kill Red and blame the murder on Reno. The real Reno has just arrived outside and prevents Martin from escaping. Later, the recovered Molly and Johnny dine with Reno at the Duchess' house and share a laugh with her as Red tricks Little Beaver into eating Johnny's spinach. *Circumstantial evidence. Frame-ups. Land rights. Lawyers. Sheriffs.* Attempted murder. Aunts. Chases. Disguise. Fights. Gunshot wounds. Indians of North America. Medicine. Poverty. Prison escapes. Railroads. Reputation. Revenge. Wards and guardians. Women ranchers.

Note: Although some contemporary reviews announced that *Sheriff of Redwood Valley* would mark Wild Bill Elliott's last appearance as "Red Ryder," Elliott's last film in the series was actually *Conquest of Cheyenne*, which was released in Jul 1946. Modern sources include Tex Cooper in the cast. For more information about the "Red Ryder" series, please consult the Series Index and see the entry below for *Tucson Raiders.*
DV 5 Apr 1946, p. 3. *HR* 13 Jul 1945, p. 12. *HR* 24 Jul 1945, p. 12. *HR* 5 Apr 1946, p. 3. *MPHPD* 29 Dec 1945, p. 2778. *MPHPD* 13 Apr 1946, p. 2938.

THE SHERIFF'S DAUGHTER *see* A TICKET TO TOMAHAWK

SHE'S TOO MEAN FOR ME (African Americans)
Goldmax Productions. *Dist* Toddy Pictures Co. 1949?. Sd; b&w. 7 reels, 5,982 ft.
Exec prod Ted Toddy.
Cast: Mantan Moreland (*Mantan*), Johnny Lee, F. E. Miller.

African American, Comedy. [*Not viewed*]. While making dinner for his wife, Mantan, a former comic star of radio and screen, is visited by an old show business friend, Stevie, and Stevie's sidekick, Blabber. Mantan tries desperately to get rid of the pair before his shrewish wife returns, and they respond by teasing him for being henpecked. When Mantan turns his back, Blabber quickly gobbles down the dinner. Mantan's wife does not believe his story that the cat ate her dinner and she comes after him, sending Mantan running from the house in abject fear. Mantan takes refuge in the rehearsal hall where Stevie and Blabber are preparing a new show, but his wife tracks him down, declaring that when she finishes with him he will think "the atomic bomb is a cap pistol." Mantan escapes his wife's clutches and ends up being hired as a chauffeur to the wealthy Dave Clark, who is about to be married to Clara York, a glamourous actress. When Clark learns that he is being blackmailed by a former fiancée, he has Mantan drive his car to the city, where Clara awaits and makes plans to meet him later. Because they want to bring their theatrical production to the city, Stevie and Blabber invite themselves along for the ride. Shortly after Mantan drops them off, he wrecks the car and is hospitalized in serious condition. Because Mantan was wearing his boss's clothes and driving his car, everyone mistakenly assumes he is Clark. Although Stevie warns that the injured man is not Clark, Rex, a theatrical manager to whom Clara was under contract prior to her engagement, devises a publicity stunt in which Clara will marry her intended on his deathbed. Clara reluctantly agrees to the marriage, but asks not to see her beloved's face because she wants to remember him as he once was. Meanwhile, Clark manages to rid himself of his conniving ex-fiancée by buying the embarrassing love letters he wrote to her and then heads by plane to meet Clara in the city for their impending wedding. Mantan wakes up in the hospital and Clara is immediately summoned, but upon hearing that his wife is coming, Mantan escapes the hospital clad only in his white gown. Mantan is finally caught by the police, but is so fearful of going back to the hospital that the policemen bring him to a doctor to have his head examined. After a lengthy examination during which Mantan's antics almost succeed in driving the doctor mad, the doctor determines that Mantan is mentally sound, but manifests a pathological fear of his wife. Clara arrives to see her husband, and is shocked to see that she is married to Mantan. After Clara is reunited with Clark and Rex's publicity ploy is revealed, Mantan is sent to jail on bigamy charges. The charges are quickly dismissed, though, when Rex declares that the marriage license was a phony. Mantan, however, sure that his wife will catch up with him soon, begs to stay in jail. His pleas are ignored, and an enraged Mrs. Mantan forces her way to Mantan's cell and collars her wayward husband, sending the entire jail into an uproar. *Comedians. Henpecked husbands. Mistaken identity. Publicity stunts.* Actors and actresses. Automobile accidents. Bigamy. Blackmail. Chauffeurs. Engagements. Hospitals. Jails. Love letters. Marriage. Physicians. Shrews. Theatrical managers.

Note: The above plot summary is taken from a dialogue continuity deposited with the NYSA. Although modern sources provide a release year of 1948, the picture was approved for exhibition in New York state in 1949.

SHIFTING SANDS (German Americans)
Triangle Film Corp. *Dist* Triangle Distributing Corp. 11 Aug **1918**. Si; b&w. 5 reels.
Dir Albert Parker. *Asst dir* Amy E. Sacker. *Scen* Catherine Carr. *Story* Charles Turner Dazey. *Cam* Pliny Horne.
Cast: Gloria Swanson (*Marcia Grey*), Joe King (*John Stanford*), Harvey Clark (*Von Holtz, also known as Sir George Denby*), Leone Carton (*Minnie Grey*), Lillian Langdon (*Mrs. Stanford*), Arthur Millett (*Major Willis*).

Espionage, World War I, Drama. Marcia Grey struggles to support herself and her ailing sister as an artist but finds no market for her work in New York. When Marcia rejects a lustful German named Von Holtz, he angrily frames her for robbery, and she is sent to Blackwells Island prison for several months. Upon her release, she finds that her sister has died and considers suicide, but decides instead to work for the Salvation Army. Soon she becomes acquainted with philanthropist John Stanford, and in time they marry. After the United States formally joins with the Allies in World War I, John becomes attached to the Secret Service. Von Holtz, now a spy for the Germans, visits the Stanfords in the guise of English nobleman Sir Robert Denby, but when Marcia recognizes him, he threatens to reveal her past to John unless she assists him in securing secret

documents from John's office. Marcia pretends to acquiesce but immediately tells her husband everything, and soon Von Holtz is behind bars. *Blackmail. Frame-ups. German Americans. Secret Service. Spies. Artists. English. Impersonation and imposture. Imprisonment. Lechery. New York City. Nobility. Philanthropists. Salvation Army. Secret documents. Sisters. World War I.*

Note: In a print of this film re-issued after World War I, the villain is not a German spy but a British counterfeiter. The later version credits Myrtle Rishell with the role of Joan and names Leone Carton's character Cora Grey.

ETR 10 Aug 1918, p. 783. *ETR* 17 Aug 1918, p. 928. *MPN* 17 Aug 1918, p. 1043. *MPN* 24 Aug 1918, p. 1257. *MPW* 17 Aug 1918, p. 1003, 1020. *MPW* 24 Aug 1918, p. 1155. *NYDM* 31 Aug 1918, p. 319. *Var* 30 Aug 1918, p. 38. *Wid's* 11 Aug 1918, p.18.

A SHIP COMES IN (Slovakian Americans)

De Mille Pictures Corp.; A William K. Howard Production. *Dist* Pathé Exchange, Inc. 4 Jun 1928 [©Pathé Exchange, Inc.; 10 May 1928; LP25281]. Si; b&w. 7 reels, 6,902 ft. Passed by the National Board of Review.

Dir William K. Howard. [*Asst dir* Emile De Ruelle]. *Orig story and scen* Julien Josephson. *Scen* Sonya Levien. *Titles* John Krafft. *Photog* Lucien Andriot. *Art dir* Anton F. Grot. *Film ed* Barbara Hunter. [*Cost* Adrian].

Cast: RUDOLPH SCHILDKRAUT (*Peter Pleznik*), LOUISE DRESSER (*Mrs. Pleznik*), Milton Holmes (*Eric*), Linda Landi (*Marthe*), Evelyn Mills (*Katinka*), Virginia Davis (*Katinka*), Fritz Feld (*Sokol*), Robert Edeson (*Judge Gresham*), Lucien Littlefield (*Dan [Casey]*), Louis Natheaux (*Gregor*).

Drama. [*Not viewed*]. The Slovakian family of Peter Pleznik emigrates to the United States, and there, despite protests from Sokol, a radical countryman he meets in a restaurant, Peter applies for American citizenship. Five years later, assisted by kindly Judge Gresham, Peter receives his citizenship papers, and soon after, his son Eric goes to fight for America in the war. Judge Gresham, meanwhile, has sentenced a radical to ten years hard labor for treason, and Sokol is chosen by his revolutionary comrades to kill Gresham. After Sokol substitutes a time bomb for a cake Peter's wife has made for the judge, Peter unwittingly brings the box with the bomb to the judge. Gresham is seriously wounded and his secretary is killed as the bomb explodes. Peter is blamed, convicted, and jailed, but he is later freed when Sokol, as he is dying after being hit by a truck, confesses to the crime. Eric is killed in the war. Despite all this, Peter's patriotism never wavers, and he returns to his job as a janitor feeling that he has given all to his country. *Citizenship. Family life. Immigrants. Patriotism. Slovakian Americans. World War I. Bombs. False arrests. Janitors. Judges. Murder. Revolutionaries.*

Note: The working title of this film was *His Country*. The onscreen credits were taken from a cutting continuity deposited at the NYSA.

Other language version(s):

Das Grosse Glueck (German language)

Mit Benutzung des Filmes *Der Patriot* von Wm. K. Howard. 1929. Sd (RCA Photophone System); b&w. 6 reels. Passed by the National Board of Review. German language.

Regie [*Dir*] Leo Birinski. *Manuskript* [*Scr*] Sonya Levien. *Dialog* [*Dial*] Leo Birinski. *Kuenstlerischer beirat* [*Artistic adv*] Frank Reicher.

Rudolf Schildkraut [(*Peter Pleznik*)], Luise Dresser [(*Mama Pleznik*)], Fritz Feld. [*German version not viewed*].

FD 1 Jul 1928. *NYT* 4 Sep 1928, p. 21. *Var* 5 Sep 1928, p. 28.

SHIR HASHIRIM (Yiddish language)

Empire Film Co.; A Henry Lynn Production. *Dist* Globe Pictures. **1935**; New York opening: 10 Oct 1935; Prod: ended late Sep 1935, in New York [©Globe Pictures; 13 Dec 1935; LP6008]. Sd; b&w. 9 reels, 7,900 ft. 70 min. Yiddish language with English subtitles.

Dir Henry Lynn. *Scr* Henry Lynn. *Mus comp and cond by* Joseph Rumshinsky.

Source: Based on the play *Shir Hashirim* by Anshel Shorr (production undetermined).

Cast: Samuel Goldenberg (*Professor Leon Oppenheimer*), Dora Weissman (*Anna Oppenheimer*), Max Kletter (*Dave Oppenheimer*), Merele Gruber (*Lily*), Yudel Dubinsky, Ruben Wendorff (*Grandfathers*), Hannah Toback (*Rose*), Seymour Rechtzeit.

Yiddish, Domestic, Melodrama. [*Not viewed*]. Professor Leon Oppenheimer, a composer, his wife Anna, their son Dave and Anna's eighty-year-old father Aaron, a middle-class Jewish family from New York, have invited Aaron's twin brother Moses and his orphaned granddaughter Lily to their summer house in the mountains. Leon, who suffers from eye problems, has been composing his new opera, *Shir Hashirim*, or "Song of Songs," while Dave has fallen in love with the beautiful Lily. After two weeks, Dave complains to Anna that Lily is planning to return to the city because he thinks that Leon dislikes her. Anna tells Dave that she is sure Leon is pleased when Lily sings his new songs. When Leon returns from a visit to the doctor, Anna tries to get him to stop working so that he will not strain his eyes, and they argue, but soon reconcile. When Lily sings as Leon plays, he exclaims that his soul is rejuvenated through her singing, and she tells him that she desires to melt her soul with his melodies. Anna and Rose, a friend who is secretly in love with Dave, see Lily and Leon together and realize that they are deeply in love. Anna worries, not only for herself and Dave, but for Leon, who could become blind from the least excitement. She resigns herself, however, to face the future and tells Rose that troubles have made her strong. When Dave tells his father that he loves Lily and wants to marry her, Leon says he won't allow it. Seeing that Leon is upset by Dave, Anna sends Dave out of the room, and Leon appreciatively says she is like a mother to him. Anna bridles at this and reminds Leon that she was once his "shining star," but that she became old and gray caring for him while he was in the hospital with bandages over his eyes. Leon promises that in three months, after the opera is produced, they will be happy again. Sometime later, Leon and Lily go for a walk in the forest, and after they both confess that they have been inspired by the other, Lily wants to kiss him, but Leon, extremely agitated, calls her a vampire and a siren. Back at the cottage, Dave finds Lily crying, and after he confesses his love, she refuses his proposal. Leon, meanwhile, tells Anna that he is afraid of himself and that they should go back to the city. Leon has now decided that Lily and Dave should marry, but Lily finds Leon alone and expresses her love to him. When he says that she is destroying his spirit and accuses her of trapping him, she starts to cry, whereupon Leon, very moved, asks her forgiveness. In a moment of extreme passion, he decides that they should love each other and not worry about tomorrow, and they leave together. Three months later, in the city, Rose, who has turned down a suitor because she still loves Dave, tries to talk Dave into going to the première of his father's *Shir Hashirim* and says that Leon and Lily have lived apart although sometimes they see each other. Dave, who rages against his father, confesses that he loves Lily even more than before. After the successful performance, Leon and Lily go to a cabaret, where he tells her that he is suffering and encourages her to stop loving him and to marry Dave. Lily tells Leon she loves him and offers him her youth, dreams, love and life. Leon thinks that maybe he can still be happy with her, and they plan to go away together. Just then, Dave arrives and shoots Lily to avenge his mother. Lily is only wounded slightly in the arm, but Leon goes blind from the excitement. He cries out that he wants to go home, and after a visit to the doctor, Dave brings him home. When Leon learns that Lily has disappeared, he takes Dave's hand and tells him that only words passed between him and Lily. He asks for forgiveness, and Dave says he believes him. When Leon expresses misery that he will be alone and blind, Anna, who has been listening silently, tells him that her eyes will be his and that she will take care of him. *Composers. Family life. Family relationships. Jews. Love affairs. Marriage. Self-sacrifice. Blindness. Brothers. Cabarets. Forests. Grandfathers. Mountains. New York City. Opera. Proposals (Marital). Revenge. Shootings. Twins. Unrequited love. Vacations.*

Note: The plot summary was based on a dialogue continuity at NYSA. The English language title of this film was *Song of Songs*. According to the *Var* review, which was printed in both English and Yiddish, Joseph Rumshinsky was the leading Yiddish composer of the time. The film was re-released later by Cinema Service Corp.

FD 14 Oct 1935, p. 7. *NYT* 11 Oct 1935, p. 31. *Var* 23 Oct 1935, p. 13.

SHOLOM ALEICHEM'S TEVYA see TEVYA

SHOOTING STAR see ANNIE OAKLEY

A SHOT IN THE NIGHT (African Americans)

Dist State Rights. **1923**; New York State license: 24 Mar 1923; Prod: ended 15 Feb 1922. Si; b&w. 5 reels.

Prod Ben Strasser and William Scales.

Cast: Walter Holeby, Walter Long, Ruth Freeman, Tom Amos, Tolliver Brothers, Bobby Smart.

African American, Comedy-drama. "The story tells of a man called 'The Masked Terror' a professional criminal and leader of a

gang who kills a financier and steals $500,000. A little boy playing detective finds the gang's den and hides there. He is discovered, tied in a bag and about to be flung into a pond, when he is rescued by the district attorney. The murdered financier's daughter is then abducted by the gang. She is gagged, maltreated, then bound and tied to the railroad tracks. She is rescued by the district attorney who catches 'The Masked Terror' and the gang by smoking them out with poisoned gas." (NYSA records.). *Abduction. African Americans. Children. District attorneys. Gangs. Murder.*

Note: Local New York State distribution was handled by American Colored Film Exchange.

Billboard 4 Mar 1922, p. 45.

SHOTGUN (Native Americans, Apache)

Allied Artists Pictures Corp.; Commander Films Corp. *Dist* Allied Artists Pictures Corp. 24 Apr **1955**; Prod: mid-Aug—mid-Sep 1954 [©Allied Artists Pictures Corp.; 3 Mar 1955; LP4448]. Sd; col (Technicolor). 7,227 ft. 80 min. PCA cert no. 17258.

Prod John C. Champion. *Dir* Lesley Selander. *Asst dir* Bud Andrews. *2d unit dir* Austen Jewell. *Wrt* Clark E. Reynolds and Rory Calhoun. *Addl dial* John C. Champion. *Photog* Ellsworth Fredericks. *Asst cam* Bud Davidson. *Spec eff* Milton Rice. *Art dir* David Milton. *Supv film ed* Lester Sansom. *Film ed* John Fuller. *Set dresser* Allan Beatty. *Mus comp and cond* Carl Brandt. *Sd* Frank McWhorter. *Rec* Joe Lapis. *Makeup artist* Carl E. Taylor. *Hair stylist* Mary Smith. *Prod mgr* Allen K. Wood. *Grip foreman* Cecil F. Haverty. *Props* Max Frankel.

Cast: Sterling Hayden (*Clay Hardin*), Yvonne De Carlo (*Abby*), Zachary Scott (*Reb Carleton*), Angela Greene (*Aletha*), Robert Wilke (*Bentley*), Harry Harvey, Jr. (*Davey*), Lane Chandler (*Mark Fletcher*), Guy Prescott (*Ben Thompson*), Ralph Sanford (*Chris*), John Pickard (*Perez*), Ward Wood (*Ed*), Rory Mallinson (*Frank*), Paul Marion (*Delgadito*), Robert E. Griffin (*Doctor*), Al Wyatt (*Greybar*), Bob Morgan (*Sam*), Peter Coe (*Apache*), Charles Morton, James Parnell (*Cavalrymen*), Richard Cutting (*Holly*), Fiona Hale (*Midge*), Francis McDonald (*Dishwasher*).

Western. [*Not viewed*]. In Arizona, after marshal Mark Fletcher is killed by a shotgun wielded by ruthless killer Ben Thompson, Clay Hardin, Mark's deputy and a former outlaw, sets out with a shotgun to avenge his death. Along the way, Clay encounters Bentley, Thompson's henchman, and Abby, a former dance hall hostess, who have been left to die in an Apache snake trap. Clay frees them, but has to kill Bentley when he tries to take his gun. Clay then travels on with Abby, who is heading for California to make a new start. Later, Clay rescues bounty hunter Reb Carleton from the Apaches and discovers that he, too, is pursuing Thompson, who has been selling guns to the Indians. At a stage depot, the trio is ambushed by two of Thompson's gunmen, whom they kill. Clay decides to go on alone but Abby and Reb follow him and are attacked by a small band of Apaches. Hearing the gunfire, Clay returns to help them, but finds Reb near death, pinned to a tree by arrows shot through his body, and learns that Abby has been taken prisoner by the Indians. Reb commits suicide with Clay's gun. Clay fearlessly enters the Apache camp and finds both Abby and Thompson. Impressed by Clay's courage, the tribal chief orders him and Thompson to fight a traditional Apache duel with shotguns. During the duel, Thompson loses his nerve, attempts to escape and is killed, as a coward, by an Apache spear in his back. The chief allows Clay and Abby to go free, and they head for Clay's ranch to begin a new life together. *Apache Indians. Bounty hunters. Deputies. Duels. Gunrunners. Revenge. Ambushes. Cowardice. Dance hall girls. Marshals. Murder. Rattlesnakes. Romance. Saloons. Suicide.*

Note: *Shotgun* was filmed in Sedona, Arizona and in California. The *HR* reviewer commented about the picture that, "Selander is the first director to my knowledge who has succeeded in presenting the absolutely chilling heartlessness of the tribe [The Apache] and its noble attitude on the screen at the same time. 'Apache' in the Indian tongue meant 'Enemy' and this was the word by which other tribes referred to them. Yet the Apaches never unleashed their cold-blooded ferocity against the white man until they had been provoked by savagery as unprincipled as, but less fiendishly ingenious, than their own. After that, they never relented." In a *HR* news item of Aug 1967, producer John C. Champion claimed outright ownership of *Shotgun*, which reportedly was made for $260,000 and which grossed $1,650,000.

Box 2 Apr 1955. *DV* 24 Mar 1955, p. 3. *Exh* 6 Apr 1955, p. 3941. *FD* 12 Apr 1955, p. 3. *Har* 2 Apr 1955, p. 54. *HR* 24 Mar 1955, p. 3 *HR* 2 Aug 1967. *MPHPD* 2 Apr 1955, p. 386. *Var* 30 Mar 1955, p. 8.

SHOULD A BABY DIE? (Jewish Americans)

Charles K. Harris Feature Film Co. *Dist* State Rights; Hanover Film Co. Jan—Feb **1916?**. Si; b&w. 5 reels.

Dir Perry N. Vekroff. *Scen* Charles K. Harris. *Cam* Harold L. Miller.

Cast: Arthur Donaldson (*Jacob Cohen*), Gazelle Marche (*Lydia*), J. W. Johnston (*Burton*), Florence Hackett (*Burton's ex-sweetheart*), Baby Christine (*Lydia as a baby*), Sonia Marcelle (*Rachel Cohen*), Camille Dalberg, Mrs. Donaldson, George Henry.

Drama. Burton, the son of a wealthy family, falls in love with Jacob Cohen's daughter Lydia, but because Burton is not Jewish, Jacob refuses to consent to a marriage. Similarly, Burton's family is alarmed because of Lydia's religion and also because her family is too impoverished to be socially acceptable. Then, Lydia discovers that she really is not Jewish at all. Her natural parents died when she was just a baby and Jacob and his wife adopted the girl, who was near death at the time, to raise as their own daughter. After the removal of the religious obstacle, the social one vanishes, too, when Lydia learns that her real parents were millionaires, and, as a result, she and Burton get married. *Class distinction. Cultural conflict. Foster parents. Jews. Parentage. Infants.*

Note: The working title for this film was *For Sale, A Baby*. Production began at the Kinemacolor studio in Whitestone, Long Island in the fall of 1915. The film, under the early title, was to be released by World Film Corp. and according to one news item, the film was released by World under the early title, but this has not been confirmed. This film was re-released by Arista Film Corp. in 1922 under the title *Orphans of the Ghetto*. Donald L. Buchanon, an assistant director and cutter, listed this film in his credits in the 1918 *Motion Picture Studio Directory*.

Motog 16 Oct 1915, p. 786. *Motog* 12 Feb 1916, pp. 375-76. *MPN* 16 Oct 1915, p. 68. *MPN* 23 Oct 1915, p. 60. *MPN* 29 Jan 1916, p. 533. *MPN* 12 Feb 1916, p. 868. *MPN* 4 Sep 1920, p. 1901. *MPW* 12 Feb 1916, p. 975. *Var* 3 Mar 1916, p. 22.

SHOW BOAT (African Americans)

Universal Pictures Corp. 28 Jul **1929**; World premiere in Palm Beach, FL: 16 Mar 1929 [©Universal Pictures Corp.; 27 Apr 1929; LP339]. Talking and singing sequences, sd eff, and mus score (Movietone); b&w. 14 reels, 11,650 ft. 126 min. [Also si; 10,290 ft.].

Pres Carl Laemmle. *Dir* Harry Pollard. *Addl dir* Arch Heath. *Asst dir* Robert Ross. *Scen* Charles Kenyon. *Story supv* Edward J. Montagne. *Dial* Harry Pollard. *Dial and titles* Tom Reed. *Photog* Gilbert Warrenton. *Spec eff photog* Frank H. Booth. *Art dir* Charles D. Hall. *Ed supv* Maurice Pivar. *Film ed* Daniel Mandell and Edward Cahn. *Cost* Johanna Mathieson. *Mus dir* Joseph Cherniavsky. *Rec eng* C. Roy Hunter. *Makeup* Jane Rene. *Unit mgr* Joseph C. Wright. *Singing voice for Laura La Plante* Eva Olivotti.

Music: "Love Sings a Song in My Heart" by Joseph Cherniavsky; "Down South" by William H. Myddleton.

Song(s): "Can't Help Lovin' Dat Man" and "Ol' Man River," music by Jerome Kern, lyrics by Oscar Hammerstein II, "Bill," music by Jerome Kern, lyrics by Oscar Hammerstein II and P. G. Wodehouse; "The Lonesome Road," music by Nathaniel Shilkret, lyrics by Gene Austin; "Here Comes The Show Boat," music and lyrics by Billy Rose and Maceo Pinkard; "Coon, Coon, Coon," music by Leo Friedman, lyrics by Gene Jefferson; "Deep River" and other spirituals.

Source: Based on the novel *Show Boat* by Edna Ferber (Garden City, NY, 1926) and the musical of the same name by Edna Ferber, Jerome Kern and Oscar Hammerstein II (New York, 27 Dec 1927).

Cast: Prologue: Otis Harlan, Helen Morgan, Jules Bledsoe, Tess "Aunt Jemima" Gardella, The Jubilee Singers, Carl Laemmle, Florenz Ziegfeld, **Cast:** Laura La Plante (*Magnolia*), Joseph Schildkraut (*Gaylord Ravenal*), Otis Harlan (*Capt. Andy Hawks*), Emily Fitzroy (*Parthenia Hawks*), Alma Rubens (*Julie*), Elsie Bartlett (*Elly*), Jack McDonald (*Windy*), Jane La Verne (*Magnolia as a child/Kim*), Neely Edwards (*Schultzy*), Theodore Lorch (*Frank*), Stepin Fetchit (*Joe*), Gertrude Howard (*Queenie*), Ralph Yearsley (*The Killer*), George Chesebro (*Steve*), Harry Holden (*Means*), Max Asher (*Utility man*), Jim Coleman (*Stagehand*), Carl Herlinger (*Wheelsman*), The Billbrew Chorus.

Historical, Show business, Musical. Brought up on a showboat, Magnolia Hawks, the star of her family's river-going revue, marries Gaylord Ravenal, a charming river gambler. Magnolia's father, Captain Andy, is swept overboard in a storm, and Magnolia and Gaylord, harassed by Magnolia's strict, overbearing mother, sell their interest in the showboat to the widow and go to Chicago. Gaylord loses the money at the gambling tables, and, following the suggestion of Magnolia's mother, leaves his family, convinced that they would be

better off without him. To support herself and her child, Magnolia goes on the variety stage and makes a success singing Negro spirituals. Magnolia's mother dies, and Magnolia returns to the showboat to be reunited with the reformed Gaylord. *African Americans. Chicago (IL). Desertion (Marital). Gamblers. Mississippi River. Showboats. Singers. Spirituals (Songs). United States–South.*

Note: Universal Pictures acquired the rights to the Jerome Kern-Oscar Hammerstein score after the film had been shot as a part-talking drama. Several scenes were then reshot to include songs, and an eighteen-minute sound prologue was added. The prologue included short speeches by Carl Laemmle and Florenz Ziegfeld and songs from the stage production were performed by Helen Morgan, Jules Bledsoe and Tess "Aunt Jemima" Gardella. Two other filmed versions of the play were made, in 1936 and 1951 (see below). *FD* 5 May 1929. *NYT* 18 Apr 1929, p. 32. *Var* 24 Apr 1929, p. 13.

SHOW BOAT (African Americans)

Universal Productions, Inc.; A James Whale Production. *Dist* Universal Productions, Inc. 17 May **1936**; World premiere in New York: 14 May 1936; Prod: 9 Dec 1935—11 Mar 1936 [©Universal Productions, Inc.; 13 May 1936; LP6347]. Sd (Western Electric Noiseless Recording); b&w. 12 reels. 110, 112 or 115 min. PCA cert no. 2043.

Pres CARL LAEMMLE. *Prod* Carl Laemmle, Jr. *Dir* James Whale. [*Dial dir* Leighton Brill]. *Asst dir* Joseph A. McDonough, [Harry Mieneke and Joe Torillo]. *Stage play, screen play and lyrics by* Oscar Hammerstein II. [*Story* Billie Burke]. [*Contr wrt* Zoë Akins]. *Cine* John J. Mescall. [*2d cam* Alan Jones]. *Special cinematographer* John P. Fulton. *Art dir* Charles D. Hall. *Film ed* Ted Kent and Bernard Burton. [*Ed supv* Maurice Pivar]. [*Cost* Western Costume Company]. [*Ward* Carl Leas]. *Cost des by* Doris Zinkeisen. *Cost exec by* Vera West. [*Designer* Ed Brymer]. *Mus dir* Victor Baravalle. [*Musical arr* Russell Bennett]. *Dance numbers staged by* LeRoy Prinz. *Sd supv* Gilbert Kurland. [*Rec of mus* Mike McLaughlin]. [*Rec of production* William Hedgecock]. [*Hair* Doris Carico]. [*Makeup* Jack Pierce and Charles Gorman]. *Tech dir* Leighton Brill. [*Scr clerk* Helen McCaffrey]. [*Stand-in for Irene Dunne* Katherine Stanley]. [*Stand-in for Allan Jones* Jack Latham]. [*Stand-in for Helen Morgan* Mary Stewart*].

Music: "Why Do I Love You?" and "I Have the Room Above Her" by Jerome Kern.

Song(s): "Make Believe," "Ol' Man River," "Can't Help Lovin' Dat Man," "You Are Love," "Gallavantin' Around" and "Ah Still Suits Me," music by Jerome Kern, lyrics by Oscar Hammerstein II; "Bill," music by Jerome Kern, lyrics by Oscar Hammerstein II and P. G. Wodehouse; "After the Ball," music and lyrics by Charles K. Harris; "Goodbye My Lady Love," music and lyrics by Joe Howard.

Source: Based on the novel *Show Boat* by Edna Ferber (Garden City, NY, 1926) and the musical of the same name by Edna Ferber, Jerome Kern and Oscar Hammerstein II (New York, 27 Dec 1927).

Cast: Irene Dunne (*Magnolia*), Allan Jones ([*Gaylord*] *Ravenal*), Charles Winninger (*Cap'n Andy Hawks*), Paul Robeson (*Joe*), Helen Morgan (*Julie* [*LaVerne*]), Helen Westley (*Parthy*), Queenie Smith (*Elly*), Sammy White (*Frank* [*Schultz*]), Donald Cook (*Steve* [*Baker*]), Hattie McDaniel (*Queenie*), Francis X. Mahoney (*Rubber Face* [*Smith*]), Marilyn Knowlden (*Kim, as a child*), Sunnie O'Dea (*Kim, at eighteen*), Arthur Hohl (*Pete* [*Gavanaugh*]), Charles Middleton ([*Sheriff*] *Vallon*), J. Farrell MacDonald (*Windy*), Clarence Muse (*Janitor* [*Sam*]), Patricia Barry (*Kim, as a baby*)], [Charles Wilson (*Jim Green*), [Mae Beatty (*Landlady*)], [Stanley Fields (*Jeb, Hillbilly patron*)], [Stanley J. Sandford (*Backwoodsman*)], [Mary Bovard (*Daughter*)], [William Alston (*Young man*)], [Marguerite Warner (*Young girl*)], [Bobs Watson (*Lost child*)], [Jane Keckley (*Mrs. Ewing*)], [Isabelle LaMal (*Companion*)], [Betty Brown, Kathleen Ellis, June Glory (*Girls*)], [Tom Ricketts (*Minister*)], [Gunnis Davis (*Doctor*)], [Harold Nelson (*Postmaster*)], [Patti Patterson (*Banjo player*)], [Betty Roche (*Tall girl*)], [Grace Cunard, Maidel Turner, Anna Demetrio (*Mothers*)], [Marilyn Harris (*Little girl*)], [Jimmy Jackson (*Young man*)], [Ricca Allen (*Old woman*)], [Maxine Cook (*Thin girl*)], [Monte Montague (*Old man*)], [Lois Verner (*Small girl*)], [Artye Folz, Barbara Bletcher (*Fat girls*)], [Helen Hayward (*Mrs. Brencenbridge*)], [Harry Barris (*Jake, pianist*)], [Maude Allen (*Fat woman*)], [Frank Whitson (*Dealer*)], [Eddy Chandler, Lloyd Whitlock, Lee Phelps, Frank Mayo, Edward Peil, Sr., Edmund Cobb, Al Ferguson (*Gamblers*)], [Daisy Bufford (*Maid*)], [Dorothy Grainger, Barbara Pepper, Renee Whitney, Alma Ross, Jeanette Dickson (*Chorus girls*)], [Arthur Housman (*Drunk*)],

[Forrest Stanley (*Theater manager*)], [Selmer Jackson (*Hotel clerk*)], [George Hackathorne (*YMCA worker*)], [Max Wagner, James P. Burtis (*Soldiers*)], [Billy Watson, Delmar Watson, Harry Watson (*Boys*)], [Ernest Hilliard, Jack Mulhall, Brooks Benedict (*Race fans*)], [Elspeth Dudgeon (*Mother superior*)], [E. E. Clive (*Englishman*)], [Helen Jerome Eddy (*Reporter*)], [Don Briggs (*Press agent*)], [LeRoy Prinz (*Dance director*)], [Harold Waldridge (*Office boy*)], [Georgia O'Dell (*School teacher*)], [George H. Reed (*Old black man*)], [Eddie Anderson (*Young black man*)], [Theodore Lorch (*Simon Legree*)], [Matthew Jones (*Bartender*)], [Jack Latham (*Juvenile*)], [Flora Finch], [Helen Dickson], [D'Arcy Corrigan].

Historical, Show business, Musical, Comedy-drama. [*Print viewed*]. Cap'n Andy Hawks's show boat the *Cotton Blossom* arrives in New Orleans. Andy's daughter Magnolia, a gifted singer, meets Gaylord Ravenal and they make believe they are in love. While rehearsing, 'Nolia's good friend, Julie LaVerne, and her husband, Steve Baker, are accused of miscegenation and are forced to quit the show and leave town. 'Nolia and Gay take their places and, because their romantic involvement onstage mimics their real feelings, they are a hit. Pete Gavanaugh, who caused Julie's ostracism when she refused his advances, then writes to Andy to expose Gay as a murderer who was let off on a verdict of self-defense. After a successful run of their show, Gay and 'Nolia marry with Andy's blessing, even though 'Nolia's mother Parthy objects to the marriage because of Gay's questionable past. A year later, 'Nolia gives birth to Kim during a storm while Gay is away playing cards. Gay returns the next morning and asks 'Nolia to move to Chicago. Initially, the family lives well at the Palmer House while Gay bets on horses, but his money quickly runs out and they are forced to move. When Elly and Frank, former members of the show boat, inquire about a shabby room for rent from which the present tenants are being evicted, they discover the tenants are 'Nolia and Gay. Gay then deserts 'Nolia because he is ashamed that he cannot provide for her and Kim. 'Nolia then performs at the Trocadero after Julie, now an alcoholic, quietly quits so that her old friend 'Nolia can get work. Parthy and Andy then arrive at the Palmer House on New Year's Eve in search of the Ravenals, and Andy discovers 'Nolia singing at the Trocadero. Although the crowd is not receptive to 'Nolia's lyrical voice, Andy gives her support from the audience and she is a success. Soon 'Nolia is an international star. Years pass and she retires from the stage, after which Kim follows in her footsteps. When Kim opens on Broadway, 'Nolia recognizes Gay, who is posing as the stage doorman. After the encore, Kim invites her mother to join Gay in song. *African Americans. Desertion (Marital). Showboats. Singers. Theatrical troupes. United States–South. Alcoholics. Chicago (IL). Family relationships. Friendship. Miscegenation. Mississippi River. Ostracism. Poverty. Reunions. Self-sacrifice. Spirituals (Songs).*

Note: This film's title card reads "Edna Ferber's *Show Boat*." Ferber's novel was serialized in *Woman's Home Companion* (Apr-Aug 1926). Many actors from the 1927 Florenz Ziegfeld-produced Broadway musical recreated their roles for the film, including Charles Winninger, Helen Morgan, Francis X. Mahoney, and Sammy White, who made his film debut in this production. According to modern sources, Paul Robeson was originally wanted for the role of "Joe" in the 1927 stage version but was unavailable. He did, however, appear in the 1928 London production with Cedric Hardwicke and Colin Clive, and the 1932 Ziegfeld Broadway revival. "Ol' Man River" later became Robeson's signature song. Irene Dunne, Allan Jones and Hattie McDaniel also starred in earlier productions.

This film was the last feature presented by Universal president and founder Carl Laemmle, who then sold his interest in the company to J. Cheever Cowdin and Charles R. Rogers. *HR* announced on 12 Oct 1935 that Universal was negotiating with M-G-M to borrow Dave Gould to stage the dances in this film, however, LeRoy Prinz was eventually hired. According to the Call Bureau Cast Service, Prinz also appeared in the film in the role of a dance director. In 1933, Universal began negotiating for Winninger and Robeson to appear in this film. According to a modern source, production was originally planned for 1933 under Frank Borzage's direction, with a script by Jo Swerling. Dunne, Winninger, Robeson and Russ Columbo were set to star. Reportedly, in 1935, initial screenplays by Zoë Akins were scrapped, and the final shooting script was completed by Oscar Hammerstein II. Akins is listed as contributing writer in Universal production files at the USC Cinema-Television Library. According to *DV*, this film started production on 9 Dec 1935 without a male lead. Wilbur Evans, John Boles, Michael Bartlett and Francisco Del Campo were still being considered for the role of "Ravenal" as of 6 Dec. Universal had hoped to borrow Nelson Eddy from M-G-M, but negotiations fell through. According to a news item in *FD* on 16 Dec 1935, three hundred African-American actors were used in this production. Cameraman Alan Jones is not to be confused with actor Allan Jones.

In an interview in the *NYT* on 17 May 1936, Irene Dunne said she regretted

that her rendition of the song "Why Do I Love You?," sung during an automobile ride on a bumpy road, was cut from the film; her location rendition was much too "jerky," while her studio performance was much too smooth to match the scene. "Why Do I Love You?" remains in the film's orchestral background, however. Dunne made a personal appearance at the film's opening at the Radio City Music Hall in New York on 14 May 1936. The songs "I Have the Room Above Her," "Gallivantin' Around" and "Ah Still Suits Me" were original songs written by Jerome Kern and Oscar Hammerstein II for the film. According to a modern source, "Got My Eye on You" and "Negro Peanut Vendor's Street Cry," also written by Kern and Hammerstein for the film, were not used.

Modern sources also claim that W. C. Fields was considered for the role of "Cap'n Andy Hawks." Modern sources list Leon Shamroy as an uncredited cinematographer. Irene Dunne and Charles Winninger performed a radio version of *Show Boat* in a *Lux Radio Theatre* broadcast on 24 Jun 1940. Universal made a 1929 adaptation of the Ferber story, directed by Harry A. Pollard and starring Laura La Plante and Joseph Schildkraut (see above). In 1951, M-G-M made a feature version of *Show Boat*, directed by George Sidney, that starred Kathryn Grayson, Ava Gardner, Howard Keel and Joe E. Brown (see below).

DV 6 Dec 1935, p. 7. *DV* 9 Dec 1935, p. 3. *DV* 12 Mar 1936, p. 8. *DV* 27 Apr 1936, p. 3. *FD* 16 Dec 1935. *FD* 30 Apr 1936, p. 6. *HR* 18 Sep 1933, p. 2. *HR* 21 Sep 1933, p. 1. *HR* 12 Oct 1935, p. 1. *HR* 27 Apr 1936, p. 3. *HR* 17 Jun 1936, p. 5. *MPD* 14 Apr 1936, p. 10. *MPH* 1 Feb 1936, p. 44. *MPH* 18 Apr 1936, pp. 16-17. *MPH* 9 May 1936, p. 39. *MPSI* Jan 1937, p. 7. *NYT* 15 May 1936, p. 29. *NYT* 17 May 1936. *Var* 20 May 1936, p. 12.

SHOW BOAT (African Americans)

Metro-Goldwyn-Mayer Corp.; controlled by Loew's Inc. *Dist* Loew's Inc. Jul **1951**; World premiere in Hollywood: 17 Jul 1951; *Prod*: Began: mid-Nov 1950 [©Loew's Inc.; 11 Jun 1951; LP996]. Sd (Western Electric Sound System); col (Technicolor). 9,695 ft. 106-08 min. Passed by the National Board of Review. PCA cert no. 15118.

Prod Arthur Freed. *Assoc prod* Ben Feiner, Jr. *Dir* George Sidney. [*Asst dir* George Rhein]. *Scr* John Lee Mahin. *Dir of photog* Charles Rosher. *Spec eff* Warren Newcombe. *Mont seq* Peter Ballbusch. *Technicolor color consultant* Henri Jaffa and James Gooch. *Art dir* Cedric Gibbons and Jack Martin Smith. *Film ed* John Dunning. *Set dec* Edwin B. Willis. *Assoc* Richard A. Pefferle. *Cost* Walter Plunkett. *Mus dir* Adolph Deutsch. *Orch* Conrad Salinger. *Vocal arr* Robert Tucker. *Addl orch* Alexander Courage. *Dances by* Robert Alton. *Rec supv* Douglas Shearer. *Hair styles designed by* Sydney Guilaroff. *Make-up created by* William Tuttle. *Ava Gardner's voice double* Annette Warren.

Song(s): "Cotton Blossom," "Where's the Mate for Me?" "Make Believe," "Can't Help Lovin' Dat Man," "I Might Fall Back on You," "Ol' Man River," "You Are Love," "Why Do I Love You?" "Life on the Wicked Stage," and "Ballyhoo," music by Jerome Kern, lyrics by Oscar Hammerstein, II; "After the Ball," music and lyrics by Charles K. Harris; "Bill," music by Jerome Kern, lyrics by Oscar Hammerstein II and P. G. Wodehouse.

Source: Based on the novel *Show Boat* by Edna Ferber (Garden City, NY, 1926) and the musical of the same name by Edna Ferber, Jerome Kern and Oscar Hammerstein, II (New York, 27 Dec 1927).

Cast: Kathryn Grayson [(*Magnolia Hawks*)], Ava Gardner [(*Julie LaVerne*)], Howard Keel [(*Gaylord Ravenal*)], Joe E. Brown [(*Captain Andy Hawks*)], Marge Champion [(*Ellie May Shipley*)], Gower Champion [(*Frank Schultz*)], Robert Sterling [(*Stephen Baker*)], Agnes Moorehead [(*Parthy Hawks*)], Lief [sic] Erickson [(*Pete*)], William Warfield [(*Joe*)], [Adele Jergens (*Cameo McQueen*)], [Owen McGiveney (*Windy McClain*)], [Frances Williams (*Queenie*)], [Regis Toomey (*Sheriff Ike Vallon*)], [Frank Wilcox (*Mark Hallson*)], [Chick Chandler (*Herman*)], [Emory Parnell (*Jake Green*)], [Sheila Clark (*Kim*)], [Ian MacDonald (*Drunk sport*)], [Fuzzy Knight (*Troc piano player*)], [Norman Leavitt (*George, the caliope player*)], [Anne Marie Dore, Christina Lind, Lyn Wilde, Marietta Elliott, Joyce Jameson, Bette Arlen, Helen Kimbell, Tao Porchon, Mitzi Uehlein, Judy Landon, Nova Dale, Mary Jane French, Marilyn Kinsley, Alice Markham, Michael Dugan, Robert Fortier, George Ford, Casse Jaeger, Boyd Ackerman, Roy Damron, Joseph Roach (*Showboat cast members*)], [George Lynn (*Dealer*)], [Melford Jones (*Black man*)], [Louis Mercier (*Dabney*)], [Lisa Ferraday (*Renee*)], [Peter Camlin (*Croupier*)], [Gil Perkins (*Player*)], [Edward Keane (*Hotel manager*)], [George Sherwood (*Trainer*)], [Tom Irish (*Bellboy*)], [Allan Ray (*Elevator operator*)], [Robert Stebbins (*Bellhop*)], [John Crawford (*Hotel clerk*)], [Jim Pierce (*Doorman*)], [Marjorie Wood (*Landlady*)], [Carol Brewster (*Girl*)], [William Tannen (*Man with Julie*)], [Anna Q. Nilsson (*Seamstress*)], [Sue Casey, Meredith Leeds, Jean Romaine (*Cuties*)], [Bert Roach (*Drunk*)], [Frank Dae (*Doctor*)], [Harry Seymour (*Piano player*)], [William "Bill" Hall (*Bouncer*)],

[Earl Hodgins (*Bartender*)], [Dan Foster (*Deckhand*)], [Ida Moore (*Little old lady*)], [Alphonse Martell (*Headwaiter*)], [Al Rhein], [Charles Regan], [Carl Sklover], [Len Hendry].

Historical, Show business, Musical. [*Print viewed*]. In the late nineteenth century, Magnolia Hawks, daughter of Cap'n Andy, the owner of the Mississippi show boat the "Cotton Blossom," falls in love with gambler Gaylord Ravenal while touring in a small town. Magnolia's strict mother Parthy disapproves of her daughter's friendship with the show's leading actress, Julie LaVerne, whom she calls a "hussy." Despite Julie's protective feelings towards Magnolia, Parthy forbids Magnolia from spending any more time with her. Meanwhile, a jealous suitor whom Julie has spurned exacts his revenge by providing the local sheriff with birth records proving that Julie is a mulatto. Seeing that the sheriff is about to board the ship to charge Julie with miscegenation and arrest her, Stephen, Julie's white husband, deliberately cuts his finger and exchanges blood with his wife so that the he, too, will have black blood in him. No longer able to justify Julie's arrest, the sheriff departs, but not before advising her to leave the ship to avoid the wrath of the townspeople. Steve leaves the troupe to join Julie, and Gaylord later takes Steve's place as the leading man in the show. Gaylord then suggests that Magnolia replace Julie, and the two prove a hit with audiences all along the Mississippi. In time, the two stars fall deeper in love, and, after marrying, they spend their honeymoon in Chicago. There Gaylord resumes his heavy gambling and loses all his money. Suspecting that Magnolia no longer loves him, Gaylord leaves her, unaware that she is pregnant. Magnolia becomes distraught, but two of her friends, dancers Ellie May Shipley and Frank Schultz, take her to audition for stage manager Jake Green. Julie, who has turned to heavy drinking after Steve left her, is a singer in Green's variety show, but quietly leaves the show when she hears Magnolia auditioning. Magnolia performs her first show on New Year's Eve, and although she very nervously starts to sing "After the Ball," she later gains the confidence needed to sing beautifully when she sees her proud father in the audience. While Gaylord continues his obsessive gambling, Magnolia gives birth to a girl, whom she names Kim Ravenal. Time passes, and Julie, accidentally meeting Gaylord on a show boat, tells him that he has a five-year-old daughter. Gaylord finds his daughter in the town of Natchez, where she is performing with her mother and grandfather, and he takes her into his arms. Much to Julie's delight, Magnolia and Gaylord reconcile, and Gaylord gives up his gambling to rejoin his wife and family on the "Cotton Blossom." *Actors and actresses. African Americans–Mixed blood. Desertion (Marital). Gamblers. Miscegenation. Showboats. Theatrical troupes. African Americans. Alcoholics. Chicago (IL). Children. Dancers. Family relationships. Fistfights. Friendship. Honeymoons. Marriage. Mississippi River. New Year's Eve. Ostracism. Poverty. Reunions. Revenge. Self-sacrifice. Sheriffs. Shrews. Singers. Theatrical producers. United States–South.*

Note: Onscreen credits incorrectly spell actor Leif Erickson's name as "Lief." Edna Ferber's novel *Show Boat* was serialized in *Woman's Home Companion* (Apr-Aug 1926). M-G-M's plan to film an adaptation of *Show Boat* was publicized as early as Jun 1942. According to news items in *HR* in Jun and Jul 1942, Oscar Hammerstein, II had planned to direct a revival of the play to feature M-G-M's popular operetta stars Jeanette MacDonald and Nelson Eddy, and the studio was planning to buy the film rights from Universal. Zeke Colvan was also said to be staging the revival and possible film. In May 1944, a *HR* news item announced that producer Arthur Freed had chosen Judy Garland for the part of "Julie." In Dec 1945, a *HR* news item noted that production was set to begin in mid-summer with Walter Huston in the role of "Cap'n Andy." According to a Dec 1949 *DV* news item, Ethel Barrymore, who was originally slated to play the role of "Parthy," had to withdraw because of a previous commitment. Mildred Natwick was then considered for that part. Eddie Foy Jr. was a candidate for the role of "Capt. Andy" according to the same news item. A 1950 *NYT* news item noted that M-G-M would go ahead with its plans to include the miscegenation aspect of the story, despite objections from the Production Code Administration, which explicitly forbade the depiction of miscegenation. The news item indicated that M-G-M planned to defend its decision by pointing to the precedent set by the PCA in allowing the subject to remain in the 1936 film adaptation of *Show Boat*. According to a 22 Feb 1950 news item in *DV*, an additional problem was caused by a revision in Garland's contract, which allowed her four months off between films and would delay production until Aug 1950.

According to studio publicity material contained in the file for the film in the AMPAS Library, some "atmospheric shots" were filmed on location in Natchez, Mississippi. A Nov 1950 *NYT* article indicates that a $100,000 replica of the *Cotton Blossom* was constructed on the M-G-M backlot and placed in the studio's 1,200-foot river. A 1972 *DV* news item noted that the replica, which was used in more than twenty films since it appeared in *Show Boat*, was sold in an auction to a Kansas City company that planned to display it at a recreation

center. The film was nominated for Academy Awards in the categories of Cinematography and Music Score.

A 30 Nov 1981 article in *People* magazine contains a statement by African American actress and former M-G-M contract player Lena Horne in which she claimed that she was passed over for the role that eventually went to Ava Gardner. Horne played the role in the 1948 M-G-M film *Words and Music*, and commented on her experience in the 1994 documentary *That's Entertainment III*. In a 19 Dec 1981 published letter to the editor of the *LAT*, director George Sidney denied Horne's claim, stating that he tested only Gardner and Dinah Shore for the role. Sidney did note, however, that he used a recording of Horne's voice for playback purposes during Gardner's screen test. The Turner Entertainment Co. restored the film in 1991. This picture marked the third motion picture adaptation of Ferber's *Show Boat*. The previous versions, both produced by Universal Pictures, were the 1929 adaptation, directed by Harry A. Pollard and starring Laura La Plante and Joseph Schildkraut; and the 1936 picture, directed by James Whale and starring Helen Morgan (see above). Included among the many stage revivals of *Show Boat* are: the 1928 London production starring Cedric Harwicke, Colin Clive and Paul Robeson, the 1946 Broadway production starring Buddy Ebsen and Jan Clayton, and the 1994 Broadway production directed by Harold Prince and starring John McMartin and Elaine Stritch.

AmCin Aug 1951, pp. 304-05, 323-28. *Box* 9 Jun 1951. *DV* 29 Dec 1949, p. 4. *DV* 22 Feb 1950, p. 6. *DV* 28 Feb 1950, p. 3. *FD* 5 Jun 1951, p. 5. *HR* 3 Jun 1942, p. 1. *HR* 29 Jun 1942, p. 2. *HR* 20 Jul 1942, p. 2. *HR* 12 May 1944, p. 1. *HR* 28 Dec 1945, p. 2. *HR* 5 Nov 1950. *HR* 17 Nov 1950, p. 12. *HR* 5 Jan 1951, p. 10. *HR* 5 Jun 1951, p. 3. *HR* 24 Nov 1951. *LAT* 19 Dec 1981. *MPHPD* 9 Jun 1951, p. 877. *NYT* 20 Jul 1951, p. 14. *Var* 6 Jun 1951, p. 6.

THE SHOW GOES ON see LET'S SING AGAIN

SHOW OFF YOUR BEAUTY see JENG YIEN DOE LEE

SHOWDOWN AT GUN HILL see LAST TRAIN FROM GUN HILL

SHOWDOWN IN DEADWOOD see THE LAWLESS EIGHTIES

DI SHTIME FUN YISROEL see THE VOICE OF ISRAEL

SHUANG FENG CHEO HUANG (Chinese language)

Grandview Film Co. **1949?**; Hong Kong showing: 1949? Sd; b&w. Length undetermined. Chinese language.

Dir Joseph Sunn. [*Not viewed*]. [No information concerning the plot of this film has been located.].

Note: The Cantonese transliterated title is *Seng Fung Keo Fung*. This film was probably made in the U.S.

SHULAMITH (Yiddish language)

Judea Films, Inc. *Dist* Judea Films, Inc. **1931** [©Judea Films, Inc.; 13 May 1931; LU2259]. Sd; b&w. 5 reels, 4,114 ft. 46 min. Yiddish language.

Author Abraham Goldfaden.

Yiddish, Historical, Drama. [*Not viewed*]. In Biblical times, a Jewish man of wealth and noble standing leads a yearly pilgrimage of Jews to Jerusalem, which the Jews occupy. His beautiful daughter Shulamith, left behind, becomes lost as she wanders. She reaches a well, and having no bucket, climbs down a ladder to quench her thirst, but the ladder breaks, and she falls to the dry bottom, where she is stranded. The great hero Absolem, on his way to Jerusalem, hears Shulamith's call for help and rescues her. They subsequently meet many times, and he takes an oath that he will marry her when he returns from Jerusalem. However, in Jerusalem, he marries Avigail, the richest woman in the Holy Land. After a number of years, Shulamith becomes ill from waiting. She refuses to reveal the cause until her father finally persuades her to tell him about Absolem's oath. He then prays that Shulamith will be avenged, and according to the oath, Absolem's two children die. Absolem realizes that he has broken the oath and tells Avigail, who sends him to keep his word with Shulamith, whom he marries upon his return. *Biblical characters. Breach of promise. Jews. Pledges. Fathers and daughters. Jerusalem (Palestine). Marriage. Pilgrims and pilgrimages. Prayer. Rescues. Wealth. Wells.*

Note: The running time was calculated from footage given in NYSA records. No reviews were located for this film. According to modern sources, the film was based on the operetta *Shulamis* by Abraham Goldfaden, and was produced by Joseph Seiden and directed by Sidney Goldin.

SHUT MY BIG MOUTH (Native Americans)

Columbia Pictures Corp. *Dist* Columbia Pictures Corp. 19 Feb **1942**; Prod: 6 Nov—4 Dec 1941 [©Columbia Pictures Corp.; 18 Feb 1942; LP11067]. Sd (Western Electric Mirrophonic Recording); b&w. 6,386 ft. 71 min. PCA cert no. 8006.

Prod Robert Sparks. *Dir* Charles Barton. [*Asst dir* Gene Anderson]. *Scr* Oliver Drake, Karen DeWolf and Francis Martin. *Story* Oliver

Drake. [*Contr to dial* Warren Wilson]. *Dir of photog* Henry Freulich. *Art dir* Lionel Banks. *Assoc* Jerome Pycha. *Film ed* Gene Havlick. *Mus* John Leipold. *Mus dir* M. W. Stoloff. *Dance dir* Edward Prinz. [*Sd eng* Ed Bernds].

Cast: JOE E. BROWN (*Wellington Holmes [also known as Henrietta Oglethorpe]*), Adele Mara (*Conchita [Elena] Montoya*), Victor Jory (*Buckskin Bill*), Fritz Feld (*Robert Oglethorpe*), Don Beddoe (*Hill*), Lloyd Bridges (*Skinny*), Forrest Tucker (*Red*), Will Wright (*Long*), Russell Simpson (*Mayor Potter*), Pedro de Cordoba (*Don Carlos Montoya*), Joan Woodbury (*Maria*), Ralph Peters (*Butch*), Joe McGuinn (*Hank*), Noble Johnson (*Chief Standing Bull*), Chief Thunder Cloud (*Indian interpreter*), [Art Mix, Blackjack Ward (*Bandits*)], [Hank Bell (*Stagecoach driver*)], [Earle Hodgins (*Stagecoach guard*)], [Eddy Waller (*Happy*)], [Fern Emmett (*Maggie*)], [Lew Kelly (*Westerner*)], [Dick Curtis (*Joe*)], [Edmund Cobb (*Stage agent*)], [Bob Folkerson (*Boy*)], [Clay De Roy (*Spanish driver*)], [Ed Peil, Sr. (*Hotel proprietor*)], [Al Ferguson (*Pursuer*)], [John Tyrrell], [Georgia Backus].

Comedy, Western. [*Print viewed*]. Horticulturist Wellington Holmes and his companion, Robert Oglethorpe, are on a mission to beautify the West. When their stagecoach is attacked by masked bandit Buckskin Bill and his gang, Holmes, who believes that the West has been tamed, thinks that the holdup is a prank. After realizing that Buckskin Bill is deadly serious, Holmes keels over, pulling his potted plants down on the bandits' heads. The posse, who has been chasing the bandits, arrives just in time to see the dazed outlaws gallop away. Hailing Holmes as a hero for foiling the robbery, the posse members appoint him the new marshal of Big Bluff. Once they are ensconced in their hotel room in town, Holmes assures the terrified Oglethorpe that they will be leaving on the next stage. He has a change of plans, however, when a rock comes crashing though their window with a note from Buckskin Bill, warning him that he will be watching every stagecoach for the new marshal. When the hotel maid tells Holmes that Buckskin Bill is unfailingly courteous to all ladies, Holmes decides to diguise himself as a woman, pose as Ogelthorpe's wife Henrietta, and board the next stage out of town. Also onboard the stage is Elena Montoya, the daughter of Don Carlos Montoya, the owner of the Big Bluff gambling and entertainment palace. Soon after leaving town, the stage is stopped by Buckskin Bill, who informs Elena that he is holding Don Carlos prisoner at his hacienda. After climbing onto the coach to escort Elena to her father, Buckskin Bill thoughtfully designates Henrietta and her "husband" Elena's chaperones. Upon arriving at the hacienda, Buckskin Bill demands $50,000 for Don Carlos' release. At a party that night, Buckskin Bill asks Holmes to dance, and the exuberant dancers spend the evening slamming each other to the ground. At bedtime, Buckskin Bill assigns Holmes and Elena to sleep in the same room. As Elena starts to disrobe, Holmes begins to scream hysterically. Rushing to the room to quiet Holmes, Bill decides to send Elena and Oglethorpe back to town to raise the ransom while the hysterical Holmes remains behind. After Elena and Oglethorpe leave, Bill tells his maid, Maria, to put Holmes to bed. When Holmes refuses to allow Maria to undress him, she begins to rip off his clothes. Saved when Maria faints at the sight of a mouse, Holmes bolts into an empty bedroom, dons men's clothes and climbs out the window and over a wall. After trudging along the trail all night long, Holmes sits on a rock to rest. When a rider gallops past, warning of approaching Indians, Holmes sticks the wig back on his head. Soon after, the Indians appear, and the chief demands Holmes's scalp. Offering to scalp himself, Holmes slices off his wig, thus winning the chief's respect. Dubbing Holmes "Chief Cave in the Face," the Indians make him a blood brother and offer him a ride back to Big Bluff. Upon returning to town, Holmes is introduced to Elena, who begs him to save her father and Oglethorpe's wife. Soon after, the maskless Buckskin Bill and two of his men gallop into town, their guns blazing, and commandeer the saloon. At the urging of the townsfolk, Holmes slinks into the saloon, intending to sneak out the back door. Spotting Holmes, Buckskin Bill throws a dagger at him but hits the rope supporting a chandelier instead. The chandelier falls on Buckskin Bill's head and knocks him unconscious. Holmes jails the outlaws, but because no one has ever seen Buckskin Bill without his mask, he fails to realize that he has actually captured the gang's leader. As the town honors their marshal at a ceremony, Buckskin Bill throws a rock from the jail window, with a note from the masked bandit, threatening to kill Don Carlos unless the prisoners are

released. When Holmes suggests freeing the outlaws and offering them a reward to lead the posse to their hideout, Buckskin Bill proposes that the marshal, Elena and Oglethorpe accompany the bandits on the mission. After drawing the posse a fake map to follow to the hideout, Buckskin Bill and the others ride off. Upon arriving at the hacienda, Buckskin Bill dons his mask and informs Oglethorpe that his wife has disappeared. Fleeing from the outlaws, Holmes runs into a bedroom, pulls on a dress and becomes Henrietta. When he accidentally lights his dress on fire, the bandits realize that Henrietta is Holmes and begin to chase him. Jumping over the balcony, Holmes throws his burning dress onto a haystack. In the distance, the Indians see the smoke and, thinking that it is a signal, ride to Holmes's rescue. Believing that the Indians are attacking the hacienda, the posse follows them there and arrives just as Holmes overpowers Bill. After Elena kisses Holmes in gratitude, he decides to stay in Big Bluff and finish beautifying the West. *Female impersonation. Horticulturalists. Masked bandits. The West.* Dance parties. Fathers and daughters. Fires. Indians of North America. Kidnapping. Maids. Marshals. Mexicans. Posses. Ransom. Wigs.

Note: The working titles of this picture were *I'm No Cowboy* and *Cowboy Joe.* Although the character played by Adele Mara is listed as "Conchita Montoya" in onscreen credits, she is called "Elena Montoya" in the film. This was Joe E. Brown's first screen appearance since suffering a serious injury in a car accident two years earlier, according to a *HR* news item.

Box 21 Feb 1942. *DV* 16 Feb 1942, p. 3. *FD* 19 Feb 1942, p. 8. *HR* 14 Oct 1941, p. 7. *HR* 16 Feb 1942, p. 3. *MPHPD* 21 Feb 1942, p. 517. *Var* 25 Feb 1942, p. 8.

SHYLOCK OF WALL STREET *see* **NONE SO BLIND**

SI EL EMPERADOR LO SUPIERA *see* **OLIMPIA**

SI L'EMPEREUR SAVAIT ÇA! *see* **OLIMPIA**

THE SIEGE AT DANCING BIRD *see* **THE UNFORGIVEN**

SIEGE AT RED RIVER (Native Americans)
Panoramic Productions; controlled by Twentieth Century-Fox Film Corp. *Dist* Twentieth Century-Fox Film Corp. 2 Apr **1954**; *Prod:* 2 Sep—5 Oct 1953 [©Twentieth Century-Fox Film Corp.; 18 Feb 1954; LP4050]. Sd (Western Electric Recording); col (Technicolor). 9 reels, 7,773 ft. 87 min. PCA cert no. 16772.
Prod Leonard Goldstein. *Dir* Rudolph Maté. [*2d unit dir* Charles Gould]. *Asst dir* Sid Sidman and [Don Torpin]. [*2d unit, 1st asst* Harbert Glaser]. [*Dial dir* Joan Hathaway]. *Scr* Sydney Boehm. *Story* J. Robert Bren and Gladys Atwater. *Dir of photog* Edward Cronjager. [*Cam tech* Al Cline]. [*Gaffer* Charlie Graham]. [*2d unit 1st cam* Art Arling]. [*Spec eff* Milt Greene and Milton Olsen]. [*Eff man* George Cones]. *Technicolor color consultant* Leonard Doss. *Art dir* Lyle Wheeler and George Patrick. *Ed supv* Paul Weatherwax. *Film ed* Betty Steinberg. *Set dec* Claude Carpenter. [*Drapery* Russ Cutter and Henry Glaesner]. *Ward dir* Charles LeMaire. *Cost des* Renie. [*Ward man* Henry West]. [*Ward girl* Vida Carroll]. *Mus* Lionel Newman. *Sd* W. D. Flick and Harry M. Leonard. *Makeup artist* Don Cash. [*Makeup* Larry Butterworth]. [*Hairdresser* Dortha Hippe and Josephine Sweeney]. [*Unit mgr* Bill Eckhardt]. [*Scr supv* Stanley Scheuer]. [*Props* Stan Detlie]. [*Asst props* Bob McLaughlin]. [*Casting dir* Millie Gussie]. [*Casting asst* Ernestine White and Frank Roderick]. [*Tech adv* John Peters]. [*2d unit scr supv* Bill Hole]. [*Stock man* Jimmy Loucks]. [*First-aid man* John Leber]. [*Auditor* Frank Turner]. [*Stunt man double for Van Johnson* Terry Wilson]. [*Stunt man—"Mail wagon"* Jim Van Horn]. [*Stunt man double for Richard Boone* Leonard Gear]. [*Stunt man—"Lumber wagon"* Ed. Jauregi and Guy Teague].
Song(s): "Tapioca," lyrics by Ken Darby, music by Lionel Newman.
Cast: VAN JOHNSON [(*Capt. James S. Simmons, also known as Jim Farraday*)], JOANNE DRU [(*Nora Curtis*)], Richard Boone [(*Brett Manning*)], Milburn Stone [(*Sgt. Benjamin Guderman, known as Benjy*)], Jeff Morrow [(*Frank Kelso*)], Craig Hill [(*Lt. Braden*)], Rico Alaniz [(*Chief Yellow Hawk*)], Robert Burton [(*Sheriff*)], Pilar Del Rey [(*Lukoa*)], [Ferris Taylor (*Anderson Smith*)], [John Cliff (*Sgt. Jenkins*)], [Robert Adler, John McKee, Carl Andre (*Raiders*)], [Ed. Rand (*Harper*)].
Western, War, Drama. [*Print viewed*]. In November 1864, at Greensburg, Ohio, a Gatling gun, on its way by train to be tested by the Union army, is stolen by Confederates, who hope to use it to change the course of the war. Boxes containing the parts of the gun, which fires 250 shots per minute, are hidden in the piano of a

traveling medicine show wagon driven west by Captain James S. Simmons, of the Georgia volunteers, masquerading as Jim Farraday, a traveling salesman from Boston, and his cohort Benjy, really Sgt. Benjamin Guderman of Jim's unit. As they perform the code song "Tapioca" in the towns they visit, they receive messages from fellow conspirators with instructions on where to go next. Upon arriving at a stream in the west, they find Nora Curtis, a Yankee nurse to whom they are both attracted, in a hospital wagon stuck in the water. Nora is trying to take her patient, an Indian woman named Lukoa, to Nora's home in Baxter Springs, where she keeps one room as a hospital ward. Nora explains that Lukoa's husband cannot join them, as the Union army has made it a hanging offense for an Indian to cross the river because Confederates, whom she despises, have taught rebellion to the Indians so they will fight the Union army. Jim and Benjy take the women to Baxter Springs, but although Nora is attracted to Jim, when he says he has hired a substitute to fight in the war, she begins to snub him. When Jim and Benjy sing "Tapioca" in Baxter Springs, shopkeeper Anderson Smith writes a message to give them, but he swallows it when Union soldiers, led by Pinkerton detective Frank Kelso, ride into town in search of the stolen Gatling gun. The soldiers raid Smith's store, and he wounds Kelso before he is shot to death. Suspecting Jim, Kelso, after Nora nurses him, sends a telegram to the Boston Pinkerton office and searches the medicine wagon, but does not find the Gatling gun. After Jim hears a dance hall girl sing the "Tapioca" song, he learns that her new beau, Brett Manning, instructed her to sing it. Manning, who mistreats the girl, tells Jim that he worked for Smith bringing horses through Indian territory for the Confederate forces, but says he is not from the South and has only helped them for the money. He offers to take Jim and the gun through Union lines and they agree on a price. After learning that all vehicles leaving town will be searched, Jim and Benjy hide the gun in Nora's hospital wagon, aware that she plans to take Lukoa and her newborn baby back to her village. The next day, Jim's scheme works, as the baby's cries and Nora's snippiness lead the sheriff to let her go without a thorough search. Jim sends Benjy and Manning to catch up to the wagon and plans to rendezvous with them the next day. After Benjy and Manning stop Nora's wagon, Manning shoots and kills Benjy and has Nora drive to Lukoa's village, where he plans to sell the gun to Chief Yellow Hawk. Jim finds his friend's body and buries him, then pursues the hospital wagon on horseback. Kelso, upon receiving word from Boston that the real Jim Farraday was killed in battle two years ago, leads soldiers in pursuit of Jim. After Manning convinces Yellow Hawk that the gun will give his tribe the strength of ten tribes, Yellow Hawk buys it, then hires Manning to operate the gun in an attack on nearby Fort Smith with many other tribes that he hopes to lead. Jim arrives at the Indian village after the warriors have left. He plans to take Nora back to Baxter Springs and then return to his own home, and although she is grateful, she protests that they should warn the fort. He argues that the people at the fort are the same kind as those who burned his home in Atlanta and killed his brother in battle. They sleep next to each other on the same blanket and are abruptly woken up by Kelso and the Union soldiers. Nora warns about the attack on Fort Smith, and Kelso reveals, to Jim's chagrin, that women and children live with the soldiers at the fort. Outside the fort, Manning and the Indians set up the Gatling gun behind cover. The Indians attack at dawn, setting fire to the fort and mowing down soldiers with the Gatling gun as they attempt to leave. After an Indian scout at the fort reports to the commanding colonel that smoke signals reveal that perhaps a thousand Indians are approaching from other tribes, the colonel refuses to signal for his major on the other side of the ridge because he fears a rout. Kelso and the Union soldiers arrive with Jim and Nora. After locating the Gatling gun, Jim jumps Manning, and Kelso fights the two Indians operating the gun with Manning. As Manning is about to crush Jim's scull with a rock, Jim knifes him to death. Jim and Kelso turn the Gatling gun on the Indians, and when the fort's colonel sees this, he signals his major to attack. The Union forces, supported by the Gatling gun, force the Indians to retreat. After the battle, Nora argues that Kelso should take into consideration Jim's actions. Kelso, who has learned that General's Lee's forces are in full retreat, allows Jim to leave. Jim tells Nora that he plans to return to Georgia and fix up his home before he travels west again, but that he will make Baxter Springs his first stop. Nora says she plans to make it his last, and he counters that it will be his next to last and that she will like Atlanta. They embrace and he

rides off as she watches. *Confederate States of America. Army. Espionage. Gatling guns. Impersonation and imposture. Loyalty. Nurses. Burial. Drunkenness. Fights. Forts. Medicine shows. Murder. Ohio. Romance. Sheriffs. Songs. Storekeepers. Telegrams. Tribal chiefs.*

Note: The working titles of this film were *Arapaho Trail* and *Gatling Gun*. *Time* noted that the film's production unit, Panoramic Productions, was set up in 1953 by Twentieth Century-Fox with Leonard Goldstein as head "to fall back on, if CinemaScope should prove a failure" when the rest of the studio was converted to CinemaScope production. This was Goldstein's first production for the studio. In an inter-office memo to Twentieth Century-Fox production head Darryl Zanuck, included in the Twentieth Century-Fox Produced Scripts Collection at the UCLA Arts—Special Collections Library, Goldstein described the Gatling gun as "America's first machine gun" and "the atom bomb of a century ago." The portrayal of the Indians in the film was discussed during a conference between Goldstein and Zanuck: "It was decided to make them a renegade gang of Indians, rather than a 'legitimate' tribe of Sioux. This is an outlaw band of Indians who prey even on their own people.... These people are not fighting for their land or for their rights or anything noble like that. They want horses and guns and money. They are raiders. They steal from both the North and the South. They are taking full advantage of the fact that the North and the South are at war with one another." According to news items, Dale Robertson was originally scheduled for the lead, and Jean Peters was a possible co-star. Tyrone Power was later scheduled to star. According to *NYT*, M-G-M loaned Van Johnson for the role; he had wanted to do a Western in the twelve years he had been with M-G-M, but they wouldn't put him in one. Information in the Produced Scripts Collection credits Irving Wallace with a revised script and Leo Townsend with a continuity, but it is not known if any of their material was used in the final film. Writer Sydney Boehm was loaned from Paramount. Location shooting was done at Moab, UT and Durango, CO, and some filming was shot at the RKO-Pathé lot. According to information in the MPAA/PCA Collection at the AMPAS Library, PCA officials objected to some "breast exposure" shots in a dance hall sequence and refused to grant the film a Code seal until they were "corrected." The studio eliminated one shot and had the Technicolor lab print one other sequence "four points darker (using Technicolor terminology)."

Box 20 Mar 1954. *DV* 24 Oct 1952. *DV* 12 Dec 1952. *DV* 19 Mar 1954, p. 3. *Exh* 7 Apr 1954, p. 3728. *FD* 12 Apr 1954, p. 6. *Har* 27 Mar 1954, p. 51. *HCN* 13 May 1954. *HR* 24 Oct 1952. *HR* 19 Mar 1954, p. 3. *LADN* 13 May 1954. *LAEx* 13 May 1954. *LAT* 10 Oct 1952. *LAT* 29 Dec 1952. *LAT* 20 Jul 1953. *LAT* 13 May 1954. *MPD* 19 Mar 1954. *MPHPD* 27 Mar 1954, pp. 2237-38. *NYT* 3 Apr 1954, p. 19. *NYT* 4 Jul 1954. *Time* 12 Apr 1954. *Var* 24 Mar 1954, p. 6.

SIERRA BARON (Latino)

Regal Pictures, Inc. *Dist* Twentieth Century-Fox Film Corp. Jul 1958; *Prod*: late Jan—late Feb 1958 [©Twentieth Century-Fox Film Corp.; 23 Jul 1958; LP11689]. Sd (RCA Sound Recording); col (DeLuxe); CinemaScope; CinemaScope Lenses by Bausch & Lomb. 10 reels, 7,176 ft. 80 min. PCA cert no. 19025.

Prod Plato A. Skouras. *Dir* James B. Clark and [Raphael J. Sevilla]. *Scr* Houston Branch. *Dir of photog* Alex Phillips. *Art dir* John Mansbridge and [Edward Fitzgerald]. *Film ed* Frank Baldridge. *Mus ed* Leon Birnbaum. *Sd eff ed* John Cornall. *Cost supv* Georgette Somohano. *Mus* Paul Sawtell and Bert Shefter. *Sd* Terry Kellum, Rafael Esparza and [Joel Moss]. *Makeup* Rosa Guerrero. *Prod mgr and asst dir* Harold E. Knox. [*In charge of production* Alberto A. Ferrer]. *Crew* "Aguila" *Scr supv* Pat Miller.

Source: Based on the novel *Sierra Baron* by Thomas Wakefield Blackburn (New York, 1955).

Cast: Brian Keith (*Jack McCracken*), Rick Jason (*Miguel Delmonte*), Rita Gam (*Felicia Delmonte*), Mala Powers (*Sue Russell*), Steve Brodie (*Rufus Bynum*), Carlos Múzquiz (*Andrews*), Lee Morgan (*Frank Goheen*), Allan Lewis (*Hank Moe*), Pedro Galván (*Judson Jeffers*), Fernando Wagner (*Crandall*), "Ferrusquilla," José Angel Espinosa (*Felipe*), Enrique Lucero (*Anselmo*), Alberto Mariscal (*Lopez*), Lynne Ehrlich (*Vicky Russell*), Michael Schmidt (*Ralph*), Tommy Riste (*Ralph's father*), Reed Howes (*Sheriff*), Robin Glattley (*Baker*), Enrique Iñigo (*Assayer*), Faith Ferry (*Young Sue*), Doris Contreras (*Young Felicia*), Marc Lambert (*Cart driver*), Stilman Segar (*Butcher*), Alicia del Lago (*Juanita*), José Trowe (*Major domo*), Armando Saenz (*Eduardo*), Lola Dávila (*Emmy*), Ricardo Adalid (*1st playboy*), Roy Fletcher (*2nd playboy*), John Courier (*Express rider*), Mark Zachary (*1st miner*), Paul Arnett (*2nd miner*), Bob Janis (*Henchman*), [Relampago (*Palamino*)].

Western. [*Print viewed*]. In 1848, eighty-seven years after the Princessa Grant, comprising 43,000 acres of land in California, was given to Rafael Delmonte by Charles III, King of Spain, his descendant, Miguel, while visiting Mexico, receives word that his father has been shot and killed. As the new *padrone* of the Princessa, Miguel returns to find that gold has been discovered on the land and "Yankees" have built a town on the north mesa. Accompanied by his vaqueros, Miguel rides to the Yankees' town and puts up a notice of

trespassing. Real estate agent Rufus Bynum, who has sold land to the settlers there, assures them that the Senate will not ratify a pending peace treaty that allows owners of Spanish land grants to keep them; however, because he thinks that Miguel's interference could slow land sales, he offers hired gun Jack McCracken $1,000 to kill Miguel. Jack rides to the Princessa hacienda, where he meets Miguel's attractive sister Felicia. When she mistakes him for a Yankee, he informs her he is a Texan, and that he has contempt for the Yankees. Meanwhile, Miguel finds a Yankee skinning a cattle hide and orders him to pay twenty dollars. Two other Yankees draw their guns, but Jack, who has followed Miguel, kills them. Miguel invites Jack to the hacienda for a drink, and Jack reveals with a smile that he was sent to kill Miguel. Despite her brother's objections, Felicia invites Jack to stay the night at the hacienda. She comes to his room and offers a gold cross, a wedding gift from the king to her grandmother to buy his services. After Jack offers himself as an extra gun to Miguel, Bynum's men lasso Jack, drag him through water and beat him up, but Miguel and his vaqueros arrive before they can kill him. Felicia tends to Jack's wounds at the hacienda, and Jack, in his delirium, says he loves her. When a wagon train of tired, starving settlers from the East plead with Miguel to let them stay until the fall and plant a crop, he graciously gives them good grassland to use, along with food and blankets. When he is told that a young mother, Sue Russell, remained on the desert to tend to her husband after a Pawnee Indian attack, he rides out with two vaqueros and comforts Sue, who has just buried her husband, with news that her young daughter is safe with the wagon train. As Jack recovers, he spends time with Felicia and explains that he became a "pistolero" after seeing his father gunned down. Sometime later, Miguel and Jack find miners setting explosives on the land. When Miguel gives them one hour to leave, one of the men attempts to shoot him, but Jack guns the man down, then learns that the man was a professional gunslinger. Bynum next tries to encourage the members of the wagon train to file claims on the land, saying a new law supporting them will take effect as soon as the Senate refuses to ratify the pending treaty with Mexico. When Felicia confronts Jack about the words he spoke while he was delirious, he admits that he does love her, but walks away saying they cannot be together. At the Yankee town, news arrives that the Senate has recognized the Spanish land grants as valid. Bynum and a group decide to kill Miguel before he learns the news and ride to the hacienda with torches. Meanwhile, Miguel courts Sue at the wagon train. He proposes and kisses her passionately, but she cannot forget what happened in the desert. Bynum and his followers begin their raid at the hacienda; however, they stop when they see the settlers' wagons approach. Miguel tells the Yankees that he never intended to dispossess them and that they can keep their homes, but that he will press his claim against Bynum when new courts are established. After Jack shoots one of Bynum's men, the new marshal arrests Bynum for inciting violence, but he escapes. Jack is about to leave, to Felicia's displeasure, when Miguel offers him a partnership. Jack says he is not the man for Felicia, then drinks to Miguel for giving away the town and calls him the "Sierra Baron." When Bynum pulls a gun on them, Miguel shoots him, using a trick that Jack had taught him. Jack, however, is hit by Bynum's bullet. He tells Felicia that he has loved her since he first saw her, and gives her the golden cross, which they both kiss. Sue decides that she does not want to leave Miguel and they embrace. In the present day, two girls visit a cemetery, where they find a headstone for John McCracken Delmonte, the first son of Miguel and Sue, who died at Gettysburg, and also headstones for Sister Felicia of the Cross, who became a nun, and for Jack, buried beside her, who died in 1849. *California–History–1846-1850. Gold miners. Hired killers. Latino. Land grants. Real estate agents. Settlers. Unrequited love. Brothers and sisters. Cemeteries. Cowboys. Deserts. Gunfights. Haciendas. Nuns. Proposals (Marital). Texans. United States. Marshals. Wagon trains.*

Note: According to *HR*, Plato Skouras, the youngest son of Twentieth Century-Fox president Spyros P. Skouras, acquired the film rights to the novel in Jun 1956. This was his first film as a producer. His first production company that was involved in the production was called Artys Corp. According to information in the MPAA/PCA Collection at the AMPAS Library, director André De Toth and Skouras conferred with PCA officials concerning this film in Jul 1957. It is unclear if De Toth was planning to direct the film at that time. Principal photography took place near Mexico City. Some scenes were shot at Cortez Pass in La Marquesa Mountains. According to the film's pressbook, the palamino "Relampago" was loaned to Skouras for the film in the name of the Mexican government by director Emilio Fernandez. Relampago, who was originally presented by the president of Cuba to the president of Mexico, developed pneumonia during shooting and died.

Box 14 Jul 1958. DV 27 Jun 1958, p. 3. Exb 9 Jul 1958, pp. 4487-88. FD 2 Jul 1958, p. 8. Har 28 Jun 1958, p. 103. HR 24 Jan 1958, p. 17. HR 25 Jun 1956. HR 21 Feb 1958, pp. 10-11. HR 27 Jun 1958, p. 3. MPHPD 19 Jul 1958, p. 911. Var 2 Jul 1958, p. 6.

THE SIGN OF THE POPPY (Chinese Americans)

Bluebird Photoplays, Inc. Dist Bluebird Photoplays, Inc. 4 Dec 1916 [©Bluebird Photoplays, Inc.; 24 Nov 1916; LP9597]. Si; b&w. 5 reels.

Dir Charles Swickard. Scen J. Grubb Alexander. Cam Harry Maguire.

Cast: Hobart Henley (Alvin Marston/Chang), Gertrude Selby (Edith Marston), Mina Cunard (Helen Durant), Wilbur Higby (Jerry Marston), Robert Clark (Rex Durant), Garland Briden (Hop Li).

Drama. Returning from their honeymoon, Alvin and Edith Marston discover that Alvin's father Jerry has been killed by a Chinatown gang. Then, Alvin's long-lost twin brother, who became a drug addict after Hop Li kidnapped him and renamed him Chang, secretly comes back in order to claim his father's fortune. As part of his plan, Chang abducts Alvin and takes his place, after which he begins brutalizing Edith, who is shocked at the change in her husband. Finally, however, Alvin, who has lost his memory, is able to find his way back home. Chang tries to shoot him, but the bullet hits a vase, which restores Alvin's memory when it falls on his head. Then, suddenly realizing the extent of his sins against his own family, Chang commits suicide. Amnesia. Brothers. Chinese Americans. Doubles. Impersonation and imposture. Long-lost relatives. Twins. Attempted murder. Chinatowns. Drug addicts. Gangs. Kidnapping. Murder. Newlyweds. Suicide.

Note: The working title for the film was The Lie.

ETR 9 Dec 1916, p. 58. MPN 30 Sep 1916, p. 2029. MPN 9 Dec 1916, p. 3666. MPW 9 Dec 1916, p. 1508, 1552. NYDM 2 Dec 1916, pp. 26-27. Wid's 7 Dec 1916, p. 1156.

THE SIGN OF THE ROSE (1915) see THE ALIEN

THE SIGN OF THE ROSE (Italian Americans)

George Beban Productions. Dist American Releasing Corp. 3 Sep 1922 [©American Releasing Corp.; 1 Sep 1922; LP18749]. Si; b&w. 6 reels, 6,200 ft. ft.

Pres Harry Garson. Supv George Beban. Dir Harry Garson. Scen J. A. Brocklehurst and Carroll Owen. Wrt George Beban. Titles Coral Burnette. Photog Sam Landers. Art dir Floyd Mueller. Film ed Violet Blair.

Source: Based on the play The Sign of the Rose by George Beban and Charles T. Dazey (New York, 11 Oct 1911).

Cast: Helene Sullivan (Lillian Griswold), Charles Edler (William Griswold), Jeanne Carpenter (Dorothy Griswold), Gene Cameron (Philip Griswold), Louise Calmenti (Rosa), Stanhope Wheatcroft (Cecil Robbins), Arthur Thalasso (Detective Lynch), George Beban (Pietro Balletti), Dorothy Giraci (Rosina Balletti), M. Solomon (Moses Erbstein).

Melodrama. In need of cash, Philip Griswold kidnaps the daughter of his brother, William, and shifts the blame to Pietro Balletti, who is seen delivering a Christmas tree to the Griswold home. While frantically searching for his child, William kills Pietro's beloved daughter, Rosina, with his automobile. Philip conspires with Cecil Robbins to frame Pietro with the aid of a white rose but finally confesses to the abduction. Pietro receives a substantial gift from the Griswolds and is reunited with his wife, whom he believed to be dead. Brothers. Christmas. Italian Americans. Kidnapping.

Note: According to the Var review, during the film's pre-released engagements (1921—22), George Beban and three other cast members gave a live stage presentation, elaborated from the original vaudeville sketch upon which the play (and the film?) were based; it was interspersed about reel 4, lasted approximately eighteen minutes minutes as against approximately 60 minutes of film, and took place in a florist shop set copied from one used in the film. The original play apparently combined film and live action, with the latter dominant. Beban starred in an earlier film based on the same source, the 1915 New York Motion Picture Corp. production entitled The Alien (see above), produced and directed by Thomas H. Ince. In that version also, a live stage presentation was included at large theaters around the country.

ETR 12 Aug 1922, p. 767. FD 12 Mar 1922. Var 10 Mar 1922, p. 42.

THE SIGN OF ZORRO (Latino)

Walt Disney Studios. Dist Buena Vista Film Distribution Co., Inc. Jun 1960; Los Angeles opening: 22 Jun 1960 [©Walt Disney Productions; 18 Aug 1958; LP16374]. Sd; b&w. 8,081 ft. 90-91 min. PCA cert no. 19091.

Prod William H. Anderson. Dir Norman Foster and Lewis R. Foster. Asst dir Vincent McEveety and Russ Haverick. Scr Norman Foster, Lowell S. Hawley, Bob Wehling and John Meredyth Lucas. Dir of photog Gordon Avil. Matte artist Peter Ellenshaw. Art dir Marvin

Aubrey Davis. Film ed Roy Livingston, Stanley Johnson, Cotton Warburton and Hugh Chaloupka. Set dec Emil Kuri and Hal Gausman. Cost Chuck Keehne. Mus William Lava. Sd Robert O. Cook. Makeup Pat McNalley. Fencing master Fred Cavens. Unit mgr Roy Wade. Prod coordinator Louis Debney.

Song(s): Zorro's theme song, words by Norman Foster, music by George Bruns.

Source: Based on the serial story The Curse of Capistrano by Johnston McCulley in All-Story Weekly (9 Aug–6 Sep 1919).

Cast: GUY WILLIAMS (Zorro [Diego de la Vega]), Henry Calvin [(Sgt. Garcia)], Gene Sheldon [(Bernardo)], Romney Brent, Britt Lomond [(Monastario)], George J. Lewis [(Don Alejandro de la Vega)], Tony Russo [(Martinez)], Jan Arven, Than Wyenn, John Dehner (Viceroy), [Lisa Gaye (Constancia, the viceroy's daughter)], [Elvira Corona], [Eugenia Paul].

Historical, Adventure. [Print viewed]. In 1820, Diego de la Vega returns to Spanish California from his studies in Spain after receiving an urgent message from his father, the wealthy landowner Don Alejandro de la Vega. Alejandro has requested his son's help in fighting the despotic Capitan Monastario, commandante of the Pueblo de Los Angeles, who is taxing landowners unmercifully. With his trusty valet, Bernardo, Diego, an exceptionally skilled fencer, comes up with a plan whereby he will pose as an ineffectual bookworm in order to deflect any suspicion about his activities, while the mute Bernardo will pretend to be deaf to better serve as Diego's spy. At the de la Vega hacienda, Alejandro calls for immediate action against Monastario, who has arrested his old friend, Nacho Torres, for treason. Fearing for his father's safety, however, Diego urges restraint. That night, Diego reveals to Bernardo his plan to transform himself into El Zorro ("The Fox") and, donning his disguise, he rescues Torres in the nick of time. Torres heads to Monterey to seek protection from the governor, after which Monastario takes Torres' wife and daughter hostage. Alejandro wants to intercede, but again Diego tries to dissuade him, leading Alejandro to feel ashamed of his son's apparent cowardice. Don Alejandro attempts a rescue of the Torres women, but is wounded by Monastario. Zorro arrives to carry him to safety and places him under the protection of the soldiers who have escorted Torres back to Los Angeles to ensure that he receives a fair trial. However, Monastario devises a ruse to delay the governor's judge and installs his henchman, the corrupt lawyer Lucensiado, in the rightful judge's place. Zorro shows up and, using his sword, forces Lucensiado to pronounce Torres and Alejandro not guilty. A furious Monastario vows to capture the mysterious Zorro, who has earned the admiration of the populace, so he devises a plan in which the thief Martinez, a skilled swordsman, will rob the townspeople and steal a precious religious icon from the local mission while disguised as Zorro. After Zorro foils both attempts by the impostor, Monastario kills Martinez to keep him from talking and then arrests Diego, claiming he is Zorro. When word arrives that the Spanish viceroy is coming to Los Angeles, Monastario makes plans to impress his superior by revealing that he has captured the infamous Zorro. Zorro is unmasked in the presence of the viceroy and his daughter Constancia, who are surprised to see Diego, an old friend from Spain. Diego denies he is Zorro, and the enraged Monastario starts a swordfight during which Diego must pretend to be inept in order to protect his secret identity. Finally, with a sword at Diego's throat, Monastario demands that Diego tell the truth or die, but before Diego can answer, Bernardo makes a brief appearance dressed as Zorro. The identity of Zorro remains a mystery and, much to the delight of the townspeople, the viceroy has Monastario arrested. California–History–To 1846. Despotism. Impersonation and imposture. Rescues. Aristocrats. Bookishness. Bumblers. Fathers and sons. Flamenco dancers. Governors. Hostages. Jails. Lawyers. Robbery. Ruses. Servants. Soldiers. Sword fights. Trials. Valets.

Note: This film is comprised of segments taken from nine episodes of Walt Disney's Zorro television series, which premiered on ABC in the fall of 1957 and ran for three seasons for a total of seventy-eight episodes. The nine episodes featured in The Sign of Zorro aired from 10 Oct 1957 to 2 Jan 1958. George Lewis, who plays Diego's father in the film, appeared as "Zorro" in the 1944 Republic serial Zorro's Black Whip. According to a modern source, author Johnston McCulley served as a consultant on the writing of Disney's television episodes. This source lists a total of thirty-six feature films based on McCulley's Zorro stories, nine of which are U.S. productions. New World Productions reprised Zorro for television during the 1989-90 season with seventy-five episodes starring Duncan Regehr as Zorro. For information on other films featuring Zorro, see entries above for The Bold Caballero and for the 1920 and 1940 versions of The Mark of Zorro.

Box 8 Aug 1960. *LAHE* 23 Jun 1960. *LAMirror-News* 23 Jun 1960. *MPH* 9 Jul 1960. *NYT* 5 Sep 1961, p. 37.

THE SILENT ENEMY (Native Americans, Chippewa)

Burden-Chanler Productions. *Dist* Paramount-Publix Corp. 2 Aug **1930**; New York premiere: 19 May 1930 [©Paramount-Publix Corp.; 1 Aug 1930; LP1459]. Talking sequence, mus score, and sd eff (Movietone); b&w. 9 reels, 7,551 ft.

Prod W. Douglas Burden and William C. Chanler. *Dir* H. P. Carver. *Asst dir* Earl M. Welch. *Scen* Richard Carver. *Titles* Julian Johnson. *Ch Camera* Marcel Le Picard. *Addl photog* Frank M. Broda, Horace D. Ashton, William Casel and Otto Durkoltz. *Synchronized mus score* Massard Kur Zhene. *Tech* L. A. Bonn.

Song(s): "Rain-Flower," music by Massard Kur Zhene, lyrics by Leo Robin; "Song of the Waters," music and lyrics by Sam Coslow and Newell Chase.

Cast: Chief Yellow Robe (*Chetoga, tribe leader*), Chief Long Lance (*Baluk, mighty hunter*), Chief Akawanush (*Dagwan, medicine man*), Spotted Elk (*Neewa, Chetoga's daughter*), Cheeka (*Cheeka, Chetoga's son*).

Documentary, Drama. In a spoken prologue, Chief Yellow Robe introduces the film: "This is the story of my people. Now the White Man has come; his civilization has destroyed my people.... But now this same civilization has preserved our traditions before it was too late; now you will know us as we really are. Everything that you will see here is real; everything as it always has been. ..." With winter approaching and food scarce, Chetoga, chief of the Ojibwa, calls a council to decide the tribe's course. Baluk, the hunter, wishes to take the hunters south; in spite of Dagwan's protests, Chetoga agrees to the plan. When winter comes and the hunters return empty-handed, Baluk decides to move the tribe northward into the path of the migrating caribou, though Dagwan, a rival for the chief's daughter, taunts him with cowardice. After days without food, camp is pitched, and Baluk goes forth to a mountain to pray to the Great Spirit. He then kills a bull moose besieged by timber wolves, but Chetoga dies, leaving Baluk chief of the tribe. After weeks of fruitless travel, Dagwan calls a ritualistic meeting. During his medicine dance, a snow-flurry is taken as a sign of Dagwan's supernatural power, and he tells them the Great Spirit requires the sacrifice of Baluk. Baluk chooses to die by fire, and a funeral pyre is built; as he mounts it, word reaches the camp of a caribou stampede. Baluk takes charge, great numbers of caribou are slain, and there is feasting. As a result of his treachery, Dagwan is condemned to go forth without food, water, or weapons, and Baluk takes Neewa for his wife. *Canadian Northwest. Caribou. Chippewa Indians. Famines. Hunters. Medicine men. Ontario (Canada). Religion.*

Note: Filmed largely on the Temagami Forest Reserve in northern Ontario, the film is a by-product of an expedition sponsored by the Museum of Natural History in New York.

FD 18 May 1930. *NYT* 20 May 1930, p. 32. *Var* 21 May 1930, p. 19.

SILK LEGS (*foreign version*) see **PIERNAS DE SEDA**

SILKS AND SATINS (French Americans)

Famous Players Film Co. *Dist* Paramount Pictures Corp. 12 Jun **1916** [©Famous Players Film Co.; 25 May 1916; LU8354]. Si; b&w. 5 reels.

Dir J. Searle Dawley. *Scen* Betty T. Fitzgerald. *Cam* H. Lyman Broening.

Cast: Marguerite Clark (*Félicité*), Vernon Steel (*Jacques Desmond*), Clarence Handysides (*Marquis*), W. A. Williams (*Henri*), Thomas Holding (*Felix Breton*), Fayette Perry (*Annette*).

Historical, Drama. On the day before she obeys her father's edict to give up her real sweetheart and marry a man she does not love, Félicité reads the diary of a French ancestor from Napoleonic times, another Félicité, whose story parallels her own. The first Félicité is engaged to the foppish Felix Breton, but Henri, a cousin who wants to marry her, holds her captive. Felix sends the swordsman, Jacques Desmond, on a rescue mission, not knowing that Félicité loves Jacques even though she has only seen him once. Jacques takes Félicité away from Henri, but instead of returning to Felix, they get married and sail to America. Inspired by the diary, the modern-day Félicité slips out of her father's house and leaves town to marry the man she really loves. *Diaries. France–History–1789-1815. French. French Americans. Heredity. Marriage–Forced. Cousins. Dandies. Elopement. Rescues.*

Note: The film was also called *Her Romance.* Although Hugh Ford was listed in the copyright entry as "author," there is no evidence that he wrote the story for this film. Ford was Famous Players' Director-General, and in this capacity may have been assigned the "author" for copyright purposes.

Motog 24 Jun 1916, p. 1450. *MPN* 24 Jun 1916, p. 3932. *MPW* 24 Jun 1916, p. 2260. *NYDM* 17 Jun 1916, p. 28. *Var* 16 Jun 1916, p. 23. *Wid's* 15 Jun 1916, p. 653.

SILLY BILLIES (Native Americans)

RKO Radio Pictures, Inc. *Dist* RKO Radio Pictures, Inc. 20 Mar **1936**; Prod: Dec 1935 [©RKO Radio Pictures, Inc.; 20 Mar 1936; LP6240]. Sd (RCA Victor System); b&w. 7 reels. 63 or 65 min. PCA cert no. 1866.

Assoc prod Lee Marcus. *Dir* Fred Guiol. [*Asst dir* Jean Yarbrough]. *Scr* Al Boasberg and Jack Townley. *Story* Thomas Lennon and Fred Guiol. *Photog* Nick Musuraca and J. Roy Hunt. *Photog eff* Vernon Walker. *Art dir* Van Nest Polglase. *Art dir assoc* Feild Gray. *Ed* John Lockert. *Mus dir* Roy Webb. *Rec* John E. Tribby.

Song(s): "Tumbleweed," music and lyrics by Dave Dreyer and Jack Scholl.

Cast: BERT WHEELER [(*Roy Banks*)], ROBERT WOOLSEY [(*Dr. Philip "Painless" Pennington*)], Dorothy Lee [(*Mary Blake*)], Harry Woods [(*Hank Bewley*)], Ethan Laidlaw [(*Trigger*)], Chief Thunderbird [(*Chief Cyclone*)], Delmar Watson [(*Morton*)], Richard Alexander [(*John Little*)], [Willie Best (*Willie*)], [Lafe McKee (*Settler*)], [Maurice Black (*Leader of outlaws*)].

Historical, Comedy, Western. [*Print viewed*]. In 1851, dentist Philip "Painless" Pennington and his assistant, Roy Banks, are on their way to settle in Little Town, unaware that the entire town is about to leave on a gold rush wagon train. After extracting an outlaw's tooth at gunpoint, Roy and Pennington, who use generous amounts of chloroform on their patients, arrive in Little Town and immediately are accosted by founding father John Little. Impressed by the bustle of the town, Pennington and Roy are easily duped into buying one of Little's buildings for their new practice and join Little in repeated toasts. The next day, however, the hungover duo is shocked to discover that the town has been deserted. As they bemoan their bad fortune, a wagon carrying a dead scout pulls into town. In the scout's hand, the duo finds a note that states that the Little Town wagon train is being led into an Indian ambush. Roy, anxious to protect Mary Blake, the Little Town schoolteacher with whom he is infatuated, insists that they find the wagon train before the attack. The duo soon catches up to the train, but Hank Bewley and Trigger, the crooked leaders of the wagon train, publicly dismiss their warnings. Roy and Pennington, however, overhear Trigger confessing to the scout's death and also learn of Hank's plans to change the train's course to throw off suspicion. Before they can expose the leaders, Pennington and Roy are accused by Hank of being renegades. As they are about to be lynched by the group, Roy and Pennington sink into a bed of quicksand and elude their executioners. The next morning, Chief Cyclone and his men find the dentists and take them to their camp. After threatening to kill the duo, Chief Cyclone dresses them in Indian garb and insists that they participate in a tribal "race for life." Still dressed as Indians, Roy and Pennington escape from the chief and rush back to the wagon train. Once again, the group refuses to believe the duo's warnings until Chief Cyclone and his tribe encircle the train with blasting rifles. Inspired by the slingshot of Morton, a young prospector, Roy and Pennington begin shooting dental sponges dipped in chloroform at the attacking Indians. As the Indians fall victim to the chloroform bombs, Roy volunteers to ride for the cavalry, which finally routs the Indians. After Roy and Pennington are declared heroes, they discover that rocks from Little Town that Morton had been carrying are filled with gold. The soon-to-be-rich Roy, Pennington and Mary embrace. *Dentists. Fraud. Gold rushes. Indians of North America. United States–History–19th century. Wagon trains. Children. Chloroform. Drunkenness. Escapes. Gold. Lynching. Massacres. Murder. Outlaws. Quicksand. Rites and ceremonies. Romance. Schoolteachers. United States. Army. Cavalry.*

Note: The working title of this film was *Wild West* or *The Wild West. HR* production charts add Nelson McDowell, Jim Thorpe and John Ince to the cast, but their participation in the final film has not been confirmed.

DV 22 Feb 1936, p. 3. *FD* 4 Apr 1936, p. 4. *HR* 7 Dec 1935, pp. 6-7. *HR* 30 Dec 1935, p. 10. *HR* 22 Feb 1936, p. 4. *MPD* 25 Feb 1936, p. 11. *MPH* 18 Jan 1936, p. 27. *MPH* 7 Mar 1936, p. 46. *NYT* 6 Apr 1936, p. 18. *Var* 8 Apr 1936, p. 17.

SILVER BULLETS *see* **FURY AT FURNACE CREEK**

THE SILVER DOLLAR *see* **OVERLAND PACIFIC**

SILVER SPURS (Latino)

Doubleday Productions. *Dist* Western Pictures Exploitation Co. 1 May **1922.** Si; b&w. 5 reels, 4,500 ft.

Supv Charles W. Mack. *Dir* Henry McCarty and Leo Meehan.

Cast: Lester Cuneo.

Western. "The title comes from a pair of lucky spurs which is given to the hero, a writer of Western stories and general all-round adventurer, by a crowd of his New York club friends. With the spurs as a good luck symbol he goes West in search of romance. In California he meets and falls in love with a Spanish girl, who has been defrauded of her estate by an unscrupulous half-breed. After many fights with the villain and his cohorts, he gets back the girl's property and returns to New York with her as his bride." (*MPNBG* 3 Oct 1922, p. 63). *Authors. California. Fraud. Indians of North America–Mixed blood. New York City. Pulp fiction. Spaniards.*

SILVER TRAILS (Latino)

Monogram Pictures Corp. *Dist* Monogram Pictures Corp. 22 Aug **1948;** Prod: late Jun 1948 [©Monogram Pictures Corp.; 22 Aug 1948; LP1854]. Sd (Western Electric Recording); b&w. 4,771 ft. 53 min. PCA cert no. 13297.

Prod Louis Gray. *Dir* Christy Cabanne. *Asst dir* Eddie Davis and [Harry Jones]. *Orig scr* J. Benton Cheney. *Dir of photog* Harry Neumann. *Settings* Vin Taylor. *Film ed* John C. Fuller. *Mus dir* Edward Kay. *Rec eng* Tom Lambert.

Song(s): "Serenade" and "Silver Trails," composers undetermined.

Cast: JIMMY WAKELY [(*Jimmy Wakely*)], "Cannonball" Taylor [(*"Cannonball"*)], Christine Larson [(*Diane Chambers*)], George Lewis [(*José*)], George Meeker [(*Willard Jackson*)], Pierce Lyden [(*Ramsay*)], Wm. Norton Bailey [(*John Chambers*)], Connie Asins [(*Conchita*)], Fred L. Edwards [(*Sturgis*)], Robert Strange [(*Don Esteban*)], Bob Woodward [(*Dirk*)], and introducing Whip Wilson (*Whip*).

Western, with songs. [*Print viewed*]. Jimmy Wakely and his pal "Cannonball" are on their way to work for California settler John Chambers when they discover the body of Don Manuel, a member of an old Californian family. Don Manuel has been killed by Ramsay and Sturgis, two men on the payroll of crooked county surveyor Willard Jackson. They have taken land grant documents that Manuel was carrying so that Jackson can make copies and claim the land for himself. José, a young Mexican land owner, accuses Jimmy of killing Manuel and challenges him to a gunfight, but Jimmy beats him to the draw. Just then, José's uncle, Don Esteban, an old friend of Jimmy's, arrives on the scene and vouches for Jimmy, but José still regards him as a land grabber. At Don Esteban's hacienda, where Jimmy and Cannonball meet ranch hand Whip, Esteban tells Jimmy that José's father was killed by unidentified settlers who took over his ranch. Although José suspects that John may have been involved in the killing, Jimmy is convinced of his friend's innocence. John and his daughter Diane, meanwhile, visit Jackson's office to collect a survey of land he has bought via a deed. When Johnny and Cannonball show up, they are welcomed by John and Jackson, but Jimmy becomes involved in a fistfight with Jackson's men. Afterward, Jackson explains to Jimmy that the native Californians whose land was confiscated by settlers could not prove title to their land and had not established property lines. After Jimmy and Cannonball head out to John's ranch, Jackson sends another gunman, Dirk, to shoot them but they return fire and kill him. When Jimmy learns that José used to court Diane, he suggests to John that he and Esteban should meet to try to discuss their differences. On their way to church the next day, the two families meet up and attend the service, for which Jimmy has asked the padre to preach a particular sermon. After church, José and Diane reunite, and John and Esteban plan a meeting involving the other settlers. Later, John informs Jackson that Esteban is about to receive a court decision as to the validity of records contained in family bibles as proof of land ownership. As John and José talk in John's ranch house, Ramsay shoots John through an open window, and José is accused of the crime but escapes. Jimmy catches José and turns him over to the sheriff, but on his death bed, John tells Jimmy that José did not shoot him. John's death incites the settlers against the Californians, and Jackson adds more acreage to his holdings. When Jimmy, Cannonball

and Whip learn that José is about to be lynched, they ride to his rescue, free him and escape. Later, Diane hires Jackson's men to hunt for José, whom she believes to be guilty, and follows Whip to where Jimmy is hiding José, who was wounded in the escape. Diane draws a gun on them but Whip lashes it out of her hand. Esteban, meanwhile, has decided to sell his hacienda and has gone to Santa Cruz to collect the documents. He is ambushed, however, and robbed of the papers. Later, Jimmy arrives at Jackson's office just in time to prevent him from burning Esteban's land grant. Diane draws her gun on Jimmy, but he is able to prove to her that Jackson has been behind all the trouble and hands him over to the sheriff. Diane and José plan to marry and with peace restored, Jimmy and Cannonball head off to another adventure. *California. Land rights. Mexican Americans. Robbery. Settlers. Surveyors. Churches. Courtship. Fathers and daughters. Fistfights. Gunfights. Gunshot wounds. Haciendas. Hired killers. Land rights. Lynching. Murder. Nephews. Ranches. Uncles. Whips and whippings.*

Note: Although contemporary reviews list other song titles, only those cited above were heard in the print viewed, which was complete. This picture marked the screen debut of "Whip" Wilson, who later starred in a number of Western films. Some sources list actress Connie Asins' name as Consuelo Asnis.

MPHPD 4 Sep 1948, p. 4303. *MPHPD* 19 Mar 1949, p. 4538. *Var* 16 Mar 1948, p. 11.

SIN (Italian Americans)

Fox Film Corp. *Dist* Fox Film Corp. Oct **1915**? [©William Fox; 3 Oct 1915; LP6523]. Si; b&w. 5 reels.

Dir Herbert Brenon. *Scen* Herbert Brenon. *Cam* Philip E. Rosen.

Cast: Theda Bara (*Rosa*), Warner Oland (*Pietro*), William E. Shay (*Luigi*).

Drama. When Rosa, an Italian peasant girl, meets the attractive, wealthy Pietro, the head of the Camorra, a New York crime syndicate, she deserts Luigi, her fiancé, and departs for America. Hurt but determined, the simple, pious Luigi follows his sweetheart to New York. To prove his love, Pietro tells Rosa that he will steal the jewels of the Madonna for her. Impressed by this seeming devotion, Rosa informs Luigi of Pietro's boast and he, not to be outdone, decides to steal the jewels himself. After Luigi presents her with the coveted gems, Rosa makes her way through the Festival of the Madonna to find Pietro at Camorra headquarters. When she arrives, the theft has been discovered, and a mob is forming to hunt the culprit. Rosa begs protection from Pietro, who throws her out into the street. Overcome by religious guilt, Rosa collapses in a deranged stupor, then after returning the jewels, Luigi kills himself on the church steps. *Guilt. Italians. Religion. Rivalry. Robbery. Churches. Country girls. Festivals. Fidelity. Insanity. Italy. Jewelry. Mafia. Mobs. New York City. Suicide.*

Motog 23 Oct 1915, p. 880. *MPN* 7 Aug 1915, p. 46. *MPN* 2 Oct 1915, pp. 26-27. *MPN* 16 Oct 1915, p. 46. *MPW* 16 Oct 1915, p. 465. *Var* 8 Oct 1915, p. 21.

SINCE YOU WENT AWAY (African Americans, Polish Americans)

Selznick International. *Dist* United Artists Corp. 20 Jul **1944**; Los Angeles premiere: Jun 1944; Prod: 19 Sep 1943—9 Feb 1944 [©Vanguard Films, Inc.; 14 Sep 1944; LP12953]. Sd (Western Electric Mirrophonic Recording); b&w. 15,480 ft. 172 min.

Pres DAVID O. SELZNICK. *Dir* John Cromwell. *Asst dir* Lowell J. Farrell and [Edward F. Mull]. [*Fill-in dir* David O. Selznick]. [*Dir of crowd seq* Tay Garnett]. [*Dir of comedy seq* Eddie Cline]. [*Scr* David O. Selznick]. *Based on the adpt of her book* Margaret Buell Wilder. *Photog* Stanley Cortez, Lee Garmes, [George Barnes and Robert Bruce]. [*Cam op* Edward P. Fitzgerald and Harry Webb]. [*Asst cam* Kenneth Meade and Harvey L. Slocomb]. *Stills* Marty Crail. *Spec eff* Jack Cosgrove. [*Assoc* Clarence Slifer]. [*Montage* Andre De Toth]. *Prod des* William L. Pereira. *Supv film ed* Hal C. Kern. *Assoc film ed* James E. Newcom. [*Film ed* John D. Faure, Arthur Fellows and Wayland M. Hendry]. [*Sd ed* Charles L. Freeman]. *Int dec* Victor A. Gangelin. *Settings* Mark Lee Kirk. [*Consultant for the Hilton home* Tom Douglas]. [*Props* Arden Cripe and Fred M. Widdowson]. [*Green* Roy A. McLaughlin]. [*Draperies* James A. Forney]. [*Wardrobe dir* Elmer Ellsworth]. [*Assoc* Adele Sadler]. *Mus dir* Max Steiner. *Assoc mus dir* Louis Forbes. [*Dance dir* Charles Walters]. *Rec* Percy Townsend. [*Re-rec* Arthur Johns]. [*Makeup supv* Robert Stephanoff]. [*Assoc* William Riddle]. [*Hair stylist* Peggy Higgins]. [*Associate* Margaret Martin]. *Prod asst* Barbara Keon. *Tech adv* Lt. Col. J. G. Taylor, U.S. Army. [*Prod mgr* Fred R. Ahern, Raymond A. Klune and Richard L. Johnston]. [*Prod artist* Joseph McMillan Johnson, A. Leslie Thomas and Frederick Robinson]. [*Unit mgr* John E. Burch and George Yohalem]. [*Head script clerk* Lydia Schiller]. [*Research* A. Joan

O'Brien and Sarah Catherine Haney]. *Casting mgr* Ruth Burch. [*Construction superintendent* Harold M. Fenton]. [*Chief draftsman* Alfred Ybarra]. [*Draftsman* Robert Ashton, Frank Pereu and William Connor]. [*Chief electrician* James Potevin]. [*Chief grip* Morris Rosen]. [*Tech adv Red Cross scenes* Jack Beaman and Iris Taylor].

Music: "The Emperor Waltz," by Johann Strauss; "Together," by B. G. De Sylva, Lew Brown and Ray Henderson.

Song(s): "Oh, My Darling Clementine," words and music by Percy Montrose; "The Dipsy Doodle," words and music by Larry Clinton.

Source: Based on the novel *Since You Went Away; Letters to a Soldier from His Wife* by Margaret Buell Wilder (New York, 1943).

Cast: Claudette Colbert [(*Anne Hilton*)], Jennifer Jones [(*Jane Hilton*)], Joseph Cotten [(*Lt. Tony Willett*)], Shirley Temple [(*Bridget "Brig" Hilton*)], Monty Woolley [(*Col. William G. Smollett*)], Lionel Barrymore [(*Clergyman*)], Robert Walker [(*William G. "Bill" Smollett II*)], Hattie McDaniel [(*Fidelia*)], Agnes Moorehead [(*Emily Hawkins*)], Nazimova [(*Zofia Koslowska*)], Albert Basserman [(*Dr. Sigmund Gottlieb Golden*)], Gordon Oliver [(*Marine officer*)], Keenan Wynn [(*Lt. Solomon*)], Guy Madison [(*Harold Smith*)], Craig Stevens [(*Danny Williams*)], Lloyd Corrigan [(*Mr. Mahoney*)], Jackie Moran [(*Johnny Mahoney*)], [Jane Devlin (*Gladys Brown*)], [Robert Anderson (*Patron at bar*)], [Irving Bacon (*Bartender*)], [Leonide Mostovoy (*Headwaiter*)], [Cindy Garner (*Sugar*)], [James Carlisle (*Sugar's officer friend*)], [George Chandler (*Taxi driver*)], [John James (*Friendly sergeant at dance*)], [Mary Anne Durkin (*Frightened girl at dance*)], [Joyce Horne (*Swenson's girl friend*)], [Anne Gillis (*Becky Anderson*)], [Grady Sutton (*Southerner*)], [Ruth Valmy (*Tony's friend*)], [Buddy Gorman (*Short soldier*)], [Patricia Peters (*Tall WAC*)], [Andrew McLaglen (*Former plowboy*)], [Addison Richards (*Major Sam Atkins*)], [George Lloyd (*Motorcycle policeman*)], [Barbara Pepper (*Pin girl*)], [Jill Warren (*Waitress*)], [Byron Foulger (*Principal*)], [Harry Hayden (*The conductor*)], [Edwin Maxwell (*Businessman*)], [Russell Hoyt (*One-armed sailor*)], [Loudie Claar (*Young mother*)], [Don Najarian, Jon Najarian (*Babies*)], [Helen Koford (*Refugee child*)], [Florence Bates (*Hungry woman*)], [Conrad Binyon (*Page boy*)], [Theodore Von Eltz (*Desk clerk*)], [Adeline deWalt Reynolds (*Elderly woman*)], [Christopher Adams, Jimmy Dodd, Martha Outlaw, Verna Knopf, Robert Cherry, Kirk Barron (*Train passengers*)], [Earl Jacobs (*One-armed boy*)], [Cecil Ballerino (*Patient at Potters Wheel*)], [Jack Gardner (*Patient in wheelchair*)], [Doodles Weaver, Paul Esburg, Richard C. Wood, Ralph Reed, James Westerfield, Warren Hymer (*Convalescents*)], [Dorothy Adams (*Nurse*)], [Willard Jillson (*Marine lover*)], [Dorothy Mann (*His girl friend*)], [Peggy Maley (*Another girl friend*)], [Robert Johnson (*Black officer*)], [Dorothy Dandridge (*His wife*)], [Shelby Bacon (*Their child*)], [Eddie Hall (*Eager sailor*)], [Warren Burr (*Serious soldier*)], [Lela Bliss (*Gabby woman*)], [Eilene Janssen (*Sergeant's child*)], [Harlan Miller (*M.P.*)], [Mrs. Ray Feldman (*Soldier's grandmother*)], [Neyle Marx (*Her grandson*)], [Johnny Bond (*AWOL*)], [Ruth Roman (*Envious girl*)], [Betsy Howard (*Friend of envious girl*)], [Stephen Wayne (*Bearded sailor*)], [William B. Davidson (*Taxpayer*)], [Tom Dawson (*Tough Bronx soldier*)], [Marilyn Hare (*Merchant Marine's wife*)], [Jonathan Hale (*Conductor*)], [Walter Baldwin (*Gateman*)], [Eric Sinclair (*Voice in convalescent ward*)], [Jerry Revell (*Foreman*)], [James Clemons, Jr. (*Caroler*)], [Dick Whittington, a dog (*Soda*)], [Neil Hamilton (*Photo of Tim Hilton*)], [John Derek], [Florence Allen], [Lulu Mae Bohorman], [Dulce Daye], [Rhonda Fleming], [Aileen Pringle], [Charles Williams], [Wallis Clark], [Neila Hart].

Homefront, World War II, Drama. [*Print viewed*]. On 12 January 1943, Anne Hilton returns home after seeing her husband Tim off to war. Lonely, Anne bitterly questions her husband's decision to leave his family and his lucrative job as an advertising executive in order to serve his country. After comforting her daughters "Brig" and Jane, Anne bids a reluctant farewell to Fidelia, the family's devoted black housekeeper. The loss of Tim's salary has created a financial hardship for the family, and consequently, they can no longer afford to pay Fidelia. When Mr. Mahoney, a sympathetic shopkeeper, extends credit to the Hiltons, Anne pledges Tim's help in finding a job for Johnny, Mahoney's serviceman son, after the war ends. The country is in the grip of a housing shortage, and when Brig, Anne's youngest daughter, insists that it is their patriotic duty to take in a boarder, Anne surrenders her own room. Col. William G. Smollett, a stern retired army officer, answers the Hiltons' ad and rents the room,

forcing the family to adjust to his demands. Soon after, Fidelia asks to move back into the house, offering her housekeeping services as rent. Anne warmly welcomes her home, but refuses to accept her offer. Later, at a crowded cocktail lounge, Anne meets her friend, Emily Hawkins, a self-centered divorcee. As the women talk, Anne is surprised by the arrival of Lt. Tony Willett, an old friend of the Hiltons', who worked as an illustrator in civilian life. After escorting Anne out of the bar, Tony asks her for a place to stay, and Anne decides to move in with her daughters to make room for Tony. Jane, a high school senior, soon develops a crush on the suave Tony. One day, Smollett's grandson Bill, an enlisted man, pays a surprise visit to his grandfather, who brusquely dismisses him. Overhearing their exchange, Jane feels compassion for Bill. Emily, meanwhile, contributes to the war effort by organizing a dance to entertain the servicemen, and enlists Jane as one of the hostesses. Nervous and unsure of herself, Jane is asked to dance by Bill. She reluctantly accepts, regarding Bill as only a "boy" next to the dashing Tony. Anne attends with Tony, and there meets Johnny Mahoney, who thanks her for offering to help him find a job. Johnny is leaving for a training flight, and soon after he departs, word comes that his plane has crashed, and for the first time, the tragedy of war is personalized for Anne. As time passes, the irascible colonel mellows and becomes a member of the family, even accepting the Hiltons' lumbering bull dog Soda. On the day that Tony is to leave, he presents Fidelia with a handsome sketch that he has drawn of her. Jane, who has contracted the mumps, bids Tony a tearful farewell. While bowling one evening, Bill and Jane become friends with a sailor after he bandages Jane's injured finger. After walking the sailor to his bus, Bill invites Jane to the soda fountain, and there Jane questions him about his timidity. In explanation, Bill relates how he bitterly disappointed his grandfather by being expelled from West Point, and then shows her a pocket watch that his grandfather had given him, inscribed with a reference to the Smollett family's proud military history. When Bill concludes that his failure resulted from personal weakness, Jane comes to his defense. The next morning, Jane informs her mother that she wants to find a job after graduation rather than attend college, but Anne refuses. Over breakfast, Jane criticizes the colonel's treatment of Bill, angering the old man. After Jane's graduation ceremony, the family receives word from Tim that he will be stopping between trains at a nearby city. Boarding the next train to the city, the family eagerly anticipates their reunion with Tim. Their train is delayed, however, and by the time they arrive, Tim has already had to leave. On the trip home, the family then meets a woman whose granddaughter was reported missing at the Battle of Corregidor. Touched by the woman's sacrifice, Anne agrees to let Jane work as a nurse's aide that summer. One day soon after, Anne is notified that Tim is missing in action. Devastated by the news, the family prays for his safety, and later, Anne tearfully reviews their scrapbook. [An intermission divides the story at this point.]

One Sunday after church, Bill tells Jane that he has been ordered to leave at midnight. As Jane and Bill spend their last hours together in the countryside, Anne implores Smollett to see Bill off at the train station that evening. Claiming that he has a previous engagement with representatives from the British army, the colonel promises to try to finish in time and asks Anne to wish Bill good luck. Meanwhile, in the country, Jane and Bill seek shelter from a sudden downpour and there dream of marrying after the war ends. At the train station, Anne conveys to Bill his grandfather's concern, and as the train pulls out, Bill presents his watch to Jane as an engagement gift. Too late, the colonel arrives at the station. Some time later, Anne breaks the news of Bill's death in battle to Jane. Filled with self-recrimination, the colonel blames himself for driving the boy too hard, and Anne tries to comfort him. On the colonel's birthday, Tony returns and is surprised by how quickly Jane has grown up. Emily then pays an unexpected visit and voices disapproval of Jane's hospital work, causing Jane to berate her for her selfishness. When Emily criticizes Jane's behavior, Anne castigates her for her lack of patriotism and, realizing that she also has been remiss in serving her country, decides to work as a welder in a shipyard. In the factory, Anne is moved when she meets an immigrant woman who recalls her thrill at reading the inscription on the Statue of Liberty and likens Anne to the embodiment of that spirit. On Christmas Eve, Jane returns Bill's watch to the colonel, bringing the old man pride and comfort. Somberly, Fidelia places the gifts under the tree that Tim sent before his

disappearance. Anne tearfully opens her gift, a music box that plays "We'll Be Together Always." As she begins to sob, the phone rings. Upon answering it, Anne's expression turns to joy, and she hurries to the staircase to announce to her daughters that their father is safe and coming home. *Family life. Housing shortages. Patriotism. Rationing in wartime. Self-sacrifice. World War II. Adolescents. African Americans. Birthdays. Christmas Eve. Dances. Dogs. Engagements. Graduations. Grandsons. Housekeepers. Immigrants. Infatuation. Lodgers. Mumps. Music boxes. Nurses. Officers (Military). Sailors. Soldiers. Transformation. War refugees. Watches. Welders. Women defense plant workers.*

Note: Before the onscreen production credits appear, the title *Since You Went Away*, followed by the word "overture" is flashed onscreen while orchestral music plays under the title. The screen then goes black, after which the Selznick logo is projected. The logo is followed by the legend "David O. Selznick presents his production of *Since You Went Away*". The onscreen writing credits: "based on the adaptation of her book by Margaret Buell Wilder," with "screenplay by the producer," although Selznick's name is not listed onscreen as the writer. The film opens with the following written prologue: "This is a story of the Unconquerable Fortress: the American Home..." An intermission divides the picture just after "Anne" is notified that her husband is missing in action. According to a modern source, Selznick began his search for a home-front drama in Jun 1942. Production materials on the film contained in the AMPAS Library reveal that Selznick settled on Wilder's book, which was largely a reprint of a column that she wrote for the *Dayton Journal Herald*. The column was written in story form as a series of letters from the writer to her husband. Portions of Wilder's book were also published in the Jun 1943 *Ladies Home Journal*. A modern source adds that after buying the story rights for $30,000, Selznick brought Wilder in to write the adaptation. After Wilder finished her adaptation, Selznick, thinking that the characters were too sketchy, took the basic structure and wrote the screenplay himself, focusing on the three principal characters of the Hilton family to create a "panorama of the home front." Selznick had originally planned to credit the screenplay to Jeffrey Daniel, a *nom de plume*, but later changed his mind, according to a 1944 *LAT* news item. According to an Aug 1943 *HR* news item, Selznick initially planned to direct the production.

To lend an air of authenticity to his drama, Selznick used five different units to film background shots of hospitalized soldiers, laborers at the Kaiser Shipyards in Richmond, CA, and Red Cross workers, according to a *NYHT* news item. A Jan 1944 *HR* news item adds that Selznick hired twenty female steelburners and nine tons of welding tools from the Wilmington Shipyard in order to lend verisimilitude to the shipyard scene. In the film's printed program, Selznick acknowledged the "technical assistance rendered by Dr. Walter L. Treadway, Medical Director of U. S. Public Health Service; Mr. Ulrie Bell and Mr. William S. Cunningham of the Office of War Information; Commander Alfred J. Bolton U. S. Navy; Mr. Allyn Butterfield of the War Dept.; Mr. Jack Beaman, liaison officer for the American Red Cross and May E. Romm, M. D.

News items in *HR* yield the following information about the production: Although George Barnes is credited with photography in the Sep 1943 production charts, he is not credited onscreen. According to modern sources, Selznick fired Barnes after two weeks of work because he was dissatisfied with the way Claudette Colbert was being photographed. In late Nov 1943, Tay Garnett was borrowed from M-G-M to direct Robert Walker's scenes, and Lee Garmes was hired to photograph them. Director Andrew De Toth worked on special montage scenes between 8 Dec—22 Dec 1943. When director John Cromwell fell ill, Selznick took over the directorial reigns from 23—26 Dec 1943. The sequence at the railroad depot was filmed at the Pathe lot on a site that once served as the rolling lawn of Tara in *Gone With the Wind*. The hangar dance was shot in a reproduction of an Army aviation hangar that encompassed two sound stages, over 20,000 square feet of floor space and utilized 100 electricians. The church scene was filmed at the Church of the Angels in Pasadena, CA. After its initial editing in Feb 1944, the film ran four and a half hours long. By early Mar 1944, Selznick had trimmed the picture to three hours twenty-eight minutes. According to a 21 Mar 1944 news item, by late Mar Selznick had cut the film to three hours, ten minutes. After its initial engagement, Selznick trimmed the film by another twenty-five minutes, according to a modern source. By the time the 127-day shoot was completed, the film had amassed a budget of nearly $3,000,000, according to a 1944 news item. A *Var* 1949 news item adds that when the film was re-released by Eagle Lion in 1949, it was cut another thirty-seven minutes.

According to a memo from Selznick reprinted in a modern source, stage actress Katharine Cornell wanted to play the role of "Anne," but Selznick desired a bigger star. In addition to Cornell, Ann Harding, Irene Dunne, Helen Hayes and Rosalind Russell were also considered for the role, according to *HR* news items. An Oct 1944 *LAT* news item adds that Colbert, when approached about playing the part of "Anne," was at first reluctant because she didn't want to play the mother of two adolescent daughters. Shirley Temple returned to the screen after a two-year absence to play the role of "Brig". Although a 17 Sep 1943 production chart places Vicci Style in the cast, Styles' participation in the completed film has not been confirmed. According to a modern source, Selznick offered Ruth Gordon the role of "Emily," but she turned it down. *HR* news items add the following actors to the cast: George Beban, Jr.; Rudolph Friml, Jr.; Michael Owen; Phyllis Adair; Clyde Fillmore; Charles Halton; Sam McDaniel; Virginia Wick; Charles King, Jr.; William Bronson; Wing Foo; Minta Durfee Arbuckle; Eva Novak; Matt Moore; Jill Browning; Buddy Yarus; Harland Briggs; Carlyle Blackwell, Jr. and Grady Thomas. Their participation in the completed film has not been confirmed, however. This picture marked the screen debut of John Derek, Guy Madison and Wilfred Jillson and the last film appearance of Nazimova. Robert Walker, who was borrowed from M-G-M to appear in this film, had recently separated from his wife Jennifer Jones, who played his sweetheart in the film. Jones and Selznick were later married.

Since You Went Away was named as the fourth most popular of the year by the National Board of Review. Post-release *HR* news items note that the lines at the film's New York opening were so long that the police ordered that the theater must open an hour-and-a-half before show time to prevent traffic jams. The film was nominated for an Academy Award for Best Picture. Claudette Colbert was nominated for Best Actress, Monty Woolley was nominated for Best Supporting Actor and Jennifer Jones was nominated for Best Supporting Actress. The picture was also nominated for Academy Awards in the following categories: Best Cinematography, Best Film Editing, Best Special Effects and Best Art Direction-Interior Decoration. Max Steiner won an Academy Award for his scoring of the film.

Box 29 Jul 1944. *DV* 19 Jul 1944, p. 3. *FD* 19 Jul 1944, p. 8. *HR* 26 May 1943. *HR* 2 Jun 1943, p. 6. *HR* 2 Aug 1943, p. 7. *HR* 10 Aug 1943, p. 1. *HR* 17 Sep 1943, p. 9. *HR* 1 Nov 1943, p. 7. *HR* 3 Nov 1943, p. 8. *HR* 4 Nov 1943, p. 6. *HR* 5 Nov 1943, p. 11. *HR* 12 Nov 1943, p. 10. *HR* 15 Nov 1943. *HR* 22 Nov 1943, p. 10. *HR* 24 Nov 1943, p. 6. *HR* 29 Nov 1943, p. 9. *HR* 30 Nov 1943, p. 5, 7, 10. *HR* 3 Dec 1943, p. 2. *HR* 15 Dec 1943, p. 33. *HR* 20 Dec 1943, p. 3, 4. *HR* 24 Dec 1943, p. 3. *HR* 27 Dec 1943, p. 4. *HR* 1 Jan 1944, p. 4. *HR* 28 Jan 1944, p. 15. *HR* 11 Feb 1944, p. 9. *HR* 8 Mar 1944, p. 3. *HR* 21 Mar 1944, p. 5. *HR* 17 Jul 1944, p. 2. *HR* 19 Jul 1944, p. 3. *HR* 24 Jul 1944, p. 6. *HR* 28 Jul 1944, p. 3. *HR* 4 Aug 1944, pp. 5-44, 48. *HR* 14 Mar 1949. *LAT* 9 Apr 1944. *LAT* 29 Oct 1944. *MPHPD* 20 Nov 1943, p. 1635. *MPHPD* 22 Jul 1944, p. 2095. *NYHT* 20 Feb 1944. *NYT* 21 Jul 1944, p. 16. *Var* 19 Jul 1944, p. 13.

SING YUN SIN NIAN (Chinese language)
Grandview Film Co. **1947?**; Hong Kong showing: 1947? Sd; b&w. Length undetermined. Chinese language.
Dir Joseph Sunn. [*Not viewed*]. [No information concerning the plot of this film has been located.].
Note: The Cantonese transliterated title is *Hen Wen Sen Neng*. The English language title is *The Lucky Bride*. This film was probably made in the U.S.

SINGIN' IN THE CORN (Native Americans)
Columbia Pictures Corp. *Dist* Columbia Pictures Corp. 26 Dec **1946**; Prod: 18 Jul—7 Aug 1946 [©Columbia Pictures Corp.; 26 Dec 1946; LP731]. Sd; b&w. 64-66 min. PCA cert no. 11961.
Prod Ted Richmond. *Dir* Del Lord. *Asst dir* Thomas Flood. *Orig scr story* Richard Weil. *Scr* Isabel Dawn and Monte Brice. *Addl dial* Elwood Ullman. *Cam* George B. Meehan. *Art dir* Sturges Carne. *Film ed* Aaron Stell. *Set dec* William Calvert. *Mus dir* George Duning. *Sd tech* George Cooper.
Song(s): "An Old Love Is a True Love," "I'm a Gal of Property," "Pepita Chiquita" and "Finale of Ghost Town," music and lyrics by Allan Roberts and Doris Fisher; "Ma (He's Making Eyes at Me)," music by Con Conrad, lyrics by Sidney Clare.
Cast: Judy Canova ·(*Judy McCoy*), Allen Jenkins (*Glen Cummings*), Guinn "Big Boy" Williams (*Hank*), Alan Bridge (*Honest John Richards*), Charles Halton (*Obediah Davis*), Robert Dudley (*Gramp McCoy*), Nick Thompson (*Indian chief*), Frances Rey (*Ramona*), George Chesebro (*Texas*), Ethan Laidlaw (*Silk Stevens*), Frank Lackteen (*Medicine man*), The Singing Indian Braves, Guy Beach (*Judge*), Silver Heels Smith, Rod Redwing (*Braves*), Mary Gordon (*Mrs. O'Rourke*), Si Jenks (*Old man*), Pat O'Malley (*O'Rourke*), Chester Conklin (*Austin driver*), Dick Stanley, Charles Randolph (*Indians*).
Western, with songs. [*Not viewed*]. When carnival fortune-teller Judy McCoy inherits her grandfather's estate, she discovers that his will stipulates that she must first return the town of McCoy's Gulch to the Indians from whom he had stolen the land years earlier before she can collect on her fortune. Judy must return the land within twenty-four hours, or it will become the property of Honest John Richards, her grandfather's former business partner. With help from Glen Cummings, her former carnival partner, Judy makes preparations to deliver the town to the Indians. Her efforts are soon thwarted, however, by Richards and his henchmen, who have convinced the Indians that the town is haunted. When the Indians refuse to accept the town, Judy and Glen attempt to generate interest in the property by disguising themselves as a wealthy Mexican couple seeking to invest money in the town. Once Judy and Glen realize that the Indians are eavesdropping on them, they try to force Richards to admit that he fabricated the stories about the town being haunted. Their plan fails, though, when Richards discovers their trap. Judy eventually succeeds in forcing a confession from Richards and his men by threatening to drown them. Afterward, the Indians accept the property, and Judy is satisfied that she has met the terms of her grandfather's will. *Duplicity. Fortune-tellers. Impersonation and imposture. Indians of North America. Land claims. Wills. Confession*

(Law). Drowning. Ghosts. Granddaughters. Mexicans. Musicians. Reputation. Small town life. Traps.

Note: *HR* production charts list Dusty Anderson in the cast, but her appearance in the released film has not been confirmed. According to a Jul 1946 *HR* news item, some filming was to take place at the Iverson and Columbia ranches in Southern California.

HR 15 Jul 1946, p. 12. *HR* 19 Jul 1946, p. 22. *MPHPD* 16 Nov 1946, p. 3312. *MPHPD* 23 Nov 1946, p. 3322. *Var* 23 Nov 1946, p. 38.

SINGIN' SPURS (Native Americans)
Columbia Pictures Corp. *Dist* Columbia Pictures Corp. 23 Sep 1948; Prod: 19 Apr—20 Apr 1948 [©Columbia Pictures Corp.; 30 Aug 1948; LP1780]. Sd; b&w. 7 reels. 61-62 min. PCA cert no. 13171.

Prod Colbert Clark. *Dir* Ray Nazarro. *Asst dir* Milton Feldman. *Orig scr* Barry Shipman. *Dir of photog* Rex Wimpy. *Art dir* Robert Peterson. *Film ed* Paul Borofsky. *Mus dir* Mischa Bakaleinikoff.

Cast: Kirby Grant (*Jeff Carter*), Patricia White (*Joan Dennis*), Lee Patrick (*Clarissa Bloomsbury*), Jay Silverheels (*Abel*), Dick Elliott (*Mr. Miggs*), Bill Wilkerson (*Chief Wolfpack*), Fred Sears (*Mr. Hanson*), Chester Clute (*Mr. Totter*), The Hoosier Hot Shots, Marion Colby, Red Enger, Billy Hill, The Shamrock Cowboys, Rod Redwing (*Baker*), Shooting Star (*Old Indian*), Gertrude Chorre (*Old Indian woman*), Kathleen O'Malley.

Western, with songs. [*Not viewed*]. At the Lazy Dollar Dude Ranch, Hoosier Hot Shots Ken, Gil, Gabe and Hezzy promise to help ranch owner Jeff Carter raise money for a neighboring tribe of Indians so that they may obtain the electric power necessary to irrigate their farms. With help from his sweetheart, Joan Dennis, Jeff plans to obtain the money by organizing an Indian Fair. To raise the $2,000 needed to pay for advertising costs, Ken, Gil and Gabe insist that Hezzy marry Clarissa Bloomsbury, a wealthy woman who wants desperately to marry Hezzy. Although Hezzy objects to the marriage, his pals ignore his concerns and propose for him. Hezzy's pals then assure him that after he borrows $2,000 from Clarissa, they will stage a fake kidnapping of him just before the wedding. Complications arise, however, when Hezzy learns that Clarissa will not come into her inheritance until after she marries. Things look bad for the Hots Shots' scheme until the Indians themselves are able to raise the necessary money and give it to Clarissa to give to Jeff. Instead of giving the $2,000 to Jeff, though, Clarissa hands it over to Hezzy, who tries to make off with it. A wild chase across the plains ensues when the Indian chief sends his tribesmen on the warpath after the Hot Shots, who have fled in an old jalopy which they cannot stop. The chase ends when the jalopy crashes into the side of a mountain. Jeff eventually receives the $2,000, and Clarissa finds happiness by marrying an old suitor. The Hot Shots celebrate by playing a concert for Jeff and Joan, who are free to resume their romance. *Fortune hunters. Indians of North America. Marriage–Forced. Musicians. Ruses. Automobile accidents. Chases. Dude ranches. Electricity. Embezzlement. Fairs. Fund-raising. Inheritance. Kidnapping. Ranchers. Romance.*

Exb 13 Oct 1948, p. 2485. *HR* 23 Apr 1948 p. 18. *HR* 30 Apr 1948 p. 14. *MPHPD* 21 Aug 1948, p. 4283.

THE SINGING BLACKSMITH (Yiddish language)
Collective Film Producers, Inc. *Dist* Yankel The Blacksmith, Inc.; New Star Films, Inc. **1938**; New York opening: week of 1 Nov 1938. Sd (Variray Blue Seal Recording); b&w. 11-12 reels, 10,320 ft. 116 min. PCA cert no. 02307. Yiddish language with English subtitles.

Exec prod Roman Rebush. *Prod supv* Ludwig Landy. *Dir* Edgar G. Ulmer. [*Director's*] *Collaborators* Ben-Zvi Baratoff and Ossip Dymow. *Asst dir* Louis Brandt and Sol Chodrow. *Titles* Charles Cooper. *Adpt* David Pinski. *Photog* William J. Miller. *Operative cam* William J. Kelley. *Film ed* Jack Kemp. *Cost* Nathan Gaiptman. *Orig mus and songs* Jacob Weinberg. *Mus dir and violin solo* Yasha Fishberg. *Rec* Edwin Schabbehar and Edward Fenton. *Makeup* Fred Ryle. [*Scr supv* Shirley Ulmer].

Source: Based on the play *Yankel der Schmid* by David Pinski (New York, 1909).

Cast: Moishe Oysher (*Yankel*), Miriam Riselle (*Tamara*), Florence Weiss (*Rivke*), Anna Appel (*Chaye-Peshe*), Ben-Zvi Baratoff (*Bendet*), Michael Goldstein (*Raffuel*), Lea Noemi (*Mariashe*), Max Vodnoy (*Simche*), Luba Wesoly (*Frumeh*), Yudel Dubinsky (*Reb Aaron*), Luba Rymer (*Sprintze-Gnesye*), B. Fishbein (*Froike*), R. Wendroff (*Elia*), Ray Schneier (*Chaika*), R. Shanock (*Leah*), Hershel Bernardi (*Young Yankel*), [Sophie Bressler (*Maid*)], [Libby Charney

(*First girl*)], [Clara Deutschmann (*Chalke*)], [Janet Deutschmann (*Second girl*)], [Riesa Halpern (*Seamstress*)].

Yiddish, Rural, Drama, with songs. [*Print viewed*]. The blacksmith Bendet's argument with his wife, Sprintze-Gnesye, is interrupted by the entrance into his shop of Simche with his son Yankel, who at nearly fifteen has lost interest in his studies. Hoping that the blacksmith will take the boy on as an apprentice, Simche agrees to Bendet's terms of three years work with no wages and the right to slap Yankel if he deserves it. After they seal the contract with a drink, Yankel promises to keep his father's wish that he grow up to be a good Jew. The years pass and Bendet, whose wife and son have died, presents Yankel with the smithy, then takes his bottle and goes on his way. Yankel lives a lustful life of singing, drinking heavily and cavorting with women. At matchmaker Chaye-Peshe's meeting place for the young, Rivke, a woman recently married to Raffuel, a sheepish man whom she met through a matchmaker, sees Yankel. When she reminds him that they once danced together at Chaika's Inn, a somewhat disreputable gathering place for travelers, they dance again, but Raffuel interrupts them and insults Yankel. The men are about to fight, when Chaye-Peshe stops them, and Yankel then goes off with another woman. Sometime later, at the dressmaker's shop, where Yankel is a frequent visitor, Rivke flirts with him, and they sing together, but Raffuel arrives and tells her to come home. When Chaye-Peshe encourages Yankel to settle down with a wife, the lothario replies, "Why eat stale bread when I can get fresh rolls." He is soon attracted to a new customer at the dressmaker's, Tamara, an orphan living with a mean aunt, who treats her worse than a servant. Seeing his interest in Tamara, Rivke tells him that Raffuel won't be coming today, but Yankel refuses her offer of company. At night, Yankel walks and sings, thinking of Tamara, and she lies in bed thinking of him. He goes to Chaye-Peshe and, despite her skepticism because of his reputation with women, convinces her to arrange a match for him with Tamara. When Tamara learns that Yankel wants to marry her, she accepts. Reb Aaron, Tamara's uncle, is not happy with the match, but Tamara stops him from insulting Yankel and says that she prefers him to the *yeshive bocher*, or student, who earlier courted her. She vows to make a man of Yankel. When they are alone, Tamara asks Yankel what made him want to marry her, and he confesses that since he met her, he has become ashamed of himself. He promises that he will become a new man and that she will be his princess. After they marry, Tamara, whose friends have deserted her because they think she married beneath her class, lets Yankel know that she is pregnant, and he is overjoyed. Meanwhile, Rivke tells Raffuel that she no longer can live with him and vows to force him to divorce her. She moves out and asks Yankel's parents if they will rent her a room. They refuse, not trusting their son, and when Rivke tauntingly says they are afraid she will lead Yankel astray, Tamara, taken aback, shows her the room. When Yankel, in defiance of his parents, agrees to give Rivke the room, his parents leave in disgust. Yankel, greatly agitated, says to Tamara that they don't really know him or her. She then asks him if he knows himself and resignedly states that people know so little of themselves. Yankel suspects Tamara is testing him by allowing Rivke to live in the house. After Tamara gives birth to a son, Rivke visits Yankel, who has had a few drinks to celebrate, in his shop. Although Yankel calls her a temptress, she seductively removes her shawl and they kiss. His parents then come and see them drunkenly dancing, and when Tamara enters, she quietly asks him to go, and Yankel leaves in shame. He wanders in despair and finds Bendet, who tells him that Tamara will understand if he says he is sorry and urges him, using himself as an example, not to break up his family and ruin his life. Rivke, meanwhile, tells Tamara about the kiss and vows to fight for Yankel. Tamara is about to leave, but Yankel interrupts them and tells Rivke to go. When Reb Aaron tries to persuade Rivke to go with Raffuel to the country, she agrees and mysteriously says she wants to go where there is a mill and a deep river. Tamara is hurt and Yankel is ashamed, but she comforts him and says that a man who feels shame is not yet lost. They kiss and then look at their son. *Blacksmiths. Jews. Manhood. Marriage. Orphans. Philanderers. Small town life. Transformation. Aunts. Childbirth. Class distinction. Dancing. Dressmakers. Drunkenness. Family relationships. Infidelity. Inns. Matchmakers. Reputation. Seduction. Separation (Marital). Temptresses. Tests of character. Uncles.*

Note: The Yiddish title of this film was *Yankel der Schmid* and its working title was *Jacob the Blacksmith*. According to *Var*, the play was "one of the

greatest works in Yiddish dramaturgy'' and ''served to give David Kessler, the late great Jewish tragedian, one of his outstanding roles.'' This was the second film of Collective Film Producers, whose film *Green Fields* was a success the previous year. *Var* notes that cast members Ben-Zvi Baratoff, Michael Goldstein and Anna Appel were members of the Yiddish Art Players. According to *NYMirror*, the film was shot near Newton, NJ in Sussex County, five miles from Camp Nordland, a Nazi camp, and close to both a nudist camp and the Shrine of the Little Flower at the Monastery of the Benedictine Order. In an interview, director Edgar G. Ulmer stated that while looking for a suitable location in which to build both a Jewish *shtetl*, or village, for this film and Ukrainian backgrounds for his film *Cossacks in Exile* (see *AFI Catalog of Feature Films, 1931-40*; F2.0820), he found some land and a lake that were ideal, which belonged to the monastery. The monk he dealt with was exceedingly cooperative and offered the use of the monastery's brothers, who had beards, for extras. Ulmer stated that he shot *Cossacks in Exile* right after this film. Although the film includes songs, no information concerning their identity has been located.

FD 14 Nov 1938, p. 6. *Forward* 12 Nov 1938. *HR* 8 Dec 1937, p. 2. *Kansas City Jewish Chronicle* 30 Dec 1938. *Morgn Fraybayt* 7 Nov 1938. *Morning Journal* 7 Nov 1938. *MPH* 17 Dec 1938, p. 54. *NYHT* 3 Nov 1938. *NYMirror* 18 Sep 1938. *NYP* 2 Nov 1938. *NYT* 3 Nov 1938, p. 27. *Var* 9 Nov 1938, p. 17.

SINGING IN THE DARK (Jewish Americans)

A.N.O. Productions, Inc. *Dist* Budsam Distributing Co. **1956**; New York opening: 7 Mar 1956; Prod: began early May 1954 at Fox Movietone Studios, NYC. Sd; b&w. 7,277 ft. 84 min.

Pres ADOLPH HOFFMAN. *Exec prod* Joey Adams. *Assoc prod* Leonard Anderson. *Dir* Max Nosseck. *Asst dir* Boris Serratore. *Dial dir* Mickey Knox. *Story* Aben Kandel. *Based on an orig idea by* Moishe Oysher and Max Nosseck. *Scr* Aben Kandel, Ann Hood and Stephen Kandel. *Dir of photog* Boris Kaufman. *Location photog* Arndt Von Rautenfeld. *Film ed* Leonard Anderson and Marc Sorkin. *Scenic des* Nikki Eastman. *Men's wardrobe* Eagle Clothes. *Gowns* Florence Lustig. *Mus dir* Abraham Ellstein. *Sd* James Gleason. *Makeup* Fred Ryle. *Asst to prod* Theodora Oysher. *Psychiatric supervision* George Kayman, M.D. *Unit mgr* Herr S. Michoeiles. *Continuity* Lee Gordon.

Song(s): by Moishe Oysher.

Cast: Moishe Oysher [(*Leo*)], Joey Adams [(*Joey Napoleon*)], Lawrence Tierney [(*Biff Lamont*)], Kay Medford [(*Luli*)], Phyllis Hill [(*Ruth*)], Mickey Knox [(*Barry*)], Al Kelly [(*Monsieur La Fontaine*)], Cindy Heller [(*Fran*)], Dave Starr [(*Larry*)], Abe Simon [(*Thug*)], Henry Sharpe [(*Dr. Neumann*)], Stan Hoffman [(*Stan*)], Paul Andor [(*Refugee*)].

Drama, with songs. [*Print viewed*]. As World War II rages, a young Jew and his mother line up for the selection process at a European concentration camp. The young man's mother is sent to her death, and he is struck on the head by a guard. After the Allies liberate the camps eight months later, the young man, now called Leo, goes to an immigration office, where another refugee from the camp tells Ruth, an American woman who works there, that Leo has no memory of his previous life, adding that the inmates named him Leo because he has the heart of a lion. Ruth befriends Leo, and on the boat to America she tells him that her uncle, Dr. Neumann, is a great psychiatrist who can help Leo recover his memory. Leo settles in Philadelphia and begins therapy with Dr. Neumann, but he remains fearful of both his past and his future. Although he and Ruth have fallen in love, Leo feels he can not ask her to marry him yet. Later, at the hotel where Leo works as a desk clerk, two gangsters show up looking for Joey Napoleon, a comedian in the hotel's nightclub. Joey tells Leo about his gambling debts and borrows some money from him. Joey's girl friend Luli, who owns the nightclub, tells him that she is putting the club up for sale because business is dead. Joey idly speculates that the kind-hearted Leo may really be a millionaire, with money stashed away in Europe, and soon convinces himself that this is true. At the club that night, Leo arrives for dinner with Ruth and Dr. Neumann just as Joey is assuring the gangsters that Leo's fortune is due to arrive any day. Reluctantly, Leo goes along with Joey's lie that he is going to lend the comic a large sum of money. Joey and the gangsters get Leo drunk, whereupon Leo launches into a musical number, revealing an operatically trained voice. No one is more surprised by this than Leo, who had no idea he could sing. The next morning, Dr. Neumann explains that the alcohol relaxed Leo's inhibitions to the point where his true self broke free. Meanwhile, Joey has started planning Leo's singing career, despite Luli's warning that Leo is a risky proposition because of his amnesia. That night, Joey pours Leo a big drink and persuades him to sign a contract making Joey his manager. Joey goes on to give a magnificent performance in the club, attracting the attention of mobster Biff

Lamont, who decides he wants a share in Leo's career. Leo becomes a huge success, but Ruth is concerned about his dependence on alcohol. Looking at Ruth, Leo at last finds his voice without being drunk and declares his love for her in song. Joey goes to see Dr. Neumann, who tells him that Leo will still be able to sing when he recovers his memory, but he will be a new person and may choose a new life. At one of their sessions, Dr. Neumann injects Leo with a narcotic to hypnotize him, then leads him through a memory of being a small boy and watching his father sing in the temple. Joey tells Biff that Leo is regaining his memory and might decide to quit singing for them, noting that the contract he had Leo sign would not stand up in court. Biff decides to hire an out-of-town thug to keep Leo in line and asks Joey to make the arrangements, stressing that there must be no connection between Biff and the enforcer. The guilt-stricken Joey is unable to betray Leo, however, and when the thug from New Jersey shows up, Joey gives him Biff's address. Later, at the club, Biff's henchmen haul Joey into Leo's dressing room and start to beat him up. Leo intervenes and one of the men breaks a bottle over Leo's head, releasing a flood of memories, including his beating by the Nazi guard. He remembers that his real name is David and that he is a cantor, like his father. Later, as Ruth puts candles in a menorah, Leo speaks of the miracle of finding himself. He quits show business and becomes a cantor again, no longer singing in the dark. Amnesia. Jews. Memory. Singers. War refugees. Cantors, Jewish. Comedians. Concentration camps. Gambling. Gangsters. Hotel clerks. Hypnotism. Immigrants. Liquor. Nightclub entertainers. Nightclub owners. Philadelphia (PA). Psychiatrists. Show business. Synagogues. World War II.

Note: The film opens with an onscreen introduction by Joey Adams in the character of ''Joey Napoleon,'' suggesting that the following story actually happened. Although Moyshe Oysher is credited onscreen with writing the songs performed in the film, no song titles were listed. A news item in *NYT* reported that *Singing in the Dark* was the first English-speaking film role for Moishe Oysher, who was a star in the Yiddish theater. Joey Adams was a successful nightclub comedian when this film was made. His wife, Cindy Heller, later changed her name to Cindy Adams and became a gossip columnist for the *New York Post*.

According to news items in *Var* and *DV*, Steve Cochran was sought for a top role in the film. Although the screen credits include a 1954 copyright statement, the film was not officially registered with the Copyright Office. According to news items, the picture was to be shot at Fox Movietone Studios in New York. Various horrific scenes of the Holocaust are shown under the credits, and while these scenes appear to be stock footage, the *NYT* review stated that filming was also done in Berlin and Hollywood.

DV 21 Apr 1954. *NYT* 7 Feb 1954. *NYT* 8 Mar 1956, p. 32. *Var* 21 Apr 1954. *Var* 14 Mar 1956, p. 22.

THE SINGING VAGABOND (Native Americans)

Republic Pictures Corp. *Dist* Republic Pictures Corp. 16 Dec **1935** [©Republic Pictures Corp.; 28 Dec 1935; LP6200]. Sd (RCA High Fidelity Sound System); b&w. 6 reels. 52 or 55 min. Passed by the National Board of Review.

[*Prod* Nat Levine]. *Supv* Armand Schaefer. *Dir* Carl Pierson. *Scr* Oliver Drake and Betty Burbridge. *Story* Oliver Drake. *Photog* William Nobles and [Ed Lyons]. *Film ed* Lester Orlebeck. *Supv film ed* Joseph H. Lewis. [*Sd* John Stransky]. *Sd eng* Terry Kellum. *Sd eff* Roy Granville.

Song(s): ''Wagon Train'' and ''Farewell, Friends of the Prairie,'' words and music by Gene Autry and Smiley Burnette; ''Honeymoon Trail'' and ''Singing Vagabond,'' words and music by Oliver Drake and Herbert Myers.

Cast: GENE AUTRY [(*Captain Tex Autry*)], Ann Rutherford [(*Lettie Morgan, also known as Mary Varden*)], Smiley Burnette [(*Frog*)], Barbara Pepper [(*Honey*)], Champion [(*Himself*)], Niles Welch [(*Judge Forsythe Lane*)], Grace Goodall [(*Hortense*)], Allan Sears [(*Utah Joe*)], Warner Richmond [(*Buck LaCrosse*)], Henry Roquemore [(*Otto*)], Frank LaRue [(*Colonel Seward*)], [Tom Brower (*Old scout*)], [Robinson Neeman (*Jerry Barton*)], [Ray Benard (*Private Hobbs*)], [Bob Burns (*Buffalo*)], [Charles King (*Red*)], [Celia McCann (*Dolly*)], [Chief Big Tree (*White Eagle*)], [Chief Thunder Cloud (*Young Deer*)], [June Thompson, Junice Thompson, Marion O'Connell, Marie Quillan, Elaine Shepherd (*Show girls*)].

Historical, Western, with songs. [*Print viewed*]. In June, 1860, at a St. Louis opera house, Jerry Barton, ''King of the Minstrels,'' performs in blackface. Backstage, he asks his sweetheart, Lettie Morgan, to elope with him that night. Lettie's bossy aunt interrupts the couple and, fearing that Jerry is a fortune hunter, tells Lettie she

is not the heiress she thought she was and has been living off her aunt's charity. After Jerry tells Lettie that an artist cannot be burdened with the responsibility of a wife, she sadly leaves the theater. Outside, Lettie bumps into a chorus girl named Honey, who is meeting her theatrical troupe, which is taking a caravan West. When the troupe's producer mistakes Lettie for the star, who is late, she joins the group as "Mary Varden." The troupe's wagon train is being escorted by Captain Tex Autry of the U.S. Cavalry and his singing plainsmen. The troupe misses the wagon train, however, and must travel solo. They reach California safely, but while en route to San Francisco, they are ambushed by a gang of thieves. Tex and his men arrive on the scene and scare off the gang with a gunfight. After Tex saves the producer and Lettie from a runaway wagon, he comments on the foolishness of his men and him risking their lives for a bunch of "crazy showgirls." His insolence angers Lettie, and she decides to walk rather than ride with Tex. Eventually tiring, Lettie asks Tex if she may ride with him, and the troupe arrives safely at Fort Henry, which is run by Colonel Seward. A friendly Indian named Young Deer warns Tex that Chief White Eagle is preparing to wage an attack on the army. When horses are stolen from the fort by a renegade named Buck LaCrosse, Tex follows to save the horses. Utah Joe, in league with White Eagle, accuses Tex of complicity with the Indians, and he is arrested for treason, a crime punishable by death. Lettie's aunt arrives with Judge Forsythe Lane, who hopes to marry Lettie and use her money to run for president. Her aunt then tells Lettie that she is not penniless and advises her to marry Lane. Lettie appeals to Lane on Tex's behalf, intimating that she will marry him if he will save Tex. As the wagon train prepares to leave, Lettie sadly says goodbye to Tex, and Lane promises to join Lettie after the trial. Lane double-crosses Lettie, however; at the trial he secures Tex's conviction by saying, "Benedict Arnold was also a distinguished soldier." After he is found guilty and sentenced to death, Tex escapes with the help of his friends, Buffalo, Idaho Kid and Frog. Suspicious that Utah Joe has promised to supply White Eagle with ammunition, Tex orders Frog to join the wagon train to spy on Utah Joe. While the caravan camps, Frog tells Lettie that Lane encouraged Tex's conviction. Honey, who has fallen in love with Frog, tells Lettie that Lane was probably jealous of Lettie's feelings for Tex, but Lettie denies loving the soldier. When Utah Joe announces plans to take a new route through Kern Valley, Frog asserts that the valley is filled with renegades and unfriendly Indians, but is rebuffed by Lane. In the night, Tex arrives and overhears Utah Joe direct White Eagle to the wagons stocked with gunpowder. Tex pulls his gun on them, and a fight ensues during which LaCrosse arrives. As Frog and Tex try to fight off the renegades, the soldiers ride up. White Eagle is shot during the scuffle, but Utah Joe escapes. LaCrosse is arrested and, under the threat of a firing squad, confesses that Utah Joe instigated the horse stealing at the fort, while he let loose the clever black stallion who opened the corral gate. LaCrosse also warns the caravan that Utah Joe is leading them into an ambush. As the caravan packs to flee, Utah Joe, now dressed as an Indian, sends a smoke signal, and the Indians encroach. Frog is grazed by a bullet and inadvertently attaches himself to the underside of the runaway powder wagon. Tex saves him and ignites the wagon, sending it, blazing, into a throng of Indians. The arrival of the plainsmen causes the Indians to retreat. As the wagon train departs, Tex and Lettie kiss, and Honey nurses Frog behind the embracing couple. *False arrests. Indians of North America. Renegades. Romantic rivalry. Theatrical troupes. United States–History–19th century. United States. Army. Cavalry. Wagon trains. Ammunition. Aunts. Betrayal. Fortune hunters. Gunfights. Gunshot wounds. Heiresses. Horse thieves. Impersonation and imposture. Jailbreaks. Judges. Marriage–Arranged. Minstrel shows. Mistaken identity. Rescues. Runaways. Show girls. Singers. St. Louis (MO). Trials.*

Note: Republic's 1935-36 season line-up as announced in the 1935 *Film Daily Product Guide* includes a Gene Autry film called *Tex Comes A-Singin'*, which may have been a working title for this film. Allan Sears was a bass opera singer prior to appearing in this film; *HR* referred to him as "Allan Sears of the sepulchral voice." According to press material in copyright records, among the North American Indian tribes represented in the film are the Apache, Black Feet, Cherokee, Choctaw, Creek, Hopi, Mission, Navajo, Nez Perce, Osage, Ojibway, Pawnee, Penobscot, Pueblo and Sioux. A modern source adds Edmund Cobb and George Letz to the cast and credits Bill Witney with the story.

DV 7 Dec 1935, p. 3. *FD* 11 Dec 1935, p. 4. *FD* 23 Jul 1936, p. 7. *HR* 7 Dec 1935, p. 3. *MPD* 11 Dec 1935, p. 7. *MPH* 7 Dec 1935, p. 29. *MPH* 14 Dec 1935, p. 62. *Var* 29 Jul 1936, p. 15.

SINS OF MAN (Austrian Americans)

Twentieth Century-Fox Film Corp.; Darryl F. Zanuck in charge of production. *Dist* Twentieth Century-Fox Film Corp. 19 Jun **1936**; New York opening: 18 Jun 1936; Prod: Mar 1936 [©Twentieth Century-Fox Film Corp.; 19 Jun 1936; LP6491]. Sd (Western Electric Noiseless Recording); b&w. 9 reels, 7,100 ft. 79 or 85 min. PCA cert no. 2153.

[*Pres* Joseph M. Schenck]. *Assoc prod* Kenneth Macgowan. *Dir* Otto Brower and Gregory Ratoff. *Asst dir* Robert Webb. *Scr* Samuel G. Engel. *Adpt* Frederick Kohner and Dr. Ossip Dymow. [*Contr to dial* Allen Rivkin]. [*Contr to scr const* Gregory Ratoff]. *Photog* Sidney Wagner. *Art dir* Hans Peters. *Settings* Thomas Little. *Film ed* Barbara McLean. [*Ed asst* Robert Fritch and Richard Billings]. *Cost* Royer. *Mus dir* Louis Silvers. *Mus score* Alexis Archangelsky. *Sd* Bernard Freericks and Roger Heman. [*Publicity dir* Harry Brand]. [*Stunt flyer* Paul Mantz].

Source: Based on the novel *Hiob, roman eines ein fachen mannes* by Joseph Roth (Berlin, 1930), translated by Dorothy Thompson as *Job* (New York, 1931).

Cast: JEAN HERSHOLT (*Christopher Freyman*), Don Ameche (*Karl Freyman/Mario Singarelli*), Allen Jenkins (*Crusty*), J. Edward Bromberg (*Anton Engel*), Ann Shoemaker (*Anna Engel*), De Witt Jennings (*Twitcheleske*), Fritz Leiber (*Father Prior*), Francis Ford (*Town drunk*), Christian Rub (*Fritz*), Adrian Rosley (*Singarelli's butler*), Gene Reynolds (*Karl Freyman, as a boy*), Mickey Rentschler (*Gabriel Freyman, as a boy*), John Miltern (*Mr. Hall*), Paul Stanton (*Minister*), Edward Van Sloan (*Austrian Army doctor*), Egon Brecher (*Doctor*), Fred Kohler, Jr. (*Town bully*), Maxine Reiner (*Bella Twitcheleske*), Ruth Robinson (*Freida Freyman*), [Paul McVey (*Army doctor*)], [Julius Tannen (*Advertising man*)], [John Marston (*Immigration officer*)], [Roland Varno (*Consul clerk*)], [Richard Powell (*Beanery man*)], [Herbert Heywood (*Stage door man*)], [Charles Tannen (*Steamship clerk*)], [Nina Campana (*Cook*)], [Ben F. Hendricks, Jack Byron, Jack Curtis, Pat West (*Bums*)], [Charles Coleman (*Doorman*)], [Ernie Alexander], [Joe Ray], [Francesca Rotoli].

Domestic, Religious, Melodrama. [*Print viewed*]. Among the Alps on the Austrian-Italian border in Tyrol in 1900, Christopher Freyman rings the church bells of Zenbruck. His wife dies after giving birth to a quiet baby boy. After a year, an Austrian Army doctor discovers that the boy, named Gabriel, has been born deaf and will never learn to speak. Anton Engel, a neighbor, suggests that Chris take Gabriel to a Catholic monastery across the border, which is known for its miracles. Although Chris goes reluctantly, being a Protestant, Father Prior tells him that Gabriel will be healed. However, ten years later, Gabriel is still deaf, although much beloved by his father and elder brother, Karl. Meanwhile, Chris and Karl quarrel bitterly over the lad's determination to be a scientist, as Chris wants Karl to follow him in his church activities. Weary of Chris's verbal abuse and provincialism, Karl abruptly leaves home. Chris decides that Karl is dead to him and burns the unopened letters from his son, who is now in America. Later, Chris notices that Gabriel can hear the high-pitched sound of a spoon hitting a glass. The local doctor says that specialists in New York and Berlin could help Gabriel, but this is too far for Chris to travel. When Chris overhears Anton and his wife Anna read a letter from Karl, in which he explains that he is working as an aeronautical engineer and asks their help in conveying to his father that he loves him and that he goes to church every week, Chris begins to communicate with his son. Sometime later, Chris announces to the townsfolk that he is leaving for New York, thanks to a ticket Karl has sent, to arrange for Gabriel to follow for treatment. Father and son are joyfully reunited, but the next day, Karl is killed on a test flight of a new airplane. Within days, World War I breaks out, and Chris is unable to return to Zenbruck, which he learns has been destroyed by bombs. Gabriel is listed as dead. Shocked, Chris walks aimlessly until he enters a church, where he hears a sermon on Job's faith in God despite tribulations. Years later, Chris works as a menial. He hears a record of a symphony of bells by Mario Singarelli and recognizes a variation on the tune he used to play on the bells at his old church. Despite his advanced age, Chris earns money for a ticket to a Singarelli concert by wearing heavy sandwich boards as advertisements. He tries unsuccessfully to see Singarelli backstage and later at the Savoy, until Singarelli learns that a man from Zenbruck has tried to see him and goes to Chris. Singarelli explains that he was

one of the few survivors of the town and that he was adopted by an Italian family. He tells Chris that he never knew his real name because he was born deaf and that the bombing restored his hearing. Realizing that Singarelli, despite his Italian accent, is actually Gabriel, Chris is reunited with his son. At the next concert, Chris plays the bells in the symphony. *Alps. Deafness. Fathers and sons. Long-lost relatives. Music. Religion. Reunions. Widowers. Accidental death. Aeronautics. Airplane accidents. Austrian Americans. Bells. Bible. Old Testament. Book of Job. Churches. Concerts. Death in childbirth. Engineers. Immigrants. Italians. Letters. Missing persons, Assumed dead. Monasteries. New York City. Physicians. Recordings. Small town life. Tyrol (Austria). World War I.*

Note: The working titles of this film were *Job* and *Turmoil*. At the conclusion, a note reads "This picture has introduced to you a new Twentieth Century-Fox screen personality Mr. Don Ameche." In reviews, Ameche was described as the "star of the 'First Nighter' radio programs" and "a semi-obscure Chicago radio actor." According to *HR*, Zanuck bought the novel for Twentieth Century-Fox for $10,000 from Gregory Ratoff, who had "treasured" it for the three years since its publication and had planned to produce it the previous winter in England. In a separate deal, according to *HR*, Ratoff was hired in an advisory capacity during preparation of the film; he subsequently became co-director. According to *NYT*, it took Jean Hersholt nearly three hours every day to put on his makeup. According to Twentieth Century-Fox publicity at the AMPAS library, stunt flyer Paul Mantz built a 1912-vintage "pusher" plane of silk and bamboo to fly and crash for the film.

Box 16 May 1936. *DV* 5 May 1936, p. 3. *FD* 12 May 1936, p. 12. *HR* 18 Sep 1935. *HR* 6 Feb 1936, p. 2. *HR* 9 Mar 1936, p. 31. *HR* 23 Mar 1936, p. 11. *HR* 5 May 1936, p. 3. *HR* 17 Oct 1936, sect. II, p. 69. *MPD* 6 May 1936, p. 14. *MPH* 18 Apr 1936, p. 45. *MPH* 16 May 1936, p. 29. *NYT* 3 May 1936. *NYT* 19 Jun 1936, p. 17. *Var* 24 Jun 1936, p. 29.

SINS OF THE CHILDREN (German Americans)

Cosmopolitan Productions. *Dist* Metro-Goldwyn-Mayer Distributing Corp. 28 Jun **1930** [©Metro-Goldwyn-Mayer Distributing Corp.; 23 Jun 1930; LP1374]. Sd and si versions (Movietone); b&w. 9 reels, 7,775 ft.

Dir Sam Wood. *Adpt* Samuel Ornitz. *Dial* Elliott Nugent and Clara Lipman. *Titles* Leslie F. Wilder. *Photog* Henry Sharp. *Art dir* Cedric Gibbons. *Film ed* Frank Sullivan and Leslie F. Wilder. *Ward* David Cox. *Rec eng* Douglas Shearer.

Source: Based on the short story "Father's Day" by J. C. Nugent and Elliott Nugent (publication undetermined).

Cast: Louis Mann (*Adolf*), Robert Montgomery (*Nick Higginson*), Elliott Nugent (*Johnnie*), Leila Hyams (*Alma*), Clara Blandick (*Martha Wagenkampf*), Mary Doran (*Laura*), Francis X. Bushman, Jr. (*Ludwig*), Robert McWade (*Joe Higginson*), Dell Henderson (*Ted Baldwin*), Henry Armetta (*Tony*), Jane Reid (*Katherine*), James Donlan (*Bide Taylor*), Jeane Wood (*Muriel Stokes*), Lee Kohlmar (*Dr. Heinrich Schmidt*).

Drama. Adolf, a German-American barber, is about to invest his savings in a building and loan association in the growing town in which he lives; instead, he sends one of his beloved children, in poor health, to a sanatorium, and his friend Joe Higginson becomes powerful in the growing community, while he remains a barber. As the children grow up, Adolf sacrifices to provide his son, Ludwig, with a medical education and later mortgages the shop to set him up in a local office. Johnnie becomes a collector for an electrical company, and his father gives up the last of his savings to cover a shortage in collections; unable to continue his employment there, Johnnie disappears. Alma falls in love with Higginson's ne'er-do-well son, Nick, who compromises her, then refuses to marry her because of their social inequality. In consequence, Adolf denounces his former friend. On Christmas Eve, having seen the mortgage foreclosed on his shop, he is reunited with all his children, including Johnnie, who finally has met success as an inventor. *Barbers and barbershops. Christmas. Family life. Fatherhood. German Americans. Physicians. Sanitariums. Self-sacrifice. Upper classes.*

Note: This film was originally released and reviewed under the title *The Richest Man in the World.*

FD 27 Jul 1930. *NYT* 26 Jun 1930, p. 16. *Var* 30 Jul 1930, p. 16.

SINS OF THE FATHERS (German Americans)

Paramount Famous Lasky Corp. 29 Dec **1928** [©Paramount Famous Lasky Corp.; 28 Dec 1928; LP25953]. Singing sequence, sd eff, and mus score (Movietone); b&w. 10 reels, 7,845 ft. [Also si; 7,724 ft.].

Dir Ludwig Berger. *Adpt and cont* E. Lloyd Sheldon. *Story* Norman Burnstine. *Titles* Julian Johnson. *Photog* Victor Milner. *Film ed* Frances Marsh. *Mus score* Hugo Riesenfeld.

Cast: Emil Jannings (*Wilhelm Spengler*), Ruth Chatterton (*Gretta*), Barry Norton (*Tom Spengler*), Jean Arthur (*Mary Spengler*), Jack

Luden (*Otto*), ZaSu Pitts (*Mother Spengler*), Matthew Betz (*Gus*), Harry Cording (*The Hijacker*), Arthur Housman (*The Count*), Frank Reicher (*The Eye Specialist*), Douglas Haig (*Tom, as a boy*), Dawn O'Day (*Mary, as a girl*).

Drama. Wilhelm Spengler, a German-American restaurateur, falls for Gretta, an unprincipled adventuress, and Wilhelm's wife, already sick from overwork, dies of a broken heart. With the advent of Prohibition, Gretta persuades Wilhelm to become a bootlegger; he amasses a fortune, sending his son, Tom, to the best schools. Upon graduation from college, Tom, who celebrates by getting drunk, goes blind drinking his father's bootleg hooch. Wilhelm is arrested in a raid, and Gretta runs off with his money and another man. His fortune gone, his son blind, and himself serving a prison term, Wilhelm's spirit is broken. He wins an early release for good behavior and becomes a waiter in a beer garden. One day he comes across his son, cured of blindness, and they are happily reunited. *Adventuresses. Beer gardens. Blindness. Bootleggers. Fatherhood. German Americans. Infidelity. Restaurateurs. Waiters.*

FD 3 Feb 1929. *NYT* 28 Jan 1929, p. 21. *Var* 30 Jan 1929, p. 26.

SIOUX BLOOD (Native Americans, Dakota)

Metro-Goldwyn-Mayer Corp.; controlled by Loew's Inc. *Dist* Metro-Goldwyn-Mayer Distributing Corp. 20 Apr **1929** [©Metro-Goldwyn-Mayer Distributing Corp.; 5 Mar 1929; LP185]. Si; b&w. 6 reels, 4,811 ft.

Dir John Waters. *Scen* George C. Hull. *Adpt* Houston Branch. *Story* Harry Sinclair Drago. *Titles* Lucille Newmark. *Photog* Arthur Reed. *Film ed* William Le Vanway. *Ward* Lucia Coulter.

Cast: Tim McCoy (*Flood*), Robert Frazer (*Lone Eagle*), Marian Douglas (*Barbara Ingram*), Clarence Geldert (*Miles Ingram*), Chief Big Tree (*Crazy Wolf*), Sidney Bracy (*Cheyenne Jones*).

Western. Two brothers are separated during an Indian uprising; one is reared by whites, the other by Indians. Years pass. One of the brothers, Flood, becomes a scout who is known as the scourge of the redskins; the other, known as Lone Eagle, becomes the meanest foe of the white man. Flood befriends Miles Ingram and his daughter, Barbara. Miles is captured by the Indians, and Barbara and Flood give themselves up to the Indians in return for the release of the elder Ingram. Flood fights with Lone Eagle, and they recognize each other. Flood, Lone Eagle, and Barbara then escape from the Indians and make their way back to freedom and the white world. *Abduction. Brothers. Dakota Indians. Scouts (Frontier).*

FD 18 Aug 1929. *Var* 22 May 1929, p. 24.

SIOUX UPRISING *see* THE GREAT SIOUX UPRISING

A SISTER OF SIX (Latino)

Fine Arts Film Co. *Dist* Triangle Film Corp. 29 Oct **1916.** Si; b&w. 5 reels.

Dir C. M. Franklin and S. A. Franklin. *Scen* Bernard McConville. *Cam* David Abel.

Cast: Ben Lewis (*Amos Winthrop*), Bessie Love (*Prudence*), George Stone (*Jonathan*), Violet Radcliffe (*Eli*), Carmen De Rue (*Priscilla*), Francis Carpenter (*Benjamin*), Beulah Burns (*Abigail*), Lloyd Pearl (*Allan*), Ralph Lewis (*Caleb Winthrop*), Frank Bennett (*Joaquin Sepulveda*), A. D. Sears (*Don Francisco Garcia*), Charles Gorman (*John Longstreet*), Charles Stephens (*Diego*), Alberta Lee (*Miss Ruth*).

Drama. A few years after the Gold Rush and following the death of Amos Winthrop, her father, Prudence leaves California as well as her sweetheart, Joaquin Sepulveda, and takes her six brothers and sisters to New England to live with her Uncle Caleb. Gold has been discovered on Caleb's land, however, so Caleb brings the family back to California to work the claim. The wealthy Don Francisco Garcia wants to add the land to his own holdings, and as a result, while Caleb and Joaquin are away, he sends his vaqueros out to capture it. Prudence and the children manage to hold off Garcia's army until the United States cavalry arrives to defeat the vaqueros, after which Joaquin and Prudence, with their fortune now assured, make plans to get married. *California–History. Cowboys. Mines. Mining claims. Uncles. Family life. Mexicans. New England. United States. Army. Cavalry.*

Note: *Var* lists the film at six reels. The working title of this film was *The Defenders*. Battle scenes in this film were shot at Sunland, CA.

Motog 21 Oct 1916, p. 937. *MPN* 23 Sep 1916, p. 1858. *MPN* 21 Oct 1916, p. 2555. *MPN* 21 Oct 1916, p. 379. *MPW* 4 Nov 1916, p. 758. *NYDM* 14 Oct 1916, p. 26. *NYT* 9 Oct 1916, p. 12. *Var* 13 Oct 1916, p. 29. *Wid's* 12 Oct 1916, p. 1031.

SITTING BULL (Native Americans, Dakota)

W. R. Frank Productions; Tele Voz de Mexico, S. A. *Dist* United Artists Corp. Oct **1954**; Prod: late Feb—late Mar 1954. Sd (Western Electric Sound System); col (Eastman Color); CinemaScope. 8,697 ft. 105 min. PCA cert no. 17128.

Pres W. R. Frank. *Assoc prod* Alfred Strauss. [*Prod* Miguel Aleman]. *Dir* Sidney Salkow. *Mexican dir* Rene Cardona. *Asst dir* Richard Dixon. *Scr* Jack DeWitt and Sidney Salkow. *Dir of photog* Charles J. Van Enger. *Mexican photog* Victor Herrera. *Spec eff* Harry Redmond, Jr. *Supv film ed* Richard L. Van Enger. *Mus* Raoul Kraushaar. *Prod supv* C. M. Florance. *Tech adv and Indian cost* Iron Eyes Cody. *Mexican prod mgr* Anthony Guerrera Tello.

Song(s): "Great Spirit," music and lyrics by Max Rich.

Cast: Dale Robertson [(*Bob Parrish*)], Mary Murphy [(*Kathy Howell*)], J. Carrol Naish [(*Sitting Bull*)], John Litel [(*General Howell*)], Iron Eyes Cody [(*Crazy Horse*)], Douglas Kennedy [(*Colonel George Armstrong Custer*)], Bill Hopper [(*Charles Wentworth*)], Joel Fluellen [(*Sam*)], John Hamilton [(*President Ulysses S. Grant*)], William Tannen [(*O'Connor*)], Tom Brown Henry [(*Webber*)], [Felix Gonzalez (*Young Buffalo*)], [Al Wyatt (*Swain*)].

Historical, Biography, Western. [*Print viewed*]. In the Black Hills of the Dakotas, Sitting Bull, leader of a large Sioux Indian tribe, watches with anger as one wagon train after another brings in white prospectors looking for gold. The prospectors are cutting through Indian territory, despite attempts by the U.S. Cavalry to divert them to the east or south. After breaking up a skirmish between the Sioux and some prospectors, Major Bob Parrish returns to his fort, where he and Colonel George Armstrong Custer argue over the role of the Cavalry in the territory. Parrish's insistence on keeping the peace with the Indians by going after the trouble-making prospectors results in his reassignment by General Howell to the Red Rock Indian Agency. Howell's daughter and Parrish's fiancée Kathy, who wants a husband with a future in the Army, decides to break off the engagement when she learns of the reassignment. When Parrish arrives at Red Rock, he is appalled at the living conditions that have been forced on the Indians, and complains to Webber, the cruel civilian agency head. Though sent to the agency to police the camp, Parrish refuses to order his men to shoot the Indians when they break out of the stockade. Webber, frustrated by the Cavalry's inaction, shoots and kills the Indian Young Buffalo. Later, cavalrymen arrive with orders to arrest Parrish, who is being sent to Washington to be court-martialed for sympathizing with the Indians and allowing the prisoners at Red Rock to escape. In Washington, Parrish meets with President Ulysses S. Grant, who demotes him to captain but assigns him to arrange a meeting with Sitting Bull. Parrish returns to the Black Hills, only to discover that Kathy is now engaged to Charles Wentworth, a war correspondent. With the help of Sam, a black runaway slave, Parrish is taken to Sitting Bull. The chief agrees to a temporary truce and a meeting with Grant, but he refuses to go to Washington, so Parrish asks the President to come to the Dakotas. Grant consents to the meeting, but before the peace treaty meeting can convene, Custer, ignoring Parrish's pleas to keep his distance, spoils the truce by provoking an Indian attack. The ensuing battle results in the death of Custer and the massacre of his regiment at Little Big Horn. Following the massacre, Parrish, determined to prevent further bloodshed, warns Sitting Bull that an Army unit is approaching, and guides the Sioux to a safe place. For his role in the evacuation, Parrish is later convicted of treason and ordered to die by firing squad. Kathy, who still loves Parrish and who has broken off her engagement to Wentworth, meets with Grant and tries unsuccessfully to prevent Parrish's execution. With only a short time to spare before Parrish's set execution, Kathy, realizing that the only testimony that can save her sweetheart is that of Sitting Bull, finds the chief and brings him to the execution site. After convincing Grant of Parrish's patriotism and preventing the captain's execution, Sitting Bull returns to his people, hopeful that now peace will prevail. *Dakota Indians. Prospectors. Sitting Bull. Tribal chiefs. United States. Army. Cavalry. African Americans. Battles. Black Hills (SD and WY). Burial. Courts-martial and courts of inquiry. General George Armstrong Custer. Engagements. Escapes. Gold. Ulysses Simpson Grant. Indian agents. Knife fighting. Little Big Horn, Battle of the, 1876. Massacres. Officers (Military). Prisoners. Reporters. Slaves. Treason.*

Note: An Apr 1953 *DV* news item noted that the film's title role was originally set for Boris Karloff, and that Dennis Morgan was to co-star. The majority of this picture was filmed in Mexico, with Mexicans playing many of the Indian roles. Although *HR* production charts include Bill Cannon in the cast, his participation in the completed film has not been determined.

As depicted in the film, Sitting Bull became the leader of the Teton Sioux after they had agreed to reside on a large reservation in the Black Hills. Also known as a mystic, Sitting Bull refused government orders to gather on the reservation in response to tensions created by the influx of white prospectors, who flocked to the area after gold was discovered in 1874. In the spring of 1876, the U.S. Army sent troops to the area, and Sitting Bull rallied members of various Sioux tribes to resist their presence. During the Battle of the Little Big Horn, he stayed in camp, fasting and praying. Following the Army's retaliation for Col. George Armstrong Custer's overwhelming defeat, Sitting Bull retreated to Canada, but eventually was forced south and surrendered on 19 Jul 1881. He was confined to the reservation, but in 1885, he toured briefly with Buffalo Bill's Wild West Show. With the emergence of the Ghost Dance in 1890, Indian agent James McLaughlin feared that Sitting Bull would re-emerge as a leader, and the Indian police were sent to arrest him. Sitting Bull was shot dead during the ensuing struggle.

Letters contained in the MPAA/PCA Collection at the AMPAS Library indicate that, just prior to the start of production, an effort was made by representatives of the Sioux tribe to pressure W. R. Frank Productions into filming the picture in Sitting Bull's native land. One letter contained a formal resolution calling the decision to film the picture in Mexico an action "not befitting our great Sioux Chief," and pointed out that the Sioux people in the Dakotas "desire an opportunity to take part in making a picture of his life." According to news items and the *Var* review, *Sitting Bull* was the first independently produced picture to be filmed in CinemaScope. For more information about the life of George Armstrong Custer and the Battle of the Little Big Horn, see entry below for *They Died with Their Boots On.*

Box 18 Sep 1954. *DV* 6 Apr 1953. *DV* 8 Sep 1954, p. 6. *FD* 8 Sep 1954, p. 6. *HR* 26 Feb 1954, p. 10. *HR* 26 Mar 1954, p. 10. *HR* 8 Sep 1954, p. 3. *MPHPD* 11 Sep 1954, p. 137. *NYT* 26 Nov 1954, p. 24. *Var* 15 Sep 1954, p. 6.

SITTING BULL AT THE "SPIRIT LAKE MASSACRE" *see* **WITH SITTING BULL AT THE SPIRIT LAKE MASSACRE**

SITTING BULL—THE HOSTILE SIOUX INDIAN CHIEF (Native Americans, Dakota)

American Rotograph Co. Jan **1914**? [©American Rotograph Co.; 23 Jan 1914; LU2018]. Si; b&w. 5 reels.

Drama. Settler Frank Randall and his family leave their home in the Black Hills of Montana in a covered wagon. They are attacked by Chief Crazy Horse and a band of Indians, but escape with the aid of Caribou, an Indian Scout. Six years later, the family is again besieged by Indians but are aided by Lieutenant Scott who is engaged to young Ruth Randall. After a tragic turn of events, many of the family members are killed and their cabin, only a few miles from the site of Sitting Bull's camp, is destroyed. Only Ruth and her younger sister Bess survive when they are rescued by Scott. *Chief Crazy Horse. Dakota Indians. Indians of North America. Massacres. Rescues. Settlers. Soldiers.* Black Hills (SD and WY). Covered wagons. Montana. Sitting Bull.

Note: No additional information about the production or release date of this film is known. Certain elements of the plot, particularly the involvement of Sitting Bull's daughter Wanda, are obscured due to a deterioration of the plot synopsis in the copyright files. The American Rotograph Co. was located in Syracuse, NY.

SIX GUNS AND A GAVEL *see* **RAIDERS OF OLD CALIFORNIA**

16 FATHOMS DEEP (Greek Americans)

Monogram Pictures Corp.; An Arthur Lake Production. *Dist* Monogram Pictures Corp. 25 Jul **1948**; Prod: late Oct—mid-Nov 1947 [©Monogram Pictures Corp.; 25 Jul 1948; LP1842]. Sd (RCA Sound System); Col (Ansco Color). 7,059 ft. 78 min. PCA cert no. 12946.

Prod James S. Burkett and Irving Allen. *Dir* Irving Allen. *Asst dir* Charles S. Gould. *Scr* Max Trell. *Adpt* Forrest Judd. *Photog* Jack Greenhalgh. [*Cam op* Paul Burress]. [*Stills* Charles O'Rourke]. *Spec eff* Ray Mercer. *Col dir* M. Peter Keane. *Film ed* Charles Craft. *Mus dir* Lud Gluskin. *Mus* Lucien Maroweck and Rene Garriguene. *Rec* Josh Westmoreland. *Prod mgr* Belmont S. Gottlieb. [*Scr supv* Mary Gibson]. [*Grip* Grant Tucker]. [*Stand-in* John Gonatos].

Source: Based on the short story "Sixteen Fathoms Under" by Eustace L. Adams in *American Magazine* (Nov 1932).

Cast: Lon Chaney [(*Dimitri*)], Arthur Lake [(*Pete*)], Lloyd Bridges [(*Lloyd Douglas*)], Eric Feldary [(*Alex*)], Tanis Chandler [(*Simi*)], John Qualen [(*Athos*)], Ian MacDonald [(*Nick*)], Dickie Moore [(*George*)], Harry Cheshire [(*Mike*)], John Bleifer [(*Captain Briacos*)], [Grant Means (*Joe*)], [John Gonatos (*Johnny*)], [Allen Mathews (*Bus driver*)].

Sea, Adventure. [*Print viewed*]. Deep sea diver Lloyd Douglas, formerly of the U.S. Navy, arrives in Tarpon Springs, Florida, looking for work on the sponge boats that have been run by generations of

Greek-Americans, whose families came to the rich Gulf of Mexico when the beds in the Mediterranean became depleted. Lloyd is sent to see Dimitri, owner of the sponge exchange at which catches are auctioned and backer of many boats, but Dimitri turns him down. When a father and son team, Athos and George, return to port empty handed and face losing their boat to Dimitri, Alex, an ambitious diver on one of the most successful boats, makes a deal with Dimitri to take over Athos' boat, against the advice of his girl friend Simi, who works for Dimitri and knows how he operates. Alex then hires Lloyd, along with divers Johnny and Nick, and gives jobs to Athos, George and Pete, a photographer, who is hired to cook. The day before the fleet is to sail, the waters and men are blessed by an archbishop. The next day, Alex's boat sets off for a month's voyage. He has a hunch that he can find sponges in certain areas at a depth of fifteen to sixteen fathoms. However, many days pass without the crew finding any sponge beds, and Alex is pressured to return to port for the next auction or risk losing his investment to Dimitri. Eventually, Alex locates a perfect spot and the crew gathers many sponges. When Lloyd goes down in the diving suit, Nick, who has been paid by Dimitri to sabotage the voyage, cuts away the wire guards around the boat's propeller in a futile attempt to cut Lloyd's air line. When Alex orders Nick to go down next, he refuses and Alex slugs him. Athos goes instead, and his air line becomes entangled with the propeller at the same time as the other end is wedged between some rocks. He loses his air supply and George dives in, without a diving suit, to rescue his father, but his leg becomes trapped by a giant clam. Alex manages to get Athos to the surface and to free George, but discovers George has drowned. Nick confesses that he is responsible and, although Athos is very distraught, he insists that Alex continue to work so that Dimitri cannot take over the boat. Athos returns with George's body to Tarpon Springs and accuses Dimitri of killing his son and of attempting to kill Alex. Dimitri tries to pin the blame on Alex and sends several henchmen in a speed boat to bust up Alex's boat. However, Alex, Lloyd and the others fight them off. Nick is killed in the fight, and Alex sends Pete in the speed boat to slow up the auction until his boat can return to harbor. On shore, Lloyd, Athos and Alex go after Dimitri and, while many from the various boats watch, Alex and Dimitri fight. Dimitri wins and runs off, but is pursued by Johnny. During their fight, Johnny knocks Dimitri down and he falls, fatally impaling himself on a sponge-gathering hook. Alex, Lloyd and the crew leave port once again. *Divers and diving. Florida. Greek Americans. Sabotage. Sponges. Auctions. Boats. Buses. Clams. Drowning. Entrepreneurs. Fathers and sons. Fights. Photographers. Rescues. Rites and ceremonies. Ship crews. Treachery.*

Note: The opening titles state that "All scenes in this motion picture were filmed in Tarpon Springs, Florida. The underwater sequences were filmed in Rainbow Springs, Florida and Marineland Studios, St. Augustine, Florida." This was the first American feature film to be shot using the Ansco Color process. According to a *HR* news item, John Gonatos, who plays Johnny in the film, was a "world-renowned sponge diver." Another version of Eustace Adams' story was released in 1934 (see *AFI Catalog of Feature Films, 1931-40*; F3.4116). In that film, Lon Chaney (who then acted under his real name, Creighton Chaney), also played the lead.

Box 12 Jun 1948. *DV* 7 Jun 1948, p. 3. *FD* 11 Jun 1948, p. 12. *HR* 15 Sep 1947, p. 1. *HR* 7 Jun 1948, p. 3, 11. *HR* 11 Oct 1948, p. 10. *LAT* 5 Aug 1948. *MPHPD* 8 May 1948, p. 4155. *MPHPD* 12 Jun 1948, p. 4197. *MPHPD* 28 Aug 1948, p. 4290. *NYT* 7 Oct 1948, p. 35. *Var* 9 Jun 1948, p. 12.

THE SKY DRAGON (Chinese Americans)

Monogram Pictures Corp. *Dist* Monogram Pictures Corp. **1949**; Prod: Dec 1948 [©Monogram Pictures Corp.; 1 May 1949; LP2407]. Sd (Western Electric Recording); b&w. 63-64 min. PCA cert no. 13645.

Series: Charlie Chan.

Prod James S. Burkett. *Dir* Lesley Selander. *Asst dir* Wesley Barry and [Ed Morey, Jr.]. *Scr* Oliver Drake and Clint Johnston. *Story* Clint Johnston. *Photog* William Sickner. [*Cam op* John Martin]. [*Gaffer* Bob Campbell]. [*Stills* Bud Graybill]. *Spec eff* Roy Mercer. *Tech dir* David Milton. *Film ed* Roy Livingston and [Ace Herman]. [*Set dec* Raymond Boltz, Jr.]. *Mus dir* Edward J. Kay. *Rec* Tom Lambert and [John Kean]. [*Makeup* Webb Overlander]. [*Hair stylist* Lela Chambers]. *Prod mgr* Allen K. Wood. [*Scr supv* Ilona Vas]. [*Grip* Harry Lewis].

Source: Based on characters created by Earl Derr Biggers.

Cast: Roland Winters (*Charlie Chan*), Keye Luke [(*Lee Chan*)], Mantan Moreland [(*Birmingham Brown*)], Noel Neill [(*Jane Marshall*)], Tim Ryan [(*Lt. Mike Ruark*)], Iris Adrian [(*Wanda LaFern*)], Elena Verdugo [(*Marie Burke, also known as Connie Barrett*)], Milburn Stone [(*Tim Norton*)], Lyle Talbot [(*Andy Barrett*)], Paul Maxey [(*John Anderson*)], Joel Marston [(*Don Blake*)], John Eldredge [(*William E. French*)], Eddie Parks [(*Jonathan*

Tibbetts)], Louise Franklin [(*Lena Franklin*)], [Lyle Latell (*Ed Davidson*)], [Gaylord Pendleton (*Ben Edwards*)], [Emmett Vogan (*Doctor*)], [Edna Holland (*Old maid*)], [Joe Whitehead (*Doorman*)], [Lee Phelps (*Plainclothesman*)], [Charlie Jordon (*Assistant stage manager*)], [Suzette Harbin (*Strange girl*)], [George Eldredge (*Stacey*)], [Bob Curtis (*Watkins*)], Frank Cady.

Detective, Drama. [*Print viewed*]. Inside the cockpit of a commercial jetliner, pilots Tim Norton and Don Blake talk with insurance couriers Ben Edwards and Ed Davidson, who are carrying a $250,000 settlement. Tim walks to the back of the cabin for some coffee, just as flight attendant Marie Burke begins serving the passengers. Marie, a former racketeer whose real name is Connie Barrett, notices that two of her accomplices, Andy Barrett and follies star Wanda LaFern, are among the passengers. When they accuse her of stealing $60,000 from them, Marie denies it and begs them not to ruin her chance at a new life. Minutes after drinking the coffee, everyone on board the plane falls asleep, including the crew. Passenger Lee Chan, the first to awaken, notices a limp hand protruding from the cockpit door, then discovers that Davidson has been knifed to death and the insurance money stolen. After Lee's father, Charlie Chan, the renowned detective, is awakened, passenger John Anderson introduces himself as an investigator for the insurance company. When the plane lands in San Francisco, police lieutenant Mike Ruark and the owner of the insurance company, William E. French, question the passengers and crew. Later, at the theater where Wanda performs, Tim and Don eavesdrop as Wanda accuses Marie of stealing the insurance money. Meanwhile, Chan, Lee, Ruark and Chan's chauffeur Birmingham Brown go to the theater, where they find Don, whose skull has been fractured. When Ruark sees Tim running away, he arrests him, while Don is rushed to the hospital. After being questioned by Chan, Barrett breaks into the detective's house, but is shot by Anderson, who had been following him. Later, Chan and Lee go to the home of Jonathan Tibbetts, the justice of the peace who officiated at the Barretts' wedding. They ask to see the negatives of the wedding photos, but when Tibbetts goes into the garage to get them, a shadowy figure knocks him out, then lights the negatives on fire. After Chan and Lee rescue Tibbetts, he checks his order book and notes that he sent prints to the LaFern sisters, Connie and Wanda. Later, Chan and Lee find a photograph of the LaFern sisters in the newspaper and recognize Connie as Marie. With Ruark's help, Chan summons all of the remaining suspects back onto the plane. Chan then asks Connie, Wanda and Tim to take their places next to the coffee cart, where they had been standing just prior to the robbery. After Chan tells them about Don's attack, a heavily bandaged Lee impersonates Don and boards the plane. As he raises his arm to point toward the thief, Connie grabs a gun from her purse. Before Connie can fire, however, Anderson shoots her, then Chan reveals that Anderson passed the money to French, his accomplice, after the plane landed. When Ruark tries to arrest them, French also draws his gun. Anderson, an experienced pilot, locks the cabin door and takes off. With the plane's sole parachute on his back, Anderson shuts off the plane's fuel and locks the cockpit door. Realizing that he has been double-crossed, French struggles with Anderson, but both are grabbed by the police. After the cockpit key is found and fuel restored to the engines, the plane lands safely. *Airplanes. Chinese Americans. Murder. Stewardesses. Thieves. African Americans. Air pilots. Arrests. Betrayal. Chauffeurs. Coffee. Eavesdropping. Fathers and sons. Garages. Impersonation and imposture. Insurance–Investigators. Justices of the peace. Keys. Money. Photographs. Police. Racketeers. Shootings. Sisters. Sleeping potions. Theaters.*

Note: The working title of this film was *Murder in the Air*. The film's title card reads: "Charlie Chan in *The Sky Dragon*." Although Roy Livingston is credited onscreen as editor, *HR* production charts credit Ace Herman as editor. For additional information on the "Charlie Chan" series, please consult the Series Index and see the entry above for *Charlie Chan Carries On*.

Box 23 Jul 1949. *DV* 28 Apr 1949, p. 3. *HR* 10 Dec 1948, p. 14. *HR* 24 Dec 1948, p. 12. *HR* 28 Apr 1949, p. 3. *MPHPD* 7 May 1949, p. 4598. *Var* 4 May 1949, p. 11.

SKY HIGH (Chinese Americans)

Fox Film Corp. *Dist* Fox Film Corp. 22 Jan **1922** [©William Fox; 15 Jan 1922; LP17480]. Si; b&w. 5 reels, 4,546 ft.

Pres William Fox. *Dir* Lynn Reynolds. *Asst dir* George Webster. *Story and scen* Lynn Reynolds. *Photog* Ben Kline.

Cast: Tom Mix (*Grant Newburg*), J. Farrell MacDonald (*Jim Halloway*), Eva Novak (*Estelle, his daughter*), Sid Jordan (*Bates*), William Buckley (*Victor Castle*), Adele Warner (*Marguerite*), Wynn Mace (*Patterson*), Pat Chrisman (*Pasquale*).

Western. Grant Newburg, an immigration officer, is dispatched to uncover the men behind the smuggling of Chinese across the Mexican border. While Newburg is scouting, he comes upon Estelle, a stranger who has lost her companions in the canyon; he sets up a camp and steals some food for her, but he is captured and bound by Bates, the leader of the smugglers, who knows of his mission. With the aid of Estelle he escapes and returns with assistance; meanwhile, Bates threatens her, unaware that she is the ward of Halloway, his employer. Newburg returns in an airplane, leaps into a stream, and swims to the place where Estelle is being held captive. Estelle is rescued; and though her guardian is arrested for smuggling, Newburg agrees to care for her until his term is served. *Airplanes. Chinese Americans. Mexican-American border region. Smuggling. United States. Dept. of Immigration. Wards and guardians.*

FD 18 Dec 1921. *MPW* 31 Dec 1921, p. 1126. *MPW* 7 Jan 1922, p. 108. *Var* 27 Jan 1922, p. 40.

SKY LINE (Fox Film Corp., 1931, David Butler) *see* **DELICIOUS**

SKYFIRE *see* **BLAZING ARROWS**

SKYLINE (Fox Film Corp., 1931, David Butler) *see* **DELICIOUS**

SKYLINE (Irish Americans)
Fox Film Corp.; Sam Taylor Production. *Dist* Fox Film Corp. 11 Oct **1931**; New York opening: week of 3 Oct 1931; Prod: 1 Jun—mid-Jun 1931 [©Fox Film Corp.; 20 Aug 1931; LP2456]. Sd (Western Electric System); b&w. 7 reels, 6,279 ft. 57 or 70 min. Passed by the National Board of Review. PCA cert no. 1285-R [22 Aug 1935].
Assoc prod John W. Considine, Jr. *Dir* Sam Taylor. [*Asst dir* Walter Mayo]. *Scr and dial* Kenyon Nicholson and Dudley Nichols. *Addl dial* Wm. Anthony McGuire. [*Contr wrt* Jack O'Donnell, Thomas Meighan and Herbert Ashton]. *Photog* John Mescall. *Art dir* Duncan Cramer. [*Film ed* Harold Schuster]. [*Cost* Dolly Tree]. *Mus score* George Lipschultz. *Sd rec* W. W. Lindsay, Jr. [*Bus mgr* O. O. Dull].
Source: Based on the novel *East Side, West Side* by Felix Riesenberg (New York, 1927).
Cast: Thomas Meighan [(*Gordon A. McClellan*)], Hardie Albright [(*John Breen*)], Maureen O'Sullivan [(*Kathleen Kearny*)], Myrna Loy [(*Paula Lambert*)], Stanley Fields [(*Captain Breen*)], Jack Kennedy [(*Mike Kearny*)], Robert McWade [(*Judge Scott*)], [Donald Dillaway (*Gerry Gaige*)], [Alice Ward (*Mrs. Kearny*)], [Dorothy Peterson (*Rose Breen*)], [Minna Gombell].
Drama. [*Print viewed*]. Rose Breen, lying sick in bed aboard her husband's barge in the East River, tells her son John that her husband, the abusive, drunken captain of the barge, is not his father. After Rose dies, John fights the captain when he insults the memory of his mother. After knocking him cold, John, who wants to build skyscrapers like those he sees from the water, swims to shore. He falls into the back of a truck, which dumps him onto a street, and then wanders until he comes to a construction site, where he faints and falls into a hole. He is about to be lifted up in a back hoe, when the hoe's operator, Mike Kearny, spots him and brings him to consciousness. Learning that John is Irish like himself and that he wants to work on a skyscraper, Kearny brings John home, where he becomes friends with Kearny's daughter Kathleen. When Kearny's boss, engineer Gordon A. McClellan, inspects the fortieth floor of a building under construction, John bribes a messenger to let him bring some plans up to McClellan. Not used to the height, John starts to faint. McClellan catches him, but they both fall on some boards below. McClellan berates John and orders him to leave, but John later convinces McClellan of his desire to work. After he hires John as a laborer on the ground, McClellan grows to like him. When Judge Scott declines McClellan's invitation to watch the fights, McClellan asks John, who is extremely delighted. John soon begins night school at an engineering college. When he tells "Mac," as he now calls McClellan, about his past and shows him his mother's locket, Mac, who was Rose's first husband, realizes he is John's father, but he refrains from admitting it when he sees how angry John gets when he talks about the father he never knew. John, who had planned to marry Kathleen after he finished school, becomes infatuated with Paula Lambert, whom he does not know is Mac's ex-lover. Mac lends John money to go to Columbia University's School of Engineering in the fall. When John tells Kathleen that he plans to move into Mac's Park Avenue apartment, Kathleen becomes upset. Upon learning of John's love for Paula, Mac tries to tell him that she isn't right for him, but John

ignores Mac's advice. After Mac insults her, Paula, who still loves Mac, threatens to take John away from Kathleen. Judge Scott then suggests to Mac that he take Paula away from John to save him from her. After buying an engagement ring for Paula, John finds Mac in her room. Hurt and angry, he vows not to trust anyone again and makes plans to leave town. Mac then confesses to being John's father. John demands that he leave him, and when Mac refuses, John hits him. Judge Scott mollifies John and tells him that Mac lost track of his wife after his father died and he had to leave her; he made every effort to find her, and has not really loved anyone else since. Feeling guilty about the way he acted, John goes to the construction site, but learns that Mac has fallen from the third floor. When Mac revives, John is there. He asks forgiveness and calls him "Dad," which Mac appreciates. Later, Mac listens over the radio to the ceremony honoring the opening of the skyscraper. His firm is now called McClellan and Son, and Kathleen, who is with him, calls him "Dad." *Ambition. Construction workers. Engineers–Civil. Fathers and sons. Long-lost relatives. Lure of the city. New York City. Parentage. Skyscrapers. Alcoholics. Barges. Battered women. Falls from heights. Fights. Infatuation. Irish Americans. Judges. Mothers and sons. Phobias. Students.*

Note: Although the screen credits state that the film was based on Felix Riesenberg's novel, it may also have been based on a 1927 play derived from the novel written by Riesenberg and Fay Pulsifer, as the file for the film in the Twentieth Century-Fox Produced Scripts Collection at the UCLA Theater Arts Library includes a copy of the play. The working title of the film was *East Side West Side*. The "dialogue taken from the screen" dated 20 Aug 1931 in the Produced Scripts Collection contains a different ending than the one in the viewed print; in the first ending, McClellan dies from his injuries, and after Judge Scott dedicates the skyscraper as a monument to McClellan, John tells Kathleen that he could not have stood losing his father if he had not found her. According to a May 1931 pre-production news item in *FD*, J. M. Kerrigan, William Holden (d. 1932) and Kendall McComas were to have featured parts, but their participation in the final film has not been confirmed. *Skyline* was the working title of both *Delicious* (see above) and *Quick Millions* (see *AFI Catalog of Feature Films, 1931-40*; F3.3583) two other Fox releases of 1931.

FD 22 May 1931, p. 8. *FD* 11 Oct 1931, p. 10. *HF* 11 Jul 1931, p. 20. *MPH* 24 Jan 1931, p. 44. *MPH* 22 Aug 1931. *NYT* 5 Oct 1931, p. 17. *Var* 6 Oct 1931, p. 29.

THE SLACKER (German Americans, Multi-ethnic)
Metro Pictures Corp. *Dist* Metro Pictures Corp. 16 Jul **1917** [©Metro Pictures Corp.; 10 Jul 1917; LP11071]. Si; b&w. 6-7 reels.
Dir William Christy Cabanne. *Scen* William Christy Cabanne. *Cam* William E. Fildew. *Tech dir* William H. Stevens. *Film ed* Mildred Richter.
Cast: Emily Stevens (*Margaret Christy*), Walter Miller (*Robert Wallace*), Leo Delaney (*John Harding*), Daniel Jarrett (*Henry Wallace*), Eugene Borden (*George Wallace*), Millicent Fisher (*Virginia Lambert*), Sue Balfour (*Mrs. Christy*), Mathilde Brundage (*Mrs. McAllister*), Baby Ivy Ward (*Child with flag*), Charles Fang (*Valet*), Belle Bruce, Dorothy Hydell, W. E. Lawrence, Jr. G. P. Hamilton, Evelyn Converse.
War preparedness, Drama. Robert Wallace, the elder son of a rich and indulgent father, marries Margaret Christy, a spirited patriot, so that he can escape the call to war. Discovering the reason for Robert's haste to get married, Margaret is appalled and resolves to bring home to her husband a sense of his personal responsibility. In order to instill patriotism in Robert, Margaret contrasts him with John Harding, the man who gave her up to go to war. When Robert protests his wife's tactics, Margaret accuses him of being a contemptible coward. The next day a German insults the American flag, and Robert, his sense of justice aroused, makes him salute it. He then bids Margaret farewell and marches off to war. Margaret sees him off without divulging the secret that she is pregnant, thus sacrificing her own welfare for that of her country. *Cowardice. Moral reformation. Patriotism. Self-sacrifice. Slackers. World War I. Flags. Germans. Pregnancy.*

Note: This film, highly praised by the Army, was used to stimulate recruiting efforts. According to a contemporary news item, John M. Mallace, a young Chicago man, was so impressed by the film that he enlisted in the Army after viewing it. Included in the news report was a reprint of a letter that Mallace wrote to Metro thanking them for making the inspirational film. According to the 1918 *MPSD*, Ben Lyon played the juvenile lead in this film, however, no information concerning his participation in the film was found in reviews, news items or the copyright descriptions. *Var* commented, "Now that drafting has become a reality and many young Americans are drawn but are sure to claim exemptions, they won't feel so sure of the exemption plea after they have seen *The Slacker.*" *MPW* noted, "A representative from every race is shown on the screen, and then the heads of all, grouped together, dissolve into the fabric of an immense Unites States flag, the true 'melting-pot' of the nations."

ETR 4 Aug 1917, p. 715. ETR 18 Aug 1917, p. 852. MPN 11 Aug 1917, p. 979, 1020, 1170. MPW 11 Aug 1917, p. 956. MPW 18 Aug 1917, p. 1118. NYDM 4 Aug 1917, p. 19. Var 3 Aug 1917, p. 25. Wid's 23 Aug 1917, p. 537.

THE SLACKER (African Americans)
Peter P. Jones Film Co. 1917. Si; b&w. 5 reels.
World War I, African American, Drama. A young African American, who evades military service during World War I proves himself to be a hero thanks to the inspiration of his sweetheart, a Red Cross nurse. The film includes a scene in which an old veteran of two previous wars appears in a vision. [No other information concerning the plot of this film is available.]. *African Americans. Heroism. Nurses. Slackers. World War I. Veterans. Visions.*
Note: This film is probably the second all-black feature made by a black production company. It may have been exhibited infrequently.
ChiDef 16 Jun 1917.

SLAUGHTER TRAIL (Native Americans, Navajo)
Justal Productions, Inc. *Dist* RKO Radio Pictures, Inc. Oct **1951**; Los Angeles opening: 11 Oct 1951.; Prod: late-Jan—mid Feb 1951 at Motion Picture Center Studios. Retakes 1 Jun—7 Jun 1951 at Corriganville Ranch and Motion Picture Center Studios. [©RKO Radio Pictures, Inc.; 10 Oct 1951; LP1421]. Sd (RCA Sound System); col (Cinecolor). 7,016 ft. 78 min. PCA cert no. 15273.
Prod Irving Allen. *Dir* Irving Allen. *Asst dir* Jack Berne and Cy Roth. [*Asst dir on retakes* George Loper]. *Scr* Sid Kuller. [*Contr wrt* Oliver Crawford]. *Dir of photog* Jack Greenhalgh. *Spec eff* Howard Anderson. *Color consultant* Wilton R. Holm and Clifford D. Shank. *Art dir* George Van Marter. *Film ed* Fred Allen. *Mus dir* Darrell Calker. [*Dance dir* Val Raset]. *Sd* Ben Winkler. *Makeup artist* David Newell. *Prod mgr* Harold Knox. [*Welfare worker* Rose Carter]. [*Stunts* Cliff Lyons]. [*Stand-in* June Davies, Jimmy Dase and Fred Vleck].
Song(s): "Hoofbeat Serenade" and "Ballad Bandelier," words and music by Lynn Murray and Sid Kuller; "The Girl in the Wood," words and music by Terry Gilkyson and Neal Stuart; "Everyone's Crazy 'Ceptin Me," words and music by Terry Gilkyson and Sid Kuller; "Jittery Deer-Foot Dan," words and music by Terry Gilkyson; "I Wish I Was a Mole in the Ground," traditional.
Cast: Brian Donlevy [(*Capt. Dempster*)], Gig Young [(*Vaughn*)], Virginia Grey [(*Lorabelle Larkin*)], Andy Devine [(*Sgt. McIntosh*)], Robert Hutton [(*Lt. Morgan*)], Terry Gilkyson [(*Singalong*)], [Lew Bedell (*Hardsaddle*)], [Myron Healey (*Heath*)], [Ken Koutnik (*Levering*)], [Eddie Parks (*Rufus Black, drummer*)], [Ralph Peters (*Matt McGroot, stagecoach driver*)], [Ric Roman (*Chief Paako*)], [Lois Hall (*Susan Wilson*)], [Robin Fletcher (*Nancy Dempster*)], [Ralph Volkie (*Sentry*)], [Fenton Jones (*Dance caller*)], [Emmett Lynn (*Old timer*)], [Frank McGrath (*Jamora, Indian scout*)], [Jody Gilbert (*Fat lady*)], [Chuck Hayward (*Wounded Indian*)], [Don Frost (*Corporal*)], [Miles Shepard (*Orderly*)], [Sherry Atkins, Joanne Franklin, Gene François, Eric Neilson, Richie Kuller (*Children*)], [Sid Brokaw, Rudolph Friml, Jr., William Wright, Earl Colbert, Eugene Englund (*Musicians*)], [Jimmy Ames, Earl Hodgins (*Poker players*)], Dorinda Clifton.
Western, with songs. [*Print viewed*]. In 1882, a stagecoach bound for San Francisco, carrying U.S. mail down the "Slaughter Trail" through New Mexico, is held up by three masked bandits who kill the guard. Vaughn, the bandits' leader, takes jewels from a package in the mail sack and hands them to his accomplice, Lorabelle, who has been posing as a passenger, for safekeeping. During their escape, Vaughn, Heath and Levering steal fresh horses from Navajo Indians whom they kill, save for one who escapes, wounded. When the stage arrives at Fort Marcy, Captain Dempster, the commanding officer, informs Lorabelle that he is delaying the stage's onward journey until the guard can be replaced. Dempster, suspecting that the Vaughn gang may be responsible for the holdup, assigns Lt. Morgan to bring them in. Lorabelle persuades Dempster to allow the stage to proceed by telling him that her grandmother is dying in San Francisco. Meanwhile, the wounded Navajo reports the attack to Chief Paako, who declares war and attacks the stagecoach. However, Morgan and his troop come to the rescue and all return to the fort. Dempster is surprised by the Indians' attack as he and Paako have been friends for a long time. In an attempt to get away from the fort, Lorabelle strikes up a friendship with Dempster's young daughter Nancy. Morgan and Dempster ride out to meet Paako, who tells them that white men have killed his brothers, that their treaty has been broken and that he will seek revenge. When Dempster promises

Paako that he will catch the culprits, Paako allows him two days to do so. In the meantime, Vaughn returns to the fort to rescue Lorabelle, posing as a cattleman. Dempster informs him that all civilians are confined to the fort due to the uprising. After Vaughn tells Lorabelle that they will sneak away at night, Lorabelle apologizes to Dempster for her behavior, and he thanks her for her kindness to his daughter whose mother was killed during the last Navajo war. Dempster tells Lorabelle that he can only appease Paako by handing over the three outlaws, but that he could not do that even if they were proven guilty by a federal court. At the regular Saturday night social, a travelling companion of Lorabelle recognizes Vaughn's laugh from the stagecoach robbery and informs Dempster. As Lorabelle participates in a vigorous square dance, the small bag of jewels fall out of her dress. Vaughn takes it and, at gunpoint, makes Nancy his hostage and orders the fort gates to be opened. Lorabelle, however, refuses to go with him. Vaughn escapes, dropping Nancy off outside the fort, and meets up with Heath and Levering. However, they are seen by the Indian they wounded, and Paako attacks, forcing them to return to the fort where they are arrested. Paako comes to the fort under a flag of truce and demands that Dempster hand over Vaughn and his men within a few minutes. Dempster sends an Indian scout to another fort for reinforcements, but the scout is killed by the Navajo. Dempster then has three volunteer soldiers, along with the Vaughn gang, go outside the fort to create a perimeter of defense. When the Navajo attack, Lorabelle helps to defend the children inside the fort. The Navajo kill Vaughn and his men and call off the attack. Lorabelle walks back into her cell and refuses to come out. When Dempster visits her, he finds Nancy there, and she asks her father not to send Lorabelle away. Dempster tells Lorabelle that she is free to go, and although an amorous feeling has developed between them, she leaves reluctantly. She is hopeful, however, that she may meet Dempster and Nancy again some day. *Deception. Forts. Navajo Indians. New Mexico. United States. Army. Cavalry. Arizona. Bandits. Cards. Fathers and daughters. Flags of truce. Folk songs. Horse thieves. Jewelry. Moral reformation. Murder. Officers (Military). Postal service. Salesmen. Schoolteachers. Scouts (Frontier). Songs. Square dances. Stagecoach robberies. Women outlaws.*
Note: According to an undated credit sheet submitted to the PCA, this independent production by Irving Allen was to be "An Eagle-Lion Classics Release," presented by Joseph Justman. Scenes involving Howard da Silva, originally cast as Capt. Dempster, had to be reshot when he was replaced after testifying as an unfriendly witness before the House Un-American Activities Committee. The *DV* review mentions reuse of footage from Irving Allen's earlier film *New Mexico* in *Slaughter Trail*. Much of the film is accompanied by songs from folk singer Terry Gilkyson and a male chorus. One song, heard only briefly in the film, "The Girl in the Wood," became a hit recording for Frankie Laine.
DV 15 May 1951. *DV* 11 Oct 1951. *Exh* 24 Oct 1951, p. 3174. *Har* 13 Oct 1951, p. 162. *HR* 11 Oct 1951. *LAT* 12 Oct 1951. *MPHPD* 18 Oct 1951.

THE SLAVE MARKET (Italian Americans)
1921?. Si; b&w. 5 reels.
Cast: James Cruze (*Jack Standing*), Marguerite Snow (*Maria*).
Drama. After arriving in New York, Maria, a poor, innocent Italian immigrant, loses her aunt in a crowd and falls prey to a gang of white slavers. Before any harm is done, however, she is rescued by wealthy Jack Standing, who soundly thrashes the gang. The love that soon develops between Jack and Maria is jeopardized when Jack takes Maria to a cabaret where a series of Eastern tableaux depicting scenes of white slavery is being presented. Dismayed by Jack's obvious enjoyment of the performance, Maria is distressed further by the arrival of Jack's former lover. Convinced that Jack prefers the other woman and the decadent life style she represents, Maria leaves, dressed in her old rags. Jack, however, realizing his deep love for her, renounces his old ways and begs her to return. *Immigrants. Innocents. Italian Americans. Moral reformation. Upper classes. Aunts. Cabaret performers. Cabarets. Fights. New York City. Rescues. White-slave traffic.*
Note: This film was reviewed in Jul 1920 by the British publication *Kinematograph Weekly* with a projected release date in Great Britain of Jul 1921. The reviewer commented on the "old-fashioned" aspects of the story, which suggests that the film might have been made sometime earlier. The only reference to the production that has been located in American journals is a listing made by the Community Motion Picture Bureau. It was viewed by the Bureau under the title *The Slave Mart*. Cruze and Snow made a number of films for Thanhouser Film Corp. between 1910 and 1916, and it is possible that Thanhouser produced this picture as well. A six-reel film entitled *The Slave Mart* is listed in release charts as available for release in Sep 1917 through Victoria Feature Films, a state rights distributor located in New York.

KW 8 Jul 1920, p. 102.

THE SLAVE MART *see* **THE SLAVE MARKET**

SLAVE SHIP (African Americans)

Twentieth Century-Fox Film Corp.; Darryl F. Zanuck in charge of production. *Dist* Twentieth Century-Fox Film Corp. 2 Jul **1937**; World premiere at New York: 17 Jun 1937; Prod: 22 Dec 1936—mid-Feb 1937; added scenes: 11 Mar—27 Mar 1937 [©Twentieth Century-Fox Film Corp.; 2 Jul 1937; LP7310]. Sd (RCA High Fidelity Recording); b&w. 10 reels, 8,315 ft. 92 min. PCA cert no. 3087.

Assoc prod Nunnally Johnson. *Dir* Tay Garnett. [*2d unit dir* Otto Brower]. *Asst dir* Booth McCracken, [Gordon Cooper and Bob Herndon]. *Scr* Sam Hellman, Lamar Trotti and Gladys Lehman. *Story* William Faulkner. [*Revisions* Walter Ferris]. *Photog* Ernest Palmer. [*2d cam* Don Anderson]. [*Asst cam* Robert Mack and Red Crawford]. [*Gaffer* Dave Anderson]. *Art dir* Hans Peters. *Film ed* Lloyd Nosler. *Set dec* Thomas Little. *Cost* Royer. [*Ward man* Bob Lee]. [*Ward girl* Carrie O'Neil]. *Mus score* Alfred Newman. *Sd* Alfred Bruzlin and Roger Heman. [*Sd rec* H. A. Root]. [*Boom man* Bob Bertrand]. [*Cableman* W. Grefrath]. [*Hair* Buddy King]. [*Makeup* Bill Cooley and Tony Carnagle]. [*Tech dir* Gilbert Pratt]. [*Prod mgr* Ed. Ebele]. [*Unit mgr* Sid Bowen]. [*Scr clerk* Helen Parker]. [*Grip* Jack Percy]. [*Props* Joe Behm]. [*Asst prop* Elmer Poggi]. [*Best boy* Charlie Graham]. [*Casting dir* Phillip Moore]. [*Technical man* Chris Christensen].

Song(s): "Lilly Dale," words and music by H. S. Thompson; "De Camptown Races," words and music by Stephen Foster; "Hades," words and music by Alfred Newman.

Source: Based on the novel *The Last Slaver* by George S. King (New York, 1933).

Cast: Warner Baxter (*Jim Lovett*), Wallace Beery (*Jack Thompson*), Elizabeth Allan (*Nancy Marlowe*), Mickey Rooney (*Swifty*), George Sanders (*Lefty*), Jane Darwell (*Mrs. Marlowe*), Joseph Schildkraut (*Danelo*), Miles Mander (*Corey*), Arthur Hohl (*Grimes*), Douglas Scott (*Boy*), Minna Gombell (*Mabel*), Billy Bevan (*Atkins*), Francis Ford (*Scraps*), Jane Jones (*Ma Belcher*), J. Farrell MacDonald (*Proprietor*), J. P. McGowan (*Helmsman*), De Witt Jennings (*Snodgrass*), Paul Hurst (*Drunk*), Dorothy Christy (*Blonde*), Charles Middleton (*Slave dealer*), Dewey Robinson (*Bartender*), Holmes Herbert (*Commander*), Edwin Maxwell (*Auctioneer*), Herbert Heywood (*Old man*), Winter Hall (*Minister*), Marilyn Knowlden (*Girl*), Arthur Aylesworth (*Stranger*), [Scotty Beckett (*Boy*)], [Chester Gan, Bull Anderson, Sven Borg, Bobby Dunn, John Wallace, Frank Meredith, Bob St. Angelo, Jack Low, Jack Stoney, John Bleifer, Len Powers, Richard Clark, Jack Byron, Dale Van Sickle, George Bruggeman, Larry Dodds, Remy Oldstead, Art Dupuis, George Du Count, Charles Griffin (*Members of crew*)], [James Burtis, James C. Morton (*Waiters*)], [Stymie Beard (*Black man on pier*)], [Otto Fries, Mel Kalish (*Singers*)], [Tom Kennedy (*Bartender*)], [Anita Brown (*Slave woman*)], [Eddie Dunn (*Ostler*)], Lionel Pape (*Commander*), [John Burton (*Officer*)], [Landers Stevens (*Owner*)], [Russ Clark, Lon Chaney, Jr. (*Laborers*)], [Fred Kelsey].

Sea, Drama. [*Print viewed*]. The barque *Wanderer* gets the reputation of being a "blood ship" after a worker is killed at its launch in Salem, Massachusetts in 1857. In the next three years, a plague and an explosion kill many others aboard. Bought in an auction by Jim Lovett and renamed the *Albatross*, the ship is used in the slave trade, which by 1860 has become outlawed everywhere. Jim and his crew, who are also shareholders, risk hanging for large profits, as their ship is one of only three slave ships still operating. After landing in Virginia with a load of slaves, Jim meets Nancy Marlowe of Norfolk. Two months later, after he orders his first mate and friend, Jack Thompson, to get rid of the crew and hire new men who would not work on a slave ship, Jim marries Nancy and brings her aboard to travel to Jamaica, where he plans to buy a plantation and settle down. However, the crew, including Thompson and Swifty, the cabin boy, mutiny and take the ship to Africa. When Jim explains his past to Nancy, she turns away in disappointment. During the trip, Jim stays drunk. In Africa, Nancy reconciles with Jim, but after slaves are selected and sent to the ship, Thompson and crew member Lefty leave Jim ashore to face the unpaid slave dealer Danelo, who tries to kill Jim for tricking him. Jim escapes and reaches the ship where he takes control of the guns and wheel. Knowing that he cannot hold off the men for long, Jim heads for St. Helena, a British island in the Atlantic. When the crew realizes Jim's plan, they send Swifty with food to

relieve Jim, who has not slept for seventy-two hours, at the wheel. Although at first Jim suspects a trick, after Nancy takes Swifty's side, Jim gives him a gun and says that he needs another man. Swifty, who all along has rebelled against the viewpoint that he is still a child, is won over, and when the crew approaches, he battles them with Jim and Nancy. When Thompson sees that St. Helena is in sight, he orders the chained slaves thrown overboard, weighted with an anchor, so that no evidence will exist to convict him. As the boat catches fire from a fallen lantern, Jim has the slaves freed so that they can swim to safety. When Thompson is about to attack him, Jim shoots him, but he is then is knocked out after falling for a ruse. When the crew abandons ship, Thompson decides that he cannot leave Jim to hang and puts him in a boat with Swifty and Nancy before he dies as the ship explodes in flames. At the trial, Nancy pleads for Jim, explaining that he freed the slaves even though he knew their existence would be proof against him. Later, on their plantation in Jamaica, Jim and Nancy's enjoyment of the quiet life is momentarily disrupted as Swifty fights with Scraps, the ship's drunken cook who rescued Nancy's dog, for a piece of pie. Cabin boys. Curses. Deception. Friendship. Mutiny. Ship crews. Ship owners. Ships. Slave traders. Africa. Auctions. Cooks. Dogs. Drowning. English. Fights. Jamaica. Manhood. Marriage. Norfolk (VA). Plantations. Ship fires. Slavery–Emancipation. St. Helena. Trials.

Note: The working title of this film was *The Last Slaver*. Notes from a conference with Darryl Zanuck concerning the second revised treatment, in the Twentieth Century-Fox Produced Scripts Collection at the UCLA Theater Arts Library, reveal a number of his concerns: "While in all probability the picture will be produced on a large scale, it is unlikely that we will have a name like [Clark] Gable, for instance, to cover up any of its possible weaknesses. Therefore, Mr. Zanuck feels that he cannot stress too much the fact that we must concentrate on the writing of an expert script that stands completely on its own....Watch, too, that the British are not made to appear stupid....Note: It is very important for censorship purposes that we indicate very plainly that the South is as radically opposed to slave-running as the North." Correspondence in the Twentieth Century-Fox Records of the Legal Department, also at UCLA, indicates that although William Faulkner is credited onscreen with the story, he actually only contributed "additional original dialogue" to a screenplay by Sam Hellman and Gladys Lehman. A note in the files states, "Mr. Zanuck and the producer decided to give Faulkner screen credit and this was the only way they could do it, as Lehman, Hellman and Trotti had been given credit for screenplay, which is the Academy limit." At the time, AMPAS limited screen credits for screenplay to three names. Faulkner is quoted in a modern source concerning his contribution: "I'm a motion picture doctor. When they run into a section they don't like, I rework it and continue to rework it until they do like it. In *Slave Ship*, I reworked sections. I don't write scripts. I don't know enough about it." According to a *HR* news item, Trotti was assigned to the film after the proposed film *The Siege of Alcazar* had been canceled due to numerous protests.

According to news items, Wallace Beery and Mickey Rooney were borrowed from M-G-M for the film. According to *MPH*, the actual filming took 102 days. *NYT* noted that the production costs exceeded $1,000,000. According to news items, Otto Brower, with a camera and technical crew, took a thirty-day trip to the Florida Keys and Bermuda to shoot offshore scenes, and a company of forty traveled to Catalina Island to shoot sea scenes. According to a Aug 1936 *HR* news item, John Ford was originally scheduled to direct, but he asked to be excused in order to take a vacation trip to Europe following the production of three films he directed in quick succession, and Howard Hawks was announced as director. According to *NYT*, in Nov 1936, Tay Garnett, who had acquired the assignment of director, was suddenly switched to *Love Is News* (see *AFI Catalog of Feature Films, 1931-40*; F3.2604). When that film was completed, he began shooting this one. According to a *HR* news item, Peter Lorre was signed on 15 Dec 1936 to play the role of the slave dealer, which ultimately went to Joseph Schildkraut, who was signed a few days before production began. John Carradine, who was not in the released film, was added to the cast on 18 Dec 1936, according to *HR*. Mary Rogers, the daughter of the late Will Rogers, was signed for the role of Nancy Marlowe but took sick with the flu during production, and Elizabeth Allan, on the day M-G-M agreed to a severance of their contract with her, signed to replace Rogers, according to news items. Tay Garnett, in his autobiography, related that the script was devised to co-star Clark Gable with Wallace Beery and Mickey Rooney, but M-G-M would not let Gable go. In the legal records, correspondence dated 22 Feb 1937, after the initial shooting was completed, states that Granville Bates played the "old man." As screen credits list Herbert Heywood in that role, it is possible that during the shooting of added scenes in Mar 1937, Bates was replaced by Heywood. According to a *Los Angeles Evening News* news item, the barquentine *Lottie Carson* was used in this film. According to a modern source, blacks who were servants and chauffeurs to Hollywood stars and producers were hired to play slaves.

Box 19 Jun 1937. *DV* 12 Jun 1937, p. 3. *FD* 17 Jun 1937, p. 7. *HR* 22 Aug 1936, p. 1. *HR* 15 Dec 1936, p. 1. *HR* 18 Dec 1936, p. 3. *HR* 19 Dec 1936, p. 3. *HR* 22 Dec 1936, p. 2. *HR* 9 Jan 1937, p. 3. *HR* 20 Jan 1937, p. 3. *HR* 27 Jan 1937, p. 6. *HR* 10 Feb 1937, p. 4. *HR* 11 Feb 1937, p. 17. *HR* 15 Feb 1937, p. 11. *HR* 11 Mar 1937, p. 3. *HR* 30 Mar 1937, p. 1. *HR* 12 Jun 1937, p. 3. *HR* 19 Nov 1937, p. 1, 4. *Los Angeles Evening News* 27 Jul 1937. *MPD* 4 Jun 1937, p. 4. *MPH* 13 Mar 1937, pp. 16-17. *MPH* 19 Jun 1937, p. 56, 58. *NYT* 8 Nov 1936. *NYT* 10 Jan 1937. *NYT* 17 Jun 1937, p. 19. *NYT* 24 Oct 1937. *Var* 23 Jun 1937, p. 3.

THE SLAVER (African Americans)

Morris R. Schlank Productions. *Dist* Anchor Film Distributors. **1927**; New York showing: 7 Dec 1927. Si; b&w. 6 reels, 5,500-5,900 ft.

Dir Harry Revier. *Scen* Mabel Z. Carroll. *Story* James Oliver Curwood. *Photog* Dal Clawson.

Cast: Pat O'Malley (*Dick Farnum*), Carmelita Geraghty (*Natalie Rivers*), John Miljan (*Cyril Blake*), J. P. McGowan (*"Iron" Larsen*), Billie Bennett (*Mrs. Rivers*), William Earle (*Gumbo*), Leo White, Phil Sleeman.

Sea, Drama. Sources vary—if not disagree—in describing the action in this film. According to *FD* (20 Nov 1927, p. 7), "hero shanghaied aboard a disreputable tramp steamer; girl lured aboard nifty yacht and to top it off there's a dirty and wicked sea captain to make life miserable for the pair." *Var* (14 Dec 1927, p. 26), on the other hand, describes only "a negro tribal chief on the coast of Africa making a deal with a dissolute white sea captain to buy a white girl. Supposed to be 'squared' by a negro cabin boy sacrificing his life, saving the girl from the black nabob" and "an abundance of fist fighting and hairy-chested sea-going deviltry." *Africa. African Americans. Sea captains. Shanghaiing. Slavery. Tribal chiefs.*

FD 20 Nov 1927, p. 7. Var 14 Dec 1927, p. 26.

SLEEP, MY LOVE (Chinese Americans)

Triangle Productions, Inc. *Dist* United Artists Corp. Jan **1948**; Los Angeles opening: 27 Jan 1948; Prod: 27 May—late Jul 1947 at Roach Studios, Inc. [©Triangle Productions, Inc.; 14 Jan 1948; LP1453]. Sd (Western Electric Recording); b&w. 10 reels, 8,666 ft. 96 min. PCA cert no. 12726.

Pres MARY PICKFORD. *Prod* Chas. Buddy Rogers and Ralph Cohn. *Assoc prod* Harold Greene. *Dir* Douglas Sirk. *Asst dir* Clarence Eurist. *Scr* St. Clair McKelway and Leo Rosten. *Dir of photog* Joseph Valentine. [*Cam op* Edward Colman]. [*Stills* Milton Gold]. *Art dir* William Ferrari. *Film ed* Lynn Harrison. *Set dec* Howard Bristol. *Miss Colbert's gowns by* Sophie. [*Ward* Margaret Jennings]. *Mus supv* David Chudnow. *Mus comp and cond* Rudy Schrager. *Sd rec* William Randall. [*Makeup* Burris Grimwood]. [*Hair stylist* Marjorie Lund]. *Prod mgr* Robert M. Beche. [*Tech adv* Dr. Marcel Frym and Fred Tang]. [*Scr supv* Mary Gibsone Whitlock]. [*Stand-in for Claudette Colbert* Carol Deane].

Source: Based on the novel *Sleep, My Love* by Leo Rosten (New York, 1946).

Cast: CLAUDETTE COLBERT [(*Alison Courtland*)], ROBERT CUMMINGS [(*Bruce Elcott*)], DON AMECHE [(*Richard Courtland*)], Rita Johnson [(*Barby*)], George Coulouris [(*Charles Vernay*)], Queenie Smith [(*Mrs. Vernay*)], Ralph Morgan [(*Dr. Rhinehart*)], Keye Luke [(*Jimmie*)], Fred Nurney [(*Haskins*)], Raymond Burr [(*Sgt. Strake*)], Maria San Marco [(*Jeannie*)], Lillian Bronson [(*Helen*)], and presenting Hazel Brooks by arrangement with Enterprise Productions, Inc. (*Daphne*), [Lillian Randolph (*Maid*)], [Syd Saylor (*Milkman*)], [Eddie Dunn (*Bartender*)], [Murray Alper (*Drunk*)], [Anne Triola].

Melodrama. [*Print viewed*]. Alison Courtland, who is from a wealthy family and married to architect Richard Courtland, wakes up hysterical on board a train from New York to Boston with no idea of how she got there. At the airport on her way back to New York, she meets an old friend, Barby, there to see off explorer Bruce Elcott, who joins Alison's flight. Richard, meanwhile, has informed police sergeant Strake about Alison's unexplained absence and because she has disappeared before, he is arranging for her to see an eminent psychiatrist, Dr. Rhinehart. After Richard tells Alison that she shot a gun at him the night before, she overcomes her reluctance to be examined. However, when a photographer, Charles Vernay, comes to Alison's house claiming to be Dr. Rhinehart and acts threateningly then suddenly disappears, Alison faints and is found by Bruce and Barby. When Richard arrives with the real Dr. Rhinehart, they all wonder if Alison imagined the earlier visitor. Later, Richard is unable to escort Alison to a party due to a business meeting, so she asks Bruce to take her. Bruce says that he would rather take her to his brother's wedding, and she is startled when his "brother" Jimmie turns out to be Chinese. Bruce explains that he spent a long time in China and Jimmie's family made him an honorary brother. While Alison enjoys the wedding reception, Richard enjoys a secret tryst with his girl friend Daphne, to whom he gives an emerald bracelet. Richard and Daphne, with Vernay's help, are planning to get Alison out of the way so that they can be married and divide up her wealth. When Alison returns home from the wedding, she sees the phony Dr. Rhinehart

lurking about again, but Bruce and Richard can find no one. Later, Richard drugs Alison's bedtime drink, and while she is asleep, makes hypnotic suggestions to her and prompts her to jump off a high balcony. Bruce, who is not convinced that Alison has been having hallucinations, returns to the house in time to prevent her from jumping. The next day, when Bruce asks Alison not to take any more bedtime drinks, she is shocked by his insinuation, but agrees after he tells her what almost happened the night before. Bruce goes to Richard's office that night and, while nosing around, finds a bill for the emerald bracelet. Soon after, at a party, Bruce tells the Courtlands that he is leaving the next day on a year-long trip. However, he does not leave and follows Richard to Vernay's studio, where he meets Daphne and notices that she is wearing an emerald bracelet. When Bruce realizes that Vernay may have been the man impersonating Dr. Rhinehart, he takes Vernay's distinctive eyeglasses and a book on hypnosis and asks Jimmie to take them to Sgt. Strake. However, before Bruce can confront Richard, Vernay knocks him out. Claiming he wants to celebrate the completion of a business deal, Richard offers Alison a large glass of drugged wine, which she drinks. Vernay arrrives and, unknown to him, is used as part of a set-up to have Alison charged with murder. While she is drugged, Richard persuades her by hypnosis that she must go downstairs and shoot "Dr. Rhinehart." Richard helps her pull the trigger, and they shoot Vernay. Alison wakes up as Richard is phoning the police, but Vernay is still alive and draws a gun on Richard, explaining to Alison about Richard's plan to replace her with Daphne. Vernay shoots Richard, intending to frame Alison for it then make her death look like a suicide. However, Bruce arrives in time to save Alison and chases Vernay upstairs. While trying to escape through a skylight, Vernay falls to his death. Later, Bruce comforts Alison. *Drugging. Hypnotism. Infidelity. Murder. Psychological torment. Airplanes. Architects. Boston (MA). Bracelets. Chinese Americans. Eyeglasses. Falls from heights. Femmes fatales. Gunshot wounds. Impersonation and imposture. New York City. Parties. Photographers. Police. Psychiatrists. Roadhouses. Set-ups. Trains. Weddings.*

Note: The novel *Sleep My Love* first appeared in serial form in *Colliers* magazine (27 Jul—24 Aug 1946) and was credited to Leonard Q. Ross, a pseudonym for Leo Rosten. The *Var* review noted that this film was "the first to carry the Mary Pickford name in about 12 years." A 15 Oct 1947 *HR* news item reported that the partnership between Pickford, husband Buddy Rogers and Ralph Cohn would be dissolved after the completion of only one production, *Sleep, My Love*. According to a Feb 1948 *New Yorker* article, United Artists arranged a private screening of *Sleep, My Love* for a group of hypnotists, psychiatrists and medical students, who were to discuss whether hypnotists could make criminals out of honest men. A demonstration of hypnotism by Dr. Franz Polgar of Budapest turned into a flurry of name-calling and intense arguing among members of the audience.

AmCin Feb 1948, pp. 46-47, 55. Box 17 Jan 1948. DV 12 Jan 1948, p. 3. FD 13 Jan 1948, p. 6. HR 16 May 1947, p. 16. HR 23 May 1947, p. 17. HR 15 Oct 1947, p. 1. HR 12 Jan 1948, p. 3, 7. HR 25 Feb 1948, p. 6. MPHPD 17 Jan 1948, p. 4017. NYT 19 Feb 1948, p. 29. New Yorker 28 Feb 1948. Var 14 Jan 1948, p. 10.

THE SLEEPING LION (Italian Americans)

Universal Film Mfg. Co. *Dist* Universal Film Mfg. Co. 23 Jun **1919** [©Universal Film Mfg. Co.; 11 Jun 1919; LP13821]. Si; b&w. 6 reels, 5,204 ft.

Dir Rupert Julian. *Asst dir* Rex Hodge. *Scen* Elliott J. Clawson. *Story* Bernard McConville. *Cam* Eddie Kull.

Cast: Monroe Salisbury (*Tony*), Pat Moore (*Little Tony*), Rhea Mitchell (*Kate Billings*), Herschel Mayall (*Durant*), Alfred Allen (*Colonel Doharney*), Alice Elliott (*Carlotta*), Marion Skinner (*Her mother*), Sidney Franklin (*Her father*), Frank Leigh.

Western. Italian potter Tony adopts an Italian waif, little Tony, and takes him from New York to the West to realize a long-held dream of owning a ranch. Once settled in the Western town, Tony manages to make an enemy of Durant, the town's chief gambler, by refusing to drink whiskey and by freely admiring Durant's girlfriend Kate Billings. A year later Tony is well-adapted as a cowboy. While he is away from home one day, Durant shoots at a shadow in the window that he believes is Tony's, but actually belongs to Little Tony, who is stunned but only slightly injured. Tony gets revenge and also manages to rescue Kate, who has eloped with Durant. After learning that Carlotta, his intended wife back East, has married one of his rivals, Tony wins Kate's love and they marry. *Adoption. Cowboys. Gamblers. Italian Americans. Waifs. Elopement. Gunshot wounds. Pottery. Rescues. Revenge.*

Note: A working title of the film was *The Open Roads*. One source incorrectly lists Bernard McConville as McCormick.

ETR 29 Mar 1919, p. 1300. *MPN* 7 Jun 1919, p. 3847. *MPN* 14 Jun 1919, p. 4031. *MPW* 31 May 1919, p. 1393. *VAR* 27 Jun 1919, p. 45. *Wid's* 1 Jun 1919, p. 11.

THE SLICKS *see* **GUNMAN'S WALK**

SLIGHTLY SCANDALOUS (Latino)

Universal Pictures Co., Inc. *Dist* Universal Pictures Co., Inc. 2 Aug 1946; Prod: late Apr–mid-May 1946 [©Universal Pictures Co., Inc.; 14 Aug 1946; LP498]. Sd (Western Electric Recording); b&w. 61-63 or 66 min. PCA cert no. 11802.

Exec prod Marshall Grant. *Assoc prod* Stanley Rubin. *Dir* Will Jason. [*Asst dir* William Tummell]. *Orig scr* Erna Lazarus and David Mathews. *Addl dial* Joel Malone and Jerry Warner. *Dir of photog* George Robinson. *Spec photog* D. S. Horsley. *Art dir* Jack Otterson and Harold H. MacArthur. *Film ed* Fred R. Feitshans, Jr. *Set dec* Russell A. Gausman and Ruby R. Levitt. *Cost supv* Vera West. *Mus dir* Milton Rosen. *Dir of sd* Bernard B. Brown. [*Sd*] *tech* John W. Rixey. *Hair stylist* Carmen Dirigo. *Dir of makeup* Jack P. Pierce. [*Double for Fred Brady* Robin Short].

Song(s): "I Couldn't Love You Anymore," "When I Fall in Love," "Same Old Routine," "The Mad Hatter" and "Baa Baa to You," music and lyrics by Jack Brooks; "Negra Leona," music and lyrics by Antonio Fernandez.

Cast: Fred Brady [(*Jerry, John and James Roberts*)], Sheila Ryan [(*Christine Wright*)], and introducing Paula Drew [(*Trudy Price*)], Walter Catlett [(*Mr. Wright*)], Jack Marshall [(*Erwin*)], Louis DaPron [(*Rocky*)], Isabelita [(*Lola Montez*)], Anne O'Neal [(*Minerva Wright*)], Moro and Yaconelli, The Guadalajara Trio, [Dorese Midgley, Georgann Smith (*Specialty dancers*)], [Harry Tyler (*Hotel desk clerk*)], [Charles Sylber, Jr. (*Waiter*)], [Frank McGlynn (*Graves*)], [Alan Edmiston (*Patron*), Ethyl May Halls (*Patrons*)], [Mel Jordan (*G. I. Joe's wife*)], [Nancy Marlow (*Receptionist*)], [Mary Jo Ellis (*Girl*)], [Carol Andrews (*Pretty blonde*)], [Helen O'Hara (*Page girl*)], [Gary Gray (*Little boy*)], [Tom Pilkington (*Jewelry salesman*)], [John J. White (*Taxi driver*)], [William H. O'Brien (*Waiter*)], [Diane Stewart (*Showgirl*)], [Billy Engle (*Husband*)], [Genevieve Bell (*Wife*)], [Dewey Robinson, Wilbur Mack, Mary Emery, Vangie Beilby (*Relatives*)].

Musical comedy. [*Print viewed*]. At the end of World War II, radio producer Jerry Roberts tries to convince Mr. Wright, a Boston fountain pen magnate, to sponsor a television show starring ex-USO entertainer Trudy Price. Though initially agreeable to the sponsorship, Wright is overruled by his spinster sister Minerva, so Jerry invites the businessman to New York City to see Trudy perform. In order to put on Trudy's radio show, Jerry forces his identical brother John, a conservative insurance agent, to lend him the necessary funds. In the midst of auditions for the show, Jerry is abducted by a group of Mexican musicians, so John is forced to take his brother's place in business discussions with Wright and his beautiful daughter Christine. When Wright insists on seeing the New York night life, John takes the Wrights to the Club Aztec, unaware that Jerry is being held there by Mexican singer Lola Montez, a former client to whom he owes money. Jerry convinces Lola and her friends to release him by promising to have Lola star on his planned television show. After the brothers switch places, John runs into a jealous Trudy, who, having seen him with Christine, threatens to quit the radio show. Still pretending to be his brother, John then becomes engaged to Trudy. Jerry insists that John persist with the ruse, so while John goes with Trudy to pick out an engagement ring, Jerry continues to romance Christine. Just as the Wrights are about to sign the television contract, Minerva arrives in New York and tells the newly engaged Christine that Jerry is already engaged to Trudy. Christine then goes to Jerry's apartment, where she runs into Trudy. They are soon joined by Lola, who tells them about Jerry and John's ruse. Trudy and Christine then decide to get even with the two brothers by having Christine pretend that she married Jerry the night before during a drunken spree. Their plan backfires, however, as Jerry attempts to exercise his marital rights with Christine, while the once-meek John actively pursues Trudy, having fallen in love with her. After the first television show airs, John goes to see Christine to straighten things out, only to be forced into a wedding ceremony before the Wright family. Jerry and Trudy arrive just in time to stop the wedding, and the two couples are correctly united. As they kiss, James, a third Roberts brother, arrives in search of Jerry and John. *Brothers. Impersonation and imposture.*

Insurance–Agents. Mistaken identity. Singers. Television programs. Television sponsors. Twins. Auditions. Brothers and sisters. Businessmen. Dancing. Debt. Engagements. Fathers and daughters. Jealousy. Jewelers. Mexicans. Musicians. Nightclub entertainers. Radio programs. Rehearsals. Seals (Animals). Taxicab drivers. Timidity. Transformation. Triplets.

Note: The working title of this film was *Oh Say Can You Sing*. According to *DV* news items in Oct 1950, playwright Frederick Jackson won a $17,500 suit against Universal for the unauthorized use of the title *Slightly Scandalous*. The California State Supreme Court, in upholding a lower court judgment from Jul 1948, ruled that Jackson held the legal rights to that title, even though his play had been produced.

DV 26 Jul 1946, p. 3. *DV* 2 Oct 1950. *DV* 4 Oct 1950. *FD* 1 Aug 1946, p. 10. *HR* 26 Apr 1946, p. 19. *HR* 26 Jul 1946, p. 3. *MPHPD* 8 Jun 1946, p. 3031. *MPHPD* 3 Aug 1946, p. 3125. *Var* 31 Jul 1946, p. 16.

SLIGHTLY SCARLET (*foreign version*) *see* **AMOR AUDAZ**

SLIGHTLY TERRIFIC (Czech Americans)

Universal Pictures Co., Inc. *Dist* Universal Pictures Co., Inc. 5 May 1944; Prod: 29 Nov–mid-Dec 1943 [©Universal Pictures Co., Inc.; 31 Mar 1944; LP12626]. Sd (Western Electric Recording); b&w. 5,222 ft. 61 min. PCA cert no. 9911.

[*Exec prod* Joseph Gershenson]. *Assoc prod* Alexis Thurn-Taxis. *Dir* Edward F. Cline. [*Asst dir* Seward Webb]. *Scr* Edward Dein and Stanley Davis. *Orig story* Edith Watkins and Florence McEnany. *Dir of photog* Paul Ivano. *Spec photog* John P. Fulton. *Art dir* John B. Goodman and Abraham Grossman. *Film ed* Norman A. Cerf. *Set dec* R. A. Gausman and L. R. Smith. *Gowns* Vera West. *Dir of sd* Bernard B. Brown. [*Sd*] *tech* Charles Carroll.

Song(s): "Me and My Whistle," "Stars and Violins," "A Dream Said Hello," "Rhythm's What You Need," "Hold That Line" and "The Happy Polka," music by Milton Rosen, lyrics by Everett Carter; "Put Your Arms Around Me, Honey," music by Albert von Tilzer, lyrics by Junie McCree; "The Blue Danube," music by Johann Strauss, new lyrics by Katherine Bellamann; "Come Back to Ireland," composer undetermined.

Cast: Leon Errol ([*James P. Tuttle/John P.*] *Tuttle*), Anne Rooney (*Julie Bryant*), Eddie Quillan (*Charlie* [*Young*]), Richard Lane (*Mike Hamilton*), Betty Kean (*Marie Mason*), Ray Malone (*Joe* [*y*] *Bryant*), Lillian Cornell [(*Gypsy singer*)], The Stardusters, Maritza Dancers, The 8 Rhythmeers, Donald Novis [(*Patrick Michael O'Toole*)], Lorraine Krueger [(*Peggy*)], Jayne Forrest [(*Valerie*)], [Lee Bennett (*Freddie Jordan*)], [Ralph Peters (*Butch*)], [Harry Woods (*Gypsy leader*)], [Robert Emmett Keane (*Brannerton*)], [William Haade (*Olaf*)], [Syd Saylor (*Sammy*)], [Franklin Parker (*Marty*)], [Dolly Miller (*Usherette*)], [Herbert Evans (*Valet*)].

Musical comedy. [*Print viewed*]. The musical revue "Stars of Tomorrow" opens to an empty house until James P. Tuttle is tricked into attending the show by automobile mechanic Joey Bryant, the younger brother of the show's star, Julie Bryant. Joey mistakenly believes that James is a millionaire, when, in reality, he is a soon-to-be unemployed car salesman. The penniless James still agrees to back the show, and asks his tycoon twin brother, John P. Tuttle, to give him the money. John refuses and orders his brother to return to their hometown in Illinois, after the local Czechoslovakian folk festival is over. Thinking that his brother is going to be in Washington, D.C. at that time, James decides to impersonate his brother and takes the show to Illinois to appear in the festival. Charlie Young, the show's producer, then convinces theatrical agent Mike Hamilton to advance the show's travel expenses if he agrees to take Mike's trouble-making client Peggy with him. While the troupe heads to Illinois in James's mobile home, Mike learns how rich John is and heads for Illinois himself with his top client, band leader Freddie Jordan. James's plan is scuttled, however, when his brother arrives at the festival, which leads to a series of mistaken identities. James finally tells Mike the truth about his identity and personal finances, but the agent, arguing that he has a blank contract signed by "J. P. Tuttle," states that he still intends to sue the shipping and steel tycoon if Freddie and his band do not perform at the festival. In a desperate attempt to convince his brother to finance the revue, James dresses up as John's long-lost love, but John discovers his brother's plot. He nevertheless agrees to allow the struggling musical revue to perform at the festival. After the performance, John is so impressed that he agrees to hire the revue as entertainment for his factory workers. *Brothers. Impersonation and imposture. Musical revues. Theatrical troupes. Twins. Youth. Band*

leaders. Brothers and sisters. Czechs. Dancers. Female impersonation. Garages. Gypsies. Hotels. Jazz music. Mechanics. Mistaken identity. Police. Rehearsals. Singers. Theatrical agents.

Note: The working title of this film was *Rhythm on Parade*.

Box 29 Apr 1944. *DV* 14 Apr 1944, p. 3. *FD* 27 Apr 1944, p. 11. *HR* 2 Nov 1943, p. 2. *HR* 26 Nov 1943, p. 11. *HR* 29 Nov 1943, p. 9. *HR* 14 Apr 1944, p. 3. *MPHPD* 4 Mar 1944, p. 1785. *MPHPD* 22 Apr 1944, p. 1858. *Var* 19 Apr 1944, p. 12.

SMART MONEY (Greek Americans)

Warner Bros. Pictures, Inc. *Dist* Warner Bros. Pictures, Inc.; The Vitaphone Corp. 11 Jul **1931** [©Warner Bros. Pictures, Inc.; 3 Jun 1931; LP2277]. Sd; b&w. 9 reels. 67 or 81 min. PCA cert no. 2308-R [26 May 1936].

Dir Alfred E. Green. *Scr, story and dial* Kubec Glasmon, John Bright, Lucien Hubbard and Joseph Jackson. *Photog* Robert Kurrle. *Art dir* Robert Haas. *Ed* Jack Killifer. *Gowns* Earl Luick. *Vitaphone Orch cond* Leo F. Forbstein.

Cast: Edward G. Robinson [(*Nick Venezelos*)], James Cagney [(*Jack*)], Evalyn Knapp [(*Irene*)], Ralf Harolde [(*Sleepy Sam*)], Noel Francis [(*Marie*)], Margaret Livingston [(*Blonde*)], Maurice Black [(*Greek barber*)], William House [(*Salesman*)], Paul Porcasi [(*Mr. Amenoppopolus*)], Gladys Lloyd [(*Cigar stand clerk*)], Polly Walters [(*Lola*)], [Boris Karloff (*Sport Williams*)], [Morgan Wallace (*District attorney*)], [Clark Burroughs (*Schultz*)], [Edwin Argus (*Two-Time Phil*)], [Mae Madison (*Small time girl*)], [Walter Percival (*Dealer Barnes*)], [John Larkin (*Snake Eyes*)], [Ben Taggart (*Hickory Short*)], [Billy House (*Salesman gambler*)], [Charles Lane (*Desk clerk*)], [Edward Hearn (*Reporter*)], [Eddie Kane (*Tom*)], [Clinton Rosemond (*George*)], [Eulalie Jensen (*Matron*)], [Wallace MacDonald (*Cigar stand clerk*)], [Charles O'Malley (*Machine-gunner*)], [Gus Leonard (*Joe*)], [John George (*Dwarf on train*)], [Larry McGrath], [Spencer Bell].

Gangster, Drama. [*Print viewed*]. Nick Venezelos, a Greek barber in a small town, is a lucky gambler who has a weakness for blondes. He has such a lucky reputation that his customers pool their resources to send him to a big poker game in the city. There, he is taken in by crooked gamblers and a deceptive blonde and loses his bankroll. He returns to barbering until he acquires a new bankroll. With the new money, he defeats the crooks, and soon his barber shop is a front for a successful gambling club. Despite the fact that he runs an honest game, the district attorney decides to put him out of business. After forcing Irene, a young woman befriended by Nick after she tried to commit suicide, to frame him in order to avoid being arrested for blackmail herself, the police arrest Nick. Prior to the arrest, Jack, Nick's friend from home, accuses Irene of framing Nick, and during the following fight, Nick accidentally kills Jack. The district attorney sends Nick to jail for manslaughter, but Nick, who is never down for long, bets the reporters that he will be out of jail before his sentence is up. *Barbers and barbershops. Gamblers. Greek Americans. Luck. Revenge. Accidental death. Attempted suicide. Blackmail. Cheating. District Attorneys. Frame-ups. Gangsters. Manicurists. Manslaughter. Poker (Game). Police. Trains.*

Note: Hubbard and Jackson received an Academy Award nomination for Best Original Story. Gladys Lloyd, who played the role of the cigar stand clerk, was the wife of Edward G. Robinson from the mid-1920s through 1956.

FD 21 Jun 1931, p. 10. *MPH* 16 May 1931, p. 34. *NYT* 19 Jun 1931, p. 21. *Var* 23 Jun 1931, p. 18.

SMILING HATE (African Americans)

Superior Art Motion Pictures, Inc. **1924**; Prod: began Apr 1924. Si; b&w. 5 reels.

Cast: Harry Henderson, Josephine Tally, Howard Augusta, George Graham, Gus Dail, Ethel Smith, Anne Kennedy, William Milton, Peggy Vance, William Smith, Estelle Kennedy, Arline Mickey, Mary Townsend, Leah Miles, Willie Meekins.

African American, Drama. [*Not viewed*]. When nefarious highgrading activity threatens to ruin his gold mine, wealthy Warren Headley sends William Bane, the fiancé of his daughter Aline, to find out who is behind the theft. Headley's son Bob, an artist who has shown no interest in his father's business, agrees to accompany William. Bob falls in love with a canteen girl, Ruth Wine, though his family is upset that her past is a mystery. A deformed individual known as "Smiling Hate" helps Bob in his investigations. After a number of adventures, William, attracted to Ruth, attacks her. She is found and carried to the Headley residence, where William's stickpin, which had become lodged in her hair during their struggle, identifies

him as the culprit. Outraged, Bob finds William and fights him. Smiling Hate, actually James Randall, an old college friend of Bob's, whose own mine had earlier been ruined by highgraders, reveals that he has been posing as a deformed man. He and Bob obtain evidence that William is the leader of the highgraders. *Abnormalities, Human. African Americans. Artists. Gold mines. Impersonation and imposture. Rape. Thieves. Canteens (War-time, emergency, etc.). Engagements. Evidence. Fathers and daughters. Fathers and sons. Fights. Romance. Wealth.*

Note: Superior Art Motion Pictures, Inc. was located in Philadelphia, PA. It was earlier known as Superior Art Productions Co., and had been located in Houston, TX.

ChiDef 24 May 1924, p. 6. *PittsC* 19 Apr 1924, p. 9.

SMILING IRISH EYES (Irish Americans)

First National Pictures, Inc. *Dist* First National Pictures, Inc. 28 Jul **1929** [©First National Pictures, Inc.; 18 Sep 1929; LP740]. Sd (Vitaphone); b&w. 8 reels, 8,550 ft. [Also si, 22 Sep 1929; 7,932 ft.].

Prod John McCormick. *Dir* William A. Seiter. *Asst dir* James Dunne. *Story, scen, dial and art titles* Tom J. Geraghty. *Photog* Sid Hickox and Henry Freulich. *Film ed* Al Hall. *Set des* Anton Grot. *Ward* Edward Stevenson. *Mus* Louis Silvers. *Choreography* Larry Ceballos, Walter Wills and Carl McBride.

Song(s): "Smiling Irish Eyes," words by Herman Ruby, music Ray Perkins; "A Wee Bit o' Love," "Then I'll Ride Home With You" and "Old Killarney Fair," words by Herman Ruby, music by Norman Spencer.

Cast: Colleen Moore (*Kathleen O'Connor*), James Hall (*Rory O'More*), Robert Homans (*Shamus O'Connor*), Claude Gillingwater (*Michael O'Connor*), Tom O'Brien ("*Black Barney*" *O'Toole*), Robert E. O'Connor (*Sir Timothy Tyrone*), Aggie Herring (*Grandmother O'More*), Betty Francisco (*Frankie West*), Julianne Johnston (*Goldie De Vere*), Edward Earle (*George Prescott*), Fred Kelsey (*County fair manager*), Barney Gilmore, Charles McHugh (*His assistants*), Madame Bosocki (*Fortune-teller*), George Hayes (*Taxi driver*), Anne Schaefer (*Landlady*), John Beck (*Sir Timothy's butler*), Oscar Apfel (*Max North*), Otto Lederer (*Izzy Levi*), William Strauss (*Moe Levi*), Dave Thursby (*Scotch barker*), Dan Crimmins (*The Trouble-maker*).

Comedy-drama. Rory O'More, a musician who works in an Irish peat bog, comes to the United States, leaving his sweetheart, Kathleen, behind. He promises to send for her as soon as he makes good. Although he writes letters daily to Kathleen, he does not post them, determined to hold them until he has good news to go with them. Finally, he gets a job playing the violin in a theatrical production. Despondent at not hearing from him, Kathleen borrows money to go to America and to bring Rory back to Ireland. She returns to Ireland in a huff when she sees Rory on stage playing their song, "Darlin' My Darlin'," while a blonde girl kisses him. They are reconciled when Rory appears in Ireland and explains everything to Kathleen's satisfaction, and the whole family emigrates to the States. *Immigrants. Ireland. Irish. Irish Americans. Letters. Musicians. Theater. Violinists.*

FD 28 Jul 1929. *NYT* 24 Jul 1929, p. 23. *Var* 31 Mar 1929, p. 17.

SMILING TO PLEASE *see* YEE SIO BO LAAN SIN

SMOKE SIGNAL (Native Americans, Apache, Ute)

Universal-International Pictures Co., Inc. *Dist* Universal Pictures Co., Inc. Feb **1955**; Prod: late May—mid-Jul 1954 [©Universal Pictures Co.; 10 Jan 1955; LP4372]. Sd (Western Electric Recording); col (Technicolor); 2:1. 7,897 ft. 87-88 min. PCA cert no. 17162.

Prod Howard Christie. *Dir* Jerry Hopper. *Asst dir* Joseph E. Kenny and [Gordon McLean]. *Story and scr* George F. Slavin and George W. George. *Dir of photog* Clifford Stine. *Technicolor consultant* William Fritzsche. *Art dir* Alexander Golitzen and Richard H. Reidel. *Film ed* Milton Carruth. *Set dec* Russell A. Gausman and James M. Walters. *Cost* Bill Thomas. *Mus supv* Joseph Gershenson. *Sd* Leslie I. Carey and Robert Pritchard. *Makeup* Bud Westmore. *Hair stylist* Joan St. Oegger.

Cast: Dana Andrews (*Brett Halliday*), Piper Laurie (*Laura Evans*), Rex Reason (*Lieutenant Wayne Ford*), William Talman (*Captain Harper*), Milburn Stone (*Sergeant Miles*), Douglas Spencer (*Garode*), Gordon Jones (*Corporal Rogers*), William Schallert (*Private Livingston*), Robert Wilke (*First Sergeant Daly*), Bill Phipps (*Private Porter*), Pat Hogan (*Delche*), Peter Coe (*Ute prisoner*), [Jerry Sheldon].

Western. Upon arriving at a small U.S. Cavalry outpost on the banks of the Colorado River, Captain Harper finds most of the fort's soldiers dead after a series of attacks by Ute Indians. Among the nine survivors are Laura Evans, the daughter of the dead commander, and her suitor, the arrogant Lieutenant Wayne Ford, who has temporarily taken charge of the remaining soldiers. The source of the trouble with the Ute tribe is assumed to be the fort's prisoner, Captain Brett Halliday, who, a few years previously, had defected to the Ute and is now awaiting a court-martial on charges of treason and murder. Halliday defends himself, explaining that when captured by the Army, he was escaping the Ute in order to reach an Apache chief with the power to stop the Ute's progressively violent attacks against the whites. However, no one believes Halliday's story, and Harper, whose brother was killed in a skirmish with the Ute while Halliday was aligned with the tribe, vows to bring the former Army captain to justice. When it becomes obvious that they can no longer remain in the fort, the soldiers, along with Laura, Halliday and Garode, a fur trader, build makeshift boats and take the only escape route possible, the treacherous and uncharted Colorado River. Ute warriors follow the two boats from the cliffs of the canyon and manage to kill a number of men, while others are nearly lost in the rapids. Halliday succeeds in a daring rescue of the helpless Private Livingston, who had earlier been blinded in a Ute attack, leading Sergeant Miles, whose life was once saved by Halliday, to defend his former captain to Harper. However, Harper and Ford, who is jealous of Laura's apparent interest in Halliday, continue to insist he is a traitor and cannot be trusted. After one of the boats breaks apart in the rapids and Halliday attempts more selfless rescues, Halliday finds himself briefly alone with Laura, who wants to know the truth behind his defection from the Army. Halliday reluctantly reveals that Laura's father, Commander Evans, was a brutal and intolerant man who treated the Ute Indians with great cruelty and injustice. Halliday was unwilling to carry out Evans' orders and defected to the Ute in the hope that he could protect them while he worked for a peaceful end to Evans' campaign of terror. Later, the Ute chief became as intolerant and warmongering as Evans, and Halliday tried to reach the Apaches for assistance in ending the violence. Though she must now face the truth about her father, Laura believes Halliday and falls in love with him. After Laura rebuffs Ford's advances, Ford angrily claims that Halliday is a "squawman" with a Ute wife awaiting him, but later Halliday explains to Laura that his wife was killed in the same battle in which Harper's brother died. An increasingly bitter Ford attempts to kill Halliday, but stumbles over a cliff and falls to his death. Finally, the small and exhausted band of survivors near the safety of a U.S. fort and spy a band of peaceful Apaches on the shore. The two remaining soldiers and Garode want Harper to release Halliday so that he can carry out his plan to attain peace and clear his name. However, Harper, an honorable man who cannot shirk his military duty, insists that he must deliver Halliday to the court. Nevertheless, Harper has come to trust and respect Halliday, so he subtly encourages him to make an escape, after which the soldiers dutifully shoot in Halliday's direction, purposefully missing him. As they watch Halliday swim to shore, Harper assures the grateful Laura that the man she has come to love will return to prove his innocence. *Colorado River (CO–Mexico). Desertion, Military. Escapes. Prisoners. United States. Army. Cavalry. Ute Indians. Apache Indians. Attempted murder. Blindness. Boats. Canyons. Disillusionment. Duty. Fathers and daughters. Forts. Fur traders. Loyalty. Rescues. Romantic rivalry. Sieges. Widowers.*

Note: This film opens with a title card stating that it was shot in the "Grand Canyon of the Colorado, known as one of the most dangerous rivers in the world." According to information contained in the file on this film in the MPAA/PCA Collection at the AMPAS Library, additional location shooting was done near Moab, Utah. *HR* and *Var* news items dated 7 Apr 1953 reported that Richard Alan Simmons was hired to write the film's screenplay based on an original story by Harold Jack Bloom; however, neither of these writers are credited onscreen and their participation in the finished film has not been confirmed. On 4 May 1954, *DV* reported that the producers had pushed back the start of production in the hopes of getting Charlton Heston for the role of "Brett Halliday." In a modern interview, producer Howard Christie dubbed *Smoke Signal* "the first seagoing Western in history" and stated that the film was shot on stretches of the San Juan and Colorado Rivers located between Mexican Hat, Utah and Marble Canyon, Arizona. A modern source adds John Day to the cast.

Box 12 Feb 1955. DV 4 May 1954. DV 3 Feb 1955, p. 3. Exb 9 Feb 1955, pp. 3916-17. FD 10 Feb 1955, p. 10. Har 5 Feb 1955, p. 24. HR 7 Apr 1953. HR 28 May 1954, p. 17. HR 9 Jul 1954, p. 6. HR 3 Feb 1955, p. 3. LAT 10 Mar 1955. MPD 3 Feb 1955. MPHPD 5 Feb 1955, p. 314. Var 7 Apr 1953. Var 9 Feb 1955, p. 10.

THE SNAIL (Chinese Americans)
W. H. Clifford Photoplay Co.; Shorty Hamilton Series. *Dist* State Rights; Ernest Shipman. Jun **1918?**. Si; b&w. 5 reels.
Cast: Shorty Hamilton.
Comedy-drama. A wealthy young American in China falls in love with a young Chinese woman who is subsequently sold into servitude and transported to America. The young man follows her to America and seeks the aid of a Chinese secret society in finding his sweetheart. A prominent American tries to arrange a marriage between his daughter and the young man, though he knows that each is in love with another. When the young man discovers the whereabouts of his sweetheart, he seeks the help of the prominent man, who betrays him by trying to have the Chinese girl deported. Before the plan can be executed, however, the young man learns that the prominent man is the Chinese girl's father and that he had delivered her to her captor. The prominent man, under threat of exposure, agrees to the marriage of the young American to the Chinese girl and of his American daughter to the poor cowboy whom she loves. *Child selling. Chinese Americans. Marriage–Arranged. Parentage. Upper classes. Americans in foreign countries. Betrayal. Blackmail. China. Deportation. Secret societies.*

Note: The W. H. Clifford Photoplay Co. first announced the film as available for the state rights market in Dec 1917, but it is unclear whether the film was released at that time. Ernest Shipman, formerly the sales manager of Clifford Photoplay, took over the distribution of the Shorty Hamilton series in mid-1918 and announced *The Snail* as a Jun release. No reviews of the film have been discovered, however. Victor Kremer, general manager of Clifford Photoplay when the film was first announced, bought the distribution rights to the Hamilton series in early 1919 and placed *The Snail* on the state rights market again later that year. A modern source states that Ethel Grey Terry was Hamilton's co-star.

MPW 5 Jan 1918, p. 150. MPW 6 Jul 1918, p. 128. MPW 22 Mar 1919, p. 1694. NYDM 15 Dec 1917, back cover. NYDM 29 Dec 1917, p. 19, back cover.

SNAKE RIVER DESPERADOES (Native Americans)
Columbia Pictures Corp. *Dist* Columbia Pictures Corp. May **1951**; Prod: 18 Oct–26 Oct 1950 [©Columbia Pictures Corp.; 1 May 1951; LP878]. Sd (RCA Sound System); b&w. 4,885 ft. 54-55 min. PCA cert no. 15009.
Series: The Durango Kid.
Prod Colbert Clark. *Dir* Fred F. Sears. [*Asst dir* Paul Donnelly and William Reinicke]. *Wrt* Barry Shipman. *Dir of photog* Fayte Brown. *Art dir* Charles Clague. *Film ed* Paul Borofsky. *Set dir* George Montgomery. *Mus dir* Ross Di Maggio. *Mus supv* Paul Mertz. *Sd eng* Jack Goodrich.
Song(s): "Brass Band Polka," music and lyrics by Smiley Burnette.
Cast: CHARLES STARRETT [(*The Durango Kid, also known as Steve Reynolds*)], Don Reynolds "Brown Jug" [(*Little Hawk*)], Tommy Ivo [(*Billy*)], Monte Blue [(*Jim Haverly*)], Smiley Burnette [(*Smiley Burnette*)], [Boyd "Red" Morgan (*Brandt*)], [George Chesebro (*Josh "Dad" Haverly*)], [John Pickard (*Dodds*)], [Charles Horvath (*Black Eagle*)], [Sam Flint (*Jason Fox*)], [Duke York (*Pete*)].
Western. [*Print viewed*]. Little Hawk, an Indian boy, is determined to stop the fighting that has broken out between his father, Black Eagle, and white settlers. Little Hawk goes in search of the Durango Kid, the secret identity of Steve Reynolds, an officer for the Department of Indian Affairs, to ask the Kid to stop the men who are selling guns to the Indians. Meanwhile, a stage coach conveying cornet player Smiley Burnett, and Jason Fox, a government man investigating the sale of guns to the Indians, is held up by a group of whites dressed as Indians. Soon after Fox is shot and killed, Steve arrives and discovers in Fox's jacket pocket a letter addressed to Jim Haverly, a friend to the Indians and the owner of the Stardale Idaho Trading Post. Steve visits the Trading Post where he finds Jim teaching his nephew Billy how to do the Indian buffalo hunt dance. Jim reports that when Black Eagle showed him his recently procured rifles, he had gone to the government in the hope of averting blood shed. When news of the stage coach raid reaches Stardale, a vigilante group forms. A townsman tries to convince Steve to join them, and when he declines, the man tells the others that Steve belongs to the Department of Indian Affairs and should be watched. Little Hawk and Billy, who are good friends, meet outside town, and when they discover a cache of rifles, they alert the Durango Kid. When the vigilantes attack an Indian village, the Kid goes after them and captures two of the leaders. Meanwhile, Billy goes back to town and tells Smiley, who is performing with his Silver Cornet Band, that he

must get the rifles before the Indians find them. Smiley follows directions, but is captured by Black Eagle's men. Steve asks Jim to take him to see Black Eagle, and meanwhile, Jim, who is revealed to be the leader of the gang selling weapons to the Indians as well as the mastermind behind the stage coach attack, plans another "Indian" raid in which he plans to get rid of Steve. When the men attack Steve and Jim on their way to Black Eagle's camp, they believe that they have killed Steve, but, dressed as the Kid, he arrives at the Indian village and overhears Jim trying to scare Black Eagle into buying rifles by telling him stories of white aggression. When Jim departs, Steve assures Black Eagle that Jim is a liar and that no white man will attack the Indians again. Jim then negotiates Smiley's release, and Smiley returns to Stardale with a peace treaty signed by Black Eagle. Jim immediately denounces the document and says that Steve was killed in an Indian ambush, but Steve arrives and disproves the traitor's words. Jim then angrily confronts his man Brandt for not shooting Steve and says that they must convince the town that the treaty is a fake by staging an "Indian" raid on Stardale. That evening, during a party celebrating the peace, someone announces the Indian raid. Jim and the vigilantes respond by reporting that they will raise an army and strike back against Black Eagle. Steve tries to convince the townspeople that the raid was done by whites, but is unsuccessful. Meanwhile, Billy goes into the wilderness and sends smoke signals to warn the Indians of the imminent attack. Jim sees the smoke signals and, recognizing Billy's work, captures the boy and then Little Hawk. Billy gets away and tells George, his father, and Steve about Jim's machinations. When George arrives to talk sense into his brother Jim when Steve, dressed as the Kid, arrives and shoots Jim dead. At Black Eagle's village, George apologises to Black Eagle and the Indian says that he hopes the two groups can live together like Steve Reynolds and the Durango Kid. Finally, Billy and Little Hawk share a peace pipe. *Deception. Gunfights. Impersonation and imposture. Indians of North America. Rifles. United States. Bureau of Indian Affairs. Children. Dances. Idaho. Peace pipes. Raids. Snake River (NW United States). Stagecoaches. Treaties.*

Note: Although reviews refer to actor Don Reynolds as Don "Brown Jug" Reynolds, onscreen credits list him as Don Reynolds "Brown Jug."

Box 26 May 1951. *DV* 11 May 1951, p. 4. *Exh* 23 May 1951, p. 3077. *FD* 31 May 1951, p. 7. *HR* 20 Oct 1950, p. 14. *HR* 11 May 1951, p. 3. *MPD* May 22, 1951. *MPHPD* 12 May 1951, p. 846. *Var* 16 May 1951, p. 6

THE SNEAK (Gypsies)

Fox Film Corp.; A Victory Picture. *Dist* Fox Film Corp. 20 Jul **1919** [©William Fox; 27 Jul 1919; LP14007]. Si; b&w. 5 reels.

Dir Edward J. Le Saint. *Scen* Ruth Ann Baldwin. *Story* J. Grubb Alexander. *Cam* Friend F. Baker.

Cast: Gladys Brockwell (*Rhona*), William Scott (*Wester Churen*), Alfred Hollingsworth (*King Panuel*), John Oaker (*Francisco Buckley*), Harry Hilliard (*Roger Barrington*), Irene Rich (*Enid Granley*), Gerrard Grassby (*Her mother*).

Drama. Rhona, daughter of the gypsy king and next in line to succeed him, chooses Wester Churen for her husband and thereby inflames her other suitor Francisco Buckley. While visiting near the gypsy camp, artist Roger Barrington is so taken by Rhona's beauty that he asks her to pose for a portrait. Francisco induces Rhona to steal Roger's valuables, and Rhona is so ashamed after Roger catches her, that she agrees to pose for him. Francisco has told Wester of Rhona's whereabouts, and in a fit of jealousy he finds his wife at Roger's home. Rhona is expelled from the gypsy camp, but her father later believes in his daughter's innocence and sends Wester for her. Rhona arrives as her father is about to die. Francisco stabs Wester, and Rhona then challenges Francisco to a knife duel. Francisco falls on his own knife and dies. The dying king gives his blessing to Rhona and the recovering Wester. *Gypsies. Jealousy. Marriage. Romantic rivalry. Duels. Fathers and daughters. Knife wounds. Models. Painters (Of paintings). Robbery. Royalty.*

Note: The location of the story is unclear from contemporary sources. *MPW* commented that the film is "commendable for its excellent atmosphere of Romany life."

ETR 21 Jun 1919, p. 217. *MPN* 21 Jun 1919, p. 4219. *MPW* 21 Jun 1919, p. 1829. *Var* 13 Jun 1919, p. 49. *Wid's* 8 Jun 1919, p. 7.

SNOWDRIFT (Native Americans)

Fox Film Corp. *Dist* Fox Film Corp. 22 Apr or 29 Apr **1923** [©William Fox; 23 Apr 1923; LP19127]. Si; b&w. 5 reels, 4,617 ft.

Pres William Fox. *Dir* Scott Dunlap. *Scen* Jack Strumwasser. *Story* James B. Hendryx. *Photog* George Schneiderman.

Source: Based on the novel *Snowdrift* by James B. Hendryx (New York, 1922).

Cast: Prologue: Bert Sprotte (*Jean McLaire*), Gertrude Ryan (*Margot McFarlane*), Colin Chase (*Murdo McFarlane*), Evelyn Selbie (*Wananebish*), Annette Jean (*Little Margot*), **Cast—Story:** Charles Jones (*Carter Brent*), Irene Rich (*Kitty*), G. Raymond Nye (*Johnnie Claw*), Dorothy Manners (*Snowdrift*), Lalo Encinas (*Joe Pete*), Lee Shumway (*John Reeves*), Charles Anderson.

Melodrama. Renegade mining engineer Carter Brent loses his money gambling in the Yukon. He falls in love with Snowdrift, a girl believed to be a half-breed who is actually an orphan of white parents though reared by an Indian squaw. Brent is regenerated through his association with Snowdrift and eventually rescues her from a dance hall manager who has made her a prisoner. *Engineers. Gambling. Indians of North America–Mixed blood. Miners. Orphans. Yukon Territory.*

FD 27 May 1923. *MPW* 9 Jun 1923.

SO BIG (Dutch Americans)

First National Pictures, Inc. 28 Dec **1924** Si; b&w. 9 reels, 8,562 ft.

Supv Earl Hudson. *Dir* Charles Brabin. *Scen* Adelaide Heilbron. *Adpt* Earl Hudson. *Editorial dir* Marion Fairfax. *Photog* T. D. McCord. *Art dir* Milton Menasco. *Film ed* Arthur Tavares.

Source: Based on the novel *So Big* by Edna Ferber (Garden City, NY, 1924).

Cast: Colleen Moore (*Selina Peake*), Joseph De Grasse (*Simeon Peake*), John Bowers (*Pervus DeJong*), Ben Lyon (*Dirk DeJong*), Wallace Beery (*Klass Poole*), Gladys Brockwell (*Maartje Poole*), Jean Hersholt (*Aug Hempel*), Charlotte Merriam (*Julie Hempel*), Dot Farley (*Widow Paarlenburg*), Ford Sterling (*Jacob Hoogenduck*), Frankie Darrow (*Dirk DeJong as boy*), Henry Herbert (*William Storm*), Dorothy Brock (*Dirk DeJong as baby*), Rosemary Theby (*Paula Storm*), Phyllis Haver (*Dallas O'Meara*).

Drama. After graduating from a fashionable finishing school and touring Europe with her father, Selina Peake returns to the United States, where her father is accidentally killed after losing his fortune in a gambling den. Selina is reduced to teaching in a high school in the Dutch community at High Prarie near Chicago. She boards in the farmhouse of Klass Poole, a dull-witted market gardener, and finally marries Pervus DeJong, a poor and backward farmer. She shares the drudgery of her husband's futile life and finds happiness only in their small son, Dirk, whom she calls "So-Big." Pervus dies from the strain of hard work, and Selina is reduced to abject poverty, eking out a marginal existence selling the few vegetables she can raise. When she meets Julie Hempel, an old school friend, Julie's father lends her enough money to begin to farm her land successfully. After eighteen years of stinting and hard work, Selina sees Dirk educated as an architect, but Dirk's promising career is then threatened by scandal. William Storm, the husband of the woman with whom Dirk has been having an affair, threatens to name him as corespondent in a divorce suit. Selina appeals to Storm not to ruin her son's life, and Storm relents. Dirk returns to his true love, Dallas, and Selina looks forward to a serene old age. *Architects. Chicago (IL). Dutch. Farmers. Illinois. Motherhood. Schoolteachers. Truck farmers.*

FD 11 Jan 1925. *NYT* 5 Jan 1925, p. 19. *Var* 7 Jan 1925, p. 37.

SO BIG (Dutch Americans)

Warner Bros. Pictures, Inc. *Dist* Warner Bros. Pictures, Inc.; The Vitaphone Corp. 30 Apr **1932**; Prod: mid-Jan—mid-Feb 1932 [©Warner Bros. Pictures, Inc.; 29 Mar 1932; LP2944]. Sd; b&w. 8 reels. 80 or 82-83 min.

Dir William A. Wellman. *Adpt* J. Grubb Alexander and Robert Lord. *Photog* Sid Hickox. [*Cam op* Richard Towers]. [*Asst cam* Wesley Anderson]. *Art dir* Jack Okey. *Ed* William Holmes. *Gowns* Earl Luick. *Vitaphone Orch cond* Leo F. Forbstein. [*Sd* Robert Lee]. [*Still photog* William Walling, Jr.].

Source: Based on the novel *So Big* by Edna Ferber (Garden City, NY, 1924).

Cast: BARBARA STANWYCK (*Selina Peake*), George Brent [(*Roelf Pool*)], Dickie Moore [(*Dirk, as a boy* ["*So Big*"])], Bette Davis [(*Dallas O'Mara*)], Mae Madison [(*Julie Hemple*)], Hardie Albright (*Dirk, grown*), Alan Hale [(*Klaus Pool*)], Earle Fox [(*Pervus De Jong*)], Robert Warwick [(*Simeon Peake*)], Dorothy Peterson [(*Maartje*)], Noel Francis, Dick Winslow [(*Roelf, age 14*)], [Guy

Kibbee (*August Hemple*)], [Arthur Stone (*Jan Steen*)], [Dawn O'Day (*Selina, as a girl*)], [Harry Beresford (*Adam Ooms*)], [Eulalie Jensen (*Mrs. Hemple*)], [Elizabeth Patterson (*Mrs. Tibbits*)], [Rita La Roy (*Paula Storm*)], [Blanche Frederici (*Widow Paarlenburg*)], [Willard Robertson (*The doctor*)], [Martha Mattox, Emma Ray (*Maiden aunts*)], [Olin Howland (*Jacob*)], [Andre Cheron (*The general*)], [Harry Holman (*Country doctor*)], [Lionel Belmore (*Reverend Dekker*)].

Historical, Rural, Drama. [*Print viewed*]. After her mother dies, Selina Peake's father takes her to Chicago, where she attends a finishing school. When her father is killed, leaving her penniless, Selina's friends learn that he was a gambler and drop her. Only Julie Hemple helps her, persuading her father, August Hemple, to get Selina a job as a schoolteacher in a small Dutch community near Chicago. There, Selina lives with a farm family, helping their adoring son Roelf with his lessons. Eventually, she marries farmer Pervus De Jong and gives birth to a son, Dirk, who becomes the center of all her hopes and dreams. As he grows, she measures him daily and nicknames him "So Big." Pervus dies, leaving Selina the struggling farm. Determined, she makes the farm pay, which enables Dirk to go away to school and eventually establish himself as an architect. Over the years, everyone comes to love the hardworking, idealistic Selina. Dirk, however, does not have his mother's strength. He falls in love with a married woman who persuades her husband to give him a job as a bond salesman in his office. He is embarrassed by his mother's farm, even though her excellent asparagus paid for his education. When he falls in love with Dallas O'Mara, a talented artist, she refuses to marry him because he is unwilling to work at something worth while. Meanwhile, Roelf has become a great sculptor. He meets Dirk, and learning that he is Selina's son, asks to see her again. At the meeting, Selina compares Roelf and Dirk, acknowledging her son's faults, while at the same time, rejoicing in Roelf's talent and good character. *Farmers. Idealism. Mothers and sons. Architects. Artists. Asparagus. Businessmen. Chicago (IL). Children. Churches. Dutch Americans. Friendship. Infidelity. Love affairs. Lure of riches. Ministers. Physicians. Prostitution. Salesmen. Sculptors. Teachers. United States–Midwest. Widows.*

Note: Edna Ferber's novel won the Pulitzer Prize. According to *FD*, Joseph Jackson wrote the adaptation with J. Grubb Alexander. The exact nature of his contribution to the final film has not been determined. Ferber's story was first filmed in 1924 by First National with star Colleen Moore, (see *AFI Catalog of Feature Films, 1921-30*; F2.5201). Warner Bros. remade the novel in 1953 with Jane Wyman as Selina. That version was directed by Robert Wise.

FD 1 May 1932, p. 11. *HR* 3 Mar 1932, p. 2. *IP* May 1932, p. 32. *MPH* 19 Mar 1932, p. 42. *NYT* 30 Apr 1932, p. 19. *Var* 3 May 1932, p. 14.

SO BIG (Dutch Americans)
Warner Bros. Pictures, Inc.; A Warner Bros.—First National Picture. *Dist* Warner Bros. Pictures, Inc. 31 Oct **1953**; Prod: mid-Feb—1 Apr 1953 [©Warner Bros. Pictures, Inc.; 4 Nov 1954; LP4107]. Sd (RCA Recording System); b&w. 9,154 ft. 101 or 104 min. PCA cert no. 16405.

Prod Henry Blanke. *Dir* Robert Wise. *Asst dir* Russ Saunders. [*2d asst dir* Fred Sheld]. *Dial dir* Anthony Jowitt. *Scr* John Twist. *Dir of photog* Ellsworth Fredricks. [*Cam op* Harry Davis]. [*Asst cam* Stewart Higgs]. *Art dir* John Beckman. *Film ed* Thomas Reilly. *Set dir* George James Hopkins. [*Props* Bud Friend]. [*Asst props* George Sweeney]. *Ward* Milo Anderson, Howard Shoup, [Rudy Harrington and Jack Delaney]. *Mus* Max Steiner. *Orch* Murray Cutter. *Sd* Oliver S. Garretson. *Makeup artist* Gordon Bau. [*Makeup* Edward Allen]. [*Hair stylist* Betty Lou Delmont]. [*Scr supv* Irva Mae Ross]. [*Gaffer* Paul Burnett]. [*Best boy* Ed Rike]. [*Grip* Hershal Brown].

Source: Based on the novel *So Big* by Edna Ferber (Garden City, NY, 1924).

Cast: Jane Wyman [(*Selina Peake DeJong*)], Sterling Hayden [(*Pervus DeJong*)], Nancy Olson [(*Dallas O'Mara*)], Steve Forrest [(*Dirk "So Big" DeJong*)], Elisabeth Fraser [(*Julie Hempel*)], Martha Hyer [(*Paula Hempel*)], Walter Coy [(*Roelf Pool*)], Richard Beymer [(*Roelf Pool, age 12-16*)], Tommy Rettig [(*Dirk DeJong, age 8*)], Roland Winters [(*Klaas Pool*)], Jacques Aubuchon [(*August Hempel*)], Ruth Swanson [(*Maartje Pool*)], Dorothy Christy [(*Widow Paarlenberg*)], Oliver Blake [(*Adam Ooms*)], Lily Kemble Cooper [(*Miss Fister*)], [Noralee Norman (*Geertje Pool*)], [Jill Janssen (*Jozina Pool*)], [Kerry Donnelly (*Paula Hemple, age 8*)], [Kenneth Osmond (*Eugene Hemple, age 9*)], [Lotte Stein (*Meena*)], [Jon Provost (*Dirk DeJong, age 2*)], [Arthur Fox (*Dirk DeJong, age 3*)], [Vera Miles, Evan

Loew, Frances Osborne, Jean Garvin, Carol Grei (*Schoolgirls*)], [Grandon Rhodes (*Bainbridge*)], [Anthony Jochim (*Accountant*)], [Herb Vigran (*Boss*)], [Joe Duval (*Jakob*)], [Frank Kreig, Bob Stephenson, Paul Brinegar, Billy Vincent, Joe Brooks, Mike Lally, Jack Henderson, Ralph Volkie, Steve Stephan, Al Lloyd, John Konorez, Dan Dowling, Dick Alexander, James Dime (*Bidders*)], [George Selk (*Johnnes Ambuul*)], [Spec O'Donnell (*Man in chair*)], [John Maxwell (*Rev. Dekker*)], [Bud Osborne (*Wagon driver*)], [Ray Bennett (*Al*)], [Jennings Miles (*Seller*)], [Frank Chase, Phil Tead, John Logan, James F. Stone (*Buyers*)], [Marjorie Bennett (*Woman servant*)], [Bill O'Brien (*Man servant*)], [David McMahon, Chalky Williams (*Policemen*)], [Charlicie Garrett (*Cook*)], [Joy Hallward (*Maid*)], [Bill Grimes, Thor Holmes, Michael Pierce, Clay Bennett, Cathy Creighton, Sue George, Gloria Moore, Jeanetta Lewis (*Children*)], [Frank Ferguson (*Assistant*)], [Tom Royal (*Eugene Hemple*)], [Lillian Culver (*Mrs. Robinson*)], [Douglas Evans (*Richard Hollis*)], [Mary Alan Hokanson (*Secretary*)], [Abdullah Abbas (*Hawker*)], [Sara Taft], [Dorothy Granger], [Elizabeth Russell].

Historical, Rural, Drama. [*Print viewed*]. In the late 1890's, Selina Peake, a student at a posh boarding school, is informed of the death of her wealthy father, who has left her penniless as a result of a botched business deal. Since the proud Selina refuses all offers of charity, August Hemple, the kindly father of Selina's best friend, Julie, obtains a teaching position for Selina in New Holland, a tiny Dutch farming community outside Chicago which has remained virtually unchanged for seventy-five years. In New Holland, Selina takes a room in the home of Klaas Pool, a crude farmer who scoffs at Selina's idealism and eye for beauty, and his overworked and miserable wife Maartje. Selina finds a kindred soul in Klaas and Maartje's son Roelf, a bright, but troubled adolescent who is unable to attend school because he must work on the farm. After discovering that Roelf has a talent for music, Selina gives him nightly piano lessons and encourages his artistic leanings, gradually leading him away from juvenile delinquency. At a charity auction, Selina catches the eye of the town's most eligible bachelor, Pervus DeJong, and later accepts his proposal of marriage. Roelf is devastated to learn that Selina, who represents to him the beauty of the world outside his hated hometown, is to marry a lowly truck farmer. However, Selina consoles him by explaining that she needs both "emeralds" and "wheat" in her life, emeralds being those people, like Roelf, who appreciate and create beauty, and wheat, those who work the land, providing the necessities of life. Selina settles into the laborious routine of a farmer's wife and gives birth to a son Dirk, who, as he grows, earns the nickname "So Big." Dirk soon displays signs of being an emerald in the rough, and although Pervus, who has never fully understood his wife, is mildly disapproving, Selina encourages her son's nascent artistic talent. Maartje dies and, shortly after, Klaas makes plans to wed the simpering Widow Paarlenberg. The grieving Roelf decides to leave New Holland forever and tearfully bids Selina goodbye. When Dirk is eight years old, Pervus dies from the strain of his hard work, and Selina, refusing offers of help from her neighbors, labors to keep the farm going on her own. Much to the shock of the denizens of conservative New Holland, Selina and Dirk travel unescorted to the Chicago Haymarket to sell their produce, but no one will buy from a woman. When all seems lost, Selina runs into her old friend Julie, now a divorced mother of two, and August, who offers to invest in Selina's proposal to grow exotic vegetables. Selina's "DeJong" asparagus is a huge success and, ten years later, she proudly sends Dirk off to college to study architecture. After college, Dirk begins work as a draughtsman in an architectural firm and maintains his involvement with his childhood sweetheart, Julie's spoiled daughter Paula. Paula, a manipulative social climber, pushes Dirk to earn more money and later convinces him to forgo his dream of becoming an architect in order to attain more immediate financial success. Dirk accepts a job in sales and promotion arranged for him by Paula, greatly disappointing Selina, who demonstrates her dismay by no longer referring to him as "So Big." Later, Dirk falls in love with the talented artist, Dallas O'Mara, who cares nothing for money and social status, and proposes marriage. Although she is fond of him, Dallas refuses, declaring that she could never marry a man whose hands are unscarred by real work. Roelf, now a renowned composer, has a triumphant return to Chicago, where he visits Dallas, an old friend from Paris. Accompanied by Dirk, Roelf takes Dallas to his reunion with Selina, and the two women, very much alike, become friends.

After Roelf and Dallas leave, Dirk, fearing that he has lost both of the women he loves, expresses his dismay at how his life has turned out. However, Selina takes him in her arms and, calling him "So Big," reminds him that it is never too late to pursue his dream of creating beauty. *Dutch Americans. Farmers. Idealism. Mothers and sons. Adolescents. Architects. Artists. Asparagus. Auctions. Boarding schools. Businessmen. Chicago (IL). Children. Composers. Friendship. Idle rich. Jealousy. Lure of riches. Neighbors. Proposals (Marital). Romance. Salesmen. Schoolteachers. Self-made men. Small town life. Snobs and snobbishness. Social climbers. Transformation. Truck farmers. United States–Midwest. Unrequited love. Widows.*

Note: This was the third film based on Edna Ferber's Pulitzer Prize winning novel. The first was a 1924 film starring Colleen Moore, and the second was a Warner Bros.' 1932 version directed by William Wellman and featuring Barbara Stanwyck as "Selina" (see above). According to a modern source, Warner Bros.' misleading ad campaign for *So Big*, which suggested that the title referred to the strapping farmer played by Sterling Hayden ("He stood there So Big...she was ready to forget she'd ever been a lady"), touched off a storm of protest and the studio became the target of a mail campaign to pull the ads.

Box 10 Oct 1953. *DV* 30 Sep 1953, p. 3. *FD* 6 Oct 1953, p. 8. *Har* 3 Oct 1953, p. 159. *HR* 20 Feb 1953, p. 13. *HR* 3 Apr 1953, p. 9. *HR* 30 Sep 1953, p. 3. *LAHE* 4 Nov 1953, p. 14. *LAT* 4 Nov 1953. *MPD* 1 Oct 1953. *MPHPD* 3 Oct 1953, p. 2013. *Newsweek* 9 Nov 1953. *NYT* 22 Oct 1953, p. 34. *Var* 30 Sep 1953, p. 6.

SO RED THE ROSE (African Americans)

Paramount Productions, Inc. *Dist* Paramount Productions, Inc. 22 Nov **1935**; Prod: 19 Jun—9 Aug 1935 [©Paramount Productions, Inc.; 22 Nov 1935; LP5970]. Sd (Western Electric Noiseless Recording); b&w. 9 reels. 90-91 min. Passed by the National Board of Review. PCA cert no. 1173.

Pres ADOLPH ZUKOR. *Prod* Douglas MacLean. *Dir* King Vidor. [*Fill-in dir* Elizabeth Hill]. [*Asst dir* Vernon Keays]. *Scr* Laurence Stallings, Maxwell Anderson and Edwin Justus Mayer. *Photog* Victor Milner. *Art dir* Hans Dreier and Ernst Fegte. *Ed* Eda Warren. *Miss Sullavan's cost des* Travis Banton. *Mus score* W. Franke Harling. *Sd rec* Harold C. Lewis and Louis H. Mesenkop.

Source: Based on the novel *So Red the Rose* by Stark Young (New York, 1934).

Cast: MARGARET SULLAVAN (*Valette Bedford*), Walter Connolly (*Malcolm Bedford*), Randolph Scott (*Duncan Bedford*), Janet Beecher (*Sally Bedford*), Elizabeth Patterson (*Mary Cherry*), Robert Cummings (*Archie Pendleton*), Harry Ellerbe (*Edward Bedford*), Dickie Moore (*Middleton Bedford*), Charles Starrett (*George McGehee*), Johnny Downs (*Yankee boy*), Daniel Haynes (*William Veal*), Clarence Muse (*Cato*), [James Burke (*Major Rushton*)], [Warner Richmond (*Confederate sergeant*)], [Alfred Delcambre (*Charles Tolliver*)], [Emma Reed (*Old servant*)], [Edward Gargan (*Cavalryman*)], [Alex Hill (*Scipio*)], [Luke Cosgrove (*Prophet*)], [Leroy Broomfield, Oscar Smith, Kid Herman (*Slaves*)], [John Larkin (*Cato's companion*)], [Charles Morris (*Officer*)], [Billy McClain (*Servant in kitchen*)], [E. H. Calvert (*Cavalry major*)], [Stanley Andrews (*Cavalry captain*)], [David Newell, Alden Chase, Paul Parry, Baron Lichter, Hal Craig, Duke York (*Soldiers*)], [Lloyd Ingraham (*Officer*)], [Dick Allen (*Confederate officer*)].

Historical, Romance, War, Drama. [*Print viewed*]. In 1861 at the Portobello plantation in Mississippi, Valette Bedford is in love with her cousin Duncan and flirts incessantly with him to draw his attention. Duncan plays cool, however, treating her as if she were a young child. Out of spite, Valette pretends to fall madly in love with her brother Edward's Texan friend, Archie Pendleton. When Archie proposes to her, she is flabbergasted and does not respond definitively, but as he is dashing off to the Civil War, he assumes that she will be waiting for him. Edward stays behind at the urging of his family, but later comes to regret his decision when he finds out Archie has been honorably killed in battle. Edward then leaves with his father's blessing. Duncan, however, refuses to fight his Northern neighbors on the grounds that many of them are friends and Americans should not fight Americans. Valette becomes disgusted by his attitude and believes it only covers cowardice. After some Yankees kidnap Valette's father Malcolm as a guide, he returns determined to go to war. After Malcolm leaves, his wife Sally has a vision of her son Edward dead on the battlefield, and accompanied by Duncan and her faithful black slave, she goes to find his body. Prior to his leaving, Valette had apologized to Duncan and had pledged her love for him. Moved by the sight of the battlefield strewn with slain Confederate soldiers, Duncan marches off to war with a battle cry, leaving Sally

and William to return Edward's body. News reaches the Bedford slaves that General Ulysses S. Grant has taken Vicksburg, and their excitement leads them to revolt against their work. A wounded Malcolm then arrives home and dies, after which Sally, heartbroken, frees their slaves. Sally, her little son Middleton, Valette and their cousin Mary maintain the house, helped by William, until Yankee soldiers invade the mansion. Valette takes pity on one young Yankee soldier who, although originally intending to rob them, has been injured and is being hunted by Confederate soldiers. She dresses him in her brother's uniform and puts him to bed, and is astonished to discover that one of the pursuing Confederate soldiers is Duncan. Duncan has changed markedly—he is no longer a pacifist—and Valette must plead for the boy's life. Although Duncan protects him, the boy dies and the family is thrown out of their own house when the Yankees set fire to it. Duncan then rejoins his troops. By the war's end, the much-reduced family is living in a small house and cooking on an outdoor stove. One day, Valette hears Duncan calling to her, and they reunite in the woods. *Pacifism and pacifists. Slavery. Southern belles. United States–History–Civil War, 1861-1865. African Americans. Arson. Cousins. Cowardice. Fathers and daughters. Flirtation. Kidnapping. Mississippi. Plantations. Proposals (Marital). Uprisings. Visions. War injuries.*

Note: A *DV* news item noted that in an effort to hasten production, director King Vidor had his wife, writer Elizabeth Hill, direct some scenes with Margaret Sullavan, while he directed crowd scenes. According to copyright records, William G. Beymer acted as Southern adviser, and William H. Hazell, who served in the Civil War, reproduced antiques from that era. The film reportedly cost $1,000,000 to produce. The United Daughters of the Confederacy contributed information for the production. Paramount borrowed Margaret Sullavan from Universal for this film. According to a *DV* news item, some scenes were shot on location at Sherwood Lake, CA.

DV 19 Jun 1935, p. 1. *DV* 2 Aug 1935, p. 3. *DV* 4 Nov 1935, p. 3. *FD* 9 Nov 1935, p. 7. *HR* 10 Aug 1935, p. 4. *HR* 4 Nov 1935, p. 3. *MPD* 5 Nov 1935, p. 6. *MPH* 17 Aug 1935, p. 41. *MPH* 16 Nov 1935, p. 63. *NYT* 28 Nov 1935, p. 39. *Var* 4 Dec 1935, p. 15.

SO YOUNG, SO BAD (Latino)

Individual Pictures, Inc. *Dist* United Artists Corp. 26 May **1950**; Prod: began 5 Jul 1949 in New York City [©Individual Pictures, Inc.; 15 Feb 1950; LP2878]. Sd (Western Electric Sound System); b&w. 10 reels, 8,169 ft. 88 or 90-91 min. PCA cert no. 14049.

Prod Edward J. Danziger and Harry Lee Danziger. *Dir* Bernard Vorhaus. *Asst dir* Sal Scoppa, Jr. and James De Gangi. *Story and scr* Jean Rouverol and Bernard Vorhaus. *Dir of photog* Don Malcames. *Film ed* Carl Lerner. *Ward* Edith Lutyens. *Mus* Robert W. Stinger. [*Mus score* Vernon Duke]. *Rec dir* David Polak. *Makeup* Fred Pyle. *Tech adv* Hon. Milton A. Gibbons.

Cast: PAUL HENREID (*Dr. [John H.] Jason*), Catherine McLeod (*Miss [Ruth] Levering*), Cecil Clovelly (*Mr. Riggs*), Grace Coppin (*Mrs. Beubler*), Anne Francis (*Loretta*), Rosita Moreno (*Dolores [Guerrero]*), Anne Jackson (*Jackie*), Enid Pulver (*Jane*).

Psychological, Prison, Melodrama. [*Print viewed*]. When three young girls escape from the Elmview Corrective School for Girls, the institute's psychiatrist, Dr. John H. Jason, is ordered to resign. The three escapees, Jane, Jackie and Loretta, are former runaways who have been sent to the school for rehabilitation. Thinking of his first day on the job, Jason reflects over his entire tenure at Elmview and tries to determine what he could have done to prevent his dismissal: Soon after his arrival at Elmview, Jason finds that the institution is demoralizing the girls rather than helping them, and that the girls are desperate to escape. When Dolores Guerrero, who was sent to the school on vagrancy charges, tries to make a break from Elmview, she is caught and promptly returned to school. Dolores then tells Jason that she is being tormented by her teacher and some other students. Jason's proposed reforms are met with disapproval by other staff members at Elmview, including Miss Ruth Levering, who opposes his work and claims that he is making promises to the girls that he cannot keep. Later, Jason is disturbed by Jane and Jackie's claims that they were recently sent to solitary confinement for attacking a supervisor, and that they are being forced to work ten hours a day. When Jason discovers that none of his recommendations have been carried out, he complains to Riggs, the head of the institution, but Riggs merely defends the school's strict disciplinary policies. In a private meeting with Jason, Miss Levering shows sympathy for Jason's efforts and confesses that she has compromised her beliefs by working within the school's corrupt framework. Another severe punishment given by Riggs results in the girls's attempting to burn down the school down.

Their attempt is squashed, however, and they are punished by the sadistic Mrs. Beuhler, who turns a high-powered fire hose on the helpless girls. News of the punishment soon reaches Jason and Miss Levering, who rush to the girls's aid. Determined to put an end to the school's tolerance of such actions, Jason threatens to report Mrs. Beuhler, but Riggs persuades Jason into reconsidering his actions. Instead of filing the complaint, Jason strikes up a deal with Riggs that will allow Riggs to stay employed with Elmview and would give Jason the power to make policy decisions for the school. Shortly after taking over Riggs' duties, Jason implements his new program, which includes new classes, recreation time and other freedoms, and the girls show remarkable improvement. Time passes, and with new budgetary difficulties setting in, Riggs decides to stir up trouble for Jason in the hope that the school board will fire him. A rumor is circulated by Loretta, one of the girls, that Miss Levering is having an affair with Jason, and when Loretta taunts Miss Levering with the claim, she loses her temper and strikes the girl. Jason witnesses the incident, and although Miss Levering submits her resignation over the matter, Jason refuses to accept it. One day, Dolores is found dead of a hanging and Jason is immediately suspended. Mrs. Beuhler is put in charge of running the school, at which point Loretta, Jane and Jackie steal a truck and try to escape. Unable to come up with the answer to his question, Jason's thoughts drift back into the present, and he leaves Elmview disheartened. Later, Jane, finds Jason and Mrs. Levering and tells them that Mrs. Beuhler was responsible for Dolores' suicide. Jason and Miss Levering deliver this information to the board members, but as Jane and other girls have been intimidated by Mrs. Beuhler and Riggs, their accusations go unconfirmed. Jason and Miss Levering's hope for justice seems lost until Jackie, who has been on the run until now, bursts into the meeting and reveals the truth. Justice is delivered to Riggs and Mrs. Beuhler, who are placed under arrest, and Jason and Miss Levering celebrate their success with marriage vows. *Girls' schools. Juvenile delinquents. Psychiatrists. Reformatories. Sadism. Arson. Blackmail. Corruption. Dismissal (Employment). Escapes. Frame-ups. Marriage. Romance. Social workers. Suicide. Teachers.*

Note: According to an 11 Feb 1949 *HR* news item, star Paul Henreid and Bernard Vorhaus were originally planning to make this film through their company, Monica Productions (named after Henreid's daughter Monica), under the title *Runaway.* On 17 Jun 1949, before the property was acquired by Individual Productions, Inc., *HR* reported that Monica Lewis was being considered for a role, but her participation in the completed film has not been confirmed. A copy of the film's cutting continuity deposited with the copyright records lists the title as *Escape If You Can;* according to a *DV* news item, the title was changed to *So Young, So Bad* in Mar 1950. A Jul 1949 *NYT* news item noted that the first scenes of the film were shot in Yonkers, NY, and that additional location shooting was set to take place in Manhattan, Long Island and Connecticut. The film marked the motion picture debut of actress Anne Jackson. Reviews commented on the similarities between this film and the 1950 Warner Bros. film *Caged,* and the *Var* review pointed out that several sequences were the same. A Sep 1952 *HCN* article reported that the parents of a missing twenty-year-old Italian girl named Marisa Biffignandi identified their daughter from an Italian movie magazine still photograph of the film's dormitory scene. During a special screening arranged for the girl's parents, they identified their daughter as an extra. The girl's mother then made a public appeal on an NBC radio program for her daughter to return home. The outcome of the search is not known.

Box 3 Jun 1950. *DV* 26 May 1950, p. 3. *FD* 1 Jun 1950, p. 5. *HCN* 3 Sep 1952. *HR* 11 Feb 1949, p. 10. *HR* 17 Jun 1949, p. 2. *HR* 6 Jul 1949, p. 3. *HR* 26 May 1950, p. 4. *HR* 21 Jul 1950, p. 3. *MPHPD* 3 Jun 1950, pp. 321-2. *NYT* 10 Jul 1949. *NYT* 24 Jul 1950, p. 15. *Var* 31 May 1950, p. 6.

SOBRE SU ESPALDA see **ESCLAVAS DE LA MODA**

THE SOCIAL BUCCANEER (Jewish Americans, Chinese Americans)
Bluebird Photoplays, Inc. *Dist* Bluebird Photoplays, Inc. 16 Oct 1916 [©Bluebird Photoplays, Inc.; 25 Sep 1916; LP9184]. Si; b&w. 5 reels.
Dir Jack Conway. *Scen* Fred Myton. *Cam* Ed Kull.
Source: Based on the novel *The Social Buccaneer* by Frederic Stewart Isham (Indianapolis, 1910).
Cast: J. Warren Kerrigan (*Chattfield Bruce*), Louise Lovely (*Marjorie Woods*), Maud George (*Miss Goldberg*), Harry Carter (*Caglioni*), Marc Robbins (*Nathan Goldberg*), Hayward Mack (*Sir Archibald Bamford*), W. T. Horne.
Drama. While working in China for Nathan Goldberg, a New York Jewish importer, Chattfield Bruce comes to admire the Robin Hood philosophy of Wong Lee, who gives to the poor all the food, clothing and money that he steals from the rich. After Chattfield informs Wong

Lee of a betrayal among his gang, Wong Lee gives him a ring that is guaranteed to give the wearer the allegiance of any Chinese throughout the world. After returning to New York, Chattfield decides to redistribute the nation's wealth with the help of Wong Lee's son, who opens a store in Chinatown as the base of operations for Chattfield's work. Goldberg, who cheats his customers of thousands of dollars annually, has social aspirations for his daughter. Chattfield arranges for Wong Lee's son to be a waiter at a lawn party Goldberg gives for his daughter's friend, Marjorie Woods, so that he can substitute a fake necklace for an expressive one belonging to Miss Goldberg. In plotting the robbery, Chattfield begins a romance with Marjorie. Nevertheless, he steals the necklace, but then confesses everything to Marjorie, who convinces him to give up his illegal philanthropy for a safer, although less charitable profession, marriage. *China. Jews. Robbery. Social reform. Thieves. Chinese. Chinese Americans. Importers. Jewelry. Merchants. New York City–Chinatown.*

Note: *MPW* commented, "One of the best impersonations, that of the Hebrew merchant, has been done by Marc Robbins."

MPN 21 Oct 1916, p. 2557. *MPW* 14 Oct 1916, p. 223. *MPW* 21 Oct 1916, p. 448. *NYDM* 14 Oct 1916, p. 26. *Var* 6 Oct 1916, p. 27. *Wid's* 5 Oct 1916, p. 1013.

THE SOCIAL HIGHWAYMAN (Italian Americans)
Shubert Film Corp. *Dist* World Film Corp. 17 Apr **1916** [©World Film Corp.; 25 Apr 1916; LU8148]. Si; b&w. 5 reels.
Dir Edwin August. *Scen* Frances Marion.
Source: Based on the play *A Social Highwayman* by Mary Stone (New York, 24 Sep 1895).
Cast: Edwin August (*John Jaffray/Curtis Jaffray*), John Sainpolis (*Hanby*), Ormi Hawley (*Countess Rossi*), Alice Clair Elliott (*Eleanore Hilton*), Noah Beery (*Hugh Jaffray*).
Drama. Curtis Jaffray's mother, an Italian peasant, must steal to support herself, but genetic tendencies as well as economic necessity contribute to her penchant for robbery, as it is inherited by her son. After John, his British nobleman father, catches him stealing, Curtis runs away, but rather than try to change his nature, he decides to put his mother's legacy to good use. As a result, after he has risen to a prominent position in the United States, he starts stealing from those who belong to his own wealthy social set and then distributing the money among the poor. Even though they can afford it, however, this sort of forced philanthropy terrifies Curtis' friends, and so they enlist the aid of the police, who finally manage to corner the criminal and kill him. *Hereditary tendencies. Italian Americans. Social reform. Thieves. English. Italians. Nobility. Peasantry. Police. Runaways.*

Motog 29 Apr 1916, p. 1000. *MPN* 29 Apr 1916, p. 2556. *MPW* 22 Apr 1916, p. 574 (ad insert). *MPW* 29 Apr 1916, p. 818, 868. *Var* 14 Apr 1916, p. 26. *Wid's* 20 Apr 1916, p. 522.

SOCIETY DEBUT see **COMING OUT PARTY**

SOCIETY SNOBS (Italian Americans)
Selznick Pictures Corp. *Dist* Select Pictures. Feb **1921** [©Selznick Pictures Corp.; 4 Feb 1921; LP16083]. Si; b&w. 5 reels, 4,234 ft.
Pres Lewis J. Selznick. *Dir* Hobart Henley. *Scen* Lewis Allen Browne. *Story* Conway Tearle. *Photog* Jack Brown.
Cast: Conway Tearle (*Lorenzo Carilo/Duke d'Amunzi*), Vivian Forrester (*Martha Mansfield*), Ida Darling (*Mrs. Forrester*), Jack McLean (*Ned Forrester*), Huntley Gordon (*Duane Thornton*).
Society, Melodrama. Italian American Lorenzo Carilo, failing at clerical work, becomes a waiter and falls under the charms of Vivian Forrester, a society girl contemptuous of her social inferiors. She rejects the suit of wealthy Duane Thornton, and in retaliation he presents Carilo to Vivian as the Duke d'Amunzi. Abetted by her ambitious mother, she responds to Carilo's advances. On their wedding night he confesses the deception, and Vivian promptly leaves him to make arrangements to have the marriage annulled. She does forgive him, however, and they are reunited. *Impersonation and imposture. Italian Americans. Marriage. Snobs and snobbishness. Upper classes. Waiters.*

ETR 9 Apr 1921, p. 1711. *FD* 20 Mar 1921. *Var* 18 Mar 1921, p. 34.

SOLD AT AUCTION (African Americans)
Balboa Amusement Producing Co.; Gold Rooster Plays. *Dist* Pathé Exchange, Inc. 11 Feb **1917**. Si; b&w. 5 reels.
Prod H. M. Horkheimer and E. D. Horkheimer. *Dir* Sherwood MacDonald. *Scen* Daniel Whitcomb. *Cam* Joseph Brotherton.
Cast: Lois Meredith (*Nan*), William Conklin (*Richard Stanley*), Marguerite Nichols (*Helen*), Frank Mayo (*Hal Norris*), Charles

Dudley (*William Raynor*), Lucy Blake (*Raynor's sister*).

Drama. Because he wants to remove anything that will remind him of his wife's infidelity, Richard Stanley sends his infant daughter Nan to a woman named Mrs. Hopkins. Stanley sends money for Nan's support, but never visits her and thus is unaware that she is treated as a slave by Mrs. Hopkins, who keeps all of the money herself. Nan's only happiness comes from her love for Hal, a young reporter. Fearful of losing her servant, Mrs. Hopkins tells Nan that there is mulatto blood in her veins. Crushed by the lie, Nan flees from the only home she has ever known. Ignorant of the world, she is carried by the tide of events unknowingly into what is termed a "matrimonial" agency, but which is in reality something worse. Nan is placed at auction and her own father bids for her against other millionaires. As he outbids them, Hal, who has traced her, enters just in time to reveal to Stanley that Nan is his own daughter. *Drudges. Prostitution. Reporters.* African Americans–Mixed blood. *Infants. Infidelity. Parentage. Runaways.*

ETR 3 Feb 1917, p. 632. *MPN* 10 Feb 1917, p. 921. *MPW* 10 Feb 1917, p. 798 (ad insert), 867, 912. *NYDM* 3 Feb 1917, p. 26. *Wid's* 25 Jan 1917, p. 61.

SOLD FOR MARRIAGE (Russian Americans)

Fine Arts Film Co. *Dist* Triangle Film Corp. 16 Apr **1916** [©Triangle Film Corp.; 10 Apr 1916; LP8702]. Si; b&w. 5 reels.

Dir William Christy Cabanne. *Scen* William E. Wing. *Cam* William E. Fildew.

Cast: Lillian Gish (*Marfa*), Frank Bennett (*Jan*), Walter Long (*Colonel Gregioff*), A. D. Sears (*Ivan*), Pearl Elmore (*Anna*), Curt Rehfelt (*Dimitri*), William E. Lowery (*George*), Fred Burns (*A policeman*), William Siebert (*The undesirable suitor*), Frank Brownlee (*Nicholas*).

Drama. Determined to sell their niece to a wealthy bachelor, Marfa's Aunt Anna and Uncle Ivan refuse to let her marry Jan, a young Russian peasant. As headstrong as Ivan and Anna, however, Marfa turns down the proposal of the district governor, Colonel Gregioff, and then knocks him senseless with a club. As a result, Ivan and Anna decide that they should leave Russia, so they sail with Marfa to the United States. On board, Marfa once again sees Jan, who has also decided to come to America. Then, when they arrive in Los Angeles, Ivan and Anna sell Marfa to a wealthy Russian immigrant. Anna finally gives in, but on the wedding day, Jan has the police stop the ceremony on the grounds that it is illegal to sell women into marriage. As a result, because Anna and Ivan finally have to yield to a higher authority, Marfa and Jan can begin making plans for their marriage. *Aunts. Immigrants. Marriage–Forced. Russia. Russian Americans. Russians. Uncles. Peasantry.*

Note: *MPN* cites the working title of the film as *Marja of the Steppes*.

Motog 25 Mar 1916, p. 717. *Motog* 15 Apr 1916, p. 881. *MPN* 15 Apr 1916, p. 2217. *MPW* 15 Apr 1916, p. 458. *MPW* 6 May 1916, p. 1042. *NYDM* 8 Apr 1916, p. 28. *NYT* 10 Apr 1916, p. 11. *Var* 7 Apr 1916, p. 23. *Wid's* 6 Apr 1916, p. 483.

SOLOMON IN SOCIETY (Jewish Americans)

Cardinal Pictures. *Dist* American Releasing Corp. 31 Dec **1922** or 28 Jan **1923**; New York premiere: week of 25 Dec 1922. Si; b&w. 6 reels, 5,600 ft.

Pres Carl Krusada. *Dir* Lawrence C. Windom. *Story and scen* Val Cleveland. *Photog* Edward Paul.

Cast: William H. Strauss (*I. Solomon*), Brenda Moore (*Rosie Solomon*), Nancy Deaver (*Mary Bell*), Charles Delaney (*Frank Wilson*), Fred T. Jones (*Orlando Kolin*), Lillian Herlein (*Mrs. Levy*), Charles Brook (*The Butler*).

Domestic, Drama. I. Solomon, a humble tailor on New York's East Side, dreams of being a designer with a shop on Fifth Avenue, but he makes no headway until a dress that he designs for Mary Bell, a laundress who suddenly becomes a movie star, attracts attention and becomes popular. Three years later Solomon has a successful Fifth Avenue shop, but his prosperity is too much for his wife, Rosie, who succumbs to a scheming Greenwich Village pianist, Orlando Kolin. Resigned to giving Rosie her freedom, Solomon, with Mary's help, stages evidence to give Rosie a reason for divorce. Fortunately, Rosie realizes her mistake in time and falls into Solomon's arms; Mary resumes her romance with Solomon's lawyer. *Actors and actresses. Couturiers. Divorce. Jews. Laundresses. Lawyers. Motion pictures. New York City–East Side. New York City–Fifth Avenue. Pianists. Tailors.*

Note: This film was advertised under the working title *House of Solomon*.

FD 21 Dec 1922. *Var* 5 Jan 1923, p. 41.

SOMBRAS DE GLORIA (Spanish language)

Sono-Art Productions, Inc. *Dist* Sono-Art World Wide Pictures, Inc. Jan **1930**; World premiere in Los Angeles: 25 Jan 1930; Prod: Oct 1929 at Metropolitan Studios, Hollywood, CA [©Sono-Art World Wide Pictures, Inc.; 4 Apr 1930; LP1216]. Sd (Western Electric System); b&w. 11 reels, ca. 9,500 ft. 106 min. Passed by the National Board of Review. Spanish language.

Presentan [*Pres*] O. E. GOEBEL and GEO. W. WEEKS. *Supervisada personalmente por* [*Personally supervised by*] O. E. Goebel and Geo. W. Weeks. *Dirección* [*Dir*] Andrew Stone. [*Asst dir* Ray Heinz]. *Argumento* [*Story*] Thomas Boyd. [*Scr* Renaud Hoffman and Henry McCarthy]. *Versión castellana* [*Castillian version*] Fernando C. Tamayo. *Fotografía* [*Photog*] Arthur Martinelli. *Editor del film* [*Film ed*] Arturo Tavares. *Acompanamientos musicales* [*Mus accompaniment*] Carlos Molina. *Arreglos musicales* [*Mus arr*] Robert A. Shepherd. *Dirección musical* [*Mus dir*] Loren Powell. *Coreografía* [*Choreography*] Don Summers. *Fonografía* [*Rec*] Ben Harper and J. G. Greger. *Dirección Tecnica* [*Tech dir*] Chas. Cadwallader. *Gerente de la producción* [*Prod mgr*] J. R. Crone.

Song(s): "Arrullo militar (Dough-boy's Lullaby)" by Eddie Dowling, James Brockman and James F. Hanley, Spanish lyrics by Fernando C. Tamayo and Genaro Veiga; "Si la vida te sonríe (Put a Little Salt on the Bluebird's Tail)" by Eddie Dowling, James Brockman and James F. Hanley, Spanish lyrics by José Bohr and Genaro Veiga; "Rosa roja de amor (Wrapped in a Red, Red Rose)" by Eddie Dowling, Joe McCarthy and James F. Hanley, Spanish lyrics by Fernando C. Tamayo and Genaro Veiga; "Then We Canoe-dle-oodle Along," by Harry Woods, Charles Tobias and José Bohr; "Noche de paz (Silent Night)" by Franz Xaver Gruber, Spanish lyricist undetermined; "Oh, Paris" and "Bienvenidos," composers undetermined.

Source: Based on the short story "The Long Shot" by Thomas Alexander Boyd in *Points of Honor* (New York, 1925).

Cast: JOSÉ BOHR [(*Eddie Williams*)], Mona Rico [(*Helen Williams*)], Francisco Marán [(*Dr. Castelli*)], César Vanoni [(*District attorney*)], Ricardo Cayol [(*Jean*)], Demetrius Alexis [(*Carl Hummel*)], Tito Davison [(*Jack*)], Juan Torena [(*Judge*)], Roberto Saa Silva, Federico Godoy, [Jorge Crespo (*Chaplain*)], [Agustín Aragón (*Reporter*)], [Ernesto Piedra], [Carlos Molina], [Juan Duval], [María Miceli], [Marina Ortiz].

Legal, Drama, with songs. [*Not viewed*]. In a courtroom, Eddie Williams is on trial for the murder of Carl Hummel, his wife Helen's employer. Jean, Eddie's nine-year-old adopted son, is the only witness to the killing. When the district attorney attempts to have Jean testify, the boy does not want to betray Eddie, and Eddie stops his testimony by admitting to the killing. However, Dr. Castelli, Eddie's lawyer, reviews Eddie's background for the jury, explaining that he was a prominent singer in Broadway shows. In the past, Helen, Eddie's girl friend, brings him news that World War I has been declared. Eddie immediately decides to enlist, and just before he embarks for Europe, he and Helen marry. In the trenches, at Christmas, Eddie disobeys an order from his captain to shoot a German soldier who is attempting to cut a Christmas tree. Later, in a similar act of compassion, Eddie again spares the same German's life during a poison gas attack which leaves Eddie severely incapacitated. While Eddie attempts to recuperate in a hospital, peace is declared. Upon returning to America, Eddie is unable to resume his theatrical career due to the effects of the gas, which has impaired his lungs, and he becomes very despondent. Adding to his troubles is the news that his wife is being courted by her employer, Carl Hummel. Castelli continues his address to the jury by telling them that Helen has been posing as a single woman in order to get work so that she can look after Eddie. One night, Eddie discovers Hummel and Helen embracing and shoots Hummel. Eddie is unaware, however, that the embrace he witnessed was one of joy and gratitude resulting from their realization that Eddie is the American soldier who had saved his life during the war. Hummel had come to America to repay his debt by locating the soldier and arranging to have him treated by an important German doctor. Castelli also reveals that the district attorney was the former captain whom Eddie had disobeyed. The jury finds Eddie innocent and he, Helen and Jean are reunited. *Entertainers. Gases, Asphyxiating and poisonous. Germans. Murder. Self-sacrifice. Trials. World War I. Adoption. Christmas. Confession (law). District attorneys. Fathers and sons. Italian Americans. Juries. Lawyers. Marriage. Newsboys. Parks. Soldiers. Theaters. Trench warfare. Unemployment. War injuries. Witnesses.*

Note: This was a simultaneously shot, Spanish-language version of the 1930 film *Blaze O' Glory* (see *AFI Catalog of Feature Films, 1921-30*, F2.0459), which was directed by Renaud Hoffman and George J. Crone, and starred Eddie Dowling and Betty Compson. The credits, cast and summary were derived from a post-production dialogue continuity submitted as part of the film's copyright registration.

The countries of origin of some of the production personnel and actors were included on the onscreen credits: Tamayo—Venezuelan; Tavares—Portuguese; Molina—Colombian; Bohr—Argentinian; Rico—Mexican; Marán—Italian; Vanoni—Argentinian; Cayol—Spanish; Alexis—Greek; Davison—Chilean; Torena—Spanish; Acosta—Mexican; Saa Silva—Chilean and Godoy—Peruvian. Modern sources, however, report that Juan Torena was born in the Philippine Islands and not in Spain. Juan Duval and María Miceli (María Calvo) were natives of Spain. Some sources include Rodolfo Galante, Gaby Arnold and Allan Wardell in the cast, but their participation has not been confirmed. It is possible that the song "Bienvenidos" is a Spanish version of "Welcome Home," words by Ballard Macdonald, music by James F. Hanley. José C. Barros is credited with contributing to the songs but his precise contributions have not been determined.

Sombras de gloria was previewed at a private screening in the Sono-Art projection room at Metropolitan Studios on 30 Dec 1929. The film began with a prologue spoken by Baltasar Fernández Cué, Hollywood correspondent for many Spanish-language magazines. Cué later worked on foreign-language adaptations of a number of Hollywood productions, including *Drácula* and *Resurrección*. In the prologue, he praised *Sombras de gloria* as a worthy precursor of many more Hollywood films to be produced in Spanish.

Cinl Mar 1930, p. 42. *FD* 16 Feb 1930. *Var* 19 Feb 1930, p. 33.

SOMBRAS DEL CIRCO (Spanish language)

Films Paramount; controlled by Paramount Publix Corp. *Dist* Paramount Publix Corp. **1931**; Bilbao, Spain opening: 22 Apr 1931; San Juan, Puerto Rico opening: 27 Jun 1931; Prod: Oct—Nov 1930 at Paramount studios, in Joinville, France. Sd; b&w. Length undetermined. *Country of origin* France. Spanish language.

Dir Adelqui Millar. *Scr* George Abbott.

Source: Based on the novel *Here Comes the Bandwagon* by Henry Leyford Gates (New York, 1928).

Cast: Amelia Muñoz (*Greta Nelson*), Tony D'Algy (*Ned Lee*), Félix de Pomés (*Nick Pogli*), Miguel Ligero (*Slim*), Antonia Arévalo (*Señora Elsie*), Alfredo Hurtado "Pitusín" (*Eric Lee*), Rafael Calvo (*Empresario*), Carmen Jiménez (*Señora Lee*), José María Blanco (*Tony*), Feliciano Catalán (*Blackie*), María Rosa de García (*Doris*).

Show business, Drama. [*Not viewed*]. Greta, Nick and Tony are trapeze artists in the Dixon Circus, and apart from their professional bonds, they are also involved in a love triangle. Greta and Tony are good friends, while Nick, in love with Greta, is jealous. While performing their "Leap from the Sky" routine, Nick lets Tony fall to his death, and although it appears to have been an accident, all the circus people give Nick the cold shoulder. The image of Tony lying dead in the ring is enough to make the circus pack up and move on to another city. During the train trip, Greta continues to suffer the hounding of Nick and, when the train is held up, she escapes into the countryside, unable to stand any more of the tension. Sometime later, the circus director engages Ned Lee to replace Tony, and by coincidence, he is the same man who fell in love with Greta when he found her lost near his farm after she left the train. Greta is afraid that Nick will repeat the "accident" during the act, but Ned confronts him and forces him to give up. From then on, the two new trapeze stars are the perfect team both in and out of the ring. *Aerialists. Circuses. Murder. Romantic rivalry. Circus performers. Farmers. Jealousy. Romance. Trains.*

Note: The working title of this film was *En mitad del camino del cielo*. This was the Spanish language version of the 1929 Paramount film *Half-Way to Heaven*, which was directed by George Abbott and starred Jean Arthur and Charles "Buddy" Rogers (see *AFI Catalog of Feature Films, 1921-30*, F2.2298). No reviews were located for the Spanish language version, but it is likely that it was shown in the U.S. Three other foreign language versions were produced in the Paramount studios at Joinville, France: a French version entitled *A mi-chemin du ciel*, directed by Alberto Cavalcanti and starring Enrique de Rivero and Janine Merrey; a German version, entitled *Der Sprung ins Nichts*, directed by Leo Mittler and starring Cilly Feindt and Aribert Mog; and a Swedish version, entitled *Halvvägs till himlen*, directed by Rune Carlsten and starring Haakon Hjelde and Elisabeth Frisk. No information has been located concerning any exhibition of these versions in the U.S.

SOMBRAS HABANERAS (Spanish language)

Hispania Talking Film Corp. *Dist* All-Star Exchange. Dec **1929**; World premiere in Los Angeles: 4 Dec 1929; Prod: Sep 1929 at Tec-Art Studios. Sd; b&w. 5 reels. Spanish language.

Prod René Cardona and Rodolfo Montes. *Dir* Cliff Wheeler. *Scr* René Nestor. *Mus comp* Ernesto Piedra.

Cast: René Cardona (*Ramón García*), Jacqueline Logan (*María*), Paul Ellis (*Pierre Dupont*), Juan Torena (*Pedro*), Pablo Alvarez (*Sr. García*), Manuel Conesa (*José*), Joyzelle (*Dancer*).

Melodrama. [*Not viewed*]. Ramón García, possessed by an uncontrollable passion for gambling, forges the signature of his father, a judge, in order to pay off his debts. Pierre Dupont, a professional gambler who wants to marry Ramón's sister María, discovers the fraud and threatens to reveal it. When María begs Dupont not to destroy her brother, he takes advantage of the situation and forces himself upon her. Ramón, armed with a revolver, witnesses the scene. A shot is heard and moments later Dupont is found dead. Despite all the evidence against him, Ramón declares his innocence. Pedro, María's journalist fiancé, succeeds in discovering the real killer, José, a waiter, who is madly in love with a dancer whom Dupont has also been pursuing. *Brothers and sisters. Cubans. Debt. Fathers and sons. Gambling. Investigations. Murder. Blackmail. Cabarets. Dancers. Engagements. Firearms. Forgers and forgery. Judges. Reporters. Waiters.*

Note: This film's working title was *Noches habaneras*. It was the first feature-length North American film to be shot in Spanish. Havana-born René Cardona's production company was originally called Cuban International Film Prod., but became Hispania Talking Film Corp. when he went into partnership with Rodolfo Montes. It is assumed that the story is set in Cuba. According to contemporary sources, part of the film's negative was destroyed in a fire at the Consolidated Laboratory on 24 Oct 1929. A private preview was held at Eastman's theater on 19 Nov 1929.

Information in *La Opinión*, Los Angeles's Spanish-language newspaper, indicates that the film's first public showing, at the Teatro Mexico in Los Angeles on 4 Dec 1929, had to be abandoned due to sound problems and was rescheduled for 6 Dec. Later, the film played the Teatro Hidalgo in mid-May 1930, in an improved version with changes in editing and sound synchronization. A news item in *FD* of 6 Oct 1929, reported that a silent version and an English version, titled *Havana Shadows*, were also planned, but their production has not been confirmed. Jacqueline Logan's voice was dubbed by an unidentified Cuban actress. The film played in San Juan, Puerto Rico in Feb 1930 under the title *Bajo el cielo de La Habana*.

Cinl Jan 1930, p. 4. *FD* 6 Oct 1929. *La Opinión* 14 Nov 1929, p. 6. *La Opinión* 20 Nov 1929, p. 7. *La Opinión* 24 Nov 1929, p. 14. *La Opinión* 4 Dec 1929, p. 6. *La Opinión* 5 Dec 1929, p. 6.

SOMETHING FOR THE BOYS (Latino)

Twentieth Century-Fox Film Corp. *Dist* Twentieth Century-Fox Film Corp. Nov **1944**; Los Angeles opening: 23 Nov 1944; New York opening: week of 29 Nov 1944; Prod: completed 26 Jun 1944 [©Twentieth Century-Fox Film Corp.; 16 Nov 1944; LP13222]. Sd (Western Electric Recording); col (Technicolor). 10 reels, 7,817 ft. 84 or 87 min.

Prod Irving Starr. *Dir* Lewis Seiler. [*Asst dir* Arthur Jacobson]. [*Dial dir* Hugh Cummings]. *Scr* Robert Ellis, Helen Logan and Frank Gabrielson. *Dir of photog* Ernest Palmer. [*2d cam* Bud Mautino]. *Spec photog eff* Fred Sersen. *Technicolor dir* Natalie Kalmus. *Assoc* Richard Mueller. *Art dir* Lyle Wheeler and Albert Hogsett. *Mus settings des by* Joseph C. Wright. *Film ed* Robert Simpson. *Set dec* Thomas Little. *Assoc* Walter M. Scott. [*Props* Mack Elliott]. *Cost* Kay Nelson and Yvonne Wood. *Mus dir* Emil Newman and Charles Henderson. *Dances staged and dir by* Nick Castle. *Sd* W. D. Flick and Roger Heman. [*Mus mixer* Murray Spivack and Vinton Vernon]. *Makeup artist* Guy Pearce. [*Tech dir* Sid Bower]. [*Tech adv* Phillip W. Booker]. [*Research dir* Frances Richardson]. [*Research asst* Katherine Lambert].

Song(s): "Something for the Boys," music and lyrics by Cole Porter; "Boom-Brrachee-Boom," "Eighty Miles Outside of Atlanta," "I Wish We Didn't Have to Say Good Night," "Samba-Boogie," "Wouldn't It Be Nice?" and "In the Middle of Nowhere," music by Jimmy McHugh, lyrics by Harold Adamson; "Batuca Nega," music and lyrics by Ary Barroso.

Source: Based on the musical *Something for the Boys*, book by Herbert and Dorothy Fields, songs by Cole Porter (New York, 7 Jan 1943).

Cast: CARMEN MIRANDA [(*Chiquita Hart*)], MICHAEL O'SHEA [(*Staff Sgt. Ronald "Rocky" Fulton*)], VIVIAN BLAINE [(*Blossom Hart*)], Phil Silvers [(*Harry Hart*)], Sheila Ryan [(*Melanie Walker*)], Perry Como [(*Sgt. Laddie Green*)], Glenn Langan [(*Lt. Ashley Crothers*)], [Roger Clark (*Lieutenant*)], [Cara Williams (*Secretary*)], [Thurston Hall (*Col. Jefferson L. Calhoun*)], [Clarence Kolb (*Col. Grubbs*)], [Paul Hurst (*Supervisor*)], [Andrew Tombes (*Southern colonel*)], [Jimmy Dodd (*Gambling soldier*)], [William "Red" Murphy, Russell Hoyt, Garry Owen, Robin Short, Gordon Wynne

(*Soldiers*)], [Larry Thompson (*Sergeant*)], [The Banda Da Lua (*Carmen Miranda's Orchestra*)], [Frank McCown], [Mary Stewart], [Esther Brodelet], [Grace Davies], [Evelyne Eager], [Billie Lane], [Valerie Traxler], [Bernice Lynne], [Doris Schaffer], [Janet Graves], [Jean McClure], [Jo Ann Dean], [Mabel Boehlke], [Midgie Dare], [Nancy Hale], [Maxine Carole], [Peggy Lou Neary], [Riley Thompson].

Homefront, Musical comedy. [*Print viewed*]. After cousins actress Blossom Hart, defense plant worker Chiquita Hart and inventor Harry Hart each learn that they are heirs to a large plantation in Masonville, Georgia, they travel separately to Masonville, and in the office of lawyer Col. Jefferson L. Calhoun, meet for the first time. As they are all poor, they are thrilled by the inheritance, but when Calhoun takes them to Magnolia Manor, they discover that the once glorious plantation house is now a ruin. In addition, paying the plantation's various property and inheritance taxes will put them deeply in debt. While the cousins are bemoaning their fate, Staff Sgt. Ronald "Rocky" Fulton, who was a well-known orchestra leader before joining the military, arrives with some of his men, including Sgt. Laddie Green. Rockie explains that the married service men of nearby Camp Dixon want to rent rooms in the manor for their wives, who have been unable to live close to their husbands due to a lack of available housing. The men pitch in and help the cousins fix up the manor, although Chiquita is continually bothered by the fact that she can pick up radio programs on the fillings in her teeth. Rocky, who has begun a romance with Blossom, suggests that they put on a musical show to raise funds for the renovations. On the day that "The Old Southern Corn Revue" is to open, Blossom is stunned by the arrival of Melanie Walker, a snobbish, rich woman, who Rocky is forced to admit is his fiancée. Melanie, believing that Rocky has arranged for the manor to be let just for her, imperiously announces the changes she intends to make, and the infuriated Blossom refuses to speak to Rocky. Before the show, Rocky explains to a disapproving Chiquita that he loves only Blossom. The show is a big success, and the next morning, Chiquita advises Blossom to fight for Rocky if she loves him. The snooty Melanie ends up covered with eggs after she tries to work one of Harry's new inventions, and she seeks solace from Lt. Ashley Crothers. While the lieutenant is there, he discovers that Harry is hosting a dice game for some of the soldiers, none of whom have wives staying at the manor. Crothers arrests the soldiers and recommends that the house be posted as off-limits for all military personnel. Col. Grubbs approves Crother's suggestion, and soon the wives are packing to leave. Meanwhile, after Harry learns that carborundum from the defense plant got into Chiquita's fillings and is causing her to receive radio programs, he decides to build an invention around the idea. One afternoon, Rocky comes to the house to try to talk to Blossom, who refuses to see him. Rocky is supposed to be on duty for war games, and is captured by the "enemy" army, which has taken over the manor as its headquarters. Hoping to save both his stripes and the manor, Rocky enlists the aid of Chiquita and Harry, who begin building a transmitter to send a message to Rocky's unit via Chiquita's teeth. The message is sent, and the cousins distract the "enemy" army with a song and dance show while Rocky's army assembles for its attack. Soon after, Rocky's side has prevailed in the manuevers, and in appreciation of Blossom, Chiquita and Harry's help, the off-limits sign is removed and the manor is once again the site of much happiness for the military men and their wives. At a celebratory party, Rocky announces that he has been selected for officer's candidate school, and the happy Blossom reconciles with him. *Brazilian Americans. Cousins. Entertainers. Inheritance. Inventors. Romance. Soldiers.* Debt. Gambling. Georgia. Jealousy. Manors. Military life. Morse code. Musical revues. Officers (Military). Radio beams. Snobs and snobbishness. Southerners. Teeth. War games. Wives. Women defense plant workers.

Note: According to information in the Twentieth Century-Fox Records of the Legal Department, located at the UCLA Arts—Special Collections Library, in Nov 1942, the studio advanced $62,500 to Michael Todd and Savoy Productions for production of the musical, then purchased the screen rights to it in 1943. Although the legal records give the purchase price as $265,000, a 12 Mar 1943 *HR* news item lists the amount paid by Fox as $305,000. Per the agreement with Todd, Fox could not release the film until at least the summer of 1944, which, as *HR* noted, was to "enable the stage original to play the key cities and tour without competition from the celluloid version." Only one of Cole Porter's songs for the musical was included in the film version. *HR* news items note that William Perlberg was originally slated to produce this film, Irving Cummings was to direct it and Betty Grable was to star in it. In Jan 1944, Bruce Humberstone was assigned to direct the picture and Brenda Marshall was set for

the female lead. According to *HR*, Humberstone auditioned The Jeepers, a seven-piece novelty orchestra, but they do not appear in the finished film. Although a 23 Feb 1944 *HR* news item noted that dance director Nick Castle was working with Carmen Miranda to prepare a "four-movement, symphonic treatment" of the popular song "Mairzy Doats," the number was not included in the film. In Apr 1944, *HR* noted that Scott Elliott had been tested for the film, but his participation in the finished picture has not been confirmed. Although a *HR* news item and studio press releases include Billie Seward, Stanley Prager, Chester Conklin, Harry Seymour and Jo-Carroll Dennison in the cast, they do not appear in the completed film. The picture marked the screen debuts of popular singer Perry Como and actor Rory Calhoun, who appeared under the name Frank McCown. Modern sources include Judy Holliday in the cast. A studio credit sheet lists the film's running time as 78 min.

According to information in the legal records and the Twentieth Century-Fox Produced Scripts Collection, the following writers worked on various versions of the screenplay: Harry Segall, Marian Spitzer, Eddie Welch, Snag Werris, Samuel Hoffenstein and Betty Reinhardt. The extent of their contributions to the completed film has not been confirmed, however. Notes from a 12 Jan 1944 studio conference reveal that production head Darryl F. Zanuck wanted the same writers who wrote *Greenwich Village*, a 1944 Twentieth Century-Fox picture starring Carmen Miranda, to write Miranda's dialogue for this film, because "they wrote especially for her, with mispronunciations, etc., and she is very funny when she is given this style of writing." The *Greenwich Village* screenwriters did not contribute to *Something for the Boys*, but Miranda's trademark mangling of the English language is included in the film. The studio records also note that the "Southland Routine," which is performed by Phil Silvers, includes excerpts from the following songs: "Southland" by Silvers, Harold Adamson and Jimmy McHugh; "Dixie's Land" by Dan Emmet; "All Over God's Heaven," traditional spiritual; "Shortnin' Bread," words by Jacques Wolfe, music traditional; "Indian Dance" by Urban Theilman; and "Climin' Up Dem Golden Stairs" by McHugh and Adamson. The studio records contain letters from songwriters Jule Styne and Sammy Cahn, who stated that the "Southland Routine" was based on their work. In early 1945, Twentieth Century-Fox paid the composers three thousand dollars not to pursue their claim. According to a 3 Feb 1943 *HR* news item, owners of the radio show *The Court of Missing Heirs* filed an infringement of copyright lawsuit against the producers and owners of the play *Something for the Boys*. The owners of the radio program alleged that the play infringed on their show's premise. The disposition of the suit is unknown.

Box 11 Nov 1944. *DV* 31 Oct 1944, p. 3, 8. *FD* 1 Nov 1944, p. 6. *HCN* 24 Nov 1944. *HR* 17 Nov 1942, p. 1. *HR* 11 Jan 1943, p. 3. *HR* 2 Feb 1943, p. 1. *HR* 3 Feb 1943, p. 9. *HR* 11 Feb 1943, p. 1. *HR* 18 Feb 1943, p. 1. *HR* 12 Mar 1943, p. 1. *HR* 8 Jun 1943, p. 1. *HR* 10 Jun 1943, p. 2. *HR* 18 Jun 1943, p. 8. *HR* 14 Oct 1943, p. 1. *HR* 19 Jan 1944, p. 1. *HR* 28 Jan 1944, p. 5. *HR* 31 Jan 1944, p. 8. *HR* 23 Feb 1944, p. 3. *HR* 27 Apr 1944, p. 4. *HR* 2 May 1944, p. 9. *HR* 5 May 1944, p. 21. *HR* 16 Jun 1944, p. 13. *HR* 27 Jun 1944, p. 3. *HR* 31 Oct 1944, p. 3. *HR* 4 Dec 1944, p. 8. *MPHPD* 26 Aug 1944, p. 2071. *MPHPD* 4 Nov 1944, p. 2165. *NYT* 28 Feb 1944. *NYT* 30 Nov 1944, p. 29. *Var* 1 Nov 1944, p. 10.

THE SON-DAUGHTER (Chinese Americans)

Metro-Goldwyn-Mayer Corp.; controlled by Loew's, Inc.; Clarence Brown's Production. *Dist* Metro-Goldwyn-Mayer Distributing Corp. 23 Dec 1932; *Prod:* 10 Oct—early Dec 1932 [©Metro-Goldwyn-Mayer Distributing Corp.; 29 Dec 1932; LP3514]. Sd (Western Electric Sound System); b&w. 9 reels. 80 min. Passed by the National Board of Review.

Dir Clarence Brown. [*Fill-in dir* Robert Z. Leonard]. [*Asst dir* Harry Bucquet]. *Scr* John Goodrich and Claudine West. *Dial* Leon Gordon. *Photog* Oliver T. Marsh. *Art dir* Cedric Gibbons. *Film ed* Margaret Booth. *Gowns* Adrian. *Score* Herbert Stothart. *Rec dir* Douglas Shearer. *Sd* Robert Shirley.

Song(s): by Anselm Goetzl and Herbert Stothart.

Source: Based on the play *The Son-Daughter* by George M. Scarborough and David Belasco (New York, 19 Nov 1919).

Cast: HELEN HAYES (*Lien Wha*), RAMON NOVARRO (*Tom Lee* [*also known as Prince Chun*]), Lewis Stone (*Dr. Dong Tong*), Warner Oland (*Fen Sha* [*also known as The Sea Crab*]), Ralph Morgan (*Fang Fou Hy*), Louise Closser Hale (*Toy Yah*), H. B. Warner (*Sin Kai*).

Melodrama. [*Print viewed*]. As the rebellion against oppression rages in China, Chinese-American sympathizers in San Francisco prepare a shipment of war materiel to be smuggled to their homeland. Faced with losing the shipment unless he can raise $100,000 in four days, Sin Kai appeals to his people for urgent help, even though his nemesis, The Sea Crab, the secret identity of wealthy merchant Fen Sha, will stop at nothing to prevent the ship's sailing. Despite their concern for China, Dr. Dong Tong and his beautiful daughter Lien Wha have a happy life. When Lien Wha falls in love with a poor young university student named Tom Lee, Tong's affection for his daughter outweighs his concerns for traditional Chinese courtship and he gives permission for them to marry. Soon, however, Sin Kai tells Tong that he must obtain a $25,000 marriage settlement for Lien Wha to give to the cause in compensation for the fact that he has no son to offer. Sadly, Tong agrees, as does Lien Wha, though she and Tom Lee are

heartbroken. Even the revelation by Sin Kai that Tom Lee is really Prince Chun, the heir to an important position in the rebellion, cannot alter their duty. After hearing that three other girls have come to an unfortunate end in similar situations, Tong has a change of heart, but Lien Wha encourages her suitors to bid more for her until Fen Sha offers $100,000. Because of her sacrifice, Tong calls her his "son-daughter," a title she accepts proudly. After the wedding, Fen Sha arranges for Tong to be robbed and murdered, then, because Sin Kai has poisoned himself after his capture, Fen Sha only needs to kill Tom Lee to prevent the arms shipment. Tom Lee secretly goes to Lien Wha, and they both overhear the details of Tong's murder. He then steals the money from Fen Sha's safe, but is wounded by a knife before escaping back to Lien Wha. Ater his death, Lien Wha strangles Fen Sha with his queue in their bridal chamber and sails to China with the arms shipment, having avenged her loved ones. *Chinese Americans. Fathers and daughters. Love. Marriage–Forced by circumstances. San Francisco (CA)–Chinatown. Self-sacrifice. Auctions. China–History. Dowry. Engagements. Munitions. Murder. Physicians. Poisoning. Princes. Strangling. Students. Suicide. Torture.*

Note: According to news items in *FD* and *HR*, Jacques Feyder was originally announced as the film's director, and M-G-M contract players Robert Young and Robert Montgomery had at various times been named as the male lead. Other news items mentioned that Richard Cromwell was going to be borrowed from Columbia for the lead. Actresses mentioned as possible leads included Anna May Wong and Lupe Velez. About ten days before the start of production, it was announced that Helen Hayes would be replaced as the lead so that she could appear in *The White Sister*, however, that production was postponed and Hayes was able to appear in both films. Other actors mentioned as possible cast members were Edmund Lowe and John Miljan, but the specific parts for which they were considered has not been determined. *HR* production charts and news items included Sumner Getchell, Frederick Burt, Ben Bard, Edward McWade and Bodil Rosing in the cast, however, their participation in the released film has not been confirmed. Other news items note the following information: Robert Z. Leonard took over as director for about ten days while Clarence Brown was ill with a bad case of flu; special lighting techniques and sets were specifically designed for "day" and "night" scenes so that Chinatown would look gaudy by day and drab by night; shortly after production began four hundred Chinese extras went on a food strike until they were given the kind of food they liked; and in early Dec 1932 ten days of new scenes were added to make the picture "a special." A 10 Nov *FD* news item erroneously reported that the picture starring Roman Novarro and Helen Hayes, entitled *Let's Go*, had been renamed *Fast Life*. *Fast Life* actually starred Madge Evans and William Haines (see *AFI Catalog of Feature Films, 1931-40*; F3.1287). According to a 24 Dec *HR* news item, playwright George Scarborough filed a lawsuit against M-G-M over script alterations in the film, however, no additional information on the suit has been located.

FD 4 Oct 1932, p. 7. *FD* 10 Nov 1932, p. 8. *FD* 31 Dec 1932, p. 4. *FD* 3 Jan 1933, p. 6. *HF* 22 Oct 1932, p. 16. *HF* 5 Nov 1932, p. 1. *HR* 14 Sep 1932, p. 3. *HR* 24 Sep 1932, p. 4. *HR* 27 Sep 1932, p. 7. *HR* 28 Sep 1932, p. 1. *HR* 29 Sep 1932, p. 1. *HR* 30 Sep 1932, p. 1. *HR* 3 Oct 1932, p. 1. *HR* 5 Oct 1932, p. 1. *HR* 10 Oct 1932, p. 1. *HR* 13 Oct 1932, p. 18. *HR* 14 Oct 1932, p. 1. *HR* 17 Oct 1932, p. 6. *HR* 3 Nov 1932, p. 1. *HR* 2 Dec 1932, p. 2. *HR* 24 Dec 1932, p. 3. *HR* 8 Dec 1932, p. 3. *MPH* 7 Jan 1933, p. 27. *NYT* 2 Jan 1933, p. 29. *Var* 3 Jan 1933, p. 27.

A SON OF BATTLE *see* **MY FIGHTING GENTLEMAN**

SON OF COCHISE *see* **TAZA, SON OF COCHISE**

A SON OF ERIN (Irish Americans)

Pallas Pictures. *Dist* Paramount Pictures Corp. 9 Nov **1916** [©Julia Crawford Ivers; 18 Oct 1916; LP9381]. Si; b&w. 5 reels.

Dir Julia Crawford Ivers. *Story and scen* Julia Crawford Ivers. *Cam* J. O. Taylor.

Cast: Dustin Farnum (*Dennis O'Hara*), Winifred Kingston (*Katie O'Grady*), Tom Bates (*Patrick O'Grady*), Jack Livingston (*Brian Trelawney*), Wilfred McDonald (*Terence*), Wallace Pyke (*Dan O'Keefe*), Lee Willard (*George Harding*), Mabel Wiles (*Florence Harding*), Hugh B. Koch (*John D. Haynes*).

Comedy-drama. Unable to make ends meet in Ireland, Dennis O'Hara decides to go to New York to become a policeman, after which he plans to send for his fiancée, Katie O'Grady. Dennis manages to pass his police examination, but then, just before he wires Katie to join him, some crooks looking for a scapegoat implicate him in a graft scheme. This alleged involvement would make it impossible for Dennis to remain a policeman, but he finally clears his name and is allowed to rejoin the force. Then, Katie comes to the United States to marry Dennis, but as excited as she is to become his wife, she is just as thrilled to see him in his policeman's uniform. *Frame-ups. Immigrants. Irish. Police. Reputation.* Graft. Ireland. New York City.

MPN 11 Nov 1916, p. 3020. *MPW* 11 Nov 1916, p. 845. *NYDM* 4 Nov 1916, p. 27. *Wid's* 2 Nov 1916, p. 1074.

A SON OF HIS FATHER (Irish Americans)

Famous Players-Lasky Corp. *Dist* Paramount Pictures. 21 Sep **1925**; San Francisco premiere: ca15 Aug 1925 [©Famous Players-Lasky Corp.; 13 Oct 1925; LP21903]. Si; b&w. 7 reels, 6,925 ft.

Pres Adolph Zukor and Jesse L. Lasky. *Dir* Victor Fleming. *Scr* Anthony Coldeway. *Photog* C. Edgar Schoenbaum.

Source: Based on the novel *A Son of His Father* by Harold Bell Wright (New York, 1925).

Cast: Bessie Love (*Nora*), Warner Baxter ("*Big Boy*" *Morgan*), Raymond Hatton (*Charlie Grey*), Walter McGrail (*Holdbrook*), Carl Stockdale (*Zobester*), Billy Eugene (*Larry*), James Farley (*Indian Pete*), Charles Stevens (*Pablo*), Valentina Zimina (*Dolores*), George Kuwa (*Wing*).

Western. "Big Boy" Morgan, a "real westerner" like his father, has lost a controlling interest in his ranch to Holdbrook, who has come under the influence of a gang of gamblers and smugglers led by Zobester. They wish to take over the property for illicit purposes. Nora O'Shea, fresh from Ireland, shows up at the Morgan ranch looking for her brother, Larry, who has been lured into becoming a member of the gang. Morgan keeps the truth from her, but she eventually learns it from Holdbrook and goes to her brother. The gang kidnaps her, but Morgan, with the aid of the U. S. Cavalry, comes to her rescue. The gang is broken up, Holdbrook gives Nora his share in the ranch, Nora and Morgan marry, and Larry is put on probation. *Brothers and sisters. Gambling. Gangs. Immigrants. Irish Americans. Ranchers. Smuggling. United States. Army. Cavalry.*

FD 11 Oct 1925. *MPW* 10 Oct 1925. *NYT* 29 Sep 1925, p. 31. *Var* 30 Sep 1925, p. 43.

SON OF INGAGI (African Americans)

Hollywood Productions; A Richard C. Kahn Production. *Dist* Sack Amusement Enterprises, Inc. **1940**. Sd; b&w. 7 reels, 5,940 ft. 70 min. PCA cert no. 5981.

[*Prod* Richard C. Kahn]. *Supv of prod* Dr. Herbert Meyer. *Dir* Richard C. Kahn. *Story and cont* Spencer Williams, Jr. *Cine* Roland Price and Herman Schapp. *Film ed* Dan Milner. *Sd eng* Cliff Ruberg. *Prod mgr* Dick L'Estrange.

Cast: Zack Williams (*N'Gina*), Laura Bowman (*Dr. [Helen] Jackson*), Alfred Grant (*Robert Lindsay*), Daisy Bufford (*Eleanor Lindsay*), Arthur Ray (*Zeno Jackson*), Spencer Williams, Jr. (*Nelson*), Earl J. Morris (*Bradshaw*), Jesse Graves (*Chief of Detectives*), "The [Four] Toppers".

African American, Horror, Mystery, Comedy-drama. [*Print viewed*]. Moments after the wedding of Robert and Eleanor Lindsay, wealthy old skinflint Dr. Helen Jackson asks the lawyer Bradshaw to draw up her will. While the wedding reception is in full swing, Helen, an African missionary who introduced Eleanor's parents, both of whom died shortly after Eleanor's birth, secretly observes the festivities through a window. The reception is interrupted by an explosion at the foundry where Bob works, which results in the loss of his job. When Helen arrives at her home, she finds her criminal brother Zeno waiting for her, so she rings her Oriental gong, summoning the strange ape-man N'Gina, who frightens Zeno away. That night, Helen completes her drug experiments and creates the greatest medicine ever made. However, when N'Gina drinks from one of the test tubes, he becomes enraged and kills her. The Lindsays find Helen's body, and because they are named as the beneficiaries in her will, they are initially suspected of murdering her. Eventually, though, the Lindsays are acquitted of the crime, and they move into Helen's manor, where Eleanor soon discovers that food is mysteriously disappearing. Bradshaw, the executor of the will, comes to urge them to sell the house, and while rummaging through the desk, he carelessly rings the gong, which summons N'Gina from his hiding place in the cellar. Angry at finding a stranger in Helen's chair, N'Gina brutally kills Bradshaw. After the comical detective Nelson, assigned to solve the case of the mystery manor, moves into the home, Zeno breaks into the couple's bedroom, but escapes when Eleanor accidentally hits Bob instead of Zeno. After seeing N'Gina emerge from the cellar, Zeno goes downstairs to seize Helen's gold. Zeno finds the gold, and when N'Gina catches him, he fires his gun at the beast, but N'Gina survives and drags Zeno upstairs to Nelson. N'Gina then carries Eleanor downstairs, and she faints upon seeing him. When Nelson wakes up and sees Zeno's body, his shouts awaken Bob, who searches for Eleanor. N'Gina accidentally starts a fire, and Eleanor's screams draw Bob and Nelson into the cellar, where Nelson fails to arrest N'Gina. Bob, however, succeeds in locking the beast in

a cell, and as the house and N'Gina go up in flames, Nelson emerges from the shrubbery with the bags of gold, and Bob and Eleanor escape unharmed. *African Americans. Apemen. Manors. Murder. Police detectives. Africa. Brothers. Brothers and sisters. Bumblers. Cellars. Dismissal (Employment). Explosions. False accusations. Fires. Foundries. Gold. Lawyers. Medicine. Missionaries. Scientists. Weddings. Wills.*

Note: A working title for this film was *Horror House*. Although onscreen credits state that the picture was copyrighted in 1940, no copyright registration has been found.

Exh 24 Jan 1940, p. 457. *FD* 24 Jan 1940, p. 7. *MPD* 15 Jan 1940, p. 8.

A SON OF SATAN (African Americans)

Micheaux Film Corp. **1924**; License application: New York State: 18 Sep 1924; Prod: began 26 Mar 1923. Si; b&w. 6 or 7 reels.

Prod Oscar Micheaux. *Dir* Oscar Micheaux. *Wrt and adpt* Oscar Micheaux.

Cast: Andrew S. Bishop, Lawrence Chenault, Emmet Anthony, Edna Morton, Monte Hawley, Shingzie Howard, Ida Anderson, E. G. Tatum, Dink Stewart, W. B. F. Crowell, Olivia Sewall, Mildred Smallwood, Blanche Thompson, Margaret Brown, Professor Hosay.

African American, Melodrama. Depiction of the experiences of an ordinary black person going to a haunted house to stay all night as the result of an argument. "This picture is filled with scenes of drinking, carousing and shows masked men becoming intoxicated. It shows the playing of crap for money, a man [Captain Tolston] killing his wife by choking her, the killing of the leader of the hooded organization and the killing of a cat by throwing a stone at it." (NYSA records.). *African Americans. Cats. Drunkenness. Ghosts. Haunted houses. Superstition.*

Note: The working title of this film was *The Ghost of Tolston's Manor*. Shooting began 26 Mar 1923 at a Bronx studio, then moved to an outdoor location in Roanoke, VA, according to a news item. The house used in the film was more than two hundred years old and was located at Clason's Point, NY. Twenty thousand feet of film was shot, and the film was edited in Charleston, WV. Critic D. Ireland Thomas, writing in the African-American newspaper *ChiDef*, commented concerning this film, "Some may not like the production because it shows up some of our Race in their true colors. They might also protest against the language used.... I must admit that it is true to nature, yes, I guess, too true. We have got to hand it to Oscar Micheaux when it comes to giving us the real stuff."

Billboard 7 Apr 1923, p. 48. *Billboard* 5 May 1923, p. 50. *ChiDef* 31 Jan 1925, p. 7. *New York Age* 31 Mar 1923, p. 6.

SON OF THE GODS (Chinese Americans)

First National Pictures, Inc. *Dist* First National Pictures, Inc. 9 Mar **1930** [©First National Pictures, Inc.; 17 Mar 1930; LP1218]. Sd (Vitaphone); b&w with col seq (Technicolor). 9 reels, 8,344 ft. [Also si.].

Dir Frank Lloyd. *Scen, dial and titles* Bradley King. *Photog* Ernest Haller.

Song(s): "Pretty Little You," words by Ben Ryan, music by Sol Violinsky.

Source: Based on the short story "Son of the Gods" by Rex Beach in *Hearst's International Cosmopolitan* (Oct–Dec 1928; Jan–Mar 1929).

Cast: Richard Barthelmess (*Sam Lee*), Constance Bennett (*Allana*), Dorothy Mathews (*Alice Hart*), Barbara Leonard (*Mabel*), James Eagle (*Spud*), Frank Albertson (*Kicker*), Mildred Van Dorn (*Eileen*), King Hoo Chang (*Moy*), Geneva Mitchell (*Connie*), E. Alyn Warren (*Lee Ying*), Ivan Christie (*Cafe manager*), Anders Randolf (*Wagner*), George Irving (*Attorney*), Claude King (*Bathurst*), Dickey Moore (*Boy*), Robert Homans (*Dugan*).

Romance. Sam Lee, reared by a wealthy Chinese merchant in San Francisco's Chinatown, is tolerated in college only because of his money. Determined to prove himself, he works his way to the Riviera, where he is befriended by Bathurst, a novelist. The writer introduces him to Allana, a sophisticated American girl. She falls hopelessly in love with him and refuses to hear anything of his past or background; however, when she learns he is Chinese, she denounces him and lashes him with her riding crop. Sam returns home, heartbroken, to see his dying father; through Eileen, his dearest friend, he learns that he was orphaned by white parents. The repentant Allana returns to the United States, and the lovers are happily reunited. *Chinese Americans. Courtship. Novelists. Racism. Riviera (France). San Francisco (CA)–Chinatown. Students. Whips and Whippings.*

FD 2 Feb 1930. *NYT* 31 Jan 1930, p. 24.

THE SON OF THE WOLF (Native Americans)

R-C Pictures Corp. 11 Jun **1922** [©R-C Pictures Corp.; 11 Jun 1922; LP17957]. Si; b&w. 5 reels, 4,970 ft.

Dir Norman Dawn. *Scen* W. Heywood.

Source: Based on the short story "The Son of the Wolf" by Jack London in *Tales of the Far North* (New York, 1900).

Cast: Wheeler Oakman (*Scruff Mackenzie*), Edith Roberts (*Chook-Ra*), Sam Allen (*Father Roubeau*), Ashley Cooper (*Ben Harrington*), Fred Kohler (*Malemute Kid*), Thomas Jefferson (*Chief Thling Tinner*), Fred Stanton (*The Bear*), Arthur Jasmine (*The Fox*), William Eagle Eye (*Shaman*).

Melodrama. Scruff Mackenzie, arriving at his quarters in the Yukon, announces his intentions of seeking a wife. Later, he meets Father Roubeau and his Indian ward, Chook-Ra, whom Scruff comes to love, but the priest forbids their marriage until the arrival of her father, Chief Tinner. When Scruff goes to a nearby town to buy gifts for Chook-Ra, he becomes infatuated with a dance hall girl. Chook-Ra follows and, determined to win him, takes some dancing lessons and surprises him at the local ball. Chief Tinner arrives, however, and forces Chook-Ra to return to her own people. Scruff follows to the Indian camp and after much bargaining wins the girl, but the minor chiefs decree that he must first fight The Bear, who also is her suitor. The latter is killed in the ensuing conflict, and the couple depart for civilization. *Clergy. Courtship. Dance hall girls. Indians of North America. Yukon Territory.*

ETR 24 Jun 1922, p. 237. *FD* 18 Jun 1922. *MPW* 24 Jun 1922, p. 737. *Var* 14 Jul 1922, p. 40.

SOÑADORES DE LA GLORIA (Spanish language)

Imperial Art Films. *Dist* United Artists Corp. **1932**; Los Angeles opening: 8 Jan 1932; Prod: at Tec-Art Studios. Sd; b&w. 11 reels, 10,200 ft. 113 min. Spanish language.

Prod Miguel Contreras Torres and Alfred T. Mannon. *Dir* Miguel Contreras Torres. *Orig story and scr* Miguel Contreras Torres. *Photog* M. A. Anderson. *Mus* Juan Aguilar, Rafael Gama, Federico Ruiz and Otero y Arcos. *Mus adpt* Pryor Moore.

Cast: Miguel Contreras Torres (*Juan Montes*), Lia Torá (*Rosario*), Manuel Granado (*Rafael Jiménez*), Medea de Movarry ("*La Dama de la Gardenia*"), Alfredo del Diestro (*Don Manuel*), José Peña "Pepet" ("*Currito*"), Emma Roldán, Antonio Cumellas, Rafael Valverde, Araceli Rey, Luis Montes, Eumenio Blanco, Hipólito Mora.

War, Drama. [*Not viewed*]. Two inseparable school friends, Rafael Jiménez and Juan Montes, meet in Seville after several years. Rafael is a popular matador, while Juan has become a distinguished writer. After a successful year abroad, Rafael has returned to reclaim his reputation in front of the bullfighting fans of Seville, where Juan enjoys an excellent social standing and shortly plans to be married. Juan welcomes his childhood friend without realizing that he will soon become his fiancée Rosario's lover. When the newspapers announce that the Moors have occupied Spanish territory in North Africa, Juan feels that he should volunteer for military service. Rafael and Rosario are then left alone, but Rafael can't solve the dilemma of losing Rosario or betraying his friend, so he too goes to the front. When Juan reads a letter from Rosario, he feels that she is being faithful to him at the expense of finding happiness with Rafael. Because he wants Rosario to be happy above all else, Juan sets out on a suicide mission, then disappears and is assumed dead. Months later, Juan, a war invalid, attends the wedding of Rafael and Rosario incognito, concealing his misfortune so as not to spoil the happiness of those he loves most. *Africa, North. Authors. Bullfighters and bullfighting. Friendship. Self-sacrifice. Spaniards. Engagements. Invalids. Missing persons, Assumed dead. Seville (Spain). War injuries. Weddings.*

Note: Contemporary sources state that prior to filming at the Tec-Art studios in Hollywood, some exteriors were shot in Seville, Spain, and in Morocco.

CM Apr 1932, p. 263. *NYT* 10 Dec 1938, p. 13.

SONG OF SONGS *see* **SHIR HASHIRIM**

SONG OF TAHITI *see* **TAHITI NIGHTS**

SONG OF THE BANDIT *see* **NORTH OF THE GREAT DIVIDE**

SONG OF THE BORDER see SOUTH OF THE RIO GRANDE

SONG OF THE CABALLERO (Latino)

Ken Maynard Productions. *Dist* Universal Pictures Corp. 29 Jun **1930** [©Universal Pictures Corp.; 20 Jun 1930; LP1377]. Sd (Movietone); b&w. 7 reels, 6,524 ft.

Pres Carl Laemmle. *Dir* Harry J. Brown. *Adpt* Bennett Cohen. *Story* Kenneth C. Beaton and Norman Sper. *Dial* Lesley Mason. *Photog* Ted McCord. *Film ed* Fred Allen. *Rec eng* C. Roy Hunter.

Cast: Ken Maynard (*Juan*), Doris Hill (*Anita*), Francis Ford (*Don Pedro Madera*), Gino Corrado (*Don José*), Evelyn Sherman (*Doña Luisa*), Josef Swickard (*Manuel*), Frank Rice (*Andrea*), William Irving (*Bernardo*), Joyzelle (*Conchita*), Tarzan (*Himself, a horse*).

Western. In California, sometime before annexation, Juan, accompanied by two followers, becomes known as a bandit who preys only on the Madera family, because of ill treatment accorded his mother by Pedro Madero. He robs Don José at a tavern celebration while his father is away escorting the beautiful Anita, betrothed to José. Juan meets the party, and, as a reward for saving Anita's life, is invited to the rancho for the fiesta. The guests are alarmed to hear that Juan is actually the bandit enemy of the family; Anita, attracted to Juan, resents her coming marriage all the more when she surprises José in the arms of a former sweetheart. Juan fights a desperate sword battle until Don Pedro learns he is his nephew; they are reconciled, José is discredited, and Anita is betrothed to Juan. *Bandits. California–History–To 1846. Courtship. Family relationships. Horses. Mexicans. Ranches. Revenge.*

FD 13 Jul 1930. *Var* 9 Jul 1930, p. 31.

SONG OF THE CITY (Italian Americans)

Metro-Goldwyn-Mayer Corp.; controlled by Loew's Inc. *Dist* Loew's Inc. 2 Apr **1937**; Prod: late Jan—20 Feb 1937 [©Metro-Goldwyn-Mayer Corp.; 29 Mar 1937; LP7018]. Sd (Western Electric Sound System); b&w. 7 reels. 65, 68-69 or 73 min. Passed by the National Board of Review. PCA cert no. 3183.

Prod Lucien Hubbard and Michael Fessier. *Dir* Errol Taggart. [*Asst dir* Marvin Stuart]. *Orig story and scr* Michael Fessier. *Photog* Leonard Smith. *Mont eff* Slavko Vorkapich. *Art dir* Cedric Gibbons. *Art dir assoc* Eddie Imazu and Edwin B. Willis. *Film ed* John B. Rogers. *Ward* Dolly Tree. *Rec dir* Douglas Shearer. [*Singing double for Margaret Lindsay* Devona Doxie].

Song(s): "Tonight Will Never Come Again," music by Dr. William Axt, lyrics by Gus Kahn; additional Italian lyrics by Enrico Ricardi.

Cast: Margaret Lindsay (*Angelina [Romandi]*), Jeffrey Dean (*Paul Herrick*), J. Carroll Naish (*Mario*), Nat Pendleton (*Benvenuto [Romandi]*), Stanley Morner (*Tommy*), Marla Shelton (*Jane Lansing*), Inez Palange (*Mrs. Romandi*), Charles Judels (*Mr. [Pietro] Romandi*), Edward Norris (*Guido [Romandi]*), Fay Helm (*Marge*), Frank Puglia (*Tony*), [Edna Callahan (*Mary*)], [Marc Kramer (*Stephen*)], [June Wilkins (*Susan*)], [Otto Yamaoka (*Wilbur*)], [Walter Miller (*Captain Hodges*)], [Paul Hurst, James Blaine (*Detectives*)], [Leonard Pennario (*Fisherboy*)], [Nick Thompson (*Fisherman*)], [Bobby Watson (*Waiter*)], [Ernie Alexander (*Steward*)], [Alan Bridge (*Captain*)], [Robert E. Homans (*Policeman*)], [Sam Hayes (*Radio announcer*)], [Evelyn Selbie (*Screaming woman*)], [Robert Billaud (*Boy soprano*)], [St. Luke's Choristers].

Domestic, Drama. [*Print viewed*]. Feeling guilty because he has lost fifty thousand dollars of her money on a stock deal, Paul Herrick doesn't want to marry multi-millionairess Jane Lansing. She insists, though, so he takes the ferry to her Marin County estate. Drunk, he falls off the ferry in the fog and is saved by the Romandi family, who think that he tried to commit suicide. They take him in to recuperate and, thinking that he is down on his luck, offer him a job fishing on their boat. He is impressed with the warmth of the family, as well as their daughter Angelina, so he decides to stay for a while. The first day out, he wants to quit because the work is so hard, but Angelina encourages him to keep at it. Meanwhile, her father, Pietro is trying to keep racketeer Tony from forcing him to pay protection money. Several weeks later, Jane receives a report from a detective she has hired to find Paul and becomes jealous of Angelina, even though Angelina plans to marry community leader Mario after he pays for her singing lessons in Milan. When Mario learns about Tony's "protection" ploy against the Romandis, he advises Tony to stay away from them and slugs him to make his point. That same night, the family learns that their son Guido plans to turn down the Rhodes

scholarship he has just won to remain with his girlfriend Marge, and Angelina tells them that she won't go to Milan and marry Mario because of her feelings for Paul. The oldest son, Benvenuto, is bitter against Paul and they fight on the boat the next day, but after Paul saves Benvenuto from drowning Paul decides that he should leave. On shore, Jane is waiting for him with a phony warrant so Paul decides to use it as a way to leave the Romandis without hurting them. Soon Marge, who has married Guido, tells Benvenuto that she is planning to leave him so that he can take the scholarship and be happy. Some time later, Angelina and Mario board the steamship *Rosalina* for Milan just as Paul and Jane board her yacht. That night, while Jane's yacht is being repaired, they hear that the *Rosalina* is on fire a short distance from them. Paul borrows a tug boat and rushes with his friends to help rescue the passengers. The fire, which started with a bomb delivered to Mario by Tony, looks fatal from a distance, but Paul manages to get aboard and rescue Angelina and Mario. Jane then invites the Romandis to her home in Marin County and she, Mario and Benvenuto convince him that he is a "rat" not to marry Angelina. *Investors. Italian Americans. Rescues. Romantic rivalry. San Francisco (CA). Singers. Bombs. Finance–Personal. Fires. Fishermen. Heiresses. Marin County (CA). Nurses. Private detectives. Rhodes scholars. Shipwrecks.*

Note: The actor Jeffrey Dean is more commonly known as Dean Jagger. Jagger was only billed as Jeffrey Dean in this film. A *HR* production chart also listed him as Dean Jeffries; it is unclear whether this is a typographical error or a name which he briefly used during the film's production. Stanley Morner changed his name to Dennis Morgan in 1939. Margaret Lindsay was borrowed from Warner Bros. for this picture. According to news items in *HR*, director Errol Taggart and two camera crews filmed backgrounds in San Francisco for the film, including a sequence featuring thirty local fishing boats.

Box 3 Apr 1937. *DV* 16 Mar 1937, p. 3. *FD* 7 May 1937, p. 12. *HR* 16 Jan 1937, p. 3. *HR* 19 Jan 1937, p. 7. *HR* 28 Jan 1937, p. 3. *HR* 1 Feb 1937, p. 18. *HR* 16 Mar 1937, p. 3. *MPD* 18 Mar 1937, p. 2. *MPH* 20 Mar 1937, p. 35 *MPH* 27 Mar 1937, p. 43. *Var* 5 May 1937, p. 16.

SONG OF THE EAGLE (German Americans)

Paramount Productions, Inc.; A Charles R. Rogers Production. *Dist* Paramount Productions, Inc. 28 Apr **1933** [©Paramount Productions, Inc.; 2 May 1933; LP3852]. Sd (Western Electric Noiseless Recording); b&w. 8 reels. 65, 70 or 83 min. Passed by the National Board of Review.

Assoc prod Harry Joe Brown. *Dir* Ralph Murphy. [*Asst dir* Tommy Atkins]. *Scr* Casey Robinson. *Orig story* Gene Towne and Graham Baker. *Addl dial* Willard Mack. *Photog* Henry Sharp. [*Cam op* Fred Mayer]. [*Asst cam* Lloyd Ahern and John Eckhardt]. [*Art dir* David Garber]. [*Film ed* Joseph Kane]. [*Ed asst* Lynn Harrison and John Link]. [*Rec eng* V. E. Vernon and Phil G. Wisdom]. [*Asst rec eng* G. B. Rayburn]. [*Chief elec* Al Holton]. [*Chief grip* Irving Newmeyer]. [*Props* William Carr]. [*Still photog* Elwood Bredell].

Song(s): "Hey, Hey, We Gonna Be Free," music by Harold Lewis, lyrics by Bernie Grossman.

Cast: Charles Bickford ([*Joe*] *Nails Anderson*), Richard Arlen (*Bill Hoffman*), Mary Brian (*Elsa Kranzmeyer*), Jean Hersholt (*Otto Hoffman*), Louise Dresser (*Emma Hoffman*), Andy Devine (*Mud*), George E. Stone (*Gus*), Gene Morgan (*Charlie*), Bert Sprotte (*Emil Kranzmeyer*), George Meeker (*August Hoffman*), Julie Haydon (*Gretchen*), Harry Walker (*Nolly*), James Bradbury, Jr. (*Slats*).

Drama. [*Print viewed*]. In 1916, Otto Hoffman takes his sons, Bill and August, into his successful beer brewing business. Unfortunately, World War I robs the Hoffmans of their son August, but Bill returns with three good buddies, Charlie, Mud and Gus, whose lives he saved. At the close of the war, Prohibition closes the brewery, and there is little work for the returning soldiers. Gus is hired by bootlegger Joe Anderson, who used to be one of the Hoffman's favorite truck drivers. Otto and Bill start producing "near beer" to maintain some kind of profit for the brewery. Now a gangster, Joe tries to intimidate Otto into selling the brewery to him, but Otto refuses to cooperate. Bill marries Elsa, daughter of family friend Emil Kranzmeyer, after the 1929 stockmarket crash, and the Hoffmans are forced to sell their home, while Joe shows off his car with bulletproof glass. After the election of Franklin Delano Roosevelt to the presidency, Prohibition is finally repealed, and the Hoffmans gleefully send out their first truckload of beer, while Joe, now also known as "Nails," plans his protection racket. Joe and his thugs intimidate bar and store owners into selling his beer instead of the Hoffmans' by intimidation and violence. Many of the Hoffman employees quit out of fear, and after

Elsa's father is killed by Joe's thugs for refusing to quit his job, Bill hires a group of unemployed ex-soldiers who are ready for good pay and a good cause. On Armistice Day, Bill celebrates with the soldiers at his brewery when Gus comes to warn him that he is on Joe's hit list. Unknown to Bill, Gus was sent to kill him and has sacrificed his life to save Bill, who once saved his life on the battlefield. Otto is killed the same night that he is to be made president of the United Brewmasters Association, and Bill is forced to break the news to his mother, Emma. Later, Bill gets the approval of the police chief in his fight against the gangsters, who deputizes Bill's workers. After Elsa tells Emma that Joe is the gangster who killed Otto, Emma goes to Joe's office, which is in her former home, and kills him. At the same time, Bill and his men are about to be shot by Joe's thugs when the rest of Bill's employees come out of hiding to fight. The workers win and throw the thugs into trucks headed for the police station. Although the police find Emma's German bible at the scene of Joe's death, they think it had been left over from when she lived there and dismiss the case as having been an inside job. Although Emma prays for her sins, peace is restored to the Hoffman home as they welcome Bill and Elsa's new baby boy into the world. *Bootleggers. Brewers and breweries. German Americans. Murder. Prohibition.* Family life. Fathers and sons. Fights. Friendship. Justifiable homicide. Racketeers. Self-sacrifice. Unemployment. War heroes. World War I.

Note: *Var* mentions that the screenplay erred in one scene in which the Jess Willard-Jack Dempsey fight in Toledo is discussed, as prohibition did not occur until after the fight. *NYT* notes the film opened with a dedicatory note to President Franklin Delano Roosevelt, which was not in the print viewed.

FD 27 Apr 1933, p. 4. *HR* 13 Apr 1933, p. 7. *IP* May 1933, p. 27. *MPD* 27 Apr 1933, p. 6. *MPH* 29 Apr 1933, p. 26. *NYT* 29 Apr 1933, p. 14. *Var* 2 May 1933, p. 13.

SONG OF THE GRINGO (Latino)

Boots and Saddles Pictures, Inc.; An Edward F. Finney Production. *Dist* Grand National Films, Inc. 22 Nov **1936** [©Grand National Films, Inc.; 10 Nov 1936; LP6960]. Sd; b&w. 6 reels. 62 min. PCA cert no. 2791.

Pres EDWARD L. ALPERSON. *Supv* Lindsley Parsons. *Dir* John McCarthy. *Scr* John McCarthy, Robert Emmett and Al Jennings. *Story* John McCarthy and Robert Emmett. [*Contr to scr const* Lindsley Parsons]. *Photog* Gus Peterson. *Art dir* Charles Clague. *Film ed* Frederick Bains. *Mus* Frank Sanucci. *Rec* Cliff Ruberg. *Prod mgr* Robert Tansey.

Song(s): "Out on the Lone Prairie," music and lyrics by Harry Miller; "My Sweet Chiquita" and "Rye Whiskey," music and lyrics by Tex Ritter; "You Are Reality," music and lyrics by Joan Woodbury; "Marta" and "Blanca Rosa," traditional Mexican waltzes arranged by Jose Pacheco; "Sam Hall," an old English folk song; other songs by Harry Revel and Frank Sanucci.

Cast: TEX RITTER [(*Tex*)], Joan Woodbury [(*Lolita Valle*)], Fuzzy Knight [(*Slim*)], Monte Blue [(*Sheriff*)], Warner Richmond [(*Cherokee*)], Al Jennings [(*Judge*)], Martín Garralaga [(*Don Estaban Valle*)], William Desmond [(*Court clerk*)], Forrest Taylor, Robert Fiske, Rosa Rey, Jose Pacheco, and his Continental Orchestra, [Richard T. Adams (*Evans*)], [White Flash, the horse (*Himself*)].

Western, with songs. [*Print viewed*]. Lawman Tex goes undercover as an outlaw by holding up miners Robert Henderson and Norman Conklin as they turn in gold from their mine. During a storm, Tex is chased by the sheriff and his deputies to the hacienda of Don Estaban Valle, where Tex hides. Hoping to capitalize on Tex's talents as an outlaw by hiring him, Señor Evans, Don Estaban's business partner, convinces the sheriff to give up his search for Tex in the house. When Tex emerges from his hiding place, he finds himself in the bedroom of Lolita, Don Estaban's daughter, and she nurses his wound and falls in love with him. Evans then recruits Tex to help him steal the profitable Henderson-Conklin mine. Evans and Don Estaban have recently financed a string of mine owners who have run into trouble. Mysteriously, all those who have accepted Evans' help have been killed, after which their property has been seized by Evans and Don Estaban. Unaware that Evans has been hiring men to kill the miners, Don Estaban has innocently profited. Soon Evans becomes jealous of Tex's favor with Lolita, whom Evans desires, while Cherokee begins to suspect Tex's loyalty to Evans. Forcing Tex to prove himself, Evans instructs him to dynamite the Henderson-Conklin mine, then orders Tex to kill the miners. While Cherokee watches nearby, Tex successfully fakes the murders, making it look as if Henderson and Conklin shot each other, then orders them to go into

hiding. After the newspapers report Henderson and Conklin's death as part of a growing list of tragedies associated with Don Estaban, he vows to extricate himself from Evans' crime ring. At Lolita's birthday fiesta, to which the sheriff has been invited, Lolita, alone with Tex, warns him to leave before he is killed. Don Estaban then catches the couple embracing and, denouncing Tex for bringing shame to his house, orders him to leave. During their argument, Don Estaban is shot, and Tex is blamed. Following Evans' orders, the Estaban maid identifies Tex as the outlaw whom the sheriff chased the night of the storm, and Tex is arrested for the miners' murders and stands trial. Tex proves his innocence by arranging for Henderson and Conklin to enter the courtroom. In a panic, Evans shoots Tex in the arm, and himself is shot by the sheriff and Tex. Later Tex returns to Lolita's room with a wounded arm, and she tells him her father, now recovered, has given them permission to marry. *Hired killers. Impersonation and imposture. Mexicans. Miners. Murder. Partnership. Undercover operations.* Birthdays. Cowboys. Duplicity. Fathers and daughters. Fights. Frame-ups. Gold mines. Greed. Moral reformation. Outlaws. Ranchers. Romantic rivalry. Storms.

Note: This film marked Tex Ritter's film debut and was, according to exploitation materials, the first in a series of "romantic action western musicals" produced by Edward F. Finney for Grand National starring Ritter and his horse "White Flash." Although the onscreen credits list Frank Sanucci and Harry Revel as two of the film's songwriters, press material found in copyright records does not credit them with specific song titles. Modern sources list the following additional cast members: Glenn Strange, Budd Buster, Murdock McQuarrie, Ethan Laidlaw, Charles "Slim" Whittaker, Edward Cassidy, Earl Dwire, Jack Kirk and Bob Burns.

FD 10 Nov 1936, p. 7. *HR* 13 Nov 1936, p. 15. *MPD* 10 Nov 1936, p. 14. *MPH* 14 Nov 1936, p. 64.

SONG OF THE ISLANDS (Hawaiians)

A Miller-Nagel Production. **1934**; Prod: on the islands of Maui, Kauai, Oahu and Hawaii and at the Lalani Hawaiian Village, Honolulu, HI. Sd; b&w (Vericolor). 40 min. Passed by the National Board of Review.

Prod Palmer Miller and Curtis F. Nagel.

Song(s): "My Little Grass Shack in Kaelakehua, Hawaii," words and music by Bill Cogswell, John Avery Noble and Thomas J. Harrison; "Aloha Oe," words and music by Queen Liliuokalani; "Kakali Nei Au (The Hawaiian Wedding Song)," words and music by Charles E. King; and other songs.

Cast: Don Blanding [(*Narrator*)], Harry Owens and his Royal Hawaiian Orchestra, With Bob Cutter, Hawaiian Girls Glee Club, Ray Kinney and his Hawaiians, Joe Kamakau Singers, Minerva Patten, Soloists Sam Kapu (*Prince*), Pualani Mokimana (*Pualani*), James Kamakaiwi (*Moku*), Joe Kamakau (*Chief*), Sam Kapu (*Chief*).

Drama, Documentary. [*Print viewed*]. Bandleader Harry Owens and His Royal Hawaiian Orchestra perform several numbers for tourists in Honolulu, Hawaii. As a steamer departs for the mainland, a woman asks Hawaiian resident Don Blanding to explain the custom of throwing leis into the water. Blanding explains that its roots lay in a story of Old Hawaii: Princess Pualani, whose name means "Flower of Heaven," is an island girl who loves Moku, a young native who is not of royal blood. Like all Hawaiians, Moku and Pualani love the water. They spend their time together like happy children and Moku makes a lei of shells for Pualani, a symbol of their eternal love. In those days, the Hawaiians practiced the old crafts, including weaving, netting and carving cocoanuts. One day, large canoes approach the island and Pualani's father, the chief of the village, greets a prince traveling from a neighboring island. The prince, who is looking for a wife, and has heard stories of Pualani's beauty, wants her for his bride. The chief accepts the prince's gifts and tells his daughter that she must marry him. She does not want to marry the prince and leave her home, but her father insists that it is her duty. Even though Pualani knows that she will one day be a queen, she still loves Moku. Though her heart is broken, Pualani returns the lei to Moku. During a sumptuous wedding feast, traditional foods are served, including fish and poi, which is made from Taro root and prepared by the men. The pig brought by the prince has been wrapped in banana leaves and cooked in a pit for three days. As Pualani dances the traditional Hula, Moku can no longer bear to watch the ceremony and leaves. Later, he makes a special lei for her and gives it to her as she departs in the prince's canoe. As the canoe goes farther away from the island, Pualani lovingly kisses the lei and places it into the water. For hours Moku sadly looks toward the sea until the lei drifts onto the shore.

Now knowing that Pualani still loves him, Moku prayers to the gods that, like the lei, Pualani will someday return to him. At the end of the story, Blanding tells his companion that it explains the reason why tourists throw leis into the water as they sail away from Hawaii, promising that someday they will return. *Hawaiians. Honolulu (HI). Rites and ceremonies. Romance. Fathers and daughters. Fish. Flowers. Hula. Pigs. Princes. Tribal chiefs. Weddings.*

Note: The opening title card to the film reads: "Song of the Islands, photographed and produced by Palmer Miller and Curtis F. Nagel." Although there is a copyright statement on the film, it was not registered for copyright. The film's opening credits list Sam Kapu and Minerva Patten as "Soloists," but Kapu is also listed separately as "Chief." Joe Kamakau is also listed twice, first with the Joe Kamakau singers, and later as "Prince." The opening credits also read: "Photographed and recorded on the islands of Maui, Kuai, Oahu and Hawaii of the beautiful Hawaiian Group." Below the cast list, the credits read "Native settings by Lalani Hawaiian Village," followed by the written prologue: "Honolulu—crossroads of the Pacific—where rainbows, flowers and music blend into a modern rhapsody of the tropics."

Some of the customs shown within the story of Pualani and Maku were anachronistic or inaccurate. According to historical sources, the custom of throwing the flowered lei into the water began in the 1920s. Additionally, cloth that is shown in the film is of Samoan, rather than native Hawaiian origin. According to modern sources, the film was produced for the Hawaii Tourist Bureau by local filmmaker George Tahara, and actress Pualani Mokimana was a member of the Mossman family, owners of the Lalani Hawaiian Village in Honolulu. No reviews have been located for the film, which is preserved in the Bishop Museum Archive in Honolulu, Hawaii.

SONG OF THE ISLANDS (Hawaiians)

Twentieth Century-Fox Film Corp. *Dist* Twentieth Century-Fox Film Corp. 13 Mar **1942**; World premiere in Miami Beach, FL: 5 Feb 1942; Prod: 20 Oct—mid-Dec 1941 [©Twentieth Century-Fox Film Corp.; 13 Mar 1942; LP11537]. Sd (Western Electric Mirrophonic Recording); col (Technicolor). 8 reels, 6,716 ft. 73 or 75 min. PCA cert no. 7884.

[*Exec prod* Darryl F. Zanuck]. *Prod* William LeBaron. *Dir* Walter Lang. [*Loc unit dir* Otto Brower]. [*Asst dir* Barney Carr]. [*Location asst dir* Fred Fox]. *Orig scr* Joseph Schrank, Robert Pirosh, Robert Ellis and Helen Logan. *Dir of photog* Ernest Palmer. *Technicolor dir* Natalie Kalmus. *Assoc* Morgan Padelford. *Art dir* Richard Day and Joseph C. Wright. *Film ed* Robert Simpson. *Set dec* Thomas Little. [*Prop dir* Eddie Jones]. *Cost* Gwen Wakeling. *Mus dir* Alfred Newman. *Dances staged by* Hermes Pan. *Sd* E. Clayton Ward and Roger Heman. *Makeup artist* Guy Pearce. *Tech dir* Hilo Hattie. [*Tech adv* John Reasin, Jimmie Lono and Harry Owens]. [*Prod mgr* William Koenig]. [*Pub dir* Harry Brand]. [*Head nurseryman* Nick Kaltenstatler]. [*Singing double for Victor Mature* Ben Gage].

Music: "Killarney," music by Michael William Balfe.

Song(s): "Down on Ami, Ami, Oni, Oni Isle," "O'Brien Has Gone Hawaiian," "Sing Me a Song of the Islands," "Maluna, Malolo, Mawaena," "Blue Shadows and White Gardenias" and "What's Buzzin' Cousin," music and lyrics by Mack Gordon and Harry Owens; "Song of the Islands," music and lyrics by Charles E. King; "Hawaiian War Chant (Ta-Hu-Wa-Hu-Wai)," music and lyrics by Johnny Noble and Leleiohaku; "Hu'I Mai," music and lyrics by Sol Hoopii; "Home on the Range," music by Dr. Brewster M. Higley, lyrics by Daniel E. Kelly, special lyrics by Mack Gordon, Harry Owens and Sol Hoopii; "Cannibal Chant," music and lyrics by Satini Pualioa; "The Cockeyed Mayor of Kaunakakai," music by R. Alex Anderson, lyrics by R. Alex Anderson and Al Stillman.

Cast: BETTY GRABLE (*Eileen O'Brien*), VICTOR MATURE (*Jefferson Harper*), JACK OAKIE (*Rusty Smith*), Thomas Mitchell (*Dennis O'Brien*), George Barbier (*Harper*), Billy Gilbert (*Palola's father*), Hilo Hattie (*Palola*), Harry Owens and his Royal Hawaiians, Lillian Porter (*Palola's cousin [Paulani]*), Hal K. Dawson (*John Rodney*), [Amy Cordone (*Specialty*)], [Bruce Wong (*House boy*)], [Bobby Stone, Rudy Robles (*Native boys*)], [Alex Pollard (*Valet*)], [Harold Lishman (*Old Native*)], [Kahala Bray], [Mary Stewart], [Virginia Hogen], [Ruth Riley], [Geraldine Fisette], [Peggy Lou Neary], [Marie Bodie], [Sheila Rae], [Edith Haskins], [Valerie Traxler], [Evelyne Eager], [Dona La Barr], [Alma Pappas], [Eleanor Peterson], [Louise Allen], [Grace Davies], [Penny Gill], [Belle Richard], [Vanita Wade], [Tani Marsh], [Pearlie May Norton], [Virginia Davies], [Dorothy Harris], [Pet Meyer], [Patsy Perrin].

Island, Musical comedy. [*Print viewed*]. On the tiny Hawaiian island of Ahmi-Oni, Irish beachcomber Dennis O'Brien lives an idyllic life with the native Hawaiians on his beachfront property. Everyone is overjoyed by the return of O'Brien's daughter Eileen, who has been

away at school for three years. Eileen, who was reared by the natives as one of their own, is equally happy to be home. The night of Eileen's welcome-home luau, the island also sees the arrival of Jefferson Harper, whose father owns the cattle ranch that occupies the majority of Ahmi-Oni. With Jeff is his Texan pal, Rusty Smith, who has a full-time job keeping Jeff from constantly pursuing pretty girls. Jeff instantly falls for Eileen, who temporarily misleads him into thinking that she is a native. Eileen escorts them to the Harper ranch, where they are greeted by foreman John Rodney. Rodney explains that they need O'Brien's land, which has the only deep-water harbor on the island, to build a pier for more productive shipping of their cattle. Harper, who has never visited Ahmi-Oni, has been trying to buy the land for years, but O'Brien wishes to keep it as a sanctuary for the natives, whom he believes Harper does not understand. Jeff and Rusty spend the next three weeks on the island, during which Jeff and Eileen fall in love, and Rusty tries to avoid the attention of native singer Palola, while pursuing her cousin Paulani. When Jeff declares his intention to stay and run the ranch, a disgruntled Rusty tells Rodney, who in turn calls Harper. Harper immediately flies out from Chicago to stop what he believes is his son's foolishness. Harper declares that the O'Briens are fortune hunters, but once Jeff makes him meet them, Harper likes them. He nonetheless spoils the party they give him by insisting that O'Brien sell him his land. Soon harsh words are exchanged, with even Jeff and Eileen joining in the argument. The Harpers try to return to their side of the island, but the only connecting bridge is washed out during a storm. Jeff and his father must stay with the O'Briens, and although Jeff is unable to reconcile with Eileen, Harper finally becomes friends with O'Brien. Soon after, Harper buys O'Brien's land, which is up for sale by the government due to nonpayment of taxes. Harper intends this as a gesture to reunite the children, but Rodney sends the O'Briens an eviction notice without consulting him. Everyone is furious with Harper, but he is able to explain the situation to O'Brien. During a luau that evening to celebrate St. Patrick's Day, Rusty, Harper and O'Brien connive to convince Eileen that Jeff has left. Eileen rushes out to see the departing plane, but Jeff is on the beach waiting for her. The quarreling lovers are reunited, and everyone sings as the families are assured of a peaceful and prosperous future together. *Cattlemen. Hawaii. Hawaiians. Ranches. Romance. Businessmen. Cousins. Eviction. Fathers and daughters. Fathers and sons. Harbors. Hula. Idealists. Irish Americans. Luaus. Rainstorms. Ranch foremen. St. Patrick's Day. Texans.*

Note: According to *HR* news items and the Twentieth Century-Fox Records of the Legal Department and the Produced Scripts Collection, both housed at the UCLA Arts—Special Collections Library, the studio had been trying since late 1937 to develop a screenplay for the title *Song of the Islands*. In late 1937, Joan Davis was intended as the star, while in early 1938, the story as then written, was to be a vehicle for the Ritz Brothers, Alice Faye and Don Ameche. Various subsequent versions were also written for Alice Faye. In Jan–Feb 1940, Gene Markey was to produce a picture entitled *Song of the Islands*, while by May 1940, Milton Sperling was to be the producer. Among the writers who worked on various treatments and screenplays entitled *Song of the Islands*, although they did not contribute to the finished film, were: Eleanor Harris, Edith Skouras, Howard Ellis Smith, Kenneth Earl, Alfred Cohn, Rian James, Hal Hudson, M. M. Musselman, Jack Andrews, Betty Hopkins, Edwin Blum, Jules Furthman and Don Ettlinger. Writers Milton Raison, Fidel La Barba and Hilary Lynn also worked on treatments, but the extent of their contribution to the released picture has not been confirmed. According to a 22 Sep 1941 studio press release, John Payne was to have the lead opposite Betty Grable. A 6 Aug 1941 *LAEx* news item stated that producer William LeBaron wanted to cast Robert Cummings opposite Grable. *HR* news items and studio records indicate that Otto Brower headed a location unit that obtained background shots in Honolulu and the Hawaiian islands. Studio records note that background scenes were also filmed on location at Catalina Island, CA. According to a 16 Jan 1942 *HR* news item, the film's premiere, to be held on 5 Feb at Miami Beach, FL, was to benefit the Navy Relief Fund. The film marked the screen debut of popular performer Hilo Hattie.

Box 7 Feb 1942. *DV* 4 Feb 1942, p. 3. *FD* 4 Feb 1942, p. 6. *HR* 4 Nov 1937, p. 1. *HR* 16 Feb 1940, p. 1. *HR* 20 Mar 1941, p. 1. *HR* 7 Aug 1941, p. 7. *HR* 20 Aug 1941, p. 4. *HR* 8 Sep 1941, p. 2. *HR* 22 Sep 1941, p. 4. *HR* 14 Oct 1941, p. 6. *HR* 17 Oct 1941, p. 17. *HR* 28 Nov 1941, p. 9. *HR* 2 Dec 1941, p. 2. *HR* 15 Dec 1941, p. 2. *HR* 29 Dec 1941, p. 6. *HR* 16 Jan 1942, p. 2. *HR* 4 Feb 1942, p. 3. *LAEx* 6 Aug 1941. *LAT* 6 May 1940. *MPHPD* 7 Feb 1942, p. 493. *NYHT* 8 Mar 1942. *NYT* 12 Mar 1942, p. 24. *Var* 18 Jun 1941. *Var* 4 Feb 1942, p. 8.

SONG OF THE OVERLAND TRAIL *see* OLD OVERLAND TRAIL

SONG OF THE SOUTH (African Americans)

Walt Disney Productions. *Dist* RKO Radio Pictures, Inc. 20 Nov **1946**; World premiere in Atlanta, GA: 12 Nov 1946 [©Walt Disney

Productions; 12 Aug 1946; LP1379]. Sd (RCA Sound System); col (Technicolor). 11 reels, 8,493 ft. 93-95 or 98 min. PCA cert no. 11163.

Pres WALT DISNEY. [*Exec prod* Walt Disney]. *Assoc prod* Perce Pearce. *Cartoon dir* Wilfred Jackson. *Photoplay dir* Harve Foster. [*Asst dir* Bill McGarry and Jack Atwood]. *Scr* Dalton Reymond, Morton Grant and Maurice Rapf. *Orig story* Dalton Reymond. *Cartoon story* William Peed, Ralph Wright and George Stallings. *Photog* Gregg Toland. *Spec processes* Ub Iwerks. *Technicolor color dir* Natalie Kalmus. *Assoc* Mitchell Kovalski. *Art dir* Perry Ferguson. *Art trmt* Elmer Plummer. *Cartoon art dir* Kenneth Anderson, Charles Philippi, Harold Doughty, Hugh Hennesy and Philip Barber. *Film ed* William M. Morgan. *Dir anim* Milt Kahl, Eric Larson, Ollie Johnston, Les Clark, Marc Davis and John Lounsbery. *Anim* Don Lusk, Harvey Toombs, Tom Massey, Ken O'Brien, Murray McClellan, Al Coe, Jack Campbell, Hal Ambro, Hal King, Cliff Nordberg and Rudy Larriva. *Eff anim* Josh Meador, George Rowley, Blaine Gibson and Brad Case. *Background and col stylist* Claude Coats and Mary Blair. *Background artist* Ralph Hulett, Brice Mack, Ray Huffine, Edgar Starr and Al Dempster. *Cost des* Mary Wills. *Mus dir* Charles Wolcott. *Photoplay score* Daniele Amfitheatrof. *Cartoon score* Paul J. Smith. *Voc dir* Ken Darby. *Orch* Edward Plumb. *Sd dir* C. O. Slyfield. *Sd rec* Fred Lau and Harold Steck. [*Tech adv* Wilbur G. Kurtz and Annie Laurie Fuller Kurtz]. [*Stand-in for Anita Brown* Myrtle Anderson]. [*Stand-in for Hattie McDaniel* Elizabeth Spratley].

Song(s): "Song of the South," music by Arthur Johnston, lyrics by Sam Coslow; "Look at the Sun" and "Uncle Remus Said," music and lyrics by Johnny Lange, Hy Heath and Eliot Daniel; "Zip-A-Dee-Doo-Dah" and "Ev'rybody Has a Laughing Place," music by Allie Wrubel, lyrics by Ray Gilbert; "Who Wants to Live Like That?" and "Let the Rain Pour Down," music and lyrics by Ken Darby and Foster Carling; "How Do You Do?" music and lyrics by Robert MacGimsey; "Sooner or Later," music by Charles Wolcott, lyrics by Ray Gilbert; "All I Want," music traditional, lyrics by Ken Darby.

Source: Based on the book *Uncle Remus: His Songs and Sayings, The Folk-Lore of the Old Plantation* by Joel Chandler Harris (New York, 1881).

Cast: Ruth Warrick [(*Sally*)], Bobby Driscoll [(*Johnny*)], James Baskett [(*Uncle Remus/Voice of Brer Fox*)], Luana Patten [(*Ginny Favers*)], Lucile Watson [(*Miss Doshy*)], Hattie McDaniel [(*Aunt Tempy*)], Eric [sic] Rolf [(*John*)], Glenn Leedy [(*Toby*)], Mary Field [(*Mrs. Favers*)], Anita Brown [(*Chloe*)], George Nokes, Gene Holland [(*Favers boys*)], "Nicodemus" Stewart [(*Voice of Brer Bear*)], Johnny Lee [(*Voice of Brer Rabbit*)].

Animation, Children's works, Historical, Comedy-drama, Musical. [*Print viewed*]. In the late nineteenth century, newspaperman John and his wife Sally travel from their home in Atlanta to the rural plantation of Sally's mother, Miss Doshy, accompanied by their young son Johnny and his black nursemaid, Aunt Tempy. Johnny is excited about meeting Uncle Remus, a legendary black storyteller who amused John and Sally during their childhood, but is confused by his parents' anger toward each other. John, whose controversial writings have strained his marriage, returns to Atlanta alone, and Sally remains at the plantation with Johnny. Hurt by what he perceives as his father's desertion of him, Johnny sneaks out of the house with the intention of running away. As he walks along, Johnny finds the elderly Uncle Remus telling stories to a group of black children. Johnny stops to listen but runs off when Tempy and another servant, Chloe, come looking for him. Remus catches Johnny in the woods and agrees to run away to Atlanta with him, but insists on stopping at his cabin for provisions. While there, Remus tells Johnny a story of Brer Rabbit, who also tried to run away despite Remus' warning that there is no place far away enough to escape trouble: Brer Rabbit is captured by Brer Fox and Brer Bear, who intend to make a tasty meal of him, but the rabbit easily outwits them, escapes and returns to his briar patch. Strengthened by the story's moral, Johnny goes home with Toby, the young black servant assigned to look after him. Sally is devastated by his attempt to run away, however, and unfairly blames his behavior on Uncle Remus. Later, Sally orders Johnny to wear a suit with a lace collar, and while the boy wanders about miserably, he is taunted by Joe and Jake Favers, poor white youngsters who are threatening to drown their sister Ginny's puppy. Ginny and Johnny become friends, and she gives him the puppy, Teenchie. Sally refuses to let him keep the puppy, however,

and orders him to return it. Instead, Johnny takes Teenchie to Uncle Remus, who agrees to keep it for him, but the next day, the Favers boys threaten Johnny with violence unless he returns the puppy. Uncle Remus tells the distressed Johnny about the time Brer Fox and Brer Bear used a tar baby to trap Brer Rabbit, but were once again outwitted by Brer Rabbit, who begged them not to fling him into the briar patch. Johnny uses the lesson of reverse psychology to get the Favers boys to complain to their mother about the puppy, and Mrs. Favers gives them a sound whipping. The angry boys then tell Sally their story, and Sally accuses Uncle Remus of "warping" Johnny with his stories and orders him to stop telling them to her son. Heartbroken, Uncle Remus returns Teenchie to the Favers boys, then roughly tells Johnny to leave him alone. A week later, Sally throws a birthday party for Johnny and allows him to invite Ginny, despite her misgivings about Ginny's humble upbringing. Johnny happily skips to Ginny's house, but her brothers muddy her only good dress. After fighting with the boys and becoming disheveled himself, Johnny tries to placate Ginny but only makes her cry more. Uncle Remus cannot resist comforting the children with a story and tells them about the time Brer Rabbit again freed himself from the clutches of Brer Fox and Brer Bear by leading them to his "laughing place." The wise old man informs the children that everyone has a laughing place, and when they run off to look for theirs, Sally finds them and chastises them for missing the party. Sally then upbraids Uncle Remus and orders him to stay away from Johnny completely. The old man decides that he is of no use anymore and, after packing his few belongings, prepares to depart. Johnny, who has realized that Uncle Remus' cabin is his laughing place, sees his friend leaving and cuts through a field to stop him. The bull in the field chases Johnny and knocks him down, and the unconscious child is rushed to the plantation house. John immediately comes down from Atlanta, but even his presence does not help his delirious son, who calls for Uncle Remus. Miss Doshy sends for him, and as Uncle Remus holds Johnny's hand and tells him another story, the child revives. Finally realizing that they must set aside their problems for the sake of their son, John and Sally decide to stay at the plantation. Later, Uncle Remus contentedly watches Johnny, Ginny and Toby play with Teenchie. He is amazed to see Brer Rabbit and his other story folk join the children, but soon runs after them and enters their joyous world. African Americans. Children. Friendship. Maturation. Southerners. Storytellers. United States–History–19th century. Allegory. Bears. Birthdays. Brothers and sisters. Bullies. Class distinction. Dogs. False accusations. Farm hands. Foxes. Frogs. Georgia. Grandmothers. Mothers and sons. Plantations. Poverty. Rabbits. Separation (Marital). Servants. Wounds and injuries.

Note: [*Note from the Editors*: Due to the large amount of available and often contradictory information about *Song of the South*, a comprehensive discussion of all aspects of the film is not possible here. The reader is advised to consult the citations listed below for additional information on the film.] The working title of this film was *Uncle Remus*. The film's opening title cards read: "Walt Disney Presents *Song of the South* with Uncle Remus and his tales of Brer Rabbit." Actor Erik Rolf's name is misspelled as "Eric" in the onscreen credits.

Joel Chandler Harris' numerous and very popular "Uncle Remus" stories first appeared in his *AtlC* column in 1876. With his son Julian, Harris, whose stories were collected in several books, established *Uncle Remus's Magazine* in 1907, after his retirement from *AtlC*. According to a modern source, Disney first purchased the rights to Harris' stories in 1939, for ten thousand dollars. Contemporary studio publicity noted that the "Uncle Remus" stories were a childhood favorite of Disney. According to a 23 Aug 1946 *AtlJ* editorial, the studio's decision to change the film's title from *Uncle Remus* to *Song of the South* displeased many Southerners, including Harris' son, Joel Harris, who protested the change in a letter to Disney. In his reply to Harris, quoted in the editorial, Disney stated that "*Song of the South* better presented our picturization of the story than did the original title." According to modern sources, the studio changed the title in order to distance the film from potential criticism from African Americans concerned about the use of the "Uncle Remus" tales.

While Harris' stories identify "Uncle Remus" as a former slave, the film does not clearly establish Remus' status nor the exact time period of the story. According to the film's file in the MPAA/PCA Collection at the AMPAS Library, PCA officials advised the studio that in order to minimize "adverse reactions from certain Negro groups," they should "be certain that the frontispiece of the book (appearing in the opening credits) establishes the date in the 1870s." Despite Breen's admonition, the frontispiece does not specify the time period, and both contemporary and modern sources disagree as to whether the film is set before or after the Civil War. In response to a 14 Jul 1944 screenplay submitted by the studio, PCA official Joseph I. Breen suggested that before proceeding further, the studio "secure the services of a competent person to advise you concerning the...acceptability of this story from the standpoint of the American Negroes. These good people, in recent months, have become most

critical regarding the portrayal on the motion picture screen of the members of their race.''

According to the program for the world premiere, the Harris family had hoped for many years that Disney would dramatize the ''Uncle Remus'' stories, perhaps as two-reel animated shorts, but ''during the years of discussion leading up to final negotiation [in 1939], the idea of full-length animated cartoon pictures interested the Disney studios and later gripped the public.'' Pre-production news items indicated that Disney originally intended to produce the film as an all-animation feature, but by the time production began, it was decided to have the picture feature live action. Although the Disney Studio had previously experimented with mixing animation and live action in *The Reluctant Dragon*, *Saludos Amigos* and *The Three Caballeros*, *Song of the South* was the first feature-length Disney picture to integrate animation fully with live actors in a dramatic storyline. According to an article in the 5 Dec 1980 issue of *Disney Newsreel*, when Disney was asked why so much live action was included in *Song of the South*, he replied, ''In this case, a living cast was absolutely necessary to get the full emotional impact and the entertainment value of the animated legends.'' Other modern sources assert that economic necessity prompted the studio to place more emphasis on live action, which could be produced more quickly and less expensively than animation.

Contemporary press materials stated that before beginning work on the animated sequences, artists from the studio visited Atlanta and neighboring regions to sketch the countryside. A 4 Oct 1944 *AtlC* article noted that studio artist Mary Blair was consulting with Atlanta artists and historians Wilbur G. and Annie Laurie Fuller Kurtz on ''matters of architecture, costumes, natural background...and 'just props.' '' According to a contemporary press release, the animated sequences and characters were being worked on ''months previous'' to the beginning of live action filming, and then the integration of the two was accomplished ''during the filming of the live action on location and on studio sets.'' Studio publicity materials for the later re-releases, however, state that the animation, while planned ahead of the live action, did not actually begin until the live sequences were completed. According to a modern interview with cartoon art director Kenneth Anderson, ''The positions where Uncle Remus looked were predetermined by placing concealed sticks which indicated the cartoon character. These sticks were covered later by the addition of an overlay painted cel. The character animation was also done later with the animators working with frame blowups of the live action film.''

A 3 Nov 1946 *AtlJ* article stated that Disney originally considered shooting the live action footage on location in Georgia but was prevented from doing so by ''technical difficulties.'' Instead, the exteriors were shot on a ranch in Phoenix, AZ, while studio scenes were filmed at the Goldwyn Studio, according to contemporary news items. Location filming began in Nov 1944.

H. C. Potter was first hired to direct the live action, but according to a 24 Jan 1945 *LAT* news item, he was replaced ''since he and Walt [Disney] couldn't see eye to eye on handling of the story.'' A 29 Jan 1945 *HCN* item noted that Harve Foster, who had been acting as assistant director, would take over as director. Although it appears that Potter did direct some sequences, it is not known whether any of his work was included in the finished film. According to a 27 Oct 1944 *HR* news item, Disney originally signed Robert MacGimpsey to score *Song of the South*. [MacGimpsey did contribute one song to the film.]

On 8 Nov 1944, *HR* noted that ''John Loder has been signed by Walt Disney to play Uncle Remus in *The Three Caballeros*.'' The character of Uncle Remus does not appear in *The Three Caballeros*, however, nor does it seem likely that Loder was seriously considered for that role, although apparently he was considered for the part of ''John.'' A 4 Oct 1944 *LAT* item stated that Loder would be starring in the picture with Janet Gaynor and Eddie ''Rochester'' Anderson. A 25 Nov 1944 *PittsC* news item reported that Anderson would be unable to accept the part offered to him, however, due to personal appearance commitments. A modern source states that Disney first offered the part of Uncle Remus to Rex Ingram, who turned it down.

According to contemporary sources, Clarence Muse was involved with the production early on, either as an adviser on the screenplay or a potential cast member. According to a 6 Jan 1946 *DW* news item, both Muse and band leader Tiny Bradshaw turned down roles in the film because they felt the picture would be ''detrimental to the cultural advancement of the Negro people.'' Bradshaw and Muse publicly expressed their discomfort with the screenplay's extreme dialect, and numerous groups contacted the Disney Studio with their concerns that the African-American characters would be portrayed in a stereotypical fashion. According to a 26 Aug 1944 *PittsC* article, when reporter Herman Hill contacted a studio representative about the growing concerns over the picture and the dialect, the representative stated that ''it would not be plausible or realistic to use 'Oxford English' in a picture laid in 1850.'' A 24 Aug 1944 *LASent* article reported that Ben Carter turned down a role in the film, as did Mantan Moreland, Monte Hawley, Ernest Whiteman and Tim Moore.

Other contemporary sources noted that James Baskett was cast when he came to the studio to audition for a vocal role. According to *LASent* news items, Helen Crozier was originally signed for the role of ''Chloe.'' Feb 1945 *LASent* news items add the following actors to the cast, although their participation in the completed film has not been confirmed: Phil Jones (*Coachman*); Walter Knox (*Gardner*); and Daisy Bufford, Anna Marby, Theo Washington and Virgil Sanchies. *HCN* news items include Marylin Gwaltney and the B. C. Singers in the cast, but their participation in the completed picture has also not been confirmed. A 1 Mar 1945 *LAT* item reported that Mary Young had been cast in the role of ''Aunt Margaret, a meanie, who is the *bete noir* of little Johnny,'' but no such character appears in the finished film.

Child stars Bobby Driscoll and Luana Patten were the first actors signed by Disney to long-term contracts, and contemporary news items noted that Disney intended to feature the young actors together as a team in future films. They

appeared in two more films together, *So Dear to My Heart* and *Melody Time*, as well as individually in several films for the studio. Driscoll's last film for the studio was 1953's *Peter Pan*, for which he supplied the voice of the title character. After a troubled adolescence, Driscoll died in 1968, at the age of thirty-one, from long-term effects of drug addiction. Patten, who had previously been a model, made her screen acting debut in *Song of the South*. After appearing in several other Disney pictures, she took time off from acting to pursue academic studies, then returned to the studio in 1957 to appear in *Johnny Tremain* and in 1966 for *Follow Me, Boys!* At the time of filming *Song of the South*, Ruth Warrick and Erik Rolf were married, but by the picture's premiere, they were divorced. This was the only film in which they appeared together.

The film marked the debut of young Glenn Leedy, who, according to studio publicity, was ''discovered'' at a school playground during location shooting in Phoenix. Although many contemporary sources asserted that Baskett made his screen debut in *Song of the South*, he had appeared in several African-American films during the 1930s under the name ''Jimmy Baskette.'' Mainly a stage and radio performer, Baskett was well-known at the time of filming for his portrayal of lawyer ''Gabby Gibson'' on the popular *Amos 'n' Andy* radio series. *Song of the South* was Baskett's last film, however; he died on 9 Jul 1948 of a heart attack and complications from diabetes. According to modern sources, Baskett replaced Johnny Lee as the voice of ''Brer Rabbit'' during the ''Laughing Place'' segment because Lee was on a USO tour. A modern source notes that the cast included Ernestine Jones, who supplied the voice of a butterfly, while other modern sources state that Baskett provided the butterfly's voice.

According to contemporary news items, the studio made elaborate preparations for the picture's premiere and general release. In order to publicize the premiere, four reporters from *AtlC* and *AtlJ* visited the studio in early Oct 1946 to begin a series of stories that would run daily in Atlanta newspapers until the premiere. Many recording artists released versions of the film's music in advance of the premiere, including Dinah Shore, the Merry Macs, Woody Herman and the Modernaires, according to a 25 Sep 1946 *HR* news item. On 1 Nov 1946, artists Fred Moore and Dick Mitchell, along with ''production expert'' Frank Bresson and Clarence Nash (the vocal artist who was the voice of Donald Duck) opened a ''miniature studio'' at the Belle Isle Arcade in Atlanta. The exhibit included Moore and Mitchell drawing sketches for visitors, demonstrations of the animation process and showings of a preview of the picture and scenes from the 1941 Disney film *The Reluctant Dragon*, which contains a tour of the actual Walt Disney Studios.

Other festivities preceding the premiere included the dedication by Walt Disney of an Uncle Remus cabin at Wren's Nest, the former home of Harris, and an Armistice Day parade on 11 Nov 1946, which showcased characters from the film. *HR* news items noted that radio shows participating in the film's premiere included *Queen for a Day*, *Bride and Groom*, Art Linkletter's *GE Houseparty* and *Vox Pop*. The premiere, which benefitted charities overseen by Atlanta's Junior League and the Uncle Remus Memorial Society's renovation of Wren's Nest, was attended by over five thousand people. Cast members Warrick, Driscoll and Patten attended, as well as Walt Disney and voice artists Nash, Pinto Colvig (Goofy), Adriana Caselotti (Snow White) and Cliff Edwards (Jiminy Crickett). In describing the premiere, local newspapers recounted the actions of Atlanta's mayor, William B. Hartsfield, who urged Disney to wire Baskett with news of the city's appreciation for his enactment of Uncle Remus. Although some Southern newspapers stated that Baskett could not be present due to his commitment to the *Amos 'n' Andy* radio show, none of the African-American cast members attended the premiere. Harold Martin, an *AtlC* columnist, pointed out that it was Atlanta's strict segregation laws that prevented Baskett and the other black cast members from attending the premiere. In a 15 Oct 1946 article, Martin noted that to bring Baskett to Atlanta, where he would not have been allowed to participate in any of the festivities, ''would cause him many embarrassments, for his feelings are the same as any man's.''

The film was a box-office success, showing a profit of $226,000 during its initial release, according to modern sources. [Modern sources list the production's cost as $2,125,000.] The picture received mixed reviews, however, with some critics applauding the animated sequences and acting while criticizing the live-action story. Bosley Crowther, the influential *NYT* critic, commented, ''the ratio of 'live' to cartoon action is approximately two to one—and that is approximately the ratio of its mediocrity to charm.'' The *Time* reviewer stated, ''Artistically, *Song of the South* could have used a much heavier helping of cartooning. Technically, the blending of two movie mediums is pure Disney wizardry. Ideologically, the picture is certain to land its maker in hot water.''

On 27 Nov 1946, Walter White, the executive secretary of the NAACP, sent telegrams to newspapers describing the NAACP's objections to the film. While expressing approval of the film's technical achievements, White stated that the NAACP ''regrets, however, that in an effort neither to offend audiences in the North or South, the production helps to perpetuate a dangerously glorified picture of slavery....[the film] unfortunately gives the impression of an idyllic master-slave relationship which is a distortion of the facts.'' A 4 Dec 1946 *Var* article about the NAACP's view of current films contained a statement from a Disney spokesperson who ''expressed surprise over objections to the film. Picture, he said, did not take place during slavery days but after the Civil War and the most sympathetic character in it is a Negro.''

The picture generated much controversy among African-American newspapers, some of which supported it while others did not. The reviewer for *The Afro-American* declared that he was ''thoroughly disgusted'' by the film, while the reviewer for *PittsC* stated that ''the truly sympathetic handling of the entire production from a racial standpoint [would] prove of inestimable goodwill in the furthering of interracial relationships.'' The chief complaints leveled at the film concerned the subservient status, costuming and dialect of

the African-American characters. In another *NYT* article, Crowther accused Disney of committing "a peculiarly gauche offense in putting out such a story in this troubled day and age." Upon the film's release, groups such as The National Negro Congress, The American Youth for Democracy, The United Negro & Allied Veterans and the American Jewish Council organized racially integrated pickets at theaters in New York City, Los Angeles, San Francisco and Boston, as well as other cities. In New York, Broadway actors such as Kenneth Spencer and Sam Wanamaker joined the picket lines.

A scrapbook for the film held in the Walt Disney Archives contains an original handbill distributed by the National Negro Congress during its picket of the film at a Los Angeles theater. The handbill proclaims that the picture contains "dangerous stereotyping [that] creates an impression of Negroes in the minds of their fellow Americans which make them appear to be second class citizens." According to a 12 Dec 1946 *Var* news item, the NAACP declined to join the National Negro Congress in its picket of a New York City theater "because it feels nothing can be gained by it." The Boston chapter of the NAACP did participate in picketing the film's exhibition there, however, according to a 24 Dec 1946 *Boston Globe* article. An 18 Jan 1947 *ChiDef* news item noted that although the film was being shown at the "white theaters" in Washington, D.C., it would not be exhibited by the "six theaters catering to Negroes."

The picketing sparked even more debate among African-American supporters and detractors of the film. *Ebony* magazine stated that the picture would "disrupt peaceful race relations and set back Negro progress," while the *PittsC* reviewer, discussing negative statements made by *Ebony*, Muse and Bradshaw, found their comments to be "unadulterated hogwash symptomatic of the unfortunate racial neurosis that seems to be gripping so many of our humorless brethren these days." In a Feb 1947 interview, printed in *The Criterion*, Hattie McDaniel defended the film by saying, "If I had for one moment considered any part of the picture degrading or harmful to my people I would not have appeared therein." In the same article, Baskett commented, "I believe that certain groups are doing my race more harm in seeking to create dissension than can ever possibly come out of the *Song of the South*."

Although Baskett was occasionally criticized for accepting such a "demeaning" role, his acting was almost universally praised, and columnist Hedda Hopper was one of the many journalists who declared that he should receive an Academy Award for his work. Baskett was not nominated for Best Actor, but received a special Oscar in 1948, a few months prior to his death. Baskett's Oscar, which honored his "able and heart-warming characterization of Uncle Remus in *Song of the South*, friend and storyteller to the children of the world," was the first Academy Award received by an African-American actor. [Baskett's Oscar was an honorary one; Sidney Poitier was the first African-American actor to win an Oscar for his performance in the 1963 picture *Lilies of the Field*. The first African-American actress to win an Oscar was Hattie McDaniel, for her work in *Gone With the Wind* in 1939.] *Song of the South* also received an Academy Award nomination for Best Scoring of a Musical Picture and won an Oscar for the song "Zip-A-Dee-Doo-Dah" by Allie Wrubel and Ray Gilbert.

Although *Song of the South* proved a financial success every time it was reissued (1956, 1972, 1980 and 1986), it has not been reissued as often as most Disney films, which are re-released every seven years. On 25 Feb 1970, *Var* reported that the Disney studio had put the film "permanently on the shelf as offensive to Negroes and present concepts of race." In 1972, however, the studio stated that the picture had never been shelved and would be re-released due to the large numbers of requests from the public. During its 1972 reissue, the picture became the highest grossing Disney re-release up to that time. The 1986 reissue included a 15 Nov 1986 "re-premiere" held in Atlanta to celebrate the film's fortieth anniversary. By gubernatorial proclamation, the day of the premiere was declared *Song of the South* day in Georgia. Proceeds from the 1986 premiere, which was attended by Warrick, benefitted the preservation of Wren's Nest. The reissues have sparked criticism of the film from some reviewers, and the picture has never been released on video in the United States, although it was released on laser disc in Japan.

The film's music was the focus of a 1946 lawsuit brought against the studio by the Southern Music Publishing Co., which claimed that it had the exclusive rights to publish all works by songwriter Ray Gilbert, who cowrote "Zip-A-Dee-Doo-Dah," "Sooner or Later" and "Ev'ry Body Has a Laughing Place." Disney had assigned all rights to the film's music to the Santly-Joy publishing company. The suit was settled out of court in 1948 when the film studio offered Southern a percentage of its royalties from the songs in contention. In 1980, Judge E. Peterson filed a ten million dollar lawsuit against the studio, claiming that he and his partner, James A. Payton, were the true authors of the song "Zip-A-Dee-Doo-Dah." The studio denied their allegations, stating that there "was no question Ray Gilbert was the author of the song." The disposition of the suit is not known.

In 1956, a one-hour show, "A Tribute to Joel Chandler Harris," was broadcast on the *Disneyland* television show. In 1975, Bryanston Pictures released director/animator Ralph Bakshi's live action/animated film *Coonskin*, an R-rated feature that satirized *Song of the South*. In 1996, Danny Glover narrated "Brer Rabbit & Boss Lion," an animated featurette made for the Showtime cable network.

Afro-American (Baltimore) 23 Nov 1946. *Afro-American (Baltimore)* 30 Nov 1946. *Afro-American (Baltimore)* 18 Jan 1947. *Afro-American (Baltimore)* 8 Feb 1947. *AtlC* 4 Oct 1944. *AtlC* 15 Oct 1944. *AtlC* 3 Oct 1946. *AtlC* 15 Oct 1946. *AtlC* 10 Nov 1946. *AtlC* 12 Nov 1946. *AtlC* 13 Nov 1946. *AtlJ* 23 Aug 1946. *AtlJ* 4 Oct 1946. *AtlJ* 3 Nov 1946. *AtlJ* 13 Nov 1946. *AtlJ* 30 Dec 1946. *Augusta Chronicle* 17 Nov 1946. *Birmingham News* 31 Oct 1946. *Birmingham News* 27 Nov 1986, pp. 8-9. *Boston Globe* 24 Dec 1946. *Box* 2 Nov 1946. *California Eagle* 29 Oct 1944. *California Eagle* 16 Jan 1947. *California Eagle* 30 Jan 1947. *California Eagle* 13 Feb 1947. *California Eagle* 27 Mar 1947. *ChiDef* 30 Nov 1946. *ChiDef* 14 Dec 1946. *ChiDef* 18 Jan 1947. *Criterion (Los Angeels)* 10 Feb 1947, p. 1. *Dallas Times Herald* 13 Nov 1946. *Disney Newsreel* 5 Dec 1980, pp. 5-6. *DV* 26 Oct 1944. *DV* 26 Sep 1946. *DV* 29 Oct 1946, p. 3, 10. *DV* 12 Dec 1946. *DV* 21 Jan 1947. *DV* 2 May 1980. *DW* 6 Jan 1946. *DW* 4 Dec 1946. *East Point Georgia Suburban Reporter* 25 Oct 1946. *Emory Wheel* 21 Nov 1986. *FD* 1 Nov 1946, p. 7. *HCN* 29 Jan 1945. *HCN* 10 Feb 1945. *HCN* 19 Feb 1945. *HR* 27 Oct 1944, p. 3. *HR* 8 Nov 1944, p. 9. *HR* 9 Jan 1946, p. 2. *HR* 25 Sep 1946, p. 4. *HR* 3 Oct 1946, p. 13. *HR* 28 Oct 1946, p. 14. *HR* 29 Oct 1946, p. 3. *HR* 4 Nov 1946, p. 12. *HR* 8 Nov 1946, p. 9. *HR* 15 Nov 1946, p. 1. *HR* 2 Dec 1946, p. 6. *HR* 31 Dec 1946, p. 15. *HR* 11 Mar 1947, pp. 15-16. *HR* 18 Mar 1947, p. 11. *HR* 10 Mar 1972. *LADN* 31 Jan 1947. *LAEx* 28 Apr 1946. *LAEx* 21 Feb 1947. *LASent* 10 Aug 1944, p. 13. *LASent* 24 Aug 1944. *LASent* 21 Dec 1944, p. 19. *LASent* 18 Jan 1945. *LASent* 1 Feb 1945. *LASent* 15 Feb 1945. *LASent* 8 Mar 1945. *LASent* 24 Jan 1946. *LASent* 7 Nov 1946. *LAT* 4 Jul 1944. *LAT* 4 Oct 1944. *LAT* 24 Jan 1945. *LAT* 1 Mar 1945. *LAT* 31 Jan 1947. *LAT* 30 Jan 1972. *LAT* 2 Jan 1981. *LAT* 2 Aug 1981. *LAT* 27 Dec 1986, p. 1, 5. *MPD* 29 Oct 1946, p. 1, 7. *MPHPD* 2 Nov 1946, p. 3285. *Newsweek* 22 Dec 1986, p. 63. *NYT* 26 Oct 1941. *NYT* 14 Dec 1946. *NYT* 28 Nov 1946, p. 40. *NYT* 8 Dec 1946. *People's Voice (New York)* 30 Nov 1946. *People's World (San Francisco)* 1 Feb 1947. *People's World (San Francisco)* 19 Apr 1947. *Phoenix Gazette* 14 Dec 1944. *Phoenix Gazette* 17 Feb 1945. *PittsC* 26 Aug 1944. *PittsC* 25 Nov 1944. *PittsC* 9 Nov 1946. *PittsC* 16 Nov 1946. *PittsC* 8 Feb 1947. *PittsC* 22 Feb 1947. *PM* 28 Nov 1946. *PM* 29 Nov 1946. *PM* 17 Dec 1946. *Southline (Atlanta)* 12 Nov 1986, pp. 18-19. *Time* 18 Nov 1946, p. 101. *Var* 11 Jul 1945. *Var* 2 Oct 1946. *Var* 6 Nov 1946, p. 18. *Var* 4 Dec 1946, p. 7, 25. *Var* 11 Feb 1948. *Var* 25 Feb 1970, p. 7, 20.

SONG OF THE WEST *see* LET FREEDOM RING

SONORA KID *see* SONORA STAGECOACH

SONORA STAGECOACH (Native Americans)

Monogram Pictures Corp. *Dist* Monogram Pictures Corp. 10 Jun 1944; Prod: mid-Dec 1942 [©Monogram Pictures Corp.; 6 May 1944; LP12657]. Sd; b&w. 4,639 ft. 51 min.

Series: The Trail Blazers.

Prod Robert Tansey. *Dir* Robert Tansey. *Asst dir* Art Hammond. *Orig story* Robert Emmett. *Scr* Frances Kavanaugh. *Cine* Edward Kull. *Film ed* John C. Fuller. *Mus dir* Frank Sanucci. *Sd eng* Glen Glenn. *Prod mgr* Fred Hoose.

Cast: HOOT GIBSON [(*Hoot Gibson*)], BOB STEELE [(*Bob Steele*)], CHIEF THUNDERCLOUD [(*Chief Thundercloud*)], Rocky Camron [(*Rocky Camron*)], Betty Miles [(*Betty Miles*)], Glenn Strange [(*Paul Kenton*)], Geo. Eldridge [(*Larry Payne*)], Karl Hackett [(*Joe Kenton*)], Henry Hall [(*Sheriff Hampton*)], Chas. King [(*Blackie Reed*)], Bud Osborn [(*Steve Martin*)], Chas. Murray, Jr. [(*Weasel*)], John Bridges [(*Pop Carson*)], Forrest Taylor [(*Judge Crandall*)], Al Ferguson [(*Red*)].

Western. [*Print viewed*]. Fearing for the safety of his prisoner, Rocky Camron, Sheriff Hampton asks the U.S. Marshals known as the Trail Blazers, Bob Steele, Hoot Gibson and Chief Thundercloud, to escort Rocky to trial in Sonora. After warning the marshals that a gang of outlaws are determined that Rocky will never reach Sonora alive, the sheriff declares that he believes that Rocky, who is accused of murder, is innocent but will never receive a fair trial. Accepting the sheriff's judgment, the marshals give Rocky a gun to defend himself and decide to help him prove his innocence. The marshals and their prisoner then head for Sonora, and in the hills, a gang led by Blackie Reed waits to ambush their coach. Spotting their assailants, Chief Thundercloud takes over the reins to the coach, while Rocky and the others mount their horses and gallop away. Blackie and the gang follow the stage, but when they notice the three horsemen in the distance, they take out after them. Rocky and the others then rejoin the coach and ride to safety at the relay station. Realizing that they have lost their prey, Blackie instructs Steve Martin, a member of the gang and a driver for the stage line, to proceed to the relay station and keep a watchful eye on the marshals and their prisoner. At the station, the marshals are greeted by Pop Carson, the manager of the stage line, and Betty Miles, Rocky's sweetheart. Over dinner, Rocky relates how he got in trouble with the law: Rocky was working in the Sonora express office managed by Paul Kenton when a cash shipment was delivered late in the day by Steve. After depositing the money in the safe, Rocky went to call on Betty. Later, after passing Blackie in the street, Rocky noticed that the safe was open and the money missing. Blackie accused Rocky of the robbery, so the sheriff and two deputies searched his house and found some money that had been planted in his mattress. In the ensuing fight, the deputies were killed and Rocky fled the scene of the crime. Betty then surmises that Blackie and Steve were working for Paul and his banker brother Joe, and that they framed Rocky for robbery and murder. Concluding that Steve can establish Rocky's innocence, Hoot formulates a plan to trick him into revealing the truth. After announcing that he is satisfied that the outlaws have been thwarted, Hoot asks Steve to drive Betty and Rocky to Sonora while the marshals ride on alone. In Sonora, meanwhile, Joe

nervously awaits the arrival of the bank examiner, fearful that the man will discover that he and his brother have embezzled the $40,000 that Rocky was accused of stealing. When the sheriff sees Blackie on the street, he orders him to remain in town, and Blackie then warns the Kentons that the sheriff is watching them. As the coach approaches a narrow pass on the trail, meanwhile, Rocky jumps off and is met by the marshals, who plan a showdown with the outlaws. Noticing a group of horsemen waiting to attack, Betty aims her gun at Steve and orders him to continue driving. After Weasel and Red, two of the gang, shoot Steve, the marshals apprehend them and threaten them with hanging unless they reveal who robbed the safe and framed Rocky. When Weasel confesses that Blackie murdered the deputies and the Kentons masterminded the plot, the marshals tie up the outlaws and leave them for the sheriff. Soon after, Steve, wounded and near death, drives the coach into town, making the brothers even more anxious. While the sheriff rides to the pass to investigate, Paul orders Blackie and his men to watch for the arrival of the marshals. Under cover of nightfall, Betty, Rocky and the marshals ride into Sonora. After sending Rocky and Betty to Judge Crandall's house, the marshals ready to confront the gunmen. Soon after, the sheriff arrives in town with his prisoners. Inside the jail, Weasel promises to turn state's evidence and the sheriff uncuffs him. Weasel overpowers the lawman, however, and escapes out the back door, but is shot by Blackie for betraying the gang. The marshals then descend upon the Kentons' office. Hearing the sound of gunfire, Betty, Rocky and the judge join the mêlée and bring the outlaws to justice. With Rocky exonerated and their mission accomplished, the marshals ride out of town. *Frame-ups. Murder. Outlaws. Prisoners. Robbery. United States. Marshals. Bankers. Brothers. Confession (Law). Embezzlement. Gunfights. Indians of North America. Jailbreaks. Sheriffs. Stagecoach drivers. Stagecoaches.*

Note: The working titles of this film were *Sonora Kid* and *The Roaring West*. The *HR* production chart mistakenly lists the character names "Joe Kenton," "Paul Kenton" and "Larry Payne" as actor names. Modern sources add Frank Ellis, Hal Price, Rodd Redwing, John Cason and Horace B. Carpenter to the cast. For additional information on the "Trail Blazer" series, please consult the Series Index.

Box 2 Sep 1944. *DV* 8 Sep 1944, p. 3. *FD* 28 Aug 1944, p. 13. *HR* 10 Dec 1943, p. 12. *HR* 17 Dec 1943, p. 10. *HR* 8 Sep 1944, p. 3. *MPHPD* 13 May 1944, p. 1890. *MPHPD* 26 Aug 1944, p. 2066. *Var* 23 Aug 1944, p. 18.

S.O.S. ALASKA see **RED SNOW**

THE SOUL OF KURA-SAN (Japanese Americans)

Jesse L. Lasky Feature Play Co. *Dist* Paramount Pictures Corp. 30 Oct 1916 [©Jesse L. Lasky Feature Play Co.; 26 Oct 1916; LP9406]. Si; b&w. 5 reels.

Pres Jesse L. Lasky. *Dir* E. J. Le Saint. *Asst dir* Captain Ford. *Scen* Charles Sarver. *Story* Frances E. Guihan. *Cam* Allan M. Davey. *Art dir* Wilfred Buckland.

Cast: Sessue Hayakawa (*Toyo*), Myrtle Stedman (*Anne Willoughby*), Tsuru Aoki (*Kura-San*), George Webb (*Herbert Graham*), Thomas Kurihara (*Naguchi*), George Kuwa (*Oki*).

Drama. In Japan, Naguchi, the proprietor of a tea room, disapproves of a match between his daughter Kura-San and Toyo, an impoverished artist. To make enough money to be able to marry Kura-San, Toyo travels to America to work for his uncle, a wealthy merchant. Meanwhile, Naguchi convinces Kura-San that Toyo has married someone else. A despondent Kura-San then models for American artist Herbert Graham. Following in love, she travels with him to America and lets him seduce her. When she returns to Japan and finds that Toyo has married, having earned a lot of money, she commits suicide. Vowing revenge, Toyo returns to America with plans to humiliate Herbert by raping the artist's fiancée, Anne Willoughby. Toyo convinces Anne to come and see him, then, in front of a painting of Kura-San, he attacks her, but he lets Anne go and gives up on gaining revenge when he feels the painting's eyes looking at him, imploring him to stop. *Artists. Attempted rape. Japan. Japanese. Japanese Americans. Models. Painters (Of paintings). Revenge. Suicide. Fathers and daughters. Paintings.*

Note: Captain Ford is probably Starrett Ford.

Motog 11 Nov 1916, p. 1091. *MPN* 11 Nov 1916, p. 3020. *MPN* 23 Dec 1916, p. 4023. *MPW* 11 Nov 1916, p. 838, 846. *NYDM* 4 Nov 1916, p. 27. *Var* 3 Nov 1916, p. 29. *Wid's* 9 Nov 1916, p. 1085.

SOULS AT SEA (African Americans)

Paramount Pictures, Inc. *Dist* Paramount Pictures, Inc. 3 Sep **1937**; Prod: began early Nov 1936 [©Paramount Pictures, Inc.; 3 Sep 1937; LP7396]. Sd (Western Electric Mirrophonic Recording); b&w. 10 reels. 90 or 92-93 min. Passed by the National Board of Review. PCA cert no. 3029.

Pres ADOLPH ZUKOR. [*Exec prod* William LeBaron]. *Dir* Henry Hathaway. [*Asst dir* Hal Walker]. *Scr* Grover Jones and Dale Van Every. *Story* Ted Lesser. *Contr spec seq* Richard Talmadge. *Photog* Charles Lang, Jr. and Merritt Gerstad. *Spec photog eff* Gordon Jennings. *Art dir* Hans Dreier and Roland Anderson. *Ed* Ellsworth Hoagland. *Int dec* A. E. Freudeman. *Cost* Edith Head. *Mus dir* Boris Morros. *Orig mus* W. Franke Harling, Milan Roder and [Bernard Kaun]. [*Orchestrations* John Leipold]. *Sd rec* Harry Mills and John Cope.

Song(s): "Susie Sapple" and "Hang Boys Hang," words and music by Ralph Rainger and Leo Robin.

Cast: GARY COOPER ([*Michael*] *"Nuggin" Taylor*), GEORGE RAFT (*Powdah*), Frances Dee (*Margaret Tarryton*), Henry Wilcoxon (*Lieut.* [*Stanley*] *Tarryton*), Harry Carey (*Captain of "William Brown"*), Olympe Bradna (*Babsie*), Robert Cummings (*George Martin*), Porter Hall (*Court prosecutor*), George Zucco ([*Barton*] *Woodley*), Virginia Weidler (*Tina*), Joseph Schildkraut (*Gaston de Bastonet*), Gilbert Emery (*Capt. Martisel*), Lucien Littlefield (*Toymaker*), Paul Fix (*Violinist*), Tully Marshall (*Pecora*), Monte Blue (*Mate*), [Stanley Fields (*Granley*)], Fay Holden (*Mrs. Martin*), [Jameson Thomas (*Pelton*)], [Cecil Cunningham (*Lady Tarrington*)], [Grace Hampton (*Old lady knitter*)], [Colin Tapley (*Donaldson*)], [Clyde Cook (*Hendry*)], [Luana Walters (*Eloise*)], [Stanley Andrews (*First mate*)], [George Lloyd, G. Pat Collins, Mathew Betz, Francis Ford (*Slavers*)], [Rollo Lloyd (*Parchy*)], [Wilson Benge (*Doctor*)], [Colin Kenny (*Military guard*)], [Craufurd Kent (*Navy clerk*)], [Robert Warwick (*Vice admiral*)], [John Elliott, J. M. Sullivan, Allan Cavan, Phillips Smalley (*Dignitaries*)], [Lionel Braham (*Lord Mayor*)], [Gloria Williams, Ethel Clayton (*Passengers*)], [Phyllis Godfrey (*Housemaid*)], [Frank Benson (*Gardener*)], [David Clyde (*Butler*)], [Mary Gordon (*Cook*)], [Herbert Clifton (*Ticket clerk*)], [Carlyle O'Rourke, Paul Walton (*Puppeteers*)], [Rolfe Sedan, Eugene Borden (*Friends of de Bastonet*)], [George Andre Beranger (*Henri*)], [Lee Shumway (*Mate*)], [Ward Bond (*Sailor*)], [Viva Tattersall (*Queen Victoria*)], [Arthur Blake (*Prime minister*)], [Harvey Clark (*Court clerk*)], [Forbes Murray (*Associate justice*)], [Davison Clark (*Bailiff*)], [Charles Middleton (*Jury foreman*)], [Olaf Hytten (*Proprietor*)], [Belle Mitchell (*Fortune teller*)], [Henry Mowbray (*Bus man*)], [Gunnis Davis (*Barber*)], [Forrester Harvey (*Pub proprietor*)], [Jane Weir (*Barmaid*)], [Lina Basquette (*Brunette*)], [Pauline Haddon (*Blonde*)], [Lowell Drew (*Jury foreman*)], [William Stack (*Judge*)], [Paul Stanton (*Defense attorney*)], [Leslie Francis (*Woolsey's secretary*)], [George MacQuarrie (*Doctor*)], [Edward Van Sloan, Ben Taggart (*Ship's officers*)], [Norman Ainsley (*Ticket taker*)], [Alonzo Price], [Lee Phelps], [Ted Oliver], [Dick Rich], [Bob McKenzie], [Jane Keckley], [Earl Pingree], [Marty Faust], [Fritzi Brunette], [Margaret Daggett], [Betty Lorraine], [Erin La Bissoniere], [Virginia Kami], [Lillian Dean], [Don Rowan], [Agnes Ayres], [Beth Hartman], [Peggy Montgomery].

Adventure. [*Print viewed*]. In 1842 in Philadelphia, sailor Michael "Nuggin" Taylor faces trial on allegations that he caused the deaths of nineteen people from the ship *William Brown*. His trial is witnessed by Barton Woodley, a British secret service agent who intends to come to Michael's defense if the verdict should find against him. In court Michael's story is told: When slaves attack Granley, a renowned slaver and the brutal captain of the *Blackbird*, his dying command is that seaman Powdah captain the vessel and Michael, a passionate abolitionist and friend of Powdah, keep the ship on course to meet with the slave traders. Michael advises Powdah to steer the ship toward a British patrol vessel in order to keep tabs on them, and along the way, they release the slaves onto the coast. The patrol ship captures the *Blackbird*, and when Michael and Powdah refuse to reveal what happened to the slaves, they are hanged by their thumbs from the halyard. While they are hanging, Powdah confesses to Michael that although he is a seaman, he is afraid of the water, and is now afraid he will fall into the ocean. In order to save his friend, Michael tells his captors, including Lieutenant Stanley Tarryton, that they will confess. Later, Powdah tries to protect Michael by telling them that although he has worked slaving ships for years, Michael

only recently came aboard and did not realize it was a slave ship. The captain is suspicious that the *Blackbird* was caught so easily and suspects that Michael deliberately steered toward them so they would be captured. In Liverpool, Michael and Powdah are acquitted for their actions, and Woodley, who is out to end slavery, takes an interest in Michael, as every ship Michael has worked on has encountered trouble and has seen the release of its slaves. Unknown to Powdah, Woodley enlists Michael to work for British intelligence and entrap the ring of slavers. At the same time, Tarryton meets with his business partner, Pecora, and they plan to take on Granley's established slave trading route. In order to do this, they immediately purchase the ship *William Brown*, which is departing the next morning for Philadelphia and Savannah, Georgia, and is considered the fastest packet on the seas. Michael also boards the *William Brown* at dawn carrying Granley's secret plans, and is met on board by Powdah. Tarryton is suspicious of Michael and is especially hostile when Michael falls in love with his sister Margaret. When Tina, the young daughter of immigrants traveling to the United States, knocks over an oil lamp below deck, a fire breaks out and ignites gunpowder, causing massive explosions. Michael struggles with Tarryton for the plans and knocks Tarryton out. The rest of the ship catches fire, and Powdah finds his girl friend, Babsie, with whom he had only just fallen in love, pinned under a fallen beam just before she dies. As Michael helps people into a lifeboat, Tarryton attacks him, but drowns after they struggle in the water. Bereft, Powdah stays on board to be with Babsie as the ship sinks, and knocks Michael into the lifeboat he will not stop him. A mast falls into the lifeboat, and when Michael revives, he urges his fellow survivors to hang onto the edges of the boat so that it will not founder. Unfortunately, the boat is overcrowded, and the desperate people are causing it to sink. Michael shoots several people, who fall into the ocean to their death, in order to save the lives of the others. At the trial, Michael clearly feels remorse for the actions he was forced to take, and refuses to defend himself against accusations that he is a slaver. After a violent argument erupts in the courtroom when several of the survivors deny the accusations against Michael, the courtroom is cleared. Woodley suddenly appears to defend Michael and reveals enough evidence in Michael's favor to change the court's initial decision of guilty and call for a retrial. Michael and Margaret then reunite. Abolitionists. Sailors. Self-sacrifice. Slave traders. Trials. United States–History–19th century. African Americans. Drowning. Explosions. Fires. Great Britain. Intelligence Service. Great Britain. Navy. Lawyers. Philadelphia (PA). Romance. Sea rescues. Secret documents. Ships.

Note: An opening prologue states that the "story was inspired by a trial for mass murder on the high seas [which] a century ago made legal and maritime history." According to the pressbook, the trial is recorded in the Philadelphia Public Ledger and is based on an incident that occurred on 19 Apr 1841 when the *William Brown* struck an iceberg and capsized. After crew and passengers got into the two available lifeboats, leaving thirty-one aboard the ship to drown, "seaman Alexander William Holmes assumed command and dumped excess [persons] overboard." A *HR* news item noted that Jo Swerling was to write "epilog scenes" for this film. Swerling's contribution to the final film has not been determined. A news item in *HR* noted that Frances Farmer was considered for the lead role. Additional news items in *HR* reveal that George Raft terminated his contract with Paramount in Nov 1936 due to a dispute over the roles he was given, including his role in *Souls at Sea*. Although production was scheduled to begin in late Oct, it was postponed due to the threat of a strike by the Pacific Coast Maritime workers, according to *HR*, and by Paramount's search for a co-star. *HR* noted that Lloyd Nolan was first considered, but later Anthony Quinn was selected to replace Raft. At this time, however, Raft and Paramount amended their rift, Raft's contract was renewed and he accepted the role of Powdah. Production was scheduled to resume on 21 Nov 1936.

Press releases claimed the following about the production: Paramount constructed a special set with a huge tank of water and the quarterdeck of a ship for shipboard scenes. For further authenticity, the studio chartered sailing ships for ocean shots and dock scenes, and the square-rigger *Star of Finland* was used as the *William Brown*. Grant Leenhauts hired sailors who knew how to work a square-rigger to appear aboard ship. Some scenes were filmed off Santa Catalina Island, CA. According to modern sources, the film was originally intended to rival M-G-M's *Mutiny on the Bounty* and to be released as a road-show, however, the plans were scaled down, as was the film. Although an actress portraying Queen Victoria is credited in the CBCS, modern sources note that the scene of Queen Victoria's court was one of many deleted from the film before its general release in theaters. The film was nominated for the following Academy Awards: Best Assistant Director, Hal Walker; Best Interior Decorations, Hans Dreier and Roland Anderson; and Music (Best Score), Paramount Studio Music Dept., Boris Morros, head score by W. Franke Harling and Milan Roder. Also based on a similar story is the 1956 British film *Seven Waves Away*, known in the United States as *Abandon Ship!*, directed by Richard Sale and starring Tyrone Power, Mai Zetterling and Lloyd Nolan.

DV 6 Aug 1937, p. 3. *FD* 10 Aug 1937, p. 6. *HR* 28 Oct 1936, p. 1. *HR* 30 Oct 1936, p. 4. *HR* 9 Nov 1936, p. 4. *HR* 14 Nov 1936, p. 1, 4. *HR* 16 Nov 1936, p. 14. *HR* 17 Nov 1936, p. 1. *HR* 18 Nov 1936, p. 2. *HR* 20 Nov 1936, p. 1. *HR* 13 Mar 1937, p. 1. *HR* 6 Aug 1937, p. 3. *Life* 16 Aug 1937. *MPD* 7 Aug 1937, p. 2. *MPD* 10 Aug 1937, pp. 1-2. *MPH* 30 Jan 1937, p. 16-17. *MPH* 11 Jul 1937, p. 19. *MPH* 14 Aug 1937, p. 58. *NYT* 10 Aug 1937, p. 23. *Var* 11 Aug 1937, p. 19.

SOULS OF SIN (African Americans)
Alexander Productions. **1949**; Prod: 1948. Sd (RCA); b&w. 5,759 ft. 64 min.
Prod William D. Alexander. *Prod supv* Harriette B. Miller. *Dir* Powell Lindsay. *Wrt* Powell Lindsay. *Dir of photog* Louis Andres. *Film ed* Walter Cruter.
Song(s): "The Things You Do to Me," music and lyrics by Savannah Churchill and Henry Glover; "Disappointment Blues" and "Lonesome Blues," music and lyrics by William Greaves.
Cast: Savannah Churchill (*Regina*), Jimmy Wright ([*William*] *Dollar Bill* [*Button*]), Billie Allen (*Etta* [*Mason*]), William Greaves ([*Isiah*] *Alabama* [*Lee*]), Emory Richardson (*Roberts*), Louise Jackson (*Mrs. Sands*), Powell Lindsay (*Bad Boy George*), Charlie Macrae (*Mac*), Bill Chase (*The Newspaper editor*), Jessie Walker (*Cool Breeze*), Harris and Scott.
African American, Drama, with songs. [*Print viewed*]. One day, William Button, a smartly dressed but down on his luck black promoter who is known to his friends as "Dollar Bill," enters his Harlem basement apartment and awakens his roommate Roberts, a writer, with a kick. Roberts barely comes to life as Mrs. Sands, Bill and Roberts' landlady, introduces the two men to their new roommate, Isiah "Alabama" Lee, a musician newly arrived from the South. Bill and Roberts complain to Mrs. Sands about crowding another person into their small room, but she tells them that he will not be there long because he is destined for success. Bill and Alabama nearly get into a brawl when Alabama starts tinkering with Roberts' typewriter, but Bill manages to diffuse the tension by asking the new roommate to play a song on his guitar. Soon after Alabama leaves the apartment to look for a job, Bill calls Roberts an "imbecile" for suggesting another one of his dumb ideas for a story. Bill then goes to a bar, where he throws a beer at a drunken patron who laughs openly at him for being so poor. When the bartender refuses to serve Bill until he shows that he can pay his tab, Bill starts a fight. The fight is soon broken up by Etta Mason, who offers to pay for Bill's drink. Later, when Etta visits Bill in his room, he is rude to her, and she leaves, her eyes filled with tears. Returning with a gift of food for everyone, Etta explains to Roberts that she has idolized Bill ever since she was young girl, when he used to give her dollar bills. Roberts knows that Bill has changed and is heading for a fall, and urges Etta to forget him. In his desperate attempt to achieve success, Bill takes a job hawking stolen jewelry for Bad Boy George, but the scheme goes bad when Bill botches a fur heist and falls in love with George's girl friend Regina. When George finds Bill and Regina kissing in a bar, a fight ensues and George winds up getting a severe beating. Following the fight, Bill takes Regina back to his apartment, where they listen to Alabama play his guitar. Regina is so impressed with Alabama's musical talent that she later takes him to an audition at the nightclub where she sings. Bill becomes increasingly hostile and, one day, tries to rape Etta. He then has an angry encounter with one of the men to whom he tried to sell a stolen ring. During the argument, Bill is shot, and as he falls to the ground, he shoots and kills the other man. Badly wounded, Bill returns to his apartment, where Alabama and the others are celebrating Alabama's new television show contract. Bill dies moments after he arrives, and Roberts is later asked to write a series of articles about his longtime friend. African Americans. Attempted rape. Authors. Boardinghouses. Musicians. New York City–Harlem. Roommates. Bars. Fistfights. Gamblers. Gangsters. Gunshot wounds. Jealousy. Jewel thieves. Landladies. Murder. Ne'er-do-wells. Romance. Singers. Television.
Note: Powell Lindsay's onscreen credit reads: "Written and directed by Powell Lindsay."
New York Age 8 Jan 1949, p. 12.

THE SOURCE (Swedish Americans)
Famous Players-Lasky Corp. *Dist* Famous Players-Lasky Corp.; Paramount Pictures. 1 Sep **1918** [©Famous Players-Lasky Corp.; 6 Aug 1918; LP12759]. Si; b&w. 5 reels, 4,637 ft.
Pres Jesse L. Lasky. *Dir* George H. Melford. *Asst dir* Claude Mitchell. *Scen* Monte M. Katterjohn. *Cam* Paul Perry. *Art dir* Wilfred Buckland.

Source: Based on the novel *The Source* by Clarence Budington Kelland (New York, 1918).

Cast: Wallace Reid (*Van Twiller Yard*), Ann Little (*Svea Nord*), Theodore Roberts (*Big John Beaumont*), Raymond Hatton (*Pop Sprowl*), James Cruze (*Langlois*), Noah Beery (*John Nord*), Nina Byron (*Ruth Piggins*), Charles West (*Paul Holmquist*), G. Butler Clonblough (*Ekstrom*), Charles Ogle (*"Sim-Sam" Samuels*).

Espionage, World War I, Drama. Van Twiller Yard, the alcoholic son of a prominent Bostonian, is shanghaied while on a drunken spree and taken to a lumber camp in New York's Green Mountains. Under the influence of hard work and the superintendent's daughter, Svea Nord, Van Twiller gives up drinking and soon earns the respect of his fellow lumbermen. When Big John Beaumont, the owner of the yard, witnesses a fight in which Van Twiller prevents Langlois, the foreman, from inciting the men to rebellion, he decides to place the former alcoholic in charge of the entire camp, to the displeasure of Svea's father. Secretly in the employ of the Swedish Power Company, owned by German spies, Langlois bribes Nord to prevent the opening of a dam that will allow the transport of Beaumont's logs to the mills. Van Twiller organizes the lumberjacks, and following a fierce battle, the floodgates are opened and the logs begin their trip down the river. As a result of his courage, Van Twiller wins Svea's love as well as the position of general manager of the lumber company. *Bostonians. Heroism. Lumber camps. Regeneration. Swedish Americans. Traitors. Abduction. Alcoholics. Conspiracy. Dams. Fights. Germans. Green Mountains. Lumber camp foremen. Lumberjacks. Rivers. Spies. Uprisings. World War I.*

Note: Kelland's novel was serialized in *The Saturday Evening Post* beginning on 4 Aug 1917. G. Butler Clonblough was the name assumed by well-known actor Gustav von Seyffertitz during World War I. Some sources for this film call him Gustav Seyffertitz. A 1941 item in the Paramount studio records lists James Neill as a cast member.

ETR 24 Aug 1918, p. 1017. *ETR* 21 Sep 1918, p. 1332. *MPN* 24 Aug 1918, p. 1214, 1257. *MPW* 24 Aug 1918, p. 1155. *MPW* 14 Sep 1918, pp. 1615-16. *MPW* 21 Sep 1918, p. 1772. *NYDM* 7 Sep 1918, p. 371. *NYT* 9 Sep 1918, p. 9. *Var* 16 Aug 1918, p. 35. *Wid's* 18 Aug 1918, pp. 23-24.

SOUS LES VERROUS *see* **PARDON US**

SOUTH OF MONTEREY (Latino)

Monogram Pictures Corp. *Dist* Monogram Pictures Corp. 10 Jul 1946; *Prod:* late Mar 1946 [©Monogram Pictures Corp.; 29 Jun 1946; LP389]. Sd (Western Electric Mirrophonic Recording); b&w. 63 min. PCA cert no. 11623.

Series: The Cisco Kid.

Prod Scott R. Dunlap. *Dir* William Nigh. *Asst dir* Eddie Davis. *Orig story and scr* Charles S. Belden. *Dir of photog* Harry Neumann. *Tech dir* Ernest Hickox. *Film ed* Richard Heermance. *Set dec* Vin Taylor. *Ward* Harry Bourne. *Mus dir* Edward J. Kay. *Rec eng* Frank McWhorter. *Makeup* Harry Ross. *Prod mgr* Charles Bigelow.

Song(s): "Tacos de amor," "Anoche hable con la luna," and "Tu chulita," words by Gladys Flores, music by Edward J. Kay; "Ride, Amigos, Ride," words by Eddie Cherkose, music by Charles Rosoff; "Cielito lindo," traditional.

Source: Based on the character created by O. Henry.

Cast: Gilbert Roland [(*The Cisco Kid*)], Martin Garralaga (*Arturo* [*Morales*]), Frank Yaconelli (*Baby*), Marjorie Riordan (*Maria* [*Morales*]), Iris Flores (*Carmelita*), George J. Lewis (*Carlos* [*Mandreno*]), Harry Woods (*Bennet*), Terry Frost (*Morgan*), Rosa Turich (*Indian woman*), [Wheaton Chambers (*Padre*)].

Historical, Drama, with songs. [*Print viewed*]. During the mid-nineteenth century, when The Cisco Kid and his gang hear that Indians and poor people are being robbed by tax collectors and land sharks in a town south of Monterey, California, he rides to their aid. Meanwhile, Carlos Mandreno, a young rancher, tells his sweetheart, Maria Morales, that he has paid his taxes and sold his cattle and now owns his ranch. Although the sale will enable them to get married, Maria tells Carlos that her brother Arturo, the chief of police, wants her to marry Bennet, the tax collector. Later, when Maria informs Arturo that she loathes Bennet for exploiting the poor, he reminds her that their house was a gift from Bennet and suggests that she not worry about the poor. Bennet, who has been foreclosing on property and selling it or giving it to his friends, prevents Carlos from interfering in his schemes by ordering Arturo to frame him for stealing cattle. Shortly after Cisco arrives in town, the money for the cattle that Carlos sold is stolen by a thief, who is known as "The Silver Bandit"

because he rides on a silver saddle. When the posse sees Cisco, his silver-covered saddle causes them to suspect that he is The Silver Bandit. During the ensuing chase, Cisco is wounded and makes his way to Maria's house. She bandages his wound and hides him from her brother. Later, in the cantina, Cisco is flirting with Carmelita, the singer, when Maria arrives in search of Arturo, who is in love with Carmelita. Maria agrees to marry Bennet if Arturo will release Carlos. A short time later, a fight breaks out when Arturo slaps Carmelita, and Cisco comes to her defense. Carmelita inadvertently reveals Cisco's identity, and Arturo arrests him. Later, Cisco and Carlos escape from jail with the help of Carmelita, who steals the key to Cisco's cell from Arturo. Carlos discloses that Bennet has a hideout in the mountains, and the two men ride there in the morning. At the hideout, the men discover that Arturo is The Silver Bandit. From their hiding place, they see Bennet kill Arturo when he refuses to split the stolen money. Cisco then struggles with Bennet and kills him. Later, Cisco tells Maria that Arturo died while defending himself and killed Bennet, The Silver Bandit. He returns the stolen money and then bids the townspeople goodbye. *Brothers and sisters. California–History. Fights. Gunshot wounds. Land rights. Police corruption. Robbery. Romance. Hideouts. Indians of North America. Jailbreaks. Marriage–Forced. Singers. Spaniards. Taxation.*

Note: For additional information on the series, consult the Series Index and see the entry above for *The Cisco Kid.*

DV 22 Aug 1946, p. 3. *FD* 27 Sep 1946, p. 10. *HR* 22 Mar 1946, p. 12. *HR* 29 Mar 1946, p. 22. *HR* 22 Aug 1946, p. 3. *MPHPD* 3 Aug 1946, p. 3127. *MPHPD* 28 Sep 1946, p. 3224.

SOUTH OF SAN ANTONE *see* **SAN ANTONE**

SOUTH OF THE RIO GRANDE (Latino)

Monogram Pictures Corp. *Dist* Monogram Pictures Corp. 15 Sep 1945; *Prod:* mid-May—early Jun 1945 [©Monogram Pictures Corp.; 25 Aug 1945; LP13702]. Sd; b&w. 5,544 ft. 61-62 min.

Series: The Cisco Kid.

[*Prod* Lindsley Parsons]. *Dir* Lambert Hillyer. [*Asst dir* Eddie Stein]. *Scr* Victor Hammond and Ralph Bettinson. *Orig story* Johnston McCulley. *Photog* William Sickner. *Tech dir* David Milton. *Ed* William Austin. [*Set dresser* Vin Taylor]. *Mus dir* Edward J. Kay. *Rec* Glen Glenn. *Prod mgr* Glenn Cook.

Source: Based on the character created by O. Henry.

Cast: Duncan Renaldo [(*The Cisco Kid*)], Martin Garralaga [(*Pancho*)], Armida [(*Pepita*)], The Guadalajara Trio, George J. Lewis [(*Miguel Sanchez*)], Lillian Molieri [(*Dolores Gonzales*)], Francis McDonald [(*Torres*)], Charles Stevens [(*Sebastian*)], Pedro Regas [(*Luis*)], Soledad Jimenez [(*Mama Maria*)], Tito Renaldo [(*Manuel Gonzales*)], [Escamillo Fernandez (*Padre*)], [Loti Parker, Diane Quillan (*Senoritas*)], [Elias Gamboa (*Anton*)], [Jerry Gomez, Matty Roubert, Augie Gomez (*Corporales*)], [Dick Botiller (*Gomez*)], [Johnny Romero (*Tonete*)], [Joe Dominguez (*Garcia*)], [Dimas Sotello (*Sergeant of Rurales*)], [Fernando Alvarado (*Child*)].

Western, with songs. [*Print viewed*]. The notorious Mexican bandit, The Cisco Kid, is interrupted by his friend Pancho while serenading the latest object of his affections. Pancho gives him a letter from Stephen, an old childhood friend, pleading for Cisco's help in fighting false charges of cattle rustling. Cisco and Pancho arrive in the bandit's old hometown just in time to save Manuel Gonzales, another innocent rancher, from a firing squad, then learn that Stephen and his family were killed the night before by Miguel Sanchez, the corrupt district officer who falsely accuses the ranchers of rustling in order to steal their cattle. Meanwhile, Dolores, Manuel's sister, is abducted by Sanchez' men and forced to sing for the district officer at a local saloon, much to the chagrin of Pepita, a jealous saloon performer who desires Sanchez. Later, Cisco and some of the ranchers discover Dominguez, a government inspector, murdered by Sanchez' men, so Cisco decides to impersonate the dead official and rides into town. Pretending to be afraid of the newly organized outlaw ranchers, Cisco accepts the protection and hospitality of Sanchez, and agrees to stay at his hacienda. In the meantime, Pepita discovers Dolores' true identity, but she is held captive by Luis and Mama Maria, the saloon's proprietors, in order to stop her from telling Sanchez. Pepita escapes, however, and rushes to Sanchez' hacienda, but before the district officer can act, Cisco steps in and orders Pancho to "execute" Dolores and leave her body where the fugitive ranchers can find it. Cisco then meets alone with the love-starved Pepita, who tells him all about Sanchez' vast cattle rustling. Pepita also informs Cisco that

Sanchez has hidden his ill-gotten gains in a buried chest. Learning that his corruption has been exposed, Sanchez and Torres, his henchman, make plans to kill Cisco and the others, then escape across the border to the United States. Sanchez' scheme backfires, however, and he is captured by Cisco. Cisco orders Sanchez to write a confession, but Sanchez instead pulls out a hidden gun and is killed in a gunfight by Cisco. With the ranchers' help, Sanchez' men are then quickly captured and turned over to the new, honest district officer. *Bandits. Government officials. Impersonation and imposture. Mexicans. Political corruption.* Abduction. Brothers and sisters. Escapes. False arrests. Firing squads. Haciendas. Jealousy. Mexico. Murder. Musicians. Ranchers. Rescues. Rustlers. Saloons. Shootouts. Singers. Watches.

Note: The title card on the viewed print reads "The Cisco Kid in *South of the Rio Grande.*" The working title of this film was *Song of the Border.* The viewed print contained five unidentified Spanish-language songs, which were referred to as "Mexican folk songs" in the Monogram pressbook. For additional information about this series, consult the Series Index and see the entry above for *The Cisco Kid.*

DV 9 Nov 1945, p. 3. *HR* 11 May 1945, p. 10. *HR* 18 May 1945, p. 10. *MPHPD* 9 Nov 1945, p. 2757. *Var* 12 Dec 1945, p. 12.

SOUTHERN PRIDE (Creoles)
American Film Co.; Mutual Star Productions. *Dist* Mutual Film Corp. 8 Oct **1917**. Si; b&w. 5 reels.

Dir Henry King. *Scen* Julian Louis Lamothe.

Cast: Gail Kane (*Lucie De Montrand*), Cora Drew (*Tante Jeanne*), Jack Vosburgh (*François De Montrand*), Robert Klein (*Gaspar La Roche*), Spottiswoode Aitken (*Father Moret*), George Periolat (*James Morgan*), Lewis J. Cody (*Robert Orme*).

Drama. The only remaining members of New Orleans' proud but poor Creole family are Lucie De Montrand, her brother François and their aunt, Tante Jeanne. Two men are in love with Lucie: James Morgan, a wealthy plantation owner whom her aunt wishes her to marry, and the impoverished Robert Orme, whose love Lucie returns. Desperate to win the favor of the town vampire, François gives her the jewels that Gaspar La Roche, an old antique dealer, had earlier given to Lucie. Then, when Lucie fails to wear them as the queen of the Knights of Consus Ball, Gaspar refuses to believe that she is ignorant of their whereabouts. If she marries him, he suggests, she may keep the jewels, but otherwise, she must return them immediately. Lucie learns from Corinne, the cook, that François has taken the gems, whereupon she visits his sweetheart and demands their return. As she walks home, Gaspar insults her, but she is defended by François and Robert. In the confusion, the gun that Gaspar had pointed at François is discharged and the antique dealer is killed. Repentant, François abandons the vampire and assumes his position as the head of the family, while Lucie, through the mediation of Father Moret, finally is allowed to marry Robert. *Antique dealers. Creoles. Jewelry. New Orleans (LA).* Balls (Parties). Clergy. Cooks. Family life. Plantation owners. Vamps.

MPN 13 Oct 1917, p. 2531. *MPN* 27 Oct 1917, p. 2953. *MPW* 13 Oct 1917, pp. 291-92.

THE SOUTHERNER *see* VIRGINIA

SOYONS GAIS (French language)
Metro-Goldwyn-Mayer Corp.; controlled by Loew's, Inc. *Dist* Culver Export, Inc. **1931**; Prod: mid-Jan 1931. Sd (Western Electric Sound System); b&w. 88 min. French language.

Réalisation de [*Dir*] Arthur Robison. [*Asst dir* Al Shenberg]. *Scénario et dialogue* [*Scr and dial*] Frances Marion. *Dialogue additionnel de* [*Addl dial*] Lucile Newmark. *Adaptation française de* [*French adpt*] Jacques Deval. *Photographie de* [*Photog*] Harold Rosson. *Décorateur* [*Art dir*] Cedric Gibbons. *Editeur* [*Ed*] Hélène Warne. *Costumes de* [*Cost*] Adrian. *Ingénieur du son* [*Sd eng*] Douglas Shearer.

Source: Based on the play *Let Us Be Gay, a Comedy* by Rachel Crothers (New York, 19 Feb 1929), as produced by John Golden.

Cast: LILY DAMITA (*Kitty Brown*), ADOLPHE MENJOU (*Bob*), Françoise Rosay (*Mme. Boucijon*), Marcel André (*Townley*), Tania Fédor (*Madge*), Mona Goya (*Diane*), Roland Caillaux (*Bruce*), André Nicolle (*Wallace*), Marcelle Corday (*Perkins*), Jean del Val (*Whitman*), Albert Petit (*Struthers*), [Lya Lys].

Comedy. [*Not viewed*]. [The following plot summary is based on the English-language version of this film, *Let Us Be Gay*; character names refer to that version. For further information regarding the English-language version, please see the note below and the entry for *Let Us Be Gay* in the *AFI Catalog of Feature Films, 1921-30.*] Kitty

and Bob Brown part when he begins to take her for granted and engages in a flirtation with a vivacious blonde. Three years later, Mrs. Bouccicault, a wealthy and scheming socialite, finds that her granddaughter, Madge, is infatuated with Bob, though she is engaged to Bruce. The society matron calls on Kitty, whom she has met in Paris, to enlist her help in breaking up the infatuation. After mistaking many other men for her prey, Kitty discovers him to be none other than her divorced husband. Difficulties ensue, however, as Kitty becomes the focus of attention for all the male guests, and Mrs. Bouccicault spends most of her time chasing them away, finally sending for Kitty's children as a last resort. Consequently, Madge gives up her romance with Bob; and after some persuasion, he regains the affections of his former wife. *Children. Divorce. Flirtation. Grandmothers. Marriage. Socialites.*

Note: The English-language version, *Let Us Be Gay*, which was released on 11 Jul 1930, was directed by Robert Z. Leonard and starred Norma Shearer and Rod La Rocque (see *AFI Catalog of Feature Films, 1912-30*; F2.3045). The working title for the French version was *Gai, gai, démarions-nous.* A production chart in *HF* lists the director of *Soyons gais* as André Luguet.

HF 17 Jan 1931, p. 24.

SPAWN OF THE NORTH (Native Americans, Native Alaskans)
Paramount Pictures, Inc. *Dist* Paramount Pictures, Inc. 26 Aug **1938**; Prod: 21 Mar—18 Jun 1938. Sd (Western Electric Mirrophonic Recording); b&w. 12 reels, 9,867 ft. 105, 110 or 112 min. Passed by the National Board of Review. PCA cert no. 4255.

Pres ADOLPH ZUKOR. *Prod* Albert Lewin. *Dir* Henry Hathaway. *Assoc dir* Richard Talmadge. [*Asst dir* John H. Morse]. *Scr* Jules Furthman and Talbot Jennings. [*Contr to scr const* Dale Van Every]. *Photog* Charles Lang. [*Process photog asst* Loyal Griggs]. *Spec photog eff* Gordon Jennings. *Process photog* Farciot Edouart. [*Spec photog eff asst* Jan Domela, Dev Jennings, Irmin Roberts and Art Smith]. *Art dir* Hans Dreier and Roland Anderson. *Ed* Ellsworth Hoagland. *Int dec* A. E. Freudeman. *Mus dir* Boris Morros. *Mus* Dimitri Tiomkin. [*Ceremonial dance staged by* Michio Ito]. *Sd rec* Harry Mills and Walter Oberst. [*Sd eff* Loren Ryder]. [*Sd eff asst* Louis Mesenkop].

Song(s): "I Wish I Was the Willow" and "I Like Hump-backed Salmon," words by Frank Loesser, music by Burton Lane.

Source: Based on the novel *Spawn of the North* by Florence Barrett Willoughby (Boston, 1932).

Cast: George Raft (*Tyler Dawson*), Henry Fonda (*Jim Kimmerlee*), Dorothy Lamour (*Nicky Duval*), Akim Tamiroff (*Red Skain*), John Barrymore (*Windy [Turlon]*), Louise Platt (*Dian [Turlon]*), Lynne Overman (*Jackson*), Fuzzy Knight (*Lefty Jones*), Vladimir Sokoloff (*Dimitri*), Duncan Renaldo (*Ivan*), John Wray (*Doctor Sparks*), Michio Ito (*Indian dancer*), Stanley Andrews (*Partridge*), Richard Ung (*Tom*), [Slicker (*A seal*)], [Alex Woloshin (*Gregory*)], [Archie Twitchell, Lee Shumway, Wade Boteler, Galan Galt, Rollo Lloyd, Arthur Aylesworth (*Fishermen*)], [Guy Usher (*Grant*)], [Henry Brandon (*Davis*)], [Egon Brecher (*Erickson*)], [Harvey Clark (*Purser*)], [Monte Blue, Irving Bacon (*Cannery officials*)], [Robert Middlemass (*Davis*)], [Eddie Marr (*First Red's gang*)], [Frank Puglia (*Second Red's gang*)], [Leonid Snegoff (*Third Red's gang*)], [Adia Kuznetzoff (*Vashia*)], [Edmund Elton (*Minister*)].

Drama. [*Print viewed*]. Alaskan salmon fisherman Jim Kimmerlee encounters his old buddy, Tyler Dawson, who has been away hunting seal to earn enough money to buy his own steam schooner. When Russian fisherman Red Skain ties up to Jim's fish traps, Jim cuts his line so that he will be unable to steal from him. Tyler defends Jim from Red, and Red leaves the scene. Later, Tyler returns to town and to his girl friend Nicky Duval, who owns the local hotel. Newspaper reporter Windy Turlon reports that local fishermen, including Jim, Lefty, Skaggs and Partridge, are joining forces to retaliate against the pirates who have been stealing from their traps. Soon thereafter, Dian Turlon returns after an eight-year absence and reunites with her childhood friends, Jim and Tyler. City life has made Dian haughty and reserved. Her father senses trouble between Jim and Tyler, due to the piracy controversy, as Jim is on the side of the law, and Tyler is not. At the Indian salmon dance that night, Dian warms up, and re-ignites her love for Jim. Tyler invites Jim to join him in a partnership, but Jim refuses as he has already owns a cannery that takes up his time. One day, Jim's friend Dimitri's ship is destroyed by an iceberg, and Jim saves Dimitri's life. Later Jim notices that Tyler's fish do not have net marks and realizes his friend has been stealing from traps. He warns him that anyone stealing from traps will be killed, but Tyler scoffs at his

warning. One day, Jim, Lefty, Skaggs and Partridge sight Red stealing from their traps, but they arrive too late to catch him. He has left behind Dimitri and Ivan, however, who were working for Red and are killed for the theft. Jim and his friends return the bodies to Red's cabin, where Jim discovers to his dismay that Tyler has joined with Red. Dian makes a cake for Jim's birthday, but Tyler does not celebrate with them, as he is planning a final raid on the traps with Red. The celebration is interrupted by the arrival of the fishermen who have discovered Lefty murdered where he was guarding their traps. Hoping to protect his friend, Jim asks Dian to advise Nicky not to let Tyler leave the hotel that night. Tyler is adamant about going out, however, presuming that he can evade Jim and his friends. Desperate to protect Tyler, Nicky sabotages his boat, but he simply takes another boat instead. Tyler catches up with Red, who leaves him with Boris and Serge, members of his gang, to finish cleaning out the traps. After they are caught in the act by Jim, Tyler begins firing on Jim's boat. Jim is compelled to return the fire, and he shoots Tyler. Boris and Serge are killed. The deaths of his friends embitters Red, who becomes determined to force Jim out of the area. When Jim goes to Red's cabin, he finds it deserted, except for Tyler, who has been left unconscious and unattended. Jim takes Tyler to town, where he is operated on by a doctor. Jim is heartbroken and plagued by guilt for shooting his friend. When Tyler reawakens and learns how he was shot, he tells Jim he never wants to see him again, but confesses to Nicky that he is not mad at Jim and that he plans to leave him all he owns. Although he is not fully healed, Tyler goes on a last outing with Red, who believes they are out to revenge themselves on Jim. Jim encounters their boat, but finds that Tyler has deceived Red and locked him in his cabin. Near death, Tyler blows the boat's whistle, causing an avalanche, and steers the boat into the cliffs, crashing it underneath the avalanche, which kills them. Turlon's newspaper reports that Tyler's death "ennobled his life," and that he made fishing safe for all. *Alaska. Fishermen. Friendship. Murder. Thieves. Avalanches. Birthdays. Dances. Deception. Gunshot wounds. Hotels. Indians of North America. Operations, Surgical. Reporters. Reunions. Romance. Russians. Sabotage. Salmon. Sea rescues. Seals (Animals). Suicide. Vigilantes.*

Note: Florence Barrett Willoughby's novel was serialized in *Hearst's International-Cosmopolitan* (Sep 1935—Jan 1936). Information in the Paramount story files at the AMPAS library reveals that Willoughby's novel was previously considered as material for a film, but was rejected due to its similarity to RKO's *The Silver Horde*. Early scripts were authored by Robert M. Yost and Stuart Anthony. Also included in the files are a story authored by Kurt Siodmak and a screen story written by Thames Williamson. Their contribution to the final film has not been determined. Early scripts cast Georges Rigaud in the lead, however, according to a news item in *HR*, he was replaced by Henry Fonda after shooting began because his French accent was too strong for the role. In addition, in other scripts, Fred MacMurray was cast as "Jim," and Frances Farmer as "Dian." *HR* news items reported the following: Randolph Scott was cast in a lead role, but left due to a commitment to another film. Maine sailor Captain Simray Graves was brought to Hollywood for the film, Porter Hall was testing for a role in the film, and Beulah Bondi and Polly Moran were cast, however, they did not appear in the released film. As early as 1936, director Henry Hathaway was preparing the film, which was originally to be shot in color. According to a later news item in *HR*, Paramount sent a camera crew headed by Richard Talmadge to Ketchikan, Alaska to film the opening scenes of a salmon run. In a contemporary educational supplement to the film, Hathaway stated that the expedition to Alaska lasted fourteen weeks and resulted in 80,000 ft. of film shot.

Paramount constructed a steel and concrete tank on the studio lot which held 375,000 gallons of water, in which fishing boats and power cruisers were launched for close range shots. In addition, some scenes were filmed on location at Lake Arrowhead, Lake Tahoe, Balboa Island and the coast of Southern California where a fishing village was built. A news item in *MPH* mentioned that two women were injured in the crush of the crowd awaiting the preview in Westwood, CA. In 1938, the following were given Academy Awards for outstanding achievement in creating special photographic and sound effects: Gordon Jennings for special effects, assisted by Jan Domela, Dev Jennings, Irmin Roberts and Art Smith; transparencies by Farciot Edouart, assisted by Loyal Griggs; sound effects by Loren Ryder, assisted by Harry Mills, Louis H. Mesenkop and Walter Oberst.

Var commented, "Merit of the film is in the persuasive and authentic photographic record of Alaskan life and customs. Highly interesting views of Indian ritual are shown as a new spawning season begins." In 1954, Paramount released *Alaska Seas*, a remake of *Spawn of the North*, directed by Jerry Hopper and starring Robert Ryan, Jan Sterling and Brian Keith..

DV 16 Aug 1938, p. 3. FD 9 Sep 1938, p. 15. HR 8 Jun 1936, p. 5. HR 22 Jun 1936, p. 2. HR 7 Jan 1938, p. 7. HR 8 Feb 1938, p. 33. HR 21 Mar 1938, p. 1. HR 12 Apr 1938, p. 9. HR 30 Apr 1938, p. 15. HR 23 Jun 1937, p. 8. HR 16 Aug 1938, p. 3. MPD 17 Aug 1938, p. 2. MPH 4 Jun 1938, p. 43. MPH 20 Aug 1938, p. 46. NYT 8 Sep 1938, p. 27. Var 24 Aug 1938, p. 12.

LE SPECTRE VERT (French language)

Metro-Goldwyn-Mayer Corp.; controlled by Loew's, Inc. *Dist* Metro-Goldwyn-Mayer Distributing Corp. May **1930**; Paris opening: 7 May 1930. Sd; b&w. 10 reels. 90 min. French language.

Dir Jacques Feyder. *Scr* Edwin Justus Mayer. *Adpt* Dorothy Farnum. *Story* Ben Hecht. *French version* Yves Mirande. *Photog* William Daniels. *Art dir* Cedric Gibbons. *Sd* Douglas Shearer.

Cast: André Luguet (*Lord Montague*), Jetta Goudal (*Lady Efra*), Pauline Garon (*Lady Vi*), Georges Renavent (*Dr. Ballou*), Jules Raucourt (*Sir James Ramsay*).

Mystery, Melodrama. [*Not viewed*]. [The following plot summary is based on the English-language version of this film, *The Unholy Night*: character names refer to that version. For further information regarding the English-language version, please see the note below.] Perceiving a pattern in the mysterious deaths of four members of an English regiment, Sir James Ramsey of Scotland Yard calls together the surviving members of the regiment in the hope of solving the murders. While they are assembled at the Montague mansion, Lady Efra, the daughter of the late Marquis of Cavendar, who was thrown out of the regiment for misconduct, arrives with her father's will. Dividing his vast fortune among Efra and the members of the regiment, and making them guardians of his daughter, Cavendar hoped to harvest his lifelong hatred by causing the regiment to fight over his money and his daughter. Each officer is suspected of being the murderer until Ramsey discovers, through a fake séance, that Efra and Mallory, one of the officers, plan to murder the whole regiment and take possession of the fortune. *Detectives. Great Britain. Army. Heirs. London (England). Murder. Scotland Yard (London, England). Spiritualism. Wills.*

Note: This was a French-language version of the 1929 film *The Unholy Night*, which was directed by Lionel Barrymore and starred Ernest Torrance, Roland Young and Dorothy Sebastian (see *AFI Catalog of Feature Films, 1921-30*; F2.5964).

NYT 8 Jun 1930, p. 6. Var 21 May 1930, p. 19.

SPEED TO BURN (Irish Americans, Italian Americans)

Twentieth Century-Fox Film Corp. *Dist* Twentieth Century-Fox Film Corp. 26 Aug **1938**; Prod: 10 Mar—early Apr 1938 [©Twentieth Century-Fox Film Corp.; 26 Aug 1938; LP8428]. Sd (Western Electric Mirrophonic Recording); b&w. 6 reels, 5,572 ft. 62 min. PCA cert no. 4212.

Series: Sports Series.

Assoc prod Jerry Hoffman. *Dir* Otto Brower. [*Asst dir* Saul Wurtzel and Hal Herman]. *Scr* Robert Ellis and Helen Logan. *Orig story* Edwin Dial-Torgerson. [*Contr wrt* Joseph Krumgold]. *Photog* Edward Snyder. [*Cam op* Kenny Green]. [*Asst cam* Maynard Rugg]. [*Gaffer* Al Baker]. *Art dir* Bernard Herzbrun and Chester Gore. *Film ed* Fred Allen. [*Asst cutter* Murray Abrams]. *Cost* Helen A. Myron. [*Ward man* Bob Martien]. [*Ward girl* Gladys Isaacson]. *Mus dir* Samuel Kaylin. *Sd* Bernard Freericks and William H. Anderson. [*Sd rec* Emmet O'Brien]. [*Boom man* Harry Kornfield]. [*Cableman* Bob Braggins]. [*Prod mgr* Ed. Ebele]. [*Unit mgr* Sam Schneider]. [*Scr clerk* Jack Vernon]. [*Grip* James Riemer]. [*Asst grip* Bruce Hunsaker]. [*Props* Frank Sullivan]. [*Best boy* D. B. Redd]. [*Livestock supv* Sid Jordan]. [*Casting* Virgil Hart]. [*Stand-in* Carl Meyers].

Song(s): "My Wild Irish Rose," music and lyrics by Chauncey Olcott.

Cast: Michael Whalen (*Matt Kerry*), Lynn Bari (*Marion Clark*), Marvin Stephens (*Tim Turner*), Henry Armetta (*Papa Gambini*), Chick Chandler (*Sport Fields*), Sidney Blackmer ([*W. R.*] *Hastings*), Johnnie Pirrone (*Tony Gambini*), Charles D. Brown (*Pop Williams*), Inez Palange (*Mrs. Gambini*), [Eleanor Virzie, Betty Greco (*Gambini children*)], [Edward Emerson (*Marti*), [Lon Chaney, Jr., Harold Goodwin (*Mugs*)], [Gloria Roy (*Nurse*)], [Edwin Stanley (*Detective*)], [Paul McVey (*Clerk*)], [Dick Rush, William Newell, Eddie Dunn, Fred Kelsey (*Policemen*)], [Hooper Atchley (*Baxter*)], [Ivan Miller (*Racing secretary*)], [Stanley Andrews, Edward Keane (*Police chiefs*)], [Wilfred Lucas (*Paddock steward*)], [Ralph Dunn, James Flavin, Eddie Hart, Jerry Storm (*Radio car policemen*)], [James C. Morton (*Bartender*)], [Emmett Vogan (*Radio announcer*)], [Chester Gan (*Chung*)], [Dave Thursby (*Groom*)], [Cliff Clark (*Auctioneer*)], [J. Anthony Hughes, John Gibson, Pat O'Malley (*Stablemen*)], [Bill Cartledge (*Jockey*)], [Ky Robinson, Bud Wiser, Hal Craig (*Motor policemen*)], [Harrison Greene], [Tom McGuire], [Jack Byron], [Phil Smalley].

Horse race, Drama. [*Print viewed*]. After his veteran horse, War Paint, comes in last in a race, Pop Williams vows to auction the horse. War Paint's jockey and trainer, young Tim Turner, quits and tries to talk delicatessen owner Papa Gambini, the father of his friend Tony, to buy the horse, but Papa refuses. Tim then visits W. R. Hastings, a wealthy horseman known for his success in bringing old horses back as stake winners, and offers to work for nothing for Hastings if he buys the horse. Hastings, who is impressed with Tim's knowledge and remembers his father, who was a great rider, sends his secretary, Marion Clark, to the auction to bid for the horse. When the auctioneer puts War Paint in with six other horses that Williams is selling, Marion, flustered, is outbid by Matt Kerry, an Irish-American policeman, who buys the group for his department. Hastings, it turns out, had arranged for War Paint to lose the earlier race by having Swipe, a boy who works at the track, give the horse a lot of water; Hastings then planned to make a killing with the horse in the upcoming Cloverdale Handicap. He now is angry with Marion, but he plans to get the horse at a later date. Tim is upset because he thinks that it is demeaning for War Paint to be a police horse. However, when he sees Matt effectively control the horse after Sport Fields, who works for Hastings, instructs a cab to backfire near the horse, Tim tells Matt he is glad War Paint has someone like him. Tony invites Matt to dinner at the delicatessen, and Matt brings Marion, with whom he has become infatuated. Later, Tim sees Sport drive a motorcycle in front of the horse and throw powder in its face. As War Paint tips over a cart and throws Matt, Tim chases Swipe, who was with Sport, and tackles him in an alley. Swipe reveals Hastings' plan and says that Sport and Marion are in on it. After learning that Matt has suffered a concussion, Tim overhears an officer say that War Paint should be shot. With Tony's help, Tim then substitutes Papa's horse Betsy for War Paint. When Tim visits Matt in the hospital, he finds Marion there and tells of Hastings' scheme and Marion's part in it. Marion walks out disturbed, and when the police find that War Paint is in Papa's stall, Marion reveals that she bought the horse from the police. She tells Tim that she is through with Hastings and really cares about Matt and asks Tim to ride the horse. They keep the horse at Papa's stall and train him early in the morning in the park so that Hastings will not locate them, while Marion works as a waitress at the deli to earn money for the entry fee. Sport finds out about the workouts, and one morning comes to the park with another mug. After slugging Tim, Sport takes the horse; however, Tim had substituted Betsy for War Paint. On the day of the Cloverdale Handicap, two police officers, not knowing that their radio microphone is on, repeat Matt's tip to bet on War Paint if he ever raced again. Officers throughout the city overhear the conversation and place bets on War Paint. Matt also hears the "broadcast" and leaves the hospital. After Sport's mug kidnaps Tim, Matt calls in a report, and when the police learn that War Paint's jockey is missing, they go on alert. Seeing the kidnapper's car go through a stop sign, the police chase it, and it goes over an embankment. The police rush Tim to the track, and although he is hurt, he wins the race before collapsing. Later, in the deli, Papa sings, as Matt is happy with Marion, and Tim feeds War Paint and Betsy. *Deception. Horses. Jockeys. Police. Secretaries.* Auctions. Automobile accidents. Delicatessens. Falls from heights. Horseracing. Irish Americans. Italian Americans. Kidnapping. Moral reformation. Romance. Waitresses.

Note: The working titles of this film were *Lucky Day, Sporting Chance* and *Racing Blood*. The opening screen credits read, "Twentieth Century-Fox presents Another Adventure in the World of Sports *Speed to Burn*." This was the first film in Twentieth Century-Fox's "Sports Series." According to news items, Jerry Hoffman, a former newspaper motion picture critic, was promoted from story adviser at the studio to producer in Oct 1937, in line with studio head Darryl Zanuck's policy of taking executives from within the studio's ranks. Hoffman was signed to produce three sports features a year with Marvin Stephens in the lead. Stephens actually only appeared in this film, but the fictional family of his friends, "The Gambinis," played by Henry Armetta, Inez Palange, Johnnie Pirrone, Eleanor Virzie and Betty Greco, are supporting characters in all the films. The series included two other films dealing with other sports, *Road Demon*, about auto racing (see above), and *Winner Take All*, about boxing (see below). According to information in the Twentieth Century-Fox Records of the Legal Department at the UCLA Theater Arts Library, some scenes in the film were shot in Griffith Park in Los Angeles and at Santa Anita Racetrack in Arcadia, CA. The legal files reveal that a solicitor for an English racehorse trainer named David Hastings claimed that his client was grossly libelled by the fact that the villainous horseman in the film was also named "Hastings." Fox paid the man £110.10 in damages and added two introductory cards to prints of the film which stated that all incidents and names of characters are fictitious, and that the names do not relate to any person bearing the same name.

Box 11 Jun 1938. *DV* 2 Jun 1938, p. 3. *FD* 7 Jun 1938, p. 14. *HR* 27 Oct 1937, p. 1. *HR* 8 Feb 1938, p. 3. *HR* 7 Mar 1938, p. 3. *HR* 14 Mar 1938, p. 7. *HR* 28 Mar 1938, p. 7. *HR* 2 Jun 1938, p. 3. *LAT* 5 Oct 1938. *MPD* 24 Jun 1938, p. 5. *MPH* 11 Jun 1938, pp. 38-39. *NYT* 9 Sep 1938, p. 25. *Var* 8 Jun 1938, p. 26.

SPEED WILD (Chinese Americans)

Harry Garson Productions. *Dist* Film Booking Offices of America. 10 May **1925** [©R-C Pictures Corp.; 10 May 1925; LP21521]. Si; b&w. 5 reels, 4,700 ft.

Dir Harry Garson. *Scen* Frank S. Beresford. *Story* H. H. Van Loan. *Photog* William Tuers.

Cast: Lefty Flynn (*Jack Ames*), Ethel Shannon (*Mary Bryant*), Frank Elliott (*Wendell Martin*), Ralph McCullough (*Charles Bryant*), Raymond Turner (*Ulysses*), Fred Burns (*Red Dugan*), Charles Clary (*Herbert Barron*).

Melodrama. For the sake of adventure, Jack Ames joins the police department as a motorcycle cop and is immediately assigned to the vice squad, which is investigating the smuggling of Chinese picture brides into the United States. When he rescues Mary Bryant after an automobile accident, Jack falls in love with her and soon promises to help straighten out her brother, Charles, who has become involved with the gang of smugglers. Jack goes to Chinatown, where he finds Charles, whom he is forced to knock out when the boneheaded boy won't leave of his own accord. Wendell Martin, the smugglers' leader, is in love with Mary and lures her aboard a yacht by telling her that Charles is held prisoner below deck. Jack learns of Mary's peril and gives chase, fighting with Martin and his gang until the police arrive. The gang is captured, and Jack wins Mary. *Brothers and sisters. Chinese Americans. Police. San Francisco (CA)–Chinatown. Smuggling. Yachts and yachting.*

FD 10 May 1925. *MPW* 23 May 1925.

THE SPELL OF CHINDI *see* TALE OF THE NAVAJOS

THE SPENDER (English Americans, Irish Americans)

Pathé Exchange, Inc.; Gold Rooster Plays. *Dist* Pathé Exchange, Inc. 1 Oct **1915** [©Pathé Frères; 6 Oct 1915; LU6566]. Si; b&w. 5 reels. *Dir* Donald McKenzie. *Scen* George Brackett Seitz.

Cast: George Probert (*Peter Lobert*), James McCabe (*Bagley*), Sam Ryan (*Patrick McCabe*), Alma Martin (*Nellie*), Paul Panzer (*Jim Walsh*).

Comedy-drama. Because of his spending excesses, Peter Lobert, the son of a wealthy Englishman, is disinherited and dismissed from his home by his father. With his faithful servant Bagley, Peter ventures to America to court the newly rich Nellie McCabe. Posing as a prince, Peter succeeds in winning Nellie's hand, but troubles begin when Nellie's father Patrick announces that Peter must support his new wife without aid from him. After confessing to the pregnant Nellie the truth about his poverty, Peter takes a job in McCabe's factory. Labor unrest leads to a violent strike, and McCabe is ambushed by his workers. With much daring, Peter holds off the seething mob and rescues his father-in-law and the factory from fiery destruction. Hearing of his impending grandfatherhood, McCabe happily embraces the young couple. *Disinheritance. English. Fortune hunters. Heroism. Impersonation and imposture. Irish Americans. Nouveaux riches. Arson. English. Factory workers. Fathers-in-law. Labor violence. Mobs. Royalty. Spendthrifts. Strikes and lockouts. Valets.*

Note: *Var* described the character of the nouveau-riche Irish American Patrick McCabe as "a broadly exaggerated Celtic character, a type entirely inconsistent with the accompanying situations.... [McCabe] is cast as a prosperous manufacturer who has retained for his castle the proverbial clay pipe and woolen socks of his younger days when hod carrying was classified as an art rather than a trade. McCabe and his wife have lifted to the height of aristocracy the mannerisms and 'bogue' of former times, the conversational sub-titles gathering occasional laughs, but coming as they do from an exaggerated character, they can hardly be construed as legitimate."

Motog 9 Oct 1915, p. 751, 768. *MPN* 8 May 1915, p. 84. *MPN* 25 Sep 1915, p. 55. *MPN* 2 Oct 1915, p. 82. *MPN* 9 Oct 1915, pp. 12-13, 14. *MPW* 2 Oct 1915, p. 92. *MPW* 16 Oct 1915, p. 518. *NYDM* 29 Sep 1915, p. 28. *Var* 15 Oct 1915, p. 21.

THE SPIDER AND THE ROSE (Latino)

B. F. Zeidman Productions. *Dist* Principal Pictures. 15 Feb **1923** [©B. F. Zeidman Productions; 19 Nov 1923; LP19620]. Si; b&w. 7 reels, 6,800 ft.

Dir John McDermott. *Story* Gerald C. Duffy. *Photog* Charles Richardson and Glen MacWilliams.

Cast: Alice Lake (*Paula*), Richard Headrick (*Don Marcello, as a child*), Gaston Glass (*Don Marcello*), Joseph J. Dowling (*The Governor*), Robert McKim (*Mendozza*), Noah Beery (*MafFitre Renaud*), Otis Harlan (*The Secretary*), Frank Campeau (*Don Fernando*), Andrew Arbuckle (*The Priest*), Alec Francis (*Good Padre*), Edwin Stevens (*Bishop Oliveros*), Louise Fazenda (*Dolores*).

Historical, Adventure. The story is set in southern California during the Mexican regime. Don Marcello, son of the governor of the territory, returns home to find that Mendozza, his father's secretary, has taken over and has aroused the anger of the revolutionary faction. Don Marcello affiliates himself with the revolutionists, who rid the community of Mendozza and reinstate the governor. *California-History-To 1846. Revolutions.*

FD 25 Mar 1923. *MPW* 24 Mar 1923. *Var* 26 Jul 1923, p. 29.

THE SPIDER'S WEB (African Americans)

Micheaux Film Corp. **1927**; Harlem opening: 8 Jan 1927. Si; b&w. 7 reels, 6,913 ft.

Dir Oscar Micheaux.

Cast: Evelyn Preer (*Norma Shepard*), Lorenzo McLane, Edward Thompson (*Martinez*), Grace Smythe, Marshall Rodgers, Henrietta Loveless, Billy Gulfport, Dorothy Treadwell.

African American, Melodrama. On a visit to her aunt in a small Mississippi delta town, Norma Shepard, a young black girl, is accosted on the street by Ballinger, the lecherous son of a white planter. Ballinger later comes to the home of Norma's aunt and attempts to force his attentions on the young girl. Elmer Harris, a Justice Department investigator who is in Mississippi looking into peonage conditions there, then arrests Ballinger. Norma and her aunt return to Harlem, where the old lady loses every penny she possesses playing the numbers. When she finally picks the winning number, she goes to the office of Martinez, a Cuban numbers banker, for the payoff and finds him dead. She takes the amount of her winnings from his safe and is later arrested for his murder. Elmer Harris, working undercover, discovers that Madame Boley, a wealthy woman from Oklahoma, killed Martinez in a fit of passion. Norma's aunt is freed, and Elmer wins Norma. *African Americans. Cubans. Gambling. Government agents. Lechery. Mississippi. Murder. New York City-Harlem. Numbers racket. Oklahoma. Plantation owners.*

Note: This film is based on the story "The Policy Player," the authorship of which has not been determined.

ChiDef 15 Jan 1927, p. 6. *New York Age* 8 Jan 1927, p. 6.

THE SPIRIT OF KNUTE ROCKNE *see* **KNUTE ROCKNE—ALL AMERICAN**

THE SPIRIT OF '76 (Native Americans)

Continental Producing Co. *Dist* State Rights. Jan **1917** Si; b&w. 9-12 reels.

Prod Robert Goldstein. *Dir* Frank Montgomery. *Asst dir* Carl LeViness. *Scen* Robert Goldstein and George L. Hutchin. *Cam* J. C. Cook.

Cast: Adda Gleason (*Catherine Montour*), Howard Gaye (*Lionel Esmond*), George Chesborough (*Walter Butler*), Chief Dark Cloud (*Joseph Brant*), Doris Pawn (*Madeline Brant*), Jack Cosgrove (*George III*), Norval McGregor (*Lorimer Steuart*), Jane Novak (*Cecil Steuart*), William Colby (*Sir John Johnson*), Lottie Cruez (*Peggy Johnson*), Chief Big Tree (*Gowah*), William Freeman (*Lord Chatham*), William Lawrence (*Captain Boyd*), William Beery (*George Washington*), Ben Lewis (*Benjamin Franklin*), Jack McCready (*Tim Murphy*).

Historical, Drama. Half-breed Catherine Montour and her brother, Lionel Esmond, are separated at childhood. Catherine then goes to England where she becomes mistress to George III. Aspiring to become queen of America, Catherine enlists George in her cause. When the colonies go to war with England, Paul Revere announces the arrival of the British, colonists and British troops exchange fire at the Battle of Lexington, and the Declaration of Independence is signed. The winter at Valley Forge, the Cherry Valley massacre and the surrender of Cornwallis occur, during which Catherine and her brother fall in love with each other. They are about to be married when they learn that they are siblings. Catherine, her ambitions crushed, attempts to return to the king's grace but fails. *Ambition. Americans in foreign countries. Brothers and sisters. England. George III, King of England, 1738-1820. Mistresses. United States-History-Revolutionary War, 1776-1783. Cherry Valley Massacre, 1778. Charles Cornwallis. The Declaration of Independence. Great Britain. Army. Incest. Indians of North America-Mixed blood. Lexington, Battle of, 1775. Valley Forge (PA).*

Note: Producer Robert Goldstein supplied the costumes for D. W. Griffith's *The Birth of a Nation* and invested in it. Griffith, in turn, promised not to make a film about the Revolutionary War during the time that Goldstein was making

his film. George Seigmann was scheduled to direct this film. It was shot in Hollywood and at Yosemite Valley, CA. This film, which reportedly cost $200,000 to make, was scheduled to have its premiere in Chicago on 7 May 1917, but was banned by Major Metallus Lucullus Cicero Funkhouser, the head of the Chicago censor board. When Goldstein attempted to show it on 14 May 1917, after cutting several thousand feet, police raided the theater and confiscated the film. It was later shown for a limited engagement in Chicago after objectionable scenes were omitted. Goldstein took control of the film from the creditors of his corporation and presented it at Clune's Auditorium in Los Angeles beginning 27 Nov 1917. After a few showings, the film was confiscated by the Federal Department of Justice, and Goldstein was charged with espionage. It was judged that scenes critical of England during the Revolutionary War could arouse bitterness and sectional feeling against England, which could endanger its alliance with the U.S. during World War I. The battlefield scenes were also deemed offensive on the grounds that they might mitigate against troop recruitment. Specific scenes regarded as objectionable included the bayoneting of a baby by an English officer, the stabbing of an old Quaker by a Hessian, the dragging of a woman by the hair by English soldiers and the carrying of a young woman by an English officer into his chambers. Goldstein was sentenced to prison for ten years. Through the efforts of Harry C. Pearce and H. C. McClung, the film was recut to nine reels and used for propaganda purposes. According to a modern source, President Woodrow Wilson commuted Goldstein's sentence to three years in 1919 and Goldstein was released after having served less than two years of his term.

ETR 9 Jun 1917, p. 56. *ETR* 18 May 1918, p. 1904. *Motog* 23 Jun 1917, p. 1342. *MPN* 7 Oct 1916, p. 2220. *MPN* 14 Oct 1916, p. 2365. *MPN* 26 May 1917, p. 3300. *MPW* 24 Jun 1916, p. 2220. *MPW* 7 Oct 1916, p. 59. *MPW* 22 Dec 1917, p. 1786. *MPW* 29 Dec 1917, p. 1947. *MPW* 11 May 1918, p. 865. *MPW* 25 May 1918, p. 1145. *MPW* 29 Jun 1918, p. 1847.

SPIRIT OF YOUTH (African Americans)

Globe Pictures Corp. *Dist* Grand National Films, Inc. 1 Apr **1938**; Washington, D.C. premiere: 20 Jan 1938. Sd (RCA Photophone); b&w. 5,659 ft. 65-66 min. PCA cert no. 3980.

Prod Lew Golder. *Assoc prod* Edward Shanberg. *Supv* Clarence Muse. *Dir* Harry Fraser. *Asst dir* Gordon Griffith. *Orig scr* Arthur Hoerl. *Photog* Robert Cline. *Art dir* F. Paul Sylos. *Film ed* Carl Pierson. *Mus sup* Lee Zahler. *Orig score* Clarence Muse and Elliot Carpenter. *Rec eng* Farrell Redd. *Tech adv* Julian Black and John Roxborough. *Prod mgr* Mack Wright.

Song(s): "Blue, What For?" "Little Things You Do," "No More Sleepy Time," "Magic Lover" and "Spirit of Youth," music and lyrics by Clarence Muse and Elliot Carpenter.

Cast: Joe Louis [(*Joe Thomas*)], Clarence Muse [(*Frankie Walburn*)], Edna Mae Harris [(*Mary Bowdin*)], Mae Turner [(*Flora Bailey*)], Cleo Desmond [(*Nora Thomas*)], Mantan Moreland [(*Creighton "Crickie" Fitzgibbons*)], Jewel Smith, Tom Southern, Jesse Lee Brooks, Margaret Whitten, Clarence Brooks [(*Speedy*)], The Plantation Choir, The Creole Chorus, The Big Apple Dancers, [Anthony Scott (*Joe Thomas, as a child*)], [Janette O'Dell (*Mary Bowdin, as a child*)].

African American, Boxing, Drama, with songs. [*Print viewed*]. In Birmingham, Alabama in 1920, Jefferson Thomas, a black foundry worker, is seriously injured when a heavy castor falls on his legs. Because Jefferson can no longer work to support his family, his young son Joe decides to leave school and find work. Joe bids a tearful farewell to his playmate, Mary Bowdin, the daughter of Jefferson's doctor. Many years later, Joe, now grown, gives his family all his savings and leaves Birmingham to make something of himself. Joe hitchhikes to Detroit, where he gets a job as a dishwasher and meets Creighton "Crickie" Fitzgibbons. When Crickie and Joe lose their jobs, they find work at a storage and shipping company, but are soon fired from the job when a foreman hits Crickie and Joe knocks him out with one punch. Impressed with his fighting abilities, Crickie encourages Joe to enter the Golden Gloves boxing tournament, and he is soon billed in the newspapers as the "Dark Destroyer." After winning the finals, manager Frankie Walburn offers to handle him as a professional. Joe accepts after consulting with his mother Nora, who now lives in the city, and who tells him to be honest and fair. As Joe wins bouts, Flora Bailey, a nightclub singer at the Bluebird Café, who is in cahoots with gambler Duke Emblin, takes an interest in him. Their involvement worries Frankie, whose concern that he is ignoring his training antagonizes Joe. When Mary and Joe's sister Eleanor, visit Flora, they implore her to help get Joe back on track, but because Duke is now betting against Joe, Flora encourages his nightlife and drinking. Joe is knocked out in a match, and as he prepares for the heavyweight championship bout against Jack Stanley, he confesses to Flora that he loves Mary. When Flora sees that he does not have his heart in the fight, she brings Mary, now a schoolteacher, to the ring, and her presence spurs Joe to defeat Stanley in a knockout.

Afterwards, he and Mary are guests of honor at a banquet at which Flora sings. *African Americans. Boxers. Boxing managers. Childhood sweethearts. Moral reformation. Mothers and sons. Singers. Accidents. Alcoholics. Birmingham (AL). Detroit (MI). Dismissal (Employment). Dissipation. Fights. Foundries. Gamblers. Nightclubs. Sisters.*

Note: This picture marked the film debut of boxer Joe Louis, who, according to an Oct 1937 *HR* news item, was set to do a series of six pictures with Clarence Muse. *HR* also noted that Edward Shanberg and Martin Finkenstein were the president and vice-president respectively of Globe Pictures Corp., which was formed to produce this film. Some aspects of Louis's career were fictionalized in the film. Born in Lexington, AL, Louis began boxing in Detroit and became a Golden Gloves title holder. On 22 Jun 1937, he won the world heavyweight title by knocking out James Braddock in Chicago. According to the file for the film in the MPAA/PCA Collection at the AMPAS Library, in Dec 1937 PCA director Joseph Breen informed Globe Pictures Corp. that the story was "questionable from the standpoint of policy, because it shows, among other things, several scenes of a black man victorious in a number of fistic encounters with white men." Breen later warned producer Edward Shanberg that he might "run into serious difficulty in the distribution of this film, especially in a number of states in the South."
Var mistakenly credits Edna Mae Harris with the role of the nightclub singer. A 2 Mar 1938 *FD* news items noted that the release of the picture was being rushed due to the knockout by Louis of fighter Nathan Mann. Some modern sources call the film *The Spirit of Youth*, while contemporary reviews call it *Spirit of Youth*. According to a modern source in which columnist Noble "Kid" Chissell recalled his participation in the film in the bit role of a reporter, Seal Harris appeared as a sparring partner and Willie Callahan, a New Jersey heavyweight, played an opponent. Chissell also noted that Callahan, hoping to get a shot at the title by "accidentally" knocking out Louis, staggered Louis with an unexpected blow before Louis knocked him out, and that the fight scenes were shot at the Old Hollywood Legion Stadium. Modern sources complete the following character names: Jesse Lee Brooks (*Joe's father, Jeff Thomas*); Tom Southern (*Dr. Dowdin*); Jewel Smith (*Duck Emerald*); and Margaret Whitten (*Eleanor Thomas*). Other films based on the life of Joe Louis include the 1953 United Artists film *The Joe Louis Story*, directed by Robert Gordon and starring Coley Wallace and Paul Stewart, and a TCF telefilm entitled *Ring of Passion*, directed by Robert Michael Lewis and starring Bernie Casey and Stephen Macht, which aired on the NBC network on 4 Feb 1978.

DV 6 Oct 1937. *FD* 30 Dec 1937, p. 7. *FD* 2 Mar 1938, p. 6. *HR* 6 Oct 1937, p. 3. *HR* 11 Jan 1938, p. 3. *MPD* 29 Dec 1937, p. 2. *MPH* 8 Jan 1938, p. 50. *MPH* 19 Feb 1938, p. 82. *NYT* 28 Feb 1938, p. 19. *Var* 5 Jan 1938, p. 16.

SPITFIRE (African Americans)
Reol Productions Corp. **1922** [©Reol Productions Corp.; 24 Jul 1922; LU18085]. Si; b&w. 5 reels.
Copyright author Osborne Williams.
Cast: Lawrence Chenault, Edna Morton, G. Edward Brown, Daisy Martin, Mabel Young, Bob Slater, Mme. Robinson, Arthur Robinson, Sam Cook, Ed Williams, "Texas"
Melodrama, African American. Guy Rogers, the son of a well-known publisher, sets out to prove his father's racist critics wrong by putting Booker T. Washington's philosophy into practice. He goes to a little Maryland Hills town where through his efforts a school and a library are built. He falls in love with Ruth Hill, whose recently widowed father, an ex-schoolteacher, is killed after being involved in horse thievery. "Buck" Bradley, the local dealer in hay and feed, who put Ruth's father up to the crime, has been made her guardian, and he beats up Guy when he tries to defend her. She nurses Guy back to health, love blooms, and they marry. *African Americans. Horse thieves. Libraries and librarians. Maryland. Publishers and publishing. Racism. Schoolteachers. Booker T. Washington.*
Note: Outdoor scenes were shot in Englewood, NJ. Reol's studio was located in New York.
Billboard 26 Aug 1922. *ChiDef* 26 Aug 1922, p. 7.

SPOILERS OF THE NORTH (Native Americans, Native Alaskans)
Republic Pictures Corp. *Dist* Republic Pictures Corp. 24 Apr **1947**; Prod: ended mid-Aug 1946 [©Republic Pictures Corp.; 17 Mar 1947; LP901]. Sd (RCA Sound System); b&w. 66 min. Passed by the National Board of Review. PCA cert no. 11917.
Assoc prod Donald H. Brown. *Dir* Richard Sale. [*Asst dir* Jack Lacey]. *Orig scr* Milton Raison. *Photog* Alfred Keller. *Spec eff* Howard Lydecker and Theodore Lydecker. *Art dir* Paul Youngblood. *Film ed* William Thompson. *Set dec* John McCarthy, Jr. and Perry Murdock. *Mus dir* Mort Glickman. *Sd* Richard Tyler. *Makeup supv* Bob Mark.
Cast: Paul Kelly [(*Matt Garraway*)], Adrian Booth [(*Jane Koster*)], Evelyn Ankers [(*Laura Reed*)], James A. Millican [(*Bill Garraway*)], Roy Barcroft [(*Moose McGovern*)], Louis Jean Heydt [(*Inspector Cal Winters*)], Ted Hecht [(*Joe Taku*)], Harlan Briggs [(*Salty*)], Francis McDonald [(*Pete Koster*)], Maurice Cass [(*Doctor*)], Neyle Morrow [(*Johnny*)], [Bobby Barber (*Steward*)], [Charles Morton (*Slim*)], [Ethan Laidlaw, Marshall Reed, Tex Terry (*Fishermen*)].

Drama. [*Not viewed*]. Arrogant Alaskan fishery tycoon Matt Garraway has been exploiting the commercial helplessness of the local Indian tribes as well as abusing the devotion of his younger brother Bill and the love of an alluring half-breed named Jane Koster. During a promotional trip to a fish products company in Seattle, Washington, Matt meets the beautiful executive secretary of the company, Laura Reed. Using his charm, Matt persuades Laura to help him obtain a large cash advance against a delivery of salmon which is far beyond his capabilities to deliver. Laura is so taken by Matt that she promises to come to Alaska to marry him at some point in the future. After Matt returns to Alaska, he finds that Bill has become sullen and angry. Bill complains about Matt's refusal to grant him a badly needed rest and a fair share of the profits. Matt, who needs Bill to keep the cannery workers in line for the upcoming push to deliver the salmon, pretends that a minor injury to his ribs is actually much worse so that Bill will feel obliged to stay and work hard. Bill postpones his long-awaited vacation, but then becomes suspicious about Matt's injury and rebels again. Matt wires Laura saying that he is seriously ill and needs to see her. When Laura arrives, Jane tries to keep Matt interested in her by helping him with an illegal scheme to use the Indians' special fishing privileges to deliver the salmon that he has promised. Jane's boyfriend, Joe, however, intrudes on Matt's night fishing scheme, so Jane kills him. The murder precipitates a police investigation, but Matt decides to attempt a bold move: a large night catch of salmon right under the noses of the U.S. Fisheries police patrol. Jane, who has realized that Matt has rejected her for Laura, kills him with a salmon harpoon. Later, Jane is sent to prison for the murders, and after Bill marries Laura and takes over the cannery, the couple runs it with fairness and honesty. *Alaska. Brothers. Canneries. Tycoons. Duplicity. Engagements. Fishing rights. Indians of North America–Mixed blood. Marriage. Murder. Native Alaskans. Pledges. Police. Romantic rivalry. Salmon. Seattle (WA). Secretaries. Wounds and injuries.*
Note: Onscreen credits were taken from an unviewable print. Information about the plot was taken from the copyright record and reviews. According to the *HR* review, the film includes "stock footage having to do with salmon runs in Northern waters."
Box 10 May 1947. *FD* 13 May 1947, p. 10. *IFJ* 17 Aug 1946, p. 39. *MPHPD* 10 May 1947. *Var* 7 May 1947, p. 18.

SPOILERS OF THE WEST (Native Americans)
Metro-Goldwyn-Mayer Corp.; controlled by Loew's Inc. *Dist* Metro-Goldwyn-Mayer Distributing Corp. 10 Dec **1927** [©Metro-Goldwyn-Mayer Distributing Corp.; 22 Nov 1927; LP24745]. Si; b&w. 6 reels, 4,784 ft.
Dir W. S. Van Dyke. *Scen* Madeleine Ruthven and Ross B. Wills. *Story* John Thomas Neville. *Titles* Joe Farnham. *Photog* Clyde De Vinna. *Film ed* Dan Sharits. *Ward* Lucia Coulter.
Cast: Tim McCoy (*Lieutenant Lang*), Marjorie Daw (*The Girl*), William Fairbanks (*The Girl's Brother*), Chief Big Tree (*Red Cloud*), Charles Thurston.
Western. Supported by a handful of Indian police, an Army lieutenant is assigned, under threat of war from the Indians, to clear out the trappers and white squatters from some Indian land. The settlers are all driven off, except for a young girl who owns a trading post. The girl realizes her foolishness, moves from the land, and later weds the lieutenant. Generals Sherman and Custer are depicted. *General George Armstrong Custer. Indians of North America. Police. William Tecumseh Sherman. Squatters. Trappers. United States. Army. Cavalry.*
Var 21 Mar 1928, p. 23.

THE SPORT OF THE GODS (African Americans)
Reol Productions Corp. **1921**; Washington showing: ca23 Apr 1921; Prod: at Tolden Studios, Bronx, New York. Si; b&w. 6-7 reels.
Pers supv Robert Levy. *Dir* Henry Vernot.
Source: Based on the novel *The Sport of the Gods* by Paul Lawrence Dunbar (New York, 1902).
Cast: Elizabeth Boyer (*Kitty Hamilton*), Edward R. Abrams (*Jim Skaggs*), George Edward Brown (*Joe Hamilton*), Leon Williams (*Berry Hamilton*), Lucille Brown (*Fannie Hamilton*), Lindsay J. Hall (*Maurice Oakley*), Jean Armour (*Julia Oakley*), Stanley Walpole (*Francis Oakley*), Walter Thomas (*Thomas*), Lawrence Chenault ("*Sadness*"), Ruby Mason (*Mrs. Jones*), Edna Morton Wilson (*Hattie Sterling*), Jim Burris (*Manager*), Dink Stewart.

African American, **Drama**. A black Virginian named Hamilton is unjustly sent to prison to save the reputation of his white employer's son, a gambler. Hamilton's family moves to New York to escape the scorn and gossip of their neighbors. The son falls in with evil companions, and the daughter becomes a singer in an underworld cabaret. Hamilton man is released from jail due to the ingenuity of his daughters' lover and follows his family to New York, only to discover that his wife, convinced that a penitentiary sentence is the same as a divorce, has remarried. After numerous complications, all ends well. *African Americans. Bigamy. Cabarets. Family relationships. Injustice. New York City. Reputation. Self-sacrifice. Singers. Virginians.*

Note: According to modern sources, Clarence Muse wrote the screenplay for this film.

SPORTING CHANCE *see* **SPEED TO BURN**

SPOTLIGHT SADIE (Irish Americans)

Goldwyn Pictures Corp. *Dist* Goldwyn Distributing Corp. 6 Apr **1919** [©Goldwyn Pictures Corp.; 29 Mar 1919; LP13544]. Si; b&w. 5 reels.

Pres Samuel Goldwyn. *Dir* Laurence Trimble. *Scen* Charles J. Wilson, Jr. *Story* Lewis Allen Browne. *Cam* Edward W. Willat.

Cast: Mae Marsh (*Sadie Sullivan*), Wallace MacDonald (*Dick Carrington*), Mary Thurman (*Hazel Harris*), Betty Schade (*Dollie Delmar*), Alec B. Francis (*Reverend John Page*), Walter Hiers (*Jack Mills*), P. M. McCullough (*Reggie Delmar*), Wellington Playter (*O'Keefe*), Lou Salter (*Nancy O'Keefe*), Richard Carlyle, Alice Davenport.

Comedy. Sadie Sullivan leaves Ireland to live with her married sister in New York. Upset at her worthless brother-in-law and her low paying five-and-ten-cent store job, Sadie, who has just read a story about a chorus girl who married a millionaire, joins a musical comedy company. Having befriended Reverend John Page, a mission clergyman, Sadie, surprised at the other girl's loose morals, is seen reading a Bible backstage. Her "saintly" reputation among the others inspires press agent Jack Mills, looking for a new angle, to devise a routine built around Sadie, now billed as "The Saintly Show Girl." After millionaire Dick Carrington switches his attentions from leading lady Dollie Delmar to Sadie, their subsequent engagement arouses Dollie to attempt to tarnish Sadie's image. Dollie sends Sadie a letter, supposedly from a friend, to meet her at a roadhouse that Dollie knows will be raided, but after Reverend Page explains Sadie's presence there satisfactorily to the police and Dick, Dick marries her. *Clergy. Irish Americans. Musical revues. Reputation. Show girls. Bible. Brothers-in-law. Frame-ups. Jealousy. Millionaires. New York City. Police raids. Press agents. Roadhouses. Sisters.*

Note: This film was originally entitled *The Saintly Show Girl*.

ETR 26 Apr 1919, p. 1607. *MPN* 3 May 1919, p. 2905. *MPW* 3 May 1919, p. 715. *Var* 25 Apr 1919, p. 80. *Wid's* 20 Apr 1919, p. 27.

THE SPREADING EVIL (German Americans)

James Keane Feature Photo-play Productions. *Dist* State Rights. Dec **1918** [©James Keane; 30 Dec 1918; LU13209]. Si; b&w. 7 reels.

Prod James Keane. *Dir* James Keane. *Scen* James Keane.

Cast: Leo Pierson (*Karl Hartsell*), Irene Wylie (*Alice Keller*), Howard Davies (*Emil Hartsell*), Carlyn Wagner (*Lennon Morrett*), Joseph Clancy (*Adolph Keller*), William A. Hackett (*Dr. John Carey*), G. B. Williams (*Jules Le Moyne*), Quex Bellamy (*M. Saccard*), Hon. Josephus Daniels (*Himself*), James Keane (*Himself*).

Social, **Drama**. Dr. John Carey, a noted blood specialist, convinces philanthropist Jules Le Moyne to finance Berlin chemist Emil Hartsell's search for a cure for syphilis. Hartsell's research proves successful, but following Le Moyne's death, the chemist breaks his pledge to give the formula to society and contracts with New York profiteer Adolph Keller to sell the drug at a price prohibitive to the poor. Representing his father in New York, Karl Hartsell becomes engaged to Keller's daughter Alice. Meanwhile, Lennon Morrett, an artist's model, contracts syphilis from roué M. Saccard, but can't afford the drug for her. When Dr. Carey is about to intercede and obtain the drug for her, Keller instead sells it to Saccard. Believing that society is responsible for her fate, Lennon sleeps with a lot of men. She blames Karl because his father has made the drug too expensive, and during his bachelor's fling before the wedding, she gives him the disease. Dr. Carey meets the elder Hartsell in Holland and pleads for the drug to be distributed cheaply in America, but Hartsell says America means nothing to him. Although Dr. Carey finally persuades

the greedy scientist of his son's illness, Hartsell refuses to give Carey the formula and arranges to treat Karl himself in New York. Because the United States and Germany are at war, Hartsell's submarine is torpedoed off the New York coast, whereupon Karl walks into the waves to join his drowned father. Later, U.S. scientists discover a cure superior to the German formula. *Chemists. Fathers and sons. German Americans. Germans. Greed. Medicine. Syphilis. Bachelor parties. Berlin (Germany). Holland. Models. New York City. Philanthropists. Physicians. Submarine boats. Suicide. Torpedoes. World War I.*

Note: Secretary of the Navy Josephus Daniels appears at the end of the film to present James Keane with a letter of endorsement. The film was shown on 29 Jun 1918 at B. F. Keith's Theatre in Washington, D.C. and early in Jul 1918 at Senator James Phelan's home, for various government officials.

ETR 14 Dec 1918, p. 157. *MPW* 30 Nov 1918, p. 987. *MPW* 4 Jan 1919, p. 120. *Var* 22 Nov 1918, p. 46.

SPRINGTIME (Creoles, French Americans)

Life Photo Film Corp. *Dist* Alco Film Corp. 28 Dec **1914**. Si; b&w. 5 reels.

Prod Edward M. Roskam. *Dir* William S. Davis. *Cam* John Arnold.

Source: Based on the play *Springtime* by Booth Tarkington and Harry Leon Wilson (New York, 19 Oct 1909).

Cast: Florence Nash (*Madeline De Valette*), Adele Ray (*L'Acadienne*), William H. Tooker (*Val De Valette*), Edward F. Roseman (*Wolf*), Bert Gardner (*Gilbert Steele*), Mrs. Sue Balfour (*Marguerite*), Frank Holland (*Raoul De Valette*), E. F. Flannigan (*Father O'Mara*), Charles Travis (*Richard Steele*), Warner P. Richmond (*Crawley*), Armin Tooker (*Louise*).

Historical, **Drama**. Val De Valette betrothed his daughter Madeline to his wealthy cousin Raoul De Valette during her childhood. Raoul is in love with L'Acadienne, a faithful Creole girl, but when he must meet Madeline, he leaves her. She follows him and tells Val about their affair, but Val does nothing. Madeline is disappointed in Raoul, but is willing to do her duty until she meets Gilbert Steele, a neighbor whose father has bought most of Val's property. When Gilbert leaves to join Andrew Jackson's forces during the War of 1812, Madeline follows him but eventually suffers a breakdown. Hearing of Madeline's state, Raoul gets out of the marriage and is free to return to L'Acadienne. When Gilbert returns home, he wants to marry Madeline and Val finally agrees. *Cousins. Creoles. Fathers and daughters. Marriage. Marriage–Arranged. Andrew Jackson. Neighbors. Nervous breakdown. United States–History–War of 1812.*

Note: *Springtime* was filmed on location in New Orleans, LA and in St. Augustine, FL. Some sources list Charles Travers for the character of Richard Steele.

Motog 2 Jan 1915, p. 25. *Motog* 6 Feb 1915, p. 195, 232. *MPN* 14 Nov 1915, p. 33. *MPN* 2 Jan 1915, p. 44. *MPW* 2 Jan 1915, p. 55. *NYDM* 23 Dec 1914, p. 37. *Var* 25 Dec 1914, p. 37.

SQUARE JOE (African Americans)

Colored Feature Photoplay Co. **1922**; Harlem opening: 18 Jun 1922. Si; b&w. Length undetermined.

Dir J. Harrison Edwards. *Scr* J. Harrison Edwards.

Cast: Joe Jeanette, John Lester Johnson, Marion Moore, Charles Fouchee, Bob Slater, Mrs. Fred R. Moore, Fred Miller, Bobby Fitzgerald, Mrs. Eugene L. Moore, Frederica Washington, Minnie Summer.

Melodrama, **African American**. An innocent man is convicted of shooting and killing a policeman during a raid of a neighborhood gambling house. Evidence obtained by a beautiful, winsome woman exonerates the man, and the real murderer is captured and punished. During the story, a prizefight occurs between the innocent man and his opponent. *African Americans. False arrests. Murder. Boxing. Evidence. Gambling houses. Police. Police raids.*

Note: According to *New York Age*, this was the first production of the Colored Feature Photoplay Co. The film was shot in Harlem. Joe Jeanette, a prizefighter, trained George Carpentier for his 1921 match with Jack Dempsey. John Lester Johnson was also a boxer.

New York Age 17 Jun 1922, p. 6. *New York Age* 24 Jun 1922, p. 6.

THE SQUAW MAN (Native Americans, English Americans)

Jesse L. Lasky Feature Play Co. *Dist* State Rights. 15 Feb **1914**. Si; b&w. 6 reels.

Dir Oscar C. Apfel and Cecil B. DeMille.

Source: Based on the play *The Squaw Man* by Edwin Milton Royle (New York, 23 Oct 1905).

Cast: Dustin Farnum (*Capt. James Wynnegate/Jim Carston*), Monroe Salisbury (*Earl of Kerhill*), Winifred Kingston (*Diana, Countess of Kerhill*), Mrs. A. W. Filson (*The Dowager Lady Kerhill*), Haidee Fuller (*Lady Mabel Wynnegate*), Dick La Reno (*Big Bill*), Billy Elmer (*Cash Hawkins*), Princess Red Wing (*Nat-U-Ritch*), Foster Knox (*Sir John*), Joseph E. Singleton (*Tabywana*), Fred Montague (*Mr. Petrie*), Baby De Rue (*Hal*), Dick Le Strange (*Grouchy*).

Drama. James Wynnegate is made executor of funds raised by members of his regiment for the families of men killed in battle. His cousin, the Earl of Kerhill, embezzles the funds, but Kerhill's wife Diana, with whom Wynnegate is in love, convinces the latter to take the blame and leave England in order to save the family's honor. Wynnegate eventually goes to Wyoming and buys a ranch using the name Jim Carston. He is saved from an attack by Cash Hawkins by the Indian maiden Nat-U-Ritch and he marries her when he learns that she is pregnant. Some time later, Diana comes West with news that Kerhill is dead, but that he had admitted his theft shortly before death. Nat-U-Ritch, knowing that her husband will send their young son Hal away, and hearing that she will be arrested for killing Hawkins, commits suicide. At the end, Diana embraces Hal. *Embezzlement. Executors. Family honor. Indians of North America. Marriage. Self-sacrifice. Children. Confession (Law). England. Murder. Nobility. Ranches. Suicide. Wyoming.*

Note: One-act versions of the play were produced as early as 1904. Modern sources credit the screenplay to DeMille and Apfel, the photography to Alfred Gandolfi, the editing to Mamie Wagner, and the art direction to Wilfred Buckland. This was the first release of the Jesse L. Lasky Feature Play Co. Although this was not the first motion picture to be filmed in Hollywood, *The Squaw Man* was the first Hollywood-made feature-length production. In addition to the 1918 version of the film, DeMille directed another version for M-G-M in 1931, starring Warner Baxter, and a 1917 sequel, entitled *The Squaw Man's Son.* (see entries below).

THE SQUAW MAN (Native Americans, English Americans)

Famous Players-Lasky Corp. *Dist* Famous Players-Lasky Corp.; Artcraft Pictures. 15 Dec **1918** [©Famous Players-Lasky Corp.; 26 Oct 1918; LP13020]. Si; b&w. 6 reels, 5,897 ft.

Pres Jesse L. Lasky. *Prod* Cecil B. DeMille. *Dir* Cecil B. DeMille. *Asst dir* Sam Wood and Ann Bauchens. *Scen* Beulah Marie Dix. *Cam* Alvin Wyckoff and King D. Gray.

Source: Based on the play *The Squaw Man* by Edwin Milton Royle (New York, 23 Oct 1905).

Cast: Elliott Dexter (*Jim Wynnegate*), Ann Little (*Naturich*), Theodore Roberts (*Big Bill*), Katherine MacDonald (*Diana, Countess of Kerhill*), Thurston Hall (*Henry, the Earl of Kerhill*), Jack Holt (*Cash Hawkins*), Tully Marshall (*Sir John Applegate*), Pat Moore (*Little Hal*), Edwin Stevens (*Sheriff Bud Hardy*), Herbert Standing (*Dean of Trentham*), Helen Dunbar (*Dowager Countess*), Winter Hall (*Fletcher*), Julia Faye (*Lady Mabel*), Noah Beery (*Tabywana*), Jim Mason (*Grouchy*), Monte Blue (*Happy*), William Brunton (*Shorty*), Charles Ogle (*Bull Cowan*), Guy Oliver (*Kid Clarke*), Jack Herbert (*Nick*), M. Hallward (*Lord Tommy*), Clarence Geldart (*Solicitor*).

Western. Jim Wynnegate is so deeply in love with Diana, the wife of his cousin Henry, the Earl of Kerhill, that when Henry embezzles an orphanage trust fund, Jim saves Diana from shame by assuming the blame himself and disappearing. Soon after settling on a ranch in Wyoming, Jim saves an Indian girl named Naturich from the cruel Cash Hawkins, thereby incurring the outlaw's enmity. Later Cash attacks Jim, but Naturich ambushes Cash and kills him. Jim gratefully marries the Indian, and soon Naturich gives birth to little Hal, who is deeply loved by his parents and idolized by the ranch hands. Several years later, Henry is mortally wounded on a hunting trip, but before he dies, he confesses his part in the embezzlement, exonerating his cousin. Diana visits Jim, who, although loath to leave his loyal wife, agrees to allow the woman he still loves to rear Hal to his rightful station in England. Overhearing the conversation, Naturich realizes that she is about to lose her son and commits suicide. Her death overwhelms Jim, but after several years, he assumes the title of earl and finally marries Diana. *Cousins. Indians of North America. Indians of North America–Mixed blood. Self-sacrifice. Suicide. Accidental death. Confession (Law). Cowboys. Embezzlement. English. Marriage–Mixed. Nobility. Outlaws. Ranches. Rescues. Wyoming.*

Note: Modern sources credit Anne Bauchens as the editor, and Wilfred Buckland as art director. For information on other versions of the film, see entry below for DeMille's 1931 *The Squaw Man.*

ETR 16 Nov 1918, p. 1925. *ETR* 21 Dec 1918, pp. 231-33. *MPN* 16 Nov 1918, p. 2984. *MPW* 16 Nov 1918, p. 759. *MPW* 21 Dec 1918, p. 1390. *NYDM* 21 Dec 1918, p. 918. *NYT* 30 Dec 1918, p. 7. *Var* 8 Nov 1918, p. 41. *Wid's* 12 Jan 1919, pp. 15-16.

THE SQUAW MAN (Native Americans, English Americans)

Metro-Goldwyn-Mayer Corp.; controlled by Loew's, Inc. *Dist* Metro-Goldwyn-Mayer Distributing Corp. 5 Sep **1931**; Prod: early Feb—early Apr 1931 [©Metro-Goldwyn-Mayer Distributing Corp.; 7 Sep 1931; LP2451]. Sd (Western Electric Sound System); b&w. 12 reels. 105-106 min. Passed by the National Board of Review.

Prod Cecil B. DeMille. *Dir* CECIL B. DeMILLE. *Asst dir* Mitchell Leisen and Earl Haley. *Scr* Lucien Hubbard and Lenore Coffee. *Dial* Elsie Janis. *Photog* Harold Rosson. *Art dir* Mitchell Leisen. *Film ed* Anne Bauchens. *Incidental mus by* Herbert Stothart. *Rec dir* Douglas Shearer.

Source: Based on the play *The Squaw Man* by Edwin Milton Royle (New York, 23 Oct 1905).

Cast: WARNER BAXTER [(*Capt. James Wyngate, later known as Jim Carsten*)], LUPE VELEZ [(*Naturich*)], ELEANOR BOARDMAN [(*Lady Diana*)], CHARLES BICKFORD [(*Cash Hawkins*)], ROLAND YOUNG [(*Sir John Applegate Kerhill*)], PAUL CAVANAUGH [(*Henry, Earl of Kerhill*)], Raymond Hatton [(*Shorty*)], Julia Faye [(*Mrs. Chichester Jones*)], De Witt Jennings [(*Sheriff Hardy*)], J. Farrell MacDonald [(*Big Bill*)], Mitchell Lewis [(*Tabywana*)], Dickie Moore [(*Little Hal*)], Victor Potel [(*Andy*)], Frank Rice [(*Grouchy*)], Eva Dennison [(*Dowager Lady Kerhill*)], Lilian Bond [(*Babs*)], Luke Cosgrave [(*Shanks*)], Frank Hagney [(*Clark*)], Lawrence Grant [(*General Stafford*)], Harry Northrup [(*Butler*)], Ed Brady [(*McSorley*)], Chrispin Martin, [Desmond Roberts (*Hardwick*)].

Western, **Society**, **Drama.** [*Print viewed*]. In England, the wealthy Capt. James Wyngate contributes £100 to a collection for orphans of the regiment to which his cousin Henry, Earl of Kerhill, belonged. When Henry, who has been embezzling the funds, learns that his accomplice Hardwick committed suicide after being caught stealing the money, he too decides to kill himself. Henry attempts suicide, but is talked out of it by James, who is in love with Henry's wife Diana and sets himself up as the embezzlement suspect in order to save Diana from shame. When an announcement is made of the missing money, James plans an immediate departure for America. Diana tries to stop him from leaving and pleads with him to stay and prove his innocence, but her protestations prove to be ineffective, and he leaves. In America, James adopts a new name, Jim Carsten, and takes up residence on a ranch in Arizona. However, he soon finds himself at odds with a local tough named Cash Hawkins, who wants to buy Jim out and get his land. Jim and his friends, Shorty and Big Bill, manage to ward off an unfriendly visit by Hawkins and his entourage, who have come to persuade Jim to sell to them. Later, at a local tavern, the unscrupulous Hawkins nearly gets an Indian, Tabywana, to give him his cattle by bribing him with liquor, until Naturich, an Indian girl who witnesses the offense, tears up the contract. Hawkins grabs Naturich by the hair, but she is saved by Jim. After Hawkins receives a mild reproach for his crime from the sheriff, he swears revenge upon Jim. Meanwhile, when Jim reads an article in an English journal containing highlights of the polo season, he sees a picture of Diana, becomes melancholy and gets drunk. When the angry Hawkins shows up at Jim's looking for trouble, Jim is so drunk and upset that he shows little interest in the outlaw's murder threats. As Hawkins prepares to shoot Jim, who makes no attempt to defend himself, a shot rings out and Hawkins is killed. The sheriff arrives, and although he sniffs everyone's guns looking for the killer, he is unable to find the murder weapon. Later, when Jim goes into the desert, he is followed by Naturich, who confesses that she killed Hawkins out of gratitude. Seven years after Jim's departure from England, Henry dies in a riding accident, and Diana learns that he had been unfaithful to her. When Diana receives word of Jim's whereabouts from the Baldwin Investigating Co., which she had commissioned to find him, she and her brother, Sir John Applegate Kerhill, go to America to find him. Upon their arrival, John and Diana discover that Jim has married a squaw and that he had a child named Little Hal. John tells Jim that, before his death, Henry told the truth about his embezzlment scheme and the cover-up, and that he is now a hero in London. Though Jim is eager to return to England, he refuses to leave Naturich, who would have no place there. Instead, he agrees to let John and Diana take the boy back with them in order to give him a proper upbringing. Naturich resists the visitors' attempts to take her child away and is

forced into hiding when the sheriff comes looking for her with evidence that she murdered Hawkins. Naturich shoots herself after watching her son being taken away by the foreigners, and Jim holds her until she dies. *Embezzlement. English in foreign countries. Indians of North America. Miscegenation. Self-sacrifice. Suicide.* Accidental death. Arizona. Child custody. Cousins. Deserts. Drunkenness. England. Fox hunts. Gratitude. Infidelity. Land sales. Murder. Polo. Ranches. Sheriffs. Snobs and snobbishness.

Note: William Faversham and William S. Hart played the leading roles in the 1905 stage production of *The Squaw Man.* This film was Cecil B. DeMille's third version of the play. His first, also his first directorial effort, was released in 1914 and starred Dustin Farnum and Monroe Salisbury (see above). DeMille followed the 1914 production with a 1918 remake, also entitled *The Squaw Man,* which starred Elliott Dexter and Ann Little (see above) A sequel to the original, *The Squaw Man's Son,* was released in 1917, was directed by E. J. Le Saint and starred Wallace Reid and Anita King (see below). According to a contemporary *NYT* article, filming of the fox hunt sequences took place at the 16,000 acre Agoura ranch, fifty miles from Hollwood, in an area known as the "Lake Sherwood" region. The *Var* review mistakenly listed Charles Bickford's character as "Big Bill," and J. Farrell McDonald's as "Cash Hawkins." According to a biography of writer Lenore Coffee, DeMille brought her to work with Elsie Janis on the script because he felt that Janis, a former musical comedy star, was "talented but had no idea of story structure." Modern sources also relate that DeMille was less than enthusiastic about making this picture (the last film to satisfy his contract with M-G-M), a fact that has been attributed in part to poor revenue prospects and Loew's, Inc. president Nicholas Schenck's request that he cancel the production before it had begun. DeMille, in his autobiography, notes that he eventually got permission to shoot the doomed picture after arguing that the studio would have to pay as much to halt the picture as it would to continue it. As predicted, *The Squaw Man* lost nearly $150,000, according to DeMille. Following this disappointing experience with this production, DeMille wrote, "I do not know whether M-G-M or I was more relieved that my contract had come to an end." Most of this picture was filmed at Hot Springs Junction, Arizona, which was near the location that DeMille had rejected for his 1914 version.

FD 20 Sep 1931, p. 10. *HF* 14 Feb 1931, p. 24. *HF* 4 Apr 1931, p. 24. *MPH* 14 Jun 1931, p. 28. *NYT* 19 Sep 1931, p. 10. *NYT* 24 Apr 1932. *Var* 22 Sep 1931, p. 26.

THE SQUAW MAN'S SON (Native Americans, English Americans)

Jesse L. Lasky Feature Play Co. *Dist* Paramount Pictures Corp. 26 Jul **1917** [©Jesse L. Lasky Feature Play Co.; 3 Jul 1917; LP11050]. Si; b&w. 5 reels.

Dir E. J. Le Saint. *Asst dir* Sterrett Ford. *Scen* Charles Maigne. *Cam* Allen M. Davey.

Source: Based on the novel *The Silent Call* by Edwin Milton Royle (New York, 1910).

Cast: Wallace Reid (*Lord Effington, also known as Hal*), Anita King (*Wah-na-gi*), Dorothy Davenport (*Edith, Lady Effington*), Donald Bowles (*John McCloud*), C. H. Geldert (*David Ladd*), Frank Lanning (*Appah*), Ernest Joy (*Lord Kerhill*), Lucien Littlefield (*Lord Yester*), Mabel Van Buren (*Lady Stuckley*), Raymond Hatton (*Storekeeper*).

Western. Hal, now fully grown, leaves his wife Edith and his estate in England to return to the land of his Indian mother. There he works for the rights of Indians in a land deal which pits him against David Ladd, the wily reservation agent who is secretly in collusion with the asphalt trust which is trying to rob the Indians. Hal falls in love with Wah-na-gi, the Carlisle graduate who has returned to teach at the agency school, but he is too honorable to conceal that he is already married. Upon the death of his father, Hal returns to England as Lord Effington to discover that Edith loves Lord Yester and wants a divorce. Hal gladly agrees, but when the family physician informs him that Edith is addicted to morphine and his presence may save her life, Hal consents to stay. Returning to America to testify in a lawsuit against the asphalt trust, Hal regretfully informs Wah-na-gi that he cannot leave his wife. The Indian maiden goes off in the snow to kill herself by the grave of Hal's mother when Hal receives a message that Edith has died from an overdose of morphine. Hal rushes into the snow, overtakes Wah-na-gi and asks her to marry him. *Drug addicts. England. Indians of North America. Indians of North America–Mixed blood. Indians of North America–Reservations. Nobility. Schoolteachers. Self-sacrifice. Suicide.* Asphalt industry. Divorce. Graves. Indian agents. Lawsuits. Morphine. Physicians. Snow storms. Trusts and trustees.

Note: This film was a sequel to the 1914 filmed version of *The Squaw Man.* A memo included in the Paramount studio records indicates that Myrtle Stedman was to co-star in the film in the role which Anita King played. For additional information on other versions of the *The Squaw Man* see entry above for the 1931 film.

ETR 11 Aug 1917, p. 787. *MPN* 4 Aug 1917, p. 827. *MPN* 11 Aug 1917, p. 1021. *MPW* 11 Aug 1917, p. 956. *MPW* 18 Aug 1917, p. 1117. *NYDM* 4 Aug 1917, p. 19. *Var* 3 Aug 1917, p. 24. *Wid's* 2 Aug 1917, p. 489.

STAGE STATION see **APACHE TRAIL**

STAGECOACH KID (Latino)

RKO Radio Pictures, Inc. *Dist* RKO Radio Pictures, Inc. Jun **1949**; Prod: 18 Oct—late Oct 1948 [©RKO Radio Pictures, Inc.; 7 Jul 1949; LP2462]. Sd (RCA Sound System); b&w. 5,371 ft. 60 min. PCA cert no. 13483.

Prod Herman Schlom. *Dir* Lew Landers. [*Asst dir* Sam Ruman and Harry Templeton]. *Story and scr* Norman Houston. *Dir of photog* Nicholas Musuraca. [*Cam op* Fred Bentley]. [*Gaffer* Frank Eucker]. [*Stills* Ollie Sigurdson]. *Art dir* Albert S. D'Agostino and Feild Gray. *Film ed* Les Millbrook. *Set dec* Darrell Silvera and Jack Mills. *Mus dir* C. Bakaleinikoff. *Mus* Paul Sawtell. *Sd* Earl Wolcott and Terry Kellum. [*Makeup* Jack Barron]. [*Hair stylist* Fay Smith]. [*Scr supv* Mercy Weireter]. [*Grip* Tom Clement and Harry Dagleish].

Cast: TIM HOLT [(*Dave Collins*)], Richard Martin [(*Chito Rafferty*)], Jeff Donnell [(*Jessie Arnold*)], Joe Sawyer [(*Thatcher*)], Thurston Hall [(*Arnold*)], Carol Hughes [(*Birdie*)], Robert Bray [(*Clint*)], Robert B. Williams [(*Parnell*)], Kenneth MacDonald [(*Sheriff*)], Harry Harvey [(*Dabney*)].

Western. [*Print viewed*]. As they ride in a stagecoach to their Arizona ranch, railroad magnate Arnold and his spoiled daughter Jessie argue about her recent involvement with a man in San Francisco. Strong-willed Jessie insists that she be allowed to return to San Francisco, while her father demands that she forget the affair. At the Arnold ranch, meanwhile, foreman Thatcher receives a telegram announcing Arnold's imminent arrival. Worried that his absentee employer will discover that he and his two ranch hands, Parnell and Clint, have been bilking the operation for years, Thatcher orders Clint and Parnell to murder Arnold on the stagecoach. The subsequent attack on the stage is detected by Dave Collins and Chito Rafferty, the owners of the stage line, who chase off Clint and Parnell before any harm is done. While the stage is stopped in Casco City, Jessie sneaks away from her father and buys some cowboy clothes, deciding to pose as a man in order to flee. Jessie then reboards the stage, which is now being driven by Dave and Chito, leaving her distraught father behind. Just outside of town, Clint and Parnell ambush the stage a second time, but upon discovering that Arnold is not on board, rob a strongbox containing $20,000 in cash. During the robbery, Jessie inadvertently unmasks Parnell for a moment, while Dave notes the brand on Parnell's horse. As Dave is about to drive back to Casco City, Jessie, who is determined to catch the next train to San Francisco, grabs his gun to stop him, but accidentally fires a round, causing the horses to run off with the stage. Now stranded in the desert, Chito, Dave, passenger Birdie, a saloon girl who is Chito's sweetheart, and an unhappy Jessie walk to Chito and Dave's nearby ranch. Later, at their ranch, Dave and Chito entrust Birdie to watch Jessie, while they ride to Casco City. In town, Dave spots Parnell's horse outside the saloon and, after brawling with him, hands him over to the sheriff. Dave and Chito then ride back to their ranch to retrieve Jessie for identification purposes, but learn that she has taken off on foot. Clint, meanwhile, reports Parnell's arrest to Thatcher, who decides that Jessie must be killed before she implicates Parnell. In the desert, Dave catches up to Jessie, lassos her to the ground and, without letting on that he is aware of her impersonation, spanks her. After a humiliated Jessie vows revenge on Dave, she is shot at by Clint and Thatcher. Hiding among some rocks, Dave exchanges gunfire with Clint and Thatcher, but it is Jessie who wounds Clint with a blind shot. Although the crooks ride off, Dave insists on remaining among the rocks until Chito finds them. Back in Casco City, Arnold finally deduces Jessie's impersonation and tells the sheriff and Chito that she must be found. While Chito, Arnold and the sheriff's posse head for the desert to find Jessie, Thatcher and Clint take advantage of their absence and break Parnell out of jail. Later that night, in their desert camp, Jessie is compelled to reveal her true identity to Dave in order to avoid a potentially compromising situation. She also tells Dave, who confesses he knew about the ruse from the beginning, about her San Francisco sweetheart. After Chito and Arnold finally locate them, however, Jessie announces to her father that she is now in love with Dave, and he encourages her to pursue the young rancher. When Jessie reveals her feelings to Dave, he questions her sincerity and insists that she is still a spoiled child. As the two argue, Parnell happens by and starts firing on them. Chased off by Dave, Parnell goes to the Arnold ranch and tries to claim his share of the strongbox money, but is told by the double-crossing Thatcher that the money

was used to hide their embezzlement from Arnold. Parnell shoots Thatcher, then with Clint, takes Arnold hostage after Dave and Chito arrive and start firing at them. After agreeing to Parnell's hostage deal, Dave sneaks to the ranch house roof and jumps on the crooks as they lead Arnold outside. Dave and Chito eventually overwhelm and capture Clint and Parnell. Later, after Arnold blesses Jessie and Dave's engagement, Birdie shows off the wedding veil she bought in Tucson, causing confirmed bachelor Chito to drive off in alarm. *Attempted murder. Embezzlement. Fathers and daughters. Male impersonation. Ranchers. Romance. Arizona. Betrayal. Deserts. Fights. Gunfights. Hostages. Jailbreaks. Mexican Americans. Ranch foremen. Sheriffs. Spanking. Stagecoach lines. Stagecoach robberies.*

Note: According to a *HR* news item, Carol Hughes was originally cast as the female lead in this picture, but was reassigned to the second lead because of a scheduling conflict. Some scenes were shot in Lone Pine, CA, according to *HR*.

Box 18 Jun 1949. *DV* 14 Jun 1949, p. 3. *FD* 27 Jun 1949, p. 6. *HR* 18 Oct 1948, p. 4. *HR* 29 Oct 1948, p. 15. *HR* 14 Jun 1949, p. 3. *MPHPD* 18 Jun 1949, p. 4649. *Var* 15 Jun 1949, p. 13.

STALLION CANYON (Native Americans)

Kanab Pictures. *Dist* Astor Pictures Corp. 1949. Sd; col (Trucolor). 72 min.

Dir Harry Fraser. *Scr* Hy Heath. *Photog* Jack McCloskey and Kenneth Green. *Art dir* H. R. Brandon. *Mus dir* Emil Velazco. *Sd* Lyle Welles.

Song(s): "The Hills of Utah," music and lyrics by Hy Heath.

Cast: Introducing Thunderbred The Miracle Stallion, Ken Curtis (*Curt Benson*), Carolina Cotton (*Ellen [Collins]*), Shug Fisher (*Red*), Forrest Taylor ([*Tom*] *Larsen*), Billy Hammond (*Little Bear*), Roy Butler (*Breezy, sheriff*), Alice Richey (*Aunt Millie*), L. H. Larsen (*Steve*), E. N. "Dick" Hammer (*Luke*), Clark Veater (*Dobie*), D. C. Swapp (*Judge*), Gail Bailey (*Laramie*), Bud Gates (*Idaho*), Bob Brandon (*Johnny Adams*), Daughters of the Utah Pioneers, [Ted Adams (*Wolf Norton*)].

Western. [*Print viewed*]. At Aunt Millie's Curly Q Ranch, foreman Curt Benson corrals a herd of wild horses, which he plans to sell in order to pay a $3,000 lien held by Tom Larsen, who owns the neighboring Bar 6 Ranch. Just then, Larsen's gang of rustlers, led by henchman Wolf Norton, releases a wild stallion Curt previously captured and trained to open a corral gate with his mouth. From a nearby hilltop, an Indian named Little Bear watches as the stallion gallops toward the corral, opens the gate and frees the herd, which the gang later captures. Before the gang can recapture the stallion, however, he gallops to Little Bear, who gently strokes his back. Later, Wolf tells Larsen that their new recruit, Johnny Adams, recently vowed to quit the gang, so they decide to shoot him. After Little Bear goes to the Curly Q to tell Curt what he has seen, Millie's niece, Ellen Collins, urges Curt to enter their old horse Rowdy into this year's stockmen's race. Later, Wolf sees Little Bear sneaking into the Bar 6 stables in search of the rustled horses. He follows Little Bear inside and knocks him unconscious with the butt of his gun. The next day, the sheriff, Breezy, tells Curt that Little Bear has been accused of shooting Johnny. Breezy then shows Curt the bullet recovered from Johnny's corpse, a .45 hollow point called a "dumdum." Later, Larsen learns that Curt and his men have rounded up a huge herd of cattle. When Curt, his men and the herd approach the ranch, Wolf and his gang start a stampede and rustle the herd. With help from Little Bear, Curt captures the stallion and plans to enter him in the race. Later, however, Breezy, Larsen and the posse arrive at the Curly Q and accuse Curt of harboring a fugitive. As Breezy arrests Little Bear, Curt threatens to kill Larsen if anything should happen to Little Bear on his way to jail. Fuming, Larsen pulls his gun and shoots at Curt, hitting the barn door behind him instead. After they leave, Curt removes the bullet, which turns out to be a dumdum. For weeks, Curt and one of his ranch hands try unsuccessfully to mount and ride the stallion. On the day of the race, Rowdy becomes lame, so Curt enters the stallion instead. In town, under the mistaken impression that Millie is entering Rowdy in the race, Larsen offers her a wager of $1,000. The arrogant Larsen is so sure that Millie's horse will lose that he throws in the lien for the ranch, and she quickly accepts. Realizing that Little Bear is the only one who can ride the stallion, Curt persuades Breezy to help him stage an escape. The race then begins, and the stallion, ridden by Little Bear, pulls ahead of the pack. Larsen recognizes Little Bear and orders Wolf to kill him, after which Larson is shot by Breezy. After the stallion wins, Curt gives Little Bear the stallion as payment

for riding, and Little Bear releases him to rejoin his herd in the wild. *Indians of North America. Ranch foremen. Rustlers. Wild horses. Animal trainers. Bullets. Debt. Frame-ups. Fugitives. Horseracing. Jails. Mountains. Murder. Nieces. Posses. Ranchers. Roundups. Sheriffs. Shootings. Wagers. Women ranchers.*

Note: The onscreen credits include a credit for sound effects, but the name, which did not appear in other sources, was unreadable. The *Var* review notes that the picture was the first Kanab Pictures production and was shot on location in Kanab, UT.

Box 11 Jun 1949. *FD* 2 Jun 1949, p. 10. *MPHPD* 4 Jun 1949, p. 4634. *Var* 1 Jun 1949, p. 11.

STAMBOUL (*foreignversion*) *see* **EL HOMBRE QUE ASESINÓ**

THE STAND AT APACHE RIVER (Native Americans, Apache)

Universal-International Pictures Co., Inc. *Dist* Universal Pictures Co., Inc. Sep **1953**; Prod: early Dec 1952—3 Jan 1953 [©Universal Pictures Co.; 25 Jun 1953; LP2784]. Sd (Western Electric Recording); col (Technicolor). 8 reels, 6,912 ft. 76-77 min. PCA cert no. 16354.

Prod William Alland. *Dir* Lee Sholem. *Asst dir* Jesse Hibbs and [Gordon McLean]. [*Dial dir* Harold Goodwin]. *Story and scr* Arthur Ross. *Dir of photog* Charles P. Boyle. *Technicolor color consultant* William Fritzsche. *Art dir* Bernard Herzbrun and Hilyard Brown. *Film ed* Leonard Weiner. *Set dec* Russell A. Gausman and Oliver Emert. *Cost* Bill Thomas. *Mus* Frank Skinner. *Sd* Leslie I. Carey and Richard De Weese. *Hair stylist* Joan St. Oegger. *Makeup* Bud Westmore. [*Unit prod mgr* Lew Leary].

Source: Based on the novel *Apache Landing* by Robert J. Hogan (New York, 1951).

Cast: Stephen McNally (*Lane Dakota*), Julia Adams (*Valerie Kendrick*), Hugh Marlowe (*Colonel Morsby*), Jaclynne Greene (*Ann Kenyon*), Hugh O'Brian (*Tom Kenyon*), Russell Johnson (*Greiner*), Jack Kelly (*Hatcher*), Edgar Barrier (*Cara Blanca*), Forrest Lewis (*Deadhorse*).

Western. [*Print viewed*]. In the desert hills, Sheriff Lane Dakota captures Grenier, accused of murdering an Indian agent named Wylie, after Grenier is about to be killed by an Apache Indian. Two Indians are killed during the struggle. Promising that Grenier will hang, Dakota takes him thirty miles to the ferry at Apache River. They cross with a stagecoach carrying cavalry officer Colonel Morsby and lovely Valerie Kendrick, who is traveling from Abilene to Salado to meet the man she plans to marry. At the stage station, Apache Landing, run by Ann Kenyon and her absent husband Tom, Morsby relates that a week ago, fifty Apaches escaped from the San Carlos reservation and killed a family of settlers nearby. Deadhorse, the ferryboat driver, notices Apaches across the river with their leader, Cara Blanca. The colonel, an Indian fighter, argues that they should send someone to bring troops, but Dakota does not think the Apaches will attack unless they are stirred up and accuses the army of scattering them from Mexico to California. Cara Blanca comes across the river in peace. He explains that his people were moved to the desert of San Carlos when white men wanted their land for farms; now, after three years in the desert, they want to return. They have come to the station only to trade for food and salt, and the whites oblige him. Although Cara Blanca agrees to leave by the next morning, the Indians remain, wanting the colonel to accompany them so that troops will not attack. Cara Blanca contends that his group did not kill the family of settlers, but that Indians who separated from them did. The colonel demands that the Apaches return to the reservation, and a gun battle ensues. When night comes, Dakota sends the women to the barge to escape, while he goes to the stable to protect his horse. He kills an Apache in the stable, then rides to the barge, and kills another Apache trying to climb in. Valerie is knocked into the water, and while Dakota rescues her, an Apache rides away on Dakota's horse. At the station house, Ann, who does not love her husband, tries to talk Dakota into escaping with her in a small flatboat hidden under a rock ledge, but Dakota is concerned about Valerie. As Apaches fire into the house, Greiner gets a gun and tries to escape, but Dakota takes it from him. When he threatens to kill Greiner, Valerie berates him. The Apaches now shoot burning arrows at the building. When a flaming arrow hits Valerie's shirt sleeve setting it on fire, Dakota rips it off and carries her to a bed, where she gently touches his face and he strokes her hair. The Apaches stop the siege temporarily, but the next day, when an Apache goes to help Cara Blanca, who is wounded, Morsby shoots and kills him, then is about to fire at Cara Blanca, until Dakota gets his rifle away. The Indians hold their fire as Dakota brings Cara Blanca to the

station house. The Apache leader says his people will not stop fighting now because they are lost. Although Morsby wants to kill Cara Blanca, because he says the women will not be safe with an Indian inside, Valerie nurses him. Greiner overhears Ann convince Hacker, a boarder who secretly loves her, to leave with her in the flatboat, but just then, Ann's husband Tom rides up. At night, Valerie sits with Dakota, and she says she has decided not to marry the rancher. They kiss, and Dakota relates that after Indians killed his father, Wylie, whom Greiner murdered, raised him. After most of the house is asleep, Greiner hears Ann and Hatcher preparing to leave. He demands to go with them, but after they take the group's guns, leaving them defenseless, Hatcher is shot and killed by the Apaches. In the commotion, Dakota awakens and recovers his gun from Greiner. Ann follows Tom to the barn to apologize, and as she says she loves him, the barn goes up in flames from burning arrows, killing them. Some Apaches then enter the station house and kill the colonel. With only a half-dozen bullets left, Dakota helps Cara Blanca to the door to tell his people that the colonel is dead. When an arrow almost hits them, Dakota calls the Indians "savages," to which Cara Blanca says Dakota would do the same if revenge were his only reason to live or die. When Greiner says that the Apaches were responsible for the inhumanities inflicted on them by whites, Dakota goes to kill him, but Valerie yells at him accusing him of only hating. Apaches then enter the house, and during the subsequent fight, Dakota throws a knife and hits an Indian about to attack Valerie. After the battle, Apache women lead Cara Blanca off. Valerie decides she will stay in Salado. She accuses Dakota of having no love in him, but after he says he is through with revenge, she kisses him as a new stage arrives. *Apache Indians. Bigotry. Revenge. Romance. Sieges. Tribal chiefs.* Ferryboats. Fires. Marriage. Murder. Officers (Military). Rescues. Sheriffs. Stables. Stagecoaches. United States. Army. Cavalry.

Note: The working title of this film was *Apache Landing*. According to modern sources, Henry Wills and Frankie Darro were in the cast. *LADN* complained that the film portrayed "the old, old story again about the Indians getting a raw deal. And while stories about Indians are here to stay, there surely must be more novel ways to deal with the problem." *LAEx* commented, "It is the traditional outdoor picture, but it seems more like a stage play in the compact way it is presented."
Box 15 Aug 1953. *DV* 11 Aug 1953, p. 3. *Exb* 12 Aug 1953, p. 3576. *FD* 11 Aug 1953, p. 6. *Har* 15 Aug 1953, p. 131 *HR* 11 Aug 1953, p. 3. *LADN* 13 Aug 1953. *LAEx* 13 Aug 1953, sec. II, p. 8. *MPD* 11 Aug 1953. *MPHPD* 15 Aug 1953, p. 1949. *Var* 12 Aug 1953, p. 6

STAND UP AND CHEER! (African Americans)
Fox Film Corp. *Dist* Fox Film Corp. 4 May **1934**; New York opening: week of 19 Apr 1934; Prod: completed late Jan 1934 [©Fox Film Corp.; 23 Mar 1934]. Sd (Western Electric Noiseless Recording); b&w. 9 reels, 7,300 ft. 80-81 min. Passed by the National Board of Review. PCA cert no. 1246-R [17 Aug 1935].
Prod Winfield Sheehan. *Assoc prod* Lew Brown. *Dir* Hamilton MacFadden. *Collaborator on story and dial* Lew Brown. *Story idea suggested by* Will Rogers and Philip Klein. *Dial* Ralph Spence. [*Contr wrt* Rian James, Edward T. Lowe, Jr., Malcolm Stuart Boylan and Hamilton MacFadden]. *Photog* Ernest Palmer and L. W. O'Connell. *Art settings* Gordon Wiles and Russell Patterson. [*Ed* Margaret Clancy]. *Cost* Rita Kaufman. *Mus dir* Arthur Lange. *Dances staged by* Sammy Lee. *Sd* E. F. Grossman. [*Location mgr* Ray Moore].
Song(s): "We're Out of the Red," "I'm Laughin'," "Baby Take a Bow," "Broadway's Gone Hill-Billy" and "This Is Our Last Night Together," music and lyrics by Lew Brown and Jay Gorney; "Stand Up and Cheer," music and lyrics by Harry Akst and Lew Brown; "She's Way Up Thar (I'm Way Down Yar)," music and lyrics by Lew Brown.
Cast: Warner Baxter (*Lawrence Cromwell*), Madge Evans (*Mary Adams*), James Dunn (*Jimmy Dugan*), Sylvia Froos (*Herself*), John Boles (*Himself*), Arthur Byron (*John Harly*), Shirley Temple (*Shirley Dugan*), Ralph Morgan (*Secretary to the president*), "Aunt Jemima" (*Herself*), Frank Mitchell (*Senator Danforth*), Jack Durant (*Senator Short*), Nick Foran (*Himself*), Nigel Bruce ([*Eustace*] *Dinwiddie*), "Skins" Miller (*Hill-Billy*), Stepin Fetchit (*Himself* [*George Bernard Shaw*]), [Frank Melton (*Fosdick*)], [Lila Lee (*Zelda*)], [Frances Morris, Lurene Tuttle, Dorothy Gulliver, Bess Flowers, Lillian West (*Stenographers*)], [Selmer Jackson, Clyde Dilson (*Correspondents*)], [Edward Earle (*Secret Service man*)], [Gayne Whitman (*Voice for president*)], [Frank Sheridan, Paul Stanton, Wallis Clark, Arthur Stuart Hull (*Senators*)], [Si Jenks (*Rube farmer*)], [Aggie Herring (*Irish washerwoman*)], [Phil Tead (*Vaudevillian*)], [Randall Sisters (*Trio*)],

[George K. Arthur (*Dance director*)], [Baby Alice Raetz (*Child*)], [Ruth Beckett (*Child's mother*)], [Bobby Caldwell (*General Lee*)], [Wilbur Mack (*Beamish*)], [Elspeth Dudgeon, Jessie Perry, Harry Northrup (*Reformers*)], [John Davidson (*Sour radio announcer*)], [Harry Dunkinson, Gilbert Clayton, Herbert Prior, Carl Stockdale (*Quartette*)], [Lucien Littlefield (*Professor Hi De Ho*)], [Joe Smith Marba (*Elephant trainer*)], [Carlton E. Griffin, Paul McVey, Rolin Ray, Reginald Simpson, Dora Clemant, Peggy Watts, Dorothy Dehn, Ruth Clifford (*Secretaries*)], [Arthur Vinton (*Turner*)], [Sam Hayes (*Radio announcer*)], [Tina Marshall (*Boy's mother*)], [Glen Walters (*Hillbilly's wife*)], [Nora Lane, Dorothy Dayton (*Toe dancers*)], [Dorothy Thompson, Amy Sureau, Toddy Peterson, Inez Mortensen, Mildred Morris, Laura Morse, Crystal Keate, Margaret Harding, Earlene Heath, Martha Fields, Grace Davies, Zita Baca, Angela Blue, Dorothy Andree, Dorothy White, Zelda Webber, Jean Allen, Deslys Barnes, Mary Jane Carey, Lorena Carr, Audrene Brier, Mary Blackwood, Dixie Dean, Dale Dee, Betty Dotson, Margaret Ehrlich, Celeste Mari Edwards, Eleanor Edwards, Harriette Haddon, Eve Kimberly, Ruth Jennings, Zumetta Garnett, Diane Gardner, Helen Fairweather, Eula Love, Lucille Miller, Anne Nagel, Marjean Roach, Marjean Rogers, Gale Ronn, Marion Shelton (*Dancers*)], [Arthur Loft], [Jack Richardson], [Dagmar Oakland], [Vivian Winston].

Social, Musical. [*Print viewed*]. Lawrence Cromwell, a noted Broadway producer and authority on feminine beauty, is appointed Secretary of Amusement, and assigned the responsibility of raising the spirits of the American people so that they can lick the Depression. At a meeting with his assistant secretaries, Lawrence's eye is caught by Mary Adams, head of the children's division, and they begin dating. Some time later, Lawrence's secretary Fosdick announces that George Bernard Shaw is there to see him, but George turns out to be a shimmy-sham dancer whom Lawrence hires as Fosdick's assistant. In another part of Washington, John Harly meets with fellow businessmen to complain about Lawrence. They have made many business deals that depend on the continuance of the Depression, and they are worried that Lawrence's plans will succeed. To stop Lawrence, Harly initiates a giant smear campaign against him. Back at Amusement Headquarters, Jimmy Dugan and his little daughter Shirley wait to see Lawrence. Shirley wanders off and is brought to Mary, who sends for Jimmy. When Lawrence arrives, Jimmy asks for an exemption to the new law that a child under seven may not work. Lawrence gives his permission and the Dugans perform their act for him. Elsewhere, members of the Senate discuss Lawrence's extravagance, with the result that Senators Danforth and Short are assigned to investigate. They talk with Lawrence and tour the facilities with Eustace Dinwiddie, Lawrence's general scout. Later that day, Lawrence goes aboard Harly's yacht, where Harly unsuccessfully attempts to bribe him into giving up. The next morning, in another meeting with his assistants, Lawrence complains about the department's slow progress, the result of an unseen foe spreading discord. The majority of the assistants stand behind Lawrence, but one, Turner, tells him that the department must be closed. After the meeting, Lawrence tells Mary that he is quitting because he cannot handle the pressures from Congress, reporters and investigators, as well as from the public. She says that he is wrong to quit, but that she loves him and will support him regardless. While Mary then watches an audition for Lawrence, George helps a penguin that talks like Jimmy Durante. That afternoon, Lawrence becomes incensed by a radio report that his incompetence is forcing his resignation, which will be a victory for solid citizens everywhere. Mary comes in to inform him that the children's division is a huge success, but before she can, he tells her that he is sticking to his guns. He warns her that the drastic budget cuts he must make will result in the cancellation of the children's division, but as they are talking, they hear another radio news flash about the Amusement Department's success, which is attributed largely to Mary's division. The president calls Lawrence to congratulate him, and Lawrence humbly tells him about Mary's contribution. After the phone call, Lawrence and Mary are notified that the Depression is officially over, and they participate in a gigantic celebration parade featuring people from all walks of life. *Bribery. Businessmen. The Depression, 1929. Entertainers. Optimism.* African Americans. Auditions. Beauty, Personal. Children. Fathers and daughters. Hillbillies. Parades. Penguins. Radio broadcasting. Romance. United States. Congress. Senate. United States. Presidents. Washington (D.C.). Yachts and yachting.

Note: The working titles of this film were *Fox Movietone Follies for 1933,* *Fox Movietone Follies for 1934, Fox Movietone Follies* and *Fox Follies.* According to information in the Twentieth Century-Fox Records of the Legal Department at the UCLA Arts—Special Collections Library, in 1970, Lincoln Perry, known professionally as Stepin Fetchit, filed a three-million dollar suit charging that Twentieth Century-Fox conspired with CBS to invade his privacy and defame his character when CBS aired clips of the films *Stand Up and Cheer!* (see below) and *In Old Kentucky* (see *AFI Catalog of Feature Films, 1931-40;* F3. 2119) on a documentary entitled "Black History: Lost, Stolen or Forgotten." Perry claimed he was depicted "as a tool of the white man who betrayed the members of his race and [who] earned two million dollars portraying Negroes as inferior human beings." Information pertaining to the disposition of the suit has not been located.

Although Shirley Temple is listed third in the film's opening onscreen cast credits, she is listed seventh in the ending credits. According to *HR* news items, Edward Sutherland was originally scheduled to direct the picture, and Lilian Harvey and Winnie Shaw were set for the cast. Sutherland may have been replaced because of illness, while the reasons behind Harvey and Shaw's withdrawals from the film have not been determined. *HR* also noted that Dorothy Stone had been tested for a role in the picture. Although a *FD* news item reported that Florence Desmond had been signed for the film, her participation in the completed picture has not been confirmed. According to the Twentieth Century-Fox Produced Scripts Collection, also at the UCLA Arts-Special Collections Library, actors considered for inclusion in the film were: Will Rogers, Lew Ayres, Spencer Tracy, Sid Silvers, Sally Eilers, Clara Bow, director David Butler, Victor Jory and Janet Gaynor, for whom a special number entitled "My Favorite Doll" was written by Lew Brown, Sammy Lee and Hans Kraly. The *Var* review noted that Brown provided the voice of the Jimmy Durante penguin. *Stand Up and Cheer!* marked the feature film debuts of singer Nick Foran, who later changed his name to Dick Foran, and comedians Frank Mitchell and Jack Durant. According to the Twentieth Century-Fox legal records, the studio rented a Kellett auto-gyro from R. V. H. Mather, and the sequence in which the device was used was filmed on location at Busch Gardens in Pasadena, CA. The legal records note that in 1935, a lawsuit was filed against Fox by Paul Blanton for infringement on a patent for "the art of producing mannikin actors" by painting faces on the legs of dancers. The case was settled out of court for $1,500.

According to a modern interview with Jane Withers, she was asked by Fox to read for a part in this picture, but after her audition, "in walked the most beautiful child I had ever seen—Shirley Temple. My heart sank to my toes. I knew she'd get the part, and I was right." Another modern source asserts that after seeing Temple in a "Frolics of Youth" short entitled *Pardon My Pups,* songwriter Jay Gorney requested that she audition for *Stand Up and Cheer!.* In her autobiography, Temple notes that producer Winfield Sheehan gave her a contract with Fox on the second day of filming her "Baby Take a Bow" number. Contemporary reviewers praised Temple's performance, and the *Var* reviewer referred to her as a "sure-fire potential kidlet star" and "the unofficial star" of the picture.

Box 28 Apr 1934. *DV* 22 Feb 1934, p. 1. *DV* 19 Mar 1934, p. 3. *FD* 16 Nov 1933, p. 8. *FD* 20 Apr 1934, p. 9, 11. *HR* 13 Jun 1933, p. 2. *HR* 16 Nov 1934, p. 2. *HR* 14 Dec 1933, p. 1. *HR* 16 Dec 1933, p. 7. *HR* 18 Jan 1934, p. 3. *HR* 22 Jan 1934, p. 6. *HR* 19 Mar 1934, p. 19. *HR* 28 Mar 1934, pp. 4-9. *MPD* 29 Mar 1934, p. 7. *MPH* 28 Apr 1934, p. 38. *NYT* 20 Apr 1934, p. 17. *Var* 24 Apr 1934, p. 14.

STAND UP AND FIGHT (African Americans)

Metro-Goldwyn-Mayer Corp.; controlled by Loew's Inc. *Dist* Loew's Inc. 6 Jan **1939**; *Prod:* began Sep 1938 [©Loew's Inc.; 3 Jan 1939; LP8538]. Sd (Western Electric Sound System); b&w. 97 or 99 min. PCA cert no. 4870.

Prod Mervyn LeRoy. [*Assoc prod* J. Walter Ruben]. *Dir* W. S. Van Dyke II. [*2d unit dir* Richard Rosson]. [*Asst dir* Hugh Boswell and Horace Hough]. *Scr* James M. Cain, Jane Murfin and Harvey Fergusson. *Story* Forbes Parkhill. [*Addl dial* Laurence Stallings]. *Photog* Leonard Smith. *Art dir* Cedric Gibbons. *Art dir assoc* Urie McLeary. *Film ed* Frank Sullivan. *Set dec* Edwin Willis. *Women's cost* Dolly Tree. *Men's cost* Valles. [*Mus score* Dr. William Axt]. *Rec dir* Douglas Shearer. *Makeup* Jack Dawn. [*Unit mgr* Frank Messenger].

Cast: WALLACE BEERY (*Captain Boss Starkey*), ROBERT TAYLOR (*Blake Cantrell*), Florence Rice (*Susan Griffith*), Helen Broderick (*Amanda Griffith*), Charles Bickford (*Arnold*), Barton MacLane (*Crowder*), Charley Grapewin (*Old Puff*), John Qualen (*Davey*), Robert Glecker (*Sheriff Barney*), Clinton Rosemond (*Enoch*), Cy Kendall (*Foreman Ross*), Paul Everton (*Allan*), Claudia Morgan (*Carolyn Talbot*), Selmer Jackson (*Whittingham P. Talbot*), Robert Middlemass (*Harkrider*), Jonathan Hale (*Colonel Webb*), [Minor Watson (*Marshall Cole*)], [Frank Darien (*Daniels*)], [William Tannen (*Lewis*)], [Edward Hearn (*Joe*)], [Edward Keane (*Donnelly*)], [John Dilson (*Auctioneer*)], [Ben Welden (*Foreman*)], [Louise Springer (*Violet*)], [Eddy Waller (*Conductor*)], [Victor Potel (*Coachdriver*)], [Harry Allen (*Engineer*)], [Walter Soderling (*Passenger*)], [Frank Jaquet (*Bartender*)], [Mitchell Lewis (*Sport*)], [Harry Cording (*Blacksmith*)], [Everett Brown (*Big black man*)], [Henry Hastings (*Old black man*)], [Ted Oliver (*Deputy Cochran*)], [Harry Strang (*Deputy Thomas*)], [Clem Bevans (*Bum*)], [Syd Saylor (*Stooge*)], [Al

Ferguson (*First teamster*)], [Sam Ash (*Second teamster*)], [Trevor Bardette (*Mob leader*)], [Jack Grey (*Stage coach passenger*)], [John Ince (*Man at auction*)], [Lee Tung-Foo (*Chinese cook*)], [James Kilgannon (*Fireman*)], [Murdock MacQuarrie (*Engineer*)], [George Ovey (*Conductor*)], [Theodore Lorch], [Hal Price], [Forrest Taylor], [Sidney D'Albrook], [George Cooper], [Claire McDowell].

Historical, Drama. [*Print viewed*]. Blake Cantrell, a Maryland aristocrat and well-bred cad, uses the occasion of his hunt to announce his impending bankruptcy. In order to pay his debts, Blake is forced to sell his slaves, thus incurring the disapproval of his house guest, Northerner Susan Griffith. Later, when Blake tries to seduce Susan, she denounces him and leaves for the Cumberland Gap with her Aunt Amanda, who owns the Bullet Stage Line there. In Cumberland, Susan meets Captain Starkey, an old friend of Amanda and manager of the Bullet Line. To keep the line solvent, Starkey has been renting stages to Arnold, who claims to be transporting fugitive slaves to freedom. Soon afterwards, Blake arrives in Cumberland to ask Colonel Webb, the construction head of the Baltimore and Ohio Railroad and an old friend of his father, for a job. Webb, who is in competition with the Bullet Line, offers Blake a job spying on Starkey, but Blake refuses. Later that night, Blake meets Starkey in a drunken brawl and Starkey, short-handed since his men have quit in order to work on the railroad, frames Blake, has him thrown in jail and then arranges for him to work off his fine on the stage line. Hard, honest work makes Blake a new man, and he and Susan are about to begin a romance when Blake sees his old slave Enoch gunned down while trying to escape from Arnold's clutches. Realizing that Starkey is involved in slave running, Blake quits the line and accepts Webb's offer. Hoping to expose Morgan, the brains behind the slave racket, Blake pretends to be a highwayman and infiltrates the gang. When a routine shipment turns into a slave massacre, Blake rides off to file charges against the stage line and Arnold, who is really Morgan. Because he is missing a crucial piece of incriminating evidence, Blake rides back to the scene of the massacre, where he comes into conflict with Arnold and Starkey, who has escaped from jail. In the ensuing shootout, Arnold dies, and Blake and Starkey survive to brave a life threatening snowstorm. During the storm, the two men come to understand each other, and when they are finally rescued, Blake conceals the incriminating evidence. After Susan sells the stage line to Starkey, she joins Blake as he goes West to open up the territory to the railroad. *Business competition. Slave traders. Slavery-Emancipation. Southerners. United States–History–19th century. Aunts. Cads. Nieces. Railroads. Snow storms. Stagecoaches.*

Note: The working title of this picture was *Give and Take,* which was also the working title of Robert Taylor's 1938 film, *The Crowd Roars. Stand Up and Fight* was also the working title of *The Crowd Roars.* According to *HR* news items, Taylor and Wallace Beery were assigned to this film when production was delayed on *Northwest Passage,* in which they were both to appear (see above). Although a news item in *HR* noted that Selznick player Margaret Tallichet was loaned out to M-G-M to appear in this picture, her participation in the project is unconfirmed. According to another news item in *HR,* Ann Morriss was considered for the lead in this film. The picture was partially shot on location at Chico, CA.

DV 30 Dec 1938, p. 3. *FD* 4 Jan 1939, p. 7. *HR* 19 Aug 1938, p. 1. *HR* 26 Aug 1938, p. 2. *HR* 24 Sep 1938, p. 10. *HR* 25 Sep 1938, p. 2. *HR* 10 Oct 1938, p. 6. *HR* 13 Oct 1938, p. 6. *HR* 30 Dec 1938, p. 3. *MPD* 4 Jan 1940, p. 10. *MPH* 19 Nov 1938, p. 57. *MPH* 7 Jan 1939, p. 36, 38. *NYT* 27 Jan 1939, p. 17. *Var* 11 Jan 1939, p. 12.

STAR FOR A NIGHT (Austrian Americans)

Twentieth Century-Fox Film Corp. *Dist* Twentieth Century-Fox Film Corp. 28 Aug **1936**; *Prod:* 1 Jun—6 Jul 1936 [©Twentieth Century-Fox Film Corp.; 28 Aug 1936; LP6838]. Sd (Western Electric Noiseless Recording); b&w. 8 reels, 6,850 ft. 76 min.

Exec prod Sol M. Wurtzel. *Dir* Lewis Seiler. *Asst dir* Sidney Bowen. *Scr* Frances Hyland and Saul Elkins. [*Contr to trmt* Lamar Trotti]. *Photog* Ernest Palmer. *Art dir* Duncan Cramer. *Film ed* Alex Troffey. *Cost* Herschel. *Mus dir* Samuel Kaylin. *Dances staged by* Sammy Lee. *Sd* George Leverett and Harry M. Leonard. [*Dancing double for Claire Trevor* Bobbie Woods].

Song(s): "Over a Cup of Coffee," "Down Around Malibu Way," "Holy Lie Production Routine #1" and "At the Beach at Malibu (Hullabaloo at Malibu)," music and lyrics by Harry Akst and Sidney Clare; "You're My Favorite One," music by Lew Pollack, lyrics by Sidney Clare.

Source: Based on the play *Die heilige Lüge* by Karin Michaelis (copyrighted 1 Apr 1915).

Cast: Claire Trevor (*Nina Lind*), Jane Darwell (*Mrs. [Martha] Lind*), Arline Judge (*Mamie DeLaMont*), Evelyn Venable (*Anna Lind*), J. Edward Bromberg (*Dr. Spellmeyer*), Dean Jagger (*Fritz Lind*), Alan Dinehart (*James Dunning*), Joyce Compton (*Ellen Romaine*), Susan Fleming (*Mildred La Rue*), Adrienne Marden (*Katherine Lind*), Frank Reicher (*Dr. Hellmkin*), Dickie Walters (*Paul Lind*), Chick Chandler (*Eddie*), Astrid Allwyn (*Josephine Hall*), Hattie McDaniel (*Hattie*), [Doris Brenwald (*Helen*)], [Wally Albright, Jr. (*Hans*)], [Moyer Bupp (*Fritz*)], [Otto Fries (*Chauffeur*)], [Kathryn Sheldon (*Gretchen*)], [Christian Rub (*Postmaster*)], [Constance Purdy (*Townswoman*)], [Torben Meyer (*Saddle maker*)], [Annette Lake (*Saddle maker's wife*)], [Frank Mills (*Taxi driver*)], [Lew Harvey, Fred Wallace, Fred Sylva (*Men in taxi office*)], [Eddie Tamblyn (*Messenger*)], [Claudia Coleman (*Landlady*)], [Eddie Anderson (*Maid's boyfriend*)], [Daisy Bufford (*Maid*)], [Phyllis Fraser, Mary Bovard (*Flappers*)], [Grace Durkin (*Salesgirl*)], [Herbert Ashley (*Piano mover*)], [Jean Houghton, Mary Mersch (*Neighbors*)], [Marvin Stephens, Georgie Billings (*Children*)], [James T. Mack (*Stage doorman*)], [Emmett Vogan (*Radio announcer*)], [Matty Roubert (*Newsboy*)], [Fred Kelsey, George Magrill (*Moving men*)], [Bobby Dale, Chuck De Shon, Jim Blair, Emmett O'Brien, George Bruggerman, James Gonzalez, Frank Erickson, Perk Lazelle, Fred Mayon, Sol Haines, Jimmy Grant, Jimmy Notarro, Jack Morton, Tom Thompson, Eddie Daniels, Gus Hyland, Don Ackerman, Eddie Foy, Bobbie Woods, Frank Phillips (*Dancers*)], [Harriette Haddon], [Inez Mortensen], [Elouise Rozelle], [Lillian Lock], [Diane Dorsey], [Colleen Ward], [Helen Seamon], [Eve Reynolds], [Rhea Neissen], [Louise Larabee], [Dale Dee], [Pokey Champion], [Lorraine Gray], [Nanci Lyon], [Doreen McKay], [Lucille La Marr], [Betty Gordon], [Kay Gordon], [Jeannette Warren], [Dorothy Haas], [Virginia Ray], [Valerie Traxler], [Norah Gale], [Martha Manning], [Kathryn Barnes], [Paul Stanton].

Domestic, Drama, with songs. [*Print viewed*]. In a village in the Austrian Tyrol, the neighbors of the blind frau Martha Lind give her a going away party as she prepares to go to New York to visit her three children: Anna, whom she says is a concert pianist; Fritz, whom she thinks owns an automobile factory; and Nina, whom she believes is a famous singer and dancer. In reality, Anna plays the piano at a music store, Fritz drives a cab, and Nina is a chorus girl. When the children receive their mother's cable that she is coming for a visit, Nina convinces them that they must keep up their deception because their mother would be ashamed to know that they have spent money that they really could not afford to send her to eye specialists in Europe. Because of Mrs. Lind's blindness, the ruse works, but it is endangered when Dr. Spellmeyer, a former student of Mrs. Lind's doctor from Austria, arrives at Anna's small Third Avenue apartment to examine Mrs. Lind. After listening to Anna's story about the charade, he calls her courageous and does not let on. Dr. Spellmeyer's operation to restore Mrs. Lind's vision is successful, and when Nina learns that her mother will be able to see in a few days, she breaks down and cries during a number, which angers the self-centered star, Josephine Hall, who wants to have Nina fired. Nina's two friends on the chorus line, Mamie DeLaMont and Mildred La Rue, convince a ditsy blonde friend, Ellen Romaine, to let Nina borrow her fancy clothes and large apartment that her wealthy beau has given her. After Mrs. Lind is able to see, the ruse continues in Ellen's apartment. Because Mrs. Lind wants to see Nina's show, Mamie, Mildred and Ellen ask Josephine to pretend to be sick one night so that Nina, Josephine's understudy, can go on in her place. When Josephine indignantly refuses, they lock her in her liquor closet, and when she does not appear at the theater, Nina is starred in the show. Mrs. Lind sees the performance, but at the end of the first act, Josephine, who has been let out by her maid, comes onstage and slaps Nina. The audience is unsure if the disruption is part of the act, and during intermission, when the producer learns what happened, he gives Josephine's role to Nina. Hoping to capitalize on the story, the producer calls the newspapers, and the next day, which is Thanksgiving, Ellen, Mamie and Mildred awaken to read about it in the headlines. They call Nina, who then plans with Anna to keep their mother from reading the papers. They find, however, that she has left the apartment. Mrs. Lind goes to the Third Avenue apartment, and later in the day, Anna's landlady calls to have the whole family come at once. They find that their mother has prepared a Thanksgiving meal and has learned about the ruse. Rather than being upset, Mrs. Lind says that she is prouder of her children

than she would have been if they had really been what they pretended to be. When Mamie, Mildred and Ellen come to join the family, Mrs. Lind says grace and blesses them all. *Austrian Americans. Austrians. Blindness–Temporary. Chorus girls. Deception. Family relationships. Friendship. Motherhood. Austria. New York City. Newspapers. Pianists. Surgeons. Taxicab drivers. Thanksgiving Day. Theatrical producers. Understudies.*

Note: The working title of this film was *The Holy Lie*. According to information in the Twentieth Century-Fox Records of the Legal Department at the UCLA Theater Arts Library, producer Sol Wurtzel wanted to buy the rights to the play early in 1935, but the deal was held back until the next year because National-Film A.G., a Berlin-based production company, held the silent film rights for ten years from the time of acquisition. In a note, Wurtzel commented, "I consider that *The Holy Lie* has the basis of a story that can be just as important as the picture *Four Sons* which we made about six years ago, and as important as *Over the Hill*' (see *AFI Catalog of Feature Films, 1931-40*; F3.1459 and F3.3329). Later correspondence indicates that the studio planned to rewrite the story, "retaining the basic idea." The legal records indicate that Harry Akst and Sidney Clare wrote an additional song for the film, "Argentine Swing," which was cut. That song remained the property of Twentieth Century-Fox and it was subsequently used in their 1937 film *Big Town Girl* (see *AFI Catalog of Feature Films, 1931-40*; F3.0335), which also starred Claire Trevor. The National-Film silent film based on the play was released in 1927 and entitled *Die heilige Lüge*.

Box 29 Aug 1936. DV 6 Jul 1936, p. 4. DV 6 Aug 1936, p. 3. FD 14 Aug 1936, p. 6. HR 2 Jun 1936, p. 7. HR 29 Jun 1936, p. 9. HR 6 Aug 1936, p. 3. MPD 7 Aug 1936, p. 10. MPH 18 Jul 1936, p. 60, 62. MPH 15 Aug 1936, p. 62. NYT 5 Sep 1936, p. 7. Var 26 Aug 1936, p. 20.

THE STAR PACKER (Native Americans)

Lone Star Productions; Monogram Pictures Corp.; A Paul Malvern Production. *Dist* Monogram Pictures Corp. 30 Jul **1934**; Prod: began 8 May 1934 at General Service Studios [©Monogram Pictures Corp.; 15 Aug 1934; LP5280]. Sd (Balsley & Phillips Recording System); b&w. 6 reels. 52 or 54 min.

Dir R. N. Bradbury. *Story and scr* R. N. Bradbury. *Photog* Archie Stout. *Film ed* Carl Pierson. *Rec* J. A. Stransky, Jr. *Tech dir* E. R. Hickson.

Cast: John Wayne [(*John Travers*)], Verna Hillie [(*Anita Matlock*)], George Hayes [(*Matt Matlock, also known as The Shadow*)], Yakima Canutt [(*Yak*)], Billy Franey, Ed Parker [(*Parker*)], Earl Dwire [(*Mason*)], Tom Lingham [(*Sheriff*)], [Artie Ortego (*Deputy*)], [George Cleveland (*Pete*)], [Davie Aldrich (*Boy*)].

Western. [*Print viewed*]. Before The Shadow and his gang of outlaws execute a stagecoach robbery, John Travers, a United States Marshal, and his Indian friend Yak intercept the coach and rob it themselves. Two of The Shadow's henchmen brutally murder the coach's driver and guard, and the horses bolt and run away with the coach. Travers saves passenger Anita Matlock, who is on her way to claim the ranch left to her by her recently murdered father, and escorts the coach into the town of Little Rock. Soon after the coach arrives, the sheriff is shot and killed, and Travers learns from Matlock, Anita's uncle and a respected rancher, that Little Rock's two previous sheriffs also were murdered. With the help of Yak, Travers begins an investigation and discovers that the killer's instructions are coming from a voice behind a phony safe in the saloon. Travers and Yak follow the gunmen and find a hideout that is near Matlock's ranch, full of notorious outlaws. After warning Matlock and Anita, who is visiting her uncle for the first time, about the outlaws, Travers and Yak jail two of The Shadow's men. That night, they further investigate the saloon, finding a secret tunnel that leads to a hollow stump in the middle of the main street. Anita, meanwhile, learns from a ranch hand named Jake that Matlock is The Shadow and that he killed her father and uncle and has assumed her uncle's identity. She tries to warn Travers, but is taken hostage by the gang as they head for town with a machine gun. Travers deputizes the townsmen and, following a daring chase, captures Matlock and the gang. Eventually, Anita and Travers marry. *Impersonation and imposture. Murder. Outlaws. Ranchers. United States. Marshals. Chases. Hostages. Indians of North America. Machine-guns. Nieces. Rescues. Romance. Safes. Saloons. Sheriffs. Stagecoach robberies.*

Note: Modern sources note that scenes in the film were shot in Newhall, CA, and that actors Ed Parker and Yakima Canutt also performed as stuntmen in the production. Canutt "stunted" for Wayne and several of the "outlaws," including George Hayes. Modern sources add Glenn Strange, Tex Palmer and Frank Ball to the cast. Abe Meyer is credited in modern sources as musical director.

DV 8 May 1934, p. 4. Box 14 Jul 1934. FD 3 Jul 1934, p. 8. HR 14 May 1934, p. 11. MPD 5 Jul 1934, p. 22. Var 23 Oct 1934, p. 25.

STARDUST AND SWEET MUSIC see CALENDAR GIRL

STARLIGHT CANYON see DESERT PURSUIT

THE STARS ARE SINGING (Polish Americans)

Paramount Pictures Corp. *Dist* Paramount Pictures Corp. Mar **1953**; Prod: early Jun—mid-Jul 1952 [©Paramount Pictures Corp.; 1 Mar 1953; LP2402]. Sd (Western Electric Recording); col (Technicolor). 8,915 ft. 97 min. PCA cert no. 16079.

Prod Irving Asher. *Dir* Norman Taurog. *Asst dir* Edward Salven. *Scr* Liam O'Brien. *Based on a story by* Paul Hervey Fox. *Dir of photog* Lionel Lindon. *Process photog* Farciot Edouart. *Spec photog eff* Gordon Jennings. *Technicolor color consultant* Monroe W. Burbank. *Art dir* Hal Pereira and Henry Bumstead. *Ed* Arthur Schmidt. *Set dec* Sam Comer and Ray Moyer. *Cost* Edith Head. *Mus dir* Victor Young. *Dance numbers staged by* Jack Baker. *Sd rec* Harold Lewis and John Cope. *Makeup supv* Wally Westmore.

Song(s): "Ah, Forsè lui che l'anima," from the opera *La Traviata*, music by Guiseppe Verdi, libretto by Francesco Maria Piave; "My Kind O' Day," "Haven't Got a Worry," "I Do! I Do! I Do!" "Woof," "Lovely Weather for Ducks," and "My Heart is Home," music and lyrics by Jay Livingston and Ray Evans; "Because," music by Guy D'Hardelot, lyrics by Edward Teschemacher.

Cast: Anna Maria Alberghetti (*"Katri"* [*Walenska*]), Rosemary Clooney (*"Terry"* [*Brennan*]), Lauritz Melchior [(*Jan Poldi*)], Bob Williams [(*Homer Tirdell*)], Tom Morton [(*Buddy Fraser*)], Fred Clark [(*McDougall*)], John Archer [(*Dave Parish*)], Mikhail Rasumny [(*Ladowski*)], Lloyd Corrigan [(*Miller*)], Don Wilson [(*Himself*)], Otto Waldis [(*Capt. Goslak*)], Henry Guttman [(*Mate*)], Paul E. Burns [(*Henryk, the messboy*)], Freeman Lusk [(*Conway*)], and Red Dust [a dog], [Danny Arnold (*Zaleski*)], [Joe Ploski (*Butcher*)], [Frank Ferguson (*Doorman*)], [Hayden Rorke (*Congressman Nolte*)], [Peter Potter, Gene Norman, Ira Cook (*Disc jockeys*)], [Ross Bagdasarian (*Song promoter*)], [Leonard Bremen (*Truck driver*)], [Hans Schumm (*Secretary to Ladowski*)], [Phillip Milton Tully (*Policeman*)], [Herbert Lytton, Len Hendry (*Immigration officers*)], [Mike Mahoney (*Reporter*)], [Hazel Boyne (*Flower woman*)], [Glen Vernon], [Robert Carson], [Anthony Warde], [Dario Piazza].

Show business, Musical. [*Print viewed*]. As the Polish Communist ship S.S. *Podolski* enters New York Harbor, a fifteen-year-old orphan stowaway, Katri Waleska, jumps into the water and swims to shore in the hope of finding freedom in America. With little more than a street address in hand, Katri seeks refuge with an old family friend, the opera star Jan Poldi. When Katri arrives, however, she is disappointed to discover that Poldi has become a down-and-out alcoholic and does not remember her. While U.S. Immigration officer McDougall and a malevolent Polish government representative, Lodowski, set out to find Katri, who has a magnificent voice. She befriends Poldi's neighbors, Terry Brennan, a singer; Homer Tirdell, a hapless Texas dog act performer and piano player; and Buddy Fraser, a dancer. Terry, Homer and Buddy eventually discover that the young girl is the sought-after Polish stowaway, but after Terry persuades the others that Katri's talents as a singer will help propel them to fame and open the way to successful stage careers of their own, they decide to risk a jail sentence and hide her. While Terry's doting boyfriend, teacher Dave Parish, tries to find a legal way to keep Katri in the country, Terry takes the girl to the Britt Recording Studios, where she makes several recordings. Terry sends the records to disc jockeys around the country, and then tries to interest television talent show host Don Wilson in having Katri appear on his show under the billing "Mamie Jones." Wilson initially rejects Terry's proposal but later changes his mind when Terry threatens to take Katri to a competing show. Katri is a big hit on the show, but immediately following her performance, she reveals her real name, which causes a furor at the studio. In a short time, however, radio listeners all across the country rally to Katri's defense and show their support for her through picketing and letter-writing. When Katri learns that Poldi has been arrested in connection with harboring an illegal alien, she gives herself up and resigns herself to her inevitable deportation. To her surprise, though, Katri receives a telephone call from President Eisenhower, who, responding to the public outcry, has arranged to let her stay in America. *Missing persons. Opera singers. Polish Americans. Refugees, Political. Singers. United States. Dept. of Immigration. Waifs. Alcoholics. Contests. Dancers. Detectives. Disc jockeys. Dogs. Dwight David Eisenhower. New York City. Publicity stunts. Radio programs. Self-*sacrifice. Stowaways. Talent agents. Tap dancing. Teachers. Washington (D.C.).*

Note: The working title for this film was *Reach for the Stars*. Only Anna Maria Alberghetti and Rosemary Clooney are listed in the end credits. The screen credit for Jay Livingston and Ray Evans reads "New songs by." The picture marked popular singer Rosemary Clooney's motion picture debut. Ross Bagdasarian, who portrayed a song promoter in the film, created the popular "Alvin and the Chipmunks" records. According to *Paramount News*, some scenes were filmed on location in New York City, on Broadway, in Greenwich Village and at the Washington Produce Market.

Box 25 Jan 1953. *DV* 27 Jan 1953, p. 3. *Exh* 28 Jan 1953, p. 3455. *FD* 27 Jan 1953, p. 6. *Har* 31 Jan 1953, pp. 18-19. *HR* 29 May 1952, p. 13. *HR* 17 Jul 1952, p. 8. *HR* 27 Jan 1953, p. 3. *MPHPD* 31 Jan 1953, p. 1701. *NYT* 12 Mar 1953, p. 24. *Var* 28 Jan 1953, p. 6.

STARS IN MY CROWN (African Americans)

Metro-Goldwyn-Mayer Corp.; controlled by Loew's Inc. *Dist* Loew's Inc. 11 May **1950**; Prod: 10 May—late Jun 1949; Addl scenes mid-Nov 1949 [©Loew's Inc.; 18 Jan 1950; LP2882]. Sd (Western Electric Sound System); b&w. 9 reels, 8,014 ft. 89 or 91 min. Passed by the National Board of Review. PCA cert no. 14046.

Prod William H. Wright. *Dir* Jacques Tourneur. [*Asst dir* Arvid Griffin and Al Jennings]. *Scr* Margaret Fitts. *Adpt* Joe David Brown. *Dir of photog* Charles Schoenbaum. *Spec eff* Warren Newcombe. *Art dir* Cedric Gibbons and Eddie Imazu. *Film ed* Gene Ruggiero. *Set dec* Edwin B. Willis. *Assoc* Alfred E. Spencer. *Cost* Walter Plunkett. *Mus score* Adolph Deutsch. *Vocal arr* Robert Tucker. *Rec supv* Douglas Shearer. *Hair styles des by* Sydney Guilaroff. *Makeup created by* Jack Dawn. [*Unit mgr* Serge Petschnikoff].

Song(s): "Will There Be Any Stars?" "Shall We Gather at the River?" "Beulah Land" and "Nut Brown Maiden," traditionals.

Source: Based on the novel *Stars in My Crown* by Joe David Brown (New York, 1947).

Cast: Joel McCrea (*Josiah Doziah Gray*), Ellen Drew (*Harriet Gray*), Dean Stockwell (*John Kenyon*), Alan Hale (*Jed Isbell*), Lewis Stone (*Dr. Daniel Kalbert Harris, Sr.*), James Mitchell (*Dr. Daniel Kalbert Harris, Jr.*), Amanda Blake (*Faith Radmore Samuels*), Juano Hernandez (*Uncle Famous Prill*), Charles Kemper (*Prof. Sam Houston Jones*), Connie Gilchrist (*Sarah Isbell*), Ed Begley (*Lon Backett*), Jack Lambert (*Perry Lokey*), Arthur Hunnicutt (*Chloroform Wiggins*), Marshall Thompson (*Narrator*), [Norman Ollestad, Jr. (*Chase Isbell*)], [Ben Watson (*Gene Caldwell*)], [Adeline de Walt Reynolds (*Granny Gailbraith*)], [Polly Bailey (*Mrs. Belsher*)], [Jim Arness (*Rufe Isbell*)], [Bill Clauson (*Cade Isbell*)], [Ralph Hodges (*Tom Isbell*)], [Charles Courtney (*Jed Isbell*)], [Jimmy Moss (*Bobby Sam Carroll*)], [Jessie Grayson (*Bessie*)], [Wilson Wood (*Thad Carroll*)], [Connie Van, Helen Eby-Rock, Margaret Bert, Patsy O'Byrne, Carl Petti, Frank Pharr, Howard Mitchell, Buddy Roosevelt, Fred Datig, Jr., Robert Cherry, Baron Lichter, Tex Terry (*Townspeople*)], [Snub Pollard (*Fat bartender*)], [Rhea Mitchell (*Mrs. Backett*)], [Blaine Metz (*Boy*)], [Jessie Arnold (*Annie's voice*)], [Edmund Glover (*Clyde Chapman*)], [Patricia Miller (*Mrs. Chapman*)], [Victor Kilian (*Ned*)], [Philo McCullough], [Jim Pierce], [Eula Guy], [Al Kunde], [Alice Richey], [Matilda Caldwell], [Helen Brown].

Historical, Religious, Drama, with songs. [*Print viewed*]. In 1865, Parson Josiah Doziah Gray arrives in the small Southern town of Walsburg and begins preaching to the townspeople. The town has become so dangerous over the years that Josiah gives his first sermon at the local saloon while holding the patrons at gun point. Josiah leads the effort to build the town's first church, and soon falls in love with and marries Harriet, the church organist. Josiah also befriends Uncle Famous Prill, a black man with whom he often goes fishing. Famous owns mica-rich property, which the nefarious general store owner Lon Backett is trying to wrest from him. Time passes, and the Grays adopt John Kenyon, Josiah's nephew, who has been orphaned. Nearly a decade after his arrival in Walsburg, Josiah learns that Daniel Kalbert Harris, Jr., a recent medical school graduate and the son of one of Josiah's friends, is planning to leave Walsburg because the townspeople are hesitant to accept a young doctor with modern schooling as their physician. The doctor rejects Josiah's piety, and while looking for work outside the town, falls in love with Faith Radmore Samuels, a Walsburg schoolteacher. Daniel tries to persuade Faith to move away with him, but just as they are about to leave, an epidemic of typhoid breaks out and John falls ill. Daniel stays to care for the ill, but he soon comes to suspect that Josiah is unwittingly spreading the disease at his sermons. Hoping to prevent further

infections, Josiah consents to the doctor's suggestion that he go into a self-imposed quarantine. When Faith contracts typhoid and is given a poor prognosis by Daniel, Josiah stuns the doctor and others by saving her life through prayer. Humbled by the experience, Daniel apologizes to Josiah for not believing in the healing power of prayer, and the two make amends. Later, Daniel again demonstrates the power of divine guidance when, through prayer, he single-handedly disperses an angry mob seeking to take away Famous' land. *Faith. Parsons. Physicians. Typhoid fever. United States–South.* African Americans. Bible. Children. Churches. Death and dying. Fathers and sons. Fishing. Healers. Hymns. Lynching. Medicine shows. Mines. Mobs. Organists. Orphans. Prayer. Quarantine. Religion. Romance. Saloons. Schoolteachers. Wards and guardians. Wills.

Note: Although Lionel Barrymore is listed in the *CBCS* as the narrator, the film was actually narrated by Marshall Thompson. According to a Feb 1948 *LAT* news item, Robert Taylor was originally set to star in the film. A Mar 1948 *HR* news item noted that William Wright was set to direct the picture, and that Van Heflin was being considered for the male lead. The film received a number of awards for exellence by many organizations, including an official citation of merit by the National Conference of Christians and Jews, and a special plaque proclaiming *Stars in My Crown* as the "Best Picture of the Year" by the editor of the *Christian Herald* magazine.

Box 4 Mar 1950. *DV* 16 Nov 1949, p. 6. *DV* 1 Mar 1950, p. 3. *FD* 6 Mar 1950, p. 6. *HR* 17 Mar 1948, p. 1. *HR* 29 Apr 1949, p. 11. *HR* 16 May 1949, p. 10. *HR* 3 Jun 1949, p. 10. *HR* 10 Jun 1949, p. 11. *HR* 17 Jun 1949, p. 16. *HR* 1 Mar 1950, p. 3. *LAT* 6 Feb 1948. *LAT* 15 Jan 1951. *MPHPD* 4 Mar 1950, p. 213. *NYT* 22 Dec 1950, p. 19. *Var* 1 Mar 1950, p. 6. *Var* 21 Aug 1950.

STARS IN MY POCKET see TONIGHT WE SING

STARS ON PARADE (African Americans)

All American News, Inc. *Dist* State Rights. **1946.** Sd; b&w. 3,900 ft. 43 min.

Prod E. M. Glucksman. *Dir* Joseph Seiden. *Orig story* Madeline Woods. *Scr* Vincent Valentini. *Photog* Bergi Contner. *Film ed* H. Seiden. *Sets* Onam Bobrink. *Makeup* Dr. Liszt.

Music: "Eddie's Blues," composer undetermined.

Song(s): "So Long," music and lyrics by Vincent Valentini; "Talk to Me," music by Bill Bird and Bob Howard, lyrics by Martin Hickey; "I've Got the Blues So Bad" ("Dead Man Blues"), music and lyrics by Shifte Henri, arrangement by Phil Moore; "The Animal Fair," music and lyrics by Frederick Johnson, Harry La Forrest and Harley Russo, arrangement by Phil Moore; " 'Taint Yours," music by Una Mae Carlisle, lyrics by Barney Young; "Oh My Deedle Dee Dum Dum Dee" and "Teasin' Me," composers undetermined.

Cast: Milton Wood (*Johnny Bennett*), Jane Cooley (*Jane Bennett*), Francine Everett (*Patti Lyon*), Bob Howard (*Station superintendent*), Duke Williams (*Don De Haven*), Clarice Graham (*Lucille Nestor*), Ray Greene (*Ira Lyon*), Lou Swarz (*Operatic star*), Jimmy Willis (*Sound engineer*), Dan Michaels (*Tragedian*), Radio Stars: Una Mae Carlisle, Bob Howard, Eddie South, Phil Moore, and The Phil Moore Four.

African American, Musical. [*Print viewed*]. Johnny Bennett has gone to war and left his sister Jane in charge of their radio station. Ira Lyon of the Glow-Tan cosmetic company is unhappy with his program and cancels it. When Johnny returns from duty and meets his sweetheart Patti Lyon, Ira's daughter, they both manage to persuade her father to attend an audition of new talent with a view to starting his program again. Meanwhile, famous radio stars Lucille Nestor and Don De Haven are stranded outside Johnny's studio when their car runs out of gas. After Lucille flirts with Johnny and Don does the same with Jane, they decide to stay on and help to create the new radio show, which Lyon has agreed to sponsor on a trial basis. However, Patti is very upset by Lucille's interest in Johnny. When Johnny finally tells Lucille that he is engaged to Patti, Lucille leaves. After Johnny hears a recording Patti has made, he makes her the star of the show, while Don convinces some major radio stars from New York to appear on the program. The broadcast begins with a song from Patti, after which she and Johnny reconcile. The show continues with appearances by swing violinist Eddie South, singer/pianists Bob Howard and Una Mae Carlisle, and numbers by the Phil Moore Four. Lyon and his partners are pleased with the show and agree to sponsor a series of broadcasts. Jane and Don have become romantically involved. *African Americans. Radio performers. Radio sponsors. Radio stations. Swing music. Veterans.* Auditions. Brothers and sisters. Fathers and daughters. Jazz music. Pianists. Romance. Singers. Violinists.

Note: Onscreen credits note that the film was "produced at the All American

Studios, Fort Lee, NJ." The film carries a 1946 copyright statement, but it was not registered for copyright. It is probable that some of the musical performances in this film were reused in *The Joint is Jumpin'* (see entry above), which was also produced by E. M. Glucksman. Although some modern sources include the Benny Carter Choir and the King Cole Trio in this film, they were not in the cast, but did appear in a 1944 Lew Landers-directed Columbia picture of the same name.

STATZIONE TERMINI see INDISCRETION OF AN AMERICAN WIFE

THE STEEL HELMET (Japanese Americans)

Deputy Corp. Productions. *Dist* Lippert Productions, Inc. 2 Feb **1951**; Los Angeles premiere: 11 Jan 1951; Prod: mid-Oct—late Oct 1950 [©Deputy Corp.; 15 Feb 1951; LP783]. Sd; b&w. 9 reels, 7,545 ft. 84 min. PCA cert no. 14901.

Pres ROBERT L. LIPPERT. *Assoc prod* William Berke. *Prod* Samuel Fuller. *Dir* Samuel Fuller. *Asst dir* John Francis Murphy. *Wrt* Samuel Fuller. *Dir of photog* Ernest Miller. *Spec eff* Ben Southland. *Optical eff* Ray Mercer. *Art dir* Theobold Holsopple. *Film ed* Philip Cahn. *Set dec* Clarence Steenson. *Ward* Alfred Berke. *Mus comp and cond by* Paul Dunlap. *Sd eng* William Lynch. *Makeup* George Bruce. *Dial coach* Stanley Price.

Cast: Robert Hutton [(*Private Bronte*)], Steve Brodie [(*Lieutenant Driscoll*)], James Edwards [(*Corporal Thompson*)], Richard Loo [(*Sergeant Tankaka*)], Sid Melton [(*G. I.*)], Richard Monahan [(*Private Baldy*)], William Chun [(*Short Round*)], Harold Fong [(*The Red*)], Neyle Morrow [(*G. I.*)], and introducing Gene Evans ([*Sergeant*] *Zack*), [Lynn Stallmaster (*Second Lieutenant*)].

War, Drama. [*Print viewed*]. Sergeant Zack, a hard-bittten U.S. Army Infantryman battling Communist North Koreans in the Korean War, is the sole survivor of an enemy attack on his regiment. A bullet hole in Zack's helmet serves as a grim reminder that he narrowly escaped death. When the sergeant regains consciousness, he finds a young Korean boy with an M-1 rifle surveying the scene of the massacre. The boy, an orphan from South Korea, whom Zack names "Short Round," wants to be Zack's friend and insists on scouting for him on his search for the enemy lines. Zack is reluctant to let the boy travel with him, but he consents to the arrangement until he can deliver Short Round to safety. On their dangerous journey through the war-torn territory, Zack and Short Round come under attack from two Communist guerrilla soldiers disguised as women praying at a religious site. After killing the two guerrillas, Zack and his charge encounter Corporal Thompson, a black medic who is also the sole survivor of a North Korean attack on his platoon. Thompson joins Zack and Short Round and the three continue their search for the front lines. They eventually encounter an American patrol regiment under the command of Lieutenant Driscoll, whom Sergeant Zack knows and dislikes. As Driscoll is in need of an experienced soldier to help his patrol set up an observation post at the front, he offers to put aside his differences with Zack and asks him to join his regiment. Zack initially refuses to join the patrol but changes his mind following a sniper attack by Communist guerrillas. Zack continues, however, to hold his opinion that the men in Driscoll's unit are mere amateurs, especially Private Baldy, who carries a music box with him, and Private Bronte, a conscientious objector in World War II. Soon after Driscoll's unit and Sergeant Zack's companions set up their observation post at an apparently deserted Buddhist temple, they come under a surprise guerrilla attack. In the ensuing battle, a Communist officer from Manchuria is taken prisoner by Driscoll, who intends to deliver his prized capture to his base. During his captivity at the observation post, the Manchurian officer tells Driscoll's Japanese-American sergeant, Sergeant Tanaka, that he should be ashamed of his allegiance to a country that interned his people during World War II. Sergeant Tanaka ignores the prisoner's words, prompting the prisoner to call him a "dirty Jap rat." While the Driscoll's unit prepares to clear out of the observation post and return to camp, they are attacked by snipers and Short Round is killed. Motivated by a desire to avenge the boy's death, Sergeant Zack kills the Manchurian officer in cold blood. The situation looks bad for the Americans, as a large Communist force is making its way to the temple, but they are saved by the arrival of a U.S. Infantry platoon. In the ensuing battle, however, Driscoll is killed and Sergeant Zack is injured. Following the defeat of the Communists in the battle, the Infantry division escorts Sergeant Zack, Corporal Thompson and the remaining men in Driscoll's unit back to camp. *African Americans.*

Japanese Americans. Korean War, 1950-1953. Koreans. Officers (Military). Soldiers. United States. Army. Ambushes. Baldness. Battles. Buddhism. Children. Communists. Death and dying. Gunshot wounds. Massacres. Murder. Orphans. Prisoners of war. Temples.

Note: The following written, onscreen dedication appears before the credits: "This story is dedicated to the United States Infantry." Samuel Fuller's onscreen credit reads: "Written, produced and directed by Samuel Fuller." The film ends with the written statement, "there is no end to this story." This was the first American feature-length film about the Korean War, which began in late 1950.

According to material contained in the MPAA/PCA Collection at the AMPAS Library, in Oct 1950, the Breen Office raised a number of objections, from the standpoint of the Production Code, to certain details in the script. The criticisms ranged from the inclusion of offensive expressions, such as "gook," which appeared in the final film, to the insensitive portrayal of Buddhism and the disregard for the sanctity of the Buddhist temple. In this matter, the Breen Office urged producer Robert L. Lippert to confine the violent scene in the temple to an ante-chamber so as not to show the wanton destruction of Buddhist religious icons. Notes in the MPAA/PCA file also indicate that the Breen Office informed Lippert that it did not approve of the story's unpunished murder of the North Korean prisoner of war, as it was a direct violation of the Geneva Convention code. In response to the Breen Office complaints, associate producer William Berke assured them that the only destruction to the temple would be done by enemy fire, and that "Zack" would be punished more severely for murdering the North Korean prison of war. While the U.S. Department of Defense refused to grant the production its offical approval, it did furnish the production with some stock military footage of artillery fighting and tank manaeuvers. A Feb 1951 *DV* news item notes that although the Pentagon raised objections to the film's unfair depiction of American officers, the film was booked, uncensored, for the entire circuit of Army and Air Force camps in the United States. An Oct 1951 *Var* news item noted that the exhibition of the film in Iran had been marked by Communist demonstrations, which resulted in the barring of the film there.

According to modern sources, the film was shot in only ten days, including a day and a half of exterior scenes in Griffith Park in Southern California. Modern sources also note that the unexpected success of the film led to a contract for Fuller with Twentieth Century-Fox.

AmCin Feb 1951, pg. 78. *Box* 13 Jan 1951. *DV* 28 Dec 1950, p. 3. *DV* 10 Jan 1951. *DV* 14 Feb 1951. *FD* 15 Jan 1951, p. 6. *HR* 20 Oct 1950, p. 14. *HR* 27 Oct 1950, p. 14. *HR* 28 Dec 1950, p. 3. *HCN* 17 Jan 1951. *MPHPD* 6 Jan 1951, p. 653. *NYT* 25 Jan 1951, p. 21. *Var* 3 Jan 1951, p. 67. *Var* 10 Oct 1951.

THE STING OF THE SCORPION (Native Americans)

Ashton Dearholt Productions. *Dist* Arrow Film Corp. 1 Oct **1923** [©Arrow Film Corp.; 9 Oct 1923; LP19485]. Si; b&w. 5 reels, 4,629 ft.

Dir Richard Hatton. *Story and scen* Daniel F. Whitcomb.

Cast: Edmund Cobb, Ashton Dearholt, Helene Rosson, Joseph Girard, Arthur Morrison, Harry Dunkinson.

Western. "Young rancher befriends Indian who has found valuable gold mine. Saloon keeper, coveting the mine and rancher's sweetheart, plots against both. Hero is accused of killing Indian but girl aids him to clear himself, and the Indian makes them a present of the mine." (*MPNBG* 6 Apr 1924, p. 65.). *Gold mines. Indians of North America. Ranchers. Saloon keepers.*

Var 17 Jan 1924, p. 27.

STORM OVER AMERICA see CONFESSIONS OF A NAZI SPY

STORM OVER THE ANDES (foreignversion) see ALAS SOBRE EL CHACO

STORM OVER WYOMING (Latino)

RKO Radio Pictures, Inc. *Dist* RKO Radio Pictures, Inc. 22 Apr **1950**; Prod: 20 Jul—early Aug 1949 [©RKO Radio Pictures, Inc.; 31 Dec 1949; LP2814]. Sd (RCA Sound System); b&w. 5,436 ft. 60 min. PCA cert no. 14034.

Prod Herman Schlom. *Dir* Lesley Selander. [*Asst dir* John Pommer]. *Wrt* Ed Earl Repp. *Dir of photog* J. Roy Hunt. [*Cam op* Richard DuValle]. [*Gaffer* Orville Beckett]. [*Stills* Ollie Sigurdson]. *Art dir* Albert S. D'Agostino and Feild Gray. *Film ed* Robert Swink. *Set dec* Darrell Silvera and Jack Mills. *Mus dir* C. Bakaleinikoff. *Mus* Paul Sawtell. *Sd* John Cass and Clem Portman. [*Makeup* Mel Berns]. [*Hair stylist* Larry Germain]. [*Scr supv* Charles Morton]. [*Grip* Frank Williams].

Song(s): "While Strolling Through the Park One Day," words and music by Ed Haley and Robert A. Keiser.

Cast: TIM HOLT [(*Dave Saunders*)], Noreen Nash [(*Chris Marvin*)], Richard Powers [(*Tug Caldwell*)], Betty Underwood [(*Ruby*)], Bill Kennedy [(*Jess Rawlins*)], Kenneth MacDonald [(*Dawson*)], Holly Bane [(*Scotty*)], Leo McMahon [(*Zeke*)], Richard Keane [sic] [(*Watson*)], Don Haggerty [(*Marshal*)], and Richard

Martin (*Chito Rafferty*), [Griff Barnett (*Telegraph operator*)].

Western. [*Print viewed*]. While riding across Wyoming sheep grazing land, out-of-work cowhands Dave Saunders and Chito Rafferty see a group of sheepherders on horseback chasing a cowboy. Investigating, Dave comes across the sheepherders, led by Jess Rawlins, the foreman of the Big M sheep ranch, as they are about to lynch the man, Tug Caldwell, for rustling. Taking the sheepherders by surprise, Dave prevents the lynching and flees with Tug and Chito to the nearest town. There, in a "cowboys only" saloon, a grateful Tug introduces Dave and Chito to his boss, Dawson, while Chito is reunited with saloon singer Ruby, one of his many sweethearts. With guns drawn, Rawlins and his men then burst into the saloon and disarm all of the cowboys. Accusing Dawson of theft and duplicity, Rawlins is about to fire on him when Ruby slips Dave a pistol and he shoots the gun out of Rawlins' hand. After the cowboys chase off the sheepmen, Dawson hires Dave and Chito as ranch hands. Later, in the town's telegraph office, Chito discovers that Rawlins has received a message from Chris Marvin, the absentee owner of the Big M, who is on her way to Wyoming. Confident that he can clear up matters with Chris, Dawson sends Chito and Dave to meet her stagecoach. On the way, however, the cowboys notice Scotty, one of Rawlins' men, driving sheep onto Dawson's land. Realizing that Scotty is trying to frame Dawson as a rustler, Dave and Chito tie him to a tree, then drive the sheep back toward the Big M. Rawlins, meanwhile, intercepts the stage outside of town and informs Chris of Dawson's "duplicity." As Chris and Rawlins ride to the Big M, they see Dave and Chito herding their sheep. Rawlins and his men pursue Dave and Chito, who ride to retrieve Scotty, whom they believe will prove their innocence to Chris. Rawlins stumbles upon Scotty before the cowboys do, however, and shoots him in cold blood, then claims that Dave and Chito did the deed. Although Rawlins tries to have the cowboys lynched, Chris insists that they receive a fair trial and sends for the marshal. After Chris imprisons Dave and Chito in her bunkhouse, Ruby hides a gun in Chito's guitar, then gives him the instrument with Chris's permission. Chito and Dave escape and, with Dawson, head for the local undertaker, where they hope to obtain proof that the bullet that killed Scotty did not come from their guns. The undertaker reveals that the fatal bullet came from a rifle, a type of gun that neither Dave nor Chito own, but as the undertaker is assuring the cowboys that he will testify on their behalf, Rawlins shoots him through an open window and flees. With no witnesses, Dave and Chito decide to confront Rawlins at the Big M. Before they reach the ranch, however, they meet up with Chris, who upon hearing about the undertaker, agrees to question her foreman herself. Chris, Dave and Chito surprise Rawlins as he is about to abscond with Chris's money, but while Chito is holding him prisoner, Rawlins manages to escape once again. Dave, meanwhile, demonstrates to Chris that Rawlins' rifle fired the bullet that killed Scotty. Finally convinced of the cowboy's innocence, Chris leads them to a place near the Colorado border where she had earlier discovered some mysterious sheep hoof marks. Chito then remembers that Rawlins had sent a telegram to a man in Colorado, and Chris deduces that her foreman has been herding her sheep across the Colorado border and selling them. At the border, Chito, Dave, Dawson and Chris engage in a gunfight with Rawlins and his men. After the sheepmen surrender, Dave knocks Rawlins unconscious with one punch. With peace restored, Ruby then proposes to Chito, who flees in a panic from his would-be bride. *Cowboys. Frame-ups. Ranchers. Range wars. Rustlers. Sheepherders. Chases. Escapes. Fights. Lynching. Mexican Americans. Murder. Ranch foremen. Saloons. Singers. Telegrams. Undertakers and undertaking.*

Note: The working title of this film was *Range War*. Actor Richard Kean's surname is misspelled "Keane" in the onscreen credits. *HR* production charts and news items add Glen McCarthy, Carl Andre, Art Felix, Herman Nowlin, Bob Burrows, Sun High Tower and Edward Cassidy to the cast, but their participation in the final film has not been confirmed. According to a *HR* news item, some scenes in the picture were shot in Bridgeport in central California.

Box 18 Feb 1950. *FD* 6 Feb 1950, p. 7. *HR* 20 Jul 1949, p. 4. *HR* 22 Jul 1949, p. 13. *HR* 1 Aug 1949, p. 6. *HR* 1 Feb 1950, p. 4. *MPHPD* 11 Feb 1950, p. 186. *Var* 16 Aug 1950, p. 11.

STORMY WEATHER (African Americans)

Twentieth Century-Fox Film Corp. *Dist* Twentieth Century-Fox Film Corp. 16 Jul **1943**; Prod: 21 Jan—late Feb 1943 [©Twentieth Century-Fox Film Corp.; 16 Jul 1943; LP12206]. Sd (Western Electric Recording); Sepiatone. 9 reels, 6,980 ft. 78 min. PCA cert no. 9101.

Prod William Le Baron and Irving Mills. *Dir* Andrew Stone. *Scr* Frederick Jackson and Ted Koehler. *Adpt* H. S. Kraft. *From an orig story by* Jerry Horwin and Seymour B. Robinson. *Dir of photog* Leon Shamroy. *Spec photog eff* Fred Sersen. *Art dir* James Basevi and Joseph C. Wright. *Film ed* James B. Clark. *Set dec* Thomas Little and Fred J. Rode. *Cost des* Helen Rose. *Supv* Fanchon. *Mus dir* Emil Newman. *Dances staged by* Clarence Robinson. *Sd* Alfred Bruzlin and Roger Heman. *Makeup artist* Guy Pearce. [*Stand-in for Lena Horne* Maggie Hathaway].

Music: "The Darktown Strutters' Ball," music by Shelton Brooks; "Margie," music by Con Conrad and J. Russel Robinson; "Ja-Da," music by Bob Carleton; "At a Georgia Camp Meeting," music by Kerry Mills; "De Camptown Races," music by Stephen Collins Foster.

Song(s): "There's No Two Ways About Love," words by Ted Koehler, music by James P. Johnson and Irving Mills; "Linda Brown," words and music by Alvis Cowens; "That Ain't Right," words and music by Nat King Cole and Irving Mills; "Ain't Misbehavin'," words by Andy Razaf, music by Thomas (Fats) Waller and Harry Brooks; "Diga Diga Doo," words by Dorothy Fields, music by Jimmy McHugh; "I Lost My Sugar in Salt Lake City," words and music by Leon René and Johnny Lange; "I Can't Give You Anything But Love," words by Dorothy Fields, music by Jimmy McHugh, special lyrics by Eddie Jones; "Geechy Joe," words and music by Cab Calloway, Jack Palmer and Andy Gibson; "Stormy Weather," words by Ted Koehler, music by Harold Arlen; "My, My, Ain't That Somethin'," words and music by Harry Tobias and Pinky Tomlin; "The Jumpin' Jive (Jim Jam Jump)," words and music by Cab Calloway, Frank Froeba and Jack Palmer; "African Dance," words by Langston Hughes, music by Clarence Muse and Connie Bemis.

Cast: Lena Horne [(*Selina Rogers*)], Bill Robinson [(*Bill "Corky" Williamson*)], Cab Calloway and His Band, Katherine Dunham and Her Troupe, Fats Waller [(*Himself*)], Nicholas Brothers [(*Themselves*)], Ada Brown [(*Ada Brown*)], Dooley Wilson [(*Gabe Tucker*)], The Tramp Band [*Themselves*], [Babe Wallace (*Chick Bailey*)], [Ernest Whitman (*Jim Europe*)], [Zutty Singleton (*Zutty*)], [Mae E. Johnson (*Mae*)], [Flournoy E. Miller (*Miller*)], [Johnny Lee (*Lyles*)], [Robert Felder (*Cab Calloway, Jr.*)], [Nicodemus Stewart (*Jake, chauffeur*)], [William Sneed (*Bill*)], [Fred Tomago Williams, Wilhelmina Gray (*Dancers*)], [The Shadracks: Johnny Horace, and Ned Stanfield], [Ruby Golden (*Fat girl*)], [Florence O'Brien (*Waitress*)], [Tomiwitta Moore (*Flower girl*)], [Lena Torrence, Judy Carol, Jeni LeGon (*Chorus girls*)], [Stymie Beard (*Call boy*)], [Coleman Hawkins (*Saxophone player in Jim Europe's 15th New York Regiment Band*)], [Taps Miller (*Horn player in Jim Europe's 15th New York Regiment Band*)].

African American, Musical. [*Print viewed*]. On a pleasant day in Hollywood, California, Bill "Corky" Williamson, a semi-retired tap dancer, is teaching his craft to a group of neighborhood children when the mailman delivers a special edition of "Theatre World." The magazine is celebrating "the magnificent contribution of the colored race to the entertainment of the world during the past twenty-five years" and features Bill on the cover. As Bill reads the various dedications from his old friends, he reminisces about the early days of his career. One such dedication from Noble Sissle inspires Bill to remember the hero's welcome he and fellow members of Jim Europe's 15th New York Regiment band received when they returned from France after World War I: Bill and his best friend Gabe live it up in high style in New York City, and Gabe pretends to be a rich talent manager in order to impress his scatterbrained girl friend. At a hall set up as a nightclub for the returning servicemen, Bill sees a beautiful woman and discovers to his amazement that she is Selina Rogers, the sister of a close friend who died in the war. After Selina and Bill dance together, Selina is introduced as the evening's star and joins Jim Europe's band in a song. Selina and Bill are attracted to each other, but her manager, Chick Bailey, gets jealous and intervenes. Selina tries to convince Bill to stay in New York and pursue a dancing career, but Bill says he has a job waiting for him in Memphis and plans to stay there until he can make something of himself. In Memphis, Bill finds work on a riverboat, but when he dances with a group of talented minstrels on board, they encourage him to go down to Beale Street to secure a job as a dancer. One night at Ada Brown's Beale Street café, where Bill has been hired as a waiter, Bailey and Selina stop by looking for new talent to star in Bailey's new show. After Bailey offers roles to Ada, a singer, Fats, a piano player and the café's band, Selina

begs him to take Bill, too. Bailey reluctantly agrees and hires Bill as an extra tom-tom player in a dance number. One evening, Bill, frustrated with his assigned role, performs a complex stair-step dance on the drums while Bailey sings. The crowd goes wild, and it takes several seconds before Bailey realizes that they are applauding Bill. When he discovers Bill's ruse, he kicks him out of the theater, but Bill punches Bailey and then has the last word when Selina agrees to go with him for a sandwich in defiance of Bailey. Back in the present, Bill is pleased to read a dedication from former enemy Bailey, who pompously has written that he was the first to recognize Bill's talent. Bill then wonders about his old friend Gabe: As Bill is about to put on his own show, he runs into Gabe, who is working as a bootblack in Harlem. Bill's show is in danger of failing because the chorus girls, who have not been paid, are threatening to quit before the first performance. To help Bill, Gabe shows up at the theater pretending to be a rich impressario and tricks the group into performing. When one of the performers, however, recognizes Gabe as the man who has shined his shoes many times, the group once again turns on him and Bill. Fortunately, Gabe's hired driver has just won money at the races. He agrees to pay the performers' salaries, and the show goes on. Later, Bill, who has earlier married Selina, asks her to move to a little house with him and raise children, but Selina tells him that she must continue to work. She goes to Paris, where she becomes a renowned star. In the present, as Bill is relaxing on his front porch with the neighborhood children, Cab Calloway stops by to pick him up for a big party, which will honor the men who are going overseas to fight in World War II. At the show, Bill reunites with a jive-talking Gabe, who is now working for Cab, and sees Selina perform. Later, she tells him that she wants to return to him and start a family. After several performances by Cab, Gabe and others, Bill and Selina appear together and all ends on a happy note. *African Americans. Dancers. Romance. Show business. Singers. Benefit performances. Blues music. Chorus girls. Dismissal (Employment). Jealousy. Memphis (TN). New York City–Harlem. Reunions. Ruses. Soldiers. Veterans. World War I. World War II.*

Note: The working title of this film was *Thanks, Pal.* According to contemporary sources, the film was loosely based on Bill "Bojangles" Robinson's life and was advertised as a "cavalcade of Negro entertainment." Robinson, who was born in 1878, began dancing professionally when he was eight and became a vaudeville and musical stage star before appearing in his first film, *Dixiana*, in 1930. He was the originator of the stair tap routine and enjoyed a reputation as one of the world's leading tap dancers. *Stormy Weather* marked Robinson's return to the screen after a five-year absence, and was his last film. He died in 1949.

Stormy Weather was the second all-black cast film made by a major studio in the 1940's; M-G-M's *Cabin in the Sky* was released just prior to *Stormy Weather* and also starred Lena Horne (see above entry). The famous comedy team of Miller & Lyles was recreated for the film, with Flournoy E. Miller playing himself and Johnny Lee replacing the deceased Aubrey Lyles. According to a 12 Nov 1942 *HR* news item, Louis Armstrong was sought for a role in the picture. Irving Mills, a composer and publisher of Harlem musical artists, who is credited onscreen as producer and William Le Baron's assistant, was hired because of his experience with "negro shows," according to a 24 Sep 1942 *HR* news item. News items in *The California Eagle* include Lucille Battle, Anise Boyer and Cleo Herndon in the cast and note that Nadine Cole, Nat King Cole's wife, dances in the picture. News items also list the following musicians as members of Jim Europe's band: Charles Wellan, Ulysses Banks, Earl Hale, Maxwell Davis, Theodore Shirley, Lawrence Lassiter, Bert Brooks, Leo McCoy Davis, Herman Pickett, Eddie Myart, Rabon Tarrant, Barron Morehead, Happy Johnson, John Haughton, James Johnson, Carl George, Eddie Hutchinson, James Porter and Ted Buckner. The participation of these performers in the final film has not been confirmed, however.

According to memos in the MPAA/PCA Collection at the AMPAS Library, some lyrics in the following songs were deemed unacceptable by the PCA: "That Ain't Right," "Yeah Man! [Linda Brown]," "Diga Diga Doo," "Geechy Joe," "Nobody," "That Man of Mine Is Dynamite," and "Good for Nothin' Joe." The last three songs were not heard in the final film. In "Diga Diga Doo," certain suggestive lyrics were changed, and in "Geechy Joe," the phrase "his jimson blues" was changed to "the lonesome blues." A few seconds of an instrumental, "Moppin' and Boppin'" by Fats Waller, Benny Carter and Ed Kirkeby, are heard at the beginning of the Memphis café sequence.

According to a Feb 1943 editorial in *The California Eagle*, William Grant Still, who was a famous African-American composer, was hired as the film's music supervisor, but resigned "because [his] conscience would not let [him] accept money to help carry on a tradition directly opposed to the welfare of thirteen million people." In the editorial, Still accused the studio of labeling "Negro" music and dancing as cruder and rougher than the quality numbers that he was producing and that his musical arrangements were thus unrealistic. He also stated that one member of the crew declared that " 'Negro bands didn't play that well.' " Still called on the black public to write letters to Twentieth Century-Fox and other major studios pointing out the faults in their representations of black culture and society. Despite Still's protest, *Stormy Weather* was praised by the mainstream press for its music and dancing. *Var*

lauded its "all-colored cast" and the fact that it had not been "permitted to engage in any grotesque or theatrically 'typed' concepts of Negro behaviourism."

The *Var* review also mentioned the "intra-trade concern" over the age difference between the film's romantic leads, Horne and Robinson, who was some forty years her senior, but noted that "the illusion comes off quite well." However, *The California Eagle* reported on 8 Apr 1943 that a "highly indignant" Robinson was set to sue "several publications" for printing the story that *Stormy Weather* would be remade with another, presumably younger, male romantic lead.

According to studio production notes on the film, the film's principal performers broadcast their musical numbers to servicemen overseas using short-wave radio. *Stormy Weather* and *Cabin in the Sky* were released during three of the nation's worst race riots. According to modern sources, the riots, which took place in Harlem, Detroit and Los Angeles (the latter known as the "zoot suit" riots) almost caused Twentieth Century-Fox to pull the film from theaters. Even though half of all first-run theaters refused to book it, the picture was a box office hit, according to an Aug 1943 *HR* news item.

Box 29 May 1943. *California Eagle* 3 Feb 1943, p. 2. *California Eagle* 17 Feb 1943, p. 2. *California Eagle* 3 Mar 1943. *California Eagle* 8 Mar 1943, p. 2. *California Eagle* 8 Apr 1943. DV 27 May 1943, p. 3. FD 28 May 1943, p. 7. HR 12 Nov 1942, p. 6. HR 7 Jan 1943, p. 1. HR 21 Jan 1943, p. 1. HR 9 Aug 1943, p. 1. HR 10 Aug 1943, p. 1. HR 27 May 1943, p. 3. HR 26 Jul 1943, p. 8. MPHPD 6 May 1943, p. 1192. MPHPD 29 May 1943, p. 1337. MPHPD 17 Jul 1943, p. 1432. NYT 22 Jul 1943, p. 15. Var 2 Jun 1943, p. 8. Var 6 Jun 1943.

THE STORY OF A GREAT PEACE *see* **THE BIRTH OF A RACE**

THE STORY OF EDDIE CANTOR *see* **THE EDDIE CANTOR STORY**

THE STORY OF JOLSON *see* **THE JOLSON STORY**

THE STORY OF KNUTE ROCKNE *see* **KNUTE ROCKNE—ALL AMERICAN**

THE STORY OF SEABISCUIT (Irish Americans)

Warner Bros. Pictures, Inc.; A Warner Bros.—First National Picture. *Dist* Warner Bros. Pictures, Inc. 12 Nov 1949; New York opening: 11 Nov 1949; Prod: early Apr—20 May 1949 [©Warner Bros. Pictures, Inc.; 15 May 1950; LP110]. Sd (RCA Sound System); col (Technicolor). 92 or 96 min.

Prod William Jacobs. *Dir* David Butler. [*Dial dir* Arthur Shields]. [*Asst dir* Phil Quinn]. [*2d asst dir* Carter Gibson]. *Wrt* John Taintor Foote. *Dir of photog* Wilfrid M. Cline. [*Cam op* George Nogle]. [*Asst cam* Paul Hill and Harry Marsh]. [*Stills* Mac Julian]. *Spec eff dir* Roy Davidson. *Spec eff* H. F. Koenekamp. *Technicolor col consultant* Mitchell Kovaleski. *Art dir* Douglas Bacon. *Film ed* Irene Morra. *Set dec* Lyle R. Reifsnider. [*Props* Gilbert Kissel]. [*Asst props* Harold Winterbottom]. *Ward* Leah Rhodes, [Clay Brackett, Ted Schultz and Mina Willowbird]. *Orch* Maurice de Packh. *Mus* David Buttolph. *Sd* Oliver S. Garretson. *Makeup artist* Perc Westmore. [*Makeup* Karl Herlinger]. [*Hair* Myrle Stoltz]. *Tech adv* Sonny Greenberg and [Clyde Hudkins]. [*Scr supv* Jean Baker]. [*Gaffer* Frank Flanagan]. [*Best boy* Gilbert Germaine]. [*Grip* Chuck Harris].

Cast: SHIRLEY TEMPLE [(*Margaret O'Hara*)], BARRY FITZGERALD [(*Shawn O'Hara*)], Lon McCallister [(*Ted Knowles*)], Rosemary De Camp [(*Mrs. Charles S. Howard*)], Donald MacBride [(*George Carson*)], Pierre Watkin [(*Charles S. Howard*)], William Forrest [(*Thomas Millford*)], Hal Moore, Joe Kennedy, Clem McCarthy (*Race commentaries*), ["Sugarfoot" Anderson (*Murphy*)], [Emmett Smith (*Porter*)], [Madame Sul-te-wan (*Libby*)], [Howard Washington, Clinton Rosemond, Ernest Wilson, Bobby Johnson, James Simmons, Eugene Jackson, Lawrence LaMarr (*Swipes*)], [Ted Williams (*Auctioneer*)], [Lew Harvey, Forbes Murray, Edward Keane, Herman Cantor (*Buyers*)], [Joe Gilbert, Hershel Dougherty, Walden Boyle, Terry Frost (*Reporters*)], [Majorie Eaton (*Miss Newsome*)], [Ezelle Poule (*Miss Finch*)], [Dee Carroll (*Nurse Talbot*)], [Joe Hernandez, Cal Frederick, John Alvin (*Announcers*)], [Alan Foster, Jack Lomas, Frank Mitchell, Charles Marsh (*Spectators*)], [Gertrude Astor (*Wife*)], [Creighton Hale (*Husband*)], [Don Forbes (*Fred Baker*)], [Ralph Volkie (*Photographer*)], [Cy Malis (*Attendant*)], [Joe Wong (*Wong*)], [Joe Smith, Bert Hanlon (*Trainers*)], [Ray Erlenborn (*Cameraman*)], Gil Warren (*Radio announcer*), [Claudia Barrett (*Girl*)], [William J. Cartledge (*Jockey George Woolf*)], [Charles Lind].

Horse race, Drama. [*Print viewed*]. Upon arriving at Millford Farms in Kentucky, Irish horse trainer Shawn O'Hara and his niece Margaret, who is studying to be a nurse, are greeted by Thomas Millford and his other trainer, George Carson. Millford has hired Shawn because of his reputation for judging the potential of racehorses early in their development. Shawn left Ireland after the death of his nephew, Margaret's brother, during a steeplechase race

made him reluctant to train jumping horses. One night, when Margaret is home from nursing school, Shawn shows her a trick for appraising a horse: He holds out a carrot to a group of yearlings and looks for the first one to claim the reward. This night, as on several previous occasions, the winner is an unprepossessing horse named Seabiscuit. Later, when Shawn, Carson and Millford cull the yearlings, Shawn begs Millford to keep Seabiscuit, but on Carson's advice, Millford turns him down. Meanwhile Millford's jockey, Ted Knowles, flirts with Margaret, but she has determined never to fall in love with a jockey and rebuffs his advances. Ted asks Shawn to intervene on his behalf, and Shawn agrees, provided Ted will buy Seabiscuit. When Ted approaches Millford with an offer, however, Millford suspects that Shawn is behind it and agrees to keep the horse for his stubborn employee. Despite Shawn's faith in Seabiscuit, his initial performance is poor. Shawn tries many tricks to increase the horse's speed, but finally Millford refuses to spend more time on the horse. After Shawn takes ill, Margaret takes him to California. Shawn convinces racehorse owner Charles S. Howard and his wife to buy Seabiscuit from Millford. He also persuades the Howards to buy Ted's contract. Using a new training method, Shawn finally makes Seabiscuit a winner. After Ted is injured in a race at Santa Anita, Shawn arranges for Margaret to be his nurse. Margaret admits that she returns Ted's love and agrees to marry him if he will give up racing. While Ted is recuperating, jockey George Woolf rides Seabiscuit in more winning races. Disaster strikes, however, when the horse develops a career-ending problem in one leg. At the request of Mrs. Howard, Shawn agrees to attempt to cure Seabiscuit, and against all odds, he succeeds. Shawn offers Ted a position as his assistant, and Ted accepts so that he can marry Margaret; however, when George is unavailable to ride a recovered Seabiscuit, Ted takes over. Furious, Margaret breaks her engagement. Ted then tells her that he is willing to leave racing, but that he wants to leave as a winner. Now that she understands, Margaret relents, and Seabiscuit wins the Santa Anita Handicap on 2 March 1940, establishing a new track record. A statue of Seabiscuit is later erected at the track, and Ted leaves racing to marry Margaret and become a trainer. *Horse trainers. Horseracing. Racehorse owners. Racehorses. Seabiscuit (Horse). Accidents. California. Charles S. Howard. Irish. Jockeys. Kentucky. Ted Knowles. Nieces. Nurses. Racetracks. Romance. Statues. Uncles. George Woolf.*

Note: The film's working title was *Always Sweethearts*. The real Seabiscuit won a record-breaking total of $437,730 in his racing career. He was purchased by C. S. Howard for $8,000 in 1934 and won the Santa Anita Handicap in 1940. Portions of the film were shot at Willits, CA, where Howard's farm was located, according to a *HR* news item. The film incorporates black-and-white newsreel footage of actual races, including the $15,000 match between Seabiscuit and War Admiral at Pimlico, as well as color footage of the Santa Anita Handicap.

Box 29 Oct 1949. DV 25 Oct 1949, p. 3. FD 26 Oct 1949, p. 8. HR 28 Mar 1949, p. 7. HR 29 Mar 1949, p. 7. HR 8 Apr 1949, p. 11. HR 29 Apr 1949, p. 13. HR 20 May 1949, p. 4. HR 25 Oct 1949, p. 3. MPHPD 29 Oct 1949, p. 65. NYT 12 Nov 1949, p. 8. Var 2 Nov 1949, p. 11.

STRAIGHT IS THE WAY (Jewish Americans)

Metro-Goldwyn-Mayer Corp.; controlled by Loew's, Inc. *Dist* Metro-Goldwyn-Mayer Corp. 10 Aug 1934; Prod: 15 Jun—9 Jul 1934 [©Metro-Goldwyn-Mayer Corp.; 7 Aug 1934; LP4888]. Sd (Western Electric Sound System); b&w. 6 reels. 59-60 or 65 min. Passed by the National Board of Review. PCA cert no. 108.

Prod Lucien Hubbard. *Dir* Paul Sloane. [*Asst dir* Harry Sharrock]. *Scr* Bernard Schubert. *Photog* Lucien Andriot. *Art dir* Cedric Gibbons. *Art dir assoc* Stanley Rogers and Edwin B. Willis. *Film ed* William S. Gray. *Ward* Dolly Tree. *Mus score* Dr. William Axt. *Rec dir* Douglas Shearer.

Source: Based on the play *Four Walls* by Dana Burnet and George Abbott (New York, 19 Sep 1927).

Cast: Franchot Tone (*Benny [Horowitz]*), May Robson (*Mrs. Horowitz*), Karen Morley (*Bertha*), Gladys George (*Shirley*), Nat Pendleton (*Skippy*), Jack LaRue (*Monk*), C. Henry Gordon ([*Chief*] *Sullivan*), Raymond Hatton (*Mendel*), William Bakewell (*Dr. Wilkes*), [Al Hill (*Body guard*)], [Jack Cheatham, Leonid Kinsky (*Mechanics*)], [Guy Usher (*Father*)], [Claudia Coleman (*Mother*)], [Gloria Fisher (*Girl to cry*)], [Delmar Watson (*Boy to cry*)], [Harry Depp (*Violin teacher*)], [Minerva Urecal, Madame Bonita, Lillian Castle (*Eastside women*)], [John M. Qualen (*Mr. Clapman*)], [Jackie Coombs (*Little boy*)], [Sherry Hall (*Radio man*)], [Isabelle La Mal (*Customer*)], [Grace Hayle (*Mrs. Clapman*)], [Max Davidson (*Old clothes man*)], [Florence Dudley, Jill Dennett, Velma Gresham

(*Molls*)], [Robert Homans, Davison Clark, Frank O'Connor (*Policemen*)], [Ernie Alexander (*Milk wagon driver*)], [Jack Baxley (*Grocery store proprietor*)], [Adrian Rosley (*Greek proprietor*)], [R. Chrysler (*Truck driver*)], [Edith Conrad], [Sunny Boyne].

Crime, Domestic, Drama. [*Print viewed*]. When he returns to his mother and his home in the Jewish section of New York City, Benny Horowitz, who has spent the last five years in prison, vows to remain free and honest. However, soon after his reunion with his mother and Bertha, a young woman with whom he grew up, Benny is approached by Monk, the neighborhood gang leader. Monk, who was responsible for tempting the once-studious Benny into a life of crime, informs Benny that not only is he now the head of a lucrative protection racket, but is the lover of Shirley, Benny's former girl friend. To the relief of Mrs. Horowitz, who suffers from heart disease, Benny scoffs at the suggestion of gang member Skippy that he rejoin the gang and rejects the advances of the still enamored Shirley. When he fails to find a job after weeks of searching, however, Benny grows despondent and confides in Bertha that he is thinking of leaving the city. After Bertha begs Benny to stay, Skippy announces that, through a bit of brute force, he has secured a mechanics job for the ex-convict at a local garage. Though his pay is low, Benny works hard at the garage and earns the respect of its owner, who confides in him one night that Monk's protection racket is driving him to bankruptcy. Determined to help his boss, Benny challenges Monk and his gang and tells them that they will not be receiving any more money from the garage. Stymied by Benny's bold defiance, Monk backs down from his demands and loses the respect of his cohorts. Later that night, Benny, buoyed by his victory over Monk, flirts with Shirley and boasts that, if he wanted, he could have Monk's woman as well as his gang. Benny then throws a matchmaker, who has come with a marriage proposition for Bertha, out of his mother's apartment after he scathingly insinuates that Bertha is in love with an ex-convict. Later, Mrs. Horowitz chides Benny about his bachelorhood and suggests that Bertha would make a good wife for him. Convinced that she deserves a better man than he, however, Benny refuses Bertha's love but fights an urge to reclaim Shirley. Benny is overwhelmed by his conflicting emotions and retreats to his tenement's rooftop. He is soon joined by Shirley, who throws herself at him in hysterical passion. As Shirley is about to force Benny into a kiss, Monk bursts onto the rooftop and threatens Benny with his gun. During the ensuing fight, the gun is fired and tossed, and Monk accidentally falls from the roof to his death. Shirley seizes on the incident and tries to force Benny into returning to her by threatening to tell the police that he murdered Monk. With Bertha's loving support, Benny decides to resist Shirley and confess to the police. However, when the police are unable to find Monk's gun, which would prove Benny's innocence, Shirley's story appears accurate. Before he is arrested, Benny is saved by Skippy, who having located Monk's gun in the back of a milk truck, presents the vindicating evidence to the police. Thus cleared, Benny embraces Bertha and reassures his mother that all is well. *Criminals–Rehabilitation. Gangsters. Jews. Love affairs. Mothers and sons. New York City–East Side. Blackmail. Extortion. Falls from heights. Fights. Firearms. Flirtation. Garages. Heart disease. Matchmakers. Mechanics. Milk trucks. Molls. Neighbors. Police. Rooftops. Tenement-houses.*

Note: The working title of this film was *Four Walls*. In May 1934, M-G-M announced in *HR* that production on the film was to be pushed up three months so that Clark Gable could play the lead. Gable, however, did not start in the production, which began in mid-Jun 1934. Mae Clarke was first assigned to play the part of "Shirley," but left the production to appear in Columbia's *Captain Hates the Sea*, according to a *HR* news item. Also in May 1934, Wells Root was reported as the assigned writer, and Edwin L. Marin as the projected director. Although Marin did not direct any part of the film, it is not known if Root contributed to the script. In addition to Gable and Clarke, Christian Rub and Henry Wadsworth were announced as cast members in *HR* news items, but neither of these actors appeared in the film. In 1928, William Nigh directed John Gilbert and Joan Crawford in *Four Walls*, the first M-G-M version of Dana Burnet and George Abbott's play (see *AFI Catalog of Feature Films, 1921-30*; F2.1942).

DV 20 Jul 1934, p. 3. *FD* 29 Aug 1934, p. 7. *HF* 16 Jun 1934, p. 8. *HR* 28 May 1934, p. 1. *HR* 16 Jun 1934, p. 7. *HR* 18 Jun 1934, p. 2, 3. *HR* 12 Jul 1934, p. 4. *HR* 20 Jul 1934, p. 4. *MPH* 28 Jul 1934, p. 45, 48. *NYT* 29 Aug 1934, p. 13. *Var* 4 Sep 1934, p. 19.

THE STRAIGHT ROAD (Irish Americans)
Famous Players Film Co. *Dist* Paramount Pictures Corp. 12 Nov 1914. Si; b&w. 4 reels.
Pres Daniel Frohman. *Dir* Allan Dwan.

Source: Based on the play *The Straight Road* by Clyde Fitch (New York, 7 Jan 1907).
Cast: Gladys Hanson (*Mary "Moll" O'Hara*), William Russell ("*Bill*" *Hubbell*), Iva Shepard (*Lazy Liz*), Arthur Hoops (*Douglas Aines*), Lorraine Huling (*Ruth Thompson*).
Drama. Mary "Moll" O'Hara, a girl of the slums, loves alcohol and fighting, a condition caused by her upbringing. One day, in "Bill" Hubbell's saloon, a disreputable woman named Liz attacks Moll and the two are arrested. On their way to jail, the women are seen by Ruth Thompson, a wealthy settlement worker, and her fiancé, Douglas Aines. They arrange to have the women brought to the settlement and Moll gives up drinking at the urging of Ruth and Mike Finnerty, a little crippled boy. Moll goes to live with Mrs. Finnerty and Bill, impressed with Moll's change of character, begins a romance with her. Aines makes advances at Moll, however, and when they are interrupted by Ruth, he convinces her that Moll is to blame. Eventually, Moll is able to convince both Ruth and Bill of her innocence by trapping Aines. *Class distinction. Infidelity. Moral reformation. Slums. Drunkenness. Fights. Handicapped. Irish Americans. Saloons. Settlement workers.*
MPW 21 Nov 1914, p. 1089, 1152. *NYDM* 18 Nov 1914, p. 32. *Var* 14 Nov 1914, p. 25.

STRAIGHT TO HEAVEN (African Americans)
Million Dollar Productions, Inc.; Domino Productions, Inc. *Dist* Sack Amusement Enterprises, Inc. **1939**; Brooklyn, New York opening: 12 Dec 1939. Sd (Variray Blue Seal Recording); b&w. 6 reels, 4,733 ft. PCA cert no. 5624.
Pres HARRY M. POPKIN. *Prod* Arthur Leonard. [*Assoc prod* Arthur A. Brooks]. *Dir* Arthur Leonard. *Orig story* Cyrus Wood, Jr. and Buddy Freeman. *Photog* Jay Rescher. *Ed* S.A. Datlowe and Willard DuBrul. *Ward* Doris Ostrow. *Music under supv* of Henry Silvern. *Sd supv* Dean Cole. *Makeup* Richard Willis. *Script boy* Sol Dashew. *Still photog* Frank Seajack.
Song(s): "Straight to Heaven," "You Can Count on Me," "When the Dark Became Dawn" and "Don't Stop," music and lyrics by Joseph Myrow and Bob Maxwell.
Cast: NINA MAE McKINNEY (*Ida Williams*), Jack Carter (*Stanley Jackson*), Percy Verwayne ("*Lucky*" *John Simon*), Jackie Ward (*Jimmy Williams*), [Lionel Monogas (*Joe Williams*)], [Bernice Vincent (*Helen*)], [Pearl Bains (*Millie*)], [The Three Peppers (*Musical specialty*)], [Millie and Bubbles (*Dance specialty*)], [Jimmy Baskette (*1st detective*)], [George Williams (*2nd detective*)], [Teddy Hale (*Meatball*)], [James Fuller (*Waiter*)], [Thomas Moseley (*Coroner*)], [Sherman Dirkson (*Fingerprint expert*)], [Emery Evans (*Officer Smith*)], [Jili Smith (*Police sergeant*)], [Martin and Williams (*Comedy team*)], [Alonzo Tucker (*Ace*)], [Tuffy Hawkins (*Gus*)].
African American, Crime, Domestic, Drama, with songs. [*Print viewed*]. Singer Jimmy Williams' father Joe is a chemist who recently lost his job to George Elliott. Since then, Joe has been investigating the "Adam and Even" brand of canned goods sold in Harlem. Soon after Joe tells his friend, lawyer Stanley Jackson, that racketeers are forcing storekeepers to sell the rotten canned food, he is framed for the murder of George. When the police find cyanide in Joe's laboratory, they believe that it was used to kill George. Stanley tells Joe's wife Ida that she must get a job and fight for Joe's freedom, but when offered a job by "Lucky" John Simon, the head of the racketeers distributing the food, she refuses it. Jimmy, however, decides to take a job from Lucky and goes to the Trocadero, where he performs a song and dedicates it to his mother. When Joe's appeal fails, Stanley offers to quit as his lawyer because the only piece of evidence he has found to prove Joe's innocence, an Apex salt shaker, has led them nowhere. Ida, who knows that Lucky is fond of her, gathers evidence on her own, while Stanley agrees to join Lucky's racketeers as an undercover agent. At the Trocadero, Ida sings a song and then goes to Lucky's office, where she accepts his gift of pearls. Jimmy witnesses the act and, misunderstanding his mother's intentions, commits a minor theft in order to be jailed with his father. Stanley finally breaks the case when he learns that Lucky is a former owner of the Apex Café in St. Louis, and thus connects him with the salt shaker clue and with the murder. The police return Jimmy to the Trocadero, but when Stanley tells Lucky what he knows, Lucky abducts him and Jimmy and takes them to his estate, where he and the gang force Jimmy to pace back and forth without water. The police eventually arrive and rescue them, and Stanley gets the truth out of Lucky, who is exposed in the newspapers. Reunited, the Williamses proudly listen to their son sing a song on the radio. *African Americans.*

Family relationships. Food, Canned. Frame-ups. New York City–Harlem. Racketeers. Singers. Abduction. Chemists. Estates. Lawyers. Nightclubs. Poison. Police. Radio broadcasting. Salt. Undercover operations.

Note: According to a Jun 1939 *HR* news item, this film had a preview showing in New York during the week of 27 Jun 1939. The news item stated that Domino Productions was a new company.

HR 27 Jun 1939. *MPH* 1 Jul 1939, p. 45.

A STRANGE CARAVAN *see* THE FIGHTING KENTUCKIAN

STRANGE VICTORY (African Americans)

Target Films, Inc. *Dist* Target Films, Inc. **1948**; New York opening: week of 25 Sep 1948. Sd; b&w. 72-73 min.

Prod Barnet L. Rosset, Jr. *Dir* Leo Hurwitz. *Scr* Leo Hurwitz. *Narr wrt by* Saul Levitt. *News cam* Peter Glushanok and George Jacobsen. *Film ed* Leo Hurwitz. *Ed asst* Faith Elliott. *Mus score* David Diamond. *Orch cond* Lehman Engel.

Cast: Alfred Drake, Muriel Smith, Gary Merrill (*Narrators*), Virgil Richardson, Cathy McGregor, Sophie Maslow, Jack Henderson, Robert P. Donley.

Compilation, Documentary. [*Not viewed*]. The film discusses post-war religious and racial bias, particularly against Catholics, Jews and African Americans, and maintains that this discrimination makes the recent war-time victories seem hollow. The roots of World War II and Hitler's rise to power are traced. Footage from the war's end is shown, as well as scenes depicting the Nazi concentration camps and other atrocities of war. Because of Jim Crow attitudes, the film states, African Americans will find little or no place in medicine, aviation, architecture, engineering or big business. *African Americans. Antisemitism. Bigotry. Racism. United States–History–Social life and customs.* Catholics. Concentration camps. Adolf Hitler. Jews. World War II.

Note: This film was apparently the only one produced by Target Films, Inc. The film's title comes from the narrator's statement that the United States' victory in the war was "a strange victory with the ideas of the loser still active in the land of the winner." According to the *NYT* review, compiled footage was taken from "newsreels, fact films and Russian pictures." According to the *Var* review, new material was shot in and around New York City. The *Var* reviewer also noted that the "menace of Communism" is not addressed by the film. An updated version of *Strange Victory* was released in 1964. That version added the voices of Martin Luther King, John Lewis, Boyard Rustin and other civil rights leaders.

Box 24 Jun 1948. *FD* 20 Jul 1948, p. 8. *FD* 10 Jul 1963. *NYT* 27 Sep 1948, p. 27. *Var* 21 Jul 1948.

STRANGE VOYAGE (Latino)

Signal Pictures. *Dist* Monogram Pictures Corp. 6 Jul **1946** [©Monogram Pictures Corp.; 2 Apr 1946; LP308]. Sd (RCA Sound System); b&w. 69-70 min.

Prod L. B. Appleton, Jr. *Dir* Irving Allen. *Asst dir* Harold Knox. *Orig scr* Andrew Holt. *Dir of photog* Jack H. Greenhalgh, Jr. [*Spec eff* Larry Glickman and Mario Castegnaro]. *Art dir* Ralph Berger. *Film ed* Irving A. Applebaum. *Set dec* Sydney A. Moore and Tommy Thompson. *Mus dir* Lud Gluskin. *Mus score* Lucien Moraweck. *Dir of sd* Percy J. Townsend. [*Re-rec and eff mixer* Joseph I. Kane]. [*Mus mixer* William H. Wilmarth].

Cast: Eddie Albert (*Chris Thompson*), Forrest Taylor (*Skipper*), Ray Teal (*Captain Andrews*), Matt Willis ([*The*] *Hammer*), Martin Garralaga (*Manuel*), Elena Verdugo (*Carmelita* [*Lopez*]), Bobby Cooper (*Jimmy* [*Trask*]), Clyde Fillmore ([*Barrier*], *Sportsman*), Daniel Kerry (*Ben*), Henry Orosco (*Father*), Junior, the monkey (*Himself*).

Adventure. [*Print viewed*]. When a sportsman named Barrier asks to rent a sailboat, Skipper, the owner, tells him the story of Chris Thompson, the previous man to rent the boat: Some time in the past, Chris puts together a crew consisting of Captain Andrews, Ben, Manuel and The Hammer and sails toward Mexico. At sea, they discover Jimmy Trask, who has stowed away with his pet monkey, and Chris allows him to stay. When the monkey runs off with a pouch belonging to Chris, Chris gets very upset and Andrews and Hammer try to discover what is inside. One day, Manuel states that his guitar cannot play—a bad omen. Shortly afterward, Ben falls overboard, and despite Chris's attempts to save him, is attacked by sharks. Later, Chris and Jimmy witness a battle between an octopus and a shark. Ignoring Manuel's prediction that two more will die, Chris orders Andrews to sail into a nearby bay. After they anchor the boat, Carmelita Lopez comes aboard to warn them that they will not find the treasure they

are seeking. She begs them not to go ashore, but shows them two coins her grandfather found before he died while searching for the treasure. The next day, Chris shows the rest of the crew a treasure map and a letter. He explains that the gold was buried by a dying monk and that he intends to give the money to the religious order that reared him when he was orphaned. If the others want to accompany him, he says that he will split his portion of the treasure with them. Despite Carmelita's warning, they all agree to go into the desert with Chris. Manuel is the first to feel the effects of heat and thirst. The others chase him when he runs off into the desert and find him near some natural gas fires that, according to the map, indicate that they are close to the treasure. They bring Manuel back to camp, but the next morning he is gone. Later, they find his body and bury him. Then Jimmy becomes ill, and Chris wants to turn back, but Jimmy insists that they continue, pointing out that a lake is marked on the map and they can refill their canteens. Later, they see a mirage, and realize that this is what is drawn on the map. Andrews and Hammer wander off together, and Andrews finds the treasure, which he and Hammer plot to steal. Jimmy overhears, and to prevent him from telling Chris, Andrews and Hammer tie him up in the desert. When Jimmy does not return to camp, Chris becomes concerned and searches for him. He finds Jimmy near death, but brings him back to camp and then takes off after Andrews and Hammer. During the ensuing shootout, Hammer is killed. While Andrews and Chris fight each other, a wind comes up and buries the treasure. Chris overcomes Andrews, but is near death from the sun when he is found by Carmelita and her father. Skipper then explains that he is waiting for Chris to return for the boat. Barrier is skeptical, but as Skipper finishes his story, Chris, Jimmy and a monkey come aboard. As if to confirm the story, the monkey is wearing a necklace of gold coins. *Buried treasure. Deserts. Betrayal. Fathers and daughters. Lure of riches. Mexico. Monkeys. Octopi. Romance. Sailboats. Sharks. Stowaways. Superstition. Thirst. Whales and whaling.*

Note: This was apparently the only production of Signal Pictures, an independent production company formed by film industry ex-servicemen, L. B. Appleton, Irving Allen, Jack H. Greenhalgh, Andrew Holt, Harold Knox and Eddie Albert.

Box 22 Dec 1945. *DV* 13 Dec 1945, p. 3. *FD* 20 Dec 1945, p. 8. *HR* 13 Dec 1945, p. 3. *MPHPD* 2 Mar 1946, p. 2870. *Var* 19 Dec 1945, p. 18.

STRANGE WIVES (Russian Americans)

Universal Pictures Corp.; A Stanley Bergerman Production. *Dist* Universal Pictures Corp. 10 Dec **1934**; Prod: 13 Oct–29 Oct 1934 [©Universal Pictures Corp.; 26 Nov 1934; LP5121]. Sd; b&w. 8 reels. 73 or 75 min. PCA cert no. 400.

Pres Carl Laemmle. *Dir* Richard Thorpe. *Asst dir* Phil Karlstein and Harry Mancke. *Adpt and scr* Gladys Unger. *Addl dial* Barry Trivers and James Mulhauser. *Contr wrt* Elliott Gibbons. *Cam* George Robinson. *Process photog* John P. Fulton. *Art dir* Alberto D'Agostino. *Film ed* Edward Curtiss. *Ed supv* Maurice Pivar. *Sd supv* Gilbert Kurland. *Makeup* Otto Lederer. *Tech dir* Nicholas Kobliansky. *Prod mgr* M. F. Murphy. *Scr clerk* Jean Raymond. *Secy to prod* Billy Moritz. *Utility secy* Ed Haskett. *Utility secy* Arthur Moss.

Source: Based on the short story "Bread upon the Waters" by Edith Wharton in *Hearst's International-Cosmopolitan* (Feb 1934).

Cast: Roger Pryor (*Jimmy King*), June Clayworth (*Nadia*), Esther Ralston (*Olga*), Hugh O'Connell (*Warren*), Ralph Forbes (*Paul*), Cesar Romero (*Boris*), Francis L. Sullivan (*Bellamy*), Valerie Hobson (*Mauna*), Leslie Fenton (*Svengaart*), Ivan Lebedeff (*Dimitry*), Doris Lloyd (*Mrs. Leeper*), Claude Gillingwater, Sr. (*Guggins*), Carrie Daumery (*Princess*), Greta Meyer (*Hilda*), Harry Cording (*Tribesman*), Olaf Hytten (*Jim's butler*), Walter Walker (*General Kourajine*), William Roberts (*Singer*), Buster Phelps, Dickie Jones (*Twins*), Phyllis Brooks (*Actress*), Leonid Snegoff (*Head waiter*), Anne O'Neal, Jean Fenwick (*Jim's secretaries*), Bobby Gordon (*Elevator boy*), Father Neal Dodd (*Minister*), Joseph Crehan (*Immigration official*), George Hackathorne (*Guggins' secretary*), Nicholas Kobliansky (*Waiter*), Victor De Linsky (*Russian priest*), Ralph Brooks (*Chauffeur*), Cortez and Galante (*Dance team*), Harry Cornell.

Comedy. [*Not viewed*]. Successful New York stockbroker Jimmy King, a confirmed bachelor, goes against the warnings of his friend Warren and marries wiley Russian refugee Nadia, who poses as a princess. Soon, Jimmy is supporting Nadia's family, which includes Olga, an ambitious interpretive dancer, Paul, an ambitious violinist,

Boris, a loafer, and Mauna, a gold digger. Nadia's father, General Kourajine, dreams only of a revolution taking place in Russia that would counteract the Bolshevik Revolution. In order to rid himself of his in-laws, Jimmy tries to exploit their Russian idiosyncrasies to make them all famous, and eventually, they all find other sources of income besides Jimmy. Jimmy also rids himself of a nervous former suitor of Nadia and finally establishes himself as head of the household with a tirade on marriage and home wreckers, leaving he and Nadia more compatible than ever. *Immigrants. In-laws. Marriage. Russian Americans. Bachelors. Bolshevists and Bolshevism. Dancers. Deception. Gold diggers. Impersonation and imposture. Infidelity. Ne'er-do-wells. New York City–Ellis Island. Princesses. Revolutionaries. Romantic rivalry. Stockbrokers. Violinists.*

DV 13 Oct 1934, p. 3. *DV* 18 Oct 1934, p. 9. *DV* 24 Nov 1934, p. 3. *FD* 1 Feb 1935, p. 13. *HR* 24 Nov 1934, p. 7. *MPH* 8 Dec 1934, p. 46. *Var* 5 Feb 1935, p. 31.

THE STRANGER FROM WAY OUT YONDER *see* **YOU CAN'T KEEP A GOOD MAN DOWN**

STREET GIRL *see* **THAT GIRL FROM PARIS**

STREET SCENE (Multi-ethnic)

Feature Productions, Inc. *Dist* United Artists Corp. 5 Sep **1931**; New York opening: 26 Aug 1931; Prod: completed late Jul 1931 [©Feature Productions, Inc.; 5 Sep 1931; LP2534]. Sd (Western Electric Sound System); b&w. 9 reels. 80 min. PCA cert no. 1321-R [29 Aug 1935].

Pres SAMUEL GOLDWYN. *Prod* Samuel Goldwyn. *Dir* King Vidor. [*Asst dir* Lucky Humberstone]. *Adpt* Elmer Rice. *Photog* George Barnes. [*2d cam* Stuart Thompson and George Nogle]. [*Asst cam* Judson Curtiss, Hal Carney and Harvey Gould]. *Settings* Richard Day. *Film ed* Hugh Bennett. *Mus dir* Alfred Newman. *Sd tech* Charles Noyes. [*Prod asst* Robert McIntyre]. [*Still photog* Kenneth Alexander].

Source: Based on the play *Street Scene* by Elmer Rice (New York, 10 Jan 1929).

Cast: Sylvia Sidney [(*Rose Maurrant*)], William Collier, Jr. [(*Sam Kaplan*)], Estelle Taylor [(*Anna Maurrant*)], Beulah Bondi [(*Emma Jones*)], David Landau [(*Frank Maurrant*)], Matt McHugh [(*Vincent Jones*)], Russell Hopton [(*Steve Sankey*)], Greta Granstedt [(*Mae Jones*)], Eleanor Wesselhoeft [(*Greta Fiorentino*)], Allan Fox [(*Dick McGann*)], Nora Cecil [(*Alice Simpson*)], Margaret Robertson, Walter James [(*Marshal James Henry*)], Max Montor [(*Abe Kaplan*)], Walter Miller, T. H. Manning [(*George Jones*)], Conway Washburne [(*Danny Buchanan*)], John M. Qualen [(*Karl Olsen*)], Anna Konstant [(*Shirley Kaplan*)], Adele Watson [(*Olga Olsen*)], Lambert Rogers [(*Willie Maurrant*)], George Humbert [(*Filippo Fiorentino*)], Helen Lovett [(*Laura Hildebrand*)], Richard Powell [(*Officer Harry Murphy*)], Jane Mercer, Monti Carter, [Louis Natheaux (*Easter*)], [Virginia Davis (*Mary Hildebrand*)], [Kenneth Seiling (*Charlie Hildebrand*)], [Howard Russell (*Dr. John Wilson*)], [Harry Wallace (*Fred Cullen*)], [Florence Enright], [Renee Shearing], [Marcia Mae Jones], [Lawrence Wagner], [Samuel S. Bonnell], [William Higbee].

Drama. [*Print viewed*]. On a hot evening in a New York tenement, neighbors gossip about each other as they return home. The main object of comment is the sadly romantic Anna Maurrant, who is having an affair with married milk collector Steve Sankey. Anna's brutish husband Frank is often away, and while he is suspicious, he has no proof of the affair. Frank comes home and yells at Anna for not knowing where their children Willie and Rose are, while social worker Alice Simpson reprimands poverty-stricken Laura Hildebrand, who is about to be evicted, for taking her children, Mary and Charlie, to the movies. Kindly Filippo Fiorentino, who longs to have children with his wife Greta, gives the Hildebrands money for the show, and socialist Abe Kaplan argues with Frank about the negative effects of capitalism. Abe's son Sam tells the building's most active gossiper, Emma Jones, to mind her own business when she passes along a juicy tidbit about Anna to Greta, and later, Rose comes home. She is accompanied by her married office manager, Mr. Easter, who wishes to set her up in an apartment. Although Rose desperately wishes to escape her dirty, mean-spirited surroundings, she refuses to become Easter's mistress. After Easter leaves, Rose talks with Sam, whom she regards as a best friend even though he is in love with her. She encourages Sam to believe in himself and nourish his individuality. The next morning, Sam's sister Shirley, a schoolteacher who has sacrificed everything so that her brother might succeed in life, asks him why he wants to get involved with Rose, as she is not Jewish. Sam tells Shirley to forget her race prejudices, after which Frank yells at

Anna as he leaves for work. The Hildebrands are evicted, and Shirley asks Rose not to encourage Sam's romantic ideas about her, because Shirley wants him to go to law school. Rose assures her that she does not want to be married yet, and she leaves with Easter for the funeral of their employer. Sam sees Sankey arrive to visit Anna, then watches in horror as Frank comes home unexpectedly. Sam yells a warning to Anna, but it is too late, for Frank has caught the lovers together. Frank shoots his wife and Sankey, then rushes away. Rose arrives home as Anna is taken away in an ambulance. While the neighborhood thrives on the scandal, Rose returns from the hospital, where she saw her mother die. Easter offers to help her, but Rose states that she will be able to care for herself and Willie. After Rose has packed her clothes, the police capture Frank, who tells Rose that he meant to be a better father. Sam wants to go away with Rose, but she tells him that they are too young to be married, and that it is important for him to fulfill his goals first. Rose hugs Sam and Shirley, tells them that she will see them again, and then leaves to begin a new life away from the tenement. *Family relationships. Gossip. Infidelity. Murder. Neighbors. Tenement-houses. Childbirth. Christopher Columbus. Danish Americans. Drunkenness. Leif Ericsson. Eviction. Flirts. German Americans. Idealists. Immigrants. Italian Americans. Jews. Love. Milkmen. New York City. Police. Racism. Schoolteachers. Social workers. Socialism.*

Note: Elmer Rice's play won a Pulitzer Prize for the 1928-1929 season, and according to a *NYT* article, was purchased by producer Samuel Goldwyn for $157,000. The actors reprising their roles from the Broadway production were: Beulah Bondi, Matt McHugh, Eleanor Wesselhoeft, T. H. Manning, Conway Washburne, John M. Qualen, Anna Konstant and George Humbert. Bondi made her screen-acting debut in this film. According to a *FD* news item, Nancy Carroll was originally set for the part of "Rose Maurrant."

According to the MPAA/PCA Collection at the AMPAS Library, Rice's play was considered controversial because of the characterization of social worker "Alice Simpson." Rice received many complaints from social agencies, including the Welfare Council of New York City. In a 2 Oct 1929 letter, a New York based Hays Office official warned Jason S. Joy, the Director of the Studio Relations Office of the AMPP, about the controversy and suggested that he keep it in mind in case the play was turned into a film. On 23 Mar 1931, the Welfare Council wrote to the MPPDA, requesting that they advise the production company working on the film about the protests over the social worker character. The letter warned: "...if the film presents the social worker in the light in which she appeared on the New York stage the film will undoubtedly meet with vigorous protests throughout the country." In response, Joy cautioned Goldwyn: "...we suggest that, unless some radical change be made in the characterization of Miss Simpson, it be definitely indicated that she is an agent for the party who is dispossessing the unfortunate family." Rice was very displeased with this and other changes suggested by Joy, and wrote a memo to Goldwyn's production executive Arthur Hornblow, Jr. suggesting various mock alterations. Among them, he proposed: "The charity worker can be changed to a Soviet agent, who is dispossessing the Hildebrands in order to precipitate a social revolution in America and make Clarence Darrow president. As she makes her exit, she drops her hand-bag and the bomb which it contains—destined for Will Hays—explodes and blows her to smithereens; and serves her damn—excuse me, darn—right, too." The problem was apparently resolved, and the picture received a seal of approval and a certificate when it was re-issued in 1935.

Street Scene was named one of the ten best pictures of 1931 by *FD*'s Nation Wide Poll. In a modern interview, director King Vidor stated that some second unit photography was done in New York, and that cinematographer Gregg Toland, not George Barnes, who is credited on screen, worked with him on the production. According to a modern source, the picture was produced for less than its $584,000 budget. Rice wrote the book for a musical version of *Street Scene*, with music by Kurt Weill and lyrics by Langston Hughes, which opened in New York on 24 Feb 1966 with Catherine Christensen and William Lewis in the starring roles. Rice's play has also been dramatized on television three times.

FD 3 Jun 1931, p. 6. *FD* 30 Aug 1931, p. 10. *HF* 15 Aug 1931, p. 14. *HR* 24 Jul 1931, p. 1. *HR* 13 Aug 1931, p. 3. *HR* 28 Aug 1931, p. 1. *IP* 31 Oct 1931, p. 29. *MPH* 22 Aug 1931, p. 32. *MPH* 10 Oct 1931, p. 41. *NYT* 27 Aug 1931, p. 22. *Var* 14 Jan 1931, p. 2, 4. *Var* 1 Sep 1931, p. 21.

A STREETCAR NAMED DESIRE (Polish Americans)

Warner Bros. Pictures, Inc.; Charles K. Feldman Group Productions; An Elia Kazan Production; A Charles K. Feldman Group Production. *Dist* Warner Bros. Pictures, Inc. 22 Mar **1951**; Prod: mid-Aug—mid-Oct 1950 [©Charles Feldman Group Productions; 15 Oct 1951; LP1240]. Sd (RCA Sound System); b&w. 10,977 ft. 125 min. PCA cert no. 14871.

Prod Charles K. Feldman. *Dir* Elia Kazan. [*1st asst dir* Don Page]. [*2d asst dir* John Prettyman]. *Scr* Tennessee Williams. *Adpt* Oscar Saul. *Dir of photog* Harry Stradling. [*2d cam* Fred Mandl]. [*Asst cam* Stu Higgs]. *Art dir* Richard Day. [*Supv art dir* Bertram Tuttle]. *Film ed* David Weisbart. *Set dec* George James Hopkins. [*Props* Scotty More]. [*Asst props* George Sweeney]. *Ward* Lucinda Ballard,

[Marguerite Royce, Lillian House and Robert O. Odell]. *Orig mus* Alex North. *Mus dir* Ray Heindorf. *Sd* C. A. Riggs. [*Boom* Frank Stahl]. *Makeup artist* Gordon Bau. [*Makeup* Otis Malcolm]. [*Body* Pat O'Grady]. [*Hair* Hazel Rogers and Ray Forman]. [*Scr clerk* Polly Craus]. [*Cableman* Frank Weixel]. [*Gaffer* Bob Campbell]. [*Best boy* Paul Butner and Harry Whittingham]. [*Grip* Truman Joiner].

Source: Based on the play *A Streetcar Named Desire* by Tennessee Williams, as presented by Irene Mayer Selznick (3 Dec 1947).

Cast: Vivien Leigh (*Blanche* [*DuBois*]), Marlon Brando (*Stanley* [*Kowalski*]), Kim Hunter (*Stella* [*Kowalski*]), Karl Malden (*Mitch*), Rudy Bond (*Steve*), Nick Dennis (*Pablo*), Peg Hillias (*Eunice*), Wright King (*A collector*), Richard Garrick (*A doctor*), Ann Dere (*The matron*), Edna Thomas (*The Mexican woman*), Mickey Kuhn (*A sailor*), [Chester Jones (*Street vendor*)], [Marietta Canty (*Black woman*)], [John B. Williams, Ira Buck Woods, John Gonatos (*Vendors*)], [Charles Wagenheim, Maxie Thrower (*Passersby*)], [Lyle Latell (*Policeman*)], [Mel Archer (*Foreman*)].

Domestic, Drama. [*Print viewed*]. Blanche DuBois arrives in New Orleans by train, and follows a sailor's directions to take a streetcar named "Desire" to her sister Stella Kowalski's apartment at Elysian Fields in the French Quarter. Blanche, an aging Southern belle, is horrified by the dilapidated building in which her sister lives with her husband Stanley, but is delighted to reunite with Stella, whom she feels abandoned her after their father's death. Blanche explains that she was given a leave of absence from her teaching job because she had become a little "lunatic," and now makes herself at home in the cramped apartment, which affords little privacy. Blanche is immediately offended by Stanley's coarse manners, and he is infuriated when he learns that Blanche has lost the family home at Belle Reve. Stanley rants about the "Napoleonic code," which he claims decrees that what belongs to the wife belongs to the husband. Unimpressed by Blanche's genteel manners, Stanley reveals that his wife is pregnant, and at his insistence, Blanche reluctantly digs out the papers which document the many unpaid loans written against the Belle Reve estate. That night, Stanley's poker game runs late, and when Stella and Blanche return from an outing together, Blanche meets Stanley's best friend Mitch, a bachelor who looks after his sick mother. Blanche turns on the radio and dances by herself, but Stanley is distracted by the music and flies into a drunken rage, during which he beats Stella. Stella and her terrified sister run up to their neighbor Eunice's apartment, but later, when Stanley calls up to her in remorse, Stella is drawn back to her husband and makes up with him. Blanche, horrified by Stanley's brutality, lingers in the street with Mitch. The next day, Stanley overhears Blanche encourage Stella to leave Stanley, whom she calls an "animal" and "subhuman," but she is unable to shake Stella's devotion to her husband. Stanley reveals that he has heard some unsavory gossip about Blanche, and his apparent secret knowledge unnerves her. That night, Blanche and Mitch go out on a date, and she resists his amorous advances by telling him that she is old-fashioned. After avoiding Mitch's questions about her age, she reveals that she drove her first young husband to suicide by mercilessly demeaning him because their marriage was not consummated. She then accepts Mitch's kiss. Five months later, when Mitch reveals his plans to marry Blanche, he and Stanley fight after Stanley tells him about her sordid past. Stanley then tells Stella that he has learned that Blanche was fired for seducing a seventeen-year-old student, and that she has a notorious reputation. Mitch stands Blanche up on her birthday and refuses to take her calls. When Stanley tells Blanche that she has overstayed her welcome, she insults him by calling him a "Polack." Stanley defends his Polish heritage, and then gives her a birthday gift of a one-way bus ticket home. Blanche then becomes hysterical and shuts herself in the bathroom. Stella and Stanley start to fight, but she goes into labor and Stanley takes her to the hospital. Later, Mitch comes to see Blanche, who is hearing music in her head, and calls her a hypocrite. Blanche truly loves Mitch, but admits that she has had "many meetings with men." Mitch forces a kiss on Blanche, but breaks their engagement and is run out of the apartment by her. She then dresses up as if she were attending a ball, and when Stanley returns home, claims that Mitch has apologized and that she has received an invitation to a cruise. Stanley accuses Blanche of lying and assaults her. When Stella returns home with her baby, she finds that Blanche has gone insane and now lives under the delusion that she is going on a Caribbean cruise. Stella has reluctantly arranged for her sister to be sent to a sanatorium, but when the doctor and

matron arrive, Blanche goes completely berserk. Mitch attacks Stanley, who vows that he never touched Blanche. Blanche finally calms down, and is touched by the doctor's gentlemanly manner, telling him that she has "always depended on the kindness of strangers." After they leave, Stella rebuffs Stanley and runs to Eunice's apartment with her baby, vowing never to return. *Battered women. Deception. Insanity. New Orleans (LA). Rape. Seduction. Sisters.* Bowling and bowling alleys. Cards. Drunkenness. Engagements. Fistfights. Polish Americans. Pregnancy. Snobs and snobbishness. Streetcars. Widows.

Note: The opening credits read: "Warner Bros. Pictures present the Pulitzer Prize and New York Critics Award Play *A Streetcar Named Desire*." The 1949 Broadway production of Tennessee Williams' play was directed by Elia Kazan and starred Jessica Tandy as "Blanche." The New York production featured Kim Hunter, Marlon Brando and Karl Malden, as well as Rudy Bond, Nick Dennis, Peg Hillias and Edna Thomas, all of whom appeared in the film. The play's London premiere was held on 11 Oct 1949, with Vivien Leigh starring as "Blanche." In Aug 1949, *HR* and *DV* news items reported that Paramount was planning to buy the screen rights to the play with the intention of featuring Bette Davis in a lead role, under William Wyler's direction. In Oct 1949, however, Charles K. Feldman bought the rights to the play. According to modern sources, Warner Bros. insisted that a "star" play the lead role of "Blanche," and therefore rejected Kazan's casting of Jessica Tandy.

Information in the MPAA/PCA Collection at the AMPAS Library reveals the following information about the production: In a 28 Apr 1950 letter, the MPAA office notified Warner Bros. that the script posed "three principal problems" with regard to the Production Code. These problems were cited as "an inference of sex perversion...[with] reference to the character of Blanche's young husband, Allan Gray, [as] there seems little doubt that this young man was a homosexual;" "an inference of nymphomania with regards to the character of Blanche herself;" and the "reference to the rape which is both justified and unpunished." The MPAA offered various plot alterations to resolve these violations of the Production Code. In the first they suggested that the filmmakers "affirmatively establish...some other reason for [Allan Grey's] suicide which will get away entirely from sex perversion." Secondly, the MPAA suggested that Blanche appear to be "searching for romance and security, and not for gross sex" and frequently call for "Allan," so that she would appear to be "seeking for the husband she has lost in any man she approaches." The MPAA also recommended that all inferences to the rape be entirely eliminated and merely be Blanche's hallucination, brought on by her "dementia." In a 2 May 1950 memo, the MPAA noted that both Kazan and Williams were telephoned after receiving their comments, and "were inclined to make speeches about the integrity of their art and their unwillingness to be connected with a production which would emasculate the validity of their production. Mr. Williams actually signed off in a great huff, declaiming that he did not need the money that much."

Negotiation continued between the MPAA and the filmmakers; however, a 24 May 1950 note written by Joseph I. Breen, head of the MPAA, noted that "we are not entirely out of the woods on this particular production....we still have some things to do by way of straightening out the characterization of the girl and the disposal of Stanley at the end of the script." A 25 Jul 1950 memo recorded a meeting between the MPAA and Warner Bros. representatives, in which they specifically discussed the "so-called rape scene," which the MPAA continued to reject. "A solution was suggested...that the indication of rape be simply abolished, and that in its place it be indicated that Stanley struck Blanche quite violently, and from this blow she collapsed. This would mean that his very pointed line, 'We've had this date with each other from the beginning,' would be simply eliminated."

According to a *NYT* article, Kazan began shooting the film in mid-Aug 1950. As of 24 Aug 1950, the matter of the rape scene was still unresolved. Actor Marlon Brando noted in a 21 Aug 1950 *NYT* article that the MPAA office would not allow him "to pick Miss Leigh up and carry her off to bed." In addition, an 8 Sep 1950 letter written by Breen suggests that he still found inferences in the script that "Blanche's" first husband was homosexual. Kazan responded to Breen's concern in a 14 Sep 1950 letter by stating that "I wouldn't put homosexuality back in the picture, if the Code had been revised last night and it was now permissible....I prefer the delicately suggested impotence theme; I prefer debility and weakness over any kind of suggestion of perversion." On 20 Oct 1950, Williams wrote the following to Breen about the rape scene: "*Streetcar* is an extremely and peculiarly *moral* play, in the deepest and truest sense of the term....The rape of Blanche by Stanley is a pivotal, integral truth in the play, without which the play loses its meaning, which is the ravishment of the tender, the sensitive, the delicate by the savage and brutal forces in modern society." Williams went on to praise Leigh's performance as "Blanche," and continued with "Please remember, also, that we have already made great concessions which we felt were dangerous to attitudes which we thought were narrow." Indeed, Williams rewrote the end of the screenplay to indicate, somewhat ambiguously, that Stella leaves her husband, whereas in the play she returns to him after her sister is removed.

The film was completed and ready for release by Jul 1951, when the Catholic Legion of Decency condemned it. That same month, as reported in a *Var* news item, a Chicago federal judge refused "to permit an extension of the two-week limitation in the Loop" for the run of the film, and declared that "he would not 'condone any picture which dealt with sex nymphomania and liquor' as its basic theme." According to Kazan, quoted in a 24 Oct 1951 *Var* news item, Warner Bros. feared that a condemnation by the Legion of Decency would ruin their chances of getting an audience for the film. Without consulting Kazan,

studio officials worked with the MPAA to make cuts in the film that would meet the MPAA's and Legion of Decency's approval. The editing was supervised by Martin Quigley (as identified in modern sources), a film trade magazine publisher and Catholic layman, who reportedly was "invited" by Warner Bros. In the 24 Oct 1951 *Var* article (which reprinted an interview with Kazan from a 21 Oct 1941 *NYT* article), Kazan noted that twelve cuts were made in the film, which resulted in a total of "three or four minutes of film." Kazan noted the cuts as follows: "a trivial cut of three words;" "a recutting of the wordless scene in which Stella...comes down the stairway to Stanley after a quarrel;" Stanley's line "You know, you might not be bad to interfere with," which is spoken shortly before he rapes Blanche; and a few other cuts "of like nature."

Kazan noted that the scene in which Stella descends the stairway "was carefully worked out...to show Stella's conflicting revulsion and attraction to her husband....It was explained to me that both the close shots and the music made the girl's relation to her husband 'too carnal.'" In addition, Kazan noted that the elimination of Stanley's line before he attacks Blanche "removes the clear implication that only here, for the first time, does Stanley have any idea of harming the girl. This obviously changes the interpretation of the character, but how it serves the cause of morality is obscure to me, though I have given it much thought."

After the cuts were made, the Legion of Decency awarded the film a "B" rating, and it was released to great critical acclaim. In 1993, Warner Bros. re-released the film with the cuts restored. The film won Academy Awards in the following categories: Best Supporting Actor (Karl Malden), Best Actress (Vivien Leigh), Best Supporting Actress (Kim Hunter), and Best Art Direction (black & white). The film was also nominated for the following Academy Awards: Best Picture, Best Direction, Best Actor (Marlon Brando), Best Cinematography, Best Costume Design, Best Music (scoring dramatic or comedy picture), Best Sound Recording (Warner Bros. Studio Sound Dept.; Nathan Levinson, sound director), and Best Writing (Screenplay). In 1984, a television version of the play was aired featuring Ann-Margret, Treat Williams, Beverly D'Angelo and Randy Quaid; and in 1992, the play was revived on Broadway starring Jessica Lange and Alec Baldwin. That version was also adapted for television.

AmCin Oct 1951, pp. 400, 424-25, 428. *Box* 16 Jun 1951. *DV* 12 Oct 1949. *DV* 14 Jun 1951, p. 3. *FD* 14 Jun 1951, p. 7. *HR* 15 Jun 1949. *HR* 11 Aug 1950, p. 9. *HR* 13 Oct 1950, p. 13. *HR* 14 Jun 1951, p. 4. *MPHPD* 16 Jun 1951, pp. 885-86. *NYT* 28 May 1950. *NYT* 21 Aug 1950. *NYT* 30 Sep 1951, p. 27. *Var* 20 Jun 1951, p. 6. *Var* 4 Jul 1951. *Var* 3 Oct 1951. *Var* 24 Oct 1951.

STREETS OF LAREDO (Latino)

Paramount Pictures, Inc. *Dist* Paramount Pictures, Inc. 27 May **1949**; New York opening: 11 May 1949; Prod: 13 Jul—26 Aug 1948; added scenes and retakes: 27 Aug—31 Aug 1948, 15 and 17 Sep 1948 [©Paramount Pictures, Inc.; 27 May 1949; LP2314]. Sd (Western Electric Recording); col (Technicolor). 10 reels, 8,346 ft. 92 min. Passed by the National Board of Review.

Prod Robert Fellows. *Dir* Leslie Fenton. *Asst dir* Francisco Day. [*Dial dir* Jim Vincent]. [*Asst dir* Harry Caplan]. [*2d asst dir* Mickey Moore and Al Mann]. *Scr* Charles Marquis Warren. *Story* Louis Stevens and Elizabeth Hill. *Dir of photog* Ray Rennahan. [*Asst cam* Charles Leahy, Robert Hosler, Phil Eastman and Harry Marsh]. [*Cam op* Archie Dalzell, Guy Bennett, John Hamilton, William Cline and Bill Rand]. [*Stills* Don English]. [*Gaffer* Howard Kelly]. *Process photog* Farciot Edouart. [*Transparencies* Wallace Kelley]. *Technicolor color dir* Natalie Kalmus. *Assoc* Monroe W. Burbank. *Art dir* Hans Dreier and Henry Bumsted. *Ed* Archie Marshek. *Set dec* Sam Comer and Bertram Granger. [*Props* Carl Camp and Bob Goodstein]. [*Asst props* Carl Coleman]. *Cost* Mary Kay Dodson. [*Ward* Ed Fitzharris, Frank Delmar and Hazel Hegarty]. *Mus score* Victor Young. *Sd rec* Harry Lindgren and Walter Oberst. *Makeup supv* Wally Westmore. [*Makeup artist* Carl Silvera and Roland Ray]. [*Hair* Hedvig Mjorud and Lavaughn Speer]. [*Asst prod mgr* C. Kenneth DeLand and Andy Durkus]. [*Scr clerk* Marvin Weldon and Claire Behnke]. [*Grip* Darrell Turnmire]. [*Double for William Holden* Frank Cordell]. [*Double for Macdonald Carey* Bob Miles]. [*Double for William Bendix* Hy Nowlin].

Song(s): "Streets of Laredo," traditional, arrangement and new lyrics by Jay Livingston and Ray Evans.

Cast: WILLIAM HOLDEN (*Jim Dawkins*), MACDONALD CAREY (*Lorn Reming*), MONA FREEMAN (*Rannie Carter*), WILLIAM BENDIX (*Wahoo Jones*), Stanley Ridges (*Major Bailey*), Alfonso Bedoya (*Charley Calico*), Ray Teal (*Cantrel*), Clem Bevans (*Pop Lint*), James Bell (*Ike*), Dick Foote (*Pipes*), Joe Dominguez (*Francisco*), Grandon Rhodes (*Phil Jessup*), Perry Ivins (*Mayor Towson*), [Mike Lally, William Hamel, Carl Andre (*Townsmen*)], [Wade Crosby, Julian Rivero (*Bartenders*)], [Alex Montoya, Joaquin Elizondo (*Mexicans*)], [Marguerite Martin (*Maria*)], [James Davies, Bob Kortman, Frank Cordell, Pat Lane, Hank Worden (*Rangers*)], [Byron Foulger (*Artist*)], [Frank Hagney (*Cowhand*)].

Western. [*Print viewed*]. In 1878, outlaws Jim Dawkins, Lorn Reming and Wahoo Jones rob a stagecoach, but later save teenager Rannie Carter from ruthless tax collector Charley Calico, who has murdered her uncle and stolen his cattle. When orphan Rannie tags along, Wahoo tells her that they are cattle inspectors. To get rid of Rannie, Lorn pays elderly rancher Pop Lint $500 to pretend that he is a family friend and take Rannie in as a boarder. Lorn is then separated from Jim and Wahoo when Calico and his gang chase them. Over the course of the next year, Lorn earns a reputation as a notorious outlaw. In order to save Lorn's life, Jim and Wahoo foil his attempt to rob a stagecoach carrying Texas Rangers, and are reluctantly sworn in as Rangers. Jim and Wahoo are quickly tested, however, after Lorn escapes, apparently due to their negligence. After the Rangers are assigned to protect a large cattle herd being driven to Mexico, Lorn steals a portion of the herd, then allows Jim and Wahoo to capture the herd to regain their standing with the Rangers. From then on, Jim and Wahoo give Lorn advance notice of all cattle drives. Not long after, Rannie, now a young woman, asks the Rangers to protect her and Pop Lint from Calico, who controls the territory. By law, the Rangers can only respond to a request made by the mayor of a town, so Jim and Wahoo convince Lorn to help. Lorn agrees to get rid of Calico, but secretly intends to take over Calico's domain. Lorn first forces the sheriff to file a formal request for help with the Rangers. Jim and Wahoo then head out to arrest Calico, whose ranch is near Pop's, and find that Calico and his gang have burned down Pop's stables, causing Pop to die of a heart attack. Jim kills Calico after he brutally tortures one of the Rangers, and Jim is declared a hero. Now determined to go straight, Jim calls off his arrangement with Lorn, who agrees to stay out of the territory. Lorn starts pursuing Rannie, however, becoming Jim's rival for her affection. Rannie rejects Jim's marriage proposal in favor of the suave Lorn, but soon realizes her mistake when Lorn tries to force himself on her. Thrown out by Rannie and rejected by his friends, Lorn busies himself with making trouble for the Rangers. When Lorn is shot and wounded after falling into a Ranger trap, he escapes to Rannie's house, where Jim removes the bullet. Rannie takes care of Lorn while he convalesces, and becomes so convinced of Lorn's evil nature as she is of Jim's goodness. Jim resigns from the Rangers after a manhunt is mounted to find Lorn, but is then arrested for his prior crimes. Wahoo goes after Lorn alone, but is killed in cold blood. Jim demands to be released so he can avenge Wahoo's death, and after Lorn takes Rannie hostage, having promised to leave Jim unharmed, Jim tracks him down in Laredo and refuses to let him escape. The former friends are forced into a gunfight, but it is Rannie who ultimately kills Lorn and avenges Wahoo's death. Betrayal. Friendship. Loyalty. Murder. Outlaws. Romantic rivalry. Texas Rangers. Attempted rape. Criminals–Rehabilitation. Extortion. Gunfights. Gunshot wounds. Laredo (TX). Ranchers. Revenge. Rustlers. Sheriffs. Stagecoach robberies. Texas. Torture.

Note: This film is a remake of Paramount's 1936 film *The Texas Rangers*, directed by King Vidor and starring Fred MacMurray, Jack Oakie, Jean Parker and Lloyd Nolan (see *AFI Catalog of Feature Films, 1931-40*; F3.4519). Although *The Texas Rangers* was based in part on a Walter Prescott Webb book of the same name, *Streets of Laredo* is based on Louis Stevens and Elizabeth Hill's screenplay for *The Texas Rangers*, and they are given onscreen story credit for *Streets of Laredo*. According to an Aug 1947 *HR* news item, Paramount bought the rights to a Norman Reilly Raine story titled "Streets of Laredo," intending to produce a film from it "on a major scale." However, although Raine is listed in connection with this film along with writers Charles Marquis Warren and Lynn Root in papers in the Paramount Collection at the AMPAS Library, and Warren and Root collaborated on a draft of the script, neither Raine nor Root are credited in any other source, and the extent of their contribution to the final film has not been determined. Although Paramount initially hoped to shoot the film "against the panorama of Texas," location filming was done in Gallup, NM, according to *HR*. Some scenes were shot at the Corrigan Ranch in the San Fernando Valley, CA.

Box 12 Feb 1949. *DV* 7 Feb 1949, pp. 3-4. *FD* 10 Feb 1949, p. 6. *HR* 18 Aug 1947, p. 1. *HR* 7 Apr 1948, p. 2. *HR* 13 Jul 1948, p. 3, 5. *HR* 11 Aug 1948, p. 3. *HR* 7 Feb 1949, p. 3. *MPHPD* 12 Feb 1949, pp. 4493-94. *NYT* 12 May 1949, p. 28. *Var* 9 Feb 1949, p. 13.

THE STRONG MAN (Belgian Americans, German Americans)

Harry Langdon Corp. *Dist* First National Pictures, Inc. 19 Sep **1926**; New York opening: week of 5 Sep 1926; Prod: early May—late Aug 1926 [©First National Pictures, Inc.; 31 Aug 1926; LP23063]. Si; b&w. 7 reels, 6,882 ft. 75 min.

Pres RICHARD A. ROWLAND. *Dir* Frank Capra. *Asst dir* J. Frank Holliday. *Story* Arthur Ripley. *Story and titles* Harry Langdon. *Titles* Clarence Hennecke and Bob Eddy. *Adpt* Hal Conklin. *Wrt* Frank Capra, Tim Whelan, J. Frank Holliday and Murray Roth. *Photog* Elgin Lessley and Glenn Kershner. *Art dir* Lloyd Brierly. *Film ed* Harold Young. *Prod mgr* William H. Jenner. *Elec* Denver Harmon.

Cast: HARRY LANGDON (*Paul Bergot*), Priscilla Bonner (*Mary Brown*), Gertrude Astor (*"Gold Tooth"*), William V. Mong (*Parson Brown*), Robert McKim (*Roy McDevitt*), Arthur Thalasso (*Zandow the Great*).

Comedy. [*Viewed print incomplete*]. Paul Bergot, a Belgian soldier during World War I, drives away a German soldier with his slingshot, then reads the latest letter from his pen pal, Mary Brown, an American with whom Paul has fallen in love, even though they have never met. While he is reading, Paul is captured by the same German soldier, who, after the Armistice, takes Paul along when he emigrates to America to become Zandow the Great, a vaudeville strong man. After their arrival, Paul searches for Mary by comparing a poor photograph of her with women he passes on the street. He is spotted by "Gold Tooth," who slips some stolen money into Paul's coat to elude the detective following her. The detective is fooled, but when "Gold Tooth" attempts to retrieve the money, she discovers that it has slipped into the lining of Paul's coat. She then tells him that she is the "Little Mary" for whom he is looking, and although he is dismayed by her worldly behavior, she lures him to her apartment building. Outside the building, however, Paul attempts to flee, and so "Gold Tooth" pretends to faint, after which Paul gets her up a stairway by holding her on his lap and scooting up the stairs one at a time, backwards. In her apartment, "Gold Tooth" chases Paul, trying to get the money, while he assumes that she is burning with passion for him. She gets the money, and Paul leaves to rejoin Zandow, who has been engaged to perform in Cloverdale. Paul enrages his fellow bus passengers with his ministrations to his cold, but eventually he and Zandow arrive in Cloverdale, where Mary's father, Parson Brown, is leading the fight against Roy McDevitt, a bootlegger and owner of the Palace Music Hall. Paul soon learns that Mary is in Cloverdale and presents himself to her, after which he is stunned by her confession that she is blind. Despite his shock, the couple are soon holding hands and sharing jokes. Zandow, meanwhile, has become drunk and cannot perform, so in order to prevent the audience from rioting, McDevitt dresses Paul in Zandow's costume and thrusts him onto the stage. Paul entertains the crowd for a while, but when one of the audience makes a rude reference to Mary, Paul begins a fight which soon escalates beyond his control. Paul takes refuge on the trapeze onto which Zandow was to be shot from a cannon, grabs a stage backdrop and covers the crowd with it. When they free themselves, he shoots at them with the cannon, and after many shots, one of which propels McDevitt into a garbage can, the Palace is destroyed. Soon after, Cloverdale has returned to its former peaceful state, and Paul, now a police officer, begins to walk his beat. Mary asks to come with him, and when she cries after his refusal, Paul relents and takes her along. He trips and she helps him up, after which they continue, arm in arm. *Belgian Americans. Blindness. German Americans. Romance. Strong men. Vaudeville. World War I.* Bootleggers. Detectives. Drunkenness. Fights. Impersonation and imposture. Letters. Music halls. Photographs. Prisoners of war. Soldiers.

Note: The film's working title was *The Yes Man*. The print viewed was a video presentation by Thames Television, in which Gertrude Astor, known as "Gold Tooth" in contemporary reviews, is called Lily, and Robert McKim, called Roy McDevitt in the same reviews, is called Mike McDevitt. Modern sources indicate that even in contemporary prints there are discrepencies in these character names, and so "Gold Tooth" was also called Lily of Broadway, and Parson Brown was also called Holy Joe. Modern sources list two more adaptors, Tay Garnett and James Langdon, and an additional titles writer, Reed Heustis. Modern sources list cast members Brooks Benedict (*Bus passenger*) and Tay Garnett. This was the first of two films starring Langdon which Capra directed, after previously co-directing Langdon in *Tramp, Tramp, Tramp*, and marked his debut as a feature director. According to modern sources, when the film was released in New York, First National placed a forty foot tall neon sign over the marquis which showed Harry lifting a barbell. According to reviews and news items, the picture was an enormous critical and financial success. According to Capra's autobiography, the picture was voted one of the ten best of 1926 by critics. Modern sources state that Zandow's vaudeville act was based on the act of a real vaudeville star, Eugene Sandow. The gag in which Langdon holds "Gold Tooth" on his lap, scoots up the stairs backwards and then falls over a ladder was repeated in Capra's 1959 film *A Hole in the Head*.

FD 9 May 1926, p. 12. *FD* 4 Jun 1926, p. 7. *FD* 12 Sep 1926, p. 6. *MPN* 18 Sep 1926, p. 1101. *MPW* 15 May 1926, p. 237. *MPW* 4 Sep 1926, p. 21, 37. *MPW* 18 Sep 1926, p. 166. *NYT* 7 Sep 1926, p. 44. *Var* 8 Sep 1926, p. 16.

STUDS LONIGAN (Irish Americans)

Longridge Enterprises, Inc. *Dist* United Artists Corp. Sep **1960**; Prod: late Feb—early Apr 1960 at Hal Roach Studios [©Longridge Enterprises, Inc.; 15 Jun 1960; LP17175]. Sd; b&w. 8,544 ft. 95 min.

Prod Philip Yordan. *Assoc prod* Leon Chooluck. *Dir* Irving Lerner. *Asst dir* Louis Brandt and Eugene Anderson, Jr. *Scr* Philip Yordan. *Photog* Arthur H. Feindel. *Spec photog consultant and prod asst* Haskell Wexler. *Spec eff* J. W. Erickson. *Art dir* Jack Poplin. *Film ed* Verna Fields. *Assoc ed* Melvin Shapiro. *Eff ed* Kay Rose. *Mus ed* Richard Berres. *Set dec* Edward G. Boyle. *Props* Richard M. Rubin. *Men's cost* Forrest T. Butler. *Women's cost* Sabine Manela. *Mus* Gerrald Goldsmith. *Sd* Ben Winkler. *Makeup artist* Fred Phillips. *Chief lighting tech* Lloyd L. Garnell. *Chief set operation tech* Frederick C. Russell. *Scr supv* Hope McLachlin. *Lab and optical eff* Consolidated Films, Inc.

Source: Based on the novel *Studs Lonigan* by James T. Farrell (New York, 1935).

Cast: Christopher Knight (*Studs Lonigan*), Frank Gorshin (*Kenny Killarney*), Venetia Stevenson (*Lucy Scanlon*), Carolyn Craig (*Catherine Banahan*), Jack Nicholson (*Weary Reilly*), Robert Casper (*Paulie Haggerty*), Dick Foran (*Patrick Lonigan*), Katherine Squire (*Mrs. Lonigan*), Jay C. Flippen (*Father Gilhooey*), Helen Westcott (*Miss Julia Miller*), Kathy Johnson (*Frances Lonigan*), Jack Kruschen (*Charlie the Greek*), Suzi Carnell (*Eileen*), Mme. Spivy (*Mother Josephine*), James Drum (*Jim Doyle*), Ben Gary, Rita Duncan (*Kitty*), Stanley Adams, Steven Ritch, George Keymas (*Gangsters*), Opal Eurard (*Mrs. Reilly*), Mavis Neal (*Mrs. Haggerty*), Phil Arnold (*Dentist*), John Graham (*Judge*), Don Garrett, Casey MacGregor (*Policemen*), Brian O'Hara (*Funeral mourner*), Val Hidey (*Stripper*), Snubby Pollard (*Newspaper vendor*), Marty Crail (*Bartender*), Darlene Hendrix, Josie Lloyd, Suzanne Sidney (*Girls at New Year's Eve party*), Kathie Browne, Judy Howard, Elaine Walker, Lorelei Vitek (*Girls at wild party*).

Drama. [*Not viewed*]. On New Year's Eve in 1919, in Chicago, eighteen-year-old Studs Lonigan looks to 1920 with feelings of fear and uncertainty. Studs is torn between his love for sixteen-year-old Lucy Scanlon and his loyalty to a gang of fellow jobless delinquints comprised of Kenny Killarney, Weary Reilly and Paulie Haggerty. When Lucy, a "good girl," leaves the New Year's Eve party early, Studs gets drunk at his gang's wild party. Stud's father Patrick, angry at his son's irresponsibility, tries to convince him to join his painting firm, while his mother has dreams of him becoming a priest. Two unproductive years pass in which Studs spends his time playing pool, drinking and chasing girls. One day, Studs's father slaps him in frustration and the boy leaves home and asks two gangsters to give him a job. After the gangsters humiliate him with a practical joke, however, Studs returns home. Studs is soon diverted from job hunting by a burlesque show, and stimulated by drink and a stripper, visits pretty spinster Julia Miller, his former teacher. After tearing Julia's dress during an attempted rape, Studs breaks down in tears. Studs is sobered by his actions, and when Julia comforts him, they form a strong emotional bond and begin an affair. Finally realizing that their relationship is wrong, Julia stops seeing Studs, who then decides to join his father's firm, although he continues to fraternize with his gang. The death of Paulie, now married and a father, shakes Studs from his complacency, and he stops drinking when he learns that Lucy has moved from Chicago. When Studs witnesses Weary being arrested for rape during a wild party, he becomes frightened and visits Julia, who introduces him to her pretty niece, Catherine Banahan. Although he begins dating Catherine, Studs believes that he is still in love with Lucy. When Kenny, the last of the gang, leaves town to become a traveling vaudeville comedian, Studs realizes that he must mature and face his problems alone. After the crash of 1929 ruins his father's business and leaves Studs jobless, he turns to his priest, Father Gilhooey, for advice. After the priest tells him that Catherine is pregnant and lectures him on his responsibilities, Studs rushes to Catherine and begs her to marry him. *Attempted rape. Drunkenness. Gangs. Juvenile delinquency. Maturation.* Chicago (IL). Fathers and sons. Gangsters. House painters. Irish Americans. Mothers and sons. New Year's Eve. Nieces. Priests. Romance. Stock market crash of 1929. Teachers. Unemployment.

Note: Although the running time for the film is listed as 103 minutes in the *DV* and *Var* preview reviews, later reviews list the running time as 95 minutes. According to a Sep 1953 *NYT* news item, publicist Stephen Strassberg initially optioned the film rights to James T. Farrell's novel. The 1935 novel was comprised of three short novels written by Farrell: *Young Lonigan* (1932); *The Young Manhood of Studs Lonigan* (1934) and *Judgement Day* (1935). In the items, Strassberg stated that Ben Hecht was interested in writing the screenplay and Marlon Brando and Elia Kazan were being sought for the production. In Sep

1955, a *DV* news item noted that Lew Kerner, who was now slated to produce the film for United Artists release, had signed David Dortort to write the script. In an Apr 1960 letter to the *NYT*, author Farrell expressed great dissatisfaction with the film adaptation and announced his desire to sell his rights to the production as soon as possible and thus sever all connections to the project. Farrell decried the fact that "Studs" does not die in the film, as he does in the novel, stating that "the Studs Lonigan trilogy was conceived from the standpoint of Studs' death. Without it, the work would have been stupid and foolish." Farrell continued that "it is obvious that [the filmmakers] do not understand the Irish and do not know what life was like in the 1920's." In a 1986 letter addressed to AMPAS, writer Bernard Gordon stated that he was hired to write the film's narration after the production was completely shot and edited. Gordon noted that he worked with the film's director and editor to give it a stronger sense of continuity. Many reviews comment on the picture's unusual visual style and its "arty" feel. Although this was not Jack Nicholson's first screen appearance, it marked his first significant role. In Mar 1979, NBC broadcast a six-hour miniseries based on Farrell's novel, starring Harry Hamlin and Colleen Dewhurst and directed by James Goldstone.

AmCin Dec 1960, p. 736, 758-61. *Box* 1 Aug 1960. *DV* 30 Sep 1955. *DV* 15 Apr 1960. *DV* 27 Jul 1960, p. 3. *Har* 30 Jul 1960. *HR* 29 Feb 1960. *HR* 1 Apr 1960. *HR* 27 Jul 1960, p. 3. *MPHPD* 20 Aug 1960, p. 811. *NYT* 27 Sep 1953. *NYT* 10 Apr 1960. *NYT* 15 Dec 1960, p. 59. *Var* 27 Jul 1960, p. 6.

A STUDY OF NEGRO ARTISTS (African Americans)

The Harmon Foundation, Inc. **1937**. Si; b&w. 4 reels.

Educational/Cultural, Documentary. [*Print viewed*]. A black artist is shown painting a seascape from a waterfront dock of New York City. Unidentified artists are shown working in various other occupations, earning livings until recognition comes. The occupations depicted include subway car inspectors and drivers, street sweepers, typists, telephone operators, office workers, postal workers, elevator operators and window washers. A number of black New York artists are shown with their works, including sculptors Richmond Barthé, Augusta Savage and William Ellisworth Artis; photographer James Latimer Allen; painters Aaron Douglas, Palmer Hayden, Benjamin Spurgeon Kitchin and the late Malvin Gray Johnson; textile designer Lois Mailou Jones; and Georgette Seabrooke, who does ink drawings. Sculpture derived from "African primitives" is shown, and it is stated, "Beautifying useful objects was the African's creed. His designs have influenced such modern artists as Picasso and Matisse." In Harlem, the New York Public Library, 135th St. Branch, which houses the Division of Negro Literature, History and Prints, is seen. At the library, a landscape painting by Robert S. Duncanson is shown, as are murals by Aaron Douglas. Black artist-teachers are seen working with their students; the teachers include Charles Alston and Susie Maribel McIver. At the 7th Avenue and West 135th Street YMCA, artist-teachers Richard Wilson Lindsey and William Ellisworth Artis are shown, as is university professor Hale A. Woodruff. Also depicted are some of the professional New York galleries that welcome work by black artists, including Delphic Studios, which is presenting an exhibition of paintings by Suzanna Ogunjani. The Harmon Foundation, at which the opening reception for a show of paintings by Cuban Negro artist Pastor Argudin y Pedroso is also seen. Examples of fine arts found in the homes of prominent American blacks include "The Governor's House in Tangier" by Henry O. Tanner, etchings by Albert Alexander Smith, and "Sammy" by Sargent Johnson. Finally, the Whitney Museum of American Art is shown as a representative of galleries housing black works in permanent exhibits with representative American art. *African Americans. Libraries and librarians. Museums. New York City–Harlem. Painters (Of paintings). Sculptors. Photographers.*

Note: This film was listed in the 1936 *Education Film Catalog* under the title *Negro Artists at Work*; its producer at the time was listed as Religious Motion Picture Foundation, Inc.

SU NOCHE DE BODAS (Spanish language)

Films Paramount; controlled by Paramount Publix Corp. *Dist* Paramount Publix Corp. **1931**; Madrid, Spain opening: 4 Apr 1931; Los Angeles opening: 22 May 1931; Prod: Jan–Feb 1931 at Paramount studios in Joinville, France. Sd; b&w. 9 reels, 7,486 ft. 83 min. *Country of origin* France. Spanish language.

Dir Louis Mercanton. *Dial dir* Florián Rey. *Scr* Henry Myers. *Adpt and Spanish dial* Luis Fernández Ardavín. *Photog* Enzo Riccioni.

Song(s): "Recordar," "Cantares que el viento llevó," "Trabajar es mi divisa," "Blancaflor," "A la mujer a quien digas" and "Entre todas te busqué."

Source: Based on the play *Der Gatte des Fräuleins* by Gábor Drégely (Vienna, 1916) and the English-language adaptation, *Little Miss Bluebeard,* by Avery Hopwood (New York, 28 Aug 1923).

Cast: Imperio Argentina (*Gisèle Landry*), Pepe Romeu (*Claude Mallet*), Miguel Ligero (*Adolphe Latour*), Manuel Russell (*Francis Calvet*), Rosita Díaz Gimeno (*Loulou*), Emilia Barrado (*Simone*), Olga Valéry (*Colette*), Antonio Monjardin (*Pemper*), Antonia Arévalo (*Madame Marchal*).

Comedy, with songs. [*Not viewed*]. [The following plot summary is based on the English-language version of this film, *Her Wedding Night*; character names refer to that version. For further information regarding the English-language version, please see the note below and the entry for *Her Wedding Night* in the *AFI Catalog of Feature Films, 1921-30*.] Norma Martin, an American film actress vacationing in Paris, weary of male admirers, leaves with her friend Gloria Marshall for the south of France. On the same train is Larry Charters, a famous composer of popular songs, and his friend, Bob Hawley, Gloria's fiancé; to escape pursuing worshipers, he persuades Bob to exchange identities during the trip. When Norma and Bob are left behind at a station, the mayor mistakes them for two elopers thought to be on the train, and before they know it they are married, Bob still masquerading as Larry. Norma and Bob then arrive at their originally intended destination, and complications ensue when Bertie Bird and Mrs. Marshall take Norma and Larry to be man and wife. In spite of the humorous confusion, they decide to let the marriage remain legal, and Bertie gets to sleep after two nights of farcical madness. *Actors and actresses. Composers. Courtship. Elopement. France. Impersonation and imposture. Motion pictures. Paris (France).*

Note: Paramount made four foreign versions of *Her Wedding Night*, which was directed by Frank Tuttle and starred Clara Bow and Ralph Forbes ((see *AFI Catalog of Feature Films, 1921-30*, F2.2457). The running times listed were calculated from footage given in NYSA records. The *Var* review of the French version lists a running time for the Paris showing of 103 min. Although the 1930 English-language version was made in the U.S., the foreign-language versions were produced at the Paramount studios in Joinville, France. In addition to Spanish and French versions, German and Portuguese versions were also produced, but no information has been located concerning showings in the U.S. of these latter versions. The German version, entitled *Ich heirate meinen Mann*, was directed by E. W. Emo and starred Trude Berliner and Kurt Vespermann; the Portuguese version, entitled *A minha noite de núpcias*, was also directed by Emo and starred Beatriz Costa and Leopoldo Froes. Some sources include Enriqueta Serrano, Carlos Díaz de Mendoza and Geneviève Félix in the cast of the Spanish version, but they were not listed in the credits of the film and their participation has not been confirmed.

Other language version(s):
Marions-nous (French language)

1931; Paris opening: 6 Mar 1931; New York opening: 4 Apr 1931; Prod: at Paramount studios in Joinville, France. Sd (Western Electric); b&w. 8,700 ft. 97 min. French language.

Dir Louis Mercanton. *Wrt* Saint-Granier. *Photog* René Guissart.

French-language cast: Alice Cocéa (*Gisèle Landry*), Fernand Gravey (*Francis Latour*), Marguerite Moreno (*Madame Marchal*), Robert Burnier (*Claude Mallet*), Pierre Etchepare (*Adolphe*), Jacqueline Delubac (*Simone*), Hélène d'Algy (*Lolita*), Véra Flory (*Maroussia*), Marcelle Lucas, Loute Isnard, Odette Laigre, Lise Hestia, Janine Mirande, Marcel Carpentier, André Siméon, Jean Mercanton, Durafour, Handrey Bodson, Jean Granier, M. Fretel. [*French version not viewed*].

La Cinematographie Française 26 Dec 1931. *Var* 25 Mar 1931, p. 71.

SU ÚLTIMA NOCHE (Spanish language)

Metro-Goldwyn-Mayer Corp.; controlled by Loew's, Inc. *Dist* Culver Export, Inc. **1931**; San Juan, Puerto Rico opening: 1 May 1931; Los Angeles opening: 17 Jul 1931; Prod: mid-Oct—early Nov 1930. Sd; b&w. 9 reels, 7,005 ft. 78 min. Spanish language.

Prod George Kann. *Dir* Chester M. Franklin. *Dial dir* Carlos F. Borcosque. *Asst dir* Al Shenberg. *Scr* Leonard Praskins. *Spanish version wrt* Eduardo Ugarte. *Photog* Ray Binger. *Art dir* Cedric Gibbons. *Film ed* Peggy O'Day. *Rec dir* Douglas Shearer.

Source: Based on the play *Patachon* by Maurice Hennequin and Félix Duquesnel (Paris, 1907) and the English-language adaptation, *Toto*, by Achmed Abdullah (New York, 21 Mar 1921).

Cast: Ernesto Vilches (*Mario Albertini*), Conchita Montenegro (*Luisa*), María Alba (*Elena Desano*), Juan de Landa (*Aquiles Desano*), Romualdo Tirado (*Pedro*), Manuel Granado (*Roberto Rivarol*), Luz Segovia (*Clara*), Julio Abadía (*Armando*), Fernando Morán.

Domestic, Comedy-drama. [*Not viewed*]. [The following plot summary is based on the English-language version of this film, *The Gay Deceiver*; character names refer to that version. For further

information regarding the English-language version, please see the note below and the entry for *The Gay Deceiver* in the *AFI Catalog of Feature Films, 1921-30.*] Antoine de Tillois leaves his puritanical wife and in Paris becomes known as King Toto, leader of the bohemian set. Their daughter, Louise, spends 8 months of each year with her mother in Blois and 4 in Paris with her father, her sole concern being to see them reunited. Although Louise has fallen in love with Robert Le Rivarol, she vows not to marry until she accomplishes her aim; consequently, Toto pretends to reform and announces he is giving up his Paris life to return to his wife. Merinville, her accountant, and his nephew—both after Louise's money—discover that Toto has been corresponding with the Countess de Sano, his latest mistress; they try to blackmail Toto and scheme to get an annulment of Louise's marriage, but Toto thwarts their plot. When the countess absconds with her husband's secretary, Toto and his wife are happily reconciled. *Bohemians and bohemianism. Courtship. Family relationships. Infidelity. Marriage. Paris (France).*

Note: The working title of this film was *Toto*. The English-language original of this film, *The Gay Deceiver*, which was released in Sep 1926, was directed by John M. Stahl and starred Lew Cody and Marceline Day. The Spanish version was primarily adapted by Miguel de Zárraga in a form faithful to the original, and subsequently reworked with variations by Eduardo Ugarte According to some sources, José López Rubio also worked on the screenplay, but his participation in the released film has not been confirmed.

Cinl Mar 1931, p. 36. *HF* 18 Oct 1930, p. 23. *HF* 25 Oct 1930, p. 23.

SU ÚLTIMO AMOR *see* MI ÚLTIMO AMOR

SUBMARINE RAIDER (Japanese Americans)

Columbia Pictures Corp. *Dist* Columbia Pictures Corp. 4 Jun 1942; Prod: 27 Feb–12 Mar 1942 [©Columbia Pictures Corp.; 14 May 1942; LP11330]. Sd (Western Electric Mirrophonic Recording); b&w. 5,792 ft. 65 min. PCA cert no. 8234.

Prod Wallace MacDonald. [*Exec prod* Irving Briskin]. *Dir* Lew Landers. [*Asst dir* Seymour Friedman]. *Orig scr* Aubrey Wisberg. *Dir of photog* Franz Planer. *Art dir* Lionel Banks. *Assoc* Paul Youngblood. *Film ed* William Lyon. *Mus dir* M. W. Stoloff. [*Sd eng* John Goodrich].

Cast: John Howard (*Chris Warren*), Marguerite Chapman (*Sue Curry*), Bruce Bennett (*First Officer Russell*), Warren Ashe (*Bill Warren*), Eileen O'Hearn (*Vera Lane*), Nino Pepitone (*Captain Yamanada*), Philip Ahn (*First Officer Kawakami*), Larry Parks (*Sparksie*), Rudy Robles (*Steward Seffi*), Roger Clark (*Grant Duncan*), Forrest Tucker (*Pulaski*), Eddie Laughton (*Shannon*), Stanley Brown (*Levy*), Jack Shay (*Oleson*), Gary Breckner (*Brick Brandon*), [Hans von Morhart (*Granz*)], [Allen Jung (*Bardo*)], [Richard Loo (*Suji*)], [Paul Fung (*Suguye*)], [Chester Gan (*Yoshiwara*)], [Roland Got (*Kenichi*)], [Keye Luke (*Tesei*)], [Juan Varro (*Duke Kahola*)], [John Holland (*Bryan*)], [Lal Chand Mehra (*Disu*)], [Alma Carroll (*Marge*)], [James Leong (*Toramatsu*)], [George Lee (*Tsuruji*)], [Beal Wong (*Hayaka*)], [Eddie Lee (*Takeo*)], [George Walcott (*Hank*)], [John Tyrrell (*Blake*)], [Bruce Wong (*Shinji*)], [Luke Chan (*Hitoshi*)].

World War II, Drama. [*Print viewed*]. On the afternoon of 6 Dec 1941, a Japanese aircraft carrier, the *Hiranamu*, drifts quietly in the South Pacific when a message from Tokyo suddenly brings the vessel to life. Ordering full steam ahead, Capt. Yamanada looks at his map and draws a circle around Pearl Harbor. That afternoon, in the same waters, Grant Duncan entertains some friends on the yacht *Vayu*, while the American submarine *Sea Serpent*, under the command of Chris Warren, is taking a routine cruise. When the watch on the *Hiranamu* spies the *Vayu*, Capt. Yamanada informs his aides that there are to be no witnesses to the carrier's presence and orders the yacht shelled. The yacht sinks and only Sue Curry and two other passengers survive. Sue and the others are relieved to see a plane flying overhead until its Japanese pilot rakes their lifeboat with his guns. Sue escapes by jumping over the side and is later picked up by the *Sea Serpent*. Shortly after the Japanese pilot returns and reports that all the survivors are dead, the *Hiranamu* picks up the submarine's attempt to radio Sue's story to the mainland. Knowing that the pilot failed, Yamanada orders him to kill himself. Then he dispatches another plane, piloted by his own son, to sink the submarine. At the same time, the radio operator aboard the carrier jams the airwaves to prevent the submarine's message from reaching the mainland. When the plane attacks the sub, Chris saves his craft by making a crash dive. In the return fire, the pilot is wounded, sending the plane crashing out of control to a watery death. With night

approaching, the *Hiranamu* steals ahead. As darkness covers Pearl Harbor, Bill Warren, Chris's brother and a government agent, senses impending disaster. Early in the evening, an attempt is made on Bill's life. Later, at a café, Bill notices some strange signaling being sent from a room in the café to an offshore ship. Sneaking into the office from which the signals emanate, Bill is struck from behind by a Japanese operative and left unconscious. The next morning, Bill awakens to the sound of Japanese bomber planes buzzing overhead. Bill tries to phone the local news broadcaster to warn him, but he is cut off. Meanwhile, the men onboard the *Sea Serpent* are listening to the news broadcast over their damaged radio set when there is a dramatic interruption and the announcer exclaims that Pearl Harbor is being bombed. Listening unemotionally as his brother's death is announced, Chris hatches a plan to trap the Japanese carrier. Knowing that the *Hiranamu* is somewhere in the vicinity, Chris instructs a Japanese speaking sailor to impersonate the downed pilot, hoping to lure the carrier to the submarine. After the planes responsible for the attack on Pearl Harbor return to the carrier, Capt. Yamanada steers the ship toward the submarine. As the carrier nears, the *Sea Serpent* torpedoes the ship, thus avenging Pearl Harbor. *Aircraft carriers. Battles. Japan. Navy. Pearl Harbor (HI), Attack on, 1941. Sea captains. Submarine boats. United States. Navy. Air pilots, Military. Attempted murder. Bombs. Brothers. Cafes. Fathers and sons. Government agents. Hara-kiri. Lifeboats. Sea rescues. Torpedoes. Traps.*

Note: The working title of this film was *Missing Submarine*. Although a *HR* chart places William Wright in the cast, his participation in the released film has not been confirmed. Another *HR* news item notes that the Hawaiian scenes were filmed at Rancho Santa Ana in Southern California. To lend authenticity to the Pearl Harbor scenes, the film utilized footage taken near the U.S. Naval base that was originally shot for the picture *Honolulu Lu*, but was then held back for inclusion in this film, according to another *HR* news item. For additional films dealing with the attack on Pearl Harbor, see entry below for *Wake Island* and consult the Subject Index.

Box 4 Jul 1942. *HR* 3 Mar 1942, p. 10. *HR* 5 Mar 1942, p. 4. *HR* 6 Mar 1942, p. 6. *HR* 1 Oct 1942, p. 4. *MPHPD* 27 Jun 1942, p. 738. *NYT* 22 Jun 1942, p. 19. *Var* 24 Jun 1942, p. 8.

SUBMARINE SCHOOL *see* CRASH DIVE

SUBMARINE ZONE *see* ESCAPE TO GLORY

SUCH IS LIFE (1931) *see* COSÌ È LA VITA

SUCH IS LIFE (Greek language)

Hellenic Cinema Corp. **1931**; Prod: recorded by Powers Cinephone at the Recording Laboratories of America [©Anthony J. Danas; 28 Feb 1931; LU2014]. Sd; b&w. 9 reels, ca. 11,000 ft. Greek language.

Supv James Vincent. *Dir* James Vincent. *Story* Dr. Orpheus Caravias.

Song(s): "Students' Song," "Yolanda's Song," "Cabaret Song," composer[s] unknown.

Cast: Rea Durey (*Yolanda*), Aristides Lukas (*Andreas Holmes*), Gerassimos Courounlis (*Pindarus*), Lambi Vasilaki (*Evangelis*), Myra Mirora (*Yolanda's mother*), Loukianos Cavadias (*Music publisher*), Margaret Canneri (*Landlady*), Alex Anastasiades (*Tsaldes*), Lola Papas (*Doris*), Pofi Athanasiou.

Melodrama, with songs. [*Not viewed*]. In an Athens University, students await the famous Professor Andreas Holmes, who will present his latest scientific discovery, the ability to revive a dead human heart. When Andreas enters the amphitheatre and removes the sheet from the waiting corpse, however, he loses his composure and cries out, as he has recognized the lifeless corpse as his former lover, Yolanda. As Andreas watches in disbelief, Yolanda's corpse begins to speak and then transform into a skeleton. Shocked at Andreas' strange behavior, the students watch in disbelief as the doctor recalls the happy days of his courtship of Yolanda: Yolanda and Andreas recline on the grass before a ruined convent, and Yolanda is shocked at the passion in Andreas' kiss. Pindarus, a befuddled trustee of the university who befriends the students, calls the couple away to the tavern where their friends await them. At the tavern, Yolanda sings a song about men's fickle natures and then confesses to Andreas that she is afraid of her love for him. At home, Yolanda's hard-working mother and low-class uncle Evangelis argue about the money Yolanda will need to finish her studies. Evangelis believes that Yolanda is wasting her time at the university and should come work at his café, but Yolanda's mother believes that such a job will taint her daughter's reputation and prevent her from becoming a respectable wife or a doctor. Yolanda arrives home and, seeing her distraught mother, insists that they do not need Evangelis' money. Yolanda then goes to

a music publisher to try to sell some songs that she has written and thus raise the five-hundred dollars needed for her registration fees. The music publisher tells her that the market is "jazz mad" and offers the dejected Yolanda a pittance for her songs. On registration day at the university, Pindarus convinces Andreas, who is without money, to give up his own scientific experiments and take a job at a local clinic. Upon discovering Andreas' plan, Yolanda insists that she will pay his registration fees with money that an uncle sent from America. Yolanda goes to her uncle's cabaret, a dump called "The House of Paradise," and she asks for a job, finally accepting an advance of five-hundred dollars instead of the one-thousand she had originally requested. Sacrificing her own education, Yolanda uses the money to register Andreas at the university. On Halloween Eve, Andreas, unaware of Yolanda's new job, tries to study but a group of friends burst into his room and carry him out to Evangelis' cabaret. Finally in the festive spirit, Andreas leads the revelry, and as he offers drinks to the musicians, he sees Yolanda at the piano. He screams that she is a liar, as she has been claiming to have had headaches every night. Evangelis insists that Yolanda keep playing after Andreas runs away. After closing, when he forces himself on her, she gives him a mortal blow to the head with a hammer. At a Greek prison, Pindarus and Andreas visit Yolanda, and Andreas, who now understands all, pledges his love. Back at the lab, Andreas, driven, continues his work on pig corpses and neglects to visit Yolanda, who is ill and suffering from a broken heart. Eventually becoming renowned for his experiments on regenerating human life, Andreas gives a lecture with the President of the Republic of Greece in attendance and then meets a rich philanthropist, Mr. Tsaldes, who offers him money to conduct his experiments and a trip to America with the Tsaldes family. At the prison, Pindarus tells Yolanda that Andreas is no longer one of them and that her love for him will entail sacrificing herself for his happiness. Sometime later, after an acquittal and a move to another city, Yolanda goes back to the apartment building where both she and Andreas once lived, and she overhears Pindarus tell the landlady that Andreas has married Doris Tsaldes, daughter of the rich philanthropist. Ten years later, after learning that Andreas has returned to Greece, Pindarus reads in the newspaper about an unidentified dying woman who is donating her body to science. Believing the woman to be Yolanda, he goes to her and realizes that only Andreas' expertise can save her. Andreas does not arrive in time and Yolanda dies crying out for one last look at her lost lover. Back in the university in the present, Andreas nearly faints and is carried out into the lobby. When he comes to his senses, he cries out that he will save Yolanda. But Pindarus, stoic and ennobled by the sight of death's inexorability, looks at Yolanda's corpse and states with sagacity, "Such is life." *Athens (Greece). Love affairs. Revivification. Scientists. Self-sacrifice. Universities. Acquittals. Attempted rape. Cabarets. Corpses. Experiments, Human. Halloween. Hallucinations. High society. Justifiable homicide. Money. Musicians. Philanthropists. Poverty. Presidents. Transplantation of organs, tissues, etc.. Women prisoners.*

Note: The plot summary and cast credits were taken from a pre-shooting script, written in Greek with side-by-side English translations, deposited with the NYSA. A news item in the 31 Jan 1931 *MPH* states that Anthony Danas was president of Hellenic Cinema Corporation. The article also states that the film was the first talking feature ever made "with the exclusive use of Greek."

MPH 31 Jan 1931, p. 43.

THE SUDDEN GENTLEMAN (Irish Americans)
Triangle Film Corp. *Dist* Triangle Distributing Corp. 2 Dec **1917**. Si; b&w. 5 reels.
Dir Thomas N. Heffron. *Scen* Joseph Anthony Roach. *Story* R. Cecil Smith. *Cam* R. E. Irish and Edward Gheller.
Cast: William Desmond (*Garry Garrity*), Mary McIvor (*Louise Evans*), Jack Richardson (*Count Caminetti*), Margaret Shillingford (*Mrs. Hawtry*), Alfred Hollingsworth (*George Douglas*), Donald Fuller (*Edward Douglas*), Alberta Lee (*Mrs. Burns*), Walter Perry (*Rafferty*), Percy Challenger (*Old Miles*).
Comedy-drama. Garry Garrity, an Irish blacksmith, receives word from America that he has fallen heir to his uncle's millions. Arriving in Chicago to take charge of his estate, Garry's awkward ways incur the enmity of his cousin and ward, Louise Evans, but after Louise sees through the rough surface to Garry's sterling qualities, the two fall in love. This disturbs Count Caminetti, who had designs on both Louise and the fortune. The count schemes with Mrs. Hawtry, who has

visions of becoming a wealthy countess, to frame Garry in a compromising situation, thus forcing him to marry Mrs. Hawtry, who would then divorce him and sue for alimony. When Louise hears the scandalous rumors generated by the count, she insists that Garry marry Mrs. Hawtry until an innkeeper admits that it has been a frame-up. Garry rushes to confront the count and as he is choking a confession from him, Louise enters. After overhearing everything, Louise begs Garry's forgiveness. *Blacksmiths. Cousins. Frame-ups. Inheritance. Irish. Nobility. Wards and guardians. Chicago (IL). Fights. Innkeepers. Ireland. Rumors. Widows.*

Note: Sources disagree concerning the cameraman of this film.

Motog 8 Dec 1917, p. 1208. *MPN* 8 Dec 1917, p. 4040. *MPW* 8 Dec 1917, p. 1481. *MPW* 15 Dec 1917, p. 1679. *NYDM* 1 Dec 1917, p. 19. *Var* 30 Nov 1917, p. 46. *Wid's* 29 Nov 1917, p. 764.

SUEGRA PARA DOS see **CHÉRIE**

SUGAR HILL BABY (African Americans)
Creative Cinema Co. *Dist* International Road Shows, Inc. 1 Jan **1938**. Sd; b&w. 6 reels, 5,928 ft. 66 min.
Dir Irwin R. Franklyn.
African American, Gangster, Drama. [*Not viewed*]. In Harlem, Winnie Caswell helps loan shark Jeff Babcock dupe his clients into taking out fake loans. One day, Roger Carter, the newly appointed activities director of the Harlem Settlement house, gives a speech in which he pledges to continue striving toward the "upliftment" of his race. To this end, Carter promises to provide guidance, jobs and an education to the people of Harlem and make it the "cleanest, happiest, and most prosperous community in America." Later, at Winnie's party, Jeff tells Winnie that he regrets having made a deal with her to outfit her Sugar Hill apartment in exchange for sending him new "suckers" to borrow from his high interest lending firm. He complains that the upkeep on her apartment has taken the profits out of his earnings. When Winnie tries to defend her lavish spending by telling Jeff that she is trying to get Harrison, the owner of the Unity Club, to take out a loan, Jeff accuses her of having romantic interests in Morgan, Harrison's employee. Winnie calms Jeff's nerves by reassuring him that he is the only man in her life. After reading about Roger's plan to clean up Harlem and his crusade against the Sugar Hill residents, Winnie tells her friends that he will not succeed in his goal and insists that he is only a "four-flusher" looking to chisel in on her racket. Some of Winnie's guests disagree with her and wager that she will not be able to get Roger to come to one of her parties, as she says she will do. Roger, meanwhile, proposes marriage to Mildred Porterfield, an employee of his, and she accepts. Later, at an assembly of Harlem residents, Roger gives another speech, detailing his plans to improve the community, and secures pledges from audience members to contribute money to finance a youth center. Winnie, who has been listening to Roger's speech, introduces herself to the reformer and offers to help him, but her true motives become apparent when she convinces Jeff that she can get Roger to "hang himself" with a plan she has devised. As part of the plan, Winnie asks Roger to meet his new "supporters" at her apartment later that week, which he does. After introducing Roger to her guests, Winnie and Jeff cleverly snare Roger into accepting a loan rather than a contribution to finance his youth center. When Roger returns home, Mildred sees the names on the check and realizes that he has been had and that he may have lost his property, which he put up as collateral. Soon after Roger hires Winnie to work for him as his social service director, he falls in love with her and she leads him astray. Roger loses his property and is accused by his committee of having connived with thieves and mobsters to ruin the settlement. Unable to contain their anger, some members of the committee attack Roger as he tries to explain the situation. Mildred, meanwhile, rushes to Winnie's and forces her to go to the settlement house and tell the crowd that it was she who concocted the scheme. Jeff and the other racketeers are soon convicted for their crimes, and Roger is reinstated as the director of the settlement and marries Mildred. *African Americans. Loan sharks. New York City—Harlem. Racketeers. Reformers. Bill collectors. Confession (Law). Engagements. Molls. Moral corruption. Mothers and daughters. Parties. Settlers. Speeches. Wagers.*

Note: The above plot summary was taken from a dialogue script of the film contained in the New York State Archives. According to credits in the script, Nita Rio was the president of Creative Cinema Company, which produced the film.

THE SULLIVANS (Irish Americans)

The U.S.S. The Sullivans, Inc.; Twentieth Century-Fox Film Corp. *Dist* Twentieth Century-Fox Film Corp. Feb **1944**; New York opening: 9 Feb 1944; Los Angeles opening: 23 Feb 1944; Prod: early Sep—mid-Nov 1943 [©Twentieth Century-Fox Film Corp.; 9 Feb 1944; LP12840]. Sd (Western Electric Recording); b&w. 12 reels, 10,091 ft. 111-112 min. PCA cert no. 9650.

Prod Sam Jaffe. *Assoc prod* Robert T. Kane. *Dir* Lloyd Bacon. [*Asst dir* Percy Ikerd]. [*Dial dir* Hugh Cummings]. *Scr* Mary McCall, Jr. *Story* Edward Doherty and Jules Schermer. *Dir of photog* Lucien Andriot. *Special photog eff* Fred Sersen. *Art dir* James Basevi and Leland Fuller. *Film ed* Louis Loeffler. *Set dec* Thomas Little. *Assoc* Fred J. Rode. *Cost* Rene Hubert. *Mus dir* Alfred Newman. *Mus* Cyril J. Mockridge. *Sd* George Leverett and Harry M. Leonard. [*Tech adv* Thomas F. Sullivan, Alleta Sullivan, Genevieve Sullivan, Katherine Mary Sullivan, Chaplain William Muenster, Lt. Charles N. Wang and Dr. J. A. Wickstrom]. [*Unit mgr* Booth McCracken]. [*Loc mgr* R. L. Hough].

Music: "You'll Never Know" by Harry Warren; "Anchors Aweigh" by Charles A. Zimmerman.

Song(s): "Who Threw the Overalls in Mistress Murphy's Chowder," music and lyrics by George L. Giefer.

Cast: Anne Baxter [(*Katherine Mary*)], Thomas Mitchell [(*Thomas F. Sullivan*)], Selena Royle [(*Alleta Sullivan*)], Edward Ryan [(*Albert Leo Sullivan*)], Trudy Marshall [(*Genevieve "Gen" Sullivan*)], John Campbell [(*Francis Henry Sullivan*)], James Cardwell [(*George Thomas Sullivan*)], John Alvin [(*Madison "Matt" Abel Sullivan*)], George Offerman, Jr. [(*Joseph Eugene Sullivan*)], Roy Roberts [(*Father Francis*)], Ward Bond [(*Commander Robinson*)], [Mary McCarty (*Gladys*)], [Bobby Driscoll (*Al, as a child*)], [Nancy June Robinson (*Genevieve, as a child*)], [Marvin Davis (*Frank, as a child*)], [Buddy Swan (*George, as a child*)], [Billy Cummings (*Matt, as a child*)], [Johnny Calkins (*Joe, as a child*)], [John Nesbitt (*Admiral*)], [Selmer Jackson (*Damage control officer*)], [Harry Shannon, Harry Strang (*C.P.O.s*)], [Barbara Brown (*Nurse*)], [Larry Thompson (*Yeoman*)], [Addison Richards (*Naval captain*)], [Ronnie Harris (*Chauncey Griffin*)], [Betty Farrington (*Mrs. Griffin*)], [Bobby Larson, Gerald Mackey, Eddie Nichols, Merrill Rodin, Leon Tyler, Gene Collins, Charles Bates (*Boys*)], [Elsa Peterson (*Nun*)], [Stephen Barclay, John Whitney (*Naval talkers*)], [Mel Schubert, Mike Kilian (*Junior officers*)], [Grandon Rhodes (*Naval doctor*)], [Frank Wilcox, George Lynn (*Officers*)], [Knox Manning (*Commentator*)], [Joe Haworth, Bernie Sell (*Stretcher bearers*)], [Mae Marsh].

Biography, Domestic, Drama. [*Print viewed*]. In the small town of Waterloo, Iowa, Thomas and Alleta Sullivan spend the early years of their married life happily attending the christenings of the latest additions to their Irish-American, Catholic family: George Thomas in 1914, Francis "Frank" Henry in 1916, Joseph Eugene in 1918, Madison "Matt" Abel in 1919 and Albert Leo in 1922. As the boys grow, they are doted upon by their mother and sister Genevieve and given stern but loving guidance by their father, who is a railroad freight conductor. The day before Al's first communion, the youngster persuades Alleta to let him wear his new suit to attend confession. The suit is ruined, however, when the boys, who do everything together, brawl with some neighborhood kids over their new dog, Chiefie. Alleta is dismayed by their conduct, but Father Francis allows Al to take communion after the boys assure him that they bear no grudge against their rivals. Later, the boys get into more mischief when they find a broken-down boat and caulk its holes with mud. The vessel stays afloat until it reaches the middle of a lake, then begins to sink. Chiefie aids in rescuing Al, thereby assuring his place in the family. Upset by Al's near-drowning, Alleta makes her sons promise that they will not set foot in a boat again until they are adults. Later, the youngsters are complaining about fetching wood for Alleta's stove when Tom makes an offhand remark about building a wood box in the kitchen wall. Wanting to help Alleta and save themselves some work, the boys obtain lumber on credit and begin building the wood box. George becomes irritated by Frank's imperious manner, however, and leaves the project. The boys then break a water pipe and the kitchen is flooded. George rushes to help, and when Tom arrives and surveys the damage, he assumes that George, as the eldest, is responsible. Before George can explain their good intentions, Tom slaps him, and the boy runs off. Frank confesses all to Tom, and as the evening wears on, each family member invents an excuse to search for the runaway.

George reappears the next morning, and after reconciling with his son, Tom declares that this should teach the Sullivans to stick together. Years later, in 1939, the boys are grown and only Al is still in high school. On the day that George wins a motorcycle race, Al meets Katherine Mary, an only child who lives with her father. Despite their youth, Al and Katherine Mary fall in love, and soon Al shows Gen the engagement ring that he has purchased. Believing that Al is too young for marriage, his brothers tease Katherine Mary when she comes for dinner and convince her that Al has many girl friends. After Katherine Mary leaves in tears and Al sinks into despair, the brothers realize the damage they have done, and with Gen, Tom and Alleta in tow, they apologize to Katherine Mary. Soon after, Katherine Mary and Al are married, and ten months later, are expecting a baby. Al is fired for taking the afternoon off to escort his wife to the doctor, but his brothers vow to help them out. Later, months after little Jimmy has been welcomed into the family, the family is lolling about on Sunday, 7 December 1941, when they hear a radio report about the attack on Pearl Harbor. The boys realize that one of their friends was on the *Arizona* and resolve to join the Navy to avenge him. Al decides that he cannot go with his brothers, due to his family responsibilities, but when Katherine Mary sees his despondent face, she tells him to accompany the others to the recruiting station. The brothers tell Commander Robinson that they want to serve on the same ship, but Robinson states that the Navy can make no such guarantees. The brothers leave, but later, after George receives his draft notice, he writes to the Navy Department and obtains official permission for the boys to serve together. Later, Tom, Alleta and Katherine Mary eagerly await letters from their loved ones, who are serving aboard the *Juneau* in the Pacific. The fighting in the Pacific grows more intense as a battle rages off the Solomon Islands, and one day, the *Juneau* is hit. Four of the brothers find each other, then realize that George is below in sick bay. They rush down to get him, and when George insists they leave him behind, Al replies, "We can't go swimming without you." Soon after, Robinson visits the Sullivan home and tells Katherine Mary, Tom, Alleta and Gen that all five of the brothers were killed in action. Stunned, Tom goes to work and salutes the water tower on which his sons used to stand and wave to him. Sometime later, Tom, Katherine Mary and Gen, who has joined the WAVES, watch with pride while Alleta christens a new destroyer, the U.S.S. *The Sullivans*. As Tom and Alleta watch the ship sail away, Alleta declares, "Tom, our boys are afloat again." *Brothers. Family life. Maturation. Military service, Voluntary. Sullivan family. World War II. Catholics. Dogs. Fistfights. Grief. Guadalcanal Island (Solomon Islands), Battle of, 1942-1943. Heroism. Iowa. Irish Americans. Motorcycle racing. Newlyweds. Officers (Military). Pearl Harbor (HI), Attack on, 1941. Pregnancy. Priests. Self-sacrifice. Ships. Sisters. Smoking. United States. Navy. Weddings. Whistling.*

Note: This film was retitled *The Fighting Sullivans* two months after its initial release. According to a 4 Apr 1944 *HR* news item, after the picture failed to attract large audiences, Twentieth Century-Fox executives changed its title, emulating "a successful New Jersey showman with a genius for redundancy." The film is based on the lives of the Sullivan brothers—George, Francis, Joseph, Madison and Albert—who were killed in action during the battle of Guadalcanal in Nov 1942 while serving aboard the cruiser *Juneau*. George and Francis, who had served a previous tour in the Navy, enlisted with their younger brothers after the attack on Pearl Harbor in order to avenge a lost friend. The brothers obtained special permission to serve together, but after their deaths, for which the entire nation mourned, the Navy officially declared that family members could not serve on the same vessel during wartime. Only ten seamen survived the attack on the *Juneau*. The brothers' parents, Mr. and Mrs. Thomas Sullivan, traveled extensively after their sons's deaths, visiting defense plants and selling war bonds. On 4 Apr 1943, Mrs. Sullivan christened a destroyer named in honor of her sons, and in Aug 1995, Al's granddaughter christened another destroyer named after the Sullivans.

A 15 Mar 1943 *HR* news item announcing producer Sam Jaffe and director Lloyd Bacon's intention to make the film indicated that Jules Schermer would be the picture's producer. According to *HR* news items, the film was made with the cooperation of the Navy and the Sullivan family. A 12 Jul 1943 *HR* news item stated that the Sullivans would "share in the proceeds of the picture." Later news items and press releases indicate that Mr. and Mrs. Sullivan, their daughter Genevieve and daughter-in-law Katherine Mary, who was Al's widow, were all present during parts of the filming and acted as technical advisers. According to a 28 Oct 1943 *HR* news item, Jaffe also secured the services of Chaplain William Muenster to supervise the wedding sequence. The news item further stated that in real life, Muenster had officiated at the marriage of Al and Katherine Mary. A studio press release noted that Lt. Charles N. Wang, who was George's superior officer when the *Juneau* was sunk, would be acting as a technical adviser, along with Guadalcanal veteran Dr. J. A. Wickstrom, of the Marine Corps.

Due to the shortage of available actors during the war, producers Jaffe and

Robert T. Kane conducted an extensive search for the film's leads, and actors considered for parts included Dane Clark, Richard Crane, Harry Patterson and Jimmie Martin. According to a 5 Aug 1943 *HR* item, the producers limited the initial tests to fifty feet in order to conserve film, and grouped the actors in fives. Jaffe also announced that he was "combing the ranks of discharged servicemen to play the adult characters, feeling that their military experience [would] give reality to the yarn." Actresses considered for the role of Mrs. Sullivan included Phyllis Povah and Dale Winter. A 27 Sep 1943 *HR* news item noted that Roger Clark, Sally Yarnell and Gerrie Noonan had been added to the cast, but their participation in the released film has not been confirmed. John Alvin was borrowed from Warner Bros. for the production, which was largely filmed on location in Santa Rosa, CA. A 24 Oct 1943 *NYT* article reported that by agreement with the Chamber of Commerce, the studio would not employ Santa Rosa residents as extras on the film unless they "carried cards from the Chamber testifying that they had volunteered to help in the harvesting of Santa Rosa's seasonal crops." The production company also had to agree to give at least three days notice for large purchases of food. According to a 9 Nov 1943 *HR* news item, the producers canceled a location shooting trip to the San Diego naval base when they decided to limit the war scene footage to the sinking of the *Juneau*, and not include any other scenes of the brothers in uniform. Another Nov 1943 news item noted that the filming of the ship's sinking was shot on the first anniversary of the actual event. The picture marked the screen debuts of John Campbell, James Cardwell, Nancy June Robinson, Marvin Davis and Billy Cummings.

According to the *NYT* review, Mr. and Mrs. Sullivan attended the film's opening in New York and sold war bonds in the lobby. The Hollywood premiere, which benefitted the Naval Aid Auxiliary, was attended by *Juneau* officer Lt. Cmdr. Roger O'Neill, according to a *LAT* article. O'Neill offered a "splendid tribute" to his lost shipmates.

Box 12 Feb 1944. *DV* 23 Aug 1943. *DV* 3 Feb 1944, p. 3. *FD* 3 Feb 1944, p. 9. *HR* 18 Feb 1943, p. 3. *HR* 15 Mar 1943, p. 1, 6. *HR* 27 May 1943, p. 4. *HR* 12 Jul 1943, p. 6. *HR* 15 Jul 1943, p. 4, 11. *HR* 16 Jul 1943, pp. 1-2. *HR* 22 Jul 1943, p. 9. *HR* 26 Jul 1943, p. 6. *HR* 4 Aug 1943, p. 8. *HR* 5 Aug 1943, p. 6. *HR* 12 Aug 1943, p. 6. *HR* 16 Aug 1943, p. 4. *HR* 3 Sep 1943, p. 1. *HR* 10 Sep 1943, p. 11. *HR* 20 Sep 1943, p. 2. *HR* 24 Sep 1943, p. 6. *HR* 27 Sep 1943, p. 12. *HR* 28 Oct 1943, p. 3. *HR* 9 Nov 1943, p. 9. *HR* 12 Nov 1943, p. 9. *HR* 15 Nov 1943, p. 2. *HR* 3 Feb 1944, p. 3, 11. *HR* 14 Feb 1944, p. 14. *HR* 22 Feb 1944, pp. 6-9. *HR* 23 Feb 1944, p. 2. *HR* 4 Apr 1944, p. 8. *MPD* 3 Feb 1944, p. 1, 3. *MPHPD* 5 Feb 1944, p. 1741. *LAT* 24 Feb 1944. *LAT* 13 Aug 1995. *NYT* 13 Jan 1944, p. 10. *NYT* 4 Apr 1943, p. 11. *NYT* 24 Oct 1943. *NYT* 10 Feb 1944, p. 19. *NYT* 28 May 1944. *Var* 9 Feb 1944, p. 12

SULLIVAN'S TRAVELS (African Americans)

Paramount Pictures, Inc. *Dist* Paramount Pictures, Inc. **1941**; New York opening: 28 Jan 1942; Prod: 12 May—22 Jul 1941 [©Paramount Pictures, Inc.; 4 Dec 1941; LP11049]. Sd (Western Electric Mirrophonic Recording); b&w. 9 reels, 8,126 ft. 90-91 min. Passed by the National Board of Review. PCA cert no. 7382.

[*Exec prod* B. G. DeSylva]. *Assoc prod* Paul Jones. *Dir* Preston Sturges. [*1st asst dir* John Morse]. [*2d asst dir* Barton Adams]. *Wrt* Preston Sturges. [*Asst wrt* Ernst Laemmle]. *Dir of photog* John Seitz. *Process photog* Farciot Edouart. [*2d cam* Otto Pierce]. [*Asst cam* Francis Burgess]. [*Stillman* Talmage Morrison]. *Art dir* Hans Dreier and Earl Hedrick. *Ed* Stuart Gilmore. [*Asst cutter* Chandler House]. [*Set dresser* Ray Moyer]. [*1st prop* Oscar Lau]. [*2d prop* Robert Goodstein]. *Cost* Edith Head. [*Ladies' ward* Hazel Hagarty]. [*Men's ward* Clayton Brackett]. *Mus dir* Sigmund Krumgold. *Mus score* Leo Shuken and Charles Bradshaw. *Sd rec* Harry Mills and Walter Oberst. [*Rec* Grant Rymal]. *Makeup artist* Wally Westmore. [*Hair supv* Leonora Sabine]. [*Hairdresser* Merl Reeves]. [*Makeup* Harold Lierly]. [*Unit mgr* Joe Youngerman]. [*Loc mgr* N. Lacey]. [*Casting* Robert Mayo]. [*Scr clerk* Nesta Charles]. [*Scenario misc* Isabelle Sullivan]. [*Secy* Marie Morris]. [*Pub* Teet Carle]. [*Stage eng* Wally Nogle]. [*Company grip* Walter McCloud]. [*Mike grip* George Ziegler]. [*Gaffer* Earl Crowell]. [*Elec* James Tait]. [*Casting office* B. McKay, B. Greenwald and Alice Thomas]. [*Secy to Mr. Sturges* Edwin Gillette]. [*Stunt double for Joel McCrea* Wes Hopper]. [*Stunt double* Allan Pomroy and John Sinclair].

Cast: Joel McCrea (*John L. Sullivan*), Veronica Lake (*The Girl*), Robert Warwick (*Mr. LeBrand*), William Demarest (*Mr. Jones*), Franklin Pangborn (*Mr. Casalsis*), Porter Hall (*Mr. Hadrian*), Byron Foulger (*Mr. Valdelle*), Margaret Hayes (*Secretary*), Robert Greig (*Sullivan's butler*), Eric Blore (*Sullivan's valet*), Torben Meyer (*The doctor*), Victor Potel (*Cameraman*), Richard Webb (*Radio man*), Charles Moore (*Colored chef*), Almira Sessions (*Ursula*), Esther Howard (*Miz Zeffie*), Frank Moran (*Tough chauffeur*), Georges Renavent (*Old tramp*), Harry Rosenthal (*The Trombenick*), Alan Bridge (*The Mister*), Jimmy Conlin (*Trusty*), Jan Buckingham (*Mrs. Sullivan*), Robert Winkler (*Bud*), Chick Collins (*Capital*), Jimmy Dundee (*Labor*), Harry Hayden (*Mr. Carson*), [Willard Robertson (*Judge*)], [Pat West (*Counterman, roadside lunch wagon*)], [J. Farrell MacDonald (*Desk sergeant*)], [Edward Hearn (*Cop, Beverly Hills station*)], [Roscoe Ates (*Counterman, Owl Wagon*)], [Paul

Newlan (*Truck driver*)], [Arthur Hoyt (*Preacher*)], [Gus Reed (*Mission cook*)], [Robert Dudley (*One-legged bum*)], [George Anderson (*Sullivan's ex-manager*)], [Monte Blue (*Cop in slums*)], [Harry Tyler (*R. R. information clerk*)], [Dewey Robinson (*Sheriff*)], [Madame Sul-te-wan (*Harmonium player*)], [Jesse Lee Brooks (*Black preacher*)], [Perc Launders (*Man at R. R. shack*)], [Emory Parnell (*Man at R. R. shack*)], [Julius Tannen (*Public defender*)], [Edgar Dearing (*Cop, mud gag*)], [Howard Mitchell (*Railroad clerk*)], [Harry Seymour (*Entertainer in air-raid shelter*)], [Billy Bletcher (*Entertainer in hospital ward*)], [Sheila Sheldon (*Child on "Poor Street"*)], [Esther Michelson (*Woman on "Poor Street"*)], [Chester Conklin (*Old bum*)], [Frank Mills (*Drunk in theatre*)], [Jester Hairston, "Hot Shot" Thomas, Joan Douglas, Arie Lee Branche, Inez Hatchett, Mary Reed, War Perkins, LeRoy Edwards, Grace Boone, Anita Brown, Maggie Thomas, Gladys Davis, Ervin Smith, Notable Vines, Artie Overstreet, Elizabeth Gray, Fay Fifer, Elizabeth Ashley, Myrtle Anderson, Frances Driver, Ruth Byers, Mark Carnahan, John Criner, Jack Winslow, James Davis, Lillian Taylor, Matilda Caldwell, William Broadus, Pearl Lancaster, Ruth Bias, Cora Lang, A. Downs (*Churchgoers*)], [Preston Sturges (*Director on movie set*)].

Road, Show business, Social, Comedy-drama. [*Print viewed*]. Hollywood film director John L. Sullivan dreams of making a film called *Brother, Where Art Thou*, dealing with the misery of the poverty-stricken, and convinces the studio executives to allow him to do research by traveling cross-country disguised as a hobo. As "Sully" treads the road dressed in a hobo outfit from the studio costume department, a fully-equipped "land yacht," complete with physician, photographer, reporter, secretary and chauffeur, follows him to take care of his every need. Hampered by their presence, Sully insists on traveling alone and arranges to meet the land yacht in Las Vegas. After working as a hired hand for a widow who has more in mind for him than chopping wood, he sneaks out of her house at night and hitchhikes, but the truck he gets a ride with lands him back in Hollywood. Frustrated by his failure, Sully wanders into a diner to buy a cup of coffee with his last dime, and a beautiful blonde actress, down on her luck, takes pity on him and buys him breakfast. Sully and "The Girl" are later arrested for stealing his own car, but they return to his palatial home after his valet and butler bail them out. The Girl dresses as a boy and joins him for his experiment, and the next morning they hop an outbound freight car. Sully and The Girl live like true hoboes, wandering through shantytowns, lining up for food at soup kitchens and listening to midnight sermons in order to secure beds at missions. In Kansas City, Sully declares his mission complete, but The Girl saddens at the thought of losing him to Hollywood. He admits to her that although he cares for her, his greedy wife will not release him from their marriage of convenience, arranged by his business manager to lower his taxes. That night, Sully wanders the streets handing out $5,000 worth of five-dollar bills to the needy. A hobo wearing Sully's stolen shoes which contained his only identification, follows Sully and robs him, and after knocking him unconscious, drags his body onto a freight car. The hobo dies shortly thereafter when he is hit by a train, and Sully awakens the next day at an unknown train station. Disoriented, Sully is arrested after an unintentional altercation with a railroad employee, and because he cannot recall his identity due to the severe blow to his head, he is called "Richard Roe" and sentenced to a hard labor camp. Sully finally recalls his identity but is beaten by the warden for speaking out of turn. At work on the chain gang, Sully is befriended by an elderly trustee, who helps him survive. He is placed in the sweatbox because of his outburst after seeing a front-page article reporting his presumed death. One evening, the convicts are allowed to see a Mickey Mouse cartoon at a black church. The parishioners are gracious, and Sully the sophisticate surprises himself when he joins in the uproarious laughter of the audience at the antics on the screen. In order to get his picture in the newspaper, Sully confesses to his own murder. The Girl, hard at work on a film, sees his photo in the newspaper and brings it to the attention of the studio heads. Overjoyed that he is alive, Sully's friends and coworkers meet him after he is released from the labor camp. Sully is pleased to hear that his wife, believing he was dead, married his business manager immediately, and that he is free to marry The Girl. Aware of the powerful misery of the poor and disadvantaged, Sully abandons his idea of directing a tragedy and is determined to produce a film that will make people laugh. *Hoboes. Impersonation and imposture.*

Mistaken identity. Motion picture directors. Accidental death. African Americans. Butlers. Chain gangs. Churches. Diners (Restaurants). Hitchhiking. Labor camps. Mickey Mouse (Cartoon character). Motion picture actors and actresses. Motion picture producers. Motion picture theaters. Photographers. Poverty. Preachers. Prison trustees. Prison wardens. Robbery. Shantytowns. Trains. Valets. Widows.

Note: The film opens with the following dedication: "To the memory of those who made us laugh: the motley mountebanks, the clowns, the buffoons, in all times and in all nations, whose efforts have lightened our burden a little, this picture is affectionately dedicated." Scripts in the Preston Sturges Collection at the UCLA Special Collections Library reveal that the above dedication, with the inclusion of the underlined phrase, "whose efforts lightened our burden a little *in this cock-eyed caravan...*", was initially the epilogue to the film, to be spoken by "Sully" as if it were the prologue of the comedy he plans to make. Sturges originally intended for the film to open with the following prologue: "This is the story of a man who wanted to wash an elephant. The elephant darn near ruined him." Sturges initially had been hoping to use a clip from a Charles Chaplin film for the scene in the church; however, modern sources note that Chaplin declined to give permission for the use of his films. In one scene in *Sullivan's Travels*, actor Joel McCrea parodies Chaplin's signature "Little Tramp" character. The Walt Disney Productions cartoon that is shown is the 1934 short "Playful Pluto."

The film cost $689,665.16 to produce and went $86,665.16 over budget. In a personnel sheet in the Sturges Collection, writer Ernst Laemmle is listed as "assistant writer." Information in the Paramount Collection at the AMPAS Library indicates that Laemmle was paid to complete the script, although Laemmle is mentioned as a co-writer with Sturges in many pre-release news items. The full extent of his contribution to the screenplay has not been determined. According to *FD*, Barbara Stanwyck was originally considered to co-star with Joel McCrea. Letters from the PCA indicate that, among other things, the Hays Office suggested that the word "bum" would be considered unacceptable by the British censors and that the filmmakers must be careful not to show "any suggestion of sexual intimacy" between "Sully" and "The Girl" in the scenes in which they are sleeping together at the mission.

According to information in the National Archives in Washington, D.C., the U.S. government's World War II Office of Censorship in New York formally disapproved exporting this film during wartime because of the "long sequence showing life in a prison chain gang which is most objectionable because of the brutality and inhumanity with which the prisoners are treated." This disapproval conformed with the department's policy of not exporting any film that could be turned into enemy propaganda. The department suggested deletions which would have made the picture acceptable under their guidelines, however, the producers declined this opportunity.

The following information is from the Paramount Collection at the AMPAS Library: Paramount purchased Sturges's original story for $10,000; Frances Farmer was tested for the role of "The Girl." Further information reveals that Paramount contracted with the Schlesinger Corp. to produce an animated main title sequence, however, for reasons not stated in the file, Paramount re-shot the main title. It is has not been determined if Schlesinger Corp. ever actually created an animated main title sequence. The "Poverty Montage" took seven hours to film, four hours longer than anticipated. An early cast list has Richard West as "Young man with earphones," but his participation in the final film has not been confirmed. Some scenes were shot on location in Canoga Park, San Marino, Castaic, Los Angeles and at Lockheed Airport, CA.

Actress Veronica Lake was six months pregnant when shooting began on this film, and, according to her autobiography, refrained from telling director Sturges until after filming began. Sturges consulted with Lake's physician regarding the strenuous nature of the part. According to modern sources, former Rose Bowl queen Cheryl Walker performed as Lake's double and associate producer Paul Jones appeared as the late husband of "Miz Zeffie" in a photograph in which the man's expression changes. Modern sources also report that Sturges wrote the film with Joel McCrea in mind for the lead.

A letter from Walter White, Secretary of the National Association for the Advancement of Colored People, to Sturges, is included in the Sturges Collection and reads as follows: "I want to congratulate and thank you for the church sequence in *Sullivan's Travels*. This is one of the most moving scenes I have seen in a moving picture for a long time. But I am particularly grateful to you, as are a number of my friends, both white and colored, for the dignified and decent treatment of Negroes in this scene. I was in Hollywood recently and am to return there soon for conferences with production heads, writers, directors, and actors and actresses in an effort to induce broader and more decent picturization of the Negro instead of limiting him to menial or comic roles. The sequence in *Sullivan's Travels* is a step in that direction and I want you to know how grateful we are."

In his autobiography, Preston Sturges noted that he wrote *Sullivan's Travels* as a reaction to the "preaching" he found in other comedy films "which seemed to have abandoned the fun in favor of the message." *NYT* called the film "the most brilliant picture yet this year" and noted that while most of Hollywood seemed to be calling for purely escapist fare because of World War II, Sturges managed to combine escapist fun with an underlying significance. However, *Sullivan's Travels* did not escape harsher criticism. *HR* noted that the film lacked the "down to earth quality and sincerity which made [Sturges's] other three pictures a joy to behold" and that "Sturges...fails to heed the message that writer Sturges proves in his script. Laughter is the thing people want—not social studies." The *New Yorker* simply stated that "anyone can make a mistake, Preston Sturges, even. The mistake in question is a pretentious number called *Sullivan's Travels*."

This film was selected for the National Film Registry by the National Film Preservation Board. Veronica Lake reprised her role in a *Lux Radio Theatre* broadcast on 9 Nov 1942, co-starring Ralph Bellamy. In the 1993 film *Amos and Andrew*, "Andrew's" Pulitzer Prize winning play was called *Yo, Brother, Where Art Thou.*

Box 13 Dec 1941. *DV* 5 Dec 1941. *FD* 14 Jan 1941, p. 2. *FD* 5 Dec 1941, p. 5. *HR* 24 Jan 1941, p. 1. *HR* 16 May 1941, p. 6. *HR* 15 Sep 1941, p. 7. *HR* 5 Dec 1941, p. 4. *Los Angeles Eagle* 18 Jun 1942. *Life* 26 Jan 1942. *MPHPD* 13 Dec 1941, p. 405. *NewRep* 26 Jan 1942. *New Yorker* 31 Jan 1942. *NYT* 29 Jan 1942, p. 25. *NYT* 1 Feb 1942. *Var* 10 Dec 1941, p. 8.

SUM HUN (Chinese language)

Cathay Pictures Ltd. **1936**; Prod: completed 16 Dec 1935 at Reliable Studios. Sd; b&w with col seq. 9 reels, 7,827 ft. PCA cert no. 1906. Cantonese language.

Prod Bruce Wong. *Dir* Frank Tang. *Co-dir* Bill Nolte. *Scr* Frank Tang and Henry Tung. *Photog* Paul Ivano.

Cast: Beal Wong, Way Kim Fong.

Drama. [*Not viewed*]. In San Francisco's Chinatown, a talented young singer, Fan, embarks on a bright career. One day, her friend, Mr. Wong, offers to take her to the local aviation school to meet some of the young Chinese-American men who are training to fight for their ancestors' country. Jung, Fan's manager, is angry that she is taking time off from her art, but the independent young woman tells him that her private life is her own business. At the aviation field, Fan is introduced to Chan and some other students who are all big fans of her singing. As they talk, they notice Lee, the most talented and ambitious of the school's students, doing a series of loop-de-loops in his plane. After his daring flight, Lee, who is very shy, meets Fan, and sometime later, Chan and a hesitant Lee go to see Fan perform. The two friends love the show, and Lee, emboldened, offers to take Fan on a ride in Golden Gate Park. As the pair gazes at the unfinished bridge in the moonlight, they declare their love for each other. After Jung orders Fan to end her relationship with Lee, another friend whom she trusts, Ming, also advises her to break off her relationship, stating that she and Lee will risk ruining their careers for romantic love, something that never lasts. Fan is too distraught to end things with Lee face-to-face, and so, in Lee's presence, she and Ming pretend to be lovers. As hoped, Lee drops her, then wanders like a dead man toward the home that he shares with his hard-working uncle, Lee Tai, a jeweler. Upon arriving home, he sees an ambulance in the street and discovers that Lee Tai has had a heart attack and died. Later, a lawyer tells Lee that although his uncle worked hard to put him through aviation school, he has died leaving nothing but debts. Lee goes to the director of the aviation school, Mr. Chang, and says that he must quit school. Chang responds by urging him to fight back and be like Charles Lindbergh, adding that the money will be found. Chang then calls Chan and tells him that he has convinced Lee to stay at the school, whereupon Chan reveals that the money for Lee's continuing education will come from Fan. Sometime later, Fan reads a newspaper article announcing Lee and Chan's departure for China, where they will fight in the Shanghai War. Before their ship sails, Chan goes to see Fan and thanks her, and she reminds him not to tell Lee that she has been his benefactress since his uncle's death. In China, Lee leads a squadron into battle and then rescues Chan when his plane crashes. Then one day, Fan, as she prepares for a benefit concert to aid the Shanghai War effort, receives a letter informing her that Lee will return to the United States with his new wife. Fan cancels the concert so that she can meet Lee's ship, but conceals herself in the crowd. Having accompanied Lee and his wife to San Francisco, Chan goes to see Fan and discovers her sick and distraught over Lee's marriage. He insists on telling Lee about her generosity, but Fan implores him to keep her secret. Later, at a banquet given by the Chinese Chamber of Congress to celebrate Lee's heroism, Chan receives a note from a doctor, who has found her address in Fan's handbag. After he discovers that Fan is dying, Chan brings Lee to her deathbed, and the reunited couple embraces. Fan then smiles as if to God and dies as her former lover weeps. *Air pilots. Chinese Americans. Romance. San Francisco (CA)–Chinatown.* Actors and actresses. Airplane accidents. Benefactors. Chambers of Commerce. China. China–History. Death and dying. Flight training. Golden Gate Bridge (San Francisco, CA). Heart disease. Immigrants. Jealousy. Jewelers. Managers (Entertainment). Rescues. Reunions. Self-sacrifice. Singers. Uncles. War heroes.

Note: The NYSA lists the film's translated title as *Heartaches*. A 17 Dec 1935 *HR* news item states that *Sum Hun* was the first Chinese picture to be made in Hollywood. No exact release date was found, although a 1 Jan 1936 release in San Francisco's Chinatown district was announced in *HR*. The film was submitted to the NYSA on 4 May 1936 by Walter Kofitt. Two reels of the film

were shot in color, according to unidentified, contemporary news items and publicity materials found in the papers of cinematographer Paul Ivano at the AMPAS Library.

HR 17 Dec 1935, p. 3.

THE SUN SHINES BRIGHT (African Americans, German Americans)
Argosy Pictures Corp.; John Ford and Merian C. Cooper's Argosy Production. *Dist* Republic Pictures Corp. 2 May **1953**; New York opening: 16 Mar 1953; Prod: late Aug—mid-Sep 1952 [©Republic Pictures Corp.; 13 Mar 1953; LP2708]. Sd (RCA Sound System); b&w. 9,129 ft. 90 min. PCA cert no. 16222.

Pres HERBERT J. YATES. *Dir* John Ford. *Asst dir* Wingate Smith. *Scr* Laurence Stallings. *Dir of photog* Archie Stout. *Opt eff* Consolidated Film Industries. *Art dir* Frank Hotaling. *Film ed* Jack Murray. *Set dec* John McCarthy, Jr. and George Milo. *Cost des* Adele Palmer. *Mus* Victor Young. *Sd* T. A. Carman and Howard Wilson.

Song(s): "My Old Kentucky Home," words and music by Stephen Foster; "Dixie," words and music by Dan D. Emmett; "Swing Low, Sweet Chariot," "Deep River," "Tenting on the Old Camp Ground" and "Marching Through Georgia," traditionals; "Hail, Hail, the Gang's All Here," words by D. A. Esrom, music by Theodore Morse and Arthur Sullivan,.

Source: Based on the short story "The Sun Shines Bright" by Irvin S. Cobb in *Hearst's International-Cosmopolitan Magazine* (Apr 1931); his short story "The Mob from Massac" included in the collection *Back Home: Being the Narrative of Judge Priest and his People* (New York, 1912); and his short story "The Lord Provides" in *The Saturday Evening Post* (9 Oct 1915).

Cast: Charles Winninger [(*Judge William "Billy" Pittman Priest*)], Arleen Whelan [(*Lucy Lee*)], John Russell [(*Ashby Corwin*)], Stepin Fetchit [(*Jeff*)], Russell Simpson [(*Dr. Lake*)], Ludwig Stossel [(*Herman Felsburg*)], Francis Ford [(*Feeney*)], Paul Hurst [(*Sgt. Jimmy Bagby*)], Mitchell Lewis [(*Andy Redcliffe*)], Grant Withers [(*Buck Ransey*)], Milburn Stone [(*Horace K. Maydew*)], Dorothy Jordan [(*Lucy's mother*)], Elzie Emanuel [(*You Ess*)], Henry O'Neill [(*Habersham*)], Slim Pickens [(*Sterling*)], James Kirkwood [(*Gen. Fairfield*)], Ernest Whitman [(*Uncle Pleasant "Pleas" Woodford*)], Trevor Bardette [(*Rufe Ramseur*)], Eve March [(*Mallie Cramp*)], Hal Baylor [(*Ramseur, Jr.*)], Jane Darwell [(*Mrs. Aurora Ratchitt*)], Ken Williams [(*Maydew's benchman*)], Clarence Muse [(*Uncle Zach*)], Mae Marsh [(*G.A.R. lady*)], [Allene Roberts (*Ramseur's girl*)], [Almira Sessions, Elizabeth Slifer (*Gossips*)], [Everett Glass (*Editor*)], [Jack Pennick (*Blackjack*)], [James Lilburn (*Cadet leader*)], [Mickey Simpson (*Assistant blacksmith*)], [Marcoreta Hellman, Ruth Clifford (*Mallie's girls*)], [Louis Mason (*Court clerk*)], [Willa Pearl Curtis, Myrtle Anderson (*Washerwomen*)], [Joe Rickson (*Dink*)], [Philip Kieffer (*Jansen*)], [James P. Jackson (*James*)], [Dan Borzage (*Townsman*)], [Barry Regan (*Tally clerk*)], [Jack Mower (*Guard*)], [Cliff Lyons, Chuck Hayward (*Deputies*)], [Frank Connor (*Dock walloper*)], [Mimi Doyle], [Mrs. Bennie Washington].

Historical, Comedy-drama, with songs. [*Print viewed*]. In a small riverside town in turn-of-the-century Fairfield County, Kentucky, kindly old Judge William "Billy" Pittman Priest is running for re-election. As the judge prepares for a day in court, the morning steamboat arrives, to the delight of the black residents who work and play along the levee. One of the town's prodigal sons, young Ashby Corwin, is returning home and greets his friends in his usual happy-go-lucky style. When he sees old Dr. Lake's ward, Lucy Lee, however, he is momentarily dumbfounded by her beauty At the courthouse, Judge Priest's black servant Jeff snores through the pompous declarations of Prosecutor Horace K. Maydew, who is Priest's competition in the upcoming election. Things get more lively, though, when elderly Uncle Pleasant "Pleas" Woodford complains on the witness stand that his nephew, U. S. Grant Woodford, spends more time at his banjo than at a useful job. Young Woodford plays "Dixie" for the court, and soon the room is filled with toe-tapping, sentimental old Confederate soldiers. After Priest gets Woodford a job in a Tornado District tobacco field, he visits the ancient Fairfield in the former Confederate officer's stately mansion. To the judge's sorrow, Gen. Fairfield still refuses to admit that Lucy Lee is his granddaughter. Lucy is ridiculed in the street by Buck Ransey and his friends, prompting Ashby to challenge him to a whip fight. Priest soon separates the men and sends them home. Later, however, he informs Ashby that the rumors about Lucy's mother are true and that Fairfield's

son was killed in a fight over the woman. Late that night, a very ill woman makes her way from the docks to the center of town, and when she collapses, Ashby and his black employee, old "Uncle Zach," carry her to the home of Dr. Lake. The woman sobs that she wants to see her baby before she dies, and after Lucy briefly appears in the room, she smiles contentedly. At her request, the men then carry her to a house of disrepute run by her old friend and employer, Mallie Cramp. Lucy rushes to see the judge, where she glimpses a portrait of her father and a woman whom she closely resembles. "Now I know who I am," she gratefully tells the judge. The next day, young Woodford is arrested for raping a white girl, and although Priest considers the evidence against him flimsy, a white lynch mob led by Ransey and the girl's father, Rufe Ramseur, soon appears at the jail. The judge draws his gun and orders the crowd to disperse, but as the angry men leave, they declare that Priest will regret his actions. Aging German storekeeper Herman Felsburg sadly muses that the judge and all of his office-holding friends surely will be turned out of office. The situation worsens when Mallie is seen visiting the judge's home. Lucy's mother has died, she reveals, and she is determined to fulfill the poor woman's request for a fine funeral. The next evening, Ashby takes Lucy to a cadets' ball, but she is embarrassed and asks to be taken home. Just then, Rufe's daughter appears and identifies Ransey as her attacker as the assembled townspeople look on. Ransey leaps into Lucy's carriage and Ashby pursues them on horseback. An elderly Confederate soldier manages to shoot Ransey, and Lucy faints as her carriage races out of control. Ashby finally manages to stop the carriage and rescue Lucy. Early on election day, Priest joins Mallie and her friends in a small but ornate funeral procession for Lucy's mother. This shocks some of the townspeople and tickles Maydew, but as the hearse makes its way down Main Street, more and more citizens join the procession. The service is held in a black-run church, and after Priest speaks touchingly of Lucy's mother, Fairfield takes a seat next to his granddaughter. In a close election, the votes of the would-be lynchers, who are grateful to the judge for "saving us from ourselves," tie the race. Jeff reminds the judge that he himself has not yet voted, and this enables the kindly old man to win the election with his own vote. That evening, a parade of well-wishers, including residents of the Tornado District and the black community, as well as Lucy, Ashby and the Woodfords, files by the home of the happily weeping judge. *African Americans. Aged men. Elections. Judges. Mobs. Small town life. United States–South. Balls (Parties). Brothels. Civil War Veterans. Courage. False arrests. Friendship. Funerals. German Americans. Illegitimacy. Kentucky. Loyalty. Lynching. Physicians. Political campaigns. Rape. Romance. Soldiers. Storekeepers.*

Note: Irvin S. Cobb's characters were also the basis of director John Ford's 1934 Fox picture, *Judge Priest* (see above), which featured Will Rogers and Stepin Fetchit. About *The Sun Shines Bright*, the *NYT* reviewer remarked: "After parading a handful of Negroes to and fro in quaking servility, the picture foists an inexcusably synthetic sequence about a near-lynching...No wonder our old friend, Stepin Fetchit, still dancing attendance on his Honor twenty years later, seems more bent than ever." The *Var* review noted that the characters included such "stereotyped figures as julep-drinking southerners, comic-opera darkies and bigoted poor white trash." In an interview, Ford called this his favorite film, although he claimed that Herbert J. Yates "fooled around with it...and almost ruined it." The film was cut from 90 to 65 minutes, and modern sources state that its financial failure contributed to the demise of Argosy Pictures. Modern sources list Barbara Ford as assistant editor.

Box 16 May 1953. *DV* 1 May 1953, p. 4. *Exb* 6 May 1953, p. 3516. *FD* 6 May 1953, p. 6. *Har* 9 May 1953, p. 76. *HR* 22 Aug 1952, p. 10. *HR* 19 Sep 1952, p. 14. *HR* 1 May 1953, p. 3. *MPHPD* 9 May 1953, p. 1830. *NYT* 18 Mar 1954, p. 25. *Var* 6 May 1953, p. 16.

SUN VALLEY CYCLONE (Native Americans)
Republic Pictures Corp. *Dist* Republic Pictures Corp. 10 May **1946**; Prod: early Sep—mid-Sep 1945 [©Republic Pictures Corp.; 8 Apr 1946; LP323]. Sd (RCA Sound System); b&w. 55-56 min. Passed by the National Board of Review. PCA cert no. 11176.

Series: Red Ryder.

Assoc prod Sidney Picker. *Dir* R. G. Springsteen. *2d unit dir* Yakima Canutt. [*Asst dir* Edward Stein]. *Orig scr* Earle Snell. *Photog* Bud Thackery. [*2d cam* Enzo Martinelli]. [*Special opt eff* Howard Lydecker and Theodore Lydecker]. [*Matte paintings* Lewis Physioc]. [*Transparency projection shots* Gordon Schaefer]. *Art dir* James Sullivan. *Film ed* Harry Keller and Charles Craft. *Set dec* John McCarthy, Jr. and Marie Arthur. *Mus dir* Richard Cherwin. *Sd* Victor Appel. [*Re-rec and eff mixer* Thomas A. Carman and Howard Wilson]. [*Mus mixer* John Stransky, Jr.]. *Makeup supv* Bob Mark. [*Horse wrangler* Helen Griffith].

Source: Based on the comic strip "Red Ryder" by Fred Harman (1938—1964), by special arrangement with Stephen Slesinger.

Cast: WILD BILL ELLIOTT (*Red Ryder*), Bobby Blake [(*Little Beaver*)], Alice Fleming [(*The Duchess*)], Roy Barcroft [(*Blackie Blake*)], Kenne Duncan [(*Dow*)], Eddy Waller [(*Major Harding*)], Tom London [(*Sheriff*)], Edmund Cobb [(*Luce*)], Edward Cassidy [(*Teddy Roosevelt*)], Monte Hale [(*Jeff*)], George Chesebro [(*Shorty*)], Rex Lease [(*Sergeant*)], Thunder [(*Red's horse*)], [Jack Kirk (*Townsman*)], Frank O'Connor (*Doctor*)], Jack Sparks (*Junior officer*)], [Hal Price (*Marshal*)].

Western. [*Print viewed*]. When Red Ryder and his Indian ward, Little Beaver, arrive in Los Palos, Arizona, in search of an outlaw, they ask the local U. S. marshal for help. As Red is talking to the marshal, an Hispanic man aims a gun at him through an open window. The man is prevented from shooting, however, by Red's horse Thunder, who attacks him. The man protests his innocence and declares that Thunder must be destroyed. The marshal also insists that Thunder be killed, but Red demands that his horse be given a "trial," and describes how they met: Six months earlier, Red rides to a recruiting station to join Col. Theodore Roosevelt's Rough Riders. The station's sergeant has rounded up a herd of wild horses, but thinks that one of them, a magnificent black stallion, will never be tamed. Red succeeds in riding the bucking animal, and his prowess is admired by Roosevelt. The colonel, who is an old friend of Red's, asks him to return to his home in Sun Valley, Wyoming, and investigate a gang of horse thieves that have been stealing herds intended for army use. After swapping his horse for the stallion, whom he names Thunder because he is as black as a thundercloud, Red returns to Sun Valley, where he finds his aunt, The Duchess, in a feud with her new neighbor, fellow horse rancher Major Harding. The neighbors are arguing about the position of a line fence, and the Duchess suspects Harding of being behind a recent rash of horse rustlings. When one of her stolen horses returns home with an altered brand, Red and Little Beaver go to town to talk to the sheriff. In town, Red notices a distinctive saddle, the owner of which is conversing with Harding's tough foreman, Blackie Blake. Unknown to Harding, Blake and his men, including Dow, the saddle's owner, are the rustlers, and are stirring up the feud as a distraction. When Red asks Blake about the returned horse, Blake starts a fistfight, which Red quickly finishes. Red insists that the warring factions meet at the Duchess' house for a peace talk, and while the meeting is being held, Blake's men rustle Harding's horses. Harding accuses the Duchess of organizing the raid and their feud is renewed. Red becomes concerned when he notices that Thunder is also missing and sets out to find him. The stallion, who had pursued one of Harding's mares, is captured by the gang, but after Dow saddles him, Blake attempts to ride him and is bucked off. Blake viciously beats the animal, who escapes while still wearing Dow's saddle. Recognizing the saddle, Red realizes that Dow and Blake must be involved in the rustling, and later that night, Dow attempts to retrieve his saddle. Thunder almost tramples the culprit to death, but Red reaches him in time and takes him to the sheriff. Worried that Dow will talk, Blake and his men storm the jail to release him. Meanwhile, Thunder has gone back to the mare and released Harding's herd, which he leads through the town's streets as Red is engaged in a shootout with Blake's men. The gang is rounded up with the exception of Blake, who escapes. Back in Los Altos, Red concludes his story by pointing out that Thunder has a particular enmity toward the man he just attacked, and when the man's disguise is removed, he is revealed to be Blake. Thunder then rewards Red and Little Beaver with a nuzzle. *Frame-ups. Horses. Ranchers. Rivalry. Rustlers. Arizona. Aunts. Chases. Cruelty to animals. Disguise. Fights. Indians of North America. Ranch foremen. Theodore Roosevelt. Rough Riders. Saddlery. Sheriffs. Shootouts. United States. Marshals. Wards and guardians. Wyoming.*

Note: For more information on the "Red Ryder" series, please consult the Series Index and the entry below for *Tucson Raiders.*

DV 3 Jun 1946, p. 3. HR 7 Sep 1945, p. 17. HR 31 May 1946, p. 3. MPHPD 11 May 1946, p. 2987. MPHPD 15 Jun 1946, p. 3042.

SUN VALLEY SERENADE (Norwegian Americans)

Twentieth Century-Fox Film Corp. *Dist* Twentieth Century-Fox Film Corp. 29 Aug **1941**; Salt Lake City, UT and Atlantic City, NJ openings: 21 Aug 1941; Prod: 24 Mar—late May 1941 [©Twentieth Century-Fox Film Corp.; 29 Aug 1941; LP10689]. Sd (Western Electric Mirrophonic Recording); b&w. 9 reels, 7,732 ft. 85 min. PCA cert no. 7218.

[*Exec prod* Darryl F. Zanuck]. *Prod* Milton Sperling. *Dir* H. Bruce Humberstone. [*2d unit and fill-in dir* Malcolm St. Clair]. [*Asst dir* Charles Hall]. [*Dial dir* Arthur Berthelet]. *Scr* Robert Ellis and Helen Logan. *Story* Art Arthur and Robert Harari. [*Contr wrt* Allan Scott, Bert Granet and Milton Sperling]. *Dir of photog* Edward Cronjager. *Art dir* Richard Day and Lewis Creber. *Film ed* James B. Clark. *Set dec* Thomas Little. *Cost* Travis Banton. *Ski clothes* F. A. Picard. *Mus dir* Emil Newman. *Dances staged by* Hermes Pan. *Sd* Alfred Bruzlin and Roger Heman. [*Sonja Henie's hairdresser* Ann Barr]. *Tech dir of skiing seq* Otto Lang. [*Prod mgr* Ben Silvey]. [*Unit mgr* Robert E. "Duke" Goux]. [*Tech dir* Bert Clark]. [*Ski instructor* Ragnar Qvale]. [*Ice skating rink designer* William Webster]. [*Sonja Henie's harmonica instructor* Ray Hoback]. [*Pub dir* Harry Brand]. [*Stand-in for Sonja Henie* Teddy Blue]. [*Singing voice double for Lynn Bari* Pat Friday]. [*Trumpet double for George Montgomery* Steve Lipkin]. [*Piano double for Cesar Romero* Chummy MacGregor]. [*Bass double for Jackie Gleason* Don Goldberg].

Music: "Moonlight Serenade," music by Glenn Miller; "In the Mood," music by Joe Garland.

Song(s): "I Know Why (And So Do You)," "It Happened in Sun Valley," "Chattanooga Choo Choo" and "The Kiss Polka," music by Harry Warren and lyrics by Mack Gordon.

Cast: SONJA HENIE (*Karen Benson*), JOHN PAYNE (*Ted Scott*), Glenn Miller and His Orchestra (*Phil Corey*), Milton Berle (*Jerome K.] Nifty Allen*), Lynn Bari (*Vivian Dawn*), Joan Davis (*Miss Carstairs*), Nicholas Brothers (*Specialty*), William Davidson (*[Jack] Murray*), Dorothy Dandridge (*Specialty*), Almira Sessions (*Nurse*), Mel Ruick (*Band leader [Jimmy Norton]*), Ralph Dunn (*Customs officer*), Chester Clute (*Process server*), [Harrison Thompson (*Sonja Henie's skating partner*)], [Gary Gray (*Child refugee*)], [Forbes Murray (*Headwaiter*)], [The Modernaires: Bill Conway], [Hal Dickson], [Ralph Brewster], [Chuck Goldstein], [and Paula Kelly], [Ralph Sanford (*Doorman*)], [Lillian Porter, Sheila Ryan (*Telephone operators*)], [Lynne Roberts (*Receptionist*)], [Dora Clemant (*Wife*)], [William Forrest (*Husband*)], [Bette Gene Moore, Ann Ray (*Children*)], [Walter "Spec" O'Donnell (*Western Union boy*)], [Ann Doran (*Waitress*)], [Fred Toones (*Porter*)], [John "Skins" Miller (*Sleigh driver*)], [Bruce Edwards (*Ski instructor*)], [Herbert Gunn, Kenneth Alexander (*Ski patrol*)], [Fred Cass, Walter Daniel, Ian Grey, Jimmy Kelly, Alex Lindgren, Walter Mitchell, Paul Shuman, Bud Stark, William Fletcher, Bob Campbell, Claud Allred, Norman Tarpenning (*Skaters*)], [Edward Kane], [Edward Earle], [Ernie Alexander], [Angela Blue].

Romantic comedy, Show business, Musical. [*Print viewed*]. When famed Idaho ski resort Sun Valley puts out a call for a band to back up singer Vivian Dawn, Phil Corey takes his band, the Dartmouth Troubadors, to the audition in New York City. Vivian throws a temper tantrum after bandleader Jimmy Norton plays an arrangement not to her liking, and Phil steps in. Phil's piano player, Ted Scott, quickly becomes enamoured of the singer, and makes a date with her after the band is engaged by Sun Valley's agent, Jack Murray. While the band members and their publicist, Jerome K. "Nifty" Allen, are congratulating each other, they receive a telegram announcing that the war refugee they volunteered to sponsor will be arriving soon. Ted, whose name Nifty put on the application, is angry, for it was only to be a publicity stunt, but the band members decide to pitch in and care for the refugee, whom they assume will be a small child. When they go to Ellis Island to greet their ward, however, they find Karen Benson, an adult Norwegian woman who had to flee her homeland after her father was killed. Karen, grateful for Ted's sponsorship, decides that she will return the favor by marrying him, but he tries to dampen her romantic aspirations. When Karen finds out that the band will be traveling to Sun Valley while she is to be sent to Nifty's aunt for safekeeping, she asks Nifty to sneak her aboard the train to Idaho. Nifty, who has a crush on Karen, reluctantly agrees, and upon reaching Sun Valley, Karen surprises Ted with her skiing expertise. Ted loves to ski and, disappointed that Vivian will not ski with him, is happy to have Karen as a partner. Vivian grows jealous though, and one evening, surprises everyone at dinner by announcing that she has decided to accept Ted's standing marriage proposal. Karen is crushed but devises a scheme to win Ted over when the two of them begin to ski down from the restaurant to the lodge below. By knocking his skiis down the mountain and then pretending that she has hurt her knee, Karen contrives for them to spend the evening in an emergency cabin.

By the time Phil, Vivian and Nifty arrive with the ski patrol to rescue them, Ted has figured out Karen's scheme. He has also realized that he does love the persistent Norwegian, and when Vivian delivers an ultimatum to choose between the two of them, Ted chooses Karen. Vivian storms out as Ted dances with Karen, and later, the Dartmouth Troubadors are the hit of Sun Valley when they accompany Karen in an ice-skating extravaganza. *Band leaders. Musicians. Norwegians. Romance. Sun Valley (ID). War refugees. African Americans. Auditions. Dancers. Gratitude. Hotels. Ice skaters and ice skating. Innocents. Jealousy. New York City-Ellis Island. Polka (Dance). Publicists. Rehearsals. Singers. Skiing.*

Note: The working titles of this film were *Passport to Life, Passport to Love* and *Sun Valley*. According to the *Var* review, the film was "the spontaneous brainchild of Darryl Zanuck, 20th-Fox production chief, who got the background inspiration during a vacation sojourn at the resort [Sun Valley, Idaho] several months ago." According to the Twentieth Century-Fox Records of the Legal Department, located at the UCLA Arts—Special Collections Library, the screenplay was based on an "original story outline" by producer Milton Sperling. The legal records and *HR* news items indicate, however, that the original story *Passport to Life* was written by Allan Scott and Bert Granet. A memorandum attached to the *SAB*, located in the picture's clippings file at the *AMPAS* Library, noted that "the studio had bought a story without any obligation to give credit to either title or authors and that Art Arthur and Robert Harari had done so much work in preparing it that they were giving them screen story credit, but that even though no other source was given, they definitely did *NOT* do an ORIGINAL screen story." A 22 Sep 1939 *HR* news item announced that Tyrone Power and Linda Darnell were to star in Scott and Granet's original story *Passport to Life*, which was to be produced by Ray Griffith. Arthur and Harari were assigned to do the treatment, and on 8 Apr 1940, *HR* stated that Sperling was to rewrite their screenplay, *Passport to Love*, for producer Griffith. In Jul 1940, Sperling was assigned production duties, his first for Twentieth Century-Fox. The legal records note that Ralph Freed and Captain Richard Carroll filed a law suit against Twentieth Century-Fox in which they claimed that the studio had plagiarized their story, "Pigtails," but the suit was later dropped.

According to a 3 Jul 1940 *HR* news item, Sun Valley ski instructor Ragnar Qvale was expected to have a role in the picture. Although he does not appear in the released film, studio publicity noted that Qvale taught extras how to ski. *Sun Valley Serenade* was Sonja Henie's first film since *Everything Happened at Night*, released by Twentieth Century-Fox in 1939, and also marked Glenn Miller's first film as an actor, although he had appeared as himself in earlier pictures. Child actor Gary Gray made his screen debut in the film, as did Miller's popular singing group The Modernaires. *HR* news items indicate that Jack Oakie was to have a leading role, Cobina Wright, Jr. and Carole Landis were considered for the part of "Vivian Dawn," and Ralph Rainger and Leo Robin were originally assigned to write songs for the picture. *HR* also noted that Janis Carter was to be tested for a role, although she does not appear in the finished film, and that second unit director Mal St. Clair briefly filled in for director H. Bruce Humberstone after he was injured in a car accident at the beginning of May 1941. *HR* news items, studio publicity and legal records note that parts of the picture were shot on location at Sun Valley and at a railroad station in Salt Lake City, Utah. According to studio records and publicity and the MPAA/PCA Collection at the AMPAS Library, three songs written by Harry Warren and Mack Gordon did not appear in the released film. They were titled: "At Last," "The World Is Waiting to Waltz Again" and "I'm Lena, the Ballerina." Although it has not been determined if the first two songs were recorded, "I'm Lena, the Ballerina" was recorded by Joan Davis, and the sequence featuring her singing it was photographed. The PCA objected to certain lyrics in the song, although it has not been determined if that was the reason for the number being deleted from the release print. The film opened in several other cities after its premieres in Salt Lake City and Atlantic City on 21 Aug 1941 and before its general release on 29 Aug 1941. The picture received Academy Award nominations for Best Cinematography, Best Music (Scoring of a musical picture) and Best Song ("Chattanooga Choo Choo"). "Chattanooga Choo Choo," as recorded by Glenn Miller and his orchestra with a vocal by Tex Beneke, was a huge hit, and was the first record in fifteen years to sell over a million copies. To commemorate the achievement, RCA Victor presented Miller with a solid gold record, which was an actual disc of the song. It was the first time a gold record was presented to a recording artist, although the Record Industry Association of America did not start awarding "official" gold records until 1958. In a 27 Nov 1948 *SEP* article, Sonja Henie stated that "Karen Benson" was the role she "liked best" and that it was the "liveliest role of [her] screen career." According to a 24 Nov 1952 *LAT* news item, Darryl Zanuck hoped to remake the film as *It Happened in Sun Valley* with Dan Dailey as the star. According to a 10 Sep 1988 *Var* news item, Broadway producer Martin Stager also planned to remake the film as a stage musical with a script written by Steve Allen and Sheldon Keller. As with the Zanuck project, the stage musical was never realized.

Box 26 Jun 1941. *Down Beat* 1 Oct 1942, p. 6. *DV* 25 Jul 1941, p. 3, 5. *FD* 24 Jul 1941, p. 6. *HR* 22 Sep 1939, p. 1. *HR* 8 Apr 1940, p. 1. *HR* 3 Jul 1940, p. 4. *HR* 28 Oct 1940, p. 2. *HR* 3 Dec 1940, p. 6. *HR* 18 Dec 1940, p. 5. *HR* 27 Dec 1940, p. 1. *HR* 20 Jan 1941, p. 8. *HR* 3 Feb 1941, p. 4. *HR* 7 Feb 1941, p. 3. *HR* 17 Feb 1941, p. 9. *HR* 21 Feb 1941, p. 4. *HR* 10 Mar 1941, p. 4. *HR* 11 Mar 1941, p. 2. *HR* 12 Mar 1941, p. 9. *HR* 13 Mar 1941, p. 1. *HR* 19 Mar 1941, p. 7. *HR* 21 Mar 1941, p. 9. *HR* 24 Mar 1941, p. 2. *HR* 16 Apr 1941, p. 9. *HR* 18 Apr 1941, p. 4. *HR* 1 May 1941, p. 2. *HR* 2 May 1941, p. 15. *HR* 9 May 1941, p. 2. *HR* 22 May 1941, p. 7. *HR* 25 Jul 1941, p. 3. *HR* 13 Aug 1941, p. 7. *HR* 18 Aug 1941, p. 8. *HR* 21 May 1941, p. 5. *LAT* 24 Nov 1952. *MPD* 28 Jul 1941. *MPH* 2 Aug 1941. *MPHPD* 17 May 1941, p. 137. *MPHPD* 6 Sep 1941, p. 251. *NYT* 1 Jun 1941. *NYT* 6 Sep 1941, p. 20. *SEP* 27 Nov 1948. *Var* 23 Jul 1941, p. 8. *Var* 10 Sep 1988.

SUNBONNET SUE (Irish Americans)

Monogram Pictures Corp. *Dist* Monogram Pictures Corp. 8 Dec **1945**; Prod: late Apr—late May 1945 [©Monogram Pictures Corp.; 24 Oct 1945; LP13662]. Sd; b&w. 8,030 ft. 89 min.

Exec dir Trem Carr. *Prod* Scott R. Dunlap. *Dir* Ralph Murphy. *Asst dir* Robert Ray and Eddie Davis. *Adpt for the scr* Ralph Murphy and Richard A. Carroll. *Orig story* Paul Gerard Smith and Bradford Ropes. *Prolog wrt by* Sidney Sutherland. *Photog* Harry Neumann. *Second cam* William Margulies. *Matte paintings and minatures* Ray Mercer. *Transparencies* Mario Castegnaro. *Tech dir* Ernest R. Hickson. *Art dir* Dave Milton. *Film ed* Richard Currier. *Set dec* Charles Thompson. *Ward* Harry Bourne. *Miss Storm's cost* Fritzi Ehrens. *Mus dir* Edward Key. *Prod numbers staged by* Jack Boyle. *Sd eng* Tom Lambert. *Re-rec and eff mixer* Jack Noyes. *Mus mixer* William H. Wilmarth. *Prod mgr* William Stohbach.

Song(s): "School Days," and "Sunbonnet Sue," music by Gus Edwards, lyrics by Will Cobb; "The Bowery," music and lyrics by Charles H. Hoyt and Percy Gaunt; "Yip-I-Addy-I-Ay," music and lyrics by Will Cobb and John H. Flynn; "Yoo Hoo" and "Ain't You Comin' Out Tonight?" music and lyrics by Carson Robinson; "By the Light of the Silvery Moon," music by Gus Edwards, lyrics by Ed Madden; "If I Had My Way," music and lyrics by Lou Klein and James Kendis; "While Strolling Through the Park One Day," music and lyrics by Ed Haley and Robert A. Keiser; "Donegal," "Roll Dem Bones" and "Look for the Rainbow," music and lyrics by Ralph Murphy and C. Harold Lewis.

Cast: Gale Storm (*Sue Casey*), Phil Regan (*Danny Dooley*), George Cleveland (*Casey*), Minna Gombell (*Mrs. Fitzgerald*), Raymond Hatton (*Joe Feeney*), Alan Mowbray (*Jonathan*), Charles Judels (*Pete Milano*), Billy Green (*Flaherty*), Charles D. Brown (*Father Hurley*), Edna Holland (*Julia Ross*), Gerald Oliver Smith (*Masters*), Jerry Franks, Jr. (*Burke*), Michael Raffetto (*Commentator*).

Drama, with songs. [*Not viewed*]. Sue Casey is a singer at her father's saloon in the Bowery section of New York City in the 1890s. Julia Ross, her social-climbing aunt, fears that her standing will be ruined if her friends learn about her humble family backround as a result of Sue's performing. Matters escalate when Julia, her friend Jonathan and her butler Masters, are thrown out of Casey's saloon by Flaherty, Casey's right-hand man, after the three create a disturbance while trying to force Sue to leave the Bowery. Meanwhile, as local election day approaches, the district becomes politically divided. Casey and the Irish immigrants back Danny Dooley, and the Italian immigrants back Pete Milano, while Julia throws her support to the corrupt Tammany Hall candidate, Joe Feeney, who wins the election. The political bosses then revoke Casey's liquor license and close the saloon down. Father Hurley, the local Catholic priest, informs Sue that her father's saloon will be allowed to reopen if she agrees to leave the Bowery and move in with Julia at her Fifth Avenue home. Sue agrees, and Julia holds a coming-out party for her niece, which turns into a brawl when Casey and Danny crash the party and attempt to take Sue back to the Bowery. Julia is convinced that her social standing has been destroyed beyond repair after Governor Fitzgerald and his wife arrive in the midst of the fight, only to learn that Mrs. Fitzgerald is an old friend of Casey's and also grew up in the Bowery. After Sue is then allowed to return home, Casey's license is reinstated, and Julia retains her social standing. *Aunts. Fathers and daughters. Saloon keepers. Singers. Snobs and snobbishness. Socialites. Elections. Fights. Governors. Irish Americans. Italian Americans. New York City-Bowery. New York City–Fifth Avenue. Parties. Police. Political campaigns. Priests.*

Note: According to a Oct 1944 *HR* news item, actress Elyse Knox was originally cast in the lead role of this film. Edward J. Kay's music score was nominated for an Academy Award in 1944, but lost to Georgie Stoll's work on the M-G-M film *Anchors Aweigh*.

Box 29 Sep 1945. *DV* 24 Sep 1945, p. 3. *FD* 27 Sep 1945, p. 7. *HR* 9 Oct 1944, p. 2. *HR* 27 Apr 1945, p. 10. *HR* 24 Sep 1945, p. 3. *MPHPD* 19 May 1945, p. 2454. *MPHPD* 29 Sep 1945, p. 2661. *Var* 10 Oct 1945, p. 8.

SUNDAY PUNCH (Swedish Americans)

Metro-Goldwyn-Mayer Corp.; controlled by Loew's Inc. *Dist* Loew's Inc. 8 May **1942**; Prod: 15 Jan—19 Feb 1942 [©Loew's Inc.; 17 Apr 1942; LP11270]. Sd (Western Electric Sound System); b&w. 8 reels, 6,836 ft. 74-76 or 78 min. Passed by the National Board of Review. PCA cert no. 8244.

Prod Irving Starr. *Dir* David Miller. [*Asst dir* Al Raboch]. *Scr* Fay Kanin, Michael Kanin and Allen Rivkin. *Orig story* Fay Kanin and Michael Kanin. *Dir of photog* Paul Vogel. *Art dir* Cedric Gibbons. *Assoc* Gabriel Scognamillo. *Film ed* Albert Akst. *Set dec* Edwin B. Willis. [*Assoc* Keogh Gleason]. *Gowns* Kalloch. [*Mus score* David Snell and Daniele Amfitheatrof]. *Rec dir* Douglas Shearer.

Cast: William Lundigan (*Ken Burke*), Jean Rogers (*Judy Galestrum*), Dan Dailey, Jr. (*Olaf* [*Ole*] *Jensen*), Guy Kibbee (*"Pops" Muller*), J. Carrol Naish (*Matt Bassler*), Connie Gilchrist (*Ma Galestrum*), Sam Levene (*Roscoe*), Leo Gorcey (*"Biff"*), "Rags" Ragland (*"Killer"*), Douglass Newland (*"Baby" Fitzroy*), Anthony Caruso (*Nat Cucci*), Tito Renaldo (*Jose*), Michael Browne (*Al*), [Bernard Zanville (*Bill*)], [Dick Wessel (*Moxie*)], [Dave Willock (*Milkman*)], [Lester Matthews (*Smith*)], [Alfred Hall (*Butler*)], [Floyd Shackelford (*Doorman*)], [Duke York, Sammy Shack (*Fighters*)], [Edward Earle (*Clerk*)], [Marcia Ralston (*Blonde*)], [George Offerman (*Elevator boy*)], [Pat West, Tom Hanlon (*Announcers*)], [Bob Ryan, Ernie Alexander (*Spectators*)], [Eddie Simms (*Tiger*)], [Cyrus W. Kendall (*Promoter*)], [Lester Dorr (*Cameraman*)], [Frank Richards (*Bystander*)], [Syd Saylor (*Cabby*)], [Gaylord Pendleton (*Ken's cabby*)], [Al Hill (*Bassler's cabby*)], [Matt McHugh (*Flint*)], [Sam Ash (*Reporter*)], [Russ Clark, Frank Hagney (*Referees*)], [John Raitt (*Trotter*)], [Robin Raymond (*Vivian*)], [John Roche], [Carl Leviness].

Boxing, Comedy-drama. [*Print viewed*]. At Ma Galestrum's Brooklyn boardinghouse, only male boxers reside, under the guidance of their trainer, Roscoe, who subscribes to the "no dames allowed" rule set by Matt Bassler, the boxers' owner. An exception is made, however, when Ma's niece Judy, a singer whom she reared, returns home. Judy's difficult tour of Europe at the start of World War II has convinced her that marriage to a nice wealthy man is the only thing for her, and she determines to find one. Ma's janitor, Olaf "Ole" Jensen, develops a serious crush on Judy, as does boxer Ken Burke, a former medical student. Though Ken pretends to dislike Judy because of her gold-digging, they soon fall in love. That same night, when Ole learns from Ken how much money fighters earn, he determines to become a wealthy man for Judy. Bassler refuses to consider an amateur like Ole, but "Pops" Muller, a down-on-his-luck manager, decides to take him when Ole's "Sunday Punch" knocks out a professional boxer. Pops also arranges a road trip for Ole, despite Ken's concern that Ole needs to develop his boxing skills. Not realizing Ole's true feelings for her, Judy kisses him goodbye and gives him a flower, strengthening his resolve to marry her. Meanwhile, Bassler, who fears that Judy will ruin Ken's boxing career, offers her a singing contract that includes an out-of-town trip. Ken is angry and disappointed in her for accepting the job, and when he receives his acceptance letter from Johns Hopkins Medical School, he tears it up and continues boxing. Months later, Ken has become a contender for the title, as has Ole. Bassler and Pops try to arrange a bout between the two, but both fighters refuse the $30,000 offer because of their friendship. Desperate to have a winning fighter, Pops convinces Ole that the money will help him win Judy, so he reluctantly agrees to fight. On the night of the fight, "Biff," another fighter, overhears Bassler and Roscoe discussing what they have done to Ken and Ole. Because Biff's allergies are forcing him to quit the ring and move to Arizona, he convinces Bassler to allow him to manage some local fighters in exchange for his silence. At the arena, Biff receives a draft notice and starts to feel guilty about his actions, so he tells Judy everything. She goes to Ken's dressing room, but when he refuses to listen, she goes to Ole and tells him that although she loves Ken, she wants him to lose so that Ken will give up the ring and return to school. Ole is hurt, but realizes that Judy and Ken belong together and promises to do his best. During the grueling fight, neither boxer can knock the other out. Judy begs Ken to throw in the towel, but he refuses, just as Ole refuses Pops's request to do the same. Finally, Olaf lands a "Sunday Punch" and wins the match, after which he helps Ken to his chair. In his dressing room, Ole tells a confused Ken that "the best man won," and Judy follows Ken out of the arena. A short time later, Ken and Judy are married at Ma's boardinghouse. As they are about to enter a taxi, the cab driver starts a fight with another driver, and Roscoe is happy that he has found a good replacement for Ken, who is going back to school. *Aunts. Boardinghouses. Boxers. Friendship. Romance. Unrequited love. Allergy. Extortion. Gold diggers. Janitors. Medical students. New York City. Photographs. Promoters. Ruses. Self-sacrifice. Singers. Swedish Americans.*

Note: According to an unidentified 25 Feb 1942 news item contained in the AMPAS Library file on the film, professional boxers Eddie Simms, Fred Seel, Abie Bain, Tommy Garland and Cy Schindell were to be in the cast; only Simms is credited elsewhere, and the participation of the other men in the released film has not been confirmed. *HR* news items include John Indrisano, Henry Jordan, Frankie Grandetta, Rio Punay, Mickey Phillips, Cliff Danielson, Sig Frolich, Rudy Cameron, Louis Matheaux, Robin Raymond, Lew Smith and Edward Kilroy in the cast, but their participation in the released film has not been confirmed. *Sunday Punch* marked the screen debut of actor Dane Clark, who appeared as "Bill." At the time of the film's production, Clark was acting under his real name, Bernard Zanville.

Box 18 Apr 1942. *DV* 15 Apr 1942, p. 3. *Exh* 22 Apr 1942. *FD* 17 Apr 1942, p. 8. *HR* 12 Jan 1942, p. 6. *HR* 16 Jan 1942, p. 4, 14. *HR* 10 Feb 1942, p. 12. *HR* 13 Feb 1942, p. 7, 10. *HR* 2 Mar 1942, p. 4. *HR* 5 Mar 1942, p. 4. *HR* 9 Mar 1942, p. 6. *HR* 15 Apr 1942, p. 3. *MPD* 15 Apr 1942. *MPHPD* 18 Apr 1942, p. 611. *NYT* 11 May 1942, p. 19. *Var* 15 Apr 1942, p. 8.

SUNDAY SINNERS (African Americans, Chinese Americans)
Colonnade Pictures Corp.; An Arthur Dreifuss Production. 1941. Sd; b&w. 7 reels, 5,928 ft. 66 min.

Dir Arthur Dreifuss. *Asst dir* Chuck Wasserman. *Orig story* Frank Wilson. *Scr adpt* Vincent Valentini. *Cine* George Webber. *Art dir* William Salter. *Ed* Robert Crandall. *Cost* Al Stevens. *Orch arr* Ken Macomber. *Sd* Ed Fenton. *Unit mgr* Irvin C. Miller.

Song(s): "Same Old Moon," "I'll Do Anything for Love" and "This Is the Life for Me," music and lyrics by Donald Heywood.

Cast: Cristola Williams (*Creola*), Norman Astwood (*Gene* [*Aiken*]), Edna Mae Harris (*Corrine* [*Aiken*]), Earl Sydnor (*Reverend* [*Jesse*] *Hampton*), Thelma Norton (*Peggy* [*Hampton*]), Harold Norton (*Earl* [*Winters*]), Alberta Perkins (*Mama Jay*), Ernie Ransom (*Ray* [*Hampton*]), Mamie Smith (*Midge*), Alex Lovejoy (*Eli*), Sidney Easton (*Bootsie*), Percy Verwayen (*Tack* [*Adams*]), Al Young (*Chin* [*Lee*]), Gus Smith (*Deacon*), Herman Green (*Roscoe*), George Williams (*Crackerjack*), and The Sunkissed Brown Skin Chorus.

African American, Show business, Comedy-drama, with songs. [*Print viewed*]. The Sunday night business of the Club Harlem, which draws the local young people away from church services, greatly upsets some members of Reverend Jesse Hampton's black church, and the reverend agrees to deliver a sermon on the topic. Gene Aiken, the club's owner, is sympathetic to the church's concern, but his avaricious wife Corrine, who is having an affair with his partner, Tack Adams, talks him out of closing down on Sundays because it is their most profitable night. Gene, who has had Corrine and Tack trailed to a roadhouse, fires Tack, and when Tack implies that Gene and Creola, a singer at the café, are romantically inclined toward each other, Gene hits him and tells Corrine that from now on their relationship will be strictly a business one. After Corrine comes up with an idea for the club to hold a dance contest to attract more young people, the reverend's daughter Peggy and her boyfriend, Earl Winters, practice so they can get married with the fifty-dollar first-prize money. When Reverend Hampton finds them dancing, they explain that the winners are promised a professional engagement, so he encourages them to "go to it." Corrine, learning that Peggy's handsome brother Ray is looking for a job, hires him as her chauffeur. Meanwhile, Eli, the reverend's brother-in-law and a frequenter of the café, tells his drinking buddy Bootsie about a money-making scheme, one of many he has had. Earlier, while Eli was in the country talking to nature to clear his conscience, as the reverend had suggested, he saw men surveying some swamp land and learned that a bus company wants to run a line into town. He now tells Bootsie that they need capital to buy the swamp land so they can sell it to the bus company. As part of the land belongs to Chin Lee, a Chinese-American launderer, they devise a plan to convince Chin, who is a friend of Bootsie's, to put up the money so they can buy the adjoining property by telling the skeptical Chin that he will be able to own every laundry in the country. Peggy and Earl win the contest, which attracts many customers. When Gene accuses Corrine of attempting to seduce Ray, who has since been fired because of her, she castigates him for running after Creola. After he slaps her, she goes to the club's bar, where she and Creola get into a fistfight. Tack throws a knife from a window at Gene and wounds him, then steals the night's take of $2,000. Before taking off, Tack leaves a pin belonging to Ray on Gene's desk, so the police arrest Ray for the crime. Meanwhile, as Eli, Bootsie and Chin investigate a shack in the swamp, they fall through the rotten wooden floor into green mud. Chin excitedly recognizes it as the rare "Confucius" mud used for facial mud packs, and they realize they have stumbled into a fortune. In town, Reverend

Hampton offers to resign after church members criticize him for going to the club to investigate, but his mother-in-law, Mama Joy, convinces him to "get hot" in his final sermon. As the congregation participates responsively in the sermon, the reverend says it is time to shed their "humble cloak" for one of righteous indignation and leads the group in a march to the club. Gene returns to the club to find that Corrine has hired underworld thugs Roscoe and Crackerjack to bring in their gang for "protection." Gene orders the gang to leave and calls the police, and when Creola, who listened to the reverend's sermon, warns Gene of the congregation's approach, he is overjoyed. Desperate, Corrine offers Roscoe and Crackerjack fifty percent of the ownership if they will help her fight the churchgoers. When one of the men starts to attack the reverend, he fights back and a brawl begins. Corrine aims a gun at her husband, but Creola is grazed instead. The police arrest the gang and Corrine. Gene then comes to an agreement with Reverend Hampton that the club will not be open on Sunday nights and will be run in a clean and orderly manner. Later, on the night that Peggy and Earl dance in their first professional appearance, Eli, Bootsie and Chin attend and celebrate their success. Ray has been released because Creola's sister Maisie, a cigarette girl at the club, overheard the thugs say that Tack planted the pin. Ray now has a good job at the club and has married Maisie. *African Americans. Business ethics. Nightclub owners. Reverends. Youth. Attempted murder. Chinese Americans. Cigarette girls. Dance contests. Dismissal (Employment). False arrests. Family relationships. Fistfights. Get-rich-quick schemes. Greed. Infidelity. Laundries. Lawyers. Marriage. Partnership. Robbery. Ruffians. Sermons. Singers. Sisters. Swamps.*

Note: Although the credits of this film state that it was copyrighted in 1941 by Colonnade Pictures Corp., the film is not listed in the copyright register. Although some modern sources state that Jack Goldberg or Goldberg Productions produced the film, neither Goldberg's name nor that of the production company was in the credits. The film was released in New York through Lou Goldberg's exchange.

SUNNY SKIES (Jewish Americans)

Tiffany Productions, Inc. 12 May **1930** [©Tiffany Productions, Inc.; 1 May 1930; LP1266]. Sd (Photophone); b&w. 8 reels, 6,994 ft.

Dir Norman Taurog. *Addl dir* Ralph De Lacy. *Scen* Earl Snell. *Story* A. P. Younger. *Dial* George Cleveland. *Photog* Arthur Reeves. *Film ed* Clarence Kolster. *Rec eng* John Buddy Myers.

Cast: Benny Rubin (*Benny Krantz*), Marceline Day (*Mary Norris*), Rex Lease (*Jim Grant*), Marjorie "Babe" Kane (*Doris*), Greta Granstedt (*College widow*), Wesley Barry (*Sturrle*), Robert Randall (*Dave*), James Wilcox (*Smith*).

Musical comedy. Jim Grant, a smartly-dressed athlete at Standtech, takes an interest in modest Mary Norris, who has scholastic ambitions but is claimed by Dave, her hometown sweetheart. Jim's roommate is Benny Krantz, a shy, blundering son of a delicatessen keeper. Jim promises Benny's father, Isadore, that he will take care of his son, while Doris, a co-ed friend of Mary's, teaches Benny what "It" is all about. Mary becomes infatuated with Jim, but he falls from grace after she discovers him intoxicated with a "fast" girl; he is also disqualified from the football team for failing in his studies. Jim tries to win Mary back, bringing on a fight with Dave, whose arm Jim breaks. Benny tries to emulate Jim, and Mary gains a reputation for dating. When Benny is critically injured during a spree, Jim saves his life with a transfusion; called back on the team, he scores the winning touchdown. *Blood–Transfusion. College life. Courtship. Football. Jews. Students.*

FD 18 May 1930. NYT 17 May 1930, p. 21. Var 21 May 1930, p. 27.

SUNSET IN THE WEST (Latino)

Republic Pictures Corp. *Dist* Republic Pictures Corp. 25 Sep **1950**; Prod: Mar 1950 [©Republic Pictures Corp.; 23 Oct 1950; LP449]. Sd (RCA Sound System); col (Trucolor). 5,993 ft. 67 min. PCA cert no. 14502.

Assoc prod Edward J. White. *Dir* William Witney. [*Asst dir* Jack Lacey]. *Wrt* Gerald Geraghty. *Dir of photog* Jack Marta. [*Cam op* Joe Novak]. [*Gaffer* Austin Heric]. [*Stills* Mickey Marigold]. *Spec eff* Howard Lydecker, Theodore Lydecker and [Jack Caffee]. *Optical eff* Consolidated Film Industries. [*Trucolor col consultant* Sam Cohen]. *Art dir* Frank Hotaling. *Film ed* Tony Martinelli. *Set dec* John McCarthy, Jr. and George Milo. *Cost supv* Adele Palmer. *Mus* R. Dale Butts. *Sd* T. A. Carman. *Makeup supv* Bob Mark. [*Makeup* Steve Drumm]. [*Hair stylist* Lynne Burke]. [*Scr supv* Marie Messinger]. [*Grip* Gary Lambrecht].

Song(s): "Sunset in the West," music and lyrics by Foy Willing, Spanish lyrics by Aaron Gonzales; "Rollin' Wheels" and "When a Pretty Girl Passes By," music and lyrics by Jack Elliott.

Cast: Roy Rogers [(*Roy Rogers*)], Trigger *The Smartest Horse in the Movies*, Estelita Rodriguez [(*Carmelita*)], Penny Edwards (*Dixie Osborne*)], Gordon Jones [(*Splinters*)], Will Wright [(*Sheriff Tad Osborne*)], Pierre Watkin [(*Gordon MacKnight*)], Charles LaTorre [(*Nick Corella*)], William J. Tannen [(*John Kimball*)], Gaylord Pendleton [(*Walter Kimball*)], Paul E. Burns [(*"Blinky" Adams*)], Dorothy Ann White [(*Dot*)], Foy Willing, and The Riders of the Purple Sage, [Rusty Wescoatt (*Wrestler*)], [Karl "Killer" Davis (*Tough wrestler*)], [Bobby Barber (*Customer*)], [Monte Montague (*Posseman*)], [Tony Roux (*Mexican vendor*)], [Tina Menard (*Felicia*)], [John De Simone (*Sailor*)], [Stanley Blystone], [Gail Bonney], [Eva Novak].

Western, with songs. [*Print viewed*]. When California sheriff Tad Osborne and his men are sent to investigate a train which an outlaw gang hijacked and then accidentally wrecked, they discover the train's cache of smuggled guns. Some weeks later, rancher and former deputy sheriff Roy Rogers waits to load his cattle onto another train, but it speeds past without stopping. Roy follows the train on his horse Trigger, jumps aboard, wrestles with one of the hijackers and is tossed from the train. He then heads for the jail in nearby Bordertown, where his friend Tad faces a mob of angry citizens complaining about the smugglers. When Tad expresses his concern that he may be voted out of office in the upcoming election, Roy promises to help him. Meanwhile, at the cantina, a Mexican American singer named Carmelita notices two suspicious-looking patrons, smugglers John and Walter Kimball. After she rushes outside to look for Splinters, a deputy, Roy wanders into the cantina. A few minutes later, Splinters enters with his dog Sherlock, mistakes two other patrons for the smugglers and begins accusing them in a loud voice. The real smugglers creep out quietly, but are followed by Roy and Sherlock. While Sherlock growls and tries to bite John, Roy fights with Walter. John then brutally wounds Sherlock and escapes, after which Roy arrests Walter. Later, Roy surmises that the smugglers have been transporting the guns to a deserted beach, where they are subsequently picked up by Mexico-bound boats. At the jail, after Splinters shaves off Walter's beard, Roy recognizes him as a wanted man. Just then, the gang bursts in and frees Walter, after which they blindfold and kidnap Roy. On the way to their hideout, a ranch belonging to their leader, lawyer Gordon MacKnight, the gang meets up with an outlaw named Nick Corella. Nick asks to join the gang, but John refuses, so Nick exacts revenge by slipping a small blade into Roy's hand. After the gang takes Roy to the edge of a steep cliff to throw him off, he cuts his ropes and escapes on Trigger, who waits nearby. Roy returns to Tad's house, where he learns that Tad has been told by a veterinarian that Sherlock will not recover and has taken him outside to "put him out of his misery." Roy rushes outside to stop Tad and learns that Sherlock has just discovered Nick's corpse in the bushes. Later, the coroner removes an antique bullet from Nick's body, and Tad mentions that MacKnight collects antique guns. Roy and his men decide to ride out to MacKnight's ranch, but MacKnight sees them coming and escapes. After Roy enters the house and notices a bird cage, he recalls hearing some birds chirping while he was being held captive. Later, the smugglers load guns onto another hijacked train, while Tad, Roy and Splinters go to the beach. There, they spot the smugglers' boat waiting offshore, just as MacKnight and the rest of the gang arrive. A shootout ensues, and although the smugglers onboard the boat escape, MacKnight is captured. The next day, Tad is re-elected in a landslide victory. *Deputies. Gunrunners. Sheriffs. Birds. Boats. California. Cantinas. Dogs. Elections. False accusations. Fistfights. Gunfights. Hideouts. Hijackers. Investigations. Jails. Kidnapping. Lawyers. Mexican Americans. Outlaws. Ranchers. Revenge. Singers. Train wrecks. Trains. Veterinarians.*

Note: The working title for this film was *Sunset in the Sierras*, which was also the title of another 1950 Roy Rogers picture. Although reviews list Paul E. Burns's character name as "Blink," he is called "Blinky" in the film.

Box 30 Sep 1950. *DV* 22 Sep 1950, p. 3. *FD* 27 Sep 1950, p. 14. *HR* 22 Sep 1950, p. 3. *MPH* 30 Sep 1950. *MPHPD* 30 Sep 1950, p. 502. *Var* 27 Sep 1950, p. 8.

SUNSET PASS (Latino)

RKO Radio Pictures, Inc. *Dist* RKO Radio Pictures, Inc. 1 Oct **1946**; Prod: late Nov–mid-Dec 1945 [©RKO Radio Pictures, Inc.; 29 Jul 1946; LP558]. Sd (RCA Sound System); b&w. 5,392 ft. 58-60 min. PCA cert no. 11337.

Exec prod Sid Rogell. *Prod* Herman Schlom. *Dir* William Berke. [*Asst dir* Harry Mancke and Doran Cox]. *Scr* Norman Houston. *Dir of photog* Frank Redman. [*2d cam* James Daly]. *Spec eff* Vernon L. Walker. [*Opt eff* Lynn Dunn]. [*Transparency projection shots* Harold Wellman]. *Art dir* Albert S. D'Agostino and Lucius O. Croxton. *Ed* Samuel E. Beetley. *Set dec* Darrell Silvera and William Stevens. *Mus dir* C. Bakaleinikoff. *Mus* Paul Sawtell. *Sd* Jean L. Speak and Roy Granville. [*Mus mixer* Earl B. Mounce].

Song(s): "Walking Arm in Arm with Jim" and "Annabella's Bustle," words by Harry Harris, music by Lew Pollack.

Source: Based on the novel *Sunset Pass* by Zane Grey (New York, 1931).

Cast: James Warren [(*Rocky*)], Nan Leslie [(*Jane Preston*)], John Laurenz [(*Chito Rafferty*)], Jane Greer [(*Helen Baxter*)], Robert Barrat [(*Rand Curtis*)], Harry Woods [(*Cinnabar*)], Robert Clarke [(*Ashton Preston*)], Steve Brodie [(*Slagle*)], Harry Harvey [(*Doab*)], [Slim Balch, Roy Bucko, Steve Stevens, George Plues, Clem Fuller, Bob Dyer, Artie Ortego, Buck Bucko (*Posse members*)], [Slim Hightower, Boyd Stockman, Glen McCarthy (*Robbers*)], [Robert Bray, Dennis Waters (*Bank clerks*)], [Florence Pepper, Vonne Lester (*Dancers*)], [Frank O'Connor (*Station agent*)], [Maria Dodd, Dorothy Curtis (*Women at station*)], [Carl Faulkner (*Passenger*)].

Western, with songs. [*Print viewed*]. Soon after railroad detectives Chito Rafferty and Rocky board a train in Arizona, it is robbed by a gang of masked bandits, who make off with a shipment of express company money. Rocky is about to shoot one of the fleeing robbers when fellow passenger Jane Preston deliberately ruins his shot by jostling his arm. Upon arriving at the next stop, Wagontongue, Rocky and Chito report to Doab, the local banker, who angrily discharges them for losing his money. Determined to retrieve the money, Rocky questions Jane about her behavior on the train, but Jane, who has just returned from the East, insists that the jostle was accidental. Overhearing Rocky's charges, Jane's brother Ashton engages him in a fistfight, which Rocky quickly wins. Later, while Rocky rides out to investigate the robbery area, girl-crazy Chito stays in town to watch Slagle, a bank cashier whom Rocky suspects is working with the outlaws. Near the robbery site, Rocky comes across an unusual horseshoe print, as well as a piece of torn cloth. Back in the Wagontongue saloon, Chito eavesdrops on a conversation between Slagle and Cinnabar, the leader of the outlaws, and convinces singer Helen Baxter to cozy up to Slagle and coax information out of him. The next day, Rocky encounters rancher Rand Curtis, who tells him that his son Range became mixed up in Ash's dubious activities and disappeared one day near the Preston ranch in Sunset Pass. Rocky then sees a black horse roaming the Preston range and recognizes it as belonging to the robber he almost shot. At the Preston ranch house, meanwhile, Jane drills her brother about the holdup, and Ash finally confesses that he became involved in Cinnabar's gang to pay for her boarding school and repay some debts. Having captured the black horse, Rocky bursts into the ranch house and forces Ash to admit that he is the animal's owner. Rocky then matches the piece of cloth he found at the robbery site with Ash's torn hatband and accuses him of the holdup. Rocky tries to convince Ash to reveal the money's whereabouts, but Ash refuses to cooperate. As Rocky is escorting Ash back to Wagontongue, he is shot by Cinnabar, who overheard Rocky's interrogation at the ranch house. Ash returns fires, scaring Cinnabar off, then takes Rocky back to the ranch house, where he and Jane tend to his wound. While delirious with fever, Rocky calls out Chito's name, prompting Ash to ride to town to find the detective. Before Ash can speak with Chito, Cinnabar threatens to implicate Ash in Range's murder, a crime Cinnabar actually committed, if he tries to leave the gang. As Chito eavesdrops, Cinnabar then tells Ash that he buried the money under one of the Prestons' many cottonwood trees. Chito goes with Ash to Rocky's side, and two weeks later, Rocky has recovered enough to take Ash for trial in Tucson. Anxious to help the repentant Ash, Rocky gives him another chance to talk, but Ash remains silent. Chito, meanwhile, stumbles upon the stolen money when Helen becomes stuck in Cinnabar's cottonwood tree. Rocky then insists that Ash return the money directly to Doab, who is impressed by Ash's honesty and tells him and Slagle about a replacement shipment of money that has just arrived. Slagle reports the news to Cinnabar, who plots to steal the money by telling Curtis that Range is buried on Preston land and inciting the townsmen to form a posse. After Range's body is found,

an enraged Curtis accuses Ash of killing his son. Ash, however, convinces Curtis that Range was killed by Cinnabar because he knew too much. Ash then informs Rocky and Chito about the new money shipment, and the detectives race to town to stop the gang from robbing the bank. After a fierce fight, Rocky and Chito apprehend all of the outlaws. Later, Rocky exonerates Ash and accepts Jane's marriage proposal, while Chito remembers that he left Helen dangling in the cottonwood and dashes off to rescue her. *Brothers and sisters. Criminals–Rehabilitation. Outlaws. Railroad detectives. Ranchers. Train robberies. Arizona. Bankers. Confession. Fistfights. Frame-ups. Gunshot wounds. Horses. Mexican Americans. Money. Nursing back to health. Posses. Romance. Saloons. Singers.*

Note: Zane Grey's novel *Sunset Pass* was published serially in *American* magazine, beginning in Apr 1928. Although actor John Laurenz sings a third song in this film, its title and composer have not been identified. It is possible that Laurenz, who also wrote songs, was the composer. According to a *HR* news item, Edward Killy was first slated to direct the film. *HR* also noted that exteriors for *Sunset Pass* were shot in Lone Pine, CA. Paramount produced two earlier versions of Grey's novel, both titled *Sunset Pass*. The first was released in 1929, and was directed by Otto Brower and starred Jack Holt (see *AFI Catalog of Feature Films, 1921-30*; F2.5473). Henry Hathaway directed the second, which was made in 1933 with Tom Keene and Randolph Scott (see *AFI Catalog of Feature Films, 1931-40*; F3.4404). Despite their common source, the plots of the three versions bear little resemblance to one another.

Box 29 Jul 1946. *DV* 17 Jul 1946, p. 3. *FD* 18 Jul 1946, p. 6. *HR* 18 Oct 1945. *HR* 23 Nov 1945, p. 12. *HR* 30 Nov 1945, p. 20. *HR* 14 Dec 1945, p. 18. *HR* 17 Jul 1946, p. 6. *MPHPD* 13 Jul 1946, p. 3090. *MPHPD* 20 Jul 1946, p. 3102. *Var* 17 Jul 1946, p. 8.

SUNSHINE AND GOLD (Gypsies)

Balboa Amusement Co. *Dist* Pathé Exchange, Inc. 29 Apr **1917** [©Pathé Exchange, Inc.; 24 Apr 1917; LU10624]. Si; b&w. 5 reels.

Dir Henry King. *Scen* Henry King. *Story* Will M. Ritchey. *Cam* Joseph Brotherton.

Cast: Baby Marie Osborne (*Little Mary*), Henry King (*The chauffeur*), Daniel Gilfether (*James Andrews*), Neil Hardin (*Dr. Andrews, his son*).

Comedy-drama. Wandering away from the excitement of a party and stage play given at her house in honor of her fifth birthday, Little Mary falls into the hands of gypsies. When she overhears their chief discuss a ransom demand for her, Mary escapes into the woods during the still of the night. The next morning, she discovers an old cabin where she meets elderly James Andrews, who, years earlier, hid himself and all his wealth in this uninhabited woodland after a quarrel with his son. The next day, when the distraught chauffeur whose negligence had been responsible for Mary's disappearance arrives, Andrews realizes that Mary is his son's daughter and decides to accompany her home. Thus, the old man and child return to the Andrews home where the whole family is reunited. *Children. Grandfathers. Gypsies. Parentage. Birthdays. Chauffeurs. Escapes. Kidnapping. Parties. Ransom.*

ETR 21 Apr 1917, p. 1388. *MPN* 28 Apr 1917, p. 2683-84. *MPW* 28 Apr 1917, p. 633. *MPW* 5 May 1917, p. 854. *NYDM* 21 Apr 1917, p. 26. *Var* 13 Apr 1917, p. 27. *Wid's* 26 Apr 1917, pp. 265-66.

THE SUNSHINE MAID *see* UNKNOWN 274

SUPERSTITION MOUNTAIN *see* LUST FOR GOLD

THE SUPREME PASSION (Irish Americans)

Dist Film Market; Playgoers Pictures, Inc. 10 May **1921**? Si; b&w. 6 reels.

Dir Samuel Bradley. *Story* Robert McLaughlin and Charles Turner Dazey. *Photog* Ben Reynolds.

Source: Inspired by the poem "Believe Me If All Those Endearing Young Charms" by Thomas Moore in *Irish Melodies*, music arranged by Sir John Stevenson (London, 1807).

Cast: Robert Adams (*Jerry Burke*), William Mortimer (*Judge Burke*), Daniel Kelly (*Dan Manning*), Mrs. Charles Willard (*Mrs. Manning*), George Fox (*Gardner*), Cecil Owen (*James Lacey*), Florence Dixon (*Mary Manning*), Madelyn Clare (*Clara*), Selmer Jackson (*Clara's beau*), Edward Keane (*Dr. Jennings*).

Melodrama. Jerry Burke is engaged to marry Mary Manning, daughter of a wealthy old Irishman, but his father opposes the match and disowns him. Meanwhile, Lacey, a successful but crooked politician, returns to Ireland and persuades the retired Manning to emigrate with Mary to the United States. Jerry follows and finds a position on a newspaper, but he is disheartened to hear that Mary plans to marry Lacey. While she is preparing for the ceremony, her veil catches on fire and a doctor announces that her beauty is

impaired, whereupon Lacey withdraws his suit. Returning to Ireland, she reveals that Jerry and reveals that the fire was a pretext to prevent her marriage to Lacey, and the lovers are reunited. *Immigrants. Ireland. Irish. Irish Americans. Marriage. Politicians. Reporters.*

Note: Although the 1923 copyright (and distribution) were by Playgoers Pictures, there appears to have been no change in length or story.
ETR 19 Mar p. 1480. *Var* 15 Mar 1923, p. 32.

SUTTER'S GOLD (German Americans, Latino)
Universal Productions, Inc.; Carl Laemmle, President; An Edmund Grainger Production. *Dist* Universal Productions, Inc. 13 Apr **1936**; Prod: 19 Nov 1935—25 Jan 1936 [©Universal Productions, Inc.; 9 Apr 1936; LP6261]. Sd (Western Electric Noiseless Recording); b&w. 10 reels. 94-95 min. PCA cert no. 2007.

Pres CARL LAEMMLE. *Dir* James Cruze. [*Asst dir* William Reiter, Vernon Keays and Fred Frank]. *Scr* Jack Kirkland, Walter Woods and George O'Neil. [*Contr wrt* Gene Fowler and Dr. L. Gutstein]. *Cine* George Robinson. *Spec cine* John P. Fulton. *Art dir* Albert S. D'Agostino. *Film ed* Philip Cahn. [*Ed supv* Maurice Pivar]. *Gowns* Brymer. *Mus score* Franz Waxman. *Sd supv* Gilbert Kurland. *Tech dir* Tito Davison. [*Script clerk* Morree Clark]. [*Horseman* Jimmy Phillips]. [*Spec horseman* Jack Boyle]. [*Prod secy* Camille Collins].

Source: Based on the novel *L'Or; la merveilleuse histoire du général Johann August Suter* by Blaise Cendrars, by arrangement with Bruno Frank (Paris, 1925).

Cast: Edward Arnold, by arrangement with B. P. Schulberg (*Johan Sutter*), Lee Tracy (*Pete Perkin*), Binnie Barnes (*Countess Elizabeth Bartoffski*), Katharine Alexander (*Anna Sutter*), Montague Love (*Captain Kettleson*), Addison Richards ([*James*] *Marshall*), John Miljan (*General [Juan Bautista] Alvarado*), Harry Carey (*Kit Carson*), William Janney (*Sutter's son, [John Sutter, Jr.]*), Nan Grey (*Sutter's daughter, [Ann Eliza Sutter]*), Robert Warwick (*General Rotscheff*), Morgan Wallace (*General Fremont*), Allen Vincent (*Alvarado's son*), [Mitchell Lewis (*King Kamehameha*)], [Frank Reicher (*Governor Felipe Vega*)], [Harry Stubbs (*John Jacob Astor*)], [Harry Cording (*Lars*)], [William Gould (*Captain Jensen*)], [George Irving (*Dr. Billings*)], [Gaston Glass (*Lieutenant Bacalenakoff*)], [William Gilbert (*General Vallejo*)], [Joanne Smith (*Ann Eliza Sutter, age 3*)], [Ronald Cosbey (*John Sutter, Jr., age 8*)], [Billy Gilbert (*General Ramos*)], [Aura de Silva (*Señora Alvarado*)], [Sidney Bracey (*Smythe*)], [Bryant Washburn (*Captain Petroff*)], [William Ruhl (*Aide*)], [Pedro Regas (*De la Cruz*)], [Russell Hopton (*Crazed sailor*)], [John King (*Alvarado, Jr.*)], [George Lloyd (*Bo'sun*)], [Walter Long, Ed Brady (*Sailors*)], [John Bleifer], [Russ Powell], [Jim Thorpe], [Paul Weigel], [Priscilla Lawson], [Jose Rubio], [Oscar Apfel], [Albert J. Smith], [Neely Edwards], [Charles Farr], [Don Briggs], [Clarence H. Wilson].

Historical, Drama. [*Print viewed*]. When Johan Sutter is falsely accused of murder in 1833 in his native Switzerland, he leaves his wife Anna, daughter Annaliese and son Johan, Jr. for America. He is immediately offered a job as a cable car driver in New York, but both he and Pete Perkin, who was hired with him, are beset by strikebreakers and are hospitalized. While recuperating, Johan decides to go to California, which has been described to him as paradisial, and upon his release, he and Pete head West. For two years they run a successful general store in Missouri until they have saved enough money to continue their travels. Pete reluctantly follows Johan to Vancouver, where they board Captain Kettleson's California-bound ship just in time to avoid being trapped in wintery Canada. The ship stops first in the Sandwich Islands, where King Kamehameha treats Kettleson, Pete and Johan to a feast, after which Pete decides to stay. Back on the ship, Johan discovers that Kettleson has secretly taken over two hundred Kanakas as slaves. Johan tries to get off the ship, but Kettleson takes him hostage, and when Pete decides to return, Kettleson holds him and steals their savings. Upon running out of water, the crew mutinies and shackles Kettleson and the first mate. Johan takes over as captain, frees the slaves, and gives everyone a last sip of water. The ship arrives on the coast of California, where Johan immediately makes himself known to General Juan Bautista Alvarado, who arranges for Johan and the Kanakas to settle the land around Fort Ross to dissuade the Russians from taking the land. Johan names the colony New Helvetia, but after three years without money for supplies, the colonists face starvation. Just in time, Russian General Rotscheff offers to sell Johan his fort, ship and farm animals, in exchange for yearly payments. Johan completes the deal and makes

the acquaintance of beautiful English-born Countess Elizabeth Bartoffski. She helps him herd the animals to the settlement, and then promises to follow his career when she is back in Russia. The colony flourishes, and eventually Johan takes final ownership of Fort Sutter. Having grown bored with the life of Russian royalty, Elizabeth visits Johan in California. He falls in love with her and proposes, but Pete protests that Johan has a wife and children and warns him that Elizabeth is only after his wealth. Johan refuses to listen, and Elizabeth stays on until gold is discovered on the land and he is robbed of everything by greedy prospectors. Elizabeth leaves Johan, who then becomes destitute until his wife and grown children arrive, having been summoned by Pete. Anna dies shortly thereafter from tropical fever, but has bound Johan to a promise to fight the loss of his land and finish New Helvetia. After many years, Johan's lawyer son, Johan, Jr., wages a court battle to reclaim his father's land. During this time, Annaliese becomes engaged to Juan Bautista Alvarado, Jr., and when Juan is fired upon because of Johan's land fight, Johan sends them out of the country for their own protection. During Johan's Admission Day speech in San Francisco, it is announced that the Supreme Court has returned Johan's land to him. The crowd of landowners riots, and Johan, Jr. is shot and killed, just as another announcement comes that the Supreme Court has reversed its decision in favor of the prospectors. Johan is mortified that the greed of the people has caused his son's death and vows to fight them for the rest of his life. By 1876, however, Johan is an elderly man waging a lost battle in Washington, with his faithful companion, Pete, by his side. One day in a park, some newsboys shout jokingly that Congress has awarded Johan his land. He rushes to the Capitol, where he buys a paper and reads the truth, that Congress has adjourned. Johan collapses on the Capitol steps and dies. *California–History–1846-1850. Settlers. John Sutter. Sutter's Fort (Sacramento, CA). Juan Bautista Alvarado. Canada. Kit Carson. Colonies. Desertion (Marital). False accusations. Friendship. Hunger. Loyalty. James Marshall. Mexicans. Mistresses. Murder. Mutiny. Prospectors. Reunions. Russians. Slave traders. Slavery–Emancipation. Streetcars. Strikebreakers. Thirst.*

Note: Although Sutter's first name is generally spelled "Johann," onscreen credits list it as "Johan." Correspondence in the MPAA/PCA files at the AMPAS Library reveals that as early as 1928, Universal was considering a production based on the life of Johann Sutter, although at that time, there was some concern that their production would be too similar to the 1929 M-G-M film *Tide of Empire*, which was also concerned with the gold rush of 1848 (see *AFI Catalog of Feature Films, 1921-30;* F2.5718). According to modern sources, in 1930, Sergei Eisenstein chose the story of Johann Sutter to be one of his early projects with Paramount, after his plans for another film, *The Glass House*, fell through. Using Blaise Cendrars' novel as his foundation, Eisenstein added to the story with research from other materials, including a personal tour of Sutter's original land in northern California, according to modern sources. The project was shelved, however. Universal's interest in the story apparently continued, as evidenced by a 1931 letter in the MPAA/PCA files to the MPPDA. The letter, authored by the Society of California Pioneers, protested the proposed Universal production, as it was their contention that Blaise Cendrars' novel was "full of historical inaccuracies, besmirching the name and character of both General John A. Sutter and James W. Marshall."

The project was not taken up again until 1934, when, in a Jul news item, *HR* reported that Howard Hawks was to direct a version of it for Universal with a screenplay by William Faulkner. According to a 1935 *HR* news item, however, William Anthony McGuire was to prepare a treatment in Jun 1934. Although there was no mention of an alteration of the Hawks directorial assignment, in Aug 1935, Universal considered assigning William K. Howard to direct the film. Howard, however, was already committed to another film. *HR* notes in Aug 1935 that producer Edmund Grainger went searching for locations in Northern California, and production was expected to begin 1 Sep 1935 with Hawks directing. In the Universal shooting schedules at the USC Special Collections Library, Hawks is credited with direction along with James Cruze, and Hawks and William Faulkner are included among the writers of this production. The exact nature of Hawks's and Faulkner's contribution to the final film has not been determined. Although the *HR* review gives adaptation credit to Gene Fowler, pre-release studio correspondence in the *SAB* questions, rather than confirms, this credit. In addition, a letter from writer Walter Woods in the *SAB* file at the AMPAS Library indicates that while he used various historical reference works, he, personally, did not use any specific incidents from Cendrars' novel.

An unidentified news item dated 15 Dec 1935 noted that 250 Hawaiian extras were hired for this film. According to correspondence in the MPAA/PCA collection, although the AMPP felt that the script conformed to the requirements of the Production Code, they recommended that Universal take "care with the portrayal of the Mexicans in this picture, to avoid burlesquing them and thus causing an unfavorable reaction in Mexico and other Spanish American countries." Further correspondence reveals that in Sep 1936, "all the sequences dealing with Mexico and Mexicans and the annexation of California by the United States" were eliminated before submitting the film to the Mexican Board of Censors, "since this fact still remains a sore spot with the

Mexican people." The film was passed by the censors. A Mar 1936 article in *HR* notes that the picture's world premiere was held in Sacramento, where a parade was held featuring 5,000 citizens in period costumes, Carl Laemmle, twenty-nine Universal actors and studio personnel, Governor Frank Merriam of California and Sacramento mayor Arthur Ferguson.

A 1935 news item in *DV* reports that Luis Trenker, a director with German Roto Films of Berlin, photographed backgrounds of Northern California for a German-language version of *Sutter's Gold*, called *Der Kaiser von Kalifornien* (*The Kaiser of California*). The German production was written and directed by Luis Trenker, photographed by Albert Benitz and Heinz von Jaworsky, and starred Luis Trenker and Viktoria v. Ballasko. The German film won an award in the Mussolini Competition for Best Foreign Film at the 1936 Venice Film Festival. According to a modern source, however, Allied forces later forbade the exhibition of the film in Germany.

DV 25 Apr 1934, p. 2. *DV* 7 Aug 1935, p. 1. *DV* 26 Mar 1936, p. 3. *FD* 28 Mar 1936, p. 7. *HR* 6 Jul 1934, p. 5. *HR* 19 Aug 1935, p. 5. *HR* 22 Aug 1935, p. 4. *HR* 26 Mar 1936, p. 3. *MPD* 27 Mar 1936, p. 4. *MPH* 11 Jan 1936, p. 27. *MPH* 15 Feb 1936, pp. 14-15. *MPH* 28 Mar 1936, p. 41. *NYT* 27 Mar 1936, p. 25. *Var* 1 Apr 1936, p. 16.

SUZANNA (Latino)

Mack Sennett Productions. *Dist* Allied Producers and Distributors. 15 Feb **1923**; Los Angeles premiere: ca. 24 Dec 1922 [©Mack Sennett; 4 Jan 1923; LP18621]. Si; b&w. 8 reels, 6,500 ft.

Pres Mack Sennett. *Supv* Mack Sennett. *Dir* F. Richard Jones. *Asst dir* Ray Grey. *Adpt* Mack Sennett. *Photog* Homer Scott, Fred W. Jackman and Robert Walters. *Lighting expert* Paul Guerin. *Art dir* Sanford D. Barnes. *Film ed* Allen McNeil. *Cost* Madame Violet.

Source: Based on the short story "Suzanna" by Linton Wells (publication undetermined).

Cast: Mabel Normand (*Suzanna*), George Nichols (*Don Fernando*), Walter McGrail (*Ramón*), Evelyn Sherman (*Doña Isabella*), Leon Bary (*Pancho*), Eric Mayne (*Don Diego*), Winifred Bryson (*Dolores*), Carl Stockdale (*Ruiz*), Lon Poff (*Alvarez*), George Cooper (*Miguel*), Indian Minnie (*Herself*), Black Hawk (*Himself*).

Romance, Comedy-drama. Hoping to consolidate their adjoining ranches, Don Fernando and Don Diego betroth their children, Ramón and Dolores, although Ramón is in love with Suzanna, the daughter of a peon on his father's ranch, and Dolores is interested in Pancho, a toreador. When Suzanna learns that she was kidnapped in infancy and is really Don Diego's daughter, she keeps silent; but Ramón finally rebels and steals Suzanna from the altar as she is about to marry Pancho. There are explanations, Ramón marries Suzanna, and Dolores marries Pancho. *Bullfighters and bullfighting. California. Parentage. Peasantry. Ranchers.*

FD 1 Apr 1923. *NYT* 26 Mar 1923 p. 16. *Var* 29 Mar 1923, p. 36.

SVENKST I OCH OMKRING NEW YORK (Swedish language,
    Swedish Americans)

Scandia Films, Inc. **1943**. Sd; b&w. 5 reels. Swedish language.

Song(s): "Du Gamla, Du Friska, du Fjellhoga Nord (Swedish National Anthem)," traditional.

Documentary. [*Not viewed*]. This documentary offers a tour of Swedish landmarks in and around New York City. The tour begins at Rockefeller Center, where the Swedish Consulate, News Exchange, Chamber of Commerce, Tourist Bureau and coffee bureau are located. Next, a Swedish massage establishment, restaurants, jewelers and Gustaf Adolf's church, the oldest Swedish church in New York City are shown. Locations important to the Swedish community are visited in Brooklyn, including the Augusta Home for the Aged and the Kallmans Orphanage. Other locations include points of interest in the Bronx, Long Island, Staten Island and New Jersey. The tour concludes at the annual Swedes' Day festival, where renowned Swedish individuals play soccer, perform traditional dances, and commemorate the old country. *New York City. Swedish Americans. Long Island (NY). New Jersey. New York City–Bronx. New York City–Brooklyn. New York City–Staten Island.*

Note: The title translates as *Swedes In and Around New York*. Film credits and the plot summary are based on a translated dialogue continuity deposited with the NYSA. According to NYSA records, the film was approved for exhibition in New York state in May, 1943. The film was shot in the New York City area and features prominent individuals from the Swedish-American community. Among the noteworthy Swedish Americans who appear in the film are Anna Lindelof Olsson, head of the Swedish division of the American Red Cross, Per Henrik Ling and Kjell Peterson, founders of the Swedish Gymnastic League in Brooklyn, Dr. Ewald Lawson, Dean of Upsala College in East Orange, and Swedish Consul General Martin Kastengren.

In the entertainment field, John Hellberg, popular singer, Ernest Mattsson, owner of Scandia Films, and Eddie Jarl, a radio announcer, are featured. Swedish-American sports figures who appear in the film include Olympic runner John Svanberg, former soccer stars Cairo Schylander and Bagar'n Levin,

Hans Lagerloef, termed "the sportsmen's best friend," and "Old man" Hjertberg, author of the cheer used at the 1912 Stockholm Olympic Games. In one scene a young Swedish woman reads the August Strindberg poem titled *Lordagskvall*, translated as *Saturday Eve*, and in another scene, John Ericsson, founder in 1861 of the *Monitor*, is commemorated.

THE SWAMP (Chinese Americans)

Hayakawa Feature Play Co. *Dist* R-C Pictures. 30 Oct **1921** [©R-C Pictures; 30 Oct 1921; LP17174]. Si; b&w. 6 reels, 5,560 ft.

Dir Colin Campbell. *Scen* J. Grubb Alexander. *Story* Sessue Hayakawa. *Photog* Frank D. Williams. *Art dir* W. L. Heywood.

Cast: Sessue Hayakawa (*Wang*), Bessie Love (*Mary*), Janice Wilson (*Norma*), Frankie Lee (*Buster*), Lillian Langdon (*Mrs. Biddle*), Harland Tucker (*Spencer Wellington*), Ralph McCullough (*Johnnie Rand*).

Melodrama. In "The Swamp," the slum quarter of a great city, live Mary, a deserted wife, and her small son Buster, struggling for an existence. They meet Wang, a Chinese vegetable peddler, when the peddler gets a black eye defending the boy. When Mary and Buster are about to be evicted, Wang saves them by peddling his horse, Bimbo; and he then becomes a fortune-teller, assisted by Buster. Rand, the new rent collector, proves to be Mary's childhood sweetheart. Through one of Wang's clients, she obtains a letter revealing that her husband, Spencer Wellington, is about to remarry. Wang, who is engaged to entertain at Norma's wedding reception, there reveals Spencer's past, thus breaking the engagement. Mary divorces Spencer and goes with Rand, while Wang, after redeeming his horse, returns to the home of his ancestors where a girl awaits him. *Chinese Americans. Divorce. Fortune-tellers. Horses. Motherhood. Peddlers and peddling. Slums.*

ETR 5 Nov 1921, p. 1627. *FD* 30 Oct 1921. *Var* 4 Nov 1921, p. 43.

SWAMP FIRE (Cajuns, French Americans)

Pine-Thomas Productions, Inc.; A Pine-Thomas Production. *Dist* Paramount Pictures, Inc. 6 Sep **1946**; New York opening: 24 Aug 1946; Prod: 25 Oct—early Nov 1945 at PRC Studios [©Paramount Pictures, Inc.; 25 Aug 1946; LP567]. Sd (Western Electric Mirrophonic Recording); b&w. 69 min. Passed by the National Board of Review.

[*Exec prod* William H. Pine and William C. Thomas]. *Assoc prod* L. B. Merman. *Dir* William H. Pine. *Asst dir* Harold Knox. *Orig scr* Geoffrey Homes. *Dir of photog* Fred Jackman, Jr. [*Spec eff* Howard A. Anderson]. [*Transparencies* Ray Smallwood]. *Art dir* F. Paul Sylos. *Supv ed* Howard Smith. *Ed* Henry Adams. *Set dec* Louis Diege. *Mus score* Rudy Schrager. *Sd rec* Max Hutchinson. [*Re-rec and eff mixer* Walter H. Oberst]. [*Mus mixer* Philip G. Wisdom].

Cast: Johnny Weissmuller (*Johnny Duval*), Virginia Grey (*Janet Hilton*), Buster Crabbe (*Mike Kalavich*), Carol Thurston (*Toni [Rousseau]*), Pedro de Cordoba (*Tim Rousseau*), Marcelle Corday (*Grandmere [Rousseau]*), William Edmunds (*Emile [Ledoux]*), Edwin Maxwell ([*Captain*] *Pierre Moise*), Pierre Watkin (*P. T. Hilton*), Charles Gordon (*Hal Payton*), Frank Fenton (*Captain Pete Dailey*), ["Ponchartrain Billy," an alligator].

Rural, Drama. [*Print viewed*]. Just after World War II, bar pilot Johnny Duval returns home to the bayous of the delta country of Louisiana after serving in the Coast Guard. Johnny has unsteady nerves after being responsible for a wartime shipwreck in which many men's lives were lost. While Johnny was away, a Cajun named Mike Kalavich courted his sweetheart, Toni Rousseau. On his way up the Mississippi River to Cypress Point, Johnny meets Janet Hilton, a wealthy society girl, who is immediately impressed with his rugged manliness. Johnny's old captain, Pierre Moise, is eager to rehire Johnny, who used to be his top bar pilot, but Johnny refuses to accept the job. A pilot friend of Johnny fakes an illness in order to get him to pilot Janet's father's yacht in the fog. Johnny successfully steers the boat to safety, and his commission as lieutenant in the Coast Guard Reserve is restored. At a town dance, Mike picks a fight with Johnny, but he refuses to fight back. Toni willingly fights Janet, however, who now rivals Toni for Johnny's affections. The night before Johnny and Toni are to marry, he is called to rescue a ship in the fog and rams into a boat, killing Toni's brother Tim. After the funeral, Johnny turns to drink and is injured in a traffic accident. He lies unidentified for weeks in a charity hospital; finally, Janet has him moved to her house on Delta Island to take care of him. When Toni and Captain Moise visit the Hiltons, she upbraids them for forcing Johnny to be a bar pilot and refuses to let them see him. After Johnny recovers, Janet gets him a job

with Hilton, who now owns the formerly free lands of the bayous where the locals hunt, fish and trap for their livelihood. Mike, who is a trapper, disdainfully disregards Hilton's posted warning signs. One day, Johnny and Janet catch Toni illegally hunting and accidentally hit her canoe with their motorboat. Toni is thrown from her boat, and Johnny wrestles an alligator to save her. Later, on Delta Island, Janet and Johnny hear a shot, and Johnny discovers that Mike and his friend Alex were trying to run a trap and were fired upon. Alex accuses Johnny of complicity with the Hiltons in breaking the tradition of bayou rights and tells him that every effort Toni made to see him was thwarted by Janet. Johnny confronts Janet, and she admits she intercepted Toni's letters and calls. After unsuccessfully trying to incite a riot among the trappers, Mike starts a swamp fire, and Toni races to the island to warn Johnny. As the fire spreads, Johnny and Toni call for each other, but when they finally embrace, Mike shoots Toni. Johnny knocks out Mike then rescues him and Toni from the engulfing flames. Later, Toni recovers and Johnny pilots a tanker for Captain Moise. *Bayous (LA). Louisiana. Mississippi River. Post-traumatic stress disorder. River boats. Romantic rivalry. Sea captains. Tests of character. Accidental death. Alligators. Attempted murder. Boating accidents. Cajuns. Dances. Engagements. Fights. Fires. Fog. Grandparents. Gulf of Mexico. Hospitals. Islands. Land rights. Manhood. Rescues. Socialites. Swamps. Trappers. United States. Coast Guard. Veterans.*

Note: A written foreword to the film states: "Here in the delta country of Louisiana where the Mississippi merges with the Gulf, at Pilot Town ninety river miles below New Orleans lives a courageous and colorful group of men, the associated bar pilots....Always members of the Coast Guard Reserve, the bar pilots enlisted for active duty during the war...." This film marked former Olympic swimming champion Johnny Weissmuller's first starring role in thirteen years in which he did not portray "Tarzan." The picture's opening credits list his character's name as "Johnny Duval," while the forewarod spells the name "Duvalle." According to the film's pressbook, the alligator that Weissmuller wrestles in the film, "Ponchartrain Billy," was brought to Hollywood in 1909 from Lake Ponchartrain near New Orleans and had previously appeared in many films. Portions of the film were shot on location in New Orleans, LA.

Box 11 May 1946. *DV* 10 May 1946, p. 3. *FD* 17 May 1946, p. 8. *HR* 9 Jan 1945, p. 3. *HR* 15 Oct 1945, p. 15. *HR* 25 Oct 1945, p. 5. *HR* 26 Oct 1945, p. 14. *HR* 9 Nov 1945, p. 16. *HR* 10 May 1946, p. 3. *HR* 30 Aug 1946, p. 10. *MPHPD* 27 Apr 1946, p. 2963. *MPHPD* 11 May 1946, p. 2986. *NYT* 26 Aug 1946, p. 21. *Var* 15 May 1946, p. 8.

SWANEE SHOWBOAT (African Americans)
Ajax Pictures. *Dist* Ajax Pictures. **1947?.** Sd; b&w. 5 reels.
Music: "Old Folks at Home" by Stephen Foster; "Boogamania," composer undetermined.
Song(s): "De Camptown Races," music and lyrics by Stephen Foster; "Lazybones," music and lyrics by Johnny Mercer and Hoagy Carmichael; "Nobody Knows de Trouble I've Seen" and "Ezekial Saw de Wheel," spirituals; "When I Married L'ooziana Lou," "I'm in Love with the Band," "Good News Jackson" and "Chicken Shack Shuffle," composers undetermined.
Cast: Nina Mae McKinney, Dewey "Pigmeat" Markham, Mabel Lee.
African American, Variety. [*Not viewed*]. This film is composed of a series of comedy and musical sketches. In one, a group of men discuss and act out being drafted, fighting in France, and dying on the battlefield, with their conversation interspersed with songs and spirituals. In another, entitled "Pigmeat Throws the Bull," Dewey "Pigmeat" Markham and Mabel Lee talk about Pigmeat's recent visit to a dude ranch, where he met Frank Sinatra, Bob Hope and Bing Crosby. *Battles. Dude ranches. France. Military service, Compulsory. Military service, Voluntary. Minstrel shows.*

Note: Although a print of this film was not viewed, the above plot and song information was taken from a cutting continuity deposited with the NYSA. No release date information was found, but according to NYSA records, the picture was submitted for censorship review in New York on 25 Mar 1947. NYSA records from 1947 list the film's footage as 3,876 feet (43 minutes), "with eliminations." According to a Nov 1949 NYSA memo, written by Motion Picture Inspector Arthur F. Boyce, a projectionist alerted Boyce to a trailer for this film which "displayed colored girl in dance that showed improper movements of the body." Boyce mentioned the incident to illustrate his contention that previews "should come under our review service," but added that under the current laws, no action could be taken on the questionable preview. Modern sources add Helen Barys, The Eight Black Streaks, The Lindy Hoppers, Scott and Whaley and the Swanee Swingsters to the cast.

SWEET DADDIES (Jewish Americans)
First National Pictures, Inc. *Dist* First National Pictures, Inc. 13 Jun **1926** [©First National Pictures, Inc.; 12 May 1926; LP22715]. Si; b&w. 7 reels, 6,562 ft.

Pres M. C. Levee. *Dir* Alfred Santell. *Asst dir* James F. O'Shea. *Adpt* W. C. Clifford. *Titles* George Marion, Jr. *Photog* Arthur Edeson. *Art dir* Jack Okey. *Film ed* Frank Lawrence.
Cast: George Sidney (*Abie Finkelbaum*), Charlie Murray (*Patrick O'Brien*), Vera Gordon (*Rosie Finkelbaum*), Jobyna Ralston (*Mariam Finkelbaum*), Jack Mulhall (*Jimmy O'Brien*), Gaston Glass (*Sam Berkowitz*), Aggie Herring.
Comedy-drama. Noted stage comedian Pat O'Brien prematurely celebrates his son's graduation from college and is fired from his act for being intoxicated; later, at a café where father and son continue their celebration, Jimmy sees Mariam Finkelbaum, whom he has met at a school prom. Abie (her father) and Pat become friends and enter into a business arrangement to import a mysterious product from the Bahamas, and they are arrested on a rum-running charge after Berkowitz, Mariam's jealous suitor, tips off prohibition officers. Jimmy meets their ship in a hydroplane and is also arrested. They are all released when it is learned that they are importing molasses; and Mariam's plans to marry Berkowitz are canceled when it is learned that he is a leading Florida bootlegger. All ends happily with Jimmy engaged to Mariam. *Actors and actresses. Bootleggers. Drunkenness. Family relationships. Florida. Irish. Jews. Molasses. Partnership. Seaplanes.*
FD 18 Jul 1926. *NYT* 23 Jun 1926, p. 28.

SWEET ROSIE O'GRADY (Jewish Americans)
Columbia Pictures Corp. *Dist* Columbia Pictures Corp. 5 Oct **1926**; trade showing: 17 Sep 1926 [©Columbia Pictures Corp.; 22 Nov 1926; LP23366]. Si; b&w. 7 reels, 6,108 ft.
Supv Harry Cohn. *Dir* Frank R. Strayer. *Scen* Harry O. Hoyt. *Photog* J. O. Taylor.
Source: Suggested by the song "Sweet Rosie O'Grady" by Maude Nugent (1896).
Cast: Shirley Mason (*Rosie O'Grady*), Cullen Landis (*Victor McQuade*), E. Alyn Warren (*Uncle Ben Shapiro*), William Conklin (*James Brady*), Lester Bernard (*Kibitzer*), Otto Lederer (*Friend*).
Comedy-drama. Rosie, an orphan, grows to womanhood under the care of Uncle Ben, a genial pawnbroker, and Brady, an Irish policeman. One day Rosie rescues Victor McQuade, a youth of the fashionable set, from some ruffians, and tends his wounds in the pawnshop. The next day, Victor, in a uniform borrowed from his chauffeur, calls to take Rosie for a ride; at his home he is detained by his sister, Muriel, who is giving a "poverty party." Rosie accidentally gets shoved in among the guests and wins first prize for having the most comical costume. Angry and mortified, she flees from Victor to Uncle Ben, who consents to her going to live with Brady in his comfortable home. Victor, intent on marrying Rosie, abducts her from Brady's home, and when they are stopped by a policeman, they have him perform the marriage ceremony. *Irish. Jews. Orphans. Pawnbrokers. Police. Poverty. Upper classes. Wealth.*
FD 26 Sep 1926. *MPW* 2 Oct 1926. *NYT* 9 Dec 1926, p. 33.

THE SWIFT SEASON *see* **WILD RIVER**

SWING! (African Americans)
Micheaux Pictures Corp.; An Oscar Micheaux Production. *Dist* Micheaux Pictures Corp. **1938.** Sd (Blue Seal Noiseless Recording); b&w. 7 reels, 6,500 ft.
Pres A. BURTON RUSSELL. *Dir* Oscar Micheaux. *Wrt* Oscar Micheaux. *Photog* Lester Lang. *Ed* Patricia Rooney. *Rec eng* Ed Fenton and E. A. Schabbehor.
Song(s): "Bei Mir Bist du Schön," music by Sholom Secunda, English lyrics by Sammy Cahn and Saul Chaplin; "Heaven Help This Heart of Mine," music and lyrics by Leonard Whitcup, Walter Samuels and Teddy Powell; and other songs.
Cast: Cora Green ([*Amanda*] *"Mandy"* [*Jenkins*]), Larry Seymour (*Cornell* [*Jenkins*]), Hazel Diaz (*Eloise* [*Jackson*]/*Cora Smith*), Alec Lovejoy (*Lem Jackson/Big Jones*), Mandy Randolph (*Liza*), Trixie Smith (*Lucy*), Carman Newsome (*Ted Gregory*), Nat Reed, Sammy Gardiner (*His assistants*), Dorothy Van Engle (*Lena* [*Powell*]), Doli Armena (*Trumpet player*), The Tyler Twins (*Tap dancers*), Columbus Jackson (*A "hustler"*), George R. Taylor (*Theatrical backer*), Leon Gross' orchestra.
African American, Show business, Drama, with songs. [*Print viewed*]. As Amanda "Mandy" Jenkins wakes up to go to work as a cook for the white Hewitt family in Birmingham, Alabama, her husband Cornell returns home from a night of gambling. When Ethel

and Liza, Mandy's friends, learn that Cornell is having an affair with Eloise Jackson, the wife of Lem, they agree that wives should stick together when men two-time them. Cornell takes Mandy's money to pay for his entertainment and diverts suspicion by telling his wife that he is an automobile salesman. Liza, however, reveals the truth about Cornell when she informs Mandy that her husband is being driven around in Eloise's car. Mandy goes to a nightclub looking for her husband, and when she finds him dancing with Eloise, a fight ensues. Months later, Eloise is living in Harlem, where she is singing under the assumed name Cora Smith. Although Eloise works for producer Ted Gregory, she pushes him around and intimidates him. When Lena Powell, Gregory's secretary, suggests to her boss that her old friend, Mandy, be hired as the wardrobe mistress, he consents to it. After punching Eloise when she is drunk, Lem delves into New York's underworld, where he soon learns that he can go on relief and be paid for not working. Three days before the show's opening, Eloise becomes intoxicated and breaks her leg, and Gregory replaces her with Mandy. Mandy, who has seen Cornell penniless, has a change of heart and takes her husband back. As Cornell soaks Mandy's tired feet, he realizes that he must stray no more. When the show finally opens it is a huge success. *Moral reformation. Philanderers. Singers. Vaudeville. Wives. Auditions. Automobiles. Birmingham (AL). Cooks. Drunkenness. Fistfights. Gambling. Gossip. Impersonation and imposture. Jealousy. New York City–Broadway. New York City–Harlem. Nightclubs. Seamstresses. Secretaries. Tap dancing. Theatrical producers. Trumpets. Welfare fraud.*

Note: According to the screen credits, the story on which this film was based was titled "Mandy." Other songs featured in the film, the titles of which have not been confirmed, are "Once I Did" and "I Got Rhythm."

THE SYMBOL OF THE UNCONQUERED (African Americans)
Micheaux Film Corp. *Dist* Micheaux Film Corp. 29 Nov **1920**. Si; b&w. 8 reels.

Prod Oscar Micheaux. *Dir* Oscar Micheaux. *Scen* Oscar Micheaux.

Cast: Iris Hall (*Evon Mason*), Walker Thompson (*Hugh Van Allen*), Lawrence Chenault, Jim Burris, Mattie Wilkes, E. G. Tatum, Leigh Whipper, James Burrough, George Catlin.

African American, Drama. [*Not viewed*]. After the death of her grandfather, Evon Mason, a young black woman from Selma, Alabama, travels to the Northwest to identify the mine claim she had been willed. There, Evon meets Hugh Van Allen, a black man seeking his fortune. Hugh, who loves Evon but thinks that she is white, discovers oil, thereby arousing the enmity of Tom Cutschawl, a racist Southerner, and Jefferson Driscoll, a black man passing for white who hates his own race. These two provoke an attack of the Ku Klux Klan to drive Hugh off the land, but Evon rescues Hugh, and the Klan is routed. Evon and Hugh eventually resolve their misunderstanding and live happily ever after. [No other information concerning the plot has been discovered]. *African Americans. Ku Klux Klan. Racism. The West. Inheritance. Mines. Oil. Racial impersonation. Rescues. Southerners.*

Note: This black independent film was shot in Fort Lee, NJ under the working title *The Wilderness Trail*. The first public screenings of the film were held in late 1920, but many contemporary and modern sources list it as a 1921 film. Some modern sources state that "Evon," not "Hugh," owns the oil lands that the Ku Klux Klan attacks, but this is probably an error. One source spells the villain's name as "Drescola" instead of "Driscoll."

ChiDef 27 Nov 1920, p. 5. *ChiDef* 8 Jan 1921, p. 4, 5. *New York Age* 25 Dec 1920, p. 6. *New York Age* 1 Jan 1921, p. 6.

SYMPHONY OF SIX MILLION (Jewish Americans)
RKO Radio Pictures, Inc. *Dist* RKO Radio Pictures, Inc. 29 Apr **1932**; New York premiere: 14 Apr 1932 [©RKO Radio Pictures, Inc.; 12 Apr 1932; LP2974]. Sd (RCA Photophone System); b&w. 10 reels. 92 or 94 min. Passed by the National Board of Review. PCA cert no. 2286-R [15 May 1936].

Exec prod David O. Selznick. *Assoc prod* Pandro S. Berman. *Dir* Gregory La Cava. *Story* Fannie Hurst. *Scr and dial* Bernard Schubert and J. Walter Ruben. *Addl dial* James Seymour. *Photog* Leo Tover. [*Cam op* Edward Henderson and Russell Metty]. [*Asst cam* Willard Barth and James Daly]. *Art dir* Carroll Clark. *Film ed* Archie F. Marshek. *Mus* Max Steiner. *Rec* George Ellis. [*Still photog* Fred Hendrickson].

Cast: Ricardo Cortez ([*Dr.*] *Felix* [*Klauber*]), Irene Dunne (*Jessica*), Anna Appel (*Hannah* [*Klauber*]), Gregory Ratoff (*Meyer* ["*Lansman*" *Klauber*]), Noel Madison (*Magnus* [*Klauber*]), Lita Chevret (*Birdie* [*Klauber*]), John St. Polis (*Dr. Schiffen*), Julie

Haydon [(*Miss Grey*)], Helen Freeman (*Miss Spencer*), Josephine Whittell [(*Mrs. Gifford*)], Oscar Apfel [(*Doctor*)], Eddie Phillips [(*Lipton*)], [Lester Lee (*Felix, as a boy*)], [Maurice Black (*Patient*)].

Domestic, Medical, Drama. [*Print viewed*]. As a boy in the Jewish ghetto of New York, Felix Klauber dreams of becoming a surgeon, while his brother Magnus devises ways to make quick money. After many years of study, Felix earns his medical degree and becomes a physician in the local clinic, where his unorthodox but successful methods earn him the respect of both his patients and his peers. Magnus, however, convinces Felix's mother Hannah that Felix should quit the clinic and open a lucrative private practice on the Upper West Side to better provide for the family, which includes Felix's aging father Meyer and his unmarried sister Birdie. Although troubled by Magnus' plan, Hannah uses her maternal influence and talks Felix into changing his practice. Soon Felix moves to Park Avenue and establishes himself as the doctor "with the million-dollar hands," whose patients' complaints are more imaginary than real. Trapped by his financial success, Felix neglects his family and ignores Jessica, his crippled childhood sweetheart who teaches at the Braille Institute for the Blind. When Felix fails to show up to perform a lifesaving operation on one of her impoverished blind students, Jessica denounces him as a traitor to his heritage and to his profession. Humbled and confused, Felix attends the "Redemption of the First Born" ceremony given in his baby nephew's honor and witnesses the sudden collapse of his father. At his family's urging, Felix agrees to perform surgery on his father, who has an advanced brain tumor, but loses his patient shortly into the operation. Devastated by his father's death, Felix vows never to practice medicine again and falls into a deep depression. However, when Jessica, whose spinal condition has worsened, announces that she is going to take a chance on a dangerous operation that may end her lameness, Felix offers his services and perfectly executes the operation. His confidence restored, Felix returns to medicine and to his ghetto roots. *Family relationships. Idealism. Jews. Materialism. New York City. Surgeons. Blindness. Braille Institute for the Blind. Disillusionment. Handicapped. Hospitals. Hypochondria. Medical students. Operations, Surgical. Rites and ceremonies. Slums. Upper classes.*

Note: The title frame of the viewed print read, "Fannie Hurst's Symphony of Six Million." Gregory Ratoff made his film debut in the picture. In New York, the film was screened twice daily at the Gaiety theater, which charged up to $1.50 for a single ticket, and had a four-week run "with options." According to *Var*, this film cost $270,000 to produce. In a letter to Katharine Brown, RKO's New York story editor, associate producer Pandro Berman stated that he was interested in hiring actor Maurice Moscovitch to play the role of the father in the film. The part was eventually played by Ratoff, however. He suggested to Brown that she avoid "the usual conception of Jewish characters, as for instance Buster Collier in *Street Scene*, or Vera Gordon" (a popular vaudeville, stage and screen actress who frequently played "Jewish mother" roles). The *Var* review noted that this film was one of the few pictures to feature a Reform rabbi. In a letter to RKO head David O. Selznick, Jason S. Joy of the MPAA warned that censors in Ohio might object to the film's operating scenes because "such scenes are too realistic if not actually gruesome" for a general audience. Modern sources include Harold Goodwin in the cast as an intern.

FD 10 Apr 1932, p. 10. *IP* Apr 1932, p. 29. *MPH* 2 Apr 1932, p. 35. *MPH* 30 Apr 1932, p. 35. *MPH* 28 May 1932, p. 87. *NYT* 15 Apr 1932, p. 23. *Var* 19 Apr 1932, p. 14.

SYNCOPATION (African Americans)
RKO Radio Pictures, Inc.; A William Dieterle Production. *Dist* RKO Radio Pictures, Inc. 22 May **1942**; *Prod:* 13 Oct–5 Dec 1941; addl scenes 11 Dec and 17 Dec 1941; jam session shot at Fox Movietone Studios, New York City on 23 Feb 1942 [©RKO Radio Pictures, Inc.; 22 May 1942; LP11371]. Sd (RCA Sound System); b&w. 9 reels, 7,915 ft. 88 min. PCA cert no. 7830.

Prod William Dieterle. *Assoc prod* Charles L. Glett. *Dir* William Dieterle. *Asst dir* Dewey Starkey. *Dial dir* Peter Berneis. *Scr* Philip Yordan and Frank Cavett. *From the orig story "The Band Played On"* by Valentine Davies. *Dir of photog* J. Roy Hunt. [*Background photog* Russ Cully]. *Spec eff* Vernon L. Walker. *Mont* Douglas Travers. *Art dir* Albert D'Agostino and Al Herman. *Ed* John Sturges. *Set dec* Darrell Silvera. *Cost* Edward Stevenson. *Mus dir* Leith Stevens. *Vocal dir* Hall Johnson. [*Dance dir* Ernst Matray]. *Rec* Richard Van Hessen and James G. Stewart. John Pommer. Michael Audley.

Music: "American Rhapsodie" by Leith Stevens.

Song(s): "Under a Falling Star," words by Rich Hall, music by Leith Stevens.

Cast: Adolphe Menjou (*George Latimer*), George Bancroft (*Mr.* [*Steve*] *Porter*), Todd Duncan (*Rex Tearbone*), Connie Boswell (*Cafe*

singer), Ted North (*Paul Porter*), Frank Jenks (*Smiley Jackson*), Jessie Grayson (*Ella* [*Tearbone*]), Mona Barrie (*Lillian*), Lindy Wade (*Paul Porter as a child*), Peggy McIntyre (*Kit Latimer as a child*), and Jackie Cooper (*Johnny* [*Schumacher*]), Bonita Granville (*Kit Latimer*), The All American Dance Band, with Charlie Barnet, Benny Goodman, Harry James, Jack Jenny, Gene Krupa, Alvino Rey, Joe Venuti selected from among leaders in *The Saturday Evening Post* poll, [Hall Johnson Choir], [Robert Benchley (*Doakes*)], [Walter Catlett (*Spelvin*)], [Charles Collins (*Fred Freddy*)], [Jack Thompson (*Reggie Tearbone*)], [Sherrill Luke (*Reggie's friend*)], [Walter Baldwin (*Tom Jones*)], [Jeff Corey (*Kit's attorney*)], [Rex Stewart (*King Jeffers*)], [Clinton Rosemond (*Professor Topeka*)], [Frank McGlynn (*Simon Goodwill*)], [Maurice Cass (*Archibald Travers*)], [Edwin Stanley (*Goodwill's attorney*)], [Bob McKenzie (*Bartender at party*)], [Thelma White (*Singer at party*)], [Martha Bamattre (*Polish woman*)], [Al Roberts (*Juggler*)], [James Clemens (*Dancer*)], [Emory Parnell (*Judge*)], [Frank Darien (*Court bailiff*)], [Madam Borget (*Jury woman*)], [Billy Reed (*Drunk dancer*)], [Charles Flynn (*Army officer*)], [Frank O'Connor (*Railroad conductor*)], [J. Louis Johnson (*Preacher*)], [Ralph Dunn, Bill Lally (*Police officers*)], [Sonny Bupp (*Boy*)], [Mimi Doyle (*Jackson's secretary*)], [Eddie Hart (*Military policeman*)], [John Hamilton (*Mr. Ames*)], [Lillian West (*Ames's secretary*)], [Michael Audley, Robert Dudley (*Bartenders*)], [Tommy Quinn (*Man in guard house*)], [Jane Patten (*Girl in canteen*)], [Dick Paxton (*Joe*)], [Sidney Miller (*Herbert*)], [Joe Brown, Jr. (*Bill*)], [Jack Finch (*Al*)], [Joe Bernard (*Old bobo*)], [Reginald Barlow (*Hobo reading paper*)], [Bobby Stebbins (*Page boy*)], [Hollis Jewell (*Young hobo*)], [William J. O'Brien (*Singing hobo*)], [Frank Mills (*Taxi driver*)], [Mickey Simpson (*Policeman at country club*)], [Joe Devlin (*House detective*)], [Spec O'Donnell (*Messenger boy*)], [Hallene Hill, John Tettemer (*Salvation Army workers*)], [Dudley Dickerson (*Musician*)], [Gordon Hart (*Eddie*)], [Armando and Lita (*Dance team*)], [Leith Stevens (*Ted Browning*)], [Effie Parnell (*Woman in bookstore*)], [Jerry Housner (*Cockeye*)], [Dewey Robinson (*Henchman*)], [Earle Hodgins (*Slave auctioneer*)], [Gus Glassmire (*Floor walker*)], [Kenneth Terrell, Edward Dew, Max Wagner, Charles Sullivan, Sammy Stein (*Gangsters*)], [Jeanette Bradley (*Cockeye's girl*)], [Gertrude Messinger (*Bride*)], [Jack Stewart (*Doorman*)], [Dolly Jarvis (*Potter's girl*)], [Francisco Maran (*Mario*)], [Charles Moore], [Sunny Boyne], [Louis Adlon].

Historical, Drama, with songs. [*Print viewed*]. In New Orleans in 1906, the Congo Square Building, formerly the site of slave auctions, now serves as an African-American employment bureau. Nearby, in an African-American college of music, an instructor is teaching his pupils to play Bach. Seven-year-old Reggie Tearbone, who is learning to play the cornet, is unable to follow the sheet music, however, and after playing a few bars, begins to improvise a jazz composition. Reggie lives with his mother Ella, who is employed as a servant in the home of architect George Latimer, a member of the once aristocratic but now impoverished Latimer family. One day, Latimer's old friend, Steve Porter, comes to visit from Chicago, accompanied by his son Paul. Upon learning of Latimer's financial problems, Porter persuades the architect and his young daughter Kit to go back home to Chicago with him. Ella accompanies the family, but Reggie, who has secured a job playing in King Jeffers' Basin Street Band, remains in New Orleans. As the family travels up the Mississippi River, they hear the music of Memphis and St. Louis. By 1916, a new style of jazz has developed out of Ragtime. On Kit's seventeenth birthday, Latimer and the Porters leave her to celebrate alone while they entertain some clients. Lonely, Kit wanders out onto the street and there meets Johnny Schumacher, a struggling young cornetist. Johnny takes Kit to a party at the apartment of musical promoter Smiley Jackson, and when Kit incites a riot with her New Orleans-style piano playing, she is arrested. At her trial, she is acquitted when she wins over the jury with a rousing rendition of boogie-woogie piano. The advent of World War I transforms both American music and the Latimer family. When the war forces the closure of Basin Street, Reggie, now known as "Rex Tearbone, King of the Cornet," travels to Chicago with Jackson, now a successful music impresario. Paul, now engaged to Kit, bids her farewell as he goes off to war. After Paul is killed in combat, Johnny and Kit realize that they love each other. Soon after the war ends, they are married, and Johnny gets a job on the road, playing in a large jazz orchestra. Kit, protesting that he will never be happy playing the circumscribed repetoire of the orchestra, refuses

to travel with him. Becoming disillusioned when he is denied his promised featured spot in the band, Johnny quits and, after wandering around finds new musical inspiration in the hobo "jungles." He receives an offer from Smiley, who is now a successful booker for whom Kit is working, to come to New York. There he reconciles with Kit, while Smiley arranges some bookings for his new band. At first, Johnny's new sound is a failure, then his audience realizes its dance potential. Dubbed "swing," Johnny's music revolutionizes the sound of jazz, and all ends happily for Kit and Johnny as they listen to a jam session featuring several great jazz musicians. *African Americans. Jazz music. Musicians. United States–History–Social life and customs. Architects. Chicago (IL). Dancing. Fathers and daughters. Gangsters. Maids. Mothers and sons. New Orleans (LA). New York City. Reconciliation. Separation (Marital). Servants. World War I.*

Note: The working title of this film was *The Band Played On*. In the opening onscreen credits, the actors are listed as "In front of the camera," and the names of the production crew are listed, without their specific jobs, as working "In back of the camera." Specific credits appear at the end of the film. According to pre-production news items in *HR*, RKO originally allotted seventy-two days to shoot this film, but had to speed up production so that Ted North and Adolphe Menjou could start shooting the Twentieth Century-Fox film *Roxie Hart*. Jack Briggs was tested for one of the leads in the picture, according to another *HR* news item, and Ethel Waters was signed to appear, according to a *DV* news item. Neither actor appeared in the released film, however. Other news items in *HR* note that background shots were filmed in Chicago and New York. According to a Feb 1942 *HR* news item, writer Philip Yordan was originally hired to work only as technical adviser on one sequence of the film, but was granted screen credit with Frank Cavett after it was established that he contributed to the entire screenplay.

According to materials contained in the RKO Archives Production Information Files at the UCLA Arts Library—Special Collections, legendary trumpet player Bunny Berigan was hired, early in Jan 1942, to dub the cornet passages which had been filmed earlier using guide tracks. However, that was not an easy task to perform and a modern source suggests that Berigan, who was battling alcoholism and would die six months later, may have had part or all of his work redone by George Thow. Rex Stewart, cornet player with the Duke Ellington band, appears in the film in a role apparently modeled on Joe (King) Oliver. The film's musical director, Leith Stevens, appears in the film as orchestra leader "Ted Browning." Among the many compositions performed in part in the film are "You Made Me Love You," "St. Louis Blues," "Copenhagen," "Jazz Me Blues," "Sugarfoot Stomp" and "Blow Your Trumpet, Gabriel."

The RKO Script Collection, also at UCLA, contains a dialogue continuity, dated 29 Nov 1941, which appears to be a record of a first cut, made as the film was finishing shooting, and is minus titles, montages and the climactic jam session. That assembly ran 13,118 feet or 146 minutes. As evidenced by the inclusion in the *CBCS* list of several characters who do not appear in the film including those portrayed by Robert Benchley and Walter Catlett, the film was severely cut before its release at a running time of 88 minutes. Among the sequences filmed, but cut, was one in which "Johnny" finds his musical inspiration while living with hoboes.

An *LAT* news item adds that a nationwide contest in *SEP* determined which jazz musicians would perform in this film. This picture is not related to the 1929 RKO film *Syncopation* (see *AFI Catalog of Feature Films, 1921-30*; F2.5510).

Box 9 May 1942. *DV* 8 Aug 1941. *FD* 7 May 1942, p. 6. *HR* 30 Jul 1941, p. 1. *HR* 26 Aug 1941, p. 2, 4. *HR* 28 Aug 1941, p. 7. *HR* 31 Oct 1941, p. 23. *HR* 11 Nov 1941, p. 1. *HR* 28 Nov 1941, p. 9. *HR* 2 Dec 1941, p. 2. *HR* 9 Feb 1942, p. 2. *HR* 6 May 1942, p. 4. *LAT* 12 Sep 1941. *MPHPD* 9 May 1942, p. 645. *NYT* 29 May 1942, p. 13. *Var* 6 May 1942, p. 8.

THE SYRIAN IMMIGRANT (Syrian Americans)

Eastern Star Film Co. Sep **1921**; Prod: May 1921. Si; b&w. 8 reels.
Cast: Nicholas S. Haber, Estella Mackintosh.

Documentary. This film is an educational picture showing the historical points of Syria, Palestine, and Egypt, and includes a story of the Syrian progress in the United States. *Egypt. Immigrants. Palestine. Syria. Syrians.*

TAHITI HONEY (French Americans)

Republic Pictures Corp. *Dist* Republic Pictures Corp. 6 Apr **1943**; Prod: 4 Jan–late Jan 1943 [©Republic Pictures Corp.; 23 Mar 1943; LP11945]. Sd (RCA Sound System); b&w. 7 reels, 6,295 ft. 68-69 min. Passed by the National Board of Review. PCA cert no. 9106.

Assoc prod John H. Auer. *Dir* John H. Auer. [*Asst dir* Harry Knight]. *Scr* Lawrence Kimble, Frederick Kohner and H. W. Hanemann. *Orig story* Frederick Kohner. *Photog* Jack Marta. *Art dir* Russell Kimball. *Film ed* Richard Van Enger. *Set dec* Otto Siegel. *Ward* Adele Palmer. *Mus dir* Morton Scott.

Song(s): "Tahiti Honey," music and lyrics by Jule Styne, George H. Brown and Sol Meyer; "This Gets Better Ev'ry Minute," "You Could Hear a Pin Drop," "Koni Plenty Hu-Hu," "Any Old Port in a Storm," "I'm a Cossack" and "In a Ten Gallon Hat," music by Lew Pollack,

lyrics by Charles Newman; "Clap Hands! Here Comes Charley!" music and lyrics by Billy Rose, Ballard MacDonald and Joseph Meyer; "Anchors Aweigh," music by Charles A. Zimmermann, lyrics by A. H. Miles and R. Lovell.

Cast: Simone Simon [(*Suzette Durand*)], Dennis O'Keefe [(*Mickey Monroe*)], Michael Whalen [(*Lt. John Barton*)], Lionel Stander [(*Pinkie*)], Wally Vernon [(*Maxie*)], Tom Seidel [(*Wally*)], Dan Seymour [(*Fats*)], Edward Gargan [(*George, the bartender*)], Tommye Adams [(*Linda*)], [Jeraldine Jordan (*Cigarette girl*)], [Harry Burns (*Joe*)], [Eleanor Counts (*Girl with sailor*)], [Earl Audet (*Sailor*)], [Forbes Murray (*Commander*)], [Eddie Kane (*Manager, Miami hotel*)], [Mary Bertrand (*Mother*)].

Romantic comedy, with songs. [*Print viewed*]. In 1941, pianist Mickey Monroe and his band, The Brooklyn Bombshells, become stranded in Tahiti after their female singer deserts the group. Business is so bad that the club owner threatens to fire them unless they get some "oomph," like that of by French-American singer Suzette Durand, who performs in a neighboring club. Despite the objections of trombone player Pinkie, who reminds his bandmates of how many times the group has been "busted up" because of a woman, the men vote to include Suzi in the group until they earn enough money to return to the United States. Womanizer Mickey is chosen as their envoy, and he persuades Suzie to join the band, by promising her that she can accompany them to America. With Suzie as their singer, the Bombshells are a big hit, but their successful run is cut short by the arrival of a boat bound for home. The men, believing that Suzie is to remain behind, bid her farewell, but as she has fallen in love with Mickey, she has faith that he will keep his promise. Desiring to please all concerned, Mickey concocts a story that Suzie must go to America to be reunited with "Charley," her Naval officer fiancé whom she has not seen in three years. The others are taken in by Mickey's sentimental pleas, and Suzie accompanies them to San Francisco. Their songs do not strike a pleasing chord there, however, and business in New Orleans is even more abysmal. Despite their travails, the men become fond of the thoughtful Suzie and engrossed in the continuing saga provided by her letters from "Charley," which are actually written by Mickey. When Pinkie complains to the others that Suzie is bad luck, she convinces them to adopt a softer style, and they finally become a hit in Miami as Eleven Jacks and a Queen. After the band signs a big contract, Mickey angers Suzie by flirting with a cigarette girl named Linda. He convinces her that he was only trying to prevent the band from uncovering their own romance, but Suzie gets her revenge when Maxie, the bass player, mistakes Navy Lt. John Barton for "Charley." Instantly attracted to Suzie, John plays along with the charade and falls in love with her as the weeks pass. Suzie is upset by Mickey's apparant lack of jealousy and so tells John that he must ask each band member's permission when he proposes to her. Even Mickey, who has realized that he loves Suzie, gives his consent, for he believes that John will make a better husband than he could. On the night of 6 December 1941, John and Mickey meet in a bar, and while getting drunk, deduce that they are rivals for Suzie's affections. As they selflessly insist that the other should marry her, Suzie walks in and, believing that neither one wants her, breaks off with both of them. Soon after, Suzie is packing to leave when Pinkie tells her that because of Pearl Harbor, she should stay and help entertain the men. Just then, Suzie receives a letter from "Charley," stating that he still loves her and is about to leave for active duty. Suzie goes to the ship to which "Charley" has been assigned and there finds Mickey and the band, who have all joined the Navy. After Suzie and Mickey reconcile, the band performs "Anchors Aweigh," much to the delight of the crowd. *Deception. Musicians. Officers (Military). Romance. Singers. Americans in foreign countries. Buttons. Cigarette girls. Drunkenness. French. Jealousy. Letters. Miami (FL). Military service, Voluntary. New Orleans (LA). Pearl Harbor (HI), Attack on, 1941. San Francisco (CA). Tahiti. Womanizers.*

Note: According to *HR* news items, this film was originally to have starred Ruth Terry, but when Terry temporarily retired to have a baby, the lead was given to Simone Simon. A 18 Jan 1943 *HR* news item noted that Nika Fisher was to make her screen debut in the picture, but her participation in the completed film has not been confirmed.

Box 10 Apr 1943. *DV* 25 Mar 1943, p. 3. *FD* 2 Apr 1943, p. 7. *HR* 21 Sep 1942, P. 5. *HR* 17 Nov 1942, p. 4. *HR* 31 Dec 1942, p. 6. *HR* 4 Jan 1943, p. 7. *HR* 18 Jan 1943, p. 10. *HR* 22 Jan 1943, p. 8. *HR* 25 Mar 1943, p. 3. *MPD* 31 Mar 1943. *MPH* 3 Apr 1943. *MPHPD* 6 Mar 1943, p. 1191. *MPHPD* 3 Apr 1943, p. 1238. *Var* 31 Mar 1943, p. 8.

TAHITI NIGHTS (Polynesian Americans)

Columbia Pictures Corp. *Dist* Columbia Pictures Corp. 28 Dec **1944**; Prod: 28 Aug—26 Sep 1944 [©Columbia Pictures Corp.; 28 Dec 1944; LP13124]. Sd (Western Electric Mirrophonic Recording); b&w. 5,680 ft. 63 min. PCA cert no. 10531.

Prod Sam White. *Dir* Will Jason. *Asst dir* Ray Nazarro. *Orig scr* Lillie Hayward. *Dir of photog* Benjamin Kline. *Art dir* George Brooks. *Film ed* Jerome Thoms. *Set dec* George Montgomery.

Song(s): "Huapala," "Garden in Tahiti" and "Luana," music and lyrics by Harry Owens; "Let Me Love You Tonight," music and lyrics by Mitchell Parrish and Rene Touzet; "The Cockeyed Mayor of Kaunakakai," music by R. Alex Anderson, lyrics by R. Alex Anderson and Al Stillman. Silverman.

Cast: Jinx Falkenburg [(*Luana*)], Dave O'Brien [(*Jack*)], Mary Treen [(*Mata*)], Florence Bates [(*Queen Liliha*)], Cy Kendall [(*Chief Enoka*)], Eddie Bruce [(*Chopstick, also known as Cyril Stonewall*)], The Vagabonds, Hilo Hattie [(*Temata*)], [Pedro de Cordoba (*Tonga*)], [Carole Mathews (*Betty Lou*)], [Satini Puailoa, Al Kikume (*Betrothal hut guards*)], [Isabel Withers (*She wolf*)], [Peter Cusanelli (*Native treasurer*)], [Clyde Fillmore (*High priest*)], [Christine Gibson, Mildred Law, Kay Dowd (*Hand maidens*)], [J. W. Cody (*Kua*)], [Silverheels Smith (*Lua*)], [Charles Opunui, Chris Willow Bird, John Pumau, Charles Soldani (*Privy counselors*)], [Bobby Frasco (*Native boy*)], [James Ilikini, Bob St. Angelo (*Enoka guards*)], [Victor Travers (*Native servant*)].

Comedy, Island, Musical. [*Print viewed*]. Soon after Jack and his Four Vagabonds band conclude their engagement at a Honolulu hotel, Jack takes the band on a trip to the Tahitian island ruled by his mother, Queen Liliha. Jack, a light-skinned native of Tahiti, is in love with Betty Lou, the band's singer, who has remained in America. Soon after arriving at the Tahitian village, Jack's pal, Cyril Stonewall, also known as "Chopstick," is forced to contend with the unwanted attentions of Temata, an elderly Tahitian woman. At the same time, Jack's mother tells him that she has arranged his marriage to Luana, Chief Enoka's daughter. Though both Jack and Luana protest the arranged marriage, Lilihua and Enoka remain firm in their resolve to see the two take over the throne as husband and wife. As dictated by Tahitian custom, Luana is confined to a betrothal hut so that Jack cannot see what she looks like until the wedding. Luana is put under the care of a handmaid and two guards, but she manages to break out one day to take a private swim. The bride-to-be finds herself stranded in the water, however, when a monkey runs off with her sarong. Jack, who happens to be passing by the swimming hole, sees Luana's distress and rushes to her aid. Unaware of the identity of the beautiful young woman, Jack falls in love with Luana, who is also unaware of her new friend's identity. A romance between Jack and Luana soon flourishes, as they meet secretly, often bemoaning the fact that they are unable to marry each other. Later, when Jack discovers Luana's identity, he reverses himself and tells her that she should go ahead with the wedding. On the day of the wedding, Luana dresses her handmaid in her veil and sends her out of the hut in her stead so that she can escape. The Four Vagabonds save the day, however, when they bring Luana to Jack and introduce her to the man she loves. *Band leaders. Bands (Music). Marriage–Arranged. Romance. Tahiti. Escapes. Hawaii. Imprisonment. Mistaken identity. Monkeys. Mothers and sons. Queens. Rites and ceremonies. Tribal chiefs. Weddings.*

Note: The working title for this film was *Song of Tahiti*.

Box 30 Dec 1944. *DV* 22 Jan 1945, p. 3. *FD* 5 Feb 1945, p. 7. *HR* 29 Aug 1944, p.7 *HR* 22 Jan 1945, p. 3. *MPHPD* 18 Nov 1944, p. 2186. *MPHPD* 27 Jan 1945, p. 2290. *Var* 31 Jan 1945, p. 10.

TAILS OF MANHATTAN see **TALES OF MANHATTAN**

TAKE A GIANT STEP (African Americans)

Sheila Productions, Inc.; Hecht-Hill-Lancaster. *Dist* United Artists Corp. Feb **1960**; Los Angeles opening: 9 Dec 1959; Prod: early Nov— early Dec 1958 at Universal-International Studios [©Sheila Productions, Inc.; 9 Dec 1959; LP15665]. Sd (Westrex Recording System); b&w. 9,000 ft. 99-100 min. PCA cert no. 19178.

Prod Julius J. Epstein. *Dir* Philip Leacock. *Asst dir* Philip Bowles and Ray DeCamp. *Scr* Louis S. Peterson and Julius J. Epstein. *Dir of photog* Arthur Arling. *Art dir* Edward Carrere. *Ed supv* Frank Gross. *Set dec* Russell Gausman and Oliver Emert. *Cost* Bill Thomas. *Mus* Jack Marshall. *Sd rec* Leslie I. Carey and Joe Lapis. *Makeup* Monty Westmore. *Hair stylist* Elizabeth Searcy. *Unit prod mgr* Tom Shaw.

Song(s): "Take a Giant Step," music and lyrics by Jay Livingston and Ray Evans, sung by Johnny Nash.

Source: Based on the play *Take a Giant Step* by Louis S. Peterson, as produced by Lyn Austin and Thomas Noyes (New York, 24 Sep 1953).

Cast: Johnny Nash (*Spence [Scott]*), Estelle Hemsley (*Gram [Martin]*), Ruby Dee (*Christine*), Frederick O'Neal (*Lem [Scott]*), Beah Richards (*May [Scott]*), Ellen Holly ([*Carol*] *The girl in the bar*), Pauline Meyers (*Violet*), Royce Wallace (*Rose*), Frances Foster (*Poppy*), Sherman Raskin (*Alan*), Frank Killmond (*Gussie*), Joseph Sonessa (*Johnny*), Dell Erickson (*Bobby*), Dee Pollack (*Tony*), William "Bill" Walker (*Frank*).

Teenage, Drama. [*Print viewed*]. Seventeen-year-old black high school student Spence Scott storms out of his history class and heads for the washroom, where he defiantly lights up a cigar. That afternoon, he admits to his sickly grandmother, Mrs. Martin, whom he calls "Gram," and to Christine, the housekeeper who looks after the old woman, that he has been expelled from his predominantly white New England school. His teacher, Miss Bailey, had declared that Southern Negroes of the Civil War period were "backwards" and needed the help of Northern whites to gain their freedom. Spence had therefore told her off and left. Gram, whose illness has diluted neither her temper nor her sarcastic sense of humor, argues with her grandson, saying, "There are ways, and there are ways." When Spence's white friends drop by, he chastises them for not defending him in class, and when they accidentally mention that because he is black, he has not been invited to a Polish-American classmate's party, he orders them from the house. He then bursts into tears and calls himself an "outcast." Gram tries to comfort the lad, but when she expresses her distaste for "wops and pollacks," Spence's anger flares up once again. On the pretext of buying small gifts for his parents, Spence packs a bag and leaves the house. Intending to flee the white, middle-class neighborhood in which he has grown up, he takes a bus to a black neighborhood and sits down in a bar. Three unsavory women named Violet, Rose and Poppy offer him a seat at their table, where he learns to his discomfort that they are penniless prostitutes. After they leave, Spence joins an attractive young woman named Carol, to whom he confesses that Gram is his only friend. Carol is amused when Spence cites a Kinsey Report statement that boys his age are "sexy." When he proposes to her, however, she gently informs him that she is already married to an unskilled worker who is never at home. Carol then announces that she is going to accompany the flirtatious stranger at the bar for a few hours of fun. This angers Spence, but Carol nevertheless kisses him gently and leaves with the other man. Back in the street, Spence encounters the three prostitutes, and Violet invites him to her room for a meal. Meanwhile, Spence's parents are both worried and infuriated by their son's absence from home. Gram tries to defend him, but Spence's father Lem threatens to "break his neck." At the prostitute's small apartment, Violet dons a dressing gown and tries to kiss Spence, but he decides to leave. Violet keeps the boy's $2.39 but lends him the bus fare to return home. Spence's parents, who have learned about their son's expulsion, angrily order him to apologize to his teacher, but he refuses to do so. Lem argues that even though those "crumbs" at the bank make jokes about "niggers," he must endure their comments to keep his job. When Spence angrily criticizes his parents' seeming passivity, Gram descends from her room and accuses Lem of bullying Spence, describing his teacher as a "nasty little hussy." After Gram reminds Lem and May that their high expectations for their son always included self-respect, Lem tries to have a talk with his son, but his remarks are awkward and superficial. At that moment, Gram calls for Spence and falls to the floor. After advising Spence to respect himself, she dies. Spence falls into his father's arms and weeps. For days after the funeral, Spence refuses to eat or talk. Christine finally badgers him into eating and then discusses her own troubled adolescence. After leaving her Southern family, Christine explains, she came north and married. When her husband died and her baby was born dead, she decided that despite the pain, there was still a lot of living to be done. Touched by this story, Spence confesses that he wants to "be with a girl" and suggests that the two of them might find happiness together for a time. Christine is amused at first, but her own loneliness causes her to "think about it." Some time later, Spence's mother discharges Christine, explaining that the family no longer needs a maid for Gram. After Christine's departure, Spence's

mother informs him that she has invited his friends over for cake. Spence reacts with anger, the two argue, and Spence runs after Christine. "I hate being black," he declares. Christine assures him that life has wonderful things to offer him and adds that if he were not black, he would never have known his grandmother. Spence returns home to find his parents in awkward conversation with his white friends. Spence announces that because he plans to attend college in the fall, this party is his farewell. After they leave, he explains to his mother that he must learn to live with the fact that his friendships with whites have limits. Spence and his mother then declare their mutual love and embrace. *Adolescence. African Americans. Bigotry. Family relationships. Grandmothers. Loneliness. Premarital sex. Self-respect. Bars. Betrayal. Class distinction. Depression, Mental. Expulsion. Friendship. Grief. Invalids. Maids. Maturation. Parties. Polish Americans. Prostitution. Racism. Runaways. Suburban life. Urban life.*

Note: The above cast is listed as it appears in the film's opening credits; however, the actors are listed in the reverse order in the end credits, which begin with William (Bill) Walker and end with Johnny Nash. Lyn Austin and Thomas Noyes' 1953 off-Broadway stage production, which starred Louis Gossett, also featured Estelle Hemsley, Frederick O'Neal and Pauline Meyers, who reprised their roles for the film.

Information in the MPAA/PCA Collection at the AMPAS Library indicates that in Apr 1958, the PCA rejected the film's original script because of the "illicit sex" between "Spencer" and "Christine." The PCA insisted that a "voice for morality" be woven into the story, "since the affair is the most important single element in the play." By Mar 1959, the producers were still unsure whether the film would be awarded a PCA seal because of the subject matter and dialogue. A *Var* news item indicates that two versions of various scenes were shot in anticipation of cuts required by the PCA. The news item also notes that the producers were hoping that rave reviews for the Broadway play, *A Raisin in the Sun*, a black family drama starring Sidney Poitier and Claudia McNeil, which opened 11 Mar 1959, would help their own box-office sales.

A pre-production news item included Larry Larson, Douglas Nash and Leo Castillo in the cast, but their participation in the released film was not confirmed. Critical reactions to the film were generally lukewarm, although reviewers complimented the performances. The *NYT* reviewer wrote: "In spite of some earnest performing by the youngster, Johnny Nash, a currently favored 'pop' singer who plays the leading role, this little tale of the boy's confusions over racial prejudice and the urges of sex is like a cross between a social justice brochure and a Negro Andy Hardy film....Mr. Leacock lost the quality of sensitivity and dignity it should have." The *Var* reviewer added that the "scenes between Nash and his white friends are awkward and stagey without real insight. The conclusion is unclear and appears to recommend an 'Uncle Tom' philosophy." In addition, Stanley Kauffman of the *New Republic* noted that, "In a negative way, *A Raisin in the Sun* and *Take a Giant Step* are milestones in the social history of the American Negro. Both films are shoddy...[*Take a Giant Step*] is not worth the time of anyone, Negro, white, Oriental or Martian." Echoing the producers' fears about the language, the *Var* review noted that "the language used, with such words as 'bastard,' 'Prostitute,' 'behind,' numerous 'damns' and 'hells,' may be sound realistically. But because they are not so commonly heard on the screen, their use could give the impression that such are inherent only to Negro households..." The picture won two awards at Switzerland's Film Locarno Film Festival. Johnny Nash was awarded for his performance and the film was voted "most humane." The then seventeen-year-old Nash was a pop and rhythm and blues singer, and in the 1950s, a regular member of the *Arthur Godfrey Talent Scouts* show on radio and television. He is best known for his 1972 hit song, "I Can See Clearly Now."

Box 14 Dec 1959. *DV* 4 Dec 1959, p. 3. *DV* 2 Aug 1960. *Exh* 16 Dec 1959, p. 4663. *FD* 7 Dec 1959, p. 8. *Har* 5 Dec 1959, pp. 194-95. *HR* 14 Nov 1958, p. 10. *HR* 5 Dec 1958, p. 8. *HR* 4 Dec 1959, p. 3. *MPHPD* 12 Dec 1959, p. 517. *NewRep* 20 Mar 1961. *NYT* 6 Mar 1961, p. 28. *Var* 18 Mar 1959. *Var* 9 Dec 1959, p. 6.

TAKE MY LIFE (African Americans)

Million Dollar Productions; A Golden Seal Production. *Dist* Consolidated National Film Exchanges. **1942**; New York opening: week of 3 Jul 1942; *Prod:* began late Mar 1941. Sd; b&w. 6,644 ft. 70 or 74 min.

Exec prod Harry M. Popkin. *Prod* Clifford Sanforth. *Dir* Leo Popkin. *Asst dir* Eddie Saeta and Bobby Ray. *Scr* Billie Myers and Edward Dewey. *Orig story* Billie Myers. *Cam* Clark Ramsey. *Ed* Martin J. Cohn. *Prod mgr and casting dir* Alfred Weston. *Tech adv on military seq* Norman O. Houston.

Cast: Harlem Dead End Kids: Freddie Baker (*Johnny Thurman*), Eugene Jackson (*Bill*), Paul White (*Icky*), Eddie Lynn (*Stinky*), and DeForrest Covan (*Shadow*), Monte Hawley (*Dr. Bob Thurman*), Jeni Le Gon (*Helen Stanley*), Lovey Lane (*Renie De Vere*), Robert Webb (*Ace Baldwin*), Jack Carter (*Sergeant Holmes*), Harry Levette (*Corporal Mack*), Guernsey Morrow (*Dr. Moore*), Herbert Skinner (*Dr. Johnson*), Arthur Ray (*Reverend Wyman*).

African American. [*Not viewed*]. Ace Baldwin, a small-time hood, has manipulated a group of impressionable youths into forming a gang of petty thieves. Johnny Thurman, a member of the gang, has

convinced his brother, Dr. Bob, to rent them a clubhouse, which is actually a front for the gang's illicit enterprise. Helen Stanley, sister of another gang member, Bill, tells Bob that she is suspicious of the boys' activities at the clubhouse, but when the two visit the place, Bob is unconvinced. Meanwhile, Renie De Vere, Bob's fiancée, has been spending time with Ace, and at her apartment, she tells him that she plans to marry the doctor so that she can give up her stage career and relax. Bob, who earlier had learned that Renie and Ace had been seen together around town, arrives unexpectedly, forcing Renie to hide Ace in her bedroom. Bob becomes suspicious of Renie, who is acting nervous, and tests her to see if she knows Ace. Although she denies it, Bob soon finds Ace's hiding place and storms out, breaking their engagement. Renie vows revenge, and Ace says he will help her by framing Johnny. Back at the clubhouse, Johnny, who has been acting as Ace's right-hand man, chides the gang for their meager earnings as thieves. When Stinky, one of the gang members, says that he has the jitters and thinks that Ace should stop pressuring them for awhile, Ace overhears Johnny defending him and then offers to help him "graduate" into the big time. After Ace explains the job, however, Johnny protests he is not ready for such a major heist. Ace bullies him to agreeing by threatening to reveal to the gang his cowardice. Later that day, the boys pass a recruiting office, where Sergeant Holmes tells them about the glory of the U.S. Army. He argues that they are not real Americans just because they were born in America, but that they must fight for their country. The boys dismiss the idea of enlisting until Holmes shows them a film depicting military heroism. Afterward, Holmes gives Johnny one of his medals. Bob and Helen return to the clubhouse and discover stolen radios, proof that the boys have been engaging in foul play. When the gang, led by Bill, arrives, Bob and Helen learn about Johnny's job and convince the boys that Ace will double-cross their friend. Johnny meets Ace and tries to tell the gangster that he has learned about the Constitution and its rules against stealing, but Ace forces him to go through with the job. During the robbery, Ace kills a watchman and leaves Johnny to take the blame. The police arrive and shoot the innocent boy, who escapes back to the clubhouse, where his brother Bob performs an emergency operation on him. Despite his family and friends' support, Johnny is convicted and faces the death penalty, but Bob promises to get him a reprieve. Meanwhile, the boys desperately search for Ace, and finally spot him driving with Renie. As the boys chase Ace's car, Ace crashes and the boys have him rushed to the hospital where Bob works. The attending physician, Dr. Moore, says that operating on the nearly dead Ace will kill him, but Bob insists, hoping that he can save Ace and get a confession out of him before Johnny goes to the electric chair that night. Ace has lost all of his motor skills, but Bob and Helen still try to get him to confess. Meanwhile, Johnny is terror-stricken as he sits on death row. As a last resort, Bob decides to recite to Ace what he terms his "Hymn of Hate." While describing in grueling detail what Johnny is experiencing at that very moment, he wheels in the electrocardiac machine, pretending he is about to perform Ace's own execution. Ace, believing he is about to be electrocuted, confesses to having killed the watchman, and Johnny is saved. Shortly after, Johnny, Bill and the boys, decked out in their new uniforms, bid goodbye to Bob and Helen and follow Holmes into service for their country. *African Americans. Frame-ups. Gangs. Gangsters. Juvenile delinquents. Moral reformation. Patriotism.* Automobile accidents. Automobile chases. Brothers. Capital punishment. Confession (Law). Gunshot wounds. Hospitals. Infidelity. Military service, Voluntary. Murder. Physicians. Robbery. Stay of execution.

Note: According to a modern source, the film may also have been released under the title *Murder Rap.* Although a print of this film was not viewed, the above plot and credits were taken from a dialogue continuity deposited with the NYSA. The *Var* review lists Harry M. Popkin as director, but all other sources credit Leo Popkin. The "Harlem Dead End Kids" were formerly known as the "Harlem Tuff Kids." According to a 13 Mar 1941 news item in the *California Eagle,* Pete Webster was first considered for the role of "Dr. Bob Thurman." According to an Apr 1941 *California Eagle* news item, the following actors were cast in the picture: Irving Smith, Earl Hall, Harold "Slickum" Garrison, Earl Morris, Sammy Warren, Curry Lee Calmes, Millie Munroe, Phil Jones, Mildred Boyd, Louise Franklin, Willie Williams, Noble Blake, Curtis Hamilton, Edward Tiney, Jack Carr and Clarence Brooks. The participation of these actors has not been confirmed, however. CThe *California Eagle* notes that Dr. E. I. Robinson was hired to work on the "men and women in white" scenes, but the exact nature of his contribution is not known. The *California Eagle* review commented that "of all the many patriotic films produced in Hollywood...this is the first one extolling the traditional patriotism of the Negro and the long,

glorious record of colored soldiers in all the country's wars." The review concluded with the following appeal to the black movie-going public: "your presence at this prerelease will strengthen the feeling in all present that motion pictures provide the greatest avenues for revealing the modern Negro in his true light." The *Var* review, however, called the film a "talky, unimaginative meller" that was "strictly limited in appeal, even for colored audiences."

California Eagle 13 Mar 1941. *California Eagle* 20 Mar 1941. *California Eagle* 27 Nov 1941, p. 3. *MPHPD* 11 Jul 1942, p. 767. *Var* 8 Jul 1942, p. 16.

TAKE THE HEIR (English Americans)

Screen Story Syndicate. *Dist* Big 4 Film Corp. 15 Jan **1930**. Talking seq and mus score (Photophone); b&w. 6 reels, 5,700 ft. [Also si.].

Dir Lloyd Ingraham. *Scen and cont* Beatrice Van. *Photog* Allen Siegler. *Mus score and synchronization* J. M. Coopersmith.

Cast: Edward Everett Horton (*Smithers*), Dorothy Devore (*Susan*), Frank Elliott (*Lord Tweedham*), Edythe Chapman (*Lady Tweedham*), Otis Harlan (*John Walker*), Kay Deslys (*Muriel Walker*), Margaret Campbell (*Mrs. Smythe-Bellingham*).

Comedy. Lord Tweedham, a tipsy Englishman, falls heir to his deceased uncle's estate in the United States. Upon his arrival there, his valet, Smithers, is forced to impersonate Tweedham because of his master's drunken state. At the home of the uncle's executor, John Walker, Smithers falls in love with the maid, Susan, though he is pursued by the executor's fat daughter, Muriel. After numerous complications, Smithers admits his identity and marries Susan, while Lord Tweedham falls victim to the wiles of Muriel. *Drunkenness. English. Impersonation and imposture. Inheritance. Maids. Nobility. Valets.*

TAKE THIS WOMAN see THE LADY FROM SHANGHAI

TAKU (Native Americans, Native Alaskans)

Norman Dawn Productions. *Dist* Monogram Pictures Corp. **1940** [©Monogram Pictures Corp.; 23 Jul 1940; LP9819]. Sd; b&w. 6 reels. 44 min. PCA cert no. 5929.

Prod Norman Dawn. *Assoc prod* Fred McConnell and George Merrick. *Dir* Norman Dawn. *Story and cont* Susan Denis. *Photog* Norman Dawn. *Film ed* Charles Hunt, Jr. *Sd* Glen Glenn. *Narr* Norman Dawn.

Cast: Bob Webster (*Bedrock Brown*), Mary Joyce (*Taku Mary*), Ann Henning (*Little Joy*), Eleanor Phillips (*Joy's mother*), John Pool (*Trapper*).

Northwest, Drama. [*Print viewed*]. Bedrock Brown, an old prospector, combs the great Alaskan wilderness accompanied by his friends, bear cubs Tom and Jerry, in search of gold and his missing friend, Hank Jones, who has failed to return from a prospecting expedition. Running out of supplies, Bedrock returns to the Taku River Trading Post, which is run by Taku Mary, to earn money by helping with the salmon run. Also at the post is Little Joy, Hank's daughter, who has never given up hope that her father will return. After the salmon run ends, Bedrock returns to the hills and Little Joy also decides to search the hills for her father. Soon after, Little Joy's mother notices the girl's absence, and Taku Mary takes off in her plane to look for her. In the wilderness, Little Joy is saved from the jaws of a wolf pack by an itinerant trapper who decides to hold her for ransom. Meanwhile, Bedrock loses his boat when it is capsized by melting glaciers, and he and the bears swim to land, where he discovers the lost mine that has become Hank's burial ground. While Bedrock strikes gold, Little Joy escapes her captor and is led to Bedrock by his wandering bears. The old prospector promises Little Joy he will take her home, but without a boat they must cross the treacherous ice caps. As the ice floes begin to break apart and a blizzard approaches, Mary sees Bedrock and Little Joy and returns to the settlement for help. Returning with the sled dogs, Mary arrives just in time to rescue Little Joy, but is too late for Bedrock, who dies in her arms. *Alaska. Missing persons. Prospectors. Runaways.* Airplanes. Bears. Blizzards. Boats. Dogsledding. Fathers and daughters. Fishing. Gold mines. Ice floes. Kidnapping. Mothers and daughters. Rescues. Salmon. Trading posts.

Note: The working title of this film was *Orphans of the North.* According to the *FD* review, the picture was filmed entirely on location in the Taku River country of Alaska by explorer-producer Norman Dawn and used native, non-professional actors.

FD 18 Sep 1939, p. 18.

TALE OF THE NAVAJOS (Native Americans, Navajo)

Leo Productions. *Dist* Loew's Inc.; Metro-Goldwyn-Mayer Corp. Apr 1949 [©Loew's Inc.; 18 Nov 1948; LP2205]. Sd (RCA Sound System); col (Technicolor). 5,268 ft. 52-53 or 58 min. Passed by the National Board of Review. PCA cert no. 12104.

Prod John A. Haeseler. *Story* Harry Chandlee and John A. Haeseler. *Mus dir* Jack Shaindlin. *Mus* Lan Adomian. *Prod aide* Jane Haeseler and Curly Twiford.

Cast: Edwin Jerome (*Narrator*), [Jimmie Palmer (*Jimmie*)].

Documentary, Travelogue. [*Print viewed*]. Around 50,000 Navajo, the largest tribe in the United States, live on 25,000 square miles near Monument Valley on the Utah-Arizona border and make their living as herdsmen. One young Navajo, Ziki, is apprenticed to a silversmith, with whom he studies the art of making the silver and turquoise jewelry that has spiritual significance for his people. The Navajo especially prize blue turquoise because it is the color of the sky that is home to the friendly gods. In hopes of placating the gods and ending a long drought that threatens the sheep on which the Navajo depend for their livelihood, Ziki's sister wears a blue blouse and all the family jewelry. Ziki's oldest sister spins wool in the traditional way, which was taught to her by Spider Woman. She sells the blankets that she weaves at a nearby trading post. Jimmie, the trader's son, is Ziki's best friend. When Ziki remembers that his grandfather knew about a pasture far away in the mountains, the two boys seek his guidance. Ziki's grandfather, who is waiting to participate in a healing ceremony, tells the boys the following story that happened to him years earlier: He travels with two friends in search of a rich land above red cliffs, which can only be reached through a rainbow of stone. They find a cache of sacred turquoise near the home of the "mystic people," an ancient tribe of cliff dwellers. Because they know that the spirits of the dead, or chindi, haunt the stones, they leave them behind. After grandfather's two friends fall to their death, he leaves without discovering the mountain pasture. His story finished, grandfather advises the boys that they should make the journey in reverence, being careful not to disturb the spirits of the dead. He then gives them an eagle feather to guide their journey. Following grandfather's instructions, Ziki and Jimmie pass Winged Rock, which in ancient times was the home of the bird monsters. When the monsters were killed by the Twin Warriors, one monster was turned into an eagle and now provides feathers for warriors. As they travel, the boys see a coyote, the mischief maker, which can mean either good or bad luck. They pass a blue bird, which indicates good luck. They ride by stones and rock formations that embody Navajo history. After crossing the river, Jimmie and Ziki arrive at Canyon de Chelly, where many Navajo took refuge from Indian hunter Kit Carson. On the canyon walls they see petroglyphs drawn by an ancient people. They continue to follow grandfather's directions to the red cliffs where the mystic people lived. Watched by owls, who sometimes carry the spirits of the dead, Ziki and Jimmie discover the pot of turquoise which grandfather described and, remembering that the spell of the chindi can only be removed by a special ceremony, they leave most of it behind. With great effort, they continue up the cliffs. One night while they sleep, the evil raven steals the eagle feather from Ziki's headband. Because grandfather warned them that they would lose their way without a feather, the boys must replace it. The feather must be taken from a live bird because a found feather might be chindi. With the help of the new feather, the boys find a rainbow-shaped rock. On the other side, they discover a wonderful pasture with lakes, grass and flowers. Ziki and Jimmie return home and lead the sheep and the tribe to the new pastures. A special ceremony is held to banish the chindi from the turquoise, and Ziki is able to use it to make new jewelry. *Droughts. Friendship. Navajo Indians. Religion. Tribal life.* Brothers and sisters. Canyon de Chelly (AZ). Coyotes. Eagles. Feathers. Grandfathers. Jewelry. Legends. Monument Valley (AZ and UT). Mythical characters. Owls. Ravens. Rites and ceremonies. Sheepherders. Spells. Spiritualism. Storytellers. Trading posts. Turquoise.

Note: The film's working title was *The Spell of Chindi*. A cutting continuity contained in Copyright Records gives a copyright date of 1946, however, the film itself was not registered with the Copyright Office until 1948. According to a *DV* news item, M-G-M acquired the film in Aug 1948, but Loew's filed a cutting continuity with the NYSA that is dated 17 Apr 1947. Opening credits state that the film is "A story of the American Indians with every element and detail based on the authentic lore and legends of the Navajo Indians." The film begins with the following foreword: "This story of youth and adventure

comes from a land hidden between America's West and its Southwest—Indian land, where the Navajo still live the tribal life, still worship their tribal gods. It is the story of two boys and of the legends and sacred chants that led them on a great quest through this land of turquoise skies, this land of Eagle and Owl, of Raven and Coyote."

The Navajo are linguistically and culturally related to the Apache. Many still farm and raise livestock and live in hogans, houses built of earth and stone which are designed to resemble the Navajo sacred mountain. In 1863, Kit Carson led an expedition against the Navajos, killing hundreds and destroying their homes and livestock. The Navajos were then forced to march to Fort Sumner, NM. The government plan to turn the Navajo into farmers failed, and after four years, they were allowed to return to their old territory in Utah, Northern Arizona and New Mexico. The march to and from Fort Sumner is referred to as The Long Walk by the Navajos. On the reservation, sheepherding, weaving and silversmithing became the major livelihoods. In 1975, the Navajos numbered about 160,000, making them the largest single group of Native Americans.

The Twin Warriors are Navajo culture heroes, who helped stabilize the earth and taught the Indians many features of their culture. The cliff dwellings of the "mystic people" that "Jimmie" and "Ziki" visit in the film are probably those built by the Anasazi, which means "ancient ones" in the Navajo language. The Anasazi lived in the Southwest centuries before the Navajo and shared many traits with later Southwestern Indian cultures.

According to the *DV* review, with the exception of Jimmie Palmer, the cast consisted of Navajos living on the reservation. The reviewer also commented that the film had been made to "cash in on the plight of the Navajo a few years ago" but added that the film was no longer timely. Although it is not clear to which specific problems the reviewer referred, during the 1930s and 1940s the U.S. government had required the Navajos to reduce their livestock by ten percent, a program that was strongly resisted by many Navajos. By 1947, the Navajos were suffering from disease and poverty and much of their grazing land was heavily eroded. In the winter of 1947-1948, a severe blizzard worsened the situation and generated national publicity about the Navajo condition. In response, the Indian Service developed a controversial plan to relocate some groups of Navajos.

Box 19 Mar 1949. *DV* 26 Aug 1948. *DV* 28 Feb 1949, p. 4. *FD* 4 Mar 1949, p. 8. *HR* 1 Mar 1949, p. 3. *MPHPD* 5 Mar 1949, p. 4522. *Var* 2 Mar 1949, p. 8.

A TALE OF TWO WORLDS (Chinese Americans)

Goldwyn Pictures Corp.; Eminent Authors. Mar **1921** [©Goldwyn Pictures Corp.; 17 Mar 1921; LP16286]. Si; b&w. 6 reels, 5,649 ft.

Dir Frank Lloyd. *Asst dir* Harry Weil. *Scen* J. E. Nash. *Story* Gouverneur Morris. *Photog* Norbert Brodin.

Cast: J. Frank Glendon (*Newcombe*), Leatrice Joy (*Sui Sen*), Wallace Beery (*Ling Jo*), E. A. Warren (*Ah Wing*), Margaret McWade (*Attendant*), Togo Yamamoto (*One Eye*), Jack Abbe (*The Worm*), Louie Cheung (*Chinaman*), Chow Young (*Slave girl*), Etta Lee (*Ah Fah*), Ah Wing (*Servant spy*), Goro Kino (*Windlass man*), Arthur Soames (*Dr. Newcombe*), Edythe Chapman (*Mrs. Newcombe*), Dwight Crittenden (*Mr. Carmichael*), Irene Rich (*Mrs. Carmichael*).

Melodrama. Carmichael, an American dealer in antiques who gains possession of the priceless Ming scepter, is slain, with his wife, by Boxers in China, but their infant daughter is saved by a servant, Ah Wing. Years later, the girl, brought up by Ah Wing as his daughter, is known as Sui Sen in San Francisco's Chinatown. Though loved by Ah Wing's assistant, the Worm, she is coveted by Ling Jo, a Boxer leader, who obtains the Ming scepter as a condition for their betrothal. However, Sui Sen falls in love with Newcombe, a wealthy young American. Newcombe rescues her from Ling Jo, who dies in a windlass trap actually prepared for his rival. *China–History–Boxer Rebellion, 1899-1901. Chinese Americans. Parentage. San Francisco (CA)–Chinatown.*

Note: The working title of this film was *The Water Lily*.

FD 20 Mar 1921. *NYT* 14 Mar 1921, p. 9. *Var* 22 Apr 1921, p. 41.

TALES OF MANHATTAN (African Americans)

Twentieth Century-Fox Film Corp.; A Julien Duvivier Film. *Dist* Twentieth Century-Fox Film Corp. 30 Oct **1942**; World premiere in Hollywood: 5 Aug 1942; New York opening: 24 Sep 1942; Prod: 22 Oct 1941—5 Feb 1942; retakes began early Mar 1942 [©Twentieth Century-Fox Film Corp.; 30 Oct 1942; LP12023]. Sd (Western Electric Mirrophonic Recording); b&w. 12 reels, 10,663 ft. 117-118 min. PCA cert no. 7887.

Prod Boris Morros and S. P. Eagle. [*Assoc prod* Sam Rheiner]. *Dir* Julien Duvivier. *Asst dir* Robert Stillman and [Charles Hall]. [*Dial dir* Don Brodie and Alan Campbell]. *Orig stories and scr by* Ben Hecht, Ferenc Molnar, Donald Ogden Stewart, Samuel Hoffenstein, Alan Campbell, Ladislas Fodor, L. Vadnai, L. Gorog, Lamar Trotti and Henry Blankfort. *Dir of photog* Joseph Walker. *Art dir* Richard Day and Boris Leven. *Film ed* Robert Bischoff. *Set dec* Thomas Little.

[*Props* Phil D'Esco]. *Cost* Dolly Tree, Bernard Newman, Gwen Wakeling and Irene. *Mus dir* Edward Paul. *Orig mus* Sol Kaplan. *Orch* Clarence Wheeler, Charles Bradshaw and Hugo Friedhofer. *Vocal arr* Hall Johnson. *Sd* W. D. Flick and Roger Heman. *Makeup artist* Guy Pearce. *Unit mgr* J. H. Nadel. [*Prod mgr* William Koenig]. [*Paul Robeson's vocal coach, accompaniest and arr* Lawrence Brown].

Music: "Bacchanale Moderne" by Sol Kaplan.

Song(s): "Glory Day," music and lyrics by Leo Robin and Ralph Rainger.

Cast: Charles Boyer ([*Paul*] *Orman*), Rita Hayworth (*Ethel* [*Halloway*]), Ginger Rogers (*Diane*), Henry Fonda (*George*), Charles Laughton (*Charles Smith*), Edward G. Robinson ([*Avery L. "Larry"*] *Browne*), Paul Robeson (*Luke*), Ethel Waters (*Esther*), Eddie "Rochester" Anderson (*Rev. Lazarus*), Thomas Mitchell ([*John*] *Halloway*), Eugene Pallette (*Luther*), Cesar Romero (*Harry* [*Wilson*]), Gail Patrick (*Ellen*), Roland Young (*Edgar*), Marion Martin (*Squirrel* [*Miss Gray*]), Elsa Lanchester (*Mrs. Smith*), Victor Francen (*Arturo Bellini*), George Sanders (*Williams*), James Gleason ("*Father*" *Joe*), Harry Davenport (*Professor Lyons*), James Rennie (*Hank Bronson*), J. Carrol Naish (*Costello*), The Hall Johnson Choir (*Themselves*), Frank Orth (*Second-hand clothes dealer*), Christian Rub (*Wilson*), Sig Arno (*Piccolo player*), Harry Hayden ([*Soupy*] *Davis*), Morris Ankrum (*Judge* [*Barnes*]), Don Douglas (*Henderson*), Mae Marsh (*Molly*), Clarence Muse (*Grandpa*), George Reed (*Christopher*), Cordell Hickman (*Nicodemus*), Paul Renay ("*Spud*" *Johnson*), Barbara (*Lynn*), Adeline DeWalt Reynolds (*Grandmother*), Helene Reynolds (*Actress*), [Robert Greig (*Lazar*)], [Jack Chefe (*Martelli the tailor*)], [William Halligan (*Evan Webb*)], [Charles Williams (*Agent*)], [Eric Wilton (*Halloway butler*)], [Connie Leon (*Mary*)], [Forbes Murray (*Dignified man*)], [Buster Brodie (*Call boy*)], [Frank Jaquet (*Musician*)], [Will Wright (*Skeptic*)], [Frank Dae (*Elderly man*)], [Rene Austin (*Susan*)], [Frank Darien (*Grandpa*)], [Dewey Robinson (*Proprietor*)], [Tom O'Grady (*Latecomer*)], [Alex Pollard (*Waiter*)], [Joseph Bernard (*Postman*)], [Don Brodie (*Whistler*)], [Ted Stanhope (*Chauffeur*)], [John Kelly (*Monk*)], [Lonnie Nichols (*Brad*)], [Charles Gray (*Rod*)], [Phillip Hurlic (*Jeff*)], [Alberta Gary (*Black girl*)], [Charles Tannen (*Pilot*)], [Esther Howard], [Archie Savage], [Rita Christiani], [Laura Vaughn], [Ella Mae Lashley], [Olive Ball], [Maggie Dorsey].

Comedy-drama. [*Print viewed*]. Just before the opening of his new Broadway show, famed actor Paul Orman is fitted with a new formal tail coat by his tailor. The tailor nervously admits that the coat was cursed by a dismissed cutter, who swore that it would bring misfortune to anyone who wore it, but Orman does not care. After a well-received performance, Orman instructs his valet, Luther, to drive him to the country estate of Ethel Halloway. Ethel was once Orman's paramour, but after the end of their affair, she married John Halloway, a rich big-game hunter. Luther believes that Orman is better off without Ethel, but the actor cannot resist engineering an impromptu rendezvous with her. Orman and Ethel alternately declare their love and suspicions about each other's motives, until he admits that he should never have broken with her, then persuades her to go to Brazil with him. Just after Orman calls his manager and instructs him to close the play, Halloway enters and menacingly shows Orman his favorite rifle. Halloway shoots Orman, and after stating that he did so accidentally, convinces Ethel to promise to testify that it was an accident. Ethel also tells Orman that she will support his version, that the shooting was deliberate, and Orman finally realizes that she lies to everyone and has no intention of ever leaving her husband for him. After asserting that Halloway missed him and that he was only pretending to be shot in order to reveal Ethel's false nature, Orman collapses in his car and instructs Luther to take him to the hospital. Soon after, Luther takes the tail coat, with its bullet hole intact, and gives it to his friend, Edgar, as security for a ten-dollar loan. Edgar is the butler for Harry Wilson, a Manhattan playboy who is to be married that evening to Diane. While Harry recovers from his wild bachelor party of the previous night, Diane receives a visit from her friend Ellen, who is determined to divorce her husband after finding evidence of his infidelity in his tail coat pocket. Diane advises her not to search her husband's clothes, then takes her to Harry's apartment. As they are waiting for Harry, Ellen urges Diane to look in his tail coat pocket, where she finds a torrid love letter from "Squirrel." Harry overhears the devastated Diane reading aloud the letter and calls his best friend, George, whom he implores to come immediately. Using

the tail coat that Luther gave to Edgar, George tells Diane that he took Harry's coat when he left the night before, and that the coat she has searched is actually his. Diane is satisfied with the explanation and allows George to keep her company while Harry finishes dressing. The intimate letter makes Diane see timid George in a new light, however, and she falls in love with him as they flirt. George, who has always loved Diane, is thrilled by her response, but when Miss Gray, the "Squirrel" of the letter, arrives to castigate Harry for getting married, George still tries to cover up for him. Diane sees through the charade, and after returning Harry's ring, leaves with George.

Luther and Edgar then pawn the tail coat in order to get Edgar's money. Mrs. Smith sees the coat in the shop and tells the proprietor that she would love to buy it for her husband Charles, who is an accomplished musician and composer. At that moment, Charles, who is playing piano in a saloon, leaves his degrading job to watch the famed conductor Arturo Bellini at a rehearsal. Charles' friend, Wilson, convinces Bellini to see Charles, and despite his fright, Charles plays his "Bacchanale Moderne" for the conductor. Bellini is impressed with the piece and offers Charles the opportunity to conduct it at his next concert. On the night of the event, Wilson tells Charles that he must wear a formal tail coat. As Charles rushes to the theater, Mrs. Smith returns to the pawnshop and buys the coat, which is much too small for Charles. Nothing can be done, however, so Charles goes onstage and conducts his symphony. The coat tears twice as Charles moves vigorously, and the audience begins to laugh. One of the musicians finally informs Charles, who removes his coat, but the laughter continues to swell. As Charles sobs onstage, Bellini stands in his box and slowly removes his own coat. Ashamed of their behavior, the other men in the audience remove their coats and applaud as Bellini gestures for Charles to resume. Charles' music is then a success, and after he leaves the hall with his wife and Wilson, he gives the coat to a worker for the Society to Aid the Friendless.

The tail coat is given to "Father" Joe, a dedicated helper of Bowery bums. Joe receives a letter for Avery L. Browne, a downtrodden fellow whom Joe knows as Larry. Joe takes the letter to Larry, and it is revealed to be an invitation to the twenty-fifth anniversary reunion of his law class. Larry, drunken and dirty as usual, refuses to attend, but Joe cleans him up, dresses him in the tail coat and sends him to the Waldorf-Astoria for the dinner. As Larry greets his old comrades, including his English teacher, Professor Lyons, he becomes more like his former, jovial self. He tells his friends that he was away on an important job in China and enjoys himself until the arrival of Williams, his ex-partner in their Chicago law firm. During the evening, Henderson, one of the attendees, believes that his wallet has been stolen, and when Larry, who is wearing a dickey and a cheap shirt, refuses to take his coat off and be searched, Williams accuses him of the crime. Williams stages a mock trial to prove that due to his low character, Larry must be guilty. Larry pleads his case, telling how he fought in World War I, married a lovely girl and entered partnership with Williams. During Prohibition, Larry had a successful practice protecting clients of doubtful occupations, but afterward, his practice fell apart and he was disbarred, probably through Williams' machinations. After losing his wife, Larry became a drifter and has wandered the streets of New York for the past six years. Finally removing his coat, Larry offers to be searched, then leaves when none of his friends speak. Henderson's chauffeur then enters and produces his wallet, which was left in the car. Completely dispirited, Larry gets drunk and returns to Joe's mission the following morning. Also arriving, however, are Larry's friends, Soupy Davis, Hank Bronson and Judge Barnes, who have come to offer him a job. Joe promises that he will send Larry right away, then tells his wife to sell the coat to the Santelli Brothers, a pair of second-hand clothes dealers.

The coat is stolen from the shop by Costello and Monk, hoodlums who want to rob a fancy gambling club. Properly attired, Costello is able to enter the club, then robs its patrons. He makes a getaway in a small plane, but when sparks from the cockpit set the coat on fire, Costello tosses it out before remembering that he hid the stolen $50,000 in it. The coat falls in fields worked by Luke and Esther, two black, Southern sharecroppers. Esther insists that they take the money to Reverend Lazurus, their preacher, who declares that it is manna from heaven. Wishing to help everyone in their poverty-stricken community, Lazurus declares that he will divide up the money to fulfill people's prayers. Esther, who has prayed for a cow, receives

sixty dollars, while Luke is given almost eight hundred dollars for a new tractor. Children receive a few dollars each for shoes and toys, and everyone gets some money for presents, for it is Christmas Eve. Even after all the prayers have been accounted for, there is a large sum of money left, and Esther declares that it should be used to build a new church and to buy tools, land and seed so that none of them will go hungry again. Everyone is satisfied until they remember old Christopher, the poorest one of all. They rush to see him, and after explaining the situation, ask what he wants for Christmas. The old man declares that all he desires is something to keep away the pesky crows, and the once glorious tail coat becomes a scarecrow in Christopher's field. *Actors and actresses. African Americans. Clothes. Composers. Curses. Homelessness. New York City. Romance. Transformation.* Airplanes. Auditions. Bachelor parties. Christmas Eve. Conductors (Music). Duplicity. Engagements. Femmes fatales. Gunshot wounds. Homelessness. Hunters. Infidelity. Jealousy. Lawyers. Letters. Missions. Mock trials. Money. New York City–Bowery. Pawnbrokers. Playboys. Poverty. Prayer. Reunions. Reverends. Scarecrows. Servants. Tailors. Thieves. Waldorf-Astoria Hotel (New York City). Whistling. Wives.

Note: The working title of this film was *Tails of Manhattan*. According to a 4 Jun 1941 *HR* news item, producer Boris Morros originally was to make the picture at Paramount, with Dalton Trumbo and Aben Kandel preparing a screenplay based on an original story written by Billy Wilder and Walter Reisch. Morros planned to use seven different directors on the seven planned episodes. No other contemporary source mentions Wilder and Reisch's involvement, and it is unlikely that they, or Trumbo and Kandel, contributed to the completed picture. A 26 Oct 1941 *NYHT* article reported that Morros had been "planning his picture ever since a year ago when a friend of his named Eagle brought the idea to him." Several other contemporary sources credit co-producer S. P. Eagle (pseudonym of Sam Spiegel) with the original story idea, although the Twentieth Century-Fox Records of the Legal Department, located at the UCLA Arts—Special Collections Library, contains a memo from Spiegel in which he states that the idea of tying the individual sequences together "by means of a tail coat was based on an original idea" found in a 1931 book of German stories by Max Nossek. Spiegel did not use any of Nossek's stories, however, just his basic premise, to which Nossek sold the rights to George Marton, who in turn assigned the rights to Spiegel.

Further information in the legal records indicates that the first sequence was based on *Marsall*, a one-act play by Ferenc Molnar, which was performed as *The Field Marshall* in Budapest on 19 Oct 1929; the second sequence was based on a play entitled *Sextette* by Ladislas Fodor, the production dates of which have not been determined; and the rest of the sequences were based on original story ideas. Contemporary sources note that director Julien Duvivier also had a hand in shaping the screenplay. Besides Duvivier, Marton, Morros and Spiegel, none of whom received onscreen writing credit, the studio's legal records indicate that writer Nicholas Jory and dialogue director Don Brodie may have contributed to the script. A 5 Feb 1942 *HR* news item noted that the production would feature writing credits for twelve of the twenty writers who worked on the screenplay. The news item also commented: "The tangle of original story credits has not yet been worked out. A total of 40 original stories and ideas were purchased for its variegated sequences."

The legal files and contemporary news items note that Irene Dunne and Joel McCrea were originally set for the leads of the second sequence, although a 23 Nov 1941 *NYT* item stated that Dunne would play Thomas Mitchell's wife in the first sequence. Walter Huston was considered for a role before Morros and Spiegel signed a distribution deal with Twentieth Century-Fox in Sep 1941, and Frances Dee was considered for one of two sequences. According to a *HR* news item, Buster Keaton was signed to play "Hiawatha" in the film, although he is not in the finished picture. Other *HR* news items state that the singing group Deep River Boys and Gene Austin were cast, but their participation in the completed picture has not been confirmed. Rita Hayworth was borrowed from Columbia for the production. Although the legal files contain a 3 Dec 1941 memo from Spiegel requesting a $2,500 salary payment to Jean Levy-Strauss, the exact nature of Levy-Strauss' contribution to the completed picture has not been determined.

The legal records, in addition to the Twentieth Century-Fox Produced Scripts Collection and other contemporary sources, note that an entire sequence featuring W. C. Fields, Phil Silvers and Margaret Dumont was filmed and deleted from the finished picture. The sequence was written primarily by Bert Lawrence, Anne Wigton, William Morrow and Edmund Beloin, although a *HR* news item stated that Eddie Welch was to collaborate with Morrow and Beloin. *HR* also noted that director Mal St. Clair worked with Duvivier on this sequence, "advising on gags and comedy routines for Fields and other comics." In the sequence, which was to be placed between the ones starring Edward G. Robinson and Paul Robeson, Fields played a confidence man who speaks before a temperance society headed by Dumont and accidentally gets his audience drunk. A 3 May 1942 *NYT* article reported that the sequence was deleted because "the producers, having shown it at sneak previews, feel that it is not in keeping with the other five sections." On 8 May 1942, an ad placed by Fields appeared in *HR*, in which he quoted from positive reviews of his sequence and rebutted a radio report that he was going to sue the studio for deleting his sequence. Fields asserted that he had no intention of suing Twentieth Century-Fox or the producers. The legal records indicate that the studio considered using Fields' sequence in its 1944 compilation film *Take It or Leave It*. In May 1996, the Fields sequence was included in the video version of *Tales of Manhattan* released by the studio.

According to a studio press release, Morros commissioned the "Bacchanale Moderne" by Sol Kaplan after hearing him play his piano concertos at a recital in Los Angeles. In a contemporary article entitled "Film Music Notes," contained in the film's file at AMPAS, the young composer noted that "Morros was so impressed with this piece that the picture in this particular sequence was shot to the music." A 9 Feb 1942 press release stated that actor Jean Gabin provided Duvivier with "a roughed out musical theme for the [second] sequence, based on a popular French ballet," but Gabin's contribution to the musical score has not been confirmed. On 18 Nov 1941, *HR* noted that Robert Katcher had reported to the studio "to prepare musical scores," but the extent of his contribution to the finished picture also has not been confirmed. In Aug 1942, *HR* noted that Kaplan's score would be broken up into five popular songs, with Paul Webster supplying the lyrics.

According to *HR* news items, the studio had trouble devising a trailer for the film due to the unusual number of starring actors, until it was decided to have a trailer "in which only speaking voices [would] be heard and no images" of the actors would be shown. Charles Boyer's voice was to be used to open the trailer, although a Jul 1942 *HR* news item stated that Walter Winchell had narrated the trailer. According to a 6 Oct 1944 *HR* news item, *Tales of Manhattan* was the first film shown to civilians in Paris after the city was liberated by the Allies.

Tales of Manhattan marked the last film appearance of actor/singer Paul Robeson, although his singing voice was featured in the 1954 East German film *Das Lied der Ströme*. According to a 23 Sep 1942 *NYT* article, Robeson announced he was "through with Hollywood until movie magnates found some other way to portray the Negro besides the usual 'plantation hallelujah shouters.'" In the interview, Robeson stated that he was "particularly despondent" over his role in *Tales of Manhattan* because "in the end it turned out to be the same old thing—the Negro solving his problem by singing his way to glory." Robeson asserted that this "very offensive" depiction was the result of "Hollywood [saying] you can't make the Negro in any other role because it won't be box office in the South."

Information in the legal files reveals that Mexican writer Francisco Rojas Gonzales sued Twentieth Century-Fox for plagiarism, claiming that Spiegel had read his story "History of a Full Dress Coat," which was published in a book of short stories in 1931, and stolen the premise. The disposition of the suit is not known, however. Another plagiarism claim was pursued by Peter J. Fabry and Raoul E. White, the authors of a book entitled *Ever Yours...Casanova*. The disposition of their suit also is not known.

Box 8 Aug 1942. *DV* 4 Aug 1942, p. 3. *FD* 5 Aug 1942, p. 7. *HR* 4 Jun 1941. *HR* 28 Aug 1941, p. 1. *HR* 3 Sep 1941, p. 4, 10. *HR* 9 Sep 1941, p. 2, 4. *HR* 11 Sep 1941, p. 2. *HR* 14 Oct 1941, p. 4. *HR* 16 Oct 1941, p. 3. *HR* 17 Oct 1941, p. 1. *HR* 21 Oct 1941, p. 6. *HR* 23 Oct 1941, p. 6. *HR* 24 Oct 1941, p. 11. *HR* 29 Oct 1941, p. 10. *HR* 10 Nov 1941, p. 1. *HR* 12 Nov 1941, p. 4. *HR* 18 Nov 1941, p. 2. *HR* 19 Nov 1941, p. 4. *HR* 24 Nov 1941, p. 1. *HR* 27 Nov 1941, p. 2. *HR* 19 Dec 1941, p. 2. *HR* 23 Dec 1941, p. 2. *HR* 6 Jan 1942, p. 10. *HR* 13 Jan 1942, p. 6. *HR* 16 Jan 1942, p. 2. *HR* 23 Jan 1942, p. 11. *HR* 28 Jan 1942, p. 1, 7. *HR* 30 Jan 1942, p. 2. *HR* 5 Feb 1942, p. 7. *HR* 23 Feb 1942, p. 7. *HR* 3 Mar 1942, p. 1. *HR* 8 May 1942, p. 16. *HR* 8 Jun 1942, p. 3. *HR* 8 Jul 1942, p. 9. *HR* 20 Jul 1942, p. 1. *HR* 28 Jul 1942, p. 8. *HR* 4 Aug 1942, p. 3. *HR* 5 Aug 1942, p. 3. *HR* 6 Aug 1942, p. 4. *HR* 10 Aug 1942, p. 1. *HR* 11 Aug 1942, p. 1. *HR* 18 Aug 1942, p. 13. *HR* 25 Sep 1942, p. 1. *HR* 28 Sep 1942, p. 6. *HR* 6 Oct 1944, p. 1. *LAEx* 23 Nov 1941. *MPD* 4 Aug 1942. *MPH* 26 Sep 1942. *MPHPD* 8 Aug 1942, p. 825. *NYHT* 26 Oct 1941. *NYT* 23 Nov 1941. *NYT* 3 May 1942. *NYT* 23 Sep 1942. *NYT* 25 Sep 1942, p. 25. *Var* 5 Aug 1942, p. 8.

TALL, TAN AND TERRIFIC (African Americans)

Astor Productions, Inc. *Dist* Astor Pictures Corp. **1946**. Sd; b&w. 4,346 ft. 48 min. Passed by the National Board of Review.

Pres R. M. Savini. *Exec prod* R. M. Savini. *Prod* Bud Pollard. *Dir* Bud Pollard. *Asst dir* Ed. Kelly. *Orig scr story* John E. Gordon. *Photog* Jack Etra. *Sets* Billy. *Ed* Bud Pollard and Shirley Stone. *Cost* Variety. *Spec mus arr by* Emile Vlasco. *Dance numbers arr by* Art Selectman. *Sd tech* Nels Mindlin.

Song(s): "Stop This Tune" and "The Sweetness of You," music and lyrics by Eugene Roland and Mickey Castle; "Teasing Me," music and lyrics by Eugene Roland, Mickey Castle and Le Roy S. Hodges; "88 Reasons Why," "Let's Get Down to Business," "You're Only Cheatin' on Yourself When You're Cheatin' on Me" and "I've Got to Go to Camp to See My Man," music and lyrics by Eugene Roland.

Cast: Monty Hawley (*Handsome Harry*), Francine Everett (*T. T.&T.* [*Tall, Tan and Terrific*]), Dots Johnson (*Duke*), Rudy Toombs (*Lefty* [*Gomez*]), Barbara Bradford (*Butterbeans*), Milton Woods (*M.C.*), MANTAN MORELAND (*Himself*), Lou Swarz, Thelma Cordero, The Two Fat Men, The Gorgeous Astor Debutantes, and the All Girl Golden Slipper Band.

African American, Show business, Comedy-drama, with songs. [*Viewed print incomplete*]. Handsome Harry, owner of the Golden Slipper nightclub, loses $5,000 to crooked gambler Duke at a craps table, which raises his debt to Duke to $10,000. Duke intends to ruin Harry financially and take the Glass Slipper, which he calls the "best money-making spot in Harlem," away from him. When Duke makes his intentions known to Harry, Harry warns Duke that he would not stand a chance of succeeding, as all the best performers are under contract to him. Among Harry's big-name acts are comedian Mantan Moreland and the lovely singer T.T. & T. known as "Tall, Tan and Terrific," both of whom appear at the club later that night. During the show, Duke and his associate, Lefty Gomez, try to lure Tall, Tan and

Terrific away from Harry and offer her a contract to sing in Chicago for $500 more than she makes working for Harry. She rejects the offer outright and tells Gomez and Duke that she will remain loyal to Harry because he gave her her big break in television. When Tall, Tan and Terrific tells Harry about Duke's offer, he reaches for his gun and vows revenge. The gun remains in Harry's possession for only a short time, though, as Lefty secretly removes it from him while he and Duke are engaged in a conversation. Harry returns to the craps table that night and, after replacing the loaded dice with real ones, wins back his losses. Soon after Harry leaves the craps table with his winnings, the lights go out and a shot rings out. Duke is killed in the darkened gambling hall, and newspaper headlines the next day report that the owner of the murder weapon is being sought as the prime suspect in the killing. The gun that was used to kill Duke, it turns out, is Harry's, and he is soon arrested and placed in jail. Devastated by the news of the murder, Tall, Tan and Terrific leaves town. When Mantan visits Harry at his cell, Harry insists that he is innocent and sends Mantan to get the money he won from Duke, which he hid in his desk drawer. Mantan follows Harry's instructions and goes to his office, where he is startled by an ugly autograph-seeker. While trying to get rid of the autograph-seeker, Mantan discovers that she has a picture of him seated at a table with Harry and Lefty, which was taken just as Lefty was sneaking the gun away from Harry. The picture provides clear evidence that Harry's gun was not in his possession at the time of the murder, and he is released from jail. Shortly thereafter, Lefty confesses to the killing and admits that the bullet, which was intended for Harry, hit Duke accidentally. Harry and his talented friends soon throw a grand reopening party at the Golden Slipper. The party is well underway when a surprise guest, Tall, Tan and Terrific, takes the stage and sings a song. After the song, she and Harry embrace, which prompts Mantan to kiss the ugly autograph-seeker. *African Americans. Business competition. Comedians. Debt. False arrests. Gambling. Murder. New York City–Harlem. Nightclub owners. Autographs. Confession (Law). Dancers. Firearms. Jails. Jazz music. Loyalty. Nightclubs. Parties. Photographs. Singers.*

Note: Although the viewed film contained a copyright statement, the title does not appear in the copyright register. Modern sources list "Johnny and George," Myra Johnson and Edna Mae Harris in the cast, but their participation in the released film has not been confirmed.

THE TALL TARGET (African Americans)

Metro-Goldwyn-Mayer Corp.; controlled by Loew's Inc. *Dist* Loew's Inc. Aug 1951 [©Loew's Inc.; 30 Jul 1951; LP1098]. Sd (Western Electric Sound System); b&w. 6,998 ft. 75 or 78 min. Passed by the National Board of Review. PCA cert no. 15130.

Prod Richard Goldstone. *Dir* Anthony Mann. [*Asst dir* Jerry Thorpe]. *Scr* George Worthing Yates and Art Cohn. *Story* George Worthing Yates and Geoffrey Homes. *Dir of photog* Paul C. Vogel. *Spec eff* A. Arnold Gillespie and Warren Newcombe. *Art dir* Cedric Gibbons and Eddie Imazu. *Film ed* Newell P. Kimlin. *Set des* Edwin B. Willis and Ralph S. Hurst. *Rec supv* Douglas Shearer. [*Sd* John Williams]. *Hairstyles des by* Sydney Guilaroff. *Makeup created by* William Tuttle.

Cast: Dick Powell [(*John Kennedy*)], Paula Raymond [(*Ginny Beaufort*)], Adolphe Menjou [(*Col. Caleb Jeffers*)], Marshall Thompson [(*Lance Beaufort*)], Ruby Dee [(*Rachel*)], Richard Rober [(*Lt. Coulter*)], Leif Erickson [(*The stranger*)], Will Geer [(*Homer Crowley*)], Florence Bates [(*Mrs. Charlotte Alsop*)], [Victor Kilian (*John K. Gannon*)], [Katharine Warren (*Mrs. Gibbons*)], [Peter Brocco (*Fernandina*)], [Barbara Billingsley (*Young mother*)], [Will Wright (*Thomas I. Ogden*)], [Regis Toomey (*Tim Rielly*)], [Jeff Richards (*Policeman*)], [Tom Powers (*Simon G. Stroud*)], [Leslie Kimmell (*Abraham Lincoln*)], [James Harrison (*Allan Pinkerton*)], [Dan Foster (*Dapper man*)], [Brad Morrow (*Winfield*)], [Percy Helton (*Beamish*)], [Lou Nova (*Zouave Sergeant*)], [Clancy Cooper (*Brakeman*)], [Robert Malcolm (*Patrolman*)], [Ken Christy, Bert Roach (*Politicians*)], [Emmett Lynn (*News vendor*)], [Charles Wagenheim (*Telegraph clerk*)], [Jonathan Hale (*Professional Southerner*)], [Cameron Grant (*Portly man*)], [Robert Easton (*Young Southerner*)], [John Butler (*Miller*)], [John Call, Frank Conlan (*Clerks*)], [Dan White (*Texan*)], [Stapleton Kent (*New Brunswick station master*)], [Erville Alderson (*Minister*)], [Frank Sully (*Telegraph boy*)], [Mickey Martin (*Messenger*)], [Alvin Hammer (*Telegraph operator*)], [John Damler (*Division manager*)], [Jack Sterling, Phil Schumacher, Tom Monroe, Bob Rich, Tom Murray,

Robert Spencer (*Zouaves*)], [Budd Fine (*Pinkerton man*)], [Wilson Wood (*Dispatcher*)], [Clarence Hennecke, Robert Stephenson, Olive Ball, Napoleon Whiting, Frank Billy Mitchell, Irving Smith, George Bunny, Bill Sundholm (*Hawkers*)], [Rodney Wooton, Wilfred Jackson, Thomas Porter (*Newsboys*)], [James Mason (*Teamster*)], [Roger Moore], [Nikki Juston], [Robert Strong], [Estelle Ettere], [Lucile Curtis], [Marjorie Jackson], [Sherry Hall], [Harry Cody].

Historical, **Drama**. [*Print viewed*]. In 1861, as the country seethes with unrest in the wake of the Presidential election, John Kennedy, a New York police officer who briefly served as Abraham Lincoln's bodyguard, becomes convinced that there will be an attempt on the newly elected President's life as Lincoln's train passes through Baltimore on his way to his inauguration in Washington, D.C. When Kennedy's report is rebuffed by Simon G. Stroud, his supervisor at the police department, he angrily resigns his post, sends his report to the War Department and then boards the Night Flyer Express bound for Baltimore and Washington. Kennedy's friend, Inspector Tim Rielly, was to meet him onboard with his ticket and suitcase, but when Kennedy arrives, Rielly is nowhere to be found, although Kennedy's suitcase has been delivered. Scrambling to buy a ticket at the ticket office, Kennedy discovers that there are none left. As the train pulls out of the station, Kennedy makes a mad dash and jumps onboard. While scouring the train for Rielly, Kennedy finds his friend's body dangling from an observation platform. After Rielly's body slips from the onrushing train, Kennedy stalks the train corridors and encounters Col. Caleb Jeffers, a Northern militia officer who is traveling to Baltimore to lead his troops in a procession. Upon returning to his seat, Kennedy sees a stranger wearing his coat and holding his ticket and gun. When the stranger tells conductor Homer Crowley that he is Kennedy, Kennedy takes Crowley to Caleb's compartment, where Caleb identifies him as the real Kennedy and offers to share his compartment. As Kennedy prowls the corridors in search of a gun, he feels a pistol pressed against his back. The stranger then escorts Kennedy to the rear of the train, and when the train stops, ushers him off. Kennedy overpowers the stranger and wrests the gun from him. As the train powers up to depart, Caleb hears the sounds of the scuffle and shoots the stranger. After Kennedy rejoins Caleb onboard, Caleb hands him a pistol and Kennedy then tells him that before dying, the stranger divulged that he was to meet his contact in car 27. Proceeding to car 27, a club car, Kennedy and Caleb find Mrs. Charlotte Alsop, an abolitionist novelist, interviewing Rachel, the slave of Lance and Ginny Beaufort. Resentful of Mrs. Alsop's intrusive questions, Lance, an officer in the Confederate Army, voices his hatred for Lincoln and storms out of the car. After he leaves, Lance's sister Ginny explains that the family plans to detrain in Atlanta so that Lance can resign his commission. When the train stops in Philadelphia, Caleb and Kennedy return to their compartment. After Kennedy stretches out on his berth, his head shrouded in a newspaper, Caleb tries to shoot him, but Kennedy has emptied his pistol. Now realizing that the stranger was Caleb's accomplice, and that Caleb was aiming at Kennedy but hit his own man by mistake, Kennedy takes Caleb into custody and turns him over to a Philadelphia police officer. When Caleb shows the officer his military credentials, Kennedy asserts that Lt. Coutler at police headquarters can vouch for his authority. As Coulter is summoned, orders come to delay the train until a package can be delivered. While the train is waiting, Mrs. Gibbons, a mysterious passenger who has been closeted in her compartment with her invalid husband, steps out for air. Soon after, Lt. Coulter arrives with a message from Stroud denying that Kennedy is a member of the police force. Overpowering Coulter, Kennedy flees and hides on the roof of the train. Once the package is delivered, the train starts moving and Kennedy slips back inside. As the train speeds into the night. Rachel motions for Kennedy to come to her cabin and confides to him that Lance is carrying a rifle with a scope. As Rachel hands Lance's gun to Kennedy, Ginny overhears them whispering, slaps Rachel and then grabs the gun from Kennedy. Ginny then summons Lance, and after striking Kennedy unconscious, he admits that he is one of the assassins plotting to kill Lincoln as his train passes through Baltimore. Lance drags Kennedy to Caleb's compartment, where the conspirators bind and gag him. When the train stops at Wilmington so that a team of horses can pull it into Baltimore, a barber boards to shave Caleb. The barber, an accomplice, explains the details of the assassination plot. As the train pulls into Baltimore, word comes that Lincoln's train has been diverted. Leaving

Kennedy in Lance's custody, Caleb detrains, and soon after, realizes that the delayed package was only a ruse to hide Lincoln in Mrs. Gibbons' compartment. As the train slowly pulls out, Caleb scrawls "the man is on the train" on the dust of Lance's car window. Noticing the message, Lance places Kennedy in Crowley's custody and leaves to retrieve his rifle. After reading the message, Kennedy overpowers his guard and runs after Lance. As they struggle, Kennedy pushes Lance off the train and onto the tracks. Soon after, Mrs. Gibbons appears and identifies herself as an undercover agent with the War Department. After congratulating Kennedy on saving Lincoln's life, she states that Kennedy's report spurred the War Department to undertake measures to secure Lincoln's safety. *Abolitionists. Assassination. Abraham Lincoln. Trains. United States–History–1815-1861. African Americans. Baltimore (MD). Brothers and sisters. Impersonation and imposture. Murder. Officers (Military). Police. Slaves. Train conductors. Undercover agents. United States. War Department.*

Note: The working title of this film was *Man on the Train.* The picture opens with the following written prologue: "90 years ago a lonely traveler boarded the night train from New York to Washington, D.C., and when he reached his destination, his passage had become a forgotten chapter in the history of the United States. This motion picture is a dramatization of that disputed journey." John Kennedy was a real New York police officer.

Box 4 Aug 1951. *DV* 1 Aug 1951, p. 3. *Exb* 15 Aug 1951, p. 3126. *FD* 7 Aug 1951, p. 6. *Har* 4 Aug 1951, p. 122-23. *HR* 5 Jan 1951, p. 10. *HR* 9 Feb 1951, p. 14. *HR* 1 Aug 1951, p. 3. *MPHPD* 4 Aug 1951, p. 966. *NYT* 28 Sep 1951, p. 26. *Var* 1 Aug 1951, p. 6.

TAMBOURINE *see* HOT BLOOD

TAN DOU QAI YEN *see* TAN DOW JIA JEN

TAN DOW JIA JEN (Chinese language)
1953?; Hong Kong showing: 1953? Sd; b&w. Length undetermined. Chinese language.

Dir Wu Dip-ying. [*Not viewed*]. [No information concerning the plot of this film has been located.].

Note: The film's Cantonese transliterated title is *Tan Dou Qai Yen.* According to available contemporary information, the film was made in Honolulu, HI.

TANGO BAR (Spanish language)
Exito Productions, Inc. *Dist* Paramount Pictures, Inc. **1935**; New York opening: 5 Jul 1935; Prod: Feb 1935 at Eastern Service Studios, Inc. in Astoria, Long Island [©Exito Productions, Inc.; 9 Jun 1935; LP5607]. Sd (Sistema Sonoro Western Electric a prueba de ruidos [Western Electric Sound System]); b&w. 7 reels, 5,578 ft. 62 min. PCA cert no. 947. Spanish language.

Dirección de [*Dir*] John Reinhardt. *Por* [*Wrt*] Alfredo Le Pera. *Fotógrafo* [*Photog*] William Miller. *Dirección musical de* [*Mus dir*] Terig Tucci. *Supervisor técnico* [*Tech supv*] Samuel E. Piza.

Song(s): "Arrabal amargo," "Lejana tierra mía" and "Por una cabeza," music by Carlos Gardel, lyrics by Alfredo Le Pera; "Los ojos de mi moza," music by Carlos Gardel and Terig Tucci, lyrics by Alfredo Le Pera.

Cast: CARLOS GARDEL (*Ricardo* [*Fuentes*]), ROSITA MORENO (*Laura* [*Montalbán*]), Enrique de Rosas (*Comandante*), Tito Lusiardo (*Puccini*), José Luis Tortosa (*Capitán*), Collette D'Arville (*Chichita*), Manuel Peluffo (*Manuel González*), Suzanne Dulier (*La criada de Laura*), William Gordon (*Mister Cohen*), Carmen Rodríguez (*Mrs. Cohen*), José Nieto (*Inspector*), Juan D'Vega (*Ramos*), Fernando Adelantado.

Musical. [*Viewed print incomplete*]. Singer Ricardo Fuentes, about to sail to Barcelona, where he hopes to recoup his lost fortune, says goodbye to his faithful friend, Puccini. At the docks, Ricardo notices the beautiful Laura Montalbán and approaches her, but she rebuffs him. Puccini hides in the ship as a stowaway and, when caught, is given the job of guarding Laura's dogs. Also on the ship is Comandante, with whom Laura was associated in gambling enterprises, and who is now blackmailing her into helping him swindle the ship's wealthy passengers. When Ricardo catches Comandante stacking the deck in a poker game with Mr. and Mrs. Cohen, he insists upon cutting the deck, causing Comandante to lose. Later, during a concert on deck, Comandante filches Mrs. Cohen's diamond bracelet and signals Laura, who sends her dog leaping over the deck to retrieve it. When the captain stops the dog to pet him, Ricardo distracts him until the bracelet is safely in Laura's hands. Although she tries to thank him, Ricardo is cold to her. Later, however, in Barcelona, he gives her a job singing at his nightclub, the Tango Bar. After learning that the American Embassy suspects that he

stole the bracelet, Ricardo pays a large sum to a pawnbroker named González, with whom Comandante hocked it, retrieves the bracelet and puts it in his safe. González and Comandante doublecross Ricardo and call the police, but when they search the safe, the bracelet is missing. Meanwhile, Laura tries to shoot González. Ricardo then tells Laura and Puccini that his safe is a double one, and has the bracelet returned to the Cohens. Disillusioned by Laura's crimes, Ricardo gives the Tango Bar to Puccini and abandons her, then boards a ship. She follows and convinces Ricardo of her reformed nature and her love for him. *Diamonds. Nightclubs. Singers. Tango (Dance). Thieves. Americans in foreign countries. Barcelona (Spain). Dancers. Dogs. Moral reformation. Poker (Game). Rescues. Sea captains. Ships. Stowaways.*

Note: The onscreen credits were taken from an incomplete print of the film, while the plot summary was based on material in the Paramount story files at the AMPAS Library. The *Var* review for a New York "projection room" screening of the film gives a length of 87 min., although NYSA records list the film's length as 5,578 feet, suggesting a running time of about 62 min. South American film star Carlos Gardel was killed in a plane accident on 24 Jun 1935, a few days before the film's opening in New York.

CinI Aug 1935, p. 6. *CM* Aug 1935, p. 477. *FD* 9 Jul 1935, p. 7. *NYT* 6 Jul 1935, p. 16. *Var* 17 Jul 1935, p. 27.

EL TANGO EN BROADWAY (Spanish language)
Exito Corp. *Dist* Paramount Productions, Inc. **1934**; New York opening: 28 Dec 1934; Prod: 5 Jul–late Jul 1934 at Eastern Service Studios, New York [©Exito Corp., Inc.; 19 Oct 1934; LP5036]. Sd; b&w. 9 reels, 7,682 ft. 85 min. Spanish language.

[*Supv* Robert Snody]. *Dirección de* [*Dir*] Louis Gasnier. [*Asst dir* Warren Murray and Jack DeLacy]. *Argumento, adaptación y letra de* [*Story, adpt and lyrics*] Alfredo Le Pera. *Fotógrafo* [*Photog*] William Miller. [*Asst cam* George Hinners]. [*Stills* Frank Serjack]. [*Art dir* Walter Keller]. *Dirección musical de* [*Mus dir*] Alberto Castellanos. [*Sd* Frank Tuthill]. *Supervisor técnico* [*Tech supv*] Samuel E. Piza.

Song(s): "Rubias de New York," "Golondrinas," "Caminito soleado" and "Soledad," music by Carlos Gardel, lyrics by Alfredo Le Pera. "Gaucho," "¡Qué me importa!" and "Chinita," by Agustín Cornejo.

Cast: CARLOS GARDEL (*Alberto Bazán*), Trini Ramos (*Celia*), Blanca Vischer (*Laurita*), Vicente Padula (*Juan Carlos*), Jaime Devesa (*Indalecio*), Susanne Dulier (*Susana*), Manuel Peluffo (*El hombre blanco*), "Don Alberto" (*Morales*), Agustín Cornejo (*Cornejo*), Carlos Spaventa (*Carlos*), [Carlos Gianotti (*El gaucho*)], [José Moriche (*Piñata*)], [Guillermo Moreno], [Manuel de Moya].

Romantic comedy, with songs. [*Print viewed*]. An extremely suspicious tightwad arrives in New York to verify that his nephew, Alberto Bazán, has invested the money entrusted to him in a legitimate business. Soon he discovers that all of the money has been invested in a theatrical agency involved in show business. The uncle adapts rapidly to the new environment, however, and soon steals Alberto's fiancée. Alberto quickly recovers and ends up marrying his ex-stenographer, a shy, unassuming woman, who had never thought of marriage before. *Investments. Romantic rivalry. Sideshows. Uncles. Marriage. New York City. Stenographers.*

Note: The working titles of this film were *His Unofficial Fiancée, Love Among Skyscrapers* and *Amor entre rascacielos.* A pre-production *FD* news item lists Fred Scheld as the assistant director and George Webber as the cameraman, but their participation in the completed film has not been confirmed.

FD 21 Jun 1934, p. 10. *FD* 6 Jul 1934, p. 6. *FD* 25 Jul 1934, p. 16. *FD* 19 Sep 1934, p. 7. *HR* 16 Jul 1934, p. 7. *NYT* 29 Dec 1934, p. 11.

DER TANZ GEHT WEITER *see* LOS QUE DANZAN

TAP ROOTS (African Americans, Native Americans, Choctaw)
Universal-International Pictures Co., Inc.; Walter Wanger Pictures, Inc.; A George Marshall Production. *Dist* Universal Pictures Co., Inc. **Aug 1948** Sd (Western Electric Recording); col (Technicolor). 108-109 min. PCA cert no. 12947.

Prod Walter Wanger. *Dir* George Marshall. *Asst dir* Aaron Rosenberg. *2d unit dir* George Templeton. *Scr* Alan LeMay. *Addl dial* Lionel Wiggam. *Dir of photog* Lionel Lindon and Winton C. Hoch. *Technicolor color dir* Natalie Kalmus. *Assoc* Morgan Padelford. *Prod des* Alexander Golitzen. *Art dir* Frank A. Richards. *Film ed* Milton Carruth. *Set dec* Russell A. Gausman and Ruby R. Levitt. *Cost* Yvonne Wood. *Mus* Frank Skinner. *Orch* David Tamkin. *Sd* Leslie I. Carey and Glenn E. Anderson. *Hair stylist* Carmen Dirigo. *Makeup* Bud Westmore.

Source: Based on the novel *Tap Roots* by James Street (New York, 1942).

Cast: VAN HEFLIN (*Keith Alexander*), SUSAN HAYWARD (*Morna Dabney*), Boris Karloff (*Tishomingo*), Julie London (*Aven Dabney*), Whitfield Connor (*Clay MacIvor*), Ward Bond (*Hoab Dabney*), Richard Long (*Bruce Dabney*), Arthur Shields (*Reverend Kirkland*), Griff Barnett (*Dr. MacIntosh*), Sondra Rodgers (*Shellie* [*Dabney*]), Ruby Dandridge (*Dabby*), Russell Simpson ([*"Big"*] *Sam Dabney*), [Jack Davis (*Militia captain*)], [Gregg Barton (*Captain*)], [George Hamilton (*Quint*)], [Jonathan Hale (*General Johnston*)], [Arthur Space, Kay Medford (*Callers*)], [William Haade (*Mob leader*)], [Harry Cording (*Leader*)], [George Lewis, Jack Worth (*Confederates*)], [Joe Whitehead (*Printer*)], [William Challee (*Sergeant*)], [John James (*Pete*)], [Charles Flynn (*Murphy*)], [Keith Richards, Bill Neff (*Lieutenants*)], [Hank Worden, Robert O'Neil (*Croppers*)], [Jack Shutta (*Carpenter*)], [Frank White (*Corporal*)], [Dick Dickinson (*Field hand*)], [Monte Montague (*Piroqueman*)], [John Beck (*Refugee*)], [Henry Vroom (*Artillery gunner*)], [Elmo Lincoln (*Sergeant*)], [Shepherd Houghton (*Orderly*)], [Helen Mowery].

Historical, War, Melodrama. [*Print viewed*]. In 1860, "Big Sam" Dabney, the founder of the Dabney plantation in Levington, Mississippi, urges his granddaughter Morna to marry her military officer beau, Clay MacIvor, before he dies. Morna begins to feel her elderly grandfather's urgency when she realizes her younger sister Aven is also interested in Clay. Clay, however, feels that they should delay their wedding, as civil war is imminent. Learning that Mississippi plans to leave the Union upon Lincoln's election, Big Sam collapses and dies. Incensed by an editorial about his grandfather, Morna's brother Bruce is later stopped from challenging Keith Alexander, the rakish publisher and editor of *The Mississippi Whig*, to a duel by Tishomingo, Big Sam's Choctaw Indian friend. Keith rides to the Dabney plantation on the pretext of making amends and quickly runs afoul of Clay. Upon Lincoln's election, Clay leaves Levington for Washington, refusing Morna's pleas to marry. With Clay away, Keith begins his courtship of Morna. Meanwhile, Morna's father Hoab makes plans to annex Levington Valley from Mississippi and declare it a neutral area, and, though skeptical, Keith agrees to give Hoab his newspaper's support. Later, Morna is paralyzed in a horseback riding accident, so the illegitimate Keith, having fallen in love with her, writes his powerful father in Washington to request an emergency leave for Clay. Upon his return to Levington, Clay refuses to break his engagement to the invalid Morna, yet begins a romance with Aven. As the secession of the southern states from the Union begins, Hoab and his supporters rally to the neutral Levington, and Clay, a Confederate loyalist, is ordered to leave the valley. He and Aven then elope, breaking Morna's heart. Though Dr. MacIntosh declares Morna's disability untreatable, Tishomingo begins Indian massage therapy, and months later, Morna begins to regain movement in her legs. Keith then makes his now honorable intentions clear, but Hoab warns him that Morna is still hopelessly in love with Clay. In the meantime, Clay uses his knowledge of the Dabneys' land to prepare for a Confederate assault on Levington, which includes blockading of the valley's supply lines to the Gulf of Mexico. As the rainy season begins, Keith heads south with three hundred men in hopes of bringing new supplies to Levington by mule trains. Tishomingo and Bruce, however, capture one of Clay's men, and learn that a Confederate attack upon the valley from the north is imminent. Knowing that Keith is twelve hours away, Morna rides to the Confederate camp to meet with Clay. Upon learning of Morna's plan, Tishomingo rides ahead to stop her, but is shot and killed by a Confederate sentry. Morna then seduces Clay, delaying the attack long enough for Keith's men to be recalled to Levington. The next morning, Morna tells Clay why she seduced him, but he, in turn, informs her that he used the time to move his cannons forward, realizing with her arrival that a surprise attack was impossible. As the Confederate attack begins, Keith orders his men to retreat into the swamps from the cannon fire. The Levington men are defeated nevertheless, but the sharpshooter Keith manages to kill Clay before the battle ends. Afterward, Morna returns to her family, and Hoab accuses her of disloyalty. Keith, however, states that her actions were heroic and openly proclaims his love. Finally realizing his responsibility in the destruction of the Dabney plantation, Hoab collapses and dies in his wife Shellie's arms. Keith then tells Morna

that her family legacy will survive, as long as the tap root upon which Big Sam proclaimed his ownership lives on. *Editors. Family relationships. Plantations. Romantic rivalry. United States–History–Civil War, 1861-1865. Unrequited love. African Americans. Betrayal. Choctaw Indians. Confederate States of America. Army. Cures. Elopement. Engagements. Illegitimacy. Jealousy. Medicine men. Mississippi. Officers (Military). Paralysis. Physicians. Rescues. Reverends. Seduction. Self-sacrifice. Servants. Swamps.*

Note: The film begins with the following spoken foreword: "This is the story of a Mississippi family, a family whose pioneer men and women had carved their broad plantations out of the wilderness itself. By 1860, their pleasant valley had become almost a state within a state, its people very willing to risk their lives on any chance, rather than to acknowledge the authority of any conscience but their own. These were the famous Dabneys of Levington." According to the film's press book, Universal filmed portions of *Tap Roots* in the Great Smoky Mountains and the Blue Mountains near Asheville, NC. The press book notes that as there were no real white oak trees near Ashton which met the film's requirements, the Universal special effects department in California constructed an artificial one, which was then shipped to the North Carolina location. Further, in order to match location shots with those made on the Universal back lot, twenty barrels of North Carolina red clay were shipped back to the studio in California. During the film's production, actress-singer Julie London eloped to Las Vegas with Jack Webb, later known as the star-producer of the radio and television series of *Dragnet*. The two were married until 1954. London later appeared on the NBC television series *Emergency*, which Webb produced from 1972 to 1977. According to *HR* news items, Universal borrowed London from Sol Lesser's company and Van Heflin from M-G-M for the film. A radio version of *Tap Roots*, with Van Heflin, Susan Hayward and Richard Long reprising their film roles, was broadcast by the *Lux Radio Theatre* on 27 Sep 1948.

Box 3 Jul 1948. *DV* 24 Jun 1948, p. 3, 8. *FD* 24 Jun 1948, p. 3. *HR* 13 May 1947, p. 6. *HR* 21 May 1947, p. 5. *HR* 29 May 1947, p. 19. *HR* 3 Jun 1947, p. 10. *HR* 15 Jul 1947, p. 6. *HR* 24 Jun 1948, p. 3. *HR* 3 Sep 1948, p. 4. *MPHPD* 10 Jan 1948, p. 4010. *MPHPD* 3 Jul 1948, p. 4226. *NYT* 26 Aug 1948, p. 16. *Var* 30 Jun 1948, p. 10.

TAXI (Irish Americans)

Twentieth Century-Fox Film Corp. *Dist* Twentieth Century-Fox Film Corp. Mar **1953**; *Prod*: mid-Jul–late Aug 1952 [©Twentieth Century-Fox Film Corp.; 22 Jan 1953; LP2354]. Sd (Western Electric Recording); b&w. 8 reels, 6,912 ft. 76-77 min. PCA cert no. 16062.

Prod Samuel G. Engel. *Dir* Gregory Ratoff. *Asst dir* Ad Schaumer. *Scr* D. M. Marshman, Jr. and Daniel Fuchs. *Screen story* Hans Jacoby and Fred Brady. *Dir of photog* Milton Krasner. *Spec photog eff* Ray Kellogg. *Art dir* Lyle Wheeler and Richard Irvine. *Film ed* Hugh S. Fowler. *Set dec* Fred J. Rode. *Ward dir* Charles LeMaire. *Cost des* Renie. *Mus* Leigh Harline. *Mus dir* Lionel Newman. *Orch* Edward Powell. *Sd* Winston H. Leverett and Harry M. Leonard. *Makeup artist* Ben Nye.

Source: Based on the motion picture story *Sans laisser d'adresse* written by Alex Joffe and Jean Paul Le Chanois (Les Films Raoul Ploquin, Silver Film, and Hoche Productions, 1950).

Cast: DAN DAILEY [(*Ed Nielson*)], CONSTANCE SMITH [(*Mary Turner*)], Neva Patterson [(*Miss Millard*)], Blanche Yurka [(*Mrs. Nielson*)], Kyle MacDonnell [(*Dottie*)], Walter Woolf King [(*Business man*)], Anthony Ross [(*Mr. Alexander*)], Mark Roberts [(*Jim Turner*)], [Harry Clark (*Riso*)], [Jack Diamond (*Chick*)], [Stubby Kaye (*Morris*)], [B. S. Pulley (*Amchy*)], [Bert Thorn (*Clerk*)], [Curtis Cooksey (*Captain Skavlon*)], [Bill Neil (*Pier guard*)], [Frank McNellis (*Ship's officer*)], [Elliott Sullivan (*Delivery man*)], [Hilda Haynes (*Mabel*)], [James Little (*Policeman*)], [Ann Dere (*Mrs. Albert*)], [Geraldine Page (*Florence Albert*)], [Rex O'Malley (*Butler*)], [Bruno Wick (*Pawnbroker*)], [Art Hannes (*Jenkins*)], [De Forest Kelley (*Fred*)], [Melville Ruick (*George*)], [Henry Jones (*Thorndike*)], [Ralph Dunn (*Rafferty*)], [Betty Buehler (*Frances*)], [Virginia Vincent (*Hortense*)], [Mario Siletti], [John "Red" Kullers (*Cabbie*)], [Glenn Hardy (*Newscaster*)], [Jonathan Hale (*Mr. Barker*)], [Al Eben (*Cab driver*)], [John J. Joyce, Jr. (*Baby*)], [Dulcy Jordan, Barbara McKenzie (*Girls in office*)], [John Cassavetes].

Romance, Comedy-drama. [*Print viewed*]. At the beginning of the day, New York taxi driver Ed Nielson greets his mother in his usual crabby mood, complaining that he has to make a payment on his cab today. Mrs. Nielson, who believes that marriage will help her grouchy son, informs him that her neighbor, Mrs. Albert, and her daughter Florence are coming for dinner that night. Ed growls that he is happy without a wife. On his first fare, Ed tries to take a longer route than needed, but the passenger informs Ed he used to live in New York and gives Ed only a nickel tip. He then loses two fares at the Brooklyn docks, but a policeman informs him that a passenger freighter is unloading. At the U.S. Immigration Office on the dock, Mary Turner,

arriving from Dublin, is given a landing card and an advance of five dollars on wages she has earned washing dishes on the trip over, then is told she must be back by five o'clock. Ed takes her on a roundabout route through Coney Island and New Jersey before arriving at the Manhattan address she has given him, which turns out to be an empty lot. Mary is trying to find her husband Jim, a traveling writer she met in Ireland a year ago and married after knowing him only a week. When Ed learns that she has only $5 to pay the $12.20 bill, he explodes, but then agrees to help find her husband so that he can get his money. After speaking with an Italian delicatessen owner, they find the wife of the janitor who used to work at the demolished building, an African-American woman who gives Mary a box of Jim's clothes and letters Mary had written that never reached him. Her only lead as to Jim's whereabouts is a pawn ticket. The pawnbroker on Park Row finds an overcoat that Mary excitedly remembers as Jim's. She is further encouraged when she sees a statue of St. Anthony and buys it for $1, as the saint is known to help find things that are lost. Sure enough, the pawnbroker notices a coatroom stub fall from the pocket of the overcoat. The stub is from Billy's Grill, a hangout for reporters. As they return to the taxi, they find a cop writing a parking ticket. Noticing that the cop looks Irish, Mary talks to him about the town his ancestors came from and, using "a bit of the blarney," succeeds in getting him to stop writing the ticket. At Billy's, Mary learns the name of Jim's publisher, Leggett & Millard. In the publisher's office, Miss Millard informs Mary that Jim went West to finish a novel and suggests she return to Ireland, causing Mary to cry. When Ed's taxi doesn't start, he takes the St. Anthony statue out to get his tools, then unknowingly leaves the statue on the curb after getting the car to run. At the pier, Mary thanks Ed and tells him that the ship's captain will give him his money. Ed is about to pick up another fare, but as he opens the trunk, he sees Mary's box of letters and runs after her. On the ship, he finds her with her infant son Kevin. She relates that she came to America to find Jim so that the baby would not wind up in an orphan asylum. Impressed with her dedication, Ed tries to bribe an immigration official to let Mary stay until her husband arrives. Insulted, the official says Ed must come up with a $500 bond to insure that she appears at an immigration hearing and suggests that he use the cab to get a loan for the money. Despite the pain this creates, Ed arranges for the loan, then brings Mary and the baby to his apartment. They arrive as Mrs. Nielson is visiting with the Alberts, who leave in outrage when Ed says he has brought Mary and Kevin there to live. While Mrs. Nielson questions her son, Mary sneaks out with the baby. Ed finds the baby in a Catholic Church, and thinking Mary has jumped into the East River, he is about to break down in tears, when he hears her praying to St. Anthony for help in finding Jim. Ed brings Mary home, where Mrs. Nielson takes a liking to her, as she herself had a broken first marriage. Mary sees a news story on television about the St. Anthony statue, which has been found across from St. Patrick's Cathedral. As the reporter interviews bystanders, Mary recognizes Jim, who gives his address. Ed drives her there and waits below with the baby. Mary finds that the apartment belongs to Miss Millard, who admits she was once married to Jim herself. This upsets Mary, as she would not have married him if she had known because of her Catholic beliefs. Miss Millard reveals that Jim is now broke and has asked her to marry him again. She says she doesn't want him now, and sends Mary to see him in another room. When she returns to the cab, Mary tells Ed that Jim was happy to see her. Taking Kevin, she kisses Ed on the cheek and blesses him. She goes into the building, but after Ed drives off, she comes back out. He pulls in front of her and tells her to get in, saying he couldn't believe her phony story, and Mary realizes she has never seen him so happy. *Bachelors. Deception. Faith. Immigrants. Innocents. Irish. Mothers and sons. New York City. Romance. Searches. Taxicab drivers. African Americans. Authors. Catholic Church. Government officials. Infants. Irish Americans. Italian Americans. Loans. Pawnshops. Police. Prayer. Publishers and publishing. Reporters. Restaurants. Separation (Marital). Statues. Television programs.*

Note: The working title of this film was *Mr. Kopolpeck.* According to the film's pressbook, director Gregory Ratoff's wife saw the French film, *Sans laisser d'address,* on which *Taxi* was based, in Paris and told her husband it would be an excellent vehicle for him. Ratoff acquired the story rights in 1950 and sold them to Twentieth Century-Fox in 1951. Although Ratoff was originally slated to star in the film with Debra Paget, according to a *LAT* news item, after the story was reworked with a New York setting, Ratoff was considered too old for the rewritten leading role. The original French title was

translated as *Without a Forwarding Address.* The French film was produced by Ray Ventura, directed by Jean Paul Le Chanois, and starred Bertrand Blier and Daniele Delorme.

The pressbook for *Taxi* states that except for Dan Dailey and Constance Smith, all cast members were hired in New York. Many of the cast were stage actors from recent hit shows, including Geraldine Page, from *Summer and Smoke*; B. S. Pulley and Stubby Kaye, from *Guys and Dolls*; Anthony Ross, from *A Streetcar Named Desire*; Harry Clark, from *Wish You Were Here*; Jack Diamond, from *Kiss Me Kate*; and Neva Patterson, from *The Seven Year Itch.* The film was shot mostly outdoors, in Manhattan, Queens, Brooklyn and Bronx locations, including Wall Street, LaGuardia Airport, Radio City Music Hall, Fifth Avenue, Jackson Heights, Long Island, and St. Patrick's Cathedral. Location shooting took six weeks.

According to information in the MPAA/PCA Collection at the AMPAS Library, in the film's first outline, Mary was an unwed mother; when the outline was read by PCA officials in Mar 1952, PCA director Joseph I. Breen stated that the story appeared to be in violation of the Production Code because it "involves illicit sex and bastardy without any recognition of the moral problems involved in such a situation"; also, the fact of Mary's illegitimate child "appears to be taken in stride by all the characters in the story." Breen suggested that the filmmakers establish "that Mary and Jim had been married in Ireland and that he had come to America, leaving Mary behind and promising to send for her 'when the time was right.' Mary, not hearing from him, decides to come to America to surprise him." Breen went on to suggest that they make Jim already married when he meets Mary "therefore, so far as Mary is concerned, although she believes she was married, no marriage actually existed." Breen's first suggestion was used in the final film, while his second suggestion was changed substantially.

Box 17 Jan 1953. *Cue* 24 Jan 1953. *DV* 13 Jan 1953, p. 3. *Exh* 28 Jan 1953, p. 3456. *FD* 13 Jan 1953, p. 6. *Har* 17 Jan 1953, p. 11. *HR* 25 Jul 1952, p. 10. *HR* 22 Aug 1952, p. 11. *HR* 13 Jan 1953, p. 3. *LADN* 5 Mar 1953. *LAT* 20 Feb 1952, p. 3. *LAT* 5 Mar 1953. *MPD* 13 Oct 1952. *MPHPD* 17 Jan 1953, p. 1685. *Newsweek* 2 Feb 1953. *NYT* 13 Jul 1952. *NYT* 22 Jan 1953, p. 20. *Time* 2 Feb 1953. *Var* 28 Nov 1951. *Var* 2 Jul 1952. *Var* 14 Jan 1953, p. 6.

TAZA, SON OF COCHISE (Native Americans, Apache)
Universal-International Pictures Co., Inc. *Dist* Universal Pictures Co., Inc. Feb **1954** [©Universal Pictures Co.; 18 Feb 1954; LP3713]. Sd (Western Electric Recording); col (Technicolor). 7,109 ft. 79-80 min. PCA cert no. 16741.

Prod Ross Hunter. *Dir* Douglas Sirk. *Asst dir* Tom Shaw. [*Dial dir* Jack Daniels]. *Scr* George Zuckerman. *Story and adpt* Gerald Drayson Adams. *Dir of photog* Russell Metty. *Technicolor col consultant* William Fritzsche. *Art dir* Bernard Herzbrun and Emrich Nicholson. *Film ed* Milton Carruth. *Set dec* Russell A. Gausman and Oliver Emert. *Cost* Jay Morley, Jr. *Mus dir* Frank Skinner. *Sd* Leslie I. Carey and Glenn E. Anderson. *Hair stylist* Joan St. Oegger. *Makeup* Bud Westmore. [*Unit prod mgr* James Vaughn].

Cast: Rock Hudson (*Taza*), Barbara Rush (*Oona*), Gregg Palmer (*Captain Burnett*), Bart Roberts (*Naiche*), Morris Ankrum (*Grey Eagle*), Gene Iglesias (*Chato*), Richard Cutting (*Cy Hegan*), Ian MacDonald (*Geronimo*), Robert Burton (*General Crook*), Joe Sawyer (*Sgt. Hamma*), Lance Fuller (*Lt. Willis*), Brad Jackson (*Lt. Richards*), James Van Horn (*Skinya*), Charles Horvath (*Kocha*), Robert Hoy (*Lobo*), Barbara Burck (*Mary*), Dan White (*Tiswin Charlie*), [Jeff Chandler (*Cochise*)], [William Leslie (*Cavalry sergeant*)], [Edna Parrish, Seth T. Bigman (*Indians*)], [John Kay Hawks (*Soldier*)].

Western. [*Print viewed*]. In 1872, Chiricahua Apache chief Cochise and Gen. Howard sign a treaty, which brings a long sought peace to Arizona. The Chiricahua live quietly on a mountain reservation for three years, and as Cochise's death approaches, he bestows the leadership of his people on his son Taza. Cochise bids both Taza and his younger son Naiche to maintain the peace and defend the Chiricahua, but soon after the old chief's death, Naiche tries to kill Taza and angrily threatens to follow Geronimo in making war on the whites. Naiche wants to wed the beautiful Oona, a match that would please her warlike father Grey Eagle, but she is deeply in love with Taza, which further heightens the tension between the two brothers. Taza places a guard on Naiche, but Grey Eagle's renegades set him free. Naiche and his followers massacre a family of settlers, but Taza catches them and has them tied to posts and hanged in the sun. This Apache punishment is not sufficient for a Cavalry unit from nearby San Carlos Reservation, however. Capt. Burnett reminds Taza that under the terms of the treaty, the Chiricahua must go the San Carlos Reservation if any one of them attacks a white man. He then moves the prisoners to Fort Apache. Furious, Taza and his Chiricahua capture the fort. Speaking with Gen. Crook, Taza agrees to settle on San Carlos, but only if his people are given tools and seed, as well as the right to police themselves. Burnett's support of this idea earns him Taza's loyalty, and soon the Chiricahua leave their "beloved

mountains" to settle on the new reservation. Taza, wearing a Cavalry uniform, heads a group of Apache reservation police, and before long, Geronimo and some forty of his hungry and weary people also come to San Carlos. Geronimo and Grey Eagle, however, are determined to escape, and Grey Eagle tells Taza that he may only have Oona in exchange for guns and ammunition. Taza refuses this demand, and when he presents the old man with jewelry and other riches instead, Grey Eagle announces that Naiche has offered him a better gift—money with which to buy weapons and bullets. Unwilling to betray his father's memory and his people, Taza gives up his beloved Oona. Soon afterward, word comes that Geronimo has broken out of the reservation. Taza wants the Apache police to capture Geronimo, but Gen. Crook readies his own troops to subdue the rebel and confines Taza to the reservation. After rejecting the uniform for his own Apache apparel, Taza defies this order. Geronimo arms his followers and, with several other bands of Apaches, awaits the arrival of Gen. Crook and Capt. Burnett. Disregarding Burnett's warning, Crook leads the troops into a narrow and dangerous mountain pass, where they are attacked by Geronimo's combined forces. During the fierce battle that ensues, Grey Eagle is killed. Taza decides to aid the Cavalry, whereupon he and Geronimo fight. Taza ultimately forces Geronimo and the rest of the Apaches to surrender, and when Naiche refuses to throw down his weapons, it is Geronimo who shoots him. Taza extracts from Crook both an apology and a promise to send Geronimo to a faraway reservation. With his Apaches now able to live in peace, Taza embraces his future wife, Oona. *Apache Indians. Brothers. Hate. Indians of North America–Reservations. San Carlos Indian Reservation (AZ). Tribal chiefs. Ambushes. Arizona. Battles. Cochise. George Crook. Escapes. Fathers and daughters. Fort Apache Indian Reservation (AZ). Geronimo. Indians of North America. Knife fighting. Loyalty. Marriage. Massacres. Officers (Military). Romantic rivalry. Self-sacrifice. Treaties. United States–History–Indian campaigns. United States. Army. Cavalry. United States. Army. Military Police.*

Note: The working title of this film was *Son of Cochise.* Onscreen credits acknowledge the contribution of the National Park Service of the U.S. Dept. of the Interior, which cooperated with filming at Arches National Monument Park, near Moab, UT. Exteriors were also filmd in California, according to contemporary sources. The picture was available to exhibitors in 3-D, 2-D, and Moropticon 3-D, single-strip. Jeff Chandler, who plays Cochise in the film, also played him in Twentieth Century-Fox's 1950 film *Broken Arrow* and Universal's 1952 picture *Battle at Apache Pass* (see above entries). Although there is no evidence that Cochise had a son named Taza, in 1882, his son Nachise joined Geronimo, Chato, and other Apache leaders in repeatedly breaking out of reservations, conducting raids, and eluding generals George Crook and Nelson Miles. In 1886 Geronimo and his followers surrendered for the last time.

Box 30 Jan 1954. *DV* 20 Jan 1954, p. 3. *Exh* 27 Jan 1954, pp. 3689-90. *FD* 10 Jan 1954, p. 6. *Har* 23 Jan 1950, p. 14. *HR* 20 Jan 1954, p. 3. *MPHPD* 30 Jan 1954, pp. 2165-66. *Var* 20 Jan 1954, p. 6.

TE QUIERO CON LOCURA (Spanish language)
Fox Film Corp. *Dist* Twentieth Century-Fox Film Corp. **1935**; New York opening: 1 Nov 1935; Prod: 18 Mar–9 Apr 1935 [©20th Century-Fox Film Corp.; 29 Sep 1935; LP5823]. Sd (Western Electric Noiseless Recording); b&w. 7 reels, 6,312 ft. 70 min. Passed by the National Board of Review. PCA cert no. 882. Spanish language.
[*Prod* John Stone]. *Dirección de* [*Dir*] John J. Boland. [*Dial dir* Enrique de Rosas]. *Adaptación cinematográfica* [*Scr*] José López Rubio and Paul Perez. *Diálogo* [*Dial*] José López Rubio. [*Photog* Joseph MacDonald]. *Dirección musical* [*Mus dir*] Edward Kilenyi.
Song(s): "No están todos los que son," "Do re me fa sol por ti" and "La locumba," words and music by Raúl Roulien; "Sueños de princesa," words by José López Rubio, music by Troy Sanders.
Source: Based on the play *La cura de reposo* by Enrique García Velloso (Madrid, 22 Oct 1927).
Cast: ROSITA MORENO [(*Norma Carter*)], Raúl Roulien [(*Alberto Foster*)], Enrique de Rosas [(*Hugo Rock*)], Juan Torena [(*Harry*)], Carlos Villarías [(*Doctor Nutts*)], Romualdo Tirado [(*El juez*)], Lucio Villegas [(*Tío Daniel*)], Nenette Noriega [(*Sonia*)], Martín Garralaga [(*Manager*)], [Vernon Steele (*Doctor Preston*)], [Emilia Leovalli (*Tía Carolina*)], [Manuel Peluffo (*Willy McRay*)], [Enrique Acosta (*Coronel*)], [Ramón Muñoz (*El guardián*)], [José López Rubio (*El borracho*)], [Hermine Sterler (*Leontine*)], [Rudolf Carl (*Jefe de sección*)], [Elena Durán (*La enfermera*)], [Mildred Harris], [Bernice Mason].
Screwball comedy, with songs. [*Not viewed*]. Betrothed to her bilious and neurasthenic cousin, Willy McRay, Norma Carter feigns

insanity before her rich aunt and uncle in order to be committed to Dr. Nutts's sanitarium so that she can escape the union. Alberto Foster, another patient, pretends to be insane in order to avoid the wrath of his former mistress' husband, who has vowed to kill him as soon as Alberto is well enough to be a worthy opponent. Alberto meets Norma and invites her for drinks on his parked airplane, as alcohol is not permitted on the sanitarium grounds. Dr. Nutts learns of Alberto's flirtations and tells Norma that the clinic is filled with spies looking for people who are not really insane. Fearing that Alberto may be a spy, Norma behaves like a lunatic for him, but he is more charmed than ever by her madcap behavior and sneaks her out of the sanitarium for an evening on the town. The couple go to a cabaret in New York, and when Nutts discovers their absence, he pursues them with Harry, a sanitarium attendant and friend of Alberto. Hugo Rock, the jealous husband, appears at the club, and Alberto disguises himself with a false moustache. When the moustache falls off while he and Norma dance, Hugo screams and chases Alberto. Nutts arrives and joins the chase, and the couple are later found by police at Alberto's flat. At a court hearing, the greedy Dr. Nutts declares that Norma needs permanent care at his clinic and that Alberto is perfectly sane. The judge decides to have the couple observed by state "alienists" to determine their sanity or insanity. The alienists, who watch Alberto and Norma on a closed-circuit television monitor, report that they suffer from "incandescent love" and are quiet and harmless, but should be isolated. The cabaret owner, who wants restitution for his ruined business, Dr. Nutts, Norma's uncle, Harry and Hugo await the verdict, and when they begin to argue, the alienists accidentally change the channel and observe the group, whom they diagnose as furiously mad. The cabaret owner, Norma's uncle, and Hugo are then all committed. Later, Norma and Alberto, in a peaceful sanitarium-like setting, sing with their brood of lovely children about the sanity of insanity in a world filled with war and fascism. *Deception. Insanity. Romance. Sanitariums. Airplanes. Aunts. Cabarets. Chases. Disguise. Engagements. Infidelity. Judges. New York City. Psychiatrists. Spies. Television. Trials. Uncles.*

Note: The plot was based on a dialogue continuity in the Twentieth Century-Fox Produced Scripts Collection, and the onscreen credits were taken from a screen credit sheet in the Twentieth Century-Fox Records of the Legal Department, both of which are at the UCLA Theater Arts Library. The working title of the film was *Rest Cure.* The title was translated in reviews variously as *I Love You Madly* and *I'm Crazy About You.* According to information in the legal records, Enrique García Velloso, in collaboration with Pedro Muñoz Seca, revamped his play six months after it was produced. The new version, entitled *La cura,* was not used by the writers of the film. Also, in the correspondence in the legal records, producer John Stone states that he and Louis F. Moore, the head of Fox's Spanish Department, developed the plot line. A *DV* news item notes that with this film, Fox was trying out John J. Boland, formerly an assistant director, as a director and that they planned to try out at least two other assistant directors as directors of Spanish language films.

CM Aug 1935, p. 478. *DV* 15 Mar 1935, p. 4. *DV* 19 Mar 1935, p. 3. *FD* 5 Nov 1935, p. 7. *NYT* 4 Nov 1935, p. 24.

TEARING THROUGH (Chinese Americans)
Richard Talmadge Productions. *Dist* Film Booking Offices of America. 12 Apr **1925** [©Carlos Productions, Inc.; 17 Apr 1925; LP21361]. Si; b&w. 5 reels, 4,714 ft.
Pres A. Carlos. *Dir* Arthur Rosson. *Cont* Frederick Stowers. *Photog* William Marshall.
Cast: Richard Talmadge (*Richard Jones*), Kathryn McGuire (*Constance Madison*), Herbert Prior (*District attorney*), Frank Elliott (*Mr. Greer*), Arthur Rankin (*Bob Madison*), Marcella Daly (*Polly*), Dave Morris (*Chester*).
Crime, Melodrama. When District Attorney Johnson is seemingly unable to break up a gang of dope smugglers, his assistant, Richard Jones, sets out on his own to investigate the lawbreakers. In the course of his snooping, he discovers that Bob Madison, his sweetheart's brother, is a drug addict, caught in the clutches of a gang. Richard is responsible for Bob's regeneration, and together they find that Greer, who is Richard's rival for the affections of Constance Madison, is, in fact, the proprietor of an opium den in Chinatown. Constance is kidnapped by Greer, and Richard rescues her from a narcotics hellhole in Chinatown. Richard proves that the D. A. is being bribed by the drug peddlers, and, as a reward for his good work, Richard is appointed the new district attorney. *Brothers and sisters. Chinatowns. Chinese Americans. District attorneys. Drug addicts. Opium. Smuggling.*

FD 3 May 1925. MPW 9 May 1925.

THE TELEGRAPH TRAIL (Native Americans)

Warner Bros. Pictures, Inc.; A Four Star Western. *Dist* Vitagraph Pictures, Inc. 18 Mar **1933** [©Vitagraph Pictures, Inc.; 15 Mar 1933; LP3740]. Sd (Western Electric System); b&w. 5,090 ft. 54 or 59-60 min. Passed by the National Board of Review. PCA cert no. 2587-R [27 Aug 1936].

Pres LEON SCHLESINGER. *Assoc prod* Sid Rogell. *Dir* Tenny Wright. *Scr and dial* Kurt Kempler. *Photog* Ted McCord. *Film ed* Wm. Clemens. *Mus score* Leo F. Forbstein.

Cast: JOHN WAYNE (*John Trent*), DUKE [(*A horse*)], Frank McHugh (*Tippy*), Marceline Day (*Alice*), Otis Harlan (*Zeke Keller*), Albert J. Smith (*Gus Lynch*), Yakima Canutt (*High Wolf*), Lafe McKee (*Lafe*), [Clarence Geldert].

Western. [*Print viewed*]. A team of men working on a cross-country telegraph line are attacked by Indians. Just before he is killed, one of the linemen manages to get a message through to the fort, indicating that a white man is behind the attacks. When Zeke Keller and his niece Alice pass the scene of the attack, Alice agrees to deliver a package of letters belonging to one of the dying men. Scout John Trent and Tippy, one of the soldiers, are sent to capture the white leader. Gus Lynch, the man behind the Indian attacks, is determined to maintain his shipping monopoly by preventing the completion of the telegraph. He also tries to force Alice to marry him, but she protests that she is already engaged. To prove it, she pulls out the picture of John that was included in the dead man's packet. Right after she makes that announcement, John and Tippy walk into Zeke's store. John is convinced she is crazy when she throws her arms around his neck. That night, John calls a meeting asking for volunteers to bring supplies to the telegraph workers. Despite Lynch's efforts to dissuade them, the men plan to leave in the morning. Alice overhears Lynch plan an Indian raid and tries to warn John, but remembering their last encounter, he runs in the other direction. Hiding from Lynch, Alice stows away. She pins a note to one of the boxes in the wagon warning of the raid. With this information, John is able to ward off the attack. When Alice is discovered, Tippy thinks she is a spy for Lynch, but John recognizes her handwriting and realizes they owe her some thanks. Lynch convinces a large band of Indians to attack the train, telling them that the telegraph lines will bring soldiers who will kill them. In the midst of the attack, John manages to get a message through to the fort. The Indians are about to claim victory when the soldiers arrive. High Wolf, Lynch's Indian henchman, is wounded. When Lynch refuses to stop and help him, High Wolf kills him. The telegraph line is completed, and John is given an award, but his real reward comes when Alice agrees to become his "commanding officer." *Indians of North America. Murder. Scouts (Frontier). Telegraph. The West. Deception. Horses. Letters. Nieces. Romance. Soldiers. Wagon trains.*

Note: Press notes in the copyright records indicate that Indians from various western reservations were used in the battle scenes. Western Union Telegraph Co. loaned an early telegraph instrument to the filmmakers. Modern sources list Slim Whitaker, Frank Ellis and Jack Kirk in the cast.

FD 29 Mar 1933, p. 8. MPD 29 Mar 1933, p. 5. Var 4 Apr 1933, p. 38.

THE TELL-TALE STEP (Italian Americans)

Thomas A Edison, Inc. *Dist* K-E-S-E Service. 28 May **1917** [©Thomas A. Edison, Inc.; 26 Apr 1917; LP10675]. Si; b&w. 5 reels, 4,698 ft.

Dir Burton George. *Scen* William Addison Lathrop. *Cam* Charles Gilson.

Cast: Pat O'Malley (*Hugh Graham*), Shirley Mason (*Lucia*), Guido Collucci (*Giovanni Pallazzi*), Charles Sutton (*Luigi*), Bob Huggins (*Pietro*), Nellie Grant (*Rosetta*), Bigelow Cooper (*Dimitri*), Sally Crute (*Beverly Winton*), Jessie Stevens (*Hugh's mother*), Leonora Von Ottinger (*Mrs. Arbuthnot*), Grace Morrissey (*Miss Stryver*), Robert Brower (*Doctor Oppenheim*).

Crime, Drama. Giovanni Pallazzi, a former member of the Black Hand, an Italian criminal organization, comes to America with his blind daughter Lucia and prospers. Hearing of his success, his former associates demand that he aid in their support. Giovanni refuses, and the organization decrees that he shall die. Luigi, the leader, comes to America and tries to force Lucia to marry him, but she refuses. While praying one night, her father is killed. Though blind, her hearing is acute and she notices a peculiar cadence in the walk of her father's slayer. Luigi now takes charge and forces her into the street to play her violin for gratuities. After she is picked up by the prosecuting attorney, her eyesight is restored by physicians. When the police apprehend Luigi, Lucia puts on a blindfold and is able to identify him as her father's killer by the sound of his step. *Black Hand (United States). Blindness. Criminals. Immigrants. Italians. Cures. Operations, Surgical. Prayer. Street entertainers. Violinists.*

Note: Working titles for this film were *Lucia* and *Blind Justice*.

ETR 2 Jun 1917, p. 1824. Motog 16 Jun 1917, p. 1339. MPW 9 Jun 1917, p. 1625. MPW 16 Jun 1917, p. 1837. NYDM 2 Jun 1917, p. 29. Var 2 Jun 1917, p. 23. Wid's 31 May 1917, pp. 348-49.

THE TEMPLE OF DUSK (Japanese Americans)

Haworth Pictures Corp. *Dist* Mutual Film Corp. 20 Oct **1918** [©Haworth Pictures Corp.; 16 Sep 1918; LU12866]. Si; b&w. 5 reels.

Dir James Young. *Story* Frances Marion. *Art dir* Milton Menasco.

Cast: Sessue Hayakawa (*Akira*), Jane Novak (*Ruth Vale*), Lewis Willoughby (*Edward Markham*), Mary Jane Irving (*Blossom*), Sylvia Bremer (*Adrienne Chester*), Henry Barrows (*Pembroke Wilson*).

Drama. Akira, a Japanese poet descended from an old samurai family, loves American Ruth Vale, who was placed in the care of Akira's father when her missionary parents died. Ruth returns Akira's affections until she meets Edward Markham, but the American proves an unfaithful husband. Three years after their marriage, Ruth becomes gravely ill while Edward amuses himself with his new lover, Adrienne Chester, but Akira comforts the dying woman with the promise that he will protect her little daughter Blossom. Later Edward marries his mistress, and, with Akira in charge of Blossom, they return to America, where Adrienne renews her old affair with Pembroke Wilson. One evening, Edward discovers Pembroke making love to his wife and kills him, but Akira accepts the blame to shield Blossom from humiliation. Troubled by a presentiment that Blossom needs him, Akira breaks out of his cell one stormy night and, although a guard shoots him, he manages to reach the girl's home. Carrying her in from the rain, Akira plays with the child until, his strength finally deserting him, he dies. *Foster parents. Infidelity. Japanese. Japanese Americans. Self-sacrifice. Americans in foreign countries. Disease. Gunshot wounds. Japan. Missionaries. Mistresses. Murder. Poets. Prison escapes. Samurai.*

Note: The 1920 *MPSD* lists this film among the credits of William Worthington, who directed many films for Haworth Pictures Corp. According to an early news item, Worthington and Young planned to alternate directorial chores for the company.

ETR 12 Oct 1918, p. 1615. MPN 28 Sep 1918, pp. 1946-47. MPN 5 Oct 1918, p. 2259. MPW 28 Sep 1918, p. 1919. MPW 19 Oct 1918, p. 452. NYDM 19 Oct 1918, p. 591. Var 1 Nov 1918, p. 38.

TEMPTATION (African Americans)

Micheaux Pictures Corp. *Dist* Micheaux Pictures Corp. **1936**. Sd; b&w. Length undetermined.

Pres Oscar Micheaux.

Cast: Andrew S. Bishop, Ethel Moses, Lorenzo Tucker, Hilda Rogers, "Slick" Chester.

African American, Drama. [*Not viewed*]. [No contemporary information about the plot of this film has been found.]. *African Americans.*

Note: Although no information on the length of this film has been found, it is presumed to be a feature. According to modern sources, this production, directed by Oscar Micheaux, had a cast including Bernice Gray, Ida Forest, Larry Seymour, Lillian Fitzgerald, the Pope Sisters, Dot and Dash, and Bobby Hargreaves and his Kit Kat Club Orchestra. Modern sources note that the plot concerns a light-skinned black model who tries to change her life and live morally, despite underworld involvement and a gangster who is determined to stop her reformation. A biography on actor Lorenzo Tucker indicates that the movie was shot at Fort Lee, NJ, and that Micheaux delayed production until star Andrew Bishop was on vacation from a job he had taken with the city of Cleveland, OH. The picture reportedly cost about $15,000 to produce, with $2,000 going for actors' salaries.

TEN CENTS A DANCE (*foreign version*) see **CARNE DE CABARET**

TEN MINUTES TO KILL *see* **TEN MINUTES TO LIVE**

TEN MINUTES TO LIVE (African Americans)

Micheaux Pictures Corp. *Dist* State Rights. Mar **1932**. Sd; b&w. Length undetermined.

Pres A. BURTON RUSSELL. *Dir* OSCAR MICHEAUX. *Asst dir* A. B. Comathiere. *Adpt and dial* Oscar Micheaux. *Photog* Lester Lang. *Master of Ceremonies* Donald Heywood. *Mus arr and floor show staged by* Donald Heywood.

Source: Based on the short stories "The Faker," "The Killer," and "Harlem After Midnight" (author and publication undetermined).

Cast: Lawrence Chenault, A. B. Comathiere, Laura Bowman, Willor Lee Guilford [(*Letha Watkins*)], Tressie Mitchell, Mabel Garrett, Carl Mahon, Galle De Gaston, George Williams, Lorenzo Tucker, [William A. Clayton, Jr. (*Morvis*)].

African American, Drama. [*Print viewed*]. In response to Gary Martin's inquiry for a girl to appear in a cowboy picture, Bess suggests he contact Ida Morton at the Lybia Club. That evening, at the club, during the Primetime Revue's chorus girl dance, Anthony proposes marriage to young Letha Watkins, despite her godfather's disapproval. Two songs are performed, one formal, the other in exotic costume. When Martin learns that both the singers are named Ida, he chooses the latter girl, even though she was not the one whom Bess recommended. Meanwhile, the godfather tells Martin to expect to see a murder in the club and explains his prediction by telling him Letha's story: Fifteen years ago, Letha had a baby and was spurned by a philandering, jobless man named Morvis, to whom she thought she was married. After telling Letha that theirs was a dog license, not a marriage license, they had a struggle and he shot her. Morvis' fake alibi led to his acquittal, and today he continues to lure girls to their ruin. As the godfather is finishing the story, Letha approaches Morvis' table and shoots him, but only slightly wounds him. Afterward, Letha receives a note from Morvis which says that she has "ten minutes to live." Letha tells Anthony that Morvis has followed her across the country and is intent on killing her because he thinks that she had framed him earlier. While preparing to kill Letha, Morvis drinks with his mistress, Charlotte Evans. Morvis abandons his plans to kill Letha when a letter from his mother explains that it was Charlotte, not Letha, who betrayed him, and that Charlotte has mentioned his presence to the police for an anticipated reward. Morvis strangles Charlotte, and Letha and Anthony leave the nightclub safely. *Marriage. Murder. Nightclubs. Philanderers. Revenge. Actors and actresses. Ambition. Chases. Chorus girls. Godparents. Letters. Proposals (Marital). Prostitution. Singers. Threats.*

Note: Although the onscreen credits contain a copyright statement, records show that the picture was not registered for copyright. Much of the film was shot silent. Willor Lee Guilford as the "Escape King" and Wm. A. Clayton, Jr. as "Morvis" are introduced in silent-film style titles. According to modern sources, one of the short stories on which the film is based was titled "The Father." On 1 Feb 1932, *FD* announced that photography on *Ten Minutes to Live* had been completed, and noted that the film was the second in a planned series of six Micheaux Pictures Corp. features with an all-black cast. The first in the series was *Veiled Aristocrats* (see below). The film may also have been known under the title *Ten Minutes to Kill.*

FD 1 Feb 1932, p. 2.

TEN NIGHTS IN A BARROOM (African Americans)

Colored Players Film Corp. **1926?;** Prod: Jun 1926. Si; b&w. 7 reels, 6,700 ft.

Cast: Charles Gilpin (*Joe Morgan*), Myra Burwell, Lawrence Chenault (*Simon Slade*), Harry Henderson (*Judge's son*), William A. Clayton, Jr. (*His rival for Slade's daughter*), Ethel Smith (*Slade's daughter*), Arline Mickey, Edward Moore, William Johnson, Florence Kennedy, William Milton, Sam Sadler, Roxanna Mickelby.

African American, Melodrama. In the small town of Cederville, Joe Morgan loses his gin mill and other property to Simon Slade, who then becomes a vice lord. Morgan becomes a drunkard as a result. Slade is also responsible for the downfall of other respectable townsfolk. When Slade throws a glass at Morgan's head, it hits Morgan's little daughter instead and she dies. Morgan pursues Slade, who also dies. The deaths lead Morgan to change, and after he stops drinking, he is elected mayor. *African Americans. Alcoholics. Death and dying. Fathers and daughters. Moral corruption. Regeneration. Saloons. Small town life. Elections. Mayors.*

Note: The film was shot at the Colored Players' Film Corp. studio in Philadelphia. A license for exhibition in New York state was granted on 27 Dec 1926, according to information in the NYSA, although an exact release date has not been determined. According to a *California Eagle* news item, the film had its western premiere on 28 Oct 1928 in Los Angeles.

California Eagle 25 Jun 1926, p. 7. *California Eagle* 26 Oct 1928.

TEN YEARS A COUNTERSPY see MAN ON A STRING

TENDER COMRADE (German Americans)

RKO Radio Pictures, Inc. *Dist* RKO Radio Pictures, Inc. **1944;** World premiere in Los Angeles: 29 Dec 1943; Prod: 13 Aug—27 Oct 1943; retakes 12 Dec 1943, 7 Jan—9 Jan 1944, 20 Jan 1944 [©RKO

Radio Pictures, Inc.; 19 Dec 1943; LP12590]. Sd (RCA Sound System); b&w. 9,204 ft. 101-102 min. PCA cert no. 9586.

Prod David Hempstead. *Assoc prod* Sherman Todd. *Dir* Edward Dmytryk. *Asst dir* Harry Scott. *Wrt* Dalton Trumbo. *Dir of photog* Russell Metty. *Spec eff* Vernon L. Walker. *Art dir* Albert S. D'Agostino and Carroll Clark. *Ed* Roland Gross. *Set dec* Darrell Silvera and Al Fields. *Miss Rogers' cost des by* Edith Head. *Gowns* Renie. *Mus dir* C. Bakaleinikoff. *Mus* Leigh Harline. *Rec* Roy Meadows. *Re-rec* James G. Stewart. *Makeup artist* Mel Berns. [*Stand-in* J. Vernon, P. McCoy, R. Campbell, D. Panter, Bob Wright, Mel Merrihugh, George Spencer, William Swingley, N. Harden, G. Bank and L. Lang].

Cast: Ginger Rogers [(*Jo Jones*)], Robert Ryan [(*Chris Jones*)], Ruth Hussey [(*Barbara Thomas*)], Patricia Collinge [(*Helen Stacey*)], Mady Christians [(*Manya*)], Kim Hunter [(*Doris White Dumbrowski*)], Jane Darwell [(*Mrs. Henderson*)], Richard Martin [(*Mike Dumbrowski*)], [Mary Forbes (*Jo's mother*)], [Richard Gaines (*Waldo Pierson*)], [Patti Brill (*Western Union delivery person*)], [Euline Martin (*Baby*)], [Edward Fielding (*Doctor*)], [Claire Whitney (*Nurse*)], [Donald Davis, Bobby Anderson (*Boys*)], [Jane Farrar], [Tom Burton], [Michael Road], [Fred Mercer].

Homefront, Drama. [*Print viewed*]. Granted a one-night leave before being shipped out for overseas duty, soldier Chris Jones visits his wife Jo. After an affectionate reunion, Jo and Chris bid farewell at the train station and dream of the day that Chris will return home. Jo collapses, sobbing, as Chris's train departs, but composes herself enough to go to her job at the Douglas Aircraft Factory. While eating lunch with three of her fellow workers, Jo proposes that they pool their resources and rent a house together. The three women: Barbara Thomas, an embittered, unfaithful wife whose husband Pete is in the Navy; Doris Dumbrowski, whose sudden wedding to her soldier boyfriend on the eve of his overseas departure prevented them from consummating their marriage; and Helen Stacey, whose husband and son are both in the service, accept Jo's idea, and they move in together, vowing to run their household as a democracy. Alone in her bedroom that night, Jo looks longingly at Chris's photograph and fondly remembers the day he proposed: Jo is drying her hair in her parents' backyard when Chris comes to ask her to marry him. Although sweethearts since childhood, Jo accuses Chris of flirting with other girls and picks a fight with him. As Jo furiously brushes her hair, Chris finally convinces her to say yes. Jo's thoughts then return to the present and she drifts off to sleep. The next day, as the women struggle to clean house, they decide to advertise for a housekeeper. Manya, a German woman who left her homeland because her people "murdered democracy," applies for the job. When Manya tells them that her husband is fighting in the U.S. Army and that she views keeping house for the four defense workers as part of her contribution to the war effort, the women decide to hire Manya and pool their earnings, splitting in five parts whatever is left after paying expenses. When the butcher sends the women an extra pound of bacon, Manya becomes indignant and denounces the idea of hoarding. After Barbara questions the necessity of rationing and preaches isolationism, Jo accuses her of not considering the consequences of her ideas. Their argument is interrupted when Barbara's date arrives. Although the others disapprove of Barbara's infidelity, she ignores their objections. Barbara is about to leave on her date when a radio broadcast announces the sinking of the aircraft carrier *Yorktown* during the Battle of Midway and names Pete as one of the sailors who is missing in action. The news upsets Barbara, who cancels her date, and makes Jo feel guilty about her harsh words. Later that night, while she talks to Chris's photograph, Jo confesses her regrets about snapping at Barbara and remembers the time her quick temper was aimed at her husband: One night after dinner, Jo feels ignored because Chris is reading a newspaper article. In a bid for attention, she tries to dig a splinter out of his hand with a needle, and when he suggests that she sew the missing buttons on his shirt instead, Jo has a tantrum and complains about his working long hours. After Chris explains that he is trying to save some money to insure her financial security when he goes to war, Jo issues him an ultimatum: either he works less or she will get a job. When Chris agrees to Jo's terms, they make up and Jo's thoughts return to the present. One afternoon, Jo skips work and when she returns home, she announces that she is pregnant. After giving birth to her son, whom she names Chris Jr., Jo gazes at Chris's photo and remembers the time that she was practicing diaper folding: After Jo explains to her surprised husband that she is

not pregnant but bought the diapers for a friend's baby shower, Chris confides that he wants to postpone having a child because he fears that he will soon be drafted and wants to be present when the baby is born. Jo is brought back to the present by the sound of her baby's cries. When Jo returns home from the hospital, Barbara tells her that Pete has been located in a Honolulu hospital and vows to renew their marriage. Soon after, Helen receives a letter from her husband with the proud news that their son has been promoted to major. Next, Mike surprises Doris by coming home for an unexpected leave. Mike's presence reminds the other women of their missing husbands, and they scramble to cook him a meal consisting of their husbands' favorite dishes. As Mike and Doris share their first married evening together, the doorbell rings. Jo answers it and immediately knows that something is wrong when she is handed a telegram. Upstairs in her bedroom, Jo opens the telegram and reads the news that Chris has been killed in battle. Cradling her infant son, Jo remembers Chris's farewell words and shows the baby the photograph of his father. After comforting little Chris with the thought that his father died so that he could live in a better world, Jo leaves the room and tells herself that "she'll take it on the chin like a good guy, like a soldier's wife should." *Marriage. Patriotism. War preparedness. Women defense plant workers. Democracy. Germans. Hospitals. Housekeepers. Infants. Infidelity. Photographs. Rationing in wartime. Telegrams. Transformation. Widows.*

Note: The film opens with the following poem titled "My Wife" written by Robert Louis Stevenson: "Teacher, Tender Comrade, Wife. A fellow farer true through life. Heart-whole and soul-free. The August Father gave to me." A news item in *HR* credits Harold Lewis as assistant director, but his participation in the released film has not been confirmed. Materials contained in the RKO Archives Production Files at the UCLA Arts Library-Special Collections add that Katina Paxinou was originally slated to play the role of "Manya." Ruth Hussey was borrowed from M-G-M and Kim Hunter from David O. Selznick's company to appear in this film. Modern sources credit John Miehle with still photography. According to materials contained in the RKO Archives Script Files at the UCLA Arts Library-Special Collections, RKO shot several different endings for this film. The picture originally concluded with "Jo's" "Little Guy" speech to her baby. According to the *LAT* review and the final script dated 4 Sep 1943, this ending was shown at the film's Los Angeles premiere on 29 Dec 1943. Although the film was not nationally released until mid-1944, RKO screened the film in Los Angeles in 1943 in order to qualify Rogers' performance for an Academy Award. (She did not receive an award or nomination.)

According to a news item in *HR*, in Jan 1944, the studio decided to shoot new footage to emphasize the "chin-up" qualities that motivate "Jo" to continue her job as a war-worker despite the tragedy that has befallen her. In one of the endings contained in the Script Files, after learning of "Chris's" death, Jo joins her fellow workers at the plant. The final released version of the film ends with Jo's "chin-up speech" on the stairs followed by a long shot of "Jo" and "Chris" walking hand-in-hand on a hilltop. An Aug 1943 news item in *HR* notes that the studio considered changing the title for fear that the audience would think that the film was a story about Russia.

In 1947, Rogers' mother, Lela Rogers, testifed at a HUAC hearing that screenwriter Dalton Trumbo was a Communist and that the film was an example of Communist propaganda. According to a 1947 *NYT* article, at that hearing, Robert Stripling, the committee investigator, testified that Rogers refused to say the lines "share and share alike-that's democracy" because she believed they contained Communist overtones. Trumbo and director Edward Dmytryk were members of the so-called "Hollywood 10," who refused to testify about Communist infiltration in the motion picture industry. For their refusal to cooperate, they were convicted of contempt of Congress and sentenced to one year in prison and a $1,000 fine. After his release from prison, Dmytryk went into self-imposed exile in England, where he directed three films. In 1951, he returned to the United States and gave testimony in the second round of committee hearings. As a result of that testimony, he was removed from the industry's blacklist. For additional information about HUAC, see above entry for *Crossfire*. Olivia De Havilland and June Duprez starred in a 22 Jan 1945 *Lux Radio Theatre* broadcast of the story.

Box 8 Jan 1944. DV 29 Dec 1943, pp. 3, 15. FD 29 Dec 1943, p. 8. HR 31 Aug 1943, p. 3, 9. HR 26 Nov 1943, p. 5. HR 29 Dec 1943, p. 3. HR 13 Jan 1944, p. 2. HR 5 Jun 1944, p. 6. LAT 30 Dec 1943. MPH 1 Jan 1944. MPHPD 25 Dec 1943, p. 1635. MPHPD 1 Jan 1944, p. 1693. NYT 2 Jun 1944, p. 21. NYT 15 May 1947. Var 29 Dec 1943, p. 8.

TENDERFEET (African Americans)
Midnight Productions. **1928.** Si; b&w. Length undetermined. [Feature length assumed.].
Dir Spencer Williams. *Orig story and asst title wrt* Spencer Williams.
Cast: Spencer Bell, Mildred Washington, Flora Washington, John Turner, Richard Frazier, Onest Conley, Douglas Carter, Cliff Ingram, Oscar Morgan, James Robinson, Spencer Williams.
Comedy, African American. [No information about the precise nature of the plot has been found.]. *African Americans.*

Note: This film was also known as *Tender Feet*. According to a news item in *California Eagle*, it was made on the Pacific coast.
California Eagle 27 Jul 1928.

THE TENDERFOOT (Native Americans)
Vitagraph Co. of America; A Blue Ribbon Feature. *Dist* Greater Vitagraph (V-L-S-E). 3 Dec **1917** [©Vitagraph Co. of America; 30 Nov 1917; LP11775]. Si; b&w. 5 reels.
Dir William Duncan. *Scen* George H. Plympton. *Cam* W. Steve Smith, Jr.
Source: Based on the short story "The Tenderfoot" by Alfred Henry Lewis.
Cast: William Duncan (*Jim*), Carol Halloway (*Cynthia of the West*), Joe Ryan ("*Smiling Jack*" *Douglas*), Florence Dye (*Ellen of the East*), Walter L. Rodgers (*Mr. Rogers*), Charles Wheelock (*Rogers' partner*), Hattie Buskirk (*Mrs. Rucker*), Fred Forrester (*The exhorting evangelist*).
Western. To escape the pain of a failed love affair, Jim goes to Wolfville, a rough Western town populated by gamblers and Indians. Shortly after he meets Cynthia, a sweet-natured local girl, Ellen, his former lover, arrives from the East and flirts with an Indian to make him jealous. The Indian, who takes Ellen's attentions seriously, sends her some ponies, which she accepts unwittingly as a gift. When she discovers that by Indian custom her acceptance amounts to a marriage agreement, she turns to Jim, promising to marry him in exchange for a way out. Jim kills the Indian in a duel, but Ellen reneges on the deal and jilts him once again. In the gambling saloon, "Smiling Jack" Douglas plots to kill Jim, but Cynthia intercedes by replacing his gun's bullets with blanks. To "Smiling Jack's" surprise, Jim resists his shots and charges him, eventually driving him from the town. His courage proven, the tenderfoot wins the heart and hand of Cynthia. *Dudes. Fights. Indians of North America. Duels. Gifts. Horses. Miscegenation. Saloons.*

Note: This film was the second of Alfred H. Lewis' "Wolfville" stories to be brought to the screen. *Dead Shot Baker*, released in 1917, was the first (see *AFI Catalog of Feature Films, 1911-20*; F1.0969). "Wolfville" stories were first collected and published in New York in 1897. Many of the same cast members were used in both productions, including William Duncan, who was also the director of both, and Carol Halloway.
ETR 8 Dec 1917, p. 59. Motog 15 Dec 1917, p. 1265. MPN 15 Dec 1917, p. 4225, 4228. MPW 15 Dec 1917, p. 1642, 1679. NYDM 8 Dec 1917, p. 22. Wid's 6 Dec 1917, p. 780.

THE TENDERFOOT (1948) *see* **THE DUDE GOES WEST**

TENGO FE EN TI (Spanish language)
Victoria Films, Inc. *Dist* RKO Radio Pictures, Inc. Jul **1940.** Sd; b&w. 66 min. Spanish language.
Prod Melville Shauer and William Gordon. *Dir* John Reinhardt. *Scr* Paul Gerard Smith and Archibald Anderson. *Orig story* Carmen V. Brown and John Reinhardt. *Adpt and addl dial* José López Rubio and Paco Moreno. *Photog* Arthur Martinelli. *Film ed* George McGuire.
Song(s): "Margaritas" and "Canción de cuna," music by Melville Shauer and Rosita Moreno, lyrics by Paco Moreno.
Cast: Rosita Moreno (*Anna Tabor/María Ratyani*), José Crespo (*Rodolfo Rey*), Romualdo Tirado (*León León*), Franco Puglia (*Enrico Buriani*), Ascension Moreno, Emilia Leovalli, Martín Garralaga, Carlos Villarías, José Peña "Pepet", Leonid Kinsky, Rosita Granada, José Luis Tortosa.
Drama. [*Not viewed*]. Enrico Buriani, surpised by the camera in his garden in the Hollywood hills, relates the story of his lost love: A generation before, he was a great dance master at the Royal Opera House in Budapest. There he trained and fell in love with his best ballet pupil, Anna Tabor. In the middle of her debut, she fainted and fell, breaking her ankle and Buriani's heart. Not only would she never be able to dance again, but the accident also resulted in the revelation that she had secretly married a young guard officer. Heartbroken Buriani leaves Budapest at once. Six years later, in Paris, he finds María, the orphaned daughter of Anna. Buriani adopts the little girl, who grows to resemble her beautiful mother. In order to serve his everlasting love for Anna, Buriani decides to make María the great ballerina that her mother might have been. After years of wandering in Europe, they come to Hollywood, where Buriani sets up a fifth-rate dancing academy and works as an extra at the studios. María, tempted by the rhythms she hears from a dancing school across the street, and wanting to help support the household, decides to register with an agent and auditions at a low-class café, where she attracts the interest of Rodolfo Rey, a successful young motion picture

director. Rey convinces the girl to work towards a career in motion pictures, but María finds it difficult to conceal her duplicity from her foster father. While working as an extra one day, Buriani discovers María taking a screen test. Furious, he locks her out of the house, but María decides to continue with Rey's plan, hoping that her foster father will eventually come to support her endeavors. When she and Rey fall in love and decide to marry, they go to tell Buriani the good news, only to discover that he has been dispossessed for non-payment of rent. María pays the rent, and begins to search for Buriani, but without success. Meanwhile, Buriani learns from his landlady that María has paid the rent and, blinded with rage, sets out for the studio to kill Rey. Entering the set, Buriani sees Maria playing the role of Anna, dancing her mother's ballet in the setting of the Royal Opera House at Budapest. The vision of María as Anna dispels Buriani's anger, and when he sees María faltering in her dance, he helps her. Overjoyed at the reunion, María dances magnificently, fulfilling Buriani's dream and vindicating Rey's judgement. From his garden today, Buriani concludes his story by revealing that María and Rey are now happily married, just as a message arrives that Maria has given birth to a baby daughter. *Dance teachers. Dancers. Foster parents. Unrequited love. Adoption. Ballerinas. Budapest (Hungary). Hollywood (CA). Landladies. Motion picture actors and actresses. Motion picture directors. Orphans.*

Note: According to a 1937 news item in *HR*, Victoria Films was organized by actress Rosita Moreno in order to produce this picture, and modern sources indicate that the film may have been filmed partially at that time at the Educational Studios in Hollywood, then resumed in 1939. The *Var* review notes that Melville Shauer, the head of Victoria Films and husband of Rosita Moreno, was a former associate producer at Paramount. This was his only Spanish language production. The film, which cost $60,000 to produce, was shown in Spanish without English subtitles. The title was translated as "I Believe in You."

FD 3 May 1937, p. 6. *HR* 19 Feb 1937, p. 4. *HR* 8 Jul 1940, p. 4. *HR* 9 Sep 1940, p. 3. *Var* 17 Jul 1940, p. 18.

TENNESSEE WILLIAMS' BABY DOLL *see* **BABY DOLL**

EL TENORIO DEL HAREM (Spanish language)

Universal Pictures Corp.; A Stanley Bergerman Production. *Dist* Universal Pictures Corp. 1931; San José, Costa Rica opening: 25 Jun 1931; San Juan, Puerto Rico opening: 15 Aug 1931; Prod: Jan—Feb 1931. Sd; b&w. 7 reels. 65 min. Spanish language.

Pres Carl Laemmle. *Supv* Paul Kohner. *Dir* Kurt Neumann. *Dial dir* Eduardo Arozamena. *Story* Francis J. Martin and James Mulhauser. *Spanish dial* Gabriel Argüelles. *Photog* Harry Neumann. *Art dir* Thomas F. O'Neill. *Sd supv* C. Roy Hunter.

Cast: Slim Summerville (*El corneta*), Lupita Tovar (*Fátima*), Tom Kennedy (*El sargento*), Manuel Arbó (*El capitán*), Eduardo Arozamena (*El mercader*), José Peña "Pepet" (*Un soldado*).

Comedy. [*Not viewed*]. During World War I, a bugler and a sergeant are great friends, except when they are both after the same woman. After swearing eternal love to all their girl friends in Russia, they leave for a new base in Arabia, where just touching a young woman is a crime punishable by marriage or death. During their free time, the two friends decide to take a look at the city and, elbowing their way through a crowd of soldiers watching a performance by a fakir, discover Fátima, the most delightful woman they could possibly imagine. The bugler and sergeant engage in a private war to win Fátima and the bugler wins. However, Fátima's irate father demands that the army officials hand over the bugler to him as he must marry Fátima. On hearing mention of marriage, the bugler takes off and the sergeant wins Fátima. However, nine months later, a baby arrives looking remarkably like the losing suitor. *Arab countries. Officers (Military). Philanderers. Romantic rivalry. Soldiers. Fakirs. Fathers and daughters. Infants. Marriage. Russia. World War I.*

Note: Universal originally intended to make Spanish-language versions of two short English-language films, *Arabian Knights* and *Let's Play*, which were directed by Stephen Roberts and starred Slim Summerville and Tom Kennedy. In Jan 1931, after production of the Spanish version of the former film, which was called *Caballeros árabes*, was completed and shooting of the latter film was in progress, the studio decided to combine the two Spanish-language versions into a feature production and shoot additional footage to make the film 65 minutes. Additional scenes were shot in Feb 1931. While it appears that the two-reel *Caballeros árabes* was edited, it does not seem likely that a Spanish-language version of *Let's Play* was ever edited. It seems that the feature, *El tenorio del harem*, contains nearly all of the unreleased Spanish version of *Let's Play*, but only a few scenes from *Caballeros árabes*. With the exception of the dialogue director and cast, all credits listed above were taken from production records of *Caballeros árabes*.

TERESA (Italian Americans)

Coliseum Films; Loew's International Corp.; controlled by Loew's Inc.; Metro-Goldwyn-Mayer Presents; A Fred Zinnemann Production. *Dist* Loew's Inc. Jul **1951**; New York opening: 5 Apr 1951; *Prod*: early May—mid-Jul 1950 [©Loew's Inc.; 24 May 1951; LP945]. Sd (Western Electric Sound System); b&w. 9,413 ft. 101-103 min. PCA cert no. 14867.

Prod Arthur M. Loew. *Dir* Fred Zinnemann. *Scr* Stewart Stern. *From an orig story by* Alfred Hayes and Stewart Stern. *Photog* William J. Miller. *Art dir* Leo Kerz. *Film ed* Frank Sullivan. *Assoc film ed* David Kummins. *Mus dir* Jack Shaindlin. *Mus* Louis Applebaum. *Rec supv* James Shields. *Scr supv* Arnold Laven. *Tech adv* Bill Mauldin, Capt. James B. Anders and Sgt. Walter R. Malott.

Cast: PIER ANGELI (*Teresa*), JOHN ERICSON (*Philip [Cass]*), Patricia Collinge (*Philip's mother*), Richard Bishop (*Philip's father*), Peggy Ann Garner (*Susan [Cass]*), Ralph Meeker (*Sgt. Dobbs*), Bill Mauldin (*Grissom*), Ave Ninchi (*Teresa's mother*), Edward Binns (*Sgt. Brown*), Rod Steiger (*Frank*), Aldo Silvani (*Professor Crocce*), Tommy Lewis (*Walter*), Franco Interlenghi (*Mario*), Edith Atwater (*Mrs. Lawrence*), Lewis Cianelli (*Cheyenne*), William King (*Boone*), Richard McNamara (*G.I. Cook*), [John Day (*G.I.*)], [Augusta Venturi (*Townswoman*)].

Psychological, Social, War, Drama. [*Print viewed*]. Philip Cass, a disturbed young war veteran, runs from an unemployment line in New York City to see his counselor Frank at the Veterans Administration. He complains his parents don't understand him and says he wishes Dobbs, a friend from the army, had been his father. At the East Side tenement apartment he shares with his parents and sister Sue, when his father invites him to listen to a ballgame, Philip rudely walks away and goes into a bedroom, then ignores his mother's aggressive fawning and after she leaves him alone, holds his head and calls out "Dobbs!" He remembers arriving with two other replacements at a village in Italy during the war, where Sgt. Dobbs throws him to the ground to protect him from a bomb attack. Later, as the soldiers eat in the center of town among the hungry children, Teresa, an attractive adolescent, brings a statuette to trade for food. When a soldier expresses a sexual interest in her, her brother Mario leads her away. Philip and the other two replacements are assigned to Teresa's home to sleep. In the middle of the night, Philip trades his watch for a dozen cans of "C" rations and leaves them upstairs for the family. Teresa sees this and smiles. The next day, when Philip does not respond aggressively enough to training, his new commanding officer, Sgt. Brown, humiliates him in front of the townspeople until Dobbs arrives. Realizing he has to teach Philip to get mad, Dobbs takes him to a secluded area, then grabs his nose and slaps his face until he fights with vigor. Afterwards, Dobbs encourages Philip to join the other soldiers who have gathered around the women doing their wash. After Teresa runs from a soldier and hides behind Philip, he offers to carry her bucket of water. She invites him to meet her family and a visiting professor from nearby Bologna, where she has learned to speak English. Her mother toasts Philip, but when Teresa asks if she can go with him for a walk, Mario, bitter about the occupation, objects. Teresa's mother, however, sends her young son Sergio with them. Sitting on a wrecked tank, they talk about love, and he is about to kiss her, when she says they must go back. At her door, he asks for a kiss using the Italian word *bacio*, and she laughs then kisses him good-bye. On a combat patrol, the Americans come to a stream below a mountain, where they set up an ambush. Dobbs gives Philip the job of firing a flare pistol after the last German passes. As he waits alone, Philip panics and leaves his position to find Dobbs, and when the Germans approach, Brown knocks Philip down to get his flare pistol, then shoots a flare. As the Americans start firing, Philip cries on the ground. Later, in a state of shock, Philip is taken to a cathedral serving as a hospital, where he learns that Dobbs is dead. After the war ends in Europe, Philip returns to Teresa's village, and Mario invites him to sleep on the couch downstairs. In the middle of the night, neither Philip nor Teresa can sleep. She comes down, and as they talk, he learns she is only thirteen. She says she fears he will disappear before she is old enough to marry, and they kiss before she breaks away to go upstairs. They soon get married outside a ruined church and spend their honeymoon in Rome. When Philip has to leave, Teresa cries, but he assures her that the army will take care of everything. At home, Philip's domineering mother relates that she worried he might have been taken advantage of by a woman in

Europe, fearing that he would turn out to be a "jellyfish" like her husband. Philip hides his wedding photo above a bureau, but when his mother finds it, she lets out a shriek and then sobs uncontrollably. After receiving a telegram from the War Brides Office authorizing her transport, Teresa arrives in New York. Sensing Philip's mother's uneasiness, Teresa asks if they can get their own room, but he defensively says he has to get a job first. After a heated argument, he prepares to start a job selling pressure cookers, and though his mother contends he'll never be a salesman, Teresa gives him encouragement. He fails, however, in his first nervous attempt, as Teresa learns at Bellevue hospital that she is pregnant. At Jones Beach on a family outing, Philip sits morosely at the water's edge and won't listen when Teresa tries to tell him about her pregnancy. Looking over the family, he is disturbed by voices in his mind, then yells, looking at his father, "I'm just like him!" and runs off. Teresa tries to calm him, but he criticizes her for calling him "Filipo." He returns home drunk to find Teresa on the roof. She insists they leave that night, but he argues it would kill his mother. When Teresa relates she is going to have a baby, Philip says she can't, and she asks if he is afraid his mother won't like it. He warns her never to say that again, and when she says he is afraid to be a father, he yells for her to leave, then watches from the roof as she walks off. Back in the present, Philip gets up from the bed when his mother comes in singing a Christmas carol and goes to see Frank. He realizes that he let himself get paralyzed because he believed he was like his father and feels that his mother wanted him to stay a baby, yet he understands they were only trying to do their best. Now he begins to feel that he is growing up. He gets a job at the YMCA and decides to leave home, but his mother accuses him of killing her. His father forcefully leads him out, however, over her objections. One night, Philip's father comes to get him after learning that Teresa has checked into Bellevue Hospital. She has been living in a furnished room and working in an Italian grocery. After the baby is born, Philip shakes his father's hand. The next day, Philip brings Teresa flowers and she says the baby's name is "Filipo." After her hospital stay, Philip brings Teresa and the baby to a modest apartment he has rented. *Fathers and sons. Italian Americans. Italians. Italy. Mothers and sons. New York City—East Side. Veterans. War brides. Bellevue Hospital (New York City). Brothers. Combat. Courtship. Hunger. Infants. New York City—Central Park. New York City—Jones Beach. Officers (Military). Panic. Pregnancy. Professors. Psychologists. Rome (Italy). Salesmen. Separation (Marital). Soldiers. Unemployment. Village life. Weddings. Young Men's Christian Association.*

Note: This was the first production of Coliseum Films, a producing subsidiary of distributor Loew's International Corp., whose president, Arthur M. Loew, was the son of the founder of the firm's parent company, Loew's, Inc. According to a *HR* news item, this was to be the first of a series of "low budgeted, locale-photographed stories which Arthur Lowe plans to make in Europe and other parts of the world." In a pre-release *NYT* article by director Fred Zinnemann, he states that Loew, with whom he earlier worked on the 1948 release *The Search*, suggested doing a film "on the plight and problems of those boys who had come back from war to a confusing, overcrowded world, which they must face 'on their own,' without superior officers and military rules and regulations to direct their lives." They decided to use an approach similar to that of *The Search*, of "letting the experiences of one ex-soldier tell the story of all his fellows, and filming the picture in its natural settings, with unknown players in the leading roles." Zinnemann had previously directed Montgomery Clift and Marlon Brando in their first films (*The Search* and *The Men*, respectively.) After writers Stewart Stern, who had also worked on *The Search*, and Alfred Hayes became involved, the story began to focus on the experiences of a foreign war bride in addition to those of a returning soldier, according to Zinnemann's article. (In his autobiography, Zinnemann states that Stern was hired to write a screenplay loosely-based on Hayes's novel *The Girl on the Via Flaminia*; however, that book, which was the source for the 1954 United Artists release *Act of Love*, seems to bear little resemblance to *Teresa*, other than the fact that it also deals with a love affair between an American G.I. and an impoverished European girl.)

A May 1950 *NYT* article noted that the film was being made "in the Italian tradition—unknown actors, and the Italian part of the story...shot in the actual bombed-out villages on the route of the Fifth Army, in which the G.I. is supposed to have served." In the article, Zinnemann noted that using unknown actors has succeeded in Europe, where costs are low enough to allow for extended time for a director to work with the cast. Stern was sent to Italy ahead of the production crew for research and to recruit potential cast members. According to the film's pressbook, the mother of seventeen-year-old actress Anna Maria Pierangeli learned of the casting call from Silvio Damico, the head of Rome's Academy of Dramatic Art, who urged her to send her daughter for a screen test. The test, sent to New York, impressed Zinnemann, who knew when he met her in Rome that she was right for the role. The actress, whose name was changed to Pier Angeli, had earlier starred in the Italian films *Domani é troppo tardi (Tomorrow Is Too Late)* and *Domani é un altro giorno (Tomorrow Is*

Another Day), both directed by Léonide Moguy. Zinnemann, in the pressbook, stated, "She is the most talented girl I have ever worked with—bar none. She combines talent with a very different kind of personality. She is quite childlike at one moment, surprisingly mature the next. She has the emotions of a little girl but a mind beyond her years by about a decade—and all this happens without her realizing it. If she is properly handled and gets good scripts, not just trash to exploit her versatility, she can climb to the absolute top and become one of the outstanding stars of her generation."

Teresa was John Ericson's first film. According to *LAT*, he previously had been with the Barter Theater in New York and had done some radio and television work. *NYT* noted, "In appearance and even in his voice use, he resembles Marlon Brando, who played in *The Men* under Mr. Zinnemann's direction—which may by significant." This also marked the film debuts of Rod Steiger, Ralph Meeker and *Stars and Stripes* celebrated war cartoonist Bill Mauldin, who also served as a technical adviser on the film. Mauldin had been wounded in the Italian campaign. According to Zinnemann's autobiography, Stern was responsible for suggesting Steiger, a personal friend. Italian village scenes were shot in the small town of Scascoli, near Bologna in the Apennines, at the foot of Mount Adone, which Zinnemann called "the pivot of the German Gothic line during the war," and the wedding ceremony was shot at Livergnano. Battle scenes were filmed where actual fighting had taken place, the hospital scene was shot in Siena and the honeymoon scenes were shot in Rome. By the time of filming, Scascoli, which had a population of 350, had been rebuilt, so the filmmakers hired townspeople to wreck it again and included many as extras in the cast. The stone watering trough was built in the main square for the film. According to news items, forty ex-G.I.s, who were studying in Italy, were cast as Fifth Army extras and bit roles. Shooting in New York took place near the Third Avenue "el" on the East Side, in Central Park, at Jones Beach, at Bellevue Hospital and at M-G-M's home office, which was used for the unemployment office scene; because the script depicted the clerk at the office as "unfriendly," the actual New York unemployment office would not allow filming on their premises, according to a *NYT* article.

According to information in the MPAA/PCA Collection at the AMPAS Library, PCA director Joseph I. Breen objected to a number of lines in the script where, he wrote, "Teresa is offering herself, sexually, for food" and "the soldiers set out to seduce the Italian girls with Hershey bars." Breen's objections led to a number of changes in the dialogue, including the alteration of a scene in the script in which Sgt. Dobbs gives Philip a Hershey bar and says, "Here now, you're all set. Do I have to teach you how to do this too?"

The film was nominated for an Academy Award for motion picture story. Some reviews commented that the film would probably appeal to art-house patrons, as opposed to general audiences. *MPD* stated, "Exhibitors operating so-called 'art theatres' might do quite a thing with this picture as proof that an American producing outfit can take a crew to Italy and come back with a picture as good, in the same ways, as the Italian outfits export to us. Such advertising might induce controversy and attendance. But the commercial exhibitor is likely to find it much more difficult to persuade his regular customers to turn out in force for a 103-minute feature unprovocatively titled, thin as to names, and decidedly scrambled in point of subject matter." A number of reviews objected to the mixture of themes in the film. *HR* called it "an arty and dull story" containing an "absurd hodge podge of melodramatic cliches." They complained that the story "seems to be a totally unnecessary effort to create a problem where none exists."

Archer Winston of *NYP* suggested that rather than center on the veteran's psychological maladjustments, the film would have done better to "look to the international romance angle, the marriage between plain people. Differences of language, background, and family would supply an abundance of plot." In his autobiography, Zinnemann acknowledged that the film was unbalanced and "split in its purpose" and that the New York scenes were far inferior to those shot in Italy. Zinnemann stated that Stern drew on his own experiences in writing the screenplay, and thus, "There was too great an emphasis on a minor facet of the story—the mother's dominance over her son. Taken too far, it diluted the force of the main theme and weakened the 'hero' to an ominous degree." Unable to postpone the shooting, Zinnemann had no choice but to go ahead with a screenplay he believed was flawed, although Bill Maudlin did try to work on it. Bosley Crowther of *NYT*, however, praised the film as meriting "the rare appreciation of all who are interested in honest, mature films" and lauded Stern and Zinnemann for having "evolved a film that places these two real young people in a world that is equally real." In a later commentary on this film and another which also dealt with a domineering mother (*Fourteen Hours*), Crowther noted that "more forthright producers are reaching for more solid motivations for their films. Aspects of human behavior which psychologists run into regularly are slowly being presented in place of the mossy cliches, thus giving more plausible reasons for characters acting as they do. And thus, to the limits erected by the stiff, obscurantist Production Code, we are watching our bolder filmmakers pushing further into the complex facts of life."

Box 3 Mar 1951. *Cue* 7 Apr 1951. *DN* 30 May 1950. *DV* 28 Feb 1951, p. 3. *Exb* 28 Feb 1951, pp. 3033-34. *FD* 28 Feb 1951, p. 6. *Har* 3 Mar 1951, p. 34. *HCN* 16 Aug 1951. *HR* 5 Dec 1949. *HR* 19 Jan 1950. *HR* 16 Jun 1950, p. 10 *HR* 14 Jul 1950, p. 10. *HR* 28 Feb 1951, pp. 3-4. *LADN* 16 Aug 1951. *LAEx* 16 Aug 1951. *LAT* 16 Apr 1950. *LAT* 17 Sep 1950 ("This Week" magazine). *LAT* 16 Aug 1951. *Life* 19 Mar 1951. *MPD* 6 Mar 1951. *MPHPD* 10 Mar 1951, p. 750. *NYDM* 6 Apr 1951. *NYJournal American* 6 Apr 1951. *NYP* 6 Apr 1951. *NYT* 14 May 1950. *NYT* 13 Aug 1950. *NYT* 11 Feb 1951. *NYT* 25 Mar 1951. *NYT* 6 Apr 1951, p. 31. *NYT* 15 Apr 1951. *NYTr* 6 Apr 1951. *SatRev* 14 Apr 1951. *Time* 9 Apr 1951. *Var* 29 Nov 1950. *Var* 28 Feb 1951, p. 13.

TERMINAL STATION *see* **INDISCRETION OF AN AMERICAN WIFE**

EL TERROR DE TORREÓN *see* **AMOR Y VIDA**

TERROR IN A TEXAS TOWN (Swedish Americans, Latino)
Seltzer Films, Inc. *Dist* United Artists Corp. 25 Aug **1958**; Prod: mid-Nov—late Nov 1957 at Hal Roach Studios [©Seltzer Films, Inc.; 10 Sep 1958; LP12208]. Sd (Western Electric); b&w. 7,250 ft. 80 min. PCA cert no. 18924.

Prod Frank N. Seltzer. *Assoc prod* Carrol Sax. *Dir* Joseph H. Lewis. *Asst dir* Richard Dixon. *Orig scr* Ben L. Perry. *Dir of photog* Ray Rennahan. *Spec eff ed* Carl Brandon. *Art dir* William Ferrari. *Film ed* Frank Sullivan and Stefan Arnsten. *Asst film ed* James T. Hecker. *Film ed* George Brand. *Set dec* Rudy Butler. *Prop master* Arnold Goode. *Mus* Gerald Fried. *Sd* Charles Althouse and Tom Renning. *Makeup* Sid Perell. *Hair stylist* Shirley Madden.

Cast: STERLING HAYDEN [(*George Hansen*)], Sebastian Cabot (*McNeil*), Carol Kelly (*Molly*), Eugene Martin (*Pepe* [*Mirada*]), Ned Young ([*Johnny*] *Crale*), Victor Millan ([*José*] *Mirada*), Frank Ferguson [(*Holmes*)], Marilee Earle [(*Monsy*)], [Ann Varella (*Rosa Mirada*)], [Sheb Wooley (*Baxter*)], [Fred Kohler (*Weed*)], [Steve Mitchell (*Keeno*)], [Jamie Russell (*Johnson*)], [Tyler McVey (*Sheriff Stoner*)], [Ted Stanhope (*Sven Hansen*)], [Gil Lamb (*Barnaby*)], [Hank Patterson (*Brady*)].

Western. [*Print viewed*]. After an arson fire destroys a farmer's house and barn, the other farmers meet to discuss efforts by hotel owner McNeil to drive them off their land. Meanwhile, at the hotel in nearby Prairie City, McNeil tells gunfighter Johnny Crale that the farmers are squatters who refuse to leave even though he has offered to pay for the land. McNeil now wants Crale to drive them away. Soon after farmer José Mirada shows his neighbor, Swedish-born Sven Hansen, that there is oil on their land, Crale arrives. Urging Mirada and his son Pepe to hide in a nearby shed, Hansen, armed with a whale harpoon, speaks with Crale. Crale asks him to transfer his land grant to McNeil, and when Hansen refuses, kills him. Mirada intends to tell the others about the oil discovery and Crale's murder of Hansen, but his wife Rosa begs him to remain silent. Some time later, Hansen's son George arrives in Prairie City, but when he asks about transportation to the Hansen farm, Crale reveals that his father has been killed. George, who had gone to sea to help pay for the farm, then asks the sheriff what is being done to catch his father's killer. The sheriff, who is one of McNeil's men, informs George that his father did not own the land, and that he will arrest him if he trespasses on the farm. George agrees to stay in the hotel, but adds that although he is a foreigner, he understands justice and will get it. After George turns down his offer to buy the land, McNeil orders Crale to get rid of him by any means short of murder. Despite the sheriff's warning, George visits the farm and talks to Mirada, who pretends to know nothing. He then gives George his father's harpoon. While they talk, Crale and his men arrive and order the Miradas to leave town. When George wonders why McNeil wants the land, Mirada again keeps silent. Later, in the hotel saloon, George offers a drink to Molly, Crale's wife, and then questions her. Although Molly reveals nothing, Hansen deduces that Crale murdered his father. Moments later, Crale and his men beat George and put him, unconscious, on a train. When George regains consciousness, he struggles back toward town. The Miradas take him in, and this time, Rosa tells him about the oil. After George informs the sheriff that there was a witness to his father's murder, Crale kills Mirada. Believing Crale's work to be done, McNeil pays him, but Crale, who was deeply affected by the courage with which Mirada faced death, turns on McNeil and kills him. When George learns of Mirada's murder, he takes his father's harpoon and heads for a showdown with Crale. Meanwhile, Molly decides to leave Crale. She interrupts a farmers' meeting at the church to tell them that George intends to face Crale with the harpoon as his only weapon. While the farmers watch, Crale shoots and wounds George, but the Swede kills Crale with the harpoon. *Courage. Farmers. Land rights. Mexican Americans. Oil. Swedish Americans. Arson. Childbirth. Children. Fights. Gunfighters. Harpoons. Hotels. Marriage. Meetings. Murder. Sailors. Saloons. Sheriffs.*

Note: The film's working title was *Hard as Nails*. The scene leading up to the climatic showdown between "George Hansen" and "Johnny Crale" is played before before the film's titles. Sheb Wooley is best known for his recording of the novelty song "Purple People Eater." Modern sources add Chuck Roberson and Emory Parnell to the cast. According to modern sources, the film was made

in ten days for $80,000. Modern sources reveal that screenwriter Ben L. Perry fronted for blacklisted writers John Howard Lawson, Mitch Lindeman and Dalton Trumbo. Trumbo, who was originally approached by producer Frank N. Seltzer to write the script, was involved in other projects and recommended Lawson and Lindeman, according to a biography of Trumbo. Later, at Seltzer's request, Trumbo rewrote the script.

Box 8 Sep 1958. *DV* 20 Aug 1958, p. 3. *FD* 25 Aug 1958, p. 6. *Har* 23 Aug 1958. *HR* 15 Nov 1957, p. 13. *HR* 22 Nov 1957, p. 13. *HR* 20 Aug 1958, p. 4. *MPHPD* 30 Aug 1958, p. 960. *Var* 20 Aug 1958, p. 6.

TEVYA (Yiddish language)
Maymon Film, Inc. *Dist* Maymon Film, Inc. **1939**; New York opening: 21 Dec 1939; Prod: began Jul 1939 at the Biograph Studios. Sd (RCA The Magic Voice of the Screen); b&w. 8,099 ft. 93 min. PCA cert no. 02645. Yiddish language with English subtitles.

Prod Henry Ziskin and [Maurice Schwartz]. *Dir* Maurice Schwartz. *Scr* Maurice Schwartz. *Titles by* Leon Chrystal. *Adpt* Marcy Klauber. *Photog* Larry Williams. *Settings* William Saulter. *Ed* Sam Citron. *Mus* Sholom Secunda. *Sd rec* Paul Robillard.

Source: Based on the Yiddish play *Tevye der Milkhiker* by Sholom Aleichem (New York, 1919), which was based on his short story "Khavah" from the series *Tevye der Milkhiker* (1896-1914).

Cast: MAURICE SCHWARTZ (*Tevya*), Miriam Riselle (*Chavah*), Rebecca Weintraub (*Goldie*), Paula Lubelski (*Zeitel*), Leon Liebgold (*Fedya* [*Galagan*]), Vicki Marcus (*Shloimele*), Betty Marcus (*Perele*), Julius Adler (*Priest* [*Aleksei*]), David Makarenko (*Mikita*), Helen Grossman (*Mikita's wife*), Morris Strassberg (*Starosta*), Al Harris (*Zazuli*), Louis Weisberg (*Shtarsina*), Boas Young (*Uradnick, officer*).

Yiddish, **Social**, **Rural**, **Historical**, **Drama**. [*Print viewed*]. Chavah, a Jewish farm girl living in the Ukraine around the turn of the century, is secretly in love with Fedya Galagan, a Russian who gives her books to read by Maxim Gorky, which she is delighted to receive. Zeitel, Chavah's sister, who has married and moved away, returns for a visit with her two young children. During the family meal, the village priest, Father Aleksei, visits and tells Tevya the dairyman, Chavah's father, that one of the daughters of Tevya's friend Mendel has fallen in love with a Gentile and is marrying into the Christian faith. When Tevya, a simple man who usually comments with philosophic humor on his life and that of his people, says that he would rather die or see his child dead than to see his daughter betray their faith, Chavah falls faint from crying. At night, on the porch of Tevya's home, Fedya tells Chavah that their love is above all faiths and brings her another book by Gorky. When he hears Tevya approach, Fedya kisses Chavah and dashes off. Tevya, who has seen Fedya leave, warns Chavah that should a pogrom occur, their supposed friends from the village wouldn't hesitate to join in. When she says she doesn't believe that they would, Tevya, suspicious of her, asks would she ever do anything to drive him and his wife Goldie to their graves, and Chavah, in tears, answers no. She marries Fedya, however, and on the day of the wedding, Tevya and Goldie go to the priest's house to try to get her back, but they are turned away. Chavah hears her parents from inside and cries out to them. At home, Tevya proclaims that Chavah is dead and questions where is God. In a town council meeting, when Fedya's brutish father Mikita argues to drive Tevya out of town, the mayor stands up for Tevya, and the discussion turns into a brawl. Sometime later, Chavah learns that Goldie is ill. Although Fedya offers to drive her home, she worries that her presence would only hasten her mother's death. As Goldie lies on her sickbed with the family gathered around, Chavah, outside in the rain, peers in through a window. Goldie then says she remembers everything and dies as she looks at Chavah. When Tevya travels to the nearby town of Boyberik, Chavah, who has been reduced to a servant by Fedya's mother, sees him through the window and runs out to him. Tevya acts horrified when he sees her and whips his old horse to race away as she calls "Father." When the council members visit Tevya to tell him that he and his family must leave town within twenty-four hours because the Tsar has decreed that Jews must be driven from all the villages, Tevya asks was there ever a time or place when the Jews were not driven out and signs their edict in resignation. Planning to go to the land of Israel, Tevya sells the belongings that he cannot keep, and he is about to sell his horse, to whom he has often talked during his journeys, but he decides that he cannot do it. When Chavah sees that a man has bought Goldie's Sabbath dress, she takes it and returns to her home. She tells Zeitel that she never gave up her faith, and when Fedya arrives to take her back, she says that she will always think kindly of

run when he sees Chavah and then orders her out. Chavah protests that she did not betray the faith and pleads to be allowed to make their plight hers. Tevya sobs and considers whether he should forgive her. He expresses worry about her sin against God, but reasons that God doesn't need his help and, seeing Goldie's dress, embraces his daughter. The family then sadly leaves their home and village. *Antisemitism. Fathers and daughters. Jews. Marriage–Mixed. Milkmen. Ostracism. Religiosity. Russia. Death and dying. Farm life. Fights. Maxim Gorky. Horses. Meetings. Mothers and daughters. Priests. Sisters. Village life. Weddings.*

Note: The title card in the opening credits reads, "Sholom Aleichem's *Tevya*." According to *Var*, the Yiddish play on which this film was based had been one of Maurice Schwartz's greatest successes. *NYT* commented concerning the production, "To the purely professional mind, the most amazing technical feature about *Tevya* is the fact that all of its exteriors were filmed around Jericho, L.I. [Long Island], for nobody has ever seen a more typically Russian locale, even in Soviet pictures, than *Tevya* boasts." According to a news item, the film, which cost $70,000, was financed by Maurice Schwartz and a group of friends. The news item states that the film was rehearsed by Schwartz and his Yiddish Art Theatre for three weeks on the Theatre's stage before production began and had a twenty-two day shooting schedule. *Var* called the film "one of the best Yiddish films made to date." The Yiddish papers *Forward*, which praised the film highly, and *Morgn Frayhayt* contended that the film diverged greatly from the Sholom Aleichem original. The *Morgn Frayhayt* reviewer was particularly critical of the film's portrayal of its non-Jewish characters. According to modern sources, in 1936, Schwartz proposed the production of a film based on the play to Joseph Green, who was planning to produce a series of Yiddish films in Poland; however, Green was reluctant to deal with the subject of intermarriage in the anti-Semitic climate in Poland at the time. In 1919, Zion Films, Inc. produced *Broken Blossoms* (also known as *Khavah*), which was based on the Sholom Aleichem story "Khavah." That film was directed by Charles E. Davenport and starred Alice Hastings, Alexander Tenenholtz and Giacomo Masuroff (see *AFI Catalog of Feature Films, 1911-20;* F1.0499). An Israeli film based on the Aleichem stories, entitled *Tuvya Hakholev*, was produced in 1968 by Menachem Golan. The stage musical *Fiddler on the Roof*, based on the Aleichem stories, opened in New York on 22 Sep 1964; it had music and lyrics by Sheldon Harnick and Jerry Bock, and was written by Joseph Stein, directed and choreographed by Jerome Robbins and starred Zero Mostel as "Tevya." The film version of the musical, which was produced in 1971, was directed by Norman Jewison and starred Topol.

FD 28 Dec 1939, p. 11. *Forward* 25 Dec 1939. *HR* 12 Jul 1939. *LAT* 17 Dec 1945. *Morgn Frayhayt* 22 Dec 1939. *MPH* 13 Jan 1940, p. 40. *NYT* 30 Jul 1939, sec. 9, p. 3. *NYT* 22 Dec 1939, p. 15. *Var* 27 Dec 1939, p. 45. *Var* 17 Jan 1940.

TEX COMES A-SINGIN' see **THE SINGING VAGABOND**

THE TEXANS (Native Americans, Comanche)

Paramount Pictures, Inc.; A Lucien Hubbard Production. *Dist* Paramount Pictures, Inc. 15 Jul **1938**; *Prod*: mid-Feb—late Apr 1938 [©Paramount Pictures, Inc.; 12 Aug 1938; LP8203]. Sd (Western Electric); b&w. 10 reels. 90 or 92 min. Passed by the National Board of Review. PCA cert no. 4258.

Pres ADOLPH ZUKOR. [*Exec prod* William LeBaron]. *Dir* James Hogan. [*Asst dir* Harry Scott]. *Scr* Bertram Millhauser, Paul Sloane and William Wister Haines. *Photog* Theodor Sparkuhl. *Spec photog eff* Farciot Edouart and Dewey Wrigley. *Art dir* Hans Dreier and John Goodman. *Ed* LeRoy Stone. *Int dec* A. E. Freudeman. *Cost* Edith Head. *Mus dir* Boris Morros. *Sd rec* Charles Hisserich and Richard Olson.

Song(s): "Silver on the Sage," words and music by Leo Robin and Ralph Rainger; "I'll Come to the Wedding," words and music by Frank Loesser.

Source: Based on the novel *North of 36* by Emerson Hough (New York, 1923).

Cast: JOAN BENNETT (*Ivy Preston*), RANDOLPH SCOTT (*Kirk Jordan*), May Robson (*Granna*), Walter Brennan (*Chuckawalla*), Robert Cummings (*Alan Sanford*), Raymond Hatton (*Cal Tuttle*), Robert Barrat ([*Major*] *Isaiah Middlebrack*), Harvey Stephens (*Lt. David Nichols*), Francis Ford (*Uncle Dud*), Bill Roberts (*Singin' Cy*), [Clarence Wilson (*Sam Boss*)], [Jack Moore (*Slim*)], [Chris Martin (*Juan Rodriguez*)], [Anna Demetrio (*Rosita Rodriguez*)], [Richard Tucker (*General Corbett*)], [Ed Gargan (*Sergeant Grady*)], [Otis Harlan (*Henry*)], [Spencer Charters (*Chairman*)], [Archie Twitchell (*Corporal Thompson*)], [William Haade (*Sergeant Cahill*)], [Irving Bacon (*Private Collins*)], [William Davidson (*I. J. Jessup*)], [Richard Denning (*Corporal Parker*)], [Frank Cordell, John Eckert, Slim Hightower, Scoop Martin, Slim Talbot, Whitey Sovern (*Cowboys*)], [James Kilgannon, Edward Brady, Carl Harbaugh, Dutch Hendrian (*Union soldiers*)], [Ernie Adams, Edward LeSaint, James Guinn (*Confederate soldiers*)], [Oscar Smith (*Black soldier*)], [Harry Woods (*Cavalry officer*)], [Vera Steadman, Virginia Jennings (*Women on street*)], [Kay Whitehead (*Stella*)], [Wheeler Oakman (*U. S. Captain*)], [Jack Perrin (*Private soldier*)], [Everett Brown (*Man with watches*)], [Margaret McWade (*Middle-aged lady*)], [James Kelso (*Snorer*)], [J. Manley Head (*Fanatic*)], [Philip Morris (*Fen*)], [James Burtis (*Swenson*)], [Esther Howard (*Madame*)], [Pat West (*Real estate man*)], [John Qualen (*Swede*)], [Harry Holman (*Town lawyer*)], [Lon Poff, James T. Mack (*Moody citizens*)], [Laurie Lane, Helaine Moler (*Girls*)].

Historical, Western. [*Print viewed*]. In Texas after the Civil War, Ivy Preston delivers a shipment of guns to her fiancé, Alan Sanford, who then leaves to raise an army with Mexican Emperor Maximilian and resume the fight against the Yankees. When Kirk Jordan, a Southerner who believes in the peaceful co-existence of the North and South, rescues Ivy from arrest by Major Isaiah Middlebrack, the entire town joins in the fight. Back at her poverty-stricken ranch, Ivy, her "Granna" and foreman Chuckawalla are confronted again by Middlebrack, who has brought with him the cavalry, led by Lieutenant David Nichols. Middlebrack slyly agrees not to arrest Ivy. Instead, he intends to tax all of her 10,000 head of cattle, and accepts land scrip for their ranch as payment. Determined to outsmart the major, Granna gets Middlebrack drunk, while Ivy mobilizes her ranch hands with the help of Kirk and his fur-trapping sidekick, Cal Tuttle. Later that night, Ivy, Kirk and Cal head the herd toward the Rio Grande River. After Granna and Chuckawalla catch up, they evade the cavalry by crossing the river. At Kirk's suggestion, a reluctant Ivy agrees to herd the cattle on a dangerous trek up to Abilene, Kansas, where she will be able to sell the cattle at a high price due to the introduction of the railroad. Middlebrack goes to the state capital and receives the authority to arrest Ivy and her troupe for tax evasion and treason, and the cavalry follows in pursuit. After the herd endures a blizzard and Granna fights illness, Alan arrives exhausted at the campsite and informs them that his plans to build a rebel army were destroyed when the emperor was dethroned and executed. When Ivy and Alan announce their engagement, there is a celebration, but Kirk is disappointed. Confronted by Comanches, who ask for one steer in exchange for peaceable passage through their land, Alan refuses their request despite Kirk's advice. After a dust storm, the herd is attacked by Comanches, who retreat when the cavalry approaches. Middlebrack arrests everyone and takes command of the wagon train, but Kirk and Cal manage to slip away unnoticed. They follow the herd for three days, but ride to the rescue when Comanches set the grasses on fire around the herd. Cal kills Middlebrack, and after the dust is settled, Lieutenant Nichols honors the death of a ranch hand and escorts the herd to the Kansas border. On arrival at Abilene, Alan disappears and the Preston herd saves the town from losing the railroad's business. Kirk confesses his love to Ivy and says goodbye. When Ivy discovers Alan is helping to form the Ku Klux Klan, she realizes the error of his ways and runs after Kirk, catching up with him in time to join Cal and him on a beaver-trapping trip. *Deception. Gunrunners. Ranchers. Texas. United States–History–Reconstruction, 1865-1898. Abilene (KS). Blizzards. Cattlemen. Comanche Indians. Drunkenness. Engagements. Indians of North America. Ku Klux Klan. Maximilian, Emperor of Mexico, 1832-1867. Railroads. Taxation. United States. Army. Cavalry.*

Note: According to Paramount story files at the AMPAS library, the film's working title was *Marching Herds*. According to the pressbook, the town of Indianola was reconstructed on the Paramount set. Paramount filmed some scenes at the La Mota Ranch, a 35,000-acre spread between San Antonio and Laredo, TX. The stampede scene used 25,000 Longhorn steer. Some props were from the Pony Express Museum in Arcadia, CA. In 1924, Paramount released *North of 36*, based on the same source, directed by Irvin Willat, and starring Jack Holt, Ernest Torrence and Lois Wilson (see above).

DV 14 Jul 1938, p. 3. *FD* 29 Jul 1938, p. 11. *HR* 21 Feb 1938, pp. 6-7. *HR* 25 Apr 1938, pp. 10-11. *HR* 14 Jul 1938, p. 3. *MPD* 15 Jul 1938, p. 5. *MPH* 16 Apr 1938, p. 27. *MPH* 23 Jul 1938, p. 39. *NYT* 28 Jul 1938, p. 23. *Var* 3 Aug 1938, p. 15.

TEXAS see **THE LAST COMMAND**

THE TEXAS LEGIONNAIRES see **THE LAST COMMAND**

TEXAS MANHUNT see **PHANTOM OF THE PLAINS**

TEXAS PIONEERS (Native Americans)

Monogram Pictures Corp.; A Trem Carr Production. *Dist* Monogram Pictures Corp. 15 Feb **1932**. Sd (Western Electric Noiseless Recording); b&w. 54 or 56 min. Passed by the National Board of Review.

Dir Harry Fraser. *Story and adpt* Harry Fraser. [*Adpt* Wellyn Totman]. *Photog* Faxon Dean. *Settings* Ernest R. Hickson. *Ed* J. Logan Pearson. [*Mus synchronized by* Abe Meyer]. *Rec* Balsley & Phillips. *Sd eng* D. S. Stoner. *Prod mgr* Paul Malvern.

Cast: BILL CODY [(*Captain Bill Clyde*)], ANDY SHUFORD [(*Andy Thomas*)], Leroy Mason [(*Mark Collins*)], Sheila Mannors [(*Nancy Thomas*)], John Elliott [(*Colonel Thomas*)], Harry Allen [(*Corporal*)], Chief Standing Bear [(*Chief*)], Iron Eyes [(*Little Eagle*)], Ann Ross [(*Squaw*)], [Frank Lackteen (*Scout*)].

Western. [*Print viewed*]. Captain Bill Clyde of the U. S. cavalry, is eager for a promotion so that he can marry his commanding officer's daughter, Nancy. He goes undercover, and after pretending to have a disagreement with the colonel, he is courtmartialed and removed from service. Bill's special mission is to determine which trader is providing the Indians with guns. Bill and the colonel both suspect Mark Collins, a romantic rival for Nancy's love. Collins indeed is dealing with the Indians, who plan with him to attack a wagon train of settlers and steal their weapons. The chief's son Little Eagle distrusts Collins, however, and protests the scheme. The cavalry's Indian scout works in cahoots with Collins and brings back a false report to the colonel, but Bill has trailed the trader and verifies that he is their suspect. Andy, the colonel's son who idolizes Bill, follows him when he rides to prevent the raid. They are too late, however, and many settlers are killed, except for those who followed a different trail and found safety at the cavalry fort. Bill finds Little Eagle lying among the wounded and brings him to the fort, since Little Eagle saved his life and they are blood brothers. Little Eagle identifies Collins as the trader who arranged the raid. Indians suddenly attack the fort. Andy manages to escape and ride for reinforcements, while Bill struggles with Collins. Little Eagle once again saves Bill's life by killing Collins, but dies in the effort. Andy brings another unit of the cavalry, who save the fort. The Indians and the cavalry have peace talks, while Nancy accepts Bill's proposal, now that he will be promoted for his work. *Friendship. Gunrunners. Indians of North America. Self-sacrifice. Traders. United States. Army. Cavalry. Courts-martial and courts of inquiry. Deception. Forts. Raids. Romantic rivalry. Scouts (Frontier). Settlers. Wagon trains.*

Note: A modern source includes Hank Bell in the cast. Iron Eyes later became known as Iron Eyes Cody.

FD 19 Jan 1932, p. 4. *FD* 31 Jan 1932, p. 4. *FD* 18 Jun 1932, p. 4. *Var* 14 Jun 1932, p. 17.

THE TEXAS RANGER *see* **THE RANGER**

A TEXAS STEER (African Americans)

Selig Polyscope Co.; A Red Seal Play of Quality. *Dist* V-L-S-E, Inc. 26 Jul 1915 [©Selig Polyscope Co.; 10 Jul 1915; LP5779]. Si; b&w. 5 reels.

Dir Giles R. Warren. *Scen* Giles R. Warren.

Source: Based on the play *A Texas Steer* by Charles Hale Hoyt (1890, first production undetermined).

Cast: Tyrone Power (*Maverick Brander*), Grace Darmond (*Bossy Brander*), Francis Bayless (*Mrs. Brander*), John Charles (*Captain Fairleigh Bright*), Mrs. Tyrone Power (*Mrs. Campbell*), Walter Roberts (*Major Yell*), Frank Weed (*Colonel Brassy Gall*).

Comedy. When Texas cattle king Maverick Brander refuses to move to Washington, D.C., where his daughter Bossy's fiancé, Captain Fairleigh Bright, will be stationed, Bossy, Bright and political boss Mayor Yell connive to have Brander elected to Congress. Brander reluctantly accepts and leaves for Washington, where he is suspicious of gentleman valets and elevators. After Bright breaks a date with Bossy because the gown that she designed is out of place in Washington society, Bossy refuses to see him. The black political boss, Mr. Fish, whom Yell promised to make Minister of Dahomey if he delivered the black vote, is disappointed when Brander cannot accommodate his dream. Later he is proud to be superintendent of the dumping of the House wastebaskets. When a committee from Texas arrives to investigate Brander's supposed ties to the railroads, Brander's secretary tries to get them drunk, but they return carrying the soused secretary. In their exuberance, they shoot bullets into the room above. After the police pursue them back to their train, Bossy reconciles with Bright. *City-country contrast. Texans. United States. Congress. Washington (D.C.). African Americans. Cattlemen. Drunkenness. Janitors. Police. Political bosses. Political corruption. Secretaries. Snobs and snobbishness.*

Note: The first New York production of the play was on 8 Jan 1894. The film was made in Selig's Chicago studio. It was re-issued in 1927 at the same time that another new production based on the play was released. The 1927 version was made by Sam E. Rork Productions, released by First National Pictures, and starred Will Rogers and Douglas Fairbanks, Jr. (see *AFI Catalog of Feature Films, 1921-30*; F2.5588). *Var* noted, "Much stress was laid upon the character of the negro who was sure of being appointed Minister to Dahomey. His talks with Brander via the captions provoked laughs where the camera enactment fell down with a thud."

Motog 24 Jul 1915, pp. 159-60, 186. *MPN* 13 Mar 1915, p. 42. *MPN* 24 Jul 1915, p. 65. *MPW* 24 Jul 1915, p. 665, 730, 732. *NYDM* 21 Jul 1915, p. 30. *Var* 6 Aug 1915, p. 18.

THE TEXAS TERROR (1945) *see* **THE NAVAJO TRAIL**

TEXAS TERROR (Native Americans)

Lone Star Productions; Monogram Pictures Corp.; A Paul Malvern Production. *Dist* Monogram Pictures Corp. 1 Feb **1935**; Prod: began 15 Nov 1934 [©Monogram Pictures Corp.; 8 Feb 1935; LP5367]. Sd (Balsley and Phillips Recording System); b&w. 6 reels. 45 or 51 min.

Dir R. N. Bradbury. *Story* R. N. Bradbury. *Photog* William Hyer and [Archie J. Stout]. *Ed* Carl Pierson. *Sd rec* Dave Stoner and [Ralph Shugart]. *Tech dir* E. R. Hickson.

Cast: JOHN WAYNE [(*Sheriff John Higgins*)], Lucille Brown [(*Beth Matthews*)], LeRoy Mason [(*Joe Dickson*)], Fern Emmett [(*Aunt Martha Hubbard*)], George Hayes [(*Sheriff Ed Williams*)], Buffalo Bill, Jr. [(*Chief Black Eagle*)], John Ince, Henry Rocquemore, Jack Duffy, [Lloyd Ingraham (*Dan Matthews*)], [Bert Dillard (*Red*)].

Western. [*Print viewed*]. Rancher Dan Matthews has withdrawn his life savings to spruce up his ranch, the "Lazy M," for the arrival of his daughter Beth from the East. That very day, robbers take refuge in Dan's house and kill him as they are pursued by his best friend, Sheriff John Higgins. Following a gun battle at the house, the outlaws flee. John believes that he accidentally killed Dan and turns his badge over to the previous sheriff, Ed Williams. John then withdraws from civilization to avenge himself on outlaws. He rescues the son of Chief Black Eagle and becomes a confidant of the tribe, who give him the symbolic gift of a ring. Later, unkempt and resembling a wild man, John rescues a young woman and her driver, Blake, from the new stagecoach, an automobile. The woman turns out to be Beth, ready to take over the "Lazy M," and Sheriff Ed convinces John he can make up for the past by becoming her foreman so that the ranch will flourish. John reluctantly agrees, even though he knows that she will eventually discover the truth. As time passes, Beth comes to appreciate western life, and soon she and John are in love. Attending a Halloween dance with the cook, Aunt Martha Hubbard, Beth meets Joe Dickson, who informs her that John killed her father. At the dance the Martin brothers spend some of the money taken from Dan, and John tricks them into leading him to their confederate, who turns out to be Dickson. They plan to steal Beth's horses, which John and the Indians prevent. One of the outlaws confesses that it was Dickson who shot Dan, and he is captured by John. Recognizing Dickson's duplicity, Beth then looks for John, with whom she is now in love. *False accusations. Ranch foremen. Ranches. Thieves. Automobiles. Dances. Gunfights. Indians of North America. Rescues. Rustlers. Sheriffs. Stagecoaches.*

Note: Modern sources also list Yakima Canutt, Bert O'Hara and Bobby Nelson in the cast. *Var* noted that the Indians "this time are allied on the law's side to combat the cattle rustlers and highway bandits."

Exh 15 Feb 1935, p. 36. *DV* 16 Nov 1934, p. 3. *Var* 3 Apr 1935, p. 30.

THANK YOU, MR. MOTO (Japanese Americans)

Twentieth Century-Fox Film Corp. *Dist* Twentieth Century-Fox Film Corp. 24 Dec **1937**; Prod: late Oct—mid-Nov 1937 [©Twentieth Century-Fox Film Corp.; 24 Dec 1937; LP7960]. Sd (Western Electric Mirrophonic Recording); b&w. 7 reels, 6,100 ft. 67-68 min. PCA cert no. 3828.

Series: Mr. Moto.

Exec prod Sol M. Wurtzel. *Dir* Norman Foster. *Asst dir* William Eckhardt. [*2d asst dir* Jerry Braun]. *Scr* Willis Cooper and Norman Foster. [*Contr wrt* Jerry Cady]. *Photog* Virgil Miller. [*2d cam* L. B. Abbott]. [*Asst cam* Ted Weisbarth and W. E. Meinardus]. [*Gaffer* Fred Hall]. *Art dir* Bernard Herzbrun and Albert Hogsett. *Film ed* Irene Morra and Nick DeMaggio. [*Asst cutter* Eleanor Morra]. *Cost* Herschel. [*Ward man* John Hassett]. [*Ward woman* Gladys Isaacson]. *Mus dir* Samuel Kaylin. *Sd* Joseph E. Aiken and William H. Anderson. [*Asst sd* J. Sigler]. [*Boom man* Harry Kornfield]. [*Cable man* E. J. La Valla]. [*Hair* Wilma Ryan]. [*Makeup* Ben Nye]. [*Prod mgr* Ed. Ebele]. [*Unit mgr* Sam Wurtzel]. [*Scr clerk* Jack Vernon]. [*Grip* Rodney Murphy].

[*Asst grip* Harry R. Jones]. [*Props* Duke Abrahams]. [*Asst prop* Ralph Hearst and Stanley Detlie]. [*Best boy* John Grady]. [*Still photog* Jerry Milligan]. [*Stunts* Jack Woody].

Source: Based on the novel *Thank you, Mr. Moto* by John P. Marquand (Boston, 1936).

Cast: PETER LORRE (*Mr. Moto*), Thomas Beck (*Tom Nelson*), Pauline Frederick (*Madame Chung*), Jayne Regan (*Eleanor Joyce*), Sidney Blackmer (*Herr [Eric] Koerger*), Sig Rumann (*Colonel Tchernov*), John Carradine (*Pieriera*), William Von Brincken (*Schneider*), Nedda Harrigan (*Madame Tchernov*), Philip Ahn (*Prince Chung*), John Bleifer (*Ivan*).

Detective. [*Print viewed*]. In the Great Gobi Desert, a Mongolian named Ning attempts to murder a man in his sleep who recently joined his camel caravan, but the man instead kills Ning. At Peiping, when an ancient scroll is found by police hidden in the man's staff, he escapes to the Grand Hotel where he changes clothes and reveals himself to be Mr. Moto, known as a mysterious adventurer, explorer and soldier of fortune. Moto attends a party given by Colonel Tchernov in honor of Eleanor Joyce, the daughter of a famous importer. After Prince Chung refuses to sell Colonel Tchernov a set of scroll paintings from the Yu'an Dynasty, Tchernov pulls a gun on him. Eleanor sees the prince angrily leave with his mother, Madame Chung, and then finds Tchernov dead. When Moto arranges the death to look like a suicide, Eleanor objects but he warns her that the incident could provoke an international incident. At Chung's home, the prince thanks Moto for saving his life, as Tchernov was about to shoot the prince, when Moto entered and killed Tchernov with a knife. In gratitude, the prince shows Moto the scrolls, which one of his ancestors painted. If placed in the proper order, the seven original scrolls, five of which the prince has, reveal a map to a great treasure in the hidden tomb of Ghengis Khan. The prince says that a sixth scroll is hidden in the Gobi desert, while the last has recently disappeared from a museum where the Chungs lent it for exhibition. After Moto reveals that he was sent to recover the treasure, Madame Chung rebukes her son for showing the scrolls and explains that it is their duty to see that the tomb is not despoiled. When Moto accuses an antique dealer, Pieriera, of stealing the scroll from the museum, Pieriera is about to name the man who paid him when he is shot from a passing car. In Moto's hotel room, he finds his belongings rifled, and when he perceives that the would-be thief is hiding, he places a gun loaded with blanks on a counter for the thief to find. He then takes out his scroll, which the thief, Schneider, steals after shooting Moto with the gun. Moto pretends to die, but then follows Schneider to the Tchernov home, where Eleanor, who is suspicious of Moto, is staying. Eleanor observes Madame Tchernov remove a scroll from her safe and leave with Schneider after speaking on the telephone with someone she calls "darling." Moto then reveals to Eleanor that he is really a detective for an importers' association. He traces the call to the Chung house and prepares to go there, but he is knocked out by the Tchernov butler Ivan. Schneider and his cohort, Eric Koerger, try to torture the prince, who refuses to reveal the hiding place of the scrolls. However, when they strike Madame Chung, the prince succumbs and the scrolls are found. Ashamed of her son, Madame Chung tries to attack the thieves with a dagger, but Koerger shoots and kills her. The thieves, having now obtained all seven scrolls, leave and take Eleanor hostage before Moto arrives with Tom Nelson, a member of the American Legation who has been courting Eleanor. After the prince, believing that he has shamed his ancestors, commits hara-kiri, Moto pledges that no one shall desecrate the tomb. He and Tom follow the thieves to a river where aboard a junk, Moto reveals that the scroll stolen from his room is an imitation. With Eleanor's help, he convinces Madame Tchernov that Koerger planned to get rid of her in favor of Eleanor. A fight breaks out during which Schneider and Koerger are killed. Moto then burns the scrolls thus keeping his promise to Prince Chung, whom, he says, can now face his ancestors without shame. *Detectives. Japanese Americans. Maps. Paintings. Soldiers of fortune. Tombs. Treasure. Undercover agents.* Americans in foreign countries. Antique dealers. Attempted murder. Butlers. Camels. Caravans. Family honor. Fathers and daughters. Fights. Gobi Desert (Mongolia and China). Hara-kiri. Hotels. Importers. Junks. Mongols. Mothers and sons. Murder. Officers (Military). Parties. Peking (China). Pledges. Princes. Rivers. Ruses. Thieves.

Note: The novel originally appeared as a serial in *The Saturday Evening Post* (8 Feb–14 Mar 1936). This was the second film in the "Mr. Moto" series.

For information about the series, please see the entry below for *Think Fast, Mr. Moto* and consult the Series Index.

Box 18 Dec 1937. *DV* 22 Nov 1937, p. 3. *FD* 26 Nov 1937, p. 7. *HR* 25 Oct 1937, p. 7. *HR* 8 Nov 1937, p. 9. *HR* 22 Nov 1937, p. 3. *MPD* 24 Nov 1937, p. 5. *MPH* 20 Nov 1937, p. 54. *NYT* 3 Jan 1938, p. 16. *Var* 12 Jan 1938, p. 15.

THANKS, GOD, I'LL TAKE IT FROM HERE *see* **WITHOUT RESERVATIONS**

THANKS, PAL *see* **STORMY WEATHER**

THAT BEDSIDE MANNER *see* **EMERGENCY WEDDING**

THAT GIRL FROM PARIS (French Americans)
RKO Radio Pictures, Inc.; A Pandro S. Berman Production. *Dist* RKO Radio Pictures, Inc. 1 Jan **1937**; New York opening: week of 31 Dec 1936; Prod: 19 Sep–mid-Nov 1936 [©RKO Radio Pictures, Inc.; 31 Dec 1936; LP6867]. Sd (RCA Victor System); b&w. 12 reels. 102 or 104-105 min. PCA cert no. 2686.

Dir Leigh Jason. *Scr* P. J. Wolfson and Dorothy Yost. *Story* Jane Murfin. *Adpt* Joseph A. Fields. [*Contr to scr const* Harold Kusell]. *Photog* J. Roy Hunt. *Art dir* Van Nest Polglase. *Art dir assoc* Carroll Clark. *Ed* William Morgan. *Set dresser* Darrell Silvera. *Gowns* Edward Stevenson. *Mus dir* Nathaniel Shilkret. *Cond* Andre Kostelanetz. *Rec* Hugh McDowell, Jr. [*Research* Elizabeth McGaffey].

Song(s): "Una voce poco fa," from the opera *The Barber of Seville*, music by Gioacchino Antonio Rossini, libretto by Cesare Sterbini; "Tarantella," music and lyrics by Heinrich Panofka; "Call to Arms," "Love and Learn," "Seal It with a Kiss," "Nephew from Nice" and "Moonface," music by Arthur Schwartz, lyrics by Edward Heyman; "Blue Danube Waltz," music by Johann Strauss, added lyrics by Ralph Freed.

Source: Suggested by the short story "Viennese Charmer" by W. Carey Wonderly in *Young's Magazine* (Mar 1928).

Cast: LILY PONS [(*Nicole "Nikki" Martin*)], JACK OAKIE [(*Whammo*)], GENE RAYMOND [(*Windy McClean*)], Herman Bing [(*Hammacher*)], Mischa Auer [(*Butch*)], Lucille Ball [(*Clair Williams*)], Frank Jenks [(*Frank, Laughing Boy*)], [Patricia Wilder (*Coat-room girl*)], [Vinton Haworth (*Reporter*)], [Willard Robertson (*Immigration officer*)], [Gregory Gaye (*Paul DeVry*)], [Ferdinand Gottschalk (*Uncle*)], [Rafaela Ottiano (*Marie*)], [Harry Jans (*Purser*)], [Landers Stevens (*Ship's captain*)], [Edward Price (*Photographer*)], [Alec Craig (*Justice of the peace*)].

Musical comedy. [*Print viewed*]. In the middle of her arranged wedding to financier Paul DeVry, Parisian opera star Nicole "Nikki" Martin suddenly rebels and takes off in search of love and adventure in the country. While hitchhiking, Nikki meets handsome American musician Windy McClean and, although he spites her, makes up her mind to follow him back to New York. Without revealing her identity, Nikki stows away on the ship on which Windy and his group, "McClean's Wildcats," are performers and is later discovered in their room by a steward. Nikki is locked up, and Windy, Whammo, Butch and Frank, "McClean's Wildcats," are fired. Still determined to be with Windy, Nikki escapes the ship in New York and locates the band's apartment a few steps ahead of the immigration officials. Once they turn away the authorities, the men demand that Nikki leave, but she stubbornly refuses until the men start undressing in front of her. At that moment, however, policemen are spotted outside, and afraid that they will be implicated, the quartet hauls the fleeing singer back to the apartment. The next morning, dancer Clair Williams, Windy's girl friend, shows up with a Mr. Hammacher, who offers them a low-paying job performing at his roadhouse. Anxious to depart, Windy and company accept the offer and, with Nikki in tow, leave the city. At the roadhouse, Nikki stuns the crowds with her singing, but a jealous Clair informs on her and sends the group running once again. To solve Nikki's problem, all of the men volunteer to marry her, then at Whammo's suggestion, they cut cards for her. Whammo cheats and wins but, seeing Windy's genuine love, bows out to his friend. At the impromptu marriage ceremony, however, Nikki finds out about the card cutting and runs back to the waiting arms of Paul DeVry. The group gags and ties Windy and, in the middle of Nikki's second lavish wedding, ambushes her and the minister, who then marries the new couple in the getaway limousine. *Deportation. French. Immigrants. Musicians. Opera singers. Romance.* Clergy. Dancers. Gambling. Hitchhiking. Jealousy. Marriage–Arranged. New York City. Ocean liners. Paris (France). Police. Roadhouses. Weddings.

Note: The working title of this film was *Street Girl*. Sources differ on the film's release date. *MPH*'s release charts give 22 Jan 1937 as the release date, while RKO studio records list 1 Jan 1937 as the release. Although Hugh McDowell, Jr. received screen credit for sound recording, John O. Aalberg, the head of RKO's sound department, was nominated for an Academy Award for this film. Modern sources give the following additional cast credits: Pat Hartigan as "Immigration officer," and Michael Mark, Louis Mercier and Richard Carle as bit players. In 1929, Wesley Ruggles directed Betty Compson and John Harron in RKO's first version of W. Carey Wonderly's story called *Street Girl* (see *AFI Catalog of Feature Films, 1921-30*; F2.5436). Jack Hively directed Anne Shirley, Desi Arnaz and Ray Bolger in a 1941 RKO version of the story, *Four Jacks and a Jill*.

DV 14 Dec 1936, p. 3. *FD* 22 Dec 1936, p. 10. *HR* 19 Sep 1936, p. 4. *HR* 12 Nov 1936, p. 13. *HR* 12 Dec 1936, p. 3. *HR* 31 Dec 1936, pp. 7-11. *MPD* 14 Dec 1936, p. 12. *MPH* 24 Oct 1936, p. 41, 44. *MPH* 19 Dec 1936, p. 56. *NYT* 1 Jan 1937, p. 19. *Var* 6 Jan 1937, p. 40.

THAT GIRL MONTANA (Native Americans)
Pathé Exchange, Inc. *Dist* Pathé Exchange, Inc. Jan **1921** [©Pathé Exchange, Inc.; 22 Dec 1920; LU15951]. Si; b&w. 5 reels.
Pres Jesse D. Hampton. *Dir* Robert Thornby. *Scen* George H. Plympton. *Photog* Lucien Andriot.
Source: Based on the novel *That Girl Montana* by Marah Ellis Ryan (New York, 1901).
Cast: Blanche Sweet (*Montana Rivers*), Mahlon Hamilton (*Dan Overton*), Frank Lanning (*Jim Harris*), Edward Peil (*Lee Holly*), Charles Edler (*Akkomi*), Claire Du Brey (*Lottie*), Kate Price (*Mrs. Huzzard*), Jack Roseleigh (*Max Lyster*).
Western. Lee Holly, a cardsharp, has brought up his daughter, Monte, in boys' clothing, She escapes to an Indian village when Holly is chased out of town and remains there two years with her friend Akkomi, resuming feminine attire and taking the name Tana. Dan Overton, a young prospector, becomes interested in her and takes her to live with white people in a boardinghouse. She is introduced by Dan to his mining partner Harris as Montana Rivers, the daughter of a partner of his, but Harris recognizes her as "Lee Holly's brat" and denounces her. Dan defends her, and after Harris suffers a paralyzing stroke he relents and makes her a partner in their mine. Holly comes to their camp after they strike gold and is killed by Harris, who learns that Tana is the daughter stolen from him. Dan's unfaithful wife is killed by a jealous lover, freeing him to marry Tana. *Cardsharping. Fatherhood. Indians of North America.*
ETR 8 Jan 1921, p. 571.

THAT I MAY LIVE (Jewish Americans)
Twentieth Century-Fox Film Corp. *Dist* Twentieth Century-Fox Film Corp. 30 Apr **1937**; Prod: late Jan-mid Feb 1937 [©Twentieth Century-Fox Film Corp.; 30 Apr 1937; LP7202]. Sd (Western Electric Mirrophonic Recording); b&w. 7 reels, 6,300 ft. 70 min. PCA cert no. 3089.
Exec prod Sol M. Wurtzel. *Dir* Allan Dwan. [*Dial dir* George Wright]. *Asst dir* Aaron Rosenberg and [Tom Dudley]. *Scr* Ben Markson and William Conselman. [*Story* David Lamson]. [*Contr wrt* Helen Logan, Robert Ellis and Saul Elkins]. *Photog* Robert Planck. [*Cam op* Harry Webb]. [*Asst cam* Lou Kunkle and Frank McDonald]. [*Gaffer* Jack McAvoy]. [*Process photog* Sol Halprin and Joe Farley]. *Art dir* Lewis Creber. *Film ed* Louis Loeffler. *Cost* Herschel. [*Ward* LaVon Larson and Claude Lampman]. *Mus dir* Samuel Kaylin. *Sd* George Leverett and Harry M. Leonard. [*Asst sd* Harold Hobson]. [*Boom* Jim Burnette]. [*Hair* Wilma Ryan]. [*Makeup* Ernie Young]. [*Prod mgr* Ed. Ebele]. [*Unit mgr* Sam Wurtzel]. [*Scr clerk* Stanley Scheuer]. [*Grip* George Carpenter]. [*Props* Frank Sullivan]. [*Best boy* Bill Barrett]. [*Asst prop* Bob McLaughlin and Monroe Liebgold]. [*Casting* Virgil Hart]. [*Still photog* Joe Milligan]. [*Stand in* Bob Johnson and Emily Baldwin].
Song(s): "On a Sunday Afternoon," words and lyrics by Harry Von Tilzer.
Cast: Rochelle Hudson (*Irene Howard*), Robert Kent (*Dick Mannion*), J. Edward Bromberg (*Tex Shapiro*), Jack La Rue (*Charlie*), Frank Conroy (*Pop*), Fred Kelsey (*Abner Jenkins*), George Cooper (*Mack*), De Witt Jennings (*Chief of police*), Russell Simpson (*Bish Plivens*), William Benedict (*Kurt Plivens*), [William Pawley (*Tom*)], [Frank McGlynn, Sr. (*Dr. Curtis*)], [Eily Malyon (*Cally Plivens*)], [Frank McGlynn, Jr. (*Ben Jenkins*)], [Paul Kruger, James Flavin (*Policemen*)], [Russ Clark, Lon Chaney, Jr. (*Engineers*)], [Mary Gordon (*Mrs. Healy*)], [E. W. Borman (*Bald-headed man*)], [Lillian Lawrence (*Sharp-faced woman*)], [Gloria Roy (*Nurse*)], [Almeda Fowler, Mary Alden, Jane Keckley, Laura Treadwell (*Women in auto*

camp)], [Armand "Curly" Wright (*Barber*)], [Ivan Miller (*Deputy*)], [Paul Porcasi (*Mr. Scaffa*)], [Eddie Dunn (*Prison guard*)], [Carl Stockdale (*Man who sees robbery*)], [Joseph E. Bernard (*Night watchman*)], [Paul McVey (*Desk clerk*)], [Heinie Conklin (*Hobo*)], [Baby Mondshine], [Blanche Payson], [Betty Farrington], [Rita Owin], [Vera Steadman], [Mary McCarty].
Crime, Road, Rural, Drama. [*Print viewed*]. Safecracker Richard Mannion is released from prison after serving three years. He plans to go straight, but three of his former gang members, Charlie, Pop and Mack, threaten to kill him if he doesn't help them rob a bank in the town of Ranville. At the bank, Dick refuses to open the safe. The nightwatchman shines a flashlight on them, and Charlie, who was about to shoot Dick, kills the nightwatchman and knocks Dick cold with his revolver. He then puts the gun into Dick's hand and leaves with Pop and Mack. As Dick is being led away by the police, Charlie shoots at him, but misses and wounds an officer. Dick escapes, then jumps a train and gets off at another small town, where he attempts to rob the cash register at a restaurant. The waitress, Irene Howard, recognizes that Dick's concealed weapon is only a monkey wrench and offers him a meal in exchange for it, then gets her boss Tom to hire Dick as a dishwasher. Two months later, as Dick and Irene cry while peeling onions, they confess their love for each other. Later, when Dick breaks a dish, Tom, drunken and jealous of Irene's affection for Dick, fires him. When Tom starts to grab Irene, Dick fights him. Irene quits, and although Dick tells her that she better go without him, she vows to remain with him. After they are unable to get a ride hitchhiking, they find a broken-down truck belonging to Tex Shapiro, a Jewish peddler. Dick fixes the engine, and Tex gives them a ride to an auto camp, where Irene and Dick demonstrate better sales techniques than Tex. At night, Tex convinces Dick to propose to Irene, but Dick changes his mind and tells her that it would be best if he continued on alone. Tex interrupts them, and when he asks if he has proposed yet, Irene takes the initiative and accepts. Before the marriage ceremony, Irene sees Dick's picture on a "wanted for murder" poster. She marries Dick anyway and later says she doesn't care what he did, but insists that he does not lie to her. Dick explains how he got mixed up with Charlie, Pop and Mack and what happened at the bank. Soon, Dick and Irene travel as Tex's partners. When Irene has a baby girl, Tex learns that Dick is wanted by the police, and after Dick explains his past, Tex, who is convinced that the Ranville chief of police will treat Dick fairly, drives them to Ranville, where Dick is arrested. Tex conceives of a plan whereby Irene will go to San Francisco and get a job at the restaurant that Charlie, Pop and Mack frequent. A month later, after she repeatedly spurns Charlie's flirtations, Irene agrees to go in with the gang to rob Tex, who is posing as a dealer of Oriental art, of $50,000 locked in a warehouse vault. The gang then reads that Dick has escaped from jail, and when Dick locates them, they agree to cut Dick in if he opens the vault. Charlie, however, plans to kill Dick and escape with Irene and all the money. At the warehouse, after Dick opens the vault, he pulls a gun on Charlie and demands his cut. Charlie admits that he killed the watchman, and police, waiting to hear this confession, close in and apprehend the gang after a gunfight. The chief of police says that he will recommend leniency for Dick, and afterward, Dick, Irene, Tex and the baby continue their travels in their truck. *Ex-convicts. Frame-ups. Fugitives. Gangs. Peddlers and peddling. Romance. Safecrackers. Waitresses. Auto camps. Bank robberies. Confession (Law). Dishwashing. Fistfights. Gunfights. Hitchhiking. Impersonation and imposture. Infants. Jews. Marriage. Police. Proposals (Marital). Restaurants. San Francisco (CA). Small town life. Threats. Trucks. Watchmen. Weddings.*
Note: Although the screen credits give no information regarding the source of the story, according to the Twentieth Century-Fox Records of the Legal Department at the UCLA Theater Arts Library, the studio paid David Lamson $2,000 for his unpublished, uncopyrighted story. Allan Dwan, in a modern biography, commented concerning this film, "I saw that again recently—it was horrible."
Box 13 Mar 1937. *DV* 27 Feb 1937, p. 3. *FD* 11 May 1937, p. 9. *HR* 25 Jan 1937, p. 11. *HR* 8 Feb 1937, p. 11. *HR* 27 Feb 1937, p. 3. *MPD* 2 Mar 1937, p. 6. *MPH* 13 Feb 1937, p. 50. *MPH* 6 Mar 1937, p. 45. *NYT* 10 May 1937, p. 23. *Var* 12 May 1937, p. 13.

THAT MAN OF MINE (African Americans)
Associated Producers of Negro Motion Pictures, Inc.; An Alexander Production. *Dist* Astor Pictures Corp. **1946**. Sd (RCA Sound System); b&w. 5,450 ft.

Prod William D. Alexander. *Dir* Leonard Anderson. *Orig story* Powell Lindsey. *Scr* Les Hafner. *Dir of photog* Don Malkames. *Film ed* Theodore H. Markovic. *Sd* Nelson Minnerly. *Makeup* Fred Ryle.

Song(s): "Breaking My Heart," music and lyrics by Joe Liggins; "How About That Jive," music by Ernestine "Tiny" Davis; "Jam Session," "Don't Get It Twisted," "Vi Vigor," "The Thing," "Standing Room Only" and "That Man of Mine," music and lyrics by Maurice King; "Woode Would," music by Bob MacRae; "It's Just Like That" and "Dear One," music and lyrics by Henri Woode and Marion Marlowe.

Cast: Betty Haynes (*Chris*), Ruby Dee (*Joan*), Powell Lindsey (*Sid [Thomas]*), Tommie Moore (*Honey Diamond [previously known as Jenny]*), Flo Hawkins (*Nicky*), Rhina Harris (*Ruth Dubois*), Kenneth Broomes, Billie and Millie (*Dancers*), The International Sweethearts of Rhythm, featuring Anna Mae Winburn, Henri Woode and His Sextet.

African American, Show business, Romance, with songs. [*Print viewed*]. At his office at the Associated Motion Picture Studios, Lem Coles, a black film producer and the leading actor in his next film, engages his director, Sid Thomas, in an argument over who should play the feminine lead. While Sid wants Joan, Lem's fiancée, to star, Lem insists that they find a new talent. Joan arrives at the office during the argument, and Lem tells her that she will not be getting the role she had hoped for. Angered by the news, Joan returns Lem's engagement ring and storms out of the office. Lem and Sid choose the beautiful Jenny to take the leading role, but they soon realize that although she has plenty of "experience," none of it involved acting. Desperate to begin rehearsals, Lem and Sid ignore Jenny's inability to act and keep her on. Hoping to capitalize on Jenny's "diamond-in-the-rough" appeal, Lem decides to change his leading lady's name to "Honey Diamond." Honey's initial appearances before the cameras prove disastrous, however. Upset that Honey ruined the love scenes by wriggling too much, and accusing the actress of being more sexy than romantic, Lem leaves the production. Sid and Joan then pull together to get Lem back to work on the film. When Lem admits that he has muddled things at the studio and apologizes to Joan for his behavior, she gives him another chance and accepts the role for which she was initially rejected. With Joan playing the romantic lead opposite Lem, the film is brought back to life and the love scenes become more believable. His love for Joan, both on and off the screen, restored, Lem carefully slips the engagement ring back on the actress' hand and looks forward to a happy future with her. *Actors and actresses. African Americans. Motion picture directors. Motion picture producers. Motion pictures. Auditions. Bands (Music). Engagements. Rehearsals. Romance. Singers. Talent agents. Tap dancing.*

Note: Although there is a 1946 copyright statement on the film, the title is not included in the copyright records.

THAT MIDNIGHT KISS (Italian Americans)

Metro-Goldwyn-Mayer Corp.; controlled by Loew's Inc. *Dist* Loew's Inc. Sep 1949; World premiere in Philadelphia, PA: 2 Sep 1949; New York opening: 22 Sep 1949; Prod: 10 Jan—mid-Mar 1949 [©Loew's Inc.; 23 Aug 1949; LP2504]. Sd (Western Electric Sound System); color (Technicolor). 10 reels, 8,873 ft. 96 or 99 min. Passed by the National Board of Review. PCA cert no. 13767.

Prod Joe Pasternak. *Dir* Norman Taurog. [*Asst dir* Dolph Zimmer]. *Scr* Bruce Manning and Tamara Hovey. *Dir of photog* Robert Surtees. [*Cam op* A. Lindsley Lane]. [*Stills* Durward Graybill]. *Technicolor color consultant* Henri Jaffa and James Gooch. *Art dir* Cedric Gibbons and Preston Ames. *Film ed* Gene Ruggiero. *Set dec* Edwin B. Willis. *Assoc* Arthur Krams. *Cost* Helen Rose. *Men's cost by* Valles. *Mus dir* Charles Previn. *Orch* Leo Arnaud and Conrad Salinger. *Mus supv* Jose Iturbi. *Rec supv* Douglas Shearer. [*Sd* Conrad Kahn]. *Hair styles des* Sydney Guilaroff. *Makeup created by* Jack Dawn. [*Prod mgr* Sergei Petschnikoff]. [*Dir of publicity* Howard Dietz]. [*Scr supv* Les Martinson]. [*Grip* Albert Hunter].

Music: Concerto No. 1 in E Flat Major by Franz Liszt; Concerto in B Flat Minor by Peter Illyich Tchaikovsky; "Revolutionary Etude" by Frédéric Chopin.

Song(s): "They Didn't Believe Me," music by Jerome Kern, lyrics by Herbert Reynolds; "I Know, I Know, I Know," music by Bronislau Kaper, lyrics by Bob Russell; "Caro nomé" from the opera *Rigoletto*, music by Guiseppe Verdi, libretto by Francesco Maria Piave; "Celeste Aida" from the opera *Aida*, music by Guiseppe Verdi, libretto by A. Ghislanzoni; selection from the opera *Lucia di Lammermoor*, music by Gaetano Donizetti, libretto by Salvatore Cammarano; "Mama mia,

che vo sapé" from the opera *Cavalleria rusticana*, music by Pietro Mascagni, libretto by Guido Menasci and Giovanni Targioni-Tozzetti; "O sole mio" by Eduardo Di Capua; "Down Among the Sheltering Pines," music by Abe Olman, lyrics by James Brockman; "Una furtiva lagrima" from the opera *L'elisir d'amore*, music by Gaetano Donizetti, libretto by Felice Romani; Overture from the opera *Semiramide*, music by Gioacchino Antonio Rossini, libretto by Gaetano Rossi; "Russian Nightingale," music and lyrics by Alexander Alabieff; "Judaline," music and lyrics by Don Raye and Gene De Paul; "Love Is Music," music based on The Fifth Symphony by Peter Illyich Tchaikovsky, lyrics by William Katz.

Cast: Kathryn Grayson (*Prudence Budell*), José Iturbi (*Himself*), Ethel Barrymore (*Abigail Trent Budell*), and introducing Mario Lanza (*Johnny Donnetti*), Keenan Wynn (*Artie Geoffrey Glenson*), J. Carrol Naish (*Papa Donnetti*), Jules Munshin (*Michael Pemberton*), Thomas Gomez (*Guido Russino Betelli*), Marjorie Reynolds (*Mary*), Arthur Treacher (*Hutchins*), Mimi Aguglia (*Mamma Donnetti*), Amparo Iturbi (*Herself*), Bridget Carr (*Donna*), Amparo Ballester (*Rosina*), Ann Codee (*Mme. Bouget*), Edward Earle (*Jason*), George Meader (*Paul*), Sheila Stein (*Peanuts*), [Joe Rocca, Frank Donia, Jerry Lascoe, Jr., Al Thompson, Michael Kostrick (*Truck drivers*)], [Charles Smith, George Boyce, Dwight Martin, Robert Cherry (*G.I. Quartette*)], [Anne O'Neal (*Charwoman*)], [Richard Lane (*Radio interviewer*)], [Wilson Wood (*Disc jockey*)], [Ed Gargan (*Traffic cop*)], [Dewey Robinson (*Waiter*)], [Stanley Blystone (*Customer*)], [Lee Phelps, Gregg Barton (*Stagehands*)], [Patty Kate Johnston (*Infant*)].

Musical, Romantic comedy. [*Print viewed*]. Abigail Trent Budell, a wealthy resident of Philadelphia and a generous patron of the arts, hopes to launch the singing career of her young granddaughter Prudence by introducing her to friend and noted musical conductor Jose Iturbi. Jose auditions Prudence for an upcoming opera and compliments her singing voice, but when he criticizes her style, she angrily storms out of the house. Abigail, whose own mother denied her the opportunity to sing professionally when she was young, is determined to help Prudence realize her dreams. To do so, Abigail finances the construction of an opera house in Philadelphia, and hires Jose to direct the new company. While Abigail begins a radio campaign to publicize the new concert hall, Jose casts Prudence in the company's first opera, opposite tenor Signor Guido Russino Betelli. During rehearsals, Jose realizes that Prudence has trouble looking directly at Betelli when she is singing to him, and tries to solve the problem through coaching. The coaching proves ineffective, however, as Prudence rejects Jose's instructions and complains that Betelli is too fat to look at. A short time later, Prudence meets Johnny Donnetti, a handsome former New York opera star who left the stage to become a truck driver for Artie Geoffrey Glenson's trucking company. While a romance blossoms between Johnny and Prudence, Jose discovers Johnny's singing abilities and introduces him at one of the concerts. After winning a standing ovation from the audience, Johnny is invited to join the company and sing with Prudence and Betelli. Complications soon arise, however, when Betelli objects to the presence of another tenor in the program and tears up his contract. Betelli's departure pleases most of the company, especially Prudence, who immediately asks Jose to replace Betelli with Johnny. Jose grants her request, but Prudence's hope of a continuing romance with Johnny is soon dashed when she discovers that Johnny intends to marry his former sweetheart Mary. Unaware that Johnny is not in love with Mary and that his marriage proposal was a result of a misunderstanding, Prudence grows increasingly despondent and her performance begins to suffer. Confusion ensues when Johnny quits the opera mistakenly believing that Abigail hired him to marry Prudence. Desperate to fill Johnny's role, Jose recalls Betelli, but is disappointed to find that Prudence is still unable to look at him when she sings. Things look bad for the opera until Mary overhears Johnny tell Jose that he does not love his fiancée, and he breaks off the engagement. The success of the opera is ensured only moments before its opening, when Betelli is tricked into quitting, and Johnny agrees to go on in his place. Prudence is delighted to have Johnny back, and the two celebrate their reunion with a kiss. *Conductors (Music). Opera houses. Opera singers. Romance. Art patronage. Auditions. Concerts. Engagements. Fathers and sons. Granddaughters. Italian Americans. Jealousy. Obesity. Philadelphia (PA). Pianists. Proposals (Marital). Radio programs. Truck drivers. Wealth.*

Note: The film's world premiere was held in Philadelphia, PA to honor Philadelphia native Mario Lanza, who made his motion picture debut in *That Midnight Kiss*. Lanza, who had appeared on the concert stage both prior to and after his service in the armed forces during World War II, made several popular musical films for M-G-M during the early 1950s. His recordings of operatic and popular music selections were also very successful. His best-known role was that of Enrico Caruso in the 1951 M-G-M film *The Great Caruso* (see above). According to biographical sources, Lanza's career was damaged by a chronic weight problem as well as alcoholism. In 1959, while in Rome, Italy, Lanza suffered a heart attack and died at age thirty-eight. According to M-G-M publicity material, Patty Kate Johnston, the infant who appeared in the film with Kathryn Grayson in a park sequence, was Grayson's newborn daughter.

Box 27 Aug 1949. *DV* 24 Aug 1949, p. 3. *FD* 25 Aug 1949, p. 6. *HR* 10 Jan 1949, p. 10. *HR* 14 Jan 1949, p. 12. *HR* 11 Feb 1949, p. 5. *HR* 4 Mar 1949, p. 12. *HR* 6 Jun 1949, p. 9. *HR* 24 Aug 1949, p. 4. *HR* 25 Aug 1949, p. 4. *MPHPD* 27 Aug 1949, p. 4730. *NYT* 23 Sep 1949, p. 28. *Var* 24 Aug 1949, p. 18.

THAT OLD MAGIC *see* **THE LUCK OF THE IRISH**

THEIR FIRST MISTAKE *see* **PARDON US**

THEIR MAD MOMENT (*foreign version*) *see* **MI ÚLTIMO AMOR**

THEY CAME TO BLOW UP AMERICA (German Americans)
Twentieth Century-Fox Film Corp. *Dist* Twentieth Century-Fox Film Corp. 7 May **1943**; Prod: 5 Dec 1942—late Dec 1942 [©Twentieth Century-Fox Film Corp.; 7 May 1943; LP12416]. Sd (Western Electric Recording); b&w. 8 reels, 6,586 ft. 73 min. PCA cert no. 9036.

Vice President in Charge of Studio Operations William Goetz. *Prod* Lee Marcus. *Dir* Edward Ludwig. [*Dial dir* Thomas Z. Loring]. [*Asst dir* William Eckhardt]. *Scr* Aubrey Wisberg. *Orig story* Michel Jacoby. *Dir of photog* Lucien Andriot. *Spec photog eff* Fred Sersen. *Art dir* James Basevi and John Ewing. *Film ed* Nick DeMaggio. *Set dec* Thomas Little and Al Orenbach. *Cost* N'Was McKenzie. *Mus dir* Hugo W. Friedhofer. *Mus dir* Emil Newman. *Sd* W. D. Flick and Harry M. Leonard.

Cast: George Sanders [(*Carl Steelman*)], Anna Sten [(*Frau Reiker*)], Ward Bond [(*Chief Craig*)], Dennis Hoey [(*Colonel Taeger*)], Sig Ruman [(*Dr. Herman Baumer*)], Ludwig Stossel [(*Julius Steelman*)], Robert Barrat [(*Captain Kranz*)], Poldy Dur [(*Helga Lorenz*)], Ralph Byrd [(*Gebhardt*)], Elsa Janssen [(*Mrs. Steelman*)], [Egon Brecher (*Kirschner*)], [Rex Williams (*Eichner*)], [Charles McGraw (*Zellerbach*)], [Sven-Hugo Borg (*Hauser*)], [Kurt Katch (*Schonzeit*)], [Otto Reichow (*Fritz*)], [Walter O. Stahl (*Taeger's aide*)], [Andre Charlot (*Zugholtz*)], [Arno Frey (*Kranz's aide*)], [Sam Wren (*Jones*)], [Etta McDaniel (*Theresa*)], [Peter Michael (*Gertzer*)], [Dick Hogan (*Coast guardsman*)], [Lisa Golm (*Saleslady*)], [Wolfgang Zilzer (*Schlegel*)], [Charles Tannen (*Smith*)], [Eula Guy (*Anna, a nurse*)], [Lane Chandler (*Reynolds*)], [Frederick Giermann, William Yetter, John Banner (*Gestapo officers*)], [Pierre Watkin, Forbes Murray (*Diplomats*)], [Torben Meyer (*Gottwald*)], [George Lynn (*Herman*)], [Henry Guttman (*Fiertag*)], [Sigurd Tor (*Holtzfeld*)], [Walter Sande (*Boatswain's mate*)], [Frederick Brunn, Albert d'Arno (*German soldiers*)], [Arthur Space, Bruce Warren, Hugh Prosser (*F. B. I. agents*)], [John Epper (*Dispatch rider*)], [Bob Stephenson (*Sentry*)], [Fred Nurney (*Ernst Reiker*)], [Jack Lorenz (*Marine sentry*)], [Bud Geary, Fred Graham (*Policemen*)], [John Mylong (*German officer*)], [Ruthe Brady (*Secretary*)].

Espionage, World War II, Drama. Carl Steelman, a German-American attorney for a mining company, is implicated in a German sabotage operation when he and seven other men are arrested shortly after arriving in a German U-Boat on the shores of New York. Following the trial of the saboteurs, Chief Craig of the F. B. I. answers a question posed by one of his men about Carl's involvement in the group by telling the story of Carl's first exposure to the German-American Bund: Despite his parents' protests, Carl, a youth, attends Bund meetings and gets into trouble with the law. Unknown to his family and the Nazi Bund leaders, however, Carl is an American agent on a top secret mission to infiltrate the higher echelons of the Nazi organization and investigate their training school for saboteurs. As part of the government's investigation of the school, Carl is given a passport belonging to a German enlisted man, Ernst Reiker, whose identity he is to assume, and is sent to Hamburg, Germany. There, Carl befriends Helga Lorenz, a Nazi operative who is suspected by the Germans of being a double agent. Given orders by the Nazis to determine Helga's loyalties, Carl soon discovers for himself that she is a double agent when he finds fake candles containing anti-Nazi propaganda in her home. Confident that Helga can be trusted, Carl confesses that he has been sent by the Nazis to spy on her and suggests that she flee before they send her to a concentration camp. Before Carl can dispose of the candles, however, Nazi agents confiscate them and Helga is immediately captured. During Helga's interrogation, she confesses to being a double agent and is ordered to do time in a detention camp. Carl cleverly saves Helga, though, by using his skills as a saboteur to sabotage the vehicle in which she is being transported. Carl then takes Helga to a boat that is waiting for them on a river and sends her to a safer place. Meanwhile, Frau Reiker, the wife of the real Reiker, causes trouble for Carl and his mission when she decides to pay a surprise visit to her husband and finds Carl in his hotel room. Though confused and angry, Frau Reiker consents to Carl's request that she give him twenty-four hours to find out what happened to her husband. Having stalled Frau Reiker, Carl rushes to his German commander, Colonel Taeger, and tells him that his wife has gone mad and that she is convinced that he is an impostor. Arguing that her delusion poses a security threat, Carl persuades the colonel to have Frau Reiker sent to a sanitarium. Meanwhile, back in America, Carl's father Julius, who never completely recovered from the shock of his son's apparent involvement with the Bund, has become seriously ill. To save Julius, the F. B. I. sends an agent to the Steelmans, and after swearing him to an oath of absolute secrecy, the agent tells Julius that his son is on a top secret mission. Julius rejoices at the news and makes a speedy recovery, but is unable to contain his excitement and pride and tells his physician, Dr. Herman Baumer, about Carl. Baumer, a Nazi sympathizer, informs on Carl, and orders are placed in Germany to have the American arrested. Carl, however, has already left Germany, and is en route to America on his first mission of sabotage. Although it is now clear to Taeger that Frau Reiker was telling the truth about Carl, Taeger kills her in her jail cell because she might expose his mistake if she is released. When the submarine on which Carl is traveling comes under attack from U.S. war planes, Carl escapes in a rubber raft and watches as the submarine explodes. After landing on American soil, Carl is arrested along with eight other saboteurs, but he is soon released when his identity is learned. Six of the eight saboteurs are tried and executed, and Dr. Baumer is exposed as a Nazi agent and is arrested. *Espionage. German Americans. Impersonation and imposture. Nazis. Sabotage. Secret agents. United States. Federal Bureau of Investigation. Bombs. Concentration camps. Disease. Escapes. Explosions. False accusations. Fathers and sons. Germany. Germany. Intelligence Service. Gestapo. Long Island (NY). Murder. Physicians. Police. Rescues. Sanitariums. World War II.*

Note: Working titles for this film were *School for Sabotage* and *School for Saboteurs*. Although information contained in the Produced Scripts Collection at the UCLA Art–Special Collections Library notes that Ben Ray Redman co-authored a 3 Aug 1942 draft of the screenplay with Michel Jacoby, Redman's contribution to the released film has not been determined. Contemporary *HR* news items note that Bryan Foy was originally set to produce the film, and that the Sheriff's Camp for Boys in Calabasas, CA, and the industrial sector of Compton, CA were selected as sites for location shooting.

AmCin May 1943, p. 184. *Box* 1 May 1943. *DV* 21 Apr 1943, p. 3. *FD* 23 Apr 1943, p. 8. *HR* 6 Jul 1942, p. 1. *HR* 24 Aug 1942, p. 7. *HR* 23 Sep 1942, p. 2. *HR* 23 Oct 1942, p. 3. *HR* 7 Dec 1942, p. 3. *HR* 16 Dec 1942, p. 3. *HR* 24 Dec 1942, p. 7. *HR* 21 Apr 1943, p. 3. *HR* 25 May 1943, p. 4. *MPH* 24 Apr 1943. *MPHPD* 13 Feb 1943, p. 1162. *MPHPD* 24 Apr 1943, p. 1273. *NYT* 15 May 1943, p. 13. *Var* 21 Apr 1943, p. 8.

THEY DARE NOT LOVE (Austrian Americans)
Columbia Pictures Corp. *Dist* Columbia Pictures Corp. 30 Apr **1941**; Prod: 6 Jan—22 Feb 1941 [©Columbia Pictures Corp.; 30 Apr 1941; LP10754]. Sd; b&w. 6,788 ft. 75 min.

Prod Samuel Bischoff. *Dir* James Whale. *Fill-in dir* Charles Vidor. *Asst dir* William Mull. *Scr* Charles Bennett and Ernest Vajda. *Story* James Edward Grant. *Dir of photog* Franz F. Planer. *Art dir* Lionel Banks. *Film ed* Al Clark. *Gowns* Saltern. *Mus dir* M. W. Stoloff. *Sd eng* Ed Bernds.

Cast: George Brent (*Prince Kurt von Rotenburg*), Martha Scott (*Marta Keller*), Paul Lukas (*Baron von Helsing*), Egon Brecher (*Professor Keller*), Roman Bohnen (*Baron Shafter*), Edgar Barrier (*Captain Wilhelm Ehrbardt*), Kay Linaker (*Barbara Murdoch*), Frank Reicher (*Captain*), Gregory Gaye (*Von Mueller*), Georges Renavent (*Belgian captain*), Peter Cushing (*English lieutenant*), Cy Kendall (*Major Kenlein*), Leon Belasco (*Pierre*), Bodil Rosing (*Leni*), Erwin Kalser (*Klaus*), Leslie Denison (*English father*), Brenda Henderson (*English girl*), Richard Lyon (*English boy*), Stanley Brown (*Michael*), Hans Schumm (*Bruckner*), Walter Stahl (*Count Marlik*), Marguerita Sylva (*Countess Marlik*), Phil Taylor

(*Hugo*), Sig Arno (*Louis*), Georgia Backus (*German secretary*), Lloyd Bridges (*Blonde officer*), Fredrik Vogeding (*Carl Schmidt*), Philip Van Zandt (*Radio operator*), John Rogers (*Noncommissioned officer*), Charles Wagenheim (*Valet*), Nicholas Bela, Don Beddoe (*Sailors*), Gerald Pierce (*Messenger boy*), Olga Borget (*Stewardess*), Poppy Wild (*Society girl*), Paul Power (*Society man*), Jack Gardner, Philo McCullough, Richard Fiske, David Oliver (*Photographers*), Jack Chefe (*Deck steward*), Ed Fetherston (*Reporter*), Jac George (*Orchestra leader*), Paul Deno (*Doorman*), Fred Wolff, Hans Fuerberg (*Waiters*), Robert Heller (*German attendant*), Harry C. Bradley.

World War II, Drama. [*Not viewed*]. On the eve of the Anschluss, Prince Kurt von Rotenburg is preparing to leave his native Austria. While pausing for one last look at his favorite restaurant, the Café Weinergarten, Kurt encounters his old friend Professor Keller, the professor's daughter Marta and her fiancé, Wilhelm Erhardt. When Kurt and Marta fondly recall their childhood friendship, Wilhelm, a secret member of the Nazi party, becomes jealous and notifies the Gestapo that the prince is at the restaurant. After narrowly escaping the ensuing Nazi raid, the prince crosses the Czechoslovakian border and is reunited with the Kellers on a ship bound for America. Also aboard the vessel is Baron von Helsing, a covert Gestapo agent who feigns sympathy for the exiled prince while secretly working to spirit him back to Germany. As the prince and Marta begin to rekindle their childhood romance, the professor reminds his daughter of her pledge to marry Wilhelm, whom they believe has been incarcerated in a concentration camp. As the boat docks in New York, Marta, heeding her father's wishes, shuns Kurt. When the prince is besieged by a group of socialites led by the title-seeking Barbara Murdoch, Marta seizes the opportunity to depart without Kurt seeing her. Having fallen deeply in love with Marta, Kurt desperately searches for her. One day, while returning from a party with Barbara, Kurt spots Marta. After ordering his limousine to stop, Kurt jumps out and persuades Marta to allow him to drive her home. At the restaurant that Marta now runs with her father, Kurt finds a group of Austrian refugees, who criticize him for his frivolous life and for his neglect of his country and his people. When Kurt promises to help and pledges his support, they hand him a list of prisoners whose freedom they have been trying to win. The next day, Kurt receives an invitation to meet von Helsing at the German Travel Office. There, von Helsing promises to release all the prisoners on the list, including Wilhelm, if Kurt surrenders himself to Germany. Accepting von Helsing's terms, Kurt agrees to sail that night. Von Helsing leads Kurt to believe that he is sailing on a Belgium ship headed for Antwerp, when in reality the boat has been purchased by the Nazis and is destined for Hamburg. That evening, when Marta calls Kurt's hotel and learns that he has gone to the German Travel Office, she begins to suspect that something is amiss and hurries to the office herself. Bursting into the rooms, Marta is shocked to encounter Wilhelm. When Wilhelm boasts of his part in the ruse to trick Kurt into returning to Germany, Marta dashes to the boat to warn Kurt. After phoning the ship's captain to alert him of Marta's arrival, Wilhelm reaches for a gun and kills himself. Allowed to board the ship, Marta hurries to Kurt's stateroom and brokenly tells him that he has been tricked. When they try to leave the boat, they discover that the stateroom door has been locked, and they are now both prisoners bound for Germany. Later they are married by the sympathetic Belgium captain and resign themselves to their grim fate. Soon after, a radiogram arrives, notifying the captain that England has declared war on Germany and ordering him to change his course. Resentful of his treatment by the Nazis, the captain destroys the message, sending the vessel into enemy waters. As the boat sails into British seas, shots from a British destroyer halt the boat, which is then boarded by English officers, who announce that England is at war with Germany. After seizing command of the German craft, the English crew sail Marta and Kurt to the safety of British soil. *Austrians. Betrayal. Impersonation and imposture. Nazis. War refugees. World War II. Austria. Fathers and daughters. Germany. Gestapo. New York City. Nobility. Patriotism. Prisoners of war. Restaurants. Ships. Social climbers. Socialites. Suicide.*

Note: The working title of this film was *We Dare Not Love*. According to a Mar 1940 *HR* news item, Columbia purchased James Edward Grant's story for $10,000 as a vehicle for Jean Arthur. In Jun 1940, the studio assigned Charles Vidor to direct the picture, which was now to star Brian Aherne and Joan Bennett, according to a *MPD* news item. A Jul 1940 *HR* news item noted that Columbia was now negotiating with Luise Rainer to star in the picture.

According to a 5 Jan 1941 *HR* news item, the studio was considering Louise Campbell as the second lead. Martha Scott, who was finally cast as the female lead, was borrowed from Sol Lesser to appear in the picture. According to a *NYT* news item, the loan was part of a deal in which Columbia, which jointly owned Melvyn Douglas' contract with M-G-M, allowed Douglas to appear in the 1941 United Artists picture *That Uncertain Feeling*), in exchange for Scott's appearance in this film. George Brent was borrowed from Warner Bros. to appear in this film. Toward the end of production, Vidor took over as director from James Whale, who had fallen ill with the flu, according to a 30 Jan 1941 *HR* news item. This picture marked the screen debut of Richard Lyon.

Box 10 May 1941. *DV* 29 Apr 1941. *FD* 16 May 1941, p. 11. *HR* 18 Mar 1940. *HR* 12 Jul 1940. *HR* 13 Dec 1940, p. 2. *HR* 5 Jan 1941, p. 6. *HR* 30 Jan 1941, p. 3, 5. *HR* 29 Apr 1941, p. 3. *MPD* 5 Jun 1940. *MPH* 3 May 1941. *MPHPD* 5 Apr 1941, p. 98. *NYT* 10 Mar 1941. *NYT* 16 May 1941, p. 21. *Var* 30 Apr 1941, p. 16.

THEY DIED WITH THEIR BOOTS ON (Native Americans, Dakota)
Warner Bros. Pictures, Inc.; A Warner Bros.—First National Picture. *Dist* Warner Bros. Pictures, Inc. 1 Jan 1942; *Prod*: 2 Jul–30 Sep 1941 [©Warner Bros. Pictures, Inc.; 3 Jan 1942; LP10933]. Sd (RCA Sound System); b&w. 12,563 ft. 138 or 140 min.
Exec prod Hal B. Wallis. *Assoc prod* Robert Fellows. *Dir* Raoul Walsh. *Dial dir* Eddie Blatt. [*Asst dir* Russ Saunders]. [*2nd asst dir* Claude E. Archer]. [*2nd unit dir* B. Reeves Eason]. *Orig scr* Wally Kline [sic] and Aeneas MacKenzie. [*Addl dial* Lenore Coffee]. *Dir of photog* Bert Glennon. [*2nd cam* Ellsworth Fredericks]. [*Asst cam* Benny Cohen]. [*Stills* Fred Morgan]. [*Gaffer* Ralph Owen]. [*Mont* Don Siegel]. *Art dir* John Hughes. *Film ed* William Holmes. [*Props* Eddie Edwards]. [*Asst props* Buddy Friend, Bill Wallace and R. Cooper]. *Gowns* Milo Anderson. [*Ward* Dick Moder and Katherine Grams]. *Mus dir* Leo F. Forbstein. *Mus* Max Steiner. *Sd* Dolph Thomas. [*Sd rec* Ned O. Nair]. [*Boom boy* Dick H. Williams]. *Makeup artist* Perc Westmore. [*Makeup* Ward Hamilton and Harlan Phillips]. [*Hair* Nellie Manley]. *Tech adv* Lt. Col. J. G. Taylor, retired, U.S. Army. [*Unit mgr* Frank Mattison]. [*Scr clerk* Eugene Busch]. [*Cable man* Everett A. Hughes]. [*Best boy* Mickey Moran]. [*Grip* William Classen]. [*Double* Yakima Canutt, Cliff Lyons, Jane Bill, Bruce Gailbraith and John Hoffman]. [*Stunts* Bill Yrigoyne, Joe Yrigoyne and Howard Hill].
Song(s): "Garry Owen," military traditional.
Cast: ERROL FLYNN (*George Armstrong Custer*), OLIVIA DE HAVILLAND (*Elizabeth* [*Libby*] *Bacon*), Arthur Kennedy (*Ned Sharp*), Charley Grapewin (*California Joe*), Gene Lockhart (*Samuel Bacon, Esq.*), Anthony Quinn (*Crazy Horse*), Stanley Ridges (*Major Romulus Taipe*), John Litel (*General Phil Sheridan*), Walter Hampden (*William Sharp*), Sydney Greenstreet (*Lt. General Winfield Scott*), Regis Toomey (*Fitzhugh Lee*), Hattie McDaniel (*Callie*), George P. Huntley, Jr. (*Lt. "Queen's Own" Butler*), Frank Wilcox (*Captain Webb*), Joseph Sawyer (*Sergeant Doolittle*), Minor Watson (*Senator Smith*), [Byron Barr (*Lieutenant Roberts*)], [John Ridgely (*Second Lieutenant Davis*)], [Joseph Crehan (*President Grant*)], [Aileen Pringle (*Mrs. Sharp*)], [Anna Q. Nilsson (*Mrs. Taipe*)], [Harry Lewis (*Youth*)], [Michael Ames (*Cadet Brown*)], [Walter Brooke (*Rosser*)], [Selmer Jackson (*Captain McCook*)], [Bob Perry, Garland Smith, Roy Barcroft, Dick French, Marty Faust, Paul Kruger, Steve Darrell (*Officers*)], [De Wolfe Hopper (*Frazier*)], [Eddie Acuff (*Corporal Smith*)], [Sam McDaniel (*Waiter*)], [George Reed (*Charles*)], [Pat McVeigh (*Jones*)], [James Seay (*Lieutenant Walsh*)], [George Eldredge (*Captain Riley*)], John Hamilton (*Colonel*), [Renie Riano, Edna Holland, Minerva Urecal, Virginia Sale (*Nurses*)], [Vera Lewis (*Head nurse*)], [Spencer Charters (*Station master*)], [Frank Orth, Ray Teal (*Barflies*)], [Hobart Bosworth (*Clergyman*)], [Joe Devlin, Fred Kelsey, Wade Crosby (*Bartenders*)], [Dick Wessel (*Staff Sergeant Brown*)], [Weldon Heyburn (*Staff officer*)], [Harry Strang, Max Hoffman, Jr., Frank Mayo (*Orderlies*)], [Sol Gorss, William Forrest, Addison Richards (*Adjutants*)], [Irving Bacon (*Salesman*)], [Russell Hicks (*Colonel of 1st Michigan*)], [Victor Zimmerman (*Colonel of 5th Michigan*)], [Ian MacDonald (*Soldier*)], [Jack Mower (*Telegrapher*)], [Alberta Gray (*Jane, kitchen maid*)], [Annabelle Jones (*Maid*)], [Hugh Sothern (*Major Smith*)], [Arthur Loft (*Tillaman*)], [Lane Chandler, Ed Parker (*Sentries*)], [Carl Harbaugh (*Sergeant*)], [G. Pat Collins (*Corporal*)], [Walter Baldwin (*Settler*)], [Clancy Cooper (*Conductor*)], [Herbert Heywood (*Newsman*)], [Joseph King (*Chairman*)], [Ed Keane (*Congressman*)], [Francis Ford (*Veteran*)], [Frank Ferguson (*Grant's secretary*)], [Virginia Brissac (*Jack Budlong*)], [George Murphy].
Biography. [*Print viewed*]. The new group of cadets at West Point in 1857 includes George Armstrong Custer, a flamboyant dresser with long curls, who wants to experience the glory of war. During his time

at the military academy, Custer commits many infractions and his classroom performance leaves much to be desired. When Abraham Lincoln is elected president, and civil war breaks out, Custer is eager to graduate and join the battle. While on a punishment tour, Custer meets pretty Elizabeth Bacon, known as Libby, and arranges to meet her later that evening. Before their rendezvous, Custer, like many other cadets, is graduated early and sent to Washington, D.C. to wait for a commission. In Washington, Custer's bad reputation prevents him from receiving an immediate commission. Tired of waiting, he charms Lt. General Winfield Scott into inviting him to lunch and then confesses his dilemma. Scott has him assigned to the Second U.S. Cavalry. At the Battle of Bull Run on 21 July 1861, Custer disregards orders and leads his men in an attack on the enemy. He is wounded in battle and sent home, but later receives a medal. While on leave, Custer plans a visit to Libby to apologize for standing her up at West Point. Before he arrives at her house, Custer encounters Samuel Bacon and, not knowing that he is Libby's father, quarrels with him. Libby is delighted to see Custer and readily forgives him, but when she introduces him to her father, he angrily throws Custer out. Custer and Libby meet secretly that night, and Custer promises to marry her when he becomes a general, reasoning that her father could not possibly object to him then. Custer rejoins his regiment and by mistake is made a general of the Michigan Brigade. At the Battle of Gettysburg, in Pennsylvania, Custer again attacks against orders and the brigade loses many men, but Confederate general Jeb Stuart is driven back. Custer continues to distinguish himself in the war, and after it is over, Bacon agrees to Libby's marriage. With the end of the war, however, Custer is out of work. Ned Sharp, one of Custer's fellow cadets, offers him the presidency of a corporation he has formed with his father to develop the Dakota Territory, but when Custer learns he will only be a figurehead, he turns down the offer. Once again General Scott comes to the rescue, this time at Libby's request, and Custer is posted to Fort Lincoln in the Dakota Territory. The fort is in total disarray when Custer and Libby arrive. Sharp has opened a trading post that sells rifles to the Indians and also runs a bar that has resulted in a drunken corps of cavalrymen. Custer whips the soldiers into shape, closing both the bar and the trading post. Under his leadership, the Seventh U.S. Cavalry wages war on the Indians. When Crazy Horse's Sioux agree to move away from their land as the U.S. government has ordered, on condition they are allowed to retain the sacred land in the Black Hills, Custer promises he will defend their rights there. The Sharps's corporation, however, has plans to run a railroad through there in order to bolster its failing business, and the Sharps work behind the scenes to have Custer relieved of his command. In response, Custer accuses Major Romulus Taipe of falsely announcing the discovery of gold in the Black Hills. Learning of an approaching battle with the Indians under the leadership of Sitting Bull, Custer begs to be returned to his command. On 25 June 1876, to save Brigadier General Alfred Terry from certain defeat, Custer sacrifices the entire Seventh Cavalry in the Battle of Little Big Horn. Afterward, Libby presents a letter sent to her by Custer before his death. In his dying declaration, Custer renews his accusations against Taipe, who is forced to resign and return the Black Hills to the Sioux. *General George Armstrong Custer. Indians of North America. United States–History–Civil War, 1861–1865. United States–History–Reconstruction, 1865–1898.* Black Hills (SD and WY). Chief Crazy Horse. Dakota Indians. Fathers-in-law. Gold. Little Big Horn, Battle of, 1876. Maids. Marriage. Michigan. Nurses. Self-sacrifice. Sitting Bull. Soldiers. Superstition. Tailors. United States Military Academy. United States. Army. Wagon trains. The West. Wounded Knee Creek, Battle of, 1890.

Note: Screenwriter Wally Klein's surname is spelled Kline in the onscreen credits. Biographical sources give the following information about George Armstrong Custer: Custer had a distinguished career during the U.S. Civil War, ending as the army's youngest major-general, and was known for his relentless pursuit of General Robert E. Lee. In 1865 Custer was court-martialed and suspended without pay for one year for harsh treatment of his troops. He was reinstated to counter the increased hostility of the Plains Indians, and in 1875 he took command of Ft. Abraham Lincoln in the Dakota Territory. In 1874, Custer led an expedition to confirm the rumored existence of gold in the Black Hills region of South Dakota. The character of Romulus Taipe was invented for the film. When the Sioux did not comply with a government order directing all Indians to move onto reservations by 31 Jan 1876, war broke out. Custer, under the command of General Alfred Terry, led his soldiers to total defeat at the Battle of Little Big Horn. Not a single soldier of the 250 men under his command survived. Custer was buried with military honors at West Point on 10 Oct 1877. Following his death, his widow wrote and lectured about his life and championed his deeds. Controversy over Custer's conduct at Little Big Horn

continues to this day.

Papers included in the Warner Bros. Collection at the USC Cinema-Television Library add the following information about the production: Joan Fontaine, Olivia De Havilland's sister, turned down the role of "Libby" and Priscilla Lane, Elizabeth Fraser and Nancy Coleman were all tested for the part. Michael Curtiz was the studio's original choice to direct. Writer Lenore Coffee was hired to strengthen the romantic scenes between Errol Flynn and De Havilland. A number of people were injured during the battle scenes; Jack Budlong, a twenty-eight-year-old stuntman, died after falling from his horse on to his sword, and untrained rider George Murphy was killed when he fell from his horse while drunk. Scenes were shot on location at Busch Gardens in Pasadena, the Warner Ranch, the Iverson Ranch in Chatsworth, CA and at nearby Lasky Mesa. Second unit director B. Reeves Eason directed much of the Battle of Little Big Horn footage. He had previously co-directed (with Michael Curtiz) the final battle scene in Warner Bros.' 1936 film *The Charge of the Light Brigade* (see *AFI Catalog of Feature Films, 1931-40;* F3.0655). An *HR* news item reports that a shortage of Native Americans in Hollywood led Warner Bros. to import Sioux from a reservation in the Dakotas. The USC files note that sixteen Dakota Indians worked in the film. The film was completed twenty-six days behind schedule. In his autobiography Raoul Walsh states "I tried to show [the Indian] as an individual who only turned vindictive when his rights as defined by treaty were violated by white men." This was the eighth and last film in which De Havilland and Flynn starred together. Some modern sources state that Eleanor Parker played a bit role in this film, but her name does not appear on the CBCS.

Among the other films about Custer are the 1909 Selig Polyscope film *On the Little Big Horn or Custer's Last Fight,* starring Paul McCormick, Jr.; the 1916 Vitagraph film *Britton of the Seventh,* directed by Lionel Belmore and starring Darwin Karr and Charles Kent (see above); *Custer's Last Fight,* a 1925 re-issue of a Thomas Ince film, and the 1926 Universal film *The Flaming Frontier,* directed by Edward Sedgwick and starring Hoot Gibson and Anne Cornwall (see above); the 1936 Weiss Productions film *Custer's Last Stand,* directed by Elmer Clifton and starring Rex Lease (see above); the 1968 U.S.–Spanish co-production *Custer of the West,* directed by Robert Siodmak and starring Robert Shaw, Mary Ure and Robert Ryan; and the 1991 ABC Television film *Son of the Morning Star,* directed by Mike Robe and starring Gary Cole, Rosanna Arquette and Dean Stockwell.

Box 22 Nov 1941. *FD* 21 Nov 1941, p. 6. *HR* 16 May 1941, p. 1. *HR* 27 May 1941, p. 4. *HR* 10 Jul 1941, p. 6. *HR* 31 Jul 1941, p. 13. *HR* 25 Sep 1941, p. 2. *HR* 19 Nov 1941, p. 3. *MPHPD* 22 Nov 1941, p. 373. *NYT* 21 Nov 1941, p. 23. *Var* 19 Nov 1941, p. 9.

THEY DREAM OF HOME see **TILL THE END OF TIME**

THEY KNEW WHAT THEY WANTED (Italian Americans)

RKO Radio Pictures, Inc. *Dist* RKO Radio Pictures, Inc. 25 Oct **1940**; San Francisco premiere: 8 Oct 1940; New York opening: 11 Oct 1940; Prod: 10 Jun—31 Jul 1940 [©RKO Radio Pictures, Inc.; 25 Nov 1940; LP10045]. Sd (RCA Victor System); b&w. 10 reels. 90 min. PCA cert no. 6449.

Prod Erich Pommer. *Exec prod* Harry E. Edington. *Dir* Garson Kanin. *Asst dir* Ruby Rosenberg. *Scr* Robert Ardrey. *Dir of photog* Harry Stradling. *Spec eff* Vernon L. Walker. *Art dir* Van Nest Polglase. *Art dir assoc* Mark-Lee Kirk. *Ed* John Sturges. *Set dec* Darrell Silvera. *Ward* Edward Stevenson. *Mus score* Alfred Newman. *Rec* John L. Cass. [*Publicity* Terry Turner].

Source: Based on the play *They Knew What They Wanted* by Sidney Howard (New York, 24 Nov 1924).

Cast: CAROLE LOMBARD (*Amy Peters*), CHARLES LAUGHTON (*Tony Patucci*), William Gargan (*Joe*), Harry Carey (*A doctor*), Frank Fay (*Father McKee*), Joe Bernard (*R.F.D.*), Janet Fox (*Mildred*), Lee Tung-Foo (*Ah Gee*), Karl Malden (*Red*), Victor Kilian (*Photographer*), Paul Lepere (*Hired hand*), Marie Blake (*Waitress*), [Millicent Green, Patricia Oakley (*Waitresses*)].

Drama. [*Print viewed*]. While visiting San Francisco, Tony Patucci, a simple grape grower from the Napa Valley, sees waitress Amy Peters and falls in love. Returning home without ever meeting Amy, Tony persuades his foreman Joe, an incorrigible womanizer and wanderer, to write a letter to Amy in Tony's name. Tony's courtship by mail culminates with his proposal to Amy, and when she requests a picture of him, Tony sends her one of Joe. Amy, destitute and willing to do anything to escape poverty, accepts the proposal and journeys to Napa to be married. Horrified to discover that her prospective husband is not the handsome young man in her photo, but rather the portly, earthy Tony, Amy reluctantly decides to go through with the alliance. However, during a celebration on the eve of the wedding, Tony falls from a rooftop and breaks both his legs, and as he lies in bed recuperating, Amy and Joe succumb to their carnal desires. Two months later, Tony is able to walk again, and as he joyously plans the wedding, Amy discovers that she is pregnant. Upon learning of his betrayal, Tony pummels Joe, who leaves the vineyards in shame. As he leaves, Joe passes Father McKee, the village priest who has come to drive Amy and Tony to their wedding, and tells the priest the awful

truth. The big-hearted Tony forgives Amy and insists that they still be married, but Amy is unable to forgive herself and, repentant, drives off with Father McKee as Tony looks on, hoping that she will return one day. *Impersonation and imposture. Infidelity. Italian Americans. Marriage of convenience. Pregnancy. Falls from heights. Farmers. Letters. Ministers. Napa Valley (CA). Proposals (Marital). San Francisco (CA). Waitresses.*

Note: The working title of this film was *The Other Man*. Materials contained in the MPAA/PCA Collection at the AMPAS Library note that PCA Director Joseph I. Breen originally forbade the studio to use the title of the play for their production, and hence RKO changed the title to *The Other Man*. The film's writers, along with director Garson Kanin and actress Carole Lombard successfully lobbied Breen to allow the film to maintain the title *They Knew What They Wanted*. Breen insisted however, that the sinners be punished at the end of the film. According to an article in *Look*, after Italy entered the war, the studio wanted Kanin to change the nationality of the character played by Charles Laughton. Kanin refused, however, and received permission from the British Embassy to allow Laughton to play an Italian-American. News items in *HR* add that the film was shot on location in the Napa Valley, CA. Modern sources note that RKO paid Sidney Howard $50,000 for the rights to his Pulitzer Prize winning play. Other filmed versions of the play are Paramount's 1928 production *The Secret Hour*, which was directed by Roland V. Lee and starred Pola Negri; and M-G-M's 1930 picture *A Lady to Love*, which was directed by Victor Seastrom and starred Vilma Banke and Edward G. Robinson (see *AFI Catalog of Feature Films, 1921-30*; F2.4881 and F2.2944). The 1956 musical play *The Most Happy Fella* produced by Kermit Blomgarden and Lynn Loesser was also based on Howard's play.

DV 9 Oct 1940, p. 3. *FD* 9 Oct 1940, p. 8. *HR* 9 May 1940, p. 10 *HR* 27 Jun 1940, p. 4. *HR* 5 Jul 1940, pp. 12-13. *HR* 26 Sep 1940, p. 4. *HR* 4 Oct 1940, p. 2. *HR* 9 Oct 1940, p. 3. *Oct* 23 Oct 1940, p. 1, 3. *MPD* 9 Oct 1940, p. 1, 3. *MPH* 12 Oct 1940, p. 46. *NYT* 11 Oct 1940, p. 25. *Var* 9 Oct 1940, p. 16.

THEY LIVE IN FEAR (German Americans)
Columbia Pictures Corp. *Dist* Columbia Pictures Corp. 15 Jun **1944**; Prod: 13 Mar—30 Mar 1944 [©Columbia Pictures Corp.; 19 Jun 1944; LP12705]. Sd (Western Electric Mirrophonic Recording); b&w. 5,884 ft. 65-66 min. PCA cert no. 10102.

Prod Jack Fier. *Dir* Josef Berne. [*Asst dir* William O'Connor]. [*Dial dir* Mel Ferrer]. *Scr* Michael L. Simmons and Sam Ornitz. *Story* Wilfrid Pettitt. *Based upon an idea by* Hilda Stone and Ruth Nussbaum. *Dir of photog* George Meehan. *Art dir* Lionel Banks and Carl Anderson. *Film ed* James Sweeney. *Set dec* Joseph Kish. [*Sd eng* Lodge Cunningham].

Cast: Otto Kruger [(*Matthew Van Camp*)], Clifford Severn [(*Paul Graffen*)], Pat Parrish [(*Pat Daniels*)], Jimmy Carpenter [(*Johnny Reynolds*)], Erwin Kalser [(*Jan Dorchik*)], [Danny Jackson (*Googy*)], [Jimmy Zaner (*Joe*)], [Jimmy Clark (*Olie Swanson*)], [Danny Desmond (*Jack*)], [Billy Benedict (*Mac*)], [Kay Dowd (*Ann*)], [Eileen McClory (*Judy*)], [Douglas Wood (*John Elwood*)], [Frederick Giermann (*Kapitan Moeller*)], [Joe McGuinness (*Anderson*)], [Betty Jane Graham (*Marta*)], [Olga Fabian (*Frau Graffen*)], [Hermine Sterler (*Frau Stoesen*)], [Anna Frenke (*Elsa*)], [William Yetter, Jr. (*Helmut*)], [George Sorel (*Kommandant*)], [Egon Brecher (*Herr Graffen*)], [John Nelson (*Frederick*)], [Phil Van Zandt (*Provost Marshal*)], [Mary Bovard (*Girl*)], [Peggy Leon (*Mrs. Van Camp*)], [Paul Andor (*Old man*)], [Hugh Beaumont (*Instructor*)], [Jean Russell, Conrad Wiedell (*Jitterbugs*)], [Alameda Fowler (*Mrs. Daniels*)].

Homefront, Teenage, Drama. [*Print viewed*]. In Nazi Germany, a teacher indoctrinates his impressionable students with the glories of Hitler and evils of democracy. Becoming agitated when one of his classmates denounces his own mother for criticizing Hitler's policies, Paul Graffen, a student in the class, returns home and begs his parents to speak out against the Reich. In response, Mr. and Mrs. Graffen remind their son that the safety of their family depends on their silent cooperation with the Nazi oppressors. The next day, Paul and his classmates are sent on a field trip to Dachau. There the boys are ordered to kill a group of prisoners by striking them with a shovel. Conscience-stricken, Paul comes to the aid of one of the outspoken victims. The man, Dr. Brower, is mortally wounded, but before dying, he instructs Paul to flee to America and gives him a letter addressed to Matthew Van Camp, the principal of Ashland High School. Paul crosses the ocean to America, and when he presents Van Camp with the letter, the principal fondly recalls his studies in Germany under the tutelage of Dr. Bower. Van Camp welcomes Paul and offers the boy refuge. At a meeting of the student council, Paul raptly watches as council president Pat Daniels lectures the students about accepting responsibility for their actions. Later, Paul joins the other students in class and excels in math. When Johnny Reynolds, the school's star

football player, loses interest in his studies and seems in danger of failing, Pat asks Paul to tutor him. Johnny resents Paul's interest in Pat, however, and the two boys argue. Pat pleads with Paul to continue his instruction, and Paul successfully coaches Johnny to pass his exams. Rather than being grateful, however, Johnny continues to resent Paul. To earn extra money, Paul starts a baby sitting service and Pat teaches him the fundamentals of child care. Before leaving to meet Johnny at a party that night, Pat convinces Paul to speak on the evils of Nazism at a benefit she is organizing for the blood bank. At the party, Johnny begins to criticize Paul, causing Pat to decide to leave early and take Paul some ice cream. Johnny follows her and accuses Paul of being a Nazi. When the two boys begin to fight, Pat orders Johnny to leave. In the locker room the next day, Johnny sees in Paul's pocket a letter written in German and steals it. Before Paul's speech that night, the boy's druggist friend, Jan Dorchik, a refugee like himself, mentions that Paul's words may reach Germany over the shortwave radio. The idea arouses Paul's concerns for his family's safety, and when Johnny phones Paul and anonymously warns him that his family will suffer if he goes through with his speech, Paul begins to have second thoughts. Approaching the microphone, Paul nervously begins to defend Hitler and Germany, thus engendering boos from the audience. In a trance, Paul stumbles off stage and goes to Van Camp's darkened office. Meanwhile, Johnny, suffering pangs of guilt, shows Van Camp the letter addressed to Paul's parents. When Van Camp translates Paul's words, expressing devotion to his new country and friends, Johnny confesses that he made a threatening phone call to Paul. Meanwhile, Paul, tortured by the feeling that he has violated the trust of his friends, conducts an imaginary dialogue with his mother and concludes that he must finish his speech. Stepping back to the microphone, Paul condemns Hitler's policies and rallies the audience to defeat the Nazis in the defense of democracy. That June, the students graduate, and as Pat and Paul walk arm in arm, Paul tells her that he has won his citizenship and plans to enlist in the military and defend his country. *Democracy. Germans. High school students. Romantic rivalry. Baby sitters. Germany. Letters. Nazis. Patriotism. School superintendents and principals. Speeches. Tutors and tutoring.*

Note: The working title of this film was *America's Children*. Although a *HR* production chart places Howard Freeman in the cast, his participation in the released film has not been confirmed. Prior to *They Live in Fear*, Joseph Berne directed silent short films. Until this film, actor Paul Andor used the name Wolfgang Zilzer. A modern source adds Frederic Brum to the cast.

DV 20 Sep 1944, p. 4. *FD* 6 Oct 1944, p. 11. *HR* 21 Feb 1944, p. 3. *HR* 17 Mar 1944, p. 18. *MPHPD* 13 May 1944, p. 1890. *MPHPD* 14 Oct 1944, pp. 2138-39.

THEY MET IN COLLEGE *see* **MY LUCKY STAR**

THEY PASSED THIS WAY *see* **FOUR FACES WEST**

THEY RODE WEST (Native Americans, Comanche, Irish Americans, Kiowa)
Columbia Pictures Corp. *Dist* Columbia Pictures Corp. Nov **1954**; Los Angeles opening: 10 Nov 1954; Prod: 17 Nov—7 Dec 1953 [©Columbia Pictures Corp.; 22 Sep 1954; LP4064]. Sd (Western Electric Recording); col (Technicolor); 1.85. 7,580 ft. 84 or 90 min. Passed by the National Board of Review. PCA cert no. 16879.

Prod Lewis J. Rachmil. *Dir* Phil Karlson. *Asst dir* Sam Nelson. *Scr* DeVallon Scott and Frank Nugent. *Based upon a story by* Leo Katcher. *Dir of photog* Charles Lawton, Jr. *Technicolor color consultant* Francis Cugat. *Art dir* Cary Odell. *Film ed* Henry Batista. *Set dec* Frank Tuttle. *Mus score* Paul Sawtell. *Sd eng* Josh Westmoreland.

Song(s): "Kiss Me Quick, and Go," words and music by F. Buckley.

Cast: Robert Francis [(*Dr. Allen Seward*)], Donna Reed [(*Laurie MacKaye*)], May Wynn [(*Manyi-ten*)], Phil Carey [(*Capt. Peter Blake*)], Onslow Stevens [(*Col. Ethan Walters*)], Peggy Converse [(*Mrs. Martha Walters*)], Roy Roberts [(*Sgt. Creever*)], Jack Kelly [(*Lt. Raymond*)], Stuart Randall [(*Satanta*)], Eugene Iglesias [(*Red Leaf*)], Frank DeKova [(*Isatai*)], John War Eagle [(*Chief Quanab*)], Ralph Dumke [(*Dr. Gibson*)], [Julia Montoya (*Maria*)], [James Best (*Lt. Finlay*)], [George Keymas (*Torquay*)], [Maurice Jara (*Spotted Wolf*)], [Edmund Cobb, Ben Corbett (*Sergeants*)], [Carl Andre (*Bugler*)], [Morgan Jones, Glen Thompson, J. P. "Bill" Catching, Don Harvey (*Troopers*)], [John Damler (*Corporal*)], [Myron Healey (*Maj. Vandergrift*)], [Fred Letuli (*Pakawa*)], [William P. Wilkerson (*Brave*)], [Frosty Royce (*Soldier*)], [Harry Lauter (*Orderly*)], [James Anderson (*Wounded man*)].

Western. [*Print viewed*]. In removing a Comanche arrow from an officer's leg, Fort McCullough's drunken Dr. Gibson severs his patient's femoral artery. Capt. Peter Blake watches the young man die and then attacks the doctor, calling him a "murdering butcher." Later, Col. Ethan Walters, commander of the post, complains in a letter to the U.S. Surgeon General that the last three medical officers assigned to the fort have been alcoholic incompetents. Some time later, a train arrives from the East, carrying the colonel's wife, Martha Walters, her pretty and flirtatious niece, Laurie MacKaye, and the fort's new surgeon, Dr. Allen Seward. Distrustful of all physicians, Blake is unrelentingly hostile toward Seward, who is not only very young, but completely inexperienced at handling horses and firearms. During the two-day ride back to the fort, Seward asks Sgt. Creever, an Irish immigrant with a fondness for "rare old Irish whiskey," if the local Kiowa Indians are "tame." Creever explains that although the Kiowa now live on a reservation, they successfully resisted the Cavalry's attempts to get them there for many years. That evening, Creever is knocked unconscious by some Indians, who quietly enter the camp to steal rifles and cartridges. Seward catches a glimpse of them and then attends to Creever. Back at the fort, some of the men show their appreciation for the skill and determination with which Seward treats his patient and cleans up the filthy fort hospital. Blake is unconvinced, however, and at the Kiowa reservation, treats the Indians roughly. He demands that Seward identify the gun thieves, but the doctor does not comply because he is too preoccupied with a young malaria patient, the son of Manyi-ten, a white woman married to Chief Satanta's son Red Leaf. Seward addresses Isatai, the medicine man, with respect, thereby earning the trust of the Kiowa healer. Later, Seward learns that the illness has spread. Disregarding orders, Seward again visits the reservation, where Isatai, himself sick, takes the doctor's quinine in order to convince the others of its efficacy. Manyi-ten, who reveals that she was reared by the Kiowa after her white parents drowned, tells Seward that the reservation's water supply is bad, but that up in the hills, the water is clean. Seward advises the tribe to go there, but Blake arrives and orders him back to the fort at gunpoint. At that moment, Red Leaf, who refused to take Seward's medicine, dies. As they are returning to the fort, Blake and Seward are attacked by the gun thieves, who turn out to be Comanches. A Cavalry unit arrives in time to save the two men, but the Comanches get away. The colonel again orders Seward to avoid the reservation, but the doctor refuses to comply, protesting that the Kiowa are ill only because they must live on a poorly situated reservation. Seward is arrested but ordered to join Blake in locating the Comanches. While searching the area, they discover that the Kiowa have left the reservation. Blake's men spot the Comanches, but the Kiowa, heading toward the hills, see that Blake is about to ambush them. In the fierce battle that follows, the Kiowa lend the Comanches their assistance, and many soldiers are killed. The injured troopers, who blame Seward for the Kiowa revolt, refuse his treatments, calling him by the nickname Blake has pinned on him, "Woodhawk," a bird that turns against its own kind. Manyi-ten warns Seward that the Kiowa, now formally allied with the Comanches, are planning a major attack, and shortly afterward, a patrol races into the fort just ahead of a crowd of charging warriors. The soldiers try to defend the fort, but one of the soldiers is ill, and soon half of the men are stricken with malaria. They blame Seward for this, too, but Laurie defends and encourages him. Seward steals away to the Indian camp to persuade the Kiowa to make peace, but Blake, assuming the doctor is a traitor, hides behind a tree and fires at him. By mistake, the captain hits Spotted Wolf, Satanta's only surviving son and Manyi-ten's new husband. Seward returns to the fort with an ultimatum from the Indians: Either let Seward use the hospital to operate on Spotted Wolf or face immediate attack by the allied Kiowa and Comanche tribes. Col. Walters admits the doctor, his patient, and the two Indian chiefs, and then waits worriedly while Seward operates. Finally, the chiefs emerge from the hospital, and Satanta praises Seward not only for having saved his son, but for treating the Indians as brothers. Col. Waters promises to help move the Kiowa to the high country, and the men shake hands. Seward takes Laurie's arm, and the couple returns to the hospital. *Indians of North America–Reservations. Insubordination. Kiowa Indians. Medical ethics. Physicians. Racism. United States. Army. Cavalry. Alcoholics. Arrests. Battles. Betrayal. Comanche Indians. Flirtation. Forts. Irish Americans. Malaria. Marriage–Mixed. Medicine men. Military discipline. Officers*

(Military). Renegades. Romantic rivalry. Tribal chiefs. United States–History–Indian campaigns.

Note: The working titles of this film were *The Wood Hawk* and *White Feather.* "The Wood Hawk," which was sometimes spelled as "Woodhawk," was also the title for Leo Katcher's original screen story. According to a Jun 1954 *DV* news item, Columbia changed the title from *White Feather* to *They Rode West* after the MPAA gave title priority to Panoramic Productions, which released a picture called *White Feather* in 1955. A 4 Nov 1952 *DV* news item announced that Columbia was seeking James Stewart for the leading role and that Vincent Sherman was slated to produce this film. Robert Francis and May Wynn had previously appeared together in the 1954 Columbia picture *The Caine Mutiny,* and according to modern sources, were a "fan magazine item" at the time. The film's copyright record, which was deposited in Sep 1954, lists a running time of 90 minutes, suggesting that before its Oct 1954 trade showings, the picture was cut by six minutes.

Box 16 Oct 1954. *DV* 4 Nov 1952. *DV* 10 Jun 1954. *DV* 15 Oct 1954, p. 3. *Exb* 20 Oct 1954, pp. 3853-54. *FD* 22 Oct 1954, p. 14. *Har* 16 Oct 1954, p. 167. *HR* 15 Oct 1954, p. 3. *LAT* 14 Jun 1952. *MPHPD* 23 Oct 1954, p. 185. *Var* 20 Oct 1954, p. 6.

THIEVES' HIGHWAY (Greek Americans, Italian Americans)
Twentieth Century-Fox Film Corp. *Dist* Twentieth Century-Fox Film Corp. Oct **1949**; Los Angeles opening: 20 Sep 1949; Prod: early Nov—late Dec 1948 [©Twentieth Century-Fox Film Corp.; 20 Sep 1949; LP2716]. Sd (Western Electric Recording); b&w. 10 reels, 8,437 ft. 93 min. PCA cert no. 13530.

[*Exec prod* Darryl F. Zanuck]. *Prod* Robert Bassler. *Dir* Jules Dassin. [*Asst dir* Henry Weinberger and Joe Rickards]. [*Dial dir* W. E. Watts]. *Scr* A. I. Bezzerides. *Dir of photog* Norbert Brodine. [*Cam op* Roger Shearman]. [*Asst cam* D. S. McEwen and Bud Brooks]. [*Stills* Ray Nolan]. *Spec photog eff* Fred Sersen. *Art dir* Lyle Wheeler and Chester Gore. *Film ed* Nick DeMaggio. *Set dec* Thomas Little and [Fred Rode]. *Ward dir* Charles LeMaire. *Cost des* Kay Nelson. *Mus dir* Lionel Newman. *Mus* Alfred Newman. *Orch* Earle Hagen. *Sd* Alfred Bruzlin and Harry M. Leonard. *Makeup artist* Ben Nye and [Pat McNally]. [*Hair stylist* Esperanza Corona]. [*Prod mgr* Gene Bryant]. [*Loc mgr* W. F. Fitzgerald]. [*Prod asst* Tom Pryor, F. L. McGarry and Paul Helmick]. [*Scr supv* Stanley Scheuer]. [*Gaffer* Ray Jones]. [*Grip* Leo McCreary].

Song(s): "The Kleftman," Greek folk song.

Source: Based on the novel *Thieves' Market* by A. I. Bezzerides (New York, 1949).

Cast: RICHARD CONTE [(*Nick Garcos*)], VALENTINA CORTESA [(*Rica*)], LEE J. COBB [(*Mike Figlia*)], BARBARA LAWRENCE [(*Polly Faber*)], Jack Oakie [(*Slob*)], Millard Mitchell [(*Ed Kinney*)], Joseph Pevney [(*Pete*)], Morris Carnovsky [(*Yanko Garcos*)], Tamara Shayne [(*Parthena Garcos*)], Kasia Orzazewski [(*Mrs. Polansky*)], Norbert Schiller [(*Polansky*)], Hope Emerson [(*Midgeon*)], [George Tyne (*Charles*)], [Edwin Max (*Dave*)], [David Clarke (*Mitch*)], [Walter Baldwin (*Policeman at market*)], [David Opatoshu (*Frenchy*)], [Ann Morrison (*Mable*)], [Percy Helton (*Bar proprietor*)], [Maurice Samuels (*Mario*)], [Saul Z. Martell (*Stukas*)], [Howland Chamberlin (*Mr. Faber*)], [Irene Tedrow (*Mrs. Faber*)], [Dick Wessel (*Cab driver*)], [Frank Kreig (*Clerk*)], [Mario Siletti (*Pietro*)], [Jim Nolan, Robert Foulk (*Policemen*)], [Harry Wilson (*Man at lunch counter*)], [Vincent Gaspari], [Silvio Giannini], [Charles Chackerian], [Vincent Sbragia], [John Lorriea], [Salvatore Daniele], [Gino Bomben], [John Gorman], [Earl Nutter], [Anthony Dentoni], [Raymond Brunetti], [Arthur Fidgeon], [Antone Silvestri], [Andrew Quock], [Joseph Scarpa], [Eddie Vinci].

Drama. [*Print viewed*]. Nick Garcos returns to his home in Fresno after a long sea voyage working as a mechanic and is welcomed home by his parents and girl friend, Polly Faber. Nick, who has saved a lot of his pay and plans to go into business with Polly's father, is unaware that his father has lost his legs in a truck accident, which appears to have been arranged by Mike Figlia, a crooked fruit and produce dealer in San Francisco. Money allegedly paid to Mr. Garcos by Figlia was also "lost" in the accident. Unable to work, Nick's father sold his damaged truck to Ed Kinney, who patched it together but still owes money on it. Nick suggests that he and Ed go into business together to truck a new crop of apples into San Francisco, and Ed cancels an agreement he made with two other truckers, Slob and Pete. Nick and Ed acquire another truck and head for the apple orchard. When Ed tries to cheat the orchard owners, Nick tells him to honor the deal he made. Slob and Pete then show up at the orchard and, not pleased about the new partnership, follow Nick and Ed with a load of their own. Nick's truck blows a tire and, as he tries to jack the truck up, it falls on him. Ed stops, pulls Nick out and repairs the flat, and they continue on. Nick arrives first at the San Francisco produce market

and goes to see Figlia. After Nick's truck is sabotaged in front of Figlia's place, he meets Rica, a girl who works for Figlia, at a lunch counter in the market. She invites him to rest in her nearby apartment, and while he is there, Figlia has Nick's truck unloaded and begins to sell the apples on consignment. However, when Nick discovers that Figlia is selling the load at $6.50 a box but intends to pay him substantially less, he demands and receives cash and a check for the full amount. He then phones Polly and asks her to come to San Francisco so they can be married. Nick buys Rica a drink to celebrate his sale, and she tells him that Polly is probably marrying him for his money. As they walk back to the market, Nick is attacked by two of Figlia's thugs, Mitch and Frenchy, and Rica picks up his wallet and runs off. Nick, thinking that Rica was in league with the thugs, goes looking for her. However, the thugs find Rica first and take the wallet. Meanwhile, Ed's truck starts to fall apart on a steep downhill slope, then crashes and bursts into flames with Ed trapped inside. When Polly arrives in San Francisco, she is met by Rica and is unhappy to learn that Nick is resting in her room. Slob and Pete then try to sell their load of apples to Figlia, but Slob angers Pete when he ghoulishly offers to go back to pick up the apples around Ed's crash site. After Rica tells Polly that Nick has been robbed of all his money, Polly walks out on him. Confused by Rica's behavior, Nick accuses her of setting him up. She warns him that Mitch and Frenchy may try to kill him, as she knows they have arranged truck accidents before. Early the next morning, Nick goes to the market and meets Slob, who tells him that Ed is dead and that Figlia and his henchmen are scavenging his cargo. As Nick and Slob head out to the crash scene, Rica phones the police. Figlia and Pete are celebrating in a bar when Nick and Slob show up. After Pete discovers that Figlia has underpaid him, Figlia tries to leave, but Nick grabs him and beats him up, forcing him to say that he has a check for Nick's father and that he will make up all the other losses. The police arrive, take Figlia into custody and warn Nick about taking the law into his own hands. Nick returns to Rica and they plan a life together. *Apple growers. Criminals. Fresno (CA). Produce trade. San Francisco (CA). Truck drivers. Bars. Engagements. Fights. Partnership. Police. Robbery. Romance. Sabotage. Seduction. Truck accidents.*

Note: The working titles of this film were *Hard Bargain* and *Collision.* According to documents in the Twentieth Century-Fox Records of the Legal Department Collection in the Arts—Special Collections Library at UCLA, the studio purchased the rights to A. I. Bezzerides' unpublished novel *The Red of My Blood* in Jan 1948 for $37,500. Bezzerides was hired at $1,000 per week, with a ten-week guarantee, to write the screenplay. The film started production, in the San Francisco produce market, through the cooperation of the Wholesale Fruit and Produce Dealers Association. Later, however, when the novel was scheduled to be published under the title *Thieves' Market* and the studio decided to use that title for the film, the Dealers Association protested vigorously. Twentieth Century-Fox production head Darryl F. Zanuck was reluctant to change the title and, in a memo to the Legal Department, wrote, "We state definitely that *Thieves' Market* pertains only to [character] Mike Figlia's market and we go out of our way to clean up the rest of the market. Therefore it seems to me that we are not guilty in any respect of damaging anyone...You can talk to Mr. Skouras [the studio's president] about it when he gets out here but I refuse to be put in the position of costing the Company added revenue. If we had committed a wrong or if we were harming someone then I would feel differently but this is not the case."

Early casting suggestions for the leading role included Dana Andrews and Victor Mature. Actors Frank Richards, Al Eben and Joe Haworth are credited in some cast lists in minor roles, but their participation in the released film is doubtful.

According to the file on the film in the MPAA/PCA Collection at the AMPAS Library, the film encountered problems with the PCA. In Feb 1949, the PCA stated that it could not "approve this picture in its present form because of the characterization of the girl Rica as a prostitute...Some extensive eliminations must be made as well as the addition of several new scenes." Producer Robert Bassler agreed, in late Feb, to shoot a new scene introducing Rica and indicating that she had regular, paid employment as a fortune teller. Bassler also agreed that excisions would be made, in dialogue and action, in scenes between Rica and Nick. Retakes were scheduled for early Mar 1949. The PCA issued a certificate in Jun "with the understanding that all prints are to be identical with the cut version shown in our projection room on June 13th." It is assumed that this is the version released, but in neither of the two prints viewed is there a scene in which Rica is established as anything other than a prostitute until the very end when she is seen reading cards in a bar. Additionally, the dialogue continuity, dated 18 Jul 1949, submitted with the copyright registration, does not include the strong anti-vigilantism dialogue spoken by a policeman to Nick after he has beaten up Figlia: "You know you can't take the law into your own hands. Taking care of guys like Figlia is our job."

Box 10 Sep 1949. *DV* 2 Sep 1949, p. 3. *FD* 8 Sep 1949, p. 8. *HR* 2 Sep 1949, p. 3. *MPHPD* 3 Sep 1949, p. 1. *NYT* 24 Sep 1949, p. 8. *Var* 7 Sep 1949, p. 11.

THIEVES' MARKET *see* **THIEVES' HIGHWAY**

THINK FAST, MR. MOTO (Japanese Americans)

Twentieth Century-Fox Film Corp. *Dist* Twentieth Century-Fox Film Corp. 27 Aug **1937**; Prod: early Feb—early Mar 1937 [©Twentieth Century-Fox Film Corp.; 27 Aug 1937; LP7440]. Sd (Western Electric Mirrophonic Sound System); b&w. 5,961 ft. 66 or 70 min. PCA cert no. 3199.

Series: Mr. Moto.

Exec prod Sol M. Wurtzel. *Dir* Norman Foster. [*Dial dir* George Wright]. *Asst dir* Saul Wurtzel, [Sol Michaels and Tom Dudley]. *Scr* Howard Ellis Smith and Norman Foster. [*Revisions and addl orig dial* Willis Cooper]. [*Contr wrt* Charles Kenyon]. *Photog* Harry Jackson. *Cam op* Johnny Schmitz. [*Asst cam* Eddie Collins and Tom Dowling]. [*Process* Sol Halprin and Joe Farley]. *Art dir* Lewis Creber. *Film ed* Alex Troffey. [*Set dresser* Walter Scott]. *Cost* Herschel. [*Ward man* Sam Benson]. [*Ward woman* Adele Farnum]. *Mus dir* Samuel Kaylin. *Sd* George Leverett and Harry M. Leonard. [*Cableman* Hal Lombard]. [*Boom man* Jim Burnette]. [*Hair* Babe Carey]. [*Makeup* Ray Romero]. [*Prod mgr* Edward Ebele]. [*Grip* Al Thayer]. [*Asst grip* J. Van Antwerp]. [*Props* Duke Abrahams]. [*Best boy* Ferdinand Meine]. [*Gaffer* Lou Johnson]. *Script clerk* Jack Vernon. [*Unit mgr* Sam Wurtzel]. [*Asst prop man* Aaron Wolf]. [*Still photog* Ray Nolan]. [*Stunts, stand-in and double for Peter Lorre* John Kascier]. [*Stand-in* Beulah Hutton and Charlie Carroll].

Song(s): "The Shy Violet," words and music by Sidney Clare and Harry Akst.

Source: Based on the short story "That Girl and Mr. Moto" by John P. Marquand in *The Saturday Evening Post (12 Sep—17 Oct 1936).*

Cast: PETER LORRE (*Mr. [Kentaro] Moto*), Virginia Field (*Gloria Danton [also known as Tanya]*), Thomas Beck (*Bob Hitchings*), Sig Rumann (*Nicolas Marloff*), Murray Kinnell (*Joseph Wilkie*), John Rogers (*Carson*), Lotus Long (*Lela Liu*), George Cooper (*Muggs Blake*), J. Carrol Naish (*Adram*), Fredrik Vogeding (*Curio dealer*), [George Hassell (*Mr. Hitchings*)], [Sam Tong (*Chee*)], [Tom Ung (*Scar-faced man*)], [Ray Hendricks (*Soloist*)], [Howard Wilson (*Jack, second boy*)], [Charles Irwin (*Steward*)], [Virginia Sale (*Stewardess*)], [Tom Herbert, Isabel La Mal (*Tourists*)], [Frank Mayo (*Ship's officer*)], [Lee Phelps (*Detective*)], [Bert Roach (*Ship's bartender*)], [Dick Alexander (*Doorman*)], [Sam Labrador (*Menial*)], [Paul Fung (*Chauffeur*)], [Soo Yong (*Telephone operator*)], [William Law (*Chief of police*)], [Charles Tannen].

Detective. [*Print viewed*]. In San Francisco's Chinatown on Chinese New Year's Day, a rug merchant spies a man with an English flag tattoo emerging from a curio shop. The rug merchant enters the shop and offers to sell the store owner $20,000 worth of diamonds. While the store owner examines the diamonds, the rug merchant finds a dead body inside a wicker basket. The police arrive and attempt to arrest the rug merchant for selling rugs without a license, but he manages to escape. The rug merchant removes his disguise, and it is revealed that he is actually Mr. Kentaro Moto. Moto makes a reservation on the *Marco Polo* ocean liner, which leaves for the Orient that night. Aboard the ship, Moto meets Bob Hitchings, son of the liner's owner. Bob is given an important letter to deliver to Joseph Wilkie, the manager of the liner's Shanghai office. Moto then notes that their steward Carson has an English flag tattoo. Bob and Moto become fast friends, as they learn that they were members of the same fraternity at Stanford University. The ship arrives in Honolulu, where Gloria Danton comes aboard and immediately attracts Bob's attention. The two fall in love, but Gloria warns Bob that he knows little about her. Moto finds Carson searching Bob's cabin and tells him that he recognizes the steward from the curio shop. The two men fight, and Moto throws Carson overboard. Arriving in Shanghai, Bob is distressed to learn that Gloria has left without him. When he gives Wilkie the important letter, the envelope is discovered to be empty. The two men call the elder Hitchings, who informs them that smugglers have been using their ships to bring contraband jewels and narcotics into the United States, and that the shipping line has already been fined $200,000 for this activity. Bob agrees to help Wilkie find the smugglers, but only after the two men search for Gloria. Meanwhile, Moto goes to the East India Bazaar where he meets Adram, who works for smuggler Nicolas Marloff. Adram immediately suspects Moto. That night, Bob receives a note telling him that Gloria works as an entertainer at the International Club. Wilkie warns Bob that the club is in a dangerous part of Shanghai, but the young Hitchings insists on

going there. Moto and his female assistant, Lela Liu, also head for the club, but they are abducted along the way. Adram attempts to kill Moto, but instead is shot himself. At the club, Bob confronts Gloria backstage, and she confesses to really being Tanya, a White Russian emigrant employed by Marloff to discover Hitchings' plans. Marloff overhears her confession and takes them both as prisoners. Back at their table, Moto, Lela and Wilkie are greeted by Marloff, who offers to take Moto to his private gambling den. Moto tells Lela in Japanese to call the police for help, but she is shot by an unknown assailant just as she reaches the chief of police. Inside the gambling room, Moto tells Marloff that he is a smuggler, too, and suggests they join forces. Shown Marloff's prisoners, Moto suggests that Bob be ransomed and Gloria killed as a traitor. Wilkie enters the room and demands that Bob be released. The wounded Adram then arrives and identifies Moto as a police informant. As Moto tries to shoot Adram, Wilkie interferes, and Moto is shot instead. Just as Marloff is about to finish Moto off, the police arrive, and Moto shoots Adram dead. As Wilkie reaches for Marloff's gun, it discharges and kills Marloff. Moto then arrests Wilkie as the leader of the smugglers, as he killed Marloff to keep from being identified. When Moto is informed that Lela has been wounded, he finds the "smoking gun" on Wilkie. With the case solved, Moto tells all that he is actually the owner of the Dai Nippon Trading Company, the Hitchings' best customer, and a "sometime amateur detective." Bob and Moto then share a fraternal handshake as Gloria looks on. *Amateur detectives. Impersonation and imposture. Japanese Americans. Murder. Romance. Shipping magnates. Smuggling. Abduction. Chinese New Year. Confession. Curio dealers. Drunkenness. Fathers and sons. Fights. Fraternities. Gambling houses. Gunshot wounds. Honolulu (HI). Importers. Jewelry. Letters. Nightclubs. Ocean liners. Police. Romance. Rugs. Russians. San Francisco (CA)–Chinatown. Shanghai (China). Ships. Singers. Stewards. Tattoos.*

Note: According to the Twentieth Century-Fox Records of the Legal Department at the UCLA Theater Arts Library, author J. P. Marquand was paid $7,000 for the film rights to his story "That Girl and Mr. Moto" on 1 Jun 1936, previous to its publication in *The Saturday Evening Post*. The legal records also note that writer Sonya Levien was charged to the project for a short time, but she did no actual writing for it. This film was the first in a series of eight Mr. Moto vechiles by Twentieth Century-Fox, all starring Peter Lorre in the lead role. The series ended in 1939 with *Mr. Moto's Last Warning* (see entry above). Twentieth Century-Fox attempted to revive the series in 1965 with the British-made *The Return of Mr. Moto* starring Henry Silva and Terence Longdon and directed by Ernest Morris (see *AFI Catalog of Feature Films, 1961-70,* F6.4080). For additional information on the series, consult the Series Index.

Box 17 Apr 1937. *DV* 2 Apr 1937, p. 3. *FD* 6 Apr 1937, p. 8. *HR* 8 Feb 1937. *HR* 2 Apr 1937, p. 3. *MPD* 5 Apr 1937, p. 4. *MPH* 20 Mar 1937, p. 35. *MPH* 17 Apr 1937, p. 42, 44. *NYT* 16 Aug 1937, p. 15. *Var* 6 Apr 1937, p. 27.

THIRD AVENUE see **EASY COME, EASY GO**

THE THIRD GLORY see **CHIP OFF THE OLD BLOCK**

THE THIRD WOMAN (Native Americans)
Robertson-Cole Co. *Dist* Robertson-Cole Distributing Corp.; Superior Pictures. Apr **1920.** Si; b&w. 5 reels.
Dir Charles Swickard. *Scen* J. Grubb Alexander. *Story* Raymond L. Schrock.

Cast: Carlyle Blackwell (*Luke Halliday*), Louise Lovely (*Eleanor Steele*), Gloria Hope (*Marcelle Riley*), Winter Hall (*Judson Halliday*), George Hernandez (*James Riley*), Walter Long (*Scar Norton*), Frank Lanning (*Tonawanna*), Myrtle Owen (*Mo-Wa*).

Drama. Although fond of childhood playmate Marcelle Riley, Luke Halliday, whose father made his fortune as an Arizona miner, becomes engaged to Eleanor Steele, a New York society belle. When Scar Norton arrives from Arizona and discloses that Luke's mother was an Indian, Luke is so traumatized that he breaks his engagement and ventures West to live among his mother's people. About to marry the Indian maiden Mo-Wa, Luke discovers that he cannot go through with the ceremony and retreats to the Settlement of Lost Hope, where he again encounters Scar Norton. Enraged when Scar taunts him over being a half-breed, Luke is about to kill his accuser when Marcelle and her father arrive and prevent him from committing the crime. Returning home with the Rileys, Luke finally realizes that Marcelle's pure love transcends all boundaries of race. *Arizona. Indians of North America. Indians of North America–Mixed blood. Parentage. Racism. Attempted murder. New York City. Socialites. Weddings. The West.*

Note: The working title of this film was *The Innocent Cheat*. Some scenes were shot in the desert of Arizona and in and around an authentic Pueblo Indian village. Sources conflict on the name of the actress playing Mo-Wa, one calling

her Myrtle Kelso, another Maym Kelso. Maym Kelso, a known film player, may have had her own unspecified part in this film, but probably did not play "Mo-Wa."

ETR 20 Mar 1920, p. 1664. *MPN* 6 Mar 1920, p. 2324. *MPN* 27 Mar 1920, p. 2987. *MPN* 17 Apr 1920, p. 3473. *MPW* 28 Feb 1920, p. 1495. *MPW* 6 Mar 1920, p. 1616. *MPW* 27 Mar 1920, p. 2174. *Var* 19 Mar 1920, p. 53. *Wid's* 21 Mar 1920, p. 19.

THIRTEEN STEPS (Chinese Americans)
Congress Pictures Corp. *Dist* State Rights. **1932.** Sd; b&w. Length undetermined.
Dir John Tansey.

Cast: Franklyn Farnum, Sheldon Lewis, Cornelius Keefe, Barbara Bedford.

Newspaper, Drama. [*Not viewed*]. When the evil Scorpion discovers that William Holt, owner of the *Globe* newspaper, is responsible for the death of his blood brother, Sing Toy, he asks his followers if they will aid him in his revenge. At the newspaper, editor Carl Gregg is plotting to take over from Holt. Holt and his wife worry that their daughter Mildred might be in danger because of the Scorpion. When Carl tries to persuade reporter Gerry Kane to cover the Scorpion story, Gerry explains that Holt has given him another story to cover. In pursuing his story, Gerry and photographer Snappy Carter interview a man named Morse in a bar. After coaxing the story from Morse, the two return to Holt's office, where Gerry's old friend Berger offers to help him with the Scorpion problem. Berger tells him to meet a man named Handsome Kelly, who takes them to a club, where Carl has a "vamp" try to distract Gerry from his pursuit of the Scorpion story. She fails, however, and Gerry and Snappy leave. At his office, Holt receives a threat from the Scorpion, and when he calls on Snappy to help him, Snappy is shot and killed. Later that evening at a hotel, Holt holds a meeting disguised as a dinner party. Mildred consoles Gerry, saying that she is worried about her father. Holt calls the meeting to order, but the lights go out and another one of Holt's men is killed. Gerry calls the police, and after several hours of questioning, the women retire for the night. As she prepares for bed, Mildred is kidnapped and taken from the hotel by the Scorpion's men. Holt receives a message from the Scorpion regarding Mildred, and a detective calls the squadron, while Gerry and the others follow an escape route out of the hotel. They raid the Scorpion's lair and arrest his men, but cannot find the Scorpion himself. In the Scorpion's private room, the Scorpion's henchman, Little Flower, explains that Mildred has been kidnapped as the atonement for the death of Sing Toy. As they prepare to kill her, Gerry bursts in, shoots the Scorpion, rescues Mildred, then takes her into his arms. *Murder. Police. Reporters. Revenge. Chinese Americans. Fathers and daughters. Hotels. Kidnapping. Photographers. Rescues. Vamps.*

Note: The plot synopsis is based on a dialogue continuity from NYSA. The film was submitted to New York censors on 19 Sep 1932 and was approved with some eliminations. The only reviews located for the film were in the British journals *The Cinema* and *KW*, which identified the director and cast members listed above. They both identified the film as being American and listed a British release length of 4,628 ft.

The Cinema 21 Mar 1934, p. 7. *KW* 22 Mar 1934, p. 41.

THIRTEEN WOMEN (Indo-Americans)
RKO Radio Pictures, Inc. *Dist* RKO Radio Pictures, Inc. 16 Sep **1932** [©RKO-Radio Pictures, Inc.; 1 Oct 1932; LP3298]. Sd (RCA Photophone System); b&w. 7 reels. 73-74 min. Passed by the National Board of Review. PCA cert no. 1429-R [4 Sep 1935].
Exec prod David O. Selznick. *Dir* George Archainbaud. [*Asst dir* Tommy Atkins]. [*2nd asst dir* Doran Cox]. *Scr* Bartlett Cormack and Samuel Ornitz. *Photog* Leo Tover. *Art dir* Carroll Clark. *Film ed* Charles L. Kimball. *Mus* Max Steiner. *Rec* Hugh McDowell, Jr.

Source: Based on the novel *Thirteen Women* by Tiffany Thayer (New York, 1932).

Cast: Irene Dunne [(*Laura Stanhope*)], Ricardo Cortez [(*Sergeant Clive*)], Jill Esmond [(*Jo*)], Myrna Loy [(*Ursula Georgi*)], Mary Duncan [(*June Raskob*)], Kay Johnson [(*Helen Frye*)], Florence Eldridge [(*Grace Coombs*)], C. Henry Gordon [(*Swami Yogadachi*)], Peg Entwistle [(*Hazel Cousins*)], Harriet Hagman [(*May Raskob*)], Edward Pawley [(*Burns*)], Blanche Friderici [(*Teacher*)], Wally Albright [(*Bobby Stanhope*)], [Julie Haydon (*Mary*)], [Elsie Prescott (*Nan*)], [Marjorie Gateson (*Martha*)], [Lloyd Ingraham (*Inspector*)], [Edward Le Saint (*Police chief*)], [Kenneth Thomson], [Leon Waycoff], [Clarence Geldert], [Violet Seaton].

Drama. [*Print viewed*]. After trapeze artist June Raskob receives a letter from Swami Yogodachi in which he predicts that her sister May

will soon die, she becomes so obsessed with fear that she allows May to fall to her death during their circus act. Later, Hazel Cousins, a friend of the now insane June and a fellow member of the exclusive St. Albans Seminary alumnae group, who also has received a horoscope, murders her husband just as the Swami had foretold. When another sorority member, Helen Frye, receives a letter in New York warning her that she will commit suicide before Christmas, she contacts group leader Laura Stanhope, who suggests that the remaining women reunite at her home in Beverly Hills. On the train there, Helen meets Ursula Georgi, a half-Indian mystic and St. Albans alumna. Ursula, who had worked for the Swami and had used her considerable hypnotic powers to control and then murder him in order to further her revenge against the group, which had ostracized her at school because of her race, subtly influences Helen to shoot herself that night. At the news of Helen's death, the normally calm Laura begins to fret about her own horoscope, which states that her young son Bobby will meet with a terrible accident on his upcoming birthday. Laura's fears become concrete when she discovers in the nick of time that candy that was sent anonymously to Bobby is poisoned, and she seeks the aid of police detective Sergeant Clive. After Clive connects Ursula to the Swami and the prior incidents, he sets a trap for her on a train to New York on which he has planted Laura. On the train, Laura almost falls victim to Ursula's hypnosis but is saved by Clive. Trapped by the police, Ursula throws herself from the caboose, thereby fulfilling the Swami's last prediction about her own death. *Astrology. East Indians. Hypnotism. Murder. Predictions. Racism. Revenge.* Aerialists. Beverly Hills (CA). Circuses. Falls from heights. Half-castes. Letters. Mothers and sons. Mysticism. New York City. Poisoning. Police detectives. Suicide. Trains. Traps.

Note: In a foreword, the film quotes a statement from *Applied Psychology* by "Professors Hollingsworth and Hoffenberger of Columbia University" about the power of suggestion. According to RKO inter-department memos, Myrna Loy replaced Zita Johann during the production. Because of Johann's firing and the fact that the script was being written and rewritten during shooting, the film went over budget. British actress Peg Entwistle, who played the role of "Hazel Cousins," committed suicide on 18 Sep 1932 by throwing herself off the "Hollywoodland" sign cliff, which is located in the Hollywood Hills. Contemporary reviewers commented on the fact that only ten women, not thirteen, were featured in the story. A comparison between onscreen and trade paper cast lists and modern source cast lists suggests that a few characters were edited out of the final film. Although modern sources include Phyllis Fraser, Betty Furness and Louis Natheaux in the cast, these actors were not seen in the viewed print. *FD* news items note that "more than a dozen famous circus acts," including Eddie DeComa, Buster Bartell, Clayton Behee, Eddie Viera and Teddy Mangean were signed to appear in the film. Their participation in the final film has not been confirmed. Modern sources state that Teddy Mangean was a wire walker, and the rest were trapeze artists. *FD* also adds James Donlan, Mitchell Harris, Allen Pomeroy and Oscar Smith to the cast, but their participation in the final film has not been confirmed. According to modern sources, David Selznick delayed the release of the film in order to capitalize on the expected success of Irene Dunne in Universal's 1932 production *Back Street.* Modern sources add the following cast members: Audrey Scott and Aloha Porter (*Equestriennes*), Cliff Herbert (*Circus act*) and Lee Phelps (*Conductor*).

FD 8 Jul 1932, p. 21. *FD* 28 Jul 1932, p. 7. *FD* 1 Aug 1932, p. 6. *FD* 15 Oct 1932, p. 4. *HR* 9 Aug 1932, p. 3. *MPH* 3 Sep 1932, p. 42. *NYT* 15 Oct 1932, p. 13. *Var* 18 Oct 1932, p. 15.

THIRTY A WEEK (Irish Americans)
Goldwyn Pictures Corp. *Dist* Goldwyn Distributing Corp. Oct—Nov **1918** [©Goldwyn Pictures Corp.; 12 Oct 1918; LP12977]. Si; b&w. 5 reels.
Dir Harry Beaumont. *Scen* J. Clarkson Miller. *Cam* George Webber. *Art dir* Hugo Ballin.
Source: Based on the play *Thirty a Week* by Thompson Buchanan (production undetermined).
Cast: Tom Moore (*Dan Murray*), Tallulah Bankhead (*Barbara Wright*), Alec B. Francis (*Mr. Wright*), Brenda Fowler (*Mrs. Wright*), Warburton Gamble (*Freddy Ruyter*), Grace Henderson (*Mrs. Murray*), Ruth Elder (*Minnie Molloy*).
Comedy-drama. Although she is engaged to the wealthy Freddy Ruyter, Barbara Wright prefers her father's handsome Irish chauffeur, Dan Murray, and marries him. The newlyweds struggle to survive on Dan's meager income, but Barbara's father, furious with them both, nearly destroys their happiness by securing Dan's dismissal from several jobs. Dan wins $300 in an auto race but immediately gives it to Minnie Molloy, whose ailing husband has been ordered West for his health. Unaware of the reason for Dan's actions, Barbara sadly returns to her triumphant father. Mr. Wright's lawyer offers Dan a large sum of money to have the marriage annulled, and when Dan refuses, the

lawyer discovers the truth about his "other woman." Touched by Dan's generosity, Mr. Wright accepts him into the family, and Barbara happily returns to her husband. *Chauffeurs. Irish Americans. Marriage. Newlyweds.* Automobile racing. Dismissal (Employment). Fathers and daughters. Generosity. Lawyers. Marriage–Annulment.

Note: The influenza epidemic may have delayed the film's general release until mid-November. Some scenes were shot in New York's Fifth Avenue shopping district, and at an automobile racetrack in Sheepshead Bay, NY. *Var* commented about actor Tom Moore, "As a young Irishman with a characteristic Gaelic smile he is an ideal type."

ETR 26 Oct 1918, p. 1771. *ETR* 2 Nov 1918, p. 1814. *MPN* 26 Oct 1918, p. 2711. *MPW* 26 Oct 1918, p. 546. *MPW* 23 Nov 1918, p. 861. *NYT* 14 Oct 1918, p. 15. *Var* 18 Oct 1918, p. 39. *Wid's* 17 Nov 1918, pp. 3-4.

THIRTY DAYS (Italian Americans)
Famous Players-Lasky Corp. *Dist* Paramount Pictures. 8 Jan **1923**; New York premiere: 10 Dec 1922 [©Famous Players-Lasky Corp.; 14 Nov 1922; LP18525]. Si; b&w. 5 reels, 4,930 ft.
Pres Jesse L. Lasky. *Dir* James Cruze. *Adpt* Walter Woods. *Photog* Karl Brown.
Source: Based on the play *Thirty Days* by A. E. Thomas and Clayton Hamilton (New York, 1923).
Cast: Wallace Reid (*John Floyd*), Wanda Hawley (*Lucille Ledyard*), Charles Ogle (*Judge Hooker*), Cyril Chadwick (*Huntley Palmer*), Herschel Mayall (*Giacomo Polenta*), Helen Dunbar (*Mrs. Floyd*), Carmen Phillips (*Carlotta*), Kalla Pasha (*Warden*), Robert Brower (*Professor Huxley*).
Comedy. After being innocently friendly with an Italian woman, John Floyd tries to escape the wrath of Giacomo, her jealous husband, by having himself sentenced to jail for thirty days. But Giacomo also is sent to jail, and both are released at the same time. John explains matters to his fiancée, Lucille, and Giacomo is put on a ship before he can harm John. *Italian Americans. Jails. Jealousy.*
ETR 23 Dec 1922. *FD* 17 Dec 1922. *MPW* 23 Dec 1922. *NYT* 11 Dec 1922, p. 22.

31ST STAR *see* **REBELLION**

THIRTY YEARS LATER (African Americans)
Micheaux Pictures. **1928** [©Oscar Micheaux; 25 Feb 1928; LU25007]. Si; b&w. 7 reels.
Dir Oscar Micheaux. *Wrt* Oscar Micheaux.
Source: Based on the short story "The Tangle" by Henry Francis Downing (publication undetermined).
Cast: William Edmonson (*George Eldridge Van Paul*), A. B. De Comathiere (*Habisham Strutt*), Mabel Kelly (*Hester Morgan*), Ardella Dabney (*Clara Booker*), Gertrude Snelson (*Mrs. Van Paul*).
Melodrama, African American. George Eldridge Van Paul, the son of a white father and a black mother, is brought up to believe that he is completely white. He falls in love with Hester Morgan, a black girl, but when she learns that he is white, she refuses to see him. George is later told by his mother of his black heritage, and he becomes proud of his race. Hester then accepts his proposal of marriage. *African Americans. African Americans–Mixed blood. Miscegenation.*

THIS GIRL IS MINE *see* **THIS WOMAN IS MINE**

THIS IS AMERICA *see* **AN AMERICAN ROMANCE**

THIS IS HEAVEN (Hungarian Americans)
Samuel Goldwyn, Inc. *Dist* United Artists Corp. 22 Jun **1929** [©Samuel Goldwyn; 15 Jun 1929; LP505]. Talking sequences, mus score, and sd eff (Movietone); b&w. 8 reels, 7,948 ft. [Also si; 7,859 ft.].
Pres Samuel Goldwyn. *Dir* Alfred Santell. *Scr* Hope Loring. *Story* Arthur Mantell. *Dial and titles* George Marion, Jr. *Photog* George Barnes and Gregg Toland. *Film ed* Viola Lawrence. *Mus score* Hugo Riesenfeld.
Song(s): "This Is Heaven," music by Harry Akst, lyrics by Jack Yellen.
Cast: Vilma Banky (*Eva Petrie*), James Hall (*James Stackpoole*), Fritzi Ridgeway (*Mamie Chase*), Lucien Littlefield (*Frank Chase*), Richard Tucker (*E. D. Wallace*).
Romantic comedy. At Ellis Island in New York, Eva Petrie, a Hungarian immigrant, meets her uncle, Frank Chase, a subway motorman, and his daughter, Mamie, with whom she will reside in the Bronx. Mamie gets Eva a job as a cook and waitress at Child's Restaurant on Fifth Avenue, and tries, unsuccessfully, to interest her

in wealthy men. Eva spots Jimmy on the subway one morning; he is wearing a chauffeur's cap, though he is actually a millionaire. Later, she is sent to preside over a griddle at a charity bazaar, where she becomes reacquainted with Jimmy—while pretending to be an exiled Russian princess. He realizes the deception and pretends to be a chauffeur. Eva and Jimmy, following a romantic courtship, are married, and she insists he go into the taxi business. Uncle Frank, however, gambles their last payment on a taxi, and Eva is forced to borrow money from Mamie's wealthy lover. Jimmy then drops the pretense, revealing his true position in life, and Eva realizes "this ees Heaven." *Bazaars. Chauffeurs. Cooks. Courtship. Hungarian Americans. Immigrants. Impersonation and imposture. Millionaires. New York City. New York City–Ellis Island. Restaurants. Subways. Uncles.*

FD 31 Mar 1929. *NYT* 27 May 1929, p. 22. *Var* 3 Apr 1929, p. 23.

THIS IS THE LIFE *see* **IT'S A GREAT LIFE**

THIS LOVE OF OURS *see* **PRIDE OF THE MARINES**

THIS REBEL BREED (African Americans, Latino)

All God's Children Co. *Dist* Warner Bros. Pictures, Inc. 19 Mar 1960; Prod: late May—early Jun 1959 at Ziv Studios [©All God's Children Co.; 19 Mar 1960; LP20181]. Sd (Westrex Recording System); b&w. 10 reels, 8,305 ft. 90 min. PCA cert no. 19411.

Prod William Rowland. *Exec prod* Robert H. Yamin. *Dir* Richard L. Bare. *Asst dir* Bert Glazer. [*2d asst dir* Gil Mandelik]. *Scr* Morris Lee Green. *Story* William Rowland and Irma Berk. *Story ed and consultant* A. B. Guthrie, Jr. *Dir of photog* Monroe Askins. *Art dir* Jack T. Collis. *Film ed* Tony Martinelli. *Sd ed* Larry Kaufman. *Mus ed* Milton Lustig. *Set dec* Lou Hafley and George Sawley. *Mus* David Rose. *Rec supv* Robert Post. *Sd* Ryder Sound Service, Inc. *Makeup* Ted Coodley. *Prod mgr* Joe Wharton. *Chief set elec* Joe Wharton. *Scr supv* Larry Lund. [*Stunts* Patricia Saunders, Mike Donovan, Russell Gillam, Marvin Willens, Bill Shannon and Loren James].

Cast: Rita Moreno [(*Lola Montalvo*)], Mark Damon [(*Frank Serano*)], Gerald Mohr [(*Lt. Robert Brooks*)], Jay Novello [(*Papa Montalvo*)], Eugene Martin [(*Rudy Montalvo*)], Tom Gilson [(*Muscles*)], Richard Rust [(*Buck Madison*)], Douglas Hume [(*Don Walters*)], Richard Laurier [(*Manuel Montalvo*)], Don Eitner [(*Jimmy Wallace*)], Diane Cannon [(*Wiggles*)], Kenny Miller [(*Winnie*)], Al Freeman [(*Satchel*)], Charles Franc [(*Elliott, also known as Scratch*)], Ike Jones [(*Latimer*)], Shirley Falls [(*Josie*)], Stevie Perry [(*George*)], Hari Rhodes [(*Claude*)], [Tol Avery (*Mr. Drake*)], [Adrienne Marden (*Mrs. Drake*)], [Lennie Bremen (*Counterman*)], [John Newton (*Mr. Hanes*)], [Ford Dunhill (*First Moray*)], [Joe Kelsay (*Joe*)], [Byron Morrow (*A teacher*)], [Flicka McKenna (*Connie, girl at swimming pool*)], [Gloria Tennes (*Helen, girl with sandwich*)], [Sandy Freeman (*Helen's girl friend*)], [Jacquelyn Durant (*Lillian*)], [Lovyss Bradley (*Librarian*)], [Jerry Brent (*Jimmy Smith*)].

Youth, Social, Drama. [*Print viewed*]. After an altercation between members of the Ebonies, an African-American teenage gang, and Buck Madison, leader of the Anglo gang, the Royals, and his girl friend Wiggles, police lieutenant Robert Brooks of the juvenile division assigns rookies Frank Serano and Don Walters to infiltrate the gangs at Bailey Union High School. Frank is of mixed Mexican and African-American heritage, while Don is white. At the school, a social science teacher assigns Lola Montalvo, an attractive Mexican-American student, to argue, on the same side as Frank, in a debate that racial hatred is a mark of ignorance. Although Lola snubs Frank at first, they begin to study together, which provokes her brother Manuel, leader of the Mexican-American gang, the Caballeros, to warn Frank, whom he calls a "black monkey," to keep away from Lola. Aided his gang, Manuel then beats up Frank as he leaves the library with Lola. When Lola's father learns about the attack, he reprimands her for sneaking off to meet blacks and for "making eyes at Anglos." Papa, though, tries to convince Manuel to learn tolerance, but Manuel bitterly blames the death of his white mother on the fact that her family would not speak to her after she married Papa. When Buck approaches Manuel about joining forces to sell marijuana in the "spic" market, they have a scuffle, and Manuel loses a religious necklace, which Buck pockets. Meanwhile, Frank speaks with Satchel, the leader of the Ebonies, about joining, but Satchel refuses because Frank is half-Mexican. After Buck tries to kiss Lola in the school hallway, Frank trips Buck, who calls him a "dirty nigger," but their fight is interrupted by a school official. During a party, Buck buys drugs from a white racist named Elliott, who has urged Buck to

push the stuff in the Mexican neighborhood. Elliott, who wants to stir up trouble between the Ebonies and the Caballeros, tells Buck about Lola's secret love affair with a member of the Royals, Jimmy Wallace. After Brooks and a black narcotics officer raid the party, Buck's cohort Muscles accuses Jimmy of calling the police, and they take him to a deserted railroad yard. There, Jimmy falls onto a spike as he struggles with Buck and Muscles, and when Jimmy dies, Buck leaves Manuel's necklace near the body. After arresting Manuel, Brooks interrogates Lola, who blames Buck and determines to obtain evidence against him. When Lola presents her side of the racial question in class, she emphasizes the loss to society when people do not allow others to function as equals. After class, Don asks Buck if he can join the Royals, and Buck, to intimidate him, sends Muscles to fight him at an abandoned lot. During the fight, Don convinces Muscles, who is unhappy with Buck, to join him in a drug deal without Buck. Frank trails Lola to a doctor's office, and when she leaves dejectedly, he tends to her and surmises that she is pregnant. Meanwhile, Buck has given Satchel's little brother George and his friends some marijuana cigarettes. When Frank and Lola find George, sick from the drugs, Frank carries him to Satchel. In back of Gabby's Grill, the Royals' hangout, Buck and his gang interrogate one of the Ebonies responsible for the attack on Buck and Wiggles. When the captive reveals that Wiggles is black, Buck becomes enraged. He rips open the African American's shirt, slops white paint over him and declares that they are "integrating" him. Inside Gabby's, Buck insults Wiggles, and after she becomes hysterical, he propositions Lola in front of her. Lola accepts and the gang go to a party at the home of Winnie, a rich boy who is trying get into the gang. At the party, Buck attempts to take Lola into a bedroom, but is interrupted when Elliott arrives. Meanwhile, Lola's little brother Rudy, who has learned she is in trouble, runs through the black neighborhood to get the Caballeros to help. He is stopped by George, but upon learning that Rudy is trying to help Lola, George tells Satchel, who gathers together the Ebonies. Manuel, released from jail, assembles the Caballeros. After Elliott sells drugs to Buck, he meet privately with Muscles and Don and agrees to return with more for them to buy. Frank, who has learned Winnie's address from Wiggles, sneaks in a window and tries to get Lola to leave. When Papa, who has tracked down Lola after learning of her pregnancy, arrives, Lola confesses it is Jimmy's baby and accuses Buck of murdering him. Buck, however, blames Muscles, and as Muscles runs out, Don identifies himself as a police officer. Elliott comes in with a gun, but the black and Mexican gangs arrive and agree to fight together against the Royals. Brooks and the narcotics officer then arrive and break up the brawl. While the officer is capturing Elliott, Frank throws Buck through a window, then bandages his injuries. After Brooks castigates the gang for not considering members of other races as human beings, Frank takes Lola home and they admit that they need each other. *Adolescents. African Americans. Gangs. Mexican Americans. Racism. Undercover operations. Accidental death. Brothers. Drug dealers. Family relationships. Fights. Frame-ups. High schools. Libraries and librarians. Marihuana. Necklaces. Parties. Pregnancy. Racial impersonation. Restaurants.*

Note: The working titles of this film were *Juvenile Jungle, Fuzz* and *All God's Children*. According to information in the MPAA/PCA Collection at the AMPAS Library, in Jul 1956, a contract was being negotiated between Bob Hope Enterprises and the International Association of Chiefs of Police for a yearly feature and a television series to be produced that would be based on police cases. Producer William Rowland was involved in these negotiations. The feature, which became *This Rebel Breed*, was based on a story that appeared in the Los Angeles Police Department's magazine *Beat*, which had been chosen by the I.A.C.P. as the outstanding police story of the year. By May 1957, the agreement had been executed between the I.A.C.P. and a company called Police Hall of Fame, Inc., in which Rowland and Monte Brice were executive producers and A. B. Guthrie, Jr. had an interest. Bob Hope, associated with the company, had discussed a distribution deal with United Artists by the time a script was submitted to the PCA for approval.

Although the PCA deemed the script unacceptable due to "excessive violence and brutality among juveniles," by 22 May 1958 a revised script was judged to meet the PCA's requirements. In May 1959, a week before filming began, Rowland wrote to the PCA regarding the film on Paramount Pictures letterhead; it is not known, however, if Paramount was involved with the production or financing of this film. By this time, the producers had negotiated a distribution deal with Warner Bros. Prior to filming, the PCA pointed out three troublesome areas in the final screenplay: the violence and brutality; "excessive use of the words 'spic' and 'nigger' "; and the "casual" treatment of "Lola's" pregnancy. Concerning the use of racial invective, a PCA official wrote, "Since these words are obviously offensive to certain people their use should be limited to those situations where the words have dramatic validity."

The film was not exhibited in the cities of Memphis, Atlanta, Dallas and Fort

Worth. According to a *DV* article, the film was booked for a 30 Mar 1960 opening in Memphis, but withdrawn after the head of the censor board and a second member objected to the film, saying it "shows teenagers selling drugs, and unfavorably portrays white, Negro and Mexican races." Though they did not ban it, as they could not with fewer than three votes, Rowland filed an equity suit in the Memphis Federal Court in May 1960 against the censor board, but withdrew the suit following a request by Warner Bros. A *Var* article states that the theater manager in Memphis said the film had never been booked. The censor boards in Atlanta, Dallas and Fort Worth rejected the film for exhibition. In 1965, Rowland, who had regained the film's rights, began releasing it under the title *Lola's Mistake*.

HR called *This Rebel Breed* the first theatrical film to be "completely 'serviced'" by Ziv-TV. Location shooting was done in East Los Angeles. Publicity stated that this was Dyan Cannon's first film. Cannon, who used the spelling "Diane" at that time, had previously appeared on television. [*The Rise and Fall of Legs Diamond*, in which she also appeared, was released prior to *This Rebel Breed*, but shot later.] *NYT* commented that the film "substitutes action for insight but maintains enough excitement to place it a cut or two above the usual sensationalized products of the genre." *Var* stated, "Its aims may be lofty, to promote some racial common sense through horrible example, but its narrative means are suspect. A brief lecture at the film's conclusion does not quite wash away repeated use of crude racial terms or explicit scenes of inter-racial cruelty and violence."

Box 22 Feb 1960. *DV* 1 Oct 1959. *DV* 4 Feb 1960, p. 3. *DV* 23 May 1960. *DV* 2 Jun 1965. *Exh* 17 Feb 1960, p. 4679. *FD* 17 Feb 1960, p. 46. *Har* 6 Feb 1960, p. 24. *HR* 4 Feb 1960, p. 3. *HR* 22 May 1959, p. 13. *HR* 5 Jun 1959, p. 14. *HR* 2 Jun 1965. *LAT* 25 May 1960. *LAT* 18 Jun 1960. *MPHPD* 5 Mar 1960, p. 612. *NYT* 5 May 1960, p. 41. *Var* 10 Feb 1960, p. 6. *Var* 1 Jun 1960.

THIS WEEKEND IS YOURS *see* **THE TOAST OF NEW ORLEANS**

THIS WOMAN IS MINE (Native Americans, Scottish Americans)
Universal Pictures Co., Inc.; Frank Lloyd Productions, Inc. *Dist* Universal Pictures Co., Inc. 22 Aug **1941**; Prod: early May—early Jul 1941 [©Universal Pictures Co., Inc.; 25 Aug 1941; LP10679]. Sd (Western Electric Mirrophonic Recording); b&w. 8,241 ft. 91-92 min. PCA cert no. 7568.

Prod Frank Lloyd. *Assoc prod* Jack H. Skirball. *Dir* Frank Lloyd. *Asst dir* Fred Frank. *Dial dir* Franklin Gray. *Scr* Seton I. Miller and Frederick Jackson. *Dir of photog* Milton Krasner. *Spec photog eff* John P. Fulton. *Art dir* Jack Otterson. *Assoc* John B. Goodman. *Film ed* Edward Curtiss. *Set dec* R. A. Gausman. *Gowns* Vera West. *Mus dir* Charles Previn. *Mus score* Richard Hageman. *Sd supv* Bernard B. Brown. [*Sd*] *tech* William Hedgcock. [*Unit pub wrt* Alanson Edwards].
Song(s): "Crossing the Bar in the Morning," "I'm Far too Young to Marry," music by Richard Hageman, lyrics by Bernie Grossman; "Song of the Voyageurs," music by Charles Previn, lyrics by Richard Hageman.
Source: Based on the novel *I, James Lewis* by Gilbert Wolf Gabriel (New York, 1932).
Cast: Franchot Tone (*Robert Stevens*), John Carroll (*Ovide de Montigny*), Walter Brennan (*Captain Jonathan Thorn*), Carol Bruce (*Julie Morgan*), Nigel Bruce (*Duncan MacDougall*), Paul Hurst (*2nd Mate Mumford*), Frank Conroy (*1st Mate Fox*), Leo G. Carroll (*Angus McKay*), Abner Biberman (*Lamazie*), Sig Ruman (*John Jacob Astor*), Morris Ankrum (*Roussel*), Louis Mercier (*La Fantasie*), Philip Charbert (*Franchere*), Ignacio Saenz (*Matouna*), Ray Beltram (*Chief Nakoomis*), Charles Judels (*Cafe proprietor*), [Chief Yowlachie (*Chief "One-Eye" Comcomly*)], [Sidney Bracey, Ernie Alexander (*Clerks*)], [Dick Humphreys, Conrad Binyon, Voyt Williams (*Boys*)], [Franklyn Farnum].
Historical, Adventure, with songs. [*Print viewed*]. In 1810 in New York, John Jacob Astor plans a two-year fur expedition into the Oregon wilderness. He tells Scottish fur traders Duncan MacDougall and Angus McKay that he is sending with them his top man, Robert Stevens, a seemingly mousy accountant. The crew of the expedition is to be manned by a group of rough-and-tumble French-Canadian voyagers led by Ovide de Montigny. At a local café, Ovide meets naïve singer Julie Morgan, whom he seduces by promising to take her to Paris. When she asks to go with him when he sails the next day, he lies simply tells her that the ship is too small, without revealing its true destination. The ship *Tonquin* sets sail, under the stern discipline of Captain Jonathan Thorn. Once at sea, Robert discovers that Julie has stowed away on the ship, still thinking it is going to France. Thorn discovers Julie and, refusing to listen to the truth, announces to the crew that she was smuggled aboard by Robert and that she is to be treated like a cabin boy. Ovide fails to admit his involvement in the matter, and bitter rifts develop between Robert and Ovide, and between Robert and Thorn. Later in the voyage, Julie finally confronts Ovide, and he uses his manly charms to convince her to meet him on

deck that night. When Thorn sends Robert to summon Julie, she falls overboard, but is saved by Ovide. Thorn soon becomes infatuated with Julie, and changes course to the Falkland Islands to take on water. At first, Thorn refuses to allow Julie ashore, but Robert, MacDougall and McKay convince the captain to let her go with them. Ovide and Julie sneak off together, and she asks him to marry her. When he refuses, she realizes the truth about the French-Canadian's intentions and runs off. Thorn decides to sail without them, and when he refuses to listen to Robert's pleas to wait, the young accountant threatens to kill the captain. After Ovide and Julie are safely aboard the ship, Robert is arrested for mutiny. Ovide then confesses all to Thorn and states that he will finally agree to marry the singer. When Thorn questions his motives, Ovide suggests that the captain may be more interested in her than he wishes to acknowledge. Upon arriving at the mouth of the Columbia River in Oregon, Thorn agrees to release Robert, but warns him not to return to the ship unless he wants to face trial for mutiny. After two months, the fort is almost completed, but the fur trading is going very slowly. Thorn tells Julie that she can live ashore, as Robert, Ovide and McKay are leading an expedition into the interior. Before they leave, however, Robert and Ovide get into a fight over Julie, during which Ovide falls, breaking his leg. After three months without word from Robert's river party, Thorn decides to take command of the expedition and moves the ship two hundred miles north to deal with another tribe of Indians. In the meantime, Robert returns, only to learn that Thorn is heading into a trap devised by the deceitful Indian Lamazie. Realizing that Julie is aboard the ship, Robert and Ovide travel overland to try to warn the ship. Robert is injured trying to traverse a waterfall, but continues with Ovide, despite his impairment. Their canoe arrives just as Lamazie's tribe is about to spring their trap. Robert sneaks Julie off the ship, then warns Thorn just as the Indians attack. In the ensuing mêlée, Ovide and Thorn are mortally wounded. Realizing that defeat and death are imminent, Thorn blows up the ship once Robert and Julie are safely ashore. *Expeditions. French Canadians. Fur traders. Sailors. Sea captains. Stowaways. Ambushes. John Jacob Astor. Bagpipes. Canoes and canoeing. Chess. Deception. Docks. Falkland Islands. Fights. Flogging. Forts. Indians of North America. Infatuation. Mutiny. New York City. Oregon. Pigs. Rescues. Romantic rivalry. Scottish Americans. Singers. Waterfalls.*

Note: The working titles of this film were *I, James Lewis* and *This Girl Is Mine*. An undated contemporary *HR* news item found in AFI Library files indicates that the Gilbert Gabriel novel was purchased in 1936 by Paramount, which planned it as a "vehicle" for actress Claudette Colbert, with Frank Lloyd as director. In Nov 1940, Lloyd, with his partner, Jack Skirball, purchased the unproduced property from Paramount, planning it as his first production for Universal. *LAEx* reported that Lloyd borrowed actor John Carroll from M-G-M and unsuccessfully attempted to borrow actress Priscilla Lane from Warner Bros. for the role of "Julie." This was the first film for actress Carol Bruce, who had previously been a musical star on Broadway in such productions as *Louisiana Purchase*. According to Universal press materials, portions of the film were shot on location in Lake Tahoe, California, and a log fort was constructed, similar in design to the actual fort built by the Astor expedition in 1810. This recreated fort was built by the Washoe Indian tribe of Carson City, Nevada, on land rented from Harry Comstock, heir to the Comstock Lode fortune. In compliance with conservation laws, Universal was required to plant five hundred new trees to replace those used in the construction of the fort. Press materials also state that noted Indian opera singer Chief Yowlachie acted in the film in the role of "Chief 'One-Eye' Comcomly," as well as teaching the Chinook Indian language to the actors in the film. The *MPHPD* review mistakenly identifies actor Roger Imhof in the role of "John Jacob Astor." Imhof is listed in the cast in early *HR* production charts; thus, it is possible that he was replaced by Sig Ruman during production. This film is a highly fictionalized account of the 1810-1811 expedition, financed by John Jacob Astor, which established the Pacific Fur Company fur-trading post at Ft. Astoria on the bank of the Columbia River. The film was re-released in 1949 by Realart under the title *Fury at Sea*.

Box 23 Aug 1941. *DV* 20 Aug 1941, p. 3. *HR* 11 Nov 1940, p. 5. *HR* 9 May 1941, p. 25. *HR* 23 May 1941, p. 9. *HR* 13 Jun 1941, p. 11. *HR* 20 Aug 1941, p. 3. *LAEx* 19 Apr 1941. *MPHPD* 28 Jun 1941, p. 171. *NYT* 13 Oct 1941, p. 21. *Var* 27 Aug 1941, p. 8.

THOSE WHO DANCE (*foreign version*) *see* **LOS QUE DANZAN**

THOU SHALT NOT KILL (1932) *see* **O FESTINO O LA LEGGE**

THOU SHALT NOT KILL (1935) *see* **NO MATARÁS**

THE THOUSAND DOLLAR HUSBAND (Swedish Americans)
Jesse L. Lasky Feature Play Co. *Dist* Paramount Pictures Corp. 29 May **1916** [©Jesse L. Lasky Feature Play Co.; 13 May 1916; LP8282]. Si; b&w. 5 reels.

Dir James Young. *Asst dir* E. L. Hollywood. *Scen* James Young. *Story* Margaret Turnbull. *Cam* Paul Perry.

Cast: Blanche Sweet (*Olga Nelson*), Theodore Roberts (*Uncle Sven Johnson*), Tom Forman (*Douglas Gordon*), James Neill (*Stephen Gordon*), Horace B. Carpenter (*Lawyer Judson*), Lucille La Varney (*Mme. Batavia*), E. L. Delaney (*Jack Hardy*), Camille Astor (*Maggie, Olga's friend*).

Comedy-drama. Olga Nelson, a Swedish maidservant, working at a boarding house that caters to college students, is particularly fond of one of them, wealthy Tom Gordon. When Tom receives word that his father has lost his fortune and he must quit school, he loses the remainder of his money in a poker game. Meanwhile, Olga inherits her Uncle Sven's fortune when he dies, but the will stipulates that she will receive the money only if she marries before her next birthday. She marries Gordon to get him out of debt but he spurns her affections because he thinks that she is socially inferior. They soon separate, and she goes out West where she falls into the clutches of nefarious fortune hunters who say that they will make a lady of her. Gordon returns to school and later, when she has become a "lady," they meet again. Through a misunderstanding they quarrel, but eventually Gordon realizes that she is being used by criminals and he saves her, after which they start their marriage over. *Boardinghouses. Class distinction. College students. Debt. Inheritance. Servants. Swedish Americans. Transformation. Wills. Criminals. Fortune hunters. Gambling. Poker (Game).*

Note: The film opened in New York on 28 May 1916.

Motog 10 Jun 1916, p. 1336. *MPN* 19 Jun 1916, p. 3599. *MPW* 10 Jun 1916, p. 1903. *NYDM* 3 Jun 1916, p. 30. *NYT* 29 May 1916, p. 9. *Var* 26 May 1916, p. 22. *Wid's* 1 Jun 1916, pp. 613-14.

THREADS OF DESTINY (Jewish Americans)
Lubin Mfg Co. *Dist* General Film Co.; Special Features Dept. 21 Oct 1914 [©Lubin Manufacturing Co.; 8 Oct 1914; LU3484]. Si; b&w. 5 reels.

Dir Joseph W. Smiley. *Scen* William H. Clifford.

Cast: Evelyn Nesbit Thaw (*Miriam Gruenstein*), Bernard Siegel (*Isaac Gruenstein*), Jack Clifford (*Fedor Tomspky, her husband*), Margaret Risser (*Rachel Shapiro*), William Cahill (*Alexis Movak, her husband*), Joseph W. Smiley (*Ivan Russak*), Russell William Thaw (*Russell, Fedor's son*), Joseph Standish (*Abraham Solman*), Marguerite Marsh (*The nun*).

Drama. Ivan Mussak of the Russian secret police massacres thousands of Jews and exiles many more. Everyone in Isaac Gruenstein's family is killed except himself and his baby daughter Miriam. Isaac is exiled to Siberia, but Miriam becomes Mussak's ward and is reared in a convent. Eighteen years later, Isaac is befriended by fellow exile Rachel Shapiro who is able to escape carrying a note written by Isaac to Miriam shortly before his death. Through chance, Rachel finds that Miriam has become Mussak's mistress, but when Miriam reads Isaac's warning about Mussak in the note, she decides to accompany Rachel and her new husband, Alexis Mayok, to America. Miriam marries Fedor Tomspky, then Mussak comes to the United States on a mission and stays with Fedor who turns out to be his cousin. Mussak wants Miriam to go away with him, but in the end, he is killed by the loyal community of Russian Jews who fear that Mussak will continue his evil work in America. *Fathers and daughters. Jews. Murder. Pogroms. Russia. Secret Police. Wards and guardians. Convents. Cousins. Escapes. Exile. Immigrants. Letters. Mistresses. Recognition. Siberia.*

Note: This film marked the screen debut of Evelyn Nesbit Thaw. Her son Russell played her son in the film.

Motog 31 Oct 1914, pp. 585-86, 611. *MPW* 7 Nov 1914, P. 846. *NYDM* 19 Aug 1914, p. 25. *NYDM* 28 Oct 1914, p. 33. *Var* 24 Oct 1914, p. 22.

THREADS OF FATE (Italian Americans)
Columbia Pictures Corp. *Dist* Metro Pictures Corp. 22 Jan 1917 [©Columbia Pictures Corp.; 22 Jan 1917; LP10053]. Si; b&w. 5 reels.

Dir Eugene Nowland. *Scen* June Mathis. *Story* Richard Barry. *Cam* John Arnold.

Cast: Viola Dana (*Dorothea*), Augustus Phillips (*Tom Wentworth*), Richard Tucker (*Dr. Grant Hunter*), Fred Jones (*Marquis Giovanni del Carnacacchi*), Helen Strickland (*Sarah Wentworth*), Nellie Grant (*Marcella*), Robert Whittier (*Jim Gregory*).

Drama. After Marcella, the wife of coal miner Jim Gregory, elopes with her Italian lover Giovanni, Jim leaves their baby daughter on the doorstep of Tom and Sarah Wentworth and sets out upon a life of wandering. Because the Wentworths bring the child up in ignorance of her history, Dorothea believes that she is their daughter. Dorothea falls in love with Dr. Grant Hunter, but when Tom inherits his father's coal mines, his wife Sarah opposes the courtship, hoping for a more advantageous match. About this time, Giovanni returns, posing as a marquis, and proposes to Dorothea. Sarah is delighted and invites the Marquis del Camachi and Marcella, who is posing as his sister, to stay with them. Dorothea refuses his proposal, however, and in a fit of rage, Giovanni plans to abduct the girl and kill Wentworth. Meanwhile Gregory has returned to lead a strike of the miners and learns that Dorothea is actually his daughter. Together he and Marcella thwart Giovanni's scheme, and in the struggle for Dorothea, Gregory is shot. The police arrest Giovanni; then Gregory, mortally wounded, dies, giving his blessing to Dorothea without revealing that he is her father. *Coal miners. Foster parents. Impersonation and imposture. Italians. Parentage. Wanderers. Coal mines. Desertion (Marital). Inheritance. Labor agitators. Nobility. Physicians. Strikes and lockouts.*

ETR 3 Feb 1917, p. 635. *Motog* 20 Jan 1917, p. 122. *MPN* 3 Feb 1917, p. 760. *MPW* 27 Jan 1917, p. 589. *MPW* 3 Feb 1917, p. 705. *NYDM* 20 Jan 1917, p. 33. *NYDM* 27 Jan 1917, p. 50. *Wid's* 1 Feb 1917, p. 69.

THREE CAME TO KILL *see* **INSIDE THE MAFIA**

THREE CHEERS FOR THE IRISH (Irish Americans, Scottish Americans)
Warner Bros. Pictures, Inc.; A Warner Bros.—First National Picture; Jack L. Warner in charge of production. *Dist* Warner Bros. Pictures, Inc. 16 Mar **1940**; New York opening: week of 9 Mar 1940; *Prod:* began mid-Dec 1939 [©Warner Bros. Pictures, Inc.; 16 Mar 1940; LP9483]. Sd (RCA Victor Sound System); b&w. 10 reels. 100 min. PCA cert no. 6007.

Exec prod Hal B. Wallis. *Assoc prod* Samuel Bischoff. *Dir* Lloyd Bacon. *Dial dir* Hugh Cummings. *Asst dir* Dick Mayberry. *Orig scr* Richard Macaulay and Jerry Wald. *Photog* Charles Rosher. *Art dir* Esdras Hartley. *Ed* William Holmes. *Ward* Milo Anderson. *Mus dir* Leo F. Forbstein. *Mus* Adolph Deutsch. *Orch arr* Ray Heindorf. *Sd* Stanley Jones. *Makeup* Perc Westmore. *Tech adv* Robert Watson.

Song(s): "Mi caballero," words and music by Jack Scholl and M. K. Jerome.

Cast: Priscilla Lane (*Maureen Casey*), Thomas Mitchell (*Peter Casey*), Dennis Morgan (*Angus Ferguson*), Alan Hale (*Gallagher*), Virginia Gray (*Patricia Casey*), Irene Hervey (*Heloise Casey*), William Lundigan ([*Michael*] *Flaherty*), Frank Jenks (*Ed McKean*), Henry Armetta (*Tony*), Morgan Conway (*Joe Niklas*), Alec Craig (*Callahan*), J. M. Kerrigan (*Scanlon*), Cliff Clark (*Mara*), William Davidson (*Police commissioner*), Joe King (*Police captain*), [Ferike Boros (*Tenement woman*)], [Ed Gargan (*Policeman*)], [Walter Miller (*Sergeant*)], [William Gould (*Desk sergeant*)], [Wade Boteler (*Lieutenant*)].

Drama. [*Print viewed*]. After twenty years of devoted service to the police force, Irish police officer Peter Casey finds himself pensioned off and replaced by rookie Angus Ferguson, whom Casey considers a "contemptuous Scottishman". While delivering a complaint one night to the Casey apartment, Angus meets Casey's eldest daughter Maureen, who runs the motherless Casey household, and a mutual attraction arises between the young people. After retiring, Casey begins to get underfoot, and so Maureen and her sisters Patricia and Heloise encourage him to run for the post of alderman. Casey accepts the challenge, and with the help of his hooligan friend Gallagher, launches his campaign. Meanwhile, Maureen and Angus have been courting, and on the night that they are secretly married, Casey pleads with Maureen to never see the Scotsman again and tries to interest her in Michael Flaherty, a nice Irishman. When Casey's campaign runs short of funds, Heloise naïvely solicits a donation from her bookie friend, Joe Niklas. Upon learning the identity of his benefactor, Casey asks his constituency to elect his opponent, and his announcement sparks a barroom brawl in which Angus arrests him for disturbing the peace. After being pardoned by the judge, Casey chastises Maureen for her friendship with the Scotsman, and when Angus announces their marriage, the furious Casey orders the newlyweds to leave his house. Casey loses his daughter but wins the election as the voters, who admire his honesty, elect him alderman. On Christmas eve, he finally wins back Maureen when the familiy is reconciled at Maureen's bedside as she gives birth to twins. *Fathers and daughters. Irish*

Americans. Marriage–Secret. Police. Pride and vanity. Bars. Bookies. Childbirth. Christmas. Elections. Fights. Political campaigns. Retirement. Scottish Americans. Sisters.

Note: The working title of this film was *You Can't Beat the Irish.* According to news items in *HR*, Geraldine Fitzgerald and Jane Bryan were slated to star in this film and Warners planned to borrow Fred MacMurray from Paramount for the lead. Songwriters Jack Scholl and M. K. Jerome were awarded an ASCAP award for their work on this picture.
DV 6 Mar 1940, p. 3. *FD* 8 Mar 1940, p. 8. *HR* 22 May 1939, p. 2. *HR* 16 Dec 1939, pp. 6-7. *HR* 5 Jan 1940, p. 6. *HR* 16 Jan 1940, p. 5. *HR* 11 Feb 1940, p. 1. *HR* 7 Mar 1940, p. 3. *HR* 24 Jul 1940, p. 7. *MPD* 11 Mar 1940, p. 3. *MPH* 16 Mar 1940, p. 34, 36. *NYT* 9 Mar 1940, p. 19. *Var* 13 Mar 1940, p. 16.

THREE DAUGHTERS (Jewish Americans, Yiddish language)
Cinema Service Corp. *Dist* Cinema Service Corp. **1950?**. Sd; b&w. Length undetermined. Yiddish language with English subtitles.
Dir Joseph Zeiden.
Source: Based on the play *Dray Tekhter* by Abraham Blum (New York, 1939).
Cast: Michel Rosenberg [(*Abe Zablinsky*)], Anatol Winogradoff, Charlotte Goldstein [(*Bertha Gottlieb Zablinsky*)], Max Wilner, Esta Saltzman [sic], Leon Schacter [(*David Gottlieb*)], Zelda Kaplan, Barney Ward, Salcia Shoor.
Yiddish, Domestic, Comedy-drama. [*Print viewed*]. David Gottlieb, a longtime accountant at a New York firm run by Abe Zablinsky and his partner, is concerned about the future of his three daughters and worries that he might lose his job if he makes a mistake. His daughter Anna suspects that her out-of-work husband Charlie is cheating, while daughter Bertha, who is in love with Robert Hoffman, a musician who has been absent for a long time, has rejected other suitors for years. The only happiness David enjoys is when his devoted wife Esther tells him that their youngest daughter Lucy is about to be married. Although Abe's partner wants to fire David, Abe, a jovial jokester, gives David a six-dollar raise after he meets Bertha, to whom he is attracted. David invites Abe to his home, hoping that Bertha will give up her romance with Robert and marry Abe. David tells her that although she does not love Abe now, love will come, especially if they have children. Bertha is repulsed, however, by the balding, plump, crude man, who liberally mixes his Yiddish with English, and when Abe proposes, she begs for more time. That evening, the mother of Lucy's husband-to-be tells Bertha that she will not allow the marriage because both families are poor, and she wants her son to marry someone with money. Bertha breaks the news to Lucy, who collapses in tears and says she must now commit suicide rather than disgrace her parents. To save her pregnant sister, Bertha decides to marry Abe, who can provide money for the family. A few years later, Bertha, despite having a daughter and plenty of money, is unhappy with her marriage and bitter because of her sacrifice. When Robert, now a renowned composer and musician, returns to town, Bertha reunites with him and is entranced with his elegant manner and cultured discourse. One day, Abe finds the two of them together and is humiliated, suspecting that Bertha prefers Robert. Following an argument, he tries to embrace Bertha, but she pushes him away, causing him to tear her dress. In his anger, he screams that everything she has is his. Later, at their little girl's birthday party, Abe is chagrined to find that Bertha is absent from the family gathering and complains to David. When she finally arrives, David talks to his daughter on Abe's behalf, but she insists that she has a right to her own happiness. Despite her words, Bertha refuses Robert when he shows up to ask her to run away with him, saying she is bound by family ties. Before Robert can leave, an intoxicated Abe sees him with Bertha and accuses Bertha of coming to her daughter's birthday party with her "lover." Abe then accuses Robert of destroying his home and orders him to take Bertha and get out. A suddenly remorseful Abe tries to take back what he said, but Bertha replies that she is only his "luxury" and vows to take her child and go. Abe, who is devoted to his daughter, tells Bertha he cannot live without the girl, but she shocks the whole company by revealing that the child is not Abe's. As she is about to tell the truth about the girl, Lucy stops her. The day before the divorce trial, Robert complains to Bertha that the scandal is going to ruin his career, forcing Bertha to realize that he wants her only as a lover. After Robert leaves, Lucy tries to convince Bertha to go back to Abe, and Bertha, admitting that Abe loves her, finally agrees to return to him. Bertha confesses to her father that a foolish dream blinded her to Abe's wonderful sincerity, and as David is taking an unsuspecting Abe to see Bertha, Abe, who has decided to take the

blame at the trial so that his wife will bear no shame, tells David that losing the baby means everything to him. After David declares that not only will he have the child, but his wife also, Abe tearfully states that he can never forget that the child is not his. At that moment, Lucy reveals that she is the mother and relates that two months after Bertha and Abe's wedding, she and Bertha went to Florida together and returned with her baby. Abe recognizes that Bertha's deed required a "heart like a mountain," and the couple are reconciled amidst crying, hugging and kissing. Sometime later, Bertha is expecting Abe's child and is finally in love with her husband. *Fathers and daughters. Infidelity. Jews. Marriage–Forced by circumstances. Romance. Secrets. Self-sacrifice. Sisters. Accountants. Birthdays. Businessmen. Class distinction. Composers. Drunkenness. Employer-employee relations. Family life. Illegitimacy. Musicians. New York City. Parentage. Partnership. Proposals (Marital). Unemployment.*

Note: The Yiddish-language title of this film is *Dray Tekhter*. The viewed print included a copyright statement dated 1961; however, no listing of this film has been located in the copyright registry. Esta Salzman's name is misspelled as "Saltzman" in the onscreen credits. Although no contemporary information regarding the film's release has been found, modern sources list the release year as 1950. According to a modern source, Michel Rosenberg originated his role in the stage version, and Leon Schachter was a coproducer of the film.

THREE FACES WEST (Austrian Americans)
Republic Pictures Corp. *Dist* Republic Pictures Corp. **3 Jul 1940**; Prod: began late Mar 1940 [©Republic Pictures Corp.; 12 Jul 1940; LP9796]. Sd; b&w. 9 reels. 79 or 81 min. PCA cert no. 6239.
Assoc prod Sol C. Siegel. *Dir* Bernard Vorhaus. [*Asst dir* Kenneth Holmes]. *Scr* F. Hugh Herbert, Joseph Moncure March, Samuel Ornitz and [Doris Anderson]. *Photog* John Alton. *Spec eff* Howard Lydecker. *Art dir* John Victor Mackay. *Ed* William Morgan. *Supv ed* Murray Seldeen. *Ward* Adele Palmer. *Mus score* Victor Young. *Prod mgr* Al Wilson.
Cast: JOHN WAYNE (*John [Phillips]*), SIGRID GURIE (*Leni Braun*), Charles Coburn (*Dr. [Karl] Braun*), Spencer Charters (*Nunk*), Helen MacKellar (*Mrs. Welles*), Sonny Bupp (*Billy Welles*), Wade Boteler (*Harris*), Trevor Bardette (*Higgins*), Russell Simpson (*Minister*), Charles Waldron (*Dr. Thorpe*), Wendell Niles (*Radio announcer*), [Roland Varno (*Eric*)], [Frederick Vogeding (*Schmidt*)], [Wolfgang Zilzer (*Dr. Preussner*)].
Drama. [*Print viewed*]. The "We the People" radio program is devoting a broadcast to the story of refugee doctors, driven from their homeland and looking for positions in the doctorless towns of America when Dr. Karl Brau one of the physicians, relates the tale of how he and his daughter Leni were driven from their homeland in Vienna. As a result of the broadcast, father and daughter are summoned to the town of Asheville Forks, North Dakota by John Phillips, the leader of the farmers' organization there. They arrive in the midst of a dust storm, and Leni, distressed by the hardships she has suffered and by the death of her fiancé Eric, wants to leave the town immediately. Her father, however, insists on staying to aid the ailing and impoverished farmers who must helplessly watch as their fortunes are blown away by the wind. Leni soon adapts to the farm community, and love comes to her and John. Soon afterward, word arrives from Eric that he is alive and coming to America, and Leni, out of gratitude, agrees to meet him in San Francisco and marry him. John's troubles mount as a dust storm devastates the land, and he convinces the farmers to follow him to a new home in Oregon. Along the way, Higgins, a troublemaker, attempts to agitate the farmers to venture to California instead, but John, after a bout of disillusionment, rallies the farmers on to Oregon. Meanwhile, in San Francisco, Leni and her father are shocked to learn that Eric has joined forces with the Nazis, and father and daughter leave Eric to rejoin John in Oregon. *Austrian Americans. Dust storms. Engagements. Farmers. Fathers and daughters. Missing persons, Assumed dead. Physicians. Refugees, Political. Nazism. North Dakota. Oregon. Radio broadcasting. Romance. San Francisco (CA). World War II.*

Note: The working titles of this film were *Doctors Don't Tell* and *The Refugee.* Although the *MPH* review credits Doris Anderson with screenplay, she is not credited onscreen or in other sources.
FD 14 Jun 1940, p. 6. *HR* 30 Mar 1940, pp. 6-7. *HR* 12 Jun 1940, p. 3. *MPH* 4 May 1940, p. 46. *MPH* 15 Jun 1940, p. 42. *NYT* 19 Aug 1940, p. 13. *Var* 19 Jun 1940, p. 14.

3 GODFATHERS (Latino)

Argosy Pictures Corp.; A Metro-Goldwyn-Mayer Picture. *Dist* Loew's Inc. Jan **1949**; World premiere in Washington, D.C. 25 Nov 1948; Prod: early May—early Jun 1948 [©Argosy Pictures Corp.; 17 Nov 1948; LP1958]. Sd (Western Electric Recording); col (Technicolor). 9,551 ft. 105-107 min.

Pres JOHN FORD and MERIAN C. COOPER. *Dir* John Ford. *Asst dir* Wingate Smith and Edward O'Fearna. *Scr* Laurence Stallings and Frank S. Nugent. *Dir of photog* Winton Hoch. *2d unit photog* Charles Boyle. [*Cam op* Harvey Gould]. [*2d unit cam op* Edward Fitzgerald]. [*Stills* Alex Kahle]. *Sd eff* Patrick Kelley. *Spec eff* Jack Caffee. *Technicolor color dir* Natalie Kalmus. *Assoc* Morgan Padelford. *Art dir* James Basevi. *Film ed* Jack Murray. *Set dec* Joe Kish. [*Props* Jack Golconda]. *Cost research* D. R. O. Hatswell. *Men's ward* Michael Meyers. *Women's ward* Ann Peck. *Mus score* Richard Hageman. *Arr and cond* Lucien Cailliet. *Sd* Frank Moran and Joseph I. Kane. *Makeup* Don Cash. *Hair dresser* Anna Malin. *Asst to dir* Lowell Farrell. *Props* Jack Golconda. [*Scr supv* Meta Sterne]. [*Grip* Thomas Griffin].

Music: "Silent Night, Holy Night," music by Franz Gruber.

Song(s): "Bringing in the Sheaves," music and lyrics by George A. Minor; "Beautiful River," music and lyrics by Robert Lowry; "Streets of Laredo (Cowboy's Lament)," traditional.

Source: Based on the novel *The Three Godfathers* by Peter B. Kyne (New York, 1913).

Cast: John Wayne [(*Robert Marmaduke Sangster Hightower*)], Pedro Armendariz [(*Pedro Roca Fuerte*)], and introducing Harry Carey, Jr. [(*William Kearny, "The Abiline Kid"*)], Ward Bond [(*"Buck" Perley Sweet*)], Mae Marsh [(*Mrs. Perley Sweet*)], Mildred Natwick [(*The mother*)], Jane Darwell [(*Miss Florie*)], Guy Kibbee [(*The judge*)], Dorothy Ford [(*Ruby Latham*)], Ben Johnson [(*Member of posse*)], Charles Halton [(*Mr. Latham*)], Hank Worden [(*Deputy sheriff*)], Jack Pennick [(*Luke, the train conductor*)], Fred Libby [(*Deputy sheriff*)], Michael Dugan, Don Summers [(*Members of posse*)], [Francis Ford (*Drunk*)].

Western. [*Print viewed*]. Texas outlaws Robert Marmaduke Sangster Hightower, Pedro Roca Fuerte and William Kearny, "The Abiline Kid," arrive in the small town of Welcome, Arizona, to rob a bank. After first meeting Sheriff Buck Perley Sweet and his wife, the three bandits encounter Mrs. Sweet's niece, Ruby Latham, the wife of the town's bank president. The outlaws then proceed to shoot their way into Latham's bank, just as Buck discovers that they are wanted men. The Abiline Kid is wounded in the ensuing shootout with the sheriff and his posse, but he manages to escape into the desert with Pedro and Robert. Back in town, Buck deputizes members of his posse and organizes a manhunt to capture the three desperados who are on horseback. The deputies are sent by train to the Mojave water tank, the nearest source of desert water, where Buck hopes the three outlaws will go. As Pedro, Robert and The Kid approach the water tank, they discover Buck's trap and plan an alternate course. Suspecting that Buck also has men waiting for them at Apache Wells, the next water source, Robert instead plans to head north to Terrapin Tanks and cross the Mexican border at a more remote location. The three bandits soon find themselves in a sandstorm, and later are forced to continue on foot after their horses escape. Meanwhile, Buck and his posse arrive at Apache Wells, and wait for the robbers. When the robbers fail to show up, Buck realizes that they must have doubled back, and goes in search of them. Robert and his men arrive at Terrapin Tanks only to discover that the tanks have been dynamited and contain no water. However, near the water tanks, the three bandits find a pregnant woman alone in a covered wagon. Unknown to the bandits, the woman is Buck's daughter. The bandits take pity on her and help her deliver her child, after which the mother makes the baby's godparents promise to keep her baby from harm. The mother dies a short time later, and the three desperadoes find themselves responsible for the care of the infant. Realizing that by continuing their journey to the Mexican border they will be endangering the infant's life, the bandits decide instead to risk arrest and return to Welcome. While making the dangerous desert crossing, The Kid collapses and dies of thirst. Pedro later breaks his leg in a fall, and shoots himself to relieve Robert of the burden of having to care for him. Braving the punishing desert heat with the infant in his arms, Robert presses onward, stumbling over rocks and finding inspiration in the Bible he carries with him. Soon after arriving in Welcome,

Robert enters a saloon and collapses at the feet of Buck and his deputies. Robert and the infant quickly recover from the arduous journey and are taken in by Buck and his wife. A jury finds Robert guilty of robbery, but he receives a light sentence in light of his heroic deed. *Bank robberies. Desert survival. Good Samaritans. Gunshot wounds. Outlaws. Self-sacrifice. Arizona. Bible. Childbirth. Death and dying. Heroes. Infants. Judges. Mexican Americans. Nieces. Pledges. Posses. Sandstorms. Sheriffs. Suicide. Thirst. Water.*

Note: The onscreen credits contain the following written dedication: "To the memory of Harry Carey, bright star of the early western sky." Carey, who died on 24 Sep 1947, was a longtime friend of both John Wayne and John Ford, and starred in two previous screen versions of the story. Peter B. Kyne's short story "Broncho Billy and the Baby," which appeared in *The Saturday Evening Post* in 1910, is identified in some sources as the basis for his novel *The Three Godfathers*. The novel first appeared in the same magazine on 23 Nov 1912. Pre-production news items in *HR* noted that Argosy Pictures negotiated a one-picture releasing contract with M-G-M for this film, and that it marked the first time that M-G-M accepted a distrubution deal without a financial investment or creative input in the production.
According to an Apr 1948 *HR* news item, director John Ford initially planned to film the picture in Mexico. The film was shot on location in Death Valley, CA. *HR* also notes that some filming was set to take place at RKO's Culver City studios. As noted above, other screen adaptations of Kyne's story include the 1916 Bluebird film *The Three Godfathers*, directed by Edward J. Le Saint and starring Harry Carey and Stella Razeto; the 1919 Universal picture *Marked Men*, directed by John Ford and also starring Carey (see *AFI Catalog of Feature Films, 1911-20*; F1.4453 and F1.2823); a 1930 Universal picture called *Hell's Heroes*, directed by William Wyler and starring Charles Bickford (see *AFI Catalog of Feature Films, 1921-30*; F2.2414); and a 1936 M-G-M film directed by Richard Boleslawski and starring Chester Morris and Lewis Stone (see *AFI Catalog of Feature Films 1931-40*; F3.4609). A television version entitled *The Godchild* appeared on the ABC network in 1974, and was directed by John Badham and starred Jack Palance.

Box 4 Dec 1948. *DV* 1 Dec 1948, p. 3. *FD* 1 Dec 1948, p. 6. *HR* 27 Jan 1948, p. 2. *HR* 3 Feb 1948, p. 12. *HR* 13 Apr 1948, p. 2. *HR* 30 Apr 1948, p. 2. *HR* 7 May 1948, p. 12. *HR* 4 Jun 1948, p. 14. *HR* 24 Nov 1948, p. 6. *HR* 1 Dec 1948, p. 3. *HR* 26 Jan 1949, p. 3. *MPHPD* 9 Oct 1948, p. 4342. *MPHPD* 4 Dec 1948, p. 4405. *NYT* 4 Mar 1949, p. 25. *Var* 1 Dec 1948, p. 11.

THREE HEARTS FOR JULIA (Refugees)

Metro-Goldwyn-Mayer Corp.; controlled by Loew's Inc. *Dist* Loew's Inc. **1943**; Prod: 4 Sep—17 Oct 1942 [©Loew's Inc.; 5 Jan 1943; LP11801]. Sd (Western Electric Sound System); b&w. 9 reels, 8,086 ft. 89 min. Passed by the National Board of Review. PCA cert no. 8967.

Prod John W. Considine, Jr. *Dir* Richard Thorpe. [*Asst dir* Bert Spurlin]. *Story and scr* Lionel Houser. *Dir of photog* George Folsey. *Art dir* Cedric Gibbons. *Assoc* Howard Campbell. *Film ed* Irvine Warburton. *Asst ed* Tom Conlon. *Set dec* Edwin B. Willis. *Assoc* Helen Conway. *Cost supv* Irene. *Mus score* Herbert Stothart. *Rec dir* Douglas Shearer.

Music: "I've Been Working on the Railroad," traditional.

Cast: ANN SOTHERN (*Julia Seabrook*), MELVYN DOUGLAS (*Jeff Seabrook*), Lee Bowman (*David Torrance*), Richard Ainley (*Philip Barrows*), Felix Bressart (*Anton Ottoway*), Marta Linden (*May Elton*), Reginald Owen (*John Girard*), Marietta Canty (*Mattie*), [Frank Faylen (*Meek gateman*)], [Chester Clute (*Homer, man in balcony*)], [Dick Elliott (*Smith, rewrite man*)], [Russell Hicks (*Colonel Martin*)], [Robert Greig (*Cairns, the butler*)], [Jacqueline White (*Kay*)], [Kay Medford (*Thelma*)], [Ann Richards (*Clara*)], [Elvia Allman (*Miss Stickney*)], [Charles LaTorre (*Bureau chief*)], [Marek Windheim (*Perfume clerk*)], [Bill Lally (*Customs man*)], [William Tannen, Rudolph Cameron, Hooper Atchley, Art Belasco, George Lollier, Anthony Warde, Estelle Etterre (*Reporters*)], [Dick Rich (*Mug attendant*)], [Oscar O'Shea (*Doorman*)], [Phyllis Cook (*Western Union woman*)], [Joe Yule (*Cab driver*)], [Fred Rapport, Bill Dill (*Waiters*)], [Leigh Sterling, Michael Butler, Cliff Danielson, Bert Hicks (*Ushers*)], [Ernie Alexander (*Johnson*)], [James Davis (*Wheller*)], [Russell Gleason (*Jones*)], [Max Willenz (*Bartender*)], [Nell Craig (*Maid*)], [Howard Hickman (*Mr. Doran*)], [James Warren (*Program vendor*)], [Hans Von Morhart, John Van Eyck, Curt Furberg, Nicholas Vehr, Jack Deery (*Nazis*)], [Dick Wessel (*Soldier*)], [Mary Field (*Miss Wheeler*)], [Aileen Haley, Eve Whitney, Marie Windsor, Mary Benoit, Natalie Draper (*Orchestra members*)].

Romantic comedy. [*Print viewed*]. In the summer of 1941, Lisbon-based foreign correspondent Jeff Seabrook, who has been away from home for two years, turns down a job to head the Berlin bureau of his newspaper, in the hope that he and his wife Julia can spend more time together. In New York, Julia, who is a concert violinist in an all-female orchestra, has a hard time concentrating on her work

because she has filed for divorce and is nervous about letting Jeff know. When Jeff learns about the impending divorce, he goes to their home to effect a reconciliation, but finds that several of Julia's fellow musicians are houseguests and hence they have no time to be alone. Soon Jeff learns that Julia, who is fed up with his long absences and broken promises, is being pursued by two men, the orchestra's manager, David Torrance, and music critic Philip Barrows. Jeff's boss, Johnny Girard, convinces him that the best way to win Julia back is to pretend to go along with the divorce, and to prove his acceptance, Jeff tells her that he will help her select his successor. Despite his pretense, Jeff finds every opportunity to pit David and Philip against each other so that he can win Julia back. Meanwhile, the orchestra works hard with its new conductor, refugee Anton Ottoway, who is chagrined to find that he is reduced to dealing with an all-female orchestra. One afternoon, Jeff picks Julia up at the concert hall, ostensibly to drive her to their lawyer's office, but instead "kidnaps" her and takes her to a country retreat where she can think things over. The next morning, Jeff gets word that he is being called up for active duty in the Army, but does not tell Julia. While Jeff is outside, Julia finds the cabin's hidden telephone and calls Philip to come and get her. When Philip arrives, he sees Julia's slippers in Jeff's room and assumes the worst, not knowing that she had actually thrown them at Jeff the night before. Now even more angry at Jeff, Julia goes through with the divorce and stops seeing Philip. On the day that they are to sign the final divorce papers, Jeff goes to see Julia at the concert hall, and they argue, then passionately kiss. Julia still will not take him back, and he leaves without telling her that he is going into the Army the next day. After the concert, Ottoway goes to a local bar to unload his troubles with the female musicians and meets Jeff, whom he immediately likes. After they play a duet on a saw, Ottoway takes an intoxicated Jeff to his place to spend the night. The next morning, as Jeff leaves for active duty, he tells Ottoway that he will be staying with "his uncle" at Fort McHenry. When Ottoway later learns what Jeff meant, he determines to help reunite him with Julia. After hearing that the USO is seeking musicians, Ottoway insists on taking the orchestra on tour and arranges for them to stop at Fort McHenry when he learns that David and Julia plan to marry at the end of the tour. Just before the performance at Fort McHenry, Julia confides in Ottoway, and he tells her that she is still in love with Jeff. She takes his advice to see Jeff, but learns from his commanding officer that it is impossible because Jeff is leaving the next day for overseas. As the concert is about to begin, Julia argues with David over playing what he considers "low-brow" music and breaks off their engagement. During the concert, Julia spontaneously bursts into a solo of "I've Been Working on the Railroad" as Jeff, who is in the wings, happily blows kisses to her. *Divorce. Foreign correspondents. Musicians. Orchestras. Romantic rivalry. Vocational obsession. Abduction. Bars. Conductors (Music). Cultural elitism. Drunkenness. Fort McHenry (MD). Houseguests. Mice. Military posts. New York City. Singing telegrams. Subpoena. United Service Organizations. War refugees.*

Note: According to news items in *HR*, the film was originally scheduled to be directed by Edward Buzzell, who became ill and was replaced by Richard Thorpe. A 22 Sep 1942 news item includes Dink Trout in the cast, but his appearance in the released film has not been confirmed. Another *HR* news item noted that Electra Simonini was to "strum the harp" as a member of the all-female orchestra, but it is unclear whether she was to be in the cast or provide harp music for the off-screen orchestra. No other contemporary sources include her in the film's credits. *Three Hearts for Julia* was one of several M-G-M films that were backlogged in late 1942 and may not have been shown throughout the country until early 1943.

Box 2 Jan 1943. *DV* 6 Jan 1943, p. 3. *FD* 6 Jan 1943, p. 5. *HR* 13 Aug 1942, p. 1. *HR* 4 Sep 1942, p. 3. *HR* 22 Sep 1942, p. 7. *HR* 8 Oct 1942, p. 4. *HR* 13 Oct 1942, p. 7. *HR* 20 Oct 1942, p. 4. *HR* 25 Nov 1942, p. 4. *HR* 6 Jan 1943, p. 3. *HR* 16 Dec 1943, p. 3. *MPH* 9 Jan 1943. *MPHPD* 14 Nov 1942, p. 1009. *MPHPD* 9 Jan 1943, p. 1101. *NYT* 21 May 1943, p. 22. *Var* 6 Jan 1943, p. 50.

THREE MEN IN WHITE (Chinese Americans)
Metro-Goldwyn-Mayer Corp.; controlled by Loew's Inc. *Dist* Loew's Inc. Jun **1944**; New York opening: 26 May 1944; Prod: 20 Nov 1943–6 Jan 1944 [©Loew's Inc.; 26 Apr 1944; LP12671]. Sd (Western Electric Sound System); b&w. 9 reels. 85-86 min. Passed by the National Board of Review. PCA cert no. 9939.
Series: Dr. Gillespie.
[*Prod* Carey Wilson]. *Dir* Willis Goldbeck. [*Asst dir* Al Raboch]. *Orig scr* Martin Berkeley and Harry Ruskin. *Dir of photog* Ray June. *Art dir* Cedric Gibbons and Harry McAfee. *Film ed* George Hively. *Set dec* Edwin B. Willis. *Assoc* Helen Conway. *Cost supv* Irene. *Mus score* Nathaniel Shilkret. *Rec dir* Douglas Shearer.

Source: Based on characters created by Max Brand.
Cast: Lionel Barrymore (*Dr. Leonard Gillespie*), Van Johnson (*Dr. Randall ["Red"] Adams*), Marilyn Maxwell (*Ruth Edley*), Keye Luke (*Dr. Lee Wong How*), Ava Gardner (*Jean Brown*), Alma Kruger (*Molly Byrd*), "Rags" Ragland (*Hobart Genet*), Nell Craig (*Nurse Parker*), Walter Kingsford (*Dr. Walter Carew*), George H. Reed (*Conover*), Celia Travers (*Nurse Slidell*), [Hope Landin (*Nurse Evans*)], [Chester Clute (*Mr. Burns*)], [Patricia Barker (*Mary Jones*)], [Violette Wilson (*Mrs. Jones*)], [Shimen Ruskin (*Martinelli, tailor*)], [Franco Corsaro (*Headwaiter*)], [George Chandler (*Parking lot attendant*)], [James Burke, Eddie Dunn, William Haade (*Policemen*)], [Mary Currier (*Nurse Workman*)], [Jane Green (*Nurse Walker*)], [Byron Foulger (*Technician*)], [Addison Richards (*George Brown*)], [Barbara Brown (*Mrs. Brown*)], [Sam McDaniel (*Phone operator*)], [Billy Cummings (*Boy on street*)], [Richard Hall (*Boy on tricycle*)].

Medical, **Drama**. [*Print viewed*]. After warning ambitious intern Randall "Red" Adams about the dangers of "blondes," noted Blair Hospital physician Dr. Leonard Gillespie confers with Red and fellow intern Dr. Lee Wong How about their future. Both Red and Lee want to be Gillespie's assistant and, hoping to impress him, each takes turns bragging about his latest diagnostic accomplishments. Torn between the two men, the irascible Gillespie, whose self-imposed deadline for making the decision is fast approaching, announces that he will be assigning a special case to each one. The wheelchair-bound Gillespie then asks Red to attend a medical forum with him later that week, and while they are at the forum's hotel, they notice a beautiful young woman stagger to her car, apparently drunk. The woman then hits a parked car and, while she is being questioned by an angry policeman, passes out. Red intervenes on the woman's behalf and, with Gillespie's help, convinces the officer to allow him to take her to a hospital. On the way there, the woman reveals to Red that she was only pretending to be unconscious but insists that she is not drunk. After the woman passes out in earnest, Red checks her into the hospital, and the next morning, informs the policeman that she had no alcohol in her system. Although Red expresses concern about the woman's health, she checks herself out without having given her name. Later, however, Red tells Gillespie about the woman and suggests that she become his test case. Gillespie, who has just assigned Lee to find out why young patient Mary Jones went into convulsions after eating candy, at first disapproves of Red's choice, but then gives him the woman's purse, which she had tossed out her car window on the way to the hospital. From her driver's license, Red discovers the woman's name is Jean Brown and goes to see her. To his surprise, Jean lives with her father and invalid mother, who has been crippled by incurable spinal arthritis. Pressed by Red, Jean confesses that she went to a party the previous night, hoping for a temporary escape from caring for her mother, and took someone else's prescription medicine, which Red deduces caused her inebriated state. After Jean reveals that she broke up with her fiancé because of her mother's condition, Red pledges to reexamine Mrs. Brown. Later, Red confers with Gillespie about Mrs. Brown's disease and learns that her arthritis is indeed incurable. Though discouraged, Red undertakes to lighten Jean's load by finding a way to make her mother mobile. The hard-working Lee, meanwhile, has put Mary on a sugar-free, vitamin-supplemented diet and is confident that he will soon have her cured. On the eve of Gillespie's deadline, Red agrees to drop by the rich, marriage-hungry Ruth Edley's apartment, but asks Lee to make a phony emergency call to him to ensure that he will not succumb to her charms. Lee calls Red at Ruth's as planned, and on their way back to the hospital, Lee takes his rival to watch a little boy hopping playfully down the street with one leg on the sidewalk, the other in the street. Lee explains to a confused Red that Mrs. Brown's arthritis may have caused one of her legs to become shorter than the other, which would account for the extreme pain she feels while walking. Having solved Red's case, Lee then takes the final step in resolving Mary's problem. Prepared to administer insulin, Lee orders Mary to eat several candies and waits to see if she has an adverse reaction to them. She doesn't, and the next morning, Lee proudly reveals to Gillespie that Mary was suffering from a mineral deficiency that caused her to crave sugar and have convulsions. Gillespie informs Lee that, although he was unaware of it at the time, he aided him in much the same way Lee helped Red. Gillespie then discovers that Red has suddenly withdrawn himself from the "competition"

and goes in search of him. At the Browns's, Red presents Mrs. Brown with orthopedic shoes and watches with satisfaction as she begins to walk for the first time in years. As he is leaving the Browns's, Red is intercepted by Gillespie, who, having spied Mrs. Brown walking, offers him the assistant's job. The intern turns him down, however, saying that Lee is the more worthy physician. Later, however, Lee learns that Gillespie has arranged for him to join the Chinese Red Army medical corps, an assignment for which he has long yearned, and vows to help bring back Red. As Red is preparing to depart for Chicago, Ruth connives to meet with him one last time at the hotel and is pleasantly surprised when Hobart, having been sent by Lee, knocks him out in the parking lot. *Hospitals. Physicians. Rivalry. Tests of character. Ambulance drivers. Arthritis. Automobile accidents. Candy. Children. Chinese Americans. Diets. Handicapped. Invalids. Mothers and daughters. Nurses. Police. Romance. Shoes. Socialites.*

Note: The film's opening title card reads: "Metro-Goldwyn-Mayer presents A New Dr. Gillespie Adventure *Three Men in White*." According to a mid-Dec 1943 *HR* news item, production shut down temporarily because of a "flu epidemic," which laid up Van Johnson, Lionel Barrymore and uncredited producer Carey Wilson. Although *HR* news items add Bobby Blake, later known as Robert Blake, to the cast, his participation in the final film has not been confirmed. As with many M-G-M films in 1944, *Three Men in White* was shown to overseas troops before its release in the U.S. For more information on the "Dr. Kildare/Dr.Gillespie" series, consult the Series Index and see entry for the 1938 film *Young Dr. Kildare* in *AFI Catalog of Feature Films, 1931-40* (F3.5251).

Box 6 May 1944. *DV* 1 May 1944, p. 3. *FD* 10 May 1944, p. 12. *HR* 19 Nov 1943, p. 18. *HR* 22 Nov 1943, p. 14. *HR* 10 Dec 1943, p. 2. *HR* 30 Dec 1943, p. 14. *HR* 5 Jan 1944, p. 2. *HR* 1 May 1944, p. 3. *HR* 18 May 1944, p. 1. *HR* 29 May 1944, p. 10. *MPHPD* 4 Mar 1944, p. 1786. *MPHPD* 6 May 1944, p. 1877. *NYT* 26 May 1944, p. 23. *Var* 3 May 1944, p. 23.

THREE OF MANY (Austrian Americans, Italian Americans)
New York Motion Picture Corp.; Kay-Bee. *Dist* Triangle Film Corp. Dec **1916**. Si; b&w. 5 reels.
Prod Thomas H. Ince. *Dir* Reginald Barker. *Story and scen* C. Gardner Sullivan. *Cam* Charles Kaufman.
Cast: Clara Williams (*Nina Antinni*), Charles Gunn (*Emil Vorstman*), George Fisher (*Paul Cardoza*).
World War I, Drama. Three friends meet at a boardinghouse in Harlem. One is Nina Antinni, an Italian maidservant; another is Paul, an Italian; and the third is Emil, an Austrian. Paul and Emil vie for the affections of Nina, but Paul wins out. When World War I breaks out, Paul and Emil go to war on opposite sides, and Nina becomes a nurse with the Italian Army. She visits Paul and is shocked by his brutality. When the Austrian army invades the town where Nina is working, Emil, who has also been brutalized by war, plans to rape Nina, who manages to restore his humanity by speaking about the sacredness of their friendship, their past together, and international brotherhood. Meanwhile, Paul's army retakes the town and he rescues Nina from captivity. Friendship wins out in the end, and he allows Emil to escape. *Austrians. Friendship. Italians. War. World War I. Attempted rape. Austria. Army. Boardinghouses. Italy. Army. New York City–Harlem. Nurses. Rivalry. Servants.*

Note: Contemporary sources disagree as to whether the film was released on 17 Dec 1916, 23 Dec 1916 or 24 Dec 1916.

ETR 16 Dec 1916, p. 134. *Motog* 30 Dec 1916, p. 1448. *MPN* 16 Dec 1916, p. 3861. *MPW* 16 Dec 1916, p. 1653. *MPW* 23 Dec 1916, pp. 1752-53. *MPW* 6 Jan 1917, p. 142. *NYDM* 9 Dec 1916, p. 22. *Wid's* 7 Dec 1916, p. 1152.

THREE WHO LOVED (Swedish Americans)
RKO Radio Pictures, Inc. *Dist* RKO Radio Pictures, Inc. 3 Jul **1931** [©RKO Radio Pictures, Inc.; 4 Jul 1931; LP2341]. Sd (RCA Photophone System); b&w. 7 reels. 63, 72 or 78 min. Passed by the National Board of Review.
Prod William LeBaron. *Assoc prod* Bertram Millhauser. *Dir* George Archainbaud. [*Asst dir* Tommy Atkins]. [*Wrt by* Martin Flavin. *Adpt and dial* Beulah Marie Dix. *Photog* Nick Musuraca. [*2d cam* Joe Biroc, Harry Wild and Edward Henderson]. [*Asst cam* George Diskant, Harold Wellman and James Daly]. *Photog eff* Lloyd Knechtel. *Film ed* Jack Kitchin. *Scenery* Max Rée. *Cost* Max Rée. *Rec* Clem Portman. [*Still photog* Robert Coburn].
Cast: Betty Compson [(*Helga Larson Hanson*)], Conrad Nagel [(*John Hanson*)], Robert Ames [(*Phil Wilson*)], Robert Emmet O'Connor [(*Tom Rooney*)], Bodil Rosing [(*Aunt Annie*)], Dickie Moore [(*Sonny Hanson*)], Freddie Santley.
Melodrama. [*Print viewed*]. John Hanson, the head teller at a bank, sends for his fiancée, Helga Larson, from Sweden and moves her into his boardinghouse, which is run by Swedish immigrant Aunt Annie.

Because he spends all of his nights studying for his bar exam, John neglects the innocent Helga and makes her a ripe target for Phil Wilson, his philandering co-worker. Sure that Phil's interest in Helga is strictly friendly, John allows Helga to go out with him, and a romance soon blossoms. Eventually, Aunt Annie warns a still oblivious John about Phil and encourages him to proceed with his marriage plans. Although Phil assures John that he has no interest in Helga, he continues to see her and, after a long afternoon together, seduces her with promises of marriage. At the same time, John, who has been speculating on the stock market, learns that, unless he finds $10,000 immediately, he will lose all of the money that he had been saving up to buy a house for Helga. Desperate to please Helga, John steals $10,000 from Phil's money drawer and then hears from Helga that she and Phil are engaged. The next day, Phil, who is about to leave town to escape Helga, is picked up by Tom Rooney, John's police detective friend, and is questioned about the missing bank funds. For a moment, John considers admitting his crime but finally allows Phil to take the blame. Five years later, Helga, who has married the now successful John, grows despondent after the birthday party of their son Sonny, and abandons John to attend a wild party. When she and her socialite friends return, John confronts Helga and finally forces her to admit that she still loves Phil, who is serving a five-year sentence in Sing Sing Prison. Overcome with guilt, John writes a confession of his crime and then asks Rooney to come by his house. At the same time, Phil escapes from prison and hides himself in John's house. While John prepares to leave for prison, Phil surprises Helga and, filled with spite, tells her that he never had intended to marry her. Crushed, Helga joins Rooney in trying to convince John to remain silent about his theft, but John insists on clearing his conscience. After Rooney leaves, an angry Phil confronts John, then runs outside to avoid capture. In John's yard, the police kill Phil, and a loving Helga tells John that she will wait for him. *Betrayal. Conscience. Philanderers. Romantic rivalry. Self-sacrifice. Swedish Americans. Bank tellers. Birthdays. Boardinghouses. Children. Confession (Law). Engagements. False arrests. Immigrants. Lawyers. Police detectives. Prison escapees. Seduction. Sing Sing Prison (NY). Socialites. Speculation. Thieves.*

Note: The working title of this film was *Helga*. According to the copyright synopsis, the character of "Phil" is killed by falling into a deep pool. "Phil's" demise is not shown or described on screen, however. RKO borrowed Conrad Nagel from M-G-M for this production. According to *FD*, Arline Judge was cast in the picture, but her participation in the final film has not been confirmed.

FD 18 Mar 1931, p. 7. *FD* 5 May 1931, p. 6. *FD* 21 Jun 1931, p. 11. *HR* 1 Jun 1931, p. 3. *IP* Aug 1931, p. 27. *MPH* 13 Jun 1931, p. 28. *Var* 11 Aug 1931, p. 22.

THREE WISE FOOLS (Irish Americans, Immigrants)
Metro-Goldwyn-Mayer Corp.; controlled by Loew's Inc. *Dist* Loew's Inc. 29 Aug **1946**; Prod: 12 Nov 1945–11 Jan 1946 [©Loew's Inc.; 13 Jun 1946; LP384]. Sd (Western Electric Sound System); b&w. 89-90 or 92 min. Passed by the National Board of Review. PCA cert no. 11463.
Prod William H. Wright. *Dir* Edward Buzzell. [*Asst dir* Marvin Stuart]. *Scr* John McDermott and James O'Hanlon. *Story* John McDermott. *Dir of photog* Harold Rosson. [*2d cam* Robert Martin]. [*Matte paintings* Warren Newcombe]. [*Matte paintings, cam* Mark Davis]. [*Transparency projection shots* A. Arnold Gillespie]. *Art dir* Cedric Gibbons and Edward Imazu. *Film ed* Gene Ruggiero and [Theron Warth]. *Set dec* Edwin B. Willis. *Assoc* Hugh Hunt. *Cost supv* Irene. *Cost des* Valles. *Mus score* Bronislau Kaper. *Rec dir* Douglas Shearer. [*Unit mixer* John A. Williams]. [*Re-rec and eff mixer* Ralph A. Pender, Newell Sparks, William Steinkamp and Michael Steinore]. [*Mus mixer* Peter P. Decker, M. J. MacLaughlin and William Saracino]. *Makeup created by* Jack Dawn. [*Research dir* George Richelavie]. [*Research asst* Inger Norswing].
Source: Based on the play *Three Wise Fools* by Austin Strong, as staged by Winchell Smith and presented by John Golden (Ottawa, 1919).
Cast: Margaret O'Brien (*Sheila O'Monahan*), Lionel Barrymore (*Dr. Richard Gaunght*), Lewis Stone (*Judge James Trumbell*), Edward Arnold (*Theodore Findley*), Thomas Mitchell (*Terence Aloysius O'Davern*), Ray Collins (*Judge Watson*), Jane Darwell (*Sister Mary Brigid*), Charles Dingle (*Paul Badger*), Harry Davenport (*The Ancient*), Henry O'Neill (*Horace Appleby*), Cyd Charisse (*Rena Fairchild*), Warner Anderson (*The O'Monahan*), Billy Curtis (*Dugan*), [Michael Kirby (*Jimmy Trumbull*)], [Tim Murdoch (*Dick Gaunght*)], [John Carlyle (*Ted Findley*)], [Henry Sylvester (*Corby*)], [Teddy Infuhr (*Johnny, the Grunt*)], [Charles Bates (*Eddie*

Oakleaf)], [Bob Alden (*O'Davern as a youth*)], [Gary Gray (*Willie, the Squeak*)], [George McDonald (*Tumbleweed*)], [Emmet Vogan, Bud Harrison (*Bailiffs*)], [William Tannen (*Prosecutor*)], [Olin Howlin (*Witness*)], [Marjorie Davies (*Secretary*)], [Cameron Grant (*Assistant*)], [Hans Hopf (*Pixie*)], [Jerry Maren (*Sir Boulder*)], [John Sheehan (*Murphy*)], [Betsy Stoddard (*Miss Emert*)], [Lee Phelps (*Policeman*)], [Marissa O'Brien (*Sister Veronica*)], [Barbara Billingsley (*Sister Mary Leonard*)], [Ray Teal (*Foreman*)], [Robert Emmet O'Connor (*Chief of police*)], [Martin Ashe (*Photographer*)], [Ernie Adams], [Garry Owen].

Historical, Comedy-drama, Fantasy. [*Print viewed*]. A group of young pixies gathered under a large oak tree listen to a story told by an old Irish leprechaun known as The Ancient. The story, about humans, begins in the garden in 1870: Under the oak tree, a young Irish musician known as The O'Monahan plays a song of love to his American sweetheart, Rena Fairchild, who lives on the other side of the garden wall. Hearing the song, Rena enters the garden and kisses The O'Monahan. Rena is followed to the oak tree by her three American suitors, Richard Gaunght, a young medical student; James Trumbell, a lawyer; and Theodore Findley, a banker. Rena rejects all three of her suitors, and instead decides to live with The O'Monahan in Ireland. Before leaving for Ireland, The O'Monahan blesses the three men and wishes them all the success they desire. Forty years pass, and the three suitors, now at the pinnacle of their careers, are friendless and live together in a large house. One day, the three old bachelors donate part of the property that Rena gave to them years earlier to the local university as a site for a future amphitheater. Soon after, they are surprised by the arrival of Sheila O'Monahan, the young granddaughter of The O'Monahan and Rena. Sheila, accompanied from Ireland by the O'Monahans' servant, Terence Aloysius O'Davern, explains that her parents are dead and that she is to become the ward of the three men. When the men reject Sheila, she and O'Davern are left with no alternative but to live in Rena's old, dilapidated house. Meanwhile, complications arise in the proposed amphitheater construction when it is discovered that the deed that Rena gave the three men is to her swamp property, not the property on which the old house stands. The three men realize that their only hope in getting the deed to the main estate is through Sheila. While tearfully considering her desperate situation, Sheila, meanwhile, suddenly remembers a story her grandmother told her about the old oak tree on the property. Sheila goes to the tree and requests the help of the fairies, and at that moment, the three bachelors arrive and invite her to live with them. Believing the invitation to be an act guided by the fairies, Sheila gladly becomes their ward. However, when Sheila learns that the men intend to tear down the old house and destroy the old oak tree, she decides to take back the deed. The three men attempt to change her mind by promising to move the oak tree to a different location, but she refuses, insisting that the leprechauns would be killed if the tree were moved. Determined to get the deed, the three men hire circus midgets to pose as leprechauns and pretend to abandon the tree. Sheila falls for the trick, and later gives the deed to the three men. When O'Davern exposes the ruse, however, the judge who gave the men custody of Sheila removes her from their home and places her in an orphanage. One day, Sheila escapes from the orphanage, enters a convent and tells her story to Sister Mary Brigid. Sister Mary then visits the three bachelors, upbraids them for mistreating Sheila and demands that they save the old oak tree. As demolition crews begin tearing down the old house, Gaunght chains himself to the tree and refuses to move. Trumbell eventually joins Gaunght in his protest, and the tree is finally saved when Findley spends all his money to prevent the tree from being torn down. The good deeds of the three old men restore Sheila's faith in mankind, and all are happily reunited. *Bachelors. Disillusionment. Fairies. Orphans. Trees. Wards and guardians. Adoption. Bankers. Convents. Deeds. Drunkenness. Dwarfs. Editors. Greed. Hoaxes. Irish. Irish Americans. Judges. Leprechauns. Nuns. Physicians. Regeneration. Servants. Spells. Superstition. Universities.*

Note: Pre-production news items in *HR* indicate that Frank Morgan was originally set for a starring role in the film. A late Nov *HR* production chart lists Theron Warth as film editor, although Gene Ruggiero is credited as editor onscreen. This picture is a remake of the 1923 Goldwyn Pictures film *Three Wise Fools*, directed and written by King Vidor and starring Claude Gillingwater and Eleanor Boardman (see *AFI Catalog of Feature Films, 1921-30*; F2.5678). Margaret O'Brien and Lionel Barrymore recreated their roles for a *Lux Radio Theatre* broadcast of the story on 1 Sep 1947.

Box 15 Jun 1946. *DV* 11 Jun 1946, p. 3. *FD* 14 Jun 1946, p. 8. *HR* 28 Nov 1944, p. 2. *HR* 16 Oct 1945, p. 1. *HR* 8 Nov 1945, p. 1. *HR* 12 Nov 1945, p. 6. *HR* 7 Dec 1945, p. 12. *HR* 11 Jan 1946, p. 13. *HR* 11 Jun 1946, p. 3. *HR* 30 Sep 1946, p. 6. *MPHPD* 23 Mar 1946, p. 2907. *MPHPD* 22 Jun 1946, p. 3055. *NYT* 27 Sep 1946, p. 19. *Var* 12 Jun 1946, p. 6.

THE THREEPENNY OPERA *see* **DIE DREIGROSCHENOPER**

THROUGH THE BACK DOOR (Belgian Americans)

Mary Pickford Co. *Dist* United Artists Corp. 17 May **1921** [©Mary Pickford Co.; 21 Jun 1921; LP16691]. Si; b&w. 6-7 reels.

Dir Alfred E. Green and Jack Pickford. *Scen* Marion Fairfax. *Photog* Charles Rosher. *Lighting eff* William S. Johnson.

Cast: Mary Pickford (*Jeanne Bodamere*), Gertrude Astor (*Hortense Reeves*), Wilfred Lucas (*Elton Reeves*), Helen Raymond (*Marie*), C. Norman Hammond (*Jacques Lanvain*), Elinor Fair (*Margaret Brewster*), Adolphe Menjou (*James Brewster*), Peaches Jackson (*Conrad*), Doreen Turner (*Constant*), John Harron (*Billy Boy*), George Dromgold (*Chauffeur*).

Comedy. When Hortense Bodamere, a Belgian widow, marries wealthy New Yorker Elton Reeves, she is persuaded to leave her daughter Jeanne behind in the care of her nurse, Marie. Five years later Mrs. Reeves sends for Jeanne, but Marie, who has married a farmer and brought up Jeanne as her own daughter, tells Hortense that the child is dead. With the outbreak of war, Marie sends Jeanne with two orphan boys to New York to the Reeves home. Jeanne is unable to reveal her identity and is given a job as maid. When she discovers that her stepfather is about to be victimized by the wiles of Margaret Brewster, however, Jeanne reveals herself; and Reeves, having recognized his error, becomes reconciled with his wife. *Belgian Americans. Belgium. Maids. Nursemaids. Orphans. Parentage. War refugees. Widows. World War I.*

FD 22 May 1921. *NYT* 6 May 1921, p. 20.

THUNDER BAY (Cajuns)

Universal-International Pictures Co., Inc. *Dist* Universal Pictures Co., Inc. Aug **1953**; New York opening: 20 May 1953; Prod: late Sep—mid-Nov 1952 [©Universal Pictures Co.; 8 May 1953; LP2785]. Sd (Western Electric Recording); col (Technicolor); 1.85. 9,237 ft. 102-103 min. PCA cert no. 16159.

Prod Aaron Rosenberg. *Dir* Anthony Mann. *Asst dir* John Sherwood. *Scr* Gil Doud and John Michael Hayes. *Story* John Michael Hayes. *Based on an idea by* George W. George and George F. Slavin. *Dir of photog* William Daniels. *Technicolor color consultant* William Fritzsche. *Art dir* Alexander Golitzen and Richard H. Riedel. *Film ed* Russell Schoengarth. *Set dec* Russell A. Gausman and Oliver Emert. *Gowns* Rosemary Odell. *Mus* Frank Skinner. *Sd* Leslie I. Carey and Joe Lapis. *Hair stylist* Joan St. Oegger. *Makeup* Bud Westmore. [*Unit prod mgr* Lew Leary].

Song(s): "Guégué Solin Gaie," French Creole lullaby, arranged by Milton Rosen.

Cast: JAMES STEWART [(*Steve Martin*)], JOANNE DRU [(*Stella Rigaud*)], GILBERT ROLAND [(*Teche Bossier*)], DAN DURYEA [(*Johnny Gambi*)], Jay C. Flippen [(*Kermit MacDonough*)], Marcia Henderson [(*Francesca Rigaud*)], Robert Monet [(*Philippe Bayard*)], Antonio Moreno [(*Dominique Rigaud*)], Henry Morgan [(*Rawlins*)], Fortunio Bonanova [(*Sheriff Antoine Chighizola*)], Mario Siletti [(*Louis Chighizola*)], [Antonio Filauri (*Joe Sephalu*)], [Frank Chase (*Radio technician*)], [Allen Pinson, Dale Van Sickel, Ted Mapes, Elvin C. Alford (*Oilmen*)], [Ben Welden, Jean Hartelle, Jack Tesler, Adrine Champagne, Donald Green, Joseph Cefalu, Lee Vaccari (*Fishermen*)], [George F. Kelly, Jr., Laurie J. Vining (*Technicians*)], [Emanuel Russo (*Radioman*)], [Joseph Guidry (*Oil worker*)], [Milton Schneider (*Ralph Parker*)], [Louis Topham].

Social, Drama. [*Print viewed*]. Penniless but full of ideas, Steve Martin and Johnny Gambi, engineers who served in the Navy during World War II, walk down a quiet road on the gulf coast of Louisiana. Teche Bossier, owner of the Port Felicity Fish Co., agrees to drive them into the shrimping town of Port Felicity in exchange for five dollars. Upon reaching their destination, Gambi rents a shrimp boat from Dominique Rigaud, although the fisherman's daughter Stella distrusts the strangers immediately. Gambi and Steve use the boat to show potential investor Kermit MacDonough the location in which they plan to drill for offshore oil. Claiming that he has designed a drilling platform that can withstand any storm, Steve estimates that by investing one million dollars now, they will soon tap an oil reserve worth two billion. His enthusiasm is so infectious that MacDonough

agrees to fund the project against the advice of his secretary, Rawlins. MacDonough warns Steve, however, that he must discover oil within three months, or his company, due to huge investments made in an offshore oil lease, will put them both out of work. Several weeks later, Gambi meets and falls for Stella's younger sister Francesca, but, according to custom, she has been betrothed since childhood to Philippe Bayard. After singing a love song in the Bon Chance, a local gathering place, Philippe is distressed to see Francesca enter with Gambi. Teche, who good-naturedly calls the oilmen "foreigners," agrees to help Steve and Gambi, but Stella, claiming that she learned about "their kind" during her stay in Chicago, refuses to accept Steve's statement that oil will be good for the town. Nevertheless, the outsiders hire a crew and begin their search for oil. When Teche sees them drop dynamite charges into the gulf, he begs them to stop, believing that the explosions will kill the shrimp and worsen an already dismal shrimping season. Steve maintains that the charges are safe, but Teche returns to town and incites the fishermen to form an angry mob. Steve finally scares them away by exploding sticks of dynamite behind them, and he placates Stella by warning Gambi to stay away from Francesca. "Go back to your people," Steve gently advises Francesca. With one month gone, Steve drives the building crew relentlessly, and the platform and rig are completed on schedule. Steve immediately orders the drilling crew to get started, and the exhausted Gambi is relieved when a hurricane warning gives the men an excuse to take the night off. Gambi and his men enter the Bon Chance with Francesca, and Philippe, furious, punches his rival and starts a brawl. The sheriff arrests the oilmen, and Francesca angrily denounces all the men. Determined to have Gambi fired, Stella visits Steve at the rig, where he explains that if he could pull up a resource that has been in the earth for millions of years, then he will truly have accomplished something. Stella finally abandons her suspicion and kisses Steve, but back in town, Philippe persuades Teche to help him destroy the oil rig. With the hurricane winds rising, Philippe climbs onto the platform and lights a bundle of dynamite, but Steve sees him and the two men fight. Philippe trips and disappears under the waves, and Steve, horrified, assumes that Stella was involved in Philippe's plot. The rig survives the storm, and in the morning, drilling begins. Eight days before the deadline, however, MacDonough visits Steve and sadly delivers the news: The board of his company, fearing a penalty for non-payment on their lease, has voted to stop the drilling operation on the following day. MacDonough has already spent all of his own money, and the crew is unable to work for no pay. At that moment, Gambi returns from town, announcing that he has just married Francesca. Steve punches Gambi, who loudly chastises Steve for having driven him and the men too hard. Steve tells them all to leave, intending to do the drilling himself, whereupon Gambi hesitates and then persuades the crew to remain. While the men are drilling, they discover that the troublesome shrimp that have been clogging the valves are actually the huge golden shrimp that have so long eluded the local fishermen. Later Steve takes Francesca to the rig, infuriating Dominique, who inflames the fisherman by declaring that the oilmen will steal their daughters and destroy the town. At Stella's request, Teche warns Steve that every boat in town is on its way to the rig. Feigning ignorance about the golden shrimp, Steve asks Teche if he can help him get rid of the creatures and then addresses the furious mob. Francesca's marriage is a happy one, he assures the men, and moreover, oil will bring progress to Port Felicity. Despite these words, the fishermen decide to destroy the structure, but at that moment, oil explodes through the rig and onto the platform. The fishermen discover that the golden shrimp bed is huge; consequently, the conflict between the oilmen and the fishermen is resolved. Teche then convinces Steve that Stella was not involved in Philippe's plot, and the lovers finally come together. Cajuns. Cultural conflict. Oil. Oil prospectors. Progress. Shrimpers (Persons). Bars. Drowning. Dynamite. Elopement. Fathers and daughters. Fishing boats. Fishing villages. Friendship. Gulf of Mexico. Hurricanes. Idealists. Jealousy. Louisiana. Marriage–Arranged. Mobs. Oil magnates. Sheriffs. Sisters. Vocational obsession.

Note: According to reviews, *Thunder Bay* was the first wide-screen release in Technicolor. Although not as wide as CinemaScope, which has an aspect ratio of 2.55 to 1, the *NYT* reviewer commented that the 1.85 aspect ratio of *Thunder Bay* was "pleasingly effective." The film also marked Universal's first use of stereophonic sound, which at the time was usable only in select theaters. Some contemporary reviewers complained that the sound, with its use of three speakers, was loud and distracting. Publicity material indicates that the picture

was originally planned as a 3-D production. Although the character played by Jay C. Flippin is listed as "MacDonald" in reviews and CBCS, he is called "MacDonough" in the film. Similarly, Henry Morgan's character is listed as "Rawlings" in offscreen cast lists, but is called "Rawlins" in the picture. According to the *HR* review, most of the picture was shot in Morgan City, LA, and on an oil-drilling barge thirty miles out in the Gulf of Mexico. The ethnicity of the local fishermen in the story is not identified in the film, but a few reviewers referred to them as Cajuns. Several reviewers did note that offshore oil drilling was a "headline subject" at the time.

AmCin May 1953, p. 212. *Box* 9 May 1953. *DV* 5 May 1953, p. 3. *Exh* 20 May 1953, pp. 3524-25. *FD* 5 May 1953, p. 6. *Har* 9 May 1953, p. 74. *HR* 26 Sep 1952, p. 11. *HR* 7 Nov 1952, p. 11. *HR* 5 May 1953, p. 3. *MPHPD* 9 May 1953, p. 1829. *NYT* 21 May 1953, p. 39. *Var* 6 May 1953, p. 6.

THUNDER IN THE SUN (Basque Americans, French Americans)

Seven Arts Productions, Inc. *Dist* Paramount Pictures Corp. May **1959**; New York opening: 8 Apr 1959; Prod: late Jul—late Aug 1958 [©Seven Arts Productions, Inc. and Carrollton, Inc.; 25 Mar 1959; LP13398]. Sd (Westrex Recording); col (Eastman Color); VistaVision; prints by Technicolor. 7,271 or 8,187 ft. 81 min. PCA cert no. 19121.

Prod Clarence Greene. *Asst to prod* Paul Stone. *Dir* Russell Rouse. *2d unit dir* Winston Jones. *Asst dir* Willard Reineck and Bert Chervin. *2d unit asst dir* Erich von Stroheim. *Scr* Russell Rouse. *Adpt* Stewart Stern. [*Orig story* Guy Trosper and James Hill]. *Dir of photog* Stanley Cortez. *2d unit photog* William F. Whitley. *Spec eff* Frank B. Wolff. *Spec photog eff* Jack Rabin and Louis DeWitt. *Prod des* Boris Leven. *Film ed* Chester Schaeffer. *Mus ed* Lloyd Young. *Set dec* Alfred E. Kegerris. *Miss Hayward's cost* Charles LeMaire. *Cost* Richard Chaney, Molly Briggs and Ann Helfgott. *Mus dir* Cyril Mockridge. *Miss Hayward's dance number choreography* Pedro de Cordoba. *Sd eff* Walter G. Elliott. *Sd rec* Frank Goodwin. *Sd re-rec* William Montague. *Hair stylist* Emmy Eckhardt and Lillian Shore. *Makeup artist* Tom Tuttle and Frank Fitz-Gibbon. *Prod mgr* Herbert E. Stewart.

Song(s): "Mon Petit" and "Thunder in the Sun," words by Ned Washington, music by Cyril Mockridge.

Cast: SUSAN HAYWARD [(*Gabrielle Dauphin*)], JEFF CHANDLER [(*Lon Bennett*)], Jacques Bergerac [(*Pepe Dauphin*)], Blanche Yurka [(*Louise Dauphin*)], Carl Esmond [(*Andre Dauphin*)], Fortunio Bonanova [(*Fernando Christophe*)], Bertrand Castelli [(*Edmond Duquette*)], Albert Carrier, Felix Locher [(*Danielle*)], Michele Marly, Albert Villasainte.

Western, with songs. [*Print viewed*]. In 1847, a group of fifty-two French Basques travel to America to escape the unrest and famine of post-Napoleonic France and set out for the West. One of their seven wagons carries the Pyrenees grapevines they hope to plant in the fertile soil of California. In Independence, Missouri, they hire a hard-drinking, womanizing scout named Lon Bennett, who delays their journey by a week with his carousing. When he finally joins the group, Lon is initially bewildered by some of the customs of the French Basques. The battle cry used by the men to communicate with one another over vast distances he finds harrowing, and considers their practice of keeping their hearth fires burning in pots so that the spirits of their ancestors will be warm superstitious and impractical. He is most baffled, however, by the Basque custom of childhood betrothal. Instantly attracted to the fiery Gabrielle Dauphin, who respects but does not love her aging husband Andre, Lon aggressively pursues her, even though she rebuffs his advances. One evening, as Lon attempts to kiss Gabrielle, Andre rushes to her aid. The young man on night guard, following Lon's orders to "shoot anything that moves," fires at Andre and kills him. Thoroughly disheartened by the death of their leader, the group decides to turn back. Gabrielle, however, compares them to sheep and reminds them about the dream for which they have traveled thousands of miles to achieve. Realizing that the people need a new leader, Gabrielle invokes the Basque custom of betrothing a widow to the deceased husband's next of kin, and in so doing, becomes engaged to Andre's younger brother Pepe. Lon refuses to drink to their happiness and several days later, tries to climb into Gabrielle's wagon as she is undressing. Gabrielle protests his boldness, stressing the importance of the family in Basque culture. At that moment, Pepe appears with a rifle and orders Lon away from the wagon. As the wagon train enters the desert, Lon warns the travelers that they will die of thirst if they persist in trying to keep the grapevines watered. Gabrielle and the others ignore Lon, but one by one, the horses begin to die. When Lon commands the Basques to leave most of their belongings in the desert, Pepe loses his patience, and the two men fight. Pepe uses his feet as well as his fists in the

brawl, but Lon proves victorious nonetheless. Gabrielle decides that the party should head for the nearby mountains, where they are sure to find water. Lon, however, adamantly refuses to lead the group into Indian territory. Exasperated, Gabrielle trains a rifle on Lon, confiscates his guns and directs the wagon train toward the mountains. There they do, indeed, find water, but they are seen by an Indian scout. As the Basques continue their journey, a hearth pot falls from a wagon, and the prairie catches fire. The travelers race toward the river, but when the wagon carrying the vines overturns, Gabrielle rushes to save the precious cargo. The fire soon surrounds her, however, and Lon sweeps her up on his horse just in time. Later, as the Basques empty their hearth pots into the river, Gabrielle thanks him for risking his life to save her. At that moment, one of the children sees smoke signals emanating from the hills above them. Lon scouts the area and discovers that Indians await them in the pass. When Pepe calmly suggests that their small group lead an attack on the far more numerous Indians, Lon reminds him that they have never fought Indians before. Pepe insists that the Basques are skilled mountain fighters, however, and that night, the men ascend to hiding places among the rocks. Before they go, Pepe catches sight of Gabrielle kissing Lon. Admitting that she belonged to Lon from the beginning, Gabrielle worriedly watches him leave and then prepares to lead the wagons through the pass. As the wagons approach, an Indian scout informs the warriors who are waiting to attack about their presence. The Basque men see this, and with a series of frightening war cries, they begin shooting. A long and fierce battle follows, and some of the Basque men are killed. In the end, though, they rout the Indians and rejoin the women on the other side of the pass. At the sight of several women bemoaning the loss of their men, Gabrielle, assigning the blame to herself, wildly tears at the vines. Lon reminds her that the men shared her dream and would have wanted to see it fulfilled. Lon leads Gabrielle and Pepe to a cliff and shows them the green valley below, declaring that they have arrived at their destination. Pepe remarks that in their new country, love comes first, and then, slapping Lon on the back, he leaves Gabrielle's side and returns to the group. Lon and Gabrielle embrace, and the wagons enter the valley. *Basque Americans. Cultural conflict. Scouts (Frontier). Transformation. Wagon trains. Accidental death. Ambushes. Battles. California. Dances. Deserts. Fires. Fistfights. French Americans. Immigrants. Independence (MO). Indians of North America. Marriage– Arranged. Mountains. Philanderers. Prairies. Romantic rivalry. Thirst. Wine and wine making.*

Note: The working titles of this film were *The Gun and the Arrow* and *Between the Thunder and the Sun*. Although not credited in the film, Guy Trosper and Jim Hill are listed in reviews and news items as the authors of the original story. Erich von Stroheim, Jr., who is listed in the onscreen credits without the ''Jr.,'' was the famous director's son.

Pre-production news items announced that the picture would be filmed in Missouri, California, Colorado, Arizona, Nevada and New Mexico. According to an Aug 1958 *NYT* article, some scenes were filmed near Mt. Whitney in the Sierra Nevada Mountains of California. The same item stated that files of the *Desert News* in Salt Lake City and Army records at Fort Laramie, WY, were consulted during the writing of the film's story. A *chistera*, a hook-shaped basket used to hurl rocks to deadly effect, is shown briefly during the film's battle scenes. Also featured are scenes depicting traditional Basque dancing and singing. In addition to Basque actor Jacques Bergerac, "fifty French players for authenticity of dialect," were cast in the picture, according to the *NYT* article. The *Var* reviewer complained about Susan Hayward's awkward French accent, noting that the Basques do not speak French, but Basque (also called the Euskara language). Although Basque is, indeed, spoken in southwestern France as well as in the Basque provinces of Spain, some Basques do speak French. According to a Feb 1958 *DV* news item, United Artists was originally set to distribute the picture.

Box 6 Apr 1959. *DV* 7 Feb 1958. *DV* 6 Aug 1958. *DV* 23 Mar 1959, p. 3. *FD* 23 Mar 1959, p. 10. *Har* 28 Mar 1959, p. 50. *HR* 25 Jul 1958, p. 7. *HR* 29 Aug 1958, p. 8. *HR* 23 Mar 1959, p. 3. *MPHPD* 28 Mar 1959, p. 204. *NYT* 10 Aug 1958. *NYT* 9 Apr 1959, p. 37. *Var* 25 Mar 1959, p. 6.

THUNDER MOUNTAIN (Latino)

RKO Radio Pictures, Inc. *Dist* RKO Radio Pictures, Inc. Jun **1947**; *Prod*: mid-Oct—early Nov 1947 [©RKO Radio Pictures, Inc.; 21 May 1947; LP1072]. Sd (RCA Sound System); b&w. 5,428 ft. 60 min. PCA cert no. 12067.

Prod Herman Schlom. *Dir* Lew Landers. [*Asst dir* John Pommer]. *Scr* Norman Houston. *Dir of photog* Jack MacKenzie. *Spec eff* Russell A. Cully. *Art dir* Albert S. D'Agostino and Charles F. Pyke. *Film ed* Philip Martin. *Set dec* Darrell Silvera. *Mus dir* C. Bakaleinikoff. *Mus* Paul Sawtell. *Sd* John C. Grubb and Roy Granville.

Source: Based on the novel *To the Last Man* by Zane Grey (New York, 1922).

Cast: TIM HOLT [(*Marvin Hayden*)], Martha Hyer [(*Ellen Jorth*)], Richard Martin [(*Chito Rafferty*)], Steve Brodie [(*Chick Jorth*)], Virginia Owen [(*Ginger Kelly*)], Jason Robards [(*Jim Gardner*)], Harry Woods [(*Trimble Carson*)], Richard Powers [(*Johnny Blue*)], Robert Clarke [(*Lee Jorth*)], Harry Harvey [(*Sheriff Bagley*)], [Dick Elliott (*Express agent*)], [Richard Foote (*Eddie*)], [Allen Lee (*Jim, stagecoach driver*)].

Western. [*Print viewed*]. In 1890, in the Grass Valley, Arizona saloon, ranch hand Chito Rafferty happily informs alcoholic lawyer Jim Gardner that their old friend, Marvin Hayden, is returning to his family's ranch after a long absence. Saloon operators Johnny Blue and Trimble Carson, who desperately want to buy the Hayden ranch, panic at the news and, aware that the Hayden family has been involved in a bloody feud with the neighboring Jorth family, tell brothers Chick and Lee Jorth about Marvin's return. Their old hatreds rekindled, Lee and Chick rush off to intercept Marvin's stagecoach, but are outridden by Chito, who stops the coach in time to prevent Marvin's death. Marvin, meanwhile, has been enjoying a flirtation with his attractive fellow passenger and is dismayed to learn that she is Lee and Chick's sister Ellen. The equally upset Ellen reminds Marvin that, years before, his father killed her father. After Marvin accuses the Jorths of murdering his father, Ellen threatens to kill Marvin unless he leaves Grass Valley immediately. Marvin, however, plans to stay, especially after he is told that the Hayden ranch is to be auctioned in a week unless $6,000 in back taxes are paid to Sheriff Bagley. While Chito discusses the situation with a now-sober Jim, who is the Hayden family lawyer, the crooked sheriff apprises Carson and Johnny that Marvin intends to save his ranch. Carson and Johnny want to buy the ranch so that they can sell it to an irrigation company, whose plans to build a dam in the area they have kept a secret. To prevent Marvin from interfering in their scheme, Johnny tells Lee and Chick that, despite Ellen's warnings, Marvin is still in the area. Chito, meanwhile, has retrieved Jim from the saloon and has also offered a housekeeping job to saloon girl Ginger Kelly, who was fired by Johnny after she helped Chito rescue Marvin. At the Hayden ranch, Jim informs Marvin that his father had $4,000 in a Phoenix bank account and hands him a pair of Marvin's father's guns. Marvin rejects the weapons, and when Lee and Chick ride up looking for a confrontation, he tells the brothers he never carries a gun. Marvin fights hand-to-hand with Chick, then is warned by Ellen not to trespass on Jorth land. Later, while Jim picks up the $4,000 that has been sent from Phoenix, Marvin drives some lost Jorth cattle back to their range and is met by a gun-wielding Ellen. Marvin fools Ellen into believing that she has accidentally killed him with a warning shot, then playfully spanks her. Their hostilities momentarily abated, Ellen and Marvin ride to the dusty canyon that was the source of their parents' feud. Anxious to prove that her father, who wanted to build a dam in the canyon, truly owned the land he claimed was his, Ellen searches for the survey marker that indicates the boundaries between Jorth and Hayden land. Just as she and Marvin stumble on a marker inserted by the irrigation company, they are shot at by Carson and Johnny, who are hiding above the canyon. Although neither is hurt, Marvin assumes Ellen's brothers attacked him and accuses Ellen of setting him up. After Ellen denies Marvin's charges, Chick finds his rival and convinces him of his innocence. Chick then comes upon Johnny and Carson and accuses them of the shooting. While Johnny and Chick fight, Carson kills Chick with a large rock, confident that the gunless Marvin will be accused of the crime. Marvin's joy at receiving Jim's money, which includes a $2,000 bank loan, is curtailed when Bagley arrives to arrest him. Unsure of Marvin's guilt, Ellen agrees to help Jim, Ginger and Chito find the real killer and takes them to the canyon, where they make a close inspection of the irrigation marker. Jim deduces the significance of the marker and instructs Chito, Ellen and Ginger to look for a spent shell from the earlier attack. and they find a .45 calibre bullet. Within earshot of Bagley, Jim then tells the jailed Marvin that he has found some helpful evidence and presents the sheriff with the ranch money. Bagley stalls Jim, however, and rushes over to the saloon, where Chito overhears him, Johnny and Carson plotting Jim's demise. Before they can execute their plan, Ginger tricks Johnny into allowing her to demonstrate her phony Annie Oakley-style shooting act and grabs Carson's .45 calibre gun. Ginger manages to flee with the gun, but she

and Jim are pursued by Carson and Johnny, who then kill Jim and retrieve the gun. After Chito breaks Marvin out of the jail, the two men join forces with Lee and confront Bagley, Carson and Johnny in the now-deserted saloon. During the ensuing gunfight, Bagley and Johnny are killed by Chito and Lee, while Marvin finally outdraws Carson. His name cleared, Marvin then reunites with Ellen. *Feuds. Frame-ups. Land sales. Murder. Ranchers. United States–History–19th century. Alcoholics. Arizona. Brothers. Brothers and sisters. Dance hall girls. Debt. Dismissal (Employment). Firearms. Fistfights. Gunfights. Lawyers. Mexican Americans. Annie Oakley. Regeneration. Saloon keepers. Sharpshooters. Sheriffs. Spanking.*

Note: The working title of this film was *To the Last Man*. In the opening credits, Zane Grey's name appears above the title. Modern sources state that because of competition with a proposed Liberty Films production, RKO was forced to change the picture's title from *To the Last Man* to *Thunder Mountain*. Although Grey's novel *Thunder Mountain* is listed as the film's source in some publications, onscreen credits do not specify a particular Grey work, and the film's plot more closely resembles that of *To the Last Man* than *Thunder Mountain*. With Tim Holt's return to filmmaking following four years of service in the Army Air Corps, RKO reinstated its "Tim Holt" western series, which it had started in 1940. Richard Martin's "Chito Rafferty" character was the only character from the studio continued from the earlier series. According to *HR*, James Warren was originally set to star in the picture and Lesley Selander, who directed many later Tim Holt Westerns, was to direct. In 1923, Victor Fleming directed Richard Dix and Lois Wilson in a silent Paramount version of Grey's novel, called *To the Last Man* (see *AFI Catalog of Feature Films, 1921-30*; F2.5749). In 1933, Henry Hathaway directed Egon Brecher and Fuzzy Knight in a second Paramount adaptation of the novel, also titled *To the Last Man* (see *AFI Catalog of Feature Films, 1931-40*; F3.4670).

Box 24 May 1947. *DV* 14 May 1947. *HR* 20 Sep 1946, p. 1. *HR* 11 Oct 1946, p. 11. *HR* 1 Nov 1946, p. 17. *HR* 14 May 1947, p. 3. *IFJ* 26 Oct 1946, p. 51. *Var* 14 May 1947, p. 15.

THUNDER OVER THE PRAIRIE (Native Americans)

Columbia Pictures Corp. *Dist* Columbia Pictures Corp. 30 Jul **1941**; Prod: 6 Jun—16 Jun 1941 [©Columbia Pictures Corp.; 30 Jul 1941; LP10781]. Sd; b&w. 5,424 ft. 59-60 min. PCA cert no. 7512.

Series: The Medico.

Exec prod Irving Briskin. **Prod** William Berke. **Dir** Lambert Hillyer. **Asst dir** Milton Carter. **Scr** Betty Burbridge. **Dir of photog** Benjamin Kline. **Film ed** Burton Kramer.

Song(s): "Saddle Tramps," "Diggin in the Cold, Cold Ground" and "Headin' for Home," words and music by Billy Hughes and Cal Shrum.

Source: Based on the novel *The Medico Rides* by James L. Rubel (New York, 1935).

Cast: Charles Starrett (*Dr. Steven Monroe*), Cliff Edwards (*Bones Malloy*), Eileen O'Hearn (*Nona Mandan*), Stanley Brown (*Roy Mandan*), Danny Mummert (*Timmy Wheeler*), David Sharpe (*Clay Mandan*), Joe McGuinn (*Hartley*), Donald Curtis (*Taylor*), Ted Adams (*Dave Wheeler*), Jack Rockwell (*Henry Clayton*), Budd Buster (*Judge Merryweather*), Cal Shrum and His Rhythm Rangers, Murdock MacQuarrie (*Mandan*), John Tyrrell (*Messenger boy*), Steve Clark (*Sheriff*), Eddie Laughton (*Prosecutor*), Francis Sayles (*Corbin*).

Medical, Western, with songs. [*Not viewed*]. Steven Monroe, a young frontier doctor, is taking a post-graduate course at the state university. Steve's roommate is Roy Mandan, an Indian youth who is planning to return to his home in Rock City and practice medicine among his people. On the day that Steve receives an offer to be an assistant staff doctor at Bellevue Hospital. In New York, Roy receives a letter from his brother, notifying him that his father is near death. Roy leaves school to return home without completing his degree and finds that the countryside surrounding Rock City has been ruined by the drought and dust storms. Roy's brother Clay is working on an irrigation project, digging ditches and paying the project's crooked boss, Henry Clayton, for the privilege. Roy decides to join his brother on the project while Steve, unhappy in New York, decides to return West to practice. In Rock City, Steve meets Bones Malloy, who has been taking a medical correspondence course and becomes Steve's apprentice. Steve treats the area's impoverished population, receiving little financial remuneration, and even delivers a litter of puppies for Timmy Wheeler, the son of Dave Wheeler, an educated but poor Indian. Meanwhile, Roy and Clay argue with Clayton's henchmen, Taylor and Hartley, and are fired from the project. To earn money, the brothers decide to hunt wild horses, hoping to sell the animals to the Midwest Construction Company. When the brothers return with the herd, however, the Midwest brand is found on two of the horses and the brothers are accused of theft, even though the animals are strays. The brothers flee from the law, but when Roy is

wounded by the posse, his sister Nona summons Steve to the fugitives' hideout, where the doctor operates on Roy. Steve tries to convince the brothers to surrender and prove their innocence, but they refuse. Soon after, a violent storm strikes, and the dam begins to fail, due to the inferior construction materials used by Clayton. Seeking to protect himself, Clayton orders the dam dynamited and then throws suspicion on Roy and Clay. Following Clayton's orders, Wheeler, now working as a night watchman, testifies that he saw Clay and Roy set the explosion. When Steve is summoned to treat little Timmy, the doctor forces a confession from the boy's father and then convinces Roy to surrender and stand trial. Believing that his brother will be railroaded into jail, Clay enlists the help of his Indian friends, rounds up another herd of horses and stampedes the animals into town while the trial is in progress. In the ensuing chaos, Roy fatally wounds Hartley, while Timmy is injured and dies in Steve's arms. With his dying breath, Hartley exposes Clayton and his gang as criminals. After the brothers are exonerated, Steve and Bones move on to new territory. *Brothers. Corruption. Frame-ups. Indians of North America. Physicians. Brothers and sisters. Confession (Law). Dams. Dismissal (Employment). Ditch diggers. Droughts. Explosions. Fathers and sons. Fugitives. Horses. Irrigation. New York City. Stampedes. Trials. Universities.*

Note: The working title of this film was *The Medico Rides*. Modern sources include Horace B. Carpenter in the cast. For additional information on the "Medico" series, please consult the Series Index.

Box 6 Sep 1941. *DV* 25 Jul 1941. *FD* 12 Sep 1941, p. 7. *HR* 25 Jul 1941, p. 3. *MPH* 2 Aug 1941. *MPHPD* 26 Jul 1941, p. 195. *Var* 30 Jul 1941, p. 20.

THUNDER PASS (Native Americans, Kiowa, Comanche)

William F. Broidy Pictures Corporation. *Dist* Lippert Pictures, Inc. 20 Aug **1954**; Prod: began mid-May 1954 [©Lippert Pictures, Inc.; 24 Sep 1954; LP4056]. Sd; b&w. 7,027 ft. 76 or 78 min. PCA cert no. 17081.

Prod A. Robert Nunes. **Assoc prod** William Calihan. **Dir** Frank McDonald. **Asst dir** William Beaudine, Jr. **Dial dir** Patrick Betz. **Scr** Tom Hubbard and Fred Eggers. **Story** George Van Marter. **Dir of photog** John Martin. **Spec eff** Ray Mercer. **Art dir** George Troast. **Supv film ed** Ace Herman. **Ward** Charles Keehne. **Mus dir** Edward J. Kay. **Rec** Al Overton. **Makeup** Charles Huber. **Hairdresser** Josephine Sweeney. **Prod supv** A. R. Milton. **Set cont** Joyce Upson. **Prop master** James Harris. **Chief elec** Lloyd Garnell.

Cast: Dane Clark [(*U.S. Cavalry Capt. Storm*)], Dorothy Patrick [(*Murdock*)], Andy Devine [(*Injun*)], Raymond Burr [(*Tulsa*)], Charles Fredericks, Mary Ellen Kay [(*Charity*)], John Carradine [(*Bergstrom*)], Raymond Hatton, Nestor Paiva, Tom Hubbard, Rick Vallin, Tommy Cook, Paul McGuire, Elizabeth Harrower, William Wilkerson, Gordon Wynne [(*Dalstead*)], Fred Gabourie, Kenneth Alton.

Historical, Western. [*Print viewed*]. In 1876, a U.S. Cavalry troop under the command of Capt. Storm prepares to evacuate white settlers from the Buffalo Valley region in the Southwest in advance of a possible Comanche and Kiowa Indian attack. Once enemies, the Comanche and Kiowa tribes, have ended their feud and are now banded together to fight the injustices of the "white man." Hoping to avert bloodshed, Storm meets with Indian chiefs Growling Bear and Black Eagle, but the "powwow" turns violent when Growling Bear's son, Running Deer, engages the captain in a knife fight to defend his father's honor. Storm quickly subdues the young Comanche, and then secures a promise from Growling Bear to hold off his planned attack for two more days. Storm believes that two days is sufficient time to evacuate the area of settlers if negotiations between the Indians and a soon-to-arrive U.S. Government emissary end in failure. With the help of "Injun," a white scout reared by Sioux Indians, Storm and his cavalrymen begin gathering the settlers of Buffalo Valley for the treacherous journey to safety across Thunder Pass. Among those being escorted out of the valley are Tulsa, a prospector; Charity, a pretty young woman who falls in love with Corporal Riga; Murdock, an embittered and rebellious woman whose father was killed in a previous Indian massacre; a seriously wounded man named Dalstead; and Bergstrom, a mysterious St. Louis skin trader. Soon after leaving Buffalo Valley, Bergstrom secretly signals some Indians who are trailing the caravan to attack the gun wagon and steal the horses. The situation for evacuees grows worse when it is discovered that their water supply has been salted. Some members of the caravan protest Storm's decision to carry the unconscious Dalstead across the pass,

insisting that it will cause the caravan to slow down. Storm, however, begins to distrust Bergstrom's motives, and suspects that Dalstead may be the government emissary sent to negotiate the peace treaty. As the caravan approaches Thunder Pass, Bergstrom leads some of the others in a rebellion against Storm, challenging his leadership and his decision to take Dalstead along at all costs. Bergstrom's attempt to take over command of the caravan ends in failure when Storm, the only one who knows the way to safety, refuses to guide the group if Dalstead is left to die. When the caravan finally reaches the pass, only a hostile Indian war party is waiting for them. A fierce gun battle ensues, during which Dalstead regains consciousness long enough to tell Storm that he is, indeed, the government agent, and that the food shipment for which the Indians are waiting has been sent to Fort Terahawk. Bergstrom is exposed as the actual gunrunner and a traitor when he is caught trying to shoot Dalstead, and Tulsa shoots and kills Bergstrom as he tries to flee. Shortly afterward, Growling Bear arrives and orders a halt to the Indian attack. With Storm's reassurance that the food shipment will be at Fort Terahawk, Growling Bear offers the caravan a guarantee of safe passage to the fort. Nearing the end of the journey, Storm looks forward to his next assignment and insists that Murdock accompany him. *Caravans. Comanche Indians. Evacuations. Gunrunners. Gunshot wounds. Kiowa Indians. Settlers. United States. Army. Cavalry. Uprisings. Ambushes. Attempted murder. Gunfights. Impersonation and imposture. Knife fighting. Oaths. Prospectors. Romance. Sabotage. Salesmen. Scouts (Frontier). Toothache. Treaties. United States–Southwest.*

Note: According to *HR* news items and production charts, filming of this picture took place at KTTV television studios in Hollywood and on location in Apple Valley, CA.

DV 28 Aug 1954. *HR* 22 Apr 1954. *HR* 21 May 1954, p. 6, 7. *HR* 9 Aug 1954, p. 3. *MPHPD* 25 Sep 1954, p. 154.

THUNDERBOLT (African Americans)

Paramount Famous Lasky Corp. 22 Jun 1929 [©Paramount Famous Lasky Corp.; 20 Jun 1929; LP487]. Sd (Movietone); b&w. 8 reels, 8,571 ft. [Also si; 7,311 ft.].

Assoc prod B. P. Fineman. *Dir* Josef von Sternberg. *Story and scr* Charles Furthman. *Story* Jules Furthman. *Dial* Herman J. Mankiewicz. *Titles* Joseph Mankiewicz. *Photog* Henry Gerrard. *Film ed* Helen Lewis. *Settings* Hans Dreier. *Rec eng* M. M. Paggi.

Song(s): "Thinkin' About My Baby" and "Daddy Won't You Please Come Home," music and lyrics by Sam Coslow.

Cast: George Bancroft (*Thunderbolt Jim Lang*), Fay Wray (*"Ritzy"*), Richard Arlen (*Bob Morgan*), Tully Marshall (*Warden*), Eugenie Besserer (*Mrs. Morgan*), James Spottswood (*Snapper O'Shea*), Fred Kohler (*Bad Al Frieberg*), Robert Elliott (*Prison chaplain*), E. H. Calvert (*District Attorney McKay*), George Irving (*Mr. Corwin*), Mike Donlin (*Kentucky Sampson*), S. S. Stewart (*Negro convict*), William L. Thorne (*Police inspector*).

Crime, Melodrama. Thunderbolt Jim Lang, wanted on robbery and murder charges, ventures out with his girl, "Ritzy," to a Harlem nightclub, where she informs him that she is going straight. During a raid on the club, Thunderbolt escapes. His gang shadows Ritzy and reports that she is living with Mrs. Morgan, whose son, Bob, a bank clerk, is in love with Ritzy. Fearing for Bob's safety, Ritzy engineers a police trap for Thunderbolt; he escapes but is later captured, tried, and sentenced to be executed at Sing Sing. From the death house, he successfully plots to frame Bob in a bank robbery and killing. Bob is placed in the facing cell, and guards frustrate Thunderbolt's attempts to get to his rival. When Ritzy marries Bob in the death house, Thunderbolt pretends repentance, confessing his part in Bob's conviction. He plots to kill the boy on the night of his execution, but instead his hand falls on his shoulder in a gesture of friendship. *Bank clerks. Capital punishment. Criminals–Rehabilitation. Gangsters. New York City–Harlem. Sing Sing Prison (NY).* African Americans.

Note: A pressbook for this film calls it "a story of a hard-fighting man who lives outside the law in the hidden places of the Negro district." Quoting director Josef von Sternberg on casting the Harlem scenes, the pressbook continues, "we were fortunate that Los Angeles has a miniature Harlem of its own in its Central Avenue district. A thorough search gave us scores of Negroes who have really lived in Harlem. Harlem, which extends from 125th to 140th streets, New York, brings heart-beats of southern plantations to metropolitan civilization. Sensation-seeking Broadwayites make these cafés possible, coming to dance shoulder-to-shoulder with habitues of this black metropolis to the beat of staccato jazz."

FD 30 Jun 1929. *NYT* 21 Jun 1929, p. 17. *Var* 26 Jun 1929, p. 22.

THE THUNDERING HERD (1914) *see* **IN THE DAYS OF THE THUNDERING HERD**

THE THUNDERING HERD (Native Americans)

Famous Players-Lasky Corp. *Dist* Paramount Pictures. 7 Mar **1925** [©Famous Players-Lasky Corp.; 23 Feb 1925; LP21180]. Si; b&w. 7 reels, 7,187 ft.

Pres Adolph Zukor and Jesse L. Lasky. *Dir* William K. Howard. *Scen* Lucien Hubbard. *Photog* Lucien Andriot.

Source: Based on the novel *The Thundering Herd* by Zane Grey (New York, c1925).

Cast: Jack Holt (*Tom Doan*), Lois Wilson (*Milly Fayre*), Noah Beery (*Randall Jett*), Raymond Hatton (*Jude Pilchuk*), Charles Ogle (*Clark Hudnall*), Col. Tim J. McCoy (*Burn Hudnall*), Lillian Leighton (*Mrs. Clark Hudnall*), Eulalie Jensen (*Mrs. Randall Jett*), Stephen Carr (*Ory Tacks*), Maxine Elliott Hicks (*Sally Hudnall*), Edward J. Brady (*Pruitt*), Pat Hartigan (*Catlett*), Fred Kohler (*Follansbee*), Robert Perry (*Joe Dunn*).

Western. In 1876, a band of buffalo hunters assembles at Sprague's Trading Post and is joined by Tom Doan, fresh from a Kansas farm. At the post, Tom meets, and falls in love with, Milly Fayre, the stepdaughter of Randall Jett, the leader of a gang of notorious outlaws who make a brutal living robbing buffalo hunters. Milly and Tom are separated, and there is an Indian uprising sparked by the irresponsible slaughtering of the buffalo herds by white adventurers. Jett is killed by his own men, and Milly escapes, attempting to make her way back to civilization. She is chased by a party of hostile Indians and falls in front of a herd of stampeding buffalo. Tom rescues her. The buffalo hunters subdue the Indians, and Tom and Milly head back to civilization. *Bandits. Bison, American. Indians of North America. Kansas. Stepfathers.*

MPW 7 Mar 1925. *Var* 25 Feb 1925, p. 30.

THUNDERING HERD (Native Americans)

Paramount Productions, Inc. *Dist* Paramount Productions, Inc. 24 Nov **1933** [©Paramount Productions, Inc.; 23 Nov 1933; LP4265]. Sd (Western Electric Noiseless Recording); b&w. 6 reels. 56-58 min. PCA cert no. 1369-R [31 Aug 1935].

[*Prod* Harold Hurley], [*Exec prod* Emanuel Cohen]. *Dir* Henry Hathaway. [*Asst to dir* Neil Wheeler]. *Scr* Jack Cunningham. *Cont* Mary Flannery. *Photog* Ben Reynolds. [*Art dir* Earl Hedrick].

Source: Based on the novel *The Thundering Herd* by Zane Grey (New York, 1925).

Cast: Randolph Scott (*Tom Doane*), Judith Allen (*Milly Fayre*), Buster Crabbe (*Bill Hatch*), Monte Blue (*Joe Billings*), Harry Carey (*Clark Sprague*), Raymond Hatton (*Jude Pilchuck*), Noah Beery (*Randall Jett*), Blanche Friderici (*Mrs. [Jane] Jett*), Barton MacLane [(*Pruitt*)], [Al Bridge (*Catlee*)], [Dick Rush (*Middlewest*)], [Frank Rice (*Blacksmith*)], [Buck Connors (*Buffalo hunter*)], [Charles McMurphy (*Andrews*)], [Francis Ford], [Tom London], [Marie Elliott].

Western. [*Print viewed*]. In 1874, Tom Doane and Bill Hatch work for trader Clark Sprague, who makes most of his money from selling buffalo skins. Tom is engaged to Milly Fayre, whose brutal stepfather, Randall Jett, has other than a fatherly interest in her. Jett's gang, while disguised as Indians, has been attacking and stealing wagons carrying buffalo hides. A wagon driven by Tom's friend Jude Pilchuck is attacked by what seem to be Indians, but Tom comes along to rescue him and the robbers escape. Jude realizes Jett is behind the robberies after he finds a tire rim from one of Jett's wagons. Milly and Tom plan to marry one night, but Jett takes her hostage and decamps. Tom angrily follows their wagons and tries to rescue Milly, but Jett brutally beats him unconscious, and ties him to his horse. Tom and his horse arrive at Sprague's, and Jude tends to Tom's injuries as they drive to find buffalo. After a month, Tom is unable to forget Milly, although they successfully skin thousands of buffalo. One of their men is robbed and killed by Jett's gang when he rides back to town with the hides. The Indian tribes on whose land the white men are hunting view the decimated buffalo herds with disgust, and band together to declare war against the killers. Smiley, a fellow hunter, warns Sprague and Tom of the dangers of both the Indians and an oncoming snowstorm, and they pack up to return to town. Meanwhile at Jett's camp, his violent wife Jane murders two of the gang who attempt to steal hides, then, although she is jealous of Milly, defends her from Jett, in a fight which results in both her own death and Jett's. Tom then rescues Milly just before she is trampled in a buffalo stampede.

On their return to town, they see Sprague's wagon train attacked by Indians and ride for Smiley's help. Smiley rallies his wagon train, and together, the two wagon trains fight off their attackers. After a terrible battle, the Indians depart, and Tom and Milly are safe together. *Bison, American. Fur traders. Kidnapping. Robbery. Stepfathers. Disguise. Engagements. Fistfights. Incest. Indians of North America. Jealousy. Murder. Stampedes. Thieves. Wagon trains.*

Note: The title on the screen was *Buffalo Stampede*, however, the credits note that the title was "formerly *Thundering Herd*." Although copyright records indicate Paramount had to receive permission from the U.S. government to round up buffalo to be used in this film, a *Var* review notes that the buffalo hunt scenes seem to be gleaned from 1920s footage. The footage may be from the 1925 Famous Players-Lasky Corp. film *The Thundering Herd*, based on the same source, directed by William K. Howard and starring Jack Holt and Lois Wilson, and Raymond Hatton as "Jude Pilchuk" (see *AFI Catalog of Feature Films, 1921-30*; F2.5710). Some scenes were filmed on location at Lone Pine, CA, according to copyright records.

DV 4 Nov 1933, p. 3. *FD* 31 Mar 1934, p. 4. *HR* 12 Sep 1933, p. 3. *Var* 5 Jun 1934, p. 29.

A TICKET TO TOMAHAWK (Native Americans, Arapaho, Chinese Americans)

Twentieth Century-Fox Film Corp. *Dist* Twentieth Century-Fox Film Corp. May **1950**; World Premiere in Denver, CO: 18 Apr 1950; Prod: 15 Aug—21 Oct 1949 [©Twentieth Century-Fox Film Corp.; 18 Apr 1950; LP207]. Sd (Western Electric Recording); col (Technicolor). 10 reels, 8,118 ft. 90 min. PCA cert no. 14098.

[*Exec prod* Darryl F. Zanuck]. *Prod* Robert Bassler. *Dir* Richard Sale. [*Asst dir* Henry Weinberger and Joe Rickards]. *Wrt* Mary Loos and Richard Sale. *Dir of photog* Harry Jackson. [*Cam op* Irving Rosenberg]. [*Stills* Anthony Ugrin]. *Spec photog eff* Fred Sersen. *Technicolor col consultant* Richard Mueller. *Art dir* Lyle Wheeler and George W. Davis. *Film ed* Harmon Jones. *Set dec* Thomas Little and Fred J. Rode. *Ward dir* Charles LeMaire. *Cost dir* Rene Hubert. *Mus* Cyril Mockridge. *Mus dir* Lionel Newman. *Orch* Herbert Spencer and Earle Hagen. [*Orch arr* Urban Thielman]. *Dances staged by* Kenny Williams. *Sd* W. D. Flick and Harry M. Leonard. *Makeup artist* Ben Nye. [*Makeup* Frank Prehoda]. [*Hair stylist* Alma Johnson, Lillian Hokom and Marie Walters]. [*Prod mgr* William Eckhardt]. [*Loc liaison* Pat O'Hara]. [*Scr supv* Stanley Scheuer]. [*Tech adv* Jennifer Chatfield].

Song(s): "A Ticket to Tomahawk (On the Colorado Trail)," music by Harry Warren, lyrics by Mack Gordon; "Paddy Works on the Erie," music and lyrics by Richard Sale; "Oh, What a Forward Young Man You Are," music by John Read, special lyrics by Ken Darby.

Cast: DAN DAILEY [(*Johnny Jameson*)], ANNE BAXTER [(*Kit Dodge, Jr.*)], Rory Calhoun [(*Dakota*)], Walter Brennan [(*Terence Sweeny*)], Charles Kemper [(*Chuckity Jones*)], Connie Gilchrist [(*Madame Adelaide*)], Arthur Hunnicutt [(*Sad Eyes Tatum*)], Will Wright [(*Marshal Kit Dodge*)], Chief Yowlachie [(*Pawnee*)], Victor Sen Young [(*Long Time*)], [Mauritz Hugo (*Dawson*)], [Raymond Greenleaf (*Mayor*)], [Harry Carter (*Charley*)], [Harry Seymour (*Velvet fingers*)], [Robert Adler (*Bat*)], [Lee MacGregor (*Gila*)], [Raymond Bond (*Station master*)], [Charles Stevens (*Trancas*)], [Chief Thundercloud (*Crooked Knife*)], [Marion Marshall (*Annie*)], [Joyce MacKenzie (*Ruby*)], [Marilyn Monroe (*Clara*)], [Barbara Smith (*Julie*)], [Jack Elam (*Fargo*)], [Paul Harvey (*Mr. Bishop*)], [Charles Soldani (*Black Wolf*)], [John War Eagle (*Lone Eagle*)], [Shooting Star (*Warrior*)], [William Self (*Telegrapher*)], [Guy Wilkerson (*Dr. Brink*)], [Edward Clark (*Jeb*)], [Olin Howlin (*Conductor*)], [George Melford (*Stationmaster*)], Robert Filmer (*Deputy sheriff*), [John Horan (*Undertaker*)], [John Merton (*Clayton*)], [Paul Brinegar], [Herbert Heywood], [Joe Forte], [William Gould], [Tim Graham], [Dick Ryan], [Jim Toney], [Jerry Sheldon], [Clarence Straight].

Comedy, Western, with songs. [*Print viewed*]. In 1876, Johnny Jameson, a "drummer," or traveling salesman, is the only passenger on the inaugural run of the Tomahawk and Western Railroad's narrow gauge train through the Colorado Rockies. During the ride, the conductor tells Johnny that certain people, stagecoach operators for example, would like to see the railroad's franchise fail. Soon after, Dakota, Trancas and Gila, who work for Colonel Dawson, the area stageline operator, cause a giant boulder to fall directly in the path of the train. Engineer Terence Sweeny manages to stop the train in time, and he and the crew then disembark to move the rock. Johnny decides to walk to the town of Epitaph and hitches a ride with Trancas and Gila. At the sheriff's office, when Johnny tries to report the train's

delay to deputy Chuckity Jones, he is knocked out Trancas. U.S. Marshal Kit Dodge, meanwhile, prepares to welcome the train with help from his tomboyish, knife-wielding granddaughter Kit. As they are leaving for the depot, however, the marshal and Kit are surprised by Trancas and Gila. The marshal shoots Trancas but is wounded by Gila. Kit suspects that Johnny may be one of the gang and, before Chuckity can intervene on his behalf, orders him to leave town. After Kit is deputized as a U.S. Marshal by her grandfather, she and an Indian named Pawnee are assigned to escort the train to Tomahawk. Colonel Dawson orders Dakota to join the posse that is escorting the train, while other gang members plot to blow up the engine during a night stop, which will be disrupted after Indian Black Wolf stirs up the local Arapahos. On the way to Tomahawk, local businessman Bishop informs Sweeny that there is no track laid for the next forty miles because the rails, which were shipped from England, have been lost at sea. Bishop explains that as the train must reach Tomahawk to fulfill the requirements of the franchise contract, he has arranged for the engine car to be hauled by teams of mules over the next forty miles. Another condition of the franchise contract is that the train must reach Tomahawk by a rapidly approaching deadline with at least one paying passenger. Although Johnny buys a ticket, he must sit alongside the train's boiler while the mules pull the locomotive, and Kit has to ensure his safe journey. Before the train departs, Chinese laundry man Long Time joins the group with laundry for Tomahawk. Madame Adelaide, her dancing girls and a musician also join up. As planned, Dawson's men Bat, Charley and Fargo show up at a night stop claiming to be telegraph men who are there to repair lines cut by the Arapahos and Kit gives them permission to bunk in the camp. Gradually, Kit softens her opinion of Johnny. When all are asleep, Bat and Charley leave while Fargo tosses sticks of dynamite under the engine. Johnny, who is sleeping alongside the train, smells the lit fuse and alerts the others. Kit then cuts the fuse with a shot and disables Fargo. Before Fargo can talk, however, Dakota kills him. Some time later, about five miles from where the track restarts, Bat and Charley place dynamite charges on a trestle bridge. They are then attacked by Indians and the dynamite is set off prematurely. Johnny knows the Arapaho chief, Crooked Knife, and after the Indians attack the train and accompanying wagons, Johnny volunteers to talk peace with him. Johnny has learned that Long Time is carrying a load of fireworks and develops a plan. He is welcomed by Crooked Knife, who agrees to allow the train safe passage. However, some of the braves distrust Johnny and ask him to produce a sign that he is "big medicine." Johnny sets off a rocket, signaling Kit and Dakota to set off the rest of the fireworks on a nearby hill, and the Indians are impressed. As the bridge is out, Kit intends to take the thirty-three-ton locomotive over a mountain by dismantling it and carrying it in sections. Dawson, meanwhile, thinks he has been double-crossed and shoots Black Wolf. He then rounds up his men for a final showdown. After Kit discovers that Dakota has sabotaged a water tower, Dakota slugs Johnny, orders the fireman to start the engine rolling and takes off at high speed down the tracks. Kit jumps into the cabin but is knocked out by Dakota. Johnny revives and while he and Dakota fight on top of the cabin, Kit recovers and throws a knife, causing Dakota to fall into a ravine. Dawson and his gang then try to ambush the train but cannot catch up with it. However, the boiler develops several leaks and the train slows to a halt. Dawson and his gang are driven off by the Indians, who ride to the rescue, and Pawnee throws a tomahawk at Dawson. As the train has stopped just short of its goal, Johnny talks the mayor of Tomahawk into extending the town limits, thereby fulfilling the requirements of the franchise. By now Kit has fallen in love with Johnny and jokingly threatens to cripple him to stop his wandering ways. Some time later, Johnny limps off to his job as train conductor, waving to his wife, Kit, and five daughters. *Arapaho Indians. Business competition. Colorado. Railroad companies. Sabotage. Stagecoach lines. Traveling salesmen. United States. Marshals. Women sheriffs. Bridges. Businessmen. Chinese. Contracts. Dynamite. Grandfathers. Mayors. Mule trains. Posses. Railroad engineers. Railroad stations. Sheriffs. Show girls.*

Note: According to documents in the Twentieth Century-Fox Records of the Legal Department at the UCLA Arts—Special Collections Library, the studio bought Mary Loos and Richard Sale's original screenplay for $30,000 in Feb 1949. A studio press release in the AMPAS Library reveals that the husband and wife team were "rabid model railroaders" and had spent two years researching narrow-gauge railroads before writing the script. According to the files, the studio made a deal with the Rio Grande and Western Railroad to film on their

track, which ran from Durango to Silverton in Colorado. In the film, Silverton doubled as both of the fictional towns of Epitaph and Tomahawk. The Durango to Silverton line, a civil engineering feat, was built to haul silver and gold ore from the San Juan Mountains.

The railroad made its inaugural run in early Jul 1882 and operated for many years. Another film, Paramount's *The Denver & Rio Grande*, shot a spectacular head-on collision of two engines on the line in Jul 1951. In Jun 1967 the National Park Service officially designated the railroad a Registered National Historical Landmark, and the following year the American Society of Civil Engineers designated it as a National Historic Civil Engineering Landmark. In the early 1980s, after four years of negotiations, Charles E. Bradshaw, Jr., a Florida citrus grower, bought the Silverton Line for $2.2 million in cash. The railroad, restored with total authenticity, reopened on 23 May 1981 as a tourist attraction. According to a *HR* news item, the *A Ticket to Tomahawk* company was scheduled to return to the studio on 23 Sep 1949 after six weeks of location filming in Colorado. Shooting of interiors at the studio ran into mid-Oct 1949.

Several reviews of the film incorrectly spell the names of the characters played by Walter Brennan, Lee MacGregor, Charlie Stevens and Edward Clark. Shortly after the film opened, *MPH* reported that some exhibitors were dissatisfied with its title. Executives of the Orpheum Theatre in Tulsa advertised the film as *The Sheriff's Daughter* (albeit the principal female character is a marshal's granddaughter). *Var* reported that Fox would test the new title in Memphis, but by that time, the film had already played in most key cities. A radio version of the film, featuring Dan Dailey and Anne Baxter, was broadcast on the *Lux Radio Theatre* on 4 Jun 1951.

Box 22 Apr 1950. DV 17 Apr 1950, p. 3. FD 21 Apr 1950, p. 6. HR 22 Sep 1949, p. 3 HR 17 Apr 1950, p. 3. MPHPD 22 Apr 1950, p. 269. MPH 1 Jul 1950. NYT 20 May 1950, p. 8. Var 19 Apr 1950, p. 8. Var 23 Jun 1950

TIDAL WAVE *see* **PORTRAIT OF JENNIE**

TIES OF BLOOD (African Americans)
Reol Productions Corp. **1921**. Si; b&w. Length undetermined. [Feature length assumed.].

Cast: Inez Clough, Arthur Ray, Harry Pleasant.
Melodrama (?), African American. No information about the precise nature of this film has been found. *African Americans.*

THE TIGER LILY (Italian Americans)
American Film Co. *Dist* Pathé Exchange, Inc. 27 Jul **1919** [©American Film Co.; 11 Jul 1919; LP13935]. Si; b&w. 5 reels, 4,784 ft.

Dir George L. Cox. *Story and scen* Joseph Franklin Poland.
Cast: Margarita Fisher (*Carmina*), Emory Johnson (*David Remington*), George Periolat (*Luigi*), E. Alyn Warren (*Giovanni*), J. Barney Sherry (*Philip Remington*), Mme. Rosita Marstini (*Mrs. Philip Remington*), Beatrice Van (*Dorothy Van Rensselaer*), Frank Clark (*Antonio*).
Drama. The clientele at Luigi's Little Italy inn come frequently because of his personable niece Carmina, known as "The Tiger Lily," who is never hesitant in rebuking her ill-mannered admirers. Giovanni, in America to kill the man who married his brother's fiancée, falls in love with Carmina. When David Remington, the son of the inn's landlord, comes to inquire about publicized knife fights there, Giovanni, seeing Carmina's attraction to David, pays Luigi for her hand in marriage. Running away, Carmina is picked up by David and taken to his home, to the dismay of his mother, the woman who was to marry Giovanni's brother. Although Mrs. Remington warns David against marrying beneath him, when he sees Carmina among society girls, he admires her more. After Mrs. Remington convinces her to leave, Carmina learns that Giovanni plans to kill Mrs. Remington and her husband. She contacts the police and after a fight, Giovanni is subdued. The Remingtons now accept Carmina as their future daughter-in-law. *Class distinction. Inns. Italian Americans. Mothers and sons. New York City–Little Italy. Revenge. Fights. Italians. Police. Socialites.*

Note: According to the copyright records and some reviews, the title of the film is *The Tiger-Lily*.
ETR 26 Jul 1919, p. 641. MPN 26 Jul 1919, p. 939. MPW 26 Jul 1919, p. 575. NYMT 20 Jul 1919. Wid's 20 Jul 1919, p. 17.

TIGER SHARK (Portuguese Americans)
First National Pictures, Inc.; controlled by Warner Bros. Pictures, Inc. *Dist* First National Pictures, Inc.; The Vitaphone Corp. 24 Sep **1932** [©First National Pictures, Inc.; 3 Sep 1932; LP3228]. Sd; b&w. 8 reels. 78 or 80 min.
[*Supv* Bryan Foy]. *Dir* Howard Hawks. *Asst dir* Richard Rosson. *Scr* Wells Root. *Story* Houston Branch. *Photog* Tony Gaudio. [*2d cam* Frank Kesson]. [*Asst cam* Carl Guthrie]. *Art dir* Jack Okey. *Marine supv by* Captain Guy Silva. *Ed* Thomas Pratt. *Gowns* Orry-Kelly.

Vitaphone Orch cond Leo F. Forbstein. [*Sd* C. A. Riggs and A. D. Mair]. [*Still photog* Mac Julian].

Cast: EDWARD G. ROBINSON (*Mike Mascarenhas*), Richard Arlen (*Pipes Boley*), Zita Johann (*Quita Silva*), Leila Bennett (*Muggsey* [*The barber*]), J. Carroll Naish (*Tony*), Vince Barnett (*Fishbone*), William Ricciardi (*Manuel Silva*).

Adventure, Romance. [*Print viewed*]. After surviving a shipwreck, San Diego tuna fisherman Mike Mascarenhas, an immigrant from Portugal, loses a hand to a shark. The following season, one of his crew, Manuel Silva, falls overboard and is killed by the sharks following the boat. Mike brings the bad news to Quita, Manuel's daughter. Moved by Quita's beauty as well as her lonely situation, Mike, who is unpopular with women, takes care of her, bringing her food and money. When he asks her to marry him, Quita confesses that she does not love him, but he insists that this does not matter to him and he will accept her as she is. Touched by his generosity, Quita agrees to marry him. At the wedding, however, she falls in love with Pipes Boley, a fellow fisherman who is Mike's best man. When Quita tells Pipes of her love, he plans to leave town, but before he does, he catches a fishing hook on the back of his neck and Mike brings him home to recover. While Quita nurses him, she and Pipes fall deeper in love. Quita accompanies Mike and Pipes on a fishing trip, where, overcome by her feelings, she embraces Pipes, unaware that Mike is watching. Angry, Mike punches Pipes and dumps his unconscious body into a leaking boat, where, he gloats, the sharks will enact justice. As Mike watches the sharks surround Pipes, his foot is caught in a line and he is dragged overboard, where the sharks attack him. The men pull him out and he dies of his injuries after apologizing to Pipes and Quita. *Fishermen. Portuguese Americans. Romantic rivalry. Sharks. Marriage. Prostheses and artificial limbs. San Diego (CA). Shipwrecks. Tuna. Weddings.*

Note: According to copyright records the title of Houston Branch's unpublished short story was "Tuna." The plot of this film strongly resembles that of the 1936 Warner Bros. film *Bengal Tiger* written by Roy Chanslor and Earl Felton (see *AFI Catalog of Feature Films, 1931-40*; F3. 0287). Outdoor sequences were filmed on location in Monterey, CA. Modern sources name John Lee Mahin and Howard Hawks as uncredited writers.
FD 23 Aug 1932, p. 9. HR 12 Aug 1932, p. 2. IP Sep 1932, p. 32. MPH 27 Aug 1932, p. 38. NYT 23 Sep 1932, p. 22. Var 27 Sep 1932, p. 17.

THE TIGER'S COAT (Latino)
Dial Film Co. *Dist* W. W. Hodkinson Corp., through Pathé Exchange, Inc. Nov **1920**. Si; b&w. 5 reels.
Dir Roy Clements. *Scen* Jack Cunningham. *Cam* R. E. Irish. *Art dir* E. P. Hunziker. *Cont man* Paul Schofield.
Source: Based on the novel *The Tiger's Coat* by Elizabeth Dejeans (Indianapolis, 1917).
Cast: W. Lawson Butt (*Alexander MacAllister*), Tina Modotti (*Jean Ogilvie*), Myrtle Stedman (*Mrs. Carl Mendall*), Myles McCarthy (*Andrew Hyde*), Frank Weed (*Frederick Bagsby*), Jiquel Lanoe (*Carl Mendall*), Nola Luxford (*Clare Bagsby*), Charles Spere, Helene Sullivan.
Drama. Engaged to his ward, a wealthy man learns that she is not Scottish, as he had believed, but Mexican. After he breaks the engagement, the girl leaves town, only to return later as a dancer. The man has by that time realized that he loves the girl after all, and they are reconciled. *Racism. Wards and guardians. Dancers. Mexicans. Scots.*
Note: The novel was also serialized in *The Pictorial Review* between Nov 1916 and Feb 1917. The film was shot at the Robert Brunton Studios in Los Angeles.
MPN 3 Jul 1920, p. 264. MPN 14 Aug 1920, p. 1373. MPN 16 Oct 1920, p. 3008. MPN 13 Nov 1920, p. 3667, 3721. MPN 18 Dec 1920, p. 4610.

TILL THE END OF TIME (African Americans)
RKO Radio Pictures, Inc.; A Dore Schary Production. *Dist* RKO Radio Pictures, Inc. 1 Aug **1946**; New York opening: 23 Jul 1946; Prod: 15 Oct 1945—22 Jan 1946 [©RKO Radio Pictures, Inc.; 23 Jul 1946; LP559]. Sd (RCA Sound System); b&w. 9,441 ft. 105 min. PCA cert no. 11260.
Dir Edward Dmytryk. *Dial dir* William E. Watts. *Asst dir* Ruby Rosenberg. *Scr* Allen Rivkin. *Dir of photog* Harry Wild. [*2d cam* Charles Straumer]. [*Spec eff* Vernon L. Walker]. [*Optical eff* Lynn Dunn]. [*Transparency projection shots* Clifford Stine]. *Art dir* Albert S. D'Agostino and Jack Okey. *Film ed* Harry Gerstad. *Set dec* Darrell Silvera and William Stevens. *Miss McGuire's clothes des by* Fred Guinn. *Mus dir* C. Bakaleinikoff. *Mus score* Leigh Harline. *Sd* Richard

Van Hessen and Clem Portman. [*Mus mixer* Earl B. Mounce]. *Prod asst* Edgar Peterson.

Song(s): "Till the End of Time," words and music by Buddy Kaye and Ted Mossman, based on *Polonaise in A Flat Major* by Frédéric Chopin.

Source: Based on the novel *They Dream of Home* by Niven Busch (New York, 1944).

Cast: Dorothy McGuire by arrangement with David O. Selznick (*Pat Ruscomb*), Guy Madison by arrangement with David O. Selznick (*Cliff Harper*), Robert Mitchum (*William Tabeshaw*), Bill Williams (*Perry Kincheloe*), Tom Tully (*C. W. Harper*), William Gargan (*Sgt. Gunn Watrous*), Jean Porter (*Helen Ingersoll*), Johnny Sands (*Tommy*), Loren Tindall (*Pinky*), Ruth Nelson (*Amy Harper*), Selena Royle (*Mrs. Kincheloe*), Harry Von Zell (*Scuffy*), Richard Benedict (*The boy from Idaho*), [Dickie Tyler (*Jimmy Kincheloe*)], [Stan Johnson (*Captain Jack Winthrop*)], [Billy Newell (*Warrant officer*)], [Lee Slater (*Burton*)], [Robert Lowell (*Epstein*)], [Peter Varney (*Franks*)], [George Burnett (*Gilman*)], [Bill Barnum (*Jackson*)], [Jack Parker (*Collector*)], [Paul Theodore, Oliver Hinsdell, John S. Roberts, Anthony Marsh, John Bailey, Michael Kostrick (*Interviewers*)], [Dick Benjamin, Alan Ward (*Sergeants*)], [Bill "Red" Murphy, Paul Smith, Drew Allan (*Marines*)], [Ernest Mishens, Tom Sutherland, Fleet White (*Paymasters*)], [Richard Slattery (*Captain*)], [Tim Ryan (*Steve Sumpter*)], [Harry Hayden (*Ed Tompkins*)], [Margaret Wells (*Mrs. Ingersoll*)], [Fred Howard (*Zeke Ingersoll*)], [Ellen Corby (*Mrs. Sumpter*)], [Mary Worth (*Mrs. Tompkins*)], [Teddy Infuhr (*Freddie Stewart*)], [Warren Jackson (*Cab driver*)], [William Forrest (*Detective*)], [Arthur Loft (*Doctor*)], [Cindy Garner (*Nurse*)], [Al Murphy (*Counterman*)], [Robert Manning (*Ex-seaman*)], [Paul Stader (*Lifeguard*)], [Tito Renaldo (*Mexican*)], [Blake Edwards (*Foreman*)], [James Logan (*Norman*)], [Caleb Peterson (*Black G.I.*)], [Stubby Kruger (*Practical lifeguard*)], [Dick Elliott, Steve Taylor (*Bartenders*)], [Alex Pope (*Mitchell*)], [Howard Negley (*Prager*)], [Jack Lee (*Lawson*)], [Jack Chapman (*Russell*)], [Warren Smith (*Citizen*)], [Eddie Craven (*Waiter*)].

Post-war life, Drama. [*Print viewed*]. After he is discharged from the Marines, twenty-one-year-old Cliff Harper returns to his home in Los Angeles. At his parents' empty house, Cliff meets his new neighbor, Helen Ingersoll, a vivacious college freshman, who is immediately starstruck by the decorated hero. Anxious to be with friends, Cliff heads for Scuffy's, his favorite pre-war soda shop. At Scuffy's, which has been transformed to a bar, friend and fellow ex-serviceman Pinky introduces Cliff to Pat Ruscomb, and instantly attracted to her, Cliff asks her to dance. In a romantic daze, Cliff abandons Pinky, goes to Pat's apartment and kisses her impetuously. When he professes his passion, however, Pat withdraws from him and talks about her husband, who was killed during the war. Depressed by Pat's mourning, Cliff returns home and is greeted ecstatically by his parents. That night, the Harpers host a barbeque, and Cliff is subjected to a variety of questions about the war. At odds with the prevailing mood of the party, Cliff tries to call Pat, who is out, then cries himself to sleep. The next day, Pinky invites Cliff to go ice skating with him and Pat, and Cliff asks an eager Helen to be his date. In the skating rink café, Cliff and Pat see a lonely soldier shaking from post-traumatic stress disorder and approach him. Cliff commiserates with the veteran, while Pat talks about her own painful past to give him courage. The next morning, Cliff is questioned by his father about his future plans and disappoints him by answering that he is unsure about what he wants to do with his life. Cliff then goes with Helen and platoon mate William Tabeshaw, who has just arrived from New Mexico, where he works as a cowboy, to see Perry Kincheloe, a fellow veteran and former boxer. Though happy to see Cliff and Bill, who has a metal plate in his skull from a war injury, the legless Perry rejects their attempt to cheer him up and politely rejects the advice of Sergeant Gunny Watrous, his discharge officer, to wear his artificial legs. Later, Cliff sees Pat drinking with an army captain at Scuffy's and then fights with his parents, who accuse him of behaving like a stranger. Unhappy and jealous, Cliff passes up the lovesick Helen and waits for Pat's return outside her apartment. After he spies Pat drunkenly kiss the captain goodnight, he calls her a tramp and leaves in a jealous huff. Once calm, Cliff returns to apologize to Pat, who reveals that she went out with the captain only because he was her husband's co-pilot. Ashamed, Cliff comforts Pat and admits that he, too, is lonely and confused. At Pat's suggestion, Cliff then takes an inspection job at the radio factory where she works as a secretary, but soon picks a fight with his supervisor. After another discouraging visit with Perry, Cliff proposes to Pat, but she rejects him for not taking charge of his life. Angry, Cliff goes drinking with Bill, who reveals that he lost his job as a cowhand in New Mexico after the metal plate in his skull began causing him unbearable pain. Concerned about Bill, who refuses to see a doctor, Cliff telephones Perry on the pretext of asking him to invest in a ranch deal that Bill has proposed. By the time that Perry, who finally finds the courage to don his artificial legs, arrives at the bar, however, Cliff has become drunk and is discussing the ranch as a serious proposition. Cliff also telephones Pat and insists that she go with him to New Mexico, but she refuses the offer and tries to talk him out of it. Cliff, Bill and Perry are then approached by a group of men who invite them to join their veterans' organization. When the group's spokesman smugly states that no "Catholics, Jews or Negroes" are admitted to the organization, Bill knocks him out and instigates a brawl. During the mêlée, Perry happily discovers that he can still throw a punch, while Bill is hit on his head and is sent to the hospital. Once Bill's condition has stabilized, Cliff comes to terms with his parents and, after declaring his intention to stay in Los Angeles, reunites with Pat. *Family relationships. Post-war life. Romance. Veterans. Widows. Amputees. Barbeques. Bars. Bigotry. Boxers. College students. Cowboys. Depression, Mental. Drunkenness. Factories. Fights. Grief. Handicapped. Hospitals. Ice skaters and ice skating. Jealousy. Los Angeles (CA). Officers (Military). Post-traumatic stress disorder. Radios. Secretaries. Unrequited love.*

Note: The working titles of this film were *They Dream of Home* and *The Dream of Home*. Modern sources note that all of the main characters in Niven Busch's novel were either American Indian or black, and that the only racial incident of the book to be retained in the film was the final bar scene. *HR* news items and RKO production files from the UCLA Arts Library—Special Collection add the following information about the production: In May 1945, producer Dore Schary received script approval from two Marine generals assigned to the project. The picture began as a Vanguard Pictures production, but was taken over by RKO in Jul 1945 along with *Notorious* (see above) and *The Spiral Staircase*. Shirley Temple and Don DeFore were considered for leading roles in the film, and John Lund was tested with Guy Madison for a "top role," but was not cast. Also tested for parts were Chris Drake and twenty-six other "recently discharged servicemen," but their participation in the final film has not been confirmed. Sam Levene was announced as a cast member, but he was not in the viewed print and his participation in the final film is doubtful. RKO borrowed Johnny Sands, who made his screen debut in the picture, Dorothy McGuire and Guy Madison from David Selznick's company. Steve Dunhill, Howard Negley and Deborah Allen, who was publicized as a recent high school graduate and beauty contest winner, were announced as cast members, but their participation in the final film has not been confirmed. Some scenes for the production were shot at the San Diego Marine Base, in Beverly Hills and Sawtelle, CA (now a part of West Los Angeles), the Westwood Ice Gardens, and at Vermont Avenue and 4th Street and the Packard-Bell plant on Wilshire Boulevard in Los Angeles. RKO purchased the film rights to the title and title song for $15,000. Robert Mitchum reprised his role in a *Lux Radio Theatre* broadcast on 6 Jan 1947, co-starring Laraine Day and Bill Williams.

Box 15 Jun 1946. *DV* 12 Jun 1946, p. 3. *FD* 14 Jun 1946, p. 8. *HR* 18 May 1945, p. 10. *HR* 9 Jul 1945, p. 9. *HR* 13 Jul 1945, p. 1. *HR* 23 Jul 1945, p. 2. *HR* 25 Jul 1945, p. 3. *HR* 31 Jul 1945, p. 8. *HR* 16 Aug 1945, p. 6. *HR* 22 Aug 1945, p. 1. *HR* 5 Oct 1945, p. 9. *HR* 19 Oct 1945, p. 15. *HR* 26 Oct 1945, p. 10. *HR* 29 Oct 1945, p. 11. *HR* 8 Nov 1945, p. 4. *HR* 21 Nov 1945, p. 8. *HR* 26 Nov 1945, p. 14. *HR* 5 Dec 1945, p. 12. *HR* 4 Jan 1946, p. 10. *HR* 18 Jan 1946, p. 14. *HR* 12 Jun 1946, p. 3, 5. *HR* 29 Jul 1946, p. 6. *MPHPD* 15 Jun 1946, p. 3041. *NYT* 24 Jul 1946, p. 24. *Var* 12 Jun 1946, p. 6.

TIME AND TIDE *see* **WILD RIVER**

TIME LOCK NUMBER 776 (Jewish Americans)
Photo Drama Co. *Dist* Photo Drama Co. Jan **1915** [©Photo Drama Co., Inc.; 6 Jan 1915; LU4255]. Si; b&w. 6 reels.
Dir Hal Reid. *Story* Hal Reid.

Cast: Joe Welch (*Isaac Abrahams*), Dora Dean (*Helen Abrahams*), David Wall (*Jack Wayne*), Edwin Carewe (*Nathan Stattler*), Mae Georgina (*Madge Melbourne*), Hal Reid (*Henry Morton*), Adella Barker (*Mrs. Mallachi*), Edward Sullivan (*Pietro*), Fred MacKaye (*Jem*), John Starkey (*Secret Service man*), Mae Trado, Jack Murray.

Crime, Drama. Isaac Abrahams, a Jewish pawnbroker and engraver in New York's East Side, patents a new time lock, but he needs capital to begin production. When Jack Wayne, an unscrupulous broker, learns about the lock, he forms a partnership with an underworld gang who want Isaac to finish a plate for the production of counterfeit one-hundred-dollar bills. Isaac's daughter Helen, who wants to become an actress, is persuaded by Wayne's cohort, Madge, to leave home. After Helen is kidnapped, Isaac agrees to finish the plate and to hand over the patent. When he demands to see Helen before

completing the job, the two are reunited briefly. As the gang drunkenly celebrates, Isaac scratches the plate, thus making it useless. Although Wayne wants to kill Helen in revenge, one of the gang members objects, so she is placed into a time-locked vault. After Secret Service men and Helen's lover, Nathan Stattler, who is also Jewish, capture the crooks, Isaac opens the vault in time to save Helen from suffocating. The uncle of Isaac's two adopted children then finances the lock, and they both become millionaires. Helen and Nathan are married by a rabbi. *Counterfeiters and counterfeiting. Engravers. Extortion. Inventions. Jews. Kidnapping. Asphyxia. Brokers. Locks. New York City–East Side. Pawnbrokers. Secret Service. Vaults.*

Note: This film was shot at the Centaur Film Co. studio in Bayonne, NJ. Fred MacKaye was also known as a professional boxer.

Motog 6 Feb 1915, p. 232. *MPN* 9 Jan 1915, p. 42. *MPN* 23 Jan 1915, p. 34, 46. *MPW* 23 Jan 1915, p. 522. *MPW* 30 Jan 1915, p. 734. *NYDM* 27 Jan 1915, p. 54.

THE TIME OF YOUR LIFE (Arab Americans, Italian Americans, Irish Americans, Greek Americans, African Americans, Chinese Americans, Polish Americans)

Cagney Productions, Inc. *Dist* United Artists Corp. 3 Sep **1948**; World Premiere in New York: 26 May 1948; *Prod:* early May—early Aug 1947; mid-Apr 1948. [©Cagney Productions, Inc.; 27 May 1948; LP1752]. Sd (Western Electric Recording); b&w. 12 reels, 9,853 ft. 109 min. PCA cert no. 12768.

Prod William Cagney. *Dir* H. C. Potter. *Asst dir* Harvey Dwight. *Adpt for the screen by* Nathaniel Curtis. *Dir of photog* James Wong Howe and [Joseph Valentine]. [*Cam op* Wilbur Bradley]. *Still photog* Madison S. Lacy. *Prod des* Wiard Ihnen. *Film ed* Walter Hanneman and Truman K. Wood. *Set dec* A. Roland Fields. *Ward* Courtney Haslam. *Mus* Carmen Dragon. *Piano compositions* Reginald Beane. *Sd rec* Earl Sitar. *Makeup* Otis Malcolm. *Hair stylist* Scotty Rackin. *Prod mgr* Dan Keefe. *Unit prod mgr* John W. Kirston. *Talent dept* Irving R. Kumin. [*Scr supv* Kay Phillips]. [*Grip* Robert Dabke]. [*Tech adv on Salvation Army scenes* Lloyd Docter].

Song(s): "Wait 'till the Sun Shines, Nellie," music by Harry Von Tilzer, lyrics by Andrew B. Sterling; "When Irish Eyes Are Smiling," music by Ernest R. Ball, lyrics by Chauncey Olcott and George Graff, Jr.

Source: Based on the play *The Time of Your Life* by William Saroyan (New York, 25 Oct 1939), as produced by the Theater Guild, Inc. in association with Eddie Dowling.

Cast: James Cagney (*Joe...whose hobby is people*), William Bendix (*Nick...his hobby is horses*), Wayne Morris (*Tom...Joe's disciple, errand boy, stooge and friend*), Jeanne Cagney (*Kitty Duval...a young woman with memories [also known as Katerina Koronovski]*), Broderick Crawford ([*Krupp*] *A bewildered cop*), Ward Bond (*McCarthy, a "blatherskite"*), James Barton ([*Kit Carson*] *A cigar store Indian fighter*), Paul Draper ([*Harry*] *"A natural born dancer"*), Gale Page ([*Mary L.*] *A woman of quality*), James Lydon ([*Dudley Raoul Bostwick*] *A frantic young man in love*), Richard Erdman ([*Willie*] *Marble game maniac*), Pedro de Cordoba (*Arab philosopher*), Reginald Beane ([*Wesley*] *Plays a mean piano*), John "Skins" Miller (*A tippler*), Tom Powers ([*Freddy Blick*] *A stool-pigeon and frame-up artist*), Natalie Schafer (*Society lady*), Howard Freeman (*Society gentleman*), Renie Riano ([*Lorene Smith*] *Blind date*), Nanette Parks ([*Elsie Mandelspiegel*] *Girl in love*), Grazia Narciso (*Nick's mother*), Claire Carleton (*"Killer"*), Gladys Blake (*Side-kick*), Lanny Rees (*Newsboy*), Marlene Aames ([*Anna*] *Nick's daughter*), [Moy Ming (*Cook*)], [Donald Kerr (*Bookie*)], [Ann Cameron (*"B" girl*)], [Floyd Walters (*Sailor*)], [Eddie Borden (*Salvation Army man*)], [Rena Case (*Salvation Army woman*)].

Comedy-drama, with songs. [*Print viewed*]. A sign in front of Nick's Pacific Street saloon, restaurant and entertainment palace in San Francisco invites customers to come in and be themselves. Among the motley group that frequents Nick's saloon are: Joe, a wealthy man who helps lonely drifters who take refuge in the saloon; Joe's faithful friend Tom, who three years before Joe had nursed back to health, and who now runs errands for him; and Willie, who endlessly plays a marbles pinball machine. One day at Nick's, a woman who calls herself Kitty Duval wanders in and is befriended by Joe. She tells Joe that her real name is Katerina Koronovski, but became Kitty Duval when she toured the country as a burlesque singer and dancer. Joe asks Tom to dance with Kitty, and they fall in love. Meanwhile, Dudley Raoul Bostwick, a lovesick young man desperately trying to

reach his girl friend, Elsie Mandelspiegel, on the telephone, dials the wrong number, and ends up telling a strange, lonely woman that he is going to kill himself if she does not marry him. The woman, Lorene Smith, eagerly arrives at Nick's, but when Dudley sees that she is a homely, middle-aged spinster, he pretends to be somebody else. Kitty and Tom go out, and while they are away, an informer named Freddy Blick questions Nick about a blonde named Kitty Duval who has a police record in Chicago. Next, Joe tells a beautiful stranger with the initials "M. L." that he was once in love with a woman named Mary, whom he met in Mexico City, but who was engaged to another man. For a moment, the woman imagines that she is Joe's Mary, and he admits that he is still in love with Mary before she says goodbye. Later, Tom returns, and after he tells Joe that he wants to marry Kitty, Joe sends him out to buy a gun. Kit Carson, an old cowboy, then enters and tells Joe fantastic tales of adventure from his youth and comments that Joe is the first person ever to believe them. Elsie finally arrives and agrees to marry Dudley, and they leave together. After Willie finally wins his perpetual game of marbles, he leaves the bar. When Tom returns with a gun, Joe sends him on a job interview as a truck driver. Kitty then comes back and confesses to Joe that she was never in burlesque, but was involved in "other" things that make her unworthy of Tom. While Joe is away collecting poetry to cheer up Kitty, Blick returns and accuses her of being Katerina Koronovski, an ex-convict who spent two years in prison. Kit comes to Kitty's defense, but Blick beats him up and throws him out of the saloon. Blick then forces Kitty to prove she was a burlesque dancer by insisting she perform her routine on the stage. After Blick orders her to take off her clothes, she admits who she really is, defiantly asking Blick if he has the courage to admit the same. After Joe returns, a fight starts in which Joe tries to shoot Blick with his defective gun, then knocks him out with his fists. Nick enters and throws Blick out, and Tom announces that he got the job and will marry Kitty. Nick then tears up his sign, saying "Enough is enough." *Good Samaritans. Hoboes. Impersonation and imposture. Saloon keepers. Saloons. Bartenders. Burlesque dancers. Candy. Champagne. Chewing gum. Chinese. Comedians. Confession. Cooks. Cowboys. Dancers. Drunkenness. Entertainers. Ex-convicts. Firearms. Fistfights. Frame-ups. Friendship. Gambling. Horseracing. Informers. Irish Americans. Liars. Loneliness. Loyalty. Marbles (Game). Marriage. Newsboys. Pianists. Pinball machines. Police. Polish Americans. Prostitution. Salvation Army. San Francisco (CA). Secrets. Singers. Slumming. Tap dancing. Toys. Unemployment. Wagers.*

Note: The prologue to the film states: "This is a motion picture of many stories and plots...a living part of life itself." The onscreen credit state that the play was awarded a Pulitzer Prize and a Drama Critics Circle Award (although, as noted in *Var*, playwright William Saroyan refused to accept the Pulitzer award). In 1942, James Cagney and his brother William formed Cagney Productions. Actress Jeanne Cagney was their sister. According to the film's file in the MPAA/PCA Collection at the AMPAS Library, PCA officers insisted that the play's tragic ending be revised for the film. Consequently, in the film's original script, "Blick" is shot dead by "Kit" in the alley behind the saloon. "Joe" then accompanies "Kit" to the police station to face arrest, and the film fades out. The *Var* review states: "After shooting a Johnston office version of the original finale, it was discovered in sneak previews that it didn't play.' The heavy Saroyanism left audiences bewildered." Thus, the closing scenes were reshot. At the PCA's request, "Blick," who was originally a police detective, was made into an informer and blackmailer. Regarding the character of "Kitty," the PCA ordered that no reference to prostitution be made; thus, she is depicted as a "B" girl in the film, and the circumstance surrounding her criminal record in Chicago are never fully explained.

Box 22 May 1948, p. 8. *DV* 25 May 1948, p. 3, 10. *FD* 26 May 1948, p. 6. *HR* 9 May 1947, p. 21. *HR* 1 Aug 1947, p. 15. *HR* 25 May 1948, pp. 3-4. *HR* 1 Jun 1948, p. 6. *MPD* 25 May 1948. *MPHPD* 22 May 1948, p. 4174. *MPHPD* 29 May 1948, p. 4182. *NYT* 27 May 1948, p. 29. *Var* 26 May 1948, p. 8.

THE TIN STAR (Native Americans)

Perlsea Co.; Paramount Pictures Corp.; The Perlberg-Seaton Production. *Dist* Paramount Pictures Corp. 6 Nov **1957**; New York opening: 23 Oct 1957; *Prod:* 22 Oct–6 Dec 1956 [©Perlsea Co. & Paramount Pictures Corp.; 1 Nov 1957; LP9397]. Sd (Westrex Sound Recording); b&w; VistaVision. 8,354 ft. 92-93 min. Passed by the National Board of Review. PCA cert no. 18468.

Prod William Perlberg and George Seaton. *Dir* Anthony Mann. *Asst dir* Michael D. Moore. *Scr* Dudley Nichols. *From a story* Barney Slater and Joel Kane. *Dir of photog* Loyal Griggs. *Art dir* Hal Pereira and Joseph MacMillan Johnson. *Ed* Alma Macrorie. *Set dec* Sam Comer and Frank McKelvy. *Cost* Edith Head. *Mus score* Elmer Bernstein. *Sd rec* Hugo Grenzbach and Winston Leverett. *Makeup supv* Wally

Westmore. *Hair style supv* Nellie Manley. *Asst to the prod* Ric Hardman. [*Unit mgr* Dick Blaydon].

Cast: HENRY FONDA [(*Morgan Hickman*)], ANTHONY PERKINS [(*Sheriff Ben Owens*)], BETSY PALMER [(*Nona Mayfield*)], MICHEL RAY [(*Kip Mayfield*)], Neville Brand [(*Bart Bogardus*)], John McIntire [(*Dr. Joe McCord*)], Mary Webster [(*Millie Parker*)], Peter Baldwin [(*Zeke McGaffey*)], Richard Shannon [(*Buck Henderson*)], Lee Van Cleef [(*Ed McGaffey*)], James Bell [(*Judge Thatcher*)], Howard Petrie [(*Harvey King*)], Russell Simpson [(*Clem Hall*)], Hal K. Dawson [(*Andy Miller*)], Jack Kenney [(*Sam Hodges*)], Mickey Finn [(*Posse member McCall*)], [Frank Cady (*Abe Pickett*)], [Bob Kenaston (*Posse member Hardman*)], [Allen Gettel (*Posse member Sloan*)], [Frank Cordell (*Posse member*)], [Frank McGrath (*Jim Clark*)], [Tim Sullivan (*Virgil Hough*)].

Western. [*Print viewed*]. Morgan Hickman, a bounty hunter, is treated coldly when he brings the body of a dangerous outlaw into a small western town to claim his reward. Ben Owens, the town's timid temporary sheriff, must verify the outlaw's identity before giving Morg the money, so the bounty hunter heads to the livery barn, where he befriends little Kip Mayfield. Morg accompanies Kip to his home outside of town, and the boy's widowed mother Nona agrees to put him up. That night, Morg sadly reveals to Nona that he lost his own wife and son. Nona then remarks that her deceased husband was an Indian. When Morg looks surprised, Nona angrily tells him that he may leave in the morning. The next day, Ben's sweetheart, Millie Parker, whose father was the sheriff for twenty years, angrily reminds Ben that he promised to turn in his badge as soon as a permanent sheriff is located, but he admits that he hopes to remain in the job. Old Dr. Joe McCord assures her that Ben will be fine, but she is certain that he will be killed, as was her father. Morg returns to town, and soon afterward, Bart Bogardus, the dead outlaw's cousin, repeatedly shoots a "half-breed" in the street, then claims that the killing was in self-defense. Ben nervously demands Bogardus' weapons, but he threatens the sheriff with his gun. Morg shoots the gun out of Bogardus' hand, and later, Ben asks Morg, who has revealed that he was once a sheriff, how to handle troublemakers. Morg replies that a sheriff must always shoot to kill. That night, Morg admits to Nona that, while he wants to continue his stay in her home, he, like most white people, were reared to hate Indians. Her husband, she replies, was killed for having the courage to stand up for himself as an equal, and since then, she adds bitterly, the townspeople have turned their hatred on her and her son. Ben worriedly tells Morg the next day that the judge has released Bogardus, and Morg agrees to coach him on handling guns and outlaws. When the stagecoach driver is later shot by two gunmen outside of town, Ben organizes a posse, but Morg refuses to participate, claiming that he will never again wear a badge. Having received his reward money, Morg buys Kip a pony and prepares to leave town. That night, Doc McCord delivers a baby, but on his way home, he is stopped by Ed McGaffey, whose brother Zeke has been shot in a "hunting accident." At daybreak, the doctor heads for home, but Ed is certain he knows that the two brothers are the killers sought by the posse. Zeke begs Ed to let the doctor go, but Ed grabs his gun and pursues him. The whole town has turned out for "McCord Day," the doctor's seventy-fifth birthday, but the singing and clapping stop as everyone realizes that the beloved doctor has been killed. As was his custom, Doc McCord had described Zeke's injury in his notebook, and when the mayor reads this, he places a dead-or-alive reward on the brothers' heads. An angry mob then charges off to the McGaffey homestead to seek revenge. As the men pass his house, Kip decides to chase them on his pony, and shortly afterward, as Morg prepares to pursue the McGaffey brothers on his own, he and Nona realize that the boy is gone. The McGaffey brothers are absent by the time the posse arrives, but Bogardus, who has assumed control of the mob, orders them to set fire to the house. Soon after they leave, Kip arrives, and when his dog runs into the canyon behind the house, the child follows. Morg and Ben follow the hoof prints, arriving near the McGaffeys' cavern hideout just as Ed begins shooting at the boy. Kip is led to safety, whereupon Ben swears he will take the outlaws in alive. Just as Morg predicts, however, Ed shoots at Ben when he attempts to approach the cave. Morg lights a fire by the cave's entrance, and soon the two brothers are forced to surrender. Bogardus, who wants Ben's job, is furious that Ben and Morg have captured the outlaws, and he orders the mob to lynch the McGaffeys. Ben tries to enlist the help of the town officials, but none

of them supports his decision to give the McGaffeys a fair trial, and Ben finds himself facing Bogardus and his lynch mob alone. This time, Ben stands up to Bogardus and is surprised when Morg appears at his side with a star on his chest. When Ben approaches Bogardus and slaps him, Bogardus draws his gun and fires. Ben shoots back, killing Bogardus. Their leader slain, the mob loses its fury. Ben asks Morg to remain in town as a lawman, but Morg assures the sheriff that he can handle the job alone, and Millie decides that she will marry Ben. Morg, Nona and Kip then leave town to begin a new life together. *Bounty hunters. Indians of North America–Mixed blood. Mothers and sons. Outlaws. Sheriffs. Tenderfoots. Bullies. Gunfights. Hideouts. Indians of North America. Mobs. Murder. Physicians. Posses. Racism. Revenge. Transformation. Widows.*

Note: According to a *LAT* article, this film was shot on location at two ranches in the San Fernando Valley and near the Prado Dam in Riverside, CA. This film was nominated for an Academy Award for Best Story and Screenplay (written for the screen).
Box 19 Oct 1957. *DV* 15 Oct 1957, p. 3. *Exb* 16 Oct 1957, p. 4390. *FD* 22 Oct 1957, p. 6. *Har* 19 Oct 1957, p. 166. *HR* 19 Oct 1956, p. 7, 12. *HR* 7 Dec 1946, p. 6. *HR* 15 Oct 1957, p. 3. *LAT* 9 Dec 1956. *MPHPD* 19 Oct 1957, p. 569. *NYT* 24 Oct 1957, p. 37. *Var* 16 Oct 1957, p. 6.

TIRE GANGSTER see **RUBBER RACKETEERS**

TISA see **MY GIRL TISA**

TKIES KAF see **THE RABBI'S POWER**

TO HAVE AND HAVE NOT see **THE BREAKING POINT**

TO THE LAST MAN see **THUNDER MOUNTAIN**

TO THE VICTOR see **MAN OF THE PEOPLE**

THE TOAST OF NEW ORLEANS (French Americans)
Metro-Goldwyn-Mayer Corp.; controlled by Loew's Inc. *Dist* Loew's Inc. 29 Sep **1950**; *Prod*: late Dec 1949—early Mar 1950 [©Loew's Inc.; 23 Aug 1950; LP350]. Sd (Western Electric Sound System); col (Technicolor). 8,716 ft. 96-98 ft. min. Passed by the National Board of Review. PCA cert no. 14504.

Prod Joe Pasternak. *Dir* Norman Taurog. [*Asst dir* Reggie Callow]. *Wrt* Sy Gomberg and George Wells. *Dir of photog* William Snyder. [*Cam op* Lathrop Worth]. [*Stills* J. Frank Shugrue]. *Spec eff* A. Arnold Gillespie and Warren Newcombe. *Technicolor col consultants* Henri Jaffa and James Gooch. *Art dir* Cedric Gibbons and Daniel B. Cathcart. *Film ed* Gene Ruggiero. *Set dec* Edwin B. Willis. *Assoc* Richard A. Pefferle. *Women's cost* Helen Rose. *Men's cost* Walter Plunkett. *Mus dir* Georgie Stoll. *Operatic numbers cond* Johnny Green. *Orch* Conrad Salinger and Robert Franklyn. *Dances staged by* Eugene Loring. *Rec supv* Douglas Shearer. *Hair styles des* Sydney Guilaroff. [*Hair stylist* Jane Garten]. *Makeup created by* William J. Tuttle. [*Prod mgr* Sergei Petschnikoff]. [*Scr supv* Grace DuBray]. [*Grip* Dick Borland]. [*Gaffer* Jimmie James]. [*Opera sequences stage by* Armando Agnini].

Song(s): "O luce di quest' anima," music and lyrics by Gaetano Donizetti; "Je suis Titania" from the opera *Mignon*, music by Ambroise Thomas, libretto by Jules Barbier and Michel Carré; "Là ci darem la mano" from the opera *Don Giovanni*, music by Wolfgang Amadeus Mozart, libretto by Lorenzo da Ponte; "Brindisi" and "Libiamo ne'lieti callici" from the opera *La traviata*, music by Giuseppe Verdi, libretto by Francesco Maria Piave; "Flower Song" from the opera *Carmen*, music by Georges Bizet, libretto by Henri Meilhac and Ludovic Halévy; duet from the opera *Madame Butterfly*, music by Giacomo Puccini, libretto by Guiseppe Giacosa and Luigi Illica; "M'appari tutt amor" from the opera *Martha der oder Der Markt von Richmond*, music by Friedrich von Flotow, libretto by Friedrich Wilhelm Riese; "The Toast of New Orleans," "Be My Love," "The Tina-lina," "Boom Biddy Boom Boom," "I'll Never Love You" and "Bayou Lullaby," music by Nicholas Brodszky, lyrics by Sammy Cahn.

Cast: KATHRYN GRAYSON (*Suzette Micheline*), MARIO LANZA (*Pepe Abellard Duvalle*), DAVID NIVEN (*Jacques Riboudeaux*), J. Carrol Naish (*Nicky Duvalle*), James Mitchell (*Pierre*), Richard Hageman (*Maestro P. Trellini*), Clinton Sundberg (*Oscar*), Sig Arno (*Mayor*), Rita Moreno (*Tina*), Romo Vincent (*Manuelo*), [George Davis (*Stooge*)], [Marietta Canty (*Angelique*)], [Alex Gerry (*Headwaiter*)], [Wallis Clark (*Mr. O'Neill*)], [Paul Frees (*Narrator*)], [Henry Cordon, Nick Thompson (*Fishermen*)], [Carmella Restivo (*Fat*

woman)], [Charles Mauu (*Passerby*)], [George Nardelli (*Chauffeur*)], [Jacques George (*Priest*)], [Ernesto Morelli (*Father*)], [George Meader (*Stage door man*)], [Jean Del Val (*Dominique*)], [Bethe Douglas (*Woman in cafe*)], [Gene Brown (*Pretty woman*)], [Guy DeVestal, Dino Bolognese, Eduard Moreno (*Waiters*)], [Robert Emmett Keane (*Chairman*)], [Nino Pipitone (*Store clerk*)], [Fred Essler (*Emile*)], [Leon Belasco (*Orchestra leader*)], [Louise Bates (*Dowager*)], [Andre Charlot (*Dignified man*)], [Sandy Lawrence (*Secretary*)], [Loulette Sablon (*Costumer*)], [Helen Dickson (*Dowager*)], [Betty Daniels], [Mary Benoit], [John Piffle], [Mitchell Lewis], [Michael Kostrick], [Mike Tellegen], [Paul Bryar], [George Humbert].

Historical, Comedy-drama, Musical. [*Print viewed*]. In the early 1900s, in the swamplands of Louisiana, the Cajun fishing village of Bayou Minou is buzzing with activity as it prepares for the annual celebration of the blessing of the fishing fleet. During the festival, the village hosts two guests of honor from New Orleans: opera star Suzette Micheline and opera director Jacques Riboudeaux. Soon after arriving in Bayou Minou, Suzette, who has a romantic understanding with Jacques, meets the handsome and uncouth Pepe Abellard Duvalle, the nephew of fisherman Nicky Duvalle. Though Suzette is initially attracted to Pepe, she soon becomes perturbed by his crude manners, and is angered when he interrupts her musical recital at the festival and turns her solo into a duet. Jacques, however, is greatly impressed with Pepe's beautiful tenor voice, and invites Pepe to train in New Orleans and sing in his opera. Pepe initially rejects the offer, but later changes his mind when a ferocious storm sinks his uncle's fishing boat. Pepe and Nicky leave Bayou Minou in the hope that Pepe will be able to make enough money to buy a new boat. Soon after Pepe arrives in New Orleans, Jacques decides he must make Pepe more presentable in public, and enlists the help of Suzette to soften his "rough edges." Jacques also hires his well-heeled friend Oscar to teach Jacques some high society manner. Jacques later takes Pepe to Maestro P. Trellini, who is amazed at Pepe's voice and agrees to train him. One evening, Pepe and Nicky join Jacques and Suzette for an elegant dinner at a fancy restaurant, but they nearly spoil the evening with their crude country manners. While Oscar continues to teach Pepe about social graces, Trellini makes great progress training Pepe's voice. Jacques eventually becomes so confident in his new tenor that he makes plans to include Pepe in a worldwide tour of his opera. Suzette takes great pleasure in refining Pepe's behavior and tastes, and a romance appears inevitable. Suzette, however, is torn between her attraction to Pepe and her desire to please Jacques, who is responsible for advancing her singing career. One day, when Pepe tries to kiss Suzette, she rejects him and then hurriedly asks Jacques to marry her. Nicky, meanwhile, becomes homesick and impatient with his nephew's efforts to become rich and vows to return to Bayou Manou. Later, Pepe tells Jacques that he is in love with Suzette and that he intends to leave New Orleans because she has spurned him. Although Jacques now realizes that Suzette proposed to him only to save her career, he encourages Pepe to stay in New Orleans and continue his opera training. Tina and Pierre, two of Pepe's friends from Bayou Manou, visit Pepe one day, but they are disappointed when they discover that their fun-loving friend has become cold and rigid. Eventually, Suzette and Jacques, too, become alarmed at the change in Pepe's personality. After rejecting a marriage proposal from Pepe, Suzette explains to Jacques that she was in love with Pepe before he became so refined, but no longer has feelings for him. When Tina and Pierre leave New Orleans because they are bored, Pepe finally realizes that he has changed for the worse. During a performance of *Madame Butterfly*, Pepe reverts to his natural behavior and, as a result, is able to reignite his romance with Suzette. *Cajuns. Class distinction. Opera singers. Romance. Transformation. Bayous (LA). City-country contrast. Etiquette. Festivals. Fishermen. Madame Butterfly (Opera). New Orleans (LA). Proposals (Marital). Restaurants. Shipwrecks. Storms. Superstition. Teachers. Uncles.*

Note: The working titles for this film were *Serenade to Suzette, Kiss of Fire* and *This Weekend Is Yours*. The film marked the motion picture acting debut of composer and conductor Richard Hageman. According to a Dec 1949 *DV* news item, Armando Agnini, who staged the opera sequences in the film, worked for the Metropoitan Opera.

Box 26 Aug 1950. *DV* 15 Dec 1949, p. 6. *DV* 24 Aug 1950, p. 3. *FD* 24 Aug 1950, p. 5. *HR* 14 Jun 1949, p. 7. *HR* 19 Aug 1949, p. 1. *HR* 1 Sep 1949, p. 2. *HR* 6 Jan 1950, p. 10. *HR* 24 Feb 1950, p. 12. *HR* 24 Aug 1950, p. 3. *MPHPD* 26 Aug 1950, p. 450. *NYT* 30 Sep 1950, p. 13. *Var* 30 Aug 1950, p. 6.

TOBY'S BOW (African Americans)
Goldwyn Pictures Corp. *Dist* Goldwyn Distributing Corp. 20 Dec **1919** [©Goldwyn Pictures Corp.; 5 Nov 1919; LP14381]. Si; b&w. 5 reels.

Pres Samuel Goldwyn. *Dir* Harry Beaumont. *Scen* Edward T. Lowe, Jr. *Cam* Norbert Brodin.

Source: Based on the play *Toby's Bow* by John Tainter Foote (New York, 12 Mar 1919).

Cast: Tom Moore (*Tom Blake*), Doris Pawn (*Eugenia*), Macey Harlam (*Dubois*), Arthur Housman (*Bagby*), Colin Kenny (*Bainbridge*), Augustus Phillips (*Paige*), Catherine Wallace (*Valerie*), Violet Schram (*Mona*), Ruby La Fayette (*Grandmother*), George K. Kuwa (*Jap*), Nick Cogley (*Toby*).

Comedy. Because the wild Bohemian life style of Greenwich Village has destroyed successful novelist Tom Blake's ability to write, his publisher refuses to advance him more money until he forsakes that environment. A friend of Tom's arranges for him to become the boarder of her Southern friend Eugenia, a fledgling writer inspired by Tom's first novel, so he can find the quiet he needs for work. Using an assumed name, Tom is introduced to Eugenia's proud, aristocratic grandmother as a guest, since she would never condescend to taking in boarders. The black servant Toby defers to Tom, but does not give the elaborate, courtly bow he reserves for family members. After Tom helps turn Eugenia's poor manuscript into a novel by virtually rewriting it himself, the book's success allows Eugenia to pay the estate's mortgage, but, when she learns Tom's identity, she furiously declares that she wants no charity. After experiencing Greenwich Village however, Eugenia returns, forgives Tom, and they marry. Tom then receives his long awaited bow from Toby. *Bohemians and Bohemianism. City-country contrast. Family life. Impersonation and imposture. New York City–Greenwich Village. Novelists. United States–South. African Americans. Aristocrats. Books. Grandmothers. Mortgages. Publishers and publishing. Servants.*

Note: The annual Pagan Rout ball given in Webster Hall in Greenwich Village, New York, which prominent artists, singers, players, and authors attended, was reproduced in a scene in this film. According to *ETR*, the character Eugenia's surname is "Fairchild," while *MPW* calls her "Vardaman." An unidentified reviewer stated that author John Tainter Foote's "understanding of the psychology of the Southern negro has resulted in some of the most delightful characterizations in modern American fiction." *ETR* commented, "Nick Cogley plays the part of Toby, the old colored servitor whose bow is sacred to family members only, and his performance is remarkable for its clever pantomime, aided by an ancient darky makeup which could not be improved upon."

ETR 27 Dec 1919, p. 419. *MPN* 27 Dec 1919, p. 271. *MPW* 27 Dec 1919, p. 1189. *NYMT* 21 Dec 1919. *NYT* 15 Dec 1919, p. 20. *Wid's* 28 Dec 1919, p. 9.

TODA UNA VIDA (Spanish language, Latino)
Paramount Famous Lasky Corp. *Dist* Paramount-Publix Corp. Dec **1930**; Valencia, Spain, opening: 15 Dec 1930; Los Angeles opening: 19 Dec 1930.; Prod: at Paramount studios in Joinville, France. Sd; b&w. 9 reels, 7,647 ft. 85 min. *Country of origin* France. Spanish language.

Dir Adelqui Millar. *Scr* Zoë Akins. *Spanish version* Ceferino Palencia.

Source: Based on the novel *Sarah and Son* by Timothy Shea (New York, 1929).

Cast: Carmen Larrabeiti (*Lola Murillo*), Tony D'Algy (*Paul Vanning*), Carlos Díaz de Mendoza (*Juan Grey*), Félix de Pomés (*John Ashmore*), Isabel Barrón (*Sra. Ashmore*), Luis Peña Illescas (*Bobby*), Joaquín Carrasco.

Social, Melodrama. [*Not viewed*]. As the result of an unfortunate marriage with Juan Grey, a layabout who refuses to work, Lola Murillo and her son Bobby live in miserable conditions in one of New York's worst neighborhoods. Formerly, the couple were a song-and-dance act in minor theaters, but when Lola became pregnant, the act folded. The situation has deteriorated so badly that Lola is forced to beg for food for Bobby. After a violent argument, Juan leaves, taking Bobby with him, but he later leaves him in the care of the Ashmores, a well-to-do family. When World War I begins, Juan enlists and is sent to Europe. Later, when Lola is entertaining wounded soldiers in hospitals, she discovers Juan at death's door. During his last moments, Lola is able to cajole information from him about Bobby's whereabouts. On returning to New York, Lola attempts to regain custody of her son, but the adoptive parents resist, threatening a long, costly legal procedure that Lola is not likely to win. Years later, Lola, now a famous singer, tries once again to reclaim her son with the help

of lawyer Paul Vanning, who had previously represented the adoptive family but is now filled with admiration for her. Bobby runs away from the Ashmores and makes his way to Vanning's home. Lola and Bobby tip over while in a racing boat, and she saves her son's life. Bobby falls asleep in her arms, as she sings a lullaby she used to sing to him when he was a baby. *Adoption. Desertion (Marital). Lawyers. Mothers and sons. Singers. Hospitals. New York City. Soldiers. Vaudeville. War injuries. World War I.*

Note: The film's working title was *Corazones de plomo.* After Paramount filmed the English-language original, *Sarah and Son,* which was directed by Dorothy Arzner and starred Ruth Chatterton and Fredric March in the U.S. (see *AFI Catalog of Feature Films, 1921-30;* F2.4801), the studio then made versions in Spanish, French, Italian, Swedish, Portuguese and Polish at its Joinville studio in Paris, France. Some sources include Cecilio Rodríguez de la Vega and Ana Adamuz in the cast of the Spanish version, but their participation has not been confirmed. In Sweden, while a number of reviewers criticized the script, Rune Carlsten's direction was praised for pacing and camera movement, in comparison with other sound films released in Sweden at the time, which, a reviewer noted, gave the impression of poor theater.

Other language version(s):
Toute sa vie (French language)

1930; Paris opening: early Nov 1930; San Francisco opening: 25 Dec 1930; New York opening: 16 Jun 1931. Sd (Western Electric); b&w. 7,782 ft. 86 or 90 min.; Country of origin: France. French language.

Dir Alberto Cavalcanti. *French adpt and dial* Jean Aragny.

French-language cast: Marcelle Chantal (*Suzanne Valmond*), Pierre Richard-Willm (*Stanley Vanning*), Fernand Fabre (*Jim Grey*), Paul Guidé (*Mr. Ashmore*), Elmire Vautier (*Mrs. Ashmore*), Jean Mercanton (*Le petit Jimmy*), Paul Cervières (*Cyril Belloc*), Carlos Avril (*Le vieux domestique*), Luce Jolly (*La bonne*), Pierre Zimmerman. [*French version not viewed*]

Il richiamo del cuore (Italian language)

1931; New York opening: 1 Mar 1931. Sd (Western Electric); b&w. 8,447 ft. 94 min.; Country of origin: France. Italian language.

Dir Jack Salvatori. *Italian adpt* Oreste Biancoli. *Photog* Harry Stradling.

Italian-language cast: Carmen Boni (*Suzanne Sandi*), Anna Fontana (*Signora Ashmore*), Carlo Lombardi (*Stanley Vanning*), Alessandro Salvini (*Signore Ashmore*), Alfredo Robert (*Cyril Belloc*), Dino di Lucca (*Jim Gray*), Ello Cosci (*Bobby*), Ada Cristina Almirante (*Elena*), Cesare Zoppetti (*Il maggiordomo*). [*Italian version not viewed*]

Hjärtats röst (Swedish language)

1930; Stockholm opening: 26 Nov 1930; New York opening: 23 Jun 1931. Sd. b&w. 8,185 ft. 91 min.; Country of origin: France. Swedish language.

Dir Rune Carlsten. *Swedish adpt* Per Stille.

Swedish-language cast: Margit Manstad (*Birgit Storm*), Ragnar Billberg (*Jim Grey, vaudeville performer*), Richard Lund (*Stanley Vanning*), Ivan Hedqvist (*Cyril Brown*), Mathias Taube (*John Ashmore*), Jessie Wessel (*Mrs. Ashmore*), Leopold Rosensohn (*Bobby*), Stellan Windrow (*Wells*), Helga Fredriksson (*Sally*), Inger De Friis (*Ashmore's girl friend*). [*Swedish version not viewed*]

A canção do berço (Portuguese language)

1931; Sd. b&w. 7,346 ft. 82 min.; Country of origin: France. Portuguese language.

Dir Alberto Cavalcanti.

Portuguese-language cast: Corina Freire, Raúl De Carvalho, Ester Leão, Alexandre de Azevedo. [*Portuguese version not viewed*]

Glos serca (Polish language)

1930; 9 reels. Country of origin: France. Polish language.

Dir Ryszard Ordyński. *Polish adpt* Jana Lechonia.

Polish-language cast: Janina Romanówna, Aleksander Żabczyński, Tadeusz Olsza, Wiktor Biegański, Stefek Rogulski. [*Polish version not viewed*].

FD 8 Mar 1931, p. 11. *FD* 21 Jun 1931, p. 11. *FD* 28 Jun 1931, p. 10. *FD* 28 Oct 1933. *NYT* 2 Mar 1931, p. 19. *NYT* 23 Oct 1933, p. 18. *Var* 23 Jul 1930, p. 19. *Var* 26 Nov 1930, p. 19. *Var* 18 Mar 1931, p. 38. *Var* 23 Jun 1931, p. 20. *Var* 30 Jul 1931, p. 20.

TOINETTE'S PHILIP *see* **RAINBOW ON THE RIVER**

A TOKIO SIREN (Japanese Americans)

Universal Film Mfg. Co. *Dist* Universal Film Mfg. Co. Jun **1920** [©Universal Film Mfg. Co.; 1 Jun 1920; LP15225]. Si; b&w. 5 reels.

Dir Norman Dawn. *Scen* Doris Schroeder. *Cam* Thomas Rae.

Source: Based on the short story "Sayonara" by Gwendolyn Logan (publication undetermined).

Cast: Tsuru Aoki (*Asuti Hishuri*), Jack Livingston (*Dr. Niblock*), Goro Kino (*Hakami*), Toyo Fujita (*Hishuri*), Arthur Jasmine (*Ito*), Peggy Pearce (*Ethel*), Florence Hart (*Amelia Niblock*), Frederick Vroom (*Mr. Chandler*), Dorothy Hipp (*Matsu*), Eleanor Hancock (*Mrs. Chandler*), Eugenie Forde.

Drama. Dr. John Niblock is conducting research in Japan when he is called to revive the bride Asuti Hishuri, who has fainted during her wedding ceremony. Upon learning that Asuti is being forced into a loveless marriage, the chivalrous Niblock offers to marry the girl in name only and take her to America where she can be free. When Niblock and his Japanese bride arrive in San Francisco, the doctor's former sweetheart appears heartbroken and Asuti realizes that she is in love with Ito, her husband's secretary. Thereupon Asuti stages a love scene between Ito and herself so that her husband may find an excuse for denouncing her. Asuti's scheme works, thus making the happiness of all four possible. *Americans in foreign countries. Japanese. Japanese Americans. Marriage of convenience. Marriage–Arranged. Japan. Physicians. San Francisco (CA). Weddings.*

Note: Some scenes for this film were shot in the Catalina Islands, CA.

ETR 26 Jun 1920, p. 386. *MPN* 3 Apr 1920, p. 3128. *MPN* 12 Jun 1920, p. 4807. *MPN* 26 Jun 1920, p. 145. *MPN* 3 Jul 1920, p. 242. *MPW* 10 Jul 1920, p. 253. *NYMT* 6 Jun 1920. *Var* 18 Jun 1920, p. 34. *Wid's* 13 Jun 1920, p. 11

TOLD IN THE HILLS (Native Americans)

Famous Players-Lasky Corp. *Dist* Famous Players-Lasky Corp.; Paramount-Artcraft Pictures. 21 Sep **1919** [©Famous Players-Lasky Corp.; 15 Aug 1919; LP14112]. Si; b&w. 5-6 reels.

Pres Jesse L. Lasky. *Dir* George Melford. *Scen* Will M. Ritchey. *Cam* Paul Perry and Henry Kotani.

Source: Based on the novel *Told in the Hills* by Marah Ellis Ryan (Chicago, 1891).

Cast: Robert Warwick (*Jack Stuart*), Ann Little (*Rachel Hardy*), Tom Forman (*Charles Stuart*), Wanda Hawley (*Ann Belleau*), Charles Ogle (*Davy MacDougall*), Monte Blue (*Kalitan*), Margaret Loomis (*Talapa*), Eileen Percy (*Tillie Hardy*), Hart Hoxie (*Henry Hardy*), Jack Herbert (*Skulking Brave*), Guy Oliver (*Captain Holt*).

Western. A Kentucky woman's dying request that her sons care for her ward, Ann Belleau, is disregarded by the younger brother, Charles Stuart, who makes love to her and marries another woman in New Orleans. The elder brother Jack marries Ann so that her child will have a name, but then leaves her his possessions and becomes a prospector and guide in Montana. Although known as "Genesee Jack," and wanting to keep away from white women, Jack meets Rachel Hardy and they fall in love. Even when she sees a squaw in Jack's cabin and he says he is an Indian himself, her love remains strong. After a young Kootenai chieftain is accidentally killed bringing a message of good will to the U.S. Cavalry, Jack, unjustly imprisoned, escapes with Rachel's help. He then leads the soldiers, who are surrounded by Indians in a mine, through a hidden tunnel to safety. Although wounded, Jack marries Rachel, after Charles repentently tells of Ann's death. *Brothers. False arrests. Indians of North America. Marriage–Forced by circumstances. Montana. Rescues. Seduction. Accidental death. Guides. Kentucky. Mines. Prison escapes. Prospectors. Tribal chiefs. United States. Army. Cavalry. Wards and guardians.*

Note: Some of this film was shot at Kaniah, ID in the Lapaway Indian Agency near Lewiston. Director Melford persuaded Indians to appear in the film. According to a modern source, James Wong Howe was an assistant cameraman on this film.

ETR 20 Sep 1919, p. 1383. *MPN* 20 Sep 1919, p. 2469. *MPW* 20 Sep 1919, p. 1865. *NYMT* 14 Sep 1919. *Var* 12 Sep 1919, p. 52. *Wid's* 10 Aug 1919, p. 23.

TOM SAWYER (Native Americans)

Paramount-Publix Corp. 15 Nov **1930** [©Paramount-Publix Corp.; 17 Nov 1930; LP1736]. Sd (Movietone); b&w. 9 reels, 7,648 ft.

Dir John Cromwell. *Scr* Sam Mintz, Grover Jones and William Slavens McNutt. *Photog* Charles Lang. *Film ed* Alyson Shaffer. *Rec eng* Harold C. Lewis.

Source: Based on the novel *The Adventures of Tom Sawyer* by Mark Twain (San Francisco, 1896).

Cast: Jackie Coogan (*Tom Sawyer*), Junior Durkin (*Huckleberry Finn*), Mitzi Green (*Becky Thatcher*), Lucien Littlefield (*Teacher*), Tully Marshall (*Muff Potter*), Clara Blandick (*Aunt Polly*), Mary Jane

Irving (*Mary*), Ethel Wales (*Mrs. Harper*), Jackie Searle (*Sid*), Dick Winslow (*Joe Harper*), Jane Darwell (*Widow Douglass*), Charles Stevens (*Injun Joe*), Charles Sellon (*Minister*), Lon Poff (*Judge Thatcher*).

Youth, Comedy-drama. Tom Sawyer has a falling-out with Becky Thatcher, his sweetheart, and seeks comfort in the forbidden company of Huck Finn, the town ragamuffin. Huck tells him of a mysterious cure for warts that requires them to visit the town graveyard at midnight. There they see Injun Joe, a treacherous half-breed, murder one of his companions. Muff Potter, also there, but in a drunken state, is made to believe he committed the crime. Tom and Huck swear a blood oath that they will not divulge what they have seen. Wrongfully rebuked by his Aunt Polly, Tom runs away from home, joining Huck and Joe Harper on an expedition to an island on the Mississippi, where they live for three days in carefree abandon. Getting homesick, Tom returns to find he is thought drowned, and the boys attend their own obsequies at the church. Tom confesses the truth about the murder at Muff Potter's trial, but Injun Joe eludes a posse. At the school picnic near a cavern, Tom and Becky get lost in the cave and stumble on Injun Joe unearthing a chest of gold; he pursues them, but falls into a crevasse to his death. Huck finds Tom and Becky and leads them to safety, retrieving the chest of gold. *Aunts. Children. Courtship. Funerals. Indians of North America–Mixed blood. Mississippi River. Missouri. Murder. Small town life. Treasure. Waifs.*

FD 23 Nov 1930. *NYT* 20 Dec 1930, p. 20. *Var* 24 Dec 1930, p. 20.

TOMAHAWK (Native Americans, Cherokee, Dakota)
Universal-International Pictures Co., Inc. *Dist* Universal Pictures Co., Inc. Feb **1951**; Prod: late May—late Jun 1950 [©Universal Pictures Co.; 9 Jan 1951; LP620]. Sd (Western Electric Recording); col (Technicolor). 81-82 min. PCA cert no. 14766.

Prod Leonard Goldstein. *Dir* George Sherman. [*Asst dir* Jesse Hibbs, Tom Shaw and Mickey Bennett]. *Scr* Silvia Richards and Maurice Geraghty. *Suggested by a story by* Daniel Jarrett. *Dir of photog* Charles P. Boyle. *Addl photog* Marvin W. Spoor. *Technicolor color consultant* William Fritzsche. *Art dir* Bernard Herzbrun and Richard H. Riedel. *Film ed* Danny B. Landres. *Set dec* Russell A. Gausman and Oliver Emert. *Cost* Bill Thomas. *Mus* Hans J. Salter. *Sd* Leslie I. Carey and Corson Jowett. *Hair stylist* Joan St. Oegger. *Makeup* Bud Westmore. *Indian tech adv* David H. Miller. [*Tech adv* John War Eagle]. [*Unit prod mgr* Bernard McEveety].

Cast: Van Heflin (*Jim Bridger*), Yvonne DeCarlo (*Julie Madden*), Alex Nicol (*Lt. Rob Dancy*), Preston Foster (*Col. Carrington*), Jack Oakie (*Sol Beckworth*), Tom Tully (*Dan Castello*), John War Eagle (*Red Cloud*), Rock Hudson (*Burt Hanna*), Susan Cabot (*Monahseetah*), Arthur Space (*Capt. Fetterman*), Russell Conway (*Maj. Horton*), Ann Doran (*Mrs. Carrington*), Stuart Randall (*Sgt. Newell*), [Raymond Montgomery (*Blair Streeter*)], [John Peters (*Pvt. Osborne*)], [Dave Sharpe (*Pvt. Parr*)], [David H. Miller (*Captain Ten Eyck*)], [Sheila Darcy], [James A. Hermstad], [Harry Peterson], [Robert J. T. Simpson], [Abner George], [Archie N. MacVicar], [Floyd Sparks], [Edward Tullis], [Adiel F. Wahl].

Historical, Western. [*Print viewed*]. In 1866, in Wyoming, Sioux chiefs and officials of the U.S. Army meet to discuss a treaty that will enable the government to open the Bozeman trail through Sioux territory. Jim Bridger, a frontier scout and fur trader, speaks out passionately against the trail, arguing that it will destroy hunting ground crucial to the Sioux's survival. After Bridger reveals his knowledge that the government is already building a fort along the proposed trail, Chief Red Cloud angrily ends the meeting, but he promises that he will not go to war unless the Sioux are attacked first. Col. Carrington, the commander of Fort Phil Kearny, the Army's new installment, offers Bridger and his partner, Sol Beckworth, positions as scouts, but Bridger at first declines. He changes his mind, however, when Monahseetah, a young Cherokee girl to whom Bridger serves as guardian, points out Lt. Rob Dancy and whispers her suspicion that he participated in the massacre in which her entire tribe was killed. Shortly after, while escorting a wagon carrying vaudeville performers Dan Castello and his niece, Julie Madden, the Indian-hating Dancy shoots a Sioux teenager and keeps the murder a secret. Dan is seriously wounded by an arrow when the Sioux retaliate, but back at the fort, Dancy claims that the attack was unprovoked. Dancy attempts to impress Julie with tales of his Indian fighting days with the infamous Reverend Shivington and his renegade militia, the Colorado Volunteers. However, Julie is attracted to Bridger, who has

saved her uncle's life by removing the arrow. Jealous, Dancy denounces Bridger as an Indian spy and "squaw man," claiming that Monahseetah is Bridger's common-law wife. Bridger returns from a scouting expedition to report that the Sioux are preparing for a full-scale war, and, although Dancy and the like-minded Capt. Fetterman want to go on the offensive, Carrington orders everyone to remain in the fort. Disobeying orders, Julie sneaks out of the fort to go riding and ends up being chased by Sioux warriors, forcing Bridger to kill Red Cloud's favorite son in the effort to rescue her. After Julie expresses her mistaken belief that Monahseetah is Bridger's wife, Bridger explains with great sorrow and anger that Monahseetah is the sister of his beloved Cherokee wife, who was killed along with her infant son in a massacre carried out by the bigoted Shivington and his Colorado Volunteers. Julie then informs Bridger of her knowledge of Dancy's participation in the Volunteers, confirming Monahseetah's and Bridger's suspicions. In the meantime, the soldiers at the fort are becoming more and more anxious to fight after being subjected to the drone of Sioux war drums for four days. After Dancy convinces Fetterman and his men to disobey orders by following a small band of Sioux, the soldiers ride straight into a trap laid by the Sioux. All are killed, save for Dancy, who escapes into the woods where he is tracked down by Bridger. Bridger confronts Dancy as the murderer of his wife and child and they begin to fight. Before he is killed with a Sioux arrow, Dancy admits to the massacre, but claims he was only following orders. Carrington's troops go to battle using the "breechloading" weapons shipped to them by the government. The soldiers quickly prevail over the Sioux, whose methods of battle cannot succeed against the new guns, which can be reloaded with lightning speed. To Bridger's relief, Carrington allows Red Cloud to pick up his dead and leave the battlefield in peace. However, Red Cloud ultimately wins the battle when word arrives from Washington that a new treaty will be signed, closing the trail and the fort. Once Carrington's men are gone, Red Cloud's warriors burn down the fort, erasing all traces of the white man's presence in their land. *Bozeman Trail (MT). Dakota Indians. Fort Phil Kearny (WY). Racism. Scouts (Frontier). United States. Army. Cavalry. Cherokee Indians. Duplicity. Firearms. Fur traders. Marriage–Mixed. Massacres. Red Cloud. Rescues. Sisters-in-law. Treaties. Tribal chiefs. Vaudevillians.*

Note: This film opens with a narrated prologue providing the historical background to the meeting between the Sioux Indians and the U.S. Army. An epilogue states that the Sioux continued to live on their lands in peace for thirty years after the burning of the U.S. fort. Rumored to be the first white man to see the Great Salt Lake, the real-life James Bridger (1804-1881) was famous as a frontier guide and the founder of Fort Bridger. Although he surveyed the Bozeman Trail for the U.S. government, he was not involved in the Sioux uprising of 1866. The climax of *Tomahawk* is based on the Fetterman Massacre of 21 Dec 1866. No one among Col. William J. Fetterman's detachment of eighty men survived after being lured into an ambush carefully planned by Sioux, Cheyenne and Arapaho warriors. The fiasco caused a public furor which ended Col. Henry B. Carrington's military career; however, a number of historians have found Carrington's claim that Fetterman disobeyed orders, as depicted in the film, quite plausible. Red Cloud was a highly respected warrior and the principal planner of the strategy leading to the Fetterman Massacre. In Nov 1868, Red Cloud signed the Treaty of Fort Laramie, in which a promise of peace was exchanged for the removal of U.S. forts from the Powder River area.

According to correspondence dated 30 Jun 1950 and contained in the file on the film in the MPAA/PCA Collection at the AMPAS Library, Universal executives promoted their project as one which would "contribute greatly to the program of the Association on American Indian Affairs." While *Tomahawk* received mixed reviews, critics did take note of its sympathetic portrayal of the Sioux, with *MPD* praising the film for "present[ing] the Indian in a mature and intelligent perspective." Location shooting for *Tomahawk* was done near Rapid City, South Dakota. A modern source adds the following actors to the cast: Chief American Horse, Chief Bad Bear and Regis Toomey in the role of "Smith."

Box 13 Jan 1951. *DV* 8 Jan 1951. *Exb* 17 Jan 1951, p. 3011. *FD* 8 Jan 1951, p. 6. *Har* 13 Jan 1951, p. 7. *HR* 8 Jan 1951, p. 3. *MPD* 8 Jan 1951. *MPHPD* 13 Jan 1951, p. 662. *NYT* 19 Feb 1951, p. 19. *Var* 10 Jan 1951, p. 13.

TOMAHAWK TRAIL (Native Americans, Apache)
Bel-Air Productions. *Dist* United Artists Corp. Feb **1957**; Prod: mid-May—early Jun 1956 [©Sunrise Pictures, Inc.; 21 Dec 1956; LP7626]. Sd (Western Electric Recording). b&w. 60-61 min.

Exec prod Aubrey Schenck. *Prod* Howard W. Koch. *Dir* Lesley Selander. *Asst dir* Paul Wurtzel. *Story* Gerald Drayson Adams. *Scr* David Chandler. *Photog* William Margulies. *Operations cam* Ben Colman. *Photog eff* Jack Rabin and Louis DeWitt. *Prod des* Jack T. Collis. *Supv ed* John F. Schreyer. *Ed* John A. Bushelman. *Mus ed* Sam Waxman. *Set dec* Clarence Steenson. *Property master* Arden Cripe.

Ward Wesley V. Jeffries and Angela Alexander. *Mus* Les Baxter. *Sd mixer* Joe Edmondson. *Re-rec* Charles Cooper. *Rec* Sound Services Inc. *Makeup artist* Ted Coodley. *Hairstyles* Mary Westmoreland. *Key grip* Herschel Brown. *Lighting tech* Robert J. Campbell.

Cast: Chuck Connors [(*Sgt. Wade McCoy*)], John Smith [(*Pvt. Reynolds*)], Susan Cummings [(*Ellen Carter*)], Lisa Montell [(*Tula*)], George Neise [(*Lt. Jonathan Davenport*)], Robert Knapp [(*Pvt. Barrow*)], Eddie Little [(*Johnny Dogwood*)], Frederick Ford [(*Pvt. Macy*)], Dean Stanton [(*Pvt. Miller*)].

Western. [*Print viewed*]. During a U.S. Cavalry patrol mission to Ft. Bowie, Lt. Jonathan Davenport, the newly appointed West Point-trained commander of the troop, clashes with his second-in-command, Sgt. Wade McCoy, a seasoned veteran of the "tomahawk trail." Davenport, ignorant of the ways of the West, cloaks his weakness with a mask of arrogance and contempt. Due to Davenport's misjudgment, the platoon loses its ammunition and supply wagons during an attack by the Apache Indians. That night, the Indians return and steal the troop's horses, forcing the men to proceed on foot through the desert to Ft. Bowie. The men resent Davenport's incompetence and his condescending attitude, and tensions mount when Davenport accuses McCoy of cowardice because of his constant criticisms. Suffering from sunstroke, Davenport then collapses. Aroused by the sound of rifle fire in the distance, signaling that Fort Bowie is under attack, Davenport orders his men to shoot on sight, despite McCoy's protests. Continuing on, the troop is drawn into a skirmish with a band of Indians, and after driving off the braves, they capture two young women. One is Ellen Carter, the daughter of the commander of Fort Defiance, who was taken prisoner by the Indians after a massacre at the fort. The other is Tula, the daughter of Victorio, the chief of the Apaches. When Davenport, raving from the heat, accuses Ellen of being an Apache squaw and orders both women bound, McCoy rebels and assumes command. That night, Pvt. Barrow, one of the enlistees, attacks Tula, and the sergeant comes to her aid, thus earning Barrow's enmity. Throughout the assault, Tula remains silent, having promised McCoy that she would not cry out and alert the Indians. On the trek back to the fort, Davenport begins to regain his equilibrium, causing McCoy to fear a court-martial, but McCoy's friend, Pvt. Reynolds, assures him that he has done the right thing. Upon reaching Ft. Bowie, the patrol discovers that the garrison has been massacred. Davenport, raving once again, addresses the dead commander and then collapses, and Miller, his orderly, blames McCoy for his superior's condition. After first issuing orders to continue to Fort Benson, McCoy decides to stay and secure the fort. That night, as Apache drums drone in the distance, Barrow assaults Ellen and she kills him while protecting herself. Later, Ellen confides to Tula that she has fallen in love with McCoy and implores her to plead with her father to end the warfare. Soon after, a band of Indians attack and fell Davenport with an arrow. After McCoy and his men drive off the first wave of Indians, Johnny Dogwood, the troop's scout, listens to the drums and warns that the braves have told Victorio that Tula has defected to the white man. Tula decides to risk her life to meet with her father. As soon as she climbs the fort wall, she is captured by two braves, who take her to Victorio. After hugging his daughter, Victorio calls off the attack and the Indians ride away. Miller then promises to support McCoy at the inquiry, and Ellen and McCoy embrace in relief. *Apache Indians. Massacres. Officers (Military). Romance. United States. Army. Cavalry. Attempted rape. Easterners. Fathers and daughters. Forts. Insanity. Prisoners. Raids. Scouts (Frontier). Tribal chiefs.*

Note: The working title of this film was *Mark of the Apache*. Although the *FD* review credits Robert Parry as director, Lesley Selander is credited in onscreen credits and in all other sources.

Box 12 Jan 1957. *DV* 26 Dec 1956, p. 3. *Exb* 26 Dec 1956, p. 4270. *FD* 3 Jan 1957, p. 5. *Har* 29 Dec 1956, p. 208. *HR* 1 Jun 1956, p. 11. *HR* 26 Dec 1956, p. 3. *MPHPD* 5 Jan 1957, p. 210. *Var* 2 Jan 1957, p. 16.

TOMORROW THE WORLD! (German Americans, Jewish Americans)

Lester Cowan Productions, Inc. *Dist* United Artists Corp. 29 Dec 1944; Prod: 19 Jun–3 Aug 1944 [©Lester Cowan Productions, Inc.; 29 Dec 1944; LP13177]. Sd; b&w. 7,797 ft. 86 min. PCA cert no. 10491.

Assoc prod David Hall. [*Prod* Lester Cowan]. *Dir* Leslie Fenton. *Asst dir* Joseph Lefert. [*Dial dir* Leon Charles]. *Scr* Ring Lardner, Jr. and Leopold Atlas. *Dir of photog* Henry Sharp. [*Still photog* Ned Scott].

Art dir James Sullivan. *Film ed* Anne Bauchens. *Set dec* Edward G. Boyle. *Cost* Odette Myrtil. *Mus score* Louis Applebaum. *Mus dir* Ann Ronell. *Mixer* Max Hutchinson. *Makeup artist* Ern Westmore. *Prod mgr* Ray Heinz. [*Pub* Lou Smith and Ralph A. Houston].

Source: Based on the play *Tomorrow the World* by James Gow and Arnaud D'Usseau (New York, 14 Apr 1943).

Cast: FREDRIC MARCH [(*Mike Frame*)], BETTY FIELD [(*Leona Richards*)], Agnes Moorehead [(*Jessie Frame*)], Joan Carroll [(*Pat Frame*)], Edit Angold (*Frieda*), and introducing Skippy Homeier in his prize winning role from the Theron Baumberger Broadway Production [(*Emil Bruckner*)], [Rudy Wissler (*Stan*)], [Boots Brown (*Ray*)], [Marvin Davis (*Dennis*)], [Patsy Ann Thompson (*Millie*)], [Mary Newton (*School principal*)], [Tom Fadden (*Mailman*)].

Social, Drama. [*Print viewed*]. The household of widower Mike Frame, a chemistry instructor at a Midwest university who is also engaged in secret war work, is anxiously awaiting the arrival of Emil Bruckner, the twelve-year-old son of Mike's late sister, who married and lived in Germany with the great German liberal leader Karl Bruckner. Both Bruckner and his wife perished in a German concentration camp, and consequently, Emil, now orphaned, is being sent to live with his American uncle. Mike's daughter Pat eagerly anticipates the arrival of her cousin, while Mike's spinster sister Jessie, an ardent anti-Nazi, disapproves of the boy joining their household. Frieda, their German housekeeper, is happy to welcome her fellow countryman, and Leona Richards, a Jewish schoolteacher and Mike's sweetheart, is warmly supportive of Mike's decision to accept him. When Emil fails to arrive on the train, Pat and Frieda become worried. Having just proposed to Leona, Mike invites her home for lunch, and soon after they arrive, Emil appears and calmly announces that he has come by plane. The extremely formal boy is suspicious of his new family's friendliness and voices a loathing for his father, who has once Mike's teacher. Thunderstruck upon discovering that Leona is Jewish, Emil makes an antisemitic remark and then goes to his room. After he leaves, Mike and Leona discuss getting married, even though their marriage would mean that Leona must refuse a lucrative offer from a Chicago school. In his room, Emil changes into his Hitler Youth uniform and later savagely attacks Frieda when she rejects his attempt to recruit her to the Nazi cause. Terrified by the boy's aggressiveness, Frieda calls for help, causing Leona and Mike to have a serious talk with the boy. After answering their questions with Nazi stock answers, Emil accuses his father of being a traitor because the liberals caused Germany to lose the war in 1918. After Mike and Leona leave the room, Emil viciously slashes the portrait of his father that is hanging on the wall. At school, Emil is assigned to Pat's class, which is being taught by Leona. With his arrogance and intolerance, Emil quickly engenders the hate of his classmates. Upon learning of Mike's impending marriage, Emil launches a campaign to divide the family and manipulates Jessie into feeling that Leona is breaking up her home. When Emil gets into a fight with Stan, a boy of Polish descent, Millie, a classmate whose American father is being held prisoner in a German camp, testifies that Stan attacked Emil. Later, Millie confesses that Emil threatened to write to Germany and have her father executed unless she testified for him. Forced to apologize before the class, Emil screams that he is being persecuted and, after running out of the classroom, he uses a piece of chalk to scrawl on the sidewalk that Leona is a "Jewish tramp." Emil then runs home and shrewdly apologizes to Mike. When Leona demands that Emil be punished for his actions, Mike, who believes Emil's insincere apology, defends the boy, causing Leona to break their engagement and accept the job in Chicago. Soon after, Pat catches Emil rifling Mike's desk in search of secret papers from the War Department, and when she threatens to tell Mike, Emil attacks her with a poker. When Pat is discovered unconscious, Emil flees and Mike sends the police after him. The incident brings Leona back to the house and she reconciles with Mike and Jessie. Stan and several of Pat's friends chase Emil, and after Stan thrashes him, the boys take him back to the house. Insane with rage, Mike almost chokes the boy to death before Leona stops him. After sending Mike out of the room, Leona talks to the boy and finds him subtly changed. When Emil discovers that Pat has borrowed a year's advance on her allowance to buy him a watch for his birthday, he breaks down and cries. Mike calls the police to take Emil away, but Pat, now conscious, and Leona urge him to give the boy another chance. When Emil stammers that he now realizes that his father was a brave man and recalls the beatings he

suffered at the hands of the Nazis, Mike understands that the boy has been an innocent victim of the Nazis and allows him to stay. *Antisemitism. Children. Family relationships. Germans. Nazis. Transformation. Aunts. Cousins. Engagements. Fathers and daughters. Housekeepers. Jews. Maids. Nephews. Orphans. Spinsters. Teachers. Widowers.*

Note: News items in *HR* yield the following information about this production: Producer Lester Cowan bought the rights to James Gow and Arnaud D'Usseau's stage play for $75,000 plus 25% of the gross, not to exceed a total of $350,000. Cowan initially considered Elliott Nugent and Leo McCarey to direct the film, and playwright Victor Wilson was first hired to write the screenplay. The contributions of Wilson to the completed film, if any, have not been confirmed. In May and Jun 1944, Cowan wanted to cast "Quiz Kid" Ruth Duskin as "Pat" and tested Scotty Beckett and Claude Binyon for the role of "Emil." Skippy Homeier, who was finally cast as "Emil," also played the role on Broadway. This marked Homeier's screen debut. Edit Angold also appeared as "Frieda" in the Broadway production. Although Jul 1944 news items add Voyt Williams, Frances Norris, Ruth Warren, Fred Chapman and Ralph Hoops to the cast, their participation in the released film has not been confirmed.

In Aug 1944, Cowan announced that he was changing the title of the film to *The Intruder*, initiating protests from Gow and D'Usseau. Cowan decided to retain the original title *Tomorrow the World* after a group of exhibitors voted in favor of that title. The picture was awarded the first "Writer's Award" by the Hollywood Writer's Mobilization, a group of radio and screenwriters who contributed their part-time services to the Office of War Information. The honor was awarded "in recognition of [the film's] superior merit as dramatic entertainment, blended with timely and significant idea content, representative of the best in current thought." Certain screenings of the film were followed by "town meetings" featuring a general audience discussion of the issues.

Box 23 Dec 1944. *DV* 15 Dec 1944, p. 3. *FD* 18 Dec 1944, p. 8. *HR* 1 Nov 1943. *HR* 20 Dec 1943, p. 1. *HR* 20 Jan 1944, p. 3. *HR* 4 May 1944, p. 3. *HR* 1 Jun 1944, p. 12. *HR* 5 Jun 1944, p. 8. *HR* 12 Jun 1944, p. 2. *HR* 14 Jun 1944, p. 4. *HR* 16 Jun 1944, p. 3, 10. *HR* 3 Jul 1944, p. 3. *HR* 27 Jul 1944, p. 13. *HR* 28 Jul 1944, p. 13. *HR* 18 Aug 1944, p. 4. *HR* 29 Aug 1944, p. 4. *HR* 31 Aug 1944, p. 3. *HR* 13 Nov 1944, p. 10. *HR* 15 Dec 1944, p. 3. *HR* 27 Dec 1944, p. 14. *MPHPD* 22 Jul 1944, p. 2007. *MPHPD* 23 Dec 1944, p. 2237. *NYT* 22 Dec 1944, p. 12. *Var* 20 Dec 1944, p. 8.

THE TONG MAN (Chinese Americans)

Haworth Pictures Corp. *Dist* Robertson-Cole Co. through Exhibitors Mutual Distributing Corp. 14 Dec 1919 [©The Haworth Pictures Corp.; 26 Nov 1919; LU14478]. Si; b&w. 5 reels, 4,975 ft.

Dir William Worthington. *Scen* Richard Schayer. *Cam* Frank D. Williams. *Art dir* Milton Menasco.

Source: Based on the novel *The Dragon's Daughter* by Clyde C. Westover (New York, 1912).

Cast: Sessue Hayakawa (*Luk Chan*), Helen Jerome Eddy (*Sen Chee*), Marc Robbins (*Ming Tai*), Toyo Fujita (*Louie Toy*), Jack Abbe (*Lucero*).

Drama. San Francisco "hatchet man" Luk Chan is in love with Sen Chee, the daughter of Louie Toy, a merchant who has become wealthy from a traffic in opium. Ming Tai, who rules the powerful Chinatown secret society Bo Sing Tong, desires Sen Chee and her father's fortune. When Louie Toy refuses to pay protection money to the Bo Sing Tong, Ming Tai arranges to have Louie Toy killed, and Luk Chan, the most feared assassin of the Tong, is chosen to carry out the crime. Luk Chan lures Louie Toy to a den, but after raising the hatchet, cannot carry out the deed. When Ming Tai is informed of the failure of the execution, he sends an assassin to kill Luk Chan. Ming Tai kills Louie Toy and then notifies the police that Luk Chan is responsible. Lucero, Louie Toy's faithful friend, informs Luk Chan that Ming Tai has captured Sen Chee. Luk Chan jumps through a skylight, and he and Lucero rescue Sen Chee. Ming Tai pursues and corners Luk Chan and Sen Chee, but Lucero arrives in time to kill Ming Tai, and the lovers and Lucero board a ship bound for China. *Chinese Americans. Drug dealers. Hired killers. San Francisco (CA)-Chinatown. Tongs (Secret societies). Assassination. False accusations. Fathers and daughters. Jumps from heights. Opium. Rescues. Ships.*

Note: The Chinese government and various Asian-American associations objected to the film's depiction of the Chinese, and the film's exhibition was impeded or prevented in several communities.

ETR 20 Dec 1919, p. 275. *MPN* 20 Dec 1919, p. 4533. *MPW* 20 Dec 1919, p. 1009. *Var* 19 Dec 1919, p. 44. *Wid's* 14 Dec 1919, p. 15.

TONGUES OF FLAME (Native Americans)

Bluebird Photoplays, Inc. *Dist* Bluebird Photoplays, Inc. 2 Dec 1918 [©Bluebird Photoplays, Inc.; 25 Nov 1918; LP13078]. Si; b&w. 5 reels.

Dir Colin Campbell. *Scen* Lanier Bartlett.

Source: Based on the short story "In the Carquinez Wood" by Bret Harte in his *In the Carquinez Woods and Other Tales* (London, 1883).

Cast: Marie Walcamp (*Teresa*), Al Whitman (*L'Eau Dormant*), Alfred Allen (*Sheriff Dunn*), Hugh Sutherland (*Jack Brace*), J. P. Wilde (*Rev. Wynn*), Lilly Clarke (*Nellie Wynn*).

Western. Teresa, a dance hall girl who stabbed her lover in a quarrel, escapes from Sheriff Dunn and his deputy and wanders into the redwood forest of Carquinez, California. She is assisted by L'Eau Dormant, an educated half-breed Indian who lives in a hollow tree trunk and with whom she soon falls in love. Dormant imagines himself in love with Nellie Wynn, the preacher's daughter, who flirts with him merely because he is different. When Sheriff Dunn, who also loves Nellie, learns that she and Dormant often meet in the forest, he hurries into the woods in a jealous rage. Teresa rushes to Dormant's tree to warn him, but because the young man discovered that Dunn is his father, he refuses to fight him. Just as the three confront one another, a fire sweeps through the woods, killing them all. *California. Dance hall girls. Forest fires. Indians of North America. Indians of North America–Mixed blood. Parentage. Redwood forests. Sheriffs. Clergy. Fights. Jealousy. Murder. Trees.*

Note: The pre-release title of this film was *In the Carquinez Woods.* Some sources give a release date of 25 Nov 1918. According to *Var*, Dormant rescues Teresa from the forest fire. Fine Arts Film Co. produced a film based on the same source in 1916 entitled *The Half-Breed* (see above).

MPN 9 Nov 1918, p. 2889. *MPN* 16 Nov 1918, p. 2988. *MPW* 18 Jan 1919, p. 390. *Var* 20 Dec 1918, p. 37.

TONGUES OF FLAME (Native Americans, Siwash)

Famous Players-Lasky Corp. *Dist* Paramount Pictures. 15 Dec 1924 [©Famous Players-Lasky Corp.; 17 Dec 1924; LP20920]. Si; b&w. 7 reels, 6,763 ft.

Pres Adolph Zukor and Jesse L. Lasky. *Dir* Joseph Henabery. *Scr* Townsend Martin. *Photog* Faxon M. Dean.

Source: Based on the novel *Tongues of Flame* by Peter Clark MacFarlane (New York, 1924).

Cast: Thomas Meighan (*Henry Harrington*), Bessie Love (*Lahleet*), Eileen Percy (*Billie Boland*), Berton Churchill (*Boland*), John Miltern (*Scanlon*), Leslie Stowe (*Hornblower*), Nick Thompson (*Adam John*), Jerry Devine (*Mickey*), Kate Mayhew (*Mrs. Vickers*), Cyril Ring (*Clayton*).

Melodrama. The town of Edgewater, built on land formerly belonging to "Siwash" Indians, owes its prosperity to its wealthy developer, Boland. When he attempts to buy the remainder of the Siwash Reservation, the Indians, led by Lahleet, their beautiful schoolteacher, are distrustful, and Boland refers them to Henry Harrington, a respected young lawyer under whose command some of their number served in the Great War. Harrington advises them to accept Boland's generous offer and draws up the necessary papers. After the sale, Boland sinks oil wells on the land; angered at this duplicity and fraud, Harrington exposes him as a common swindler. Boland then has Harrington jailed on a false charge of robbery. Meanwhile, an action instituted by Hornblower, a shyster, on the Indians' behalf results in a court decision awarding the tribe the entire town of Edgewater, owing to irregularities in Boland's original surveys. The townspeople, angered at Boland, set fire to his properties. Released from jail when the fires burn out of control, Harrington organizes the Indians and saves the town. The Indians get back their reservation and return Edgewater to its grateful citizens. Harrington declares his love for Lahleet. *Fires. Indians of North America. Land rights. Oil wells.*

FD 21 Dec 1924. *NYT* 16 Dec 1924, p. 28. *Var* 17 Dec 1924, p. 37. .

TONIGHT WE SING (Russian Americans, Jewish Americans)

Twentieth Century-Fox Film Corp. *Dist* Twentieth Century-Fox Film Corp. Apr **1953**; New York opening: 12 Feb 1953; Prod: 18 Apr—12 Jun 1952 [©Twentieth Century-Fox Film Corp.; 12 Feb 1953; LP2620]. Sd (Western Electric Recording); col (Technicolor). 12 reels, 9,831 or 10,149 ft. 109 or 113 min. PCA cert no. 15936.

Prod George Jessel. *Dir* "Mitele" Leisen. *Asst dir* Arthur Lueker. *Scr* Harry Kurnitz and George Oppenheimer. *Dir of photog* Leon Shamroy. *Spec photog eff* Ray Kellogg. *Technicolor color consultant* Leonard Doss. *Art dir* Lyle Wheeler and George W. Davis. *Film ed* Dorothy Spencer. *Set dec* Thomas Little and Walter M. Scott. *Ward dir* Charles LeMaire. *Cost des* Renie. *Mus dir* Alfred Newman. [*Spec asst to mus dir* Edward Rebner]. *Choral dir* Ken Darby. *Ballet choreographed by* David Lichine. *Sd* Winston Leverett and Murray Spivack. *Makeup artist* Ben Nye. *Tech adv* Sol Hurok, Armando Agnini and Sergei Malavsky. [*Publ* Harry Bland]. *Singing voice double for Byron Palmer* Jan Peerce.

Music: "Autumn Leaves," by Frédéric Chopin; "Schoen Rosmarin," by Fritz Kreisler; "The Swan," by Camille Saint-Saëns; Violin Concerto No. 2, by Henryk Wieniawski; "Valse Caprice," by Anton Rubinstein; "Mattinata," by Ruggiero Leoncavallo; "Zigeunerweisen," by Pablo Martín Meliton Sarasate y Navascuez; Violin Concerto by Felix Mendelssohn.

Song(s): "Moonlight" and "The Volga Boatman," Russian folk songs; "Sweet and Low," by Joseph Barnby; "Menuetto," by Franz Schubert; "Pas De Deux," by Léon Mincus; Excerpts from the operas: *Madame Butterfly* by Giacomo Puccini; *Boris Godunov* by Modest Moussorgsky; *La Traviata* by Giuseppe Verdi; *Faust* by Charles Gounod.

Source: Based on the book *Impresario* by Sol Horuk and Ruth Goode (New York, 1946).

Cast: David Wayne (*S. Hurok*), Ezio Pinza (*Feodor Chaliapin*), Roberta Peters (*Elsa Valdine*), Tamara Toumanova (*Anna Pavlova*), Anne Bancroft (*Emma Hurok*), Isaac Stern (*Eugene Ysaye*), Byron Palmer (*Gregory Lawrence*), and The Voice of Jan Peerce [(*Singing voice of Gregory Lawrence*)], Oscar Karlweis [(*Benjamin Golder*)], Mikhail Rasumny [(*Nicolai*)], Steven Geray [(*Prager*)], Walter Woolf King [(*Gritti*)], [Serge Perrault (*Allbrecht*)], [John Meek (*Sol Hurok, age 10*)], [Eda Reis Merin (*Mrs. Golder*)], [Russell Cantor (*Eddie Golder*)], [Alexander Zakin (*Eugene Ysaye's accompanist*)], [Alex Steinart (*Conductor*)], [Oscar Beregi (*Dr. Markoff*)], [Leo Mostovoy (*Petlukoff*)], [Ray Largay (*Charles Dillingham*)], [Clemence Gifford (*Mme. Schumann-Heink*)], [Jeanne Determann (*Mme. Butterfly*)], [Wolfgang Fraenkel (*Jules Massenet*)], [Judith Bland (*Cellist in Paris*)], [Lela Bliss (*Mrs. Granek*)], [Harry Hayden (*Mr. Granek*)], [Les O'Pace (*Stage manager*)], [Ann Ware (*Pianist at Settlement House*)], [Bertha Rosemond (*Singer*)], [Tamara Shayne (*Customer*)], [Clinton Rosemond (*Father*)], [Peter Camlin (*Hotel manager*)], [Roy Regnier (*Doorman*)], [Zoia Karabanova (*Anna Pavlova's maid*)], [Isabel Withers (*Maid*)], [Rudy Rama (*Janitor*)], [Pedro Regas (*Greek*)], [James Adamson, Dudley Dickerson (*Porters*)], [Gregg Martell (*Guard*)], [Leslie Denison, Maurice Marsac, Victor Desny (*Aides*)], [Nelson Welch (*Butler*)], [Sergei Malavsky (*Russian*)], [Dolores Mann (*Secretary*)], [Joan Arnold (*Ballerina*)], [Camillo Guercio (*Doctor*)], [Ben Astar, Lester Sharpe, John Diggs, Wilson Millar, George E. Stone (*Impresari*)].

Biography, Musical. [*Print viewed*]. In 1895, in the village of Pogar in the Ukraine, young Solomon Solomonavich Hurok is told by his music teacher that he lacks talent. Fifteen years later, in the winter in St. Petersburg, Sol is reprimanded by his boss at a hardware store for leading a choral group in the backroom. He goes that night with his fiancée Emma to see Feodor Chaliapin in Moussorgsky's *Boris Godunov* and they are enthralled. At the opera's conclusion, Sol reveals to Emma that he has quit his job. Inspired by Chaliapin's performance, Sol goes to his dressing room, where he overhears Chaliapin's manager talk the singer out of doing an American tour. Sol wins Chaliapin's favor by encouraging him to go to the U.S. and convinces him to let him manage the tour. Sol tells Emma he must leave for America immediately and says he will send for her as soon as he arranges Chaliapin's first concert. In New York, Sol boards with Ben Golder, a Jewish jeweler, and his family, and becomes a trolley car conductor, while Chaliapin fails to answer some seventy letters. Sol arranges a pupils' recital at the Bronx Settlement House and becomes impressed that so many working people in the audience appreciate the music so much. He dreams of finding a way to bring the best in opera, ballet and music to such an audience. Emma soon arrives and the two marry in Golder's store. As a present, Golder gives them tickets to the Hippodrome, where, following an elephant act, they see a magnificent performance of Saint-Saëns' *The Swan* by the ballerina Anna Pavlova. Entranced, Sol goes backstage, where he connives his way into seeing the dancer. He says he wants to assemble the greatest company in the history of ballet around her, but when he admits that he has no money, Pavlova has her maid push him out. He returns to Golder's store late to find Emma crying in bed behind a locked door, and though she castigates him for ruining their honeymoon, she soon opens the door and embraces him. Golder interrupts with a telegram from Chaliapin requesting that Sol come at once to his hotel in Paris. Sol tears up the telegram, telling his wife that he has given up his ambitions, but Emma insists that she loves him because of his dreams. In Paris, Sol learns, to his chagrin, that Chaliapin wired him only to win a bet. Chaliapin reimburses Sol for

the expense of the trip, then introduces Gregory Lawrence as his American protegé and has Gregory sing for Sol, who rips up Chaliapin's check and leaves in disgust. Gregory follows and confesses that he is not Chaliapin's pupil but a hotel doorman. Impressed with Sol's integrity, Gregory asks him to be his manager and Sol agrees. On the ship to America, Sol meets virtuoso violinist Eugene Ysaye and encourages him to play the Hippodrome, so that large working-class audiences can see him. Sol explains that many immigrants cannot come to Carnegie Hall or other high-class theaters because of shabby clothes, advertisements only in English, and advance sales requiring an extra trip uptown for tickets. Ysaye agrees it will be an honor to play for such an audience if Sol will handle the booking. Following Ysaye's success, Sol presents many artists at the Hippodrome, including Madame Luisa Tetrazzini, Isadora Duncan, Madame Ernestine Schumann-Heink, and Gregory Lawrence in Puccini's *Madame Butterfly*. After the U.S. enters World War I, Sol presents shows to American troops in France. In Russia, when Chaliapin's hotel room is shot up, he orders Nikolai to write to Sol. At a gathering following the armistice, Sol announces that he and Emma will now take their long overdue honeymoon. When a phone call from the U.S. Immigration Office interrupts them, Sol realizes that Chaliapin has arrived, and Emma knows that their honeymoon is off again. Sol convinces Chaliapin to sign a ten-year contract, luring him with a description of the luxurious life at the Waldorf presidential suite. Chaliapin appears in Gounod's *Faust* and, to the chagrin of Golder, now in charge of financing, insists on extravagance in clothes, scenery and props. After the critics hail Chaliapin's success, Pavlova wires Sol that she wants to come under his management. Although Golder advises Sol to wait until the opera tour is over, Sol insists on creating a dance company to star her. Pavlova tours the country, but in San Francisco, one year later, on the evening of Sol and Emma's wedding anniversary, Emma is distraught when he shows her a beautiful jewelled pin in the shape of a swan that he bought for the dancer. He promises to come right back after giving Pavlova the pin, but becomes engrossed in her performance and forgets. When he returns late, he finds Emma gone and realizes he forgot their anniversary. When Chaliapin, in Boston with laryngitis, calls and insists that Sol come immediately, Sol refuses, saying he has lost something more important that Chaliapin's voice. After searching in vain all over the country, Sol returns to the opera company in Philadelphia, where they face bankruptcy as they prepare to open in New York. Signore Gritti, a rival impresario, has offered to buy Chaliapin's contract, but does not want the rest of the company, and Chaliapin accepts despite Sol's concerns for the others. Emma returns when she learns that Sol has lost the company and says that although he hurt her, she hurt herself more by staying away. Chaliapin interrupts their reunion, and when he blames the bankruptcy on Sol, Emma castigates Chaliapin. The singer then gives Sol a satchel of money and admits he has left Gritti because he realized Gritti has no taste. Chaliapin extols Sol for his friendship and allows him to call him "Feodor" just once. The opera company puts on a full season of grand opera at popular prices. At long last, Sol and Emma, in a horse and carriage, plan their honeymoon; however, they find that the driver has a beautiful voice, and Emma instructs her husband to do something about it. Sol replies, "Mrs. Hurok, I love you." Ambition. Sol Hurok. Immigrants. Impresarios. Marriage. Opera singers. Russian Americans. Ballet. Bankruptcy. *Boris Godunov* (Opera). Feodor Chaliapin. *Le Cigne* (Ballet). Deception. Charles Dillingham. Dismissal (Employment). Doormen. Elephants. *Faust* (Opera). Hardware stores. Hippodrome (New York City). Honeymoons. Jewelers. Jews. Maids. Music teachers. New York City. New York City–Bronx. Ocean liners. Paris (France). Anna Pavlova. Recitals. Reconciliation. Separation (Marital). St. Petersburg (Russia). Ukraine. Wagers. Wedding anniversaries. Weddings. World War I. Eugène Ysaye.

Note: "Mitele" Leisen is the name used by director Mitchell Leisen in the onscreen credits. Studio publicity for this film states that Sol Hurok introduced more great European concert artists to the U.S. and more American artists to the rest of the world than any other person in this century. According to the publicity, in 1945, producer George Jessel read galley proofs of Hurok's autobiography, written with Ruth Goode, which was used for the basis of the script. The publicity states that the film "makes no pretense of portraying Hurok's life story." In conference notes concerning a draft of a script, located in the Twentieth Century-Fox Produced Scripts Collection at the UCLA Arts—Special Collections Library, studio production head Darryl Zanuck stated, "We must remember that a great part of our audience will never have heard of Hurok, and thus it won't do us a bit of good to stick to the facts of his life if they

are not presented in an entertaining manner." Publicity for the film states, "Hurok feels it conveys the essence of his rise from a poverty-stricken, music-struck Russian immigrant to his present preeminence as a concert star-maker." Scenes depicting Hurok's bombardment of Feodor Chaliapin with letters and his persuasion of Anna Pavlova to star in her own company were based in fact, according to publicity.

It was Zanuck's idea, according to a 16 Nov 1945 letter by Gregory Ratoff in the Produced Scripts Collection, to characterize Hurok "as a man who is madly in love with art of any kind, who loves music as life itself, who cannot live without it but has no talent and can only express himself as an artist by associating himself with the greatest." Ratoff was involved with Jessel in early plans to produce the film. Ratoff's letter also reveals that Zanuck suggested including a sequence in which Hurok discovers African-American singer Marian Anderson performing in an empty concert hall in Paris and then fights for the right to put her in a place like Carnegie Hall. Ratoff wrote, "Here we can put in Hurok's mouth words of freedom and equality in the world of music and art, etc., etc." (In 1939, Anderson was not allowed to sing at Constitution Hall in Washington, D.C. by the Hall's owners, the Daughters of the American Revolution; subsequently, Eleanor Roosevelt arranged a concert featuring Anderson on the steps of the Lincoln Memorial.)

In 1946, treatments and scripts were written for this project by Eugenie Leontovich and George S. George under the titles *Heaven for Sale* and *Stars in My Pocket*. Other suggested titles during this period were "Symphony," "Sing for Me" and "The New World Symphony." It is not known whether any of Leontovich and George's work was used in the final film. In a *NYT* article, Jessel stated that the project was dormant until the success of *The Great Caruso*, another music biography, in 1951 (see above). Titles suggested by Harry Kurnitz in his script of 1951 were *The Music Maker* and *The Music Master*. The title *Tonight We Sing* was used in Feb 1951 as the title of a proposed RKO musical. It was first used for this project in Nov 1951.

Danny Thomas and Jose Ferrer were considered in 1951 for the role of Hurok. Zanuck, in conference notes, stated, "Danny Thomas may not be the best actor in the world, but he has a kind of appealing, pleading quality which might do just as well." According to information in the Produced Scripts Collection and in the MPAA/PCA Collection at the AMPAS Library, Jean Negulesco was originally assigned to direct. Mitchell Leisen's name as director first appears on material dated 22 Apr 1952. In Leisen's biography, he stated that Oscar Karlweis, who ultimately played the role of Golder, was originally scheduled to play Hurok, but Hurok wanted an actor more handsome and famous than Karlweis. According to publicity, Leisen designed the jewelled swan pin used in the film.

According to publicity, Armando Agnini, who was the technical director for all the operatic sequences, had previously been the stage manager of the Metropolitan Opera for fifteen years and had been with the San Francisco Opera for thirty-five years. Pianist-conductor Sergei Malavsky was the technical adviser for the Russian operatic scenes. Dancer and choreographer David Lichine had been Anna Pavlova's dance partner. Composer, conductor and pianist Edward Rebner, the special assistant to music director Alfred Newman, had once been Ezio Pinza's concert accompanist. Isaac Stern's own accompanist, Alexander Zakin, played the accompanist to Stern's character, Eugene Ysaye. Stern played on his own 250-year-old Guarnerius violin in the film. According to a *NYT* article, Stern's role was originally conceived with Artur Rubinstein in mind to play himself. Serge Perrault, who played Pavlova's dance partner, was from the Paris Opera Ballet. Roberta Peters, who debuted at the Metropolitan Opera on 17 Nov 1951, was their youngest soprano. Pinza, Stern, Peters, Tamara Toumanova and Jan Peerce all had been under Hurok's management.

According to PCA material and a *NYT* pre-release article, the character of Hurok is Jewish; however, this is not explicitly mentioned in the final film. Leisen, in his biography, stated that a proposed ballet sequence for Pavlova was not filmed because of a disagreement between him and Zanuck, and the "Autumn Leaves" ballet sequence was cut in the editing room by Zanuck; shots from that sequence survive in the opening prologue to the film. Leisen also stated that sets were rented from the San Francisco Opera company.

Box 31 Jan 1953. *Cue* 14 Feb 1953. *DV* 5 Dec 1951. *DV* 26 Jan 1953, p. 3. *Down Beat* 25 Mar 1953, p. 5. *Exb* 28 Jan 1953, p. 3456. *FD* 26 Jan 1953, p. 7. *Har* 31 Jan 1953, p. 18. *HR* 18 Apr 1952, p. 4. *HR* 26 Jan 1953, p. 3. *LAEx* 11 Apr 1953. *LAT* 11 Apr 1953. *MPD* 26 Jan 1953. *MPHPD* 31 Jan 1953, p. 1701. *Newsweek* 23 Feb 1953. *NYT* 6 Jul 1952. *NYT* 13 Feb 1953, p. 17. *Time* 2 Mar 1953. *Var* 28 Jan 1953, p. 6.

TONIO, SON OF THE SIERRAS (Native Americans, Apache, Navajo, Latino)

Dist Davis Distributing Division. Dec **1925**. Si; b&w. 5 reels.

Dir Ben Wilson. *Photog* Alfred Gosden.

Source: Based on the novel *Tonio, Son of the Sierras; a Story of the Apache War* by General Charles King (New York, 1906).

Cast: Ben Wilson (*Lt. Booth*), Neva Gerber (*Miss Brower*), Chief Yowlache (*Tonio*), Jim Welch (*Colonel Brower*), Bob Walker (*Lt. Downs*), Ruth Royce, Fay Adams.

Western. [*Viewed print incomplete*]. Tonio, the son of a Navajo chief, is the Indian scout at Fort Almy. When the Apaches go on the warpath, he disappears from the fort. During a battle, Lieutenant Booth is wounded while he rescues the married daughter of the fort's commander, Colonel Brower. Booth and Lieutenant Downs are rivals for Colonel Brower's other daughter. After a stagecoach robbery and murder has occurred at Piney Point, Tonio, who has been accused by Downs of treachery, returns to the fort and, through a window,

observes Booth, who had defended Tonio, give Downs some money. After Downs leaves, Tonio follows him to a cabin and sees him plant Booth's kerchief near a a hidden bag that was taken during the stage holdup. The next day, Tonio brings his father, the Navajo chief, to meet the colonel, who arranges for the chief to have his warriors get ready for the fight against the Apaches. Later, Downs meets with a cohort, Sanchez, at a bar to give him the bag of coins. The paymaster for the district, who is drinking there, notices that the bag is a U.S. government pay sack. Downs says that Booth loaned him $300 to pay a debt he owes to Sanchez and that the money was in the bag when he gave it to him. Realizing that the bag was stolen from the stagecoach, the paymaster goes with Sanchez and Downs to the fort to report to Colonel Brower. At the fort, Downs asks Miss Brower if she will go riding with him that afternoon, and she agrees, if Booth does not return by then. Believing Booth to be above suspicion, Colonel Brower vows to personally investigate and returns the money to the paymaster. Sanchez rides off, after inviting Downs to bring Miss Brower for a visit that afternoon. Downs then tells the colonel that he followed Tonio to the cabin, where he found the stolen money. The colonel asks Downs to take him there. Meanwhile, Tonio sends Booth a smoke signal, and when he arrives, relates that he followed Downs to the cabin, where he opened a box and took a sack of gold away. Hoping he is wrong, Booth follows Tonio to the cabin. The colonel and Downs arrive first, and the colonel recognizes the kerchief as belonging to Booth. Downs says he distrusted Booth all along. When Tonio and Booth arrive, the colonel arrests Booth and Tonio for murder and the holdup at Piney Point. They are imprisoned at the fort, and a guard sadistically has Booth watch Downs ride off with Miss Brower. Booth asks the guard to give a note to Miss Brower, and when the guard takes it, Booth grabs his rifle and keys through the bars. Tonio gets out and hits the guard over the head with the rifle, and they escape on horses. The colonel calls out his men to pursue them. Meanwhile, Sanchez commands some Apaches not to hurt "the white squaw," whom he says is for him, after they plan to attack Downs. Sanchez reveals that he now plans to enjoy both the money and the girl. Downs fights Sanchez, but an Apache hits him over the head with a rifle, then they ride off with Miss Brower and their horses. After seeing the Apaches riding with the colonel's daughter, the Navajo chief goes to his village and sends his braves with rifles to save her. Booth and Tonio come upon Downs, who says that Sanchez and "the red devils" have the girl. Booth and Tonio join the Navajos pursuing the Apaches, who have been instructed by Sanchez to bring the girl to his cabin. The colonel and his men find Downs unconscious and revive him, then set off to save his daughter. The cavalry reaches the Navajo and the chief coordinates his attack with them. As the Navajo fight the Apaches, Booth chases down and fights the Apache carrying Miss Brower and throws him from a high rock. She faints and Booth carries her off. Tonio knocks Sanchez off his horse and they fight. Sanchez draws his knife and in their struggle, he is stabbed. Tonio brings the mortally wounded man to the colonel, and Sanchez confesses that his Indians held up the stage, and tells that Downs found the strongbox and tried to frame Booth before dying. The colonel then confronts Downs and orders a subordinate to take him away. Booth carries Miss Brower to her father, and when she revives, the colonel gives Booth her hand. They embrace, as Tonio looks on. *Apache Indians. Fathers and daughters. Fathers and sons. Forts. Frame-ups. Latino. Officers (Military). Romantic rivalry. Scouts (Frontier). United States–History–Indian campaigns. Cabins. Jailbreaks. Murder. Rescues. Stagecoach robberies. Tribal chiefs.*

Note: The plot summary is based primarily on an incomplete print of the film, of which only reels 3-5 of 5 exist. Reviews suggests a number of plot points that were not in the print viewed.

FD 20 Dec 1925. *MPN* 19 Dec 1925, p. 3042.

TONKA (Native Americans, Dakota)

Walt Disney Productions. *Dist* Buena Vista Film Distribution Co. 25 Dec **1958**; Prod: 4 Jun–25 Jul 1958 [©Walt Disney Productions; 14 Nov 1958; LP13958]. Sd (RCA Sound Recording); col (Technicolor). 10 reels, 8,746 ft. 96-97 min. PCA cert no. 19127.

Pres WALT DISNEY. *Prod* James Pratt. *Dir* Lewis R. Foster. *Asst dir* Horace Hough. [*2d asst dir* Herb Hirst and Mickey McCardle]. *Scr* Lewis R. Foster and Lillie Hayward. *Dir of photog* Loyal Griggs. [*Cam op* Judd Curtis and Harry Underwood]. [*Asst cam* Dick Kelly, Bob McGowan and Robert Morrison]. [*Gaffer* John C. Bella]. [*Stills* Eddie Jones]. [*Spec eff* Clarence Burke, Max Luttenberg, Chuck Spurgeon

and Edwin Tillman]. *Art dir* Robert E. Smith. *Matte artist* Peter Ellenshaw. *Film ed* H. Ellsworth Hoagland. *Mus ed* Evelyn Kennedy. *Set dec* Emile Kuri and Oliver Emert. [*Painter* Harry Bogart, Eldon Hall and William Powky]. [*Drapery* Fred Price and Norman Smith]. [*Propmaker* Stuart Brown and Willard Marty]. [*Carpenter foreman* Marty Buryan]. [*Construction* Ellis Coleman]. *Cost* Chuck Keehne, Gertrude Casey, [Pat Cummings, Pat Kelly and Pete Saldutti]. *Mus* Oliver Wallace. *Orch* Clifford Vaughan. *Sd supv* Robert O. Cook. *Sd mixer* Harry M. Lindgren. [*Sd rec* Art Smith]. [*Boom man* Thomas Goldrick]. [*Cable man* Mal Rennings]. *Makeup* Pat McNalley. [*Makeup artist* Bill Wood]. *Hair stylist* Ruth Sandifer and [Hedvig Mjorud]. [*Prod mgr* John Grubbs]. [*Unit mgr* Russ Haverick]. [*Scr supv* Lois Thurman]. [*Key grip* Garrett Lambrecht]. [*Grip* Elmer Balogh, Henry Convertino, Robert Fleming, Erwin Jones, Frank Kauffman, Stanley Miller and Richard Sutton]. [*Best boy* Knox K. Kelly]. [*Property master* Lou Wildey]. [*Propman* Charles Chrisman and Jim Treanor]. [*Lamp op* Ivan Bauerle, Harold Hazelbush, James H. Murray and Samuel A. Wierman]. [*Horse trainer* Les Hilton and Jack Sanders]. [*Ramrod* Bill Jones]. [*Wrangler* L. E. Ballard, Joe Craigmaile, Ed Duarte, Alton Galbreith, Leroy Kennedy, Frank Sanders and Joe Lomax]. [*American Humane Association man* Paul Ridge]. [*Generator op* Jess Salais]. [*Laborer* Landis Davis]. [*Swing gang* Ted Deardorf]. [*Publ* John Ormonde]. [*Timekeeper* Charles Leist]. [*Loc auditor* Chuck Gabbert]. [*First aid man* Ken Gillmore]. [*Leadman* Elmer Grether]. [*Greensman* Clifford Shoir and Abe Siegal]. [*Driver capt.* Henry Thornsberry]. [*Stretchout driver* Dominic Battaglia]. [*Driver* Roy Benson, Ted De Moss, Cecil Moon, Joe Didier, Wilber Freese, Ed Goodman, Robert Kent, George Lucas, Roy Nelson, Nick Potskoff, John Williams, Cecil Wynn and Albert Zarro]. [*Craft service* Ed Meece, C. E. Sheehan, Jr. and Clarence Soper]. [*Stunt rider for Sal Mineo* Gene White]. [*Stunt double for Sal Mineo* Bob Finn]. [*Stand-in for Sal Mineo* Junior Bernard]. [*Stunts* Clyde "Acey" Hudkins and Red Morgan].

Song(s): "Tonka," lyrics by Gil George, music by George Bruns.

Source: Based on the novel *Comanche* by David Appel (Cleveland, 1951).

Cast: Sal Mineo [(*White Bull*)], Philip Carey [(*Captain Myles Keogh*)], Jerome Courtland [(*Lt. Henry Nowlan*)], H. M. Wynant [(*Yellow Bull*)], Joy Page [(*Prairie Flower*)], Britt Lomond [(*George Armstrong Custer*)], Rafael Campos [(*Strong Bear*)], Herbert Rudley [(*Captain Benteen*)], Sydney Smith [(*General Terry*)], John War Eagle [(*Sitting Bull*)], Gregg Martell [(*Cpl. Korn*)], Slim Pickens [(*Ace*)], Robert Buzz Henry [(*Lt. Crittenden*)], [Eddie Little Sky (*Spotted Tail*)], [Johnny Guerin, Harold Green, Chester Von Pelt (*Indians*)], [Leland Thompson (*Indian boy*)], [Al Wyatt (*Trooper*)], [Pat Castor, Claude Brennan, Alvin Grimes (*Officers*)], [Stan Frank (*Indian scout*)], [Ed Saluskin (*Scout*)], [Conrad Well (*Orderly*)], [W. C. Yeomans (*Kellogg*)], [George Bernier, Hugh Porter, Tom Bride, Rod Rosebrook, Walt Smead (*Ace's men*)], [Monroe Carlson (*Major Marcus A. Reno*)], [Alba Shawaway (*Scout for Custer/War dance drummer/Indian*)], [Chuck Fite, Wayne Houston, Harry Welch, Charles Biles, Robert Patrick, Bob Patterson, C. R. Yount, Leroy Ditmore, Jim Alderman, Karl Kleint, Red Reynolds, Frank Stoul, Jim Smith, Larry Baxter, Gard Safley (*Cavalrymen*)], [Dallas Quick, Clem Klink (*Dignitaries*)], [Peggy Jaques, Renee Jaques (*Pioneers*)], [Wallace Lee Hug, Levi Von Pelt (*Children*)], [Morton Remmels], [Nettie Shawaway], [Harry Miller], [Myrtle Brashear], [Lynn Burke], [Alma Armstrong], [Walter Schenck], [Armond Delmar], [Jack Dusick], [Bob Marx], [Gus Norin], [Roland Ray], [Glen Wright], [Jack Muhs], [O. Hensel], [Cliff Burdette], [Leroy Johnson].

Western. [*Print viewed*]. In the Montana Territory of 1876, two young braves, White Bull and his friend, Strong Bear, watch as their elders chase after a herd of wild horses. One horse in particular, a strong and swift stallion, catches their attention. White Bull, in an abortive attempt to capture this horse, loses his cousin Yellow Bull's prized rope. Back at the Indian village, White Bull's uncle, Sioux Chief Sitting Bull, is angry with him for not only losing the rope, but also for losing the quiver, bow and arrows that the chief gave him. He forbids White Bull from hunting until he has proven himself worthy of trust. The next morning when White Bull goes searching for the missing items, he captures the horse and names it Tonka Wakan, meaning "The Great One." After weeks of working with Tonka and gradually gaining his trust, White Bull returns to his people, who have fled to a new village to escape certain destruction by the U.S. Cavalry.

When Sitting Bull rewards White Bull for his courage, ingenuity and tenacity, Yellow Bull becomes envious and demands that Tonka be given to him. Regretfully, the chief concedes that it is Yellow Bull's right to have Tonka, given his senior status in the tribe. One night, White Bull, appalled at the way Yellow Bull has been treating Tonka, sets the horse free. Tonka is soon captured by some horse traders, who sell him to Captain Myles Keogh of the Cavalry. Appreciative of Tonka's speed, strength and beauty, Keogh takes pride in the horse and treats him with great care. Meanwhile, White Bull is sent on a mission with some other braves to find out how many soldiers threaten the Indians. While scouting Fort Lincoln, White Bull is relieved to discover Tonka safely residing in the fort's stable. When Keogh finds that White Bull was Tonka's owner, he praises him for training Tonka so gently and so well. After White Bull is questioned by General George Armstrong Custer, he is allowed to ride Tonka once before he is set free. Custer, expressing a great desire to massacre the Indians, begins to lay plans for the big attack. He does not realize that a legion of Indians, Sioux as well as many other tribes, are planning their own war against him. When the day of the assault arrives, Custer and his men are completely surprised as they are surrounded by continuing waves of Indians. As the bloody battle ensues, White Bull is beaten unconscious, while his good friend, Strong Bear, is killed during an attempt to save him. Custer, raging and defiant until the end, is shot through the head. After killing Keogh, Yellow Bull is trampled to death by Tonka before he can claim Keogh's scalp. White Bull eventually revives and is tending to Tonka when a group of soldiers appear. One of the soldiers, upon recognizing White Bull from Fort Lincoln, prevents his man from shooting the Indian. He takes both White Bull and Tonka back to the fort. On 10 April 1878, a proclamation is made recognizing Tonka as the only survivor of Custer's Last Stand and retiring him from further duty. Tonka is to reside at Fort Lincoln, living the remainder of his days in comfort and with the only person who will ever be able to ride him again, his exercise boy, White Bull. Adolescents. Cousins. General George Armstrong Custer. Dakota Indians. Horses. Little Big Horn, Battle of the, 1876. Manhood. Montana. Sitting Bull. Cruelty to animals. Envy. Fort Lincoln (NE). Horse trading. Officers (Military). Self-sacrifice. United States. Army. Cavalry.

Note: The working title of this film was *Comanche*. The pressbook for the film stated that this was "the first full-scale movie attempt to tell the battle story [of Custer's Last Stand] from the Indian viewpoint." For more information about Custer and the Battle of Little Big Horn, please see the entry above for *They Died With Their Boots On*. David Appel's novel was purchased by Disney in Oct 1956, according to news items, and in Apr 1958, as production was being planned, it had still not been decided whether it would be a feature-length theatrical film, or a two-part feature for the ABC television series *Disneyland*.

Fess Parker was originally scheduled for the role of "Captain Myles Keogh" and tested for the part on 27 May 1958, according to production reports at the Walt Disney Archives. Parker subsequently refused the second-billed role, however, and was placed on suspension, according to *Var*. Studio publicity states that over five hundred Indians were used as warriors in Sitting Bull's army, and two hundred and fifty residents of Bend and Madras, Oregon, were used as cavalry soldiers. According to the *San Francisco News*, the role of Sitting Bull was originally to have been played by an Indian actor named Blue Eagle, but after receiving the news that he had won the role, Blue Eagle died from a heart attack.

According to an article in the *Rapid City Daily Journal* included in a studio scrapbook, Disney chose Northern and Central Oregon locations for filming over locations scouted in South Dakota. Studio publicity adds the following information about Oregon location sites: the re-enactment of the Battle of Little Big Horn was shot at the Warm Springs Reservation; Custer's command headquarters was built near the town of Bend; and an Indian village was constructed on the Deschutes River. Shooting also took place at Madras, Oregon, according to production reports, and process shots were completed at M-G-M Studios.

Reviews generally praised the film, and a few applauded the studio for its concern with historical accuracy. The film was criticized, however, for evading issues concerning the causes of the Little Big Horn conflict. *HR* stated, "The re-enactment of the historic Indian fight is spectacular and exciting. And in one point, at least, it is accurate. A lone quartet of warriors did offer the first opposition to Custer's advancing column as it approached the Sioux encampment." *Var* commented that the film was "probably somewhat romantic in its view of the Sioux, but seeing the whole thing through Indian eyes, and the eyes of an Indian youth, at that, gives the story a fresh approach.... As with all Disney pictures, the research into such things as costumes and background is authentic and helpful." The *Christian Science Monitor* criticized the film for making "no attempt to explore the rights and wrongs of the situation between the redskins and whites in the 1870's." *NYT* noted that the film "rarely suggests the basic causes of Indian-white friction."

The film was telecast as *Comanche* in two parts, on 18 Feb and 25 Feb 1962, on *Walt Disney's Wonderful World of Color*. In 1977, the film was retitled *A Horse Called Comanche*, according to *LAT*.

Bend (OR) Bulletin 21 May 1958. *Bend (OR) Bulletin* 4 Jun 1958. *Bend (OR) Bulletin* 5 Jun 1958. *Bend (OR) Bulletin* 25 Jun 1958. *Bend (OR) Bulletin* 1 Jul 1958. *Bend (OR) Bulletin* 15 Jul 1958. *Bend (OR) Bulletin* 24 Jul 1958. *Bend (OR) Bulletin* 23 Oct 1958. *Bend (OR) Bulletin* 24 Jan 1959. *BHCN* 6 Jan 1959. *Box* 27 Oct 1956. *Box* 29 Dec 1958. *Capital Journal (Salem, OR)* 28 Jun 1958. *Central Oregonian* 24 Jul 1958. *Central Oregonian* 26 Jul 1958. *Christian Science Monitor* 30 Dec 1958. *Cue* 7 Mar 1959. *DV* 1 Apr 1958. *DV* 1 May 1958. *DV* 27 May 1958. *DV* 28 May 1958. *DV* 20 Jun 1958. *DV* 15 Jul 1958. *DV* 16 Dec 1958, p. 3. *Enterprise-Courier (Oregon City, OR)* 25 Jul 1958. *Eugene (OR) Register-Guard* 22 Jun 1958. *Exb* 24 Dec 1958, p. 4548. *FD* 16 Dec 1958, p. 6. *Har* 20 Dec 1958, p. 203. *HCN* 26 Dec 1958. *HR* 30 Apr 1958. *HR* 16 Dec 1958, p. 3. *LAEx* 23 Oct 1956. *LAT* 23 Jan 1977. *Madras (OR) Pioneer* 22 May 1958. *Madras (OR) Pioneer* 10 Jul 1958. *Madras (OR) Pioneer* 24 Jul 1958. *MPD* 22 Dec 1958. *MPHPD* 20 Dec 1958, p. 92. *Newsweek* 5 Jan 1959. *NYP* 1 Oct 1958. *NYT* 18 May 1958. *NYT* 26 Mar 1959, p. 27. *Oregon Journal* 17 Jul 1958. *Oregon Journal* 22 Jan 1959. *Oregon Journal* 2 May 1958. *The Oregonian* 25 May 1958. *The Oregonian* 22 Jun 1958. *The Oregonian* 2 Jul 1958. *Rapid City (SD) Daily Journal* 21 May 1958. *Redwood City, California Tribune* 9 Feb 1959 *San Francisco News* 26 May 1958. *Var* 17 Dec 1958, p. 6. *Yakima Morning Herald* 10 Jun 1958.

TONY AMERICA (Italian Americans)

Triangle Film Corp. *Dist* Triangle Distributing Corp. 6 Oct **1918**. Si; b&w. 5 reels.

Dir Thomas N. Heffron. *Scen* Doris Schroeder. *Story* Evelyn Campbell. *Cam* C. H. Wales.

Cast: Francis McDonald (*Tony America*), Yvonne Paris (*Rosa Picciano*), Rae Godfrey (*Mamie Dean*), Dorothy Giraci (*Giulia*), Mrs. Harry Davenport (*Mrs. Picciano*), Harold Holland (*Hans*), Ludwig Lowry (*Angelo*), Dick Loreno (*Vincenzio*).

Social, Drama. Lured to the United States by a greedy *padrone*, a young Italian arrives in New York and dubs himself "Tony America." Hoping to make his fortune, Tony becomes a fruit peddler, but because the *padrone* holds him in debt for his passage to America, he remains poor. In order to brighten his difficult existence, Tony marries Rosa Picciano, his landlady's daughter, unaware that the girl merely wishes to escape her strict mother. Soon after the birth of their daughter Giulia, Tony learns that Rosa has carried on an affair with a German butcher for several years, and later, she divorces him on an unjust charge. When Tony's friends scornfully suggest that the butcher fathered his baby, he nearly kills the German, but the sight of Giulia clutching the American flag stops him. Tony's friend, Marie Dean, promises to help him regain custody of Giulia, whom he dearly loves, and in the end, the two succeed in winning her back. *Child custody. Employer-employee relations. Immigrants. Infidelity. Italians. Marriage of convenience. New York City. Peddlers and peddling. Butchers. Debt. Divorce. Flags. Fruit. Germans. Greed. Landladies. Parentage.*

MPN 19 Oct 1918, p. 2591. *MPW* 28 Sep 1918, p. 1923. *MPW* 12 Oct 1918, p. 257. *MPW* 19 Oct 1918, p. 444. *NYDM* 22 Nov 1918, p. 663. *Var* 11 Oct 1918, p. 44. *Wid's* 6 Oct 1918, p. 15.

TOO GOOD TO BE TRUE see **EASY COME, EASY GO**

TOO MANY GIRLS (Latino)

RKO Radio Pictures, Inc. *Dist* RKO Radio Pictures, Inc. 8 Oct **1940**; Prod: began 22 Jun 1940 [©RKO Radio Pictures, Inc.; 1 Nov 1940; LP10056]. Sd (RCA Victor System); b&w. 9 reels. 85 min.

Prod George Abbott. *Exec prod* Harry E. Edington. *Dir* George Abbott. [*2d unit dir* Ray McCarey]. *Asst dir* Dewey Starkey. *Scr* John Twist. *Dir of photog* Frank Redman. [*Fill-in dir of photog* Russell Metty]. *Spec eff* Vernon L. Walker. *Art dir* Van Nest Polglase. *Art dir assoc* Carroll Clark. *Ed* William Hamilton. *Cost* Edward Stevenson. *Mus score* George Bassman. *Mus cond* Frank Tours. *Orch arr* George Bassman and Gene Rose. *Vocal dir* Hugh Martin. *Dance numbers* LeRoy Prinz. *Rec* Earl A. Wolcott.

Song(s): "You're Nearer," "I Don't Know What Time It Was," "Spic and Spanish," "Love Never Went to College," " 'Cause We All Got Cake," "Heroes in the Fall," "Pottawatomie," music by Richard Rodgers, lyrics by Lorenz Hart.

Source: Based on the musical *Too Many Girls* by George Marion, Jr., music by Richard Rodgers, lyrics by Lorenz Hart (New York, 18 Nov 1939).

Cast: Lucille Ball (*Connie Casey*), Richard Carlson (*Clint Kelly*), Ann Miller (*Pepe*), Eddie Bracken (*Jojo Jordan*), Frances Langford (*Eileen Eilers*), Desi Arnaz (*Manuelito*), Hal LeRoy (*Al Terwilliger*), Libby Bennett (*Tallulah Lon*), Harry Shannon (*Mr. [Harvey] Casey*), Douglas Walton (*Beverly Waverly*), Chester Clute (*Lister*), Tiny Person (*Midge Martin*), Ivy Scott (*Mrs. Tewksbury*), Byron Shores (*Sheriff Andaluz*), Van Johnson (*Chorus boy*).

Musical comedy. [*Print viewed*]. Connie Casey, a high-spirited, headline-chasing heiress, keeps her manufacturing-tycoon father busy worrying about her. Deported from Europe for her antics, Connie decides to enroll in her father's alma mater, Pottawatomie College, in Stop Gap, New Mexico, in order to be near her latest heart throb, British playwright Beverly Waverly. In desperation, Mr. Casey hires Clint Kelly, Jojo Jordan, Manuelito and Al Terwilliger, the pride of the Ivy League college football teams, to act as Connie's bodyguards. After signing an "anti-romantic" clause in their contracts, the boys arrive at Pottawatomie to discover the worst football team in the West. Unable to resist the game, Manuelito joins the team, soon followed by Clint, Jojo and Al. After a short time, the Pottawatomie team begins to wipe up the field with their opponents and headlines of the team's success reach the East. Meanwhile, Clint begins to fall in love with Connie and decides that he must resign from his contract with Mr. Casey. Soon after, Connie learns the terms of Clint's business arrangement with her father and angrily insists that her bodyguards leave town before the day of the big game. Learning of their players' plans, the townfolk pursue the boys, who are caught by Beverly and returned just in time for the game. Encouraged by Connie's declaration of love, Clint leads the team to victory and wins the girl's heart. *College life. College students. Courtship. Football players. Heiresses. Latino. Romance. Bodyguards. Contracts. Fathers and daughters. Football players. New Mexico. Tycoons.*

Note: According to a news item in *HR*, RKO paid $100,000 for the rights to the play. Another item in *HR* notes that cameraman Russell Metty briefly took over shooting for Frank Redman when Redman had to attend a funeral. Eddie Bracken, Desi Arnaz, Hal LeRoy, Libby Bennett, Ivy Scott, Byron Shores and Van Johnson all reprised their stage roles for this picture, which marked the screen debut of all but LeRoy, and director George Abbott produced the original stage version. Modern sources add that Desi Arnaz and Lucille Ball, who were married in 1941, met while filming this picture.

DV 4 Oct 1940, p. 3. *FD* 4 Oct 1940, p. 10. *HR* 13 Feb 1940, p. 3. *HR* 24 Jun 1940, p. 3. *HR* 18 Jul 1940, p. 2. *HR* 25 Jul 1940, p. 6. *HR* 4 Oct 1940, p. 3. *MPD* 8 Oct 1940, p. 7. *MPH* 12 Oct 1940, p. 49. *NYT* 21 Nov 1940, p. 43. *Var* 9 Oct 1940, p. 16.

TOO MUCH OF EVERYTHING see **THE BELOVED BRAT**

TOO YIEN FEN FONG (Chinese language)

Grandview Film Co. **1948?**; Hong Kong showing: 1948? Sd; b&w. Length undetermined. Chinese language.

Cast: Lai Yee. [*Not viewed*]. [No information concerning the plot of this film has been located.].

Note: The film's Cantonese transliterated title is *Tou Yin Fen Fong*. Available contemporary information indicates that the film was probably made in the United States.

THE TOP O' THE MORNING (Irish Americans)

Universal Film Mfg. Co. 4 Sep **1922** [©Universal Film Mfg. Co.; 18 Aug 1922; LP18169]. Si; b&w. 5 reels, 4,627 ft.

Pres Carl Laemmle. *Dir* Edward Laemmle. *Scen* George Randolph Chester and Wallace Clifton. *Story* Anne Caldwell. *Photog* Charles Stumar.

Source: Based on the play *Top o' the Mornin'* by Anne Caldwell (ca 1913).

Cast: Gladys Walton (*"Jerry" O'Donnell*), Harry Myers (*John Garland*), Doreen Turner (*Dot Garland*), Florence D. Lee (*Jerry's aunt*), William Welsh (*Dermott O'Donnell*), Don Bailey (*Mulrooney*), Dick Cummings (*Father Quinn*), Margaret Campbell (*Mrs. O'Donnell*), Ralph McCullough (*Eugene O'Donnell*), Ethel Shannon (*Katherine Vincent*), Harry Carter (*Blakely Stone*), William Moran (*Thomas Wilson*), Sally Russell (*Katie McDougal*), Martha Mattox (*Miss Murdock*).

Romance. An Irish girl, Jerry, comes to her father in America. But finding life unpleasant with her stepmother, Jerry leaves home and encounters John Garland, a millionaire, now a widower, whom she knew in Ireland. Garland hires her to be governess to his daughter. Jerry's brother, Eugene, a cashier in Garland's bank, is implicated in a robbery of his employer; and Jerry is also involved, apprehended, and jailed. Garland, however, clears the O'Donnells and declares his love for Jerry. *Bank clerks. Brothers and sisters. Governesses. Irish Americans. Millionaires. Robbery. Stepmothers. Widowers.*

FD 3 Sep 1922. *MPW* 9 Sep 1922. *MPW* 7 Oct 1922.

TOP O' THE MORNING (Irish Americans)

Bing Crosby Enterprises, Inc. *Dist* Paramount Pictures, Inc. 5 Sep **1949**; New York opening: 31 Aug 1949; Prod: early Nov—22 Dec 1948 [©Bing Crosby Enterprises, Inc.; 5 Sep 1949; LP2572]. Sd (Western Electric Recording); b&w. 98-99 min. Passed by the National Board of Review. PCA cert no. 13550.

Prod Robert L. Welch. *Dir* David Miller. *Asst dir* Oscar Rudolph. *Wrt* Edmund Beloin and Richard Breen. *Dir of photog* Lionel Lindon. [*Cam op* William Rand]. [*Stills* Don English]. *Spec photog eff* Gordon Jennings. *Process photog* Farciot Edouart. *Art dir* Hans Dreier and Henry Bumstead. *Ed* Arthur Schmidt. *Set dec* Sam Comer and Emile Kuri. *Cost* Mary Kay Dodson. *Mus dir* Robert Emmett Dolan. *Vocal arr* Joseph J. Lilley. *Mus assoc* Troy Sanders. *Spec orch arr* Van Cleave. *Dances by* Eddie Prinz. *Sd rec* Philip Wisdom and Gene Garvin. *Makeup supv* Wally Westmore. [*Makeup artist* Sidney Perell]. [*Hair* Gertrude Reid]. *Tech adv* Arthur Shields. [*Prod mgr* Curtis Mick and James Cottrell]. [*Scr supv* Harry Hogan]. [*Grip* Dominic Seminerio]. [*Gaffer* Stanley Williams].

Song(s): "You're in Love with Someone" and "Top O' the Morning," music by James Van Heusen, lyrics by Johnny Burke; and traditional Irish airs.

Cast: Bing Crosby (*Joe Mulqueen*), Ann Blyth (*Conn McNaughton*), Barry Fitzgerald (*Officer Briany McNaughton*), Hume Cronyn (*Hughie Devine*), Eileen Crowe (*Biddy O'Devlin*), John McIntire (*Inspector Fallon*), Tudor Owen (*Cormac Gillespie*), Jimmy Hunt (*Pearse O'Neill*), Morgan Farley (*Edwin Livesley*), John Eldredge (*E. L. Larkin*), John "Skins" Miller (*Dowdler*), John Costello (*Village gossip*), Dick Ryan (*Clark O'Ryan*), Bernard Cauley, Paul Connelly, John O'Brien (*Boys*), Gus Taillon (*Caretaker*), Mary Field (*Maid*), [Olin Howlin (*Barfly*)], [G. Pat Collins (*Bartender*)], [Laura Elliot (*Office secretary*)], [John Sheehan (*Driver*)], [Dick Keene (*Post office clerk*)], [Edward Emerson, Murray F. Yeats (*Assistants*)], [Pat Lane (*Guide*)], [Gene Ackerman (*Boy*)], [Kathleen Kennedy (*Specialty dancer*)], [Jimmy O'Brien], [William O'Leary].

Musical. [*Print viewed*]. In a small town near Cork, Ireland, civic guard Sergeant Briany McNaughton alerts his assistant, Hughie Devine, that the famous Blarney Stone has been stolen from the castle. This marks a big day for the village, as there has been no comparable crime in over thirty years. When Briany and Hughie investigate, they learn that villager Cormac Gillespie was seen near the castle the night before. Chief Inspector Fallon, from the Irish police force, orders Briany off the case because he does not consider him a professional, but Briany nevertheless determines to solve the crime. Meanwhile, in New York City, insurance investigator Joe Mulqueen is assigned to work undercover to find the Blarney Stone because his parents were Irish and his company insured the Stone for $500,000. Joe spends his first day in Ireland near Blarney Castle posing as a painter, and is befriended by some boys, who introduce him to Briany's beautiful daughter Conn, as she washes clothes in the castle's stream. Conn is stunned by Joe's presence, as he seems to fulfill a well-known prophesy about the theft of the Stone. However, suspicious Hughie arrests Joe and brings him to Briany for questioning. Although they lock Joe up when he refuses to give them any information about why he is there, they release him after he wins them over by singing an Irish ballad. Although Briany considers Joe a prime suspect, he invites him to his house for a party. That night at the party, Conn consults with wise woman Biddy O'Devlin, who is the keeper of the Stone's legend, and confirms that so far, Joe has fulfilled the conditions of the prediction, down to the coat he is wearing that night, and the fact that Conn is falling in love with him. When Joe returns from the party, he finds Briany and Hughie searching his room, and they learn that Joe is an investigator and hear his dictaphone recording, in which he says that Briany is not effective. Briany considers throwing Joe out of town but resists when he hears about the insurance company's $5,000 reward. Although everyone suspects that Cormac is the thief, Fallon tells Joe that the only fingerprints found on the castle wall belong to Hughie. Joe becomes more suspicious of the deputy when Hughie shows little remorse after his only relative dies in a cart accident. Joe starts to link together the accidents and recent unusual events that have been blamed on the theft, and formulates a secret plan with Fallon. One night, Joe and Conn enjoy their first kiss, but their joy is crushed when Briany arrives home with news that Fallon has fired him because Joe intimated that he might impede their investigation. Conn throws Joe out because he deceived her about his work, and because she hoped her father would find the Stone in order to restore his pride. Biddy warns her that the predictions indicate that the stranger of legend will be killed in the Killeen forest if his loved one abandons him. The next day, Joe investigates the site where Hughie's cousin died and realizes from tracks in the ground that someone tipped the cart over while it was stationary. Joe insists that Briany be reinstated, and arranges to meet Fallon and Briany that night at Biddy's cabin in the Killeen woods. Biddy then tells the police that the Stone was stolen to cover up the murder of Hughie's cousin. Everyone deserts Biddy to chase Cormac when he suddenly appears, but Hughie is disturbed by a comment Biddy made about his soul, and knocks out the boy sentry, Pearse O'Neill, to get her alone. Hughie is about to strangle Biddy when Joe and Briany stop him, and he reveals that he murdered his cousin for the money. Hughie is arrested, and before he is taken away, he vows never to reveal where he hid the Stone. Biddy realizes that although Joe did not die, the final prediction has come true, as it says that the singer, who is Pearse, will be struck down by violence, and the song will not be finished by a man. Pearse revives and everyone wanders away from Biddy's cabin, taking a path past a 700-year-old chapel. When Briany sits down upon a large stone that moves, Conn marvels that a stone set so long ago suddenly come loose. Joe realizes that Briany has discovered the Blarney Stone, and Briany is now hailed as a hero. *The Blarney Stone. Insurance–Investigators. Ireland. Legends. Police. Romance. Aged women. Castles. Cousins. Dictograph. Fathers and daughters. Forests. Impersonation and imposture. Irish Americans. Murder. New York City. Parties. Predictions. Recordings. Rewards. Singers. Songs.*

Note: The working titles of this film were *Diamond in the Haystack* and *Needle in a Haystack*. According to information in the copyright records, traditional Irish airs heard in the film are: "Believe Me If All Those Endearing Young Charms," "As Beautiful Kitty," "The Donovans," "Oh! 'Tis Sweet to Think," "In a Shady Nook One Moonlight Night" and "My Lagan Love."

Box 6 Aug 1949. *DV* 5 Aug 1949, p. 3, 9. *FD* 5 Aug 1949. p. 7. *HR* 23 Dec 1948, p. 3. *HR* 5 Aug 1949, p. 3. *MPHPD* 6 Aug 1949, p. 4705. *NYT* 1 Sep 1949, p. 25. *Var* 20 Jul 1949, p. 6.

TOPSY AND EVA (African Americans)

Feature Productions, Inc. *Dist* United Artists Corp. Aug **1927**; Los Angeles premiere: 16 Jun 1927 [©Feature Productions, Inc.; 13 Jul 1927; LP24175]. Si; b&w. 8 reels, 7,456 ft.

Prod consultant Myron Selznick. *Dir* Del Lord. *Adpt* Lois Weber. *Cont* Scott Darling. *Titles* Dudley Early. *Photog* John W. Boyle.

Source: Based on the play *Topsy and Eva* by Catherine Chisholm Cushing (New York, 23 Dec 1924).

Cast: Rosetta Duncan (*Topsy*), Vivian Duncan (*Eva*), Gibson Gowland (*Simon Legree*), Noble Johnson (*Uncle Tom*), Marjorie Daw (*Marietta*), Myrtle Ferguson (*Aunt Ophelia*), Nils Asther (*George Shelby*), Henry Victor (*St. Claire*).

Melodrama. Topsy, a little black imp, is offered for sale by Simon Legree at an auction on the Shelby estate. When no one bids, Eva St. Claire gets her for a nickel; Topsy, Uncle Tom and other slaves are then turned over to Aunt Ophelia for correction and cleaning. When St. Claire is unable to pay his debt to Legree, the latter reclaims his property, but Topsy escapes while Legree and Shelby engage in a furious battle. Struggling against great drifts of snow, she finds a pair of skis and later a horse equipped with snowshoes; she reaches the river before Legree and his dogs and finds a graveyard where runaway slaves have sought refuge. Later, learning that Eva is gravely ill, Topsy prays for her recovery. Eva revives, and the two friends are happily reunited. *African Americans. Children. Miracles. Slavery. Uncle Tom's Cabin* (Novel).

FD 21 Aug 1927. *NYT* 8 Aug 1927, p. 10. *Var* 22 Jun 1927, p. 30.

EL TORBELLINO DEL JAZZ see CARNE DE CABARET

TORMENTO (Italian language)

Bruno Valletty. **1932**; *Prod:* ended mid-Feb 1932. Sd; b&w. Length undetermined. Italian language.

Dir Bruno Valletty. *Orig story* Alessandro Ciardelli Cerrai. *Cam* Ernest Miller. *Tech art and sets* Vincent Palmentola. *Theme song and incidental mus* Aldo Franchetti. *Prod mgr* Arthur Barbera-Rubin.

Cast: Livia Maracci, Rino Naldi, César Vanoni, Paul Cremonesi, Louis Colombo.

Drama?. [*Not viewed*]. [No information on the plot of this film could be located.]. *Italians.*

Note: No reviews or information on the film's release could be found. However, a Jul 1932 *FD* news item, originating from Hollywood, noted that producer/director Bruno Valletty was in New York negotiating for the release of the film, which an earlier news item indicated had just been completed. The film was listed in a release chart in the 1933 *FDYB*.

FD 16 Feb 1932, p. 4. *FD* 16 Jul 1932, p. 2.

TORTILLA FLAT (Latino, Portuguese Americans)

Metro-Goldwyn-Mayer Corp.; controlled by Loew's Inc.; Victor Fleming's Production. *Dist* Loew's Inc. May **1942**; New York opening: 21 May 1942; Prod: 23 Nov 1941—12 Feb 1942; retakes Feb 23—24 Feb 1942 [©Loew's Inc.; 23 Apr 1942; LP11274]. Sd (Western Electric Sound System); sepia. 11 reels, 9,457 ft. 105 min. Passed by the National Board of Review. PCA cert no. 8103.

Prod Sam Zimbalist. *Dir* Victor Fleming. [*Fill-in dir* Sam Zimbalist]. [*Asst dir* Robert Golden]. *Scr* John Lee Mahin and Benjamin Glazer. *Dir of photog* Karl Freund. [*Photog* Harold Rosson]. [*Monterey exteriors* Jack Smith]. *Spec eff* Warren Newcombe. *Art dir* Cedric Gibbons. *Assoc* Paul Groesse. *Film ed* James E. Newcom and [Robert J. Kern]. *Set dec* Edwin B. Willlis and [Keogh Gleason]. *Gowns* Kalloch. *Men's cost by* Gile Steele. *Mus score* Franz Waxman. [*Choir dir* Robert Mitchell]. [*"Varsoviana" dance dir* Ramon Ros]. *Rec dir* Douglas Shearer. *Make-up created by* Jack Dawn.

Song(s): "Ay, Paisano!" music by Franz Waxman, lyrics by Frank Loesser.

Source: Based on the novel *Tortilla Flat* by John Steinbeck (New York, 1935).

Cast: SPENCER TRACY (*Pilon*), HEDY LAMARR (*Dolores Sweets Ramirez*), JOHN GARFIELD (*Danny [Alvarez]*), Frank Morgan (*The Pirate*), Akim Tamiroff (*Pablo*), Sheldon Leonard (*Tito Ralph*), John Qualen (*Jose Maria Corcoran*), Donald Meek (*Paul D. Cummings*), Connie Gilchrist (*Mrs. Torelli*), Allen Jenkins (*Portagee Joe*), Henry O'Neill (*Father [Juan] Ramon*), Mercedes Ruffino (*Mrs. Marellis*), Nina Campana (*Senora Teresina [Cortez]*), Betty Wells (*Cesca*), Arthur Space (*Mr. Brown*), Harry Burns (*Torelli*), [Roque Ybarra (*Alfredo*)], [Nina Campana (*Señora Teresina Cortez*)], [Tim Ryan (*Rupert Hogan*)], [Charles Judels (*Joe Machado*)], [Yvette Duguay (*Little girl*)], [Harry Strang (*Fireman*)], [Tito Renaldo (*Boy*)], [Louis Jean Heydt (*Young doctor*)], [Walter Sande (*Foreman*)], [Jack Carr (*Owner*)], [Shirley Warde (*Nurse*)], [Emmett Vogan (*Doctor*)], [Bob O'Connor, George Magrill (*Cannery workers*)], [Sammy Fong (*Squid owner*)], [St. Brendan's Boys Choir], [Georgia Stark (*Whistling solo*)].

Comedy-drama. [*Print viewed*]. In Monterey, California, paisano Danny Alvarez inherits a gold watch and two houses in the area known as Tortilla Flat from his grandfather. Because Danny is in jail for public drunkenness, his friends, Pilon and Pablo, convince jailer Tito Ralph to "parole" Danny to celebrate and invite Tito to come along. Pilon warns Danny that property and watches bring unwanted responsibilities and cajoles him into selling the watch for some wine. On the way to celebrate in one of the houses, Danny meets Dolores Ramirez, a "Portagee" girl to whom Danny is attracted and names "Sweets." During the party, Pilon talks Danny into renting the other house to him, then convinces Pablo to live with him and pay the fifteen dollars rent. The next day, while Danny serves out the rest of his jail term, Pilon and Pablo find Portagee Joe and Jose Maria Corcoran drunk in the back yard and invite them to live in the house for the three dollars which Jose Maria has. That night, Danny goes to see Sweets, who likes Danny, but has ambitions for a husband, a home and children who don't have to pick beans for a living. When Pablo summons Danny because Pilon's house is on fire, Danny does not care and passionately kisses Sweets, but she throws him out after threatening him with a knife. After the fire, Pilon and the other paisanos, accompanied by a young widower with a baby they met watching the fire, go to Danny's house. Because the baby is starving, Danny goes to Sweets to get milk from her goats and, seeing how gentle Sweets is with the baby, Danny becomes even more smitten. The next morning, Pilon worries about paying his rent and becomes intrigued by The Pirate, a shabby old man who lives with several dogs in a chicken coop. Pilon surmises that Pirate must be a miser because he sells twenty-five cents worth of wood each day, yet never spends anything. Hoping to get Pirate's money, Pilon convinces the old man to come and live at Danny's, saying that his friends worry about him. Meanwhile, Danny visits Sweets at the sardine cannery where she works and gets into a scuffle with the foreman when he is told to leave. Walking by the bay, Danny sees a small fishing boat for sale for $210, then goes to pawn his guitar in exchange for a vacuum cleaner for Sweets. Back at home, Danny is not happy that Pirate and "his boys" are new tenants until Pilon tells him about Pirate's money. Danny then confesses to Pilon that he needs money to buy a boat. The next day, when Pirate reveals that he needs one thousand quarters to

buy a gold candlestick for St. Francis, which he had promised the saint if one of his dogs recovered from a serious illness, Pilon is ashamed and resolves to safeguard Pirate's bag of quarters. Now knowing that he has no other choice, Danny gets a job at the cannery. When Pilon finds out, he knows that it is because of Sweets and fears that she will make the paisanos leave the house if she marries Danny. Pilon lies to Danny that she has been bragging that they are engaged, then steals the vacuum and uses it to buy wine. That night, Sweets angrily accuses Danny of the theft and he counters by accusing her of spreading a story about their engagement. She then slaps him and orders him out. Meanwhile, at the house, after Portagee Joe takes six quarters from Pirate's bag, an angry Pilon recounts the money and discovers that Pirate has more than enough to buy the candlestick. When Danny comes home, he knocks Pilon down when Pilon insults Sweets, then grabs a jug of wine and leaves. The next day, after washing and grooming Pirate, the paisanos take him to church to see the candlestick and hear Father Juan Ramon, who gives a sermon about the candlestick and the miracle of Pirate's dog's recovery. That same morning, a drunken Danny goes to the cannery to see Sweets and is again told to leave. In a fight with several foremen, Danny is accidentally crushed in one of the machines. Later, at the hospital, Pilon learns that Danny's lung has been punctured and he is near death. When Sweets hysterically lashes out at Pilon, he goes to the woods and overhears Pirate telling his dogs about the sermon. Pilon then goes to the church, where his prayers to St. Francis are overheard by Father Juan, who is touched when Pilon offers to buys another candlestick if Danny gets well. Some time later, Father Juan finds Pilon cutting squid and tells him that "someone's prayers have been answered" because Danny is much better. Father Juan adds that Sweets is sorry for her anger and that all of his friends are worried. As the priest leaves, he says that St. Francis does not need another candlestick but would be grateful if Danny somehow had a boat. Some time later, Danny and Sweets are married and a raffle is held for Danny's guitar. Unknown to all but Father Jaun, Pilon himself paid for the tickets, and the money was used to buy Danny the boat. That night, as Pilon and the paisanos drink in Danny's house, Pilon concludes that it was the house that caused all of Danny's troubles. When a fire accidentally starts, the paisanos decide to sleep on the beach and let the house burn. *Friendship. Mexican Americans. Monterey (CA). Romance. Accidents. Candlesticks. Canneries. Dogs. False accusations. Fires. Guitars. Infants. Inheritance. Jails. Pawnshops. Portuguese Americans. Prayer. Priests. Raffles. Recluses. Robbery. Vacuum cleaners. Weddings. Widowers. Wine and wine making.*

Note: The opening title card reads, "Metro-Goldwyn-Mayer presents Spencer Tracy Hedy Lamarr John Garfield in Victor Fleming's Production of John Steinbeck's *Tortilla Flat*." The following written prologue precedes the story: "In the California hills just outside the old seaport town of Monterey live warmhearted people of laughter and kindness—the paisanos. They, and their ancestors, have lived there for a hundred or two years, in a little world of their own called Tortilla Flat." The term "paisano," which literally means a friend or compatriot, also refers to persons of Hispanic or mixed Hispanic and Native American ancestry who resided in the country towns of Northern California.

According to news items, M-G-M had wanted to borrow Rita Hayworth from Columbia to play the role of "Sweets Ramirez," and actors Desi Arnaz and Rags Ragland were both tested for parts in the film. John Garfield was borrowed from Warner Bros. for the film. Actor Robin Raymond was included in the cast in a *HR* news item, but his appearance in the released film has not been confirmed. According to a pre-production news item, actress Maria Montez was tested for a role in the film. Other news items indicate that some exteriors and backgrounds for the film were shot on location in Monterey, CA, and Mario Castelnuevo-Tedesco was to have written five new musical sequences for the film. The extent of Castelnuevo-Tedesco's participation in the released film has not been determined.

According to a 1935 *HR* news item, Paramount initially bought the screen rights to Steinbeck's novel. M-G-M had acquired the rights to the novel by 1940, however, as verified in a 1940 short produced by Frank Whitbeck for the studio that announced the film as "coming" and starring Spencer Tracy. Although the film included many of the characters and situations of the novel, several aspects of the story were changed. In the novel, Sweets is a minor character and does not marry "Danny," who dies after a fall. In the novel, it is "Danny," a recently discharged veteran, who dwells on the responsibilities of property and sinks into an alcoholic depression that ultimately leads to his death. In the novel, "Danny" and "Pilon" do work seasonally, while in the film, much dialogue is devoted to a discussion of their loathing of work.

DV 12 Dec 1942. *DV* 22 Apr 1942, p. 3. *Box* 25 Apr 1942. *FD* 22 Apr 1942, p. 6. *HR* 4 Nov 1935, p. 2. *HR* 17 Sep 1941, p. 1. *HR* 3 Nov 1941, p. 6. *HR* 12 Nov 1941, pp. 2-3. *HR* 18 Nov 1941, p. 7. *HR* 21 Nov 1941, p. 6, 8. *HR* 26 Nov 1941, p. 6. *HR* 13 Jan 1942, p. 4. *HR* 23 Feb 1942, p. 3. *HR* 24 Mar 1942, p. 3. *HR* 10 Apr 1942, p. 2. *HR* 22 Apr 1942, p. 3. *Life* 1 Jun 1942, pp. 39-41. *MPHPD* 25 Apr 1942, p. 621. *NYT* 22 May 1942, p. 27. *Var* 22 Apr 1942, p. 8.

TOTO see **SU ÚLTIMA NOCHE**

TOU YIN FEN FONG see **TOO YIEN FEN FONG**

TOUCH OF EVIL (Latino)

Universal-International Pictures Co., Inc. *Dist* Universal Pictures Co., Inc. Feb **1958**; Los Angeles opening: 23 Apr 1958; Prod: 18 Feb—early Apr 1957 [©Universal Pictures Co., Inc.; 15 Mar 1958; LP10314]. Sd (Westrex Recording System); b&w. 95 min. PCA cert no. 18506.

Prod Albert Zugsmith. *Dir* Orson Welles. *Asst dir* Phil Bowles. *Scr* Orson Welles. *Dir of photog* Russell Metty. *Art dir* Alexander Golitzen and Robert Clatworthy. *Film ed* Virgil Vogel, Aaron Stell and [Edward Curtiss]. *Set dec* Russell A. Gausman and John P. Austin. *Gowns* Bill Thomas. *Mus* Henry Mancini. *Mus supv* Joseph Gershenson. *Sd* Leslie I. Carey and Frank Wilkinson. *Makeup* Bud Westmore.

Source: Based on the novel *Badge of Evil* by Whit Masterson (New York, 1956).

Cast: CHARLTON HESTON [(*Ramon Miguel "Mike" Vargas*)], JANET LEIGH [(*Susan Vargas*)], ORSON WELLES [(*Hank Quinlan*)], Joseph Calleia [(*Pete Manzies*)], Akim Tamiroff [(*"Uncle" Joe Grandi*)], Joanna Moore [(*Marcia Linnekar*)], Ray Collins [(*Adair*)], Dennis Weaver [(*The night man*)], Valentin De Vargas [(*Pancho*)], Mort Mills [(*Schwartz*)], Victor Millan [(*Manuelo Sanchez*)], Lalo Rios [(*Risto*)], Michael Sargent [(*Pretty boy*)], Phil Harvey [(*Blaine*)], Joi Lansing [(*Blonde*)], Harry Shannon [(*Gould*)], Marlene Dietrich [(*Tana*)], Zsa Zsa Gabor [(*Strip-club owner*)], [Joseph Cotten (*Coroner*)], [Rusty Wescoatt (*Casey*)], [Mercedes McCambridge (*Gang leader*)], [Wayne Taylor, Ken Miller, Raymond Rodriguez (*Gang members*)], [Arlene McQuade (*Ginnie*)], [Dominick Delgarde (*Lackey*)], [Joe Basulto (*Young delinquent*)], [Jennie Dias (*Jackie*)], [Yolanda Bojorquez (*Bobbie*)], [Eleanor Dorado (*Lia*)], [Keenan Wynn].

Film noir. [*Print viewed*]. While passing through the seedy border town of Los Robles, newlyweds Mike and Susan Vargas witness a car bomb explosion in which Rudy Linnekar, a local construction magnate, and his female companion are killed. Suspecting that the bomb was planted on the Mexican side of the border and may be the work of the Grandi narcotics ring, Vargas, the Mexican head of the Pan-American Narcotics Commission, offers his assistance to the Los Robles officials investigating the case. The lead detective, the obese and lumbering Capt. Hank Quinlan, rudely rebuffs Vargas's offer and makes subtly racist remarks. However, Quinlan's partner, the loyal Sgt. Pete Menzies, and Adair, a district attorney, apologize for Quinlan's behavior and invite Vargas to observe their investigation because of his status as a highly placed Mexican government official. In the meantime, a group of young Mexican men working for "Uncle" Joe Grandi, a small-time crime boss with a bad toupee, bring Susan, an American, to Grandi's headquarters in a sleazy hotel. Grandi warns Susan of dire consequences if her husband continues his prosecution of Grandi's brother, an imprisoned drug dealer awaiting trial in Mexico, but Susan, unimpressed, insults Grandi by calling him a "lopsided Little Caesar." While investigating the case on the Mexican side of the border, Quinlan visits the tawdry brothel run by Tana, a former lover, and the place fills him with nostalgic yearnings. Tana, who at first does not recognize him, looks upon Quinlan with pity and suggests that he "lay off the candy bars" which he has substituted for liquor since going on the wagon several years before. Upon learning of Susan's encounter with Grandi, Vargas decides that she will be safer stashed in a motel on the American side of town while he continues working on the Linnekar case. However, unbeknownst to Vargas, the motel is owned by Grandi, managed by a disturbed night clerk, and in the middle of the desert. Quinlan soon tracks down a suspect, a Mexican shoe clerk who was having an affair with Linnekar's daughter, Marcia, and later married her in a secret ceremony. Sanchez claims he is innocent and appeals to Vargas for help, infuriating Quinlan, who demands that they stop speaking in Spanish. After a prolonged search, Quinlan declares that Menzies has found damning evidence of Sanchez's guilt concealed in a shoe box. Vargas, who had earlier seen that the box was empty, accuses Quinlan of planting dynamite in the box to frame Sanchez, but Quinlan claims that Vargas is only trying to protect his own kind and has a "natural prejudice" for Mexicans. Grandi approaches Quinlan to suggest that they work together to ruin Vargas and after Quinlan has downed several drinks at Grandi's prodding, they plot to destroy Vargas professionally and personally by framing Susan. Grandi's gang of young hoodlums, led by a sadistic woman clad in black leather, take over the motel and accost the terrified Susan, who is shot up with drugs and then transported to a room in Grandi's hotel. When Vargas meets with Police Chief Gould and District Attorney Adair to discuss his suspicions about Quinlan, the faithful Menzies doggedly tracks down his partner to inform him of the meeting and is devastated when he finds Quinlan drunk in a bar. Quinlan storms in on the meeting and, furious that Gould is not defending him, makes a show of throwing down his badge. Uncomfortable with the fact that Vargas is an outsider making accusations against a star detective, Gould and Adair placate Quinlan by telling Vargas to stay out of police business. Al Schwartz, a young assistant D.A., stands by Vargas and secretly gains him access to Quinlan's case files, which strongly suggest that Quinlan, tortured by the fact that he was unable to find enough evidence to convict the "half-breed" who strangled his wife, has been framing suspects for years. Unable to accept that his partner and best friend is crooked, Menzies attempts to defend Quinlan, blaming Vargas for Quinlan's binge after years of sobriety. Unable to reach Susan by phone, Vargas finally makes it to the motel to find the night clerk sitting in the dark and seemingly speechless with fear. To Vargas's horror, all that remains in Susan's room are the stench of marijuana smoke and the debris of a wild party. Meanwhile, Quinlan arrives at Grandi's hotel and enters the room where Susan lies naked and unconscious, the smell of marijuana clinging to the clothing strewn about the floor. After calling Menzies to report that he has found Vargas's wife surrounded by evidence of a drug party, Quinlan, who wants to ensure that he will not be a victim of blackmail, strangles Grandi with one of Susan's stockings. Soon after, Vargas, who has launched a desperate search for his wife, learns that Susan has been jailed on suspicion of drug use, prostitution and the murder of Grandi. Knowing that Quinlan is behind the frame-up and feeling helpless to stop him, Vargas explodes with rage, but Menzies takes him aside and reveals that he found Quinlan's cane at the murder scene. Although he is devastated by the fall of his idol, Menzies agrees to help Vargas amass more incontrovertible evidence of Quinlan's criminal activities and consents to being wired in the hopes that Quinlan will confess to his trusted partner. Quinlan, still on a binge, has holed up at Tana's place where, in a drunken haze, he asks her to read his fortune. Tana, however, sadly declares that his future is "all used up" and advises him to go home. As he reels out the door, Quinlan is confronted by Menzies, who begins asking questions about the Grandi murder while, nearby, Vargas records the conversation. As they walk towards a bridge spanning a murky canal, Menzies accuses Quinlan of betraying his loyalty by setting him up as the stooge who always found the planted evidence. The argument is interrupted when Quinlan hears the sound of their voices on Vargas's tape and finally realizes that Menzies is wired. When Menzies tries to stop Quinlan from harming Vargas, who is clinging to the side of the bridge, Quinlan shoots him and then, in shock at what he has done, stumbles down to the canal to wash the blood from his hands. Vargas confronts Quinlan with the evidence he now has on tape, and Quinlan prepares to kill him so that he can pin the Menzies murder on him. However, Menzies, on the brink of death, manages to crawl to the edge of the bridge and shoot Quinlan. Schwartz arrives with Susan, who has been released from jail, and Vargas departs to take her home to Mexico City, knowing that he is leaving behind enough evidence to prove that Quinlan framed Susan, Sanchez and many others. Ironically, however, Sanchez has ended up confessing to the murder of Rudy Linnekar. Tana arrives at the edge of the canal and gazing with Schwartz at Quinlan's large frame floating in the black water, she sadly remarks that Quinlan was "some kind of man." *Frame-ups. Investigations. Mexican-American border region. Mexicans. Police detectives. Racism.* Alcoholics. Betrayal. Blackmail. Brothels. District attorneys. Drug dealers. Drugs. Dynamite. False arrests. Friendship. Gangs. Loyalty. Marriage–Mixed. Mexican Americans. Motels. Murder. Newlyweds.

Note: The working title of this film was *Badge of Evil*. The following information is from modern sources, except as noted: After Universal purchased Whit Masterson's novel in 1956, producer Albert Zugsmith assigned Paul Monash to write a screenplay based on the book, although the project was shelved after Monash completed his screenplay. Descriptions differ as to how Orson Welles, who had not directed a film in the United States since the 1948 Republic picture *Macbeth*, became involved in the Zugsmith production. Some

writers state that Welles became friends with Zugsmith during production of *Pay the Devil*, in which Welles appeared as an actor, and after that film wrapped, Welles offered to direct the "worst" script Zugsmith had, which was *Badge of Evil*. Other sources state that Welles had been signed as an actor only for *Badge of Evil*, but that when Charlton Heston was contacted about appearing in the film, he suggested that Welles also direct it. Heston, who agreed to star in the picture for seven and a half percent of the gross, cited *Citizen Kane* as one of his favorite films, and Universal, in order to please Heston, who was a top box-office draw at the time, agreed to hire Welles as the director.

Welles was signed to rewrite and direct the film, but was only compensated the $125,000 he had been offered as an actor. Some modern sources claim that Welles did not read Masterson's novel and completely rewrote Monash's script, while other sources state that Welles did include parts of the novel and original adaptation in his finished screenplay. Among the significant ways in which Welles departed from the novel and the Monash screenplay were to change the character played by Heston from a white district attorney to a Mexican narcotics agent; to change the nationality of Janet Leigh's character from Mexican to American; and to set the film in a Mexican-American border town rather than in a Southern California town. Welles also heightened racial and sexual tensions in his screenplay.

Welles originally wanted to shoot the picture on location in Tijuana, but was unable to do so. Some sources note that Universal ordered Welles to shoot closer to the studio so that his shooting schedule could be closely monitored, while other sources state that Mexican government censors, concerned over the depiction of drug use and violence, refused Welles permission to film in Mexico. Welles decided to shoot instead at Venice, CA, where most of the filming took place at night. While scouting the location, Welles fell into a canal and suffered painful injuries that required the use of a sling and a cane while he was off camera. Just prior to filming, Leigh was also injured and the cast on her broken left arm had to be hidden during shooting. During more revealing scenes, such as those set in the motel, Leigh's cast was sawn off and her arm re-splinted after filming. Although, according to a modern interview, Welles originally wanted Lloyd Bridges to play "Pete Menzies," he was "more than happy with Calleia" and considered himself "very lucky with that cast." Welles prevailed on several friends—Joseph Cotten, Marlene Dietrich, Mercedes McCambridge and Keenan Wynn—to act in the picture for union scale wages, although when the studio decided to include Dietrich in the onscreen billing, they were required to pay her more money. Most sources note that Welles wrote Dietrich's part after filming had already begun, and after calling her the night before he wished to film her scenes, shot all of her sequences in one night. Some sources, however, report that her scenes took more than one night to film. Although modern sources refer to the character played by Dietrich as "Tanya," her name in the film is "Tana." Dietrich considered this role "Tana" one of her favorites, and in a 4 Sep 1960 *NYT* article, claimed that she did her "best dramatic acting" in the last scene, in which she declares, "What does it matter what you say about people?" Some modern sources also include John Dierkes, Billy House and Gus Schilling in the cast. Maurice Seiderman, who was Welles's makeup man on *Citizen Kane*, is often credited with helping transform Welles into "Quinlan," for which he was padded with an extra sixty pounds. Although most modern sources credit John Russell as the camera operator who assisted director of photography Russell Metty, some list Phil Lathrop as the operator. Terry Nelson is listed as assistant director, along with Phil Bowles, who received an onscreen credit, and F. D. Thompson is credited as the production manager.

The famous opening sequence, in which a camera follows the bomb placed in "Rudy Linnekar's" car and introduces "Mike Vargas" and his wife, has become one of the most frequently cited examples of Welles's talent for unusual camera work. Another well-known long take in the film is the interrogation of "Sanchez" in his apartment, which Welles reportedly filmed on the first day of shooting as proof of his ability to make the film quickly and efficiently. The picture was completed in early Apr 1957, and in a 10 Jun 1977 *NYT* article, Heston is quoted as saying that the film "had an $825,000 budget and [a schedule of] 38 shooting days...and Orson brought it in for $900,000 in 39 days."

Edward Curtiss, who is credited on *HR* production charts as the editor, was fired by Welles when they did not agree on the cutting of the film, but Welles did work well with the next editor assigned to the picture, Virgil M. Vogel. The post-production phase of the project was complicated, and after several months, Vogel was replaced by Aaron Stell, who was later assisted by studio executive Ernest Nims. Modern sources offer conflicting accounts concerning why control over the film's final edit was taken away from Welles, but note that eventually, Harry Keller was brought in to direct one day's worth of additional scenes, which the studio felt were necessary to provide a more linear narrative. Keller worked with cameraman Cliff Stein and writer Franklin Coen for the added scenes. Heston was reluctant to appear in the sequences to be shot by Keller rather than Welles and caused production to be held up for a day, although he did reimburse the studio approximately eight thousand dollars for the delay. Another change imposed by the studio was the printing of the credits over the opening sequence. Welles had intended for the credits to appear at the film's end, so that the audience's attention would not be diverted from the long and narratively important tracking shot at the beginning.

The studio finally released the film in Apr 1958 with little advertising, and it was a box-office failure in the United States. Criticism of the film varied, with some writers praising Welles's innovative style, while others disliked the story and "artsy" direction. The picture was better received in Europe, however, and Welles accepted the award for best international film at the World's Fair in Brussels in 1958. Despite the critical success of the film in Europe, Welles never again directed a picture in the United States. [Although Welles did work

on some independent projects in the U.S., he was never hired by a studio to direct in America after 1957, nor did he complete any independent films there.] In 1975, another version of the film was discovered and preserved by the American Film Institute. The 1975 version contains approximately fifteen minutes of additional footage, although modern sources conflict as to whether the longer version contains any of Keller's footage, and how close this version is to the one originally edited by Welles. Over the years, the picture's stature among critics and audiences has grown, and it has become one of Welles's most analyzed and highly praised films. Often discussed are Welles's innovative use of sound, lighting and the camera, as well as his depiction of racism and sexuality. Many modern critics assert that the the motel scenes in *Touch of Evil* influenced Alfred Hitchcock, whose 1960 film *Psycho* starred Leigh and featured work by cameraman John Russell and art director Robert Clatworthy.

Box 24 Mar 1958. *Cue* 10 May 1958. *DV* 17 Mar 1958, p. 3, 14. *Exh* 19 Mar 1958, p. 4447. *FD* 2 Apr 1958, p. 6. *Har* 22 Mar 1958, p. 47. *HR* 15 Feb 1957, p. 12. *HR* 29 Mar 1957, p. 52. *HR* 17 Mar 1958, p. 3. *LAT* 24 Apr 1958. *MPD* 19 Mar 1958. *MPHPD* 22 Mar 1958, p. 765. *MPH* 22 May 1958, p. 25. *NYT* 4 Sep 1960. *NYT* 10 Jan 1977. *Var* 19 Mar 1958, p. 16. *Var* 25 Jun 1975.

TOUTE SA VIE *see* **TODA UNA VIDA**

THE TOY WIFE (French Americans)
Metro-Goldwyn-Mayer Corp.; controlled by Loew's Inc. *Dist* Loew's Inc. 10 Jun **1938**; Prod: mid-Mar—27 May 1938 [©Loew's Inc.; 6 Jun 1938; LP8078]. Sd (Western Electric Sound System); b&w. 10 reels. 93 or 96 min. Passed by the National Board of Review. PCA cert no. 4249.

Prod Merian C. Cooper. *Dir* Richard Thorpe. [*Asst dir* Robert A. Golden]. *Scr* Zoë Akins. *Photog* Oliver T. Marsh. *Art dir* Cedric Gibbons. *Art dir assoc* Harry McAfee and Edwin B. Willis. *Film ed* Elmo Veron. *Women's costumes* Adrian. *Men's costumes* Gile Steele. *Mus score* Edward Ward. *Rec dir* Douglas Shearer.

Source: Based on the play *Frou-frou* by Henri Meilhac and Ludovic Halévy (Paris, 30 Oct 1869) and the play *Frou Frou* by Augustin Daly (New York, 15 Feb 1870).

Cast: LUISE RAINER (*Gilberte Brigard, Frou Frou*), Melvyn Douglas (*Georges Sartoris*), Robert Young (*Andre Vallaire*), Barbara O'Neil (*Louise Brigard*), H. B. Warner (*Victor Brigard*), Alma Kruger (*Madame Vallaire*), Libby Taylor (*Suzanne*), Theresa Harris ("*Pick*"), Walter Kingsford (*Judge Rondell*), Clinton Rosemond (*Pompey*), Clarence Muse (*Brutus*), Leonard Penn (*Gaston Vincent*), Alan Perl (*Georgie*), [Margaret Irving (*Madame DeCambri*)], [Rafaela Ottiano (*Felicianne*)], [Beulah Hall Jones (*Sophie*)], [George H. Reed (*Gabriel*)], [Madame Sul-te-wan (*Eve*)], [Hal Le Seur (*First brother*)], [Tom Rutherford (*Jacques*)], [Douglas McPhail (*Second brother*)], [Edward Van Sloan (*Dr. Martine*)], [Albert Morin (*Emile*)], [Edward Keane (*Auctioneer*)], [D'Arcy Corrigan (*Actor*)], [Natalie Garson (*Woman in Spanish costume*)], [George Regas (*Man in court*)], [Charles Albin (*Priest*)], [Esther Muir (*Blonde woman*)], [Priscilla Lawson (*Dark woman*)], [Brent Sargent (*Young man*)], [Marguerite Whitten (*Rose*)], [Billy McClain (*Black orchestra leader*)], [George Humbert (*Italian organ grinder*)], [Henry Roquemore (*Proprietor of toy shop*)], [Robert Spindola (*Italian boy*)], [Barbara Bedford (*Woman in doctor's office*)], [Ruby Elzy (*Mulatto at fruit stand*)], [Myrtle Anderson (*Therese*)], [Willa Curtis (*Marguerite*)], [Gertrude Saunders (*Yellow Marie*)], [Violet McDowell (*Brown Marie*)], [Cora Lang (*Yvonne*)], [Irene Allen (*Agathe*)], [Olive Ball, Geneva Williams, Mary Luster, Edna Franklin, Charles Andrews, Ernest Wilson, Henry Thomas, Louise Robinson, Fannie Washington (*Servants*)].

Historical, **Drama**. [*Print viewed*]. In the early 1800's, sixteen-year-old coquette Gilberte Brigard, called "Frou Frou," returns from school in France to her Louisiana plantation. Craving excitement, Frou Frou feigns a toothache so that she can visit the dentist in New Orleans. Although her travelling chaperone, Madame Vallaire, tries to watch over Frou Frou, she sneaks away to attend a ball where she meets Madame Vallaire's wastral son Andre, with whom she is infatuated. Upon their return home, Frou Frou and her more stable older sister Louise attend Georges Sartoris, a family friend who is recovering from a knife wound received while prosecuting a white man accused of killing a young slave. Although Louise is in love with Georges, she encourages him to marry her sister when she learns that he is in love with Frou Frou. Five years later, as Georges and Frou Frou's son Georgie is celebrating his fourth birthday, Georges has become concerned that Frou Frou's youthful playfulness has not decreased during their marriage. Because he fears that their marriage will be destroyed because she is unable to run their household, he asks Louise to stay with them and take charge, telling her that Frou

Frou is merely a "toy wife." While Louise runs the household, Frou Frou happily begins rehearsing an amateur play with Andre with whom she become reacquainted after a chance meeting. Soon, however, she begins to realize that Louise has supplanted her position within the household. When even little Georgie seems to prefer Louise to his mother, Frou Frou confronts Louise, who still loves Georges, but has only been trying to save Frou Frou's marriage. When Louise tells her sister why Georges wanted her to come into their home, Frou Frou decides to leave with Andre, who has asked her to elope with him. Six months later, after Madame Vallaire tells Frou Frou's father Victor that the pair has gone to New York, he dies of a heart attack. Because Frou Frou turns her inheritance over to Georgie, she and Andre are soon destitute due to his gambling debts. They then return to New Orleans after which Georges challenges Andre to a duel. Although Andre is known to be the better shot, he is killed by Georges. Frou Frou and her maid "Pick" soon are impoverished and she is weakened by pneumonia. One evening, after Frou Frou offers prayers in a small church, Louise finds her. Georges refuses to see her or allow their son to see her, until Louise makes him realize that Frou Frou only became his toy wife because that was what he really wanted. Georges finally goes to Frou Frou and brings her home where she dies after telling him that Louise loves him and will make him a good wife. *Flirts. French Americans. Infidelity. Marriage. New Orleans (LA). Sisters. Children. Duels. Heart disease. Pneumonia. Traveling companions. United States–History–Social life and customs. United States–South.*

Note: The film's pre-production title was *Mlle. Froufrou*. A written prologue following the opening credits reads: "Gone is the flag of France from Louisiana, but until the Civil War the life of its French residents in New Orleans and on the great plantations was under the old regime of France." Although Zoë Akin's screenplay was based on the French and American versions of the play *Froufrou,* no underlying dramatic or literary work is credited on screen. *SAB* notes that the screenplay was "not original" but does not mention the source which "could not be shown," according to a hand-written notation on the *SAB* form. Richard Thorpe had to be replaced as the director of M-G-M's *The Shopworn Angel* (see *AFI Catalog of Feature Films, 1931-40;* F3.4038) because of a scheduling conflict with this film. According to a *HR* news item, portions of the film were shot on location at Sherwood Forest, California. Other versions of the same story include a 1914 Thanhouser film entitled *Frou Frou,* directed by Lloyd Lonergan and starring Maude Fealy, and a 1917 Peerless production called *A Hungry Heart* directed by Emile Chautard and starring Alice Brady (see *AFI Catalog of Feature Films, 1911-20;* F1.1493 and F1.2101), a 1918 Italian film and a 1923 French film, both called *Frou-Frou.*

DV 1 Jun 1938, p. 3. *FD* 6 Jun 1938, p. 6. *HR* 12 Mar 1938, p. 3. *HR* 21 Mar 1938, p. 18. *HR* 28 Mar 1938, p. 2. *HR* 1 Jun 1938, p. 3. *MPD* 2 Jun 1938, p. 5. *MPH* 30 Apr 1938, p. 25. *MPH* 4 Jun 1938, p. 32. *NYT* 24 Jun 1938, p. 15. *Var* 8 Jun 1938, p. 17.

TOYS OF FATE (Gypsies)

Screen Classics, Inc. *Dist* Metro Pictures Corp. May **1918** [©Metro Picures Corp.; 25 May 1918; LP12458]. Si; b&w. 7 reels.

Supv Maxwell Karger. *Dir* George D. Baker. *Scen* June Mathis. *Titles* Ferdinand Pinney Earle. *Cam* Eugene Gaudio.

Cast: Mme. Nazimova (*Zorah/Hagar*), Charles Bryant (*Henry Livingston*), Irving Cummings (*Greggo*), Edward J. Connelly (*Howard Belmont*), Dodson Mitchell (*Bruce Griswold*), Frank Currier (*Pharos*), Nila Mac (*Blanche Griswold*).

Drama. Hagar, a gypsy living in the United States, deserts her husband Pharos and daughter Zorah for Bruce Griswold, who in turn, abandons her. She commits suicide, while Griswold attains wealth and power. After Zorah has grown to womanhood, her gypsy band passes through Griswold's town, and he becomes fascinated with her and sends her to school. Zorah loves Henry Livingston, but because he is engaged to someone else, she finally consents to marry Griswold. When Pharos tells Zorah the truth about Griswold and Hagar, she decides to take poison, but Griswold finds the potion and, in a drunken stupor, drinks it and dies. Zorah is tried for Griswold's murder, but with the help of Livingston, is eventually acquitted. Livingston's fiancée, horrified that he would represent a gypsy, breaks the engagement, leaving him free to marry Zorah. *Attempted suicide. Gypsies. Poisoning. Desertion (Marital). Drunkenness. Racism. Suicide. Trials.*

Note: Some sources call the character of Pharos, Maspero, and the character of Zorah, Azah. The working title of the film was *Fate Decides.* It had its premiere in New York on 11 May 1918.

ETR 6 Apr 1918, p. 1461. *ETR* 18 May 1918, pp. 1896-97, 1935. *MPN* 25 May 1918, p. 3097. *MPN* 1 Jun 1918, p. 3306. *MPW* 1 Jun 1918, p. 1330, 1337. *NYDM* 25 May 1918, p. 739. *NYDM* 6 Jul 1918, p. 965. *Wid's* 19 May 1918, p. 7.

TRADITIONS ALTAR *see* LI TING LANG

TRAFFIC IN SOULS (Immigrants)

Imp (Independent Moving Picture Co.). *Dist* Universal Film Mfg. Co. Nov **1913** [©Universal Film Mfg. Co.; 2 Dec 1913; LU1767]. Si; b&w. 6-7 reels.

Dir George Loane Tucker. *Scen* Walter MacNamara and George Loane Tucker.

Cast: Jane Gail (*Mary Barton*), Ethel Grandin (*Lorna Barton*), William Turner (*Isaac Barton*), Matt Moore (*Officer Larry Burke*), William Welsh (*William Trubus*), Mrs. Hudson Lyston (*Mrs. Trubus*), Irene Wallace (*Alice Trubus*), William Cavanaugh (*Bill Bradshaw*), Howard Crampton (*The Go-Between*), Arthur Hunter (*Procurer*), William Burbidge (*Mr. Smith*), Laura Huntley (*Emigrant girl*), William Powers (*Emigrant girl's brother*).

Social, Drama. Mary and Lorna, the lovely daughters of Isaac Barton, an elderly inventor, work in a fashionable confectionary. Nice mannered procurer Bill Bradshaw lures Lorna to drink with him, after which he imprisons her in an abandoned house. When news of Lorna's supposed fall from grace reaches the shop, Mary's reputation is also tainted. She loses her job and is hired by Mr. Trubus, a renowned philanthropist and secretly the leader of a prosperous gang of white slavers, who prey on newly-arrived immigrant girls. After Mary discovers that Bradshaw is working for Trubus, she and her sweetheart, officer Larry Burke, who earlier rescued several girls from the same ring, gather evidence against Trubus using an invention of Barton that records his dealing onto a cylinder. After a rooftop chase, Bradshaw is shot and falls to his death, while Mary rescues Lorna. The ensuing scandal brings on the death of Trubus' wife and the insanity of his daughter. *Abduction. Falls from heights. Immigrants. Moral corruption. Phonographs. Pimps. Police. Saleswomen. Sisters. White-slave traffic. Chases. Confectioners and confectionaries. Dismissal (Employment). Insanity. Philanthropists. Reputation. Rescues. Scandal.*

Note: Advertisements for the film said that it was based on the Rockefeller White Slavery Report and on the investigation of the Vice Trust by District Attorney Whitman. In a news item in 17 Dec 1913 *NYDM,* John D. Rockefeller, Jr. denied that any films about white-slave traffic had his sanction or were in any way approved by the Bureau of Social Hygiene, through which he conducted his investigations of white-slave traffic. Furthermore, he stated that "the use of my name in any such connection is absolutely unauthorized, and that I and those associated with me in this work regard this method of exploiting vice as not only injudicious but positively harmful." *Var* commented, "there's a laugh on the Rockefeller investigators in the play in the personality of one of the white slavers, a physical counterpart of John D., himself so striking as to make the observer sit up and wonder whether the granger of Pocantico Hills really came down to pose for the Universal." According to modern sources, the film was cast by Imp editor Jack Cohn and was made without the knowledge of Imp officials. Director Tucker quit Imp and went to the London Film Company in England after *Traffic in Souls* was shot. Jack Cohn cut it from ten to six reels. The popularity of the film (modern sources claim that it cost $5,700 to make and that it grossed approximately $450,000) touched off a wave of white-slave pictures. The National Board of Censorship of Motion Pictures viewed the film on 27 Oct 1913 and passed it with five minor alterations.

Motog 15 Nov 1913, p. 339. *Motog* 29 Nov 1913, pp. 397-98. *MPN* 22 Nov 1913, p. 34. *MPW* 22 Nov 1913, p. 849. *NYDM* 19 Nov 1913, p. 33. *NYDM* 17 Dec 1913, p. 30. *Var* 28 Nov 1913, p. 12.

TRAGEDIA D'AMORE *see* LA CARTA

LA TRAGEDIA DEL CIRCO *see* LA JAULA DE LOS LEONES

TRAGEDIAS DE LA VIDA BOHEMIA *see* LA VIDA BOHEMIA

THE TRAGEDY OF CARPATHO-UKRAINE (Ukrainian language, Ukrainian Americans)

Kobzar Film Corporation. *Dist* Kobzar Film Corporation. **1940**; Prod: filmed in New York City. Sd; b&w. 8 reels, 7,474 ft. Ukrainian language.

Prod Vasile Avramenko.

Song(s): "Ukraine Has Not Perished" (national anthem of Carpatho-Ukraine), traditional; and other songs, composers undetermined.

Documentary, Political. [*Not viewed*]. In the city of Khust, leaders of the recently formed Carpatho-Ukrainian government meet at their new capital building. Prime Minister Dr. Augustin Woloshyn is meeting with other statesmen in a conference in which they plan to negotiate with leaders from the surrounding Slavic nations, including the Ukraine's former occupiers, Czechoslovakia and Poland. Hordes of young people, anxious to support the fledgling nation, volunteer for the army, which sadly has no weapons. As the

men train, their discipline and professionalism grows. News of the establishment of Carpatho-Ukraine is met with great joy by Ukrainian Americans who offer support and money to their struggling brothers in the old country. Meanwhile, in Khust, the Carpatho-Ukraine Sojm (congress) meets to hasten the declaration of its independence. The Sojm's Oath of Office is read in Ukrainian, Czech, and Roumanian, and the twelfth of February is established as the Day of Independence. The Sojm passes laws, sings the Ukrainian national anthem, and by secret ballot unanimously elects Dr. Woloshin as its president. Woloshin gives a rousing acceptance speech, which includes his principle that "Faith is the strength of the individual and the strength of the people." The Sojm then makes several decrees: Ukrainian is established as the national language; a flag is adopted, as is an emblem, the trident of St. Vladimir the Great; and a national anthem is selected. Woloshin vows that the Ukraine's strength to repel her enemies will come and that aggressors of the new nation will be fought until vanquished. *Elections. Nationalism. Parliament. Ukraine. World War II. Carpathian Mountains. Czechoslovakia. Military Service, Voluntary. Poland. Politicians.*

Note: According to NYSA records, this film was made in New York City. Although a print was not viewed, the above credits and plot summary were taken from a translated dialogue continuity deposited with the NYSA. The film recounts the brief period of the independent Ukrainian state, Carpatho-Ukraine, established in 1938 when Czechoslovakia granted the region autonomy. At the time independence was proclaimed in Carpatho-Ukraine, Hungary had already begun an occupation that was to last throughout World War II. The film opens with a history of the Ukraine from the ancient state of Kiev to the establishment of Carpatho-Ukraine and depicts the customs, religion and culture of the Ukrainian people.

It is not clear from the cutting continuity whether the scenes of the Carpatho-Ukrainian "Sojm," or congress, located in the city of Khust, are re-enactments or documentary footage of the proceedings. The leaders of the Carpatho-Ukrainian state that the film features include Prime Minister Dr. Augustin Woloshin, Minister Julian Revai, Augustin Stephan, Dr. Mihailo Brasschaiko, Dr. Stephen Kotcherhan, Dr. Stephan Rossocha, Colonel Yefframeev, Feodor Revai, Captain Belay, and Dr. Vladimir Kamarinsky. The narrator states that the film seeks to assist "general Ukrainian striving for national emancipation" and that the current Ukrainian independence movement is neither "pro-German, nor anti-American, nor anti-British."

THE TRAGEDY OF LIFE see **CHIJLKU WO MAWASURU CHIKARA**

TRAIL OF THE ARROW (Native Americans, Osage)

William F. Broidy Productions, Inc. *Dist* Monogram Pictures Corp. 2 Nov **1952** [©William F. Broidy Productions, Inc.; 15 Dec 1951; LP2214]. Sd; b&w. 4,777 ft. 54 min. PCA cert no. 16323.

Prod Wesley Barry. *Dir* Thomas Carr. *Asst dir* Melville Shyer. *Scr* Melvin Levy and Maurice Tombragel. *Photog* Harry Newmann. *Spec eff* Ray Mercer. *Supv ed* Ace Herman. *Set des* Dave Milton. *Mus dir* Edward J. Kay. *Sd rec* John Carter. *Set cont* Anita Speer.

Cast: Guy Madison (*Wild Bill Hickok*), Andy Devine (*Jingles*), Wendy Waldron (*Jeannie*), Raymond Hatton (*Rossen*), Monte Blue (*Thunderbird*), Rory Mallinson (*Owens*), Anthony Sydes (*Ned*), Steve Pendleton (*Matthews*), Neyle Morrow (*Taloga*), Francis Ford (*Zeke*), Ferris Taylor (*Gorman*), Dick Rich (*Dillon*), Tom Steele (*Falk*), Dave Sharpe (*Lonny*), Tito Renaldo (*Little Deer*), Rod Redwing (*Red Horse*).

Western. [*Not viewed*]. When Johnson, an agent of the Department of the Interior who has been assigned to secure food for the Indians, is murdered, U. S. Marshal Wild Bill Hickok and his sidekick Jingles are sent to investigate. After Matthews, a local rancher, blames the Osage Indians for Johnson's murder and confides that he fears the new agent, Rossen, a neighboring rancher, may share the same fate, Hickok and Jingles decide to interview Rossen. As they near Rossen's ranch, the two lawmen witness a trio of Indians attacking two Indian riders. After killing one of the Indians and wounding the other, the three depart, and Hickok and Jingles come to the wounded man's aid. The injured man is a young brave named Taloga, and Hickok and Jingles hoist him onto a horse and take him to the Rossen ranch. At the ranch, meanwhile, the three marauders, who are in reality employees of Rossen, discard their Indian disguises and report to their boss. Rossen and his henchmen have been rustling the cattle that the government had arranged to buy for the Indians, while implicating the Indians in their crimes. Rossen then sells the cattle for his own reward and appropriates the government funds for himself. Hickok, Jingles and Taloga arrive at Rossen's ranch, and as Rossen dresses Taloga's wounds, his three hechmen enter and accuse the Indians of rustling

the herds earmarked for feeding. Matthews then gallops into the ranch in a furor, exclaiming that his herd has been stolen by the Indians and demanding that the government pay for the animals. When Rossen refuses to pay him because the cattle were never delivered, Matthews threatens to take the law into his own hands and raise an army of ranchers to confront the Indians. Upon discovering that the murdered Indian was Red Feather, chief of the Osage people, and that Taloga is his son, Hickok and Jingles ride to the reservation to meet with the Osage leaders. There, Indians convince Hickok of their innocence and tell him that Red Feather had come to town to inform Johnson that his people were starving, not to wreak havoc. After leaving the reservation, Hickok and Jingles are ambushed by Rossen's fake Indians. Fending off their attackers, Jingles and Hickok return to Rossen's ranch and unearth the Indian disguises. Realizing that Rossen and his men have been impersonating Indians, Hickok and Jingles, aided valiantly by Taloga, vanquish the greedy rancher and his henchmen. *Frame-ups. Impersonation and imposture. Indian agents. Osage Indians. Ranchers. United States. Marshals. Disguise. Indians of North America–Reservations. Murder. Rustlers.*

Note: According to a modern source, this theatrical release was a compilation of two episodes from the 1950's television series, *The Adventures of Wild Bill Hickok*, which starred Guy Madison and Andy Devine. One of the episodes was "The Indian Bureau"; the other has not been identified. The series began as a syndicated program for local broadcast from 1951 to 1954. From 1955 to 1956, it was broadcast on the CBS network, and on ABC from 1957 to 1958. A radio version, also starring Madison and Devine, was broadcast on the Mutual network from 1951 to 1956. For biographical information about Hickok, please see the entry above for *The Plainsman*. Modern sources add Terry Frost and Jack Reynolds to the cast.

Exb 9 Sep 1953, pp. 3593-94. *MPHPD* 5 Sep 1953, p. 1981.

TRAILS WESTWARD see **LAST OF THE COMANCHES**

TRAIN TO TOMBSTONE (Native Americans)

Lippert Productions, Inc.; A Donald Barry Production. *Dist* Lippert Productions, Inc. Aug **1950**; *Prod:* late Apr—early May 1950 [©Lippert Productions, Inc.; 19 Sep 1950; LP357]. Sd (Glen Glenn Sound Company); b&w. 6 reels, 5,113 ft. 56 or 58 min. PCA cert no. 14642.

Pres ROBERT L. LIPPERT. *Exec prod* Murray Lerner. *Prod* William Berke. *Assoc exec* Jack Leewood. *Dir* William Berke. *Asst dir* Melville Shyer. *Orig story* Donald Barry. *Scr* Orville Hampton and Victor West. *Dir of photog* Ernest Miller. *Cam op* Archie Dalzell. *Art dir* Fred Preble. *Film ed* Carl Pierson. *Ward* Alfred Berke. *Mus dir* Albert Glasser. *Sd eng* Harry Smith and Harry Eckles. *Makeup* Ted Coodley. *Prod mgr* Betty Sinclair. *Scr supv* Mary Chaffee. *Dial coach* Dean Reisner.

Cast: Donald Barry [(*Len Howard*)], Robert Lowery [(*Staley*)], Wally Vernon [(*Clifton Gulliver*)], Tom Neal [(*Dr. Willoughby*)], Judith Allen [(*Belle*)], Barbara Stanley [(*Doris Clayton*)], Minna Phillips [(*Abbie*)], Nan Leslie [(*Marie*)], Claude Stroud [(*Brown*)], Ed Cassidy [(*George, the Conductor*)].

Western. [*Print viewed*]. In the 1880s, at a train station in Albuquerque, New Mexico, passengers wait for the train to Tombstone, Arizona, which has been delayed due to the threat of an Indian ambush. Sitting on the platform waiting to board is a lovely paraplegic, Doris Clayton, who sits in a wheelchair next to her aunt Abbie. When they meet a reverend also waiting to board, Doris reveals that she is on her way to marry her fiancé, Lt. Gary Landell of the U. S. Cavalry. Later, Abbie tells another passenger, Dr. Willoughby, that Doris' doctor believes that her paralysis is psychological in nature. Farther down the platform is a young gambling hall owner named Marie, who is accompanying her friend Belle to Tombstone, having hired her to work in her establishment. After Willoughby carries Doris onto the train, the nervous train conductor, George, receives his orders to begin their journey. As the train is pulling away from the station, traveling salesman Clifton Gulliver jumps onboard, spilling his suitcase of corsets all over the aisle. Suddenly, two cowboys, who are shooting at each other, begin chasing the train. One of them, Len Howard, jumps onto the back of the train, evading his pursuer, then tells George that he wants to buy a ticket. When Abbie goes to the back of the train, Len takes her seat and begins talking with Doris. Doris reveals that she is paralyzed and that her upcoming marriage to Gary was arranged when she was a little girl. In the baggage compartment, a marshal, who has been placed aboard the train to guard a shipment of gold worth $250,000, tells George that they suspect one of the passengers of being a lookout for a gang of robbers, who use local Indian braves to help them ambush trains. George says

that he checked out all the passengers except Len, after which the train's engineer, Tim, finds a "Wanted" circular offering $5,000 for Len's capture. After the marshal accuses Len of being the lookout and handcuffs him to his seat, a herd of sheep rush onto the tracks ahead. Len announces that they are about to become the victims of an Indian trick and orders George to remove his handcuffs, which he does. Len and George then quickly pass out rifles to all of the male passengers, who begin firing when the Indians attack. Tim manages to get the train through the sheep, but not before he, George, and the reverend are shot. When the marshal tries to place the handcuffs back onto his wrists, Len pulls his gun, so George intervenes, ordering that Len remain unshackled in the event of another attack. A short time later, the train comes to an incline, and Doris sees the marshal, who is really the lookout, trying to signal to the gang. After another shootout with the braves, Gary, who is secretly working with the gang, jumps aboard, where he is shot and killed. Doris is so surprised to see Gary that she jumps out of her seat, finding herself cured of her paralysis. Later, Len, who reveals that he is actually an undercover agent, announces his engagement to Doris, and the reverend agrees to perform their wedding ceremony in Tombstone. *Impersonation and imposture. Indians of North America. Train robberies. Trains. Albuquerque (NM). Ambushes. Cures. Engagements. Gold. Marshals. Nieces. Officers (Military). Paraplegics. Physicians. Railroad engineers. Reverends. Rifles. Sheep. Shootings. Tombstone (AZ). Train conductors. Train stations. Traveling salesmen.*

Note: According to news items, the picture was shot on location in Carson City, NV. Modern sources include Bill Kennedy and Jack Perrin in the cast.
Box 16 Sep 1950, p. 8. *HR* 22 Mar 1950, p. 8. *HR* 27 Apr 1950, p. 5. *HR* 28 Apr 1950, p. 14. *HR* 5 May 1950, p. 10. *HR* 1 Sep 1950, p. 3. *MPHPD* 9 Sep 1950, p. 477-8. *Var* 6 Sep 1950, p. 8.

THE TRAITOR (Latino)
Excelsior Pictures Corp. *Dist* Puritan Pictures Corp. 29 Aug 1936. Sd; b&w. 60 min. Passed by the National Board of Review. PCA cert no. 2332.

Prod Sig Neufeld and Leslie Simmonds. *Dir* Sam Newfield. *Asst dir* William O'Connor. *Story* John Neville. *Story ed* Joseph O'Donnell. *Photog* Jack Greenhalgh. *Film ed* Jack English. *Sd rec* Hans Weeren.

Cast: TIM McCOY (*Tim [Vallance]*), Frances Grant (*Mary [Allen]*), Frank Melton (*Jimmy [Allen]*), Pedro Regas (*[Pedro] Moreno*), Frank Glendon (*Big George*), Carl Hackett (*Captain [John Hughes]*), Dick Curtis (*Morgan*), Roger Williams (*Sheriff*), [Jack Rockwell (*Smoky*)], [Dick Botiller (*Remos*)], [Wally Wales (*Hunk*)], [Ed Cobb (*Joe*)], [Wally West (*Bud*)], [Tina Menard (*Maria*)], [Soledad Jiménez (*Juana*)].

Western. [*Print viewed*]. Although Texas Ranger Tim Vallance helps capture bandit Pedro Moreno's bucking horse Thunder, Moreno remains at large. Tim then mollifies Thunder and is the first man other than Moreno who is able to ride him. Ranger captain John Hughes then sends Tim to the small town of Plainview to stop a lynching of Moreno and his young accomplice, who refuses to give his name. Tim successfully saves the criminals, securing their right to a trial, then lets them go, hoping they will lead him to their boss Big George and he will be able to apprehend them all legally. In order to allow Tim to go undercover, Hughes publicly dismisses him for cowardice. Moreno and his accomplice arrive at the Flying A Ranch to lay low for awhile and the accomplice is revealed as Jimmy, brother to Mary Allen, who offered Tim a job on the ranch. Moreno poses as "Pedro Gonzalez," but Mary's servant, Juana, warns her he is the bandit Moreno. Tim then arrives for work and, seeing Jimmy in a photograph with Mary, is forced to reveal that her brother is a bandit called "The Texas Kid" who runs with Moreno. To avoid the criminals, Tim tells Mary he was kicked out of the Rangers, even though Hughes's letter to her refutes it, and he leaves the ranch. In town, at the Blue Cat Cantina, Big George's cover business, Tim gets himself recruited into the gang of contrabanders by returning Moreno's horse to him. Big George continues to move contraband over the border and the Rangers, believing Tim has gone crooked, try to catch him. At the cabin of sheepherder Jose Ramos, who will act as liaison between Hughes and Tim, Hughes urges Tim to call off his undercover work, but Tim is undaunted. Then, while the gang's pilot prepares a $100,000 shipment of drugs, Tim gets their fingerprints. Later, Ranger Smoky shoots Tim off his horse. After Smoky removes Tim's bullet at his request and leaves to get help, Tim escapes on his horse to the

Ramos' cabin, where he collapses, delirious. Mary, having learned Tim's true mission from Hughes, nurses him. Meanwhile, Big George has become suspicious of Tim and surrounds the cabin. Jimmy goes in to save Mary and helps Tim fight the outlaws. The Rangers join the gunfight and Moreno, Jimmy and Hughes are all fatally wounded. Jimmy dies, sorry for his crimes. Smoky then arrests Tim, unaware of his innocence. Tim goes to trial and is convicted and jailed, but eventually Smoky unearths a letter Hughes wrote that vindicates Tim. Although Tim is free to leave his cell, Smoky puts Mary behind bars with him. *False arrests. Rangers. Smuggling. Undercover agents. Brothers and sisters. Drugs. False accusations. Gunfights. Gunshot wounds. Horses. Justice. Letters. Lynching. Mexican Americans. Moral reformation. Ranches. Saloons. Self-sacrifice. Servants. Texas. Trials.*

Note: Although a 1936 copyright statement appears on the viewed print, the title is not listed in the copyright registry. *Var* and press material list Joseph O'Donnell as film editor, although the onscreen credits list him as story editor. A modern source erroneously lists Holdbrook Todd as editor. *Var* erroneously credits producer Sig Neufeld with direction. A modern source lists the following additional cast members: Frank Ellis (*Ranger*), Jimmy Aubrey (*Bus driver Slim*), Charles "Slim" Whitaker (*Plainview man/Ranger*), George Chesebro (*Lynch leader*), Art Dillard (*Roadblock man*), Frank McCarroll (*Lyncher at fence*), Oscar Gahan (*Outlaw in cantina*), Julian Rivero (*Jose Ramos*), Jack Kirk and Al Taylor (*Outlaws*), Jack King, Ray Henderson (*Rangers*), and Buck Morgan (*Lyncher*).
FD 6 Nov 1936, p. 13. *Var* 4 Nov 1936, p. 19.

TRANSGRESSION *(foreign version)* see **NUIT D'ESPAGNE**

THE TRAP (Chinese Americans)
Monogram Pictures Corp. *Dist* Monogram Pictures Corp. 30 Nov 1946; *Prod*: late Jul—mid-Aug 1946 [©Monogram Pictures Corp.; 26 Nov 1946; LP728]. Sd (Western Electric Sound System); b&w. 69 min.

Series: Charlie Chan.

Prod James S. Burkett. *Dir* Howard Bretherton. *Asst dir* Harold Knox. *Orig scr* Miriam Kissinger. *Dir of photog* James Brown. *Tech dir* Dave Milton. *Supv film ed* Richard Currier. *Ed* Ace Herman. *Set dec* Raymond Boltz, Jr. *Mus dir* Edward J. Kay. *Rec* Tom Lambert. *Makeup* Harry Rose. *Prod mgr* William Calihan, Jr.

Source: Based on characters created by Earl Derr Biggers.

Cast: Sidney Toler [(*Charlie Chan*)], Mantan Moreland [(*Birmingham*)], Victor Sen Young [(*Jimmy Chan*)], Tanis Chandler [(*Adelaide*)], Larry Blake [(*Rick Daniels*)], Kirk Alyn [(*Sergeant Reynolds*)], Rita Quigley [(*Clementine*)], Anne Nagel [(*Marcia*)], Helen Gerald [(*Ruby*)], Howard Negley [(*Cole King*)], Lois Austin [(*Mrs. Thorn*)], Barbara Jean Wong [(*San Toy*)], Minerva Urecal [(*Mrs. Weebles*)], Margaret Brayton [(*Madge Mudge*)], Bettie Best [(*Winifred*)], Jan Bryant [(*Lois*)], [Walden Boyle (*George "Doc" Brandt*)].

Detective, Show business, Comedy-drama. [*Print viewed*]. Cole King's variety troupe, along with press agent Rick Daniels, and Mrs. Thorn, the wardrobe mistress, occupy a Malibu, California beach house. When Adelaide, a showgirl, criticizes Marcia, the imperious star of the show and King's girl friend, Marcia threatens to reveal that Adelaide is secretly married to physician George Brandt and also hints that she knows Brandt's real identity. Marcia then forces showgirl Lois to steal letters from Adelaide's trunk by threatening to tell King that Lois is under eighteen. Later, Marcia disappears and Lois' body is discovered by Chinese troupe member San Toy. Because Lois has been strangled, a murder technique said to be favored by the Chinese and the French, both San Toy and Adelaide are under suspicion. When Daniels suggests that they try to make Lois' death appear to be a drowning, San Toy, who is a friend of Jimmy, the son of Chinese detective Charlie Chan, asks Chan to investigate. During the course of the investigation, both Chan's assistant Birmingham and San Toy are attacked. Later troupe member Clementine finds Marcia's body, a silk cord wrapped around her neck, washed up on the beach. Later, Chan discovers Daniels burying Marcia's bathrobe. When Chan reveals that the cord from the robe was used in one of the murders, Daniels claims that the robe was planted on King to frame him. Then King accuses Daniels of murdering the women and trying to hide the evidence. Privately, Chan reveals that he knows that Brandt was once accused of his wife's murder, and although he was exonerated, his career was ruined. He went to war and met and married Adelaide in Paris, where Marcia first met them. Brandt admits that he found Lois' body and removed the letters, but denies killing her. Chan then decides to set a trap for the killer. That night, King confesses that he took a box from

Brandt's suitcase that contained incriminating papers. Jimmy later finds the missing box in the furnace. Jimmy then sees someone try to strangle San Toy and intervenes, inadvertently spoiling Chan's trap. Chan, Jimmy and Birmingham chase her attacker, who is revealed to be Mrs. Thorn. Mrs. Thorn had deserted King, her husband, and when she wanted to return to him, he humiliated her by offering her a job as his wardrobe mistress. She then killed the two women and framed King in order to make him suffer. Her letters were in the box that King stole from Brandt. Later, Chan assures Brandt that the Board of Medical Examiners will reinstate his license and he will be free to practice under his own name. *Chinese Americans. Entertainers. Frameups. Murder. Private detectives. African Americans. Blackmail. Fathers and sons. Letters. Malibu (CA). Physicians. Press agents. Secret passageways. Strangling. Traps. Wives.*

Note: *The Trap* marked the last film appearance of Sidney Toler, who died in Feb 1947. Roland Winters assumed the role of "Charlie Chan" in the 1947 film *The Chinese Ring*. For more information on the "Charlie Chan" series, consult the Series Index and see the entry above for *Charlie Chan Carries On*.

DV 27 Dec 1946, p. 3. *HR* 2 Aug 1946, p. 18. *HR* 16 Aug 1946, p. 18. *HR* 27 Dec 1946, p. 3. *MPHPD* 2 Nov 1946, p. 3287.

THE TRAVELING SALESWOMAN (Native Americans)

Columbia Pictures Corp.; A Joan Davis Production. *Dist* Columbia Pictures Corp. 5 Jan **1950**; Prod: 5 Aug–20 Aug 1949 [©Columbia Pictures Corp.; 3 Jan 1950; LP2731]. Sd (Western Electric Recording); b&w. 6,712 ft. 74-75 min.

Prod Tony Owen. *Dir* Charles F. Riesner. *Asst dir* Jack Corrick. *Story and scr* Howard Dimsdale. *Dir of photog* George L. Diskant. *Spec eff* Fred Wolff. *Art dir* Carl Anderson. *Film ed* Viola Lawrence. *Set dec* George Montgomery. *Gowns* Jean Louis. *Mus dir* Mischa Bakaleinikoff. [*Sd* Josh Westmoreland].

Song(s): "Every Baby Needs a Da Da Daddy" and "He Died with His Boots On," words and music by Allan Roberts and Lester Lee.

Cast: JOAN DAVIS [(*Mabel King*)], Andy Devine [(*Waldo*)], Adele Jergens [(*Lilly*)], Joe Sawyer [(*Cactus Jack*)], Dean Riesner [(*Tom*)], John Cason [(*Fred*)], Chief Thundercloud [(*Running Deer*)], [Harry Hayden (*J. L. King*)], [Charles Halton (*Clumhill*)], [Minerva Urecal (*Mrs. Owen*)], [Eddy Waller (*Mr. Owen*)], [Teddy Infuhr (*Homer*)], [Robert Cherry (*Simon*)], [William Newell (*Bartender*)], [Ethan Laidlaw (*Mike*)], [Harry Woods (*Jenkins*)], [Harry Tyler (*Jasper North*)], [Alan Bridge (*P. Carter*)], [Fred Aldrich (*Cowpuncher*)], [George McDonald (*Bob*)], [Gertrude Chorre (*Squaw*)], [Louis Mason (*Livery stableman*)], [Emmett Lynn (*Desert rat*)], [B. G. Norman (*Charlie*)], [Jessie Arnold (*Lady customer*)], [Bob Wilke (*Loser*)], [Stanley Andrews (*Banker*)], [George Chesebro (*Horseman*)], [Bill Wilkerson (*Tony*)], [Chief Yowlachie (*Sam*)], [Nick Thompson (*Indian Itch*)], [Heinie Conklin].

Historical, Comedy, with songs. [*Print viewed*]. In a small Eastern town in 1889, Mabel King tries desperately to obtain a loan to keep her father's soap factory in business. To that end, she invites Clumhill, the banker, to see the factory for himself. Mabel's father J. L. is aghast when he learns this news because the company no longer has the employees needed to run the factory. Mabel suggests that she and Waldo, her fiancé, run the machinery so that Clumhill will believe that they are still in business. The machinery runs amok, but Clumhill reports that King Soap removed an old spot from his hat, and consequently, he will renew their note if they can produce some orders before the old note comes due in three weeks. Mabel is convinced that she will be a better salesperson than Waldo, and finally, J. L. agrees to allow her to go on the road. Waldo, however, is concerned about the dangers of the road and surreptitiously follows her. At her first stop out West, Mabel learns that the saloon is the biggest soap user in town and, in an effort to seem friendly, she gets drunk there. A gunfight breaks out between cowboy Mike and rustler Cactus Jack, and before he is shot, Mike slips a phony bill of sale into Mabel's pocket. Cactus Jack searches Mike's body for the bill of sale, which is proof of his nefarious deeds, and when he fails to find it, divines what happened and goes looking for Mabel. In the meantime, Mabel resolves to create a demand for the soap by selling it door-to-door. At one house, the Owen family asks her to dinner and then to stay the night, but when they learn that she is a traveling saleswoman, they decide to keep her apart from their oldest son Simon, because their daughter ran away with a traveling salesman. As a practical joke, Homer, their youngest son, sets traps for Mabel. She evades them, but members of Cactus Jack's gang, who are trying to retrieve the bill of

sale, are thwarted by them. Later, when Mabel prepares for bed, she discovers the phony bill of sale, but does not understand its significance. The following morning, the gunmen spot a group of Indians on the horizon and decide to let them dispose of Mabel. Their plan fails when the Indian chief, the notorious Running Deer, spares Mabel's life after she accidentally eats a bar of soap and blows bubbles. In the next town, Waldo waits anxiously for Mabel. There, a store owner decides to create a demand for his surplus soap by starting a rumor that there is a diamond in one of the boxes. Mabel hears the rumor, and believing that it is her father's ring, buys all the soap herself. Later, the town is warned that the Indians are on the war path, and Mabel offers to intercede with Running Deer if everyone in town will agree to buy King Soap. Cactus Jack and his cohorts then dress up as Indians, planning to kill Mabel and blame her death on them. She is saved by the arrival of the real Indians, and after the townspeople recognize Cactus Jack, Mabel displays the bill of sale, and Cactus Jack is arrested. Then Running Deer vows to remain peaceful if the town supplies him with King Soap, the only thing that can cure his itchy scalp. Now that the factory is saved, Mabel and Waldo return home. *Indians of North America. Soap. Traveling salesmen. The West. Women in business. Bankers. Children. Drunkenness. Fathers and daughters. Gunfights. Hoaxes. Murder. Saloons. Stores. Retail. Traps.*

Box 31 Dec 1949. *DV* 28 Dec 1949, p. 3. *HR* 5 Aug 1949, p. 12. *HR* 12 Aug 1949, p. 12. *HR* 28 Dec 1949, p. 3. *MPHPD* 18 Feb 1950, p. *NYT* 6 Jan 1950, p. 25. *Var* 28 Dec 1949, p. 6.

TREACHERY RIDES THE RANGE (Native Americans, Cheyenne)

Warner Bros. Pictures, Inc. *Dist* Warner Bros. Pictures, Inc. 2 May **1936**; Prod: ended 24 Dec 1935 [©Warner Bros. Pictures, Inc.; 25 Apr 1936; LP6303]. Sd; b&w. 6 reels. 56 or 58 min. PCA cert no. 1870.

[*Prod* Bryan Foy]. *Dir* Frank McDonald. *Story and scr* William Jacobs. *Photog* L. William O'Connell. *Art dir* Ted Smith. *Ed* Frank MaGee. *Mus dir* Leo F. Forbstein.

Song(s): "Ridin' Home" and "Leather and Steel," music and lyrics by M. K. Jerome and Jack Scholl.

Cast: Dick Foran (*Capt. Red Taylor*), Paula Stone (*Ruth Drummond*), Craig Reynolds (*Wade Carter*), Monte Blue (*Col. Drummond*), Carlyle Moore, Jr. (*Little Big Wolf*), Henry Otho (*Burley Barton*), Jim Thorpe (*Chief Red Smoke*), Monte Montague [(*Nebraska Bill*)], Don Barclay [(*Corporal Bunce*)], Frank Bruno [(*Little Big Fox*)], Milt Kibbee [(*Eph Billings*)], Tom Wilson [(*Denver*)], Bud Osborne [(*Pawnee Pete*)], Nick Copeland [(*Neal*)], [Dick Botiller (*Antelope Boy*)], [Gene Alsace (*Scout Blackbourne*)], [William Desmond (*Driver*)], [Tom Brower (*Marshal*)], [Ferdinand Schumann-Heink (*Cliff*)], [Bob Burns (*Nevins*)], [Larry Kent (*Clerk*)].

Western, with songs. [*Print viewed*]. A treaty between the United States government and the Cheyenne Indians makes it a criminal offense for white hunters to shoot buffalo. Col. Drummond and Capt. Red Taylor are entrusted with enforcing the treaty. Buffalo hunter Wade Carter asks Drummond for permission to hunt buffalo in the Texas panhandle, and when Drummond refuses, Carter decides to force the Indians to break the treaty by having his men shoot the two sons of Chief Red Smoke while dressed as army officers. One of the sons, Little Big Wolf, survives and brings his dead brother home. Blaming the army, the Cheyenne go on the warpath for revenge. By doing so, they break the treaty and Drummond decides to arrest Red Smoke despite Red's defense of the Indians' actions. Drummond's daughter Ruth writes that she will soon return to the fort from Dodge City. Red rides through an Indian attack to warn her of the danger, but she thinks that he is overcautious and arranges to travel with Carter's men. Carter goads Red until he starts a fight and then has him arrested so he cannot interfere with their plans. Meanwhile, Indians attack Carter's wagon train. Burley Barton, Carter's partner, attacks Ruth, who runs off and is captured by the Indians. Red Smoke plans to torture her in revenge for the murder of his son, but Red manages to prove that Carter is guilty of the murder and peace returns. *Bison, American. Cheyenne Indians. United States. Army. Cavalry. Hostages. Hunters. Murder. Treachery. Treaties.*

Note: The film's working title was *Treachery Rides the Trail*. Foran's billing on screen was "Dick Foran The Singing Cowboy."

DV 24 Dec 1935, p. 2. *FD* 29 May 1936, p. 8. *HR* 28 Feb 1936, p. 3. *MPD* 2 Mar 1936, p. 6. *MPH* 1 Feb 1935, p. 44. *MPH* 7 Mar 1936, p. 50. *NYT* 30 May 1936, p. 7. *Var* 3 Jun 1936, p. 54.

TREASURE OF LOS ALAMOS see BORDER TREASURE

A TREE GROWS IN BROOKLYN (Irish Americans)
Twentieth Century-Fox Film Corp. *Dist* Twentieth Century-Fox Film Corp. Feb **1945**; New York opening: 28 Feb 1945; Prod: 1 May— 2 Aug 1944 [©Twentieth Century-Fox Film Corp.; 28 Feb 1945; LP13224]. Sd (Western Electric Recording); b&w. 13 reels, 11,583 ft. 128 or 132 min. PCA cert no. 10160.

Prod Louis D. Lighton. *Dir* Elia Kazan. [*Asst dir* Saul Wurtzel]. [*Dial dir* Arthur Pierson and Nicholas Ray]. *Scr* Tess Slesinger and Frank Davis. [*Contr to dial* Anita Loos]. *Dir of photog* Leon Shamroy. [*2d cam* Curtis Fetters]. *Spec photog eff* Fred Sersen. [*Transparency projections shot* Edwin Hammeras. *Transparency projection shots* Edward Snyder]. *Art dir* Lyle Wheeler. *Film ed* Dorothy Spencer. *Set dec* Thomas Little. *Assoc* Frank E. Hughes. *Cost* Bonnie Cashin. *Mus* Alfred Newman. *Orch arr* Edward Powell. *Sd* Bernard Freericks and Roger Heman. [*Mus mixer* Murray Spivack and Vinton Vernon]. *Makeup artist* Guy Pearce. [*Research dir* Frances Richardson]. [*Research asst* Gertrude Kingston]. [*Head of landscape dept* Nick Kalten].

Song(s): "Annie Laurie," music by Lady John Scott, lyrics by William Douglas; "Sweet Molly Malone" and "The First Noël," traditional; "Silent Night, Holy Night," music by Franz Gruber, lyrics by Joseph Mohr; "Joy to the World," music by Joseph Handel, lyrics by Isaac Watts; "Away in a Manger," music by James Ramsey Murray, lyrics anonymous; "Adeste fideles (O, Come All Ye Faithful)," music by John Francis Wade, lyrics by Frederick Oakeley.

Source: Based on the book *A Tree Grows in Brooklyn* by Betty Smith (New York, 1943).

Cast: Dorothy McGuire (*Katie Nolan*), Joan Blondell (*Aunt Sissy*), James Dunn (*Johnny Nolan*), Lloyd Nolan (*Officer McShane*), James Gleason (*McGarrity*), Ted Donaldson (*Neeley Nolan*), Peggy Ann Garner (*Francie [Nolan]*), Ruth Nelson (*Miss McDonough*), John Alexander (*Steve Edwards*), B. S. Pully (*Christmas tree vendor*), [Ferike Boros (*Grandma Rommely*)], [Charles Halton (*Mr. Barker*)], [J. Farrell Macdonald (*Carney, the junkman*)], [Adeline deWalt Reynolds (*Mrs. Waters*)], [George Melford (*Mr. Spencer*)], [Mae Marsh, Edna Jackson (*Tynmore sisters*)], [Vincent Graeff (*Henny Gaddis*)], [Susan Lester (*Flossie Gaddis*)], [Johnnie Berkes (*Mr. Crackenbox*)], [Lillian Bronson (*Librarian*)], [Alec Craig (*Werner*)], [Al Bridge (*Cheap Charlie*)], [Joseph J. Greene (*Hassler*)], [Virginia Brissac (*Miss Tilford*)], [Harry Harvey, Jr. (*Herschel Knutsen*)], [Robert Anderson (*Augie*)], [Art Smith (*Charlie, the iceman*)], [Norman Field, George Meader (*Principals*)], [Erskine Sanford (*Undertaker*)], [Martha Wentworth (*Sheila's mother*)], [Francis Pierlot (*Priest*)], [Al Eben (*Union representative*)], [Peter Cusanelli (*Barber*)], [Harry Seymour (*Floorwalker at the 5 & 10*)], [Paul Graeff, Gerald Mackey, Robert Ferrero, Mickey McGuire, Danny Shaw (*Raiders*)], [Paul Weigel (*Candy store proprietor*)], [Walt Robbins (*Junkman*)], [Nancy June Robinson, Mary Lou Harrington, Sally Brown, Jacqueline Larkin, Joy Duguay, Eva Lee Kuney, Janice Hood, Sheilah Brown, Linda Bieber, Joyce Tucker (*Girls*)], [Teddy Infuhr, Boots Brown, Mickey Kuhn, Gordon Rader, Elvin Field, Paul Hilton, Ronnie Pattison (*Boys*)], [Jack Lawrence, Nicholas Ray (*Bakery clerks*)], [Patricia McFadden (*Sheila*)], [Robert Strange, George Carleton, Robert Malcolm (*Doctors*)], [Jessie Arnold, Edythe Elliott (*Nurses*)], [Tony Santoro (*Waiter*)], [Robert Tait (*Street singer*)], [Sue Moore], [Ethel May Halls], [Fernanda Eliscu], [Cecil Weston], [Ruth Rickaby], [Constance Purdy], [Harry Denny], [Jean Fowler], [Charles Marsh], [Dink Trout], [James B. Carson], [Jack Carr], [Irving Gump].

Domestic, Melodrama, with songs. [*Print viewed*]. During the early part of the century, in the Irish-American section of Brooklyn, the poor Nolan family struggles to make ends meet in their tenement flat. Johnny Nolan, an infrequently employed singing waiter, is an alcoholic whose jovial, impractical nature is the delight and despair of his hard-working wife Katie, who serves as the tenement's scrubwoman. Their two children, the ever-hungry Neeley and the wistful, teenaged Francie, help Katie by selling rags. Francie idolizes her father, who encourages her to daydream about better times to come. One afternoon, Francie notices with dismay that the tree growing in the tenement courtyard is being ruthlessly trimmed. She is distracted, however, by the arrival of insurance agent Barker, who collects Katie's weekly premiums. Barker, a notorious gossip, reveals that Katie's sister Sissy has married for the third time. Katie is furious

but the children are delighted that they will have another uncle Bill, for Sissy always calls her husbands Bill. Later that evening, Johnny comes home and learns from Francie that "their" tree has been cut. Johnny assures her that the tree will grow back in the spring, then leaves for a job singing at a wedding. When Sissy arrives soon after for a visit, Katie castigates her for marrying again without obtaining a divorce from her last husband. The earthy Sissy protests that she waited for seven years before re-marrying, and insists that she really loves her new man, who is a milkman named Steve Edwards. Sissy then joins the children on the sidewalk, and when a neighborhood woman complains about the Nolans borrowing her daughter's roller skates, police officer McShane breaks up the loud discussion. McShane, who is new to the neighborhood, is charmed by Katie's loveliness, but she is nonplussed by his attraction. Afraid that Sissy is a bad influence on the children, Katie forbids her to visit again. Johnny returns home late that night and is thrilled to see Katie waiting up for him. Francie and Neeley awaken, and Johnny regales them with tales of the wedding. After the children return to bed, Johnny promises Katie that he will make a "fresh start," but the pragmatic Katie knows that nothing will come of his big talk. The next morning, Francie and Neeley are on their way to school when they see the drunken Johnny staggering home. McShane escorts him up the stairs and is stunned to learn that he is Katie's husband. Later, Francie confides in Johnny her dream to attend a nicer school in a better neighborhood. Even though it means lying about their address, Johnny convinces Katie to let Francie go, and Francie becomes a member of Miss McDonough's class at the new school. Soon after, Katie moves the family to a tiny, less expensive apartment on the top floor of the tenement. Believing that Katie made the move out of stinginess, Johnny forlornly sings "Annie Laurie," accompanying himself on a piano left by the former occupant. On Christmas Eve, Miss McDonough encourages Francie to become a writer, and after class is over, Francie and Neeley obtain a leftover tree from a Christmas tree vendor. The children carry their prize home, and the Nolans are joined by Steve and Sissy, whose pregnancy has reconciled her with Katie. Katie confides in Sissy that she is pregnant also, and later that night, tells Johnny. Finally realizing why Katie moved them to the cheaper apartment, Johnny is further crushed when Katie insists that Francie will have to quit school before her graduation from eighth grade, so that she can go to work. Determined to keep Francie in school, Johnny leaves to find a job, but after he has been missing for over a week, Katie begins searching for him. Later, McShane brings her news that Johnny died from pneumonia while looking for work, and at his funeral, many people lament his loss. So grief-stricken that she cannot cry, Francie stoically agrees to work with Neeley in McGarrity's bar after school to help provide for the family. Katie is relieved that Francie can stay in school but is aware that Francie blames her for Johnny's death. After Sissy's baby is born safely in a hospital, Katie asks Francie to remain close by until her time comes, for they cannot afford a hospital. One afternoon, Katie goes into labor, and as Francie comforts her, Katie reveals how much she misses Johnny, and mother and daughter draw closer. They name the baby Annie Laurie, and the little family continues. Graduation day arrives, and while Katie attends Neeley's ceremony at the old school, Sissy goes with Francie. On her desk, Francie discovers a bouquet paid for with money Johnny gave to Sissy before Christmas, and also a card he wrote to her. The gesture finally enables Francie to release her grief, and after a good cry, she receives her diploma with her class. Afterward, the family has ice cream at the drugstore, and a neighborhood boy asks Francie out on her first date. When the Nolans return to their apartment, they find McShane helping Steve babysit Annie Laurie. Sissy and Steve leave, and McShane asks Katie if he can keep company with her, intending to marry her as soon as she feels that a decent interval has passed. Touched by McShane's kindness, Katie agrees, and Francie, as the eldest, also gives her consent. McShane promises to be a good friend to the two oldest children and asks permission to adopt Annie Laurie. When Francie and Neeley go outside to leave the courting couple alone, they remark that while their sister's life will be easier than theirs, she will not have as much fun. Francie then notices that her tree is growing again, just as Johnny promised it would. *Disillusionment. Family life. Fathers and daughters. Grief. Idealists. Maturation. New York City–Brooklyn. Poverty. Adolescence. Alcoholics. "Annie Laurie" (Song). Childbirth. Christmas Eve. Courtship. Death and dying. Education. Gossip. Graduations.*

Grandmothers. Infants. Insurance–Agents. Irish Americans. Marriage. Mothers and daughters. Neighbors. Police. Reconciliation. Saloon keepers. Schoolteachers. Scrubwomen. Sisters. Tenement-houses. Trees. *Troilus and Cressida* (Play).

Note: The opening title card reads "Twentieth Century-Fox presents Betty Smith's *A Tree Grows in Brooklyn*." The screen rights to Smith's novel became the focus of a bidding war among several studios before the book was even published, according to a 24 Jun 1943 *HR* news item. Twentieth Century-Fox obtained the rights to the best-seller for $55,000, and intended to star Alice Faye as "Katie Nolan," according to later *HR* news items. When Faye proved unavailable, Gene Tierney was tested for the role. On 31 Mar 1944, *HR* stated that actors "not officially announced but strongly rumored for roles" included Mary Anderson, Jeanne Crain and Fred MacMurray. The studio carried out an extensive search for an actor to play "Johnny Nolan," and on 16 Dec 1943, *HR* noted that Phil Regan was the "leading contender." James Dunn, who won the role in the film, was signed in Apr 1944, and a *HR* news item commented that "Dunn was tested twice, once at the beginning of the search, and again after all other possibilities had been abandoned and it was certain no top boxoffice name would be available." Dorothy McGuire, who was only thirteen years older than Peggy Ann Garner at the time of filming, was borrowed from David O. Selznick's company for the production. Ted Donaldson was borrowed from Columbia, and John Alexander was borrowed from Warner Bros.

A 19 May 1944 *HR* news item described one of the film's sets as "the most elaborate and, mechanically speaking, costly set to be used" on the studio's lot in several years. A full stage was taken up with the four-story replica of the Nolans' Brooklyn tenement house, and in one scene, "the cameras [were to] work on elevators to capture action in sequence on all of the floors during one take."

According to information in the film's file in the MPAA/PCA Collection at the AMPAS Library, the PCA initially refused to approve the screenplay due to "the bigamous characterization of Sissy." The PCA also disapproved of the light tone taken by the characters toward Sissy's marital escapades, and on 26 Apr 1944, suggested that the portrayal of Sissy as a much-married woman would be acceptable if it were clearly established that her previous husbands had died before she remarried. On 4 May 1944, the PCA approved the script, although the Office did issue further warnings that Sissy's "false philosophy" regarding the nature of love and marriage should be toned down.

Smith's book and the film were the subjects of libel lawsuits brought by Smith's cousin, Sadie Grandner. Grandner alleged that Smith based the character of "Aunt Sissy" on her, but with malicious and slanderous implications upon her character, and that following the book and film's release, she had become the object of scorn and ridicule by her acquaintances. According to information in the Twentieth Century-Fox Records of the Legal Department, located at the UCLA Arts–Special Collections Library, Grandner filed suit against Smith and her publishing company first, before the film was produced. The studio, worried that she would hold them liable as well, deliberately "toned down" the portrayal of Sissy. The legal records reveal that in Feb 1946, Grandner, who filed suit against the studio under the name Sadie Kandler, dropped her claim in exchange for $1,500. The disposition of her suit against Smith and the publishing company is not known.

A Tree Grows in Brooklyn, which benefitted the Naval Aid Auxiliary with its gala West Coast premiere, was first seen by U.S. troops in Manila, according to a 7 Feb 1945 *HR* news item. The picture garnered much critical praise and excellent boxoffice receipts, and marked the dramatic film debut of director Elia Kazan, a renowned stage director who had previously worked on two film documentaries. When Kazan came to Hollywood for the production, he was accompanied by Nicholas Ray, with whom he had worked on the stage. *A Tree Grows in Brooklyn* was the first film on which Ray worked, and he also makes a brief appearance in the picture as a bakery clerk. Although some modern sources list Ray as Kazan's assistant director, studio legal records credit him as a dialogue director. According to one modern source, Ray aided Alfred Newman in preparing the film's musical score. The picture marked a return to production by producer Louis D. Lighton, who had not personally supervised a film since the 1939 M-G-M film *Lucky Night*. *A Tree Grows in Brooklyn* was a personal triumph for Dunn, whose superb notices helped revitalize his career. Garner and Nolan also received much praise, and critics commented warmly on McGuire's transition from the childlike bride in the 1943 Twentieth Century-Fox production *Claudia* to the hardworking "Katie Nolan." The film was named one of the ten best films of the year by *FD*, the National Board of Review, *Time* and *NYT*. The picture also received an Academy Award nomination for Tess Slesinger and Frank Davis' screenplay. The screenplay was Slesinger's last, however, as she died on 21 Feb 1945. Slesinger and Davis were married and frequently worked together. Dunn was awarded a Best Supporting Actor Oscar and Garner received a special Oscar as "the outstanding child performer of 1945." According to a 3 Jun 1945 *NYT* article, the picture was among "the first selections for inclusion in the film section of the Library of Congress." The article quotes acting librarian Dr. Luther H. Evans as saying that "the chief purpose of the library in its film selections was to preserve those 'which faithfully record...the contemporary life and tastes and preferences of the American people.' "

Smith cowrote a musical play version of her novel with George Abbott, and it opened in New York on 19 Apr 1951, with lyrics by Dorothy Fields and music by Arthur Schwartz. Joan Blondell also starred as "Sissy" in the road company version of the musical play, which opened on 9 Oct 1952. In 1974, the NBC network broadcast a television film based on Slesinger and Davis' adaptation of the novel, also entitled *A Tree Grows in Brooklyn*. The 1974 production was directed by Joseph Hardy and starred Cliff Robertson, Diane Baker and James Olson.

Box 3 Feb 1945. *DV* 24 Jan 1945, p. 3, 5. *FD* 24 Jan 1945, p. 11. *HCN* 2 Mar 1945. *HR* 24 Jun 1943, p. 1. *HR* 1 Jul 1943, p. 1. *HR* 5 Oct 1943, p. 1. *HR* 16 Dec 1943, p. 1. *HR* 31 Mar 1944, p. 6. *HR* 17 Apr 1944, p. 3. *HR* 28 Apr 1944, p. 4. *HR* 5 May 1944, p. 21. *HR* 19 May 1944, p. 10. *HR* 28 Jul 1944, p. 15. *HR* 3 Aug 1944, p. 10. *HR* 24 Jan 1945, p. 3. *HR* 7 Feb 1945, p. 1. *HR* 27 Feb 1945, p. 4. *HR* 1 Mar 1945, p. 1, 6. *HR* 5 Mar 1945, p. 3. *HR* 6 Mar 1945, p. 10. *HR* 13 Mar 1945, p. 15. *HR* 20 Mar 1945, p. 11. *LAT* 2 Mar 1945, p. 8. *Look* 6 Feb 1945, pp. 47-51. *MPD* 24 Jan 145, p. 1, 14. *MPHPD* 3 Jun 1944, p. 1923. *MPHPD* 27 Jan 1945, p. 2289. *NYT* 1 Mar 1945, p. 25. *NYT* 4 Mar 1945. *NYT* 3 Jun 1945. *PM* 14 May 1944. *Var* 24 Jan 1945, p. 10.

TRES AMORES (Spanish language)

Goldsmith Productions, Ltd.; A Ken Goldsmith Production. *Dist* Universal Pictures Corp. **1934**; New York opening: 2 Nov 1934; Prod: Jul—Aug 1934 at the Talisman Studios. Sd; b&w. 7,801 ft. 87 min. Spanish language.

Prod Moe Sackin. *Dir* Aubrey Scotto. *Dial dir* Jesús Topete. *Scr* Paul Gangelin and Luther Reed. *Orig story* Al Boasberg. *Adpt and Spanish dial* René Borgia. *Art dir* Lewis J. Rachmil and Paul Palmentola. *Ed* Lou Sackin.

Cast: José Crespo (*Arturo Rosales*), Anita Campillo (*Gloria Shelton*), Mona Maris (*Lola Duval*), Mimi Aguglia (*Adela Gardin*), Paul Ellis (*Duque Carlos*), Andrés de Segurola (*El juez*), Carlos Villarías (*Abogado Nelson*), Soledad Jiménez (*Señora Morán*), María Borello (*La criada*), Paco Moreno (*Alfonso*), Ralph Navarro (*Abogado*), Enrique Acosta (*Presidente*), Carlos Montalbán (*Pedro*), Juan Duval (*Paco*), Movita Castañeda (*Doris*), Jesús Topete (*Olsen*), Alma Real, Rosa Rey, Ramón Muñoz, Emilia Leovalli, Tina Menard.

Melodrama. [*Not viewed*]. [The following plot summary is based on the English-language version of this film, *Bachelor Mother*; character names refer to that version. For further information regarding the English-language version, please see the note below and the entry for *Bachelor Mother* in the *AFI Catalog of Feature Films, 1931-40*; F.3.0204] When Joe Bigelow, a rich youth with companions of questionable character, is arrested for reckless driving, his lawyer and supposed friend pleads to the judge on behalf of Joe's "poor old mother" not to send him to jail. As Joe has no living mother, the lawyer convinces him to obtain one at an old ladies' home. He finds a kindly spinster, Cynthia Wilson, who is happy that Joe wants to "adopt" her as a mother. Joe is not sent to jail, and soon he develops a real fondness for Cynthia, while becoming romantically involved with Mary Somerset, the young woman in charge of the old ladies' home. When the lawyer and his girl friend, Lola Butler, scheme to get Joe's money by claiming that Joe and Lola got engaged, Cynthia, to save Joe from marrying Lola, confesses to the judge that she is not really Joe's mother, and he is sent to jail for thirty days. After Joe is paroled, he refuses to marry Lola. She pulls a gun on him, but during their altercation, Cynthia shoots Lola. In court, both Cynthia and Joe attempt to sacrifice themselves for the other; however, Cynthia is acquitted and Joe is reunited with Mary. Adoption. Aged women. Mothers and sons. Self-sacrifice. Spinsters. Youth. Deception. Gold diggers. Gunshot wounds. Imprisonment. Lawyers. Marriage–Forced. Retirement homes. Romance. Traffic violations. Wealth.

Note: This is a Spanish-language version of the 1933 film *Bachelor Mother*, which was directed by Charles Hutchison and starred Evalyn Knapp and James Murray. The working titles of the Spanish-language version were *La madre adoptiva* and *Feliz accidente*. The running time was calculated from footage given in NYSA records. The Spanish version, unlike the English-language version which was distributed on a states rights basis, was distributed by Universal Pictures Corp. It is possible that Julia Bejarano and Filomena Liñán were in the Spanish version, but their participation has not been confirmed.

CM Dec 1934, p. 680.

TRIAL (Latino)

Metro-Goldwyn-Mayer Corp.; controlled by Loew's Inc. *Dist* Loew's Inc. 7 Oct **1955**; Prod: early Apr—16 May 1955 [©Loew's Inc.; 15 Aug 1955; LP5314]. Sd (Western Electric Sound System); b&w. 105 or 109 min. Passed by the National Board of Review. PCA cert no. 17532.

Prod Charles Schnee. *Assoc prod* James E. Newcom. *Dir* Mark Robson. *Asst dir* Robert Saunders. *Wrt* Don M. Mankiewicz. *Dir of photog* Robert Surtees. *Spec eff* Warren Newcombe. *Art dir* Cedric Gibbons and Randall Duell. *Film ed* Albert Akst. *Set dec* Edwin B. Willis and Fred MacLean. *Mus* Daniele Amfitheatrof. *Rec supv* Wesley C. Miller. [*Sd* Wallace A. Wallace]. *Hairstyles by* Sydney Guilaroff. *Makeup created by* William Tuttle. [*Tech adv* Al Rothman].

Source: Based on the novel *Trial* by Don M. Mankiewicz (New York, 1955).

Cast: Glenn Ford (*David* [*Blake*]), Dorothy McGuire (*Abbe* [*Nyle*]), Arthur Kennedy (*Barney* [*Castle*]), John Hodiak (*District Attorney* [*John*] *Armstrong*), Katy Jurado (*Mrs.* [*Consuela*] *Chavez*), Rafael Campos (*Angel Chavez*), Juano Hernandez (*Judge Theodore Motley*), Robert Middleton (*A. A. "Fats" Sanders*), John Hoyt [(*Ralph Castillo*)], Paul Guilfoyle [(*Cap Grant*)], Elisha Cook [(*Finn*)], Ann Lee [(*Gail Wiltse*)], Whit Bissell [(*Sam Wiltse*)], Richard Gaines [(*Dr. Schacter*)], Barry Kelley [(*Jim Backett*)], [Frank Cady (*Canford*)], [Charles Tannen (*Bailiff*)], [David Leonard (*County clerk*)], [John Rosser (*Asst district attorney*)], [James Todd (*Minister*)], [Sheb Wooley (*Butteridge*)], [Charlotte Lawrence (*Mrs. Webson*)], [Percy Helton (*Youval*)], [Dorothy Green (*Mrs. Ackerman*)], [Everett Glass (*Dean*)], [Grandon Rhodes (*Terry Bliss*)], [Charles Evans, Frank Wilcox (*Lawyers*)], [John McKee, Robert Forrest (*Policemen*)], [Anthony Merrill (*Workman*)], [Wilson Wood (*Checker*)], [Robert Bice (*Abbott*)], [John Maxwell (*Benedict*)], [Michael Dugan (*Pine*)], [Bob Stratton (*Attendant*)], [Eddie Baker (*Electrician*)], [Vince Townsend (*Dr. Abraham Tenfold*)], [Gloria Moore (*Girl*)], [Frank Ferguson (*Kiley*)], [Robert Forest, Mort Mills, Heinie Brock, Leonard Freeman, Joe Locke (*Reporters*)], [Robert Haines (*Stenotype operator*)], [Joe McGuinn (*Sgt. Walter O'Flair*)], [Richard Tyler (*Johnson*)], [Mitchell Lewis (*Jury foreman*)], [Jean Wong (*Chinese girl*)], [Don Orlando (*Italian man*)], [Joe Flynn (*Speakers bureau*)], [Natalie Masters (*Rally chairman*)], [Rodney Bell (*Lew Bardman*)], [Lois Kimbrell (*Publicity girl*)], [Hal K. Dawson (*Nervous man*)], [Isabel Campo (*Mexican specialty dancer*)], [J. Peter Lloyd].

Legal, Drama. [*Print viewed*]. After being informed that his lack of trial experience threatens his chances of achieving tenure, State University law professor David Blake decides to spend his summer vacation interning for a local attorney. In the nearby resort town of San Juno, California, David is unsuccessful until he happens into the small law office of Barney Castle. Barney enthusiastically offers to pay David's expenses in exchange for assistance on his biggest case to date, the *pro bono* defense of Angel Chavez, a Mexican-American teenager accused of murdering Marie Wiltse, a local white girl. Marie's body was discovered the evening before on San Juno's private beach after beachgoers heard her screams. Nearby, police found a trembling and frightened Angel and immediately hauled him off to jail. Angel admits that he trespassed onto the beach and ran into Marie, an acquaintance from school. According to Angel, he and Marie kissed, but Marie suddenly became frightened of getting caught and bolted. Noting that Marie suffered from a serious heart condition, Barney declares the state's case weak and refuses to accept District Attorney John Armstrong's offer of a plea bargain. Meanwhile, the simmering racial tension between San Juno's white and Mexican-American communities threatens to explode, leading Barney and David to visit the dead girl's grieving parents to request that they hold a small, private funeral. Mrs. Wiltse agrees to their request, but the following day, two of the town's most outspoken racists, Ralph Castillo and Cap Grant, show up at Marie's funeral and incite the crowd with calls for vengeance and racial segregation. Transformed into a lynch mob, the crowd heads over to the town jail to demand that Angel be handed over. Barney and David, aware that the jailer, A. A. "Fats" Sanders, is sympathetic to the mob, rush to the jail to demand Angel's protection. Eventually, Sanders convinces the assembled townspeople to disperse by promising them a "legal hanging." David begins preparing for the upcoming trial, working after hours at Barney's beach house with Abbe Nyle, Barney's attractive secretary. Meanwhile, in order to raise funds for Angel's defense, Barney travels to New York City with Consuela Chavez, Angel's mother. Judge Theodore Motley, a black man, is assigned to preside over the case, arousing David's suspicion that the choice of judge has been influenced by the powerful town bigots in an attempt to give the trial the appearance of fairness. When David cautiously approaches Judge Motley with his concerns, the judge, greatly insulted, accuses David of racism. Jury selection begins, after which Barney summons David to New York in order to make a speech at a fundraising rally for Angel. David suspects that Barney's New York colleagues are Communists and confronts Barney with his suspicions. In response, Barney cynically proclaims that he does not care whether the money he raises for Angel is "clean, American money." At the Madison Square Garden rally, David reluctantly delivers the short speech Barney has prepared for him, but when he attempts to speak

out against Communism, he is drowned out by a large, brass band. Back in California, a disillusioned David is furious with Abbe for not warning him about Barney's political leanings and, to make matters worse, his presence at the New York rally catches the attention of the zealous Senator Battle, chairman of the State Un-American Activities Committee. David soon confronts Abbe, with whom he was beginning to fall in love, with his suspicion that both she and Barney are Communist Party members. Abbe admits that Barney is a Communist, and confesses that she was a "fellow traveler" in her idealistic college days, but insists that she no longer supports the Party. David accepts Abbe's tearful apology and their romantic involvement deepens. With jury selection completed, Angel's trial begins. In his opening statement, Armstrong asks for the death penalty, declaring that Marie died in the act of defending herself from a sexual assault by Angel. David decides against calling defense witnesses, preferring instead to raise doubts about the prosecution's case, a strategy which proves successful as he rigorously cross-examines first Marie's cardiologist and then an eyewitness. Barney returns from New York and, over David's objections, inexplicably insists that Angel take the stand. Soon realizing that Barney plans to sabotage any chance of Angel's acquittal in order to make the boy a martyr for the Communist cause, Abbe advises David to resign from the case, but David refuses to abandon Angel. On the stand, Angel is convincing under David's gentle questioning, but begins to falter when Armstrong catches him in a number of lies, most notably concerning the extent of his sexual education. The jury returns a guilty verdict and David begins preparing an appeal, but Barney promptly fires him. Later, David and Abbe visit Mrs. Chavez hoping to convince her to dismiss Barney from the case, but Barney has successfully manipulated her into believing that the sacrifice of her son will benefit the fight for racial equality. The next morning, as Angel's sentencing commences, David bursts into the courtroom and demands to be heard as a "friend of the court." After Barney's attempts to silence him fail, David makes an impassioned speech revealing Barney's plan to engineer Angel's execution in order to drum up support for the Communist Party. The judge believes David, as do the prosecutor and assembled townspeople, who greatly fear becoming pawns in a Communist plot. Judge Motley sentences Angel to a short term in reform school, causing Barney to denounce him as an "Uncle Tom." Barney's outburst earns him a thirty-day sentence for contempt, while David learns that Sen. Battle's committee is no longer investigating him. A relieved David and Abbe leave the now empty courtroom arm in arm, as a pensive Judge Motley looks on. *Communists. Lawyers. Mexican Americans. Racism. Trials. African Americans. Death by shock. District attorneys. Duplicity. Funerals. Judges. Juries. Law (Concept). Love affairs. Mobs. Mothers and sons. Murder. New York City. Physicians. Professors. Rallies. Secretaries. Subpoena. Witnesses.*

Note: Opening credits note that Don Mankiewicz's screenplay was adapted from his "Harper's Prize Novel." According to the *HR* review and a *NYMirror-News* news item, the prestigious award, given to Mankiewicz in 1954 for his unpublished manuscript of *Trial*, carried with it $10,000 and guaranteed publication of the novel by Harper's Publishing. Mankiewicz was subsequently paid $25,000 for screen rights and hired to write the film adaptation of his work. The *HR* review indicates that Mankiewicz gave the screenplay a happier ending and developed the love story in more detail than in the novel. According to studio publicity material, Grosset and Dunlap published a special edition of *Trial* to tie-in with the release of the film. The film's closing credits provide character names for the principle players accompanied by clips from the film featuring the respective actors. According to news items in *NYMirror-News* and in *NYT*, the New York City rally scene was shot at the Shrine Auditorium in Los Angeles. Filmed over three days at a cost of $110,000, the scene used 2,000 extras, 750 of whom were students from the nearby University of Southern California. Correspondence dated March 1955 and contained in the MPAA/PCA Collection at the AMPAS library indicates that M-G-M executives were concerned that the script might appear as a "subtly Communist vehicle" given the negative comments made by the protagonist about the fictitious Senator's zealous pursuit of Communists and the sympathy accorded his love interest, a former Party member. However, correspondence to studio executives from PCA officials makes no mention of any suggestion of pro-Communist sentiment and the above plot elements remain in the filmed version. The PCA office was highly critical of the script's intimation that David and Abbe spend the night together and of oblique references to Abbe's prior affair with her boss, both of which remain in the film. *Trial* received generally laudatory reviews and was praised for its historical significance and depiction of race relations. The *HR* review declared not only that "every American should see it," but also "every European" since this film would "prove...that Americans, in their approach to history, are not stupid, not children, and not naïve." The feature article in *Life* magazine emphasized the timeliness of the film by noting that at a Harlem rally protesting the acquittal of two white men accused of murdering fourteen-year-

old Emmett Till for whistling at a white woman, one African-American speaker warned the crowd not to accept any help from the Communist Party because "their support is the kiss of death." The *DV* review proclaimed the film's depiction of Judge Motley a notable advance in the representation of black characters, adding that if the *Birth of a Nation* "was the Negro race's greatest misfortune," *Trial* may be its "greatest break in terms of a fully felt, many-sided, warm human being."

Box 6 Aug 1955. *DV* 2 Aug 1955, p. 3. *Exh* 10 Aug 1955, p. 4006. *FD* 3 Aug 1955, p. 10. *Har* 6 Aug 1955, p. 126. *HR* 1 Apr 1955, p. 46. *HR* 13 May 1955, p. 7. *HR* 2 Aug 1955, p. 3. *LAT* 4 Sep 1955, p. 1, 4. *Life* 17 Oct 1955. *MPD* 4 Aug 1955. *MPHPD* 6 Aug 1955, p. 545. *NYMirror-News* 2 Sep 1955. *NYT* 15 May 1955. *NYT* 14 Oct 1955, p. 21. *Var* 3 Aug 1955, p. 6.

THE TRIAL OF MARY DUGAN (*foreign version*) *see* **EL PROCESO DE MARY DUGAN**

THE TRIAL OF SERGEANT RUTLEDGE *see* **SERGEANT RUTLEDGE**

TRIGGER FINGERS (Gypsies)
Victory Pictures Corp. *Dist* State Rights; Victory Pictures Corp. Dec 1939; Prod: began mid-Apr 1939. Sd; b&w. 55 min.
Series: Lightning Bill Carson.
Prod Sam Katzman. *Dir* Sam Newfield. *Orig scr* Basil Dickey. *Photog* Bill Hyer. *Film ed* Holbrook Todd.
Cast: Tim McCoy (*"Lightning" Bill Carson*), Ben Corbett (*Magpie*), Jill Martin (*Jessie Bolton*), Joyce Bryant (*Margaret*), Carleton Young (*Lee*), John Elliott (*Jim Bolton*), Bud McTaggart (*Jerry*), Ralph Peters (*Mort*), Forrest Taylor (*Crane*), Kenne Duncan (*Johnson*), Ted Adams (*Jeff*).
Western. [*Not viewed*]. Assigned to investigate a rash of cattle rustling, government agents "Lightning" Bill Carson, Magpie and Margaret arrive in town posing as gypsies. Their first stop is the Bolton ranch where Jim Bolton and his daughter Jessie have been robbed of the proceeds from their cattle sale. Bill suspects the Bolton's foreman, Crane, of being in league with the rustlers, but in reality, it is Lee, a respected citizen, who is the leader of the gang. Uneasy about the arrival of the gypsies, Lee orders his henchmen Johnson and Mort to watch them. By telling fortunes with playing cards, Bill obtains a set of fingerprints of the men he suspects, but wants more. With his pals, he visits the gang's hideout and deals a set of cards. This convinces Lee that Bill is a government agent, and in an ensuing fight, Mort is killed and Jeff, one of the gang, wounded. After the "gypsies" escape in their wagon, Lee decides to frame them for Mort's murder. His plan succeeds, and a posse, led by Lee and Crane, is organized to capture the agents. Meanwhile, Bill compares the new fingerprints with those already in his possession and discovers that they are identical. He sends Magpie and Margaret to town with the evidence, while he rides to the Bolton ranch. There, Jessie accuses him of murder, but he convinces her of his innocence. When Jerry, the deputy marshal, arrives, he and Bill join forces to aid Magpie and Margaret, who are unarmed. They arrive just as Lee and Crane are in hot pursuit of the gypsy wagon. After Bill and Jerry shoot down Crane, Bill captures the fleeing Lee and forces the rest of the gang to surrender. Deputies. Government agents. Gypsies. Impersonation and imposture. Rustlers. Undercover operations. Fathers and daughters. Fights. Fingerprints. Fortune-tellers. Frame-ups. Posses. Ranch foremen.
Note: Modern sources add Carl Mathews to the cast and credit Bert Sternbach as assistant director and Marcel Le Picard as cameraman. For additional information about the series, see entry for *Lightnin' Bill Carson* in *AFI Catalog of Feature Films, 1931-40*; F3.2489.
HR 15 Apr 1939, p. 3. *Exh* 6 Sep 1939, p. 381. *Var* 20 Dec 1939, p. 47.

IL TRIONFO DELL'INNOCENZA *see* **AMORE E MORTE**

A TRIP THROUGH THE ARCTIC WITH UNCLE SAM (Native Americans, Native Alaskans)
19??. Si; b&w. 4 reels.
Educational/Cultural. [*Not viewed*]. Views of Eskimo life along the coast of Alaska and Siberia. Titles are: Part I—On the U.S.S. Cutter Bear; Part II—In the Land of the Midnight Sun; Part III—Uncle Sam Moves His Eskimo Family; Part IV—Queer Industries of the Arctic. Alaska. Native Alaskans. Siberia.
Note: This film was listed in an educational film catalog. No year of production or release was given.

A TRIP TO CHINATOWN (Chinese Americans)
Fox Film Corp. *Dist* Fox Film Corp. 6 Jun 1926 [©William Fox; 6 Jun 1926; LP22832]. Si; b&w. 6 reels, 5,594 ft.

Pres William Fox. *Supv* George E. Marshall. *Dir* Robert P. Kerr. *Asst dir* Horace Hough. *Scen* Beatrice Van. *Photog* Barney McGill.
Source: Based on the short story "A Trip to Chinatown" by Charles Hale Hoyt in *The Dramatic Works of Charles H. Hoyt* (New York, ca 1901).
Cast: Margaret Livingston (*Alicia Cuyer*), Earle Foxe (*Welland Strong*), J. Farrell MacDonald (*Benjamin Strong*), Anna May Wong (*Ohtai*), Harry Woods (*Norman Blood*), Marie Astaire (*Rose Blood*), Gladys McConnell (*Marion Haste*), Charles Farrell (*Gayne Wilder*), Hazel Howell (*Henrietta Lott*), Wilson Benge (*Slavin*), George Kuwa (*Tulung*).
Comedy. Millionaire and hypochondriac Welland Strong is given only six months to live and decides to take a trip. Aboard a Pullman, he runs afoul of a jealous bridegroom who mistakenly believes that Strong has been making love to his wife. John then arrives in San Francisco's Chinatown. There he meets a charming widow, and the excitement of pursuing her cures him. In the end, he wins the widow. Chinese Americans. Courtship. Hypochondria. Jealousy. Millionaires. San Francisco (CA)–Chinatown. Widows.
FD 20 Jun 1926.

THE TRIUMPH OF INNOCENCE *see* **AMORE E MORTE**

EL TRIUNFO DE UN AMOR *see* **CARNE DE CABARET**

EL TRIUNFO DE UNA MUJER VENCIDA *see* **LA CAUTIVADORA**

TROOPER HOOK (Native Americans, Apache)
Fielding Productions, Inc.; Filmaster Productions, Inc.; A Sol Baer Fielding Production. *Dist* United Artists Corp. Jun 1957; Los Angeles opening: 26 Jun 1957; Prod: early Sep—early Oct 1956 [©Fielding Productions, Inc.; 7 Jun 1957; LP9145]. Sd (Westrex Recording System); b&w; 1.85. 7,386 or 8,111 ft. 80-81 min. PCA cert no. 18447.
Pres SOL BAER FIELDING. *Prod* Sol Baer Fielding. [*Prod exec* Robert Stabler]. *Dir* Charles Marquis Warren. *Asst dir* Nathan Barragar. [*2d asst dir* Nat Holt, Jr.]. *Scr* Martin Berkeley, David Victor and Herbert Little, Jr. *Cine* Ellsworth Fredericks. [*Art dir* Nick Remisoff]. *Film ed* Fred W. Berger. *Set dec* G. W. Berntsen. *Prop master* Mike Gordon. *Ward* Robert Odell. [*Women's ward* Voulee Giokaris]. *Mus comp and cond* Gerald Fried. *Sd* Fred A. Kessler. *Makeup* William D. Woods and John Holden. *Hair stylist* Madine Danks. *Prod mgr* Glenn Cook. *Casting* Lynn Stalmaster. *Scr supv* May Wale.
Song(s): "Trooper Hook," music by Gerald Fried, lyrics by Mitzi Cummings, sung by Tex Ritter.
Source: Based on the short story "Sergeant Houck" by Jack Schaefer in *Collier's* (14 Jul 1951).
Cast: JOEL McCREA [(*Sgt. Clovis Hook*)], BARBARA STANWYCK [(*Cora Sutliff*)], EARL HOLLIMAN [(*Jeff Bennett*)], Edward Andrews [(*Charlie Travers*)], John Dehner [(*Fred Sutliff*)], Susan Kohner [(*Consuela*)], Royal Dano [(*Mr. Trude*)], Celia Lovsky [(*Señora Sandoval*)], Stanley Adams [(*Salesman*)], Introducing Terry Lawrence [(*Quito*)], Rudolfo Acosta (*Nanchez*), Richard Shannon [(*Ryan*)], Sheb Wooley [(*Cooter Brown*)], Jeanne Bates [(*Ann Weaver*)], Patrick O'Moore [(*Col. Weaver*)], Cyril Delivanti [sic] [(*Junius*)], Rush Williams [(*Corp. Stoner*)], Alfred Linder, Paul Newlan, D. J. Thompson [(*Tess*)], Mary Gregory, Charles Gray.
Historical, Western. [*Print viewed*]. Led by Sergeant Clovis Hook, the U.S. Cavalry finally captures Apache chief Nanchez, described by one of the soldiers as "the worst butcher in the territory." As the troops are rounding up the families of the killed and captured braves, they discover that the mother of Nanchez's small son Quito is Cora Sutliff, a white woman captured by the tribe some years earlier. Cora, refusing to speak to anyone, accompanies her boy and the other prisoners to the fort, where Colonel Weaver, after suggesting that Cora should have killed herself rather than be taken as Nanchez's squaw, conducts a search and finally locates the woman's white husband Fred. As Nanchez looks on, Hook leaves the fort with Cora and the boy, intending to deliver them to Fred in San Miguel, a small town near Tucson. While the three await the stagecoach at a nearby station, a local settler insults Cora and grabs her son, whereupon she breaks her silence, screaming that the man is an animal and that she will kill anyone who harms the boy. Hook punches the troublemaker and secures food and clothing for his charges, and Cora begins to tell Hook about her experiences with Nanchez. In order to survive, she

explains, she adopted Apache ways and finally became accustomed to life with the tribe. Cora describes her husband Fred as a kind man who surely will learn to accept Quito as his own son. While riding on the stage, Hook and Cora befriend Jeff Bennett, a young cowboy who has lost his horse in a poker game. At one of the stagecoach's stops, Jeff disembarks while a rancher named Charlie Travers, a Hispanic woman named Señora Sandoval and her pretty granddaughter Consuela climb aboard. The driver, a hardened character named Mr. Trude, takes the stage into open country, but shortly afterward, Jeff learns that Nanchez and some of his braves have escaped from the fort. Certain that Nanchez will come for his son, Jeff borrows a horse and rides out to warn Hook about the escaped Apache. When the stagecoach overturns in an accident, Nanchez appears and demands his son, but Hook refuses to give him up. Travers claims the boy is more Indian than white and should be turned over to the chief, but Jeff and the other passengers sympathize with Cora and order the rancher to be silent. While the men repair the stagecoach, Travers unsuccessfully tries to bribe Cora to give up her son, and the next morning, when Nanchez appears again, Travers offers the chief the same bribe. Nanchez kills Travers, whereupon Hook threatens to shoot little Quito unless Nanchez lets them all go. Nanchez agrees but threatens to match wits with Hook again one day. After bidding farewell to Jeff, who has fallen in love with Consuela, Hook, Cora and Quito take a wagon to Fred's ranch, but Fred refuses to accept Quito into his home. Cora decides to take Quito and depart with Hook, but Fred, pointing a gun at Hook, orders her off the wagon and back into the house. At that moment, Nanchez and his braves attack. Leaping onto the wagon, Fred begins shooting at the Apaches, and after he is hit by a bullet from Nanchez, he kills the Apache and then dies. With nowhere to go, Cora reluctantly supposes she and Quito might live with relatives back East, but Hook, who has grown to love Cora and her son, suggests that they remain with him. Quito winks his approval, and all three break into broad smiles. *Apache Indians. Bodyguards. Indians of North America–Mixed blood. Mothers and sons. Prisoners. Racism. United States–History–Indian campaigns. United States. Army. Cavalry. Arizona. Battles. Bribery. Cowboys. Latino. Marriage. Mutes. Ranchers. Romance. Settlers. Stagecoach drivers. Stagecoaches. Threats.*

Note: The working title of this film was *Sergeant Houck.* The film's opening credits appear on pages of a book opened to reveal the words, "A Chronicle of the West." According to news items and information in the MPAA/PCA Collection at the AMPAS Library, M-G-M purchased the screen rights to Jack Schaefer's short story in 1952 and assigned the property to producer Hayes Goetz. The PCA, however, informed the studio that a film based on the story as written could not be approved by them because the cavalry officer, at the end, "is going off to live with this woman who is still, in fact, the wife of another man." In Dec 1955, *LAT* reported that the story was to be "packaged to Paramount" by Charles Marquis Warren, who was to write the script as well as direct. In Feb 1956, Sol Baer Fielding, who had been a producer at M-G-M, purchased the rights to the story from his former studio and made a deal with United Artists to finance and distribute the film, which became the first production of his newly formed Fielding Productions. According to the pressbook, filming was done in Kanab, Utah. The title song was sung throughout the film by Tex Ritter. The *Var* reviewer commented that Ritter's singing was an attempt to emulate the use of the song in *High Noon* (which was also sung by Ritter), but that in *Trooper Hook*, "It's not too successful, since it intrudes more than informs."

Box 6 Jul 1957. *DV* 21 Jul 1952. *DV* 24 Jun 1957, p. 3. *Exh* 26 Jun 1957, pp. 4343-44. *FD* 27 Jun 1957, p. 10. *Har* 29 Jun 1957, p. 102. *HR* 21 Feb 1956. *HR* 19 Jul 1956. *HR* 14 Sep 1956, p. 13. *HR* 5 Oct 1956, pp. 16-17. *HR* 24 Jun 1957, p. 3. *LAEx* 27 Jun 1957. *LAT* 7 Dec 1955. *LAT* 27 Jun 1957. *MPHPD* 6 Jul 1957, p. 441. *NYT* 13 Jul 1957, p. 11. *Var* 26 Jun 1957, p. 6.

TROPENNÄCHTE (German language)

Films Paramount; controlled by Paramount Publix Corp. *Dist* Paramount Publix Corp. **1931**; New York opening: 23 May 1931; Prod: at Paramount studios in Joinville, France. Sd; b&w. 65 min. *Country of origin* France. German language.

Dir Leo Mittler. *Story* William Slavens McNutt and Grover Jones. *Adpt and dial* Egon Eis and Rudolph Katscher. *Photog* René Guissart.

Source: Based on the novel *Victory* by Joseph Conrad (London and New York, 1915).

Cast: Dita Parlo, Robert Thoeren, Werner Hollmann, Fritz Greiner, Fritz Rasp, Manfred Furst.

Musical, Drama. [*Not viewed*]. [The following plot summary is based on the English-language version of this film, *Dangerous Paradise;* character names refer to that version. For further information regarding the English-language version, please see the note below and the entry for *Dangerous Paradise* in the *AFI Catalog*

of Feature Films, 1921-30.] Alma, a member of Zangiacomo's all-female orchestra, playing at Schomberg's hotel in Sourabaya, is frightened by the men's advances; attracted by the kindness of Heyst, a hotel guest, she hides on his boat to escape her tormentors. Heyst, who has retreated to a remote island following an unhappy love affair, discovers her and grudgingly allows her to remain at his cabin. Meanwhile Zangiacomo and Schomberg fight over her, resulting in Zangiacomo's death; Schomberg is then held prisoner by Mr. Jones, Ricardo, and Pedro, three desperadoes, who convert the hotel into a gambling house. To divert them, Schomberg tells them of gold on the island; and after killing and robbing Schomberg, the men depart. In a desperate confrontation with Heyst, Pedro and Ricardo are killed and Alma is wounded; but Heyst is grateful for the awakening of courage and love. *Gambling. Hotels. Murder. Outlaws. Seduction. South Sea Islands. Violinists.*

Note: Portions of Joseph Conrad's novel appeared in *Munsey's Magazine* (Feb 1915). While the 1930 English-language version, entitled *Dangerous Paradise,* which was directed by William Wellman and starred Nancy Carroll and Richard Arlen, was made at the Paramount studios in Hollywood, foreign-language versions were produced at Paramount's studios in France. In addition to a German version, whose New York showing in May 1931 was reviewed, and an Italian version, which was approved by the New York State censors in 1931, French, Swedish and Polish versions were produced in France, but do not appear to have been released in the U.S. Although *Var* lists Paul Rino as cameraman, *FD* and modern sources list René Guissart. As Paul Reno is listed as production manager for another Paramount German film made at Joinville, *Sonntag des Lebens,* the man listed in the *Var* review may have been the production manager for this film. The French version, entitled *Dans une île perdue,* was directed by Alberto Cavalcanti and starred Danièle Parola and Enrique de Rivero. The Swedish version, entitled *Farornas paradis,* was directed by Rune Carlsten and starred Elisabeth Frisk and Knut Martin. The Polish version, entitled *Niebezpieczny raj,* was directed by Ryszard Ordynski and starred Maria Malicka and Adam Brodzisz. According to NYSA records, an alternate title of the Italian version was *Domini senza Dio.*

Other language version(s):
La riva dei bruti (Italian language)

1931; Prod: at the Paramount studios in France. Sd; b&w. Italian language.

Dir Mario Camerini.

Camillo Pilotto, Carlo Lombardi, Carmen Boni. [*Italian version not viewed*].

FD 31 May 1931, p. 11. *Var* 27 May 1931, p. 57.

UN TROU DANS LE MUR see **UN HOMBRE DE SUERTE**

THE TROUBLE BUSTER (Romanian Americans)

Pallas Pictures. *Dist* Paramount Pictures Corp. 8 Oct **1917** [©J. C. Ivers; 19 Sep 1917; LP11423]. Si; b&w. 5 reels.

Dir Frank Reicher. *Story and scen* Gardner Hunting. *Story* Tom Forman. *Cam* James C. Van Trees.

Cast: Vivian Martin (*Michelna Libelt*), James Neill (*Franz Libelt*), Paul Willis ("*Blackie*" *Moyle*), Charles West (*Tip Morgan*), Louise Harris (*Mrs. Camden*), Mary Mersch (*Ruth Camden*), Vera Lewis (*Mrs. Westfall*).

Drama. Soon after their arrival in America, Romanian immigrant Franz Libelt dies, leaving his daughter Michelna an orphan. Michelna is befriended by Blackie Moyle, another orphan, who offers the girl his home, a large piano box in a vacant lot, and teaches her to be a "newsie." A friendship springs up between the two, and Michelna cuts off her curls, dresses as a boy and changes her name to Mike. After Blackie is blinded while protecting the girl from a thief, Mike is forced to find a way to support them both. It occurs to her that two clay statuettes sculpted by herself and Blackie might be valuable, and so she takes them to an art exhibit. When Mike's statue, known as the "trouble buster," sells immediately, she helps her friend by claiming that the artist is really Blackie. He then becomes the sensation of the art world and is sent to Paris to have his sight restored. Finally able to see again, Blackie understands Mike's deception and returns to America to set things right. When he finally finds Michelna, she asks him why he came back and he replies, "for the love of Mike." *Blindness. Friendship. Male impersonation. Orphans. Romanian Americans. Sculpture. Art galleries. Cures. Immigrants. Newsboys. Paris (France). Thieves.*

Note: Early titles for the film were *Love O' Mike* and *The Dogy.* Tom Forman wrote the original story, which was revised by Gardner Hunting.

Motog 27 Oct 1917, p. 889. *MPN* 27 Oct 1917, p. 2950. *MPW* 27 Oct 1917, p. 519, 579. *NYDM* 20 Oct 1917, p. 17. *NYDM* 27 Oct 1917, p. 2. *Var* 12 Oct 1917, p. 40. *Wid's* 18 Oct 1914, p. 671.

TROUBLE IN TEXAS see **MASKED RAIDERS**

EL TROVADOR DE LA RADIO (Spanish language)
  Dario Productions, Inc. *Dist* Paramount Pictures, Inc. **1939**; San Juan, Puerto Rico opening: 26 Jan 1939; Prod: 18 Oct—late Nov 1938. Sd; b&w. 9 reels, 7,346 ft. 82 min. PCA cert no. 4887. Spanish language.
  Prod Dario Faralla. *Dir* Richard Harlan. *Dial dir* Gabriel Navarro. *Asst dir* Herman Webber. *Scr* Arthur Vernon Jones. *Orig story* Bernard Luber and Nenette Noriega. *Spanish vers* Gabriel Navarro. *Photog* Harry Hallenberger. *Art dir* Ralph Berger. *Mus dir* Dr. Hugo Riesenfeld. *Mus supv* Abe Meyer. *Sd* Hugo Grenzbach. *Makeup* Max Factor. *Prod mgr* Irving Applebaum.
  Song(s): "Sueño de amor," "Presumida," "Mujeres latinas," "Cantor del pueblo" and "Trovador," music by Tito Guízar and Rafael Gama, lyrics by Nenette Noriega.
  Cast: Tito Guízar (*Mario del Valle*), Robina Duarte (*Nina*), Tana (*Alba*), Paul Ellis (*Doctor Marco Caballero*), Paco Moreno (*Pepe*), Barry Norton (*Reporter*), Carlos Villarías (*Sánchez*), Lucio Villegas (*Head doctor*), Martín Garralaga (*Store manager*), José Peña "Pepet" (*Furniture man*), Sarita Wooton (*Rosita*), Luz Segovia (*Head nurse*), María Borello (*First nurse*), Elena Martínez (*Second nurse*), Rosita Granada (*Third nurse*), El Charro Gil, y sus Caporales.
  Drama, with songs. [*Not viewed*]. Mario del Valle, a popular radio singer who is visting Los Angeles, has been the victim of embezzlement by his secretary and his physician. When Mario takes out an insurance policy, his secretary withholds the check to cover her embezzling. Mario, meanwhile, has fallen in love with a nurse named Nina, and when he catches a bad cold one evening, he insists on being taken to the hospital where she works. While Mario is in the hospital, his secretary announces to the press that they are engaged, hoping that Mario's fear of bad publicity will prevent him from prosecuting her. When Mario tries to collect on his insurance, he discovers what has happened, and also finds that his secretary's crimes have left him penniless. After he confronts her, she secretly switches his gargling medicine with disinfectant, and when Nina comes to give him the medicine, his vocal chords are damaged and he can no longer sing. Nina is then dismissed from her job for carelessness. Some time later, the secretary argues with the doctor, and in revenge, she tells Mario the whole story. Mario then confronts the doctor, and in his anger, he discovers that his voice has returned to what it was. Mario then looks for Nina, they are reconciled, and he returns to sing on the radio. *Embezzlement. Mutes. Nurses. Radio performers. Singers. Hospitals. Los Angeles (CA). Poison. Secretaries.*
  Note: Some sources refer to the film under the English-language title, *Radio Troubadour*. A modern source includes Pilar Arcos, Manuel París and César Miró as possible cast members, and notes that a connection between this film and a Jul 1934 press report, which said that Tito Guízar was returning to New York after having spent several weeks in Hollywood filming *El trovador de la radio*, a Spanish-language picture, has not been determined.
  HR 31 Mar 1938, p. 6. *HR* 5 Oct 1938, p. 3. *HR* 22 Oct 1938, p. 6. *HR* 29 Oct 1938, p. 6. *HR* 30 Nov 1938, p. 3. *Imparcial Films* 8 May 1939. *MPD* 8 Dec 1938, p. 5. *MPH* 3 Dec 1938, p. 36.

THE TRUE NORTH (Native Americans, Native Alaskans)
  Dist Robertson-Young. 18 Oct 1925. Si; b&w. 7 reels.
  Dir Capt. Jack Robertson. *Photog* Wylie Wells Kelly.
  Cast: Personages:, Capt. Jack Robertson, Arthur H. Young.
  Travelogue. A trip through Alaska to Siberia and back, which includes such highlights as caribou and bear; Young killing and skinning a moose, then making a canoe of its hide; Mount McKinley; the Yukon River rapids and the breaking up of two thousand miles of ice; the Bering Sea; Eskimos; the midnight sun; Mount Kalmai; kodiak bears; and spawning salmon. *Alaska. Bears. Bering Sea. Caribou. McKinley, Mount (AK). Moose. Native Alaskans. Salmon. Siberia. Yukon River (Yukon and AK).*
  FD 18 Oct 1925.

TRUMPET TO THE MORN see **TWO FLAGS WEST**

TSVEY SHVESTER see **TWO SISTERS**

TU AMOR O LA VIDA see **EL CABALLERO DE LA NOCHE**

TUCSON RAIDERS (Native Americans)
  Republic Pictures Corp. *Dist* Republic Pictures Corp. 14 May **1944**; Los Angeles opening: 11 May 1944; Prod: 28 Feb—early Mar 1944 [©Republic Pictures Corp.; 3 May 1944; LP12653]. Sd (RCA Sound System); b&w. 6 reels. 55 min. Passed by the National Board of Review. PCA cert no. 9892.
  Series: Red Ryder.
  Assoc prod Eddy White. *Dir* Spencer Bennet. *2d unit dir* Yakima Canutt. [*Asst dir* Harry Knight and Leonard Kunvely]. *Orig story* Jack O'Donnell. *Scr* Anthony Coldewey. *Photog* Reggie Lanning. *Art dir* Gano Chittenden. *Film ed* Harry Keller. *Set dec* Otto Siegel. *Mus score* Joseph Dubin. *Sd* Tom Carman.
  Source: Based on the comic strip "Red Ryder" by Fred Harman (1938—1964), by special arrangement with Stephen Slesinger.
  Cast: WILD BILL ELLIOTT (*Red Ryder*), George "Gabby" Hayes [(*Gabby Hayes*)], Bobby Blake [(*Little Beaver*)], Alice Fleming [(*The Duchess*)], Ruth Lee [(*Hannah Rogers*)], Peggy Stewart [(*Beth Rogers*)], LeRoy Mason [(*Jeff Stark*)], Stanley Andrews [(*Governor York*)], John Whitney [(*Tom Hamilton*)], Bud Geary [(*One Eye*)], Karl Hackett [(*Reverend George Allen*)], Tom Steele [], Marshall Reed (*Deputies*), Tom Chatterton [(*Judge James Wayne*)], Edward Cassidy [(*Sheriff Kirk*)], [Edward M. Howard (*Logan*)].
  Western. [*Print viewed*]. In the late 1800s, the citizens of Painted Valley rebel against the tyranny of territorial governor York by preparing a petition asking the President to admit them to the Union. York's thugs attempt to break up the meeting at which citizen Gabby Hayes is discussing the petition, but they are chased away by Red Ryder. Red, a well-known law-and-order man, has been summoned to Painted Valley by his aunt, The Duchess, who is a respected rancher. Gabby accompanies Red to the Duchess' ranch, where Red introduces her to his Indian ward, Little Beaver, who was rescued by Red when a dam burst and drowned his tribe. Also visiting the ranch are Jeff Stark, the president of the territorial bank, Hannah Rogers and her niece Beth, who is in love with Tom Hamilton, the Duchess' foreman. Unknown to the townspeople, Stark is in league with York, who has misappropriated public funds from Stark's bank in order to buy a monopoly on all transportation lines. Hannah, a weak-willed woman who covets her niece's ranch, is under Stark's control. The Duchess explains to Red that she has requested help from an old friend, James Wayne, who is an influential judge. Fearing that Wayne's investigation will uncover his wrongdoing, Stark orders Sheriff Kirk and Deputy Logan to kill whoever is on the next incoming stage. Logan and another deputy attack the stage and wound the passenger, then are chased off by Red. Believing the passenger to be Wayne, Red takes him to the town doctor, but after the man dies, discovers that he is Reverend George Allen. The sheriff then arrests Red for Allen's murder and claims that the stage driver saw him do it. Stark is not sure that Red will be convicted though, so he orders Hannah to visit Red in jail and slip him a gun loaded with blanks, after which Kirk will shoot Red while he tries to escape. Little Beaver finds the blanks, however, and switches the doctored gun with the sheriff's. Red escapes from Kirk and Logan, but Stark decides to use the jailbreak to his advantage by robbing the stage coming from Tucson and blaming it on Red. Stark gives Hannah a coded message to pass to the sheriff, who is searching for Red at the Duchess' ranch. Gabby and Red grow suspicious when Hannah gives the note to Kirk and blinks three times. Gabby steals the note, and by reading every third word, Red learns of Stark's plan. Red then rides to nearby Rockland, where the stage carrying the mine company's payroll is to change horses. Red stops the coach, which is carrying Judge Wayne, and explains the situation. Wayne agrees to Red's plan, which is to switch the payroll box with one filled with explosives. Red and the judge watch as the gang robs the coach, but Red's plan is derailed when Little Beaver, who followed him, arrives and is captured by the gang. Afraid that Little Beaver will be harmed, the Duchess beats Hannah until she admits that Stark and York are the leaders of the gang, and reveals the location of their hideout. Red, Gabby and Tom ride to the hideout to rescue Little Beaver, and both Kirk and Stark are killed during the ensuing shootout. Stark drops the doctored box as he falls, and a huge explosion kills the rest of the gang. Later, after watching Judge Wayne officiate at Beth and Tom's wedding, Red, Little Beaver and Gabby ride off in search of more adventures. *Bankers. Cowboys. Duplicity. Indians of North America. Territorial governors. Women ranchers. Aunts. Chases. Deputies. Embezzlement. Explosions. False arrests. Jealousy. Murder. Petitions. Ranch foremen. Reverends. Secret codes. Sheriffs. Shootouts. Stagecoach robberies. Wards and guardians.*
  Note: Fred Harman's popular comic strip was distributed by the NEA Service from 1938 until the 1950s, after which it was distributed by the McNaught

Syndicate and then by King Features until 1964. "Red Ryder" was voted "favorite comic strip" by the Boys' Clubs of America in the 1940s, and the cartoon hero became the "spokesman" for the Daisy BB Gun Company. A radio show based on Harman's characters began in 1942, and the strip was first put on the screen by Republic in the studio's 1940 serial entitled *Adventures of Red Ryder*. The twelve-chapter serial starred Don "Red" Barry as the red-haired cowboy, Tommy Cook as "Little Beaver" and Maude Pierce Allen as "The Duchess." *Tucson Raiders* was the first entry in Republic's feature-length series. Wild Bill Elliott starred as Red in sixteen of the twenty-three Republic features, and was applauded by critics for his portrayal of the cowboy who declared himself to be "a peaceable man." Appearing with Elliott were Bobby Blake as Little Beaver, Red's Indian ward, and Alice Fleming as his aunt, the Duchess. Frequent co-stars included Peggy Stewart, Roy Barcroft and Kenne Duncan. Comic western actors George "Gabby" Hayes and Emmett Lynn were each briefly featured in the series.

Each film opened with a shot of Elliott and Blake stepping out of a Red Ryder book, followed by opticals of Elliott riding, with his name and character name superimposed, and of Blake riding, with his name featured. Occasionally, other co-stars were featured in the book logo or riding opticals. In 1946, Elliott made his last appearance as Red in *Conquest of Cheyenne*, and Allan Lane took over the role in *Santa Fe Uprising*. Blake continued as Little Beaver, but Alice Fleming was replaced as the Duchess by actress Martha Wentworth. (By coincidence, the Duchess' "real" name was Martha Wentworth.) Lane played Red in seven films for Republic.

In 1949, Equity acquired the rights to Harman's comic strip. Jim Bannon starred as Red in four films for Equity, with Don Kay Reynolds playing Little Beaver and Marin Sais as the Duchess. Emmett Lynn returned to the series, which continued to feature Peggy Stewart. Allan Lane reprised his role as Red in the 1956 syndicated television series, which lasted for thirty-nine episodes. The series featured Louis Letteri as Little Beaver and Elizabeth Slifer as the Duchess. M-G-M's 1984 film, *A Christmas Story*, which was based on Jean Shepherd's book *In God We Trust, All Others Pay Cash*, illustrated the enormous popularity of Red Ryder in the 1940s in its story of young "Ralphie Parker," whose only Christmas wish was for a "Genuine Red Ryder Carbine Action Two Hundred Shot Lightning Loader Range Model Air Rifle." Modern sources include the following actors in the cast of *Tucson Raiders*: Fred Graham, Frank McCarroll, Frank Pershing, Bert LeBaron, Joe Yrigoyen, Charles Sullivan, Neal Hart, Ted Wells, Carey Loftin, Foxy O'Callahn, Ken Terrell and Tommy Coats. For more titles in the "Red Ryder" series, please consult the Series Index.

Box 3 Jun 1944. *DV* 12 May 1944, p. 3. *FD* 25 May 1944, p. 4. *HR* 24 Nov 1943, p. 1. *HR* 28 Feb 1944, p. 11. *HR* 3 Mar 1944, p. 46. *HR* 12 May 1944, p. 3. *MPD* 22 May 1944. *MPHPD* 13 May 1944, p. 1890. *MPHPD* 20 May 1944, p. 1898.

TULIP TIME *see* **SEVEN SWEETHEARTS**

TULSA (Native Americans)

Walter Wanger Pictures, Inc.; A Walter Wanger Production. *Dist* Eagle Lion Films, Inc.; controlled by Pathe Industries, Inc. 13 Apr 1949; World premiere in Tulsa, OK: 13 Apr 1949; Prod: late Jun—17 Aug 1948 [©Pathe Industries, Inc.; 13 Apr 1949; LP2305]. Sd (RCA Sound System); col (Technicolor). 88 or 90 min. PCA cert no. 13400.

Prod Walter Wanger. *Assoc prod* Edward Lasker. *Dir* Stuart Heisler. *Asst dir* Howard W. Koch. *Scr* Frank Nugent and Curtis Kenyon. *Suggested by a story by* Richard Wormser. *Dir of photog* Winton Hoch. [*Cam op* Harvey Gould]. [*Gaffer* Bob Campbell]. [*Stills* George Hommel]. *Spec photog eff* John Fulton. *Technicolor color dir* Natalie Kalmus. *Assoc col dir* Richard Mueller. *Art dir* Nathan Juran. *Film ed* Terrell Morse. *Dec* Armor Marlowe and Al Orenbach. *Cost des* Herschel. *Mus* Frank Skinner. *Mus cond* Charles Previn. *Orch* David Tamkin. *Mus dir* Irving Friedman. *Sd* Howard Fogetti. *Makeup* Ern Westmore and Del Armstrong. *Hair styling* Joan St. Oegger and Helen Turpin. *Prod supv* James T. Vaughn. [*Scr supv* Arnold Laven]. [*Casting dir* Owen McLean]. [*Grip* Charles Rose].

Song(s): "Tulsa," music by Allie Wrubel, lyrics by Mort Greene.

Cast: Susan Hayward [(*Cherry "Cherry" Lansing*)], Robert Preston [(*Brad "Bronco" Brady*)], Pedro Armendariz [(*Jim Redbird*)], Lloyd Gough [(*Bruce Tanner*)], Chill Wills [(*Pinky Jimpson and narrator*)], Edward Begley [(*"Crude" Johnny Brady*)], Jimmy Conlin [(*Homer Triplette*)], Roland Jack [(*Cowboy*)], [Harry Shannon (*Nelse Lansing*)], [Pierre Watkin (*Winters*)], [Lois Albright (*Candy*)].

Drama, with songs. [*Print viewed*]. In the early 1920s, in the oil-rich plains of Tulsa, Oklahoma, three ranchers, Native American Jim Redbird, Nelse Lansing and his one-quarter Native American daughter Cherokee, who is known as "Cherry," discover that some of their cattle have died after drinking from polluted streams. Jim and Nelse go to the neighboring Tanner Petroleum Corp. to complain, when suddenly one of the wells explodes, and Nelse is crushed to death by the well platform. Later, at refinery owner Bruce Tanner's hotel room, Tanner's adviser, Winters, refuses Cherry's demand for $20,000 to replace some prize cattle killed in the explosion. On her way out,

Cherry encounters her cousin, hotel employee Pinky Jimpson, who walks her out to the curb. There, drunken oilman "Crude" Johnny Brady hands Cherry a packet of papers, hops into a cab and speeds away. When Pinky tries to return the papers to Johnny the following morning, he learns that Johnny was killed in a brawl the previous night. Pinky then gives Cherry the news and explains that the papers are oil leases which grant her the right to drill on land belonging to Jim and another Native American rancher named Charlie Lightfoot. Later, Tanner arrives, apologizes to Cherry for Winters' behavior and offers her a check for $20,000 in exchange for her newly-acquired drilling rights. When Jim arrives and complains about the pollution, Cherry decides to form her own oil company and take Jim on as a partner. One day, Cherry receives a visit from Johnny's son and heir, famous Princeton athlete Brad "Bronco" Brady. Soon after, in Tulsa, Tanner overhears Brad encouraging Cherry to continue drilling and offers to put up the additional money, with one stipulation: If she does not strike oil within three weeks, the leases will become his. Cherry accepts the challenge and soon strikes oil, but Charlie and some of the other ranchers are dissatisfied with their royalties. At an oil drillers' meeting, they demand additional drilling, dismissing Brad's warning against spoiling their grasslands. When Cherry hosts an opera company reception at her new mansion, the governor attends, and Brad persuades him to appoint a commission on environmental conservation. Later, Tanner persuades Cherry to merge her company with his to form a conglomerate called Tel Oil. Without Jim's approval, Cherry signs an agreement granting additional drilling on his property. Later, when Jim bars Tel Oil workers from his property, Tanner contacts his friend, Judge McKay, who holds an informal hearing in his office. The judge threatens to appoint a guardian for Jim, who is a ward of the state, after which Jim returns home. There, he finds the carcasses of some of his cattle on the banks of a polluted stream. To test the water for oil, Jim strikes a match, and the stream immediately erupts in flames. After the fire creeps upstream toward the refinery, Pinky, Cherry and Brad arrive. The wells begin exploding one by one, and Jim is injured while attempting to save his remaining cattle. After Cherry rushes to his aid, and they are both trapped, Brad bravely rescues them. Later, Jim apologizes for starting the fire, and when he hears Cherry vow to rebuild with spaced wells and fences to protect the cattle, he gratefully kisses her. *Indians of North America. Nature conservation. Oil companies. Oklahoma. Ranchers. Tulsa (OK). United States–History-20th century. Athletes. Cattle. Cousins. Drunkenness. Explosions. Fathers and daughters. Fires. Governors. Heirs. Hotels. Judges. Kisses. Mansions. Oil wells. Parties. Partnership. Rescues. Rivers. Threats. Tulsa (OK).*

Note: The film opens with offscreen narration, and the opening credits include a dedication to the governor and the people of Oklahoma. *HR* news items note that actor Rocco Lanzo and violinist Roger Haines had been added to the cast, but their participation in the released film has not been confirmed. According to a 17 Jun 1948 *Var* news item, some exteriors were shot at the ranch of Oklahoma Governor Roy J. Turner, near the town of Sulpher, Oklahoma. An 18 Aug 1948 *HR* news item reported that other location shooting took place in Tulsa. According to information contained in the file for the film in the MPAA/PCA Collection at the AMPAS Library, the oil well fire scene was shot in a remote section of Oklahoma. The *SAB* credits Walter Wanger with the original idea, but no other source lists him that way. A 12 Feb 1954 *HR* news item noted that Carroll Pictures had acquired the film for re-issue, but no further information about this company has been located.

Box 26 Mar 1949. *DV* 21 Mar 1949, p. 3. *FD* 21 Mar 1949, p. 7. *HR* 25 Jun 1948, p. 20. *HR* 26 Jul 1948, p. 11. *HR* 4 Aug 1948, p. 3. *HR* 13 Aug 1948, p. 14. *HR* 18 Aug 1948, p. 3. *HR* 21 Mar 1949, p. 4. *HR* 24 Mar 1949, p. 7. *MPHPD* 19 Mar 1949, p. 4537. *NYT* 27 May 1949, p. 25. *Var* 17 Jun 1948. *Var* 23 Mar 1949, p. 8.

TUMBLEWEED (Native Americans, Yaqui)

Universal-International Pictures Co., Inc. *Dist* Universal Pictures Co., Inc. 3 Dec **1953**; Prod: early Mar—early Apr 1953 [©Universal Pictures Co.; 2 Dec 1953; LP3170]. Sd (Western Electric Recording); col (Technicolor). 7,090 ft. 79 min.

Prod Ross Hunter. *Dir* Nathan Juran. *Asst dir* John Sherwood. *Scr* John Meredyth Lucas. *Dir of photog* Russell Metty. *Technicolor col consultant* William Fritzsche. *Art dir* Bernard Herzbrun and Richard H. Riedel. *Film ed* Virgil Vogel. *Set dec* Russell A. Gausman and John Austin. *Cost* Bill Thomas. *Mus dir* Joseph Gershenson. *Sd* Leslie I. Carey and Glenn E. Anderson. *Hair stylist* Joan St. Oegger. *Makeup* Bud Westmore.

Source: Based on the novel *Three Were Thoroughbreds* by Kenneth Perkins (New York, 1939).

Cast: Audie Murphy (*Jim Harvey*), Lori Nelson (*Laura [Saunders]*), Chill Wills (*Sheriff Murchoree*), Roy Roberts (*Nick Buckley*), Russell Johnson (*Lam [Blanden]*), K. T. Stevens (*Louella Buckley*), Madge Meredith (*Sarah [Blanden]*), Lee Van Cleef (*Marv*), I. Stanford Jolley (*Ted*), Ross Elliott (*Seth [Blanden]*), Ralph Moody (*Aguila*), Eugene Iglesias (*Tigre*), Phil Chambers (*Trapper Ross*), Lyle Talbot (*Weber*), King Donovan (*Wrangler*), Harry Harvey (*Prospector*), [Edmund Cobb (*Fred, driver*)], [Belle Mitchell (*Indian*)], [Ezelle Poule (*Mrs. Clark*)], [Felipe Turich (*Mexican*)], [Gregg Barton (*Miner*)], [Roy Butler (*Driver*)], [Emile Avery, Jennings Miles (*Brush men*)], [Clem Fuller (*Townsman*)], [Eddie Dew], [Don Nagel], [Lee Roberts], [Tommy Hart].

Western. [*Print viewed*]. While riding across the desert, guide Jim Harvey encounters Tigre, a wounded Yaqui Indian. Jim stops to help him and learns that he was shot by a white man. After Jim removes the bullet and washes the wound, Tigre explains that he is the son of Aguila, a fierce Yaqui leader, and warns Jim to leave the area before Aguila arrives. Later, near the town of Mile High, Jim joins a wagon train led by Seth Blanden, which he will guide to Borax, where Seth shares a ranch with his brother Lam. Also in the group are Seth's wife Sarah and her sister, Laura Saunders. To avoid the Yaqui, whom he knows are in the area, Jim directs the wagons to travel by a roundabout route. Along the way, Sarah, noticing Laura's interest in Jim, expresses her wish that Laura marry Seth's brother Lam and share the ranch with them. While scouting ahead of the train, Jim spots a smoke signal and hurriedly rejoins the wagons. In the shelter of the nearby cliffs, Jim hides the women behind the chaparral. After a preliminary attack by the Indians, Jim decides to try to bargain with Aguila, believing that he might succeed because he saved Tigre's life. Aguila, insisting that his son has no white friends, ties Jim to a stake in the sun and leaves him to die, but later, Tigre's mother, who is grateful to Jim for saving Tigre's life, cuts him loose. When Jim arrives in Borax, the townspeople greet him with hostility, and he discovers that with the exception of the women, the entire Blanden party was killed. Jim tries to tell his side of the story, but the crowd, led by Lam, demands his life for abandoning the party. To protect Jim, Sheriff Murchoree takes him to jail. Later, Tigre sneaks into the jail and frees Jim. As they escape, Tigre reveals that his father learned about the location of the wagons from a white man. Before he can reveal more, Tigre is killed, and Jim runs for his life. He makes it as far as Nick Buckley's ranch before his injured horse collapses. Jim intends to steal a horse, but is spotted by one of the ranch hands, who takes him to Buckley. While Jim tells his story, he collapses from his wounds, and Buckley's wife Louella asks her husband to help him, reminding him of a similar incident in his past. Buckley lends Jim an awkward-looking horse named Tumbleweed, saying that he is the best horse in his stable. He then stalls the posse while Jim heads into Yaqui territory in search of Aguila. When Jim stops to rest he discovers a saddle bag filled with silver ore hidden in a clearing, which, unknown to Jim, is on Blanden land. Meanwhile, in town, Louella tells Sarah that she and her husband have helped Jim because Buckley was once falsely accused of a crime. She helped him then and later married him. When Lam decides to join the posse, Laura insists on joining him. After crossing some alkali flats, Jim and Tumbleweed reach Coyote Springs, only to discover that it is dry, but Tumbleweed digs down to water and saves their lives. Jim sees Murchoree arrive without the posse and almost leaves him to die, but finally turns back and shows the sheriff the water hole that Tumbleweed dug. Jim is about to tell Murchoree about finding the ore when the rest of the posse arrives and stops him. Suddenly, the Yaqui attack, and Jim suggests that they "play possum" to lure Aguila into the open. The ploy works, but Aguila is badly wounded. Jim begs him to reveal the name of the white man who betrayed the wagon train, and when Lam and his party approach, Aguila accuses Lam of betraying his brother so that he could profit from the silver. Using Laura as a shield, Lam escapes into Yaqui territory. Jim chases him on Tumbleweed, who is faster than he looks. The two men struggle on some cliffs, and Lam falls to his death. When the others join Jim, Buckley gives Tumbleweed to Jim and Laura as a wedding present. *Betrayal. False accusations. Horses. Yaqui Indians.* Brothers. Deserts. Fathers and sons. Guides. Gunshot wounds. Jailbreaks. Mothers and sons. Posses. Ranchers. Romance. Ruses. Sheriffs. Silver. Sisters. Water.

Box 21 Nov 1953. *DV* 17 Nov 1953, p. 3. *Exh* 18 Nov 1953, p. 3644. *FD* 3 Dec 1953, p. 6. *Har* 21 Nov 1953, p. 187. *HR* 13 Mar 1953, p. 9. *HR* 3 Apr 1953, p. 9. *HR* 17 Nov 1953, p. 3. *MPD* 18 Nov 1953. *MPHPD* 21 Nov 1953, p. 2077. *Var* 18 Nov 1953, p. 6.

TUNA CLIPPER (Scottish Americans, Portuguese Americans)
Monogram Pictures Corp. *Dist* Monogram Pictures Corp. 10 Apr **1949**; World premiere in San Pedro, CA: 9 Mar 1949; Prod: began early Nov 1948 [©Monogram Pictures Corp.; 10 Apr 1949; LP2276]. Sd; b&w. 6,953 ft. 77 min. PCA cert no. 13547.

Prod Lindsley Parsons. *Assoc prod* Roddy McDowall and Ace Herman. *Dir* William Beaudine. *Asst dir* Wesley Barry. *Orig scr* W. Scott Darling. *Cam* William Sickner. *Cam op* John Martin. *Gaffer* Lloyd Garnell. [*Stills* Eddie Jones]. *Tech dir* David Milton. *Film ed* Leonard W. Herman. *Mus score* Edward J. Kay. *Rec* Tom Lambert. *Makeup* Webb Overlander. *Tech dir* David Milton. *Tech adv* R. L. "Doc" Puccinelli. *Scr supv* Ilona Vas. [*Grip* Bill Johnson].

Cast: Roddy McDowall (*Alec McLennan*), Elena Verdugo (*Bianca Pereira*), Roland Winters (*Ransome*), Rick Vallin (*Silvestre Pereira*), Dickie Moore (*Frankie Pereira*), Russell Simpson (*Fergus*), Doris Kemper. [*Mrs. McLennan*], Peter Mamakos (*Manuel*), Richard Avonde (*Peter*), Michael Vallon (*Papa Pereira*).

Drama. [*Not viewed*]. Alec McLennan, who comes from a family of Scottish American tuna fishermen, has hopes of someday becoming a lawyer. Alec's boyhood friend, Frankie Pereira, whose Portuguese family, including brother Silvestre, are also tuna fishermen, decides to make some money by booking bets at the racetrack. After accepting a bet from an insurance salesman, a bully named Ransome, Frankie neglects to place the wager, and instead, pockets the money. When Ransome's horse wins, paying 10-to-1, Frankie flees, leaving Alec to answer for the debt. In order to earn the money to pay Ransome the $2,000 Frankie owes him, Alec leaves home and takes a job on a boat owned by the Pereira family. Later, Alec's father becomes angry that Alec is working on the boat and disowns him, forcing Alec to become a boarder in the Pereira home. There, Alec incurs the wrath of Silvestre, who torments him while he is at work on the boat. When he later saves Silvestre's life, however, Alec wins his friendship. Papa Pereira notices that Alec's pocketbook is often empty, despite the money that he is paid after each trip, and becomes suspicious. When Frankie's sister Bianca also becomes suspicious, she tells a fisherman named Manuel about it. Later, Manuel forces a confession from Ransome, who admits that he has been extorting Frankie's debt from Alec. Meanwhile, Frankie, who has been working as an exercise boy and jockey at a racetrack, has also been paying off Ransome. Later, Ransome is forced to return Alec's money, and when Alec's family learns why he left home, they forgive him. *Debt. Family relationships. Fishermen. Self-sacrifice.* Boats. Bookies. Bullies. Gambling. Horseracing. Insurance. Jockeys. Lodgers. Portuguese Americans. Racetracks. Rescues. Rivalry. Salesmen. Scottish Americans.

Note: The film was shot in San Diego, San Pedro and off the coast of Southern California, according to news items.

Box 19 Mar 1949. *DV* 10 Mar 1949, p. 3. *FD* 15 Mar 1949, p. 8. *HR* 13 Oct 1948, p. 1. *HR* 5 Nov 1948, p. 8. *HR* 19 Nov 1948, p. 14. *HR* 14 Jan 1949, p. 10. *HR* 17 Feb 1949, p. 6. *HR* 10 Mar 1949, p. 3. *MPHPD* 19 Mar 1949, p. 4538. *Var* 16 Mar 1949, p. 11.

TUNDRA (Native Americans, Native Alaskans)
Burroughs-Tarzan Pictures, Inc. *Dist* Burroughs-Tarzan Pictures, Inc. 24 Aug **1936**; Prod: completed mid-Jun 1936. Sd; b&w. 75 or 78 min. PCA cert no. 2313.

Pres Ashton Dearholt. *Prod* George W. Stout. *Dir* Norman Dawn. *Asst dir* Glenn Cook. *Orig story* Norman Dawn. *Cont and dial* Norton S. Parker. *Adpt* Charles F. Royal. *Photog* Norman Dawn, Jacob Kull and Edward Kull. *Art dir* Charles Clague. *Film ed* Walter Thompson and Thomas Neff. *Mus dir* Abe Meyer.

Cast: Del Cambre (*Dr. Jason Barlow, The Flying Doctor*), Wm. Merrill McCormick, Wally Howe (*Trappers*), Earl Dwire (*Storekeeper*), Jack Santos (*Half breed*), Fraser Acosta (*Eskimo father*), Mrs. Elsie Duran (*Eskimo woman*), Bertha Maldanado (*Eskimo girl*).

Adventure, Animal, Drama. [*Print viewed*]. Dr. Jason Barlow, a flying doctor in the Alaskan tundra, flies to a remote Eskimo village in Solitude Bay and saves a sick child through surgery. Two Eskimos then travel four hundred miles by dog sled to bring Barlow back to their pestilence-ridden village of Noonak. Because the men's dogs are half-starved and exhausted, Barlow must take his plane farther than he has ever traveled across frozen land. Barlow is forced to descend when he has engine trouble, and the plane crashes and burns in a bank of snow surrounded by frigid water. Barlow narrowly escapes an avalanche and a polar bear, and swims to land, carrying only a pencil, a notebook, three cigarettes, and a lighter. He continues to log his

journey in his notebook and manages to start a fire in a mountain cave, which is the home of two brown bear cubs and their fierce mother. Barlow names the friendly cubs "Tom" and "Jerry" and together they elude the mother bear. Barlow and the cubs survive on muskrat and salmon, but endure prolonged periods of hunger. When a herd of musk-oxen surrounds the camp, Barlow is forced up a tree, until the cubs' growling distracts the oxen and he escapes. When Barlow has been missing three weeks, an Eskimo finds his plane propeller and a team of fliers goes out to find him. Barlow hears one of the fliers' plane, but it passes over him. Barlow then finds a group of snowshoe rabbits and catches one for dinner. Tom and Jerry get entangled with a lion cub, and when Barlow is forced to defend himself against the mother lion, he and the cubs end up in the river. Meanwhile, having no luck in the planes, the search team goes out on sleds and kayaks. The bears then start a fire as Barlow hunts porcupine and fears that he will have to kill Tom or Jerry in order to survive. He then arrives at Noonak, which has been wiped out by the plague, and finds a note from the last survivor stating that he feared he would be killed by the starving wild dogs outside his cabin. The herd of dogs arrives and the cubs are forced up a tree pole. Barlow then climbs to the top of a shack and lights a fire to smoke out the dogs. Soon the mother bear arrives and scares away the dogs, and Barlow's friend Mac arrives in a kayak. Barlow then says good-bye to Tom and Jerry, whom he says kept him from going crazy in the tundra. *Airplane accidents. Alaska. Bears. Hunger. Physicians. Arctic regions. Diaries. Dogs. Feats of strength. Fires. Forests. Glaciers. Loneliness. Musk oxen. Native Alaskans. Plague. Porcupines. Rescues. Snow. Snowshoe rabbits.*

Note: The viewed print was missing credits. The foreword to this film describes "that mighty wilderness known as the Alaskan tundra...abounding with life and sudden death," and dedicates this picture to "that dauntless brotherhood of mercy flyers [who] fly to remote settlements, annihilating time and space, carrying food, supplies, and precious medical aid to combat pestilence." The forward also describes the film as a "photographic record of a dramatic chapter in the life of one of those heroic riders of the sky, a young physician known as the 'Flying Doctor.'" The film's working title was *Alaska Bound.* According to *HR,* the film was started by Carl Laemmle, but was dropped by Universal when the studio passed to new owners. This film was shot on location in Alaska for seven months, after which, according to a *HR* news item, director Norman Dawn made a deal with Universal for the rights to the footage and took it to Burroughs-Tarzan for editing, who distributed it in Jul 1936 as a "roadshow special." A modern source states that the film contains large portions of stock shots from Universal's 1933 film *S.O.S. Iceberg* (see *AFI Catalog of Feature Films, 1931-40;* F3.5456) and other pictures. In 1949, Del Cambre starred in the RKO remake of this film called *Arctic Fury.* According to a modern source, that film included sequences from *Tundra.*

DV 21 Aug 1936, p. 3. *Exb* 1 Sep 1936. *FD* 25 Aug 1936, p. 4. *HR* 16 Jun 1936, p. 6. *HR* 21 Aug 1936, p. 3. *HR* 22 Aug 1936, p. 1. *MPD* 22 Aug 1936, p. 3. *MPH* 29 Aug 1936, p. 48, pp. 68-69. *Var* 9 Dec 1936, p. 13.

TURKISH DELIGHT (Turkish Americans)

De Mille Pictures Corp. *Dist* Pathé Exchange, Inc. 11 Nov **1927** [©Pathé Exchange, Inc.; 3 Nov 1927; LP24612]. Si; b&w. 6 reels, 5,397 ft.

Supv C. Gardner Sullivan. *Dir* Paul Sloane. *Asst dir* William J. Scully. *Scen* Tay Garnett. *Adpt* Albert Shelby Le Vino. *Story* Irvin S. Cobb. *Titles* John Krafft. *Photog* Jacob A. Badaracco. *Art dir* Max Parker. *Film ed* Margaret Darrell.

Cast: Julia Faye (*Zelma*), Rudolph Schildkraut (*Abdul Hassan*), Kenneth Thomson (*Donald Sims*), Louis Natheaux (*Achmet Ali*), May Robson (*Tsakran*), Harry Allen (*Scotty*), Toby Claude (*Nassarah*).

Comedy. Abdul Hassan, a pompous Turkish rug dealer in New York, disdains all womenkind, excepting his American-born niece Zelma, to whom he turns for counsel. Meanwhile, in Tamboustan, the sultan dies, and his violent and officious widow rules, for the seven male heirs have met violent deaths. Villainous Achmet Ali brings the sultana news of Abdul, now rightful heir, and she orders him brought for her inspection as a mate. Aboard their ocean liner, Zelma meets and falls in love with Donald Sims, a wealthy American adventurer; despite Abdul's protests, Donald follows them to Tamboustan. Achmet has Donald captured, and while Abdul courts a member of the harem, Zelma plans to rescue Donald, instigating a revolt in the harem and thwarting the sultana's henchmen, who are after Abdul. The quartet escapes and returns to the United States, where all is well. *Adventurers. Courtship. Harems. Imaginary lands. Misogyny. New York City. Royalty. Rugs. Turkish Americans. Turks. Widows.*

TURMOIL *see* **SINS OF MAN**

TURNING THE EARTH'S AXIS *see* **CHIJLKU WO MAWASURU CHIKARA**

TUSKEGEE FINDS THE WAY OUT (African Americans)

Crusaders Film Co. **1923**; New York showing: Jun 1923. Si; b&w. 7 reels.

African American, Educational/Cultural. The life and vision of African-American educator Booker T. Washington is presented. *African Americans. Tuskegee Institute. Booker T. Washington.*

Note: The Crusaders Film Co. was located in New York City. According to an article in *Billboard,* this educational film was shown at Columbia University in early Jun 1923 and was to be exhibited throughout the country following its screenings in New York.

Billboard 9 Jun 1923, p. 50.

TWELVE ANGRY MEN (Latino)

Orion-Nova Productions. *Dist* United Artists Corp. Apr **1957**; Prod: mid-Jun—mid-Jul 1956 [©Orion-Nova Twelve Angry Men; 10 Apr 1957; LP8463]. Sd; b&w; 1.85. 8,615 ft. 90 or 95 min. PCA cert no. 18206.

Prod Henry Fonda and Reginald Rose. *Assoc prod* George Justin. *Dir* Sidney Lumet. *Asst dir* Donald Kranze. *Story and scr* Reginald Rose. *Dir of photog* Boris Kaufman. *Cam op* Saul Midwall. *Art dir* Robert Markel. *Film ed* Carl Lerner. *Mus comp and cond* Kenyon Hopkins. *Sd* James A. Gleason. *Makeup* Herman Buchman. *Scr supv* Faith Elliott.

Source: Based on the teleplay *Twelve Angry Men* by Reginald Rose on *Studio One* (CBS, 20 Sep 1954).

Cast: Henry Fonda [(*Juror 8*)], Lee J. Cobb [(*Juror 3*)], Ed Begley [(*Juror 10*)], E. G. Marshall [(*Juror 4*)], Jack Warden [(*Juror 7*)], Martin Balsam [(*Juror 1, the foreman*)], John Fiedler [(*Juror 2*)], Jack Klugman [(*Juror 5*)], Edward Binns [(*Juror 6*)], Joseph Sweeney [(*Juror 9*)], George Voskovec [(*Juror 11*)], Robert Webber [(*Juror 12*)], [Rudy Bond (*Judge*)], [James A. Kelly (*Guard*)], [Bill Nelson (*Court clerk*)], [John Savoca (*Defendant*)].

Legal, Drama. [*Print viewed*]. At the close of a murder trial conducted in a New York City courtroom, the judge gives the jury its final instructions, reminding them that a guilty verdict will mean an automatic death sentence for the defendant, a Puerto Rican youth accused of killing his father. Once in the stiflingly hot jury room, Juror 3, a middle-aged businessman who is estranged from his own son, loudly proclaims that the boy is guilty and that all ghetto youths are criminals, while Juror 7, a fast talking salesman, wants the jury to reach a decision quickly because he wishes to attend a baseball game that evening. Juror 1, the foreman, who is a genial high school football coach, conducts a preliminary ballot and, without hesitation, eleven jurors vote for conviction. Juror 8, a sensitive and thoughtful architect, casts the only dissenting vote, stating that he has doubts about the case and wishes to give the boy, who has had a difficult life in the ghetto, a fair hearing. Juror 10, approximately sixty-years-old and the owner of a garage, gruffly declares that the architect is a weak-willed "bleeding heart" before launching into a diatribe against slum dwellers. Wishing to restore calm, Juror 12, a young advertising executive, suggests that each juror present the reasons behind his verdict as a means of convincing Juror 8. The salesman, the garage owner and the businessman all suggest that the boy's ethnicity and class have been enough to convince them he murdered his father, while Juror 2, a shy and stammering bank clerk, appears to be maintaining his guilty verdict because he feels intimidated by the more outspoken jurors. Juror 4, a middle-aged and articulate stockbroker, and Juror 6, a young blue-collar worker, go over the evidence which determined their verdicts with much detail and thought. The prosecution has presented two seemingly reliable eyewitnesses, and motivation for the murder was suggested by the youth's frequent fights with his father. In addition, a shopkeeper identified the murder weapon as identical to an unusual and ornately carved knife he had sold the boy shortly before the murder. Finishing his exposition, Juror 4 offhandedly remarks that "everyone knows slums breed criminals," leading Juror 5, who until this point has remained silent, to declare with great dignity that he was raised in a slum. After Juror 8 points out inconsistencies in the prosecution's case and raises a number of questions, he throws down a cheap knife he bought nearby the courthouse which appears almost identical to the murder weapon. As many of the jurors begin to grow frustrated

with the discussion, Juror 8 suggests that the foreman take a secret ballot from which he will abstain, promising that if all of them vote guilty this time, he will go along with them on the final ballot. Now, however, one juror out of the eleven votes "not guilty." Most of the jurors believe that Juror 5 has changed his mind, but the "not guilty" vote turns out to be that of Juror 9, an elderly and frail man to whom the jurors have, until now, paid little attention. After tempers have cooled down, Jurors 8 and 9 point out the inconsistencies in the prosecution's version of events on the night of the murder, and Juror 9 is especially convincing when he notes problems with the testimony of a prosecution witness who, like himself, is elderly. The two men manage to sway Jurors 5 and 11 to their side, for a total of four "not guilty" verdicts. Juror 10 now explodes with anger over what he views as "nitpicking" and Juror 3 harrasses Juror 11, an Eastern European refugee, for changing his mind. After tempers subside, the weary jury continues its deliberations and when another ballot is taken, the tally is six to six, with Jurors 2 and 6 changing their original verdicts. Now at a complete standstill, some of the jurors want to declare a hung jury, but know that the judge will not accept the declaration without further deliberations. When Juror 11, who takes his duty as a citizen very seriously, questions whether all of the jurors have a clear understanding of "reasonable doubt," the obnoxious Juror 7 makes an angry speech full of anti-immigrant invective. Next, the newly confident Juror 2 asks how a 5'6" boy could have made a downward stab wound on a man who stood 6'2", leading Juror 5, who saw many a knife fight in the tough neighborhood in which he was raised, to convincingly demonstrate that the boy would most likely have held the knife underhanded, making a downward wound impossible. The foreman and Juror 12 eventually vote "not guilty," as does Juror 7, whose lack of concern over the case and desire to do whatever is most expedient greatly angers Juror 11, the immigrant. When Juror 8 asks the three remaining jurors to explain their continued insistence on a guilty verdict, Juror 10 makes an angry speech so full of hate and bigotry that everyone is shocked into silence. Juror 4, earlier so confident that the boy was guilty, admits he has reasonable doubt when the astute Juror 9 suddenly remembers that a female prosecution eyewitness had impressions on the sides of her nose of the sort left by eyeglasses. In support of their "not guilty" verdicts, the jurors realize that the witness deceived the court by taking off her glasses prior to her court appearance and they surmise that she was most likely not wearing them in bed the night she claimed to have witnessed the murder. Since Juror 10, who remains separated from the group because of shame over his outburst, has indicated he will change his vote, Juror 3 now stands alone in his conviction that the boy is guilty and he becomes increasingly belligerent and stubborn. When a picture of his son, who is only a few years older than the accused, unexpectedly falls out of his wallet, he suddenly breaks down into sobs and exclaims that all children are rotten ingrates. Overcome with emotion and guilt at the memory of his son, who rejected his harsh and authoritarian manner, he finally whispers "not guilty." As the jurors silently file out of the jury room, Juror 8 gently hands the distressed man his jacket. On the courthouse steps, Juror 8 and Juror 9 bid farewell, secure in the knowledge that they helped to ensure that personal prejudices did not determine the fate of the accused. *Bigotry. Juries. Law (Concept). Trials. Aged men. Architects. Bank clerks. Businessmen. Class distinction. Fathers and sons. Immigrants. Knives. Murder. Poverty. Puerto Ricans. Stockbrokers.*

Note: The television production of *Twelve Angry Men*, which starred Robert Cummings and Franchot Tone, was awarded an Emmy for Best Television Play of the 1954-55 season. According to a modern source, Reginald Rose had cut twenty minutes from his original play for its television performance and did not add any additional material for the film version. Henry Fonda and Reginald Rose combined the names of their companies, Orion and Nova respectively, for the production of this film. *Twelve Angry Men* was shot entirely in New York City and the opening and closing exteriors depict Foley Square. According to an *HR* article dated Apr 1957, the film was rehearsed and shot in a little over a month, at a cost of $340,000. *Twelve Angry Men* marked Sidney Lumet's directing debut. According to a biography of Fonda, Fonda hired Lumet because he had extensive experience in television and had a reputation for staying on schedule and within a budget. Both Fonda and Rose deferred their salaries for the film. *DV* reported that although a year and a half after the film's release the two producers had yet to receive even half of their fees, they had been successful in selling European theatrical rights to producer Lars Schmidt.

Although the film received rave reviews and was nominated for three Academy Awards (Best Picture, Best Director and Best Screenplay), it did only modest business, grossing a total of $1,000,000, according to a *Var* news item

dated Mar 1958. *Twelve Angry Men* won the Writer's Guild of America Award for Best Film and was also exceptionally popular with foreign critics. It won top awards from the British Film Academy, as well as from the Italian and Polish Film Critics Associations and the Berlin Film Festival. In addition, the film was honored by the American Bar Association for "contributing to greater public understanding and appreciation of the American system of justice." An *HR* news item, dated May 1966, noted that *Twelve Angry Men* had long been used as an industrial training aid for corporate managers studying the interaction, emotions and prejudices of group decision making. According to his autobiography, Fonda was disappointed with United Artists's distribution strategy and felt that the studio's approach had deprived the film of a chance at financial success. In particular, Fonda noted that United Artists placed *Twelve Angry Men* in theaters too large for a "small" film to fill and, in addition, did not rerelease it after it won numerous awards.

AmCin Dec 1956, pp. 724-725. *Box* 9 Mar 1957. *DV* 27 Feb 1957, p. 3. *DV* 26 Dec 1958. *DV* 26 Jan 1960. *FD* 27 Feb 1957, p. 6. *Har* 2 Mar 1957, p. 35. *HCN* 10 Feb 1958. *HR* 20 Jul 1956, p. 11. *HR* 26 Mar 1957, p. 3. *HR* 11 Apr 1957. *HR* 22 Aug 1958. *HR* 19 May 1966. *LAT* 31 Mar 1957. *MPD* 27 Feb 1957. *MPHPD* 2 Mar 1957, p. 281. *NYT* 24 Jun 1956. *NYT* 15 Apr 1957, p. 24. *Var* 27 Feb 1957, p. 6. *Var* 5 Mar 1958.

12 MILE REEF *see* **BENEATH THE 12-MILE REEF**

TWENTY FATHOMS BELOW *see* **DOWN TO THE SEA**

TWENTY-SEVEN WAGON LOADS OF COTTON *see* **BABY DOLL**

TWIN BEDS (Russian Americans)
Edward Small Productions, Inc. *Dist* United Artists Corp. 24 Apr 1942; Prod: late Sep—late Oct 1941 [©Edward Small Productions, Inc.; 6 Apr 1942; LP11196]. Sd (Western Electric Recording); b&w. 5 reels, 7,554 ft. 83-84 min. Passed by the National Board of Review. PCA cert no. 7949.

Pres by Edward Small. *Assoc prod* Stanley Logan. *Dir* Tim Whelan. *Asst dir* Rollie Asher. *Scr* Curtis Kenyon, Kenneth Earl and E. Edwin Moran. *Dir of photog* Hal Mohr. *Art dir* John DuCasse Schulze. *Supv film ed* Grant Whytock. *Film ed* Francis D. Lyon. *Set dec* Edward Boyle. *Miss Bennett's ward des by* Irene. *Miss Merkel's and Miss Farrell's ward des by* René Hubert. *Mus score* Dimitri Tiomkin. [*Conga dance supv* Ramon]. *Sd* Earl Sitar. *Sd eff ed* T. K. Wood. *Makeup artist* Don Cash. *Asst to prod* Grant Whytock. *Prod mgr* Max H. Golden.

Song(s): Excerpts from *I pagliacci*, music and libretto by Ruggiero Leoncavallo.

Source: Based on the play *Twin Beds* by Margaret Mayo and Salisbury Field (New York, 14 Aug 1914).

Cast: GEORGE BRENT (*Mike Abbott*), JOAN BENNETT (*Julie Abbott*), Mischa Auer (*Nicolai Cherupin*), Una Merkel (*Lydia*), Glenda Farrell (*Sonya [Cherupin]*), Ernest Truex (*Larky*), Margaret Hamilton (*Norah*), Charles Coleman (*Butler*), Charles Arnt (*Manager*), Thurston Hall (*Horace Touchstone*), Cecil Cunningham (*Miss MacMahon*), George Carleton (*Minister*), [*Toto, a dog*].

Domestic, Comedy. [*Print viewed*]. As they walk down the aisle during their wedding ceremony, Julie and Mike Abbott argue about Julie's involvement with the USO, which will prevent them from taking a honeymoon. Mike soon becomes dissatisfied with his marriage because Julie is too busy with work to spend any time with him, and the tabloids publish lurid reports about the various men who are pursuing her. One night, Julie throws an engagement party for Larky, her former suitor, who is engaged to her friend, Lydia, even though she promised Mike a quiet dinner together at home. Mike is repelled by the snobby crowd in his apartment and becomes jealous when their neighbor, Russian opera singer Nicolai Cherupin, pursues Julie. Cherupin's wife Sonya apprises Mike of the key warning signs indicating that her errant husband is falling for another woman. When Nicolai brings him a gourmet meal, which is the third sign, Mike throws him out of the apartment. Later that night, Julie snubs Mike because she thinks he distrusts her, and he declares that they may as well have twin beds. Mike and Julie make up until Nicolai is heard singing *I pagliacci*, the fourth sign, which means he is about to make a conquest. Mike insists that they move to another apartment building, but unknown to them, Lydia, who caught Julie and Larky in an innocent embrace during the party, has insisted that they move, and Sonya, who is jealous of Nicolai's flirtation with Julie, has also decided to move. All three couples end up in the same building, and Mike is dismayed to find that his casual remark during his fight with Julie has resulted in separate beds. Nicolai believes that Julie has purposely followed him to the new building, and starts to sing to her in his apartment. When Mike hears him singing, he leaves Julie. Nicolai then tries to woo Julie, who angrily insists that he never call

her again. Nicolai gets drunk and when he returns to the building, the security guard mistakenly lets him into the Abbotts' apartment. Nicolai collapses in Mike's bed, and Julie is horrified to find him there in the morning. Mike, meanwhile, has boarded a train for Canada, but decides to return to Julie after receiving sage marital advice from an avowed bachelor. When Mike returns, Julie is trying to get rid of Nicolai, who is suffering from a severe hangover, and she forces Nicolai to hide in a trunk. As the maid, Norah, has mistaken Nicolai's suit for Mike's and taken it to be cleaned, Nicolai borrows one of Mike's suits. Every time he tries to dress, however, someone comes in the room, forcing him to hide, and the maid eventually removes the clothes. Nicolai then tries to flee by the fire escape, but Lydia thinks he is a burglar so he runs back into Julie's bedroom. Larky then chases him, but Nicolai turns the tables, steals his clothes and locks him in a closet. Nicolai still has not dressed when Sonya arrives at the apartment with a detective who has been tracking Nicolai. As the detective insists that Nicolai is in the apartment, Lydia appears demanding the return of her husband. Julie is shocked when Larky is released from the closet, but once he explains how he got there, Nicolai is found in the trunk. Once again the angry spouses vow to move. Later that night, Mike and Julie make up and decide to move back to their old apartment. *Apartments. Infidelity. Marriage. Romantic rivalry. Drunkenness. Hangovers. I pagliacci (Opera). Landlords. Maids. Parties. Private detectives. Russians. Trains. United Service Organizations. Weddings.*

Note: News items reveal the following information about the production: Director Ralph Murphy was to have been borrowed from Paramount for this film; Binnie Barnes and Dick Powell were to star; and Walter DeLeon and Stephen Morehouse Avery were to work on the script. DeLeon and Avery's contribution to the final film has not been determined. First National released two earlier American versions of Margaret Mayo and Salisbury Field's play, both titled *Twin Beds*: the 1920 release was directed by Lloyd Ingraham and starred Carter and Flora De Haven (see *AFI Catalog of Feature Films, 1911-20*; F1.4596); the 1929 release was directed by Alfred Santell and starred Jack Mulhall and Patsy Ruth Miller (see *AFI Catalog of Feature Films, 1921-30*; F2.5897). In 1934, Warner/First National released a British version of the play titled *Life of the Party*, directed by Ralph Dawson and starring Jerry Verno.
Box 7 Mar 1942. *FD* 21 Apr 1942, p. 10. *HR* 5 Mar 1941, p. 1. *HR* 26 Mar 1941, p. 10. *HR* 23 Apr 1941, p. 1. *HR* 5 Sep 1941. *HR* 24 Oct 1941. *HR* 16 Apr 1942, p. 3. *MPHPD* 25 Apr 1942, p. 621. *NYT* 1 May 1942, p. 23. *Var* 26 Feb 1941. *Var* 22 Apr 1942, p. 8.

THE TWIN TRIANGLE (Gypsies)

Balboa Amusement Co. *Dist* Equitable Motion Pictures Corp.; World Film Corp. 1 May **1916** [©Equitable Motion Pictures Corp.; 20 May 1916; LU8397]. Si; b&w. 5 reels.

Dir Harry Harvey. *Scen* Bess Meredyth. *Cam* Joseph Brotherton.

Cast: Jackie Saunders (*Czerta/Madeline*), Mollie McConnell (*Mrs. Van Schuyler*), Ruth Lackaye (*Marco's mother*), Edward J. Brady (*Marco*), William Conklin (*MacCanley Byrnes*), Robert Grey (*Lord Fitz Henry*), Joyce Moore.

Drama. Czerta, a gypsy waif, lives with Marco and his old mother. After Marco's mother dies, Czerta discovers that as a baby she was stolen. When Marco tries to force his attentions upon her, she stabs him; then, leaving Marco for dead, she meets MacCanley Byrnes, a distinguished artist, visiting the area on a camping trip. She asks Byrnes to take her away with him, and he takes her to New York City where she receives an education. Byrnes is commissioned to paint Madeline Van Schuyler's portrait, and finds himself very attracted to her because she resembles Czerta. Czerta becomes jealous when she sees them together and flees. Many years later, Madeline, her mother, and Byrnes attend a theater dance performance starring Czerta. Mrs. Van Schuyler recognizes Czerta as her long-lost daughter and welcomes her into the family. Marco, who survived the stabbing incident years earlier, is also at the theater seeking revenge. Byrnes realizes that he truly loves Czerta thus, when Marco attempts to fulfill his vengeance, Byrnes kills him and saves Czerta. *Artists. Gypsies. Knife wounds. Theater.* Attempted rape. Camping. Dancers. Education. Jealousy. Kidnapping. New York City. Portraits (Paintings). Revenge. Self-defense. Waifs.

Note: Jackie Saunders was formerly an artist's model. This film was the second feature made at the Long Beach, CA studios of the Horkheimer Brothers.
Motog 6 May 1916, p. 1066. *Wid's* 18 May 1916, p. 578.

TWIN TRIGGERS (Chinese Americans)

Action Pictures, Inc. *Dist* Weiss Brothers Artclass Pictures. 13 Apr **1926**. Si; b&w. 5 reels, 4,368 ft.

Pres Lester F. Scott, Jr. *Dir* Richard Thorpe. *Scen* Betty Burbridge. *Story* Jack Townley.

Cast: Buddy Roosevelt (*Bud Trigger/Kenneth Trigger*), Nita Cavalier (*Gwen, Kenneth's fiancée*), Frederick Lee (*Dan Wallace, Gwen's uncle*), Laura Lockhart (*Muriel Trigger, the twins' mother*), Lafe McKee (*Silas Trigger, Muriel's ex-husband*), Charles Whitaker (*Kelly, the garage proprietor*), Clyde McClary (*Bugs, the radio nut*), Togo Frye (*The Cook*), Hank Bell (*The Law*).

Western. "Twin brothers are pitted against each other as one is engaged in smuggling Chinese and other is out to stop practice. The law and order chap accomplishes his task and also wins brother's girl." (*MPNBG* 11 Oct 1926, p. 52.). *Brothers. Chinese Americans. Smuggling. Twins.*

TWO CAPTAINS WEST see THE FAR HORIZONS

TWO FLAGS WEST (Native Americans, Apache, Kiowa)

Twentieth Century-Fox Film Corp. *Dist* Twentieth Century-Fox Film Corp. Nov **1950**; New York opening: 12 Oct 1950; Prod: 11 Apr—late May 1950 [©Twentieth Century-Fox Film Corp.; 11 Oct 1950; LP605]. Sd (Western Electric Recording); b&w. 10 reels, 8,258 ft. 92 min. PCA cert no. 14543.

Prod Casey Robinson. *Dir* Robert Wise. [*2d unit dir* Richard Talmadge]. [*Asst dir* William Eckhardt]. [*Dial dir* Anthony Jowitt]. *Scr* Casey Robinson. *Based on a story by* Frank S. Nugent and Curtis Kenyon. *Dir of photog* Leon Shamroy. [*Cam op* Bud Mautino]. [*Gaffer* Charles Graham]. [*Stills* Anthony Ugrin]. *Spec photog eff* Fred Sersen. *Art dir* Lyle Wheeler and Chester Gore. *Film ed* Louis Loeffler. *Set dec* Thomas Little and Fred J. Rode. *Ward dir* Charles Le Maire. *Cost des* Edward Stevenson. *Mus dir* Alfred Newman. *Mus* Hugo Friedhofer. *Orch* Earle Hagen and Maurice de Packh. *Sd* Alfred Bruzlin and Harry M. Leonard. *Makeup artist* Ben Nye. [*Makeup* Allan Snyder]. [*Hair stylist* Lillian Hokom]. [*Tech adv* Major Philip J. Kieffer]. [*Prod mgr* Sam Wurtzel]. [*Loc mgr* R. A. Klune]. [*Scr supv* Irving Cooper]. [*Grip* Leo McCreary]. [*Horse handler* Popovi Da]. [*Stunts* Dave Sharp, Billy Jones, Terry Wilson, Fred Kennedy and Paul Stader].

Song(s): "Dixie's Land," words and music by Daniel Decatur Emmett; "I'm a Good Old Rebel," traditional; "Battle Hymn of the Republic," words by Julia Ward Howe, music by William Steffe.

Cast: Joseph Cotten [(*Col. Clay Tucker*)], Linda Darnell [(*Elena Kenniston*)], Jeff Chandler [(*Maj. Henry Kenniston*)], Cornel Wilde [(*Capt. Mark Bradford*)], Dale Robertson [(*Lem*)], Jay C. Flippen [(*Sgt. Terrance Duffy*)], Noah Beery [(*Cy Davis*)], Harry Von Zell [(*Ephraim Strong*)], John Sands [(*Lt. Adams*)], Arthur Hunnicutt [(*Sgt. Pickins*)], [Jack Lee (*Courier*)], [Harry Carter (*Lt. Reynolds*)], [Ferris Taylor (*Dr. Magowan*)], [Sally Corner (*Mrs. Magowan*)], [Everett Glass (*Reverend Simpkins*)], [Marjorie Bennett (*Mrs. Simpkins*)], [Roy Gordon (*Capt. Stanley*)], [Aurora Castillo (*Maria*)], [Stanley Andrews (*Col. Hoffman*)], [Don Garner (*Ash Cooper*)], [Jimmy Spencer (*Indian*)], [Robert Adler (*Hank*)], [Lee MacGregor (*Cal*)], [Hilliard Crown], [George K. Hundley], [Fabian Chevez, Jr.], [Donald Curtis], [Brinton Turkles], [William McCarter], [Donald Cox], [Jose Baca], [Fred Holm], [Joseph Droege], [Charity Holt], [Bill Burch], [Don Nevitt], [Hank Potts], [Allen B. Church], [Ed Pulliam], [Ferguson Pollycutt], [Sam Tafoya], [William H. Doyle, Jr.], [Bertha Brennan].

Historical, Drama. [*Print viewed*]. At a prison camp at Rock Island, Illinois, in the autumn of 1864, Captain Mark Bradford, who became the camp commander after injuries ended his fighting career, offers Confederate prisoners the chance to be paroled. In order to be freed, the prisoners must agree to serve as Union soldiers and protect frontier forts against Indians. The Confederates' leader, Colonel Clay Tucker of Georgia, knows that there will be no further exchanges of prisoners and so considers the offer. After seeing one of his men die in the prison, Clay gets Mark's word that the men will not be asked to fight against their own, then breaks a tie vote among the prisoners in favor of going. Clay is demoted to 2nd lieutenant, and the unit joins the 3rd Cavalry of the Army of the Republic at Fort Thorn, New Mexico. Fort Thorn is commanded by the stern, rebel-hating Major Henry Kenniston, who is frustrated that an injury suffered during his first battle has kept him from the war. At dinner, the major's sister-in-law Elena, a Mexican-American from Monterey, breaks down in tears when Clay relates that he fought at Chancellorsville, where her husband, the major's brother, lost his life. Mark, who fell in love with Elena on the day of her wedding, is surprised to find her there, and she states that Kenniston wrote her that she could reach the fort with an Army supply train, then travel to Monterey with an escorted wagon. She has now been at the fort for six months, and in addition to

becoming frustrated with Kenniston's excuse that he cannot spare a wagon escort, she is tired of his over-protective attitude and romantic aspirations. When the Southerners chase some Indians into a mountain pass, Kenniston orders "retreat" sounded, then reprimands Clay in the presence of his men for almost riding into a trap. After the Southerners, obeying Kenniston's orders, execute two men for running whiskey and guns to the Indians, they find out that the men were agents of the Confederate government. Feeling that Kenniston has broken their agreement, Clay joins his disgruntled men in planning to desert. Kenniston then sends the Southern troops to escort a wagon train West, hoping that if they desert, they will do it then, while he is expecting it. Although Kenniston takes Elena's name off the lists of passengers, she hides in the parson's wagon and when Mark spots her hiding, he says nothing. Along the way, Clay learns that Elena has come along, and after he allows her to stay, they grow fond of each other during the trip. The night before the troops plan to bolt for Texas, Ephraim Strong, a Confederate agent who has masqueraded as a merchant, tells Clay of his plan to link Confederate Texas with the Pacific Ocean. Strong hopes to defeat the blockade that is strangling the South and make Californian gold available to the Confederacy. Strong urges Clay not to desert, but to return and gain Kenniston's confidence, as Fort Thorn is the only block between Texas and Tucson, and also bring Elena back, so as not to antagonize Kenniston. After their return, Kenniston still does not trust Clay even though he brought Elena back, and when suspicious wagon tracks are spotted in the vicinity, Clay is not chosen for the patrol. When the son of the feared Kiowa chief Satank is captured, the chief and his warriors approach the fort to demand the boy's return. Kenniston, calling the son a "rebel," orders him shot, whereupon Satank issues a threat and leaves. Meanwhile, Clay has received orders to take his troops to rendezvous with a wagon train and proceed with it to California. Clay takes over command of the patrol from Mark, who had come to regard him as a friend, but when he learns that the fort is surrounded by Satank and his braves, Clay and his men decide to go back, as they know that women and children will die if they desert. During the fight with the Indians, Mark is wounded, and Clay rescues him when an Indian tries to kill him. After fighting has temporarily ceased for the night, Clay apologizes to Elena, who is helping to nurse the wounded, for bringing Mark back, and she sadly relates that before he died, Mark confessed he loved her. A note attached to a flaming arrow arrives with a message that the Indians demand the lives of the officers in revenge for the murder of Satank's son, but that they will spare the others. Kenniston then decides to go alone to his death and turns over command to Clay, who is now respectful of Kenniston's integrity. When he leaves the fort and the gates close, Kenniston issues an agonizing scream, and his body is recovered the following day after the Indians leave. A rider then arrives with the news that General Sherman has completed his march to the sea and that Savannah is surrounded, leaving the Confederacy cut in half. As the Union soldiers whoop at the news and sing "The Battle Hymn of the Republic," the rebels proudly sing "Dixie." With the news that the war will soon be over, Elena comforts Clay, who despairs that there is now nothing left to go home to. She asks for help to rebuild her home at the fort, and in Spanish, tells him it will all seem better tomorrow. *Confederate States of America. Army. Cultural conflict. Loyalty. United States–History–Civil War, 1861-1865. United States–History–Indian campaigns. United States. Army. Cavalry. Kiowa Indians. Massacres. Mexican Americans. Military posts. Murder. New Mexico. Obsession. Prisons. Revenge. Rock Island (IL). Self-sacrifice. Sisters-in-law. Spies. Stowaways. Uprisings. Wagon trains. Widows.*

Note: The working title of this film was *Trumpet to the Morn.* The opening credits contain the following statement: "On December 8th, 1863, President Abraham Lincoln issued a Special Proclamation, whereby Confederate Prisoners of War might gain their freedom, provided they would join the Union Army to defend the frontier West against the Indians." In correspondence included in the Twentieth Century-Fox Records of the Legal Department at the UCLA Arts–Special Collections Library, writer Frank S. Nugent stated that he came up with the idea for this film while he was working on the screenplay of *She Wore a Yellow Ribbon* (see above) in the fall of 1948. While doing research, Nugent read a brief statement in the book *Fighting Indians of the West,* by Dee Brown and Martin F. Schmitt (New York, 1948) concerning the use of paroled Confederate soldiers to man frontier forts at the end of the Civil War. After a futile attempt to locate confirming information, Nugent wrote to Schmitt at the University of Oregon. Schmitt and Brown responded with further information regarding sources of the information, in particular, the seventy-odd volumes of the *Official Records of the War of the Rebellion.* Nugent noted that over six thousand former Confederate soldiers, after taking a loyalty oath, were

"galvanized," and that late in 1864, there was a Confederate conspiracy to open a road from El Paso to California so that Southern sympathizers in California could fight in the war. Nugent's story was originally entitled "The Yankee from Georgia." He submitted it to the Goldwyn Studios and to M-G-M, but although those studios expressed interest, they made no offer until it could be more fully developed.

According to *LAEx,* Twentieth Century-Fox bought the story with the intention of starring Victor Mature in the role of "Col. Clay Tucker." Richard Basehart subsequently was signed for the role, before being replaced by Joseph Cotten, who was borrowed from Selznick. Kathryn Sheldon was originally scheduled to play "Mrs. Magowan." Location scenes were shot at the Pueblo of San Ildefonso, a community of Tewa Indians twenty-two miles from Santa Fe, NM. According to publicity for the film, buildings in the pueblo date from the 1500s. The filmmakers agreed not to come near the tribal kiva (the underground council room), the graveyard or sacred shrines.

In 1951, R. W. Alcorn, a producer, claimed in correspondence with Twentieth Century-Fox that in Sep 1949 he purchased a story entitled "Between Two Flags" by William Lippman, which, he stated, was very similar to this film. Alcorn claimed to have contacted Nugent to work on the story outline, but Nugent denied this, saying he had never been given a copy of Lippman's story. No further information regarding Alcorn's claim has been located.

In Apr 1957, the *Twentieth Century-Fox Hour* broadcast a remake of *Two Flags West* entitled "The Still Trumpet," starring Dale Robertson, who appeared in a supporting role in the original version. The teleplay was written by Curtis Kenyon and the show was directed by Lewis Allen.

Box 14 Oct 1950. *Cue* 14 Oct 1950. *DN* 30 May 1950. *DV* 9 Oct 1950. *Exh* 11 Oct 1950, pp. 2952-53. *FD* 10 Oct 1950, p. 6. *Har* 14 Oct 1950, p. 164. *HR* 9 Oct 1950, p. 3, 8. *LADN* 2 Nov 1950. *LAEx* 23 Sep 1949. *LAT* 2 Nov 1950. *MPD* 10 Oct 1950, p. 14. *MPHPD* 14 Oct 1950, p. 518. *NYT* 13 Oct 1950, p. 23. *Var* 11 Oct 1950, p. 8.

TWO GUN MAN FROM HARLEM (African Americans)

Merit Pictures, Inc. *Dist* Sack Amusement Enterprises, Inc. 1 May **1938.** Sd; b&w. 66 min.

Dir Richard C. Kahn. *Wrt* Richard C. Kahn. *Photog* Marcel LePicard and Harvey Gould. *Art dir* Vin Taylor. *Film ed* Wm. Faris. *Mus* Herbert Jeffrey, and the Four Tones. *Sd eng* Cliff Ruberg. *Prod mgr* Al Lane.

Cast: Herbert Jeffrey [(*Bob Blake/The Deacon*)], Margaret Whitten [(*Sally Thompson*)], Clarence Brooks [(*John Barker*)], Mantan Moreland [(*Bill*)], Stymie Beard [(*Jimmy Thompson*)], Spencer Williams, Jr. [(*Butch Carter*)], Mae Turner, Jesse Lee Brooks [(*The sheriff*)], Rose Lee Lincoln, Tom Southern, The Cats and the Fiddle, The Four Tones, Paul Blackman [(*himself*)], [Faithful Mary].

African American, Western, with songs. [*Print viewed*]. After spending a pleasant evening with pretty Sally Thompson and her talkative young brother Jimmy, Bob Blake returns to John Steel's Wyoming ranch, where he works as a cowboy. At the ranch, Bob discovers that Steel has been murdered by a man with whom his wife Ruth was having an affair, and whom she refuses to name. As Bob inspects the body, Ruth substitutes her lover's gun with Bob's, and Bob subsequently is accused of the crime by the sheriff. During the sheriff's interrogation, Bob's friend Bill, the ranch cook, turns off the lights, and the sheriff, believing that Bob has escaped, rides off with his men. Once alone with Bob, Ruth confesses to framing him and insists that he leave the area to avoid arrest. Bob hitchhikes across the country and eventually arrives in Harlem, where he meets a man known as The Deacon, a killer who was once a preacher, and gets an idea to assume a new identity and return to Wyoming disguised as a church elder. Back in Wyoming, Bob, now known as The Deacon, allies himself with Butch Carter, a miner who has been paid by the well-to-do John Barker, Steel's killer, to kidnap and murder Ruth. After Bob and Carter rob Barker on the road, Carter rides to Sally's ranch, where he forces himself on the young woman. Bob, who has been told by Jimmy that Sally is being pressured into marrying Barker to avoid foreclosure on her father's ranch, saves Sally from Carter's advances. With Carter's money, Bob pays Sally two thousand dollars, which she happily gives to Barker to pay off her father's loan. Soon after, Bob confers with an angry, confused Ruth, who has been locked in a shed, and again robs and fights with Barker. While Jimmy rushes to find the sheriff, Barker and Carter descend on the old mine where Bob has taken Sally for protection. Just as the sheriff arrives, Bob overwhelms Barker and takes the lawman to Ruth, who finally exposes Barker as her husband's killer. After revealing his true identity, Bob leaves with a smitten Sally. *African Americans. Cowboys. Disguise. Frame-ups. Impersonation and imposture. Murder. Outlaws. Brothers and sisters. Clergy. Fights. Foreclosure. Hitchhiking. Infidelity. Kidnapping. Loans. Marriage–Forced by circumstances. Miners. New York City–Harlem. Ranchers. Rescues. Robbery. Romance. Sheriffs. Wyoming.*

Note: Onscreen credits indicate the film was copyrighted in 1938; however no registration has been located in the copyright records. Although a song is performed in the picture, its title and composer have not been determined. Actor Herbert Jeffrey used the name Herb Jeffries when appearing as a singer.

Box 30 Apr 1938. *Exh* 1 Jul 1938, p. 156.

TWO SHALL BE BORN (Polish Americans)

Twin Pictures Corp. *Dist* Vitagraph Co. of America. 7 Dec **1924** [©Twin Pictures Corp.; 13 Nov 1924; LP29811]. Si; b&w. 6 reels, 5,443 ft.

Dir Whitman Bennett. *Story* Marie Conway Oemler. *Photog* Edward Paul.

Source: Inspired by the short story "Two Shall Be Born" by Susan Marr Spaulding in *An American Anthology, 1787—1900* (Boston, ca 1900).

Cast: Jane Novak (*Countess Mayra Zuleska*), Kenneth Harlan (*Brian Kelly*), Sigrid Holmquist (*Janet Van Wyck*), Frank Sheridan (*Dominick Kelly*), Herman Lieb (*Baron von Rittenheim*), Fuller Mellish (*Count Florian*), Joseph Burke (*Wenceslaus*), Blanche Craig (*Aunt Honora Kelly*), Josseffa De Bok (*Franciska*), Catharine Evans (*Widow Callaghan*), Walter James (*Hund*).

Melodrama. As he lies dying, Count Florian Zuleski of Poland, the head of a committee working for perpetual peace among European nations, entrusts his daughter, Mayra, with the dangerous mission of delivering some important documents to New York. Arriving in the United States, Mayra is unable to establish contact with the Polish representative and goes to live with her aunt. She soon meets Brian Kelly, who is working as a traffic cop after being disinherited by his irate millionaire father for not entering into a marriage of convenience with patrician Janet Van Wyck. Brian and Mayra are secretly married, and she is finally able to deliver the papers, but she is immediately kidnapped by the Polish traitor, Baron von Rittenheim, who takes her to a deserted house in the slums. Mayra is severely beaten but refuses to divulge the whereabouts of the vital documents. She is rescued by Brian, von Rittenheim is turned over to the police, and Brian is reconciled with his father. *Abduction. Disinheritance. New York City. Peace. Poles. Police. Polish Americans. Secret documents.*

FD 8 Feb 1925.

TWO SISTERS (Yiddish language)

Graphic Pictures Corp. *Dist* Foreign Cinema Arts, Inc. **1938**; New York opening: 29 Nov 1938; Prod: in the Bronx, NY. Sd (RCA The Magic Voice of the Screen); b&w. 8 reels, 6,865 ft. 79-80 min. Passed by the National Board of Review. Yiddish language with English subtitles.

Prod Ben K. Blake. *Dir* Ben K. Blake. *Asst dir* Moe Goldman. *Orig story and adpt* Samuel H. Cohen. *Photog* George F. Hinners. *Art dir* William Saulter. *Ed* Harry Foster. *Mus score and dir* Yosef Rumshinsky. *Rec eng* Paul Robillard.

Cast: JENNIE GOLDSTEIN (*Betty Glickstein*), Sylvia Dell (*Sally Glickstein*), Celia Boodkin (*Mrs. Gershon [Rachel] Glickstein*), Betta Bialis (*Betty Glickstein, as child*), Joan Carroll (*Sally Glickstein, as child*), Muni Seroff (*Dr. Max Feinberg*), Harvey Kier (*Dr. Jack Glickstein*), Abraham Teitelbaum (*Gershon Glickstein*), Jack Wexler (*Laibush Glickstein*), Rebecca Weintraub (*Channa Glickstein*), Michael Rosenberg (*Chyimitcha*), Betty Jacobs (*Dubrish*), Yudel Dubinsky (*Shatchin*), Ida Adler (*Supervising nurse*), Anna Levine (*First customer*), Anetta Hoffman (*Second customer*).

Yiddish, Melodrama. [*Print viewed*]. On her deathbed, Rachel Glickstein asks her twelve-year-old daughter Betty to educate and watch over her younger sister Sally, and Betty swears that she will. Because their father Gershon goes to work very early every morning, he asks his brother Laibush, a butcher in the Bronx, if he and the girls can live with him, his wife Channa and their son Jack. Laibush and Channa are happy to oblige, and they soon all move into a large apartment. Eighteen years later, Jack, a dentist, has fallen in love with Sally, who is now a nurse, while Betty, who has continually put her sister's welfare above her own, plans to marry Jack's friend, Dr. Max Feinberg, a young intern. Gershon has moved to Denver because of an illness. One day, Jack complains to Max that Sally doesn't love him and expresses envy that Max has Betty, who dotes on the man she loves. Max responds that Betty, who encouraged him to become a doctor and supported him financially while he was at school, loves with the feeling of a mother. When an emergency operation is needed and Sally cannot locate a doctor, she convinces the head nurse to let her call Max. With Sally at his side to give him confidence, Max

successfully performs his first major operation. When Betty offers Max $1,000 to open a new office, he at first refuses to accept it, but she insists. At the opening of Max's office, Sally gets drunk, and Max publicly thanks Betty and vows to take care of her happiness and future. However, Max and Sally, who have been working together frequently, realize that they have fallen in love with each other. They are reluctant, however, to acknowledge their feelings. Betty buys a house for her and Max to move into after they marry, and she has wedding invitations printed. Seeing the invitations, Sally breaks down and cries, and when Betty questions her, she says that she wants to leave New York. Thinking that Sally has had a minor spat with Jack, Betty makes her sister swear to remain. Sally then convinces Max that love is stronger than duty or gratitude and that Betty will understand this when they break the news of their love to her. Jack sees them together and confronts them, concerned more for Betty's feelings than for his own wounded ones. Max then confesses to Betty that he loves Sally. Betty is flooded with anguish, and she accuses Sally of robbing her not only the best years of her life, but now her heart and soul. Sally refuses to acknowledge that she owes her sister anything and stands firm in her resolve to love Max. When Sally argues that Max, if he married Betty, would be ashamed of her because she is not educated, Betty points out that she sacrificed her own life to take care of her and sent her to nursing college instead of pursuing her own education. Betty pleads with Sally to give Max up, and when Sally instead attempts to jump from a window, Betty finally understands how strong their love is. She resigns herself to continue to fulfill the duties of a mother, as Sally and Max now prepare to marry. When Gershon arrives for what he thinks will be Betty's wedding and finds Sally in the wedding dress, he orders her to remove it, and Sally is about to comply when Betty falsely asserts that she broke the engagement because she stopped loving Max. Before the ceremony, Max asks for Betty's forgiveness, and she tells him that she forgave him a long time ago. When they hear music, she asks him to dance with her. After the dance, Betty swoons, and then sends Max to Sally to begin the ceremony. Alone, Betty looks at the portrait of her mother and says that she has kept her oath. *Jews. Mothers and daughters. Nurses. Physicians. Romantic rivalry. Self-sacrifice. Sisters. Attempted suicide. Aunts. Butchers. Cousins. Drunkenness. New York City. Pledges. Uncles. Weddings.*

Note: Because the print viewed had no English subtitles, the plot summary above was taken from a dialogue continuity in the NYSA, while the credits came from the print. The Yiddish title of this film was *Tsvey Shvester*. This was the only film produced by Graphic Pictures Corp. and the first and perhaps only film of Jennie Goldstein, whom *Var* called "one of the great dramatic stars of the Yiddish theatre." *Var* went on to call this "one of her typical roles," and noted "this gives her excellent opportunities for emoting, but unlike her lachrymal moments on the Yiddish stage, when she has shown heed for restraint, Miss Goldstein has been wisely checked by Blake in most of the dramatic moments." Most reviews praised the performance of Michel (also called "Michael") Rosenberg in the film's comedic interludes.

Box 24 Dec 1938. *Exh* 14 Dec 1938. *FD* 7 Dec 1938, p. 6. *NYT* 1 Dec 1938, p. 29. *Var* 14 Dec 1938, p. 15.

TYRANT OF RED GULCH (Russian Americans)

FBO Pictures. 25 Nov **1928** [©F.B.O. Productions, Inc.; 25 Nov 1928; LP20]. Si; b&w. 5 reels, 4,778 ft.

Dir Robert De Lacy. *Story and cont* Oliver Drake. *Titles* Randolph Bartlett. *Cam* Nick Musuraca. *Film ed* Jay Joiner.

Cast: Tom Tyler (*Tom Masters*), Frankie Darro (*"Tip"*), Josephine Borio (*Mitza*), Harry Woods (*Ivan Petrovitch*), Serge Temoff (*Boris Kosloff*), Barney Furey (*Anton*).

Melodrama. While looking for an old friend, Tom and his pal, Tip, come upon a little mining settlement under the despotic rule of a Russian, Ivan Petrovitch, and save Mitza and her little brother from his cruelty. Later, they are ambushed, and when Tom is separated from the party, Mitza and her brother are recaptured. Tom and Tip follow Petrovitch into a cave; the Russian escapes, leaving a half-wit to dynamite the cave, but Tip overpowers him, and Tom arrives at the mine to lead the inmates against the guards. Tom finds a friend among the prisoners, and they overtake Petrovitch, who has escaped with Mitza. *Dictators. Friendship. Mining towns. Russian Americans.*

FD 16 Feb 1928. *Var* 12 Dec 1928, p. 31.

LA ÚLTIMA CITA (Spanish language)

Columbia Pictures Corp. *Dist* Columbia Pictures Corp. **1936**; San José, Costa Rica opening: 24 Nov 1935; New York opening: 17 Jan 1936; Prod: began 7 Jun 1935. Sd; b&w. 8 reels. PCA cert no. 1771. Spanish language.

Prod Moe Sackin. *Dir* Bernard B. Ray. *Story and scr* René Borgia. *Mus* Willy Stahl.

Cast: José Crespo (*Alvaro Soler*), Luana Alcañiz (*Yolanda*), Andrea Palma (*Magda Soria*), Romualdo Tirado (*Crispín*), Soledad Jiménez (*Doña Luisa*), Rafael Storm (*Enrique Soria*), Paul Ellis (*Paul Albir*).

Romance, Melodrama. [*Not viewed*]. Alvaro Soler, a violinist on the road to fame, is invited to a café where Yolanda, the adopted daughter of his good friend, the Bohemian Crispín, is dancing. As the pianist has not shown up, Alvaro accompanies Yolanda's dance on his violin, and they are a great hit. Alvaro falls in love with the dancer to the extent of canceling all his concerts just to be with her. Enrique Soria, an old friend of Alvaro's, suggests that he appear in a benefit concert organized by his wife Magda to ensure that the artist's name is not forgotten. Magda becomes infatuated with the violinist and dominates him remorselessly. Obliged to fight a duel with Enrique and then abandoned by Magda, the wretched Alvaro also loses Yolanda, who marries a well-to-do admirer. About twenty-five years later, Alvaro, now performing all over the world, has finally triumphed as an artist. He returns to New York, where he is visited by a young lady who looks like Yolanda. The woman, Yolanda's daughter, reminds Alvaro of his true love. *Dancers. Romance. Violinists. Adoption. Bohemians and bohemianism. Cabarets. Duels. Fame. Infatuation. Infidelity. Marriage. New York City. Seduction. Socialites.*

Note: Reviews and news items translated the title as *The Last Date* and *The Last Rendezvous*. Although no information regarding the running time of this film has been located, the film was approved by the New York State censors at 6,595 feet after censorship eliminations had been made. A film of that length runs 73 minutes.
FD 23 Jan 1936, p. 8. *HR* 8 Jun 1935, p. 11. *HR* 7 Mar 1936, p. 5. *HR* 13 Nov 1936, p. 15. *NYT* 22 Jan 1936, p. 15.

EL ÚLTIMO DE LOS VARGAS (Latino, Spanish language)

Fox Film Corp. *Dist* Fox Film Corp. Oct **1930**; New York opening: 3 Oct **1930**; Prod: Aug 1930. Sd; b&w. 7 reels. 61 min. Passed by the National Board of Review. Spanish language.

Presenta [*Pres*] William Fox. *Supervisión de* [*Supv*] William Goetz. *Dirección de* [*Dir*] David Howard. [*Scr* Ernest Pascal]. [*Spanish version* Francisco Moré de la Torre]. [*Photog* Sidney Wagner]. [*Film ed* Al Dripps]. [*Sd* Eugene Grossman].

Source: Based on the short story "The Last of the Duanes" by Zane Grey in *Argosy* (Sep 1914).

Cast: Jorge Lewis [(*José Vargas*)], Luana Alcañiz [(*Elvira Núñez*)], Vicente Padula [(*Blanco*)], Carmen Rodríguez [(*Sr. Vargas*)], Christina Montt [(*Lola*)], Martín Garralaga [(*Erche*)], Juan de Landa [(*Capitán de los Rurales*)], Max Wagner [(*Estévez*)], Hipólito Mora [(*Yucca*)], Pablo Arenas [(*Luke Ramos*)], Nelly Fernández, [Amadeo Alcañiz (*Sr. Núñez*)], [Nelly Fernández], [Carlos Villarías], [María Teresa Renner].

Western. [*Not viewed*]. After being away for a long time, José Vargas returns to his home town of Llanos, Texas, to discover that his father has been shot and killed. José promises his mother that he will not take the law into his own hands, but in a confrontation, is forced to kill the assassin and become a fugitive from the law. During his flight, José learns that Elvira Núñez, one of his lady friends, has been kidnapped by Blanco and his gang after they have killed her father. José rescues Elvira, captures Blanco and turns him over to the authorities, then is cleared of the charges against him. *Fugitives. Latino. Mothers and sons. Murder. Rustlers. Self-defense. Texans. Bandits. Gangs. Kidnapping. Rescues. Romance. Texas Rangers.*

Note: This was a Spanish-language version of the 1930 film *Last of the Duanes*, which was directed by Alfred L. Werker and starred George O'Brien and Myrna Loy (see *AFI Catalog of Feature Films, 1921-30*; F2.2980). The story was first filmed by Fox in 1919 as *The Last of the Duanes*. That version was directed by J. Gordon Edwards and starred William Farnum (see *AFI Catalog of Feature Films, 1911-20*; F1.0028). A 1924 film with the same title was directed by Lynn Reynolds and starred Tom Mix and Marian Nixon (see *AFI Catalog of Feature Films, 1921-30*; F2.2979). Twentieth Century-Fox remade the story again in 1941 as *Last of the Duanes*. That version was directed by James Tinling and starred George Montgomery and Lynne Roberts.

EL ÚLTIMO DE SU SEXO see IT'S GREAT TO BE ALIVE

EL ÚLTIMO VARÓN SOBRE LA TIERRA see IT'S GREAT TO BE ALIVE

DI UMGLIKLIKHE KALE see THE UNFORTUNATE BRIDE

UNASHAMED (German Americans)

Metro-Goldwyn-Mayer Corp.; controlled by Loew's, Inc. *Dist* Metro-Goldwyn-Mayer Distributing Corp. 2 Jul **1932**; Prod: began late May 1932 [©Metro-Goldwyn-Mayer Distributing Corp.; 6 Jul 1932; LP3126]. Sd (Western Electric Sound System); b&w. 8 reels. 74 or 77 min. Passed by the National Board of Review.

Dir Harry Beaumont. [*Asst dir* Sandy Roth]. *Orig scr* Bayard Veiller. *Photog* Norbert Brodine. *Art dir* Cedric Gibbons. *Film ed* William S. Gray. *Gowns* Adrian. *Rec dir* Douglas Shearer. [*Sd* Paul Neal].

Cast: Helen Twelvetrees (*Joan Ogden*), Robert Young (*Dick Ogden*), Lewis Stone (*Henry Trask*), Jean Hersholt (*Mr. [Heinrich] Schmidt*), John Miljan (*District Attorney Harris*), Monroe Owsley ([*August Schmidt, also known as*] *Harry Swift*), Robert Warwick (*Mr. Ogden*), Gertrude Michael (*Marjorie*), Wilfred North (*Judge Ambrose*), Tommy Jackson (*Captain Riorden*), Louise Beaver (*Amanda*), [Rolfe Sedan (*Florist*)], [Herman Bing (*Hans*)], [Robert Dudley (*Spectator in courtroom*)].

Domestic, Drama. [*Print viewed*]. Joan Ogden is in love with Harry Swift, a gambler and polo player, who is not in the same social class as Joan's family. Her brother Dick, who, though younger than Joan, is very protective of her, doesn't want her to associate with Harry. Joan's father, who has lovingly reared Joan since his wife's death, warns her to keep away from Harry because "he's no good," but Joan is too much in love to give him up. When delicatessen owner Heinrich Schmidt goes to visit Mr. Ogden a few days later, Ogden is startled to learn that Schmidt is Harry's father. Schmidt wants Joan to stop seeing his son, whose real name is August Schmidt, so that he will go back to live with his father in their old neighborhood and forget about his acquired taste for luxury. Despite Mr. Schmidt's plea, Joan remains adamant about Harry. Later, Harry goes to see his father to ask for two thousand dollars so he can open an office. Although Schmidt is financially successful, he refuses to give Harry any more money. After they quarrel and make up, however, Schmidt agrees. The next night, Harry goes to see Ogden and shows him the money, pretending that he has made it from business deals. Ogden still is unimpressed, however, and tells him not to see Joan any more. A short time later, Joan and Harry check into a hotel and spend the night together. The next morning, Harry tells Joan that her father will insist that they marry to save her reputation, and that the three million dollars she is due to inherit will soon be theirs. He also tells her that he may have to put on an act in front of her family, but no matter what happens, he loves her. Meanwhile, at the Ogden house, Dick is nearly hysterical when he discovers that Joan has been out all night. Though his father is certain everything is all right, Dick goes looking for her. While he is out, Joan and Harry arrive and tell Ogden what has happened. Instead of insisting on their marriage, however, he tells Joan that he will not let her make another mistake and that they will keep things quiet. Dick then comes home and confronts Harry, with whom he has a violent argument when Harry says that he will tell everyone that Joan spent the night with him. During the argument, Dick goes to get a gun and when he returns, he shoots Harry. After Dick's arrest, his attorney, Henry Trask, wants to use the "unwritten law" defense, but Dick refuses to allow Joan to be humiliated in court. Joan, who now blames both Dick and her father for Harry's death, coldly refuses to help. During the trial, District Attorney Harris warns the all-male jury that there is no such thing as the unwritten law, and evidence seems to point to pre-meditated murder. When Joan is on the witness stand, she testifies that Dick shot Harry, "for no reason at all," after which Dick tells her whatever she has done, he still loves her. That night, Trask goes to Joan and describes what will happen if Dick is convicted and sent to the electric chair. Despite his words, she will not help Dick until she reads about executions in the newspaper. Remorseful, she then goes to Trask to beg him to let her help. He warns her that by saving Dick she may ruin herself for life, but she says she must do whatever is necessary. On the stand, Joan pretends to be callous and amoral and makes the jury believe that Dick was merely punishing a man who had degraded his sister. When she leaves the stand, people in the courtroom shout insults at her, and the jury acquits Dick. Finally, Trask explains to Ogden and Dick that through Joan's sacrifice, Dick can go free, and the Ogdens are a family again. *Brothers and sisters. Class distinction. Family relationships. German Americans. Murder. Reputation. Delicatessens. District Attorneys. Fortune hunters. Hotels. Judges. Maids. Millionaires. New York City. Parties. Trials. Widowers.*

Note: Working titles of the film were *Compromised* and *Without Shame*. According to *Var*, actress Helen Twelvetrees was borrowed from RKO for this picture. The *HR* review notes that the film was based on an actual murder case, however, no details of the real case have been located.

FD 15 Jul 1932, p. 7. *HF* 21 May 1932, p. 8. *HF* 28 May 1932, p. 8. *HR* 17 Jun 1932, p. 2. *MPH* 23 Jul 1932, p. 42. *NYT* 15 Jul 1932, p. 13. *Var* 19 Jul 1932, p. 25.

THE UNBELIEVER (German Americans)
Thomas A Edison, Inc.; Perfection Pictures. *Dist* George Kleine System. Feb **1918** [©Thomas A. Edison, Inc.; 15 Feb 1918; LP12062].
Si; b&w. 7 reels, 6,468 ft.
Pres George Kleine. *Prologue supv* Lieut. Frederick Kensel, U.S.M.C. *Dir* Alan Crosland. *Cam* Philip Tannura.
Source: Based on the novel *The Three Things* by Mary Raymond Shipman Andrews (Boston, 1915).
Cast: Marguerite Courtot (*Virginie Harbrok*), Raymond McKee (*Philip Landicutt*), Erich von Stroheim (*Lieut. Kurt von Schnieditz*), Kate Lester (*Margaret Landicutt*), Frank de Vernon (*Uncle "Jemmy" Landicutt*), Mortimer Martini (*Eugene Harbrok*), Blanche Davenport (*Madam Harbrok*), Harold Hallacher (*Pierre Harbrok*), Darwin Karr (*"Lefty"*), Earl Schenck (*Emanuel Muller*), Gertrude Norman (*Marianne Marnholm*), Lew Hart (*Hoffman*), Maj. Thomas Holcomb (*The commanding officer*), Lieut. J. F. Rorke (*Lieut. Terence O'Shaughnessy*), Sergt. Moss Gill (*Albert Mullins*), Maj. Ross E. Rowell, Capt. Thomas Sterett, Percy Webb, Cpl. Bob Ryland.
World War I, Drama. Distressed by her son Philip's class and racial prejudice, as well as his disbelief in God, wealthy New Yorker Margaret Landicutt encourages him to enlist in the United States Marine Corps during World War I. In the trenches, Philip witnesses such heroism and suffering that his viewpoint begins to change. Across the lines in Belgium, the German forces, led by the brutal Lieut. Kurt von Schnieditz, execute Madam Harbrok and her little son, believing them guilty of aiding the enemy, but because of Virginie Harbrok's beauty, the lieutenant spares the young woman. Philip rescues Virginie and, learning that she has lost her family, sends her to live with his mother in America. Shortly afterwards, "Lefty," Philip's old chauffeur and close friend on the battlefield, sacrifices his life for Philip, whereupon the young man's notions of class and racial distinctions are forever dismissed. Philip is seriously injured in the battle, and as he lies on the field, he sees Jesus walking among the wounded and abandons atheism. Upon his return home, Philip, a new man, is united with Virginie. *Atheists. Class distinction. Combat. Racism. Religious conversion. World War I. Belgium. Chauffeurs. Executions. Friendship. Germany. Army. Jesus Christ. Military service, Voluntary. New York City. Officers (Military). Orphans. Self-sacrifice. United States. Marine Corps. War injuries.*
Note: The picture was produced with the co-operation of the United States Marine Corp. Battle scenes were filmed at the U.S. M.C. Cantonment at Quantico, VA. Modern sources include Lew Hart and Moss Gill in the cast. Erich von Stroheim was called Karl von Stroheim in most reviews and publicity. The men of the third Battalion, Sixth Regiment, United States Marine Corps also appeared in the film.

ETR 26 Jan 1918, p. 696. *ETR* 23 Feb 1918, p. 992. *MPN* 2 Feb 1918, p. 710. *MPN* 2 Mar 1918, p. 1320. *MPW* 9 Feb 1918, p. 875. *MPW* 2 Mar 1918, pp. 1267-68. *NYDM* 16 Feb 1918, p. 20. *NYDM* 23 Feb 1918, p. 18. *NYT* 12 Feb 1918, p. 9. *Var* 15 Feb 1918, p. 52. *Var* 3 May 1918, p. 40. *Wid's* 28 Feb 1918, p. 967.

UNCHARTED CHANNELS (Russian Americans)
Jesse D. Hampton Productions. *Dist* Robertson-Cole Distributing Corp. Jun **1920**. Si; b&w. 6 reels.
Pres Jesse D. Hampton. *Dir* Henry King. *Story* Kenneth B. Clarke and Eugene B. Lewis. *Cam* Victor Milner.
Cast: H. B. Warner (*Timothy Webb, Jr.*), Kathryn Adams (*Sylvia Kingston*), Sam de Grasse (*Nicholas Schonn*), Evelyn Selbie (*Elsa Smolski*), William Elmer (*Jim Baker*), Percy Challenger (*Roger Webb*), Thomas H. Persse (*Peter Hines*), J. P. Lockney (*Thomas Empey*).
Drama. Timothy Webb's wealthy father, objecting to his son's reckless mode of living, cuts him out of his will. Donning overalls, Tim goes to work in the factory left by his father to Tim's uncle and becomes a plumber. Joining the labor union, Tim discovers that Nicholas Schonn, an opportunistic Bolshevik pretending to be in sympathy with the workmen, is sowing the seeds of labor unrest, aided by feminist Elsa Smolski. Pretending to join their ranks, Tim foils Schonn's scheme to bilk heiress Sylvia Kingston out of $50,000, winning Sylvia's love in the process. Sylvia then offers the check to

Tim, who uses the money to buy back his father's factory and, after granting raises to all the employees, proves his worthiness and succeeds in ejecting the trouble making radicals from the plant. *Bolshevists and Bolshevism. Disinheritance. Fathers and sons. Labor agitators. Moral reformation. Employer-employee relations. Factory workers. Feminism. Russian Americans. Spendthrifts. Trade unions.*

ETR 3 Jul 1920, p. 485. *MPN* 26 Jun 1920, p. 147. *MPW* 24 Jul 1920, p. 506. *Wid's* 13 Jun 1920, p. 15.

UNCLAIMED CARGO *see* WOMAN IN THE DARK

UNCLE JASPER'S WILL (African Americans)
Micheaux Film Corp. **1922**. Si; b&w. 6 reels.
Cast: William E. Fountaine, Shingzie Howard.
Melodrama (?), African American. No information about the precise nature of this film has been found. *African Americans. Wills.*
Note: This film was also known also as *Jasper Landry's Will*.

UNCLE MOSES (Yiddish language)
Yiddish Talking Pictures, Inc. *Dist* Yiddish Talking Pictures, Inc. **1932**; New York opening: 20 Apr 1932; Prod: late Mar—early Apr 1932; recorded at Metropolitan Studios, Fort Lee, N.J. Sd; b&w. 9 reels, 7,902 ft. 88 min. Passed by the National Board of Review. Yiddish language with English subtitles.
Pres LOUIS WEISS. *Supv* Louis Weiss. *Dir* Aubrey Scotto and Sidney Goldin. *Asst dir* Shimen Rushkin and Frank Melford. *Dial* Maurice Schwartz. *Photog* Frank Zucker and Buddy Harris. *Art dir* Anthony Continer. *Film ed* Bob Snody. *Gowns* Brenner Bros., N.Y. *Mus dir* Samuel Polonsky. *Rec eng* Marc S. Asch, Gerre Barton and Armond Schettini. *Tech dir* Charles Nasca.
Music: "Kamenoi Ostro" by Anton Rubinstein.
Source: Based on the novel *Uncle Moses* by Sholom Asch (New York, 1918) and the play of the same name, as adapted by Maurice Schwartz (New York, 28 Nov 1930).
Cast: MAURICE SCHWARTZ (*Uncle Moses*), Rubin Goldberg (*Alter Melnick*), Judith Abarbanell (*Masha*), Zvee Scooler (*Charlie*), Mark Schweid (*Aaron [Melnick]*), Sally Schor (*Rosie*), Rebecca Weintraub (*Gnendel*), Jacob Mestel (*Berel*), Sam Gertler (*Sam*), Leon Seidenberg (*Mannes*), Wolf Goldfaden (*Nachman*), Abe Sincoff (*Zalmen Shoichet*), Shirley Zelazo (*Zierele*), Michael Gibson (*Moishe Gross*), Ben-Zion Katz (*Schmiel-Yossel*), [Michael Rosenberg].
Yiddish, Social, Comedy-drama. [*Print viewed*]. The owner of a New York Lower East Side sweatshop and clothing store, who is called "Uncle Moses" by his employees, is a philanderer who continually complains that everyone comes to him for money, while his employees, whom he brought over from his village of Kuzmin in Europe, complain about their fourteen-hour work day. When Masha, the eighteen-year-old daughter of his former employee Aaron Melnick, asks Uncle Moses for money so that her father could open a business, Uncle Moses angrily refuses because Aaron has ridiculed his "fat belly." Incensed, Masha insults Uncle Moses, which only increases his desire for her. After she leaves, Uncle Moses gives her father back his job with a raise and talks Aaron into asking him to dinner. When Uncle Moses gives Masha a bracelet, her mother, who is against her match with Charlie, who works in the shop, embraces her. As Uncle Moses continues to give presents to Masha, his nephew Sam, who runs the shop, fears that his uncle will marry Masha and that he will lose his inheritance. Sam gets gangster Mannes to try to create scandals involving Uncle Moses with a restaurant proprietress and a Polish woman, with whom he has been involved, but their efforts fail. To inure himself with Masha, Uncle Moses, over the next year, exercises to get rid of his paunch, shaves his beard, gives her parents presents and sends her dresses and fur coats. He continues, however, to dream of his deceased wife. When labor organizer Moishe Gross urges the shop workers to strike, Uncle Moses increases their salaries substantially and orders improvements in the shop. Moishe, however, refuses to budge from his demand of setting up a union shop. After Uncle Moses shows Masha a house for them to share once they marry and confesses his love, she cries in despair. He then complains that she has led him on has and deceived him, and because she is unwilling to ruin her parents' happiness, she says that she now loves him and will marry him. After the wedding celebration, the image of Uncle Moses' first wife in a photograph glares at him as he prepares for the wedding night. Later, while Masha is in the maternity hospital, Charlie orders the workers to go on strike. Although Uncle Moses

wants to give the workers more money, Sam refuses and gets Mannes to send thugs to interrupt the workers' meeting. In the midst of the strike, a son is born to Masha. Masha, who is unhappy with her life, tells Uncle Moses that she was happier washing dishes and going to concerts in Jackson Park with Charlie than with her life of luxury. She tells Uncle Moses that she loves him, but that she must go away, and he sadly offers to send for a lawyer to get a divorce. When he learns that the thugs beat the workers and that Charlie has been arrested, Uncle Moses sends Sam to get him out and rebukes Sam for using thugs. Pushing him away, Uncle Moses stumbles and falls. During his recovery, Uncle Moses sends word to the strikers that he will agree to an eight-hour day, a twenty percent raise and electric machines, among other things, and Moishe becomes the union delegate. Uncle Moses makes out his will, leaving his estate to Masha and his son, who are going to Europe, to his workers, and to Sam. He also leaves money for hospitals and to be sent to Kuzmin. His wife's image now shows a concerned expression. When he gets well, Uncle Moses visits the shop and relates that upon driving around the city, which is something he never took the time to do before, he overheard a sermon at a great synagogue which defined man. He then wondered, "What is man?" After a life of accomplishments, he realizes, only the grave awaits. Uncle Moses then asks one of the workers to sing a melody that his father used to sing. *Clothing industry. Employer-employee relations. Family relationships. Jews. Marriage of convenience. New York City–East Side. Philanderers. Sweatshops. Childbirth. Divorce. Dreams. Family life. Gangsters. Labor agitators. Labor violence. Nephews. Polish Americans. Restaurants. Strikes and lockouts. Trade unions. Weddings.*

Note: The running time listed above was calculated from the footage given in NYSA records. According to a pre-production news item, this film was going to be made by Yiddish Talking Pictures, Inc. in association with Weiss Bros. Weiss Bros. is not credited on the film, although Louis Weiss is listed as presenter and supervisor. According to news items, the film was planned to be completed in time for release during the Passover week in 1932. The film includes shots taken at Delancey and Orchard Streets in New York's Lower East Side. Modern sources note that Sholem Asch (whose name is spelled "Sholom" in the screen credits) was America's most popular "serious" Yiddish writers and that Maurice Schwartz was the country's leading Yiddish actor. Modern sources also state that Asch's novel was first serialized in the *Forward*.

Detroit Jewish Chronicle 27 Jan 1939. *FD* 14 Mar 1932, p. 2. *FD* 24 Mar 1932, p. 30. *FD* 28 Mar 1932, p. 8. *FD* 3 Apr 1932, p. 5. *FD* 23 Sep 1932, p. 4. *Forward* 25 Apr 1932. *Kansas City Jewish Chronicle* 22 Apr 1938. *Morgn Fraybayt* 27 Apr 1932. *Morning Journal* 25 Apr 1932. *Der Tag* 28 Apr 1932. *Var* 4 Sep 1935.

UNCLE REMUS *see* **SONG OF THE SOUTH**

UNCLE SAM PREPARES *see* **HOW UNCLE SAM PREPARES**

UNCLE TOM'S CABIN (African Americans)
World Producing Corp. *Dist* World Film Corp. 10 Aug **1914** [©World Producing Corp.; 14 Aug 1914; LU3361]. Si; b&w. 5 reels.
Prod J. V. Ritchey. *Dir* William Robert Daly.
Source: Based on the novel *Uncle Tom's Cabin* by Harriet Beecher Stowe (Boston, 1852) and the play of the same name by George L. Aiken (New York, 18 Jul 1853).
Cast: Sam Lucas (*Uncle Tom*), Walter Hitchcock (*George Shelby*), Hattie Delaro (*Mrs. Shelby*), Master Abernathy (*George Shelby, Jr.*), Teresa Michelena (*Eliza*), Irving Cummings (*George Harris*), Paul Scardon (*Haley*), Marie Eline (*Little Eva St. Clair*), Garfield Thompson (*St. Clair*), Roy Applegate (*Simon Legree*), Boots Wall (*Topsy*).
Drama. George Shelby is forced to sell his faithful slave Uncle Tom and the baby son of Eliza Harris to Haley, a slave trader who holds the mortgage to his farm. Eliza escapes with the child and is able to join her husband George, and Vance, both runaway slaves, even though she is pursued by Haley's bloodhounds. Meanwhile, Uncle Tom saves little Eva St. Clair from drowning on the boat ride to Haley's plantation. Her kindly father then buys Tom, but, when Little Eva dies and St. Clair is killed trying to stop a fight, Tom and the other slaves are sold to the brutal Simon Legree. Legree mercilessly beats Tom when Casey, his housekeeper, escapes with Emmeline, his favorite slave, then leaves the old man to die. Just before Tom dies, however, he is found and comforted by George Shelby, Jr. who had been searching for the slave in fulfillment of a promise he had made as a young man. *Escapes. Infants. Pledges. Rescues. Slavery. Chases. Dogs. Plantations.*
Note: The novel was first serialized in *The National Era*, 1851-52. Sam Lucas, a seventy-two-year-old black actor, recreated his role from the Broadway production of the novel. Modern sources note that this was the first "white"

film in which a black actor was the star. In addition to the 1918 Paramount version (see below), many other films have been based on the novel including two 1903 films by Edison and Lubin; two 1910 films by Thanhouser and Pathé; a 1927 film by Universal (see below); and a 1955 CBS-TV version.
Motog 22 Aug 1914, p. 264. *MPN* 29 Aug 1914, p. 56. *MPW* 22 Aug 1914, p. 1077, 1152. *NYDM* 12 Aug 1914, p. 29. *Var* 4 Sep 1914, p. 13.

UNCLE TOM'S CABIN (African Americans)
Famous Players-Lasky Corp. *Dist* Famous Players-Lasky Corp.; Paramount Pictures. 15 Jul **1918** [©Famous Players-Lasky Corp.; 5 Jul 1918; LP12635]. Si; b&w. 5 reels.
Pres Adolph Zukor. *Dir* J. Searle Dawley. *Scen* J. Searle Dawley. *Cam* H. Lyman Broening. *2d cam* Chester A. Lyons.
Source: Based on the novel *Uncle Tom's Cabin* by Harriet Beecher Stowe (Boston, 1852) and the play of the same name by George L. Aiken (New York, 18 Jul 1853).
Cast: Marguerite Clark (*Little Eva St. Clair/Topsy*), J. W. Johnston (*Haley*), Florence Carpenter (*Eliza Harris*), Frank Losee (*Uncle Tom*), Phil Ryley (*Marks*), Harry Lee (*Jeff*), Walter Lewis (*Simon Legree*), Augusta Anderson (*Mrs. St. Clair*), Ruby Hoffman (*Cassy*), Susanne Willis (*Aunt Chloe*), Mrs. Priestley Morrison (*Ophelia*), Thomas Carnahan, Jr. (*George Shelby, Jr.*), Jere Austin (*George Harris*), Henry Stamford (*Mr. St. Clair*).
Social, Drama. When Kentucky plantation owner George Shelby is forced to sell several of his slaves, one of them, Eliza Harris, escapes across the icy Ohio River with her child. Kindly old Uncle Tom, however, is sold to a Southern slave trader and begins his voyage down the Mississippi River. During the trip, he rescues little Eva St. Clair from the river, and out of gratitude, the girl's father buys him. At the St. Clair home in New Orleans, Uncle Tom, Little Eva, and a mischievous little slave named Topsy become such close friends that Eva extracts a promise from her father to free the slave. The delicate Eva becomes ill and dies, and because her father is killed soon afterwards, St. Clair's promise goes unfulfilled, and Uncle Tom is sold to the brutal Simon Legree. Continually beaten, Uncle Tom finally dies just as George Shelby, Jr. arrives offering to repurchase the slave and take him home. Before his death, Uncle Tom sees a vision of Eva beckoning him to join her in heaven. *Children. Mississippi River. New Orleans (LA). Sadism. Slavery–Emancipation. Slaves. Southerners. Disease. Escapes. Heaven. Kentucky. Ohio River. Plantation owners. Pledges. Rescues. Slave traders. Visions.*
Note: The picture was filmed in Louisiana, Maine and New York City. The novel was first serialized in *The National Era*, 1851-52. For information on remakes, see entry above.
ETR 29 Jun 1918, p. 320. *ETR* 13 Jul 1918, p. 474. *MPN* 13 Jul 1918, p. 256. *MPW* 25 May 1918, p. 1168. *MPW* 20 Jul 1918, p. 453, 458. *Var* 9 Aug 1918, p. 33. *Wid's* 7 Jul 1918, pp. 29-30.

UNCLE TOM'S CABIN (African Americans)
Universal Pictures Corp. 2 Sep **1928**; New York premiere: 4 Nov 1927 [©Universal Pictures Corp.; 10 Nov 1927; LP24673]. Music score (Movietone); b&w. 13 reels, 13,000 ft. [Also a silent version.].
Pres Carl Laemmle. *Supv* Edward J. Montagne and Julius Bernheim. *Dir* Harry Pollard. *Scen* Harvey Thew and Harry Pollard. *Titles* Walter Anthony. *Photog* Charles Stumar and Jacob Kull. *Film ed* Gilmore Walker, Daniel Mandell and Byron Robinson. *Mus score* Hugo Riesenfeld. *Tech adv* Col. George L. Bryam.
Source: Based on the novel *Uncle Tom's Cabin* by Harriet Beecher Stowe (Boston, 1852).
Cast: James Lowe (*Uncle Tom*), Virginia Grey (*Eva St. Clare*), George Siegmann (*Simon Legree*), Margarita Fisher (*Eliza*), Eulalie Jensen (*Cassie*), Arthur Edmund Carew (*George Harris, a slave*), Adolph Milar (*Haley*), Jack Mower (*Mr. Shelby*), Vivian Oakland (*Mrs. Shelby*), J. Gordon Russell (*Tom Loker*), Skipper Zeliff (*Edward Harris, a slaveowner*), Lassie Lou Ahern (*Little Harris*), Mona Ray (*Topsy*), Aileen Manning (*Miss Ophelia*), John Roche (*St. Clare*), Lucien Littlefield (*Lawyer Marks*), Gertrude Astor (*Mrs. St. Clare*), Gertrude Howard (*Uncle Tom's wife*), Geoffrey Grace (*The Doctor*), Rolfe Sedan (*Adolph*), Marie Foster (*Mammy in St. Clare house*), Francis Ford (*Lieutenant*), Martha Franklin (*Landlady*), Nelson McDowell (*Phineas Fletcher*), Grace Carlisle (*Mrs. Fletcher*), C. E. Anderson (*Johnson*), Dick Sutherland (*Sambo*), Tom Amardares (*Quimbo*), Bill Dyer (*Auctioneer*).
Melodrama. Mulattoes George and Eliza, the "beloved slaves" of neighboring Kentucky plantation owners, are about to be married when their plans are scotched by Edward Harris, George's master. Over the next years, the Shelbys, Eliza's kindly masters, incur a

deepening debt to a blackguard named Haley, forcing them to surrender their slaves Tom and Harry, Eliza's young son. Eliza, overhearing the plans, escapes with Harry across the border. She is pursued by Lawyer Marks and his companion, Loker, and, although harbored by Quaker Phineas Fletcher, is extradited by dint of the new Dred Scott Decision. Returning home, they find themselves on a riverboat with Haley, Tom, and George, who had escaped from Harris' clutches and obtained work as a stoker. Haley's presence forces George into a watery escape and Marks and Loker into stealthy evasion until they can sell Harry to yet another slave owner; meanwhile, Eliza's grief drives her to near self-destruction. White northerner Augustus St. Claire and his young daughter, Eva, intervene on Tom's behalf and buy him, leaving Eliza to be sold downriver at a New Orleans slave auction. A deep friendship develops between Eva and Topsy, a scurvy black imp who becomes her servant, but the little white girl dies, soon followed by her father. Tom is then sold to Simon Legree, a villainous northerner who also buys Eliza. He brings her into his home, usurping the place of Cassie, an older mulatto slave, who jealously confides to Tom her bitter and tortuous history at the hands of Legree. The story reveals Cassie to be Eliza's mother; reunited, they try to escape, ending up in Legree's attic. Though Tom is beaten to death, their whereabouts are concealed until Legree happens upon them. A fight ensues, in which Legree, drunk, hysterical, and tormented by visions of the goodly Tom, falls from the attic to his death. George, who has found and claimed little Harry, emerges from a passing band of refugees, and the long-sought reunion takes place. *African Americans. African Americans–Mixed blood. Dred Scott Decision, 1857. Drunkenness. Extradition. Family relationships. Kentucky. Lawyers. Marriage. New Orleans (LA). Plantation owners. Plantations. Quakers. River boats. Slaves.*

Note: According to a *Var* news story in Sep 1952, this film was released in 1950 illegally in a sound version in which a narrator read the original titles. The perpetrator, Howard G. Underwood of Pine Grove, KY, removed the original Universal credits and substituted credits which read, "Howard G. Underwood presents *Uncle Tom's Cabin*. Produced by Howard G. Underwood, Copyrighted 1950." Universal sued for damages, an injunction against exhibition, seizure of prints and destruction of prints and negatives. In Sep 1952, a U.S. Marshal in Lexington, KY seized and impounded three prints of the film from Underwood's garage, in accordance with a court order. *Var* noted, "Strange aspect of the case is that the film has been showning in hundreds of theatres and drive-ins and has been doing tremendous biz, often outgrossing many present-day pictures." According to an audio transcription at NYSA, the 1950 version opened with the following statement: "Please do not form an opinion of this great motion picture from the opening scenes. Remain here in this theatre during its complete showing. We assure you you will be rewarded by its greatness."

FD 13 Nov 1927. *MPW* 12 Nov 1927. *NYT* 5 Nov 1927, p. 16. *Var* 9 Nov 1927, p. 18. *Var* 10 Sep 1952.

UNCONQUERED (African Americans)

Jesse L. Lasky Feature Play Co. *Dist* Paramount Pictures Corp. 31 May 1917 [©Jesse L. Lasky Feature Play Co.; 12 May 1917; LP10756]. Si; b&w. 5 reels.

Dir Frank Reicher. *Asst dir* Charles Watt. *Story and scen* Beatrice C. de Mille and Leighton Osmun. *Cam* Dent Gilbert.

Cast: Fannie Ward (*Mrs. Jackson*), Jack Dean (*Richard Darcier*), Hobart Bosworth (*Henry Jackson*), Tully Marshall (*Jake*), Mabel Van Buren (*Mrs. Lenning*), Jane Wolfe (*Voodoo queen*), Billy Jacobs (*Little Billy*).

Drama. Mrs. Jackson endures the cruelty of her husband Henry for the sake of her son Billy. Mr. Jackson is so unfeeling that he insists upon his wife inviting his mistress, Mrs. Lenning, to visit them at their Florida home. Although Mr. Jackson desires a divorce, he will not consider it without the custody of his son. While in Florida, Mrs. Jackson meets Richard Darcier, who sympathizes with her plight. Mr. Jackson seizes upon their friendship to frame his wife in a compromising situation with Darcier and then sues for divorce, winning custody of his son. Meanwhile, Darcier's caretaker Jake, an African-American voodoo worshipper, has been warned by a voodoo priestess that he must provide their group with a victim or die himself. Crazed by the threat, he kidnaps Billy and offers the boy's life as a sacrifice. Mrs. Jackson finds the sacrificial cave and offers her life in exchange for that of her son's. At that moment, Mr. Jackson arrives with a rescue party, saves both their lives and, realizing the strength of his ex-wife's mother love, restores her son to her. Mrs. Jackson then marries Darcier and the reconstituted family begins life anew. *Child custody. Children. Divorce. Florida. Human sacrifice. Marriage. Motherhood. Self-sacrifice. Voodoo. Abduction. African Americans. Frame-ups. Mistresses. Rescues.*

Note: The title of the original story was "The Conflict." "Unconquered" was the title of an original story, also by Beatrice C. de Mille and Leighton Osmun, that was the source for the 1916 film entitled *Unprotected*, which was also produced by the Jesse L. Lasky Feature Play Co.

ETR 2 Jun 1917, p. 1824. *Motog* 2 Jun 1917, p. 1177. *MPN* 2 Jun 1917, p. 3459. *MPW* 2 Jun 1917, p. 1457, 1500. *NYDM* 25 May 1917, p. 29. *Wid's* 24 May 1917, p. 323.

UNCONQUERED (Native Americans, Ottawa)

Paramount Pictures, Inc. *Dist* Paramount Pictures, Inc. 4 Feb **1948**; Denver, CO opening: 4 Nov 1947; Prod: 2d unit photography: began early Jun 1946; principal shooting: 29 Jul—8 Nov 1946; addl scenes: 25-26 Nov 1946; 10 Dec 1946; 30 Dec 1946; 5 May 1947. [©Paramount Pictures, Inc.; 3 Oct 1947; LP1539]. Sd (Western Electric Recording); col. (Technicolor). 13,188 ft. 146-147 min. Passed by the National Board of Review.

Prod CECIL B. DeMILLE. *Dir* CECIL B. DeMILLE. *2d unit dir* Arthur Rosson. *Asst dir* Edward Salven. *Rehearsal dir* Arthur Pierson. *Dial dir* Robert Foulk. [*Asst dir/company clerk* George Reese]. [*Asst dir* Mickey Moore, Danny McCauley and Eddie Morse]. [*2d unit asst dir* Richard McWhorter]. [*2d unit 2d asst dir* Bud Brill]. *Scr* Charles Bennett, Fredric M. Frank and Jesse Lasky, Jr. [*Scen* Jeanie Macpherson and N. Rains]. *Dir of photog* Ray Rennahan. [*Cam dept staff* Archie Dalzell, Bob Reilly, John Hamilton and Phil Eastman]. [*Still photog* G. E. Richardson]. [*2d unit cam* Wally Kelly]. [*2d unit 2d cam* Guy Bennett and Art Lane]. [*2d unit asst cam* Bob Hosler]. [*2d unit still cam* Jack Coffman]. *Dir of photog eff* Gordon Jennings. *Dir of process photog* Farciot Edouart and Wallace Kelley. *Spec photog eff* Paul Lerpae and Devereux Jennings. [*Spec eff cam* F. Finger and I. Roberts]. [*Spec eff cam op* F. Barber]. [*Spec eff asst cam* E. Wahrmann]. [*2d unit spec eff asst* William Kislingbury]. *Technicolor color dir* Natalie Kalmus. *Assoc* Robert Brower. [*2d unit Technicolor cam* Bill Snyder]. [*2d unit Technicolor tech* Roger Mace and Fred Ditmar]. [*2d unit Technicolor asst* Wilet Martin, George Gall and Charles Termini]. [*2d unit Technicolor loader* Cecil Myers]. [*2d unit Technicolor mechanic* Adolph Prautsch]. *Art dir* Hans Dreier and Walter Tyler. [*Art dept staff* Al Roeloff and Bill Teel]. *Ed* Anne Bauchens. [*Cutting* Gladys Carley]. [*Script cutting* Claire Benke and Bill Shanks]. *Set dec* Sam Comer and Stanley Jay Sawley. [*Painter* Lee Price]. [*2d unit painter* Ted Roland and Jim Daraio]. [*Set const* Russ Brown]. [*Set dresser* Jay Sawley, Morry Goodman and Jack Gosnell]. [*Prop* Joe Thompson, Frank Lindsay, Jr. and Jack Leys]. [*Prop shop* Dick Webb]. [*2d unit prop shop* James Roe]. [*2d unit prop* Carl Coleman]. [*2d unit 2d prop* Dwight Thompson]. *Cost* Gwen Wakeling. [*Cost*] exec by Madame Barbara Karinska. [*Ward supv* F. Richardson]. [*Ward* Eric Seelig, Edna Shotwell, Julie Cockerill, Joe Caplan and King Greenwood]. [*2d unit ward* Ed Fitzharris]. [*2d unit 2d ward* John Johnson]. *Mus score* Victor Young. [*Mus dept* Phil Boutelje, Louis Lipstone and Roy Fjastad]. *Dances staged by* Jack Crosby. [*Dance dept* Al Mann and Bob Goodstein]. *Sd rec* Hugo Grenzbach, John Cope and [William Sosteleo]. [*Boom* Wallace Nogle]. [*Cable man* Ross Howe]. [*2d unit sd tech* George Tallian]. *Makeup supv* Wally Westmore. [*Makeup* Glen Alden, Charles Huber, Max Asher and Charles Hansen]. [*Makeup secy* Reine Van Gelder]. [*Hair supv* Nellie Manley]. [*Hair* Gertrude Reed, Mabelle Carey and Maudlee McDougall]. [*2d unit hair* Doris Roland]. [*Prod staff* Donald Hayne, Jesse Lasky, Jr., Fred Frank and Bernice Mosk]. *Tech supv* [*ship*] Capt. Fred F. Ellis, B.M.M. (Ret.). *Indian language adv* Iron Eyes Cody. [*Research* Henry Noerdlinger]. [*Bus mgr* Roy Burns]. [*Asst bus mgr* Andy Durkus]. [*2d unit bus mgr* C. Kenneth DeLand]. [*Casting* Joe Egli, Tish Morgan, Billy Greenwald, Marge Graham, Tony Reagan and Bob Osterman]. [*Coordinator* Howard David and Ted Holderness]. [*Elec* Hubert H. Graham and Lorne P. Netten]. [*Boom grip* Buck Walters]. [*Grip* Ted Powell, Colie Kessinger and Whitie Reed]. [*2d unit grip* Miles Seminero, V. Bratton, E. Hazel, Earl Miller, Bill Geiger, Murray Young, Bob West, C. Goettman, W. H. Newson, F. Goff, Al Lipsey, C. Kelly, Jake Boumeister and K. Smith]. [*Horseman* Bill Hurley]. [*Illustrator* Dwight Franklin]. [*Prod dept* George Bertholon, Frank Caffey and Don Robb]. [*Pub* Phil Koury]. [*P.A. operator and chair asst* Russell Martin and James Cassin]. [*Secy to Cecil B. DeMille* Florence Cole]. [*Secy to Donald Hayne* Katherine Arruda]. [*Secy to Roy Burns and Edward Salven* Evelyn Faber]. [*Secy to Jeanie Macpherson* Virginia Terrill]. [*Secy* Bernice Mosk and D. Hayne]. [*Company clerk* G. Reese]. [*Receptionist* Evelyn Sullivan]. [*Restaurant* P. Kessinger]. [*Lab tech* C. Gemora]. [*Scr clerk* Claire Behnke and S. Freedle]. [*2d unit scr clerk* Harry Hogan]. [*2d unit auditor* Frank Parmenter]. [*2d unit timekeeper* Bob Kegg]. [*2d unit nurseryman* Wesley Jones]. [*2d unit machine shop* Jerry Gerard]. [*2d*

unit double for Gary Cooper Frank Cordell]. [*2d unit double* Henry Wills, Iron Eyes Cody, Fred Zendar, Frank McMahon, Ned Winchester and Leila Finn].

Source: Based on the novel *Unconquered: A Novel of the Pontiac Conspiracy* by Neil H. Swanson (New York, 1947).

Cast: GARY COOPER (*Captain Christopher Holden*), PAULETTE GODDARD (*Abby [Hale]*), Howard Da Silva (*[Martin] Garth*), Boris Karloff (*Guyasuta, Chief of the Senecas*), Cecil Kellaway (*Jeremy Love*), Ward Bond (*John Fraser*), Virginia Campbell (*Mrs. John Fraser*), Katherine DeMille (*Hannah*), Henry Wilcoxon (*Captain Steele*), Sir C. Aubrey Smith (*Lord Chief Justice*), Victor Varconi (*Captain Simeon Ecuyer*), Virginia Grey (*Diana*), Mike Mazurki (*Bone*), Porter Hall (*Leach*), Richard Gaines (*Colonel George Washington*), Gavin Muir (*Lieut. Fergus McKenzie*), Jane Nigh (*Evelyn*), Alan Napier (*Sir William Johnson*), Marc Lawrence (*Sioto, medicine man*), Raymond Hatton (*Venango scout*), John Mylong (*Colonel Henry Bouquet*), George Kirby (*Charles Mason, London astronomer*), Leonard Carey (*Jeremiah Dixon, London astronomer*), Frank R. Wilcox (*Richard Henry Lee*), Davison Clark (*Mr. Carroll of Virginia*), Griff Barnett (*Brother Andrews of Pennsylvania*), Lloyd Bridges (*Lieut. Hutchins*), Oliver Thorndike (*Lieut. Baillie*), Nan Sunderland (*Mrs. Pruitt*), Rus Conklin (*Mamaultee*), Iron Eyes Cody (*Red Corn*), Julia Faye (*Widow Swivens*), Paul E. Burns (*Dan McCoy*), Mary Field (*Maggie*), Diane Wadelow (*Lancashire lass*), Clarence Muse (*Jason*), [Robert Warwick (*Pontiac, chief of the Ottawas*)], [Sanders Clark (*Ben*)], [Matthew Boulton (*Captain Brooks*)], [Willa Pearl Curtis (*Mammy*)], [Jeff York (*Wide-shouldered youth*)], [Frank Moran (*Burly ruffian*)], [Olaf Hytten (*Star of London purser*)], [Alec Harford (*Shifty-eyed cutthroat*)], [Fred Zendar (*Trapper*)], [Dick Alexander, William Meader, Wallace Earl (*Slaves*)], [Barbara Morrison, Lloyd Whitlock, Boyd Irwin (*Ship's passengers*)], [George Magrill (*Ship's agent/Royal American officer*)], [Budd Fine (*Ship's mate*)], [Valmere Barman (*Ship's girl*)], [Kenneth Gibson, Carl Saxe, Sam Ash, James Flavin, Al Murphy, Harlan Miller, Fred Zendar, Byron Foulger, Joe Whitehead, Walter Baldwin, Bill Wallace, Jasper Palmer, Jim Nolan, Jim Drum, Don Lynch, Bill Murphy, Ted Mapes, George Anderson, Gil Sullivan, George Anderson, Trevor Bardette, Chuck Hamilton, George Bunny, James Carlisle (*Townsmen*)], [Llorna Jordan, Ethel Wales, Besse Wade, Betty Farrington, Jane Everett, Donya Dean, Dorothy Adams (*Townswomen*)], [Syd Saylor (*Spieler for Dr. Diablo*)], [John Harmon (*Spieler for Boukabokabus*)], [Eddie Dunn, Bill Sundholm, Francis Ford, Francis McDonald, Guy Wilkerson, Jack Clifford, John Northpole, Bob Kortman, Ray Spiker (*Frontiersmen*)], [June Harris (*Frontierswoman*)], [Jack Weatherwax (*Man with dog act*)], [Earle Hodgins (*Spieler for mermaid*)], [Alan Bridge (*Militiaman*)], [Hope Landin (*Joshua's mother*)], [Richard Reeves (*Joshua*)], [Si Jenks (*Farmer*)], [Crane Whitley (*Plantation agent*)], [Robert Barron (*Overseer*)], [Louise Saraydar (*Girl*)], [Eric Alden (*Zeke/Indian*)], [Frank Hagney (*Jake*)], [Hugh Prosser, Ray Teal (*Gilded Beaver soldiers*)], [Edgar Dearing (*Gilded Beaver soldier/Frontiersman*)], [Noble Johnson (*Big Ottowa Indian*)], [Chief Thundercloud (*Chief Killbuck*)], [Sally Rawlinson (*Brunette girl*)], [Larry Thompson, Russ Clark, John James (*Officers*)], [Bill Hall, John Merton (*Corporals*)], [Constance Purdy (*Buxom woman*)], [Geraldine Wall (*Mrs. Bitt*)], [Donna Courter, Greta Granstedt (*Ballroom women*)], [James Horne, Ted Allan, David Ralston, Gilbert Wilson, Lex Barker, Gus Taute (*Royal American officers*)], [Clancy Cooper (*Sentry*)], [Fred Coby (*Royal American soldier*)], [Lee Phelps (*Royal American sergeant*)], [Charles Victor (*Royal American officer/Officer/Court clerk*)], [Jerry James (*Captain Clark/Royal American officer/Officer/Court clerk/Townsman*)], [Larry Lawson (*Royal American officer/Trapper*)], [Charles Middleton (*Mulligan*)], [Ottola Nesmith (*Guest*)], [Fred Kohler, Jr. (*Sergeant*)], [Forrest Taylor (*Trader*)], [Jack Lee (*Major Trent*)], [Karolyn Grimes (*Little girl*)], [Beatrice Gray (*Ballroom girl*)], [Fred Datig, Jr., Christopher Clark (*Boys*)], [Buddy Roosevelt, Dwight Butcher (*Guards*)], [Bill Haade, Erville Alderson, John Mallon, Mike Lally, Charles Sullivan, Jeff Corey (*Trappers*)], [Len Hendry (*Trapper/Indian*)], [Eigene R. Eberle, Calvin Ellison (*Drummer boys*)], [Bert Moorhouse, Mike Kilian (*Virginia militia officers*)], [Carl Mathews (*Trapper witness/Indian*)], [William Bailey (*Townsman witness*)], [Lane Chandler (*Pennsylvania militia officer*)], [John Miljan (*Prosecutor*)], [J. W. Cody, Chuck Hamilton (*Lesser chiefs*)], [Maxine

Chevalier, Claire DuBrey, Mimi Aguglia, Nenette Vallon, Inez Palange, Rose Higgins (*Squaws*)], [Chabing, Charmienne Harker (*Young squaws*)], [Roderic Redwing, Jay Silverheels, Vaughn Anthony, Bob Kortman, Albert Cavigga (*Indians*)], [Belle Mitchell, Fernanda Eliscu (*Old crone squaws*)], [Boyd Davis (*Dr. Boyd*)], [Charles Flynn (*Ensign Price*)], [Jack Overman, Harry Cording, Bill Hunter (*Ramparts soldiers*)], [Jack Pennick (*Joe Lovat*)], [Allan Ray (*Soldier*)], [Henry Mowbray, John Goldsworthy (*Old Bailey tipstaffs*)], [Montague Shaw (*Old Bailey undersheriff*)], [Crauford Kent (*Old Bailey chaplain*)], [Gordon Richards (*Old Bailey sheriff*)], [Arthur Gould Porter (*Old Bailey personal clerk*)], [Colin Kenny, Leyland Hodgson (*Old Bailey warders*)], [Arthur Blake (*Old Bailey visiting noble*)], [Leslie Denison (*Old Bailey usher*)], [Dick Elmore (*Young officer*)], [Bob Baughman (*Regimental drummer*)], [Anna Lehr], [Gertrude Valerie], [Al Ferguson], [Maria Tavares], [Frances Sanford].

Historical, War, Drama. [*Print viewed*]. In 1763 at the Old Bailey in London, Abigail Hale is sentenced to death for helping her brother fight the press gang which was attempting to forcibly press him into service at sea. To avoid hanging, Abby agrees to fourteen years of indentured service in the colonies and boards a ship bound for Norfolk, Virginia. The ship's brutish captain, Martin Garth, who is transporting munitions for the Indians of the Ohio Valley, bids for Abby, but is outbid by Captain Chris Holden from Virginia. When the ship reaches Norfolk, Chris, who is about to be married, grants Abby her freedom. After learning that an edict has forbidden the sale of guns, Garth buys every indentured servant on the ship, including Abby, who thinks Chris has double-crossed her. Meanwhile, Chris's fiancée Diana leaves him for his brother. In Peakestown, colonial leaders who are planning to seize Pittsburgh from the Indians meet with Chris and Garth. Garth, who is a blood brother to Guyasuta, the chief of the Senecas, and has married Guyasuta's daughter Hannah in order to trade the Indians guns for furs, claims the Indians gave him the land deeds to Pittsburgh. Under Pontiac, chief of the Ottawas, Indians from the Ottawa, Seneca, Delaware, Shawnee and other tribes, meanwhile, have been circulating a war belt to enlist the tribes to fight the colonists and drive them to the sea. Chris's friend, John Fraser, found the belt on a dead Indian and gave it to him. Since the colonialists have no army, Chris offers to carry peace belts to the Indians. Chris's two scouts are quickly killed by Indians sent by Garth to steal the peace belts. Chris arrives at Fort Pitt, where Abby is a barmaid in Garth's saloon, and she helps him retrieve the belts. Armed with two pistols, Chris makes his escape with Abby to John's blacksmith shop. At a ball at Fort Pitt in honor of King George III's birthday, Garth exposes Abby to Captain Simeon Ecuyer, who was at her trial, and Chris lays claim to her in order to force Garth into a duel. Ecuyer determines Garth to be Abby's legal owner and, unaware that Garth is a traitor, forbids Chris from pursuing him and Abby. When Indian envoys alert Garth that the war has started and that they need weapons, he places Abby in the care of the Indians and goes to Guyasuta's camp, where plans are being made to burn the forts after the settlers are convinced to surrender. Meanwhile, at Fort Pitt, a widowed settler enters the ball carrying her wounded daughter and reports an Indian massacre. Ecuyer orders Chris to clear the town of people and burn it down, but he instructs John to carry out the order so that he can save Abby. Garth leaves Guyasuta's camp for Fort Pitt, forsaking Abby, who is tortured and burned by the Senecas. In a cloud of smoke, Chris arrives and convinces Guyasuta and Sioto, his medicine man, that his compass is the "medicine of death." He and Abby escape, but are pursued in canoes. By going over a mammoth waterfall, Abby and Chris convince the Senecas that they are dead, and they escape on foot to the outskirts of Venango to a cabin belonging to a family that has been killed. In Venango, all the settlers have been massacred except an old man, who warns Chris and Abby not to be tricked by the Indians into surrender. Meanwhile, Garth advises Ecuyer and Captain Steele, the officer in command, to raise a white flag at Fort Pitt, and relates Guyasuta's promise that all will be set free. Chris warns the settlers not to surrender, but is court-martialed for defying Ecuyer's earlier orders and sentenced to death. Abby agrees to stay with Garth of her own volition if he will free Chris, and Hannah, who had earlier arranged for Abby to be kidnapped by the Indians because she was jealous of Garth's interest in her, sacrifices herself by crossing the moat disguised as Chris and taking gunfire meant for him. Chris arrives at the fort at Bushy Run, held by Colonel

Henry Bouquet and his 42nd Infantry, hoping his garrison will rescue Fort Pitt, but a quarter of Bouquet's men have been massacred. As the Indians begin their assault on Fort Pitt, Chris gathers a handful of the 42nd's surviving infantrymen and wagons full of dead soldiers and marches on Fort Pitt. The Indians, believing the garrison is alive, retreat. Chris kills Garth before he can escape with Abby, and is pardoned by Ecuyer. Ecuyer then marries Abby and Chris and orders Chris to go west with the frontier. *Fort Pitt (PA). Indentured servants. Indians of North America. Pontiac's Conspiracy, 1763-1765. Settlers. Traitors. United States–History–Colonial period, ca. 1600-1775. Balls (Parties). Barmaids. Bushy Run, Battle of. Courts-martial and courts of inquiry. Escapes. False arrests. George III, King of England, 1738-1820. Great Britain. Army. Gunrunners. London (England). Marriage. Massacres. Medicine men. Miscegenation. Ottawa Indians. Pittsburgh (PA). Profiteering. Romantic rivalry. Scouts (Frontier). Sea captains. Self-sacrifice. Seneca Indians. Ships. Torture. Tribal chiefs. Virginians. George Washington. Waterfalls. The West.*

Note: The title card to the film reads "Cecil B. DeMille's *Unconquered.*" A spoken narration opens the film, establishing the period and giving some historical background and motivation for the story. It begins, "At the forks of the Ohio stands an American city, a colossus of steel, whose mills and furnaces bring forth bone and sinew for a nation. Not so long ago, a lowly outpost guarded this very spot. It was called Fort Pitt...."

According to a 25 Sep 1947 article in *DV*, this film, which cost $4.2 million to make, was DeMille's most expensive film to date. Referring to the Sep 1947 subpoenaing of forty-seven members of the film community by the House Un-American Activities Committee to appear at hearings in Washington, D.C., DeMille, about to embark on a publicity tour for this film, is quoted in the article as having said "I'm also going to try to correct the impression that Hollywood is a nest of Communism." According to the Paramount Collection contained in the AMPAS Library, in Jun 1946, the Production Code Administration suggested a rewrite of "Abby's" wedding scene to eliminate its "objectionable flavor," stating "the present offhand handling of this marriage seems unduly light and undignified."

Portions of this film were shot at the Conejo Grade, forty-five miles west of Los Angeles, CA. According to the Paramount Collection, a second unit photographed up and down the north fork of Clearwater River in Idaho, eighty-two miles from the closest town of Orofino on 4 Jul 1946. Big Mesa Falls in Ashton, ID (near Boise) was filmed for the waterfall scenes, and the rapids river sequence was shot in McCall, ID (also near Boise). The exteriors of the log fort and Wolf Creek were shot in a state forest in New York. Extensive filming took place in the Kiskiminetas River country in western Pennsylvania and in Cook's Forest, sixty miles from Pittsburgh, PA. According to a 1 Jul 1946 *Par News* item, after three weeks of shooting in Cook's Forest, part of Cook's National Park, heavy rains and floods forced the second unit to move 250 miles east to a scenic plateau north of the Allegheny Mountains. DeMille had fifteen fifty-foot birch trees shipped from Pennsylvania forests to Hollywood for the Peakestown spring fair scene in the film. According to *ParNews*, DeMille used dozens of real fireballs and flaming arrows in the battle scene; eight persons suffered burns and one extra's hair was burned.

A *ParNews* item noted that DeMille bowed to the PCA by using soapsuds in Paulette Goddard's barrel bath scene, even though there was no bubblebath in 1763. Several reviews mentioned DeMille's depiction of Goddard in a crude wooden barrel as uncharacteristic of DeMille's traditionally lavish bath scenes, and an article in the *NYT* on 28 Jul 1946 stated that "a reliable piece of DeMille glamour—the bath scene—is going to find itself thrown for a loss in the showman's budget-heavy venture." According to a *HR* news item, between three and four thousand extras were used for the film in one hundred and ten days of shooting. Although Paramount circulated much press about DeMille's authentic and sensitive use of Native Americans in this film, an article in the *NYT* on 19 Oct 1947 said "it is deplorably evident that *Unconquered*, in this year of grace, is as viciously anti-redskin as *The Birth of a Nation* was anti-Negro long years back." The *NYT* review of the film, in reference to the depiction of "villainous Indians," stated that "all of them [were] incontrovertible Caucasians"; but, according to an article in *Picturegoer*, one hundred and fifty Native Americans ranging from Navajos to Cherokees were used in the assault on Fort Pitt. The film's technical adviser, Iron Eyes Cody, was of Seneca-Cherokee ancestry. Cody began working with DeMille as an actor in 1914 in *The Squaw Man*.

This film was nominated for a 1947 Academy Award for Special Effects. Included in the nomination were Farciot Edouart, Devereux Jennings, Gordon Jennings, Wallace Kelley and Paul Lerpae for visual effects, including miniatures, transparency process projection, and optical effects for the long boat sequence, the water falls and canoe escape sequence and the battle sequence. George Dutton was nominated for sound, and George Dutton for sound effects.

AmCin Oct 1946, p. 348 *Box* 4 Oct 1947. *DV* 20 Aug 1947. *DV* 24 Sep 1947. *DV* 25 Sep 1947. *FD* 24 Sep 1947, p. 8. *HR* 2 Jan 1947, p. 6. *HR* 24 Sep 1947, p. 3. *HR* 20 Oct 1947, p. 2. *HR* 6 Nov 1947, p. 10. *IFJ* 12 Oct 1946, p. 40. *Life* 24 Nov 1947, pp. 116-17. *MPHPD* 27 Sep 1947, p. 3849. *NYT* 22 Sep 1946. *NYT* 28 Jul 1946. *NYT* 11 Oct 1947, p. 11. *Picturegoer* Nov 1947. *Var* 24 Sep 1947, p. 11.

UNDER ARIZONA SKIES *see* WESTERN HERITAGE

UNDER FALSE COLORS (Russian Americans)

Thanhouser Film Corp.; Gold Rooster Plays. *Dist* Pathé Exchange, Inc. 23 Sep **1917**. Si; b&w. 5 reels.

Dir Emile Chautard. *Story* Lloyd Lonergan.

Cast: Frederick Warde (*John Colton*), Jeanne Eagles ("*Countess Olga*"), Robert Vaughn (*Jack Colton*), Anne Gregory (*Vera*), Carey Hastings.

Drama. At the first rumblings of revolution, a Russian countess flees the country with the assistance of Jack Colton, a young American in Russia to arrange a loan from her father. On the ship to America, Countess Olga meets Vera, a young girl who is also fleeing the advancing danger of revolution to live with her father's friend, John Colton, Jack's father. En route, the ship is torpedoed and Vera dies, leaving Olga a letter to deliver to Colton. After she is rescued by a lifeboat, Olga decides to assume Vera's identity and calls upon Colton, who receives the girl as his old friend's daughter. All goes well for Olga until a secret band of revolutionaries enlist her aid by promising to help the poor left behind in Russia. Soon after, Colton discovers that Olga is not who she pretends to be, but remains silent. His confidence in Olga is rewarded when she foils the revolutionaries' scheme to kill Colton. Realizing that the band of revolutionaries are working for their own self-interest rather than that of the oppressed, Colton infiltrates the organization and exposes their leader's greed. The avaricious leader is then disposed of and Jack Colton returns from Russia. Once home, he falls in love with Olga and the two are married. *Exiles. Impersonation and imposture. Nobility. Revolutionaries. Russia–History–Revolution, 1917-1921. Russian Americans. Americans in foreign countries. Greed. Lifeboats. Loans. Ships. Torpedoes.*

Motog 13 Oct 1917, 781. *MPW* 29 Sep 1917, p. 2004. *MPW* 6 Oct 1917, p. 132. *NYDM* 22 Sep 1917, p. 16. *Var* 12 Oct 1917, p. 40.

UNDER FIESTA STARS (Latino)

Republic Pictures Corp. *Dist* Republic Pictures Corp. 25 Aug **1941**; Prod: began early Jul 1941 [©Republic Pictures Corp.; 25 Aug 1941; LP10709]. Sd (RCA Sound System); b&w. 7 reels, 5,566 ft. 62 min. Passed by the National Board of Review.

Assoc prod Harry Grey. *Dir* Frank McDonald. [*Asst dir* Art Siteman]. *Scr* Karl Brown and Eliot Gibbons. *Story* Karl Brown. *Photog* Harry Neumann. *Film ed* Tony Martinelli. *Mus supv* Raoul Kraushaar. *Prod mgr* Al Wilson.

Song(s): "Under Fiesta Stars," words and music by Gene Autry and Fred Rose; "Purple Sage in the Twilight," words and music by Jule Styne, Sol Meyer and Gene Autry; "Keep It in the Family," words and music by Smiley Burnette; "When You're Smiling, (the Whole World Smiles with You)," words and music by Mark Fisher, Joe Goodwin and Larry Shay; "I've Got No Use for Women," words and music by Sol Meyer; "The Man on the Flying Trapeze," words and music by Walter O'Keefe.

Cast: GENE AUTRY [(*Gene Autry*)], Smiley Burnette [(*Frog Millhouse*)], Carol Hughes [(*Barbara Erwin*)], Frank Darien [(*Benjamin Peabody*)], Joseph Strauch, Jr. [(*Tadpole Millhouse*)], Pauline Drake [(*Kitty Callahan*)], Ivan Miller [(*Arnold*)], Sam Flint [(*Fry*)], Elias Gamboa [(*Jose Ortega*)], John Merton [(*Tommick*)], Jack Kirk [(*Sheriff*)], Inez Palange [(*Mrs. Ortega*)], [Champion (*Gene's horse*)].

Western, with songs. [*Print viewed*]. When rodeo rider Gene Autry's foster father, Henry "Dad" Erwin dies, Gene is bequeathed a half-interest in Dad's mine and ranch. The other half is left to Dad's niece, Barbara Erwin, who arrives from the East with her friend, Kitty Callahan. Barbara wishes to sell the mine, as she desperately needs the money, but Gene wants to continue Dad's work, for the mine employs Mexican rancheros whose land was ruined by dust storms. Gene explains to Barbara that although all the profits are currently put back into operations, the mine eventually will provide her with an income, and that without it, the rancheros will starve. Because they do not have enough money to return East, Barbara and Kitty stay and vow to use their feminine wiles on Gene and his pal, Frog Millhouse, in order to change Gene's mind. After her sweet-talking fails to win Gene over to her side, Barbara hires attorneys Arnold and Fry to sell the mine for her. Unknown to Barbara, the unscrupulous lawyers have been trying for years to gain control of the mine, and they order their henchmen Tommick to deal with Gene. Tommick and his gang fail in their

attempt to kill Gene, but his troubles only increase when Barbara and Kitty draw a line down the middle of Dad's ranch house, thereby dividing it exactly in half. Later, Barbara begins to waver in her determination to sell the mine when one of the rancheros names his newborn daughter after her out of gratitude for keeping the mine open. Tommick continues his work, however, and rigs an explosion which seriously injures ranchero Jose Ortega. Mrs. Ortega blames Gene, and after Barbara rises to his defense, she realizes that she is in love with him and cannot sell the mine. Barbara tells Arnold and Fry that she wants to pull out, but they tell her to send Gene alone to meet them at the mine the next day to discuss the matter. The following afternoon, Gene, Barbara, Frog and Kitty enjoy a picnic, during which Barbara tells Gene about the meeting. After Gene leaves, the others are joined by Benjamin Peabody, Dad's lawyer, who, upon hearing about Barbara's dealings with Arnold and Fry, is worried about Gene's safety. They all rush to the mine, where Gene has just won a fistfight with Arnold. Before they can escape though, Gene and the others are forced back into the mine when Fry arrives with Tommick and his gang. While Gene and Frog shoot it out with the gang, Frog's young brother Tadpole crawls out through a ventilation shaft and rides for help. Tadpole returns with the rancheros just as Gene is running out of ammunition, and the criminals are captured. Soon after, at a fiesta, Tadpole watches in disgust as Gene and Frog romance Barbara and Kitty, but he quickly changes his mind about women when he is smitten with a pretty señorita. *Cowboys. Inheritance. Lawyers. Mines. Romance. Ambushes. Brothers. Cooperatives. Easterners. Explosions. Fiestas. Foster parents. Gunfights. Horses. Mexicans. Nieces. Picnicking.*

Note: The Republic official billing sheet located in the film's production file at the AMPAS Library lists Burr Caruth in the cast, but his name is crossed off the players' listing and Inez Palange's name is handwritten on the list. It has not been determined if Caruth is in the picture. This was the first film in which Joseph Strauch, Jr. starred as Smiley Burnette's younger brother "Tadpole." Modern sources include the following actors in the cast: Curley Dresden, Hal Taliaferro, Frankie Marvin and Pascale Perry.

Box 30 Aug 1941. *FD* 28 Aug 1941, p. 6. *DV* 13 Oct 1941. *HR* 11 Jul 1941, p. 6. *HR* 18 Jul 1941, p. 8. *MPHPD* 23 Aug 1941, p. 218. *MPHPD* 30 Aug 1941, p. 234.

UNDER FIRE (Native Americans)
Clifford S. Elfelt Productions, Inc. *Dist* Davis Distributing Division, Inc. **1926** [©Clifford S. Elfelt Productions, Inc.; 1 Jan 1926; LP22255]. Si; b&w. 5 reels.
Prod Albert I. Smith. *Dir* Clifford S. Elfelt. *Adpt* Frank Howard Clark.
Source: Based on the novel *Under Fire* by Capt. Charles King (Philadelphia, 1895).
Cast: Bill Patton, Jean Arthur, Cathleen Calhoun, Norbert Myles, William Bertram, Harry Moody, W. Cassel, H. Renard.
Western. Lieutenant Tom Brennan is cashiered from the 7th Cavalry on two charges, both unjust: that of deserting his men in the face of a cruel Indian attack, and of entertaining a married woman in his quarters after hours. Tom wanders into the desert and is picked up half-dead by Yuba Bill, a prospector with whom he goes into partnership. The Indians go on the warpath, and Tom rides to the fort and warns the colonel. Tom's innocence is established by the confession of an enlisted man, and Tom is reinstated to the service with full honors, renewing his engagement with Margaret Cranston. *Courts-martial and courts of inquiry. Forts. Indians of North America. Infidelity. Prospectors. United States. Army. Cavalry.*

UNDER SOUTHERN SKIES (African Americans)
Universal Film Mfg. Co.; A Broadway Universal Feature. *Dist* Universal Film Mfg. Co. 20 Sep **1915** [©Universal Film Mfg. Co.; 7 Sep 1915; LP6301]. Si; b&w. 5 reels.
Dir Lucius Henderson. *Scen* William Addison Lathrop.
Source: Based on the play *Under Southern Skies* by Lottie Blair Lathrop (New York, 12 Nov 1901).
Cast: Mary Fuller (*Lelia Crofton*), Charles Ogle (*Major Crofton*), Clara Byers (*Stella Crofton*), Bert Bushy (*Col. Mavor*), Milton Sills (*Burleigh Mavor*), William Heidloff (*Ambrose Mavor*), John Ridgway (*Col. Daubeney*), Paul Panzer (*Steve Daubeney*), Marie Shotwell (*Mrs. Hampton*), Mary Moore (*Fifi Hampton*), Harry Blakemore (*Uncle Joshuaway*), Nellie Slattery (*Aunt Doshey*), Margaret Wall (*Anner Lizer*), Marie Weirman (*Phinney*).
Historical, Drama. Lelia Crofton, a Louisiana belle of the 1860's, loves Burleigh Mavor. By chance, she sees one of her father's black

stablemen making love to a neighbor's maid, whom she supposed was white. The incident shocks Lelia and leaves a great impression upon her. When she rejects suitor Steve Daubeney, he threatens to expose a damaging secret about her mother, whom she has never met. Remembering the incident with the neighbor's maid, Lelia worries that her mother might be black, and when Daubeney learns of her fears, he leads her to believe that they are well-founded. To keep Daubeney quiet, she agrees to marry him. On her wedding day, however, Mrs. Crofton appears at the church to beg her daughter's forgiveness, and the marriage is halted as Lelia sees she is white. Colonel Crofton swears revenge on Daubeney, but the young man has already disappeared from the plantation. At Fort Sumter, Daubeney, a Confederate private, captures Burleigh, an officer, and ties him to a tree to tar and feather him. Informed of the misdeed, Lelia rescues Burleigh, and both escape from Daubeney and his gang. Later, as Burleigh and Lelia are about to exchange wedding vows, Daubeney attempts to kill his rival but is shot as a deserter before he can pull the trigger. *Rivalry. Soldiers. Southern belles. United States–South. African Americans. Attempted murder. Blackmail. Desertion, Military. Fort Sumter (SC). Marriage–Forced. Parentage. Plantations. Reputation. United States–History–Civil War, 1861-1865.*

Note: This film was shot in Savannah, GA.
Motog 25 Sep 1915, pp. 640-41, 659. *MPW* 3 Jul 1915, p. 87. *MPW* 28 Aug 1915, p. 1492. *MPW* 2 Oct 1915, p. 146. *MPN* 28 Aug 1915, p. 72. *MPN* 18 Sep 1915, p. 2. *MPN* 2 Oct 1915, p. 90.

UNDER THE TONTO RIM (Latino)
RKO Radio Pictures, Inc. *Dist* RKO Radio Pictures, Inc. 1 Aug **1947**; *Prod:* began mid-Jan 1947 [©RKO Radio Pictures, Inc.; 26 Jun 1947; LP1145]. Sd (RCA Sound System); b&w. 5,512 ft. 61 min. PCA cert no. 12238.
Prod Herman Schlom. *Dir* Lew Landers. [*Asst dir* John Pommer]. *Scr* Norman Houston. *Dir of photog* J. Roy Hunt and [George Diskant]. *Spec eff* Russell A. Cully. *Art dir* Albert S. D'Agostino and Charles F. Pyke. *Film ed* Lyle Boyer. *Set dec* Darrell Silvera and John Sturtevant. *Mus dir* C. Bakaleinikoff. *Mus* Paul Sawtell. *Sd* Jack Gross and Terry Kellum.
Source: Based on the novel *Under the Tonto Rim* by Zane Grey (New York, 1926).
Cast: TIM HOLT [(*Brad Canfield*)], Nan Leslie [(*Lucy Dennison*)], Richard Martin [(*Chito Rafferty*)], Richard Powers [(*Dennison*)], Carol Forman [(*Juanita*)], Tony Barrett [(*Roy Patton*)], Harry Harvey [(*Sheriff*)], Jason Robards [(*Captain McLean*)], Robert Clarke [(*Hooker*)], Jay Norris [(*Andy*)], Lex Barker [(*Joe, deputy*)], Steve Savage [(*Curly*)], [Richard Foote (*Henry, deputy*)], [Lee Frederick, Graham Covert (*Hostlers*)], [Bud Osborne (*Steve*)], [George Magrill (*Guard*)], [Jack Gordon (*Bartender*)].
Western. [*Print viewed*]. After Brad Canfield, the owner of the Rim Rock Stage Line of Arizona, picks up a woman stranded in the desert and delivers her to the nearest outpost, his stagecoach is besieged by outlaws. During the attack, the leader of the masked outlaws, Dennison, shoots and kills Andy, one of Brad's drivers, and snatches the woman from the stage. Determined to bring in their friend's killer, Brad and his sidekick, Chito Rafferty, go to Wicksburg and confer with Captain McLean of the Territorial Rangers. McLean informs them that the outlaws have been eluding capture by hiding somewhere in the Tonto Rim wilderness, but that one of their gang, Roy Patton, is incarcerated in the Tonto jail. Hoping to extract information about the gang from Patton, Brad and Chito go to Tonto, but there learn that the outlaw has refused to talk and will be hanged in the morning. By impersonating a Ranger, Chito is able to convince the Tonto sheriff that Brad is a dangerous fugitive and "arrests" him in the Tonto saloon. After Brad is thrown in a cell adjoining Patton's, the outlaws try to break Patton out but are unsuccessful. Chito, however, slips Brad two pistols through the cell window, and Brad helps Patton to escape. As he and Patton are fleeing, Brad is shot, and Patton, believing Chito's stories that Brad has hidden $10,000 in stolen money, offers to take him to his gang's hideout. Brad follows Patton to the hideout, the entrance of which is obscured by large rocks, and there is nursed by Lucy, the woman from the stage. Although sympathetic to Brad, Lucy refuses to name the gang's boss and advises Brad to leave. When Brad tries to go, however, Patton insists that he wait to meet the "boss," and Brad is forced to continue his impersonation. Several days later, while Chito sits in jail for his part in Brad's escape, Brad pretends that his wound is festering so that

he can see Lucy again and meet Dennison. While Brad is proving himself to the cautious Dennison, he sees the grey spotted bandana worn by Andy's killer and confirms his suspicions that Dennison is the murderer. Later, Lucy reveals that she is Dennison's sister and, for that reason, cannot betray him. After Dennison welcomes Brad into the gang, Brad convinces Patton that he needs to go to Tonto to keep an eye on his partner. Unknown to Brad, Juanita, a Mexican servant who is in love with Dennison, follows him to Tonto and sees him enter the sheriff's office. After Brad tells the sheriff how to find the gang, he rides back to the hideout. Although Lucy tries to warn Brad about Juanita, he is caught and tied up by Dennison. While the sheriff's posse rides toward the hideout, Dennison prepares to raid the town. Brad breaks free and fights with Juanita, then shoots her. After this, he sneaks up on the gang and initiates a gunfight, which the posse soon joins. In the end, Brad shoots and kills Dennison and says a temporary goodbye to an understanding Lucy. *Brothers and sisters. Hideouts. Impersonation and imposture. Outlaws. Revenge. Stagecoach drivers. Arizona. Deserts. Gunfights. Gunshot wounds. Jailbreaks. Mexican Americans. Mexicans. Murder. Posses. Sheriffs.*

Note: The opening credits read: "RKO Radio Pictures, Inc. presents Tim Holt in Zane Grey's *Under the Tonto Rim.*" According to a *HR* news item, Virgil Caywood and Robert Bray were cast members, but their participation in the final film has not been confirmed. Although J. Roy Hunt is credited onscreen as director of photography, George Diskant is listed in an *HR* production chart in that capacity. Some scenes for the picture were shot near Victorville, CA, according to a *HR* news item. Modern sources add Herman Hack to the cast. Herman C. Raymaker directed and Richard Arlen and Mary Brian starred in the first film version of Grey's novel, which was released in 1928 by Paramount (see *AFI Catalog of Feature Films*; F2.5948). In 1933, Henry Hathaway directed and Stuart Erwin and Verna Hillie starred in the first sound version of the novel, also titled *Under the Tonto Rim* and produced by Paramount (see *AFI Catalog of Feature Films*; F3.4853). Modern sources comment that the 1947 version bears little resemblance to Grey's novel.

Box 14 Jun 1947. *DV* 4 Jun 1947. *FD* 5 Jun 1947, p. 4. *HR* 8 Jan 1947, p. 4. *HR* 10 Jan 1947, p. 18. *HR* 13 Jan 1947, p. 13. *HR* 17 Jan 1947, p. 18. *HR* 4 Jun 1947, p. 3. *IFJ* 18 Jan 1947, p. 44. *Var* 4 Jun 1947, p. 16.

THE UNDERCOVER MAN (Italian Americans)
Columbia Pictures Corp.; A Robert Rosen Production. *Dist* Columbia Pictures Corp. Apr **1949**; New York opening: 20 Apr 1948; *Prod:* 4 May–16 Jun 1948 [©Columbia Pictures Corp.; 15 Mar 1949; LP2161]. Sd (Western Electric Recording); b&w. 84-85 min. PCA cert no. 13250.

Dir Joseph H. Lewis. *Asst dir* Wilbur McGaugh. *Written for the screen by* Sydney Boehm. *Addl dial* Malvin Wald. *Dir of photog* Burnett Guffey. *Art dir* Walter Holscher. *Film ed* Al Clark. *Set dec* William Kiernan. *Gowns* Jean Louis. *Mus score* George Duning. *Mus dir* M. W. Stoloff. *Sd eng* Jack Goodrich.

Source: Based on the article "Undercover Man: He Trapped Capone" by Frank J. Wilson in *Colliers* (26 Apr 1947) and a story outline by Jack Rubin.

Cast: GLENN FORD [(*Frank Warren*)], Nina Foch [(*Judith Warren*)], James Whitmore [(*George Pappas*)], Barry Kelly [(*Edward O'Rourke*)], David Wolfe [(*Stanley Weinberg*)], Frank Twiddell [(*Inspector Herzog*)], Howard St. John [(*Joseph S. Horan*)], John F. Hamilton [(*Sergeant Shannon*)], Leo Penn [(*Sidney Gordon*)], Joan Lazer [(*Rosa Rocco*)], Esther Minciotti [(*Maria Rocco*)], Angela Clarke [(*Theresa Rocco*)], Anthony Caruso [(*Salvatore Rocco*)], Robert Osterloh [(*Manny Zanger*)], Kay Medford [(*Gladys LaVerne*)], Patricia White [(*Muriel Gordon*)], [Peter Brocco (*Johnny*)], [Everett Glass (*Judge Parker*)], [Joe Mantell (*Newsboy*)], [Michael Cisney (*Fred Ferguson*)], [Marcella Cisney (*Alice Ferguson*)], [Sidney Dubin (*Harris*)], [William Vedder (*Druggist*)], [Jim Drum, Robert Malcolm, Allen Mathews (*Policemen*)], [Esther Zeitlin (*Woman in window*)], [Tom Coffey, William Rhinehart (*Gunmen*)], [Ralph Volkie (*Big Fellow/Man in white*)], [Al Murphy (*Middle-aged man*)], [Lynn Whitney (*Blonde*)], [Ronnie Ralph, Billy Gray (*Boys*)], [Cy Malis, Jack Gordon (*Sluggers*)], [Silvio Minciotti (*Vendor*)], [Virginia Farmer (*Housewife*)], [John Butler (*Grocer*)], [Rose Plumer (*Woman tenant*)], [Richard Bartell (*Court attendant*)], [Ben Erway (*Court clerk*)], [Franklyn Farnum (*Federal judge*)], [Frank Mayo (*Jury foreman*)], [Wheaton Chambers (*Male secretary*)], [George Douglas (*District attorney*)], [Helen Wallace (*Mrs. O'Rourke*)], [Sam LaMarr (*Customer*)], [Peter Virgo (*Cigar store proprietor*)], [Pat Lane (*Deputy*), Brian O'Hara, Joe Palma (*Deputies*)], [Paul Marion (*Young hoodlum*)], [Edwin Max (*Manager*)], [Billy Nelson (*Bouncer*)], [Billy Stubbs (*Crap dealer*)],

[Ted Jordan (*Thug*)], [Glen Thompson, Roy Darmour, Wally Rose, Harlan Warde, Saul Gorss (*Hoodlums*)], [Stella LeSaint (*Storekeeper's wife*)], [Tom Hanlon (*Newsreel announcer*)], [Ken Harvey (*Big Fellow*)], [Daniel Meyers], [Franklin Parker], [Alma Maison], [Irene Martin], [Ann Cameron], [Bernard Sell], [Ed Randolph].

Crime, Drama. [*Print viewed*]. Treasury agent Frank Warren attempts to contact Manny Zanger, a man with access to information that would prove that mobster "The Big Fellow," the head of a major crime syndicate, is guilty of tax evasion, but Zanger is killed before the meeting takes place. Although the police capture the killer, they are unable to hold him because none of the witnesses will testify against him. The Treasury Department hopes to apprehend The Big Fellow on tax evasion charges, and to this end, confiscates bookkeeping records from his low-level associates. The T-men then arrest all the bookkeepers who work for the syndicate in order to compare their signatures to those on certain bank deposit cards. Before the T-men can complete this effort, however, Edward O'Rourke, the syndicate lawyer, obtains the bookkeepers' release. In frustration, Inspector Herzog, a police captain, quits the force. Sergeant Shannon, a policeman who, years earlier, abandoned his attempt to fight The Big Fellow, then shows Frank the record of Salvatore Rocco, a bookkeeper for the mob, whom he arrested before he was demoted to a desk job. When Frank learns that Rocco lives in the same neighborhood as Zanger's contact, he visits the apartment. Rocco's wife, angry because he has left her for another woman, admits that Rocco knew Zanger, but adds that she does not know Rocco's current whereabouts. She shows Frank a letter from Rocco, and Frank is pleased to discover that Rocco's handwriting matches that on the bank deposit cards. Frank and his associate persuade Rocco's girlfriend, Gladys LaVerne, to talk to Rocco. Gladys tells Frank that Rocco will testify if he gets federal protection and the reward. In exchange, Rocco asks his young daughter Rosa to bring him a notebook he had hidden at his former apartment, which contains the records of deposits he made for the mob. Before she can deliver it, however, Rocco is killed by the mob. When Frank returns from Rocco's funeral, his room has been searched and two waiting men beat him severely. Later, O'Rourke tries to make a deal with The Big Fellow and subtly threatens Judy, Frank's wife, who is staying at her parent's nearby farm. Deeply disturbed, Frank takes the next train to visit Judy and tells her that he intends to quit his job. After Frank's return to the city, Rosa and her grandmother visit Frank. Rosa's grandmother tells Frank that her husband died defying the Mafia in Italy, then gives him Rocco's book. A contrite Frank agrees to stay and fight The Big Fellow. The book contains almost all the evidence the Treasury Department needs to prosecute The Big Fellow. They then track down Sidney Gordon, another mob bookkeeper, in Los Angeles, and arrest him and his wife Muriel. Gordon agrees to cooperate and his testimony leads to the indictment of The Big Fellow and his associates. O'Rourke then sets out to buy off the grand jury. After O'Rourke is subpoenaed, he meets secretly with Frank and offers him a complete account of The Big Fellow's financial arrangements and also reveals that the jury has been bought. The mobsters discover his betrayal and kill him. Frank then uses O'Rourke's information to substitute a new jury for the corrupt one and The Big Fellow is sentenced to twenty years in prison. *Bookkeepers. Gangsters. Lawyers. Murder. United States. Treasury Department. Betrayal. Bribery. Farms. Fathers and daughters. Grandmothers. Italian Americans. Juries. Marriage. Police. Subpoena. Suicide. Tax evasion. Witnesses.*

Note: The film's working title was *Chicago Story*, according to an 11 Mar 1948 *LAT* article, and it was to be shot on location in Chicago. The film begins with the following written and spoken foreword: "In the cracking of many big criminal cases—such as those of the John Dillinger, Lucky Luciano and Al Capone, among others—the newspaper headlines tell only of the glamorous and sensational figures involved. But behind the headlines are the untold stories of ordinary men and women, acting with extraordinary courage. This picture concerns one of these men." This film marked James Whitmore's film debut. A 4 May 1948 *LAT* news item reported that some scenes were shot at Union Station in Los Angeles. Contemporary reviews noted that this film was loosely based on the events surrounding the arrest of Al Capone. CBCS credits both Ralph Volkie and Ken Harvey with the role of "The Big Fellow."

Box 26 Mar 1949. *DV* 18 Mar 1949, p. 3. *FD* 21 Mar 1949, p. 11. *HR* 11 Jun 1948, p. 12. *HR* 18 Mar 1949, p. 3. *LAT* 11 Mar 1948. *LAT* 4 May 1948. *MPHPD* 26 Mar 1949, p. 4549. *NYT* 21 Apr 1949, p. 30. *Var* 23 Mar 1949, p. 8.

UNDERGROUND SPY *see* **THE RED MENACE**

UNDERWORLD (African Americans)

Micheaux Pictures Corp. *Dist* Sack Amusement Enterprises, Inc. Sep 1937; New York opening: 30 Sep 1937. Sd; b&w. 8,697 ft.

Pres ALFRED N. SACK. *Prod* Oscar Micheaux. *Dir* Oscar Micheaux. [*Wrt* Oscar Micheaux]. *Cont* Jack Kemp. *Photog* Lester Lang. *Ed* Nathan Cy Braunstein.

Song(s): "It Don't Mean a Thing," music by Duke Ellington, lyrics by Irving Mills; "I'll Never Say 'Never Again' Again," music and lyrics by Harry Woods.

Source: Based on the short story "Chicago After Midnight" by Edna Mae Baker (publication undetermined).

Cast: Bee Freeman [(*Dinah Jackson*)], Sol Johnson [(*Paul Bronson*)], "Slick" Chester [(*LeRoy Giles*)], Ethel Moses [(*Evelyn Martin*)], Oscar Polk [(*Sam Brown*)], Lorenzo Tucker, Dottie Salters, The Pope Sisters, Bobby Hargreaves Orchestra, [Larry Seymour (*Tim Sharkey*)], ["Stringbeans"], [Clara Bell Powell], [Harlem's Apache Chorus], [The Six Sizzlers].

African American, Crime, Drama. [*Print viewed*]. After Paul Bronson graduates from a black college in the South, he accepts the invitation of Chicago gambler LeRoy Giles to vacation in Chicago. LeRoy, who has been having a secret affair for three years with singer Dinah Jackson, the wife of Sam Brown, owner of the Red Lily nightclub, has brought Paul to Chicago to fleece him, but Paul attracts Dinah's attention and they become involved during the next month. Paul wants to marry Dinah, but she refuses, saying she only wants their affair to continue as it is. After Paul refuses money offered by Dinah, he meets Evelyn Martin, who recognizes him from college and who is trying to run a beauty parlor. Evelyn and Paul have lunch together and are seen by LeRoy, whom Dinah has supported financially and who is upset about her affair with Paul. LeRoy tells Dinah about Evelyn, and she threatens to ruin Paul. After Paul tells Dinah that he has decided to go home, she arranges for LeRoy to drug and rob him. LeRoy doubles the dose and almost kills Paul. After Paul overhears LeRoy and Dinah discussing his money, he gets it back from LeRoy and, still groggy from the drug, goes to the Red Lily. Meanwhile, Sam's detectives tell him about Dinah's affair with LeRoy. When Sam catches them together, he orders her bank accounts closed and charge accounts canceled. LeRoy shoots Sam and puts the gun by his body. After Paul comes in dazed and picks up the gun, Dinah accuses him of killing Sam. She pays LeRoy to leave town and is able to keep Paul in town and away from Evelyn because of his confusion about the murder. However, Paul, now the manager of the Red Lily, meets Evelyn again, and after he tells Dinah he is through with her, she reports him to the police. After Dinah, on drugs and intoxicated, has a mental breakdown, her car is hit by a train and she is killed. Her affidavit seems certain to convict Paul when Ching Li, a Chinese man who worked and lived at the Red Lily, confesses to police that he witnessed the murder. Paul is freed and leaves the city with Evelyn. *African Americans. Chicago (IL). City-country contrast. Confidence men. Duplicity. False accusations. Infidelity. Singers. Accidental death. Automobile accidents. Beauty operators. College students. Detectives. Drugging. Murder. Nervous breakdown. Nightclub owners. Nightclubs. Pawnbrokers. Thieves. Trains.*

Note: *Underworld* played at the Harlem Opera House in New York 30 Sep-3 Oct 1937. The only contemporary source located for the film is an unidentified review in the George P. Johnson Negro Collection at UCLA.

UNDISPUTED EVIDENCE (African Americans)

Cotton Blossom Film Corp. **1922.** Si; b&w. 5 reels.

Melodrama (?), African American. No information about the precise nature of this film has been found. *African Americans.*

Note: According to information in the George P. Johnson Collection at the UCLA Special Collections Library, a pre-production announcement stated that the film was to be shot in and around San Antonio, TX.

THE UNFORGIVEN (Native Americans, Kiowa)

Hecht-Hill-Lancaster; A James Productions, Inc. Picture. *Dist* United Artists Corp. Apr 1960; New York opening: 6 Apr 1960; Prod: mid-Jan—early Feb 1959; early Mar—early May 1959 [©James Productions, Inc.; 6 Apr 1960; LP16849]. Sd; col (Technicolor); Panavision. 10,859 ft. 119-120 or 125 min.

Prod James Hill. *Dir* John Huston. *Asst dir* Tom Shaw. *Scr* Ben Maddow. *Dir of photog* Franz Planer. [*Spec eff* Dave Koehler]. *Art dir* Stephen Grimes. *Assoc* Ramon Rodriguez Granada. *Ed* Russell

Lloyd. [*Prop master* Ross Burke]. *Cost des* Dorothy Jeakins. *Mus* Dimitri Tiomkin. *Rec by* Santa Cecilia Orchestra. *Sd rec* Basil Fenton-Smith. *Sd ed* Leslie Hodgson. *Makeup* Frank McCoy and Frank LaRue. *Exec prod mgr* Gilbert Kurland.

Source: Based on the novel *The Unforgiven* by Alan LeMay (New York, 1957).

Cast: BURT LANCASTER [(*Ben Zachary*)], AUDREY HEPBURN [(*Rachel Zachary*)], Audie Murphy [(*Cash Zachary*)], John Saxon [(*Johnny Portugal*)], Charles Bickford [(*Zeb Rawlins*)], Lillian Gish [(*Matilda Zachary*)], Albert Salmi [(*Charlie Rawlins*)], Joseph Wiseman [(*Abe Kelsey*)], June Walker [(*Hagar Rawlins*)], Kipp Hamilton [(*Georgia Rawlins*)], Arnold Merritt [(*Jude Rawlins*)], Doug McClure [(*Andy Zachary*)], Carlos Rivas [(*Lost Bird*)].

Western. [*Print viewed*]. In the Texas Panhandle sometime after the Civil War, young Rachel Zachary is enjoying a free-spirited gallop on the open range, when she is disturbed by the sight of a strange man. The old man lifts his saber aloft, tells her she is "no Zachary" and shouts that he is "the sword of God." Later, the man appears outside the Zachary cabin, prompting Rachel's mother Matilda, who recognizes the man, to aim her gun at him and chase him off. Soon after, Rachel's brother Ben, who has been on a long trip to Wichita, joins his two younger brothers Cash and Andy, as they round up horses for the next drive to Kansas. Ben's partner, Zeb Rawlins, brings his family to the Zachary ranch for a visit, during which young Georgia Rawlins announces her interest in Ben, and shy Charlie Rawlins admits he hopes to marry Rachel. Over dinner, the families also discuss their various victories over the "Kiowa devils," Indians from the nearby hills who killed Will Zachary some years earlier. Ben and Cash later search for the mysterious old man, whom Ben knows to be "a Kelsey," but he disappears into a wind storm. One day three Kiowa Indians appear on the Zachary ranch. A young man named Lost Bird offers several horses in exchange for Rachel, who, Abe Kelsey has informed him, is his long-lost sister. Ben angrily replies that Rachel was adopted by the Zacharys after her white parents were massacred in their wagon by Kiowas. The Indians ride away, but after they begin frequenting the area, the local cowboys and their families start to gossip among themselves. When Charlie finally proposes to Rachel, she kisses him in the hope of arousing jealousy in Ben, whom she loves. On his way home, however, Charlie is killed by Kiowas as Kelsey looks on. Rachel attempts to comfort Charlie's mother, but the grief-stricken woman screams that it was Rachel, "a red-hide nigger," who caused his death. Anxious to settle the ugly rumors about Rachel, Ben and his men capture Kelsey and lead him before Charlie's bereaved parents with a noose around his neck. When Zeb demands the truth, Kelsey reveals that years before, he and Will Zachary had killed many Kiowas in revenge for an Indian-led massacre. Zachary took a crying Kiowa baby back to Matilda, who reared the child as her own, then later, when the Indians had kidnapped Kelsey's son Aaron, Zachary refused to swap little Rachel for Aaron. Kelsey had hounded the Zachary family for years after his boy was killed. At this public disclosure of Rachel's secret identity, Matilda beats Kelsey's horse, causing the old man to be hanged. The settlers all shun the Zachary family, and when Matilda later admits that Will had taken the Kiowa infant to replace the baby girl Matilda had just lost, Cash insults Rachel, calls the Zacharys "Injun lovers" and rides away in a drunken stupor. Lost Bird and two warriors approach the Zachary cabin under a sign of peace while dozens of Kiowas wait on the far side of the river. To prevent a battle, Rachel insists on joining them. Finally exhibiting his love for Rachel, Ben orders her to stay in the cabin and has young Andy kill one of the warriors. The shooting leads to a full-scale battle, and the four Zacharys kill many Indians. Rachel, who had wondered if she could kill her "own kind," is assured by Ben that they are similar in blood only. At the Rawlins ranch, Cash hears gunshots and prepares to respond, but Georgia begs him to stay and marry her. The Kiowas send cattle to stampede the Zachary cabin, whereupon Ben sets the house on fire and retreats to the root cellar with Andy, Rachel and his mortally wounded mother. As the fire subsides and the Indians prepare to enter the cellar, Cash arrives, and he and Ben shoot the remaining Kiowas. Lost Bird, however, quietly enters the cellar and looks questioningly at Rachel. In response, she shoots him dead. The Zacharys climb out of the cellar and survey their burned home, their dead mother and a landscape littered with Kiowa bodies. Then, however, their attention is drawn skyward as a flock of birds takes flight. *Brothers and sisters. Family relationships. Hate.*

Kiowa Indians. Parentage. Racism. Revenge. Battles. Chases. Cowboys. Family honor. Flutes. Foundlings. Gossip. Grief. Horses. Indians of North America. Insanity. Jealousy. Kidnapping. Loyalty. Lynching. Murder. Pianos. Ranchers. Settlers. Texas. Wind storms.

Note: The film's working titles were *The Siege at Dancing Bird* and *The Siege at Dancing Burg*. LeMay's novel, *The Unforgiven*, was serialized in *The Saturday Evening Post* under the title *Kiowa Moon* (6 Mar—27 Apr 1957). Onscreen credits state that Dimitri Tiompkin's music was "Recorded in Rome, Italy with the Santa Cecelia Orchestra." On 29 Jan 1957, *Var* reported that J. P. Miller had been assigned to write the screenplay version of Alan LeMay's novel, but his contribution to the final film has not been confirmed. Contemporary news items list a number of actors and actresses who were considered for parts in the film: Richard Burton, Kirk Douglas and Robert Mitchum (probably for the role of "Cash Zachary"), Eva Le Gallienne (for the role of "Matilda Zachary") and Natalie Wood (for the role of "Rachel Zachary"). An Apr 1958 item in *DV* noted that Delbert Mann was set to direct the picture, but by Aug 1958, Huston had been signed. According to publicity items, the film was shot entirely in Durango, Mexico. A 27 Feb 1959 *HR* item reports that production was halted when Audry Hepburn was thrown from a horse during filming. According to a 9 Mar 1959 article in *LAT*, Huston recruited Mexican director Emilio Fernandez to work on the production as the supervisor of the outdoor action scenes. The article stated that Fernandez would also play the role of a "bloodthirsty Kiowa Indian." The extent of his contribution to the completed film is undetermined.

Box 4 Apr 1960. *Box* 11 Apr 1960. *DV* 30 Mar 1960, p. 3. *Exb* 30 Mar 1960, p. 4690. *FD* 30 Mar 1960, p. 6. *Har* 2 Apr 1960, p. 54. *HR* 9 Jan 1959, p. 13. *HR* 27 Feb 1959, p. 6. *HR* 1 May 1959, p. 17. *HR* 8 May 1959, p. 30. *HR* 30 Mar 1960, p. 3. *MPHPD* 2 Apr 1960, p. 643. *NYT* 7 Apr 1960, p. 46. *Var* 30 Mar 1960, p. 6.

THE UNFORTUNATE BRIDE (Yiddish language)

Lynn Productions, Inc. *Dist* Judea Films, Inc. **1932**; Prod: 1932 sound version incorporates a 1926 silent film made by The Jaffe Art Film Corp.. Sd (Seiden Sound System); b&w. Length undetermined. Yiddish language with English subtitles.

New version dir Henry Lynn. *Photog* Sam Rosen. *Literary ed* Abraham Armband. *Mus arr* Art Shryer. *Sd tech* Leonard A. Herzig. *Tech dir* Solomon Krause.

Source: Based on the Yiddish play *Di Gebrokhene ertser oder Libe un Flikht* by Zalmen Libin (New York, 1903).

Cast: [*1926 film*]: Maurice Schwartz (*Benjamin Resanov*), Lila Lee (*Ruth Esterin*), Wolf Goldfaden (*Cantor Esterin*), Bina Abramowitz (*Mama Esterin*), Isadore Cashier (*Victor Kaplin*), Anna Appel (*Shprinze*), Charles Nathanson (*Mr. Kruger*), Liza Silbert (*Mrs. Kruger*), Theodore Silbert (*Milton Kruger*), Miriam Ellias (*Miriam*), Morris Strassberg (*The marriage broker*), Henrietta Schnitzer (*Esther*), Betty Ferkouf (*Benjamin's mother*), Leonid Snegoff (*Captain of the Cossacks*), Julius Adler (*David Adler*), Cast—Prologue: Michael Rosenberg [(*The grandfather*)], Lillian Karen [(*Rachel*)], Bernard Holtzman [(*Moishe*)].

Yiddish, Melodrama. [*Print viewed*]. As an elderly Jewish man sits in his dressing gown and opens a book, his two grandchildren, Rachel, a girl of about fifteen, and Moishe, her younger brother, arrive for a visit. After the children say that they came despite their mother's admonition against going out alone in the dark, their grandfather talks to them about the *Torah*, the Bible, and he cautions Rachel that what she sees with her young eyes is not necessarily the truth, as she does not yet understand about the heart. He then tells the following story, which begins in the years before World War I: Mr. Kruger, the president of a New York synagogue, wants to arrange for his son Milton to marry Ruth Esterin, the daughter of the synagogue's cantor, but Rachel thinks that Milton is a "fathead." Benjamin Resanov, a newly-arrived immigrant, wanders in the city destitute and penniless. David Adler, an acquaintance from Russia, recognizes Ben in the park, and Ben tells David that he escaped from Russia after the Cossacks searched for him because of his writings. David arranges for Ben to get a job, and Ben soon begins to live with a family in the same tenement as Ruth. They meet when she comes to babysit one night while he is studying, and they soon fall in love, as she teaches him English and learns Russian from him. One Sunday, when the Krugers, who have become wealthy and moved to Riverside Avenue, visit Ruth's family, Milton tries to flirt with Ruth, but she rebukes him. When her father asks if she can choose a better husband than Milton, she reveals that she has already chosen one. Ruth then goes to Ben's apartment to tell him that her father is forcing her to marry, and when the cantor arrives to talk to Ben alone, Ruth overhears him ask Ben to sacrifice his love for her because he has little to offer her. Ruth intrudes and confesses that she cannot be happy without Ben, and her father warns that if she disobeys him, he will disown her. Even though Ben had

been married in Russia, he marries Ruth, as he believes his wife Esther to be dead. Sometime later, Ben has become a successful journalist and Ruth is pregnant. Her father, heartbroken that she has rebelled, will not forgive her. Ben receives a letter from Esther saying that she has been taken to a prison in Kiev. As the Czar's reign is on the verge of collapse, she asks for him to return. Ruth is shocked, and after Ben tells her about his escape, she says that he must return because Esther's need is greater than her own. At the boat, as he is to leave for Russia, Ruth holds back the words that might keep Ben with her and instead kisses him goodbye. To avenge Ruth's rebuke of his son, Kruger compels the cantor to officiate at his son's lavish wedding. The cantor imagines Ruth as the bride, then, when Kruger taunts him that Ruth married a man who already had a wife, Esterin quits his job. Ruth, who is depressed, leaves her home because of neighbors' gossip. She finds work in a sewing factory and has her baby. Later, she returns to her parents' home with her baby and reconciles with her father. They go to the synagogue, where Ruth mouths the words of the service as she dies. Although Moishe has fallen asleep, Rachel is greatly affected by the story. Her grandfather comforts her and tells her, as the *Torah* commands, to listen to her mother, then she'll understand the world, which has so much that is terrible and difficult in it. Bigamy. Cantors. Jewish. Fathers and daughters. Jews. Refugees. Political. Romance. Self-sacrifice. Cossacks. Gossip. Grandfathers. Mothers and daughters. New York City. Reporters. Revenge. Russia. Sweatshops. Synagogues. Weddings.

Note: The Yiddish title of this film is *Di Umgliklikhe Kale*. This film is a re-release of a 1926 Yiddish film entitled *Broken Hearts (Di Tsebrokhene Hertser)* [see above] with a synchronized score, narration and a few additional scenes. Although no reviews have been located for the 1932 version, the film is listed in the *MPH* release charts from 12 Mar through 30 Jul 1932. According to a *FD* news item in Mar 1932, Maurice Schwartz announced that he had begun legal action to prevent the re-release of *Broken Hearts*. No further information has been located regarding this. According to modern sources, in the original 1926 film, the character "Ben" returns to "Ruth," as he has learned during his travels that his first wife "Esther" has died.

FD 7 Mar 1926. *FD* 14 Mar 1932, p. 2. *NYT* 3 Mar 1926, p. 26.

THE UNHOLY NIGHT (*foreign version*) *see* LE SPECTRE VERT

[UNIDENTIFIED FILM] (AfricanAmericans)

1921?; Prod: in San Antonio. Si; b&w. 5 reels.

Dir B. L. Teycer.

African American, Documentary. African Americans living in San Antonio, Texas, including doctors, lawyers, teachers, businessmen and women, school children, police officers, preachers and other well-known people are shown. Douglass High School defeats Waco High School in a sporting event. A parade is held of African-American churches to celebrate the advent of Protestantism in San Antonio. African-American notable personages from other spots in Texas and the rest of the South are shown. *African Americans. San Antonio (TX). Churches. High schools. Parades. Protestantism.*

Note: The only information concerning this film was found on an undated and unidentified ad for a showing at the Dreamland Theatre in San Antonio, TX. The ad, which listed no title for the film, is included in the George P. Johnson Collection at the UCLA Special Collections Library. As the ad also listed the showing of the 1921 release *No Woman Knows*, it is assumed that the unidentified film was shown in 1921. The ad called the unidentified film the "First Colored Picture ever made here by a colored man." B. L. Teycer, who made the film, is credited as cameraman for the 1922 two-reel film *The Wild Hunters*, which was also made in San Antonio.

UNITED STATES SMITH (Russian Americans)

Gotham Productions. *Dist* Lumas Film Corp. 15 Jun **1928** [©Lumas Film Corp.; 21 Jul 1928; LP25480]. Si; b&w. 7 reels, 7,022 ft.

Pres Sam Sax. *Prod* Harold Shumate. *Dir* Joseph Henabery. *Scr* Curtis Benton. *Scen* Louis Stevens. *Story* Gerald Beaumont. *Photog* Ray June.

Cast: Eddie Gribbon (*Sgt. Steve Riley*), Lila Lee (*Molly Malone*), Mickey Bennett (*Ugo* [*U. S. Smith*]), Kenneth Harlan (*Cpl. Jim Sharkey*), Earle Marsh (*Danny*).

Melodrama. Marine Sgt. Steve Riley is returning to the States to box Army Cpl. Jim Sharkey for the championship. Aboard ship, Steve meets a poor Russian boy named Ugo who has no family, and Steve takes him into the service as a sort of mascot, calling him U. S. Smith. After Ugo saves Steve's life, the sergeant decides to give him a good education, agreeing to throw the fight to obtain the money for his plan. Ugo begs him not to do so, and Steve, after seeing Sharkey wearing his girl friend Molly's charm (which Ugo has placed on him

purposely in order to rile Steve), wins the fight out of anger. Everything is worked out, however, and all ends happily. *Boxing. Jealousy. Orphans. Russian Americans. United States. Army. United States. Marine Corps.*

NYT 24 Jul 1928, p. 13.

THE UNKNOWN SOLDIER SPEAKS (African Americans)

Lincoln Productions, Inc. *Dist* State Rights; Lincoln Productions, Inc. 2 Jun 1934 [©Lincoln Productions, Inc.; 28 Mar 1934; MU4704]. Sd; b&w. 6,998 ft. 67 or 70 min.

Dir Jack Goldberg. *Dial* Robert Rossen. *Narr* Alan Bunce.

African American, Compilation, Documentary. [*Not viewed*]. Using newsreel and previously released documentary footage, this film focuses on the life of the common soldier, from the conflicts of World War I to those of Nazi Germany and Italy under Mussolini. Narrated by a voice representing the spirit of the "unknown soldier," the film intercuts shots of assorted political events and military leaders with footage of troop movements and actual battles. Scenes include the funeral of Archduke Ferdinand of Austria, the German invasion of Sarajevo in Yugoslavia, the sinking of the German battleship *Blucher*, the Italian military advance through the Alps, and the German incursion into the North African desert. The World War I activities and sacrifices of the highly decorated all-black 369th Infantry of the U.S. Army are highlighted, as are the various methods of military destruction, from the simple horse and gun, to the sophisticated airplane and battleship. Life behind the battle lines is also shown. *African Americans. Soldiers. United States. Army. United States. Navy. War. Aerial combat. Africa, North. Battleships. Combat. Francis Ferdinand, Archduke of Austria, 1863-1914. Germany. Army. Italy. Army. Military invasion. Benito Mussolini. Nazism. Sarajevo (Yugoslavia). World War I.*

Note: Some sources list the film's title as *Unknown Soldier Speaks*. One source credits Jack Goldberg as editor, not director. Alan Bunce was a well-known Broadway actor. The film was labeled as propaganda in some reviews. According to one reviewer, unacknowledged footage from Lewis Milestone's 1930 Universal film, *All Quiet on the Western Front*, was also used. Reviewers commented that the film juxtaposed World War I and contemporary footage for thematic effect. According to a May 1934 *FD* news item, two versions of the picture were distributed in New York, a "Negro version," which was to be shown in Harlem and other "colored communities," and a white version, which was booked at the Mayfair Theatre. Modern sources state that Lincoln Productions was forced to make "compilation" films because they lacked the funds for original all-black movies. Some modern sources refer to the production company as Goldberg Brothers.

FD 18 May 1934, p. 4. *FD* 26 May 1934, p. 3. *HR* 26 May 1934, p. 3. *MPH* 2 Jun 1934, p. 43, 75. *NYT* 26 May 1934, p. 12. *Var* 29 May 1934, p. 12.

UNKNOWN 274 (Immigrants)

Fox Film Corp. *Dist* Fox Film Corp. 16 Dec 1917 [©William Fox; 9 Dec 1917; LP11819]. Si; b&w. 5 reels.

Dir Harry Millarde. *Scen* Adrian Johnson. *Story* George Scarborough. *Cam* David Mills and Ollie Leach.

Cast: June Caprice (*Dora Belton, in later life*), Kittens Reichert (*Dora Belton, as a child*), Florence Ashbrook (*Miss Stegal*), Inez Marcel (*Her assistant*), Dan Mason (*Professor Jim*), Richard Neill (*Pete Davis*), Tom Burroughs (*Franz Marsh*), Jean Armour (*Mme. Gordon*), William Burns (*Paul Windsor*), Alexander Shannon.

Drama. Dora Belton's father flees the hounding of his father, an influential foreign official, by coming to the United States where he supports his infant daughter by playing the violin. One day, he is kidnapped, taken back to his native country, and his daughter is deposited at an orphanage. She is registered as "unknown 274," and her only possession is an old violin of her father's. Sixteen years later, Mme. Gordon, a popular Broadway modiste, visits the orphanage and adopts Dora. Planning to sell the girl to a millionaire to reap the benefit of her investment, Mme. Gordon decides to educate the girl, taking her to an old music teacher. The old man is actually her father, who fails to recognize his now grown up baby. Later, the rich young man whom Dora was to entice really falls in love with her and rescues her from her predicament. When the old musician recognizes his old violin and regains his daughter, all ends happily. *Child selling. Fathers and daughters. Kidnapping. Millionaires. Violinists. Adoption. Couturiers. Immigrants. Music teachers. New York City. Orphanages. Recognition.*

Note: Contemporary sources disagree on whether Mills or Leach was the cinematographer. One modern source credits Lady as the dog in the film. It is possible that this film was made under the title *The Sunshine Maid*. Some contemporary sources list the film's length as six reels.

ETR 5 Jan 1918, p. 450. *MPW* 29 Dec 1917, p. 1997. *MPW* 5 Jan 1918, p. 91. *Wid's* 27 Dec 1917, pp. 827-28.

THE UNPAINTED WOMAN (Swedish Americans)

Universal Film Mfg. Co. *Dist* Universal Film Mfg. Co.; A Universal Special Attraction. 26 May 1919 [©Universal Film Mfg. Co.; 9 May 1919; LP13698]. Si; b&w. 6 reels, 5,427 ft.

Dir Tod Browning. *Asst dir* K. C. Stewart and Fred Tyler. *Scen* Waldemar Young. *Titles* Allen Siegler. *Story* Sinclair Lewis. *Cam* Al Siegler and Alfred Gosden. *Props* E. Dyer and Wecker (full name unknown).

Cast: Mary MacLaren (*Gudrun Trygavson*), Thurston Hall (*Martin O'Neill*), David Butler (*Charley Holt*), Laura Lavarnie (*Mrs. Holt*), Fritzie Ridgway (*Edna*), Willard Louis (*Helnie Lorber*), Carl Stockdale (*Pliny*), Lydia Yeamans Titus (*Mrs. Hawes*), Mickey Moore (*Olaf*).

Rural, Drama. Gudrun Trygavson works in the American wheat country as a hired girl to Mrs. Hawes. Charley Holt, the son of a rich family, takes the Swedish girl to a dance where she is snubbed by his mother and sister. Enraged at his snobbish relatives, Charley marries Gudrun and gets a menial job as a mill worker. A child is born, but Gudrun's life is unhappy because Charley becomes an alcoholic. After five years of marriage Charley dies in a saloon fight. Gudrun then buys a small farm and works the wheat fields. When tramp Martin O'Neill comes to the farm, Mary feeds him and he works for her. Martin later saves Gudrun and her child from a burning barn but is suspected of starting the fire himself and narrowly escapes a lynching. Finally, it is disclosed that the fire was actually started by Heine, a jealous rival, and Gudrun and Martin are married. *Alcoholics. Farmers. Swedish Americans. Tramps. Arson. Factory workers. Fights. Jealousy. Lynching. Marriage. Rescues. Romantic rivalry. Saloons. Snobs and snobbishness. Wheat.*

Note: Lewis' story was originally caled "Prairie Gold." Contemporary sources conflict on whether Stewart or Tyler was the film's assistant director. Production charts in contemporary trade journals indicate that Siegler replaced Gosden as cinematographer, and that Wecker replaced Dyer as properties supervisor. Mid-production trade articles announced that the film's company planned to shoot location scenes in the Imperial Valley, CA and in Kentucky.

Camera 23 Feb 1919, p. 9. *Camera* 2 Mar 1919, p. 6. *Camera* 30 Mar 1919, p. 7, 9. *MPN* 10 May 1919, p. 3089. *MPN* 17 May 1919, p. 3271. *MPW* 10 May 1919, p. 938. *Var* 30 May 1919, p. 77. *Wid's* 4 May 1919, p. 7.

UNPROTECTED (African Americans)

Jesse L. Lasky Feature Play Co. *Dist* Paramount Pictures Corp. 13 Nov 1916 [©Jesse L. Lasky Feature Play Co.; 21 Oct 1916; LP9375]. Si; b&w. 5 reels.

Pres Jesse L. Lasky. *Dir* James Young. *Asst dir* W. S. Van Dyke. *Story* Beatrice C. de Mille and Leighton Osmun or James Hatton. *Cam* Paul P. Perry.

Cast: Blanche Sweet (*Barbara King*), Theodore Roberts (*Rufus Jamison*), Ernest Joy (*Governor John Carroll*), Tom Forman (*Gordon Carroll*), Walter Long (*Joshua Craig*), Mrs. Lewis McCord (*Mattie Rowe, a convict*), Robert Gray (*Tony Salvarro*), Jane Wolff (*The mulatto*).

Social, Drama. After her parents die, Barbara King, a Southerner, lives with her uncle Rufus Jamison, who rails that Barbara's mother ruined her life by marrying an artist and forces Barbara to do domestic work. Barbara enters her father's last work in an exhibition and meets artist Gordon Carroll and his father, the governor. When Jamison discovers Barbara's secret attic studio and destroys her father's statue, Barbara hits him with a candlestick, whereupon he falls through a trap door and dies. Barbara is convicted, sentenced and sent to work at Joshua Craig's turpentine plant where black prisoners labor under harsh conditions. After she attempts to protect convict Tony Salvarro from a beating, she is tied to a tree. Taken into Craig's house to replace his convict mistress, Barbara plots a mutiny with the other prisoners. When the governor inspects the camp, Craig hides Barbara's identity. Later, Craig drunkenly attacks her, but Gordon, who is hunting nearby, arrives to rescue her. Tony sacrifices his life for Barbara, while the prisoners mutiny and kill Craig. Barbara then convinces the governor to have the conditions of the camp ameliorated. Pardoned, she marries Gordon and they have a child. *Convicts. Mutiny. Penal colonies. Prison life. Self-sacrifice. United States–South. African Americans. Artists. Governors. Mistresses. Murder. Pardons. Rape. Turpentine industry and trade. Uncles.*

Note: According to the Community Motion Picture Bureau, the film was based on New York Governor Whitman's statement against the farming of

prisoners to private parties. A genuine turpentine plant in the South was used in the film. No reviews were located for this film. Sources conflict concerning the author of the story on which this film was based: material in the Paramount studio records indicates that it was based on a story by Beatrice C. de Mille and Leighton Osmun entitled "Unconquered," while information in the copyright descriptions indicates that James Hatton was the author. *Unconquered* was the title of a film released in 1917, which was based on a story by de Mille and Osmun entitled "The Conflict."

MPN 4 Nov 1916, p. 2836. *MPW* 28 Oct 1916, p. 573. *MPW* 18 Nov 1916, p. 949. *NYDM* 21 Oct 1916, p. 33.

UNSEEN ENEMY (Italian Americans)

Universal Pictures Co., Inc. *Dist* Universal Pictures Co., Inc. 10 Apr **1942**; Prod: 4 Feb—mid-Feb 1942 [©Universal Pictures Co., Inc.; 16 Mar 1942; LP1149]. Sd (Western Electric Mirrophonic Recording); b&w. 5,481 ft. 60-61 min.

Assoc prod Marshall Grant. *Dir* John Rawlins. [*Asst dir* Melville Shyer]. *Dial dir* Harold Erickson. *Orig scr* Roy Chanslor and Stanley Rubin. *Based on an idea by* George Wallace Sayre. *Dir of photog* John W. Boyle. *Art dir* Jack Otterson. *Assoc* Harold H. MacArthur. *Film ed* Edward Curtiss. *Set dec* R. A. Gausman. *Gowns* Vera West. *Mus dir* Charles Previn. *Sd dir* Bernard B. Brown. [*Sd*] *tech* William Fox.

Song(s): "Who Is Sylvia?" words by William Shakespeare, music by Franz Schubert.

Cast: Irene Hervey (*Gen [Rand]*), Don Terry (*Bill [Flynn Hancock, also known as Bill Flynn, Capt. Wilhelm Roering and Capt. Von Ritter]*), Leo Carrillo (*Nick*), Andy Devine (*Sam [Dillon]*), Lyonel Royce ([*Capt. Willhelm*] *Roering*), Turhan Bey (*Ito*), Frederick Gierman ([*Franz*] *Muller*), William Ruhl (*Callaban*), Clancy Cooper ([*Alan*] *Davies*), Eddie Fetherston (*Badger*), [Hugh Beaumont (*Narrator*)], [George Eldredge (*Marshal*)], [Rico De Montez (*Waiter*)], [Charles Sullivan (*Bartender*)], [Francis Sayles (*Chef*)], [Ed Peil, Sr. (*Patron*)].

Espionage, War, Drama. [*Print viewed*]. On the night of 20 Nov 1941, two high-ranking Nazi naval officers escape from a prisoner of war camp on the Canadian border. When one man is shot, he orders the other to go to San Francisco to meet with their confederates. In San Francisco, the escapee runs into harbor detective Sam Dillon, but the officer, not recognizing him, lets him go. The German then goes to "The Schooner Club," a waterfront café where an anniversary party is being held for its Italian American owner, Nick, by his stepdaughter, Gen Rand. The escapee, using the name Bill Flynn, asks Gen to sing "Who Is Sylvia?" in order to signal his cohorts of his arrival. The café's Asian waiter Ito tells Bill to go to Warehouse C on Pier 46, and Gen follows him there. Bill meets with Nick, a hired hand of the Axis powers, and tells the café owner that he is actually Captain Wilhelm Roering. Nick then arranges a meeting between Bill and the head of the local German spy ring. Gen later meets with Sam and tells him about the Nazi's arrival at the club. After Bill takes Gen out to dinner, Nick warns him to stay away from his stepdaughter. Bill then meets with Franz Muller, president of the German American Exporting Co., who offers to put him in command of a captured Japanese ship currently being held in San Francisco Bay. It is Muller's plan to free the ship, man it with German, Italian and Japanese loyalists and use it to raid American vessels in the Pacific. Meanwhile, Sam tells police inspector Alan Davies of Muller's true allegiance, and they scheme to capture the Axis agents that night. Unfortunately, Gen inadvertently tells Nick of those plans, and he warns the spies. Despite this, Muller refuses to pay Nick the $10,000 he is owed unless he agrees to hide some Italian nationalists in his club until they can commandeer the Japanese ship. Using a rowboat, Nick and Muller smuggle the men out of the warehouse, but are discovered by Sam as they make their escape. Nick is wounded, but the spies manage to flee the police in a power boat. After arriving safely at the Schooner Club, Bill visits Gen, who has been informed of his identity, and Sam arrests Bill, but later learns that Bill is actually Capt. William Flynn Hancock, a Canadian intelligence officer. Bill tells Inspector Davies that he impersonated captured German officer Capt. Von Ritter at Roering's prison camp, then convinced the German that he was under orders to accompany him on his escape to San Francisco; when Roering was killed in the escape, he then assumed the dead Nazi's identity in order to discover his mission. That night, however, the real Roering arrives at the Schooner Club, and unsure of his identity, Nick and Ito send for Muller. Gen sends a warning note to her father, but the spies intercept it and capture Bill. Learning that the Nazis plan to abduct Gen as well,

Nick goes to her rescue, but is knocked unconscious by Ito after Gen convinces him to turn his employers over to the police. As the spies capture the Japanese ship, Sam and the harbor patrol arrive. The spies are captured, but Nick is killed in the shootout, along with Roering and Ito. Gen is later consoled by Sam, and Bill agrees to marry her after the war is over. *Cafés. Canadians. Government agents. Impersonation and imposture. Nazis. San Francisco (CA). Spies. Stepfathers. Waterfronts. Canadian-American border region. Chases. Escapes. Gunfights. Gunshot wounds. Italian Americans. Prison escapees. Prisoners of war. Ships. Singers. Traps. Waiters.*

Note: The film does not contain any opening credits; instead, it opens with an extended voice-over narration, which warns Americans to beware of the "unseen enemy," German, Italian and Japanese spies who may be living "right next door" in order to sabotage the U.S. war effort. According to *HR*, the original idea for this film was based on the true story of German spy Captain Fritz Duquesne, who was captured by the FBI in Jun 1941. According to a 1939 *LAT* article, Duquesne first came to world attention when he waged "a one-man war against the British in South Africa as a means of revenge for the death of his wife and sister" following the Boer War. When Universal considered making the film in 1939, Burt Kelly was assigned to the project as its associate producer. After Duquesne's arrest in 1941, Universal reportedly considered updating the original script it had purchased two years earlier from Arthur D. Howden Smith, who had acted as a second for Duquesne in a duel and who admitted to informing on the German. Smith received no official writing credit, and it has not been determined if any of his work was used in the final film. Universal publicity materials state that this picture marked the screen debut of actor Rudolph Friml, Jr., the son of the noted composer; however, his participation in the released film has not been confirmed.

Box 4 Apr 1942. *DV* 26 Mar 1942, p. 3. *FD* 10 Apr 1942, p. 8. *HR* 1 Jul 1941, p. 9. *HR* 28 Jan 1942, p. 1. *HR* 29 Jan 1942, p. 3. *HR* 6 Feb 1942, p. 11. *HR* 26 Mar 1942, p. 3. *MPHPD* 4 Apr 1942, pp. 585-86. *Var* 1 Apr 1942, p. 8.

UNSEEN HANDS (Native Americans)

Encore Pictures. *Dist* Associated Exhibitors, Inc. 25 May **1924** [©Associated Exhibitors, Inc.; 12 May 1924; LU20192]. Si; b&w. 6 reels, 5,382 ft.

Prod Walker Coleman Graves, Jr. *Dir* Jacques Jaccard. *Wrt* Walker Coleman Graves, Jr.

Cast: Wallace Beery (*Jean Scholast*), Joseph J. Dowling (*Georges Le Quintrec*), Fontaine La Rue (*Madame Le Quintrec*), Jack Rollins (*Armand Le Quintrec*), Cleo Madison (*Matoaka*), Jim Corey (*Wapita*), Jamie Gray (*Nola*).

Melodrama. At the insistence of his wife, Le Quintrec, a wealthy mine owner, hires wandering adventurer Jean Scholast as a reward for gallantry. When Quintrec dies as a result of Jean's plotting, his widow marries Jean, giving him power of attorney. Jean sells her property and flees to Arizona, where he marries an Indian squaw. Pursued by Armand, Le Quintrec's son, Jean dies of heart failure when Le Quintrec's spirit appears. *Arizona. Bigamy. Ghosts. Indians of North America. Land rights. Miners. Miscegenation. Vagabonds. Wills.*

FD 7 Sep 1924. *Var* 27 Aug 1924, p. 25.

UNTAMED (Latino)

Triangle Film Corp. *Dist* Triangle Distributing Corp. 1 Sep **1918**. Si; b&w. 5 reels.

Dir Cliff Smith. *Story and scen* Kenneth B. Clarke. *Cam* Steve Rounds.

Cast: Roy Stewart (*Jim Jason*), Ethel Fleming (*Ruth Allen*), May Giraci (*Carmelita*), H. N. Dudgeon (*Don Felipe Arrello*), H. C. Simmons (*Prof. David Allen*), Graham Pettie (*Pancho*), John Lince (*Mike*), Elvira Weil (*Dolores*), Eagle Eye (*Pedro*).

Western. On the Mexican border, Jim Jason forms a partnership with Don Felipe Arrello, even though he is troubled by a clause in their contract which states that if one of the partners dies, the other will inherit their ranch. When the ranch begins to prove profitable, Felipe hires an assassin to kill Jim, but the cowboy discovers the plan and gives the killer a sound beating. Jim's sweetheart, Ruth Allen, who has come to the area with her father to restore the old Spanish architecture, sees the fight and assumes that he is mistreating his men, but his concern for little Carmelita, who is suffering from typhoid fever, convinces Ruth of Jim's kindness. Felipe tries once again to kill Jim, who leads his cowboys in pursuit of the villain. Upon reaching Felipe's hideout, however, they learn that Dolores, his betrayed lover, has already killed him. *Attempted murder. Contracts. Cowboys. Mexican Americans. Mexicans. Partnership. Ranches. Children. Fistfights. Hired killers. Mexican-American border region. Murder. Typhoid fever.*

Note: Some sources credit the role of Dolores to Jimmy Weil. One reviewer states that Clarke's story appeared in *The Saturday Evening Post.*

ETR 31 Aug 1918, p. 1046. *ETR* 7 Sep 1918, p. 1179. *MPN* 7 Sep 1918, p. 1604. *MPW* 7 Sep 1918, p. 1462. *MPW* 14 Sep 1918, pp. 1608-09. *Var* 13 Sep 1918, p. 41. *Wid's* 1 Sep 1918, pp. 19-20.

UNTAMED FURY (African Americans)

Danches Bros. Productions. *Dist* Producers Releasing Corp.; controlled by Pathe Industries, Inc. 22 Mar 1947 [©Pathe Industries, Inc.; 22 Mar 1947; LP889]. Sd (RCA Sound System); b&w. 61-62 or 65 min. PCA cert no. 11570.

Prod Ewing Scott. *Dir* Ewing Scott. *Asst dir* Daniel D. Doran. *Scr* Taylor Caven and Paul Gerard Smith. *Story* Ewing Scott. *Photog* Ernest Miller. *Film ed* Robert Crandall. *Mus score and dir* Alexander Laszlo. *Rec* Cuyler Tuthill. *Prod supv* Georges Danches. *Alligator hunts cond by* Ross Allen.

Cast: Gaylord Pendleton [(*Jeff Owens*)], Mikel Conrad [(*"Gator Bait" Blair*)], Leigh Whipper [(*Uncle Gabe*)], Mary Conwell [(*Judie Blair*)], Althea Murphy [(*Patricia Wayburn*)], Jack Rutherford [(*Nubie Blair*)], Charles Keane [(*Rufe Owens*)], Rodman Bruce [(*Lige*)], Paul Savage [(*Swamper*)], E. G. Marshall [(*Pompano*)], Norman MacKay [(*John Bradbury*)].

Drama. [*Not viewed*]. When writer John Bradbury reveals that he has come to Florida's Okefenokee Swamp for inspiration, Uncle Gabe, a wise old black man, relates the following story: Years before, alligator hunter Nubie Blair, his son "Gator Bait," so called because he loves to lure alligators into his father's nets by jumping into the swamp, and daughter Judie enjoy their simple, rural life. Rufe Owens and his son Jeff also hunt the swamp, but unlike Blair, Owens sends his son to school and has high hopes for his future. The two fathers continually pit the boys against each other, and Jeff and Gator grow up as intense rivals. Eventually, Jeff leaves Okefenokee to continue his education, while the more athletic Gator remains in the swampland. Years later, Jeff, now a civil engineer, returns to Okefenokee, bursting with plans for roads, hospitals and other improvements. Despite Jeff's genuine concern for their well-being, the local residents, including Blair, Gator and Owens, are suspicious of his ideas. Only Judie, who has grown into an attractive young woman, appreciates Jeff's efforts. Gator's animosity toward Jeff increases when he realizes that Patricia Wayburn, the sophisticated owner of the tourist camp where he works as a guide, was once involved with the engineer. Pat, who enjoys a flirtatious relationship with Gator, immediately expresses a desire to resume her romance with Jeff, but he rebuffs her. Later, Jeff presents his plans at a meeting and is soundly rejected by the townspeople, who fear that his proposed "improvements" will result in the destruction of their simple lifestyle. Calling Jeff "uppity," Gator then hurls his surveying equipment into the river, and the engineer is carried bodily to the edge of town. That night, Judie swims to retrieve Jeff's equipment from the river bottom. Knowing how much Judie fears alligators, Jeff is deeply touched by her help and gives her a passionate kiss. The next day, Jeff confers with his boss, Sprague, about the town's resistance, and Sprague warns Blair and Lige that if they try to stop Jeff again, he will call in the state police. Jeff then hosts a dance, hoping to alleviate some of the tension in the town, but Gator uses the situation to provoke a fight with his rival. When Gator pulls a knife on Jeff during the fight, Blair rushes in to stop him and insists that he apologize to Jeff. Gator does apologize and agrees to act as Jeff's swamp guide the next morning, but as soon as he gets Jeff alone in the swamp, he tries to strangle him with a loose vine. After a fierce struggle, Jeff knocks Gator out and saves him from an attacking alligator. Jess drags the still unconscious Gator back to shore and lies to Blair, telling him that his son slipped and hit his head. Despite Jeff's forgiving gesture, Gator, Blair and Lige lead an armed attack on Jeff's road construction crew and force him to stop work. Later, Jeff criticizes Pat for teasing the impressionable Gator, but she insists that her feelings for the swampman are genuine. After blessing his budding romance with Judie, Pat gives Jeff a farewell kiss, unaware that Gator is watching her from a distance. Misunderstanding the kiss, a jealous Gator throws Pat into the river and later vows to kill Jeff. Judie hears Gator's threat and runs to Owens for help. The unsuspecting Jeff, meanwhile, is out on the swamp marking trees for felling, when Gator fires at him. Gator misses and eventually falls into some quicksand. Once again Jeff saves Gator's life and, when a frantic Judie and Owens arrive on the scene, he once again protects Gator with a lie. His anger spent, Gator finally admits that he was wrong, and the two men shake hands. *Engineers-Civil. Okefenokee Swamp*

(FL). Progress. Rivalry. Romance. Swamps. African Americans. Alligators. Attempted murder. Authors. Children. City-country contrast. Construction workers. Dances. Education. Family relationships. Fathers and sons. Fights. Hunting. Jealousy. Quicksand. Rescues. Tour guides. Tourists.

Note: The working title of this film was *The Outlander*. Ewing Scott's screen story was titled "Gaitor Bait." According to the *HR* review, Scott tried to sell his story in Hollywood for "several years" before obtaining backing from the Danches brothers. Prior to their involvement with Scott, the Danches brothers, Abe, Ralph and George, ran a wholesale produce business in Cleveland and during World War II specialized in dehydrated and powdered eggs. Some of the above character names, which were taken from a copyright cutting continuity, are listed differently in the reviews. The family name "Blair" is listed as "Kirk" in reviews and "Owens" is listed as "Owen." In reviews, Owens' and Blair's first names are listed as "Crane" and "Sam," respectively, not "Rufe" and "Nubie." According to a Nov 1946 *HR* news item, the picture was made on location in Florida, in the southern section of the Okefenokee Swamp. In Sep 1951, *Var* reported that George Danches of Danches Productions filed a breach of contract lawsuit against Eagle Lion and Pathe Industries, the parent distribution companies, demanding $250,000 in damages. Danches claimed that the defendants made improper deductions and failed to use "the best efforts" to distribute the picture. The disposition of the lawsuit is not known.

Box 5 Apr 1947. *DV* 1 Apr 1947. *FD* 27 Mar 1947. *HR* 25 Nov 1946, p. 16. *HR* 1 Apr 1947, p. 3. *NYT* 26 Apr 1947, p. 10. *NYT* 9 May 1948. *Var* 26 Mar 1947, p. 12. *Var* 18 Sep 1951.

UNTAMED YOUTH (Gypsies)

R-C Pictures Corp. *Dist* Film Booking Offices of America. 5 May 1924 [©R-C Pictures Corp.; 18 Apr 1924; LP20105]. Si; b&w. 5-6 reels, 4,558 ft.

Dir Emile Chautard. *Scen* Charles Stillson and Charles Beahan. *Photog* Joseph A. Dubray and Pierre Collings.

Source: Based on the play *Born of the Cyclone* by G. Marion Burton (production date undetermined).

Cast: *Cast—Release version:* Derelys Perdue (*Marcheta*), Lloyd Hughes (*Robert Ardis*), Ralph Lewis (*Joe Ardis*), Emily Fitzroy (*Emily Ardis*), Josef Swickard (*Pietro*), Joseph J. Dowling (*Reverend Loranger*), Tom O'Brien (*Jim Larson*), Mickey McBan (*Ralph*). *Cast—Copyright version:* Derelys Perdue (*Lila*), Lloyd Hughes (*François*), Ralph Lewis (*Antoine*), Max Davidson (*Pierre*), Mickey McBan (*Raoul*), Josef Swickard (*Gorgio*), Emily Fitzroy (*Manon*), Caroline Rankin (*Madame Guernette*).

Melodrama. Robert Ardis, a small-town youth studying for the ministry, encounters a visiting Gypsy, Marcheta, and is displeased by her pagan conduct. When she saves the life of his younger brother, however, Robert becomes fascinated with her. Though scorning his religion, she saves his life during a storm by praying for a miracle, and in rescuing him she comes to believe in God. *Brothers. Gypsies. Miracles. Paganism. Religion. Theological seminaries. Youth.*

Note: In the release version the story and the characters were altered to introduce the idea of religious conversion. The working title of this film was *Beware the Woman.*

MPW 10 May 1924.

UP IN CENTRAL PARK (Irish Americans)

Universal-International Pictures Co., Inc. *Dist* Universal Pictures Co., Inc. Jul 1948; New York opening: 26 May 1948; Prod: early Oct—mid-Dec 1947 [©Universal Pictures Co., Inc.; 8 Jun 1948; LP1918]. Sd (Western Electric Recording); b&w. 86-87 min. PCA cert no. 12938.

Prod Karl Tunberg. *Dir* William A. Seiter. *Asst dir* William Holland. *Wrt for the scr by* Karl Tunberg. *Dir of photog* Milton Krasner. *Spec photog* David S. Horsley. *Prod des* Howard Bey. *Film ed* Otto Ludwig and [Russell Schoengarth]. *Set dec* Russell A. Gausman and Ted Offenbecker. *Cost* Mary Grant. *Mus arr and dir by* Johnny Green. [*Mus score* Sigmund Romberg]. *Dances and mus seq staged by* Helen Tamiris. *Sd* Leslie I. Carey and Joe Lapis. *Hair stylist* Carmen Dirigo. *Makeup* Bud Westmore.

Song(s): "When She Walks in the Room," "Carousel in the Park" and "Oh Say, Can You See (What I See)," music by Sigmund Romberg, lyrics by Dorothy Fields; "Pace, pace mio Dio" from the opera *La forza del destino* by Giuseppe Verdi, libretto by Francesco Maria Piave.

Source: Based on the musical *Up in Central Park*, music by Sigmund Romberg, book by Herbert and Dorothy Fields, as produced by Michael Todd (New York, 27 Jan 1945).

Cast: DEANNA DURBIN (*Rosie Moore*), DICK HAYMES (*John Matthews*), VINCENT PRICE (*Boss* [*William*] *Tweed*), Albert Sharpe (*Timothy Moore*), Tom Powers (*Rogan*), Hobart Cavanaugh (*Mayor*

[*Joe*] *Oakley*), Thurston Hall (*Governor Motley*), Howard Freeman (*Myron Schultz*), Mary Field (*Miss Murch*), Tom Pedi (*O'Toole*), Moroni Olsen (*Big Jim Fitts*), William Skipper, Nelle Fisher (*Dancers*), [Patricia Alphin, Nina Lunn, Bunny Waters (*Guests*)], [Wayn Tredway, Frank McFarland, Harry Denny, Hal Taggart, Ed Peil, Sr., Mike Lally (*Politicians*)], [Curt Bois (*Maitre d'*)], [G. Pat Collins, Brick Sullivan, J. G. McMahon (*Ward heelers*)], [George Spaulding (*Barton*)], [Billy Newell (*Stage manager*)], [Martin Garralaga (*Bertolli*)], [Thomas Jackson, Tom P. Dillon (*Officials*)], [Harold Goodwin (*Spencer*)], [Al Murphy (*Doorman*)], [Richard Kipling (*Waiter with trick tray*)], [Paul Peter Szemere, Robert Verdaine, Rod De Medici (*Immigrants*)], [Alice Backes (*Swedish immigrant girl*)], [Charles Miller (*Jones*)], [Tudor Owen (*Footman*)], [Clarence Straight (*Reporter*)], [Bert Moorhouse (*Democrat*)], [John Valentine (*Butler*)], [Erich von Schilling (*Porter at Stetson House*)], [Billy Kimbley (*Alfred*)], [Carol Dawn Pierson (*Little dancing girl*)], [Art Thompson, Stuart Holmes (*Judges*)], [William H. O'Brien (*Waiter*)], [Charles Meakin (*Alderman*)], [Boyd Ackerman, Leslie Sketchley (*Policemen*)], [Eddie Scarpa (*Attendant*)], [Carl Sepulveda (*Carriage driver*)], [Eva Pearson (*Ticket seller*)], [David Newell].

Musical, Drama. [*Print viewed*]. In the 1870s, as election time rolls around in New York City, the political organization Tammany Hall, led by its corrupt political boss, William Tweed, is once again working hard to re-elect its candidates, including the mayor, Joe Oakley, in order to continue its raids upon the coffers of the city and state. The lone voice against Tweed's organization is John Matthews, a young, naïve reporter for the *New York Times*. Meanwhile, Irish immigrants Timothy Moore and his singing daughter Rosie arrive in New York with stars in their eyes, only to be set upon immediately by Rogan, one of Tweed's men. After the illiterate Timothy votes twenty-three times for the Tammany ticket, he is rewarded with $50 and an invitation to Tweed's victory party. There, Rosie wanders upstairs, where she inadvertently overhears Tweed's latest plan to embezzle the city's monies through the unnecessary renovation of Central Park. Fearful that Rosie may know about his plan, Tweed appoints the guileless Timothy to the post of Park Superintendent. Later, John meets Timothy, and the new city official, not knowing that John is a reporter, tells him that some of the park's zoo animals are actually being raised for Tweed's consumption. After the story appears in the paper, Timothy is fired, but when Rosie asks the infatuated Tweed to give her father another chance, he agrees. John is also enraptured with Rosie, so he, in turn, offers Timothy a job with his paper. Once alone, John tries to convince Rosie of Tweed's dishonesty, but has little success. Rosie almost becomes aware of Tweed's true character later that night, however, when he makes numerous, lecherous advances toward her during dinner, but is interrupted by Timothy, who mistakenly believes that he was invited for supper as well. Rosie then arranges a meeting between John and Tweed. When the political boss offers to sponsor John's proposed novel if he agrees to quit his position at the *New York Times*, John refuses the bribe. Later, John discovers Timothy attending grammar school classes, and with the help of Miss Murch, a schoolteacher, the old man learns of Tweed's corruption. Timothy tries to tell Rosie about Tweed, but she refuses to listen, having become romantically involved with him even though he is married. With Tweed's help, Rosie auditions for an opera company, and though she is offered a role in an upcoming production, Tweed insists that she be cast in the current show. An upset Timothy then offers to help John gain evidence against Tweed by breaking into city hall and examining the city's financial records. They are caught when Oakley wanders into his office, but the drunken mayor is tricked into giving his copies of Tweed's financial dealings to the newspaperman. Their corruption exposed, Tweed and his associates quickly make plans to flee the country, but Tweed makes no apologizes to Rosie for his actions, stating his belief in the rights of the strong over the weak. After he leaves her, Rosie wanders through Central Park, where she is discovered by Timothy and John. She then asks her father's forgiveness and is reunited with John. *Fathers and daughters. Immigrants. Irish Americans. Political bosses. Political corruption. Reporters. William Marcy "Boss" Tweed. Assimilation (Sociology). Auditions. Bribery. Chimpanzees. Dancers. Dismissal (Employment). Drunkenness. Elections. Governors. Literacy. Mayors. Merry-go-rounds. New York City–Central Park. The New York Times (Newspaper). Opera houses. Opera singers. Restaurants. Schools. Schoolteachers. Zoos.*

Note: According to *HR*, Universal purchased the film rights to the Sigmund Romberg-Herbert Fields-Dorothy Fields musical in Feb 1946. The studio originally intended the production to be shot in Technicolor and produced by Felix Jackson. *NYT* reported in Oct 1946 that actor-dancer Fred Astaire considered making his screen directorial debut with *Up in Central Park*; however, he had just opened a chain of dance schools at the same time which may have prevented him taking on this production. According to *HR* news items, the film's production start date was delayed from Dec 1946 to Jul 1947 because of Technicolor difficulties. In Sep 1947, William Goetz, the production chief at Universal, told *NYT* that the studio was filming *Up in Central Park* in black and white because of a "bottleneck" at the Technicolor laboratory, which would delay the release of the film by nearly one year. Later, in Oct 1947, another *NYT* news item stated that Universal had chosen William Seiter as the film's director and planned to film *Up in Central Park* in black and white, rather than Technicolor, in order to keep production costs down. *NYT* also noted that the musical number "The Birds and the Bees" from the original stage production would not be filmed, as it did not meet PCA code restrictions. According to *LAT*, because of bad previews, Universal cut several musical numbers out of the picture, including the song "Close as Pages in a Book." *LAT* estimated that the excised footage cost the studio over $200,000 to produce. Karl Tunberg's onscreen credit reads: "Produced and Written for the Screen by."

Up in Central Park is loosely based on events surrounding New York's Tammany Hall political scandal of 1871. William Marcy "Boss" Tweed, portrayed by actor Vincent Price in the film, was a corrupt political boss, who headed what would later be known as the "Tweed Ring." Tweed began his career in politics as a volunteer fireman, and was elected city alderman in 1850. While still an alderman, Tweed served in the U.S. Congress from 1853 to 1855, and began to take control of the political organization known as Tammany Hall. After losing his re-election bid as alderman in 1855, Tweed was elected to the city's Board of Supervisors in 1856. With the help of A. Oakley Hall, mayor of New York City, Richard B. Connolly, the city controller, and Peter Barr Sweeny, a city chamberlain, Tweed then gained control of the political graft system throughout New York. By 1868, Tweed had been elected to the state senate, as well as holding the posts of school commissioner, deputy commissioner of public works, and deputy street commissioner for New York City. For nearly twenty years, the city's coffers were systematically looted by the Tweed Ring through bribery, the padding of all city bills by eighty-five percent and phony check writing.

Tweed's undoing began in 1870, when political cartoonist Thomas Nast attacked him and his men in *Harper's Weekly*, and Samuel J. Tilden fought him for control of their political party. Tweed was then tried and convicted of larceny and forgery, but in Dec 1875, he escaped prison and fled the country. He was recognized in Spain on the basis of a Nast cartoon and returned to New York, where he died in prison on 12 Apr 1878. It is estimated that the Tweed Ring stole between 30 and 200 million dollars during its political reign.

Box 5 Jun 1948. *DV* 26 May 1948, p. 3. *FD* 3 Jun 1948, p. 8. *HR* 21 Feb 1946. *HR* 9 Dec 1946, p. 3. *HR* 3 Oct 1947, p. 15. *HR* 26 May 1948, p. 5. *HR* 1 Jun 1948, p. 6, 10. *LAT* 28 Jun 1948. *MPHPD* 10 Jan 1948, p. 4010. *MPHPD* 29 May 1948, pp. 4181-82 *NYT* 20 Oct 1946. *NYT* 28 Sep 1947. *NYT* 12 Oct 1947. *NYT* 27 May 1948, p. 29. *Var* 26 May 1948, p. 8.

UP JUMPED THE DEVIL (African Americans)
Dixie National Pictures, Inc. *Dist* Consolidated National Film Exchanges. **1941.** Sd; b&w. 6,100 ft. 68 min.

Prod Jed Buell.

Song(s): "Dreams of You" and "Jump Off the Springboard," composers undetermined.

Cast: Mantan Moreland (*Washington*), Shelton Brooks (*Jefferson*), Maceo Sheffield (*Bad News Johnson, also known as Swamee Reever*), Earl Morris (*A tramp*), Lawrence Criner (*Sheriff*), Myrtle Fortune, Patsy Hunter, Millie Monroe, Suzette Harbin, Avanelle Harris, Doris Akes.

African American, Comedy, with songs. [*Not viewed*]. Recent parolees Jefferson and Washington are desperate to find jobs so that they will not be picked up for vagrancy. When they see that the wealthy Mrs. Wendell Brown is hiring a butler and a maid, Jefferson convinces Washington to dress up as a woman and take the maid's job while he performs the duties of the butler. Washington is reluctant and uncooperative, but finally agrees to keep his dress on, as the alternative is to run around nude. As Jefferson and Washington hitchhike to Mrs. Brown's, where they are to work at her "Aid to Abyssinia" bazaar, they are picked up by Bad News Johnson, a crook whom they met in jail. Bad News offers to let the two in on a scam he is planning to put over on Mrs. Brown, but they decline, saying that they have had enough of prison life. At the bazaar, the male guests flirt with Washington, while Bad News, dressed as "Swamee Reever," a soothsayer, pretends to read the women's fortunes as he is stealing their jewels. Washington, who is an unregenerate dice shooter, gets in a game of craps and wins the men's fancy clothes with his "crooked dice." Now dressed as a man, Washington observes Bad News telling Mrs. Brown's fortune and then stealing her pearl necklace. Bad News threatens Washington if he tells anyone about the theft, and when

Mrs. Brown's husband searches both men to no avail, Washington keeps quiet. Jefferson shows Washington where the necklace has been hidden, and the two steal it and then refuse to return it to the angry Bad News until the police arrive and catch him red-handed. *African Americans. Female impersonation. Fortune-tellers. Jewel thieves. Parole. Servants. Charity bazaars. Craps (Game). Hitchhiking. Necklaces. Police. Upper classes.*

Note: Although a print of this film was not viewed, the above plot was taken from a dialogue continuity deposited with the NYSA. Some character names were deduced from photographs and descriptions within the cutting continuity. Exact release date information was not found, but according to a *NYAms* news item, the film was ready for distribution on the East Coast as of 30 Aug 1941. NYSA records indicate that by the time the film was submitted for censorship approval in 1945, Dixie National Pictures had been taken over by Toddy Pictures Co., which became the film's distributor. According to an 18 Sep 1941 news item in the African-American journal *California Eagle*, Earl Morris, who played a tramp in the picture, broke his leg during shooting. Modern sources credit William Xavier Crowley as the film's director and include Florence O'Brien and Clarence Brooks in the cast.

Amsterdam News (New York) 30 Aug 1941, p. 21. *California Eagle* 14 Aug 1941, p. 2. *California Eagle* 18 Sep 1941, p. 4.

THE VAGABOND LOVER *see* **ARSHIN MAL ALAN**

EL VAGABUNDO *see* **EL OTRO SOY YO**

THE VALIANT (*foreign version*) *see* **EL VALIENTE**

THE VALIANT HOMBRE (Latino)
Inter-American Productions, Inc. *Dist* United Artists Corp. **1949** [©Inter-American Productions, Inc.; 21 Jan 1949; LP2479]. Sd (RCA Sound System); b&w. 8 reels, 5,520 ft. 60-61 min. PCA cert no. 13395.
Series: The Cisco Kid.
Pres PHILIP N. KRASNE. *Prod* PHILIP N. KRASNE. *Assoc prod* Duncan Renaldo. *Dir* Wallace Fox. *Asst dir* Ben Chapman. *Orig scr* Adele Buffington. *Cine* Ernest Miller. [*Cam op* Edward Coleman]. [*Stills* Bill Crosby]. *Film ed* Martin Cohn. [*Set dec* Tom Thompson]. *Mus comp and dir* Albert Glasser. *Sd eng* Ferroll Redd. [*Makeup* Ted Larson]. *Prod mgr* Dick L'Estrange. [*Scr supv* Bobby Sierkes]. [*Grip* Stanley Levine].
Source: Based on the character created by O. Henry.
Cast: Duncan Renaldo ([*The*] *Cisco* [*Kid*]), Leo Carrillo (*Pancho*), John Litel [(*Lon Lansdell*)], Barbara Billingsley [(*Linda Mason*)], Guy Beach, Stanley Andrews [(*Sheriff Dodge*)], Lee "Lasses" White [(*Old prospector*)], John James [(*Paul Mason*)], Eugene Roth, Ralph Peters, Frank Ellis, Terry Frost, George De Normand, Daisy.
Western. [*Print viewed*]. In Brownsville, Texas, cowboys PAncho and "The Cisco Kid" meet a man named Joe Haskins, while he is trying to feed a heartbroken dog named Daisy, who has lost her appetite as well as her master, gold prospector Paul Mason. After Cisco gets Daisy to eat a bite, he sends Pancho to the café to get some more meat, then listens while Joe recounts the events leading up to Paul's disappearance: One day, Paul swaggered into the saloon, ordered champagne for himself, Joe and Daisy and announced that he had struck a vein. Paul showed Joe some of his nuggets and said that he planned to record the claim in the morning. Joe then got drunk, passed out and, when he woke up later, Paul was gone. Back on the street, Joe is suddenly shot by a gunman firing from the saloon, so Cisco runs inside with his gun drawn. By the time Sheriff Dodge and Deputy Clay arrive, Joe is dead, and Cisco and Pancho are arrested for his murder and jailed. While guarding Cisco and Pancho, Clay falls asleep, so Cisco tells Daisy to fetch the keys for them. As they are sneaking out, Clay wakes up, but Cisco manages to lock him in the cell. After Cisco persuades the undertaker to accompany him to the sheriff's office, Cisco demonstrates that the fatal bullet's calibre differs from Pancho's pistol. The sheriff lets them go, and is forced to arrest the real culprit, an outlaw named Pete, who is murdered shortly thereafter by an unseen shooter. On his way back to the jailhouse, Cisco meets his friend, Whiskers, whose stagecoach, which is carrying Paul's sister Linda to town, has become stuck in a river. Meanwhile, Lon Lansdell, a saloon keeper who is working with the gang, goes to the shack where Paul is being held and threatens to harm Linda unless he reveals the location of his claim. When Daisy comes up to Lansdell and sniffs enthusiastically at him, Cisco and Pancho surmise that he has been near Paul. After Cisco goes to Linda's hotel room and tells her that she is not safe in town, she rudely slams the door in his face. Cisco then gets Pancho to tell Linda that he is

there to take her to the Murdocks' ranch, where she is expected to arrive tomorrow, saying that her hosts refused to allow her to stay in a hotel even for one night and have sent a carriage. When they arrive at the shack, she realizes that she has been tricked and tries to escape, but Cisco picks her up and carries her inside. Shortly thereafter, Lansdell and the gang arrive and burst in with their guns drawn. Lansdell then tells Linda that they have found the gang's hideout and offers to take her there. After they leave, Cisco and Pancho wrestle with their guards and tie them up, purposely leaving their knots loose, so that they can escape and lead them to the hideout. When Cisco and Pancho arrive, the outlaws begin firing on them. Eventually, the henchmen surrender, and when he tries to escape across a suspension bridge, Lansdell falls from the cliff to his death below. Later, Cisco and Pancho say farewell to Paul, Linda and Daisy. *Cowboys. Gold. Kidnapping. Mexican Americans. Prospectors. Bridges. Brownsville (TX). Cafes. Champagne. Deputies. Dogs. Drunkenness. Escapes. Falls from heights. False arrests. Gold miners. Gunfights. Hideouts. Hotels. Jailbreaks. Keys. Ranches. Rivers. Ruses. Saloon keepers. Saloons. Sheriffs. Stagecoaches. Threats.*

Note: According to *NYT*, this film was shot on location in the San Fernando Valley. Although the onscreen credits list the copyright date as 1948, the copyright catalog lists it as 1949. Modern sources include the following in the cast: Herman Hack, Hank Bell, Budd Buster, Eddie Parker and Dave Sharpe. For additional information on the "Cisco Kid" series, please consult the Series Index and see above entry for *The Cisco Kid*.

DV 14 Dec 1948, p. 3. *FD* 15 Dec 1948, p. 5. *HR* 14 Dec 1948, p. 3. *MPHPD* 25 Dec 1948, p. 4434. *NYT* 17 Oct 1948. *Var* 15 Dec 1948, p. 6.

EL VALIENTE (Spanish language)
Fox Film Corp. *Dist* Fox Film Corp. Nov **1930**; New York opening: 7 Nov 1930; Prod: between Jul and Sep 1930. Sd; b&w. 8 reels.
Supv John Stone. *Dir* Richard Harlan. *Asst dir* Eli Dunn. *Scr* Tom Barry and John Hunter. [*Spanish version wrt* Paul Perez, Francisco Moré de la Torre, Manuel Paris, Salvador Martin and Juan Puerta]. *Photog* Sidney Wagner. *Sd* Eugene Grossman.
Source: Based on the play *The Valiant* by Holworthy Hall and Robert Middlemass (copyrighted 29 Sep 1920).
Cast: Juan Torena (*Carlos Douglas, also known as Jaime Daik*), Angelita Benítez (*María Douglas*), Carlos Villarías (*Prison warden*), María Calvo (*Sra. Douglas*), Ralph Navarro (*Buck*), Rafael Callol (*Chaplain*), Max Wagner (*First sergeant*), Juan de Landa (*Police sergeant*), Julio Villarreal (*Judge*), Jacinto Jaramillo (*Luis*), Guillermo del Rincón (*Roberto*), Raúl Lechuga.
Melodrama. [*Not viewed*]. At the end of World War I, soldier Carlos Douglas returns to America and kills an old friend who had betrayed a confidence, then turns himself in to the police using the name Jaime Daik. Eventually, he is sentenced to die. Carlos' aged mother, having no idea of his whereabouts, thinks she recognizes him from a published photograph of Daik and, anxious to know the truth, begs her daughter María to visit the prison. Carlos manages to convince María that he is not the man she is looking for, but is instead a friend of her brother whom he saw killed, fighting courageously, during the war. *Aliases. Brothers and sisters. Capital punishment. Missing persons. Mothers and sons. Murder. Prisons. Judges. Long-lost relatives. Revenge. Self-sacrifice. Trials. World War I.*

Note: This was a Spanish-language version of the 1929 Fox film *The Valiant*, which was directed by William K. Howard and starred Paul Muni and Marguerite Churchill. The Spanish version was originally intended to be a three-reel short, and shooting on that was concluded in Aug 1930. However, the studio then expanded the short to feature length with additional scenes that were shot between 27 Aug and 4 Sep 1930. In 1940, Twentieth Century-Fox released a remake of *The Valiant*, entitled *The Man Who Wouldn't Talk*, directed by David Burton and starring Lloyd Nolan and Jean Rogers (see *AFI Catalog of Feature Films, 1931-40*; F3.2726). *El valiente* played in Mexico City in Apr 1931 under the title *El patíbulo*.

CM Feb 1931, p. 133.

THE VALLEY OF DECISION (Irish Americans)
Metro-Goldwyn-Mayer Corp.; controlled by Loew's Inc. *Dist* Loew's Inc. Jun **1945**; New York opening: week of 3 May 1945; Prod: 19 Sep—early Dec 1944; added scenes began 16 Jan 1945 [©Loew's Inc.; 13 Apr 1945; LP13232]. Sd (Western Electric Sound System); b&w. 10,520 ft. 111 or 118 min. Passed by the National Board of Review. PCA cert no. 10665.
Prod Edwin H. Knopf. *Dir* Tay Garnett. [*Asst dir* Marvin Stuart]. [*Fill-in dir of added scenes* George Cukor]. *Scr* John Meehan and Sonya Levien. *Dir of photog* Joseph Ruttenberg. [*2d cam* Herbert Fischer]. *Spec eff* A. Arnold Gillespie and Warren Newcombe. [*Matte*

paintings, cam Mark Davis]. [*Miniatures* Don Jahraus]. *Art dir* Cedric Gibbons and Paul Groesse. *Film ed* Blanche Sewell. *Set dec* Edwin B. Willis. *Assoc* Mildred Griffiths. *Cost supv* Irene. *Assoc* Marion Herwood Keyes. *Mus dir* Herbert Stothart. *Rec dir* Douglas Shearer. [*Unit mixer* John F. Dullam]. [*Re-rec and eff mixer* James Z. Flaster, Standish J. Lambert, Robert W. Shirley, Newell Sparks, William Steinkamp, Michael Steinore and John A. Williams]. [*Mus mixer* Earl Cates and M. J. McLaughlin]. *Makeup created by* Jack Dawn. *Hair styles created by* Sydney Guilaroff. [*Unit mgr* Walter Strohm].

Song(s): "Molly Baun," traditional Irish ballad.

Source: Based on the novel *Valley of Decision* by Marcia Davenport (New York, 1942).

Cast: GREER GARSON (*Mary Rafferty*), GREGORY PECK (*Paul Scott*), Donald Crisp (*William Scott*), Lionel Barrymore (*Pat Rafferty*), Preston Foster (*Jim Brennan*), Marsha Hunt (*Constance Scott*), Gladys Cooper (*Clarissa Scott*), Reginald Owen (*McCready*), Dan Duryea (*William Scott, Jr.*), Jessica Tandy (*Louise Kane*), Barbara Everest (*Delia*), Marshall Thompson (*Ted Scott*), Geraldine Wall (*Kate Shannon*), Evelyn Dockson (*Mrs. Callahan*), John Warburton (*Giles*), Russell Hicks (*Mr. Laurence Gaylord*), Mary Lord (*Julia Gaylord*), Arthur Shields (*Callahan*), Dean Stockwell (*Paulie*), Mary Currier (*Mrs. Laurence Gaylord*), [Moroni Olsen (*Richard Kane*)], [Norman Ollestad (*Callahan's son*)], [Connie Gilchrist (*The cook*)], [Wayne Farlow, Warren Farlow (*Timmy*)], [Willa Pearl Curtis (*Black maid*)], [Jesse Graves (*Sweeper*)], [Lee Phelps, Harry Strang (*Guards*)], [William O'Leary (*O'Brien*)], [Richard Abbott (*Minister*)], [Joy Harrington (*Stella*)], [Bryn Davis (*Maid*)], [Lumsden Hare (*Dr. McClintock*)], [Anna Q. Nilsson (*Nurse*)], [Sherlee Collier (*Clarrie*)], [Fred Chapman, Timmy Hawkins, Gerald Mackey, Vincent Graeff (*Irish boys*)], [Pat Ryan, Mike Ryan (*Timmy, seven years*)], [Jim Farley], [George Sherwood], [Kernan Cripps].

Historical, **Romance**. In 1873, Irish immigrant Mary Rafferty lives with her wheelchair-bound father Pat and her widowed sister, Kate Shannon, in a small shack in an area of Pittsburgh known as "The Flats." One day, Mary tells her father that she has accepted a job as a live-in maid at the home of steel mill owner William Scott. Patrick, who lost his legs in an accident at Scott's mill and is embittered toward the family, angrily disapproves of Mary's decision. Soon after starting her job, Mary endears herself to William's wife Clarissa, his daughter Constance, and his three sons, Ted, William, Jr., and Paul. Mary falls instantly in love with Paul, who has just returned home from London and has big plans to modernize the furnace at the Scott mill. A romance soon flourishes between Paul and Mary, much to the consternation of Louise Kane, a cunning snob who is determined to marry Paul for his money. One year passes, and Paul proposes to Mary, but Mary rejects the idea because it would be improper for her, a servant, to marry her master's son. Constance, meanwhile, secretly marries Giles, the Earl of Moulton. After announcing the marriage to her parents, Constance asks her mother for permission to take Mary with them to England. Clarissa consents to the arrangement, and Mary leaves Pittsburgh without bidding farewell to Paul. Two years pass, and when William learns that Paul is in love with Mary, he recalls Mary to Pittsburgh and gives his blessing to their marriage. Paul and Mary resume their romance, but Mary's happiness is soon dampened by the discovery that her father has been leading a crippling and violent strike against William's mill. When she overhears William's plan to send in strikebreakers, Mary negotiates a temporary truce and arranges a meeting between the strikers and William. Ted is sent by his father to meet the arriving strikebreakers at the train station and send them home, but he gets drunk and fails to deliver his father's message. As a result, the strikebreakers arrive at the meeting, and a bloody riot ensues. Patrick and William are killed in the fight, and their deaths fill Mary with so much grief that she concludes that she and Paul can never marry. The passage of ten years finds Paul in a loveless marriage with Louise, and the father of a young boy. One day, the aged and ailing Clarissa sends for Mary, her truest friend, and tells her that she is willing her share of the mill to her. Following Clarissa's death, Ted, William, Jr. and Constance decide to sell the Scott mill, despite Paul's impassioned pleas to keep it in the family. Paul nearly loses the family mill until Mary sides with him and persuades Constance to change her allegiances. Paul then leaves Louise, who has only shown an interest in his money, and goes to Mary. *Class distinction. Family life. Irish Americans. Maids. Romance. Steel mills.*

Death and dying. Drunkenness. Fathers and daughters. Fathers and sons. Feuds. Friendship. Grief. Gunfights. Handicapped. Heart disease. Immigrants. Inheritance. Jealousy. Marriage–Secret. Pittsburgh (PA). Proposals (Marital). Riots. Steel magnates. Steel workers. Strikebreakers. Strikes and lockouts. Trade unions. Widows.

Note: According to a Feb 1943 *HR* news item, M-G-M paid $75,000 for the rights to Marcia Davenport's novel. A 21 Feb 1945 *HR* news item notes that George Cukor took over direction of added scenes from Tay Garnett when Garnett became ill. A pre-production news item in *HR* notes that John Hodiak was originally slated for the part played by Gregory Peck. The initial *HR* production chart for the film lists Hume Cronyn in the cast, but he did not appear in the released film. According to modern sources, Cronyn was originally cast in the part of "Ted Scott," but was later replaced by Marshall Thompson because Cronyn appeared too short when standing beside Peck in the film. Early *HR* production charts list Sara Allgood, Mary Phillips and Edith Leach in the cast, and *HR* news items include Alec Craig, Dorothy Russell and Robert and Richard Ganieri in the cast. The appearance of these actors in the final film has not been confirmed. Actor Dean Stockwell made his motion picture debut in the film. Greer Garson was nominated for an Academy Award for Best Actress, and Herbert Stothart was nominated for Best Scoring of a Dramatic or Comedy Picture. The film received *Photoplay*'s Best Picture award. On 20 Mar 1960, the CBS network aired a television version of *The Valley of Decision*, directed by Tom Donovan and starring Nancy Wickwier and Lloyd Bridges.

Box 21 Apr 1945. *DV* 10 Apr 1945, p. 3. *FD* 10 Apr 1945, p. 6. *HR* 2 Feb 1943, p. 1. *HR* 28 Aug 1944, p. 4. *HR* 31 Aug 1944, p. 3. *HR* 15 Sep 1944, p. 15, 16. *HR* 19 Sep 1944, p. 1. *HR* 20 Sep 1944, p. 10. *HR* 29 Sep 1944, p. 14. *HR* 6 Oct 1944, p. 11. *HR* 13 Oct 1944, p. 14. *HR* 26 Oct 1944, p. 6. *HR* 10 Nov 1944, p. 31. *HR* 1 Dec 1944, p. 8. *HR* 16 Jan 1945, p. 6. *HR* 21 Feb 1945, p. 1. *HR* 10 Apr 1945, pp. 3-4. *HR* 14 May 1945, p. 13. *HR* 11 Jan 1946, p. 3. *MPHPD* 16 Dec 1944, p. 2230. *MPHPD* 14 Apr 1944, p. 2401. *NYT* 4 Mar 1945, p. 23. *Var* 11 Apr 1945, p. 14.

VALLEY OF HUNTED MEN (German Americans)

Republic Pictures Corp. *Dist* Republic Pictures Corp. 13 Nov **1942**; Los Angeles opening: 22 Oct 1942; Prod: late Aug–early Sep 1942 [©Republic Pictures Corp.; 13 Nov 1942; LP11733]. Sd (RCA Sound System); b&w. 6 reels, 5,022 ft. 59-60 min. Passed by the National Board of Review. PCA cert no. 8904.

Series: The Three Mesquiteers.

Assoc prod Louis Gray. *Dir* John English. [*Asst dir* George Blair]. *Scr* Albert DeMond and Morton Grant. *Based on an orig idea by* Charles Tedford. *Photog* Bud Thackery. *Art dir* Russell Kimball. *Film ed* William Thompson. *Set dec* Otto Siegel. *Mus score* Mort Glickman.

Cast: Bob Steele (*"Tucson" Smith*), Tom Tyler (*"Stony" Brooke*), Jimmie Dodd (*"Lullaby" Joslin*), Edward Van Sloan [(*Dr. Heinrich Steiner*)], Roland Varno [(*Captain Carl Baum*)], Anna Marie Stewart (*Laura Steiner*), Edythe Elliott [(*Elizabeth Schiller*)], Arno Frey [(*Von Breckner*)], Richard French [(*Franz Toler*)], Robert Stevenson [(*Kruger*)], George Neise [(*Paul Schiller*)], [Duke Adlon (*Willie Schmidt*)], [Charles Flynn (*S. W. Tomsen*)], [Dutch Hendrian (*Wessel*)], [Kenne Duncan (*Curley*)], [Hal Price (*Clem Parker*)], [Kermit Maynard (*Roberts*)], [Jack Kirk (*Hank Carlson*)], [Charles Graham, Henry Morris, Jim Mitchell, Tex Terry (*Posse*)], [John Frazer (*Radio announcer*)], [Budd Buster (*Jud Carson*)], [Mickey Rentschler (*Danny*)], [Arvon Dale (*Reporter*)].

Western. [*Print viewed*]. In 1941, three German airmen, led by Captain Carl Baum, escape from a Canadian prisoner of war camp and cross into Wyoming. Local ranchers grow nervous as radio reports of the Nazis' murderous flight southward are broadcast daily, and one in particular, Clem Parker, theorizes that other Germans in the country are aiding them. "Tucson" Smith, "Stony" Brooke and "Lullaby" Joslin, ranchers known as The Three Mesquiteers, try to calm Parker, especially when he casts aspersions on Dr. Heinrich Steiner, a German refugee scientist who, along with his daughter Laura, is developing a chemical that will aid in extracting rubber from culebra plants. One afternoon, after Lullaby admires an expensive gun in Jud Carson's general store, the Germans sneak into town, steal the gun and shoot Carson. Carson alerts the townsfolk before dying, and they assemble a posse to pursue the Nazis. One is killed during the chase, while another is picked up as a hitchhiker by the unsuspecting Steiners. The man forces the Steiners to take him to their home and then to shoot at the posse. The man is killed while trying to escape, and Parker, realizing that the Steiners were unwilling accomplices, agrees to participate in Heinrich's experiment. Meanwhile, Baum has hitched a ride from Paul Schiller, Heinrich's nephew. Paul, who has not seen Heinrich in many years, has come to Wyoming to help with the Steiners' work. Baum kills the young man, then presents himself as Paul in order to steal Heinrich's formula for Germany. Baum is welcomed by the Steiners and the ranchers, but shortly after his

arrival, he is abducted by a group of secret Nazi sympathizers, led by German consul Von Breckner, who are unaware of his identity. Baum's Nazi tattoo proves his true loyalties, and the men agree to help in his plan to kidnap the doctor. The Mesquiteers foil their attempt, however, and become suspicious of Baum, especially when they find the gun used to kill Carson in his possession. Hoping to uncover the truth, the Mesquiteers and Steiner quietly send for Paul's mother, Elizabeth Schiller, but Laura, unaware of their intentions, tells Baum that she is coming for a surprise visit. Baum reports to his cohorts, who arrange to meet Elizabeth before she enters town. They warn her that they are holding Paul captive and threaten to kill him unless she pretends that Baum is her son. Elizabeth acquiesces, and the Mesquiteers are mystified when she warmly greets Baum. The day after her arrival, Heinrich prepares to conduct his experiment, but Baum contaminates the formula with acid to ruin the crops and turn the ranchers against the doctor. The first round of spraying is a disaster, with the crops dying almost instantaneously. While Heinrich struggles to determine what went wrong, the ranchers grow angrier. Curious about why Elizabeth has not come to watch the experiment, the Mesquiteers question her, and the frightened woman confides in them. They rush to the experiment site, as the ranchers, who have just heard on the radio that the Japanese have attacked Pearl Harbor, are about to lynch the doctor. The Mesquiteers forestall them with Elizabeth's story, and Baum and his cohorts, who have been inciting the ranchers, attempt to flee. The men are captured, however, and Baum confesses to killing Paul. Soon after, the American government offers to help the ranchers recover from the damage done by Baum, and everyone pitches in to help Heinrich use his formula to support the war effort. *Chemical formulas. Germans. Impersonation and imposture. Ranchers. Sabotage. Chases. Crop dusters. Escapes. Family relationships. Firearms. Foreign agents. Hitchhiking. Murder. Officers (Military). Prisoners of war. Rubber. Scientists. Tattoos. Threats. War refugees. World War II. Wyoming.*

Note: The opening title card reads "Republic Pictures presents The Three Mesquiteers in *Valley of Hunted Men*," followed by pictures of Bob Steele, Tom Tyler and Jimmie Dodd with their names and character names superimposed. For more information about the series, consult the Series Index and the entry for *The Three Mesquiteers* in *AFI Catalog of Feature Films, 1931-40*; F3.4617.

DV 23 Oct 1942, p. 3. *HR* 28 Aug 1942, p. 11. *HR* 23 Oct 1942, p. 10. *MPHPD* 6 Mar 1943.

VALLEY OF THE SUN (Native Americans)

RKO Radio Pictures, Inc. *Dist* RKO Radio Pictures, Inc. 6 Feb **1942**; Prod: 22 Sep—mid-Nov 1941 [©RKO Radio Pictures, Inc.; 30 Jan 1942; LP11056]. Sd (RCA Sound System); b&w. 7,131 ft. 78-79 or 84 min. PCA cert no. 7764.

Prod Graham Baker. *Dir* George Marshall. *Asst dir* Edward Donahue. *Scr* Horace McCoy. *Dir of photog* Harry Wild. *Spec eff* Vernon L. Walker. *Art dir* Albert S. D'Agostino and Walter E. Keller. *Ed* Desmond Marquette. *Cost* Edward Stevenson. *Mus dir* C. Bakaleinikoff. *Mus* Paul Sawtell. *Rec* Bailey Fesler and John C. Grubb.

Source: Based on the short story "Valley of the Sun" by Clarence Budington Kelland in *The Saturday Evening Post* (16 Dec 1939—3 Feb 1940).

Cast: Lucille Ball [(*Christine Larson*)], James Craig [(*Jonathan Ware*)], Sir Cedric Hardwicke [(*Warrick*)], Dean Jagger [(*Jim Sawyer*)], Peter Whitney [(*Willie*)], Billy Gilbert [(*Justice of the peace*)], Tom Tyler [(*Geronimo*)], Antonio Moreno [(*Chief Cochise*)], George Cleveland [(*Bill Yard*)], Hank Bell [(*Shotgun*)], [Richard Fiske, Don Terry (*Lieutenants*)], Indians from the pueblos of Taos, Santa Clara, Jemes, San Juan and Tesuque, [Chris Willow Bird (*Apache Indian*)], [Fern Emmett (*Spinster*)], [Carleton Young (*Nolte*)], [Carl Sepulveda (*Pickett*)], [George Melford (*Dr. Thomas*)], [Pat Moriarty (*Mickey Maguire*)], [Stanley Andrews (*Major*)], [Chester Clute (*Secretary*)], [Al St. John, Harry Lamont, Al Ferguson, Chester Conklin, Ed Brady, Lloyd Ingraham, Frank Coleman (*Men on street*)], [Ethan Laidlaw (*Johnson*)], [Steve Clemento (*Knife thrower*)], [George Lloyd (*Sergeant*)], [Bud Osborne (*Rose*)], [Tom London (*Parker*)], [Francis McDonald (*Interpreter*)], [Harry Hayden (*Governor*)].

Historical, Western. [*Print viewed*]. In 1868, in Arizona, frontier scout Jonathan Ware is court-martialed for allowing three innocent Indians to escape from an Army jail. After Jonathan is sentenced to a five-year prison term, a friendly sergeant who understands the scout's concern for the injustices suffered by the Indians allows him to escape. Jonathan then hitches a ride on a stagecoach carrying Indian

agent Jim Sawyer and a justice of the peace, who is accompanying the agent to the town of Desert Center to marry Sawyer and Christine Larson, the proprietor of the Busy Bee Café. When Sawyer discovers his non-paying passenger, he throws Jonathan off the stage, and the scout hitches a ride to town with an Indian. At the Busy Bee Café, Chris is awaiting the arrival of the coach when Willie, her simple-minded but kindhearted friend, warns her that Sawyer doesn't love her. Willie's instincts are correct, for in reality, Sawyer is a dishonorable man who has been cheating the Indians of their cattle. After the stage arrives, Sawyer and Chris dress for the wedding ceremony. Attired in his wedding finery, Sawyer goes to the café, and when he finds Jonathan there, a fistfight erupts in which the bridegroom is soundly beaten. Warrick, an English settler who detests the corrupt Sawyer, offers Jonathan refuge at his house, but when Sawyer's men track the scout there, they beat him up and throw him out of town. Finding Jonathan unconscious in the desert, Willie takes him to Chris for medical aid. Jonathan is attracted to Chris, and upon recovering, he joins forces with Willie and Warrick to stop the wedding. Crawling into the attic above the chapel, the three drop red ants on the bridegroom until he runs, scratching, out of the chapel. When Willie abducts the judge to prevent the wedding, Chris and Sawyer take the stage to Tucson, where they plan to marry. Along the trail, Jonathan, who has decided to travel to Washington to plead the case of the Indian, and the judge board the stage. With the judge on board, Chris and Sawyer decide to marry in the coach, but their nuptials are interrupted by an Indian attack. Recognizing his friend Jonathan, Chief Cochise takes the four passengers to his camp, where a meeting of the tribes is being held. To protect Chris, Jonathan tells the Indians that she is his wife. When Geronimo recognizes Sawyer as the man who has been stealing cattle from the Indians, he demands his life. After promising to return the cattle, Jonathan challenges Geronimo to a contest for Sawyer's life. When Jonathan wins the contest, the Indians set their four prisoners free, and while riding along a mountain trail, they see several cavalry officers riding the trail below. Sawyer calls to the men, but by the time the soldiers arrive, Jonathan has disappeared and Lieutenant Burke informs them that there is a bounty on the scout. Back in town, Chris, who has fallen in love with Jonathan, calls off her wedding. When a jealous Sawyer discovers Jonathan visiting Chris at the café, he calls the soldiers to arrest the scout. Soon after, Cochise visits Sawyer to demand the return of the cattle, but the agent reneges on his promise and takes Cochise prisoner instead. That night, Jonathan and his captors are camped along the trail when Chris, Willie, the judge and Warrick surprise his guards and free him. Determined to make Sawyer keep his word, Jonathan threatens to turn him over to the Indians unless he returns the cattle. As they are driving the herd toward the Indian camp, Jonathan sees war smoke signals and Sawyer admits to holding Cochise prisoner. The Indian war party is converging on the town just as Jonathan and Sawyer gallop in and free Cochise, halting the attack. After witnessing Jonathan's good deeds, the lieutenant lets him go free. Jonathan and Chris then marry and are bound for their honeymoon via stagecoach when Sawyer, in a hurry to leave the state, boards the coach. After knocking the intruder unconscious, Jonathan kisses his bride. *Duplicity. Indian agents. Indians of North America. Romantic rivalry. Scouts (Frontier). Ants. Arizona. Café owners. Cochise. Deserts. English in foreign countries. Escapes. Fistfights. Geronimo. Jailbreaks. Justices of the peace. Stagecoaches. United States. Army. Cavalry. Weddings.*

Note: According to a 1940 news item in *HR*, Robert Sisk was originally slated to produce this film, Bartlett Cormack was to have written the screenplay and Joel McCrea was to play the male lead. A Jul 1941 news item in *HR* notes that Dorothy Comingore was slated as the female lead, but illness forced her replacement by Lucille Ball. Another pre-production news item in *HR* adds that soundman Bailey Fesler was transferred from this film to *The Magnificent Ambersons* at the request of Orson Welles. According to the *HR* review, the film was shot on location in Arizona and in Santa Fe and Taos, NM, and employed Indians from the Taos, Santa Clara, Jemes, San Juan and Tesuque pueblos in New Mexico. Another news item in *HR* adds that actor Tom Tyler was borrowed from Republic to appear in this film.

Box 10 Jan 1942. *DV* 8 Jan 1942, p. 3. *FD* 8 Apr 1942, p. 7. *HR* 30 Apr 1940, p. 2. *HR* 31 Jul 1941, p. 7. *HR* 8 Sep 1941, p. 4. *HR* 22 Sep 1941, p. 13. *HR* 30 Oct 1941, p. 9. *HR* 14 Nov 1941, p. 8. *HR* 8 Jan 1942, p. 3. *MPHPD* 17 Jan 1942, p. 463. *NYT* 19 Mar 1942, p. 29. *Var* 14 Jan 1942, p. 8.

VAMPING VENUS (Irish Americans)

First National Pictures, Inc. *Dist* First National Pictures, Inc. 13 May **1928** [©First National Pictures, Inc.; 19 Apr 1928; LP25165]. Si; b&w. 7 reels, 6,021 ft.

Pres Richard A. Rowland. *Dir* Eddie Cline. *Adpt* Howard J. Green. *Story* Bernard McConville. *Titles* Ralph Spence. *Photog* Dev Jennings. *Film ed* Paul Weatherwax.

Cast: Charlie Murray (*Michael Cassidy/King Cassidy of Ireland*), Louise Fazenda (*Maggie Cassidy/Circe*), Thelma Todd (*Madame Vanezlos, the dancer/Venus*), Russ Powell (*Pete Papaglos/Bacchus*), Joe Bonomo (*Simonides, the strongman/Hercules*), Big Boy Williams (*Mars*), Spec O'Donnell (*Western Union boy/Mercury*), Fred O'Beck (*Vulcan*), Gustav von Seyffertitz (*Jupiter*), Gus Partos (*Shopkeeper*), Janet MacLeod (*Juno*), Yola D'Avril (*Stenographer*).

Comedy-drama. Irish American Michael Cassidy sneaks out one evening to join his buddies at their annual dinner at the Silver Spoon Night Club. There he is knocked unconscious by Simonides, strongman in a troupe of performers, who resents Cassidy's flirting with Madame Vanezlos, another member of the troupe. Cassidy dreams of himself as king of Ireland, cavorting in ancient Greece among the gods and goddesses: Venus, actually Madame Vanezlos; Circe, in real life his wife; and Hercules, in reality Simonides. In time, he becomes ruler of the country by introducing many marvels of modern machinery. Then a rebellion is started against Cassidy and his buzzers, telephones, tanks, and machine guns. In the midst of the battle, Cassidy sees Hercules abducting Venus, and rescues her with the aid of his troops. Cassidy regains consciousness and realizes it was all a dream. *Dreams. Greece–History. Irish. Irish Americans. Mythical characters. Strong men. Technology. Theatrical troupes.*

FD 11 Nov 1928. *Var* 27 Jun 1928, p. 34.

DER VANDERER YID *see* **THE WANDERING JEW**

THE VANISHING AMERICAN (Native Americans, Navajo)

Famous Players-Lasky Corp. *Dist* Paramount Pictures. 15 Feb **1926**; New York premiere: 15 Oct 1925 [©Famous Players-Lasky Corp.; 16 Feb 1926; LP22402]. Si; b&w. 10 reels, 9,916 ft.

Pres Adolph Zukor and Jesse L. Lasky. *Dir* George B. Seitz. *Scr* Ethel Doherty. *Adpt* Lucien Hubbard. *Photog* C. Edgar Schoenbaum and Harry Perry. *Tech adv* Louisa Wetherill.

Source: Based on the novel *The Vanishing American* by Zane Grey (New York, 1925).

Cast: Richard Dix (*Nophaie*), Lois Wilson (*Marion Warner*), Noah Beery (*Booker*), Malcolm McGregor (*Earl Ramsdale*), Nocki (*Indian boy*), Shannon Day (*Gekin Yashi*), Charles Crockett (*Amos Halliday*), Bert Woodruff (*Bart Wilson*), Bernard Siegel (*Do Etin*), Guy Oliver (*Kit Carson*), Joe Ryan (*Jay Lord*), Charles Stevens (*Shoie*), Bruce Gordon (*Rhur*), Richard Howard (*Glendon*), John Webb Dillon (*Naylor*).

Western. After a prologue unfolding the history of the Navajo in the West, the story is told of Nophaie, a strong, righteous Indian, who thrashes Booker, an evil Indian agent, for attempting to force his attentions on Marion Warner, the white schoolteacher with whom Nophaie is in love. Nophaie flees into the hills in order to escape Booker's vengeance and returns only to persuade his people to give over their horses to Earl Ramsdale, an Army procurement agent needing horses for the war. Nophaie enlists and saves Ramsdale's life during the fighting, learning then that Ramsdale is in love with Marion. After the war Nophaie returns to his people and finds that they are living in squalor. The Indians go on the warpath, and Nophaie rides to warn the whites. Nophaie and Booker die in the fighting, and Nophaie's only comfort is to die in the arms of Marion. *Indian agents. Indians of North America. Navajo Indians. Schoolteachers. United States. Army. Cavalry.*

Note: For information on the 1955 adaptation of Zane Grey's novel, see entry below.

FD 5 Oct 1925. *MPW* 24 Oct 1925. *NYT* 16 Oct 1925, p. 18.

THE VANISHING AMERICAN (Native Americans, Navajo, Apache)

Republic Pictures Corp. *Dist* Republic Pictures Corp. 17 Nov **1955** [©Republic Pictures Corp.; 16 Sep 1955; LP5868]. Sd (RCA Sound System); b&w; 1.66. 8,100 ft. 90 min. PCA cert no. 17589.

Pres Herbert J. Yates. *Assoc prod* Joe Kane. *Dir* Joe Kane. *Asst dir* A. J. Vitarelli. *Scr* Alan LeMay. *Photog* John L. Russell, Jr. *Spec eff* Howard Lydecker and Theodore Lydecker. *Art dir* Walter Keller. *Film*

ed Richard L. Van Enger. *Set dec* John McCarthy, Jr. *Mus* R. Dale Butts. *Sd* Melvin M. Metcalfe, Jr. and Howard Wilson. *Makeup supv* Bob Mark. *Optical eff* Consolidated Film Industries.

Source: Based on the novel *The Vanishing American* by Zane Grey (New York, 1925).

Cast: Scott Brady (*Blandy*), Audrey Totter (*Marian Warner*), Forrest Tucker (*Morgan*), Gene Lockhart (*Blucher*), Jim Davis (*Glendon*), John Dierkes (*Friel*), Gloria Castillo (*Yashi*), Julian Rivero (*Etenia*), Lee Van Cleef (*Jay Lord*), George Keymas (*Coshonta*), Charles Stevens (*Quah-Tain*), Jay Silverheels (*Beeteia*), James Millican (*Joe Walker*), Glenn Strange (*Beleanth*), Francis McDonald (*Stage driver*), Fred Graham (*Larkin*), Hank Worden (*Shoie*), Augie Gomez (*Old Folks*).

Western. [*Not viewed*]. High-spirited Marian Warner comes to New Mexico to claim the ranch left to her by her uncle and meets Blandy, a Navajo Indian and decorated veteran of the Spanish-American War. Blandy is bitter toward his own people for rejecting him because he was brought up by whites, and toward the whites for rejecting him when he came home from the war. After angrily telling Marian that the land she has inherited has belonged to the Navajos for seven hundred years, Blandy takes her to Morgan's trading post. Morgan and Blucher, a corrupt Indian agent, have been persecuting the Navajos and stealing their land, with the help of renegade Apaches led by Coshonta. Morgan is eager to acquire Marian's land and valuable water rights, and he tries unsuccessfully to pressure her into selling them to his accomplice, a rancher named Friel. At the trading post's guest house, Marian encounters Yashi, a young Navajo woman being held captive by Morgan. Yashi tells Marian about Morgan's treacherous deeds, including his practice of having Blucher deliver Navajo girls to his living quarters. Yashi's plight confirms Marian's suspicions about Morgan, and she helps the girl escape. In retaliation, Morgan sends his henchmen, Jay Lord and Glendon, to beat up the Navajo chief Etenia, Yashi's father. Marian finds Blandy and convinces him that she wants to align herself with his people in their fight against Morgan. She and Blandy raid Blucher's safe for incriminating evidence, which they send to U.S. Marshal Joe Walker via Etenia. The Apaches kill Etenia after he completes his mission, leading to a full-scale Navajo uprising. The marshal arrives and arrests Morgan and Blucher after Blandy persuades the Navajos to release them. In return, the marshal promises to advocate for fairer land rights for the Navajos. Blandy and Marian, who have fallen in love, plan their future together. *Apache Indians. Indians of North America–Reservations. Land rights. Navajo Indians. Battles. Escapes. Indian agents. Inheritance. New Mexico. Romance. Trading posts. Treachery. United States. Marshals. Uprisings. Veterans.*

Note: Before being published as a novel in 1925, Zane Grey's *The Vanishing American* was serialized in *Ladies Home Journal* (22 Nov 1922—23 Apr 1923). According to modern sources, the magazine version, with its interracial love story and negative portrayal of a Christian missionary, caused a public uproar. *Ladies Home Journal* received thousands of letters of protest, and Grey's publisher, Harper's, refused to release the book until he changed the ending. Zane complied, and in the novel version, the Navajo hero was shot to death at the end. *HR* production charts indicate that the crew was based in St. George, Utah. In 1925, George B. Seitz directed Richard Dix and Lois Wilson in Paramount Pictures' *The Vanishing American*, the first filmed version of Zane Grey's novel (see above). Modern sources report that, because Grey was writing novels faster than Harper's could publish them, Lucien Hubbard, adaptor of the 1925 film, drew on material from the prolific author's other works.

Exb 30 Nov 1955, pp. 4066-67. *Har* 26 Nov 1955, p. 190. *Box* 26 Nov 1955. *DV* 17 Nov 1955, p. 3. *FD* 23 Nov 1955, p. 10. *HR* 17 Nov 1955, p. 3. *MPD* 22 Nov 1955. *MPHPD* 26 Nov 1955, p. 681. *Var* 23 Nov 1955, p. 6.

THE VANISHING FRONTIER (Latino)

Larry Darmour Productions; Paramount Publix Corp. *Dist* Paramount Publix Corp. 29 Jul **1932** [©Paramount Publix Corp.; 28 Jul 1932; LP3174]. Sd (RCA Photophone Recording); b&w. 7 reels. 65 or 70 min. Passed by the National Board of Review. PCA cert no. 1732-R [29 Oct 1935].

Dir Philip E. Rosen. [*Wrt*] by Stuart Anthony. *Photog* James S. Brown.

Cast: JOHNNY MACK BROWN (*Kirby Tornell*), Evalyn Knapp (*Carol Winfield*), ZaSu Pitts (*Aunt Sylvia*), Raymond Hatton (*Hornet*), Ben Alexander (*Lucien Winfield*), J. Farrell Macdonald (*Waco*), Wallace MacDonald (*Captain Roger Kearney*), George Irving (*General Winfield*), Joyzelle (*Dolores*), "Deacon" McDaniels (*Whistlin' Six*).

Historical, Military, Romance, Drama. [*Print viewed*]. In California in 1850, a military government under governor General Winfield executes its laws by force against the Spanish people. One of them, Juan Valdez, loses his land when he refuses to take an oath of allegiance to the United States. Bandit Kirby Tornell leads a group of guerillas, who rob a coach carrying Winfield's men. In the town square, two of the robbers, Waco and Hornet, are sentenced to hang by Captain Roger Kearney. That night, while Kearney is en route to a masked ball in San Vicente, Kirby jumps him and steals his costume and arrives at the ball, which takes place in a mill that was once the Tornell home. At the dance, Kirby poses as himself, the bandit Tornell, and charms Winfield's daughter Carol, who calls him a "hillbilly Napoleon." In a back room, Kirby forces Winfield to sign an order releasing Waco and Hornet. Kearney then arrives and announces that the bandit Tornell is at the ball, but Kirby escapes and frees Waco and Hornet. Later, Kirby swears his love to Carol. Winfield and Kearney then receive word from Washington, D.C. that an investigator will be arriving in California to consider adjudging civil law. Carol and Kirby rendezvous and he assures her military rule will cease as soon as Washington knows about Winfield's atrocities. Their romance is complicated, however, when Carol's personal maid, Dolores, covers for her while she meets with Kirby, and Dolores' brother Juanito suspects Dolores of hiding her lover, Lucien, who is Carol's brother. When Lucien is later found dead, Kirby is accused, and Winfield orders his execution. Carol, believing Kirby killed her brother, agrees to help her father capture him by telling him she is meeting Kirby that night. When the lovers meet, Kirby is wounded. A court trial follows and testimony reveals that Lucien knew Kirby was having an affair with Carol. Kirby is sentenced to hang in twenty-four hours. Carol then learns that Juanito killed Lucien for impregnating Dolores and fled to Mexico. Carol is instrumental in helping Kirby escape from his prison boat. By morning, Winfield has received orders from the Secretary of War to end all military activities. The cavalry, unaware of the mandate, pursues Kirby, and Hornet is killed in the crossfire. A retreat is finally sounded and the guerillas are granted amnesty. The Winfield army leaves town, but Carol stays with Kirby. *Bandits. California–History–1846-1850. Latino. Military government. Revolutionaries. Romance.* Betrayal. Boats. Brothers and sisters. Escapes. Executions. False arrests. Gunshot wounds. Impersonation and imposture. Land rights. Masked balls. Pregnancy. San Vicente (CA). Stagecoach robberies. Trials. United States. Army. Cavalry.
FD 17 Sep 1932, p. 22. *MPH* 23 Jul 1932, p. 48. *Var* 20 Sep 1932, p. 15.

THE VANISHING VIRGINIAN (African Americans)
Metro-Goldwyn-Mayer Corp.; controlled by Loew's Inc.; A Frank Borzage Production. *Dist* Loew's Inc. Feb **1942**; World premiere in Lynchburg, VA: 23 Jan 1942; Prod: 2 Sep—mid-Oct 1941; addl scenes began early Nov 1941 [©Loew's Inc.; 2 Dec 1941; LP11403]. Sd (Western Electric Sound System); b&w. 10 reels, 8,707 ft. 95-97 min. Passed by the National Board of Review. PCA cert no. 7860.
Prod Edwin Knopf. *Dir* Frank Borzage. [*Asst dir* Lew Borzage]. *Scr* Jan Fortune. *Dir of photog* Charles Lawton. *Art dir* Cedric Gibbons. *Assoc* William Ferrari. *Film ed* James E. Newcom. *Set dec* Edwin B. Willis. *Gowns* Kalloch. *Men's cost* Gile Steele. *Mus score* David Snell. *Mus adpt* Earl Brent. *Mus dir* Lennie Hayton. *Spiritual arr* Jester Hairston. [*Addl mus* Franz Waxman]. *Rec dir* Douglas Shearer. *Makeup created by* Jack Dawn.
Song(s): "Steal Away," traditional Negro spiritual; "The World Was Made for You," music by Johann Strauss, adapted with English lyrics by Earl K. Brent and Minnaletha White; "Bill Bailey, Won't You Please Come Home," music and lyrics by Hughie Cannon; "Auld Lang Syne," music, Scottish traditional, lyrics by Robert Burns.
Source: Based on the book *The Vanishing Virginian* by Rebecca Yancey Williams (New York, 1940).
Cast: Frank Morgan (*Robert* [*"Cap'n Bob*] *Yancey*), Kathryn Grayson (*Rebecca Yancey*), Spring Byington (*Rosa Yancey*), Natalie Thompson (*Margaret Yancey*), Douglass Newland (*Jim Shirley*), Mark Daniels (*Jack Holden*), Elizabeth Patterson (*Grandma*), Juanita Quigley (*Caroline Yancey*), Scotty Beckett (*Joel Yancey*), Dickie Jones (*Robert Yancey, Jr.*), Leigh Whipper (*Uncle Josh* [*Preston*]), Louise Beavers (*Aunt Emmeline* [*Preston*]), J. M. Kerrigan (*John Phelps*), Harlan Briggs (*Mr. Rogard*), Katharine Alexander (*Marcia Marshall*), [Dolores Hurlic (*Sugar*)], [Marcella Moreland (*Baby*)], [Cleo Desmond (*Aunt Mandy Brown*)], [Barbara Bedford (*Mildred Simpson*)], [Dudley Dickerson (*Alexander*)], [Howard Hickman (*Dr.*

Edwards)], [Alfred Grant (*Jefferson Brown*)], [Arie Lee Branche (*Edith Brown*)], [Erville Alderson (*Judge Fred Stuart*)], [Edward Hearn, Hooper Atchley (*Jurymen*)], [Francis Ford (*Mountaineer*)], [William Forrest (*Wm. Harrison Jordon*)], [Matt Moore (*Chas. Inglestadt*)], [George Irving (*Roger Payson*)], [Clinton Rosemond (*Black minister*)], [Keith Copland, Charles Bates, Margaret Campbell, Anelle McCarthy, Dickie McCoy (*Grandchildren*)], [Lee Bennett (*Joe, as an adult*)], [Rita Quigley (*Caroline, as an adult*)], [Cliff Danielson (*Robert, as an adult*)], [Jester Hairston (*Mover*)], Rex Downing (*Newsboy*), [Helen Blizzard (*Robert, Sr.'s wife*)], [Myrtle Anderson (*Maid*)], [Lois Hodnutt, Clifford Holland (*Soloists in "Steal Away"*)], [Clarence Badger, Jr., Phyllis Cooke (*Soloists in "Bill Bailey, Won't You Please Come Home?"*)].
Domestic, Biography, Comedy-drama, with songs. [*Print viewed*]. In 1913, district attorney Robert "Cap'n Bob" Yancey, the patriarch of a large, eccentric Lynchburg, Virginia family, has definite ideas about what his independently-spirited children should be. While teenager Rebecca wants to be an writer, Bob wants her to be an artist, and while his eldest daughter Margaret wants to be a lawyer, Bob wants her to be a singer. Bob plans to run for his seventh term as district attorney, but his loving wife Rosa prefers that he does not. One day, when he hears from his trusted old friend and family servant, Uncle Josh Preston, that Jefferson Brown, a black man and the son of Aunt Mandy Brown, who had worked for Bob's father, is about to go on trial for murder, Joshua is incensed, and convinced that Jefferson "has no murder in his heart." Bob respects Uncle Joshua's feeling, but as the district attorney he must prosecute. When Aunt Mandy comes to see Bob and says that Jefferson struck the dead man in anger because he had been with his wife, Bob assures her that her son will get a fair trial and promises to find a good lawyer. Bob is so impressed by young criminal attorney Jim Shirley, a new tenant in his building, that he asks him to defend Jefferson. As he soon learns, Jim is the son of Marcia Marshall, a childhood friend of Bob's. Meanwhile, Margaret's beau, Jack Holden, who is about to become a Stanley Steamer salesman, proposes, but Margaret turns him down, still determined to be a lawyer. That evening, Bob brings Jim home for dinner, and although the children are rambunctious and everything seems to go wrong, Jim feels comfortable with the family and develops a crush on Margaret. Some time later, when Jefferson's trial begins, Bob mops up spilled ink with his handkerchief and a few moments later wipes his face, using the same cloth. Seeing Bob's black, ink-stained face, the entire courtroom erupts in laughter, except for Jim and the presiding judge, Fred Stuart, who are angry and accuse Bob of doing the stunt on purpose. When Bob refuses to apologize, the judge jails him for contempt of court. That night, while Bob is in jail, Jim and Margaret argue over the issue and Jim leaves. When Bob is released, he learns that Jefferson has been convicted, but only of manslaughter, which resulted in a five-year sentence. Bob then happily reveals that he intended to disrupt the court because he knew that Jefferson was facing a "hanging" jury and the stunt would soften them. Soon Becky, who stood up for Jim in his argument with Margaret, gets flowers from him, and Rosa wants the family to take its vacation at their plantation outside of Lynchburg. During a political meeting, Bob later learns that his chief rival, Rogard, openly opposes Prohibition but is secretly stockpiling liquor for the time when the county "goes dry." Bob, who truly is against Prohibition, thinks that a man like Rogard should not be in office and decides to run for an eighth term, against Rosa's wishes. She forgives him for breaking his promise, but is very worried that he is tempting fate and will be defeated. That same day, Uncle Joshua saves little Caroline Yancey's life when a bull attacks the younger children while they are foolishly playing in the pasture. When it looks as though Joshua is going to have a heart attack, Bob starts to take a stick to the children, but Joshua recovers. The next day, Jack arrives at the plantation and tells Margaret that he does not mind if she becomes a lawyer and still wants to marry her. When the rest of the family goes with Jack in his car, Bob stays behind and discovers Joshua dead. A few days later, he eulogizes his old friend in the black church, saying that God may have allowed Joshua to stay on earth so long because he was needed to save Caroline's life. Some time later, Jack and Margaret are about to marry and a now more mature Becky and Jim become interested in each other. Marcia, who returns to town as a celebrity because she is traveling the country championing women's suffrage, tells Rosa how jealous she has always been of her, and Rosa softens toward her, even

though a photograph of the two women appears in the newspaper and implies that Rosa, too, is a suffragette. After several more elections, in 1929, Bob is running for his eleventh term and Rosa is so worried that a defeat might devastate him that she writes all of their now-grown children to return home for a visit. Despite his popularity, Bob loses the election. The next day, the entire family, including Margaret, Jack and their family and Jim, Becky and her family, expects Bob to be depressed, but he is very cheerful because of his family and friends, and on his way to the office, he is touched when his supporters serenade him with "Auld Lang Syne." *African Americans. District attorneys. Family life. Lynchburg (VA). United States–History-Social life and customs. Aging. Automobiles, Antique. Bulls. Cigarettes. Clergy. Elections. Farms. Funerals. Grandparents. Handkerchiefs. Heart disease. Ink. Jealousy. Lawyers. Racial impersonation. Servants. Singers. Trials. Women's suffrage. Working women.*

Note: A working title of the film was *Mr. Yancey of Virginia*. The film opens with the following written prologue: "This is the story of a vanishing era when simple men so loved their country, their families and their friends that America became a better place in which to live. Such a man was 'Cap'n Bob' Yancey." Some reviews list a preview running time of 101 minutes. Rebecca Yancey Williams' book was based on the lives of her own family. According to the *Exh* review, the character of "Marcia Marshall" was loosely based on Nancy Astor, who made a newsworthy return to her native Virginia in the 1920s, after becoming the first woman member of the British House of Commons. This film marked the motion picture debut of actor Douglass Newland and also marked the first onscreen speaking part of choir director and actor Jester Hairston. Hairston is best known for his roles in the television series *Amos 'n Andy* in the 1950s and *Amen* in the 1980s.

Box 6 Dec 1941. *DV* 3 Dec 1941. *Exh* 10 Dec 1941. *FD* 3 Dec 1941, p. 6. *HR* 5 Sep 1941, p. 10. *HR* 17 Oct 1941, p. 16. *HR* 6 Nov 1941, p. 4. *HR* 7 Nov 1941, p. 2. *HR* 3 Dec 1941, p. 6. *HR* 18 Dec 1941, p. 1. *HR* 26 Jan 1942, p. 9. *MPD* 3 Dec 1941. *MPHPD* 6 Dec 1941, p. 394. *NYT* 28 May 1942, p. 13. *STR* 6 Dec 1941. *Var* 3 Dec 1941, p. 8.

VAQUERO see **RIDE, VAQUERO!**

VEILED ARISTOCRATS (African Americans)

Micheaux Pictures Corp.; A Micheaux Production. *Dist* Micheaux Pictures Corp. Feb **1932**. Sd; b&w. Length undetermined.

Dir Oscar Micheaux.

Source: Based on the novel *Veiled Aristocrats* by Charles W. Chesnutt (publication undetermined).

Cast: Laura Bowman, Lorenzo Tucker (*John Walden*).

African American, Drama, with songs. [*Viewed print incomplete*]. Twenty years after leaving home, John Walden returns to Fayettesville after having achieved his ambition to become a lawyer. He and his mother Molly, who is glad to be reunited with her son, discuss the problem of his sister Rena. A dark-skinned black man, Frank Fowler, has proposed marriage to her, while Molly had picked out a more light-skinned man for Rena. John also does not want the refined Rena, who has been reared not to associate with colored people, to marry any man who is black, as the family is light-skinned. As well, John has heard Frank say that he and Rena would marry immediately if it were not for Molly. Rena overhears her mother ask John to break up the match, and he promises to do so. At a nightclub, a woman indicates she will tell the story of the Waldens, and a waitress sings with piano accompaniment. *African Americans. Brothers and sisters. Motherhood. Racism. Gossip. Lawyers. Marriage. Nightclubs. Singers.*

Note: Although the length of this film has not been determined, it is believed to have been released as a feature. The credits and plot synopsis are based on a surviving trailer and fragments from two reels preserved in the Library of Congress. No song titles for this film have been found. According to a news item in *FD*, the picture was finished by the beginning of the year and was the first of six planned all-black cast films to be produced for the current season by the Micheaux Pictures Corp. A later news item in *FD* indicates that retakes on the movie were completed in Jan 1932. According to modern sources, the film was produced during the summer of 1931 at the home of actress Alice B. Russell's mother in Montclair, NJ, which was known as "The Homestead." Miss Russell was Micheaux's wife. Modern sources note that the cast included Barrington Guy, Lawrence Chenault and Walter Fleming, and that Micheaux wrote, directed and produced the film.

FD 8 Jan 1932, p. 2. *FD* 1 Feb 1932, p. 2.

LA VENDA EN LOS OJOS see **NADA MÁS QUE UNA MUJER**

VENGANZA EN MONTE CARLO see **DOS NOCHES**

VENGEANCE see **RANGE WARFARE**

VERBENA TRÁGICA (Spanish language)

Cantabria Films. *Dist* Columbia Pictures Corp. **1939**; Panama opening: 13 Dec 1938; Los Angeles opening: 7 Mar 1939; Prod: May-Jun 1938. Sd (Western Electric Sound System); b&w. 8 reels. 85 min. PCA cert no. 4425. Spanish language.

Producida [*Prod*] Jaime Del Amo. *Dirigida* [*Dir*] Charles Lamont. *Ayudante director* [*Asst dir*] Ralph Slosser. *Argumento original y adaptación cinematográfica* [*Orig story and scr*] Jean Bart. *Versión española* [*Spanish version*] Miguel de Zárraga. *Fotografía* [*Photog*] Arthur Martinelli. *Escenografía* [*Art dir*] Edward Jewell. *Compilación* [*Ed*] Guy V. Thayer, hijo. *Supervisión musical* [*Mus supv*] Lee Zahler. *Sonido* [*Sd*] William R. Fox. *Gerente de producción* [*Prod mgr*] Frederick A. Spencer.

Song(s): "El patrón" and "El coronel," words and music by Sergio de Karlo; "Gitanerías," words and music by Pilar Arcos.

Cast: FERNANDO SOLER (*Mateo Vargas*), Luana de Alcañiz (*Blanca* [*Vargas*]), Juan Torena (*Claudio*), Pilar Arcos (*Mamita* [*Vargas*]), Cecilia Callejo (*Lola* [*Vargas*]), y el niño [and the boy] Jorge Mari (*Pepito* [*Vargas*]), Carlos Villarías (*Manuel*), Romualdo Tirado (*Pérez*), Sergio de Karlo (*Luis*), Danton Ferrero (*Doctor*), Leonor Turich (*Tensita*), Lou Hicks (*Pat* [*the policeman*]), Carlos Ruffino (*Tomara*), Israel García (*José*), Fred Gonzalez (*Ventura*), Pedro Viñas (*Vendedor de globos* [*salesman*]).

Drama. [*Print viewed*]. In New York's Spanish neighborhood, residents happily prepare for a festival on the eve of Columbus Day. The friends and family of boxer Mateo Vargas, who have missed him over the past eight months, are eager for his return after serving a term in jail for striking a policeman. When Mateo receives a parole and arrives unexpectedly at his apartment, his mother, Mamita, little brother Pepito, and sister Lola prepare a celebration. His wife Blanca, however, faints when she sees her husband. After a worried Mateo summons a doctor, he learns that Blanca is a few months pregnant. Mateo is shocked at the news and, knowing that he cannot be the father, he becomes bitter and suspicious. He asks the doctor not to tell anyone about Blanca, then goes to a friend's tavern to drink. His manager, Manuel, wants Mateo to go back into training for a shot at the championship, but Mateo is too preoccupied with Blanca's infidelity to concentrate on his career. During Mateo's absence, Blanca had secretly been seeing Claudio, Lola's fiancé. Though they have tried to hide their relationship, Lola suspects that Claudio is more interested in Blanca than her, but when she tells her mother, Mamita slaps her. Later that day, Mateo confronts Blanca about her pregnancy and demands to know who is responsible. Though he tells Blanca that he feels partially responsible for her infidelity, she will not reveal the name of her lover. As the evening approaches, Mateo drinks more and becomes obsessed with discovering his wife's lover's identity. When he runs into Claudio on the street, he demands to know who has been seeing Blanca, but a frightened Claudio tries to tell him that his suspicions are groundless. Claudio then secretly goes to the Vargas apartment to see Blanca. Claudio convinces her to meet him in the basement later by riding down on the dumb waiter. When Claudio enters the basement, he is secretly observed by Lola, who sees him checking the ropes on the dumb waiter. Lola then runs upstairs and confronts Blanca. As they argue, a very drunk Mateo comes home with Lola and tells him that Claudio is Blanca's lover and that she was just about to leave on the dumb waiter. He runs to the dumb waiter shaft and yells for Claudio, but Claudio, concerned that Blanca has taken too long to meet him, goes up to the apartment, unaware that Mateo is there. When Claudio arrives, the two men have a violent argument. Fearful, Claudio moves to the fire escape, but is followed by Mateo. As the festival revelers dance on the street, they see the men on the fire escape just before Mateo strikes Claudio, causing him to fall to the pavement. Because Claudio dies in the fall, Pat, the neighborhood policeman is summoned. As Pat takes Mateo away, Blanca screams that she is responsible and still loves Mateo, but he will not listen. Just before he leaves the building, she tells him that she will always love him. Finally, when Mamita comes, she comforts Blanca, who says that she will spend the rest of her life repaying Mamita's kindness. *Boxers. Family relationships. Latino. Infidelity. Jealousy. Columbus Day. Drunkenness. Dumb-waiters. Engagements. Fire-escapes. Hotels. Imprisonment. Manslaughter. New York City. Police.*

Note: According to information in the file on the film in the MPAA/PCA Collection at the AMPAS Library, the English-language title of the film was *Block*

Party. The Hays Office issued a certificate to the film's producer after a warning that the subject of adultery should be given "proper treatment." Although there is a copyright statement in the film's opening, it is not listed among copyright records. Opening credits list the actor portraying Pepito as Jorge Mari, while the end credits list him as George Mari.

CM Nov 1938, p. 560. *HR* 6 Aug 1938, p. 3. *Imparcial Films* 5 Aug 1938. *NYT* 13 Mar 1939, p. 12.

LA VEUVE JOYEUSE (French language)

Metro-Goldwyn-Mayer Corp.; controlled by Loew's Inc.; An Ernst Lubitsch Production. *Dist* Loew's Inc. **1934**. Sd; b&w. 10 reels. 105 min. Passed by the National Board of Review. French language.

Mise en scène [Dir] Ernst Lubitsch. *Scénario de [Scr]* Ernest Vajda and Samson Raphaelson. *Version française de [French version by]* Marcel Achard. *Photographie de [Photog]* Oliver T. Marsh. *Décorateur [Art dir]* Cedric Gibbons. *Associé [Assoc]* Fredric Hope and Edwin B. Willis. *Montage de [Ed]* Adrienne Fazan. *Robes de Mlle. MacDonald dessinées par [Miss MacDonald's gowns designed by]* Adrian. *Costumes de [Ward]* Ali Hubert. *Adaptation musicale de [Mus adpt]* Herbert Stothart. *Lyrics de [Lyr]* André Hornez. *Choregraphie [Choreog]* Albertina Rasch. *Ingénieur du son [Sd eng]* Douglas Shearer.

Source: Based on the operetta *Die lustige Witwe* music by Franz Lehar, book and lyrics by Victor Leon and Leo Stein (Vienna, 28 Dec 1905):

Cast: MAURICE CHEVALIER (*Danilo*), JEANETTE MacDONALD (*Missia*), Danièle Parola (*La reine*), André Berley (*Le roi*), Fifi D'Orsay (*Marcelle*), Marcel Vallée (*L'ambassadeur*), Emile Dellys (*Zizipoff*), Georges Davis (*L'ordonnance*), Pauline Garon (*Loulou*), Jean Perry (*Le valet*), [Barbara Leonard (*Maid*)], [Akim Tamiroff (*Turk*)], [Georges Renavent (*Adamovitch*)], [Albert Petit (*Manager of Maxim's*)], [Jules Raucourt (*Prosecuting attorney*)], [Eugene Borden (*Defense attorney*)], [Georgette Rhodes, Anita Pike, Odette Duval (*Missia's maids*)], [Fred Cavens, Sam Ash, Harry Lamont (*Policemen*)], [André Cheron (*Presiding judge*)], [André Verrier (*Jailer*)], [Gene Gouldeni (*Nondescript priest*)], [August Tollaire (*Orthodox priest*)], [Jacques Lory (*Newsboy/Coatman*)], [Lee Tin (*Excited man*)], [George Nardelli, Constant Franke, Jacques Venaire, George Jackson, George Renault, Marcel Ventura (*Escorts*)], [Juliet Dika (*Wardrobe mistress*)], [Eugene Beday (*Doorman*)], [Carrie Daumery (*Animal woman*)], [Alice Ardell (*Kiki*)], [Max Barwyn, Georges De Gombert, Gino Corrado, Arthur de Ravenne (*Waiters*)], [Lya Lys (*Maxim's girl*)], [Adrienne d'Ambricourt (*Newspaper woman*)], [Rolfe Sedan], [Albert Pollet (*Head waiter*)], [Paul Ellis (*Dancer*)], [Fred Malatesta, George Colega (*Ambassadors*)].

Historical, Musical, Romance. [*Not viewed*]. [The following plot summary is based on the English-language version of this film, *The Merry Widow*; character names refer to that version. For further information regarding the English-language version, please see the note below and the entry for *The Merry Widow* in the *AFI Catalog of Feature Films, 1931-40*.] In 1885, in the tiny European kingdom of Marshovia, playboy Count Danilo, the captain of the royal guard, admires the veiled rich widow Sonia during a military parade and later slips into her gardens to woo her. Obeying a Marshovian edict that stipulates that widows must always wear veils in public, the surprised Sonia covers her face before Danilo sees her and, in spite of his begging, refuses to lift it. Sonia then firmly rejects Danilo's deft flirtations but, over the next few days, is filled with confused thoughts about him. Unable to deal with her emotions, Sonia declares her one-year Marshovian widowhood over and moves to Paris. Because Sonia owns fifty-two percent of every cow in Marshovia and therefore controls the economy, her departure alarms the king, Achmed II, who frantically confers with his wife, Queen Dolores, about possible local suitors for the widow. After Dolores vetoes all of his suggested suitors, Achmed catches the queen entertaining Danilo in her bedroom. As punishment for his philandering, Achmed orders Danilo to go to Paris and marry Sonia. Before reporting to the Marshovian embassy for further instructions, Danilo decides to visit Maxim's, a favorite cabaret where all of the can-can dancers know and adore him. As Danilo leaves his rooms, Sonia, his neighbor, sees him and, abandoning her horde of insincere suitors, follows him to Maxim's. There Danilo runs into the bumbling Ambassador Popoff, who relates his "top secret" plan of ensnaring the coveted widow during the next night's embassy ball. When Sonia arrives at Maxim's, she is mistaken for a cabaret "girl" and is engaged by the unsuspecting Danilo. Irritated by Danilo's casual romantic attitudes,

Sonia, who calls herself Fifi, flirts with various men in front of the count and laughs at his jealous indignation. In one of Maxim's private dining rooms, Sonia then drives Danilo to distraction by acting seductive and indifferent in turn. However, when Danilo confesses to her that he prefers cabaret girls because they never ask about "tomorrow," Sonia reveals that she is a "lady" and leaves in a wounded huff. Devastated by Sonia's exit, Danilo fails to show up at the embassy ball as expected and is found by Mishka, his orderly, in a drunken stupor at Maxim's. In his intoxicated state, Danilo reveals his diplomatic mission to the Maxim's women and is dragged to the ball under protest. After Popoff threatens to court-martial him if he refuses to woo the widow, the lovesick Danilo prepares to do his duty and meet Sonia. When Danilo discovers that Sonia and Fifi are one in the same, he is overjoyed but covers his feelings when she coolly rebuffs him. Eventually Danilo convinces Sonia of his sincere desire to give up his playboy ways and marry. Danilo's victory is short-lived, however, when Sonia overhears Popoff telling Danilo that, because the Marchovian newspapers are about to print a story exposing the marriage scheme, he must wed Sonia that night. Although Danilo refuses to participate further in the scheme and is put on trial for treason in Marchovia, Sonia continues to condemn him as a cold-blooded womanizer. Shortly before his execution is to take place, however, Sonia visits Danilo in jail, and while aware that Popoff is still conniving to bring them together, the couple finally gives in to love and embraces. Duty. Economics. Mythical lands. Playboys. Romance. Widows. Balls (Parties). Cabarets. Can-can (Dance). Courts-martial and courts of inquiry. Dancers. Diplomats. Drunkenness. Embassies. Flirtation. Infidelity. Jails. Jealousy. Mistaken identity. Nobility. Officers (Military). Parades. Paris (France). Royalty. Treason.

Note: The onscreen credits for this French version of the 1934 film *The Merry Widow*, which was directed by Ernst Lubitsch and starred Maurice Chevalier and Jeanette MacDonald, were taken from a studio cutting continuity. *La veuve joyeuse* was produced simultaneously with the English version ((see *AFI Catalog of Feature Films, 1931-40*; F3.2839). According to a 19 Jun 1934 *Var* news item, four versions of the film were being shot simultaneously by director Ernst Lubitsch for American, French, English and Belgian markets. The article states that while only two languages, French and English, were being used, certain scenes in the picture were being "emphasized for the English speaking audiences and others played down for foreign consumption." A one-reel version of Lehar's operetta, starring Alma Rubens, was filmed in 1912 by Reliance-Majestic. The 1925 von Stroheim version featured Mae Murray and John Gilbert (see *AFI Catalog of Feature Films, 1921-30*; F2.3568). In 1952, Curtis Bernhardt directed Lana Turner, Fernando Lamas and Una Merkel, playing the part of Sonia's companion, in an M-G-M Technicolor remake of the operetta.

Var 19 Jun 1934, p. 2.

VI TVÅ *see* **DOÑA MENTIRAS**

VIAJE DE PLACER *see* **NO DEJES LA PUERTA ABIERTA**

VICTIMS OF PERSECUTION (Jewish Americans, African Americans)

Bud Pollard Productions, Inc.; William Goldberg Productions. *Dist* Bud Pollard Productions, Inc. 16 Jun **1933**; *Prod*: in Grantwood, N.J.. Sd; b&w. 6 reels, 5,522 ft. 60 min.

Pres William Goldberg. *Dir* Bud Pollard. *Photog* Frank Zucker and Don Malkames.

Source: Based on the play *Victims of Persecution* by David Leonard (production undetermined).

Cast: Mitchell Harris (*Judge Aaron Margolies*), Betty Hamilton (*Ruth Margolies*), Judah Bleich (*Judah Rosenbach*), Shirling Oliver (*Frederick Morgenstern*), John Willard (*John McLean Carter*), Anna Lowenwirth (*Sarah*), Dan Michaels (*Henry*), Charles Adler (*Doctor*), David Leonard (*Herschel*).

Social, Drama. [*Not viewed*]. Judge Aaron Margolies of New York prepares a speech for a rally in which Jews and Gentiles plan to show solidarity to halt intolerance and religious persecution, which is engulfing Europe, from spreading in the United States. Aaron's daughter Ruth and one of her suitors, John Carter, interrupt Aaron and his secretary Herschel, who is secretly fond of Ruth, with the news that John's father George, the state chairman of a major political party, is going to nominate Aaron to run for governor. Just then, Aaron receives a radiogram from his eighty-two-year-old father-in-law, Judah Rosenbach, stating that he is coming for a visit from the Holy Land, where he went to live ten years earlier after his wife died. Frederick Morgenstern, a wealthy backer of the march, arrives and when he gets Ruth alone, proposes. Ruth is miffed when he says that he plans to contribute to her father's campaign because of his love for her.

Sometime after the rally, Aaron and Herschel prepare for a controversial case concerning a black man, Peter Johnson, who, Aaron feels, has been wrongly convicted of murder by a lower court. George arrives to speak with Aaron, and a few bigots, who think he is Aaron, harass him as he enters the house. Aaron's black servant Henry shows Herschel a note that was stuck by the kitchen door with a knife, which reads: "Take warning—Don't play God to the niggers—If he don't hang, you will." Unaware of the note, George warns Aaron that he cannot put through the nomination unless Aaron gives up the Johnson case. Later, Aaron discusses the situation with Judah and delineates his dilemma: if he withdraws from the case, Johnson will probably be sent to death; yet if he persists, his action will arouse increased persecution against his own people, the Jews. A gunshot from a passing car nearly hits Judah. Early in the morning, Judah hears ticking in a bag of groceries that has just been delivered. He immerses it in water, and as a cloud of smoke encircles his head, his eyes are damaged. When it is examined, the bag is found to have contained enough nitroglycerine to blow up the house. George, John, Frederick and Ruth argue with Aaron to give up the case, but Judah takes Aaron's side when Aaron says that justice is the most precious of God's gifts to mankind. To illustrate his reasoning, Judah tells the following story: In the small European principality of Bedenitz, Prince Karl refused to sign a document, which his anti-Semitic chancellor had drawn up, to drive the Jews into exile. Karl warned Mendel, formerly the royal collector of taxes among the Jews, of the chancellor's intention, and Mendel's daughter Leah offered herself to him to save her people. Mendel, when he learned of Leah's actions, was greatly saddened because he felt that she was lost to God. Karl, who fell in love with Leah, destroyed the chancellor's edict, and the chancellor rallied soldiers for a march on the palace. As the battle raged, Karl abdicated and fled with Leah. They climbed to a high spot, and Leah revealed to him her plot. Karl forgave her, and they died together. Mendel, although he lost everything, still praised God. At the completion of the story, Judah states that Leah's sacrifice was in vain. Now, Ruth, George, John and Frederick all tell Aaron that they will support him no matter what he decides. When Aaron and Judah are alone, Judah speaks of a vision of a new day of peace and brotherhood, with no more hatred, envy or ignorance, and Aaron asserts that only through righteousness and justice will they reach that day. *Antisemitism. Fathers and daughters. Fathers-in-law. Jews. Judges. Racism. Abdication. African Americans. Attempted murder. Bombs. Cooks. Fathers and sons. Imaginary lands. Millionaires. Mobs. New York City. Political candidates. Princes. Proposals (Marital). Romantic rivalry. Secretaries. Self-sacrifice. Sieges. Soldiers. Suicide. Threats. Unrequited love.*

Note: The plot summary was based on a dialogue continuity in NYSA records. According to reviews and news items, this film was planned as the first of a series of "Jewish dramas done entirely in English," to be produced by William Goldberg Productions and directed by Bud Pollard. No information has been located concerning other films of the series. The story that the character "Judah" relates near the end of the film is two reels in length, according to the dialogue continuity. *Var* states that this part is a "clip from some old picture." No information has been located concerning the identity of the earlier film. The film also appears, from the dialogue continuity, to have contained stock footage of a protest rally and of World War I.

Exb 25 Jun 1933, p. 4, 15. *FD* 14 Jun 1933, p. 6. *FD* 17 Jun 1933, p. 4. *MPD* 15 Jun 1933, p. 2. *MPD* 17 Jun 1933, p. 4. *MPH* 24 Jun 1933, p. 43. *NYT* 17 Jun 1933, p. 16. *Var* 20 Jun 1933, p. 11.

THE VICTOR (English Americans)
Universal Pictures Corp. 22 Jul **1923** [©Universal Pictures Corp.; 5 Jul 1923; LP19183]. Si; b&w. 5 reels, 4,880 ft.
Dir Edward Laemmle. *Scen* E. Richard Schayer. *Photog* Clyde De Vinna.
Source: Based on the short story "Two Bells for Pegasus" by Gerald Beaumont in *Redbook Magazine* (Feb 1922).
Cast: Herbert Rawlinson (*Hon. Cecil Fitzhugh Waring*), Dorothy Manners (*Teddy Walters*), Frank Currier (*Lord Waring*), Otis Harlan (*J. P. Jones*), Esther Ralston (*Chiquita Jones*), Eddie Gribbon (*Porky Schaup*), Tom McGuire (*Jacky Williams*).
Romantic comedy. The Honorable Fitzhugh Waring, eldest son of Lord Waring, comes to America on his father's advice to marry Chiquita Jones, the daughter of J. P. Jones, a rich chewing gum king, and save the family estate. Almost starving because he is too proud to carry out his original plan, Fitzhugh meets Teddy, a poor but pretty actress, who shares her meal of doughnuts with him. Fitzhugh becomes a prizefighter to earn some money and is so successful that

he wins the British middleweight crown. The money saves Lord Waring's finances, and Fitzhugh gets the old man's approval of his marriage to Teddy. *Actors and actresses. Boxers. Chewing gum. English. Finance–Personal.*

FD 22 Jul 1923. *MPW* 28 Jul 1923. *Var* 26 Jul 1923, p. 29.

VICTOR HERBERT'S NAUGHTY MARIETTA *see* **NAUGHTY MARIETTA**

LA VIDA BOHEMIA (Spanish language)
Cantabria Films. *Dist* Columbia Pictures Corp. **1938**; Panama opening: 16 Feb 1938; San Juan, Puerto Rico opening: 12 Aug 1938; New York opening: Feb 1939; Prod: began 17 Aug 1937 at Hollywood Studios. Sd (R.C.A.); b&w. 10 reels. 89 min. Spanish language.
Producida por [*Prod*] Jaime del Amo. *Dirigida por* [*Dir*] Josef Berne. *Ayudante del director* [*Asst dir*] Miguel de Zárraga, Jr. *Adaptación cinematográfica* [*Scr*] José López Rubio. *Fotógrafo* [*Photog*] John Alton. *Director artístico* [*Art dir*] F. Paul Sylos. *Compilador* [*Ed*] Irving Applebaum. *Vestuario especial para Rosita Díaz y Gilbert Roland, diseñado por* [*Wardrobe specially designed for Rosita Díaz and Gilbert. Roland*] Martha Austin, *Vestuario especial para Rosita Díaz y Gilbert Roland, diseñado por* [*Wardrobe specially designed for Rosita Díaz and Gilbert. Roland*] Jack Mosser. *Música original de* [*Orig mus*] Alexander Borisoff. *Ingeniero de sonido* [*Sd eng*] George Ellis. *Maquillaje por* [*Makeup*] Max Factor. *Gerente de producción* [*Prod mgr*] Bartlett Carré. [*Research* Stanley Blyth].
Source: Based on the novel *Scènes de la vie de bohème* by Henri Murger (Paris, 1849).
Cast: ROSITA DÍAZ (*Mimi*), Gilbert Roland (*Rodolfo*), Miguel Ligero (*Schaunard*), José Crespo (*Vizconde*), Romualdo Tirado (*Colline*), Juan Torena (*Marcelo*), Blanca Poza (*Eufemia*), Anita Campillo (*Musette*), Tina Menard (*Denise*), Carlos Villarías (*M. Bernard*), José Peña Pepet (*Durand*).
Drama. [*Print viewed*]. Mimi, a poor seamstress, comes to live in the same lodgings as Rodolfo, a struggling writer. Rodolfo is intrigued by Mimi's beauty and introduces her to his Bohemian friends. Later, when Rodolfo writes for a periodical without realizing that it is no longer publishing, Mimi fakes delivery of the articles and substitutes her earnings for the fee. A viscount, in love with Mimi, is persuaded by her to commission Rodolfo to write a play. However, although he is now in love with her, Rodolfo believes that Mimi, his inspiration, is deceiving him with the viscount and throws her out. Later, Mimi takes work making artificial flowers but becomes ill. One of Rodolfo's friends encounters her and invites her back to the lodgings for a meal. Although Rodolfo, now successful, no longer lives there, she returns for the dinner and reunites with Mimi. However, she is now very ill and is moved to a hospital where she dies with Rodolfo at her side. *Bohemians and bohemianism. Jealousy. Playwrights. Poverty. Romance. Seamstresses. Death and dying. Deception. Eviction. False accusations. Nobility. Self-sacrifice. Theatrical producers.*

Note: This film was released as *Tragedias de la vida bohemia* in Santiago, Chile. According to *FD* and *HR* news items beginning in May 1937, Jaime del Amo and Josef Berne, co-directors of Cantabria Productions, signed Rosita Díaz to star in a series of twelve Spanish films to be made in Hollywood. The company's first film was to be *El camino de Hollywood*; however, in Jun 1937, the company shelved plans for that film because of story difficulties and substituted *La vida bohemia*. Cantabria produced only one other film, the 1938 *Verbena trágica* (see above), which did not star Díaz. A *HR* news item stated that actor Miguel Ligero was known as "the Charlie Chaplin of Spain" and that he was married to Blanca Poza, who was also in the cast. The film, in a revised edition, was approved for exhibition by the New York State censors at a length of 7,647 feet. *NYT*, in reviewing the Feb 1939 New York screening, remarked, "Thanks to the high moral standards obtaining in Hollywood's film factories, Mimi, the unfortunate heroine of *La Boheme*, has been made an 'honest woman' at last." The review noted the insertion of two or three English titles between scenes, "assuring the spectators that Rodolfo and Mimi were married right away and that, when tempted later, she was a guest of the handsome Viscount for only 12 hours and that her love for her husband prevented her from 'falling.'" Among the many film adaptations of Henri Murger's novel or of the 1896 opera *La Boheme* by Giacomo Puccini, which was inspired by the novel, are the following: the 1916 Paragon Film *La Vie de Boheme*, directed by Albert Capellani and starring Alice Brady and Paul Capellani (see *AFI Catalog of Feature Films, 1911-20*; F1.4743); the 1926 M-G-M film *La Boheme*, directed by King Vidor and starring Lillian Gish and John Gilbert (see *AFI Catalog of Feature Films, 1921-30*; F2.0508); the 1935 British production *Mimi*, directed by Paul Stein and starring Douglas Fairbanks, Jr. and Gertrude Lawrence; the 1945 French film *La Vie de Boheme*, directed by Marcel L'Herbier and starring Louis Jordan; and the 1965 Italian-French opera film *La Boheme*, directed by Franco Zeffirelli.

FD 6 May 1937, p. 6. *FD* 4 Aug 1937, p. 9. *HR* 15 May 1937, p. 2. *HR* 18 Jun 1937, p. 19. *HR* 10 Aug 1937, p. 12, 13. *HR* 17 Aug 1937, p. 17. *NYT* 6 Feb 1939, p. 8.

THE VIEW FROM POMPEY'S HEAD (African Americans)

Twentieth Century-Fox Film Corp. *Dist* Twentieth Century-Fox Film Corp. Nov **1955**; New York opening: 4 Nov 1955; *Prod*: 6 Jun—early Jul 1955; addl scenes and retakes late Aug 1955 [©Twentieth Century-Fox Film Corp.; 4 Nov 1955; LP5715]. Sd (Western Electric Recording); col (De Luxe); CinemaScope; Lenses by Bausch & Lomb. 11 reels, 8,718 ft. 97 min. PCA cert no. 17585.

[*Exec prod* Darryl F. Zanuck]. *Prod* Philip Dunne. *Dir* Philip Dunne. *Asst dir* Eli Dunn. *Wrt for the screen by* Philip Dunne. *Dir of photog* Joe MacDonald. *Spec photog eff* Ray Kellogg. *Color consultant* Leonard Doss. *Art dir* Lyle R. Wheeler and Leland Fuller. *Film ed* Robert Simpson. *Set dec* Walter M. Scott and Paul S. Fox. [*Prop dir* Walter Scott]. [*Props* Duke Abrahams]. *Ward dir* Charles LeMaire. [*Miss Wynter's dresser* Kay Nelson]. *Mus* Elmer Bernstein. *Cond* Lionel Newman. *Orch* Fred Steiner. *Sd* E. Clayton Ward and Harry M. Leonard. *Makeup* Ben Nye. *Hair styling* Helen Turpin. [*Tech adv* Marguerite Brown]. [*Painter of portrait* Emil Kosa].

Source: Based on the novel *The View from Pompey's Head* by Hamilton Basso (New York, 1954).

Cast: Richard Egan [(*Anson "Sonny" Page*)], Dana Wynter [(*Dinah Blackford Higgins*)], Cameron Mitchell [(*Mickey Higgins*)], Sidney Blackmer [(*Garvin Wales*)], Marjorie Rambeau [(*Lucy Wales*)], Dorothy Patrick Davis [(*Meg Page*)], Rosemarie Bowe [(*Kit Robbins Garrick*)], Jerry Paris [(*Ian Garrick*)], Ruby Goodwin [(*Esther*)], [Pamela Stufflebeam (*Julia Higgins*)], [Evelyn Rudie (*Cecily Higgins*)], [Howard Wendell (*John Duncan*)], [Dayton Lummis (*Charles Barlowe*)], [Bess Flowers (*Miss Mabry*)], [Cheryl Calloway (*Debbie Page*)], [Charles Herbert (*Pat Page*)], [De Forest Kelley (*Hotel clerk*)], [Florence Mitchel (*Garrick's secretary*)], [Robert Johnson (*Bellhop*)], [Anna Mabry (*Maid*)], [Wilma Jacobs (*Betty Jo Ann*)], [Bill Walker (*Pullman porter*)], [Frances Driver (*Servant*)], [Jack Mather (*Policeman*)], [Charles Watts (*Police sergeant*)], [Wade Dumas (*Groom*)], [Tom Wilson (*Trainman*)], [Lesley Harrison (*Miss Harmon*)], [Charles Andrews (*Manservant*)], [Otis Greene (*Hotel servant*)], [George Chester (*Hotel waiter*)], [Kenneth Gibson (*Guest at party*)], [Jim Butler (*Cleon Pyle*)].

Drama. [*Print viewed*]. The partners of a New York law firm are puzzled by a lawsuit that has been filed against their client, a publishing company once headed by the now-deceased Phillip Greene. The lawsuit, brought by Lucy Wales, the wife of famous Southern writer Garvin Wales, contends that Greene, Garvin's editor, withdrew thousands of dollars from the author's account and gave the money to a woman named Anna Jones. Remembering Greene as an honest man who took Wales "from the gutter," and introduced him to a life of wealth and fame, lawyer Anson Page decides to visit Pompey's Head, a Southern town situated close to the author's island estate. As his wife Meg packs his bags, Anson reminisces about his own youth in Pompey's Head, especially the many days he spent at Mulberry, a fine old house belonging to the family of his friend, Dinah Blackford. Just before he left Pompey's Head for a New York law career ten years earlier, Anson had realized that Dinah, whom he had always treated as a kid sister, was truly in love with him. The Blackford family, having lost its money, had been forced to leave Mulberry, but as young Mickey Higgins, a poor "kid from the Channel," packed up the truck for the family, Dinah had sworn that she would get the house back. As he checks into the gracious old Marlborough Hotel, Anson notes that the town, once a thriving seaport, has not changed. Anson, known as "Sonny" by his childhood friends, visits his old chum, Ian Garrick, now a local lawyer. He then drives out to the Wales's beachfront estate, but the entrance to the property is locked. Back at the hotel, Anson is surprised by a visit from Dinah, who promises to arrange a meeting between him and Lucy. Dinah drives Anson to Mulberry, where she now lives with her children and husband, Mickey. The owner of a successful company, Mickey had bought and renovated the property to please Dinah. Lucy, who is waiting in the sitting room, explains that she has filed the lawsuit for her husband, a blind man who will never write again. After Lucy leaves, Mickey asks Anson to represent his new company, Consolidated Enterprises, but Anson stiffly refuses the offer. Later, Anson and Dinah dance together at a party in his honor, and on the terrace, they admit they still care for each other. Mickey suspects their mutual affection and drunkenly accuses Anson's grandfather of

having been a carpetbagger. Anson leaves, whereupon Mickey bursts into Dinah's room and forces himself on her. The next day, Lucy complains that her husband's writings are "sordid and disgraceful," and that his friendship with Greene was to blame. Anson suspects that Garvin secretly asked Greene to pass money to Anna Jones and that it is Lucy, not Garvin, who is pressing the suit. When Anson declares that if Garvin formally denies his suspicions, Anson will give Lucy a large check. Lucy promises that Garvin will make the statement on the following day. That afternoon, while Anson and Dinah walk on the beach, Dinah explains that she married Mickey purely in order to regain Mulberry, and he married her for the respect accompanying her family name. Anson kisses Dinah repeatedly but wonders aloud whether their love should cause the breakup of both of their families. After discovering that Anna Jones lived in an all-black town, Anson questions Garvin, who is sitting by the beach behind his home. Unaware that Lucy is listening from behind a tree, Garvin reluctantly admits that Anna, a light-skinned black woman who is now dead, was his mother. Lucy, whose Devereaux family was one of the most important in Pompey's Head, never knew about her husband's background: Garvin's father, a white sharecropper from Alabama and a brute, reared him after his mother dropped him "in a corn patch" and moved to Pompey's Head. Garvin won fame as a writer and then returned to the South, where Anna threatened to reveal their relationship to him unless he "paid her off." Greene quietly made the payments for Garvin to prevent the world from learning that he was "not only trash, but black trash." Astounded, Anson assures Garvin that regardless of his parentage, he has given the world great writing. He then gives Garvin the check and leaves, catching sight of the horrified Lucy as he walks away. Later, Lucy returns the check, telling Anson that Garvin has explained everything: Because Garvin came from a family of wealthy landowners, he was too ashamed to tell her that he gave money to their "old colored maid." Anson tells Dinah that Lucy, whose view of life simply precludes the truth, will probably come to believe this story. My father, he adds, called it "the view from Pompey's Head." Dinah plans to leave Mickey for Anson, but Mickey points out that Dinah will never be able to give up Mulberry. Dinah admits that she, like Lucy, is trying to "hold onto something," and that Anson still loves his wife. At the train station, Dinah tearfully kisses Anson goodbye. *Class distinction. Lawyers. Miscegenation. Racism. Small town life. United States–South. African Americans. African Americans–Mixed blood. Authors. Blackmail. Blindness. Childhood sweethearts. Embezzlement. Family honor. Infidelity. Lawsuits. Mansions. Marriage. New York City. Recluses. Southern belles. Upper classes.*

Note: According to materials contained in Twentieth Century-Fox Records of the Legal Department and Produced Scripts Collection at the UCLA Arts—Special Collections Library, Fox paid $75,000 for the rights to Hamilton Basso's novel. The studio originally wanted Gregory Peck to play "Anson;" Jean Simmons, Maggie McNamara or June Allyson to portray "Dinah;" Basil Ruysdael to play "Garvin;" and Eva LeGalliene or Ethel Barrymore to portray "Lucy," according to materials in the Fox files. An Aug 1954 *HR* news item stated that Julian Blaustein was slated to produce this film. Although publicity materials contained in the AMPAS Library files note that silent film stars Cleo Ridgely, Dorothy Phillips, Lulu Betz, Helen Foster and Anne Cornwall appeared in this film and Maria Cimarusti played "Dinah" and "Mickey's" sixteen-month old child, their participation in the released film has not been confirmed. According to publicity materials, locations were filmed around Brunswick and Savannah, GA. Brunswick's Ogelthorpe Hotel served as the Marlborough Hotel and the 18th-century plantation Wormsloe provided the exterior of "Mulberry." The beach scenes were shot at Jekyll Island, Sea Island and St. Simmons Island.

According to materials contained in the film's MPAA/PCA Files at the AMPAS Library, approval of the script was initially refused because of its inclusion of adultery. To satisfy the PCA, the adulterous relationship between "Anson" and "Dinah" was changed to a love affair that stops just short of infidelity. The *MPHPD* review noted, "As an attack on present-day systems of caste—among the whites themselves as well as for the Negro—this picture treads but lightly on Southern toes. It is more of a gentle reprimand than a vigorous assault....This placement of emphasis is all to the good, since it is what the paying customers prefer." This picture marked the American screen debut of English actress Dana Wynter and the first time that Dorothy Patrick was billed as Dorothy Patrick Davis.

Box 29 Oct 1955. *DV* 26 Oct 1955, p. 3. *Exh* 2 Nov 1955, p. 4055. *FD* 26 Oct 1955, p. 5. *Har* 29 Oct 1955, p. 175. *HR* 8 Nov 1954. *HR* 8 Jul 1955, p. 12. *HR* 26 Oct 1955, p. 3. *MPHPD* 29 Oct 1955, p. 649. *NYT* 5 Nov 1955, p. 22. *Var* 26 Oct 1955, p. 6.

VIGILANTES OF BOOMTOWN (Native Americans)

Republic Pictures Corp. *Dist* Republic Pictures Corp. 15 Feb **1947**; *Prod*: early May—mid-May 1946 [©Republic Pictures Corp.; 22 Jan 1947; LP870]. Sd (RCA Sound System); b&w. 56 min. Passed by the National Board of Review. PCA cert no. 11767.

Series: Red Ryder.

Assoc prod Sidney Picker. *Dir* R. G. Springsteen. [*Asst dir* Ed Stein]. *Orig scr* Earle Snell. *Photog* Alfred Keller. *Art dir* Fred A. Ritter. *Film ed* Wm. P. Thompson. *Set dec* John McCarthy, Jr. and Earl Wooden. *Mus dir* Mort Glickman. *Sd* Fred Stahl. *Makeup* Bob Mark.

Source: Based on the comic strip "Red Ryder" by Fred Harman (1938—1964), by special arrangement with Stephen Slesinger.

Cast: ALLAN LANE (*Red Ryder*), Bobby Blake [(*Little Beaver*)], Martha Wentworth [(*The Duchess*)], Roscoe Karns [(*Billy Delaney*)], Roy Barcroft [(*McKean*)], Peggy Stewart [(*Molly McVey*)], George Turner [(*James John "Gentleman" Corbett, also known as "Jim McVey"*)], Eddie Lou Simms [(*Sparring partner*)], George Chesebro [(*Dink*)], Bobby Barber [(*Sparring partner*)], George Lloyd [(*Thug*)], Ted Adams [(*Sheriff*)], John Dehner [(*Bob Fitzsimmons*)], Earle Hodgins [(*Governor*)], [Harlan Briggs (*Judge, Seth*)], [Budd Buster (*Goff*)], [Jack O'Shea (*Referee*)].

Western. [*Print viewed*]. In 1897, after prizefighting is legalized by the Nevada legislature, the governor of Carson City announces that he will support a boxing match scheduled between fighters James John "Gentleman" Corbett and Bob Fitzsimmons. Corbett, who now goes by the name Jim McVey, is a rancher and father of a grown daughter named Molly. Along with her henchmen, Curly and Jake, Molly criticizes the governor for his stance because she does not want her father to return to boxing. She then sends her men to stop the fight. Meanwhile, Jim talks with a group of men preparing a fighter to challenge Sullivan, the world champion. At the hotel, Molly learns that Jim has gone to see his old boxing manager, Billy Delany. The next morning at the training camp, Red sees Fitzsimmons arguing with Jim as reporters look on and mistakes the fracas for a sincere fight. When he attempts to stop them, they explain that they hoping to create some hype for the press. When Fitzsimmons solicits outlaws to come to the under-policed city, one man, McKean, joins up because he wants to even the score with Red. While Jim continues his training, Billy meets secretly with McKean and his men to plan their strategy. Later, Red and Jim spar in the ring, when the lights suddenly go out. Lurking outside, McKean fires at Red through the window. Mistaking McKean for one of Molly's henchmen, Red goes to the judge, Seth, who sets bail for Molly's men at $10,000. When Little Beaver reports that he has seen McKean and his men rustling cattle nearby, Red and Jim go to look for them, and Little Beaver follows. Red recovers the herd, but the rustlers chase Jim and Little Beaver into a cabin and surround them. The sheriff shows Red a picture of McKean, and he recognizes him as an outlaw he has arrested before. They announce their plan to ship the gambling money out in hay wagons, but fill the bags with iron washers instead of gold. Meanwhile, Molly's men kidnap Jim and plan to hold him at their mine until the fight has been canceled. In order to assure a good night's sleep for Jim before his fight the next morning, Red suggests that Jim take the bed inside the cabin, while he sleeps in the bunkhouse. That night, when Molly's men break in to kidnap Jim, they take Red by mistake. The next morning, Molly sees Jim warming up for the fight, and realizes that her men have kidnapped Red instead of Jim. Dink, who had been chosen to load the wagon with washers, tells McKean and the gang when the real gold transport will take place. Molly sets Red free so that he can stop the outlaws from getting away with the $25,000 in gold. McKean and his men attack the wagon, shoot Dink and get away with the money. Later, after Jim has zost the championship, Billy reminds him that there will be another fight soon. *Boxing. James J. Corbett. Fathers and daughters. Gambling. Outlaws. Retirement. Rustlers. Abduction. Aunts. Camps. Carriages and carts. Carson City (NV). Deputies. Bob Fitzsimmons. Gambling. Gold mines. Governors. Hideouts. Judges. Lassoes. Law (Concept). Nephews. Ranchers. Sheriffs.*

Note: This film was very loosely based on the life of prizefighter James John "Gentleman Jim" Corbett. Corbett won the world heavyweight championship in 1892 and lost it to Bob Fitzsimmons in 1897. For more information about Corbett's life, please see the note to *Gentleman Jim* above. Modern sources include Tom Steele, Pascale Perry, Herman Nolan, Herman Hack and Harlan Briggs in the cast. For additional information on the "Red Ryder" series, please consult the Series Index and see the entry above for *Tucson Raiders*.

AmCin Sep 1946, p. 332. *Box* 8 Mar 1947. *DV* 10 Feb 1947. *FD* 18 Mar 1947, p. 10. *HR* 10 May 1946, p. 11. *HR* 10 Feb 1947, p. 3. *Var* 12 Feb 1947, p. 22.

VIGILANTES OF DODGE CITY (Native Americans)

Republic Pictures Corp. *Dist* Republic Pictures Corp. 15 Nov **1944**; Los Angeles opening: 26 Oct 1944; Prod: early Jul—mid-Jul 1944 [©Republic Pictures Corp.; 17 Oct 1944; LP13000]. Sd (RCA Sound System); b&w. 6 reels, 4,986 ft. 54-55 min. Passed by the National Board of Review. PCA cert no. 10316.

Series: Red Ryder.

[*Exec prod* William J. O'Sullivan]. *Assoc prod* Stephen Auer. *Dir* Wallace Grissell. *2d unit dir* Yakima Canutt. [*Asst dir* John Grubbs]. *Scr* Norman S. Hall and Anthony Coldewey. *Orig story* Norman S. Hall. *Photog* William Bradford. [*2d cam* Edward P. Fitzgerald]. [*Transparency projection shots* Gordon C. Schaefer]. *Art dir* Fred A. Ritter. *Film ed* Charles Craft. *Set dec* Earl Wooden. *Mus score* Joseph Dubin. *Sd* Ed Borschell. [*Re-rec and eff mixer* John Stransky, Jr.]. [*Re-rec, eff and mus mixer* Howard Wilson].

Source: Based on the comic strip "Red Ryder" by Fred Harman (1938—1964), by special arrangement with Stephen Slesinger.

Cast: WILD BILL ELLIOTT (*Red Ryder*), Bobby Blake [(*Little Beaver*)], Alice Fleming [(*The Duchess*)], Linda Stirling [(*Carol Franklin*)], LeRoy Mason [(*Luther Jennings*)], Hal Taliaferro [(*Walter Bishop*)], Tom London [(*Denver Thompson*)], Stephen Barclay [(*Captain James Glover*)], Bud Geary [(*Ross Benteen*)], Kenne Duncan [(*Dave Brewster*)], Bob Wilke [(*Bill*)], [Stanley Andrews (*General Wingate*)].

Western. [*Print viewed*]. Dodge City horse rancher Red Ryder, his Indian ward Little Beaver and their pal, Denver Thompson, are inspecting the herd when they hear gunshots. The friends are too late to stop the robbery of a freight wagon carrying a large sum of money. Before driver Jim Evans dies, he tells Red that the same men who robbed him the previous month are responsible. Red goes to town, where he informs the Duchess, his aunt and owner of the freight line, of the grim news. The Duchess is devastated because the frequent robberies have led to heavy insurance premiums and are bankrupting her. Banker Luther Jennings is also upset about the loss of his money shipment and once again offers to buy the freight line. The Duchess refuses to sell, however, because of Jennings' low offer. Unknown to the Duchess and Red, Jennings is plotting with Walter Bishop, the Duchess' insurance salesman, to drive the freight line into bankruptcy and then take it over. They have hired Ross Benteen and his gang to perpetrate the robberies, all of which are of Jennings' own shipments. Jennings and Bishop go to Benteen's cave hideout, where they divide up the loot with the gang. Jennings correctly surmises that Red's support is what is keeping the Duchess' morale up and preventing her from selling out, and so he orders Benteen to rustle Red's herd of horses, which have been raised for the cavalry. Jennings hopes to frame Red for the disappearance of the horses and then have him arrested for defrauding the government. The next afternoon, Benteen's men steal Red's horses, and Jennings intimates to Captain James Glover, the investigating calvary officer, that Red is about to sell his horses to another bidder and is responsible for the freight line robberies. Glover arrests Red, but while they are stopped on the way to the fort, Benteen tries to kill Glover and make Red look responsible. When Red saves the officer, however, Glover realizes that Red is innocent. Glover convinces his commanding officer, General Wingate, to let him return with Red to Dodge City, where they hope to uncover the real culprits. Meanwhile, Little Beaver, determined to help Red, nurses back to health a colt that is the last remaining member of the missing herd. Little Beaver then frees "Little Papoose," and follows the colt as he goes through the gang's secret cave to the valley beyond, where the other horses are being held. While he is in the cave, Little Beaver overhears the gang's plan to commit another robbery and frame Red for it when he returns. When Red and Glover reach Dodge City, Little Beaver tells Red about his discoveries, and Red goes with him to the cave. There, Red fights with Dave Brewster, one of Benteen's henchmen, and gets him to confess his crimes and reveal Jennings and Bishop's complicity. Red takes Brewster back to town, where Glover then confronts Jennings and Bishop, who take Little Beaver hostage during an escape attempt. Red rescues his ward, and the two crooks are killed as the wagon they are riding in careens off a cliff. Later, Dodge City is declared safe once more, and Red is awarded another contract by the cavalry. *Fistfights. Frame-ups. Freight lines. Horses. Robbery. Rustlers. Aunts. Bankers. Caves. Chases. Duplicity. Generals. Hideouts. Indians of North America. Insurance. Rumors. United States. Army. Cavalry. Wards and guardians.*

Note: Modern sources include Horace B. Carpenter in the cast. For more information about the ''Red Ryder'' series, please consult the Series Index and the entry above for *Tucson Raiders*.

DV 27 Oct 1944, p. 3. *HR* 7 Jul 1944, p. 11. *HR* 27 Oct 1944, p. 3. *MPHPD* 4 Nov 1944, pp. 2165-66.

A VILNA LEGEND *see* **THE RABBI'S POWER**

THE VIOLENT LAND *see* **RAIDERS OF OLD CALIFORNIA**

VIOLENT SATURDAY (Amish)

Twentieth Century-Fox Film Corp. *Dist* Twentieth Century-Fox Film Corp. Apr 1955 [©Twentieth Century-Fox Film Corp.; 20 Apr 1955; LP5029]. Sd; col (De Luxe); CinemaScope; CinemaScope lenses by Bausch & Lomb. 8,130 ft. 90-91 min.

Prod Buddy Adler. *Dir* Richard Fleischer. *Asst dir* Joseph E. Rickards. *Scr* Sydney Boehm. *Dir of photog* Charles G. Clarke. *Spec photog eff* Ray Kellogg. *Col consultant* Leonard Doss. *Art dir* Lyle Wheeler and George W. Davis. *Film ed* Louis Loeffler. *Set dec* Walter M. Scott and Chester Bayhi. *Ward dir* Charles LeMaire. *Cost des* Kay Nelson. *Mus* Hugo Friedhofer. *Cond by* Lionel Newman. *Orch* Edward B. Powell. *Sd* E. Clayton Ward and Harry M. Leonard. *Makeup artist* Ben Nye. *Hair styling by* Helen Turpin.

Source: Based on the novel *Violent Saturday* by William L. Heath (New York, 1955).

Cast: Victor Mature [(*Shelley Martin*)], Richard Egan [(*Boyd Fairchild*)], Stephen McNally [(*Harper*)], Virginia Leith [(*Linda Sherman*)], Tommy Noonan [(*Harry Reeves*)], Lee Marvin [(*Dill*)], Margaret Hayes [(*Emily Fairchild*)], J. Carrol Naish [(*Chapman*)], Sylvia Sidney [(*Elsie Braden*)], Ernest Borgnine [(*Stadt*)], Dorothy Patrick [(*Helen*)], Billy Chapin [(*Steve Martin*)], Brad Dexter [(*Gil Clayton*)], [Donald Gamble (*Bobby*)], [Raymond Greenleaf (*Mr. Fairchild*)], [Rickey Murray (*Georgie*)], [Robert Adler (*Stan*)], [Harry Carter (*Bart*)], [Ann Morrison (*Mrs. Stadt*)], [Kevin Corcoran (*David Stadt*)], [Donna Corcoran (*Anna Stadt*)], [Noreen Corcoran (*Mary Stadt*)], [Boyd ''Red'' Morgan (*Slick*)], [Florence Ravenel (*Miss Shirley*)], [Eilene Bowers (*Bank teller*)], [Dorothy Phillips (*Bank customer*)], [Virginia Carroll (*Marion, secretary*)], [Ralph Dumke (*Sidney*)], [Robert Osterloh (*Roy, bartender*)], [Joyce Newhard (*Dorothy*)], [Helen Mayon (*Mrs. Pilkas*)], [Harry Seymour (*Conductor*)], [Mack Williams (*Drug clerk*)], [Fred Shellac (*Signalman*)], [John Alderson (*Amish farmer*)], [Esther Somers (*Amish woman on train*)], [Jeri Weil, Patricia Weil (*Amish children*)], [Sammy Ogg].

Crime, Drama. [*Print viewed*]. Harper, a bank robber who is posing as a costume jewelry salesman, checks into a hotel in Bradenville, a small town adjacent to a mine. Harper's associates, Chapman and Dill, soon arrive aboard the train and surreptitiously observe the bank's daily procedures. At the Bradenville library, librarian Elsie Braden steals a pocketbook after receiving a notice from banker Harry Reeves that her loan payments are past due. At the same time, mine manager Shelley Martin rescues his son Steve from a fistfight. Later at work, Shelley finds that the mine owner's son, Boyd Fairchild, is too obsessed with his wife Emily's infidelity and his own sense of failure to do any work. That night at home, Shelley and his wife discover that Steve has been fighting because he is jealous that his best friend's father fought at the front, while Shelley was enlisted by the government to increase his copper production during the war. Harper, meanwhile, discovers a small Amish farm outside town, and realizes that the hospitable farmer, Stadt, has no phone or other means of modern communication or transportation. That night, Boyd gets drunk and becomes friendly with Linda Sherman, a new nurse in town. Linda is sympathetic to Boyd and helps him home, although she resists his advances because he is married. When Emily arrives home, Linda warns her to stop humiliating Boyd, or she will accept his offer to run away with him. At her own apartment, Linda is unaware that Reeves is lurking in an alley and watching her undress through the window. Harry then catches Elsie throwing away the stolen purse, but she threatens to expose him as a voyeur if he tries to implicate her. Just before dawn, Emily awakens Boyd, and after a heartfelt discussion, they decide to renew their love and take a vacation together. In the morning, Chapman and Dill kidnap Shelley and take him to the farm. There they imprison him and Stadt's family in the barn's hayloft, while they take Shelley's car to town. After Chapman calls in a false traffic accident to distract the police, they rob the bank. Harry attempts to shoot the robbers, but is killed by Dill, who

also shoots Emily. The robbers escape to the farm, where Shelley has managed to free himself, Stadt and his family. Stadt refuses to help Shelley defend them because the Amish are avowed pacifists. Shelley initially refuses to turn over the keys to a truck, but decides to relent out of respect for Stadt. However, after Chapman rams Shelley's car through the barn door, Shelley shoots and kills him. Harper sets the car on fire, and Shelley and the family push it outside to prevent the barn from burning. When one of the children is wounded by Harper's gunfire, Shelley kills Harper and is shot in the leg by Dill. As Dill reloads his gun, Stadt stabs him to death with a pitchfork, then asks God's forgiveness. Later in the hospital, Harry confesses to Linda that he has watched her, and she forgives him. Linda then consoles Boyd about Emily's death, but he sends her away when he starts to cry. Now that his father is a hero, Steve's faith in him is renewed. *Amish. Bank robberies. Conscience. Mine foremen. Murder. Small town life. Children. Debt. Drunkenness. Explosions. Farmers. Fathers and sons. Fistfights. Golf. Gunshot wounds. Heroism. Impersonation and imposture. Inferiority complexes. Infidelity. Kidnapping. Marriage. Nurses. Pacifism and pacifists. Peeping Toms.*

Note: William L. Heath's novel, which appeared in *Cosmopolitan* in Feb 1955 as one of their ''complete mystery novel'' features, was published in conjunction with the release of the film. The film was shot on location in Bisbee and at the Tucson Country Club in Tucson, AZ. In addition, some exteriors were shot at the 20th Century-Fox ranch in Malibu, CA. According to news items, 20th Century-Fox originally planned to have the film's premiere in Lancaster, PA, an Amish community. However, after the town's mayor, Kendig Bare, read the original story, he refused to permit the screening because he deemed the film ''too violent and sexy.'' No information about subsequent premieres has been found. The *Time* reviewer noted that in the scene in which ''Stadt'' murders the robber, ''the morality of violence is brought vividly into question, and the question has seldom been answered with more pith and natural majesty.'' The *NYT* reviewer commented that ''Ernest Borgnine as the Amish farmer is a joke. In flat black hat and chin whiskers, he acts as though he's just off the Ark.'' In another *NYT* article about violence in films, the same writer declared that the violence in *Violent Saturday* ''has no moral purpose or point'' and ''the fact that the farmer, by his nature and religion, deeply abhors violence is the only remotely philosophical—and then defeatist—point in the film.''

Box 23 Apr 1955. *DV* 10 Mar 1955. *DV* 13 Apr 1955, p. 3. *Exh* 20 Apr 1955, pp. 3951-52. *FD* 27 Apr 1955, p. 6. *Har* 16 Apr 1955, p. 62. *HR* 13 Apr 1955, p. 3. *LAEx* 21 Apr 1955. *MPHPD* 16 Apr 1955, p. 401. *NYT* 12 May 1955, p. 32. *NYT* 15 May 1955. *Time* 16 May 1955. *Var* 13 Apr 1955, p. 8.

THE VIRGIN OF SEMINOLE (African Americans)

Micheaux Film Corp. **1922**; Chicago opening: 5 Dec 1922. Si; b&w. 6 or 7 reels, 5,400 or 7,000 ft.

Pres Oscar Micheaux. *Dir* Oscar Micheaux.

Cast: William E. Fountaine, Shingzie Howard.

African American, Northwest, Drama. [*Not viewed*]. A young Black man from the South enters the Canadian wilds. By virtue of his strength and daring, he is made a member of the Canadian mounted police. Through his admirable work as an officer, and especially through his gunfight with a desperado, the young man becomes rich and famous, then purchases a ranch and finds true love. *African Americans. Canada. North West Mounted Police. Romance. Gunfights. Ranchers.*

ChiDef 25 Nov 1922, p. 7. *ChiDef* 2 Dec 1922, p. 6. *New York Age* 24 Mar 1923, p. 6. *New York Age* 31 Mar 1923, p. 6.

VIRGINIA (African Americans)

Paramount Pictures, Inc. *Dist* Paramount Pictures, Inc. 21 Feb **1941**; New York premiere: 22 Jan 1941; Prod: 17 Jul—2 Oct 1940 [©Paramount Pictures, Inc.; 21 Feb 1941; LP10269]. Sd (Western Electric Mirrophonic Recording); col (Technicolor). 12 reels. 107 or 110 min. Passed by the National Board of Review.

[*Exec prod* William LeBaron]. *Prod* Edward H. Griffith. *Dir* Edward H. Griffith. [*Asst dir* Roland Asher]. *Scr* Virginia Van Upp. *Story* Edward H. Griffith and Virginia Van Upp. *Dir of photog* Bert Glennon and William V. Skall. *Process photog* Farciot Edouart. *For the Technicolor Company: Color art dir* Natalie Kalmus. *Assoc* Henri Jaffa. *Art dir* Hans Dreier and Ernst Fegte. *Ed* Eda Warren. *Cost* Edith Head. *Sd rec* Hugo Grenzbach and Don Johnson. [*Tech adv* Edward S. de Butts].

Cast: Madeleine Carroll (*Charlotte Dunterry*), Fred MacMurray (*Stonewall [Jackson] Elliott*), Stirling Hayden (*Norman Williams*), Helen Broderick (*Theo Clairmont*), Carolyn Lee (*Pretty Elliott*), Marie Wilson (*Connie Potter*), Paul Hurst (*Thomas*), Tom Rutherford (*Carter Francis*), Leigh Whipper (*Ezechial*), Louise Beavers (*Ophelia*), Darby Jones (*Joseph*), [Edward Van Sloan, John

Hyams (*Ministers*)], [William D. Russell (*Loafer*)], [Thomas Louden (*First butler*)], [Wilson Benge (*Second butler*)], [Wanda McKay (*Girl*)], [George Melford, Jan Buckingham (*Guests*)], [Sam McDaniel (*First servant*)], [Charles R. Moore (*Second servant*)], [Edward S. de Butts (*Overseer*)].

Rural, **Romance**. [*Print viewed*]. Charlotte Dunterry returns to her family home in Fairville, Virginia after having lived in New York City most of her life. "Charlie," a city sophisticate who is ignorant of Southern ways, is appalled at the rundown condition of her family home, a 150-year-old mansion built by Thomas Jefferson, which she has inherited and plans to sell. She becomes reacquainted with Stonewall Jackson Elliott, a former family friend who, having lost his ancestral home, now lives in a modest cottage with his cousin Theo Clairmont and his little daughter, Pretty Elliott, while his wife leads the life of an adventuress abroad. Through the influence of Stoney and Joseph, a former black servant who has returned to the Dunterry estate so that he can die at home, Charlie comes to appreciate Southern customs and history, and she reworks her land as a farm so that she can earn income rather than sell the house. Charlie is assisted by Joseph, and Ophelia and Ezechial, kindhearted descendants of slaves who chose to remain at the Dunterry estate. Charlie and Stoney fall in love, but when he rebuffs her because he is married, she accepts the marriage proposal of Norman Williams, a handsome Northerner who is her next-door neighbor and has been wooing her. Stoney nevertheless continues to work Charlie's farm. One day during a horse race, Charlie's horse accidentally kicks Pretty in the head, but Charlie gives her own blood for a transfusion for Pretty and the child recovers. The near-tragedy cements Stoney and Charlie's love and, in time, Charlie believes that Stoney will marry her. She becomes embittered, however, when Stoney receives word that his wife is returning home for good, and Charlie then returns to New York. Stoney's wife returns in a coffin, however, and Norman withholds the news of her death from Charlie so that there will be no obstacles to their marriage. Charlie hears the news on the day of her wedding and is deeply touched when Stoney arrives to "give the bride away," since he is the closest thing she has to a relative. Standing before the altar, Norman is swayed by Stoney's goodwill, and he releases Charlie from their engagement so that she and Stoney can marry. With this union, Charlie finally embraces her Southern heritage. *City-country contrast. Romance. Southerners. Virginia. African Americans. Children. Crypts. Cultural conflict. Death and dying. Drunkenness. Fathers and daughters. Horseracing. Inheritance. Legends. Picnicking. United States–South. Weddings.*

Note: The working title of this film was *The Southerner*. This film marks the acting debut of Sterling Hayden, whose first name was changed temporarily to "Stirling" by the studio. *HR* called Hayden's debut "amazing." According to his autobiography, Hayden's debut in this picture was dependent upon the approval of his co-star, Madeleine Carroll, who had the right of cast approval. Carroll and Hayden married in 1942 and were married for four years.

According to Paramount press information, *Virginia* was shot on location in Albermarle County near Charlottesville, VA. The exteriors of the following historical homes were used in the film: "Monticola," near Howardsville, VA, as the "Dunterry" estate; "Bremo," the home of General Cocke, co-founder along with Thomas Jefferson of the University of Virginia, as the "Williams" estate; "Estouteville," the home of the Randolphs of Virginia; and the Farmington Country Club. Scenes of Jefferson's home, "Monticello," and the rotunda of the University of Virginia appear behind the title credits. *HR* news items reported the following: Some scenes were filmed on location at Elk Hill, VA; trotting races were filmed in Pomona, CA; barn-style dances were led by Mr. and Mrs. Elswood Graham, who were "exponents of old-fashioned barn dances"; Cleo and Edward, a Creole New Orleans ballroom dance team, were to appear in the film; Lucy Ville Sommers was "discovered" by director Edward H. Griffith in *Virginia* and signed to a contract. Her appearance in this film has not been confirmed. While the *HR* review called this film "one of the truly fine pictures of this or any year," *NYT* noted that it depicted "a wholly incredible someplace where little Confederate flags still hang under family portraits, where a Yankee is a person to be watched and the colored folks all behave as though there never had been any 'freedom.'" A *HR* news item noted that a print of the film was shipped to Rear Admiral Richard E. Byrd, a Virginia native who was a friend of director Griffith, at Little America, Antarctica.

AmCin Feb 1941, p. 65. *Box* 18 Jan 1941. *DV* 10 Jan 1941. *FD* 14 Jan 1941, p. 4. *HR* 16 Jul 1940, p. 2. *HR* 1 Aug 1940, p. 10. *HR* 6 Aug 1940, p. 8. *HR* 22 Aug 1940, p. 7. *HR* 16 Sep 1940, p. 8. *HR* 17 Sep 1940, p. 3. *HR* 3 Oct 1940, p. 6. *HR* 9 Dec 1940, p. 2. *HR* 23 Dec 1940, p. 7. *HR* 10 Jan 1941, p. 3. *MPH* 18 Jan 1941, p. 3. *MPHPD* 11 Jan 1941, p. 38. *NYT* 29 Jan 1941, p. 21. *Var* 15 Jan 1941, p. 14.

VISA *see* **A LADY WITHOUT PASSPORT**

UNA VIUDA ROMÁNTICA (Spanish language)

Fox Film Corp. *Dist* Fox Film Corp. **1933**; New York opening: 1 Sep 1933; Prod: Feb 1933. Sd; b&w. 8 reels, 6,537 ft. 73 min. Passed by the National Board of Review. Spanish language.

[*Prod* John Stone]. *Supervisión de* [*Supervision by*] Gregorio Martínez Sierra. *Dirección de* [*Direction by*] Louis King. *Adaptación cinematográfica de* [*Screenplay by*] José López Rubio and Paul Perez. [*Photog* Robert Planck]. [*2d cam* Arthur Arling]. [*Asst cam* Joe Farley and H. C. Smith].

Source: Based on the play *Sueño de una noche de agosto* by Gregorio Martínez Sierra (Madrid, 20 Nov 1918).

Cast: CATALINA BÁRCENA (*Rosario* [*Castellanos*]), Gilbert Roland (*Luis Felipe de Córdoba* [*also known as Prudencio González*]), Mona Maris (*Estrella* [*Polar*]), Juan Torena (*Mario* [*Castellanos*]), Julio Peña (*Pepe* [*Castellanos*]), Fernando de Toledo (*Emilio* [*Castellanos*]), Julia Bejarano (*Doña Barbarita*), María Calvo (*María Pepa*), Romualdo Tirado (*Un policía*), Juan Martínez Plá (*Don Juan* [*Medina*]), Paco Moreno (*Guillermo*), [Mimi Aguglia (*Encarna*)], [Enrique Jardiel Poncela (*Encargado*)], [José López Rubio (*Speaker*)], [Enrique Acosta], [Antonio Vidal].

Romantic comedy. [*Not viewed*]. After her brothers Mario, Pepe and Emilio have gone out and her grandmother, Doña Barbarita, has gone to bed, the young widow, Rosario Castellanos sits down to read a book by her favorite author, Luis Felipe de Córdoba. Outside a storm begins to blow, and a man's hat sails into her open window. Thinking that no one is at home, the owner of the hat climbs through the window to retrieve it and startles Rosario. He puts her at ease and introduces himself as Prudencio González, and they discuss the book she is reading. Although Felipe de Córdoba is Prudencio's pseudonym, he does not tell this to Rosario, but says only that he is a friend of Felipe and that Felipe is looking for a secretary. When Rosario's eyes light up, he agrees to arrange a meeting between the two the following morning. They hear the brothers arriving home, and in his haste to leave, Felipe forgets his hat. When the brothers press Rosario for an explanation, she faints. The next morning, when Felipe arrives at his office to meet with Rosario, she asks the secretary, Guillermo, to kick him out because of the position into which she was forced due to his forgetfulness. As a confused Guillermo looks on, Felipe explains the use of his pseudonym, and then to Rosario's further astonishment, he hires her as his secretary. Her first assignment, Felipe tells her, is to have lunch with him. The first restaurant they choose has to be abandoned when two of her brothers arrive, and the second one is rejected when Felipe spies his lover, Estrella Polar, an American dancer. They decide to return to his office to eat and begin work on their new novel. As they work, Estrella bursts in and reminds him that they have plans for the evening. When she leaves, Rosario, in a fit of jealousy, walks out as well. At her house, as the brothers prepare to attend a costume party where Estrella will be, Rosario chides them for desiring her, but when they leave, she sneaks out and goes to the costume shop where she sees an outfit to wear. Having no money of her own, she exchanges her diamond ring as a deposit for use of the costume, which was made specially for Estrella. At the ball, Rosario catches the eye of Felipe, who does not recognize her. They dance and the judges award her the prize for best costume, as Estrella expresses her outrage. The next morning, as her frantic family searches for her, Rosario wakes up in Felipe's bed. Felipe, sleeping on the den couch, awakens to explain that he did not wish her family to see her in her condition, so he brought her to his home. Estrella arrives and as she and Felipe argue, Rosario slips out to return to her home. In her anger, Estrella tears the beautiful costume to pieces. When Pepe hears a voice on the phone, Mario investigates. He finds Rosario, who tells them she was kidnapped. As she relates her story, a delivery boy brings her costume award. The owner of the costume store, who is furious about the condition of his costume, follows, and as Rosario tries to explain, Felipe's hat sails into the room. He is brought in by the police, who noticed him lurking about, and Rosario claims that he is her kidnapper. Felipe confirms her claim, and she joins them to lodge a complaint at the police station. As they ride in the police car, the officer sees that Rosario's only intention is to win Felipe's affection. He lets the couple out, and they immediately hail a cab. In the cab, Felipe asks Rosario to let him love her for the rest of his life. She answers by throwing his hat out the window, and they snuggle in the corner of the taxi. *Novelists. Romance. Secretaries. Widows. Brothers and sisters.*

Costumes. Dancers. Grandmothers. Hats. Masked balls. Rainstorms. Restaurants.

Note: The plot summary was based on a screen continuity in the Twentieth Century-Fox Produced Scripts Collection, and the onscreen credits were taken from a screen billing sheet in the Twentieth Century-Fox Records of the Legal Department, both of which are at the UCLA Theater Arts Library. *NYT* reviewed the film as *La viuda romántica* and gave the translation of the title as "The Romantic Widow." The film's running time was calculated from the footage listed in the records of the NYSA. The play was translated into English and adapted by Helen and Harley Granville Barker, and under the title *The Romantic Young Lady*, opened in London on 18 Sep 1920 and in New York on 4 May 1926.

CM Jul 1933, p. 380. *IP* Mar 1933, p. 21. *NYT* 4 Sep 1933, p. 9.

VIVA CISCO KID (Latino)

Twentieth Century-Fox Film Corp. *Dist* Twentieth Century-Fox Film Corp. 12 Apr **1940**; Prod: Late Dec 1939—early Feb 1940 [©Twentieth Century-Fox Film Corp.; 12 Apr 1940; LP9842]. Sd (Western Electric Mirrophonic Recording); b&w. 6,315 ft. 65 or 70 min. PCA cert no. 5992.

Series: The Cisco Kid.

Exec prod Sol M. Wurtzel. *Dir* Norman Foster. [*Asst dir* Saul Wurtzel and Sam Schneider]. *Scr* Samuel G. Engel and Hal Long. [*Contr wrt* Frances Hyland]. *Dir of photog* Charles Clarke. *Art dir* Richard Day and Chester Gore. *Film ed* Norman Colbert and [Fred Allen]. *Set dec* Thomas Little. *Cost* Herschel. *Mus dir* Samuel Kaylin. *Sd* Bernard Freericks and William H. Anderson. [*Prod mgr* William Koenig].

Song(s): "La Cucaracha," Mexican folk song.

Source: Based on the character created by O. Henry.

Cast: Cesar Romero ([*The*] *Cisco Kid*), Jean Rogers (*Joan Allen*), Chris-Pin Martin (*Gordito*), Minor Watson (*Jesse Allen*), Stanley Fields (*Boss*), Nigel de Brulier (*Moses*), Harold Goodwin ([*Hank*] *Gunther*), Francis Ford (*Proprieter* [*of eating house*]), Charles Judels (*Pancho*), [Harrison Greene (*Frank Snodgrass Benson*)], [LeRoy Mason (*Outlaw leader*)], [Tom London (*Town marshal*)], [Jim Mason (*Lem*)], [Hank Worden (*Deputy*)], [Eddy Waller (*Stage driver*)], [Ray Teal (*Josh*)], [Bud Osborne (*Kennedy*)], [Paul Sutton (*Joshua*)], [Mantan Moreland (*Memphis*)], [Paul Kruger (*Jack*)], [Willie Fung (*Wang*)], [Frank Darien (*Express man*)], [Jacqueline Dalya (*Helena*)], [Margaret Martin (*Helena's mother*)], [Inez Palange (*Mexican mother/Gordito's sister*)].

Western. [*Print viewed*]. In her upstairs room, Helena makes love to her sweetheart, the Cisco Kid, and after pledging her undying love, signals out the window with her handkerchief. Her mother rushes in to warn Cisco that American policemen are on the way. Knowing Helena has betrayed him, Cisco ties her up in the curtain and jumps out the window. Cisco learns that his cohort, Gordito, is getting married to the twice-widowed sister of Señor Pancho. Cisco breaks up the wedding by convincing Pancho that Gordito is another dying man. Out on the range, Cisco tells Gordito that they are adventurers, not the marrying kind, and pledges to give up women forever. Witnessing the holdup of a stagecoach, however, Cisco immediately falls for one of the passengers, Joan Allen. When the robbers fail to find the $25,000 the stage is supposedly carrying, they shoot the driver and prepare to rob and kill the passengers. Cisco and Gordito break up the holdup and take the stage safely into the town of Towash. In town, the express agent finds the money in a hidden compartment under the driver's seat. The robbers arrive at the "Garden of Eden" saloon, where they tell their leader, Hank Gunther, the bad news. After he finds out the money has actually arrived, Hank orders Jesse Allen, their inside man, to rob the express office that night. Jesse learns that his daughter Joan has arrived in town. Joan is taken to Jesse's home by Cisco, who agrees to dine with her that night. When Jesse arrives at home, he tells his daughter that he is no good for her, and then leaves for town when Cisco shows up for dinner. Cisco tells Joan that he has fallen in love with her, but as he is an outlaw, he must leave her before he hurts her. Cisco and Gordito agree to leave for Arizona the next day. Moses, a wandering preacher, sees Jesse hold up the express office. The posse takes out after Jesse, but he hears their hoof beats, and eludes them. Hank, realizing that Moses can identify Jesse, kills him that night. Jesse tells Joan what he has done and rides across the state border to Grande, agreeing to wait for her there. Cisco and Gordito run across Joan on their way to Grande, only to be captured by the posse. When Moses' murder is discovered, the posse wants to lynch the two men. They escape, with the posse in quick pursuit, leaving Joan with Hank and his henchmen. Hank takes Joan to the Sugar Loaf Mine, the Boss's hideout. The Boss, a practical joker, holds Joan hostage and sends Hank out to find Jesse. After escaping the posse, Cisco and Gordito are saved from arrest in Grande by Jesse. The three go to the mine to rescue Joan. Cisco and Gordito convince the Boss that they want to join his gang. They are about to rescue Joan when Hank arrives with the captured Jesse. The boss takes all four into the mine, placing them in a tunnel. The boss has his thug, Joshua, collapse the tunnel entrance, but the explosion collapses the mine as well, killing the entire gang. As they wait in the tunnel to die, Gordito finds a rabbit and uses it to locate a small hole to the outside. With dynamite, they then blast their way out of the mine. Jesse decides to return the money to Towash, and Joan kisses Cisco goodbye. As he and Cisco ride off, Gordito lights one of the Boss's trick cigars, which blows up in his face. *Bandits. Fathers and daughters. Mexicans. Mines and mineral resources. Outlaws. Rescues. Stagecoach robberies. Betrayal. Cigars. Dynamite. Friendship. Lynching. Murder. Posses. Practical jokes. Preachers. Rabbits. Saloons. Stagecoach drivers. Weddings.*

Note: The working titles for this film were *Romance in New York*, *The Cisco Kid in New York*, *Romance in Chicago*, *The Cisco Kid in Chicago*, and *Cisco Kid No. 2*. Materials found in the the Twentieth Century-Fox Produced Script Collection at the UCLA Theater Arts Library demonstrate that the original concept for this film included taking the Cisco Kid to either New York or Chicago. This work, done in the outline and treatment stages by writers M. M. Musselman and Leonard Hoffman, was rejected and the final product was created by the credited writers Samuel G. Engel and Hal Long. In a *HR* production chart, Fred Allen was listed as the film editor and Sam Schneider was listed as the assistant director, but their participation in the final film has not been confirmed. *HR* also reported that studio filming ended 2 Jan 1940, with the cast and crew then moving to Sedonia Basin, Arizona for two weeks of location shooting. According to a *NYT* article, John Igual de Montijo filed suit against a number of film companies, including Twentieth Century-Fox, arguing that his work "Viva Madero" was plagiarized by Paramount's *Northwest Mounted Police* and *Viva Cisco Kid*. According to Twentieth Century-Fox legal records, the lawsuit was dismissed in September 1941. For more information on the Cisco Kid series, see the entry above for *The Cisco Kid* and consult the Series Index.

Box 23 Mar 1940. *DV* 15 Mar 1940, p. 3. *FD* 25 Mar 1940, p. 5. *HR* 3 Jan 1940, p. 2. *HR* 30 Dec 1939, p. 6. *HR* 16 Mar 1940, p. 3. *MPD* 19 Mar 1940, p. 3. *MPH* 24 Feb 1940, p. 33. *MPH* 23 Mar 1940, p. 42, 44. *NYT* 22 Mar 1940, p. 23. *NYT* 20 Jul 1941. *Var* 20 Mar 1940, p. 16.

¡VIVA MI TIERRA! see LAS FRONTERAS DEL AMOR

THE VOICE OF ISRAEL (Yiddish language)

Judea Films, Inc. *Dist* Judea Films, Inc. **1931**; approved by Pennsylvania State Board of Censors 21 Sep 1931; Prod: ended mid-Aug 1931 [©Judea Films, Inc.; 5 Dec 1931; LU2691]. Sd; b&w. 10 reels, 8,439 ft. 93 min. Yiddish language with singing in Hebrew.

Song(s): "Hayum Harth (Today the World Is Called into Existence)," "V'al Y'dei Avodecho (Let Thy Prophets Speak Thy Words)," "Av Horachamim (Father of Mercy, Grant Us Everlasting Deliverance)," "Shim Shalom (Grant Us Peace)," "Adonoi Zecho Ronu (Oh God, Thou Hast Always Been Mindful of Us)," "U-Ba Shofar Godol (The Sound of the Shofar)," "Kol Nidre (Forgive Our Vows and Iniquities)," "Socho Hoisho" and "Yism'chu B'Malchuscho (Rejoice Ye in the Sabbath)," traditionals.

Cast: Cantor Mordechai Hershman, Cantor Joseph Shapiro, Cantor Shaile Engelhardt, Cantor David Roitman, Cantor Louis Waldman, Cantor Joseph Rosenblatt, Cantor Joseph Shlisky, Cantor Adolph Katchko, Cantor Seidel Rovner, Cantor Meyer Machtenberg, Choir.

Yiddish, Compilation, Musical. [*Not viewed*]. Aspects of the history of the Jewish people, emphasizing their persecution and martyrdom, are presented in ten scenes, each culminating with the singing by a famous cantor of an appropriate prayer. The scenes are entitled "The Tree of Israel," "The Tower of Babel," "Sodom and Gomorrah," "Israel in Bondage," "The Burning Bush," "The Redemption of Israel," "The Wilderness," "The Wailing Wall," "Modern Pogroms" and "The Sabbath." The first seven scenes present Biblical occurrences, while the last three present contemporary settings. The film ends with the statement that the Jewish people remain committed to the principles of faith, hope and charity, the three virtues that earlier were shown to branch out from the Tree of Israel. In addition, they visualize a united world that recognizes the sacred rights of all peoples to live in peace. *Biblical characters. Cantors, Jewish. Faith. Jews. Martyrs. Religiosity. Religious persecution. Babel, Tower of. Bible. Old Testament. Book of Exodus. Egypt–History. Jews–History. Kishinev (Russia). Palestine. Pogroms. Western Wall (Jerusalem).*

Note: The Yiddish title of this film is *Di Shtime fun Yisroel*. The running time was calculated from footage given in NYSA records. No reviews for this film have been located. According to an interview in 1948 with Joseph Seiden, one of the owners of Judea Films, *The Voice of Israel*, which featured the best known cantors of the day, was budgeted at $20,000. In a poster, the film is advertised as presenting "Four Generations of the World's Greatest Cantors," and a photograph of Shaile Engelhardt is captioned the "World's Youngest Cantor," while one of Seidel Rovner is captioned the "World's Oldest Cantor." According to modern sources, the film consisted, in addition to scenes of the cantors singing, excerpts from a number of silent films, some of which were made before World War I.

Detroit Jewish Chronicle 18 Dec 1931. *FD* 12 Aug 1931, p. 3.

VOICE OF STEPHEN WILDER *see* **THE LAWLESS**

THE VOICE OF THE WIND *see* **NAVAJO**

THE VOLCANO (Jewish Americans)

Harry Raver, Inc.; Four Star Pictures; Artco Productions, Inc. *Dist* W. W. Hodkinson Corp. through Pathé Exchange, Inc. 24 Aug **1919**. Si; b&w. 6 reels.

Pres Harry Raver. *Dir* George Irving. *Story* Augustus Thomas. *Cam* Ned Van Buren.

Cast: Leah Baird (*Ruth Carroll*), Edward Langford (*Captain Nathan Levison*), W. H. Gibson (*Davy Carroll*), Jacob Kingsbury (*Alexis Minski*), Harry Bartlett (*Grandpa Carroll*), William Fredericks (*Michael*), Elivra Amazar (*Olga Petrovitch*), Becky Bruce (*Mrs. Van Leiden*), Governor Alfred E. Smith (*Himself*).

Social, Drama. Ruth Carroll, a schoolteacher in New York's Lower East Side, meets Bolshevist Alexis Minski at her grandfather's bookstore. After Ruth complains to her superintendent about undernourished schoolchildren, Minski's ravings cause her suspension, and she joins the Reds. Meanwhile, Captain Nathan Levison, returning from the Argonne, is assigned by the Secret Service to investigate New York's radicals. While visiting the Carrolls to announce the imminent arrival of Ruth's brother Davy, who saved Levison's life but lost his foot, Levison falls in love with Ruth. Chagrined, Minski convinces Ruth that Levison plans to arrest her and her grandfather, whereupon Ruth furiously requests that Levison be killed. After Governor Alfred E. Smith signs a bill making it illegal to display the Red flag, the Bolshevists plot to assassinate him, the Mayor of Seattle, and Attorney General Alexander Palmer, but Davy, with other soldiers, break up the meeting. Davy convinces Ruth of Minski's perfidy, and they save Levison. Ruth marries Levison, and at a wedding attended by the governor, Davy marries a reformed Bolshevist. *Assassination. Bolshevists and Bolshevism. Brothers and sisters. Jews. New York City–Lower East Side. Schoolteachers. Secret Service. War heroes. Alexander Mitchell Palmer. Amputees. Booksellers and bookselling. Dismissal (Employment). Flags. Self-sacrifice. Alfred E. Smith. Weddings.*

Note: This film was shot at the Biograph studios in New York. According to *Var*, Governor Alfred E. Smith, who appears in the film, and Assistant Secretary of the Navy Franklin D. Roosevelt, withdrew their official sanction and endorsement after complaints were made from a Yiddish daily that the film was strongly anti-Semitic. Because of this, producer Harry Raver and author Augustus Thomas made the villain "Minski," whose appearance and gestures were stereotypically Jewish, say in a subtitle, "I am not a Jew; I am a Bolshevik." Raver and Thomas also changed the name of the hero from "Captain Garland" to "Captain Nathan Levison." The film had a pre-release special showing by the National Press Club in Washington, D.C. to government and political leaders at midnight, 4 Jul 1919. There was also a pre-release special showing to editors of the leading Jewish newspapers and periodicals.

ETR 30 Aug 1919, p. 1079. *MPN* 23 Aug 1919, p. 1687. *MPW* 16 Aug 1919, p. 1024. *NYMT* 10 Aug 1919. *Var* 15 Aug 1919, p. 71. *Wid's* 17 Aug 1919, p. 15.

LA VOLUNTAD DEL MUERTO (Spanish language)

Universal Pictures Corp. *Dist* Universal Pictures Corp. Nov **1930**; San José de Costa Rica opening: 16 Nov 1930; New York opening: 12 Dec 1930.; Prod: Jul—Aug 1930. Sd (Sistema Western Electric [Western Electric Sound System]); b&w. 9 reels, 7,856 ft. 87 min. Spanish language.

Presenta [*Pres*] Carl Laemmle. *Producida por* [*Prod*] Carl Laemmle, Jr. *Productor asociado* [*Assoc prod*] Paul Kohner. *Dirigida por* [*Dir*] George Melford. [*Asst dir* Jay Marchant]. [*Dial dir* Enrique Tovar Avalos]. *Guión y diálogo por* [*Scr and dial*] B. Fernández Cué. *Operador* [*Cam*] George Robinson. *Director artístico* [*Art dir*] Walter R. Koessler. *Editor del film* [*Film ed*] Arthur Tavares. *Supervisor de la edición del film* [*Supv film ed*] Maurice Pivar. *Supervisor de acústica* [*Sd supv*] C. Roy Hunter.

Source: Based on the play *The Cat and the Canary* by John Willard (New York, 7 Feb 1922).

Cast: Antonio Moreno (*Pablo*), Lupita Tovar (*Anita*), Soledad Jiménez (*Mammy*), Andrés de Segurola (*Crosby*), Manuel Granado (*Carlos*), Roberto Guzmán (*Enrique*), Conchita Ballesteros (*Cecilia*), María Calvo (*Susana*), Lucio Villegas (*Doctor*), Agostino Borgato (*Hendricks*), [Nicolás Ruiz], [Manuel Ballesteros], [Pablo Alvarez].

Mystery. [*Not viewed*]. Exactly twenty years after the death of the lonely, eccentric millionaire Cyrus West, his descendents are summoned to meet one midnight in his gloomy, old mansion for a very belated reading of his will. West's closest relatives are dismayed to learn that they have been disinherited due to the fact that they believed him to be crazy. Anita, a distant relative, is revealed as the only heir to West's fortune and properties as long as her mental state remains stable. However, the subsequent disappearance of West's lawyer, an attack on cousin Pablo by a "monster" and several other inexplicable events combine to place a great strain on Anita's sanity. Eventually, the police determine that Carlos, another relative and a potential heir, is responsible for the campaign of terror. *Fear. Heiresses. Inheritance. Insanity. Millionaires. Murder.* Haunted houses. Investigations. Lawyers. Police. Threats. Wills.

Note: This film was a simultaneously shot Spanish version of the 1930 film *The Cat Creeps*, which was directed by Rupert Julian and starred Helen Twelvetrees and Raymond Hackett (see *AFI Catalog of Feature Films, 1921-30*, F2.0798). The cast and technical credits for the Spanish-language version were annotated from a studio cutting continuity. The play, *The Cat and the Canary*, had been filmed in 1927 in a version directed by Paul Leni and starring Laura La Plante and Creighton Hale (see *AFI Catalog of Feature Films, 1921-30*, F2.0797) and was again filmed in 1939 with Bob Hope and Paulette Goddard, directed by Elliott Nugent (see *AFI Catalog of Feature Films, 1931-40*, F3.0626) and, in 1978, as a British production directed by Radley Metzger. *La voluntad del muerto* was retitled *La heredera de Mr. West* when exhibited in Buenos Aires, Argentina, in Jul 1931.

Cinl Nov 1930, p. 30.

VOODOO *see* **DRUMS O' VOODOO**

VU IZ MAYN KIND? *see* **WHERE IS MY CHILD?**

EL VUELO DEL AMOR *see* **LAS FRONTERAS DEL AMOR**

LA VUELTA DEL HIJO PRÓDIGO *see* **EL OTRO SOY YO**

THE WAGES OF SIN (African Americans)

Micheaux Film Corp. **1928**. Si; b&w. Length undetermined. *Prod* Oscar Micheaux. *Dir* Oscar Micheaux.

Source: Based on the short story "Alias Jefferson Lee."

Cast: Lorenzo Tucker

African American, Drama. After his mother dies, African-American motion picture producer Winston Le Jaune returns to his home for the burial. His older sister reveals to him that their mother's dying wish was for him to take care of their younger brother, J. Lee, a ne'er-do-well who has shown himself to be a coward during World War I in France. After returning to the city, Winston sends for J. Lee and gives him a job in the company. J. Lee promptly steals money from the company, putting it into financial trouble, and spends it in cabarets and at wild parties, and on women. Winston fires his brother and is forced to make numerous trips to try to raise money for the company. While away, he meets and falls in love with a woman. They plan to marry, but she suddenly disappears. In Chicago, Winston meets J. Lee and offers him his job back. J. Lee now intentionally destroys the company and betrays his brother. [The only information regarding the conclusion of this film that has been found is that a new and unusual character is introduced at this point; the denouement involves thrills and heroism; and the ending is a happy one.]. *African Americans. Brothers. Motion picture producers. Ne'er-do-wells. Betrayal. Brothers and sisters. Cabarets. Chicago (IL). Cowardice. Dismissal (Employment). Funerals. Parties. Robbery.*

Note: Modern sources list the film's title as *Wages of Sin* and list the following additional cast members: Sylvia Birdsong, William A. Clayton, Jr., Katherine Noisette, Alice B. Russell, William Baker, Bessie Gibbens, Gertrude Snelson and Ethel Smith.

ChiDef 8 Dec 1928, p. 6. *New York Age* 2 Feb 1929, p. 6.

WAGON TRACKS WEST (Native Americans, Pawnee)

Republic Pictures Corp. *Dist* Republic Pictures Corp. 19 Aug **1943**; Prod: mid-May—late May 1943 [©Republic Pictures Corp.; 13 Jul 1943; LP12163]. Sd (RCA Sound System); b&w. 6 reels, 4,946 ft. 54-55 min. Passed by the National Board of Review. PCA cert no. 9416.

Assoc prod Louis Gray. *Dir* Howard Bretherton. [*Asst dir* Kenneth Holmes]. *Orig scr* William Lively. *Photog* Reggie Lanning. *Art dir* Russell Kimball. *Film ed* Charles Craft. *Set dec* Charles Thompson. *Mus score* Mort Glickman. *Sd* Tom Carman.

Cast: Wild Bill Elliott [(*Wild Bill Elliott*)], George "Gabby" Hayes [(*Gabby Whittaker*)], Tom Tyler [(*Clawtooth*)], Anne Jeffreys [(*Moonbush*)], Rick Vallin [(*John Fleetwing*)], Robert Frazer [(*Robert Warren*)], Roy Barcroft [(*Laird*)], Charles Miller [(*Brown Bear*)], Tom London [(*Lem Martin*)], Cliff Lyons [(*Matt*)], Jack Rockwell [(*Sheriff Summers*)], [Bill Nestell (*Burns*)], [Kenne Duncan (*Gregg*)], [J. W. Cody (*Blue Feather*)], [Jack Ingram (*Joe*)], [Hal Price (*Townsman*)], [Minerva Urecal (*Mrs. Perkins*)], [Roy Butler (*Cattleman*)], [Bryant Washburn (*College superintendant*)].

Western. [*Print viewed*]. In 1891, Pawnee John Fleetwing is the first Indian to graduate from the Cumberland Indian College medical school, and is congratulated by the school superintendent for being valedictorian of his class. While Fleetwing is returning to his home in Six Gun County, wandering cowboys Wild Bill Elliott and "Gabby" Whittaker, who are going in the same direction as Fleetwing, flee from an Indian attack. They jump from a cliff into a lake, not seeing a warning sign that the water is unsafe. Gabby, who swallowed some of the water, begins to feel ill as he and Bill reach town. While Bill tends to the horses, Gabby tries to get some food at the local saloon, but his feverish actions convince the scornful cowboys that he is drunk. Fleetwing, who has just arrived by stagecoach, attempts to help Gabby, but the cowboys, led by bully Laird, attack him as well. Bill comes to the saloon and beats up Laird, then allows Fleetwing to treat Gabby. They take him to a hotel, where they learn that the Indians have been dying from the same fever for the past year, ever since the local ranchers installed an irrigation system. Bill then accompanies Fleetwing to his tribe's camp, where his father, Brown Bear, lies ill with the fever. Fleetwing's quick treatment is about to save Brown Bear's life, but Clawtooth, the corrupt medicine man, kills Brown Bear so that he, not Fleetwing, can assume control of the tribe. Clawtooth is in league with Robert Warren, the territorial Indian Commissioner, who, along with Laird, wants to drive the Indians off their valuable land. Warren has promised Clawtooth money and guns in exchange for his help, and has also fomented the ranchers' hatred of the Indians. Bill tells the ranchers that it is the backwash from their irrigation that is poisoning the Indians' water and spreading the fever, but they do not care, even when Fleetwing warns them that they, too, will be hit by the fever when the rainy season starts. Wanting to get rid of Fleetwing, Warren and Laird plan to poison head rancher Lem Martin's water and frame Fleetwing for it. Warren shoots Martin during the raid, and Fleetwing is blamed when his medical school pin is found on the scene. Bill and Gabby help Fleetwing escape when he is arrested, for it is obvious that he will not get a fair trial. While Fleetwing hides out in a cave, Bill and Gabby uncover the connection between Warren, Laird and Clawtooth. After Fleetwing is captured by the sheriff, Bill and Gabby confront Laird and Clawtooth, and Clawtooth is killed. Laird unknowingly drinks some of the poisoned water, and convinced that only Fleetwing can save him, confesses that Warren killed Martin. Bill and Gabby rush him to town, arriving just in time to save Fleetwing from hanging and prevent a battle between the Indians and the ranchers. After Warren is arrested, the sheriff and ranchers admit that they have done the Indians a great injustice and plan to outfit Fleetwing with an office in town. As everyone shakes hands, Bill and Gabby leave in search of further adventures. *Cowboys. Pawnee Indians. Physicians. Racism. Ranchers. Caves. Fever. Frame-ups. Gunfights. Indian agents. Irrigation. Medical colleges. Poisoning. Racial impersonation. Sheriffs. Water.*

Note: Modern sources include the following actors in the cast: Frank Ellis, Hank Bell, Jack O'Shea, Ray Jones, Curley Dresden, Frank McCarroll, Marshall Reed, Ben Corbett, Jack Montgomery and Tom Steele.

DV 23 Jul 1943, p. 3. *FD* 28 Oct 1943, p. 6. *HR* 21 May 1943, p. 11. *HR* 23 Jul 1943, p. 3. *MPH* 31 Jul 1943. *MPHPD* 26 Jun 1943, p. 1391. *MPHPD* 31 Jul 1943, p. 1455. *Var* 27 Oct 1943, p. 10.

WAGON WHEELS (Native Americans)

Paramount Productions, Inc. *Dist* Paramount Productions, Inc. 14 Sep **1934**; New York premiere: 3 Oct 1934; Prod: began 8 Aug 1934 [©Paramount Productions, Inc.; 21 Sep 1934; LP4956]. Sd (Western Electric Noiseless Recording); b&w. 6 reels. 55-56 min. Passed by the National Board of Review. PCA cert no. 196.

Pres ADOLPH ZUKOR. *Prod* Harold Hurley. *Dir* Charles Barton. *Scr* Jack Cunningham. *Adpt* Charles Logue and Carl A. Buss. *Photog* William C. Mellor. [*Art dir* Earl Hedrick]. [*Ed* Jack Dennis]. *Vocal interpolations: "Estrellita"* Lorraine Bridges. *Vocal interpolations: "Under the Daisies"* Jan Duggan. *Vocal interpolations: "Wagon Wheels"* Earl Covert and The Singing Guardsmen. [*Sd* Phil G. Wisdom].

Song(s): "Wagon Wheels," words and music by Peter DeRose and Billy Hill; "Estrellita," words and music by Manuel Ponce, adapted by Frank LaForge; "Under the Daisies," composer unknown.

Source: Based on the novel *Fighting Caravans* by Zane Grey (New York, 1929).

Cast: Randolph Scott (*Clint Belmet*), Gail Patrick (*Nancy Wellington*), Billy Lee (*Sonny Wellington*), Monte Blue ([*Kenneth*] *Murdock*), Raymond Hatton (*Jim Burch*), Jan Duggan (*Abby Masters*), Leila Bennett (*Hetty Masters*), Olin Howland (*Bill O'Meary*), Howard Wilson ([*Permit*] *officer*), Julian Madison (*Lester*), Eldred Tidbury (*Chauncey*), Colin Tapley (*Mountaineer*), J. P. McGowan (*Couch*), James A. Marcus (*Jed*), Helen Hunt (*Mrs. Jed*), James B. "Pop" Kenton (*Masters*), John Marston (*Orator*), Sam McDaniels (*Negro coachman*), Michael Visaroff (*Russian*), E. Alyn Warren (*The Factor*), [Alfred Delcambre (*Ebe*)].

Western, with songs. [*Print viewed*]. On May 1, 1840, a wagon train leaves Independence, Missouri, for Oregon, led by old scouts Bill O'Meary and Jim Burch and the young Clint Belmet, whom they reared. Joining them are the beautiful widow Nancy Wellington and her little boy Sonny, whom Nancy kidnapped from her in-laws after they took custody of Sonny when his father died. Clint warns Nancy about the arduous trip West, but she is determined and buys a sturdy rig from the half-Indian fur trapper Kenneth Murdock. Fearing the white man will destroy his prosperous fur trade in the Northwest, Murdock conspires with other trappers to prevent the settlers from reaching Powder River. Meanwhile, the elderly Abby Masters, who is keeping a journal of the trip, falls in love with Jim and records the caravan's two week fight with roving bands of Indians. After the fifth man dies, Murdock tries to convince the train to turn back, but Clint refuses. While Sonny celebrates his fourth birthday, Nancy confides her past to Clint and the two fall silently in love. When the train reaches the Beaver Parks Trading Post, the men spend two weeks drinking and gambling, until Clint, disappearing for four days, spies Murdock conspiring with Indians and rallies the women to force their men back on the trail. When they reach Powder River, the Indians attack; Abby's sister Hetty and scout Bill are killed before Clint sets the kerosene wagon on fire and creates a cloud of smoke, forcing the Indians to retreat. While the hand of Bill's ghost joins them in a pledge, Jim and Clint promise to lead the train safely to Oregon. There Jim and Abby decide to marry, and Clint asks Sonny if he would like him for a father. *Fur traders. Indians of North America. Indians of North America-Mixed blood. Murder. Renegades. Scouts (Frontier). Settlers. Wagon trains. Abduction. Child custody. Diaries. Friendship. Oregon. Proposals (Marital). Widows.*

Note: Zane Grey's novel was serialized in *Country Gentleman* between Nov 1928 and Mar 1929. The title card on the viewed print read "Zane Grey's *Wagon Wheels.*" This film's working title was *Fighting Caravans*, the title of a 1931 Paramount film also based on Zane Grey's story (see above). A modern source states that footage from *Fighting Caravans* was used in this film. According to press material found in copyright records, portions of this film were shot at the ranch of Al Gatesman, located near Cooperstown, CA, thirty miles from Sonora. The title song for this film was first used in the *Ziegfeld Follies of 1934*. Modern sources list the following additional cast members: Pauline Moore, Lew Meehan, Fern Emmett, Clara Lou Sheridan, Harold Goodwin and Howard Wilson.

DV 17 Jul 1934, p. 1. *DV* 8 Aug 1934, p. 7. *DV* 1 Sep 1934, p. 3. *FD* 5 Oct 1934, p. 8. *HR* 1 Sep 1934, p. 2. *MPH* 8 Sep 1934, p. 38. *NYT* 4 Oct 1934, p. 19. *Var* 9 Oct 1934, p. 18.

WAGONS WEST (Native Americans, Cheyenne)

Monogram Pictures Corp.; Silvermine Productions. *Dist* Monogram Pictures Corp. Jun **1952**; Prod: late Sep—mid-Oct 1951 [©Monogram Pictures Corp.; 27 Jun 1952; LP1796]. Sd; col (Cinecolor). 6,303 ft. 70 min. PCA cert no. 15681.

Prod Vincent M. Fennelly. *Dir* Ford Beebe. *Asst dir* William Calihan, Jr. *Dial dir* Jack Reitze. *Wrt by* Dan Ullman. *Dir of photog* Harry Neumann. *Col consultant* Wilton R. Holm and Clifford D. Shank. *Art dir* Martin Obzina. *Film ed* Walter Hannemann. *Mus ed* Eve Newman. *Settings* Bob Priestley. *Set cont* Ilona Vas. *Mus* Marlin Skiles. *Rec eng* Charles Cooper. *Makeup artist* Lou Phillips. *Hair stylist* Lenora Sabine.

Cast: ROD CAMERON [(*Jeff Curtis*)], Noah Beery, Jr. [(*Arch Lawrence*)], Peggie Castle [(*Ann Wilkins*)], Michael Chapin [(*Ben Wilkins*)], Henry Brandon [(*Clay Cook*)], Sarah Hayden [(*Mrs. Cook*)], Frank Ferguson [(*Cyrus Cook*)], Anne Kimbell [(*Alice Lawrence*)], Wheaton Chambers [(*Sam Wilkins*)], Riley Hill [(*Gaylord Cook*)], Effie Laird [(*Old maid*)], I. Stanford Jolley [(*Slocum*)], Almira Sessions [(*Old maid*)], Harry Tyler [(*Old man*)], [Glenn Strange (*Joplin marshal*)], [Harry Strang (*Territorial marshal*)], [John Parrish (*Chief Black Kettle*)], [Charles Stevens (*Kaw chief*)], [Forrest Taylor (*Johnson*)], [Ken Cooper (*Outrider*)], [Ralph Moody)].

Western. [*Print viewed*]. As Jeff Curtis is on his way to Joplin to lead a wagon train west, he picks up a runaway boy, Ben Wilkins, and Ben's dog, Buzz. Jeff takes the boy back to the Wilkins family in Joplin, and there meets Ben's pretty sister Ann. Young Ben had run away because Cyrus Cook, the organizer of the train, had ordered the dog killed. Jeff takes an immediate disliking to Cook, and Cook's two braggart nephews, Clay and Gaylord, and gets into a fierce fight with Clay. Some days after the wagon train starts, two U.S. marshals overtake it, looking for wagoneers who have been smuggling rifles to the Cheyennes. A day or so later the Cooks, in a sudden flare of anger, leave the train and drive ahead into Indian territory. Jeff follows the Cooks, and with the help of Ben, who has trailed Jeff, finds hidden rifles in one of the Cooks's wagons. Jeff forces the rifle-carrying wagon back to the main camp. The Indians, believing they have been cheated out of their rifles, attack the camp. Clay tries to shoot and kill Jeff during the battle but Ben saves Jeff's life. Cook and Clay both are killed by Indian arrows, and the Indians are driven off. Jeff, alone, follows them and succeeds in making peace with Black Kettle, the chief. The wagon train is given safe passage and proceeds, with Ann proudly at Jeff's side. *Cheyenne Indians. Dogs. Runaways. Scouts (Frontier). Wagon trains. Battles. Brothers and sisters. Fights. Gunrunners. Nephews. Rifles. Sisters. United States. Marshals.*

Box 21 Jun 1952. *DV* 16 Jun 1952, p. 3. *HR* 28 Sep 1951, p. 22. *HR* 12 Oct 1951, p. 14 *HR* 16 Jun 1952, p. 3. *MPHPD* 21 Jun 1952, p. 1418. *Var* 18 Jun 1952, p. 6.

WAGONS WESTWARD see MAN OF CONQUEST

WAIKIKI WEDDING (Hawaiians)

Paramount Pictures, Inc. *Dist* Paramount Pictures, Inc. 26 Mar 1937; Prod: 17 Dec 1936—23 Feb 1937 [©Paramount Pictures, Inc.; 26 Mar 1937; LP7031]. Sd (Western Electric Noiseless Recording); b&w. 10 reels. 88-90 min. Passed by the National Board of Review. PCA cert no. 3135.

Pres ADOLPH ZUKOR. *Prod* Arthur Hornblow, Jr. [*Exec prod* William LeBaron]. *Dir* Frank Tuttle. [*Asst dir* Richard Harlan]. *Scr* Frank Butler, Don Hartman, Walter DeLeon and Francis Martin. *Orig story* Frank Butler and Don Hartman. *Photog* Karl Struss. *Hawaiian exteriors* Robert C. Bruce. *Spec photog eff* Farciot Edouart. *Art dir* Hans Dreier and Robert Usher. *Ed* Paul Weatherwax. *Int dec* A. E. Freudeman. *Cost* Edith Head. *Mus dir* Boris Morros. *Orch* Victor Young. *Arr by* Al Siegel and Arthur Franklin. *Dance dir* LeRoy Prinz. *Sd rec* Gene Merritt and Louis Mesenkop.

Song(s): "Sweet Leilani," music and lyrics by Harry Owens; "Okolehao," "In a Little Hula Heaven," "Blue Hawaii" and "Sweet Is the Word for You," music and lyrics by Leo Robin and Ralph Rainger; "Nani Ona Pua," "Lani's Song" and "Momi Pele," music by Ralph Rainger, Hawaiian lyrics by Jimmy Lowell.

Cast: Bing Crosby (*Tony Marvin*), Bob Burns (*Shad Buggle*), Martha Raye (*Myrtle Finch*), Shirley Ross (*Georgia Smith*), George Barbier (*J. P. Todhunter*), Leif Erikson (*Victor*), Grady Sutton (*Everett Todhunter*), Granville Bates (*Uncle Herman*), Anthony Quinn (*Kimo*), Mitchell Lewis (*Koalani*), George Regas (*Muamua*), Nick Lukats (*Assistant Purser*), Prince Lei Lani (*Priest*), Maurice Liu (*Kaiaka*), Raquel Echeverria (*Mahina*), Iris Yamaoka (*Secretary*), [Wafford the pig], [Lotus Liu (*Suki*)], [Nalani De Clercq (*Maile*)], [Kuulei De Clercq (*Lani*)], [Miri Rei, Augie Goupil (*Specialty dancers*)], [Spencer Charters (*Frame*)], [Alexander Leftwich (*Harrison*)], [Ralph Remley (*Tomlin*)], [Harry Stubbs (*Keith*)], [Pierre Watkin (*Durkin*)], [Jack Chapin (*Photographer*)], [Pedro Regas (*Driver*)], [George Kaluna, Harry Field, George Herrera, Joe Molina, Manuella Kalili, Tony Urchel (*Members of Kimo's gang*)], [Victor Wong, Lee Tung-Foo (*Gardeners*)], [Henry Roquemore, Ethel Clayton, Gloria Williams (*Tourists*)], [David Newell (*Radio operator*)], [Emma Dunn, Nina Campana (*Old women*)], [Ray Kinney (*Singer*)], [Harry Vejar (*Desk sergeant*)], [Robert O'Connor (*First policeman*)], [Lalo Encinas (*Second policeman*)], [Sojin, Jr. (*Bellboy*)], [Richard Terry (*Taxi driver*)], [Alfonso Pedroza (*Doorman*)], [Harry Tyler (*Sailor*)], [Harold Entwistle].

Musical comedy. [*Print viewed*]. Tony Marvin, who works in advertising at J. P. Todhunter's Imperial Pineapples in Hawaii, designs a publicity stunt involving the selection of an "Imperial Pineapple Girl," who is to come to Hawaii for three weeks of romance and then publish her impressions of the trip. After Georgia Smith, the chosen girl, threatens to return home early when her glamorous trip to Hawaii proves uneventful, Tony is picked to romance her. As Georgia leaves her hotel for the home-bound ship, a stranger, hired by Todhunter, asks her to smuggle a necklace to San Francisco for his sister. Inside the necklace is a stolen, sacred black pearl, which the stranger says must be returned to the islanders in order to appease the goddess of their volcano, which has started to smoke. Georgia and her stenographer, Myrtle Finch, and Tony and his friend, Shad Buggle, are all obliged to sail to a nearby island and return the pearl. The island ceremonies and moonlight enchant Georgia, and she falls in love with Tony, unaware that he works for the pineapple company. Tony, meanwhile, has been calling in installments of the Pineapple Girl's impressions for the island's newspapers, which he has written himself. After the High Priest prays for the acceptance of the pearl by the goddess, Tony and his friend Kimo order the islanders to create a fire beneath the volcano to make it look as if the pearl was fake and the goddess is still angry, thereby promoting further adventures for Georgia. Eventually, Tony, Georgia, Shad and Myrtle escape from the island in Tony's boat and head for the mainland. Tony tries many times to confess to Georgia his part in the pearl scheme, but cannot get up the nerve. As they approach the mainland, he proposes to Georgia and tells her to put on her best dress for an immediate wedding. Meanwhile, Georgia's hometown fiancé Victor, a dentist, and her Uncle Herman have flown to Hawaii to save Georgia from the duplicitous Tony and the dangerous islands. Although by now Tony is pleading with Todhunter to publicly deny the authenticity of the Pineapple Girl's articles so that Georgia will accept him, Victor convinces Georgia that Tony deliberately exploited her. Todhunter refuses to cooperate with Tony, and he is forced to quit. Georgia refuses to believe Tony is in love with her and, oblivious to his attempts to win back her trust, boards the ship for home. Finally, Tony sends an old woman onto the ship to pose as his mother. The woman asks Georgia if she loves Victor and tells her not to let her pride keep her from the man she really loves. Georgia runs off the ship just in time and, although she discovers the woman was a hoax, kisses Tony anyway. *Adventures. Hawaii. Publicity stunts. Romance. Advertising. Businessmen. Contests. Dentists. Engagements. Hawaiians. Hoaxes. Honesty. Pearls. Pigs. Police. Pride and vanity. Proposals (Marital). Rites and ceremonies. Ships. Stenographers. Volcanoes.*

Note: According to news items, Bing Crosby initially turned down the starring in role in this film because the story wasn't right for him, and Paramount rewrote the script to get him to accept the role. *HR* announced on 7 Jan 1937 that a unit led by Robert Bruce had left to shoot background scenes in Honolulu, Hawaii. According to a news item in *HR*, the owner of "Wafford the Pig," used in various scenes in this film, demanded a payraise for the animal from $60-a-week to $1,000-a-week. Harry Owens won a 1937 Academy Award for Best Song for "Sweet Leilani."

DV 4 Aug 1936, p. 3. *DV* 6 Aug 1936, p. 6. *DV* 20 Mar 1937, p. 3. *FD* 23 Mar 1937, p. 7. *HR* 5 Aug 1936, p. 3. *HR* 18 Dec 1936, p. 2. *HR* 21 Dec 1936, p. 18. *HR* 7 Jan 1937, p. 4. *HR* 11 Jan 1937, p. 1. *HR* 24 Feb 1937, p. 3. *HR* 26 Feb 1937, p. 13. *HR* 20 Mar 1937, p. 3. *MPD* 22 Mar 1937, p. 4. *MPH* 6 Mar 1937, p. 49, 52. *MPH* 3 Apr 1937, p. 41. *NYT* 25 Mar 1937, p. 29. *Var* 31 Mar 1937, p. 17.

WALK LIKE A DRAGON (Chinese Americans)

Paramount Pictures Corp. *Dist* Paramount Pictures Corp. 26 Sep 1960; New York opening: 15 Sep 1960; Prod: late Dec 1959—late Jan 1960 [©Paramount Pictures Corp.; 20 May 1960; LP16377]. Sd; b&w. 8,538 ft. 95 min. PCA cert no. 19561.

Prod James Clavell. *Dir* James Clavell. *Asst dir* Richard Caffey. *Wrt* James Clavell and Daniel Mainwaring. *Dir of photog* Loyal Griggs. *Art dir* Hal Pereira and Roland Anderson. *Film ed* Howard Smith. *Set dec* Sam Comer and Robert Benton. *Mus scored by and cond by* Paul Dunlap. *Sd rec* Gene Merritt and Winston Leverett. *Mus supv* Wally Westmore. *Hair style supv* Nellie Manley. *Tech adv* Benson Fong. *Unit prod mgr* Don Robb.

Song(s): "Walk Like a Dragon," words and music by Mel Torme, sung by Mel Torme.

Cast: Jack Lord (*Linc Bartlett*), Nobu McCarthy (*Kim Sung*), James Shigeta (*Cheng Lu*), Mel Torme (*The Deacon*), Josephine Hutchinson (*Ma Bartlett*), Rudolph Acosta (*Sheriff Marguelez*), Benson Fong (*Wu*), Michael Pate (*Will Allen*), Lilyan Chauvin (*Mme. Lili Raide*), Don Kennedy (*Masters*), Donald Barry (*Caleb Cabot*), Natalie Trundy (*Susan*), Lester Matthews (*Peter Mott*), Michael Ross (*Taffy*), Charles Irwin (*Angus*), Tom Kennedy (*Jethro, the bartender*), Tony Young (*Cabot*), Kam Tong (*San*), Cicely Walper (*Mrs. O'Leary*), Paul Maxey (*Barber*), Peter Gordon (*Rorke*), Peter Humphreys (*Mason*), Jerry Groves (*Auctioneer*), Clarence Lung (*Pat Eurasian*), Max Power (*Juror*), Dee Cooper (*Stage coachdriver*).

Western. [*Not viewed*]. Shocked when he sees a lovely Chinese girl, Kim Sung, being sold into prostitution in a San Francisco slave market, Linc Barlett buys her, intending to set her free. Kim has nowhere to go, however, and so he is forced to take her home to the mining town of Jerico. Accompanying them on their journey is Cheng Lu, a young Chinese immigrant who speaks perfect English and has come to America to join his uncle Wu, a laundryman in Jerico. Immediately the two men clash, Linc because he feels that the Chinese are an inferior race, and Cheng because he resents his countrymen having to grovel in front of white men. Their antagonism grows as they both discover that they desire Kim. In Jerico, the love triangle has violent repercussions. Linc, whose mother, Ma Bartlett, will not let him keep Kim as his mistress, announces his intention of marrying her. Linc tries to make the citizens accept Kim as an equal, but they refuse. Afraid of Linc's prowess with a gun, they strike at him economically, bent on destroying his freight line business. Lili Raide, the owner of the gambling hall and Linc's former sweetheart, also turns against him. The town also turns on Cheng when the young Chinese, discovering that he can kill legally in self-defense, hires a gunfighter known as The Deacon to make him the fastest draw in town, intending to shoot it out with Linc. Cheng soon discovers, however, that the white man's laws do not apply to Chinese, when he is forced to kill his teacher in a fair fight and then is promptly arrested for murder. Only though the intervention of Linc, whose love for Kim has taught him tolerance, is Cheng's life spared. Linc, a moral man who believes in justice, goes to Cheng's defense and makes the town accept that there is one law for all. Upon his release, Cheng, determined to win Kim, challenges Linc to a gunfight. Kim, who by now realizes that women are not slaves and have a freedom of choice, steps between them. Cheng then tells Kim that he wants to marry her and orders her to cut off his pigtail, a symbol of revolt against his ancient customs of servitude, stating that from now on, he will "walk like a dragon." After Linc reiterates his love, Kim chooses Cheng and they walk off together. Bigotry. Chinese Americans. Immigrants. Romantic rivalry. Gunfighters. Gunfights. Laundries. Mining towns. Mothers and sons. Prostitution. San Francisco (CA). Self-defense. Slavery. Transformation. Uncles.

Box 6 Jun 1960. *DV* 2 Jun 1960, p. 3. *Exb* 8 Jun 1960, p. 4710. *FD* 2 Jun 1960, p. 7. *Har* 4 Jun 1960, pp. 90-91. *HR* 31 Dec 1959, p. 8. *HR* 4 Jan 1960, p. 8. *HR* 22 Jan 1960, p. 16. *HR* 2 Jun 1960, p. 3. *MPHPD* 4 Jun 1960, p. 724. *NYT* 16 Sep 1960, p. 24. *Var* 8 Jun 1960, p. 6.

WALK SOFTLY, STRANGER *see* **GAMBLING HOUSE**

WALK TALL (Native Americans, Shoshoni)
Associated Producers, Inc. *Dist* Twentieth Century-Fox Film Corp. Oct **1960**; *Prod*: 6 Jun—11 Jun 1960 [©Twentieth Century-Fox Film Corp.; 31 Aug 1960; LP17108]. Sd; col (DeLuxe); CinemaScope; CinemaScope lenses by Bausch & Lomb. 6 reels, 5,435 ft. 60 min. PCA cert no. 19695.

Prod Maury Dexter. *Dir* Maury Dexter. *Asst dir* Frank Parmenter. [*2d assist dir* Willard Kirkham]. *Story and scr* Joseph Fritz. *Dir of photog* Floyd Crosby. [*Cam op* Nelson Cordes]. [*1st asst cam* Bob Holser]. [*2d asst cam* Ken Peach]. [*Stills* Milt Gold]. [*Gaffer* Lloyd Garnell]. [*Cam equipment* Mark Armistead]. [*Spec eff* Rocky Cline]. *Supv film ed* Edward Dutko. [*Asst cutter* Eddie Campbell]. [*Ward man* Wes Jeffries]. *Mus comp and cond* Richard D. Aurandt. *Sd* Jack Solomon. *Sd facilities by* Continental Sound Corp. [*Sd rec* Bruce Greiner]. [*Sd boom man* Bill Flannery]. [*Sd cable man* Al Yaylian]. *Makeup* Don Cash. *Scr supv* Mary Yerke. *Property master* Leigh Carson. *Asst to the prod* Leonard A. Schwartz. [*Best boy* Norman McClay]. [*Elec* Georgie Breslow, Herb Kammerer, William Kane and Les Holt]. [*Generator op* Mike Huff]. [*Key grip* Carl Reed]. [*2d grip* Bert Brown]. [*Grip* Cliff Brown]. [*Asst prop man* Bob Eaton]. [*Transportation* Dave Lesser]. [*Driver* Jim Foote, Ike Danning, Pat

Hustis, Gil Casper, George Greiner and C. Wynn]. [*Head wrangler* Jeff Flores]. [*First aid man* John W. Leber]. [*Craft service* Jim Hicks]. [*Prod secy* Julie Arden]. [*Publ* Dave Epstein]. [*Payroll* Jan Kelly]. [*Catering* Ed Michelson]. [*Casting of extras* Allied Casting]. [*Stunts (Trask)* Bob Morgan]. [*Stunts (Carter)* George Robotham].

Cast: Willard Parker [(*Captain Ed Trask*)], Joyce Meadows [(*Sally Medford*)], Kent Taylor [(*Frank Carter*)], Russ Bender [(*Colonel Stanton*)], Ron Soble [(*Leach*)], Bill Mims [(*Jake*)], Alberto Monte [(*Carlos*)], Felix Locher [(*Chief Black Feather*)], Dave DePaul [(*Buffalo Horn*)].

Western. [*Print viewed*]. Bounty hunter Frank Carter, with his gang of three, Leach, Jake and Carlos, attack a Shoshone Indian village on the Secora River, occupied by only squaws and old men, to capture scalps to sell for forty dollars each. Chief Black Feather meets with Colonel Stanton of the 33rd Cavalry to protest the violation of the peace treaty signed ten months earlier and says that Shoshones who lose their scalp cannot join their fathers in the council fire until the one who took the scalp is dead. Learning that Young Buffalo Horn, whose bride was murdered by the bounty hunters, has already gone on the warpath with seven others, the colonel assigns Captain Ed Trask to capture Carter and his gang. Trask, a Civil War hero whom the chief respects as one of the white men who "walk tall among his people," had been a fellow officer to Carter, who was cashiered from the service. The colonel emphasizes that Carter should be brought back alive, so that he could stand trial and die by the firing squad to prove to the Shoshone Nation, who are ready to rise up in war, that the white man's brand of justice is as effective as theirs. Carter is to rendezvous with his men after he collects the bounty in Holcolm, an abandoned mining town in the Black Hills. Because Holcolm is outside of the colonel's jurisdiction, Trask must go there alone. At the mining town, Trask captures Carter before his gang gets there, but Carter is able to hide the bounty money. After Trask and Carter leave, Leach, Jake and Carlos arrive, and because Leach deduces that only one man captured Carter, they set off in pursuit to recover their money. Trask leads Carter relentlessly on, not allowing him to make a fire, which he thinks may attract Carter's gang or Buffalo Horn. At night as Trask sleeps, Carter tries to escape, but Trask, having tied a string from Carter's leg to his own wrist, awakens in time. After seeing from a distance a group of Indians attack and burn a covered wagon, Trask and Carter find an injured woman and her dead grandfather. The woman, Sally Medford, explains that she and her grandfather were heading to Arizona from Pennsylvania to prospect for gold. When she expresses a virulent hatred for "murdering Red savages," Carter proudly tells her that he has dedicated his life to killing every Indian he finds. Sally rides with them on Trask's pack horse, and when Carter's gang arrive at the overturned wagon, Leach, noticing the deeper tracks and a perfumed scarf, deduces that they now are traveling with a woman, the idea of which greatly excites Jake. When they stop for the night and Sally learns that Carter might be executed for killing Indians, she says he should instead be given a medal. Carter then vows that when he is free, he will kill the Indians who murdered her grandfather. Trask chains Carter to a fallen tree trunk for the night, and in the morning, Carter is bitten on the leg by a rattlesnake. Trask shoots the snake then sucks the poison from Carter's leg, but when they are ready to leave, Sally protests that moving Carter will be risking his life. Trask tells her that if they remain, their lives will be in danger from Carter's men or from Buffalo Horn. After Carter falls from his horse twice and goes into convulsions, Sally vows to report Trask for mistreatment of his prisoner. Trask decides to start a fire to make a hot stimulant for Carter, but as he covers Carter with blankets, Carter, who had been feigning illness, chokes Trask with his chain and threatens to kill him if Sally doesn't get Trask's keys and unlock his handcuffs. She does this, and the men struggle. Trask knocks out Carter, but then Leach, Jake and Carlos arrive and knock out Trask. After Carter tells them that the money is back at Holcolm, Carter shoots Trask from a distance with a rifle. Sally sees this, then sneaks off. Carter sends Carlos and Jake, who eagerly wants the "sweet smelling filly," to capture her and the pack horse she took, planning to meet them on the trail to Holcolm. When Jake and Carlos encounter Sally, Jake assures her he will escort her to Colonel Stanton as soon as they get their money. Meanwhile, Trask revives and finds his hat and gun. Jake and Carlos lead Sally, who now appears to have been attacked, to Leach and Carter, who berates the two for forgetting about the pack horse. Trask finds the pack horse and follows the

group to Holcolm, where he silently subdues Carlos. Sally hugs Trask, who tells her he has to bring Carter back alive to avert an Indian war. He hides her, then comes upon Leach, and after both draw, Leach falls dead. After Trask shoots a gun from Carter's hand, Jake runs off in fright. As Carter, who has now recovered his gun, is about to shoot Trask, he is killed by an arrow. Indians then approach and drop Jake's body on the ground. Buffalo Horn tells Trask that he will tell Black Feather that the Shoshone and "one who walks tall" brought justice together. As the Indians ride off in peace, Trask and Sally smile at each other. *Bounty hunters. Gangs. Justice. Murder. Officers (Military). Racism. Revenge. Shoshoni Indians. Black Hills (SD and WY). Gunshot wounds. Mining towns. Prospectors. Scalping. Snake bites. Treaties. Tribal chiefs. United States. Army. Cavalry.*

Note: The working title of this film was *The Black Hills*. The opening credits for this film contain the following statement: "This motion picture was filmed with the cooperation of the California Forest Service, Department of Agriculture in the San Bernardino National Forest."

Box 24 Oct 1960. *DV* 20 Oct 1960, p. 3. *Exb* 26 Oct 1960, p. 4762. *FD* 27 Oct 1960, p. 8. *Har* 22 Oct 1960, p. 170. *HR* 20 Oct 1960, p. 3. *LAT* 6 Jan 1961, pt. II, p. 10. *MPHPD* 12 Nov 1960, p. 917. *Var* 26 Oct 1960, p. 17.

WALK THE PROUD LAND (Native Americans, Apache)

Universal-International Pictures Co., Inc. *Dist* Universal Pictures Co., Inc. Sep **1956**; Prod: 21 Nov—late Dec 1955 [©Universal Pictures Co.; 27 Jun 1956; LP6823]. Sd (Westrex Recording System); col (Technicolor); CinemaScope. Length undetermined.

Prod Aaron Rosenberg. *Dir* Jesse Hibbs. *Asst dir* Paul Bowles. *Scr* Gil Doud and Jack Sher. *Dir of photog* Harold Lipstein. *Spec photog* Clifford Stine. *Technicolor color consultant* William Fritzsche. *Art dir* Bill Newberry. [*Supv art dir* Alexander Golitzen]. *Film ed* Sherman Todd and [Ted Kent]. *Set dec* Russell A. Gausman and Ray Jeffers. *Cost* Bill Thomas. *Mus supv* Joseph Gershenson. *Sd* Leslie I. Carey and Frank H. Wilkinson. *Hair stylist* Joan St. Oegger. *Makeup* Bud Westmore.

Source: Based on the book *Apache Agent* by Woodworth Clum (Boston, 1936).

Cast: AUDIE MURPHY [(*John P. Clum*)], ANNE BANCROFT [(*Tianay*)], PAT CROWLEY [(*Mary Dennison*)], Charles Drake [(*Tom Sweeny*)], Tommy Rall [(*Taglito*)], Robert Warwick [(*Chief Eskiminzin*)], Jay Silverheels [(*Geronimo*)], Eugene Mazzola [(*Tono*)], Anthony Caruso [(*Disalin*)], Victor Millan [(*Santos*)], Ainslie Pryor [(*Captain Larsen*)], Eugene Iglesias [(*Chato*)], Morris Ankrum [(*General Wade*)], Addison Richards [(*Governor Safford*)], Maurice Jara [(*Alchise*)], Frank Chase [(*Stone*)], Ed Hinton [(*Naylor*)], Marty Carrizosa [(*Pica*)], [George Keymas (*Ponce*)], [John Pickard (*Sheriff*)], [Natividad Vacio (*Compos*)], [Clem Fuller (*Stagecoach driver*)], [William Forrest (*Mr. Dennison*)], [Rankin Mansfield (*Banker*)], [Francis McDonald (*Shaman*)], [Paul McGuire (*Neely*)], [William O'Neal (*Bartender*)], [Jack Lomas (*Snyder*)], [Tyler McVey (*Lang*)], [Jack Mather (*Chandler*)], [Jean Andren (*Mrs. Dennison*)], [Bernie Gozier, Jerry Eskow (*Drunken Indians*)], [Herold Goodwin (*Telegrapher*)], [Vi Ingraham (*Woman that cries*)].

Western. [*Print viewed*]. John P. Clum, an Indian agent, arrives in Tucson to take up his new job as adviser to the San Carlos Apache reservation and meets with his superiors, Governor Safford and General Wade. Clum's humanist tendencies disturb the belligerent Wade, who believes that the only way to deal with the Indians is through military might. In response, Clum states that the Department of the Interior currently believes it has a duty to protect the Indian bands that have surrendered and will no longer seek to wipe them out. When Clum arrives at the reservation and sees a group of Apache men being brought back from the work fields in chains, he demands that Captain Larsen, head of the San Carlos cavalry, unchain them. Larsen is angry, but complies, and later, Tianay, an Indian woman in mourning for her husband, thanks Clum for his act of kindness. Later, when Clum hears some braves making war cries, he approaches the men and a scuffle ensues. Chief Eskiminzin arrives and scolds his braves for fighting with the man who set their chief free, and instead of allowing the cavalry to punish them, Clum instructs the chief to punish the braves as he sees fit. Acting on orders from President Ulysses S. Grant, Clum tells Larsen to leave San Carlos, and then instructs the Apaches to set up their own police and judicial system. After the chief chooses Taglito, Alchise and Chato as the new keepers of the peace, Clum returns to his cabin to find that Tianay has moved in with her young son Tono. Clum tells her that he is already engaged to another, but she begs him not to send her back as it will disgrace

her in the eyes of the chief. Meanwhile, when food supplies do not arrive from Tucson, Clum agrees to procure guns for the Indians so that they can hunt. Later, the Apache police force bring in two scoundrels, whom Clum had earlier met in Tucson hawking Apache scalps. Clum takes the men into Tucson to be jailed for poaching, but while having a drink with Tom Sweeny, a former Army man from San Carlos, the scoundrels, having been released, show up and a brawl ensues. Afterward, Clum finally succeeds in convincing Sweeny to take a job training the Apache police force. Back at the reservation, Taglito tells Clum that he wants to marry her and is jealous of Clum. When Taglito's brother decides to shoot at Clum with his newly acquired rifle, however, Taglito shoots him dead, and later, the chief tells Clum that Taglito wishes to make him his blood brother. Tianay tries to convince Clum to have more than one wife, and when Clum, who is weakening, receives a letter from Mary Dennison, his fiancée, he decides that they will marry upon her arrival. Clum invites the governor, the general and other officials to the wedding ceremony, but no one shows up, except Sweeny's Apache police force, who give a gun salute, much to the governor's chagrin. Despite this gaffe, Clum persuades the governor to attend an Apache dance performance that night, as an act of cultural exchange, and the governor agrees, eventually warming to Clum's ways. During the dance, Clum introduces Mary to Tianay and Tono, and Mary is shocked when she discovers that Tianay has been living with her husband. Just then, infamous Apache renegade Geronimo arrives at San Carlos and calls on Taglito and another brave, Santo, to join him. Clum offers the braves the freedom to go, but they decline. Clum then tells Geronimo that he can stay on the reservation, if he follows the rules, and the renegade departs to think about the proposal. Later, Mary tells Tianay to leave the couple's cabin, and Clum scolds her for not being sensitive to the Apache's ways. Tono is sad that Clum will not be his father and convinces a young friend, Pica, to go with him into the wilderness to find Geronimo. Later, Mary encourages her husband to search for the boy, and Tianay and Clum eventually find the children asleep in some bushes. The four then witness Geronimo attacking a wagon train, and the Cavalry rides in. Back at San Carlos, Taglito wants to take the rifles and join Geronimo, but Clum says that they will have to kill him first. Clum announces that he will talk to Geronimo, and after a terrified Mary tries to stop him, Clum, Sweeny and the Apache police head for the wilderness. Clum says that he will deal with Geronimo in the same way that the Bible's Gideon fought his enemy: They will trick Geronimo into thinking that they have more forces than they do by shooting rifles into the air. Geronimo laughs when he hears from his scout that Clum is approaching with only twenty men, but after Clum fails to convince Geronimo to surrender, the remaining men shoot their rifles and the echo scares Geronimo's men, who flee. Clum brings in Geronimo and his men in chains, while the Cavalry returns to San Carlos. When Wade proclaims that he is now in control, Clum quits his job in disgust and disappointment. Taglito and the chief, however, convince Clum not to run away, but to stay and continue to fight for their rights. Even Mary encourages him to carry on his good works. Tono, having given up Geronimo as his hero, wields his toy gun, calling, "I am Mister, I capture my enemies." *Apache Indians. John Philip Clum. Geronimo. Indian agents. Indians of North America–Reservations. Tucson (AZ). Ambushes. Bible. Children. Dances. Generals. Governors. Heroism. Marriage. Rifles. Romantic rivalry. Scalping. United States. Army. Cavalry. Weddings.*

Note: This film's working title was *Apache Agent*. The written prologue states that the story is true and that it began in 1874. The words of the prologue are also spoken, by Woodworth Clum, the son of John Philip Clum and author of the biography on which the film is based. A written epilogue and voice-over narration state: "John Clum spent the rest of his life fighting for the welfare of his Indians, but his dream of self government for them was not realized until long after his death. In November 1955, the United States Government turned the administration of the San Carlos reservation over to the Apaches themselves..." Clum, an Indian agent, was, according to *Var*, "the first white man to force the surrender of the notorious Geronimo." Geronimo's final surrender took place on 3 Sep 1886 to General Nelson Miles.

According to a *HR* news item, location shooting took place in Tucson, AZ. The *HR* reviewer praised the picture as being "one of the most interesting stories of the American frontier" in that it is "based on a true story of an important part of U.S. history, the turning point in the treatment of the Indian by the white conqueror." The *Saturday Review*, however, maligned the film, saying that "like other serious efforts, it is an earnest, dreary exercise in naïve anthropology, Hollywood's vulgar apology for all 'the only good injun' films."

Box 14 Jul 1956. *DV* 10 Jul 1956, p. 3. *Exb* 25 Jul 1956, p. 4192. *FD* 12 Jul 1956, p. 7. *Har* 14 Jul 1956, p. 111. *HR* 16 Nov 1955, p. 3. *HR* 30 Dec 1955, p. 11. *HR* 10 Jul 1956, p. 3. *LAT* 2 Aug 1956. *MPD* 10 Jul 1956. *MPHPD* 14 Jul 1956, p. 969. *NYT* 8 Sep 1956, p. 20. *Saturday Review* 25 Aug 1956. *Var* 11 Jul 1956, p. 6.

WANDERER OF THE WASTELAND (Latino)

RKO Radio Pictures, Inc. *Dist* RKO Radio Pictures, Inc. **1945**; New York opening: 28 Sep 1945; Prod: late May—9 Jun 1945 [©RKO Radio Pictures, Inc.; 28 Sep 1945; LP13668]. Sd (RCA Sound System); b&w. 6,069 ft. 67 min. PCA cert no. 10956.

Exec prod Sid Rogell. *Prod* Herman Schlom. *Dir* Edward Killy and Wallace Grissell. *Asst dir* Sam Ruman. *Dial dir* Leslie Urbach. *Scr* Norman Houston. *Dir of photog* Harry J. Wild. [*2d cam* Charles Straumer]. [*Spec optical eff* Lynn Dunn]. [*Spec optical eff and matte paintings* Vernon L. Walker]. *Art dir* Albert S. D'Agostino and Lucius Croxton. *Ed* J. R. Whittredge. *Set dec* Darrell Silvera. [*Gowns* Renie]. *Mus* Paul Sawtell. *Mus dir* C. Bakaleinikoff. *Sd* Richard Van Hessen and Roy Granville. [*Mus mixer* Earl B. Mounce].

Source: Based on the novel *The Wanderer of the Wasteland* by Zane Grey (New York, 1923).

Cast: James Warren [(*Adam Larey*)], Richard Martin [(*Chito Rafferty*)], Audrey Long [(*Jeannie Collinshaw*)], Robert Barrat [(*Uncle James Collinshaw*)], Robert Clarke [(*Jay Collinshaw*)], Harry Woods [(*Guerd Eliott*)], Minerva Urecal [(*Mama Rafferty*)], Harry D. Brown [(*Papa Mike Rafferty*)], Tommy Cook [(*Chito, as a boy*)], Harry McKim [(*Adam, as a boy*)], Jason Robards [(*Dealer*)], [Sammy Blum (*Bartender*)], [Larry Wheat (*Station master*)], [Fred Aldrich, Sam Lufkin, Ethan Laidlaw, Sam Shack, Lou Palfy (*Gamblers*)], [Cecil Stewart (*Piano player*)], [Gordon Jones (*Sheriff*)], [Myrna Dell (*Girl with gambler*)], [Beverly Bushe (*Girl*)], [Allan Lee (*Stage driver*)], [Dick Elliott (*Record clerk*)], [Budd Buster (*Hotel proprietor*)], [Tanis Chandler], [Nan Leslie], [Jimmy Jordan].

Western. [*Print viewed*]. While crossing the Mojave Desert in 1880, the Rafferty family, little Chito, Chito's Irish father, Papa Mike, and Spanish mother Mama, hear cries for help and find a boy stumbling alone through the sands. The boy, Adam Larey, recounts the story of his mother's sudden death and father's subsequent murder and directs the Raffertys to his parents' wagon. There, beside the bodies, they find the murderer's dead horse, and when Adam notices the brand of the Crescent J ranch on the animal's flank, he vows to avenge his father's death. Adam is adopted by the Raffertys, and ten years later, the family owns a sheep ranch in Randsburg, California and the boys have grown to adulthood. Since the age of fifteen, Adam has wandered the wastelands in search of his father's killer. Upon returning to Randsburg from an expedition, Adam sees the Crescent J brand on a suitcase owned by Jeannie Collinshaw, who is passing through town. After Jeannie's stage leaves town, Adam learns from the station master that her destination is Pichacho, Arizona. Accompanied by Chito, Adam follows Jeannie to the town of Pichacho where, outside the saloon, he sees a horse bearing the Crescent J brand. Upon discovering that the animal belongs to Jay Collinshaw, Jeannie's brother, Adam approaches Jay, who is immersed in a game of poker. Resentful at being interrupted by a sheep rancher, Jay pulls a gun on Adam and begins to shoot at his feet, causing Adam to draw his own weapon and shoot Jay in the wrist. After leaving the saloon, Adam and Chito register at the local hotel. Later, Jeannie visits Adam to extend an invitation from her uncle James to visit their ranch the next day. The next morning, Jeannie meets Adam on the trail to the ranch and questions him about his interest in their brand. When an unseen assailant fires at them, Adam accuses Jeannie of setting up an ambush for him. At the ranch, Adam meets Jeannie's wheelchair-bound uncle, who offers him a job keeping Jay out of trouble. Adam accepts on the condition that he hire Chito, too. After Adam departs, Collinshaw extracts a photograph from his desk drawer and lovingly gazes at it. On his way back to town, Adam, meanwhile, locates the spent gunshells fired by his assailant. In town, Adams visits the county clerk's office and asks to see the deed to the Collinshaw ranch. By examining the bill of sale, Adam ascertains that Collinshaw paid $10,000 for the property ten years earlier, the exact amount of money stolen from the Larey wagon. At a party held in honor of Jeannie's birthday that evening, Guerd Eliott, the ranch foreman, accuses Jeannie of being in love with Adam. As Jeannie and Eliott quarrel on the porch, Jay slips into his uncle's office, steals $1,000 from the strongbox and rides into town to gamble. Soon after, Adam and Chito arrive at the party. Confronting Collinshaw alone in his office, Adam accuses him of killing his father and produces the empty shell, which fits Collinshaw's rifle. After confessing to the crime, Collinshaw explains that he killed for revenge because Adam's father had stolen the only woman he had ever loved. Handing over the photograph of

Adam's mother, Collinshaw admonishes Adam that he has learned the hard lesson that revenge resolves nothing. Adam's love for Jeannie renders him impotent to kill her uncle, and so he decides to foresake her and return to California. For Jeannie's sake, Collinshaw asks Adam to recover the money stolen by Jay, and he consents. After Adam leaves the room, Eliott enters and Collinshaw produces his confession to the murder of Adam's father. He also shows Eliott his new will leaving Adam his entire estate and asks him to sign as a witness. When Eliott protests and reminds Collinshaw that he had previously ordered Adam shot, Collinshaw fires Eliott and accuses him of contributing to Jay's death by fostering his gambling. Aware that Collinshaw's confession would implicate Adam if Collinshaw were murdered, Eliott pulls his gun, kills Collinshaw and then assembles a posse to apprehend Adam. At the saloon, meanwhile, Adam accuses the dealer of cheating with marked cards and demands he return the money that Jay lost. After the dealer complies, Adam rides out of town but is soon apprehended and jailed by the posse. While visiting Adam in jail, Jeannie reveals that Jay has admitted to stealing the money and then pleads with him to tell the truth and save himself. When she leaves, Chito appears and breaks Adam out of jail. After bidding his friend goodbye, Adam declares his intention to wander the wastelands once again. He then goes to Eliott's room, and at gunpoint, forces him to accompany him on foot. Defeated by thirst and exhaustion, Eliott confesses to Collinshaw's murder just as the posse, led by Jeannie and Chito, catch up to them. After producing the confession he found on her uncle's desk, Jeannie turns it over and reads a note on the back written by her uncle, attesting that Adam declined to kill him. Thus exonerated, Adam returns to the Rafferty ranch with Chito and his new wife Jeannie, and there announces that he is home to stay. *Murder. Revenge. Sheep ranchers.* Adoption. Arizona. Brothers and sisters. California. Cheating. Confession (Law). False accusations. Gambling. Jealousy. Mexican Americans. Nieces. Paralysis. Posses. Ranch foremen. Uncles. Wills.

Note: Zane Grey's novel was published serially in *McClure's* magazine, beginning in May 1920. A silent two-strip Technicolor version of Grey's story was made by Famous Players-Lasky in 1924. It was directed by Irvin Willat and starred Jack Holt, Noah Beery and Billie Dove (see *AFI Catalog of Feature Films, 1921-30*; F2.6087). The novel was also the source of a 1935 Paramount film directed by Otho Lovering and starring Dean Jagger and Gail Patrick (see *AFI Catalog of Feature Films, 1931-40*; F3.4950).

Box 22 Sep 1945. *DV* 28 Sep 1945, p. 3. *FD* 18 Oct 1945, p. 7. *HR* 25 May 1945, p. 15. *HR* 8 Jun 1945, p. 14. *HR* 28 Sep 1945, p. 3. *MPHPD* 29 Sep 1945, p. 2662. *NYT* 29 Sep 1945, p. 12. *Var* 26 Sep 1945, p. 14.

THE WANDERING JEW (Yiddish language)

Jewish American Film Arts, Inc. *Dist* Jewish American Film Arts, Inc. 20 Oct **1933**; Prod: 20 Jul—early Aug 1933 at Atlas Soundfilm Recording Studios, Long Island. Sd; b&w. 7 reels, 6,688 ft. 66, 68 or 70 min. Yiddish language with English subtitles.

Dir George Roland. *Story, adpt and dial* Jacob Mestel. *Photog* Frank Zucker and J. Burgi Contner. *Mus dir* I. J. Hochman.

Cast: Jacob Ben-Ami (*Arthur Levi*), Natalie Browning (*Gertrude*), M. B. Samuylow (*The Wanderer*), Ben Adler (*Paul Von Eisenon*), Jacob Mestel (*The servant*), Abraham Teitelbaum (*The reporter*), William Epstein (*Messenger*).

Yiddish, Social, Drama. [*Not viewed*]. Arthur Levi, an assimilated Jewish painter living in Berlin, dreams that his deceased father, whom he has used as the prototype for his latest work, "The Eternal Wanderer," responds to his own query of "Whither, father," with the admonition, "To the end of the goal....To eternity." As Levi finishes the painting, his servant, also a Jew, questions whether at the present time, when the country is agitated against the Jews, the Art Academy, where Levi teaches, will accept a painting with a Jewish subject. Levi, however, does not believe that current events have anything to do with art. As Levi leaves to visit his sweetheart Gertrude, who is not Jewish, a street orator rages against the Jews and asserts that Germany must be free of them. Later, as a Jewish reporter interviews Levi, Paul Von Eisenen, who calls himself Levi's friend, expresses to Gertrude both his fear for her future should she marry Levi and his own desire to marry her. Gertrude, however, rebukes Paul. Levi, meanwhile, explains to the reporter that the painting depicts the Jew as the eternal wanderer among nations. Levi's servant notices a determination in the eyes of the subject, and when Levi equates the look with the vengeance of his father's God, Jehovah, the servant retorts that a feeling of mercy, rather than vengeance, inspired the patriarch Abraham to open the eyes of brutal, idol-worshipping nations to Jehovah's mercy. Levi cynically points out that religious

nations recently sent their sons to horrible deaths in the world war, but the servant argues that the war was not Jehovah's fault and relates Abraham's efforts to avoid a war between his shepherds and those of Lott. After the reporter leaves, Paul casually remarks that he believes the Jews rule the world through an international secret clan, whereupon Levi berates Paul. After Paul leaves, Levi confesses to Gertrude that she brings him greater happiness than his art. The next day, the committee of the Art Academy rejects the painting and discharges Levi from his professorship. Levi, who says that he has made an effort to cleanse himself of his Jewish background, fumes at this turn of events. Paul warns Gertrude that whoever does not join the upcoming attack against the Jews will be crushed, but she again refuses to listen. Levi goes out to view for himself the burning of Jewish books and works. As a Nazi mob throws stones at his studio, Levi, afraid that they will destroy his painting, raises his knife to it, but the painting speaks to him in the voice of his father and admonishes him that the Jewish spirit must not be destroyed because it belongs to all humanity. The "Wanderer" tells Levi that when people don't want the contributions of the Jews, they must be taught in sleep to understand, and he relates that the Jews earlier were threatened with destruction during the Babylonian siege of Jerusalem, the Crusades in the Middle Ages, the Spanish Inquisition and the pogroms during the rule of the Russian czars. In the present day, the Wanderer tells Levi, a new order has been established in Russia; Jews are welcome to contribute to the culture of Spain; and in the Holy Land, Jewish cities and villages are blossoming. Gertrude arrives with a warning that Jews are being attacked in the street and that their houses are being burned, and she tells Levi goodbye, saying that although she loves him, she cannot stand up against a whole nation. In despair, Levi asks his father where to go, and the Wanderer predicts that, as in the past, a leader will arise to save the Jews. He relates that Moses led the Jews out of Egypt, and that later, a new Moses, Theodor Herzl, devised a plan for a Jewish Congress in Jerusalem. The Wanderer says that millions of people around the world are protesting against the racial hatred in Germany, and as he proclaims his dream for the Jews to be a nation among nations, Levi, now convinced that the Jewish spirit cannot be destroyed, vows "To eternity!" *Antisemitism. Assimilation (Sociology). Conversion (Religious). Fathers and sons. Germany. Jews. Jews–History. Nazism. Painters (Of paintings). Paintings. Religious persecution. Transformation. Wanderers. Biblical characters. Book burning. Crusades. Dismissal (Employment). Dreams. Egypt–History. Theodor Herzl. Inquisition–Spain. Jerusalem–Siege, 586 B.C.. Mobs. Palestine. Pogroms. Reporters. Russia. Servants. World War I.*

Note: The plot summary was based on a dialogue continuity at NYSA and reviews. The Yiddish title is *Der Vanderer Yid*. According to a *FD* news item dated 13 Jun 1933, Herman Ross, who owned a non-theatrical film business, organized a production company called Mammoth Pictures Co. to make this film. Subsequent sources, including NYSA records, call the production company Jewish American Film Arts, Inc. According to *FD* news items, this was to be the first of a series of films directed by George Roland and starring Jacob Ben-Ami, in Yiddish and English that would deal with current problems of Jewish life in Germany. A *MPD* news item noted that the company was organized by Ross to produce "Jewish art pictures." According to reviews, the film included footage from newsreels showing scenes from World War I, Nazi storm troops, the burning of Jewish books in Berlin, an anti-Hitler protest meeting in Madison Square Garden, the Soviet Union, Palestine, and from earlier dramatic films depicting past scenes in Jewish history.

According to NYSA information, after the New York State censors licensed the film on 13 Oct 1933, they were asked to approve English-language titles, which were to be superimposed on the film. After viewing the film with the new titles on 18 Oct, Irwin Esmond, the director of the censor board's motion picture division, in a memorandum commented, "it was our opinion that the superimposing of these English titles actually changed the situation for the reason that the picture, as originally presented in the Jewish dialogue and titles, contained an appeal merely to the Jewish people to maintain their religious ideals and standards through whatever difficulties, as had been their history in the past. By putting English titles on the picture it became a propaganda picture, being an appeal to the English speaking people in a partisan way, and might create a good deal of friction and trouble, and possibly violence." The censor board reserved the right to revoke the license at any time and to require that eliminations be made in the future.

According to a *FD* news item, the film was re-edited "to meet with the objections of religious groups" in Oct 1934 by Olympic Pictures, which planned to release it. According to NYSA records, in Oct 1937, the film, in a cut version of 5,710 feet, was retitled *A Jew in Exile*. *Exh* reviewed the film under this title in Jun 1938. In Dec 1939, the film's title was changed to *Nazi Terror* and in Jan 1941 to *The Jew in Germany*.

Exb 10 Nov 1933. *Exb* 15 Jun 1938. *FD* 13 Jun 1933, p. 2. *FD* 19 Jul 1933, p. 8. *FD* 27 Jul 1933, p. 4. *FD* 1 Aug 1933, p. 5. *FD* 4 Aug 1933, p. 6. *FD* 7 Aug 1933, p. 10. *FD* 21 Oct 1933, p. 4. *FD* 19 Oct 1934, p. 8. *Har* 4 Nov 1933, p. 175. *MPD* 12 Jul 1933, p. 2. *MPD* 21 Oct 1933, p. 4. *MPH* 28 Oct 1933, p. 59. *NYT* 21 Oct 1933, p. 11. *Spectator* 24 Nov 1933, p. 768. *Var* 24 Oct 1933, p. 2.

WANTED, A MOTHER (Italian Americans)
World Film Corp. *Dist* World Film Corp. 18 Mar **1918** [©World Film Corp.; 5 Mar 1918; LU12146]. Si; b&w. 5 reels.
Pres William A. Brady. *Dir* Harley Knoles. *Scen* Virginia Tyler Hudson. *Story* Julia Burnham. *Cam* René Guissart.
Cast: Madge Evans (*Eileen Homer*), George MacQuarrie (*Dr. Homer*), Gerda Holmes (*Dr. Thelma Winter*), Alec B. Francis (*Dr. Thayer*), Lionel Belmore (*Guiseppe*), Tom Evans (*Guiseppe's son*), Rosina Henley (*Marie*), Harry Bartlett (*James*).
Drama. Neglected by her grief-stricken father, a doctor, after the tragic death of his wife, little Eileen Homer changes the wording of her father's ad for a governess to read: "Wanted, a mother." A laborer named Guiseppe asks Dr. Homer to operate on his ailing son, but when the boy dies, the enraged father attacks the doctor. Eileen meets her father's friend, Dr. Thelma Winter, and that night, while dreaming that Dr. Winter has become her fairy mother, she walks in her sleep to the edge of the lake. Wandering aimlessly in his grief, Guiseppe rescues the girl and takes her home to fill the void left by the loss of his son. In trying to return home, Eileen falls from the fire escape and is rushed to the hospital, where Dr. Winter saves her life. Afterwards, the grateful Dr. Homer becomes a more loving father with the help of his new wife, Dr. Winter, and Guiseppe becomes the family's gardener. *Children. Fathers and daughters. Italians. Laborers. Neglected children. Physicians. Widowers. Advertisements. Dreams. Fairies. Falls from heights. Gardeners. Governesses. Hospitals. Lakes. Operations, Surgical. Somnambulism.*

Note: One source attributes the story to Helen Bearé.
ETR 16 Mar 1918, p. 1233. *MPN* 9 Mar 1918, p. 1450. *MPN* 23 Mar 1918, p. 1766. *MPW* 23 Mar 1918, p. 1701. *MPW* 30 Mar 1918, p. 1872, 1874. *Wid's* 4 Apr 1918, p. 1057.

WANTED FOR MURDER, OR BRIDE OF HATE *see* **THE BRIDE OF HATE**

WAR ARROW (Native Americans, Kiowa, Seminole)
Universal-International Pictures Co., Inc. *Dist* Universal Pictures Co., Inc. Jan **1954**; Prod: early Mar—early Apr 1953 [©Universal Pictures Co.; 3 Jan 1954; LP3255]. Sd (Western Electric Recording); col (Technicolor). 7,239 ft. 78 min. PCA cert no. 16563.
Prod John W. Rogers. *Dir* George Sherman. *Asst dir* Frank Shaw. *Wrt* John Michael Hayes. *Dir of photog* William Daniels. *Technicolor color consultant* William Fritzsche. *Art dir* Bernard Herzbrun and Alexander Golitzen. *Film ed* Frank Gross. *Set dec* Russell A. Gausman and Joseph Kish. *Cost des* Edward Stevenson. *Mus dir* Joseph Gershenson. *Sd* Leslie I. Carey and Richard DeWeese. *Makeup* Bud Westmore. *Hair stylist* Joan St. Oegger.
Cast: Maureen O'Hara (*Elaine Corwin*), Jeff Chandler (*Major Howell Brady*), John McIntire (*Col. Jackson Meade*), Suzan Ball (*Avis*), Noah Beery (*Sgt. Augustus Wilks*), Charles Drake (*Sgt. Luke Schermerhorn*), Henry Brandon (*Maygro*), Dennis Weaver (*Pino*), Jay Silverheels (*Satanta*), James Bannon (*Capt. Roger* [*G.*] *Corwin*), Steve Wyman (*Captain Neil*), Brad Jackson (*Lieutenant*), [Lance Fuller, Kermit Maynard, Bill Ward (*Troopers*)], [Dee Carroll (*Hysterical mother*)], [Ezelle Poule (*Mother*)], [Roy Whaley (*Lieutenant*)], [Darla Ridgeway (*Crying child*)], [Dick Fortune (*Lieutenant*)], [Emile Avery (*Sentry*)], [Jack Torneck (*Adjustment*)], [Sally Yarnell].
Historical, Western. [*Print viewed*]. Major Howell Brady of the U.S. Cavalry is sent to Fort Clark, Texas, with his two sergeants, Luke Schermerhorn and Augustus Wilks, to put down bloody raids on settlers by Kiowa Indians. Brady's arrival is greeted with little enthusiasm by Col. Jackson Meade, the commanding officer at Fort Clark, who sees Brady's presence as a threat to his authority. Meade balks at Brady's plan to use the peaceful Seminole Indians to keep the Kiowas at bay, but Brady goes ahead with his plan and meets with Chief Maygro, chief of the Seminoles. Maygro initially resists Brady's plan, but later changes his mind after seeing the ease with which Brady and his men fight off raiding Kiowas with their high-powered Henry repeating rifles. In exchange for Maygro's help in stopping Kiowa raids, Brady gives him $500, food and a promise that the Seminoles will be given the fertile Santa Media Valley. Brady's decision to quarter the Seminoles at Fort Clark is met with resistance by Meade and many others, and he soon finds that his only ally at the

fort is Elaine Corwin, a widow whose husband was killed on a scouting mission. Brady and Elaine soon fall in love, and Avis, Maygro's daughter, becomes jealous of the romance. The training of the Seminoles proves a success, and they repel the Kiowa raids. During one of the attacks, Brady sees a white man flee with the Indians. Although he is unable to get a good look at the man, Brady finds the sword he dropped, which bears the name "R. G. Corwin." Later, while questioning Elaine about her husband, Brady learns that he was only presumed dead, and that he was associated with a Mexican group determined to incite the Kiowas to battle. Brady nearly loses his Seminole support when Meade fails to deliver a food supply promised to the Seminoles. Maygro leads his tribesmen out of the fort, but Brady manages to win them back after stealing the food and delivering it himself. Meade jails Brady and his sergeants for the theft, but they are freed by Elaine and some of the Seminoles. Soon after the jailbreak, Brady discovers that the Kiowas are preparing a massive assault on the fort, and he returns to warn Meade. Meade disregards the warning and is about to return the men to jail when one of his own patrols arrives with the same news. A fierce battle ensues between the Kiowas and those inside the fort, but Brady outwits the attackers by sneaking out of the fort and firing on the Kiowas from behind. Among the many killed at the fort is Corwin, who revealed himself to be a traitor by fighting on the side of the Seminoles. Having saved the fort from destruction, Brady looks forward to his next mission with Elaine at his side. *Battles. Forts. Kiowa Indians. Raids. Romance. Seminole Indians. Texas–History. United States–History–Indian campaigns. United States. Army. Cavalry. Fathers and daughters. Jailbreaks. Jealousy. Missing persons, Assumed dead. Rifles. Settlers. Swords. Traitors. Tribal chiefs. Widows.*

Note: A working title for this film was *Brady's Bunch.*

Box 12 Dec 1953. *DV* 17 Jun 1953. *DV* 8 Dec 1953, p. 3. *FD* 17 Dec 1953, p. 3. *HR* 6 Mar 1953, p. 23. *HR* 3 Apr 1953, p. 9. *HR* 8 Dec 1953, p. 3. *MPHPD* 12 Dec 1953, p. 2101. *Var* 9 Dec 1953, p. 6.

WAR CLOUDS *see* **THE YELLOW TOMAHAWK**

WAR CRY *see* **INDIAN UPRISING**

WAR DANCE *see* **APACHE DRUMS**

WAR DRUMS (Native Americans, Apache, Latino)

Bel-Air Productions. *Dist* United Artists Corp. Apr **1957**; *Prod:* mid-Jul—early Jul 1956 [©Palm Productions, Inc.; 9 Apr 1957; LP8459]. Sd (Westrex Recording System); col (DeLuxe). 75 min. PCA cert no. 18278.

Exec prod Aubrey Schenck. *Prod* Howard W. Koch. *Dir* Reginald LeBorg. *Asst dir* Paul Wurtzel. *Wrt* Gerald Drayson Adams. *Photog* William Margulies. *Operative cam* Ben Colman. *Spec photog eff* Jack Rabin and Louis DeWitt. *Prod des* Jack T. Collis. *Supv ed* John S. Schreyer. *Ed* John A. Bushelman. *Set dec* Clarence Steenson. [*Set dec* Arden Cripe]. *Joan Taylor's cost des* Paula Giokaris. *Ward* Wesley V. Jefferies and Angela Alexander. *Mus* Les Baxter. [*Mus ed* Carl Lodato and Sam Waxman]. *Sd ed* Joe Edmondson. *Re-rec* Charles Cooper. *Makeup artist* Ted Coodley. *Hair styles* Mary Westmoreland. *Scr supv* Kathleen Fagan. *Key grip* Herschel Brown. *Lighting tech* Joe Edesa.

Music: "The Mexican Hat Dance," arranged by F. A. Partichela.
Song(s): "Cielito lindo," traditional.

Cast: Lex Barker [(*Mangas Colorado*)], Joan Taylor [(*Riva*)], Ben Johnson [(*Luke Fargo*)], Larry Chance [(*Ponce*)], Richard Cutting [(*Judge Bolton*)], John Pickard [(*Sheriff Bullard*)], James Parnell [(*Arizona*)], John Colicos [(*Chino*)], Tom Monroe [(*Dutch Herman*)], Jil Jarmyn [(*Nona*)], Jeanne Carmen [(*Yellow Moon*)], Mauritz Hugo [(*Clay Staub*)], Ward Ellis [(*Delgadito*)], [Fred Sherman (*Dr. Gordon*)], [Paul Fierro (*Fiero*)], [Alex Montoya (*Manuel*)], [Stuart Whitman (*Johnny Smith*)], [Barbara Parry (*Mary Smith*)], [Jack Hupp (*Lt. Roberts*)], [Red Morgan (*Trooper Teal*)].

Western. [*Print viewed*]. When Mangas Colorado and his band of Apaches raid a camp of Mexican bandits who have stolen their horses, they retrieve their property and also take Riva, a half-Mexican, half-Comanche Indian girl whose father was killed by the horse thieves during a raid on his ranch. Mangas, pulling Riva along by a leash, and his band visit the camp of trader Luke Fargo, Mangas' old friend. When Judge Bolton, who is in the area to make a peace treaty with the Apaches, asks about the girl, Fargo explains that the Apaches kidnap Mexican girls to sell to white saloon owners. The judge is disgusted

at the Indians' blatant practice of white slavery, but Fargo compares their actions to the U.S. government's placing of Indians on reservations as well as to the Southern states' legalized slavery. Around the campfire Riva sings and dances with Fargo, and smitten, he offers to trade guns for the girl, but Mangas refuses. The Apaches return to their village, where Mangas announces that he wishes to make Riva his wife. The Apaches, including Mangas' best friend Ponce, are distressed, and the medicine man Chino says that the spirits will retaliate if Mangas marries outside of the Apaches' customs. Although Ponce changes his position, two other warriors challenge Mangas, who fights them to the death. Mangas' cousin Yellow Moon and his sister Nona do not easily accept Riva, and when they attempt to force her to do squaw's labor, including building a wicky for her husband-to-be, Riva brawls with them and then tells Mangas that she will be treated as his equal. Mangas agrees, and then teaches Riva to shoot and hunt. At the wedding ceremony, Fargo, disappointed that he has lost Riva, nonetheless offers her a horse as a wedding present, and on the couple's wedding night, Riva teaches Mangas to kiss like an American. Later on, gold miners violate the American peace treaty by panning in Apache territory, and when Nona confronts them, they beat her and then shoot and injure her son, Little Owl. Mangas tries to convince the miners to go away peacefully, but they capture him and whip his backside, leaving humiliating scars. The enraged Apache chief then alerts Riva and the other warriors, and they raid the camp, killing all but one of the men. Later, Judge Bolton and Fargo meet at the site of the recent raid, and Sheriff Bullard announces his intent to teach the Apaches a lesson. Fargo asks that he may be permitted to go see Mangas to ascertain the truth, before they resort to violence. The judge agrees, but insists that the troops be shown the Apaches' hiding place. With the troops behind him, Fargo approaches the Apache band with a white flag, but as Mangas leaves his cover, Riva, spotting the troops assembled, cries out a warning. Ponce, in a panic, fires the first shot and kills Judge Bolton. During the ensuing battle, Fargo is wounded, and Riva nurses his wounds. When Mangas shows up, he recounts his humiliation at the hands of the miners, and Fargo says farewell. As the Apaches continue their raids on miners' camps, wagon trains and settlements, the Civil War breaks out, and Fargo becomes a U.S. Army major. Mangas is shot in a skirmish, and Riva, refusing to entrust her beloved husband to Chino, has him taken to a white settlement where an American doctor can treat him. After the doctor has finished tending Mangas' wounds, Fargo and his troops arrive at the settlement, and Fargo goes to see Riva and Mangas. Fargo explains that he has received orders to kill the Apache warriors and send the women and children to Fort Stanton, unless the Apaches put down their weapons and go peacefully to the reservations. Mangas refuses that option, but makes peace with his old friend Fargo. Fargo, realizing that Mangas will never give up, calls a temporary truce in order to allow the Apaches to seek refuge in the mountains. Riva, Mangas and their band of warriors depart with dignity. *Apache Indians. Battles. Friendship. Gunfights. Mangas Coloradas. United States. Army. Cavalry. Ambushes. Brothers and sisters. Childbirth. Cousins. Gold miners. Horse thieves. Indians of North America–Mixed blood. Indians of North America–Reservations. Kidnapping. Marriage–Mixed. Medicine men. Mexicans. Peace. Physicians. Romantic rivalry. United States–History–Civil War, 1861-1865. Wounds and injuries.*

Note: The film's working title was *Chief Red Sleeves.* The Apache Chief Mangas Coloradas (who is called Mangas Colorado in the film), along with Cochise, led much of the warfare against U.S. outposts during a twenty-five year period of Apache unrest beginning in the early 1860s. Coloradas was also the father of one of Cochise's wives. The scene in the film in which "Riva" and the warriors force the white doctor to tend to "Mangas'" wounds was based on a true incident, in which Mangas' warriors brought their chief, who had been shot in the chest, to a doctor in Janos, Mexico, and forced the man at gunpoint to remove the bullet. *War Drums* was shot on location in Kanab, UT. Although in the film Riva states that she is half Mexican, half Comanche, ads for the film describe her as a "White Warrior Woman." "Mangas" was also a character in the 1955 film *Fort Yuma* (see above).

Box 4 May 1957. *DV* 28 Mar 1957, p. 10. *Exh* 3 Apr 1957, pp. 4308-09. *FD* 1 Apr 1957, p. 3. *Har* 30 Mar 1957, pp. 50-51. *HR* 13 Jul 1956, p. 11. *HR* 27 Jul 1956, p. 13. *HR* 28 Mar 1957, p. 9. *MPD* 29 Mar 1957. *MPHPD* 30 Mar 1957, p. 322. *Var* 3 Apr 1957, p. 6.

THE WAR OF THE TONGS (Chinese Americans)

Universal Film Mfg. Co.; Red Feather Photoplays. *Dist* Universal Film Mfg. Co. 19 Feb **1917** [©Universal Film Mfg. Co.; 7 Feb 1917; LP10147]. Si; b&w. 5 reels.

Cam George W. Lawrence.

Cast: Tom Hing (*Chin Ting*), Hoo Ching (*Lee Hoy*), Lee Gow (*Wong Wing*), Lin Neong (*Suey Lee*).

Drama. Wong Wing, a clerk in Sam Hop's tea shop, loves Suey Lee but her father's landlord, Chin Ting, a Tong leader, wants the girl for himself. When Suey refuses Ting's proposal of marriage, Lee gives his daughter permission to marry Wong Wing, provided he can raise a dowry of $900. Wong Wing attempts to win the money at Chin Ting's gambling house but instead is cheated of his entire savings. Wing's accusations of trickery precipitates a war between his tong and that of Chin Ting. After several clashes between the tongs, Wong Wing disposes of his rival and wins Suey Lee. *Chinese Americans. Gang wars. Gangs. Landlords. Salesclerks. Tongs (Secret societies). Cheating. Dowry. Gambling houses. Tea.*

Note: This film, according to news items, was written by a Chinese writer, and its principal actors were members of the Imperial Chinese players. Although *MPW* stated that the film was directed "by an American," they praised the film for giving "an insight into Oriental life impossible to obtain when the actors are Americans." At some length, *MPW* applauded the film's depiction of Chinese-American life: "For the first time in the history of screen productions, the customs of the Chinese in their homes, stores and secret societies are shown by native performers. The inner workings of the tongs and the Chinese gambling houses are vividly and faithfully depicted. Every phase of Chinese home life, including the strange marriage rites, is depicted.... The celebrated Chinese lottery, which is shrouded in much mystery, is exposed, as are the methods of the tongs. A secret meeting of a warring tong, with all the strange rites of the members, has been photographed, and every ceremony performed in the lodge rooms is declared to be exactly reproduced as it occurs in actual life. Chinese are noted for their honesty in business transactions and this phase of their lives is carefully brought out in the development of the story, as some of the action takes place in a large Chinese mercantile house, where their business methods are also carefully depicted. The strange system of accounting used by Chinese merchants, which is baffling to a member of another race but most simple to themselves, is only one of the many bits of atmosphere used in this unusual film production."

ETR 24 Feb 1917, p. 835. *MPN* 24 Feb 1917, p. 1258. *MPW* 24 Feb 1917, p. 1245. *Wid's* 15 Feb 1917, p. 103.

WAR OF THE WILDCATS *see* IN OLD OKLAHOMA

WAR PAINT (Native Americans, Arapaho)

Metro-Goldwyn-Mayer Corp.; controlled by Loew's Inc. *Dist* Metro-Goldwyn-Mayer Distributing Corp. 10 Oct **1926** [©Metro-Goldwyn-Mayer Corp.; 18 Oct 1926; LP23231]. Si; b&w. 6 reels, 5,034 ft,

Dir W. S. Van Dyke. *Story* Peter B. Kyne. *Cont* Charles Maigne. *Titles* Joe Farnham. *Photog* Clyde De Vinna.

Cast: Tim McCoy (*Lieut. Tim Marshall*), Pauline Starke (*Polly Hopkins*), Charles French (*Major Hopkins*), Chief Yowlache (*Iron Eyes*), Chief Whitehorse (*White Hawk*), Karl Dane (*Petersen*).

Western. Iron Eyes, a medicine man, foments discontent among his people during the early 1880s. Young Lieut. Tim Marshall arrests him, following a knife duel in which both are wounded and from which Tim is saved by Chief Fearless Eagle (White Hawk?), a friend of the whites. Tim meets Polly, daughter of Major Hopkins, picking flowers outside the fort, and forces her to return to safety. Meanwhile, Iron Eyes escapes from the guardhouse and vows vengeance on the whites. At a dance, where Tim declares his love for Polly, a wounded messenger arrives telling of his escape from Iron Eyes. Major Hopkins then delivers an ultimatum to Fearless Eagle: unless Iron Eyes is delivered up in twenty-four hours, American troops will destroy his tribe. Iron Eyes stages an attack on the fort, but Tim escapes and persuades Fearless Eagle to rout the attackers and save the women and children of the garrison. *Arapaho Indians. Forts. Frontier and pioneer life. Medicine men. United States. Army.*

Var 20 Oct 1926, p. 63.

WAR PAINT (1950) *see* BROKEN ARROW

WAR PAINT (Native Americans)

K-B Productions, Inc. *Dist* United Artists Corp. 28 Aug **1953**; Prod: late Feb—mid-Mar 1953 at Motion Picture Center Studios [©K-B Productions, Inc.; 28 Jul 1953; LP2993]. Sd (Western Electric Recording); col (Pathé Color). 84-86 or 89 min. PCA cert no. 16482.

Pres AUBREY SCHENCK. *Prod* Howard W. Koch. *Dir* Lesley Selander. *Asst dir* Gilbert L. May. *Scr* Richard Alan Simmons and Martin Berkeley. *Based on a story by* Fred Freiberger and William Tunberg. *Dir of photog* Gordon Avil. [*Stills* George Hommel]. *Spec eff* Daniel Hays. *Photog eff* Jack Rabin and David Commons. *Art dir* Wiard B. Ihnen. *Film ed* John F. Schreyer. *Set dec* Victor A. Gangelin. *Ward* Wesley V. Jefferies. *Mus* Emil Newman and Arthur Lange. *Sd*

Ben Winkler. *Hair stylist* Mary Smith. *Makeup artist* Stanley Campbell. *Lighting tech* Joseph Edesa. *Scr supv* Ted Schilz.

Song(s): "Elaine," words and music by Johnny Lehmann and Emil Newman.

Cast: Robert Stack [(*Lt. Billings*)], Joan Taylor [(*Wanima*)], Charles McGraw [(*Sgt. Clarke*)], Keith Larsen [(*Taslik*)], Peter Graves [(*Trooper Tolson*)], Robert Wilke [(*Grady*)], Walter Reed [(*Allison*)], John Doucette [(*Trooper Charnofsky*)], Douglas Kennedy [(*Clancy*)], Charles Nolte [(*Cpl. Hamilton*)], James Parnell [(*Martin*)], Paul Richards [(*Trooper Perkins*)], William Pullen [(*Jeb*)], Richard Cutting [(*Lt. Kirby*)].

Western. [*Print viewed*]. On their way back to Fort Kirk from patrol duty, Lt. Billings and Sgt. Clarke are informed that they must deliver a treaty to the nearby trading post, where it will be picked up by a waiting lieutenant named Kirby. The treaty, which contains terms of peace that are satisfactory to both the Indians and the U.S. government, must be delivered to Chief Gray Cloud within nine days, or there will be war. The men, particularly Trooper Perkins, whose wife has just had a baby, are unhappy, and when they reach the trading post, they are dismayed to learn that Kirby has not arrived. Unknown to Billings and his men, Kirby and his men have been killed by Gray Cloud's son Taslik, an embittered warrior who believes the treaty will further weaken his people. When Taslik arrives at the post, Billings asks him to guide the troop to Gray Cloud's village. That night, as the soldiers listen to Trooper Charnofsky's stories about life in Poland, Taslik applies war paint and glares at them. When one of the men suspiciously inquires about the war paint, Taslik asks, "Do you not wear war clothes?" After a day's ride through desert terrain, heavy boulders destroy all but one of the soldiers' water barrels, and the next day, Billings is horrified to learn that the remaining barrel has sprung a leak. Taslik leads them to a spring, but it is dry. While the men sleep, Taslik steals away and receives water from his sister Wanima, who has been secretly accompanying the party and helping her brother to sabotage the water supply. Several mishaps later, Billings begins to suspect Taslik, and when all the horses are set loose, he finally confronts the brave. Taslik states that although his father considers white men honorable, he is certain the treaty will be broken. Determined to deliver the treaty, Billings order the men to continue, but it soon becomes apparent that Taslik has been leading them in circles. Exasperated and thirsty, a trooper named Tolson kills Taslik. Because the men are weak from thirst, Billings decides to send one man, Clancy, ahead to the village, but Wanima follows and shoots him. Before Clancy dies, he wounds her, however, and the detachment later stumbles onto the two fallen bodies. The soldiers want to kill Wanima, but Billings opts to take her along as proof that they want peace. Wanima leads the men not to water, but to a deserted gold mine. Grady, one of the soldiers, tries to kill Wanima, and when Billings defends her, Tolson shoots him in the arm. Realizing that Billings is sincere in his desire for peace, Wanima takes the party to a spring, thereby postponing a mutiny. That night, Tolson and two others decide to kill the loyal members of the troop so that they may plunder the gold mine. Clarke sends Billings and Wanima on to the village while he fends off the mutineers, but after the stabbing and shooting are over, only Tolson remains alive. As Billings and Wanima approach Gray Cloud's village, the soldier attacks them. A brutal fight ensues, but in the end, Billings stabs Tolson. Exhausted, Wanima and the lieutenant slowly enter the village together. *Desert survival. Guides. Indians of North America. Sabotage. Treaties. United States. Army. Cavalry. Ambushes. Gold mines. Greed. Gunfights. Gunshot wounds. Knife fighting. Murder. Mutiny. Officers (Military). Polish Americans. Sabotage. Self-sacrifice. Soldiers. Suicide. Thirst. Trading posts.*

Note: The closing credits include the following written acknowledgement: "*War Paint* was photographed in its entirety in beautiful Death Valley National Monument, California, with the cooperation of the U.S. Department of the Interior and the National Park Service. Without their help, this picture would not have been possible." *HR* production charts include Neville Brand in the cast, but his participation in the released film has not been confirmed. The pressbook for the film erroneously boasts that it was the first feature-length picture ever to be filmed in Death Valley. According to news items, *War Paint* was the first production of Howard Koch's company, K-B Productions, Inc. According to correspondence in the MPAA/PCA Collection at the AMPAS Library, an early draft of the screenplay contained a mercy killing scene to which PCA Director Joseph I. Breen objected.

Box 4 Jul 1953. *DV* 29 Jun 1953, p. 3. *Exb* 15 Jul 1953, p. 3560. *FD* 14 Jul 1953, p. 6. *Har* 4 Jul 1953, p. 107. *HCN* 26 Sep 1953. *HR* 11 Feb 1953. *HR* 20 Feb 1953, p. 13. *HR* 13

Mar 1953, p. 9. *HR* 25 May 1953. *HR* 29 Jun 1953, p. 3. *IP* Jun 1953, pp. 8-9. *LAEx* 26 Sep 1953. *LAT* 26 Sep 1953. *MPD* 7 Jul 1953. *MPHPD* 4 Jul 1953, p. 1903. *Var* 8 Jul 1953, p. 6.

WAR PARTY *see* **FORT APACHE**

WARBONNET *see* **THE SAVAGE**

WARPATH (Native Americans, Dakota)

Nat Holt Productions. *Dist* Paramount Pictures Corp. Aug **1951**; Prod: late Aug–late Sep 1950 [©Paramount Pictures Corp.; 1 Aug 1951; LP1127]. Sd (Western Electric Recording); col (Technicolor). 8,564 ft. 95 min. PCA cert no. 14913.

Prod Nat Holt. *Assoc to the prod* Harry Templeton. *Dir* Byron Haskin. *Asst dir* James Paisley. *Story and scr* Frank Gruber. *Dir of photog* Ray Rennahan. *Technicolor col consultant* Richard Mueller. *Art dir* John Goodman. *Film ed* Philip Martin. *Set dec* Robert Priestly. *Ward* Elmer Ellsworth. *Mus comp and cond* Paul Sawtell. *Sd rec* Gene Merritt. *Makeup artist* Norman Pringle. [*Tech adv* Col. Brice C. Custer].

Source: Based on the novel *Broken Lance* by Frank Gruber (New York, 1949).

Cast: EDMOND O'BRIEN (*John Vickers*), DEAN JAGGER (*Sam Quade [previously known as Morrison]*), FORREST TUCKER (*Sgt. O'Hara [previously known as Bly]*), HARRY CAREY, JR. (*Capt. Gregson*), Polly Bergen (*Molly Quade*), James Millican (*General [George] Custer*), Wallace Ford (*Private Potts*), Paul Fix (*Private Fiore*), Louis Jean Heydt (*Herb Woodson*), Paul Lees (*Corp. Stockbridge*), Walter Sande (*Sgt. Parker*), Charles Dayton (*Lieut. Nelson*), Bob Bray (*Major Comstock*), Douglas Spencer (*Kelso*), James Burke (*Old-Timer*), Chief Yowlachie (*Chief*), John Mansfield (*Sub-chief*), Monte Blue (*1st Emigrant*), Frank Ferguson (*Marshal*), Cliff Clark (*Bartender*), Paul Burns (*Bum*), Charles Stevens (*Courier*), John Hart (*Sgt. Plennert*).

Western. [*Print viewed*]. Newly arrived in town, John Vickers confronts Herb Woodson on the street and challenges him to draw his gun. When Woodson asks John why he has been following him for eight years, John reminds him that he and two other men killed his fiancée Helen. Woodson fires and misses, but John's bullet finds its target, and as Woodson dies, he reveals that the other two killers, Morrison and Bly, have joined the U.S. Cavalry. Shortly afterward, John, enroute to Bismarck, North Dakota, to enlist in General George Custer's Seventh Regiment, defends Molly Quade, an attractive young woman who is being harassed by a drunken sergeant. The sergeant, O'Hara, is furious at the intrusion, and after the train arrives in Bismarck, he is pleased to learn that John has been assigned to his company at Fort Lincoln. John befriends some of the other Company M men, but O'Hara torments him, ordering him to perform stable duty and other loathsome tasks. Meanwhile, Molly, who has come to Fort Lincoln to help her father run the general store, tells the elder Quade that she has met an interesting man, but Quade, upon meeting John, is inexplicably rude to the recruit. O'Hara overhears John asking a soldier if Bly and Morrison are in the Seventh Regiment. Several days later, Company M is ordered to subdue a band of Sioux that has attacked a wagon train. At Nelson's Island, miles from the fort, the company finds itself outnumbered and under attack by the Indians. Following a furious battle, John volunteers to return to the fort for help, but as he disappears into the trees, someone takes a shot at him. John arrives at the fort just as General Custer rides up. Custer remarks that he remembers John's years as an outstanding Union officer. Then the general and his men, to the great relief of the besieged troopers, accompany John to Nelson's Island. Having helped to save the surviving soldiers of Company M from slaughter, John is promoted to the rank of first sergeant. That day, John accuses O'Hara of having shot at him on the island and reveals his suspicions that O'Hara is one of his fiancée's murderers. Worried, O'Hara visits Quade and advises him that John has discovered his identity, whereupon Quade persuades him to flee for his life. New information convinces John that O'Hara is, in fact, Bly, but after strapping on his gun, John learns that the sergeant has deserted. After advising John to pursue the killers through legal channels, Captain Gregson orders him and his men to escort a wagon train through Sioux country. Quade and Molly, having sold their store, join the wagon train and are captured along with John and several others when the party is attacked. At the Sioux village, where O'Hara is also being held captive, the prisoners learn that Custer unknowingly is leading his men into an impossible battle

with ten thousand Sioux and Cheyenne at Little Big Horn. To help the others escape, O'Hara disrupts the tribe's spirited powwow with gunfire, sacrificing his life in the process. John, Quade and Molly seize the opportunity to steal away from the village, and that night, John tells Molly that although he knows that her father is also one of the killers, he is no longer obsessed with a desire for revenge. While the sweethearts talk, Quade rides off to warn Custer about the Indian forces at Little Big Horn. The next day, John and Molly rejoin Captain Gregson's detachment, which succeeds in winning a battle against the Sioux. Realizing that Custer and most of the Seventh Regiment have probably been wiped out, Gregson persuades John to become an officer so that he and his future wife Molly can live in the officer's quarters. *Military life. Revenge. United States–History–Indian campaigns. United States. Army. Cavalry. Aliases. Attempted murder. Battles. Bismarck (ND). General George Armstrong Custer. Dakota Indians. Desertion, Military. Escapes. Fathers and daughters. Forts. Gunfights. Heroism. Indians of North America. Little Big Horn, Battle of the, 1876. Massacres. North Dakota. Obsession. Rescues. Rites and ceremonies. Romance. Self-sacrifice. Settlers. Storekeepers. Wagon trains.*

Note: A condensed version of Frank Gruber's novel was published in Jul 1948 in *Mammoth Western* magazine. Onscreen credits include the following dedication: "This picture is dedicated as a living memorial to the Seventh U.S. Cavalry, whose immortal fame has added so richly to the heritage of our country." An acknowledgment at the end of the film expresses appreciation to the Dept. of the Interior, Office of Indian Affairs; to Robert Yellowtail and the Crow Indian tribe; to the Yellowstone County Fair Board; and to the city of Billings, Montana. According to contemporary sources, some scenes were filmed at the County Inland Empire Fair building in Billings, MT, and at other Billings locations. The film depicts some of the events that led to the famous 1876 Battle of Little Big Horn, in which George Armstrong Custer and all of his men were killed. Gold had been discovered in the Black Hills of the Dakotas in 1874, and white prospectors flooded the region earlier granted to the Dakota (Sioux) Indians. Both the Sioux and the Cheyenne were opposed to these incursions, and in 1876, the U.S. Seventh Cavalry was ordered to launch a large-scale campaign to end the resistence. Custer located Chief Sitting Bull's camp on the Little Big Horn River, but he greatly underestimated the size of the combined Sioux and Cheyenne forces. Col. Brice C. Custer, who served as technical adviser on the picture, was Custer's grandnephew, according to a Sep 1950 *Par News* item. For information on other pictures on General Custer and the Battle of the Little Big Horn, see the entry above for *They Died With Their Boots On.*

DV 1 Jun 1951. *HCN* 3 Aug 1951. *HR* 18 Aug 1950, p. 13. *HR* 28 Sep 1950, p. 12. *HR* 1 Jun 1951. *LADN* 13 Oct 1950. *LAEx* 3 Aug 1951. *LAT* 3 Aug 1951. *MPD* 5 Jun 1951. *MPHPD* 2 Jun 1951. *NYT* 23 Nov 1951, p. 32. *Var* 6 Jun 1951, p.

WARRIOR GAP (Native Americans, Dakota)

Davis Distributing Division, Inc. *Dist* Vital Exchanges. **1925**; New York State license: 4 Dec 1925. Si; b&w. 5 reels, 4,900 ft.

Dir Alvin J. Neitz. *Scen* George W. Pyper. *Photog* Alfred Gosden.

Source: Based on the novel *Warrior Gap, a Story of the Sioux Outbreak of '68* by Capt. Charles King (New York, c1897).

Cast: Ben Wilson (*Captain Deane*), Neva Gerber (*Elinor Folsom*), Robert Walker (*Major Burleigh*), Jim Welch (*Colonel Stevens*), Aline Goodwin (*Mrs. Hal Folsom*), Lafe McKee (*John Folsom*), Dick Hatton (*Hal Folsom*), Alfred Hewston (*Sergeant Casey*), Ruth Royce (*Mrs. Fletcher*), Len Haynes (*Chief Red Cloud*), William Patten (*Courier*).

Western. Captain Deane and Major Burleigh are returning with their troops from a frontier post when they are attacked by hostile Indians. The men have been ordered to avoid a direct military confrontation, but Major Burleigh, prompted by military vainglory, insists on counterattacking. Deane refuses and parts company with the major and his men, later defending Elinor Folsom from an Indian attack on her isolated ranch. Deane is arrested for insubordination and cowardice, but he is cleared of these charges, is released, and whips Burleigh in a fight. Deane is then ordered to convey a military payroll, and Burleigh incites a band of Indians to intercept him. Elinor learns of this plot and rides to warn Deane, and the two are soon compelled to fight for their lives. They are rescued by the cavalry, and Burleigh is shot. Elinor and the captain are wed. *Dakota Indians. Indians of North America. Red Cloud. United States. Army. Cavalry.*

THE WARS FOR CIVILIZATION IN AMERICA *see* **THE INDIAN WARS**

THE WATER LILY *see* **A TALE OF TWO WORLDS**

WATERFRONT (Irish Americans)

Warner Bros. Pictures, Inc. *Dist* Warner Bros. Pictures, Inc. 15 Jul 1939; Prod: 11 Feb—mid-Mar 1939 [©Warner Bros. Pictures, Inc.; 15 Jul 1939; LP8976]. Sd; b&w. 6 reels. 59-60 min. PCA cert no. 5226.

[*Prod* Bryan Foy]. [*Exec prod* Jack L. Warner and Hal B. Wallis]. *Dir* Terry Morse. *Dial dir* Arthur Ripley. [*Asst dir* Les Guthrie]. *Scr* Lee Katz and Arthur Ripley. [*Contr to trmt* Fred Niblo, Jr.]. [*Contr to scr const* Don Ryan]. *Photog* James Van Trees. *Art dir* Charles Novi. *Film ed* Louis Hesse. *Gowns* Milo Anderson. *Sd* Stanley Jones.

Source: Based on the play *Blindspot* by Kenyon Nicholson (production undetermined).

Cast: Gloria Dickson (*Ann Stacey*), Dennis Morgan (*Jim Dolen*), Marie Wilson (*Ruby Waters*), Sheila Bromley (*Marie Cordell*), Larry Williams [(*Frankie Donahue*)], Aldrich Bowker [(*Father Dunn*)], Frank Faylen [(*Skids Riley*)], Ward Bond [(*Mart Hendler*)], Arthur Gardner [(*Dan Dolen*)], George Lloyd [(*Joe Becker*)], [Dutch Hendrian (*Pete*)], [Lee Phelps (*Turnkey Martin*)], [Jerry Fletcher (*Elevator operator*)], [Eddie Marr (*Fat man*)], [Charles Sullivan (*Bouncer*)], [Elliott Sullivan, Joe Devlin, Max Wagner, Paul Bryar (*Committeemen*)], [Alice Connor (*Girl*)], [Jack Goodrich (*Girl's partner*)], [Sally Sage (*Fay Simmons*)], [John Ridgely (*Orchestra leader*)], [Eddy Chandler (*Official*)], [Tommy Bupp (*Boy*)], [John Hamilton (*Detective captain*)], [Ralph Dunn, Cliff Saum (*Detectives*)], [William Gould (*Sergeant Walsh*)], [Sam Bernard (*Drunk*)], [Al Downing, Jack Mower, Charles Delaney, Frank Mayo, Hal Craig (*Policemen*)], [Philip Morris (*Police announcer*)], [Charles Trowbridge (*Judge*)], [Al Lloyd].

Drama. [*Print viewed*]. Longshoreman Jim Dolen, the hot-tempered president of the Waterfront Club in New York City, an association of dockworkers, gets into a fight with Mart Hendler, his opponent in the election for president, when Hendler refuses to comply with an order. When Jim's friend, Frankie Donahue, tries to stop the fight, Jim slugs him, and Frankie's head hits an anchor as he falls. Jim is jailed for assault and is relieved to learn while in jail that Frankie has revived and soon will be sent home. Jim's fiancée, Ann Stacey, who is deeply worried about his propensity for fighting, speaks with the new parish priest, Father Dunn, who then visits Jim in jail. When Jim explains that his father taught him never to let others make a "sap" of him, Father Dunn calls him a coward and says that he is afraid that if he does not take advantage of others, they will take advantage of him. Father Dunn's rebukes have an effect on Jim, and when he gets out of jail, he promises Ann to try to understand what Father Dunn told him. Jim and Ann get married and plan to move to a ranch. At the Annual Longshoremen and Stevedore's Ball, Jim graciously suggests that Hendler be made the new president. After a very drunk Hendler insults Jim during his acceptance speech, Jim tells the gathering that Hendler will make a good president even though he is drunk. At the laughter this remark provokes, Hendler throws a bottle at Jim, and Jim's brother Dan pushes him out of the way. Dan is killed by the bottle, and Hendler's girl friend, Marie Cordell, gets him away before the police arrive. Jim threatens to kill Hendler if the police fail to arrest him in twenty-four hours. After Dan's funeral, Father Dunn learns that Jim has gone after Hendler with a gun and tells the police, and an all-cars bulletin is put out for Jim. When he sees a police car, Jim surreptitiously gives his gun to Frankie, who has forgiven him for the earlier incident. Jim is picked up, but the captain of detectives cannot hold him because he has broken no law. Meanwhile, Hendler, terrified to give himself up and face the punishment of death for something he didn't mean to do, implores Marie to get enough money for them to leave the country. When the police break into Marie's apartment, Hendler escapes through a window. Because none of Hendler's "friends" will give Marie money to pay the skipper of a boat on which they plan to escape the country that night, Marie gets Ann to give her the money by convincing her that Hendler is no more a killer than Jim would have been if Frankie had died, and that if Hendler does not escape, Jim will either kill him outright or in a courtroom. Jim's friend, Skids Riley, overhears their conversation and tells Jim, who angrily confronts Ann. Just then, Frankie tells Jim that he has learned that Hendler is hiding above the Mariner's Restaurant. To stop Jim, Ann pulls a gun on him, but he slugs her and takes it away. Ann gets the police, who then arrest Jim for carrying a concealed weapon. However, with Frankie's help, Jim escapes from his cell. When Ann hears about the escape on the radio, she goes to the Mariner's Restaurant. Thinking that she is

double-crossing him, Hendler slugs Ann and puts her in a closet. When Jim arrives, Hendler hides outside the window. Marie tells Jim that Hendler has left, but when Jim hears Ann fall over in the closet, he thinks it must be Hendler and raises his gun to shoot. Marie stops him, and Jim and Ann embrace, while the wire supporting Hendler on the ledge gives way, and he falls to his death. Marie cries over his body. Father Dunn convinces the judge to commute Jim's sentence to probation and then blesses him and Ann as they leave for their ranch. *Accidental death. Fights. Irish Americans. Longshoremen. Marriage. Revenge. Balls (Parties). Brothers. Clubs. Docks. Drunkenness. Friendship. Fugitives. Jailbreaks. Loyalty. Lure of the country. New York City. Pledges. Police. Priests. Restaurants.*

Note: According to a news item in *HR*, this picture was filmed on location in San Pedro, CA. This was the first time that the actor previously known as Stanley Morner and Richard Stanley used the name Dennis Morgan.

DV 12 Oct 1939, p. 3. *FD* 25 Jul 1939, p. 8. *HR* 11 Feb 1939, p. 3. *HR* 12 Oct 1939, p. 12. *MPH* 22 Jul 1939, p. 50, 52. *NYT* 17 Jul 1939, p. 10. *Var* 19 Jul 1939, p. 19.

WATERFRONT (German Americans)

Alexander-Stern Productions. *Dist* Producers Releasing Corp. 15 Jul 1944; Prod: mid-Mar—late Mar 1944 [©Producers Releasing Corp.; 27 May 1944; LP12688]. Sd (Western Electric Mirrophonic Recording); b&w. 5,816 ft. 65-66 min.

Prod Arthur Alexander. *Dir* Steve Sekely. *Asst dir* Lou Perlof. [*Fill-in dir* Elmer Clifton]. *Orig scr* Martin Mooney and Irwin R. Franklyn. *Dir of photog* Robert Cline. *Art dir* Paul Palmentola. *Film ed* Charles Henkel, Jr. *Set dec* Harry Reif. *Mus dir* Lee Zahler. *Sd eng* Arthur B. Smith.

Cast: JOHN CARRADINE (*Victor Marlow*), J. CARROL NAISH (*Dr. Carl Decker*), Maris Wrixon (*Freda Hauser*), Edwin Maxwell (*Max Kramer*), Terry Frost (*Jerry Donovan*), John Bleifer ([*Oscar*] *Zimmerman*), Marten Lamont (*Mike Gorman*), Olga Fabian (*Mrs. [Emma] Hauser*), Claire Rochelle (*Maisie*), Billy Nelson (*Butch*).

Espionage, World War II, Drama. [*Print viewed*]. As optometrist Dr. Carl Decker leaves his office at the San Francisco docks, a man follows and then robs him. Through the dark mist, two drunks witness the theft and summon the police. By the time the officers arrive, however, the thief has fled and Decker denies that a crime has been committed. Later, at Decker's office, a man enters and asks for a lens replacement. After uttering an odd phrase that identifies him as a German agent, the man, Victor Marlow, hands Decker a message to decipher. When Decker informs Marlow that his book containing the secret codes and the names of all the German agents operating on the West Coast has just been stolen, the two set out to retrieve it. Before beginning their search, Decker directs Marlow to rent a room at Mrs. Emma Hauser's boardinghouse and explains that although Mrs. Hauser is not a member of the spy ring, her daughter Freda works as a secretary for Max Kramer, a covert member of the ring. When Decker points out his assailant, dock worker Adolph Mertz, Marlow follows him, and the next morning, Mertz's body is found floating in the bay. The newspaper account of Mertz's death sends Kramer to the Anchor Café to question Oscar Zimmerman, the man he hired to procure the book. Kramer accuses Zimmerman of murdering Mertz and declares that he must acquire the code book to protect his family in Germany from the Gestapo. To calm Kramer, Zimmerman accuses Decker's operatives of murdering Mertz. After Kramer leaves, Zimmerman, who had obtained the book from Mertz before he was killed, sends Decker a message, offering to sell the book and directing him to a meeting at the café the following night. Meanwhile, Mrs. Hauser's boarders are all sitting down to breakfast when Marlow rings the doorbell and requests a room. When Mrs. Hauser states that she has no vacancies, Marlow threatens her family in Germany unless she accommodates him, after which she agrees to give him her own room. After breakfast, Freda's fiancé Jerry Donovan, a ship chandler, drives her to work, where he seess his old friend, police officer Mike Gorman. Later that day, Decker receives Zimmerman's note and shows it to Marlow, who begins to suspect that Kramer is connected to the theft. The next day, Decker keeps his appointment with Zimmerman, who offers to sell the book for $5,000 and instructs Decker to deliver the cash to the café the following evening. Jerry, meanwhile, visits Kramer at his office to ask for a loan so that he can close a contract with a shipping company. Agreeing to lend Jerry the money, Kramer tells him to return the following day. That night, Marlow barges into Zimmerman's office and demands the book's return. After Zimmerman extracts it from his safe and hands it to Marlow, Marlow

pulls out a pistol and forces Zimmerman to admit that Kramer hired Mertz to steal the book. Marlow then shoots Zimmerman and takes the book to Decker, who denounces his homicidal behavior. Upon reading the report of Zimmerman's murder in the paper, Kramer, conscience-stricken and fearing for his life, pens a confession naming Decker as a spy. He then phones Freda at home and after explaining that he is planning a trip, instructs her to remove two envelopes from his bank vault and deposit them at the office. Overhearing the conversation, Marlow realizes that Kramer is planning to betray him and decides to take action. At Kramer's office later that evening, Marlow shoots him just as Jerry arrives to remind him of the loan. The police are summoned, and upon finding Jerry in the building, arrest him for murder. Mike is assigned to the case, but is perplexed when he learns that both Kramer and Zimmerman were killed by the same German revolver. Mike's only other clue is a sketch found on Kramer's desk, but when he shows it to Freda, she is unable to identify the artist. The next day, Marlow reads a newspaper story detailing Decker's escape from the police and the exposure and arrest of nineteen other German agents. After receiving a message directing him to the pier, Marlow goes there and finds Decker hiding in a fisherman's shack. When Decker begs for Marlow's help, Marlow coldly pulls out his revolver, shoots him and then returns to the Hauser house. After he arrives, Freda notices a sketch drawn by Marlow and realizes that he is the murderer. When Marlow takes Freda and her mother hostage and locks them in their room, the other boarders notify the police. Soon after, Mike and several officers arrive to apprehend Marlow. With the real murderer under arrest, Jerry is exonerated and is happily reunited with Freda. *Codes. Germans. Murder. Robbery. Spies. Boardinghouses. Dock workers. Engagements. False arrests. Firearms. Hostages. Insurance. Mothers and daughters. Optometrists. Piers. Police. San Francisco (CA). Secretaries. Ship crews.*

Note: Although a *HR* production chart places Tony Carson in the cast, his participation in the released film has not been confirmed. According to a *HR* news item, Elmer Clifton stepped in to direct when Steve Sekely fell ill with the flu.

Box 20 May 1944. *DV* 10 May 1944, p. 3. *FD* 25 May 1944, p. 9. *HR* 17 Mar 1944, p. 18. *HR* 24 Mar 1944, p. 1, 14. *HR* 10 May 1944, p. 3. *MPHPD* 15 Apr 1944, p. 1850. *MPHPD* 13 May 1944, p. 1887. *Var* 2 Aug 1944, p. 20.

WAY DOWN SOUTH (African Americans)
Principal Productions, Inc.; Bobby Breen Productions, Inc. *Dist* RKO Radio Pictures, Inc. 21 Jul **1939**; Prod: 26 Apr—19 May 1939 [©Bobby Breen Productions, Inc.; 21 Jul 1939; LP9176]. Sd (RCA Victor Sound System); b&w. 62-63 min.
Prod Sol Lesser. *Assoc prod* Barney Briskin. *Dir* Bernard Vorhaus. *Asst dir* John Sherwood and [Lee Sholem]. *Orig story and scr* Clarence Muse and Langston Hughes. *Photog* Charles Schoenbaum. *Spec eff* Vernon L. Walker. *Art dir* Lewis J. Rachmil. *Ed* Arthur Hilton. *Ward* Albert Deanno. *Mus dir* Victor Young. *Vocal arr* Hall Johnson. [*Dance dir* Clarence Muse]. *Sd tech* Richard Van Hessen. [*Tech adv* Clarence Muse].
Song(s): "Louisiana" and "Good Ground," words and music by Clarence Muse and Langston Hughes.
Cast: BOBBY BREEN (*Timothy Reid, Jr.*), Alan Mowbray (*Jacques Bouton*), Ralph Morgan (*Timothy Reid, Sr.*), Steffi Duna (*Pauline*), Clarence Muse (*Uncle Catan*), Sally Blane (*Claire Bouton*), Edwin Maxwell (*Martin Dill*), Charles Middleton (*Cass*), Robert Greig (*Judge Ravenal*), Lillian Yarbo (*Janie*), Stymie Beard (*Gumbo*), The Hall Johnson Choir, [Jack Carr (*Luke*)], [Marguerite Whitten (*Lulu*)].
Historical, Drama, with songs. [*Print viewed*]. In pre-Civil War Louisiana, plantation owner Timothy Reid is a generous man who values kindness to his slaves over the pursuit of profit. When Timothy dies in a carriage accident, the executorship to Timothy's nearly bankrupt estate is assigned to unscrupulous attorney Martin Dill. Dill, goaded by his greedy mistress Pauline, decides to sell the slaves and other assets of the plantation and depart for Paris with the proceeds. Meanwhile, Timothy's son Tim, who has inherited his father's good nature, appeals to innkeeper Jacques Bouton for help. Bouton befriends the boy and presents his case to Judge Ravenal. Upon hearing the facts, the judge intervenes to prevent the sale of the slaves, relieves Dill of his power, and thus saves the plantation. *Greed. Inheritance. Plantation owners. Slavery. Southerners. United States–History. Accidental death. Judges. Lawyers. Mistresses. Plantations. Slavery.*

Note: According to a news item in *HR*, Clarence Muse signed a contract for his services as actor, technical adviser and dance director on this film. Another

news item in *HR* adds that the film was shot on location at Rancho Providencia, Uplifters, and at the Stratton Ranch in Calabasas, CA.

DV 19 Jul 1939, p. 3. *FD* 25 Jul 1939, p. 8. *HR* 30 Mar 1939, p. 4. *HR* 12 Apr 1939, p. 5. *HR* 27 Apr 1939, p. 12. *HR* 10 May 1939, p. 8. *HR* 12 May 1939, p. 4. *HR* 20 May 1939, p. 5. *HR* 19 Jul 1939, p. 3. *MPD* 21 Jul 1939, p. 5. *MPH* 3 Jun 1939, p. 35. *MPH* 22 Jul 1939, p. 52. *Var* 23 Aug 1939, p. 14.

WAY FOR A SAILOR *(foreign version)* see **EN CADA PUERTO UN AMOR**

THE WAY OF ALL FLESH (German Americans)
Paramount Famous Lasky Corp. 1 Oct **1927**; New York premiere: 25 Jun 1927 [©Paramount Famous Lasky Corp.; 1 Oct 1927; LP24471]. Si; b&w. 9 reels, 8,486 ft.
Pres Adolph Zukor and Jesse L. Lasky. *Dir* Victor Fleming. *Scr* Jules Furthman. *Adpt* Lajos Biro. *Titles* Julian Johnson. *Photog* Victor Milner.
Source: Based on the short story "The Way of All Flesh" by Perley P. Sheehan (publication undetermined).
Cast: Emil Jannings (*August Schiller*), Belle Bennett (*Mrs. Schiller*), Phyllis Haver (*Mayme*), Donald Keith (*August, Junior*), Fred Kohler (*The Tough*), Philippe De Lacey (*August, as a child*), Mickey McBan (*Evald*), Betsy Ann Lisle (*Charlotte*), Carmencita Johnson (*Elizabeth*), Gordon Thorpe (*Karl*), Jackie Coombs (*Heinrich*), Dean Harrell, Anne Sheridan, Dorothy Kitchen.
Drama. The world of bank cashier August Schiller centers chiefly on his patient wife and six children, and he prides himself on being an ideal father, a faithful worker, and a loyal husband. For the first time since his honeymoon, August leaves Milwaukee to deliver some bonds in Chicago, and on the train he innocently becomes involved with Mayme, an adventuress. She seduces him and during a drunken revel steals his bonds; her lover, The Tough, and his gang beat him and attempt to take his watch, but August in his fury grapples with The Tough, who is killed by a passing train. August changes clothing with The Tough and is reported as having died a hero's death defending his employer's trust. Years later, a broken derelict, he learns that his oldest son has become a famous violinist, and he hoards to buy a gallery seat at a concert. He follows the boy home on Christmas Day, catching furtive glimpses of his happy family, who fail to recognize him. *Adventuresses. Bankers. Chicago (IL). Christmas. Family life. Fatherhood. German Americans. Milwaukee (WI). Robbery. Seduction. Tramps. Violinists.*

FD 3 Jul 1927. *NYT* 27 Jun 1927, p. 25. *Var* 29 Jun 1927, p. 19.

THE WAY OF ALL FLESH (Hungarian Americans)
Paramount Pictures, Inc. *Dist* Paramount Pictures, Inc. 5 Jul **1940**; New York opening: week of 6 Jun 1940; Prod: began mid-Nov 1939 [©Paramount Pictures, Inc.; 5 Jul 1940; LP9760]. Sd (Western Electric Mirrophonic Recording); b&w. 9 reels. 86 min. Passed by the National Board of Review. PCA cert no. 5978.
[*Exec prod* William LeBaron]. [*Assoc prod* Eugene J. Zukor]. *Dir* Louis King. [*Asst dir* Joseph Lefert]. *Scr* Lenore Coffee. *Story* Lajos Biro and Jules Furthman. *Dir of photog* Theodor Sparkuhl and [Henry Sharp]. *Art dir* Hans Dreier and John Goodman. *Ed* Stuart Gilmore. *Int dec* A. E. Freudeman. *Mus score* Victor Young. *Sd rec* Hugo Grenzbach and Don Johnson.
Source: Based on the short story "The Way of All Flesh" by Perley P. Sheehan (publication undetermined).
Cast: *The Krizia Family*: Akim Tamiroff (*Paul [Kriza Sr.]*), Gladys George (*Anna [Kriza]*), William Henry (*Paul, Jr.*), John Hartley (*Victor [Kriza]*), Marilyn Knowlden (*Julie [Kriza]*), Betty McLaughlin (*Mitzi [Kriza]*), *As Children:* James West (*Paul Jr.*), Darryl Hickman (*Victor*), June Hedin (*Julie*), Norma Nelson (*Mitzi*), Tommy Bupp (*Timothy*), Muriel Angelus (*Mary Brown*), Berton Churchill (*Reginald L. Morten*), Fritz Leiber (*Max*), Roger Imhof (*Franz Henzel*), James Seay (*Varno*), Douglas Kennedy (*Timothy*), James Burke (*Frisco*), Stanley Price (*Lefty*), John Harmon (*Pete*), Leonard Penn (*Joe*), [Torben Meyer (*Sandor Nemzetti*)], [Robert C. Fischer (*Baker*)], [Ethel May Halls (*Mother*)], [Cullen Johnston (*Boy*)], [George Anderson (*Hotel manager*)], [John Laird (*Hotel clerk*)], [Joyce Mathews (*Telegraph girl*)], [Wallace Rairden (*Bellhop*)], [Sam Ash, Allen Fox (*Cigar clerks*)], [Lester Scharff, Marty Faust (*Waiters*)], [Wanda McKay, Dorothy Dayton (*Cigarette girls*)], [Janet Waldo (*Hat check girl*)], [Oscar Smith (*Porter*)], [Jack Norton (*Barber*)], [Paul E. Burns (*First hobo*)], [Jimmy Conlin (*Second hobo*)], [Wade Boteler, Howard Mitchell, James Flavin (*Policemen*)], [Billy Engle (*Newspaper owner*)], [Galan Galt (*Foreman*)], [Guy Bellis

(*Minister*)], [Sam Flint (*First director*)], [Frank Darien (*Second director*)], [Henry Roquemore (*Third director*)].

Melodrama. [*Print viewed*]. In 1925, in Linzua, Pennsylvania, Hungarian immigrant Paul Kriza makes an honest living as a bank cashier, content to support his devoted wife Anna and four children on a meager salary. Paul's boss, Franz Henzel, sends him to New York to deliver $100,000 cash to client Sandor Nemzetti. Varno, a spy in Henzel's bank, has notified crook Reginald L. Morten of Paul's arrival at the Hotel Empress. When Nemzetti is delayed, Morten's moll, Mary Brown, poses as a journalist and seduces Paul into drinking until he passes out. Upon awakening the next morning, Paul realizes that he has been robbed and accuses Mary, but she pretends not to know him. Morten's men then knock him out and put him on the railroad tracks. While one of them picks his pockets, Paul wakes and defends himself, and the thug is killed by an oncoming train. The police find Paul's inscribed watch on the tracks and assume that the mutilated corpse is Paul, and the papers report that a cashier died a hero's death while defending his trust. Although Paul recognizes his picture in the paper, no one believes that he is Paul Kriza because Mary had him shave off his beard, and his badly beaten body makes him look like a hobo. Suffering from psychological devastation and partial amnesia, Paul wanders the streets of New York for years, unsure of who he is. Meanwhile, his son Paul, Jr. grows up and becomes a world-class violinist. When Paul, Jr. makes his New York debut, his father is in the audience and cries when he plays his father's favorite piece for his encore. Paul, Jr. returns home to Linzau for Christmas and his father follows. He watches as his family visits his grave, then follows them home and peers in the window as they sing Christmas carols. When a policeman tries to arrest him, Paul, Jr. and Anna invite the stranger inside, but he declines and walks away into the snowy night. *Amnesia. Bank clerks. Hoboes. Hungarian Americans. Innocents. Missing persons, Assumed dead. Thieves. Violinists. Attempted murder. Christmas. Concerts. Drunkenness. Family life. Fathers and sons. Gangsters. Graves. Impersonation and imposture. Molls. New York City. Pride and vanity. Reporters. Seduction. Trains.*

Note: A silent version of this story was made by Paramount in 1927 starring Emil Jannings and Belle Bennett and directed by Victor Fleming (see above). Jules Furthman wrote the screenplay for the 1927 film, and Lajos Biro wrote the adaptation. That film credits the story "The Way of All Flesh" by Perley P. Sheehan as its literary source. The 1940 version does not credit the Sheehan story as a literary source, but instead credits Furthman and Biro with story.

DV 24 May 1940, p. 3. FD 11 Jun 1940, p. 6. HR 11 Nov 1939, p. 6. HR 25 Nov 1939, pp. 6-7. HR 24 May 1940, p. 3. MPD 28 May 1940, p. 9. MPH 6 Jan 1940, p. 48. MPH 1 Jun 1940, p. 41. NYT 6 Jun 1940, p. 33. Var 29 May 1940, p. 14.

THE WAY OF ALL MEN (*foreign version*) see **DIE MASKE FÄLLT**

THE WAY TO LOVE (*foreign vesion*) see **L'AMOUR GUIDE**

WE AMERICANS (German Americns, Italian Americans, Jewish Americans)

Universal Pictures Corp.; Universal-Jewel. 25 Mar or 6 May **1928** [©Universal Pictures Corp.; 20 Mar 1928; LP25092]. Si; b&w. 9 reels, 8,700 ft.

Supv Carl Laemmle, Jr. *Dir* Edward Sloman. *Adpt and cont* Alfred A. Cohn. *Cont* Edward Sloman. *Photog* Jackson J. Rose. *Film ed* Robert Jahns.

Source: Based on the play *We Americans: A New Play* by Milton Herbert Gropper and Max Siegel (New York, 12 Oct 1926).

Cast: George Sidney (*Mr. Levine*), Patsy Ruth Miller (*Beth Levine*), George Lewis (*Phil Levine*), Eddie Phillips (*Pete Albertini*), Beryl Mercer (*Mrs. Levine*), John Boles (*Hugh Bradleigh*), Albert Gran (*Mr. Schmidt*), Michael Visaroff (*Mr. Albertini*), Kathlyn Williams (*Mrs. Bradleigh*), Edward Martindel (*Mr. Bradleigh*), Josephine Dunn (*Helen Bradleigh*), Daisy Belmore (*Mrs. Schmidt*), Rosita Marstini (*Mrs. Albertini*), Andy Devine (*Pat O'Dougal*), Flora Bramley (*Sara Schmidt*), Jake Bleifer (*Korn*).

Society, Drama. Hugh Bradleigh, the son of a socially prominent family, falls in love with Beth Levine, whose parents are Russian Jewish immigrants. Pete Albertini, the son of an Italian American family, is affianced to Sara Schmidt, whose parents are German immigrants. When war with Germany breaks out, Hugh, Pete, and Beth's brother Phil all enlist. Overseas, Phil loses his life in order to save Hugh's, and Pete loses a leg. When the survivors return from Europe, Pete marries Sara; Hugh announces his engagement to Beth, but his parents object. All objections are dropped, however, when the Bradleighs meet Beth's parents and learn of Phil's sacrifice for Hugh.

German Americans. Immigrants. Italian Americans. Jews. Russians. Upper classes. Veterans. World War I.

FD 25 Mar 1928 MPW 5 May 1928. NYT 29 Mar 1928, p. 25. Var 4 Apr 1928, p. 28.

WE DARE NOT LOVE see **THEY DARE NOT LOVE**

WE WERE DANCING (Polish Americans, Austrian Americans)

Metro-Goldwyn-Mayer Corp.; controlled by Loew's Inc. *Dist* Loew's Inc. **1942**; New York premiere: 30 Apr 1942; Prod: 29 Sep—26 Nov 1942; added scenes late Dec 1941 [©Loew's Inc.; 5 Feb 1942; LP11370]. Sd (Western Electric Sound System); b&w. 9 reels, 8,452 ft. 93-94 min. Passed by the National Board of Review. PCA cert no. 7883.

Prod Robert Z. Leonard and Orville O. Dull. *Dir* Robert Z. Leonard. [*Asst dir* Hugh Boswell]. *Scr* Claudine West, Hans Rameau and George Froeschel. [*Contr wrt* Lenore Coffee]. *Dir of photog* Robert Planck. *Dir of photog for added scenes* Harold Rosson. *Art dir* Cedric Gibbons. *Assoc* Daniel B. Cathcart. *Film ed* George Boemler. *Set dec* Edwin B. Willis. *Mus score* Bronislau Kaper. *Rec dir* Douglas Shearer. *Hair styles by* Sydney Guilaroff. [*Tech adv* Milton Schwartz].

Source: Based in part on the play *Tonight at 8:30* by Noël Coward (London, 9 Jan 1936).

Cast: NORMA SHEARER (*Vicki Wilomirska*), Melvyn Douglas ([*Baron Nicholas*] *Nicki Prax* [*also known as Mr. Manesque*]), Gail Patrick (*Linda Wayne*), Lee Bowman (*Hubert Tyler*), Marjorie Main (*Judge Sidney Hawkes*), Reginald Owen (*Major Tyler-Blane*), Alan Mowbray (*Grand Duke Basil*), Florence Bates (*Mrs. Vanderlip*), Heather Thatcher (*Mrs. Tyler-Blane*), Connie Gilchrist (*Olive Ransome*), Nella Walker (*Mrs. Bentley*), Florence Shirley (*Mrs. Charteris*), Russell Hicks (*Mr. Bryce-Carew*), Norma Varden (*Mrs. Bryce-Carew*), [Paul Porcasi (*Manager Duquesne*)], [John Piffle (*Dutchman*)], [Lionel Pape (*Englishman*)], [George H. Reed (*Butler, Blane's house*)], [Ottola Nesmith (*Mrs. Quimby*)], [Mary Forbes (*Mrs. Sandys*)], [Thurston Hall (*Senator Quimby*)], [Douglas Wood (*Colonel Sandys*)], [Alan Napier (*Captain Blackstone*)], [Martin Turner, John "Buddy" Williams (*Red Caps*)], [Pierre Watkin (*Mr. Tom Bentley*)], [Bryant Washburn, Sr. (*Mr. Lambert*)], [Nella Walker (*Mrs. Janet Bentley*)], [Helene Millard (*Mrs. Lambert*)], [Florence Wix (*Sporting woman*)], [Alfred Hall (*Butler*)], [Alex Callum, Fred Santley, Harry Hayden (*Clerks*)], [Dick Elliott (*Mr. Platt*)], [Jessamine Newcombe (*Mrs. Platt*)], [Betty Hayward, June Millarde (*Debutantes*)], [Dorothy Morris (*Claire Bentley*)], [John Roche (*Mr. Fox*)], [Duncan Renaldo (*Sam Estrella*)], [Anthony Marsh (*Tommy Brooke*)], [Willy Castello (*Felucci*)], [Emmett Vogan (*Bailiff*)], [Polly Bailey (*Flower woman*)], [Harold Minjir (*Beverly*)], [Barlowe Borland (*McDonough*)], [Dick Alexander (*Moving man*)], [Alex Pollard (*Ransome's butler*)], [Jacques Vanaire (*Beverly's assistant*)], [Gino Corrado (*Headwaiter in inn*)], [Esther Michelson (*Headwaiter's wife*)], [Meeka Aldrich (*Housemaid*)], [Henry Roquemore (*Mr. Ransome*)], [Charles Sullivan (*Train announcer*)], [Bill Fisher (*Train conductor*)], [John Holland, Herbert Rawlinson (*Friends*)], [Jean Fenwick].

Romantic comedy. [*Print viewed*]. At a Charleston, South Carolina party celebrating her forthcoming marriage to wealthy lawyer Hubert Tyler, Polish princess Victoria Wilomirska dances with impoverished Viennese aristocrat Baron Nicholas Prax and the two fall in love. Vicki's friends cannot dissuade her from marrying the charming Nicki, who survives by playing bridge and living off the rich. The pair elope to New York, where Nicki's friend, Basil, a phony grand duke, who, like Nicki, is a "professional guest," warns them that a married couple cannot flourish in the profession. Vicki suggests that they keep their marriage secret and take advantage of her invitations as well as his. When she runs into Hubert at Grand Central Station, she lies about her marriage to Nicki, then goes on to the home of the wealthy Bentleys. During the weekend, interior decorator Linda Wayne, Nicki's suspicious former lover, arrives, incurring Vicki's jealousy. Hubert also arrives, and the next morning, when most of the guests are leaving for a shooting party, Linda insists that they awaken Nicki. They are shocked to discover Nicki and Vicki asleep in his room, and, rather than cause a scandal, the pair reveal their marriage and decide to be the perfect "couple" of houseguests. Unfortunately, many of Nicki's former hostesses are uninterested in a married man, and they are forced to make new wealthy friends. For the next year, Nicki and Vicki travel to a variety of unsophisticated towns in middle America. While staying with the Ransomes in St. Louis, Hubert, Mr.

Ransome's lawyer, arrives. The men play bridge that evening, and Nicki, who has had too much to drink, loses $1,200 to Hubert and covers the loss with a bad check. Vicki goes to Hubert and says that without Nicki's knowledge, she used all the money in their checking account to buy a sable coat. Hubert knows that she is covering for Nicki and tears up the check, then offers her money, but she refuses. When Nicki finds out, he feels so badly that he determines to return to New York and find a real job. Ninety miles from New York, they stop at an inn and run into Basil, who invites them to join him at the hunting lodge of the wealthy Bryce-Carews. When Nicki decides to accept "just for a few days," Vicki is concerned, both because she doubts his sincerity in wanting to find real work and because Linda is also a guest. Some time later, Vicki phones Hubert and asks him to help her get a divorce. At the proceedings, Hubert is distressed that the male judge has been replaced by a female, Judge Sidney Hawkes, who is charmed by Nicki. On the witness stand, Vicki discusses Nicki's effect on wealthy women and, although Nicki reminds her of her love for him, she refuses to stop the divorce. Hubert then calls Linda to the stand, and it is revealed that she loves Nicki and Vicki found them in a compromising position during a parlor game called "Sardines." Nicki's sincere profession of love for Vicki moves the judge to tears, but she still grants the divorce. After spending six months in South America, Nicki returns to New York and goes to see Linda, on her invitation. He is cool to her, but she offers him a job. When she reveals that a competitor, Mrs. Vanderlip, is remodeling Hubert's Long Island mansion because he is marrying Vicki, Nicki asks her to get him a job with the decorator. At the mansion, Nicki, who is using the name Manesque, shows up to display fabric samples. After a private talk with Hubert, Nicki is retained, and tells a shocked Vicki that he needs the job because he plans to marry again. At the end of the decorating assignment, Nicki reveals to Vicki that he has accepted a job from a Hollywood friend of Tyler-Blane and will be going West shortly. He pretends that he is happy about her impending marriage and has no hard feelings, but when she starts to cry, he admits that he still loves her and has been trying to get her back. Vicki says that it is too late, then leaves for Charleston with Hubert. Desperate, Nicki follows them. The night before the wedding, Nicki finds Vicki on the terrace and offers her his best wishes, then convinces her to dance one more waltz. They kiss, and a short time later, Hubert tells his aunt that the pair has gone, with his blessings. Finally, Nicki and Vicki happily settle in Hollywood in a small cottage. *Austrian Americans. Elopement. Houseguests. Lawyers. Marriage. Nobility. Polish Americans. Aunts. Charleston (SC). Cottages. Dancing. Divorce. Engagements. Furniture. Hats. Hollywood (CA). Inns. Interior decorators. Jealousy. Judges. New York City. Parties. Rifles. Social climbers. St. Louis (MO).*

Note: Noël Coward's *Tonight at 8:30* consists of nine one-act plays. In the original London production, the plays were performed in increments of three on successive nights. According to a *HR* news item on 18 Apr 1941, M-G-M had purchased the rights to all nine plays and *We Were Dancing* incorporated elements from several. Actors Sig Ruman and Dennis Hoey, listed in the CBCS respectively as "Baron Prax" and "Prince Wilomirsky," were not in the released film, although their characters, the fathers of "Nicki" and "Vicki," are referred to in the film. Several additional actors included in the CBCS but not seen in the released film were Philip Ahn, Ian Wolfe and Tim Ryan. An unidentified, but contemporary news item contained in the AMPAS Library file on the film noted that "Ian Hunter will be the guy who gets jilted...twice," but that role was played by Lee Bowman. A *HR* news item on 14 Nov 1941 indicated that Lennie Hayton was doing "prerecordings," for the film, but the extent of his contribution to the completed film has not been determined.

Box 17 Jan 1942. *DV* 14 Jan 1942, p. 3. *FD* 19 Jan 1942, p. 8. *HR* 14 Nov 1941, p. 2. *HR* 24 Nov 1941, p. 7. *HR* 23 Dec 1941, p. 11. *HR* 14 Jan 1942, p. 4. *HR* 23 Jan 1942, p. 11. *MPD* 15 Jan 1942. *MPHPD* 17 Jan 1942, p. 461. *NYT* 1 May 1942, p. 23. *STR* 17 Jan 1942. *Var* 21 Jan 1942, p. 8.

WE WERE STRANGERS (Latino)
Horizon Pictures. *Dist* Columbia Pictures Corp. May **1949**; Prod: 30 Aug—26 Oct 1948 [©Columbia Pictures Corp.; 2 May 1949; LP2310]. Sd (Western Electric Recording); b&w. 105-106 min. PCA cert no. 13563.
Prod S. P. Eagle. *Asst prod* Jules Buck. *Dir* John Huston. *Asst dir* Carl Hiecke. *Dial dir* Gladys Hill. *Scr* Peter Viertel and John Huston. *Dir of photog* Russell Metty. *Spec scenes* Lawrence W. Butler. *Art dir* Cary Odell. *Film ed* Al Clark. *Set dec* Louis Diage. *Miss Jones' cost by* Jean Louis. *Mus score* George Antheil. *Mus dir* M. W. Stoloff. *Sd eng* Lambert Day. *Hair styles* Larry Germain.
Source: Based on the episode "China Valdez" by Robert Sylvester in his novel *Rough Sketch* (New York, 1948).

Cast: JENNIFER JONES *by arrangement with David O. Selznick* [(*China Valdes*)], JOHN GARFIELD *by arrangement with Roberts Productions* [(*Tony Fenner*)], PEDRO ARMENDARIZ [(*Armando Ariete*)], Gilbert Roland [(*Guillermo Mantilla*)], Ramon Novarro [(*Chief*)], Wally Cassell [(*Miguel*)], David Bond [(*Ramon Sanchez*)], Jose Perez [(*Toto Berenguer*)], Morris Ankrum [(*Bank manager*)], [Tito Renaldo (*Manolo Valdes*)], [Paul Monte (*Roberto*)], [Leonard Strong (*Bombmaker*)], [Robert Tafur (*Rubio*)], [Alexander McSweyn, Alfonso Pedroza (*Sanitation men*)], [Ted Hecht (*Enrico*)], [Santiago Martinez (*Waiter*)], [Joel Rene (*Student*)], [Argentina Brunetti (*Mother*)], [Mimi Aguglia (*Mama*)], [Robert Malcolm (*Priest*)], [Roberta Haynes (*Lolita*)], [Lelia Goldoni (*Consuelo*)], [Paul Marion (*Truck driver*)], [Felipe Turich (*Spy*)], [Fred Chapman (*Altar boy*)], [Julian Rivero (*Flower vendor*)], [Jack Clisby (*Guard*)], [Salvador Baguez (*Cart driver*)], [Alex Montoya (*Chauffeur*)], [Peter Virgo (*Contreras' chauffeur*)], [Federico Godoy (*Contreras*)], [Harry Vejar (*Watchman*)], [Albert Morin (*Sanchez*)], [Rod Redwing], [Charles Granucci], [Herschel Graham], [Abdullah Abbas], [Gertrude Chorre], [Thomas Quon Woo], [Spencer Chan], [Edwin Rochelle], [Rodolfo Hoyos], [Billy Wilson], [Tina Menard], [Joe Sawaya].

Drama. [*Print viewed*]. In 1933, Cuba has suffered seven years of terror perpetrated by a regime of corrupt politicians led by President Gerardo Machado. Threatened by a growing revolutionary underground, the senate passes a bill making all public gatherings a crime. One day a group of students, including Manolo Valdes, is caught distributing anti-government leaflets and chased by the political police called the Porra. Manolo escapes, but one student is shot and captured. Manolo, fearful that his identity will be revealed, goes into hiding, but first arranges with his sister China to signal him if the police do not come for him. The following day, China indicates that all is well, but as Manolo enters the university, he is killed by the police while China watches in horror. Later, China joins the underground, determined to take revenge on her brother's killer. At one of the group's meetings, she meets Tony Fenner, an American, and volunteers to participate in his plan to assassinate the Cuban leadership. Her first assignment is to withdraw money from Tony's account at the bank where she works. That same day at the bank, Porra agent Armando Ariete asks to examine all American accounts. China recognizes him as the man who killed Manolo, but maintains her composure. Later, Tony reveals his plan: The volunteers, consisting of Guillermo Mantilla, Ramon Sanchez, Toto Berenguer and Miguel, will tunnel from China's house to the cemetery. Tony will then assassinate a popular member of the government, and while all the other government officials attend his funeral, will explode a bomb underground, killing all of them. China warns Tony that because Contreras, the man he intends to kill, has a reputation for being better than the rest of the government, some members may object to his murder, but Tony will not make another choice. After the meeting, China and Tony, who have begun to fall in love, have breakfast and are seen by Ariete, who recognizes Tony's name from the bank. While work begins secretly on the tunnel, Ariete keeps close watch on China. One night, Ariete arrives at China's house, bringing food and flowers. Under the influence of too much rum, Ariete plays Russian roulette and then begs China to make love to him. Although Tony is prepared to intervene, Ariete passes out. As the digging continues, Ramon, a student, has second thoughts about killing Contreras when he remembers how, as a small boy, he used to play with his son. He becomes increasingly disturbed and wanders around the streets, begging people to prevent the murder. China and Guillermo find him, but he breaks away from them and is hit by a truck and killed. Later, at the bank, Ariete questions China about Tony, whose family was Cuban, and threatens to arrest her if she does not turn him in. Finally, the tunnel is completed, and Contreras is killed. Tony's plans fail, however, when Contreras' family decides to bury his body at a different cemetery. China offers to withdraw Tony's money from the bank so that he can leave the country, even though Tony, who is angry at his failure, does not want to leave. When China cashes Tony's check, she is fired, but before she leaves, she secretly gives the money to another employee to deliver to Tony. When she returns home, however, Tony is waiting for her, and when China tells him that Ariete is outside, he decides to die fighting and a gunfight ensues. Using dynamite that was intended for the bomb, Tony and China are able to drive the police away, but Tony is fatally wounded in the battle.

Before he dies, however, he hears the city bells ringing, indicating that the revolution has begun. *Cuba. Cuban Americans. Police. Political corruption. Revolutionaries. Accidental death. Assassination. Banks. Bills, Legislative. Brothers and sisters. Cemeteries. Dynamite. Gerardo Machado y Morales. Murder. Nervous breakdown. Revenge. Romance. Shootouts. Students. Tunnels.*

Note: The film's working title was *Rough Sketch*. When the film was released, some viewers protested that the picture was Communist propaganda. The *HR* review called it "the heaviest dish of Red theory ever served to an audience outside the Soviet" and "a shameful handbook of Marxian dialectics." In a 12 May 1949 *LAEx* article, the Los Angeles district of the Federation of Women's Clubs is quoted as saying to Columbia head Harry Cohn that the film "can certainly be interpreted as a call to direct action by revolution against today's governments that are friendly to the United States." Modern sources report a rumor that Gene Kelly was slated to star in the film. Director John Huston and producer Sam Spiegel, whose pseudonym was S. P. Eagle, were partners in Horizon Pictures.

Box 7 May 1949. *DV* 22 Apr 1949, p. 3. *FD* 21 Apr 1949, p. 8. *HR* 22 Apr 1949, pp. 3-4. *LAEx* 12 May 1949. *MPHPD* 30 Apr 1949, p. 4589. *NYT* 28 Apr 1949, p. 28. *Var* 27 Apr 1949, p. 11.

WE WORK AGAIN (African Americans)

Works Progress Administration. **1937.** Sd; b&w. Length undetermined.

African American, Social, Documentary. [*Not viewed*]. This film documents the activities of blacks under the Works Progress Administration. The black point of view is presented, examining the black as a citizen and taxpayer, living among fellow blacks who are professionals and laborers alike. *African Americans. Employment.*

Note: According to a contemporary (but unidentified) source, this film was made to enlist black support for federal employment programs. As the running time has not been found, this film may have been a short.

THE WEDDING NIGHT (Polish Americans)

Howard Productions, Inc. *Dist* United Artists Corp. 8 Mar **1935**; Prod: early Nov—early Dec 1934 [©Samuel Goldwyn; 4 Mar 1935; LP5366]. Sd (Western Electric Noiseless Recording); b&w. 9 reels. 81-82, 85 or 90 min. Passed by the National Board of Review. PCA cert no. 640.

Prod Samuel Goldwyn. *Dir* King Vidor. [*Asst dir* Walter Mayo]. *Scr* Edith Fitzgerald. *Orig story* Edwin Knopf. *Photog* Gregg Toland. *Art dir* Richard Day. *Film ed* Stuart Heisler. *Mus dir* Alfred Newman. *Sd rec* Frank Maher.

Cast: GARY COOPER [(*Tony Barrett*)], ANNA STEN [(*Manya Novak*)], Ralph Bellamy [(*Fredrik*)], Helen Vinson [(*Dora Barrett*)], Siegfried Rumann [(*Mr. Novak*)], Esther Dale [(*Mrs. Kaise Novak*)], Leonid Snegoff [(*Sobieski*)], Eleanor Wesselhoeft [(*Mrs. Sobieski*)], Milla Davenport [(*Grandmother*)], Agnes Anderson [(*Helena*)], Hilda Vaughn [(*Hezzie*)], Walter Brennan [(*Bill Jenkins*)], [Hedi Shope (*Anna*)], [Otto Yamaoka (*Taka*)], [Violet Axelle (*Frederika*)], [Ed Eberle (*Uncle*)], [Robert Louis Stevenson II, Auguste Tollaire, Dave Wengren, George Magrill, Bernard Siegel, Harry Semels (*men at party*)], [Miami Alvarez, Constance Howard, Jay Eaton, Jay Belasco (*Guests at party*)], [Richard Powell (*Truck driver*)], [Douglas Wood (*Heywood*)], [George Meeker (*Gilly*)], [Robert Bolder (*Doctor*)], [Alphonse Martell (*Waiter*)].

Drama. [*Print viewed*]. Novelist Tony Barrett and his wife Dora have huge bills to pay because of their fast New York lifestyle, so he is eager to get an advance on his newest novel. When his publisher tells him that success has gone to his head and the novel is unpublishable, however, Tony has no choice but to move to his family's run-down farm in Connecticut. Shortly after he and Dora arrive, Polish farmer Mr. Novak and his attractive daughter Manya visit and offer Tony $5,000 for a field bordering the Novak farm. Dora is delighted with the money and wants them both to go back to New York, but Tony decides to stay and write another novel, using the Novaks and their neighbors as models. After some weeks, Tony, who has been drinking heavily, tells Manya that she is not in love with Fredrik, the young man whom her father has chosen as her husband, and makes suggestive remarks that anger her. The next day he goes to apologize and the two begin a close friendship. After Tony's servant Taka quits to return to New York, Manya begins spending more time at Tony's farm and the two fall in love, like "Stephen" and "Sonya," the characters in his story. When Fredrik learns from a neighbor that Manya has been seen "laughing" in Tony's parlor, he and her father forbid her to see him again. She secretly continues to see Tony, however, and when a blizzard prevents her from returning home one night, her father angrily confronts Tony at his farm the next morning.

As Manya and Novak return home, he demands that she marry Fredrik the following Monday. She protests that she will not spend her life being an unpaid servant like her mother, but Novak slaps her. The same day, Tony is surprised by the return of Dora, who has missed him terribly during their separation. She hears stories about the previous night, but hopes that they mean nothing until she reads his manuscript. On the night before her wedding, Manya goes to see Tony, but finds Dora instead. The two speak of the book and how it will end, but both realize that they are really speaking about their own lives. After Dora gently tells Manya that she is sure that "Daphne," the wife in Tony's novel, would not give up "Stephen," but would feel very sorry for "Sonya," Manya tells her about the wedding, then leaves. Later, when Tony returns home, he and Dora talk and he asks for a divorce, but she refuses and tells him that the end of his story should have "Sonya" marry her Polish fiancé. When Tony learns the next evening that Manya and Fredrik are being married, he goes to the wedding party and dances with her, then leaves. Later, when a very drunk Fredrik is angered by Manya's lack of responsiveness, he storms out of their bedroom and goes to Tony's house. Manya follows, and as she tries to stop Fredrik from fighting with Tony on the stairs, she falls. Tony carries her to the parlor, where he tells her he loves her. After Manya dies and her grieving family leaves, Dora goes to Tony to tell him that he can now see Manya privately. As he looks out the window, he tells Dora about how full of life Manya was and imagines that she is waving to him. When he turns around, he sees that Dora has gone. *Farmers. Fathers and daughters. Infidelity. Marriage. Novelists. Polish Americans. Battered women. Connecticut. Debt. Farmers. Japanese Americans. New York City. Servants. Tobacco. Weddings.*

Note: *MPH* lists a preview running time of 90 min. According to a pre-production chart in *HF*, the film was originally entitled *Broken Soil*. Another *HF* chart credits Edwin Knopf and "Richmond" as the writers, however, Richmond's name does not appear elsewhere and neither that person's full name or participation in the released film has been confirmed. An *HR* news item in Jul 1936 noted that Samuel Goldwyn had just won the Mussolini Cup for *The Wedding Day*, which was presented to him by Los Angeles' Italian consul, Ernesto Arrighi.

DV 15 Feb 1935, p. 3. *FD* 19 Feb 1935, p. 6. *HF* 8 Sep 1934, p. 8. *HF* 27 Oct 1934, p. 8. *HF* 1 Dec 1934, p. 8. *HR* 16 Oct 1934, p. 11. *HR* 26 Oct 1934, p. 7. *HR* 15 Feb 1935, p. 3. *HR* 8 Jul 1936, p. 4. *MPD* 16 Feb 1935, p. 4. *MPH* 19 Jan 1935, p. 67. *MPH* 23 Feb 1935, p. 54. *NYT* 16 Mar 1935, p. 19. *Var* 20 Mar 1935, p. 17.

WEDDINGS AND BABIES (Italian Americans, Swedish Americans)

Morris Engel Associates. *Dist* Morris Engel Associates. 5 Oct **1960**; Prod: 1957. Sd; b&w. 7,293 ft. 81 min.

Prod Morris Engel. *Dir* Morris Engel. *Orig story* Morris Engel. *Story treatment* Mary-Madeleine Lanphier, Blanche Hanalis and Irving Sunasky. *Photog* Morris Engel. *Film ed* Stan Russell and Michael Alexander. *Mus ed* Eddy Manson.

Cast: Viveca Lindfors (*Bea*), John Myhers (*Al*), Chiarina Barile (*Mama*), Leonard Elliott (*Ken*), Joanna Merlin (*Josie*), Chris (*Tony*), Gabriel Kohn (*Carl*), Mary Faranda (*Mrs. Faranda*).

Drama. [*Not viewed*]. Al is an Italian American photographer whose specialty is weddings and baby pictures. He lives in his small New York City studio with his Swedish girl friend Bea, who also serves as his model and assistant. They have been together for some time, and although Bea is eager to get married and have babies of her own, Al is reluctant to make such a commitment. Al is also distracted by problems with his elderly mother, who speaks almost no English and is rapidly declining into senility. When Mama shows up at the studio after having been evicted for accidentally setting a fire, Al and Bea sadly put her into a nursing home. The matter of their own future remains unresolved, however, and just before her thirtieth birthday, Bea threatens to leave. Al agrees to marry Bea and buys her an engagement ring, but is soon beset by difficulties when his expensive new camera breaks and his mother disappears from the home. Al searches the city for his mother, and finally finds her by his father's grave. Bea, fearing that Al still does not know what he wants, returns his ring. After photographing yet another wedding, Al calls Bea to tell her that he now realizes that he really does want to marry her. *Italian Americans. Love affairs. Mothers and sons. Photographers. Swedish Americans. Aged women. Cemeteries. Jealousy. Marriage. New York City. Nursing homes. Senility.*

Note: *Weddings and Babies* featured star Viveca Lindfors' five-year-old son by director Don Siegel, Chris Siegel, who is identified in reviews simply as Chris. He later changed his name to Kristoffer Tabori before embarking on his own career as an actor and director. According to *Time*, Chiarina Barile, who

played "Mama," was an Italian immigrant whom Morris Engel discovered sitting on her front steps on Sullivan Street a few days after shooting started. The film was shot on location in New York City. According to modern sources, the film was shot with a portable synchronous sound camera of Engel's own design. Although the film was made in 1957, it did not open in the United States until 1960. In a *NYT* interview, Engels said that after trying for two years to come to a satisfactory arrangement with a distributor, he decided to try booking the film into theaters himself. In 1958, *Weddings and Babies* shared the Critics Award at the Venice Film Festival with Ingmar Bergman's *Wild Strawberries*. The subsequent critical reception in the United States was mixed, but Lindfors received unanimously glowing reviews. Engel's work was highly regarded in France, where, according to news items, he was regarded as a forerunner of the "New Wave."

Cue 8 Oct 1960. *Exb* 9 Nov 1960, p. 4768. *Har* 29 Oct 1960, p. 176. *McCalls* Oct 1960. *NYT* 26 Jun 1960. *NYT* 6 Oct 1960. *New Yorker* 22 Oct 1960. *Time* 14 Nov 1960. *Var* 17 Sep 1958. *Var* 1 Jun 1960.

WELCOME DANGER (Chinese Americans)

Harold Lloyd Corp. *Dist* Paramount Famous Lasky Corp. 12 Oct 1929 Sd (Movietone); b&w. 10 reels, 9,955 ft.

Dir Clyde Bruckman. *Story* Clyde Bruckman, Lex Neal and Felix Adler. *Dial* Paul Gerard Smith. *Photog* Walter Lundin and Henry Kohler. *Rec eng* George Ellis.

Song(s): "Billie" and "When You Are Mine," music and lyrics by Lynn Cowan and Paul Titsworth.

Cast: Harold Lloyd (*Harold Bledsoe*), Barbara Kent (*Billy Lee*), Noah Young (*Clancy*), Charles Middleton (*John Thorne*), William Walling (*Captain Walton*), James Wang (*Doctor Gow*), Douglas Haig (*Roy*).

Comedy. Harold Bledsoe, the son of a former chief of police in San Francisco, is called to the city to quell the flourishing crime among Asian and American gangsters. En route, Harold, a meek botanist, stops to examine some flowers and misses his train, but he gets a ride with Billy Lee and her young crippled brother, who are going to San Francisco for an operation on the boy's leg. Dr. Gow, a kindly physician, complains of the evil of narcotics to Captain Walton, as does John Thorne, a supposed reformer but actually an underworld leader. Harold promises action, and, disguised as a Chinese man, he infiltrates a flower shop to rescue the doctor from the villains. The criminals escape, but by matching a set of fingerprints, Harold proves Thorne's guilt and forces a confession from him. *Botanists. Chinese Americans. Drugs. Gangsters. Handicapped. Physicians. Police. San Francisco (CA).*

Note: Copyrighted as 12 reels. Also si; 10,796 ft.

Var 23 Oct 1929, p. 17.

WELCOME STRANGER (Jewish Americans)

Belasco Productions, Inc. *Dist* Producers Distributing Corp. 24 Aug 1924 [©Belasco Productions, Inc.; 24 Aug 1924; LP20575]. Si; b&w. 7 reels, 6,618 ft.

Dir James Young. *Adpt* James Young and Willard Mack. *Titles* Katherine Hilliker and H. H. Caldwell. *Photog* George Benoit.

Source: Based on the play *Welcome Stranger* by Aaron Hoffman (New York, 13 Sep 1920).

Cast: Dore Davidson (*Isadore Solomon*), Florence Vidor (*Mary Clark*), Virginia Brown Faire (*Essie Solomon*), Noah Beery (*Icabod Whitson*), Lloyd Hughes (*Ned Tyler*), Robert Edeson (*Eb Hooker*), William V. Mong (*Clem Beemis*), Otis Harlan (*Seth Trimble*), Fred J. Butler (*Gideon Tyler*), Pat Hartigan (*Detective*).

Comedy-drama. Isadore Solomon, a Jew, is driven from the small New England town of Valley Falls by the mayor and some leading citizens when he arrives to open a general store. Clem Beemis, a handyman at the hotel, befriends Solomon and Mary Clark, another newcomer to Valley Falls, and persuades them to invest in an electric light plant which would provide illumination for the whole town. Banker's son Ned Tyler, who falls in love with Mary, gets a bank's assistance for the project while the mayor and his henchmen attempt to thwart it. Eventually the power plant is erected, and the townspeople honor Clem, Solomon, and Mary at a great celebration. *Bigotry. Electricity. Jews. Mayors. New England. Small town life.*

FD 19 Oct 1924. *MPW* 25 Oct 1924. *NYT* 14 Oct 1924, p. 21. *Var* 15 Oct 1924, p. 30.

THE WELL (African Americans)

Cardinal Pictures, Inc.; A Harry M. Popkin Production. *Dist* United Artists Corp. 10 Sep 1951; Prod: began late Sep 1950 [©Cardinal Pictures, Inc.; 29 Sep 1951; LP1717]. Sd (RCA Sound System); b&w. 7,697 ft. 84-85 min. PCA cert no. 15138.

Pres HARRY M. POPKIN. *Prod* Clarence Greene and Leo Popkin. *Dir* Leo Popkin and Russell Rouse. *Asst dir* Ralph Slosser and Leon Chooluck. *Wrt for the screen by* Russell Rouse and Clarence Greene. *Dir of photog* Ernest Laszlo. *Prod des* Rudolph Sternad. *Film ed* Chester Schaeffer. *Mus ed* George C. Emick. *Set dec* Murray Waite. *Women's ward* Maria Donovan. *Men's ward* Jack Masters. *Mus comp and dir* Dimitri Tiomkin. *Sd* Ben Winkler and Mac Dalgleish. *Sd eff* Fred Maguire. *Makeup* Gus Norin. *Prod supv* Joseph H. Nadel.

Cast: *in order of appearance:* Gwendolyn Laster (*Carolyn*), Richard Rober (*Ben Kellog*), Maidie Norman (*Mrs. Crawford*), George Hamilton (*Grandfather*), Ernest Anderson (*Mr. Crawford*), Dick Simmons (*Mickey*), Lane Chandler (*Stan*), Pat Mitchell (*Peter*), Margaret Wells (*Schoolteacher*), Wheaton Chambers (*Woody*), Michael Ross (*Frank*), Russell Trent (*Chet*), Allen Mathews (*Hal*), John Philips (*Fred*), Walter Morrison (*Art*), Christine Larson (*Casey*), Jess Kirkpatrick (*Quigley*), Roy Engel (*Gleason*), Alfred Grant (*Gaines*), Ed Max (*Milkman*), Guy Beach (*Baggage man*), Robert Osterloh (*Wylie*), Henry Morgan (*Claude Packard*), Barry Kelly (*Sam Packard*), Walter Kelly (*Chip*), Mary Ellen Kay (*Lois*), Beverly Jons (*Sally*), Elzie Emanuel (*Student*), Tom Powers (*Mayor*), Bill Walker (*Dr. Billings*), Douglas Evans (*Lobel*), Sherry Hall (*Manners*).

Social, Drama. [*Print viewed*]. As Carolyn Crawford, a five-year-old African-American girl, skips through a vacant field on her way to school, she slips and falls into a well. Her mother and grandfather give her description to sheriff Ben Kellog, who then learns that three classmates saw a man speaking with her in front of Woody's flower shop. Woody tells of a white man who bought flowers for the girl, whom he had never seen before. Word soon spreads in the black community that a white man abducted Carolyn. A crowd of blacks and whites gathers at the police station, where Gaines, Carolyn's uncle, accuses Ben of not doing everything he can because the suspect is white. Ben indignantly says that color has nothing to do with it. Ben learns that the suspect, Claude Packard, is the nephew of construction company owner Sam Packard, an influential man in town. When Claude is found at the bus station and questioned, he admits that he bought Carolyn flowers, but says he then sent her off to school. He explains that he was passing through town on his way to a new mining project where he hoped to get a job, and thought he would visit his uncle. Worried that the scandal could ruin him, Sam tries to coerce Claude into saying they were together all morning. Ben had been about to book Claude, but he now hesitates and keeps the search open. Word spreads among blacks that Sam is going to get his nephew freed. As he leaves the police station, Sam is questioned by Gaines and Carolyn's father, and when Sam falls and the two black men run, a rumor circulates among the whites that Sam has been beaten up by blacks. Incidents of racial fighting begin to occur in the town. Ben and his deputy Mickey search in the vacant field where Carolyn fell, but they are interrupted when an officer informs them of the fighting. Ben sends Mickey to take Claude to the county seat until things cool off. At a citizen's committee meeting, Ben requests that the mayor get the state militia, but both black and white citizens think that is extreme. When Ben warns that they will soon have a race riot, a black man describes a riot he experienced in which his father's body was dragged through the streets and a white child was beaten to death. Upset at the description, the mayor goes to see the governor. As violence continues unabated, Sam's assistant Wylie and other whites beat up Gaines. Mobs race through streets, as groups gather weapons. A Packard warehouse is burned down, and talk spreads of running "these niggers" out of town. At a gathering at Sam's, he vows to drive out the blacks even if he has to kill every one of them. Ben warns that he will shoot anyone who tries to kill a black. In the field, a dog barks at the hole into which Carolyn fell. The dog's owner, a boy, finds Carolyn's school book and jacket and runs off. During a meeting of blacks, Gaines advocates killing two "ofays" for every black killed, and Crawford agrees. Mickey brings Claude back to town after being attacked at a road block. The boy brings Carolyn's things to her mother, and as word spreads that the girl has been found, tensions are eased. At the well, Gleason, a white racist who owns a radio and electronics service, lowers a microphone into the hole and hears Carolyn's voice. Ben lowers a rope, but when Carolyn does not tie it around her waist, her mother explodes in tears. After township records are examined, it is decided to dig sixty-three feet, then cut a tunnel across to Carolyn. A white-owned company offers lumber to

shore up the tunnel as they go. When Sam arrives, he realizes they will never get to Carolyn in time by digging and suggests they sink a shaft using his company's crane. As the cars of the townspeople shine their headlights into the field for light, the men begin to work. Sam asks Claude, who has worked in mines, to tunnel across once they reach Carolyn's depth, but Claude, hating the town, leaves. As they pump water out of the hole, a cave-in occurs trapping Wylie. Gaines rescues him, but then another wall caves in. Finally, Claude, who has returned, pulls Carolyn out, with Gaines's help. An African-American doctor takes her to an ambulance, as the crowd anxiously awaits word on her condition. Ben comes out and tells Mrs. Crawford that Carolyn is going to be alright, then Gleason announces the news to the assembled group, who rejoice. Sam winks at Crawford as the ambulance pulls out. *African Americans. Personality change. Racism. Rescues. Riots. Sheriffs. Small town life. Strangers. Wells. Accidents. Children. Committees. Construction industry. Dogs. False accusations. Family relationships. Mayors. Nephews. Physicians. Tunnels.*

Note: The working title of this film was *Deep Is the Well*. Harry and Leo Popkin, Clarence Greene and Russell Rouse of Cardinal Productions had previously made the film *D.O.A.*. The filmmakers acknowledged that they were influenced in making *The Well* by the 1949 tragedy of Kathy Fiscus, a child from Pasadena, CA, who fell into a pipe sunk into an abandoned oil field and died before help could reach her. Her plight was broadcast on live television, marking the first time a news event became a dramatic national focal point through the fledgling medium of television. In May 1950, a *LAEx* news item stated that Harry Popkin "almost popped when he read...that Billy Wilder had an idea for a picture based on the tragic Kathy Fiscus rescue....[Popkin] does not intend for anyone to beat him to the screen with the picture." Wilder's film *Ace in the Hole* (also known as *The Big Carnival*) was, in fact, released before *The Well* in Jul 1951 (as was the Warner Bros., Robert Wise-directed film *The Three Secrets*, which was released in Oct 1950 and inspired by the Fiscus tragedy.) *LAEx*, in their review, stated, "The final sequence of *The Well* is reminiscent in many ways of the tragic Kathy Fiscus case, and as the desperate operations continue through the night, the heartbreaking suspense (remembering little Kathy's fate) becomes almost unbearable."

In a *NYT* article, Greene stated that the filmmakers used "authentic, factual material drawn from actual race-riots in American cities, notably one in Detroit on June 20, 1943, in which thirty-four persons died." Location work was done in the northern California towns of Marysville and Grass Valley, and the film was completed at the Motion Picture Center Studio in Hollywood on a $450,000 budget. According to *DV*, a week before the film was to open in Cincinnati in Oct 1951, the Ohio Film Censor Board notified the distributor, United Artists, that they needed more time to deliberate. The censor board did not grant the film a seal of approval until Feb 1952. *DV* stated that "the presence of Negro characters in the plot" had been of concern to the board.

The *Pittsburgh Courier*, an African-American newspaper, chose the film as the best picture of the year, and the Foreign Language Press Film Critics Circle awarded the filmmakers a special mid-season citation. Some reviewers criticized the film's dramatic handling of the story. *NYT* criticized the first part of the film as a "presumptuous concoction of suddenly inspired race hate and wildly explosive race rioting that is easier to rue than to believe." *NYr* complained that in the denouement, "the transformation of the rioters from hoodlums into upstanding, cooperative, and ingenious citizens, all united to save a child, is effected so suddenly that the spectator has quite a time reorienting his ideas about the virtuous and the wicked." *Var*, however, lauded the film's "frank and ofttimes brutal approach" to race relations.

Box 8 Sep 1951. *DV* 5 Sep 1951, p. 3. *Exh* 12 Sep 1951, p. 3152. *FD* 7 Sep 1951, p. 10. *Har* 8 Sep 1951, p. 144. *HR* 28 Sep 1950, p. 12. *HR* 29 Sep 1950. *HR* 4 Oct 1950. *HR* 18 Oct 1950. *HR* 27 Oct 1950, p. 14. *HR* 5 Sep 1951, p. 3. *LAEx* 2 May 1950. *LAT* 5 May 1950. *LAT* 23 Sep 1950. *MPHPD* 8 Sep 1951, p. 1005. *NYT* 27 Sep 1951, p. 37. *Var* 5 Sep 1951, p. 6.

WEN HEI QUEI LOI *see* **HOON SI GWAY LAI**

THE WERNHER VON BRAUN STORY *see* **I AIM AT THE STARS;**
    THE WERNHER VON BRAUN STORY

WEST OF NEVADA (Native Americans)
    Colony Pictures, Inc. *Dist* State Rights. 22 Jun **1936.** Sd; b&w. 5,335 ft. 59 or 63 min. PCA cert no. 2254.
    Prod Arthur Alexander. *Dir* Robert Hill. *Asst dir* Glen Cook. *Scr* Rock Hawkey. *Orig story* Charles Kyson. *Photog* Robert Cline. *Settings* Fred Breble [sic]. *Film ed* Dan Milner. *Sd* Corson Jowett.
    Cast: REX BELL (*Jim Lloyd [later known as Jim Carden]*), Joan Barclay (*Helen Haldain*), Al St. John (*Walla Walla [Wiggins]*), Steve Clark (*Milt Haldain*), Georgia O'Dell (*Rose Gilbury*), Dick Botiller (*Bald Eagle*), Frank McCarrol (*Slade Sangree*), Forrest Taylor (*Steven Cutting*).
    Western. [*Print viewed*]. Jim Lloyd and his friend, Walla Walla Wiggins, rescue Milt Haldain and Bald Eagle when they are attacked by a gang of bandits. Jim tends to Bald Eagle's gunshot wound, then he and Walla Walla accompany the two men to Haldain's trading post, where they meet Haldain's daughter Helen and her friend, Rose

Gilbury. Haldain tells Jim that he is a taxidermist, and his wagon does contain stuffed specimens, but when Jim and Walla Walla carry them inside, they discover that the specimens are too heavy to be what they seem. Meanwhile, Slade Sangree, the leader of the gang that attacked Haldain, informs banker Steven Cutting that Haldain and the gold he was carrying got away. Cutting tells Slade that he has embezzled $20,000 of bank funds and therefore needs the gold immediately. Slade promises to get it and leaves, after which Jim arrives to pick up the mail sent to him care of the bank. He reads a letter from his father, who tells him that Haldain is working a gold mine with the local Indians, and that they are in danger from claim jumpers. Jim finds Walla Walla, and as they are riding, they see Slade and his gang, who have taken Bald Eagle prisoner and are questioning him. Slade frees Bald Eagle after he refuses to work for him, and soon after, Jim and Walla Walla tangle with Slade's gang and best them. Sometime later, Cutting steams open another letter from Jim's father, who informs Jim that Cutting is under federal investigation. Cutting substitutes that letter with one intimating that Jim is a claim jumper and shows the fake letter to Helen, who panics and rides to Haldain's hideout to warn him. At the hideout, Slade's gang has already taken Haldain and Bald Eagle prisoner when Helen and Rose arrive. Cutting arrives as well, on the pretense of wanting to help Helen, and Slade pretends to take him prisoner after Helen writes him a $20,000 ransom check. Cutting orders Slade to follow Haldain and the others to their mine while he goes to the bank and cashes the check, after which Jim and Walla Walla arrive at the now-empty hideout. Slade's gang rob Haldain and the others of the gold they have just mined, and the theft is witnessed by Jim and Walla Walla. After freeing Haldain, Helen and the others, Jim explains that he is really Jim Carden, son of Senator Carden, and is there on behalf of his father to protect the Indians and capture Cutting. Just then, Slade, Cutting and more of their gang return to finish off the Haldains. While the Indian miners ride after the gang, Walla Walla gets Cutting and Jim goes after Slade. Jim makes Cutting tell Helen the truth about the phony letter and she happily apologizes to Jim. *Bankers. Claim jumpers. False accusations. Gold mines. Indians of North America. Undercover agents. Bankers. Embezzlement. Gangs. Gunshot wounds. Hideouts. Letters. Romance. Senators. Skunks. Taxidermy.*

Note: According to the film's onscreen credits, the name of Charles Kyson's original story was "Raw Gold." Although there is a copyright statement on the opening title card of the film, the title is not listed in the copyright catalog. Set designer Fred Preble's name is spelled Breble in the onscreen credits. Contemporary sources indicate that Normandy Pictures Corp. may have been connected to Colony, and that it may have been involved in the production of this film. Modern sources note that Rock Hawkey was director Robert Hill's pseudonym and include Bob Woodward in the cast.

FD 21 Jul 1936, p. 11. *Var* 22 Jul 1936, p. 34.

WEST OF THE ROCKIES *see* **CALL OF THE ROCKIES**

WEST TO GLORY (Latino)
    PRC Pictures, Inc.; controlled by Pathe Industries, Inc. *Dist* PRC Pictures, Inc.; controlled by Pathe Industries, Inc. 22 Apr **1947** [©Pathe Industries, Inc.; 22 Apr 1947; LP951]. Sd; b&w. 61 min.
    Prod Jerry Thomas. *Dir* Ray Taylor. *Dial dir* Gloria Welsch. *Asst dir* F. O. Collings. *Orig scr* Elmer Clifton and Robert B. Churchill. *Dir of photog* Milford Anderson. *Spec eff* Ray Mercer. *Film ed* Joseph Gluck. *Supv ed* Norman A. Cerf. [*Sets* Louis Diage]. *Orch by* Walter Greene. *Sd eng* Glen Glenn. *Rec* Glen Glenn Sound Co. *Dir of makeup* Austin Bedell. *Prod mgr* William L. Nolte.
    Song(s): "Cry, Cry, Cry" and "West to Glory," music and lyrics by Eddie Dean and Hal Blair; "In the Shadow of the Mission," music and lyrics by Pete Gates.
    Cast: EDDIE DEAN [(*Eddie Dean*)], and his horse FLASH, Roscoe Ates [(*Soapy*)], Dolores Castle [(*Maria*)], Gregg Barton [(*Barrett*)], Jimmy Martin [(*Cory*)], Zon Murray [(*Avery*)], Alex Montoya [(*Juan*)], Harry Vejar [(*Don Lopez*)], Casey MacGregor, Billy Hammond, Ted French, Carl Mathews [(*Vincente*)], and The Sunshine Boys.
    Western, with songs. [*Print viewed*]. Eastern cattle buyer Barrett arrives in the Southwest in order to steal the Lopez Diamond, which has been in the Lopez family for generations, before Señor Lopez can restore the diamond to the Mexican people. At a party at his hacienda, attended by United States marshals Eddie Dean and Soapy, Lopez exposes a bag of gold that is his life savings. The next day, one of Lopez' ranch hands is killed in an ambush as he takes the gold to town. Eddie and Soapy find his body and report the incident to

Barrett, hoping to intimidate him. At the hacienda, while Dean and Soapy visit Lopez and Maria, his beautiful young friend, Barrett makes Lopez an offer to buy the diamond, and Lopez takes it out of the safe to show it to him. Soapy, standing guard outside, is hit by a water pump and dreams he finds the gold in a buffalo head in the town saloon. Later, Eddie catches Barrett's men at the hacienda, but they escape. Maria appears genuinely loyal to Lopez and befriends Eddie, but later she asks Barrett to help her steal the diamond. He refuses in order not to expose his true motives, then tries to kidnap her and steal the key to the safe, but she is rescued by Eddie. Barrett forces Juan, a Lopez ranch hand, to frame Eddie for the murder of the ambushed ranch hand by showing Lopez his gold bag and a few coins found among Eddie's possessions. Barrett's men then shoot Juan dead, and Eddie and Soapy find him. Later Eddie catches Maria opening the safe, and Lopez hits Eddie in order to defend Maria, who pulls a gun on Soapy. The bandits then enter, however, and Eddie comes to Lopez and Maria's rescue. After the bandits confess they are working for Barrett, and Eddie admits that he and Soapy are marshals, Maria reveals herself to be a government agent on assignment to protect the diamond. Eddie and Soapy go after Barrett, and during a gunfight at the saloon, Soapy shoots the buffalo head, which falls, spilling out the gold. Eddie finds the Lopez diamond on Barrett and arrests him. Lopez and Maria ride west with Eddie and Soapy as their chaperones. *Diamonds. Government agents. Mexicans. Thieves. Undercover agents. United States. Marshals. Cattlemen. Gunfights. Haciendas. Murder. Ranches. Saloons.*

Note: Although *MPA* lists the release date as 22 Apr 1947, the *FDYB* and *Har* give the date as 12 Apr 1947. The *DV* and *HR* reviews list Hugh Winn as the film's editor, although Joseph Gluck and Norman A. Cerf are credited onscreen.

Box 3 May 1947. *DV* 25 Jul 1947. *FD* 25 Apr 1947, p. 9. *HR* 25 Jul 1947, p. 3. *Var* 30 Apr 1947, p. 26.

WESTERN HERITAGE (Latino)

RKO Radio Pictures, Inc. *Dist* RKO Radio Pictures, Inc. 24 Jan **1948**; Prod: Aug 1947 [©RKO Radio Pictures, Inc.; 11 Feb 1948; LP1495]. Sd (RCA Sound System); b&w. 5,477 ft. 61 min. PCA cert no. 12674.

Prod Herman Schlom. [*Exec prod* Sid Rogell]. *Dir* Wallace A. Grissell. [*Asst dir* John Pommer]. *Orig scr* Norman Houston. *Dir of photog* Alfred Keller. *Spec eff* Russell A. Cully. *Art dir* Albert S. D'Agostino and Lucius O. Croxton. *Film ed* Desmond Marquette. *Set dec* Darrell Silvera and Adolph Kuri. *Mus dir* C. Bakaleinikoff. *Mus* Paul Sawtell. *Sd* Jean L. Speak and Terry Kellum.

Song(s): "Did You Happen to Find a Heart?" words by Herb Magidson, music by Lew Pollack.

Cast: TIM HOLT [(*Ross Daggett*)], Nan Leslie [(*Beth Winston*)], Richard Martin [(*Chito Rafferty*)], Lois Andrews [(*Cleo Raymond*)], Tony Barrett [(*Trigg McCord*)], Walter Reed [(*Joe Powell*)], Harry Woods [(*Arnold*)], Richard Powers [(*Spade*)], Jason Robards [(*Judge Henry Winston*)], Robert Bray [(*Pike*)], Perc Launders [(*Sheriff Claiborne*)], [Bud Osborne, Monte Montague, Dick Rush (*Citizens*)], [Emmett Lynn (*Doctor S. Stevens*)], [Rita Lynn (*Dance hall girl*)].

Western. [*Print viewed*]. In a Tucson, Arizona saloon, ex-convict Joe Powell confesses to singer Cleo Raymond that he is involved in an illegal scheme and shows her a stolen wallet containing valuable papers. Cleo is disappointed that Joe, her former lover, has refused to go straight and bids him goodbye. As Joe is leaving the saloon, he is jumped by his three cohorts, Arnold, Pike and Trigg McCord, who try to steal the wallet from him. Joe is saved by passing rancher Ross Daggett, but refuses to report the attack. The next day, Ross and his partner, the half Irish, half Mexican Chito Rafferty, return to their home town and make a $6,000 land payment at the recorder's office, where Ross's girl friend, Beth Winston, works. As they head for their ranch, they see Arnold, Trigg and Pike pursuing Joe and, after an exchange of gunfire, force them to flee. The fatally wounded Joe instructs Ross to deliver the wallet to Cleo and dies without identifying himself. Ross is then ambushed by Arnold, Trigg and Pike, who steal the contents of the wallet and leave the rancher for dead. When Ross awakens, he finds Joe's body missing and is unable to identify his killers to the sheriff. Arnold, meanwhile, appears in the recorder's office claiming to be Joe and presents Beth's uncle, Judge Henry Winston, with a Spanish land grant naming Joe as the rightful owner of most of the surrounding land. Henry is unable to dispute the claim, but assures Beth and Ross that he is going to confirm its legality in Santa Fe, New Mexico. Chito and Ross then ride off to search for

Joe's body and are followed by Pike, who begins shooting at them. Pretending to be hit, Ross outsmarts Pike and soon overwhelms him. After Ross and Chito deliver Pike to Sheriff Claiborne, Arnold shows up at the jail demanding that the lawman serve eviction notices to the local ranchers. When Claiborne refuses to comply, Arnold orders Trigg to shoot him and then releases Pike. Later, at Ross and Chito's ranch, Pike attempts to claim the land and cattle, but is lassoed by Ross and hauled into town. There Ross informs Arnold that no one will be evicted until a court rules on the land grant. Ross and Chito then attend a ranchers meeting that Henry, who has just returned from Santa Fe, has arranged. Also at the meeting is Spade, the local saloon owner and a silent partner of Arnold's. After Henry reveals that the grant appears to be legal, the doctor announces that, before dying, Claiborne named Trigg as his killer. The suspicious Chito follows Spade to his saloon and sees Trigg, who is told of Claiborne's confession, leaving town. Chito intercepts Trigg on the way to Mexico and takes him to jail. When Trigg refuses to talk, Ross and Chito allow Arnold and his gang to break him out of jail and follow Trigg and Pike to Joe's hidden body. The ranchers confront the outlaws over Joe's body, and Ross eventually kills Pike, while Trigg escapes and rushes back to Arnold. Ross and Chito present Henry with Joe's body and tell him that, in order to identify him, he must go to Tucson to find Cleo. While Henry is gone, Spade orders two of his henchmen to kill Ross and Chito as they are leaving the recorder's office, but once again, the ranchers outmanuever the outlaws and escape. In Tucson, meanwhile, Cleo identifies the empty wallet as belonging to Joe and reveals that her ex-lover was an accomplished forger. Henry convinces Cleo to identify Joe's body and sends a telegram to Beth informing her of their impending arrival. Arnold and his gang steal the telegram from Beth and rush to stop Cleo's stage, but are intercepted by Ross, who engages them in a gun battle. Eventually, Ross captures Arnold, while a posse formed by Chito rounds up the remaining outlaws. Later, Chito flirts with Cleo, while Ross and Beth drive a wagon across their now-secure range. *Arizona. Eviction. Land claims. Murder. Ranchers. Fights. Forgers and forgery. Gunfights. Irish Americans. Jailbreaks. Judges. Mexican Americans. Nieces. Robbery. Romance. Saloons. Sheriffs. Tucson (AZ).*

Note: The working title of this film was *Under Arizona Skies*. Carol Foreman is listed in *HR* production charts as a cast member, but her participation in the final film has not been confirmed.

Box 14 Feb 1948. *DV* 30 Jan 1948, p. 3. *FD* 2 Feb 1948, p. 6. *HR* 8 Aug 1947, p. 21. *HR* 22 Aug 1947, p. 13. *HR* 30 Jan 1948, p. 12. *MPHPD* 7 Feb 1948, p. 4051. *Var* 4 Feb 1948, p. 20.

WESTERN UNION (Native Americans, Dakota)

Twentieth Century-Fox Film Corp. *Dist* Twentieth Century-Fox Film Corp. 21 Feb **1941**; New York premiere: 31 Jan 1941; Prod: late Sep—28 Nov 1940; addl scenes 6 Dec—7 Dec and 13 Dec 1940 [©Twentieth Century-Fox Film Corp.; 21 Feb 1941; LP10385]. Sd (Western Electric Mirrophonic Recording); col (Technicolor). 10 reels, 8,570 ft. 93 or 95 min. PCA cert no. 6715.

[*Exec prod* Darryl F. Zanuck]. *Assoc prod* Harry Joe Brown. *Dir* Fritz Lang. [*2d unit dir* Lynn Shores and Otto Brower]. [*Asst dir* Saul Wurtzel and Hal Herman]. [*2d asst dir* Henry Weinberger]. *Scr* Robert Carson. [*Contr to dial* Horace McCoy and Jack Andrews]. [*Contr wrt* George Bruce]. *Dir of photog* Edward Cronjager and Allen M. Davey. [*Cam op* Joe MacDonald]. [*Asst cam* Henry Cronjager]. [*Cam tech* Nelson Cordez]. [*Asst cam tech* Paul Uhl]. [*Cam maintenance* Joe Noecker]. [*Cam loader* William Cline]. [*Gaffer* Fred H. Hall]. [*Stills* Frank Powolny]. [*Process cam* Harry Jackson]. [*Process technician* Roger Mace]. [*Mechanical eff* William Mittlestedt and Ben Southland]. *Technicolor dir* Natalie Kalmus. *Assoc* Morgan Padelford. *Art dir* Richard Day and Albert Hogsett. *Film ed* Robert Bischoff. *Set dec* Thomas Little. [*Props* Don Greenwood]. [*Asst props* William Sittel, Max Goldman and Lemuel Tribe]. *Cost* Travis Banton. [*Ward* Robert Martien, Tom Clark, Marguerite Royce and Steve Brandt]. *Mus dir* David Buttolph. *Sd* Bernard Freericks and Roger Heman. [*Asst mixer* W. R. Snyder]. [*Stageman* Arthur Wright]. [*Cableman* Carl W. Daniels]. [*Extra cableman* Clarence Schiffer]. [*Makeup* Bob Cowan and Ray Lopez]. [*Hairdresser* Buddy King]. [*Prod mgr* William Koenig and Fred Fox]. [*Unit mgr* Duke Goux]. [*Asst unit mgr* Jerry Bryan]. [*Pub dir* Harry Brand]. [*Pub* Gordon Gordon]. [*Robert Young's riding instructor* Fay Hamblin]. [*Scr clerk* Stanley Scheuer]. [*Livestock man* Russel Crane]. [*Key grip* Bruce Hunsaker]. [*Grip* H. B. Romey and Harry R. Jones]. [*Carpenter* Roy Pierce]. [*Painter* Charles King]. [*Landscape man* Max Lauer].

Source: Based on the novel *Western Union* by Zane Grey (New York, 1939).

Cast: Robert Young (*Richard Blake*), Randolph Scott (*Vance Shaw*), Dean Jagger (*Edward Creighton*), Virginia Gilmore (*Sue Creighton*), John Carradine (*Doc Murdoch*), Slim Summerville (*Herman*), Chill Wills (*Homer [Kettle]*), Barton MacLane (*Jack Slade*), Russell Hicks (*Governor*), Victor Kilian (*Charlie*), Minor Watson (*Pat Grogan*), George Chandler (*Herb*), Chief Big Tree (*Chief Spotted Horse*), Chief Thundercloud (*Indian leader*), Dick Rich (*Porky*), Addison Richards (*Captain Harlow*), Irving Bacon (*Barber*), [Harry Strang (*Henchman*)], [Charles Middleton (*Stagecoach passenger*)], [Francis Ford, Eddy Waller (*Stagecoach drivers*)], [Reed Howes, Tom London (*Bandits*)], [Steve O'Brien (*Office boy*)], [Paul Burns (*Bert*)], [Arthur Aylsworth (*Woody*)], [Cliff Clark (*Sheriff*)], [Russ Clark], [Frank Mills], [Ralph Dunn], [James Flavin], [Kermit Maynard], [Herman Nowlin], [John Epper], [Tom Forman], [Larry Dodds], [Sid Jordan], [Robert Clarke], [Captain Anderson], [Bill Beauman], [George Plues], [Hank Bell], [Earl Dobbins], [Cecil Kellogg], [Merlyn Nelson], [Ed Warren], [Frank Ellis], [Tommy Coates], [Joe P. Smith], [Clint Sharp], [Frank McGrath], [Boone Hazlett], [Joe Molina], [Tony Urchel], [James I. Spencer], [Iron Eyes Cody], [Harold A. Malendez], [Clarence Chorre], [Sonny Chorre], [Harry "Silverheels" Smith], [Bahe Denetdeel], [Jack Henry Fritz], [J. W. Cody].

Historical, Western. [*Print viewed*]. In 1861, Western Union engineer Edward Creighton is surveying a telegraph line when he is severely wounded in an accident. Bank robber Vance Shaw, on the run from a posse, comes upon Creighton and saves his life while eluding his pursuers. After Creighton recovers, he returns to Omaha, Nebraska, where he intends to build a telegraph line to Salt Lake City, Utah. There is much opposition to the line from Confederate soldiers, Indians and outlaws, but Creighton intends to get the job done with the help of his sister Sue, foreman Pat Grogan and assistant Homer Kettle. Unaware of Shaw's past, Grogan hires him as a scout, and Creighton allows him to stay, as Shaw has professed a desire to reform. They are joined by tenderfoot Richard Blake, a Harvard-educated engineer whom Creighton hires as a favor to Blake's father. Blake and Shaw compete for the affections of Sue, but their romantic rivalry is short-lived, for on 4 July 1861, construction of the line begins. The work is arduous, but the company makes progress until a mysterious attack, reportedly by Indians, devastates the camp. Shaw is suspicious, however, saying that he does not think Indians would be interested in their cattle, which have been stolen. Shaw leaves to investigate and follows the culprits' trail to the camp of Jack Slade, his former cohort. Slade and his gang, which Shaw quit after the bank robbery, admit to dressing as Indians to rustle the company's cattle. Unable to betray his former comrades, Shaw tells Creighton that a large band of Dakota Indians stole the cattle, and that it would be better to replace them than to risk a fight. Soon after, men working on the forward line are approached by a band of drunken Indians, and the nervous Blake shoots one despite Shaw's orders to remain calm. While they are distracted by the Indians, who mean no real harm, the main camp is attacked by Slade's men, who are again disguised as Indians. The company discovers the ruse when one of the wounded "Indians" is revealed to be white, and Creighton grows suspicious of Shaw's involvement when they are forced to buy back their stolen horses from Slade, whom Shaw admits knowing. Creighton then must convince Chief Spotted Horse to allow them to build the line through Indian territory, even though the man Blake wounded was Spotted Horse's son. After Creighton persuades the Indians, work continues until the company is almost at Salt Lake City. Slade's men strike again, however, after luring Shaw from the camp and tying him up. Shaw escapes and returns to the company's camp, which has been nearly destroyed. Convinced of Shaw's complicity, Creighton fires him, but before he leaves, Shaw reveals to Blake that Slade is his brother. Shaw then finds Slade and his men in a nearby town and is killed in a gunfight with them. Shaw's death is avenged by Blake, who follows him and kills Slade. Soon after, the line is completed, and as Creighton and Sue celebrate, he tells her that Shaw can hear them. Criminals–Rehabilitation. Dakota Indians. Loyalty. Outlaws. United States–History–Civil War, 1861-1865. The West. Western Union. Arson. Brothers and sisters. Construction workers. Cooks. Drunkenness. Engineers. False accusations. Fourth of July. Fugitives. Gunfights. Innovations. Omaha (NE). Racial impersonation. Revenge. Romantic rivalry. Salt Lake City (UT). Scouts (Frontier). Stagecoach drivers. Tenderfoots. Wounds and injuries.

Note: The film's opening title card reads "Twentieth Century-Fox Presents Zane Grey's *Western Union*." Although some modern sources assert that Grey did not write a novel entitled *Western Union*, and claim that the film was instead based on an original story by studio writers, the Twentieth Century-Fox Records of the Legal Department, located at the UCLA Arts—Special Collections Library, indicate that Grey did write the novel, which was published on 20 Oct 1939, three days before his death. Both Grey's novel, his last, and the film present a fictional account of the real Edward Creighton, a Western Union engineer who helped survey and build the telegraph line from Omaha, NE to Salt Lake City, UT. A 26 Jan 1941 *NYHT* article commented about the film: "In 1861 it cost $212,000 to extend the telegraph from Omaha to Salt Lake City, and the crew took four months and eleven days, covering 1,100 miles, to do the job. To reproduce their feat in 1940, a company of 300 traveled 2,000 miles in ten months at a cost of more than $1,000,000."

According to a 26 Oct 1939 *HR* news item, Paramount attempted to acquire rights to Grey's novel. Grey's son, Romer, reportedly revealed that before his father's death, "negotiations had been on for Gary Cooper to star in the production which [Grey] was to produce for either United Artists or RKO release." Twentieth Century-Fox obtained the rights to Grey's novel in Nov 1939 for $25,000, and according to a *HR* news item, the studio also purchased an original story by Ward Wing about the history of the Western Union company. Apparently the studio did not intend to use Wing's material, but purchased it "to forestall any conflict with the Zane Grey yarn." A modern source states that executive producer Darryl F. Zanuck originally considered assigning Irving Pichel as the film's director. Studio legal records indicate that writers Albert Shelby LeVino, Curtis Kenyon and Kenneth Earl worked on early drafts of the film's screenplay, but the extent of their contribution to the completed picture has not been confirmed.

A 12 Aug 1940 *HR* news item announcing the signing of Fritz Lang as director also noted that Brenda Joyce had been cast in the feminine lead, and Don Ameche and Lloyd Nolan had been assigned to leading roles. On 11 Sep 1940, however, *HR* noted that Twentieth Century-Fox was borrowing Robert Young from M-G-M to replace Ameche. Other *HR* news items stated that Laird Cregar would be in the cast, then announced that because he was being held up by his work in *Hudson's Bay*, he was to be replaced by George "Gabby" Hayes, but illness prevented Hayes from appearing in the finished film. Lucille Miller and Esther Brodelet were included in the cast by *HR* news items, but their participation in the completed film has not been confirmed. A *HR* news item also included Mary Astor in the cast, but she does not appear in the released picture. Actor Chill Wills was borrowed from M-G-M for the production.

A 21 Oct 1940 *HR* news item noted that during principal photography, the film's script was sent "back to writer George Bruce with instructions to build up the part of Virginia Gilmore." The extent of Bruce's contribution to the released film has not been determined, however. The picture was largely shot on location at Kanab and Zion National National Park, UT, and House Rock Canyon, AZ. According to a 26 Sep 1940 *HR* news item, fourteen Native Americans traveled from Hollywood to the Kanab location because "any arrangements for use of government reservation Indians in that territory [would involve] too much 'red tape.'" A 1 Dec 1940 *NYT* article reported that Lang did not cast the local Piute Indians in the picture "because of their stature [which meant that] they didn't look like the customers' conception of Indians." The article stated that instead, Lang "ordered a shipment of Hollywood Indians from Central Casting—tall, high cheek-boned fellows who look like aborigines are supposed to look." According to a studio press release, Twentieth Century-Fox actor Henry Fonda, who had once worked as a lineman and in telegraph laboratories in Minneapolis, served as a technical adviser on the production.

According to a *HR* news item, in Dec 1940, the studio purchased J. Hyatt Downing's novel *Sioux City*, intending to produce it as a "follow-up" to *Western Union*. Randolph Scott and Laird Cregar were to star in the picture, but it was never made.

AmCin Mar 1941, p. 128. *Box* 8 Feb 1941. *DV* 31 Jan 1941, pp. 3-4. *FD* 7 Feb 1941, p. 7. *HR* 26 Oct 1939, p. 1. *HR* 7 Nov 1939, p. 3. *HR* 8 Nov 1939, p. 3. *HR* 12 Aug 1940, p. 1. *HR* 9 Sep 1940, p. 5. *HR* 10 Sep 1940, p. 4. *HR* 11 Sep 1940, p. 7. *HR* 12 Sep 1940, p. 9. *HR* 16 Sep 1940, p. 2. *HR* 20 Sep 1940, p. 7. *HR* 24 Sep 1940, p. 7. *HR* 26 Sep 1940, p. 4. *HR* 27 Sep 1940, p. 7. *HR* 18 Oct 1940, p. 2. *HR* 21 Oct 1940, p. 3, 6. *HR* 25 Oct 1940, p. 6. *HR* 29 Oct 1940, p. 3. *HR* 12 Nov 1940, p. 5. *HR* 14 Nov 1940, p. 1. *HR* 16 Nov 1940, p. 1. *HR* 22 Nov 1940, p. 9. *HR* 28 Nov 1940, p. 5. *HR* 6 Dec 1940, p. 4. *HR* 13 Dec 1940, p. 3. *HR* 17 Dec 1940, p. 4. *HR* 24 Dec 1940, p. 4. *HR* 24 Jan 1941, p. 4. *HR* 28 Jan 1941, p. 3. *HR* 31 Jan 1941, p. 3. *MPD* 3 Feb 1941. *MPH* 8 Feb 1941. *NYHT* 26 Jan 1941. *NYT* 1 Dec 1940. *NYT* 26 Jan 1941. *NYT* 7 Feb 1941, p. 23. *Var* 5 Feb 1941, p. 12.

THE WESTERNERS (Native Americans)

Benjamin B. Hampton Productions; Great Authors' Pictures, Inc. *Dist* W. W. Hodkinson Corp. through Pathé Exchange, Inc. Aug **1919**. Si; b&w. 7 reels.

Supv Benjamin B. Hampton. *Dir* Edward Sloman. *Scen* E. Richard Schayer. *Titles* Stewart Edward White. *Cam* John Seitz. *Tech adv* Clark Comstock.

Source: Based on the novel *The Westerners* by Stewart Edward White (New York, 1901).

Cast: Roy Stewart (*Cheyenne Harry*), Robert McKim (*Michael "Black Mike" Lafond*), Wilfred Lucas (*Jim Buckley*), Mildred Manning (*Prue Welch/Molly Lafond*), Mary Jane Irving (*Little Molly Welch*), Graham Pettie (*Prof. Welch*), Frankie Lee (*Dennis, the kid*), Clark Comstock (*Lone Wolf*), Dorothy Hagar (*Bismarck Annie*).

Western. Half-breed Indian Michael Lafond vows vengeance after scout Jim Buckley forces him off a wagon train for insulting a white woman. Michael kills Prue Welch, the wife of a New England professor, and kidnaps her baby daughter Molly. Michael raises Molly as his own daughter, then, fifteen years later, he opens a dance hall, and forces Molly to becomes a dance hall girl. He plots to ruin Jim, now a leading citizen of the Black Hills community, and his scheming causes Jim to have to fight his way out of the settlement. Jim is aided in the struggle by Cheyenne Harry, Molly's suitor. Michael overtakes Jim on horseback, but is thrown over an embankment by Jim and killed. Jim returns to find Molly happy with Cheyenne Harry. *Frontier and pioneer life. Indians of North America–Mixed blood. Kidnapping. Scouts (Frontier). Dance hall girls. Falls from heights. Murder. New Englanders. Professors. Revenge. Wagon trains.*

Note: White's novel was first published in serial form in *Munsey's Magazine.* The film had several pre-release exhibitions, the earliest of which began on 15 Jun 1919 in Los Angeles and 3 Aug 1919 in New York.

ETR 16 Aug 1919, p. 909. *MPN* 16 Aug 1919, p. 1495. *MPW* 16 Aug 1919, p. 1020. *NYT* 4 Aug 1919, p. 8. *Var* 6 Jun 1919, p. 50. *Var* 8 Aug 1919, p. 49. *Wid's* 10 Aug 1919, p. 5.

WESTWARD HO THE WAGONS! (Native Americans, Pawnee, Dakota)

Walt Disney Productions. *Dist* Buena Vista Film Distribution Co. 25 Dec **1956**; Prod: 16 Jan–23 Mar 1956; retakes on 26 May 1956 [©Walt Disney Productions; 20 Sep 1956; LP8882]. Sd (RCA Sound Recording); col (Technicolor); CinemaScope. 9 reels, 7,753 ft. 86 min. PCA cert no. 18089.

Pres WALT DISNEY. [*Exec prod* Walt Disney]. *Prod* Bill Walsh. *Dir* William Beaudine. *2d unit dir* Yakima Canutt. *Asst dir* William Beaudine, Jr. and [Albert Whitlock]. [*2d asst dir* Vincent McEveety]. *Dial dir* Ralph Maxheimer. *Scr* Tom Blackburn. *Photog* Charles P. Boyle. [*Cam op* Jack Whitman]. *Spec process* Ub Iwerks. *Matte artist* Peter Ellenshaw. *Art dir* Marvin Aubrey Davis. *Ed* Cotton Warburton. *Set dec* Emile Kuri and Bertram Granger. [*Props* Jack Golconda]. *Cost* Chuck Keehne and Gertrude Casey. *Mus* George Bruns. *Orch* Edward Plumb. [*Dance dir* Ralph Maxheimer]. *Sd supv* Robert O. Cook. *Sd rec* Dean Thomas. [*Rec* Lou Skelton]. [*Cable man* Malcolm Rennings]. *Makeup* David Newell. *Hair stylist* Lois Murray. *Unit mgr* Ben Chapman. [*Tech adv* Iron Eyes Cody]. [*Prod mgr* Bill Anderson]. [*Scr clerk* Fred Hartsook]. [*1st grip* Garrett Lambrecht]. [*Pub* Leonard Shannon]. [*Caterer* Rolly Harper]. [*Stunts* Joe Yrigoyen, Robert Buzz Henry, Edward C. Canutt, Joe Canutt, John Eppers, Jerry Brown, Red Morgan, A. C. Hudkins, Al Wyatt, Chuck Courtney, Bob Folkerson, Gene White, Forrest Burns, Boyd Stockman, John J. Hudkins, Cliff Lyons, Bob Woodward, Don Happy, Rocky Shahan, Edward Juaregi, L. Johnson, Robert Whitey Hughes and George Steele].

Song(s): "Westward Ho the Wagons!" and "The Ballad of John Colter," music by George Bruns, lyrics by Tom Blackburn; "Wringle Wrangle," music and lyrics by Stan Jones; "I'm Lonely My Darlin'," new arrangement of "Green Grow the Lilacs," music and lyrics by George Bruns and Fess Parker; "Pioneer's Prayer," music by Paul Smith, lyrics by Gil George; and traditional Indian songs, including a Sioux medicine chant.

Source: Based on the novel *The Children of the Covered Wagon* by Mary Jane Carr (New York, 1934).

Cast: Fess Parker [(*John "Doc" Grayson*)], Kathleen Crowley [(*Laura Thompson*)], Jeff York [(*Hank Breckenridge*)], David Stollery [(*Dan Thompson*)], Sebastian Cabot [(*Bissonette*)], George Reeves [(*James Stephen*)], Doreen Tracey [(*Bobo Stephen*)], Barbara Woodell [(*Mrs. Stephen*)], John War Eagle [(*Wolf's brother*)], Cubby O'Brien [(*Jerry Stephen*)], Tommy Cole [(*Jim Stephen*)], Leslie Bradley [(*Spencer Armitage*)], Morgan Woodward [(*"Obie" Foster*)], Iron Eyes Cody [(*Many Stars*)], Anthony Numkena [(*Little Thunder*)], Karen Pendleton [(*Myra Thompson*)], Jane Liddell [(*Ruth Benjamin*)], Jon Locke [(*Ed Benjamin*)], [Brand Stirling (*Tom Foster*)], [Beulah Archuletta (*White Antelope*)], [George Ross, Sandy Sanders, Max Wagner, Pete Kellett, Chuck Courtney, Buff Brady, Ray Berwick (*Wagon men*)], [Dorothy Crider, Gertrude Astor (*Wagon women*)], [Eddie Little (*Pawnee brave*)], [Dewey Drapeau (*Pawnee chief*)], [Grey Eagle (*Indian*)], [Kathleen Beaudine, Clancy Hurrell (*Children*)], [Carl Mathews].

Western, with songs. [*Print viewed*]. In 1844, a wagon train heading for Oregon stops for the day before leaving Pawnee territory and entering the lands of the friendly Sioux. During the break, Hank Breckenridge, the wagon's gruff scout, complains about the restrictions of majority rule to his friend, John "Doc" Grayson. That night, the wagon train's children listen intently as Doc sings about a trapper whose courage and speed enabled him to race away from maurading Blackfeet Indians. The next day, the children are playing on a ridge when four Pawnee war party scouts spot the eldest, Dan Thompson. In order to protect the others, Dan gives himself up, and after the warriors take him away, the children remain in hiding until dark in case there are more Pawnee in the area. At the Pawnee camp, Dan is able to escape while the Indians dance, but in order to out run his last pursuer, Dan must shove some large rocks down a hillside to crush him. When Dan reaches the wagon train, he tells them that hundreds of Pawnees were at the camp, and Hank realizes that it must be a war party, which will attack the wagons at daybreak. Doc and Hank give orders to the group to unload all but bare necessities, so that they can reach Sioux territory before dawn. The Indians attack at daybreak, although a rear guard repels the first wave and gives the wagons time to take cover in the hills. After a few more attacks, however, Hank realizes that the major thrust is about to come and that the Indians will prevail. Doc then asks farmer Obie Foster and speculator Spencer Armitage to release their extra horses because the Pawnees are more interested in the animals than in collecting scalps. Armitage balks, as he hopes to make a profit from the horses, but Foster releases them and the Indians retreat after rounding them up. The wagons move on and soon reach Fort Laramie in Sioux territory, where Hank learns from Bissonette, the French fort boss, that the Sioux may no longer be friendly because the last wagon train killed two braves from the tribe of Chief Wolf's Brother. As the travelers set up camp, Doc sends Armitage and some of the children to the fort to trade for buffalo robes. At the fort, medicine man Many Stars is captivated by the blonde hair of Dan's little sister Myra and tells Wolf's Brother that the child is good luck. Armitage pushed the chief away when he touches Myra, and although Bissonette calms the angry chief, he refuses to let his son Little Thunder roughhouse with Dan. Upon hearing of the childrens' interactions with the Indians, Doc, Hank and wagonmaster Jim Stephens decide to leave in the morning. That night, however, Wolf's Brother arrives at the camp and offers to trade valuable ponies, a sacred white buffalo robe and a ceremonial whistle for Myra, who, along with Dan and their older sister Laura, is fatherless. Wolf's Brother assures them that he will rear the girl as a princess, but Stephens and Laura angrily reject his offer. The next day, Doc confers again with the dissatisfied Indians, then decides that it would be safer to stay close to the fort rather than leave. As the Indians are departing, Little Thunder falls from his horse and is seriously injured. The Indians refuse Doc's offer to help, and soon Little Thunder is near death. Doc and Laura go to the Indian encampment, where Little Thunder's mother begs her husband to accept the white man's help. Doc diagnoses a bone splinter that has punctured a vein in the boy's neck, and despite Wolf's Brother's antagonism, Doc is able to operate and relieve the pressure. Soon after, Little Thunder recovers and the Indians bring gifts to the whites. Wolf's Brother tells Doc that he is his friend and that his tribe will escort them on their journey, after which Dan rides with Little Thunder and Doc joins Laura on her wagon. *Children. Cultural conflict. Dakota Indians. Oregon Trail. Physicians. Wagon trains. Abduction. Bison, American. Books. Bow and arrow. Brothers and sisters. Dances. Escapes. Farmers. Fathers and sons. Fort Laramie (WY). French Americans. Hair. Horses. Medicine men. Mothers and sons. Operations, Surgical. Pawnee Indians. Religion. Riding accidents. Romance. Scouts (Frontier). Sign language. Speculation. Traders. Tribal chiefs.*

Note: The working title of this film, which was Walt Disney's first western feature, was *Children of the Covered Wagon.* According to a story in the *Oswego Review* (from Oswego, OR), Disney bought the rights to the novel in 1949 on the suggestion of Hollywood columnist Jimmy Fiddler. Author Mary Jane Carr find "considerable change" in the film, but was "well satisfied" with it, according to the news story. Several contemporary newspaper stories pointed out that historical accuracy was important to Disney and the actors. The film featured four "Mouseketeers" from the "Mickey Mouse Club" television series: Tommy Cole, Doreen Tracey, Cubby O'Brien and Karen Pendleton. Expecting a large number of children to see the film, Disney, in a *Denver Post* article, stated, "We're not going to have a lot of loving and smooching. There's too much of that in pictures. Kids resent it." According to publicity for the film, the outdoor scenes were shot at Conejo Ranch near Thousand Oaks, CA. Although three western states were scouted for locations, the heavy Disney production schedule resulted in the mid-winter start date, so the Thousand Oaks location was used. Lodge-pine poles for the tepees built for the sets were bought from the Blackfoot reservation in Montana and painted with Sioux tribal designs, according to publicity.

A one-hour *Disneyland* telecast on 14 Nov 1956, entitled "Along the Oregon

Trail," included a behind-the-scenes look at the filming of *Westward Ho the Wagons!*. On the day of the film's opening, the first segment of a four-part series about Indians, entitled "The First Americans" began on the *Disneyland* series. The film was shown in two parts on the *Disneyland* television program on 19 Feb and 26 Feb 1961.

Box 22 Dec 1956. *Christian Science Monitor* 6 Mar 1956. *Denver Post* 6 Jan 1957. *Detroit Times* 18 Jan 1957. *DV* 18 Dec 1956, p. 3. *Exb* 26 Dec 1956, p. 4265. *FD* 20 Dec 1956, p. 12 *Glendale News Press* 24 Mar 1956. *Har* 29 Dec 1956, p. 207. *HCN* 17 Dec 1956. *HR* 18 Dec 1956, p.3. *LAEx* 1 Apr 1956, p. 8, 11. *LAEx* 26 Dec 1956. *LAT* 31 Oct 1955. *LAT* 19 Apr 1956. *LAT* 27 Sep 1956. *LAT* 26 Dec 1956, p. 8. *LAMirror-News* 27 Dec 1956. *McKeesport News* 14 Jan 1957. *Menasba Twin City News Record* 3 Jan 1957. *MPD* 27 Dec 1956, p. 3. *MPHPD* 22 Dec 1956, p. 195. *Oswego Review* 28 Feb 1957 *Post-Advocate* 25 Jan 1956. *Time* 4 Feb 1957. *Var* 19 Dec 1956, p. 7.

WESTWARD THE WOMEN (French Americans, Italian Americans, Japanese Americans)

Metro-Goldwyn-Mayer Corp.; controlled by Loew's Inc. *Dist* Loew's Inc. 11 Jan **1951**; *Prod*: mid-Apr—late Jun 1951 [©Loew's Inc.; 21 Nov 1951; LP1346]. Sd (Western Electric Sound System); b&w. 116 or 118 min. Passed by the National Board of Review. PCA cert no. 15385.

Prod Dore Schary. *Dir* William A. Wellman. [*Asst dir* Reggie Callow]. *Scr* Charles Schnee. *Story* Frank Capra. *Dir of photog* William Mellor. *Art dir* Cedric Gibbons and Daniel B. Cathcart. *Film ed* James E. Newcom. *Set dec* Edwin B. Willis and Ralph S. Hurst. *Cost* Walter Plunkett. *Ward* Tommy McCoig. *Mus* Jeff Alexander. *Rec supv* Douglas Shearer. [*Sd eng* Conrad Kahn]. [*Unit mgr* Ruby Rosenberg]. [*Animal trainer* Johnny Indrisano]. *Tech adv* Jim Louck.

Music: "To the West! To the West! by Henry Russell.

Cast: Beverly Dennis (*Rose [Meyers]*), Renata Vanni (*Mrs. Maroni*), John McIntire (*Roy [E.] Whitman*), Julie Bishop (*Laurie [Smith]*), Hope Emerson (*Patience [Hawley]*), Marilyn Erskine (*Jean [Johnson]*), Lenore Lonegan (*Maggie [O'Malley]*), Henry Nakamura (*Ito*), Denise Darcel ([*Fifi*] *Danon*), Robert Taylor (*Buck [Wyatt]*), [Guido Martufi (*Tony Maroni*)], [Bruce Cowling (*Cat*)], [Patrick Conway (*Sid Cutler*)], [Chubby Johnson (*Jim Stacey*)], [Mary Alan Hokanson (*Cora*)], [Raymond Bond (*Preacher*)], [Terry Wilson (*Lon*)], [Michael Dugan (*Outrider*)], [Edith Mills (*Sadie*)], [John Cason (*Margaret's man*)], [Mikel Conrad (*Rose's man*)], [Lou Nova (*Blacksmith*)], [Frankie Darro (*Jean's man*)], [Z. Yaconelli (*Mrs. Maroni's man*)], [Ted Adams, Gene Roth (*Bartenders*)], [George Chandler (*Mackerel face*)], [Earl Hodgins (*Drunk*)], [Stanford Jolley (*Gambler*)], [John War Eagle (*Indian Chief*)], [Bert LeBaron (*Ken*)], [Elmer Napier (*Walt*)], [Ann Roberts, Lucille House, Shirley Lucas, Pat Paul, Donna Hall, Opal Erne, Norma Santillo, Norma Young, Jody Smith, Mary Murphy, Sharon Lucas, Mary Casiday, Cornelia Flores, Stevie Myers, Alice Wills, Edith Happy, Karen Hale, Claire Andre, Maxine Garrett, Marilyn Lindsey, Marlyn Gladstone, Fiona O'Shiel, Alice Markham, Polly Burson, Evelyn Finley, Kathleen O'Malley, Doris Lee Cole (*Pioneer women*)], [Henry Wills, Ed Juaregui, Archie Butler, Bill Cartledge, Carl Pitti, Pat Ford, Frank McGrath, Don House, Ray Thomas, Clem Fuller, Clint Sharp, Gene Coogan (*Outriders*)], [Claire Carleton, Dorothy Granger, Mil Patrick, Joan Valerie (*Flashy girls*)], [Tom Greenway (*Bart*)], [Tom Monroe] (*Tennese Jim*).

Western. [*Print viewed*]. By 1851, Roy Whitman has established a growing ranching community in his California valley. The one thing missing is women for the men to marry, which would enable them to set down roots in the valley. Whitman hires scout Buck Wyatt to travel with him to Chicago, where he hopes to recruit enough women to provide wives for one hundred men. Buck thoroughly disapproves of the idea, believing that the journey across the country is too hard for women, but when Whitman offers him double his usual salary, he reluctantly agrees. The 140 women whom Whitman recruits are a varied group, including Patience Hawley, the aging widow of a New England sea captain; farm girl Maggie O'Malley, an expert with a gun; Rose Meyers, who is pregnant with an illegitimate child; Mrs. Maroni, an Italian widow traveling with her nine-year-old son Tony; and French-born Fifi Danon and Laurie Smith, two former prostitutes looking for a new life. Buck also hires fifteen men to help him get the women to California, warning both the men and the women against fraternization. After a quick lesson in mule driving, the journey begins. Buck immediately has to send one of the men away when he behaves familiarly with one of the women, and promises that he will kill the next man he catches breaking the rules. The journey is every bit as difficult as Buck had predicted. Indians circle the wagon train and, although they do not attack, they announce their intention to return later. When Laurie is raped by a man who believes that her

former profession allows him to treat her any way he wants, Buck carries through with his promise and kills the man. That night, many of the men leave, taking some of the women with them. Jim Stacey, who has fallen in love with Rose, asks her to leave with him, but when she refuses to abandon the train, he stays with her. The next morning, Buck discovers the defections, but rather than turn back, he announces that he will make the women into men. The first step is to teach them how to use a gun. During the practice Tony is accidentally shot and killed. Mrs. Moroni becomes temporarily insane, and Buck must drag her off her son's grave and put her in Patience's care. The women negotiate a difficult pass, clearing the rocks and trees before lowering the wagons with ropes, and one woman is killed in the process. Later, the mules stampede when Danon fires a gun at a rabbit. In reaction to Buck's anger at her, Dannon rides away from the train, and he chases after her. After an argument, they admit they love each other. When they return to the train, they find it under attack from Indians. After the attack, a roll call of the casualties reveals the deaths of Whitman, Jim and several of the women. Buck and Ito, the Japanese cook, are the only men left. Later, Laurie is killed when her wagon is washed away during a thunderstorm. The last big obstacle facing the women is the desert. Rose goes into labor during the crossing, and when a wheel falls off the wagon in which Patience is caring for her, the women hold it up until after the birth of her baby boy. Finally, the train reaches its destination, but the women refuse to meet their future husbands until they have had time to clean up. When they are ready they drive into town to meet the waiting men. Buck is now the admiring champion of these plucky women and warns the men to be good to them. As the women choose their husbands, Danon stops Buck before he can leave, and they join the line of couples waiting to be married. *Mail order brides. Romance. United States–History–Social life and customs. Wagon trains. The West. Accidental death. Childbirth. French Americans. Indians of North America. Italian Americans. Japanese Americans. Prostitution. Weddings. Widows.*

Note: The film's pre-release title was *Pioneer Women*. The opening credits list Robert Taylor and Denise Darcel first, with several other cast members listed after them. The end credits show various members of the cast, with their character names, and end with Robert Taylor, followed by the words "and the women." According to *IP*, the film was shot on location in Suprise Valley, Paria Canyon and Johnson Creek, Utah. The location camp was in Kanab, Utah. *Time* noted that M-G-M made a short about the production's location shoot.

IP also noted that actor Henry Nakamura's role was written especially for him after director William Wellman and producer Dore Schary were impressed by his performance as the lovable "Tommy" character in the 1951 M-G-M film *Go for Broke!*. *M-G-M News* noted that Wellman cast Navajos, Utes and Piutes as Indians in the film. Contemporary reviews and news items variously stated that 100, 140, 200 and 400 women took part in the film, although the film itself refers to 140 women. According to his autobiography, Frank Capra had planned to direct the film hmself and cast Gary Cooper in the lead, but later sold his story to his neighbor, Wellman.

AmCin Jan 1952, pp. 14-15, 42-43, 45. *Box* 24 Nov 1951. *DV* 15 Nov 1951, p. 3. *FD* 20 Nov 1951, p. 14. *HR* 6 Apr 1951, P. 3. *HR* 13 Apr 1951, p. 10. *HR* 15 Jun 1951, p. 8. *HR* 21 Nov 1951. *IP* Nov 1951, pp. 8-9. *LAT Magazine* 8 Jul 1951. *MPHPD* 24 Nov 1951, p. 1118. *NYT* 1 Jan 1952, p. 21. *Time* 14 Jan 1951, p. 82. *Var* 21 Nov 1951, p. 6.

WETBACKS (1949) *see* **BORDER INCIDENT**

WETBACKS (Latino)

Banner Pictures, Inc. *Dist* Gibraltor Motion Picture Distributors, Inc. Feb **1956**; Los Angeles opening: 22 Feb 1956; Prod: 4 May—mid-May 1955. Sd; col (Eastman Color); 1.85. 9 reels, 7,883 or 7,908 ft. 86 or 88-89 min. PCA cert no. 17686.

Prod Hank McCune. *Assoc prod* Byron Roberts. *Dir* Hank McCune. *Scr* Pete La Roche. [*Story* Hank McCune]. *Dir of photog* Brydon Baker. *Film ed* Ronald V. Ashcroft. *Set des* Robert Haver. [*Props* Ralph Hanson]. *Mus dir* Les Baxter. *Sd* Lyle Willey. *Lighting* Charles Beckett. *Tech equipment* Charles Hannawalt. *Tech dir* Lt. Commander R. C. Cannon, USCGR.

Cast: Lloyd Bridges [(*Jim Benson*)], Nancy Gates [(*Sally Parker*)], Barton MacLane [(*Karl Shanks*)], John Hoyt [(*Steve Bodine*)], Harold Peary [(*Juan Ortega*)], Nacho Galindo [(*Alphonso*)], Robert Keys [(*Reeser*)], David Colmans [(*Pedro*)], Jose Gonzales Gonzales [(*Wetback*)], Louis Jean Heydt [(*Coast Guard commander*)], Scott Douglas [(*Immigration officer*)], Wally Cassell [(*Coast Guard lieutenant*)], Richard Powers [(*Highway Patrol inspector*)], Salvador Baguez [(*Mexican policeman*)], Joe Dominguez, Roy Gordon, I. Stanford Jolley, Maury Dexter, Gene Roth.

Crime, Sea, Adventure. [*Print viewed*]. Immigration officers engage in a gun battle when smugglers try to unload a boatful of

illegal immigrants onto a U.S. beach. Later, at the U.S. Immigration Bureau, an officer complains to his superior that although illegal immigrants, or "wetbacks," are being smuggled across the borders of Texas, California and Arizona, the bureau has no idea where the operation is based. Describing the smugglers as "the most vicious kind of human scavengers," the official remarks that they take in four to five thousand dollars per week from families who often give up their life savings in order to get one of their members into the United States. Once there, the immigrants are hired out as farm labor, while the smugglers, who have promised their customers good jobs and homes, simply disappear. The official, however, has a plan. Jim Benson, an ex-Coast Guard officer and present owner of a nearly bankrupt charter fishing business, persuades the man to whom he is deeply in debt to let him take his vessel on one more trip. As Jim tears the "Sheriff's Sale" notice from his boat, two men, one of them Mexican, approach him with a business offer, but he ignores them. At that moment, Karl Shanks and Sally Parker, Jim's obnoxious customer and his date, arrive for their Mexican fishing trip. While Jim makes coffee, Karl quietly tinkers with his fishing rod, and during the trip, he complains constantly. Finally, he offers Jim twice his fee if he can locate a fish, but threatens to pay nothing if they return from the trip empty-handed. A huge marlin bites, but because Karl has tampered with the rod, the fish gets away. Realizing he has been tricked, Jim threatens to strangle Karl if he refuses to pay. Karl demands to be taken to the nearest town, promising to give Jim the money. When they arrive in Delgado, Mexico, however, Karl secretly pours beer in the gas tank and runs away. The two men from the dock, who described themselves as importer/exporters, again try to hire Jim, but he is suspicious of them and refuses. Alphonso, the owner of the local cantina and inn, has neither the gasoline nor the money to help his stranded friend, and even Sally, sitting dejectedly at the bar, declares that she is broke. Jim and Sally talk until late, whereupon she retires and Jim returns to the boat. The two men, who identify themselves as Steve Bodine and Juan Ortega, admit that they want Jim to carry a number of Mexican men across the border, claiming that the work that awaits them there will give them and their families "a chance." Because he so desperately needs the money, Jim reluctantly agrees to make the run, but when Sally questions him, he changes his mind. Bodine and Ortega, however, threaten Jim with a gun and begin to load men onto the boat. The wife of one of the laborers, not believing that her husband will be paid a fortune just for picking cotton, begs him not to go, but he insists on making the trip. During the run, Jim tries to change course, but Bodine's henchman notices this and punches him. A Coast Guard vessel calls to Jim, but because the crew knows him, they allow his boat to pass. When Jim returns to Delgado, Bodine informs him that he must continue making the runs. Frustrated and scared, Jim confesses to Sally, but when he refuses to admit his crime to the police, she reveals that she is a U.S. Immigration Bureau agent. Jim reacts with fury to the news that she has been planted in Delgado to help uncover the smugglers. They argue, and Sally leaves, but Ortega sees her peering into the smugglers' headquarters and locks her up. Back in the U.S., an Immigration inspector learns that Jim is being used and angrily orders his men to get him out. Meanwhile, Sally frees herself and finds Jim in Delgado's main street, where they find temporary safety from the smugglers by blending in with the crowds of a local fiesta. Jim's little friend Pedro secretly siphons gas from the town taxi and pours it into the tank of Jim's boat. The smugglers beat the boy, but Jim and Sally escape to the boat, which has been loaded with a single immigrant. Their vessel is closely pursued by the smugglers, and while hiding with Jim in a small cove, Sally explains that she became an agent after her father, a boatman, was killed by wetback smugglers. Bodine and Ortega chase the couple through the waves, and Jim tries to take cover from their bullets by weaving around a large freighter. The arrival of a Coast Guard boat sends the smugglers running, but they are soon caught. Shanks reveals that he, too, is an agent, and that he has deposited a large sum of money in Jim's account. On Jim's boat, Sally and Jim kiss. *Aliens, Illegal. Delgado (Mexico). Mexicans. Sea captains. Smuggling. Undercover operations. United States. Dept. of Immigration. Americans in foreign countries. Bartenders. Chases. Children. Escapes. Festivals. Fishing. Freighters. Immigrants. Impersonation and imposture. Mexican Americans. Mexican-American border region. Motorboats. Romance. United States. Coast Guard.*

Note: According to a 24 May 1955 *DV* news item, filming began on 4 May

1955 on Catalina Island, but was halted after approximately two weeks due to a labor dispute between producer Hank McCune and the actors. The actors protested that according to their SAG contracts, McCune owed them nine hundred dollars in back salaries. McCune was not allowed to resume shooting until the back salaries were paid, and certified checks for advanced salaries for the actors as well as other guild and union members were issued. Production restarted in early Jul 1955. According to the film's pressbook, additional filming took place in Mexico. The technical director, Lt. Commander R. C. Cannon, was an officer in the United States Coast Guard Reserve. Contemporary sources note that the Coast Guard provided the production with technical advice and equipment.

Box 9 Jun 1956. *DV* 24 May 1955. *DV* 25 May 1955. *DV* 23 Feb 1956, p. 3. *Exb* 31 Oct 1956, p. 4246. *Har* 3 Mar 1956, pp. 34-35. *MPHPD* 9 Jun 1956, p. 929. *NYT* 5 May 1956, p. 13. *Var* 7 Mar 1956, p. 6.

WE'VE COME A LONG, LONG WAY (African Americans)

Negro Marches On, Inc. **1944**; U.S. Premiere in New York: 24 Jun 1944. Sd; b&w. 6,200 ft.

Dir Jack Goldberg. *Narr* Elder Lightfoot Solomon Michaux. *Addl narr* Mary McLeod Bethune and Major Wright.

Song(s): "We've Come a Long, Long Way," composer unknown.

African American. [*Not viewed*]. On the occasion of a memorial service for Lt. Lester Collins, an African-American officer, who gave his life for his country after the attack on Pearl Harbor, achievements of African Americans during the seventy-five years since emancipation are highlighted. The narrator suggests what would happen to black culture, society, and politics if Nazism was allowed to dominate the world. Prominent twentieth-century African Americans are shown flourishing in education, business, science, the military, and sports, among them actor and singer Paul Robeson, opera singer Marian Anderson, dancer Bill Robinson, boxer Joe Louis, educator and scientist George Washington Carver, Olympic athlete Jesse Owens, band leader Duke Ellington and singer Lena Horne. *African Americans. Clergy. Nazism. World War II. George Washington Carver. Nationalism. Pearl Harbor (HI), Attack on, 1941. Slavery. United States–History.*

Note: Although a print of this film was not viewed, the above credits and summary were taken from a dialogue continuity deposited with the NYSA. The dialogue continuity indicates that either a voiceover or an on-screen prologue states: "December 7th —A day that will go down in infamy. The United States of America was deliberately and cruelly attacked by the Empire of Japan. No matter how long it may take and no matter what the cost may be, we will win through to absolute victory." The film opens with a speech by President Franklin D. Roosevelt. The film's principle narrator, Elder Solomon Lightfoot Michaux, was the pastor of the Radio Church in Washington, D. C. Additional narrators included Dr. Mary McLeod Bethune, president of Bethune Cookman College and the National Council of Negro Women, and Major Wright, a banker and former college president. Wright's narration states that he was the sponsor of a bill that would commemorate the 1st of February, 1864 as the day that Congress adopted the resolution proposing the ratification of the 13th Amendment, which prohibited slavery in the United States. Portions of the film were shot in New York City's Harlem.

FD 6 Jun 1944, p. 9. *NYT* 26 Jun 1944, p. 21. *Var* 28 Jun 1944, p. 16.

WHAT A GUY (African Americans, Chinese Americans)

Lucky Star Productions. *Dist* Toddy Pictures Co. **1947?**. Sd; b&w. 4,855 ft.

Cast: Mantan Moreland (*What-a-Hotel Manager* [*also known as Mantan*]), Monte Hawley (*Police Officer Fixem*), Ruby Dee (*Hotel owner, maybe* [*Mrs. Ruby Dawson*]), Lawrence Criner (*Smokey and Toughie* [*Gat Dawson*]), Jo Rhetta (*Working girl, and how*), Al Curtis (*One-Lung*), John Bouie (*House detective* [*also known as J. B.*]), Ken Freeman (*No-Talkie*).

African American, Comedy. [*Not viewed*]. After getting in a fight with his buddy and convincing the policeman not to press charges, a penniless Mantan takes a job from Mrs. Ruby Dawson, owner of a quaint country inn. Mantan is attracted to Ruby and is quite content with his job as clerk. Just as his friend J. B. arrives and shows Mantan his monogrammed wallet stuffed with five one-hundred dollar bills, a young woman in the lobby yells for the police, saying that she has been robbed of her monogrammed wallet. The policeman gives the wallet to the young woman along with J. B.'s new watch, which she also claims to be hers. When Ruby returns, Mantan brags that he and J. B. fought off seventeen gun-toting burglars, and Ruby, impressed, hires the now destitute J. B. to be the house detective. One-Lung, a Chinese laundry owner, then arrives and says that he needs to rent a room, as his entire shop has burned down, incinerating all of his customers' clothes, including Mantan's. Mantan cannot understand One-Lung's English, but when the launderer dances like Bill Robinson, Mantan decides he is a "hep-cat" after all. Meanwhile, Gat Dawson, Ruby's husband, returns home after spending seven years at

the penitentiary. When he meets Mantan, he informs him that he was in show business before becoming a mobster, and the two take turns doing impersonations and recitations. When Gat and Ruby reunite, Gat demands to know if she has been faithful and declares that he will kill her if she wasn't. She swears that she has been true, but the two get in a fight nonetheless. When she then informs him that he has to get a job, he is shocked and hurt. He tells her he has a better plan: they will stage his death and raise money at a wake. The wake is announced and all the hotel's residents show up. While playing cards, One-Lung sees the supposedly dead Gat sit up and tells J. B., who decides to investigate. Gat thinks Ruby, Mantan and J. B. have tried to double-cross him, and he holds them up at gunpoint. The policeman arrives and pulls a gun on Gat and promises to send him back to the penitentiary. Mrs. Dawson says she will depend on Mantan from now on, and Mantan proudly tells the policeman that the hotel now belongs to him. *African Americans. Clerks. Funerals. Inns. Swindlers and swindling. Cards. Chinese Americans. Gangsters. Impersonations (Comic). Marriage. Parole. Police. Unemployment. Watches.*

Note: Although a print of this film was not viewed, the above credits and plot summary were taken from a dialogue continuity deposited with the NYSA. Lawrence Criner's character name is listed in the continuity's credit page as "Smokey and Toughie," but is called "Gat Dawson" in the script. Exact release date information was not found, but the script was submitted to the New York censors on 7 May 1947 and, according to MPAA/PCA records at the AMPAS Library, the film was approved for distribution in Ohio in 1947. Modern sources add Anna Lucasta to the cast.

WHAT A MAN (*foreign version*) see ASÍ ES LA VIDA

WHAT A MOTHER-IN-LAW! (Yiddish language)
   Quality Film Corp. Apr? **1934**; Prod: original film made in 1927 by Thomas Productions; added scenes shot ca. 1934. Sd; b&w. 7 reels, 5,812 ft. 65 min. Yiddish language with English subtitles.
   Supv Joseph Schiller. *Dir* Harry S. Brown. [*Dir of 1927 film* Harry Garson]. *Dial* Jacob Mestel. *Photog* Robert J. Marshall. *Ed* Joseph Schiller. *Mus arrangement* Allyn B. Carrick. *Sd eng* H. Reeves.
   Source: Based on the play *The Lunatic* by H. Kalmon (production undetermined).
   Cast: [1927 film] LUDWIG SATZ [(*Hymie Moses*)], [Claire Adams (*Frances*)], [George Tobias (*One of the suitors*)], [*Cast—1934 film:*] Max Wilner [(*Max*)], Paula Klida [(*Sadie*)].
   Yiddish, Domestic, Comedy, with songs. [*Print viewed*]. After supper one evening, Max, a harangued husband, sings along to a Yiddish song on the radio. His wife Sadie, who doesn't like "The Jewish Hour," puts on some dance music, which Max despises. After he pleads for just one Yiddish song, she relents, and they hug and sing along as they reminisce about how they used to sit together in the evening. Sadie then remembers that she is late for a bridge game and goes to dress. Max's uncle arrives in a dejected state because of a quarrel with his wife. Max asserts that he is the boss in his home, but then Sadie orders him to clear the table and do the dishes before she leaves. When his uncle points out that Max also is afraid of his wife, Max says that it is his mother-in-law, not his wife, whom he fears. In revolt, Max takes off his apron, gets out a bottle of wine, offers a drink to his uncle and tells him the story of Hymie Moses, the son of the tailor, and his mother-in-law. Max begins the story before Hymie marries into the Relkin family. On a Sunday morning, Samuel Relkin makes breakfast for his bossy wife Gertrude and his attractive daughter Frances, both of whom sleep late. After Frances awakens, two of her three boyfriends arrive with theater tickets for her. The third, Hymie, a shabbily dressed, naïve *schlemiel*, is laughed at by children as he walks through the New York streets to the Relkin home. Although her mother does not approve, Frances goes for the bashful Hymie and they marry. A year later, Frances has a baby. Frances and Hymie have their first real argument as Frances, egged on by her mother, complains that she always has to stay at home with the baby. The quarrel ends with Hymie staying with the baby, while Frances goes to a wedding, despite the fact that he is completely incompetent as a babysitter. Five years pass, and the couple now have two children. Because she thinks that Hymie does not earn enough, Gertrude urges Frances to divorce him. Although Frances at first resists, when Hymie and her mother get into an argument, Frances decides to seek a divorce. Samuel tells Hymie about a man who was nagged so much by his wife that he went insane. When Frances is about to leave with the children, Hymie suddenly starts making unusual movements and gestures and attempts to jump out the

window. Both Frances and her mother are horrified, and Frances says she now will stay. When Hymie is alone with Samuel, he explains that he is only pretending to be insane. He tells Samuel to convince the doctor, who has been called, to go along with the ruse, but the doctor arrives while Samuel is away and takes Hymie to an insane asylum. Hymie escapes from his cell, but he is confronted by a huge insane person, whom he pacifies by giving him sugar. When he runs out of sugar, Hymie acts like a boss to the man, and the man becomes afraid of Hymie. When Hymie is released, he reveals to Samuel his new theory: that women, like the insane, want to have a boss. Frances now tells Hymie that she wants only him, and Hymie says that his mother-in-law will no longer have anything to say in his house. At the story's conclusion, Max and his uncle, having drunk the bottle of wine, sing and dance, chanting that they are the bosses of the house. Sadie enters and when she complains about the dishes still on the table, Max acts like he is insane. Sadie, however, realizes that he is copying Hymie's trick and increases her nagging. Max asks his uncle for help, but his uncle, newly depressed, says that he has his own troubles. *Battle of the sexes. Bumblers. Henpecked husbands. Insane asylums. Jews. Marriage. Mothers-in-law. Ruses. Baby sitters. Drunkenness. Fathers-in-law. Infants. New York City. Radio broadcasting. Romantic rivalry. Uncles.*

Note: The plot summary was based on a dialogue continuity submitted to the New York censors on 5 Apr 1934, which is at the NYSA. The running time was calculated from footage shown in NYSA records. The Yiddish title of this film is *Oy di Shviger!* The film is a re-release of a 1927 American film entitled *The Lunatic* with new scenes added. Ludwig Satz also starred in the stage version. The new scenes include some songs, the titles of which have not been identified.
   Exhibitors Daily Review 2 Apr 1927.

WHAT'S BUZZIN' COUSIN? (African Americans)
   Columbia Pictures Corp. *Dist* Columbia Pictures Corp. 8 Jul **1943**; Prod: 16 Mar—16 Apr 1943 [©Columbia Pictures Corp.; 8 Jul 1943; LP12132]. Sd (Western Electric Mirrophonic Recording); b&w. 8 reels, 6,754 ft. 75 min.
   Prod Jack Fier. *Dir* Charles Barton. [*Asst dir* Louis Germonprez]. *Scr* Harry Sauber. *Based upon a story by* Aben Kandel. *Addl dial* John P. Medbury. *Dir of photog* Joseph Walker. *Art dir* Lionel Banks. *Assoc* Paul Murphy. *Film ed* James Sweeney. *Set dec* Joseph Kish. *Mus dir* M. W. Stoloff. *Dance dir* Nick Castle. [*Sd eng* Lambert Day].
   Music: First Movement of Piano Concerto No. 1 in B-flat minor by Peter Ilyich Tchaikovsky; Hungarian Rhapsody No. 2 by Franz Liszt.
   Song(s): "Mr. President" and "By Order of the Interceptor," words and music by Walter Samuels and Saul Chaplin; "Short, Fat and 4-F," "Where Am I Without You?" and "Ain't That Just Like a Man?" words and music by Don Raye and Gene de Paul; "Nevada," words and music by Walter Donaldson and Mort Greene; "In Grandpaw's Beard," "Three Little Mosquitoes" and "They're Countin' in the Mountains," words and music by Charles Newman and Lew Pollack; "1875," words and music by Wally Anderson; "Knocked Out Nocturne," words by Eddie Cherkose, music by Jacques Press.
   Cast: Ann Miller [(*Ann Crawford*)], Rochester [(*Rochester*)], John Hubbard [(*Jimmy Ross*)], Freddy Martin and His Orchestra [(*Freddy Martin*)], [Leslie Brooks (*Josie*)], [Jeff Donnell (*Billie*)], [Carol Hughes (*May*)], [Theresa Harris (*Blossom*)], [Roy Gordon (*Jim Langford*)], [Bradley Page (*Pete Hartley*)], [Warren Ashe (*Dick Bennett*)], [Dub Taylor (*Jed*)], [Betsy Gay (*Saree*)], [Louis Mason (*Hillbilly*)], [Eugene Jackson (*Bellboy*)], [Jessie Arnold (*Mrs. Hillbilly*)], [Erville Alderson (*Gas station attendant*)], [Harry Tyler (*Harry, hotel clerk*)], [Walter Soderling (*Mr. Hayes*)], [Eddie Featherstone (*Radio delivery man*)], [John Tyrrell, Craig Woods (*Henchmen*)].
   Show business, Musical. [*Viewed print incomplete*]. Jimmy Ross, a successful lawyer and childhood friend of band leader Freddy Martin, abandons his law practice for the summer and joins the Martin band as a singer. Rochester, another member of the company, and his girl friend Blossom join Freddy, Jimmy and the band in driving across the country to a booking in New York. One day, they stop at Waverhill, a ghost town, for gas. Finding none, they decide to spend the night in the run-down, deserted Palace Hotel. The next morning, Ann Crawford, a young dancer, and her three friends, Josie, Billie and May, arrive in town and are horrified to see the condition of the property in which they all have invested. Ann explains to Rochester that, when the property was willed to her by her grandfather, there was a tax lien on it, so she and her friends pooled their resources and

paid it off. When Ann and Jimmy meet, he gets an idea about what to do with the hotel and becomes their partner. Jimmy convinces Freddy that he can renovate the hotel, put in a floor show and advertise in neighboring cities. Although Jimmy offers to put up the money, he asks Freddy and the band to commit to play the opening engagement. Freddy agrees and, in a very short time, the hotel reopens with Freddy and Ann performing. The show is poorly attended however, and while Jimmy and Ann intend to persevere, her friends want to leave. Ann admits to them that she has fallen in love with Jimmy. On a drive in the countryside, Rochester, Blossom, Jimmy and Ann get lost and come across a hillbilly family, who perform for them and later join the hotel's show. One day, Rochester is planting a Victory garden when he finds a gold nugget in the earth, and a ''gold rush'' is started in Waverhill. Hundreds of people buy up land and the town booms. Jim Langford, the real estate speculator who handled Ann's purchase, sends Pete Hartley, a confidence man, to Waverhill to buy back the property. When Hartley makes the women an offer, Ann wants to discuss it with Jimmy, as he financed the refurbishing, but the women vote to sell immediately. Later, Hartley tells Jimmy that he has bought everything and that Jimmy is now working for him. After Jimmy accuses Ann of double-crossing him, he visits an assayer for an evaluation of Rochester's nugget and is told that it is very fine gold and can be found in any dentist's office as it is a tooth inlay. Jimmy finds Rochester shooting dice with the bellboys and tells him the news, and Rochester realizes that it was one of his own fillings that started the gold rush. Meanwhile, Ann drives away, leaving Jimmy the capital he had invested in the hotel, plus interest, and a note stating that she had always intended to repay him. Langford then decides to develop Waverhill legitimately. Later, in New York, Ann and her friends reunite and they tell her that Jimmy has been looking for her. The girls then tune in a live Freddy Martin broadcast on a radio they have just acquired. After Jimmy dedicates a love song to her, Ann goes to the radio station and she and Jimmy embrace. *Dancers. Ghost towns. Gold rushes. Hotels. Nightclubs. African Americans. Band leaders. Bellboys. Dice. Dwellings-Remodeling. Hillbillies. Land developers. Lawyers. Orchestras. Radio broadcasting. Real estate agents. Romance. Singers. Speculation. Teeth. Victory gardens.*

Note: The viewed print, which ran approximately 66 minutes, may have been missing one or more musical numbers. According to an Aug 1942 pre-production news item in *HR*, Al Green was initially slated to direct this film. A Nov 1942 *HR* news item announced that Robert Haymes, a vocalist with the Freddy Martin orchestra, was to play a leading man in this film. Although Martin's orchestra appears in the picture, Haymes is not credited anywhere. The Tchaikovsky piano concerto that Martin performed in the film became a big hit for the band leader, and subsequently, lyrics were written by Bobby Worth for the piece, which was then retitled "Tonight We Love." A *HR* production chart places Adele Mara in the cast, but her participation in the released film has not been confirmed.

Box 17 Jul 1943. *DV* 12 Aug 1943, p. 3. *FD* 30 Jul 1943, p. 6. *HR* 31 Aug 1942, p. 1. *HR* 5 Nov 1942. *HR* 19 Mar 1943, p. 10. *HR* 12 Aug 1943, p. 3. *MPH* 31 Jul 1943. *MPHPD* 5 Jun 1943, p. 1351. *MPHPD* 31 Jul 1943, p. 1454. *NYT* 23 Jul 1943, p. 21. *Var* 28 Jul 1943, p. 8.

WHEEL OF CHANCE (Russian Americans)
First National Pictures, Inc. *Dist* First National Pictures, inc. 17 Jun **1928** [©First National Pictures, Inc.; 4 Jun 1928; LP25341]. Si; b&w. 7 reels, 6,813-6,895 ft.

Pres Richard A. Rowland. *Dir* Alfred Santell. *Adpt and cont* Gerald C. Duffy. *Titles* Garrett Graham. *Photog* Ernest Haller. *Film ed* Cyril Gardner.

Source: Based on the short story ''Roulette'' by Fannie Hurst in *The Vertical City* (New York & London, 1922).

Cast: Richard Barthelmess (*Nickolai Turkeltaub/Jacob Talinef [born Schmulka Turkeltaub]*), Bodil Rosing (*Sara Turkeltaub*), Warner Oland (*Mosher Turkeltaub*), Ann Schaeffer (*Hanscha Talinef*), Lina Basquette (*Ada Berkowitz*), Margaret Livingston (*Josie Drew*), Sidney Franklin (*Pa Berkowitz*), Martha Franklin (*Ma Berkowitz*).

Melodrama. The Turkeltaub family leaves Russia for the United States during the czarist regime, saddened by the apparent death of little Schmulka, fraternal twin of their other son, Nickolai. In America, the Turkeltaubs prosper; Nickolai becomes a prominent district attorney, and he is engaged to marry Ada Berkowitz. Schmulka, now known as Jacob Talinef, is revealed to have survived his childhood, having been nursed back to health by Hanscha Talinef, a midwife who brought him as a youth to New York. A young gangster and a drunkard, Jacob accidentally kills Josie Drew, a promiscuous

girl who once had a relationship with Nickolai. Nickolai, as prosecuting attorney, is influenced by his mother, who is drawn to the redheaded boy, to ask for leniency. After serving a short jail sentence, Jacob is finally reunited with his family. *Alcoholism. Brothers. Criminals–Rehabilitation. District attorneys. Immigrants. Midwives. Russian Americans. Russians. Twins.*

Note: The working title of this film may have been *Roulette*.
FD 8 Jul 1928. *NYT* 2 Jul 1928, p. 11. *Var* 4 Jul 1928, p. 16.

WHEELS OF DESTINY (Native Americans)
Universal Pictures Corp. *Dist* Universal Pictures Corp. 19 Feb **1934** [©Universal Pictures Corp.; 30 Jan 1934; LP4447]. Sd; b&w. 7 reels. 63-64 min.

Dir Alan James. *Story, scr and dial* Nate Gatzert. *Photog* Ted McCord. *Film ed* Charles Harris. *Rec eng* Earl Crain.

Song(s): ''Wheels of Destiny,'' words and music by Ken Maynard.

Cast: Ken Maynard (*Ken Manning*), Dorothy Dix (*Mary*), Philo McCullough (*Rocky*), Frank Rice (*Pinwheel*), Jay Wilsey (*Bill*), Ed Coxen (*Dad*), Fred Sale, Jr. (*''Scalp-em-alive''*), Fred McKaye (*Red*), Jack Rockwell (*Ed*), William Gould (*Deacon*), Nelson McDowell (*Trapper*), ''Tarzan,'' a horse.

Western. [*Not viewed*]. Bill, who has struck it rich mining gold in California, returns to his home town in the Midwest to organize a wagon train. On the eve of the wagon train's departure, a prayer meeting is held in town for the participants. Rocky, an outlaw, sends part of his gang to the meeting, while he and the rest of his men go to Bill's hotel room to search for gold mining maps. While Rocky batters down Bill's door, Ken Manning, Bill's mining partner, shows up and single-handedly halts the robbery. Taken with Bill's sister Mary, Ken later agrees to be an unofficial guide on the wagon train. Soon after the caravan takes off, Rocky instigates trouble by betting an old trapper that his horse can outrun the trapper's trained steer. When the steer wins, Rocky and his gang start a brawl and are thrown out of the wagon train. Later, to secure permission to cross an Indian reservation, Ken gives his word to an Indian chief that no one in the group will molest the reservation buffalo. Determined to cause trouble, however, Rocky and his men shoot at the herd and cause a stampede. Furious at the white men's betrayal, the Indians tie up Ken and begin planning a massacre. Ken's horse Tarzan, however, unties the rope, and Ken flees to warn the wagon train. Ken reaches the train's camp ahead of the Indians, and the group is able to minimize its losses. During the attack, Rocky and his men try to steal Bill's maps, but all except Rocky are killed by the Indians. To further protect themselves, the travelers set fire to the prairie and keep ahead of the pursuing Indians. That night, they ride into a thunderstorm and are forced to cross a raging stream in the dark. Just as the group appears out of danger, Rocky makes a sudden, last attempt at stealing the maps but is killed by Indians. As they near California, Mary gives Ken her heart. *Gold miners. Indians of North America. Outlaws. Thieves. Wagon trains. The West. Brothers and sisters. Buffalo (NY). Duplicity. Escapes. Fights. Fires. Horses. Hotels. Indians of North America-Reservations. Maps. Massacres. Pledges. Prairies. Prayer. Rivers. Romance. Stampedes. Storms. Trappers. United States-Midwest. Wagers.*

Note. Modern sources add Merrill McCormick, Slim Whitaker, Hank Bell, Bob Burns, Artie Ortego, Wally Wales, Helen Gibson, Jack Evans, Bud McClure, Fred Burns, Chief Big Tree, Marin Sais, Chuck Baldra, Blackjack Ward, Bobby Dunn, Arkansas Johnny and Roy Bucko to the cast. In addition, modern sources state that exteriors for the film were shot in Lone Pine, CA.

FD 28 Mar 1934, p. 9. *HR* 6 Jan 1934, p. 3. *MPD* 9 Apr 1934, p. 3. *MPH* 14 Apr 1934, p. 39, 42. *Var* 3 Apr 1934, p. 27.

WHEN A MAN'S A MAN *see* **MASSACRE RIVER**

WHEN BROADWAY WAS A TRAIL (Dutch Americans)
Shubert Film Corp.; A Shubert Feature. *Dist* World Film Corp. 26 Oct **1914** [©World Film Corp.; 27 Oct 1914; LU3722]. Si; b&w. 5 reels.

Dir O. A. C. Lund. *Scen* O. A. C. Lund.

Cast: Barbara Tennant (*Priscilla Elliott*), O. A. C. Lund (*Henry Minuet*), Edward Roseman (*Peter Minuet*), Julia Stuart (*Mistress Minuet*), Lindsay J. Hall (*Salvation Hibbins*), Mary Navarro (*Mistress Hibbins*), Alec B. Francis (*Standish Hope*), George Cowl (*Iroquois Chief*).

Historical, Drama. In 1626, Henry Minuet, the son of the governor of New Amsterdam [New York], goes to the colony of

Danvers [Salem, Mass.] to buy grain, and falls in love with Priscilla Elliott, even though they do not speak the same language. Salvation Hibbins wants to marry Priscilla and when her father dies, Salvation's mother tries to force the marriage. When Priscilla refuses, Mistress Hibbins accuses her of being a witch. Henry defends her, but both are ostracized from the colony. Eventually they reach New Amsterdam where Henry's family has difficulty accepting Priscilla. Finally, they decide to return to the forest, shunning both of their peoples. *Colonies. Cultural conflict. Dutch. New York City–History. Ostracism. Puritanism. Salem (MA). United States–History–Colonial period, ca. 1600–1775. Forests. Mothers and daughters. New York City. Witchcraft.*

MPN 31 Oct 1914, p. 49. *Motog* 31 Oct 1914, p. 612. *MPW* 31 Oct 1914, p. 656. *MPW* 7 Nov 1914, p. 840. *NYDM* 28 Oct 1914, p. 30. *Var* 24 Oct 1914, p. 22.

WHEN CAROL TOOK THE SUBWAY *see* **THE ADVENTURES OF CAROL**

WHEN EAST COMES WEST (Chinese Americans)
Phil Goldstone Productions. **1922**; New York State license: ca6 Apr 1922. Si; b&w. 5 reels, 4,450 ft.
Dir B. Reeves Eason. *Scen* Anthony Coldeway.
Cast: Franklyn Farnum, Andrew Waldron.
Western. "Jones arrives in a notorious Western town and volunteers to be sheriff. On meeting Mary Brennan, a ranchowner, he arranges for a Chinese friend of his to be her cook. Jones discovers that Mary's foreman is the leader of the gunrunners in town. After leading them to believe he is on their side, Jones captures the gang, aided by the Chinaman and later reveals to Mary that he and the Chinaman are United States marshals in disguise." (*National Film Archive Catalogue, Part III, Silent Fiction Films, 1895–1930*; The British Film Institute, London, 1966, p. 249.). *Chinese Americans. Cooks. Gunrunners. Ranch foremen. Ranchers. Sheriffs.*

WHEN LIGHTS ARE LOW *see* **WHERE LIGHTS ARE LOW**

WHEN MEN BETRAY (African Americans)
Micheaux Film Corp. **1929**; Harlem opening: 28 Sep 1929. Si; b&w. Length undetermined.
Pres A. Burton Russell. *Prod* Oscar Micheaux. *Dir* Oscar Micheaux.
Cast: Katherine Noisette, William Clayton, Jr., Alonzo Tucker.
African American, Melodrama. [*Not viewed*]. The following plot synopsis appeared in *NYA* 28 Sep 1929: "Briefly, it is the story of a beautiful girl, who was cold to the love of a good and ambitious young lad. Believing the rosy promises of a smooth-tongued stranger, she runs away and follows him to the city. The unhappiness and disaster which followed can easily be imagined. Deserted on her wedding night—alone, penniless, in a foreign city, left to the none too tender mercy of strangers. Her sad plight and the events which follow her desertion make a gripping, brutally frank, yet wonderfully, absorbing picture." *African Americans. Deception. Desertion (Marital). Lure of the city. Strangers. Weddings. Chicago (IL). New York City.*
Note: *New York Age* called this film a "melodrama of night life in Chicago and New York with an all colored cast."
New York Age 28 Sep 1929, p. 6.

WHEN THE CLOCK STRUCK NINE (Irish Americans, Italian Americans)
1921 [©Lilian Howarth; 20 Apr 1921; LU16408]. Si; b&w. Length undetermined. [Feature length assumed.].
Wrt Lillian Howarth.
Melodrama. Lower New York City's Kelly's Corners is the home of Jim Grady, who loves Maggie Murphy, the beauty and belle of the Corners, and good-natured Tony Morrillo, with whom Maggie indulges in a light flirtation. Over her mother's objections, Maggie accepts a bracelet from Tony on the night of the big Kelly Club dance, but she discards it for a necklace from Jim. *The events of the evening turn topsy-turvy the lives of all three: the necklace turns out to be stolen, Detective Jarvis catches Tony with the necklace in his possession, and Maggie's unwillingness to incriminate Jim results in a three-year prison term for Tony. By the time Tony is released, Maggie has married Jim and left him for wealthy gambler Dick Martin, and Jim has become a barroom lounger. Seeing an opportunity for revenge, Tony maneuvers Jim into burglarizing Martin's house, where he is shot by Martin. Maggie falls to Jim's side and... awakens from a bad dream.* Arriving to escort Maggie to the dance, Jim assures her that the bracelet presents no problem and slips a ring on her finger. *Courtship. Detectives. Dreams. Gamblers. Irish Americans. Italian Americans. New York City. Perjury. Revenge. Robbery.*

Note: The production and distribution companies for this film have not been determined.

WHEN THE DESERT SMILES (German Americans)
Circle H. Film Co. *Dist* State Rights; Arrow Film Corp.; Aywon Film Corp. Apr **1919?**. Si; b&w. 5 reels.
Cast: Neal Hart.
Western. After a cowboy, who loves the mistreated ward of a German rancher, buys property from an old settler which the German wants because it is rich in gold, the cowboy discovers that the German and his nephew have been working a mine on the land. The cowboy fights to save his mine and to prevent his cattle from being run off. He proves that the German's land really belongs to the ward, and then wins her love. *Cowboys. Gold mines. Land rights. Wards and guardians. Battered women. Cattle. German Americans. Nephews. Ranchers. Settlers.*
Note: Some sources list the title of this film as *When the Desert Smiled*. The film first appeared as a state rights release by Arrow Film Corp. in Apr 1919. It was later reviewed and listed as an Aywon Film Corp. release in Oct 1919.
MPW 8 Nov 1919, p. 245. *Var* 31 Oct 1919, p. 61.

WHEN THE REDSKINS RODE (Native Americans, Delaware, Huron, Miami, Ottawa)
Kay Pictures, Inc.; Columbia Pictures Corp. *Dist* Columbia Pictures Corp. May **1951**; Prod: 8 Aug–18 Aug 1950 [©Columbia Pictures Corp.; 31 May 1951; LP1029]. Sd (RCA Sound Recording); col (Supercinecolor). 7,018 ft. 78 min. PCA cert no. 14853.
Prod Sam Katzman. *Dir* Lew Landers. [*Asst dir* Wilbur McGaugh]. *Wrt for the scr by* Robert E. Kent. *Dir of photog* Lester White. *Art dir* Paul Palmentola. *Film ed* Richard Fantl. *Set dec* Sidney Clifford. *Mus dir* Mischa Bakaleinikoff. [*Sd eng* Josh Westmoreland]. *Unit mgr* Herbert Leonard.
Cast: Jon Hall [(*Prince Hannoc*)], Mary Castle [(*Elizabeth Leeds*)], James Seay [(*George Washington*)], John Ridgely [(*Christopher Gist*)], Sherry Moreland [(*Morna*)], Pedro de Cordoba [(*Chief Shingiss*)], John Dehner [(*John Delmont*)], Lewis L. Russell [(*Governor Robert Dinwiddie*)], William Bakewell [(*Appleby*)], [Gregory Gay (*St. Pierre*)], [Rusty Wescoatt (*Zuneau*)], [Milt Kibbee (*Davey*)], [Rick Vallin (*Duprez*)].
Historical, Drama. [*Print viewed*]. By 1753, after years of fighting European colonists, Indian tribes, through treaties with the English and French, have begun to live peacefully with the whites. In July, at an outdoor gathering in Williamsburg, Prince Hannoc, son of Shingiss, chief of the Delaware Nation, wins a wrestling match against a white. Elizabeth Leeds, who lives above the White Swan Inn, wins a wager betting on the prince and requests him to visit her in her room that evening. As Hannoc, who has learned to speak English just that year, waits for her, the man who lost the bet, a bigot named Appleby, calls him a "Redskin" and insults him concerning his interest in Elizabeth. Hannoc goes for Appleby's throat, and when they are separated, Appleby challenges him to a duel. As his weapon, the prince chooses a cleaver, which he throws at a portrait on the wall, splitting the face, thus scaring Appleby off. In Elizabeth's room, Hannoc is reticent to respond to her advances and says it is because he is an Indian. She then lets him know she is half-Indian, giving him an Indian friendship belt, which she says was given to her by her mother, a Shawnee. She kisses him, but he says she is more white than Indian and doubts that she could share the life of an Indian man. As she goes behind a partition to undress, he leaves. John Delmont, the largest importer in the colonies, who in reality is a French spy named Devereaux, then visits Elizabeth, his lover. After the Miamis, in league with the French, burn a settler's home and kill the inhabitants, Colonel George Washington, leading the Virginia militia, and his scout, Christopher Gist, realize that the French intend to construct forts along the Ohio River on British land to connect settlements in the south with Canada. Washington believes that the colonists' only hope is to get the powerful, but neutral, Delaware Nation on the British side and then other tribes would follow. He warns Prince Hannoc that if the French succeed, they will also take Delaware land. That night, outside the inn, three men led by Appleby attack the prince, and according to plan, Elizabeth stops the fight and takes Hannoc inside to clean his wounds. As Delmont eavesdrops, Hannoc reveals that Washington will march with forty men tomorrow to meet Shingiss. During the journey, they repel an attack by French soldiers disguised as Indians. At the Delaware village, Chief Shingiss learns that his son does not want to marry his childhood love Morna, but that

he desires a half-white woman. Angry that the white man has taken his son, Shingiss now refuses to enter into a treaty with England, saying the Delaware people will stand alone. Washington goes to Fort Le Boeuf to deliver a protest to French commander St. Pierre. He plans to hold Washington as a "guest" while his soldiers and men from the Wyandot tribe attack the Delaware village, as he does not know that Shingiss refused the treaty offer, but believes they are only waiting for the British king's signature before it takes effect. When Washington does not return, Hannoc and Gist invade the fort and capture needed rifles before leaving with Washington and blowing up the powderhouse. After the French enter the Delaware village to claim the land, Washington's men fight beside the Delaware, and the French and the Wyandots are defeated. Shingiss, now convinced that his people cannot stand alone, agrees to meet with Virginia Governor Robert Dinwiddie, but insists that Morna travel with them. Showing Williamsburg to the chief, Washington calls it a "village of peace," explaining that he desires freedom and independence for every man, and that they plan to build a country, not threatening forts. Impressed, Shingiss predicts that Washington will be a great leader. Two months later, as they are still waiting for the king's signature on the treaty, Dinwiddie receives word that the Ottawa from Canada are joining the French and Wyandot forces. Outnumbered 1,000 to 150 in the defense of the newly constructed Fort Necessity at Great Meadows, Washington asks Shingiss if his men will fight with them before the treaty arrives, but Shingiss refuses. Fearing that the Delaware will join the fight, Delmont sends assassins to kill Shingiss. They attack at night, and after Hannoc and Morna find the dying chief, Hannoc kills one assassin with a tomahawk and learns from another that they were following Delmont's orders. Morna trails a third assailant to the inn, leaving teeth from her necklace in a trail for Hannoc to follow. At the inn, Appleby, drunk, grabs Morna, but Hannoc knocks him out. Hannoc climbs up the building and, outside Elizabeth's window, sees Delmont kiss her and tell her he plans to bring St. Pierre news of Shingiss' death. Hannoc and Morna burst in and subdue the two. Meanwhile, the French and Indian tribes supporting them have surrounded Fort Necessity and begun pummeling it with cannon fire. Inside, Washington bitterly expresses the hope that this will teach England that America cannot be held with delays and the lack of arms and training of his militia. Hannoc, leading the Delaware, charges the French, who, with their Indian allies, retreat. After the battle, Hannoc promises Morna that he will return to his people when the war ends, and she says she will be there. As they kiss, Gist notes to Washington that at least the Indians have learned something from the white man. *Delaware Indians. French. Princes. Spies. United States–History–French and Indian War, 1755-1763. Virginia. George Washington. Washington's Expedition to the Ohio, 1st, 1753-1754. Washington's Expedition to the Ohio, 2d, 1754. Assassination. Bigotry. Childhood sweethearts. Robert Dinwiddie. Fort Le Boeuf (PA). Christopher Gist. Huron Indians. Impersonation and imposture. Importers. Inns. Miami Indians. Ottawa Indians. Raids. Rescues. Seduction. Treaties. Williamsburg (VA). Wrestlers and wrestling.*

Note: *Var* commented that the new three-color Supercinecolor process used in this film "is a vast improvement over the old Cinecolor, which employed only two hues. Tints in interior scenes are accurately reproduced for the most part. But some outdoor shots, notably of evergreens against the sky, have a washed-out purple effect."

Box 12 May 1951. *DV* 9 May 1951, p. 3. *Exh* 23 May 1951, p. 3077. *FD* 14 May 1951, p. 7. *Har* 12 May 1951, p. 75. *HR* 9 May 1951, p. 3. *MPD* 15 May 1951. *MPHPD* 12 May 1951, p. 846. *Var* 9 May 1951, p. 6.

WHERE COWBOY IS KING (Native Americans)
American Lifeograph Co. *Dist* State Rights; Globe Feature Picture Booking Co.; United Booking Office Feature Co. May **1915** [©American Lifeograph Co., Inc.; 16 Apr 1915; LU5042]. Si; b&w. 4 reels.
Documentary. The 1914 annual round-up at Pendleton, Oregon opens with cowgirls riding bucking horses in competition, followed by a cowboys' bucking contest. Steer roping, bulldogging, and wild bull riding are shown. Races run include cowboy and cowgirl relay races; a stagecoach race, in which one coach, pulled by mustangs, overturns, spewing out its occupants before righting itself; Indian pony and relay races; squaw races; maverick races; and cowboy and cowgirl standing races, in which contestants stand with each foot on a separate horse. Fancy roping and trick riding are also exhibited. *Cowboys. Cowgirls. Horseracing. Pendleton (OR). Riding. Rodeos. Horses. Indians of North America. Stagecoaches.*

Note: The complete title of this film as listed in the copyright descriptions is *Where Cowboy is King; or, 1914 Pendleton Oregon Round-Up*. The American Lifeograph Co. was located in Portland, OR. The round-up was an annual event. According to one review, in the riding contests pictured in this film, about twenty horses were killed. The film played at the New York Hippodrome for two weeks. While *MPN* lists the film's length as being two reels, and *MPW* states that it is a half-hour show, three other contemporary sources state that the film's length is four reels.
Motog 12 Jun 1915, p. 992. *MPN* 29 May 1915, p. 74. *MPN* 12 Jun 1915, p. 48. *MPW* 29 May 1915, p. 1442. *Var* 28 May 1915, p. 17.

WHERE DID YOU GET THAT GIRL? (Scottish Americans)
Universal Pictures Co., Inc. *Dist* Universal Pictures Co., Inc. 3 Jan **1941**; Prod: 30 Oct—mid-Nov 1940 [©Universal Pictures Co., Inc.; 26 Dec 1941; LP10134]. Sd (Western Electric Mirrophonic Recording); b&w. 7 reels, 5,833 ft. 65 min. PCA cert no. 5030.
Assoc prod Joseph G. Sanford. *Dir* Arthur Lubin. [*Asst dir* Phil Karlstein]. [*Dial dir* Joan Hathaway]. *Scr* Jay Dratler, Paul Franklin and Stanley Crea Rubin. *Orig story* Jay Dratler. *Dir of photog* John Boyle. *Art dir* Jack Otterson. *Assoc* Ralph M. DeLacy. *Film ed* Philip Cahn. *Set dec* R. A. Gausman. *Cost* Vera West. *Mus dir* H. J. Salter. *Sd supv* Bernard B. Brown. *Sd tech* Charles Carroll. [*Unit pub wrt* Louis Blaine].
Song(s): "Where Did You Get That Girl?" words by Bert Kalmar, music by Harry Puck; "Sergeant Swing" and "Rug Cuttin' Romeo," words by Everett Carter, music by Milton Rosen; "Colorín, colorado," composer undetermined.
Cast: Leon Errol ([*Alex*] *MacDevin*), Helen Parrish (*Helen* [*Borden*]), Charles Lang (*Jeff* [*Brant*]), Eddie Quillan (*Joe* [*Olsen*]), Franklin Pangborn (*Digby*), Stanley Fields (*Crandall*), Tom Dugan (*Murphy*), Joe Brown, Jr. (*Davey*), Leonard Sues (*Franky*), Kenneth Lundy (*Shrimp*), Joe Cobb (*Tubby*), Billy Jack Elliott (*Jack*), Peter Sullivan (*Pete*), Thurston Hall (*Stuyvesant*), Wade Boteler (*Connolly*), Frank Mitchell (*Crook*), Nina Orla (*Singer*), Tim Ryan (*Inspector*), Leon Belasco (*Hayden*), [George Lloyd (*Crook*)], Tom Hanlon, [Gary Breckner (*Announcers*)], [Hope Landin (*Mrs. Olsen*)], [Kay Leslie (*Secretary*)], [Elliott Sullivan, Frank Marlowe (*Cab drivers*)], [Ed Stanley (*Harper*)], [Eddie Bruce (*Seymour Murdock*)], [Philip Van Zandt (*Baxter*)], [Charlotte Treadway (*Fat woman*)], [Harold Daniels (*Wise guy*)], [Connie Leon (*Housewife*)], [Bob McKenzie (*Tubby's father*)], [Lorin Raker (*Anderson*)], Henry Martin, [David Tihmar (*Ballet dancers*)].
Musical. [*Print viewed*]. In the audience of a radio broadcast, singer Helen Borden's dress catches on a button of classical composer Jeff Brant's suit, causing a major disturbance and resulting in their ejection from the studio. Later, Helen and Jeff discover that they live in the same boardinghouse run by Mrs. Olsen, whose son Joe is attempting to start a swing band. Unknown to Jeff, Joe has been arranging Jeff's classical compositions for the band. Joe invites Helen to join the band and she, in turn, convinces Jeff to join them. The band is so poor, however, that the musicians must practice on the instruments in Scottish pawnbroker Alex MacDevin's store. Alex agrees to loan the band the instruments long enough to record a demonstration record. A band member's father is night watchman at the Four Star Record Co., and his son "borrows" his duplicate key so that they can make a record. As they finish, however, two crooks break into the studio, blow open a safe and steal bonds, forcing the band to flee without the valuable recording. MacDevin suggests that the band find a radio sponsor, but ends up agreeing to sponsor the broadcasts himself. Jeff and Joe arrange with radio station executive Digby for a slot at 5:00 a.m. Meanwhile, Stuyvesant, Four Star's president, finds out that, due to a mistake, 6,000 copies of the record have been made. As he believes that the robbers may have made the recording, he orders it to be distributed, calling the group "The Mystery Swingsters with Mademoiselle X." The band's live broadcasts generate a lot of interest but they have misunderstood the terms of the contract and MacDevin owes the station much more money than anticipated. Meanwhile, the record becomes a number one best-seller. Another band claiming to be "The Swingsters" is signed to a long-term radio contract, but they are suspected of being the safecrackers and are arrested, just before their initial broadcast, by bungling police detectives Crandall and Murphy. Jeff, Helen, Joe and the band substitute for the arrested musicians but are heard by Stuyvesant and are arrested as well. While the band is being questioned at the police station, the two burglars are brought in, having been arrested for parking next to a fire hydrant and discovered to be in possession of

the stolen Four Star bonds. Jeff, Helen, Joe and the band then sign contracts with both the record company and the radio station, with Alex acting as their very astute manager. *Bands (Music). Pawnbrokers. Recording industry. Singers. Songwriters. Swing music. Band leaders. Boardinghouses. Burglars. Impersonation and imposture. Musical instruments. Police detectives. Radio programs. Radio sponsors. Romance. Scottish Americans. Talent agents.*

DV 18 Dec 1940, p. 3. *FD* 8 Jan 1941, p. 6. *HR* 28 Oct 1940, p. 4. *HR* 1 Nov 1940, p. 9. *HR* 4 Nov 1940, p. 4, 6. *HR* 18 Dec 1940, p. 3. *MPH* 21 Dec 1940, p. 45. *MPHPD* 22 Feb 1941, p. 65. *Var 26 Mar 1941, p. 18.*

WHERE DO WE GO FROM HERE? (Dutch Americans, Native Americans)

Twentieth Century-Fox Film Corp. *Dist* Twentieth Century-Fox Film Corp. Jun **1945**; New York opening: 6 Jun 1945; *Prod*: 28 Aug—mid-Nov 1944; retakes and addl scenes began 21 Dec 1944 [©Twentieth Century-Fox Film Corp.; 29 May 1945; LP13389]. Sd (Western Electric Recording); col (Technicolor). 8 reels, 6,978 ft. 77-78 min. PCA cert no. 10525.

Prod William Perlberg. *Dir* Gregory Ratoff. [*Dir of retakes and addl scenes* George Seaton]. [*Asst dir* Ad Schaumer]. [*Dial dir* Serge Bertensson]. *Scr* Morrie Ryskind. *Story* Morrie Ryskind and Sig Herzig. *Dir of photog* Leon Shamroy. [*2d cam* Bud Mautino]. *Spec photog eff* Fred Sersen. [*Miniatures* Ralph O. Hammeras]. *Technicolor dir* Natalie Kalmus. *Assoc* Richard Mueller. *Art dir* Lyle Wheeler and Leland Fuller. *Film ed* J. Watson Webb. *Set dec* Thomas Little. *Assoc* Walter M. Scott. *Cost* Bonnie Cashin. *Mus dir* Emil Newman and Charles Henderson. *Incidental mus* David Raksin. *Orch arr* Maurice DePackh. *Dances staged by* Fanchon. [*Dance dir* Seymour Felix]. *Sd* Arthur von Kirbach and Harry M. Leonard. [*Re-rec and eff mixer* Roger Heman]. [*Mus mixer* Murray Spivak and Vinton Vernon]. *Makeup artist* Ben Nye. [*Research dir* Frances C. Richardson]. [*Research asst* Ruth Fox].

Music: "Yankee Doodle," traditional; "1776 Boogie" by David Raksin.

Song(s): "All at Once," "Morale," "If Love Remains," "Song of the Rhineland" and "Columbus," music by Kurt Weill, lyrics by Ira Gershwin.

Cast: FRED MacMURRAY [(*Bill Morgan*)], JOAN LESLIE [(*Sally/ Prudence Smith/Katrina*)], JUNE HAVER [(*Lucilla Powell/ Gretchen/Indian woman*)], Gene Sheldon [(*Ali*)], Anthony Quinn [(*Chief Badger*)], Carlos Ramirez [(*Benito*)], Alan Mowbray [(*General George Washington*)], Fortunio Bonanova [(*Christopher Columbus*)], Herman Bing [(*Hessian colonel*)], Howard Freeman [(*Kreiger*)], [Otto Preminger (*General Rahl*)], [John Davidson (*Benedict Arnold*)], [Rosina Galli (*Old lady*)], [Fred Essler, Bert Roach, Paul Weigel, Ferdinand Munier, Harry Holman, Harrison Greene (*Dutch councilmen*)], [Joseph Haworth, Scott Elliott, Robert Castaine, William Carter (*Servicemen*)], [Arno Frey (*German lieutenant*)], [Max Wagner (*Sergeant*)], [Larry Thompson (*Soldier*)], [Bob Stephenson, Will Kaufman, Walter Bonn (*Dutchmen*)], [Hans von Morhart (*Blacksmith*)], [Joe Bernard (*Burgher*)], [Hope Landin (*Elderly wife*)], [Dick Elliott (*Father*)], [Norman Field (*Minister*)], [Edward Clark (*Organist*)], [Cyril Ring (*Army doctor*)], [Sam Bernard (*Jailer*)], [Ralph Dunn, Ralph Sanford (*Policemen*)], [Edward Hyans (*Brooklyn soldier*)], [Helen Servis, Eileen Scott (*Brooklyn girls*)], [Robert Hamilton], [Buddy Moore], [Ed Stanbridge], [Richard Reed], [Hal Taggart], [Ronald Stanton], [Jack Ross], [Louis Mosconi], [John Roche], [Warren Lane], [Allan Ross], [Jack Lomas], [Dinsmore Delano], [Bill Voorhees], [William Lundy], [Joseph De Angelo], [Randolph Hughes], [Nikki Manners], [Price Samuel], [Edgar Caldwell], [Eugene Hovey], [Jean Gary], [Muriel Kearney], [Al Gallagher], [Jerry Warren], [Barbara Blain], [Betty Slabe], [Betty Leonard], [Peggy Gordon], [June Earle], [Timmy Sabor], [Lorraine Reimer], [Betty Jean Orth], [Robert Cassidy], [Lucia Rand], [JoAnn Dale], [Eleanor Peterson], [Vincent Vaux], [Joan Carey], [Blanche Taylor], [Kay Adell], [Dolly Yankee], [Joy Barlowe], [Marian Kerrigan], [Sharon Hurley], [Dona La Barr], [Bunny Carlton], [Lynne Sterling], [Margaret Westberg], [Dolly Perrin], [Perk Lazelle], [George Mann], [Billy Coull], [Neal Sinclair], [William Vaux], [Sam Ash], [James Desin], [Phil Bloom], [Johnny Reese], [Willie Bloom], [Gino Corrado], [Robert St. Angelo], [Merle L. Weaver], [Joseph Glick], [Ted Doner], [James Clemons], [William Nye], [Mishka Egan], [Bill Borzage], [Jack Perry], [Stuart Norton], [Tom Ladd], [Joe Evans], [Hansel Warner], [Adrian Altomare], [James Ford], [Grant Davis], [Russell Ash].

Historical, Homefront, Satire, Fantasy, Musical comedy. [*Print viewed*]. Bill Morgan despairs when he tries to enlist in the Navy and is rejected as a 4-F, as he was by the Army. He goes to the New York U.S.O. canteen where Lucilla Powell, with whom he is in love, works, but Lucilla only has eyes for men in uniform. Lucilla tricks Bill into washing dishes, and he is aided by Sally, a sensible young woman who cannot compete with Lucilla's glamour. Bill is unaware of Sally's feelings for him, just as he is unaware of Lucilla's true, shallow nature. After finishing the dishes, Bill tries to talk Lucilla into a date, but she snubs him for a serviceman. Dejected, Bill returns to his scrap metal yard, which he sees as his only way to contribute to the war effort. There, an elderly woman brings in a load of junk, including an antique lamp. After the woman leaves, Bill is astonished to hear a man's voice begging to be released from the lamp. When Bill drops the lamp, a genie named Ali materializes from its remains and thanks Bill for freeing him. Bill is stunned but quickly recovers when Ali promises him some wishes for his good deed. Bill states that all he wants is to be in the Army, but when he emerges from Ali's magic cloud of smoke, he finds himself at Valley Forge in 1776. The troops with which Bill marches stop at a U.S.O. canteen for coffee, doughnuts and dancing, and Bill is entranced by a hostess named Prudence Smith, who bears an uncanny resemblance to Sally. Bill is distracted from Prudence, however, by the appearance of General George Washington and Benedict Arnold. When he finally speaks to Washington alone, Bill recalls his history lessons from Miss Hockheimer of Bronx High School and assures the general that Arnold is a traitor. Bill also volunteers to spy among the Hessian troops and goes to a tavern, where he meets a flirtatious waitress named Gretchen, who reminds him of Lucilla. Bill almost gets away with his spying mission, but is caught by General Rahl, who sentences him to be shot. Just as he is about to be killed, Bill is whisked away by Ali, whose good intentions continue to be thwarted by his magic timepiece, which is still broken. Although Ali succeeds in getting Bill into the Navy, he winds up on the *Santa Maria* with Christopher Columbus in 1492. Bill arrives just as disgruntled sailor Benito leads his fellow seaman in a mutiny against Columbus, but Bill is able to persuade them to stop. They soon discover land and sets off in a sailboat for New York. He lands at Manhattan Island, where he is entranced by the sight of a curvaceous Indian woman undressing inside her tepee. Bill's happy exclamation at her show causes the woman to faint, and when Bill checks on her, he is forced to shoo away an encroaching bear. Bill is next terrified by the appearance of the woman's husband, Chief Badger, who threatens to scalp him. Bill talks the chief into selling him Manhattan for twenty-four dollars, but at the conclusion of their deal, finds that he has been swindled by the chief, his wife and their pet bear, who have perpetuated "the old badger game" on him. Bill finally realizes that the "Lucilla type" is not for him, and wishes that he could see the faces of the old Dutchmen when they discover that he owns Manhattan. Ali then transports him to Nieuw Amsterdam of the early 1600s. A respected blacksmith, Bill is enjoying the time period when he is confronted by obnoxious businessman Kreiger, who asserts that he is marrying the girl Bill loves. The woman turns out to be another Sally double named Katrina, and Bill realizes that she is indeed the woman for him. She is being forced to marry Kreiger, however, because he holds the deed to her father's farm. Determined to save Katrina, Bill approaches the city council and proves that he owns Manhattan with the deed signed by Chief Badger. He sells the island to them, but after they levy a series of taxes on him, Bill ends up owing them money and is thrown in jail. He is joined by the inebriated Ali, who helps him rescue Katrina from her wedding to Kreiger, then takes them on a ride through the centuries. When they arrive in the twentieth century, Ali kicks Bill out of the car into a recruiting station, and Katrina becomes Sally. Bill is accepted into the Marines and marches with them in a parade, although Ali at first has him marching with the Women's Marine Reserves. Safely installed among the men, Bill assures Sally of his love, while Ali is accosted by two policemen, who are suspicious of the 854 B.C. birthdate on his draft card. Ali wishes himself into the Marines, and is joined by Lucilla as he marches alongside Bill, who is accompanied by Sally. *Genies. Military service, Voluntary. Romance. Time travel. United States—History. Wishes. 4-F. Bears. Christopher Columbus. Dutch Americans. Espionage. Flirts. Indians of North America. Magic lamps. Marriage—Forced. Mutiny. New York City. Parades. Rationing in wartime. Swindlers and swindling. United Service Organizations. George Washington.*

Note: According to a Feb 1944 *HR* news item, this film originally was to be directed by Walter Lang and was to star Michael O'Shea as "Bill Morgan" and Stanley Prager as "Ali." Although a Mar 1944 news item announced that Agnes De Mille had been hired as the dance director, a May 1944 *HR* news item stated that Hermes Pan was to be the dance director. A 27 May 1944 *LAEx* item reported that Vivian Blaine would be one of the female costars. Well-known vaudeville performer Gene Sheldon, who stars as "Ali," made his American film debut in this picture. Fox borrowed Joan Leslie from Warner Bros. and Carlos Ramirez from M-G-M for the production. According to a *HR* news item, 250 Marines from the Marine Base at San Diego were hired as extras.

According to information in the Twentieth Century-Fox Produced Scripts Collection and the Records of the Legal Department, both located at the UCLA Arts—Special Collections Library, early versions of the story included adventures in which "Bill Morgan" meets Commodore Perry and Lucretia Borgia. A 27 Jan 1944 screenplay included a gag in which Bill meets Don Ameche aboard the *Santa Maria* and exclaims "I don't know if it's 1492 or 1942," after Ameche states that he is inventing the telescope. In a 5 Sep 1944 script, Ameche is replaced by Ernst Lubitsch, who glares at Bill and asks, "Who did you think I was—Christopher Columbus?" after Bill recognizes him. Although photographs of Lubitsch in costume on the set exist, the gag was not included in the released film. Writers Snag Werris and George Seaton (who directed the retakes and additional scenes as a favor to Gregory Ratoff, according to *HR*) are listed by the legal files as contributing to the script, but the extent of their contributions to the finished picture has not been determined. The studio records also reveal that Ira Gershwin and Kurt Weill wrote three additional songs that do not appear in the completed picture: "It Could Have Happened to Anyone," "Woo, Woo, Woo, Woo, Manhattan!" and "That's How It Is." [Part of the latter song was included in "Morale."] Gershwin and Weill's songs were highly praised in contemporary reviews, and the "Columbus" comic opera sequence was frequently singled out for acclaim. *Where Do We Go From Here?* was the only film in which Fred MacMurray and June Haver, who were married in 1954, appeared together. The legal files contain information about a plagiarism lawsuit filed by Vera Blanch Edens, who claimed that the studio had stolen the film's story from a scenario she wrote entitled "Hunters of the Promised Land." After her first suit was dismissed, Edens filed suit again, but the judge dismissed the case with prejudice to prevent her from filing a third time.

Box 26 May 1945. *DV* 23 May 1945, p. 3, 8. *FD* 23 May 1945, p. 10. *HR* 15 Jun 1943, p. 1. *HR* 19 Nov 1943, p. 2. *HR* 11 Feb 1944, p. 1. *HR* 14 Mar 1944, p. 13. *HR* 26 May 1944. *HR* 8 Aug 1944, p. 25. *HR* 16 Aug 1944, p. 4. *HR* 17 Aug 1944, p. 20. *HR* 24 Aug 1944, p. 7. *HR* 25 Aug 1944, p. 13. *HR* 19 Sep 1944, p. 9. *HR* 11 Oct 1944, p. 3. *HR* 9 Nov 1944, p. 17. *HR* 16 Nov 1944, p. 10. *HR* 21 Dec 1944, p. 4. *HR* 23 May 1945, p. 6. *HR* 14 Jun 1945, p. 8. *LAEx* 27 May 1944. *MPD* 24 May 1945. *MPHPD* 7 Oct 1944, p. 2131. *MPHPD* 26 May 1945, p. 2465. *NYT* 7 Jun 1945, p. 25. *Var* 23 May 1945, p. 19.

WHERE IS MY CHILD? (Yiddish language)

Menorah Productions, Inc.; Abraham Leff, President. *Dist* Menorah Productions, Inc. **1937**; New York opening: 23 Nov 1937 [©Menorah Productions, Inc.; 2 Dec 1937; LP7761]. Sd; b&w. 10 reels, 8,722 ft. 95 min. Yiddish language with English subtitles.

Pres ABRAHAM LEFF. *Dir* Abraham Leff and Henry Lynn. *Scr* Henry Lynn. *Photog* J. Burgi Contner. *Film ed* George Roland. *Mus dir* Jack Stillman. *Rec eng* Edwin Schabbehar.

Song(s): "The Lullaby Song," especially written for Celia Adler, words and music by Ludwig Satz.

Source: Based on the play *Forgotten Mothers* by Sam Steinberg and William Siegel (copyrighted 27 Jun 1937).

Cast: CELIA ADLER (*Esther [Liebman]*), Anna Lillian (*Alice [Gross]*), Morris Strassberg (*Dr. [Adolf] Reisner*), Ruben Wendorf (*Elick*), Morris Silberkasten (*Morris [Gross]*), Blanche Bernstein (*Molka*), Mischa Stutchkof (*Victor*), Ceril Arnon (*Julia [Reisner]*), Solomon Steinberg (*Anderson*), Esther Gerber (*Nurse [Margaret]*), Leo Schectman (*Young Victor*).

Yiddish, Domestic, Melodrama. [*Print viewed*]. In 1911, in New York, Esther Liebman, a destitute Jewish refugee from Russia, gives birth to a son. She and her husband Joseph had left the hardships of Russia with hopes for a happy future in America, but Joseph fell ill on the boat and died. After three months of suffering, Esther, having no friends or relations, is unable to support the child. She is about to jump into the river with the baby, when Dr. Adolf Reisner sees her from his car and stops her. Reisner deceitfully arranges for wealthy Morris Gross and his wife Alice, who have lost three children, to adopt Esther's child through a crooked orphan home. Frightened at her prospects for taking care of her child, Esther signs a card and thus relinquishes all her rights to the child, without understanding that she will not be able to get her child back later. When she returns to the orphan home and says that she cannot live without her child, she is sent away. Esther vows to search for the child door-to-door, if necessary. Six years later, Esther learns that the doctor now is at the Gross's house for a party to celebrate the entrance of their adopted son Victor into school. Realizing that Victor may be her son, Esther goes to the school and as she watches the boys play football, cries

about her lost child. When she hugs Victor, a policeman orders her away. Later, at the Gross home, as Esther peers through a window, a police officer catches her and brings her inside. Reisner denies knowing Esther, but she sees Victor's picture and collapses, and the policeman leaves her in Reisner's care. Reisner promises that she will get her child that day, but instead calls an insane asylum and arranges for the corrupt owner to send an ambulance. Twenty years later, in 1937, Victor cares for the patients in the asylum. He takes a particular interest in Esther, who often rolls up a quilt, holds it like a baby and says to her imaginary child that she is not insane and that he will help her. Fearful of the attendants, after suffering years of afflicted punishments from the staff, Esther barely responds to Victor when he questions her. As the Grosses, Reisner and his daughter Julie, who loves Victor, prepare for Victor's birthday party, Gross, who wants Victor to give up his work at the institution and open a private practice, convinces Reisner to have Julie talk Victor into quitting. Victor and Julie have an argument about it, and when Reisner and Gross join in, Victor tells of the many patients he meets who have been put into the institution by people who have benefited afterwards. Speaking of Esther, he vows to punish the person who put her there and Julie backs him up. Victor then asks Alice if he could bring the woman from the institution home so that he can help her outside of the fearful environment of the asylum. Alice agrees, and when Esther arrives, she is still afraid to talk much. After she sees herself in the mirror and cries at her changed appearance, she sees Reisner and struggles to remember. Despite Reisner's claim that she is insane, she accuses him and asks, "Where is my child?" Alice realizes who she is and tells Victor, who embraces his real mother. He yells at Reisner and threatens to have him prosecuted, and explains to Alice that Esther needs him now. Alice replies that she is satisfied to have reared a son for the true mother, as Victor embraces both Julie and Esther, who in her happiness says, "There is a God." *Charlatans. Child selling. Deception. Foster parents. Jews. Mothers and sons. Physicians. Refugees, Political. Attempted suicide. Birthdays. Insane asylums. New York City. Orphanages. Parties. Police. Postal workers. Religiosity.*

Note: The Yiddish title of this film is *Vu Iz Mayn Kind?* According to papers at NCJF, Sam Steinberg and William Siegal, authors of the play *Forgotten Mothers*, signed an agreement with Menorah Productions, Inc. to sell them the rights to the play two days after the play was copyrighted. It is not known if the play was ever performed publicly. In the screen credits, Siegal's name is listed as "S. Siegel." While the actor playing "Anderson" is credited as Solomon Steinberg in the screen credits, *Var* notes that Samuel Steinberg, one of the authors, was in the film and does not credit Solomon Steinberg.

Var 1 Oct 1937, p. 29.

WHERE LIGHTS ARE LOW (Chinese Americans)

Hayakawa Feature Play Co. *Dist* R-C Pictures Corp. 4 Sep **1921** [©Hayakawa Feature Play Co.; 7 Dec 1920; LU15855]. Si; b&w. 6 reels.

Dir Colin Campbell. *Adpt* Jack Cunningham. *Photog* Frank D. Williams.

Source: Based on the short story "East Is East" by Lloyd Osborne in *Metropolitan Magazine* (Apr 1920).

Cast: Sessue Hayakawa (*T'Su Wong Shih*), Togo Yamamoto (*Chang Bong Lo*), Goro Kino (*Tuang Fang*), Gloria Payton (*Quan Yin*), Kiyosho Satow (*Lang See Bow*), Misao Seki (*Chung Wo Ho Kee*), Toyo Fujita (*Wung*), Jay Eaton ("*Spud" Malone*), Harold Holland (*Sergeant McConigle*).

Melodrama. T'Su Wong Shih, a Chinese prince, loves Quan Yin, a gardener's daughter, though his uncle plans to marry him into a wealthy mandarin family; and before leaving for America to obtain an education, he promises the girl that he will join her soon. Following graduation from college, while visiting a slave auction in San Francisco's Chinatown, he recognizes his beloved one and bids $5,000 for her; he wins but is unable to raise the required sum. The auctioneer agrees to give him a three-year extension on the payment, and T'Su Wong Shih goes to work at various sorts of jobs but meets with little success until he wins a lottery prize. Threats from an Oriental gangster induce the auctioneer to yield his captive, but T'Su Wong Shih engages in a fight with the gangster, rescues Quan Yin, and claims her for his wife. *Chinese Americans. Gangsters. Lotteries. San Francisco (CA)–Chinatown. Slavery.*

Note: This film was also reviewed under the title *When Lights Are Low.*

FD 3 Jul 1921. *NYT* 1 Aug 1921, p. 6 or 8. *Var* 5 Aug 1921, p. 26.

WHERE THE TRAIL DIVIDES (Native Americans)

Jesse L. Lasky Feature Play Co. *Dist* Paramount Pictures Corp. 12 Oct **1914** [©Jesse L. Lasky Feature Play Co.; 30 Sep 1914; LU3451]. Si; b&w. 5 reels.

Cam Robert L. Carson.

Source: Based on the novel *Where the Trail Divides* by William Otis Lillibridge (New York, 1907).

Cast: Robert Edeson (*"How" Lander*), Theodore Roberts (*Colonel Lander*), J. W. Johnston (*Clayton Craig*), Winifred Kingston (*Bess Lander*), James Neill (*Sam Rowland*), Constance Adams (*Mrs. Rowland*), Fred Montague (*Rev. John Eaton*), Antrim Short (*Little "How"*), Mary Jane Higbee (*Little Bess*).

Western. Col. Landers adopts two children, "How," an Indian boy, and Bess, whose parents were killed in an Indian uprising. When the children are grown, How proposes to Bess, whom he has loved since his childhood. She accepts his proposal, thus angering Clayton Craig, Lander's nephew who also wants to marry her. After Lander's death, How is exiled from the ranch, so he and Bess buy new land. One day, after he has been away, How returns to his cabin to see Bess and Craig embracing. How grants Bess her freedom after which she marries Craig and moves to New York. Some time later, How discovers oil on the land that he gave Bess, so he follows them to New York. There he finds that Craig has been unfaithful to Bess. In the end, Bess rejects Craig so that she and How can remarry and find "a trail to happiness together." Divorce. Indians of North America. Indians of North America—Mixed blood. Infidelity. Orphans. Remarriage. Adoption. Nephews. New York City. Oil. Uprisings.

MPN 24 Oct 1914, p. 40. *MPW* 10 Oct 1914, p. 252. *MPW* 24 Oct 1914, p. 495. *NYDM* 21 Oct 1914, p. 30. *Var* 17 Oct 1914, p. 15.

WHERE THE WIND DIES see PASSION

WHERE'S MY MAN TO-NITE see MARCHING ON!

WHILE THOUSANDS CHEER (African Americans)

Gold Seal Productions, Inc.; Million Dollar Productions, Inc. *Dist* State Rights. **1940**; Los Angeles opening: 14 Nov 1940. Sd; b&w. 6 reels, 5,851 ft. 64 min. PCA cert no. 6350.

Pres Harry M. Popkin. *Prod* Clifford Sanforth. *Assoc prod* Sara Francis. *Supv* George D. Ringer. *Dir* Leo C. Popkin. *Asst dir* Gordon Griffith. *Orig story and scr adpt* Joseph O'Donnell. *Cam* Marcel Picard, Herman Schoff and Clark Ramsey. *Art dir* Paul Palmentola. *Film ed* Martin G. Cohn. *Sd* Cliff Ruberg. *Makeup* Harry Ross. *Prod mgr* Arthur C. Ringer. *Publicity dir* Harry Levette.

Cast: Kenny Washington (*Kenny Harrington*), Mantan Moreland (*Nash*), Pete Webster (*Downey*), Jeni Le Gon (*Myra*), Reginald Fenderson (*Phil Harrington*), Lawrence Criner (*Green*), Monte Hawley (*Johnson*), Florence O'Brien (*Daisy*), Ida Belle Kauffin (*Rose*), Bud Harris (*Coach Harding*), Earl Hall (*Jerry Stevens*), John Thomas (*Jack Saunders/Spike*), Reginald Anderson (*Umpire*), Jack Spears (*Referee*), Alfred Grant (*Radio announcer*), Edward Thompson (*Ransom*).

African American, Football, Crime, Drama. [*Not viewed*]. Kenny Harrington, the star football player of Gilmore College, leads his team to many victories, raising hopes that Gilmore will play in the "Peach Bowl," the championship playoffs of the Western conference. Unknown to Kenny, Downey, the head of a gambling syndicate, has placed a $100,000 bet against the Gilmore team and has sent his henchman, Green, to see to it that Kenny does not play in the upcoming game. When Green and Johnson, head of the west coast offices of the gambling syndicate, find Kenny at the Collegiate Café and offer him $25,000 to leave the team until after the Peach Bowl, Kenny, his pal Phil Harrington and other college students throw them out of the café. Later, Phil throws a party at Johnson's café, where a brawl breaks out when he cannot pay the bill. When Kenny and his trainer, Nash, learn of the riot, they rush to the café and help Phil and the other students escape. After Green and Johnson blackmail Kenny, threatening to reveal that he was responsible for knocking a waiter at the café unconscious, Kenny agrees to drop out of the team's game against Carlton College. Just before the game, however, Kenny decides to play, and he helps his team win. To get back at Kenny for double-crossing them, the gamblers bribe Rose, a "college widow," to lure him and Phil to their hideout, where they plan to hold them captive. As the game between Gilmore and Union gets underway, Myra, Kenny's sweetheart, and her pal Daisy confront Rose and force her to tell them where Phil and Kenny are being held. With help from

other members of Kenny's team and from the police, Myra and Daisy go to the hideout and arrive in time to save them. The gangsters are placed under arrest, and Kenny is rushed to the football field, where he eventually leads the team to victory. With Gilmore's place in the Peach Bowl playoffs assured, Kenny and Myra plan their wedding. African Americans. College life. Football. Football players. Gamblers. Gangsters. Kenny Washington. Abduction. Ambulances. Blackmail. Bookies. Cafés. Fistfights. Football coaches. Hideouts. Marriage. Police. Rescues. Romance.

Note: A working title for this film was *Gridiron Graft*. It was reviewed in *Exh* in Dec 1941 under the title *As Thousands Cheer*. The film was re-released in 1945 as *Crooked Money*. The *DV* review complimented Million Dollar Productions for having brought to the screen the story of Kenny Washington, "the colored All-American [who] put the University of California at Los Angeles on the gridiron map." Washington graduated from UCLA in 1940, and became one of the first blacks to play in the National Football League following World War II. He played with the Los Angeles Rams and other professional football teams following his record-breaking stint at UCLA.

DV 15 Nov 1940, p. 3. *Exh* 24 Dec 1941, p. 915.

WHISPERING GHOSTS (African Americans)

Twentieth Century-Fox Film Corp. *Dist* Twentieth Century-Fox Film Corp. 22 May **1942**; Prod: 8 Jan—7 Feb 1942 [©Twentieth Century-Fox Film Corp.; 22 May 1942; LP11340]. Sd (RCA Sound System); b&w. 8 reels, 6,745 ft. 75 min. PCA cert no. 8124.

Exec prod Sol M. Wurtzel. *Dir* Alfred Werker. [*Asst dir* William Eckhardt]. *Scr* Lou Breslow. *Orig story* Philip MacDonald. [*Special material for Milton Berle* Ray Singer and Joe Erens]. *Dir of photog* Lucien Ballard. [*Spec eff* Lou Witte]. *Art dir* Richard Day and Lewis Creber. *Film ed* Alexander Troffey. *Set dec* Thomas Little. *Cost* Herschel. *Mus* Emil Newman and Leigh Harline. *Sd* W. B. Delaplain and Harry M. Leonard. [*Prod mgr* William Koenig]. [*Dir of pub* Harry Brand]. [*Trainer of Jim the crow* Curly Twyfford and Dave Twyfford].

Cast: MILTON BERLE (*H. H. Van Buren*), Brenda Joyce (*Elizabeth ["Betty"] Woods*), John Shelton (*David Courtland*), John Carradine (*Norbert [also known as] Long Jack*), Willie Best (*Euclid White [Brown]*), Edmund MacDonald (*[Jerry] Gilpin*), Arthur Hohl (*Inspector Norris [alias of Manuel Dazetta]*), Grady Sutton (*Jonathan Flack*), Milton Parsons (*Dr. [Walter] Bascomb [alias of Jackson Voker]*), Abner Biberman (*Mack Wolf*), Renie Riano (*Meg [also known as Stella]*), Charles Halton (*[Mark] Gruber*), Harry Hayden (*Conroy*), [Jack Gargan (*Shadow*)], [George Offerman, Jr. (*Chuck*)], [Frank Faylen (*Curley*)], [Marvin Stephens (*Page boy*)], [Jim, a crow], [Josephine Beach, a rat].

Comedy, Mystery. [*Print viewed*]. Ten years after the unsolved murder of Captain Eli Wetherby, his grandniece Elizabeth "Betty" Woods searches his boat, the *Black Joker*, for hidden treasure with her fiancé, David Courtland. Betty's belief in the existence of the treasure comes from listening to *The Man Who Lifts the Veil*, a radio show featuring amateur detective H. H. Van Buren. Van has been dramatizing her uncle's case and has promised his listeners that he will solve the crime during next week's show. While Betty leaves the boat, which is docked in New Jersey, to return to her New York City apartment, Van is confronted by New Jersey police inspector Norris at the radio station. Norris threatens to arrest Van for obstructing justice if he does not reveal Wetherby's killer, but when Van tells him that he suspects a man known as Manuel Dazetta, Norris laughingly tells him that Wetherby's alias was Dazetta. After Norris leaves, Van's sponsor, Conroy, orders him to go to the *Black Joker* and uncover the real killer. Van departs with his black valet, Euclid Brown, but his arrival at the boat is preceded by that of two actors, Stella and Norbert, who have been hired by Van's announcer, Jerry Gilpin. Van and Gilpin are engaged in an ongoing and escalating war of practical jokes, and Gilpin has hired Stella and Norbert to enact the roles of Wetherby's crazed fiancée Meg, and Wetherby's first mate, Long Jack. Their frightful act succeeds in terrifying Euclid, but Van overhears them discussing their roles and deduces the truth. When Betty appears, however, Van thinks that she is also an actress and does not believe her when she says that her uncle's lawyer gave her two clues to finding the treasure, a dog collar and a will, stating that she must take the same trip that Wetherby took on 23 Sep 1929. As Van is searching the boat, Professor Walter Bascomb, an oceanographer, and traveling book salesman Jonathan Flack board, stating that they became lost while driving in the heavy fog. Norris also arrives, and much confusion ensues for Van as the dog collar is stolen and a dead sailor, Mack Wolf, is found. Wolf was one of Wetherby's men, and Van

eventually realizes that Bascomb is another of the former crew, then known as Jackson Voker. Bascomb is attacked, but before collapsing, he tells Van to check Wetherby's logbook. Van and Euclid use a large globe to plot out Wetherby's listed course on 23 Sep 1929, which turns out to be the combination that opens a secret compartment in the globe. Inside is what appears to be a fortune in diamonds, and Bascomb then reveals that although he did kill Wolf, it was Norris, whose real name is Manuel Dazetta, who killed Wetherby in order to get the diamonds. Norris has been searching for the stones ever since Wetherby found them and is bitterly disappointed when Jonathan states that they are merely Mexican rock crystals. Soon everyone is safely off the boat, and Van and Euclid travel back to New York City with Norris as their prisoner. *Amateur detectives. Investigations. Murder. Radio performers. Treasure.* Actors and actresses. African Americans. Boats. Fog. Impersonation and imposture. Inheritance. New Jersey. New York City. Nieces. Police inspectors. Practical jokes. Radio sponsors. Sailors. Valets.

Note: The working titles of this film were *Whispering Wires* and *Whispering in the Dark.* According to information in the Twentieth Century-Fox Records of the Legal Department and the Produced Scripts Collection, both located at the UCLA Arts—Special Collections Library, Milton Sperling wrote an original story entitled "Whispering Wires," but his work was not used for the final film. Ralph Spence, Jack Jungmeyer, Jr. and Maurice Rapf also wrote treatments for the picture, but the extent of their contribution to the completed film has not been confirmed. According to *HR* and *LAT* news items, Lynn Bari and Charlotte Greenwood were set to co-star in the picture. Bari was replaced by Brenda Joyce and appeared instead in Twentieth Century-Fox's *Secret Agent of Japan.* Although Willie Best's character is listed as "Euclid White" in the end credits, in the film he is called "Euclid Brown." Best was borrowed from Warners Bros. for the production.

Box 18 Apr 1942. *DV* 16 Apr 1942, p. 3, 8. *FD* 17 Apr 1942, p. 8. *HR* 24 Nov 1941, p. 2. *HR* 25 Nov 1941, p. 2. *HR* 18 Dec 1941, p. 6. *HR* 2 Jan 1942, p. 2. *HR* 8 Jan 1942, p. 3. *HR* 9 Jan 1942, p. 9. *HR* 19 Jan 1942, p. 6. *HR* 6 Feb 1942, p. 11. *HR* 9 Feb 1942, p. 1. *HR* 16 Apr 1942, p. 4. *LAEx* 22 Nov 1941. *LAT* 29 Dec 1941. *MPHPD* 18 Apr 1942, p. 610. *NYT* 18 May 1942, p. 19. *Var* 22 Apr 1942, p. 18.

WHISPERING IN THE DARK *see* **WHISPERING GHOSTS**

WHISPERING SAGE (Basque Americans)
Fox Film Corp. *Dist* Fox Film Corp. 20 Mar **1927** [©Fox Film Corp.; 13 Mar 1927; LP23781]. Si; b&w. 5 reels, 4,783 ft.
Pres William Fox. *Dir* Scott R. Dunlap. *Asst dir* Ted Brooks. *Scen* Harold Shumate. *Photog* Reginald Lyons.
Source: Based on the novel *Whispering Sage* by Harry Sinclair Drago and Joseph Noel (New York, 1922).
Cast: Buck Jones (*Buck Kildare*), Natalie Joyce (*Mercedes*), Emile Chautard (*José Arastrade*), Carl Miller (*Esteban Bengoa*), Albert J. Smith (*Ed Fallows*), Joseph Girard (*Hugh Acklin*), William A. Steele (*Tom Kildare*), Ellen Winston (*Mrs. Kildare*), Hazel Keener (*Mercedes' friend*), Enrique Acosta (*Old Pedro*), Joseph Rickson.
Western. Buck Kildare, searching for a killer, encounters a colony of Basques in the desert and saves them from the henchmen of Hugh Acklin, owner of an adjoining ranch, who wants to take over the immigrants' land. Discovering Acklin's duplicity, Buck soon becomes an ally of the Basques and falls in love with Mercedes, daughter of their leader. In a showdown between the factions, Buck discovers that Acklin's foreman murdered his brother, Tom. Government forces save the Basques at the last minute, and Buck is happily united with the girl. *Bandits. Basque Americans. Courtship. Land rights. Ranchers.*

FD 10 Apr 1927. *MPW* 9 Apr 1927. *Var* 6 Apr 1927, p. 24.

WHISPERING WIRES *see* **WHISPERING GHOSTS**

WHITE BIRD *see* **RENDEZVOUS**

THE WHITE DRAGON *see* **MAD HOLIDAY**

WHITE EAGLE (Native Americans)
Columbia Pictures Corp. *Dist* Columbia Pictures Corp. 7 Oct **1932**; Prod: 13 Jun—25 Jun 1932 [©Columbia Pictures Corp.; 7 Sep 1932; LP3244]. Sd (Western Electric Sound System); b&w. 7 reels. 64-65 or 67 min.
Dir Lambert Hillyer. *Scr* Fred Myton. *Photog* L. William O'Connell. *Film ed* Gene Melford. [*Sd eng* Glenn Rominger].
Cast: BUCK JONES [(*White Eagle, also known as John Harvey*)], Barbara Weeks [(*Janet Rand*)], Robert Ellis [(*Gregory*)], Jason Robards [(*Dave Rand*)], Ward Bond [(*Bart*)], Robert Elliott [(*Captain Blake*)], Bob Kortman [(*Sheriff*)], [Frank Campeau (*Gray Wolf*)], [Jimmy Howe (*Zachariah Kershaw*)], [Jim Thorpe (*Indian chief*)], [Clarence Geldert (*Doctor*)], [Silver (*White Eagle's horse*)].

Western. [*Print viewed*]. While on the stagecoach taking her to Virginia City to visit her brother Dave, Janet Rand sees White Eagle, a Pony Express rider, race by. In town, White Eagle fights with Bart over his treatment of Silver, his horse, and his young friend, Zachariah Kershaw. Bart is in league with Gregory, who poses as a Pony Express agent. Gregory orders Bart to waylay the stage carrying Janet because he fears it carries a letter that reveals he is a criminal. Shortly afterward, the townspeople receive news that Indians attacked the stage, but White Eagle discovers that the raiders were white men. When Dave and others follow White Eagle's trail, they find that he has saved Janet from a mountain lion. A month later, Dave worries that Janet is spending too much time with White Eagle and reminds her that White Eagle is an Indian. White Eagle's father, Gray Wolf, also disapproves of their friendship and advises White Eagle to return to his people. White Eagle, however, believes that peace can exist between Indians and settlers. White Eagle discovers Bart and his gang disguised as Indians, but the townspeople believe he made up the story to deceive them. Zach helps White Eagle escape from the angry settlers, but when he returns to his Indian village, he finds it burned and all the inhabitants massacred. When White Eagle warns Janet about an Indian attack, Dave tells him that he is not wanted among the settlers. White Eagle joins the Indians, saves Janet during an attack, and turns her over to Captain Blake of the cavalry. White Eagle supports Blake's offer of peace during a meeting of the chieftains and believes Blake's promise that he will see justice done. When Gray Wolf overhears White Eagle say that he will neither return to Virginia City nor forget Janet, he tells him that he was adopted as an infant, after he was saved from a burning fort. White Eagle's real father was Major Harvey, and his real name is John Harvey. White Eagle rejoins the Pony Express, and when Blake learns Gregory's plans, he sends White Eagle after him. Meanwhile, Gregory has abducted Dave and Janet and plans to force her into marriage. White Eagle leads Gregory, who has killed Bart, into an ambush, saves the Rands and is reunited with Janet. *Brothers and sisters. Indians of North America. Pony express. Racism.* Abduction. Criminals. Disguise. False accusations. Fistfights. Foster children. Fraud. Rescues. Romance. Stagecoach robberies. United States. Army. Cavalry.

Note: *White Eagle* was also the title of a 1941 Buck Jones serial. Modern sources add Alf James to the cast.

FD 24 Sep 1932, p. 6. *MPH* 1 Oct 1932, p. 54. *NYT* 24 Sep 1932, p. 18. *Var* 27 Sep 1932, p. 21.

WHITE FEATHER (1954) *see* **THEY RODE WEST**

WHITE FEATHER (Native Americans, Arapaho, Cheyenne, Crow, Dakota)
Panorama Productions; controlled by Twentieth Century-Fox Film Corp. *Dist* Twentieth Century-Fox Film Corp. Feb **1955**; Los Angeles opening: 15 Feb 1955; New York opening: 16 Feb 1955; Prod: mid-Jul—mid-Sep 1954 [©Twentieth Century-Fox Film Corp.; 8 Feb 1955; LP4574]. Sd (Western Electric Recording); col (Technicolor); CinemaScope. 12 reels. 102 min. PCA cert no. 16787.
Pres LEONARD GOLDSTEIN. *Prod* Robert L. Jacks. *Dir* Robert Webb. *Asst dir* Hal Klein. *Scr* Delmer Daves and Leo Townsend. *Dir of photog* Lucien Ballard. *Art dir* Jack Smith. *Film ed* George Gittens. *Set dec* Richard Siegel. *Cost des* Travilla. *Mus* Hugo Friedhofer. *Mus cond* Lionel Newman. *Sd* Joseph I. Kane. *Makeup artist* Lou Hippe. [*Tech adv* Iron Eyes Cody].
Source: Based on the short story "My Great-Aunt Appearing Day" by John Prebble in *Lilliput Magazine* (Jul-Aug 1952).
Cast: Robert Wagner [(*Josh Tanner*)], John Lund [(*Colonel Lindsay*)], Debra Paget [(*Appearing Day*)], Jeffrey Hunter [(*Little Dog*)], Eduard Franz [(*Chief Broken Hand*)], Noah Beery [(*Lt. Ferguson*)], Virginia Leith [(*Ann Magruder*)], Emile Meyer [(*Magruder*)], Hugh O'Brian [(*American Horse*)], Milburn Stone [(*Commissioner Trenton*)].
Western. [*Print viewed*]. In 1877, when Josh Tanner, a surveyor on his way to Fort Laramie, takes a short cut through Cheyenne territory, he finds a corpse pierced by an Indian arrow. While packing the body onto his horse under the watchful eyes of Little Dog, a Cheyenne chief's son, and his group of braves, Josh unwittingly wins a game of chance that Little Dog plays with him from afar, and his life is spared. When Josh arrives at Fort Laramie with the body, an angry Colonel Lindsay announces that the men will suffer the same fate if they persist in violating the peace treaty with the Cheyennes by crossing

into their territory to pan for gold. Later, during a ceremony in which the colonel oversees the signing of a treaty by the Sioux, Blackfeet and Arapaho tribes, which will require them to move onto reservations, the Cheyenne, who refuse to capitulate, attack. The colonel, a pacifist, will not allow the white men to retaliate. Soon after, Josh and Ann Magruder, daughter of the rough saloon owner from whom Josh rents a room, ride into the country, where they are accosted by Little Dog and his warrior band. Little Dog taunts Josh, but Josh handles the Indians well, understanding the Cheyenne warrior's codes of dignity and respect. Josh eventually wins over Little Dog by giving him his hair comb as a gift, and the warriors allow Josh and Ann, who also has deep sympathy for the Indians, to go on their way. Back at the fort, Ann's father, in a drunken fit, tells Josh to leave his daughter alone, implying that she was raped as a young girl and is now "damaged goods." The next day, upon an invitation from Little Dog and his sister, Appearing Day, Josh goes to the Cheyenne village and watches the Indian warriors' war-games. Josh gives Little Dog and the brave's closest friend, American Horse, Bowie knives and the two practice at throwing them at a target of a white man. Later, as Josh washes his face in the river, Appearing Day arrives, and when he gives her his bar of soap, she asks for a kiss. Little Dog and American Horse later steal a horse from the Crow tribe, whom they denigrate as a lesser creed, and give it to Josh as a gift. Josh finally meets Little Dog's father, Chief Broken Hand, who asks that Josh sit at a council meeting, during which Broken Hand plans to announce his decision to accept the peace treaty and leave the Cheyenne territory for a reservation in the South. After Little Dog becomes enraged at his father's decision, Broken Hand asks Josh to try to convince his son to give up the fight. In the medicine man's lodge, Josh urges Little Dog to show as much wisdom as he has courage. Still angry and humiliated, Little Dog declares that he will go alone to the hills to consult the spirits. Later, American Horse, having witnessed Josh kissing Appearing Day, hits the girl, claiming that she belongs to him. He then rides to the fort and attacks Josh for taking Appearing Day away from him. In the ensuing scuffle, a guard is killed, and American Horse is imprisoned. Appearing Day, having interpreted Josh's words of sympathy as a promise of love, shows up in his bed, unclothed. He tells her that she must go back, but then admits that he loves her and promises to talk to her father. When Little Dog sneaks into Fort Laramie to release American Horse, he kills a guard. The colonel and a group of Cavalry soldiers go to see Broken Hand, hoping that he will allow them to arrest Little Dog and American Day. Josh, who has accompanied them, wants to discuss Appearing Day with Broken Hand, but the patriarch refuses. Broken Hand does agree to sign the peace treaty, and as he does so, a brave arrives and throws a knife festooned with a white feather at the colonel's feet, indicating a challenge from Little Dog. Although Little Dog and American Horse are working alone, the colonel calls out the entire Cavalry. The inhabitants of the Cheyenne village and the Cavalry arrive at the appointed place, and the two warriors taunt the officers. Josh, realizing that he must make one of the braves shoot first, provokes American Horse by calling him a woman, and when the warrior breaks down and shoots, violating the terms of the agreement, he is in turn shot down by Broken Hand. Josh tries to convince Little Dog to save his own life, but Little Dog prefers to fight Josh to the death like a brave warrior. Appearing Day rides up and begs Little Dog to be faithful to his white friend, who has always treated him well. Little Dog shakes Josh's hand and then rushes at the troops, who shoot him dead. Josh goes to Little Dog's dead body and lovingly arranges him in a dignifed pose. After the colonel declares that they have seen the last of the Indian wars, Josh announces that he will wed Appearing Day. The couple are married in a Methodist church, and Broken Hand lives long enough to see his grandson enter the Military Academy at West Point. *Cheyenne Indians. Fort Laramie (WY). Friendship. Heroism. Indians of North America–Reservations. Treaties. United States. Army. Cavalry. Alcoholics. Arapaho Indians. Brothers and sisters. Courage. Crow Indians. Dakota Indians. Fathers and daughters. Gold miners. Horses. Murder. Rites and ceremonies. Romantic rivalry. Saloon keepers. Surveyors. Tribal chiefs.*

Note: The film's working title was *The Challenge.* Opening credits begin with an offscreen narrator who states: "What you will see actually happened; the only difference being the Indian's language..." Although an accompanying onscreen written statement establishes the story's period as 1877, the events depicted in the film appear to be based on the 1868 Fort Laramie Treaty signing, which stipulated that the Southern Cheyennes and the Arapahos would be sent to a combined reservation. The treaty negotiations were organized by a peace commission that was formed after a series of bloody and unsuccessful military campaigns. The *Var* review commented that in *White Feather* "seldom is the Redskin depicted as the villain. Rather the plot makes the white man the aggressor." Similarly, the *HR* review stated that "if [the public] is really interested in what the Indians of the frontier were like, [the film] should have great success, for it is one of the most massive and accurate screen spectacles ever put on the screen." In a *HCN* interview, director Robert Webb stated that he "tried to show the Indian in a different light" by making them intelligent and worthy. The film was shot on location in Durango, Mexico, according to *HR* production charts and news items. A Jun 1954 *LAEx* item announced that Terry Moore, Dale Robertson and Rita Moreno would star in the picture along with Robert Wagner. *White Feather* was producer Leonard Goldstein's last film.

Box 12 Feb 1955. *DV* 9 Feb 1955, p. 3. *FD* 10 Feb 1955, p. 10. *HCN* 13 Dec 1954. *HR* 16 Jul 1954, p. 1. *HR* 10 Sep 1954, p. 17. *HR* 9 Feb 1955, p. 3. *LAEx* 5 Jun 1954. *LAEx* 16 Mar 1955. *LAT* 16 Feb 1955. *MPD* 14 Feb 1955 *MPHPD* 12 Feb 1955, p. 321. *Newsweek* 21 Mar 1955. *NYT* 17 Feb 1955, p. 23. *Stage–Screen–Drama* 16 Feb 1955. *Var* 9 Feb 1955, p. 10.

THE WHITE FLOWER (Hawaiians)

Famous Players-Lasky Corp. *Dist* Paramount Pictures. 4 Mar **1923**; New York premiere: 25 Feb 1923 [©Famous Players-Lasky Corp.; 21 Feb 1923; LP18722]. Si; b&w. 6 reels, 5,731 ft.

Pres Adolph Zukor. *Dir* Julia Crawford Ivers. *Story and adpt* Julia Crawford Ivers. *Photog* James Van Trees.

Cast: Betty Compson (*Konia Markham*), Edmund Lowe (*Bob Rutherford*), Edward Martindel (*John Markham*), Arline Pretty (*Ethel Granville*), Sylvia Ashton (*Mrs. Gregory Bolton*), Arthur Hoyt (*Gregory Bolton*), Leon Barry (*David Panuahi*), Lily Philips (*Bernice Martin*), Reginald Carter (*Edward Graeme*), Maui Kaito (*Kahuna*).

Melodrama. Konia Markham, the daughter of an American father and a Hawaiian mother, is told by a sorceress that the man who presents her with a perfect white flower will be her true love. When Bob Rutherford offers a gardenia to Konia at a banquet, David Panuahi, a rejected suitor, becomes even more jealous and persuades Konia to have the *kahuna* put a death curse on Bob's fiancée, Ethel Granville. Bob's devotion to a failing Ethel softens Konia, however, and she has the curse removed. She is about to jump into a volcano when Bob—now released by Ethel from their engagement—finds her and declares his love. *Curses. Hawaii. Hawaiians. Sorcerers. Volcanoes.*

FD 4 Mar 1923. *MPW* 10 Mar 1923. *MPW* 7 Apr 1923. *Var* 8 Mar 1923, p. 30.

WHITE GOLD (Latino)

De Mille Pictures Corp. *Dist* Producers Distributing Corp. 14 Mar **1927**; New York premiere: 24 Feb 1927 [©Cinema Corp. of America; 8 Mar 1927; LP23762]. Si; b&w. 7 reels, 6,108 ft.

Supv C. Gardner Sullivan. *Dir* William K. Howard. *Adpt* Garrett Fort, Marion Orth and Tay Garnett. *Titles* John Krafft and John Farrow. *Photog* Lucien Andriot. *Art dir* Anton Grot. *Film ed* Jack Dennis.

Source: Based on the play *White Gold* by J. Palmer Parsons (New York, 2 Nov 1925).

Cast: Jetta Goudal (*Dolores Carson*), Kenneth Thomson (*Alec Carson*), George Bancroft (*Sam Randall*), George Nichols (*Carson, Alec's father*), Robert Perry (*Bucky O'Neil*), Clyde Cook (*Homer*).

Drama. Alec Carson, son of an embittered old Arizona sheepherder, marries Dolores, a Mexican dance hall girl, and takes her to the ranch, which is suffering from a drought. Carson strongly resents the girl's intrusion and tries to make his son doubt her fidelity; soon her nerves become strained from the old man's insults and her husband's failure to stand up for her. Sam Randall, a nomadic sheepherder, comes to the ranch looking for work, and Carson hires him when he notes Randall's inclination to flirt with Dolores. Alec, made suspicious by his father, quarrels with his wife, and they part in anger, Alec sleeping in the bunkhouse. That night, Randall sneaks into the girl's bedroom. The following morning, Carson declares he caught the guilty couple and killed Randall; Dolores refuses Alec an explanation because of his lack of faith in her. Destroying the evidence of her innocence, she throws the gun with which she shot Randall into a mud hole and walks away to freedom. *Arizona. Dance hall girls. Droughts. Family relationships. Jealousy. Marriage. Mexican Americans. Ranchers. Sheepherders.*

FD 6 Mar 1927. *MPW* 9 Apr 1927. *NYT* 11 Apr 1927, p. 18. *Var* 2 Mar 1927, p. 16.

WHITE HEAT (Hawaiians)

Seven Seas Corp. *Dist* State Rights; Pinnacle Productions, Inc. 15 Jul **1934**; New York opening: 15 Jun 1934. Sd; b&w. 60 or 62 min.

Prod William Fiske III. *Dir* Lois Weber. *Scr* Lois Weber. *Orig story and scr* James Bordrero. *Photog* Alvin Wyckoff and Frank Titus. *Mus supv* Abe Meyer.

Song(s): "Kuala Lullaby," words and music by Gus Kahn and Ted Fiorito.

Cast: Virginia Cherrill (*Lucille Cheney*), Mona Maris (*Leilani*), Hardie Albright (*Chandler Morris*), David Newell (*William Hawks*), Arthur Clayton (*Armia*), Robert Stevenson (*Mac*), Whitney de Rahm (*Hale*), Naomi Childers (*Mrs. Cheney*), Nani Palsa (*Adam*), Kolimau Kamai (*Lono*), Kamaunani Achi (*Mrs. Hale*), Peter Lee Hyun (*Soong*), Nohili Naumu (*Leilani's father*).

Island, Drama. [*Not viewed*]. William Hawks, the new foreman for the Cheney sugar plantation in Hawaii, works day and night at his job, all but ignoring his social and romantic life. Eventually, however, William develops an attachment to Leilani, a local woman, and takes her into his home as his housekeeper and native "wife." After he is called back to San Francisco by Cheney, William meets and falls in love with Cheney's socialite daughter Lucille. Lucille marries William and returns with him to the Hawaiian plantation, displacing Leilani in the process. Soon, Lucille grows bored and restless on the plantation, disgusted by her crude surroundings and irritated by the persistent tropical rains. After she resists the charms of a young native, Lucille's romantic desires are aroused by the arrival of her former fiancé, Chandler Morris, who sails to the island on his yacht. William, seeing Lucille's growing passion for Morris, accuses his rival of betrayal, and a vicious fight ensues. To save Morris from William's beating, Lucille starts a fire in the sugar cane, which threatens the entire crop and plantation. As William directs the fire-fighting operation and does battle with the flames, he falls from his horse and into the smoky inferno. Lucille, seizing her opportunity, escapes with Morris to his yacht, while the still devoted Leilani rescues William from the deadly flames and reunites with her true love. *Cultural conflict. Hawaii. Marriage. Miscegenation. Plantations. Socialites. Fires. Fistfights. Housekeepers. Infidelity. Jealousy. Rainstorms. Rescues. San Francisco (CA). Sugar. Yachts and yachting.*

Note: The working title of this film was *Cane Fire*. *DV* reviewed it under that title in Dec 1933. *White Heat* was Lois Weber's first "talkie" and the last film she ever directed. The noted silent film director and scenarist died on 13 Nov 1939. Sources disagree on one plot point. One source states that "Lucille" starts the crop fire to distract "William," enabling her to flee with "Morris," while another says that "Lucille" lights the fire to save "Morris" from "William's" beating. According to *MPH*, the film's fire sequence was tinted red to "increase the effect." *Var* reported that "Hawaiian music, and familiar singing, etc., are dragged into the action intermittently." According to a *HR* news item, the film was shot on location in the Hawaiian island of Kauai, and one reviewer noted that the cast was dominated by "native Hawaiians." Other *HR* news items add Martin Burton and Lani Kruse, "young Korean of the Clark Gable type," to the cast, but their participation in the final film has not been confirmed. M-G-M "released" the song "Kuala Lullaby" to this production, according to *HR*.

DV 12 Dec 1933, p. 3. *FD* 13 Apr 1934, p. 7. *FD* 15 Jun 1934, p. 16. *HR* 4 Aug 1933, p. 4. *HR* 15 Aug 1933, p. 7. *HR* 28 Aug 1933, p. 3. *MPD* 15 Jun 1934, p. 22. *MPH* 30 Jun 1934, p. 56. *MPH* 18 Aug 1934, p. 71. *NYT* 16 Jun 1934, p. 20. *Var* 19 Jun 1934, p. 27.

THE WHITE KIMONO *see* **THE CRIMSON KIMONO**

THE WHITE PIANO *see* **LOST BOUNDARIES**

THE WHITE RENEGADE (African Americans)

Dist State Rights; Artclass Pictures Corp. 1 Oct **1931**. Sd; b&w. 7 reels, 5,949 ft. 66 min.

Song(s): "Just a Song at Twilight" and "My Mother's Prayer," composer unknown.

Western, with songs. [*Not viewed*]. In a wagon train headed for California, Dr. Ezra Holt chastises his wife Hetty for flirting with young men. The wagon train stops in the town of Independence, where Wanda lives with of her husband Diamonds, who threatens to reveal her true identity if she does not stop spying on him. The lieutenant of the wagon train, Allan Grant, tells Ezra that the townspeople may be a bad influence on the youngsters aboard the train; however, Ezra believes that the townspeople are merely in need of his "Elixir of Life." In town, Ezra meets Diamonds, who challenges him to a "wrist-twisting" contest; instead Ezra sets up shop and has his slave Opium sing while he performs magic tricks for the crowd. After he has sold some of his Elixir, Ezra and Hetty go to a saloon, where Hetty begins to flirt. Ezra becomes enraged, and the next morning goes to the gambling house where Diamonds operates. While Ezra is involved in a game of faro, Diamonds visits Hetty and talks her into eloping with him. Their conversation is overheard by Wanda, who finds Ezra and tells him about the elopement. Ezra returns to his wagon, where Hetty tells him that she is leaving. When

his attempts to dissuade her fail, Ezra goes to Diamonds and makes him promise to take good care of Hetty. Wanda then goes to Hetty and explains that she also left her husband for Diamonds but came to regret it. Hetty realizes her error and searches for Ezra, planning to beg for forgiveness, but Ezra and Opium have left Independence to join a group of pioneers heading west. To support herself, Hetty becomes a singer, but she sings only sad songs. Some time later, Opium returns to Independence with the news of Ezra's death, and he tells Diamonds that before Ezra died, he had confiscated large boxes of gold that Indians had stolen from wagon trains. Opium leads Diamonds to nearby caves where, he says, the gold is hidden. As they enter a cave, Opium disappears, leaving Diamonds to wander aimlessly in the dark maze of caves. Outside, Opium tells Ezra, who is alive, that Hetty loves him and that she has taken a wagon train to find him. Ezra sends Opium to warn the wagon train of Indian attacks, and after thanking Opium for his loyal service, Ezra sets him free. He asks Opium to join the wagon train and watch over Hetty, then leaves to continue his life as a renegade. *African Americans. Flirts. Gambling houses. Marriage. Romantic rivalry. Separation (Marital). Wagon trains. Caves. Deception. Indians of North America. Medicine shows. Saloons. Singers. Slavery–Emancipation.*

Note: No reviews have been located for this film. The plot synopsis is based on a dialogue continuity from NYSA. A modern source credits Jack Irwin as the producer, director and author of the screenplay, includes Tom Santschi, Blanche Mehaffey, Philo McCullough, Reed Howes, Ted Wells, Donald Keith, Marjorie Keyes, Gene Layman, Billy Franey, Tom Murray and Mrs. Ted Wells in the cast and adds that the working title of the film was *The Empire Builders*.

THE WHITE SQUAW (Native Americans, Dakota, Scandinavian Americans)

Columbia Pictures Corp. *Dist* Columbia Pictures Corp. Nov **1956**; Prod: 14 May—24 May 1956 [©Columbia Pictures Corp.; 30 Nov 1956; LP7275]. Sd (Westrex Recording System); b&w; 1.85. 8 reels, 6,547 ft. 72-73 or 75 min. PCA cert no. 18172.

Prod Wallace MacDonald. *Dir* Ray Nazarro. *Asst dir* Sam Nelson. *Scr* Les Savage, Jr. *Dir of photog* Henry Freulich. *Art dir* Ross Bellah. *Film ed* Edwin Bryant. *Set dec* Alfred E. Spencer. *Mus cond* Mischa Bakaleinikoff. *Sd* Don McKay.

Source: Based on the novel *The White Squaw* by Larabie Sutter (Greenwich, CT, 1952).

Cast: David Brian [(*Sigrod Swanson*)], May Wynn [(*Eetay-O-Wahnee*)], William Bishop [(*Bob Garth*)], Nancy Hale [(*Kerry Arnold*)], William Leslie [(*Thor Swanson*)], Myron Healey [(*Eric Swanson*)], Robert C. Ross [(*Knute Swanson*)], Frank de Kova [(*Yellow Elk*)], George Keymas [(*Yotab*)], Roy Roberts [(*Purvis*)], Grant Withers [(*Sheriff*)], Wally Vernon [(*Faro Bill*)], [Paul Birch (*Thad Arnold*)], [Neyle Morrow (*Swift Arrow*)], [Guy Teague (*Joe Hide*)], [Vi Ingraham (*Nueva*)], [Bill Hale (*Bartender*)], [Emil Sitka (*Texas Jim*)], [Nick Thompson (*Sam*)], [Harry Strang (*Dr. Miller*)], [Robert Bice, Henry Rowland (*Cowhands*)], [Dennis Moore (*Rancher*)].

Western. [*Print viewed*]. While hiding behind some rocks one night, Yotah, Eetay-O-Wahnee and several other Sioux Indians watch as Wyoming settler Sigrod Swanson and his sons Thor, Eric and Knute, poison their reservation's water supply. Rancher Thad Arnold appears and reminds Sigrod that because he never filed a claim on the land, it was the U.S. government's right to settle the Indians there. Furious, Sigrod argues that he was too busy building his home and rearing a family to file papers with the government. Yotah suddenly fires on the ranchers, shouting, "I hate all white men," even though Eetay-O-Wahnee protests that it is Purvis, the Indian agent, who should bring Swanson to justice. In the darkness, Yotah accidentally wounds Arnold, and in the confused shooting that follows, Sigrod sees that Eetay-O-Wahnee, whom he calls "the white squaw," is among the attackers. After the Indians return to their village, old Yellow Elk reveals that Eetay-O-Wahnee's white father, whose name he once promised never to reveal, has, through Purvis, been sending her money over the years. Much to Eetay-O-Wahnee's surprise, Yellow Elk then hands her two thousand dollars. Determined to use her wealth to buy cattle for her starving people, she and Yotah ask cattleman Bob Garth if they may purchase his animals, but he claims that the herd is worth twice that much. Yellow Elk finally reveals that Arnold is Eetay-O-Wahnee's father, and she rides to his ranch seeking help. Meanwhile, Arnold, realizing he is about to die of his bullet wound, tells his daughter Kerry about her half sister Eetay-O-Wahnee, born to

him and his Sioux wife, Yellow Elk's sister, when he was a soldier in the Black Hills many years before. Afraid he would be called a "squaw man" for loving an Indian woman, Arnold placed his half-Sioux daughter in Yellow Elk's care when the child's mother died. Kerry is shocked by this news, but Arnold urges her to give Eetay-O-Wahnee half of his property upon his death. He then expires, whereupon Sigrod persuades Kerry to burn Arnold's will and keep the old man's story a secret. Just then, Eetay-O-Wahnee arrives. Accusing her of having killed Arnold during the shootout, Sigrod and Kerry turn her away. Eetay-O-Wahnee rides to town to tell Purvis that Sigrod has been poisoning the water, but Sigrod arrives and demands her arrest. Because there is no evidence implicating Eetay-O-Wahnee in Arnold's killing, Purvis and the sheriff let her go, after which Sigrod searches for Garth to forbid him from selling cattle to the Indians. Sigrod's hatred of Indians so angers Bob that he defiantly accepts Eetay-O-Wahnee's money. Driven nearly mad with fury, Sigrod attacks Bob and almost kills him. Purvis and the sheriff break up the fight, but later, as Eetay-O-Wahnee and Bob are riding to her village, they discover that Sigrod's sons have killed Bob's friend Joe and scattered the herd. As Bob convalesces in Eetay-O-Wahnee's teepee, she rides back to town and is followed by Yotah. When Sigrod's son Eric attacks Eetay-O-Wahnee, Yotah kills him and flees. Sigrod then has Eetay-O-Wahnee arrested for Eric's murder. Yotah tells Bob and Yellow Elk that Eetay-O-Wahnee must have killed Eric, whereupon the old Indian gives Bob a duplicate of Arnold's will. Realizing that the will offers Eetay-O-Wahnee her only hope for a fair trial, Bob delivers it to Purvis. Unaware that Purvis has placed the document in his pocket, Kerry tells Sigrod and his sons to destroy the will by blowing up the safe in the Indian agent's office. The dynamite blasts a hole in the jail's wall, and Sigrod takes Eetay-O-Wahnee from her cell and rides away. Bob forces Kerry to accompany him, Purvis and the sheriff to Sigrod's ranch, and when they arrive, young Knute Swanson, who is opposed to his father's brutal methods, tells them that his father intends to kill Eetay-O-Wahnee. She manages to escape Sigrod on horseback, but as she reaches her village, Sigrod arrives and begins shooting wildly. After Sigrod wounds Yotah, Yellow Eagle shoots Sigrod in the arm, but the enraged rancher begins setting fire to the teepees, screaming, "Get off my land!" Bob and Purvis ride up just as Sigrod is attacking Eetay-O-Wahnee, and in the fight that follows, Bob knocks Sigrod into a flaming teepee, where he is burned to death. Before he dies, Yotah confesses to the killings of both Arnold and Eric, and Kerry opens her heart to Eetay-O-Wahnee. The Indians then round up the cattle, and as Purvis vows to help build a new village in which the Indians can live in peace, Bob lovingly takes Eetay-O-Wahnee's hand. *Dakota Indians. Hate. Indian agents. Indians of North America–Mixed blood. Racism. Settlers. Swedish Americans. Brothers. Cattlemen. Chases. Explosions. Fathers and daughters. Fathers and sons. Fires. Fistfights. Gunshot wounds. Half sisters. Indians of North America–Reservations. Murder. Poisoning. Romance. Sheriffs. Shootings. Wills. Wyoming.*

Note: According to a *HR* news item, in Mar 1956, Columbia purchased two stories by Les Savage, Jr. (pseudonym Larabie Sutter), "The Gun Witch of Wyoming" and "The White Squaw." Although the *SAB* lists *The Gun Witch of Wyoming* as the title of this film's source novel, that story apparently was never published, or was not published under that title.

Box 20 Oct 1956. DV 3 Oct 1956, p. 3. Exb 31 Oct 1956, p. 4242. FD 9 Oct 1956, p. 10. Har 3 Oct 1956, p. 3. HR 20 Mar 1956. HR 11 May 1956, p. 20. HR 18 May 1956, p. 16. HR 6 Oct 1956, p. 159. MPD 8 Oct 1956. MPHPD 6 Oct 1956, p. 99. Var 3 Oct 1956.

WHITE YOUTH (French Americans)

Universal Film Mfg. Co. *Dist* Universal Film Mfg. Co. Dec **1920** [©Universal Film Mfg. Co.; 1 Dec 1920; LP15870]. Si; b&w. 5 reels, 4,765 ft.

Pres Carl Laemmle. *Dir* Norman Dawn. *Scen* George C. Hull. *Story* Clara Beranger and Forrest Halsey. *Cam* Thomas Rea.

Cast: Edith Roberts (*Aline Ann Belame*), Alfred Hollingsworth (*Gneral Belame*), Thomas Jefferson (*François Cayetane*), Arnold Gregg (*Burton Striker*), Hattie Peters (*Calalou*), Lucas C. Luke (*Butler*), Sam Konnella (*Pierre*), Baldy Delmont (*Monsieur Le Moyne*), Phyllis Allen (*Madame Le Moyne*), Alida D. Jones (*Madame Martin*), Gertrude Pedlar (*Mother Superior*), Olga Mojean (*Madame La Roche*).

Drama. Convent reared Aline Ann Belame has never seen her grandfather General Belame. One day a letter arrives from him summoning Aline to his plantation in order to meet the husband he has chosen for her. Elated at the anticipation of having a home and a husband, Aline arrives at the plantation only to learn that her prospective fiancé Monsieur Cayetane, is a withered old man. Aline refuses the match and soon after falls in love with Burton Striker, who is installing a vault door on the General's wine cellar. Their plans for elopement discovered, Cayetane challenges Striker to a duel. In the shooting, Cayetane's bullet goes astray and breaks the General's prized pipe, motivating him to break his granddaughter's engagement. However, the General still withholds his blessings until Striker withholds the combination to the vault, at which time the General graciously concedes defeat. *Duels. French Americans. Grandfathers. Marriage–Arranged. Elopement. Plantations. Southerners.*

Note: Some scenes in this film were shot in New Orleans and other parts of Louisiana. An unidentified review praised the film for "painting the customs and manners of the French who reside in New Orleans and vicinity."

MPW 18 Dec 1920, p. 914. MPN 13 Nov 1920, p. 3749. MPN 18 Dec 1920, p. 4679. Wid's 19 Dec 1920, p. 7.

WHO IS TO BLAME? (Japanese Americans)

Triangle Film Corp. *Dist* Triangle Distributing Corp. 19 May **1918.** Si; b&w. 5 reels.

Dir Frank Borzage. *Story* E. Magnus Ingleton. *Cam* Pliny Horne.

Cast: Jack Abbe (*Taro San*), Jack Livingston (*Grant Barton*), Maude Wayne (*Marion Craig*), Lillian West (*Tonia Marsh*), Lillian Langdon (*Mrs. Craig*).

Drama. Charmed by the bright smile of Taro San, a Japanese rickshaw boy, Grant Barton takes the young man to the United States as his valet. Grant marries Marion Craig, but when she departs for California to visit her sick mother, he becomes enamored of Tonia Marsh, a vamp. Marion discovers them together and leaves Grant, whereupon Taro resolves to help his kind employer out of his difficulties. Persuading Tonia that he is a member of the imperial family of Japan, Taro pays court to the adventuress, and when Grant finds them in each other's arms, he immediately fires Taro. Grant and Marion are reconciled, while Taro sadly returns to Japan. *Impersonation and imposture. Japanese. Rickshaw drivers. Self-sacrifice. Valets. Vamps. California. Dismissal (Employment). Royalty. Separation (Marital).*

ETR 25 May 1918, p. 2002. MPN 1 Jun 1918, p. 3253, 3304. MPW 25 May 1918, p. 1191. MPW 1 Jun 1918, p. 1332. Var 24 May 1918, p. 34. Wid's 19 May 1918, pp. 21-22.

WHO IS YOUR SERVANT? *see* WHO'S YOUR SERVANT?

WHO WILL MARRY ME? (Italian Americans)

Bluebird Photoplays, Inc. *Dist* Bluebird Photoplays, Inc. 27 Jan **1919** [©Bluebird Photoplays, Inc.; 21 Jan 1919; LP13311]. Si; b&w. 5 reels.

Dir Paul Powell. *Scen* Fred Myton. *Story* Sonya Levien.

Cast: Carmel Myers (*Rosie Sanguinetti*), Thurston Hall (*Jerome Van Tyne*), William Dyer (*Karl Kremer*), Betty Schade (*Sylvia Stone*), Kingsley Benedict (*Richard Carr*), Marian Skinner (*Rosie's mother*), Adelaide Elliott (*Charlotte Van Tyne*), Burton Law (*Antonio Mosconi, also known as Tony the Barber*).

Drama. Rosie Sanguinetti's parents arrange her marriage, against her will, to Antonio Mosconi, "Tony the Barber." At the wedding ceremony in her Little Italy, New York neighborhood, Rosie flees to the settlement house where she meets Jerry Van Tyne, a wealthy young man who agrees, in a drunken state, to marry her. The next day Jerry realizes the consequences of the situation. Spurred on by Jerry's aunt, Rosie believes that she is not Jerry's equal, and goes home to her mother. Jerry later assumes the blame for a murder in order to protect Sylvia Stone, his former girlfriend. Rosie takes the stand at the trial, and lies that Jerry committed the crime to avenge her honor. Jerry is freed, and Rosie wins his admiration and love. *Class distinction. Italian Americans. Marriage–Forced by circumstances. Runaways. Self-sacrifice. Aunts. Drunkenness. Duplicity. Missions. Murder. New York City–Little Italy. Trials. Weddings.*

ETR 21 Dec 1918, p. 246. MPN 1 Feb 1919, p. 735, 755. MPN 8 Feb 1919, p. 922. MPW 1 Feb 1919, p. 675. Var 24 Jan 1919, p. 45. Wid's 26 Jan 1919, p. 7.

WHOOPEE (Native Americans)

Samuel Goldwyn, Inc. *Dist* United Artists Corp. 7 Sep **1930** [©Samuel Goldwyn; 1 Sep 1930; LP1584]. Sd (Movietone); col (Technicolor). 12 reels, 8,393 ft.

Pres Samuel Goldwyn and Florenz Ziegfeld. *Dir* Thornton Freeland. *Asst dir* H. B. Humberstone. *Scen* William Conselman. *Photog* Lee Garmes, Ray Rennahan and Gregg Toland. *Art dir* Richard Day. *Film ed* Stuart Heisler. *Cost des* John Harkrider. *Mus dir* Alfred Newman. *Dance dir* Busby Berkeley. *Sd eng* Oscar Lagerstrom.

Song(s): "Makin' Whoopee!" "Stetson," "My Baby Just Cares for Me" and "A Girl Friend of a Boy Friend of Mine," music by Walter Donaldson, lyrics by Gus Kahn; "I'll Still Belong to You," music by Nacio Herb Brown, lyrics by Edward Eliscu.

Source: Based on the play *Whoopee* by Walter Donaldson, Gus Kahn and William Anthony McGuire (New York, 4 Dec 1928) and the play *The Nervous Wreck* by Owen Davis (New York, 9 Oct 1923).

Cast: Eddie Cantor (*Henry Williams*), Eleanor Hunt (*Sally Morgan*), Paul Gregory (*Wanenis*), John Rutherford (*Sheriff Bob Wells*), Ethel Shutta (*Mary Custer*), Spencer Charters (*Jerome Underwood*), Chief Caupolican (*Black Eagle*), Albert Hackett (*Chester Underwood*), William H. Philbrick (*Andy McNabb*), Walter Law (*Judd Morgan*), Marilyn Morgan (*Harriett Underwood*), George Olsen and his Orchestra, Jeanne Morgan, Virginia Bruce, Muriel Finley, Ernestine Mahoney, Christine Maple, Jane Keithley, Mary Ashcraft, Georgia Lerch, Betty Stockton (*Showgirls*).

Musical comedy. Though Sally Morgan has long been in love with Wanenis, an Indian boy who lives near her father's ranch, she is obliged to become engaged to the sheriff while Wanenis is away being educated to the white man's ways. Unwilling to go through with the marriage, Sally prevails upon Henry Williams, an invalid living on the ranch, to take her away in his ramshackle Ford. With her father and the sheriff in pursuit, Sally and Henry run out of gas, but they steal gasoline from a car belonging to a family whose ranch they later go for food. When the family arrives, Henry, now the cook, disguises himself in blackface. Later they narrowly escape the sheriff and take refuge in an Indian reservation. Wanenis, believing that his race makes his love for Sally impossible, has abandoned white civilization, and Sally is about to be carried off by her father when it is discovered that Wanenis is a white, abandoned at birth; Sally's father now consents to the marriage. *Automobiles. Cooks. Courtship. Elopement. Indians of North America. Invalids. Racism. Ranches. Sheriffs.*

FD 5 Oct 1930. Var 8 Oct 1930, p. 22.

WHO'S TO BLAME? *see* **HER MOMENT**

WHO'S YOUR BROTHER? (Jewish Americans)
Curtiss Pictures Corp. *Dist* State Rights. Dec **1919**. Si; b&w. 6 reels.
Dir John G. Adolfi. *Story and scen* Robert Bronson Stockbridge. *Cam* Harry Keepers.
Cast: Edith Taliaferro (*Esther Field*), Frank Burbeck (*Stephen Field*), Paul Panzer (*Stephen Field, 25 years earlier*), E. Coit Albertson (*Dr. William Morris*), Herbert Fortier (*Robert E. Graham, Sr.*), Gladden James (*Robert Graham, Jr.*), Elizabeth Garrison (*Mrs. Robert Graham*), Elizabeth Kennedy (*The kid*), Edith Stockton (*Dorothy Graham*).
Drama. Stephen Field, a Jewish financier, takes great pleasure in philanthropic work at a community service center in the U.S. His daughter Esther devotes her time to entertaining returning soldiers in a canteen. When he reads in a newspaper about massacres of Jews and Armenians in Europe, and the suffering and starvation among other peoples there, Stephen remembers having lost his own wife and young son in a massacre years earlier. At the canteen, Esther meets Robert Graham, who suffers from fainting spells, the result of a war wound. Graham falls in love with Esther, much to the chagrin of his anti-Semitic father. Esther is also courted by the brilliant Jewish surgeon, William Morris. Esther's affection for Morris leads the jealous Graham to lash out at his rival with anti-Semitic invective even though Esther gently refuses Morris' marriage proposal. Graham loses control of his high-powered car due to a fainting spell, and the car goes over a precipice and turns over on top of him. Morris is the only person who can save his life, but the surgeon hesitates, fearing that failure would be interpreted as jealousy and thus compromise his professional integrity. Esther pleads with Morris to perform the operation, and he finally consents, sacrificing his own happiness for the woman he loves. The operation is proclaimed a surgical miracle, and Esther chooses to marry the man who performed that miracle. *Immigrants. Jews. Romantic rivalry. Self-sacrifice. Surgeons. War victims. Antisemitism. Armenians. Automobile accidents. Cossacks. Fathers and daughters. Humanitarianism. Massacres. Philanthropists. Turkey.*

Note: This film was the first production of the Curtiss Pictures Corp. It was re-released in 1920 by Equity Pictures Corp. under the title *Keep to The Right.* Sources disagree about the massacre of the Field family early in the film: *MPW* states that it was a Cossack massacre in Russia, while the Community Motion Picture Bureau says it occurred in Turkey by Turkish soldiers. A report from the Community Motion Picture Bureau noted, "All through the film were generous titles impressive of the need of brotherhood and brotherly love among men, suggesting that religion should be on a broad basis that would overlook racial and social boundaries and would consist primarily and solely of a love towards one's fellow men." According to *Wid's*, the film was endorsed by the New York Federation of Churches. On actress Edith Taliaferro, critic Helen Rockwell of *ETR* wrote, "She has a dazzling smile and a wistful expression that are as magnetic and as full of personality as Mary [Pickford]'s curls or Dorothy Gish's walk."
ETR 8 Nov 1919, p. 1973. MPN 13 Dec 1919, p. 4286. MPN 9 Oct 1920, p. 451. MPN 18 Dec 1920, p. 4670, 4683. MPW 20 Nov 1920, p. 387. NYMT 26 Oct 1919. Wid's 19 Oct 1919, p. 7.

WHO'S YOUR SERVANT? (Japanese Americans)
Dist Robertson-Cole Distributing Corp. 22 Feb **1920**. Si; b&w. 5 reels, 4,950 ft.
Prod Clarence Payne. *Scen* Julian Johnson.
Source: Based on the play *Hari Kari* by Julian Johnson (New York, 5 Dec 1913).
Cast: Lois Wilson (*Madeline Bancroft*), Yukio Aoyama (*Ito Natsume*), Andrew Robeson (*Admiral Bancroft*), Albert Morrison (*Capt. Norman Sharp*), William Scott (*Lt. Clifford Bruce*), Frances Burnham (*Dorothy Taylor*).
Drama. When Rear Admiral Bancroft discovers the plans missing for his new battleship, suspicion falls on Lt. Clifford Bruce, his daughter Madeline's suitor, who was seen climbing out of the Admiral's window. In reality, Bruce, attempting to keep his courtship with Madeline a secret, was retrieving a love letter that he had written to the Admiral's daughter. Madeline, suspecting Ito, the house servant, of stealing the plans, takes advantage of the fact that the servant is in love with her and visits his room that night. He shows her the plans which he boasts will bring him a fortune so that the two can elope. Madeline then attempts to gain possession of the papers, and in the ensuing struggle, Ito is stabbed to death. The supposition that he has committed "hari kari" avoids any further investigation, the plans are returned, and the lieutenant wins the consent of the admiral to marry Madeline. *Espionage. Letters. Robbery. Secret plans. United States. Navy. Hara-kiri. Japanese Americans. Self-defense. Servants.*

Note: This film was reviewed in *Var* under the title *Who Is Your Servant?*.
ETR 6 Mar 1920, p. 1442. MPN 14 Feb 1920, p. 1712-13. MPN 13 Mar 1920, p. 2518. MPN 27 Mar 1920, p. 2838. MPW 13 Mar 1920, p. 1841. MPW 31 Jun 1920, p. 690-91. Var 27 Feb 1920, p. 47. Wid's 14 Mar 1920, p. 17.

WHY BLAME ME? *see* **HER MOMENT**

WHY BRING THAT UP? (Racial impersonation)
Paramount Famous Lasky Corp. 12 Oct **1929**; New York premiere: 4 Oct 1929 [©Paramount Famous Lasky Corp.; 14 Sep 1929; LP766]. Sd (Movietone); b&w. 10 reels, 7,882 ft. [Also si; 6,036 ft.].
Dir George Abbott. *Adpt* Hector Turnbull. *Adpt and dial* George Abbott. *Story* Octavus Roy Cohen. *Titles* George Marion, Jr. *Photog* J. Roy Hunt. *Film ed* William Shea. *Rec eng* Harry D. Mills.
Song(s): "Do I Know What I am Doing While I'm in Love?" by Leo Robin and Richard A. Whiting; "Shoo Shoo Boogie Boo," by Leo Robin, Sam Coslow and Richard Whiting.
Cast: Charles E. Mack (*Charlie*), George Moran (*George*), Evelyn Brent (*Betty*), Harry Green (*Irving*), Bert Swor (*Bert*), Freeman Wood (*Powell*), Lawrence Leslie (*Casey*), Helen Lynch (*Marie*), Selmer Jackson (*Eddie*), Jack Luden (*Treasurer*), Monte Collins, Jr. (*Skeets*), George Thompson (*Doorman*), Eddie Kane (*Manager*), Charles Hall (*Tough*).
Comedy-drama. George's partner in vaudeville quits their act, claiming that Betty has broken his heart. George then teams up with Charlie, a stranded trouper, and Irving becomes their manager. Later, in New York, the "Two Black Crows" are starred in their own revue and save to build their own theater on Broadway. Betty comes to the theater with her lover, who poses as a cousin and induces George to hire her. She showers him with jewels and money. She tries to persuade George to invest in oil stock her lover is selling, and though their act is a success, Charlie fires Betty. When Charlie and Betty's lover quarrel, Charlie is injured. Realizing that he has been duped, George is called to the hospital, and in desperation he does bits of the act for Charlie, who, as a result, regains consciousness. *Chorus girls. Musical revues. New York City–Broadway. Racial impersonation. Singers. Vaudeville.*

Note: For information about George Moran and Charles Mack, the vaudeville and burlesque black-faced comedians, please see the entry above for the 1932 film *Hypnotized.*

WIEJSKIE WESELE (Polish language)
Paf. Pictures. **1941.** Sd; col. 4 reels. Polish language.
Mus prepared by Jan Dobiński. *Choral dir* Jan Lezon.
Cast: Paul Faut, Stefania Mentkowska, Marian Mossakowski, Marian Szafnicki, Genia Jakubczak, Edmund Kreglicki.
Documentary. [*Not viewed*]. A Polish village wedding, with traditional costumes, dances and songs, is depicted. The social life and customs of the village are depicted. *Poland. Village life. Weddings. Dancing. Songs.*
Note: An English translation of this film's title is *A Country Wedding.* Called the first Polish color film, it was made in Buffalo, NY, by Paf. Pictures, a New York corporation. Paf. received financial assistance from the city of Buffalo to make the picture, according to a May 1941 article in a Polish-language Chicago newspaper. Sets were constructed at Buffalo's St. John Kanty High School, and the cast included a number of actors and singers from Buffalo and other northern U.S. cities. Technical personnel were hired out of New York and Hollywood. An announcement for a Chicago showing of the film stated, "These beautiful Polish films should be seen by all Poles, old and young, especially the youngsters born in America to get to know better the true Polish customs." Proceeds from the May 1941 Chicago screenings went to the Polish Relief Fund for Polish war victims.
Dziennik Chicagoski 16 May 1941, p. 2. *Dziennik Chicagoski* 17 May 1941, p. 9. *Dziennik Związkowy (Zgoda)* 15 May 1941.

A WIFE BY PROXY (Irish Americans)
Columbia Pictures Corp. *Dist* Metro Pictures Corp. 6 Jan **1917** [©Columbia Pictures Corp.; 9 Jan 1917; LP9935]. Si; b&w. 5 reels.
Dir John H. Collins. *Scen* John H. Collins and/or and June Mathis. *Story* John B. Clymer and Charles A. Logue. *Cam* Arthur A. Cadwell.
Cast: Mabel Taliaferro (*"Jerry" McNairn*), Robert Walker (*Norton Burbeck*), Sally Crute (*Beatrice Gaden*), Fred Jones (*Frederick Gaden*), Yale Benner (*Howard Curtis*), George Melville (*Timothy McNairn*), Ricca Allen (*Scraggs, the housekeeper*), Jerome N. Wilson (*Guyler, Burbeck's attorney*), Ed Mack (*Flynn, the butler*).
Drama. Norton Burbeck's affection for adventuress Beatrice Gaden blinds him to the fact that Beatrice is in league with Norton's cousin Howard to deprive him of his inheritance. Under the terms of their uncle's will, the estate will revert to Howard if Norton does not marry within a certain period of time. Thinking that he is engaged to Beatrice, Norton believes he has fulfilled the terms of his legacy until Beatrice tearfully confesses that she is already married. The schemers are ultimately defeated, however, because Norton, on the advice of his lawyer, has protected his holdings by marrying Jerry McNairn, a young Irishwoman he had befriended when she was orphaned. As Jerry prepares to return to Ireland, Norton comes to the realization that he really loves her and declares his love for his wife by proxy. *Adventuresses. Conspiracy. Inheritance. Irish. Marriage by Proxy. Wills. Cousins. Lawyers. Orphans.*
Note: Sources differ concerning the scenarist of this film.
ETR 27 Jan 1917, p. 565. *MPN* 30 Dec 1916, p. 4200. *MPN* 6 Jan 1917, p. 43. *MPN* 20 Jan 1917, p. 441. *MPW* 13 Jan 1917, p. 280. *MPW* 20 Jan 1917, p. 358. *NYDM* 13 Jan 1917, p. 28. *Wid's* 18 Jan 1917, pp. 46-47.

WILD BEAUTY (Native Americans)
Universal Pictures Co., Inc. *Dist* Universal Pictures Co., Inc. 9 Aug **1946**; Prod: mid-May—early Jun 1946 [©Universal Pictures Co., Inc.; 21 Aug 1946; LP512]. Sd (Western Electric Recording); b&w. 59 or 61 min. PCA cert no. 11810.
Prod Wallace W. Fox. *Dir* Wallace W. Fox. [*Asst dir* Phil Bowles]. *Orig scr* Adele Buffington. *Scr* Dorcas Cochran. *Dir of photog* Maury Gertsman. *Art dir* Jack Otterson and Abraham Grossman. *Film ed* D. Patrick Kelley. *Set dec* Russell A. Gausman and Leigh Smith. *Gowns* Rosemary Odell. *Mus dir* Paul Sawtell. *Dir of sd* Bernard B. Brown. [*Sd*] *tech* Jess Moulin. *Hair stylist* Carmen Dirigo. *Dir of makeup* Jack P. Pierce.
Song(s): "My Country 'Tis of Thee," music by Henry Carey, lyrics by Samuel Francis Smith.
Cast: Don Porter [(*Dr. David Morrow*)], Lois Collier [(*Linda Gibson*)], Jacqueline de Wit [(*Sissy*)], Robert Wilcox [(*Gordon Madison*)], George Cleveland [(*Barney*)], Dick Curtis [(*John Andrews*)], Robert "Buzzy" Henry [(*Johnny*)], [Wild Beauty, a horse (*Wild Beauty*)], [Eva Puig (*Winnie*)], [Pierce Lyden (*Roy*)], [Roy Brent (*Gus*)], [Isabel Withers (*Mrs. Anderson*)], [Hank Patterson (*Ed*)].
Western. [*Print viewed*]. Eastern schoolteacher Linda Gibson and Sissy, her companion, arrive in Flagstaff, in the Arizona territory on the same day that Dr. David Morrow, the local physician, is asked by Johnny, an orphaned Indian boy, to care for an injured wild colt.

Though convinced that the colt will die, David agrees to treat the horse, which Johnny names "Wild Beauty." Later, David tells Linda and Sissy about the hard life the Indians have on the reservation, and that Linda must understand their way of life if she is to be a successful teacher there. Johnny soon nurses Wild Beauty back to health, in hopes that the young colt will help him "becomes friends" with the herd of wild horses living on the reservation. Linda later goes to Barney, Johnny's guardian, and insists that the storekeeper take Johnny's riding privileges away from him until the young boy begins attending school. The heartbroken Johnny then runs away from home, but David and Barney find the boy by searching the frontier for Wild Beauty, whom Johnny had previously reunited with his mother. David then returns to the reservation and insists that Linda tender her resignation, but the schoolteacher stays on after Johnny accepts her apology and agrees to go to school. Later, Gordon Madison, Linda's old boyfriend, arrives at the reservation to ask Linda to return to the East with him, though she is now practically engaged to David. After seeing Gordon kiss Linda, however, David mistakenly believes that she is in love with the Easterner. Meanwhile, Gordon and John Andrews, a local rancher, make plans to slaughter the herd of wild horses and use their hides in Gordon's shoe factory. Knowing that they cannot touch the horses while they remain on the Indian reservation, Andrews and his men secretly corral the wild horses onto his property. Johnny, however, senses that Wild Beauty is in trouble and rushes out of the classroom. Linda tells David and Barney about the boy's sudden departure, and they rush off after him. Johnny is shot by one of Andrew's cowboys as he approaches the herd, and is later discovered by David and Barney. Meanwhile, Wild Beauty breaks down the corral's gate and releases the wild herd. Andrews, who has ridden off to kill the wounded Johnny, attempts to shoot David, but is instead killed by the stampeding wild horses. David then returns to the reservation, beats Gordon unconscious, and puts the Easterner on the outgoing stage. David and Linda are then united, as are Johnny and Wild Beauty. *Horses. Indians of North America. Physicians. Schoolteachers. Youth. Arizona. Attempted murder. Cowboys. Dogs. Easterners. Fights. Gunshot wounds. Indians of North America-Reservations. Orphans. Rescues. Stagecoaches. Stampedes. Trading posts.*
Note: According to a *LAT* news item, portions of the film were shot on location in Red Rock Canyon, CA.
Box 17 Aug 1946. *DV* 9 Aug 1946, p. 3. *HR* 17 May 1946, p. 11. *HR* 9 Aug 1946, p. 3. *LAT* 30 Apr 1946. *MPHPD* 29 Jun 1946, p. 3076. *MPHPD* 17 Aug 1946, p. 3150.

THE WILD BULL'S LAIR (Native Americans)
R-C Pictures Corp. *Dist* Film Booking Offices of America. 28 Jun **1925** [©R-C Pictures Corp.; 28 Jun 1925; LP21661]. Si; b&w. 6 reels, 5,280 ft.
Dir Del Andrews. *Asst dir* Al Werker. *Scen* Marion Jackson. *Photog* Ross Fisher.
Source: Based on the short story "The Wild Bull's Lair" by Frank M. Clifton (publication undetermined).
Cast: Fred Thomson (*Dan Allen*), Catherine Bennett (*Eleanor Harbison*), Herbert Prior (*James Harbison*), Tom Carr (*Henry Harbison*), Frank Hagney (*Eagle Eye*), Frank Abbot (*Yuma*), Silver King (*Himself*).
Western. Eagle Eye, an embittered Indian college graduate, disguises himself as a white man and persuades James Harbison to create a new breed of cattle by crossing cows with bison. The first of the strain, a wild bull called Diablo, escapes from Harbison's ranch and goes to Skull Mountain, headquarters of a band of savage Indians led by Eagle Eye and dedicated to the destruction of the white man. Eagle Eye trains the bull to lead away the rancher's cattle and to gore anyone who attempts to stop him. Dan Allen is sent by the government to investigate and goes to the Harbison ranch, where he falls in love with Eleanor, the rancher's pretty daughter. Eagle Eye lures Harbison and his daughter to Skull Mountain and sets Diablo loose on them; Dan arrives and overcomes the bull. The Indians are subdued, and Dan marries Eleanor. *Bison, American. Bulls. Cattle. Horses. Indians of North America. Ranches.*
FD 2 Aug 1925. *MPW* 8 Aug 1925. *Var* 26 Aug 1925, p. 26.

THE WILD DAKOTAS (Native Americans, Arapaho)
Neufeld Productions. *Dist* Associated Film Releasing Corp. Feb **1956** [©Associated Film Releasing Corp.; 6 Apr 1956; LP6412]. Sd (Glen Glenn Sound Co.); b&w. 6,437 ft. 71-73 min. PCA cert no. 17877.

Prod Sigmund Neufeld. *Dir* Sam Newfield. *Asst dir* Herbert Glazer. *Scr* Thomas W. Blackburn. *Dir of photog* Kenneth Peach. *Film ed* Holbrook Todd. *Master of props* George Bahr. *Ward* Paul Burns. *Mus comp and cond by* Paul Dunlap. *Sd rec* Jack Lilly. *Makeup artist* Lee Greenway. *Prod mgr* Bert Sternbach.

Song(s): "The Wild Dakotas," composer undetermined.

Cast: Bill Williams [(*Jim Henry*)], Coleen Gray [(*Susan "Lucky" Ruth*)], Jim Davis [(*Aaron Baring*)], John Litel [(*Morgan Wheeler*)], Dick Jones [(*Mike McGeehee*)], John Miljan [(*Chief Antelope*)], Lisa Montell [(*Ruth Murphy*)], Stan Jolley [(*Tabor*)], Wally Brown [(*McGraw*)], Iron Eyes Cody [(*Redrock*)], Bill Dix [(*Wagon scout*)].

Western. [*Print viewed*]. On their way to settle in Powder Valley, a band of wagons led by stern wagon master Aaron Baring passes a string of Indian smoke signals. When young Mike McGeehee asks Baring to stop the wagons while one of the women delivers her baby, the despotic Baring refuses, earning the ire of Susan "Lucky" Ruth, a reformed riverboat gambler seeking to start a new life in the West. That night, as the settlers map out their claims on the valley, Jim Henry, a frontier scout sympathetic to the plight of the Indian, warns that the land belongs to the Arapaho and suggests that the settlers meet with Chief Antelope to negotiate a compromise. After Jim and Mike ride out to bring Antelope to meet with the settlers, Morgan Wheeler, one of the homesteaders, urges Baring to be fair with the Indians. Baring, who has staked out the best land in the center of town, is unyielding, however, and when Jim returns with Antelope, he warns that he will shoot any Indian within ten miles of the settlement. After the incensed Indians depart, Baring accuses Jim of being a traitor and orders him lashed to a wheel and whipped. The next morning, Baring becomes jealous of Susan's concern for Jim and the two men fight. After knocking Baring unconscious, Jim commandeers two horses and gallops away with Susan. Plotting revenge, Baring forges on with the wagons. One night, Mike, who has come to respect the Indians, overhears Baring discussing with Perkins, his henchman, how he fixed the drawing to assure that the two of them would be awarded prime land. Baring then outlines his plot to incite the cavalry to war by telling them that the Indians have kidnapped Susan. As Mike rides off to warn Jim, Antelope and several braves visit Jim's camp to inform him that they plan to attack the wagons and admonish him to leave the area. Soon after the Indians depart, Mike gallops into camp and relates Baring's nefarious plot. Led by Jim, Susan and Mike ride to the Arapaho encampment, but only the two men are admitted to a conference with the chiefs. After recounting Baring's scheme, Jim promises to depose the corrupt Baring and bring a new wagon leader to meet with the chiefs and restore peace. Antelope accepts Jim's proposal on the condition that Susan remain behind as a hostage. If Jim fails to return by two hours after the next dawn, Susan will be killed and the Arapaho will go to war. Leaving Susan in Antelope's hands, Jim and Mike reach the wagons just as Baring has gone to report Susan's kidnapping to the cavalry troop trailing the settlers. When Jim and Mike attempt to contact Wheeler, the voice of reason, Perkins captures them and ties them up. Upon finding Mike's hat beside his wagon, Wheeler becomes suspicious and discovers Mike and Jim bound and gagged. While Mike stays behind, Wheeler rides with Jim to the Arapaho camp. At daybreak, as the Indians rally for war, the cavalry rides to free Susan. Just as the troops, accompanied by Baring, reach the mouth of the Arapaho camp, Jim and Wheeler appear. When Jim charges Baring with treason, the two men fight and Jim knocks Baring unconscious. Slinging Baring's body over his shoulder, Jim delivers him to Antelope, who examines him and declares him dead. Susan, dressed in Indian garb, runs to embrace Jim and praises Antelope's kind treatment. With Wheeler's appointment as the new wagon master, Jim's bargain is fulfilled and peace is restored. *Arapaho Indians. Romantic rivalry. Scouts (Frontier). Treachery. Wagon trains. Gamblers. Land rights. United States. Army. Cavalry. Whips and whippings.*

Note: The film opens with the following voice-over narration: "The end of the war between the States left the American nation undivided and rich in public land. The great territory of the West lay open to those who would claim it. And they came, from every walk of life...white collar and homespun, law abiding and the lawless, rolling the wheels of their wagons into an unknown wilderness toward the far off homeland of the Plains Tribes—the wild Dakotas, the warlike Sioux and the proud Arapaho." Although the character played by Collen Gray is addressed as "Sue 'Lucky' Ruth" in the film's dialogue, she is listed as "Sue 'Lucky' Dunneen" in the film's production records.

THE WILD FAWN *see* **THE GOOD-BAD WIFE**

WILD GEESE (Swedish Americans)

Tiffany-Stahl Productions, Inc. 15 Nov **1927** [©Tiffany-Stahl Productions, Inc.; 26 Nov 1927; LP24698]. Si; b&w. 7 reels, 6,448 ft.

Prod supv L. L. Ostrow. *Dir* Phil Stone. *Scr* A. P. Younger. *Photog* Max Dupont, Earl Walker and Joseph Dubray. *Art dir* George E. Sawley. *Film ed* Martin G. Cohn.

Source: Based on the novel *Wild Geese* by Martha Ostenso (New York, 1925).

Cast: Belle Bennett (*Amelia Gare*), Russell Simpson (*Caleb Gare*), Eve Southern (*Judith Gare*), Donald Keith (*Sven Sandbo*), Jason Robards (*Mark Jordan*), Anita Stewart (*Lind Archer*), Wesley Barry (*Martin Gare*), Rada Rae (*Ellen Gare*), Austin Jewel (*Charlie Gare*), Evelyn Selbie (*Mrs. Klovatz*), D'Arcy Corrigan (*Mr. Klovatz*), Jack Gardner (*Skuli*), James Mack (*Parson*), Bert Sprotte (*Marshal*), Bodil Rosing (*Mrs. Sandbo*), Bert Starkey.

Melodrama. Twenty-five years ago, before her marriage to Minnesota farmer Caleb Gare, Amelia, then engaged to Mark Jordan, bore Mark's child out of wedlock when he was accidentally killed. Now, Caleb, with his merciless intolerance, uses this knowledge to dominate her as well as her other children: Martin, a soft-eyed youth of twenty-one; Judith, a spirited girl of nineteen; Ellen, a stupid, nearsighted girl of sixteen; and young Charlie, a hell-raising imp. Lind Archer, a young schoolteacher, comes to live with the family and becomes friends with Judith, though she abhors Caleb's tyranny; she soon falls in love with Mark Jordan, who works at the Klovatz farm and is actually Amelia's illegitimate son. Judith, who loves Sven Sandbo, longs to be free of her oppressive yoke and rebels against Caleb, causing her mother at last to show open defiance. To expose his wife's past, Caleb summons Mark Jordan to the house; on the night of the meeting, Caleb falls into quicksand, and they are all liberated by his death. *Bigotry. Family life. Farmers. Illegitimacy. Marriage. Minnesota. Quicksand. Schoolteachers. Swedish Americans.*

FD 17 Dec 1927. MPW 10 Dec 1927. NYT 5 Dec 1927, p. 26. Var 7 Dec 1927, p. 18.

THE WILD GIRL (Gypsies)

Eva Tanguay Film Corp.; Selznick Pictures. *Dist* Lewis J. Selznick Enterprises, Inc.; Selznick Pictures; Select Pictures Corp. Sep **1917** [©Eva Tanguay Film Corp.; 14 Nov 1917; LP11715]. Si; b&w. 5 reels.

Pres Harry Weber. *Dir* Howard Estabrook. *Story* George M. Rosener. *Cam* Frank G. Kugler.

Cast: Eva Tanguay (*Firefly*), Tom Moore (*Donald MacDonald*), Stuart Holmes, Valerie Bergere, Herbert Evans, Dean Raymond, John Davidson, Norah Cecile.

Drama. In a gypsy camp a dying stranger abandons a baby girl with a note explaining that on her eighteenth birthday, she is to inherit a Virginia estate. The gypsy chief, aware of the girl's value, instructs Sabia, the tribe's matron, to dress and rear her as a boy. Years later, while the tribe is traveling in Virginia, Vosho, the chief's son, discovers the true sex of the girl, now called Firefly, and demands to marry her. Forced into marriage, Firefly flees from the camp on her wedding night and meets up with Donald McDonald, a local newspaper editor. Donald, thinking that Firefly is a boy, hires her as an errand runner and she soon falls secretly in love with him. Eventually, she unites with her uncle and lives happily on his estate until Vosho shows up to claim her. After a hard fight, Donald rescues Firefly and jails Vosho, who is later freed by Firefly's jealous cousin. When she witnesses a scene between Donald and his secretary, Firefly, convinced that he does not love her, returns to the gypsy camp. With the aid of her uncle, Donald locates Firefly and declares his undivided love for her. *Editors. Gypsies. Inheritance. Male impersonation. Virginia. Cousins. Fights. Imprisonment. Infants. Jealousy. Marriage-Forced. Newspapers. Rescues. Secretaries. Uncles.*

Note: According to news items, this film marked the screen debut of Eva Tanguay, a popular vaudeville comedienne known as the "Bombshell of Joy" and the "Eccentric Comedienne." In mid-1916, however, Tanguay made a self-promoting feature called *Energetic Eva*, which may or may not have been released theatrically. Although Selznick Pictures appears as the producing company in the advertisements, Eva Tanguay's company filed for copyright. Earlier in 1917, Tanguay announced that she was joining forces with Selznick to produce starring vehicles for herself. The film was originally released as a Selznick picture, but with the formation of the Select Pictures Corp. and the dissolution of Selznick Pictures, the film was subsequently distributed by Select.

MPW 11 Aug 1917, p. 891. MPW 18 Aug 1917, p. 1098. MPW 22 Sep 1917, p. 1872. MPW 13 Oct 1917, p. 182 (ad insert). Wid's 8 Nov 1917, p. 718.

WILD HORSE CANYON (Latino)

Monogram Pictures Corp. *Dist* Monogram Pictures Corp. 21 Dec **1938**; Prod: began mid-Nov 1938 [©Monogram Pictures Corp.; 4 Jan 1939; LP8537]. Sd; b&w. 6 reels. 51 min. PCA cert no. 4917.

Prod Robert Tansey. *Dir* Robert Hill. *Asst dir* Eddie Saeta. *Orig scr* Robert Emmett. *Photog* Bert Longnecker. *Film ed* Howard Dillinger. *Sd* Cliff Ruberg.

Cast: Jack Randall (*Jack*), Dorothy Short (*Jean Hall*), Frank Yaconelli (*Lopez*), Dennis Moore (*Pete Hall*), Warner Richmond (*Travers*), Ed Cassidy (*Tom Hall*), Walter Long (*Rosco*), Charles King (*Red*), Earl Douglas (*Valdesto*), Hal Price.

Western. [*Not viewed*]. Jack and his pal Lopez ride the Wild Horse Trail in search of the rustlers who murdered Jack's brother. While riding from one ranch to another, Jack visits a ranch owned by Jean Hall and her father Tom. Unknown to Jean and Tom, their ranch foreman Travers is stealing their horses with the help of Mr. Hall's son Pete. After Jack saves Jean from one of the rustlers, Tom hires Jack and Lopez as ranch hands. When Rosco, one of the rustlers, offers to buy 400 horses from Tom, Jack becomes suspicious because his brother was killed just after selling his horses so that the purchasers could reclaim their money. Consequently, Jack decides to mark the bills with which Rosco purchases the herd. When Tom is shot and robbed on his way to town after collecting his money, Jack traces the marked money to Pete and Travers and accuses them of rustling. In response, the rustlers take Jack captive in a mountain cabin, but with the help of his faithful horse, Rusty, who unties him, Jack escapes. When Jack confronts the rustlers in town, Travers orders Pete to shoot him in cold blood, and when Pete hesitates, Travers kills Pete. Meanwhile, Lopez asks for help from his brother, the governor of Sonoma, and when Lopez and Jack identify Travers and his gang as the ones who killed Jack's brother, the gang is arrested. With his brother's killer brought to justice, Jack decides to stay and help Jean run the ranch. *Brothers and sisters. Horse thieves. Murder. Ranchers. Revenge. Cowboys. Escapes. Fathers and daughters. Governors. Mexicans. Outlaws. Ranch foremen. Rescues. Sisters.*

Note: The working title of this film was *Wild Horse Trail*. Modern sources add Sherry Tansey and Rusty the Wonder Horse to the cast.

FD 3 Jan 1939, p. 6. *HR* 19 Nov 1938, pp. 6-7. *MPD* 3 Jan 1939, p. 6. *MPH* 7 Jan 1939, p. 40. *Var* 18 Jan 1939, p. 12.

WILD HORSE MESA (Native Americans)

Paramount Publix Corp. *Dist* Paramount Publix Corp. 25 Nov **1932** [©Paramount Publix Corp.; 28 Nov 1932; LP3442]. Sd (Western Electric Noiseless Recording); b&w. 7 reels. 60 or 72.5 min. Passed by the National Board of Review. PCA cert no. 1414-R [31 Aug 1935].

Dir Henry Hathaway. *Scr* Harold Shumate and Frank Howard Clark. *Photog* Arthur Todd.

Source: Based on the novel *Wild Horse Mesa* by Zane Grey (New York, 1928).

Cast: Randolph Scott (*Chane Weymer*), Sally Blane (*Sandy Melberne*), Fred Kohler (*Rand*), Lucille La Verne ("*Ma*" ["*The General*"] *Melberne*), Charley Grapewin (*Sam Bass*), James Bush (*Bent Weymer*), Jim Thorpe (*Indian chief*), George F. Hayes (*Slack*), Buddy Roosevelt (*Horn*), E. H. Calvert (*Sheriff*).

Western. [*Print viewed*]. In Four Corners, outlaw Rand plans to rustle horses from the Indian reservation into a barbed wire corral. Cowboy Chane Weymer blows up the fence and warns Rand not to steal from the Indians. Intimidated, Rand leaves, but his barbed wire has caught and killed a young colt, angering its father, "Panquitch," leader of the wild horses. Rand involves Ma "The General" Melberne, owner of the general store, in his scheme to capture the horses, but does not tell her that it is illegal, or that the horses will be maimed by the barbed wire. That night Chane's brother Bent locks up the store, but is knocked out by Rand and his men, who rob the safe and frame Bent for the robbery. Later, without showing his face, Chane throws money into the store and claims responsibility for the crime, but eludes the sheriff. Later that evening, he returns to the store and talks with Sandy, the General's daughter who is in love with Bent, and finds a piece of a pearl-handled gun. The General sells her store and with her brother, Sam Bass, Sandy and Bent, joins Rand for the wild horse roundup. In the desert, Sandy watches as Chane tries to capture Panquitch, but when he sees she is in the way of a stampede, he gives up Panquitch to rescue her. Since Sally has hurt her ankle, he takes her to an Indian camp where she spends the night. Chane returns her to Rand's camp the next day, and is chagrined to discover that Bent

and Sally are engaged, but stays at the camp until nightfall. In the meantime, Rand tries to turn Bent against his brother, and plots to kill Chane and plant some of the stolen money on him. After Chane matches the piece from the pearl-handled gun to Rand's gun, they fight. They "jail" Rand in the barbed wire, while the herd of horses is sent toward him by his own men, who are unaware of his situation. Rand frees himself, but Panquitch chases him until he falls off a cliff and dies. Later, the Indians gift Chane with Panquitch, but he sets him free after Sally promises to marry him if Panquitch can return to his mate. *Brothers. Duplicity. Frame-ups. Horses. Indians of North America. Rustlers. Deserts. Engagements. Falls from heights. Family relationships. Fights. Firearms. General stores. Robbery. Romantic rivalry. Roundups. Self-sacrifice. Sheriffs.*

Note: According to the copyright synopsis, "Rand" kills "Bent" just before he is killed by "Panquitch." Neither the viewed film nor the script, however, suggests that "Bent" is killed, although he does not reappear at the end of the film. According to copyright records, the film was shot on location near Flagstaff, AZ, and used 350 Navajo Indians as extras. Paramount previously made an adaptation of Grey's novel in 1925, which was directed by George B. Seitz and starred Jack Holt and Noah Beery (see *AFI Catalog of Feature Films, 1921-30*; F2.6371).

HR 10 Nov 1932, p. 3. *Var* 17 Jan 1933, p. 15.

WILD HORSE MESA (Latino)

RKO Radio Pictures, Inc. *Dist* RKO Radio Pictures, Inc. 13 Nov **1947**; Prod: late Jul—early Aug 1947 [©RKO Radio Pictures, Inc.; 19 Nov 1947; LP1334]. Sd (RCA Sound System); b&w. 5,445 ft. 60-61 min. PCA cert no. 12629.

Prod Herman Schlom. *Dir* Wallace A. Grissell. [*Asst dir* John Pommer]. *Scr* Norman Houston. *Dir of photog* Frank Redman. *Art dir* Albert S. D'Agostino and Lucius O. Croxton. *Film ed* Desmond Marquette. *Set dec* Darrell Silvera and Adolph Kuri. *Mus dir* C. Bakaleinikoff. *Mus* Paul Sawtell. *Sd* Jean L. Speak and Roy Granville.

Source: Based on the novel *Wild Horse Mesa* by Zane Grey (New York, 1928).

Cast: TIM HOLT [(*Dave Jordan*)], Nan Leslie [(*Sue Melhern*)], Richard Martin [(*Chito Rafferty*)], Richard Powers [(*Hod Slack*)], Jason Robards [(*Pop Melhern*)], Tony Barrett [(*Jim Horn*)], Harry Woods [(*Jay Olmstead*)], William Gould [(*Marshal Bradford*)], Robert Bray [(*Tex*)], Richard Foote [(*Rusty*)], Frank Yaconelli [(*Clemente*)].

Animal, Western. [*Print viewed*]. Confident they know the location of a herd of wild horses, Pop Melhern and his daughter Sue have hired a group of cowboys to help them round up the animals. When their search yields nothing, cowboy Hod Slack demands that Pop pay him and the other men immediately, but Dave Jordan, a hand who is in love with Sue, rallies the men to continue. Dave and his sidekick, Chito Rafferty, then stumble on the powerful stallion Panquich, who leads them to the rest of the enormous herd. As the cowboys are rounding up the horses, rival horse trader Jim Horn, who is working for businessman Jay Olmstead, arrives with his men. Horn tries to steal the horses at gunpoint, but loses the ensuing fight. The next morning, Slack traps Panquich in a makeshift barb-wire corral. Seeing the proud animal torn by the wire, an enraged Dave brawls with Slack, who is then fired by Pop. After Slack vows revenge, Dave comforts Panquich and prepares to break him. Horn, meanwhile, reports Pop's find to Olmstead, and the crooked Olmstead devises a plan whereby he can steal Pop's horses. He offers Pop $32,000 for the herd, then, while accompanying him back to the horse camp, murders him with the butt of his gun and steals his cash. Before Olmstead can flee, Slack, who has been following him from town, appears and blackmails him into making him his partner. Back at the horse camp, Sue realizes that Panquich cannot be tamed by Dave and sets him free. Olmstead then rides up and, presenting his bill of sale, demands the horses. Suspicious of Olmstead, Dave refuses to turn over the herd until he hears from Pop. Dave and Chito soon find Pop's abandoned body and also discover a button lying nearby that came from a gun handle. Sure that the button fits in the murder weapon, Dave rides to town and confronts Horn and Slack in the saloon. An angry Olmstead arrives with the marshal, who, while sympathetic to Dave's position, insists that he needs more evidence against Olmstead. Determined to obtain that evidence, Dave breaks into Olmstead's office that night and is discovered by the businessman. During the ensuing scuffle, Dave retrieves Olmstead's gun and knocks his foe unconscious. After Dave fits the button into the butt of Olmstead's gun, he tells Sue that he has found her father's killer. At the same time, however, Slack, who

has witnessed the fight, tells Olmstead that he should flee town immediately and then tricks him into opening his safe. Slack then kills Olmstead and steals his money. The next morning, the marshal arrests Dave for Olmstead's murder, but Chito, aware that Slack is planning to raid the camp, soon breaks Dave out of jail. Dave and Chito arrive at the camp in time to warn Sue and her cowboys, and together they confront Slack and his gun-wielding gang. After the ensuing gunfight reaches an impasse, Slack tries to charge Sue and Dave, but Dave counters by causing the herd to stampede. Panquitch then appears and starts to trample the terrified Slack. The subdued Slack is arrested by the marshal, who has since found out that Dave's gun did not kill Olmstead, and Sue and Dave's happy future is finally assured. As Sue and Dave watch, Panquitch returns to the wilderness. *Cowboys. Frame-ups. Horse traders. Murder. Robbery. Wild horses. Blackmail. Businessmen. Cruelty to animals. Dismissal (Employment). Fathers and daughters. Fights. Firearms. Gunfights. Jailbreaks. Marshals. Mexican Americans. Revenge. Romance. Roundups. Stampedes.*

Note: The opening title card reads: "RKO Radio Pictures, Inc. presents Tim Holt in Zane Grey's *Wild Horse Mesa*." Grey's novel may have been first published in a magazine, but no information regarding this publication has been found. According to *HR*, the film was shot in Lone Pine, CA, and at RKO's studio ranch in Encino, CA. In 1925, George B. Seitz directed Noah Berry and Jack Holt, Tim Holt's father, in a silent Paramount version of Grey's story, which was titled *Wild Horse Mesa* (see *AFI Catalog of Feature Films, 1921-30;* F2.6371). In 1932, Henry Hathaway directed a second Paramount version, also called *Wild Horse Mesa,* starring Randolph Scott and Verna Hillie (see below). *Box* 22 Nov 1947. *FD* 21 Nov 1947, p. 6. *HR* 23 Jul 1947, p. 4. *HR* 25 Jul 1947, p. 19. *HR* 30 Jul 1947, p. 14. *HR* 1 Aug 1947, p. 15. *HR* 14 Nov 1947, p. 3. *Var* 19 Nov 1947, p. 8.

WILD HORSE STAMPEDE *see* **KING OF THE WILD HORSES**

WILD HORSE TRAIL *see* **WILD HORSE CANYON**

WILD IS THE WIND (Italian Americans, Basque Americans)
Paramount Pictures Corp. *Dist* Paramount Pictures Corp. Feb **1958**; Los Angeles premiere: 11 Dec 1957; *Prod:* 1 May—21 Jun 1957 [©Paramount Pictures Corp., Hal B. Wallis & Joseph H. Hazen; 1 Feb 1958; LP9831]. Sd (Westrex Recording System); b&w; VistaVision High Fidelity. 10,265 ft. 110 or 114 min. PCA cert no. 18652.

Pres HAL B. WALLIS. *Prod* Hal B. Wallis. *Assoc prod* Paul Nathan. *Dir* George Cukor. *Asst dir* D. Michael Moore. *2d unit dir* Arthur Rosson. *Screen story and scr* Arnold Schulman. *Dir of photog* Charles Lang, Jr. *2d unit photog* Loyal Griggs. *Spec photog eff* John P. Fulton. *Process photog* Farciot Edouart. *Art dir* Hal Pereira and Tambi Larsen. *Ed supv* Warren Low. *Set dec* Sam Comer and Arthur Krams. *Cost* Edith Head. *Mus comp and cond* Dimitri Tiomkin. *Sd rec* Gene Merritt and Winston Leverett. *Makeup supv* Wally Westmore. *Hair style supv* Nellie Manley.

Song(s): "Wild Is the Wind," music by Dimitri Tiomkin, lyrics by Ned Washington, sung by Johnny Mathis; "Scapricciatiello," music by Fernando Albano, lyrics by Pacifico Vento, sung by Anna Magnani.

Source: Based on the novel *Furia* by Vittorio Nino Novarese (publication undetermined).

Cast: ANNA MAGNANI [(*Gioia*)], ANTHONY QUINN [(*Gino*)], ANTHONY FRANCIOSA [(*Bene*)], Dolores Hart [(*Angie*)], Joseph Calleia [(*Alberto*)], Lili Valenty [(*Teresa*)], [James Flavin (*Wool buyer*)], [Dick Ryan (*Priest*)], [Iphigenie Castiglioni, Joseph Vitale, Ruth Lee, Frances Morris, Fern Barry, Ken Hooker, Max Power, Courtland Shepard, Robert R. Stephenson, Jeane Wood, Trude Wyler (*Party guests*)].

Domestic, Drama. [*Print viewed*]. When Gino, a 'wealthy but lonely sheep rancher in Nevada, decides to marry his deceased wife's sister Gioia, she emigrates from Italy and immediately moves into her new husband's home. Gino's brother Alberto, sister-in-law Teresa, twenty-one-year-old daughter Angie and Bene, a Basque sheepherder whom Gino treats as an adopted son, welcome Gioia into the home with kindness and understanding, but Gino, who is used to exerting control over people, soon begins to criticize her for speaking Italian and for not being more like her sister. Several months after Gioia's arrival, she accompanies Gino and Bene on a tour of the rancher's property. From the jeep, Gino sees a herd of wild horses grazing on his land, and when he pulls out a rifle to kill one of them, Gioia approaches the animal and cautions it to run away. Deeply moved by the sight of the magnificent horses, Gioia asks Gino if she might have one, but when he later ropes a horse to the ground for her, she is horrified and begs him to set the beast free. Exasperated, Gino knocks

her down, and Bene, bending over her to calm her down, looks into her eyes and then, embarrassed, backs away. Later Teresa and Gioia argue about who should run the household, and Gioia complains that she has nothing to do. Soon afterwards, Gioia tries to break the wild horse herself. When the horse rears over her, Bene leaps over the fence, protectively backs Gioia into a corner, and impulsively kisses her. Shocked, Gioia slaps him and then wanders away in a daze. A week later, Gino has an elaborate birthday party for Gioia, but after Gino, raising his glass to toast his wife, calls her by her dead sister's name, Gioia, highly offended, locks him out of their bedroom. Gino, unaware of his blunder, angrily departs for Boston to visit Angie at college. While Gino is away, the lambing season begins, and after Bene and Gioia help the hired hands to deliver the little animals, Bene follows Gioia into the barn and kisses her passionately. The lovers meet often during the following weeks, and on the night before Gino comes home, Gioia visits Bene in his room. The next morning, Teresa, who knows about the affair, confronts Gioia, who defiantly declares that Bene loves her and that the two of them plan to tell Gino and go away together. Gioia finds Bene tending the sheep and the couple embraces just as Gino walks over the hill. Gino strikes Bene and accuses him of betrayal, whereupon Bene, deeply ashamed, declares that he can no longer bear to look at Gioia. Bene leaves the ranch, and Gioia, realizing that her lover has abandoned her, prepares to return to Italy. Before driving her to the airport, Alberto tries to convince Gino that in trying to force Gioia to assume his dead .wife's personality, he has never given Gioia a chance to be herself. Gino angrily orders his brother from the house, but later, he finds Gioia at the airport and asks her forgiveness. After Gino declares his love for Gioia, she takes his hand, and the two return home. *Betrayal. Immigrants. Italian Americans. Marriage. Obsession. Sheep ranchers. Widowers. Airports. Basque Americans. Birthdays. Brothers. College students. Dogs. Drunkenness. Forgiveness. Infidelity. Loneliness. Nevada. Sheep. Sisters-in-law. Wild horses.*

Note: The working titles of this film were *Furia, Obsession* and *A Woman Obsessed.* According to a *DV* news story, producer Hal Wallis signed Anna Magnani to star in a film on her condition that it would be a remake of *Furia,* a 1946 Italian film, based on an Italian novel of the same name by Vittorio Nino Novarese. That film, which starred Isa Pola and Rossano Brazzi, was directed by Magnani's then-husband, Goffredo Alessandrini, Wallis showed the film to a number of screenwriters, including Arnold Schulman, who wrote the final picture, but none of the resulting scripts were acceptable to Wallis. A May 1956 *HR* news item states that Eugene Frenke, who owned a screenplay by Philip Yordan based on *Furia,* signed a deal with Wallis to produce the film starring Magnani. It is not known if Frenke was involved with the final film. Schulman, in the *DV* news story, states that he later presented an original idea to Wallis, through his agent, which bore no similarity to *Furia* in "line of dialogue, incident or character," and that idea became the basis for *Wild Is the Wind.* Although Schulman's subsequent contract stated that he would adapt *Furia,* Wallis, in Jan 1957, publicly stated that Magnani would not appear in *Furia,* and that Schulman's work was an original screenplay. Following production, Wallis submitted credits for the film to Paramount, the distributor, listing Schulman with original screenplay; however, Paramount's legal department, recalling that Wallis' original contract with Magnani required that one of the writers of *Furia* be given credit, insisted upon this to protect themselves. Wallis then encouraged Schulman to ask the Screen Writers' Guild to arbitrate. Information at the AMPAS Library states that the Guild decided that because there had been source material, a credit reading, "Based on a story by Vittorio Nino Novarese," should be given to the Italian writer of the novel, and that Schulman should be credited with screen story and screenplay. The AMPAS Library information also states that Novarese's name was dropped from the advertising. A summary of the Italian film reveals that the plot of the earlier film does bear some resemblance to that of *Wild Is the Wind,* in that the Italian film deals with an extra-marital affair between the wife of a horse breeder and her husband's "stud-keeper."

John Sturges was originally hired to direct *Wild Is the Wind*; however, on 25 Mar 1957, a week before shooting was to begin, he withdrew from the project due to illness, according to *DV.* George Cukor, who took over direction, in a modern interview stated that Sturges left the project to replace Fred Zinnemann on *The Old Man and the Sea.* A biography on Cukor states that Sturges left when it became apparent that the film would be more of a love story than an action picture. Most of the exteriors were shot on a sheep ranch in Gardnerville, NV, and some shooting was done at the Reno airport. The film's premiere was a charity benefit for City of Hope. *DV* reported in Jan 1958 that Paramount protested the "adults only" ruling of the Chicago censor, because of the scenes showing the birth of a lamb, and of "Gioia" walking into "Bene's" bedroom. Hal Wallis, in his autobiography, states that Bill Gray was the production manager. The onscreen credit for the title song, which was nominated for an Academy Award, notes that singer Johnny Mathis was a "Columbia Records Artist." Anna Magnani and Anthony Quinn received Academy Award nominations for their performances.

AmCin Jan 1958, pp. 24-5, 54-6. *Box* 14 Dec 1957. *Cosmopolitan* Feb 1958. *Cue* 14 Dec 1957. *DV* 30 Oct 1957, p. 1, 19. *DV* 26 Mar 1957. *DV* 11 Dec 1957, p. 3. *DV* 20 Jan 1958.

Exb 25 Dec 1957, pp. 4417-18. *FD* 11 Dec 1957, p. 6. *Har* 14 Dec 1957, pp. 198-99. *HCN* 12 Dec 1957. *HR* 1 May 1956. *HR* 27 Aug 1957. *HR* 11 Dec 1957, p. 3. *LAEx* 14 Jan 1957. *LAEx* 12 Dec 1957. *LAT* 5 Jun 1957. *LAT* 12 Dec 1957. *Life* 16 Dec 1957, p. 73. *MPD* 11 Dec 1957. *MPHPD* 14 Dec 1957, p. 641. *New Yorker* 21 Dec 1957. *NYT* 12 Dec 1957, p. 35. *SatRev* 28 Dec 1957. *Time* 16 Dec 1957. *Var* 11 Dec 1957, p. 6.

WILD RIVER (African Americans)

Twentieth Century-Fox Film Corp. *Dist* Twentieth Century-Fox Film Corp. May **1960**. New York opening: 26 May 1960; Prod: 15 Oct 1959–4 Jan 1960 [©Twentieth Century-Fox Film Corp.; 22 May 1960; LP16409]. Sd (Westrex Recording System); col (DeLuxe); CinemaScope. 9,874 ft. 105, 110 or 115 min. PCA cert no. 19552.

Prod Elia Kazan. *Dir* Elia Kazan. *Asst dir* Charles Maguire. *Scr* Paul Osborn. *Dir of photog* Ellsworth Fredricks. *Color consultant* Leonard Doss. *Art dir* Lyle R. Wheeler and Herman A. Blumenthal. *Film ed* William Reynolds. *Set dec* Walter M. Scott and Joseph Kish. *Cost* Anna Hill Johnstone. *Mus comp and cond* Kenyon Hopkins. *Sd* Eugene Grossman and Richard Vorisek. *Makeup* Ben Nye. *Hair styles* Helen Turpin.

Source: Based on the novels *Mud on the Stars* by William Bradford Huie (New York, 1942) and *Dunbar's Cove* by Borden Deal (New York, 1957).

Cast: MONTGOMERY CLIFT [(*Chuck Glover*)], LEE REMICK [(*Carol Baldwin*)], Jo Van Fleet [(*Ella Garth*)], Albert Salmi [(*Hank Bailey*)], J. C. Flippen [(*Hamilton Garth*)], James Westerfield [(*Cal Garth*)], Barbara Loden [(*Betty Jackson*)], Frank Overton [(*Walter Clark*)], Malcolm Atterbury [(*Sy Moore*)], [Pat Hingle (*Narrator*)], [Robert Earl Jones (*Sam Johnson*)], [Bruce Dern (*Jack Roper*)], [Big Jeff Bess (*Joe John Garth*)], [Judy Harris (*Barbara Baldwin*)], [Jim Menard (*Jim Baldwin, Jr.*)], [James Steakley (*Mayor Tom Maynard*)], [Patricia Perry (*Mattie*)], [John Dudley (*Todd*)], [Alfred E. Smith (*Thompson*)], [Mark Menson (*Winters*)], [C. C. L. Wray (*Justice of the peace*)], [Edna Snapp (*Wife of justice of the peace*)], [Ross Apperson (*Attorney*)], [Mike Dodd (*Sheriff*)], [Mark Anthony (*Night clerk*)], [David Ferrell], [Earl Williamson], [James Hampton], [Donna Carnegie], [James Campbell].

Social, Drama. [*Print viewed*]. As part of President Franklin D. Roosevelt's New Deal, Congress creates the Tennessee Valley Authority in May 1933. The mandate of the TVA is to stop the deadly flooding of the Tennessee River and bring progress to the poverty stricken area through the construction of a series of dams. Chuck Glover, an idealistic TVA employee, arrives in a small Tennessee town to head the TVA's land purchasing office, where he will supervise relocation and land clearing operations. Chuck's first task is to convince the elderly Ella Garth, matriarch of a large family which has lived on an island in the river for generations, to sell her land to the government. Ignoring the "TVA Keep Off" signs, Chuck crosses the river to Garth Island, but Ella refuses to speak to him. Hoping Ella's three grown sons can help, Chuck approaches them, but when he clumsily suggests that Ella might be senile, Joe John Garth tosses him into the river. That evening, Joe John comes to town to apologize to Chuck and relay the message that Ella will receive him the following day. When Chuck returns to the island, he finds Ella, surrounded by her black field hands and their families, railing against Roosevelt's New Deal. To illustrate her situation, Ella pretends to attempt to force Sam Johnson, an elderly field hand, to sell her his beloved hunting dog. After making her point, Ella, who is not interested in the modern conveniences the dam will bring, declares that she cannot be forced to sell her land because to do so would be "against nature." Noticing that Ella's workers are idle and completely dependent upon her generosity for their survival, Chuck takes Sam aside and asks him to bring the men to the TVA office to discuss employment possibilities. Chuck also appeals to Ella's granddaughter, Carol Baldwin, a young and lonely widow with two small children, who moved to the island after the death of her husband. Although she is sure that Ella will die if forced to leave her land, Carol realizes that progress is inevitable and promises to help Chuck, to whom she is attracted. Carol reveals to Chuck that she is not in love with Walter Clark, the older man she is expected to marry, and after spending a night together in the house Carol once shared with her husband, Chuck and Carol become romantically involved. When Chuck hires local black laborers, including Ella's field hands, to work on the TVA's land-clearing operation, he arouses the anger of some of the locals. Sy Moore, a prominent businessman, urges Chuck to create segregated work crews and pay the black workers less than the whites, but Chuck flatly refuses to maintain such inequities, leading Moore to warn of

retaliation by less reasonable townspeople. Ella's workers and their families pack up and leave the island, and soon even Ella's sons realize that it is time to go. Ella remains on the island alone, except for the loyal Sam, who refuses to leave her. Carol begs her grandmother to leave, but Ella, who knows that Carol is in love with Chuck, angrily rejects her pleas. Walter Clark, Carol's fiancé, is alerted to Chuck's relationship with Carol by Hank Bailey, a cotton farmer who wants to take revenge on Chuck because one of his black workers left to take advantage of the higher wages offered by the TVA. Bailey enlists Clark's aid in getting Chuck away from Carol and back to his hotel room, where Bailey is waiting, but at the last minute, Clark warns Chuck. After Chuck refuses to be bullied by Bailey, who wants to be compensated for the work lost after he nearly beat his field hand to death for working for the TVA, Bailey knocks Chuck to the ground and picks his pockets. The following day, Chuck is phoned by his superiors in Washington, who tell him that time is running out and he must contact the U.S. Marshal to begin eviction proceedings against Ella. Hamilton and Cal Garth approach Chuck to propose that they sell the land themselves after having their mother declared incompetent. However, Chuck, who now understands and greatly admires Ella's pride and dignity, is disgusted with their plan and declares that he would rather have Ella removed with a gun to her head. Chuck reluctantly asks the marshal to remove Ella the next day, then goes to the island to make one last attempt to convince her to leave on her own. Even though she knows that the island will soon be under water, Ella steadfastly refuses to leave, and as Chuck heads back to the ferry, he notices that the faithful Sam continues to plow the fields. Chuck, saddened by Ella's plight and depressed by his part in it, returns to Carol's house, where Carol begs him to take her with him when he leaves, but Chuck is afraid of the emotions Carol arouses in him and is unable to give her an answer. As Carol bursts into sobs over Chuck's ambivalence, Clark arrives to warn them that the town thugs, led by Bailey, are gathering outside. As the sheriff watches from the sidelines, the crowd vandalizes Carol's home and Chuck's car. Proclaiming that he will not be run out of town, Chuck confronts Bailey, but is quickly knocked out. Carol then attacks Bailey with her fists and when Bailey knocks her down, the sheriff finally intercedes. After complimenting Carol on her fighting skills, Chuck proposes and they get married that night. The following day, Chuck and Carol accompany the marshal to Ella's island. As Ella's former workers look on, the marshal reads the eviction notice, after which the silent Ella walks to the ferry accompanied by the sounds of ax blows and falling trees. At her modern new home, Ella sits on the front porch, staring at the river and refusing to speak. A short time later, as workers finish clearing the island and prepare to burn down her farmhouse, Ella passes away. Once his work is done, Chuck and his new family fly out of the valley, first past Garth Island, now a tiny speck in a man-made lake, and then over the powerful new dam. *Aged women. Love affairs. New Deal, 1933-1939. Tennessee. United States–History–Social life and customs. African Americans. Family relationships. Floods. Idealism. Mayors. Northerners. Progress. Racism. Rivers. Romantic rivalry. Rural life. Segregation. United States–South. Widows.*

Note: The working titles for this film were *Mud on the Stars, Time and Tide, The Swift Season* and *As the River Rises.* When initial grosses for the film fell below Twentieth Century-Fox's expectations, the title was temporarily changed to *The Woman and the Wild River* to accompany an advertising campaign emphasizing the love affair between Montgomery Clift's and Lee Remick's characters. Both William Bradford Huie's *Mud on the Stars* and Borden Deal's *Dunbar's Cove* examined the impact of progress on the rural South in the decades preceding World War II. *Wild River* was the first film based on a work by Huie, whose novels had earlier been deemed too controversial for the screen. In a *NYT* interview dated Feb 1960, Huie noted that six films based on his work were currently in production, including *Wild River*, a situation made possible by "the recent liberalization of the industry's self-censorship code."

The film's prologue consists of black and white footage of a raging flood and the devastation left in its wake, followed by a newsreel-style interview with a survivor. An offscreen narrator provides the film's historical background, stating that on 18 May 1933, Congress created the Tennessee Valley Authority (TVA), a massive public works program designed to end the loss of life and property caused by the overflowing of the Tennessee River. According to a modern source, the black and white opening footage is taken from Pare Lorenz's 1930 documentary, *The River.* Although reviews for *Wild River* list Robert Earl Jones's character as "Ben," his character's name in the film is "Sam Johnson." This film marked Bruce Dern's motion picture debut.

DV news items dated Aug 1957 and Sep and Oct 1958 reported that first Ben Maddow and then Calder Willingham had been signed to adapt *Mud on the Stars* for Elia Kazan. However, these writers are not credited onscreen and the

extent of their participation in the finished film has not been determined. A modern source reports that Kazan had hoped to write the script himself, but after a number of unsuccessful drafts, worked closely with Maddow and Willingham before hiring Paul Osborn. Nine drafts of the script were written and additional working titles reportedly included *God's Valley*, *The Coming of Spring* and *New Face in the Valley*. According to *DV* and *HR* news items dated Mar 1959, Marilyn Monroe was scheduled to play the female lead. In his memoirs, Kazan recounted that Twentieth Century-Fox executives urged him to hire Monroe, an idea he called "absurd." Kazan added that he never considered anyone for the role but Lee Remick, whom he had directed in his 1956 film *A Face in the Crowd*.

Wild River was shot entirely on location in Tennessee, in the towns of Cleveland, where the cast and crew were lodged, and Charleston, and on Lake Chickamauga and the Hiwassee River. The large set used for the Garth farmhouse took two months to construct at a cost of $40,000 and was subsequently burnt down for one of the film's final scenes. Eighty percent of the film's approximately fifty speaking parts were filled by locals with no previous acting experience. According to an article published in *LAMirror-News* in Nov 1959, Kazan sparked a controversy in Cleveland after he hired extras from a slum known as "Gum Hollow" to play Depression-era Southerners. A number of prominent townspeople were angered by Kazan's casting choice and allegedly claimed that the "white trash" of Gum Hollow did not accurately depict the area's Depression unemployed. Kazan reportedly had to reshoot a few scenes, this time using "respectable, legitimate unemployed" in place of the "squatters." According to information in the file on the film in the AMPAS Library, during filming, Lee Remick's husband, television producer William Colleran, was in a serious auto accident and Remick returned to Los Angeles, causing production to shut down for one week. That delay, coupled with bad weather, put the shoot one month behind schedule.

Wild River received a number of positive reviews and was voted eighth runner-up for best picture of 1960 by the National Board of Review. A number of critics, however, felt that the romantic plot distracted viewers from the film's powerful social themes, while the *HR* review declared that *Wild River*'s exploration of racial conflict "put the real story out of focus." Other reviewers focused their criticism on Clift, with *Films in Review* declaring that Clift was "no longer capable of acting" and that "his tense form and visage devitalize[d] every scene he [was] in." In his memoirs, Kazan termed the film a commercial "disaster" and placed part of the blame for its poor showing at the box office on Twentieth Century-Fox, which, Kazan alleged, did not distribute the film widely and pulled it too quickly from the theatres. Nevertheless, the film remained one of Kazan's favorites and has received praise from modern critics, one of whom termed it Kazan's "finest and deepest film."

According to a modern source, Kazan's earliest inspiration for *Wild River* came after a visit to Tennessee in the mid-thirties and a stint working for the Department of Agriculture in 1941. In his autobiography, Kazan stated that he had planned for many years to make a film which would be "an homage to the New Deal," but that by the time he began working on the script in 1955, he had developed sympathy for the anti-progress stance represented by the character of Ella Garth, making *Wild River* his most ambivalent film in terms of its treatment of political and moral issues. A modern source reports that Kazan wanted Marlon Brando for the male lead, but he was unavailable. Kazan, who had directed Clift in a 1942 production of the play *The Skin of Our Teeth*, was at first adamantly opposed to hiring Clift because of the actor's drinking problem. Clift reportedly promised Kazan that he would stay sober for the duration of the shoot and he was accompanied to Tennessee by a secretary assigned to keep an eye on him. With the exception of one brief binge near the end of production, reported Kazan, Clift kept his promise. A modern source adds Hardwick Stuart (*Marshal Hogue*) to the cast.

Box 6 Jun 1960. *DV* 25 Jun 1956. *DV* 9 Aug 1957. *DV* 4 Sep 1958. *DV* 13 Oct 1958. *DV* 26 Mar 1959. *DV* 31 Jul 1959. *DV* 9 Sep 1959. *DV* 15 Oct 1959. *DV* 24 May 1960, p. 3. *Exh* 8 Jun 1960, p. 4710. *FD* 26 May 1960, p. 6. *FIR* Jun-Jul 1960. *Har* 28 May 1960, p. 86. *HR* 26 Jun 1956. *HR* 25 Mar 1959. *HR* 15 Oct 1959. *HR* 24 May 1960, p. 3. *LAEx* 11 Sep 1959. *LAMirror* 10 Nov 1959. *LAT* 4 Mar 1957. *MPD* 24 May 1960. *MPHPD* 28 May 1960, p. 716. *NYT* 10 Feb 1960. *NYT* 27 May 1960, p. 22. *Var* 25 May 1960, p. 6.

THE WILD WEST (1936) *see* SILLY BILLIES

WILD WEST (Native Americans)

PRC Pictures Inc.; controlled by Pathe Industries, Inc. *Dist* Producers Releasing Corp. 1 Dec **1946**; Prod: early May 1946 [©Pathe Industries, Inc.; 1 Dec 1946; LP712]. Sd (Western Electric Mirrophonic Recording); col (Cinecolor). 71-72 or 76 min. PCA cert no. 11791.

Prod Robert Emmett Tansey. *Dir* Robert Emmett Tansey. *Asst dir* Louis Germonprez. *Dial dir* Frances Kavanaugh. *Orig scr* Frances Kavanaugh. *Dir of photog* Fred Jackman, Jr. *Spec eff* Ray Mercer. *Col dir* Bill Holm. *Art dir* Edward C. Jewell. *Film ed* Hugh Winn. *Set dec* Vin Taylor. *Cost* Karlice. *Vocal and orch arr* Walter Greene. *Mus dir* Karl Hajos. *Sd eng* Ben Winkler. *Dir of makeup* Bud Westmore. *Prod mgr* Norman Cook. *Bus mgr* Jerry Thomas.

Song(s): "Ride on the Tide of a Song," "Journey's End" and "I Can Tell by the Stars," music and lyrics by Dorcas Cochran and Charles Rosoff; "Elmer the Knock-Kneed Cowboy," music and lyrics by Eddie Dean, Ruth Herscher and Louis Herscher.

Cast: EDDIE DEAN [(*Eddie Dean*)], and his horse FLASH, Roscoe Ates [(*Soapy Jones*)], Al LaRue [(*Stormy Day*)], Sarah Padden [(*Carrie Bannister*)], Robert "Buzzy" Henry [(*Skinny Bannister*)], Louise Curry [(*Florabelle Bannister*)], Jean Carlin [(*Mollie Bannister*)], Lee Bennett [(*Butler*)], Terry Frost [(*Drake Dawson*)], Warner Richmond [(*Judge Templeton*)], Lee Roberts [(*Captain Roberts*)], Chief Yowlachie [(*Chief Black Fox*)], Bob Duncan [(*Rockey*)], Frank Pharr [(*Doctor*)], Matty Roubert [(*Halfbreed Charlie*)], John Bridges [(*Constable*)], Al Ferguson [(*Kansas*)], Bud Osborne [(*Cactus*)].

Western, with songs. [*Print viewed*]. When Butler, the head of the Western Telegraph Company, is introduced to his new assistants, Eddie Dean, Stormy Day and Soapy Jones, he does not believe that the three cowboys will be much help in meeting his construction deadline. Butler's worries are heightened when local Indians, led by Chief Black Fox, go on the warpath after Drake Dawson's men illegally kill buffalo for their hides. Because Dawson believes that better communication will interfere with his profitable schemes, he adds to the tumult by convincing the Indians that the telegraph wires will bring evil spirits to the country. When Butler is informed that he will lose his contract if he does not reach Prescott by a certain time, Stormy suggests that they contact Carrie Bannister, who has great influence with Chief Black Fox. Carrie, a widow who lives with her three children, Skinny, Florabelle and Mollie, is respected by the Indians because her late husband Jim, a U.S. Ranger, negotiated a treaty between the Indians and the U.S. government. Black Fox tells Eddie that his people are angered by the slaughter of the buffalo, and Eddie agrees to stop it. Then, seeing her daughters' interest in Eddie and Stormy, Carrie suggests that the men use her ranch as headquarters for their operations. Eddie tells Butler that he, Stormy and Soapy served under Bannister in the Rangers. Ever since his murder, the three have searched for his killer. One day, while Eddie is in Prescott, some of Dawson's men try to destroy the telegraph company's headquarters. Stormy, Soapy and Butler overcome their attackers and bring them into town. Before the trial, Eddie sends Soapy to gather information about wanted criminals to use against the jailed men. Skinny begs to accompany Soapy, and against his better judgment, Eddie agrees. Meanwhile, with the help of the Indians, the men work all night to run the telegraph cable. Black Fox suggests that they hide the cable in the trees, and so they are able to reach Prescott without Dawson's knowledge. Returning from their mission, Soapy and Skinny are ambushed by Dawson's men, and Skinny is badly wounded. Near Skinny, Soapy finds an abandoned gun that was one of a pair belonging to Bannister and is convinced that one of Dawson's gang killed the ranger. Later, Eddie, Stormy and Soapy go into Prescott for the trial of the men who attacked their headquarters and learn that crooked Judge Templeton ordered their release. Eddie then asks Butler to telegraph for the Rangers, but Dawson's men hear the telegraph keys clicking and pull out the wires. Back at the Bannisters', however, a recovering Skinny hears Butler's message and relays it to the Rangers. When Eddie learns that Dawson is carrying Bannister's other gun, he arrests the outlaw and a gunfight ensues. The Rangers arrive in time to overcome Dawson's men. Skinny is made an honorary Ranger, and Eddie and Stormy vow to return soon to see Mollie and Florabelle. *Indians of North America. Profiteering. Rangers. Telegraph. Ambushes. Bison, American. Fathers and sons. Fistfights. Gunfights. Gunshot wounds. Judges. Motherhood. Physicians. Prescott (AZ). Romance. Sisters. Tomboys.*

Note: The film's working title was *Melody Roundup*. It was reissued in 1948 as *Prairie Outlaws*. That version ran 57 minutes and was in black and white.

Box 7 Dec 1946. *DV* 27 Nov 1946, p. 4. *FD* 2 Dec 1946, p. 6. *HR* 3 May 1946, p. 12. *HR* 27 Nov 1946, p. 6. *MPHPD* 10 Aug 1946, p. 3138. *MPHPD* 7 Dec 1946, p. 3347. *Var* 27 Nov 1946, p. 28.

WILD WOMEN (Hawaiians)

Universal Film Mfg. Co. *Dist* Universal Film Mfg. Co. 25 Feb **1918** [©Universal Film Mfg. Co.; 18 Feb 1918; LP12083]. Si; b&w. 5 reels.

Prod Harry Carey. *Dir* Jack Ford. *Scen* George Hively. *Story* Harry Carey and Jack Ford. *Cam* Ben F. Reynolds.

Cast: Harry Carey (*Cheyenne Harry*), Molly Malone (*The princess*), Martha Mattox (*The queen*), Edward Jones (*Pelon*), Vester Pegg (*Pegg*), E. Van Beaver (*The boss*), Wilfred Taylor (*Slugger Joe*).

Western, Comedy. In order to raise money for one of the cowpunchers whose wife is in need of a costly operation, Cheyenne Harry convinces the cowboys of the Circle-L Ranch to take part in a San Francisco rodeo. After winning most of the prizes, Harry and the boys visit a Hawaiian-style cabaret to celebrate. Several Honolulu

cocktails each finally prove too much for the cowboys, and even the gyrations of the grass-clad hula dancers cannot keep them awake. Harry dreams that he and his companions have been shanghaied and forced to scrub the deck. When the crew mutinies, Harry is cast ashore on an island, where he so enchants the Hawaiian queen that she decides to marry him. Harry manages to elude the aging queen and is about to embrace the young and pretty princess when he wakes up. Swearing off Hawaiian cocktails, Harry and the cowboys return to the ranch. *Cabarets. Cowboys. Dreams. Drunkenness. Hawaii. Castaways. Dancers. Good Samaritans. Kidnapping. Mutiny. Ranches. Rodeos. Royalty. San Francisco (CA). Ship crews. Ship owners. Ships.*

Note: Wilfred Taylor may actually be Wilton Taylor. Modern sources credit the photography to John W. Brown.

ETR 9 Mar 1918, p. 1141. *MPN* 9 Mar 1918, p. 1466. *MPW* 2 Mar 1918, pp. 1273-74. *MPW* 9 Mar 1918, p. 1409. *Var* 1 Mar 1918, p. 42. *Wid's* 7 Mar 1918, p. 988.

THE WILDERNESS TRAIL *see* **THE SYMBOL OF THE UNCONQUERED**

WILL TOMORROW EVER COME *see* **NORTHWEST OUTPOST**

WINCHESTER '73 (Native Americans)
Universal-International Pictures Co., Inc. *Dist* Universal Pictures Co., Inc. 12 Jul **1950**; New York opening: 7 Jun 1950; Prod: mid-Feb—late Mar 1950 [©Universal Pictures Co., Inc.; 9 Jun 1950; LP182]. Sd (Western Electric Recording); b&w. 8,306 ft. 92 min. PCA cert no. 14646.

Prod Aaron Rosenberg. *Dir* Anthony Mann. [*Asst dir* Jesse Hibbs]. *Scr* Robert L. Richards and Borden Chase. *From a story by* Stuart N. Lake. *Dir of photog* William Daniels. *Art dir* Bernard Herzbrun and Nathan Juran. *Film ed* Edward Curtiss. *Set dec* Russell A. Gausman and A. Roland Fields. *Gowns* Yvonne Wood. *Mus dir* Joseph Gershenson. *Sd* Leslie I. Carey and Richard DeWeese. *Hair stylist* Joan St. Oegger. *Makeup* Bud Westmore.

Cast: JAMES STEWART (*Lin McAdam*), SHELLEY WINTERS (*Lola Manners*), DAN DURYEA (*Waco Johnny Dean*), STEPHEN McNALLY (*Dutch Henry Brown* [*also known as Matthew McAdam*]), Millard Mitchell ([*Frankie*] *High Spade* [*Wilson*]), Charles Drake (*Steve Miller*), John McIntire (*Joe Lamont*), Will Geer (*Wyatt Earp*), Jay C. Flippen (*Sgt. Wilkes*), Rock Hudson (*Young Bull*), John Alexander (*Jack Riker*), Steve Brodie (*Wesley*), James Millican (*Wheeler*), Abner Biberman (*Latigo Means*), Anthony Curtis (*Doan*), James Best (*Crater*), [Gregg Martell (*Mossman*)], [Frank Chase (*Cavalryman*)], [Chuck Roberson (*Long Tom*)], [Carol Henry (*Dudeen*)], [Ray Teal (*Marshall Noonan*)], [Virginia Mullen (*Mrs. Jameson*)], [John Doucette (*Roan Daley*)], [Steve Larrell (*Bat Masterson*)], [Chief Yowlachie (*Indian*)], [Frank Conlan (*Clerk*)], [Ray Bennett (*Charles Bender*)], [Guy Wilkerson (*Virgil Earp*)], [Robert Anderson (*Bassett*)], [Larry Olsen, Tim Hawkins, Bill McKenzie (*Boys at rifle shoot*)], [Edmund Cobb (*Target watcher*)], [Forrest Taylor (*Target clerk*)], [Norman Kent (*Buffalo hunter*)], [Norman Ollestad (*Stable boy*)], [Ethan Laidlaw (*Station master*)], [Tony Taylor, Robert Winans, Jimmie Hawkins (*Boys*)], [Mel Archer, Ted Mapes (*Bartenders*)], [Monte Montague (*Posseman*)], [Gary Jackson (*Gary Jameson*)], [Bonnie Kay Eddy (*Bonnie Jameson*)], [Jennings Miles (*Stagecoach driver*)], [John War Eagle (*Indian interpreter*)], [Duke Yorke], [Bud Osborne], [Jack Curtis].

Western. [*Print viewed*]. In 1876, cowboy Lin McAdam and his good friend, Frankie "High Spade" Wilson, travel to Dodge City, Kansas to participate in the Centennial Rifle Shoot, which is being held on the Fourth of July. Lin knows that his sharpshooting brother, Dutch Henry Brown, whom he suspects murdered their father, will also be in the contest, as first prize is a rare Winchester '73 rifle. Soon after their mutual arrivals in Dodge City, Lin and Dutch Henry are stopped from killing each other by the town's famous marshal, Wyatt Earp. Later, Lin narrowly defeats his brother in the rifle contest, but Dutch Henry and his friends ambush Lin and steal the Winchester. Two days later, a penniless Dutch Henry loses the rifle in a poker game to Joe Lamont, an Indian trader. Lamont is later killed by Young Bull, an Indian chief whom Lamont had hoped to cheat with defective guns and rifles. Meanwhile, Lin learns from Jack Riker, a saloon keeper, that Dutch Henry is headed for Tascosa to meet up with Waco Johnny Dean, an outlaw. That night on the trail, Lin and High Spade run into a U.S. Cavalry unit, led by Sgt. Wilkes, which has been surrounded by Young Bull's warriors. The Indians attack the next morning, but they are repelled when Lin shoots and kills Young Bull.

After Lin and High Spade leave, Wilkes discovers the rare Winchester by the dead Indian chief and gives it to Steve Miller, the cowardly fiancé of Lola Manners, a dance hall girl. Steve and Lola then travel to Tascosa, where they accept the hospitality of the Jameson family. Waco Johnny and his men soon arrive at the Jameson home, with a posse in hot pursuit, and the outlaw uses Lola as a hostage when Steve refuses to give him the Winchester. Waco Johnny kills Steve in a gunfight, then escapes from the farmhouse with Lola and the rifle and heads for Dutch Henry's hideout in the nearby mountains. Dutch Henry quickly recognizes the Winchester and demands it back. The outlaws then plan a bank robbery, only to have Lin and High Spade arrive in Tascosa that same day. Lin kills Waco Johnny just as Dutch Henry and his men are leaving the bank, and Lola is shot and wounded in the ensuing gunfight. Lin takes off alone after his brother, who heads back toward his mountain hideout. Though he is trapped below Dutch Henry, Lin torments his brother by calling him by his given name, Matthew McAdam, then manages to sneak behind him as he reloads the Winchester. Lin then shoots and kills Dutch Henry, finally avenging their father's death. Later, Lin returns to Tascosa with the Winchester, where he is welcomed with open arms by both Lola and High Spade. *Brothers. Chases. Revenge. Rifles. Sharpshooters. Bank robberies. Contests. Cowardice. Dance hall girls. Dodge City (KS). Wyatt Earp. Engagements. Fights. Fourth of July. Gunrunners. Gunshot wounds. Hideouts. Indians of North America. Bat Masterson. Murder. Outlaws. Poker (Game). Posses. Saloon keepers. Shootouts. United States. Army. Cavalry. United States. Marshals.*

Note: The film opens with the following written foreword: "This is a story of the Winchester Rifle Model 1873 *'The gun that won the West.'* To cowman, outlaw, peace officer or soldier, the Winchester '73 was a treasured possession. An Indian would sell his soul to own one..." According to *HR* news items throughout the late 1940s, Fritz Lang planned to direct this film as an independent production released through Universal. In Dec 1946, the film was placed on Universal's production schedule, and Lang announced he would shoot the film on location at Zion City National Park, UT. According to a Jun 1947 *HR* news item, Lang then decided to film exterior scenes in Valley of Fire, NV.

A 1951 *LAT* news item reported that writer Stuart Lake sued Universal for $400,000 when the studio failed to credit him as writer of the film's original story when that story was published in an unnamed film magazine. After a magistrate ruled that Universal was at fault in the matter, Lake and the studio settled out of court. In 1952, James Stewart was named the winner of the third annual Reno Silver Spurs award as best Western actor of 1951 for his performance in *Winchester '73*. According to *LAT*, the film was also named best Western film and Anthony Mann was named best Western director.

This was the first of eight films on which Stewart and Mann worked together, the last being the 1955 Columbia film *The Man from Laramie*. According to modern sources, Stewart made *Winchester '73* as part of a two-picture agreement with Universal, in which the actor participated in the film's profits, rather than being paid his regular salary or a flat fee. Because of the box-office success of *Winchester '73*, some modern sources estimate that Stewart received $500,000. Modern sources also state that Stewart suggested that Anthony Mann replace the departed Fritz Lang as the film's director after the actor saw Mann's work on the 1950 M-G-M film, *Devil's Doorway* (see entry above). In turn, Mann brought writer Borden Chase onto the project to re-write the existing screenplay by Robert L. Richards, according to modern sources.

A radio version of *Winchester '73*, with James Stewart and Stephen McNally reprising their film roles, was broadcast on the *Lux Radio Theatre* on 12 Nov 1951. The Robert L. Richards/Borden Chase screenplay was the basis for a 1967 television movie by the same name, starring Tom Tryon and John Saxon, and directed by Herschel Daugherty. Dan Duryea, who played outlaw "Waco Johnny Dean" in the 1950 film, played Saxon's sympathetic father in the 1967 television production.

Box 10 Jun 1950. *DV* 7 Jun 1950, p. 3, 5. *FD* 8 Jun 1950, p. 7. *HR* 19 Mar 1946. *HR* 10 Dec 1946, p. 2. *HR* 20 Dec 1946, p. 1. *HR* 20 Jun 1947, p. 6. *HR* 17 Feb 1950, p. 15. *HR* 7 Jun 1950, p. 4. *LAT* 10 May 1951. *LAT* 24 Apr 1952. *MPHPD* 10 Jun 1950, p. 329. *NYT* 8 Jun 1950, p. 38. *Var* 7 Jun 1950, p. 8.

THE WINE GIRL (Italian Americans)
Bluebird Photoplays, Inc. *Dist* Bluebird Photoplays, Inc. 25 Mar **1918** [©Bluebird Photoplays, Inc.; 5 Mar 1918; LP12150]. Si; b&w. 5 reels.

Dir Stuart Paton. *Story* Harvey Gates. *Cam* Duke Hayward.
Cast: Carmel Myers (*Bona*), Rex De Rosselli (*Andrea Minghetti*), E. A. Warren (*Chico Piave*), Kenneth Harlan (*Frank Harris*), Katherine Kirkwood (*Mrs. Harris*).

Drama. Andrea Minghetti runs a California vineyard with the help of his pretty niece Bona, who cooks for the employees. A worker named Chico Piave, who belongs to a secret crime society, tries unsuccessfully to force himself on Bona, and later, he demands that Andrea give him both the young woman and a large sum in cash. Meanwhile, the wealthy Frank Harris accepts a job at the vineyard on

a dare and is so impressed with Bona's cooking that he offers her a position in his mother's kitchen. Mrs. Harris treats Bona cruelly until word comes that Bona has inherited a fortune from Andrea, who has disappeared in her absence. Mrs. Harris' sudden kindness dismays Bona, who returns home and informs the police of Chico's earlier threats. Chico is arrested, but Andrea, who merely hid to escape the criminal, returns to the vineyard, as does Frank, who declares his love for Bona. *Criminals. Extortion. Gold diggers. Italian Americans. Laborers. California. Cooks. Drudges. Inheritance. Nieces. Police. Vineyards. Wagers.*

ETR 23 Mar 1918, p. 1309. *MPN* 30 Mar 1918, p. 1927. *MPW* 30 Mar 1918, p. 1865, 1876. *NYDM* 30 Mar 1918, p. 18. *Var* 22 Mar 1918, p. 47. *Wid's* 4 Apr 1918, p. 1056.

WING TOY (Chinese Americans)

Fox Film Corp. *Dist* Fox Film Corp. 30 Jan 1921 [©William Fox; 30 Jan 1921; LP16112]. Si; b&w. 5-6 reels.
Pres William Fox. *Dir* Howard M. Mitchell. *Asst dir* Edward Dodds. *Scen* Thomas Dixon, Jr. *Story* Pearl Doles Bell. *Photog* Glen MacWilliams.

Cast: Shirley Mason (*Wing Toy*), Raymond McKee (*Bob Harris*), Edward McWade (*Wong*), Harry S. Northrup (*Yen Low*), Betty Schade (*White Lily*), Scott McKee (*The Mole*).

Melodrama. In her sixteenth year, Wing Toy learns how as an infant she was brought to Wong, a Chinese laundryman, by a former convict known as The Mole and that her father was Chinese and her mother American. Later, to give her a better home, Wong pledged her in marriage to Yen Low, a powerful and unscrupulous underworld figure, when she would come of age. Yen Low plans to divorce his American wife, White Lily, and marry Wing Toy. The intervention of reporter Bob Harris leads to the release of Wing Toy; Yen Low is killed by White Lily; and Wing Toy's engagement to the reporter becomes possible when it is revealed that she is the daughter of the district attorney. *Chinese Americans. Laundries. Marriage-Arranged. Miscegenation. New York City-Chinatown. Reporters. Waifs.*

ETR 12 Feb 1921, p. 1066. *FD* 12 Feb 1921. *Var* 11 Mar 1921, p.32.

THE WINGED MYSTERY (German Americans)

Bluebird Photoplays, Inc. *Dist* Bluebird Photoplays, Inc. 26 Nov 1917 [©Bluebird Photoplays, Inc.; 30 Oct 1917; LP11649]. Si; b&w. 5 reels.
Dir Joseph De Grasse. *Scen* William Parker. *Story* Archer McMackin.

Cast: Franklyn Farnum (*Captain August Siever/Louis Siever*), Claire Du Brey (*Gerda Anderson*), Rosemary Theby (*Shirley Wayne*), Charles Hill Mailes (*Josiah Wayne*), Sam De Grasse (*Mortimer Eddington*), T. D. Crittenden (*Henry Waltham Steele*), Frederick Montague (*Captain Bernard*).

Espionage, World War I, Drama. Louis and August Siever, the twins sons of a German father and American mother, are traveling in Europe when war breaks out. August joins the Kaiser's army, but Louis, a supporter of the United States, is practically made a prisoner in Berlin for a year while he tries to prove his American citizenship. After a violent confrontation with Louis, August steals his brother's passport and leaves for New York with Gerda Anderson, a German spy. When August and Gerda hear that the Waynes, wealthy friends of Louis, are throwing a weekend party on Long Island, they rent a nearby house and invite all of the Waynes' guests, including Louis, to a "mystery" party. Once arrived, the guests, who are mostly women, are made prisoner and ransom notes are sent to their husbands via carrier pigeons. While Shirley Wayne and Louis track down and are captured by the extortionists, Mortimer Eddington, an amateur detective, devises a method to trace the pigeons back to the house. Before Shirley and Louis come to harm, police officers close in and demand the Germans' surrender, but they choose to fight, and die in the attempt. *Brothers. Detectives. German Americans. Germans. Kidnapping. Long Island (NY). Pigeons. Ransom. Spies. Twins. Fights. Germany. Germany. Army. New York City. Parties. Passports. Police. Robbery.*

MPN 8 Dec 1917, p. 4067. *MPW* 1 Dec 1917, p. 1334, 1388. *NYDM* 24 Nov 1917, p. 19. *NYT* 12 Nov 1917, p. 11. *Var* 16 Nov 1917, p. 52.

WINGS FOR THE EAGLE (German Americans)

Warner Bros. Pictures, Inc.; A Warner Bros.—First National Picture. *Dist* Warner Bros. Pictures, Inc. 18 Jul 1942; *Prod:* 12 Jan—late Feb 1942. Sd (RCA Sound System); b&w. 7,650 ft. 84-85 min.
Prod Robert Lord. *Dir* Lloyd Bacon. *Dial dir* Hugh Cummings. [*Asst dir* Richard Mayberry]. *Orig scr* Byron Morgan and B. H. Orkow. *Addl*

dial Richard Macaulay. *Dir of photog* Tony Gaudio. *Spec eff* Byron Haskin and H. F. Koenekamp. *Art dir* Max Parker. *Film ed* Owen Marks. *Gowns* Milo Anderson. *Mus* Frederick Hollander. *Mus dir* Leo F. Forbstein. *Sd* Francis J. Scheid. *Makeup artist* Perc Westmore.

Cast: ANN SHERIDAN (*Roma Maple*), DENNIS MORGAN (*Corky Jones*), Jack Carson (*Brad Maple*), George Tobias (*Jake Hanso*), Russell Arms (*Pete Hanso*), Don DeFore (*Gil Borden*), Tom Fadden (*Tom "Cyclone" Shaw*), John Ridgely (*Johnson*), Frank Wilcox (*Stark*), George Meeker (*Personnel man*), Fay Helm (*Miss Baxter*), Billy Curtis (*Midget*), Emory Parnell (*Policeman*), Edgar Dearing (*Motorcycle officer*), [Russell Hicks (*Speaker*)], [Dorothy Vaughan (*Mrs. Shaw*)], [Billy Dawson (*Bobby*)], [Eddie Acuff (*Al*)], [Joe Devlin (*Service station owner*)], [Robert Winkler, Sonny Bupp, Harry Harvey, Jr., Barry Downing (*Kids*)], [Ted Oliver (*Guard*)], [Catherine Lewis (*Personnel clerk*)], [Jean Inness (*Personnel woman*)], [Victor Zimmerman (*F.B.I. man*)], [Frank Mayo, Charles Sullivan (*Workmen*)], [Frank Ferguson (*Personnel man*)], [Creighton Hale (*Jeweler*)], [Frank Faylen (*Leader*)], [Jerry Mandy (*Waiter*)], [Clancy Cooper (*Policeman*)], [Eddie Dew, Jack Gardner, Bill Edwards, Renny McEvoy, Charles Drake (*Customers*)], [David Willock (*Slim*)], [Emmett Vogan (*Clerk*)], [John Maxwell, Kenneth Harlan (*Supervisors*)], [Ken Christy (*Inspector*)], [Frank Coghlan, Jr. (*Mail boy*)], [Ray Montgomery (*Young man*)], [June Millarde (*Girl*)], [John Hamilton (*Executive*)], [Fred Kelsey (*Desk sergeant*)], [Knox Manning, Wen Niles (*Radio announcers*)], [Sol Gorss (*Sergeant*)], [Dick French], [Pat McVey], [Lee Phelps], [Walter Sande], [Dick Wessel], [Eddy Waller], [Jack Mower].

War preparedness, Comedy-drama. [*Print viewed*]. In 1941, when more bombers are needed for the allied war effort, workers from all over the country flock to the Lockheed Aircraft plant in Burbank, California. Among them is Corky Jones, who plans to stay with his old college friend, Brad Maple. Corky has a low draft number and intends to avoid the draft by obtaining a job in the defense industry. Brad is delighted to see Corky again, but his wife Roma is not happy about an additional mouth to feed. Brad, who does not have a job, has spent their savings on a correspondence course in aircraft engineering, only to discover that the school is a fake. The next day, Corky undergoes an extensive security check at Lockheed and soon obtains a job in the storeroom. With an advance against his salary, he buys several bags of groceries as his contribution to the household. Roma is delighted with the food, but Brad is so jealous that Corky moves out. Corky rents a room from German immigrant Jake Hanso, a supervisor at the plant, and his son Pete, Corky's co-worker, who plans to join the air corps upon his graduation from college. Later, Roma leaves Brad and gets a job in the personnel department of the plant. Pleased that she is free, Corky immediately asks her out to dinner. Things grow complicated, however, when Brad also finds employment at the plant. Eventually, the two men come to blows over Roma. At work, Jake asks the workers to donate their services to build an extra bomber, which they will then give to the English soldiers as a Christmas present. Later, Jake is fired because, although loyal to the United States, as an enemy alien, he is not allowed to work in the defense industry. Pete is angered by his father's treatment and abandons his plans to join the air corps. Although saddened by the event, Jake admits that his dismissal is his own fault, as he waited too long to apply for citizenship. Together with Corky, he helps Pete realize that he still wants to fly bombers. Jake then finds work in a diner until his citizenship application is completed. After several months, Pete completes his education and joins the air corps, and Jake becomes a citizen. Father and son vow that one will make the bombers that the other will fly—Hanso to Hanso. Afterward, at home, Corky and the Hansos hear that the Japanese have bombed Pearl Harbor. Pete returns to the base, and Corky and Jake hurry to the plant, where production is stepped up. After the Japanese attack Corky changes his mind about evading the draft. He reunites Roma and Brad and joins the air corps. Then, after Pete is killed in the Philippines, Corky promises Jake that he will down two Japanese bombers in Pete's honor, and he does. *Aircraft industry. Fathers and sons. Romantic rivalry. Aerial combat. Air pilots. Military. Citizenship. Diners (Restaurants). Dismissal (Employment). Dwarfs. Friendship. Immigrants. Jealousy. Lockheed Aircraft Plant (Burbank, CA). Patriotism. Pearl Harbor (HI), Attack on, 1941. Revenge. Separation (Marital). World War II.*

Note: The film begins with the following written dedication: "To our

airplane factory workers, whose magnificent efforts will enable the United Nations to preserve a free way of life, this motion picture is respectfully dedicated." The film's working title was *The Shadow of Their Wings*. News items in *HR* add the following information about the production: For the first time since the beginning of the war, the studio received permission to shoot some scenes at Lockheed Aircraft Plant in Los Angeles, where the crew filmed bombers waiting to be sent to England by way of Canada. Each member of the film crew was required to carry a birth certificate in order to gain entrance to the plant. Jack Carson replaced Ronald Reagan in the role of "Brad" when the latter was assigned to *Desperate Journey*. At the time of the film's release, Russell Arms was serving in the United States Army. Although there is a 1942 copyright statement on the film, no record of the picture appears in the *Copyright Catalog*.

Box 6 Jun 1942. *FD* 4 Jun 1942, p. 8. *HR* 7 Jan 1942, p. 1. *HR* 12 Jan 1942, p. 1. *HR* 16 Jan 1942, p. 1. *HR* 2 Jun 1942, p. 4. *MPHPD* 6 Jun 1942, p. 697. *NYT* 1 Aug 1942, p. 14. *Var* 3 Jun 1942, p. 9.

WINNER TAKE ALL (Italian Americans)

Twentieth Century-Fox Film Corp. *Dist* Twentieth Century-Fox Film Corp. 21 Apr **1939**; Prod: Late Nov—20 Dec 1938 [©Twentieth Century-Fox Film Corp.; 21 Apr 1939; LP9178]. Sd (Western Electric Mirrophonic Recording); b&w. 5,735 ft. 60-62 min. PCA cert no. 4941.

Series: Sports Series.

Assoc prod Jerry Hoffman. *Dir* Otto Brower. [*Asst dir* Gordon Cooper]. *Scr* Frances Hyland and Albert Kay. *Orig story* Jerry Cady. *Photog* Edward Cronjager. *Art dir* Richard Day and Haldane Douglas. *Settings* Thomas Little. *Film ed* Nick De Maggio. *Cost* Herschel. *Mus dir* Samuel Kaylin. *Sd* Alfred Bruzlin and William H. Anderson.

Cast: Tony Martin (*Steve Bishop*), Gloria Stuart (*Julie Harrison*), Henry Armetta (*Papa Gambini*), Slim Summerville (*Muldoon*), Kane Richmond (*Paulie Mitchell*), Robert Allen (*Tom Walker*), Inez Palange (*Mama Gambini*), Johnnie Pirrone, Jr. (*Tony Gambini*), Pedro de Cordoba (*Pantrelli*), Betty Greco (*Maria Gambini*), Eleanor Virzie (*Rosa Gambini*), [George Blake, Morrie Cohan (*Referees*)], [Gino Corrado, Stephen Soldi, Carlos Gionetti, John Northpole, Jack Costello (*Sons of Garibaldi*)], [Fred Kelsey (*Policeman*)], [Ralph Dunn (*Waiter*)], [Albert Pollet (*French waiter*)], [Ole Olsen (*Delivery man*)], [Spike Mason, Mickey McAvoy, Jimmy O'Gatty, Joe Gray, Harvey Parry, Pat McKee, Charles Sullivan, Dutch Hendrian (*Fighters*)], [Syd Saylor, Eddie Acuff (*Rubbers*)], [Frank Orth (*Pete*)], [Gene Morgan, John Sheehan (*Announcers*)], [Billy Wayne (*Jimmy Rooney's trainer*)], [George Magrill (*Jimmy Rooney*)], [Jockey Haefeli (*Edward Gargan*)].

Boxing, Drama. [*Print viewed*]. At Gambini's Delicatessen, Mama Gambini complains to her husband that he is working too hard, and convinces him to hire a waiter. With a long line of interviewees, Papa Gambini doesn't know what to do. Steve Bishop, an out-of-work rodeo cowboy, tells Papa that he doesn't have the eighty-six cents to pay for his dinner, so Papa hires him as the waiter. When one of the interviewees tries to punch Papa, Steve knocks him out, thus earning his first raise. At a dinner for the social club "Sons of Garibaldi," the president, Mr. Pantrelli, announces that the club needs $5,000 to finish the recreation hall it is building for the neighborhood. Sportswriter Julie Harrison arrives at the dinner with her boyfriend, fight promoter Tom Walker. Julie suggests they put on a fight, and Tom offers his fighters for free if the club can come up with a venue. After Steve spills a plate of spaghetti on Tom, he confesses to Julie that he is not a waiter, but an agriculture student from the University of Montana, stranded in New York after the rodeo went bankrupt. The preliminary fight for the benefit is billed as a "Battle Royal," six boxers in the ring at once, with Papa as referee. Steve wins the event, much to the crowd's and the Gambinis' pleasure. The main event pits Jimmy Rooney against Paulie Mitchell, a friend of Julie. When Paulie hurts his ankle, the crowd urges Steve to take his place. With Julie coaching him, Steve takes a beating, but wins the fight. Back at the delicatessen, Papa tells how they raised $1,000, but need $4,000 more. Steve is signed up to fight for Tom, with Muldoon as his manager. Tom, taking advantage of the notoriety of Steve's first victory, sets him up with fixed fights, but Steve begins to believe he really is a good fighter. Julie tries to warn Steve, but he is too drunk on champagne, women and success to listen. His fight against Paulie is fixed, too, but Julie convinces Paulie to really fight Steve, which leads to Steve's first defeat. Papa loses all the recreation hall money betting on Steve, and Tom is so angry he sells Steve's contract to Julie for twenty-five cents. Julie and Muldoon convince Steve that he can be a good fighter if he trains with them, and uses Papa as his backer.

After Steve slowly works his way back up, Julie sets up a re-match with Paulie, with Papa the promoter. Upset at losing Julie to Steve, Tom tells Papa that Paulie is all washed up and gets Papa to bet his $2,500 gate on Steve. Tom then tells Steve that Julie instructed Paulie to knock him out in the earlier match, but not why. Steve has little will to fight, but when Paulie tells him the truth about the first fight, Steve becomes rejuvenated. The fight is even until the last round, when Steve finally knocks out Paulie. When Tom enters the ring to denounce Paulie, Paulie knocks him out, and Steve raises his hand in a mock victory gesture. Gambini tells all that they finally have the money to finish the recreation center. *Boxers. Boxing. Clubs. Delicatessens. Fixed fights. Italian Americans. Reporters. Restaurateurs. Charities. Contracts. Cowboys. Drunkenness. Employer-employee relations. Family life. Gamblers. Revenge. Romance. Unemployment. Waiters.*

Note: The working titles of this film was *Golden Gloves*. According to a Twentieth Century-Fox press release, this was Tony Martin's first straight dramatic role. Prior to *Winner Take All*, Martin had preformed in twelve musicals at Fox. Press releases also note the following information: Martin had to leave the set at noon each Thursday to do radio rehearsals for his weekly coast-to-coast radio show. Martin was trained for the fight sequences by Jackie Fields, former welter-weight champion. Actress Gloria Stuart, who plays a sports reporter in this film, actually was such a writer prior to becoming an actress. This was the final film in the studio's "Sports Series." For information on the series, please see entry above for *Speed to Burn*.

Box 25 Feb 1939. *DV* 15 Feb 1939, p. 3. *FD* 12 Apr 1939, p. 9. *HR* 3 Dec 1938, p. 5. *HR* 20 Dec 1938, p. 7. *HR* 16 Feb 1939, p. 3. *MPD* 27 Feb 1939, p. 10. *MPH* 25 Feb 1939, p. 44. *NYT* 31 Mar 1939, p. 19. *Var* 5 Apr 1939, p. 15.

WINNERS OF THE WILDERNESS (Native Americans)

Metro-Goldwyn-Mayer Corp.; controlled by Loew's Inc. *Dist* Metro-Goldwyn-Mayer Distributing Corp. 15 Jan **1927** [©Metro-Goldwyn-Mayer Corp.; 24 Jan 1927; LP23585]. Si; b&w with col sequences (Technicolor). 7 reels, 6,343 ft.

Dir W. S. Van Dyke. *Cont* Josephine Chippo. *Titles* Marian Ainslee. *Photog* Clyde De Vinna. *Film ed* Conrad A. Nervig. *Settings* David Townsend. *Ward* Lucia Coulter.

Cast: Tim McCoy (*Colonel O'Hara*), Joan Crawford (*Renée Contrecoeur*), Edward Connelly (*General Contrecoeur*), Roy D'Arcy (*Captain Dumas*), Louise Lorraine (*Mimi*), Edward Hearn (*George Washington*), Tom O'Brien (*Timothy*), Will R. Walling (*General Braddock*), Frank Currier (*Governor de Vaudreuil*), Lionel Belmore (*Governor Dinwiddie*), Chief Big Tree (*Pontiac*).

Historical, Drama. Colonel O'Hara, "dashing young officer of Braddock's staff is aided to escape from the French by daughter of commandant whom he worships. When the positions are reversed and she is his prisoner of war she willingly consents to become his prisoner for life." (*MPNBG* 12 Apr 1927, p. 65.) "The costumes of the period offer a pleasing contrast to the interesting sequences ... in which are seen such historical figures as Washington and Braddock. The latter's disastrous defeat is the film's highlight and it is carried out with realism." (*MPN* 8 Apr 1927, p. 1276.). *Edward Braddock. Robert Dinwiddie. Pontiac. United States–History–French and Indian War, 1755-1763. George Washington.*

FD 3 Apr 1927. *Var* 23 Mar 1927, p. 19.

WINNING OF THE WEST (Native Americans)

Dist Aywon Film Corp. Aug **1922**. Si; b&w. 5 reels.

Western. "Tom Sherman and his family live in a stockade home in the west. When only the two children are at home, the stockade is attacked by a band of whiskey-maddened Indians. The children explode a can of powder, driving the Indians off. Years later, the boy is in the army and the girl has a daughter of her own, whose dearest playmate is an Indian girl whom they have nursed back to health. The daughter is kidnapped by the Indians and the Indian girl rescues her. A fight follows between whites and Indians, with the brother's troop riding to the rescue." (*MPNBG* 3 Oct 1922, p. 79.). *Children. Indians of North America. Kidnapping. United States. Army. Cavalry.*

THE WINNING TICKET (Italian Americans)

Metro-Goldwyn-Mayer Corp.; controlled by Loew's Inc. *Dist* Loew's Inc. 8 Feb **1935**; Prod: 14 Nov—mid-Dec 1934 [©Metro-Goldwyn-Mayer Corp.; 30 Jan 1935; LP5300]. Sd (Western Electric Sound System); b&w. 7 reels. 69-70, 72 or 74 min. Passed by the National Board of Review. PCA cert no. 560.

Prod Jack Cummings and Charles F. Riesner. *Dir* Charles F. Riesner. *Scr* Ralph Spence and Richard Schayer. *Orig story* Robert Pirosh and

George Seaton. *Photog* Charles Clarke. *Art dir* Cedric Gibbons. *Art dir assoc* David Townsend and Edwin B. Willis. *Film ed* Hugh Wynn. *Rec dir* Douglas Shearer.

Cast: Leo Carrillo (*Joe Tomasello*), Louise Fazenda (*Nora [Tomasello]*), Ted Healy (*Eddie [Dugan]*), Irene Hervey (*Mary [Tomasello]*), James Ellison (*Jimmy*), Luis Alberni (*Tony*), Purnell B. Pratt (*Mr. Powers*), Akim Tamiroff (*Guiseppe*), Betty Jane Graham (*Noreen [Tomasello]*), Billy Watson (*Joey [Tomasello, Jr.]*), Johnny Indrisano (*Lefty Costello*), Ronald Fitzpatrick (*Mickey [Tomasello]*), Frank Moran (*Bartender*)], [Lee Phelps (*Bookmaker*)], [William Stack (*Jeffries*)], [Montague Shaw (*President of insurance co.*)], [Jane Meredith, Larry Steers (*Travelers*)], [Milton Owen (*Purser*)], [Sherry Hall (*Officer*)], [Bud Harris (*Valet*)], [Wilbur Mack (*Banker*)], [Charles Dunbar (*Still cameraman*)], [Wally Maher (*Sound man*)], [James P. Burtis (*Newsreel man*)], [Sam Flint (*Captain*)], [Clara Blandick (*Aunt Maggie*)], [George Guhl (*Turnkey*)], [Al Hill (*Bookie*)], [Clarence Hummel Wilson (*Dolan*)].

Comedy. [*Print viewed*]. The Tomasellos are a poor Italian immigrant family who live in New York. At the urging of his brother-in-law Eddie, and against the wishes of his wife Nora, who objects to gambling, barber Joe Tomasello purchases an Irish sweepstakes ticket. While listening to the sweepstakes drawing on the radio, Eddie faints when Joe's ticket number is announced as the $150,000 first prize winner. Instead of telling Joe right away that he has won, Eddie tries to finagle a percentage of the winnings by ingratiating himself with the winner. Before he can succeed, though, Jeffries, a representative from Lloyd's Insurance Company of London, brings Joe the good news and offers to buy the winning ticket for $10,000 so that he can gamble the money on a bigger win. Joe accepts the offer, but complications arise when Eddie remembers that he gave his lawyer, Tony, the ticket to hold. Eddie plans to get the ticket from Tony, but in the meantime, spends most of Joe's money on a horseracing bet. After their horse, "Salome," wins, Joe and Eddie go to Tony's to get the ticket, but are shocked when they discover that Joe's baby, Mickey, was the last one seen with it. Desperate to find the missing ticket, Tony, Eddie and Joe try to get Mickey to show them what he did with the jar that contained the winning ticket. When the baby points to some loose flooring in the living room, they take apart the floor and dig a huge hole, but come up with nothing. Tony, who faces imprisonment for his outstanding debts, worries about the lost ticket and sees that their only solution is to go to Ireland by boat and try to convince the sweepstakes officials that Joe had purchased the winning ticket. Eddie, who is afraid of ships, is tricked onto the boat by Joe, but, along with the Tomasellos, he is ejected from the steamer when he is discovered to be a stowaway. Later, when the men see Mickey inserting a piece of paper into the mouth of a ceramic parrot, they think that it is a sign that the toddler has hidden the ticket inside one of his father's many ceramic parrot pieces. Tony, Eddie and Joe, with the help of the man who sold the remaining forty-five parrots to Joe, track down the owners of the ceramic birds. One of the owners is Mr. Powers, who, when visited by the three men, watches in disbelief as they destroy his parrot and find nothing. Tony and Joe are then jailed for their actions. When Nora, with her baby, visits them in jail, she brings Joe his guitar to help him pass the time. However, Nora and Joe soon quarrel, and when she breaks the guitar over his head, the missing ticket emerges from the broken guitar, and Joe suddenly remembers that the baby had been playing with the instrument. Having rescued themselves from their troubles, Nora, Joe and Tony go to "Salome's" stock farm and ride their winning thoroughbred. *Horseracing. Irish. Italian Americans. Sweepstakes. Wagers. Bankers. Barbers and barbershops. Brothers-in-law. Class distinction. Family life. Guitars. Immigrants. Infants. Insurance–Agents. Jails. Lawyers. New York City. Picnicking. Reporters. Ships. Steamboats. Stowaways.*

Note: Although *HR* pre-release news items and production charts credit Robert Hopkins with the original story, and list Clarence Muse, Tom McGuire, Jim Farley, Curley Wright and Robert Homans in the cast, their participation in the film has not been confirmed. Background scenes were filmed at the Saratoga racetrack in Saratoga Springs, New York.

DV 30 Aug 1934, p. 4. *DV* 14 Nov 1934, p. 2. *DV* 9 Jan 1935, p. 3. *FD* 9 Feb 1935, p. 4. *HR* 1 Nov 1934, p. 6. *HR* 19 Nov 1934, p. 10. *HR* 10 Dec 1934, p. 6. *HR* 14 Dec 1934, p. 8. *HR* 9 Jan 1935, p. 3. *MPD* 10 Jan 1935, p. 11. *MPH* 17 Nov 1934, p. 48. *MPH* 19 Jan 1935, p. 58. *NYT* 11 Feb 1935, p. 14. *Var* 12 Feb 1935, p. 39.

WINTER GARDEN *see* **MR. MOTO'S LAST WARNING**

WINTER TIME *see* **WINTERTIME**

WINTERSET (Italian Americans)

RKO Radio Pictures, Inc.; A Pandro S. Berman Production. *Dist* RKO Radio Pictures, Inc. 20 Nov 1936; Prod: 23 Jul—late Sep 1936 [©RKO Radio Pictures, Inc.; 3 Dec 1936; LP6751]. Sd (RCA Victor System); b&w. 8 reels. 75 or 77-78 min. PCA cert no. 2472.

Dir Alfred Santell. *Scr* Anthony Veiller. *Photog* Peverell Marley. *Spec eff* Vernon Walker. *Art dir* Van Nest Polglase. *Art dir assoc* Perry Ferguson. *Ed* William Hamilton. *Set dresser* Darrell Silvera. *Mus dir* Nathaniel Shilkret. *Rec* John L. Cass. [*Research* Elizabeth McGaffey]. [*Press rep* S. Barret McCormick].

Source: Based on the play *Winterset* by Maxwell Anderson, as produced by Guthrie McClintic (New York, 25 Sep 1935).

Cast: Burgess Meredith (*Mio [Romagna]*), Margo (*Miriamne [Esdras]*), Eduardo Ciannelli (*Trock [Estrella]*), Maurice Moscovitch (*Esdras*), Paul Guilfoyle (*Garth [Esdras]*), Edward Ellis (*Judge Gaunt*), Stanley Ridges (*Shadow*), Mischa Auer (*Radical*), Willard Robertson (*Policeman in the square*), Alec Craig (*Hobo*), John Carradine ([*Bartolomeo*] *Romagna*), Myron McCormick (*Carr*), Helen Jerome Eddy (*Mrs. Romagna*), Barbara Pepper (*Girl*), Fernanda Eliscu (*Piny*), George Humbert (*Lucia*), Murray Alper (*Louie*), Paul Fix (*Joe*).

Drama. [*Print viewed*]. In 1920, in a town near New York City, a factory paymaster is robbed and killed, and Italian radical Bartolomeo Romagna is wrongfully arrested and executed for the crime. Sixteen years later, Liggett, a law school professor, concludes that the exclusion of the testimony of a key witness, gangster Garth Esdras, during Romagna's trial, had denied the Italian his justice. News reports of Liggett's findings come to the attention of three people: Judge Gaunt, who had sentenced Romagna; mobster Trock Estrella, the real murderer; and Romagna's son Mio. Worried that Garth, who has been leading a reclusive life since the trial, will now expose him, Trock visits him in his Brooklyn tenement and warns him to be silent. That night, Garth's sister Miriamne happens to meet Mio under the Brooklyn Bridge and, unaware of their connection to each other, falls instantly in love with him. Later, the couple meets again in a square and dance to a hurdy-gurdy. During this romantic interlude, a half-crazed Gaunt arrives in the square, searching for Garth. After being soaked by a winter rain storm, Mio tells Miriamne about his father and his need to prove his innocence. Without revealing her relationship to the case, Miriamne advises him to find Garth. Then in the Esdras' tenement, Gaunt questions Garth to appease his own doubts, while Mio tries to force a confession from him. Soon Trock, who has just had Shadow, another witness to the paymaster's murder, shot, arrives and threatens both Mio and Gaunt. Wounded but alive, Shadow bursts through the door and tries to shoot Trock, but dies before he can pull the trigger. At that moment, the police show up looking for Gaunt, but because Garth has hidden Shadow's body, they discount Mio's accusations of murder. Trock leaves with more threats, but a driven Mio tells Miriamne that he is going out to tell the world his story. Torn between her love for her brother and for Mio, Miriamne finally follows Mio, who is caught in the square by Trock and his gunman. Soon after, Garth, overcome by guilt, runs into the street and is shot by the gunman. Still trapped, Mio starts to play the prohibited hurdy-gurdy to attract the police and, to his and Miriamne's relief, is arrested. The gunman then mistakenly kills Trock, at last freeing Mio and Miriamne from their pasts. *Gangsters. Guilt. Injustice. Italian Americans. Murder. Brooklyn Bridge (New York City). Brothers and sisters. Fathers and sons. Hurdy-gurdies. Insanity. Judges. Law students. New York (State). Police. Professors. Radicalism. Rainstorms. Tenement-houses. Trials.*

Note: Maxwell Anderson's play won the 1935 Drama Critics' Circle Award. Burgess Meredith and Russian-born stage actor Maurice Moscovitch made their Hollywood screen debuts in this film. Meredith, Margo, Eduardo Ciannelli and Fernanda Eliscu appeared in the original New York stage production, and Myron McCormick replaced Ciannelli in the same show. Several reviewers noted the similarities between Anderson's play and the Nicola Sacco-Bartolomeo Vanzetti case. The *NYT* review stated that the reference to the Italian Americans' infamous 1921 trial and their execution in 1927 after a reopening of the case was "thinly disguised." The play's tragic ending was altered for the film. In the play, "Garth" lives and both "Miriamne" and "Mio" are shot and killed by "Trock's" gunman. Although the film, which modern sources state was budgeted at $400,000, was billed as a successor to the critically and financially successful *The Informer*, it did not do well for RKO.

According to modern sources, Anne Shirley was first considered for the role

of "Miriamne." *MPH*'s "In the Cutting Room" includes Sidney Toler, Murray Kinnell and Bobby Caldwell as cast members, but their participation in the final film has not been confirmed. Art director Perry Ferguson and musical director Nathaniel Shilkret received Academy Award nominations for their work on the film. *FD* voted the film one of the year's ten best in its annual poll of film critics.

Modern sources add Alan Curtis (*Sailor*), Arthur Loft (*District attorney*), Otto Hoffman (*Elderly man*), Al Hill (*Gangster*), Bobby Caldwell (*Mio as a boy*) and Grace Hayle to the cast. In 1948, the Mexican subsidiary of RKO released an adaptation of *Winterset*, *A la sombra del puente*, set in Mexico and starring Ester Fernàndez and David Silva. *Winterset* was presented twice on television, in 1951 by the ABC broadcasting network, with Richard Carlyle and Eduardo Ciannelli, and in 1959 by the NBC broadcasting network and *Hallmark Hall of Fame*, with Don Murray, Piper Laurie and George C. Scott.

DV 13 Nov 1936, p. 3. *FD* 17 Nov 1936, pp. 5-9. *HR* 22 Jul 1936, p. 2. *HR* 21 Sep 1936, p. 6. *HR* 13 Nov 1936, p. 3. *MPD* 14 Nov 1936, p. 2. *MPH* 22 Aug 1936, p. 33. *MPH* 21 Nov 1936, p. 46. *NYT* 4 Dec 1936, p. 31. *Var* 9 Dec 1936, p. 12.

WINTERTIME (Norwegian Americans)
Twentieth Century-Fox Film Corp. *Dist* Twentieth Century-Fox Film Corp. 17 Sep **1943**; *Prod:* mid-Mar—mid-Jul 1943 [©Twentieth Century-Fox Film Corp.; 17 Sep 1943; LP12454]. Sd (Western Electric Recording); b&w. 9 reels, 7,418 ft. 82 min. PCA cert no. 9214.

[*Exec prod* Darryl F. Zanuck]. *Prod* William LeBaron. *Dir* John Brahm. [*Fill-in dir* Archie Mayo]. [*Asst dir* Saul Wurtzel]. [*2d unit dir* Otto Brower]. *Scr* E. Edwin Moran, Jack Jevne and Lynn Starling. *Story* Arthur Kober. *Dir of photog* Joe MacDonald. *Mus seq photog* Glen MacWilliams. [*Fill-in photog* Charles Clarke]. [*Fill-in photog* Jimmy Van Trees]. *Spec photog eff* Fred Sersen. *Art dir* James Basevi and Maurice Ransford. *Mus seq stage settings by* Joseph Wright. *Film ed* Louis Loeffler. *Set dec* Thomas Little. *Assoc* Walter M. Scott. *Cost* Rene Hubert. *Mus dir* Emil Newman and Charles Henderson. *Mus seq supv by* Fanchon. *Mus seq staged by* Kenny Williams. [*Fanchon's asst* Carlos Romero and Jimmy Gonzalez]. *Sd* Jesse Bastian and Roger Heman. *Makeup artist* Guy Pearce. [*Dir of pub* Harry Brand].

Music: "Jingle Bells" by J. S. Pierpont; excerpts from *The Nutcracker Suite* by Peter Ilyich Tchaikovsky.

Song(s): "Wintertime," "That Thing They Sing About," "Later Tonight," "Dancing in the Dawn," "Tell Me It's You," "I'm All A-Twitter Over You" and "We Always Get Our Girl," music by Nacio Herb Brown, lyrics by Leo Robin; "I Like It Here," music and lyrics by Leo Robin and Nacio Herb Brown, special lyrics by Charles Henderson.

Cast: SONJA HENIE [(*Nora*)], Jack Oakie [(*Skip Hutton*)], Cesar Romero [(*Brad Barton*)], Carole Landis [(*Flossie Fouchere*)], S. Z. Sakall [(*Hjalmar Ostgaard*)], Cornel Wilde [(*Freddy Austin*)], Woody Herman and His Orchestra, [Helene Reynolds (*Marian Daly*)], [Matt Briggs (*Russell Carter*)], [Don Douglas (*Jay Rogers*)], [Geary Steffen (*Jimmy*)], [Charles Trowbridge (*Mr. Prentice*)], [Nella Walker (*Mrs. Prentice*)], [Georges Renavent (*Bodreau*)], [Jean Del Val (*Constable*)], [Arthur Loft (*Advertising man*)], [Jean De Briac (*Moving man*)], [Henri De Soto (*Headwaiter*)], [Charles Irwin (*Drunk*)], [Dick Elliott (*Husband*)], [Buford McCusker (*Skating partner*)], [Fred Essler (*Consul*)], [Eugene Borden, Muni Seroff (*Workmen*)], [Michael Westfall (*Boy*)], [Gwen Kenyon (*Girl*)], [Gus Corrado (*Clerk*)], [Kay Linaker (*Wife*)], [Kate Harrington, Claire Whitney, Betty Roadman, Leila McIntyre (*Bridge players*)].

Musical comedy. [*Print viewed*]. Skip Hutton, the irrepressible co-owner of the Chateau Promenade in Canada, convinces his creditors to cease their foreclosure procedures for one night, when he will have Norwegian millionaire Hjalmar Ostgaard as his guest. Skip hopes that the presence of Ostgaard and his niece Nora, a world amateur skating champion, will stimulate business, despite the trepidations of his partner, Freddy Austin. Freddy is displeased that Skip has lied to Nora, who believes that they will be staying in the world-famous Chateau Frontenac, and so, upon picking her up at the train station, reveals the truth about her shabby accomodations. Nora kindly overlooks the deception as Ostgaard, sleepy from a cold, is put to bed, and joins Freddy for a cookout over the hotel fireplace. Nora and Ostgaard must remain in Canada to receive their quota numbers, with which they will emigrate to the United States, and while they wait, Nora schemes with Freddy, Skip and Brad Barton, the hotel band's wolfish singer, to trick Ostgaard into buying a fifty-percent interest in the chateau. With Ostgaard's money, Freddy is able to modernize the chateau and attract more business. Although Freddy and Nora begin to fall in love, Freddy is distracted by the appearance of Marian Daly,

a photographer for an influential winter sports magazine. Marian makes no secret of her attraction to Freddy, who is forced to spend time with her in order to get a good review for the chateau. Nora becomes intensely jealous, and her problems increase when Ostgaard's money is frozen after Germany invades Norway. With no more money coming in, Ostgaard is afraid that the hotel will be taken from him, and Nora decides to help by accepting promoter Jay Rogers' offer to star her in an ice skating show in New York City. Due to the invasion of Norway, however, Nora's quota number is no longer valid and she cannot enter the United States unless she marries a U.S. citizen. Her relationship with Freddy having deteriorated, Nora plays up to Brad, who is unaware of her dire financial state. Thinking that he is marrying an heiress, Brad accepts Nora's suggestion that they elope, but Skip, determined to reunite Freddy and Nora, interferes with their plans. Thanks to Skip's machinations, Freddy and Nora reconcile and are soon married, after which Rogers presents Nora in her big show. *Canada. Hotels. Ice skaters and ice skating. Immigrants. Norwegians. Romance. Deception. Elopement. Entrepreneurs. Financial crisis. Fortune hunters. Investments. Jealousy. Photographers. Singers. Skiing. Uncles.*

Note: The working title of this film was *Quota Girl*. According to information in the Twentieth Century-Fox Produced Scripts Collection at the UCLA Arts-Special Collections Library, executive producer Darryl F. Zanuck suggested the film's premise, based on the experiences of his maid, a Swedish national who obtained a quota number and U.S. entry visa through a stay in Canada. The following writers are listed in the scripts collection or *HR* news items as having contributed to the screenplay, but the extent of their contribution to the completed film has not been determined: Franz Spencer, Robert Carson, Francis Wallace, Frederick Jackson and Walter Bullock. *HR* news items supply the following information about the production: The picture was originally to be shot in Technicolor, be directed by H. Bruce Humberstone and feature Phil Regan. Due to wartime construction limits, the studio contemplated filming the picture entirely on location in Quebec, Canada, but instead filmed only background shots near Quebec and in Sun Valley, Idaho. For the Sun Valley location, Johnny Johnson accompanied second unit director Otto Brower, but the exact nature of Johnson's contribution to the film has not been determined. Although Joe MacDonald and Glen MacWilliams are credited onscreen as the film's photographers, *HR* news items and production charts credit Charles Clarke and note that Jimmy Van Trees replaced MacDonald when MacDonald fell ill. Bufford McCusker replaced Geary Steffen as Sonia Henie's skating partner after Steffen was drafted. During the last month of filming, Archie Mayo took over direction of the ice skating production numbers. Studio publicity includes Helene Benda and Manuel Paris in the cast, but their participation in the finished film has not been confirmed.

Box 18 Sep 1943. *DV* 9 Sep 1943, p. 3, 6. *FD* 10 Sep 1943, p. 10. *HR* 3 Dec 1941, p. 2. *HR* 6 Jan 1942, p. 2. *HR* 25 Jun 1942, p. 1. *HR* 3 Jul 1942, p. 4. *HR* 31 Jul 1942, p. 6. *HR* 25 Sep 1942, p. 8. *HR* 25 Jan 1943, p. 4. *HR* 27 Jan 1943, p. 1, 3. *HR* 24 Feb 1943, p. 1. *HR* 25 Feb 1943, p. 3. *HR* 19 Mar 1943, p. 4, 11. *HR* 6 May 1943, pp. 12-13. *HR* 12 May 1943, p. 4. *HR* 17 May 1943, p. 3. *HR* 11 Jun 1943, p. 4. *HR* 14 Jun 1943, p. 5. *HR* 15 Jun 1943, p. 3. *HR* 16 Jul 1943, p. 7. *HR* 9 Sep 1943, p. 3. *HR* 4 Oct 1943, p. 7. *MPD* 9 Sep 1943. *MPH* 11 Sep 1943. *MPHPD* 17 Jul 1943, p. 1431. *MPHPD* 11 Sep 1943, p. 1529. *MPHPD* 6 Nov 1943, p. 1617. *NYT* 30 Sep 1943, p. 27. *Var* 15 Sep 1943, p. 10.

WITCHCRAFT (French Americans, Native Americans)
Jesse L. Lasky Feature Play Co. *Dist* Paramount Pictures Corp. 16 Oct **1916** [©Jesse L. Lasky Feature Play Co.; 5 Oct 1916; LP9246]. Si; b&w. 5 reels.

Pres Frank Reicher. *Dir* Frank Reicher. *Asst dir* L. W. O'Connell. *Scen* Margaret Turnbull. *Story* Robert Ralston Reed. *Cam* Dent Gilbert.

Cast: Fannie Ward (*Suzette*), Jack Dean (*Richard Wayne*), Paul Weigel (*Makepeace Struble*), Lillian Leighton (*Nokomis*).

Historical, Drama. Suzette and her mother are Huguenot refugees living in a New England colony whose elders persecute any so-called deviant behavior, labeling it witchcraft. When Suzette's mother becomes ill, Suzette seeks the help of Nokomis, an Indian woman who has been accused of witchcraft. Suzette meets and falls in love with Richard Wayne, ward of the miserly Makepeace Struble, but Struble, who also covets Suzette, sends Richard to work for the governor so that he can marry her. By accusing her sickly mother of witchcraft, Struble blackmails Suzette into marrying him. When her mother dies, Struble becomes increasingly abusive to Suzette, and in her anger, she wishes him dead. To protect her from evil, Nokomis gives Suzette a talisman, telling her that an Indian uprising is brewing. After Suzette goes to warn Richard about the Indians, Struble, striken with apoplexy, accuses her of casting a spell on him. Although she has saved the town from attack, Suzette is sentenced to hang. Through the last minute intervention of Richard and the governor, Suzette's life is spared, and she and Richard marry. *Battered women. False accusations. New England. United States—History—Colonial period, ca.*

1600-1775. Witchcraft. Blackmail. Duplicity. Huguenots. Indians of North America. Marriage–Forced. Misers. Religious persecution. Stroke. Talismans. Territorial governors. Uprisings. Wards and guardians.

Note: The story for this film was written by Robert Ralston Reed, a New Jersey physician, and was selected as the prize-winning project of the Jesse L. Lasky training program at Columbia University. The class in photodramatics was taught by Professor V. O. Freeburg, and William C. de Mille was the judge for the competition.

Motog 28 Oct 1916, p. 993. *MPN* 28 Oct 1916, p. 2710. *MPW* 28 Oct 1916, p. 536, 606. *NYDM* 21 Oct 1916, p. 26. *Var* 20 Oct 1916, p. 25. *Wid's* 26 Oct 1916, p. 1055.

THE WITCHING EYES (African Americans)

1929 [©Ernest Stern; 26 Nov 1929; LU871]. Si; b&w. Length undetermined. [Feature length assumed.].

Prod Ernest Stern. *Wrt* Ernest Stern.

Melodrama, African American. Haitian Val Napolo, possessed of a witching hand and the evil eye, is persuaded by his friend Cortex to go to the United States and pose as a leader of his people. Napolo meets with great success and gets to know Sylvia Smith, the daughter of a recently deceased black leader. Napolo develops a burning desire for Sylvia, but she favors Ralph Irving, a gentle poet. Napolo puts a curse on them and breaks up their love affair. When Sylvia still refuses him, Napolo kidnaps her. Ralph learns of the abduction and rescues Sylvia, discrediting Napolo in the eyes of his people. *African Americans. Haiti. Kidnapping. Poets. Voodoo.*

WITH BUFFALO BILL ON THE U. P. TRAIL *see* **BUFFALO BILL ON THE U. P. TRAIL**

WITH CUSTER AT LITTLE BIG HORN *see* **GENERAL CUSTER AT LITTLE BIG HORN**

WITH SITTING BULL AT THE SPIRIT LAKE MASSACRE (Native Americans, Dakota)

Sunset Productions. 15 Jun **1927**. Si; b&w. 6 reels, 5,192 ft.

Pres Anthony J. Xydias. *Dir* Robert North Bradbury. *Adpt for the screen* Ben Allah. *Photog* James S. Brown, Jr. *Ed* Della M. King.

Cast: BRYANT WASHBURN (*Donald Keefe*), Chief Yowlache (*Sitting Bull*), Anne Schaefer (*Mame Mulcain*), Jay Morley (*Pat Mulcain*), Shirley Palmer (*Celia Moore*), James O'Neil (*Little Bear*), Bob Bradbury, Jr. (*Bob Keefe*), Fred Warren (*Happy Hartz*), Leon Kent (*John Mulcain*), Lucille Balart (*Mary Moore*), Tom Lingham (*Parson Rogers*).

Historical, Drama. [*Viewed print incomplete*]. In the Midwest, in the 1860s or 1870s, settlements of whites are growing. Although the Sioux Indians have professed their friendliness to one such settlement near Spirit Lake, Iowa, Chief Sitting Bull, whose mere name evokes terror among the whites, surveys the settlement at Spirit Lake from afar and vows to retake the land that belonged to his fathers. He informs a companion that the Great Spirit told him that if he retakes the land, the Great Spirit will send many buffalo and he, Sitting Bull, will be chief of a happy people. Donald Keefe, a resident of the Spirit Lake settlement, rides into town with his brother Bob and meets sisters Celia and Mary Moore. Seeing this, Parson Rogers predicts that there soon will be a double wedding. Meanwhile, the Mulcain family, consisting of Pat, the most disliked man in the settlement, his brother John and Mame, who is known to the Indians as the "White Witch" because of her prophesies, visit Sitting Bull, as Pat wants to trade liquor for pelts. After the trade, Sitting Bull speaks alone to Mame and offers her many pelts and his protection if she will prophesy to his chiefs that they should retake their lands. Some time later, after an attack, Parson Rogers brings Celia to the Mulcain cabin and asks if they will care for her while he goes for help. Mame agrees only after the parson pays her. Meanwhile, the Indians have captured Mary, but Sitting Bull instructs his underling not to let anything happen to her, as he may need a new squaw. At the Mulcain cabin, Pat kisses Celia, who struggles against him before Mame pulls Pat away. The parson notifies Donald, and they ride back with Bob and their pal, Happy Hartz. They find Celia and Mary's father lying dead outside his house and Mary gone. Donald believes it would be suicide to go to the Indian camp that night, so they return to the settlement. The next day, Donald leads a meeting at the settlement, then goes with a few men to Sitting Bull's camp to find Mary. When Sitting Bull and three other Indians come to the Mulcain cabin for the "White Witch" to read their prophesy, the Indian leader tells Donald to come to the camp that afternoon for proof that they do not have Mary. He then assures Mame that she will be safe in his camp during the subsequent attack

on the settlement. He gives her more pelts, then she reads her cards for the others and tells them that the Great Spirit wants Sitting Bull to lead the Indians against the white man. Pat and John Mulcain find Celia eavesdropping at the door and capture her. At the Indian camp, while the Indians do an ominous ghost dance, Donald rescues Mary and other white girls who have been captured, but Pat and his brother see them. Donald and Bob knock out the Mulcains, and Happy sends the girls to warn the settlers that the Indians are on the warpath. After the Indians capture Happy, Donald and Bob rescue him. As Sitting Bull and many braves ride off to fight, Donald sends Bob to bring back soldiers. Meanwhile, after the girls spread the word that the Indians are coming to attack, the settlers fire on the Indians as they ride through town. Bob relays the message at an army post. Sitting Bull and his braves are victorious, but when Pat asks for his share of the plunder, Sitting Bull submits him to the "vengeance of the squaws," who surround and begin to kick him. Sitting Bull's victory is short-lived, as the soldiers win the battle against him. He is shorn of his eagle feathers and put on the reservation, where he continues to dream of power. Finally, Parson Rogers' prophesy of a double wedding comes true. *Dakota Indians. Deception. Indians of North America. Prophets. Raids. Settlers. Sitting Bull. Spirit Lake (IA). Brothers. Eavesdropping. Kidnapping. Oaths. Parsons. Romance. Sisters.*

Note: This film was also known as *Sitting Bull at the "Spirit Lake Massacre"*. In the opening credits, the phrase "A Thrilling Epic of Frontier Days" follows the title. One reel of six was missing from the print viewed.

Var 3 Aug 1927, p. 19.

WITHIN OUR GATES (African Americans)

Micheaux Film Co. *Dist* Micheaux Film Co.; Quality Amusement Corp. 12 Jan **1920**. Si; b&w. 7 or 8 reels.

Prod Oscar Micheaux. *Dir* Oscar Micheaux. *Scen* Oscar Micheaux.

Cast: Evelyn Preer (*Sylvia Landry*), Flo Clements (*Alma Prichard*), James D. Ruffin (*Conrad Drebert*), Jack Chenault (*Larry Prichard*), William Smith (*Philip Gentry, a detective*), Charles D. Lucas (*Dr. V. Vivian*), Bernice Ladd (*Mrs. Geraldine Stratton*), Mrs. Evelyn (*Mrs. Elena Warwick*), William Starks (*Jasper Landry*), Ralph Johnson (*Philip Griddlestone*), E. G. Tatum (*Efrem*), Grant Edwards (*Emil*), Grant Gorman (*Armand Griddlestone*), [Mattie Edwards], [S. T. Jacks], [Jimmie Cook].

African American, Drama. [*Print viewed*]. Sylvia Landry, a young black woman from the South, visits her Northern cousin, divorcee Alma Prichard. Sylvia's fiancé, Conrad Drebert, writes to her from Brazil, where he is working, to express his joy at their forthcoming wedding and tell her that he will send a telegram with the date of his arrival. When the telegram arrives, though, Alma, who is in love with Conrad, intercepts and destroys it, then connives to have Sylvia be seen with another man when Conrad arrives. When the innocent Sylvia appears, Conrad tries to strangle her, but she is saved by Alma. Conrad storms out and breaks their engagement, much to Alma's satisfaction. In her sorrow, Sylvia takes a job at a Southern school for poor black children that is run by Reverend Wilson Jacobs and his sister Constance. When money troubles hit the establishment, however, Sylvia decides to go to Boston to find a rich benefactor. One day, depressed that she has not met any rich people to take an interest in the school's plight, Sylvia saves a little boy from being struck by the car of rich philanthropist Elena Warwick, and is herself injured. Mrs. Warwick visits her in the hospital and Sylvia tells her that the school must find $5,000 in the next ten days or it will close. Mrs. Warwick is set to give the school the money until she speaks with her friend, Mrs. Geraldine Stratton, a woman who opposes the suffragette movement because it appalls her that black women would also get the vote. Mrs. Stratton convinces the naïve Mrs. Warwick that educating blacks is a mistake, and that they are more suited to being field hands and lumberjacks. She suggests giving the money to Old Ned, a black preacher whose fiery sermons encourage blacks to remain "pure" and untainted by education, culture and politics. When Sylvia returns to collect the school's money from Mrs. Warwick, she is refused, but later, Mrs. Warwick changes her mind and sends the school fifty-thousand dollars. Sylvia returns to Piney Woods, where Jacobs proposes. Sylvia refuses the offer, however, as she has fallen in love with Doctor V. Vivian, a young Boston man deeply committed to improving blacks' social conditions, who had saved her when she was pickpocketed on the street beneath his office window. Meanwhile, Larry, Alma's stepbrother, a notorious gangster whose alias is "The Leech," is fleeing police after killing another gambler in a card game.

He escapes to Vicksburg, where he plans to swindle the poor blacks in the Piney Woods region by selling them stolen goods. Larry eventually encounters Sylvia, with whom he was once in love, and tells her that he will reveal her past to the school's administrators if she does not steal the school's money for him. Distraught, Sylvia returns to Boston. Larry, meanwhile, has also gone back North and is shot while trying to rob a bank. When Dr. Vivian goes to the Prichards' to tend Larry's wounds, he meets Alma, who tells him about Sylvia's past: Sylvia was adopted by a family of poor black southerners named Landry. When she was a young girl, the Landrys sent Sylvia to school, and the educated girl eventually realized that her father's landlord and employer, Philip Griddlestone, owed him six-hundred-twenty-five dollars. Armed with his daughter's calculations, Mr. Landry went to see Griddlestone, who rudely dismissed him. At that moment, a white laborer whom Griddlestone had earlier swindled, entered the room and shot Griddlestone, after which Efrem, Griddlestone's gossipy, meddlesome servant, screamed through the town's streets that Mr. Landry murdered his employer. A lynch mob formed and the Landry family ran away, taking refuge in the swamps. The manhunt continued for a week, and, frustrated that the Landrys had eluded them, the mob attacked and killed the traitorous Efrem, who had been gloating about how much the whites loved him. Mr. and Mrs. Landry and their young son Emil were captured on a Sunday. The parents were hanged and burned at the stake, but Emil escaped. Meanwhile, the real killer was accidentally shot by the mob, and Griddlestone's brother Armand followed Sylvia back to her refuge, the home of her parents' friends. As Armand attacked her and tried to rape her, he saw a scar on her breast and suddenly realized that Sylvia was his own daughter from his legitimate union with a black woman. Armand then paid for the girl's education but never revealed his identity, and left the house that day, without telling her that he was her father. Back in the present, Dr. Vivian finds a distraught Sylvia and tells her that they must remember that their people fought in Cuba, Mexico and France for the freedom of their great country. Confident that once married Sylvia will be an excellent wife and a confirmed patriot, Dr. Vivian is not disappointed. *African Americans. Lynching. Murder. Plantation owners. Racism. Schools. Sharecroppers. Southerners. United States–South. African Americans–Mixed blood. Attempted rape. Blackmail. Boston (MA). Brazil. Clergy. Detectives. Dreams. Engagements. Gangsters. Jealousy. Mobs. Philanthropy. Religion. Swindlers and swindling. Working women.*

Note: Ads for the film alternately list its length as seven or eight reels. The film created controversy over its scenes of lynching and racial conflict, and by Jun 1920 the film had been edited down to six reels, with much of its controversial material removed. One modern source adds LaFont Harris (*The boy*) to the cast. Other modern sources state that the film was based on the Leo M. Frank murder-lynching case, and that Oscar Micheaux's 1921 film *The Gunsaulus Mystery* (see above) is a re-edited version of *Within Our Gates*, but these claims are most likely false. Micheaux's production company is alternately listed as the Micheaux Book and Film Co. and the Micheaux Film Co. in contemporary sources. It is unclear whether the Quality Amusement Corp. distributed the film from the beginning or became the distributor after its early playdates.

New York Age 17 Jul 1920, p. 6. *New York Age* 25 Dec 1920, p. 6.

WITHOUT A MOTHER AND SWEETHEART *see* **SENZA MAMMA E'NNAMURATO**

WITHOUT HONOR *see* **HE WAS HER MAN**

WITHOUT RESERVATIONS (Latino)
Jesse L. Lasky Productions, Inc.; RKO Radio Pictures, Inc.; Mervyn LeRoy's Production. *Dist* RKO Radio Pictures, Inc. May **1946**; *Prod:* 15 Oct 1945–14 Jan 1946; addl scenes mid-Feb 1946 [©Jesse L. Lasky Productions, Inc.; 3 Jun 1946; LP433]. Sd (RCA Sound System); b&w. 105 or 107 min. PCA cert no. 11262.

Prod JESSE L. LASKY and WALTER MACEWEN. *Dir* MERVYN LEROY. *Asst dir* Lloyd Richards. *Scr* Andrew Solt. *Dir of photog* Milton Krasner. [*2d cam* Harry Davis]. *Spec eff* Vernon L. Walker, Russell A. Cully and Harold Stine. *Mont* Harold Palmer. [*Matte paintings* Al Simpson]. [*Transparency projections shots* Lynn Dunn]. *Art dir* Albert S. D'Agostino and Ralph Berger. *Ed* Jack Ruggiero. *Set dec* Darrell Silvera and James Altwies. *Miss Colbert's clothes by* Adrian. *Mus dir* C. Bakaleinikoff. *Mus* Roy Webb. *Sd* Clem Portman and Francis M. Sarver. [*Mus mixer* Earl B. Mounce]. *Prod asst* William H. Cannon. [*Advertising and pub dir* William Hebert].

Source: Based on the novel *Thanks, God, I'll Take It From Here* by Jane Allen and Mae Livingston (unpublished).

Cast: CLAUDETTE COLBERT ([*Christopher*] *Kit* [*Madden, also known as Kit Klotch*]), JOHN WAYNE ([*Captain*] *Rusty* [*Thomas*]), Don DeFore ([*Lieutenant*] *Dink* [*Watson*]), Anne Triola ([*Consuela*] *Connie* (*Callahan*)), Phil Brown (*Soldier*), Frank Puglia (*Ortega*), Thurston Hall ([*Henry*] *Baldwin*), Dona Drake (*Dolores* [*Ortega*]), Fernando Alvarado (*Mexican boy*), Charles Arnt (*Salesman*), Miss Louella Parsons [(*Herself*)], [Jack Benny, Cary Grant, Dolores Moran, Mervyn LeRoy (*Themselves*)], [Charles Evans (*Jerome*)], [Harry Hayden (*Mr. Randall*)], [Lela Bliss (*Mrs. Randall*)], [Houseley Stevenson (*Turnkey*)], [Junius Matthews (*Potter*)], [Griff Barnett (*Train conductor*)], [Will Wright, Tom Chatterton (*Pullman conductors*)], [Thelma Gyrath, Marilyn Buford (*WACs*)], [J. Louis Johnson (*Car porter*)], [Frank Dae (*Man with book*)], [Ian Wolfe (*Charlie Gibbs*)], [Grace Hampton (*Lois*)], [Minerva Urecal (*Sue*)], [Esther Howard (*Sarah*)], [Robert Espinosa, Henry Mirelez, Rose Marie Lopez, Michael Economides, José Alvarado, George Economides, Miguel Tapia (*Mexican children*)], [Dick Dickerson (*Young sailor*)], [Joel Fluellen (*Waiter in club car*)], [Jack Parker, John Crawford, Lee Bennett, Henry Vroom (*Soldiers*)], [Oscar O'Shea (*Conductor*)], [Ruth Roman (*Girl in negligee*)], [William Challee (*Corporal*)], [Sam McDaniel (*Freddy*)], [Henry Hastings, Ernest Anderson (*Waiters*)], [Tay Dunn (*Navy ensign*)], [Harold Davis, Tom Hubbard, Bob Wallace, Sid Davies, Charles Elmergreen, Fleet White, Bill Shannon, Roger Creed, Joe Haworth, Peter Michael (*Marines*)], [Ralph Hubbard, Russ Whiteman (*Sailors*)], [John Gilbreath, Bill Udell (*Navy N.C.'s*)], [Brook Hunt, Bruce Brewster, Charles Faber (*Army lieutenants*)], [Bill O'Leary (*Candy Butcher*)], [Chef Milani (*Diner captain*)], [Harry Evans, Paul Gustine (*Travelers*)], [Reid Kilpatrick, Marvin Miller (*Announcers*)], [Vincent Graeff (*Boy Scout*)], [Kernan Cripps, Charlie Moore, Dudley Dickerson (*Red Caps*)], [Charles Williams (*Bert*)], [Erskine Sanford (*Tim*)], [Jan Wiley (*Manicurist*)], [John Bleifer (*Coal heaver*)], [Charles Hall (*Window washer*)], [Art Miles (*Truck driver*)], [Warren Smith, Eric Alden (*Chauffeurs*)], [Al Kunde, George Russell, Bill Sundholm, Frank Pharr (*Abraham Lincolns*)], [Harry Holman, Wallace Scott (*Gas station attendants*)], [Lisa Golm (*Alma*)], [Blanca Vischer (*Mexican beauty*)], [John Kellogg, Robin Short, Nanette Vallon, Jean Wong (*Reporters*)], [Lois Austin (*Congresswoman*)], [Leona Maricle (*Baldwin's secretary*)], [Jean Koehler (*Western Union operator*)], [Harry Strang (*Policeman*)], [Cy Kendall (*Bond's man*)], [William Benedict (*Western Union boy*)], [Lorin Raker (*Mr. Klotch*)], [Jesse Graves (*Porter*)], [Al Rosen (*Train mechanic*)], [George Magrill (*Taxi driver*)], [Raymond Burr (*Paul Gill*)], [Fred Coby (*French officer*)], [Verne Richards (*Brakeman*)], [June Glory], [Barbara Smith], [Bob Pepper].

Road, Romantic comedy. [*Print viewed*]. Hollywood-bound author Christopher "Kit" Madden, whose best-selling novel *Here Is Tomorrow* is the talk of the nation, is about to board a train in New York when she is cabled that Cary Grant is unavailable to play the lead in the screen adaptation of her book. Although Kit initially rejects the suggestion of Arrowhead Pictures producer Henry Baldwin that an unknown be cast as the novel's post-war hero, she changes her mind when she is seated across from Captain Rusty Thomas, a handsome Marine. Immediately struck by Rusty's masculine charm, Kit finds herself lying about her identity upon hearing Rusty and his good-natured traveling companion, Lieutenant Dink Watson, denigrating *Here Is Tomorrow*. Calling herself Kit Klotch, Kit defends the book and insists on the credibility of the hero's pragmatic notions about romance. While waiting for a new train in Chicago, Kit receives a telegram from Baldwin, whom she had contacted earlier about Rusty, ordering her to keep track of him. Rusty and Dink, however, leave the station in order to purchase some rationed whiskey, and Kit ends up missing her train while chasing after them. To avoid revealing herself, the baggage-less Kit pretends that she has lost her ticket and is forced to travel in the coach section. Kit nonetheless enjoys herself with Rusty and Dink, getting drunk and silly in the dining car. When Consuela "Connie" Callahan, a talkative flirt whom Dink and Rusty refer to as a "beetle," accuses Kit of stealing her orchid, however, a scene erupts, and Kit is thrown off the train the next morning. Then, as they make plans with Kit to meet up in San Diego, where they are stationed, Rusty and Dink miss their train. Although the Marines have access to a nearby military airfield, Rusty, eager to stay with Kit, lies

that the next flight to San Diego has been canceled due to bad weather. Kit, Rusty and Dink get caught in a downpour while walking from the airfield, but are befriended by a man who eventually sells Kit his exotic, fussy Italian car. During the drive west, Rusty tries to romance Kit in a hay field, but his unabashed sexuality unnerves her and causes her to intellectualize the situation. Frustrated, Rusty starts to mope until the car runs out of water and they are forced to seek help at a New Mexican ranch. There Rusty flirts with the Mexican-American ranch owner's daughter, causing Kit to seethe with jealousy. Anxious to stop the flirtation, Kit tells the patriotic rancher that Rusty and Dink stole their uniforms and are only posing as Marines. When the enraged rancher begins firing his rifle at Dink and Rusty, the trio drives off in a frenzy. After Kit confesses her lie and thereby reveals her true feelings, she and Rusty happily reconcile. Later, at an Albuquerque hotel, Kit, who left her purse at the ranch, decides to use her notoriety to wrangle a room for the night. The scheme backfires, however, when a local newspaper reporter informs the hotel manager that according to the latest press wire, Kit has already arrived in Hollywood. Kit is thrown in jail, but is bailed out by the still ignorant Dink and Rusty. Baldwin then arrives to vouch for Kit, and upon learning of Kit's true identity, Rusty becomes irate and refuses to consider starring in her movie. While Kit then makes her mark in Hollywood, Rusty feigns indifference and tries to ignore reports about Kit's romance with an Arrowhead star. At Dink's urging, Rusty finally admits that he still loves Kit and wires her that he is coming to visit. As Rusty pulls up to her house, an overjoyed Kit looks heavenward and says, "Thanks, God, I'll take it from here." *Impersonation and imposture. Novelists. Officers (Military). Romance. Albuquerque (NM). Automobiles. Chicago (IL). Deception. Drunkenness. Grand Central Station (New York City). Hotels. Jails. Jealousy. Mexican Americans. Motion picture actors and actresses. Motion picture producers. New Mexico. Patriotism. Ranchers. Rationing in wartime. Reporters. San Diego (CA). Telegrams. Train stations. Trains. United States. Marine Corps.*

Note: The working title of this film was *Thanks, God, I'll Take It From Here.* The picture was the first that Jesse L. Lasky Productions made in conjuction with RKO. Director Mervyn LeRoy's film company was called Arrowhead Productions, the same name used for the movie company in the film, but Arrowhead was not involved in the making of this picture. RKO borrowed Don DeFore from Hal Wallis' company for the production. *HR* announced that LeRoy was testing Lieutenant Gavin Alberts and Dorothy Porter for roles in the film, but their participation in the final film has not been confirmed. Mabel Webb was announced as a cast member in *HR*, but her participation in the final film has not been confirmed. Background shots for the production were filmed in Chicago and New York, and some scenes were shot in Chatsworth, CA, according to *HR*. Some reviewers commented on the similarity between this picture and Frank Capra's 1934 Columbia hit *It Happened One Night*, which also starred Claudette Colbert (see *AFI Catalog of Feature Films, 1931-40*; F3.2181). According to modern sources, the film cost $1,683,000 to produce. Claudette Colbert reprised her role in a *Lux Radio Theatre* broadcast on 26 Aug 1946, with co-star Robert Cummings.

Box 11 May 1946. DV 8 May 1946, p. 5. FD 13 May 1946, p. 12. HR 11 May 1945, p. 8. HR 10 Jul 1945, p. 2. HR 8 Aug 1945, p. 9. HR 23 Aug 1945, p. 14. HR 9 Oct 1945, p. 3. HR 18 Oct 1945, p. 3. HR 9 Nov 1945, p. 6. HR 9 Jan 1946, p. 14. HR 15 Jan 1946, p. 2. HR 12 Feb 1946, p. 13. HR 8 May 1946, p. 3, 16. HR 12 Jun 1946, p. 8. MPHPD 9 Mar 1946, p. 2884. MPHPD 11 May 1946, p. 2985. NYT 8 Jun 1946, p. 17. Var 8 May 1946, p. 8.

WITHOUT SHAME *see* **UNASHAMED**

WOLF RIDERS (Native Americans)
Reliable Pictures Corp. *Dist* State Rights; Commodore Pictures Corp.; William Steiner. 26 Dec 1935. Sd; b&w. 6 reels, 5,311 ft. 59 min. Passed by the National Board of Review.

Pres BERNARD B. RAY. *Assoc prod* Harry S. Webb. *Dir* Harry S. Webb. *Asst dir* William Nolte. *Story* Carl Krusada. *Dial* Lewie C. Borden. *Cont* Rose Gordon. *Photog* J. Henry Kruse. *Art tech* Charles Stevens. *Ed* Fred Bain. *Sd* J. S. Westmoreland.

Cast: JACK PERRIN (*Jack Jennings*), Lillian Gilmore (*Mary Clark*), Lafe McKee (*Clark*), Nancy Deshon (*Peggy*), William Gould (*Butch Weldon*), George Chesebro (*Al Pearce*), Earl Dwire (*Red Wolf*), Starlight (*Himself*), [Slim Whitaker (*Butch's henchman*)], [Frank Ellis (*Jennings, Jack's father*)].

Western. [*Print viewed*]. Three bandits, pursued by the Indian chief Red Wolf and his warriors for stealing their furs, find the cabin of settler Jennings and demand his ammunition. Jennings, who is Red Wolf's friend, only helps the men after being threatened. When the Indians arrive, Jennings and his wife are killed in the crossfire while trying to protect their infant son Jack. Before he dies, Jennings asks Red Wolf to rear Jack. Five years pass, and Red Wolf, who has treated

Jack as his own son and taught him never to lie, takes Jack to the U.S. Customs Indian agent, Clark, and asks him to adopt Jack and send him to school. When Jack is an adult, he makes his adopted fathers proud as he works with Clark to protect the Indians. One day, Jack sees a gang robbing two Indians of their furs, and while Jack catches two of them, one escapes. The fleeing bandit, Al Pearce, goes to the Crystal Hotel, owned by local bigwig Butch Weldon, and tells Butch that Jack captured their men. Butch and Al squabble over what action to take and also over Peggy, Butch's new singer and Al's girl friend. Peggy flirts with both of them, but tells Al that she loves him best. He replies that after selling their next load of furs, he and Butch are through. Butch overhears their conversation and plans to get rid of Al. Meanwhile, Jack confides his suspicions that Butch is the gang's ringleader to Clark and Red Wolf, and they warn him that he will need solid evidence because Butch has so much influence. Jack then goes to greet his childhood sweetheart, Clark's daughter Mary, who is visiting from school. After he sees her, Jack goes on patrol and catches Al with furs bearing the company tag, which marks them as Indian and government property. Butch ambushes them as they talk and, after knocking Jack out, murders Al and shoots one shot from Jack's gun, thus making it appear that Jack killed Al. Jack regains consciousness and takes Al's body to town, where he confesses to Clark that he does not know if he killed Al or not, and that the stolen pelts are missing. Clark reluctantly arrests Jack, after which Peggy hysterically calls him a murderer. Later, Clark orders two deputies to take Jack to the county seat, as Butch's gang is threatening him. They are followed by Peggy, who shoots at Jack and believes she has hit him after he falls from his horse. Jack is not harmed though, and goes to Red Wolf for advice. Red Wolf devises a trap for Butch and sends Jack, disguised as an Indian, with Young Bear to try to sell company furs to Butch. Jack, Red Wolf and the other Indians trap Butch, and after Jack gets Butch to write a confession stating that he killed Al, Red Wolf forces Jack and Butch to exchange clothes. Red Wolf then sets Butch free, and just after he leaves, Butch is killed by Peggy, who thinks he is Jack. Before he dies, Butch confesses his guilt to Peggy, and Jack, now cleared, kisses Mary. *Bandits. Frame-ups. Fur. Indians of North America. Murder. Thieves. Confession. Hotel owners. Indian agents. Orphans. Revenge. Romantic rivalry. Wards and guardians.*

Note: Although there is a copyright statement in this film's onscreen credits, the title is not listed in the copyright register. The running time listed above was calculated from footage given in NYSA records. According to modern sources, Budd Buster, Robert Walker, George Morrell and Blackie Whiteford were also in the cast.

FD 4 Jan 1935, p. 2.

WOLF SONG (Native Americans)
Paramount Famous Lasky Corp. 30 Mar 1929 [©Paramount Famous Lasky Corp.; 29 Mar 1929; LP254]. Singing sequences, sd eff, and mus score (Movietone); b&w. 8 reels, 6,769 ft. [Also si; 6,060 ft.].

Dir Victor Fleming. *Scr* John Farrow and Keene Thompson. *Titles* Julian Johnson. *Photog* Allen Siegler. *Film ed* Eda Warren. *Mus dir* Irvin Talbot. *Supv mus rec* Max Terr.

Song(s): "Mi amado," words by Lewis and Young, music by Harry Warren; "Yo te amo Means I Love You," words by Al Bryan, music by Richard Whiting.

Source: Based on the short story "Wolf Song" by Harvey Ferguson in *Red Book* (Jul—Aug 1927).

Cast: Gary Cooper (*Sam Lash*), Lupe Velez (*Lola Salazar*), Louis Wolheim (*Gullion*), Constantine Romanoff (*Rube Thatcher*), Michael Vavitch (*Don Solomon Salazar*), Ann Brody (*Duenna*), Russ Colombo (*Ambrosia Guiterrez*), Augustina Lopez (*Louisa*), George Rigas (*Black Wolf*).

Western. Lola Salazar, the daughter of a haughty California don, elopes with Sam Lash, an unkempt Kentucky trapper of no particular means. They live together in a settlement in the mountains until Sam decides that he is sick of civilization; he rejoins his former companions in the Canadian wilderness, while Lola returns to her family. Sam soon finds the nights too long and lonely and heads home, only to be shot by a couple of braves. He drags himself to Lola's hacienda, however, and they are reunited. *California. Canada. Elopement. Indians of North America. Kentucky. Sierra Nevada Mountains (CA and NV). Spaniards. Trappers.*

Note: Filmed on location in the California Sierras.
FD 3 Mar 1929. *Var* 27 Feb 1929, p. 80.

WOLVES OF CATCLAW see THE PRESCOTT KID

WOLVES OF THE NORTH (Native Americans, Native Alaskans)
Universal Film Mfg. Co. 16 Apr **1921** [©Universal Film Mfg. Co.; 29 Apr 1921; LP16459]. Si; b&w. 5 reels, 4,404 ft.
Dir Norman Dawn. *Scen* Wallace Clifton. *Story* Norman Dawn. *Photog* Thomas Rae.
Cast: Herbert Heyes (*"Wiki" Jack Horn*), Percy Challenger (*Professor Norris*), Eva Novak (*Aurora Norris*), Starke Patterson (*David Waters*), Barbara Tennant (*Jenfau Jen*), William Eagle Eye (*Massakee*), Clyde Tracy (*Lech*), Millie Impolito (*Rose of Spain*).
Melodrama. Aurora, daughter of Professor Norris, a student of Eskimo culture in the region of Unalik on the southeast coast of Alaska, is devoted to David, a youth of weak character who has been reared in the family, and she is aloof to other men. "Wiki" Jack, primitive and passionate, sets out to win her despite her unconcealed disdain for him. After David's death in an avalanche, Aurora begins to admire Wiki's steadfast courage and submits to his overpowering love. *Alaska. Avalanches. Native Alaskans.*
Note: The working title of this film was *The Evil Half.*
FD 15 May 1921. *Var* 20 May 1921, p. 41.

THE WOMAN AND THE BEAST (Italian Americans)
Graphic Features. *Dist* Graphic Features; State Rights. Apr **1917**. Si; b&w. 5 reels.
Dir Ernest C. Warde. *Scen* Emmet Mixx. *Cam* William M. Zollinger.
Cast: Marie Shotwell (*Rosa*), Fred Eric (*John*), Alphonse Ethier (*Big Frank*), Kathryn Adams (*Marie*), J. H. Gilmour (*The priest*), Tula Belle (*The child*).
Drama. John, an Italian musician, comes to America and settles in a small Italian enclave where he courts and marries Rosa, a beautiful widow, thus incurring the enmity of Big Frank, Rosa's former suitor. John's peaceful demeanor antagonizes his hot-tempered wife, and frequent quarrels result, but their mutual love for Rosa's little daughter usually reconciles the pair. When the circus comes to town, Big Frank stabs and kills the tent man and hides in the woods. In the ruckus a lion escapes, and Rosa's little daughter, frightened by the sight of the beast, is injured in a fall. Roused by his wife's taunts of cowardice, John joins the hunt for the lion. Rosa, repenting her outburst of temper, goes in search of her husband and is attacked by Frank who runs off when a priest appears. Meanwhile John sees the lion enter a shack at the foot of a hill. Frank, seeking refuge, enters the shack and is attacked by the lion. From the ridge above, John loosens a huge rock which falls upon the shack, killing the lion and Frank. Rosa then proclaims her husband a hero, and all their differences are reconciled. *Children. Fugitives. Heroism. Immigrants. Italians. Lions. Marriage. Widows. Attempted rape. Circuses. Forests. Jealousy. Murder. Musicians. Priests. Wounds and injuries.*
Note: Animal trainer Captain Jack Bonavita, who was killed by one of his own lions before this film's release, served as Alphonse Ethier's double in the fight scene with a lion.
ETR 12 May 1917, p. 1606. *MPN* 12 May 1917, p. 3014-15. *MPW* 21 Apr 1917, p. 379. *Var* 21 Dec 1917, p. 1606. *Wid's* 13 Dec 1917, p. 795.

WOMAN AND THE LAW (Latino)
Fox Film Corp.; A Fox Standard Picture. *Dist* Fox Film Corp. 17 Mar **1918** [©William Fox; 3 Mar 1918; LP12210]. Si; b&w. 7 reels.
Pres William Fox. *Dir* Raoul A. Walsh. *Scen* Raoul A. Walsh. *Cam* Roy Overbaugh.
Cast: Miriam Cooper (*Blanquetta La Salle*), Ramsey Wallace (*Jack La Salle*), Peggy Hopkins (*Josie Sabel*), Jack Connors (*Jack La Salle, Jr.*), George Humbert (*Señor Del Castillo*), Agnes Neilsen (*Señora Del Castillo*), Lewis Dayton (*Ramon Alvarez*), John Laffe (*Col. Thomas La Salle*), Lillian Satherwaite (*Ruth La Salle*), Winifred Allen (*Blanquetta as a young woman*).
Drama. Jack La Salle marries South American heiress Blanquetta Del Castillo, and the two settle into a happy life in New York City. Following the birth of their son, Jack, Jr., however, Jack becomes involved in an affair with the notorious Josie Sabel and thereafter ignores his wife. Outraged upon learning that Jack has taken their son to Josie's apartment, Blanquetta files for divorce, the court finally ruling that the boy must live with each parent for a portion of the year. As the time of little Jack's departure from his father approaches, Jack, Sr. declares that he will never return the boy to his mother, whereupon the tortured Blanquetta shoots and kills her faithless husband. The jury, moved by Blanquetta's desire to love and protect

her son, ultimately acquits her. *Child custody. Divorce. Infidelity. Manslaughter. Mothers and sons. Fathers and sons. Heiresses. New York City. South Americans. Trials.*
Note: The film was based on a murder case in which Blanca De Saulles shot her former husband, John Longer De Saulles, on 3 Aug 1917. The film had its premiere in New York on 3 Mar 1918.
ETR 16 Mar 1918, p. 1232. *MPN* 23 Mar 1918, pp. 1670-71, 1764-65. *MPW* 23 Mar 1918, p. 1701. *Var* 15 Mar 1918, p. 43. *Wid's* 28 Mar 1918, p. 1031.

THE WOMAN AND THE WILD RIVER see WILD RIVER

THE WOMAN HE LOVED (Jewish Americans)
Dist American Releasing Corp. 1 Oct **1922**. Si; b&w. 5 reels, 5,200 ft.
Dir Edward Sloman. *Story and scen* William V. Mong. *Photog* Antonio Gaudio.
Cast: William V. Mong (*Nathan Levinsky*), Marcia Manon (*Esther Levinsky*), Eddie Sutherland (*Jimmy Danvers*), Mary Wynn (*Helen Comstock*), Charles French (*John Comstock*), Fred Malatesta (*Max Levy*), Harvey Clark (*John Danvers*), Bruce Guerin (*David Levinsky, as a child*), Lucille Ward (*Rosie Romansky*).
Drama. Suffering persecution, Russian Jews Nathan Levinsky, his wife, Esther, and his son, David, escape their homeland for the United States, where Nathan ekes out a feeble existence as a peddler. Esther despairs of her life and leaves Nathan for Max Levy, but reverses cause her to allow David to be adopted by the wealthy Danvers family. Some years later, Nathan prospers on a small California ranch, which adjoins the larger ranch of John Comstock. Comstock makes no secret of his dislike for Jews, yet he unknowingly approves when his daughter, Helen, falls in love with the Danvers' adopted son, Jimmy, whom Nathan secretly recognizes as David. Nathan loses everything in a fire, goes to San Francisco to begin anew, and is reunited with a contrite Esther. Jimmy learns the truth about his parentage and goes to San Francisco to search for Nathan; Helen and Comstock follow, and Helen disappears. Nathan saves Helen from disgrace at the hands of Max Levy, and gratitude prompts Comstock to sanction Helen's marriage to Jimmy. *Adoption. Bigotry. California. Immigrants. Jews. Marriage–Mixed. Parentage. Peddlers and peddling. San Francisco (CA).*
ETR 16 Sep 1922. FD 10 Sep 1922. *MPN* 16 Sep 1922, p. 1387. *MPW* 16 Sep 1922. *MPW* 30 Sep 1922. *Var* 8 Sep 1922, p. 41.

THE WOMAN IN BLACK (Gypsies)
Biograph Co.; Klaw and Erlanger; Special Features Dept. *Dist* General Film Co. Nov **1914** [©Klaw & Erlanger; 31 Oct 1914; LP3649]. Si; b&w. 4 reels.
Dir Lawrence Marston. *Cam* Tony G. Gaudio.
Source: Based on the play *The Woman in Black* by H. Grattan Donnelly (New York, 25 Jan 1897).
Cast: Lionel Barrymore (*Robert Crane*), Alan Hale (*Frank Mansfield*), Mrs. Lawrence Marston (*Zenda, also known as The Woman in Black*), Marie Newton (*Mary, the gypsy girl*), Millicent Evans (*Stella Everett*), Charles Hill Mailes (*Mr. Everett*), Hector V. Sarno, Jack Drumier, Frank Evans.
Melodrama. Mary, a young gypsy girl, is seduced by the immoral Robert Crane and abandoned. She is exiled from the gypsies and, along with her mother Zenda, known as "The Woman in Black," she vows revenge. Meanwhile, Crane blackmails Stella Everett's father into forcing her to marry him, even though she loves Frank Mansfield, Crane's rival for a congressional seat. Frank wins, but Stella still faces the prospect of marriage to Crane until Zenda comes to her with a plan. On their wedding day, after the vows are recited, Crane lifts the veil from his wife's face and discovers that his bride is actually Mary. Now Stella and Frank are free to marry, and Zenda has gained her revenge. *Cads. Gypsies. Marriage–Forced by circumstances. Revenge. Blackmail. Desertion (Marital). Impersonation and imposture. Mothers and daughters. Political candidates. Rivalry. Seduction. Weddings.*
Note: This film was first released in 1914 as a three-reeler; it was also released in a five reel version in 1916.
Motog 21 Nov 1914, p. 719. *Var* 20 Aug 1915, p. 21.

THE WOMAN IN 47 (Italian Americans)
Frohman Amusement Corp. *Dist* Equitable Motion Pictures Corp., releasing through World Film Corp. 7 Feb **1916** [©Equitable Motion Pictures Corp.; 27 Jan 1916; LU7557]. Si; b&w. 5 reels.
Dir George Irving. *Story* Frederick Chapin.
Cast: Alice Brady (*Viola Donizetti*), William Raymond (*Tony*), John Warwick (*Tony's cousin*), George D. Melville (*Pasquale Donizetti*), Eric Blind (*Mr. Collingswood*), Lillian Concord (*Mrs. Collingswood*), Tom McGrath (*Mr. Sharpless*), Bert Rooney (*Godfrey, his son*), Jack Sherrill (*The reporter*).

Drama. To get away from her father and the fiancé he has chosen for her, Viola Donizetti emigrates from Italy to the United States, determined to rejoin Tony, her sweetheart. Unable to find Tony, however, Viola begins a relationship with the wealthy Collingswood, but leaves him when she discovers that he has a wife. Then, Viola finally locates Tony, with whom she makes plans to get married. Before the ceremony, they check into room 47, while Collingswood, obsessed with Viola, goes to the hotel and moves into room 48. He writes a suicide note citing his failed affair with Viola as the reason for his actions and then shoots himself. When Tony reads the note, he decides to leave Viola, but the priest who has been summoned to perform the ceremony persuades him to forget about the letter, and then, finally, Tony and Viola marry. *Hotels. Immigrants. Infidelity. Italians. Suicide. Italy. Marriage–Arranged. Priests. Suicide notes.*

Note: *Motog* lists Edwin August as the director of the film, as well as an actor in it. However, no other source mentions him. The film was re-issued in late 1920 or early 1921 on a state rights basis by the Frohman Amusement Corp.
Motog 12 Feb 1916, p. 374. *MPN* 19 Feb 1916, p. 1021. *MPN* 18 Sep 1920, P. 2204. *MPN* 23 Oct 1920, p. 3206. *MPW* 12 Feb 1916, p. 886. *MPW* 19 Feb 1916, p. 1141, 1200. *Var* 4 Feb 1916, p. 25.

WOMAN IN THE DARK (Italian Americans, German Americans)
Republic Pictures Corp. *Dist* Republic Pictures Corp. 15 Jan **1952**; Prod: began early Apr 1951 [©Republic Pictures Corp.; 20 Dec 1951; LP1517]. Sd (RCA Sound System); b&w. 5,401 ft. 60 min. Passed by the National Board of Review. PCA cert no. 15285.
Assoc prod Stephen Auer. *Dir* George Blair. [*Asst dir* Johnny Grubbs]. *Scr* Albert DeMond. *Dir of photog* John MacBurnie. [*Opt eff* Consolidated Film Industries]. *Art dir* Frank Hotaling. *Film ed* John Rich. *Set dec* John McCarthy, Jr. and George Milo. *Cost supv* Adele Palmer. *Mus* Stanley Wilson. *Sd* T. A. Carman. *Makeup supv* Bob Mark.
Source: Based on the play *Moon over Mulberry Street* by Nicholas Cosentino, as produced by Standish O'Neill (New York, 4 Sep 1935).
Cast: Penny Edwards [(*Anna Reichardt*)], Ross Elliott [(*Father Tony Morello*)], Rick Vallin [(*Phil Morello*)], Richard Benedict [(*Gino Morello*)], Argentina Brunetti [(*Mama Morello*)], Martin Garralaga [(*Papa Morello*)], Edit Angold [(*Tante Maria*)], Peter Brocco [(*Nick Petzick*)], Barbara Billingsley [(*Evelyn Courtney*)], John Doucette [(*Dutch Bender*)], Richard Irving [(*Slats Hylan*)], Luther Crockett [(*Inspector Johnson*)], Carl Thompson [(*Mickey*)], Charles Sullivan [(*Bartender*)].
Gangster, Drama. [*Print viewed*]. Mama and Papa Morello, a kindly Italian-American couple, are celebrating their fortieth wedding anniversary. Attending the party are old family friends Tante Maria, a German bakery owner; her pretty young shop assistant, Anna Reichardt; and two of the couple's sons: Tony, a Catholic priest, and Gino, a ne'er-do-well who, although down on his luck, boasts that he will achieve success the quick way. Their third son Phil, a lawyer, suddenly arrives with a well-dressed young woman and surprises everyone by introducing her as his fiancée, Evelyn Courtney. Phil's announcement saddens Anna, as she is in love with him. Gino, on the other hand, reacts to the wealthy and attractive Evelyn with inappropriate boasting. When Phil chastises Gino, he storms angrily out of the building. At a nearby bar, which also serves as the unofficial headquarters for city alderman and gangster Nick Petzick, Gino fights with Petzick's two henchmen, Slats Hylan and Dutch Bender. Nick calls off his thugs, and Gino hints that he would like to become part of Petzick's operation. The corrupt politician, insisting that he entered politics solely to help people, smilingly sends Gino on his way, but Gino's request has given him an idea. Petzick orders Hylan and Bender to promise Gino ten thousand dollars for assisting them in the robbery of the "Unclaimed Cargo," a million-dollar jewel collection that is to be sold to the highest bidder by its owner, the Waldorf Jewelry Company. A Waldorf employee who owes Petzick a favor has agreed to facilitate the robbery, but the gangster had been uncertain about how to dispose of the jewels. Because the insurer of the collection, the Apex Insurance Co., is represented by Gino's brother Phil, Petzick will threaten to reveal Gino's role in the robbery unless Phil arranges for Apex to buy the jewels back for a large sum. Desperately short of money, Gino agrees to help the two thieves with the robbery. Anna, who dates Gino occasionally, becomes worried when he cancels their movie date, and when she later sees him peering into Waldorf's in the company of two known gangsters, she consults Tony. That night, Tony visits his parents' apartment, but they inform him that Gino has retired early with a cold. Tony peeks into

Gino's window, but finding the room empty, he makes a call to Inspector Johnson. Meanwhile, Gino and Petzick's henchmen commit the robbery, during which Gino knocks the night watchman unconscious. As they dash for their car, however, the police arrive. Bullets fill the air, but the robbers finally escape, and Gino returns to his room through the window. Later Tony confronts Gino, warning that if he becomes a criminal and hurts their parents, he will get tough. The next day, Tony and Anna visit Phil, whom Petzick has already ordered to buy the jewels back for the insurance company. Phil devises a plan, and Anna, worried for his safety, gives him her Saint Christopher medal for protection. Moved, he kisses her. Next, Phil confronts Gino, and when Gino realizes he has been used, he admits his crime and confesses that he has been unable to sleep since the robbery. The next evening, as Phil prepares to carry out his plan at Petzick's headquarters, Evelyn enters, furious that he forgot their opera date. Declaring that they are not compatible, she breaks off their engagement and leaves. Phil then keeps his appointment with Petzick, exchanging a suitcase full of money for the jewels while the alderman's thugs wait just outside the door. Suddenly Gino enters with a gun, and the two brothers pick up both suitcases and head for the door. "I was raised in just as tough a neighborhood as you were," Phil remarks to Petzick, "and I can be just as tough as you." The next day, the newspaper names Phil as the hero who recovered the jewels. Gino sees Phil holding Anna's hand and jokes about their friendly rivalry for her affections. Just then, a car speeds by, and Gino is shot to death while trying to shield his brother. Distressed, Phil enters Petzick's headquarters with a gun, but the thugs wrench it away from him. As they are about to kill him, the police enter with Tony and Anna. Petzick is shot, and as the other crooks are led away, Phil takes Anna in his arms and kisses her. *Brothers. Family relationships. Gangsters. Ne'er-do-wells. Political bosses. Robbery. Alibi. Bakers and bakeries. Class distinction. Engagements. Family honor. Fistfights. German Americans. Italian Americans. Jewel thieves. Jewelry stores. Lawyers. Murder. Parties. Police. Political corruption. Priests. Snobs and snobbishness. Threats. Unrequited love. Urban life.*
Note: The working title of this film was *Unclaimed Cargo*.
Box 26 Jan 1952. *DV* 14 Jan 1952, p. 3. *Exb* 20 Jan 1952. *Har* 19 Jan 1952. *HR* 6 Apr 1951. *HR* 14 Jan 1952, p. 3. *MPHPD* 2 Feb 1952, p. 1222. *Var* 16 Jan 1952, p. 6.

A WOMAN OBSESSED *see* **WILD IS THE WIND**

A WOMAN OF IMPULSE (Latino, Italian Americans, African
  Americans, Creoles)
Famous Players-Lasky Corp. *Dist* Famous Players-Lasky Corp.; Paramount Pictures. 29 Sep **1918** [©Famous Players-Lasky Corp.; 18 Sep 1918; LP12889]. Si; b&w. 5 reels, 4,440 ft.
Pres Adolph Zukor. *Dir* Edward José. *Scen* Eve Unsell. *Cam* Hal Young.
Source: Based on the play *A Woman of Impulse* by Louis K. Anspacher (New York, 1 Mar 1909).
Cast: Lina Cavalieri (*Leonora, "La Vecci"*), Gertrude Robinson (*Nina*), Raymond Bloomer (*Count Nerval*), Robert Cain (*Phillip Gardiner*), Ida Waterman (*Mme. Gardiner*), Leslie Austen (*Dr. Paul Spencer*), J. Clarence Handysides (*Mr. Stuart*), Mathilde Brundage (*Mrs. Stuart*), Corrine Uzzell (*Cleo*), Lucien Muratore, Estar Banks.
Drama. Leonora, the daughter of a poor Italian lacemaker, is unable to afford voice lessons until wealthy Americans Mr. and Mrs. Stuart adopt her and her younger sister Nina. Leonora soon wins fame as the Parisian prima donna "La Vecci," whose beauty attracts many admirers, including Phillip Gardiner and his Spanish cousin, Count Nerval. Worried by his excessive jealousy but very much in love, Leonora marries the count and travels with him to the United States. Still infatuated with her, Phillip invites Leonora to visit his family in New Orleans, and when she rebuffs him, he turns his attention to Nina. Learning that Nina's sweetheart, Dr. Paul Spencer, will join them, Leonora begs Phillip to leave the girl in peace, but he only seizes the prima donna in his arms and kisses her. Leonora faints during an attempt to stab Phillip, but on awakening, she finds him dead and herself accused of murder. Leonora's name is cleared when Phillip's Creole lover confesses that it was she who stabbed him, after which Leonora and the count renew their love. *Jealousy. Murder. Opera singers. Unrequited love. Adoption. African Americans–Mixed blood. Americans in foreign countries. Confession (Law). Creoles. False arrests. Italians. Nobility. Paris (France). Physicians. Sisters. Spaniards. Upper classes.*

Note: Lina Cavalieri's husband, famed tenor Lucien Muratore, appeared briefly in the film. *Har* commented, "There may be trouble for exhibitors situated below the Mason-Dixon line on account of the misuse of the name 'Creole' as applying to a mulatto. Besides, the violation of this mulatto by a white man is not a very pleasing situation."

ETR 28 Sep 1918, p. 1407. ETR 2 Nov 1918, p. 1812. MPN 28 Sep 1918, p. 2089. MPW 28 Sep 1918, p. 1918. MPW 28 Dec 1918, p. 1559. NYT 21 Oct 1918, p. 15. Var 27 Sep 1918, p. 43. Wid's 22 Sep 1918, p. 19.

WOMAN OF THE YEAR (Greek Americans, Refugees)

Metro-Goldwyn-Mayer Corp.; controlled by Loew's Inc. *Dist* Loew's Inc. **1942**; New York opening: 5 Feb 1942; Prod: 27 Aug—26 Oct 1941; addl scenes, early Dec 1941 [©Loew's Inc.; 13 Jan 1942; LP11036]. Sd (Western Electric Sound System); b&w. 12 reels, 10,268 ft. 112 min. Passed by the National Board of Review. PCA cert no. 7844.

Prod Joseph L. Mankiewicz. *Dir* George Stevens. [*Asst dir* Red Golden]. *Orig scr* Ring Lardner, Jr. and Michael Kanin. [*Contr wrt* John Lee Mahin]. *Dir of photog* Joseph Ruttenberg. *Art dir* Cedric Gibbons. *Assoc* Randall Duell. *Film ed* Frank Sullivan. *Set dec* Edwin B. Willis. *Gowns* Adrian. *Mus score* Franz Waxman. *Rec dir* Douglas Shearer. *Hair styles by* Sydney Guilaroff. *Sculptor of Katharine Hepburn bust* Robert McKnight.

Cast: SPENCER TRACY (*Sam Craig*), KATHARINE HEPBURN (*Tess Harding*), Fay Bainter (*Ellen Whitcomb*), Reginald Owen (*Clayton*), Minor Watson (*William J. Harding*), William Bendix (*"Pinkie" Peters*), Gladys Blake (*Flo Peters*), Dan Tobin (*Gerald Howe*), Roscoe Karns (*Phil Whittaker*), William Tannen (*Ellis*), Ludwig Stossel (*Dr. Lubbeck*), Sara Haden (*Matron*), Edith Evanson (*Alma*), George Kezas (*Chris*), [Connie Gilchrist (*Mrs. Dunlap*)], [Grant Withers (*Al Dunlap*)], [Sergio Orta (*Mr. Yea*)], [Jules Cowles (*Joe, bartender*)], [Jimmy Conlin (*Abbott*)], [Murdock MacQuarrie (*Head copy reader*)], [Jack Carr (*Fat man*)], [Michael Visaroff (*Russian*)], [Carey Harrison, Julian Rivero (*Spaniards*)], [Herbert Ashley (*Doorman*)], [Charles Sullivan (*Cabby*)], [Henry Roquemore (*Judge*)], [Cyril Ring (*Chauffeur*)], [Floyd Criswell (*Policeman*)], [Fern Emmett (*Judge's wife*)], [Walter O. Stahl (*Yugoslav consul*)], [Lisa Golm (*Yugoslav consul's wife*)], [Doris Borodin (*Leni*)], [Ben Lenny (*Ex-pug*)], [John Berkes (*Paddy Doran*)], [George Ovey (*Telegrapher*)], [Ray Teal (*Reporter*)], [Al Seymour (*Pinkie's fight stooge*)], [Curt Furberg, Ruth Cherrington (*Foreigners*)], [Amber Norman (*Showgirl*)], [Dorothy Ates (*Phone woman*)], [Winifred Harris (*Chairwoman*)], [George Guhl (*Door attendant*)], [John Sheehan (*Red face*)], [Bobby Larson (*Dickie Dunlap*)], [Ann Codee (*Madame Sylvia*)], [Eddie Simms (*Champ*)], [Duke York (*Gargantua*)], [Harry Tenbrook, Jack Raymond, Frank Mills, Harry Semels (*Mugs*)], [Bob Perry (*Referee*)].

Comedy. [*Print viewed*]. As *New York Chronicle* sports columnist Sam Craig listens to the radio quiz program *Information, Please*, he is disgusted to hear nationally-known political columnist and *Chronicle* colleague Tess Harding miss a question about baseball and suggest that the sport be abolished for the duration of the war. Sam then writes a column lambasting her, and when Tess retaliates in kind, their editor, Clayton, orders them to meet in his office and stop their intramural squabbling. Sam is immediately impressed when he catches the attractive Tess adjusting her stockings, and she is equally attracted to him. Sam invites her to a Yankees game, and by the ninth inning, novice Tess has caught onto baseball and has made friends with some of the unruly fans, thus impressing Sam even more. Tess invites Sam over to her apartment that night, but he is chagrined to find out that she is having a party with dozens of her international friends. Despite constant interruptions due to Tess's busy life and the disdain of Tess's male secretary, Gerald Howe, Sam and Tess fall in love and decide to marry. Sam wants a traditional wedding with his mother present, but to accomodate Tess's hectic schedule, she and Gerald determine that the wedding must take place almost immediately and be held in South Carolina. Tess's diplomat father, William J. Harding, and her aunt, feminist Ellen Whitcomb, are only able to stay ten minutes and Tess is called away for an important call just after the wedding, leaving Sam a bit bewildered. The wedding night is equally frenetic; just as they are about to go to bed, missing Yugoslavian political refugee Dr. Lubbeck shows up and summons a group of his fellow countrymen. In retaliation, Sam calls his buddies over for a party and the apartment is in chaos until Flo Peters, the wife of Sam's bartender friend "Pinkie" learns that it is their wedding night and spreads the word to the others. Several months later, Sam

and Tess are still very much in love, but are frequently separated due to Tess's political life and Sam's coverage of sporting events. One night, after Sam, who has been bristling over Tess's neglect, arrives home from a business trip, Tess is very solicitous, thus arousing Sam's suspicions. When she suggests that they have a child, he is ecstatic, thinking that she is pregnant, but instead she reveals that she has adopted a young Greek war refugee named Chris because she is chairwoman of a refugee committee. Though Sam likes the boy, he is angry and criticizes her for not giving even "ten percent" of her heart to matters at home. Their argument is interrupted by the news that she has just been named "America's Outstanding Woman of the Year." On the night of the banquet, Sam realizes that Chris is very lonesome for other children, and when Tess off-handedly tells Sam that the child will be alone during the banquet, they have a bitter argument and Sam stays home. After she leaves, Sam takes Chris to the Greek Children's home, where the boy is happily reunited with his friends. Following the banquet, Tess waits at the apartment with reporters who are anxious to photograph them together. She is stunned when she finds that his things are gone and deduces that he has taken Chris back to the home. She goes to retrieve him, but when she realizes that the boy does not want to be with her, she leaves. The next day, at the office, Tess gets a telegram from Ellen inviting her and Sam to Connecticut. She asks Sam to accompany her, but he refuses, and she realizes that he wants to end their "perfect marriage," which he says is neither. In Connecticut, Tess learns that Ellen and the long-widowed William are marrying, after years of silently loving each other. Tess makes an excuse about Sam's absence and is hurt when Ellen tells her how lucky she is to have Sam while she is still young because success not shared is empty. After the wedding, Tess drives back to New York to the apartment Sam has rented for himself. While he is sleeping, she decides to prove her mettle as a housewife and cook his breakfast, using recipes in a cookbook from Sam's mother. When he awakens, he silently watches as everything goes wrong for Tess, and when he finally speaks, a conciliatory Tess says that she wants to start over as a traditional wife. He is angered at her new "act," but she returns to the kitchen, determined to show him she can be domestic, until the coffeepot and waffle iron both overflow and she breaks down. Sam then embraces her and says he doesn't want to change her, he merely wants their marriage to come first and suggests that instead of being Tess Harding or Mrs. Sam Craig, she be Tess Harding Craig. She thinks that is a wonderful idea, and when Gerald arrives to take her to launch a battleship, Sam instead launches him, with Tess's approval. *Battle of the sexes. Columnists. Feminism. Marriage. Adoption. Aunts. Awards. Banquets. Bars. Bartenders. Baseball. Connecticut. Diplomats. Drunkenness. Fathers and daughters. Greeks. Hats. Information, Please* (Radio program). *New York City. New York Yankees* (Baseball team). *Newspapers. Orphanages. Pancakes, waffles, etc.. Parties. Radio programs. Reporters. Secretaries. Separation* (Marital). *Sports fans. Unrequited love. War refugees. Weddings. Yugoslavians.*

Note: According to various contemporary sources, *Woman of the Year* was written especially for Katharine Hepburn by screenwriters Ring Lardner, Jr. and Michael Kanin and was purchased by M-G-M at Hepburn's request. A feature article in *Time* on 12 Feb 1942, summarizes information from several sources and states that the screenplay was purchased for $100,000, at that time a record for an original screenplay. The article and other sources noted that the purchase price was especially surprising considering the relative youth of the two writers [Lardner was twenty-six and Kanin thirty-one] and added that Hepburn chose her own leading man, Spencer Tracy, and insisted that George Stevens, who had directed her in two RKO films, *Alice Adams* in 1935 and *Quality Street* in 1937 (see *AFI Catalog of Feature Films, 1931-40*; F3.0065 and F3.3576) be borrowed for the picture. M-G-M publicity materials contained in the AMPAS Library file on the film, however, claim that the film was expressly written for both Hepburn and Tracy.

HR news items indicate that the screenplay was purchased by M-G-M and Stevens was hired as the director in mid-Jul 1941. Some contemporary and modern sources indicate that Lardner, Jr. originally suggested to director Garson Kanin an idea for a screenplay based on the relationship between his author and sportswriter father and *New York Herald Tribune* political columnist Dorothy Thompson. Kanin then suggested that Lardner, Jr. collaborate with his brother Michael on the script.

Woman of the Year was the first of nine films in which Hepburn and Tracy co-starred. Tracy died in 1967, shortly after completion of their last film together, *Guess Who's Coming to Dinner?* (see *AFI Catalog of Feature Films, 1961-70*; F6.1975). Their film roles often re-created characterizations established in *Woman of the Year*, and included such popular films as *Adam's Rib* (1949, see above), *Pat and Mike* (1952) and *Desk Set* (1957). Many modern critics have written about the personal relationship between the two actors, and, subsequent to Tracy's death, Hepburn gave interviews and wrote about their twenty-five year love affair. She clarified an often recounted story

of their first meeting: Producer Joseph L. Mankiewicz introduced the two actors at a chance meeting on the M-G-M Culver City lot. Later, according to Hepburn, when she expressed to Mankiewicz some concern that she might appear too tall onscreen next to Tracy, Mankiewicz replied, "Don't worry, he'll cut you down to size."

Woman of the Year earned an Oscar for Lardner, Jr. and Michael Kanin for Best Original Screenplay and also earned a nomination for Hepburn for Best Actress. It was selected as one of the "Top Ten" films of the year by the *NYT* and others. Reviews generally agreed with the *NYT* review which stated "the plot is formula, but the writing, the direction of George Stevens and the acting of Miss Hepburn and Mr. Tracy are all as crisp and crackling as a brand new $1,000 bill." Some reviews and many modern sources have commented on the film's surprisingly pro-feminist statements and the fact that at the end of the film "Sam" accepts "Tess" as the strong, career-oriented woman she is.

Actor Dan Tobin made his motion picture debut in the film. The popular *Information, Please* radio quiz program, hosted by noted literary critic Clifton Fadiman, was broadcast from 1938 to 1948. A 1976 TV movie was based on the film and starred Renee Taylor and Joseph Bolgna. In 1981, Lauren Bacall portrayed "Tess" in a Broadway musical production of the story. The TV movie and play were also titled *Woman of the Year*.

Box 17 Jan 1942. *DV* 14 Jan 1942, p. 3. *FD* 19 Jan 1942, p. 8. *HR* 26 Aug 1941, p. 8. *HR* 29 Aug 1941, p. 14. *HR* 24 Oct 1941, p. 10. *HR* 3 Dec 1941, p. 2. *HR* 14 Jan 1942, p. 3. *HR* 26 May 1942, p. 6. *HR* 28 Dec 1942, p. 4. *MPHPD* 17 Jan 1942, p. 461. *NYT* 6 Feb 1942, p. 23. *NYT* 8 Feb 1942. *Time* 12 Feb 1942. *Var* 14 Jan 1942, p. 8.

A WOMAN'S HONOR (Italian Americans)

Fox Film Corp. *Dist* Fox Film Corp. 12 Jun **1916** [©William Fox; 11 Jun 1916; LP8487]. Si; b&w. 5 reels.

Dir Roland West. *Scen* Donald I. Buchanan. *Cam* Ed Wynard.

Source: Based on the short story "La Terribula" by George L. Knapp in *Snappy Stories* (4 Dec 1915).

Cast: Jose Collins (*Helena*), Arthur Donaldson (*Tochetti*), Mrs. Cecil Raleigh (*La Terribula*), Bradley Barker (*Guido Ferrari*), Armand Cortez (*Roberto*), Devore Palmer, Ruby Hoffman, Anna Reedor.

Drama. Helena, a young girl from the Italian hills goes to Naples to wait for her fiancé, who has recently gone to America, to send for her. While there, she falls prey to a "terrible woman" and to a count, Tochetti, who rapes her. The count then gives the girl enough money to go to America to meet her fiancé, but a short time later, the young man dies after toiling in the coal mines of Pennsylvania. The girl then goes to New York and meets a wealthy Italian lawyer who falls in love with her and helps her to return to Italy to avenge herself for the wrong done to her by the count and the woman. Although the lawyer discovers that his uncle is the count who they are seeking, he still helps his sweetheart, and after her vengeance is complete, he takes her back to America to start a new life. *Immigrants. Italians. Italy. Lawyers. Naples (Italy). Rape. Revenge. Coal miners. New York City. Nobility. Pennsylvania. Uncles.*

Note: Another film entitled *A Woman's Honor* was released by the Great Northern Film Co. in late 1915, but this film was a foreign production and had no relation to the 1916 Fox Film. Some scenes were shot in Jamaica.

Motog 24 Jun 1916, p. 1453. *MPN* 24 Jun 1916, p. 3932. *MPW* 1 Jul 1916, p. 100. *Wid's* 15 Jun 1916, pp. 646-47.

WOMEN LOVE ONCE (Hungarian Americans)

Paramount Publix Corp. *Dist* Paramount Publix Corp. 4 Jul **1931** [©Paramount Publix Corp.; 3 Jul 1931; LP2333]. Sd (Western Electric Noiseless Recording); b&w. 8 reels. 73-74 min. Passed by the National Board of Review.

Dir Edward Goodman. [*Wrt*] by Zoë Akins. *Photog* Karl Struss. [*Sd eng*] M. M. Paggi].

Source: Based on the play *Daddy's Gone A-Hunting* by Zoë Akins (New York, 31 Aug 1921).

Cast: Paul Lukas [(*Julien Fields*)], Eleanor Boardman [(*Helen Fields*)], Juliette Compton [(*Hester Dahlgren*)], Geoffrey Kerr [(*Allen Greenough*)], Judith Wood [(*Olga*)], Marilyn Knowlden [(*Janet Fields*)], Claude King [(*Theodore Stewart*)], Mischa Auer [(*Oscar*)], Paul Nicholson.

Domestic, Melodrama. [*Print viewed*]. In New York, Hester Dahlgren, a wealthy admirer of Hungarian-American commercial artist Julien Fields, offers to support him for a year of study in Paris so that he can become a great artist. Although Julien declines her offer, his loving wife Helen insists that he not pass up such an opportunity. While Julien is in Paris, Helen stays in New York and is introduced to the kindhearted and wealthy Allen Greenough, who looks after her and her daughter Janet. Allen's friend agrees to look at Julien's portfolio and tells Allen in confidence that Julien is a capable draughtsman, but no great talent. Helen, however, has complete faith in Julien's artistic promise. When Julien returns to New York, he

brings an unmarried Bohemian couple, Oscar and Olga, home with him, and Helen is surprised to find him a changed man. Julien immediately tells Helen she never should have made him go to Paris because he now must live the free, experimental life of an artist in search of meaning. Six months later, Julien, who rarely comes home to Helen and Janet, openly sees Hester. He still refuses to work a day job, but also does not produce paintings of any significance. Helen, meanwhile, is forced to support herself and Janet solely on her earnings as a dressmaker. Allen, now in love with Helen, tries to convince her that Julien is a talentless, lazy man who has forced her to live a half-sordid, Bohemian life, but Helen maintains her love for her husband. Allen invites her to a costume ball in a hotel and lends her his mother's jewels for her period costume. Julien is also at the ball, but Hester's husband has insisted on escorting her. When Hester invites Julien to her room, her husband, dressed in the same cape as Julien, waits for her and threatens to kill her. Hearing Hester scream, Julien enters and disarms Dahlgren, and reporters milling about the halls print the scandal. Allen, more furious with Julien than ever, asks Helen to leave Julien and marry him. In an attempt to prove Julien still cares for her, Helen keeps Allen's jewels and confesses to Julien that Allen has been making love to her. Julien is amused and nonchalantly tells her to keep the jewels. Resigned that Julien no longer cares enough for her even to be jealous, Helen tells him it is over and runs from the apartment in tears. While Janet runs after her mother, she is hit by a car and lands in the hospital. During Janet's recovery, Allen amply provides for Helen and she begins to care for him. Five months later, Janet is released from the hospital and reunites with Helen at Allen's house, as Allen has offered to stay in a hotel. When Julien comes to say goodbye to Janet, Allen tells him that Helen is seeking a divorce to marry him. That afternoon, Janet dies, and Helen, distraught with grief, tells Julien they need each other again. Julien admits to being a failure, but insists he still wants Helen, and they embrace. *Artists. Bohemians and bohemianism. Desertion (Marital). Infidelity. Irresponsibility. Romantic rivalry. Self-sacrifice. Art patronage. Attempted murder. Automobile accidents. Balls (Parties). Class distinction. Divorce. Dressmakers. Hungarian Americans. Mothers and daughters. New York City. Paris (France)–Latin Quarter. Poets. Proposals (Marital). Reconciliation. Scandal. Unrequited love. Yachts and yachting.*

Note: An early working title for this film was *Daddy's Gone A-Hunting*, which was also the title of the song "Helen" sings to "Janet" in the film. *NYT* and *FD* mistakenly credit Helen Johnson in the part of "Olga." In 1925, M-G-M made a silent version of the play under the same title, which was directed by Frank Borzage and starred Alice Joyce and Percy Marmont (see *AFI Catalog of Feature Films, 1921-30*; F2.1132).

FD 28 Jun 1931, p. 10. *HR* 11 Jun 1931, p. 6. *MPH* 4 Jul 1931, p. 34. *NYT* 27 Jun 1931, p. 20. *NYT* 5 Jul 1931, p. 3. *Var* 30 Jun 1931, p. 20.

WOMEN OF DESTINY see SAN ANTONE

WON LEE SHUEN FU (Chinese language)

1940. Sd; b&w. Length undetermined. Chinese language.

Dir Jimmy William. [*Not viewed*]. [No information concerning the plot of this film has been located.].

Note: The Cantonese transliterated title is *Mam Lei Tsun Fu.* This film was probably made in the U.S.

WONDER CHILD see LITTLE MISS ROUGHNECK

THE WONDERFUL COUNTRY (African Americans, Native Americans, Apache, German Americans)

D.R.M. Productions, Inc.; M.P.L. Productions. *Dist* United Artists Corp. Oct **1959**; Prod: early Oct–early Dec 1958 [©D.R.M. Productions, Inc.; 23 Sep 1959; LP14705]. Sd (Westrex Recording System); col (Technicolor). 10 reels, 8,784 ft. 96 min. PCA cert no. 19365.

Exec prod Robert Mitchum. *Prod* Chester Erskine. *Dir* Robert Parrish. *Asst dir* Henry Spitz. *Scr* Robert Ardrey. *Photog* Floyd Crosby and Alex Phillips. *Spec eff* Lester Swartz. *Prod des* Harry Horner. *Film ed* Michael Luciano. *Mus ed* Richard C. Harris. *Sd ed* Del Harris. *Ward des* Mary Wills. [*Ward* Reeder Boss]. *Mus comp and cond* Alex North. *Mus arr* Maurice de Packh. *Sd rec* José B. Carles. *Sd re-rec* Roger Heman. *Makeup supv* Louis LaCava. [*Hairdresser* Alma J. Clark]. [*In charge of production* Luis Sánchez Tello]. *Prod mgr* R. J. Lannan. *Properties* Arden Cripe. [*Scr supv* Bobbie Sierks]. [*Tech adv* Tom Lea]. [*Publ* Maurice Segal].

Source: Based on the novel *The Wonderful Country* by Tom Lea (Boston, 1952).

Cast: ROBERT MITCHUM [(*Martin Brady*)], JULIE LONDON [(*Ellen Colton*)], Gary Merrill [(*Major Colton*)], Albert Dekker [(*Captain Rucker*)], Jack Oakie [(*Travis Hight*)], Charles McGraw [(*Doc Stovall*)], "Satchel" Paige [(*Tobe Sutton*)], Anthony Caruso [(*Santos*)], Mike Kellin [(*Pancho Gil*)], Victor Mendoza [(*General Castro*)], Jay Novello [(*Diego Casas*)], John Banner [(*Ben Sterner*)], Max Slaten [(*Ludwig Sterner*)], Marguerito Luna [(*Captain Verdugo*)], Joe Haworth [(*Stoker*)], Tom Lea [(*Peebles*)], Chuck Roberson [(*Gallup*)], Pedro Armendáriz (*Cipriano Castro*), [Chester Hayes (*Rascon*)], [Claudio Brook (*Ruelle*)], [Judy Marsh (*Entertainer at fiesta*)].

Western. [*Print viewed*]. In the 1870s, Martin Brady, an American who has lived most of his life in Mexico, crosses the Rio Grande and comes to the Texas town of El Puerto. Martin has come north to deliver gold ore and pesos in exchange for rifles on behalf of his *padrone*, Don Cipriano Castro of the ruling family in northern Mexico. In the town, his horse is tripped by a tumbleweed, and Martin breaks his leg. Some of the townspeople think that Martin, who they believe is Mexican, stole the Andalusian stallion. Ellen Colton, the wife of the newly-arrived cavalry commanding officer, sends for Doc Stovall, who sets Martin's leg. In lieu of his fee, Stovall asks that Martin's horse Lagrimas, which is Spanish for "tears," be put to stud with his mare, and Martin, who received the horse from the Castros, agrees. Martin convalesces in the barn of Ben Sterner, a German immigrant who supplies the Castros with rifles. When Sterner's nephew Ludwig, newly-arrived from Germany, becomes friendly with Martin, Sterner warns that Martin is an assassin to be avoided. Major Colton asks Martin's help to facilitate a joint military operation between his cavalry and the Castros' forces against the southern Apaches, who hide in the Castros' territory after raiding in the north. Martin scoffs at the possibility, as the Mexicans disparagingly think of Anglos as "gringos." However, Travis Hight, a jovial agent of the Continental and Southern Railroad, plans to offer money to the Castros to get their help to wipe out the Apaches. Captain Rucker of the Texas Rangers, whom Martin has avoided, relates that he knew Martin's father and suspects that Martin, as a child, killed his father's murderer, then fled to Mexico. He wants Martin to join the Rangers and encourages him to start life anew after revealing that his father's murderer was a wanted man and that Martin did not have to flee. At a party, Martin finds Ludwig in a fight with a drunk, who has made malicious remarks about Ellen's supposed promiscuity and slurs about Martin. After the drunk breaks a bottle and viciously cuts Ludwig, Martin slugs the drunk and shoots him dead when he goes for his gun. He escapes to Mexico, where he finds that Don Cipriano has left for the capital city to see the governor. Martin meets with Don Cipriano's younger brother, Marcos, who insults Martin and sends him to the capital to explain the loss of the rifles, which had been stolen from his compatriot Diego while Martin recovered from his broken leg. At the capital, Martin finds his *padrone*, who has now taken over the government, strangely lethargic and complacent, but also autocratic. After a few weeks, Martin meets Hight, who has arranged a meeting between Colton and the Castros. During a fiesta, Ellen, in Mexico with her husband, with whom she is unhappy, goes off alone with Martin. She rebukes him for being a hired killer, and when she contends he is not a whole man without his gun, he removes the gun and kisses her. The Castros agree to a joint campaign against the Apaches with Colton's cavalry, made up of African-American soldiers. After learning that his brother plans to assassinate him, Don Cipriano sends Martin to kill Marcos. When Martin refuses, Don Cipriano insults him, calling him a "gringo." He warns that according to their law, he has the right to kill Martin if he attempts to leave his employ before the debt for the rifles is paid. Defiantly, Martin says that is not his law and rides off. When Lagrimas' hoof becomes injured, Martin takes refuge with Santiago Santos, a peasant farmer, and his family. After Apaches, challenged by the combined forces, attack a nearby ranchero, Santos is saddened that the peace of twenty years is now over. Tobe Sutton, a black U.S. officer, relates that the cavalry has been attacked and that Major Colton has been severely wounded. Despite his condition, Colton orders his men to carry him to a rendezvous with Captain Rucker and the Mexican forces 100 miles away. When scouts see Apaches below with a wagon, the major orders an attack despite Martin's objection, but after Colton passes

out, Martin joins the attack to follow Colton's wish. Following a gun battle in which the Apache leader is killed, the rifles are recovered. Before he dies, Colton asks Martin to take Ellen his ring. At the fort, Martin tells Ellen that what they feel for each other is not wrong, and she responds that if he wants her, he must come across the river. Meanwhile, Rucker returns the rifles to Marcos, who relates that Don Cipriano is dead. As the new governor, Marcos orders the Rangers to leave Mexico and demands that Rucker turn over Martin, but Rucker refuses and tells Martin that witnesses testified that he killed the drunk who attacked Ludwig in self-defense. As Martin rides towards the river, an assassin wounds Lagrimas, but Martin shoots the assassin, then kills his severely wounded horse. That accomplished, he puts down his gun, gunbelt and hat, and approaches the Rio Grande. *Cultural conflict. Expatriates. Hired killers. Mexican-American border region. Mexicans. Mexico–History–1867-1910. Personality change. Texans.* African Americans. Apache Indians. Battles. Bigotry. Brothers. Drunkenness. Farmers. Forts. Generals. German Americans. Governors. Hats. Horses. Immigrants. Infidelity. Justifiable homicide. Munitions dealers. Murder. Nephews. Officers (Military). Parties. Physicians. Railroad agents. Rio Grande. Texas. Texas Rangers. United States. Army. Cavalry. Wagons. Wounds and injuries.

Note: According to news items, director Robert Parrish met with author Tom Lea in Lea's hometown of El Paso, TX late in 1951 concerning the production of a film based on his novel, which had not yet been completed. In Nov 1953, Lea sold the film rights to Parrish and Gregory Peck, who announced the next month that they were forming an independent company to produce the film in Mexico in 1955. Parrish worked on the screenplay with Lea in El Paso in Oct 1954, and shortly after, the two formed a partnership to make the film. By Jul 1958, the film rights were owned by Lea, Parrish and Chester Erskine. According to a letter in the MPAA/PCA Collection at the AMPAS Library, in Sep 1958, D.R.M. Productions, Inc. was about to produce the film under M.P.L. (Mitchum-Parrish-Lea) Productions. Lea portrayed a barber in the film. This was Jack Oakie's first film since *Tomahawk* in 1951 (see above), aside from a brief, cameo appearance in the 1956 film *Around the World in 80 Days*. In his autobiography, Parrish stated that when he had trouble casting the role of the African-American cavalry officer, Robert Mitchum suggested "Satchel" Paige, the great baseball player from the American Negro League, who had never acted in a film before. According to news items, the film was shot entirely in Mexico. Most of the shooting was done in Durango, San Miguel de Allende and La Punta. Reviews praised the atmosphere of the film: *NYT* commented, "Practically every 'take' arrests the eye in tinting and detail. Some of the shots—quietly looming adobe villages, [a] nocturnal street festival and a frenzied onslaught of Apache riders—are spine-tingling." *Var* stated, "It compellingly conveys a sense of the period and the country" and praised the scenes of "an actual Mexican fiesta." *HR*, critical of the way the film dealt with the historical significance of the use of African-American cavalry to fight the Apaches, commented, "the script never probes the emotions of a race, recently released from slavery, being used to fight an Indian tribe desperately fighting for its freedom."

HR also questioned whether the film dealt adequately with the Apache presence in northern Mexico: "History tells us that a small group of these Indians (who seldom numbered more than 200 active warriors) kept a large group of Mexican farmers so terrorized that they could be used as a permanent base, growing crops for the savages and supplying horses and women for them. They inflicted humiliating defeats on both the Mexican and U.S. forces and were only checked when the two nations acted in common. This is such an important story that it should either be exploited to the fullest or completely ignored." A modern Mexican source adds the following actors to the cast: Alberto Pedret, Alberto Mariscal, José Chávez Trowe, Ignacio Villalbazo, Antonio Sandoval, Hernando Name and Salvador Godínez.

Box 5 Oct 1959. *DV* 29 Dec 1953. *DV* 22 Sep 1958. *DV* 29 Sep 1959, p. 3. *Exb* 7 Oct 1959, p. 4642. *FD* 29 Sep 1959, p. 10. *Har* 3 Oct 1959, pp. 158-59. *HCN* 8 Oct 1959. *HR* 29 Dec 1953. *HR* 9 Nov 1954. *HR* 31 Jul 1958. *HR* 29 Sep 1959, p. 3. *HR* 10 Oct 1958, p. 9. *HR* 5 Dec 1958, p. 9. *LAEx* 17 Sep 1958. *LAEx* 8 Oct 1959. *LAT* 3 Dec 1951. *LAT* 20 Oct 1954. *LAT* 8 Oct 1959. *MPD* 11 Sep 1959. *MPHPD* 3 Oct 1959, p. 437. *NYT* 26 Apr 1959. *NYT* 5 Nov 1959, p. 39. *Var* 30 Sep 1959, p. 6.

THE WOOD HAWK *see* **THEY RODE WEST**

THE WORLD, THE FLESH AND THE DEVIL (African Americans)

Sol C. Siegel Productions, Inc.; Harbel Productions, Inc.; Metro-Goldwyn-Mayer Corp.; controlled by Loew's Inc. *Dist* Loew's Inc. May **1959**; World premiere in Cleveland: 23 Apr 1959 [©Loew's Inc., Sol C. Siegel Productions, Inc. & Harbel Productions, Inc.; 31 Dec 1958; LP12826]. Sd (Westrex Recording System); b&w; CinemaScope; Process lenses by Panavision. 10 reels, 8,509 or 8,551 ft. 95 min. PCA cert no. 19049.

Prod George Englund. *Dir* Ranald MacDougall. *Asst dir* Al Jennings. *Scr* Ranald MacDougall. *Screen story* Ferdinand Reyher. *Dir of photog* Harold J. Marzorati. *Spec eff* Lee LeBlanc. *Art dir* William A. Horning and Paul Groesse. *Film ed* Harold F. Kress. *Set dec* Henry Grace and Keogh Gleason. *Inger Stevens' ward selected by* Kitty Mager. *Mus* Miklos Rozsa. *Rec supv* Franklin Milton. *Makeup* William Tuttle. *Hair styles by* Sydney Guilaroff.

Song(s): "Gotta Travel On," words and music by Paul Clayton; "Fifteen (Sixteen—Eighteen)" words and music by Alan Greene.

Source: Suggested by the novel *The Purple Cloud* by Matthew Phipps Shiel (London, 1901).

Cast: HARRY BELAFONTE [(*Ralph Burton*)], INGER STEVENS [(*Sarah Crandall*)], MEL FERRER [(*Benson Thacker*)].

Post-Apocalyptic, Drama. [*Print viewed*]. Ralph Burton, an black mining engineer on a job in central Pennsylvania, is trapped in a cave-in for five days. When sounds of rescue work cease, Ralph, in a rage that he is being left to die, moves rocks and boards, and digs until he reaches a ladder and climbs out. He finds the mine deserted, then sees newspaper headlines reading, "U.N. Retaliates for Use of Atomic Poison" and "Millions Flee from Cities! End of the World." In the deserted town, Ralph hotwires a car, then drives to New York City, but finds the George Washington Bridge and Lincoln Tunnel clogged with empty cars. At a shipyard, Ralph finds a motorboat, which he navigates to the city docks. His calls through empty streets bring only echoes, and at a vacant church, Ralph cries in anguish. At a radio transmitting station, he listens to a recording of a broadcast in which he learns that following a walkout from the United Nations, a nation started using radioactive isotopes. Ralph fears that he may be the only person left alive in the world, but after he surveys his domain from the top of the Empire State Building, a white woman, Sarah Crandall, surreptitiously follows him to an apartment building he uses as his new home. Over the next few weeks, Sarah watches unnoticed as Ralph fixes up the building. He acquires two mannequins, whom he names "Snodgrass" and "Betsy," and talks to them. With a generator and a truck engine, Ralph lights the street lamps on the block where he lives. When, in a fit of pique, he throws "Snodgrass" from a balcony to the pavement below, Sarah, thinking Ralph jumped, screams. He confronts her and she explains she survived the catastrophe in a decompression chamber. As time goes on, the two become friends, but when Sarah suggests she move into his building, he says facetiously that people might talk. Ralph, who spends much time rescuing books from the library, advises Sarah to stay busy also. She explodes, saying she is "free, white and 21" and will do as she pleases. Upset at the remark, Ralph is further irritated when she talks about love and marriage. He tells her not to push him, then reminds her, he is "colored," a "Negro," "nigra," or "nigger," depending on who is speaking, and that in normal circumstances she would not know him because of his race. She breaks down in tears, but a few days later, Ralph brings her a diamond from Harry Winston and a newspaper headline he has made proclaiming her birthday. That night, he plays doorman, maitre d', waiter and singer at a club to celebrate Sarah's birthday, but when she asks him to sit with her, he says he is not permitted to sit with customers and refuses her request to dance. She says she has pride also and walks out. Later, Sarah calls Ralph to tell him that she has seen a boat in the East River. On it they find Benson Thacker, arriving from the Southern hemisphere in a state of exhaustion. Once Ben recovers, following a week of care from Ralph, he gets the impression that Ralph is deliberately leaving him and Sarah together. Ben thanks Ralph for the clear field regarding Sarah, but Ralph, who dislikes Ben for his condescending attitude, says that while he will not get in his way, he also will not get out of it. Peeved at Ralph, Sarah tells Ben he can kiss or make love to her, and they kiss, but she breaks away and drives off. Two weeks later, Sarah brings Ralph flowers. Ralph admits that he loves her, but when she confides that Ben has asked her to move in with him, Ralph stoically calls Ben a good man. Angry about Ralph's complacency, Sarah invites Ben to her apartment, but when he crudely suggests they have sex, Sarah declines. Unable to decide how she feels about either man, Sarah surmises she should go away alone, but Ben, saying he will make the decision for her, goes to Ralph's apartment with a gun and orders him to move on, but Ralph refuses. Outside the building, as Ralph goes to meet Sarah, Ben shoots at him with a rifle from above. Ralph takes a rifle from a gun store, and they have a showdown until daybreak, when, near the United Nations building, Ralph reads an antiwar inscription from the Bible and disposes of his gun. Ben follows suit, then Sarah finds the two. Ralph is about to leave them, saying he has work to do saving whatever he can. She asks him not to go and puts out her hand and he takes it. She then calls out to Ben, who takes her other hand, and the three walk together. *African Americans. Miscegenation. New York City. Nuclear warfare. Survival skills. Automobiles. Boats. Engineers–Civil. Friendship. Mannequins*

(Figures). Mine accidents. Nightclubs. Pennsylvania. Radio broadcasting. Sexual harassment. Shootouts. United Nations.

Note: The working title of this film was *The End of the World*. The film ends with the words "The Beginning" on the screen. According to press material written by director Randall MacDougall, the 1901 novel *The Purple Cloud*, by Matthew Phipps Shiel, was purchased by a major studio in 1927. MacDougall called the novel "one of the first to concern itself with man's growing capacity to utterly destroy himself." According to various news items, Paramount planned to make the film in 1940 under the title *The Last Man in the World* and was negotiating for René Clair to direct and Conrad Veidt to star.

Following the atomic bombings in Japan in August 1945, a number of producers were preparing films to deal with the subject, including Frank Capra, M-G-M and Hal Wallis. When Paramount, in Dec 1945, decided to revive this project, using a script by James Hilton based on the novel, *LAEx* commented, "Stand back, boys! Now it's Paramount throwing another bomb into the atomic story ring." Zoltan Korda was to direct and Ray Milland to star. In Aug 1950, *LAT* announced that George Pal planned to make a film for Paramount based on Hilton's script. According to MacDougall, Sol Siegel purchased the rights to the novel in 1956 and decided to marry concerns about racial tensions to those in the novel about survivors in a world nearly destroyed. (The three characters in the original novel were Caucasians.) According to MacDougall, "Siegel felt strongly, as do many historians, that these two problems are interrelated and that we must solve both in order to solve either." Siegel formed an alliance with Harry Belafonte's new company, Harbel Productions, in 1957 to produce the film.

MacDougall explained the concept of the film, as worked out between himself, Siegel and producer George Englund, that "the spirit of man is indomitable, unconquerable, and impervious to either the threat, or actuality of the ultimate destruction." He wrote that the film "makes no pretense of solving the problems of man" and described the climax as "a reaffirmation of the truism that force solves nothing." In a letter published in *LAMirror-News*, following the release of the film, independent producer Arch Oboler related that he heard that an "indecisive ending" was forced on MacDougall. Oboler also pointed out that "certain aspects" of this film "are somewhat similar" to his earlier film *Five*, which also had as a character an African-American survivor of a nuclear holocaust (see entry above for more information on that film.)

Time stated that the ending "was reshot after a big front-office foofaraw." A Nov 1958 *NYT* article on the film related that location shooting had been done in New York a year earlier, and studio work in Hollywood was completed in Jun 1958, but a decision was made to return to New York to reshoot some of the material. MacDougall at that time stated, "Some of the stuff we had for our ending as well as the footage in other parts of the film done in Hollywood was not so powerful and authentic as the material we got here [in New York] last year. So, we decided to try again." In a *LAEx* article, MacDougall commented, "The precise ending must take place in the minds of those who see the picture. It was not our purpose in making the picture to tell people what to think. They must think for themselves." According to a biography of Belafonte, he and the other actors, Inger Stevens and Mel Ferrer, were not satisfied with the treatment of racial issues in the film and complained to Siegel during production.

Reviews generally admired the quality of the production, but criticized the ending and the handling of the racial conflicts. *LAMirror-News* wrote that the film "soon bogs down in a standardized Hollywood plot of racial issues and the old triangle." *Time* complained that "the grand drama of humanity's survival collapses into an irrelevant wrangle about racial discrimination that has no...real significance." *SatRev* wondered concerning the ending, "Are we to assume that some sort of polygamous arrangement has been worked out, or will the three henceforth lead entirely sexless lives, thus dooming both white and colored races to extinction? No answer being given, we must assume that the color question was injected into the story more as a gimmick than out of any real seriousness."

AmCin Jun 1959, p. 346-47, 378-80. *Box* 13 Apr 1959. *Box* 20 Apr 1959. *Cleveland Press* 22 Apr 1959. *Cue* 23 May 1959. *DV* 8 Apr 1959, p. 4 *Exh* 8 Apr 1959, pp. 4573-74. *FD* 10 Apr 1959, p. 8. *Har* 11 Apr 1959, pp. 58-59. *HCN* 30 May 1959. *HR* 5 Feb 1940. *HR* 8 Apr 1959, p. 3. *LAEx* 18 Dec 1945. *LAEx* 24 May 1959, sec. 7, p. 1, 4. *LAEx* 30 May 1959, sec. 2, p. 3. *LAT* 12 Aug 1950. *LAT* 30 May 1959, pt. I, p. 9. *LAMirror-News* 14 Mar 1959. *LAMirror-News* 1 Jun 1959. *LAMirror-News* 17 Jun 1959. *MPHPD* 11 Apr 1959, p. 219. *NYP* 21 May 1959. *New Yorker* 30 May 1959. *NYT* 2 Nov 1958. *NYT* 21 May 1959, p. 35. *SatRev* 2 May 1959. *Time* 1 Jun 1959. *Var* 8 Apr 1959, p.6.

WU LI CHANG (Spanish language)

Metro-Goldwyn-Mayer Corp.; controlled by Loew's Inc. *Dist* Metro-Goldwyn-Mayer Distributing Corp. Oct **1930**; Los Angeles opening: 31 Oct 1930; Prod: Aug 1930. Sd (Western Electric Sound System); b&w. 7 reels. Passed by the National Board of Review. Spanish language.

[*Supv* George Kann]. *Dirigida por* [*Dir*] Nick Grindé. [*Dial dir* Carlos F. Borcosque]. *Adaptación cinematográfica de* [*Scr*] Frances Marion. *Arreglo de* [*Adpt*] Madeleine Ruthven. *Versión española de* [*Spanish version by*] Salvador de Alberich. *Fotografiada por* [*Photog*] Leonard Smith. *Director artístico* [*Art dir*] Cedric Gibbons. *Editada por* [*Ed*] George Boemler. *Acústica por* [*Sd*] Douglas Shearer. [*Sd* W. G. Kennedy].

Source: Based on the play *Mr. Wu* by Henry Maurice Vernon and Harold Owen (New York, 14 Oct 1914).

Cast: ERNESTO VILCHES (*Mister Wu*), José Crespo (*Alfredo Gregory*), Angelita Benítez (*Nang Ping*), Marcela Nivón (*Mrs. Gregory*), José Soriano Viosca (*Mister Gregory*), Ura Mita (*Ah Wong*), Martín Garralaga (*Mister Holman*), Mara del Sobral (*Hilda Gregory*), Virginia Ruiz.

Drama. [*Not viewed*]. The great love of widower Wu Li Chang, a man of considerable culture, wealth and power in China, is his daughter Nang Ping, who, following tradition, has been promised in marriage to a mandarin. Ridiculing her father's vigilance, Nang Ping escapes from his palace and falls in love with Alfredo Gregory, an English gentleman, who wants to marry her. When Wu discovers this, he feels compelled to sacrifice the lives of the two lovers to appease the gods. With a broken heart, he kills his beloved daughter and, determined to fulfill the divine command, arranges a meeting with Gregory's mother, who offers her own life in place of her son's. Prepared to kill herself, she pours a powerful poison into a cup of tea which she will drink in Mr. Wu's presence. However, suspecting that she is trying to kill him, Wu switches his tea with hers and dies in horrible pain. *Chinese. Fathers and daughters. Mothers and sons. Murder. Romance. Self-sacrifice. China. English. Human sacrifice. Marriage–Arranged. Palaces. Poison. Tea. Widowers.*

Note: This film was a Spanish-language remake of the 1927 M-G-M film *Mr. Wu*, which was directed by William Nigh and starred Lon Chaney, Louise Dresser and Renée Adorée (see *AFI Catalog of Feature Films, 1921-30;* F2.3656).

Cinl Nov 1930, p. 30. *CM* Dec 1930, p. 1,210.

WUA KIO TSE GON *see* **HUA CHIO JUH GUANG**

WYOMING (Native Americans)
Metro-Goldwyn-Mayer Corp.; controlled by Loew's Inc. *Dist* Metro=Goldwyn-Mayer Distributing Corp. 24 Mar **1928** [©Metro-Goldwyn-Mayer Distributing Corp.; 24 Mar 1928; LP25190]. Si; b&w. 5 reels, 4,435 ft.
Dir W. S. Van Dyke. *Scen* Madeleine Ruthven and Ross B. Wills. *Wrt* W. S. Van Dyke. *Titles* Ruth Cummings. *Photog* Clyde De Vinna. *Film ed* William Le Vanway. *Ward* Lucia Coulter.
Cast: Tim McCoy (*Lieut. Jack Colton*), Dorothy Sebastian (*Samantha Jerusha Farrell*), Charles Bell (*Chief Big Cloud*), William Fairbanks (*Buffalo Bill*), Chief Big Tree (*An Indian*), Goes in the Lodge (*Chief Chapulti*), Blue Washington (*Mose*), Bert Henderson (*Oswald*).
Western. Big Cloud, an Indian boy, and Jack Colton, son of a pioneer, are united as children by a pledge of friendship but become enemies as adults. The son of Chief Chapulti, Big Cloud insists on fighting for what he believes is Indian territory. Violating a treaty, Big Cloud raids a wagon train. Colton, a cavalry lieutenant who is leading the party across the prairie, has a romantic interest in Samantha Farrell, a headstrong woman who would rather hasten west to stake her claim than stop to fight Indians. The raiding party attacks, is repelled by the cavalry, and is defeated when Chapulti, to stop the killing, shoots his own son. The romance between Colton and Samantha continues. *Buffalo Bill Cody. Frontier and pioneer life. Indians of North America. Murder. United States. Army. Cavalry. Wagon trains.*

FD 6 Aug 1928.

XEPOLYTO, TAGMAN *see* **BAREFOOT BATTALION**

THE YANKEE BANDIT *see* **THE CALIFORNIA TRAIL**

YANKEE DON (Latino)
Richard Talmadge Productions, Inc. *Dist* State Rights; Mercury Pictures Corp. **1931**. Sd; b&w. 5,574 ft. 60-61 min.
Dir Noel Mason. *Story* Madeline Allen. *Cont and dial* Francis Jackson.
Song(s): "My Gringo" and "Caballero Song," composer unknown.
Cast: Richard Talmadge (*Dick Carsey*), Lupita Tovar (*Juanita*), Gayne Whitman, Sam Appel, Julian Rivero, Alma Real, Victor Stanford.
Western, with songs. [*Not viewed*]. Dick Carsey leaves New York for the Barbary Coast. On the train going west, Carsey confuses the room number on his ticket and accidentally wakens Juanita, a beautiful, young Mexican woman. All during the rest of the trip, Carsey attempts to apologize to her, but she refuses to listen. At their destination, however, Carsey earns Juanita's respect when he chases a group of bandits away from the stage and prevents them from stealing a construction company payroll. Tenny, the company's owner, offers Carsey a job laying a pipeline across the land of Don Juan's ranch. Don Juan has refused Tenny access to his land, and Tenny is hoping that he will shoot Carsey for trespassing, which will send the don to jail and allow Tenny free access to his land. Don Juan's men do not shoot Carsey; instead they capture him and bring him to the don. There, Carsey learns that Juanita is the don's daughter.

Juanita tells her father that Carsey is the man who stopped the stagecoach robbery, and the don agrees to let him go. Impressed by the don's behavior, Carsey offers to work for him. His first plan foiled, Tenny sends one of his men to San Francisco to bring back a large group of hoodlums. Meanwhile, Carsey organizes the don's men into a gang. Carsey and Juanita plan to marry, and to get the money he needs for a ring, Carsey asks Tenny for the money he had promised him for laying the pipeline. Don Juan sees Carsey's horse in front of Tenny's company and assumes Carsey has been double-crossing him. He forbids Carsey to enter his house, but Carsey forces his way in and begs Juanita to let him explain. She refuses to listen to Carsey's explanations, but when Tenny's men attack, Carsey helps defend the ranch, and he and Juanita are reconciled. *California. Land rights. Mexican Americans. Outlaws. Ranches. False accusations. Fathers and daughters. New York City. Romance. Stagecoach robberies. Trains. The West.*

Note: According to *Var*, Talmadge performed a series of athletic stunts in the picture.

FD 17 May 1931, p. 10. *Var* 20 May 1931, p. 17.

YANKEE DOODLE DANDY (Irish Americans)
Warner Bros. Pictures, Inc.; A Warner Bros.—First National Picture. *Dist* Warner Bros. Pictures, Inc. 2 Jan **1943**; New York premiere: 29 May 1942; Prod: 3 Dec 1941—10 Feb 1942 [©Warner Bros. Pictures, Inc.; 2 Jan 1943; LP11830]. Sd (RCA Sound System); b&w. 11,347 ft. 125-126 min. PCA cert no. 7929.
Exec prod JACK L. WARNER and Hal B. Wallis. *Assoc prod* William Cagney. *Dir* Michael Curtiz. *Dial dir* Hugh MacMullan. [*Asst dir* Frank Heath]. [*2d asst dir* George Tobin]. *Scr* Robert Buckner and Edmund Joseph. *Orig story* Robert Buckner. [*Contr to scr* Julius J. Epstein and Philip G. Epstein]. *Dir of photog* James Wong Howe. [*Photog* Sol Polito]. [*2d cam* W. Anderson]. [*Asst cam* William Reinhold]. [*Stills* Mac Julian]. [*Gaffer* Everett Burkhalter]. *Mont* Don Siegel. *Art dir* Carl Jules Weyl. *Film ed* George Amy. *Gowns* Milo Anderson. [*Ward* Rydo Loshak, Leon Roberts and Marie Pickering]. *Orch arr* Ray Heindorf and Heinz Roemheld. *Mus dir* Leo F. Forbstein. *Dance numbers staged and dir* LeRoy Prinz and Seymour Felix. *James Cagney's dances* John Boyle. *Sd* Everett A. Brown. *Makeup artist* Perc Westmore. [*Makeup* William Cosley and William Phillips]. [*Hair* Martha Aker and Ruby Felker]. *Tech adv* William Collier, Sr.
Song(s): "Yankee Doodle Boy," "Give My Regards to Broadway," "Over There," "You're a Grand Old Flag," "Mary is a Grand Old Name," "So Long, Mary," "Larry O'Leary," "The Biggest Baby in the Bunch," "Harrigan," "Oh, You Wonderful Girl," "Blue S Gray Skies," "The Barber's Ball," "Like the Wandering Minstrel," "You Remind Me of My Mother," "In a Kingdom All our Own," "In a Love Nest Cozy and Warm," "Little Nellie Kelly," "I Was Born in Virginia," "Molly Malone," "Billie," lyrics and music by George M. Cohan. "Strictly Off the Record," by Richard Rodgers and Lorenz Hart; additional lyrics by Jack Scholl.
Cast: JAMES CAGNEY [(*George M. Cohan*)], Joan Leslie [(*Mary Cohan*)], Walter Huston [(*Jerry Cohan*)], Richard Whorf [(*Sam H. Harris*)], Irene Manning [(*Fay Templeton*)], George Tobias [(*Dietz*)], Rosemary DeCamp [(*Nellie Cohan*)], Jeanne Cagney [(*Josie Cohan*)], Frances Langford [(*Singer*)], George Barbier [(*Erlanger*)], S. Z. Sakall [(*Schwab*)], Walter Catlett [(*Theatre manager*)], Douglas Croft [(*George M. Cohan, as boy of 13*)], Minor Watson [(*Albee*)], Eddie Foy, Jr. [(*Eddie Foy*)], Chester Clute [(*Goff*)], Odette Myrtil [(*Madame Bartholdi*)], Patsy Lee Parsons [(*Josie Cohan, as a girl of 12*)], Capt. Jack Young [(*The president*)], [Pat Flaherty (*Soldier*)], [Clinton Rosemond (*Butler*)], [Dorothy Kelly, Marijo James (*Sister act*)], [Henry Blair (*George M. Cohan, age 7*)], [Jo Ann Marlowe (*Josie Cohan, age 6*)], [Thomas W. Ross (*Doctor*)], [Sailor Vincent (*Schultz*)], [Fred Kelsey (*Irish cop*)], [David Willock (*Stagehand*)], [June Millarde (*Young girl*)], [Harry Seymour (*Assistant manager*)], [Napoleon Simpson (*Porter*)], [Phyllis Kennedy (*Fanny*)], [Leon Belasco (*Magician*)], [Georgia Caine (*Woman boarder*)], [Syd Saylor (*Second boarder*)], [Ernie Stanton (*Waiter*)], [Bud McCallister (*Call boy*)], [Creighton Hale (*Telegraph operator*)], [Jean Inness (*Woman reporter*)], [Leah Baird (*Housekeeper*)], [Ernest Anderson (*Valet*)], [George Ovey (*Street cleaner*)], [Murray Alper (*Wise guy*)], [Garry Owen (*Clerk*)], [Victor Zimmerman (*Medical officer*)], [Francis Pierlot (*Dr. Lewellyn*)], [John Hamilton (*Major*)], [Harry Hayden (*Dr. Anderson*)], [Ruth Robinson (*Nurse*)], [William Forrest, Ed Keane

(*Critics*)], [Charles Smith, Dick Chandlee (*Boys*)], [Joyce Reynolds, Joyce Horne (*Girls*)], [Wallis Clark (*Theodore Roosevelt in musical number*)], [Georgia Carroll (*Betsy Ross in musical number*)], [Charles Irwin (*English announcer in musical number*)], [Fred Santley, John "Skins" Miller (*Judges in musical number*)], [Ann Edmonds, Ann Corcoran, Juanita Stark (*Soubrettes*)], [Joan Winfield, Vera Lewis (*Actresses*)], [Herbert Heywood, Edward McWade (*Doormen*)], [Spencer Charters, Thomas Jackson, William Davidson (*Stage managers*)], [Eddie Graham, Al Lloyd, Glen Cavender, Jack Mower, Hank Mann, Al Herman, Jim Toney, Charles Drake, John Sheehan, Louis Mason, Jack Wiso, Eddie Kano, Tom Dugan (*Actors*)], [James Flavin, Dick Wessel (*Veterans*)], [George Meeker, Frank Mayo (*Hotel clerks*)], [Audrey Long, Ann Doran (*Receptionists*)], [Jackie Salling, Joe Levine (*Newsboys*)], [Elliot Sullivan, Frank Sully, Frank Faylen (*Sergeant*)], [Eddie Acuff, Walter Brooke, Bill Edwards, William Hopper (*Reporters*)], [Frank Dee], [Mary Currier].

Biography, **Musical**. [*Print viewed*]. Actor and songwriter George M. Cohan is impersonating President Franklin D. Roosevelt in the musical show *I'd Rather Be Right*, by George S. Kaufman and Moss Hart, when he is summoned to meet the president at the White House. In response to the president's questions, George tells him the story of his life: George was born on the Fourth of July, 1878 to Jerry and Nellie Cohan, a pair of vaudeville actors. A short time later, his sister Josie is born and soon the family is touring the country as "The Four Cohans." The family gets a big break when they are hired to star in *Peck's Bad Boy*. At thirteen, George, the star of the play, is a success, but his self-importance is responsible for losing the Cohans several bookings. Several years later, George, now a young man, meets aspiring singer Mary when he is playing the part of an old man and she comes backstage to ask his sage advice about breaking into show business. The Cohans and Mary, who soon learns George's real age, go to New York, where George tries to sell the songs he has written. When he learns that The Four Cohans are losing work because of his reputation for imperious behavior, he pretends that his play has been sold so that the others will accept a booking without him. Later, in a bar, George overhears Sam H. Harris talking with Schwab, a potential backer, and offers him his new musical, *Little Johnny Jones*. Sam and George become partners and produce a number of plays that feature George's popular formula of success stories laced with patriotism. In the meantime, George proposes to Mary, Josie becomes engaged, and the older Cohans buy a farm and retire. It is the end of The Four Cohans and George takes this opportunity to write *Popularity*, a serious play. It fails miserably, but news of its failure is wiped out of the papers by the sinking of the *Lusitania* by the Germans in 1915. When the U.S. enters the war, George tries to enlist, but at thirty-nine, is too old to be a soldier. Unable to fight, George writes the inspirational song "Over There." After World War I, Cohan writes more shows. Josie and Nellie die and then George's father Jerry dies. Feeling his age, George dissolves his partnership with Sam so that he and Mary can take a much-needed rest. They travel to Europe and Asia, and end up on the Cohan farm. George pretends to enjoy his life, but he hates being out of the limelight. After a group of teenagers see George reading *Variety* and think that the headline "Stix Nix Hix Pix" is a form of jive talk, George realizes how much he still wants to be performing and gladly accepts Sam's offer to star in *I'd Rather be Right*. The president has listened quietly to George's story and now presents him with the Congressional Medal of Honor for his songs "Over There" and "It's a Grand Old Flag." George is the first actor to receive this honor, and he responds as he used to when he was with The Four Cohans, "My mother thanks you; my father thanks you; my sister thanks you; and I thank you." When George leaves the White House, a parade of soldiers and a band march by singing "Over There," and George proudly joins them. *Actors and actresses. George M. Cohan. Family relationships. Patriotism. Playwrights. Songwriters. Congressional Medal of Honor. Dancers. Fourth of July. Irish Americans. New York City–Broadway. Parades. Romance. Franklin Delano Roosevelt. Theatrical producers. Vaudevillians. World War I.*

Note: George M. Cohan wrote and produced more than thirty-five plays, many of them with his partner Sam H. Harris, and composed more than 500 songs. Modern critics have attributed his importance to the fact that his theatrical career survived and helped define the transition from vaudeville to the American musical play. He received the Congressional Medal of Honor in 1936 and died on 5 Nov 1942. Apart from leading an unsuccessful fight against the Actors Equity Association during their strike in 1919, his life was so oriented toward the theater that associate producer William Cagney, star James

Cagney's brother, and writer Robert Buckner complained in memos reproduced in a modern source, "He had no outside interests. His only objective was success, and he achieved it with monotonous annual regularity...." When Cohan objected to the way certain parts of his life were portrayed in the screenplay, Buckner, William Cagney and executive producer Hal B. Wallis explained in a letter dated 29 Aug 1941 that many biographical films produced by Warner Bros. took some liberty with the facts, thereby gaining dramatic interest. "Under your construction...the story is concerned largely with your chronology of productions, interspersed with personal scenes....We believe that the deep-dyed Americanism of your life is a much greater theme than the success story."

According to memos included in the Warner Bros. Collection at the USC Cinema-Television Library, Cohan was opposed to any portrayal of his private domestic life. He specifically objected to the character of "Mary," the screenwriters' largely invented romantic interest. In answer to his objections, Cagney, Buckner and executive producer Hal B. Wallis explained in the same letter "...The love story can be changed as you wish, to bring the girl in more casually and to delay the courtship and marriage very much as you have indicated...." In real life, Cohan married twice, the first time to actress Ethel Levey and the second time to Agnes Mary Nolan, a chorus girl who had been a member of his company for three years. Cohan wanted the character of "Mary" introduced late in the film so that his first wife would have no grounds for believing that the character was based on her. According to a 2 Aug 1944 *Var* article, Levey later unsuccessfully sued Warner Bros. for violation of her "rights of privacy" in making the film. New York Federal Judge William Bondy stated that "the introduction of fictional characters and a large fictional treatment of Cohan's life may hurt Miss Levey's feelings but they do not violate her rights of privacy."

In a 9 Oct 1943 letter to Joseph Karp of the Warner Bros. legal department that is included in the Warner Bros. Collection, Buckner objected to giving Julius and Philip Epstein screen credit for their contribution to the film, protesting that ninety percent of the construction and seventy percent of the dialogue had been written by him. The Epsteins eventually relinquished onscreen credit on the condition that their friend Edmund Joseph remain in the credits. According to news items in *HR*, the studio was interested in assigning a role to Philip Reed, and cinematographer Sol Polito substituted for James Wong Howe while the latter was ill. Memos in the Warner Bros. Collection add the following information about the production: Hal Wallis wanted to cast Irene Manning in the role of "Mary," and Donald Crisp was considered for the role of "The President." Makeup artist Perc Westmore planned to use masks to age the characters throughout the film. This idea was vetoed by Wallis. According to a news item in *LAT* on 28 Dec 1941, Cagney's dance instructor, Johnny Boyle, was a former member of the Cohan and Harris Minstrels.

Press notes included in the file on the film at the AMPAS Library add the following information about the production: Cagney was Cohan's own choice to play him on screen. When "Over There" was introduced by Nora Bayes at Camp Merritt, Long Island (Cohan remembered the location as Fort Myer) in 1917, all the lights went out during the performance, but the show continued after the headlights of nearby parked cars and trucks were turned on the stage. This incident is reproduced in the film, with Frances Langford, billed as "The Singer," performing the song. Technical adviser William Collier, Sr. was in many musicals with Cohan. Daily production reports note that filming was completed in fifty-eight days, ten days behind schedule. A real horse was used in the "Little Johnny Jones" number, and among the many other musical numbers in the film were extravagant productions of "Give My Regards To Broadway," "You're A Grand Old Flag," "Over There," and "Yankee Doodle Dandy," as well as Cagney's more intimate rendering of the love song "Mary." Cagney was several years older than Rosemary DeCamp, who played his mother, and actress Joan Leslie was only seventeen. This was the only film role in which Walter Huston sang and danced, and this was the first time James Cagney appeared in a film with his sister Jeanne.

Instead of tickets for the film's New York City premiere, Warner Bros. sold war bonds, ranging in price from $25 to $25,000. A 1 Jun 1942 news item notes that over 1,554 people bought bonds and raised over $5,000,000 for the war effort. The item adds that similar openings were planned for other cities, including Los Angeles and London. A premiere performance to benefit the Mexican Red Cross was held at the Palacio de Bellas Artes in Mexico City. A 27 May 1942 *HR* news item notes that the premiere would be broadcast over WMCA from 8-8:30 p.m. and members of the cast would be interviewed by actress Helen Twelvetrees.

Modern sources add the following information: Although the contract between Cohan and Warner Bros. stipulated that he compose three new songs for the film, these songs were never written. The filmmakers worked rapidly in order to complete the film before the ailing Cohan died. They held a special screening for Cohan and his wife Agnes, but Cohan lived long enough to read the film's rave reviews. The idea of a film about Cohan had made the rounds of the studios—Fred Astaire was at one time considered for the role—but Cagney, who had twice been falsely labeled a Communist, took the role of "Cohan" partly because he and his brother William believed that performing in an obviously patriotic film such as this would help deflect political criticism. Cagney recreated his role as "George M. Cohan" in the 1955 Paramount film *The Seven Little Foys*, directed by Melville Shavelson. In the film, Cagney as "Cohan," dances a duet with Bob Hope as "Eddie Foy." *Yankee Doodle Dandy* was one of The *FD* Ten Best Pictures of 1943 and was nominated for the Best Picture Oscar. Director Michael Curtiz and editor George Amy were also nominated for Oscars; Walter Huston received a nomination for Best Supporting Actor; and Robert Buckner was nominated for Best Original Story. James Cagney won his only Academy Award for his performance in this film. Ray Heindorf and Heinz Roemheld received an Oscar for Best Music Scoring, although Roemheld does

not receive a credit on the film. The film also earned an Oscar for Best Sound Recording.

Box 30 May 1942. *FD* 1 Jun 1942, p. 6. *HR* 14 Apr 1941, p. 1. *HR* 24 Dec 1941, p. 7. *HR* 22 Apr 1942, p. 1. *HR* 22 May 1942, p. 1. *HR* 27 May 1942, p. 1, 6. *HR* 1 Jun 1942, p. 3. *HR* 13 Aug 1942, p. 11. *HR* 19 Oct 1942, p. 7. *HR* 10 Feb 1943, p. 6. *MPHPD* 6 Jun 1942, p. 699. *NYT* 30 May 1942, p. 9. *Var* 3 Jun 1942, p. 8.

A YANKEE FROM THE WEST (Norwegian Americans)

Majestic Motion Picture Co. *Dist* Mutual Film Corp.; A Mutual Masterpicture. Aug **1915**. Si; b&w. 4 reels.

Dir George Siegmann. *Scen* Mary O'Connor. *Cam* B. C. Hayward.

Source: Based on the novel *A Yankee from the West* by Opie Read (Chicago, 1879).

Cast: Wallace Reid (*Billy Milford*), Signe Auen (*Gunhild*), Tom Wilson (*Jim Dorsey*), Josephine Crowell (*Mrs. Stuvic*), Chris Lynton (*Professor Emerson*), Bill Brown (*Jan Hagnerg*), Al W. Filson (*Whitney Mills*), George Siegmann (*Sheriff Dick*).

Drama. Billy Milford, a Harvard graduate, works as a stationmaster in a Western town and courts the pretty Gunhild, a Norwegian immigrant. Because of his excessive drinking, Billy is fired from his post, but retaliates by robbing the company with his friend, Jim Dorsey, who then runs off with the money. Abandoned, Billy faces the police alone and avoids arrest but leaves town and Gunhild in his shame. Two years later, Gunhild meets Billy, now the operator of an Eastern farm, and love is rekindled. Jim also reappears, and his attentions to Gunhild as well as his blackmail threats force Billy to do battle. After an unsuccessful first attempt, Billy finally knocks his rival out and then confesses to the railroad superintendant his part in the crime, handing over his savings as restitution. Moved by Billy's honesty, the superintendant refuses the money, giving it to Gunhild as a wedding present instead. *Conscience. Norwegian Americans. Railroad stations. Revenge. Robbery. Betrayal. Blackmail. Confession (Law). Drunkenness. Escapes. Farmers. Fistfights. Police.*

Motog 28 Aug 1915, p. 415, 439. *MPN* 17 Apr 1915, p. 54. *MPN* 21 Aug 1915, p. 110. *MPN* 11 Sep 1915, p. 80. *MPW* 21 Aug 1915, p. 1392. *Var* 27 Aug 1915, p. 19.

A YANKEE PRINCESS (Irish Americans)

Vitagraph Co. of America. *Dist* Vitagraph Co. of America. 21 Apr **1919** [©Vitagraph Co. of America; 1 Apr 1919; LP13562]. Si; b&w. 5 reels.

Dir David Smith. *Scen* Bessie Love. *Story* Bernard McConville.

Cast: Bessie Love (*Patsy O'Reilly*), Robert Gordon (*Larry Burke*), George Pierce (*Michael O'Reilly*), Aggie Herring (*Mrs. O'Reilly*), J. Carlton Wetherby (*Lord Windbourne*), Katherine Griffith (*Lady Windbourne*), Lydia Yeamans Titus (*Molly McGuire*), Max Asher (*The French chef*).

Comedy-drama. Ragged Patsy O'Reilly imagines herself descended from Irish nobility. When her father, an impoverished contractor, invents an ore crusher, the family becomes rich overnight and moves to New York. Patsy is enrolled in a finishing school, and her parents tour Ireland where they purchase, at Patsy's request, a coat-of-arms from the bankrupt Lord Windbourne family. After the O'Reillys return to America they are visited by Lady Windbourne and her son, the Lord, who do not mention that the adopted coat-of-arms is their own. Lord Windbourne becomes engaged to Patsy, but is later revealed as an impostor by the true heir to the Windbourne line, Larry Burke, an English officer. Larry marries Patsy and gives her an authentic ancestral name and coat-of-arms. *Immigrants. Irish Americans. Nouveaux riches. Bankruptcy. Contractors. Engagements. Finishing schools. Heirs. Heredity. Impersonation and imposture. Investors. Ireland. New York City. Nobility. Officers (Military).*

Note: The copyright holdings credit Bessie Love with the scenario, but *Wid's* gives joint credit to Love and Bernard McConville. A modern source credits Clyde de Vinna with the film's cinematography.

ETR 19 Apr 1919, p. 1527. *MPN* 19 Apr 1919, p. 2523. *MPW* 19 Apr 1919, pp. 431-32. *MPW* 26 Apr 1919, pp. 464-65. *Var* 11 Apr 1919, p. 55. *Wid's* 13 Apr 1919, p. 7.

YANKEE SPEED (Latino)

Sunset Productions. *Dist* Aywon Film Corp. 1 Jul **1924**. Si; b&w. 6 reels, 5,200 ft.

Pres Anthony J. Xydias. *Dir* Robert N. Bradbury. *Scen* Robert N. Bradbury. *Photog* L. W. McManigal.

Cast: Kenneth McDonald (*Dick Vegas*), Jay Hunt (*Don Verdugo*), Richard Lewis (*Pedro Ramírez*), Milton Fahrney (*José T. Vegas*), John Henry (*Ramón García*), Viola Yorga (*Marquita Fernández*), Virginia Ainsworth (*Inez La Velle*).

Western. A wealthy oil man, José Vegas, orders his son, Richard, shipped west in a boxcar after the boy shows considerably more interest in athletics than in business. Richard arrives in Arizona, where he is put to work in the oil fields by his father's foreman. At a nearby hacienda, Don Manuel feigns death in order to discover what his heirs will do. Dick eventually brings to justice one of Don Manuel's heirs, García, after he attempts to discover the location of the family fortune by force and cunning. Richard wins the love of Don Manuel's niece, Marquita. *Arizona. Athletes. Fatherhood. Inheritance. Mexican Americans. Oil fields.*

FD 20 Jul 1924.

YANKEL DER SCHMID *see* **THE SINGING BLACKSMITH**

YED SIU BOG LONG SEM *see* **YEE SIO BO LAAN SIN**

YEE SIO BO LAAN SIN (Chinese language)

Grandview Film Co. **1946?**; Hong Kong showing: 1946? Sd; b&w. Length undetermined. Chinese language.

Dir Jiang Wai-kwong.

Cast: Lai Yee, Wong Hok-sing. [*Not viewed*]. [No information concerning the plot of this film has been located.].

Note: The Cantonese transliterated title is *Yed Siu Bog Long Sem.* The English language title of the film is *Smiling to Please.* This film was probably made in the U.S.

YEIN DOW (Chinese language)

Grandview Film Co. **1949?**; Hong Kong showing: 1949? Sd; b&w. Length undetermined. Chinese language.

Cast: Wong Hok-sing. [*Not viewed*]. [No information concerning the plot of this film has been located.].

Note: The Cantonese transliterated title is *Yien Dou.* According to information from the Hong Kong Film Archives, this film was shot in both Hong Kong and San Francisco.

YELLOW AND WHITE *see* **BROKEN FETTERS**

YELLOW CARGO (Chinese Americans)

Condor Pictures, Inc.; A George A. Hirliman Production. *Dist* Grand National Films, Inc. 13 Oct **1936** [©Grand National Films, Inc.; 3 Dec 1936; LP6739]. Sd; b&w. 7 reels. 63 or 70 min. PCA cert no. 2188.

Series: Federal Agent.

Pres EDWARD L. ALPERSON. *Assoc prod* Samuel Diege. *Dir* Crane Wilbur. *Asst dir* Bobby Ray. *Scr* Crane Wilbur. [*Orig story* Crane Wilbur]. *Photog* Mack Stengler. *Art dir* Frank Sylos. *Ed* Tony Martinelli. *Mus supv* Abe Meyer. *Sd rec* Glen Glenn.

Cast: CONRAD NAGEL (*Allan O'Connor*), Eleanor Hunt (*Bobbie Reynolds*), Vince Barnett (*"Bulb" Callahan*), Jack La Rue (*Al Perrelli* [*also known as Jose Salazar*]), Claudia Dell (*Fay Temple*), Henry Strange (*Joe Breeze*), John Ivans (*District Commissioner*), Vance Carroll (*Burke Darrell*), [Crane Wilbur (*Monty Brace*)], [Lillian Wessner].

Drama. [*Print viewed*]. Allan O'Connor is sent by the immigration office in New York to investigate the smuggling of Chinese aliens into Los Angeles. At the same time, Bobbie Reynolds, a reporter, investigates Globe Productions in Hollywood, an independent film company that suspiciously avoids publicity. When Bobbie and her clumsy assistant, "Bulb" Callahan, meet Globe's elusive president, Monty Brace, at the airport, Bobbie befriends Allan, who poses as an aspiring actor. Meanwhile, Stuart, a border patrol officer, is badly beaten while trailing a stolen ambulance by a man who has a fetish for rolling pieces of paper. During a screen test at Globe, Allan gets Globe director Al Perrelli's fingerprints on his cigarette case and catches Perrelli nervously rolling a piece of paper. The next day, Bobbie and Allan meet Brace and Perrelli at a municipal pier, from where they carry twenty Hollywood extras dressed as Chinese to an island for filming. There, Allan takes a picture of Brace with an unidentified man. Allan then learns from an ex-convict-turned-actor that Globe has been sending their extras home early by a different route. Perrelli's fingerprints show that he is Jose Salazar, an escaped criminal from Buenos Aires. Allan and Bulb are then hired as extras for a day's shooting, and that evening, Allan waits on the island to join the cargo of real Chinese men, but is discovered and knocked out. Meanwhile, Bobbie and Bulb are caught trying to take a picture and are bound and gagged and driven to an old ranch house, where Burke Darrell, a well-known financier, is hiding. When Allan revives, he notifies the police, who stop the truckload of Chinese and identify the man in Allan's picture as Darrell. After a chase in which the

smugglers switch cars and Allan follows a trail of Bobbie's discarded shoes, Allan stops Perrelli, and Bobbie reveals herself as an officer of the Department of Justice. *Aliens, Illegal. Chinese. Hollywood (CA). Motion picture studios. Smuggling. Undercover operations.* Automobile chases. Capitalists and financiers. Fetishes. Fugitives. Impersonation and imposture. Islands. Latin Americans. Motion picture actors and actresses. Motion picture directors. Motion picture producers. Photographers. Police. Reporters. Shoes. United States. Dept. of Immigration. United States. Dept. of Justice.

Note: This film was the first in a proposed series of six George A. Hirliman films produced for Grand National featuring Conrad Nagel and Eleanor Hunt as undercover government agents. Only four films were made, the last of which was *Bank Alarm* in 1937 (see *AFI Catalog of Feature Films, 1931-40*; F3.0229). For additional information on the series, consult the Series Index.

DV 2 Jun 1936, p. 3. *Exb* 15 Jun 1936. *FD* 6 Jun 1936, p. 7. *HR* 2 Jun 1936, p. 3. *MPD* 4 Jun 1936, p. 12. *MPH* 7 Nov 1936, p. 56. *Var* 18 Nov 1936, p. 29.

THE YELLOW DOG (German Americans)

Universal Film Mfg. Co.; Universal Special. *Dist* Jewel Productions, Inc. 4 Nov 1918 [©Jewel Productions, Inc.; 2 Oct 1918; LP12953]. Si; b&w. 6 reels.

Dir Colin Campbell. *Scen* Elliott J. Clawson. *Cam* Harry Neumann.

Source: Based on the short story "The Yellow Dog" by Henry Irving Dodge in *The Saturday Evening Post* (4 May 1918).

Cast: Arthur Hoyt (*Albert Walker*), Antrim Short (*"Nosey" White*), Clara Horton (*Kate Cummings*), Frank Clark (*Alexander Cummings*), Will Machin (*Karl Schneider*), Frank Hayes (*Jones*), Fred Kelsey (*Max Kummich*), Frederick Starr (*Henry Babbitt*), Ruby Lafayette (*Mrs. Blakely*), Ralph Graves (*Tom Blakely*), Lily Clarke (*Tom's sweetheart*).

Espionage, World War I, Drama. In the small shipbuilding town of Danforth, Albert Walker realizes, to his distress, that German sympathizers, spies and draft evaders, by voicing doubts about the United States' involvement in the war, are having a disastrous effect on the patriotic spirit of the townspeople. In order to silence these "yellow dogs," Albert organizes the boys of Danforth into a club, to be headed by a young patriot called "Nosey" White. The boys pledge to challenge unpatriotic remarks by handling the speaker a card labeled "yellow dog." While Nosey is in the home of his sweetheart, Kate Cummings, one day, he overhears her father, Alexander Cummings, in conversation with a group of German spies. Learning that the agents plan to set fire to the shipyard, he informs his father, who rushes to the scene and engages one of the spies in a fight. The spy is shot, and when Albert and Nosey expose Cummings, the German is sent to prison. *Clubs. German Americans. Patriotism. Spies. World War I.* Conspiracy. Fights. Germans. Military service, Compulsory. Sabotage. Shipbuilders. Shipyards.

Note: Dodge's story was also published in book form (New York, 1918). The film had a pre-release run in New York beginning 13 Oct 1918. Inspired by Jewel's advance publicity campaign, a nationwide movement was initiated to form Anti-Yellow Dog clubs. Boys wishing to join the clubs were instructed to "ferret out pro-German sympathizers and rumor-mongers, and label them 'Yellow Dog.'" According to news items, city and state officials commonly involved themselves in the formation of these clubs. Various release dates were listed in the reviews.

ETR 28 Sep 1918, p. 1423. *MPN* 21 Sep 1918, p. 1911. *MPN* 28 Sep 1918, p. 2080. *MPW* 5 Oct 1918, p. 120. *MPW* 12 Oct 1918, p. 282, 284. *NYDM* 26 Oct 1918, p. 627. *Var* 18 Oct 1918, p. 18. *Wid's* 24 Oct 1918, p. 18.

THE YELLOW PASSPORT (Jewish Americans)

World Film Corp.; A Shubert Production. *Dist* World Film Corp. 7 Feb 1916 [©World Film Corporation; 5 Feb 1916; LU7630]. Si; b&w. 5 reels.

Dir Edwin August. *Scen* Frances Marion and Edwin August. *Story* Abraham S. Schomer. *Cam* Philip Hatkin.

Cast: Clara Kimball Young (*Sonia Sokoloff*), Edwin August (*Adolph Rosenheimer*), John Sainpolis (*Fedia*), Alec B. Francis (*Myron Abram*), John Boyle (*Carl Rosenheimer*), Mrs. Landau (*Mrs. Rosenheimer*), Edward Kimball (*David Sokoloff*), Mrs. Kimball (*Mrs. Sokoloff*), Thomas Charles (*Fiodor*), Florence Hackett (*Akulena, Fiodor's wife*), Silas Feinberg (*Alex Sokoloff*), Robert Cummings (*Ivan*), Nicholas Dunaew (*Music master*), Adolph Lestina (*Chief of police*).

Drama. Sonia Sokoloff, a voice student, is the daughter of a wealthy Russian Jewish family. Fedia, an anti-Semitic police spy, infiltrates the house as the family valet and attempts to rape Sonia, who has him fired. In revenge, Fedia incites the Black Hundred, an anti-Semitic organization to which he belongs, to an attack on the Sokoloff house

in which Sonia's parents are killed. Sonia is allowed to continue her music studies in Russia only by accepting a yellow passport, which marks her as a prostitute. Eventually she and her uncle, forced to leave the country when the police learn that she has accepted the passport under false premises, travel to America, meeting opera impresario Carl Rosenheimer and his son Adolph during the journey. Carl recognizes Sonia's talent and promotes her singing career in America, where she becomes a celebrity and Adolph's fiancée. Fedia, however, shows up in America and exposes the secret of Sonia's yellow passport. Adolph denounces her, but Akulena and Fiodor, Sonia's friends from Russia, come to America with papers that establish her innocence, and the lovers are reunited. *Antisemitism. Exile. Opera singers. Religious persecution. Russia. Secret Police.* Attempted rape. Impersonation and imposture. Impresarios. Jews. Libel and slander. Murder. Music students. Revenge. Russia. Uncles. Valets.

Note: Scenes from the film were shot on Ellis Island. It is unclear whether Schomer's story was written for the screen or another medium. The actress Mrs. Kimball is very likely Pauline Garrett Kimball; the actress Mrs. Landau is probably Mrs. David Landau. World later renamed the film *The Badge of Shame*, copyrighted it again under that title (9 Mar 1917; LU10398), and re-released it on 19 Mar 1917.

MPN 12 Feb 1916, p. 878. *MPW* 12 Feb 1916, p. 885. *MPW* 19 Feb 1916, p. 1140. *MPW* 25 Mar 1916, p. 2090. *Var* 4 Feb 1916, p. 28.

THE YELLOW TOMAHAWK (Native Americans, Cheyenne)

K. B. Productions, Inc. *Dist* United Artists Corp. May 1954; Prod: completed late Oct 1953 [©K. B. Productions, Inc.; 21 Apr 1954; LP3693]. Sd (Western Electric Sound); col (Color Corp. of America); 1.85. 7,378 ft. 82 min. PCA cert no. 16843.

Pres AUBREY SCHENCK. *Prod* Howard W. Koch. *Dir* Lesley Selander. *Asst dir* Emmett Emerson. *Scr* Richard Alan Simmons. *Based on a story by* Harold Jack Bloom. *Dir of photog* Gordon Avil. *Spec eff* Russell Shearman. *Color consultant* Clifford D. Shank. *Film ed* John Schreyer. *Ward* Wesley V. Jeffries. *Mus* Les Baxter. *Orch* Albert Harris. *Sd mixer* Ben Winkler. *Makeup created by* Eddie Polo. *Hair stylist* Mary Smith. *Prop master* Arden Cripe. *Scr supv* Theodore Shilz.

Cast: Rory Calhoun (*Adam [Reed]*), Peggie Castle (*Katherine [Bohlen]*), Noah Beery (*Tonio [Perez]*), Warner Anderson (*Major Ives*), Peter Graves ([*Walt*] *Sawyer*), Lee Van Cleef (*Fire Knife*), Rita Moreno (*Honey Bear*), Dan Riss (*Sergeant Bandini*), Walter Reed (*Keats*), Patrick Joseph Sexton (*Lieutenant Bascom*), Robert Bray (*Lieutenant Banion*), Adam Williams (*Corporal Maddock*), James Best (*Private Bliss*), Ned Glass (*Willy*).

Western. [*Print viewed*]. In the hills of the Wyoming Territory, Adam Reed, an Indian scout, arrives for a meeting with an old friend, the Cheyenne brave Fire Knife. Fire Knife asks Adam to deliver the yellow tomahawk of war to Cavalry Major Ives, who is known to the Cheyenne as "the butcher" because he was responsible for a massacre in which many Cheyenne women and children were killed. After promising Adam that the women and children living in Ives's encampment will be given time to leave before violence erupts, Fire Knife presents Adam with his father's bow as a symbol of their friendship. Despite Adam's warning, Ives, who hates the Cheyenne with a vengeance, refuses to evacuate the camp, where he is building a fort in violation of a treaty with the Cheyenne. Adam makes plans to travel to Fort Ellis in order to report Ives's illegal construction to their superior, General Faulkner, and in the meantime, meets a number of the encampment's civilian residents, including the bookish Keats, the fort's architect, and Tonio Perez, an affable Mexican adventurer being pursued by Honey Bear, an amorous young Indian woman. Adam also renews his acquaintance with Kate Bohlen, the fiancée of Lt. Bascom, who he had met earlier at a swimming hole. Later that afternoon, a prospector, Walt Sawyer, rides into camp with his seriously injured partner, Willy. Sawyer claims that the two were attacked by Cheyenne warriors, but Adam is suspicious of his story. In answer to Adam's queries, Sawyer claims that they found no gold, but when left alone briefly with Willy, Sawyer finishes him off in order to keep the gold they discovered for himself. Ives uses Sawyer's story of an unprovoked Indian attack to his advantage, declaring that the Cheyenne have already broken their promise. Adam begs Fire Knife for more time in order to reach Faulkner for help in getting Ives to leave the area, but Fire Knife is unmoved by Adam's pleas. Without informing them of the true danger of their situation, Ives gives the soldiers' wives the option of leaving the encampment with Tonio, but all of the women choose to stay with their husbands, except for Kate,

who has just broken off her engagement to Bascom and wishes to return to Boston. Ives and Keats, accompanied by two of Ives's men, Corporal Maddock and Private Bliss, ride out to the hills to retrieve a hidden cache of weapons. When Ives opens the metal box, however, he finds nothing but a tomahawk. Before Ives can return, smoke signals appear on the horizon, and the Cheyenne begin their attack, descending on the ill-prepared camp in droves. During the exceptionally violent attack, women and children are assaulted with tomahawks and chased into tents which are then set afire. Although Adam is wounded and knocked unconscious, Fire Knife makes sure his life is spared. Kate, having returned to the camp because she was unable to make it through enemy territory, grieves over the body of Bascom, crying out for vengeance, until Adam reminds her that the Cheyenne were only avenging the deaths of their own families. Tonio and Honey Bear also return, having seen the ominous smoke signals, but they are too late to help. Maddock blames Ives for the murder of his family and wants to shoot him, but Adam intervenes, suggesting that the small band of survivors attempt to make their way to Fort Ellis, where Faulkner will decide the question of Ives's guilt. On the first night of their journey, Kate and Adam reveal their feelings for each other, while Tonio remains impervious to Honey Bear's longings. The following day, the Cheyenne attack, and Keats, Maddock and Bliss are killed. Taking the friendship bow with him, Adam seeks out the warriors and attempts to return the bow to Fire Knife, who refuses it. The Cheyenne braves tell Adam that they want only that Ives be turned over to them, but Adam refuses their request, declaring that Ives must face the judgment of his own people. During the battle that follows, Sawyer, who Adam now knows killed his partner and then blamed it on the Cheyenne, is wounded and dies a slow death, clutching his gold until the end. Honey Bear manages to save Tonio's life by killing a Cheyenne who is about to attack him, and fighting valiantly, the greatly depleted group succeeds in killing all the warriors, save for Fire Knife. In abject fear, Ives calls out to Fire Knife, begging for mercy and revealing the secret explaining his pathological hatred of the Indians: he has Cheyenne blood and therefore planned the massacre as a misguided means of erasing his own past. As no ammunition remains, Adam has no choice but to fight Fire Knife one on one with his bow. After shooting Fire Knife through the heart, Adam sadly leaves the token of their friendship—the prized bow—by Fire Knife's body. Once the group safely reaches Fort Ellis, Tonio and Honey Bear, now in love, ride off in search of new adventures, while Kate remains at the fort to begin her new life with Adam. Ives warns Adam not to reveal the truth of his ancestry, but Adam replies that his only concern is that Faulkner listen to both of their stories carefully, for only the general can decide which approach will best solve the "Indian problem": total eradication of a people or fairness and the honoring of peace treaties. *Cheyenne Indians. Friendship. Massacres. Racism. United States. Army. Cavalry. Architects. Battles. Duplicity. Engagements. Forts. Greed. Indians of North America–Mixed blood. Mexicans. Prospectors. Revenge. Treaties. Unrequited love. Wyoming.*

Note: The working titles of this film were *Fire Knife* and *War Clouds.* K. B. Productions was also known as Schenck-Koch Productions. *The Yellow Tomahawk* was shot on location in Kanab, Utah.

Box 15 May 1954. *DV* 7 May 1954, p. 3. *Exh* 19 May 1954, p. 3755. *FD* 14 Jun 1954, p. 6. *Har* 8 May 1954, p. 74. *HR* 23 Oct 1953, p. 13. *HR* 7 May 1954, p. 3. *MPD* 13 May 1954. *MPHPD* 8 May 1954, p. 2285. *Var* 19 May 1954, p. 6.

THE YELLOW TRAFFIC (Chinese Americans)
Blaché Features, Inc. Jun **1914** [©Blaché Features, Inc.; 27 Jun 1914; LP3056]. Si; b&w. 4 reels.
Drama. In New England, Captain Rawley, the skipper of the *Caroline,* is heavily indebted to Edward Allen, an unscrupulous merchant who wants to possess the ship and use it to illegally traffic Chinese aliens. Allen is in love with Alice, the Captain's daughter, but she is in love with Tom Northrup, a member of the U.S. Coast Guard. When Rawley and his son Jim, who is first mate, put to sea, they are overpowered by Red Bill and his cohorts, members of Allen's gang. Jim manages to send a wireless message to Alice of their trouble, however, and she, in turn, contacts the Coast Guard. Jim is meanwhile forced to walk the plank, but swims ashore, where he joins Alice, Tom, and the Coast Guard in defeating the smugglers. Finally, Alice receives a $5,000 reward for her part in breaking up the illegal operations which she gives to her father to redeem his debt. *Gangs. Merchants. New England. Sea captains. Secret Service. Smuggling.*

United States. Coast Guard. Chinese Americans. Debt. Fathers and daughters. Rewards. Telegrams.

Note: James Johnson lists this film among his credits in the 29 Jan 1916 *MPSD,* but the nature of his participation is unclear.
MPW 20 Jun 1914, p. 1744.

YELLOWSTONE KELLY (Native Americans, Arapaho, Dakota)
Warner Bros. Pictures, Inc. *Dist* Warner Bros. Pictures, Inc. 5 Sep **1959**; Prod: early Apr—early Jun 1959 [©Warner Bros. Pictures, Inc.; 5 Sep 1959; LP17058]. Sd (RCA Sound Recording); col (Technicolor). 10 reels, 8,252 ft. 91 min. PCA cert no. 19319.
Dir Gordon Douglas. *Asst dir* Bill Kissel. *Scr* Burt Kennedy. *Dir of photog* Carl Guthrie. *Art dir* Stanley Fleischer. *Film ed* William Ziegler. *Set dec* William Wallace. *Cost des* Marjorie Best. *Mus cond* Howard Jackson. *Sd* M. A. Merrick. *Makeup supv* Gordon Bau.
Source: Based on the novel *Yellowstone Kelly* by Clay Fisher (Boston, 1957).
Cast: Clint Walker [(*Luther "Yellowstone" Kelly*)], Edward Byrnes [(*Anse Harper*)], John Russell [(*Gall*)], Ray Danton [(*Sayapi*)], Claude Akins [(*Sergeant*)], Rhodes Reason [(*Major Towns*)], Andra Martin [(*Wahleeah*)], Gary Vinson [(*Lieutenant*)], Warren Oates [(*Corporal*)], [Harry Shannon (*Captain*)], [Buff Brady (*Helmsman*)], [Nesdon Booth (*Reed*)], [Chief Yowlachie (*Medicine man*)], [Vince St. Cyr, Clyde Howdy (*Indians*)], [Foster Hood (*Drummer*)].
Western. [*Print viewed*]. Luther "Yellowstone" Kelly, trapper, surveyor and Indian scout, arrives at the Yellowstone River with skins to sell at Fort Buford in the Dakota Territory. Major Towns, the fort's commanding officer, asks Kelly to be the Army's scout through Sioux territory south of the Missouri, and Kelly reluctantly agrees, setting out with Anse, a young man he met on the steamship. As they approach the Snake River, they are captured by Sayapi, a young Sioux, and brought before Gall, chief of the Seven Nations and a hater of whites. Gall reminds Kelly that seven years earlier, Kelly had saved his life after Gall was shot by soldiers and left for dead, and he now demands that Kelly do the same for a captured Arapaho, a beautiful maiden named Wahleeah. Kelly manages to remove the bullet from her spine, and Gall allows Kelly and Anse to leave, despite Sayapi's objections. Later, Wahleeah, half-dead from fever, approaches Kelly's cabin, and when Kelly warns that she will die if she is moved, Gall orders that she remain there until the winter, provoking a jealous outburst by Sayapi. When she revives, Wahleeah asks Kelly to take her to her own people, but he refuses, unwilling to let anything interfere with his trapping. Aware that soldiers are about to cross the river, Kelly warns Major Towns that a thousand Sioux are on the other side, but Towns, eager to punish the Sioux for the massacre at Little Bighorn, orders his soldiers to drive them back to the Dakota Territory. Meanwhile, Anse decides to take Wahleeah back to her people, but Sayapi and his men stop them, and Kelly returns to find his house aflame and Anse dying. An anguished Kelly tracks Sayapi to a cave and kills him, then rescues Wahleeah and tells her he will now return her to her tribe. Kelly learns that Major Downs died in an attack by the Sioux, and the surviving soldiers are surrounded. On the open plain, Kelly goes unarmed to meet Gall. who offers Kelly his freedom in exchange for Wahleeah, but insists that the soldiers must die. Kelly refuses and Gall orders an attack. Kelly refuses, and Gall orders the Sioux to attack. When Kelly asks Gall how many more must die, proclaiming that the land no longer smiles on the Sioux people, Gall goes off in frustration. Sometime later, Kelly and Wahleeah ride mules to the river, where he signals a steamship to stop for them. *Adolescents. Arapaho Indians. Dakota Indians. Friendship. Gall (Sioux chieftain). Luther Sage Kelly. Miscegenation. Personality change. Racism. Romance. Trappers. United States–History–Indian campaigns. Yellowstone National Park (WY). Ambition. Caves. Fistfights. Gunshot wounds. Nephews. Nursing back to health. Officers (Military). Rescues. Steamboats.*

Note: According to the pressbook for the film, scenes were shot in Arizona in and around Flagstaff, the San Francisco Peaks area and Sedona, where the battle at the end was filmed. The pressbook states that 114 Navajo Indians portrayed Sioux warriors. The film featured three stars from ABC-TV series: Clint Walker of *Cheyenne;* Edward Byrnes, who played "Kookie" on 77 *Sunset Strip;* and John Russell of *Lawman.* Reviewers noted that this film would test whether stars of television would attract viewers to movie theaters.
Var commented, "Box office response to this picture will provide more data on the question of whether stars developed in teleseries can draw paying customers on the strength of their names rather than tv characters they portray. It's a good bet that they will, especially in this combination." *MPD* predicted

that the stars' "names may well bring out to theaters that part of the so-called 'lost' audience which has been lost because of TV westerns and action dramas." *Var* praised the film's "craftsmanship in every department" which, they suggested, "displayed the three tv heroes in a production framework not approachable in telefilming." *LAMirror-News* called the film "a throwback to those Technicolored cavalry versus Indian days before the movie western went somberly psychological, tense and black-and-white."

Box 24 Aug 1959. *DV* 12 Aug 1959, p.3. *Exb* 26 Aug 1959, pp. 4618-19. *FD* 20 Aug 1959, p.6. *Har* 15 Aug 1959, p. 131. *HR* 10 Apr 1959. p. 14. *HR* 5 Jun 1959, p. 11. *HR* 12 Aug 1959. *LAEx* 17 Sep 1959. *LAT* 30 Aug 1959. *LAT* 18 Sep 1959. *LAMirror-News* 17 Sep 1959. *MPD* 13 Aug 1959. *MPHPD* 15 Aug 1959, p. 373. *NYT* 12 Nov 1959, p. 27. *Var* 12 Aug 1959, p. 18.

THE YES MAN *see* THE STRONG MAN

YES SIR, MR. BONES (African Americans)

Spartan Productions, Inc. *Dist* Lippert Productions, Inc. 13 Jul 1951; Prod: ended Mar 1951 [©Spartan Productions, Inc.; 27 Jun 1951; LP990]. Sd; b&w. 6 reels, 4,855 ft. 54 min. PCA cert no. 15299.

Prod Ron Ormond. *Assoc prod* June Carr. *Dir* Ron Ormond. *Asst dir* F. O. Collings. [*Story and scr* Ron Ormond]. *Photog* Jack Greenhalgh. *Spec eff* Ray Mercer. *Art dir* F. Paul Sylos. *Ed* Hugh Winn. *Set dec* Theodore Offenbecker. *Men's ward* Alfred Berke. *Women's ward* Kitty Mager. *Mus* Walter Greene. *Sd eng* Glen Glenn and Earl Crain, Jr. *Makeup artist* Paul Stanhope, George Bruce and Harry Ross. *Prod supv* William Magginetti. *Prop master* Ernest Johnson. *Scr supv* Sam Freedle.

Song(s): "I Want to Be a Minstrel Man," by June Carr; "Is Your Rent Paid Up in Heaven," by Mildred and Jimmy Mulcahy, and Bill Anson; "Flying Saucers," by Elliott Carpenter; "Memphis Bill" and "Stay Out of the Kitchen," by Elliott Carpenter and F. E. Miller; "Southland," by Edith and Gracia Drion, and Walter Greene.

Cast: Cotton Watts, Chick Watts, Slim Williams, Ches Davis, Emmett Miller, F. E. Miller [(*Jim*)], Ned Haverly, Billy Green, Brother Bones, Elliott Carpenter, Scatman Carothers [sic], The Hobnobbers, Monette Moore, Ellen Sutton, Jimmy O'Brien, Sally Anglim, Archie Twitchell [(*Interlocutor*)], Gary Jackson [(*Billie Crane*)], Cliff Taylor, Phil Arnold, Boyce & Evans, Jester Hairston Singers, Pete Dailey and His Chicagoans.

Musical. [*Print viewed*]. At the Show Boat Rest Inn, Jim, an African-American porter, polishes a window pane and looks through the glass to a gathering of mostly white men, two of whom dance to the accompaniment of a black piano player. Impressed by the sight, Jim tells Billie Crane, an inquisitive, young white boy who comes by, that the men inside are old minstrel men. Jim takes Billie in and introduces him to the men. While Jim gets Billie some food, Billy Green, formerly an "Interlocutor," explains to the boy that a minstrel was a man who "made everybody happy," though he sometimes got into a little trouble. Green is interrupted when a fat, black cook brandishing a pot chases Jim, singing "Stay Out of the Kitchen." After she leaves to get Billie a cookie, Green describes the Interlocutor as a man with a pleasing voice and magnetic personality, who introduced the acts of minstrel shows in blackface of burnt cork. Bennie, one of the former minstrels, instructs Billie to visualize, then walks around a pole and appears on the other side in blackface and a minstrel costume to perform a song and dance. Afterwards, Green tells Billie that minstrel shows started on the Mississippi River and instructs him to visualize it. As a showboat travels along the river, slaves by a plantation cabin sing spirituals and dance. Green relates that the showboats had a ready-made audience when they docked. The performers on the decks of the boat present a "teaser," consisting of singers, dancers and juggling clowns. Inside, a blackface Interlocutor introduces tambourine girls and various acts, including blackface "end men" performing comedy routines in black dialect, blackface tap dancers, a white singing group performing nineteenth-century songs, a comedy act performed by two African Americans, a female singer, female dancers, blackface singers, a softshoe dancer doing a sand dance, an Irish tenor, a "bones" player, a piano player and a courtroom skit. After the finale, Billie's mother comes to the gathering of men. She berates Billie for wandering off and explains that she and Billie had been next door making a purchase when he left her. She says she hopes he didn't ask too many questions, but Green assures her that he didn't mind. Billie then says that he wants to be a minstrel man, and when Mrs. Crane asks what a minstrel man is, Green invites her to sit down. As he begins his tale again, the slaves at the plantation sing a spiritual. *African Americans. Minstrel shows. Racial impersonation. Showboats.* Children. Comedians. Cooks. Dancers.

Mississippi River. Mothers and sons. Plantations. Porters. Retirement homes.

Note: The following statement appears after the opening credits: "By far the most colorful era in show business was that of the Minstrels. These black-face troupes traveled in picturesque river showboats and heralded their arrival by the vibrant notes of the steam calliope. There was nothing like the excitement of a Minstrel Show: the singers, the dancers—the comedy of the end men, the dignified interlocutor—the rhythms of the banjo, the tambourines and the 'bones.' Today the Minstrels are nearly forgotten. They have 'drifted on down the river,' but have left, in their wake, a great American tradition." Scatman Crothers' name was misspelled as "Carothers" in the opening credits.

Box 4 Aug 1951. *DV* 26 Jul 1951, p. 3. *Exb* 15 Aug 1951, p. 3125. *Har* 4 Aug 1951, p. 124. *HR* 23 Mar 1951, p. 10. *HR* 26 Jul 1951, p. 3. *MPH* 11 Aug 1951. *Var* 1 Aug 1951, p. 6.

YIDDISH FATHER *see* THE YOUTH OF RUSSIA

THE YIDDISH KING LEAR (Yiddish language)

Lear Pictures, Inc. *Dist* Lear Pictures, Inc. **1935**. Sd; b&w. 8 reels, 7,848 ft. 70 min. Yiddish language with English subtitles.

Prod Johnnie Walker and Jack Rieger. *Supv* Joseph Seiden. *Dir* Harry Thomashefsky. *Screen adpt* Abraham Armband. *Photog* Joseph Freeman. *Art dir* Robert Van Rosen. *Sd eng* Murray Dichter. *Tech adv* David Van Tobin.

Source: Based on the play *Der Yiddishe Kenigen Lear* by Jacob Gordin (copyrighted 23 Nov 1889).

Cast: Maurice Krohner (*David Mosheles, the Yiddish King Lear*), Fannie Levenstein (*Hanna Lear, Mosheles' wife*), Jacob Bergreen (*Joffe*), Miriam Grosman (*Toibelle, Mosheles' youngest daughter*), Eddie Pascal (*Shomoi*), Rose Schwartzberg (*Servant*), Morris Weisman (*Abraham Chariff*), Jeannette Paskewich (*Etelle, Mosheles' eldest daughter*), Morris Tarlofsky (*Moses Chorid*), Esther Adler (*Gitelle, Mosheles' second daughter*), [Harold Schutzman].

Yiddish, Melodrama. [*Print viewed*]. In Vilna, Russia, in 1892, David Mosheles, a devout, but highly excitable Jewish father, presides over a *Purim* feast, during which he gives jewelry to his three daughters, Etelle, Gitelle and Toibelle. While her sisters bless their father, Toibelle, supported by her sweetheart, Mr. Joffe, a self-proclaimed epicure, renounces the gift saying that nature, not ornament, makes people beautiful. David announces that he will entrust his fortune to Etelle's husband, Abraham Chariff, to divide equally among his daughters and go with his wife, Hanna Lear, to Jerusalem. David then tells Toibelle that Chariff will select a husband for her, but Toibelle calls Chariff false and begs her father not to trust him, which provokes David to order him out of his house. Before Joffe leaves with Toibelle, he calls David "the Jewish King Lear." Two months later, after Chariff refuses to pay Toibelle the stipend promised by Hanna Lear, she goes with Joffe to St. Petersburg, where they study to be doctors. When David learns of Chariff's refusal and realizes that Chariff intends also to end payments to him, he and Hanna Lear return home. Soon Etelle imperially gives orders to her mother and David's clowning servant Shomoi, locks up the food and feeds David radishes and bread. Chariff sells his property to his brother so that he can keep it from David, while Gitelle's husband, Moses Chorid, spends his time drinking. Although Toibelle returns with Joffe, David refuses to forgive her. After Chariff orders Toibelle out and also tells Hanna Lear to get out when she cries, David leaves with Shomoi. Having lost his eyesight, David wanders with Shomoi asking charity. Later, at Joffe and Toibelle's wedding, Joffe refuses Chariff's gift of a gold watch and chain and orders him to leave when Chariff derides Toibelle's dream of building a hospital for the poor. After Gitelle and her husband arrive and the ceremony begins, David and Shomoi enter the house to rest. The family is reconciled and a doctor gives the opinion that David's eyesight could be restored through a slight operation. After Etelle and Chariff report that Chariff's brother has thrown them out, David forgives everyone and says that he will see that their wealth will be restored. *Fathers and daughters. Jews. King Lear* (Play). *Sisters. Sons-in-law.* Beggars. Blindness–Temporary. Drunkenness. Gifts. Greed. Jerusalem (Palestine). Physicians. Purim. Servants. St. Petersburg (Russia). Vilnius (Lithuania). Wanderers. Weddings.

Note: The opening screen credits read "Lear Pictures Inc. presents The Immortal Jacob Gordin's Classic *The Yiddish King Lear*." Gordin's play was derived from *The Tragedy of King Lear* by William Shakespeare (26 Dec 1606). Modern sources state that the Gordin play, as produced by Harry Thomashefsky, was performed throughout 1935 by the Federal Theater Project's Yiddish Drama Unit and that the picture was a filmed version of that production.

A *HR* news item dated 28 Aug 1935 stated that Johnnie Walker planned to

produce *Jewish King Lear* in the East, but the production dates and location have not been located. While written screen credits in English list Rose Rosen as playing a servant, spoken credits in Yiddish and modern sources give Rose Schwartzberg. Modern sources state that the film's New York opening was delayed until Feb 1936. Other films based on Shakespeare's play include the 1909 Vitagraph one-reeler entitled *Shakespeare's Tragedy King Lear*; the 1916 Thanhouser Film Corp. five-reeler starring Frederick Warde (see *AFI Catalog of Feature Films, 1911-20;* F1.2354); the 1970 British-Danish co-production directed by Peter Brook and starring Paul Scofield; the 1970 Russian Lenfilm production *Korol Lir*, directed by Grigori Kozintsev and starring Yuri Yarvet; the 1983 British television production starring Sir Laurence Olivier; and the 1985 Japanese production *Ran*, directed by Akira Kurosawa and starring Tatsuya Nakadai.

FD 5 Nov 1935, p. 7. *HR* 28 Aug 1935, p. 4.

THE YIDDISH MAMA see MY YIDDISHE MAMA

THE YIDDISHE FATHER *see* THE YOUTH OF RUSSIA

YIDDLE WITH HIS FIDDLE (Yiddish language)

Green-Film. *Dist* Sphinx Films Corp. **1936**; Warsaw, Poland opening: Sep 1936; New York opening: 31 Dec 1936. Sd; b&w. 8 reels, 8,466 ft. 92 min. *Country of origin* Poland. Yiddish language with English subtitles.

Dir Joseph Green and Jan Nowina-Przybylski. *Scr* Joseph Green. *Orig story* Konrad Tom. *Photog* Jack Jonitowicz. *Art dir* Jacob Kalich. *Settings* Jack Weinreich.

Song(s): "Oy Mame Bin Ich Farliebt" ("Oy Mamma I'm So in Love"), "Yidl Mitn Fidl," "Shiker," "Wedding Chant," "Teibele's Song" and "Romance," music by Abraham Ellstein, lyrics by I. Manger, English lyrics by Molly Picon.

Cast: MOLLY PICON [(*Yiddle*)], N. [i.e. Max] Bozyk [(*Isaac Kalamutker*)], S. Landau [(*Saul Gold*)], S. Fostel [(*Arye*)], M. Brin [(*Marshelik*)], D. Fakiel [(*Teibele Lipsker*)], A. Kurc [(*Bernard, restaurateur*)], L. Liebgold [(*Efraim, also known as Froim*)], A. Lewin [(*Widow*)], S. Natan [(*R. Singer, theatrical manager*)].

Yiddish, Comedy-drama, with songs. [*Print viewed*]. At Kazimierz, a small market town in Poland, a diminutive Jewish street musician plays her violin in the market place, but she is ignored until a flirt offers her two *zlotys* to dance. With the money, she buys herring and rolls for her father Arye, also a musician, but finds that he has been evicted for non-payment of rent. She has the idea that they can become traveling musicians, and when he worries that she will be annoyed by men, she disguises herself as Yiddle, a young Jewish boy. In a courtyard in a new town, Yiddle and Arye find Isaac Kalamutker, a clarinetist, and Efraim, or "Froim," another violinist, already playing. The two pairs of musicians insult each other, and their resulting racket as they compete causes the residents to close their windows. When Yiddle then plays a solo and the others join in, the people throw money down, and the two groups decide to join forces. That night, Yiddle is aroused by Froim as she listens to him playing his violin by a river. Later, Yiddle is disturbed when Froim, who has fallen asleep, puts his arm around her, and she dreams that dressed as a girl, she meets Froim, walks through the countryside with him and kisses him. As she awakens, she discovers that she is kissing a kitty. As they play throughout many towns, Yiddle falls in love with Froim, and when he rescues her after she falls in a river, Yiddle forgets herself and tries to kiss him. Shocked, Froim drops her in the water. The group plays for a wedding in a small town, where the bride, Teibele Lipsker, does not want to marry the groom, Saul Gold, an older, egotistical man who has been married twice before. After the ceremony, Teibele sneaks away with the musicians and becomes a singer with the group. She provokes the jealousy of Yiddle when she walks arm-in-arm with Froim, although, unknown to Yiddle, Teibele is only asking Froim to help her find Yosel, the man she really loves. Isaac convinces the group to go to Warsaw, where he knows a widow restaurant owner who wants to marry him. Once in Warsaw, Isaac decides to stop wandering and becomes engaged to the widow. Meanwhile, Teibele gets a contract to sing in a theater, and when she excitedly tells the group the news and that the owners want Froim to play in the band, Yiddle, disheartened, breaks down crying. She reveals to Isaac that she is a girl and that she loves Froim, whereupon Isaac assures her that Froim is only helping Teibele find Yosel. Isaac then locates Yosel and brings him to Teibele. The night of Teibele's opening, Yiddle visits her dressing room and, while no one is there, tries on Teibele's dress. She then finds a note from Teibele saying that she has left to be with Yosel. Yiddle tells the producer, who pushes her onstage and tells her to sing. In a song, Yiddle tells the story of

her masquerade as a boy, her falling in love and her heartbreak when another girl came along. When the delighted audience laughs, Yiddle walks off in tears. However, backstage, she and Froim embrace. Froim goes to buy Yiddle a ring, and when he returns, he overhears the theater manager, who wants Yiddle to tour America, say that Froim would only stand in her way. Froim then writes a note on her dressing room mirror saying that he never really loved her and goes. At the dock as they leave for America, Yiddle and Arye say goodbye to Isaac, Yosel and Teibele, who says that Gold has divorced her by letter. On the boat, as Yiddle sits with her father in the dining room, they hear Froim's violin leading the orchestra, which is playing "Yiddle with His Fiddle," the song she earlier sang. She confronts him and the two lovers then walk to the side of the boat and embrace. *Infatuation. Jews. Male impersonation. Musicians. Partnership. Poland. Romance. Rural life. City-country contrast. Divorce. Dreams. Fathers and daughters. Jealousy. Marriage–Arranged. Ocean liners. Restaurateurs. Rivalry. Rivers. Singers. Theatrical managers. Warsaw (Poland). Weddings.*

Note: The Yiddish title of this film is *Yidl mitn Fidl.* In an oral history conducted by the Hebrew University Oral History Department, producer and director Joseph Green relates that he was born in Poland and had experience in numerous Yiddish theater groups in Europe and New York before he established a production company to make Yiddish films in Poland; that this was the first of four films he made in Poland; that he was able to finance this film with money he made from the release of *Joseph in the Land of Egypt* (see above); that the film cost over $60,000; that most of the film was shot in Kazimierz, Poland, about an hour from Warsaw; that his company had offices in Warsaw and New York; that half of the orchestra of over fifty were from the Warsaw Symphony; and that the film was the first Yiddish film to play on Broadway. According to Green, Jan Nowina-Przybylski, who received screen credit as co-director, was really the technical director. Green's screenplay was originally entitled "Castles in the Air." This was American comedienne Molly Picon's first sound film, although *East and West*, a 1923 Austrian film in which she starred, had been re-released in 1932 as *Mazel Tov* (see above) with additional sound sequences in which she did not appear.

Exh 15 Jan 1937, p. 65. *FD* 4 Jan 1937, p. 5. *Kansas City Jewish Chronicle* 21 Jan 1938. *Kansas City Jewish Chronicle* 4 Feb 1938. *MPD* 5 Jan 1937, p. 3. *NYT* 2 Jan 1937, p. 15. *Var* 6 Jan 1937, p. 41.

YIDISHE TOCHTER see A DAUGHTER OF HER PEOPLE

DER YIDISHER FOTER see THE YOUTH OF RUSSIA

DER YIDISHER NIGN see THE JEWISH MELODY

YIDL MITN FIDL see YIDDLE WITH HIS FIDDLE

YIEN DOU see YEIN DOW

YIN FA CHU CHU HOI see YIN HUA CHU CHU KAI

YIN HUA CHU CHU KAI (Chinese language)

1955?; Hong Kong showing: 1955? Sd; b&w. Length undetermined. *Country of origin* Hong Kong and U.S.. Versions in Chinese (Mandarin and Cantonese), Vietnamese and English language. [*Not viewed*]. [No information concerning the plot of this film has been located.].

Note: The Cantonese transliterated title is *Yin Fa Chu Chu Hoi.* The English language title is *Cherry Blossom.* According to information from the Hong Kong Film Archive, the film was co-produced by a Hong Kong and an American company and was filmed in Hollywood and Hong Kong in four separate language versions: Mandarin, Cantonese, Vietnamese and English.

YISKOR (Yiddish language)

Gloria Films, Inc. **1932**; New York opening: midnight on 27 Apr 1932; Prod: ended early Feb 1932; recorded at Atlas Soundfilm Recording Studios; film incorporates a 1924 Austrian film produced by Jüdische Kunstfilm also entitled *Yiskor.* Sd; b&w. 8 reels, 7,500 ft. 80 min. Yiddish language.

[*Prod* William Goldberg]. [*Prod of 1924 film* Sidney M. Goldin and Ivan Abramson]. [*Dir* George Roland]. [*Dir of 1924 film* Sidney M. Goldin]. [*Screenplay of 1924 film* Harry Seckler]. [*Photog* Walter Strenge].

Source: Based on the play *Yiskor* by Harry Seckler (ca. 1923).

Cast: Maurice Schwartz [(*Leibke*)], [Oskar Beregi (*Count*)], Dagny Servaes (*The count's daughter*), [Fritz Strassny], [Bine Abramovitz], [Berta Gersten], [Anna Appel], [Lotte Stranger], [Wolf Goldfaden], [Isidor Casher], [Betty Reve], [Mark Schweid], [Carl Gotz], [Morris Strassberg], [Wolf Silberber], [Jacob Mestel], [Josef Schwartsberg].

Yiddish, Drama. [*Print viewed*]. By a grave in a cemetery, a Jewish boy asks his uncle the meaning of the *Yiskor* memorial ceremony thay they are observing. The uncle suggests that the boy asks the rabbi, and after the ceremony is completed, the rabbi explains that they are

praying for the soul of a Jewish martyr. He then tells the following story, which he says occurred in a Polish village called Ostodar, 150 years earlier: Not far from the castle of a stern count, lives a Jewish boy named Leibke, who was reared by a Christian stepmother. The count's overseer, who looks out for Leibke, gets him a position as a hunter for the count, and soon the count's daughter falls in love with him and appoints him chief huntsman. Leibke doesn't respond to her advances, and her attendant, upset that her own lover Stepan, a rabid anti-Semite, was not made chief huntsman, tells the countess that Leibke loves Kreindel, the daughter of a Jewish innkeeper. Leibke and Kreindel plan to marry, but the jealous countess calls him to come to her room, ostensibly to congratulate him on his upcoming marriage. She toasts the marriage with wine and tries to get Leibke drunk, and when he attempts to leave, she pretends to faint. Leibke carries her to her bed, but when she then hugs and kisses him, he throws her down. In response, she strikes him with a whip and accuses him of attacking her. Leibke is sent to a dungeon in the prison tower, but a hunchback, who is Leibke's friend, tells the count's overseer, and together they devise a plan to free him. After his escape, Leibke returns to the inn, where the rabbi advises him and Kreindel to marry immediately and leave the village. Following the wedding, they ride off together. Stepan, ordered by the count to bring Leibke back, interrupts the Jews' religious service and reads a decree from the count that if Leibke does not present himself in twenty-four hours, he will take ten Jews as hostages. After Stepan leaves, the rabbi asks for volunteers, and although the members of the congregation hesitate at first, after the rabbi volunteers to be the first Jewish hostage, others join him. The hunchback finds Leibke and Kreindel in a cave, and when Leibke learns of the count's decree, he gives himself up. During a celebration in which a dancing bear is whipped mercilessly, the head of the bear is removed to reveal, to the countess' horror, Leibke unconscious. She rebukes the laughing guests, as the sadistic Stepan drags Leibke off, then visits Leibke in the dungeon, where she declares her love for him. Leibke rebukes her, and she vows to force him to love her, but he says that no matter what she does, she will not succeed. She immediately swallows poison from her ring and dies. The count, grief-stricken, accepts Stepan's accusation that Leibke was responsible for his daughter's death and orders a grave to be prepared for Leibke. Although the Jews offer all their possessions to the count through his overseer to try to save Leibke's life, the count remains obstinate and does not even listen to the arguments of his own priest against executing Leibke. The Jews come to the graveyard and watch outside a gate as Leibke is buried alive in the grave. Afterward, they cut *krish*, pieces of their coats, and mourn. Back at the graveyard in the present, the rabbi, having finished telling the boy the story, leads the congregation in the *Kaddish*, or mourning prayer. *Antisemitism. Jealousy. Jews. Martyrs. Poland. Religious persecution. Rites and ceremonies. Unrequited love. Bears. Caves. Cemeteries. Dungeons. Escapes. False arrests. Fathers and daughters. Hostages. Hunchbacks. Hunters. Inns. Live burial. Nobility. Poisoning. Rabbis. Sadism. Seduction. Self-sacrifice. Suicide. Uncles. Weddings. Whips and whippings.*

Note: According to a modern source, the original play was inspired by a Jewish legend. This film is a re-release of a 1924 Austrian film with additional sequences and narration filmed and recorded in New York in 1932. The above credits come from NCJF records. According to news items in *FD*, Maurice Schwartz applied in the Brooklyn Supreme Court for a temporary injunction to prevent Gloria Films, Inc. from using his name in connection with the exploitation of this film and said he had agreed to appear in it with the understanding that it was to be a new talking film rather than a silent film with a talking prologue. The decision by the court was reserved. A news item noted that three reels of the film were shot in one day. According to NYSA records, the film was re-titled *The Holy Martyr* in 1934. The only credits on the print viewed, which was entitled *The Prince and the Pauper*, were for Schwartz and Cinema Service Corp. as the presenter. Most likely, *The Prince and the Pauper* was the title used when Cinema Service re-released the film, as the leader of the film still contains the original title *Yiskor*.

FD 8 Feb 1932, p. 6. *FD* 14 Mar 1932, p. 2. *FD* 24 Mar 1932, p. 30. *FD* 25 Apr 1932, p. 4. *MPD* 5 May 1933, p. 2. *Var* 6 Jun 1933, p. 15.

YO, TÚ Y ELLA (Spanish language)
Fox Film Corp. *Dist* Fox Film Corp. **1933**; New York opening: 29 Nov 1933; Prod: Jul 1933. Sd; b&w. 8 reels. Passed by the National Board of Review. Spanish language.

[*Prod* John Stone]. *Supervisión de* [*Supv*] Gregorio Martínez Sierra. *Dirección de* [*Dir*] John Reinhardt. *Adaptación cinematográfica de* [*Scr*] José López Rubio and John Reinhardt. [*Photog* Robert Planck].

[*Cam op* Arthur Arling]. [*Asst cam* Roger Sherman and Al Lebovitz].
Source: Based on the play *Mujer* by Gregorio Martínez Sierra (Barcelona, Jun 1925).
Cast: CATALINA BÁRCENA (*Estrella* [*Villalba*]), Gilbert Roland (*Gabriel* [*Villalba*]), Rosita Moreno (*Fernanda*), Mona Maris (*Laura*), Valentín Parera (*Eduardo*), Julio Peña (*Carlos*), Romualdo Tirado (*Mariano*), Rosita Granada (*Doncella*), José Peña Pepet (*Fotógrafo*).

Domestic, Comedy. [*Not viewed*]. In Paris, on New Year's Eve, Estrella and Gabriel Villalba and Estrella's sister Fernanda prepare for the evening's festivities. At the last minute, Gabriel informs Estrella that he will be unable to accompany her. After seeing his lover Laura, Gabriel informs Estrella that he must leave to attend to business in Biarritz. Acting on her intuition, Estrella accuses Gabriel of seeing another woman. Gabriel confesses to the affair, and after Estrella proclaims them finished, he leaves. Later, Estrella accompanies Fernanda and her new husband Carlos on their honeymoon. When they arrive in Venice, Estrella notices that Gabriel is staying at the same hotel with his new wife Laura, whom Estrella has never met. Laura, who is spoiled and ungrateful, fights with Gabriel. Seeing Estrella sitting alone by the pool, Laura, captivated by her elegance, tries to start a conversation with her; however, when she sees Gabriel on the diving board, Estrella abruptly leaves. Later that day, Laura sees Estrella at an outdoor café, and Estrella, not knowing that Laura is Gabriel's wife, agrees to join her. When Laura introduces Gabriel as her husband, Estrella's initial shock turns to glee. Calling herself a widow, she proceeds to take potshots at Gabriel's expense with ammunition supplied by his unknowing new bride. The couple leaves after Laura flirts with one of the restaurant's musicians, and in their room, Laura accuses Gabriel of being attracted to Estrella. She follows him to Estrella's room, and after he walks out in anger, Estrella reveals the truth about their previous marriage to Laura, who is aghast. Estrella, Fernanda and Carlos then travel throughout Europe pursued by telegrams from Gabriel, who wishes to talk with Estrella. After they finally reach their home in Madrid, Gabriel arrives at Estrella's house, while she prepares to leave for an engagement which, she hints, involves another man. Laura then phones him, and their ensuing argument ends with his promise to leave her forever. He goes to seek advice from a mutual friend of his and Estrella's during which time Estrella returns and retires to her bedroom. Gabriel then returns and pushes his way past the maid into Estrella's room, where he asks her to come back to him. Estrella asks him to leave, but when he refuses, she goes out followed by Gabriel, who continues to plead with her. Without a taxi in sight, Estrella enters a movie theater, and as the onscreen lovers argue about their relationship, Gabriel promises her that he will be a new man. Estrella replies that she only desires the man with whom she once fell in love. As the onscreen picture ends, Gabriel and Estrella embrace, and as the theater patrons file out, they pass the coming attraction which reads: "Don't Trust Your Husband." *Marriage. Remarriage. Spaniards. Cabarets. Cafés. Confession. Divorce. Flirtation. Honeymoons. Hotels. Infidelity. Madrid (Spain). Motion picture theaters. Musicians. New Year's Eve. Paris (France). Sisters. Swimming. Venice (Italy).*

Note: The plot summary was based on a screen continuity in the Twentieth Century-Fox Produced Scripts Collection, and the onscreen credits were based on a screen billing sheet in the Twentieth Century-Fox Records of the Legal Department, both of which are in the UCLA Theater Arts Library. The working title of this film was *Mujer*. *NYT* and *FD* erroneously list the title as *Io...tu...y...ella (I...Thou...and...She)*. A review includes Martín Garralaga and Manuel Noriega in the cast, but their names do not appear in the credits and their participation has not been confirmed.

CM Jan 1934, p. 6. *FD* 11 Dec 1933, p. 7. *IP* Aug 1933, p. 25. *NYT* 5 Dec 1933, p. 31.

A YOKE OF GOLD (Latino)
Universal Film Mfg. Co.; Red Feather Photoplays. *Dist* Universal Film Mfg. Co. 14 Aug **1916** [©Universal Film Mfg. Co.; 17 Jul 1916; LP8723]. Si; b&w. 5 reels.

Dir Lloyd B. Carleton. *Scen* Calder Johnstone. *Story* Robert Wagner. *Cam* Roy H. Klaffki.
Cast: Emory Johnson (*Jose Garcia*), Alfred Allen (*Luis Lopez*), Richard Morris (*Padre Amador*), Harold Skinner (*Castro Arrellanes*), Dorothy Davenport (*Carmen*), Gretchen Lederer.

Historical, Drama. During the days of the California missions, Jose Garcia becomes friends with Luis Lopez, a local Robin Hood determined to redistribute among the poor the loot of the rich. Inspired by Luis, Jose sets out to rob the home of wealthy landowner

Don Ortega. On the way, however, Jose gets lost in the desert and is nearly dead when he is found by Don Ortega's aristocratic cousin, Castro Arrellanes, and Castro's daughter Carmen, who take him in and nurse him back to health. Jose quickly falls in love with Carmen, and as a result renounces his plan of robbing the rich. Then, he learns that Luis has made plans to break into Don Ortega's house. Jose manages to stop him, after which Luis reforms and becomes a monk, and Jose and Carmen get married. *Aristocrats. California–History–To 1846. Class distinction. Robbery. Criminals–Rehabilitation. Deserts. Monks. Nursing back to health.*

Note: The film was also known as *In The Days of the Missions.*

MPN 5 Aug 1916, p. 788. *MPW* 5 Aug 1916, p. 944. *MPW* 19 Aug 1916, p. 1295. *Wid's* 17 Aug 1916, p. 789.

YOU CAN'T BEAT THE IRISH *see* **THREE CHEERS FOR THE IRISH**

YOU CAN'T KEEP A GOOD MAN DOWN (African Americans)
Lone Star Motion Picture Co. **1922**. Si; b&w. 6 reels.
Photog B. L. Teycer.

Melodrama (?), African American. No information about the precise nature of this film has been found. *African Americans.*

Note: The working title of this film was *The Stranger from Way Out Yonder.*

ChiDef 16 Dec 1922, p. 7.

YOU CAN'T WIN (African Americans)
Eroy C. Ware Motion Picture Studio. **1927**?. Sd; b&w. Length undetermined.
Supv Eroy C. Ware. *Dir* Eroy C. Ware.

Cast: E. M. Jackson, Flora Buttler, Mr. Ravara, Dayse Turnour, T. Dickson, Miss A. Franklin, C. Davis.

African American, Drama. [*Not viewed*]. [No information concerning the plot of this film has been located, other than a photograph of an actor in a racing car.]. *African Americans. Automobile racing.*

Note: According to a 1 Jan 1927 news item in *PittsC*, E. M. Jackson, who appears in this film, was a director in the production company and a "famous auto dirt track champion." No information has been located concerning exhibition of the film. The news item noted, "Screen tests in order to obtain new talent will be given wherever the picture is shown."

PittsC 1 Jan 1927, pt. II, p. 5.

YOUNG AMERICA (African Americans)
Twentieth Century-Fox Film Corp. *Dist* Twentieth Century-Fox Film Corp. 6 Feb **1942**; Prod: mid-Aug—mid-Sep 1942; addl scenes late Sep [©Twentieth Century-Fox Film Corp.; 6 Feb 1942; LP11081]. Sd (RCA Sound System); b&w. 7 reels, 6,552 ft. 72-73 min. PCA cert no. 7681.

Exec prod Sol M. Wurtzel. *Dir* Louis King. [*Asst dir* Jasper Blystone]. [*Dial dir* Arthur Berthelet]. *Orig scr* Samuel G. Engel. *Dir of photog* Glen MacWilliams and [Lucien Andriot]. *Art dir* Richard Day and Lewis Creber. *Film ed* Louis Loeffler. *Set dec* Thomas Little. *Cost* Herschel. *Mus dir* Cyril J. Mockridge. *Sd* Arthur von Kirbach and Harry M. Leonard. [*Pilot for flying seq* Paul Mantz]. [*Prod mgr* William Koenig].

Song(s): "We're on the Four-H Trail," sung to the tune of "We're on the Homeward Trail," composer undetermined.

Cast: JANE WITHERS (*Jane Campbell*), Jane Darwell (*Grandma [Nora] Campbell*), Lynne Roberts (*Elizabeth Barnes*), William Tracy (*Earl Tucker [alias of Ivan Leslie]*), Robert Cornell (*Jonathan Blake*), Roman Bohnen (*Mr. Barnes*), Irving Bacon (*Bart Munson*), Ben Carter (*Abraham*), Louise Beavers (*Pansy*), Darryl Hickman (*David Engstrom*), Sally Harper (*Susie [Clark]*), Carmencita Johnson (*Hazel*), Daphne Ogden (*Ellen*), Charles Arnt (*Principal [Rice]*), Myra Marsh (*Teacher*), Hamilton MacFadden (*[Jim] Benson*), [Hugh Beaumont, Charles Tannen (*G-men*)], [Arthur Loft, Don Forbes (*Announcers*)], [Paul Burns (*Farmer*)], [Conrad Binyon (*Bunny Griffith*)], [Lester Dorr (*Chamber of Commerce clerk*)], [Charles Wilson (*Roy Wilstack*)], [Cliff Clark (*Judge Howlett*)], [Robert Emmett Keane (*Wilson*)], [J. Anthony Hughes (*Judge Baker*)], [Marie Blake (*Waitress*)].

Teenage, Comedy-drama. [*Print viewed*]. Spoiled city girl Jane Campbell is furious when her widower father sends her to the rural town of Button Willow Valley to live with her grandmother, Nora Campbell. Jane and her black servant, Abraham, loathe their new surroundings, and while Abraham copes with Nora's helper, Pansy,

Jane begins attending school. Jane's arrogance drives away all potential friends except for young David Engstrom, who nominates her for membership in the local chapter of the 4-H Club. Jane, who has never heard of the youth-oriented organization, is unimpressed when she learns how it promotes agricultural skills and good citizenship. Jane declines membership but changes her mind upon discovering that handsome Jonathan Blake is the club's president. Jane's interest in Jonathan dismays quiet Elizabeth Barnes, who is in love with him. Elizabeth's weak-willed father tries to comfort her by promising to buy her a purebred Hereford calf for her 4-H state fair project, but he instead loses her money in a poker game held by shady entrepeneur Earl Tucker. When Barnes tells Earl about his dilemma, Earl obtains a mixed-breed calf, then forges papers certifying its lineage. Elizabeth is delighted with her calf, which she names "Royal Jonathan II," and happily tends to him as the months pass. Jane also chooses a calf for her project and names it "King Blake the First." Pansy and Abraham, who have struck up a quarrelsome friendship, know that Jane is interested in 4-H only as a means to ensnare Jonathan in a romance, but Jonathan still courts Elizabeth. On the day of the fair, Jane has lunch with Earl, who intimates that she will win the contest because Elizabeth's calf is not purebred. Jane refuses to believe him but promises to buy his tractor with her prize money if she wins. Elizabeth wins, but Earl, desperate for the money, sends a telegram to the judges challenging Royal Jonathan's lineage. The calf's phony papers are exposed and Jane is declared the winner, but she is horrified by the proceedings, as Earl signed her name to the telegram. Barnes confesses all to his daughter, who protects him by refusing to explain the situation to the 4-H officials. Soon after, Elizabeth is suspended from the club, while Jane is ostracized by the other members for getting Elizabeth in trouble. Jonathan stands by Elizabeth, and the despondent Jane decides to return to the city. Before leaving, she sends Abraham to Earl's office to pay a bill, and while there, Abraham overhears two government agents question Earl about a man, Ivan Leslie, who is wanted for draft evasion. Abraham also overhears when a drunken Barnes tells Earl that he wants to reveal the truth about Elizabeth's calf. Abraham repeats the information to Jane, who captures the fleeing Earl and forces him to write a confession admitting full responsibility for the forged papers. The government agents then apprehend Earl, who is the draft dodger. Soon after, Elizabeth represents the club at a national 4-H meeting held in Washington, D.C., and says a fond hello to Jane and her fellow members during a radio broadcast. *4-H clubs. Adolescents. City-country contrast. Forgers and forgery. Romantic rivalry.* African Americans. Airplanes. Cattle. Contests. Conventions (Gatherings). Fairs. Friendship. Government agents. Grandmothers. Horses. Military service, Compulsory. Ostracism. Servants. Telegrams.

Note: Following the film's opening credits is a written prologue that states, "The producers of *Young America* wish to express their gratitude and thanks to the Secretary of Agriculture Claude R. Wickard and his associates—to Mr. M. L. Wilson, Director of Extension Service of the Department of Agriculture, and to the thousands of 4-H Club leaders throughout the country, for their whole-hearted assistance and cooperation in making this motion picture possible." According to a *HR* news item, Todd Karns was originally set to play "Jonathan Blake," but was beset by a "lip infection" and was replaced by Robert Cornell. Although Glen MacWilliams receives onscreen credits as the picture's director of photography, *HR* production charts list Lucien Andriot as the photographer. A 28 Jul 1941 *HR* news item noted that the picture would have a budget of approximately $500,000, and a 16 May 1941 *LAEx* news item reported that in Jun 1941 Jane Withers would be visiting the 1941 4-H club convention in Washington, D.C.

Box 10 Jan 1942. *DV* 5 Jan 1942, p. 3. *FD* 8 Jan 1942, p. 6. *HR* 28 Jul 1941, p. 11. *HR* 15 Aug 1941, p. 9. *HR* 20 Aug 1941, p. 7. *HR* 25 Aug 1941, p. 4. *HR* 12 Sep 1941, p. 11. *HR* 22 Sep 1941, p. 4. *HR* 5 Jan 1942, p. 3. *LAEx* 16 May 1941. *MPHPD* 10 Jan 1942, p. 451. *Var* 7 Jan 1942, p. 44.

YOUNG BUFFALO BILL (Latino, Native Americans, Comanche)
Republic Pictures Corp. *Dist* Republic Pictures Corp. 12 Apr **1940**; Prod: began late Feb 1940 [©Republic Pictures Corp.; 12 Apr 1940; LP9582]. Sd (RCA "High Fidelity" Recording); b&w. 6 reels. 59 min. PCA cert no. 6134.

Assoc prod Joseph Kane. *Dir* Joseph Kane. [*Asst dir* Bill O'Connor]. *Scr* Harrison Jacobs, Robert Yost and Gerry Geraghty. *Orig story* Norman Houston. *Photog* William Nobles. *Film ed* Tony Martinelli. *Mus dir* Cy Feuer. *Prod mgr* Al Wilson.

Song(s): "Blow, Breeze, Blow" and "Rollin' Down to Santa Fe," composer unknown.

Cast: ROY ROGERS [(*Buffalo Bill Cody*)], GEORGE "GABBY" HAYES [(*Gabby*)], Pauline Moore [(*Tonia Regas*)], Hugh Sothern [(*Don Regas*)], Chief Thundercloud [(*Akuna*)], Julian Rivero [(*Panelio*)], Trevor Bardette [(*Emilio Montez*)], Gaylord Pendleton [(*Jerry Calhoun*)], Wade Boteler [(*Colonel Joe Calhoun*)], Anna Demetrio [(*Elena*)], Estelita Zarco [(*Dolores*)].

Historical, Western, with songs. [*Print viewed*]. Buffalo Bill Cody and his sidekick Gabby ride to the New Mexico territory to help Colonel Joe Calhoun of the U.S. Cavalry conduct a land survey. The military's efforts have been hampered by a series of Indian raids led by the Comanche medicine man Akuna and by the opposition of Don Regas, the largest land holder in the territory. Unknown to Don Regas, his ranch foreman, Emilio Montez, is in league with Akuna, his half brother, to wrest control of a secret gold mine located on the Regas land. Colonel Calhoun has asked Bill and Gabby to look after his tenderfoot son Jerry, who is coming from the East to complete the survey, and Bill, who is attracted to the don's granddaughter Tonia, convinces the girl to persuade her grandfather to cooperate with Jerry. Montez has other plans for Jerry, however, and after luring the boy into losing all his money gambling, Montez demands that he falsify the survey to exclude the northern section of the Regas land, the portion on which the mine is allegedly located. When Don Regas learns that he has been denied part of his land grant, he angrily denounces the survey and boards the east-bound stage to challenge the document in Washington. Montez informs Jerry that they must eliminate Don Regas, and when Jerry threatens to tell his father, Montez stabs him, takes him prisoner and orders Akuna to ambush the stage. Meanwhile, Bill, suspicious of the survey, discovers that Montez has filed a claim on the land and, anticipating trouble, rides after the stage. Arriving just after the Indians have attacked, Bill and Gabby drive the marauders away and take the injured Don Regas to his ranch. That night, Montez sneaks into the ranch house to search for the land grant documents, and Gabby and Bill follow him back to Akuna's camp. There, Jerry warns them of a planned attack on the hacienda, and Gabby rides for the cavalry as Bill and Jerry ride for the ranch. Gabby and the reinforcements arrive just in time to rout the Indians, and after Jerry admits that he made a mistake in the survey, Don Regas is accorded his entire land grant. *Buffalo Bill Cody. Duplicity. Land rights. New Mexico. Ranchers. Surveyors.* Comanche Indians. Fathers and sons. Gambling. Granddaughters. Grandfathers. Half brothers. Medicine men. Mexican Americans. Ranch foremen. Stagecoaches. United States. Army. Cavalry.

Note: The working title of this film was *Buffalo Bill, Plainsman.* The film is not based on the historical facts of William F. Cody's life. For biographical information on Cody, please see the entry above for *Buffalo Bill.* Modern sources add Hank Bell, William Kellogg, Iron Eyes Cody, Jack O'Shea, George Chesebro and Trigger to the cast.

Exb 1 May 1940, p. 513. *FD* 28 May 1940, p. 9. *HR* 18 Jan 1940, p. 6. *HR* 2 Mar 1940, pp. 6-7. *MPH* 30 Mar 1940, p. 58. *MPH* 20 Apr 1940, p. 35. *Var* 1 May 1940, p. 20.

YOUNG DANIEL BOONE (Native Americans, Iroquois, Shawnee)
Monogram Pictures Corp. *Dist* Monogram Pictures Corp. 5 Mar **1950;** Prod: mid-Oct—late Oct 1949 [©Monogram Pictures Corp.; 26 Feb 1950; LP27]. Sd (Western Electric Recording); col (Cinecolor). 6,360 ft. 71 min. PCA cert no. 14241.

Prod James S. Burkett. *Dir* Reginald LeBorg. *Asst dir* William Calihan. *Scr* Clint Johnston and Reginald LeBorg. *Story* Clint Johnson. *Photog* G. Warrenton. *Col consultant* Wilton R. Holm and Clifford D. Shank. *Ed* Charles Craft. *Supv film ed* Otho Lovering. [*Set dresser* Raymond Boltz, Jr.]. *Mus dir* Edward J. Kay. *Rec* J. Kean. *Makeup* T. Larsen. *Prod supv* Allen K. Wood. *Set cont* Mary Chaffee. *Tech adv on Indian Affairs* Nipo T. Strongheart.

Cast: David Bruce [(*Daniel Boone*)], Kristine Miller [(*Rebecca Bryan*)], Damian O'Flynn [(*Capt. Richard Fraser, also known as Maj. Antoine de Brissaque*)], Don Beddoe [(*Charlie Bryan*)], Mary Treen [(*Helen Bryan*)], John Mylong [(*Lt. Col. Baron Kurt von Arnheim*)], William Roy [(*Little Hawk*)], Stanley Logan [(*Col. Benson*)], Herbert Naish [(*Pvt. Haslet*)], Nipo T. Strongheart [(*Chief Walking Eagle*)], Richard Foote [(*Lt. Perkins*)], Stephen S. Harrison [(*Sentry*)], [Bret Hamilton (*British soldier*)], [Joe E. Molina, Tony Urchel (*Fraser's Indians*)], [Charles Soldani, Dewey Drapeau, Bob Lugo, Max Reid, Dimas Sotello (*Iroquois Indians*)], [Lalo Encinas (*Shawnee Chief*)], [Chief Yowlachie (*Indian guide*)].

Historical, Western. [*Print viewed*]. In the early 1750s, the French and British are locked in a bitter struggle for control of the Ohio Valley. To further their cause, the French incite the Iroquois

Indians to attack the British colonists, and in 1755, a British regiment is massacred by a group led by a local Indian chief. Among the few survivors are Lt. Col. Baron Kurt von Arnheim, a Hessian officer serving in the British Army, Charlie Bryan, a civilian trader from Philadelphia, and the mortally wounded Lt. Perkins. Before he dies from his injuries, Perkins tells von Arnheim that the Indians were led by whites. Von Arnheim decides that he must get this information to Col. Benson at British headquarters, but is stymied because the Indians are holding Bryan's two daughters, Rebecca and Helen, prisoner. Meanwhile, another survivor, Pvt. Haslet, has managed to reach Benson with news of the massacre, and the colonel sends Daniel Boone to scout for other survivors. Benson also assigns Capt. Richard Fraser to take dispatches to Gen. Braddock at Fort Stuart. Soon after the traitorous Fraser sets off on foot with an Indian scout, he kills the scout and then destroys Benson's request for reinforcements. Boone, accompanied by a young Indian, Little Hawk, finds von Arnheim and Bryan, but Bryan is dismayed that they have come alone. However, Boone conceives a plan to rescue Bryan's daughters by using multiple gunpowder explosions to make it appear that their force is much larger than it really is. The scheme works, and the group heads for the relative safety of an abandoned fort which has a hidden supply of food. Meanwhile, Fraser is arranging with the Indians to capture von Arnheim and follows Boone and the others to the fort, still posing as a loyal British officer. Von Arnheim insists that someone within the British command betrayed the regiment, as the Indians knew their exact route. Boone and von Arnheim set out to try to arrange for an escort troop but are attacked by Fraser's Indians. Upon returning to the fort, Boone and von Arnheim find that Fraser has taken the others prisoner. Fraser admits his treachery and reveals that he is Maj. Antoine de Brissaque of the French Colonial Office and intends to take von Arnheim, the finest tactician in the British Army, to Paris, to convince the British of the folly of pursuing their colonizing policies. As they are all about to leave, however, they are attacked by Shawnee Indians, who are hostile to both the British and the French. Fraser frees his prisoners, and they work together to temporarily drive off the Shawnee. Later, von Arnheim prepares a strategy to combat the Shawnee when they return, and Boone and Rebecca get to know each other. When the Shawnee attack again, von Arnheim fires at them with remotely controlled rifles, and the Indians retreat. Boone then turns his gun on Fraser, while von Arnheim strips him of his rank and takes him prisoner. However, a lingering Indian frees Fraser, and he takes Rebecca hostage and, once more claims the upper hand. At night, as more Indians enter the fort, Boone escapes. The next day, the others leave on foot as Fraser's and the Indians' prisoners, and Boone follows them and prepares an attack involving more gunpowder trickery. He also removes Fraser's gun while he is asleep, sabotages the Indians' bows and arrows, and substitutes the bullets in their guns with blanks. The next morning, Boone walks blithely into their camp, playing a flute. While the Indians shoot at him, he continues to play the flute, appearing immortal. He talks to them in their own language, then, from inside his shirt, removes the bullets they think they have been firing at him. Confronted by this seemingly magical display, the superstitious Indians run off. Fraser attacks Boone with a knife, and during the ensuing fight, Fraser falls on the blade. Later, after Boone has freed everyone, von Arnheim returns to Europe and Boone leaves to settle down with Rebecca. *Daniel Boone. Kentucky. Scouts (Frontier). Traitors. United States—History—Colonial period, ca. 1600-1775. United States—History—French and Indian War, 1755-1763.* Fathers and daughters. Flutes. Forts. French. Gun powder. Hessians. Hostages. Iroquois Indians. Military education. Officers (Military). Romance. Sabotage. Shawnee Indians. Superstition. Traders.

Note: According to historical records as noted in modern sources, in 1775, as part of an agreement with Richard Henderson's Transylvania company, Daniel Boone led a group of settlers, which included his wife and daughter, from Yadkin, North Carolina to the Indian territory known as Kain-tu-kee. After the American Revolution, Boone worked as a surveyor along the Ohio River, but little of the film's plot was based on actual events. Many films and television shows based on the life of Daniel Boone have been made, including the 1923 short film *Daniel Boone*, which was part of the Yale University Press's *Chronicles of America* series; *Daniel Boone Thru the Wilderness*, a 1926 Sunset Productions film starring Roy Stewart and directed by either Frank S. Mattison or Robert N. Bradbury (see *AFI Catalog of Feature Films, 1921-30*; F2.1197); *Daniel Boone*, a 1936 RKO Radio Pictures production starring George O'Brien and directed by David Howard; *Daniel Boone, Trail Blazer*, a 1956 Republic picture starring Bruce Bennett and directed by Albert C. Gannaway and Ismael Rodriguez (see entries above); and the NBC television series *Daniel Boone*, which starred Fess Parker and ran from 1964 to 1969.

Box 11 Mar 1950. *DV* 24 Feb 1950, p. 3. *FD* 8 Mar 1950, p. 10. *Har* 4 Mar 1950, p. 36. *HR* 21 Oct 1949, p. 10. *HR* 28 Oct 1949, p. 14. *HR* 24 Feb 1950, p. 3. *MPHPD* 4 Mar 1950, p. 214. *Var* 1 Mar 1950, p. 16.

THE YOUNG LAND (Latino)

C. V. Whitney Pictures, Inc. *Dist* Columbia Pictures Corp. May **1959**; Prod: began early Aug 1957 [©C. V. Whitney Pictures, Inc.; 30 Dec 1957; LP12884]. Sd (RCA Sound Recording); col (Technicolor). 10 reels, 7,960 or 7,975 ft. 89 min. PCA cert no. 18792.

Pres C. V. WHITNEY. *Prod* Patrick Ford. *Assoc prod* Lowell J. Farrell. *Dir* Ted Tetzlaff. *Asst dir* William Forsyth. *Scr* Norman Shannon Hall. *Dir of photog* Winton C. Hoch and Henry Sharp. *Spec eff* Jack Caffee. *Technicolor color consultant* Morgan Padelford. *Art dir* Jack Okey. *Supv film ed* Tom McAdoo. *Asst film ed* William Millspaugh. *Set dec* Victor Gangelin. *Men's cost* Frank Beetson. *Women's cost* Ann Peck. *Mus wrt and cond* Dimitri Tiomkin. *Re-rec supv* Gene Garvin. *Sd* Arthur Kirbach. *Mus rec supv* Lowell Frank. *Makeup* Web Overlander. *Hair stylist* Myrl Stoltz. *Properties* Arthur C. Cole. *Tech adv* Ramon Talavera and [Roberto de la Madrid].

Song(s): "Strange Are the Ways of Love," sung by Randy Sparks, music by Dimitri Tiomkin, lyrics by Ned Washington.

Source: Based on the short story "Frontier Frenzy" by John Reese in *The Saturday Evening Post* (30 Oct 1954).

Cast: Pat Wayne [(*Jim Ellison*)], Yvonne Craig [(*Elena de la Madrid*)], Dennis Hopper [(*Hatfield Carnes*)], Dan O'Herlihy [(*Judge Millard Isham*)], Roberto de la Madrid [(*Roberto de la Madrid*)], Cliff Ketchum [(*Ben Stroud*)], Ken Curtis [(*Lee Hearn*)], Pedro Gonzalez Gonzalez [(*Santiago*)], Edward Sweeny [(*Sully*)], John Quijada [(*Carlos, a vaquero*)], Miguel Camacho [(*Miguel*)], Tom Tiner [(*Court clerk*)], Carlos Romero [(*Quiroga*)], Edward Jauregui [(*Drifter*)], The Mariachis Los Reyes De Chapala, [Cliff Lyons (*Jury foreman*)], [Mario Arteaga (*Mario*)], [Charles Heard (*Clarence Tolliver*)].

Western. [*Print viewed*]. In the town of San Bartolo, California, in 1848, just after Mexico ceded California to the United States, Hatfield Carnes shoots Francisco Quiroga as Quiroga draws, then fires at him again and again until he dies. Young sheriff Jim Ellison, who prefers using his fists rather than guns because he realizes others are better shots than he, arrests Hatfield, who remarks that he "had to shoot me a Mexican." The distinguished New England judge Millard Isham, arriving with Deputy U.S. Marshal Ben Stroud to conduct the trial, is astounded to learn that Jim, formerly a corporal in the Marines, has not received his authority from the U.S. territorial government, but from Don Roberto de la Madrid, the former alcalde, who still runs most of the area. At a birthday celebration for Don Roberto's attractive daughter Elena, Ben and Jim select a jury and include a couple of new Mexican Americans citizens. When Elena asks Jim, who is shy, to dance, he first gets her father's permission. The next day, during the trial in a converted animal hide warehouse, Jim testifies that although Hatfield frequently pushed around Mexicans, no Mexican had ever tried to attack him. When Hatfield takes the stand, and uses the term "Mex," the judge reprimands him, saying that the Mexicans present would find the word distasteful. Hatfield relates his version of the events: After he told Quiroga, who had been drinking with him and his friends in a saloon, that he didn't belong with them, he assumed there would be a fight and told Quiroga to step outside; when Quiroga went for his gun, Hatfield beat him to the draw. After Hatfield admits killing four Mexicans before Quiroga, Ben contends that he deliberately taunted Quiroga. General store owner Clarence Tolliver, a witness to the killing, testifies that Hatfield told Quiroga, "You talk big, Mex. Let's see if you got guts enough to draw on a white man." Judge Isham instructs the jury they must decide that Hatfield is guilty if, knowing he was more adept with a gun than Quiroga, he goaded him into drawing through a hostile gesture. If, however, Hatfield shot in self-defense, he must be set free. Mexican vaqueros, who have gathered in town because of the trial, believe Hatfield will not be convicted because killing Mexicans has never been considered murder in the area. Seeing them, Hatfield worries about a lynching, but Jim maintains they are American citizens now and have a right to talk. Don Roberto arrives in town with Elena, and Jim takes him to meet the judge, who is honored. After Isham sends Jim to quiet a mariachi band, hired by Lee Stroud, a man Ben has recognized as an outlaw from Fort Omaha, Jim bests Lee in a fight. The judge berates Jim for leaving the prisoner alone and orders him to appoint a deputy to guard Hatfield. Jim then convinces Lee to do the job. As they eat

together, Don Roberto tells Judge Isham that the case puts American justice on trial; he wants to believe that Mexican Americans are citizens entitled to all rights, as the Treaty of Guadaloupe Hidalgo states, but he wonders if an American jury will be as stern with Hatfield as they would be if a Mexican killed a white American. Judge Isham frankly states that he does not know, but hopes the jury will be fair. When the judge apologizes for some rowdy whites in the cantina, Don Roberto acknowledges that ruffians are needed for a young land. The rowdies from the cantina circle the jail riding and shooting, and when Jim sees the vaqueros getting their guns out, he tries to send Elena home, but she refuses to go. He brings her to the jail for protection, but Hatfield embarrasses her with talk about his sexual exploits with "squaws." Lee, who sides with Hatfield, but fears the vaqueros, tells Hatfield he will help him escape when he says so. Judge Isham invites Don Roberto to join him on the bench when the jury returns its verdict, as he wants the Mexican people to feel represented. Learning that Lee is a wanted man, the judge castigates Jim for choosing him as a deputy, but Ben attests that quite a number of lawmen started out with bad records. After the jury announces its verdict of guilty, Jim disarms the whites and the vaqueros in the courtroom. Isham sentences Hatfield to twenty-five years in a federal prison, but because the crime was committed during a period of transition to constitutional law, he suspends the sentence on the condition that Hatfield never own, wear or touch a firearm. As soon as Hatfield is set free, he grabs Lee's gun and hits him over the head. Jim gets a pistol and follows Hatfield outside, while Ben stops the whites and vaqueros from following. Unhappy with the pistol, Jim makes his way to the jail to get his rifle, as Hatfield, hidden, boasts that after he kills Jim, he'll come after Elena. At the jail, Elena urges Jim not to go out, saying they could barricade the door until someone comes for help, but Jim says he would then be ashamed to look in the mirror. He kisses her for the first time, then goes out and orders Hatfield to drop his gun. After a shoot-out, Hatfield drops dead, and Judge Isham tells Don Roberto that American justice has been completely vindicated. He commends Jim, who, though slightly wounded, hugs Elena. Bigotry. California–History–1846-1850. Justice. Mexican Americans. Sheriffs. Shootouts. Trials. Birthdays. Cantinas. Courage. Deputies. Fathers and daughters. Fistfights. Jails. Judges. Juries. New Englanders. Outlaws. Romance. United States. Marine Corps. United States. Marshals.

Note: The opening credits contain the following acknowledgments: "We wish to express our appreciation to the citizens of the Republic of Mexico for their cooperation in the making of this motion picture, and to the following organizations: The Charro Association of Old Mexico; The Los Angeles Sheriff's Charro Posse." According to a *HR* news item, the story "Frontier Frenzy" was bought in Oct 1955 by C. V. Whitney Pictures, Inc. At the time, Merian C. Cooper was to be the film's executive producer, and Frank Nugent was hired to write the screenplay. It is not known if Nugent completed any work for this production. According to modern sources, Cooper earlier had talked Whitney, one of the world's leading industrialists, into forming the company. Publicity for the film noted that it was the third film in Whitney's "Americana" series, following John Ford's *The Searchers*, which Nugent also scripted (see above) and *The Missouri Traveler*. *MPH* noted that Whitney was "dedicated to films that have a common denominator, themes that embrace the people and growth of America." Release of this film was held up after Buena Vista, which had originally planned to distribute the film, dropped out following a dispute concerning the release of *The Missouri Traveler*. Warner Bros. considered releasing the film before Whitney contracted with Columbia.

Outdoor scenes were shot in a pueblo constructed in Thousand Oaks, CA. According to publicity, John Ford persuaded Roberto de la Madrid, the film's technical adviser, to act in the film. Ford's son Patrick, who had been associate producer of *The Searchers*, produced this film, which marked the first starring role for John Wayne's son Pat, who was eighteen at the time. *HR* remarked, "It's quite likely that young Wayne will learn more about acting in the years to come. But, with proper exploitation, he's got what it takes to be a star right now—a bright and easy going youthful charm, lithe and competent physical fitness, a casual self-possession in love scenes and an infectious sense of humor."

The Young Land marked the film debut of Dallas-born actress Yvonne Craig, a nineteen-year-old former ballerina. Reviews praised the work of twenty-one-year-old Dennis Hopper. *LAT* commented, "This increasingly skillful young actor brings such a depth of quirky, deadly playful malice to his role that he might be a fugitive from a far, far better script." *HR* stated that the film "is just on the threshold of being one of the great westerns" and commented that the story "develops one of history's universal themes, the necessity for a conquering race to do justice to a conquered one in order that both shall be unified into a nation." *Var*, however, criticized the film as "superficial, repetitious and awkwardly naïve."

BHCN 7 May 1959. *Box* 27 Apr 1959. *DV* 18 Jun 1958. *DV* 22 Apr 1959, p. 3. *Exb* 22 Apr 1959, pp. 4577-78 *FD* 22 Apr 1959, p. 6. *Har* 25 Apr 1959, p. 67 *HCN* 7 May 1959. *HR* 7 Oct 1955. *HR* 20 Oct 1955. *HR* 24 Jul 1958. *HR* 22 Apr 1959, p. 3. *LAEx* 16 May 1957. *LAEx* 7 May 1959. *LAT* 6 May 1959. *MPD* 23 Apr 1959. *MPHPD* 25 Apr 1959, p. 236 *Var* 22 Apr 1959, p. 6.

THE YOUNG LIONS (Jewish Americans)

Twentieth Century-Fox Film Corp. *Dist* Twentieth Century-Fox Film Corp. Apr **1958**; New York opening: 2 Apr 1958; Prod: 17 Jun–late Oct 1957 [©Twentieth Century-Fox Film Corp.; 18 Mar 1958; LP10300]. Sd (Westrex Recording System); b&w; CinemaScope; Lenses by Bausch & Lomb. 17 reels, 15,074 ft. 167 min. PCA cert no. 18687.

[*Exec prod* Buddy Adler]. *Prod* Al Lichtman. *Dir* Edward Dmytryk. *Asst dir* Ad Schaumer. *Scr* Edward Anhalt. *Dir of photog* Joe MacDonald. *Spec photog eff* L. B. Abbott. *Art dir* Lyle R. Wheeler and Addison Hehr. *Film ed* Dorothy Spencer. *Set dec* Walter M. Scott and Stuart A. Reiss. *Exec ward des* Charles LeMaire. *Cost des* Adele Balkan. *Mus* Hugo Friedhofer. *Cond* Lionel Newman. *Orch* Edward B. Powell. *Sd* Alfred Bruzlin and Warren B. Delaplain. *Makeup* Ben Nye. *Hair stylist* Helen Turpin. *Tech adv* Lt. Col Allison A. Conrad. [*Unit mgr–Europe* Ben Chapman]. [*Unit mgr–USA* Saul Wurtzel].

Song(s): "How About You?" words by Ralph Freed, music by Burton Lane.

Source: Based on the novel *The Young Lions* by Irwin Shaw (New York, 1948).

Cast: MARLON BRANDO [(*Christian Diestl*)], MONTGOMERY CLIFT [(*Noah Ackerman*)], DEAN MARTIN [(*Michael Whiteacre*)], Hope Lange [(*Hope Plowman*)], Barbara Rush [(*Margaret Freemantle*)], May Britt [(*Gretchen Hardenburg*)], Maximilian Schell [(*Captain Hardenburg*)], Dora Doll [(*Simone*)], Lee Van Cleef [(*Sergeant Rickett*)], Liliane Montevecchi [(*Françoise*)], Parley Baer [(*Brandt*)], Arthur Franz [(*Lieutenant Green*)], Hal Baylor [(*Private Burnecker*)], Richard Gardner [(*Private Cowley*)], Herbert Rudley [(*Captain Colclough*)], [John Alderson (*Corporal Kraus*)], [Sam Gilman (*Private Faber*)], [L. Q. Jones (*Private Donnelly*)], [Julian Burton (*Private Brailsford*)], [Ashley Cowan (*Maier*)], [Vaughn Taylor (*Mr. Plowman*)], [Gene Roth (*Host at party*)], [Milton Frome (*Draft board doctor*)], [Harry Ellerbe (*Draft board chairman*)], [Craig Karr (*Draft board secretary*)], [Michael Smith (*Draft board member*)], [George Meader (*Milkman*)], [Voltaire Perkins (*Druggist*)], [Ann Daniels (*Hatcheck girl*)], [Alberto Morin (*Bartender*)], [Robert Burton (*Colonel Mead*)], [Ann Codee (*French woman*)], [Mary Pierce (*Young French girl*)], [Christian Pasques (*French boy*)], [Alfred Tonkel (*German waiter*)], [Doris Wiss (*Nurse*)], [John Gabriel (*Patient in German hospital*)], [Stan Kamber (*Private Acaro*)], [Ed Rickard (*Mailman*)], [Joan Douglas (*Maid*)], [Harvey Stephens (*General Sam Rockland*)], [Paul Comi (*Private Abbott*)], [Michael Pataki (*Private Hagstrom*)], [Stephen Bekassy (*German major*)], [Ivan Triesault (*German colonel*)], [Otto Reichow (*German officer*)], [Clive Morgan (*British colonel*)], [Kurt Katch (*Concentration camp commandant*)], [Robert Ellenstein (*Rabbi Joseph Silverson*)], [John Bonner (*Mayor*)], [Jeffrey Sayre (*Drunk on subway*)], [Joe Brooks (*Corporal*)], [Henry Rowland (*Sergeant*)], [Nicholas King (*Medic*)], [Art Reichle, David Dabov, Lee Winter (*Soldiers*)], [Norbert Schiller (*Civilian*)], [Hubert Kerns].

Drama, World War II. [*Print viewed*]. On New Year's Eve, 1938, Christian Diestl, a Bavarian shoemaker and part-time ski instructor, is romancing American Margaret Freemantle at a party. When Margaret asks Christian if he is a Nazi party member, he replies that he is not at all political but believes that the Nazis stand for something hopeful in Germany. He explains that he had to abandon his medical studies due to the lack of free universities in Germany, and that Hitler has promised to change that. Margaret is dismayed by Christian's affiliation and leaves the party early. World War II begins, and on 24 Jun 1940, when France surrenders to Germany, Christian, now a Nazi lieutenant, reports to Captain Hardenburg on the steps of Sacre Coeur in Paris. In New York, singer Michael Whiteacre, hoping to be exempted from army service, is examined by the draft board and told to report for induction in about three months' time. At the draft board, Michael meets Noah Ackerman, who has recently arrived in New York from California. Michael invites Noah to a party that evening where he meets Margaret Freemantle, now Michael's girl friend, and is introduced to Hope Plowman, who is from Vermont. Noah escorts Hope to her temporary home in Brooklyn and instantly falls in love with her. In Paris, Christian's fellow officer Brandt has arranged a blind date for him with Françoise, a friend of the French woman, Simone, he is seeing. Although Françoise at first asks Christian how many Frenchmen he has killed, she later apologizes, explaining that her husband was killed in Belgium. Christian walks

her home and asks to see her again. In Vermont, Hope nervously introduces Noah to her father, having told him beforehand that Noah is Jewish. Mr. Plowman and Noah walk around the small town, steeped in Puritan tradition, and as they return to Hope, Mr. Plowman tells Noah that he has never known a Jew and agrees to their marriage. In Paris, Christian asks for a transfer as he dislikes having been assigned to round up children for labor duties and is beginning to doubt his country's purpose. Hardenburg gives Christian leave to go to Berlin and asks him to deliver a present to his wife Gretchen. Gretchen seduces Christian and tells him that she knows someone on Rommel's staff who can arrange a transfer of duty. In New York, Michael has been unable to pull any strings to keep himself out of the army and must report for basic training. Margaret, who is working for the Office of War Information, is being posted overseas and wants to get married, but Michael is unwilling. The next day, Noah leaves Hope to report to the army. In North Africa, Christian and Hardenburg execute a dawn raid on an encampment of British soldiers. Hardenburg carries the attack to excess, and orders all the wounded to be killed, but Christian finds himself unable to follow that order. Noah and Michael end up in the same army platoon, where Noah is subjected to harassment by Captain Colclough, who makes him the scapegoat for the confinement of the entire platoon to the barracks for a weekend. The other soldiers try to intimidate Noah with veiled ethnic slurs. Later, when Noah discovers that money he has been saving for a birthday present for Hope has been stolen from his footlocker, he issues a challenge to the unknown thief to fight him, and when four of the largest men in the platoon admit to the theft, Noah asks Michael to be his second. When Michael reports to Capt. Colclough that Noah has been badly beaten in three fights and asks him to put a stop to it, the captain warns Michael that he has been instructed by the colonel to approve or disapprove a request to have him transferred to Special Services in London, but should he complain to the colonel about Noah's treatment, the transfer will not go through. The transfer papers come in, but Michael elects not to leave as Noah still has one more fight. Noah wins that one and then goes A.W.O.L. In North Africa, the German troops are attacked by British and American forces, but Christian and Hardenburg escape on a motorcycle. After Christian tells him that he is sick of the "great German army," Hardenburg replies that he should have shot him earlier when he disobeyed a command. The motorcycle hits a land mine. In America, a pregnant Hope visits Noah in army detention and tells him that a lawyer has indicated to her that if he returns to his old company, he will not go to prison. Noah goes back and faces the wrath of Colclough, who fully expects to continue his persecution of Noah; however, the colonel informs him that he will be court-martialed for his actions against Noah and Michael. Noah's fellow soldiers welcome him back, present him with a copy of James Joyce's *Ulysses*, which Colclough had confiscated, and inside it, the money he lost. Christian, now a captain, visits Hardenburg in a hospital and finds him with his head totally bandaged. Hardenburg asks him to visit Gretchen again to reassure her that he is "salvageable." He also asks Christian to bring him a bayonet with which to kill a fellow patient, who is beyond hope and wants to die. In Berlin, before visiting Gretchen, Christian witnesses the devastation and misery of the city. Gretchen tells him that her husband has killed himself with a bayonet, adding that she had written to him telling him not to return, that he would be better off in a permanent veterans hospital. When Gretchen propositions him, Christian pushes her away in disgust and leaves. Christian meets Brandt again and they drive back to Paris to meet Simone and Françoise. Brandt tells Christian that Germany has lost the war and that he intends to desert. Christian tells Françoise that the thought of seeing her again kept him going through the horrors he has witnessed. She urges him to also desert, but during the night he leaves a farewell note to her, "Forgive me, I love you but I am a German soldier." In London, Michael and Margaret are together in a club during an air raid. Michael has turned down promotions, choosing to remain a private, but feeling guilt about having Noah and the others do his fighting for him, decides to return to his old company, now fighting in Normandy. He tells Margaret they will get married upon his return. In Vermont, Hope, now the mother of a baby girl, receives a letter from Noah promising to return to them. In Normandy, when they are pinned down by enemy fire, Noah, with Michael's help, rescues several of the men who had fought him. In Germany, when the retreating convoy with which Christian is now

fighting is strafed by a plane, he wanders away and comes upon the Nackerholtz concentration camp. The camp's commander complains to him about the difficulties of running such a camp and receives orders, by phone, to kill every man, woman and child in the camp, 6,000 people, before the American troops arrive. The commandant encourages Christian to face the enemy when they arrive, doing his duty for the fatherland, but Christian wanders on very distraught and despairing. Noah and Michael's company liberate the camp and bring the local mayor to witness the horror therein. A rabbi, a former prisoner, asks permission of the company's captain to hold a religious service in the camp, and the captain guarantees that he can, over the protests of the mayor who states that this will cause riots. Noah and Michael are walking in the woods around the camp when the sound of Christian destroying his machine gun against a tree stump attracts them. As Christian walks toward them, Michael shoots and kills him. The war ends and Noah returns to New York to Hope and his daughter. *Americans in foreign countries. Antisemitism. France. Germany. Jews. Nazism. Soldiers. World War II. Africa, North. AWOL. Bars. Berlin (Germany). Bigotry. Bombing, Aerial. Concentration camps. Desertion, Military. Deserts. Disillusionment. Drugstores. Duty. Fathers and daughters. Fistfights. Friendship. Infidelity. London (England). Mayors. Military bases. Military service, Compulsory. Milkmen. Mines, Military. Mothers and daughters. Motorcycles. New Year's Eve. New York City. Officers (Military). Paris (France). Parties. Postal workers. Rabbis. Romance. Scapegoats. Seduction. Singers. Skiing. Suicide. Ulysses (Book). Vermont. War crimes. War injuries.*

Note: a *NYT* news item of 3 Mar 1952 reported that director Fred Zinnemann was about to option the film rights for the best-seller, *The Young Lions*, which he intended to produce and direct independently. The item also stated that Zimmermann had made overtures to Marlon Brando and Montgomery Clift, with whom he had previously worked, to play two of the leading roles. However, on 23 Jan 1954, *NYT* announced that producers Jacques Braunstein and Robert Lord had purchased the film rights for a sum in excess of $100,000. On 25 Jan 1954, *FD* reported that Irwin Shaw was to receive a percentage of the profits and would write the screenplay. An 11 Sep 1955 *NYT* news item indicated that Braunstein and Lord would produce Shaw's screenplay for United Artists release.

According to documents in the Twentieth Century-Fox Records of the Legal Department at the UCLA Arts—Special Collections Library, in Dec 1956, the studio acquired the rights to the novel from Braunstein for $50,000 and 15% of the net profits. Additionally, Irwin Shaw was to receive $65,000 spread over ten years. The Twentieth Century-Fox Produced Scripts Collection, also at the UCLA Arts—Special Collections Library, contains a copy of Shaw's undated screenplay. All the Twentieth Century-Fox drafts were written by Edward Anhalt.

Filming began in France and Germany in Jun 1957 on a budget of $2,625,700. According to a studio press release, the Struthof concentration camp, which the French had preserved just as they found it, near Strasbourg was used as a location. When the studio ran advertisements in Strasbourg newspapers for "200 very thin, emaciated men," it found that 28 of the applicants were former inmates of Struthof. The North African desert scenes were shot at Borrego Springs, CA, supplemented by footage from the British documentary *Desert Victory*. The final confrontation, the only scene including the three principals, was filmed near Mt. Wilson CA. By the time filming was completed in late Oct, the cost had risen to $3,553,245. Two sequences paralleling that between "Christian" and "Margaret" on New Year's Eve 1938, were shot but deleted in editing. The sequence with "Michael" was set in a New York night club, while the sequence in which "Noah" watched the father he had neither known nor liked very much, die, took place in a cheap hotel in Santa Monica CA. "Noah's" father was played by noted Jewish stage actor Jacob Ben-Ami, making what would have been his Hollywood debut at the urging of Montgomery Clift, an old friend and admirer.

When the film opened, a good deal of criticism was leveled at the change from novel to film in the "Christian" character. In Shaw's novel, he was a hard-core, unregenerate Nazi, but the film presents him as a misguided "idealist" who eventually realizes the evil of the cause to which he has dedicated himself. In a 15 May 1957 memo to the producer, director and screenwriter, executive producer Buddy Adler wrote, "We need one good strong German character to speak for the German people as a whole, and to cast the guilt on the Nazis as opposed to the entire German population. A good picture today can take a million dollars out of Germany, and I am sure that unless we do something as suggested in the foregoing, this picture will not be sympathetically received in Germany."

In a 14 Apr 1958 *Life* feature on the film, it was reported that Brando delivered a fifteen-hour lecture to Dmytryk, Lichtman and Anhalt in which he gave a detailed analysis of Christian Diestl's character to convince them to make changes. Dmytryk, in a 17 Mar 1978 interview, stated, "I never spent 15 hours with Marlon.... The writer, Anhalt, and I already had these ideas about the character, and explained them to Marlon." The changes in Diestl's character enraged Irwin Shaw, who, quoted in a biography of Shaw, said that Brando "played him in a sympathetic way because he wants to be sympathetic on screen." The issue of anti-Semitism, which loomed large in the novel, was diminished in the film. Adler, in the same 15 May 1957 memo, in which he reacted to a draft in which the anti-Semitism was considerably less subtle,

wrote, "I also recommend that in the scene in the barracks in which Noah is called 'Jew-boy,' the connotation here should not be that the bullies and the captain dislike Noah because he is a Jew, but because he is sensitive etc.... The bullies are angry with Noah not because he is Jewish, but because the whole company is being punished because Noah failed in his duty to keep the windows clean." Critics also complained about loose ends and structural problems in the screenplay. However, Dmytryk has stated that he considers the film to be one of the best he made.

Producer Al Lichtman, longtime executive producer at MGM and former head of distribution for Twentieth Century-Fox, returned from a retirement due to health problems, to produce the film but died before it opened. This was Dean Martin's first dramatic role; his character's surname in the novel is "Whitacre," but was changed to "Whiteacre" for the film. Studio records indicate that Peter Brocco appeared in a deleted sequence. The *CBCS* lists Wade Cagle, Kendall Scott, Anne Stebbins and Ann Paige as cast members but their participation in the released film has not been confirmed.

Box 17 Mar 1958. *Box* 24 Mar 1958, p. 3. *DV* 23 Sep 1957, p. 16 *DV* 14 Mar 1958, p. 3. *Exh* 19 Mar 1958, pp. 4446-47. *FD* 25 Jan 1954. *FD* 17 Mar 1958, p. 8. *Har* 15 Mar 1958, p. 44. *HR* 14 Mar 1958, p. 3. *HR* 29 Oct 1958. *Life* 14 Apr 1958, pp. 65-68. *Look* 15 Apr 1958, pp. 50-55. *LAT* 11 Apr 1958. *MPHPD* 15 Mar 1958, p. 757. *NewRep* 28 Apr 1958, pp. 21-22. *NYT* 3 Mar 1952. *NYT* 23 Jan 1954. *NYT* 11 Sep 1955. *NYT* 3 Apr 1958 *Time* 14 Apr 1958. *Var* 19 Mar 1958, p. 6.

YOUNG MAN WITH A HORN (African Americans)

Warner Bros. Pictures, Inc.; A Warner Bros.—First National Picture. *Dist* Warner Bros. Pictures, Inc. 11 Mar 1950; Prod: mid-Jul—early Sep 1949 (©Warner Bros. Pictures, Inc.; 30 Apr 1950; LP124]. Sd (RCA Sound System); b&w. 10,035 ft. 111 min.

Prod Jerry Wald. *Dir* Michael Curtiz. *Dial dir* Norman Stuart. [*Asst dir* Sherry Shourds and Carter Gibson]. [*2d unit dir* David Curtiz]. *Scr* Carl Foreman and Edmund H. North. *Dir of photog* Ted McCord. [*2d cam* Ellsworth Fredericks]. [*Asst cam* Wally Meinardus]. [*Stills* Mac Julian]. *2d unit montage dir* David C. Gardner. *Art dir* Edward Carrere. *Film ed* Alan Crosland, Jr. *Set dec* William Wallace. [*Props* Herbert Plews and Robert Turner]. *Ward* Milo Anderson, Jeanette Storke and Vic Vallejo]. *Mus dir* Ray Heindorf. *Mus adv* Harry James. *Sd* Everett A. Brown. *Makeup artist* Perc Westmore. [*Makeup* John Wallace]. [*Hair* Betty Lou Delmont]. [*Scr supv* Irva Mae Ross]. [*Gaffer* Paul Burnett]. [*Best boy* Cliff Hutchinson]. [*Grip* Bill Chassen]. [*Kirk Douglas' trumpet solos* Harry James]. [*Juano Hernandez' trumpet solos* Jimmy Zito].

Music: "Moanin' Low," music by Ralph Rainger; "Get Happy," music by Harold Arlen; "Can't We Be Friends?" music by Kay Swift; "Chinatown, My Chinatown,: music by Jean Swartz; "Sweet Georgia Brown," music by Ben Bernie, Maceo Pinkard, Kenneth Casey; "Silent Night," music by Franz Gruber; "Blue Room" and "You Took Advantage of Me, music by Richard Rogers; "The Shadow Waltz" and "I Only Have Eyes for You," music by Harry Warren; "Tea for Two," music by Vincent Youmans; "The Man I Love" and "S'Wonderful," music by George Gershwin; "What Is This Thing Called Love," music by Cole Porter.

Song(s): "In the Sweet Bye and Bye," words by Vincent P. Bryan, music by Harry Von Tilzer; "The Very Thought of You," words and music by Ray Noble; "Too Marvelous for Words," words by Johnny Mercer, music by Richard A. Whiting; "I May Be Wrong, but I Think You're Wonderful," words by Harry Ruskin, music by Henry Sullivan; "Swing Low, Sweet Chariot," traditional black spiritual arranged by H. T. Burleigh; "Nobody Knows the Trouble I've Seen," traditional black spiritual; "With a Song in My Heart," words by Lorenz Hart, music by Richard Rodgers.

Source: Based on the novel *Young Man with a Horn* by Dorothy Baker (New York, 1938).

Cast: KIRK DOUGLAS [(*Rick Martin*)], LAUREN BACALL [(*Amy North*)], DORIS DAY [(*Jo Jordan*)], Hoagy Carmichael [(*Smoke Willoughby*)], Juano Hernandez [(*Art Hazzard*)], Jerome Cowan [(*Phil Morrison*)], Mary Beth Hughes [(*Marge Martin*)], Nestor Paiva [(*Louis Galba*)], Orley Lindgren [(*Rick, as a boy*)], Walter Reed [(*Jack Chandler*)], [Jack Kurschen (*Cab driver*)], [Alex Gerry (*Dr. Weaver*)], [Jack Shea (*Nurse*)], [James Griffith (*Walt*)], [Dean Riesner (*Joe*)], [Everett Glass (*Man leading song*)], [Dave Dunbar (*Alcoholic bum*)], [Robert O'Neill (*Bum*)], [Paul E. Burns, Burk Symon (*Pawnbrokers*)], [Julius Wechter (*Boy drummer*)], [Ivor James (*Boy banjoist*)], [Larry Rio (*Owner*)], [Dan Seymour (*Mike*)], [Vivian Mallah, Lorna Jordan, Lewell Enge (*Molls*)], [Paul Dubov (*Maxie*)], [Marjorie Pemberton (*Checkroom girl*)], [Murray Leonard (*Bartender*)], [Ted Eckelberry (*Elevator boy*)], [Frank Cady (*Hotel clerk*)], [Keye Luke (*Ramundo*)], [Hershel Dougherty (*Attendant*)], [Dick Cogan (*Intern*)], [Hugh Murray (*Doctor*)], [Paul Brinegar

(*Stage manager*)], [Bill Walker (*Black minister*)], [Helene Heigh (*Tweedsy woman*)], [Wilson Wood (*Young man*)], [Katharine Kurasch (*Miss Carson*)], [Bumps Meyers, George Washington, Oscar Bradley, Rocky Robinson, Zutty Singleton (*Musicians*)], [Hugh Charles], [Sid Kane], [Bridget Brown].

Drama, with songs. [*Print viewed*]. Musician Smoke Willoughby reminisces about his old friend, legendary trumpet player Rick Martin: After his mother dies when he is about nine, Rick moves in with his sister in California. One day, when she is out for the evening, Rick wanders into a mission church and is fascinated by the piano there. Having decided to take up some kind of instrument, Rick notices a trumpet in a pawn shop window and gets a job in a bowling alley to pay for it. Next to the bowling alley is an after-hours club, where Rick hears jazz for the first time. He is befriended by black trumpet player Art Hazzard, who gladly teaches his young apprentice what he knows. When Rick is older, he is able to find jobs playing for carnivals and dance marathons, but Art advises against pursuig a career as a musician, warning him that it is a hard life. Ignoring the advice of his friend, Rick follows Art to New York and there he gets a job playing trumpet for big band leader Jack Chandler and makes friends with Smoke and singer Jo Jordan. Chandler insists that Rick play the music exactly as written, but after he is finished for the night, Rick plays the jazz he loves at a small club. One night, Chandler fires Rick after he plays a jazzy number during a break, and despite Jo's efforts on his behalf, Rick refuses to go back when Chandler offers to rehire him. Later, Rick learns from Jo that Art has been sick and returns to New York. Jo gets him a job with another dance orchestra, where he becomes very popular, and after hours, he helps out Art at Louis Galba's nightclub. One night, Jo brings her friend Amy North to hear Rick play. Amy, who is studying to be a psychiatrist, blames her physician father for her mother's death by suicide and, as a result, believes that she is incapable of love. Nonetheless, Rick falls in love with her, and they are married. After their marriage, Rick and Amy are driven apart by his dedication to his music. Rick works at night and Amy goes to school in the daytime, so they seldom see each other. The situation grows steadily worse, and when Art comes looking for Rick because he hasn't been to Galba's in months, Rick lashes out at him. Later, a distraught Art is hit by a car. When he hears about the accident, Rick rushes to the hospital, but Art dies before they can be reconciled. Devastated, Rick returns home to learn that Amy has flunked her finals and wants a divorce. Rick's playing suffers, and he begins to drink heavily and finally collapses. After he recovers, he suggests to Smoke that they make their own records. Although Smoke is convinced that no one will buy them, he agrees to attempt it, but Rick is unable to complete a solo and in frustration, destroys his trumpet. Afterward, he disappears. After suffering an extended breakdown, Rick, who is ill with pneumonia, is taken by a taxi driver to a drunk tank. Smoke discovers his whereabouts and calls Jo and Amy. Amy does not come, but loyal Jo helps Rick recover. Now that he has discovered his heart, Rick is able to become a great musician. *African Americans. Jazz music. Musicians.* Automobile accidents. Brothers and sisters. California. Churches. Drunkenness. Fathers and daughters. Friendship. Funerals. Hospitals. Marriage. Nervous breakdown. New York City. Nightclubs. Nursing back to health. Regeneration. Romance. Singers. Trumpets.

Note: According to reviews, this film is loosely based on the life of cornet player Bix Beiderbecke, a renowned jazz musician of the 1920s and 1930s. Beiderbecke first learned to play the piano before taking up the cornet at fourteen. In the 1920s, he played with The Wolverines, and later joined Paul Whiteman's band. Beiderbecke drank heavily and in late 1929, he left Whiteman's band permanently and returned to Davenport to convalesce. He died in 1931, at the age of twenty-eight, from lobar pneumonia and edema of the brain. According to a news item in *HR* on 10 Oct 1941, Producer Benjamin Glazer's next production was to be an adaptation of Dorothy Baker's best-selling novel on Beiderbecke, with a screenplay to be written by himself and Theodore Reed. Reed was said to be set to direct the project, which was being offered to various studios. It has not been determined at what point Glazer and Reed's participation in the project ended.

According to contemporary sources, Warner Bros. studio musician Larry Sullivan coached Kirk Douglas so that his trumpet playing would look realistic on screen. Harry James played Douglas' trumpet solos offscreen, and Jimmy Zito dubbed those of Juano Hernandez. According to publicity material, several well-known jazz musicians of the day, including Bumps Meyers, George Washington, Oscar Bradley, Rocky Robinson and Zutty Singleton performed in the film's background bands. Scenes were filmed on location at the Aragon Ballroom in Ocean Park, the ballroom of the Beverly-Wilshire Hotel, a Skid Row midnight mission and a black church in East Los Angeles, according to publicity material. Some background scenes were filmed in New York City.

Contemporary reviews noted that James's commercial sound was out of character for a supposedly avant garde jazz musician like "Rick Martin."

Box 11 Feb 1950. *DV* 8 Feb 1950, p. 3, 9. *FD* 8 Feb 1950, p. 11. *HCN* 13 Feb 1950. *HR* 10 Oct 1941, p. 1. *HR* 8 Jul 1949, p. 9. *HR* 9 Sep 1949, p. 13. *HR* 8 Feb 1950, p. 3, 12. *MPHPD* 12 Feb 1950, p. 185. *NYT* 10 Feb 1950, p. 18. *Time* 27 Feb 1950. *Var* 8 Feb 1950, p. 11.

YOUNG SINNERS (Irish Americans)

Fox Film Corp. *Dist* Fox Film Corp. 17 May **1931**; New York opening: week of 8 May 1931 [©Fox Film Corp.; 27 Apr 1931; LP2193]. Sd (Western Electric System); b&w. 7,100 ft. 70 or 78-79 min. Passed by the National Board of Review.

Pres WILLIAM FOX. *Dir* John Blystone. [*Asst dir* Jasper Blystone]. *Stage dir* Samuel T. Godfrey. *Adpt, cont and dial* William Conselman. *Photog* John Seitz. *Art dir* Gordon Wiles. [*Film ed* Ralph Dixon]. [*Cost* Sophie Wachner]. *Sd rec* E. Clayton Ward. [*Fight double for Thomas Meighan* Sid Jordan]. [*Ski double for Hardie Albright* Sigurd Wathne]. [*Ski double for Dorothy Jordan* Eva Monrad]. [*Ski double for Thomas Meighan* H. P. Devick].

Song(s): "You Called It Love" and "Better Wait Till You're Eighteen," music and lyrics by James F. Hanley.

Source: Based on the play *Young Sinners* by Elmer Harris (New York, 28 Nov 1929).

Cast: Hardie Albright [(*Gene Gibson*)], Thomas Meighan [(*Tom McGuire*)], Dorothy Jordan [(*Constance Sinclair*)], Cecilia Loftus [(*Caroline Sinclair*)], James Kirkwood [(*John Gibson*)], Edmund Breese [(*Trent*)], Lucien Prival [(*Baron Karl Franz Josef von Konetz*)], [Edward Nugent (*Bud*)], [Gaylord Pendleton (*Reggie*)], [David Rollins (*Tommy*)], [Arnold Lucy (*Butler*)], [Nora Lane (*Maggie McGuire*)], [Joan Castle (*Sue*)], [John Arledge (*Jimmy*)], [Yvonne Pelletier (*Madge*)], [Billy Butts (*Timmy McGuire*)], [Sid Jordan (*Sleigh driver*)], [Dixie Lee].

Youth, Drama, with songs. [*Print viewed*]. Teenage sweethearts Constance Sinclair and Gene Gibson carouse on a Florida beach with a group of their high society friends. When the alcohol supply runs low, the couple go to "rum row" in Gene's speedboat, but are arrested by revenue officers as they return to the party. Connie's prim mother Caroline is furious when, as a result of the arrest, a photograph of Connie in a revealing bathing suit is published in a local newspaper. Determined to separate Connie from the dissolute Gene, Caroline takes her on to Samoa, where they meet the pretentious Baron Karl Franz Josef von Konetz, and Caroline arranges his engagement to Connie. When the Sinclairs and the baron return home to celebrate the engagement, Connie is surprised by the sudden appearance of Gene, who had not contacted her while she was away. Gene assures Connie of his love for her, and Connie rushes off to tell her mother that she will not marry von Konetz. While Connie is absent, however, Gene learns of her engagement to the baron and leaves after writing her a note of congratulations. The dissipirited Connie then agrees to go along with Caroline's plans, while Gene engages in a three-day drunken party that forces the apartment manager to summon Gene's hypocritical father John. The elder Gibson is disgusted by his son's behavior, but cannot defend himself against Gene's charges of neglect. John's adviser Trent counsels him to entrust Gene to the care of Tom McGuire, an Adirondack guide who specializes in "rebuilding rich men's sons." McGuire arrives and, after explaining to John that he will build up Gene physically, leaves with the youth, who resents his Irish tutor. At McGuire's cabin in the Airondacks, Gene vows to improve himself so that he can beat up McGuire, but as the weeks pass and his strength and clarity of mind return, he grudgingly begins to respect him. Gene is also impressed by McGuire's devotion to his wife Maggie and young son Timmy and wishes that his father had been as attentive as McGuire. The test of Gene's newfound determination comes when he convinces McGuire to attend his sister's wedding. McGuire is reluctant to leave the youth alone, but Gene assures him that he can be trusted. Once McGuire leaves, however, Connie appears. Gene is glad to see her, but insists that she return to her hotel to spend the night. When a snowstorm prevents her from leaving, Connie attempts to seduce Gene, but he locks himself in his bedroom. The next morning, an admiring Connie admits that Gene has changed for the better. When McGuire returns to the cabin before Connie leaves, he is furious upon discovering that she spent the night there. Before Gene can explain, McGuire hits him, and the two are brawling when John, Caroline and Trent arrive for a visit. Gene bests McGuire and explains that he wishes to marry Connie. John gives his consent and offers Gene a job and an

apartment, and Caroline, who learned her lesson about matchmaking when the baron was arrested for writing bad checks, also approves. McGuire pronounces that Gene has graduated and tells the sweethearts that if they make friends of their children, they will not need the likes of him. Connie calls McGuire an "old sweetie," and the grateful Gene tells him that he is a real pal. *Adirondack Mountains. Dissipation. Guides. Regeneration. Romance. Beaches. Cabins. Drunkenness. Engagements. False accusations. Fathers and sons. Fistfights. Florida. Hypocrisy. Irish Americans. Mothers and daughters. Neglected children. Nobility. Parties. Pledges. Samoan Islands. Seduction. Skiing. Snow storms. Tests of character.*

Note: The play was copyrighted under the title *Wings of Youth.* According to the contract with the playwright in the Twentieth Century-Fox Records of the Legal Department at the UCLA Theater Arts Library, Fox agreed not to release the film nationally until 1 Jan 1931, until 1 Apr 1931 in Philadelphia, Chicago, Pittsburgh, Cleveland and Detroit, and until 1 Aug 1931 in the United Kingdom, unless a run of the play in those places had already ended. The company paid the author $55,000 for the motion picture rights, which at the time was a high figure. The Twentieth Century-Fox Produced Scripts Collection at the ULCA Theater Arts Library contains an adaptation by Maurine Watkins that is dated before any material written by William Conselman. According to information in the Twentieth Century-Fox Records of the Legal Department, also at UCLA, Watkins' material was not used in the final film. According to *NYT*, this was Thomas Meighan's first film in two years. *Var* notes that Dorothy Jordan was borrowed from M-G-M and that the film included some newsreel ski shots. *Var* complained that "padding is responsible for the running time of 79 minutes" and suggested that "theatres which want to chop will find the trimming easy to do with the film in better shape at around the hour mark." The running time is, in fact, listed at 70 minutes in *MPH* release charts dated after the film's release.

FD 10 May 1931, p. 10. *HR* 20 Apr 1931, p. 2. *NYT* 9 May 1931, p. 15. *Var* 13 May 1931, p. 36.

THE YOUNG YEARS see **ALL THE FINE YOUNG CANNIBALS**

THE YOUNGER GENERATION (Jewish Americans)
Columbia Pictures Corp. *Dist* Columbia Pictures Corp. 4 Mar or 9 Mar **1929** [©Columbia Pictures Corp.; 18 Mar 1929; LP227]. Talking seq (Western Electric System with Columbia Symphony Orchestra); b&w. 8 reels, 7,866 or 8,217 ft.; also si: 7,246 or 7,394 ft. 75 or 95 min.
[*Prod* Jack Cohn]. *Dir* Frank R. Capra. [*Asst dir* Tenny Wright]. *Scr* Sonya Levien. *Dial* Howard J. Green. *Photog* Teddy Tetzlaff. [*Art dir* Harrison Wiley]. [*Film ed* Arthur Roberts]. *Mus cond* Bakaleinikoff. [*Tech dir* Edward Shulter]. [*Prod mgr* Joe Cooke].
Source: Based on the play *It Is to Laugh* by Fannie Hurst (New York, 26 Dec 1927).
Cast: JEAN HERSHOLT [(*Julius Goldfish*)], LINA BASQUETTE [(*Birdie Goldfish*)], RICARDO CORTEZ [(*Morris Goldfish*)], Rosa Rosanova [(*Tilda Goldfish*)], Rex Lease [(*Eddie Lesser*)], Martha Franklin [(*Mrs. Lesser*)], Sid Crossley [(*Butler*)], [Julia Swayne Gordon (*Mrs. Striker*)], [Julianne Johnston (*Irma Striker*)], [Jack Raymond (*Pinsky*)], [Otto Fries (*Tradesman*)].
Domestic, Drama. [*Print viewed*]. Morris Goldfish, the son of a Jewish immigrant family living on Delancey Street in New York's East Side, resides with his father Julius, a pushcart pot salesman; his mother Tilda, who toils in the kitchen all day long and resents her husband's laziness; and his sister Birdie, who is in love with their neighbor Eddie Lesser. Julius' favorite child is Birdie, while Tilda's favorite is Morris, who, she believes, will grow up to be a very successful businessman. Morris fights with his sister and then with Eddie over a piece of bread that his mother promised him for being a good son and making some money selling newspapers. The fighting results in an accident which sets their apartment ablaze, but Morris proudly tells his mother that he was able to salvage some valuables that they can now sell in a fire sale. Many years later, Tilda's prophesy is proven true when Morris makes a fortune as a successful Fifth Avenue antique dealer and is able to move his family into his swank uptown apartment. Tilda is comfortable in her new surroundings, but Julius is lonely and Birdie misses Eddie, now her sweetheart. Both admit that they are "a couple of Goldfish in the wrong fishbowl," and complain that they don't laugh anymore. Julius' pride is hurt when Morris announces that he has changed his name to Fish in order to ease his assimilation into Park Avenue society. When Birdie claims that Morris has moved his family in with him only to protect his image, Morris upbraids her for her insolence and reminds them that they should be grateful that he saved them from squalor. Morris forbids Eddie to visit Birdie, but Eddie manages to see her long

enough to plan an elopement with her. Before the rendezvous takes place, however, Eddie unwittingly becomes an accomplice to a jewelry store robbery and is forced into hiding. After a detective shows up at Morris' looking for Eddie, Birdie finds him at their planned meeting place and succeeds in convincing him to surrender himself. Eddie is jailed, but Morris is furious at the publicity his story has attracted and evicts his poor sister. Morris keeps Birdie's banishment a secret from his parents and intercepts all her letters to them, so that they worry for her safety. Two years later, Julius, fed up with being "jailed" by his own son, sets out to find his daughter, and soon learns that she has had a child and has earned enough money to support herself while awaiting Eddie's release from prison. Julius and Tilda return to Morris', where they are humiliated when their son addresses them as his servants in order to avoid social embarrassment. Unable to continue living under such conditions, Julius packs his bags, but does not get far before he becomes ill. Morris softens at the sight of his father on his deathbed and summons Birdie to be with him, and for a brief moment the family is happily reunited. Following Julius' death, Morris offers to comfort his mother with a trip to Europe, but she refuses and tells him that she is leaving to live with Birdie on Delancey Street, where she belongs. *Assimilation (Sociology). Cultural conflict. Family life. Jews. New York City–Fifth Avenue. New York City–Lower East Side. Wealth. Antique dealers. Death and dying. Eviction. Fires. Jewel thieves. Neighbors. Romance. Salesmen. Scandal.*

Note: According to modern sources, half of *The Younger Generation* was filmed at the Columbia studio with the remainder filmed on a sound stage on Santa Monica Boulevard during the winter of 1929. This was the first part-sound film for both Capra and Columbia, and there are four lip-synchronized dialogue passages. Modern sources also include Bernard Siegel (*Kruger*) and Walter Brennan in the cast. The sound cameraman was Ben Reynolds, according to Capra's autobiography, in which he also said that both he and Columbia preferred to make an all-talking film, but sound stages and equipment were at a premium, so all the dialogue scenes had to be shot together.

FD 17 Mar 1929, p. 5. *MPN* 23 Mar 1929, p. 923. *NYT* 11 Mar 1929, p. 22. *Var* 20 Mar 1929, p. 12.

YOU'RE OUT OF LUCK (African Americans)
Sterling Productions. *Dist* Monogram Pictures Corp. 20 Jan **1941**; Prod: late Nov—mid-Dec 1940 [©Monogram Pictures Corp.; 20 Jan 1941; LP10511]. Sd (Western Electric Recording); b&w. 6 reels, 5,490 ft. 62 min.
Prod Lindsley Parsons. *Dir* Howard Bretherton. [*Asst dir* Mack Wright]. *Scr and orig story* Edmund Kelso. *Dir of photog* Fred Jackman, Jr. *Art dir* Charles Clague. *Settings* David Milton. *Film ed* Jack Ogilvie. *Sd dir* William Fox.
Cast: FRANKIE DARRO (*Frankie* [*O'Reilly*]), Kay Sutton (*Margie*), Mantan Moreland (*Jeff*), Vicki Lester (*Sonya* [*Varney*]), Richard Bond (*Tom* [*O'Reilly*]), Janet Shaw (*Joyce*), Tristram Coffin ([*Dick*] *Whitney*), Willie Costello ([*Johnny*] *Burke*), Alfred Hall (*Haskell*), Paul Maxey (*Pete*), Ralph Peters (*Mulligan*), Paul Bryar, Jack Mather, [Gene O'Donnell], [Billy Snyder (*Cameraman*)].
Crime, Comedy-drama. [*Print viewed*]. Frankie O'Reilly, an elevator operator at the Carlton Arms, becomes embroiled in a murder investigation when he and his friend, parking attendant Jeff, witness the gangland murder of one of its tenants, Hal Dayton. Frankie calls his police detective brother Tom, who is under pressure from the *Star-Tribune* newspaper because his precinct has been unable to halt a recent crime wave. With Frankie's unwelcome help, Tom questions Dayton's friend, Dick Whitney, a wealthy young retiree who lives in the same building. Urged on by his girl friend, Sonya Varney, Whitney admits that Dayton was a gambler, but insists he was honest. Later, Tom takes Frankie and Jeff to the precinct to look at mug shots, and they recognize a photograph of Whitney, who was once arrested for embezzlement. After getting permission from the building manager, Haskell, Tom asks Frankie and Jeff to follow Whitney. Jeff soon learns that Whitney packs a gun, and they follow him to the Ringside gambling club, which is operated by gangster Johnny Burke. Whitney catches them following him, and asks Frankie to call the police if he does not leave the club in ten minutes. Inside, Burke is warned by Sonya, his former girl friend, that Whitney is coming after him, but Whitney disarms the gangster and demands Dayton's $60,000. Although he obtains the money, Whitney is unable to leave the club because the thugs who killed Dayton are guarding the door. Frankie and Jeff find Whitney inside, and after giving Frankie the envelope of money addressed to Dayton's sister Joyce, he

insists they call the police. By the time Tom's squad raids the club, it is completely deserted. Reporters take a candid photograph of the police reconstructing the scene and use it to humiliate Tom in print. Later, Frankie is shocked to discover the contents of the envelope, and hides it in the building's little-used furnace. When Haskell asks Frankie to fix the elevator, which appears to be stuck, Frankie and Jeff discover that Whitney's body has been thrown on top of the elevator. Bullets from Whitney's and Dayton's murders match, and while the police are searching Whitney's apartment, Tom's fiancée, switchboard operator Margie, patches through a call to Frankie from Sonya. Sonya pretends to be Joyce and asks Frankie to deliver the money to her at a certain address. Haskell then panics when he learns where Frankie hid the money because he is burning trash in the furnace. Jeff, however, has relocated the money in the washing machine, and reporters get a photograph of Tom and Frankie drying out the laundered cash. Frankie realizes that "Joyce's" call must be a trap because she could never have known about him. When he and Jeff go to Sonya's address, they find the apartment ransacked and Tom bound and gagged in a closet. Tom is demoted for bungling the investigation and losing the $60,000. Later, Frankie gets a call from the real Joyce and they arrange to meet. Joyce informs Frankie and Jeff that her brother used to mention Burke in his letters. When Jeff reveals that his girl friend is Sonya's maid, and that Sonya was Burke's former girl friend, Frankie heads for Sonya's apartment, after giving the address to Margie with instructions to call Tom. Sonya confesses that Burke murdered Dayton and Whitney because Dayton framed him by playing a longshot with inside information. Although Burke has given Sonya twelve hours to leave town, his thugs take her, Frankie and Jeff hostage until Burke arrives. Burke forces everyone into the freight elevator just as police surround the building, but on a cue from Frankie, Jeff pushes the emergency button, and the elevator halts, allowing Tom and the police to capture the gangsters. *African Americans. Amateur detectives. Brothers. Elevator operators. Murder. Apartment managers. Gambling. Gangsters. Impersonation and imposture. Money. Parking garage attendants. Police detectives. Police raids. Reporters. Telephone operators.*

Box 18 Jan 1941. DV 8 Jan 1941. HR 29 Nov 1940, p. 9. HR 6 Dec 1940, p. 8. HR 13 Dec 1940, p. 12. HR 8 Jan 1941, p. 3. MPD 13 Jan 1941. MPH 11 Jan 1941. Var 12 Mar 1941, p. 16.

THE YOUTH OF RUSSIA (Yiddish language)

Sov-Am Film Corp. *Dist* Sov-Am Film Corp. **1934**; New York opening: Nov 1934. Sd; b&w. 7 reels. 65 min. Yiddish language with English subtitles.

Dir Henry Lynn. *Wrt* Henry Lynn. *Mus* Jack Stillman.

Song(s): "Chinese Flower Song," "Bereosenka" and "The Rabbi Eleemelech," composer unknown.

Cast: Wolf Goldfaden (*Israel Slotopolsky*), Gertrude Bulman (*Kaile*), Sam Gertler, Dave Fafer, Morris Strassberg, Itzak Swerdlov, Rose Wallerstein, Boaz Young, Dora Kashinskya, Moishe Zilberstein, Louis Bakshitsyky, Morris Marcus, Valie Valentinova, Alex Balshakov, Nadia Gorel, Esta Salzman, Harry Miller, Meyer Silcezr, Chai Yaen.

Yiddish, Social, Drama, with songs. [*Not viewed*]. Israel Slotopolsky, a Jewish shoemaker in the Soviet Union who, in Czarist Russia, had been a forest contractor, has not mastered his new trade in the fifteen years since the revolution. Neither has he come to understand the new thinking of his buxom twenty-year-old daughter Kaile, now called "Catherine," regarding marriage. Kaile is about to marry for the fourth time, and Israel, whose two sons died in the war and whose wife died of grief, rages and pleads with Kaile that marrying again is immoral, as under the new system, she has not needed to get divorces from her past husbands. Kaile, however, contends that now if people do not suit or love each other, they can easily part. She promises, though, that this will be her last wedding. When Israel meets her fiancé, factory inspector and Communist Party member, Ivan Ivanowitch Goldberg, whose name used to be Itchkie, Ivan patronizingly praises Israel because he is a "worker." After Israel leaves them alone, Ivan embraces Kaile passionately, tearing her blouse, and they excitedly plan to go to a parade of the Red Army after the wedding. Israel returns and finds that Ivan has carried Kaile to her bed, and when Israel is alone with Kaile, he complains that Ivan is not her equal, but she says that she loves him. They marry, while Israel prays and weeps. Two months later, Israel spends a Sabbath eve at the home of Jews who still keep the religious tradition, albeit in secret. They reminisce about the old way of life, in which, one of them says,

despite the Czars and pogroms, they lived like kings following the Jewish rituals and customs, and they decry the new "god," endless work. Meanwhile, Kaile, without Israel's knowledge, gives a party at their home to celebrate her fifth marriage. At the party, Russian dances are danced and songs are sung, including one by a Chinese girl, who is engaged to a black man. When Israel hears about the party, he rushes home, and when he learns that Kaile has married again, he starts to faint, then berates her and grabs his hammer, threatening to kill her. After he falls exhausted, Kaile's new husband, Abrasha (formerly Abraham) Greenberg, patiently tries to explain that they are trying to build something more beautiful and wholesome than the old system and points out that under Jewish law, a woman could get a divorce only if her husband agreed; if a man deserted his wife or was a rogue, his wife was stuck in the marriage. Abrasha then relates the story of his Uncle Solomon, a religious fanatic who, during the Czarist regime, lived in Galicia: Solomon's daughter Rachel, whose husband had run off with another woman six years earlier, has become the object of gossip because she has been seen in the company of young men. Solomon warns her that under Jewish law, she must remain married until her husband dies. Rachel, however, stays away from home for two weeks, and when her mother Machle takes her side in an argument with Solomon and blames his fanaticism for the break up of their family, he attempts to throw a chair at her, then orders her out, calling her a witch. When Rachel returns and confesses that she has married a Christian, Solomon makes a mad dash at her, and she runs out. Abrasha relates that Solomon became insane. Israel, saying that he is stronger than Solomon, takes Kaile's hand, then faints. Feeling responsible, Kaile asks his forgiveness and says she will do whatever he tells her to do. Israel forgives her and, resigned that the new order is their destiny, apologizes to Abrasha and asks him to take good care of Kaile, then dies after blessing his daughter and her new husband. Kaile cries and says that her father had hoped somebody would be left to pray for his soul, but Abrasha nods his head, as if to say that that would be asking too much. *Cultural conflict. Fathers and daughters. Jews. Marriage. Russia. Women's rights. African Americans. Chinese. Communists. Fanatics. Insanity. Parties. Rites and ceremonies. Shoemakers.*

Note: The plot summary was based on a dialogue continuity at NYSA. The Yiddish title of this film is *Di Yugnt fun Rusland*. According to NYSA records, an affidavit stating that the title had been changed to *Yiddish Father* was filed on 14 Apr 1935. The Yiddish title for the re-release was *Der Yidisher Foter*. Later re-release press sheets give the title as *The Yiddishe Father* and the distributor as Cinema Service Corp.

Exh 15 Nov 1935, p. 33. FD 12 Nov 1934, p. 11. NYT 10 Nov 1934, p. 19.

YOYSEF IN MITSRAIM see **JOSEPH IN THE LAND OF EGYPT**

YU LUH SHEN PING (Chinese language)

Grandview Film Co. **1947?**; Hong Kong showing: 1947? Sd; b&w. Length undetermined. Chinese language.

Dir Jiang Wai-kwong. [*Not viewed*]. [No information concerning the plot of this film has been located.].

Note: The Cantonese transliterated title is *Ng Log Shen Ping*. This film was probably made in the U.S.

DER YUGNT FUN RUSLAND see **THE YOUTH OF RUSSIA**

YVONNE FROM PARIS (French Americans)

American Film Co. *Dist* Pathé Exchange, Inc. 13 Jul **1919** [©American Film Co.; 8 Jul 1919; LP13936]. Si; b&w. 5 reels.

Dir Emmett J. Flynn. *Scen* Frank Howard Clark. *Story* Joseph Franklin Poland. *Tech dir* S. A. Baldridge.

Cast: Mary Miles Minter (*Yvonne Halbert*), Alan Forrest (*Lawrence Bartlett*), Vera Lewis (*Aunt Marie Provost*), J. Barney Sherry (*David Marston*), Bertram Grassby (*Harley Pembroke*), Rosemary Theby (*Cecile*), E. Alyn Warren (*Luigi*), Jack Farrell (*Henri Franey*), Jeanne Robbins, Frank Clark.

Comedy-drama. Successful Parisian dancer Yvonne Halbert grows tired of the overwatchfulness of her aunt and runs away to America. Disguised and hiding out in the steerage of a boat, Yvonne meets violinist Luigi. She dances to Luigi's accompaniment in a Greenwich Village cabaret, where she is discovered by David Marston, the producer who had negotiated to bring the famous Yvonne to America. Marston signs the supposed unknown performer and intends to bill her under the name of Yvonne, whom he believes has broken her contract with him. Apache dancer Cecile claims to be the real Yvonne, but matters are straightened out with the arrival of Aunt

Marie. Yvonne marries Lawrence Bartlett, the author of the play that features her in America. *Dancers. French Americans. Immigrants. Impersonation and imposture. Mistaken identity. Paris (France). Runaways. Apache dancers. Aunts. Boats. Cabarets. New York City–Greenwich Village. Playwrights. Theatrical producers. Violinists.*

ETR 12 Jul 1919, p. 467. MPN 12 Jul 1919, p. 595. MPW 12 Jul 1919, p. 287. Var 18 Jul 1919, p. 42, 46. Wid's 6 Jul 1919, p. 23.

Z DYMEM POŻARÓW (Polish language)

1941; World premiere in Chicago: 4 Jun 1941. Sd; b&w. Length undetermined. Polish language.

Dir Tadeusz Wroński and Corey G. Cook. *Scr* Tadeusz Wroński and Stach Milewicz. *Cond of choir* A. Chrzanowski.

Song(s): "Fujarka," "Z Tamtej strony jeziora," "Hej łrozbujał się," "Kołysanda 'Śpij;dziecinko już'," "U mej matki rodzonej," "Z Dymem Pożarów," "Modlitwa," "Święty Mocny" and "Nie damy Ziemi," composers undetermined.

Source: Inspired by the book *Księgi narodu polskiego i pielgrzymstwa polskiego* by Adam Mickiewicz (1833).

Cast: Tadeusz Wroński (*Farmer*), Stach Milewicz (*Jaśka*), Helena Kubiatowski, W. łPrzybyła, Malinowski, Demantóws, Danusi Krassowska, Heerin.

Allegory, Historical, World War II, Drama, with songs. [*Not viewed*]. In a prologue, Polish kings and the Polish nation defend Christian values in foreign lands where God has been rejected and replaced with soul-less substitutes in whose name they wage war. In the main story, in August 1939, Jasiek, a young farmer, lives with his wife Jagna and his old father-in-law. After the Nazis invade Poland in September 1939, terrorizing the Poles, there is great uncertainty about the survival and freedom of the nation. Jasiek is wounded during a heroic battle, then is sent to a camp, from which he escapes. Faith in a better future becomes his only reason to live. Meanwhile, the mayor of Warsaw, Stefan Starzynski, is visited by a group of Poles from the U.S. He expresses to them his belief in the heroism, patriotism and strength of the Polish nation. Jasiek returns to his village and dies in the arms of his wife, saying the words, "for my Motherland." In an allegorical epilogue, taken from the prophetic writings of the great nineteenth century Polish poet Adam Mickiewicz, the Polish nation rises from the smoke of fires and the dust and blood of Polish patriots to make the nation grand and powerful again. It is stated that Poland will be invaded on the first day, Warsaw will collapse on the second day and the nation will be resurrected on the third day. The resurrected Poland will free all European nations from bondage, and all wars among Christians will cease. *Farmers. Invasions. Adam Mickiewicz. Nazis. Poland–History. Stefan Starzynski. War victims. Warsaw (Poland). World War II. Allegory. Christianity. Escapes. Fathers-in-law. Marriage. Mayors. Polish Americans. Prison camps. Village life.*

Note: An English translation of this film is *With the Smoke of the Fires*. According to articles from the Chicago-based Polish-language newspaper *Dziennik Związkowy (Zgoda)*, the film was produced by theater artist and singer Tadeusz Wroński, the founder of the Detroit Opera. After World War I, Wroński produced concerts and plays to collect money for hunger relief in Poland. Wroński explained in one of the articles that the Polish people's apathetic reaction to the Nazi occupation of Poland prompted him to use Adam Mickiewicz's *Księgi narodu polskiego i pielgrzymstwa polskiego* (*The Books of the Polish Nation and Pilgrimage*) as the inspiration for the film. As noted in *Zgoda*, Mickiewicz (1798-1855), called Poland's greatest poet, "foresaw the moment of doubt and despair of the Polish nation and called on Poles to unite in the fight against the evil enemy for the bright future of Poland." According to the articles, Mickiewicz "predicted the Polish National Golgotha but never lost faith in the final Polish victory."

The film was made in Hollywood, beginning in Jan 1941. One *Zgoda* article stated that production was interrupted for two months because of heavy rains in Jan and Feb 1941. Corey G. Cook, the film's director, was associated with Courtesy Ideal Pictures Corp. The film was first shown in Chicago in early May 1941 to a group of seven Polish priests, who in a published statement, commented, "The film, illustrating Hitler's invasion of Poland, presents the clash of two worlds on the Polish land, the one of overwhelming military mechanical might and one of the soul. This film helps Poles, living in America far away from the events of 1939, envision what their brothers and sisters went through. On the other hand, it also helps us understand where the Polish Nation took its strength to resist the great mechanical power without giving in, acting heroically, preferring to see the beloved Warsaw in ruins to the one intact paying homage to the brutal invader. In addition, this film gives us an answer to the question how to explain why the German occupation was unable to break the Polish spirit and the hope of Poles." The priests applauded the film's choice of Mickiewicz as the "interpreter of the horrible September 1939 events in Poland," as well as its use of "modest means" without the "gimmicks of American film technology," which might have taken away from the dignity of the

Polish suffering." The film was shown to Polish journalists in Chicago on 4 May 1941; a reviewer noted some "minor technical problems," but praised the "moral importance" of the film, the performances and the music and songs. The film had its official premiere on 4 Jun 1941 at the Holy Trinity School in Chicago; following the film, Wroński sang a number of patriotic and traditional Polish songs. One news item stated that the film was initially accused of being pro-German propaganda. Another Hollywood-made, Polish-language film dealing with the Nazi invasion of Poland, *Ten Ostatni* (see above), was shown in Chicago in Apr 1941.

Dziennik Związkowy (Zgoda) 2 Apr 1941. Dziennik Związkowy (Zgoda) 12 Apr 1941, p. 10. Dziennik Związkowy (Zgoda) 3 May 1941. Dziennik Związkowy (Zgoda) 5 May 1941. Dziennik Związkowy (Zgoda) 7 May 1941. Dziennik Związkowy (Zgoda) 24 May 1941, p. 8. Dziennik Związkowy (Zgoda) 26 May 1941. Dziennik Związkowy (Zgoda) 27 May 1941. Dziennik Związkowy (Zgoda) 28 May 1941. Dziennik Związkowy (Zgoda) 29 May 1941. Dziennik Związkowy (Zgoda) 4 Jun 1941.

ZAMBOANGA (Tagalog language)

Filippine Film Production, Inc. *Dist* Grand National Films, Inc. 15 Apr **1938** Sd; b&w. 6-7 reels. 60, or 64-65 min. Tagalog—English language.

Pres Edward L. Alperson. *Prod* George F. Harris and Edward Tait. *Dir* Eduardo De Castro. *Photog* William H. Jansen. *Ed* Ralph Dixon. *Mus score* Dr. Edward Kilenyi. *Rec* Louis R. Morse. *Narr* Frederick Lindsley.

Cast: Hadji-Razul (*Himself*).

Island, Drama. [*Not viewed*]. Danao, the head of the Moro pearl divers on a small island in the Sulu Sea, falls in love with Minda, the granddaughter of chief Datu Tanbuong. When Hadji-Razul, the cruel, polygamous chief of the Tao natives, sees Min da, he desires to take her for his wife, and kidnaps her and the other Moro women while their men are away diving for pearls. An eclipse of the sun signals a warning to the Moro men, and Danao goes to the neighboring island village to rescue his beloved. After battling his rival, Danao is eventually successful and returns Minda and the other women to their own island. *Philippines. Polygamy. Romance. Americans in foreign countries. Basketwork. Eclipses, Solar. Fights. Pearl diving. Sea captains.*

Note: *Var* noted that the "original" running time of the film was 110 minutes. The film was copyrighted three times by Filippine Film Productions, Inc. According to information in *NYT*, the picture was made by American George F. Harris and his partner, Edward Tait, in the Philippines at a small studio which they began in the early 1930s. The article also stated that the film took nine months to shoot and that the producers took the negative of the completed picture to Hollywood for scoring and editing. The film was made for American audiences, according to contemporary sources. Reviews note that English and Tagalog dialogue is heard onscreen and subtitles are used during portions of the film.

Box 24 Jul 1937. Box 23 Apr 1938. FD 12 Jul 1937, p. 9. MPD 13 Jul 1937, p. 12. MPH 17 Jul 1937, p. 48. NYT 18 Jul 1937. Var 27 Apr 1938, p. 23.

ZANE GREY'S DESERT GOLD *see* **DESERT GOLD**

ZANE GREY'S THE GOLDEN WEST *see* **THE GOLDEN WEST**

ZANE GREY'S THE RAINBOW TRAIL *see* **THE RAINBOW TRAIL**

ZANE GREY'S THUNDER MOUNTAIN *see* **THUNDER MOUNTAIN**

ZANE GREY'S UNDER THE TONTO RIM *see* **UNDER THE TONTO RIM**

ZANE GREY'S WAGON WHEELS *see* **WAGON WHEELS**

ZANE GREY'S WESTERN UNION *see* **WESTERN UNION**

ZANE GREY'S WILD HORSE MESA *see* **WILD HORSE MESA**

ZEIN WEIB'S LUBOVNICK (Yiddish language)

High Art Pictures Corp. *Dist* High Art Pictures Corp. **1931**; New York opening: 25 Sep 1931; Prod: 2 Jul—mid-Jul 1931 [©Hugh-Art Pictures Corp. [sic]; 13 Apr 1932; LU2980]. Sd; b&w. 7,195 ft. 80 or 82 min. Yiddish language with English subtitles.

Pres NATHAN HIRSH and MORRIS KLEINERMAN. *Dir* Sidney M. Goldin. [*Asst dir* Robert Sheridan]. *Story written by* Shin Ra-Chell. *Photog* Frank Zucker and [Buddy Harris]. *Ed* Joe Silverstein. *Rec* Percy Glenn.

Song(s): "Ich has alle frauen" and "Oi gite weibele," words and music by Ludwig Satz; "That Beautiful Moon" and "The Song in My Heart," composer unknown.

Cast: LUDWIG SATZ [(*Edouard Wien, also known as Herman Weingard*)], Lucy Levin [(*Golde Blumberg*)], Isidor Casher [(*Oscar Stein*)], Lillian Feinman [(*Golde's aunt*)], Zita Ma-Kar, [Michael Rosenberg], [Jacob Frank], [Anne Shapiro], [Siru Zazi].

Yiddish, Comedy, with songs. [*Print viewed*]. Backstage during rehearsals, New York matinee idol Edouard Wien bumps into Golde Blumberg, who works for costumer Oscar Stein, Eddie's uncle and the stingy manager of his show. Eddie and Golde look lovingly at each other until Oscar angrily sends her back to work. Oscar, who is still stung from been jilted by a woman, argues that women are all false, wicked and frivolous. When Eddie counters that he believes women to be more faithful than men, Oscar challenges him to bet $10,000 that Golde will not refuse to marry a man whom she does not love if he is wealthy. Eddie accepts and disguises himself as Herman Weingard, an aged, unappealing man. While Oscar plays up to Golde the advantages of a marriage to Herman, Eddie, dressed as Herman, tries to discourage her interest. The two men pester her until she agrees to marry Herman just to be left alone. Shattered, Eddie confesses to Oscar that although he has fallen in love with Golde, he has lost faith in her. Oscar suggests that they marry and then proposes a new $25,000 bet—that once married to Herman, Golde will deceive him with a younger man. After the marriage, Golde insists on sleeping alone. She and Herman go to a beach resort, where Eddie, as the elderly husband, continually pesters her with his whining about the way a "good wifey" should behave. Although she claims that she does love him, she pushes him away in disgust when he kisses her. After three weeks, "Herman" disappears, which causes Golde to worry and long for him. However, when Eddie, now dressed as himself, visits, ostensibly to see his "friend Herman," Golde encourages his flirtation. They begin a courtship and go to the beach, row on a lake and walk arm-in-arm through the woods, all the while followed by the spying Oscar. In the evening, Golde expresses her love for Eddie. Disheartened, Eddie hands Oscar a check to cover the bet, but when Golde suddenly runs away from him, saying that she is a married woman, Eddie retrieves the check. Eddie then returns as Herman, but when he tries to woo Golde, she again pushes him away. He berates her for marrying him when she was not in love with him, and she accuses him of trying to bribe her with his wealth. When he demands that they sleep in the same bedroom, she runs off. During a rehearsal, Eddie receives a letter from Golde, telling him that she does not love her husband, but loves him, Eddie, instead. Greatly upset, he decides to close the show, but before giving Oscar the check for the bet, tries a final test. When Golde suggests that they die together to resolve the conflict, Eddie refuses and encourages her to engage in a secret affair with him. Shocked, Golde says she would rather die than deceive her husband. Eddie vows to drown himself because, he says, he cannot live without her and, after leaving her room, changes into Herman. Golde confesses to her husband that Eddie tried to steal her away. He then takes off his beard and wig and says he has proven that there are decent women in the world. Feeling ridiculed, Golde tells him to go, but he sweet-talks her and they kiss. After they sing to each other from separate rooms as they prepare for their honeymoon evening, Eddie, in formal dress, enters Golde's room to find her waiting for him in bed. *Aged men. Impersonation and imposture. Infidelity. Jews. Marriage. Romance. Singers. Tests of character. Wagers. Beaches. Honeymoons. Letters. Misogyny. New York City. Resorts. Theatrical managers. Uncles.*

Note: The print viewed, a re-release print, did not have the Yiddish title, and was called *His Wife's Lover*, which is the translation *Var* and *FD* give in their reviews. *Zein Weib's Lubovnick* is the spelling of the Yiddish title given by *Var* and *FD*. Modern sources call the film *Zayn Vaybs Lubovnik*. The English language working title of this film was *Love Crazy*. This film was shown in Cleveland in Jan 1932 under the title *His Wife's Sweetheart*. According to *Var*, the film cost $20,000 to make and was filmed in nine days. According to *New York World Telegram*, the film was based on a Yiddish play in which Ludwig Satz earlier acted. Satz was one of the stars of the Yiddish popular stage. A *FD* news item, dated 2 Jul 1931, stated that Satz signed to star in a series of Yiddish films under the direction of Sidney M. Goldin, but no other films in the proposed series were produced. Another *FD* news item from Jul 1931 stated that Satz had been signed by Nathan Hirsh to star in six English language films for Avon Pictures Co., but none of these films were produced. A press sheet for this film calls it "the first Jewish musical comedy talking picture." The film contains some shots of New York's Lower East Side, specifically the corner of Orchard and Rivington Streets. It was re-released in New York beginning 29 May 1950 with newly added English subtitles by George Roland. Modern sources list the following additional cast credits: Moishe Silverstein, Sam Levenworth, William Epstein and Sidney M. Goldin, the director.

Cue 27 May 1950. *Daily Cinema* 10 Jul 1959. *Exh* 21 Jun 1950, p. 2874. *FD* 2 Jul 1931, p. 12. *FD* 14 Jul 1931, p. 2. *FD* 27 Jul 1931, p. 4. *FD* 1 Oct 1931, p. 5. *FD* 4 Oct 1931, p. 8. *Jewish Independent* 29 Jan 1932. *New York World Telegram* 26 Sep 1931. *Var* 29 Sep 1931, p. 22.

ZENG YIN DEO LEI *see* **JENG YIEN DOE LEE**

EL ZÍNGARO VAGABUNDO *see* **EL REY DE LOS GITANOS**

INTRODUCTION TO THE INDEXES

★ *Within Our Gates* has five separate indexes to assist the researcher: A Chronological Index of film titles, a Personal Name Index, a Subject Index, an Ethnic Category Index and a Foreign Language Index. Entries within all of the indexes have the same basic arrangement: alphabetical headings followed by chronological, then alphabetical listing of film titles.

CHRONOLOGICAL INDEX OF FILM TITLES

★ In this index, films are listed alphabetically under the year of release. Films that may have been released in either of two years, for example 1944 or 1945, are listed only once, under the first possible year of release. Films for which release dates cannot be definitively determined are listed under the most likely release year, followed by a question mark, for example, 1948?

CHRONOLOGICAL INDEX OF FILM TITLES

1912   The Adventures of
            Lieutenant Petrosino
        The Alaska-Siberian
            Expedition
        Atop of the World in
            Motion
1913   The Inside of the White
            Slave Traffic
        Traffic in Souls
1913?   The Call of the Blood
        Hiawatha
        The Lure of New York
1914   At the Cross Roads
        Captain F. E.
            Kleinschmidt's Arctic
            Hunt
        Dan
        The Good-for-Nothing
        The Great Diamond
            Robbery
        Hearts United
        In the Days of the
            Thundering Herd
        In the Land of the Head
            Hunters
        The Indian Wars
        John Barleycorn
        The Jungle
        Life's Shop Window
        The Little Angel of Canyon
            Creek
        The Little Jewess
        The Littlest Rebel
        The Nightingale
        Northern Lights
        An Odyssey of the North
        The Redemption of David
            Corson
        Rose of the Rancho
        Springtime
        The Squaw Man
        The Straight Road
        Threads of Destiny
        Uncle Tom's Cabin
        When Broadway Was a Trail
        Where the Trail Divides
        The Woman in Black
        The Yellow Traffic
1914?   A Boy and the Law
        The Chinese Lily
        The Lust of the Red Man
        The Mysterious Mr. Wu
            Chung Foo
        Sitting Bull—The Hostile
            Sioux Indian Chief
1915   The Adventures of a
            Madcap
        After Five
        The Alien
        An American Gentleman
        The Birth of a Nation
        Captain Courtesy
        The Cheat
        Children of the Ghetto
        Chimmie Fadden
        Chimmie Fadden Out West
        The Clemenceau Case
        Cohen's Luck
        The Danger Signal
        The Gambler of the West
        The Girl I Left Behind Me
        The Grandee's Ring
        Hearts of Men
        How Molly Malone Made
            Good
        The Immigrant
        The Italian
        Just Jim
        The Kindling

        Kreutzer Sonata
        The Lamb
        The Last of the Mafia
        The Lure of Woman
        Marse Covington
        The Melting Pot
        The Nigger
        The Pageant of San
            Francisco
        The Penitentes
        The Rosary
        The Sable Lorcha
        Sealed Valley
        The Secret Sin
        The Spender
        A Texas Steer
        Time Lock Number 776
        Under Southern Skies
        Where Cowboy Is King
        A Yankee from the West
1915?   The Beachcomber
        Chinatown Pictures
        The Jewish Crown
        Life of American Indian
            [sic]
        The Life of Sam Davis: A
            Confederate Hero of the
            Sixties
        The Period of the Jew
        Sam Davis, the Hero of
            Tennessee
        Sin
1916   Alien Souls
        Arms and the Woman
        The Aryan
        At Piney Ridge
        Betrayed
        Britton of the Seventh
        Broken Chains
        Broken Fetters
        A Child of Mystery
        Civilization's Child
        The Colored American
            Winning His Suit
        The Criminal
        The Daughter of the Don
        The Fall of a Nation
        The Flames of Johannis
        The Flower of No Man's
            Land
        Following the Flag in
            Mexico
        The Folly of Revenge
        For the Defense
        The Gilded Spider
        Gold and the Woman
        Gretchen, the Greenhorn
        The Grip of Jealousy
        The Half-Breed
        Her Debt of Honor
        The Honorable Friend
        Hop, the Devil's Brew
        Hulda from Holland
        The Innocent Lie
        The King's Game
        Light at Dusk
        Little Meena's Romance
        Lone Star
        Lord Loveland Discovers
            America
        The Love Girl
        Man and His Angel
        A Man of Sorrow
        Mixed Blood
        The Morals of Hilda
        Pasquale
        Peck O' Pickles
        Poor Little Peppina
        The Pretenders
        Pudd'nhead Wilson

        Ramona
        The Romantic Journey
        The Scarlet Oath
        The Sign of the Poppy
        Silks and Satins
        A Sister of Six
        The Social Buccaneer
        The Social Highwayman
        Sold for Marriage
        A Son of Erin
        The Soul of Kura-San
        The Thousand Dollar
            Husband
        Three of Many
        The Twin Triangle
        Unprotected
        Witchcraft
        The Woman in 47
        A Woman's Honor
        The Yellow Passport
        A Yoke of Gold
1916?   Fate's Chessboard
        Should a Baby Die?
1917   The Adventures of Buffalo
            Bill
        The Adventures of Carol
        Alaska Wonders in Motion
        The Bar Sinister
        The Barrier
        The Bond Between
        The Bottle Imp
        The Bride of Hate
        The Bronze Bride
        The Buffalo Bill Show
        The Call of Her People
        The Call of the East
        The Captain of the Gray
            Horse Troop
        Castles for Two
        The Conqueror
        Crime and Punishment
        The Flower of Doom
        Follow the Girl
        Forbidden Paths
        The Gun Fighter
        Hashimura Togo
        Her Own People
        The Hidden Children
        His Sweetheart
        How Uncle Sam Prepares
        I Will Repay
        A Jewel in Pawn
        John Ermine of the
            Yellowstone
        A Kentucky Cinderella
        The Little American
        The Little Boy Scout
        The Little Chevalier
        The Little Samaritan
        Lost in Transit
        A Love Sublime
        My Fighting Gentleman
        A Night in New Arabia
        One Law for Both
        The Peddler
        The Plow Woman
        The Primitive Call
        The Pulse of Life
        Queen X
        The Red Woman
        The Renaissance at
            Charleroi
        A Roadside Impresario
        Rosie O'Grady
        Runaway Romany
        The Secret Game
        The Secret of Eve
        The Slacker
        Sold at Auction
        Southern Pride

        The Spirit of '76
        The Squaw Man's Son
        The Sudden Gentleman
        Sunshine and Gold
        The Tell-Tale Step
        The Tenderfoot
        Threads of Fate
        The Trouble Buster
        Unconquered
        Under False Colors
        Unknown 274
        The War of the Tongs
        A Wife by Proxy
        The Wild Girl
        The Winged Mystery
        The Woman and the Beast
1917?   Barnaby Lee
1918   An Alien Enemy
        Amarilly of Clothes-Line
            Alley
        The Birth of a Race
        The Border Raiders
        The Bravest Way
        A Broadway Scandal
        Broken Ties
        The City of Dim Faces
        The City of Tears
        A Daughter of the Old
            South
        Denny from Ireland
        Doing Their Bit
        Fields of Honor
        Find the Woman
        The Firebrand
        Free and Equal
        The Girl in the Dark
        The Goddess of Lost Lake
        The Golden Wall
        Good-Bye, Bill
        The Greatest Thing in Life
        The Gypsy Trail
        The Hell Cat
        Hell's End
        Her American Husband
        Her Moment
        Hidden Pearls
        His Birthright
        Hitting the Trail
        The Honor of His House
        How Could You, Jean?
        Huck and Tom; or, the
            Further Adventures of
            Tom Sawyer
        The Hun Within
        I Want to Forget
        In Judgment Of
        Johanna Enlists
        The Kaiser's Finish
        Laughing Bill Hyde
        The Liar
        Little Red Decides
        The Little Runaway
        A Little Sister of Everybody
        Love's Law
        The Man Above the Law
        Marked Cards
        Me Und Gott
        The Midnight Patrol
        The Million Dollar Mystery
        My Cousin
        Mystic Faces
        One More American
        The Only Road
        The Ordeal of Rosetta
        Out of a Clear Sky
        The Price of Applause
        The Prussian Cur
        The Ranger
        Real Folks
        The Reckoning Day

The Red, Red Heart
Ruggles of Red Gap
Sandy
Set Free
Shifting Sands
The Source
The Spreading Evil
The Squaw Man
The Temple of Dusk
Thirty a Week
Tongues of Flame
Tony America
Toys of Fate
The Unbeliever
Uncle Tom's Cabin
Untamed
Wanted, a Mother
Who Is to Blame?
Wild Women
The Wine Girl
Woman and the Law
A Woman of Impulse
The Yellow Dog

1918? Indian Life
Rosemary Climbs the
Heights
The Snail

1919 As a Man Thinks
Auction of Souls
A Bachelor's Wife
Behind the Door
Bonnie, Bonnie Lassie
Come Out of the Kitchen
The Courageous Coward
Daughter of Mine
The Delicious Little Devil
Deliverance
Desert Gold
Diane of the Green Van
Erstwhile Susan
Evangeline
A Fallen Idol
False Evidence
A Fighting Colleen
Fighting for Gold
The Gray Horizon
The Gray Towers Mystery
A Heart in Pawn
The Heart of Wetona
Hearts of Men
His Debt
His Parisian Wife
The Homesteader
Injustice
Just Squaw
Lasca
The Last of His People
The Little Diplomat
The Lord Loves the Irish
The Lost Battalion
Love and the Law
Mandarin's Gold
A Man's Duty
The Other Man's Wife
The Red Viper
The Right to Happiness
The Scar
Scarlet Days
The She Wolf
The Sleeping Lion
The Sneak
Spotlight Sadie
The Tiger Lily
Toby's Bow
Told in the Hills
The Tong Man
The Unpainted Woman
The Volcano
The Westerners
Who Will Marry Me?
Who's Your Brother?
A Yankee Princess
Yvonne from Paris

1919? Alaska
America Was Right
The Brand of Judas
The Chosen Path
In the Land of the Setting
Sun; or, Martyrs of
Yesterday
When the Desert Smiles

1920 Before the White Man
Came
Billions
The Brute
The Cup of Fury

The Cyclone
Dangerous Days
Dangerous Hours
The Dark Mirror
Darling Mine
The Daughter of Dawn
The Devil's Claim
Dinty
Eyes of Youth
The Face at Your Window
For the Soul of Rafael
Frontier Days
The Girl of My Heart
The Good-Bad Wife
The Great Shadow
Hidden Charms
Huckleberry Finn
Humoresque
In the Depths of Our
Hearts
It's a Great Life
The Last of the Mohicans
Li Ting Lang
Lifting Shadows
Locked Lips
The Luck of the Irish
The Man Who Dared
The Mark of Zorro
The North Wind's Malice
On with the Dance
Our Christianity and
Nobody's Child
Outside the Law
Pagan Love
The Paliser Case
The Purple Cipher
The Riddle: Woman
Rio Grande
The Secret Gift
The Symbol of the
Unconquered
The Third Woman
The Tiger's Coat
A Tokio Siren
Uncharted Channels
White Youth
Who's Your Servant?
Within Our Gates

1920? Broken Hearts
The Greatest Love
Her Story
Reformation
The Scarlet Dragon

1921 Across the Divide
All Souls' Eve
Anne of Little Smoky
As the World Rolls On
The Barricade
Bits of Life
Black Roses
The Burden of Race
By Right of Birth
The Call of His People
The Cave Girl
Cheated Love
A Child in Pawn
Cotton and Cattle
Diane of Star Hollow
A Divorce of Convenience
The Double O
Fifty Candles
The First Born
A Fool's Promise
A Giant of His Race
The Girl from God's
Country
The Green-Eyed Monster
Guile of Women
The Gunsaulus Mystery
Hearts of the Woods
Hold Your Horses
The Hunger of the Blood
The Hypocrite
The Kiss
The Land of Hope
Little Italy
Little Miss Hawkshaw
Lonely Heart
Lotus Blossom
Love's Plaything
The Lure of a Woman
Made in Heaven
The Man from Texas
A Modern Cain
The Money Maniac
The Negro of Today

No Woman Knows
One Man in a Million
Puppets of Fate
The Secret Sorrow
The Shadow
Shadows of the West
Shame
Society Snobs
The Sport of the Gods
The Swamp
The Syrian Immigrant
A Tale of Two Worlds
That Girl Montana
Through the Back Door
Ties of Blood
When the Clock Struck
Nine
Where Lights Are Low
Wing Toy
Wolves of the North

1921? The Slave Market
The Supreme Passion
[Unidentified Film]

1922 Anna Ascends
Big Stakes
Blazing Arrows
Breaking Home Ties
The Bull-Dogger
A California Romance
Captain Fly-by-Night
Cardigan
Come On Over
The Crimson Skull
Cross Roads
The Crow's Nest
The Cub Reporter
The Dungeon
East Is West
Easy Money
Fair Lady
The Five Dollar Baby
Flesh and Blood
Foolish Lives
For His Mother's Sake
The Good Provider
The Great Alone
The Greatest Sin
The Guttersnipe
The Half Breed
The Hands of Nara
Head over Heels
Hungry Hearts
Little Miss Smiles
The Man with Two Mothers
The Mohican's Daughter
My Boy
Nanook of the North
One Eighth Apache
Pals of the West
Pawn Ticket 210
Peacock Alley
The Perfect Dreamer
The Power of Love
The Pride of Palomar
Saturday Night
The Schemers
The Scrapper
Second Hand Rose
Shadows
The Sign of the Rose
Silver Spurs
Sky High
Solomon in Society
The Son of the Wolf
Spitfire
Square Joe
The Top O' the Morning
Uncle Jasper's Will
Undisputed Evidence
The Virgin of Seminole
When East Comes West
Winning of the West
The Woman He Loved
You Can't Keep a Good
Man Down

1923 Anna Christie
April Showers
Backbone
Breaking into Society
Crashin' Thru
Deceit
The Devil's Match
Fashion Row
Flames of Wrath
His Great Chance
The Huntress

Jamestown
Jealous Husbands
Little Old New York
The Lone Wagon
Look Your Best
The Miracle Makers
None So Blind
Potash and Perlmutter
Purple Dawn
Regeneration
Ruggles of Red Gap
Scars of Jealousy
The Secret of the Pueblo
A Shot in the Night
Snowdrift
The Spider and the Rose
The Sting of the Scorpion
Suzanna
Thirty Days
Tuskegee Finds the Way
Out
The Victor
The White Flower

1924 Birthright
The Broken Law
California in '49
Conductor 1492
A Debtor to the Law
Defying the Law
Down by the Rio Grande
East of Broadway
Fools' Highway
The Heritage of the Desert
His Darker Self
The House Behind the
Cedars
In High Gear
In Hollywood With Potash
and Perlmutter
The Lightning Rider
The Lure of Love
The Mine with the Iron
Door
The Night Hawk
North of Nevada
North of 36
The Pell Street Mystery
Peter Pan
Racing Luck
Smiling Hate
So Big
A Son of Satan
Tongues of Flame
Two Shall Be Born
Unseen Hands
Untamed Youth
Welcome Stranger
Yankee Speed

1924? The Flaming Crisis

1925 Abie's Imported Bride
The Beautiful City
The Black Boomerang
Body and Soul
Brand of Cowardice
Braveheart
Cobra
Custer's Last Fight
A Daughter of the Sioux
The Devil's Disciple
Don Q, Son of Zorro
The Fearless Lover
Flower of Night
Friendly Enemies
Galloping Vengeance
The Gold Hunters
The Greatest Love of All
His People
Hogan's Alley
Irish Luck
Justice of the Far North
Kivalina of the Ice Lands
Lights of Old Broadway
The Man in Blue
The Manicure Girl
Marcus Garland
The Midnight Girl
My Son
Old Clothes
One of the Bravest
The Prairie Wife
Quicker'n Lightnin'
Red Love
The Red Rider
Salome of the Tenements
Scarlet Saint
The Scarlet West

A Son of His Father
Speed Wild
Tearing Through
The Thundering Herd
Tonio, Son of the Sierras
The True North
Warrior Gap
The Wild Bull's Lair

1926 April Fool
The Barrier
Blarney
Broken Hearts
Buffalo Bill on the U. P.
Trail
The Campus Flirt
The Cohens and Kellys
The Conjure Woman
Desert Gold
The Devil Horse
The Fighting Deacon
The Fighting Edge
The Flaming Frontier
The Flying Ace
The Frontier Trail
General Custer at Little Big
Horn
Into Her Kingdom
Irene
Kosher Kitty Kelly
Laddie
The Last Frontier
The Little Irish Girl
Meet the Prince
Millionaires
Pals in Paradise
The Passaic Textile Strike
A Prince of His Race
Private Izzy Murphy
Puppets
Reckless Money
Rose of the Tenements
Shadows of Chinatown
The Strong Man
Sweet Daddies
Sweet Rosie O'Grady
A Trip to Chinatown
Twin Triggers
Under Fire
The Vanishing American
War Paint

1926? The House on Cedar Hill
Ten Nights in a Barroom

1927 Aflame in the Sky
The Auctioneer
Bitter Apples
Blind Alleys
The Broken Violin
California
The Callahans and the
Murphys
Children of Fate
The Chinese Parrot
Clancy's Kosher Wedding
The Devil's Saddle
Don Mike
The Dove
Drums of the Desert
The Fighting Hombre
Finnegan's Ball
For the Love of Mike
Frisco Sally Levy
The Frontiersman
The Gay Defender
Ham and Eggs at the Front
A Harp in Hock
Heroes in Blue
His Foreign Wife
Irish Hearts
Jake the Plumber
[Japanese-American Film]
Lost at the Front
The Love Mart
McFadden's Flats
The Millionaire
Old San Francisco
Open Range
The Overland Stage
Pleasure Before Business
Poro College in Moving
Pictures
Primitive Love
The Princess from Hoboken
Red Clay
The Red Raiders
Roarin' Broncs
Rose of the Golden West

Sailor Izzy Murphy
Sally in Our Alley
The Scar of Shame
The Shamrock and the Rose
The Slaver
The Spider's Web
Spoilers of the West
Topsy and Eva
Turkish Delight
The Way of All Flesh
Whispering Sage
White Gold
Wild Geese
Winners of the Wilderness
With Sitting Bull at the
Spirit Lake Massacre

1927? El que a hierro mata
You Can't Win

1928 Absent
Anybody Here Seen Kelly?
Black Gold
Breed of the Sunsets
The Broken Mask
The Cameraman
The Canyon of Adventure
The Cavalier
Chinatown Charlie
The Cohens and the Kellys
in Paris
The Crash
Diamond Handcuffs
Eleven P.M.
Flying Romeos
George Washington Cohen
The Glorious Trail
The Great White North
The Hawk's Nest
Heart Trouble
Hold 'Em Yale
The House of Scandal
The Jazz Singer
Kit Carson
The Mating Call
The Midnight Ace
Mother Machree
The Night Bird
Orphan of the Sage
Ramona
Ransom
The Rawhide Kid
The Riding Renegade
Riley the Cop
El Robin Hood de México
The Secret Hour
A Ship Comes In
Sins of the Fathers
Tenderfeet
Thirty Years Later
Tyrant of Red Gulch
Uncle Tom's Cabin
United States Smith
Vamping Venus
The Wages of Sin
We Americans
Wheel of Chance
Wyoming

1929 Abie's Irish Rose
Chinatown Nights
The Cohens and Kellys in
Atlantic City
The Desert Rider
East Side Sadie
Evangeline
Frozen Justice
Hallelujah
Hambre
Hawk of the Hills
Hearts in Dixie
In Old Arizona
In Old California
The Invaders
Is Everybody Happy?
Die Königsloge
Love, Live and Laugh
Lucky Boy
Masked Emotions
Mister Antonio
Mother's Boy
The Overland Telegraph
The Peacock Fan
Redskin
Romance of the Rio Grande
Señor Americano
Show Boat
Sioux Blood
Smiling Irish Eyes

Sombras habaneras
This Is Heaven
Thunderbolt
Welcome Danger
When Men Betray
Why Bring That Up?
The Witching Eyes
Wolf Song
The Younger Generation

1930 Abraham Lincoln
Alma de gaucho
Amor audaz
Anna Christie
Anybody's War
The Arizona Kid
Around the Corner
Así es la vida
The Bad Man
Behind the Make-Up
Big Boy
The Big Pond
The Break Up
Las campanas de Capistrano
Una cana al aire
Cascarrabias
Charros, gauchos y manolas
Check and Double Check
Chijiku wo mawasuru
chikara
The Cohens and the Kellys
in Scotland
Cuando el amor ríe
El cuerpo del delito
A Daughter of the Congo
¡De frente, marchen!
Del mismo barro
El dios del mar
Doña mentiras
East Is West
Easy Street
Estrellados
Eternal Fools (Ewige
Naranim)
La fuerza del querer
Galas de la Paramount
Georgia Rose
The Grand Parade
Un hombre de suerte
La jaula de los leones
Kathleen Mavourneen
The Kibitzer
King of Jazz
Ladies Love Brutes
A Lady to Love
The Lash
The Last Dance
Locuras de amor
Los que danzan
The Melody Man
Monsieur le Fox
My Yiddishe Mama
Olimpia
On the Border
El precio de un beso
El presidio
El príncipe del dólar
Revista Hispano-Americana
La rosa de fuego
El secreto del doctor
Sei tu l'amore
Sevilla de mis amores
She Got What She Wanted
The Silent Enemy
Sins of the Children
Sombras de gloria
Son of the Gods
Song of the Caballero
Le spectre vert
Sunny Skies
Take the Heir
Toda una vida
Tom Sawyer
El último de los Vargas
El valiente
La voluntad del muerto
Whoopee
Wu Li Chang

1931 Aloha
The Avenger
Beyond Victory
The Black Camel
Buster se marie
Un caballero de frac
Los calaveras
Call of the Rockies
Carne de cabaret

La carta
La cautivadora
Cavalier of the West
Charlie Chan Carries On
Cheri-Bibi
Chérie
Chinatown After Dark
Cimarron
The Cisco Kid
El código penal
The Cohens and Kellys in
Africa
El comediante
¿Conoces a tu mujer?
Così è la vita
Cuerpo y alma
Dämon des Meeres
La dama atrevida
Del infierno al cielo
Delicious
Don Juan diplomático
Drácula
Die Dreigroschenoper
Echec au roi
En cada puerto un amor
Esclavas de la moda
The Exile
La fiesta del diablo
Fighting Caravans
La fruta amarga
Gente alegre
Gentleman's Fate
La gran jornada
The Great Meadow
The Guilty Generation
Hay que casar al príncipe
Huckleberry Finn
The Hurricane Horseman
El impostor
La incorregible
Jenny Lind
Kismet
Law of the Tong
La ley del harem
Little Caesar
La llama sagrada
Lo mejor es reír
Las luces de Buenos Aires
Mamá
Die Maske Fällt
Mi último amor
Mr. Lemon of Orange
Monerías
La mujer X
Noche de duendes
Nuit d'Espagne
Oklahoma Jim
Pagliacci
Pardon Us
El pasado acusa
Le père célibataire
Personal Maid
Le petit café
Politiquerías
El príncipe gondolero
El proceso de Mary Dugan
La pura verdad
Quand on est belle
Regeneración
La regina di Sparta
Resurrección
Riders of the Rio
Shulamith
Skyline
Smart Money
Sombras del circo
Soyons gais
The Squaw Man
Street Scene
Su noche de bodas
Su última noche
Such Is Life
El tenorio del harem
Three Who Loved
Tropennächte
The Voice of Israel
The White Renegade
Women Love Once
Yankee Don
Young Sinners
Zein Weib's Lubovnick

1931? La porta del destino

1932 Amor in montagna
Amor y vida
Amore e morte
L'athlète incomplet

The Black King
Le bluffeur
Border Devils
El caballero de la noche
Call Her Savage
Le cas du docteur Brenner
Charlie Chan's Chance
The Cohens and Kellys in
 Hollywood
¿Cuándo te suicidas?
Cuore d'emigrante
Dangers of the Arctic
A Daughter of Her People
Flesh
The Forty-Niners
La foule hurle
The Galloping Kid
Genoveffa
The Golden West
Harlem Is Heaven
The Hatchet Man
The Heart of New York
Hearts of Humanity
Une heure près de toi
Hidden Valley
Hollywood, ciudad de
 ensueño
El hombre que asesinó
Hombres en mi vida
Huddle
Hypnotized
Igloo
Joseph in the Land of Egypt
Law and Lawless
Ljubav i strast
Marido y mujer
The Match King
Mazel Tov
Me and My Gal
Men Are Such Fools
Mystery Ranch
No Greater Love
O festino o la legge
Out of the Crimson Fog
Parigi affascina; ovvero,
 Malavita
Le plombier amoureux
The Rainbow Trail
Riders of the Desert
Scarface
The Secrets of Wu Sin
Senza mamma e'nnamurato
So Big
The Son-Daughter
Soñadores de la gloria
Symphony of Six Million
Ten Minutes to Live
Texas Pioneers
Thirteen Steps
Thirteen Women
Tiger Shark
Tormento
Unashamed
Uncle Moses
The Unfortunate Bride
The Vanishing Frontier
Veiled Aristocrats
White Eagle
Wild Horse Mesa
Yiskor

1932?
1933
The Girl from Chicago
L'amour guide
Best of Enemies
Broken Dreams
The California Trail
Charlie Chan's Greatest
 Case
Circle Canyon
The Cohens and Kellys in
 Trouble
Counsellor at Law
Dance Hall Hostess
Diplomaniacs
Dos noches
The Emperor Jones
Espérame
The Eternal Jew
Ever in My Heart
Grand Slam
It's Great to Be Alive
King of the Wild Horses
A Lady's Profession
Let's Fall in Love
Live and Laugh
Man from Monterey
The Man Who Dared: An
 Imaginative Biography

Melodía de arrabal
La melodía prohibida
No dejes la puerta abierta
Obey the Law
Olsen's Big Moment
Primavera en otoño
Racetrack
Rafter Romance
El rey de los gitanos
Robbers' Roost
Song of the Eagle
The Telegraph Trail
Thundering Herd
Victims of Persecution
Una viuda romántica
The Wandering Jew
Yo, tú y ella

1933?
1934
Scandal
As the Earth Turns
The Battling Buckaroo
Behold My Wife!
Beloved
Blossom Time
Broadway Bill
La buenaventura
The Cactus Kid
Call of the Coyote
Un capitán de cosacos
Caravane
The Cat's-Paw
Charlie Chan in London
Charlie Chan's Courage
Cheyenne Sun Dance
Chloe: Love Is Calling You
La ciudad de cartón
Coming Out Party
La cruz y la espada
Cuesta abajo
Dos más uno, dos
Drums O' Voodoo
Eskimo
The Fighting Hero
Fighting Through
Las fronteras del amor
Granaderos del amor
The Great Flirtation
He Was Her Man
Imitation of Life
Judge Priest
Laughing Boy
Lazy River
Limehouse Blues
The Lone Defender
Massacre
Nada más que una mujer
'Neath the Arizona Skies
Operator 13
Our Daily Bread
The Prescott Kid
The Rabbi's Power
Riding Speed
She Was a Lady
Song of the Islands
Stand Up and Cheer!
The Star Packer
Straight Is the Way
Strange Wives
El tango en Broadway
Tres amores
The Unknown Soldier
 Speaks
La veuve joyeuse
Wagon Wheels
What a Mother-in-Law!
Wheels of Destiny
White Heat
The Youth of Russia

1934?
1935
Harlem After Midnight
Alas sobre el Chaco
Angelina o el honor de un
 brigadier
Annie Oakley
¡Asegure a su mujer!
Bar-Mitzvah
Black Fury
Bordertown
El cantante de Nápoles
Captured in Chinatown
Charlie Chan in Egypt
Charlie Chan in Paris
Charlie Chan in Shanghai
Chinatown Squad
Circle of Death
Cowboy Holiday
Cyclone of the Saddle
The Cyclone Ranger

De la sartén al fuego
El día que me quieras
Fighting Pioneers
Harmony Lane
His Family Tree
Un hombre peligroso
L'homme des Folies
 Bergère
The Irish in Us
Julieta compra un hijo
Lem Hawkins' Confession
The Little Colonel
The Littlest Rebel
McFadden's Flats
Melody Trail
Naughty Marietta
A Night at the Opera
A Night at the Ritz
No matarás
North of Arizona
Piernas de seda
Range Warfare
Rendezvous
Rescue Squad
Riddle Ranch
Romance in Manhattan
Rosa de Francia
Ruggles of Red Gap
Señora casada necesita
 marido
Shir Hashirim
The Singing Vagabond
So Red the Rose
Tango Bar
Te quiero con locura
Texas Terror
The Wedding Night
The Winning Ticket
Wolf Riders
The Yiddish King Lear

1935?
1936
The Irish Gringo
Aces and Eights
After the Thin Man
Amor que vuelve
Below the Deadline
The Bold Caballero
Border Phantom
Charlie Chan at the Circus
Charlie Chan at the Race
 Track
Charlie Chan's Secret
Contra la corriente
El crimen de media noche
Custer's Last Stand
Dancing Pirate
Dangerous Intrigue
Daniel Boone
Desert Gold
El diablo del mar
Dimples
Down to the Sea
Ellis Island
For the Service
General Spanky
The Glory Trail
The Green Pastures
Hair-Trigger Casey
Human Cargo
It Had to Happen
Kelly the Second
Klondike Annie
The Last of the Mohicans
Laughing Irish Eyes
Let's Sing Again
Love and Sacrifice
Mad Holiday
Muss 'Em Up
My American Wife
Paddy O'Day
The Phantom of Santa Fe
Pinto Rustlers
The Prisoner of Shark
 Island
Rainbow on the River
Ramona
Rebellion
Ride, Ranger, Ride
Robin Hood of El Dorado
Rose of the Rancho
Sea Spoilers
Show Boat
Silly Billies
Sins of Man
Song of the Gringo
Star for a Night
Sum Hun

Sutter's Gold
Temptation
The Traitor
Treachery Rides the Range
Tundra
La última cita
West of Nevada
Winterset
Yellow Cargo
Yiddle with His Fiddle

1937
Arshin Mal Alan
Bargain with Bullets
The Barrier
Big City
Black Legion
Boots and Saddles
Border Cafe
Boy of the Streets
The Californian
The Cantor's Son
El capitán Tormenta
El carnaval del diablo
Charlie Chan at the
 Olympics
Charlie Chan at the Opera
Charlie Chan on Broadway
Dark Manhattan
The Devil's Playground
Drums of Destiny
Green Fields
Harlem on the Prairie
Hills of Old Wyoming
The Holy Oath
I Want to Be a Mother
It Could Happen to You
The Jester (Der
 Purimspieler)
Law and Lead
Life Begins in College
Maid of Salem
Man of the People
Manhattan Merry-Go-Round
Music for Madame
Natalka Poltavka
Nation Aflame
Old Louisiana
One Mile from Heaven
The Plainsman
Prairie Thunder
The Riders of the Whistling
 Skull
Shadows of the Orient
Slave Ship
Song of the City
Souls at Sea
A Study of Negro Artists
Thank You, Mr. Moto
That Girl from Paris
That I May Live
Think Fast, Mr. Moto
Underworld
Waikiki Wedding
We Work Again
Where Is My Child?

1938
The Adventures of Tom
 Sawyer
The Beloved Brat
Birthright
Breaking the Ice
The Buccaneer
California Frontier
Castillos en el aire
Charlie Chan at Monte
 Carlo
City Streets
Dangerous to Know
Daughter of Shanghai
Di que me quieres
The Duke Is Tops
Gateway
God's Step Children
Gone Harlem
Happy Landing
Hawaii Calls
Hits and Bits of 1938
In Old Chicago
Josette
Life Goes On
Little Miss Roughneck
Marusia
Mis dos amores
Mr. Moto Takes a Chance
Mr. Moto's Gamble
Mr. Wong, Detective
My Lucky Star
Outlaw Express

Outside of Paradise
Passport Husband
Policy Man
The Power of Life
The Rage of Paris
Rascals
The Renegade Ranger
Road Demon
The Singing Blacksmith
Spawn of the North
Speed to Burn
Spirit of Youth
Sugar Hill Baby
Swing!
The Texans
The Toy Wife
Two Gun Man from Harlem
Two Sisters
La vida bohemia
Wild Horse Canyon
Zamboanga

1938? Amore che non torna
I due gemelli

1939 The Adventures of
Huckleberry Finn
Allegheny Uprising
Bad Lands
A Brivele der Mamen
The Bronze Buckaroo
Charlie Chan at Treasure
Island
Charlie Chan in Honolulu
Charlie Chan in Reno
The Cisco Kid and the Lady
City in Darkness
Confessions of a Nazi Spy
Cossacks in Exile
Daughter of the Tong
Daughters Courageous
The Devil's Daughter
Double Deal
Drifting Westward
Drums Along the Mohawk
The Escape
The Fighting Gringo
Fisherman's Wharf
Forged Passport
Frontiers of '49
Gang Smashers
The Girl from Mexico
Gone With the Wind
Harlem Rides the Range
Heaven with a Barbed Wire
Fence
Los hijos mandan
In Old Caliente
La Inmaculada
Judge Hardy and Son
Keep Punching
King of Chinatown
Kol Nidre
Let Freedom Ring
The Light Ahead
Lying Lips
Mamele
Man of Conquest
Miracle on Main Street
Mirele Efros
Mr. Moto in Danger Island
Mr. Moto Takes a Vacation
Mr. Moto's Last Warning
Mr. Wong in Chinatown
Moon over Harlem
Motel the Operator
Mothers of Today
My Son
The Mystery of Mr. Wong
One Dark Night
El otro soy yo
Papá soltero
Reform School
The Return of the Cisco
Kid
Stand Up and Fight
Straight to Heaven
Tevya
Trigger Fingers
El trovador de la radio
Verbena trágica
Waterfront
Way Down South
Winner Take All

1939? A Chinese Gains a Fortune
in America
1940 Am I Guilty?
Americaner Schadchen
Arizona Frontier
Behind the News
Broken Strings
Charlie Chan at the Wax
Museum
Charlie Chan in Panama
Charlie Chan's Murder
Cruise
Covered Wagon Days
Cuando canta la Ley
Doomed to Die
East of the River
Eli Eli
Elsa Maxwell's Public Deb
No. 1
Escape
Escape to Glory
The Fatal Hour
The Fighting 69th
Gang War
The Gay Caballero
George Washington Carver
Geronimo
Girl from God's Country
The Great Advisor
Hawaii
Her Second Mother
Hi-Yo Silver
Hua Chio Juh Guang
If I Had My Way
Jennie
The Jewish Melody
Kit Carson
Knute Rockne—All
American
Little Nellie Kelly
Lucky Cisco Kid
The Man I Married
The Mark of Zorro
Mexican Spitfire
Mexican Spitfire Out West
Midnight Shadow
Murder over New York
Music in My Heart
Mystery in Swing
New Moon
Northwest Passage (Book
I—Rogers' Rangers)
The Notorious Elinor Lee
Overture to Glory
Paradise in Harlem
Perfidia
Phantom of Chinatown
Prairie Schooners
The Ramparts We Watch
Rhythm of the Rio Grande
Santa Fe Trail
Son of Ingagi
Taku
Tengo fe en ti
They Knew What They
Wanted
Three Cheers for the Irish
Three Faces West
Too Many Girls
The Tragedy of
Carpatho-Ukraine
Viva Cisco Kid
The Way of All Flesh
While Thousands Cheer
Won Lee Shuen Fu
Young Buffalo Bill
1940? Mr. Washington Goes to
Town
1941 Accent on Love
Adam Had Four Sons
Belle Starr
Birth of the Blues
Caught in the Act
Charlie Chan in Rio
Come Live with Me
Dead Men Tell
Doomed Caravan
The Face Behind the Mask
Four Shall Die
The Gang's All Here
Gauchos of Eldorado
Golden Gate Girl
Hold Back the Dawn
Hurry, Charlie, Hurry
Ice-Capades
In the Land of the Navajo

King of the Zombies
Lady from Louisiana
Land of Liberty
Louisiana Purchase
Mazel Tov Yidden
The Mexican Spitfire's Baby
Min Jok Jay Hung Sing
Murder on Lenox Avenue
Mutiny in the Arctic
Mystery Ship
New York Town
Ten Ostatni
The Pioneers
Playmates
Prairie Pioneers
Ride on Vaquero
Road Agent
Romance of the Rio Grande
Saddlemates
Secret of the Wastelands
Sullivan's Travels
Sun Valley Serenade
Sunday Sinners
They Dare Not Love
This Woman Is Mine
Thunder Over the Prairie
Under Fiesta Stars
Up Jumped the Devil
Virginia
Western Union
Where Did You Get That
Girl?
Wiejskie Wesele
You're Out of Luck
Z Dymem Pożarów
1941? The Blood of Jesus
Hampton Institute: Its
Program of Education for
Life
1942 Across the Pacific
All Through the Night
American Empire
Apache Trail
Below the Border
Castle in the Desert
Cat People
Dr. Gillespie's New
Assistant
Foreign Agent
Friendly Enemies
From Across the Border
Gentleman Jim
Holiday Inn
In This Our Life
Juke Girl
King of the Stallions
Lawless Plainsmen
Let's Get Tough!
Little Tokyo, U.S.A.
Lucky Ghost
Mexican Spitfire at Sea
Mexican Spitfire Sees a
Ghost
Mexican Spitfire's Elephant
Mokey
The Navy Comes Through
Nazi Agent
North to the Klondike
Prisoner of Japan
Professor Creeps
Rio Rita
Rubber Racketeers
Secret Enemies
Seven Sweethearts
Shut My Big Mouth
Song of the Islands
Submarine Raider
Sunday Punch
Syncopation
Take My Life
Tales of Manhattan
They Died With Their Boots
On
Tortilla Flat
Twin Beds
Unseen Enemy
Valley of Hunted Men
Valley of the Sun
The Vanishing Virginian
We Were Dancing
Whispering Ghosts
Wings for the Eagle
Woman of the Year
Young America

1943 Action in the North Atlantic
Air Force
The Amazing Mrs. Holliday
Bataan
Border Patrol
Cabin in the Sky
Crash Dive
Crime Smasher
Deerslayer
Dixie
Dr. Gillespie's Criminal
Case
Doughboys in Ireland
Fighting Americans
Frontier Fury
The Gang's All Here
Gangway for Tomorrow
Gin Guo Chin Yuan
The Girl from Monterrey
Good Luck, Mr. Yates
His Butler's Sister
Hitler's Children
In Old Oklahoma
Jack London
Ladies' Day
Land of Hunted Men
The Law Rides Again
The Leopard Man
Let's Have Fun
Marching On!
Margin for Error
The Meanest Man in the
World
Mexican Spitfire's Blessed
Event
Mr. Lucky
The Outlaw
The Ox-Bow Incident
Redhead from Manhattan
Riding High
Stormy Weather
Svenskt I Och Omkring
New York
Tahiti Honey
They Came to Blow Up
America
Three Hearts for Julia
Wagon Tracks West
What's Buzzin' Cousin?
Wintertime
Yankee Doodle Dandy
1944 Address Unknown
An American Romance
Andy Hardy's Blonde
Trouble
Black Magic
Block Busters
Buffalo Bill
Charlie Chan in the Secret
Service
Chin Hai In Siong
The Chinese Cat
Chip Off the Old Block
Cry of the Werewolf
Dark Waters
Going My Way
Guon Min Guh Lu
Hi, Beautiful
Knickerbocker Holiday
Kuan Fong Lang Tyeh
Lady, Let's Dance!
Lake Placid Serenade
Lifeboat
Marshal of Reno
Minstrel Man
Mr. Skeffington
My Pal Wolf
The Negro Soldier
Outlaw Trail
The Racket Man
Riding West
The San Antonio Kid
Sheriff of Las Vegas
Since You Went Away
Slightly Terrific
Something for the Boys
Sonora Stagecoach
The Sullivans
Tahiti Nights
Tender Comrade
They Live in Fear
Three Men in White
Tomorrow the World!
Tucson Raiders
Vigilantes of Dodge City
Waterfront
We've Come a Long, Long
Way

1945
Anoush
The Bells of St. Mary's
Betrayal from the East
Between Two Women
The Cisco Kid Returns
Club Havana
Colorado Pioneers
The Dolly Sisters
Escape in the Fog
The Gay Senorita
The Great John L.
Great Stagecoach Robbery
The House on 92nd St.
I Love a Bandleader
In Old New Mexico
The Jade Mask
Jealousy
Johnny Angel
A Medal for Benny
The Mummy's Curse
El Navajo
The Navajo Trail
Nob Hill
Of One Blood
Our Vines Have Tender
   Grapes
Phantom of the Plains
Pride of the Marines
Rhapsody in Blue
Salome, Where She Danced
Samurai
The Scarlet Clue
The Shanghai Cobra
South of the Rio Grande
Sunbonnet Sue
A Tree Grows in Brooklyn
The Valley of Decision
Wanderer of the Wasteland
Where Do We Go From
   Here?

1946
Abie's Irish Rose
Bad Bascomb
Beauty and the Bandit
Beware
Border Bandits
Bringing Up Father
California Gold Rush
Canyon Passage
Cuban Pete
Dangerous Money
Dark Alibi
Dirty Gertie from Harlem,
   U.S.A.
Don Ricardo Returns
The Face of Marble
G. I. War Brides
Gas House Kids
The Gay Cavalier
The Gentleman Misbehaves
Mantan Messes Up
Notorious
The Red Dragon
Rendezvous 24
Renegade Girl
Romance of the West
The Sailor Takes a Wife
Santa Fe Uprising
Saratoga Trunk
Shadows Over Chinatown
Sheriff of Redwood Valley
Singin' in the Corn
Slightly Scandalous
Song of the South
South of Monterey
Stars on Parade
Strange Voyage
Sun Valley Cyclone
Sunset Pass
Swamp Fire
Tall, Tan and Terrific
That Man of Mine
Three Wise Fools
Till the End of Time
The Trap
Wild Beauty
Wild West
Without Reservations

1946?
Beale Street Mama
Fight That Ghost
Go Down, Death!
Harlem on Parade
House-Rent Party
Yee Sio Bo Laan Sin

1947
The Adventures of Don
   Coyote
Bells of San Fernando
Black Gold
Body and Soul
Bowery Buckaroos
Boy! What a Girl!
Buck Privates Come Home
Buffalo Bill Rides Again
The Burning Cross
Calendar Girl
California
Carnegie Hall
The Chinese Ring
Citizen Saint
Copacabana
Crossfire
Dangerous Venture
Dark Delusion
Desperate
Duel in the Sun
Easy Come, Easy Go
The Farmer's Daughter
The Foxes of Harrow
Going to Glory, Come to
   Jesus
Hi De Ho
Humoresque
It Had To Be You
Jiggs and Maggie in Society
Jivin' in Be-Bop
The Jolson Story
Juke Joint
King of the Bandits
Last of the Redmen
The Last Round-Up
Little Mister Jim
Mantan Runs for Mayor
Marshal of Cripple Creek
The Mighty McGurk
My Wild Irish Rose
New Orleans
Northwest Outpost
On the Old Spanish Trail
Oregon Trail Scouts
The Peanut Man
Pirates of Monterey
Reet, Petite and Gone
The Return of Rin Tin Tin
Ride the Pink Horse
Riding the California Trail
Robin Hood of Monterey
Rustlers of Devil's Canyon
Sepia Cinderella
Spoilers of the North
Thunder Mountain
Under the Tonto Rim
Untamed Fury
Vigilantes of Boomtown
West to Glory
Wild Horse Mesa

1947?
Bow Yu Lee Hua
Gin Fen Nee Shaan
Hai Jeow Chin Yuan
Hong Yien Fei Bo Ming
Hoon Si Gway Lai
Jia O Tien Chen
Luan Feng Heh Ming
Return of Mandy's Husband
Sing Yun Sin Nian
Swanee Showboat
What a Guy
Yu Luh Shen Ping

1948
Angel in Exile
The Arizona Ranger
The Betrayal
Big City
The Boy with Green Hair
Call Northside 777
Cry of the City
Docks of New Orleans
The Dude Goes West
The Feathered Serpent
The Fight Never Ends
Fighting Father Dunne
Flight to the Sun
Fort Apache
Four Faces West
Fury at Furnace Creek
Gentleman's Agreement
The Golden Eye
Gun Smugglers
Guns of Hate
Half Past Midnight
Harpoon
I Remember Mama

Indian Agent
Jiggs and Maggie in Court
Key Largo
Killer Diller
The Lady from Shanghai
Louisiana Story
The Luck of the Irish
Miracle in Harlem
The Miracle of the Bells
Moonrise
Music Man
My Girl Tisa
Night Wind
Old Los Angeles
Open Secret
The Paleface
Reaching from Heaven
Red River
Renegades of Sonora
Rocky
Shanghai Chest
Shep Comes Home
Silver Trails
Singin' Spurs
16 Fathoms Deep
Sleep, My Love
Strange Victory
Tap Roots
The Time of Your Life
Unconquered
Up in Central Park
Western Heritage

1948?
Boarding House Blues
Jeng Yien Doe Lee
Junction 88
Kuang Feng Juu Yien Fay
Too Yien Fen Fong

1949
Anna Lucasta
Answer for Anne
Apache Chief
Arctic Fury
Arctic Manhunt
Border Incident
Boston Blackie's Chinese
   Venture
Brothers in the Saddle
C-Man
Call of the Forest
The Clay Pigeon
Colorado Territory
The Cowboy and the
   Indians
The Cowboy and the
   Prizefighter
The Dalton Gang
The Daring Caballero
Daughter of the West
The Fighting Kentuckian
The Gay Amigo
The Girl from Jones Beach
The Golden Stallion
Harbor of Missing Men
Home of the Brave
House of Strangers
Illegal Entry
Jiggs and Maggie in Jackpot
   Jitters
Jigsaw
The Kissing Bandit
Knock on Any Door
Laramie
Lookout Sister
Lost Boundaries
Lust for Gold
Masked Raiders
Massacre River
The Mysterious Desperado
Pinky
Portrait of Jennie
The Prairie
Prejudice
The Quiet One
Ranger of Cherokee Strip
The Red Menace
Ride, Ryder, Ride!
Riders of the Range
Roll Thunder Roll!
Rose of the Yukon
Rustlers
Satan's Cradle
Shamrock Hill
She Wore a Yellow Ribbon
The Sky Dragon
Souls of Sin
Stagecoach Kid
Stallion Canyon

The Story of Seabiscuit
Streets of Laredo
Tale of the Navajos
That Midnight Kiss
Thieves' Highway
3 Godfathers
Top O' the Morning
Tulsa
Tuna Clipper
The Undercover Man
The Valiant Hombre
We Were Strangers

1949?
Come On, Cowboy!
Girl in Room 20
Harlem Follies
The Joint Is Jumpin'
Lang Hu Bee Yuh
She's Too Mean for Me
Shuang Feng Cheo Huang
Yein Dow

1950
Ambush
Annie Get Your Gun
Bandit Queen
The Baron of Arizona
Battleground
Belle of Old Mexico
The Big Hangover
Black Hand
Border Treasure
The Breaking Point
Broken Arrow
Buccaneer's Girl
The Cariboo Trail
Catskill Honeymoon
Cherokee Uprising
Chinatown at Midnight
Colt .45
Comanche Territory
Damien
The Daughter of Rosie
   O'Grady
Davy Crockett, Indian
   Scout
Deported
Devil's Doorway
Emergency Wedding
The Furies
The Girl from San Lorenzo
Give Us This Day
God, Man and Devil
I Killed Geronimo
Indian Territory
Intruder in the Dust
The Iroquois Trail
The Jackie Robinson Story
Jiggs and Maggie Out West
Jolson Sings Again
A Lady Without Passport
Last of the Buccaneers
The Lawless
The Men
The Missourians
Monticello, Here We Come!
Mystery Street
Mystery Submarine
No Way Out
North of the Great Divide
The Palomino
Panic in the Streets
Raiders of Tomahawk Creek
Riders of the Pony Express
Right Cross
Rio Grande
Rio Grande Patrol
Rock Island Trail
Rocky Mountain
Sands of Iwo Jima
So Young, So Bad
Stars in My Crown
Storm Over Wyoming
Sunset in the West
A Ticket to Tomahawk
The Toast of New Orleans
Train to Tombstone
The Traveling Saleswoman
Two Flags West
Winchester '73
Young Daniel Boone
Young Man with a Horn

1950?
Three Daughters

1951
Across the Wide Missouri
Adventures of Captain
   Fabian
Apache Drums
Cavalry Scout
Cuban Fireball

Cyclone Fury
Distant Drums
Five
Flaming Feather
Fort Defiance
Gambling House
The Girl on the Bridge
Go for Broke!
The Great Caruso
The Harlem Globetrotters
The House on Telegraph
    Hill
Hurricane Island
Jim Thorpe—All-American
The Last Outpost
Little Big Horn
The Magnificent Yankee
The Mark of the Renegade
Mask of the Dragon
Molly
Native Son
New Mexico
Oh! Susanna
Only the Valiant
Queen for a Day
The Raging Tide
Saturday's Hero
Show Boat
Slaughter Trail
Snake River Desperadoes
The Steel Helmet
A Streetcar Named Desire
The Tall Target
Teresa
Tomahawk
Warpath
The Well
Westward the Women
When the Redskins Rode
Yes Sir, Mr. Bones

1952 Anything Can Happen
Apache Country
Apache War Smoke
Arctic Flight
The Battle at Apache Pass
Battles of Chief Pontiac
The Big Sky
Brave Warrior
Bright Victory
Buffalo Bill in Tomahawk
    Territory
Bugles in the Afternoon
California Conquest
Desert Pursuit
The Fabulous Senorita
The Fighter
Fort Osage
The Half-Breed
Hiawatha
High Noon
Indian Uprising
The Iron Mistress
It's a Big Country: An
    American Anthology
Japanese War Bride
Kid Monk Baroni
My Man and I
Navajo
The Quiet Man
The Raiders
Red Ball Express
Red Snow
The Ring
Rose of Cimarron
The Savage
Trail of the Arrow
Wagons West
Woman in the Dark

1952? Call of the Navajo

1953 Ambush at Tomahawk Gap
Arrowhead
Beneath the 12-Mile Reef
Bright Road
Captain John Smith and
    Pocahontas
The Charge at Feather River
Column South
Conquest of Cochise
Cry of the Hunted
Dream Wife
The Eddie Cantor Story
Fort Ti
The Glass Wall
The Glory Brigade
The Great Sioux Uprising
Jack McCall Desperado

The Jazz Singer
The Joe Louis Story
Last of the Comanches
The Man Behind the Gun
The Man from the Alamo
The Member of the
    Wedding
The Nebraskan
Old Overland Trail
The Pathfinder
Ride, Vaquero!
San Antone
Sangaree
Seminole
So Big
The Stand at Apache River
The Stars Are Singing
The Sun Shines Bright
Taxi
Thunder Bay
Tonight We Sing
Tumbleweed
War Paint

1953? Tan Dow Jia Jen

1954 Apache
Arrow in the Dust
Barefoot Battalion
Battle of Rogue River
The Black Dakotas
Broken Lance
Carmen Jones
Cattle Queen of Montana
Dangerous Mission
Drum Beat
Drums Across the River
Go Man Go
Hell's Half Acre
Hondo
Indiscretion of an American
    Wife
Massacre Canyon
Overland Pacific
Passion
Salt of the Earth
Saskatchewan
Siege at Red River
Sitting Bull
Taza, Son of Cochise
They Rode West
Thunder Pass
War Arrow
The Yellow Tomahawk

1955 Apache Ambush
Apache Woman
Bad Day at Black Rock
Blackboard Jungle
Brevities of 1955
Chief Crazy Horse
Davy Crockett, King of the
    Wild Frontier
Day of Decision
Duel on the Mississippi
The Far Horizons
Fort Yuma
Foxfire
Good Morning, Miss Dove
The Gun That Won the
    West
Headline Hunters
Indian American
The Indian Fighter
Kentucky Rifle
Kiss of Fire
The Last Command
The Lonesome Trail
The Long Gray Line
A Man Called Peter
Marty
Murder in Villa Capri
Not As a Stranger
The Rose Tattoo
Santa Fe Passage
Seminole Uprising
Seven Angry Men
Seven Cities of Gold
Shotgun
Smoke Signal
Trial
The Vanishing American
The View from Pompey's
    Head
Violent Saturday
White Feather

1955? Yin Hua Chu Chu Kai
1956 Baby Doll
The Benny Goodman Story
The Broken Star
The Burning Hills
The Catered Affair
Comanche
Crowded Paradise
Dakota Incident
Daniel Boone, Trail Blazer
Davy Crockett and the
    River Pirates
Death of a Scoundrel
Frontier Woman
Full of Life
Ghost Town
Giant
Hot Blood
The Last Frontier
The Last Hunt
The Last Wagon
The Lone Ranger
Man from Del Rio
Mohawk
Pillars of the Sky
Quincannon, Frontier Scout
Raw Edge
Reprisal!
Rockin' the Blues
The Searchers
Secret of Treasure
    Mountain
Serenade
7th Cavalry
Singing in the Dark
Walk the Proud Land
Westward Ho the Wagons!
Wetbacks
The White Squaw
The Wild Dakotas

1957 All Mine to Give
Apache Warrior
Band of Angels
Bayou
Beau James
The Brothers Rico
Burden of Truth
The Deerslayer
Dragoon Wells Massacre
Edge of the City
Gun Battle at Monterey
The Guns of Fort Petticoat
The Halliday Brand
Joe Dakota
Journey to Freedom
The Lawless Eighties
Man in the Shadow
The Midnight Story
Naked in the Sun
The Oklahoman
Pawnee
Raiders of Old California
Raintree County
Revolt at Fort Laramie
The Ride Back
Ride Out for Revenge
Run of the Arrow
Satchmo the Great
Segregation and the South
The Tin Star
Tomahawk Trail
Trooper Hook
Twelve Angry Men
War Drums

1958 Ambush at Cimarron Pass
Apache Territory
The Badlanders
Blood Arrow
Bullwhip
The Defiant Ones
Escape from Red Rock
Flaming Frontier
Fort Bowie
Fort Massacre
Frontier Gun
Gun Fever
Gunfire at Indian Gap
Gunman's Walk
Home Before Dark
Houseboat
Kings Go Forth
The Last Hurrah
The Light in the Forest
The Lone Ranger and the
    Lost City of Gold
Machete

Marjorie Morningstar
Never Love a Stranger
Oregon Passage
The Rawhide Trail
Ride a Crooked Trail
St. Louis Blues
Seven Hills of Rome
Sierra Baron
Terror in a Texas Town
Tonka
Touch of Evil
Wild Is the Wind
The Young Lions

1959 Al Capone
Anna Lucasta
The Black Orchid
The Crimson Kimono
Cry Tough
The FBI Story
Gunmen from Laredo
The Hanging Tree
Imitation of Life
Inside the Mafia
The Jayhawkers!
John Paul Jones
The Last Angry Man
Last Train from Gun Hill
Night of the Quarter Moon
Odds Against Tomorrow
The Oregon Trail
Porgy and Bess
Shake Hands with the Devil
The Sheriff of Fractured
    Jaw
Thunder in the Sun
The Wonderful Country
The World, the Flesh and
    the Devil
Yellowstone Kelly
The Young Land

1960 The Adventures of
    Huckleberry Finn
All the Fine Young
    Cannibals
All the Young Men
Cimarron
Comanche Station
The Crowning Experience
The Dark at the Top of the
    Stairs
The Day They Robbed the
    Bank of England
Flaming Star
For the Love of Mike
Hell to Eternity
I Aim at the Stars: the
    Wernher von Braun Story
I Passed for White
Ice Palace
Key Witness
The Last Voyage
Man on a String
Oklahoma Territory
Pay or Die
The Plunderers
The Pusher
Sergeant Rutledge
The Sign of Zorro
Studs Lonigan
Take a Giant Step
This Rebel Breed
The Unforgiven
Walk Like a Dragon
Walk Tall
Weddings and Babies
Wild River

PERSONAL NAME INDEX

★ Entries in the Personal Name Index are arranged alphabetically, with film credits listed below the names of all producers, directors, writers and actors in the book in chronological, then alphabetical, order. Credits have been arranged under "Main entries," that is, the name by which a specific individual was most commonly known is used and all films for that person are listed under a single, main entry name. Alternate names or spelling of names are listed below the main entry, followed by that indidivual's filmography as reflected in *Within Our Gates*.

To arrive at a main entry, the staff ascertained what name a person used for the majority of his or her career or what name modern sources typically have used to identify that individual. While the main entry for some persons were very easy to determine, many required considerable research. Establishment of main entries were based on a variety of sources, including both published and in-progress volumes of the *AFI Catalog of Motion Pictures Produced in the United States*, *Variety* obituaries, various editions of the *Film Daily Year Book*, *The Motion Picture Almanac*, *The Motion Picture Studio Directory* and *The Players Directory*. Additional helpful sources included *The Film Encyclopedia* (original and revised editions) by Ephraim Katz, *Who Was Who on Screen* by Evelyn Mack Truitt, *Who's Who in Hollywood, 1900—1976* by David Ragan, *Black Hollywood* by Gary Null, *The Versatiles* by Alfred E. Twomey and Arthur F. McClure and *Who Is That?* by Warren B. Meyers. A number of other more specialized books on actors, writers and directors, plus books of filmmaking of ethnic groups also proved helpful.

Once the main entry name was determined, we added all of the variations of the name to the entry as same as variations. For example, under the entry for Ahn, Philip, is included the phrase same as, followed by Ahn, Phil and Ahn, Phillip. Ample cross references are supplied to direct the reader from variations to the main entries, for example, under LaRue, "Lash," the reader is directed to the main entry for LaRue, Al "Lash." We have, however, refrained from including superfluous see references, such as Ahn, Phil see Ahn, Philip. When individuals seemed to be known by two or more name variations in equal measure, we simply selected one to be the main entry.

Because films included in *Within Our Gates* were made over the course of fifty years, many problems arose while attempting to determine main entries. Sometimes two different persons of the exact same name were included in the index. For example, actor William Holden (1918—1981) and actor William Holden d. 1932. For these cases, designations were included such as birth or death dates, or other brief distinguishing phrases. To further identify some similar names we have used terms such as *actor*, *African-American actor* or *prod*, and occasionally attached dates of careers when necessary. Additional clarification among the entries is offered with the phrase not the same as when the names of two individuals were so similar that their filmographies might easily be confused.

There are some cases, however, in which exact determinations could not be made. The reader will thus notice the use of the phrase *could be same* as to direct the user to the filmography of another person who could actually be the same, but for whom definitive information was unavailable.

PERSONAL NAME INDEX

Aaker, Lee
1954   Hondo
Aames, Marlene
1948   The Time of Your Life
Abadía, Julio
1931   Monerías
          Su última noche
1935   Rosa de Francia
Abarbanel, Judith *same as*
   Abarbanell, Judith
1932   Uncle Moses
1937   The Cantor's Son
1940   Americaner Schadchen
Abarbanel, Lorraine
1937   The Cantor's Son
Abbas, Abdullah
1937   Big City
1949   We Were Strangers
1953   So Big
1956   Serenade
Abbe, Harry
1927   [Japanese-American Film]
Abbe, Jack
1918   Her American Husband
          Mystic Faces
          Who Is to Blame?
1919   The Tong Man
1920   Locked Lips
1921   Lotus Blossom
          A Tale of Two Worlds
Abbey, Leo
1941   Mutiny in the Arctic
Abbey, William
1938   Hawaii Calls
Abbot, Frank
1925   The Wild Bull's Lair
1938   The Buccaneer
Abbott and Costello *see* **Abbott,**
   Bud; Costello, Lou
Abbott, Aimee
1918   Doing Their Bit
Abbott, Bud
1942   Rio Rita
1947   Buck Privates Come
          Home
Abbott, Dorothy
1948   The Paleface
1950   Annie Get Your Gun
Abbott, George
1929   Why Bring That Up?
1931   La incorregible
          Sombras del circo
1940   Too Many Girls
Abbott, John
1942   Rubber Racketeers
1944   Cry of the Werewolf
1946   Saratoga Trunk
1947   Humoresque
Abbott, Marion
1923   Backbone
Abbott, Richard
1943   Action in the North
          Atlantic
1945   The Valley of Decision
Abbott, Robert S.
1927   The Millionaire
Abbott, Mrs. Robert S.
1927   The Millionaire
Abdo, Eddie
1939   Mr. Moto Takes a
          Vacation
1945   The Mummy's Curse

Abdul, George
1932   Hypnotized
Abdullah, Achmed
1920   Pagan Love
Abe, Utaka
1915   The Cheat
Abel, I. W.
1957   Burden of Truth
Abel, Walter
1920   The North Wind's Malice
1939   Miracle on Main Street
1941   Hold Back the Dawn
1942   Holiday Inn
1944   An American Romance
          Mr. Skeffington
1955   The Indian Fighter
1957   Raintree County
Abeles, Edward
1915   After Five
Abernathy, Master
1914   Uncle Tom's Cabin
Abraham, Jake *same as* **Abrams,**
   Jake *not the same as* **Abrams,**
   Jacob
1921   The Cave Girl
1922   Pawn Ticket 210
Abrahams, Derwin *same as*
   Abrahams, D. M.
1937   Hills of Old Wyoming
1941   Doomed Caravan
          Secret of the Wastelands
1948   Docks of New Orleans
1950   The Girl from San
          Lorenzo
Abramowitz, Bina *same as*
   Abramovitz, Bine
1926   Broken Hearts
1932   The Unfortunate Bride
          Yiskor
Abrams, Dick
1921   The Gunsaulus Mystery
Abrams, Edward R.
1921   The Sport of the Gods
Abrams, Hiram
1919   Hearts of Men
Abrams, Jacob *not the same as*
   Abraham, Jake
1916   A Man of Sorrow
Abrams, Jake *see* **Abraham, Jake**
Abrams, Leon
1945   The Mummy's Curse
Abrams, Rita
1922   The Mohican's Daughter
Abramson, Ivan
1917   One Law for Both
1932   Yiskor
Abramson, Max
1922   My Boy
Abramson, William
1917   One Law for Both
Abril, Dorothy
1916   Alien Souls
Ace, a dog
1940   Girl from God's Country
1943   Jack London
Achard, Marcel
1934   La veuve joyeuse
1935   L'homme des Folies
          Bergère
Achi, Kamaunani
1934   White Heat
Acker, Jean
1921   The Kiss
1925   Braveheart

Acker, Martha
1956   Serenade
Ackerman, Boyd
1948   Up in Central Park
1951   Show Boat
Ackerman, Don
1936   Star for a Night
Ackerman, Gene
1949   Top O' the Morning
Ackerman, Leonard
1959   Al Capone
Ackerman, Walter
1927   Aflame in the Sky
Ackerson, George
1947   Carnegie Hall
1949   Lost Boundaries
1953   The Joe Louis Story
Ackroyd, Jack
1929   Frozen Justice
Acosta, Enrique
1925   Don Q, Son of Zorro
1927   Whispering Sage
1930   Así es la vida
          Una cana al aire
          Estrellados
          Locuras de amor
          El precio de un beso
          Sombras de gloria
1931   Don Juan diplomático
          Monerías
          Pardon Us (*foreign*
            version)
          Politiquerías
1932   Hollywood, ciudad de
            ensueño
1933   Dos noches
          Una viuda romántica
1934   The Prescott Kid
          Tres amores
1935   El cantante de Nápoles
          Te quiero con locura
1936   Ramona
Acosta, Fraser
1934   Nada más que una mujer
1936   Tundra
Acosta, Manuel
1925   Flower of Night
Acosta, Rodolfo *same as* **Acosta,**
   Rudolfo; Acosta, Rudolph
1953   San Antone
1954   Drum Beat
          Hondo
          Passion
1957   Apache Warrior
          Trooper Hook
1960   Flaming Star
          Walk Like a Dragon
Acuff, Eddie
1937   Black Legion
1938   Road Demon
1939   Winner Take All
1940   Charlie Chan in Panama
1942   Dr. Gillespie's New
          Assistant
          In This Our Life
          They Died With Their
           Boots On
          Wings for the Eagle
1943   Yankee Doodle Dandy
1944   Andy Hardy's Blonde
           Trouble
1946   Bad Bascomb
1947   Buck Privates Come
           Home

Adair, Alice
1931   Cimarron
1932   Hypnotized
1935   ¡Asegure a su mujer!
Adair, Jack *not the same as* **Adair,**
   John
1936   After the Thin Man
1937   Manhattan
           Merry-Go-Round
Adair, John *not the same as* **Adair,**
   Jack
1936   Muss 'Em Up
1940   The Ramparts We Watch
Adair, Phyllis
1943   Land of Hunted Men
Adair, Robert
1934   Limehouse Blues
Adair, Virginia
1922   Second Hand Rose
Adalid, Ricardo *same as* **Black,**
   Ricardo Adalid
1955   Seven Cities of Gold
1958   Sierra Baron
Adamovic, Olga
1932   Ljubav i strast
Adams, Abigail *see* **Adams,**
   Tommye
Adams, Barton
1941   Sullivan's Travels
1946   Abie's Irish Rose
Adams, Berle
1946   Beware
1947   Reet, Petite and Gone
1949   Lookout Sister
Adams, Betty
1949   The Dalton Gang
Adams, Carol
1941   Ice-Capades
Adams, Casey
1957   Dragoon Wells Massacre
Adams, Christopher
1944   Since You Went Away
Adams, Claire
1924   The Night Hawk
1934   What a Mother-in-Law!
Adams, Constance
1914   Where the Trail Divides
Adams, Dora
1917   Queen X
Adams, Dorothy
1942   Dr. Gillespie's New
          Assistant
1944   Since You Went Away
1947   The Foxes of Harrow
1948   Unconquered
1950   The Cariboo Trail
1952   Fort Osage
1956   The Broken Star
1958   Gunman's Walk
Adams, Eadie
1937   Big City
Adams, Ernie *same as* **Adams,**
   Ernest; Adams, Ernie S.
1926   Pals in Paradise
1927   The Gay Defender
1934   Broadway Bill
          Operator 13
          The Prescott Kid
1935   Ruggles of Red Gap
1936   My American Wife
          Rose of the Rancho
1937   Man of the People
1938   California Frontier
          The Texans
1941   The Face Behind the
           Mask
          Mystery Ship

Adams, Ernie

Road Agent
1943 Jack London
1944 An American Romance
Lake Placid Serenade
1945 Escape in the Fog
Johnny Angel
Rhapsody in Blue
1946 The Gay Cavalier
The Gentleman
Misbehaves
Three Wise Fools
1947 Buck Privates Come
Home
Desperate
The Mighty McGurk
Robin Hood of Monterey
1948 Fighting Father Dunne

Adams, Eustace L.
1936 Down to the Sea

Adams, Fay
1925 A Daughter of the Sioux
Tonio, Son of the Sierras

Adams, Frankie
1931 Delicious

Adams, Gerald Drayson *same as*
Adams, Gerald
1948 Old Los Angeles
1951 Flaming Feather
1952 The Battle at Apache Pass
1954 Taza, Son of Cochise
1955 Chief Crazy Horse
Duel on the Mississippi
1957 Tomahawk Trail
War Drums

Adams, Jane *same as* **Adams, Poni**
1945 Salome, Where She
Danced
1950 The Girl from San
Lorenzo

Adams, Jimmie
1930 The Grand Parade

Adams, Jo Jo
1955 Brevities of 1955

Adams, Joe *(African-American
actor) not the same as* **Adams,
Joey**
1954 Carmen Jones

Adams, Joey *not the same as*
Adams, Joe *(African-American
actor)*
1956 Singing in the Dark

Adams, Julia
1952 Bright Victory
1953 The Man from the Alamo
The Stand at Apache
River

Adams, Kathryn *(actress), d. 1959*
1917 The Woman and the Beast
1920 Uncharted Channels

Adams, Kathryn *(actress, circa
1940s)*
1940 If I Had My Way

Adams, Lowden
1935 Rendezvous
1937 Big City

Adams, Mary
1952 Bugles in the Afternoon
1957 All Mine to Give

Adams, Nick
1956 The Last Wagon
1959 The FBI Story

Adams, Pearl
1938 The Buccaneer

Adams, Peggy
1917? Barnaby Lee

Adams, Peter
1958 Bullwhip

Adams, Phillip
1958 The Last Hurrah
1960 Sergeant Rutledge

Adams, Poni *see* **Adams, Jane**

Adams, Richard T. *see* **Adams, Ted**
1936 Song of the Gringo
1947 Buffalo Bill Rides Again
1959 The Jayhawkers!

Adams, Robert
1920 Hidden Charms
1921? The Supreme Passion

Adams, Sam
1932 The Golden West
1934 The Cat's-Paw

1941 Mutiny in the Arctic
Adams, Stanley
1957 Trooper Hook
1960 Studs Lonigan

Adams, Ted *same as* **Adams,
Richard T.; Adams, Theodore**
1931 Cavalier of the West
1934 The Battling Buckaroo
1936 Custer's Last Stand
1939 Trigger Fingers
1941 Thunder Over the Prairie
1942 King of the Stallions
1943 Dr. Gillespie's Criminal
Case
1947 The Last Round-Up
Vigilantes of Boomtown
1949 Brothers in the Saddle
Stallion Canyon
1950 I Killed Geronimo
1951 Westward the Women

Adams, Tommye *same as* **Adams,
Abigail**
1943 Tahiti Honey
1945 Our Vines Have Tender
Grapes
1947 Copacabana

Adams, Victor
1933 Counsellor at Law
1937 Charlie Chan on
Broadway

Adams, William
1945 The House on 92nd St.
1959 Odds Against Tomorrow

Adamson, Evelyn
1924 Defying the Law

Adamson, Ewart
1927 Aflame in the Sky
1935 Annie Oakley
1936 Below the Deadline

Adamson, James
1937 Dark Manhattan
1953 Tonight We Sing

Adamson, Victor *see* **Dixon,
Denver**

Adden, Margaret
1943 Dr. Gillespie's Criminal
Case

Addiss, Jus
1951 Queen for a Day

Ade, George
1915 Marse Covington

Adelantado, Fernando
1935 El día que me quieras

Adell, Kay
1945 Where Do We Go From
Here?

Adger, Jules
1943 Cabin in the Sky

Adler, Ben *same as* **Adler, Benny**
1932 Joseph in the Land of
Egypt
1933 The Wandering Jew
1939 The Light Ahead

Adler, Buddy
1951 The Harlem Globetrotters
Saturday's Hero
1953 Last of the Comanches
1955 Violent Saturday
1958 The Young Lions

Adler, Celia
1937 Where Is My Child?

Adler, Charles
1933 Victims of Persecution

Adler, E. *could be same as* **Adler,
Esther**
1940 Americaner Schadchen

Adler, Esther *could be same as*
Adler, E.
1935 The Yiddish King Lear

Adler, Felix
1929 Welcome Danger
1932 Hypnotized

Adler, Ida
1932 Joseph in the Land of
Egypt
1938 Two Sisters

Adler, Jay
1952 My Man and I
1956 The Catered Affair
1960 All the Fine Young
Cannibals

Adler, Julius
1926 Broken Hearts
1932 The Unfortunate Bride
1939 Tevya
1950 Catskill Honeymoon

Adler, Luther
1949 House of Strangers
1956 Hot Blood
1959 The Last Angry Man

Adler, Robert
1948 Cry of the City
Fury at Furnace Creek
The Luck of the Irish
1950 Broken Arrow
No Way Out
A Ticket to Tomahawk
Two Flags West
1954 Broken Lance
Siege at Red River
1955 Violent Saturday
1960 Flaming Star

Adler, Sonya
1932 Joseph in the Land of
Egypt

Adler, Stella *same as* **Ardler, Stella**
1948 My Girl Tisa

Adlon, Duke
1942 Valley of Hunted Men

Adlon, Louis
1938 Happy Landing
1942 Syncopation
1943 Action in the North
Atlantic

Adolfi, John G.
1919 Who's Your Brother?
1925 The Scarlet West

Adolphson, Edvin
1930 Doña mentiras *(foreign
version)*
Un hombre de suerte
(foreign version)

Adoree, Andre
1958 Escape from Red Rock

Adorée, Renée
1921 Made in Heaven
1924 Defying the Law
1926 Blarney
1928 The Mating Call

Adreon, Franklyn
1940 Hi-Yo Silver

Adrian, George
1943 Action in the North
Atlantic

Adrian, Iris
1941 New York Town
1943 Action in the North
Atlantic
His Butler's Sister
Ladies' Day
1948 The Paleface
1949 The Sky Dragon

Agar, John
1948 Fort Apache
1949 She Wore a Yellow
Ribbon
1950 Sands of Iwo Jima
1955 The Lonesome Trail
1958 Frontier Gun

Agee, James
1949 The Quiet One

Agnew, Robert
1922 Pawn Ticket 210

Agresti, Ed
1943 The Leopard Man

Agüeras, José
1931 Las luces de Buenos Aires

Aguglia, Mimi
1931 Mi último amor
1932 Marido y mujer
1933 It's Great to Be Alive
(foreign version)
Primavera en otoño
Una viuda romántica
1934 Tres amores
1935 Señora casada necesita
marido
1943 The Outlaw
1948 Cry of the City
Unconquered
1949 That Midnight Kiss
We Were Strangers
1950 Black Hand
Deported
Right Cross

Aguilar, Perfideo
1956 Giant

Aguvaluk
1925 Kivalina of the Ice Lands

A'Hearne, Tommy
1939 Los hijos mandan

Ahern, Lassie Lou
1928 Uncle Tom's Cabin

Ahn, Philip *same as* **Ahn, Phil;
Ahn, Phillip**
1936 Klondike Annie
1937 Thank You, Mr. Moto
1938 Daughter of Shanghai
Hawaii Calls
1939 Charlie Chan in Honolulu
King of Chinatown
1942 Across the Pacific
Let's Get Tough!
Submarine Raider
1943 The Amazing Mrs.
Holliday
1945 Betrayal from the East
1947 The Chinese Ring
1948 The Miracle of the Bells
1949 Boston Blackie's Chinese
Venture
1950 The Big Hangover
1952 Japanese War Bride
Red Snow
1954 Hell's Half Acre

Ahteenah, Princess
1935 Circle of Death

Aihara, Luis
1951 Go for Broke!

Ainley, Joe
1956 Daniel Boone, Trail
Blazer

Ainley, Richard
1942 Three Hearts for Julia

Ainslee, Marian
1927 California
Winners of the
Wilderness
1929 Hallelujah

Ainsley, Norman
1937 Charlie Chan on
Broadway
Souls at Sea
1941 Hold Back the Dawn

Ainsworth, Helen
1956 Reprisal!
1958 Bullwhip

Ainsworth, Sydney
1920 The Cup of Fury
1921 Hold Your Horses

Ainsworth, Virginia
1924 Yankee Speed

Aiston, Arthur C.
1914 At the Cross Roads

Aitken, Spottiswoode
1915 The Birth of a Nation
1917 Southern Pride
1918 How Could You, Jean?
In Judgment Of
1919 Bonnie, Bonnie Lassie
Evangeline

Akawanush, Chief
1930 The Silent Enemy

Akes, Doris
1941 Up Jumped the Devil

Akimoff, Alex
1949 Illegal Entry
1958 The Last Hurrah

Akin, Mary
1925 My Son

Akins, Claude
1956 The Burning Hills
1957 Joe Dakota
1958 The Defiant Ones
1959 Porgy and Bess
Yellowstone Kelly

Akins, Zoë
1930 Toda una vida
1931 Women Love Once
1936 Show Boat
1938 The Toy Wife

Adler, Julius
1951 Cuban Fireball
1955 The Rose Tattoo
1957 The Brothers Rico

Alana, Edward
1950   Panic in the Streets
Alana, Glenn
1950   Damien
Alaniz, Rico
1950   A Lady Without Passport
1952   California Conquest
          The Fighter
1953   Column South
          Conquest of Cochise
1954   Drum Beat
          Siege at Red River
1955   The Last Command
Alarcón, Francisco
1931   La pura verdad
Alba, Luz
1934   La ciudad de cartón
1949   Daughter of the West
Alba, María
1930   Charros, gauchos y
          manolas
          El cuerpo del delito
          La fuerza del querer
          Los que danzan
          Olimpia
1931   El código penal
          Del infierno al cielo
          La ley del harem
          Su última noche
1932   Hypnotized
Alba, Orpha
1923   Look Your Best
Albanese, Licia
1956   Serenade
Alberghetti, Anna Maria
1953   The Stars Are Singing
1955   The Last Command
Alberich, Salvador de
1930   ¡De frente, marchen!
          Estrellados
          Wu Li Chang
1931   La fruta amarga
Alberni, Luis *same as* **Alberni,
          Louis**
1915   Children of the Ghetto
1921   Little Italy
1932   The Cohens and Kellys in
          Hollywood
          Hombres en mi vida
          Hypnotized
1933   The California Trail
          Man from Monterey
1934   La buenaventura
          Caravane
          La ciudad de cartón
1935   ¡Asegure a su mujer!
          The Winning Ticket
1936   Dancing Pirate
1937   Manhattan
          Merry-Go-Round
1939   Let Freedom Ring
1940   Elsa Maxwell's Public
          Deb No. 1
1942   Mexican Spitfire's
          Elephant
Alberoni, Sherry
1960   Pay or Die
Albert, Carlos
1949   The Kissing Bandit
1951   The Mark of the
          Renegade
Albert, Don
1946?   Beale Street Mama
Albert, Eddie
1943   Ladies' Day
1946   Strange Voyage
1948   The Dude Goes West
Albert, Somer
1952   Anything Can Happen
Albertson, E. Coit
1919   Who's Your Brother?
Albertson, Frank
1930   Son of the Gods
1932   Huddle
1933   The Cohens and Kellys in
          Trouble
          Ever in My Heart
1937   The Plainsman
1940   Behind the News
1941   Louisiana Purchase
1958   The Last Hurrah

Albertson, Jack
1952   Anything Can Happen
Albertson, Mabel
1958   Home Before Dark
1960   All the Fine Young
          Cannibals
Albin, Andy
1960   Cimarron
Albin, Charles
1938   The Toy Wife
Albright, Hardie
1931   Skyline
          Young Sinners
1932   The Match King
          So Big
1934   White Heat
1945   The Jade Mask
Albright, Lois
1949   Tulsa
Albright, Lola
1949   The Girl from Jones
          Beach
1952   Arctic Flight
1957   Pawnee
1958   Oregon Passage
Albright, Wally *same as* **Albright,
          Wally, Jr.**
1932   Thirteen Women
1934   As the Earth Turns
1935   Black Fury
1936   Star for a Night
1937   Maid of Salem
          Old Louisiana
Alcaide, Chris
1954   The Black Dakotas
          Massacre Canyon
          Overland Pacific
1955   Apache Ambush
          Duel on the Mississippi
1956   The Benny Goodman
          Story
Alcaide, Rafael
1938   Castillos en el aire
Alcalde, Mario
1956   Crowded Paradise
1960   All the Young Men
Alcañiz, Amadeo
1930   El último de los Vargas
Alcañiz, Luana *same as* **De
          Alcañiz, Luana**
1930   Del mismo barro
          El presidio
          El último de los Vargas
1931   La dama atrevida
          La llama sagrada
          El pasado acusa
1933   Primavera en otoño
1934   Nada más que una mujer
1935   Julieta compra un hijo
1936   Contra la corriente
          La última cita
1939   Frontiers of '49
          Verbena trágica
Alcañiz, Marina
1930   Del mismo barro
1932   Hombres en mi vida
Alcántara, José
1931   Cuerpo y alma
          Hay que casar al príncipe
          Mamá
Alda, Manuel
1950   Black Hand
1953   Ride, Vaquero!
1960   Pay or Die
Alda, Robert
1945   Rhapsody in Blue
1959   Imitation of Life
Aldana, Elvira *could be same as*
          Aldana, Vida
1946   The Gay Cavalier
Aldana, Vida *could be same as*
          Aldana, Elvira
1946   Beauty and the Bandit
1951   The Mark of the
          Renegade
Aldao, Camilo
1930   El secreto del doctor
Alden, Bob
1946   Three Wise Fools

Alden, Eric
1938   The Adventures of Tom
          Sawyer
1944   Lake Placid Serenade
1946   Without Reservations
1948   The Paleface
          Unconquered
1953   Arrowhead
1957   Beau James
1959   The Jayhawkers!
          Last Train from Gun Hill
Alden, Mary *not the same as*
          Aldon, Mari
1915   The Birth of a Nation
1919   Erstwhile Susan
1922   The Man with Two
          Mothers
1926   April Fool
1937   That I May Live
Alderdice, Robert
1938   Birthright
Alderette, Clorinda
1954   Salt of the Earth
Alderman, Jim
1958   Tonka .
Alderson, Erville
1920   The Good-Bad Wife
1930   The Bad Man
          The Lash
1934   Lazy River
1936   Ramona
1938   The Adventures of Tom
          Sawyer
1939   The Adventures of
          Huckleberry Finn
          Judge Hardy and Son
1940   Knute Rockne—All
          American
          Santa Fe Trail
1942   The Vanishing Virginian
1943   What's Buzzin' Cousin?
1944   An American Romance
1946   Canyon Passage
1947   Desperate
1948   The Feathered Serpent
          Shanghai Chest
          Unconquered
1951   The Tall Target
Alderson, John
1955   Violent Saturday
1958   The Young Lions
Aldez, Louis
1936   Ramona
Aldon, Mari *not the same as* **Alden,
          Mary**
1951   Distant Drums
Aldrich, Davie
1934   The Star Packer
Aldrich, Fred
1945   Wanderer of the
          Wasteland
1950   The Traveling
          Saleswoman
1956   Reprisal!
Aldrich, Meeka
1942   We Were Dancing
Aldrich, Robert
1947   Body and Soul
1951   New Mexico
1954   Apache
Aldrich, Roma
1943   Frontier Fury
Aldrich, William E.
1923   Purple Dawn
Aldridge, Katharine *same as*
          Aldridge, Kay
1941   Dead Men Tell
          Louisiana Purchase
Aleman, Miguel
1954   Sitting Bull
Aler, Barbara
1959   The Black Orchid
Alexander, Arthur
1935   Cowboy Holiday
1936   West of Nevada
1937   Law and Lead
1944   Waterfront
Alexander, Ben
1917   The Little American
1923   Jealous Husbands
1932   The Vanishing Frontier
1957   Man in the Shadow

Alexander, Betty
1947   Buck Privates Come
          Home
          Dangerous Venture
Alexander, Chester A.
1925   Body and Soul
Alexander, Clifford
1918   An Alien Enemy
Alexander, Dick *same as*
          Alexander, Richard
1931   The Hurricane Horseman
          Law of the Tong
1935   Cowboy Holiday
1936   Silly Billies
1937   The Plainsman
          Think Fast, Mr. Moto
1942   We Were Dancing
1945   Salome, Where She
          Danced
1946   Canyon Passage
1947   Northwest Outpost
1948   Unconquered
1949   Lust for Gold
1950   Rock Island Trail
1953   So Big
Alexander, Edward
1918   In Judgment Of
Alexander, Ernie
1932   Hypnotized
1934   The Cat's-Paw
          Operator 13
          Straight Is the Way
1936   After the Thin Man
          Sins of Man
1937   Life Begins in College
          Song of the City
1939   Judge Hardy and Son
1941   Sun Valley Serenade
          This Woman Is Mine
1942   Dr. Gillespie's New
          Assistant
          Nazi Agent
          Sunday Punch
          Three Hearts for Julia
1943   Bataan
Alexander, J. Grubb
1916   Mixed Blood
          The Sign of the Poppy
1917   The Plow Woman
1919   The Sneak
1920   The Devil's Claim
          The Purple Cipher
          The Third Woman
1921   The Swamp
1922   One Eighth Apache
1926   Rose of the Tenements
1927   The Chinese Parrot
1932   The Hatchet Man
          So Big
Alexander, Jeffrey
1958   Flaming Frontier
Alexander, John
1944   Mr. Skeffington
1945   A Tree Grows in Brooklyn
1947   The Jolson Story
          New Orleans
1950   Winchester '73
Alexander, Katharine
1934   Operator 13
1936   Sutter's Gold
1938   Rascals
1942   The Vanishing Virginian
Alexander, Kenneth
1941   Sun Valley Serenade
Alexander, Max
1935   Cowboy Holiday
1937   Law and Lead
Alexander, Richard *see*
          Alexander, Dick
Alexander, Major-General Robert
1919   The Lost Battalion
Alexander, William D. *same as*
          Alexander, William
1946   That Man of Mine
1947   Jivin' in Be-Bop
1948   The Fight Never Ends
1949   Souls of Sin
1955   Brevities of 1955
Alexis, Demetrius *same as* **Alexis,
          Demetri; Alexis, Demetrios**
1930   Sombras de gloria
1931   The Cohens and Kellys in
          Africa

1936   Paddy O'Day
1938   The Buccaneer
1944   Lake Placid Serenade
1947   The Foxes of Harrow
1952   Anything Can Happen
"Alfalfa" see Switzer, Carl "Alfalfa"
Alford, Elvin C.
1953   Thunder Bay
Alford, Julius
1950   Panic in the Streets
Alfvén, Margita
1930   Un hombre de suerte
          (foreign version)
Algara, Gabriel
1931   Un caballero de frac
          La incorregible
1932   El hombre que asesinó
Algier, Sid
1917   My Fighting Gentleman
Ali, George
1924   Peter Pan
Ali, Hadji
1931   Politiquerías
Alison, David see Horsley, David
The All American Dance Band
1942   Syncopation
The All American Girl Band
1949?   The Joint Is Jumpin'
All Girl Golden Slipper Band
1946   Tall, Tan and Terrific
All Runner, Emily
1959   The FBI Story
Allah, Ben
1927   With Sitting Bull at the
          Spirit Lake Massacre
Allan, Drew
1946   Till the End of Time
Allan, Elizabeth
1937   Slave Ship
Allan, Hugh
1928   Hold 'Em Yale
Allan, Ted
1948   Unconquered
Alland, William
1948   The Lady from Shanghai
1952   The Raiders
1953   The Stand at Apache
          River
1955   Chief Crazy Horse
Allara, Frank
1931   Così è la vita
Allardt, Albert same as Allardt, A.
1917   The Hidden Children
1918   An Alien Enemy
Allasio, Marisa
1958   Seven Hills of Rome
Allee
1922   Nanook of the North
Allegro, Alfred
1946   The Gentleman
          Misbehaves
Allen and Allen
1946?   Beale Street Mama
Allen, Alfred
1916   A Child of Mystery
          A Yoke of Gold
1917   Follow the Girl
1918   The Girl in the Dark
          Tongues of Flame
1919   The Sleeping Lion
1922   The Pride of Palomar
1928   Anybody Here Seen Kelly?
Allen, Anistine
1948?   Boarding House Blues
Allen, Ann E.
1951   The Harlem Globetrotters
Allen, Annie Lou
1921   Hearts of the Woods
Allen, Barbara Jo see Vague, Vera
Allen, Billie
1949   Souls of Sin
Allen, Brian
1956   The Benny Goodman
          Story
Allen, Charles H. same as Allen, Charles
1920   In the Depths of Our
          Hearts
1921   The Lure of a Woman

Allen, Corey
1960   Key Witness
Allen, Diana
1920   The Face at Your Window
Allen, Dick
1935   So Red the Rose
1936   Klondike Annie
Allen, Drew see Frye, Gilbert
Allen, E. Celise
1949?   Girl in Room 20
Allen, Eddie
1936   Klondike Annie
Allen, Florence
1928   George Washington
          Cohen
1944   Since You Went Away
1950   No Way Out
Allen, Glenn
1947   The Burning Cross
1949   Lookout Sister
Allen, Harry
1927   Turkish Delight
1929   In Old California
1932   Texas Pioneers
1935   A Night at the Opera
1938   Outside of Paradise
1939   Stand Up and Fight
Allen, Irene
1938   The Toy Wife
Allen, Irving
1946   Strange Voyage
1948   16 Fathoms Deep
1951   New Mexico
          Slaughter Trail
Allen, Irwin
1954   Dangerous Mission
Allen, Jacqueline
1951   The Great Caruso
Allen, Jean
1934   Stand Up and Cheer!
Allen, Joe, Jr.
1943   Action in the North
          Atlantic
1946   Dangerous Money
Allen, Joel
1950   Battleground
Allen, John H.
1936   Charlie Chan at the Race
          Track
Allen, Joseph
1918   Good-Bye, Bill
Allen, Judith
1933   Thundering Herd
1937   Boots and Saddles
1950   Train to Tombstone
Allen, Lester
1945   The Dolly Sisters
Allen, Louise
1942   Song of the Islands
Allen, Madeline
1931   Yankee Don
Allen, Maude
1930   The Big Pond (foreign
          version)
1936   Show Boat
1939   Let Freedom Ring
Allen, Phyllis
1920   White Youth
**Allen, Ray not the same as Allen
Ray (African-American actor)**
**Allen, Ray (African-American
actor) could be same as Allen,
Roy (African-American actor)**
1946?   Fight That Ghost
Allen, Rex
1953   Old Overland Trail
1960   For the Love of Mike
**Allen, Ricca same as Allen, Ricca
K.**
1917   A Wife by Proxy
1936   Show Boat
1937   Maid of Salem
Allen, Ricky
1960   All the Fine Young
          Cannibals
Allen, Robert
1934   Broadway Bill
1938   Gateway
1939   Winner Take All

Allen, Rose
1941   Birth of the Blues
**Allen, Roy (African-American
actor) could be same as Allen,
Ray (African-American actor)**
1946?   House-Rent Party
Allen, Sam
1922   The Son of the Wolf
Allen, Steve
1956   The Benny Goodman
          Story
Allen, Steve, Jr.
1956   The Benny Goodman
          Story
Allen, Tom
1960   Flaming Star
Allen, Winifred
1918   Woman and the Law
Allgood, Sara
1947   My Wild Irish Rose
Allison, May
1917   The Hidden Children
Allister, Claude
1930   Ladies Love Brutes
Allman, Elvia
1942   Three Hearts for Julia
Allman, Sheldon
1959   Inside the Mafia
Allred, Claud
1941   Sun Valley Serenade
Allwyn, Astrid
1936   Charlie Chan's Secret
          Dimples
          It Had to Happen
          Star for a Night
1937   It Could Happen to You
Allyson, June
1946   The Sailor Takes a Wife
1950   Right Cross
**Almirante, Ada Cristina same as
Almirante, Ada C.**
1930   Toda una vida (foreign
          version)
1931   La fiesta del diablo
          (foreign version)
Alonso, Chito
1934   Las fronteras del amor
1935   Rosa de Francia
Alonzo, Gilbert
1949   The Cowboy and the
          Indians
Alper, Murray
1936   Winterset
1938   Passport Husband
          Road Demon
1940   East of the River
1943   Air Force
          Yankee Doodle Dandy
1948   Sleep, My Love
1953   The Jazz Singer
Alperson, Edward L.
1936   Song of the Gringo
          Yellow Cargo
1938   Zamboanga
1952   Rose of Cimarron
1956   Mohawk
Alperson, Edward L., Jr.
1952   Rose of Cimarron
Alpert, David
1951   The Magnificent Yankee
1952   It's a Big Country: An
          American Anthology
1953   The Charge at Feather
          River
          The Eddie Cantor Story
1955   Blackboard Jungle
          Kiss of Fire
The Alphabetical Four
1940   Paradise in Harlem
Alphin, Patricia
1947   Buck Privates Come
          Home
1948   Up in Central Park
Alsace, Gene
1935   Range Warfare
1936   Treachery Rides the
          Range
1940   Arizona Frontier
1941   The Pioneers

Alson, Martin J.
1914   The Great Diamond
          Robbery
Alston and Young
194-   Mistaken Identity
Alston, William
1936   Show Boat
Alten, Frank
1943   Action in the North
          Atlantic
Altman, Frieda
1945   The House on 92nd St.
1954   Go Man Go
Altmiller, Ernest
1952   The Big Sky
Altomare, Adrian
1945   Where Do We Go From
          Here?
Alton, Jeralyn
1952   It's a Big Country: An
          American Anthology
Alton, Kenneth
1954   Thunder Pass
Altuna, Robert
1952   The Ring
Alvarado, Don same as Page, Don
1930   Estrellados
          La rosa de fuego
1935   Rosa de Francia
1936   Amor que vuelve
          Rose of the Rancho
1940   Knute Rockne—All
          American
1942   Secret Enemies
1951   A Streetcar Named Desire
1958   Marjorie Morningstar
Alvarado, Fernando
1937   The Barrier
1945   A Medal for Benny
          South of the Rio Grande
1946   Without Reservations
1948   Angel in Exile
1955   The Last Command
1956   Giant
Alvarado, José
1945   The Gay Senorita
1946   Without Reservations
1947   The Last Round-Up
          Ride the Pink Horse
1948   Angel in Exile
1949   The Cowboy and the
          Indians
**Alvarez Rubio, Pablo not the same
as Alvarez, Pablo**
1930   Los que danzan
1931   Drácula
Alvarez, Luis
1930   Charros, gauchos y
          manolas
Alvarez, Mario
1931   Gente alegre
Alvarez, Miami
1930   The Last Dance
1935   The Wedding Night
Alvarez, Miguel Angel
1927?   El que a hierro mata
**Alvarez, Pablo not the same as
Alvarez Rubio, Pablo**
1929   Sombras habaneras
1930   Monsieur le Fox
          La voluntad del muerto
Alvarez, Rosa Elvira
1935   Angelina o el honor de
          un brigadier
Alves, Lidia
1951   Native Son
Alvin, John
1944   The Sullivans
1948   Open Secret
          Rocky
          Shanghai Chest
1949   The Story of Seabiscuit
1950   The Breaking Point
1953   Dream Wife
1955   Kentucky Rifle
Alvir, Rafael
1931   Gente alegre
          El impostor
Alvord, Adeline M.
1918   Me Und Gott

Alyn, Kirk
1943   Action in the North
        Atlantic
1946   The Trap
1951   Gambling House
1952   The Savage
Aman, Sara
1960   The Pusher
Amara, Lucine
1951   The Great Caruso
Amaral, Nestor
1953   The Man Behind the Gun
Amardares, Tom
1928   Uncle Tom's Cabin
Amargo, Henry
1960   Flaming Star
Amato, Giuseppe
1958   Seven Hills of Rome
Amauli, Giulio
1932   Genoveffa
Amaya, Carmen
1944   Knickerbocker Holiday
Amazar, Elivra
1919   The Volcano
Amazar, Mlle. Elaine
1919   As a Man Thinks
Amber, Hrach
1945   Anoush
Ambler, Jerry
1951   Fort Defiance
Ambricourt, Adrienne d' see
    D'Ambricourt, Adrienne
Ambrod, Adriano
1950   Deported
Ameche, Don
1936   Ramona
        Sins of Man
1938   Gateway
        Happy Landing
        In Old Chicago
        Josette
1948   Sleep, My Love
Amendt, Rudolf see **Davis, Robert O.**
The American G.I. Chorus
1947   Northwest Outpost
American Horse, Ben
1952   The Savage
Amerise, Francisco
1930   Alma de gaucho
Ames, Adrienne
1935   Harmony Lane
Ames, Barbara
1945   I Love a Bandleader
Ames, Dick
1956   The Benny Goodman
        Story
Ames, Enrico
1934   La cruz y la espada
Ames, Jean
1942   All Through the Night
Ames, Jimmy same as **Ames, Jim**
1947   Ride the Pink Horse
1951   Slaughter Trail
1953   The Jazz Singer
1955   Blackboard Jungle
Ames, Joy
1948   Big City
Ames, Judith
1953   Arrowhead
1958   Oregon Passage
Ames, Leon same as **Waycoff, Leon; Wykoff, Leon**
1932   Thirteen Women
1933   The Man Who Dared: An
        Imaginative Biography
1935   Rescue Squad
1937   Charlie Chan on
        Broadway
1939   Man of Conquest
        Mr. Moto in Danger
        Island
1950   Ambush
        Battleground
        The Big Hangover
1952   It's a Big Country: An
        American Anthology
Ames, Michael
1942   They Died With Their
        Boots On

Ames, Ramsay
1946   Beauty and the Bandit
        The Gay Cavalier
Ames, Robert
1930   A Lady to Love
1931   Three Who Loved
Ames, Stephen
1948   The Boy with Green Hair
1952   My Man and I
1953   Ride, Vaquero!
Amiel, Denys
1930   El secreto del doctor
        (foreign version)
Amigo, Norma
1953   The Eddie Cantor Story
Ammons, Albert
1946?   Harlem on Parade
Amo, Jaime del same as **Del Amo, Jaime**
1938   La vida bohemia
1939   Verbena trágica
Amor, Carlos
1928   Ramona
Amoroso, Angela
1932   Amor in montagna
Amos, Tom
1923   A Shot in the Night
Anastasiades, Alex
1931   Such Is Life
Anaya, Gilbert C.
1957   Burden of Truth
Anaya, María
1932   ¿Cuándo te suicidas?
Ander, Charlotte
1931   La carta (foreign
        version)
Anders, Bill
1955   The Lonesome Trail
Anders, Glenn
1948   The Lady from Shanghai
Anders, Luana
1959   The FBI Story
Anderson, A. E.
1932   The Galloping Kid
Anderson, Agnes
1935   The Wedding Night
Anderson, Allegretti
1930   Georgia Rose
Anderson, Archibald
1940   Tengo fe en ti
Anderson, Audley
1959   The FBI Story
Anderson, Augusta
1918   Uncle Tom's Cabin
1919   Come Out of the Kitchen
1935   Ruggles of Red Gap
Anderson, Axel
1944   An American Romance
Anderson, Bobby (child actor) not the same as **Anderson, Robert** (actor, circa 1916—1937) or **Anderson, Robert** b. 1923
1944   Tender Comrade
1945   Colorado Pioneers
Anderson, Bull
1937   Slave Ship
Anderson, C. E., Captain same as **Anderson, C. E.; Anderson, Cap; Anderson, Captain**
1928   Uncle Tom's Cabin
1934   Our Daily Bread
1935   The Little Colonel
1939   Let Freedom Ring
1940   Northwest Passage (Book
        I—Rogers' Rangers)
1941   Western Union
1943   The Ox-Bow Incident
Anderson, Charles (actor)
1922   A California Romance
1923   The Huntress
        Snowdrift
Anderson, Charles (writer)
1941   The Pioneers
Anderson, Claire
1918   The Price of Applause
Anderson, Corny
1937   Dark Manhattan
Anderson, D. A.
1950   Riders of the Pony
        Express

Anderson, Dave
1949   The Fighting Kentuckian
Anderson, Doris
1930   Cascarrabias
1940   Three Faces West
Anderson, Dusty
1946   The Gentleman
        Misbehaves
Anderson, Eddie same as "Rochester"; **Anderson, Eddie** "Rochester"
1934   Behold My Wife!
1936   The Green Pastures
        Rainbow on the River
        Show Boat
        Star for a Night
1937   One Mile from Heaven
1939   Gone With the Wind
1941   Birth of the Blues
1942   Tales of Manhattan
1943   Cabin in the Sky
        The Meanest Man in the
        World
        What's Buzzin' Cousin?
1945   I Love a Bandleader
1946   The Sailor Takes a Wife
Anderson, Effie
1940   Jennie
1941   Hurry, Charlie, Hurry
Anderson, Ernest
1942   In This Our Life
1943   Yankee Doodle Dandy
1946   Without Reservations
1947   The Peanut Man
1950   No Way Out
1951   The Well
1952   The Iron Mistress
Anderson, George not the same as **Anderson, George M.**
1939   King of Chinatown
1940   The Way of All Flesh
1941   Hold Back the Dawn
        Sullivan's Travels
1943   Dixie
1945   Nob Hill
1947   California
        Desperate
        My Wild Irish Rose
1948   Unconquered
Anderson, George M. not the same as **Anderson, George**
1914   The Good-for-Nothing
Anderson, Guy
1950   Battleground
        The Lawless
1951   The Magnificent Yankee
Anderson, Harry not the same as **Anderson, Harry S.**
1941   Mystery Ship
1943   Doughboys in Ireland
Anderson, Harry S. not the same as **Anderson, Harry**
1951   Saturday's Hero
Anderson, Herbert
1947   My Wild Irish Rose
1956   The Benny Goodman
        Story
Anderson, Ida
1921   The Secret Sorrow
1924   A Son of Satan
Anderson, James
1951   Five
1954   Drums Across the River
        They Rode West
1955   Seven Angry Men
Anderson, John (actor) could be same as **Anderson, John R.** (Actor)
1953   The Eddie Cantor Story
Anderson, John Murray (dir)
1930   King of Jazz
Anderson, John R. (actor) could be same as **Anderson, John** (actor)
1959   Last Train from Gun Hill
Anderson, Judith
1942   All Through the Night
1950   The Furies
Anderson, Leonard
1946   That Man of Mine
1947   Jivin' in Be-Bop
1956   Singing in the Dark

Anderson, Marion Clayton
1960   The Crowning
        Experience
Anderson, Mary silent actress
1918   His Birthright
Anderson, Mary (actress), b. 1924
1939   Gone With the Wind
1944   Lifeboat
1950   Last of the Buccaneers
Anderson, Mary (silent actress)
1922   The Half Breed
Anderson, Maxwell
1935   So Red the Rose
Anderson, Michael
1959   Shake Hands with the
        Devil
1960   All the Fine Young
        Cannibals
Anderson, Myrtle
1936   The Green Pastures
1938   The Toy Wife
1941   Sullivan's Travels
1942   The Vanishing Virginian
1953   The Sun Shines Bright
Anderson, Nellie
1918   Little Red Decides
Anderson, Philip
1929   Redskin
Anderson, Reginald
1937   Harlem on the Prairie
1940   While Thousands Cheer
Anderson, Richard
1951   Across the Wide Missouri
        Go for Broke!
        The Magnificent Yankee
1953   Dream Wife
Anderson, Robert could be same as **Anderson, Bobby** (child actor) or **Anderson, Robert** (actor), b. 1923 not the same as **Anderson, Robert** (actor, 1916—1937)
1943   The Leopard Man
Anderson, Robert (actor), b. 1923 not the same as **Anderson, Bobby** (child actor) or **Anderson, Robert** (actor, circa 1916—1937)
1943   Gangway for Tomorrow
        Mexican Spitfire's Blessed
        Event
1944   Since You Went Away
1945   Johnny Angel
        A Tree Grows in Brooklyn
1950   Winchester '73
1952   Bright Victory
1958   The Light in the Forest
1960   The Crowning
        Experience
Anderson, Robert (actor, 1916—1937) not the same as **Anderson, Bobby** (child actor)
Anderson, Robert (actor, circa 1916—1937) not the same as **Anderson, Robert** (actor), b. 1923
1918   The Hun Within
1919   The Right to Happiness
1937   It Could Happen to You
Anderson, "Sugarfoot"
1949   The Story of Seabiscuit
Anderson, Warner
1946   Bad Bascomb
        Three Wise Fools
1947   Dark Delusion
1951   Go for Broke!
        Only the Valiant
1954   Drum Beat
        The Yellow Tomahawk
1955   Blackboard Jungle
Anderson, William (actor)
1917   The Bar Sinister
Anderson, William H. (prod)
1960   The Sign of Zorro
Andes, Keith
1947   The Farmer's Daughter
1956   Pillars of the Sky
Andikian, Krish
1945   Anoush

Andor, Paul *see* **Zilzer, Wolfgang**

Andre, Carl
1944   Buffalo Bill
1948   The Paleface
1949   Colorado Territory
        Streets of Laredo
1950   Colt .45
1953   The Charge at Feather
        River
        The Great Sioux Uprising
        The Man from the Alamo
1954   Siege at Red River
        They Rode West

Andre, Charles
1949   The Fighting Kentuckian

Andre, Claire
1951   Westward the Women

Andre, Julia
1947   Pirates of Monterey

Andre, Lona
1936   Custer's Last Stand

André, Marcel
1930   Olimpia (*foreign
        version*)
1931   Le père célibataire
        El proceso de Mary
        Dugan (*foreign
        version*)
        Soyons gais

Andre, Mary
1959   The Black Orchid

Andre, Monya
1934   Imitation of Life
1937   Big City
1948   Gentleman's Agreement

Andre, Pierre
1946   The Gay Cavalier
1947   My Wild Irish Rose

Andree, Dorothy *same as* **Andre,
Dorothy**
1934   Stand Up and Cheer!
1954   Cattle Queen of Montana

Andren, Jean
1949   Anna Lucasta
1950   Belle of Old Mexico
        I Killed Geronimo
1953   Dream Wife
1955   Good Morning, Miss Dove
1956   Walk the Proud Land

Andrew, Sylvia
1947   My Wild Irish Rose

Andrews, Andy
1945   The Shanghai Cobra

Andrews, Arkansas "Slim" *see*
Andrews, Slim

Andrews, Billy (*child actor*) *not
the same as* **Andrews, William**
(*actor*)
1947   California
1948   The Paleface

Andrews, Carol
1945   Nob Hill
1946   Slightly Scandalous

Andrews, Charles
1936   The Green Pastures
1938   The Toy Wife
1939   Reform School
1940   Mystery in Swing
1955   The View from Pompey's
        Head

Andrews, Dana
1940   Kit Carson
        Lucky Cisco Kid
1941   Belle Starr
1943   Crash Dive
        The Ox-Bow Incident
1946   Canyon Passage
1955   Smoke Signal
1956   Comanche

Andrews, Del
1925   The Wild Bull's Lair
1928   The Rawhide Kid

Andrews, Edward
1957   Trooper Hook
1959   Night of the Quarter
        Moon

Andrews, Frank
1914   The Nightingale
1915   Children of the Ghetto

Andrews, Ismay
1932   The Black King

Andrews, Jack
1941   Western Union
1947   Dark Delusion

Andrews, Lois
1948   Western Heritage
1949   Rustlers

Andrews, Mark
1955   The Long Gray Line

Andrews, Robert D.
1943   Bataan

Andrews, Robert Hardy
1951   The Mark of the
        Renegade
1952   The Half-Breed

Andrews, Slim *same as* **Andrews,
Arkansas "Slim"**
1940   Arizona Frontier
        Rhythm of the Rio
        Grande
1941   The Pioneers
1952   Buffalo Bill in Tomahawk
        Territory

Andrews, Stanley
1935   So Red the Rose
1936   Dangerous Intrigue
1937   Big City
        The Devil's Playground
        The Plainsman
        Souls at Sea
1938   The Buccaneer
        Road Demon
        Spawn of the North
        Speed to Burn
1940   Geronimo
        Hi-Yo Silver
        Kit Carson
        The Mark of Zorro
1941   Dead Men Tell
1942   The Navy Comes Through
        North to the Klondike
        Valley of the Sun
1943   Crash Dive
        Dixie
        In Old Oklahoma
        The Ox-Bow Incident
        Riding High
1944   Lake Placid Serenade
        Tucson Raiders
        Vigilantes of Dodge City
1946   Bad Bascomb
1947   California
        Easy Come, Easy Go
1948   Docks of New Orleans
        I Remember Mama
        The Paleface
1949   Brothers in the Saddle
        The Valiant Hombre
1950   Colt .45
        Rock Island Trail
        The Traveling
        Saleswoman
        Two Flags West
1953   Ride, Vaquero!

Andrews, William (*actor*) *not the
same as* **Andrews, Billy** (*child
actor*)
1953   Last of the Comanches

The Anestos
1944   Minstrel Man

Angel, Daniel M.
1959   The Sheriff of Fractured
        Jaw

Angel, Heather
1933   Charlie Chan's Greatest
        Case
1936   The Bold Caballero
        Daniel Boone
        The Last of the Mohicans
1944   Lifeboat

Angeles, Consuelo de los
1930   Del mismo barro

Angeles, Marita
1931   Un caballero de frac
        La incorregible
        Las luces de Buenos Aires
        La pura verdad (*foreign
        version*)

Angeli, Pier
1951   Teresa

Angelus, Muriel
1940   The Way of All Flesh

Angie *see* **Rossitto, Angie**

Anglim, Sally
1951   Yes Sir, Mr. Bones

Angold, Edit
1940   Escape
1944   Tomorrow the World!
1951   The Great Caruso
        Molly
1952   Woman in the Dark

Angus, Katherine
1919   Just Squaw

Anhalt, Edna
1950   Panic in the Streets
1953   The Member of the
        Wedding
1955   Not As a Stranger

Anhalt, Edward
1950   Panic in the Streets
1953   The Member of the
        Wedding
1955   Not As a Stranger
1958   The Young Lions

Ankers, Evelyn
1942   North to the Klondike
1943   His Butler's Sister
1947   Last of the Redmen
        Spoilers of the North

Ankewich, Camille
1918   One More American

Ankin, Vart
1937   Arshin Mal Alan

Ankrum, Morris *same as* **Morris,
Stephen**
1937   Hills of Old Wyoming
1941   Doomed Caravan
        Road Agent
        This Woman Is Mine
1942   Tales of Manhattan
1947   Little Mister Jim
        The Mighty McGurk
1949   Colorado Territory
        We Were Strangers
1952   Fort Osage
        Hiawatha
        The Raiders
1953   The Man Behind the Gun
1954   Apache
        Cattle Queen of Montana
        Drums Across the River
        Taza, Son of Cochise
1955   Chief Crazy Horse
        The Last Command
1956   Death of a Scoundrel
        Quincannon, Frontier
        Scout
        Walk the Proud Land
1958   Frontier Gun

Ann, Anny
1931   Chérie (*foreign version*)

Annabella
1934   Caravane

Ansara, Michael
1951   Only the Valiant
1952   Brave Warrior
1956   The Lone Ranger
        Pillars of the Sky

Ansel, Armando
1931   La fiesta del diablo
        (*foreign version*)

Anson, Ina
1928   The Broken Mask

Anson, Laura
1922   The Great Alone

Antes, Jerry
1944   Chip Off the Old Block

Anthony, De Leon
1928   The Broken Mask
1929   Is Everybody Happy?

Anthony, Emmet
1924   A Son of Satan

Anthony, Jack
1927   The Fighting Hombre

Anthony, June-Ellen
1957   Band of Angels

Anthony, Mark
1960   Wild River

Anthony, Ray
1959   Night of the Quarter
        Moon

Anthony, Stuart
1932   The Vanishing Frontier
1934   Un capitán de cosacos
        Charlie Chan in London
1935   Charlie Chan in Paris
1936   Desert Gold
        Ramona
1939   King of Chinatown

Anthony, Vaughn
1948   Unconquered

Anthony, Walter
1924   The Lightning Rider
1927   The Chinese Parrot
1928   Anybody Here Seen Kelly?
        The Cavalier
        Uncle Tom's Cabin

Antiznat, Henri
1914   The Nightingale

Antoine, LeRoy
1945   Rhapsody in Blue

Anton, Karl
1931   La pura verdad (*foreign
        version*)

Antonet
1931   Un caballero de frac

Antrim, Harry
1948   The Luck of the Irish
1949   Border Incident
1950   Devil's Doorway
        Intruder in the Dust
1958   Gunman's Walk
1959   Gunmen from Laredo

Anug, Wong
1941   Min Jok Jay Hung Sing

Anzel, Hy
1957   Beau James

Aoki, Daniel T.
1954   Hell's Half Acre

Aoki, Tsuru *same as* **Aoki, Tsura;
Aoki, Tsuri; Hayakawa, Tsuru
Aoki**
1916   Alien Souls
        The Honorable Friend
        The Soul of Kura-San
1917   The Call of the East
1918   The Bravest Way
        His Birthright
1919   The Courageous Coward
        The Gray Horizon
        A Heart in Pawn
1920   Locked Lips
        A Tokio Siren
1921   Black Roses
1960   Hell to Eternity

Aoyama, Yukio *same as* **Aoyama,
U**
1918   The Bravest Way
1920   Who's Your Servant?

Apache
1938   Outlaw Express

Aparicio, Manuel
1949   Jigsaw

Apfel, Oscar *same as* **Apfel, Oscar
C.**
1914   The Squaw Man
1915   After Five
1916   A Man of Sorrow
1917   The Hidden Children
1919   Auction of Souls
        Mandarin's Gold
1929   Smiling Irish Eyes
1930   Abraham Lincoln
1931   Huckleberry Finn
1932   The Heart of New York
        Symphony of Six Million
1934   Beloved
1935   Romance in Manhattan
1936   Sutter's Gold
1937   Shadows of the Orient

Aphed Elk
1934   Laughing Boy

Apking, Fritz
1954   Dangerous Mission
1955   The Long Gray Line

Aplon, Boris
1947   Citizen Saint

Apostolof, Stephen C.
1957   Journey to Freedom

Appel, Anna
1926   Broken Hearts
1932   The Heart of New York
        Symphony of Six Million
        The Unfortunate Bride
        Yiskor

1937   Green Fields
      The Holy Oath
1938   The Singing Blacksmith

Appel, H.
1940   Americaner Schadchen

Appel, Sam
1931   Yankee Don
1936   Ramona
      Rose of the Rancho

Apperson, Ross
1960   Wild River

Applebaum, Irving
1940   Cuando canta la Ley

Appleby, Dorothy
1933   King of the Wild Horses
1934   As the Earth Turns
1935   Charlie Chan in Paris

Applegarth, Jonas, Chief
1954   Drum Beat
1959   The Sheriff of Fractured
      Jaw

Applegate, Roy
1914   Uncle Tom's Cabin

Appleton, L. B., Jr.
1946   Strange Voyage

Apus & Estrellita
1947   Sepia Cinderella

Aragny, Jean
1930   Toda una vida (*foreign
      version*)

Aragón, Agustín
1930   Sombras de gloria

Aragon, Art
1952   The Ring

Aranis, Agnes
1930   Del mismo barro

Arbó, Manuel
1930   El dios del mar
      East Is West (*foreign
      version*)
1931   Charlie Chan Carries On
      (*foreign version*)
      Cheri-Bibi
      El código penal
      El comediante
      ¿Conoces a tu mujer?
      Drácula
      Hay que casar al príncipe
      La mujer X
      El príncipe gondolero
      El tenorio del harem

Arbo, Virginia
1931   La ley del harem

Arbuckle, Andrew
1918   Denny from Ireland
1920   Darling Mine
1923   The Spider and the Rose

Archainbaud, George
1925   Scarlet Saint
1926   Puppets
1928   George Washington
      Cohen
1931   Three Who Loved
1932   Thirteen Women
1947   Dangerous Venture
1950   Border Treasure
1952   Apache Country

Archer, Claude E.
1939   Confessions of a Nazi Spy
1942   They Died With Their
      Boots On

Archer, Harry
1916   Mixed Blood
1917   The Bronze Bride

Archer, John *same as* **Bowman,
Ralph**
1941   King of the Zombies
1943   Crash Dive
1949   Colorado Territory
1953   The Stars Are Singing

Archer, Mel
1950   North of the Great Divide
      Winchester '73
1951   Distant Drums
      A Streetcar Named Desire

Archibald, Freddie
1936   The Green Pastures

Archibald, Myra
1940   The Ramparts We Watch

Archuletta, Arline
1947   The Last Round-Up

Archuletta, Beulah
1955   Foxfire
1956   The Searchers
      Westward Ho the
      Wagons!

Arco, I.
1940   Americaner Schadchen

Arco, Louis
1942   All Through the Night
1943   Action in the North
      Atlantic
      Gangway for Tomorrow
1944   Address Unknown

Arcos, Guillermo
1934   Cuesta abajo
1936   Ramona

Arcos, Pilar
1938   Castillos en el aire
1939   Miracle on Main Street
      (*foreign version*)
      El otro soy yo
      Verbena trágica
1940   Cuando canta la Ley

Ardel, Henri
1920   Lifting Shadows

Ardell, Alice *same as* **Ardelle,
Alice**
1932   Le bluffeur
1934   Imitation of Life
      La veuve joyeuse
1935   Ruggles of Red Gap

Ardell, Franklyn
1936   It Had to Happen

Ardell, Maxine
1941   Louisiana Purchase
1949   House of Strangers

Ardelle, Alice *see* **Ardell, Alice**

Arden, Eddie
1947   The Farmer's Daughter

Arden, Eve
1960   The Dark at the Top of
      the Stairs

Arden, Hunter
1916   The Innocent Lie

Arden, Mary
1945   Jealousy
1946   California Gold Rush

Arden, Sally
1933   It's Great to Be Alive

Ardito, Gino
1958   Never Love a Stranger

Ardizoni, John
1920   The Good-Bad Wife
1937   Man of the People
1950   Black Hand

Ardizoni, Rosario
1950   Black Hand

Ardler, Stella *see* **Adler, Stella**

Ardrey, Robert
1940   They Knew What They
      Wanted
1959   The Wonderful Country

Aredas, Dan
1951   Go for Broke!

Arenas, Pablo
1930   El último de los Vargas

Areu, Enrique
1931   Regeneración

Areu, José
1931   Regeneración

Areu, Roberto
1931   Regeneración

Arévalo, Antonia
1931   Sombras del circo
      Su noche de bodas

Argent, Robert
1955   Murder in Villa Capri

Argentina, Imperio
1931   Lo mejor es reír
      Su noche de bodas
1932   ¿Cuándo es suicidas?
1933   Melodía de arrabal

La Argentinita
1930   Galas de la Paramount

Argüelles, Gabriel
1931   El tenorio del harem

Argüelles, José
1932   El hombre que asesinó
1933   Espérame
      Melodía de arrabal

Argus, Edwin
1931   Smart Money

Ari, Ben
1959   Al Capone

Arias, José
1930   Las campanas de
      Capistrano

José Arias Orchestra
1930   Las campanas de
      Capistrano

Aristi Eulate, Juan
1930   Olimpia
1931   Del infierno al cielo
      Don Juan diplomático
      El impostor
      Regeneración

The "Aristo-Genes" Girls Club
1946   Beware

Ariza, Francisco J.
1938   Di que me quieres

Arkin, Ted
1940   Elsa Maxwell's Public
      Deb No. 1

Arledge, John *not the same as*
Arledge, Johnson
1931   Young Sinners
1932   Huddle
1933   Olsen's Big Moment
1934   Coming Out Party
1937   Big City
1939   Gone With the Wind

Arledge, Johnson *not the same as*
Arledge, John
1930   King of Jazz

Arlen, Bette
1950   Annie Get Your Gun
1951   Show Boat

Arlen, David
1940   Broken Strings

Arlen, Richard
1927   Sally in Our Alley
1929   Thunderbolt
1930   Galas de la Paramount
1932   Tiger Shark
1933   Song of the Eagle
1941   Mutiny in the Arctic
1947   Buffalo Bill Rides Again
1951   Flaming Feather

Arling, Charles
1918   The Ranger

Armand, Alice
1938   Josette

Armando and Lita
1942   Syncopation

Armband, Abraham *same as*
Armband, A.
1932   Mazel Tov
1933   The Eternal Jew
1935   The Yiddish King Lear
1936   Love and Sacrifice

Armena, Doli
1938   Swing!

Armendáriz, Guadalupe
1932   Amor y vida

Armendáriz, Pedro
1948   Fort Apache
1949   3 Godfathers
      Tulsa
      We Were Strangers
1959   The Wonderful Country

Armenta, F. A.
1934   La cruz y la espada
      Laughing Boy

Armetta, Enrico
1930   Sei tu l'amore

Armetta, Henry
1920   The Face at Your Window
1929   In Old Arizona
      Love, Live and Laugh
1930   A Lady to Love
      A Lady to Love (*foreign
      version*)
      Sins of the Children
1932   Huddle
      Scarface
1933   The Cohens and Kellys in
      Trouble

1934   Imitation of Life
1935   Chinatown Squad
1936   Let's Sing Again
1937   Manhattan
      Merry-Go-Round
1938   Road Demon
      Speed to Burn
1939   The Escape
      Fisherman's Wharf
      Winner Take All
1940   Three Cheers for the Irish
1941   Caught in the Act
1943   Good Luck, Mr. Yates

Armetta, Sal
1960   Pay or Die

Armida
1930   On the Border
1937   Border Cafe
1943   The Girl from Monterrey
1945   South of the Rio Grande
1949   The Gay Amigo

Armour, Jean
1917   Unknown 274
1921   The Sport of the Gods

Arms, Russell
1942   Wings for the Eagle

Armstrong, Alma
1958   Tonka

Armstrong, Audrey
1949?   Harlem Follies

Armstrong, Bill *same as*
Armstrong, William W. *not the
same as* **Armstrong, Will**
1951   Saturday's Hero
1957   Naked in the Sun

Armstrong, Byron
1938   The Adventures of Tom
      Sawyer

Armstrong, Dale
1936   My American Wife

Armstrong, David
1955   The Long Gray Line

Armstrong, Gary
1945   Colorado Pioneers
1947   California
      Humoresque
1948   Moonrise

Armstrong, Henry
1939   Keep Punching

Armstrong, Herbert
1959   The FBI Story

Armstrong, Larrie L.
1959   The Hanging Tree

Armstrong, Louis
1943   Cabin in the Sky
1957   Satchmo the Great

Louis Armstrong and His Band
1947   New Orleans

Armstrong, Lucille
1957   Satchmo the Great

Armstrong, Margaret
1935   Annie Oakley
1940   Elsa Maxwell's Public
      Deb No. 1

Armstrong, R. G.
1958   Never Love a Stranger

Armstrong, Robert
1939   Man of Conquest
1940   Behind the News
1942   Let's Get Tough!
1946   G. I. War Brides
1948   The Paleface

Armstrong, Will *not the same as*
Armstrong, Bill
1927   Clancy's Kosher Wedding
1940   Little Nellie Kelly

Arna, Lissi *same as* **Arna, Lissy**
1930   Doña mentiras (*foreign
      version*)
      Los que danzan (*foreign
      version*)
1931   Beyond Victory
      Daemon des Meeres
      Die Maske Fällt

Arnaz, Desi
1940   Too Many Girls
1942   The Navy Comes Through
1943   Bataan
1946   Cuban Pete

Arnedillo, Luis
1933   Espérame
Arness, James *same as* **Arness, Jim; Aurness, James**
1947   The Farmer's Daughter
1950   Battleground
         Stars in My Crown
1951   Cavalry Scout
1954   Hondo
Arnett, Paul
1958   Sierra Baron
Arnheim, Gus
1932   Scarface
Arno, Sig
1941   They Dare Not Love
1942   Tales of Manhattan
1943   His Butler's Sister
         Let's Have Fun
1950   The Toast of New Orleans
Arnold, Bert
1952   Red Snow
Arnold, Danny
1953   The Stars Are Singing
1955   Fort Yuma
Arnold, Edward
1936   Sutter's Gold
1939   Let Freedom Ring
1946   Three Wise Fools
1947   The Mighty McGurk
1948   Big City
1950   Annie Get Your Gun
Arnold, Edward, Jr.
1937   Life Begins in College
1942   Holiday Inn
Arnold, Frank
1946   Canyon Passage
1949   Knock on Any Door
1950   Emergency Wedding
1953   Cry of the Hunted
Arnold, Helen
1917   The Call of Her People
         One Law for Both
Arnold, Homer
1950   Intruder in the Dust
Arnold, Jack *same as* **Haworth, Vinton**
1937   That Girl from Paris
1940   Mexican Spitfire Out West
1941   The Mexican Spitfire's Baby
         New York Town
         Playmates
1942   Mexican Spitfire's Elephant
1943   Ladies' Day
1957   Man in the Shadow
Arnold, Jessie
1916   Mixed Blood
1920   The Dark Mirror
1938   The Beloved Brat
1939   The Escape
1942   Nazi Agent
1943   Frontier Fury
         What's Buzzin' Cousin?
1945   Escape in the Fog
         A Tree Grows in Brooklyn
1947   The Farmer's Daughter
         It Had To Be You
         The Jolson Story
1948   The Lady from Shanghai
1950   No Way Out
         Stars in My Crown
         The Traveling Saleswoman
Arnold, Joan
1942   Holiday Inn
1953   Tonight We Sing
Arnold, Larry
1949   House of Strangers
Arnold, Newton
1960   All the Young Men
Arnold, Phil *same as* **Arnold, Philip**
1947   Buffalo Bill Rides Again
         Jiggs and Maggie in Society
1951   Yes Sir, Mr. Bones
1953   The Jazz Singer
1960   Studs Lonigan

Arnold, Seth
1949   Lost Boundaries
Arnold, William
1935   A Night at the Ritz
1937   The Devil's Playground
Arnon, B.
1937   Green Fields
Arnon, Ceril
1937   Where Is My Child?
Arnst, Bobbie
1934   Beloved
Arnt, Charles
1936   After the Thin Man
1941   Hold Back the Dawn
1942   Twin Beds
         Young America
1943   Gangway for Tomorrow
         In Old Oklahoma
1944   My Pal Wolf
1946   Without Reservations
1947   Calendar Girl
1948   The Boy with Green Hair
1949   Boston Blackie's Chinese Venture
         Masked Raiders
1953   The Great Sioux Uprising
Arozamena, Amparo
1940   Perfidia
Arozamena, Eduardo
1931   Carne de cabaret
         Cheri-Bibi
         Don Juan diplomático
         Drácula
         Resurrección
         El tenorio del harem
1932   Hombres en mi vida
1940   Perfidia
Arriaga, Dolly
1952   It's a Big Country: An American Anthology
Arrias, Antonio
1945   The Gay Senorita
Arroyito
1939   El otro soy yo
         Papá soltero
1940   Cuando canta la Ley
Arselle, Carmen
1922   The Pride of Palomar
Arslan, Sylvia
1944   Mr. Skeffington
1945   Great Stagecoach Robbery
1947   Humoresque
Artarne, Wong
1947   Little Mister Jim
1948   The Lady from Shanghai
Artaud, Antonin
1931   Die Dreigroschenoper (*foreign version*)
Arteaga, Mario
1959   The Young Land
1960   Sergeant Rutledge
Artegas, Joaquín
1934   Un capitán de cosacos
Artero, Matilde
1933   Espérame
Arthur, Art
1937   Charlie Chan on Broadway
1941   Sun Valley Serenade
1943   Riding High
Arthur, Charlotte
1935   Rescue Squad
Arthur, Daniel V.
1914   The Great Diamond Robbery
Arthur, Dorothy
1914   The Great Diamond Robbery
Arthur, Eva
1952?   Call of the Navajo
Arthur, George K.
1925   Lights of Old Broadway
1926   Irene
1934   Stand Up and Cheer!
Arthur, Harris
1952?   Call of the Navajo
Arthur, Henry
1938   Road Demon

Arthur, Jean
1926   Under Fire
1928   Sins of the Fathers
1930   Galas de la Paramount
1937   The Plainsman
Arthur, John (*actor, circa early 1950s*) *not the same as* **Arthur, Johnny** (*actor*), 1883–1951
1952?   Call of the Navajo
Arthur, Johnny (*actor*), 1883–1951 *not the same as* **Arthur, John** (*actor, circa early 1950s*)
1935   Rendezvous
1936   Ellis Island
Arthur, Johnny (*child actor*) *not the same as* **Arthur, Johnny** (*actor*), 1883–1951
1952?   Call of the Navajo
Arthur, Lee
1915   Cohen's Luck
Arthur, Priscilla
1952?   Call of the Navajo
Arthur, Robert (*actor*)
1952   The Ring
Arthur, Robert (*prod, writer*) *not the same as* **Aurthur, Robert Alan** (*writer*)
1940   New Moon
1944   Chip Off the Old Block
1947   Buck Privates Come Home
1950   Buccaneer's Girl
1955   The Long Gray Line
1956   Pillars of the Sky
1957   The Midnight Story
Artizoni, J.
1935   A Night at the Opera
Arven, Jan
1960   The Sign of Zorro
Arvidson, Linda
1915   The Gambler of the West
Arvizu, Paulita
1938   Daughter of Shanghai
Arzner, Dorothy
1930   Galas de la Paramount
Ash, Russell
1945   Where Do We Go From Here?
1958   Marjorie Morningstar
Ash, Sam
1934   Operator 13
         La veuve joyeuse
1935   Rendezvous
1936   It Had to Happen
         Robin Hood of El Dorado
1937   Big City
         Charlie Chan on Broadway
1939   King of Chinatown
         Stand Up and Fight
1940   The Way of All Flesh
1941   The Face Behind the Mask
1942   Sunday Punch
1945   Nob Hill
         Where Do We Go From Here?
1948   Unconquered
1952   The Big Sky
Ashbrook, Florence
1917   Unknown 274
The Ashburns
1944   Block Busters
Ashcraft, Mary
1930   Whoopee
Ashcroft, Karl
1952?   Call of the Navajo
Ashdown, Nadine
1950   Battleground
Ashe, Martin
1946   Three Wise Fools
Ashe, Warren
1941   The Face Behind the Mask
1942   Submarine Raider
1943   Action in the North Atlantic
         Deerslayer
         What's Buzzin' Cousin?
1944   The Racket Man

Asher, E. M.
1926   The Cohens and Kellys
1928   Flying Romeos
1930   East Is West
Asher, Irving
1942   Nazi Agent
1953   The Stars Are Singing
Asher, Max
1919   A Yankee Princess
1927   Lost at the Front
1929   Show Boat
Asher, Roland
1928   Chinatown Charlie
Ashforth, George
1932   Hypnotized
Ashkenazy, Irvin
1956   Davy Crockett and the River Pirates
Ashley, Arthur
1918   Broken Ties
1922   Breaking Home Ties
Ashley, Edward
1941   Come Live with Me
Ashley, Elizabeth (*African-American actress*)
1941   Sullivan's Travels
Ashley, Herbert
1934   Broadway Bill
1936   Dimples
         Star for a Night
1937   Big City
         The Devil's Playground
1938   Happy Landing
1941   Belle Starr
         Ride on Vaquero
1942   Woman of the Year
1945   The Dolly Sisters
Ashley, Joel
1956   The Broken Star
         Ghost Town
Ashley, Peter
1940   Knute Rockne—All American
Ashton, Herbert
1931   Skyline
Ashton, Sylvia
1921   Hold Your Horses
1922   Saturday Night
1923   The White Flower
1928   The Crash
Asins, Connie
1947   Ride the Pink Horse
1948   Silver Trails
Askam, Earl
1937   The Plainsman
1939   Allegheny Uprising
Askins, Ida
1916   The Colored American Winning His Suit
Aslin, Edna
1929   The Invaders
Asquith, Mary
1914   Life's Shop Window
Asta, a dog *same as* **Skippy, a dog**
1936   After the Thin Man
Asta, Mrs., a dog
1936   After the Thin Man
Astaire, Fred
1942   Holiday Inn
Astaire, Marie
1926   A Trip to Chinatown
1930   The Grand Parade
Astar, Ben *same as* **Ben-Astar, Albert**
1951   Queen for a Day
1953   Fort Ti
         Tonight We Sing
Asther, Nils
1927   Topsy and Eva
1945   Jealousy
1948   The Feathered Serpent
Astor, Camille
1915   Chimmie Fadden
         Chimmie Fadden Out West
1916   For the Defense
         The Thousand Dollar Husband

Astor, Gertrude
1921　Through the Back Door
1926　The Strong Man
1928　The Cohens and the
　　　　Kellys in Paris
　　　　Uncle Tom's Cabin
1929　Frozen Justice
1941　Hold Back the Dawn
1948　Music Man
1949　The Story of Seabiscuit
1950　Jolson Sings Again
1951　Apache Drums
　　　　Queen for a Day
1952　Fort Osage
1956　Westward Ho the
　　　　Wagons!
1957　The Oklahoman

Astor, Mary
1925　Don Q, Son of Zorro
　　　　Scarlet Saint
1927　Rose of the Golden West
1930　Ladies Love Brutes
　　　　The Lash
1942　Across the Pacific

Astor, Nubar Arthur
1951　Saturday's Hero

Astwood, Norman
1940　Paradise in Harlem
1941　Murder on Lenox Avenue
　　　　Sunday Sinners

Atchley, Hooper
1934　The Prescott Kid
1937　The Plainsman
1938　Mr. Wong, Detective
　　　　Road Demon
　　　　Speed to Burn
1939　The Mystery of Mr. Wong
1940　The Fatal Hour
　　　　The Gay Caballero
　　　　Geronimo
1942　Gentleman Jim
　　　　Three Hearts for Julia
　　　　The Vanishing Virginian
1943　Action in the North
　　　　Atlantic
　　　　Gangway for Tomorrow
　　　　In Old Oklahoma

Atcitty, Thomas
1952?　Call of the Navajo

Ates, Dorothy
1942　Woman of the Year

Ates, Roscoe *same as* **Ates, Rosco**
1930　Check and Double Check
1931　Cimarron
1932　The Rainbow Trail
1939　Gone With the Wind
1941　Birth of the Blues
　　　　Sullivan's Travels
1946　Wild West
1947　West to Glory
1957　Run of the Arrow

Athanasiou, Pofi
1931　Such Is Life

Athens, Vi
1943　Good Luck, Mr. Yates

Atkins, Albert
1955　The Rose Tattoo

Atkins, Barbara
1951　Mask of the Dragon

Atkins, Sherry
1951　Slaughter Trail

The Tommy Atkins Sextette
1930　King of Jazz

Atkinson, George
1948　I Remember Mama

Atlas, Dorothy
1947　Desperate

Atlas, Leopold
1944　Tomorrow the World!

Attaway, Ruth
1957　Raintree County
1959　Porgy and Bess

Atterbury, Malcolm
1956　Dakota Incident
　　　　The Lone Ranger
　　　　Reprisal!
1960　Wild River

Atwater, Barry
1956　Man from Del Rio

Atwater, Edith
1949　C-Man
1951　Teresa

Atwater, Gladys
1942　American Empire
1953　The Great Sioux Uprising
1954　Overland Pacific
　　　　Siege at Red River

Atwell, Roy
1946　Abie's Irish Rose

Atwill, Lionel
1935　Rendezvous
1939　Mr. Moto Takes a
　　　　Vacation
1940　Charlie Chan in Panama
　　　　Charlie Chan's Murder
　　　　Cruise

Aubert, Lenore
1949　The Prairie

Aubrey, Helen
1914　The Redemption of David
　　　　Corson

Aubrey, Jimmy
1925　The Gold Hunters
1930　The Grand Parade
1935　Rescue Squad
1936　Aces and Eights
1939　Charlie Chan in Reno
　　　　Mr. Moto Takes a
　　　　Vacation
　　　　Mr. Moto's Last Warning
1940　Charlie Chan in Panama
1941　Dead Men Tell
1944　Hi, Beautiful
1946　Abie's Irish Rose
　　　　Bringing Up Father
　　　　Rendezvous 24
1947　Jiggs and Maggie in
　　　　Society
1948　Jiggs and Maggie in Court
1949　Jiggs and Maggie in
　　　　Jackpot Jitters

Aubuchon, Jacques
1953　Beneath the 12-Mile Reef
　　　　So Big

Auclair, Jacqueline
1956　Hot Blood

Audet, Earl
1943　Tahiti Honey

Audley, Eleanor
1950　No Way Out
1951　Gambling House
1956　Full of Life
1958　Home Before Dark
1959　The FBI Story

Audley, Michael
1942　Syncopation
1947　The Foxes of Harrow
1948　Cry of the City
　　　　Fury at Furnace Creek
　　　　Gentleman's Agreement
1950　Panic in the Streets

Auen, Signe
1915　A Yankee from the West

Auer, Florence
1922　Fair Lady
1925　The Beautiful City
1949　Knock on Any Door

Auer, John H.
1931　El comediante
1937　Manhattan
　　　　Merry-Go-Round
1938　Outside of Paradise
1939　Forged Passport
1943　Gangway for Tomorrow
　　　　Tahiti Honey
1954　Hell's Half Acre

Auer, Mischa
1931　Delicious
　　　　Women Love Once
1932　Call Her Savage
　　　　No Greater Love
1936　Winterset
1937　That Girl from Paris
1938　The Rage of Paris
1940　Elsa Maxwell's Public
　　　　Deb No. 1
1942　Twin Beds

Auer, Stephen
1944　The San Antonio Kid
　　　　Sheriff of Las Vegas
　　　　Vigilantes of Dodge City

1949　Rose of the Yukon
1952　Woman in the Dark

Auerbach, Peter
1943　Action in the North
　　　　Atlantic

August, Adelle
1955　Apache Ambush

August, Edwin
1916　The Social Highwayman
　　　　The Yellow Passport
1918　A Broadway Scandal
　　　　The City of Tears
1938　The Rage of Paris

Augusta, Howard
1924　Smiling Hate
1927　Children of Fate

Augustin, William
1934　Coming Out Party

Augustine, Larry
1939　Miracle on Main Street

Auld, Aggie
1938　Hawaii Calls

Aulli, Marco
1958　Seven Hills of Rome

Aumont, Geneviv
1957　Journey to Freedom

Aumont, Jean Pierre
1959　John Paul Jones

Aunt Jemima *see* **Gardella, Tess**

Aurness, James *see* **Arness, James**

Aurthur, Robert Alan (*writer*) *not
　the same as* **Arthur, Robert**
　(*prod, writer*)
1957　Edge of the City

Austen, Leslie
1918　A Woman of Impulse

Auster, Islin
1942　The Navy Comes Through

Austin, Alan
1960　Pay or Die

Austin, Albert
1922　My Boy
1933　The Cohens and Kellys in
　　　　Trouble

Austin, Angela
1959　The Black Orchid

Austin, Charlotte
1957　Pawnee

Austin, Frank
1931　Noche de duendes
1948　Jiggs and Maggie in Court

Austin, Gene
1936　Klondike Annie

Austin, Jack
1921　The Green-Eyed Monster

Austin, Jere *not the same as*
Austin, Jerry
1918　Uncle Tom's Cabin
1919　Erstwhile Susan
1922　Cardigan

Austin, Jerry *not the same as*
Austin, Jere
1946　Saratoga Trunk

Austin, Leslie
1923　Jamestown

Austin, Lois
1946　G. I. War Brides
　　　　The Trap
　　　　Without Reservations
1948　The Golden Eye
　　　　Shanghai Chest
1952　Fort Osage

Austin, Phyllis Konstam
1960　The Crowning
　　　　Experience

Austin, Rene
1942　Tales of Manhattan

Austin, William
1923　Ruggles of Red Gap
1934　Imitation of Life

Autant-Lara, Claude
1931　Buster se marie
1932　L'athlète incomplet
　　　　Le plombier amoureux

Authmar, Lee
1929　The Peacock Fan

Autry, Gene
1935　Melody Trail
　　　　The Singing Vagabond
1936　Ride, Ranger, Ride

1937　Boots and Saddles
　　　　Manhattan
　　　　Merry-Go-Round
1941　Under Fiesta Stars
1947　The Last Round-Up
1949　The Cowboy and the
　　　　Indians
1950　Indian Territory
1952　Apache Country

Avasiago, Los
1949?　Harlem Follies

Avent, John E.
1950　Intruder in the Dust

Averback, Hy
1956　The Benny Goodman
　　　　Story

Averill, Jackie
1943　The Meanest Man in the
　　　　World

Aversa, Roy
1948　Music Man

Avery, Dwayne
1955　Blackboard Jungle

Avery, Emile
1953　The Man from the Alamo
　　　　Tumbleweed
1954　War Arrow
1955　Chief Crazy Horse
1957　Run of the Arrow

Avery, Mary
1938　The Beloved Brat

Avery, Phyllis
1951　Queen for a Day

Avery, Ted
1951　Little Big Horn
1952　Kid Monk Baroni

Avery, Tol
1951　Gambling House
1955　Headline Hunters
1960　This Rebel Breed

Avery, Val
1957　Edge of the City
1959　Last Train from Gun Hill

Avil, Gordon
1931　El proceso de Mary
　　　　Dugan (*foreign
　　　　version*)

Avila, Ben
1955　Blackboard Jungle

Avila, Henry
1935　A Night at the Opera

Avonde, Richard
1949　Tuna Clipper

Avramenko, Vasile *same as*
　Avramenko, V.
1937　Natalka Poltavka
1939　Cossacks in Exile
1940　The Tragedy of
　　　　Carpatho-Ukraine

Avril, Carlos
1930　Toda una vida (*foreign
　　　　version*)

Axelle, Violet
1935　The Wedding Night

Axiotis, Giorgios
1954　Barefoot Battalion

Axman, Hanne
1949　The Red Menace

Axness, Ralph
1948　The Paleface

Axzell, Carl
1917　The Adventures of Carol

Axzell, Evelyn
1918　The Hell Cat

Axzell, Violet
1916　The Flames of Johannis

Ayars, Ann
1942　Apache Trail
　　　　Nazi Agent

Aye, Maryon
1926　Irene

Aylesworth, Arthur *same as*
Aylsworth, Arthur
1936　Dimples
　　　　Rose of the Rancho
1937　Slave Ship
1938　The Adventures of Tom
　　　　Sawyer
　　　　Spawn of the North
1939　The Adventures of
　　　　Huckleberry Finn
　　　　Drums Along the Mohawk
　　　　The Return of the Cisco
　　　　Kid

Aylesworth, Arthur
1940   Northwest Passage (Book I—Rogers' Rangers)
        Santa Fe Trail
1941   Western Union
Aylesworth, Douglas
1947   King of the Bandits
Aylsworth, Arthur see **Aylesworth, Arthur**
Ayres, Agnes
1917   The Renaissance at Charleroi
1937   Maid of Salem
        Souls at Sea
Ayres, John
1957   The Halliday Brand
Ayres, Lew
1930   East Is West
1932   The Cohens and Kellys in Hollywood
1951   New Mexico
Mitch Ayres Orchestra
1944   Lady, Let's Dance!
Ayres, Robert
1959   John Paul Jones
Azevedo, Alexandre de
1930   Toda una vida (foreign version)
Babb, Dorothy
1941   Playmates
1944   Chip Off the Old Block
Babbitt, Harry
1941   Playmates
Babcock, Dwight V.
1945   The Mummy's Curse
Baber, Vivianne
1932   The Black King
Babishwili, Wladimir
1952   Anything Can Happen
Baby Evelyn
1925   The Greatest Love of All
Baby Marie see **Osborne, Marie**
Baca, Jose
1950   Two Flags West
Baca, Zita
1934   Stand Up and Cheer!
Bacall, Lauren
1948   Key Largo
1950   Young Man with a Horn
Baccaloni, Salvatore
1956   Full of Life
Bacchus, Antony
1949   Illegal Entry
Bachelor, Stephanie
1943   His Butler's Sister
1944   Lake Placid Serenade
1946   G. I. War Brides
Bacher, William A.
1947   The Foxes of Harrow
Bachman, Lawrence P.
1942   Dr. Gillespie's New Assistant
1943   Dr. Gillespie's Criminal Case
Bachus, Michael
1959   Last Train from Gun Hill
Bacigalupi, Louis
1945   Nob Hill
1947   The Foxes of Harrow
Backer, Franklyn E.
1922   Big Stakes
Backes, Alice
1948   Up in Central Park
Backus, George
1948   Moonrise
Backus, Georgia
1941   They Dare Not Love
1942   Shut My Big Mouth
1951   Apache Drums
        The Mark of the Renegade
Backus, Henny
1955   Blackboard Jungle
Backus, Jim
1950   Emergency Wedding
1952   Bright Victory
1960   Ice Palace
Backus, Lionel
1934   Our Daily Bread

Bacon, Bob see **Bacon, Robert**
Bacon, David
1943   Crash Dive
Bacon, Frank
1916   Her Debt of Honor
Bacon, Gerald F.
1915   The Melting Pot
Bacon, Irving
1934   Broadway Bill
1937   Big City
1938   Mr. Moto's Gamble
        Passport Husband
        Spawn of the North
        The Texans
1939   The Adventures of Huckleberry Finn
        Gone With the Wind
        Heaven with a Barbed Wire Fence
1940   Jennie
1941   Accent on Love
        Ride on Vaquero
        Western Union
1942   Holiday Inn
        They Died With Their Boots On
        Young America
1943   Action in the North Atlantic
        The Amazing Mrs. Holliday
        In Old Oklahoma
1944   Chip Off the Old Block
        Since You Went Away
1948   Moonrise
        Rocky
1950   Emergency Wedding
1952   Rose of Cimarron
1953   Fort Ti
1956   Dakota Incident
1958   Ambush at Cimarron Pass
        Fort Massacre
Bacon, Jim
1959   Al Capone
1960   Pay or Die
Bacon, Lloyd
1926   Private Izzy Murphy
1934   He Was Her Man
1935   The Irish in Us
1940   Knute Rockne—All American
        Three Cheers for the Irish
1942   Wings for the Eagle
1943   Action in the North Atlantic
1944   The Sullivans
1953   The Great Sioux Uprising
Bacon, Margaret
1960   Pay or Die
Bacon, Robert same as **Bacon, Bob**
1947   Buck Privates Come Home
1948   The Miracle of the Bells
Bacon, Shelby
1942   Holiday Inn
1944   Since You Went Away
1946   Saratoga Trunk
1947   The Peanut Man
1949   Pinky
Bacon, Walter
1958   Home Before Dark
Baden, S. C.
1931   Pardon Us (foreign version)
Badger, Clarence G. same as **Badger, Clarence** not the same as **Badger, Clarence, Jr.**
1919   Daughter of Mine
1921   Guile of Women
1923   Potash and Perlmutter
1926   The Campus Flirt
1930   The Bad Man
Badger, Clarence, Jr. not the same as **Badger, Clarence G.**
1942   The Vanishing Virginian
1945   Rhapsody in Blue
Badin, Max
1940   Eli Eli
        The Great Advisor
        Her Second Mother

Baena, Carlos see **Martínez Baena, Carlos**
Baer, Buddy
1952   The Big Sky
1953   Dream Wife
Baer, John
1951   Saturday's Hero
1952   The Battle at Apache Pass
        Indian Uprising
Baer, Max
1942   The Navy Comes Through
1943   Ladies' Day
Baer, Parley
1950   Comanche Territory
1958   The Young Lions
1959   The FBI Story
1960   The Adventures of Huckleberry Finn
Bagdad, William
1956   Hot Blood
Bagdasarian, Ross
1953   The Stars Are Singing
1956   Hot Blood
Baggett, Lynne
1943   Air Force
1945   Rhapsody in Blue
Baggot, King same as **Baggott, King**
1921   Cheated Love
1928   The House of Scandal
1934   Beloved
1935   Chinatown Squad
1941   Come Live with Me
Bagley, James
1915   How Molly Malone Made Good
Bagni, John
1941   Mutiny in the Arctic
        New York Town
1947   The Foxes of Harrow
1950   Black Hand
Baguez, Salvador
1949   We Were Strangers
1952   The Iron Mistress
1956   Wetbacks
Bail, Charles
1959   The Jayhawkers!
Bailey, Bill not the same as **Bailey, William Norton**
1943   Cabin in the Sky
Bailey, Buck
1949   Satan's Cradle
Bailey, Carmen
1935   ¡Asegure a su mujer!
1936   El diablo del mar
        Ramona
1938   California Frontier
        Daughter of Shanghai
1939   Drifting Westward
        La Inmaculada
Bailey, Don
1922   The Top O' the Morning
Bailey, Frankie
1925   Flower of Night
Bailey, Gail
1949   Stallion Canyon
Bailey, Harry
1927   The Princess from Hoboken
1938   City Streets
1940   Geronimo
Bailey, Jack
1951   Queen for a Day
Bailey, Joe
1953   Column South
Bailey, John
1946   Till the End of Time
Bailey, Lee
1933   It's Great to Be Alive
Bailey, Lynn
1938   Dangerous to Know
Bailey, Oliver D.
1915   The Melting Pot
Bailey, Pearl
1954   Carmen Jones
1958   St. Louis Blues
1959   Porgy and Bess
1960   All the Fine Young Cannibals

Bailey, Polly same as **Bailey, Polly Vann; Vann, Polly**
1936   Klondike Annie
1937   Man of the People
1940   If I Had My Way
1942   Nazi Agent
        We Were Dancing
1943   The Amazing Mrs. Holliday
1945   Nob Hill
1946   Bringing Up Father
1947   Dark Delusion
        Easy Come, Easy Go
1950   Annie Get Your Gun
        No Way Out
        Stars in My Crown
Bailey, Raymond
1949   The Girl from Jones Beach
1957   Band of Angels
1959   Al Capone
Bailey, Richard
1947   The Burning Cross
1950   Ambush
Bailey, Sherwood
1934   Beloved
1936   Paddy O'Day
1937   The Plainsman
Bailey, William Norton same as **Bailey, William; Bailey, Wm. Norton** not the same as **Bailey, Bill**
1936   Charlie Chan's Secret
        Klondike Annie
1942   Nazi Agent
1944   Andy Hardy's Blonde Trouble
1947   Desperate
        The Farmer's Daughter
        The Foxes of Harrow
1948   Music Man
        Silver Trails
        Unconquered
1950   Devil's Doorway
Bain, Babette
1957   Beau James
Bainbridge, W. H. same as **Bainbridge, William H.**
1917   The Bond Between
1918   A Broadway Scandal
        Mystic Faces
1919   Desert Gold
Bains, Pearl
1939   Straight to Heaven
Bainter, Fay
1939   Daughters Courageous
1942   Woman of the Year
1944   Dark Waters
Bair, David
1946   Canyon Passage
1948   Big City
Baird, Jimmy
1959   The Black Orchid
Baird, Leah
1917   One Law for Both
1919   As a Man Thinks
        The Volcano
1923   The Miracle Makers
1942   All Through the Night
        Secret Enemies
1943   Action in the North Atlantic
        Air Force
        Yankee Doodle Dandy
1947   Humoresque
1949   The Girl from Jones Beach
1951   Queen for a Day
Baird, Michael
1956   Dakota Incident
Bajor, Gizi
1930   El secreto del doctor (foreign version)
Bakaleinikoff, Constantin
1958   St. Louis Blues
Bakalyan, Richard
1957   The Brothers Rico
Baker, Art
1946   Abie's Irish Rose
1947   Dark Delusion
        The Farmer's Daughter
1949   Massacre River

1951   Only the Valiant

Baker, Benny
1936   Rose of the Rancho
1948   My Girl Tisa
1949   Rose of the Yukon

Baker, Bob
1938   Outlaw Express

Baker, Carroll
1956   Baby Doll
        Giant

Baker, Consuelo
1933   Let's Fall in Love
1934   Coming Out Party

Baker, Doris
1920   The Secret Gift

Baker, Doyle
1955   Blackboard Jungle

Baker, Eddie
1934   Our Daily Bread
1955   Trial
1956   Dakota Incident
        Giant

Baker, Elsie
1950   Mystery Street

Baker, Fay
1946   Notorious
1951   The House on Telegraph
        Hill

Baker, Frank same as **Baker, Frank C.**
1936   Klondike Annie
1940   Escape to Glory
1951   Saturday's Hero
1957   Run of the Arrow
1958   The Last Hurrah

Baker, Freddie
1942   Take My Life

Baker, George D.
1916   The Pretenders
1918   In Judgment Of
        The Only Road
        Toys of Fate

Baker, Graham same as **Baker, C. Graham**
1925   The Beautiful City
1926   Millionaires
1927   Irish Hearts
1933   Song of the Eagle
1942   Valley of the Sun
1948   Four Faces West

Baker, Herbert
1953   Dream Wife

Baker, Hettie Gray
1914   John Barleycorn
        An Odyssey of the North

Baker, James
1937   The Plainsman

Baker, Joby
1959   The Last Angry Man
1960   Key Witness

Baker, Kenny
1943   Doughboys in Ireland
1947   Calendar Girl

Baker, Phil
1943   The Gang's All Here

Baker, Snowy
1937   Big City

Baker, Tommy
1940   Knute Rockne—All American

Bakewell, William
1931   The Great Meadow
1934   Straight Is the Way
1936   Sea Spoilers
1939   Gone With the Wind
1947   The Farmer's Daughter
        King of the Bandits
1948   Night Wind
1951   Oh! Susanna
        When the Redskins Rode
1955   Davy Crockett, King of the Wild Frontier

Bakshitsyky, Louis
1934   The Youth of Russia

Balanoff, Simchah
1934   The Rabbi's Power

Balart, Lucille
1927   With Sitting Bull at the Spirit Lake Massacre

Balázs, Béla
1931   Die Dreigroschenoper
        Die Dreigroschenoper (foreign version)
        La fiesta del diablo (foreign version)

Balch, Slim same as **Balch, Joe**
1946   Sunset Pass
1956   The Last Hunt

Balderston, John L.
1936   The Last of the Mohicans

Baldock, Alvin
1951   Saturday's Hero

Baldra, Chuck
1934   Fighting Through

Baldwin, Bill
1952   It's a Big Country: An American Anthology
1958   St. Louis Blues

Baldwin, Curley
1918   Little Red Decides

Baldwin, Dick
1937   Life Begins in College
1938   Mr. Moto's Gamble

Baldwin, Earl
1935   The Irish in Us
1942   The Navy Comes Through

Baldwin, Frank D.
1914   The Indian Wars
1917   The Adventures of Buffalo Bill

Baldwin, Jack
1934   Our Daily Bread

Baldwin, Peter
1957   The Tin Star

Baldwin, R. H. could be same as **Baldwin, Robert**
1955   Foxfire

Baldwin, Robert could be same as **Baldwin, R. H.**
1941   Caught in the Act

Baldwin, Ruth Ann
1919   The Sneak
1921   Puppets of Fate

Baldwin, Walter
1942   In This Our Life
        Syncopation
        They Died With Their Boots On
1943   Let's Have Fun
1944   Since You Went Away
1948   Cry of the City
        Unconquered
1949   The Gay Amigo
        Thieves' Highway
1953   Ride, Vaquero!
1960   Oklahoma Territory

Balfour, Sue same as **Balfour, Sue, Mrs.**
1914   Springtime
1917   The Slacker (Metro Pictures Corp.)

Balin, Ina
1959   The Black Orchid

Ball, Frank
1932   The Forty-Niners
1936   Border Phantom

Ball, Lucille
1934   Broadway Bill
1937   That Girl from Paris
1940   Too Many Girls
1942   Valley of the Sun

Ball, Marshall
1950   The Men

Ball, Olive
1938   The Toy Wife
1942   Tales of Manhattan
1951   The Tall Target

Ball, Suzan
1954   War Arrow
1955   Chief Crazy Horse

Ballantyne, Lon
1960   Flaming Star
        I Passed for White

Ballard, Rex
1921   Across the Divide

Ballard, Shirley
1950   Emergency Wedding

Ballerino, Cecil
1944   Since You Went Away

Ballester, Amparo
1949   That Midnight Kiss

Ballesteros, Conchita
1930   The Bad Man (foreign version)
        La voluntad del muerto

Ballesteros, Manuel
1930   La voluntad del muerto

Ballesteros, Rosita
1930   The Bad Man (foreign version)
        Monsieur le Fox
        Sevilla de mis amores

Ballew, Smith
1950   I Killed Geronimo

Ballin, Hugo
1919   Daughter of Mine
1920   Pagan Love
1925   The Prairie Wife

Ballin, Mabel
1918   Laughing Bill Hyde
1920   Pagan Love

Ballon, Nanette
1945   The Dolly Sisters

Ballou, Harry
1940   The Notorious Elinor Lee

Ballou, Marion
1930   The Big Pond
1934   Our Daily Bread

Balsam, Martin
1957   Twelve Angry Men
1958   Marjorie Morningstar
1959   Al Capone

Balshakov, Alex
1934   The Youth of Russia

Balshofer, Fred
1930   La jaula de los leones

Balter, Sam
1951   The Harlem Globetrotters

Bamattre, Martha
1937   It Could Happen to You
1938   Gateway
1942   Syncopation
1944   Address Unknown
1950   Battleground
1951   The Great Caruso

Bancroft, Anne
1953   Tonight We Sing
1956   The Last Frontier
        Walk the Proud Land

Bancroft, Charles
1933   La melodía prohibida

Bancroft, George
1927   White Gold
1929   Thunderbolt
1930   Ladies Love Brutes
1942   Syncopation

The Banda Da Lua
1943   The Gang's All Here
1944   Something for the Boys

Bane, Hollis same as **Bane, Holly** could be same as **Ragan, Mike**
1947   Buffalo Bill Rides Again
1948   Harpoon
        Renegades of Sonora
1949   Riders of the Range
1950   North of the Great Divide
        Storm Over Wyoming

Bankhead, Tallulah
1918   Thirty a Week
1944   Lifeboat

Banks, Charles E.
1922   A California Romance

Banks, Douglas
1952   Red Ball Express

Banks, Estar
1918   A Woman of Impulse

Banks, F. L.
1919   Injustice

Banks, Gertrude "Baby"
1955   Brevities of 1955

Banks, Joan
1952   Bright Victory

Banks, Monty
1924   Racing Luck

Banks, Otis
1919   Injustice

Banks, Mrs. Otis
1919   Injustice

Banks, Sadie
1933   Live and Laugh

Banky, Vilma
1929   This Is Heaven
1930   A Lady to Love
        A Lady to Love (foreign version)

Bannai, Paul
1951   Go for Broke!

Banner, John
1941   Accent on Love
1943   They Came to Blow Up America
1946   Rendezvous 24
1948   My Girl Tisa
1951   Go for Broke!
1959   The Wonderful Country

Bannister, Joy
1947   Citizen Saint

Bannister, Monica
1932   Hypnotized
1941   Accent on Love

Bannon, Jim same as **Bannon, James**
1945   The Gay Senorita
1949   The Cowboy and the Prizefighter
        Ride, Ryder, Ride!
        Roll Thunder Roll!
1950   Jiggs and Maggie Out West
1954   War Arrow
1959   Inside the Mafia

Bara, Nina
1945   The Gay Senorita
        The Mummy's Curse
1950   A Lady Without Passport

Bara, Theda not the same as **Barr, Theda**
1915   The Clemenceau Case
        Kreutzer Sonata
1915? Sin
1916   Gold and the Woman

Baratoff, Ben-Zvi
1938   The Singing Blacksmith

Barbash, Bob
1960   The Plunderers

Barbato, Rosa
1948   Music Man
1959   The Black Orchid

Barbé, Carlos
1930   La fuerza del querer
1943   Action in the North Atlantic
1947   The Foxes of Harrow

Barber, Bobby
1943   The Amazing Mrs. Holliday
1947   Spoilers of the North
        Vigilantes of Boomtown
1948   Big City
        The Miracle of the Bells
1949   The Girl from Jones Beach
1950   Sunset in the West
1951   Across the Wide Missouri

Barbéris, René
1930   Un hombre de suerte
        Un hombre de suerte (foreign version)

Barbi, Vince
1958   Never Love a Stranger
1960   Pay or Die

Barbier, George
1930   The Big Pond
1933   A Lady's Profession
1934   The Cat's-Paw
1935   McFadden's Flats
1937   Waikiki Wedding
1938   My Lucky Star
1942   Song of the Islands
1943   Yankee Doodle Dandy

Bárcena, Catalina
1931   Mamá
1933   Primavera en otoño
        Una viuda romántica
        Yo, tú y ella
1934   La ciudad de cartón
1935   Julieta compra un hijo
        Señora casada necesita marido

Barclay, Don
1936   Border Phantom
        Treachery Rides the
            Range
1937   Black Legion
1938   Outlaw Express
1942   Mexican Spitfire Sees a
            Ghost
        Mexican Spitfire's
            Elephant
1955   The Long Gray Line

Barclay, Jerry
1958   Gun Fever
1959   Gunmen from Laredo

Barclay, Joan same as **Greear, Geraine**
1936   The Glory Trail
        West of Nevada
1943   Ladies' Day
        Mexican Spitfire's Blessed
            Event
1945   The Shanghai Cobra

Barclay, Stephen
1944   The Sullivans
        Vigilantes of Dodge City
1946   G. I. War Brides

Barcroft, Roy
1940   East of the River
        Santa Fe Trail
1942   Below the Border
        Nazi Agent
        They Died With Their
            Boots On
1943   Dr. Gillespie's Criminal
            Case
        In Old Oklahoma
        Wagon Tracks West
1945   Colorado Pioneers
1946   Sun Valley Cyclone
1947   Marshal of Cripple Creek
        Oregon Trail Scouts
        Rustlers of Devil's
            Canyon
        Spoilers of the North
        Vigilantes of Boomtown
1948   Old Los Angeles
        Renegades of Sonora
1949   Ranger of Cherokee Strip
1950   The Missourians
        North of the Great Divide
        Rock Island Trail
1953   Old Overland Trail
1956   The Last Hunt
1957   Band of Angels

Bard, Ben
1943   The Leopard Man

Bardette, Trevor
1939   Charlie Chan at Treasure
            Island
        Let Freedom Ring
        Stand Up and Fight
1940   Murder over New York
        New Moon
        Santa Fe Trail
        Three Faces West
        Young Buffalo Bill
1941   Doomed Caravan
        Mystery Ship
        Romance of the Rio
            Grande
1942   Apache Trail
1943   Deerslayer
1947   The Last Round-Up
        Marshal of Cripple Creek
1948   The Paleface
        Unconquered
1949   Apache Chief
        Lust for Gold
1950   A Lady Without Passport
        The Palomino
1953   Ambush at Tomahawk
            Gap
        The Man from the Alamo
        The Sun Shines Bright
1954   Dangerous Mission
1957   Dragoon Wells Massacre

Bárdi, Odön
1930   El secreto del doctor
            (foreign version)

Bardot, Joe
1959   Night of the Quarter
            Moon

Bare, Richard L.
1960   This Rebel Breed

Barela, Adolfo
1954   Salt of the Earth

Eddie Barfield's Trio
1937   Bargain with Bullets

Bargy, Roy
1930   King of Jazz

Bari, Lynn
1938   Josette
        Mr. Moto's Gamble
        Speed to Burn
1939   City in Darkness
        The Return of the Cisco
            Kid
1940   Kit Carson
1941   Sun Valley Serenade

Barile, Chiarina
1960   Weddings and Babies

Baring, Mathilde
1918   Love's Law

Barker, Adella
1915   Time Lock Number 776

Barker, Bill
1957   Revolt at Fort Laramie

Barker, Bonita
1933   It's Great to Be Alive

Barker, Bradley
1916   A Woman's Honor
1919   Come Out of the Kitchen
        Erstwhile Susan
1929   Mother's Boy

Barker, Cecil
1949   Portrait of Jennie

Barker, Jess
1943   Good Luck, Mr. Yates
1955   Kentucky Rifle

Barker, Lex
1947   Crossfire
        The Farmer's Daughter
        Under the Tonto Rim
1948   Unconquered
1952   Battles of Chief Pontiac
1955   Duel on the Mississippi
1957   The Deerslayer
        War Drums

Barker, Margaret
1949   Lost Boundaries

Barker, Patricia
1943   Dr. Gillespie's Criminal
            Case
1944   Three Men in White

Barker, Reginald (dir) not the
    same as **Barker, Reginald C.**
    (writer)
1915   The Italian
1916   The Criminal
        Three of Many
1918   The Hell Cat
1920   Dangerous Days
1927   The Frontiersman

Barker, Reginald C. (writer) not
    the same as **Barker, Reginald**
    (director)
1925   Quicker'n Lightnin'

Barleon, Amelia
1919   The Scar

Barlow, Reginald
1933   Grand Slam
1934   Operator 13
1935   Romance in Manhattan
1936   The Last of the Mohicans
1942   Syncopation

Barlowe, Joy
1941   Louisiana Purchase
1945   Where Do We Go From
            Here?

Barman, Valmere
1948   Unconquered

Barnard, Harry
1934   Our Daily Bread

Barnes, Binnie
1935   Rendezvous
1936   The Last of the Mohicans
        Sutter's Gold
1938   Gateway
1948   The Dude Goes West

Barnes, Charles Mercer
1951   Saturday's Hero

Barnes, Deslys
1934   Stand Up and Cheer!

Barnes, Francis
1956   Serenade

Barnes, Gordon
1952   Red Snow

Barnes, Jane
1935   Melody Trail
        Naughty Marietta
1937   Man of the People

Barnes, Joanna
1958   Home Before Dark

Barnes, Kathryn
1936   Star for a Night
1938   In Old Chicago

Barnes, Mae
1959   Odds Against Tomorrow

Barnes, Rayford
1954   Drum Beat
        Hondo
1955   Seven Angry Men
1956   The Burning Hills
1958   Fort Massacre
1960   Cimarron

Barnes, T. Roy
1931   Aloha

Barnes, V. L.
1932   Hidden Valley

Barnes, Walter
1958   Oregon Passage

Barnet, Charlie
1942   Syncopation

Barnett, Antonina
1947   Northwest Outpost

Barnett, Griff
1946   Without Reservations
1947   Duel in the Sun
1948   Fighting Father Dunne
        Fury at Furnace Creek
        Tap Roots
        Unconquered
1949   Pinky
1950   Storm Over Wyoming

Barnett, Jackie same as **Barnett, Jack**
1950   Right Cross
1953   The Eddie Cantor Story

Barnett, Loretta
1942   Holiday Inn

Barnett, Vince same as **Barnett, Vincent**
1932   Flesh
        Scarface
        Tiger Shark
1934   The Cat's-Paw
1935   Black Fury
1936   After the Thin Man
        Down to the Sea
        Yellow Cargo
1942   Foreign Agent
1943   Crime Smasher
1947   The Mighty McGurk
1949   Knock on Any Door
1950   Border Treasure
1953   The Jazz Singer

Barney, Jay
1950   A Lady Without Passport

Barney, Marion
1919   Mandarin's Gold

Barnick, Ted
1941   New York Town

Barnum, Bill
1946   Till the End of Time

Baroja, Ricardo
1931   La incorregible

Baron, Joyce Ann
1950   Intruder in the Dust

Baron, Lita see **Isabelita**

Barón, Max see **Wagner, Max**

Baron, Rudy
1951   The Great Caruso

Baronian, Haiyastan
1945   Anoush

Barr, Anthony same as **Barr, Tony**
1949   Border Incident
        Daughter of the West
1951   Cuban Fireball

Barr, Byron see **Young, Gig**

Barr, Edna
1934   Drums O' Voodoo

Barr, Muriel
1942   Holiday Inn

Barr, Theda not the same as **Bara, Theda**
1949   Knock on Any Door

Barrado, Emilia
1931   Su noche de bodas

Barrat, Robert same as **Barrat, Robert H.**
1934   Massacre
1935   Bordertown
1936   The Last of the Mohicans
1937   The Barrier
        Black Legion
1938   Breaking the Ice
        The Buccaneer
        The Texans
1939   Allegheny Uprising
        Bad Lands
        Charlie Chan in Honolulu
        The Cisco Kid and the
            Lady
        Man of Conquest
        The Return of the Cisco
            Kid
1940   Northwest Passage (Book
            I—Rogers' Rangers)
1942   American Empire
1943   They Came to Blow Up
            America
1945   The Great John L.
        Wanderer of the
            Wasteland
1946   Sunset Pass
1949   Riders of the Range
1950   The Baron of Arizona
        Davy Crockett, Indian
            Scout
1951   Distant Drums

Barraud, George
1923   Little Old New York
1934   Charlie Chan in London

Barrera, Rolando
1948   The Paleface

Barret, Michael
1950   The Cariboo Trail

Barreto, Pedro
1931   La fiesta del diablo

Barrett, Bernice
1946   Notorious

Barrett, Claudia
1949   The Story of Seabiscuit

Barrett, Curt
1951   Mask of the Dragon

Barrett, Dorothy
1917   The Pulse of Life

Barrett, Janet
1936   Ramona
1944   Mr. Skeffington
1947   Humoresque

Barrett, Majel
1959   The Black Orchid

Barrett, Muriel
1936   Ramona

Barrett, Tony
1947   The Farmer's Daughter
        Under the Tonto Rim
        Wild Horse Mesa
1948   Guns of Hate
        Western Heritage
1950   Black Hand

Barrias, Antonia
1928   El Robin Hood de México

Barrie, Barbara
1956   Giant

Barrie, Mona
1934   Charlie Chan in London
1942   Syncopation

Barrie, Nigel
1919   Diane of the Green Van
1922   East Is West
1925   Hogan's Alley

Barrier, Edgar
1940   Escape
1941   They Dare Not Love
1945   Nob Hill
1948   Rocky
1950   Last of the Buccaneers
1951   Hurricane Island

1953 The Stand at Apache
 River
Barringer, R. E.
1931 Riders of the Rio
Barrington, Herbert
1914 The Great Diamond
 Robbery
1916 Broken Chains
Barrington, Phyllis
1931 Law of the Tong
Barris, Harry
1930 King of Jazz
1936 Show Boat
1941 Birth of the Blues
1942 Holiday Inn
1943 Dixie
Barriscale, Bessie
1914 Rose of the Rancho
1934 Beloved
Barron, Baynes
1949 Lust for Gold
1952 California Conquest
1955 Duel on the Mississippi
1958 Ambush at Cimarron Pass
Barrón, Isabel
1930 Toda una vida
Barron, Kirk
1944 Since You Went Away
Barron, Richard
1952 Red Snow
Barron, Robert
1946 Saratoga Trunk
1948 Unconquered
Barrow, Dick
1955 Brevities of 1955
Barrows, George
1959 Imitation of Life
 The Jayhawkers!
Barrows, Henry A. *same as*
 Barrows, H. A.; Barrows,
 Henry
1916 A Man of Sorrow
1917 The Captain of the Gray
 Horse Troop
 Lost in Transit
1918 The Temple of Dusk
1919 The Right to Happiness
1920 The Purple Cipher
1925 Cobra
1926 The Little Irish Girl
1930 The Kibitzer
1934 Broadway Bill
Barrows, James O. *same as*
 Barrows, James
1919 The Lord Loves the Irish
1922 The Pride of Palomar
Barrows, Nick
1928 The Night Bird
Barry, Baby Charline
1935 Riddle Ranch
Barry, Donald *same as* **Barry, Don;**
 Barry, Red
1949 The Dalton Gang
1950 Train to Tombstone
1960 Walk Like a Dragon
Barry, Eleanor
1916 The Flames of Johannis
Barry, Fern
1958 Wild Is the Wind
1959 The FBI Story
 The Hanging Tree
Barry, Jack
1958 Gunman's Walk
Barry, Jean
1936 After the Thin Man
Barry, Leon *see* **Bary, Leon**
Barry, Patricia
1936 Show Boat
Barry, Pauline
1916 Gold and the Woman
Barry, Phyllis
1933 Diplomaniacs
Barry, Richard
1917 Threads of Fate
Barry, Tom
1929 In Old Arizona
1930 El valiente
Barry, Viola
1914 John Barleycorn

Barry, Wesley
1918 Amarilly of Clothes-Line
 Alley
 How Could You, Jean?
 Johanna Enlists
1920 Dinty
1921 Bits of Life
1927 Wild Geese
1930 Sunny Skies
1943 Ladies' Day
1946 Dangerous Money
1947 Buffalo Bill Rides Again
1948 The Golden Eye
 Rocky
 Shanghai Chest
1949 The Sky Dragon
 Tuna Clipper
1952 Trail of the Arrow
Barry, William
1932 L'athlète incomplet
Barrymore, Ethel
1914 The Nightingale
1917 The Call of Her People
1947 The Farmer's Daughter
1948 Moonrise
1949 Pinky
 Portrait of Jennie
 That Midnight Kiss
1952 It's a Big Country: An
 American Anthology
Barrymore, John
1933 Counsellor at Law
1938 Spawn of the North
1941 Playmates
Barrymore, John Drew
1958 Never Love a Stranger
1959 Night of the Quarter
 Moon
Barrymore, Lionel
1914 The Woman in Black
1926 The Barrier
1930 Estrellados
1934 La ciudad de cartón
1935 The Little Colonel
1939 Let Freedom Ring
1942 Dr. Gillespie's New
 Assistant
1943 Dr. Gillespie's Criminal
 Case
1944 Since You Went Away
 Three Men in White
1945 Between Two Women
 The Valley of Decision
1946 Three Wise Fools
1947 Dark Delusion
 Duel in the Sun
1948 Key Largo
1950 Right Cross
Barsamian, Louise
1937 Arshin Mal Alan
Barsha, Leon
1940 Prairie Schooners
Barstead, Sue
1938 In Old Chicago
Bart, Jan
1950 Catskill Honeymoon
Bart, Jean
1939 Verbena trágica
Bartell, Richard *same as* **Bartell,**
 Dick
1943 Dr. Gillespie's Criminal
 Case
1949 The Girl from Jones
 Beach
 Knock on Any Door
 The Undercover Man
1952 The Iron Mistress
1958 The Badlanders
Bartels, Louis John
1931 The Cohens and Kellys in
 Africa
Bartheel, Carla
1930 Los que danzan *(foreign
 version)*
1931 Dämon des Meeres
 Die Maske Fällt
Barthelmess, Richard
1919 Scarlet Days
1925 The Beautiful City
1928 Wheel of Chance
1930 The Lash
 Son of the Gods

1934 Massacre
Bartholomae, Philip
1927 Rose of the Golden West
Bartholomew, Freddie
1947 Sepia Cinderella
Barti, Marina
1950 Deported
Bartlett, Bennie *same as* **Bartlett,**
 Benny
1937 Maid of Salem
1947 The Adventures of Don
 Coyote
Bartlett, Don
1925 The Beautiful City
Bartlett, Elsie
1927 A Harp in Hock
1929 Show Boat
Bartlett, Hall
1948 The Paleface
1952 Navajo
1960 All the Young Men
Bartlett, Harry
1918 Wanted, a Mother
1919 The Volcano
Bartlett, Lanier
1915 The Rosary
1918 The Man Above the Law
 Marked Cards
 Tongues of Flame
Bartlett, Randolph
1928 Breed of the Sunsets
 The Riding Renegade
 Tyrant of Red Gulch
Bartlett, Richard
1950 Battleground
1952 Hiawatha
1953 The Charge at Feather
 River
1955 The Lonesome Trail
1957 Joe Dakota
Bartlett, Sy
1955 The Last Command
Bartley, Nalbro Isadorah
1922 Head over Heels
Barton, Anne
1957 Pawnee
Barton, Buzz
1928 Orphan of the Sage
1934 The Lone Defender
1935 Fighting Pioneers
Barton, Charles T. *same as* **Barton,**
 Charles
1934 Wagon Wheels
1942 Shut My Big Mouth
1943 Let's Have Fun
 What's Buzzin' Cousin?
1947 Buck Privates Come
 Home
Barton, Dan
1953 Dream Wife
 The Jazz Singer
Barton, Finis
1933 Broken Dreams
1934 Coming Out Party
Barton, George
1947 Buck Privates Come
 Home
 California
1950 Rock Island Trail
1952 Anything Can Happen
Barton, Geraldine
1932 Hypnotized
Barton, Gregg
1947 West to Glory
1948 Tap Roots
1949 Massacre River
 That Midnight Kiss
1951 Distant Drums
 Gambling House
1952 Apache Country
1953 Tumbleweed
1954 Drums Across the River
1955 Seven Angry Men
1956 Raw Edge
1957 Joe Dakota
1958 The Badlanders
Barton, Irene
1957 The Guns of Fort
 Petticoat

Barton, James
1935 His Family Tree
1948 The Time of Your Life
1950 The Daughter of Rosie
 O'Grady
Barton, Joan
1946 Romance of the West
Barwyn, Max
1931 Beyond Victory
 Cimarron
1934 La veuve joyeuse
1948 My Girl Tisa
Bary, Leon *same as* **Barry, Leon**
1923 Suzanna
 The White Flower
1924 The Lightning Rider
1930 El secreto del doctor
 (foreign version)
Barzell, Wolf
1932 Joseph in the Land of
 Egypt
Barzman, Ben
1948 The Boy with Green Hair
1950 Give Us This Day
Basch, Felix
1930 Doña mentiras *(foreign
 version)*
Basehart, Richard
1951 The House on Telegraph
 Hill
1960 For the Love of Mike
Basenko, Ben
1932 A Daughter of Her People
1934 The Rabbi's Power
The Basin Street Boys
1938 The Duke Is Tops
Baskett, James *same as* **Baskette,**
 Jimmy
1932 Harlem Is Heaven
1939 Straight to Heaven
1946 Song of the South
Baskovitch, Nick
1936 Dangerous Intrigue
Basquette, Lina
1928 Wheel of Chance
1929 The Younger Generation
1937 Souls at Sea
1938 The Buccaneer
Bass, J. B.
1919 Injustice
Bass, Werner
1940 Overture to Glory
Bass, Willard
1952? Call of the Navajo
Basserman, Albert
1940 Escape
 Knute Rockne—All
 American
1943 Good Luck, Mr. Yates
1944 Since You Went Away
1945 Rhapsody in Blue
Basserman, Elsa
1940 Escape
1945 Rhapsody in Blue
Bassett, Joe
1953 The Charge at Feather
 River
Bassett, Russell
1916 Hulda from Holland
Bassing, Eileen
1958 Home Before Dark
Bassing, Robert
1958 Home Before Dark
Bassler, Robert
1949 Thieves' Highway
1950 A Ticket to Tomahawk
1951 The House on Telegraph
 Hill
1953 Beneath the 12-Mile Reef
Baston, J. Thornton
1920 The Good-Bad Wife
1951 Jim Thorpe—All-American
Basulto, Joe
1958 Touch of Evil
Bataille-Henri, Jacques *same as*
 Bataille, Henri
1930 Amor audaz *(foreign
 version)*
 The Big Pond *(foreign
 version)*
1931 Le petit café

Batanides, Arthur
1959   Cry Tough
Batcheller, George R.
1929   The Peacock Fan
1936   Below the Deadline
1941   Caught in the Act
Batchelor, Walter
1947   Copacabana
Bateman, Charles
1959   The FBI Story
Bateman, Victory
1922   Captain Fly-by-Night
Bates, Barbara
1945   Salome, Where She
          Danced
1958   Apache Territory
Bates, Charles
1942   The Vanishing Virginian
1943   In Old Oklahoma
1944   An American Romance
          The Sullivans
1946   Three Wise Fools
1947   Little Mister Jim
Bates, Florence
1942   Mexican Spitfire at Sea
          We Were Dancing
1943   His Butler's Sister
          Mr. Lucky
1944   Since You Went Away
          Tahiti Nights
1946   Saratoga Trunk
1948   I Remember Mama
1949   The Girl from Jones
          Beach
          Portrait of Jennie
1950   Belle of Old Mexico
1951   The Tall Target
Bates, George
1932   The Galloping Kid
Bates, Granville
1937   The Plainsman
          Waikiki Wedding
Bates, Jeanette (dancer)
1938   In Old Chicago
Bates, Jeanne (actress)
1944   The Racket Man
1957   Trooper Hook
1958   Blood Arrow
Bates, Kathryn
1936   Klondike Annie
1941   Birth of the Blues
Bates, Les not the same as **Bates,
    Lester**
1922   Big Stakes
1927   Irish Hearts
1928   The Glorious Trail
Bates, Lester not the same as **Bates,
    Les**
1921   By Right of Birth
Bates, Louise
1935   A Night at the Ritz
1938   The Beloved Brat
1950   The Toast of New Orleans
Bates, Richard
1940   Midnight Shadow
Bates, Tom same as **Bates, Tom D.**
1916   A Son of Erin
1918   Huck and Tom; or, the
          Further Adventures of
          Tom Sawyer
1920   Huckleberry Finn
1927   Don Mike
Batie, Franklin
1930   Big Boy
Batlle, Carlos de
1932   El hombre que asesinó
Battersby, Charles
1937   Dark Manhattan
Battista, Miriam
1920   Humoresque
1922   The Good Provider
1931   Così è la vita
Battles, Lucille
1942   Lucky Ghost
Baucum, Paul
1949   The Quiet One
Baude, Anna-Lisa
1930   Un hombre de suerte
          (foreign version)

Bauer, Arthur
1919   Love and the Law
Baugé, André
1931   Le petit café
Baughman, Bob
1948   Unconquered
Bauman, Rod
1955   Blackboard Jungle
Baumgarten, E. J.
1957   The Deerslayer
Bavuso, Salvatore
1932   Amore e morte
Baxley, Jack
1934   Straight Is the Way
1937   Man of the People
1938   Rascals
1946   Canyon Passage
1947   California
          Desperate
          The Last Round-Up
1948   The Lady from Shanghai
Baxley, Paul
1949   Knock on Any Door
1958   The Badlanders
1960   All the Young Men
Baxter, Alan
1937   It Could Happen to You
1940   Escape to Glory
          Santa Fe Trail
1942   Prisoner of Japan
1949   The Prairie
Baxter, Anne
1943   Crash Dive
1944   The Sullivans
1948   The Luck of the Irish
1950   A Ticket to Tomahawk
1960   Cimarron
Baxter, Billy
1938   Josette
Baxter, George
1934   The Great Flirtation
1957   Gun Battle at Monterey
Baxter, Joan
1949   Knock on Any Door
Baxter, Larry
1958   Tonka
Baxter, Les
1956   Hot Blood
Baxter, Warner
1925   A Son of His Father
1927   Drums of the Desert
1928   Ramona
1929   In Old Arizona
          Romance of the Rio
          Grande
1930   The Arizona Kid
1931   The Cisco Kid
          The Squaw Man
1934   Broadway Bill
          Stand Up and Cheer!
1936   The Prisoner of Shark
          Island
          Robin Hood of El Dorado
1937   Slave Ship
1939   The Return of the Cisco
          Kid
1941   Adam Had Four Sons
Bay, Dorothy
1934   The Cat's-Paw
Bayless, Francis
1915   A Texas Steer
Baylor, Hal
1952   Fort Osage
1953   The Sun Shines Bright
1956   The Burning Hills
1958   The Young Lions
Bayón Herrera, Luis
1931   Las luces de Buenos Aires
Beach, Brandon
1936   Dangerous Intrigue
1943   Gangway for Tomorrow
1947   The Farmer's Daughter
1949   Rose of the Yukon
Beach, Guy
1946   Singin' in the Corn
1949   Lust for Gold
          The Valiant Hombre
1951   The Well
1952   High Noon

Beach, John
1937   Hills of Old Wyoming
1939   The Cisco Kid and the
          Lady
Beach, Olive Mae
1951   The Great Caruso
Beach, Rex
1917   The Barrier
1920   The Cup of Fury
          Dangerous Days
          The North Wind's Malice
Beach, Richard
1937   It Could Happen to You
Beach, William
1945   The House on 92nd St.
Beady the Racoon
1949   Call of the Forest
Beahan, Charles
1924   Untamed Youth
Beaird, Barbara
1960   Flaming Star
Beaird, Pamela
1955   Good Morning, Miss Dove
1957   The Guns of Fort
          Petticoat
Beal, Charlie
1947   New Orleans
Beal, Frank
1913   The Inside of the White
          Slave Traffic
1918   Her Moment
1929   Señor Americano
1931   Cimarron
Beal, John
1937   Border Cafe
1943   Let's Have Fun
Beal, Royal d. 1969
1949   Lost Boundaries
1953   The Joe Louis Story
Beal, Scott R. d. 1973 same as **Beal,
    Scott** not the same as **Beal,
    Scotty**
1918   Her Moment
1934   Imitation of Life
Beal, Scotty not the same as **Beal,
    Scott R.** d. 1973
1952   Bright Victory
Beale, William C.
1921   The Hunger of the Blood
Beall, Barbara
1959   The FBI Story
Beamon, Clifford
1947   Juke Joint
Beane, Reginald
1948   The Time of Your Life
Bear, Mary
1949   Harbor of Missing Men
Beard, Betty
1949   Pinky
Beard, Dewey
1914   The Indian Wars
Beard, Renee
1947   The Foxes of Harrow
1949   Pinky
1953   Bright Road
Beard, Stymie same as **Beard,
    Mathew; Stymie**
1936   Rainbow on the River
1937   Slave Ship
1938   The Beloved Brat
          Two Gun Man from
          Harlem
1939   Way Down South
1940   Broken Strings
1941   Belle Starr
1943   Stormy Weather
Bearden, Bessie
1921   The Gunsaulus Mystery
Beasley, Barney
1935   The Cyclone Ranger
Beathea, David
1946?   House-Rent Party
Beaton, Kenneth C.
1930   Song of the Caballero
Beattie, Elizabeth
1958   Flaming Frontier
Beatty, Mae
1936   Show Boat

Beauchamp, D. D.
1953   The Man from the Alamo
1960   For the Love of Mike
Beaudine, Kathleen
1956   Westward Ho the
          Wagons!
Beaudine, William same as
    Beaudine, William, Sr.
1927   Frisco Sally Levy
1928   The Cohens and the
          Kellys in Paris
1942   Foreign Agent
          Professor Creeps
1946   The Face of Marble
1947   Bowery Buckaroos
          The Chinese Ring
1948   The Feathered Serpent
          The Golden Eye
          Jiggs and Maggie in Court
          Shanghai Chest
1949   Jiggs and Maggie in
          Jackpot Jitters
          Tuna Clipper
1950   Jiggs and Maggie Out
          West
1951   Cuban Fireball
1956   Westward Ho the
          Wagons!
Beaudry, Bob
1955   Blackboard Jungle
Beauman, Bill
1941   Western Union
Beaumont, Gerald
1928   United States Smith
Beaumont, Harry
1918   Thirty a Week
1919   Toby's Bow
1922   The Five Dollar Baby
1932   Unashamed
Beaumont, Hugh
1942   Unseen Enemy
          Young America
1943   Good Luck, Mr. Yates
          Mexican Spitfire's Blessed
          Event
1944   The Racket Man
          They Live in Fear
1948   Reaching from Heaven
1951   Go for Broke!
          The Last Outpost
1952   Bugles in the Afternoon
1953   The Member of the
          Wedding
1955   Indian American
Beaumont, Lucy
1937   Maid of Salem
Beauregard, Frank
1948   The Miracle of the Bells
Beaver, Louise see **Beavers, Louise**
Beaver, Walter
1955   Bad Day at Black Rock
Beavers, Louise same as **Beaver,
    Louise**
1932   Unashamed
1934   Imitation of Life
1936   General Spanky
          Rainbow on the River
1938   Life Goes On
1939   Reform School
1941   Belle Starr
          Virginia
1942   Holiday Inn
          Seven Sweethearts
          The Vanishing Virginian
          Young America
1943   Jack London
1950   The Jackie Robinson Story
1960   All the Fine Young
          Cannibals
Beban, George
1915   The Alien
          The Italian
1916   Pasquale
1917   The Bond Between
          His Sweetheart
          Lost in Transit
          A Roadside Impresario
1918   One More American
1919   Hearts of Men
1921   One Man in a Million
1922   The Sign of the Rose
1925   The Greatest Love of All

Beban, George, Jr.
1919   Hearts of Men
1921   One Man in a Million
1947   Buck Privates Come
        Home

Béby
1931   Un caballero de frac

Becerra, Francisco
1932   Amor y vida

Beche, Robert
1940   Hi-Yo Silver

Bechet, Marieluise
1939   Moon over Harlem

Bechet, Sidney
1939   Moon over Harlem

Bechtel, William same as **Betchel, William**
1919?   The Chosen Path
1920?   The Scarlet Dragon
1930   A Lady to Love (foreign version)

Beck, Danny
1941   Birth of the Blues
1947   Jiggs and Maggie in Society
1948   Jiggs and Maggie in Court

Beck, John
1921   The Cave Girl
1926   General Custer at Little Big Horn
1929   Smiling Irish Eyes
1948   Tap Roots

Beck, Kimberly
1959   The FBI Story

Beck, Thomas same as **Beck, Tom**
1935   Charlie Chan in Egypt
        Charlie Chan in Paris
1936   Charlie Chan at the Race Track
1937   Charlie Chan at the Opera
        Thank You, Mr. Moto
        Think Fast, Mr. Moto
1938   Road Demon

Becker, Arnold
1954   Go Man Go

Becker, Beatrice
1933   It's Great to Be Alive

Becker, Doris
1938   In Old Chicago

Becker, Fred G.
1921   Cheated Love

Becker, Joe
1958   Escape from Red Rock

Becker, Ken
1959   Last Train from Gun Hill

Beckett, Ruth
1934   Stand Up and Cheer!

Beckett, Scotty
1937   Slave Ship
1939   The Escape
1942   The Vanishing Virginian
1943   Good Luck, Mr. Yates
1947   The Jolson Story
1950   Battleground
1957   The Oklahoman

Beckwith, Roger see **Von Brincken, William**

Beda, Helen
1939   The Light Ahead

Beday, Eugene
1934   La veuve joyeuse

Beddoe, Don same as **Beddoe, Donald**
1940   Charlie Chan's Murder Cruise
        Escape to Glory
1941   The Face Behind the Mask
        They Dare Not Love
1942   Shut My Big Mouth
1947   Buck Privates Come Home
        California
        The Farmer's Daughter
1950   Emergency Wedding
        Young Daniel Boone
1952   The Big Sky
        The Iron Mistress
1958   Bullwhip

Bedell, Chuck
1946   Cuban Pete

Bedell, Lew
1951   Slaughter Trail

Bedell, Patsy
1938   In Old Chicago
1942   Holiday Inn

Bedford, Barbara
1920   The Last of the Mohicans
1922   The Power of Love
1928   The Broken Mask
        The Cavalier
1930   The Lash
1932   Thirteen Steps
1937   Big City
1938   The Toy Wife
1940   Little Nellie Kelly
1942   Nazi Agent
        The Vanishing Virginian
1943   Dr. Gillespie's Criminal Case
1944   Andy Hardy's Blonde Trouble

Bedoya, Alfonso
1948   Angel in Exile
1949   Border Incident
        Streets of Laredo
1952   California Conquest

Beebe, Earl
1915   The Grandee's Ring

Beebe, Ford
1928   The Canyon of Adventure
1934   The Prescott Kid
1948   Shep Comes Home
1949   The Dalton Gang
        Satan's Cradle
1950   Davy Crockett, Indian Scout
        The Girl from San Lorenzo
1952   Wagons West

Beebe, Marjorie
1932   Hypnotized

Beecher, Elizabeth
1943   Land of Hunted Men

Beecher, Janet
1935   So Red the Rose
1937   Big City
1939   Man of Conquest
1940   The Gay Caballero
        The Mark of Zorro

Beekman, Bobby
1960   The Dark at the Top of the Stairs

Beery, Noah same as **Beery, Noah, Sr.**
1916   The Social Highwayman
1918   Hidden Pearls
        The Source
        The Squaw Man
1920   Dinty
        The Mark of Zorro
1921   Bits of Life
        Lotus Blossom
1922   Flesh and Blood
        The Power of Love
1923   The Spider and the Rose
1924   The Heritage of the Desert
        North of 36
        Welcome Stranger
1925   The Thundering Herd
1926   The Vanishing American
1927   The Dove
        The Love Mart
1930   Big Boy
1933   Thundering Herd
1944   Block Busters

Beery, Noah, Jr. sometimes also known as **Noah Beery**
1920   The Mark of Zorro
1939   Bad Lands
1944   Hi, Beautiful
1948   Indian Agent
        Red River
1950   Davy Crockett, Indian Scout
        Two Flags West
1951   The Last Outpost
1952   Wagons West
1954   The Black Dakotas
        War Arrow
        The Yellow Tomahawk

Beery, Rita
1944   Dark Waters

Beery, Wallace
1918   Johanna Enlists
1919   Behind the Door
1920   The Last of the Mohicans
1921   A Tale of Two Worlds
1924   So Big
        Unseen Hands
1929   Chinatown Nights
1932   Flesh
1937   Slave Ship
1939   Stand Up and Fight
1946   Bad Bascomb
1947   The Mighty McGurk

Beery, William
1917   The Spirit of '76

Begg, Bill same as **Beggs, Bill**
1937   Charlie Chan at the Olympics

Beggs, Lee
1934   Lazy River

Begishe, Pipe Line
1956   The Searchers

Begley, Ed 1901—1970 same as **Begley, Edward**
1949   Tulsa
1950   Stars in My Crown
1957   Twelve Angry Men
1959   Odds Against Tomorrow

Begley, Martin
1948   Cry of the City
1949   House of Strangers

Begon, Blanche
1938   The Buccaneer

Beilby, Vangie
1934   The Cat's-Paw
1937   Maid of Salem
1942   Rio Rita
1943   The Amazing Mrs. Holliday
1946   Slightly Scandalous

Beirute, Yerye
1955   Seven Cities of Gold

Bejarano, Julia
1932   Hollywood, ciudad de ensueño
1933   Una viuda romántica
1934   The Lone Defender
        The Prescott Kid
1935   Cowboy Holiday
1936   El diablo del mar
        Ramona

Bejaut, Emile
1947   The Foxes of Harrow

Bekassy, Stephen
1953   The Pathfinder
1956   Serenade
1958   The Light in the Forest
        The Young Lions

Bekiaris, Apostolos
1954   Barefoot Battalion

Bel Geddes, Barbara
1948   I Remember Mama
1950   Panic in the Streets

Bela, Nicholas same as **Bela, Nick**
1931   Little Caesar
1941   New York Town
        They Dare Not Love

Belafonte, Harry
1953   Bright Road
1954   Carmen Jones
1959   Odds Against Tomorrow
        The World, the Flesh and the Devil

Belafonte, Marguerite
1959   Night of the Quarter Moon

Belanger, Juliette
1925   Don Q, Son of Zorro

Belasco, Art same as **Belasco, Arthur**
1934   Coming Out Party
1940   New Moon
1942   Nazi Agent
        Three Hearts for Julia
1944   An American Romance

Belasco, David
1914   Rose of the Rancho

Belasco, Jay
1916   The Gilded Spider
        The Grip of Jealousy
1935   The Wedding Night

Belasco, Leon
1939   Fisherman's Wharf
1941   Hold Back the Dawn
        Playmates
        They Dare Not Love
        Where Did You Get That Girl?
1942   Holiday Inn
1943   The Gang's All Here
        Gangway for Tomorrow
        Yankee Doodle Dandy
1944   An American Romance
        Chip Off the Old Block
1949   Jiggs and Maggie in Jackpot Jitters
1950   The Toast of New Orleans
1951   Cuban Fireball
1952   The Fabulous Senorita

Belasco, Walter
1916   The Grip of Jealousy
1917   A Jewel in Pawn

Belcher, Alice
1922   Second Hand Rose

Belcher, Charles
1920   The Mark of Zorro

Belcher, Frank
1915   The Danger Signal

Belden, Charles S. same as **Belden, Charles**
1937   Charlie Chan at the Opera
        Charlie Chan on Broadway
1938   Charlie Chan at Monte Carlo
        Mr. Moto's Gamble
1939   Charlie Chan in Honolulu
1946   Beauty and the Bandit
        The Gay Cavalier
        South of Monterey

Beldon, Beth
1947   The Farmer's Daughter

Belgard, Arnold
1948   Half Past Midnight
        Night Wind

Bélières, Léon
1930   Un hombre de suerte (foreign version)

Belita
1941   Ice-Capades
1944   Lady, Let's Dance!

Bell, Alicia
1930   La jaula de los leones

Bell, Amelia
1930   La jaula de los leones

Bell, Charles
1928   Wyoming

Bell, Genevieve
1946   Slightly Scandalous
1951   The Great Caruso

Bell, George
1949   Colorado Territory

Bell, Hank
1926   Twin Triggers
1930   Abraham Lincoln
1934   Fighting Through
1937   The Plainsman
1940   Geronimo
1941   Western Union
1942   Shut My Big Mouth
        Valley of the Sun
1943   The Law Rides Again
        The Ox-Bow Incident
1945   Great Stagecoach Robbery
        Salome, Where She Danced
1948   Old Los Angeles

Bell, Harold
1944   Chip Off the Old Block

Bell, Jack
1944   Chip Off the Old Block

Bell, James
1942   Holiday Inn
1943   Gangway for Tomorrow
        The Leopard Man
1949   Streets of Laredo
1952   Japanese War Bride
1957   The Tin Star

Bell, James
1959   The Oregon Trail
Bell, Mary
1956   Crowded Paradise
Bell, Monta
1925   Lights of Old Broadway
1930   The Big Pond
       The Big Pond (foreign version)
       East Is West
1931   Personal Maid
1941   Birth of the Blues
Bell, Pearl Doles
1921   Wing Toy
Bell, Ralph circa 1918
1918   Denny from Ireland
Bell, Ralph circa 1957
1957   Edge of the City
Bell, Rex
1935   Fighting Pioneers
1936   West of Nevada
1937   Law and Lead
Bell, Ricardo, Jr.
1930   Las campanas de Capistrano
Bell, Rodney
1947   My Wild Irish Rose
1955   Trial
1960   Key Witness
Bell, Rosita
1930   La jaula de los leones
Bell, Spencer
1928   Tenderfeet
1929   The Peacock Fan
1931   Smart Money
Bell, Tom
1936   Kelly the Second
Bellah, James not the same as **Bellah, James Warner**
1953   The Man Behind the Gun
Bellah, James Warner not the same as **Bellah, James**
1960   Sergeant Rutledge
Bellamy, Earl
1947   The Last Round-Up
1949   Laramie
1950   Emergency Wedding
1955   Seminole Uprising
Bellamy, Madge
1920   The Riddle: Woman
1925   The Man in Blue
1934   Charlie Chan in London
Bellamy, Quex
1918   The Spreading Evil
Bellamy, Ralph
1933   Ever in My Heart
1935   The Wedding Night
1936   Dangerous Intrigue
1940   Elsa Maxwell's Public Deb No. 1
Bellas, Roy
1936   Ramona
Bellaver, Harry
1945   The House on 92nd St.
1950   No Way Out
1956   Serenade
1957   The Brothers Rico
Belle, Tula
1917   The Woman and the Beast
1919   Deliverance
Bellew, Cosmo Kyrle
1934   Behold My Wife!
       Beloved
Bellini, Francesca
1959   The Black Orchid
Bellini, Nino
1945   The Dolly Sisters
Bellis, Guy
1940   The Way of All Flesh
Bello, Marino
1930   Monsieur le Fox (foreign version)
Bellotti, Mario
1931   La carta (foreign version)
Belmont, Gladys
1929   Redskin
Belmont, Virginia
1945   Betrayal from the East
       Johnny Angel

Belmonte, Gloria
1938   Di que me quieres
Belmonte, Hernán
1938   Di que me quieres
Belmore, Daisy
1928   We Americans
Belmore, Lionel
1916   Britton of the Seventh
1918   Wanted, a Mother
1921   Guile of Women
1922   Head over Heels
1924   Racing Luck
1927   Winners of the Wilderness
1928   Heart Trouble
1932   So Big
1936   The Last of the Mohicans
1937   Maid of Salem
Beloin, Edmund
1949   Top O' the Morning
Belser, Lee
1959   Night of the Quarter Moon
Belt, Madeline
1940   Paradise in Harlem
Beltram, Orlando
1950   Mystery Submarine
Beltram, Ray
1941   This Woman Is Mine
1949   The Cowboy and the Indians
1953   The Charge at Feather River
1960   Flaming Star
Beltran, Alma
1957   Dragoon Wells Massacre
Beltran, Lasca
1932   Amor y vida
Ben-Ami, Jacob
1933   The Wandering Jew
1937   Green Fields
Ben-Astar, Albert see **Astar, Ben**
Benadaret, Bee
1946   Notorious
Benard, Ray see **Corrigan, Ray**
Benavente, Lolita
1933   Espérame
Benchley, Robert
1933   Rafter Romance
1942   Syncopation
Bender, Don
1953   The Eddie Cantor Story
Bender, Russ
1957   Beau James
1960   Walk Tall
Bendix, William
1942   Woman of the Year
1944   Lifeboat
1948   The Time of Your Life
1949   Streets of Laredo
1951   Gambling House
1954   Dangerous Mission
Benedek, Laslo
1949   The Kissing Bandit
Benedet, Julián
1938   Di que me quieres
Benedic, Jule
1954   Go Man Go
Benedict, Billy same as **Benedict, William**
1936   After the Thin Man
       Ramona
1937   That I May Live
1943   The Ox-Bow Incident
1944   Block Busters
       They Live in Fear
1946   The Gentleman Misbehaves
       Without Reservations
1947   Bowery Buckaroos
1948   Night Wind
1950   Riders of the Pony Express
1959   The Hanging Tree
       Last Train from Gun Hill
Benedict, Brooks
1927   Lost at the Front
1934   Broadway Bill
1936   Show Boat
1937   Charlie Chan at the Olympics

1938   Josette
1939   Mr. Moto Takes a Vacation
1943   Jack London
1947   My Wild Irish Rose
1948   The Miracle of the Bells
1958   Houseboat
Benedict, Howard
1941   Hurry, Charlie, Hurry
Benedict, Kingsley
1917   The Plow Woman
1919   Who Will Marry Me?
Benedict, Richard
1946   Till the End of Time
1947   Crossfire
1948   The Arizona Ranger
1952   Woman in the Dark
Benedict, William see **Benedict, Billy**
Benet, Marianne
1959   Shake Hands with the Devil
Benét, Stephen Vincent
1930   Abraham Lincoln
Bengal, Ben
1949   Illegal Entry
Benge, Wilson
1926   A Trip to Chinatown
1928   Anybody Here Seen Kelly?
1937   Maid of Salem
       Man of the People
       Souls at Sea
1941   Virginia
1943   His Butler's Sister
1950   Emergency Wedding
Benham, Albert
1933   Dos noches
Benham, Grace
1916   Alien Souls
1938   Dangerous to Know
Beninato, George
1950   Panic in the Streets
Benítez, Angelita
1930   El valiente
       Wu Li Chang
1931   El comediante
       Monerías
Benjamin, Dick not the same as **Benjamin, Richard** (actor, director)
1946   Till the End of Time
Benner, Yale
1917   A Wife by Proxy
Bennes, John
1956   Mohawk
Bennet, Hope
1938   Life Goes On
Bennet, Spencer Gordon same as **Bennet, Spencer; Bennet, Spencer G.**
1929   Hawk of the Hills
1935   Rescue Squad
1944   Tucson Raiders
1952   Brave Warrior
Bennett, Alma
1919   The Right to Happiness
Bennett, Barbara
1929   Mother's Boy
Bennett, Belle
1918   The Reckoning Day
1924   In Hollywood With Potash and Perlmutter
1927   The Way of All Flesh
       Wild Geese
1928   Mother Machree
Bennett, Billie
1927   The Slaver
Bennett, Bruce same as **Brix, Herman**
1940   Escape to Glory
       Hi-Yo Silver
1942   Submarine Raider
1943   Frontier Fury
1950   Mystery Street
1951   The Last Outpost
1953   Dream Wife
1956   Daniel Boone, Trail Blazer
1958   Flaming Frontier

Bennett, Catherine
1925   The Wild Bull's Lair
Bennett, Charles
1941   They Dare Not Love
1948   Unconquered
1954   Dangerous Mission
Bennett, Chester
1920   The Purple Cipher
Bennett, Clay
1953   So Big
Bennett, Constance
1925   My Son
1930   Son of the Gods
1940   Escape to Glory
Bennett, Edna
1936   Klondike Annie
Bennett, Fran
1955   The Far Horizons
1956   Giant
Bennett, Frank
1916   Gretchen, the Greenhorn
       A Sister of Six
       Sold for Marriage
1917   Lost in Transit
Bennett, Irene
1937   The Plainsman
Bennett, Joan
1932   Me and My Gal
1938   The Texans
1940   The Man I Married
1942   Twin Beds
1943   Margin for Error
1945   Nob Hill
Bennett, Joe
1918   Marked Cards
       The Reckoning Day
Bennett, Lee
1942   The Vanishing Virginian
1943   The Gang's All Here
1944   Slightly Terrific
1946   Wild West
       Without Reservations
1947   The Last Round-Up
Bennett, Leila
1932   Tiger Shark
1934   Wagon Wheels
Bennett, Libby
1940   Too Many Girls
Bennett, Marilyn
1956   Rockin' the Blues
Bennett, Marjorie
1918   The Midnight Patrol
1950   Two Flags West
1953   So Big
1958   Home Before Dark
Bennett, Mickey
1926   The Cohens and Kellys
1928   United States Smith
Bennett, Ray same as **Bennett, Raphael**
1937   Drums of Destiny
       Old Louisiana
1940   Hi-Yo Silver
1941   Doomed Caravan
       Gauchos of Eldorado
       Romance of the Rio Grande
1942   Lawless Plainsmen
       Prisoner of Japan
1945   The Navajo Trail
1946   The Gay Cavalier
1949   The Dalton Gang
1950   Ambush
       Black Hand
       Winchester '73
1951   Apache Drums
1952   The Big Sky
       Bugles in the Afternoon
1953   The Great Sioux Uprising
       So Big
1956   Giant
Bennett, Richard
1932   No Greater Love
Bennett, Robert
1936   Love and Sacrifice
Bennett, Sedal
1948   Fighting Father Dunne
       The Miracle of the Bells
Bennett, Spencer Gordon see **Bennet, Spencer Gordon**

Bennett, Tommy
1940   Knute Rockne—All American
Bennett, Whitman
1922   Fair Lady
1924   Two Shall Be Born
Bennison, Andrew
1924   Defying the Law
Benny, Jack
1943   The Meanest Man in the World
1946   Without Reservations
1957   Beau James
Benoit, Mary
1942   Three Hearts for Julia
1950   The Toast of New Orleans
1951   Molly
1955   The Long Gray Line
1960   Cimarron
Benoit, Victor
1915   Children of the Ghetto
The Benoits
1941   Ice-Capades
Benroy, Tony
1952   Red Snow
Bensfield, Ray
1932   Hypnotized
Benson, Carl
1945   The House on 92nd St.
Benson, Clyde
1916   Civilization's Child
Benson, Mrs. F. D.
1949?   Girl in Room 20
Benson, Frank
1937   Souls at Sea
1940   Escape to Glory
Benson, John
1957   Beau James
Benthall, Dwinelle
1928   The Crash
Bentley, Bobette
1958   The Last Hurrah
Bentley, Robert
1923   None So Blind
Benton, Anne
1960   Flaming Star
Benton, Curtis (*actor*) *could be same as* **Benton, Curtis** (*writer*)
1936   It Had to Happen
Benton, Curtis (*writer*) *could be same as* **Benton, Curtis** (*actor*)
1927   Clancy's Kosher Wedding
1928   United States Smith
Benton, Jack
1949   Satan's Cradle
Benton, Steve
1940   Escape to Glory
1948   The Lady from Shanghai
1950   Jolson Sings Again
1956   Full of Life
1958   The Last Hurrah
Benz, Hamilton
1945   The House on 92nd St.
Beranger, André de *see* **Beranger, George Andre**
Beranger, Clara S. *same as* **Beranger, Clara**
1918   The Golden Wall
1919   Come Out of the Kitchen
1920   White Youth
Beranger, George Andre *same as* **Beranger, André de; Beranger, George; Beranger, George A.; Beringer, J. A.**
1915   The Birth of a Nation
1916   The Half-Breed
           Mixed Blood
1917   A Love Sublime
1918   Sandy
1925   The Man in Blue
1937   Souls at Sea
1946   Saratoga Trunk
1948   Cry of the City
Bercovici, Leonardo
1949   Portrait of Jennie
Bercowich, Gertrude
1932   Mazel Tov
Bercutt, Sharon
1960   Flaming Star

Beregi, Oscar 1918–1976
1952   Anything Can Happen
1953   Tonight We Sing
Beregi, Oskar 1875–1965
1932   Yiskor
Berenson, Abe
1950   Panic in the Streets
Beresford, Evelyn
1944   Buffalo Bill
1950   Annie Get Your Gun
Beresford, Frank S. *same as* **Beresford, Frank**
1918   The Border Raiders
1921   Anne of Little Smoky
1925   Speed Wild
Beresford, Harry
1931   Charlie Chan Carries On
1932   The Match King
           So Big
1933   Ever in My Heart
1936   Klondike Annie
Beresford, Vera
1918   A Daughter of the Old South
Beretta, Carmen
1945   The Dolly Sisters
Berezovska, Lydia
1937   Natalka Poltavka
Berg, Bernard
1946   Rendezvous 24
Berg, Gertrude
1951   Molly
Bergen, Edgar
1948   I Remember Mama
Bergen, Jerry
1942   Let's Get Tough!
Bergen, Polly
1950   The Men
1951   Warpath
1953   Cry of the Hunted
Berger, Bernard
1925   Lights of Old Broadway
Berger, Gustave *same as* **Berger, Gustav**
1939   My Son
1941   Mazel Tov Yidden
1950   God, Man and Devil
Berger, Ludwig
1928   Sins of the Fathers
1930   Galas de la Paramount
1931   Le petit café
Berger, Mable
1948?   Junction 88
Berger, Ricky
1948   Fighting Father Dunne
Bergerac, Jacques
1959   Thunder in the Sun
Bergère, Ouida
1916   Arms and the Woman
           The Romantic Journey
1920   On with the Dance
1922   Peacock Alley
Bergere, Valerie
1917   The Wild Girl
Bergerman, Stanley
1932   The Cohens and Kellys in Hollywood
1935   Chinatown Squad
Bergh, Joanne de
1948   Call Northside 777
Berglund, Erik "Bullen"
1930   Doña mentiras (*foreign version*)
Bergman, Helmer
1929   Señor Americano
Bergman, Henry *same as* **Bergman, Henri**
1915   The Melting Pot
1916   Man and His Angel
Bergman, Ingrid
1941   Adam Had Four Sons
1945   The Bells of St. Mary's
1946   Notorious
           Saratoga Trunk
Bergreen, Jacob
1935   The Yiddish King Lear
Beringer, J. A. *see* **Beranger, George Andre**

Berk, Ben
1932   Ljubav i strast
Berk, Irma
1960   This Rebel Breed
Berke, Irwin
1959   Night of the Quarter Moon
Berke, William
1936   Hair-Trigger Casey
1941   Thunder Over the Prairie
1942   Lawless Plainsmen
1943   Frontier Fury
1944   Riding West
1945   Betrayal from the East
1946   Renegade Girl
           Sunset Pass
1950   Bandit Queen
           Train to Tombstone
1951   The Steel Helmet
Berkeley, Busby
1943   The Gang's All Here
Berkeley, Martin
1943   Dr. Gillespie's Criminal Case
1944   Three Men in White
1953   The Nebraskan
           War Paint
1957   Trooper Hook
Berkes, John *same as* **Berkes, Johnnie**
1942   Woman of the Year
1945   Our Vines Have Tender Grapes
           A Tree Grows in Brooklyn
1946   Canyon Passage
1947   The Mighty McGurk
Berle, Milton
1941   Sun Valley Serenade
1942   Whispering Ghosts
1943   Margin for Error
Berley, André
1930   Olimpia (*foreign version*)
1931   Buster se marie
           Jenny Lind
           Le père célibataire
           Le petit café
           Quand on est belle
1934   Caravane
           La veuve joyeuse
1935   L'homme des Folies Bergère
Berlin, Irving
1942   Holiday Inn
Berliner, George
1931   El pasado acusa
Berliner, Martin
1948   My Girl Tisa
Berliner, Rudolph
1920   The Great Shadow
Berliner, Trude
1931   Chérie (*foreign version*)
1945   The Dolly Sisters
Berman, Pandro S.
1932   Symphony of Six Million
1942   Rio Rita
1955   Blackboard Jungle
Bern, Paul
1920   The North Wind's Malice
1922   Head over Heels
           The Man with Two Mothers
1925   Flower of Night
1927   The Dove
Bernard, Barney
1923   Potash and Perlmutter
Bernard, Barry
1944   Charlie Chan in the Secret Service
1955   A Man Called Peter
1960   Cimarron
Bernard, Butch
1957   All Mine to Give
Bernard, Dorothy
1916   A Man of Sorrow
1920   The Great Shadow
Bernard, Harry
1935   Ruggles of Red Gap
1937   The Devil's Playground

Bernard, Joe *same as* **Bernard, Joseph; Bernard, Joseph E.**
1935   A Night at the Ritz
1937   That I May Live
1939   The Adventures of Huckleberry Finn
1940   They Knew What They Wanted
1941   Playmates
1942   Apache Trail
           Syncopation
           Tales of Manhattan
1943   Action in the North Atlantic
1945   Nob Hill
           Where Do We Go From Here?
1947   California
           My Wild Irish Rose
           Pirates of Monterey
1949   Arctic Manhunt
           The Clay Pigeon
Bernard, Lester
1926   Sweet Rosie O'Grady
1927   Pleasure Before Business
1928   Flying Romeos
Bernard, Sam
1939   Waterfront
1942   Let's Get Tough!
1943   Crime Smasher
1945   Where Do We Go From Here?
1949   The Girl from Jones Beach
Bernardi, Hershel
1937   Green Fields
1938   The Singing Blacksmith
Bernardos, Manuel
1933   Espérame
Bernath, Shari Lee
1959   The Jayhawkers!
Bernds, Edward
1958   Escape from Red Rock
Berne, Josef *same as* **Berne, Joe**
1938   La vida bohemia
1939   Mirele Efros
1944   They Live in Fear
1950   Catskill Honeymoon
Berneis, Peter
1942   Syncopation
1949   Portrait of Jennie
Berner, Sara
1946   The Sailor Takes a Wife
1948   Jiggs and Maggie in Court
Bernerd, Jeffrey *same as* **Bernerd, Jerry**
1946   The Face of Marble
1947   Black Gold
           King of the Bandits
           Robin Hood of Monterey
Bernhard, Joseph
1952   Japanese War Bride
Bernhardt, Curtis
1942   Juke Girl
Bernheim, Julius
1928   Uncle Tom's Cabin
Bernie, Thomas S., Jr.
1940   The Ramparts We Watch
Bernier, George
1958   Tonka
Bernstein, Blanche
1937   Where Is My Child?
Bernstein, Isadore *same as* **Bernstein, I.**
1922   The Great Alone
1925   His People
           The Red Rider
1927   The Shamrock and the Rose
1928   George Washington Cohen
           The Rawhide Kid
1929   Lucky Boy
1932   No Greater Love
1936   For the Service
1938   City Streets
Bernstein, Leonard
1957   Satchmo the Great
Berquist, Harold
1934   Our Daily Bread

Berrell, George
1921   The Girl from God's Country
Berrill, Larry
1957   Burden of Truth
Berry Brothers
1948?   Boarding House Blues
Berry, Art, Sr.
1944   An American Romance
Bert, Genevieve
1922   Cross Roads
Bert, Howard
1958   Marjorie Morningstar
Bert, Margaret
1940   Little Nellie Kelly
1942   Mokey
       Nazi Agent
1947   Dark Delusion
1949   Prejudice
1950   Annie Get Your Gun
       Right Cross
       Stars in My Crown
1953   The Member of the Wedding
Berthe, Jacques
1958   Kings Go Forth
Berti, Dehl
1957   Apache Warrior
Bertini, Fernando
1931   Pagliacci
Bertram, William
1926   Under Fire
Bertrand, Mary
1943   Tahiti Honey
Berwick, Irvin
1951   The Raging Tide
Berwick, Ray
1956   Westward Ho the Wagons!
Beryl, Michele
1932   Le cas du docteur Brenner
Besbas, Peter E.
1957   Journey to Freedom
Besruchko, S.
1938   Marusia
Bess, Big Jeff
1960   Wild River
Besser, Joe
1955   Headline Hunters
Besserer, Eugenie
1915   The Rosary
1919   Auction of Souls
       Scarlet Days
1920   For the Soul of Rafael
1922   The Hands of Nara
1923   Anna Christie
1925   Friendly Enemies
1928   The Jazz Singer
1929   Mister Antonio
       Thunderbolt
Best, Bettie
1946   The Trap
Best, Deannie
1948   Shanghai Chest
Best, H. M.
1916   Ramona
Best, James
1950   Comanche Territory
       Winchester '73
1951   Apache Drums
1952   The Battle at Apache Pass
1953   Column South
       Seminole
1954   They Rode West
       The Yellow Tomahawk
1955   Seven Angry Men
Best, Willie *same as* **Best, William**
1935   Annie Oakley
       The Littlest Rebel
1936   General Spanky
       Muss 'Em Up
       Silly Billies
1939   Miracle on Main Street
       Mr. Moto in Danger Island
       Mr. Moto Takes a Vacation
1942   Juke Girl
       Whispering Ghosts
1943   Cabin in the Sky
       Dixie

1946   Dangerous Money
       The Face of Marble
       The Red Dragon
1948   Half Past Midnight
       Shanghai Chest
1949   Jiggs and Maggie in Jackpot Jitters
Bestor, Billy
1944   Chip Off the Old Block
Betchel, William *see* **Bechtel, William**
Bethea, David
1936   The Green Pastures
1946?   Fight That Ghost
1947   Hi De Ho
       Reet, Petite and Gone
Betsuie, Exactly Sonnie
1956   The Searchers
Bettger, Lyle
1953   The Great Sioux Uprising
1954   Drums Across the River
1956   The Lone Ranger
Bettinson, Ralph
1940   Doomed to Die
       Phantom of Chinatown
1945   South of the Rio Grande
Betz, Audrey
1945   The Dolly Sisters
Betz, Matthew *same as* **Betz, Mathew**
1925   Lights of Old Broadway
1926   The Little Irish Girl
1928   Sins of the Fathers
1937   Souls at Sea
Beutel, Jack *see* **Buetel, Jack**
Bevan, Billy *same as* **Bevan, William**
1928   Riley the Cop
1934   Limehouse Blues
1937   Slave Ship
1939   Let Freedom Ring
1947   It Had To Be You
Bevans, Clem
1937   Big City
1939   Stand Up and Fight
1940   Girl from God's Country
1948   Moonrise
       The Paleface
1949   Portrait of Jennie
       Streets of Laredo
1956   Davy Crockett and the River Pirates
Bever, George
1931   Chérie
Beverley, Helen
1937   Green Fields
1939   The Light Ahead
1940   Overture to Glory
1944   Black Magic
Bey, Turhan
1942   Unseen Enemy
Beymer, Richard *same as* **Beymer, Dick**
1953   So Big
1954   Indiscretion of an American Wife
Bezzerides, A. I.
1942   Juke Girl
1943   Action in the North Atlantic
1949   Thieves' Highway
1953   Beneath the 12-Mile Reef
1959   The Jayhawkers!
Bialis, Betta *could be same as* **Bialis, Rosetta**
1938   Two Sisters
Bialis, Rosetta *could be same as* **Bialis, Betta**
1939   The Light Ahead
1940   Americaner Schadchen
Bianchi, Angelo
1934   Limehouse Blues
Biancoli, Oreste *could be same as* **Bilancia, Oreste**
1930   Toda una vida (*foreign version*)
Bias, Ruth
1941   Sullivan's Travels
Biberman, Abner
1941   This Woman Is Mine
1942   Little Tokyo, U.S.A.
       Whispering Ghosts

1943   The Leopard Man
1945   Betrayal from the East
       Salome, Where She Danced
1950   Winchester '73
Biberman, Herbert J. *same as* **Biberman, Herbert**
1939   King of Chinatown
1947   New Orleans
1954   Salt of the Earth
Biberowich, L.
1939   Cossacks in Exile
Bibikov, Maria *same as* **Bibikoff, Maria**
1945   The Dolly Sisters
1951   The Girl on the Bridge
Bice, Robert
1943   Gangway for Tomorrow
1946   G. I. War Brides
1949   Illegal Entry
1952   Desert Pursuit
       Hiawatha
       Red Snow
1955   Foxfire
       The Gun That Won the West
       Trial
1956   The White Squaw
Bickford, Charles
1930   Anna Christie
1931   The Squaw Man
1933   Song of the Eagle
1936   Rose of the Rancho
1937   The Plainsman
1938   Daughter of Shanghai
1939   Stand Up and Fight
1940   Girl from God's Country
1943   Mr. Lucky
1947   Duel in the Sun
       The Farmer's Daughter
1948   Four Faces West
1951   Jim Thorpe—All-American
       The Raging Tide
1955   Not As a Stranger
1960   The Unforgiven
Biddell, Sidney
1940   Escape to Glory
Biddle, Craig, Jr.
1923   Fashion Row
Bieber, Linda
1943   The Amazing Mrs. Holliday
1945   A Tree Grows in Brooklyn
Bieber, Nita
1950   A Lady Without Passport
Biegański, Wiktor
1930   Toda una vida (*foreign version*)
Bienvenu, Mrs. E.
1948   Louisiana Story
The Big Apple Dancers
1938   Spirit of Youth
Big Tree, John, Chief *same as* **Big Tree; Big Tree, Chief**
1917   The Spirit of '76
1921   By Right of Birth
1923   The Huntress
1925   The Red Rider
1926   The Frontier Trail
1927   The Frontiersman
       Spoilers of the West
       Winners of the Wilderness
1928   Wyoming
1929   The Overland Telegraph
       Sioux Blood
1934   The Cat's-Paw
1935   The Singing Vagabond
1936   Custer's Last Stand
1937   Hills of Old Wyoming
       Maid of Salem
1939   Drums Along the Mohawk
1941   Western Union
1949   She Wore a Yellow Ribbon
1950   Devil's Doorway
Bigard, Barney
1947   New Orleans
1958   St. Louis Blues
Bigelow, Charles J.
1945   The Navajo Trail
1946   Border Bandits

Biggs, Anna Marie
1944   An American Romance
Bighead, Jack
1951   Jim Thorpe—All-American
Bigman, Seth T.
1954   Taza, Son of Cochise
Bikel, Theodore
1958   The Defiant Ones
Bilancia, Oreste *could be same as* **Biancoli, Oreste**
1930   Doña mentiras (*foreign version*)
1931   La fiesta del diablo (*foreign version*)
Bilbo, Boyd
1955   Blackboard Jungle
Bilbrew, A. C. *same as* **Billbrew, A. C. H.**
1929   Hearts in Dixie
1947   The Foxes of Harrow
The Bilbrew Chorus
1929   Hearts in Dixie
       Show Boat
Bilbrook, Lydia
1940   Mexican Spitfire Out West
1941   The Mexican Spitfire's Baby
1942   Mexican Spitfire at Sea
       Mexican Spitfire's Elephant
1943   Mexican Spitfire's Blessed Event
Biles, Charles
1958   Tonka
Bill, George *could be same as* **George, Bill**
1952   Bugles in the Afternoon
Billaud, Robert
1937   Song of the City
Billberg, Ragnar
1930   Toda una vida (*foreign version*)
Bill-Bocketts
1931   Die Dreigroschenoper (*foreign version*)
Billbrew, A. C. H. *see* **Bilbrew, A. C.**
Biller, Irene
1933   The Man Who Dared: An Imaginative Biography
Billie and Millie
1946   That Man of Mine
Billings, George *same as* **Billings, Georgie**
1934   As the Earth Turns
1936   Dangerous Intrigue
       Star for a Night
1938   The Adventures of Tom Sawyer
1940   Knute Rockne—All American
Billings, Jesse
1923   Deceit
Billingsley, Barbara
1946   Three Wise Fools
1949   Prejudice
       The Valiant Hombre
1951   Oh! Susanna
       The Tall Target
1952   Woman in the Dark
Billington, Francelia
1917   My Fighting Gentleman
1922   Blazing Arrows
Billopps, Mr.
1921   A Giant of His Race
Bilous, W.
1939   Cossacks in Exile
Bilson, Bruce
1944   Chip Off the Old Block
Bimbo, Charles
1932   Hypnotized
1934   She Was a Lady
Bing, Herman *same as* **Bing, Hermann**
1930   Anna Christie (*foreign version*)
1931   El proceso de Mary Dugan (*foreign version*)
1932   Flesh
       Hypnotized
       Unashamed

1934 Broadway Bill
      The Cat's-Paw
1935 His Family Tree
1936 Dimples
      Human Cargo
      Laughing Irish Eyes
1937 That Girl from Paris
1940 Elsa Maxwell's Public
      Deb No. 1
1945 Where Do We Go From
      Here?
1946 Rendezvous 24

Bingham, Edfrid A. *same as*
Bingham, Edfrid
1920 The Paliser Case
1921 Guile of Women

Binney, Constance
1919 Erstwhile Susan

Binney, Faire
1953 Dream Wife
      The Eddie Cantor Story

Binney, Josh
1947 Hi De Ho
1948 Killer Diller
1948? Boarding House Blues
1949? The Joint Is Jumpin'

Binns, Edward
1951 Teresa
1957 Twelve Angry Men

Binyon, Claude
1942 Holiday Inn
1943 Dixie
1950 Emergency Wedding

Binyon, Conrad
1941 This Woman Is Mine
1942 Young America
1943 Good Luck, Mr. Yates
      The Meanest Man in the
      World
1944 Since You Went Away
1950 Sands of Iwo Jima

Birch, Paul
1953 The Eddie Cantor Story
1954 Cattle Queen of Montana
1955 Apache Woman
1956 The White Squaw
1957 Joe Dakota
1958 Gunman's Walk
1959 Gunmen from Laredo
1960 The Dark at the Top of
      the Stairs
      Pay or Die

Bird, Billie
1952 Anything Can Happen

Birdhead, Chief
1917 The Conqueror

Birdsell, Donald
1960 The Crowning
      Experience

Birdsong, Amy
1925 Marcus Garland

Birdwell, Russell J.
1951 Jim Thorpe—All-American

Birell, Tala *same as* **Birrell, Tala**
1931 Don Juan diplomático
      (foreign version)
1933 Let's Fall in Love
1938 Josette

Birinski, Leo
1928 A Ship Comes In *(foreign
      version)*
1930 Olimpia *(foreign
      version)*

Biro, Lajos
1927 The Way of All Flesh
1940 The Way of All Flesh

Birrell, Tala *see* **Birell, Tala**

Bischoff, Samuel *same as* **Bischoff,
      Sam**
1935 The Irish in Us
      A Night at the Ritz
1940 Escape to Glory
      Three Cheers for the Irish
1941 They Dare Not Love
1952 The Half-Breed

Bishell, Frank
1937 Boy of the Streets

Bishop, Andrew S. *same as*
Bishop, Andrew
1924 The House Behind the
      Cedars
      A Son of Satan

1935 Lem Hawkins' Confession
1936 Temptation

Bishop, David
1956 Giant

Bishop, Elsie
1927 His Foreign Wife
1936 Ramona

Bishop, Julie *same as* **Wells,
      Jacqueline**
1938 Little Miss Roughneck
1943 Action in the North
      Atlantic
1945 Rhapsody in Blue
1947 Last of the Redmen
1950 Sands of Iwo Jima
1951 Westward the Women
1955 Headline Hunters

Bishop, Richard
1948 Call Northside 777
1951 Teresa

Bishop, Richard *(child actor)*
1956 Giant

Bishop, William
1949 Anna Lucasta
1952 The Raiders
1954 Overland Pacific
1956 The White Squaw
1959 The Oregon Trail

Bissell, Whit
1949 Anna Lucasta
1955 Not As a Stranger
      Trial
1956 Dakota Incident
      Man from Del Rio
1958 The Defiant Ones
1959 The Black Orchid

Bistagne, Emile
1938 Charlie Chan at Monte
      Carlo

Bittner, W. W.
1917 Runaway Romany

Bizub, Andrew
1940 The Ramparts We Watch

Blaché, Herbert
1917 The Peddler

Black, Buck
1925 Lights of Old Broadway

Black, Charlie
1918 The Hell Cat

Black, Dorothy
1934 Imitation of Life

Black, George
1940 The Ramparts We Watch

Black, Maurice
1931 Little Caesar
      Smart Money
1932 Scarface
      Symphony of Six Million
1933 The Cohens and Kellys in
      Trouble
      Grand Slam
1936 Ellis Island
      Laughing Irish Eyes
      Silly Billies
1937 The Californian

Black, Ricardo Adalid *see* **Adalid,
      Ricardo**

Black, Thurman
1936 Dimples

Black, Tom
1955 Headline Hunters

Black, Valerie
1946 Beware
1949 Lost Boundaries

Black, William W.
1918 The Hell Cat
      The Prussian Cur

Black Diamond, a horse
1949 Call of the Forest

Black Eagle, Chief
1916 Gold and the Woman

Black Elk, Ben
1952 The Savage

Black Fox, the Scholar Horse
1935 Cyclone of the Saddle

Black Hawk *could be same as*
      Black Hawk, Chief
1923 Suzanna

Black Hawk, Chief *could be same
      as* **Black Hawk**
1935 Range Warfare

Black Horse, Harry
1956 The Searchers

Black Jack, a horse
1948 Renegades of Sonora

Black King, a horse
1935 Riddle Ranch

Black Lizard
1919 The Heart of Wetona

Black Wolf
1919 The Heart of Wetona

Blackburn, Thomas *same as*
      Blackburn, Thomas W.;
      Blackburn, Tom
1950 Colt .45
1951 Cavalry Scout
1954 Cattle Queen of Montana
1955 Davy Crockett, King of
      the Wild Frontier
1956 Davy Crockett and the
      River Pirates
      Westward Ho the
      Wagons!
      The Wild Dakotas

Blackford, Jeanne
1952 High Noon
1953 The Member of the
      Wedding

Blackley, Douglas *see* **Kent, Robert**

Blackman, Don
1959 Gunmen from Laredo

Blackman, Paul
1938 Two Gun Man from
      Harlem

Blackmer, Sidney
1930 The Bad Man
1931 Little Caesar
1935 The Little Colonel
1937 Shadows of the Orient
      Thank You, Mr. Moto
1938 Charlie Chan at Monte
      Carlo
      In Old Chicago
      Speed to Burn
1942 Nazi Agent
1943 In Old Oklahoma
1944 Buffalo Bill
1947 Duel in the Sun
1948 My Girl Tisa
1951 Saturday's Hero
1955 The View from Pompey's
      Head

Blackwell, Carlyle
1916 Broken Chains
1918 The Golden Wall
      Hitting the Trail
1920 The Third Woman

Blackwood, George
1934 Massacre

Blackwood, Mary
1934 Coming Out Party
      Stand Up and Cheer!

Blagoi, George, Lieut. *same as* **Blagoi,
      George, Lieut.**
1926 Into Her Kingdom
1942 The Navy Comes Through
1943 Action in the North
      Atlantic
1945 Nob Hill
1947 Northwest Outpost

Blagoi, Tina
1944 Address Unknown

Blain, Barbara
1945 Where Do We Go From
      Here?

Blaine, James
1936 After the Thin Man
1937 Charlie Chan on
      Broadway
      Song of the City
1938 Gateway
      Mr. Moto's Gamble
      Passport Husband

Blaine, Ruby
1925 The Midnight Girl
1927 Bitter Apples

Blaine, Vivian
1944 Something for the Boys
1945 Nob Hill

Blair, Anthony
1952 Anything Can Happen

Blair, Betsy
1950 Mystery Street
      No Way Out
1955 Marty
1957 The Halliday Brand

Blair, Bob
1945 The Shanghai Cobra

Blair, George
1934 She Was a Lady
1939 Forged Passport
1940 Behind the News
1941 Ice-Capades
1942 Valley of Hunted Men
1944 The Negro Soldier
1946 G. I. War Brides
1949 Rose of the Yukon
1950 The Missourians
1952 Desert Pursuit
      Woman in the Dark

Blair, Henry
1940 Little Nellie Kelly
1943 Air Force
      Yankee Doodle Dandy
1947 Easy Come, Easy Go

Blair, Jim *same as* **Blair, Jimmy**
1936 After the Thin Man
      Star for a Night

Blair, Joan
1947 New Orleans

Blair, Nicky
1959 Night of the Quarter
      Moon
1960 Hell to Eternity

Blaisdell, William
1924 Racing Luck

Blake, Amanda
1950 Stars in My Crown

Blake, Arthur
1937 Souls at Sea
1948 Unconquered

Blake, Ben K.
1938 Two Sisters

Blake, Bobby *see* **Blake, Robert**

Eubie Blake and His Orchestra
1932 Harlem Is Heaven

Blake, George
1938 Mr. Moto's Gamble
1939 Winner Take All

Blake, Gladys
1934 Coming Out Party
1939 The Cisco Kid and the
      Lady
1942 Seven Sweethearts
      Woman of the Year
1944 Chip Off the Old Block
      Hi, Beautiful
1946 The Gentleman
      Misbehaves
      Shadows Over Chinatown
1948 The Time of Your Life

Blake, Joan
1952 The Fabulous Senorita

Blake, Larry
1946 The Trap
1948 Call Northside 777
1952 High Noon
1957 Band of Angels
      Beau James

Blake, Loretta
1915 The Sable Lorcha

Blake, Lucy
1917 Sold at Auction

Blake, Madge
1951 Queen for a Day
1952 The Iron Mistress
1957 All Mine to Give

Blake, Marie
1939 Judge Hardy and Son
1940 Jennie
      They Knew What They
      Wanted
1942 Dr. Gillespie's New
      Assistant
      Young America
1943 Dr. Gillespie's Criminal
      Case
1945 Between Two Women
1947 Dark Delusion

Blake, Oliver *same as* **Prickett, Oliver**
1941   New York Town
1942   Castle in the Desert
1945   A Medal for Benny
         Rhapsody in Blue
1947   The Mighty McGurk
1948   Cry of the City
         The Miracle of the Bells
         Moonrise
         The Paleface
1949   Colorado Territory
         The Girl from Jones
         Beach
1952   The Iron Mistress
1953   So Big
1954   Drum Beat
1957   Raintree County

Blake, Pamela
1942   Dr. Gillespie's New
         Assistant

Blake, Robert *same as* **Blake, Bobby**
1942   Mokey
1944   Marshal of Reno
         The San Antonio Kid
         Sheriff of Las Vegas
         Tucson Raiders
         Vigilantes of Dodge City
1945   Colorado Pioneers
         Great Stagecoach Robbery
         Phantom of the Plains
1946   California Gold Rush
         Santa Fe Uprising
         Sheriff of Redwood Valley
         Sun Valley Cyclone
1947   Humoresque
         The Last Round-Up
         Marshal of Cripple Creek
         Oregon Trail Scouts
         The Return of Rin Tin Tin
         Rustlers of Devil's
           Canyon
         Vigilantes of Boomtown
1950   Black Hand
1952   Apache War Smoke

Blake, Thomas F.
1917   Rosie O'Grady

Blake, Walter R.
1957   The Ride Back

Blakely, James
1934   Broadway Bill

Blakemore, Harry
1915   Under Southern Skies

Blakeney, Olive
1945   Nob Hill

Blakey, Ruble
1947   Sepia Cinderella
1948   Miracle in Harlem

Blalock, Ira
1950   Panic in the Streets

Blanchard, Dale
1949   Apache Chief

Blanchard, Lee
1948   The Paleface

Blanchard, Mari
1958   Machete

Blanchard, W. A.
1957   Burden of Truth

Blanchon, Jean
1931   El proceso de Mary
         Dugan (*foreign
         version*)

Blancke, Kate
1916   The Pretenders

Blanco, Eumenio
1930   El cuerpo del delito
         El precio de un beso
1932   Soñadores de la gloria
1951   Cuban Fireball
1958   Escape from Red Rock

Blanco, José María
1931   Sombras del circo

Blanco, Rafael
1930   Las campanas de
         Capistrano
         La rosa de fuego

Bland, Judith
1953   Tonight We Sing

Blandick, Clara
1930   Sins of the Children
         Tom Sawyer
1931   Huckleberry Finn
1933   Charlie Chan's Greatest
         Case
         Ever in My Heart
1934   As the Earth Turns
         Beloved
         Broadway Bill
1935   The Winning Ticket
1939   The Adventures of
         Huckleberry Finn
         Drums Along the Mohawk
1943   Dixie

Blanding, Don
1934   Song of the Islands

Blane, Sally
1932   Wild Horse Mesa
1937   One Mile from Heaven
1939   Charlie Chan at Treasure
         Island
         Way Down South

Blank, Roger
1955   Blackboard Jungle

Blanke, Henry *same as* **Blanke, Heinz**
1930   The Bad Man
         The Bad Man (*foreign
         version*)
         Los que danzan
         Los que danzan (*foreign
         version*)
1931   Dämon des Meeres
         La dama atrevida
         La llama sagrada
         Die Maske Fällt
1932   Le bluffeur
1936   The Green Pastures
1939   Daughters Courageous
1952   The Iron Mistress
1953   So Big
1956   Serenade
1960   Ice Palace

Blankfield, Eve *see* **Unsell, Eve**

Blankfort, Henry
1942   Rubber Racketeers
         Tales of Manhattan
1948   Open Secret

Blankfort, Michael
1941   Adam Had Four Sons
1950   Broken Arrow

Blasdale, Evanne
1927   The Fighting Hombre

Blass, Herman
1940   Overture to Glory

Blau, Fred, Jr.
1958   Home Before Dark

Blaustein, Julian
1950   Broken Arrow

Blay, Helen
1932   A Daughter of Her People
1940   The Great Advisor

Bledsoe, Jules
1929   Show Boat

Bleich, Judah *same as* **Bleich, Jehuda**
1930   Eternal Fools (Ewige
         Naranim)
1933   Victims of Persecution
1937   The Cantor's Son

Bleifer, John *same as* **Bleifer, Jake; Bleifer, John M.**
1928   We Americans
1935   Black Fury
1936   Sutter's Gold
1937   Slave Ship
         Thank You, Mr. Moto
1938   Charlie Chan at Monte
         Carlo
1939   Mr. Moto Takes a
         Vacation
1940   Girl from God's Country
         The Mark of Zorro
1943   Mr. Lucky
1944   Waterfront
1946   Rendezvous 24
         Without Reservations
1947   Northwest Outpost
1948   Call Northside 777
         16 Fathoms Deep
1952   Red Snow

Bletcher, Arlene
1948   The Miracle of the Bells

Bletcher, Barbara
1936   Show Boat

Bletcher, Billy
1933   Diplomaniacs
         A Lady's Profession
1934   The Cat's-Paw
1936   Desert Gold
1938   California Frontier
         Rascals
1941   Sullivan's Travels
1944   Buffalo Bill

Blin, Roger
1951   Adventures of Captain
         Fabian

Blind, Eric
1916   The Woman in 47

Blinn, B. F. *not the same as* **Blinn, Beatrice**
1925   Quicker'n Lightnin'

Blinn, Beatrice *not the same as* **Blinn, B. F.**
1936   Dangerous Intrigue

Bliss, Lela
1944   Since You Went Away
1946   Without Reservations
1948   I Remember Mama
1950   Intruder in the Dust
1953   Tonight We Sing

Bliss, Ted
1937   Black Legion

Blizzard, Helen
1942   The Vanishing Virginian

Blochman, Lawrence G.
1935   Chinatown Squad

Block, Arthur
1937   The Cantor's Son

Block, Ralph
1930   The Arizona Kid
1934   Massacre

Blodgett, Linda
1955   Murder in Villa Capri

Bloem, R. H.
1931   Delicious

Blondell, Joan
1934   He Was Her Man
1945   A Tree Grows in Brooklyn

Blood, Adele
1920   The Riddle: Woman

Bloodgood, Margaret
1936   Dimples
         It Had to Happen

Bloom, Harold Jack
1954   The Yellow Tomahawk

Bloom, Phil
1945   Where Do We Go From
         Here?

Bloom, William (*prod*)
1953   The Glory Brigade

Bloom, Willie (*actor*)
1945   Where Do We Go From
         Here?

Bloomer, Raymond
1918   Out of a Clear Sky
         A Woman of Impulse

Blore, Eric
1934   Behold My Wife!
         Limehouse Blues
1940   Music in My Heart
1941   New York Town
         Sullivan's Travels
1946   Abie's Irish Rose

Blue, Angela
1934   Stand Up and Cheer!
1941   Sun Valley Serenade

Blue, Ben
1947   My Wild Irish Rose

Blue, Monte
1918   Johanna Enlists
         The Only Road
         The Red, Red Heart
         The Squaw Man
1919   Told in the Hills
1922   Peacock Alley
1925   Hogan's Alley
1927   Bitter Apples
1933   Thundering Herd
1934   Wagon Wheels

1960   Ice Palace

1936   Desert Gold
         Ride, Ranger, Ride
         Song of the Gringo
         Treachery Rides the
           Range
1937   Souls at Sea
1938   Spawn of the North
1940   Geronimo
1941   New York Town
         Sullivan's Travels
1942   Across the Pacific
         Gentleman Jim
         North to the Klondike
         Secret Enemies
1943   Action in the North
         Atlantic
1946   Saratoga Trunk
1947   Bells of San Fernando
         Humoresque
         My Wild Irish Rose
1948   Key Largo
1949   Colorado Territory
         Ranger of Cherokee Strip
1950   The Iroquois Trail
1951   Snake River Desperadoes
         Warpath
1952   Rose of Cimarron
         Trail of the Arrow
1953   Ride, Vaquero!
1954   Apache

Blue Eagle, Chief
1958   Gunman's Walk

Bluebird, Princess
1942   King of the Stallions

Blum, Edwin
1957   The Midnight Story

Blum, Sammy *same as* **Blum, Sam**
1930   The Grand Parade
1934   Broadway Bill
1936   Rose of the Rancho
1937   The Devil's Playground
1945   Betrayal from the East
         Wanderer of the
           Wasteland

Blumenstock, Mort
1927   Rose of the Golden West
1928   Ransom

Blumenthal, Richard
1933   L'amour guide

Blumfield, Baby
1922   Little Miss Smiles

Blystone, John
1931   Mr. Lemon of Orange
         Young Sinners
1932   Charlie Chan's Chance
1934   Coming Out Party
1937   Music for Madame

Blystone, Stanley
1931   Noche de duendes
1934   Broadway Bill
1935   Fighting Pioneers
         A Night at the Opera
1936   Human Cargo
         The Prisoner of Shark
           Island
1937   Boots and Saddles
         Charlie Chan at the
           Olympics
1938   The Buccaneer
         California Frontier
         Dangerous to Know
         Mr. Moto's Gamble
         Passport Husband
1939   Charlie Chan in Reno
         Drifting Westward
         The Escape
         Mr. Moto Takes a
           Vacation
1940   Murder over New York
1941   Mutiny in the Arctic
         Mystery Ship
1943   Action in the North
         Atlantic
1946   Bringing Up Father
1947   California
1948   Big City
         Fighting Father Dunne
         The Paleface
1949   Rose of the Yukon
         Rustlers
         That Midnight Kiss
1950   Sunset in the West
1952   Fort Osage
         Indian Uprising
         The Raiders

1953　The Great Sioux Uprising
　　　　Jack McCall Desperado
Blyth, Ann
1944　Chip Off the Old Block
1949　Top O' the Morning
1951　The Great Caruso
Blythe, Betty
1918　The Little Runaway
1922　Fair Lady
1924　In Hollywood With
　　　　Potash and Perlmutter
1936　Rainbow on the River
1944　The Chinese Cat
1947　Jiggs and Maggie in
　　　　Society
1949　Jiggs and Maggie in
　　　　Jackpot Jitters
1955　The Lonesome Trail
Board, Robert
1950　Right Cross
1951　The Magnificent Yankee
Boardman, Eleanor
1928　Diamond Handcuffs
1931　The Great Meadow
　　　　The Squaw Man
　　　　Women Love Once
Boardman, Nan
1950　Battleground
1952　Red Ball Express
Boardman, Virginia True
1925　The Red Rider
Boasberg, Al
1927　Clancy's Kosher Wedding
1930　¡De frente, marchen!
1934　Tres amores
1935　A Night at the Opera
1936　Silly Billies
Boaz, Charles
1959　The Jayhawkers!
Bo-Bo, a parrot
1921　One Man in a Million
Bocignon, Iris
1946　The Gay Cavalier
Bódalo, José
1930　El secreto del doctor
Bodeen, DeWitt
1942　Cat People
1948　I Remember Mama
　　　　The Miracle of the Bells
Bodie, Marie
1942　Song of the Islands
Bodnar, E.
1939　Cossacks in Exile
Bodson, Handrey
1931　Su noche de bodas
　　　　(*foreign version*)
Boehlke, Mabel
1944　Something for the Boys
1945　Nob Hill
Boehm, Carla
1943　Hitler's Children
Boehm, David
1933　Grand Slam
1944　Knickerbocker Holiday
Boehm, Sydney
1949　The Undercover Man
1950　Mystery Street
1952　The Savage
1954　Siege at Red River
1955　Violent Saturday
Boetticher, Budd *same as*
　　Boetticher, Oscar, Jr.
1943　Good Luck, Mr. Yates
1945　Escape in the Fog
1952　Red Ball Express
1953　The Man from the Alamo
　　　　Seminole
Bogard, A. R.
1939　Mr. Moto's Last Warning
Bogart, Humphrey
1937　Black Legion
1942　Across the Pacific
　　　　All Through the Night
1943　Action in the North
　　　　Atlantic
1948　Key Largo
1949　Knock on Any Door
Bogeaus, Benedict
1944　Dark Waters
1954　Cattle Queen of Montana
　　　　Passion

Bogomoletz, Maj. Gen.
1926　Into Her Kingdom
Bogua, Julius
1934　Laughing Boy
Bohem, Endre
1957　Pawnee
Bohn, John
1943　Gangway for Tomorrow
1944　An American Romance
Bohnen, Roman
1941　They Dare Not Love
1942　Young America
1947　California
1948　Open Secret
Bohorman, Lulu Mae
1944　Since You Went Away
Bohr, José
1930　Así es la vida
　　　　Sombras de gloria
1932　Hollywood, ciudad de
　　　　ensueño
Bois, Curt
1941　Hold Back the Dawn
1946　Saratoga Trunk
1948　Up in Central Park
Bojm, Henryk
1934　The Rabbi's Power
Bojorquez, Yolanda
1958　Touch of Evil
Bok, Fuk
1939?　A Chinese Gains a
　　　　Fortune in America
Bokor, Hal
1951　Apache Drums
Boland, Eddie *same as* **Boland,**
　　Edward
1931　The Guilty Generation
1932　The Secrets of Wu Sin
1934　The Cat's-Paw
1935　Range Warfare
Boland, Jack *could be same as*
　　Boland, John J.
1927　The Auctioneer
1929　Evangeline
1932　Call Her Savage
1939　Los hijos mandan
Boland, John J. *could be same as*
　　Boland, Jack
1935　Piernas de seda
　　　　Te quiero con locura
Boland, Mary
1931　Personal Maid
1935　Ruggles of Red Gap
1940　New Moon
Bolden, Harry
1953　The Member of the
　　　　Wedding
Bolder, Robert
1935　The Wedding Night
Bolding, Bonnie
1957　The Brothers Rico
Boldrick, Betty
1933　It's Great to Be Alive
Boles, Jim
1957　Naked in the Sun
1960　The Pusher
Boles, John
1928　We Americans
1930　King of Jazz
1934　Beloved
　　　　Stand Up and Cheer!
1935　The Littlest Rebel
1936　Rose of the Rancho
Boleslawski, Richard *same as*
　　Boleslavsky, Richard
1934　Operator 13
Boley, May
1931　Fighting Caravans
Bolognese, Dino
1950　The Big Hangover
　　　　Black Hand
　　　　The Toast of New Orleans
1951　The Great Caruso
Bolster, Anita
1944　Going My Way
1945　Nob Hill
Bolton, Guy
1931　Delicious

Bolton, Patsy
1949　Shamrock Hill
Bolton, Phil
1950　Damien
Bomben, Gino
1949　Thieves' Highway
Bonanova, Fortunio
1937　El capitán Tormenta
　　　　El carnaval del diablo
1939　La Inmaculada
1940　The Mark of Zorro
1943　Dixie
1944　Going My Way
1945　Where Do We Go From
　　　　Here?
1946　The Red Dragon
　　　　The Sailor Takes a Wife
1953　Conquest of Cochise
　　　　Thunder Bay
1959　Thunder in the Sun
Bonar, Ivan
1959　Night of the Quarter
　　　　Moon
Bonavia, Humberto
1930　Alma de gaucho
Bond, Anson
1952　Japanese War Bride
Bond, David
1949　We Were Strangers
1950　Black Hand
　　　　A Lady Without Passport
1951　The Great Caruso
1958　Bullwhip
　　　　Gun Fever
Bond, Frank
1925　Hogan's Alley
Bond, Fred *not the same as* **Bond,**
　　Frederick C.
1918　Me Und Gott
Bond, Frederick C. *same as* **Bond,**
　　Fred C. *not the same as* **Bond,**
　　Fred
1945　Samurai
Bond, Johnny
1944　Riding West
　　　　Since You Went Away
Bond, Lilian *same as* **Bond, Lillian**
1931　The Squaw Man
1947　The Jolson Story
Bond, Raymond
1947　The Burning Cross
1950　A Ticket to Tomahawk
1951　Westward the Women
1953　The Man from the Alamo
Bond, Richard
1941　You're Out of Luck
Bond, Rudy
1951　A Streetcar Named Desire
1957　The Brothers Rico
　　　　Twelve Angry Men
Bond, Tommy
1938　City Streets
1941　New York Town
1950　Battleground
　　　　Intruder in the Dust
Bond, Ward
1932　Flesh
　　　　White Eagle
1933　Obey the Law
1934　Broadway Bill
1935　Black Fury
1936　Muss 'Em Up
1937　The Devil's Playground
　　　　Music for Madame
　　　　Souls at Sea
1938　Hawaii Calls
　　　　Mr. Moto's Gamble
1939　The Cisco Kid and the
　　　　Lady
　　　　Confessions of a Nazi Spy
　　　　Drums Along the Mohawk
　　　　The Girl from Mexico
　　　　Gone With the Wind
　　　　Heaven with a Barbed
　　　　Wire Fence
　　　　Mr. Moto in Danger
　　　　Island
　　　　The Return of the Cisco
　　　　Kid
　　　　Waterfront
1940　Kit Carson
　　　　Santa Fe Trail

1942　Gentleman Jim
1943　They Came to Blow Up
　　　　America
1944　The Sullivans
1946　Canyon Passage
1948　Fort Apache
　　　　Tap Roots
　　　　The Time of Your Life
　　　　Unconquered
1949　3 Godfathers
1951　Only the Valiant
1952　The Quiet Man
1954　Hondo
1955　The Long Gray Line
1956　Dakota Incident
　　　　Pillars of the Sky
　　　　The Searchers
1957　The Halliday Brand
Bondi, Beulah
1931　Street Scene
1937　Maid of Salem
1938　The Buccaneer
1950　The Baron of Arizona
　　　　The Furies
Bonelli, William
1915　An American Gentleman
Bongini, Raffaele *same as* **Bongini,**
　　R.
1920　Lifting Shadows
1932　Amore e morte
Bonham, Guy
1943　Doughboys in Ireland
Boni, Carmen
1930　Toda una vida (*foreign
　　　　version*)
1931　La fiesta del diablo
　　　　(*foreign version*)
　　　　Tropennächte (*foreign
　　　　version*)
Boniface, Patsy
1949　Pinky
Boniface, Symona
1934　Broadway Bill
Bonillas, Myrta
1930　Así es la vida
1936　Ramona
Bonita, Madame
1934　Our Daily Bread
　　　　Straight Is the Way
Bonn, Walter
1937　Charlie Chan at the
　　　　Olympics
1940　Elsa Maxwell's Public
　　　　Deb No. 1
　　　　Escape
　　　　The Man I Married
1945　Where Do We Go From
　　　　Here?
Bonne, Shirley
1959　The FBI Story
Bonnell, Lee
1942　The Navy Comes Through
1947　Jiggs and Maggie in
　　　　Society
Bonnell, Samuel S.
1931　Street Scene
Bonner, John
1958　The Young Lions
Bonner, Priscilla
1922　Shadows
1923　April Showers
　　　　Purple Dawn
1926　The Strong Man
Bonnett, Edna
1935　A Night at the Opera
Bonney, Gail
1949　The Red Menace
1950　Sunset in the West
1953　Dream Wife
　　　　The Member of the
　　　　Wedding
1958　Home Before Dark
　　　　The Last Hurrah
Bonny, Fred
1934　Drums O' Voodoo
Bonomo, Joe
1926　The Flaming Frontier
1928　Vamping Venus
Bonsato, Candido
1946　Notorious

Boodkin, Celia *same as* **Budkin, Celia**
1938   Two Sisters
1939   The Light Ahead
1940   Americaner Schadchen
1954   Go Man Go
Boodkin, M. *same as* **Budkin, Misha**
1939   The Light Ahead
1940   Americaner Schadchen
Bookasta, George
1928   The Night Bird
1936   It Had to Happen
        Rose of the Rancho
Booker, Beryl
1947   Boy! What a Girl!
Boon, Robert
1950   Battleground
1951   Go for Broke!
Boone, Daniel
1939   Mr. Moto's Last Warning
Boone, Grace
1941   Sullivan's Travels
Boone, Richard
1953   Beneath the 12-Mile Reef
1954   Siege at Red River
Booth, Adrian
1947   Spoilers of the North
1950   Rock Island Trail
1951   Oh! Susanna
Booth, Barbara
1938   In Old Chicago
Booth, Charles G.
1945   The House on 92nd St.
1948   Fury at Furnace Creek
Booth, June
1943   Gangway for Tomorrow
        Mexican Spitfire's Blessed
        Event
Booth, Karin
1948   Big City
1950   The Cariboo Trail
        Last of the Buccaneers
1955   Seminole Uprising
Booth, Katharine
1941   Hold Back the Dawn
        Louisiana Purchase
1942   Holiday Inn
1943   Dr. Gillespie's Criminal
        Case
1946   The Sailor Takes a Wife
Booth, Nesdon *same as* **Booth, Ned**
1953   The Glass Wall
1957   The Brothers Rico
        Raintree County
1958   Escape from Red Rock
1959   The FBI Story
        Yellowstone Kelly
Booth, Robert
1955   Davy Crockett, King of
        the Wild Frontier
Borcosque, Carlos F. *same as*
Borcosque, Carlos
1930   Sevilla de mis amores
        Wu Li Chang
1931   Cheri-Bibi
        En cada puerto un amor
        La mujer X
        Su última noche
1933   Dos noches
1935   Alas sobre el Chaco
1937   El carnaval del diablo
Bordeaux, Joe
1932   Hypnotized
1934   Broadway Bill
Borden, Eddie
1927   The Dove
1936   Rose of the Rancho
1943   Frontier Fury
        Gangway for Tomorrow
        Ladies' Day
        Mexican Spitfire's Blessed
        Event
1948   The Time of Your Life
1949   Knock on Any Door
Borden, Eugene
1917   The Slacker (Metro
        Pictures Corp.)
1918   The Liar
1921   The Barricade
1934   Coming Out Party
        La veuve joyeuse

1935   L'homme des Folies
        Bergère
1937   Charlie Chan on
        Broadway
        Souls at Sea
1938   Charlie Chan at Monte
        Carlo
        Happy Landing
1940   The Man I Married
        The Mark of Zorro
1941   Charlie Chan in Rio
1943   Wintertime
1944   Dark Waters
1945   The Dolly Sisters
1947   The Foxes of Harrow
        The Jolson Story
1950   Black Hand
        Last of the Buccaneers
1952   The Big Sky
        The Iron Mistress
        Red Ball Express
Borden, L. C. *same as* **Borden, Lewie C.**
1935   Wolf Riders
1940   Broken Strings
Borden, Olive
1934   Chloe: Love Is Calling
        You
Borden, Renee
1934   The Fighting Hero
Bordoni, Irene
1941   Louisiana Purchase
Bordrero, James
1934   White Heat
Borelli, Carlo
1931   La regina di Sparta
Borello, María
1934   Tres amores
1939   La Inmaculada
        El trovador de la radio
Boreo, Emile
1947   Carnegie Hall
Boretz, Allen *same as* **Boretz, Alan**
1947   Copacabana
        It Had To Be You
1948   My Girl Tisa
1949   The Girl from Jones
        Beach
Borg, Sven Hugo *same as* **Borg, Sven; Borg, Sven-Hugo**
1933   Let's Fall in Love
1937   Slave Ship
1942   The Navy Comes Through
1943   Action in the North
        Atlantic
        Jack London
        They Came to Blow Up
        America
1944   Address Unknown
1945   Nob Hill
1947   The Farmer's Daughter
1948   Music Man
Borg, Veda Ann
1939   Miracle on Main Street
1940   Behind the News
1943   The Girl from Monterrey
Borgani, Nick
1949   House of Strangers
1959   The Black Orchid
Borgato, Agostino
1929   Romance of the Rio
        Grande
1930   Behind the Make-Up
        La voluntad del muerto
1931   La gran jornada (*foreign
        version*)
1933   La melodía prohibida
        Primavera en otoño
1935   Julieta compra un hijo
1937   El capitán Tormenta
        Man of the People
1938   Daughter of Shanghai
Borget, Madam *could be same as*
Borget, Nina *or* **Borget, Olga**
1942   Syncopation
Borget, Nina *could be same as*
Borget, Madam *or* **Borget, Olga**
1936   My American Wife
Borget, Olga *could be same as*
Borget, Madam *or* **Borget, Nina**
1938   The Buccaneer
1941   They Dare Not Love

Borgia, René
1931   Carne de cabaret
        El pasado acusa
1932   Hombres en mi vida
1934   Tres amores
1935   Alas sobre el Chaco
1936   Amor que vuelve
        El crimen de media
        noche
        La última cita
1940   Perfidia
Borgnine, Ernest
1955   Bad Day at Black Rock
        The Last Command
        Marty
        Violent Saturday
1956   The Catered Affair
1958   The Badlanders
1960   Man on a String
        Pay or Die
Boring, Edwin
1918   The Birth of a Race
Borio, Josephine
1928   Tyrant of Red Gulch
Borisoff, Norman
194-   Mistaken Identity
Borland, Barlowe
1938   Dangerous to Know
1942   We Were Dancing
Borman, E. W.
1937   The Plainsman
        That I May Live
Borodin, Doris
1942   Woman of the Year
Boros, Ferike
1930   Ladies Love Brutes
1931   Gentleman's Fate
1932   Huddle
1933   Rafter Romance
1935   Black Fury
1940   Girl from God's Country
        Three Cheers for the Irish
1943   Margin for Error
1945   A Tree Grows in Brooklyn
Borowsky, Marvin
1945   Pride of the Marines
1951   Gambling House
Borzage, Bill
1943   In Old Oklahoma
1944   An American Romance
1945   Where Do We Go From
        Here?
1948   Moonrise
Borzage, Dan
1947   Easy Come, Easy Go
1953   The Sun Shines Bright
1954   Drum Beat
1956   Pillars of the Sky
1958   The Last Hurrah
1959   The Hanging Tree
Borzage, Frank
1918   Who Is to Blame?
1920   Humoresque
1922   The Good Provider
        The Pride of Palomar
1937   Big City
1942   Seven Sweethearts
        The Vanishing Virginian
1943   His Butler's Sister
1948   Moonrise
Bosan, Alonzo
1948?   Junction 88
Bosocki, Madame
1929   Smiling Irish Eyes
Bost, Herbert
1919   Injustice
Bostick, Floyd
1954   Salt of the Earth
Boswell, Connie
1942   Syncopation
Bosworth, Hobart
1914   John Barleycorn
        An Odyssey of the North
1915?   The Beachcomber
1917   The Little American
        Unconquered
1919   Behind the Door
1925   My Son
1927   The Chinese Parrot
1930   Abraham Lincoln
1932   No Greater Love
1936   General Spanky

1942   They Died With Their
        Boots On
Boteler, Wade
1920   The Cup of Fury
1921   Fifty Candles
        One Man in a Million
1922   Second Hand Rose
1928   The Crash
1931   Beyond Victory
1934   Charlie Chan's Courage
        Operator 13
1935   Black Fury
        Melody Trail
1936   Charlie Chan at the
        Circus
        Human Cargo
1938   Dangerous to Know
        In Old Chicago
        Little Miss Roughneck
        Passport Husband
        The Rage of Paris
        Spawn of the North
1939   The Adventures of
        Huckleberry Finn
1940   Knute Rockne—All
        American
        Three Cheers for the Irish
        Three Faces West
        The Way of All Flesh
        Young Buffalo Bill
1941   Birth of the Blues
        Mystery Ship
        Where Did You Get That
        Girl?
1942   Gentleman Jim
1943   The Amazing Mrs.
        Holliday
        Riding High
Botiller, Dick *same as* **Botiller, Richard**
1934   The Fighting Hero
        The Prescott Kid
1935   Circle of Death
        Range Warfare
1936   Dangerous Intrigue
        Ramona
        The Traitor
        Treachery Rides the
        Range
        West of Nevada
1937   The Californian
1939   The Fighting Gringo
1942   Across the Pacific
1943   In Old Oklahoma
1945   South of the Rio Grande
Botkin, Perry
1941   Birth of the Blues
Botollo, José *same as* **Bottolo, José**
1936   Amor que vuelve
        Ramona
Bouchey, Willis
1952   Anything Can Happen
1954   Battle of Rogue River
        Drum Beat
1955   The Long Gray Line
1956   Pillars of the Sky
1957   Beau James
1958   The Last Hurrah
1960   Sergeant Rutledge
Boudoures, Peter
1954   Barefoot Battalion
Boudreaux, Joseph
1948   Louisiana Story
Bougini, Rafaelo
1932   Cuore d'emigrante
Bouie, John
1947?   What a Guy
Boulter, Rosalyn
1957   All Mine to Give
Boulton, Matthew
1948   Unconquered
Bourg, Wilson, Jr.
1950   Panic in the Streets
Bourgeois, Philip
1950   Panic in the Streets
Boutell, Genee
1932   Hypnotized
Bovard, Mary
1936   Show Boat
        Star for a Night
1944   They Live in Fear
1946   The Sailor Takes a Wife

Bow, Clara
1925   The Scarlet West
1930   Galas de la Paramount
1932   Call Her Savage
Bowdoin, Edna
1934   Imitation of Life
Bowdon, Dorris
1939   Drums Along the Mohawk
1940   Jennie
Bowe, Rosemarie
1955   The View from Pompey's
        Head
Bowen, Harry
1935   Ruggles of Red Gap
Bower, Aubrey
1951   Adventures of Captain
        Fabian
Bowers, Cookie
1950   Catskill Honeymoon
Bowers, Eilene
1955   Violent Saturday
Bowers, Jess see Buffington, Adele
Bowers, John
1916   Hulda from Holland
1919   Daughter of Mine
1921   Bits of Life
1924   So Big
1926   Laddie
        Pals in Paradise
1927   Heroes in Blue
Bowker, Aldrich
1939   Waterfront
1940   Jennie
1941   Romance of the Rio
        Grande
Bowles, Donald
1917   The Squaw Man's Son
Bowman, Laura
1920   The Brute
1932   Ten Minutes to Live
        Veiled Aristocrats
1934   Drums O' Voodoo
1935   Lem Hawkins' Confession
1938   God's Step Children
1940   The Notorious Elinor Lee
        Son of Ingagi
Bowman, Lee
1942   Three Hearts for Julia
        We Were Dancing
1943   Bataan
Bowman, Ralph see Archer, John
Bowman, Rudy
1949   She Wore a Yellow
        Ribbon
Bowser, Aubrey
1921   The Call of His People
Bowsher, Raymond C.
1950   Battleground
Boyce & Evans
1951   Yes Sir, Mr. Bones
Boyce, Donna Jo
1950   The Breaking Point
Boyce, George
1949   That Midnight Kiss
Boyd, Bill see Boyd, William
    1898—1972
Boyd, Edward
1940?   Mr. Washington Goes to
        Town
Boyd, Kathryn
1926   The Flying Ace
1928   Black Gold
Boyd, Mildred
1928   Riley the Cop
Boyd, Mildred (African-American
    actress) not the same as **Boyd,
    Mildred**
1945   I Love a Bandleader
1946   The Red Dragon
1949   Pinky
1951   The Harlem Globetrotters
Boyd, Thomas
1930   Sombras de gloria
Boyd, William 1898—1972 same as
    Boyd, Bill not the same as
    Boyd, Bill 1910—1977 or **Boyd,
    William** (Stage)
1926   The Last Frontier
1931   Beyond Victory
1937   Hills of Old Wyoming

1941   Doomed Caravan
        Secret of the Wastelands
1943   Border Patrol
1947   Dangerous Venture
Boyer, Anise
1932   Harlem Is Heaven
Boyer, Charles
1931   El proceso de Mary
        Dugan (foreign
        version)
1934   Caravane
1941   Hold Back the Dawn
1942   Tales of Manhattan
Boyer, Elizabeth
1921   The Sport of the Gods
Boyer, Jean
1933   L'amour guide
Boyer, Richard
1959   The FBI Story
Boyett, William
1955   The Long Gray Line
Boyjan, Jack
1947   The Foxes of Harrow
Boykin
1946   Dirty Gertie from
        Harlem, U.S.A.
Boylan, Malcolm Stuart
1928   The Great White North
1933   A Lady's Profession
1934   Stand Up and Cheer!
1940   Girl from God's Country
Boylan, Mary
1959   Odds Against Tomorrow
Boyle, Eileen
1950   No Way Out
Boyle, Irene
1915   Children of the Ghetto
Boyle, John
1916   The Yellow Passport
Boyle, Walden
1936   Dangerous Intrigue
1946   Bringing Up Father
        The Trap
1947   The Burning Cross
1948   The Paleface
1949   Illegal Entry
        The Story of Seabiscuit
Boyne, Hazel
1949   Knock on Any Door
1953   The Stars Are Singing
1957   Beau James
Boyne, Sunny
1934   Straight Is the Way
1942   Syncopation
Bozán, Elena
1931   Las luces de Buenos Aires
Bozán, Sofía
1931   Las luces de Buenos Aires
Bozano, Enzo
1931   La fiesta del diablo
        (foreign version)
Bozyk, Max same as **Bozhyk, Max;
    Bozyk, Maks**
1936   Yiddle with His Fiddle
1937   The Jester (Der
        Purimspieler)
1939   A Brivele der Mamen
        Mamele
1950   Catskill Honeymoon
        God, Man and Devil
Bozyk, Rose same as **Bozhyk, Rose**
1950   Catskill Honeymoon
Brabin, Charles
1924   So Big
1931   The Great Meadow
Bracco, Baby Marie
1934   Call of the Coyote
Brace, Linda
1955   Good Morning, Miss Dove
Bracey, Clara T.
1915   The Gambler of the West
Bracey, Sidney same as **Bracy,
    Sidney**
1917   Crime and Punishment
1918   The Million Dollar
        Mystery
1923   Ruggles of Red Gap
1928   The Cameraman
1929   Sioux Blood
1931   The Avenger
1933   Broken Dreams

1934   Broadway Bill
        The Cat's-Paw
        Laughing Boy
        Our Daily Bread
1935   Rendezvous
1936   Charlie Chan at the Race
        Track
        Sutter's Gold
1937   Maid of Salem
1938   The Rage of Paris
1941   This Woman Is Mine
Bracken, Bertram
1917   The Primitive Call
1924   Defying the Law
Bracken, Eddie
1940   Too Many Girls
1949   The Girl from Jones
        Beach
Bracken, Mildred
1916   The Fall of a Nation
Bracker, Vera
1927   The Millionaire
Brackett, Charles
1934   Behold My Wife!
1936   Rose of the Rancho
1941   Hold Back the Dawn
1943   Mr. Lucky
Bracy, Sidney see Bracey, Sidney
Bradbeck, Butch
1950   No Way Out
Bradbury, Mrs.
1917   The Captain of the Gray
        Horse Troop
Bradbury, Bob, Jr. see Steele, Bob
Bradbury, James could be same as
    **Bradbury, James, Jr. [or] or
    Bradbury, James, Sr.**
1916   At Piney Ridge
Bradbury, James, Jr.
1921   Bits of Life
1928   Flying Romeos
        The Glorious Trail
1929   In Old Arizona
1931   The Cisco Kid
1933   Song of the Eagle
Bradbury, James, Sr.
1930   Abraham Lincoln
Bradbury, Robert North same as
    **Bradbury, R. N.; Bradbury,
    Robert N.**
1919   The Last of His People
1924   In High Gear
        Yankee Speed
1927   With Sitting Bull at the
        Spirit Lake Massacre
1932   Hidden Valley
        Riders of the Desert
1934   The Star Packer
1935   Texas Terror
Bradford, Barbara same as
    **Bradford, Barbara
    "Butterbeans"**
1946   Tall, Tan and Terrific
Bradford, Gardner
1920   Outside the Law
1928   Heart Trouble
Bradford, Lane
1949   The Cowboy and the
        Prizefighter
        Roll Thunder Roll!
1950   The Missourians
1952   Fort Osage
        The Raiders
1953   The Great Sioux Uprising
1954   Drums Across the River
1955   Seven Angry Men
1957   Apache Warrior
1958   The Lone Ranger and the
        Lost City of Gold
Bradford, Marshall
1949   The Red Menace
1951   The Magnificent Yankee
1957   Band of Angels
Bradford, Robert
1940   Little Nellie Kelly
1942   Rio Rita
Bradin, Jean
1930   El secreto del doctor
        (foreign version)

Bradley, Bart
1960   Pay or Die
Bradley, Bernard
1943   Cabin in the Sky
Bradley, Chuckie
1959   Imitation of Life
Bradley, Doryce
1946   Mantan Messes Up
Bradley, Grace
1934   The Cat's-Paw
1936   Rose of the Rancho
Bradley, Harry C. same as
    Bradley, Harry
1933   Grand Slam
1934   As the Earth Turns
        Broadway Bill
        Our Daily Bread
1935   Rendezvous
1936   It Had to Happen
1941   Mystery Ship
        They Dare Not Love
1943   Dixie
1944   Mr. Skeffington
Bradley, Jeanette
1942   Syncopation
Bradley, John H.
1950   Sands of Iwo Jima
Bradley, Lee
1949   She Wore a Yellow
        Ribbon
Bradley, Leslie
1955   Good Morning, Miss Dove
        Kiss of Fire
        Seven Cities of Gold
1956   Westward Ho the
        Wagons!
1958   Frontier Gun
        Marjorie Morningstar
Bradley, Lovyss
1960   This Rebel Breed
Bradley, Oscar
1950   Young Man with a Horn
Bradley, P. could be same as
    Bradley, Paul
1959   Last Train from Gun Hill
Bradley, Paul could be same as
    Bradley, P.
1948   Music Man
1949   House of Strangers
        Illegal Entry
1950   Emergency Wedding
1959   Imitation of Life
Bradley, Samuel
1921?   The Supreme Passion
Bradley, Truman
1940   Northwest Passage (Book
        I—Rogers' Rangers)
1941   Charlie Chan in Rio
        Dead Men Tell
1948   Call Northside 777
Bradley, Willard King
1920?   The Scarlet Dragon
Bradna, Olympe
1937   Souls at Sea
Bradshaw, Herbert
1919   The Scar
Bradshaw, Joan
1956   The Catered Affair
Brady, Alice
1915   The Lure of Woman
1916   The Woman in 47
1918   The Ordeal of Rosetta
1921   The Land of Hope
        Little Italy
1922   Anna Ascends
1938   In Old Chicago
Brady, Billy, Jr.
1952   Red Ball Express
Brady, Buff
1949   The Golden Stallion
1956   Westward Ho the
        Wagons!
1959   Yellowstone Kelly
Brady, Ed same as **Brady, E. J.;
    Brady, Edward; Brady, Edward
    J.; Brady, Edwin J.**
1916   The Twin Triangle
1918   Marked Cards
1919   Diane of the Green Van
1921   Cheated Love
        The Kiss

1922	The Pride of Palomar
1924	Fools' Highway
1925	Flower of Night
	The Thundering Herd
1927	Clancy's Kosher Wedding
	Lost at the Front
1931	Oklahoma Jim
	The Squaw Man
1936	Klondike Annie
	Rose of the Rancho
	Sutter's Gold
1937	Man of the People
1938	The Buccaneer
	The Texans
1939	The Adventures of
	Huckleberry Finn
1942	Valley of the Sun

Brady, Fred (actor) could be same as **Brady, Fred** (writer)
1944	An American Romance
1946	Slightly Scandalous

Brady, Fred (writer) could be same as **Brady, Fred** (actor)
1953	Taxi

Brady, H. G.
1940	The Ramparts We Watch

Brady, Jasper Ewing same as **Brady, Jasper Ewing, Col.**
1914	The Little Angel of
	Canyon Creek
1916	Britton of the Seventh

Brady, Nicholas same as **Brady, Nick**
1959	John Paul Jones
	The Sheriff of Fractured
	Jaw

Brady, Pat
1949	The Golden Stallion
1958	The Light in the Forest

Brady, Ruth same as **Brady, Ruthe**
1943	The Gang's All Here
	They Came to Blow Up
	America
1947	Little Mister Jim
	The Mighty McGurk

Brady, Scott
1955	The Vanishing American
1956	Mohawk
1958	Ambush at Cimarron Pass
	Blood Arrow

Brady, William A.
1916	The Scarlet Oath
1917	The Adventures of Carol
	The Red Woman
1918	Broken Ties
	The Golden Wall
	Wanted, a Mother

Braham, Lionel
1937	Souls at Sea

Brahm, John
1940	Escape to Glory
1943	Wintertime

Braidwood, Flora
1919	Deliverance

Braly, Hal
1951	Saturday's Hero

Bramley, Flora
1928	We Americans

Bramley, Raymond
1950	Broken Arrow

Brammall, Jack same as **Brammall, John**
1915	The Gambler of the West
1917	A Love Sublime

Branch, Houston
1929	Sioux Blood
1932	The Heart of New York
	The Match King
	Tiger Shark
1938	Mr. Wong, Detective
1941	Mystery Ship
1944	Block Busters
1958	Sierra Baron

Branch, William
1927	Pleasure Before Business

Branche, Arie Lee
1941	Sullivan's Travels
1942	The Vanishing Virginian

Brand, George
1950	Mystery Street
1958	Frontier Gun

Brand, Harry
1929	Masked Emotions

Brand, Neville
1951	Only the Valiant
1953	The Charge at Feather
	River
	The Man from the Alamo
1956	Mohawk
	Raw Edge
1957	The Tin Star
1960	The Adventures of
	Huckleberry Finn

Branden, Michael same as **Twitchell, Archie**
1938	Spawn of the North
	The Texans
1939	King of Chinatown
1940	Behind the News
	Charlie Chan at the Wax
	Museum
	Geronimo
1948	Moonrise
1951	Yes Sir, Mr. Bones

Brandenburg, Chet
1950	Broken Arrow
1957	Gun Battle at Monterey

Brandes, Alaine
1941	Louisiana Purchase
1942	Holiday Inn

Brando, Marlon
1950	The Men
1951	A Streetcar Named Desire
1958	The Young Lions

Brandon, Artie
1938	Life Goes On
1943	Cabin in the Sky

Brandon, Beverly
1951	Distant Drums

Brandon, Bob
1949	Stallion Canyon

Brandon, Clifton
1960	Sergeant Rutledge

Brandon, Edward
1937	Harlem on the Prairie
1940	Midnight Shadow

Brandon, Harry could be same as **Brandon, Henry**
1940	Doomed to Die

Brandon, Henry could be same as **Brandon, Harry**
1937	Black Legion
1938	Spawn of the North
1947	Northwest Outpost
1948	Old Los Angeles
	The Paleface
1952	Wagons West
1954	War Arrow
1956	Comanche
	The Searchers

Brands, X
1957	Band of Angels
1959	Gunmen from Laredo
1960	Oklahoma Territory

Brandt, Bill
1947	The Jolson Story

Brandt, Charles C.
1919	As a Man Thinks

Brandt, George
1945	The House on 92nd St.

Brandt, Janet
1955	Good Morning, Miss Dove
1960	Cimarron

Brandt, John
1957	Burden of Truth

Brandt, Louis
1939	Mirele Efros

Brannum, Tom
1959	John Paul Jones

Brant, Lynton
1934	Our Daily Bread

Brant, Peggy
1944	Chip Off the Old Block

Brashear, Myrtle
1958	Tonka

Brasno, George
1936	Charlie Chan at the
	Circus

Brasno, Olive
1936	Charlie Chan at the
	Circus

Brasselle, Keefe
1952	It's a Big Country: An
	American Anthology
1953	The Eddie Cantor Story

Brasseur, Pierre
1930	Un hombre de suerte
	(foreign version)
1934	Caravane

Braun, Gertrude
1918	The Birth of a Race

Braun, Judith
1952	Red Ball Express

Braus, Mortimer
1939	El otro soy yo

Bravo, Danny
1960	For the Love of Mike

Braxton, Harry
1929	Lucky Boy

Braxton, Preston
1949	Pinky

Bray, Bob see **Bray, Robert**

Bray, Kahala
1942	Song of the Islands

Bray, Robert same as **Bray, Bob**
1946	Sunset Pass
1947	Crossfire
	Desperate
	Wild Horse Mesa
1948	The Arizona Ranger
	Fighting Father Dunne
	Gun Smugglers
	Guns of Hate
	Indian Agent
	Western Heritage
1949	Brothers in the Saddle
	The Clay Pigeon
	Rustlers
	Stagecoach Kid
1951	Warpath
1953	Seminole
1954	Drums Across the River
	The Yellow Tomahawk
1958	Never Love a Stranger

Bray, William
1918	My Cousin

Brayton, Margaret
1936	My American Wife
1946	The Trap
1949	Pinky
1957	All Mine to Give

Braznick, Fedor same as **Braznick, F.; Braznick, Fedir; Braznyk, Fedor**
1937	Natalka Poltavka
1938	Marusia
1939	Cossacks in Exile

Breacher, Lorraine
1943	The Gang's All Here

Breakston, George
1939	Judge Hardy and Son

Breamer, Sylvia same as **Bremer, Sylvia**
1918	The Temple of Dusk
1922	The Man with Two
	Mothers

Brecher, Egon
1929	Die Königsloge
1934	As the Earth Turns
1935	Black Fury
1936	Charlie Chan's Secret
	Paddy O'Day
	Sins of Man
1937	Black Legion
1938	Gateway
	Spawn of the North
1939	Confessions of a Nazi Spy
	Judge Hardy and Son
1940	Knute Rockne—All
	American
	The Man I Married
1941	They Dare Not Love
1942	All Through the Night
	The Navy Comes Through
1943	Gangway for Tomorrow
	Hitler's Children
	They Came to Blow Up
	America
1944	They Live in Fear

Breckenridge, Paul
1948?	Boarding House Blues

Breckner, Gary
1938	Mr. Moto's Gamble
	Road Demon
1941	Where Did You Get That
	Girl?
1942	Submarine Raider
1943	Margin for Error

Breedlove, Philip
1956	Reprisal!

Breen, Bobby
1936	Let's Sing Again
	Rainbow on the River
1938	Breaking the Ice
	Hawaii Calls
1939	Fisherman's Wharf
	Way Down South

Breen, David
1956	7th Cavalry
1957	The Guns of Fort
	Petticoat

Breen, George
1949	Jigsaw

Breen, Hurley
1947	It Had To Be You

Breen, Joseph
1955	Apache Ambush
1959	Gunmen from Laredo

Breen, Richard L. same as **Breen, Richard**
1949	Top O' the Morning
1955	Seven Cities of Gold
1959	The FBI Story

Breen, Thomas E.
1950	Battleground

Breene, Celina same as **Breene, Baby Celina**
1932	Mazel Tov
1933	The Eternal Jew
	Live and Laugh

Breese, Edmund
1931	Chinatown After Dark
	Young Sinners
1932	The Golden West
	The Hatchet Man
	The Match King
1934	Beloved
	Broadway Bill

Bregovska, Zorka
1932	Ljubav i strast

Brehm, Richard
1950	Colt .45

Bremen, Lennie same as **Bremen, Leonard**
1945	Pride of the Marines
1947	Buck Privates Come
	Home
	The Foxes of Harrow
1949	The Girl from Jones
	Beach
1953	The Stars Are Singing
1957	Beau James
1960	Ice Palace
	This Rebel Breed

Bremer, Lucille
1947	Dark Delusion

Bremer, Sylvia see **Breamer, Sylvia**

Bren, J. Robert
1942	American Empire
1945	The Gay Senorita
1953	The Great Sioux Uprising
1954	Overland Pacific
	Siege at Red River

Bren, Milton
1929	The Desert Rider

Brendel, El
1926	The Campus Flirt
1929	Frozen Justice
1931	Delicious
	Mr. Lemon of Orange
1933	Olsen's Big Moment
1938	Happy Landing
1940	If I Had My Way

Brenes, Martha
1947	Ride the Pink Horse

Brenes, Ulysses
1958	Machete

Brengk, Ernest
1958	Houseboat

Brenlin, George
1960	Cimarron

Brenn, Doris
1938   The Beloved Brat
Brennan, Andrew *same as*
    Brennan, Andy
1953   San Antone
1954   Drums Across the River
Brennan, Bertha
1950   Two Flags West
Brennan, Claude
1958   Tonka
Brennan, Frederick Hazlitt
1944   My Pal Wolf
Brennan, Hazel
1920   The Paliser Case
Brennan, Michael
1960   The Day They Robbed the
        Bank of England
Brennan, Ruth
1951   Oh! Susanna
Brennan, Walter
1930   King of Jazz
1934   Beloved
        The Prescott Kid
1935   The Wedding Night
1938   The Adventures of Tom
        Sawyer
        The Buccaneer
        The Texans
1940   Northwest Passage (Book
        I—Rogers' Rangers)
1941   This Woman Is Mine
1948   Red River
1950   A Ticket to Tomahawk
1954   Drums Across the River
1955   Bad Day at Black Rock
Brenner, Alfred
1960   Key Witness
Brenon, Herbert
1915   The Clemenceau Case
        Kreutzer Sonata
1915?   Sin
1924   Peter Pan
Brent, Dorothy
1943   Crash Dive
Brent, Evelyn
1919   The Other Man's Wife
1927   Blind Alleys
1928   The Mating Call
1929   Why Bring That Up?
1930   Galas de la Paramount
1938   Daughter of Shanghai
        Mr. Wong, Detective
1939   Daughter of the Tong
1947   Robin Hood of Monterey
1948   The Golden Eye
Brent, George
1931   Charlie Chan Carries On
1932   So Big
1940   The Fighting 69th
1941   They Dare Not Love
1942   In This Our Life
        Twin Beds
1949   Illegal Entry
Brent, Jerry
1959   The FBI Story
1960   This Rebel Breed
Brent, Linda
1942   Below the Border
1943   In Old Oklahoma
Brent, Lynton
1930   The Last Dance
1938   Mr. Wong, Detective
1941   The Pioneers
1943   Gangway for Tomorrow
        Redhead from Manhattan
1946   The Gay Cavalier
1950   Right Cross
Brent, Mauryne
1949?   Come On, Cowboy!
Brent, Milarde
1948   Four Faces West
Brent, Romney
1960   The Sign of Zorro
Brent, Roy
1943   The Law Rides Again
1946   Wild Beauty
Brent, Rudolph
1940   Mystery in Swing
Brent, Wesley
1943   In Old Oklahoma

Brent, William
1948   Four Faces West
Brenwald, Doris
1936   Star for a Night
Breon, Edmund
1946   Saratoga Trunk
Breon, Eugene
1921   The Money Maniac
Brereton, Tyrone
1928   The Canyon of Adventure
1931   Cimarron
Bresee, R. A.
1916   Her Debt of Honor
Breslin, John
1959   Shake Hands with the
        Devil
Breslin, Pat
1954   Go Man Go
Breslow, Lou
1932   No Greater Love
1936   Charlie Chan at the Race
        Track
        Paddy O'Day
1937   One Mile from Heaven
1938   City Streets
        Mr. Moto Takes a Chance
1942   Whispering Ghosts
1943   Good Luck, Mr. Yates
Bressart, Felix
1940   Escape
1942   Three Hearts for Julia
1949   Portrait of Jennie
Bressel, Claribel
1948   The Luck of the Irish
Bressler, Sophie
1938   The Singing Blacksmith
Bret, Tom
1918   The Birth of a Race
Bretherton, Howard *same as*
    Bretherton, Howard P.
1932   The Match King
1935   El cantante de Nápoles
1941   You're Out of Luck
1942   Below the Border
1943   Wagon Tracks West
1944   The San Antonio Kid
1945   The Navajo Trail
1946   The Trap
Brewer, Betty
1942   Juke Girl
Brewer, Jameson
1956   Ghost Town
Brewster, Bruce
1946   Without Reservations
Brewster, Carol
1949   The Girl from Jones
        Beach
1951   Show Boat
Brewster, Diane
1957   The Oklahoman
Brewster, Jimmy
1936   After the Thin Man
Brewster, Ralph
1941   Sun Valley Serenade
Brewster Twins *same as* **Brewster,**
    Barbara; Brewster, Gloria
1938   Happy Landing
        My Lucky Star
Briac, Jean de *see* **De Briac, Jean**
Brian, David
1950   Intruder in the Dust
1953   Ambush at Tomahawk
        Gap
1956   The White Squaw
Brian, Donald
1938   Dangerous to Know
Brian, Edwin
1937   Boy of the Streets
Brian, Mary
1924   Peter Pan
1930   Galas de la Paramount
        The Kibitzer
1933   Song of the Eagle
1935   Charlie Chan in Paris
Briant, Roy
1927   Open Range
Brice, Monte
1942   Mexican Spitfire Sees a
        Ghost
1943   Doughboys in Ireland

1946   Singin' in the Corn
1948   The Paleface
Briceño, Hector
1935   Rosa de Francia
Bricker, Elsie
1946   Gas House Kids
Bricker, George
1939   Mr. Moto in Danger
        Island
1942   Little Tokyo, U.S.A.
        North to the Klondike
1946   Gas House Kids
1952   Arctic Flight
Bride, Tom
1958   Tonka
Briden, Garland
1916   The Sign of the Poppy
Bridge, Alan *same as* **Bridge, Al**
1932   The Forty-Niners
1933   Thundering Herd
1935   Melody Trail
        A Night at the Opera
        North of Arizona
        Rendezvous
1937   Song of the City
1938   Little Miss Roughneck
1940   If I Had My Way
        Santa Fe Trail
1941   The Face Behind the
        Mask
        Road Agent
        Sullivan's Travels
1942   In This Our Life
        Juke Girl
1945   The Jade Mask
        A Tree Grows in Brooklyn
1946   Saratoga Trunk
        Shadows Over Chinatown
        Singin' in the Corn
1947   Black Gold
        California
        The Mighty McGurk
1948   Fury at Furnace Creek
        Unconquered
1950   North of the Great Divide
        The Traveling
        Saleswoman
1951   Oh! Susanna
Bridges, John
1943   The Law Rides Again
1944   Outlaw Trail
        Sonora Stagecoach
1946   Wild West
Bridges, Lloyd
1941   They Dare Not Love
1942   Shut My Big Mouth
1944   Riding West
1946   Canyon Passage
1948   Moonrise
        16 Fathoms Deep
        Unconquered
1949   Home of the Brave
1950   Colt .45
1951   Little Big Horn
1952   High Noon
1953   Last of the Comanches
1955   Apache Woman
1956   Wetbacks
1957   Ride Out for Revenge
Bridges, Lorraine
1933   It's Great to Be Alive
1935   A Night at the Opera
1942   Seven Sweethearts
Bridges, Tom
1943   The Gang's All Here
Brier, Audrene
1933   It's Great to Be Alive
1934   Stand Up and Cheer!
Brier, Barbara
1949   Shamrock Hill
Brierre, Maurice
1934   Lazy River
1951   Across the Wide Missouri
Briggs, Donald *same as* **Briggs,**
    Don
1936   After the Thin Man
        Show Boat
        Sutter's Gold
1937   Man of the People
1938   The Beloved Brat

Briggs, Harlan
1936   After the Thin Man
        Mad Holiday
1939   The Adventures of
        Huckleberry Finn
1940   Charlie Chan's Murder
        Cruise
        Jennie
1942   The Vanishing Virginian
1946   Canyon Passage
1947   Spoilers of the North
        Vigilantes of Boomtown
1948   Fury at Furnace Creek
Briggs, Jack
1941   The Mexican Spitfire's
        Baby
1942   Mexican Spitfire's
        Elephant
1943   Ladies' Day
1951   New Mexico
Briggs, Matt
1943   The Meanest Man in the
        World
        The Ox-Bow Incident
        Wintertime
1944   Buffalo Bill
Bright, John
1931   Smart Money
1948   Open Secret
Bright, Richard
1959   Odds Against Tomorrow
Brill, Patti
1943   Gangway for Tomorrow
        Mexican Spitfire's Blessed
        Event
1944   Tender Comrade
1945   Betrayal from the East
1955   Not As a Stranger
Brin, Max *same as* **Brin, M.; Bryn,**
    Maks
1936   Yiddle with His Fiddle
1937   The Jester (Der
        Purimspieler)
1939   Mamele
Brincken, Wilhelm von *see* **Von**
    Brincken, William
Brind, Nuchim
1939   The Light Ahead
Brindel, Eugene
1955   Davy Crockett, King of
        the Wild Frontier
Brinegar, Paul
1949   Pinky
1950   A Ticket to Tomahawk
        Young Man with a Horn
1953   The Member of the
        Wedding
        So Big
Lou Bring Orchestra
1944   Lady, Let's Dance!
Brinkman, Dolores
1927   Jake the Plumber
Brinley, Charles
1924   California in '49
1934   Broadway Bill
        The Prescott Kid
Briskin, Barney
1937   The Californian
1938   Breaking the Ice
        Hawaii Calls
1939   Way Down South
Briskin, Irving
1938   City Streets
        Little Miss Roughneck
1940   Prairie Schooners
1941   The Face Behind the
        Mask
        Mystery Ship
        Thunder Over the Prairie
1942   Lawless Plainsmen
        Submarine Raider
1943   Frontier Fury
        Redhead from Manhattan
1944   Riding West
Briskin, Mort
1950   The Jackie Robinson Story
Briskin, Samuel J.
1934   Broadway Bill
1937   Border Cafe
        Music for Madame

Brissac, Virginia
1938 Gateway
1939 The Cisco Kid and the Lady
1940 If I Had My Way
1942 They Died With Their Boots On
1945 The Dolly Sisters
   The Scarlet Clue
   A Tree Grows in Brooklyn
1948 Old Los Angeles
1952 Bugles in the Afternoon

Brister, Robert
1937 Big City
1938 Dangerous to Know

Bristoff, Nestor
1947 Northwest Outpost

Bristow, Ninita
1913 The Inside of the White Slave Traffic

Brito, Phil
1948 Music Man

Britt, Elton
1949 Laramie

Britt, May
1958 The Young Lions

Britton, Barbara
1941 Louisiana Purchase
   Secret of the Wastelands
1945 The Great John L.
1950 Bandit Queen
1952 The Raiders

Britton, Ken
1948 Jiggs and Maggie in Court

Milt Britton and Band
1943 Riding High

Brix, Herman see **Bennett, Bruce**

Broadhurst, Cecil
1960 The Crowning Experience

Broadus, William
1941 Sullivan's Travels
1944 The Negro Soldier

Broadway Bill, a horse
1934 Broadway Bill

Brocco, Peter
1949 Boston Blackie's Chinese Venture
   The Undercover Man
1950 Black Hand
   The Breaking Point
   Broken Arrow
   Jolson Sings Again
1951 The Great Caruso
   The Tall Target
1952 The Ring
   Woman in the Dark
1956 Hot Blood

Brock, Dorothy
1924 So Big
1925 The Man in Blue

Brock, Geraldine
1949? Girl in Room 20

Brock, Heinie
1955 Trial
1957 Raintree County

Brocklehurst, J. A.
1922 The Sign of the Rose

Brockman, Joe
1949 Knock on Any Door

Brockwell, Gladys
1919 The Sneak
1924 So Big
1926 The Last Frontier

Brodelet, Esther
1933 It's Great to Be Alive
1935 Piernas de seda
1944 Something for the Boys

Broder, Jack
1952 Kid Monk Baroni

Broderick, Helen
1938 The Rage of Paris
1939 Stand Up and Fight
1941 Virginia
1944 Chip Off the Old Block

Broderick, Robert
1914 The Redemption of David Corson
1916 Arms and the Woman

Brodie, Buster
1942 Tales of Manhattan

Brodie, Don same as **Brody, Don**
1933 The Cohens and Kellys in Trouble
1935 Black Fury
1936 My American Wife
1937 Charlie Chan at the Olympics
   Charlie Chan on Broadway
   Man of the People
1938 Mr. Moto's Gamble
1940 Music in My Heart
1942 Tales of Manhattan
1943 Mr. Lucky
1945 Johnny Angel
1948 The Luck of the Irish
1957 Beau James

Brodie, Steve
1946 Sunset Pass
1947 Crossfire
   Desperate
   Thunder Mountain
1948 The Arizona Ranger
   Guns of Hate
1949 Brothers in the Saddle
   Home of the Brave
   Massacre River
   Rose of the Yukon
   Rustlers
1950 Winchester '73
1951 Only the Valiant
   The Steel Helmet
1953 The Charge at Feather River
1958 Sierra Baron

Brodkin, Herbert H.
1938 Happy Landing

Brodney, Oscar
1949 Arctic Manhunt
1950 Comanche Territory

Brodsky, Samuel
1920 Hidden Charms

Brody, Ann
1925 The Manicure Girl
   Red Love
1927 Clancy's Kosher Wedding
   Heroes in Blue
   Jake the Plumber
1929 Wolf Song
1932 The Heart of New York

Brody, Don see **Brodie, Don**

Brody, Dorothy
1957 All Mine to Give

Brody, Howard
1948 The Boy with Green Hair
1953 The Eddie Cantor Story

Brody, Penny
1957 All Mine to Give

Brogan, Harry
1959 Shake Hands with the Devil

Broidy, William F.
1958 Bullwhip

Brokaw, Charles
1938 The Buccaneer

Brokaw, Sid
1951 Slaughter Trail

Bromberg, J. Edward
1936 Sins of Man
   Star for a Night
1937 Charlie Chan on Broadway
   That I May Live
1938 Mr. Moto Takes a Chance
1940 The Mark of Zorro
1944 Chip Off the Old Block
1945 Salome, Where She Danced

Bromfield, John
1948 Harpoon
1950 The Furies
1954 The Black Dakotas
1956 Quincannon, Frontier Scout

Bromley, Sheila same as **Mannors, Sheila**
1932 Texas Pioneers
1934 The Prescott Kid
1939 Waterfront
1945 The House on 92nd St.

1957 The Lawless Eighties
1960 Ice Palace

Bronfeld, Jack
1950 Intruder in the Dust

Bronson, Arthur
1931 Delicious

Bronson, Betty
1924 Peter Pan
1927 Open Range

Bronson, Charles same as **Buchinsky, Charles**
1954 Apache
   Drum Beat
1957 Run of the Arrow

Bronson, George
1944 Buffalo Bill

Bronson, Lillian
1945 Rhapsody in Blue
   A Tree Grows in Brooklyn
1948 Sleep, My Love
1950 Black Hand
1952 Rose of Cimarron
1955 Foxfire

Bronsten, N. A.
1950 Give Us This Day

Bronston, Samuel
1943 Jack London
1959 John Paul Jones

Broo-Juter, Ragna
1930 Doña mentiras (foreign version)

Brook, Charles
1922 Solomon in Society

Brook, Claudio same as **Brook, Claude**
1956 Daniel Boone, Trail Blazer
1959 The Wonderful Country

Brooke, Hillary
1940 New Moon
1946 The Gentleman Misbehaves

Brooke, Michael
1938 The Buccaneer

Brooke, Myra same as **Brooks, Myra**
1918 A Daughter of the Old South
   The Liar

Brooke, Ralph not the same as **Brooks, Ralph**
1950 Mystery Submarine
1953 The Charge at Feather River

Brooke, Tyler
1934 Imitation of Life
1938 In Old Chicago

Brooke, Walter
1942 All Through the Night
   In This Our Life
   They Died With Their Boots On
1943 Yankee Doodle Dandy
1949 C-Man

Brooks, Alan
1926 Pals in Paradise

Brooks, Arthur A.
1939 Gang Smashers
   Straight to Heaven

Brooks, Barry
1950 A Lady Without Passport
1951 Gambling House
   Saturday's Hero
1952 The Half-Breed
1953 The Eddie Cantor Story

Brooks, Clarence
1919 A Man's Duty
1921 By Right of Birth
1928 Absent
1930 Georgia Rose
1935 Lem Hawkins' Confession
1937 Bargain with Bullets
   Dark Manhattan
1938 Spirit of Youth
   Two Gun Man from Harlem
1939 The Bronze Buckaroo
   Harlem Rides the Range
1940 Am I Guilty?
1944 The Negro Soldier
1950 Rock Island Trail

Brooks, Eunice
1931 The Exile
1932? The Girl from Chicago

Brooks, Gail
1917 Her Own People

Brooks, Hadda
1949? The Joint Is Jumpin'

Brooks, Hazel
1947 Body and Soul
1948 Sleep, My Love

Brooks, Irving
1914 The Nightingale

Brooks, Jean could be same as **Golm, Louise** or **Palfi, Lotte**
1939 Confessions of a Nazi Spy

Brooks, Jean name assumed by actress **Jeanne Kelly** in 1943 not the same as **Brooks, Jean** (above)
1939 Miracle on Main Street
1943 The Leopard Man

Brooks, Jess Lee same as **Brooks, Jesse; Brooks, Jesse C.; Brooks, Jesse Lee; Brooks, Jessie**
1937 Dark Manhattan
1938 Life Goes On
   Spirit of Youth
   Two Gun Man from Harlem
1940 Am I Guilty?
   Broken Strings
   Gang War
   Midnight Shadow
   Mystery in Swing
   Santa Fe Trail
1941 Four Shall Die
   Sullivan's Travels
1942 Lucky Ghost

Brooks, Joe
1953 So Big
1955 The Long Gray Line
1958 The Young Lions
1960 Flaming Star

Brooks, Leslie
1943 What's Buzzin' Cousin?
1945 I Love a Bandleader

Brooks, Lucius see **The Four Tones**

Brooks, Myra see **Brooke, Myra**

Brooks, Phyllis
1934 Strange Wives
1935 McFadden's Flats
1938 In Old Chicago
1939 Charlie Chan in Honolulu
   Charlie Chan in Reno

Brooks, Ralph not the same as **Brooke, Ralph**
1934 Strange Wives
1947 Buck Privates Come Home
1948 Fighting Father Dunne
1950 Mystery Street
1957 Beau James

Brooks, Rand
1939 Gone With the Wind
1940 Jennie
   Northwest Passage (Book I—Rogers' Rangers)
1943 Air Force
1947 Dangerous Venture
1953 The Charge at Feather River
1958 The Last Hurrah

Brooks, Renny K.
1954 Hell's Half Acre

Brooks, Richard
1948 Key Largo
1950 Mystery Street
1955 Blackboard Jungle
1956 The Catered Affair
   The Last Hunt

Brooks, Robert same as **Brooks, Robert, Pvt.**
1929 Hearts in Dixie
1944 The Negro Soldier

Brooks, Shelton
1939 Double Deal
1941 Up Jumped the Devil
1942 Professor Creeps

Brooks, Thelma
1936 El diablo del mar

Broome, Joe
1952   Buffalo Bill in Tomahawk Territory

Broome, Lee
1952   Buffalo Bill in Tomahawk Territory

Broome, Ray
1952   Buffalo Bill in Tomahawk Territory

Broomes, Kenneth
1946   That Man of Mine

Broomfield, Leroy
1935   So Red the Rose

Brophy, Edward *same as* **Brophy, Edward S.**
1931   Buster se marie
        Buster se marie *(foreign version)*
1932   Flesh
1935   Naughty Marietta
1936   Kelly the Second
1938   Passport Husband
1942   All Through the Night
1943   Air Force
1946   Renegade Girl
1958   The Last Hurrah

Broquin, Albert
1931   Die Dreigroschenoper *(foreign version)*

Brosse, Marcel de la *see* **De La Brosse, Marcel**

Brother Bones
1951   Yes Sir, Mr. Bones

Brouner, Ella
1939   Mirele Efros

Brow, Billy
1943   Hitler's Children

Brower, Dorcas
1960   Ice Palace

Brower, Otto
1930   Galas de la Paramount
1931   Fighting Caravans
1936   Sins of Man
1937   Slave Ship
1938   Road Demon
        Speed to Burn
1939   Winner Take All
1940   The Gay Caballero
1941   Belle Starr
        Western Union
1942   Little Tokyo, U.S.A.
        Song of the Islands
1943   Crash Dive
        Wintertime
1944   Buffalo Bill
1947   Duel in the Sun

Brower, Robert
1915   Cohen's Luck
1917   The Tell-Tale Step
1923   Thirty Days
1927   The Gay Defender
1930   Abraham Lincoln

Brower, Tom *same as* **Brower, Thomas L.**
1935   The Singing Vagabond
1936   Treachery Rides the Range
1937   Maid of Salem

Brown, Ada
1943   Stormy Weather

Brown, Alexander
1946?   Harlem on Parade

Brown, Alfred
1959   John Paul Jones

Brown, Anita
1935   Charlie Chan in Egypt
1937   Slave Ship
1941   Sullivan's Travels
1946   Song of the South

Brown, Anne
1945   Rhapsody in Blue

Brown, Barbara
1943   Good Luck, Mr. Yates
1944   The Sullivans
        Three Men in White

Brown, Betty
1936   Show Boat

Brown, Beverly
1950   Panic in the Streets

Brown, Bill *see* **Brown, William H.**

Brown, Billy *not the same as* **Brown, William H.**
1951   The Harlem Globetrotters

Brown, Bob *not the same as* **Brown, Robert**
194-   Mistaken Identity

Brown, Boots
1944   Tomorrow the World!
1945   A Tree Grows in Brooklyn

Brown, Bridget
1950   Young Man with a Horn

Brown, Campbell, Colonel
1955   Davy Crockett, King of the Wild Frontier

Brown, Carmen V.
1940   Tengo fe en ti

Brown, Charles D.
1938   Mr. Moto's Gamble
        Speed to Burn
1939   Charlie Chan in Reno
        Mr. Moto in Danger Island
1940   Santa Fe Trail
1944   The Racket Man
1945   Sunbonnet Sue
1946   Notorious

Brown, Clarence *same as* **Brown, Clarence L.**
1920   The Last of the Mohicans
1930   Anna Christie
1932   The Son-Daughter
1941   Come Live with Me
1950   Intruder in the Dust
1952   It's a Big Country: An American Anthology

Brown, Dolores *(actress)*
1931   Cimarron

Brown, Dolores *(African-American singer)* *see* **Pancho and Dolores**

Brown, Don *(dancer) could be same as* **Brown, Donald** *(actor)*
1942   Holiday Inn

Brown, Donald *(actor) could be same as* **Brown, Don** *(dancer)*
1935   Piernas de seda
1936   The Green Pastures

Brown, Donald H. *(prod)*
1947   Spoilers of the North

Brown, Edward *circa 1910s see* **Brown, J. Edwin**

Brown, Edward *circa early 1920s see* **Brown, George Edward** *(African-American actor)*

Brown, Eleanor
1950   Annie Get Your Gun

Brown, Ella Mae
1946   Abie's Irish Rose

Brown, Elmer *could be same as* **Brown, Elmer H.**
1945   The House on 92nd St.

Brown, Elmer H. *could be same as* **Brown, Elmer**
1933   Counsellor at Law

Brown, Evelyn S.
1941?   Hampton Institute: Its Program of Education for Life

Brown, Everett
1937   The Plainsman
1938   The Duke Is Tops
        The Texans
1939   Gone With the Wind
        Stand Up and Fight

Brown, Gene
1950   The Toast of New Orleans

Brown, George Edward *(African-American actor) same as* **Brown, Edward; Brown, G. Edward** *not the same as* **Brown, J. Edwin**
1921   The Call of His People
        The Gunsaulus Mystery
        The Secret Sorrow
        The Sport of the Gods
1922   The Schemers
        Spitfire

Brown, Gilson
1937   Boy of the Streets

Brown, Hal *not the same as* **Brown, Halbert**
1947   California

Brown, Halbert *not the same as* **Brown, Hal**
1919   The Other Man's Wife

Brown, Harry *(actor) same as* **Brown, Harry D.** *could be same as* **Brown, W. Harry** *not the same as* **Brown, Harry** *(writer)*
1934   Our Daily Bread
1945   Wanderer of the Wasteland
1949   Massacre River
1953   Ride, Vaquero!

Brown, Harry *(writer) not the same as* **Brown, Harry** *(actor)*
1950   Sands of Iwo Jima
1951   Apache Drums
        Only the Valiant
1952   Bugles in the Afternoon

Brown, Harry C. *see* **Browne, Harry C.**

Brown, Harry D. *see* **Brown, Harry** *(actor)*

Brown, Harry Joe *(prod, dir) same as* **Brown, Harry J.** *not the same as* **Brown, Harry S.** *(dir, prod)*
1924   North of Nevada
1927   The Red Raiders
1928   The Canyon of Adventure
        The Glorious Trail
1929   Señor Americano
1930   Song of the Caballero
1933   Song of the Eagle
1934   The Great Flirtation
1938   My Lucky Star
1941   Western Union
1944   Knickerbocker Holiday
1956   7th Cavalry
1957   The Guns of Fort Petticoat

Brown, Harry S. *(dir, prod) not the same as* **Brown, Harry Joe** *(prod, dir)*
1932   A Daughter of Her People
1934   What a Mother-in-Law!

Brown, Helen
1937   Big City
1938   Gateway
1949   Arctic Manhunt
1950   Stars in My Crown
1951   Molly
1954   Dangerous Mission
1958   Houseboat
1960   The Dark at the Top of the Stairs

Brown, Horace
1943   Action in the North Atlantic

Brown, J. C. *same as* **Brown, J. Rufus**
1921   The Secret Sorrow
1922   Easy Money

Brown, Mrs. J. D.
1921   The Lure of a Woman

Brown, J. Edwin *same as* **Brown, Edward** *not the same as* **Brown, George Edward** *(African-American actor)*
1917   The Pulse of Life

Brown, J. Rufus *see* **Brown, J. C.**

Brown, James *same as* **Brown, Jim L.**
1943   Air Force
1944   Going My Way
1949   Anna Lucasta
1950   Sands of Iwo Jima
1953   The Charge at Feather River
        The Man Behind the Gun
1959   Inside the Mafia

Brown, Jeanette Schiller
1932   A Daughter of Her People

Brown, Jerry
1923   Deceit

Brown, Jim L. *see* **Brown, James**

Brown, Joe *not the same as* **Brown, Joe, Jr.**
1929   In Old Arizona
1932   Charlie Chan's Chance

Brown, Joe David *(writer)*
1950   Stars in My Crown

Brown, Joe E.
1942   Shut My Big Mouth
1951   Show Boat

Brown, Joe, Jr. *not the same as* **Brown, Joe**
1941   Where Did You Get That Girl?
1942   Syncopation

Brown, Johnny Mack *same as* **Brown, John Mack**
1931   The Great Meadow
1932   The Vanishing Frontier
1945   The Navajo Trail
1946   Border Bandits

Brown, Joie, Jr. *(African-American actor) not the same as* **Brown, Joe E.** *or* **Brown, Joe, Jr.**
1935   Lem Hawkins' Confession

Brown, Karl
1941   Prairie Pioneers
        Under Fiesta Stars

Brown, Katharine
1939   Gone With the Wind

Brown, Lew *(actor) not the same as* **Brown, Lew** *(writer, prod), d. 1958*
1960   Pay or Die

Brown, Lew *(writer, prod), d. 1958 not the same as* **Brown, Lew** *(actor)*
1934   Stand Up and Cheer!

Brown, Lloyd
1916   Ramona

Brown, Lowell
1959   The FBI Story

Brown, Lucille *see* **Browne, Lucile**

Brown, Lyle
1944   Buffalo Bill

Brown, Margaret *(African-American actress) not the same as* **Brown, Marguerite**
1924   A Son of Satan

Brown, Marguerite *not the same as* **Brown, Margaret** *(African-American actress)*
1940   The Ramparts We Watch

Brown, Marie
1953   Dream Wife

Brown, Melba
1934   Judge Priest

Brown, Melville
1930   Check and Double Check

Brown, Milt
1923   Ruggles of Red Gap

Brown, Morgan
1937   It Could Happen to You

Brown, N. *could be same as* **Brown, Nancy**
1923   Deceit

Brown, Naaman
1960   Sergeant Rutledge

Brown, Nancy *could be same as* **Brown, N.**
1921   By Right of Birth

Brown, Patrick R.
1956   Reprisal!

Brown, Peter
1958   Marjorie Morningstar

Brown, Phil
1946   Without Reservations
1948   The Luck of the Irish
        Moonrise
1951   The Harlem Globetrotters
1959   John Paul Jones

Brown, R. L., Dr.
1923   Regeneration
1926   The Flying Ace

Brown, Ralph
1940   The Notorious Elinor Lee
1947   Jivin' in Be-Bop

Brown, Ray *(musician) not the same as* **Brown, Raymond** *(actor)*
1947   Jivin' in Be-Bop

Brown, Raymond *(actor) same as* **Brown, Ray** *not the same as* **Brown, Ray** *(musician)*
1957   Raintree County

Brown, Raymond (actor) (continued)
1936　Laughing Irish Eyes
1937　One Mile from Heaven

Brown, Robert *not the same as* **Brown, Bob**
1959　Shake Hands with the Devil

Brown, Roberta
1928　The Midnight Ace

Brown, Rowland
1936　Robin Hood of El Dorado
1937　Boy of the Streets

Brown, Sally
1945　A Tree Grows in Brooklyn

Brown, Sheilah
1945　A Tree Grows in Brooklyn

Brown, Stanley
1941　The Face Behind the Mask
　　　They Dare Not Love
　　　Thunder Over the Prairie
1942　Lawless Plainsmen
　　　Submarine Raider
1943　Frontier Fury
　　　Redhead from Manhattan
1944　Riding West

Brown, Steve
1948　I Remember Mama

Brown, Thelma
1934　Judge Priest

Brown, Tom
1934　Judge Priest
1938　In Old Chicago
1942　Let's Get Tough!
1944　Hi, Beautiful
1945　The House on 92nd St.
1947　Buck Privates Come Home

Brown, Vanessa
1947　The Foxes of Harrow
1952　The Fighter

Brown, Vera
1934　Judge Priest

Brown, Vivian
1950　Devil's Doorway

Brown, W. Harry *could be same as* **Brown, Harry** (*actor*)
1952　The Iron Mistress

Brown, Wally
1943　Gangway for Tomorrow
　　　Mexican Spitfire's Blessed Event
1946　Notorious
1956　The Wild Dakotas

Brown, William H. *same as* **Brown, Bill** *not the same as* **Brown, Billy**
1915　A Yankee from the West
1916　Little Meena's Romance

Brown, Willis
1914?　A Boy and the Law

Brown, Winona
1915　Captain Courtesy

Browne, Cicely
1953　Fort Ti

Browne, Harry C. *same as* **Brown, Harry C.**
1916　The Flower of No Man's Land

Browne, Kathie
1960　Studs Lonigan

Browne, Lewis Allen
1919　Spotlight Sadie
1921　Society Snobs

Browne, Lucile *same as* **Brown, Lucille**
1921　The Sport of the Gods
1935　Texas Terror

Browne, Michael
1942　Sunday Punch
1945　Pride of the Marines
1950　Battleground

Browning, Barbara
1949?　The Joint Is Jumpin'

Browning, Ivan
1952　The Iron Mistress
1953　The Member of the Wedding

Browning, Natalie
1933　The Wandering Jew

Browning, Tod
1917　A Love Sublime
1918　Set Free
1919　Bonnie, Bonnie Lassie
　　　The Unpainted Woman
1920　Outside the Law
1921　No Woman Knows
1934　Lazy River

Brownlee, Frank
1916　The Half-Breed
　　　Sold for Marriage
1918　Her Moment
　　　Me Und Gott
1919　Desert Gold
1920　The Man Who Dared

The Brox Sisters
1930　King of Jazz

Brú, María
1931　La pura verdad

Bruce, Alan
1937　Music for Madame

Bruce, Becky
1919　The Volcano

Bruce, Belle
1917　The Slacker (Metro Pictures Corp.)

Bruce, Carol
1941　This Woman Is Mine

Bruce, David 1914–1976 *could be same as* **Bruce, David** *circa 1915*
1940　Knute Rockne—All American
　　　Santa Fe Trail
1945　Salome, Where She Danced
1949　Prejudice
1950　Young Daniel Boone

Bruce, David *circa 1915 could be same as* **Bruce, David** 1914–1976
1915　Children of the Ghetto

Bruce, Eddie
1941　Where Did You Get That Girl?
1944　Chip Off the Old Block
　　　Tahiti Nights
1946　Notorious

Bruce, Gary
1943　Action in the North Atlantic

Bruce, George
1940　Kit Carson
1941　Western Union
1947　Little Mister Jim
1958　Ride a Crooked Trail

Bruce, Kate
1916　Gretchen, the Greenhorn
1918　The Greatest Thing in Life
　　　The Hun Within
1919　Scarlet Days
1924　His Darker Self

Bruce, Mary
1922　The Crow's Nest

Bruce, Nigel
1934　Coming Out Party
　　　Stand Up and Cheer!
1941　This Woman Is Mine

Bruce, Rodman
1947　Untamed Fury

Bruce, Virginia
1930　Galas de la Paramount
　　　Whoopee
1939　Let Freedom Ring

Bruckman, Clyde
1928　The Cameraman
1929　Welcome Danger

Brudie, Annabelle
1938　Happy Landing

Brudie, Marianne
1938　Happy Landing

Bruggeman, George *same as* **Bruggerman, George**
1936　Star for a Night
1937　Slave Ship

Brujó, José
1931　Lo mejor es reír
1932　El hombre que asesinó

Brulier, Nigel de *see* **De Brulier, Nigel**

Brullier, N. de *see* **De Brulier, Nigel**

Brumbach, Jeanne
1932　Le cas du docteur Brenner

Brummer, Andrew
1940　The Ramparts We Watch

Brundage, Mathilde *same as* **Brundage, M., Mrs.; Brundage, Matilda**
1916　Her Debt of Honor
1917　The Slacker (Metro Pictures Corp.)
1918　The Liar
　　　A Woman of Impulse
1920　The Good-Bad Wife
1922　My Boy
1923　Fashion Row

Bruner, Charles *could be same as* **Brunner, Charles**
1959　The FBI Story

Bruner, Irving
1939　A Brivele der Mamen

Brunette, Fritzi
1916　At Piney Ridge
1919　The Lord Loves the Irish
1937　Maid of Salem
　　　Souls at Sea

Brunetti, Argentina
1947　California
1949　House of Strangers
　　　Knock on Any Door
　　　We Were Strangers
1950　Broken Arrow
　　　The Lawless
1951　The Great Caruso
1952　Apache War Smoke
　　　The Fighter
　　　The Iron Mistress
　　　Rose of Cimarron
　　　Woman in the Dark
1953　San Antone
1955　The Far Horizons
　　　The Last Command
1957　The Brothers Rico
　　　The Midnight Story

Brunetti, Primo
1933　Primavera en otoño

Brunetti, Raymond
1949　Thieves' Highway

Brunius, Anne-Marie
1930　Doña mentiras (*foreign version*)

Brunius, John W.
1930　Doña mentiras (*foreign version*)

Brunn, Frederick
1943　Crash Dive
　　　Gangway for Tomorrow
　　　They Came to Blow Up America
1946　Rendezvous 24

Brunner, Charles *could be same as* **Bruner, Charles**
1943　Deerslayer

Bruno, Frank
1936　Treachery Rides the Range
1937　Charlie Chan at the Olympics
　　　Man of the People
1938　Mr. Wong, Detective

Bruno, the bear
1917　A Roadside Impresario

Brunton, Robert
1918　The Goddess of Lost Lake
1919　The Lord Loves the Irish

Brunton, William
1918　The Squaw Man

Bryan, Arthur Q.
1954　Broken Lance

Bryan, Marvin
1957　The Brothers Rico

Bryan, Paul
1946　Notorious
1947　Ride the Pink Horse

Bryant, Bill
1954　Battle of Rogue River

Bryant, Charles
1918　Toys of Fate
1920　Billions

Bryant, Ethel
1934　Broadway Bill
1948　The Paleface

Bryant, Jan
1946　The Trap

Bryant, John
1952　Red Snow
1958　The Last Hurrah

Bryant, Joyce
1939　Trigger Fingers

Bryant, Kurt
1957　Naked in the Sun

Marie Bryant Swing Band
1938　The Duke Is Tops

Bryant, Nana
1938　The Adventures of Tom Sawyer
1940　If I Had My Way
1948　Reaching from Heaven
1949　The Kissing Bandit
1951　Only the Valiant
1952　Bright Victory

Bryant, Paul (*child actor*)
1946　Saratoga Trunk

Bryant, Theona
1959　The FBI Story

Bryant, Willie
1939　Keep Punching

Bryar, Claudia
1956　Giant

Bryar, Paul
1939　Waterfront
1941　The Gang's All Here
　　　You're Out of Luck
1942　Foreign Agent
1946　Gas House Kids
　　　Shadows Over Chinatown
1947　The Chinese Ring
1949　Lust for Gold
1950　The Toast of New Orleans
1951　Cavalry Scout
1952　Arctic Flight
　　　Fort Osage
1955　Seven Angry Men
1958　Gunman's Walk
1959　Al Capone
1960　Cimarron

Bryn, Maks *see* **Brin, Max**

Bryson, Betty
1933　It's Great to Be Alive

Bryson, J. J.
1919　The Last of His People

Bryson, Winifred
1923　Crashin' Thru
　　　Suzanna

Buchanan, Donald I.
1916　A Woman's Honor

Buchanan, Edgar
1940　Escape to Glory
1943　Good Luck, Mr. Yates
1944　Buffalo Bill
1949　Lust for Gold
1950　The Big Hangover
　　　Devil's Doorway
1951　Flaming Feather
1955　The Lonesome Trail
1960　Cimarron

Buchanan, Elsa
1934　Charlie Chan in London

Buchanan, Morris
1952　The Iron Mistress

Buchanan, Thompson
1920　Dangerous Days

Buchinsky, Charles *see* **Bronson, Charles**

Buchman, Harold
1940　Jennie
1941　Romance of the Rio Grande

Buchman, Sidney
1934　Broadway Bill
1950　Jolson Sings Again
1951　Saturday's Hero

Buchowetzki, Dimitri
1931　La carta (*foreign version*)
1932　El hombre que asesinó

Buck and Bubbles *see also* Sublett,
　John W. "Bubbles"
1946　　Mantan Messes Up
Buck, a dog
1935　　Melody Trail
Buck, Jules
1949　　We Were Strangers
1960　　The Day They Robbed the
　　　　　Bank of England
Buck, Leon *see* The Four Tones
Buckingham, Jan
1940　　Mexican Spitfire Out
　　　　　West
1941　　Sullivan's Travels
　　　　　Virginia
Buckingham, Tom
1918　　The Reckoning Day
1934　　He Was Her Man
Buckland, Wilfred
1914　　Rose of the Rancho
Buckler, Hugh
1936　　The Last of the Mohicans
Buckles, Ann
1960　　The Crowning
　　　　　Experience
Buckley, Buz
1947　　Little Mister Jim
Buckley, Frederic Robert *same as*
　Buckley, F. R.
1917　　A Night in New Arabia
Buckley, Kay
1950　　Raiders of Tomahawk
　　　　　Creek
Buckley, Louise
1948　　Gentleman's Agreement
Buckley, Myrtle
1932　　Hypnotized
Buckley, William
1920　　The Devil's Claim
1922　　Sky High
Buckner, Robert
1940　　Knute Rockne—All
　　　　　American
　　　　　Santa Fe Trail
1942　　Gentleman Jim
1943　　Yankee Doodle Dandy
1950　　Deported
1952　　Bright Victory
1953　　The Man Behind the Gun
Buckner, Teddy
1958　　St. Louis Blues
Bucko, Buck
1946　　Sunset Pass
Bucko, Roy
1946　　Sunset Pass
1947　　Marshal of Cripple Creek
"Buckwheat" *see* Thomas, William
　"Buckwheat"
Bucquet, Harold S. *same as*
　Bucquet, Harry
1931　　El proceso de Mary
　　　　　Dugan
1932　　The Son-Daughter
Budd, Norman
1949　　The Red Menace
1950　　Battleground
Budin, A.
1922　　Hungry Hearts
Budkin, Celia *see* Boodkin, Celia
Budkin, Misha *see* Boodkin, M.
Budlong, Jack
1942　　They Died With Their
　　　　　Boots On
Buehler, Mrs. circa 1917
1917　　The Bond Between
Buehler, Betty circa 1953
1953　　Taxi
Buel, Kenean
1918　　Doing Their Bit
1919　　A Fallen Idol
Buell, Jed
1937　　Harlem on the Prairie
1940?　　Mr. Washington Goes to
　　　　　Town
1941　　Up Jumped the Devil
1942　　Lucky Ghost
　　　　　Professor Creeps
Buetel, Jack *same as* Beutel, Jack
1943　　The Outlaw
1952　　The Half-Breed
　　　　　Rose of Cimarron

Buffalo Bill, Jr. *see* Wilsey, Jay
Buffalo, Joe
1959　　The Sheriff of Fractured
　　　　　Jaw
Buffington, Adele *same as* Bowers,
　Jess
1928　　The Broken Mask
1931　　Aloha
1942　　Below the Border
1945　　The Navajo Trail
1946　　Wild Beauty
1949　　The Valiant Hombre
1950　　Jiggs and Maggie Out
　　　　　West
1958　　Bullwhip
Buffington, Sam
1958　　The Light in the Forest
　　　　　The Rawhide Trail
Bufford, Daisy
1934　　Imitation of Life
1936　　Show Boat
　　　　　Star for a Night
1940　　Son of Ingagi
Buffum, Ray
1954　　The Black Dakotas
Buford, Marilyn
1946　　Without Reservations
Buka, Donald
1951　　New Mexico
Bulawka, N.
1939　　Cossacks in Exile
Bulgakov, Leo
1938　　Marusia
Bull, Richard
1956　　Full of Life
Bullman, Gertrude *see* Bulman,
　Gertrude
Bullock, Walter
1940　　The Gay Caballero
1943　　The Gang's All Here
Bulman, Gertrude *same as*
　Bullman, Gertrude
1934　　The Youth of Russia
1935　　Bar-Mitzvah
1939　　A Brivele der Mamen
　　　　　Mamele
Buloff, Joseph
1933　　Live and Laugh
1934　　The Rabbi's Power
1947　　Carnegie Hall
1950　　Monticello, Here We
　　　　　Come!
Bunn, Earl
1936　　Dangerous Intrigue
1938　　Little Miss Roughneck
1941　　Mystery Ship
Bunn, John
1939　　Moon over Harlem
Bunny, George 1870–1952
1925　　Lights of Old Broadway
1927　　Heroes in Blue
1928　　Breed of the Sunsets
Bunny, George 1893–1958
1944　　An American Romance
1948　　Unconquered
1951　　The Tall Target
Bunston, Herbert
1932　　Charlie Chan's Chance
Bunyea, Mabel
1918　　Hitting the Trail
Bupp, Moyer
1936　　Star for a Night
Bupp, Sonny
1940　　Three Faces West
1942　　Syncopation
　　　　　Wings for the Eagle
Bupp, Tommy
1936　　It Had to Happen
　　　　　Paddy O'Day
1937　　Maid of Salem
1939　　Confessions of a Nazi Spy
　　　　　Fisherman's Wharf
　　　　　Waterfront
1940　　The Way of All Flesh
Burbank, Betty
1918　　Me Und Gott
Burbank, Leon
1948　　Fighting Father Dunne

Burbeck, Frank
1919　　Who's Your Brother?
Burbidge, William
1913　　Traffic in Souls
Burbridge, Betty
1925　　Quicker'n Lightnin'
1926　　Twin Triggers
1931　　Chinatown After Dark
1932　　The Secrets of Wu Sin
1933　　Dance Hall Hostess
1935　　Melody Trail
　　　　　Rescue Squad
　　　　　The Singing Vagabond
1941　　Thunder Over the Prairie
1943　　Frontier Fury
1945　　The Cisco Kid Returns
　　　　　In Old New Mexico
1949　　The Daring Caballero
Burch, Bill
1950　　Two Flags West
Burch, Jas.
1943　　Cabin in the Sky
Burck, Barbara
1954　　Taza, Son of Cochise
Burden, W. Douglas
1930　　The Silent Enemy
Burdette, Cliff
1958　　Tonka
Burdette, John
1928　　Chinatown Charlie
Burger, Paul
1937　　Charlie Chan at the
　　　　　Olympics
Burgère, André
1931　　Le père célibataire
　　　　　El proceso de Mary
　　　　　Dugan (*foreign
　　　　　version*)
　　　　　Quand on est belle
Burgess, Dorothy
1929　　In Old Arizona
1933　　It's Great to Be Alive
Burgess, Helen
1937　　The Plainsman
Burk, Al
1937　　The Plainsman
Burke, Billie
1936　　My American Wife
　　　　　Show Boat
1942　　In This Our Life
1960　　Sergeant Rutledge
Burke, Caroline
1945　　Rhapsody in Blue
Burke, Edwin
1929　　Love, Live and Laugh
1931　　Del infierno al cielo
　　　　　Mr. Lemon of Orange
1932　　Call Her Savage
1935　　The Littlest Rebel
Burke, Georgia
1959　　Anna Lucasta
Burke, J. Frank
1915　　The Alien
　　　　　The Italian
Burke, Jack
1953　　Beneath the 12-Mile Reef
Burke, James
1933　　A Lady's Profession
1934　　The Cat's-Paw
1935　　Ruggles of Red Gap
　　　　　So Red the Rose
1936　　It Had to Happen
　　　　　Klondike Annie
1938　　The Buccaneer
1939　　The Cisco Kid and the
　　　　　Lady
1940　　Charlie Chan's Murder
　　　　　Cruise
　　　　　Little Nellie Kelly
　　　　　The Way of All Flesh
1942　　All Through the Night
1943　　Dixie
　　　　　Riding High
1944　　Three Men in White
1945　　The Dolly Sisters
　　　　　I Love a Bandleader
1947　　Body and Soul
　　　　　California
　　　　　Easy Come, Easy Go
1948　　Night Wind
1949　　Shamrock Hill

1951　　The Last Outpost
　　　　　Warpath
1953　　Arrowhead
Burke, Joseph
1917　　The Little Chevalier
1917?　　Barnaby Lee
1918　　Good-Bye, Bill
1924　　Two Shall Be Born
Burke, Kathleen
1937　　Boy of the Streets
1938　　Rascals
Burke, Lynn
1958　　Tonka
Burke, Marie
1919　　The Gray Towers Mystery
1923　　Little Old New York
Burke, Tom
1938　　The Buccaneer
Burke, Walter
1950　　Mystery Street
1958　　Never Love a Stranger
1959　　The Crimson Kimono
Burkett, James S. *same as* Burkett,
　J. S.
1944　　Black Magic
　　　　　Charlie Chan in the
　　　　　　Secret Service
　　　　　The Chinese Cat
1945　　The Jade Mask
　　　　　The Scarlet Clue
　　　　　The Shanghai Cobra
1946　　Dangerous Money
　　　　　Dark Alibi
　　　　　Don Ricardo Returns
　　　　　The Red Dragon
　　　　　Shadows Over Chinatown
　　　　　The Trap
1947　　Bells of San Fernando
　　　　　The Chinese Ring
1948　　Docks of New Orleans
　　　　　The Feathered Serpent
　　　　　The Golden Eye
　　　　　Shanghai Chest
　　　　　16 Fathoms Deep
1949　　The Sky Dragon
1950　　Young Daniel Boone
Burkett, Ray
1948　　The Boy with Green Hair
Burkey, J. R.
1917　　The Bronze Bride
Burkhart, Monte
1960　　Flaming Star
Burlando, Joseph
1946　　The Gay Cavalier
Burley, Dan
1947　　Jivin' in Be-Bop
Burnell, Gene
1923　　None So Blind
Burnet, Dana
1929　　Love, Live and Laugh
Burnett, Don
1957　　Raintree County
Burnett, George
1946　　Till the End of Time
Burnett, Mr. Tom L.
1920　　Frontier Days
Burnett, Mrs. Tom L.
1920　　Frontier Days
Burnett, W. R.
1932　　Scarface
1943　　Action in the North
　　　　　Atlantic
　　　　　Crash Dive
1954　　Dangerous Mission
Burnette, Coral
1922　　The Sign of the Rose
Burnette, Smiley
1935　　Melody Trail
　　　　　The Singing Vagabond
1936　　Ride, Ranger, Ride
1937　　Boots and Saddles
　　　　　Manhattan
　　　　　　Merry-Go-Round
1941　　Under Fiesta Stars
1949　　Laramie
1950　　Raiders of Tomahawk
　　　　　Creek
1951　　Cyclone Fury
　　　　　Snake River Desperadoes

Burnham, Beatrice
1916   Ramona
Burnham, Frances
1920   Who's Your Servant?
Burnham, Julia
1917   The Adventures of Carol
1918   Wanted, a Mother
Burnham, Terry
1959   Imitation of Life
1960   Key Witness
Burnier, Robert
1931   Su noche de bodas
        (*foreign version*)
Burns, Beulah
1916   The Fall of a Nation
        Gretchen, the Greenhorn
        A Sister of Six
Burns, Bob *see* **Burns, Robert**
Burns, Bob 1893–1956
1935   The Singing Vagabond
1937   Waikiki Wedding
1940   Prairie Schooners
Burns, Bobby *see* **Burns, Robert**
Burns, Craig
1949   Call of the Forest
Burns, Dorothy *see* **Vernon, Dorothy**
Burns, Eddie *same as* **Burns, Edward** *not the same as* **Burns, Edmund**
1932   The Rainbow Trail
1943   The Amazing Mrs. Holliday
Burns, Edmund *same as* **Burns, Ed; Burns, Edward** *not the same as* **Burns, Eddie**
1918   The Ordeal of Rosetta
1921   Fifty Candles
        The Girl from God's Country
1922   East Is West
1923   Scars of Jealousy
1925   The Manicure Girl
1927   The Chinese Parrot
        The Princess from Hoboken
        The Shamrock and the Rose
1928   Ransom
1934   Broadway Bill
Burns, Fannetta
1923   His Great Chance
Burns, Forrest
1947   Oregon Trail Scouts
1951   Gambling House
1952   The Raiders
        Red Ball Express
Burns, Fred
1915   The Birth of a Nation
1916   Sold for Marriage
1925   Speed Wild
1927   The Overland Stage
1932   Law and Lawless
Burns, Grace
1950   Emergency Wedding
Burns, Harry
1937   Charlie Chan on Broadway
1942   Tortilla Flat
1943   Tahiti Honey
Burns, J. Walter
1952   Bright Victory
Burns, Marion
1931   Oklahoma Jim
1932   The Golden West
        Me and My Gal
Burns, Neal
1934   Behold My Wife!
1938   Little Miss Roughneck
1946   The Face of Marble
Burns, Paul E. *same as* **Burns, Paul**
1939   The Cisco Kid and the Lady
        Heaven with a Barbed Wire Fence
        The Return of the Cisco Kid
1940   New Moon
        The Way of All Flesh
1941   Belle Starr
        Western Union

1942   Juke Girl
        Young America
1943   Crash Dive
        The Meanest Man in the World
        The Ox-Bow Incident
1947   Desperate
1948   The Paleface
        Unconquered
1949   Arctic Manhunt
        Lust for Gold
1950   Sunset in the West
        Young Man with a Horn
1951   Flaming Feather
        Warpath
1953   The Stars Are Singing
1958   Gunman's Walk
Burns, Robert *same as* **Burns, Bob; Burns, Bobby** *not the same as* **Burns, Bob** 1893–1956
1917   The Captain of the Gray Horse Troop
1932   Law and Lawless
1934   Lazy River
1935   Circle of Death
1936   Treachery Rides the Range
1937   The Plainsman
Burns, Sandy
1923   His Great Chance
1935   Lem Hawkins' Confession
Burns, Thelma
1916   A Man of Sorrow
Burns, Tommy
1917   The Plow Woman
Burns, William
1917   Unknown 274
Burnside, Henrietta
1942   Cat People
Burnstine, Norman
1928   Sins of the Fathers
Burr, Ann
1946   Canyon Passage
Burr, C. C.
1928   Chinatown Charlie
Burr, Eugene
1938   City Streets
Burr, Lonny
1951   Queen for a Day
Burr, Raymond
1946   Without Reservations
1947   Desperate
1948   Fighting Father Dunne
        Sleep, My Love
1951   New Mexico
1954   Passion
        Thunder Pass
1956   Secret of Treasure Mountain
Burr, Warren
1944   Since You Went Away
Burrascano, Giovanni
1932   Amor in montagna
Burrell, Mrs. Hamer
1919   Injustice
Burrell, Stanley
1954   Go Man Go
Burrelle, Vera
1940   The Notorious Elinor Lee
Burress, Jimmy *same as* **Burris, Jim**
1920   The Symbol of the Unconquered
1921   The Sport of the Gods
1936   The Green Pastures
Burress, William
1916   A Man of Sorrow
1935   The Little Colonel
        Naughty Marietta
1936   After the Thin Man
Burris, Jim *see* **Burress, Jimmy**
Burrough, James
1920   The Symbol of the Unconquered
Burrough, Tom *same as* **Burroughs, Tom**
1917   Unknown 274
Burroughs, Benjamin
1945   The House on 92nd St.

Burroughs, Clark
1931   Smart Money
Burroughs, Tom *see* **Burrough, Tom**
Burrows, Bob
1950   Colt .45
1952   The Raiders
Burrows, John H.
1957   Dragoon Wells Massacre
1958   Oregon Passage
1959   Al Capone
Burrud, Bill
1943   Hitler's Children
Burson, Polly
1951   Westward the Women
1952   Rose of Cimarron
1953   The Man from the Alamo
1959   The Jayhawkers!
Burson, Wayne
1956   The Burning Hills
1958   Gunman's Walk
Burston, Janet
1947   The Farmer's Daughter
Burt, Benny
1952   It's a Big Country: An American Anthology
1955   Blackboard Jungle
Burt, Frank (*actor*)
1934   Operator 13
Burt, Frank (*writer*)
1949   Arctic Fury
1950   Chinatown at Midnight
Burt, Frederic *same as* **Burt, Frederick**
1931   The Cisco Kid
1934   The Cat's-Paw
Burt, Nellie
1920?   The Scarlet Dragon
Burt, William
1934   The Lone Defender
Burtis, James P. *same as* **Burtis, James**
1933   Olsen's Big Moment
1934   Charlie Chan's Courage
1935   Rendezvous
        The Winning Ticket
1936   Desert Gold
        General Spanky
        Show Boat
1937   Slave Ship
1938   The Texans
Burtis, Thomson
1943   In Old Oklahoma
Burton, Bernard W.
1944   Chip Off the Old Block
Burton, Charlotte
1916   Lone Star
Burton, Clarence
1917   My Fighting Gentleman
1919   Hearts of Men
1924   The Mine with the Iron Door
1927   A Harp in Hock
Burton, David
1931   Fighting Caravans
1933   Let's Fall in Love
1940   Jennie
Burton, Frederick
1918   Ruggles of Red Gap
1921   Bits of Life
1922   Anna Ascends
1933   Counsellor at Law
1935   McFadden's Flats
1938   My Lucky Star
1939   Confessions of a Nazi Spy
1947   The Foxes of Harrow
1948   Fury at Furnace Creek
Burton, George
1917   The Little Boy Scout
1932   The Rainbow Trail
1935   Ruggles of Red Gap
1936   Klondike Annie
Burton, John
1917   The Bond Between
1918   Hidden Pearls
        Huck and Tom; or, the Further Adventures of Tom Sawyer
1923   Flames of Wrath
1937   Slave Ship
1947   Dark Delusion

Burton, Julian
1951   The House on Telegraph Hill
1958   The Young Lions
Burton, Marie
1938   Daughter of Shanghai
1939   King of Chinatown
Burton, Martin
1933   Broken Dreams
Burton, Richard
1960   Ice Palace
Burton, Robert
1952   My Man and I
1953   Cry of the Hunted
1954   Broken Lance
        Siege at Red River
        Taza, Son of Cochise
1955   The Last Command
        A Man Called Peter
1956   Reprisal!
1958   The Young Lions
Burton, Tom
1944   My Pal Wolf
        Tender Comrade
Burton Sisters
1950   Monticello, Here We Come!
Burton-Mercur, Paul
1955   Murder in Villa Capri
Burwell, Myra
1926?   Ten Nights in a Barroom
Busacco, Josephine
1932   Amore e morte
Busatt, Ivan
1940   Overture to Glory
Busby, A. H. *same as* **Bushy, Bert**
1915   Under Southern Skies
Busby, Allison, Dr.
1950   Intruder in the Dust
Busch, Alvin
1952   Bright Victory
Busch, Ernst
1931   Die Dreigroschenoper
Busch, Mae
1934   Beloved
1938   Daughter of Shanghai
Busch, Niven
1934   He Was Her Man
1938   In Old Chicago
1941   Belle Starr
1951   Distant Drums
1953   The Man from the Alamo
Bush, Anita
1922   The Bull-Dogger
        The Crimson Skull
Bush, James
1932   Wild Horse Mesa
1935   Harmony Lane
1936   The Glory Trail
1943   Air Force
1949   Massacre River
1950   The Lawless
Bush, Nora
1949   Lust for Gold
Bushaland, Albert
1925   His People
Bushe, Beverly
1945   Wanderer of the Wasteland
Bushman, Francis X.
1952   Apache Country
Bushman, Ralph *same as* **Bushman, Francis X., Jr.**
1920   It's a Great Life
1930   Sins of the Children
1937   Big City
1939   Let Freedom Ring
Bushy, Bert *see* **Busby, A. H.**
Buskirk, Hattie
1917   The Tenderfoot
1919   Fighting for Gold
Busley, Jessie
1931   Personal Maid
1940   Escape to Glory
Buss, Carl A.
1934   Wagon Wheels
Henry Busse and His Orchestra
1944   Lady, Let's Dance!

Bussi, Solange
1931　Die Dreigroschenoper
　　　(foreign version)
Buster, Budd same as **Buster, Bud**
1935　The Cyclone Ranger
　　　Riddle Ranch
1936　Custer's Last Stand
1937　Drums of Destiny
　　　Old Louisiana
1939　Daughter of the Tong
1941　Thunder Over the Prairie
1942　Valley of Hunted Men
1943　The Law Rides Again
1945　The Mummy's Curse
　　　Salome, Where She
　　　　Danced
　　　Wanderer of the
　　　　Wasteland
1946　California Gold Rush
　　　Sheriff of Redwood Valley
1947　Marshal of Cripple Creek
　　　Vigilantes of Boomtown
Butcher, Dwight
1943　Riding High
1948　Unconquered
Buti, Carlo
1938?　I due gemelli
Butler, Archie
1950　Ambush
　　　Annie Get Your Gun
1951　Westward the Women
1953　Ride, Vaquero!
Butler, David
1918　The Greatest Thing in
　　　　Life
1919　Bonnie, Bonnie Lassie
　　　The Unpainted Woman
1924　In Hollywood With
　　　　Potash and Perlmutter
1925　The Gold Hunters
1926　Meet the Prince
1929　Masked Emotions
1931　Delicious
1935　The Little Colonel
　　　The Littlest Rebel
1940　If I Had My Way
1941　Playmates
1947　My Wild Irish Rose
1949　The Story of Seabiscuit
1950　The Daughter of Rosie
　　　　O'Grady
Butler, Eddie
1957　Naked in the Sun
Butler, Frank
1937　Waikiki Wedding
1944　Going My Way
1945　A Medal for Benny
1947　California
Butler, Fred J.
1916　Little Meena's Romance
1924　Welcome Stranger
Butler, Helen
1946?　Go Down, Death!
Butler, Hugo
1937　Big City
1939　The Adventures of
　　　　Huckleberry Finn
Butler, Jimmy same as **Butler, Jim**
1934　Beloved
1935　Romance in Manhattan
1939　The Escape
1955　The View from Pompey's
　　　　Head
Butler, John (actor) not the same
　as **Butler, John K.** (writer)
1936　After the Thin Man
1937　Black Legion
1949　House of Strangers
　　　The Undercover Man
1950　No Way Out
1951　The Tall Target
Butler, John K. (writer) not the
　same as **Butler, John** (actor)
1934　La buenaventura
1946　G. I. War Brides
1949　Harbor of Missing Men
1954　Drums Across the River
1955　Headline Hunters
1958　Ambush at Cimarron Pass
Butler, Mary Ellen
1945　Samurai

Butler, Michael
1942　Seven Sweethearts
　　　Three Hearts for Julia
Butler, Rosita
1937　Maid of Salem
Butler, Roy
1943　Wagon Tracks West
1949　Stallion Canyon
1950　Bandit Queen
　　　Devil's Doorway
　　　Indian Territory
1953　The Man from the Alamo
　　　Tumbleweed
Butler, W. J. same as **Butler,
　William**
1915　The Gambler of the West
1924?　The Flaming Crisis
Butt, Bob
1946　The Gay Cavalier
Butt, W. Lawson same as **Butt,
　Lawson**
1918　The Goddess of Lost Lake
1919　Desert Gold
1920　Dangerous Days
　　　The Tiger's Coat
Butterfield, Herbert
1951　The House on Telegraph
　　　　Hill
Butterworth, Charles
1936　Rainbow on the River
1939　Let Freedom Ring
Butterworth, Ernest, Jr.
1920　The Luck of the Irish
Butterworth, Ernest, Sr.
1916　The Fall of a Nation
1918　The Greatest Thing in
　　　　Life
Butterworth, Frank
1918　Amarilly of Clothes-Line
　　　　Alley
Butterworth, Joe
1924　North of Nevada
Butterworth, Walter
1947　Citizen Saint
Buttler, Flora
1927?　You Can't Win
Buttram, Pat
1950　Indian Territory
1952　Apache Country
Butts, Billy
1931　Young Sinners
Butts, Edward S. de
1941　Virginia
Buzard, Eddie
1936　Human Cargo
Buzby, Florence
1951　The House on Telegraph
　　　　Hill
Buzet, Marie-Antoinette
1931　Die Dreigroschenoper
　　　(foreign version)
Buzzell, Edward
1946　Three Wise Fools
1950　Emergency Wedding
Buzzi, Pietro same as **Buzzi, Signor**
1917　The Bond Between
1918　One More American
Byars, Katherine
1948　The Fight Never Ends
Byer, Charles
1929　Romance of the Rio
　　　　Grande
Byers, Clara
1915　Under Southern Skies
Byers, Ruth
1941　Sullivan's Travels
Byington, Spring
1938　The Adventures of Tom
　　　　Sawyer
　　　The Buccaneer
1942　The Vanishing Virginian
1947　It Had To Be You
　　　Little Mister Jim
1950　Devil's Doorway
Bykoff, Vladimar
1936　Klondike Annie
Byles, Louis
1960　The Crowning
　　　　Experience

Byrd, Eddie
1946　Beware
Byrd, Louis
1960　Sergeant Rutledge
Byrd, Ralph
1940　The Mark of Zorro
1943　The Meanest Man in the
　　　　World
　　　They Came to Blow Up
　　　　America
Byrd, William
1948　The Betrayal
Byrne, William
1940　Knute Rockne—All
　　　　American
Byrnes, Bobi
1959　Night of the Quarter
　　　　Moon
Byrnes, Edward
1958　Marjorie Morningstar
1959　Yellowstone Kelly
Byrnes, Patricia
1948　The Boy with Green Hair
Byron, A. S. "Pop" 1876–1943 not
　the same as **Byron, Arthur**
　1872–1943
1936　Dimples
Byron, Arthur 1872–1943 not the
　same as **Byron, A. S. "Pop"**
　1876–1943
1934　Stand Up and Cheer!
1936　The Prisoner of Shark
　　　　Island
Byron, Delma
1936　Dimples
Byron, Jack same as **Byron, John**
1923　April Showers
1936　Sins of Man
1937　Slave Ship
1938　Speed to Burn
1940　The Gay Caballero
Byron, Marion
1930　The Bad Man
1932　The Heart of New York
Byron, Nina
1918　The Source
Byron, Paul
1916　A Child of Mystery
　　　For the Defense
Byron, Walter
1933　Charlie Chan's Greatest
　　　　Case
　　　Grand Slam
1942　Nazi Agent
Bytell, William
1918　Her Moment
Cabal, Robert
1947　Ride the Pink Horse
1949　Border Incident
1953　The Man Behind the Gun
Cabanne, Bill see **Cabanne,
　William** (actor)
Cabanne, Christy (dir) same as
　**Cabanne, W. Christy; Cabanne,
　William Christy**
1915　The Lamb
1916　Sold for Marriage
1917　The Slacker (Metro
　　　　Pictures Corp.)
1921　The Barricade
1931　Carne de cabaret
1932　Hearts of Humanity
1935　Alas sobre el Chaco
1947　King of the Bandits
　　　Robin Hood of Monterey
1948　Silver Trails
Cabanne, Emilie
1936　Ramona
1953　The Jazz Singer
Cabanne, Julie
1935　¡Asegure a su mujer!
1938　In Old Chicago
Cabanne, William (actor) same as
　Cabanne, Bill
1942　Holiday Inn
1947　Jiggs and Maggie in
　　　　Society
　　　King of the Bandits
1949　Anna Lucasta
1950　Right Cross
1952　Kid Monk Baroni

Cabanne, William Christy (dir) see
　Cabanne, Christy (dir)
Cable, Richard
1956　Serenade
Cabot, Bruce
1936　The Last of the Mohicans
　　　Robin Hood of El Dorado
1950　Rock Island Trail
1952　Kid Monk Baroni
1959　John Paul Jones
　　　The Sheriff of Fractured
　　　　Jaw
Cabot, Sebastian
1956　Westward Ho the
　　　　Wagons!
1957　Dragoon Wells Massacre
1958　Terror in a Texas Town
Cabot, Susan
1951　Tomahawk
1952　The Battle at Apache Pass
1958　Fort Massacre
Cabrera, Antonio
1936　El diablo del mar
Cadell, Don
1943　Dr. Gillespie's Criminal
　　　　Case
1947　Crossfire
Cades, Russell
1950　Damien
Cady, Frank
1949　Prejudice
　　　The Sky Dragon
1950　Emergency Wedding
　　　Young Man with a Horn
1955　The Indian Fighter
　　　Trial
1957　The Tin Star
Cady, Jerry same as **Cady, Jerome**
1937　Charlie Chan on
　　　　Broadway
　　　Thank You, Mr. Moto
1938　Charlie.Chan at Monte
　　　　Carlo
　　　Mr. Moto's Gamble
1939　Winner Take All
1941　The Mexican Spitfire's
　　　　Baby
1942　Mexican Spitfire at Sea
1948　Call Northside 777
Caesar, Arthur
1924　His Darker Self
1932　The Heart of New York
1933　Obey the Law
1935　McFadden's Flats
Caffero, Rudy
1931　Delicious
Cagney, James
1931　Smart Money
1934　He Was Her Man
1935　The Irish in Us
1940　The Fighting 69th
1943　Yankee Doodle Dandy
1948　The Time of Your Life
1959　Shake Hands with the
　　　　Devil
Cagney, Jeanne
1943　Yankee Doodle Dandy
1948　The Time of Your Life
1955　Kentucky Rifle
Cagney, Tim
1955　Good Morning, Miss Dove
Cagney, William
1943　Yankee Doodle Dandy
1948　The Time of Your Life
Cahill, William
1914　Threads of Destiny
Cahn, Edward L.
1949　Prejudice
1959　Inside the Mafia
1960　Oklahoma Territory
Cahn, Sammy
1957　Beau James
Caillaux, Roland
1931　Soyons gais
Caillet, Dollie
1948　Call Northside 777
Cain, Ace
1935　The Cyclone Ranger
1935?　The Irish Gringo

Cain, James M.
1939 Stand Up and Fight
Cain, Robert
1916 The Innocent Lie
1918 A Woman of Impulse
1924 Conductor 1492
Caine, Derwent Hall
1917 Crime and Punishment
Caine, Georgia
1940 Santa Fe Trail
1941 Hurry, Charlie, Hurry
1942 Dr. Gillespie's New
       Assistant
       Gentleman Jim
1943 Yankee Doodle Dandy
1944 Mr. Skeffington
Caine, Howard
1960 Pay or Die
Cains, Ruth
1958 Machete
Cairney, John
1959 Shake Hands with the
       Devil
Cairns, Sally
1941 Playmates
1942 King of the Stallions
Caits, Joe
1936 After the Thin Man
Caizza, Alfred
1955 Good Morning, Miss Dove
Calder, Caleen
1952 The Half-Breed
       Rose of Cimarron
Caldwell, Anne
1922 The Top O' the Morning
Caldwell, Bill
1947 The Farmer's Daughter
Caldwell, Bobby
1934 Stand Up and Cheer!
Caldwell, Edgar
1945 Where Do We Go From
       Here?
1947 Calendar Girl
Caldwell, H. H.
1924 Welcome Stranger
1925 The Prairie Wife
1928 Mother Machree
Caldwell, Matilda
1941 Sullivan's Travels
1950 Stars in My Crown
Caldwell, Orville
1935 His Family Tree
1937 Big City
Caler, John
1956 Giant
Calhern, Louis
1933 Diplomaniacs
1946 Notorious
1950 Annie Get Your Gun
       Devil's Doorway
1951 The Magnificent Yankee
1952 It's a Big Country: An
       American Anthology
1955 Blackboard Jungle
Calhoun, Cathleen
1926 Under Fire
Calhoun, Jean
1922 The Cub Reporter
Calhoun, Red
1947 Juke Joint
Calhoun, Rory same as **McCown,
Frank**
1944 Something for the Boys
1945 The Great John L.
       Nob Hill
1949 Massacre River
1950 A Ticket to Tomahawk
1954 The Yellow Tomahawk
1955 Shotgun
1956 Raw Edge
1957 Ride Out for Revenge
1958 Apache Territory
Calhoun, William
1918 The Little Runaway
1925 Red Love
Calihan, William
1954 Thunder Pass
Calkins, Johnny same as **Calkins,
John**
1942 Gentleman Jim
1944 The Sullivans

1948 The Boy with Green Hair
       Moonrise
Call, John
1951 The Tall Target
1952 Indian Uprising
1953 Ride, Vaquero!
Callaghan, Andrew J.
1929 Redskin
Callahan, Bobby
1943 The Outlaw
Callahan, Edna
1937 Song of the City
Callahan, George
1944 Black Magic
       Charlie Chan in the
       Secret Service
       The Chinese Cat
1945 The Jade Mask
       The Scarlet Clue
       The Shanghai Cobra
1946 Dark Alibi
       The Red Dragon
Callahan, Harold
1921 Anne of Little Smoky
Callahan, Margaret
1935 His Family Tree
1936 Muss 'Em Up
Callahan, Mushy
1935 The Irish in Us
1949 House of Strangers
Callahan, Robert E.
1949 Daughter of the West
Callam, Alex
1942 Rubber Racketeers
Callamand, Lucien
1930 Un hombre de suerte
       (foreign version)
Callaway, Cheryl
1955 Good Morning, Miss Dove
       The Last Command
Calleia, Joseph
1936 After the Thin Man
       Robin Hood of El Dorado
1937 Man of the People
1948 Four Faces West
1950 The Palomino
1952 The Iron Mistress
1956 Hot Blood
       Serenade
1958 The Light in the Forest
       Touch of Evil
       Wild Is the Wind
1959 Cry Tough
Callejo, Cecilia
1938 Outlaw Express
       The Renegade Ranger
1939 Verbena trágica
1945 The Cisco Kid Returns
       Salome, Where She
       Danced
Callejo, María Luz
1930 Un hombre de suerte
1931 Cheri-Bibi
       La fruta amarga
       Mamá
Callender, Red same as **Callender,
George "Red"**
1947 New Orleans
1958 St. Louis Blues
Callender, Romaine
1938 Passport Husband
Calles, Angelita
1931 Regeneración
Calles, Guillermo same as **Calles,
William**
1931 Regeneración
1955 Seven Cities of Gold
1956 The Last Frontier
Calliga, George
1938 The Buccaneer
1948 Big City
Callol, Rafael
1930 El valiente
Callow, Ridgeway
1939 Gone With the Wind
1957 Raintree County
1958 The Badlanders
1959 Night of the Quarter
       Moon
1960 Cimarron

Calloway, Cab
1958 St. Louis Blues
Cab Calloway and His Band same
as **Cab Calloway and His
Cotton Club Band**
1943 Stormy Weather
1937 Manhattan
       Merry-Go-Round
1947 Hi De Ho
Calloway, Cheryl
1955 The View from Pompey's
       Head
Calloway, Ernest
1946 Beware
Calloway, Star
1932? The Girl from Chicago
Callum, Alex
1942 We Were Dancing
Calmenti, Louise
1922 The Sign of the Rose
Calmer, Lee could be same as
Calmes, Curry Lee or **Lee,
Curry**
1939 The Bronze Buckaroo
Calmes, Curry Lee could be same
as **Calmer, Lee** or **Lee, Curry**
1943 Cabin in the Sky
Calnek, Roy
1921 Hearts of the Woods
1925 Abie's Imported Bride
1926 A Prince of His Race
1927 Children of Fate
Calvert, Catherine
1917 The Peddler
Calvert, Charles
1960 All the Fine Young
       Cannibals
Calvert, E. H. same as **Calvert, E.
H., Captain**
1929 Thunderbolt
1930 Behind the Make-Up
       The Kibitzer
       Ladies Love Brutes
1931 Beyond Victory
1932 Wild Horse Mesa
1935 So Red the Rose
1936 Ellis Island
       The Glory Trail
Calvin, Henry
1956 The Broken Star
1960 The Sign of Zorro
Calvin, U. G.
1918 Denny from Ireland
Calvo, Elodia
1932 Amor y vida
Calvo, María same as **Calvo, María,
Sra.**
1930 Amor audaz
       Charros, gauchos y
         manolas
       El cuerpo del delito
       Del mismo barro
       Estrellados
       Monsieur le Fox
       Sevilla de mis amores
       El valiente
       La voluntad del muerto
1931 Carne de cabaret
       El código penal
       El comediante
       Gente alegre
       El pasado acusa
       Politiquerías
1933 Primavera en otoño
       Una viuda romántica
1934 Granaderos del amor
1935 Angelina o el honor de
         un brigadier
       El cantante de Nápoles
       Rosa de Francia
1940 Perfidia
Calvo, Rafael
1931 Charlie Chan Carries On
       (foreign version)
       ¿Conoces a tu mujer?
       Cuerpo y alma
       Esclavas de la moda
       Hay que casar al príncipe
       La ley del harem
       Mamá
       Sombras del circo

Camacho, Alberto
1938 Di que me quieres
Camacho, Miguel
1959 The Young Land
Camacho Vega, Manuel
1930 Las campanas de
       Capistrano
Camargo, Anita
1934 Granaderos del amor
1935 Alas sobre el Chaco
1936 Ramona
Camax, Valentine
1951 Adventures of Captain
       Fabian
Cambias, G. S.
1950 Panic in the Streets
Cambre, Del see **Delcambre,
Alfred**
Cambridge, Godfrey
1959 The Last Angry Man
Camden, Joan
1956 The Catered Affair
Cameo, a dog
1927 Ham and Eggs at the
       Front
Camerini, Mario
1931 Tropennächte (foreign
       version)
Cameron, Ann
1948 The Time of Your Life
1949 The Undercover Man
Cameron, Bruce
1943 Gangway for Tomorrow
       Hitler's Children
       Riding High
1956 Reprisal!
Cameron, Constance
1958 Gunman's Walk
Cameron, Gene
1922 The Sign of the Rose
Cameron, Hugh
1927 For the Love of Mike
Cameron, Patricia
1948 Gentleman's Agreement
Cameron, Rod same as **Cox,
Rodney**
1940 If I Had My Way
1943 Riding High
1945 Salome, Where She
       Danced
1947 Pirates of Monterey
1951 Cavalry Scout
       Oh! Susanna
1952 Fort Osage
       Wagons West
1953 San Antone
1955 Headline Hunters
       Santa Fe Passage
Cameron, Rudolph
1927 For the Love of Mike
1942 Three Hearts for Julia
Camilli, Bernardo
1931 La regina di Sparta
Camlin, Peter
1947 The Foxes of Harrow
1949 The Girl from Jones
       Beach
1951 Show Boat
1952 The Big Sky
       The Iron Mistress
1953 Tonight We Sing
Camp, Charles
1949 Knock on Any Door
Campagnone, Catherine
1932 Senza mamma
       e'nnamurato
Campan, Zanie
1951 Adventures of Captain
       Fabian
Campana, Ettore
1935 A Night at the Opera
Campana, Nina
1935 A Night at the Opera
1936 It Had to Happen
       Sins of Man
1937 It Could Happen to You
       Man of the People
       Waikiki Wedding
1938 Outlaw Express
1942 Tortilla Flat

Campbell, Alan
1942   Tales of Manhattan
Campbell, Alexander
1949   Jigsaw
        Lost Boundaries
Campbell, Bob
1941   Sun Valley Serenade
Campbell, Charles *could be same as* **Campbell, Charles D.**
1947   Easy Come, Easy Go
Campbell, Charles D. *could be same as* **Campbell, Charles**
1959   Al Capone
Campbell, Colin (*actor*)
1922   Cardigan
1930   Big Boy
1945   Salome, Where She Danced
Campbell, Colin (*dir*)
1914   In the Days of the Thundering Herd
1915   The Rosary
1918   Tongues of Flame
        The Yellow Dog
1921   Black Roses
        The First Born
        The Swamp
        Where Lights Are Low
Campbell, Elaine
1944   Chip Off the Old Block
Campbell, Evelyn
1918   Tony America
Campbell, Irene
1946?   Go Down, Death!
Campbell, James
1960   Wild River
Campbell, John
1944   The Sullivans
Campbell, Josephine
1933   It's Great to Be Alive
Campbell, Lois Jane
1931   Cimarron
Campbell, Louise
1938   The Buccaneer
Campbell, Margaret (*actress*), 1873–1939
1922   The Top O' the Morning
1930   Take the Heir
Campbell, Margaret (*child actress*)
1942   The Vanishing Virginian
Campbell, Ned
1951   Native Son
Campbell, Paul
1947   It Had To Be You
1952   Indian Uprising
Campbell, Tim
1940   George Washington Carver
Campbell, Virginia
1948   Unconquered
Campbell, Webster
1917   The Renaissance at Charleroi
Campbell, William *not the same as* **Campbell, William** (*African-American actor*)
1950   The Breaking Point
1959   The Sheriff of Fractured Jaw
Campbell, William (*African-American actor*)
1947   Hi De Ho
1948   Killer Diller
Campeau, Frank
1923   The Spider and the Rose
1926   The Frontier Trail
1929   In Old Arizona
1930   Abraham Lincoln
1931   Fighting Caravans
1932   White Eagle
1936   Robin Hood of El Dorado
Campeau, George
1947   My Wild Irish Rose
Campeau, Lauretta
1947   Citizen Saint
Campillo, Anita
1934   La buenaventura
        La cruz y la espada
        Cuesta abajo
        Tres amores

1935   Un hombre peligroso
        Julieta compra un hijo
1938   La vida bohemia
Campo, Del *same as* **Del Campo, Francisco**
1935   El día que me quieras
1936   Ramona
1937   The Californian
Campo, Isabel
1955   Trial
Campobasso, Alberto
1932   Senza mamma e'nnamurato
Campos, Rafael
1955   Blackboard Jungle
        Trial
1958   The Light in the Forest
        Tonka
Camron, Rocky
1944   Outlaw Trail
        Sonora Stagecoach
1946   Romance of the West
Canady, John
1947   New Orleans
Canale, Gianna
1951   Go for Broke!
Canales, Susan
1959   John Paul Jones
Candoli, Pete
1958   Kings Go Forth
Cane, Charles
1942   All Through the Night
1943   Dixie
        Mr. Lucky
1945   Nob Hill
1946   The Gentleman Misbehaves
1950   Ambush
1951   Native Son
1953   San Antone
1954   Dangerous Mission
1957   Gun Battle at Monterey
Canneri, Margaret
1931   Such Is Life
Cannon, Dyan *same as* **Cannon, Diane**
1960   This Rebel Breed
Cannon, Judy
1958   Gunman's Walk
Cannon, Pomeroy
1918   Denny from Ireland
Cannon, Raymond
1945   Samurai
Cannutt, Yakima *see* **Canutt, Yakima**
Canova, Judy
1946   Singin' in the Corn
1960   The Adventures of Huckleberry Finn
Cansino Family *see also* **Hayworth, Rita**
1936   Dancing Pirate
Cansino, Rita *see* **Hayworth, Rita**
Cansino, Vernon
1948   The Lady from Shanghai
Cantor, Al
1951   Saturday's Hero
Cantor, Eddie
1930   Whoopee
1931   Mr. Lemon of Orange
1953   The Eddie Cantor Story
Cantor, Herman
1948   Jiggs and Maggie in Court
        Music Man
1949   The Story of Seabiscuit
Cantor, Ida
1953   The Eddie Cantor Story
Cantor, Russell
1953   Tonight We Sing
Cantrell, Early
1945   Betrayal from the East
Cantú, A. J.
1931   Politiquerías
Canty, Marietta
1942   Three Hearts for Julia
1943   Mexican Spitfire's Blessed Event
1944   Lake Placid Serenade
1950   The Toast of New Orleans
1951   A Streetcar Named Desire

1955   A Man Called Peter
Canutt, Joe
1955   The Far Horizons
Canutt, Yakima *same as* **Cannutt, Yakima**
1926   The Devil Horse
1931   The Hurricane Horseman
1932   Law and Lawless
1933   The Telegraph Trail
1934   The Battling Buckaroo
        Fighting Through
        'Neath the Arizona Skies
        The Star Packer
1935   Circle of Death
        Cyclone of the Saddle
1937   It Could Happen to You
        Prairie Thunder
        The Riders of the Whistling Skull
1939   Gone With the Wind
1941   Gauchos of Eldorado
        Prairie Pioneers
1944   The San Antonio Kid
        Tucson Raiders
        Vigilantes of Dodge City
1945   Great Stagecoach Robbery
1946   Santa Fe Uprising
        Sun Valley Cyclone
1947   Northwest Outpost
1950   Rocky Mountain
1953   Last of the Comanches
1956   Westward Ho the Wagons!
Canzano, Gabriel *see* **Canzona, Gabriel**
Canzona, Gabriel *same as* **Canzano, Gabriel**
1943   The Gang's All Here
1948   My Girl Tisa
Capell, Peter
1960   I Aim at the Stars: the Wernher von Braun Story
Capellani, Paul
1917   One Law for Both
Capellani, Roger
1931   Un caballero de frac
Capo, Sidney
1951   Distant Drums
Capote, Truman
1954   Indiscretion of an American Wife
Capra, Frank *same as* **Capra, Frank R.; Capra, Frank, Col.**
1926   The Strong Man
1927   For the Love of Mike
1929   The Younger Generation
1934   Broadway Bill
1944   The Negro Soldier
1951   Westward the Women
Capreoli, A.
1935   A Night at the Opera
Capri, Marcya
1921   The Money Maniac
Caprice, June
1917   Unknown 274
Capua, Giulio de
1935   El día que me quieras
Capuano, Sam
1960   Pay or Die
Caraballo, José
1935   Alas sobre el Chaco
1936   Contra la corriente
Carabella, Angela
1950   A Lady Without Passport
Caravias, Orpheus, Dr.
1931   Such Is Life
Carbajal, Tony
1956   Comanche
Car-Bert Dancers
1945   In Old New Mexico
Carbone, Anthony
1959   Inside the Mafia
Carboni, John
1950   Black Hand
Carbuccia, H. de
1931   El proceso de Mary Dugan (*foreign version*)

Card, Bob
1931   Riders of the Rio
Card, Kathryn
1958   Home Before Dark
Cárdenas, Elsa
1956   Giant
1960   For the Love of Mike
Cárdenas, Guty
1931   La dama atrevida
Cardo, Paula de
1938   Daughter of Shanghai
1939   King of Chinatown
1940   Geronimo
Cardona, René
1929   Sombras habaneras
1930   Cuando el amor ríe
        Del mismo barro
1931   Carne de cabaret
1954   Sitting Bull
Cardwell, James
1944   The Sullivans
1945   The Shanghai Cobra
1946   Canyon Passage
1948   Harpoon
Carew, Arthur Edmund *same as* **Carew, Arthur; Carewe, Arthur**
1919   Bonnie, Bonnie Lassie
        Daughter of Mine
1920   Rio Grande
1928   Uncle Tom's Cabin
1936   Charlie Chan's Secret
Carew, Edwin *see* **Carewe, Edwin**
Carewe, Arthur *see* **Carew, Arthur**
Carewe, Edwin *same as* **Carew, Edwin**
1913   The Inside of the White Slave Traffic
1915   Marse Covington
        Time Lock Number 776
1919   False Evidence
1920   Rio Grande
1925   My Son
1928   Ramona
1929   Evangeline
1931   Resurrección
Carewe, Rita
1928   Ramona
Carey, Cappy
1959   Al Capone
Carey, Harry *same as* **Carey, Harry D.; Carey, Harry, Sr.**
1915   Just Jim
1918   Wild Women
1923   Crashin' Thru
1924   The Lightning Rider
        The Night Hawk
1926   The Frontier Trail
1931   Cavalier of the West
1932   Border Devils
1933   Thundering Herd
1936   The Prisoner of Shark Island
        Sutter's Gold
1937   Border Cafe
        Souls at Sea
1938   Gateway
1940   They Knew What They Wanted
1943   Air Force
1947   Duel in the Sun
1948   Red River
Carey, Harry, Jr.
1948   Moonrise
        Red River
1949   She Wore a Yellow Ribbon
        3 Godfathers
1950   Rio Grande
1951   Warpath
1953   Beneath the 12-Mile Reef
        San Antone
1955   The Long Gray Line
1956   The Searchers
        7th Cavalry
Carey, James
1923   Deceit
Carey, Joan
1945   Where Do We Go From Here?

Carey, Leonard
1941   Accent on Love
1948   Unconquered
Carey, MacDonald *same as* **Carey, Macdonald**
1949   Streets of Laredo
1950   Comanche Territory
         The Lawless
         Mystery Submarine
1959   John Paul Jones
Carey, Mary Jane
1934   Stand Up and Cheer!
Carey, Olive *same as* **Golden, Olive; Golden, Olive Fuller**
1932   Border Devils
1956   Pillars of the Sky
         The Searchers
1957   Run of the Arrow
Carey, Papa Mutt
1947   New Orleans
Carey, Patricia
1941   Louisiana Purchase
Carey, Phil *same as* **Carey, Philip**
1953   The Man Behind the Gun
         The Nebraskan
1954   Massacre Canyon
         They Rode West
1955   The Long Gray Line
1958   Tonka
Carey, Tim
1956   The Last Wagon
1957   Bayou
Cariguel, Claude
1951   The Great Caruso
Carillo, Leo *see* **Carrillo, Leo**
Carillo, Mario
1926   The Barrier
Carl, Rudolf
1935   Te quiero con locura
Carlan, Florine
1959   The Black Orchid
Carle, Richard
1930   The Grand Parade
         A Lady to Love
1933   Diplomaniacs
1934   Beloved
1936   Let's Sing Again
Carleton, Bob
1946   Bringing Up Father
Carleton, Claire
1944   My Pal Wolf
1948   The Time of Your Life
1949   Satan's Cradle
1951   Westward the Women
1952   The Fighter
1958   Fort Massacre
Carleton, George
1942   Twin Beds
1943   Gangway for Tomorrow
         Riding High
1945   A Tree Grows in Brooklyn
1946   Rendezvous 24
1947   The Last Round-Up
Carleton, Guy
1953   Beneath the 12-Mile Reef
Carleton, Lloyd B.
1915   The Girl I Left Behind Me
1916   The Morals of Hilda
         A Yoke of Gold
Carleton, Sue
1950   Annie Get Your Gun
Carleton, W. T.
1916   Poor Little Peppina
Carleton, William P.
1920   The Riddle: Woman
Carlie, Ed
1924   Racing Luck
Carlile, David
1957   Apache Warrior
Carlin, Jean
1946   Wild West
Carlisle, Bertha
1941   Birth of the Blues
Carlisle, Chester
1943   Gangway for Tomorrow
Carlisle, Grace
1928   Uncle Tom's Cabin
Carlisle, James
1944   An American Romance
         Since You Went Away

1948   Unconquered
1950   Emergency Wedding
Carlisle, Kitty
1935   A Night at the Opera
Carlisle, Rita
1934   Limehouse Blues
Carlisle, Una Mae
1946   Stars on Parade
1948? Boarding House Blues
1949? The Joint Is Jumpin'
Carlo, Val
1947   The Adventures of Don Coyote
Carlo, Yvonne de *see* **De Carlo, Yvonne**
Carlos y Greta
1935   No matarás
Carlos, A.
1925   Tearing Through
Carlos, Don
1955   Apache Ambush
Carlson, Monroe
1958   Tonka
Carlson, Richard
1940   Too Many Girls
1953   Seminole
1955   The Last Command
Carlson, Wamp
1943   Doughboys in Ireland
Carlsten, Rune
1930   Toda una vida (*foreign version*)
Carlton, Bunny
1945   Where Do We Go From Here?
Carlton, Rex
1949   C-Man
Carlton, Violet
1934   Broadway Bill
Carluccio, Yolanda
1932   Cuore d'emigrante
Carlyle, Aileen
1943   Mexican Spitfire's Blessed Event
1946   Notorious
Carlyle, Jack *not the same as* **Carlyle, John**
1936   Dangerous Intrigue
Carlyle, John *not the same as* **Carlyle, Jack**
1946   The Sailor Takes a Wife
         Three Wise Fools
1954   Dangerous Mission
Carlyle, Kathy
1960   The Pusher
Carlyle, Pat *same as* **Carlyle, Patrick**
1934   Call of the Coyote
1935? The Irish Gringo
Carlyle, Richard (*actor*), d. 1942
1919   Spotlight Sadie
1929   Hearts in Dixie
         In Old California
Carlyle, Richard (*actor, circa 1950s*)
1952   The Iron Mistress
Carlyle, Sidney
1920   Humoresque
Carmen, Jeanne
1957   War Drums
Carmen, Jewel
1916   The Half-Breed
1917   The Conqueror
Carmichael, Albert R.
1951   Saturday's Hero
Carmichael, Hoagy
1945   Johnny Angel
1946   Canyon Passage
1950   Young Man with a Horn
Carmona, Francisco
1938   Di que me quieres
Carnahan, Mark
1941   Sullivan's Travels
Carnahan, Suzanne *see* **Peters, Susan**
Carnahan, Thomas, Jr.
1918   Uncle Tom's Cabin

Carnegie, Dale
1947   Jiggs and Maggie in Society
Carnegie, Donna
1960   Wild River
Carnell, Suzi
1960   Studs Lonigan
Carner Ribalta, Josep *same as* **Carner-Ribalta, J.**
1930   Amor audaz
         Cascarrabias
         El cuerpo del delito
         El dios del mar
         Galas de la Paramount
1931   Gente alegre
         El príncipe gondolero
1940   Perfidia
Carney, Alan
1943   Gangway for Tomorrow
         Mexican Spitfire's Blessed Event
         Mr. Lucky
Carney, Bob
1955   Headline Hunters
Carney, Lucile
1920   The Dark Mirror
Carney, Marion
1949   Daughter of the West
Carnovsky, Morris
1944   Address Unknown
1945   Our Vines Have Tender Grapes
         Rhapsody in Blue
1949   Thieves' Highway
Carol, Jack
1959   The Crimson Kimono
Carol, Joan *see* **Carroll, Joan**
Carol, Judy
1943   Stormy Weather
Carol, Sue
1928   The Cohens and the Kellys in Paris
1930   Check and Double Check
Carole, Maxine
1944   Something for the Boys
Caron, Doria
1944   Mr. Skeffington
1945   Nob Hill
1948   My Girl Tisa
Caron, Patricia
1934   Broadway Bill
Carpenter, Betty
1922   Cardigan
Carpenter, Carleton
1949   Lost Boundaries
Carpenter, Elliott
1940   Broken Strings
1951   Yes Sir, Mr. Bones
Carpenter, Florence
1918   Uncle Tom's Cabin
Carpenter, Francis
1916   Gretchen, the Greenhorn
         A Sister of Six
Carpenter, Fred
1943   Ladies' Day
1945   Betrayal from the East
Carpenter, Grant
1922   The Pride of Palomar
Carpenter, H. C.
1918   The Border Raiders
Carpenter, Horace B. *same as* **Carpenter, H. B.; Carpenter, Horace**
1916   For the Defense
         The Thousand Dollar Husband
1917   Castles for Two
1918   One More American
1931   Riders of the Rio
1932   The Galloping Kid
         Riders of the Desert
1945   Great Stagecoach Robbery
Carpenter, Jeanne
1922   The Sign of the Rose
Carpenter, Jimmy *same as* **Carpenter, James**
1943   Doughboys in Ireland
1944   They Live in Fear

Carpenter, Josh
1945   The Navajo Trail
Carpenter, Ken
1941   New York Town
Carpenter, Madeline
1932   Hypnotized
Carpenter, Virginia
1940   Phantom of Chinatown
Carpentier, Marcel
1931   Su noche de bodas (*foreign version*)
Carper, Larry
1951   Distant Drums
Carr, Alexander
1923   Potash and Perlmutter
1924   In Hollywood With Potash and Perlmutter
1926   April Fool
1932   Hypnotized
         No Greater Love
Carr, Barney
1936   General Spanky
Carr, Bridget
1949   That Midnight Kiss
1950   Annie Get Your Gun
1951   The Mark of the Renegade
Carr, Catherine
1915   The Melting Pot
1918   Shifting Sands
Carr, Dixie
1916   The Grip of Jealousy
Carr, Gertrude
1942   All Through the Night
Carr, Harry
1947   Rustlers of Devil's Canyon
Carr, Jack *not the same as* **Carr, Jack** (*African-American actor*)
1940   East of the River
1941   New York Town
         Playmates
1942   Tortilla Flat
         Woman of the Year
1945   A Tree Grows in Brooklyn
1952   The Iron Mistress
1958   Bullwhip
Carr, Jack (*African-American actor*)
1939   Way Down South
1941   Four Shall Die
Carr, June
1948   Shep Comes Home
1949   The Dalton Gang
1951   Yes Sir, Mr. Bones
Carr, Larry
1958   Houseboat
Carr, Lorena
1931   Riders of the Rio
1932   Hypnotized
1934   Stand Up and Cheer!
Carr, Marian
1956   Ghost Town
Carr, Mary *same as* **Carr, Mary K.; Carr, Mary Kennavan; Carr, Mary Kennevan; Carr, Mrs.**
1916   The Flames of Johannis
         Light at Dusk
1917   The Barrier
1918   The Birth of a Race
1924   East of Broadway
         The Mine with the Iron Door
1925   The Gold Hunters
         Hogan's Alley
1931   Beyond Victory
         Law of the Tong
Carr, Michael
1957   Apache Warrior
Carr, Mrs. *see* **Carr, Mary**
Carr, Nat
1925   His People
1926   April Fool
         The Cohens and Kellys
         Kosher Kitty Kelly
         Millionaires
         Private Izzy Murphy
1928   The Jazz Singer
1939   Daughters Courageous

Carr, Richard
1956   Man from Del Rio
Carr, Rosemary
1916   The Flames of Johannis
Carr, Sabin W.
1937   Harlem on the Prairie
Carr, Stephen
1923   Little Old New York
1924   North of 36
1925   The Thundering Herd
Carr, Thomas *(dir)*
1952   Trail of the Arrow
Carr, Tom *(actor)*
1925   The Wild Bull's Lair
Carr, Trem
1931   Oklahoma Jim
1936   Sea Spoilers
1938   Outlaw Express
1943   Crime Smasher
1944   Lady, Let's Dance!
1945   Sunbonnet Sue
Carradine, John
1936   Daniel Boone
         Dimples
         The Prisoner of Shark
           Island
         Ramona
         Winterset
1937   Thank You, Mr. Moto
1938   Gateway
1939   Drums Along the Mohawk
         Mr. Moto's Last Warning
1941   Western Union
1942   Whispering Ghosts
1943   Gangway for Tomorrow
1944   Waterfront
1946   The Face of Marble
1949   C-Man
1954   Thunder Pass
1958   The Last Hurrah
1959   The Oregon Trail
1960   The Adventures of
           Huckleberry Finn
Carrady, Victor
1958   Machete
Carraher, Robert
1954   Dangerous Mission
Carral, Antonio
1930   Las campanas de
           Capistrano
Carrasco, Joaquín
1930   Un hombre de suerte
         Toda una vida
1931   La pura verdad
Carré, Bartlett *same as* **Carré, Bart**
1934   The Battling Buckaroo
         Call of the Coyote
1935   Circle of Death
         No matarás
1949   The Cowboy and the
           Prizefighter
1955   Apache Woman
Carreón, Polín
1932   Amor y vida
Carrera, Liane Held
1918   The Liar
Carrere, Roone
1935   A Night at the Opera
Carricart, Robert
1959   The Black Orchid
Carrick, Allyn B.
1920?   Her Story
Carrick, John
1931   Charlie Chan Carries On
Carrickson, S. B.
1925   Irish Luck
Carrier, Albert
1959   Thunder in the Sun
Carrillo, Leo *same as* **Carillo, Leo**
1929   Mister Antonio
1931   The Guilty Generation
1932   Men Are Such Fools
1933   Obey the Law
         Racetrack
1935   The Winning Ticket
1936   It Had to Happen
1937   The Barrier
         Manhattan
           Merry-Go-Round
1938   City Streets
         Little Miss Roughneck

1939   Fisherman's Wharf
1941   Road Agent
1942   American Empire
         Unseen Enemy
1949   The Daring Caballero
         The Gay Amigo
         Satan's Cradle
         The Valiant Hombre
1950   The Girl from San
           Lorenzo
Carrington, Jack
1943   Ladies' Day
Carrington, Lola
1946   Mantan Messes Up
Carrizosa, Marty
1956   Walk the Proud Land
Carroll, Alma
1942   Submarine Raider
1943   Redhead from Manhattan
Carroll, Connie
1956   Rockin' the Blues
Carroll, Dee
1949   The Story of Seabiscuit
1952   Bright Victory
1954   Drum Beat
         War Arrow
Carroll, Diahann *not the same as*
  Carroll, Diane
1954   Carmen Jones
1959   Porgy and Bess
Carroll, Diane *not the same as*
  Carroll, Diahann
1946   Cuban Pete
Carroll, Frank J.
1925   The Scarlet West
Carroll, Georgia
1943   Yankee Doodle Dandy
Carroll, Janice
1956   The Catered Affair
Carroll, Joan *same as* **Carol, Joan**
1937   One Mile from Heaven
1938   Gateway
         Two Sisters
1939   Mr. Moto's Last Warning
1944   Tomorrow the World!
1945   The Bells of St. Mary's
Carroll, John
1936   Muss 'Em Up
1941   This Woman Is Mine
1942   Rio Rita
1948   Angel in Exile
         Old Los Angeles
Carroll, Leo G. *same as* **Carroll,
  Leo**
1939   City in Darkness
1940   Charlie Chan's Murder
           Cruise
1941   This Woman Is Mine
1945   The House on 92nd St.
Carroll, Lucia
1940   Santa Fe Trail
Carroll, Mabel Z.
1927   The Slaver
Carroll, Madeleine
1941   Virginia
Carroll, Mary
1950   The Breaking Point
1955   Foxfire
         Good Morning, Miss Dove
Carroll, Mildred
1933   It's Great to Be Alive
Carroll, Nancy
1929   Abie's Irish Rose
1930   Galas de la Paramount
1931   Personal Maid
Carroll, Richard A.
1945   Sunbonnet Sue
Carroll, Terry
1931   Personal Maid
Carroll, Vance
1936   Yellow Cargo
Carroll, Virginia
1944   Lake Placid Serenade
1946   G. I. War Brides
1947   The Last Round-Up
1955   Good Morning, Miss Dove
         Headline Hunters
         Violent Saturday

Carroll, William *same as* **Carroll,
  W. A.**
1916   Lord Loveland Discovers
           America
1917   John Ermine of the
           Yellowstone
         My Fighting Gentleman
         A Roadside Impresario
1921   Fifty Candles
1924   North of 36
1926   The Fighting Edge
Carruth, Richard
1956   Man from Del Rio
Carruthers, Bruce
1950   North of the Great Divide
Carruthers, Steve
1953   Dream Wife
Carry, Jack
1944   Buffalo Bill
Carsdale, Betty
1921   The Land of Hope
Carson, Cindy
1956   Frontier Woman
Carson, Dan
1952   The Big Sky
Carson, Frances
1946   Saratoga Trunk
Carson, Fred
1953   The Charge at Feather
           River
Carson, Jack *(actor),* 1910—1963
1937   It Could Happen to You
         Music for Madame
1939   The Escape
1942   Gentleman Jim
         Wings for the Eagle
Carson, Jack *(western actor) see*
  Pendleton, Gaylord
Carson, James B.
1935   Harmony Lane
1939   Judge Hardy and Son
1945   A Tree Grows in Brooklyn
Carson, Kit
1944   Mr. Skeffington
1946   Dangerous Money
         Shadows Over Chinatown
1955   The Lonesome Trail
Carson, Renee
1945   The House on 92nd St.
Carson, Robert
1941   Western Union
1950   Indian Territory
1952   Red Snow
1953   The Man from the Alamo
         The Stars Are Singing
1956   Mohawk
1957   Band of Angels
1960   Cimarron
Carson, Willie May
1922   Big Stakes
Carter, Ann
1948   The Boy with Green Hair
1953   The Member of the
           Wedding
Carter, Ben
1941   Ride on Vaquero
1942   Young America
1943   Crash Dive
         Redhead from Manhattan
1945   The Scarlet Clue
1946   Dark Alibi
Carter, Cathy
1947   Bowery Buckaroos
         King of the Bandits
Carter, Douglas *not the same as*
  Carter, Douglas *(African-
  American actor)*
1950   Mystery Street
1951   The Great Caruso
Carter, Douglas *(African-American
  actor)*
1928   Tenderfeet
Carter, Frank *not the same as*
  Carter, Frank *(silent actor)*
1959   Last Train from Gun Hill
Carter, Frank *(silent actor)*
1922   Foolish Lives
Carter, Freddie
1947   Jivin' in Be-Bop

Carter, Harry *(actor, circa
  1940s—1950s)*
1943   Crash Dive
1948   Cry of the City
         Fury at Furnace Creek
1950   Broken Arrow
         No Way Out
         A Ticket to Tomahawk
         Two Flags West
1951   The House on Telegraph
           Hill
1954   Broken Lance
1955   Violent Saturday
Carter, Harry *(silent actor)*
1916   The Social Buccaneer
1917   A Kentucky Cinderella
1918   The Girl in the Dark
1922   The Top O' the Morning
Carter, Helena
1952   Bugles in the Afternoon
1953   The Pathfinder
Carter, Jack *not the same as*
  Carter, Jack *(African-American
  actor)*
1934   Charlie Chan's Courage
Carter, Jack *(African-American
  actor)*
1939   The Devil's Daughter
         Straight to Heaven
1942   Take My Life
1947   Sepia Cinderella
1948   Miracle in Harlem
Carter, Janis
1952   The Half-Breed
Carter, Jimmy
1959   The Jayhawkers!
Carter, Lavada
1948   Miracle in Harlem
Carter, Louise
1934   Beloved
1936   Paddy O'Day
         Rose of the Rancho
Carter, Milton
1945   The Great John L.
Carter, Monti
1931   Street Scene
Carter, Neil
1949   House of Strangers
Carter, Reginald
1923   The White Flower
Carter, Wally
1944   Chip Off the Old Block
Carter, William
1945   Where Do We Go From
           Here?
Carthay, Dan
1938   Di que me quieres
Cartier, Jacques
1930   King of Jazz
Cartier, Robert
1931   Esclavas de la moda
         Mi último amor
Cartledge, Bill *same as* **Cartledge,
  William J.**
1938   Speed to Burn
1941   Playmates
1949   The Story of Seabiscuit
1951   Westward the Women
Carton, Leone
1918   Shifting Sands
Caruso, Anthony *same as* **Caruso,
  Tony**
1942   Across the Pacific
         Sunday Punch
1943   The Girl from Monterrey
1944   The Racket Man
1945   I Love a Bandleader
         Pride of the Marines
1949   Anna Lucasta
         Illegal Entry
         The Undercover Man
1952   Desert Pursuit
         The Iron Mistress
1953   The Man Behind the Gun
1954   Cattle Queen of Montana
         Drum Beat
         Passion
         Saskatchewan
1955   Santa Fe Passage
1956   Walk the Proud Land
1957   Joe Dakota
         The Lawless Eighties
         The Oklahoman

Caruso, Anthony *(cont.)*
1958   The Badlanders
        Fort Massacre
1959   The Wonderful Country

Caruso, Enrico
1918   My Cousin

Caruso, Enrico, Jr.
1934   La buenaventura
1935   El cantante de Nápoles

Caruso, Henry
1937   Boy of the Streets

Caruso, Marie
1947   Citizen Saint

Caruso, Tony *see* **Caruso, Anthony**

Caruth, Burr
1938   Gateway

Carvalho, Claire
1933   Racetrack

Carver, George Washington, Dr.
1940   George Washington
        Carver

Carver, H. P.
1930   The Silent Enemy

Carver, Louise
1932   Riders of the Desert

Carver, Lynne
1939   The Adventures of
        Huckleberry Finn

Carver, Mary
1960   Pay or Die

Carver, Richard
1930   The Silent Enemy

Casagrande, Matilde
1931   La carta *(foreign
        version)*

Case, Kathleen
1953   The Eddie Cantor Story

Case, Rena
1948   The Time of Your Life

Caselotti, Luisa
1930   Sei tu l'amore
1931   La gran jornada *(foreign
        version)*

Casey, Dolores
1939   King of Chinatown

Casey, Emmett
1945   Salome, Where She
        Danced

Casey, Leslie *same as* **Casey,
Lesley**
1919   The Other Man's Wife
1921   Little Miss Hawkshaw

Casey, Sue
1950   Annie Get Your Gun
        The Daughter of Rosie
        O'Grady
1951   Show Boat

Cashen, Georgann
1956   Giant

Cashen, Mary Ann
1956   Giant

Cashier, Izidor *same as* **Casher,
Isidor; Casher, Izidor; Cashier,
Isadore; Cashier, Isidor;
Cashier, Isidore; Cashier,
Izidore**
1926   Broken Hearts
1931   Zein Weib's Lubovnick
1932   The Unfortunate Bride
        Yiskor
1937   The Cantor's Son
        Green Fields
1939   The Light Ahead
1940   The Jewish Melody

Cashier, Jenny
1939   The Light Ahead
        My Son

Casiday, Mary
1951   Westward the Women

Casino, Del
1946? Harlem on Parade
1947   Citizen Saint

Casino, Jimmy
1955   Foxfire

Casman, Nellie
1951   Molly

Cason, Bob
1947   The Last Round-Up
1948   Fury at Furnace Creek
1949   Laramie
1959   Gunmen from Laredo

Cason, Chuck
1955   Apache Ambush

Cason, John
1950   The Traveling
        Saleswoman
1951   Westward the Women
1954   Saskatchewan
1956   The Last Frontier
1958   Gunman's Walk
1960   Cimarron

Caspary, Vera
1941   Lady from Louisiana

Casper, Robert
1960   Studs Lonigan

Cass, Fred
1941   Sun Valley Serenade

Cass, Maurice
1937   Charlie Chan at the
        Opera
        Life Begins in College
1938   Breaking the Ice
        Josette
1942   Syncopation
1947   Spoilers of the North
1952   Kid Monk Baroni

Cass County Boys
1952   Apache Country

Cassady, James
1916   The Flames of Johannis

Cassavetes, John
1953   Taxi
1957   Edge of the City

Cassel, W. *not the same as* **Cassell,
Wally**
1926   Under Fire

Cassell, Wally *not the same as*
Cassel, W.
1942   Dr. Gillespie's New
        Assistant
1946   Bad Bascomb
1949   Arctic Manhunt
        We Were Strangers
1950   Sands of Iwo Jima
1951   Little Big Horn
        Oh! Susanna
1956   Wetbacks

Cassidy, Edward *same as* **Cassidy,
Ed**
1936   Hair-Trigger Casey
1938   Outlaw Express
        Wild Horse Canyon
1941   The Gang's All Here
1944   Tucson Raiders
1945   Colorado Pioneers
1946   Sun Valley Cyclone
1947   Buffalo Bill Rides Again
        On the Old Spanish Trail
        Oregon Trail Scouts
1950   Train to Tombstone
1953   Dream Wife

Cassidy, Ellen
1919   The Other Man's Wife

Cassidy, Robert
1945   Where Do We Go From
        Here?

Cassinelli, Dolores
1921   Anne of Little Smoky
1923   Jamestown
1925   The Midnight Girl

Casson, Christopher
1959   Shake Hands with the
        Devil

Casson, Lewis
1959   Shake Hands with the
        Devil

Castaine, Robert
1945   Where Do We Go From
        Here?

Castañeda, Movita *see* **Movita**

Casteig, Pilar
1931   La pura verdad

Castejón, Blanca de *same as*
Castejón, Blanca
1931   Charlie Chan Carries On
        (foreign version)
        Esclavas de la moda
        El impostor
        Resurrección
1937   El carnaval del diablo
1938   Mis dos amores
1939   Los hijos mandan

Castel, Freddy
1931   La pura verdad

Castelli, Bertrand
1959   Thunder in the Sun

Castelli, Silvio
1932   Amor in montagna

Castello, Jack *same as* **Costello,
Juan**
1931   La fruta amarga

Castello, William *see* **Costello,
Willy**

Casteneda, Movita *see* **Movita**

Castiglioni, Iphigenie
1958   Wild Is the Wind

Castillo, Aurora
1950   Two Flags West

Castillo, Carmen
1928   El Robin Hood de México
1930   Charros, gauchos y
        manolas

Castillo, Gloria
1955   The Vanishing American
1958   The Light in the Forest

Castillo, Mary Lou
1954   Salt of the Earth

Castillo de Bonzo, Consuelo
1931   The Cisco Kid

Castle, Dolores
1947   West to Glory
1948   Cry of the City
1949   The Girl from Jones
        Beach
        House of Strangers

Castle, Don
1940   Northwest Passage (Book
        I—Rogers' Rangers)

Castle, Joan
1931   Mr. Lemon of Orange
        Young Sinners
1938   Gateway

Castle, Lillian
1934   Straight Is the Way
1935   A Night at the Ritz
1947   My Wild Irish Rose

Castle, Mary
1951   When the Redskins Rode

Castle, Peggie *same as* **Castle,
Peggy**
1950   Buccaneer's Girl
1952   Wagons West
1954   Overland Pacific
        The Yellow Tomahawk
1956   Quincannon, Frontier
        Scout
1958   Seven Hills of Rome

Castle, Ruth
1948   Harpoon

Castle, S. *see* **Ulmer, Shirley**

Castle, Sherle *see* **Ulmer, Shirley**

Castle, William
1937   It Could Happen to You
1940   Music in My Heart
1942   North to the Klondike
1948   The Lady from Shanghai
1953   Conquest of Cochise
        Fort Ti
1954   Battle of Rogue River
1955   Duel on the Mississippi
        The Gun That Won the
        West

Castleton, Barbara
1920   Dangerous Days
        Dangerous Hours

Castor, Pat
1958   Tonka

Castro, Bob
1949   House of Strangers

Castro, Elsa de
1930   Doña mentiras *(foreign
        version)*
        Un hombre de suerte
        (foreign version)

Castro, Isabelita
1945   A Medal for Benny

Castro Blanco, Jesús
1932   El hombre que asesinó

Caswell, Nancy
1936   Custer's Last Stand

Catalán, Feliciano
1931   Sombras del circo

Catching, J. P. *same as* **Catching, J.
P. "Bill"**
1953   The Nebraskan
1954   They Rode West

Cathrey, George
1948   The Miracle of the Bells

Catlett, Big Sid
1947   Boy! What a Girl!

Catlett, Walter
1933   Olsen's Big Moment
1942   Syncopation
1943   His Butler's Sister
        Yankee Doodle Dandy
1944   Hi, Beautiful
        Lady, Let's Dance!
        Lake Placid Serenade
1945   I Love a Bandleader
1946   Slightly Scandalous
1948   The Boy with Green Hair
1956   Davy Crockett and the
        River Pirates
1957   Beau James

Catlin, George
1920   The Symbol of the
        Unconquered

Cato, Minta
1932? The Girl from Chicago

The Cats and the Fiddle
1938   The Duke Is Tops
        Two Gun Man from
        Harlem

Cauley, Bernard
1949   Top O' the Morning

Caulfield, Betty
1955   Good Morning, Miss Dove
        A Man Called Peter

Caupolican, Chief
1930   Whoopee

Cautiero, Bob
1940   The Mark of Zorro

Cavadias, Loukianos
1931   Such Is Life

Cavalcanti, Alberto
1930   Toda una vida *(foreign
        version)*

Cavalier, Nita
1926   Twin Triggers

Cavaliere, Steve
1949   House of Strangers

Cavalieri, Lina
1918   A Woman of Impulse

Cavan, Allan *same as* **Cavan, Alan;
Cavan, Allen** *not the same as*
Cavens, Al
1936   Rebellion
1937   Charlie Chan on
        Broadway
        Nation Aflame
        Old Louisiana
        Souls at Sea

Cavanagh, Paul *same as*
Cavanaugh, Paul
1931   The Squaw Man
1945   Club Havana
1947   Humoresque
1950   The Iroquois Trail

Cavanaugh, Hobart
1935   Bordertown
1939   Daughters Courageous
1940   Elsa Maxwell's Public
        Deb No. 1
        Santa Fe Trail
1941   Playmates
1943   Jack London
1947   Easy Come, Easy Go
1948   My Girl Tisa
        Up in Central Park

Page Cavanaugh Trio
1948   Big City

Cavanaugh, Paul *see* **Cavanagh,
Paul**

Cavanaugh, William
1913   Traffic in Souls
1921   Love's Plaything
1925   Red Love

Cavell, Mark
1953   The Man from the Alamo

Cavell, Maurice
1947   Citizen Saint
Caven, Jess *same as* **Cavin, Jess**
1928   Ramona
1929   The Desert Rider
1934   Chloe: Love Is Calling You
1937   The Plainsman
1939   Allegheny Uprising
Caven, Taylor
1944   Marshal of Reno
1947   Untamed Fury
Cavender, Glen
1921   Little Miss Hawkshaw
1937   Charlie Chan at the Olympics
1938   The Beloved Brat
        Gateway
1940   The Man I Married
1942   Juke Girl
1943   Yankee Doodle Dandy
Cavens, Al *not the same as* **Cavan, Allan**
1947   The Farmer's Daughter
1952   The Half-Breed
Cavens, Fred
1934   La veuve joyeuse
1935   L'homme des Folies Bergère
Caverly, Helene
1934   Broadway Bill
Cavett, Frank
1942   Syncopation
1944   Going My Way
1951   Across the Wide Missouri
Cavigga, Albert
1948   Unconquered
Cavin, Jess *see* **Caven, Jess**
Caviness, Cathryn
1941?   The Blood of Jesus
Cavitt, Jessie
1951   Queen for a Day
Cawley, Pat
1959   Night of the Quarter Moon
Cawthorn, Joseph *same as* **Cawthorne, Joseph**
1928   Hold 'Em Yale
1932   Men Are Such Fools
1933   Best of Enemies
        Broken Dreams
        Grand Slam
1934   Lazy River
1935   Harmony Lane
        Naughty Marietta
Cayol, Ricardo
1930   Sombras de gloria
Cea, Carlos
1930   El presidio
Cecil, Ed *same as* **Cecil, Edward**
1922   The Guttersnipe
1935   Charlie Chan in Paris
1938   The Buccaneer
        City Streets
1940   Elsa Maxwell's Public Deb No. 1
Cecil, Nora *same as* **Cecile, Norah**
1917   The Wild Girl
1928   The Cavalier
1931   Street Scene
1934   Laughing Boy
1936   Dancing Pirate
1939   The Adventures of Huckleberry Finn
1942   Apache Trail
Cefalu, Joseph
1953   Thunder Bay
Celano, Guido
1950   Deported
1958   Seven Hills of Rome
Celli, Teresa
1949   Border Incident
1950   Black Hand
        Right Cross
1951   The Great Caruso
Cennerazzo, Armando
1931   Così è la vita
Ceprano, Dorita
1931   Regeneración

Cerrai, Alessandro Ciardelli
1932   Tormento
Cervi, Gino
1954   Indiscretion of an American Wife
Cervi, N.
1916   Poor Little Peppina
Cervières, Paul
1930   Toda una vida (*foreign version*)
Cesana, Renzo
1950   A Lady Without Passport
1951   The Mark of the Renegade
1952   California Conquest
Cezon, Ricard
1935   Ruggles of Red Gap
Chabing
1947   The Chinese Ring
1948   Shanghai Chest
        Unconquered
Chace, C. R.
1938   Birthright
Chackerian, Charles
1949   Thieves' Highway
Chacón, Juan
1954   Salt of the Earth
Chadwell, Wallace
1941   Adam Had Four Sons
1946   Bringing Up Father
Chadwick, Cyril
1923   Thirty Days
1924   Peter Pan
1928   The Mating Call
Chadwick, Helene
1920   The Cup of Fury
1921   Made in Heaven
Chain, Mike
1960   The Dark at the Top of the Stairs
Chalif, Selmer L.
1947   The Adventures of Don Coyote
Challee, William
1946   Without Reservations
1947   Desperate
1948   Tap Roots
1951   Gambling House
1957   Raintree County
1960   Cimarron
        The Plunderers
Challenger, Percy
1917   The Sudden Gentleman
1918   Little Red Decides
1920   Uncharted Channels
1921   Wolves of the North
Chalmers, Thomas
1927   Blind Alleys
1952   Anything Can Happen
Chalyapin, Feador, Jr.
1926   Into Her Kingdom
Chamberlin, Howland
1948   Angel in Exile
1949   Thieves' Highway
1952   High Noon
Chamberlin, J. R.
1917   The Bar Sinister
Chambers, Janice
1939   The Adventures of Huckleberry Finn
Chambers, Kathleen
1924   Defying the Law
Chambers, Lyster
1915   Marse Covington
1919   A Fallen Idol
Chambers, Phil
1953   The Man from the Alamo
        Tumbleweed
1954   Drums Across the River
        Overland Pacific
1955   Foxfire
1957   Raintree County
Chambers, Robert W.
1922   Cardigan
Chambers, Wheaton
1940   Geronimo
1943   Gangway for Tomorrow
1946   South of Monterey
1947   The Mighty McGurk
        On the Old Spanish Trail
1949   The Undercover Man

1950   The Baron of Arizona
1951   The Magnificent Yankee
        The Well
1952   Wagons West
1953   The Member of the Wedding
1957   The Oklahoman
1958   Gunman's Walk
Champagne, Adrine
1953   Thunder Bay
Champion, a horse
1935   Melody Trail
        The Singing Vagabond
1936   Ride, Ranger, Ride
1937   Boots and Saddles
1941   Under Fiesta Stars
1947   The Last Round-Up
1949   The Cowboy and the Indians
1950   Indian Territory
1952   Apache Country
Champion, Gower
1951   Show Boat
Champion, John C.
1955   Shotgun
Champion, Marge
1951   Show Boat
Champion, Pokey
1936   Star for a Night
Chan, Doris
1947   Little Mister Jim
1948   The Lady from Shanghai
Chan, Frances
1944   Black Magic
1945   Samurai
Chan, George
1946   Shadows Over Chinatown
Chan, Luke
1932   The Secrets of Wu Sin
1935   Charlie Chan in Shanghai
1942   Submarine Raider
1943   Bataan
1944   The Chinese Cat
1945   Samurai
Chan, Michael
1943   The Amazing Mrs. Holliday
Chan, Spencer
1942   Across the Pacific
1945   Betrayal from the East
1947   The Chinese Ring
        Little Mister Jim
1949   We Were Strangers
1950   The Breaking Point
1951   The House on Telegraph Hill
Chance, Larry
1952   Battles of Chief Pontiac
1955   The Rose Tattoo
1957   War Drums
1958   Fort Bowie
        Fort Massacre
1959   Al Capone
1960   Flaming Star
        Pay or Die
Chandlee, Dick
1943   Yankee Doodle Dandy
Chandlee, Harry
1936   Let's Sing Again
        Rainbow on the River
1945   Rhapsody in Blue
1947   The Jolson Story
1949   Tale of the Navajos
Chandler, Anna
1934   Broadway Bill
Chandler, Bill
1952   Fort Osage
Chandler, Chick *same as* **Chandler, Chic**
1925   Red Love
1936   Star for a Night
1937   One Mile from Heaven
1938   Mr. Moto Takes a Chance
        Speed to Burn
1943   Action in the North Atlantic
1945   Nob Hill
1948   Music Man
1951   Show Boat
1953   The Eddie Cantor Story

Chandler, David
1951   Apache Drums
1953   Jack McCall Desperado
1957   Tomahawk Trail
Chandler, Eddy *same as* **Chandler, Ed; Chandler, Eddie** *not the same as* **Chandler, Edwin**
1934   Broadway Bill
1936   Show Boat
1937   Black Legion
1939   Gone With the Wind
        Waterfront
1940   East of the River
        Knute Rockne—All American
        Murder over New York
        Santa Fe Trail
1942   All Through the Night
        In This Our Life
1943   Action in the North Atlantic
        Good Luck, Mr. Yates
        In Old Oklahoma
1944   Charlie Chan in the Secret Service
1945   A Medal for Benny
1947   California
        Easy Come, Easy Go
        The Mighty McGurk
Chandler, Edwin *not the same as* **Chandler, Eddy**
1947   Easy Come, Easy Go
1957   The Guns of Fort Petticoat
Chandler, George
1930   The Last Dance
1932   Me and My Gal
1934   He Was Her Man
1937   Big City
        Charlie Chan at the Olympics
        One Mile from Heaven
1938   Gateway
        Mr. Moto's Gamble
        Rascals
1939   Mr. Moto Takes a Vacation
1941   Western Union
1942   Castle in the Desert
1943   The Amazing Mrs. Holliday
        The Ox-Bow Incident
1944   Buffalo Bill
        Since You Went Away
        Three Men in White
1945   The Shanghai Cobra
1947   It Had To Be You
1948   The Miracle of the Bells
        The Paleface
        Reaching from Heaven
1949   Knock on Any Door
1950   Battleground
1951   Across the Wide Missouri
        Westward the Women
1952   My Man and I
        Rose of Cimarron
1955   Apache Ambush
Chandler, Helen
1929   Mother's Boy
1933   Dance Hall Hostess
Chandler, Janet
1932   The Golden West
1935   Cowboy Holiday
        Cyclone of the Saddle
Chandler, Jeff
1950   Broken Arrow
        Deported
        Two Flags West
1952   The Battle at Apache Pass
        Red Ball Express
1953   The Great Sioux Uprising
1954   Taza, Son of Cochise
        War Arrow
1955   Foxfire
1956   Pillars of the Sky
1957   Man in the Shadow
1959   The Jayhawkers!
        Thunder in the Sun
1960   The Plunderers
Chandler, Joan
1947   Humoresque

Chandler, Lane
1927	Open Range
1931	The Hurricane Horseman
	Riders of the Rio
1934	The Battling Buckaroo
1935	North of Arizona
1937	Law and Lead
	The Plainsman
1938	Passport Husband
1940	Charlie Chan in Panama
	Hi-Yo Silver
	Santa Fe Trail
1942	Secret Enemies
	They Died With Their
	Boots On
1943	In Old Oklahoma
	Riding High
	They Came to Blow Up
	America
1946	Saratoga Trunk
1947	California
	Duel in the Sun
1948	The Arizona Ranger
	The Paleface
	Red River
	Unconquered
1950	Ambush
1951	The Well
1953	The Charge at Feather
	River
1955	Apache Ambush
	The Indian Fighter
	Shotgun
1956	The Lone Ranger

Chandler, Mack
1950	Mystery Street
	Right Cross
1951	Go for Broke!
1960	The Adventures of
	Huckleberry Finn

Chandler, Robert
| 1929 | Hawk of the Hills |

Chandler, Tanis
1945	Wanderer of the
	Wasteland
1946	Shadows Over Chinatown
	The Trap
1948	16 Fathoms Deep

Chandler, Warren
| 1918 | The Birth of a Race |
| 1919 | The Gray Towers Mystery |

Chaney, Bill
| 1941 | Playmates |
| 1944 | Block Busters |

Chaney, Frances
| 1951 | Saturday's Hero |

Chaney, Lon
1916	The Gilded Spider
	The Grip of Jealousy
1918	A Broadway Scandal
1920	Outside the Law
1921	Bits of Life
1922	Flesh and Blood
	Shadows

Chaney, Lon, Jr. *sometimes also
known as* **Lon Chaney**
1937	Life Begins in College
	One Mile from Heaven
	Slave Ship
	That I May Live
1938	Happy Landing
	Josette
	Mr. Moto's Gamble
	Passport Husband
	Road Demon
	Speed to Burn
1939	City in Darkness
1942	North to the Klondike
1945	The Mummy's Curse
1948	16 Fathoms Deep
1951	Only the Valiant
1952	Battles of Chief Pontiac
	High Noon
1954	Passion
1955	The Indian Fighter
	Not As a Stranger
1956	Daniel Boone, Trail
	Blazer
1958	The Defiant Ones

Chang, Anna
| 1932 | The Hatchet Man |

Chang, Key H.
| 1945 | Betrayal from the East |

Chang, King Hoo
| 1930 | Son of the Gods |

Chang, Li Ho *see* **Pablo, Juan J.**

Chang, Melie
| 1942 | Little Tokyo, U.S.A. |

Chanler, William C.
| 1930 | The Silent Enemy |

Channing, Ruth
| 1934 | Laughing Boy |
| | Lazy River |

Chanslor, Roy
| 1942 | The Navy Comes Through |
| | Unseen Enemy |

Chantal, Marcelle
1930	El secreto del doctor
	(*foreign version*)
	Toda una vida (*foreign
	version*)

Chantal, Monique
| 1951 | Go for Broke! |

Chapin, Alice
| 1921 | Anne of Little Smoky |

Chapin, Anne Morrison
| 1946 | The Sailor Takes a Wife |
| 1948 | Big City |

Chapin, Billy
| 1955 | A Man Called Peter |
| | Violent Saturday |

Chapin, Eunice
| 1935 | Señora casada necesita |
| | marido |

Chapin, Frederic *same as* **Chapin, Frederick**
1916	The Woman in 47
1917	The Peddler
1919	Auction of Souls

Chapin, Jack
| 1937 | Waikiki Wedding |
| 1940 | Geronimo |

Chapin, Michael
1947	The Farmer's Daughter
1948	Call Northside 777
	Night Wind
1952	Wagons West

Chapin, Robert
| 1938 | Passport Husband |
| 1942 | Prisoner of Japan |

Chaplin, Charles, Jr.
| 1959 | Night of the Quarter |
| | Moon |

Chaplin, Sydney
| 1956 | Pillars of the Sky |

Chapman, Bob
| 1934 | The Cat's-Paw |

Chapman, Edythe
1917	The Little American
1918	The Gypsy Trail
	Huck and Tom; or, the
	Further Adventures of
	Tom Sawyer
	The Only Road
	Sandy
1919	Deliverance
1920	Huckleberry Finn
1921	Bits of Life
	A Tale of Two Worlds
1922	Saturday Night
1923	The Miracle Makers
1930	Take the Heir

Chapman, Freddie *same as* **Chapman, Fred**
1944	Buffalo Bill
	Sheriff of Las Vegas
1945	Colorado Pioneers
	Great Stagecoach Robbery
	Nob Hill
	The Valley of Decision
1946	California Gold Rush
1947	Easy Come, Easy Go
	It Had To Be You
1948	Fighting Father Dunne
	My Girl Tisa
1949	We Were Strangers

Chapman, Helen
| 1959 | The Last Angry Man |

Chapman, Hugh
| 1941 | Belle Starr |

Chapman, Jack
| 1946 | Till the End of Time |

Chapman, Janet
| 1943 | Dr. Gillespie's Criminal |
| | Case |

Chapman, Lonny
| 1956 | Baby Doll |

Chapman, Marguerite
1940	Charlie Chan at the Wax
	Museum
1942	Submarine Raider

Charbert, Philip
| 1941 | This Woman Is Mine |

Charell, Erik
| 1934 | Caravane |

Charello, George "Shorty"
| 1948 | The Lady from Shanghai |

Charisse, Cyd
1946	Three Wise Fools
1949	The Kissing Bandit
1951	The Mark of the
	Renegade

Charles, Captain
| 1919 | His Parisian Wife |

Charles, Hugh
| 1950 | Young Man with a Horn |

Charles, John
| 1915 | A Texas Steer |

Charles, Leon
1944	Tomorrow the World!
1952	The Raiders
1955	Foxfire
1956	The Benny Goodman
	Story
1957	The Midnight Story

Charles, Lewis
1950	Panic in the Streets
1952	Anything Can Happen
1955	The Rose Tattoo
1959	Al Capone

Charles, Thomas
| 1916 | The Yellow Passport |

Charles, Wanita
| 1947 | Calendar Girl |

Charles, Zachary A.
| 1951 | Gambling House |

Charlesworth, Ellen
| 1950 | A Lady Without Passport |

Charlita
1952	Apache War Smoke
	The Iron Mistress
1953	Ride, Vaquero!
1954	Massacre Canyon

Charlot, Andre
1943	They Came to Blow Up
	America
1945	The Dolly Sisters
1947	The Foxes of Harrow
1950	Annie Get Your Gun
	The Toast of New Orleans

Charney, Kim
| 1957 | The Guns of Fort |
| | Petticoat |

Charney, Libby
| 1938 | The Singing Blacksmith |

El Charro Gil y sus Caporales
| 1939 | El trovador de la radio |

Charsky, Sonia
1951	The House on Telegraph
	Hill
1953	Cry of the Hunted

Charters, Spencer
1923	Little Old New York
1930	Whoopee
1932	The Match King
1935	Romance in Manhattan
1936	My American Wife
1937	Waikiki Wedding
1938	Breaking the Ice
	In Old Chicago
	The Texans
1939	Drums Along the Mohawk
1940	Girl from God's Country
	Lucky Cisco Kid
	Santa Fe Trail
	Three Faces West
1942	Juke Girl
	They Died With Their
	Boots On
1943	Yankee Doodle Dandy

Chase, Alden *see* **Chase, Stephen**

Chase, Bill
| 1949 | Souls of Sin |

Chase, Borden
1948	Red River
1950	Winchester '73
1958	Ride a Crooked Trail

Chase, Charley
1930	Una cana al aire
	Locuras de amor
	El príncipe del dólar
	El príncipe del dólar
	(*foreign version*)
1931	Monerías
1936	Kelly the Second

Chase, Colin
1916	The Grip of Jealousy
1917	The Bond Between
	Her Own People
1923	Snowdrift
1935	The Cyclone Ranger
1937	The Plainsman

Chase, Francis, Jr.
| 1955 | Kentucky Rifle |

Chase, Frank
1950	Winchester '73
1952	Red Ball Express
1953	Seminole
	So Big
	Thunder Bay
1954	Saskatchewan
1956	Walk the Proud Land
1958	The Rawhide Trail
	Ride a Crooked Trail

Chase, Stephen *same as* **Chase, Alden; Chase, Stephan**
1934	The Prescott Kid
1935	The Little Colonel
	So Red the Rose
1940	New Moon
1941	Hold Back the Dawn
1949	The Daring Caballero
1950	Emergency Wedding
	North of the Great Divide
1951	Cavalry Scout
	Gambling House
1952	Hiawatha
1953	The Great Sioux Uprising

Chatburn, Jean
| 1935 | Naughty Marietta |

Chatkin, David J.
| 1943 | Good Luck, Mr. Yates |

Chatman, Frank
| 1922 | Foolish Lives |

Chatterton, Ruth
| 1928 | Sins of the Fathers |

Chatterton, Tom
1940	Covered Wagon Days
1944	An American Romance
	Marshal of Reno
	Tucson Raiders
1945	Colorado Pioneers
1946	Sheriff of Redwood Valley
	Without Reservations
1947	California

Chaudet, Louis William
| 1917 | Follow the Girl |

Chautard, Emile *same as* **Chautard, Emil**
1917	Under False Colors
1918	A Daughter of the Old
	South
	The Ordeal of Rosetta
1919	His Parisian Wife
1924	Untamed Youth
1927	The Love Mart
	Whispering Sage
1930	Amor audaz (*foreign
	version*)
1931	Echec au roi
	La gran jornada (*foreign
	version*)
	Le petit café
	El proceso de Mary
	Dugan (*foreign
	version*)
1932	Le bluffeur
1933	L'amour guide
	The California Trail

Chauvin, Lilyan
| 1960 | Walk Like a Dragon |

Chavez, Ernie
1952   The Ring
Chavez, José
1956   Comanche
Chay, Betty
1949   Illegal Entry
Chayefsky, Paddy
1955   Marty
Chayes, Anita
1935   Bar-Mitzvah
Cheaney, Loia
1938   The Beloved Brat
Cheatham, Jack
1934   Straight Is the Way
1938   In Old Chicago
1946   The Gay Cavalier
Chee-ak see **Mala, Ray**
Cheeka
1930   The Silent Enemy
Cheever, Russ
1949   House of Strangers
Chefe, Jack
1935   Charlie Chan in Shanghai
1941   Accent on Love
        Louisiana Purchase
        They Dare Not Love
1942   Tales of Manhattan
1945   Rhapsody in Blue
1947   It Had To Be You
1949   Illegal Entry
1953   Dream Wife
1954   Dangerous Mission
Chehuan, Fernando
1955   Seven Cities of Gold
Cheirel, Micheline
1941   Hold Back the Dawn
Chekhov, Michael
1946   Abie's Irish Rose
Chelieu, Armán
1934   La buenaventura
Don Chema see **Gomez, Carlos**
Chenal, Pierre
1951   Native Son
Chenault, Jack
1920   Within Our Gates
Chenault, Lawrence
1920   The Brute
        The Symbol of the
            Unconquered
1921   The Burden of Race
        The Call of His People
        The Gunsaulus Mystery
        The Secret Sorrow
        The Sport of the Gods
1922   The Crimson Skull
        The Schemers
        Spitfire
1924   Birthright
        The House Behind the
            Cedars
        A Son of Satan
1925   Body and Soul
        The Devil's Disciple
1926   A Prince of His Race
1926?   Ten Nights in a Barroom
1927   Children of Fate
        The Scar of Shame
1932   Out of the Crimson Fog
        Ten Minutes to Live
Cheney, J. Benton
1941   Doomed Caravan
1948   Silver Trails
Cherkose, Eddie
1941   Gauchos of Eldorado
Chermanoff, George
1940   The Mark of Zorro
Cherney, Dick
1958   The Last Hurrah
Cheron, André
1927   Rose of the Golden West
1930   Amor audaz (foreign
            version)
        East Is West (foreign
            version)
1931   Don Juan diplomático
            (foreign version)
        El impostor
1932   Le bluffeur
        Une heure près de toi
        So Big
1934   Caravane
        La veuve joyeuse

1935   L'homme des Folies
            Bergère
1938   Charlie Chan at Monte
            Carlo
1941   Louisiana Purchase
Cherrill, Virginia
1931   Delicious
1933   Charlie Chan's Greatest
            Case
1934   White Heat
Cherrington, Ruth
1942   Rio Rita
        Woman of the Year
1943   Margin for Error
Cherry, Jack
1945   The House on 92nd St.
Cherry, Robert
1944   Since You Went Away
1947   Calendar Girl
1949   That Midnight Kiss
1950   Stars in My Crown
        The Traveling
            Saleswoman
Chesebro, George same as
    Chesboro, George;
    Chesborough, George
1917   The Spirit of '76
1919   The She Wolf
1929   Show Boat
1934   The Fighting Hero
1935   Cyclone of the Saddle
        North of Arizona
        Wolf Riders
1936   Custer's Last Stand
        Pinto Rustlers
1937   Hills of Old Wyoming
        Prairie Thunder
1939   Daughters Courageous
1941   The Pioneers
1945   Colorado Pioneers
        Salome, Where She
            Danced
1946   Santa Fe Uprising
        Singin' in the Corn
        Sun Valley Cyclone
1947   Vigilantes of Boomtown
1948   Fury at Furnace Creek
1949   Lust for Gold
        Ranger of Cherokee Strip
        Roll Thunder Roll!
1950   The Traveling
            Saleswoman
1951   Cyclone Fury
        Oh! Susanna
        Snake River Desperadoes
1952   Indian Uprising
1953   Last of the Comanches
Cheshire, Harry same as **Cheshire,**
    Harry V.
1948   Moonrise
        Night Wind
        16 Fathoms Deep
1949   Anna Lucasta
        The Clay Pigeon
1953   Cry of the Hunted
1954   Dangerous Mission
Chester, Alfred could be same as
    Chester, "Slick"
1948   Miracle in Harlem
Chester, Alma
1935   Cowboy Holiday
1937   The Devil's Playground
Chester, George (actor)
1955   The View from Pompey's
            Head
Chester, George Randolph
    (writer)
1922   The Top O' the Morning
Chester, Lila
1918   The Million Dollar
            Mystery
Chester, Marie
1924?   The Flaming Crisis
Chester, "Slick" could be same as
    Chester, Alfred
1932   Harlem Is Heaven
1935   Lem Hawkins' Confession
1936   Temptation
1937   Underworld
Cheung, Louie
1921   A Tale of Two Worlds

Chevalier, Maurice
1930   The Big Pond
        The Big Pond (foreign
            version)
        Galas de la Paramount
1931   Le petit café
1932   Une heure près de toi
1933   L'amour guide
1934   La veuve joyeuse
1935   L'homme des Folies
            Bergère
Chevalier, Maxine
1948   Unconquered
Chevez, Fabian, Jr.
1950   Two Flags West
Chevret, Lita
1932   Symphony of Six Million
1933   The Man Who Dared: An
            Imaginative Biography
1934   Charlie Chan's Courage
1940   The Fatal Hour
Chew, Frank
1926   Shadows of Chinatown
1929   Chinatown Nights
Chiang, Grace
1931   La carta (foreign
            version)
Chiarini, Luigi
1954   Indiscretion of an
            American Wife
Chiba, Hisa
1952   Japanese War Bride
Childers, Hazel
1915   The Cheat
Childers, Naomi
1921   Hold Your Horses
1934   White Heat
Childress, Alvin
1959   Anna Lucasta
Chiles, George
1930   King of Jazz
Chin, Gum
1930   A Lady to Love
        A Lady to Love (foreign
            version)
Ching, Bo
1943   The Amazing Mrs.
            Holliday
Ching, Hoo
1917   The War of the Tongs
Ching, William
1947   Buck Privates Come
            Home
1951   Oh! Susanna
Chippo, Josephine
1927   Winners of the
            Wilderness
Chirello, George
1960   Pay or Die
Chisholm, William
1917   The Conqueror
Chisney, Betty
1932   Hypnotized
Chissell, Noble "Kid"
1945   Jealousy
1949   Pinky
Chitty, Erik
1960   The Day They Robbed the
            Bank of England
Chivra, Alex
1935   Ruggles of Red Gap
Chodorov, Edward
1937   The Devil's Playground
Chodorov, Jerome
1937   The Devil's Playground
1941   Louisiana Purchase
Chong, Peter
1945   Betrayal from the East
Chong, Won Show
1948   The Lady from Shanghai
Chooluck, Leon
1960   Studs Lonigan
Chordes, Ray
1952   It's a Big Country: An
            American Anthology
Choree, Mrs. could be same as
    Chorre, Gertrude
1934   Behold My Wife!

Chorniuk, Peter
1938   Marusia
Chorre, Clarence
1941   Western Union
Chorre, Gertrude could be same as
    Choree, Mrs.
1929   Frozen Justice
1936   Ramona
1948   Singin' Spurs
1949   We Were Strangers
1950   The Traveling
            Saleswoman
Chorre, Marie
1936   Ramona
Chorre, Sonny
1936   Ramona
1937   The Plainsman
1941   Western Union
1948   The Paleface
Chouteau, Mickie
1960   Cimarron
Chow, Aen Ling
1949   Boston Blackie's Chinese
            Venture
Chow, Chin Kuang
1945   Escape in the Fog
Chow, David
1945   Samurai
Chris see **Tabori, Kris**
Chrisman, Pat
1922   Sky High
Christensen, Miss
1919   The Gray Towers Mystery
Christensen, Benjamin
1928   The Hawk's Nest
Christian, Mr.
1919   Injustice
Christian, Beulah
1946   Notorious
Christian, Carl
1959   Night of the Quarter
            Moon
1960   All the Fine Young
            Cannibals
Christian, Hattie
1921   The Gunsaulus Mystery
Christian, Tony
1950   Battleground
1951   Go for Broke!
Christiani, Rita
1942   Tales of Manhattan
1943   Cabin in the Sky
Christians, Mady
1944   Address Unknown
        Tender Comrade
Christians, Rudolph
1920   The Secret Gift
Christie, Howard
1941   Road Agent
1953   Seminole
1955   Smoke Signal
1957   Joe Dakota
Christie, Ivan see **Christy, Ivan**
Christine, Baby
1916?   Should a Baby Die?
Christine, Virginia
1943   Action in the North
            Atlantic
1945   The Mummy's Curse
        Phantom of the Plains
1948   Night Wind
1952   High Noon
1955   Good Morning, Miss Dove
        Not As a Stranger
1960   Flaming Star
Christmas, Leonard
1939   Harlem Rides the Range
1940   Mystery in Swing
1942   Lucky Ghost
Christopher, Kay
1947   Desperate
1949   Prejudice
Christopher, Robert
1959   Al Capone
1960   Pay or Die
Christy, Dorothy
1930   She Got What She Wanted
1932   The Cohens and Kellys in
            Hollywood
1937   Slave Ship

1951   Oh! Susanna
1953   So Big

Christy, Ivan *same as* **Christie, Ivan**
1930   Son of the Gods
1936   Rose of the Rancho

Christy, Ken
1942   Wings for the Eagle
1947   Jiggs and Maggie in Society
1948   Cry of the City
1950   No Way Out
1951   The Tall Target
1960   All the Fine Young Cannibals

Christy, Laclade
1935   Alas sobre el Chaco

Christy, Nora
1949   The Kissing Bandit

Chrysler, Allen
1958   Flaming Frontier

Chrysler, R.
1934   Straight Is the Way

Chrysler, Walter, Jr.
1953   The Joe Louis Story

Chryson, Kenneth
1955   Headline Hunters

Chrystal, Leon
1939   Tevya

Chuck, Kenneth
1947   The Chinese Ring

Chuen, Ko Lo
1941   Min Jok Jay Hung Sing

Chun, William
1951   The Steel Helmet

Chung, Chan Tien
1941   Min Jok Jay Hung Sing

Chung, Frances
1947   Dark Delusion

Chung, Kei Thing
1951   The House on Telegraph Hill

Chung, Lee
1926   Shadows of Chinatown

Chung, Liu
1918   Mystic Faces

Chung, Walter
1920   Dinty

Chung, Wong
1936   Klondike Annie
1939   King of Chinatown

Church, Allen B.
1950   Two Flags West

Churchill, Berton
1924   Tongues of Flame
1934   Judge Priest
1935   A Night at the Ritz
1936   Dimples
1938   In Old Chicago
1939   Daughters Courageous
1940   Elsa Maxwell's Public Deb No. 1
       The Way of All Flesh

Churchill, Blanche
1934   Broadway Bill

Churchill, Grant
1916   The Daughter of the Don

Churchill, Marguerite
1931   Charlie Chan Carries On

Churchill, Robert B.
1947   West to Glory

Churchill, Savannah
1948   Miracle in Harlem
1949   Souls of Sin

Churchill, Vicki Lee
1955   Headline Hunters

Cianelli, Eduardo *see* **Ciannelli, Eduardo**

Cianelli, Lewis
1951   Teresa

Ciannelli, Eduardo *same as* **Cianelli, Eduardo**
1931   Così è la vita
1936   Winterset
1947   California
1958   Houseboat

Cicero, Mateo
1930   La jaula de los leones

Cichy, Martin
1955   Foxfire

Cimino, Mario
1951   The Great Caruso

Ciolli, Augusta
1955   Marty

Cirici-Ventalló, Matías
1931   El código penal
       ¿Conoces a tu mujer?
       Cuerpo y alma
       Esclavas de la moda
       Hay que casar al príncipe
       El impostor
       La ley del harem

Cirillo, Charles
1958   The Last Hurrah
1960   Pay or Die

Cisar, George
1948   Call Northside 777
1957   The Brothers Rico
1960   All the Fine Young Cannibals

Cisney, Marcella
1949   The Undercover Man

Cisney, Michael
1949   Arctic Manhunt
       The Undercover Man
1950   Jolson Sings Again

Citen, Sam
1929   East Side Sadie

Claar, Loudie
1944   Since You Went Away

Clair, Fanny
1930   Un hombre de suerte (*foreign version*)

Claire, Gertrude
1916   The Aryan
       The Criminal
1926   The Little Irish Girl

Claire, Roy
1935   Circle of Death

Clancy, Carl Stearns
1922   Nanook of the North

Clancy, Ellen
1937   Prairie Thunder

Clancy, Fog Horn
1920   Frontier Days

Clancy, George
1916   Lord Loveland Discovers America

Clancy, Georgia
1950   The Furies

Clancy, Joseph
1918   The Spreading Evil

Clapham, Leonard
1924   The Heritage of the Desert

Clapp, Chester B.
1915   The Sable Lorcha

Clapp, Woodbridge
1918   Broken Ties

Clare, Madelyn
1921?   The Supreme Passion

Clare, Mildred
1933   It's Great to Be Alive

Clarendon, Hal
1914   The Redemption of David Corson

Clark Bros.
1948   Killer Diller

Clark, Anice
1949   Lookout Sister

Clark, Bert
1938   My Lucky Star

Clark, Beulah
1919   A Fighting Colleen

Clark, Camilla
1922   Second Hand Rose

Clark, Carl
1959   The Hanging Tree

Clark, Christopher
1948   Unconquered

Clark, Cliff
1938   Mr. Moto's Gamble
       Speed to Burn
1940   Knute Rockne—All American
       Santa Fe Trail
       Three Cheers for the Irish
1941   Western Union

1942   Mokey
       Secret Enemies
       Young America
1943   Ladies' Day
1944   Andy Hardy's Blonde Trouble
1947   Buck Privates Come Home
       It Had To Be You
1948   Fort Apache
       Jiggs and Maggie in Court
1949   Home of the Brave
1950   Ambush
       The Big Hangover
       The Cariboo Trail
       The Men
1951   Cavalry Scout
       Warpath
1952   The Big Sky
       High Noon
       My Man and I

Clark, Colbert
1935   Harmony Lane
1936   Laughing Irish Eyes
1948   Singin' Spurs
1949   Laramie
1950   Raiders of Tomahawk Creek
1951   Cyclone Fury
       Snake River Desperadoes

Clark, Dane *same as* **Zanville, Bernard**
1942   Sunday Punch
1943   Action in the North Atlantic
1945   Pride of the Marines
1948   Moonrise
1951   Fort Defiance
1954   Go Man Go
       Thunder Pass

Clark, Davison
1934   Straight Is the Way
1937   Souls at Sea
1938   The Buccaneer
       Gateway
1940   Geronimo
1941   Belle Starr
       Prairie Pioneers
1942   Gentleman Jim
1943   Jack London
1944   Charlie Chan in the Secret Service
1948   Cry of the City
       Four Faces West
       Unconquered

Clark, Don R.
1951   Saturday's Hero

Clark, Dort
1958   Never Love a Stranger

Clark, Edward
1917   The Bronze Bride
1926   Millionaires
       Private Izzy Murphy
1927   Sally in Our Alley
1943   The Meanest Man in the World
1945   Where Do We Go From Here?
1947   My Wild Irish Rose
1948   My Girl Tisa
1949   Illegal Entry
1950   Rock Island Trail
       A Ticket to Tomahawk
1951   Gambling House

Clark, Frank (*actor*)
1915   The Rosary
1916   At Piney Ridge
1918   The Yellow Dog
1919   Auction of Souls
       Fighting for Gold
       The Tiger Lily
       Yvonne from Paris
1921   Little Miss Hawkshaw

Clark, Frank Howard (*writer*)
1919   The Last of His People
       Yvonne from Paris
1922   Big Stakes
1924   In High Gear
1926   Under Fire
1928   The Riding Renegade
1932   Wild Horse Mesa

Clark, Fred
1947   Ride the Pink Horse
1948   Cry of the City
       Fury at Furnace Creek
1953   The Stars Are Singing

Clark, Gordon
1947   Bells of San Fernando
       The Foxes of Harrow
1948   Half Past Midnight
1952   The Big Sky

Clark, Harry
1941   Ice-Capades
1952   Anything Can Happen
1953   Taxi

Clark, Harvey *same as* **Clarke, Harvey**
1918   Marked Cards
       Shifting Sands
1921   The Kiss
1922   The Woman He Loved
1926   The Frontier Trail
1927   McFadden's Flats
       Rose of the Golden West
1928   The Night Bird
1933   Olsen's Big Moment
1934   Charlie Chan's Courage
1936   Paddy O'Day
1937   The Devil's Playground
       Souls at Sea
1938   Dangerous to Know
       Spawn of the North

Clark, Jack *same as* **Clark, Jack J.**
1915   The Last of the Mafia
1916   The Innocent Lie

Clark, James B. (*dir*)
1958   Sierra Baron

Clark, Janet Elsie
1936   My American Wife

Clark, Jimmy (*actor*)
1944   They Live in Fear

Clark, Josephine
1916   Peck O' Pickles

Clark, Judy
1944   Minstrel Man
1951   The Girl on the Bridge

Clark, Ken (*actor*)
1956   The Last Wagon

Clark, Lyle
1950   The Big Hangover
1951   The Magnificent Yankee

Clark, Mamo *same as* **Mamo**
1938   Hawaii Calls
1940   Girl from God's Country

Clark, Marguerite
1916   Silks and Satins
1918   Out of a Clear Sky
       Uncle Tom's Cabin
1919   Come Out of the Kitchen

Clark, Milas, Jr. *same as* **Clark, Milas**
1955   Good Morning, Miss Dove
1957   Band of Angels
1958   St. Louis Blues

Clark, Richard *not the same as* **Clark, Richard Dale**
1937   Slave Ship
1939   City in Darkness
1946   Notorious

Clark, Richard Dale *not the same as* **Clark, Richard**
1958   The Last Hurrah

Clark, Robert *not the same as* **Clarke, Robert**
1916   The Sign of the Poppy

Clark, Roger
1942   Submarine Raider
1944   Something for the Boys

Clark, Roy *not the same as* **Clark, Royden**
1915   The Rosary

Clark, Royden *not the same as* **Clark, Roy**
1950   Colt .45

Clark, Russ
1936   Paddy O'Day
1937   One Mile from Heaven
       Slave Ship
       That I May Live
1938   Mr. Moto's Gamble
1941   Hold Back the Dawn
       Western Union

1942	Sunday Punch
1943	Ladies' Day
1947	California
1948	Unconquered
1950	Right Cross

Clark, Sanders
1948	Unconquered

Clark, Sheila
1951	Show Boat

Clark, Steve (*western actor*)
1934	The Prescott Kid
1936	West of Nevada
1941	Thunder Over the Prairie
1942	Lawless Plainsmen
1943	Deerslayer
	Land of Hunted Men
	The Law Rides Again
1944	Riding West
1946	Border Bandits
1947	The Last Round-Up
1949	Ride, Ryder, Ride!
1953	Ambush at Tomahawk
	Gap

Clark, Steven (*actor, beginning circa early 1950s*)
1951	Saturday's Hero

Clark, Tom
1949	Illegal Entry

Clark, Vernon E.
1948	Four Faces West

Clark, Violet
1919	Bonnie, Bonnie Lassie
1920	Locked Lips

Clark, W. T.
1919	Love and the Law

Clark, Wallis *same as* **Clarke, Wallis**
1933	Ever in My Heart
1934	Beloved
	Massacre
	Stand Up and Cheer!
1936	It Had to Happen
1939	Allegheny Uprising
	Gone With the Wind
1942	Gentleman Jim
1943	Jack London
	Yankee Doodle Dandy
1944	Mr. Skeffington
	Since You Went Away
1950	The Toast of New Orleans

Clark, Wyatt
1948?	Junction 88

Clarke, Angela
1949	The Undercover Man
1951	The Great Caruso
	The Harlem Globetrotters
1952	It's a Big Country: An American Anthology
	The Savage
1953	Beneath the 12-Mile Reef

Clarke, David
1942	Foreign Agent
1948	The Boy with Green Hair
1949	Illegal Entry
	Thieves' Highway
1950	Intruder in the Dust
	A Lady Without Passport
	Sands of Iwo Jima
1951	The House on Telegraph Hill
	Only the Valiant
1957	Edge of the City

Clarke, Evelyn
1958	Home Before Dark

Clarke, George
1916	The Flames of Johannis

Clarke, Georgia
1933	It's Great to Be Alive

Clarke, Harvey *see* **Clark, Harvey**

Clarke, Kenneth B. (*writer*)
1916	Lone Star
1918	Untamed
1920	Uncharted Channels

Clarke, Kenny (*musician*)
1947	Jivin' in Be-Bop

Clarke, Lillian *same as* **Clarke, Lilly; Clarke, Lily**
1918	The Hun Within
	Tongues of Flame
	The Yellow Dog

Clarke, Mae *same as* **Langdon, Mae Clarke**
1948	Reaching from Heaven
1950	Annie Get Your Gun
1951	The Great Caruso
1955	Not As a Stranger
1956	The Catered Affair
	Mohawk

Clarke, Paul
1959	Cry Tough

Clarke, Robert *not the same as* **Clark, Robert**
1941	Western Union
1945	Wanderer of the Wasteland
1946	Sunset Pass
1947	Desperate
	The Farmer's Daughter
	Thunder Mountain
	Under the Tonto Rim
1948	Fighting Father Dunne
1949	Riders of the Range
1952	The Fabulous Senorita
1953	Captain John Smith and Pocahontas
1956	The Benny Goodman Story
1957	Band of Angels
1959	The FBI Story

Clarke, Wallis *see* **Clark, Wallis**
1935	Chinatown Squad

Clarke, Westcott B.
1927	Finnegan's Ball

Clary, Charles
1915	The Penitentes
	The Rosary
1917	The Conqueror
1925	Speed Wild
1927	His Foreign Wife

Claude, Toby
1927	Turkish Delight

Claudier, Annette
1958	The Badlanders
1959	The Hanging Tree

Clauson, Bill
1948	The Miracle of the Bells
1950	Stars in My Crown

Clavell, James
1960	Walk Like a Dragon

Clawson, Elliott J.
1917	A Kentucky Cinderella
1918	The Yellow Dog
1919	The Sleeping Lion

Claxton, William F.
1948	Half Past Midnight

Clay, Harry
1943	Gangway for Tomorrow

Clay, Velma
1919	The Little Diplomat

Clays, Lilian *same as* **Clayes, Lillian**
1948	The Miracle of the Bells
1950	Battleground

Clayton, Arthur
1926	Laddie
1934	Charlie Chan in London
	White Heat

Clayton, Buck
1956	The Benny Goodman Story

Clayton, Ethel
1916	Broken Chains
1927	The Princess from Hoboken
1928	Mother Machree
1933	Let's Fall in Love
1937	Souls at Sea
	Waikiki Wedding
1938	The Buccaneer
1939	King of Chinatown
1940	Geronimo
1941	New York Town
1943	Dixie

Clayton, Florence
1948	Fighting Father Dunne

Clayton, Gilbert
1921	Across the Divide
1934	Stand Up and Cheer!

Clayton, James
1956	Frontier Woman

Clayton, Richard
1940	East of the River
	Knute Rockne—All American

Clayton, William A., Jr. *same as* **Clayton, William A.; Clayton, William, Jr.**
1926	A Prince of His Race
1926?	Ten Nights in a Barroom
1927	Children of Fate
1929	When Men Betray
1930	Easy Street
1932	Ten Minutes to Live

Clayworth, June
1934	Strange Wives
1953	Dream Wife

Cleary, Leo
1949	The Red Menace

Cleary, Paul
1951	Saturday's Hero

Cleaver, Zelda
1957	Band of Angels

Clegg, Cy
1932	The Rainbow Trail
1934	Our Daily Bread

Clein, John
1932	Hearts of Humanity
1939	Keep Punching

Clemant, Dora *see* **Clement, Dora**

Clemens, Whitedove
1934	Behold My Wife!

Clement, Clay
1935	Chinatown Squad
1936	It Had to Happen
	Let's Sing Again
1939	Allegheny Uprising

Clement, Dora *same as* **Clemant, Dora**
1934	Laughing Boy
	She Was a Lady
	Stand Up and Cheer!
1936	My American Wife
1938	Hawaii Calls
	My Lucky Star
1941	Sun Valley Serenade

Clemente, Frank Z.
1936	Amor que vuelve

Clemente, Steve *see* **Clemento, Steve**

Clemento, Steve *same as* **Clemente, Steve**
1921	The Double O
1934	Fighting Through
1937	Hills of Old Wyoming
1942	Valley of the Sun

Clements, Flo
1920	Within Our Gates

Clements, Forrest E.
1934	Cheyenne Sun Dance

Clements, Foy
1920	The Brute

Clements, Hal (*actor*) *could be same as* **Clements, Harry** (*dir*)
1915	The Immigrant
	The Secret Sin

Clements, Harry (*dir*) *could be same as* **Clements, Hal** (*actor*)
1918	The Reckoning Day

Clements, Roy
1920	The Tiger's Coat
1921	The Double O
1926	The Devil Horse
1942	Professor Creeps

Clements, Stanley
1941	Accent on Love
1944	Going My Way

Clemons, James
1942	Syncopation
1943	Dixie
1945	Where Do We Go From Here?

Clemons, James, Jr.
1939	Miracle on Main Street
1944	Since You Went Away

Cleveland, George (*actor*)
1934	The Star Packer
1937	Boy of the Streets
1940	Hi-Yo Silver
1941	Playmates
1942	Mexican Spitfire's Elephant
	Valley of the Sun

1943	Ladies' Day
1944	My Pal Wolf
1945	Sunbonnet Sue
1946	Wild Beauty
1947	Easy Come, Easy Go
	My Wild Irish Rose
1948	Fury at Furnace Creek
1951	Flaming Feather
	Fort Defiance
1953	San Antone

Cleveland, George (*writer*)
1930	Sunny Skies

Cleveland, Val *see* **Krusada, Carl**

Clevenger, Beatrice
1914	Dan

Clever, Willy
1931	Chérie (*foreign version*)
	La fiesta del diablo (*foreign version*)

Clewes, Howard
1960	The Day They Robbed the Bank of England

Clexx, Harry
1959	The Jayhawkers!

Cliff, John
1954	Siege at Red River
1957	The Midnight Story
1960	Oklahoma Territory

Cliffe, H. Cooper
1916	Arms and the Woman
	Gold and the Woman

Clifford, Eugene
1925	Scarlet Saint

Clifford, Jack
1914	Threads of Destiny
1936	Dimples
1937	Charlie Chan on Broadway
	The Plainsman
1938	The Buccaneer
1939	Mr. Moto Takes a Vacation
1945	Salome, Where She Danced
1946	Canyon Passage
1947	California
1948	Unconquered

Clifford, Larry
1940	Little Nellie Kelly

Clifford, Mary Lou
1959	The FBI Story

Clifford, Ruth
1917	A Kentucky Cinderella
1918	The Red, Red Heart
1923	April Showers
1927	Don Mike
1934	Stand Up and Cheer!
1936	Paddy O'Day
1948	Cry of the City
	The Luck of the Irish
1949	Prejudice
1952	The Quiet Man
1953	The Sun Shines Bright
1955	A Man Called Peter
1958	The Last Hurrah
1960	Sergeant Rutledge

Clifford, W. C.
1926	Sweet Daddies

Clifford, William H. *same as* **Clifford, W. H.**
1914	Threads of Destiny
1918	Denny from Ireland
	The Ranger
1925	The Black Boomerang

Clift, Denison
1918	His Birthright
	The Midnight Patrol

Clift, Montgomery
1948	Red River
1954	Indiscretion of an American Wife
1957	Raintree County
1958	The Young Lions
1960	Wild River

Clifton, Dorinda
1950	Annie Get Your Gun
1951	Slaughter Trail

Clifton, Elmer
1914	John Barleycorn
1915	The Birth of a Nation
	The Sable Lorcha
1935	Captured in Chinatown
	Cyclone of the Saddle

Clifton, Elmer
1936	Custer's Last Stand
1938	California Frontier
1944	Waterfront
1947	West to Glory

Clifton, Emma Bell
1919	The Little Diplomat

Clifton, Frank M.
1927	Don Mike
1928	Kit Carson

Clifton, Herbert
1937	Souls at Sea

Clifton, Nat "Sweetwater"
1954	Go Man Go

Clifton, Wallace *same as* **Clifton, Wallace C.**
1917	The Secret of Eve
1921	Wolves of the North
1922	The Guttersnipe
	The Top O' the Morning

Cline, Edward F. *same as* **Cline, Eddie; Cline, Edward**
1925	Old Clothes
1928	The Crash
	Vamping Venus
1938	Breaking the Ice
	Hawaii Calls
1944	Since You Went Away
	Slightly Terrific
1946	Bringing Up Father
1947	Jiggs and Maggie in Society
1948	Jiggs and Maggie in Court
1949	Jiggs and Maggie in Jackpot Jitters
1950	Jiggs and Maggie Out West

Clinton, Walter
1951	Saturday's Hero
1958	Marjorie Morningstar

Clisby, Jack *same as* **Clissby, Jack**
1936	General Spanky
1937	Dark Manhattan
1939	Double Deal
1949	Knock on Any Door
	Lookout Sister
	We Were Strangers

Clive, E. E.
1934	Charlie Chan in London
1936	Show Boat
1937	Maid of Salem
1938	Gateway
1939	Mr. Moto's Last Warning

Clive, Henry
1918	I Want to Forget
1919	As a Man Thinks
1933	Obey the Law

Clonblough, G. Butler *see* **Seyffertitz, Gustav von**

Clooney, Rosemary
1953	The Stars Are Singing

Clork, Harry
1947	The Mighty McGurk

Close, John *same as* **Close, Johnny**
1950	The Breaking Point
1951	The Girl on the Bridge
	Jim Thorpe—All-American
1959	Al Capone
1960	Key Witness
	Pay or Die

Clough, Inez
1921	The Gunsaulus Mystery
	The Secret Sorrow
	Ties of Blood
1922	Easy Money
1932	Out of the Crimson Fog

Clovelly, Cecil
1950	So Young, So Bad

Cloy, May
1916	Peck O' Pickles

Clune, W. H.
1916	Ramona
1921	The Girl from God's Country

Clute, Chester
1938	Mr. Moto's Gamble
	Rascals
1940	Elsa Maxwell's Public Deb No. 1
	Too Many Girls
1941	Hold Back the Dawn
	Hurry, Charlie, Hurry
	New York Town
	Sun Valley Serenade

1942	All Through the Night
	Three Hearts for Julia
	Valley of the Sun
1943	The Meanest Man in the World
	Yankee Doodle Dandy
1944	Lake Placid Serenade
	Three Men in White
1946	Canyon Passage
	The Gentleman Misbehaves
	The Sailor Takes a Wife
	Saratoga Trunk
1947	Easy Come, Easy Go
1948	Singin' Spurs
1949	The Girl from Jones Beach

Clute, Sid
1952	Red Ball Express
1956	Mohawk
1959	Inside the Mafia

Clyde, Andy
1935	Annie Oakley
	McFadden's Flats
1937	The Barrier
1939	Bad Lands
1941	Doomed Caravan
	Secret of the Wastelands
1943	Border Patrol
1947	Dangerous Venture
1950	Cherokee Uprising

Clyde, David
1937	The Plainsman
	Souls at Sea
1943	Good Luck, Mr. Yates

Clyde, June
1932	The Cohens and Kellys in Hollywood

Clyde, Neil
1932	Hypnotized

Clymer, John B.
1917	His Sweetheart
	A Wife by Proxy
1920	The Riddle: Woman
1928	Anybody Here Seen Kelly?
1946	The Gentleman Misbehaves

Coakley, Marion
1919	The Lost Battalion

Coates, Phyllis
1958	Blood Arrow

Coates, Shirley
1942	Mokey

Coats, Tommy *same as* **Coates, Tommy**
1940	Geronimo
1941	Mystery Ship
	Western Union
1949	Ranger of Cherokee Strip

Cobb, Edmund *same as* **Cobb, Ed; Cobb, Eddie**
1923	The Sting of the Scorpion
1924	California in '49
1926	General Custer at Little Big Horn
1934	The Prescott Kid
1936	Show Boat
	The Traitor
1940	Prairie Schooners
	Santa Fe Trail
1941	Gauchos of Eldorado
1942	Shut My Big Mouth
1943	Frontier Fury
	In Old Oklahoma
	Jack London
1944	Marshal of Reno
1945	Escape in the Fog
	The Navajo Trail
	Salome, Where She Danced
1946	Renegade Girl
	Santa Fe Uprising
	Sun Valley Cyclone
1947	Buffalo Bill Rides Again
	Oregon Trail Scouts
1948	Fury at Furnace Creek
	The Golden Eye
1949	The Daring Caballero
	Lust for Gold
1950	Comanche Territory
	The Girl from San Lorenzo
	Winchester '73

1952	The Raiders
1953	The Great Sioux Uprising
	Tumbleweed
1954	Broken Lance
	Drums Across the River
	They Rode West
1955	Apache Ambush
1958	The Last Hurrah

Cobb, Geraldine
1948	The Golden Eye

Cobb, Irvin S.
1922	The Five Dollar Baby
1927	Turkish Delight
1938	Hawaii Calls

Cobb, Joe
1941	Where Did You Get That Girl?

Cobb, John
1921	The Lure of a Woman

Cobb, Lee J. *same as* **Cobb, Lee**
1948	Call Northside 777
	The Luck of the Irish
	The Miracle of the Bells
1949	Thieves' Highway *not the same as*
1952	The Fighter
1957	Twelve Angry Men

Cobbs, Ruth
194-	Mistaken Identity

Cobián, Rudy
1939	Los hijos mandan

Coburn, Charles
1940	Three Faces West
1942	In This Our Life
1944	Knickerbocker Holiday
1945	Rhapsody in Blue
1959	John Paul Jones

Coburn, Cleis
1956	The Last Wagon

Coburn, Gladys
1917	The Primitive Call

Coby, Fred
1946	Don Ricardo Returns
	Without Reservations
1948	Unconquered
1949	The Prairie
	Ride, Ryder, Ride!
1952	My Man and I
1953	The Man from the Alamo
1956	Dakota Incident
1959	Last Train from Gun Hill
1960	The Adventures of Huckleberry Finn
	Cimarron
	Key Witness

Cocaine, a horse
1954	Passion

Cocéa, Alice
1931	Su noche de bodas (*foreign version*)

Coch, Edward *same as* **Coch, Ed, Jr.**
1953	The Pathfinder
1955	Seminole Uprising

Cochran, Dorcas
1946	Wild Beauty

Cochran, Gifford
1933	The Emperor Jones

Cochran, Jeane
1952	The Half-Breed

Cochran, Steve
1945	The Gay Senorita
1947	Copacabana
1951	Jim Thorpe—All-American

Cockrell, Marian
1944	Dark Waters

Codee, Ann
1941	Charlie Chan in Rio
	Come Live with Me
1942	Woman of the Year
1944	Mr. Skeffington
1945	Johnny Angel
	The Mummy's Curse
1949	That Midnight Kiss
1950	A Lady Without Passport
1951	Go for Broke!
1952	The Iron Mistress
1958	Kings Go Forth
	The Young Lions

Cody, Bertha
1950	Devil's Doorway

Cody, Bill *same as* **Cody, Bill, Sr.**
1931	Oklahoma Jim
1932	Texas Pioneers
1935	The Cyclone Ranger
1939	The Fighting Gringo

Cody, Frank
1947	Bells of San Fernando

Cody, Harry
1950	Right Cross
1951	The Great Caruso
	The Tall Target

Cody, Iron Eyes *same as* **Iron Eyes**
1932	The Rainbow Trail
1941	Saddlemates
	Western Union
1947	Bowery Buckaroos
	The Last Round-Up
1948	The Dude Goes West
	Indian Agent
	The Paleface
	Unconquered
1949	Arctic Manhunt
	The Cowboy and the Indians
	Massacre River
1950	Broken Arrow
	Cherokee Uprising
	Comanche Territory
	North of the Great Divide
1952	Apache Country
	Apache War Smoke
	Fort Osage
	The Savage
1954	Sitting Bull
1955	Apache Ambush
1956	Westward Ho the Wagons!
	The Wild Dakotas
1958	Gun Fever
	The Light in the Forest

Cody, J. W. *same as* **Cody, Joe; Cody, Joseph William**
1934	Laughing Boy
1941	Western Union
1942	King of the Stallions
1943	Wagon Tracks West
1944	Tahiti Nights
1947	The Last Round-Up
1948	Unconquered
1949	Massacre River
1950	Broken Arrow
1955	Apache Ambush
1958	Bullwhip

Cody, Lew *same as* **Cody, Lewis J.**
1917	Southern Pride
1924	Defying the Law
1931	Beyond Victory

Cody, William F. *same as* **Cody, William Frederick**
1914	The Indian Wars
1917	The Adventures of Buffalo Bill
	The Buffalo Bill Show

Coe, Peter
1945	The Mummy's Curse
1950	Rocky Mountain
	Sands of Iwo Jima
1953	Arrowhead
1954	Passion
1955	Shotgun
	Smoke Signal

Coe, William E.
1938	Mr. Moto's Gamble

Coen, Franklin
1939	Forged Passport
1953	The Glory Brigade
1955	Chief Crazy Horse
	Kiss of Fire
1959	Night of the Quarter Moon

Coffee, Lenore *same as* **Coffee, Lenore J.**
1924	Fools' Highway
1931	The Squaw Man
1940	The Way of All Flesh
1942	They Died With Their Boots On
	We Were Dancing

Coffey, Jack *not the same as*
Coffey, John H.
1944   Chip Off the Old Block
Coffey, John H. *not the same as*
Coffey, Jack
1950   Panic in the Streets
Coffey, Tom
1949   The Undercover Man
Coffin, Estelle
1914   The Littlest Rebel
Coffin, Ida
1940   Am I Guilty?
1942   Lucky Ghost
Coffin, Tristram *same as Coffin,*
Tris; Coffin, Tristam
1940   Arizona Frontier
        Doomed to Die
        Rhythm of the Rio
          Grande
1941   You're Out of Luck
1943   Crime Smasher
1946   Dangerous Money
        G. I. War Brides
        The Gay Cavalier
1948   Shanghai Chest
1950   The Baron of Arizona
        The Big Hangover
1951   Queen for a Day
1952   Indian Uprising
1953   The Eddie Cantor Story
Coffman, Joe W.
1931   Pagliacci
Cogan, Dick
1950   Jolson Sings Again
        Young Man with a Horn
1951   The Great Caruso
        The Magnificent Yankee
        Saturday's Hero
1952   The Iron Mistress
Coghlan, Eileen
1944   Dark Waters
Coghlan, Frank, Jr. *same as*
Coghlan, Junior
1926   The Last Frontier
1927   A Harp in Hock
1933   Racetrack
1936   Charlie Chan at the Race
        Track
1940   Knute Rockne—All
        American
        Murder over New York
1942   Wings for the Eagle
Coghlan, Phillis
1934   Charlie Chan in London
1936   After the Thin Man
1938   Rascals
Cogley, Nick
1919   Toby's Bow
1921   Guile of Women
1929   Abie's Irish Rose
1931   The Cohens and Kellys in
        Africa
Cohan, Morrie *(actor)*
1939   Winner Take All
Cohee, Regina
1921   The Lure of a Woman
Cohen, Albert J.
1935   A Night at the Ritz
1953   The Great Sioux Uprising
Cohen, Bennett
1929   Señor Americano
1930   Song of the Caballero
1938   The Renegade Ranger
Cohen, Bennett R. *same as Cohen,*
Bennett
1947   King of the Bandits
        Robin Hood of Monterey
Cohen, Charles
1939   The Light Ahead
1940   Americaner Schadchen
Cohen, Emanuel
1933   Thundering Herd
1934   Behold My Wife!
        The Great Flirtation
        Limehouse Blues
1935   McFadden's Flats
        Ruggles of Red Gap
Cohen, Herbert S.
1936   Ellis Island

Cohen, Herman
1952   Battles of Chief Pontiac
        Kid Monk Baroni
Cohen, Martin
1950   Catskill Honeymoon
Cohen, Maury M. *(prod)*
1932   The Secrets of Wu Sin
1936   Ellis Island
1939   La Inmaculada
Cohen, Octavus Roy
1929   Why Bring That Up?
Cohen, Sammy *(actor)*
1927   The Auctioneer
1940   The Fighting 69th
Cohen, Samuel H. *(writer)*
1938   Two Sisters
Cohn, Al *same as Cohn, Alfred A.*
1923   Fashion Row
1925   Friendly Enemies
        His People
1926   The Cohens and Kellys
1927   Frisco Sally Levy
1928   The Cohens and the
        Kellys in Paris
        The Jazz Singer
        We Americans
1931   The Cisco Kid
1932   Me and My Gal
        Mystery Ranch
1933   Robbers' Roost
1939   The Return of the Cisco
        Kid
Cohn, Art
1949   Illegal Entry
1951   The Tall Target
1958   Seven Hills of Rome
Cohn, Ben *(western writer)*
1934   The Lone Defender
Cohn, Harry
1926   Sweet Rosie O'Grady
1927   Pleasure Before Business
        Sally in Our Alley
1928   Ransom
1930   Around the Corner
        The Melody Man
Cohn, Jack
1929   The Younger Generation
Cohn, Martin
1941   Caught in the Act
Cohn, Ralph
1947   The Adventures of Don
        Coyote
1948   Sleep, My Love
Cohn, Robert
1950   The Palomino
Coke, Eddie
1943   Action in the North
        Atlantic
        The Amazing Mrs.
        Holliday
1947   Buck Privates Come
        Home
1948   The Lady from Shanghai
        Shanghai Chest
Cokes, Bud
1958   The Last Hurrah
Colbert, Claudette
1927   For the Love of Mike
1930   Amor audaz *(foreign*
        version)
        The Big Pond
        The Big Pond *(foreign*
        version)
1934   Imitation of Life
1937   Maid of Salem
1939   Drums Along the Mohawk
1944   Since You Went Away
1946   Without Reservations
1948   Sleep, My Love
Colbert, Earl
1951   Slaughter Trail
Colbert, Frank
1923   Flames of Wrath
Colby, Marion
1942   Holiday Inn
1948   Singin' Spurs
Colby, Pat
1960   All the Young Men
Colby, William
1917   The Spirit of '76

Colconda, Ligio de *could be same*
as Golconda, Ligia de
1925   Brand of Cowardice
Colcord, Mable
1935   The Irish in Us
1948   The Miracle of the Bells
Coldewey, Anthony *same as*
Coldeway, A. W.; Coldeway,
Anthony
1916   The Morals of Hilda
1922   When East Comes West
1923   Ruggles of Red Gap
1925   Cobra
        A Son of His Father
1927   Old San Francisco
1934   Dos más uno, dos
1944   Marshal of Reno
        Tucson Raiders
        Vigilantes of Dodge City
Coldwell, J.
1923   Deceit
Cole, Celeste
1931   The Exile
Cole, Dona
1955   The Long Gray Line
Cole, Doris Lee
1951   Westward the Women
King Cole Trio
1948   Killer Diller
Cole, Lester
1933   Charlie Chan's Greatest
        Case
1934   Charlie Chan in London
Cole, Nat "King"
1958   St. Louis Blues
1959   Night of the Quarter
        Moon
Cole, Phyllis
1960   I Passed for White
Cole, Roger
1952   The Iron Mistress
        It's a Big Country: An
        American Anthology
Cole, Tommy
1956   Westward Ho the
        Wagons!
Colean, Charles
1949   Knock on Any Door
Colebrook, Edward *same as*
Colebrook, Ed
1937   It Could Happen to You
1953   Column South
Colee, Forrest R.
1950   Colt .45
Colega, George
1934   La veuve joyeuse
Coleman, Caryl
1947   Black Gold
Coleman, Charles
1931   Beyond Victory
1932   The Heart of New York
1933   Diplomaniacs
1935   His Family Tree
        Rendezvous
1936   Sins of Man
1938   Gateway
        The Rage of Paris
1940   Mexican Spitfire
        Mexican Spitfire Out
        West
1942   Twin Beds
1943   Mexican Spitfire's Blessed
        Event
1945   The Gay Senorita
1954   Salt of the Earth
Coleman, Cherrie
1917   Crime and Punishment
Coleman, Claudia
1934   Operator 13
        Straight Is the Way
1936   Human Cargo
        Star for a Night
1937   Man of the People
Coleman, Emil
1945   Nob Hill
Coleman, Frank
1921   The Cave Girl
1942   Valley of the Sun
Coleman, Irene
1934   Broadway Bill
1936   After the Thin Man

Coleman, J. W.
1919   Injustice
Coleman, James *could be same as*
Coleman, Jim
1939   Daughter of the Tong
Coleman, Jim *could be same as*
Coleman, James
1929   Show Boat
Coleman, Majel
1929   Romance of the Rio
        Grande
Coleman, Robert
1944   Chip Off the Old Block
Coleman, Ruth
1938   Outside of Paradise
Coleman, Tom
1946   Notorious
1948   Fighting Father Dunne
Colemans, Edward
1953   The Man Behind the Gun
1956   The Lone Ranger
Coles, Mildred
1940   Santa Fe Trail
1941   Hurry, Charlie, Hurry
Colicos, John
1957   War Drums
Coll, Max
1931   Cheri-Bibi
Colleano, Bonar
1950   Give Us This Day
Collentine, Bobbie
1956   Full of Life
Colley, Tom
1951   Saturday's Hero
Collier, Floyd
1951   Saturday's Hero
Collier, Lois
1941   Gauchos of Eldorado
1946   Wild Beauty
Collier, Lorraine
1945   Nob Hill
Collier, Marian
1960   Pay or Die
Collier, Richard
1955   A Man Called Peter
1959   Imitation of Life
Collier, Sherlee
1945   The Valley of Decision
Collier, William, Jr. *same as*
Collier, William (Buster), Jr.
1922   Cardigan
        The Good Provider
1924   Fools' Highway
        The Mine with the Iron
        Door
1930   The Melody Man
1931   Cimarron
        Little Caesar
        Street Scene
Collier, William, Sr.
1931   Mr. Lemon of Orange
1938   Josette
1939   Miracle on Main Street
Collinge, Claire
1921   Love's Plaything
Collinge, Patricia
1944   Tender Comrade
1951   Teresa
Collins, Betty
1932   Hypnotized
Collins, Charles *not the same as*
Collins, Chick
1936   Dancing Pirate
1942   Syncopation
Collins, Chick *not the same as*
Collins, Charles
1938   Daughter of Shanghai
1939   Mr. Moto Takes a
        Vacation
1941   Sullivan's Travels
1943   Dr. Gillespie's Criminal
        Case
Collins, Cora Sue
1934   As the Earth Turns
1935   Harmony Lane
        Naughty Marietta
1938   The Adventures of Tom
        Sawyer

Collins, Eddie
1938　In Old Chicago
1939　Charlie Chan in Honolulu
　　　Charlie Chan in Reno
　　　Drums Along the Mohawk
　　　Heaven with a Barbed
　　　　Wire Fence

Collins, Ervey
1937　The Plainsman

Collins, G. Pat *same as* **Collins,
　George Pat; Collins, Pat**
1934　He Was Her Man
1935　Black Fury
1936　It Had to Happen
　　　Robin Hood of El Dorado
1937　Souls at Sea
1942　They Died With Their
　　　　Boots On
1947　Easy Come, Easy Go
1948　Up in Central Park
1949　The Clay Pigeon
　　　Top O' the Morning
1950　Indian Territory
1951　Gambling House
1957　Beau James

Collins, Gene
1943　Crash Dive
1944　The Sullivans
1948　Fighting Father Dunne
　　　My Girl Tisa

Collins, Hal
1948　The Feathered Serpent

Collins, John *(actor)*
1947　Boy! What a Girl!

Collins, John H. *(dir, writer)*
1915　Cohen's Luck
1916　The Flower of No Man's
　　　　Land
1917　Rosie O'Grady
　　　A Wife by Proxy

Collins, Jose
1916　A Woman's Honor

Collins, Kathleen
1927　The Devil's Saddle
　　　The Overland Stage
1932　Border Devils

Collins, Leroy
1948　The Betrayal

Collins, Lewis D. *same as* **Collins,
　Lew; Collins, Lewis**
1931　Law of the Tong
1936　Down to the Sea
1949　The Cowboy and the
　　　　Prizefighter
　　　Ride, Ryder, Ride!
　　　Roll Thunder Roll!
1950　Cherokee Uprising

Collins, Lucille
1935　The Irish in Us

Collins, Madge
1937　Maid of Salem

Collins, Monte
1922　Come On Over
　　　The Man with Two
　　　　Mothers

Collins, Monte, Jr.
1929　Why Bring That Up?

Collins, Ray
1942　The Navy Comes Through
1946　Three Wise Fools
1953　Column South
1958　Touch of Evil

Collins, Richard
1955　Kiss of Fire
1958　The Badlanders
1960　Pay or Die

Collins, Russell
1950　Damien
1955　Bad Day at Black Rock
1956　The Last Frontier
1957　Raintree County

Collucci, Guido
1917　The Tell-Tale Step

Collum, John
1936　General Spanky

Colman, Ben
1953　The Glass Wall

Colman, Booth
1952　The Big Sky

Colmans, David
1956　Wetbacks

Colmans, Edward
1952　California Conquest
　　　The Iron Mistress
1953　Conquest of Cochise
1955　Headline Hunters
　　　The Last Command
　　　Santa Fe Passage
1957　Raiders of Old California

Colmar, Eric
1953　Captain John Smith and
　　　　Pocahontas

Colmes, Walter
1947　The Burning Cross

Colombet, Louise
1948　I Remember Mama
1950　Battleground
1960　Pay or Die

Colombo, Frances
1932　Amore e morte

Colombo, Louis
1932　Tormento

Colombo, Luigi
1930　Sei tu l'amore

Colombo, Russ
1929　Wolf Song

Colombus, Chris
1949　Lookout Sister

Colomé, Antoñita
1931　Un caballero de frac
　　　La pura verdad

Colominas, Kay
1959　The Black Orchid

Colon, Miriam
1956　Crowded Paradise

Colonna, Alex
1932　Amor in montagna

Colonna, Jerry
1941　Ice-Capades

Colt, Bobby
1950　Catskill Honeymoon

Colton, John
1919　The She Wolf
1930　Sevilla de mis amores
1934　Laughing Boy

Colton, Sam
1935　Bar-Mitzvah

Colton, Scott
1938　Little Miss Roughneck

**Christopher Columbus and his
　Swing Crew**
1939　Moon over Harlem

Colvin, George
1926　The Flying Ace

Colvin, Marion
1920　The Cup of Fury

Colvin, William
1918　The Ranger
1930　The Cohens and the
　　　　Kellys in Scotland

Colwell, James
1922　The Great Alone

Comandini, Adele
1943　Good Luck, Mr. Yates

Comathiere, A. B. *same as*
　**Comethiere, A. B.; De
　Comathiere, A. B.**
1920　The Brute
1923　Deceit
1928　The Midnight Ace
　　　Thirty Years Later
1931　The Exile
1932　The Black King
　　　Ten Minutes to Live
1934　Drums O' Voodoo

Combe, Boyce
1917　Runaway Romany

Combs, Carol
1944　An American Romance

Comerate, Sheridan
1960　Ice Palace

Comerford, Lorraine
1949　Knock on Any Door

Comethiere, A. B. *see* **Comathiere,
　A. B.**

Comi, Paul
1958　The Young Lions
1960　The Dark at the Top of
　　　　the Stairs

Comiskey, Pat
1957　Gun Battle at Monterey

Como, Perry
1944　Something for the Boys

Como, Rossella
1958　Seven Hills of Rome

Comock
1922　Nanook of the North

Comont, Mathilde
1926　Puppets
　　　Rose of the Tenements
1928　Ramona
1930　The Lash
1932　L'athlète incomplet
1936　Robin Hood of El Dorado

Compson, Betty
1918　The Border Raiders
1919　The Little Diplomat
1923　The White Flower
1930　She Got What She Wanted
1931　Three Who Loved
1936　Laughing Irish Eyes
1938　The Beloved Brat

Compton, Dorothy
1933　It's Great to Be Alive

Compton, John
1945　Pride of the Marines
1950　Rock Island Trail
1951　Oh! Susanna

Compton, Joyce
1934　Imitation of Life
1936　Ellis Island
　　　Star for a Night
1946　Dark Alibi

Compton, Juliette
1931　Women Love Once
1932　The Match King
1934　Behold My Wife!

Comstock, Clark
1919　The Westerners
1922　Blazing Arrows
1925　The Red Rider

Conaty, James
1947　The Farmer's Daughter
1950　Emergency Wedding

Conavaras, Nicholas
1952　Anything Can Happen

Concord, Lillian
1916　The Woman in 47

Conde, Carlos
1952　My Man and I

Conde, Rita
1947　Ride the Pink Horse

Condos Brothers
1938　Happy Landing

Conerly, E. S.
1954　Salt of the Earth

Conesa, Manuel *see* **Paris, Manuel**

Four Congaroos
1948　Killer Diller

Conick, Walter
1925　Body and Soul

Conklin, Charles *see* **Conklin,
　Heinie**

Conklin, Chester
1923　Anna Christie
1924　North of Nevada
1927　McFadden's Flats
1941　Sullivan's Travels
1942　Valley of the Sun
1944　Knickerbocker Holiday
1945　Betrayal from the East
1946　Singin' in the Corn
1949　The Golden Stallion
　　　Jiggs and Maggie in
　　　　Jackpot Jitters
　　　Knock on Any Door
1955　Apache Woman

Conklin, Hal
1926　The Strong Man

Conklin, Heinie *same as* **Conklin,
　Charles**
1925　Hogan's Alley
1926　The Fighting Edge
1927　Drums of the Desert
　　　Ham and Eggs at the
　　　　Front
1931　Cimarron
1935　Ruggles of Red Gap
1936　After the Thin Man
　　　My American Wife

Conklin, Russ *same as* **Conklin,
　Rus**
1947　The Foxes of Harrow
1948　Unconquered
1951　Hurricane Island
1952　Anything Can Happen
1953　Arrowhead
　　　The Pathfinder
1955　Seminole Uprising

Conklin, William
1916　The Twin Triangle
1917　Sold at Auction
1926　Sweet Rosie O'Grady
1927　Rose of the Golden West

Conlan, Frank
1948　My Girl Tisa
1949　Border Incident
1950　Devil's Doorway
　　　Winchester '73
1951　The Tall Target

Conley, Bing
1947　The Mighty McGurk

Conley, Onest
1928　Tenderfeet

Conlin, Jimmy *same as* **Conlin,
　James**
1940　The Way of All Flesh
1941　Hurry, Charlie, Hurry
　　　New York Town
　　　Sullivan's Travels
1942　Woman of the Year
1943　Dixie
1949　Knock on Any Door
　　　Prejudice
　　　Tulsa
1953　The Jazz Singer

Conn, Carole
1959　The Jayhawkers!

Conn, Irene
1920　In the Depths of Our
　　　　Hearts

Connell, Richard
1942　Rio Rita

Connelly, Bobby
1916　Britton of the Seventh
1918　Out of a Clear Sky
1920　Humoresque

Connelly, Edward J. *same as*
　Connelly, Edward
1915　Marse Covington
1918　Toys of Fate
1919　False Evidence
1927　Winners of the
　　　　Wilderness
1929　The Desert Rider

Connelly, Helen
1920　Humoresque

Connelly, Marc
1936　The Green Pastures
1943　Cabin in the Sky
1956　Crowded Paradise

Connelly, Paul
1949　Top O' the Morning

Connelly, Peggy
1958　Houseboat

Conner, Duane E.
1953　The Great Sioux Uprising

Conner, Earl
1953　The Great Sioux Uprising

Conner, Gilbert *same as* **Conner,
　Gilbert E.**
1953　The Great Sioux Uprising
1956　Pillars of the Sky

Conners, Barry
1931　The Black Camel
　　　Charlie Chan Carries On
　　　Charlie Chan Carries On
　　　　(foreign version)
1932　Charlie Chan's Chance
　　　Me and My Gal
　　　The Rainbow Trail

1937　Man of the People
　　　That I May Live
1938　Passport Husband
1945　Escape in the Fog
1948　Big City
1950　Ambush
　　　The Traveling
　　　　Saleswoman

Connolly, Barbara
1918   Little Red Decides
Connolly, Jack
1917   A Jewel in Pawn
1919   The Little Diplomat
Connolly, Mattie
1918   The Ranger
Connolly, Walter
1934   Broadway Bill
1935   So Red the Rose
1939   The Adventures of
        Huckleberry Finn
Connor, Alice
1939   Daughters Courageous
        Waterfront
Connor, Della
1915   The Danger Signal
Connor, Edward
1921   Anne of Little Smoky
Connor, Frank
1953   The Sun Shines Bright
Connor, Whitfield
1948   Tap Roots
Connors, Mrs.
1919   A Man's Duty
Connors, Buck
1933   Thundering Herd
1936   My American Wife
1937   The Plainsman
Connors, Chuck
1955   Good Morning, Miss Dove
1957   Tomahawk Trail
Connors, George
1925   The Red Rider
1927   Open Range
Connors, Jack
1918   Woman and the Law
Connors, Kay
1946   Rendezvous 24
Conover, Jean
1925   The Midnight Girl
Conover, Theresa Maxwell
1936   Rainbow on the River
Conrad, Charles *same as* **Conrad,
Charles J.**
1950   Broken Arrow
        No Way Out
        Rock Island Trail
Conrad, Connie
1949   Knock on Any Door
Conrad, Eddie *same as* **Conrad,
Eddy**
1938   Gateway
        Happy Landing
        My Lucky Star
        Road Demon
1940   Behind the News
1941   Hurry, Charlie, Hurry
Conrad, Edith
1934   Straight Is the Way
Conrad, Eugene
1944   Chip Off the Old Block
Conrad, Eve
1949   Pinky
Conrad, Frances
1918   Ruggles of Red Gap
Conrad, George
1952   It's a Big Country: An
        American Anthology
1953   The Glory Brigade
Conrad, Jack
1948   Gentleman's Agreement
Conrad, Mikel *same as* **Conrad,
Mike**
1947   Untamed Fury
1949   Arctic Manhunt
1950   Bandit Queen
1951   Westward the Women
Conrad, Paul
1948   Docks of New Orleans
Conrad, Walter
1956   Full of Life
Conrad, William (*actor, prod*),
1920–1994
1947   Body and Soul
1948   Four Faces West
1953   Cry of the Hunted
1957   The Ride Back

Conrad, William (*silent actor*)
1915   The Last of the Mafia
Conried, Hans
1943   His Butler's Sister
        Hitler's Children
1951   New Mexico
1955   Davy Crockett, King of
        the Wild Frontier
Conroy, Frank
1935   Charlie Chan in Egypt
1937   Charlie Chan at the
        Opera
        Music for Madame
        That I May Live
1941   This Woman Is Mine
1943   Crash Dive
        The Ox-Bow Incident
Conselman, William
1926   Into Her Kingdom
1930   Whoopee
1931   Young Sinners
1935   The Little Colonel
1937   That I May Live
1940   If I Had My Way
Considine, John W., Jr.
1930   Abraham Lincoln
1931   Skyline
1932   Flesh
1936   Robin Hood of El Dorado
1942   Three Hearts for Julia
Considine, Mildred
1920   The Girl of My Heart
Constant, Aina
1945   The Bells of St. Mary's
        Johnny Angel
Conte, John
1939   Confessions of a Nazi Spy
Conte, Richard *same as* **Conte,
Nicholas**
1939   Heaven with a Barbed
        Wire Fence
1948   Call Northside 777
        Cry of the City
1949   House of Strangers
        Thieves' Highway
1951   The Raging Tide
1952   The Fighter
        The Raiders
1956   Full of Life
1957   The Brothers Rico
Conte, Steve
1952   Hiawatha
1957   Gun Battle at Monterey
1959   The Black Orchid
Conti, Albert
1927   The Chinese Parrot
1930   The Melody Man
1931   Don Juan diplomático
        (*foreign version*)
1932   Men Are Such Fools
1934   Beloved
1938   Gateway
Conti, Joe
1940   East of the River
Contreras, Doris
1958   Sierra Baron
Contreras, Miguel *see* **Contreras
Torres, Miguel**
Contreras, Roberto
1958   The Badlanders
Contreras Torres, Miguel *same as*
Contreras, Miguel
1932   Soñadores de la gloria
1935   No matarás
1949   Border Incident
Converse, Evelyn
1917   The Slacker (Metro
        Pictures Corp.)
Converse, Peggy
1943   Good Luck, Mr. Yates
1954   Drum Beat
        They Rode West
Conville, Robert
1918   Laughing Bill Hyde
1921   Cotton and Cattle
Convy, Bert
1958   Gunman's Walk
Conway, Bert
1947   New Orleans
1948   Open Secret
1949   Pinky

Conway, Bill
1941   Sun Valley Serenade
Conway, Curt
1948   Gentleman's Agreement
1949   Illegal Entry
        Knock on Any Door
Conway, Jack *same as* **Conway,
John**
1915   The Penitentes
1916   The Social Buccaneer
1917   A Jewel in Pawn
1918   Little Red Decides
1921   The Kiss
1928   Flying Romeos
1939   Let Freedom Ring
1940   Northwest Passage (Book
        I—Rogers' Rangers)
Conway, Morgan
1939   Charlie Chan in Reno
1940   Three Cheers for the Irish
1943   Jack London
Conway, Patrick
1951   Westward the Women
Conway, Robert
1940   The Mark of Zorro
Conway, Russ *same as* **Conway,
Russell**
1947   Buck Privates Come
        Home
1949   Arctic Manhunt
1950   The Lawless
1951   Tomahawk
1952   Fort Osage
1957   The Midnight Story
Conway, Tom
1942   Cat People
        Rio Rita
1956   Death of a Scoundrel
Conwell, Mary
1947   Untamed Fury
Coogan, Gene
1950   Battleground
1951   Across the Wide Missouri
        Westward the Women
Coogan, Jack, Sr.
1922   My Boy
1925   Old Clothes
Coogan, Jackie
1922   My Boy
1925   Old Clothes
1930   Tom Sawyer
1931   Huckleberry Finn
1959   Night of the Quarter
        Moon
Cook, Christine Larson *see*
Larson, Christine
Cook, Clyde
1927   White Gold
1937   Souls at Sea
Cook, Corey G.
1941   Ż Dymem Pożarów
Cook, Donald
1932   The Heart of New York
1936   Ellis Island
        Show Boat
Cook, Earle Browne
1922   The Dungeon
Cook, Ed
1936   Dimples
Cook, Elisha, Jr. *same as* **Cook,
Elisha**
1937   Life Begins in College
1938   My Lucky Star
1940   Elsa Maxwell's Public
        Deb No. 1
1944   Dark Waters
1954   Drum Beat
1955   The Indian Fighter
        Trial
Cook, Ira
1953   The Stars Are Singing
Cook, Jimmie
1920   Within Our Gates
Cook, Louise
1931   The Exile
Cook, Mark
1931   Delicious
Cook, Maxine
1936   Show Boat

Cook, Myron
1957   Band of Angels
Cook, Norman
1949   Arctic Fury
Cook, Phyllis *same as* **Cooke,
Phyllis**
1942   Three Hearts for Julia
        The Vanishing Virginian
Cook, Rowena
1940   Kit Carson
Cook, Sam
1922   Spitfire
Cook, Tommy
1943   Good Luck, Mr. Yates
1945   The Gay Senorita
        Wanderer of the
        Wasteland
1947   Humoresque
1948   Cry of the City
1949   Daughter of the West
1950   Panic in the Streets
1952   The Battle at Apache Pass
        Rose of Cimarron
1954   Thunder Pass
1956   Mohawk
Cook, Warren
1924   His Darker Self
Cook, Whitfield
1946   The Sailor Takes a Wife
1948   Big City
Cooke, Baldwin
1936   After the Thin Man
Cooke, Baldy
1942   Nazi Agent
Cooke, Hal
1937   Maid of Salem
        Man of the People
1942   Nazi Agent
Cooke, Marie
1948?   Boarding House Blues
        Junction 88
Cooke, Phyllis *see* **Cook, Phyllis**
Cooke, Ray
1937   Man of the People
1939   Daughters Courageous
1941   Playmates
Cooksey, Curtis
1953   Taxi
1956   Death of a Scoundrel
Cooley, Charles
1948   The Paleface
Cooley, Hallam *same as* **Cooley,
Hal**
1916   The Daughter of the Don
1922   The Man with Two
        Mothers
Cooley, Isabelle
1957   Raintree County
1959   Anna Lucasta
1960   I Passed for White
Cooley, James
1936   Ramona
Cooley, Jane
1946   Stars on Parade
Cooley, Ron
1937   Life Begins in College
Cooley, Willard
1918   The Firebrand
Coolidge, Karl
1924   California in '49
Cooling, Maud
1918   Fields of Honor
Coombs, Carol
1948   The Boy with Green Hair
1949   Knock on Any Door
Coombs, Jackie
1927   The Callahans and the
        Murphys
        The Way of All Flesh
1928   Ransom
1934   Straight Is the Way
Coon, Gene L.
1957   Man in the Shadow
Cooney, Debbie
1958   The Last Hurrah
Coontz, Bill
1957   Raiders of Old California
Cooper, Mrs.
1914   The Nightingale

Cooper, Ashley
1922   The Hands of Nara
        The Son of the Wolf
Cooper, Ben
1955   Headline Hunters
        The Last Command
        The Rose Tattoo
Cooper, Bigelow
1917   The Tell-Tale Step
Cooper, Bobby
1943   Good Luck, Mr. Yates
1946   Strange Voyage
Cooper, Charles
1938   The Singing Blacksmith
Cooper, Clancy
1942   All Through the Night
        Juke Girl
        They Died With Their
          Boots On
        Unseen Enemy
        Wings for the Eagle
1943   Deerslayer
        Frontier Fury
        Redhead from Manhattan
1944   Riding West
1947   California
1948   Unconquered
1951   Distant Drums
        The Tall Target
1953   The Man Behind the Gun
1959   The Sheriff of Fractured
          Jaw
Cooper, Clarence
1949   The Quiet One
Cooper, Claude
1914   The Nightingale
Cooper, Dee
1946   The Gay Cavalier
1960   Walk Like a Dragon
Cooper, Dulcie
1922   The Hands of Nara
Cooper, Edna Mae
1928   George Washington
        Cohen
Cooper, Edward *not the same as*
Cooper, Edwin
1933   Diplomaniacs
1936   Human Cargo
        It Had to Happen
1938   Rascals
Cooper, Edwin *not the same as*
Cooper, Edward
1949   Lost Boundaries
Cooper, Gary
1929   Wolf Song
1930   Galas de la Paramount
1931   Fighting Caravans
1934   Operator 13
1935   The Wedding Night
1937   The Plainsman
        Souls at Sea
1946   Saratoga Trunk
1948   Unconquered
1951   Distant Drums
1952   High Noon
        It's a Big Country: An
          American Anthology
1959   The Hanging Tree
Cooper, George *(actor)*, 1892–
1943
1918   Fields of Honor
1923   Suzanna
1926   The Barrier
1931   Gentleman's Fate
1933   Ever in My Heart
        Grand Slam
1934   Broadway Bill
1937   That I May Live
        Think Fast, Mr. Moto
1939   Stand Up and Fight
Cooper, George *(actor, beginning
circa late 1940s)*
1947   Crossfire
1950   Mystery Street
Cooper, Georgia
1935   A Night at the Ritz
Cooper, Gladys
1943   Mr. Lucky
1945   The Valley of Decision

Cooper, Inez
1942   Rio Rita
1947   Riding the California
         Trail
1950   Border Treasure
Cooper, Jackie
1937   Boy of the Streets
1942   The Navy Comes Through
        Syncopation
Cooper, Jeanne
1953   The Man from the Alamo
Cooper, Joseph
1920   Humoresque
Cooper, Ken *same as* **Cooper,
Kenny**
1936   Custer's Last Stand
1937   The Plainsman
1952   Wagons West
Cooper, Mary
1952   Bright Victory
Cooper, Melville
1935   Rendezvous
1940   Escape to Glory
        Murder over New York
Cooper, Merian C.
1933   Diplomaniacs
1936   Dancing Pirate
1938   The Toy Wife
1948   Fort Apache
1949   She Wore a Yellow
         Ribbon
        3 Godfathers
1950   Rio Grande
1952   The Quiet Man
1956   The Searchers
Cooper, Miriam
1915   The Birth of a Nation
1918   The Prussian Cur
        Woman and the Law
1919   Evangeline
Cooper, Olive
1933   The Cohens and Kellys in
         Trouble
1936   Laughing Irish Eyes
1941   Ice-Capades
Cooper, Ralph
1937   Bargain with Bullets
        Dark Manhattan
1938   The Duke Is Tops
1940   Am I Guilty?
        Gang War
Cooper, Ray
1944   Mr. Skeffington
Cooper, Ted
1952   The Half-Breed
Cooper, Tex
1943   The Ox-Bow Incident
Cooper, Walter
1940   Gang War
Cooper, Willis
1937   Thank You, Mr. Moto
        Think Fast, Mr. Moto
1938   Mr. Moto Takes a Chance
Coot, Miss
1947   Going to Glory, Come to
        Jesus
Coote, Robert
1939   Bad Lands
        Mr. Moto's Last Warning
Copelan, Jodie
1958   Ambush at Cimarron Pass
Copeland, Nick
1935   Black Fury
1936   General Spanky
        Treachery Rides the
         Range
1937   The Devil's Playground
        Man of the People
1938   City Streets
1939   The Escape
        Heaven with a Barbed
         Wire Fence
1940   New Moon
Copland, Keith
1942   The Vanishing Virginian
Coppin, Douglas D.
1947   It Had To Be You
Coppin, Grace
1949   Lost Boundaries
1950   So Young, So Bad

Coral, Tito
1934   Un capitán de cosacos
1935   Señora casada necesita
        marido
Corbaley, Kate
1918   Real Folks
Corbay, Laura
1948   The Paleface
Corbell, A. G. *same as* **Corbelle, A.
G.**
1918   The Golden Wall
        My Cousin
Corbett, Ben *same as* **Corbett,
Benjamin; Corbett, Benny**
1921   Shadows of the West
1926   Shadows of Chinatown
1931   Cavalier of the West
        Riders of the Rio
1934   Fighting Through
1935   Circle of Death
1936   For the Service
1939   Trigger Fingers
1944   Buffalo Bill
1949   Colorado Territory
1950   Colt .45
1952   Indian Uprising
1953   The Charge at Feather
        River
1954   They Rode West
Corbett, Glenn
1959   The Crimson Kimono
1960   All the Young Men
        Man on a String
Corbett, Harry
1959   Shake Hands with the
        Devil
Corbett, Olive
1917   The Little Samaritan
Corbett, William
1920   The Face at Your Window
Corby, Ellen
1946   Cuban Pete
        Till the End of Time
1948   Fighting Father Dunne
        I Remember Mama
1957   All Mine to Give
Corcoran, Ann
1943   Yankee Doodle Dandy
Corcoran, Donna
1951   Apache Drums
1955   Violent Saturday
Corcoran, Kevin
1955   Violent Saturday
Corcoran, Noreen
1955   Violent Saturday
1957   Band of Angels
Corday, Andrée
1930   The Big Pond
        The Big Pond *(foreign
        version)*
Corday, Mara
1954   Drums Across the River
1955   Foxfire
1956   Raw Edge
Corday, Marcelle
1926   Into Her Kingdom
1931   Nuit d'Espagne
        Soyons gais
1935   L'homme des Folies
        Bergère
1938   Charlie Chan at Monte
        Carlo
        Happy Landing
        Rascals
1946   Swamp Fire
Corday, Rita *same as* **Corday,
Paula; Croset, Paula**
1943   Gangway for Tomorrow
        Hitler's Children
        Mexican Spitfire's Blessed
         Event
        Mr. Lucky
Cordell, Frank
1933   Robbers' Roost
1937   The Plainsman
1938   The Texans
1940   Geronimo
1944   Buffalo Bill
1947   Duel in the Sun
1949   Streets of Laredo
1952   The Savage
1953   Arrowhead

1957   The Tin Star
Corden, Henry
1952   Hiawatha
1960   The Adventures of
        Huckleberry Finn
Cordero, Thelma
1946   Tall, Tan and Terrific
Cording, Harry
1928   Sins of the Fathers
1934   Strange Wives
1935   Charlie Chan in Paris
        Naughty Marietta
1936   Daniel Boone
        Sutter's Gold
1937   Maid of Salem
1939   The Adventures of
        Huckleberry Finn
        Stand Up and Fight
1940   Santa Fe Trail
1941   Mutiny in the Arctic
1944   An American Romance
1947   California
        Dangerous Venture
1948   Tap Roots
        Unconquered
1949   Lust for Gold
1950   Last of the Buccaneers
1952   Brave Warrior
1953   Ambush at Tomahawk
        Gap
Cordoba, Pedro de *same as* **De
Cordoba, Pedro**
1917   One Law for Both
        Runaway Romany
1918   A Daughter of the Old
        South
1920   The Dark Mirror
1936   Ramona
        Rose of the Rancho
1937   Maid of Salem
1939   City in Darkness
        Man of Conquest
        Winner Take All
1940   The Mark of Zorro
1941   Romance of the Rio
        Grande
1942   Shut My Big Mouth
1944   Tahiti Nights
1945   Club Havana
        In Old New Mexico
1946   Cuban Pete
        Swamp Fire
1947   Robin Hood of Monterey
1948   The Time of Your Life
1949   The Daring Caballero
        Daughter of the West
1950   Comanche Territory
        The Lawless
1951   Cuban Fireball
        Oh! Susanna
        When the Redskins Rode
Cordon, Henry
1950   The Toast of New Orleans
Cordone, Amy
1942   Song of the Islands
Córdova, Arturo de
1939   Los hijos mandan
        Miracle on Main Street
        (foreign version)
1945   A Medal for Benny
1947   New Orleans
Cordova, Fred *(actor)*
1942   North to the Klondike
1947   Pirates of Monterey
        Robin Hood of Monterey
1948   The Feathered Serpent
Cordova, Frederick de *(dir)*
1949   Illegal Entry
1950   Buccaneer's Girl
1953   Column South
Cordova, Leander de
1945   The Gay Senorita
1949   The Mysterious
        Desperado
Cordova, Margarita
1960   Pay or Die
Cordova, Rudolph de
1918   The Birth of a Race
        A Daughter of the Old
        South

Cordovan, Joseph
1959   Night of the Quarter Moon

Cordy, Henry
1945   The House on 92nd St.

Cordy, Mita
1945   The House on 92nd St.

Corey, Eugene
1922   The Guttersnipe

Corey, Jeff
1941   Mutiny in the Arctic
1942   North to the Klondike
          Syncopation
1947   California
1948   Unconquered
1949   Home of the Brave
1950   Rock Island Trail
1951   New Mexico
          Only the Valiant

Corey, Jim
1924   Unseen Hands
1927   Open Range

Corey, Wendell
1950   The Furies
1952   My Man and I
1954   Hell's Half Acre
1958   The Light in the Forest

Corgo, Pelayo
1931   La pura verdad

Corigliano, John
1947   Carnegie Hall

Corio, Rafael
1934   Las fronteras del amor
1940   If I Had My Way
          The Mark of Zorro

Corley, Cynthia
1951   Queen for a Day

Cormack, Bartlett
1930   El cuerpo del delito
1932   Thirteen Women

Corman, Roger
1955   Apache Woman

Cormeny, Rhoda
1950   The Men

Cornejo, Agustín same as **Cornejo**
1934   Cuesta abajo
          El tango en Broadway

Cornell, Ann
1947   Boy! What a Girl!

Cornell, Dale
1944   Address Unknown

Cornell, Harry
1934   Strange Wives

Cornell, James
1947   Easy Come, Easy Go

Cornell, Lillian
1944   Slightly Terrific

Cornell, Robert
1942   Young America

Cornell, Rudolph
1935?   The Irish Gringo

Corner, Sally
1950   Two Flags West
1955   A Man Called Peter

Cornick, Walter
1928   The Midnight Ace

Cornthwaite, Robert
1951   Gambling House
          The Mark of the Renegade

Cornwall, Anne
1926   The Flaming Frontier
1949   Knock on Any Door

Corona, Elvira
1960   The Sign of Zorro

Corrado, Gino
1928   The Cohens and the Kellys in Paris
          The House of Scandal
1929   Señor Americano
1930   Song of the Caballero
1933   Obey the Law
1934   Broadway Bill
          La veuve joyeuse
1935   Charlie Chan in Paris
1936   Rebellion
1938   Dangerous to Know
          Daughter of Shanghai
          Rascals
1939   The Return of the Cisco Kid
          Winner Take All

1940   The Mark of Zorro
          New Moon
1942   We Were Dancing
1945   The Dolly Sisters
          Where Do We Go From Here?
1947   Calendar Girl
          My Wild Irish Rose

Corrado, Gus
1943   Wintertime

Correll, Charles J.
1930   Check and Double Check

Corrigan, D'Arcy
1927   Wild Geese
1935   Rosa de Francia
1936   Klondike Annie
          Ramona
          Show Boat
1938   The Toy Wife

Corrigan, Emmett
1932   The Golden West
          Me and My Gal

Corrigan, James
1923   April Showers

Corrigan, Lloyd
1926   The Campus Flirt
1930   Anybody's War
1936   Dancing Pirate
1940   Elsa Maxwell's Public Deb No. 1
1941   The Mexican Spitfire's Baby
1942   North to the Klondike
1943   Hitler's Children
1944   Lake Placid Serenade
          Since You Went Away
1949   The Girl from Jones Beach
1951   The Last Outpost
          New Mexico
1953   The Stars Are Singing

Corrigan, Ray same as **Benard, Ray; Corrigan, Ray "Crash"**
1935   The Singing Vagabond
1937   The Riders of the Whistling Skull
1943   Land of Hunted Men
1946   Renegade Girl
1955   Apache Ambush

Corsaro, Franco
1930   Monsieur le Fox (foreign version)
1931   La gran jornada (foreign version)
1940   The Mark of Zorro
1944   Three Men in White
1960   Pay or Die

Corsia, Ted de see **De Corsia, Ted**

Cortay, John
1948   Cry of the City

Cortazar, Ernesto
1940   Perfidia

Cortes, Armand same as **Cortez, Armand**
1915   How Molly Malone Made Good
1916   A Woman's Honor
1942   North to the Klondike
1945   Rhapsody in Blue

Cortés, Carlota
1930   Las campanas de Capistrano

Cortesa, Valentina
1949   Thieves' Highway
1951   The House on Telegraph Hill

Cortez and Galante
1934   Strange Wives

Cortez, Alfred could be same as **Curtis, Al**
1946?   House-Rent Party

Cortez, Anita
1918   The Birth of a Race

Cortez, Armand see **Cortes, Armand**

Cortez, Lita
1936   Ramona
          Rebellion

Cortez, Maria
1947   Ride the Pink Horse

Cortez, Ricardo same as **Cortez, Richard**
1929   The Younger Generation
1932   Flesh
          Symphony of Six Million
          Thirteen Women
1937   The Californian
1939   Charlie Chan in Reno
          The Escape
          Heaven with a Barbed Wire Fence
          Mr. Moto's Last Warning
1940   Murder over New York
1941   Romance of the Rio Grande
1942   Rubber Racketeers
1958   The Last Hurrah

Corthell, Herbert
1933   The Cohens and Kellys in Trouble

Cortland, Pat
1956   Giant

Cosbey, Ronnie same as **Cosbey, Ronald; Crosby, Ronnie**
1933   Dance Hall Hostess
          Ever in My Heart
1936   Sutter's Gold
1941   Birth of the Blues

Cosby, Jack LaVern
1935   Rosa de Francia

Cosci, Ello
1930   Toda una vida (foreign version)

Cosgrave, Jack same as **Cosgrove, Jack** could be same as **Cosgrove, John**
1917   The Spirit of '76

Cosgrave, Luke same as **Cosgrove, Luke**
1928   The Mating Call
1931   The Squaw Man
1935   So Red the Rose
1938   The Adventures of Tom Sawyer

Cosgriff, Robert
1941   Caught in the Act

Cosgrove, Douglas
1933   The Man Who Dared: An Imaginative Biography

Cosgrove, Jack see **Cosgrave, Jack**

Cosgrove, John could be same as **Cosgrave, Jack**
1919   Deliverance

Cosgrove, Luke see **Cosgrave, Luke**

Coslow, Sam
1947   Copacabana

Cossar, John
1921   Made in Heaven

Cossart, Ernest
1936   My American Wife
1944   Knickerbocker Holiday
1947   The Jolson Story

Costa, Joseph
1958   Never Love a Stranger

Costa, Ricardo
1946   Notorious

Costa, Robert
1954   Hell's Half Acre

Costanten, Ben
1956   Daniel Boone, Trail Blazer

Costello, Alan Roberts
1960   Ice Palace

Costello, Delmar
1936   Ramona
1946   The Gay Cavalier

Costello, Dolores
1926   The Little Irish Girl
1927   Old San Francisco
1938   The Beloved Brat
          Breaking the Ice

Costello, Don
1941   Ride on Vaquero
1945   Great Stagecoach Robbery
          Nob Hill
1946   The Red Dragon

Costello, Helene
1926   Millionaires

Costello, Jack could be same as **Costello, John**
1939   Winner Take All

Costello, John could be same as **Costello, Jack**
1949   Top O' the Morning
1956   The Catered Affair

Costello, Juan see **Castello, Jack**

Costello, Lou
1942   Rio Rita
1947   Buck Privates Come Home

Costello, Maurice
1923   None So Blind
1927   The Shamrock and the Rose
1941   Lady from Louisiana

Costello, Tom
1934   Broadway Bill

Costello, Willy same as **Castello, William; Castello, Willy; Costello, Willie**
1935   Melody Trail
1940   Phantom of Chinatown
1941   You're Out of Luck
1942   We Were Dancing
1943   Action in the North Atlantic

Costi, Maria
1954   Barefoot Battalion

Costo, Putro
1931   La regina di Sparta

Cota, David
1943   The Leopard Man
1949   Border Incident
1950   A Lady Without Passport

Cotera, Manuel
1932   Amor y vida

Cott, Jonathan
1953   Cry of the Hunted
          Dream Wife

Cotten, Joseph
1944   Since You Went Away
1947   Duel in the Sun
          The Farmer's Daughter
1949   Portrait of Jennie
1950   Two Flags West
1957   The Halliday Brand
1958   Touch of Evil

Cotter, Catherine
1935   Rescue Squad
1936   Pinto Rustlers

Cottman, Herman
1950   Panic in the Streets

Cotton, Carolina
1949   Stallion Canyon
1952   Apache Country

Cottrell, William
1953   Captain John Smith and Pocahontas

Couch, Robert
1929   Hallelujah

Couderc, Pierre
1931   La gran jornada (foreign version)

Coughlin, Kevin
1958   The Defiant Ones

Couillard, Jarvis
1949   Prejudice

Coull, Billy
1945   Where Do We Go From Here?

Coulouris, George
1944   Mr. Skeffington
1947   California
1948   Sleep, My Love

Coulson, Roy
1925   Don Q, Son of Zorro

Coulter, Fraser
1920   The Face at Your Window

Council, Elizabeth
1960   I Passed for White

The Country Gentlemen
1950   The Big Hangover

Counts, Eleanor
1943   Tahiti Honey

Courier, John
1958   Sierra Baron

Courounlis, Gerassimos
1931   Such Is Life
Courtenay, William
1916   The Romantic Journey
Courter, Donna
1948   Unconquered
Courtland, Jerome
1950   Battleground
       The Palomino
1958   Tonka
Courtleigh, Jr., William
1914   The Nightingale
1916   The Innocent Lie
Courtney, Chuck *same as*
   Courtney, Charles
1950   Stars in My Crown
1955   The Long Gray Line
1956   Westward Ho the
       Wagons!
Courtney, Inez
1934   Broadway Bill
1936   Let's Sing Again
Courtney, Jane
1918   The Firebrand
Courtot, Marguerite
1917   Crime and Punishment
1918   The Unbeliever
Courtright, Clyde
1942   Nazi Agent
Courtright, William
1927   Don Mike
1928   Kit Carson
Covan, DeForrest
1939   Reform School
1940?   Mr. Washington Goes to
       Town
1942   Take My Life
1954   Carmen Jones
Covan, Willie
1938   The Duke Is Tops
Covan Studio Dancers
1937   Bargain with Bullets
Coventry, Florence
1915   The Danger Signal
1918   The Golden Wall
Covert, Donald
1956   Man from Del Rio
Covert, Earl
1940   Little Nellie Kelly
Covert, Graham
1947   Desperate
       Under the Tonto Rim
Covington, Bruce
1930   On the Border
Cowan, Ashley
1955   A Man Called Peter
1958   The Young Lions
Cowan, Jerome
1943   Ladies' Day
1944   Minstrel Man
       Mr. Skeffington
1949   The Girl from Jones
       Beach
1950   Young Man with a Horn
Cowan, Karla
1931   Riders of the Rio
1932   The Galloping Kid
Cowan, Lester
1944   Tomorrow the World!
Cowan, Sada
1923   Fashion Row
Cowan, Verlie
1948   The Betrayal
Cowan, Will
1946   Cuban Pete
Cowl, George
1914   Dan
       When Broadway Was a
       Trail
Cowles, Jules
1917   The Bar Sinister
1936   Rose of the Rancho
1937   Big City
1942   Mokey
       Woman of the Year
Cowling, Bruce
1947   Dark Delusion
1950   Ambush
       Battleground
       Devil's Doorway
       A Lady Without Passport

1951   Westward the Women
1952   The Battle at Apache Pass
Cowper, William
1914   The Redemption of David
       Corson
Cox, Aileen Babs
1948   The Golden Eye
Cox, Donald
1950   Two Flags West
Cox, George L.
1919   The Tiger Lily
Cox, Jewell
1922   Foolish Lives
Cox, Morgan
1941   Road Agent
Cox, Rodney *see* **Cameron, Rod**
Cox, Virginia
1949   Brothers in the Saddle
Coxen, Edward *same as* **Coxen, Ed**
1919   Desert Gold
1934   Wheels of Destiny
1938   Little Miss Roughneck
Coy, Robert de
1957   Burden of Truth
Coy, Walter
1950   Colt .45
1952   Bugles in the Afternoon
1953   So Big
1956   Pillars of the Sky
       The Searchers
1959   Gunmen from Laredo
Coyle, James J.
1945   The House on 92nd St.
Coyle, Walter V.
1921   Love's Plaything
Coyne, Jeff
1957   All Mine to Give
Crabbe, Buster *same as* **Crabbe,**
   Larry; Crabbe, Larry "Buster"
1933   Thundering Herd
1936   Desert Gold
1938   Daughter of Shanghai
1946   Swamp Fire
1947   Last of the Redmen
1957   The Lawless Eighties
Craddock, Claudia
1933   A Lady's Profession
Craft, William James
1925   Galloping Vengeance
1929   The Cohens and Kellys in
       Atlantic City
1930   The Cohens and the
       Kellys in Scotland
Crafts, Griffin
1960   I Passed for White
Crago, Bill
1943   Action in the North
       Atlantic
       Air Force
Craig, Adeline
1935   Annie Oakley
Craig, Alan
1959   The FBI Story
Craig, Alec
1936   Winterset
1937   That Girl from Paris
1939   Confessions of a Nazi Spy
1940   Three Cheers for the Irish
1941   Ride on Vaquero
1942   Cat People
1943   Action in the North
       Atlantic
1945   A Tree Grows in Brooklyn
Craig, Blanche
1922   The Good Provider
1924   Two Shall Be Born
Craig, Carolyn
1956   Giant
1958   Apache Territory
1960   Studs Lonigan
Craig, Catherine
1940   Doomed to Die
       Murder over New York
1941   Louisiana Purchase
Craig, Charles
1919   The Gray Towers Mystery
1921   A Divorce of
       Convenience

Craig, Edith
1934   Broadway Bill
1935   Harmony Lane
1936   After the Thin Man
Craig, Hal
1922   The Scrapper
1935   So Red the Rose
1938   Speed to Burn
1939   Waterfront
1942   Gentleman Jim
1943   Action in the North
       Atlantic
Craig, James
1942   Friendly Enemies
       Valley of the Sun
1945   Our Vines Have Tender
       Grapes
1947   Dark Delusion
       Little Mister Jim
1950   A Lady Without Passport
1957   Naked in the Sun
Craig, May
1952   The Quiet Man
Craig, Nell
1931   Cimarron
1934   The Cat's-Paw
1936   Klondike Annie
1941   Birth of the Blues
       New York Town
1942   Dr. Gillespie's New
       Assistant
       Three Hearts for Julia
1943   Dr. Gillespie's Criminal
       Case
1944   Three Men in White
1945   Between Two Women
1947   Dark Delusion
Craig, Rod Scott
1951   Saturday's Hero
Craig, Yvonne
1959   The Young Land
Crail, Marty
1960   Studs Lonigan
Crain, Jeanne
1943   The Gang's All Here
1949   Pinky
Cramer, Dick *see* **Cramer, Richard**
Cramer, Marc *same as* **Kramer,**
   Marc
1937   Song of the City
1944   My Pal Wolf
1945   Johnny Angel
1947   The Adventures of Don
       Coyote
Cramer, Richard *same as* **Cramer,**
   Dick; Cramer, Rychard
1934   The Cat's-Paw
1935   Riddle Ranch
1936   After the Thin Man
       Robin Hood of El Dorado
1937   Man of the People
1938   The Buccaneer
1940   Arizona Frontier
       Northwest Passage (Book
       I—Rogers' Rangers)
Crampton, Howard
1913   Traffic in Souls
1918   The Border Raiders
Crandall, Suzi
1951   Gambling House
Crane, Beverly
1950   Emergency Wedding
Crane, Colleen
1956   Giant
Crane, Doc
1916   Mixed Blood
Crane, Frank Hall *same as* **Crane,**
   Frank
1919   The Scar
1934   'Neath the Arizona Skies
Crane, Fred
1939   Gone With the Wind
1949   The Gay Amigo
Crane, Harold
1915   The Melting Pot
Crane, Jimmy
1945   The Bells of St. Mary's
1948   Moonrise
Crane, Marlene
1956   Giant

Crane, Phyllis
1931   Aloha
1934   Broadway Bill
Crane, Richard
1943   Dr. Gillespie's Criminal
       Case
1950   A Lady Without Passport
1951   The Last Outpost
Crane, Stephen
1944   Cry of the Werewolf
Crane, Ward
1920   The Luck of the Irish
1926   The Flaming Frontier
1927   The Auctioneer
Cranwell, Peter
1953   Seminole
Cravat, Nick
1955   Davy Crockett, King of
       the Wild Frontier
Cravat, Noel
1945   Escape in the Fog
Cravath, Jeff
1937   Life Begins in College
Craven, Eddie
1946   Till the End of Time
Craven, Frank
1933   Best of Enemies
1934   He Was Her Man
1942   In This Our Life
1943   Jack London
Craven, James
1946   Sheriff of Redwood Valley
1949   The Clay Pigeon
1953   The Eddie Cantor Story
       San Antone
Craven, John
1943   Dr. Gillespie's Criminal
       Case
Crawford, Ben
1938   Little Miss Roughneck
Crawford, Broderick
1942   North to the Klondike
1948   The Time of Your Life
1949   Anna Lucasta
1953   Last of the Comanches
1955   Not As a Stranger
Crawford, Earl
1945   The Navajo Trail
Crawford, Florence
1925   The Scarlet West
Crawford, Gwen
1945   The Bells of St. Mary's
Crawford, Joan
1925   Old Clothes
1927   Winners of the
       Wilderness
1947   Humoresque
Crawford, John
1946   Without Reservations
1950   Mystery Street
       Right Cross
1951   Cuban Fireball
       Show Boat
1953   Conquest of Cochise
1954   Battle of Rogue River
1959   John Paul Jones
1960   I Aim at the Stars: the
       Wernher von Braun
       Story
Crawford, Joseph E.
1954   Carmen Jones
Crawford, Kathryn
1929   Señor Americano
1930   King of Jazz
Crawford, Lorraine
1949   The Girl from Jones
       Beach
Crawford, Nancy
1958   The Light in the Forest
Crawford, Oliver
1948   My Girl Tisa
1951   Slaughter Trail
1953   The Man from the Alamo
Crawford, Sam
1921   As the World Rolls On
Crawford, Stuart
1942   Nazi Agent
Crawley, Constance
1916   Lord Loveland Discovers
       America
1917   A Jewel in Pawn

Crean, Patrick
1958   Seven Hills of Rome
Creasman, Pauline
1952   Anything Can Happen
Creed, Roger
1946   Without Reservations
1948   The Miracle of the Bells
1952   The Savage
Crehan, Joseph *same as* **Crehan, Joe**
1934   Strange Wives
1935   Black Fury
1937   Big City
1938   Gateway
        Happy Landing
        Road Demon
1940   Elsa Maxwell's Public Deb No. 1
        Geronimo
        Little Nellie Kelly
        Music in My Heart
        Santa Fe Trail
1942   Gentleman Jim
        They Died With Their Boots On
1943   The Amazing Mrs. Holliday
        Mr. Lucky
1944   An American Romance
        Black Magic
1946   Bad Bascomb
        Dangerous Money
1947   The Foxes of Harrow
1949   Prejudice
1953   San Antone
Creighton, Cathy
1953   So Big
Cremonesi, Paul
1932   Tormento
The Creole Chorus
1938   Spirit of Youth
Creona, Dimitri *same as* **Creona, D.**
1937   Natalka Poltavka
1939   Cossacks in Exile
Crespo, Jorge Juan *same as* **Crespo, Jorge**
1930   Así es la vida
        Sombras de gloria
Crespo, José
1930   Olimpia
        El presidio
        Wu Li Chang
1931   En cada puerto un amor
        La mujer X
        El proceso de Mary Dugan
1933   Dos noches
1934   La ciudad de cartón
        Tres amores
1935   Alas sobre el Chaco
        Angelina o el honor de un brigadier
        Señora casada necesita marido
1936   La última cita
1938   Rascals
        La vida bohemia
1939   Miracle on Main Street (*foreign version*)
1940   Tengo fe en ti
Crews, Laura Hope
1933   Ever in My Heart
        Rafter Romance
1934   Behold My Wife!
1939   Gone With the Wind
1941   New York Town
Crider, Dorothy
1956   Westward Ho the Wagons!
1957   The Guns of Fort Petticoat
Crimmins, Dan
1929   Smiling Irish Eyes
Criner, Gennette *see* **Criner, Janette**
Criner, Janette *same as* **Criner, Gennette**
1919   Injustice
        A Man's Duty

Criner, John
1940   Midnight Shadow
1941   Sullivan's Travels
Criner, Lawrence *same as* **Criner, J. Lawrence; Criner, Laurence**
1926   The Flying Ace
1927   The Millionaire
1928   Black Gold
1937   Bargain with Bullets
1938   The Duke Is Tops
        Life Goes On
1939   Gang Smashers
        One Dark Night
1940   Am I Guilty?
        Gang War
        While Thousands Cheer
1941   The Gang's All Here
        King of the Zombies
        Up Jumped the Devil
1947?   What a Guy
1948   Miracle in Harlem
Crinley, William
1915   Just Jim
Cripps, Kernan
1934   Broadway Bill
1940   Mexican Spitfire Out West
1943   Gangway for Tomorrow
        Ladies' Day
        Mr. Lucky
1945   I Love a Bandleader
        Johnny Angel
        The Valley of Decision
1946   Without Reservations
1947   California
        The Last Round-Up
        My Wild Irish Rose
1949   The Clay Pigeon
Crisp, Donald *same as* **Needham, James**
1915   The Birth of a Nation
1916   Ramona
1917   The Bond Between
        His Sweetheart
        Lost in Transit
        A Roadside Impresario
1925   Don Q, Son of Zorro
1938   The Beloved Brat
1939   Daughters Courageous
1940   Knute Rockne—All American
1945   The Valley of Decision
1955   The Long Gray Line
1958   The Last Hurrah
Crist, Harry C. *see* **Fraser, Harry**
Cristal, Linda
1956   Comanche
1959   Cry Tough
Cristo, Paul
1952   Anything Can Happen
Cristy, A. J.
1931   Delicious
Criswell, Floyd
1937   One Mile from Heaven
1938   The Buccaneer
1942   Woman of the Year
Crittenden, Dwight *see* **Crittenden, T. D.**
Crittenden, T. D. *same as* **Crittenden, Dwight**
1917   The Winged Mystery
1918   Real Folks
1920   The Cup of Fury
1921   A Tale of Two Worlds
Crocker, Harry
1927   Sally in Our Alley
1942   Gentleman Jim
1945   The Great John L.
Crockett, Charles
1926   Into Her Kingdom
        The Vanishing American
1927   The Princess from Hoboken
1930   Abraham Lincoln
Crockett, Dick
1956   Davy Crockett and the River Pirates
        Full of Life
1958   Escape from Red Rock
Crockett, Lute
1948   Key Largo
1949   The Girl from Jones Beach

1950   Colt .45
Crockett, Luther
1950   I Killed Geronimo
1951   Cuban Fireball
        Saturday's Hero
1952   Woman in the Dark
Croft, Douglas
1943   Yankee Doodle Dandy
Croft, Mary
1943   In Old Oklahoma
Cromer, Dean
1957   The Brothers Rico
Cromer, Harold
1948?   Boarding House Blues
Cromwell, John
1930   Tom Sawyer
1944   Since You Went Away
Cromwell, Richard
1935   McFadden's Flats
1943   Crime Smasher
Crone, George *same as* **Crone, George J.**
1930   Así es la vida
1932   Hollywood, ciudad de ensueño
Cronin, Jim
1953   Dream Wife
Cronyn, Hume
1944   Lifeboat
1946   The Sailor Takes a Wife
1949   Top O' the Morning
1956   Crowded Paradise
Crooks, Georgette
1948   The Boy with Green Hair
Crosby, Bing
1930   King of Jazz
1937   Waikiki Wedding
1940   If I Had My Way
1941   Birth of the Blues
1942   Holiday Inn
1943   Dixie
1944   Going My Way
1945   The Bells of St. Mary's
1949   Top O' the Morning
Crosby, Cathy
1959   Night of the Quarter Moon
Crosby, Gene
1923   The Lone Wagon
Crosby, Louis
1947   The Last Round-Up
Crosby, Orma
1922   The Schemers
Crosby, Ronnie *see* **Cosbey, Ronnie**
Crosby, Wade
1942   Gentleman Jim
        They Died With Their Boots On
1943   In Old Oklahoma
1945   Johnny Angel
1947   The Peanut Man
1948   The Paleface
1949   Rose of the Yukon
        Streets of Laredo
1950   The Missourians
1952   Rose of Cimarron
1953   Old Overland Trail
Croset, Paula *see* **Corday, Rita**
Crosland, Alan
1917   The Little Chevalier
1918   The Unbeliever
1927   Old San Francisco
1928   The Jazz Singer
1930   Big Boy
1934   Massacre
Crosman, Henrietta
1915   How Molly Malone Made Good
1936   Charlie Chan's Secret
Cross, Archie
1939   Moon over Harlem
Cross, Dennis
1957   Naked in the Sun
Crossland, Marjorie
1952   Bright Victory
Crossley, Sid
1929   The Younger Generation

Crossman, Melville *see* **Zanuck, Darryl F.**
Crosson, Bob
1956   The Benny Goodman Story
Crothers, Scatman
1951   Yes Sir, Mr. Bones
1959   Porgy and Bess
Crouch, William Forest *same as* **Forest, William**
1947   Reet, Petite and Gone
Crow, Slim
1949   Illegal Entry
Crowe, Eileen
1949   Top O' the Morning
1952   The Quiet Man
1959   Shake Hands with the Devil
Crowe, H. P., U.S.M.C., Lt. Col.
1950   Sands of Iwo Jima
Crowell, Josephine
1915   The Birth of a Nation
        The Penitentes
        A Yankee from the West
1918   The Bravest Way
        Me Und Gott
1919   Diane of the Green Van
Crowell, W. B. F. (*African-American actor*) *not the same as* **Crowell, William**
1922   The Dungeon
1924   Birthright
        The House Behind the Cedars
        A Son of Satan
Crowell, William
1936   The Glory Trail
Crowley, Jane
1948   Call Northside 777
1955   Good Morning, Miss Dove
1959   The FBI Story
Crowley, Kathleen
1955   Seven Cities of Gold
1956   Westward Ho the Wagons!
Crowley, Pat
1956   Walk the Proud Land
1960   Key Witness
Crowley, William X.
1942   Lucky Ghost
        Professor Creeps
Crown, Hilliard
1950   Two Flags West
Croy, Homer
1933   The Cohens and Kellys in Trouble
Crozier, Emmet
1927   Blind Alleys
Crozier, Helen
1947   The Foxes of Harrow
Cruez, Lottie *see* **Kruse, Lottie**
Crutchfield, Les
1959   Last Train from Gun Hill
Crutchley, Rosalie
1950   Give Us This Day
Crute, Sally
1916   Light at Dusk
1917   The Peddler
        The Tell-Tale Step
        A Wife by Proxy
1920?   The Greatest Love
Cruz, Jo de la
1934   The Cactus Kid
Cruz, Joe de la *same as* **Delacruz, Joe; Dellacruz, Joe**
1932   Hidden Valley
        Law and Lawless
1934   The Battling Buckaroo
        The Prescott Kid
1936   Ramona
1939   Frontiers of '49
Cruz, Juan de la
1916   Hop, the Devil's Brew
1920   For the Soul of Rafael
Cruz, Teodoro
1932   Amor y vida
Cruze, James
1917   The Call of the East
1918   The City of Dim Faces
        Hidden Pearls
        The Million Dollar Mystery
        The Source

Cruze, James
1921?	The Slave Market
1923	Ruggles of Red Gap
	Thirty Days
1928	The Mating Call
1930	La fuerza del querer
	She Got What She Wanted
1933	Best of Enemies
	Racetrack
1936	Sutter's Gold

Cruzon, Virginia
1950	Emergency Wedding

Cryer, Jessie
1942	Lucky Ghost
	Professor Creeps
1947	The Foxes of Harrow

Cuarteto México
1935	No matarás

Cucinelli, Enrico
1931	Delicious

Cugat, Xavier
1930	Charros, gauchos y manolas

Cukor, George
1938	The Adventures of Tom Sawyer
1939	Gone With the Wind
1940	Escape
1945	The Valley of Decision
1958	Wild Is the Wind

Cullen, Captain William J.
1919	The Lost Battalion

Culler, Robert
1945	The House on 92nd St.

Cullington, Margaret
1918	Little Red Decides

Culver, Lillian
1953	Dream Wife
	So Big
1958	Home Before Dark

Cumberland, Roscoe
1951	The Harlem Globetrotters

Cumby, William
1936	The Green Pastures

Cumellas, Antonio
1932	Soñadores de la gloria
1933	Dos noches

Cumming, Dorothy
1925	The Manicure Girl

Cummings, Billy
1944	The Sullivans
	Three Men in White
1945	Colorado Pioneers
1947	Oregon Trail Scouts
1948	Fighting Father Dunne

Cummings, Charles
1917	The Hidden Children

Cummings, Constance
1931	The Guilty Generation

Cummings, Dick *see* **Cummings, Richard**

Cummings, Dwight *see* **Cummins, Dwight**

Cummings, Irving
1914	Uncle Tom's Cabin
1918	The Million Dollar Mystery
	Toys of Fate
1919	Auction of Souls
	Mandarin's Gold
	The Scar
1922	Flesh and Blood
1924	Fools' Highway
1929	In Old Arizona
1931	The Cisco Kid
1941	Belle Starr
	Louisiana Purchase
1945	The Dolly Sisters

Cummings, Jack
1935	The Winning Ticket

Cummings, Richard *same as* **Cummings, Dick**
1919	The Delicious Little Devil
1921	No Woman Knows
1922	The Great Alone
	The Top O' the Morning

Cummings, Robert 1867–1949
1914	The Jungle
1916	The Yellow Passport
1917	Crime and Punishment
1920	The Face at Your Window

Cummings, Robert 1908–1990
1935	So Red the Rose
1936	Desert Gold
1937	Souls at Sea
1938	The Texans
1948	Sleep, My Love

Cummings, Ruth
1927	California
1928	Wyoming

Cummings, Susan *could be same as* **Cummings, Suzanne**
1956	Secret of Treasure Mountain
1957	Tomahawk Trail

Cummings, Suzanne *could be same as* **Cummings, Susan**
1955	Headline Hunters

Cummings, Thomas
1922	Cardigan

Cummins, Dwight *same as* **Cummings, Dwight**
1933	El rey de los gitanos
1949	The Cowboy and the Indians

Cummins, Josephine
1957	Raintree County

Cunard, Grace
1936	Show Boat
1945	Great Stagecoach Robbery

Cunard, Myna *same as* **Cunard, Mina**
1916	The Sign of the Poppy
1943	Good Luck, Mr. Yates
1955	Good Morning, Miss Dove

Cunayou
1922	Nanook of the North

Cuneo, Lester
1917	The Hidden Children
1922	Blazing Arrows
	Silver Spurs

Cunning, Patrick Michael
1935	Julieta compra un hijo
1944	Mr. Skeffington

Cunningham, Bob
1959	John Paul Jones

Cunningham, Cecil
1937	Souls at Sea
1938	Daughter of Shanghai
1940	New Moon
1941	Hurry, Charlie, Hurry
1942	Twin Beds
1943	In Old Oklahoma

Cunningham, Jack
1918	The Border Raiders
	The Goddess of Lost Lake
	Little Red Decides
	Real Folks
1920	The Tiger's Coat
1921	Where Lights Are Low
1925	Don Q, Son of Zorro
1931	The Guilty Generation
1933	Thundering Herd
1934	Wagon Wheels
1935	Ruggles of Red Gap

Cunningham, Joe
1940	Knute Rockne—All American
1942	The Navy Comes Through
1943	Dixie

Cunningham, Pete
1956	Frontier Woman

Curci, Elvira
1960	Pay or Die

Curci, Francesco
1931	Pagliacci

Curci, Gennaro
1935	A Night at the Opera
1937	Manhattan Merry-Go-Round
1938	Charlie Chan at Monte Carlo
	Road Demon

Curdins, Harry
1935	Black Fury

Curley, Leo
1952	The Raiders

Curole, Edgar J., Jr.
1950	Panic in the Streets

Curran, Paul
1959	John Paul Jones

Curran, Thomas
1930	The Kibitzer

Currie, Finlay
1960	The Adventures of Huckleberry Finn

Currie, Louise *same as* **Curry, Louise**
1946	Wild West
1947	The Chinese Ring
1951	Queen for a Day

Currier, Frank
1918	Toys of Fate
1923	The Victor
1925	Lights of Old Broadway
1927	California
	The Callahans and the Murphys
	Winners of the Wilderness

Currier, Mary
1941	The Face Behind the Mask
1943	The Meanest Man in the World
	Yankee Doodle Dandy
1944	Three Men in White
1945	The Dolly Sisters
	The Valley of Decision
1947	Body and Soul
	Dark Delusion
	The Foxes of Harrow
1948	Angel in Exile

Curry, Louise *see* **Currie, Louise**

Curry, Mason
1959	Al Capone

Curry, Nathan
1937	Harlem on the Prairie
1940?	Mr. Washington Goes to Town
1942	Lucky Ghost

Curtis, Al *could be same as* **Cortez, Alfred** *not the same as* **Curtis, Alan**
1947?	What a Guy

Curtis, Alan *not the same as* **Curtis, Al**
1946	Renegade Girl
1949	Apache Chief

Curtis, Anthony *see* **Curtis, Tony**

Curtis, Beatrice
1934	Broadway Bill
1937	The Devil's Playground
1938	City Streets

Curtis, Billy
1942	Wings for the Eagle
1946	Three Wise Fools
1947	Buck Privates Come Home
1948	Jiggs and Maggie in Court

Curtis, Bob
1949	The Sky Dragon

Curtis, Dick *same as* **Curtis, Richard**
1936	The Traitor
1938	City Streets
	Little Miss Roughneck
1941	Mystery Ship
1942	Shut My Big Mouth
1943	Jack London
1946	California Gold Rush
	Renegade Girl
	Santa Fe Uprising
	Wild Beauty
1950	Rock Island Trail
1952	Rose of Cimarron

Curtis, Donald
1940	Knute Rockne—All American
1941	Thunder Over the Prairie
1943	Bataan
1946	Bad Bascomb
1950	Two Flags West
1956	7th Cavalry

Curtis, Dorothy
1946	Sunset Pass
1947	Buffalo Bill Rides Again
	The Farmer's Daughter

Curtis, Edward S.
1914	In the Land of the Head Hunters

Curtis, Jack
1918	Free and Equal
	Little Red Decides
	Marked Cards
1934	The Prescott Kid
1936	It Had to Happen
	Sins of Man
1950	Winchester '73

Curtis, Ken
1949	Call of the Forest
	Stallion Canyon
1950	Riders of the Pony Express
	Rio Grande
1952	The Quiet Man
1955	The Long Gray Line
1956	The Searchers
1958	The Last Hurrah
1959	The Young Land

Curtis, Lucile
1950	Mystery Street
1951	The Tall Target
1952	It's a Big Country: An American Anthology
1960	All the Fine Young Cannibals

Curtis, Nathaniel
1948	The Time of Your Life

Curtis, Tony *same as* **Curtis, Anthony**
1950	Winchester '73
1957	The Midnight Story
1958	The Defiant Ones
	Kings Go Forth

Curtis, Willa Pearl *same as* **Curtis, Willa; Curtiss, Willa Pearl**
1938	The Toy Wife
1945	The Valley of Decision
1948	Unconquered
1951	Native Son
1953	Bright Road
	The Sun Shines Bright

Curtiz, Gabriel
1956	Death of a Scoundrel

Curtiz, Michael
1931	Dämon des Meeres
1935	Black Fury
1939	Daughters Courageous
1940	Santa Fe Trail
1943	Yankee Doodle Dandy
1950	The Breaking Point
	Young Man with a Horn
1951	Jim Thorpe—All-American
1953	The Jazz Singer
1960	The Adventures of Huckleberry Finn

Curwood, James Oliver
1927	The Slaver

Cusack, Cyril
1959	Shake Hands with the Devil

Cusanelli, Peter *same as* **Cusanelli, Pete**
1944	Tahiti Nights
1945	The Dolly Sisters
	A Tree Grows in Brooklyn
1946	Saratoga Trunk
1947	The Mighty McGurk
1948	The Lady from Shanghai
1950	Black Hand

Cushing, Peter
1941	They Dare Not Love
1959	John Paul Jones

Custer, Bob
1925	Galloping Vengeance
1927	The Fighting Hombre

Custodio, Ana María
1931	Charlie Chan Carries On (*foreign version*)
	¿Conoces a tu mujer?
	Cuerpo y alma
	Mi último amor

Cuthbertson, Alan
1959	Shake Hands with the Devil

Cutler, Bunty
1940	New Moon
1948	My Girl Tisa

Cutler, Marty
1920	The Brute

Cutler, Victor
1944 My Pal Wolf
1946 Canyon Passage
Cutter, Bob
1934 Song of the Islands
Cutting, Richard *same as* **Cutting, Dick; Cutting, Richard H.**
1953 The Man from the Alamo
War Paint
1954 Drum Beat
Taza, Son of Cochise
1955 Good Morning, Miss Dove
The Gun That Won the
West
Seminole Uprising
Seven Angry Men
Shotgun
1957 War Drums
1958 Ride a Crooked Trail
Cuyas, Andre
1940 The Mark of Zorro
Dabney, Ardella *same as* **Dabney, Ardelle**
1927 The Broken Violin
1928 Thirty Years Later
Dabney, Virginia
1938 Daughter of Shanghai
Dabov, David
1958 The Young Lions
Dadmun, Leon E.
1924 The Lure of Love
Dae, Frank
1938 In Old Chicago
1941 Hold Back the Dawn
1942 Tales of Manhattan
1946 Without Reservations
1947 The Foxes of Harrow
1951 Show Boat
Daggett, Dave
1946 G. I. War Brides
Daggett, Margaret
1937 Souls at Sea
Dagmar, Florence
1915 Chimmie Fadden Out
West
The Kindling
1916 Pudd'nhead Wilson
Dague, Roswell
1923 Jamestown
Dagwell, Bill
1927 Jake the Plumber
Daheim, John
1955 Headline Hunters
Dahl, Arlene
1947 My Wild Irish Rose
1950 Ambush
1953 Sangaree
Dail, Gus
1924 Smiling Hate
Dailey, Dan *same as* **Dailey, Dan, Jr.**
1942 Mokey
Sunday Punch
1950 A Ticket to Tomahawk
1953 Taxi
Dailey, E. V., Rev.
1947 Citizen Saint
Dailey, J. Hammond
1933 Counsellor at Law
Pete Dailey and His Chicagoans
1951 Yes Sir, Mr. Bones
Daisy, a dog
1949 The Valiant Hombre
Daix, Hubert
1930 El secreto del doctor
(*foreign version*)
Dalberg, Camille
1916? Should a Baby Die?
D'Albrook, Sidney *same as* **D'Albrook, Sid; D'Albrook, Sydney**
1919 The Lost Battalion
1922 Little Miss Smiles
1927 The Princess from
Hoboken
1937 Maid of Salem
The Plainsman
1939 Stand Up and Fight
1943 Jack London
The Leopard Man
1948 The Miracle of the Bells

Dale, Allan
1927 The Princess from
Hoboken
Dale, Arvon
1942 Valley of Hunted Men
1947 Calendar Girl
Dale, Bobby
1936 Star for a Night
Dale, Charles
1932 The Heart of New York
1945 Nob Hill
Dale, Donna
1959 Inside the Mafia
Dale, E. L.
1938 City Streets
1941 The Face Behind the
Mask
Dale, Esther
1935 The Wedding Night
1943 The Amazing Mrs.
Holliday
1949 Anna Lucasta
1957 The Oklahoman
Dale, Jim
1953 The Eddie Cantor Story
Dale, JoAnn
1945 Where Do We Go From
Here?
Dale, John V.
1959 The Hanging Tree
Dale, Little "Buck"
1932 The Galloping Kid
Dale, Mike
1952 Red Ball Express
Dale, Nova
1951 Show Boat
Dale, Suzan
1940 Rhythm of the Rio
Grande
Dale, Virginia *circa* 1920
1921 Shadows of the West
Dale, Virginia (*actress, in films from 1938*)
1942 Holiday Inn
1948 Docks of New Orleans
Dale, Vivien
1932 The Cohens and Kellys in
Hollywood
Dales, Arthur
1959 The Sheriff of Fractured
Jaw
Daley, Cass
1943 Riding High
Daley, Jack *same as* **Daly, Jack**
1936 After the Thin Man
Klondike Annie
1937 Big City
Maid of Salem
1938 Little Miss Roughneck
1942 Nazi Agent
1949 Colorado Territory
1950 The Daughter of Rosie
O'Grady
No Way Out
Right Cross
1952 My Man and I
1957 Raintree County
1959 Inside the Mafia
1960 Cimarron
Key Witness
D'Algy, Helena *same as* **d'Algy, Hélène**
1930 Doña mentiras
Un hombre de suerte
1931 Su noche de bodas
(*foreign version*)
1932 El hombre que asesinó
1933 Melodía de arrabal
D'Algy, Tony
1930 El secreto del doctor
Toda una vida
1931 La fiesta del diablo
La incorregible
Lo mejor es reír
Sombras del circo
Dallzell, Paul
1915 Marse Covington
Dalmas, Herbert
1941 Saddlemates
1944 Address Unknown
An American Romance

1947 Last of the Redmen
Dalmer, John
1957 Gun Battle at Monterey
Dalton, Audrey
1954 Drum Beat
Dalton, Bernice
1950 No Way Out
Dalton, Dorothy
1916 Civilization's Child
1920 The Dark Mirror
Dalton, Robert
1938 Passport Husband
Daly, Arnold
1916 The King's Game
Daly, Jack *see* **Daley, Jack**
Daly, James
1960 I Aim at the Stars: the
Wernher von Braun
Story
Daly, Marcella
1925 Tearing Through
Daly, Tom
1947 It Had To Be You
1949 Lust for Gold
1951 The Harlem Globetrotters
Saturday's Hero
1958 Frontier Gun
Daly, William Robert
1914 Uncle Tom's Cabin
1916 At Piney Ridge
Dalya, Jacqueline *same as* **Hilliard, Jacqueline Dalya**
1940 The Gay Caballero
Viva Cisco Kid
1941 Charlie Chan in Rio
Lady from Louisiana
1950 Mystery Submarine
Dalz, John
1958 Never Love a Stranger
Damas, Antonio
1946 Beauty and the Bandit
D'Ambricato, Adrienne *same as* **Ambricourt, Adrienne d'**
1930 Amor audaz (*foreign
version*)
1931 Jenny Lind
Nuit d'Espagne
El proceso de Mary
Dugan
El proceso de Mary
Dugan (*foreign
version*)
Quand on est belle
1933 L'amour guide
Primavera en otoño
1934 La veuve joyeuse
1939 City in Darkness
1946 Saratoga Trunk
Damita, Lily
1931 Fighting Caravans
Le père célibataire
Quand on est belle
Soyons gais
1932 Une heure près de toi
The Match King
Damler, John
1951 The Tall Target
1953 The Charge at Feather
River
1954 They Rode West
1958 Ambush at Cimarron Pass
1959 The FBI Story
1960 Cimarron
Key Witness
Damon, Mark
1960 This Rebel Breed
Damonde, Renée
1931 Quand on est belle
Damone, Vic
1960 Hell to Eternity
Damron, Roy
1951 Show Boat
Damrosch, Walter
1947 Carnegie Hall
Dana, Frederick
1929 Hawk of the Hills
Dana, Leora
1958 Kings Go Forth

Dana, Viola
1915 Cohen's Luck
1916 The Flower of No Man's
Land
1917 Rosie O'Grady
Threads of Fate
1918 The Only Road
1919 False Evidence
1921 Puppets of Fate
1922 The Five Dollar Baby
1926 Kosher Kitty Kelly
Danaroff, Alex
1952 Anything Can Happen
Danches, George
1948 Harpoon
D'Ancora, Maurizio
1931 La fiesta del diablo
(*foreign version*)
D'Andrea, Tom
1945 Pride of the Marines
1947 Humoresque
Dandridge, Dorothy
1941 Four Shall Die
Lady from Louisiana
Sun Valley Serenade
1944 Since You Went Away
1951 The Harlem Globetrotters
1953 Bright Road
1954 Carmen Jones
1959 Porgy and Bess
Dandridge, Putney
1932 Harlem Is Heaven
Dandridge, Ruby
1940 Midnight Shadow
1943 Cabin in the Sky
1946 Saratoga Trunk
1947 My Wild Irish Rose
1948 Tap Roots
Dandridge, Vivian
1953 Bright Road
Dane, Karl
1925 Lights of Old Broadway
1926 War Paint
Dane, Olga
1935 A Night at the Opera
Dane, Patricia
1942 Rio Rita
Dane, Peter
1959 Al Capone
Dane, Robert
1951 The Girl on the Bridge
1952 Red Ball Express
1953 Seminole
Dangcil, Linda
1958 Escape from Red Rock
Danger, Bru
1958 The Rawhide Trail
1959 Al Capone
Dangerfield, George
1917 The Bar Sinister
Daniel, George M.
1922 One Eighth Apache
Daniel, Roberta
1945 The Dolly Sisters
Daniel, Walter
1941 Sun Valley Serenade
Daniele, Salvatore
1949 Thieves' Highway
Daniell, Henry
1942 Castle in the Desert
1950 Buccaneer's Girl
Daniels, Ann
1958 The Young Lions
Daniels, Bebe
1924 The Heritage of the
Desert
1925 The Manicure Girl
1926 The Campus Flirt
1933 Counsellor at Law
Daniels, Betty
1950 The Toast of New Orleans
Daniels, Billy
1947 Sepia Cinderella
1959 Night of the Quarter
Moon
Daniels, Dimples
1946 Beware
Daniels, Eddie
1936 Star for a Night

Daniels, Hank
1947   The Burning Cross
Daniels, Harold
1941   Where Did You Get That
        Girl?
1949   Daughter of the West
1957   Bayou
Daniels, Hon. Josephus
1918   The Spreading Evil
Daniels, Larry
1950   Monticello, Here We
        Come!
Daniels, Lyons
1926   The Flying Ace
Daniels, Mark
1942   Nazi Agent
        The Vanishing Virginian
1947   The Last Round-Up
Daniels, Victor *see* **Thunder
Cloud, Chief**
Daniels, Viola
1951   The Great Caruso
Daniels, Walter
1927   The Dove
Danielson, Cliff
1942   Nazi Agent
        Seven Sweethearts
        Three Hearts for Julia
        The Vanishing Virginian
Dano, Royal
1957   All Mine to Give
        Man in the Shadow
        Trooper Hook
1960   The Adventures of
        Huckleberry Finn
        Cimarron
Dante, Anthony *could be same as*
Dante, Tony
1950   Black Hand
Dante, Jeanne
1959   The FBI Story
Dante, Lionel
1949   Illegal Entry
Dante, Tony *could be same as*
Dante, Anthony
1960   Pay or Die
Dantine, Helmut
1940   Escape
1942   The Navy Comes Through
Danton, Joan
1949   Knock on Any Door
1955   Blackboard Jungle
Danton, Ray
1955   Chief Crazy Horse
1959   Yellowstone Kelly
1960   Ice Palace
Danziger, Abraham J.
1913?   The Lure of New York
Danziger, Edward J.
1949   Jigsaw
1950   So Young, So Bad
Danziger, Harry Lee
1949   Jigsaw
1950   So Young, So Bad
Da Prato, Emilia
1933   It's Great to Be Alive
DaPron, Louis
1946   Slightly Scandalous
DarBoggia, Henry
1951   The Great Caruso
1959   The Black Orchid
Darby, Nettie Belle
1925   The Greatest Love of All
Darby, Thomas
1946?   Fight That Ghost
        House-Rent Party
1947   Hi De Ho
D'Arc, Gizelle
1957   Band of Angels
Darcel, Denise
1950   Battleground
1951   Westward the Women
d'Arcy, Andre
1953   Dream Wife
D'Arcy, Roy
1927   Frisco Sally Levy
        Winners of the
        Wilderness
1937   El capitán Tormenta

Darcy, Sheila *same as* **Wassem,
Rebecca**
1938   Dangerous to Know
        Daughter of Shanghai
1939   King of Chinatown
1951   Tomahawk
Darden, Tasmania
1919   A Man's Duty
DaRe, Aldo *see* **Ray, Aldo**
Dare, Carla
1947   Citizen Saint
Dare, Helena
1947   Jiggs and Maggie in
        Society
1948   Open Secret
1952   Buffalo Bill in Tomahawk
        Territory
Dare, Irene
1938   Breaking the Ice
Dare, Midgie
1944   Something for the Boys
Darian, Fred
1956   Hot Blood
Darien, Frank
1931   Cimarron
1935   Charlie Chan in Shanghai
        The Little Colonel
1938   The Adventures of Tom
        Sawyer
1939   The Adventures of
        Huckleberry Finn
        Stand Up and Fight
1940   Viva Cisco Kid
        The Way of All Flesh
1941   Under Fiesta Stars
1942   Juke Girl
        Syncopation
        Tales of Manhattan
1943   The Gang's All Here
1944   Andy Hardy's Blonde
        Trouble
1946   Bad Bascomb
Darin, Robert
1959   Imitation of Life
Dark Cloud *same as* **Dark Cloud,
Chief; Darkcloud, John**
1915   The Penitentes
1917   John Ermine of the
        Yellowstone
        The Spirit of '76
Dark Cloud, Mrs.
1919   Desert Gold
Dark, Christopher
1957   The Halliday Brand
Dark, Michael
1924   Conductor 1492
1927   The Dove
Dark, Stanley
1916   Man and His Angel
Darling, Ida
1914   The Nightingale
1921   Society Snobs
1926   Irene
1928   The House of Scandal
Darling, Ro Mere *same as* **Darling,
Romiere**
1934   Laughing Boy
1949   The Cowboy and the
        Indians
Darling, W. Scott *same as* **Darling,
Scott**
1927   Topsy and Eva
1937   Boy of the Streets
        Charlie Chan at the
        Opera
1939   Mr. Wong in Chinatown
        The Mystery of Mr. Wong
1940   The Fatal Hour
1947   The Chinese Ring
1948   Docks of New Orleans
        The Golden Eye
        Rocky
        Shanghai Chest
1949   Tuna Clipper
1952   Desert Pursuit
Darmond, Grace
1915   A Texas Steer
Darmour, Larry
1937   Shadows of the Orient
1939   Frontiers of '49

Darmour, Roy
1945   I Love a Bandleader
1948   The Miracle of the Bells
1949   The Undercover Man
1953   The Jazz Singer
1957   Burden of Truth
Darnell, Linda
1940   The Mark of Zorro
1944   Buffalo Bill
1945   The Great John L.
1950   No Way Out
        Two Flags West
1956   Dakota Incident
d'Arno, Albert
1940   Escape
1943   Action in the North
        Atlantic
        They Came to Blow Up
        America
1951   Go for Broke!
1952   Anything Can Happen
        The Big Sky
Darr, Vondell
1940   Little Nellie Kelly
D'Arrast, Harry d'Abbadie
1931   Lo mejor es reír
Darrell, Steve
1942   They Died With Their
        Boots On
1947   On the Old Spanish Trail
1948   Half Past Midnight
1949   The Fighting Kentuckian
1950   Rock Island Trail
1953   Column South
        San Antone
1954   Dangerous Mission
        Drums Across the River
1955   Good Morning, Miss Dove
        The Last Command
        A Man Called Peter
1956   The Last Hunt
1957   Joe Dakota
Darren, James
1957   The Brothers Rico
1958   Gunman's Walk
1960   All the Young Men
Darrieux, Danielle
1938   The Rage of Paris
Darrin, Diana
1958   Blood Arrow
Darro, Frankie *same as* **Darrow,
Frankie**
1924   So Big
1925   The Fearless Lover
1928   Tyrant of Red Gulch
1934   Broadway Bill
1936   Charlie Chan at the Race
        Track
1941   The Gang's All Here
        You're Out of Luck
1951   Across the Wide Missouri
        Westward the Women
D'Art, E. Clement
1917   The Little Chevalier
1917?   Barnaby Lee
D'Artega, Alfonso
1947   Carnegie Hall
Darvas, Charles
1927   The Dove
Darvas, Lili
1960   Cimarron
D'Arville, Collette
1935   Tango Bar
Darwell, Jane
1914   Rose of the Rancho
1915   After Five
1930   Tom Sawyer
1931   Huckleberry Finn
1935   McFadden's Flats
1936   Paddy O'Day
        Ramona
        Star for a Night
1937   Slave Ship
1939   Gone With the Wind
        Miracle on Main Street
1942   All Through the Night
        Young America
1943   The Ox-Bow Incident
1944   Tender Comrade
1946   Three Wise Fools
1949   3 Godfathers
1950   The Daughter of Rosie
        O'Grady

1953   The Sun Shines Bright
1958   The Last Hurrah
Da Silva, Howard *same as* **da Silva,
Howard**
1942   Juke Girl
1948   Unconquered
1949   Border Incident
Dassin, Jules
1942   Nazi Agent
1949   Thieves' Highway
Datig, Fred, Jr.
1948   Unconquered
1950   Sands of Iwo Jima
        Stars in My Crown
Daube, Belle
1934   Coming Out Party
        Operator 13
d'Auburn, Denis
1939   Mr. Moto's Last Warning
Daugherty, Herschel
1958   The Light in the Forest
Daumery, Carrie
1932   L'athlète incomplet
        Le bluffeur
1934   Caravane
        Strange Wives
        La veuve joyeuse
1935   Ruggles of Red Gap
Daumery, Jean
1931   Nuit d'Espagne
1932   Le cas du docteur
        Brenner
        La foule hurle
Dauphin, Claude
1950   Deported
Davalos, Dick
1960   All the Young Men
Daven, André
1934   Caravane
1945   Nob Hill
Davenport, Alice
1918   Little Red Decides
1919   Spotlight Sadie
Davenport, Blanche
1918   The Unbeliever
1919   The Lost Battalion
Davenport, Danny
1951   Queen for a Day
1957   Beau James
Davenport, Doris
1940   Behind the News
Davenport, Dorothy
1916   A Yoke of Gold
1917   The Squaw Man's Son
Davenport, E. L.
1947   Calendar Girl
Davenport, Harry
1938   The Rage of Paris
1939   Gone With the Wind
1942   Tales of Manhattan
1943   The Amazing Mrs.
        Holliday
        Gangway for Tomorrow
        Jack London
        The Ox-Bow Incident
1946   G. I. War Brides
        Three Wise Fools
1947   The Farmer's Daughter
Davenport, Mrs. Harry *same as*
Davenport, H., Mrs.
1916   Ramona
1918   Tony America
Davenport, Milla
1921   The Girl from God's
        Country
1935   The Wedding Night
1936   Human Cargo
Davenport, Ned
1948   The Miracle of the Bells
1953   The Great Sioux Uprising
Daves, Delmer
1945   Pride of the Marines
1950   Broken Arrow
1954   Drum Beat
1955   White Feather
1956   The Last Wagon
1958   The Badlanders
        Kings Go Forth
1959   The Hanging Tree

Daves, Michael
1954   Drum Beat
Davey, Earle
1932   Hypnotized
Davi, Jana
1958   Fort Bowie
        Gun Fever
        The Rawhide Trail
1959   Gunmen from Laredo
David, John
1950   Panic in the Streets
Davidoff, Alex
1944   An American Romance
Davidovitch, Raquel
1932   Ljubav i strast
Davidson, Bert
1948   The Miracle of the Bells
1950   Battleground
        The Big Hangover
        Mystery Street
        Right Cross
1952   Brave Warrior
Davidson, Dore
1920   Humoresque
1922   The Good Provider
1923   None So Blind
1924   Welcome Stranger
Davidson, Jack
1915   The Alien
Davidson, John
1915   The Danger Signal
1917   The Wild Girl
1921   Cheated Love
        No Woman Knows
1922   Saturday Night
1934   Stand Up and Cheer!
1935   Charlie Chan in Egypt
1939   Mr. Moto Takes a
        Vacation
        Mr. Moto's Last Warning
1944   The Chinese Cat
1945   Where Do We Go From
        Here?
1948   The Luck of the Irish
Davidson, Lawford
1928   George Washington
        Cohen
1929   The Overland Telegraph
1930   Ladies Love Brutes
Davidson, Max
1918   The Hun Within
1921   No Woman Knows
1922   Second Hand Rose
1924   Fools' Highway
        Untamed Youth
1925   Hogan's Alley
        Justice of the Far North
        Old Clothes
1926   Into Her Kingdom
1927   Pleasure Before Business
1933   The Cohens and Kellys in
        Trouble
1934   Straight Is the Way
1937   The Plainsman
Davidson, Ray
1934   Broadway Bill
Davidson, Ronald
1940   Hi-Yo Silver
Davidson, William *same as*
  Davidson, William B.
1916   Her Debt of Honor
        The Pretenders
1917   The Call of Her People
1934   Imitation of Life
        Laughing Boy
        Massacre
1935   Bordertown
        A Night at the Ritz
1938   Happy Landing
        The Texans
1940   Three Cheers for the Irish
1941   Sun Valley Serenade
1942   Gentleman Jim
        In This Our Life
        Juke Girl
1943   In Old Oklahoma
        Yankee Doodle Dandy
1944   Since You Went Away
1946   Saratoga Trunk
1947   The Farmer's Daughter
        My Wild Irish Rose

Davies, Blair
1935   Rendezvous
Davies, Daniel
1917   The Hidden Children
Davies, Edna
1921   Cotton and Cattle
Davies, Grace
1934   Stand Up and Cheer!
1942   Song of the Islands
1944   Something for the Boys
Davies, Howard
1917   Her Own People
        The Hidden Children
1918   His Birthright
        The Spreading Evil
1919   Auction of Souls
1936   Ramona
1937   Maid of Salem
Davies, James *not the same as*
  Davis, Jim 1915–1981
1947   California
        Easy Come, Easy Go
1949   Streets of Laredo
1950   The Furies
1957   Beau James
Davies, Lloyd G.
1949   The Red Menace
Davies, Marion
1917   Runaway Romany
1923   Little Old New York
1925   Lights of Old Broadway
1934   Operator 13
Davies, Marjorie
1946   Three Wise Fools
Davies, Marshall
1916   The Colored American
        Winning His Suit
Davies, Richard
1941   Road Agent
1943   The Amazing Mrs.
        Holliday
1960   Cimarron
Davies, Rupert
1959   John Paul Jones
Davies, Sid
1946   Without Reservations
Davies, Valentine
1942   Syncopation
1956   The Benny Goodman
        Story
Davies, Virginia
1942   Song of the Islands
Dávila, Lola
1958   Sierra Baron
Da Vinci, Elena
1958   Escape from Red Rock
Davis, "Chicago" Carl
1949?   Harlem Follies
Davis, A. Porter, Dr.
1921   The Lure of a Woman
Davis, Alan
1937   The Barrier
1938   Passport Husband
1940   Charlie Chan in Panama
        Elsa Maxwell's Public
        Deb No. 1
        Murder over New York
Davis, Ann
1955   A Man Called Peter
Davis, Bette
1932   So Big
1935   Bordertown
1942   In This Our Life
1944   Mr. Skeffington
1956   The Catered Affair
1959   John Paul Jones
Davis, Bob *see* **Davis, Robert O.**
Davis, Bond
1934   Broadway Bill
Davis, Boyd
1943   Dr. Gillespie's Criminal
        Case
1946   Saratoga Trunk
1948   Unconquered
1950   Emergency Wedding
Davis, Bryn
1944   An American Romance
1945   The Valley of Decision
1946   Bringing Up Father

Davis, C.
1927?   You Can't Win
Davis, Carl
1951   Gambling House
Davis, Ches
1951   Yes Sir, Mr. Bones
Davis, Chick
1935   Cyclone of the Saddle
1936   Custer's Last Stand
Davis, Dolly
1930   Un hombre de suerte
        (foreign version)
Davis, Donald
1944   Tender Comrade
Davis, Dorothy Patrick *see*
  Patrick, Dorothy
Davis, Eddie
1945   The Jade Mask
        The Scarlet Clue
        The Shanghai Cobra
        Sunbonnet Sue
1946   Beauty and the Bandit
        Border Bandits
        The Gay Cavalier
        The Red Dragon
        South of Monterey
1947   King of the Bandits
        Riding the California
        Trail
        Robin Hood of Monterey
1948   Silver Trails
Davis, Frank *(actor)*
1931   The Cohens and Kellys in
        Africa
Davis, Frank *(prod, writer)*
1927   California
1930   Olimpia
        El presidio
1931   En cada puerto un amor
        La fruta amarga
        La mujer X
Davis, Frank *(writer)*
1945   A Tree Grows in Brooklyn
1948   Fighting Father Dunne
1951   Jim Thorpe—All-American
1953   The Jazz Singer
1955   The Indian Fighter
1959   Night of the Quarter
        Moon
Davis, Gail
1950   Indian Territory
Davis, George *same as* **Davis,**
  Georges; Davis, Giorgio
1926   Into Her Kingdom
1930   A Lady to Love
        A Lady to Love *(foreign
        version)*
        Monsieur le Fox *(foreign
        version)*
1931   Buster se marie
        Buster se marie *(foreign
        version)*
        Echec au roi
        La gran jornada *(foreign
        version)*
        Le petit café
        El proceso de Mary
        Dugan *(foreign
        version)*
1932   L'athlète incomplet
        Le plombier amoureux
1934   Caravane
        The Cat's-Paw
        La veuve joyeuse
1935   Charlie Chan in Paris
1938   Charlie Chan at Monte
        Carlo
        Passport Husband
1939   City in Darkness
1941   New York Town
1943   Action in the North
        Atlantic
1945   The Dolly Sisters
1948   Big City
1950   Belle of Old Mexico
        The Toast of New Orleans
Davis, Gladys
1941   Sullivan's Travels
Davis, Grant
1945   Where Do We Go From
        Here?

Davis, Gunnis *same as* **Davis, J.**
  Gunnis
1934   Broadway Bill
1936   Show Boat
1937   Souls at Sea
Davis, Harold
1946   Without Reservations
Davis, Harry
1959   The Last Angry Man
Davis, J. Gunnis *same as* **Davis,**
  Gunnis
1923   Jealous Husbands
1931   Charlie Chan Carries On
Davis, Jack
1948   Tap Roots
1956   Crowded Paradise
Davis, James *(African-American*
  actor) same as* **Davis, Jimmy**
  (African-American actor)
1937   Harlem on the Prairie
1941   King of the Zombies
        Sullivan's Travels
Davis, Jean
1944   Chip Off the Old Block
Davis, Jerry
1952   Apache War Smoke
Davis, Jim 1915–1981 *same as*
  Davis, James *not the same as*
  Davies, James
1942   Three Hearts for Julia
1950   The Cariboo Trail
1951   Cavalry Scout
        Little Big Horn
        Oh! Susanna
1952   The Big Sky
        Rose of Cimarron
1955   The Last Command
        The Vanishing American
1956   The Wild Dakotas
1957   Apache Warrior
        Raiders of Old California
1958   Flaming Frontier
Davis, Joan
1937   Life Begins in College
1938   Josette
        My Lucky Star
1941   Sun Valley Serenade
1950   The Traveling
        Saleswoman
Davis, John
1950   The Lawless
Davis, Johnny
1944   Knickerbocker Holiday
Davis, Karl *same as* **Davis, Karl**
  "Killer"
1950   The Daughter of Rosie
        O'Grady
        Sunset in the West
1951   Mask of the Dragon
1957   Apache Warrior
Davis, Lew *same as* **Davis, Lou**
1938   City Streets
Davis, Lisa
1955   The Long Gray Line
Davis, Lou *same as* **Davis, Lew**
1942   Mexican Spitfire at Sea
Davis, Luther
1950   Black Hand
Davis, Marvin
1944   The Sullivans
        Tomorrow the World!
1945   Nob Hill
Davis, Merian Margie
1945   Nob Hill
Davis, Michael
1960   All the Young Men
Davis, Nancy
1952   It's a Big Country: An
        American Anthology
Davis, Ossie
1950   No Way Out
Davis, Owen
1927   Blind Alleys
1928   Chinatown Charlie
1929   Frozen Justice
Davis, Owen, Jr.
1937   It Could Happen to You
1940   Knute Rockne—All
        American

Davis, Robert A. (*African-American actor*) *same as* **Davis, Robert** *not the same as* **Davis, Robert O.**
1949	Knock on Any Door
1950	No Way Out
1951	The Harlem Globetrotters
1952	Red Ball Express

Davis, Robert O. *same as* **Amendt, Rudolf; Amendt, Rudolph; Davis, Bob**
1933	Primavera en otoño
1934	La ciudad de cartón
	Las fronteras del amor
1935	De la sartén al fuego
	Rendezvous
1939	Confessions of a Nazi Spy
1940	Knute Rockne—All American
	The Man I Married
1942	Nazi Agent
1950	The Big Hangover

Davis, Rufe
1941	Gauchos of Eldorado
	Prairie Pioneers
	Saddlemates

Davis, Sally
| 1948 | Harpoon |

Davis, Sammy, Jr.
| 1959 | Anna Lucasta |
| | Porgy and Bess |

Davis, Sammy, Sr.
| 1956 | The Benny Goodman Story |

Davis, Spencer
| 1952 | Anything Can Happen |

Davis, Stanley
| 1941 | Ice-Capades |
| 1944 | Slightly Terrific |

Davis, Susan
| 1958 | Home Before Dark |
| 1959 | The FBI Story |

Davis, Tyrrell
| 1929 | Mother's Boy |

Davis, Virginia
| 1928 | A Ship Comes In |
| 1931 | Street Scene |

Davis, Wee Willie
1942	Gentleman Jim
1947	Calendar Girl
	The Foxes of Harrow

Davis, Will S. *same as* **Davis, William S.**
| 1918 | In Judgment Of |

Davis, William
| 1946 | Beware |

Davis, William S. *same as* **Davis, Will S.**
| 1914 | Springtime |

Davison, Tito
1930	Así es la vida
	La fuerza del querer
	Los que danzan
	El presidio
	Sombras de gloria
1931	Cheri-Bibi
	La gran jornada
1934	Granaderos del amor
1935	Rosa de Francia

Davison, Tito H. *same as* **Davison, Tito**
| 1934 | Laughing Boy |

D'Avril, Yola
1928	Vamping Venus
1930	King of Jazz
1945	Rhapsody in Blue
1952	Red Ball Express

Daw, Marjorie
1920	Dinty
1921	Fifty Candles
1922	The Pride of Palomar
1927	Spoilers of the West
	Topsy and Eva

Dawley, J. Searle
| 1916 | Silks and Satins |
| 1918 | Uncle Tom's Cabin |

Dawn, Isabel
1940	Behind the News
1941	Ice-Capades
1946	Singin' in the Corn

Dawn, Katherine
| 1925 | Justice of the Far North |

Dawn, Norman
1919	Lasca
1920	A Tokio Siren
	White Youth
1921	Wolves of the North
1922	The Son of the Wolf
1925	Justice of the Far North
1936	Tundra
1940	Taku
1949	Arctic Fury

Dawson, Billy
| 1940 | Knute Rockne—All American |
| 1942 | Wings for the Eagle |

Dawson, Diane
| 1953 | The Eddie Cantor Story |

Dawson, Doris
| 1928 | Heart Trouble |

Dawson, Douglas
| 1931 | The Hurricane Horseman |

Dawson, Frank
| 1934 | She Was a Lady |
| 1943 | Crash Dive |

Dawson, Hal K.
1936	My American Wife
	Paddy O'Day
1937	Life Begins in College
	One Mile from Heaven
1938	Gateway
1940	Elsa Maxwell's Public Deb No. 1
1942	Dr. Gillespie's New Assistant
	Song of the Islands
1943	The Meanest Man in the World
	Mr. Lucky
	Riding High
1955	Foxfire
	Trial
1956	The Benny Goodman Story
1957	The Tin Star
1958	The Last Hurrah

Dawson, Ivo
| 1921 | The Money Maniac |

Dawson, Tom
| 1944 | Since You Went Away |

Dax, Donna
| 1945 | In Old New Mexico |
| 1947 | The Jolson Story |

Day, Alice
| 1929 | Is Everybody Happy? |
| 1930 | The Melody Man |

Day, Doris
| 1950 | Young Man with a Horn |

Day, Edward
| 1928 | The Midnight Ace |

Day, John
1951	Teresa
1953	The Man from the Alamo
	Seminole
1958	The Badlanders
1959	Night of the Quarter Moon

Day, Laraine
| 1943 | Mr. Lucky |

Day, Marceline
1926	The Barrier
1927	Red Clay
1928	The Cameraman
1930	Sunny Skies
1933	The Telegraph Trail

Day, Richard
| 1958 | Never Love a Stranger |

Day, Shannon
1922	Captain Fly-by-Night
1926	The Barrier
	The Vanishing American

Day, Tom
| 1927 | The Red Raiders |

Day, Vernon
| 1914 | The Indian Wars |

Daye, Dulce
| 1944 | Since You Went Away |
| 1947 | Jiggs and Maggie in Society |

Dayle, Lucien
| 1931 | Chérie |

Dayton, Charles
| 1951 | Warpath |

Dayton, Dorothy
1934	Stand Up and Cheer!
1939	King of Chinatown
1940	The Way of All Flesh

Dayton, James
| 1921 | Shadows of the West |

Dayton, Lewis
| 1918 | Woman and the Law |

Dazey, Charles Turner
| 1918 | Shifting Sands |
| 1921? | The Supreme Passion |

Dazey, Frank Mitchell
| 1936 | Klondike Annie |

Dazie, Mlle.
| 1920? | The Scarlet Dragon |

De Navrotzki, Igor *see* **Igor and Yvette**

de Walt Reynolds, Adeline *see* **Reynolds, Adeline de Walt**

Deacon, Richard
1955	Blackboard Jungle
	Good Morning, Miss Dove
1956	Hot Blood
1958	The Last Hurrah

de Alberich, Salvador *see* **Alberich, Salvador de**

De Alcañiz, Luana *see* **Alcañiz, Luana**

Dean, Barney
1941	Louisiana Purchase
1943	Dixie
1948	The Paleface

Dean, David
| 1940 | The Ramparts We Watch |

Dean, Dixie
1933	It's Great to Be Alive
1934	Stand Up and Cheer!
1935	Piernas de seda

Dean, Don
| 1951 | Native Son |

Dean, Donya
| 1948 | Unconquered |

Dean, Dora
| 1915 | Time Lock Number 776 |

Dean, Douglas
| 1941 | Louisiana Purchase |

Dean, Eddie
1941	Gauchos of Eldorado
1946	Romance of the West
	Wild West
1947	West to Glory

Dean, Jack
1915	The Cheat
1916	For the Defense
	Witchcraft
1917	Unconquered

Dean, James
| 1956 | Giant |

Dean, Jeffrey *see* **Jagger, Dean**

Dean, Jo Ann
| 1944 | Something for the Boys |

Dean, Julia
| 1915 | How Molly Malone Made Good |

Dean, Lillian
| 1937 | Souls at Sea |

Dean, Louis
1918	The Birth of a Race
	The Kaiser's Finish
1922	Cardigan

Dean, Man Mountain
| 1937 | Big City |

Dean, Margia
1948	Shep Comes Home
1950	Bandit Queen
	The Baron of Arizona
1955	The Lonesome Trail
1958	Ambush at Cimarron Pass

Dean, Martin
| 1959 | The Black Orchid |

Dean, Priscilla
| 1920 | Outside the Law |

Dean, Ray
| 1920? | The Greatest Love |

Dean, Wally
| 1949 | The Girl from Jones Beach |

Dean, William
| 1950 | Panic in the Streets |

Deane (full name unknown)
| 1915 | The Immigrant |

Deane, Clara
| 1932 | Amor in montagna |

Deane, Dorris
| 1922 | The Half Breed |

Deane, Elaine
| 1937 | Nation Aflame |

Deane, Harold A.
| 1950 | Devil's Doorway |

Deane, Hazel
| 1923 | The Secret of the Pueblo |

Deane, Marjorie
| 1941 | New York Town |

Deane, Shirley
| 1936 | Charlie Chan at the Circus |

Deane, Sydney
| 1914 | Rose of the Rancho |
| 1920 | The Last of the Mohicans |

De Angelo, Joseph *same as* **DeAngelo, Joe**
1945	Where Do We Go From Here?
1950	Black Hand
1956	Serenade

Deanne, Marjorie
| 1943 | Riding High |

Deans, Herbert
| 1953 | The Man Behind the Gun |

Dear, Frank L.
| 1914 | At the Cross Roads |

Dearholt, Ashton
1916	Lone Star
1918	The Girl in the Dark
1923	The Sting of the Scorpion
1936	Tundra

Dearing, Dorothy
| 1935 | Piernas de seda |
| 1940 | Murder over New York |

Dearing, Edgar *same as* **Dearing, Ed; Deering, Edgar**
1930	Abraham Lincoln
	Estrellados
1934	Eskimo
1936	After the Thin Man
	Rose of the Rancho
1937	Big City
	The Plainsman
1940	Knute Rockne—All American
1941	Louisiana Purchase
	Sullivan's Travels
1942	Apache Trail
	The Navy Comes Through
	Wings for the Eagle
1943	The Meanest Man in the World
1945	Johnny Angel
1946	The Gentleman Misbehaves
1948	My Girl Tisa
	The Paleface
	Unconquered
1949	Boston Blackie's Chinese Venture
1950	Raiders of Tomahawk Creek
	Right Cross

Dearing, Peter
| 1957 | Naked in the Sun |

Dearring, Mary Lee
| 1947 | Citizen Saint |

Deary, Clarissa
| 1943 | Marching On! |

Deauville, John
| 1958 | The Last Hurrah |

Deaver, Nancy
| 1922 | The Mohican's Daughter |
| | Solomon in Society |

DeBase, Eddie
| 1941? | The Blood of Jesus |

De Bear, Peter
| 1953 | The Eddie Cantor Story |

De Bok, Joseffa
1924   Two Shall Be Born
DeBolt, Birdie
1938   Hawaii Calls
De Briac, Jean *same as* **Briac, Jean de**
1930   Behind the Make-Up
1931   Los calaveras (*foreign version*)
1934   Coming Out Party
1938   Charlie Chan at Monte Carlo
1943   Wintertime
1945   The Dolly Sisters
        Nob Hill
1947   The Foxes of Harrow
1948   Half Past Midnight
De Brulier, Nigel *same as* **Brulier, Nigel de; Brullier, N. de; De Brullier, Nigel**
1916   Pasquale
        Ramona
1917   The Bond Between
1918   Me Und Gott
1935   Charlie Chan in Egypt
1936   Down to the Sea
        Robin Hood of El Dorado
1937   The Californian
1939   Heaven with a Barbed Wire Fence
1940   Viva Cisco Kid
De Bulger, Louis
1921   The Gunsaulus Mystery
1923   Deceit
DeCamp, Rosemary
1941   Hold Back the Dawn
1943   Yankee Doodle Dandy
1945   Pride of the Marines
        Rhapsody in Blue
1949   The Story of Seabiscuit
1950   The Big Hangover
De Camp, Victor
1935   Harmony Lane
DeCarlo, Vinnie
1958   The Badlanders
De Carlo, Yvonne
1943   Deerslayer
1945   Salome, Where She Danced
1950   Buccaneer's Girl
1951   Tomahawk
1954   Passion
1955   Shotgun
1956   Death of a Scoundrel
        Raw Edge
1957   Band of Angels
De Carlton, George
1914   Northern Lights
1915   The Nigger
De Carlton, Grace
1916   Betrayed
De Carvalho, Raúl
1930   Toda una vida (*foreign version*)
De Castro Sisters
1947   Copacabana
De Castro, Eduardo
1938   Zamboanga
De Castro, Jerry
1947   Ride the Pink Horse
Decker, Harry L.
1936   Dangerous Intrigue
Decker, S. K.
1947   Bells of San Fernando
Decker, Samuel K.
1946   Renegade Girl
De Clercq, Kuulei
1937   Waikiki Wedding
De Clercq, Nalani
1937   Waikiki Wedding
De Comathiere, A. B. *see* **Comathiere, A. B.**
De Corday, Paul
1947   The Foxes of Harrow
De Cordoba, Pedro *see* **Cordoba, Pedro de**
De Cordova, Frederick *see* **Cordova, Frederick de**
DeCordova, Leander *see* **Cordova, Leander de**

De Cordova, Rudolph *see* **Cordova, Rudolph de**
De Corsia, Ted
1948   The Lady from Shanghai
1951   New Mexico
1952   The Savage
1953   Ride, Vaquero!
1956   Mohawk
1957   Gun Battle at Monterey
        The Lawless Eighties
        The Midnight Story
1959   Inside the Mafia
1960   Oklahoma Territory
Decuire, June
1943   Cabin in the Sky
De Domenicis, Mario
1930   Sei tu l'amore
Dee, Dale
1934   Stand Up and Cheer!
1936   Star for a Night
1938   In Old Chicago
Dee, Frances
1934   Coming Out Party
1937   Souls at Sea
1948   Four Faces West
Dee, Frank
1943   Yankee Doodle Dandy
Dee, George
1950   Battleground
1952   Red Ball Express
Dee, Ruby
1946   That Man of Mine
1947?   What a Guy
1948   The Fight Never Ends
1950   The Jackie Robinson Story
        No Way Out
1951   The Tall Target
1954   Go Man Go
1957   Edge of the City
1958   St. Louis Blues
1960   Take a Giant Step
Dee, Sandra
1959   Imitation of Life
Deegan, Josette
1949   Pinky
1951   Go for Broke!
Deems, Barrett
1957   Satchmo the Great
Deer Spring
1934   Laughing Boy
Deer, George
1952   Fort Osage
Deering, Edgar *see* **Dearing, Edgar**
Deering, Olive
1948   Gentleman's Agreement
Deery, Jack
1937   Maid of Salem
1942   Three Hearts for Julia
DeFore, Don
1942   Wings for the Eagle
1946   Without Reservations
De Forest, Patsey
1917   A Night in New Arabia
De Friis, Inger
1930   Toda una vida (*foreign version*)
Dega, Igor
1947   Copacabana
        My Wild Irish Rose
De Garre, Harold
1941   Louisiana Purchase
De Gaston, Galle
1932   Ten Minutes to Live
De Gaw, Boyce
1940   Behind the News
1941   Ice-Capades
DeGolyer, Mary
1949   The Red Menace
De Gombert, Georges
1934   La veuve joyeuse
De Grasse, Joseph
1916   The Gilded Spider
        The Grip of Jealousy
1917   The Winged Mystery
1918   A Broadway Scandal
1924   So Big
De Grasse, Pete
1938   Mr. Moto's Gamble

De Grasse, Sam *same as* **Grasse, Sam de**
1915   The Birth of a Nation
1916   The Half-Breed
1917   The Winged Mystery
1920   Uncharted Channels
De Grey, Sidney *same as* **De Gray, Sidney; Grey, Sydney de**
1918   His Birthright
        The Reckoning Day
1920   The Mark of Zorro
1922   The Half Breed
1925   Brand of Cowardice
1927   Bitter Apples
1934   Broadway Bill
DeHaven, Gloria
1945   Between Two Women
De Havilland, Olivia
1935   The Irish in Us
1939   Gone With the Wind
1940   Santa Fe Trail
1941   Hold Back the Dawn
1942   In This Our Life
        They Died With Their Boots On
1955   Not As a Stranger
Dehelly, Suzanne
1930   Un hombre de suerte (*foreign version*)
Dehn, Dorothy
1934   Stand Up and Cheer!
1937   The Devil's Playground
Dehn, Irene
1948   Gentleman's Agreement
Dehner, John
1944   Lake Placid Serenade
1946   Rendezvous 24
1947   Vigilantes of Boomtown
1949   Prejudice
1950   Last of the Buccaneers
        Riders of the Pony Express
1951   When the Redskins Rode
1952   California Conquest
1954   Apache
1955   Duel on the Mississippi
1957   Revolt at Fort Laramie
        Trooper Hook
1958   Apache Territory
1960   The Sign of Zorro
Deighton, Marga Ann
1942   Mokey
Dein, Edward
1943   The Leopard Man
1944   Slightly Terrific
Deione, Madame
1920   The Luck of the Irish
De Jonghe, Daniel
1943   Action in the North Atlantic
1949   The Girl from Jones Beach
Dekker, Albert
1943   In Old Oklahoma
1945   Salome, Where She Danced
1947   California
1948   Fury at Furnace Creek
        Gentleman's Agreement
1950   The Furies
1958   Machete
1959   The Wonderful Country
De Kova, Frank
1952   The Big Sky
1953   Arrowhead
1954   Drum Beat
        Passion
        They Rode West
1956   The Lone Ranger
        Pillars of the Sky
        Reprisal!
        The White Squaw
1957   Ride Out for Revenge
        Run of the Arrow
1958   Apache Territory
1959   The Jayhawkers!
De La Brosse, Marcel *same as* **Brosse, Marcel de la**
1938   Happy Landing
1945   Johnny Angel
1952   The Iron Mistress

De Lacey, Philippe *same as* **De Lacy, Philippe**
Delacruz, Joe *see* **Cruz, Joe de la**
De La Cruz, Juan *see* **Cruz, Juan de la**
DeLacy, Leigh
1937   Big City
De Lacy, Philippe
1924   Peter Pan
1927   The Way of All Flesh
1928   The Broken Mask
        Mother Machree
De Lacy, Ralph
1935   Harmony Lane
De Lacy, Robert
1928   Tyrant of Red Gulch
De La Haye, Ina
1950   Give Us This Day
DeLaire, Diane
1955   The Lonesome Trail
        The Long Gray Line
Del Amo, Jaime *see* **Amo, Jaime del**
DeLamont, Charles
1936   Dangerous Intrigue
De La Mothe, Leon
1930   Las campanas de Capistrano
De La Motte, Marguerite
1920   The Mark of Zorro
1922   Shadows
1923   Scars of Jealousy
1924   East of Broadway
1926   The Last Frontier
        Meet the Prince
        Pals in Paradise
de Landa, Juan *see* **Landa, Juan de**
Delaney, Charles
1922   Solomon in Society
1927   Frisco Sally Levy
1928   The Cohens and the Kellys in Paris
1930   Around the Corner
        Kathleen Mavourneen
1932   Hearts of Humanity
1935   Captured in Chinatown
1936   Below the Deadline
1939   Waterfront
1952   The Half-Breed
Delaney, E. L.
1916   The Thousand Dollar Husband
Delaney, Leo
1917   The Slacker (Metro Pictures Corp.)
Délano, Adriana
1931   La gran jornada
Delano, Dinsmore
1945   Where Do We Go From Here?
Delano, Edith Barnard
1916   Hulda from Holland
De Lanti, Stella
1925   Don Q, Son of Zorro
Delany, Maureen
1935   His Family Tree
Delaro, Hattie
1914   Uncle Tom's Cabin
1917   A Night in New Arabia
1922   Cardigan
DeLauer, Robert "Bob"
1951   Saturday's Hero
DeLaval, Mario
1951   The Great Caruso
DeLavalade, Herman
1920   In the Depths of Our Hearts
De Lavallade, Carmen
1959   Odds Against Tomorrow
D'Elba, Count H.
1918   Marked Cards
Delcambre, Alfred *same as* **Cambre, Del**
1934   Wagon Wheels
1935   So Red the Rose
1936   Tundra
1949   Arctic Fury
Del Campo, Francisco *see* **Campo, Del**

De Legge, Boise
1926   The Flying Ace
De Leo, Don
1940   The Notorious Elinor Lee
DeLeon, Walter
1933   A Lady's Profession
1935   Ruggles of Red Gap
1937   Waikiki Wedding
1941   Birth of the Blues
1943   Riding High
Delese, Don
1939   Lying Lips
Delevanti, Cyril *same as*
    Delavanti, Cyril
1945   The Jade Mask
        The Shanghai Cobra
1957   Ride Out for Revenge
        Trooper Hook
1958   Gun Fever
Delgarde, Domenick
1958   Touch of Evil
De Liguoro, Rina *same as* **De**
    Liguoro, Countess
1931   Politiquerías
1934   Behold My Wife!
1935   Angelina o el honor de
        un brigadier
De Linsky, Victor
1918   The Kaiser's Finish
1934   Strange Wives
1937   It Could Happen to You
1938   The Buccaneer
        Charlie Chan at Monte
        Carlo
        City Streets
        Gateway
        Happy Landing
Delius, Fritz
1930   Doña mentiras (*foreign
        version*)
Dell, Claudia
1930   Big Boy
1932   Hearts of Humanity
1936   Yellow Cargo
1944   Black Magic
Dell, Dennett
1934   Laughing Boy
Dell, Dorothy
1948   The Miracle of the Bells
Dell, Gabriel
1942   Let's Get Tough!
1944   Block Busters
1947   Bowery Buckaroos
Dell, Myrna
1943   In Old Oklahoma
1945   Wanderer of the
        Wasteland
1948   Fighting Father Dunne
        Guns of Hate
1949   The Girl from Jones
        Beach
        Lust for Gold
        Rose of the Yukon
1950   The Furies
Dell, Sylvia
1938   Two Sisters
Della Santina, Bruno
1959   The Black Orchid
1960   Pay or Die
Dellatorre, Claire
1958   The Last Hurrah
Dellys, Emile
1934   La veuve joyeuse
Delmar, Armond
1958   Tonka
Delmar, Thomas
1921   Across the Divide
Delmont, Baldy
1920   White Youth
Delmore, Herbert
1916   Broken Chains
Delmour, Jean
1931   Nuit d'Espagne
1932   L'athlète incomplet
        Le bluffeur
Deloffre, Rene
1951   Go for Broke!
deLoos, Jana *same as* **De Loos,**
    Janna
1943   Action in the North
        Atlantic

1947   Buck Privates Come
        Home
De Loos, Janna
1944   Lake Placid Serenade
De Lorez, Claire
1925   Cobra
DeLorme, Noelle
1943   Gangway for Tomorrow
Del Rey, Artie
1950   The Furies
Del Rey, Nita
1952   The Fabulous Senorita
Del Rey, Pilar
1949   Illegal Entry
1950   A Lady Without Passport
1951   The Mark of the
        Renegade
1954   Siege at Red River
1956   Giant
del Rincón, Guillermo
1930   El valiente
Del Rio, Dolores
1928   Ramona
1929   Evangeline
1937   The Devil's Playground
1960   Flaming Star
Del Rio, Evelyn
1938   Mis dos amores
Del Rio, Jack
1955   The Long Gray Line
Del Ruth, Hampton
1927   Lost at the Front
Del Ruth, Roy
1925   Hogan's Alley
1926   The Little Irish Girl
1927   Ham and Eggs at the
        Front
1935   L'homme des Folies
        Bergère
1936   It Had to Happen
1938   Happy Landing
        My Lucky Star
Delubac, Jacqueline
1931   Chérie
        Su noche de bodas
        (*foreign version*)
Delva, Rosita
1943   The Leopard Man
Delvá, Suzanne
1930   Olimpia (*foreign
        version*)
Del Val, Jean
1931   Quand on est belle
        Soyons gais
1932   L'athlète incomplet
        Le plombier amoureux
1940   The Mark of Zorro
1942   Gentleman Jim
1943   Action in the North
        Atlantic
        Wintertime
1947   Buck Privates Come
        Home
        The Foxes of Harrow
1950   Battleground
        Last of the Buccaneers
        The Toast of New Orleans
1952   The Iron Mistress
1955   Duel on the Mississippi
Del Valle, Gabriel
1959   The FBI Story
De Main, Gordon
1932   The Forty-Niners
1941   Hold Back the Dawn
1942   King of the Stallions
Demantóws
1941   Z Dymem Pożarów
De Marco, Tony
1943   The Gang's All Here
Demarest, William
1928   The Crash
        The Jazz Singer
1937   Big City
        Charlie Chan at the
        Opera
1938   Josette
1941   Ride on Vaquero
        Sullivan's Travels
1942   All Through the Night
1947   The Jolson Story
1950   Jolson Sings Again

1955   The Far Horizons
DeMario, Donna
1947   Robin Hood of Monterey
De Medici, Rod
1948   Up in Central Park
1951   The Great Caruso
DeMeo, Angelo
1959   The FBI Story
Demetri, Claude
1946?   House-Rent Party
Demetrio, Anna
1935   McFadden's Flats
1936   Show Boat
1938   The Texans
1940   Young Buffalo Bill
1950   Bandit Queen
        Black Hand
de Mille, Beatrice C.
1916   Unprotected
1917   Castles for Two
        Forbidden Paths
        Unconquered
DeMille, Cecil B.
1914   Rose of the Rancho
        The Squaw Man
1915   After Five
        The Cheat
        Chimmie Fadden
        Chimmie Fadden Out
        West
        The Kindling
1917   The Little American
1918   The Squaw Man
1922   Saturday Night
1925   Braveheart
1930   Estrellados
1931   The Squaw Man
1937   The Plainsman
1938   The Buccaneer
1941   Land of Liberty
1948   Unconquered
DeMille, Katherine
1936   Ramona
1937   The Californian
        Charlie Chan at the
        Olympics
1939   In Old Caliente
1947   Black Gold
1948   Unconquered
de Mille, William C.
1915   After Five
1917   Hashimura Togo
        The Secret Game
1918   The Honor of His House
        One More American
1930   El secreto del doctor
1933   The Emperor Jones
Deming, W. R.
1939   Mr. Moto in Danger
        Island
Deming, Walter
1918   Love's Law
De Mond, Albert
1927   His Foreign Wife
1928   Anybody Here Seen Kelly?
        The Cohens and the
        Kellys in Paris
        The Night Bird
1929   The Cohens and Kellys in
        Atlantic City
1930   The Cohens and the
        Kellys in Scotland
1931   The Cohens and Kellys in
        Africa
1935   Alas sobre el Chaco
1941   Gauchos of Eldorado
        Saddlemates
1942   Valley of Hunted Men
1949   The Red Menace
1952   Woman in the Dark
De Montez, Rico
1942   Unseen Enemy
1946   Cuban Pete
De More, H. C.
1917   The Plow Woman
Demorest, Drew *same as*
    Demarest, Drew
1937   Man of the People
1942   Nazi Agent
Demourelle, Vic
1938   The Buccaneer

Dempsey, Jack
1937   Big City
Dempsey, Pauline
1920   The Good-Bad Wife
Dempster, Carol
1919   Scarlet Days
Dench and Stewart
1941   Ice-Capades
Denetdeel, Bahe
1936   Ramona
1941   Western Union
Deneut, Dickey
1936   General Spanky
Dengate, Dennis
1952   The Big Sky
1953   The Charge at Feather
        River
Denham, Reginald
1932   El hombre que asesinó
Denham, Vera
1959   The FBI Story
        Last Train from Gun Hill
De Night, Fannie Belle
1929   Hallelujah
Denis, Susan
1940   Taku
Denise, Patricia
1958   Marjorie Morningstar
Denison, Leslie
1940   Escape to Glory
1941   Charlie Chan in Rio
        They Dare Not Love
1943   The Amazing Mrs.
        Holliday
1945   Escape in the Fog
1946   Rendezvous 24
1948   Unconquered
1952   Brave Warrior
1953   Tonight We Sing
D'Ennery, Guy
1936   Klondike Annie
1940   Covered Wagon Days
        The Mark of Zorro
1941   Prairie Pioneers
Dennett, Jill
1934   Straight Is the Way
Denning, Richard
1938   The Buccaneer
        The Texans
1939   King of Chinatown
1940   Geronimo
1941   Adam Had Four Sons
1949   Harbor of Missing Men
1954   Battle of Rogue River
1955   The Gun That Won the
        West
Denning, W. R.
1943   Gangway for Tomorrow
Dennis, Beverly
1951   Westward the Women
Dennis, Danny
1955   Blackboard Jungle
Dennis, John
1931   Delicious
Dennis, Nick
1951   A Streetcar Named Desire
1952   Anything Can Happen
        The Iron Mistress
1953   The Glory Brigade
1956   Hot Blood
Dennis, Robert C.
1957   Revolt at Fort Laramie
Dennis, Russell
1952   Bright Victory
Dennis, Walter
1936   Dimples
Dennison, Eva
1931   The Squaw Man
Dennison, Jo-Carroll
1943   The Gang's All Here
1947   The Jolson Story
Dennison, Leslie
1946   Dangerous Money
1948   The Feathered Serpent
Denny, Harry
1938   Josette
1945   A Tree Grows in Brooklyn
1947   The Farmer's Daughter
1948   Up in Central Park
1955   The Long Gray Line

Denny, Reginald
1928   The Night Bird
1950   The Iroquois Trail
Denny, Susan
1959   The Sheriff of Fractured
        Jaw
Deno, Paul
1941   They Dare Not Love
De Normand, George
1935   Melody Trail
1949   The Gay Amigo
        Satan's Cradle
        The Valiant Hombre
Dent, Vernon
1938   Little Miss Roughneck
1944   Address Unknown
        Chip Off the Old Block
1945   I Love a Bandleader
1947   It Had To Be You
Denton, Paul
1956   The Catered Affair
1959   The FBI Story
Dentoni, Anthony
1949   Thieves' Highway
De Nubila, Italia
1953   Ride, Vaquero!
DePaul, Dave
1960   Walk Tall
de Pomés, Félix see **Pomés, Félix
de**
Depp, Harry
1916   The Love Girl
1934   Straight Is the Way
1937   Charlie Chan on
        Broadway
1939   The Return of the Cisco
        Kid
1940   Elsa Maxwell's Public
        Deb No. 1
        The Man I Married
1944   Black Magic
1945   In Old New Mexico
1946   Shadows Over Chinatown
Deputy, Ted
1948   The Miracle of the Bells
De Ramey, Pierre
1932   Le bluffeur
Dere, Ann
1951   A Streetcar Named Desire
1953   Taxi
Derek, John
1944   Since You Went Away
1949   Knock on Any Door
1951   Saturday's Hero
1953   Ambush at Tomahawk
        Gap
DeRita, Joe
1946   The Sailor Takes a Wife
Dern, Bruce
1960   Wild River
De Rochemont, Louis
1940   The Ramparts We Watch
1945   The House on 92nd St.
1960   Man on a String
De Rochemont, Louis, III
1960   Man on a String
De Rochemont, Louis, Jr.
1940   The Ramparts We Watch
DeRosa, Ascanio
1931   Così è la vita
De Rosner, Gaza
1949   House of Strangers
De Rosselli, Rex
1918   The Wine Girl
De Rouen, Reed
1959   John Paul Jones
        The Sheriff of Fractured
        Jaw
DeRoux, Bernard
1945   Rhapsody in Blue
1947   The Foxes of Harrow
De Roy, Clay
1937   The Plainsman
1942   Shut My Big Mouth
De Roy, Harry
1915   Chimmie Fadden
Derr, E. B.
1931   Beyond Victory
1932   Scarface
1936   The Glory Trail
        Rebellion

1937   Drums of Destiny
        Old Louisiana
1943   Deerslayer
Derr, Richard
1941   Charlie Chan in Rio
1942   Castle in the Desert
Derrick, George
1949   Border Incident
1950   A Lady Without Passport
Dertano, Robert C.
1957   Journey to Freedom
De Rue, Carmen same as **De Rue,
Baby**
1914   The Squaw Man
1916   Gretchen, the Greenhorn
        A Sister of Six
De Ruiz, Nick
1924   The Night Hawk same as
        **De Ruiz, Nicholas; De
        Ruiz, Nicolás**
1922   East Is West
        The Half Breed
1925   The Man in Blue
1936   Robin Hood of El Dorado
De Sa, Alfredo
1946   Notorious
De Sales, Francis
1955   Headline Hunters
1957   All Mine to Give
1958   Apache Territory
De Sano, Marcel
1926   Blarney
1931   Don Juan diplomático
        (foreign version)
        El proceso de Mary
        Dugan
        El proceso de Mary
        Dugan (foreign
        version)
De Santis, Joe
1956   Full of Life
        The Last Hunt
1959   Al Capone
        Cry Tough
Desfis, Angelo
1943   Gangway for Tomorrow
Desha, Stephan
1950   Damien
Deshielle, Willard
1916   Man and His Angel
De Shon, Chuck
1936   Star for a Night
Deshon, Florence
1920   The Cup of Fury
        Dangerous Days
Deshon, Frank
1918   The Border Raiders
        The Girl in the Dark
Deshon, Nancy
1935   Wolf Riders
De Sica, Vittorio
1954   Indiscretion of an
        American Wife
De Silva, Fred
1926   Buffalo Bill on the U. P.
        Trail
De Simone, John
1950   Sunset in the West
Desin, James
1945   Where Do We Go From
        Here?
Deslys, Kay
1930   Take the Heir
1931   Cimarron
1940   Escape
Desmond, Bill
1935   Cyclone of the Saddle
1936   Custer's Last Stand
Desmond, Cleo
1923   Deceit
1927   The Millionaire
1938   Spirit of Youth
1940   Am I Guilty?
1940?   Mr. Washington Goes to
        Town
1942   Mokey
        The Vanishing Virginian
Desmond, Danny
1944   They Live in Fear
1945   The Jade Mask

Desmond, Lucille
1918   The Reckoning Day
Desmond, William
1916   The Criminal
1917   The Sudden Gentleman
1918   Hell's End
1927   Red Clay
1931   Oklahoma Jim
1936   Song of the Gringo
        Treachery Rides the
        Range
Desny, Victor
1950   Battleground
1953   Tonight We Sing
De Soto, Henri
1943   Wintertime
1945   The Dolly Sisters
De Soto, Nita
1956   Crowded Paradise
De Stefani, Joseph
1938   Gateway
De Stefano, Rosina
1932   Senza mamma
        e'nnamurato
De Stiffney, Angelo
1955   Seven Cities of Gold
d'Estournelles de Constant, Paul
1932   La foule hurle
DeSylva, B. G.
1935   The Littlest Rebel
1938   The Rage of Paris
1941   Birth of the Blues
        Louisiana Purchase
        Sullivan's Travels
1943   Dixie
        Riding High
1944   Going My Way
De Tar, Lucille
1920?   Broken Hearts
Determann, Jeanne
1953   Tonight We Sing
DeTolly, Lola
1947   Northwest Outpost
De Toth, Andre
1944   Dark Waters
1953   Last of the Comanches
1955   The Indian Fighter
1960   Man on a String
Deutchman, Clara see
    Deutschmann, Clara
Deutsch, Armand
1950   Ambush
        Right Cross
1951   The Magnificent Yankee
Deutsch, Ernst
1940   Escape
        The Man I Married
Deutsch, Helen
1952   It's a Big Country: An
        American Anthology
Deutschmann, Clara same as
    Deutchman, Clara
1938   The Singing Blacksmith
1939   Mirele Efros
Deutschmann, Janet
1938   The Singing Blacksmith
Deval, Jacques
1931   Jenny Lind
        Le père célibataire
        El proceso de Mary
        Dugan (foreign
        version)
        Soyons gais
1940   New Moon
De Valdez, Carlos
1934   The Prescott Kid
1936   The Bold Caballero
        Robin Hood of El Dorado
1937   Drums of Destiny
        Old Louisiana
De Valintine, Rudolpho see
    Valentino, Rudolph 1895—
1926
De Vargas, Valentin
1958   Touch of Evil
De Vaull, William
1915   The Birth of a Nation
1925   Lights of Old Broadway

De Vere, Gertrude
1918   Me Und Gott
De Vere, Harry
1917   His Sweetheart
        A Roadside Impresario
Devere, Lillian
1915   Cohen's Luck
Devereaux, Helen
1945   The Scarlet Clue
Deverell, Helen
1946   Abie's Irish Rose
Deverich, Nat
1922   The Power of Love
De Vernon, Frank
1918   The Unbeliever
Devesa, Jaime
1933   Espérame
        Melodía de arrabal
1934   Cuesta abajo
        El tango en Broadway
1935   Un hombre peligroso
        Julieta compra un hijo
1936   El crimen de media
        noche
DeVestal, Guy
1950   The Toast of New Orleans
Devine, Andy
1928   We Americans
1933   The Cohens and Kellys in
        Trouble
        Song of the Eagle
1935   Chinatown Squad
1938   In Old Chicago
1940   Geronimo
1941   Mutiny in the Arctic
        Road Agent
1942   North to the Klondike
        Unseen Enemy
1946   Canyon Passage
1947   On the Old Spanish Trail
1948   Old Los Angeles
1950   The Traveling
        Saleswoman
1951   New Mexico
        Slaughter Trail
1952   Trail of the Arrow
1954   Thunder Pass
1960   The Adventures of
        Huckleberry Finn
Devine, Denny
1946   Canyon Passage
Devine, James
1922   The Good Provider
Devine, Jerry
1923   Potash and Perlmutter
1924   Tongues of Flame
Devine, Tad
1946   Canyon Passage
De Vito, Angelo
1932   Cuore d'emigrante
        Senza mamma
        e'nnamurato
Devlin, Don
1956   The Catered Affair
Devlin, Jane
1944   Since You Went Away
Devlin, Joe
1939   The Mystery of Mr. Wong
        Waterfront
1942   Gentleman Jim
        Syncopation
        They Died With Their
        Boots On
        Wings for the Eagle
1944   Mr. Skeffington
1945   The Shanghai Cobra
1946   Bringing Up Father
1947   Body and Soul
        The Mighty McGurk
        My Wild Irish Rose
1949   Jiggs and Maggie in
        Jackpot Jitters
1950   The Jackie Robinson Story
1958   The Last Hurrah
De Voe, Frank
1936   It Had to Happen
De Voe, Theo
1933   It's Great to Be Alive
Devon, Richard
1958   The Badlanders

DeVonde, Chester
1920 The Good-Bad Wife
Devore, Dorothy
1925 The Prairie Wife
1930 Take the Heir
1939 Miracle on Main Street
De Vorska, Jesse *same as* **Devorska, Jess**
1926 Rose of the Tenements
1927 Jake the Plumber
1930 Around the Corner
1932 Me and My Gal
Dew, Edward *same as* **Dew, Eddie**
1941 Mutiny in the Arctic
1942 Across the Pacific
Cat People
Syncopation
Wings for the Eagle
1943 Ladies' Day
Mexican Spitfire's Blessed Event
1953 Tumbleweed
Dew, Sin Lang
1934 Blossom Time
De Wees, Jack
1932 Hypnotized
Dewey, Charlotte
1945 Nob Hill
Dewey, Earle S. *same as* **Dewey, Earle**
1941 Gauchos of Eldorado
Mystery Ship
1946 The Gentleman Misbehaves
Dewey, Edward *same as* **Dewey, Ed**
1941 Four Shall Die
1942 Take My Life
Dewey, Elmer
1926 Shadows of Chinatown
Dewey, Evelyn
1945 Nob Hill
Dewhurst, Colleen
1960 Man on a String
de Wilde, Brandon
1953 The Member of the Wedding
de Wit, Jacqueline de *see* **Wit, Jacqueline de**
De Witt, Angela
1938 Gateway
1946 Rendezvous 24
DeWitt, Jack
1946 Don Ricardo Returns
1947 Bells of San Fernando
The Return of Rin Tin Tin
1948 Rocky
1952 Battles of Chief Pontiac
1954 Sitting Bull
1958 Oregon Passage
DeWolf, Karen
1936 Ride, Ranger, Ride
1938 Passport Husband
1941 Saddlemates
1942 Shut My Big Mouth
De Wolfe, Billy
1943 Dixie
Dexter, Alan
1953 Column South
Dexter, Anthony
1953 Captain John Smith and Pocahontas
Dexter, Brad
1955 Violent Saturday
1957 The Oklahoman
1959 Last Train from Gun Hill
Dexter, Elliott
1917 Castles for Two
1918 The Squaw Man
1922 The Hands of Nara
Dexter, John
1947 Buffalo Bill Rides Again
Dexter, Maury
1956 Wetbacks
1958 Frontier Gun
1960 Walk Tall
Dexter, Sharon
1952 Buffalo Bill in Tomahawk Territory

DeYoung, Frances
1948 The Betrayal
Dezel, Albert
1931 Call of the Rockies
Di Benedetta, Maria
1925 The Greatest Love of All
Di Capua, Guido
1950 Black Hand
Di Donato, Pietro
1950 Give Us This Day
Di Fede, Luigi
1932 Amore e morte
Di Gangi, C. J.
1957 Edge of the City
Di Parma, Violetta
1932 Amore e morte
di Reda, Joe
1959 The Black Orchid
Dial-Torgerson, Edwin
1938 Speed to Burn
Diamond, Don
1957 Raiders of Old California
Diamond, Gary
1955 Blackboard Jungle
Good Morning, Miss Dove
Diamond, I. A. L.
1949 The Girl from Jones Beach
Diamond, Jack
1953 Taxi
Diamond, Jean
1931 Jenny Lind
Diamond, Robert L.
1953 Ride, Vaquero!
Diana, Clara
1932 Amore e morte
Dias, Jennie
1958 Touch of Evil
Diaz de Mendoza, Carlos
1930 Toda una vida
1931 La carta
Charlie Chan Carries On (*foreign version*)
La fiesta del diablo
Díaz Flores, Luis
1932 Hollywood, ciudad de ensueño
1935 Alas sobre el Chaco
1936 Contra la corriente
1939 La Inmaculada
Díaz Gimeno, Rosita *same as* **Díaz, Rosita**
1931 Un caballero de frac
Lo mejor es reír
Su noche de bodas
1935 Angelina o el honor de un brigadier
Rosa de Francia
1938 La vida bohemia
Diaz Lebron, Angel Luis
1956 Crowded Paradise
Diaz Lebron, Gilberto
1956 Crowded Paradise
Diaz, Hazel
1938 Swing!
Dibbs, Ken
1954 Dangerous Mission
1956 Daniel Boone, Trail Blazer
Dibrova, Olena
1937 Natalka Poltavka
Dick, Diana
1950 Annie Get Your Gun
Dick, Douglas
1949 Home of the Brave
1952 The Iron Mistress
1957 The Oklahoman
1960 Flaming Star
Dicker, Karen
1959 Imitation of Life
Dickerson, Dick
1946 Without Reservations
1947 Buck Privates Come Home
Dickerson, Dudley
1936 The Green Pastures
1940 Knute Rockne—All American
1942 Gentleman Jim
In This Our Life
Syncopation
The Vanishing Virginian

1943 Dixie
1946 Dangerous Money
Without Reservations
1947 It Had To Be You
1949 Knock on Any Door
1953 Tonight We Sing
Dickerson, Milton
1929 Hallelujah
Dickey, Basil
1926 The Frontier Trail
1932 The Secrets of Wu Sin
1937 Law and Lead
1939 Trigger Fingers
Dickey, Paul
1930 Estrellados
Dickinson, David
1940 Knute Rockne—All American
Dickinson, Dick
1932 Hidden Valley
1938 Mr. Moto's Gamble
1947 Pirates of Monterey
1948 Tap Roots
1949 Pinky
Dickinson, Homer
1936 Dimples
Klondike Annie
1937 One Mile from Heaven
1949 Knock on Any Door
1951 Gambling House
Dickson, Dick
1942 American Empire
Dickson, Florence
1935 Piernas de seda
Dickson, Gloria
1939 Waterfront
Dickson, Hal
1941 Sun Valley Serenade
Dickson, Helen
1936 Show Boat
1943 Dr. Gillespie's Criminal Case
1950 Annie Get Your Gun
The Toast of New Orleans
1951 The Great Caruso
Dickson, Jeanette
1936 Show Boat
Dickson, T.
1927? You Can't Win
Diege, Samuel
1936 Yellow Cargo
Diehl, Jim
1949 Laramie
Diener, Arpad
1960 I Aim at the Stars: the Wernher von Braun Story
Dierkes, John
1954 Passion
1955 Not As a Stranger
The Vanishing American
1957 The Guns of Fort Petticoat
The Halliday Brand
1958 Blood Arrow
The Rawhide Trail
1959 The Hanging Tree
The Oregon Trail
Diestro, Alfredo del
1930 Los que danzan
1931 El código penal
La dama atrevida
La ley del harem
La mujer X
El pasado acusa
1932 Soñadores de la gloria
1934 Nada más que una mujer
Dieterle, William *same as* **Dieterle, Wilhelm**
1930 Los que danzan (*foreign version*)
1931 Dämon des Meeres
Kismet
La llama sagrada (*foreign version*)
Die Maske Fällt
1933 Grand Slam
1942 Syncopation
1947 Duel in the Sun
1949 Portrait of Jennie

Dietrich, Marlene
1949 Jigsaw
1958 Touch of Evil
Dietrich, Ralph
1940 Charlie Chan at the Wax Museum
The Gay Caballero
1941 Accent on Love
Dead Men Tell
1942 Castle in the Desert
1943 Margin for Error
1950 Mystery Submarine
Dietz, Jack
1942 Let's Get Tough!
1944 Block Busters
Digges, Dudley
1932 The Hatchet Man
1933 The Emperor Jones
1934 Massacre
Diggins, Peggy
1942 Gentleman Jim
Diggs, John
1953 Tonight We Sing
Dika, Juliet
1934 La veuve joyeuse
Dill, Bill
1942 Three Hearts for Julia
Dill, Jack
1917 Follow the Girl
Dill, Joe
1937 The Barrier
Dill, Max M.
1916 Peck O' Pickles
Dill, Michael
1948 Moonrise
Dillard, Art
1941 Mystery Ship
1947 Marshal of Cripple Creek
Dillard, Bert
1935 Texas Terror
1949 Colorado Territory
Dillard, Bill
194- Mistaken Identity
1946? Fight That Ghost
House-Rent Party
1948 The Fight Never Ends
Dillaway, Dana
1956 Giant
Dillaway, Donald *same as* **Dillaway, Don; Dilloway, Donald**
1931 Cimarron
Mr. Lemon of Orange
Skyline
1943 Gangway for Tomorrow
Margin for Error
1953 Dream Wife
The Eddie Cantor Story
1954 Dangerous Mission
Dillion, John Webb *see* **Dillon, John Webb** (*actor*), 1877—1949
Dillon, Andrew
1923 Little Old New York
Dillon, Bobby
1945 Great Stagecoach Robbery
Dillon, Brandon
1958 Flaming Frontier
Dillon, Dickie
1943 Good Luck, Mr. Yates
1944 Sheriff of Las Vegas
1945 Great Stagecoach Robbery
1946 California Gold Rush
Dillon, Eddie
1932 The Golden West
Dillon, Edward
1950 Panic in the Streets
Dillon, Forrest
1939 Allegheny Uprising
1943 The Ox-Bow Incident
Dillon, Irving
1916 The Flames of Johannis
Dillon, Jack (*actor*), 1866—1937 *same as* **Dillon, John**
1929 In Old Arizona
1931 The Cisco Kid
Dillon, John E.
1950 Panic in the Streets

Dillon, John Francis (*dir, actor*),
  1884—1934 *same as* **Dillon,**
  Jack
  1922   The Cub Reporter
  1932   Call Her Savage
          The Cohens and Kellys in
            Hollywood
Dillon, John Webb (*actor*), 1877—
  1949 *same as* **Dillion, John**
  Webb
  1917   The Primitive Call
  1922   The Mohican's Daughter
  1926   The Vanishing American
  1934   Broadway Bill
Dillon, Pat
  1944   Chip Off the Old Block
Dillon, Robert A. *same as* **Dillon,**
  Robert
  1920   The Last of the Mohicans
  1927   Ham and Eggs at the
          Front
Dillon, Thomas P. *same as* **Dillon,**
  Thomas; Dillon, Tom P.
  1940   Little Nellie Kelly
  1944   Going My Way
  1945   Escape in the Fog
          Nob Hill
  1947   Duel in the Sun
          Easy Come, Easy Go
          The Mighty McGurk
  1948   My Girl Tisa
          Up in Central Park
  1950   Black Hand
  1956   The Catered Affair
Dillon, Tom *not the same as*
  Dillon, Thomas P.
  1938   Birthright
Dilson, Clyde
  1934   Stand Up and Cheer!
Dilson, John *same as* **Dilson, John**
  H.
  1935   Charlie Chan in Paris
  1936   It Had to Happen
  1938   My Lucky Star
  1939   Stand Up and Fight
  1940   Elsa Maxwell's Public
          Deb No. 1
  1941   The Face Behind the
          Mask
          Mystery Ship
  1943   Dr. Gillespie's Criminal
          Case
          In Old Oklahoma
          The Leopard Man
  1944   Buffalo Bill
  1945   Rhapsody in Blue
Dilson, John H.
  1940   Phantom of Chinatown
  1941   New York Town
Diltz, Hubert
  1932   Hypnotized
DiMaggio, Joe
  1937   Manhattan
          Merry-Go-Round
Dime, James *not the same as* **Dime,**
  Jimmie
  1953   So Big
  1958   The Last Hurrah
Dime, Jimmie *not the same as*
  Dime, James
  1934   Nada más que una mujer
DiMeo, Luisa
  1958   Seven Hills of Rome
Diminici, Mario
  1930   Olimpia
Dimond, Jack
  1955   Headline Hunters
Dimsdale, Howard
  1950   A Lady Without Passport
          The Traveling
          Saleswoman
Dineen, Audrey
  1956   The Benny Goodman
          Story
Dinehart, Alan
  1934   The Cat's-Paw
  1936   Charlie Chan at the Race
          Track
          Human Cargo
          It Had to Happen
          Star for a Night
  1944   Minstrel Man

Dinehart, Alan, III
  1951   Apache Drums
Dingle, Charles
  1945   A Medal for Benny
  1946   Three Wise Fools
  1947   Duel in the Sun
"Dinky Dean" *see* **Riesner, Dean**
Dinovitch, Abe
  1940   New Moon
  1947   Northwest Outpost
  1948   Call Northside 777
  1952   The Big Sky
Dion, Hector
  1918   One More American
  1919   Auction of Souls
Dione, Rose
  1921   Cheated Love
  1931   Nuit d'Espagne
Dip-ying, Wu *could be same as*
  Ying, Wu Dip
  1953?   Tan Dow Jia Jen
DiPaolo, Dante
  1944   Chip Off the Old Block
Dirkson, Sherman
  1939   Straight to Heaven
Dishmon, Alberta
  1950   Intruder in the Dust
Disney, Walt
  1946   Song of the South
  1955   Davy Crockett, King of
          the Wild Frontier
  1956   Davy Crockett and the
          River Pirates
          Westward Ho the
          Wagons!
  1958   The Light in the Forest
          Tonka
Ditline, Rene
  1915   Sealed Valley
Ditmore, Leroy
  1958   Tonka
Ditrichstein, Leo
  1915   How Molly Malone Made
          Good
Divorkin, Ida
  1939   My Son
Dix, Beulah Marie
  1917   The Call of the East
  1918   Hidden Pearls
          The Squaw Man
  1931   Three Who Loved
  1933   Ever in My Heart
Dix, Billy *same as* **Dix, Bill**
  1953   Old Overland Trail
  1955   Bad Day at Black Rock
  1956   The Wild Dakotas
Dix, Dan
  1943   The Ox-Bow Incident
Dix, Dorothy
  1934   Wheels of Destiny
Dix, Joan
  1932   Hypnotized
Dix, Marion
  1930   The Kibitzer
Dix, Richard
  1926   The Vanishing American
  1927   The Gay Defender
  1929   Redskin
  1931   Cimarron
  1937   The Devil's Playground
  1939   Man of Conquest
  1942   American Empire
Dix, Rollo
  1935   Rendezvous
Dix, Tommy
  1944   Andy Hardy's Blonde
          Trouble
Dixie Jubilee Singers
  1929   Hallelujah
Dixon, Allen
  1923   Deceit
Dixon, Alonzo
  1921   The Lure of a Woman
Dixon, Denver *same as* **Adamson,**
  Victor *see also* **Mix, Art**
  1933   Circle Canyon
Dixon, Florence
  1920   Hidden Charms
  1921?   The Supreme Passion
  1922   Anna Ascends

Dixon, Henry
  1924?   The Flaming Crisis
Dixon, Ivan
  1959   Porgy and Bess *
Dixon, Thomas
  1916   The Fall of a Nation
  1937   Nation Aflame
Dixon, Thomas, Jr.
  1921   Wing Toy
Dmytryk, Edward
  1943   Hitler's Children
  1944   Tender Comrade
  1946   Till the End of Time
  1947   Crossfire
  1950   Give Us This Day
  1954   Broken Lance
  1957   Raintree County
  1958   The Young Lions
Dobbins, Earl
  1941   Western Union
Dobbs, George
  1940   Elsa Maxwell's Public
          Deb No. 1
  1943   The Gang's All Here
Dobkin, Lawrence *same as*
  Dobkin, Larry
  1955   Kiss of Fire
  1957   Raiders of Old California
  1958   The Defiant Ones
Dockson, Evelyn
  1945   The Valley of Decision
Dockstader, George
  1950   The Jackie Robinson Story
Dockstader, Lew
  1914   Dan
Dodd, Claire
  1932   The Match King
  1934   Massacre
  1939   Charlie Chan in Honolulu
  1940   If I Had My Way
Dodd, Jimmie *same as* **Dodd,**
  James; Dodd, Jimmy
  1942   Valley of Hunted Men
  1944   An American Romance
          Hi, Beautiful
          Since You Went Away
          Something for the Boys
  1947   Buck Privates Come
          Home
Dodd, Maria
  1946   Sunset Pass
Dodd, Mike
  1960   Wild River
Dodd, Neal *same as* **Dodd, Father**
  Neal; Dodd, Reverend Neal
  1934   Strange Wives
  1940   Santa Fe Trail
Dodds, Edward
  1944   Hi, Beautiful
Dodds, Jack
  1953   The Glory Brigade
Dodds, Larry
  1937   Slave Ship
  1938   Gateway
  1941   Western Union
  1943   The Ox-Bow Incident
  1944   Buffalo Bill
Dodge, Anna
  1915   The Rosary
Dodson, Bert
  1950   Indian Territory
Doerner, William
  1960   The Pusher
Doggett, Wm.
  1949   Lookout Sister
Doherty, Edward
  1944   The Sullivans
Doherty, Ethel
  1926   The Vanishing American
  1932   Men Are Such Fools
Dohlman, Hazel
  1951   The Great Caruso
Dolan, Bobby
  1945   The Bells of St. Mary's
Dolan, Frank *same as* **Dolan,**
  Frank J.
  1932   Me and My Gal
  1937   Man of the People

Dolan, Nan
  1955   Good Morning, Miss Dove
Doland, F.
  1931   Delicious
Dolciame, Ray
  1945   Nob Hill
  1947   Bells of San Fernando
  1948   My Girl Tisa
Dole, Bert
  1945   Salome, Where She
          Danced
Dolgin, Sol
  1957   Pawnee
Dolgoruki, Igor
  1945   The Dolly Sisters
  1947   Northwest Outpost
Doll, Dora
  1958   The Young Lions
Doll, Robert M.
  1925   The Greatest Love of All
Dolling, Sally
  1934   Call of the Coyote
Dolombo, Frances
  1932   Amor in montagna
Domaine, Ted du
  1960   Ice Palace
Domb, Adam
  1934   The Rabbi's Power
Dombourajian, Elizabeth
  1950   Panic in the Streets
Domergue, Faith
  1953   The Great Sioux Uprising
  1955   Santa Fe Passage
Dominguez, Frances
  1945   A Medal for Benny
  1952   The Fabulous Senorita
Dominguez, Joe *could be same as*
  Domínguez, José
  1943   The Leopard Man
  1945   A Medal for Benny
          South of the Rio Grande
  1949   Streets of Laredo
  1950   Bandit Queen
          The Furies
  1953   Ride, Vaquero!
  1955   Headline Hunters
  1956   The Broken Star
          Wetbacks
  1957   The Ride Back
  1958   The Badlanders
Domínguez, José *could be same as*
  Domínguez, Joe
  1930   The Bad Man (*foreign*
          version)
  1932   Riders of the Desert
  1940   Geronimo
  1949   Border Incident
          The Kissing Bandit
  1950   A Lady Without Passport
"Don Alberto" *same as* **Infanta,**
  Alberto
  1934   El tango en Broadway
  1938   Di que me quieres
"Don Catarino" *same as* **Pirrín,**
  Chevo
  1931   Gente alegre
          El príncipe gondolero
  1935   El cantante de Nápoles
"Don Mario"
  1938   Di que me quieres
Don, Jack
  1934   The Cat's-Paw
Donadio, Luigi
  1932   Amor in montagna
Donahue, Patricia
  1957   The Brothers Rico
  1959   Al Capone
Donahue, Troy
  1959   Imitation of Life
Donaldson, Mrs.
  1916?   Should a Baby Die?
Donaldson, Arthur
  1915   Hearts of Men
  1916   A Woman's Honor
  1916?   Should a Baby Die?
  1917   I Will Repay
  1918   Find the Woman
Donaldson, John
  1938   Josette

Donaldson, Ted
1945   A Tree Grows in Brooklyn
Donath, Ludwig *same as* **Donath, Louis**
1943   Gangway for Tomorrow
        Margin for Error
1947   The Jolson Story
1950   Jolson Sings Again
        Mystery Submarine
1951   The Great Caruso
Donatt, Renee
1948   Moonrise
Donde, Manuel
1956   The Last Frontier
Donegan, Madeline
1940   The Notorious Elinor Lee
Doner, Ted
1945   Where Do We Go From
        Here?
Dones, Paolo
1932   Amore e morte
Dones, Sidney P. *same as* **Dones, Sidney Preston**
1919   Injustice
1920?   Reformation
Dong, David
1939   King of Chinatown
Dong, Tong Hill
1941   Min Jok Jay Hung Sing
Donia, Frank
1949   That Midnight Kiss
Doniger, Walter
1957   The Guns of Fort
        Petticoat
Donlan, James
1930   Sins of the Children
1934   The Cat's-Paw
Donlevy, Brian
1929   Mother's Boy
1936   Human Cargo
1938   In Old Chicago
1939   Allegheny Uprising
1941   Birth of the Blues
        Hold Back the Dawn
1944   An American Romance
1946   Canyon Passage
1951   Slaughter Trail
1958   Escape from Red Rock
Donley, Robert P.
1948   Strange Victory
Donlin, Mike
1928   Riley the Cop
1929   Thunderbolt
Donn-Byrne, Brian Oswald
1921   Puppets of Fate
Donnell, Jeff
1943   Doughboys in Ireland
        What's Buzzin' Cousin?
1949   Stagecoach Kid
1954   Massacre Canyon
1957   The Guns of Fort
        Petticoat
Donnelly, Donal
1959   Shake Hands with the
        Devil
Donnelly, Dorothy
1915   Sealed Valley
Donnelly, Kerry
1953   So Big
Donnelly, Leo
1923   Potash and Perlmutter
Donnelly, Ruth
1932   The Rainbow Trail
1933   Ever in My Heart
1945   The Bells of St. Mary's
1948   Fighting Father Dunne
Donovan, Gwen
1945   Nob Hill
Donovan, King
1948   Open Secret
1950   A Lady Without Passport
        Mystery Street
        Right Cross
1951   Little Big Horn
1953   Tumbleweed
1954   Broken Lance
1958   The Defiant Ones
1959   The Hanging Tree

Donovan, Michael Patrick *same as* **Donovan, Mike; Donovan, Mike Pat**
1940   Doomed to Die
1946   Bringing Up Father
1950   Mystery Street
Donte, Joseph
1957   Beau James
Dooley, Billy
1934   The Cat's-Paw
1935   Naughty Marietta
Doraine, Lucy
1931   El proceso de Mary
        Dugan (*foreign
        version*)
Doran, Ann *same as* **Doran, Ann Lee**
1936   Dangerous Intrigue
        Let's Sing Again
1937   The Devil's Playground
1938   City Streets
        Little Miss Roughneck
1941   New York Town
        Sun Valley Serenade
1943   Air Force
        Yankee Doodle Dandy
1944   Mr. Skeffington
1945   Pride of the Marines
1948   Reaching from Heaven
1949   The Clay Pigeon
1951   Gambling House
        Tomahawk
1953   The Eddie Cantor Story
1957   Band of Angels
1958   The Badlanders
        The Rawhide Trail
1959   The FBI Story
Doran, Mary
1929   Lucky Boy
1930   Sins of the Children
1933   Grand Slam
1935   Naughty Marietta
Dorando, Eleanor
1958   Touch of Evil
Dore, Ann *could be same as* **Dore, Anne Marie**
1954   Dangerous Mission
Dore, Anne Marie *could be same as* **Dore, Ann**
1951   Show Boat
Dorety, Charles
1931   Los calaveras
        Los calaveras (*foreign
        version*)
Dorf, Morris
1932   A Daughter of Her People
Dorfmann, Robert
1951   Adventures of Captain
        Fabian
Dori, Adriana
1931   Così è la vita
1932   Parigi affascina; ovvero,
        Malavita
Doria, Francesca
1932   Amor in montagna
Dorian, Charles
1918   Hell's End
Dorian, Ernest
1942   Prisoner of Japan
Dorita y Varela
1938   Di que me quieres
Dorn, Doris
1924   The Lightning Rider
Dorn, Philip
1940   Escape
1948   I Remember Mama
1949   The Fighting Kentuckian
Doro, Marie
1917   Castles for Two
Dorr, Dorothy
1925   Quicker'n Lightnin'
Dorr, Lester
1937   Big City
        Charlie Chan on
        Broadway
1938   Mr. Moto's Gamble
1939   The Cisco Kid and the
        Lady
        Mr. Moto in Danger
        Island
        Mr. Moto Takes a
        Vacation

1940   Mexican Spitfire Out
        West
1942   Gentleman Jim
        Little Tokyo, U.S.A.
        Sunday Punch
        Young America
1944   Hi, Beautiful
1945   The Jade Mask
        Nob Hill
1946   G. I. War Brides
        Notorious
1947   California
1948   Music Man
1950   The Big Hangover
1955   Seven Angry Men
1958   Marjorie Morningstar
Dorrell, Artie
1947   Body and Soul
Dorrington, Clint
1958   The Last Hurrah
Dorrington, Lucile
1917   The Little Samaritan
Dorr's St. Luke's Choristers *see* St. Luke's Choristers
D'Orsay, Fifi
1931   Mr. Lemon of Orange
1934   La veuve joyeuse
D'Orsay, Lawrence
1918   Ruggles of Red Gap
D'Orsay, Lonnie
1944   Address Unknown
Dorsen, Robert
1950   Panic in the Streets
Dorsey, Diane
1936   Star for a Night
Dorsey, Jimmy
1948   Music Man
Jimmy Dorsey's Orchestra
1948   Music Man
Dorsey, Maggie
1942   Tales of Manhattan
D'Orsey, Princess
1955   Brevities of 1955
Dortort, David
1956   Reprisal!
Doscher, Doris
1918   The Birth of a Race
Dosh, Fred
1945   Rhapsody in Blue
Doss, Tommy
1950   Rio Grande
Dotson, Betty
1934   Stand Up and Cheer!
Dotson, Ernest
1955   Good Morning, Miss Dove
Doty, Douglas *same as* **Doty, Douglas Z.**
1929   Masked Emotions
1931   Lo mejor es reír
1933   Racetrack
Doucet, Catherine *same as* **Doucet, Catharine**
1937   Man of the People
1948   The Dude Goes West
Doucet, Paul
1919   The Scar
Doucette, John
1947   The Burning Cross
        The Foxes of Harrow
        Ride the Pink Horse
1949   Lust for Gold
1950   Border Treasure
        The Breaking Point
        Broken Arrow
        The Iroquois Trail
        Winchester '73
1951   Cavalry Scout
        Only the Valiant
1952   Bugles in the Afternoon
        Desert Pursuit
        High Noon
        Rose of Cimarron
        Woman in the Dark
1953   War Paint
1955   Seven Cities of Gold
1956   The Burning Hills
        Dakota Incident
        Ghost Town
        Quincannon, Frontier
        Scout
1957   The Lawless Eighties

1958   Gunfire at Indian Gap
Doud, Gil
1953   Thunder Bay
1954   Saskatchewan
1956   Walk the Proud Land
1960   Hell to Eternity
Douday, Salo
1945   The House on 92nd St.
Dougherty, Hershel
1949   The Story of Seabiscuit
1950   Young Man with a Horn
Dougherty, Jack
1922   Second Hand Rose
1936   General Spanky
1937   Big City
        Charlie Chan on
        Broadway
Douglas, Alan *could be same as* **Douglas, Allan**
1946   Dangerous Money
Douglas, Allan *could be same as* **Douglas, Alan**
1952   Anything Can Happen
Douglas, Bethe
1950   The Toast of New Orleans
Douglas, Burt
1959   Night of the Quarter
        Moon
Douglas, Byron
1927   Red Clay
Douglas, Cathy
1950   Riders of the Pony
        Express
Douglas, Diana
1949   House of Strangers
1955   The Indian Fighter
Douglas, Don *same as* **Douglas, Donald**
1934   Lazy River
        Operator 13
1939   Mr. Moto in Danger
        Island
1940   Charlie Chan in Panama
1941   Dead Men Tell
        Hold Back the Dawn
1942   Little Tokyo, U.S.A.
        Tales of Manhattan
1943   Action in the North
        Atlantic
        The Meanest Man in the
        World
        Wintertime
1945   Club Havana
Douglas, Earl
1938   Wild Horse Canyon
1940   Rhythm of the Rio
        Grande
Douglas, George
1940   Covered Wagon Days
1947   King of the Bandits
1949   The Undercover Man
Douglas, Gordon
1936   General Spanky
        Kelly the Second
1951   Only the Valiant
1952   The Iron Mistress
1953   The Charge at Feather
        River
        The Eddie Cantor Story
1959   Yellowstone Kelly
Douglas, J. Ian
1958   Fort Bowie
Douglas, Joan
1941   Sullivan's Travels
1958   The Young Lions
Douglas, Kirk
1950   Young Man with a Horn
1952   The Big Sky
1955   The Indian Fighter
1959   Last Train from Gun Hill
Douglas, Laurie
1942   Holiday Inn
Douglas, Marian
1929   Sioux Blood
1931   Aloha
Douglas, Melvyn
1933   Counsellor at Law
1935   Annie Oakley
1938   The Toy Wife
1942   Three Hearts for Julia
        We Were Dancing

Douglas, Nathan E. see Young, Nedrick

Douglas, Paul
1950   Panic in the Streets
1957   Beau James

Douglas, Phyllis
1957   Raintree County
1959   Night of the Quarter Moon
1960   Cimarron

Douglas, Rita
1942   Foreign Agent

Douglas, Robert
1950   Buccaneer's Girl
        Mystery Submarine
1954   Saskatchewan
1955   Good Morning, Miss Dove

Douglas, Scott
1956   Wetbacks

Douglas, Susan
1949   Lost Boundaries
1951   Five

Douglas, Terrill
1959   The Hanging Tree

Douglas, Warren
1943   Action in the North Atlantic
        Air Force
1945   Pride of the Marines
1947   The Chinese Ring
1951   Cuban Fireball
1957   Dragoon Wells Massacre

Dove, Billie
1927   The Love Mart

Dover, Nancy
1931   Cimarron

Dover, Robert Foster same as Dover, Robert
1950   Broken Arrow
1952   Indian Uprising

Dovey, Alice
1916   The Romantic Journey

Dow, Edward
1943   Action in the North Atlantic

Dow, Peggy
1952   Bright Victory

Dowd, Kay
1944   Tahiti Nights
        They Live in Fear

Dowell, George B.
1936   Klondike Annie

Dowlan, William C.
1920   Locked Lips

Dowling, Constance
1944   Knickerbocker Holiday

Dowling, Danny same as Dowling, Dan
1944   Mr. Skeffington
1947   Humoresque
1953   So Big

Dowling, Edward
1920?   The Greatest Love

Dowling, J. J. see Dowling, Joseph J.

Dowling, Joseph J. same as Dowling, J. J.; Dowling, Joseph
1916   The Criminal
1917   The Gun Fighter
1918   An Alien Enemy
        Free and Equal
        The Goddess of Lost Lake
        A Little Sister of Everybody
1919   The Lord Loves the Irish
1922   The Half Breed
        The Pride of Palomar
1923   The Spider and the Rose
1924   Unseen Hands
        Untamed Youth
1925   Flower of Night
1926   The Little Irish Girl

Dowling, Marion
1935   Melody Trail

Downen, Donald
1935   A Night at the Ritz

Downes, Olin
1947   Carnegie Hall

Downey, Morton
1929   Mother's Boy

Downing, Al
1938   The Buccaneer
1939   Waterfront

Downing, Barry
1942   Wings for the Eagle

Downing, Joseph
1941   Belle Starr

Downing, Rex same as Downing, Rex Haddon
1936   General Spanky
1939   The Escape
1942   The Vanishing Virginian
1946   Gas House Kids
1948   Call Northside 777

Downing, Wilfred
1959   Shake Hands with the Devil

Downs, A.
1941   Sullivan's Travels

Downs, Cathy
1949   Massacre River
1955   Kentucky Rifle

Downs, Johnny
1935   So Red the Rose
1941   Adam Had Four Sons
1945   Rhapsody in Blue
1953   Column South

Downs, Watson
1957   The Oklahoman
1958   Gunman's Walk

Doyle, Enya
1949   Ride, Ryder, Ride!

Doyle, James D.
1923   Backbone

Doyle, John T.
1929   Mother's Boy

Doyle, Laird
1935   Bordertown
1947   Northwest Outpost

Doyle, Mary
1917   The Bar Sinister
1938   The Beloved Brat

Doyle, Mimi
1942   Syncopation
1953   The Sun Shines Bright
1955   The Long Gray Line
1958   The Last Hurrah
1960   Pay or Die

Doyle, William H., Jr.
1950   Two Flags West

Dracula, a cat
1945   Jealousy

Drago, Harry Sinclair
1929   The Desert Rider
        The Overland Telegraph
        Sioux Blood

Drake, Alfred
1948   Strange Victory

Drake, Caroline
1957   Band of Angels

Drake, Charles
1942   Across the Pacific
        Wings for the Eagle
1943   Air Force
        Yankee Doodle Dandy
1950   Comanche Territory
        Winchester '73
1952   Red Ball Express
1954   War Arrow
1956   Walk the Proud Land

Drake, Chris
1944   My Pal Wolf
1945   Betrayal from the East
1950   Battleground

Drake, Claudia
1943   Border Patrol
1946   The Face of Marble
        Renegade Girl
1947   The Return of Rin Tin Tin
1948   Indian Agent
1949   The Cowboy and the Indians

Drake, Dona
1941   Louisiana Purchase
1946   Without Reservations
1949   The Girl from Jones Beach

Drake, Douglass see Mitchell, Johnny d. 1951

Drake, Frances
1933   No dejes la puerta abierta

Drake, Jack
1952?   Call of the Navajo

Drake, Oliver
1928   Breed of the Sunsets
        Orphan of the Sage
        Tyrant of Red Gulch
1929   The Desert Rider
1931   The Hurricane Horseman
1932   Law and Lawless
1934   The Battling Buckaroo
1935   The Cyclone Ranger
        The Singing Vagabond
1937   Boots and Saddles
        Nation Aflame
        The Riders of the Whistling Skull
1938   The Renegade Ranger
1939   The Fighting Gringo
1942   Shut My Big Mouth
1945   The Mummy's Curse
1948   The Feathered Serpent
1949   The Sky Dragon
1957   Dragoon Wells Massacre

Drake, Orville
1931   Law of the Tong

Drake, Pauline
1940   The Fatal Hour
1941   Under Fiesta Stars
1944   The Racket Man

Drake, Tom
1953   Sangaree
1957   Raintree County

Drake, Willie
1946?   House-Rent Party

Drapeau, Dewey
1950   Young Daniel Boone
1953   The Great Sioux Uprising
1956   Westward Ho the Wagons!

Draper, Alice
1943   His Butler's Sister
1944   Hi, Beautiful

Draper, Billy
1952   Navajo

Draper, Natalie
1942   Three Hearts for Julia

Draper, Paul
1948   The Time of Your Life

Dratler, Jay
1941   Where Did You Get That Girl?
1948   Call Northside 777
1960   I Aim at the Stars: the Wernher von Braun Story

Dray, Rosa
1916   Ramona

Dréan, Alexandre
1932   Le cas du docteur Brenner

Dreeben, Alan
1952   My Man and I

Dreifuss, Arthur
1939   Double Deal
1940   Mystery in Swing
1941   Murder on Lenox Avenue
        Sunday Sinners
1945   The Gay Senorita
1949   Shamrock Hill

Dresher, Beatrice A.
1954   Passion

Dresser, Louise same as Dresser, Luise
1923   Ruggles of Red Gap
1928   A Ship Comes In
        A Ship Comes In (foreign version)
1933   Song of the Eagle
1937   Maid of Salem

Dresser, Luise see Dresser, Louise

Dressler, Marie
1927   The Callahans and the Murphys
1930   Anna Christie

Drevjen, Nari
1943   Action in the North Atlantic

Drew, Mrs.
1915?   The Beachcomber

Drew, Ann
1927   The Red Raiders

Drew, Cora
1917   Southern Pride

Drew, Ellen
1940   Geronimo
1950   The Baron of Arizona
        Davy Crockett, Indian Scout
        Stars in My Crown

Drew, Florence
1918   Denny from Ireland
1922   Come On Over

Drew, Lillian
1918   Ruggles of Red Gap

Drew, Lowell
1937   Souls at Sea

Drew, Norma
1934   Imitation of Life

Drew, Paula
1946   Slightly Scandalous
1950   A Lady Without Passport

Drew, Roland
1928   Ramona
1929   Evangeline
1938   The Adventures of Tom Sawyer
1942   Across the Pacific
        All Through the Night
        Secret Enemies

Drexel, Nancy same as Kitchen, Dorothy
1927   The Way of All Flesh
1928   Breed of the Sunsets
        The Riding Renegade
        Riley the Cop
1932   Hollywood, ciudad de ensueño

Drexel, Steve
1960   All the Young Men

Dreyfus, Miss
1919   Injustice

Driggers, Don
1946   The Gay Cavalier
1947   Pirates of Monterey

Driscoll, Bobby
1944   The Sullivans
1946   Song of the South

Driscoll, Tex
1943   The Ox-Bow Incident
1956   Giant

Driver, Frances
1941   Sullivan's Travels
1951   Molly
1952   The Iron Mistress
1955   The View from Pompey's Head

Droege, Joseph
1950   Two Flags West

Drohan, William J.
1952   Bright Victory

Dromgold, George
1921   Through the Back Door
1928   Hold 'Em Yale

Drouart, Hazlan
1917   A Night in New Arabia

Drouet, Robert
1915   The Gambler of the West

Droughan, Amos
1946?   Go Down, Death!

Dru, Joanne
1946   Abie's Irish Rose
1948   Red River
1949   She Wore a Yellow Ribbon
1953   Thunder Bay
1954   Siege at Red River
1958   The Light in the Forest

Drum, James could be same as Drum, Jim
1960   Studs Lonigan

Drum, Jim could be same as Drum, James
1948   Unconquered
1949   The Undercover Man
1950   Battleground
1951   The Magnificent Yankee

Drumier, Jack
1914 The Woman in Black
1917 The Adventures of Carol
1918 The Golden Wall
Drury, James
1955 Blackboard Jungle
1956 The Last Wagon
Drute, Dena
1937 Green Fields
Duane, Jack
1929 Redskin
Duane, Michael
1943 Dr. Gillespie's Criminal
Case
Redhead from Manhattan
Duarte, Arthur
1931 Die Dreigroschenoper
(foreign version)
Duarte, Robina
1939 Miracle on Main Street
(foreign version)
El otro soy yo
El trovador de la radio
Dubin, Sidney
1949 Knock on Any Door
The Undercover Man
Dubinsky, Nadja
1956 Hot Blood
Dubinsky, Yudel same as
Dubinsky, Judel
1930 Eternal Fools (Ewige
Naranim)
1933 Live and Laugh
1935 Shir Hashirim
1938 The Singing Blacksmith
Two Sisters
1939 The Light Ahead
1940 Americaner Schadchen
Dublin, Darren
1957 The Brothers Rico
DuBois, Diane
1943 The Amazing Mrs.
Holliday
1956 Dakota Incident
DuBois, William
1934 La cruz y la espada
Dubov, Paul
1942 North to the Klondike
1950 Young Man with a Horn
1952 High Noon
1955 Apache Woman
1957 The Brothers Rico
1959 The Crimson Kimono
DuBrey, Claire
1917 Follow the Girl
The Winged Mystery
1918 The Border Raiders
1920 Dangerous Hours
1921 That Girl Montana
1934 Coming Out Party
1936 Ramona
1937 Man of the People
1940 Charlie Chan's Murder
Cruise
1945 Rhapsody in Blue
1946 Don Ricardo Returns
1947 Bells of San Fernando
1948 Unconquered
1952 Rose of Cimarron
1958 Frontier Gun
DuBuc, Joseph
1959 The Hanging Tree
Du Bus, Alma
1947 Citizen Saint
Ducount, George
1936 Dangerous Intrigue
Du Count, George
1937 Slave Ship
1938 Gateway
Du Crow, Tote
1920 The Mark of Zorro
1922 The Pride of Palomar
1925 Don Q, Son of Zorro
Dudgeon, Elspeth
1934 Stand Up and Cheer!
1936 Show Boat
1949 Lust for Gold
1952 Anything Can Happen
Dudgeon, H. N.
1918 Untamed

Dudley, Charles
1917 Sold at Auction
Dudley, Florence
1934 Straight Is the Way
Dudley, Frank
1914 The Nightingale
Dudley, John
1960 Wild River
Dudley, Robert
1918 Out of a Clear Sky
1932 Unashamed
1936 Paddy O'Day
The Prisoner of Shark
Island
1941 Sullivan's Travels
1942 Syncopation
1946 Singin' in the Corn
1949 Portrait of Jennie
Dudley, Sherman H.
1922 Easy Money
Dudley, Sherman H., Jr.
1926 Reckless Money
Dudley, Susie
1921 The Lure of a Woman
Dufau, Celestino
1930 Cascarrabias
Duff, Amanda
1939 The Escape
Mr. Moto in Danger
Island
Duff, Howard
1949 Illegal Entry
1956 The Broken Star
Duff, Warren
1951 Gambling House
1955 The Last Command
Duffield, Brainard
1949 Jigsaw
Duffield, Harry S.
1920 Rio Grande
Duffy, Albert
1940 The Gay Caballero
Duffy, Dan
1921 A Divorce of
Convenience
Duffy, Gerald C.
1919 A Fighting Colleen
1921 Hold Your Horses
1922 Head over Heels
1923 The Spider and the Rose
1926 Kosher Kitty Kelly
1928 Wheel of Chance
Duffy, J. A.
1939 Frontiers of '49
Duffy, Jack
1935 Texas Terror
DuFrane, Frank
1937 Big City
DuFrayne, June
1947 Citizen Saint
Dugan, Bobby
1949 Pinky
Dugan, Jimmy
1946 Shadows Over Chinatown
Dugan, Michael
1949 She Wore a Yellow
Ribbon
3 Godfathers
1950 Annie Get Your Gun
A Lady Without Passport
1951 Across the Wide Missouri
Show Boat
Westward the Women
1955 Trial
1957 Raintree County
Dugan, Tom
1933 Grand Slam
1934 The Cat's-Paw
1935 Chinatown Squad
Rendezvous
1937 Big City
1939 Daughters Courageous
1940 The Fighting 69th
1941 Where Did You Get That
Girl?
1943 The Amazing Mrs.
Holliday
Bataan
The Meanest Man in the
World
Yankee Doodle Dandy

1944 Hi, Beautiful
1946 Bringing Up Father
1947 Easy Come, Easy Go
The Mighty McGurk
1948 Half Past Midnight
Dugas, Oscar Roy
1928 The Midnight Ace
Dugay, Yvette see **Duguay, Yvette**
Duggan, Jan
1934 Wagon Wheels
1936 The Prisoner of Shark
Island
1937 Life Begins in College
Duguay, Joy
1945 A Tree Grows in Brooklyn
Duguay, Yvette same as **Dugay,**
Yvette
1942 Tortilla Flat
1943 Dr. Gillespie's Criminal
Case
1951 The Great Caruso
1952 Hiawatha
1954 Cattle Queen of Montana
Duke, a horse
1933 Man from Monterey
The Telegraph Trail
Duke, John
1959 Al Capone
1960 Pay or Die
Duke, Maurice
1948 Music Man
Dulac, Arthur
1943 Action in the North
Atlantic
Dulier, Suzanne same as **Dulier,**
Susanne
1934 Cuesta abajo
El tango en Broadway
1935 El día que me quieras
Tango Bar
Dull, Orville O. same as **Dull, O. O.**
1942 We Were Dancing
1946 Bad Bascomb
1947 Little Mister Jim
Dumas, Wade
1939 Harlem Rides the Range
1950 No Way Out
1955 The View from Pompey's
Head
Dumbrille, Douglass same as
Dumbrille, Douglas
1933 The Man Who Dared: An
Imaginative Biography
1934 Broadway Bill
Massacre
Operator 13
1935 Naughty Marietta
1938 The Buccaneer
1939 Charlie Chan at Treasure
Island
City in Darkness
Mr. Moto in Danger
Island
1942 Castle in the Desert
1945 A Medal for Benny
1950 Buccaneer's Girl
1952 Apache War Smoke
1953 Captain John Smith and
Pocahontas
Dumke, Ralph
1950 The Breaking Point
Mystery Street
1954 Massacre Canyon
They Rode West
1955 Violent Saturday
Dumonceau, Andre
1942 Prisoner of Japan
Dumont, Dorothy Yvonne could
be same as **Dumont, Yvonne**
1919 Injustice
Dumont, Harry
1918 The Birth of a Race
Dumont, Margaret
1935 A Night at the Opera
Dumont, Yvonne could be same as
Dumont, Dorothy Yvonne
1920? Reformation
Duna, Steffi
1936 Dancing Pirate
1938 Rascals
1939 Way Down South

Dunaew, Nicholas
1916 The Yellow Passport
1917 The Flower of Doom
The Pulse of Life
1918 The Firebrand
Dunaway, Warren
1940 Geronimo
Dunbar, Charles
1934 Lazy River
1935 The Winning Ticket
Dunbar, Dave could be same as
Dunbar, David
1937 Maid of Salem
1940 Escape to Glory
1950 Young Man with a Horn
Dunbar, David
1924 North of 36
1925 Galloping Vengeance
1927 The Fighting Hombre
Dunbar, Dixie
1937 Life Begins in College
Dunbar, Dorothy
1924? The Flaming Crisis
Dunbar, Helen
1918 The Squaw Man
1923 Thirty Days
1926 Meet the Prince
Dunbar, Louise
1921 The Green-Eyed Monster
Dunbar, Robert N.
1917 The Conqueror
1918 In Judgment Of
Me Und Gott
1919 Fighting for Gold
Duncan, Ann
1949 Knock on Any Door
1951 Saturday's Hero
Duncan, Archie
1959 John Paul Jones
Duncan, Betsy
1958 Home Before Dark
Duncan, Bob
1943 Action in the North
Atlantic
1945 The Cisco Kid Returns
1946 Wild West
1951 New Mexico
Duncan, Bud
1931 Riders of the Rio
Duncan, Craig
1959 Al Capone
Duncan, David
1953 Sangaree
Duncan, Hadley J.
1921 The Burden of Race
Duncan, John
1947 It Had To Be You
1951 The Harlem Globetrotters
Duncan, Kenne same as **Duncan,**
Ken; Duncan, Kenneth
1939 Trigger Fingers
1942 Valley of Hunted Men
1943 In Old Oklahoma
The Law Rides Again
Wagon Tracks West
1944 Marshal of Reno
Sheriff of Las Vegas
Vigilantes of Dodge City
1946 California Gold Rush
Santa Fe Uprising
Sheriff of Redwood Valley
Sun Valley Cyclone
1950 Davy Crockett, Indian
Scout
Indian Territory
1952 Indian Uprising
1957 Revolt at Fort Laramie
Duncan, Leonard
1947 Juke Joint
Duncan, Mary
1929 Romance of the Rio
Grande
1932 Thirteen Women
Duncan, Melody
1947 Juke Joint
Duncan, Pamela
1957 Gun Battle at Monterey
Duncan, Renault
1946 Don Ricardo Returns
1947 Bells of San Fernando

Duncan, Rita
1960　Studs Lonigan
Duncan, Rosetta
1927　Topsy and Eva
Duncan, Sam
1939　Heaven with a Barbed
　　　　Wire Fence
Duncan, Todd
1942　Syncopation
Duncan, Veleda
1932　Hypnotized
Duncan, Vernon B. *could be same
　as* **Duncan, Vernon S.**
1948　The Betrayal
Duncan, Vernon S. *could be same
　as* **Duncan, Vernon B.**
1919　The Homesteader
Duncan, Vivian
1927　Topsy and Eva
Duncan, William
1917　The Tenderfoot
Duncan's Beauty Show Girls
1947　Juke Joint
Dundee, Jimmie *same as* **Dundee,
　James; Dundee, Jim; Dundee,
　Jimmy**
1936　It Had to Happen
1938　The Buccaneer
　　　　Daughter of Shanghai
1939　Mr. Moto in Danger
　　　　Island
1940　Lucky Cisco Kid
　　　　Murder over New York
1941　Birth of the Blues
　　　　Hold Back the Dawn
　　　　Sullivan's Travels
1944　Going My Way
1945　The Bells of St. Mary's
　　　　A Medal for Benny
1947　California
　　　　Easy Come, Easy Go
　　　　The Mighty McGurk
1952　The Savage
Dungan, Charles
1919　The Scar
**Katherine Dunham and Her
　Troupe**
1943　Stormy Weather
Dunham, Phil *(actor)*
1936　Hair-Trigger Casey
1947　California
1950　Annie Get Your Gun
Dunham, Phil *(writer)*
1937　Bargain with Bullets
1938　The Duke Is Tops
　　　　Life Goes On
1939　Gang Smashers
Dunhill, Ford
1960　This Rebel Breed
Dunhill, Steve *same as* **Jillson,
　Willard**
1944　Since You Went Away
1947　Duel in the Sun
1948　Harpoon
1950　Rocky Mountain
1951　Apache Drums
Dunkinson, Harry
1917　Follow the Girl
1923　The Sting of the Scorpion
1934　Broadway Bill
　　　　Stand Up and Cheer!
Dunlap, Scott R. *same as* **Dunlap,
　Scott**
1922　Pawn Ticket 210
1923　Snowdrift
1925　The Fearless Lover
1926　The Frontier Trail
1927　Whispering Sage
1939　The Mystery of Mr. Wong
1940　Doomed to Die
1942　Below the Border
1944　Lady, Let's Dance!
1945　Sunbonnet Sue
1946　Beauty and the Bandit
　　　　Border Bandits
　　　　The Gay Cavalier
　　　　South of Monterey
1947　Riding the California
　　　　Trail
1960　The Plunderers

Dunmore, James
1947　Hi De Ho
Dunn, Bobby
1934　Broadway Bill
1937　Slave Ship
Dunn, Eddie
1936　My American Wife
　　　　Rose of the Rancho
1937　Charlie Chan on
　　　　Broadway
　　　　Man of the People
　　　　One Mile from Heaven
　　　　Slave Ship
　　　　That I May Live
1938　Rascals
　　　　Speed to Burn
1939　The Cisco Kid and the
　　　　Lady
　　　　Let Freedom Ring
1940　Mexican Spitfire Out
　　　　West
1942　Mexican Spitfire at Sea
1943　The Amazing Mrs.
　　　　Holliday
　　　　Margin for Error
1944　Three Men in White
1945　Salome, Where She
　　　　Danced
1946　Canyon Passage
1947　Buck Privates Come
　　　　Home
1948　Call Northside 777
　　　　Sleep, My Love
　　　　Unconquered
Dunn, Emma
1931　The Guilty Generation
1932　The Cohens and Kellys in
　　　　Hollywood
1933　Grand Slam
　　　　It's Great to Be Alive
1937　Waikiki Wedding
Dunn, Frank
1934　Behold My Wife!
Dunn, George
1955　Good Morning, Miss Dove
1957　Joe Dakota
Dunn, J. Norton
1943　Margin for Error
Dunn, James *(actor)* 1901–1967
1934　Stand Up and Cheer!
1945　A Tree Grows in Brooklyn
Dunn, James circa 1919
1919　Deliverance
Dunn, Josephine
1928　We Americans
Dunn, Paul
1948　Fighting Father Dunne
　　　　The Paleface
Dunn, Pete *could be same as*
　Dunne, Peter
1957　Band of Angels
Dunn, Ralph
1937　One Mile from Heaven
1938　Gateway
　　　　Mr. Moto's Gamble
　　　　Speed to Burn
1939　Mr. Moto in Danger
　　　　Island
　　　　Mr. Moto Takes a
　　　　Vacation
　　　　The Return of the Cisco
　　　　Kid
　　　　Waterfront
　　　　Winner Take All
1940　Elsa Maxwell's Public
　　　　Deb No. 1
　　　　Murder over New York
　　　　New Moon
1941　Accent on Love
　　　　Dead Men Tell
　　　　Sun Valley Serenade
　　　　Western Union
1942　The Navy Comes Through
　　　　Syncopation
1943　Action in the North
　　　　Atlantic
　　　　Dr. Gillespie's Criminal
　　　　Case
1945　Escape in the Fog
　　　　Where Do We Go From
　　　　Here?
1946　Gas House Kids
　　　　Saratoga Trunk

1947　Buck Privates Come
　　　　Home
　　　　California
1948　Fighting Father Dunne
　　　　Fury at Furnace Creek
　　　　The Golden Eye
　　　　My Girl Tisa
1949　The Fighting Kentuckian
1950　No Way Out
1953　Taxi
1956　Crowded Paradise
Dunn, Robert A., Rev.
1949　Lost Boundaries
Dunn, Tay
1946　Without Reservations
1951　The Great Caruso
Dunn, Violet
1931　The Black Camel
Dunn, William *same as* **Dunn,
　William R.**
1917　I Will Repay
1918　I Want to Forget
　　　　The Little Runaway
Dunn, Winifred
1919　The Red Viper
1934　Las fronteras del amor
Dunne, Eithne
1959　Shake Hands with the
　　　　Devil
Dunne, Elizabeth
1942　Cat People
Dunne, Finley Peter, Jr.
1934　Imitation of Life
Dunne, George
1956　Giant
Dunne, Irene
1931　Cimarron
1932　Symphony of Six Million
　　　　Thirteen Women
1936　Show Boat
1948　I Remember Mama
Dunne, Peter
1943　Action in the North
　　　　Atlantic
　　　　Redhead from Manhattan
Dunne, Philip
1932　Me and My Gal
1936　The Last of the Mohicans
1948　The Luck of the Irish
1949　Pinky
1955　The View from Pompey's
　　　　Head
Dunne, Steve
1958　Home Before Dark
Dunning, Don
1951　Flaming Feather
1953　Arrowhead
Dunnock, Mildred
1953　The Jazz Singer
1956　Baby Doll
Dupea, Anna
1934　Laughing Boy
Dupea, Talzumbie
1944　Buffalo Bill
1951　Across the Wide Missouri
Dupont, E. A.
1935　Rendezvous
Dupont, Gertl
1950　Battleground
DuPont, Renald
1951　The Great Caruso
Dupree, Roland
1946　The Sailor Takes a Wife
Duprez, June
1942　Little Tokyo, U.S.A.
Du Puis, Art
1936　The Last of the Mohicans
Dupuis, Art
1937　The Devil's Playground
　　　　Slave Ship
1938　Charlie Chan at Monte
　　　　Carlo
　　　　Happy Landing
1940　The Mark of Zorro
1948　I Remember Mama
　　　　The Miracle of the Bells
1951　Gambling House
Dupuis, Joan
1959　The FBI Story

Dur, Poldy
1943　Margin for Error
　　　　They Came to Blow Up
　　　　America
Durafour
1931　Su noche de bodas
　　　　(foreign version)
Duran, Edna
1939　Drifting Westward
Durán, Elena
1935　Te quiero con locura
1935?　The Irish Gringo
1936　Ramona
1939　La Inmaculada
Duran, Mrs. Elsie
1936　Tundra
Duran, Larence
1938　Hawaii Calls
Duran, Ruben
1938　Hawaii Calls
Durand, David
1930　Ladies Love Brutes
1934　As the Earth Turns
Durand, Edward
1922　Anna Ascends
1923　Potash and Perlmutter
Durant, H. R.
1917　The Red Woman
Durant, Jack
1934　Stand Up and Cheer!
Durant, Jacquelyn
1960　This Rebel Breed
Durant, M.
1922　Peacock Alley
Durante, Jimmy
1932　Le plombier amoureux
1957　Beau James
Durbin, Deanna
1943　The Amazing Mrs.
　　　　Holliday
　　　　His Butler's Sister
1948　Up in Central Park
Durey, Rea
1931　Such Is Life
Durgeon, Augusta
1940　The Ramparts We Watch
Durham, Bull *see* **Durham, Louis**
Durham, G. A.
1931　Oklahoma Jim
Durham, Louis *same as* **Durham,
　Bull**
1918　Hell's End
Durkin, Grace
1936　Star for a Night
Durkin, Junior
1930　Tom Sawyer
1931　Huckleberry Finn
Durkin, Mary Anne
1944　Since You Went Away
Durlam, G. A. *same as* **Durlam,
　Arthur; Durlam, George
　Arthur**
1935　Captured in Chinatown
1936　Aces and Eights
　　　　Custer's Last Stand
Durning, Bernard
1921　Diane of Star Hollow
Durousseau, Antoine
1959　Porgy and Bess
DuRoy, Harry
1916　A Man of Sorrow
Duryea, Dan
1945　The Valley of Decision
1950　Winchester '73
1953　Thunder Bay
1955　Foxfire
Duryea, George *see* **Keene, Tom**
Dusick, Jack
1958　Tonka
D'Usseau, Léon
1931　Echec au roi
1937　Nation Aflame
Dutra, John
1950　Battleground
Dutriz, John
1947　The Foxes of Harrow
Duval, Al
1937　Bargain with Bullets
1938　The Beloved Brat

Hermanos Duval
1938   Di que me quieres
Duval, Jacqueline
1952   Red Ball Express
Duval, Joe
1949   The Red Menace
1951   The Girl on the Bridge
1953   So Big
Duval, Juan
1930   Cascarrabias
        Los que danzan
        Sombras de gloria
1931   Carne de cabaret
1933   The California Trail
1934   Un capitán de cosacos
        Tres amores
1935   No matarás
1936   Amor que vuelve
        El diablo del mar
1939   Miracle on Main Street
        (*foreign version*)
        Mr. Moto in Danger
        Island
1940   Rhythm of the Rio
        Grande
1948   The Feathered Serpent
1949   Brothers in the Saddle
1950   The Breaking Point
        The Palomino
        Right Cross
Duval, Odette
1934   La veuve joyeuse
Duval, Paulette
1926   Blarney
Duvivier, George
1956   The Benny Goodman
        Story
Duvivier, Julien
1942   Tales of Manhattan
D'Vega, Juan
1935   Tango Bar
Dvorak, Ann
1932   Scarface
1934   Massacre
1937   Manhattan
        Merry-Go-Round
Dwan, Allan
1914   The Straight Road
1916   The Half-Breed
1920   The Luck of the Irish
1929   Frozen Justice
1936   Human Cargo
1937   One Mile from Heaven
        That I May Live
1938   Josette
1942   Friendly Enemies
1947   Calendar Girl
        Northwest Outpost
1948   Angel in Exile
1950   Sands of Iwo Jima
1954   Cattle Queen of Montana
        Passion
Dwan, Dorothy
1927   McFadden's Flats
1929   The Peacock Fan
Dwire, Earl
1934   'Neath the Arizona Skies
        The Star Packer
1935   Fighting Pioneers
        Wolf Riders
1936   Pinto Rustlers
        Tundra
1937   Law and Lead
Dworshak, Lois
1941   Ice-Capades
Dwyer, Ethel
1921   Cotton and Cattle
Dwyer, Marlo
1947   Crossfire
1954   Dangerous Mission
Dye, Florence
1917   The Tenderfoot
Dyer, Bob
1946   Sunset Pass
Dyer, E. C.
1930   Georgia Rose
Dyer, William *same as* **Dyer, Bill**
1916   Broken Fetters
1917   The Pulse of Life
1919   Who Will Marry Me?
1922   The Crow's Nest
1928   Uncle Tom's Cabin

Dymow, Ossip *same as* **Dymow,
Ossip, Dr.**
1936   Sins of Man
1938   The Singing Blacksmith
1939   Mirele Efros
1940   Overture to Glory
Dynamite, a horse
1925   Old Clothes
1932   Law and Lawless
Dyrenforth, Harold
1945   The House on 92nd St.
1947   Carnegie Hall
1952   Red Ball Express
Eagan, Theodore
1948   The Fight Never Ends
Eager, Evelyne *same as* **Eager,
Evelyn**
1942   Song of the Islands
1944   Something for the Boys
Eagle Eye *could be same as* **Eagle
Eye, William**
1915   The Lamb
1918   Untamed
1922   The Pride of Palomar
Eagle Eye, William *could be same
as* **Eagle Eye**
1921   Wolves of the North
1922   The Son of the Wolf
Eagle Shirt, William
1917   The Conqueror
Eagle, Don
1957   Naked in the Sun
Eagle, James *see* **Eagles, James**
Eagle, S. P. *see* **Spiegel, Sam**
Eagles, James *same as* **Eagle,
James**
1930   Abraham Lincoln
        Son of the Gods
1934   He Was Her Man
        Massacre
1935   Charlie Chan in Egypt
1936   Charlie Chan at the Race
        Track
1943   Crash Dive
Eagles, Jeanne *same as* **Eagels,
Jeanne**
1917   Under False Colors
Ealey, June
1942   Holiday Inn
Earl, Connie
1939   Gone With the Wind
Earl, Kenneth
1942   Twin Beds
1943   Mr. Lucky
Earl, Wallace *same as* **Earl, Wally**
1948   Unconquered
1959   Anna Lucasta
Earlcott, Gladys
1917   The Red Woman
Earle, Edward *same as* **Earle,
Eddie**
1918   The Little Runaway
1923   None So Blind
1924   The Lure of Love
1926   Irene
1929   Smiling Irish Eyes
1934   She Was a Lady
        Stand Up and Cheer!
1935   Chinatown Squad
1938   City Streets
        Mr. Moto's Gamble
        The Rage of Paris
1940   If I Had My Way
1941   Mystery Ship
        Sun Valley Serenade
1942   Sunday Punch
1943   Crash Dive
        Dr. Gillespie's Criminal
        Case
        Jack London
1944   Black Magic
1945   In Old New Mexico
1946   Dark Alibi
1947   The Mighty McGurk
        Ride the Pink Horse
1949   That Midnight Kiss
1950   Annie Get Your Gun
1951   Go for Broke!
1952   The Raiders
1955   A Man Called Peter

Earle, Ferdinand Pinney
1918   Toys of Fate
Earle, Jane
1948   Gentleman's Agreement
Earle, June
1945   Where Do We Go From
        Here?
Earle, Marilee
1958   Terror in a Texas Town
Earle, Robert
1947   Jiggs and Maggie in
        Society
Earle, Walter
1946   Beware
Earle, William (*actor*)
1927   The Slaver
Earle, William P. S. (*dir*)
1917   I Will Repay
1918   The Little Runaway
Early, Dudley
1927   Topsy and Eva
Early, Margaret
1939   Judge Hardy and Son
Early, Pearl
1941   Birth of the Blues
1943   In Old Oklahoma
Earnest, Charles
1936   Charlie Chan's Secret
Earwood, Tommy
1958   The Last Hurrah
Easler, Fred
1944   Address Unknown
Easley, Elroy
1945   Of One Blood
Eason, B. Reeves *same as* **Eason, B.
Reaves; Eason, Breezy; Eason,
Reaves; Eason, Reeves**
1919   The Right to Happiness
1922   When East Comes West
1931   Cimarron
1933   Dance Hall Hostess
        Racetrack
1937   Prairie Thunder
1939   Gone With the Wind
1942   American Empire
        They Died With Their
        Boots On
1947   Black Gold
        Duel in the Sun
Eason, W. B. *same as* **Eason, Mike**
1937   Boy of the Streets
1938   Mr. Wong, Detective
1939   Mr. Wong in Chinatown
        The Mystery of Mr. Wong
1940   Covered Wagon Days
        The Fatal Hour
1947   Last of the Redmen
East, Ed
1949   Jiggs and Maggie in
        Jackpot Jitters
1950   The Baron of Arizona
East, Henry
1932   Hypnotized
East, Stewart
1959   The Black Orchid
Eastman, Janet
1934   Broadway Bill
Easton, Jack
1939   The Escape
Easton, Jane
1957   The Brothers Rico
Easton, Mark
1957   All Mine to Give
Easton, Paul
1957   All Mine to Give
Easton, Richard
1928   Ramona
Easton, Robert
1951   The Tall Target
Easton, Sid *same as* **Easton,
Sidney; Easton, Sydney**
1940   Paradise in Harlem
1941   Murder on Lenox Avenue
        Sunday Sinners
1946?   Fight That Ghost
1948   Killer Diller
1948?   Boarding House Blues
Eastwood, Clint
1958   Ambush at Cimarron Pass

Eaton, Jay
1921   Where Lights Are Low
1935   A Night at the Opera
        The Wedding Night
1950   The Big Hangover
Eaton, Marjorie
1949   The Story of Seabiscuit
1952   Rose of Cimarron
Eaton, Pearl
1936   Klondike Annie
Eaton, Winifred
1930   East Is West
Eben, Al
1942   All Through the Night
1945   A Tree Grows in Brooklyn
1948   The Lady from Shanghai
        The Miracle of the Bells
1951   The Harlem Globetrotters
1952   Fort Osage
1953   Taxi
Eberle, Ed
1935   The Wedding Night
Eberle, Eugene R.
1948   Unconquered
Eberle, Ray
1918   Me Und Gott
Eberling, June
1935   Black Fury
Eberts, John *same as* **Eberts,
Johnny**
1936   Dancing Pirate
1943   The Leopard Man
The Ebony Trio
1946?   Harlem on Parade
Ebright, Robert
1951   The Great Caruso
Ebsen, Buddy
1938   My Lucky Star
1955   Davy Crockett, King of
        the Wild Frontier
1956   Davy Crockett and the
        River Pirates
Eburne, Maude
1932   Le plombier amoureux
1933   Robbers' Roost
1934   Lazy River
1935   Ruggles of Red Gap
Eby, Earl
1935   Rendezvous
1936   The Prisoner of Shark
        Island
Eby, Lois
1940   Hi-Yo Silver
Eby-Rock, Helen
1944   Mr. Skeffington
1950   Stars in My Crown
Eccles, Robin
1959   The FBI Story
Eccles, Ted
1960   Cimarron
Echeverria, Gerald
1947   Riding the California
        Trail
1949   Border Incident
Echeverria, Raquel
1937   Waikiki Wedding
Eckelberry, Ted
1950   Battleground
        Young Man with a Horn
Eckels, Lew
1945   The House on 92nd St.
1948   Call Northside 777
Eckert, John *same as* **Eckert,
Johnny**
1937   The Plainsman
1938   The Texans
Eckhardt, Oliver
1928   The Cavalier
Eckhardt, William
1936   Charlie Chan at the
        Circus
1937   Thank You, Mr. Moto
1938   Mr. Moto Takes a Chance
1940   The Gay Caballero
        Murder over New York
1941   Accent on Love
        Charlie Chan in Rio
1942   Whispering Ghosts
1943   They Came to Blow Up
        America
1944   Buffalo Bill

1948 Fury at Furnace Creek
1949 House of Strangers
1950 No Way Out
Two Flags West

Eckstein, William
1914? A Boy and the Law

Economides, George
1946 Without Reservations
1952 It's a Big Country: An American Anthology

Economides, Michael
1946 Without Reservations

Eddinger, Wallace
1914 The Great Diamond Robbery

Eddy, Bob (*writer*) *not the same as* **Eddy, Robert** (*actor*)
1926 The Strong Man

Eddy, Bonnie Kay
1950 Winchester '73

Eddy, Helen Jerome
1916 Pasquale
1917 His Sweetheart
Lost in Transit
1918 One More American
1919 The Tong Man
1921 The First Born
One Man in a Million
1931 The Great Meadow
1932 No Greater Love
1936 Klondike Annie
Show Boat
Winterset
1938 City Streets

Eddy, Nelson
1935 Naughty Marietta
1939 Let Freedom Ring
1940 New Moon
1944 Knickerbocker Holiday
1947 Northwest Outpost

Edele, Velma
1926 Shadows of Chinatown

Edelman, Louis F.
1940 The Fighting 69th
1953 The Jazz Singer

Edelman, Merl S.
1957 Burden of Truth

Eden, Barbara
1960 Flaming Star

Edeson, Robert (*American actor*) *not the same as* **Eddison, Robert** (*English actor*)
1914 Where the Trail Divides
1915 The Girl I Left Behind Me
How Molly Malone Made Good
1924 Welcome Stranger
1925 Braveheart
The Scarlet West
1928 George Washington Cohen
A Ship Comes In
1929 Romance of the Rio Grande
1930 The Lash
1931 Aloha

Edington, Harry E.
1940 They Knew What They Wanted
Too Many Girls

Edison, Thomas A.
1915 Cohen's Luck

Edler, Charles *same as* **Edhler, Charles; Ehler, Charles; Elder, Charles**
1919 The Heart of Wetona
1920 Huckleberry Finn
1921 That Girl Montana
1922 The Sign of the Rose

Edmiston, Alan
1946 Slightly Scandalous

Edmiston, James
1954 Dangerous Mission

Edmonds, Ann
1940 East of the River
1943 Yankee Doodle Dandy

Edmonson, William
1927 The Millionaire
1928 The Midnight Ace
Thirty Years Later

Edmunds, Robert
1942 Professor Creeps

Edmunds, William
1940 Escape
Geronimo
The Mark of Zorro
1942 Juke Girl
1943 Deerslayer
1946 Swamp Fire
1950 The Lawless

Edmundson, Mr.
1915 Just Jim

Edson, Marshall
1949 Ride, Ryder, Ride!

Edward, Walter *see* **Edwards, Walter**

Edwards, Alan
1945 Salome, Where She Danced

Edwards, Bill *same as* **Edwards, William**
1942 Wings for the Eagle
1943 Action in the North Atlantic
Air Force
Riding High
Yankee Doodle Dandy

Edwards, Blake
1944 Marshal of Reno
1946 Till the End of Time

Edwards, Bruce
1941 Sun Valley Serenade
1943 Gangway for Tomorrow
1944 My Pal Wolf
1945 Betrayal from the East
1946 Dangerous Money
1949 Prejudice
1950 Sands of Iwo Jima

Edwards, Celeste Mari
1934 Stand Up and Cheer!

Edwards, Charles *same as* **Edwards, C.**
1917? Barnaby Lee

Edwards, Cliff *same as* **Ukelele Ike**
1939 Gone With the Wind
1941 Thunder Over the Prairie
1942 American Empire
Lawless Plainsmen

Edwards, Edgar
1941 Ride on Vaquero

Edwards, Elaine
1959 Inside the Mafia

Edwards, Eleanor
1934 Stand Up and Cheer!

Edwards, Fred L.
1948 Silver Trails

Edwards, Frog
1949? The Joint Is Jumpin'

Edwards, Grant
1920 Within Our Gates

Edwards, Harry D.
1943 The Girl from Monterrey

Edwards, J. Gordon
1914 Life's Shop Window

Edwards, J. Harrison
1922 Square Joe

Edwards, James
1949 Home of the Brave
1951 The Steel Helmet
1952 Bright Victory
1953 The Joe Louis Story
The Member of the Wedding
1955 Seven Angry Men
1959 Anna Lucasta
Night of the Quarter Moon

Edwards, Josephine
1940 Mystery in Swing

Edwards, LeRoy
1941 Sullivan's Travels
1947 California

Edwards, Mary Ann
1956 Giant
1959 The FBI Story

Edwards, Mattie
1920 The Brute
Within Our Gates

Edwards, Neely
1929 Show Boat
1933 Diplomaniacs
1936 Sutter's Gold
1939 Mr. Moto in Danger Island
1942 Mexican Spitfire's Elephant

Edwards, Penny
1950 North of the Great Divide
Sunset in the West
1952 Woman in the Dark

Edwards, Ralph
1937 Manhattan Merry-Go-Round
1940 George Washington Carver

Edwards, Sam
1942 Rubber Racketeers
1958 The Badlanders

Edwards, Sarah
1935 Ruggles of Red Gap
1936 Dangerous Intrigue
My American Wife
1937 Life Begins in College
1938 The Beloved Brat
1939 The Adventures of Huckleberry Finn
1940 Lucky Cisco Kid
New Moon
1941 Birth of the Blues
The Face Behind the Mask
1944 Charlie Chan in the Secret Service
1946 Saratoga Trunk

Edwards, Snitz
1921 Cheated Love
No Woman Knows
1923 The Huntress
1926 April Fool

Edwards, Thornton
1940 Lucky Cisco Kid
1947 The Chinese Ring
Robin Hood of Monterey
1948 Fury at Furnace Creek

Edwards, Vince
1952 Hiawatha
1956 Serenade
1957 Ride Out for Revenge

Edwards, Walter *same as* **Edward, Walter**
1917 The Bride of Hate
1918 The Gypsy Trail
Real Folks

Edwards, Weston *see* **Fraser, Harry**

Edwards, William *see* **Edwards, Bill**

Edwin, Walter
1915 The Danger Signal

Effe, William *see* **Ehfe, William**

Effrat, Jack
1940 The Notorious Elinor Lee

Egan, Jack (*actor*) *not the same as* **Eagan, Jack** (*cam*)
1931 Delicious

Egan, Mishka
1945 Where Do We Go From Here?

Egan, Richard
1952 The Battle at Apache Pass
Bright Victory
1953 The Glory Brigade
1955 Seven Cities of Gold
The View from Pompey's Head
Violent Saturday

Eggen, Robert
1957 The Halliday Brand

Eggers, Fred
1954 Thunder Pass

Ehfe, William *same as* **Effe, William; Ephe, William**
1916 The Daughter of the Don

Ehlers, Walter D.
1955 The Long Gray Line

Ehmig, George
1950 Panic in the Streets

Ehrhart, Eddie
1947 California

Ehrlich, Lynne
1958 Sierra Baron

Ehrlich, Margaret
1934 Stand Up and Cheer!

The 8 Rhythmeers
1944 Slightly Terrific

Eilers, Sally
1931 The Black Camel

Eiman, John
1960 The Dark at the Top of the Stairs

Einfeld, Richard
1959 The Oregon Trail

Eis, Egon
1931 Tropennächte

Eitner, Don
1960 This Rebel Breed

Ekberg, Carl
1943 Action in the North Atlantic
Gangway for Tomorrow
1944 Address Unknown

Ekström, Märta
1930 Doña mentiras (*foreign version*)

Elam, Jack
1950 A Ticket to Tomahawk
1952 The Battle at Apache Pass
High Noon
My Man and I
The Ring
1953 Ride, Vaquero!
1954 Cattle Queen of Montana
1957 Dragoon Wells Massacre

Elam, Trippy
1959 The FBI Story

Elbaum, Ruth
1939 Mirele Efros

Elder, Ruth
1918 Thirty a Week

Elders, Harry
1952? Call of the Navajo

Eldredge, Florence
1932 Thirteen Women

Eldredge, Frank
1943 Hitler's Children
1951 Saturday's Hero

Eldredge, George *same as* **Eldridge, Geo.; Eldridge, George** *could be same as* **Eldridge, Geo.**
1940 Northwest Passage (Book I—Rogers' Rangers)
1942 They Died With Their Boots On
Unseen Enemy
1944 Outlaw Trail
The Racket Man
Sonora Stagecoach
1946 Dark Alibi
The Gentleman Misbehaves
Shadows Over Chinatown
1948 Reaching from Heaven
Shanghai Chest
1949 The Sky Dragon
1952 Brave Warrior
California Conquest
1953 The Man from the Alamo
1954 Overland Pacific

Eldredge, John
1937 Charlie Chan at the Olympics
One Mile from Heaven
1946 Dark Alibi
1949 The Sky Dragon
Top O' the Morning
1957 Raintree County

Eldridge, Charles
1916 The Pretenders
1920? Broken Hearts
1921 Made in Heaven

Eldridge, George *see* **Eldredge, George**

Elfelt, Clifford S.
1922 Big Stakes
1926 Under Fire

Elhardt, Kaye
1959   The Crimson Kimono
Eline, Marie
1914   Uncle Tom's Cabin
Elinor, Carli D.
1956   The Benny Goodman
        Story
Eliot, John *see* **Elliott, John**
Eliscu, Edward
1936   Paddy O'Day
1945   The Gay Senorita
Eliscu, Fernanda
1936   Winterset
1945   A Tree Grows in Brooklyn
1948   Unconquered
1949   Harbor of Missing Men
Elison, Fernanda
1950   Black Hand
Elizondo, Joaquin
1949   Streets of Laredo
Elkas, Edward *same as* **Elkes,**
   Edward; Elkus, Edward
1918   The Birth of a Race
        Hitting the Trail
1924   Birthright
Elkins, Saul
1936   Charlie Chan at the Race
        Track
        Star for a Night
1937   That I May Live
1950   Colt .45
Ellenshaw, Peter
1958   The Light in the Forest
Ellenstein, Robert
1958   The Young Lions
1960   Pay or Die
Ellenwood, Grace
1921   By Right of Birth
Ellerbe, Harry
1935   So Red the Rose
1958   The Young Lions
Ellias, Miriam
1926   Broken Hearts
1932   The Unfortunate Bride
Ellingford, William
1919   The Lord Loves the Irish
1920   The Cyclone
Duke Ellington and his Orchestra
   same as **Duke Ellington and**
   his Cotton Club Orchestra
1930   Check and Double Check
1943   Cabin in the Sky
Ellingwood, H.
1944   Buffalo Bill
Elliot, Biff
1955   Good Morning, Miss Dove
Elliot, John *see* **Elliott, John**
Elliot, Laura
1949   Top O' the Morning
Elliot, Robert *see* **Elliott, Robert**
Elliott, Adelaide
1919   Who Will Marry Me?
Elliott, Alice *same as* **Elliott, Alice**
   Clair
1916   The Social Highwayman
1919   The Sleeping Lion
Elliott, Bill *see* **Elliott, William**
   "Wild Bill"
Elliott, Billy Jack
1941   Where Did You Get That
        Girl?
Elliott, Cecil
1936   After the Thin Man
1958   The Rawhide Trail
Elliott, Clyde
1947   Citizen Saint
Elliott, Dick *same as* **Elliott,**
   Richard "Dick"
1936   The Prisoner of Shark
        Island
1938   Mr. Moto's Gamble
1940   Behind the News
1942   All Through the Night
        Three Hearts for Julia
        We Were Dancing
1943   Wintertime
1944   An American Romance
        Hi, Beautiful
1945   Wanderer of the
        Wasteland
        Where Do We Go From
        Here?

1946   Dangerous Money
        Saratoga Trunk
        Till the End of Time
1947   Desperate
        Thunder Mountain
1948   The Dude Goes West
        The Paleface
        Singin' Spurs
1949   Rose of the Yukon
1950   Belle of Old Mexico
        Rock Island Trail
1951   Fort Defiance
1952   High Noon
Elliott, Edythe
1942   Valley of Hunted Men
1943   Gangway for Tomorrow
        Redhead from Manhattan
1945   A Tree Grows in Brooklyn
1946   Santa Fe Uprising
1948   The Lady from Shanghai
1952   Rose of Cimarron
Elliott, Frank
1923   Ruggles of Red Gap
1925   The Gold Hunters
        Speed Wild
        Tearing Through
1930   Take the Heir
1940   New Moon
1947   Humoresque
Elliott, Gordon *see* **Elliott, William**
   "Wild Bill"
Elliott, Heenan
1945   The Mummy's Curse
1948   The Lady from Shanghai
Elliott, John *same as* **Elliot, John;**
   Elliott, John H.
1931   Oklahoma Jim
1932   Call Her Savage
        Hidden Valley
        Riders of the Desert
        Texas Pioneers
1934   As the Earth Turns
        Operator 13
1935   Captured in Chinatown
        Cowboy Holiday
        Fighting Pioneers
        A Night at the Ritz
1937   Souls at Sea
1939   Trigger Fingers
1945   Escape in the Fog
1948   The Lady from Shanghai
Elliott, Leonard
1940   Overture to Glory
1960   Weddings and Babies
Elliott, Lillian
1925   Old Clothes
1943   Gangway for Tomorrow
Elliott, Marie
1933   Thundering Herd
Elliott, Marietta
1950   Annie Get Your Gun
1951   Show Boat
Elliott, Robert *same as* **Elliot,**
   Robert
1921   Lonely Heart
        The Money Maniac
1922   Fair Lady
1929   Thunderbolt
1930   Kathleen Mavourneen
1932   White Eagle
1939   Gone With the Wind
Elliott, Ross
1947   The Burning Cross
1950   Chinatown at Midnight
1952   Woman in the Dark
1953   Tumbleweed
1954   Massacre Canyon
Elliott, Scott
1945   Where Do We Go From
        Here?
Elliott, Ted
1947   Oregon Trail Scouts
Elliott, William "Wild Bill" *same*
   as **Elliot, Bill; Elliott, Bill;**
   Elliott, Gordon; Elliott, Wild
   Bill; Elliott, William
1935   A Night at the Ritz
1937   Boots and Saddles
        Boy of the Streets
1939   Frontiers of '49
1940   Prairie Schooners
1943   Wagon Tracks West

1944   Marshal of Reno
        The San Antonio Kid
        Sheriff of Las Vegas
        Tucson Raiders
        Vigilantes of Dodge City
1945   Colorado Pioneers
        Great Stagecoach Robbery
        Phantom of the Plains
1946   California Gold Rush
        Sheriff of Redwood Valley
        Sun Valley Cyclone
1948   Old Los Angeles
Ellis, A. B. *same as* **Ellis, Albert;**
   Ellis, Albert B.
1917   The Hidden Children
Ellis, Anita
1953   The Joe Louis Story
Ellis, Antony
1957   The Ride Back
Ellis, Byron
1943   Cabin in the Sky
Ellis, Edith
1931   The Great Meadow
        Quand on est belle
Ellis, Edward
1936   Winterset
1937   Maid of Salem
1939   Man of Conquest
Ellis, Evelyn
1948   The Lady from Shanghai
1953   The Joe Louis Story
Ellis, Frank
1935   Wolf Riders
1937   The Riders of the
        Whistling Skull
1941   Western Union
1949   The Cowboy and the
        Prizefighter
        The Valiant Hombre
1950   Indian Territory
1952   The Raiders
1953   The Man from the Alamo
Ellis, Jack *same as* **Ellis, John**
1929   East Side Sadie
1955   The Long Gray Line
Ellis, Jerry
1935   The Cyclone Ranger
Ellis, Juney
1953   The Glass Wall
1954   Drum Beat
1956   Giant
        The Last Wagon
1957   Joe Dakota
Ellis, Kathleen
1936   Show Boat
Ellis, Mary Jo
1946   Slightly Scandalous
Ellis, Maurice
1949   Lost Boundaries
Ellis, Patricia *not the same as* **Ellis,**
   Patti Marie
1935   A Night at the Ritz
Ellis, Patti Marie *not the same as*
   Ellis, Patricia
1953   Bright Road
Ellis, Paul *same as* **Granado,**
   Manuel; Paralupi, Benjamin
   Ingénito
1927   Bitter Apples
1929   In Old California
        Sombras habaneras
1930   Alma de gaucho
        Charros, gauchos y
        manolas
        La voluntad del muerto
1931   Monerías
        El pasado acusa
        Su última noche
1932   Hombres en mi vida
        Soñadores de la gloria
1933   Dos noches
1934   La buenaventura
        Tres amores
        La veuve joyeuse
1935   Captured in Chinatown
        Un hombre peligroso
        No matarás
1936   La última cita
1938   California Frontier
        Di que me quieres
        Mis dos amores
1939   Los hijos mandan
        Papá soltero
        El trovador de la radio

1940   Cuando canta la Ley
Ellis, Robert *(actor)*, 1933–1973
1955   The Long Gray Line
1956   Pillars of the Sky
Ellis, Robert *(actor, art dir, dir)*,
   1892–1935
1921   A Divorce of
        Convenience
1922   Anna Ascends
1931   Aloha
1932   White Eagle
Ellis, Robert *(writer)*
1935   ¡Asegure a su mujer!
        Charlie Chan in Egypt
1936   Charlie Chan at the
        Circus
        Charlie Chan at the Race
        Track
        Charlie Chan's Secret
1937   Charlie Chan at the
        Olympics
        Charlie Chan on
        Broadway
        That I May Live
1938   Charlie Chan at Monte
        Carlo
        Rascals
        Road Demon
        Speed to Burn
1939   City in Darkness
        The Escape
1940   Lucky Cisco Kid
1941   Sun Valley Serenade
1942   Song of the Islands
1944   Something for the Boys
Ellis, Ward
1957   War Drums
Ellison, Calvin
1948   Unconquered
Ellison, Curley
1948   The Betrayal
Ellison, James *same as* **Ellison,**
   Jimmy
1935   The Winning Ticket
1937   The Barrier
        The Plainsman
1941   Ice-Capades
1943   The Gang's All Here
1944   Lady, Let's Dance!
1946   G. I. War Brides
1947   Calendar Girl
1950   I Killed Geronimo
Ellison, Jennie
1919   The Scar
Ellison, Marjorie
1916   The Gilded Spider
Ellison, Samuel
1923   Flames of Wrath
Elljay, Sam
1946?   Beale Street Mama
        Go Down, Death!
Ellsler, Effie
1935   Black Fury
Ellsworth, Bob *same as* **Ellsworth,**
   Robert
1936   Charlie Chan at the Race
        Track
1937   The Plainsman
Ellsworth, Virginia
1946   Abie's Irish Rose
Ellyn, Jean
1949   C-Man
Elman, Ziggy
1956   The Benny Goodman
        Story
Elmassian, Zaruhi *same as*
   Elmassian, Zari
1933   It's Great to Be Alive
1945   Anoush
Elmer, Billy *same as* **Elmer,**
   William
1914   Rose of the Rancho
        The Squaw Man
1915   The Kindling
1916   The Honorable Friend
1917   Castles for Two
1918   The Bravest Way
1920   Uncharted Channels
1922   The Man with Two
        Mothers
1931   Cimarron

Elmergreen, Charles
1946   Without Reservations

Elmore, Dick *same as* **Elmore, Richard**
1948   Unconquered

Elmore, Pearl *same as* **Elsmore, Pearl**
1916   Sold for Marriage

Elorriaga, Luis
1930   Charros, gauchos y manolas

Elsner, Karl
1960   I Aim at the Stars: the Wernher von Braun Story

Elsom, Isobel
1942   Seven Sweethearts
1957   The Guns of Fort Petticoat

Elson, Lee
1948   Harpoon

Eltinge, Julian
1915   How Molly Malone Made Good
1940   If I Had My Way

Elton, Edmund
1938   Spawn of the North

Eltz, Theodore Von *see* **Von Eltz, Theodore**

Elvidge, June
1917   The Red Woman
1918   Broken Ties

Elviro, Pedro "Pitouto"
1931   Un caballero de frac

Elwen, Lottie
1949   C-Man

Elzy, Ruby
1933   The Emperor Jones
1938   The Toy Wife
1941   Birth of the Blues

Emanuel, Demetris
1940   East of the River

Emanuel, Elzie
1950   Intruder in the Dust
      No Way Out
1951   The Well
1953   The Sun Shines Bright

Emanuel, Manuel
1935   A Night at the Opera

Emerson, E. *not the same as* **Emerson, Edward**
1920   The Great Shadow

Emerson, Edward *not the same as* **Emerson, E.**
1938   Speed to Burn
1941   Birth of the Blues
1942   Holiday Inn
1943   Dixie
1949   Top O' the Morning

Emerson, Emmett
1952   The Fighter
1954   The Yellow Tomahawk

Emerson, Faye
1942   Juke Girl
      Secret Enemies
1943   Air Force

Emerson, Hope
1948   Cry of the City
1949   House of Strangers
      Thieves' Highway
1951   Westward the Women
1957   All Mine to Give
      The Guns of Fort Petticoat

Emerson, John
1918   Good-Bye, Bill

Emerson, Kathleen
1918   Her American Husband

Emery, Claire
1945   Nob Hill

Emery, Gilbert
1934   Coming Out Party
1935   Harmony Lane
1937   Souls at Sea
1938   The Buccaneer
1941   Adam Had Four Sons

Emery, Katherine
1952   Hiawatha

Emery, Mary
1946   Slightly Scandalous
1947   It Had To Be You
1949   Knock on Any Door
1950   Emergency Wedding
1953   The Member of the Wedding

Emery, Maude *same as* **Emory, Maud; Taylor, Maud Emery**
1920   For the Soul of Rafael

Emhardt, Robert
1952   The Iron Mistress
1958   The Badlanders

Emile, William
1941   Playmates

Emlay, Earl
1915   The Pageant of San Francisco

Emmet, Robert *see* **Tansey, Robert Emmett**

Emmett, Fern
1932   The Forty-Niners
1935   Melody Trail
      Texas Terror
1937   The Riders of the Whistling Skull
1942   Shut My Big Mouth
      Valley of the Sun
      Woman of the Year

Emmett, Robert *see* **Tansey, Robert Emmett**

Emmons, Mrs. *could be same as* **Emmons, Louise A.** *or* **Emmons, Marion**
1916   Mixed Blood

Emmons, Larry
1937   Black Legion

Emo, E. W.
1931   Lo mejor es reír

Emory, Ray *could be same as* **Emory, May**
1919?   The Chosen Path

Emory, Richard
1951   Little Big Horn
      Mask of the Dragon
1952   Red Snow
1955   Seven Angry Men
1958   Houseboat

Encinas, Lalo
1923   The Huntress
      Snowdrift
1934   The Cat's-Paw
1936   Rose of the Rancho
1937   Waikiki Wedding
1941   Hurry, Charlie, Hurry
1950   Young Daniel Boone

Endo, Shigeru Jerry
1951   Go for Broke!

Endore, Guy
1941   Lady from Louisiana

Eng, Esther
1941   Golden Gate Girl

Enge, Lewell
1950   Young Man with a Horn

Engel, Jos. W.
1941   Doomed Caravan

Engel, Mark
1955   Good Morning, Miss Dove

Engel, Morris
1960   Weddings and Babies

Engel, Roy
1951   The Well
1954   Dangerous Mission
1957   All Mine to Give

Engel, Samuel G.
1936   Sins of Man
1938   Gateway
1940   Viva Cisco Kid
1941   Charlie Chan in Rio
      Ride on Vaquero
      Romance of the Rio Grande
1942   Young America
1953   Taxi
1955   Good Morning, Miss Dove
      A Man Called Peter

Engelhardt, Cantor Shaile
1931   The Voice of Israel

Engels, Virginia
1948   Fury at Furnace Creek

Enger, Red
1948   Singin' Spurs

England, Paul
1934   Charlie Chan in London

Englander, Otto
1949   Massacre River

Engle, Billy *same as* **Engle, Bill**
1934   Our Daily Bread
1940   The Way of All Flesh
1942   Mokey
1944   An American Romance
1946   Slightly Scandalous
1948   The Paleface
1949   Lust for Gold

Engle, Paul
1955   Good Morning, Miss Dove

English, Jack (*actor*)
1953   Beneath the 12-Mile Reef

English, John (*dir*)
1940   Hi-Yo Silver
1942   Valley of Hunted Men
1947   The Last Round-Up
1949   The Cowboy and the Indians
1950   Indian Territory

English, Kay
1935   Naughty Marietta
1953   Ride, Vaquero!

English, Richard
1949   Lust for Gold

Englund, Eugene
1951   Slaughter Trail

Englund, George
1959   The World, the Flesh and the Devil

Ennis, Floyd
1959   Odds Against Tomorrow

Enright, Florence
1931   Street Scene
1934   Our Daily Bread

Enright, Ray
1943   Good Luck, Mr. Yates
1951   Flaming Feather

Enriquez, Gilbert
1938   Little Miss Roughneck

Enserro, Mike
1958   Never Love a Stranger

Entwistle, Harold
1937   Maid of Salem
      Waikiki Wedding

Entwistle, Peg
1932   Thirteen Women

Epper, John *same as* **Eppers, John**
1941   Western Union
1943   Action in the North Atlantic
      They Came to Blow Up America
1944   Buffalo Bill
1954   Broken Lance

Epstein, Julius J. *same as* **Epstein, Julius**
1939   Daughters Courageous
1943   Yankee Doodle Dandy
1944   Mr. Skeffington
1960   Take a Giant Step

Epstein, Mel
1951   Molly
1952   The Savage

Epstein, Philip G.
1939   Daughters Courageous
1943   Yankee Doodle Dandy
1944   Mr. Skeffington

Epstein, William
1933   The Wandering Jew

Erdman, Richard *same as* **Erdman, Dick**
1944   Mr. Skeffington
1948   The Time of Your Life
1950   The Men
1958   The Rawhide Trail

Eremin, Joan
1948   Renegades of Sonora
1949   Harbor of Missing Men

Erens, Joe
1942   Whispering Ghosts

Eric, Fred
1917   The Woman and the Beast

Eric, Martin
1959   The Hanging Tree

Erickson, A. F.
1935   Ruggles of Red Gap

Erickson, Carl
1935   Black Fury

Erickson, Dell *same as* **Erickson, Del**
1955   Blackboard Jungle
1960   Take a Giant Step

Erickson, Frank
1936   Star for a Night

Erickson, Harold
1931   Delicious
1942   Unseen Enemy

Erickson, Leif *same as* **Erikson, Leif**
1937   Waikiki Wedding
1951   Show Boat
      The Tall Target

Erickson, Peter
1948   The Miracle of the Bells

Ericson, Helen
1939   The Escape
1940   Charlie Chan in Panama

Ericson, John
1951   Teresa
1955   Bad Day at Black Rock
1958   Oregon Passage

Erikson, Glenn
1936   Desert Gold

Erikson, Leif *see* **Erickson, Leif**

Erkelenz, Peter
1931   El proceso de Mary Dugan (*foreign version*)

Erlenborn, Ray
1949   The Story of Seabiscuit

Erlik, Robert
1951   The Girl on the Bridge

Erman, John M.
1955   Blackboard Jungle
1956   The Benny Goodman Story

Erne, Opal
1951   Westward the Women

Ernest, Clarence
1945   Rhapsody in Blue

Ernest, George *same as* **Ernest, Georgie**
1934   Beloved
1937   The Plainsman

Ernest, Rolf
1937   It Could Happen to You

Ernst, Jessie
1935   L'homme des Folies Bergère

Errol, Leon
1939   The Girl from Mexico
1940   Mexican Spitfire
      Mexican Spitfire Out West
1941   Hurry, Charlie, Hurry
      The Mexican Spitfire's Baby
      Where Did You Get That Girl?
1942   Mexican Spitfire at Sea
      Mexican Spitfire Sees a Ghost
      Mexican Spitfire's Elephant
1943   Mexican Spitfire's Blessed Event
1944   Slightly Terrific

Ersi, Elsa
1929   Die Königsloge

Erskine, Chester
1946   The Sailor Takes a Wife
1959   The Wonderful Country

Erskine, Howard
1953   Seminole

Erskine, Marilyn
1951   Westward the Women
1953   The Eddie Cantor Story

Ervin, Diane
1947   California
      Easy Come, Easy Go

Erway, Ben
1946   Notorious
1947   The Farmer's Daughter
1948   Shep Comes Home
1949   The Undercover Man
1950   Jolson Sings Again
1959   The FBI Story
1960   The Dark at the Top of
          the Stairs

Erwin, Stuart
1938   Passport Husband
1960   For the Love of Mike

Erwin, William
1950   Battleground
1956   Man from Del Rio
1958   Gun Fever

Esburg, Paul
1944   Since You Went Away

Escalante, Henry *same as*
  Escalante, Enrique
1949   Border Incident
1955   Apache Ambush

Escobar, Jess
1936   Ramona

Esherick, Ruth
1952   Bright Victory

Eskow, Jerry
1956   Walk the Proud Land

Eskridge, John
1931   Dämon des Meeres

Esmelton, Fred *same as* **Esmelton,
  Frederick**
1919   Come Out of the Kitchen
1924   Conductor 1492
1927   The Chinese Parrot
          The Gay Defender

Esmond, Carl *same as* **Esmond,
  Charles**
1942   The Navy Comes Through
          Seven Sweethearts
1943   Margin for Error
1944   Address Unknown
1950   Mystery Submarine
1959   Thunder in the Sun

Esmond, Jill
1932   Thirteen Women
1944   My Pal Wolf
1955   A Man Called Peter

Espinosa, José Ángel *see*
  "Ferrusquilla"

Espinosa, Robert
1946   Without Reservations
1947   Ride the Pink Horse

Espiritu, Roque
1943   Bataan

Essaris, William
1950   Panic in the Streets

Essex, Estelle
1932   Hypnotized

Essex, Harry
1947   Desperate
1956   Raw Edge

Essler, Fred
1943   Wintertime
1945   Where Do We Go From
          Here?
1946   Saratoga Trunk
1950   The Toast of New Orleans
1956   The Benny Goodman
          Story

Estabrook, Howard
1917   The Wild Girl
1930   Amor audaz
          The Bad Man
          Behind the Make-Up
1931   Cimarron
          Kismet
1937   Maid of Salem
1954   Cattle Queen of Montana
          Passion

Estelita *see* **Rodriguez, Estelita**

Estelle, Fay *same as* **Estill, Fay**
1935   ¡Asegure a su mujer!

Ester, Lemist
1932   Me and My Gal

Estes, John
1943   Action in the North
          Atlantic
          Air Force
          Redhead from Manhattan

Estrada, Ester
1932   Amor y vida

Estrada, Manuel
1950   Panic in the Streets

Estrella, Esther
1941   Prairie Pioneers

Etchepare, Pierre
1931   Su noche de bodas
          (foreign version)
1932   Une heure près de toi

Ethier, Alphonse *same as* **Ethier,
  Alphonz**
1917   The Woman and the Beast
1918   I Want to Forget
1929   In Old Arizona
1932   The Match King

Ethridge, Ella
1953   The Member of the
          Wedding
1956   Giant
1959   The FBI Story
1960   The Plunderers

Etiévant, Henri
1932   La foule hurle

Etlinger, Karl *same as* **Ettlinger,
  Karl**
1930   Olimpia *(foreign
          version)*
1931   Daemon des Meeres
          Kismet
          Die Maske Fällt

Etterre, Estelle *same as* **Ettaire,
  Estella; Ettaire, Estelle; Ettere,
  Estelle**
1938   Dangerous to Know
1942   Dr. Gillespie's New
          Assistant
          Three Hearts for Julia
1951   The Tall Target

Ettinger, Eve
1932   Ljubav i strast

Ettlinger, Don
1937   Life Begins in College
1938   My Lucky Star
1940   Elsa Maxwell's Public
          Deb No. 1

Ettlinger, Karl *see* **Etlinger, Karl**

Etzkorn, Max
1937   It Could Happen to You

Eugene, Billy
1925   A Son of His Father

Eunson, Dale
1957   All Mine to Give

Eunson, Katherine
1957   All Mine to Give

Eurard, Opal
1960   Studs Lonigan

Eurist, Clarence
1946   Don Ricardo Returns
1948   Sleep, My Love
1951   Flaming Feather

Eustral, Anthony *same as* **Eustrel,
  Anthony**
1953   Captain John Smith and
          Pocahontas

Evans, Bob *see* **Evans, Robert**

Evans, Brandon
1933   The Emperor Jones
1936   Dangerous Intrigue

Evans, Brooke
1941   Louisiana Purchase

Evans, Catharine *could be same as*
  Evans, Catherine
1924   Two Shall Be Born

Evans, Charles *not the same as*
  Evans, Charles E. d 1953
1946   Without Reservations
1947   It Had To Be You
1948   Reaching from Heaven
1949   The Prairie
1950   The Big Hangover
          Colt .45
          The Furies
1951   The Great Caruso
          The Last Outpost
          The Magnificent Yankee
1952   Bugles in the Afternoon
          Indian Uprising
1953   Sangaree
1954   Battle of Rogue River
1955   Headline Hunters
          A Man Called Peter
          Trial

1960   I Passed for White

Evans, Cicely
1959   Imitation of Life

Evans, Dale
1943   In Old Oklahoma
1949   The Golden Stallion

Evans, Dick
1955   Chief Crazy Horse

Evans, Douglas
1943   Hitler's Children
1947   Dangerous Venture
          The Farmer's Daughter
1949   The Golden Stallion
1950   North of the Great Divide
1951   Cuban Fireball
          Queen for a Day
          The Well
1952   The Quiet Man
          Red Ball Express
1953   The Eddie Cantor Story
          So Big
1956   The Benny Goodman
          Story

Evans, Emery
1939   Straight to Heaven

Evans, Estelle
1949   The Quiet One

Evans, Eynon
1959   The Sheriff of Fractured
          Jaw

Evans, Frank *could be same as*
  Evans, Frankie *not the same as*
  Evans, Franck Taylor
1914   The Woman in Black

Evans, Frankie *could be same as*
  Evans, Frank
1923   Backbone

Evans, Gene
1951   The Steel Helmet
1954   Cattle Queen of Montana

Evans, Harry
1946   Without Reservations

Evans, Herbert
1917   The Wild Girl
1918   The Firebrand
1937   Maid of Salem
1944   Slightly Terrific
1946   Bringing Up Father
1947   Jiggs and Maggie in
          Society
1948   The Miracle of the Bells

Evans, Jacqueline
1956   Daniel Boone, Trail
          Blazer

Evans, Jean
1956   Hot Blood

Evans, Joan
1953   Column South

Evans, Joe
1945   Where Do We Go From
          Here?

Evans, Julius
1958   Gun Fever

Evans, Madge
1916   Broken Chains
1917   The Adventures of Carol
1918   The Golden Wall
          Wanted, a Mother
1932   Huddle
1934   Stand Up and Cheer!

Evans, Millicent
1914   The Woman in Black

Evans, Robert *same as* **Evans, Bob**
1943   Gangway for Tomorrow
1950   Black Hand

Evans, Russell *same as* **Evans, Russ**
1953   The Glory Brigade
1957   Band of Angels

Evans, Tom
1918   Wanted, a Mother

Evanson, Edith
1942   Dr. Gillespie's New
          Assistant
          Woman of the Year
1945   The Jade Mask
1948   I Remember Mama
1951   The Magnificent Yankee

Evarts, Hal G.
1931   La gran jornada

Evelyn, Mrs. *could be same as*
  Evelyn, Fay
1920   Within Our Gates

Evelyn, Judith
1956   Giant

Everest, Barbara
1945   The Valley of Decision

Everett, Francine *same as*
  Everette, Francine
1939   Keep Punching
1940   Paradise in Harlem
1946   Dirty Gertie from
          Harlem, U.S.A.
          Stars on Parade
          Tall, Tan and Terrific

Everett, Jane
1948   Half Past Midnight
          Unconquered

Everett, John
1932?   The Girl from Chicago

Everett, Munzall
1921   A Modern Cain

Everette, Francine *see* **Everett,
  Francine**

Evers, Ernest
1914   The Jungle

Evers, King
1922   The Half Breed

Everton, Paul
1938   The Beloved Brat
1939   Stand Up and Fight
1940   Mexican Spitfire Out
          West

ex-Duflos, Huguette
1931   El proceso de Mary
          Dugan *(foreign
          version)*

Eyer, Richard
1960   Hell to Eternity

Eyer, Robert
1960   The Dark at the Top of
          the Stairs

Eythe, William
1943   The Ox-Bow Incident
1945   The House on 92nd St.

Eyton, Bessie
1914   In the Days of the
          Thundering Herd

Fabares, Shelley
1958   Marjorie Morningstar

Faber, Charles
1946   Without Reservations

Fabian, Olga
1944   My Pal Wolf
          They Live in Fear
          Waterfront
1948   My Girl Tisa

Fabre, Fernand
1930   Toda una vida *(foreign
          version)*

Fábregas, Virginia
1931   La fruta amarga

Fadden, Tom
1942   Wings for the Eagle
1944   Tomorrow the World!
1945   A Medal for Benny
1947   California
          Easy Come, Easy Go
1948   The Dude Goes West
          Moonrise
1950   Devil's Doorway
1960   Flaming Star

Fadiman, William
1956   The Last Frontier

Faducha, Marion
1922   Second Hand Rose

Fafara, Tiger
1955   Good Morning, Miss Dove

Fafer, Dave
1934   The Youth of Russia

Fahey, Myrna
1959   Imitation of Life

Fahrney, Milton
1924   Yankee Speed

Fain, Elmer
1937   Bargain with Bullets

Fain, M. G.
1949   Lust for Gold

Fain, Matty
1936   Ellis Island
1937   Boy of the Streets
        Shadows of the Orient
1938   Mr. Moto's Gamble

Fair, Elinor *could be same as* **Fair, Lenore**
1921   Through the Back Door
1922   Big Stakes
1934   Broadway Bill

Fair, Lenore *could be same as* **Fair, Elinor**
1918   The Reckoning Day

Fairbanks, Douglas *same as* **Fairbanks, Douglas, Sr.**
1915   The Lamb
1916   The Half-Breed
1920   The Mark of Zorro
1925   Don Q, Son of Zorro

Fairbanks, Douglas, Jr.
1931   Little Caesar
1932   L'athlète incomplet
1938   The Rage of Paris

Fairbanks, Lucille *same as* **Fairbanks, Lucile**
1940   Knute Rockne—All American

Fairbanks, William
1924   Down by the Rio Grande
1925   The Fearless Lover
1927   Spoilers of the West
1928   Wyoming

Faire, Robyn
1957   Band of Angels

Faire, Virginia Brown *same as* **Faire, Virginia Browne**
1924   The Lightning Rider
        Peter Pan
        Welcome Stranger
1925   Friendly Enemies
        His People
1927   Pleasure Before Business
1928   The Canyon of Adventure

Fairfax, Betty
1946   Rendezvous 24

Fairfax, James
1952   Battles of Chief Pontiac

Fairfax, Marion
1915   The Immigrant
1917   Hashimura Togo
        The Secret Game
1918   The Honor of His House
1920   Dinty
1921   Through the Back Door
1924   So Big

Fairfax, Thur
1927   Rose of the Golden West

Fairfax, Virginia
1915   An American Gentleman

Fairley, Freeman
1932   The Black King

Fairlie, Gerard
1935   Charlie Chan in Shanghai

Fairweather, Helen
1934   Stand Up and Cheer!

Fakiel, D.
1936   Yiddle with His Fiddle

Falaise, Henri de la
1931   Echec au roi
        Nuit d'Espagne

Falck, Ragnar
1930   Doña mentiras (*foreign version*)

Falconi, Dino
1931   La fiesta del diablo (*foreign version*)

Falkenburg, Jinx *same as* **Falkenberg, Jinx**
1935   Rosa de Francia
1937   El carnaval del diablo
1944   Tahiti Nights
1945   The Gay Senorita

Falkenstein, Fritz
1938   Breaking the Ice

Falleur, Amelia
1937   Maid of Salem

Fallon, Charles
1935   Ruggles of Red Gap

Falls, Shirley
1960   This Rebel Breed

Fanchon and Marco
1935   A Night at the Opera

Fang, Charles *same as* **Fang, Charlie**
1916   Broken Fetters
1917   The Slacker (Metro Pictures Corp.)
1919   Mandarin's Gold
1920   Pagan Love
1923   Backbone

Fanning, Frank
1937   One Mile from Heaven
1938   Mr. Moto's Gamble
1940   Murder over New York

Fante, John
1940   East of the River
1952   My Man and I
1956   Full of Life

Far, Look Suit
1941   Min Jok Jay Hung Sing

Faragoh, Francis Edwards *same as* **Faragoh, Francis**
1931   Little Caesar
1936   Dancing Pirate
1941   Lady from Louisiana
1947   Easy Come, Easy Go

Farah, Jameel *see* **Farr, Jamie**

Faralla, Darío
1939   El otro soy yo
        Papá soltero
        El trovador de la radio
1940   Cuando canta la Ley

Faralla, William
1940   Cuando canta la Ley
1941   Hold Back the Dawn

Faranda, Mary
1960   Weddings and Babies

Farber, Jerry
1947   Buck Privates Come Home

Farfan, Robert *same as* **Farfan, Bob**
1938   Little Miss Roughneck
1947   Black Gold
1956   The Lone Ranger

Faris, Charles
1949   House of Strangers

Faris, Franco
1931   La regina di Sparta

Farjeon, Herbert
1941   Playmates

Farley, Dot *same as* **Farley, Dorothy**
1914?   The Lust of the Red Man
1924   So Big
1925   My Son
1926   The Little Irish Girl
1927   McFadden's Flats
        The Overland Stage
        The Shamrock and the Rose
1931   Law of the Tong
1942   Cat People
1948   Fighting Father Dunne

Farley, James *same as* **Farley, J. M.; Farley, Jim**
1925   A Son of His Father
1931   Charlie Chan Carries On
        Fighting Caravans
1936   Dancing Pirate
1937   The Californian
1940   Santa Fe Trail
1942   Little Tokyo, U.S.A.
1943   Gangway for Tomorrow
1945   In Old New Mexico
        The Valley of Decision
1946   Abie's Irish Rose
1947   Buck Privates Come Home

Farley, Lesley
1947   Jiggs and Maggie in Society

Farley, Morgan
1934   Beloved
1948   Gentleman's Agreement
        Open Secret
1949   Top O' the Morning
1952   High Noon

Farley, Pat *same as* **Farley, Patricia**
1935   Naughty Marietta

Farlow, La Rue
1960   Cimarron

Farlow, Warren
1945   The Valley of Decision

Farlow, Wayne
1945   The Valley of Decision

Farmer, Jacques
1920   Our Christianity and Nobody's Child

Farmer, Oliver
1938   Life Goes On

Farmer, Virginia
1941   Gauchos of Eldorado
1947   California
1949   Lust for Gold
        The Undercover Man
1950   The Men
1952   High Noon

Farnham, Joseph White *same as* **Farnham, Joe; Farnham, Joseph**
1919   Deliverance
1921   Diane of Star Hollow
1926   Blarney
        War Paint
1927   Frisco Sally Levy
        Spoilers of the West
1928   The Cameraman
        Diamond Handcuffs
1930   El presidio

Farnsworth, Dick *same as* **Farnsworth, Richard**
1948   The Paleface
1953   Arrowhead

Farnum, Dorothy
1922   Fair Lady
1930   Sevilla de mis amores
        Le spectre vert

Farnum, Dustin
1914   The Squaw Man
1915   Captain Courtesy
1916   A Son of Erin
1926   The Flaming Frontier

Farnum, Franklyn
1917   The Winged Mystery
1918   In Judgment Of
1921   The Hunger of the Blood
1922   Cross Roads
        When East Comes West
1931   Oklahoma Jim
1932   Thirteen Steps
1936   Custer's Last Stand
1937   The Plainsman
1941   This Woman Is Mine
1943   Frontier Fury
1948   I Remember Mama
        The Miracle of the Bells
        Old Los Angeles
1949   Knock on Any Door
        The Undercover Man
1950   Colt .45

Farnum, William
1914   The Redemption of David Corson
1916   A Man of Sorrow
1917   The Conqueror
1935?   The Irish Gringo
1936   Custer's Last Stand
1937   Maid of Salem
1940   Hi-Yo Silver
        Kit Carson
1942   American Empire
1945   The Mummy's Curse
1949   Daughter of the West

Farr, Charles
1936   Sutter's Gold

Farr, Felicia
1956   The Last Wagon
        Reprisal!

Farr, Hugh
1950   Rio Grande

Farr, Jamie *same as* **Farah, Jameel**
1955   Blackboard Jungle

Farr, Karl
1950   Rio Grande

Farr, Lynn
1948   Old Los Angeles
1950   Ambush

Farrar, David
1959   John Paul Jones

Farrar, Geraldine
1918   The Hell Cat
1920   The Riddle: Woman

Farrar, James
1953   Dream Wife

Farrar, Jane
1944   Tender Comrade

Farrell, Charles (*American actor*)
1926   A Trip to Chinatown
1931   Delicious

Farrell, Charles (*British actor*)
1959   The Sheriff of Fractured Jaw

Farrell, Fred, Major *same as* **Farrell, Major**
1943   Gangway for Tomorrow
1944   Address Unknown

Farrell, Glenda
1931   Little Caesar
1932   The Match King
1933   Grand Slam
1942   Twin Beds
1952   Apache War Smoke

Farrell, Jack
1918?   Rosemary Climbs the Heights
1919   Yvonne from Paris

Farrell, John W.
1949   Portrait of Jennie

Farrell, Lowell J. *same as* **Farrell, Lowell**
1944   Since You Went Away
1947   Duel in the Sun
1948   Fort Apache
1949   She Wore a Yellow Ribbon
1959   The Young Land

Farrell, Major *see* **Farrell, Fred, Major**

Farrell, Neyneen
1929   Frozen Justice

Farrell, Paul
1959   Shake Hands with the Devil

Farrell, Richard
1922   Breaking Home Ties

Farrell, Rusty
1945   Johnny Angel

Farrell, Tod
1957   The Oklahoman

Farrington, Adele
1916   The Love Girl
        The Morals of Hilda
1917   A Roadside Impresario
1920   Rio Grande

Farrington, Betty
1930   Anybody's War
1937   That I May Live
1941   Birth of the Blues
1944   The Sullivans
1945   The Dolly Sisters
1947   California
1948   Unconquered
1952   The Fabulous Senorita

Farrington, Frank
1918   The Million Dollar Mystery
1919   The Scar
1920   The Face at Your Window

Farrow, John Charles *not the same as* **Farrow, John Villiers**
1959   John Paul Jones

Farrow, John Villiers *not the same as* **Farrow, John Charles**
1927   White Gold
1929   Wolf Song
1947   California
        Easy Come, Easy Go
1953   Ride, Vaquero!
1954   Hondo
1959   John Paul Jones

Faulkner, Carl
1937   Charlie Chan on Broadway
1940   Murder over New York
1946   Sunset Pass
1947   Crossfire

Faulkner, Philip, Jr. *same as*
  Faulkner, P. J.
1950   Jolson Sings Again
Faulkner, Ralph *same as* **Faulkner,**
  Ralph C.
1918   The Prussian Cur
1921   Anne of Little Smoky
1923   April Showers
1947   The Foxes of Harrow
Faulkner, William
1937   Slave Ship
1939   Drums Along the Mohawk
Fauntelle, Diane
1948   Docks of New Orleans
1951   Queen for a Day
Faust, Bob
1947   Dangerous Venture
Faust, Edouard
1940   Escape
Faust, Marty *same as* **Faust, M.;**
  Faust, Martin
1918   Find the Woman
1935   Charlie Chan in Paris
        The Little Colonel
1936   Ramona
1937   Man of the People
        Souls at Sea
1938   Road Demon
1940   The Way of All Flesh
1941   Hold Back the Dawn
        Saddlemates
1942   They Died With Their
        Boots On
1944   An American Romance
Faust, Miguel Rocha *see* **Rocha,**
  Miguel Faust
Faust, Victoria
1945   The Scarlet Clue
Faut, Paul
1941   Wiejskie Wesele
Faversham, Phil
1952   Bright Victory
Fawcett, Bill *see* **Fawcett, William**
Fawcett, Charles
1951   Adventures of Captain
        Fabian
Fawcett, George
1918   The Hun Within
1919   Scarlet Days
1921   Little Italy
1926   The Flaming Frontier
1931   Personal Maid
Fawcett, William *same as* **Fawcett,**
  Bill
1949   Ride, Ryder, Ride!
        Roll Thunder Roll!
1952   The Raiders
        Rose of Cimarron
1955   Seminole Uprising
1956   Dakota Incident
1957   Band of Angels
Fay, E.
1952   Anything Can Happen
Fay, Frank
1940   They Knew What They
        Wanted
Fay, Lew
1951   Jim Thorpe—All-American
Faye, Alice
1938   In Old Chicago
1943   The Gang's All Here
Faye, Charles
1935   Rosa de Francia
1938   Mr. Moto's Gamble
1939   Mr. Moto's Last Warning
Faye, Francine
1948   Jiggs and Maggie in Court
Faye, Julia
1917   A Roadside Impresario
1918   Sandy
        The Squaw Man
1922   Saturday Night
1926   Meet the Prince
1927   Turkish Delight
1931   The Squaw Man
1947   California
        Easy Come, Easy Go
1948   Unconquered
1950   The Lawless

Faye, Randall
1945   Great Stagecoach Robbery
Faylen, Frank
1939   Waterfront
1941   Come Live with Me
1942   Across the Pacific
        Mokey
        Three Hearts for Julia
        Whispering Ghosts
        Wings for the Eagle
1943   The Gang's All Here
        Yankee Doodle Dandy
1944   Address Unknown
        An American Romance
        Andy Hardy's Blonde
        Trouble
1947   California
        Easy Come, Easy Go
1956   7th Cavalry
Fayth, Gloria *same as* **Faythe,**
  Gloria
1933   It's Great to Be Alive
Fazenda, Louise
1923   The Spider and the Rose
1925   Hogan's Alley
1926   Millionaires
1928   Riley the Cop
        Vamping Venus
1935   The Winning Ticket
Fealy, Margaret
1941   Gauchos of Eldorado
Fealy, Maude
1938   The Buccaneer
Fears, Tom
1951   Saturday's Hero
Feather Hat, Jr.
1956   The Searchers
Featherstone, Ed *see* **Fetherston,**
  Eddie
Featherstone, Eddie *see*
  Fetherston, Eddie
Featherstone, Edward *see*
  Fetherston, Eddie
Feder Sisters *same as* **Feder,**
  Miriam; Feder, Sylvia
1950   Catskill Honeymoon
Feder, Moishe
1937   I Want to Be a Mother
1939   Mirele Efros
1940   The Jewish Melody
Fédor, Tania
1930   Olimpia (*foreign
        version*)
1931   Don Juan diplomático
        (*foreign version*)
        Le petit café
        Soyons gais
Fee, Luk Won
1941   Golden Gate Girl
Feeney, Francis
1921   Little Miss Hawkshaw
Joel Feig Choir
1939   Kol Nidre
Feinberg, Silas
1916   The Yellow Passport
Feiner, Ben, Jr.
1951   Show Boat
Feinman, Lillian
1931   Zein Weib's Lubovnick
Feins, Bernard
1946   Cuban Pete
Feist, Felix
1952   Battles of Chief Pontiac
1953   The Man Behind the Gun
Feitshans, Fred R., Jr. *same as*
  Feitshans, Fred
1949   Arctic Fury
Feld, Fritz
1928   A Ship Comes In
        A Ship Comes In (*foreign
        version*)
1941   The Mexican Spitfire's
        Baby
1942   Shut My Big Mouth
1944   Knickerbocker Holiday
1945   The Great John L.
1948   My Girl Tisa
1950   Belle of Old Mexico
Feld, Harry
1939   My Son
1941   Mazel Tov Yidden

Feldary, Eric
1941   Hold Back the Dawn
1945   Salome, Where She
        Danced
1948   16 Fathoms Deep
1949   Illegal Entry
Felder, Robert
1943   Stormy Weather
Feldman, Charles K.
1948   Red River
1951   A Streetcar Named Desire
Feldman, Milton
1944   Cry of the Werewolf
1945   Escape in the Fog
        The Gay Senorita
1948   Singin' Spurs
1950   Jolson Sings Again
1952   Indian Uprising
1953   The Nebraskan
1956   Hot Blood
Feldman, Mrs. Ray
1944   Since You Went Away
Felice, Ernie
1948   Music Man
Felix, Art *same as* **Feliz, Art; Feliz,**
  Arturo
1935   Riddle Ranch
1952   Fort Osage
Félix, Lorenzo *same as* **Felix, L. R.**
1939   Miracle on Main Street
        (*foreign version*)
Feliz, Arturo *see* **Felix, Art**
Fellowes, Edith *see* **Fellows, Edith**
Fellowes, Rockcliffe *same as*
  Fellowes, Rockliffe; Fellows,
  Rockcliffe
1920   The Cup of Fury
        Pagan Love
1921   Bits of Life
1932   Huddle
Fellows, Arthur
1939   Gone With the Wind
1947   Duel in the Sun
1949   Portrait of Jennie
Fellows, Edith *same as* **Fellowes,**
  Edith
1932   Law and Lawless
1935   Black Fury
1938   City Streets
        Little Miss Roughneck
1940   Music in My Heart
Fellows, Robert
1940   Knute Rockne—All
        American
        Santa Fe Trail
1942   They Died With Their
        Boots On
1949   Streets of Laredo
1954   Hondo
Fellows, Rockcliffe *see* **Fellowes,**
  Rockcliffe
Felsing, Grete
1930   Doña mentiras (*foreign
        version*)
Feltcorn, Harry
1940   The Ramparts We Watch
Felton, Verna
1940   If I Had My Way
        Northwest Passage (Book
        I—Rogers' Rangers)
1950   Buccaneer's Girl
1951   New Mexico
1957   The Oklahoman
Fenderson, Reginald *same as*
  Fenderson, Reggie
1936   The Green Pastures
1937   Bargain with Bullets
1938   Life Goes On
1939   Gang Smashers
        Reform School
1940   Am I Guilty?
        Gang War
        While Thousands Cheer
1941   Four Shall Die
Fenn, Jean
1956   Serenade
Fennelly, Parker
1949   Lost Boundaries
Fennelly, Vincent M.
1950   Cherokee Uprising
1952   Wagons West

1955   Seven Angry Men
Fenner, Walter
1945   The Shanghai Cobra
Fenton, Francis (*writer*) *could be
  same as* **Fenton, Frank** (*writer*)
1928   The Broken Mask
Fenton, Frank (*actor*)
1942   The Navy Comes Through
1944   Buffalo Bill
1946   Swamp Fire
1947   The Adventures of Don
        Coyote
1948   Renegades of Sonora
1949   The Clay Pigeon
        The Golden Stallion
        Ranger of Cherokee Strip
        Rustlers
1950   The Lawless
1953   The Nebraskan
Fenton, Frank (*writer*) *same as*
  Fenton, Frank E. (*writer*) *could
  be same as* **Fenton, Francis**
  (*writer*)
1933   Dos noches
1953   Ride, Vaquero!
1955   Seven Cities of Gold
1959   The Jayhawkers!
Fenton, Leslie
1931   The Guilty Generation
1932   The Hatchet Man
1934   Strange Wives
1935   Chinatown Squad
1944   Tomorrow the World!
1949   Streets of Laredo
Fenton, Lucille
1947   Citizen Saint
Fenton, Mabel
1915   How Molly Malone Made
        Good
Fenton, Mark
1916   A Child of Mystery
1917   John Ermine of the
        Yellowstone
1925   Brand of Cowardice
Fenwick, Harry
1926   Buffalo Bill on the U. P.
        Trail
Fenwick, Jean
1934   Strange Wives
1940   New Moon
1942   We Were Dancing
1948   Jiggs and Maggie in Court
Ferdinand, Roger
1931   Quand on est belle
Ferguson, Al *same as* **Ferguson,**
  Alfred
1916   Lone Star
1936   Show Boat
1939   Frontiers of '49
        Stand Up and Fight
1942   Shut My Big Mouth
        Valley of the Sun
1943   Gangway for Tomorrow
1944   Sonora Stagecoach
1945   The Mummy's Curse
        Salome, Where She
        Danced
1946   Wild West
1947   California
        The Mighty McGurk
1948   Gun Smugglers
        Unconquered
1949   Knock on Any Door
1953   The Member of the
        Wedding
Ferguson, Casson
1918   The Gypsy Trail
        How Could You, Jean?
        The Only Road
1925   Cobra
Ferguson, Charles
1916   The Innocent Lie
Ferguson, Elsie
1919   His Parisian Wife
Ferguson, Frank
1942   They Died With Their
        Boots On
        Wings for the Eagle
1943   The Meanest Man in the
        World
1945   The Dolly Sisters
1946   Canyon Passage

1947 California
     The Farmer's Daughter
1948 Fighting Father Dunne
     Fort Apache
     The Miracle of the Bells
1950 The Furies
     The Lawless
     Right Cross
1951 Warpath
1952 The Iron Mistress
     Wagons West
1953 So Big
     The Stars Are Singing
1954 Drum Beat
1955 Trial
1957 The Lawless Eighties
1958 The Light in the Forest
     Terror in a Texas Town

Ferguson, Helen
1919 The Lost Battalion
1922 Hungry Hearts
1924 Racing Luck
1925 The Scarlet West
1929 In Old California

Ferguson, Myrtle
1927 Topsy and Eva

Ferguson, W. J.
1922 Peacock Alley

Fergusson, Harvey
1939 Stand Up and Fight

Ferkouf, Betty *same as* **Ferkauf, Betty**
1926 Broken Hearts
1932 The Unfortunate Bride

Fermas, Nicos
1954 Barefoot Battalion

Fern, Janette
1941 Hurry, Charlie, Hurry

Fernald, Bruce
1945 The House on 92nd St.

Fernández Ardavín, Luis Fernández, zx
1931 Su noche de bodas
     Fernández, zy
     Chérie (*foreign version*)

Fernández Cué, Baltasar Fernández, zy
1930 La voluntad del muerto

Fernandez, Abel
1955 Fort Yuma
     The Last Command
1956 The Last Wagon

Fernández, Antonio
1928 El Robin Hood de México

Fernández, Emilio
1934 La buenaventura

Fernandez, Escamillo
1945 South of the Rio Grande

Fernandez, Freddy
1956 Daniel Boone, Trail Blazer

Fernández, María Luisa
1931 Chérie (*foreign version*)

Fernandez, Miguel
1936 Ramona
1952 The Raiders

Fernández, Nelly
1930 Del mismo barro
     El último de los Vargas
1931 La cautivadora
     Esclavas de la moda
     Politiquerías

Fernández Cué, Baltasar *same as* **Fernández Cué, B.**
1930 The Bad Man (*foreign version*)
     East Is West (*foreign version*)
     Los que danzan
1931 Don Juan diplomático
     Drácula
     Resurrección

Fernández García, Carmelita
1930 Doña mentiras
     El secreto del doctor

Fernando, Adelantado
1935 Tango Bar

Ferney, Jeannette
1932 L'athlète incomplet
     Le plombier amoureux

Ferns, Alma
1934 Our Daily Bread

Ferny, Ernest
1932 Une heure près de toi

Ferraday, Lisa
1951 Show Boat
1952 California Conquest
1956 Death of a Scoundrel

Ferrara, Jim
1942 American Empire

Ferrell, David
1960 Wild River

Ferrell, Ray
1960 The Plunderers

Ferrer, José
1952 Anything Can Happen

Ferrer, Mel
1944 They Live in Fear
1949 Lost Boundaries
1959 The World, the Flesh and the Devil

Ferrero, Danton
1939 Verbena trágica

Ferrero, Robert
1945 Nob Hill
     A Tree Grows in Brooklyn

Ferrier, André
1931 La gran jornada (*foreign version*)
1934 Caravane

Ferris, Audrey
1927 Sailor Izzy Murphy

Ferris, Walter
1934 Imitation of Life
1937 Maid of Salem
     Slave Ship

"Ferrusquilla" *same as* **Espinosa, José Ángel**
1958 Sierra Baron

Ferry, Faith
1958 Sierra Baron

Fessier, Michael
1937 Song of the City

Fessler, Edward I.
1957 Bayou

Fetchit, Stepin
1929 Hearts in Dixie
     Show Boat
1930 La fuerza del querer
1934 Judge Priest
     Stand Up and Cheer!
1935 Charlie Chan in Egypt
1936 Dimples
1948 Miracle in Harlem
1953 The Sun Shines Bright

Fetherston, Eddie *same as* **Featherstone, Eddie; Featherstone, Edward; Fetherston, Ed; Fetherstone, Eddie**
1934 The Cat's-Paw
1936 Charlie Chan at the Race Track
1937 The Devil's Playground
     Shadows of the Orient
1938 Little Miss Roughneck
1941 They Dare Not Love
1942 Unseen Enemy
1943 Good Luck, Mr. Yates
     What's Buzzin' Cousin?
1947 Easy Come, Easy Go
     The Jolson Story
1949 Lust for Gold
1958 The Last Hurrah
1960 The Adventures of Huckleberry Finn

Feyder, Jacques
1930 Anna Christie (*foreign version*)
     Olimpia (*foreign version*)
     Le spectre vert

Fidgeon, Arthur
1949 Thieves' Highway

Fido Rover
1927 Frisco Sally Levy

Fieberling, Hal
1950 Sands of Iwo Jima
1951 Jim Thorpe—All-American

Fiedler, John
1957 Twelve Angry Men

Field, Betty
1944 Tomorrow the World!

Field, Elvin
1945 A Tree Grows in Brooklyn

Field, Esther
1939 Mothers of Today
1940 Eli Eli

Field, Florence
1936 The Green Pastures
1942 Lucky Ghost

Field, Grace *not the same as* **Fields, Gracie 1898—1979**
1948 Gentleman's Agreement
1949 Prejudice

Field, Harry
1937 Waikiki Wedding

Field, Margaret
1948 The Paleface
1952 The Raiders

Field, Mary
1939 The Fighting Gringo
1942 Mexican Spitfire at Sea
     Mokey
     Three Hearts for Julia
1944 Mr. Skeffington
1946 The Gentleman Misbehaves
     Song of the South
1948 Unconquered
     Up in Central Park
1949 Top O' the Morning
1952 Anything Can Happen
1958 Ride a Crooked Trail

Field, Norman
1945 A Tree Grows in Brooklyn
     Where Do We Go From Here?
1951 Gambling House
1952 The Fabulous Senorita

Field, Sylvia
1942 Dr. Gillespie's New Assistant
1945 Salome, Where She Danced
1957 All Mine to Give

Field, Virginia
1937 Think Fast, Mr. Moto
1938 Charlie Chan at Monte Carlo
1939 The Cisco Kid and the Lady
     Mr. Moto Takes a Vacation
     Mr. Moto's Last Warning

Fielding, Edward *same as* **Fielding, Ed**
1940 East of the River
1941 Hold Back the Dawn
1942 In This Our Life
1943 Good Luck, Mr. Yates
     Mr. Lucky
1944 Mr. Skeffington
     My Pal Wolf
     Tender Comrade
1945 A Medal for Benny
1946 Saratoga Trunk

Fielding, Gerald
1940 New Moon
1947 It Had To Be You

Fielding, Lisabith
1955 Foxfire

Fielding, Margaret
1938 City Streets

Fielding, Romaine
1927 Rose of the Golden West

Fielding, Sol Baer
1953 Bright Road
1957 Trooper Hook

Fields, Benny
1944 Minstrel Man

Fields, Don
1952 It's a Big Country: An American Anthology

Fields, Eddie *same as* **Fields, Eddy**
1945 The Gay Senorita
1951 Gambling House

Fields, Herbert
1933 Let's Fall in Love

Fields, Jackie
1937 Big City

Fields, Jerry
1945 The Cisco Kid Returns

Fields, Joseph A. *same as* **Fields, Joseph**
1935 Annie Oakley
1937 That Girl from Paris
1939 The Girl from Mexico
1940 Mexican Spitfire
1941 Louisiana Purchase

Fields, Leonard H. *same as* **Fields, Leonard**
1931 El comediante
1937 It Could Happen to You

Fields, Lew
1925 Friendly Enemies

Fields, Martha
1934 Stand Up and Cheer!

Fields, Norman
1950 The Breaking Point

Fields, Sammie (*African-American actor*) *not the same as* **Fields, Sammy**
1928 Eleven P.M.

Fields, Sidney (*actor*) *could be same as* **Fields, Sidney** (*writer*)
1937 Charlie Chan on Broadway

Fields, Sidney (*writer*) *could be same as* **Fields, Sidney** (*actor*)
1947 My Wild Irish Rose

Fields, Stanley
1930 Ladies Love Brutes
1931 Cimarron
     Little Caesar
     Skyline
1936 It Had to Happen
     Show Boat
1937 Maid of Salem
     Souls at Sea
1940 New Moon
     Viva Cisco Kid
1941 Where Did You Get That Girl?

Fier, Jack
1941 Mystery Ship
1942 Lawless Plainsmen
1943 Doughboys in Ireland
     Frontier Fury
     Let's Have Fun
     What's Buzzin' Cousin?
1944 Riding West
     They Live in Fear

Fierro, Paul
1941 New York Town
1948 Red River
1950 A Lady Without Passport
1952 The Fighter
1953 Ride, Vaquero!
     San Antone
1956 Raw Edge
1957 War Drums
1958 Oregon Passage

Fife, J. W.
1921 A Modern Cain

Fife, Jack
1937 The Plainsman

Fife, Maxine
1945 A Medal for Benny
1947 Copacabana

Fife, Shannon
1924 The Lightning Rider

Fifer, Fay
1941 Sullivan's Travels
1958 St. Louis Blues

Figarola, Raúl
1931 La ley del harem

Filauri, Antonio *same as* **Filauri, A.**
1935 A Night at the Opera
1938 Charlie Chan at Monte Carlo
     Josette
1941 Hold Back the Dawn
1944 Mr. Skeffington
1945 The Gay Senorita
     Nob Hill
1947 Easy Come, Easy Go
     King of the Bandits
1948 Cry of the City
1949 The Girl from Jones Beach

Filauri, Antonio
1950   Black Hand
1951   The Great Caruso
1953   Thunder Bay
1956   The Benny Goodman
      Story

Fillmore, Clyde
1943   Margin for Error
1944   Tahiti Nights
1946   Bad Bascomb
      Strange Voyage

Fillmore, Nellie
1920   Pagan Love

Filmer, Robert
1945   Nob Hill
1949   Colorado Territory
1950   A Ticket to Tomahawk
1956   The Lone Ranger

Filson, Mrs. A. W.
1914   The Squaw Man

Filson, Al W. *same as* **Filson, Al**
1915   A Yankee from the West
1916   At Piney Ridge
1921   The Girl from God's
      Country
      Made in Heaven

Filson, Helen
1919   Hearts of Men

Finch, Flora
1927   Rose of the Golden West
1936   Show Boat

Finch, Jack
1942   Syncopation

Finchuk, J.
1939   Cossacks in Exile

Finderson, Reggie
1942   Lucky Ghost

Findlay, David
1929   The Peacock Fan

Findlay, Ruth
1919   The Scar

Findlay, Thomas
1923   Little Old New York

Fine, Budd *same as* **Fine, Bud**
1934   Lazy River
1937   Man of the People
      The Plainsman
1941   Mystery Ship
1943   Mr. Lucky
1948   The Miracle of the Bells
      Unconquered
1950   Annie Get Your Gun
1951   The Tall Target

Fineman, B. P. *same as* **Fineman, B. P. "Bernie"**
1929   Thunderbolt
1930   Sevilla de mis amores

Fink, Henry
1930   The Kibitzer

Finkel, Abem
1935   Black Fury
1937   Black Legion

Finkel, Favish
1950   Monticello, Here We
      Come!

Finlay, Jack
1951   Saturday's Hero
1953   Seminole

Finlay, Ned *see* **Finley, Ned**

Finlayson, James *same as* **Finlayson, Jimmie**
1930   El príncipe del dólar
      El príncipe del dólar
      (*foreign version*)
1931   Pardon Us
      Politiquerías

Finley, Evelyn
1940   Arizona Frontier
1943   Jack London
1951   Westward the Women
1957   The Guns of Fort
      Petticoat

Finley, Muriel
1930   Whoopee

Finley, Natalie
1938   The Buccaneer

Finley, Ned *same as* **Finlay, Ned**
1916   Britton of the Seventh

Finn, Mickey
1957   Beau James
      The Tin Star

Finn, Sammy *same as* **Finn, Sam;**
Finn, Samuel
1936   Charlie Chan at the Race
      Track
1937   Manhattan
      Merry-Go-Round
1939   The Escape
1943   Mr. Lucky
1949   Illegal Entry
1950   The Furies
1957   The Brothers Rico

Finnegan, Mimi
1927   Finnegan's Ball

Finney, Charles
1951   Jim Thorpe—All-American

Finney, Edward F. *same as* **Finney, Edward**
1940   Arizona Frontier
      Rhythm of the Rio
      Grande
1942   King of the Stallions
1949   Call of the Forest
      The Prairie
1952   Buffalo Bill in Tomahawk
      Territory

Firestine, Beverly
1936   Ramona

Firestone, Berel
1959   The Jayhawkers!

Firestone, Edward
1955   Good Morning, Miss Dove

Fischer, Gloria *see* **Fisher, Gloria**

Fischer, Margarita *see* **Fisher, Margarita**

Fischer, Robert C. *same as* **Fischer, Bob** *could be same as* **Fisher, Robert**
1940   The Way of All Flesh

Fischter, W. D. *same as* **Fischter, Walter**
1914   Dan

Fisette, Geraldine
1942   Song of the Islands

Fishbein, Benjamin *same as* **Fishbein, B.**
1934   The Rabbi's Power
1938   The Singing Blacksmith
1940   Overture to Glory

Fisher, Bill
1942   We Were Dancing

Fisher, Diane
1940   The Man I Married

Fisher, George *not the same as* **Fisher, George "Shug"**
1916   Three of Many
1918   A Little Sister of
      Everybody
1925   Justice of the Far North

Fisher, George "Shug" *not the same as* **Fisher, George**
1947   The Last Round-Up
      On the Old Spanish Trail
1949   Stallion Canyon
1950   Riders of the Pony
      Express
      Rio Grande
1960   Sergeant Rutledge

Fisher, Gloria *same as* **Fischer, Gloria**
1934   As the Earth Turns
      Straight Is the Way
1938   The Beloved Brat

Fisher, John
1943   Jack London

Fisher, Larry
1926   Into Her Kingdom
1928   Breed of the Sunsets
1934   Charlie Chan's Courage
1936   Paddy O'Day
1938   Little Miss Roughneck

Fisher, Maggie H. *same as* **Fisher, Maggie; Fisher, Maggie Halloway**
1918   Out of a Clear Sky

Fisher, Mamie
1949?   Girl in Room 20

Fisher, Margarita *same as* **Fischer, Margarita**
1919   The Tiger Lily
1928   Uncle Tom's Cabin

Fisher, Marvin
1941   Ice-Capades

Fisher, Millicent
1917   The Slacker (Metro
      Pictures Corp.)

Fisher, Nelle
1948   Up in Central Park

Fisher, Robert *could be same as* **Fischer, Robert C.**
1915   Hearts of Men

Fisher, Steve
1945   Johnny Angel
1953   The Man from the Alamo
      San Antone
1954   Hell's Half Acre

Fishkind, Abraham
1939   The Light Ahead

Fishman, Sylvia
1940   The Great Advisor

Fishson, Misha
1939   The Light Ahead

Fisk, Warren
1950   Colt .45

Fiske, Dick *see* **Fiske, Richard**

Fiske, George
1944   Buffalo Bill
      Riding West

Fiske, Richard *same as* **Fiske, Dick**
1940   Prairie Schooners
1941   They Dare Not Love
1942   Valley of the Sun

Fiske, Robert
1936   Song of the Gringo
1937   The Devil's Playground
      Drums of Destiny
      Old Louisiana

Fiske, William, III
1934   White Heat

Fisko, Robert
1942   Gentleman Jim

Fiszer, Jakub
1937   The Jester (Der
      Purimspieler)

Fitch, Donald
1924   Down by the Rio Grande

Fite, Chuck
1958   Tonka

Fitts, Margaret
1950   Stars in My Crown

Fitzgerald, Barry
1943   The Amazing Mrs.
      Holliday
1944   Going My Way
1947   California
      Easy Come, Easy Go
1949   The Story of Seabiscuit
      Top O' the Morning
1952   The Quiet Man
1956   The Catered Affair

Fitzgerald, Betty T.
1916   Silks and Satins

Fitzgerald, Bobby
1922   Square Joe

Fitzgerald, Cissy *same as* **Fitz-
Gerald, Cissy; Fitzgerald,
Cissie**
1927   McFadden's Flats

Fitzgerald, Dallas M.
1921   Puppets of Fate
1922   The Guttersnipe

Fitzgerald, Edith
1935   The Wedding Night

Fitzgerald, Ella
1958   St. Louis Blues

Fitzgerald, Jean
1942   Juke Girl

Fitzgerald, Mike
1958   Flaming Frontier

Fitzgerald, Millie
1958   The Last Hurrah

Fitzgerald, Neil
1935   Charlie Chan in Shanghai
1939   Mr. Moto's Last Warning

Fitzgerald, Richard B.
1957   Beau James

Fitzmaurice, George
1916   Arms and the Woman
      The Romantic Journey
1920   On with the Dance
1927   The Love Mart
      Rose of the Golden West

Fitzpatrick, James
1939   Gone With the Wind

Fitzpatrick, Ronald
1935   The Winning Ticket

Fitzroy, Emily
1923   Jealous Husbands
1924   Untamed Youth
1929   Show Boat
1936   The Bold Caballero

Fitzsimmons, Charles (*actor*)
1952   The Quiet Man
1958   The Last Hurrah

Fitzsimmons, R. H.
1919   The Red Viper

Fitzsimmons, Ralph
1938   Happy Landing

Fitzsimons, Charles B. (*prod*)
1956   Mohawk

Fix, Paul
1930   Ladies Love Brutes
1936   After the Thin Man
      Charlie Chan at the Race
      Track
      The Prisoner of Shark
      Island
      Winterset
1937   Big City
      Border Cafe
      Souls at Sea
1938   The Buccaneer
      Daughter of Shanghai
      Mr. Moto's Gamble
1942   Dr. Gillespie's New
      Assistant
1943   In Old Oklahoma
1948   Angel in Exile
      Red River
1949   The Fighting Kentuckian
1951   Warpath
1954   Hondo
1956   Giant
1957   Man in the Shadow

Fjorde, Madame
1915   How Molly Malone Made
      Good

Fladwed, Henry
1953   The Eddie Cantor Story

Flaherty, Frances
1948   Louisiana Story

Flaherty, Pat
1939   Miracle on Main Street
1940   Knute Rockne—All
      American
1941   Dead Men Tell
1942   Gentleman Jim
      Juke Girl
1943   Good Luck, Mr. Yates
      Yankee Doodle Dandy
1946   G. I. War Brides
1948   Key Largo
1950   The Daughter of Rosie
      O'Grady
      The Jackie Robinson Story

Flaherty, Robert *same as* **Flaherty, Robert J.**
1922   Nanook of the North
1948   Louisiana Story

Flaherty, Vincent X.
1951   Jim Thorpe—All-American

Flame, a dog
1948   Night Wind
      Shep Comes Home

Flanagan, Bud *see* **O'Keefe, Dennis**

Flanagan, Edward James *see* **O'Keefe, Dennis**

Flannery, Mary
1933   Thundering Herd

Flannigan, E. F.
1914   Springtime

Flash, a horse
1927   Open Range
1946   Wild West
1947   West to Glory

Flateau, Georges *same as* **Flateau, George; Slatteau, George**
1951   Adventures of Captain
      Fabian

Flatley, James
1940   Escape to Glory

Flavin, Arthur
1948 The Miracle of the Bells
Flavin, James
1934 Beloved
1935 Chinatown Squad
  Rendezvous
1936 Charlie Chan at the Race
  Track
1937 Big City
  Charlie Chan on
   Broadway
  That I May Live
1938 The Buccaneer
  Gateway
  Speed to Burn
1939 The Cisco Kid and the
  Lady
  Mr. Wong in Chinatown
1940 Knute Rockne—All
  American
  Lucky Cisco Kid
  The Way of All Flesh
1941 Belle Starr
  Hold Back the Dawn
  New York Town
  Ride on Vaquero
  Western Union
1942 Gentleman Jim
  Juke Girl
1943 Action in the North
  Atlantic
  Air Force
  Riding High
  Yankee Doodle Dandy
1945 Johnny Angel
  The Shanghai Cobra
1947 Easy Come, Easy Go
  The Mighty McGurk
1948 Fury at Furnace Creek
  My Girl Tisa
  Unconquered
1950 Rock Island Trail
1951 Oh! Susanna
1953 The Eddie Cantor Story
1954 Massacre Canyon
1955 Apache Ambush
1957 Beau James
1958 The Last Hurrah
  Wild Is the Wind
Flavin, Martin
1930 El presidio
1931 Three Who Loved
Fleck, Fred
1914 The Littlest Rebel
Fleer, Harry
1957 Band of Angels
Fleischer, Richard
1949 The Clay Pigeon
1955 Violent Saturday
Fleischman, Bunky
1940 Knute Rockne—All
  American
Fleischmann, Harry *same as*
 Fleischman, Harry; Fleishman,
 Harry
1939 Let Freedom Ring
Fleming, Alice
1941 Playmates
1944 Marshal of Reno
  The San Antonio Kid
  Sheriff of Las Vegas
  Tucson Raiders
  Vigilantes of Dodge City
1945 Colorado Pioneers
  Great Stagecoach Robbery
  A Medal for Benny
  Phantom of the Plains
1946 California Gold Rush
  Saratoga Trunk
  Sheriff of Redwood Valley
  Sun Valley Cyclone
Fleming, Bob *same as* **Fleming,**
 Robert; Flemming, Bob
1915 The Immigrant
1928 The Riding Renegade
Fleming, Ethel
1918 Untamed
Fleming, Rhonda
1943 In Old Oklahoma
1944 Since You Went Away
1951 The Last Outpost
1958 Bullwhip
  Home Before Dark

Fleming, Susan
1933 Olsen's Big Moment
1934 Charlie Chan's Courage
1936 Star for a Night
Fleming, Victor
1922 Anna Ascends
1925 A Son of His Father
1927 The Way of All Flesh
1929 Abie's Irish Rose
  Wolf Song
1939 Gone With the Wind
1942 Tortilla Flat
Flemming, Bob *see* **Fleming, Bob**
Fletcher, Dusty
1948 Killer Diller
1948? Boarding House Blues
Fletcher, Jerry
1939 Waterfront
Fletcher, Lester
1960 Pay or Die
Fletcher, Robin
1951 Slaughter Trail
Fletcher, Roy
1958 Sierra Baron
Fletcher, Tom
1925 Body and Soul
Fletcher, William
1937 The Californian
1941 Sun Valley Serenade
1952 Red Snow
Flick, Pat C. *same as* **Flick, Patsy**
1937 Black Legion
Flicka, a horse
1950 Riders of the Pony
  Express
Flinn, John C.
1926 The Last Frontier
  Pals in Paradise
Flint, Helen
1934 Broadway Bill
1937 Black Legion
Flint, Sam *same as* **Flint, Samuel**
1933 Broken Dreams
1934 Broadway Bill
1935 A Night at the Ritz
  The Winning Ticket
1936 Charlie Chan at the Race
  Track
1937 It Could Happen to You
1940 The Way of All Flesh
1941 Under Fiesta Stars
1943 Dixie
1944 The Chinese Cat
1945 Nob Hill
1947 California
  It Had To Be You
1948 Four Faces West
  The Golden Eye
  Old Los Angeles
1949 The Gay Amigo
  Knock on Any Door
1950 Cherokee Uprising
  The Palomino
  Rock Island Trail
1951 Saturday's Hero
  Snake River Desperadoes
1958 Gunman's Walk
1959 The FBI Story
Flippen, Jay C. *same as* **Flippen, J.
 C.**
1950 Buccaneer's Girl
  Two Flags West
  Winchester '73
1953 Thunder Bay
1956 7th Cavalry
1957 The Deerslayer
  The Halliday Brand
  The Midnight Story
  Run of the Arrow
1958 Escape from Red Rock
1960 The Plunderers
  Studs Lonigan
  Wild River
Flood, James
1921 Bits of Life
  Guile of Women
1923 Look Your Best
1929 Mister Antonio
Flood, Redmond
1936 Rose of the Rancho

Flood, Thomas *same as* **Flood,**
 Tom; Flood, Tommy
1939 In Old Caliente
1940 Prairie Schooners
1946 Singin' in the Corn
Florelle
1931 Die Dreigroschenoper
  (foreign version)
Florence [full name unknown]
1915 Hearts of Men
Flores Brothers
1942 Rio Rita
Flores, Alberto
1950 Panic in the Streets
Flores, Carol
1934 Laughing Boy
Flores, Cornelia
1951 Westward the Women
Flores, Felipe *same as* **Flores,**
 Felipe de
1931 Carne de cabaret
1956 Comanche
Flores, Iris
1946 The Gay Cavalier
  South of Monterey
1947 Ride the Pink Horse
Flores, Joe
1917 John Ermine of the
  Yellowstone
Florey, Robert
1936 Rose of the Rancho
1938 Dangerous to Know
  Daughter of Shanghai
1941 The Face Behind the
  Mask
1951 Adventures of Captain
  Fabian
Flory, Véra
1931 Su noche de bodas
  (foreign version)
Flothow, Rudolph *same as*
 Flothow, Rudolph C.
1929 Lucky Boy
1949 Boston Blackie's Chinese
  Venture
Flournoy, Elizabeth *same as*
 Flournoy, Betty
1934 Coming Out Party
1950 Annie Get Your Gun
  Emergency Wedding
1955 Good Morning, Miss Dove
1956 Serenade
1958 Home Before Dark
Flournoy, Richard
1936 General Spanky
Flowers, Bess
1926 Irene
  Laddie
1934 Broadway Bill
  Stand Up and Cheer!
1938 City Streets
  In Old Chicago
1943 The Amazing Mrs.
  Holliday
1944 Mr. Skeffington
1947 The Farmer's Daughter
1950 The Big Hangover
1951 The Great Caruso
1955 The View from Pompey's
  Head
1959 Imitation of Life
Flowers, Theodore "Tiger"
1926 The Fighting Deacon
Fluellen, Joel
1946 Without Reservations
1947 The Burning Cross
1950 The Jackie Robinson Story
1954 Sitting Bull
1955 Seven Angry Men
1959 Imitation of Life
  Porgy and Bess
Flynn, Charles *same as* **Flynn
 Charles J.; Flynn, Chuck**
1942 Syncopation
  Valley of Hunted Men
1943 Action in the North
  Atlantic
  Air Force
1947 Desperate
1948 Fighting Father Dunne
  Tap Roots
  Unconquered

Flynn, Emmet J. *same as* **Flynn, E.
 J.**
1949 House of Strangers
1950 No Way Out
Flynn, Emmett J.
1919 A Bachelor's Wife
  Yvonne from Paris
1920 The Man Who Dared
1921 Shame
Flynn, Errol
1940 Santa Fe Trail
1942 Gentleman Jim
  They Died With Their
   Boots On
1950 Rocky Mountain
1951 Adventures of Captain
  Fabian
Flynn, Joe 1924—1974 *not the
 same as* **Flynn, Joseph** *circa
 1930s*
1955 Trial
Flynn, Lefty *same as* **Flynn, M. B.;
 Flynn, Maurice B.; Flynn,
 Maurice Bennett**
1925 Speed Wild
Flynn, Ray
1941 New York Town
1943 Mr. Lucky
1944 The Racket Man
1949 Illegal Entry
Flynn, Rita
1931 The Cisco Kid
Flynn, Roy
1938 The Buccaneer
Foch, Nina
1944 Cry of the Werewolf
1945 Escape in the Fog
1949 The Undercover Man
Fodor, Ladislas *same as* **Fodor,**
 Lázló
1942 Tales of Manhattan
Foley, Red, and His Saddle Pals
1941 The Pioneers
Foley, Romey
1945 Colorado Pioneers
Folkerson, Bob
1942 Shut My Big Mouth
1960 Flaming Star
Folks, Casey
1951 Queen for a Day
Folorance, C. M.
1956 The Lone Ranger
Foltz, Virginia
1920 The Paliser Case
Folz, Artye
1936 Show Boat
Fonda, Henry
1938 Spawn of the North
1939 Drums Along the Mohawk
1942 Tales of Manhattan
1943 The Ox-Bow Incident
1948 Fort Apache
1949 Jigsaw
1957 The Tin Star
  Twelve Angry Men
Fong, Benson
1944 Charlie Chan in the
  Secret Service
  The Chinese Cat
1945 Nob Hill
  The Scarlet Clue
  The Shanghai Cobra
1946 Dark Alibi
  The Red Dragon
1949 Boston Blackie's Chinese
  Venture
1950 Chinatown at Midnight
1960 Walk Like a Dragon
Fong, Fun
1941 Min Jok Jay Hung Sing
Fong, Harold
1945 Betrayal from the East
1949 Boston Blackie's Chinese
  Venture
1951 The Steel Helmet
Fong, Lang
1939? A Chinese Gains a
  Fortune in America
Fong, Les
1947 Little Mister Jim

Fong, Paul C. *could be same as* **Fung, Paul**
1935   Captured in Chinatown
Fong, Sammy
1942   Tortilla Flat
Fong, Wai Gim *could be same as* **Fong, Way Kim**
1939?   A Chinese Gains a Fortune in America
Fong, Way Kim *could be same as* **Fong, Wai Gim**
1936   Sum Hun
Fong, Willie *could be same as* **Fung, Willie**
1933   The Cohens and Kellys in Trouble
Fonsilli, Sergio
1930   Doña mentiras (*foreign version*)
Fontaine, Joan *same as* **Burfield, Joan**
1937   Music for Madame
1939   Man of Conquest
1956   Serenade
Fontaine, William E. *see* **Fountaine, William E.**
Fontana, Anna
1930   Toda una vida (*foreign version*)
Fontana, Gilda
1955   Seven Cities of Gold
Foo, Lee Tong *same as* **Foo, Lee Tung; Tung-Foo, Lee**
1937   Waikiki Wedding
1938   Mr. Wong, Detective
1939   Mr. Wong in Chinatown
        The Mystery of Mr. Wong
        Stand Up and Fight
1940   Phantom of Chinatown
        They Knew What They Wanted
1941   Accent on Love
        Dead Men Tell
        Secret of the Wastelands
1942   Across the Pacific
1947   The Chinese Ring
1948   The Golden Eye
1950   Annie Get Your Gun
        The Cariboo Trail
Foo, Mei Lee
1943   Jack London
Foo, Wing
1935   Captured in Chinatown
1943   Bataan
1945   Escape in the Fog
Foote, Bradbury
1944   Lady, Let's Dance!
Foote, Courtenay *same as* **Foote, Courtney**
1915   Captain Courtesy
1918   Love's Law
1919   His Parisian Wife
1923   Little Old New York
Foote, John Taintor
1940   The Mark of Zorro
1949   The Story of Seabiscuit
Foote, Richard *same as* **Foote, Dick**
1947   Thunder Mountain
        Under the Tonto Rim
        Wild Horse Mesa
1948   The Arizona Ranger
1949   Streets of Laredo
1950   Young Daniel Boone
Foran, Dick *same as* **Foran, Nick**
1934   Stand Up and Cheer!
1936   Treachery Rides the Range
1937   Black Legion
        Prairie Thunder
1939   Daughters Courageous
1940   The Fighting 69th
1941   Road Agent
1947   Easy Come, Easy Go
1948   Fort Apache
1960   Studs Lonigan
Foran, Mary
1960   I Passed for White
Foran, Nick *see* **Foran, Dick**

Forbert, Leo
1934   The Rabbi's Power
Forbes, Don
1940   Elsa Maxwell's Public Deb No. 1
1942   Young America
1949   The Story of Seabiscuit
Forbes, Glen
1942   Holiday Inn
Forbes, Mary
1930   East Is West
1934   She Was a Lady
1935   McFadden's Flats
        Rendezvous
1938   Outside of Paradise
        The Rage of Paris
1942   We Were Dancing
1943   Mr. Lucky
1944   Tender Comrade
1947   It Had To Be You
1958   Houseboat
Forbes, Ralph
1934   Strange Wives
1935   Rescue Squad
1936   Daniel Boone
Forbes, Scott
1950   Rocky Mountain
Ford, Captain *see* **Ford, Sterett**
Ford, Celeste
1934   Behold My Wife!
Ford, Constance
1956   The Last Hunt
Ford, Damon *see* **O'Flynn, Damien**
Ford, David
1960   The Pusher
Ford, Dorothy
1945   Nob Hill
1949   3 Godfathers
1950   Sands of Iwo Jima
Ford, Elsie
1917   John Ermine of the Yellowstone
Ford, Eugenie *see* **Forde, Eugenie**
Ford, Francis
1917   John Ermine of the Yellowstone
1922   Cross Roads
1925   The Red Rider
1927   The Devil's Saddle
1928   Uncle Tom's Cabin
1930   Kathleen Mavourneen
        Song of the Caballero
1933   Charlie Chan's Greatest Case
        Man from Monterey
        Thundering Herd
1934   Charlie Chan's Courage
        Judge Priest
1936   Charlie Chan at the Circus
        Charlie Chan's Secret
        Paddy O'Day
        The Prisoner of Shark Island
        Sins of Man
1937   Slave Ship
        Souls at Sea
1938   In Old Chicago
        The Texans
1939   Bad Lands
        Drums Along the Mohawk
1940   Geronimo
        Lucky Cisco Kid
        Viva Cisco Kid
1941   Romance of the Rio Grande
        Western Union
1942   They Died With Their Boots On
        The Vanishing Virginian
1943   The Ox-Bow Incident
1947   California
1948   Fort Apache
        Unconquered
1949   She Wore a Yellow Ribbon
        3 Godfathers
1952   The Quiet Man
        Trail of the Arrow
1953   The Sun Shines Bright

Ford, Frederick
1957   Revolt at Fort Laramie
        Tomahawk Trail
Ford, George
1942   Cat People
1943   Gangway for Tomorrow
1951   Show Boat
1952   Indian Uprising
1958   The Last Hurrah
Ford, Glenn
1939   Heaven with a Barbed Wire Fence
1949   Lust for Gold
        The Undercover Man
1953   The Man from the Alamo
1955   Blackboard Jungle
        Trial
1960   Cimarron
Ford, Grace
1937   Big City
Ford, Harrison 1892—1957
1917   A Roadside Impresario
1922   Shadows
1923   Little Old New York
Ford, Hugh
1916   The Innocent Lie
Ford, Jack (*dir*) *see* **Ford, John** (*dir*)
Ford, James
1945   Where Do We Go From Here?
Ford, John (*dir*) *same as* **Ford, Jack** (*dir*) *not the same as* **Ford, John** (*actor*)
1918   Wild Women
1922   Little Miss Smiles
1928   Mother Machree
        Riley the Cop
1932   Flesh
1934   Judge Priest
1936   The Prisoner of Shark Island
1939   Drums Along the Mohawk
1948   Fort Apache
1949   She Wore a Yellow Ribbon
        3 Godfathers
1950   Rio Grande
1952   The Quiet Man
1953   The Sun Shines Bright
1954   Hondo
1955   The Long Gray Line
1956   The Searchers
1958   The Last Hurrah
1960   Sergeant Rutledge
Ford, Lloyd
1947   Calendar Girl
Ford, Norman, Lt.
1944   The Negro Soldier
Ford, Pat (*actor*)
1951   Westward the Women
Ford, Patrick (*prod*)
1956   The Searchers
1959   The Young Land
1960   Sergeant Rutledge
Ford, Paul
1945   The House on 92nd St.
1949   Lust for Gold
Ford, Phil *same as* **Ford, Philip**
1928   Riley the Cop
1929   Love, Live and Laugh
1933   It's Great to Be Alive
1937   It Could Happen to You
1938   Outside of Paradise
1939   Forged Passport
1940   Girl from God's Country
1941   Lady from Louisiana
1943   In Old Oklahoma
1948   Angel in Exile
1949   Ranger of Cherokee Strip
Ford, Ross
1943   Action in the North Atlantic
        Air Force
1947   My Wild Irish Rose
Ford, Ruth
1942   Across the Pacific
        In This Our Life
        Secret Enemies
1943   Air Force

Ford, Sterrett *same as* **Ford, Captain**
1916   The Soul of Kura-San
1917   The Squaw Man's Son
Ford, Wallace *same as* **Ford, Wally**
1932   Hypnotized
1942   All Through the Night
1945   The Great John L.
1950   The Breaking Point
        The Furies
1951   Warpath
1953   The Nebraskan
1958   The Last Hurrah
Forde, Eugene *same as* **Forde, Eugene J.**
1933   Primavera en otoño
1934   Charlie Chan in London
        Charlie Chan's Courage
1937   Charlie Chan on Broadway
1938   Charlie Chan at Monte Carlo
1940   Charlie Chan's Murder Cruise
Forde, Eugenie *same as* **Ford, Eugenie**
1919   Bonnie, Bonnie Lassie
1920   A Tokio Siren
Forde, Rae
1914   At the Cross Roads
Foreman, Carl
1949   The Clay Pigeon
        Home of the Brave
1950   The Men
        Young Man with a Horn
1952   High Noon
Forest, Mary
1950   Monticello, Here We Come!
Forest, Robert
1955   Trial
Forest, William *see* **Crouch, William Forest**
Forman, Carol
1947   Desperate
        Under the Tonto Rim
1948   Docks of New Orleans
        The Feathered Serpent
1949   Brothers in the Saddle
1951   Oh! Susanna
Forman, Tom (*actor*), 1893—1926
1915   Chimmie Fadden
        Chimmie Fadden Out West
        The Kindling
1916   The Thousand Dollar Husband
        Unprotected
1917   Forbidden Paths
        Hashimura Togo
        The Trouble Buster
1919   Told in the Hills
1922   Shadows
1923   April Showers
1926   Kosher Kitty Kelly
Forman, Tom (*actor*), circa 1930s—1940s
1932   Hypnotized
1937   The Californian
1941   Western Union
1950   Ambush
Forrest, Allan *same as* **Forrest, Alan; Forrest, Allen**
1916   Peck O' Pickles
1918?   Rosemary Climbs the Heights
1919   A Bachelor's Wife
        Yvonne from Paris
1920   Li Ting Lang
        The Purple Cipher
1921   Cheated Love
1925   Old Clothes
Forrest, Ann
1920   Dangerous Days
Forrest, Arthur
1956   Crowded Paradise
Forrest, Guy
1950   Panic in the Streets
Forrest, Jayne
1944   Slightly Terrific

Forrest, Lottie Pickford *see* **Pickford, Lottie**
Forrest, Mabel
1934   Behold My Wife!
Forrest, Marguerite *same as* **Forrest, Margaret**
1917   The Renaissance at Charleroi
1921   Little Italy
Forrest, Robert
1955   Trial
1957   Raintree County
Forrest, Sally
1950   Mystery Street
Forrest, Steve
1953   Dream Wife
      So Big
1960   Flaming Star
Forrest, William
1941   Sun Valley Serenade
1942   In This Our Life
      Little Tokyo, U.S.A.
      They Died With Their Boots On
      The Vanishing Virginian
1943   Action in the North Atlantic
      Air Force
      Good Luck, Mr. Yates
      Hitler's Children
      Yankee Doodle Dandy
1944   Mr. Skeffington
1946   Till the End of Time
1947   Dark Delusion
      The Jolson Story
1948   Fort Apache
1949   The Girl from Jones Beach
      Illegal Entry
      The Story of Seabiscuit
1950   Emergency Wedding
1951   The Harlem Globetrotters
1953   The Eddie Cantor Story
1955   A Man Called Peter
1956   Walk the Proud Land
1957   Band of Angels
      Beau James
      Burden of Truth
1958   The Last Hurrah
Forrester, Fred
1917   The Tenderfoot
Forrester, Vivian
1921   Society Snobs
Forst, Emil *same as* **Forst, E.; Forst, Elmer**
1924   Fools' Highway
Förster, Rudolph
1931   Die Dreigroschenoper
Forsyne, Ida
1936   The Green Pastures
1938   Birthright
Forsyth, William *same as* **Forsyth, Bill; Forsythe, William**
1938   Josette
1939   Mr. Moto in Danger Island
1959   The Young Land
Fort, Garrett
1925   The Midnight Girl
1927   White Gold
1930   The Big Pond
      Doña mentiras
1931   La carta
      Drácula
      El impostor
1940   The Mark of Zorro
Forte, Joe *same as* **Forte, Josef; Forte, Joseph**
1948   Call Northside 777
1950   A Ticket to Tomahawk
1958   The Last Hurrah
1959   The Jayhawkers!
Forth, George J.
1917   I Will Repay
Fortier, Herbert
1919   Who's Your Brother?
Fortier, Robert
1951   Show Boat
Fortson, Robert
1919   Injustice

Fortune, Dick *same as* **Fortune, Richard**
1952   Indian Uprising
1954   War Arrow
Fortune, Jan
1939   Man of Conquest
1942   Mokey
      The Vanishing Virginian
Fortune, John
1939   Moon over Harlem
Fortune, Myrtle
1941   Up Jumped the Devil
Fortune, Richard *see* **Fortune, Dick**
Foshay, Harold
1938   Josette
Foss, Darrell
1918   Her American Husband
Fossett, Howard
1934   Call of the Coyote
Fossier, Mildred
1950   Panic in the Streets
Fostel, Simche *same as* **Fostel, S.**
1936   Yiddle with His Fiddle
1939   A Brivele der Mamen Mamele
Foster, Alan
1949   The Story of Seabiscuit
Foster, Art
1942   Gentleman Jim
1943   Action in the North Atlantic
Foster, Arthur Turner
1936   Klondike Annie
Foster, Daisy
1927   The Broken Violin
Foster, Dan
1949   The Clay Pigeon
1950   Battleground
      Devil's Doorway
1951   Show Boat
      The Tall Target
Foster, Dianne
1957   The Brothers Rico
1958   The Last Hurrah
Foster, Donald
1959   Al Capone
Foster, Edward *same as* **Foster, Eddie**
1941   The Face Behind the Mask
1943   Action in the North Atlantic
1958   Marjorie Morningstar
Foster, Frances
1960   Take a Giant Step
Foster, Harve
1936   The Glory Trail
1939   Gone With the Wind
1946   Song of the South
Foster, Helen
1928   The Mating Call
1948   Call Northside 777
Foster, Lewis R. *same as* **Foster, L. R.; Foster, Lew**
1932   Hypnotized
1951   The Last Outpost
1956   Dakota Incident
1958   Tonka
1960   The Sign of Zorro
Foster, Marie
1928   Uncle Tom's Cabin
Foster, May
1927   The Frontiersman
Foster, Morris *same as* **Foster, J. Morris**
1916   The Innocent Lie
Foster, Norman
1932   The Cohens and Kellys in Hollywood
1933   Rafter Romance
1937   Thank You, Mr. Moto
      Think Fast, Mr. Moto
1938   Mr. Moto Takes a Chance
1939   Charlie Chan at Treasure Island
      Charlie Chan in Reno
      Mr. Moto Takes a Vacation
      Mr. Moto's Last Warning
1940   Charlie Chan in Panama
      Northwest Passage (Book I—Rogers' Rangers)

      Viva Cisco Kid
1952   Navajo
1955   Davy Crockett, King of the Wild Frontier
1956   Davy Crockett and the River Pirates
1960   The Sign of Zorro
Foster, Patty
1947   Citizen Saint
Foster, Preston
1933   The Man Who Dared: An Imaginative Biography
1935   Annie Oakley
1936   Muss 'Em Up
1940   Geronimo
1942   American Empire
      Little Tokyo, U.S.A.
1945   The Valley of Decision
1951   Tomahawk
Foster, Rose Marie
1955   Brevities of 1955
Foster, Rube
1921   As the World Rolls On
Fostini, John
1947   The Burning Cross
1960   The Pusher
Fouchee, Charles
1922   Square Joe
Fougá, Bernardo
1932   Amor y vida
Foulger, Byron
1941   Mystery Ship
      Sullivan's Travels
1942   Apache Trail
1943   Dr. Gillespie's Criminal Case
      In Old Oklahoma
      Margin for Error
1944   An American Romance
      Black Magic
      Since You Went Away
      Three Men in White
1945   Nob Hill
1947   The Adventures of Don Coyote
      Bells of San Fernando
      The Chinese Ring
      Easy Come, Easy Go
1948   Unconquered
1949   The Dalton Gang
      The Kissing Bandit
      Satan's Cradle
      Streets of Laredo
1950   The Girl from San Lorenzo
1952   Apache Country
      Rose of Cimarron
1954   Cattle Queen of Montana
1957   Gun Battle at Monterey
Foulk, Robert
1948   Unconquered
1949   Thieves' Highway
1950   A Lady Without Passport
      Mystery Street
1951   Saturday's Hero
1955   Apache Ambush
      Blackboard Jungle
      Headline Hunters
1956   Hot Blood
1957   Raintree County
Fountaine, William E. *same as* **Fontaine, William E.**
1922   The Dungeon
      Uncle Jasper's Will
      The Virgin of Seminole
1923   Deceit
1929   Hallelujah
The Four Night Hawks
1931   Call of the Rockies
The Four Tones *same as* **Brooks, Lucius; Buck, Leon; Hardin, Ira; Hunter, Rudolph**
1937   Harlem on the Prairie
1938   Two Gun Man from Harlem
1939   The Bronze Buckaroo
      Harlem Rides the Range
      One Dark Night
1946   Mantan Messes Up
The Four Toppers
1940   Mystery in Swing
      Son of Ingagi

The Four V's
1945   I Love a Bandleader
Fowler, Almeda *same as* **Fowler, Alameda**
1937   That I May Live
1941   The Face Behind the Mask
1943   Dr. Gillespie's Criminal Case
1944   They Live in Fear
1946   Notorious
Fowler, Brenda
1918   Thirty a Week
1934   Judge Priest
1935   Ruggles of Red Gap
Fowler, Frank
1955   The Far Horizons
Fowler, Gene d. 1960
1933   L'amour guide
1936   It Had to Happen
      Sutter's Gold
Fowler, Gene (narrator) *could be same as* **Fowler, Gene** *or* **Fowler, Gene, Jr.**
1950   Damien
Fowler, Gene N. (actor) *could be same as* **Fowler, Gene** d. 1960 *or* **Fowler, Gene, Jr.**
1959   The Oregon Trail
Fowler, Gene, Jr.
1950   Damien
1959   The Oregon Trail
Fowler, H. Waller, Jr.
1950   Panic in the Streets
Fowler, J. C.
1945   The Dolly Sisters
Fowler, Jean
1945   A Tree Grows in Brooklyn
Fowler, John C. *same as* **Fowler, J. C.; Fowler, John**
1929   The Peacock Fan
1938   The Buccaneer
Fowler, Phyllis
1953   Fort Ti
Fowley, Douglas
1934   Operator 13
1936   Dimples
1937   Charlie Chan on Broadway
      One Mile from Heaven
1938   Mr. Moto's Gamble
      Passport Husband
1939   Charlie Chan at Treasure Island
1940   East of the River
1941   Secret of the Wastelands
1943   Dr. Gillespie's Criminal Case
      Riding High
1944   The Racket Man
1946   Rendezvous 24
1947   Desperate
1948   Docks of New Orleans
      The Dude Goes West
      Gun Smugglers
1949   Massacre River
      Satan's Cradle
1950   Battleground
      Rio Grande Patrol
1951   Across the Wide Missouri
1953   The Man Behind the Gun
1955   The Lonesome Trail
1956   The Broken Star
      Man from Del Rio
1957   Bayou
      Raiders of Old California
Fox, Allen *same as* **Fox, Allan**
1931   Street Scene
1937   Charlie Chan on Broadway
1938   Mr. Moto's Gamble
      Passport Husband
1940   Geronimo
      The Way of All Flesh
Fox, Arthur
1953   So Big
Fox, Chuck
1960   Pay or Die
Fox, Earle
1916   Alien Souls
1923   Fashion Row
1926   A Trip to Chinatown

Fox, Earle (continued)

1932 Men Are Such Fools
So Big

Fox, Finis
1919 False Evidence
1925 My Son
1928 Ramona
1929 Evangeline
1931 Resurrección

Fox, Frank
1946 Bringing Up Father
1947 Bowery Buckaroos
1949 Daughter of the West
1950 The Baron of Arizona
1956 Death of a Scoundrel

Fox, Fred
1942 Song of the Islands
1947 Buffalo Bill Rides Again

Fox, Frederic Louis
1954 Overland Pacific
1955 Headline Hunters
1956 Dakota Incident

Fox, George
1920 Hidden Charms
1921? The Supreme Passion

Fox, Janet
1940 They Knew What They
Wanted

Fox, Jesslyn
1960 All the Fine Young
Cannibals

Fox, Jimmie *same as* **Fox, Jimmy**
1953 Ride, Vaquero!
1956 The Catered Affair

Fox, John, Jr. *not the same as* **Fox, Johnny**
1926 Laddie

Fox, Johnny *not the same as* **Fox, John, Jr.**
1925 Friendly Enemies

Fox, Lucy
1921 The Money Maniac

Fox, Michael
1953 The Glass Wall

Fox, Paul Hervey
1936 Ramona
1953 The Stars Are Singing

Fox, Sidney
1932 The Cohens and Kellys in
Hollywood

Fox, Wallace W. *same as* **Fox, Wallace**
1925 My Son
1928 Breed of the Sunsets
The Riding Renegade
1936 The Last of the Mohicans
1942 Let's Get Tough!
1943 The Girl from Monterrey
1944 Block Busters
Minstrel Man
1946 Wild Beauty
1949 The Daring Caballero
The Gay Amigo
The Valiant Hombre

Fox, William (*actor*) *not the same as* **Fox, William** (*production executive*), 1879—1952
1956 Serenade

Fox, William (*production executive*), 1879—1952 *same as* **Fox, Wm.** (*production executive*), 1879—1952 *not the same as* **Fox, William** (*actor*)
1915 Children of the Ghetto
The Girl I Left Behind Me
Kreutzer Sonata
The Nigger
1918 I Want to Forget
The Prussian Cur
Woman and the Law
1920 The Face at Your Window
The Girl of My Heart
1921 Little Miss Hawkshaw
Shame
Wing Toy
1922 A California Romance
Little Miss Smiles
Pawn Ticket 210
Sky High
1923 Snowdrift
1926 A Trip to Chinatown
1927 The Auctioneer
Whispering Sage

1928 Mother Machree
Riley the Cop
1929 Frozen Justice
Hearts in Dixie
Love, Live and Laugh
Masked Emotions
Romance of the Rio
Grande
1930 The Arizona Kid
Cuando el amor ríe
El precio de un beso
El último de los Vargas
1931 The Black Camel
Cuerpo y alma
Del infierno al cielo
Esclavas de la moda
Hay que casar al príncipe
El impostor
Mr. Lemon of Orange
Young Sinners

Foy, Bryan
1929 Die Königsloge
1932 Tiger Shark
1933 Obey the Law
1936 Treachery Rides the
Range
1937 Prairie Thunder
1938 The Beloved Brat
1939 Waterfront
1940 East of the River
1942 Little Tokyo, U.S.A.

Foy, Charley *same as* **Foy, Charles**
1940 East of the River

Foy, Eddie, Jr. *same as* **Foy, Eddie**
1936 Star for a Night
1943 Dixie
Yankee Doodle Dandy

Foy, Mary
1925 Irish Luck
The Manicure Girl

Frack, Jack
1946 The Gentleman
Misbehaves

Fraction, Edward
1948 The Betrayal

Fraenkel, Heinrich
1930 Los que danzan (*foreign version*)
Olimpia (*foreign version*)
1931 La llama sagrada (*foreign version*)

Fraenkel, Wolfgang
1953 Tonight We Sing

Frakadakis, Vassilios
1954 Barefoot Battalion

Frambes, William
1946 Bringing Up Father

Franc, Charles
1960 This Rebel Breed

Francell, Jacqueline
1933 L'amour guide

Francen, Victor
1941 Hold Back the Dawn
1942 Tales of Manhattan
1951 Adventures of Captain
Fabian

Franchon, Leonard
1921 Cotton and Cattle

Franciosa, Anthony
1958 Wild Is the Wind

Francis, Alec B. *same as* **Francis, Alec**
1914 When Broadway Was a
Trail
1916 The Yellow Passport
1918 Broken Ties
Thirty a Week
Wanted, a Mother
1919 Spotlight Sadie
1920 The Paliser Case
1923 The Spider and the Rose
1927 Sally in Our Alley
1929 Evangeline
1932 No Greater Love
1934 The Cat's-Paw

Francis, Anne
1950 So Young, So Bad
1955 Bad Day at Black Rock
Blackboard Jungle

Francis, Charles
1916 Broken Fetters

Francis, Coleman
1957 Burden of Truth
1960 Cimarron

Francis, Kay
1930 Behind the Make-Up
Galas de la Paramount

Francis, Leslie
1937 Souls at Sea

Francis, Martha
1925 The Scarlet West

Francis, Noel
1931 Smart Money
1932 So Big
1934 Imitation of Life

Francis, Olin
1934 The Battling Buckaroo
1935 Circle of Death
1935? The Irish Gringo
1936 Rose of the Rancho

Francis, Robert
1954 They Rode West
1955 The Long Gray Line

Francis, Sara
1939 Reform School
1940 Gang War
While Thousands Cheer
1941 Four Shall Die

Francisco, Betty
1924 East of Broadway
1929 Smiling Irish Eyes
1931 Charlie Chan Carries On
1932 Mystery Ranch

Franciscus, James
1960 I Passed for White

Franck, J. L.
1916 Ramona
1918 Her Moment

François, Gene
1951 Slaughter Trail

Francone, Frank
1950 A Lady Without Passport
1951 Go for Broke!

Francone, Tiny
1948 Cry of the City
1952 It's a Big Country: An
American Anthology

Franey, Billy *same as* **Franey, Bill;** **Franey, William**
1927 Aflame in the Sky
1928 The Canyon of Adventure
The Glorious Trail
1934 The Star Packer

Frank, Alexander *same as* **Frank, Alexander F.**
1918 The Liar

Frank, Bert S. *could be same as* **Frank, J. Herbert**
1914 The Littlest Rebel

Frank, Bruno
1940 Northwest Passage (Book
I—Rogers' Rangers)

Frank, Carl
1948 The Lady from Shanghai

Frank, Christian J. *same as* **Frank, Chris;** **Frank, Christian** *could be same as* **Franke, Chris**
1922 The Guttersnipe
1928 The Cavalier
The Secret Hour
1934 Broadway Bill
1940 New Moon

Frank, Consuelo
1935 Rosa de Francia

Frank, Ernst L.
1931 Don Juan diplomático
(*foreign version*)

Frank, Fred (*dir*) *not the same as* **Frank, Fredric M.** (*writer*)
1934 Imitation of Life
1936 Sutter's Gold
1941 This Woman Is Mine
1945 Salome, Where She
Danced
1946 Canyon Passage
Cuban Pete
1949 Illegal Entry
1950 Buccaneer's Girl
1952 The Raiders
1953 Column South

Frank, Fredric M. (*writer*) *not the same as* **Frank, Fred** (*dir*)
1940 Escape to Glory
1948 Unconquered

Frank, Harriet, Jr.
1960 The Dark at the Top of
the Stairs

Frank, J. Herbert *same as* **Frank, Herbert** *could be same as* **Frank, Bert S.**
1918 Good-Bye, Bill
1920? The Scarlet Dragon

Frank, Jacob
1929 Mother's Boy
1931 Zein Weib's Lubovnick

Frank, Jerry
1958 Fort Bowie

Frank, John
1960 All the Fine Young
Cannibals

Frank, Melvin
1947 It Had To Be You
1959 The Jayhawkers!

Frank, Piano
1946 Dirty Gertie from
Harlem, U.S.A.

Frank, Stan
1958 Tonka

Frank, W. R.
1954 Sitting Bull

Franke, Blanche
1951 The Great Caruso

Franke, Chris *could be same as* **Frank, Christian J.**

Franke, Constant
1934 La veuve joyeuse
1937 Charlie Chan at the
Olympics
1938 Charlie Chan at Monte
Carlo
1941 Louisiana Purchase

Frankel, Fanchon
1927 Jake the Plumber

Frankel, Gene
1949 C-Man

Frankel, Isidor *same as* **Frankel, I.;** **Frankel, Isadore;** **Frankel, Izidor**
1939 Motel the Operator
1940 Eli Eli
The Great Advisor
Her Second Mother
1950 God, Man and Devil

Frankian, Misak
1945 Anoush

Franklin, A., Miss
1927? You Can't Win

Franklin, Chester *not the same as* **Franklin, Chester M.** 1890—1948
1939 Gone With the Wind
1947 Duel in the Sun

Franklin, Chester M. 1890—1948 *not the same as* **Franklin, Chester**
1916 Gretchen, the Greenhorn
A Sister of Six
1921 All Souls' Eve
1931 Le père célibataire
Su última noche

Franklin, Dean
1940 The Fighting 69th

Franklin, Edna
1938 The Toy Wife

Franklin, Harry
1951 The Girl on the Bridge

Franklin, Harry L. *not the same as* **Franklin, Harry S.**
1920 The Secret Gift

Franklin, Harry S. *not the same as* **Franklin, Harry L.**
1952 Red Snow
1958 Gun Fever

Franklin, Irene
1934 Lazy River

Franklin, Irwin R. *see* **Franklyn, Irwin R.**

Franklin, Joanne
1951 Slaughter Trail

Franklin, John E.
1918   The Prussian Cur
Franklin, Louise *same as*
Franklyn, Louise
1942   Lucky Ghost
1945   I Love a Bandleader
1946   Shadows Over Chinatown
1949   Lookout Sister
        The Sky Dragon
1953   Bright Road
Franklin, Martha
1922   Little Miss Smiles
1924   Racing Luck
1925   Don Q, Son of Zorro
1928   Uncle Tom's Cabin
        Wheel of Chance
1929   The Younger Generation
Franklin, Paul
1941   Where Did You Get That
        Girl?
1949   Ride, Ryder, Ride!
        Roll Thunder Roll!
Franklin, Rupert
1925   The Prairie Wife
Franklin, Sidney *(actor) not the*
same as **Franklin, Sidney, Jr.**
(dir), circa 1950s or **Franklin,**
Sidney A. *(dir), 1893–1972*
1919   The Sleeping Lion
1922   The Guttersnipe
1923   Fashion Row
1924   In Hollywood With
        Potash and Perlmutter
1925   His People
        One of the Bravest
1926   Rose of the Tenements
1928   Wheel of Chance
Franklin, Sidney A. *(dir), 1893–*
1972 same as **Franklin, S. A.**
(dir); **Franklin, Sidney, S. A.**
(dir); **Franklin, Sidney A.** *(dir) not*
the same as **Franklin, Sidney**
(actor) or **Franklin, Sidney, Jr.**
(dir), circa 1950s
1916   Gretchen, the Greenhorn
        A Sister of Six
1919   The Heart of Wetona
1922   East Is West
Franklin, Sidney, Jr. *(dir), circa*
1950s not the same as **Franklin,**
Sidney *(actor) or* **Franklin,**
Sidney A. *(dir), 1893–1972*
1957   Gun Battle at Monterey
Franklyn Irwin R. *same as*
Franklin, Irwin R.
Franklyn, Irwin R.
1932   Harlem Is Heaven
1938   Sugar Hill Baby
1944   Minstrel Man
        Waterfront
1949   Daughter of the West
Franklyn, Louise *see* **Franklin,**
Louise
Franks, Jerry Jr.
1943   Redhead from Manhattan
1947   The Farmer's Daughter
        Jiggs and Maggie in
        Society
Franks, Jerry, Jr.
1945   Sunbonnet Sue
Franquelli, Fely
1943   The Leopard Man
Franz, Arthur
1950   Sands of Iwo Jima
1953   The Eddie Cantor Story
        The Member of the
        Wedding
1958   The Young Lions
Franz, Eduard
1950   Emergency Wedding
1951   The Great Caruso
        The Magnificent Yankee
        Molly
1953   Dream Wife
        The Jazz Singer
1954   Broken Lance
1955   The Indian Fighter
        The Last Command
        White Feather
1956   The Burning Hills

Franz, Joseph J. *same as* **Franz, J.**
J.; **Franz, Joseph**
1921   The Cave Girl
1924   The Pell Street Mystery
Franzen, Nell
1916   Lord Loveland Discovers
        America
Frasco, Bobby
1944   Tahiti Nights
1945   The Bells of St. Mary's
1948   Fighting Father Dunne
Fraser, Dennis
1952   My Man and I
Fraser, Elisabeth
1953   So Big
Fraser, Harry *same as* **Crist, Harry**
C.; **Edwards, Weston;** **Fraser,**
Harry L.
1926   General Custer at Little
        Big Horn
1931   Oklahoma Jim
1932   Border Devils
        Texas Pioneers
1934   Fighting Through
        'Neath the Arizona Skies
1935   Fighting Pioneers
1936   Hair-Trigger Casey
1937   Bargain with Bullets
        Dark Manhattan
1938   Spirit of Youth
1949   Stallion Canyon
Fraser, Phyllis
1936   Star for a Night
Fraser, Robert *see* **Frazer, Robert**
Fraser, Stanley
1951   Apache Drums
1952   The Iron Mistress
Frasher, Jim
1950   Mystery Street
Fratellone, A.
1932   Amore e morte
Fraunholtz, Fraunie *same as*
Fraunholz, Fraunie
1917   The Little Boy Scout
Frawley, William
1916   Lord Loveland Discovers
        America
1935   Harmony Lane
1939   The Adventures of
        Huckleberry Finn
1942   Gentleman Jim
1944   Going My Way
        Lake Placid Serenade
1947   My Wild Irish Rose
Frazco, Michael
1951   The Great Caruso
Frazee, Jane
1947   Calendar Girl
        On the Old Spanish Trail
Frazer, Al *same as* **Frazier, Al** *not*
the same as **Frazer, Alex**
1937   Boy of the Streets
Frazer, Alex *not the same as*
Frazer, Alex
1949   The Cowboy and the
        Indians
Frazer, George P.
1919?   The Chosen Path
Frazer, John
1942   Valley of Hunted Men
Frazer, Robert *same as* **Fraser,**
Robert; **Frazer, Robert W.;**
Frazier, Robert
1916   Light at Dusk
1924   The Mine with the Iron
        Door
1925   The Scarlet West
1926   Desert Gold
1929   Frozen Justice
        Sioux Blood
1932   The Rainbow Trail
1936   Below the Deadline
1939   Daughter of the Tong
1943   Wagon Tracks West
Frazier, Al *see* **Frazer, Al**
Frazier, Richard
1928   Tenderfeet
Frazier, Robert *see* **Frazer, Robert**
Frederic, Norman *see* **Fredric,**
Norman

Frederic, William *same as*
Frederick, William *could be*
same as **Fredericks, William**
1922   Peacock Alley
Frederici, Blanche *see* **Friderici,**
Blanche
Frederick, Ann
1948   The Luck of the Irish
Frederick, Beatrice
1921   Across the Divide
Frederick, Cal
1949   The Story of Seabiscuit
Frederick, Freddie Burke *same as*
Frederick, Freddie
1930   Ladies Love Brutes
Frédérick, Hélène
1932   La foule hurle
Frederick, Lee
1947   Desperate
        Under the Tonto Rim
Frederick, Pauline
1918   A Daughter of the Old
        South
1920   The Paliser Case
1936   Ramona
1937   Thank You, Mr. Moto
Fredericks, Charles
1954   Thunder Pass
1960   Ice Palace
Fredericks, William *could be same*
as **Frederic, William**
1919   The Volcano
Fredric, Norman *same as* **Frederic,**
Norman
1958   Gun Fever
        The Light in the Forest
        The Lone Ranger and the
        Lost City of Gold
Fredriksson, Helga *could be same*
as **Fredricksen, Helda**
1930   Toda una vida *(foreign*
        version)
Free, Bill
1949   The Red Menace
Freed, Arthur
1940   Little Nellie Kelly
1943   Cabin in the Sky
1950   Annie Get Your Gun
1951   Show Boat
Freed, Bert
1950   Black Hand
        No Way Out
1952   Anything Can Happen
1956   Crowded Paradise
Freed, Lazar *same as* **Fried, Lazar**
1925   Salome of the Tenements
1936   Love and Sacrifice
1937   The Holy Oath
1940   Eli Eli
        The Great Advisor
        The Jewish Melody
        Overture to Glory
Freeland, George
194-   Mistaken Identity
Freeland, Thornton
1930   Whoopee
Freeman, Al *same as* **Freeman, Al**
Jr.
1960   This Rebel Breed
Freeman, Bee
1935   Lem Hawkins' Confession
1937   Underworld
Freeman, Buddy
1939   Straight to Heaven
Freeman, Charles A.
1947   Going to Glory, Come to
        Jesus
Freeman, Dusty
1947   Sepia Cinderella
Freeman, Everett
1951   Jim Thorpe—All-American
1958   Marjorie Morningstar
Freeman, Helen
1930   Abraham Lincoln
1932   Symphony of Six Million
1946   Saratoga Trunk
Freeman, Howard
1943   Margin for Error
1944   An American Romance
1945   Where Do We Go From
        Here?

1947   California
        Easy Come, Easy Go
1948   Cry of the City
        The Time of Your Life
        Up in Central Park
Freeman, Joel
1953   Cry of the Hunted
1955   Bad Day at Black Rock
        Blackboard Jungle
Freeman, Kathleen
1952   Kid Monk Baroni
1953   Dream Wife
        The Glass Wall
1957   The Midnight Story
        Pawnee
1958   Houseboat
Freeman, Kay
1946?   House-Rent Party
Freeman, Kenneth *same as*
Freeman, Ken
1947?   What a Guy
1948   Miracle in Harlem
Freeman, Leonard
1955   Trial
Freeman, Mona
1949   Streets of Laredo
1957   Dragoon Wells Massacre
Freeman, Raoul
1947   It Had To Be You
1955   The Long Gray Line
1958   The Last Hurrah
Freeman, Ruth
1921   A Giant of His Race
1923   A Shot in the Night
Freeman, Sandy
1960   This Rebel Breed
Freeman, William
1915   The Birth of a Nation
1917   The Spirit of '76
Freemanson, Carl
1940   Mexican Spitfire Out
        West
Frees, Paul
1950   The Toast of New Orleans
1952   The Big Sky
Frees, Wolf
1960   The Day They Robbed the
        Bank of England
Freeto, Ralph
1947   Calendar Girl
Fregonese, Hugo
1951   Apache Drums
        The Mark of the
        Renegade
Freiberger, Fred
1953   War Paint
1958   Blood Arrow
Freiden, Joe
1952   Red Ball Express
Freiman, Louis
1937   The Cantor's Son
Freire, Corina
1930   Toda una vida *(foreign*
        version)
Freiwald, Eric
1950   Raiders of Tomahawk
        Creek
1958   The Lone Ranger and the
        Lost City of Gold
Fremont, Al *same as* **Fremont, Al;**
Fremont, A.; **Fremont, Alfred**
1920   The Girl of My Heart
French, Caroline *same as* **French,**
Carolyn
1914   The Nightingale
French, Charles K. *same as*
French, Charles
1916   The Aryan
        The Criminal
1918   Free and Equal
        The Midnight Patrol
1922   The Woman He Loved
1926   The Flaming Frontier
        War Paint
French, Dick *same as* **French,**
Richard
1935   Black Fury
1938   Mr. Moto's Gamble
1942   Across the Pacific
        They Died With Their
        Boots On
        Valley of Hunted Men
        Wings for the Eagle

1943 Margin for Error
French, F.
1920 Lifting Shadows
French, Mary Jane
1946 The Sailor Takes a Wife
1950 Annie Get Your Gun
1951 Show Boat
French, Norma
1960 Ice Palace
French, Richard see **French, Dick**
French, Ted
1947 West to Glory
French, Valerie
1956 Secret of Treasure
    Mountain
Freney, Jeannette
1932 Le bluffeur
Frenke, Anna
1944 They Live in Fear
Fresco, David
1950 Right Cross
1959 The Black Orchid
1960 Pay or Die
Fretel, M.
1931 Su noche de bodas
    (foreign version)
Freuchen, Peter
1934 Eskimo
Frey, Annemarie
1930 Olimpia (foreign
    version)
Frey, Arno
1931 Die Maske Fällt
1933 Best of Enemies
1935 Rendezvous
1936 Human Cargo
1937 Charlie Chan at the
    Olympics
1940 Escape
    Escape to Glory
    The Man I Married
1942 Valley of Hunted Men
1943 Action in the North
    Atlantic
    They Came to Blow Up
    America
1944 Address Unknown
1945 Where Do We Go From
    Here?
1946 Rendezvous 24
Freybe, Carl
1940 The Man I Married
Frick and Frack
1944 Lady, Let's Dance!
Friderici, Blanche same as
 Frederici, Blance
1932 The Hatchet Man
    So Big
    Thirteen Women
1933 Thundering Herd
Frieburn, Milton
1948 The Paleface
Friedborn, William
1952 Bright Victory
Friedkin, Joel
1941 The Face Behind the
    Mask
1943 Frontier Fury
1945 The Great John L.
1946 California Gold Rush
1949 The Clay Pigeon
1950 The Daughter of Rosie
    O'Grady
Friedlander, Eddie
1930 Eternal Fools (Ewige
    Naranim)
1933 Live and Laugh
1940 Eli Eli
Friedman, Seymour
1941 Mystery Ship
1942 Submarine Raider
1949 Boston Blackie's Chinese
    Venture
1950 Chinatown at Midnight
1956 Secret of Treasure
    Mountain
Friedman, Vera Lee
1956 Giant
Friedrich, James K.
1940? Mr. Washington Goes to
    Town

1955 Indian American
Friend, Helene
1933 It's Great to Be Alive
Friend, Philip
1950 Buccaneer's Girl
Friendly, Fred W.
1957 Satchmo the Great
Fries, Otto same as **Fries, Otto H.**
1928 Riley the Cop
1929 The Younger Generation
1934 Broadway Bill
    She Was a Lady
1935 A Night at the Opera
1936 Human Cargo
    Star for a Night
1937 Slave Ship
Friganza, Trixie
1940 If I Had My Way
Frikin, Anatole
1944 Address Unknown
Friml, Rudolph, Jr. same as **Friml,
 Rudy**
1951 Slaughter Trail
1952 The Iron Mistress
Frings, Ketti
1941 Hold Back the Dawn
1955 Foxfire
Fritsch, Gunther von same as
 Fritsch, Gunther
1930 Olimpia (foreign
    version)
Fritz, Anna Mae
1936 The Green Pastures
Fritz, Jack Henry
1941 Western Union
Fritz, John
1958 Fort Massacre
Fritz, Joseph
1960 Walk Tall
Fritz, Shilia
1936 Ramona
Frizelle, Mildred
1931 Cimarron
Fröberg, Anna-Lisa
1930 Doña mentiras (foreign
    version)
Fröhlich, Gustav
1931 Kismet
    La llama sagrada (foreign
    version)
Froelich, Sig
1950 Right Cross
Froelick, Anne
1947 Easy Come, Easy Go
Froeschel, George
1942 We Were Dancing
1960 I Aim at the Stars: the
    Wernher von Braun
    Story
Frohlich, Elisabeth
1938 Gateway
Frohman, Daniel
1914 The Redemption of David
    Corson
    The Straight Road
Frolich, Rudy
1940 The Man I Married
Frome, Milton
1958 The Young Lions
Fromkess, Leon
1944 Minstrel Man
1945 Club Havana
Froos, Sylvia
1934 Stand Up and Cheer!
Frost, Don
1951 Slaughter Trail
Frost, Leila
1916 The Fall of a Nation
Frost, Terry
1941 Gauchos of Eldorado
1943 The Girl from Monterrey
1944 Waterfront
1946 The Gay Cavalier
    South of Monterey
    Wild West
1949 The Story of Seabiscuit
    The Valiant Hombre
1950 The Baron of Arizona
1952 The Raiders
1953 The Man Behind the Gun

1959 The FBI Story
Frostova, Janina
1944 Lake Placid Serenade
Frye, Dwight
1931 The Black Camel
1941 Mystery Ship
Frye, Gilbert same as **Allen, Drew**
1942 Prisoner of Japan
1946 The Gay Cavalier
    Rendezvous 24
1947 Bells of San Fernando
Frye, Togo
1926 Twin Triggers
Fuchs, Daniel
1950 Panic in the Streets
1953 Taxi
Fuchs, Leo
1937 I Want to Be a Mother
1940 Americaner Schadchen
1941 Mazel Tov Yidden
1950 Monticello, Here We
    Come!
Fuerberg, Hans same as **Furberg,
 Hansc; Furburg, Hans**
1936 Human Cargo
1937 Charlie Chan at the
    Olympics
1941 They Dare Not Love
1943 Action in the North
    Atlantic
1944 Address Unknown
Fuerberg, Kurt same as **Fuerberg,
 Curt von; Furberg, Curt;
 Furberg, Kurt**
1938 The Buccaneer
1942 Three Hearts for Julia
    Woman of the Year
1944 Address Unknown
Fürth, Jaro
1931 La pura verdad (foreign
    version)
Fuji
1959 The Crimson Kimono
Fujikawa, Jerry same as **Fujikawa,
 Jerry H.**
1951 Go for Broke!
1952 Japanese War Bride
Fujioshi, Kenneth
1951 Go for Broke!
Fujita, Toyo
1919 The Courageous Coward
    The Tong Man
1920 A Tokio Siren
1921 Black Roses
    Where Lights Are Low
Fukunaga, Akira same as
 Fukunaga, Akoroa
1951 Go for Broke!
1954 Hell's Half Acre
Fullback
1932 Harlem Is Heaven
Fuller, Alva
1941? The Blood of Jesus
Fuller, Barbra
1949 Harbor of Missing Men
    The Red Menace
1950 Rock Island Trail
Fuller, Clem
1946 The Gay Cavalier
    Sunset Pass
1951 Apache Drums
    Westward the Women
1952 The Raiders
1953 The Great Sioux Uprising
    Tumbleweed
1956 Walk the Proud Land
Fuller, Donald
1917 The Sudden Gentleman
Fuller, Haidee
1914 The Squaw Man
Fuller, James same as **Fuller,
 Jimmy**
1936 The Green Pastures
1939 Straight to Heaven
1947 Boy! What a Girl!
    Sepia Cinderella
Fuller, Junior
1932 Hypnotized
Fuller, Lance
1954 Cattle Queen of Montana
    Taza, Son of Cochise
    War Arrow

1955 Apache Woman
    Kentucky Rifle
1956 Frontier Woman
    Secret of Treasure
    Mountain
Fuller, Mary
1915 Under Southern Skies
Fuller, Samuel same as **Fuller, Sam**
1950 The Baron of Arizona
1951 The Steel Helmet
1957 Run of the Arrow
1959 The Crimson Kimono
Walter Fuller's Orchestra
1947 Sepia Cinderella
Fulton, Doris
1946 Shadows Over Chinatown
Fulton, James F. same as **Fulton,
 James**
1918 Ruggles of Red Gap
Fulton, Joan see **Shawlee, Joan**
Fulton, Maude
1933 Broken Dreams
    The Cohens and Kellys in
    Trouble
Fulton, Rad
1958 Marjorie Morningstar
Fung, Bill
1941 Min Jok Jay Hung Sing
Fung, Paul could be same as **Fong,
 Paul C.**
1936 Klondike Annie
1937 Think Fast, Mr. Moto
1942 Across the Pacific
    Submarine Raider
1943 The Amazing Mrs.
    Holliday
    Jack London
1945 Betrayal from the East
    Samurai
Fung, Willie could be same as
 Fong, Willie
1932 The Hatchet Man
1935 Ruggles of Red Gap
1940 Viva Cisco Kid
1942 North to the Klondike
Furberg, Curt see **Fuerberg, Kurt**
Furberg, Hans see **Fuerberg, Hans**
Furberg, Kurt see **Fuerberg, Kurt**
Furey, Barney same as **Fury,
 Barney**
1928 Tyrant of Red Gulch
1931 Cimarron
1936 Custer's Last Stand
Furey, James A. same as **Furey, J.
 A.; Furey, J. S.; Fury, J. A.**
1920 On with the Dance
Furlaud, Maxime
1949 Lost Boundaries
Furman, Roger
1948 The Fight Never Ends
Furness, Betty
1933 Let's Fall in Love
1935 McFadden's Flats
Furness, George
1960 The Last Voyage
Furst, Manfred
1931 Tropennächte
Furthman, Charles
1921 Lotus Blossom
1929 Thunderbolt
Furthman, Jules same as **Fox,
 Stephen; Furthman, Jules G.;
 Furthman, Julius G.**
1920 The Man Who Dared
1922 A California Romance
    Pawn Ticket 210
1927 The Way of All Flesh
1929 Abie's Irish Rose
    Thunderbolt
1930 Del mismo barro
1931 Cuerpo y alma
1938 Spawn of the North
1940 Northwest Passage (Book
    I—Rogers' Rangers)
    The Way of All Flesh
1943 The Outlaw
Fury, Barney see **Furey, Barney**
Fury, Ed
1956 Raw Edge

Fury, J. A. *see* Furey, J. A.
Fusier-Gir, Jeanne
1931 Chérie
Fuzzy the Bear
1949 Call of the Forest
Gaal, Franciska
1938 The Buccaneer
Gabbai, David
1953 The Glory Brigade
Gabin, Jean
1932 La foule hurle
Gable, Clark
1939 Gone With the Wind
1951 Across the Wide Missouri
1957 Band of Angels
Gabor, Eva
1941 New York Town
Gabor, Zsa Zsa
1956 Death of a Scoundrel
1958 Touch of Evil
Gabourie, Fred
1954 Thunder Pass
Gabriel, John
1958 The Young Lions
Gabrielson, Frank
1944 Something for the Boys
Gaddis, Michael *same as* **Gaddis, Mike**
1948 The Golden Eye
Gade, Svend
1926 Into Her Kingdom
Gade, William
1929 Die Königsloge
Gage, Erford
1943 Gangway for Tomorrow
   Hitler's Children
   Mr. Lucky
Gage, Linda
1941 New York Town
Gagne, Fryda
1937 Maid of Salem
Gagnon, Rene A., Pfc.
1950 Sands of Iwo Jima
Gaige, Russell
1953 Sangaree
Gail, Jane
1913 Traffic in Souls
Gailing, B.
1940 Americaner Schadchen
Gaillard, Robert
1923 Jamestown
Gaillard, Slim
1954 Go Man Go
Gaines, Al
1920 The Brute
Gaines, Charlie
1923 Regeneration
Gaines, Eugene
1960 Sergeant Rutledge
Gaines, Harris
1948 The Betrayal
Gaines, Richard
1944 Tender Comrade
1947 Humoresque
   Ride the Pink Horse
1948 Unconquered
1954 Drum Beat
1955 Trial
Gainey, Michael
1955 Good Morning, Miss Dove
Galanga, Juliet
1932 Amor in montagna
Galante, Rudolph
1934 La cruz y la espada
Galbraith, Bruce
1934 Broadway Bill
Gale, Alice
1918 The Birth of a Race
Gale, Deidre
1943 The Gang's All Here
Gale, Gladys
1936 Klondike Annie
Gale, June
1935 L'homme des Folies
   Bergère
1938 Josette
   My Lucky Star
1939 Charlie Chan at Treasure
   Island
   The Escape

Gale, Marguerite
1915 How Molly Malone Made
   Good
1919 Mandarin's Gold
Gale, Norah
1936 Star for a Night
1938 Daughter of Shanghai
   In Old Chicago
1939 King of Chinatown
Gale, Wesley
1952 The Iron Mistress
Galen, Liana
1933 It's Great to Be Alive
Galento, Mario
1956 Frontier Woman
Galeotti, Violet
1931 La gran jornada (*foreign version*)
Galezio, Leonard
1923 Deceit
Galindo, Nacho
1942 Rio Rita
1946 The Gay Cavalier
1950 Belle of Old Mexico
   Broken Arrow
   A Lady Without Passport
1951 Cuban Fireball
   Flaming Feather
1954 Broken Lance
1955 Headline Hunters
1956 Wetbacks
Galitzine, Leo
1947 The Foxes of Harrow
Gallagher, Al
1945 Where Do We Go From
   Here?
Gallagher, Carole
1943 Gangway for Tomorrow
1950 Sands of Iwo Jima
Gallagher, Don
1944 Going My Way
Gallagher, Glen
1949 The Girl from Jones
   Beach
Gallagher, Jack (*actor*) *could be same as* **Gallagher, Jack** (*prod*)
1932 Border Devils
Gallagher, Jack (*prod*) *could be same as* **Gallagher, Jack** (*actor*)
1933 Dos noches
Gallagher, Ray
1935 Riddle Ranch
Gallagher, Richard "Skeets" *same as* **Gallagher, Skeets**
1927 For the Love of Mike
1930 Galas de la Paramount
Gallant, Lorenzo
1940 The Ramparts We Watch
Gallardo, Marta
1932 Amor y vida
Gallaudet, John
1937 The Devil's Playground
1938 Little Miss Roughneck
1940 Knute Rockne—All
   American
1941 Birth of the Blues
   Road Agent
1942 Holiday Inn
1946 Bad Bascomb
   Shadows Over Chinatown
1947 The Farmer's Daughter
1948 Docks of New Orleans
1950 Right Cross
Gallaway, Howard
1946 Dirty Gertie from
   Harlem, U.S.A.
Gallery, Tom
1920 Dinty
Galli, Augusto
1930 Sei tu l'amore
Galli, Eola
1947 Carnegie Hall
Galli, Rosina
1939 Fisherman's Wharf
1941 Gauchos of Eldorado
1943 Good Luck, Mr. Yates
1945 Where Do We Go From
   Here?

Gallison, Joe
1960 All the Young Men
Gallo, Fortune
1931 Pagliacci
Gallo, Jacques
1959 The Black Orchid
Gallo, Lou
1959 Odds Against Tomorrow
Gallodoro, Al
1945 Rhapsody in Blue
Gallone, Soava
1930 El secreto del doctor
   (*foreign version*)
Gallow, Janet Ann
1946 Canyon Passage
Galloway, Howard
1946? Beale Street Mama
1947 Juke Joint
1949? Girl in Room 20
Galloway, Morgan
1934 Call of the Coyote
Galt, Galan
1938 Spawn of the North
1940 The Way of All Flesh
Galvan, Gilbert
1947 Bells of San Fernando
Galván, Pedro
1955 Seven Cities of Gold
1958 Sierra Baron
Gam, Rita
1956 Mohawk
1958 Sierra Baron
Gamas, María Estheer
1931 Las luces de Buenos Aires
Gambarelli, Eole
1932 Amor in montagna
1947 Citizen Saint
Gambaro, Teresa
1932 Amor in montagna
Gamble, Donald
1955 Violent Saturday
Gamble, Fred
1918 A Broadway Scandal *same as* Gamble, Frederick
1920 The Secret Gift
Gamble, Ralph
1957 Gun Battle at Monterey
1959 Al Capone
Gamble, Ted R.
1960 For the Love of Mike
Gamble, Warburton
1918 Thirty a Week
1919 As a Man Thinks
1920 The Paliser Case
Gamboa, Elias *could be same as* **Gamboa, Eliso**
1941 Under Fiesta Stars
1945 South of the Rio Grande
1948 Angel in Exile
1949 Border Incident
1950 Bandit Queen
Gamboa, Eliso *could be same as* **Gamboa, Elias**
1943 The Leopard Man
Gamet, Kenneth
1942 Juke Girl
1945 Betrayal from the East
1952 Indian Uprising
1953 Last of the Comanches
1957 The Lawless Eighties
Gan, Chester *same as* **Gann, Chester**
1934 Fighting Through
1936 After the Thin Man
   Klondike Annie
   Mad Holiday
1937 Slave Ship
1938 Speed to Burn
1939 King of Chinatown
   The Mystery of Mr. Wong
1942 Across the Pacific
   All Through the Night
   Submarine Raider
1943 The Amazing Mrs.
   Holliday
   Crash Dive
Ganardi, Maria
1951 The Great Caruso

Gandero, Alberto
1937 El capitán Tormenta
Gandos, Giorgio
1958 Seven Hills of Rome
Gangelin, Paul
1934 Beloved
   Tres amores
1942 Nazi Agent
Ganghorn, Jack
1929 Hawk of the Hills
Ganley, Gail
1953 The Eddie Cantor Story
1958 Marjorie Morningstar
Gann, Chester *see* **Gan, Chester**
1936 Sea Spoilers
Gann, Ernest K.
1951 The Raging Tide
Gann, Michael J. *same as* **Gann, M. J.**
1937 Natalka Poltavka
1939 Cossacks in Exile
Gannaway, Albert C.
1956 Daniel Boone, Trail
   Blazer
1957 Raiders of Old California
Gant, Harry A. *same as* **Gant, Harry**
1919 A Man's Duty
1921 By Right of Birth
1928 Absent
1930 Georgia Rose
Garbo, Greta
1930 Anna Christie
   Anna Christie (*foreign version*)
García, Adelina
1939 Miracle on Main Street
   (*foreign version*)
Garcia, Allan
1931 The Cisco Kid
   La gran jornada
1932 Marido y mujer
1933 The California Trail
Garcia, Amadita
1947 Ride the Pink Horse
García, Captain *see* **García, Fernando, Captain**
Garcia, David
1950 Belle of Old Mexico
Garcia, Ernest
1915 After Five
García, Fernando, Captain *same as* **García, Captain**
1930 Cascarrabias
1936 Ramona
1949 The Kissing Bandit
Garcia, Harry
1947 Ride the Pink Horse
1950 The Palomino
García, Israel
1930 Las campanas de
   Capistrano
1936 El crimen de media
   noche
1939 Verbena trágica
Garcia, Joe
1944 The San Antonio Kid
Garcia, John
1956 Giant
Garcia, Kenneth
1950 Black Hand
García, María Rosa de
1931 Sombras del circo
Garcia Pena, Pascual
1952 My Man and I
Garcin, Marcel de
1931 Don Juan diplomático
   (*foreign version*)
Gard, Wymer
1954 Dangerous Mission
Garde, Betty
1948 Call Northside 777
   Cry of the City
Gardel, Carlos
1931 Las luces de Buenos Aires
1933 Espérame
   Melodía de arrabal
1934 Cuesta abajo
   El tango en Broadway
1935 El día que me quieras
   Tango Bar

Gardella, Tess *same as* **Aunt Jemima**
1929   Show Boat
1934   Stand Up and Cheer!
Garden, John
1959   Odds Against Tomorrow
Gardenia, Vincent
1945   The House on 92nd St.
Gardiner, Becky
1931   El proceso de Mary Dugan
        El proceso de Mary Dugan (*foreign version*)
1934   Coming Out Party
Gardiner, Reginald
1945   The Dolly Sisters
1948   Fury at Furnace Creek
Gardiner, Sammy
1938   God's Step Children
        Swing!
Gardner, Arthur
1938   Mr. Moto's Gamble
1939   Waterfront
1942   Rubber Racketeers
1948   The Dude Goes West
Gardner, Ava
1944   Three Men in White
1951   Show Boat
1953   Ride, Vaquero!
Gardner, Bert
1914   Springtime
Gardner, Cyril
1930   Cascarrabias
        El cuerpo del delito
Gardner, Diane
1934   Stand Up and Cheer!
Gardner, Frank
1960   All the Fine Young Cannibals
Gardner, Jack 1900—1977 *not the same as* **Gardner, Jack** circa 1927
Gardner, Jack 1900—1977; some of the credits listed below may actually be for **Gardner, Jack** circa 1927
1936   Below the Deadline
1939   Daughters Courageous
1941   The Face Behind the Mask
        The Mexican Spitfire's Baby
        New York Town
        They Dare Not Love
1942   Gentleman Jim
        Juke Girl
        Wings for the Eagle
1943   Redhead from Manhattan
1944   Chip Off the Old Block
        Since You Went Away
1945   A Medal for Benny
Gardner, Jack circa 1927 *not the same as* **Gardner, Jack** 1900—1977
1927   Wild Geese
Gardner, John
1950   Battleground
1953   The Eddie Cantor Story
Gardner, Richard
1958   The Young Lions
1960   Hell to Eternity
Gardner, Virginia
1943   His Butler's Sister
Garfias, Juanita
1935   Alas sobre el Chaco
Garfield, John
1939   Daughters Courageous
1940   East of the River
1942   Tortilla Flat
1943   Air Force
1945   Pride of the Marines
1947   Body and Soul
        Humoresque
1948   Gentleman's Agreement
1949   Jigsaw
        We Were Strangers
1950   The Breaking Point
Gargan, Edward *same as* **Gargan, Ed**
1934   Behold My Wife!
        She Was a Lady

1935   The Irish in Us
        So Red the Rose
1937   Big City
1938   Gateway
        The Rage of Paris
        Rascals
        Road Demon
        The Texans
1939   Heaven with a Barbed Wire Fence
        Winner Take All
1940   Charlie Chan in Panama
        Girl from God's Country
        Northwest Passage (Book I—Rogers' Rangers)
        Three Cheers for the Irish
1943   In Old Oklahoma
        The Meanest Man in the World
        Tahiti Honey
1948   The Dude Goes West
1949   That Midnight Kiss
1950   Belle of Old Mexico
1951   Cuban Fireball
Gargan, Jack
1938   Mr. Moto's Gamble
1942   Whispering Ghosts
1943   Ladies' Day
        Mr. Lucky
1947   The Farmer's Daughter
1948   Fighting Father Dunne
        The Golden Eye
        The Miracle of the Bells
1949   Arctic Manhunt
        The Girl from Jones Beach
1951   The Great Caruso
        The Magnificent Yankee
1953   The Eddie Cantor Story
        The Member of the Wedding
1955   Blackboard Jungle
Gargan, William
1935   Black Fury
        A Night at the Ritz
1940   They Knew What They Wanted
1945   The Bells of St. Mary's
1946   Rendezvous 24
        Till the End of Time
Gari, Martine
1959   The Black Orchid
Garland, Judy
1940   Little Nellie Kelly
Garland, Richard
1952   The Battle at Apache Pass
1953   Column South
Garland, Tom *same as* **Garland, Tommy**
1949   House of Strangers
1950   Right Cross
Garmo, Alfredo
1942   Rio Rita
Garner, Cindy
1944   Since You Went Away
1946   Till the End of Time
1952   Red Ball Express
Garner, Darleen
1945   Nob Hill
Garner, Don
1950   A Lady Without Passport
        Two Flags West
1951   Saturday's Hero
Garner, Lee
1954   Go Man Go
Garner, Paullyn
1934   Imitation of Life
Garner, Peggy Ann
1945   Nob Hill
        A Tree Grows in Brooklyn
1951   Teresa
Garner, Ray
1941?   Hampton Institute: Its Program of Education for Life
Garner, Mrs. Ray
1941?   Hampton Institute: Its Program of Education for Life
Garnett, Tay
1927   Turkish Delight
        White Gold

1937   Slave Ship
1943   Bataan
1944   Since You Went Away
1945   The Valley of Decision
Garnett, Zumetta
1934   Stand Up and Cheer!
Garon, Pauline
1930   Le spectre vert
1931   Echec au roi
1934   La veuve joyeuse
1935   L'homme des Folies Bergère
1936   It Had to Happen
Garr, Eddie
1933   Obey the Law
1949   The Girl from Jones Beach
Garr, Tony
1955   Blackboard Jungle
Garralaga, Martin
1930   The Bad Man (*foreign version*)
        Charros, gauchos y manolas
        ¡De frente, marchen!
        Los que danzan
        El precio de un beso
        Sevilla de mis amores
        El último de los Vargas
        Wu Li Chang
1931   Charlie Chan Carries On (*foreign version*)
        Cuerpo y alma
        La dama atrevida
        La gran jornada
        La llama sagrada
1933   Dos noches
        No dejes la puerta abierta
        El rey de los gitanos
1934   Un capitán de cosacos
        La cruz y la espada
1935   Angelina o el honor de un brigadier
        El cantante de Nápoles
        De la sartén al fuego
        Piernas de seda
        Rosa de Francia
        Te quiero con locura
1936   Song of the Gringo
1938   Di que me quieres
        Mis dos amores
        Outlaw Express
1939   The Fighting Gringo
        El otro soy yo
        Papá soltero
        El trovador de la radio
1940   Cuando canta la Ley
        Rhythm of the Rio Grande
        Tengo fe en ti
1943   The Outlaw
1944   Going My Way
1945   The Cisco Kid Returns
        In Old New Mexico
        A Medal for Benny
        South of the Rio Grande
1946   Beauty and the Bandit
        Don Ricardo Returns
        The Gay Cavalier
        The Sailor Takes a Wife
        South of Monterey
        Strange Voyage
1947   California
        Ride the Pink Horse
        Riding the California Trail
1948   The Feathered Serpent
        Four Faces West
        Shep Comes Home
        Up in Central Park
1949   Border Incident
1950   Bandit Queen
        Jolson Sings Again
        A Lady Without Passport
1952   The Fabulous Senorita
        The Fighter
        The Ring
        Woman in the Dark
1953   San Antone
1956   Serenade
1957   Man in the Shadow
1959   Gunmen from Laredo
        The Last Angry Man

Garrard, Don
1958   Flaming Frontier
Garraway, Tom
1956   Frontier Woman
Garrett, Betty
1948   Big City
Garrett, Charlicie *same as* **Garrett, Charlcie**
1953   The Member of the Wedding
        So Big
Garrett, Don
1953   Seminole
1960   Studs Lonigan
Garrett, Gary
1948   Harpoon
Garrett, Grant
1946   Bad Bascomb
1947   The Mighty McGurk
Garrett, Mabel
1932   Ten Minutes to Live
Garrett, Maxine
1951   Westward the Women
Garrett, Michael
1959   The FBI Story
Garrett, Oliver H. P.
1929   Chinatown Nights
1939   Gone With the Wind
1940   The Man I Married
1947   Duel in the Sun
Garrett, Sam
1945   The Dolly Sisters
Garrick, Gene
1945   Salome, Where She Danced
1946   G. I. War Brides
1948   The Luck of the Irish
Garrick, Richard
1951   A Streetcar Named Desire
1955   A Man Called Peter
Garrison, Mrs.
1919   The Other Man's Wife
Garrison, Elizabeth
1919   Who's Your Brother?
Garrison, Harold *same as* **Garrison, Harold A.**
1939   Reform School
1940   Gang War
1942   Lucky Ghost
Garrison, Michael
1960   The Dark at the Top of the Stairs
Garrison, Patricia
1948   Harpoon
Garrison, Slick
1940?   Mr. Washington Goes to Town
Garson, Anthony
1952   Arctic Flight
Garson, Greer
1945   The Valley of Decision
Garson, Harry
1920   For the Soul of Rafael
1922   The Hands of Nara
        The Sign of the Rose
1925   Speed Wild
1934   What a Mother-in-Law!
Garson, Natalie
1937   Big City
1938   The Toy Wife
Garuffi, Lucino
1931   La gran jornada (*foreign version*)
Garvin, Anita
1931   Los calaveras
        Los calaveras (*foreign version*)
Garvin, Jean
1953   So Big
Garwood, William
1916   Broken Fetters
1918   Her Moment
Gary, Alberta
1942   Tales of Manhattan
Gary, Ben
1960   Cimarron
        Studs Lonigan
Gary, Erwin
1932?   The Girl from Chicago

Gary, Gene
1943   Gangway for Tomorrow
1947   Northwest Outpost
1949   Rose of the Yukon
Gary, Jean
1945   Where Do We Go From Here?
Gary, Paul
1957   Beau James
Gary, Ralph
1960   Pay or Die
Gasnier, Louis
1930   Amor audaz
        Amor audaz (foreign version)
1933   Espérame
        Melodía de arrabal
1934   Cuesta abajo
        El tango en Broadway
1939   La Inmaculada
Gaspari, Vincent
1949   Thieves' Highway
Gassman, Vittorio
1953   Cry of the Hunted
        The Glass Wall
Gaston, Mae
1917   John Ermine of the Yellowstone
Gaston, Richard F.
1952   Red Ball Express
Gastrock, Philip
1916   The Fall of a Nation
Gates, Bud
1949   Stallion Canyon
Gates, Emily
1921   The Lure of a Woman
Gates, Frank
1935   The Cyclone Ranger
Gates, Harvey
1918   A Broadway Scandal
        The Wine Girl
1924   Fools' Highway
1926   The Barrier
1930   Así es la vida
1942   Let's Get Tough!
Gates, Larry
1957   The Brothers Rico
Gates, Maxine
1948   My Girl Tisa
1956   Giant
Gates, Nancy
1943   Hitler's Children
1949   Roll Thunder Roll!
1953   The Member of the Wedding
1954   Hell's Half Acre
1956   Death of a Scoundrel
        Wetbacks
1958   The Rawhide Trail
Gates, William "Pop"
1951   The Harlem Globetrotters
1954   Go Man Go
Gateson, Marjorie
1932   Thirteen Women
1933   Let's Fall in Love
1934   Coming Out Party
        Operator 13
1935   His Family Tree
1938   Gateway
1940   Escape to Glory
        Geronimo
Gattiker, Albert
1940   The Ramparts We Watch
Gatzert, Nate
1934   Wheels of Destiny
1939   Frontiers of '49
Gavin, James
1960   Key Witness
Gavin, John
1959   Imitation of Life
Gawthorne, Peter
1931   Charlie Chan Carries On
Gay, Betsy
1938   The Adventures of Tom Sawyer
1943   What's Buzzin' Cousin?
Gay, Betty Lou
1931   Riders of the Rio

Gay, Gregory same as **Gaye, Gregory**
1937   Charlie Chan at the Opera
        That Girl from Paris
1941   They Dare Not Love
1949   Harbor of Missing Men
1951   When the Redskins Rode
Gaye, Howard
1915   The Birth of a Nation
1917   The Spirit of '76
Gaye, Lisa
1954   Drums Across the River
1960   The Sign of Zorro
Gayle, Rozelle
1949?   The Joint Is Jumpin'
Gaylord, David
1943   Action in the North Atlantic
Gaylord, Karen
1949   The Girl from Jones Beach
Gaynor, Janet
1931   Delicious
1934   La ciudad de cartón
Gaytán, Norma
1929   Hambre
Gaytzera, Anthony
1928   The Midnight Ace
Gazzaniga, Don
1951   Gambling House
Gean, Harold
1950   Intruder in the Dust
Gear, Luella
1949   Jigsaw
Geary, Bud same as **Geary, Main Bud; Geary, Maine**
1936   General Spanky
        It Had to Happen
        The Prisoner of Shark Island
1937   Big City
        The Devil's Playground
1938   Little Miss Roughneck
1940   Murder over New York
1941   Gauchos of Eldorado
1942   All Through the Night
        Cat People
        The Navy Comes Through
1943   Bataan
        Good Luck, Mr. Yates
        In Old Oklahoma
        Ladies' Day
        They Came to Blow Up America
1944   Marshal of Reno
        The San Antonio Kid
        Sheriff of Las Vegas
        Tucson Raiders
        Vigilantes of Dodge City
1945   Colorado Pioneers
        Great Stagecoach Robbery
        Phantom of the Plains
1946   Sheriff of Redwood Valley
1947   California
Geary, Richard
1958   The Rawhide Trail
Gebert, Gordon
1951   The House on Telegraph Hill
Gee, Young
1950   Panic in the Streets
Geer, Lennie same as **Geer, Leonard**
1955   Apache Ambush
1957   The Oklahoman
Geer, Will
1949   Anna Lucasta
        Answer for Anne
        Lust for Gold
1950   Broken Arrow
        Comanche Territory
        Intruder in the Dust
        Winchester '73
1951   The Tall Target
1952   Bright Victory
1954   Salt of the Earth
Gegna, Jeanette
1931   Delicious

Gehrman, Lucy
1939   A Brivele der Mamen
1950   God, Man and Devil
Gehrman, Misha
1939   A Brivele der Mamen
Geigel, Albert
1940   The Man I Married
Geiger, Myron
1937   The Plainsman
1947   Easy Come, Easy Go
Geiger, Rod E.
1950   Give Us This Day
Geise, Sugar
1933   It's Great to Be Alive
Geldert, Clarence same as **Geldart, C. H.; Geldart, Clarence**
1916   The Fall of a Nation
1917   The Squaw Man's Son
1918   The Bravest Way
        The Gypsy Trail
        Hidden Pearls
        Sandy
        The Squaw Man
1921   All Souls' Eve
1924   North of 36
1929   The Overland Telegraph
        Sioux Blood
1932   Thirteen Women
        White Eagle
1933   Broken Dreams
        Dance Hall Hostess
        The Telegraph Trail
1934   Our Daily Bread
Gelsey, Erwin
1933   Grand Slam
1936   Muss 'Em Up
1941   Birth of the Blues
1951   Gambling House
Genardi, Maria
1950   Black Hand
Gendron, Pierre
1944   Minstrel Man
General, a dog
1946   The Face of Marble
Genevois, Simone
1932   Le cas du docteur Brenner
Genge, Paul
1959   The FBI Story
Gentner, Norma
1949   The Kissing Bandit
George, Abner
1951   Tomahawk
1952   Battles of Chief Pontiac
George, Anthony
1958   Gunfire at Indian Gap
George, Beatrice
1921   By Right of Birth
George, Bill could be same as **Bill, George**
1949   Masked Raiders
George, Burton
1917   The Tell-Tale Step
George, George W.
1950   Mystery Submarine
1953   Thunder Bay
1955   Smoke Signal
1957   The Halliday Brand
1958   Apache Territory
George, Gladys
1934   Straight Is the Way
1940   The Way of All Flesh
1944   Minstrel Man
George, Jac could be same as **George, Jack** or **George, Jacques**
1941   They Dare Not Love
George, Jack could be same as **George, Jac** or **George, Jacques**
1943   His Butler's Sister
1944   An American Romance
        Mr. Skeffington
1946   The Gentleman Misbehaves
1948   Harpoon
1949   Arctic Manhunt
1951   Go for Broke!
        The Great Caruso
1953   Column South
        Dream Wife

George, Jacques could be same as **George, Jac** or **George, Jack**
1950   The Toast of New Orleans
George, James
1953   The Glory Brigade
George, John
1931   Smart Money
George, Marthe
1931   Jenny Lind
George, Mary
1951   Molly
George, Maud
1916   The Social Buccaneer
George, Ott
1950   Black Hand
George, Sue
1953   So Big
1957   Raintree County
George, William
1919   The Homesteader
Georgina, Mae
1915   Time Lock Number 776
Geraci, May see **Giraci, May**
Geraghty, Carmelita
1923   Jealous Husbands
1925   Brand of Cowardice
1927   The Slaver
1936   The Phantom of Santa Fe
Geraghty, Gerald same as **Geraghty, Gerry**
1939   In Old Caliente
1940   Young Buffalo Bill
1941   Secret of the Wastelands
1947   On the Old Spanish Trail
1949   The Red Menace
1950   Sunset in the West
Geraghty, Maurice
1937   Hills of Old Wyoming
1942   Apache Trail
1951   Tomahawk
1952   Rose of Cimarron
1956   Mohawk
Geraghty, Thomas J. same as **Geraghty, Tom; Geraghty, Tom J.**
1919   The Courageous Coward
        Diane of the Green Van
        A Heart in Pawn
1925   Irish Luck
1929   Smiling Irish Eyes
1932   Hypnotized
Gerald, Helen
1946   G. I. War Brides
        The Gay Cavalier
        The Trap
1948   Gentleman's Agreement
Gerald, Jim
1951   Adventures of Captain Fabian
Gerard, Barney
1946   Bringing Up Father
1947   Jiggs and Maggie in Society
1948   Jiggs and Maggie in Court
1949   Jiggs and Maggie in Jackpot Jitters
1950   Jiggs and Maggie Out West
Gerard, Carl same as **Gerrard, Carl**
1917   Crime and Punishment
        The Little Samaritan
1920   The Secret Gift
Gerard, Rene
1920?   The Scarlet Dragon
Gerard, Teddie
1921   The Cave Girl
Geray, Steven same as **Geray, Steve**
1942   Castle in the Desert
1949   Harbor of Missing Men
1950   A Lady Without Passport
1951   The House on Telegraph Hill
1952   The Big Sky
1953   Tonight We Sing
1955   Kiss of Fire
Gerber, David
1949   The Prairie
Gerber, Esther
1937   Where Is My Child?

Gerber, Neva
1924   California in '49
1925   A Daughter of the Sioux
         Tonio, Son of the Sierras
         Warrior Gap

Gerdes, Emma
1918   How Could You, Jean?

Gereghty, Helen
1958   The Last Hurrah

Gericke, Eugene
1950   Battleground
1951   Go for Broke!

Gerien, Ben
1943   Redhead from Manhattan

Gering, Marion
1936   Rose of the Rancho

Gering, Walter
1943   Crime Smasher

Germano, Joseph
1957   Burden of Truth

Gerner, Don
1950   The Iroquois Trail

Gerrard, Carl *see* Gerard, Carl

Gerrard, Charles
1918   The Hun Within
1922   Anna Ascends

Gerrard, Douglas
1926   Private Izzy Murphy
1948   The Luck of the Irish

Gerry, Alex
1950   The Breaking Point
         Rock Island Trail
         The Toast of New Orleans
         Young Man with a Horn
1952   Rose of Cimarron
1953   The Eddie Cantor Story
         The Jazz Singer

Gerry, Toni
1958   Oregon Passage

Gershenson, Joseph *same as*
    Gershenson, Joe
1944   Slightly Terrific
1947   Pirates of Monterey

Gerson, Betty Lou
1949   The Red Menace

Gerstad, John
1949   Lost Boundaries

Gerstad, Merritt B.
1930   A Lady to Love (*foreign
         version*)

Gersten, Berta
1932   Yiskor
1939   Mirele Efros
1950   God, Man and Devil
1956   The Benny Goodman
         Story

Gerstle, Frank
1953   The Glory Brigade
1954   Drum Beat
1958   Ambush at Cimarron Pass
1959   Inside the Mafia

Gert, Valeska
1931   Die Dreigroschenoper

Gertler, Sam
1932   Uncle Moses
1934   The Youth of Russia
1937   I Want to Be a Mother

Gessner, Robert
1934   Massacre

Gest, Inna
1947   Northwest Outpost

Getchell, Sumner
1934   Coming Out Party
1938   My Lucky Star
1948   My Girl Tisa
1950   Last of the Buccaneers

Gettel, Allen
1957   The Tin Star

Gettinger, Peter
1958   Never Love a Stranger

Gettinger, William *see* Steele,
    William

Getz, Stan
1956   The Benny Goodman
         Story

Geva, Tamara *could be same as*
    Tamara
1937   Manhattan
         Merry-Go-Round

Ghazlo, Anthony
1957   Band of Angels

Gianfredo, Michele
1932   Amor in montagna

Giannini, Silvio
1949   Thieves' Highway

Gianotti, Carlos
1934   El tango en Broadway

Gibbons, Eliot *same as* Gibbons,
    Elliott
1934   Strange Wives
1935   Alas sobre el Chaco
         Chinatown Squad
1941   Under Fiesta Stars

Gibbons, Jevere
1934   As the Earth Turns

Gibbs, Robert Payton
1914   The Jungle

Giblyn, Charles
1916   Civilization's Child
1920   The Dark Mirror
1933   Let's Fall in Love

Gibney, Sheridan
1934   Massacre
1936   The Green Pastures

Gibson, Carter
1931   Delicious

Gibson, Christine
1944   Tahiti Nights

Gibson, Don
1951   Saturday's Hero
1953   Seminole

Gibson, Donna
1950   The Breaking Point

Gibson, Helen
1932   Law and Lawless
1935   Cyclone of the Saddle
1936   Custer's Last Stand
1953   The Man from the Alamo

Gibson, Hoot
1926   The Flaming Frontier
1928   The Rawhide Kid
1943   The Law Rides Again
1944   Outlaw Trail
         Sonora Stagecoach

Gibson, James
1930   The Arizona Kid

Gibson, John
1938   Speed to Burn

Gibson, Judith
1942   Holiday Inn

Gibson, Julie
1944   Going My Way
         Hi, Beautiful
1947   Bowery Buckaroos

Gibson, Kenneth
1937   The Plainsman
1940   New Moon
1948   Unconquered
1955   The View from Pompey's
         Head

Gibson, Michael
1932   Uncle Moses

Gibson, Mimi
1957   The Brothers Rico
         The Oklahoman
1958   Houseboat

Gibson, Ralph
1953   The Eddie Cantor Story
         The Man Behind the Gun

Gibson, Tom
1930   Así es la vida
1933   Dance Hall Hostess

Gibson, W. H.
1919   The Volcano

Gibson, Wynne
1939   Miracle on Main Street

Gidding, Nelson
1959   Odds Against Tomorrow

Giebler, Al
1932   Hypnotized

Gielgud, Gwen Bagni
1956   The Last Wagon

Giermann, Frederick *same as*
    Gierman, Frederick
1940   Escape
1942   Unseen Enemy
1943   Action in the North
         Atlantic
         They Came to Blow Up
         America

1944   Address Unknown
         They Live in Fear

Gifford, Alan
1960   I Aim at the Stars: the
         Wernher von Braun
         Story

Gifford, Clemence
1953   Tonight We Sing

Gifford, Frances
1942   American Empire
1945   Our Vines Have Tender
         Grapes
1947   Little Mister Jim

Gift, Donn
1948   Fighting Father Dunne

Giglio, Alexander
1935   A Night at the Opera

Giglio, Clemente
1932   O festino o la legge

Giglio, Sandro
1951   Saturday's Hero
1955   The Rose Tattoo

Gil, Rosita
1930   Así es la vida

Gil-Spear, Adrian
1917   The Barrier

Gilbert, Billy *same as* Gilbert,
    William; Gilbert, William
    "Billy"
1931   Chinatown After Dark
1935   A Night at the Opera
1936   Kelly the Second
         My American Wife
         Sutter's Gold
1937   Music for Madame
1938   Breaking the Ice
         Happy Landing
         My Lucky Star
1939   Forged Passport
1942   Song of the Islands
         Valley of the Sun
1949   The Kissing Bandit

Gilbert, Bobby
1959   Al Capone

Gilbert, Don
1946   Dirty Gertie from
         Harlem, U.S.A.
1947   Juke Joint

Gilbert, Doris
1944   Lake Placid Serenade

Gilbert, Edwin
1942   All Through the Night
1947   My Wild Irish Rose

Gilbert, Eugenia
1922   The Half Breed
1926   Laddie

Gilbert, Florence
1923   Breaking into Society

Gilbert, Fran
1947   Buffalo Bill Rides Again

Gilbert, Jack
1917   The Bride of Hate
1919   The Red Viper

Gilbert, Jo *could be same as*
    Gilbert, Joanne
1951   Hurricane Island
1955   Good Morning, Miss Dove

Gilbert, Joanne
1957   Ride Out for Revenge

Gilbert, Jody
1948   The Paleface
1949   Knock on Any Door
1951   Slaughter Trail

Gilbert, Joe
1942   Nazi Agent
1947   California
         The Farmer's Daughter
1949   The Story of Seabiscuit
1950   Jolson Sings Again
1951   Jim Thorpe—All-American
1957   Band of Angels

Gilbert, John
1921   Shame
1922   A California Romance
1931   Gentleman's Fate

Gilbert, Maude
1915   The Alien

Gilbert, Mercedes
1921   The Call of His People
1925   Body and Soul
1939   Moon over Harlem

Gilbert, Paul
1943   Action in the North
         Atlantic

Gilbert, Raye
1940   George Washington
         Carver

Gilbert, William *see* Gilbert, Billy

Gilbreath, John *same as*
    Gilbreath, Jon
1946   Rendezvous 24
         Without Reservations

Gilchrist, Bianca
1934   Imitation of Life

Gilchrist, Connie
1942   Apache Trail
         Sunday Punch
         Tortilla Flat
         We Were Dancing
         Woman of the Year
1944   Andy Hardy's Blonde
         Trouble
1945   The Valley of Decision
1946   Bad Bascomb
1948   Big City
1950   Buccaneer's Girl
         Stars in My Crown
         A Ticket to Tomahawk
1952   The Half-Breed

Gildart, Fred
1949   Call of the Forest

Gilden, Richard
1958   Blood Arrow

Giler, Berne
1949   C-Man

Giles, Maudice
1947   The Peanut Man

Gilfether, Daniel
1917   Sunshine and Gold

Gilkyson, Terry
1951   Slaughter Trail

Gill, Frank, Jr.
1953   The Great Sioux Uprising

Gill, Gwenllian
1934   Behold My Wife!

Gill, Moss, Sergt.
1918   The Unbeliever

Gill, Penny
1942   Song of the Islands

Dizzy Gillespie and His Orchestra
1947   Jivin' in Be-Bop

Gillespie, Edward
1914   The Great Diamond
         Robbery
1915   The Alien

Gillespie, William
1943   Cabin in the Sky
1945   Rhapsody in Blue

Gillette, Ruth
1938   In Old Chicago
         Josette
1939   The Return of the Cisco
         Kid

Gillick, Tom
1950   The Men

Gillingwater, Claude *same as*
    Gillingwater, Claude, Sr.
1922   My Boy
1926   Into Her Kingdom
1929   Smiling Irish Eyes
1934   Broadway Bill
         Strange Wives
1936   The Prisoner of Shark
         Island

Gillis, Ann *same as* Gillis, Anne
1937   The Californian
1938   The Adventures of Tom
         Sawyer
1944   Since You Went Away

Gillman, Frances
1934   Laughing Boy

Gillman, Fred
1947   The Mighty McGurk
1949   The Kissing Bandit
1950   Annie Get Your Gun
1951   Across the Wide Missouri
         The Magnificent Yankee

Gillstrom, Arvid E.
1927   Clancy's Kosher Wedding

Gilman, Jack
1944　　Block Busters
Gilman, Sam
1955　　A Man Called Peter
1956　　Full of Life
1958　　The Young Lions
Gilmore, Art *not the same as*
Gilmour, Arthur
1946　　Rendezvous 24
Gilmore, Barney
1927　　Heroes in Blue
1929　　Smiling Irish Eyes
Gilmore, Helen
1918　　Huck and Tom; or, the
　　　　　Further Adventures of
　　　　　Tom Sawyer
Gilmore, John
1956　　Raw Edge
Gilmore, Lillian
1935　　Wolf Riders
Gilmore, Lowell
1945　　Johnny Angel
1954　　Saskatchewan
1956　　Comanche
Gilmore, Paul
1915　　The Penitentes
Gilmore, Stuart
1952　　The Half-Breed
Gilmore, Virginia
1940　　Jennie
1941　　Western Union
Gilmour, Arthur *not the same as*
Gilmore, Art
1959　　The FBI Story
Gilmour, J. H.
1917　　The Woman and the Beast
Gilpatric, Guy
1943　　Action in the North
　　　　　Atlantic
Gilpin, Charles
1926?　Ten Nights in a Barroom
Gilroy, Bert
1938　　The Renegade Ranger
1939　　The Fighting Gringo
1942　　Mexican Spitfire's
　　　　　Elephant
1943　　Ladies' Day
　　　　　Mexican Spitfire's Blessed
　　　　　Event
Gilson, Tom
1960　　This Rebel Breed
Gimeno, Alvaro
1931　　La dama atrevida
Gimeno, Rosita Díaz *see* **Díaz**
Gimeno, Rosita
Ginelli, Leda
1931　　La pura verdad
Gines, Henry "Gang"
1939　　Lying Lips
Ginn, Hayward
1915　　The Alien
Ginn, Maury, Jr.
1934　　Coming Out Party
Ginsberg, Henry
1956　　Giant
Gionetti, Carlos
1939　　Winner Take All
Giotopoulos, Evangelos
1954　　Barefoot Battalion
Giovanni, John
1959　　The Black Orchid
Gipson, J. C.
1954　　Go Man Go
Giraci, Dorothy
1918　　Tony America
1922　　The Sign of the Rose
Giraci, May *same as* **Geraci, May**
1916　　The Fall of a Nation
1918　　The Man Above the Law
　　　　　One More American
　　　　　Untamed
Girard, Bernard
1957　　Ride Out for Revenge
Girard, Joseph *same as* **Girard,**
Joe; Girard, Joseph W.
1923　　The Sting of the Scorpion
1924　　In Hollywood With
　　　　　Potash and Perlmutter
　　　　　The Night Hawk
1927　　Whispering Sage

1929　　Redskin
1933　　Racetrack
1936　　Aces and Eights
1942　　The Navy Comes Through
Giraud, Octavio
1939　　Drifting Westward
　　　　　Frontiers of '49
Giraud, Wesley
1937　　Boy of the Streets
　　　　　The Plainsman
Gironda, Vince
1950　　Emergency Wedding
Girosi, Marcello
1954　　Indiscretion of an
　　　　　American Wife
1959　　The Black Orchid
Girvin, Virginia
1947　　Hi De Ho
Gish, Dorothy
1916　　Gretchen, the Greenhorn
　　　　　Little Meena's Romance
1918　　The Hun Within
1925　　The Beautiful City
Gish, Lillian
1915　　The Birth of a Nation
1916　　Sold for Marriage
1918　　The Greatest Thing in
　　　　　Life
1947　　Duel in the Sun
1949　　Portrait of Jennie
1960　　The Unforgiven
Gist, Robert
1949　　Jigsaw
1959　　Al Capone
　　　　　The FBI Story
Gitlitz, Ben
1939　　Kol Nidre
Gittelson, June
1940　　New Moon
Gittens, Wyndham
1918　　Me Und Gott
Givens, Bessie
1928　　The Midnight Ace
Givot, George
1936　　Paddy O'Day
1956　　The Benny Goodman
　　　　　Story
Gladakis, John George
1953　　Beneath the 12-Mile Reef
Gladden, Arlyne
1944　　Chip Off the Old Block
Gladden, W. W. E., Chaplain
1919　　Injustice
Gladden, Mrs. W. W. E.
1919　　Injustice
Gladstone, Isaac
1939　　The Light Ahead
Gladstone, Jacob
1940　　Overture to Glory
Gladstone, Marlyn
1948　　The Paleface
1951　　Westward the Women
1959　　Al Capone
Glaser, Lulu
1915　　How Molly Malone Made
　　　　　Good
Glasheri, Terressta
1940　　George Washington
　　　　　Carver
Glasmon, Kubec
1931　　Smart Money
Glass, Everett
1949　　Pinky
　　　　　The Undercover Man
1950　　The Big Hangover
　　　　　Rock Island Trail
　　　　　Two Flags West
　　　　　Young Man with a Horn
1951　　The Magnificent Yankee
1953　　The Sun Shines Bright
1955　　Trial
1958　　Gunman's Walk
Glass, Gaston
1919　　The Lost Battalion
1920　　Humoresque
1922　　Little Miss Smiles
1923　　The Spider and the Rose
1925　　The Scarlet West
1926　　Sweet Daddies
1930　　La fuerza del querer
　　　　　She Got What She Wanted

1931　　La gran jornada (*foreign*
　　　　　version)
1933　　Racetrack
1936　　Sutter's Gold
Glass, George
1950　　The Men
1959　　Shake Hands with the
　　　　　Devil
Glass, Montague
1922　　Hungry Hearts
1924　　In Hollywood With
　　　　　Potash and Perlmutter
Glass, Ned
1940　　Prairie Schooners
1949　　Knock on Any Door
1950　　Mystery Street
1952　　It's a Big Country: An
　　　　　American Anthology
1954　　The Yellow Tomahawk
1959　　The Jayhawkers!
　　　　　The Last Angry Man
Glasser, Bernard
1958　　Escape from Red Rock
Glassman, Barnett
1959　　John Paul Jones
Glassmire, Gus
1942　　Syncopation
1943　　Gangway for Tomorrow
　　　　　In Old Oklahoma
Glath, Ellsworth
1945　　The House on 92nd St.
Glattley, Robin
1958　　Sierra Baron
Glaum, Louise
1916　　The Aryan
1918　　An Alien Enemy
　　　　　The Goddess of Lost Lake
Glazer, Benjamin
1927　　The Love Mart
1931　　Don Juan diplomático
　　　　　Don Juan diplomático
　　　　　(*foreign version*)
1933　　L'amour guide
1942　　Tortilla Flat
Gleason, Adda
1915　　The Rosary
1916　　Ramona
1917　　The Spirit of '76
Gleason, Jackie *same as* **Gleason,**
Jackie C.
1942　　All Through the Night
Gleason, James
1931　　Beyond Victory
1937　　Manhattan
　　　　　Merry-Go-Round
1942　　Tales of Manhattan
1943　　Crash Dive
1945　　A Tree Grows in Brooklyn
1948　　The Dude Goes West
1957　　Man in the Shadow
1958　　The Last Hurrah
Gleason, Lucille Webster *same as*
Gleason Lucile Webster;
Gleason, Lucille
1934　　Beloved
1936　　Klondike Annie
1938　　The Beloved Brat
Gleason, Mary Ellen
1950　　Annie Get Your Gun
Gleason, Pat
1941　　The Gang's All Here
1942　　Rubber Racketeers
1943　　Air Force
　　　　　The Amazing Mrs.
　　　　　Holliday
1944　　Lake Placid Serenade
1951　　Cuban Fireball
Gleason, Russell
1931　　Beyond Victory
1942　　Three Hearts for Julia
Gleason, Tom
1958　　Home Before Dark
Gleaves, Abraham
1936　　The Green Pastures
Gleckler, Robert *same as* **Glecker,**
Robert
1929　　Mother's Boy
1938　　Rascals
1939　　Stand Up and Fight

Glendinning, John
1949　　Lost Boundaries
Glendon, Frank *same as* **Glendon,**
J. Frank
1917　　A Night in New Arabia
　　　　　The Renaissance at
　　　　　Charleroi
1920　　For the Soul of Rafael
1921　　A Tale of Two Worlds
1925　　Lights of Old Broadway
1932　　Law and Lawless
1935　　Circle of Death
1936　　Aces and Eights
　　　　　The Traitor
Glenn, Leslie
1960　　Pay or Die
Glenn, Roy, Sr. *same as* **Glenn,**
Roy; Glenn, Roy Edwin, Sr.
1937　　Life Begins in College
1954　　Carmen Jones
1955　　A Man Called Peter
1958　　St. Louis Blues
1959　　Porgy and Bess
1960　　The Adventures of
　　　　　Huckleberry Finn
Glennon, Bert
1930　　Around the Corner
Glett, Charles L.
1942　　Syncopation
Glick, Joseph *same as* **Glick, Joe**
1934　　Limehouse Blues
1945　　Where Do We Go From
　　　　　Here?
Glickman, Marty
1954　　Go Man Go
Glines, James
1940　　Geronimo
Glisby, Neal
1937　　Big City
Gloria, Angelo
1932　　Amore e morte
Glory, June
1936　　Show Boat
1946　　Without Reservations
1948　　The Paleface
Glover, Edmund *same as* **Glover,**
Ed; Glover, Edmond
1943　　Gangway for Tomorrow
1945　　Betrayal from the East
1950　　Battleground
　　　　　Stars in My Crown
Glover, Rubeline
1937　　Dark Manhattan
Gluck, Margel
1935　　Rescue Squad
Glucksman, E. M.
1946　　Stars on Parade
1947　　Hi De Ho
1948　　Killer Diller
1948?　Boarding House Blues
1949?　The Joint Is Jumpin'
Glucksman, Laura
1932　　Mazel Tov
Gluster, Al
1947　　Boy! What a Girl!
Gockel, H. W., Rev
1948　　Reaching from Heaven
Godard, John
1958　　Gun Fever
Goddard, Paulette
1941　　Hold Back the Dawn
1948　　Unconquered
1949　　Anna Lucasta
Godderis, Albert
1941　　Louisiana Purchase
1958　　Home Before Dark
Godfrey, Everett
1922　　For His Mother's Sake
Godfrey, George
1937　　Big City
　　　　　The Riders of the
　　　　　Whistling Skull
Godfrey, Peter
1949　　The Girl from Jones
　　　　　Beach
Godfrey, Phyllis
1937　　Souls at Sea
1948　　My Girl Tisa

Godfrey, Rae
1918   Marked Cards
       Tony America
Godfrey, Samuel T.
1931   Young Sinners
1935   Charlie Chan in Paris
       A Night at the Ritz
Godoy, Federico *same as* **Godoy, Fred**
1930   Monsieur le Fox
       Sombras de gloria
1936   Ramona
1948   Gentleman's Agreement
1949   We Were Strangers
Godsoe, Harold
1932   Cuore d'emigrante
       Harlem Is Heaven
       Senza mamma
       e'nnamurato
1947   Copacabana
Goebel, O. E.
1930   Así es la vida
       Sombras de gloria
Goedeck, Edward
1943   Action in the North
       Atlantic
Goering, Alice
1950   No Way Out
Goes in the Lodge
1928   Wyoming
Goethals, Stanley
1920   Outside the Law
Goettinger, Bill *see* **Steele, William**
Goetz, Harry M.
1936   The Last of the Mohicans
Goetz, Hayes
1952   Apache War Smoke
1954   Arrow in the Dust
Goetz, Leon
1931   Call of the Rockies
Goetz, William
1930   El último de los Vargas
1931   The Cisco Kid
       La gran jornada
1935   L'homme des Folies
       Bergère
1942   Little Tokyo, U.S.A.
1943   Crash Dive
       Margin for Error
       The Meanest Man in the
       World
       The Ox-Bow Incident
       They Came to Blow Up
       America
1944   Lifeboat
Goetzke, Bernhard
1932   Le cas du docteur
       Brenner
Goff, Ivan
1949   Prejudice
1956   Serenade
1957   Band of Angels
1959   Shake Hands with the
       Devil
Goff, Lloyd
1947   Body and Soul
Golconda, Ligia de *same as*
Golconda, Lygia de *could be*
same as **Colconda, Ligio de**
1931   La dama atrevida
1933   It's Great to Be Alive
       (*foreign version*)
1935   Angelina o el honor de
       un brigadier
Gold, S.
1940   Americaner Schadchen
Gold, Zachary
1947   Humoresque
Goldbeck, Willis
1924   Peter Pan
1925   Flower of Night
1928   Diamond Handcuffs
1942   Dr. Gillespie's New
       Assistant
1943   Dr. Gillespie's Criminal
       Case
1944   Three Men in White
1945   Between Two Women
1947   Dark Delusion
1956   The Lone Ranger
1960   Sergeant Rutledge

Goldberg, Alfred
1920   Humoresque
Goldberg, Bennie
1959   Al Capone
Goldberg, Bert
1946   Dirty Gertie from
       Harlem, U.S.A.
1946? Beale Street Mama
Goldberg, Dave
1946? Harlem on Parade
Goldberg, Dina
1950   Catskill Honeymoon
Goldberg, Jack
1932   Harlem Is Heaven
1934   The Unknown Soldier
       Speaks
1939   Double Deal
1940   Paradise in Harlem
1944   We've Come a Long, Long
       Way
1946? Harlem on Parade
1947   Boy! What a Girl!
       Sepia Cinderella
1948   Miracle in Harlem
Goldberg, Lou
1940   The Notorious Elinor Lee
Goldberg, Michael
1932   Joseph in the Land of
       Egypt
Goldberg, Rube (*writer*)
1926   The Campus Flirt
Goldberg, Rubin (*actor*)
1932   Uncle Moses
Goldberg, William
1932   Yiskor
1933   Victims of Persecution
Goldburg, Jesse J.
1927   The Fighting Hombre
Golden, Alfred
1937   One Mile from Heaven
Golden, Edward A.
1943   Hitler's Children
Golden, Michael
1960   The Day They Robbed the
       Bank of England
Golden, Mickey
1956   Serenade
Golden, Olive *see* **Carey, Olive**
1915   Just Jim
Golden, Robert S.
1943   Hitler's Children
Golden, Ruby
1943   Stormy Weather
Golden, Sidney M. *see* **Goldin,
Sidney M.**
1915? The Jewish Crown
       The Period of the Jew
Goldenberg, Samuel
1935   Shir Hashirim
Golder, Lew
1938   Spirit of Youth
Goldfaden, Abraham
1931   Shulamith
Goldfaden, Wolf
1926   Broken Hearts
1932   Joseph in the Land of
       Egypt
       Uncle Moses
       The Unfortunate Bride
       Yiskor
1934   The Youth of Russia
1939   The Light Ahead
Goldin, Bertina
1929   East Side Sadie
Goldin, Pat
1946   Bringing Up Father
1947   Jiggs and Maggie in
       Society
       King of the Bandits
1948   Half Past Midnight
       Jiggs and Maggie in Court
1949   Jiggs and Maggie in
       Jackpot Jitters
1950   Jiggs and Maggie Out
       West
Goldin, Sidney M. *same as* **Golden,
Sidney M.; Goldin, S. M.;
Goldin, Sidney**
1915   The Last of the Mafia
1929   East Side Sadie
1930   Eternal Fools (Ewige
       Naranim)
       My Yiddishe Mama

1931   Zein Weib's Lubovnick
1932   Mazel Tov
       Uncle Moses
       Yiskor
1937   The Cantor's Son
Goldina, Marian
1960   Flaming Star
Golding, Samuel R.
1950   Buccaneer's Girl
Goldman, Harold
1944   Knickerbocker Holiday
Goldman, Lawrence
1924? The Flaming Crisis
Goldner, Charles
1950   Give Us This Day
Goldoni, Lelia
1949   House of Strangers
       We Were Strangers
Goldschmidt, Robert
1945   Colorado Pioneers
Goldsmith, Frank
1915   The Clemenceau Case
Goldsmith, Ken
1936   The Last of the Mohicans
Goldsmith, Martin M. *same as*
Goldsmith, Martin
1954   Overland Pacific
1958   Fort Massacre
Goldstein, Charlotte
1930   Eternal Fools (Ewige
       Naranim)
1938   The Power of Life
1950? Three Daughters
Goldstein, Chuck
1941   Sun Valley Serenade
Goldstein, Jennie
1938   Two Sisters
Goldstein, Leonard
1936   Daniel Boone
1949   Arctic Manhunt
1950   Comanche Territory
1951   Tomahawk
1952   The Battle at Apache Pass
1953   The Great Sioux Uprising
1954   Siege at Red River
1955   Chief Crazy Horse
       White Feather
Goldstein, Louis
1939   Mothers of Today
Goldstein, Michael
1937   Green Fields
1938   The Singing Blacksmith
Goldstein, Robert
1917   The Spirit of '76
Goldstein, Ruby
1953   The Joe Louis Story
Goldstein, Samuel
1932   Joseph in the Land of
       Egypt
Goldstone, Henry L.
1932   Law and Lawless
Goldstone, Richard
1951   The Tall Target
Goldsworthy, John *same as*
Goldsworthy, J. H.
1916   Her Debt of Honor
1945   The Shanghai Cobra
1948   The Luck of the Irish
       Unconquered
Goldthwaite, Rogenia
1941? The Blood of Jesus
Goldwyn, Samuel
1919   Daughter of Mine
       Spotlight Sadie
       Toby's Bow
1920   The Cup of Fury
       Dangerous Days
       The North Wind's Malice
       The Paliser Case
1923   Potash and Perlmutter
1924   In Hollywood With
       Potash and Perlmutter
1929   This Is Heaven
1930   Whoopee
1931   Street Scene
1935   The Wedding Night
1959   Porgy and Bess
Golitzen, Alexander
1945   Salome, Where She
       Danced
1946   Canyon Passage

Golm, Ernest
1944   Address Unknown
1945   Rhapsody in Blue
Golm, Lisa
1940   Escape
1942   Woman of the Year
1943   They Came to Blow Up
       America
1946   Without Reservations
1949   Anna Lucasta
Goltz, Horst von der, Capt.
1918   The Prussian Cur
Golubeff, Gregory
1945   Rhapsody in Blue
1947   Northwest Outpost
1949   The Girl from Jones
       Beach
Gombell, Minna
1931   Skyline
1932   The Rainbow Trail
1937   Slave Ship
1941   Doomed Caravan
1942   Mexican Spitfire Sees a
       Ghost
1944   Chip Off the Old Block
1945   Sunbonnet Sue
Gomberg, Sy
1950   The Toast of New Orleans
Gómez, Anna María
1955   Seven Cities of Gold
Gomez, Augie
1933   The California Trail
1945   South of the Rio Grande
1946   The Red Dragon
1948   Old Los Angeles
1955   The Vanishing American
Gómez, Carlos "Don Chema"
1930   Charros, gauchos y
       manolas
Gomez, Felipa
1948   Key Largo
Gomez, Felipe
1949   The Cowboy and the
       Indians
Gómez, Gerardo
1936   El crimen de media
       noche
Gomez, Inez
1916   Ramona
1921   Cheated Love
Gomez, Jerry
1945   South of the Rio Grande
Gomez, Ralph
1948   The Paleface
Gómez, Ramiro
1938   Di que me quieres
Gomez, Thomas
1947   Ride the Pink Horse
1948   Angel in Exile
       Key Largo
1949   That Midnight Kiss
1950   The Furies
1951   The Harlem Globetrotters
1959   John Paul Jones
Gomez, Vicente
1949   The Kissing Bandit
Gómez Cantón, Eduardo
1932   Amor y vida
Gómez Ferrer, Francisco
1931   La incorregible
Gomöry, Vilma
1930   El secreto del doctor
       (*foreign version*)
Gonatos, John
1948   16 Fathoms Deep
1951   A Streetcar Named Desire
1953   Beneath the 12-Mile Reef
Gonzales, Ernesto
1960   The Pusher
Gonzales, Jose Gonzales
1956   Wetbacks
Gonzales, Lupe
1938   The Buccaneer
Gonzales, Soledad
1936   Ramona
González, Adalberto Elías
1931   La cautivadora
1939   La Inmaculada

Gonzalez, Felix
1954   Sitting Bull
Gonzalez, Fred
1939   Verbena trágica
Gonzalez, James
1936   Star for a Night
1953   The Jazz Singer
González, María
1931   La pura verdad
González, Pedro
1931   La pura verdad
Gonzalez, Pedro Gonzalez
1959   The Young Land
Gonzalez, William E.
1956   Crowded Paradise
Good, John
1950   Black Hand
Good, Peter B.
1940   Knute Rockne—All
        American
Good, Richard
1947   Citizen Saint
Goodall, Grace
1934   Judge Priest
1935   The Singing Vagabond
1938   The Buccaneer
        City Streets
Gooding, Sally
1940   The Notorious Elinor Lee
Goodman, Benny
1942   Syncopation
1956   The Benny Goodman
        Story
**Benny Goodman and His
Orchestra**
1943   The Gang's All Here
1956   The Benny Goodman
        Story
Goodman, Daniel Carson
1921   The Barricade
Goodman, Danny
1923   April Showers
Goodman, Edward
1931   Women Love Once
Goodman, Irving
1956   The Benny Goodman
        Story
Goodman, J. Kenneth
1922   The Dungeon
Goodman, Lee
1959   Imitation of Life
Goodrich, Edna
1917   Queen X
Goodrich, Frances
1935   Naughty Marietta
1936   After the Thin Man
Goodrich, Jack
1939   Waterfront
Goodrich, John F. *same as*
Goodrich, John
1926   Puppets
1932   The Son-Daughter
Goodwin, Aline
1925   Warrior Gap
1926   Desert Gold
Goodwin, Bill
1943   Riding High
1947   The Jolson Story
1950   Jolson Sings Again
Goodwin, Harold *same as*
Goodwin, Herold
1918   Set Free
1926   The Flaming Frontier
1928   The Cameraman
1934   She Was a Lady
1935   Romance in Manhattan
1936   Robin Hood of El Dorado
1938   Happy Landing
        My Lucky Star
        Speed to Burn
1939   The Cisco Kid and the
        Lady
1940   Charlie Chan at the Wax
        Museum
        Charlie Chan in Panama
        Viva Cisco Kid
1941   Accent on Love
1947   Ride the Pink Horse
1948   Up in Central Park
1956   Walk the Proud Land

Goodwin, Ruby
1955   The View from Pompey's
        Head
Goodwins, Fred
1918   Amarilly of Clothes-Line
        Alley
Goodwins, Leslie
1939   The Girl from Mexico
1940   Mexican Spitfire
        Mexican Spitfire Out
        West
1941   The Mexican Spitfire's
        Baby
1942   Mexican Spitfire at Sea
        Mexican Spitfire Sees a
        Ghost
        Mexican Spitfire's
        Elephant
1943   Ladies' Day
        Mexican Spitfire's Blessed
        Event
1944   Hi, Beautiful
1945   The Mummy's Curse
Gorcey, Bernard
1929   Abie's Irish Rose
1944   Block Busters
1947   Bowery Buckaroos
        The Peanut Man
Gorcey, David
1942   Let's Get Tough!
1947   Bowery Buckaroos
Gorcey, Kay *same as* **Marvis, Kay**
1944   Block Busters
1947   Copacabana
Gorcey, Leo
1938   The Beloved Brat
1942   Let's Get Tough!
        Sunday Punch
1944   Block Busters
1947   Bowery Buckaroos
Gordiano, Anita
1937   El carnaval del diablo
Gordon, Mrs.
1916   Ramona
Gordon, Al *(actor)*
1931   Delicious
Gordon, Alex *(prod)*
1955   Apache Woman
Gordon, B. *could be same as*
Gordon, Bruce *(silent actor)*
1931   Delicious
Gordon, Bert
1938   Outside of Paradise
1943   Let's Have Fun
Gordon, Betty
1936   Star for a Night
Gordon, Bobby *(actor) not the*
same as **Gordon, Robert**
(actor)
1925   His People
1928   The Jazz Singer
1933   Counsellor at Law
1934   Strange Wives
Gordon, Bruce *from circa late*
1940s
1960   Key Witness
Gordon, Bruce *(silent actor) could*
be same as **Gordon, B.**
1925   Brand of Cowardice
1926   Pals in Paradise
        The Vanishing American
1928   Anybody Here Seen Kelly?
Gordon, C. Henry
1931   The Black Camel
        Charlie Chan Carries On
1932   Scarface
        Thirteen Women
1934   Lazy River
        Straight Is the Way
1937   Charlie Chan at the
        Olympics
1939   City in Darkness
        Man of Conquest
        The Return of the Cisco
        Kid
1940   Charlie Chan at the Wax
        Museum
        Kit Carson
Gordon, Charles
1939   Double Deal
1946   Swamp Fire

Gordon, Christine
1943   Action in the North
        Atlantic
Gordon, Colin
1960   The Day They Robbed the
        Bank of England
Gordon, Dick *see* **Gordon, Richard**
Gordon, Don *same as* **Gordon,**
Donald
1948   Big City
1952   It's a Big Country: An
        American Anthology
1956   The Benny Goodman
        Story
1957   Revolt at Fort Laramie
1959   Cry Tough
Gordon, Douglas
1934   She Was a Lady
1940   Escape to Glory
Gordon, Elliott *see* **Elliott, William**
"Wild Bill"
Gordon, Flash
1943   Riding High
Gordon, Fred
1947   Sepia Cinderella
Gordon, Gavin
1931   The Great Meadow
1935   Bordertown
1946   Notorious
Gordon, Glen Charles
1952   Bright Victory
Gordon, Gloria
1953   Beneath the 12-Mile Reef
1955   A Man Called Peter
Gordon, Gwendoline
1919   Injustice
Gordon, Harold
1952   The Iron Mistress
1953   The Jazz Singer
Gordon, Harris
1934   Our Daily Bread
Gordon, Huntley *same as* **Gordon,**
Huntly
1920   The Dark Mirror
1921   Society Snobs
1933   Racetrack
1935   The Irish in Us
1936   Daniel Boone
        Klondike Annie
1939   Mr. Wong in Chinatown
1940   Phantom of Chinatown
Gordon, Jack *(silent actor)*
1914   At the Cross Roads
Gordon, Jack, b. 1903
1947   Under the Tonto Rim
1949   The Undercover Man
Gordon, James *not the same as*
Gordon, James B.
1919   Behind the Door
1920   The Last of the Mohicans
1926   Rose of the Tenements
1929   Masked Emotions
Gordon, James B. *not the same as*
Gordon, James
1955   The Gun That Won the
        West
Gordon, John E.
1946   Beware
        Tall, Tan and Terrific
1949   Lookout Sister
Gordon, Julia Swayne
1920   Lifting Shadows
1925   Lights of Old Broadway
1929   Is Everybody Happy?
        The Younger Generation
1932   The Golden West
Gordon, Kay
1936   Star for a Night
Gordon, Kitty
1919   Mandarin's Gold
        The Scar
Gordon, Leo
1954   Hondo
1955   Santa Fe Passage
        Seven Angry Men
1956   7th Cavalry
1957   Man in the Shadow
1958   Apache Territory
        Ride a Crooked Trail
1959   The Jayhawkers!

Gordon, Leon
1931   ¿Conoces a tu mujer?
        Mi último amor
1932   The Son-Daughter
Gordon, Mary
1927   Clancy's Kosher Wedding
1931   The Black Camel
1932   Call Her Savage
1934   Beloved
        Our Daily Bread
1935   The Irish in Us
1936   After the Thin Man
        Laughing Irish Eyes
1937   Souls at Sea
        That I May Live
1938   City Streets
        Gateway
1939   The Escape
1940   Elsa Maxwell's Public
        Deb No. 1
1942   Gentleman Jim
1944   The Racket Man
1946   Shadows Over Chinatown
        Singin' in the Corn
1948   Fort Apache
1949   Shamrock Hill
Gordon, Maude Turner
1918   The Ordeal of Rosetta
1935   A Night at the Ritz
1936   After the Thin Man
Gordon, Paul d.1929
1916   The Pretenders
Gordon, Paul circa 1940s
1940   If I Had My Way
1944   An American Romance
Gordon, Peggy
1945   Where Do We Go From
        Here?
Gordon, Peter
1960   Walk Like a Dragon
Gordon, Richard *same as* **Gordon,**
Dick
1934   Broadway Bill
1944   Black Magic
1945   In Old New Mexico
1950   Jolson Sings Again
1952   Bright Victory
1953   The Eddie Cantor Story
Gordon, Robert *(actor) not the*
same as **Gordon, Bobby** *(actor)*
1917   The Little American
1918   Huck and Tom; or, the
        Further Adventures of
        Tom Sawyer
1919   A Yankee Princess
Gordon, Robert *(writer, dir)*
1943   The Girl from Monterrey
1953   The Joe Louis Story
1958   The Rawhide Trail
Gordon, Rose
1934   The Cactus Kid
        The Fighting Hero
1935   Wolf Riders
Gordon, Roy
1943   Jack London
        What's Buzzin' Cousin?
1944   An American Romance
1945   The Shanghai Cobra
1947   The Last Round-Up
1949   Apache Chief
        The Cowboy and the
        Indians
1950   Indian Territory
        Two Flags West
1951   Jim Thorpe—All-American
1953   Sangaree
1955   The Gun That Won the
        West
1956   Wetbacks
1959   The FBI Story
Gordon, Ruth
1943   Action in the North
        Atlantic
Gordon, Stanley
1948   Call Northside 777
Gordon, Taylor
1933   The Emperor Jones
Gordon, Vera
1920   Humoresque
        The North Wind's Malice
1920?   The Greatest Love
1922   The Good Provider

1923	Potash and Perlmutter
1924	In Hollywood With Potash and Perlmutter
1926	The Cohens and Kellys
	Kosher Kitty Kelly
	Millionaires
	Private Izzy Murphy
	Sweet Daddies
1928	The Cohens and the Kellys in Paris
1929	The Cohens and Kellys in Atlantic City
1930	The Cohens and the Kellys in Scotland
1931	The Cohens and Kellys in Africa
1946	Abie's Irish Rose

Gordon, Will *could be same as* **Gordon, William**

Gordon, William
1931	Delicious

Gordon, William *could be same as* **Gordon, Will**
1935	Tango Bar
1940	Tengo fe en ti
1946	Notorious

Gore, Rosa
1928	Anybody Here Seen Kelly?
1934	The Cat's-Paw

Gorel, Nadia
1934	The Youth of Russia

Gorgas, Alice
1920	The Brute

The Gorgeous Astor Debutantes
1946	Tall, Tan and Terrific

Gorman, Buddy
1944	Since You Went Away
1947	The Jolson Story

Gorman, Charles
1915	The Gambler of the West
1916	A Sister of Six

Gorman, Eric
1952	The Quiet Man

Gorman, Grant
1920	Within Our Gates

Gorman, Inez
1953	Dream Wife

Gorman, John dir
1915	An American Gentleman

Gorman, John (*actor*)
1949	Thieves' Highway

Gorney, Jay
1945	The Gay Senorita

Gorog, L.
1942	Tales of Manhattan

Gorshin, Frank
1959	Night of the Quarter Moon
1960	Studs Lonigan

Gorss, Saul *same as* **Gorss, Sol**
1940	East of the River
1942	Juke Girl
	Secret Enemies
	They Died With Their Boots On
	Wings for the Eagle
1943	Air Force
1944	Mr. Skeffington
1949	Knock on Any Door
	The Undercover Man
1958	Bullwhip
1960	Ice Palace

Gosden, Freeman F.
1930	Check and Double Check

Gossett, Christine
1936	Ramona

Got, Archie
1943	Action in the North Atlantic

Got, Roland
1941	Secret of the Wastelands
1942	Across the Pacific
	Submarine Raider
1943	The Amazing Mrs. Holliday

Góth, Sándor
1930	El secreto del doctor (*foreign version*)

Gottesman, Solomon J., Rev.
1959	The Last Angry Man

Gottlieb, Alex
1941	Mystery Ship
1949	The Girl from Jones Beach
1952	The Fighter

Gottlieb, Richard
1943	Riding High

Gottschalk, Ferdinand
1933	Grand Slam
1935	L'homme des Folies Bergère
1937	That Girl from Paris

Gotz, Carl
1932	Yiskor

Goudal, Jetta
1925	Salome of the Tenements
1927	White Gold
1930	Le spectre vert

Gough, Earl
1939	Moon over Harlem

Gough, Lloyd
1949	Tulsa

Goula, José
1931	Chérie (*foreign version*)

Gould, Howard
1948	Shep Comes Home

Gould, Rita
1944	An American Romance

Gould, Sandra
1949	The Girl from Jones Beach
1957	Beau James
1959	Imitation of Life

Gould, Walter (*actor*)
1917	One Law for Both

Gould, Walter (*prod*)
1951	Native Son

Gould, William *could be same as* **Gould, William Howard**
1934	Wheels of Destiny
1935	A Night at the Opera
	Wolf Riders
1936	Pinto Rustlers
	Sutter's Gold
1938	Mr. Wong, Detective
1939	Confessions of a Nazi Spy
	Mr. Moto Takes a Vacation
	Waterfront
1940	Three Cheers for the Irish
1942	Juke Girl
1946	Beauty and the Bandit
1947	My Wild Irish Rose
	Wild Horse Mesa
1950	A Ticket to Tomahawk

Gould, William Howard *could be same as* **Gould, William**
1936	After the Thin Man

Gouldeni, Gene
1934	La veuve joyeuse

Goulding, Edmund
1918	The Ordeal of Rosetta
1922	Peacock Alley
1925	The Beautiful City
1930	Galas de la Paramount
	The Grand Parade
1931	La fiesta del diablo
	La fiesta del diablo (*foreign version*)
1932	Flesh

Goupil, Augie
1937	Waikiki Wedding

Gourmet, Marcel
1950	The Iroquois Trail

Govea, Jose
1956	Serenade

Gover, Mildred
1935	Harmony Lane
1940	Santa Fe Trail

Gow, Lee
1917	The War of the Tongs

Gowland, Gibson
1919	Behind the Door
1925	The Prairie Wife
1927	Topsy and Eva
1940	Northwest Passage (Book I—Rogers' Rangers)
1941	Mutiny in the Arctic

Goya, Mona
1931	Buster se marie
	Chérie
	Jenny Lind
	Quand on est belle

	Soyons gais

Gozier, Bernie
1952	Hiawatha
1953	Dream Wife
	The Nebraskan
1955	Kiss of Fire
1956	Walk the Proud Land

Gozzo, Conrad
1956	The Benny Goodman Story

Grable, Betty
1942	Song of the Islands
1945	The Dolly Sisters

Grabowski, Norman
1959	Night of the Quarter Moon

Grace, Geoffrey
1928	Uncle Tom's Cabin

Grace, Meyer
1946	Dark Alibi

Grace-Boon, Margaret
1919	Injustice

Gradus, Ben
1956	Crowded Paradise

Grady, Billy *see* **Grady, William, Jr.**

Grady, Blanche
1941	Louisiana Purchase

Grady, William, Jr. *same as* **Grady, Billy**
1949	Arctic Manhunt
1953	Cry of the Hunted

Graeff, Diane
1948	The Boy with Green Hair

Graeff, Paul
1942	Mokey
1945	Nob Hill
	A Tree Grows in Brooklyn
1947	It Had To Be You

Graeff, Vincent
1942	Mokey
1944	Buffalo Bill
1945	Nob Hill
	A Tree Grows in Brooklyn
	The Valley of Decision
1946	Without Reservations
1947	Easy Come, Easy Go
	It Had To Be You
1948	Fighting Father Dunne
	My Girl Tisa

Graf, Max
1927	Finnegan's Ball

Graf, Peter
1935	Bar-Mitzvah

Graff, Fred *see* **Graham, Fred**

Graff, Wilton
1948	Gentleman's Agreement
1956	The Benny Goodman Story

Graffeo, Phyllis
1950	A Lady Without Passport

Grafton, Louise
1925	Irish Luck

Graham, Betty Jane
1932	Hearts of Humanity
	No Greater Love
1935	The Winning Ticket
1944	They Live in Fear

Graham, Charles
1915	An American Gentleman
1918	The Birth of a Race
1922	Cardigan
1942	Valley of Hunted Men

Graham, Clarice
1946	Stars on Parade

Graham, Eddie
1943	Yankee Doodle Dandy

Graham, Frank
1943	Crime Smasher

Graham, Fred *same as* **Graff, Fred; Grahame, Fred**
1940	East of the River
	New Moon
1943	They Came to Blow Up America
1944	Buffalo Bill
	Cry of the Werewolf
	Marshal of Reno
1945	Colorado Pioneers
	Nob Hill
	Phantom of the Plains

1947	Buffalo Bill Rides Again
	On the Old Spanish Trail
1948	The Miracle of the Bells
1949	Border Incident
	The Fighting Kentuckian
	She Wore a Yellow Ribbon
1950	No Way Out
1951	Across the Wide Missouri
1952	The Big Sky
	Fort Osage
1954	Overland Pacific
1955	The Vanishing American
1956	The Last Hunt

Graham, Garrett
1928	Wheel of Chance

Graham, George (*actor*)
1957	Journey to Freedom

Graham, George (*dir*)
1924	Smiling Hate

Graham, Herschel
1943	Action in the North Atlantic
1949	We Were Strangers

Graham, Howard
1956	The Catered Affair

Graham, John
1947	Citizen Saint
1956	Crowded Paradise
1960	Studs Lonigan

Graham, R. E.
1914	The Great Diamond Robbery

Graham, Richard
1943	In Old Oklahoma

Graham, S. Edwin
1936	El diablo del mar

Graham, Sheilah
1947	Jiggs and Maggie in Society

Graham, Tim
1949	Shamrock Hill
1950	A Ticket to Tomahawk
1951	Jim Thorpe—All-American
1952	High Noon
1958	Bullwhip

Grahame, Fred *see* **Graham, Fred**

Grahame, Gloria
1947	Crossfire
1953	The Glass Wall
1955	Not As a Stranger
1957	Ride Out for Revenge
1959	Odds Against Tomorrow

Grahame, Margot
1938	The Buccaneer

Grainger, Dorothy *see* **Granger, Dorothy**

Grainger, Edmund
1932	The Rainbow Trail
1950	Sands of Iwo Jima
1960	Cimarron

Grajciar, John W.
1957	Burden of Truth

Gramby, Joseph *see* **Granby, Joseph**

Gran, Albert
1928	We Americans
1930	The Kibitzer

Granada, Carmen *could be same as* **Granada, Rosita**
1930	Una cana al aire
	Charros, gauchos y manolas
1931	La cautivadora
	Politiquerías

Granada, Rosita *could be same as* **Granada, Carmen**
1930	Cuando el amor ríe
	¡De frente, marchen!
1931	En cada puerto un amor
	El pasado acusa
1932	Marido y mujer
1933	No dejes la puerta abierta
	Yo, tú y ella
1935	Piernas de seda
1938	The Buccaneer
1939	El trovador de la radio
1940	Tengo fe en ti

Granado, Manuel *see* **Ellis, Paul**

Granby, Joseph *same as* **Gramby, Joseph**
1921   Diane of Star Hollow
1948   The Lady from Shanghai
Grandel, Jeanine
1957   Band of Angels
Grandin, Ethel
1913   Traffic in Souls
Grandin, Robert
1954   Broken Lance
Grandon, Francis J. *could be same as* **Grandon, Frank**
1917   The Little Boy Scout
1918   Love's Law
Grandon, Frank *could be same as* **Grandon, Francis J.**
1921   Lotus Blossom
Grandpre, Jean Louise
1939   Miracle on Main Street
Grandstaff, Kathryn
1953   Arrowhead
Grandville, Marcelle
1947   Riding the California Trail
Graneman, Eddy
1936   Custer's Last Stand
Granet, Bert
1941   Sun Valley Serenade
Grange, Douglas
1950   The Furies
Grange, Maud
1917   The Bronze Bride
       John Ermine of the Yellowstone
Granger, Dorothy *same as* **Grainger, Dorothy**
1930   Una cana al aire
1931   Noche de duendes
1936   Show Boat
1940   New Moon
1942   North to the Klondike
1943   The Amazing Mrs. Holliday
1944   Chip Off the Old Block
1945   The Jade Mask
1946   Shadows Over Chinatown
1948   The Paleface
1951   Westward the Women
1953   So Big
1957   Raintree County
Granger, Michael
1952   Hiawatha
1954   Battle of Rogue River
1956   Mohawk
1958   Gunman's Walk
Granger, Stewart
1956   The Last Hunt
Granier, Jean
1931   Su noche de bodas (*foreign version*)
Granstedt, Greta
1930   Sunny Skies
1931   Street Scene
1945   Our Vines Have Tender Grapes
1948   Unconquered
1953   The Eddie Cantor Story
Grant, A. Cameron *same as* **Cameron, Grant**
1946   Three Wise Fools
1950   Annie Get Your Gun
       The Big Hangover
1951   The Tall Target
1952   It's a Big Country: An American Anthology
1953   The Eddie Cantor Story
1955   Good Morning, Miss Dove
Grant, Alfred
1939   One Dark Night
       Reform School
1940   Am I Guilty?
       Mystery in Swing
       Son of Ingagi
       While Thousands Cheer
1941   Four Shall Die
1942   The Vanishing Virginian
1951   The Well
Grant, Arthur
1934   Operator 13

Grant, Austin
1940   New Moon
Grant, Cameron *see* **Grant, A. Cameron**
Grant, Cary
1943   Mr. Lucky
1946   Notorious
       Without Reservations
1953   Dream Wife
1958   Houseboat
Grant, Corinne
1915   The Adventures of a Madcap
Grant, Frances
1919   Come Out of the Kitchen
1925   Scarlet Saint
1936   The Traitor
Grant, Helena
1934   Charlie Chan in London
Grant, Jack *not the same as* **Grant, Jack Jr.**
1931   Delicious
Grant, Jack, Jr. *not the same as* **Grant, Jack**
1940   Knute Rockne—All American
Grant, James Edward
1938   Josette
1940   Music in My Heart
1941   They Dare Not Love
1945   The Great John L.
1950   Rock Island Trail
       Sands of Iwo Jima
1954   Hondo
1956   The Last Wagon
Grant, Jimmy
1934   Coming Out Party
1936   Star for a Night
Grant, John (*actor*) *could be same as* **Grant, Johnny** *not the same as* **Grant, John** (*writer*)
1946   Beware
1951   Mask of the Dragon
Grant, John (*writer*) *not the same as* **Grant, John** (*actor*)
1942   Rio Rita
1947   Buck Privates Come Home
Grant, Johnny *could be same as* **Grant, John** (*actor*)
1957   Beau James
Grant, Kathryn
1956   Reprisal!
1957   The Brothers Rico
       The Guns of Fort Petticoat
1958   Gunman's Walk
Grant, Kirby
1948   Singin' Spurs
1950   Indian Territory
Grant, Lawrence
1929   Is Everybody Happy?
1931   The Squaw Man
1936   Klondike Annie
Grant, Marshall
1942   Unseen Enemy
1946   Slightly Scandalous
1948   Moonrise
Grant, Morton
1942   Valley of Hunted Men
1946   Song of the South
Grant, Nellie
1917   The Tell-Tale Step
       Threads of Fate
Grant, S.
1917   How Uncle Sam Prepares
Grant, Valentine
1915   The Melting Pot
1916   The Innocent Lie
Grant, Virginia
1947   The Peanut Man
Granucci, Charles
1949   We Were Strangers
Granville, Bonita
1937   Maid of Salem
1938   The Beloved Brat
1940   Escape
1942   Syncopation
1943   Hitler's Children
1944   Andy Hardy's Blonde Trouble

1956   The Lone Ranger
Granville, Charlotte
1917   The Red Woman
1934   Behold My Wife!
1936   Rose of the Rancho
Granville, Max
1949?   Harlem Follies
Grapewin, Charley
1932   Huddle
       Wild Horse Mesa
1934   Judge Priest
1935   Rendezvous
1937   Big City
1939   Stand Up and Fight
1942   They Died With Their Boots On
Grassby, Bertram *same as* **Grasby, Bertram**
1919   The Delicious Little Devil
       The Gray Horizon
       Yvonne from Paris
1920   Dangerous Days
       For the Soul of Rafael
1921   Fifty Candles
       Hold Your Horses
Grassby, Gerrard
1919   The Sneak
Grasse, Sam de *see* **De Grasse, Sam**
Grattan, Stephen *same as* **Gratton, Stephen**
1918   The Birth of a Race
1919   The Lost Battalion
Gratton, Billy
1940   Knute Rockne—All American
Gratton, Stephen *see* **Grattan, Stephen**
Gravers, Steve
1959   Al Capone
Graves, Janet
1944   Something for the Boys
Graves, Jesse *same as* **Graves, Jessie**
1936   After the Thin Man
       General Spanky
1939   The Adventures of Huckleberry Finn
1940   Son of Ingagi
1945   Rhapsody in Blue
       The Valley of Decision
1946   G. I. War Brides
       Without Reservations
1947   California
Graves, Leonard
1960   Pay or Die
Graves, Peter
1951   Fort Defiance
1953   Beneath the 12-Mile Reef
       War Paint
1954   The Yellow Tomahawk
1955   Fort Yuma
       The Long Gray Line
1957   Bayou
Graves, Ralph
1918   The Yellow Dog
1919   Scarlet Days
1922   Come On Over
1926   Blarney
1932   Huddle
Graves, Robert
1934   Caravane
1935   Charlie Chan in Paris
1938   Charlie Chan at Monte Carlo
Graves, Taylor
1924   North of Nevada
Graves, Walker Coleman, Jr.
1924   Unseen Hands
Gravey, Fernand
1931   Chérie
       Su noche de bodas (*foreign version*)
Gravina, Cesare
1916   Poor Little Peppina
1925   Flower of Night
       The Man in Blue
Gray Eyes *same as* **Gray Eyes, Pete**
1949   Colorado Territory
1956   The Searchers

Gray, Alberta
1942   They Died With Their Boots On
Gray, Beatrice
1946   G. I. War Brides
1948   Unconquered
1950   Emergency Wedding
Gray, Billy
1947   Little Mister Jim
1948   Fighting Father Dunne
1949   Lust for Gold
       The Undercover Man
1951   Jim Thorpe—All-American
Gray, Blanche
1918   Set Free
Gray, Bob *see* **Gray, Robert** b. in Houlton, ME
Gray, Charles
1942   Tales of Manhattan
1957   Trooper Hook
Gray, Coleen *same as* **Gray, Colleen**
1948   Fury at Furnace Creek
       Red River
1951   Apache Drums
1954   Arrow in the Dust
1956   Death of a Scoundrel
       The Wild Dakotas
Gray, Dolores
1944   Mr. Skeffington
Gray, Dorothy
1934   As the Earth Turns
1935   Black Fury
Gray, Elizabeth
1941   Sullivan's Travels
Gray, Ethel
1919   A Man's Duty
Gray, Gary
1941   Sun Valley Serenade
1943   The Meanest Man in the World
1944   Address Unknown
1946   Rendezvous 24
       Slightly Scandalous
       Three Wise Fools
1947   Dark Delusion
       Little Mister Jim
1948   Gun Smugglers
       Night Wind
1949   The Girl from Jones Beach
       Masked Raiders
Gray, George Arthur
1929   Hawk of the Hills
Gray, Harry *not the same as* **Grey, Harry**
1929   Hallelujah
1932   The Black King
Gray, Jamie
1924   Unseen Hands
Gray, Jenifer *same as* **Gray, Jennie**
1934   Coming Out Party
1938   The Rage of Paris
Gray, Jimmy
1953   Column South
Gray, Joe
1938   Mr. Moto's Gamble
1939   Winner Take All
1947   It Had To Be You
Gray, Lawrence
1927   The Callahans and the Murphys
1928   Diamond Handcuffs
Gray, Lorraine
1936   Star for a Night
Gray, Louis
1941   Gauchos of Eldorado
       Prairie Pioneers
       Saddlemates
1942   Valley of Hunted Men
1943   Wagon Tracks West
1944   Marshal of Reno
1945   Great Stagecoach Robbery
1948   Silver Trails
Gray, Mack
1945   Johnny Angel
Gray, Marion
1952   The Savage
Gray, Maurine
1934   Broadway Bill

Gray, Robert b. in Houlton, ME *not the same as* **Gray, Robert** *from circa 1940s or* **Grey, Robert** b. in Oakland, CA
1916   Unprotected
1918   The Ranger

Gray, Robert *from circa 1940s*
1948   The Lady from Shanghai

Gray, Roger
1935   Naughty Marietta
1936   Rebellion
1938   City Streets
1939   The Adventures of Huckleberry Finn
1943   Redhead from Manhattan

Gray, Theresa
1921   Cheated Love

Gray, Virginia *see* **Grey, Virginia**

Gray, Wilhelmina
1943   Stormy Weather

Grayham, Clarice
1946?   Fight That Ghost

Grayson, Jessie
1939   One Dark Night
1942   Syncopation
1950   Stars in My Crown

Grayson, Kathryn
1942   Rio Rita
        Seven Sweethearts
        The Vanishing Virginian
1949   The Kissing Bandit
        That Midnight Kiss
1950   The Toast of New Orleans
1951   Show Boat

Greathouse, Gean
1950   Panic in the Streets

Greaves, William
1948   The Fight Never Ends
        Miracle in Harlem
1949   Lost Boundaries
        Souls of Sin

Greaza, Walter N.
1948   Call Northside 777
1951   New Mexico

Grecco, Mike
1957   Naked in the Sun

Greco, Betty
1938   Road Demon
        Speed to Burn
1939   Winner Take All

Greear, Geraine *see* **Barclay, Joan**

Greeley, Evelyn
1918   The Golden Wall
        Hitting the Trail
1921   Diane of Star Hollow

Green, Abel
1947   Copacabana

Green, Alfred E. *same as* **Green, Alfred**
1921   Through the Back Door
1922   Come On Over
1924   In Hollywood With Potash and Perlmutter
1926   Irene
1927   The Auctioneer
1931   Smart Money
1934   As the Earth Turns
1940   East of the River
1947   Copacabana
        The Jolson Story
1948   Four Faces West
1950   The Jackie Robinson Story
1953   The Eddie Cantor Story

Green, Ben
1937   Life Begins in College

Green, Bill (*musician*)
1958   St. Louis Blues

Green, Billy *not the same as* **Green, William E.**
1945   Sunbonnet Sue
1947   My Wild Irish Rose
1949   The Fighting Kentuckian
1951   Yes Sir, Mr. Bones

Green, Cora
1938   Swing!

Green, Denis
1940   Northwest Passage (Book I—Rogers' Rangers)

Green, Donald
1953   Thunder Bay

Green, Dorothy
1920   The Good-Bad Wife
1955   Trial

Green, Duke
1936   Robin Hood of El Dorado

Green, Eddie
1946   Mantan Messes Up

Green, Edwin
1915   The Rosary

Green, George (*actor*)
1951   Native Son

Green, George (*writer*) *could be same as* **Green, George D.** (*writer, prod*)
1943   The Girl from Monterrey

Green, George D. (*writer, prod*) *could be same as* **Green, George** (*writer*)
1949   Apache Chief

Green, Gerald
1959   The Last Angry Man

Green, Griswold
1960   Flaming Star

Green, Harold (*actor*)
1958   Tonka

Green, Harrison *see* **Greene, Harrison**

Green, Harry
1929   Why Bring That Up?
1930   Galas de la Paramount
        The Kibitzer
1934   Coming Out Party
1939   The Cisco Kid and the Lady

Green, Herman
1940   Paradise in Harlem
1941   Murder on Lenox Avenue
        Sunday Sinners

Green, Howard J.
1928   Vamping Venus
1929   The Younger Generation
1930   The Melody Man
1931   Esclavas de la moda
1932   The Cohens and Kellys in Hollywood
1943   Doughboys in Ireland
1944   The Racket Man

Green, Jack
1936   Charlie Chan at the Race Track

Green, Jane
1944   Three Men in White
1946   Bad Bascomb
        The Sailor Takes a Wife
1947   The Mighty McGurk
1948   Gentleman's Agreement

Jimmie Green's Orchestra
1946?   Go Down, Death!

Green, Joe *see* **Greene, Joseph J.**

Green, Joe (*African-American actor*)
1920   Our Christianity and Nobody's Child

Green, Joseph (*dir, prod, writer*) *same as* **Greenberg, Joseph** *not the same as* **Greene, Joseph J.**
1932   A Daughter of Her People
        Joseph in the Land of Egypt
1936   Yiddle with His Fiddle
1937   The Jester (Der Purimspieler)
1939   A Brivele der Mamen Mamele

Green, Les
1960   Pay or Die

Green, Millicent
1940   They Knew What They Wanted

Green, Mitzi
1930   Galas de la Paramount
        Tom Sawyer
1931   Huckleberry Finn

Green, Morris Lee
1960   This Rebel Breed

Green, Nora
1939   Moon over Harlem

Green, Urbie
1956   The Benny Goodman Story

Green, Walter
1918   Hitting the Trail

Green, William E. *not the same as* **Green, Billy**
1950   Emergency Wedding
1951   Gambling House
1952   Indian Uprising
1959   The Jayhawkers!

Greenberg, Henry
1959   Al Capone

Greenberg, Joseph *see* **Green, Joseph** (*dir, prod, writer*)

Greene, Angela
1944   Mr. Skeffington
1947   Humoresque
        King of the Bandits
1955   Shotgun

Greene, Clarence
1951   The Well
1959   Thunder in the Sun

Greene, Clay M.
1916   Broken Chains

Greene, Eve
1934   Operator 13
1935   Alas sobre el Chaco

Greene, Harold (*prod*)
1948   Sleep, My Love

Greene, Harrison *same as* **Green, Harrison**
1934   Broadway Bill
        Our Daily Bread
1935   Charlie Chan in Shanghai
        A Night at the Ritz
1936   Sea Spoilers
1937   It Could Happen to You
1938   In Old Chicago
        Mr. Moto's Gamble
        Passport Husband
        Speed to Burn
1940   Viva Cisco Kid
1945   Escape in the Fog
        Nob Hill
        Where Do We Go From Here?

Greene, Ira
1940   George Washington Carver
        Overture to Glory

Greene, Jaclynne
1953   The Stand at Apache River
1959   The Crimson Kimono

Greene, Joe *see* **Greene, Joseph J.**

Greene, Joel
1957   Burden of Truth

Greene, Joseph J. *same as* **Green, Joe**; **Greene, Joe** *not the same as* **Green, Joseph** (*dir, prod, writer*)
1945   Nob Hill
        A Tree Grows in Brooklyn
1949   Roll Thunder Roll!
1950   The Baron of Arizona
        I Killed Geronimo
1957   Man in the Shadow
1959   Night of the Quarter Moon

Greene, Margaret
1917   One Law for Both

Greene, Marion L.
1955   Brevities of 1955

Greene, Otis
1955   The View from Pompey's Head

Greene, Ray
1946   Stars on Parade

Greene, Richard
1938   My Lucky Star

Greenfield, Darwin
1950   Panic in the Streets

Greenfield, Rose
1936   Love and Sacrifice
1937   I Want to Be a Mother
1940   Eli Eli
        The Great Advisor
        Her Second Mother
        The Jewish Melody

Greenleaf, Raymond
1949   Pinky
1950   A Ticket to Tomahawk
1955   Headline Hunters
        Violent Saturday

Greenstreet, Sydney
1942   Across the Pacific
        They Died With Their Boots On

Greenway, Tom
1950   A Lady Without Passport
1951   The Harlem Globetrotters
        Jim Thorpe—All-American
        Westward the Women
1952   High Noon
        My Man and I
1953   Ride, Vaquero!

Greenwood, Charlotte
1943   The Gang's All Here

Greenwood, Clara
1921   Cheated Love

Greenwood, Ethel
1951   Molly
1956   Giant

Greer, Allan *same as* **Greer, Allen**
1936   Custer's Last Stand
        The Glory Trail

Greer, Dabbs
1950   Devil's Doorway
1952   My Man and I
1953   Dream Wife
1955   Foxfire
        Seven Angry Men
1957   All Mine to Give
        Pawnee
1959   Last Train from Gun Hill

Greer, Jane
1946   Sunset Pass

Gregg, Arnold
1920   White Youth

Gregg, Helen
1928   Orphan of the Sage

Gregg, Reverend
1934   Imitation of Life

Gregg, Virginia
1946   Notorious
1947   Body and Soul
1948   Gentleman's Agreement
1959   The Hanging Tree
1960   All the Fine Young Cannibals

Gregor, Arthur
1931   La fruta amarga

Gregor, Nora
1930   Olimpia (*foreign version*)
1931   El proceso de Mary Dugan (*foreign version*)

Gregory, Anne
1917   Under False Colors

Gregory, Betty
1946   Abie's Irish Rose

Gregory, James
1959   Al Capone

Gregory, Mary
1957   Trooper Hook

Gregory, Paul
1930   Whoopee

Gregory, Stephan
1945   The Shanghai Cobra

Gregory, Walter
1936   General Spanky

Grei, Carol
1953   So Big

Greig, Robert
1932   The Cohens and Kellys in Hollywood
1933   It's Great to Be Alive
        Robbers' Roost
1939   Drums Along the Mohawk
        Way Down South
1941   Sullivan's Travels
1942   Tales of Manhattan
        Three Hearts for Julia
1945   Nob Hill

Greiner, Fritz
1931   Tropennächte

Grenier, Larry
1944   An American Romance

Gresham, Velma
1934   Straight Is the Way

Grey, Albert L.
1924   His Darker Self

Grey, Harry *not the same as* **Gray, Harry**
1937   Manhattan
        Merry-Go-Round
1940   Covered Wagon Days
1941   Under Fiesta Stars
1944   Lake Placid Serenade
Grey, Ian
1941   Sun Valley Serenade
Grey, Jack *same as* **Grey, Jack C.**
1937   Big City
1939   Stand Up and Fight
1941   The Mexican Spitfire's
        Baby
Grey, Jane
1916   Man and His Angel
1918   The Birth of a Race
Grey, John
1928   Chinatown Charlie
1932   Hypnotized
1945   I Love a Bandleader
Grey, Lynda
1941   Louisiana Purchase
1942   Holiday Inn
Grey, Nan
1936   Sea Spoilers
        Sutter's Gold
Grey, Patricia
1927   Bitter Apples
Grey, Robert b. in Oakland, CA *not the same as* **Gray, Robert** b. in Houlton, ME
1916   The Twin Triangle
1922   Big Stakes
Grey, Sadie
1923   Deceit
Grey, Sydney de *see* **De Grey, Sidney**
Grey, Terry
1936   El diablo del mar
Grey, Virginia *same as* **Gray, Virginia**
1928   Uncle Tom's Cabin
1940   Three Cheers for the Irish
1946   Swamp Fire
1948   Unconquered
1951   Slaughter Trail
1952   Desert Pursuit
1955   The Last Command
        The Rose Tattoo
Grey Eagle
1956   Westward Ho the
        Wagons!
Grey Shadow, a dog
1944   My Pal Wolf
Gribble, Donna Jo
1945   The Dolly Sisters
1948   The Boy with Green Hair
Gribbon, Eddie *same as* **Gribbon, Edward**
1922   Captain Fly-by-Night
1923   The Victor
1924   East of Broadway
1926   Desert Gold
        The Flaming Frontier
1927   The Callahans and the
        Murphys
1928   United States Smith
1931   Mr. Lemon of Orange
1935   The Cyclone Ranger
1937   Big City
Gribbon, Harry
1928   The Cameraman
        Chinatown Charlie
Grider, Josh
1954   Go Man Go
Griffies, Ethel
1933   A Lady's Profession
1941   Dead Men Tell
1942   Castle in the Desert
1946   Saratoga Trunk
Griffin, Alex
1920   Our Christianity and
        Nobody's Child
Griffin, Carlton E.
1934   She Was a Lady
        Stand Up and Cheer!
1936   Dangerous Intrigue
Griffin, Charles
1937   Slave Ship
1949   Rose of the Yukon

Griffin, Chris
1956   The Benny Goodman
        Story
Griffin, Denise
1955   Murder in Villa Capri
Griffin, Douglas
1924   The House Behind the
        Cedars
Griffin, Eleanore
1943   In Old Oklahoma
1944   Hi, Beautiful
1945   Nob Hill
1955   Good Morning, Miss Dove
        A Man Called Peter
1959   Imitation of Life
Griffin, Frank *(actor)*
1954   Dangerous Mission
1958   Bullwhip
Griffin, Frank *(dir, prod, writer)*
1924   Conductor 1492
1927   Lost at the Front
Griffin, Jimmy
1944   An American Romance
Griffin, Robert E. *same as* **Griffin, Robert**
1950   Broken Arrow
1951   The Magnificent Yankee
1952   Indian Uprising
1953   Conquest of Cochise
1954   The Black Dakotas
1955   Bad Day at Black Rock
        Shotgun
1957   Pawnee
1958   The Badlanders
1960   Ice Palace
Griffin, Stephanie
1956   The Last Wagon
Griffin, Ted
1916   Gold and the Woman
Griffin, William
1948   The Fight Never Ends
Griffith, Bea
1947   Reet, Petite and Gone
Griffith, Bill *see* **Griffith, William**
Griffith, Billy *see* **Griffith, William**
Griffith, Catherine
1935   Naughty Marietta
Griffith, Corinne
1917   I Will Repay
1926   Into Her Kingdom
Griffith, D. W.
1915   The Birth of a Nation
        The Lamb
        The Penitentes
        The Sable Lorcha
1916   Little Meena's Romance
1918   The Greatest Thing in
        Life
        The Hun Within
1919   Scarlet Days
1930   Abraham Lincoln
Griffith, Edward H.
1917?   Barnaby Lee
1921   The Land of Hope
1928   Hold 'Em Yale
1941   Virginia
Griffith, Eleanor
1922   Cardigan
Griffith, Gordon *same as* **Griffith, Gordon S.**
1920   Huckleberry Finn
1941   Adam Had Four Sons
1947   The Jolson Story
Griffith, Hugh
1960   The Day They Robbed the
        Bank of England
Griffith, James *same as* **Griffith, James J.**
1949   Daughter of the West
1950   The Breaking Point
        The Cariboo Trail
        Indian Territory
        Young Man with a Horn
1951   Apache Drums
1954   The Black Dakotas
        Drum Beat
1955   Apache Ambush
1957   The Guns of Fort
        Petticoat
        Raintree County
1958   Bullwhip
        Frontier Gun

Griffith, Katherine
1918   In Judgment Of
1919   A Yankee Princess
1920   Huckleberry Finn
Griffith, Kay
1938   My Lucky Star
1940   Covered Wagon Days
Griffith, Kenneth
1942   Holiday Inn
Griffith, Raymond
1935   L'homme des Folies
        Bergère
1936   It Had to Happen
1939   Drums Along the Mohawk
1940   The Man I Married
        The Mark of Zorro
Griffith, W. L.
1930   La rosa de fuego
1936   Amor que vuelve
Griffith, William *same as* **Griffith, Bill; Griffith, Billy**
1934   Operator 13
1950   Jiggs and Maggie Out
        West
1952   The Iron Mistress
Grimes, Alvin
1958   Tonka
Grimes, Bill
1953   So Big
Grimes, Chicky
1949?   Harlem Follies
Grimes, Karolyn
1948   Unconquered
1949   Lust for Gold
1950   Rio Grande
Grimes, Tom
1923   The Secret of the Pueblo
Grimes, William H.
1924?   The Flaming Crisis
Grindé, Nick
1929   The Desert Rider
1930   Wu Li Chang
1938   Mis dos amores
1939   King of Chinatown
Grindle, Richard
1952   It's a Big Country: An
        American Anthology
Grinstead, Durward
1937   Maid of Salem
Grippo, Jan
1947   Bowery Buckaroos
Grisel, Louis *same as* **Grizel, Louis**
1916   Broken Chains
1919   His Parisian Wife
Grismer, Joseph R.
1916   Broken Chains
Grissell, Wallace *same as* **Grissell, Wallace A.**
1944   Marshal of Reno
        Vigilantes of Dodge City
1945   Wanderer of the
        Wasteland
1947   Wild Horse Mesa
1948   Western Heritage
Griswold, Grace
1922   Anna Ascends
Griswold, Herbert Spencer
1925   Hogan's Alley
Grizel, Louis *see* **Grisel, Louis**
Grosman, Miriam *see* **Grossman, Miriam**
Gross, A.
1940   Americaner Schadchen
Gross, Adella
1955   Brevities of 1955
Gross, Edward
1936   Rainbow on the River
Gross, Jack J. *same as* **Gross, Jack**
1945   Johnny Angel
1948   Fighting Father Dunne
1951   The Mark of the
        Renegade
1957   Pawnee
Leon Gross' Orchestra
1938   God's Step Children
        Swing!
Gross, W. J.
1917   The Bar Sinister
        The Barrier

Grossman, F. Maury
1939   Los hijos mandan
Grossman, Helen
1939   Tevya
Grossman, Irving
1950   Catskill Honeymoon
Grossman, Miriam *same as* **Grosman, Miriam; Grossman, M.**
1935   The Yiddish King Lear
1940   Americaner Schadchen
        The Great Advisor
Grout, Austin
1931   Delicious
Grover, Leonard
1914   The Redemption of David
        Corson
Groves, Jerry
1946   Dangerous Money
1960   Walk Like a Dragon
Grozier, Bernie
1958   Fort Massacre
Gruber, Frank
1945   Johnny Angel
1950   The Cariboo Trail
1951   Flaming Feather
        Warpath
Gruber, Merele
1935   Shir Hashirim
Grudberg, Icchok
1939   A Brivele der Mamen
Gruen, James
1928   Anybody Here Seen Kelly?
        Riley the Cop
Grünbaum, Herbert
1931   Die Dreigroschenoper
Gruning, Ilka
1942   Friendly Enemies
1944   An American Romance
1946   Rendezvous 24
1947   Desperate
Grut, D. Jersey
1957   Gun Battle at Monterey
The Guadalajara Trio
1942   Rio Rita
1945   South of the Rio Grande
1946   Slightly Scandalous
Guard, Kit
1934   Broadway Bill
        The Cactus Kid
1935?   The Irish Gringo
1937   Shadows of the Orient
1951   Fort Defiance
Guardino, Harry
1958   Houseboat
The Guardsmen
1941   Playmates
Gudinsky, Bella
1930   Eternal Fools (Ewige
        Naranim)
Guedel, John
1936   General Spanky
Guedry, C. P.
1948   Louisiana Story
Guercio, Camillo
1953   Tonight We Sing
Guerin, Bruce
1922   The Woman He Loved
Guerin, Johnny
1958   Tonka
Guerra, Francesca
1916   Poor Little Peppina
Guerrero, Carmen
1930   Amor audaz
        Una cana al aire
        Cascarrabias
        Locuras de amor
1931   Carne de cabaret
        Drácula
        La gran jornada
Guerrero, Ramón
1930   Sevilla de mis amores
1936   Contra la corriente
Guerrero, Raul
1940   Perfidia
Guerrero, Tony
1940   Northwest Passage (Book
        I—Rogers' Rangers)

Guevara, Elías
1930   Las campanas de
        Capistrano
1935   El cantante de Nápoles
Guhl, George
1935   A Night at the Opera
        The Winning Ticket
1936   After the Thin Man
        My American Wife
1937   Charlie Chan on
        Broadway
1939   The Adventures of
        Huckleberry Finn
1940   Little Nellie Kelly
1941   Birth of the Blues
1942   Woman of the Year
1943   The Amazing Mrs.
        Holliday
Guidé, Paul
1930   Toda una vida (*foreign
        version*)
Guidry, Joseph
1953   Thunder Bay
Guiffre, Carlo
1958   Seven Hills of Rome
Guihan, Frances *same as* **Guihan,
Frances E.**
1916   The Soul of Kura-San
1918   His Birthright
1919   The Courageous Coward
        A Heart in Pawn
        His Debt
Guilford, Willor Lee
1930   A Daughter of the Congo
        Easy Street
1932   Ten Minutes to Live
Guilfoyle, Paul
1936   Winterset
1940   East of the River
1950   Davy Crockett, Indian
        Scout
1954   Apache
1955   Chief Crazy Horse
        Not As a Stranger
        Trial
Guillerme, Olimpio
1929   Hambre
Guillermin, John
1960   The Day They Robbed the
        Bank of England
Guinan, Texas
1919   The She Wolf
Guinn, James
1938   The Texans
Guiol, Clara
1931   Noche de duendes
Guiol, Fred
1933   The Cohens and Kellys in
        Trouble
1936   Silly Billies
1956   Giant
Guisado, Oscar
1931   Regeneración
Guise, Janine
1931   Chérie
Guise, Thomas J.
1918   Free and Equal
Guízar, Tito
1938   Mis dos amores
1939   El otro soy yo
        Papá soltero
        El trovador de la radio
1940   Cuando canta la Ley
1947   On the Old Spanish Trail
Gulfport, Billy
1927   The Spider's Web
Gullan, Campbell
1920?   Her Story
Gulliver, Dorothy
1934   Stand Up and Cheer!
1936   Custer's Last Stand
Gum, Wong
1934   Blossom Time
Gumley, Leonard
1950   Sands of Iwo Jima
Gump, Diane
1956   Serenade
Gump, Irving
1945   Nob Hill
        A Tree Grows in Brooklyn

Gunderson, Roger
1955   The Rose Tattoo
Gunn, Charles
1916   Three of Many
Gunn, Earl
1941   Secret of the Wastelands
Gunn, Fronzie
1921   Made in Heaven
Gunn, Herbert
1941   Sun Valley Serenade
Gunning, Wid
1928   The Hawk's Nest
Gurie, Sigrid
1940   Three Faces West
Gurs, Peter
1947   Northwest Outpost
Gushkin, Anna *see* **Guskin, Anna**
Gusick, John
1955   Seven Cities of Gold
Guskin, Anna *same as* **Gushkin,
Anna**
1939   The Light Ahead
1940   Americaner Schadchen
Gustafsson, Sven
1930   Un hombre de suerte
        (*foreign version*)
Gustine, Paul
1937   Hills of Old Wyoming
1946   Without Reservations
1959   Imitation of Life
Gutentag, Bertha, Madam *same as*
Guttentag, Bertha
1932   Mazel Tov
1937   The Cantor's Son
Guth, Raymond
1959   Inside the Mafia
Guthrie, A. B., Jr.
1960   This Rebel Breed
Guthrie, Jean Ann Rose
1942   American Empire
Gutiérrez, Leopoldo
1938   Di que me quieres
Gutiérrez, Olga
1955   Seven Cities of Gold
Gutiérrez, Rubí
1935   Rosa de Francia
1936   Ramona
Gutstein, L., Dr.
1936   Sutter's Gold
Guttentag, Bertha *see* **Gutentag,
Bertha, Madam**
Guttman, Henry
1943   Action in the North
        Atlantic
        They Came to Blow Up
        America
1951   Go for Broke!
1953   The Stars Are Singing
Guy, Andre
1951   Go for Broke!
Guy, Claude
1951   Go for Broke!
Guy, Eula
1943   They Came to Blow Up
        America
1948   The Boy with Green Hair
        The Miracle of the Bells
1949   Call of the Forest
1950   Mystery Street
        Stars in My Crown
1951   The Great Caruso
Guyse, Sheila
1947   Boy! What a Girl!
        Sepia Cinderella
1948   Miracle in Harlem
Guzda, O.
1939   Cossacks in Exile
Guzmán, Agustín
1936   El crimen de media
        noche
Guzman, Chinto
1951   Apache Drums
Guzmán, Gloria
1931   Un caballero de frac
        Las luces de Buenos Aires
Guzmán, Roberto *same as*
Guzmán, Roberto E.
1930   The Bad Man (*foreign
        version*)
        Del mismo barro
        Monsieur le Fox
        La voluntad del muerto

1931   La gran jornada
        El impostor
1934   Un capitán de cosacos
Gwenn, Edmund
1936   Mad Holiday
1943   The Meanest Man in the
        World
Gwynne, Anne
1941   Road Agent
Gyrath, Thelma
1946   Without Reservations
Haade, William *same as* **Haade,
Bill**
1938   The Texans
1940   Geronimo
        Knute Rockne—All
        American
1941   Accent on Love
        Hurry, Charlie, Hurry
1942   Juke Girl
        The Navy Comes Through
1943   Action in the North
        Atlantic
        Dr. Gillespie's Criminal
        Case
1944   An American Romance
        Sheriff of Las Vegas
        Slightly Terrific
        Three Men in White
1945   Nob Hill
        Phantom of the Plains
1946   Bringing Up Father
        The Gentleman
        Misbehaves
1947   Buck Privates Come
        Home
1948   Key Largo
        Tap Roots
        Unconquered
1949   Knock on Any Door
1950   Ambush
        Rock Island Trail
1951   Oh! Susanna
1953   San Antone
Haal, Renee
1941   Hurry, Charlie, Hurry
Haas, Charles
1948   Moonrise
Haas, Dorothy
1936   Star for a Night
Haas, Hugo
1945   Jealousy
1947   The Foxes of Harrow
        Northwest Outpost
1948   My Girl Tisa
1949   The Fighting Kentuckian
1951   The Girl on the Bridge
1959   Night of the Quarter
        Moon
Haber, Nicholas S.
1921   The Syrian Immigrant
Hack, Herman
1947   Marshal of Cripple Creek
Hackathorne, George
1918   Amarilly of Clothes-Line
        Alley
        Huck and Tom; or, the
        Further Adventures of
        Tom Sawyer
1920   The Last of the Mohicans
1934   Strange Wives
1936   Show Boat
1939   Gone With the Wind
Hackel, A. W.
1936   Border Phantom
1940   Am I Guilty?
Hackett, Albert *same as* **Hackett,
Albert M.**
1919   Come Out of the Kitchen
1920   The Good-Bad Wife
1930   Whoopee
1935   Naughty Marietta
1936   After the Thin Man
Hackett, Carl *see* **Hackett, Karl**
Hackett, Florence
1916   The Yellow Passport
1916?   Should a Baby Die?
1920?   Broken Hearts
Hackett, Hal
1947   Dark Delusion

Hackett, Karl *same as* **Hackett,
Carl**
1936   Border Phantom
        Down to the Sea
        The Traitor
1941   The Pioneers
1944   Sonora Stagecoach
        Tucson Raiders
1946   Canyon Passage
Hackett, Lillian
1924   In Hollywood With
        Potash and Perlmutter
Hackett, William A.
1918   The Spreading Evil
Hadden, George
1934   Charlie Chan's Courage
Haddon, Harriette
1933   It's Great to Be Alive
1934   Stand Up and Cheer!
1936   Star for a Night
1938   Daughter of Shanghai
        In Old Chicago
1939   King of Chinatown
Haddon, Pauline
1937   Souls at Sea
Haden, Sara *same as* **Haden, Sarah**
1935   Black Fury
1937   The Barrier
1939   Judge Hardy and Son
1942   Woman of the Year
1944   Andy Hardy's Blonde
        Trouble
1945   Our Vines Have Tender
        Grapes
1946   Bad Bascomb
Hadfield, Harry
1915   Chimmie Fadden Out
        West
Hadfield, Tedd
1959   Imitation of Life
Hadji-Razul
1938   Zamboanga
Hadley, Bert
1918   Her Moment
1924   The Lightning Rider
Hadley, Reed
1941   Road Agent
1945   The House on 92nd St.
1949   Riders of the Range
1950   The Baron of Arizona
1951   Little Big Horn
1952   The Half-Breed
Hadnott, William
1949   Lookout Sister
Haefeli, Charles *same as* **Haefeli,
Jockey**
1935   Charlie Chan in Shanghai
1936   The Prisoner of Shark
        Island
1937   Charlie Chan on
        Broadway
1938   Road Demon
1939   Winner Take All
Haeseler, John A.
1949   Tale of the Navajos
Hafner, Les
1946   That Man of Mine
Hagan, Dorothy *same as* **Hagar,
Dorothy**
1918   Hell's End
1919   The Westerners
Hageman, Richard
1947   New Orleans
1950   The Toast of New Orleans
1951   The Great Caruso
Hagen, George
1933   L'amour guide
Hagen, Holger
1960   Man on a String
Hagen, Jean
1950   Ambush
Hagen, Kevin
1958   The Light in the Forest
Hagenbruch, Charlotte
1931   La llama sagrada (*foreign
        version*)
        Die Maske Fällt
Hagerthy, Ron
1953   The Charge at Feather
        River

Haggerty, Don
1948   Angel in Exile
        Fighting Father Dunne
        Gun Smugglers
1949   The Cowboy and the
        Prizefighter
        Rustlers
1950   Sands of Iwo Jima
        Storm Over Wyoming
1951   Gambling House
        Go for Broke!
1958   Blood Arrow

Hagio, Taski
1937   Big City

Hagman, Harriet
1932   Thirteen Women

Hagney, Frank same as **Hagney, Frank S.**
1921   Anne of Little Smoky
1923   Backbone
1925   Braveheart
        Hogan's Alley
        The Wild Bull's Lair
1927   The Frontiersman
1928   The Glorious Trail
        The Rawhide Kid
1929   Masked Emotions
1931   Fighting Caravans
        The Squaw Man
1936   Robin Hood of El Dorado
1937   Big City
1940   Northwest Passage (Book
        I—Rogers' Rangers)
1942   Gentleman Jim
        Sunday Punch
1946   Saratoga Trunk
1947   California
1948   Harpoon
        The Paleface
        Unconquered
1949   Knock on Any Door
        Streets of Laredo
1953   Ride, Vaquero!
1955   The Last Command
1957   The Guns of Fort
        Petticoat
1959   The Jayhawkers!
        Last Train from Gun Hill

Hagood, Kenny "Pancho" see **Pancho and Delores**

Hague, Howard R.
1957   Burden of Truth

Hahn, Philip
1914   The Nightingale
1916   The Scarlet Oath

Haig, Douglas
1928   Sins of the Fathers
1929   Welcome Danger
1931   The Cisco Kid
1932   Call Her Savage

Haily, Bert
1920?   Reformation

Haines, Bob could be same as **Haines, Robert**
1932   Hypnotized

Haines, Nola
1951   The Great Caruso

Haines, Rhea
1914   An Odyssey of the North
1915?   The Beachcomber
1919   Scarlet Days

Haines, Robert could be same as **Haines, Bob**
1955   Trial

Haines, Sally
1933   It's Great to Be Alive

Haines, Sol
1936   Star for a Night

Haines, William
1930   Estrellados

Haines, William Wister
1937   Black Legion
1938   The Texans

Hainey, Betty Jean
1936   Dimples

Hairston, Jester
1941   Sullivan's Travels
1942   The Vanishing Virginian
1956   Full of Life

Jester Hairston Choir same as **Jester Hairston Singers**
1947   The Foxes of Harrow
1951   Yes Sir, Mr. Bones

Hairston, Margaret same as **Hairston, Margaret Lancaster**
1954   Carmen Jones
1959   Porgy and Bess

Halama, Loda
1951   Gambling House

Haldeman, Tim
1955   Good Morning, Miss Dove

Hale, Alan
1914   The Woman in Black
1916   Pudd'nhead Wilson
        The Scarlet Oath
1925   Braveheart
1930   She Got What She Wanted
1931   Aloha
1932   The Match King
        So Big
1934   Broadway Bill
        Imitation of Life
1937   Music for Madame
1940   The Fighting 69th
        Santa Fe Trail
        Three Cheers for the Irish
1942   Gentleman Jim
        Juke Girl
1943   Action in the North
        Atlantic
1947   My Wild Irish Rose
1948   My Girl Tisa
1950   Colt .45
        Stars in My Crown

Hale, Alan, Jr. sometimes also known as **Alan Hale**
1942   Rubber Racketeers
1948   Music Man
1952   Arctic Flight
1953   Captain John Smith and
        Pocahontas
        The Man Behind the Gun
1955   The Indian Fighter
1957   All Mine to Give

Hale, Barbara
1943   Mexican Spitfire's Blessed
        Event
1948   The Boy with Green Hair
1949   The Clay Pigeon
1950   Emergency Wedding
        Jolson Sings Again
1953   Last of the Comanches
        Seminole
1955   The Far Horizons
1956   7th Cavalry
1957   The Oklahoman

Hale, Bill
1950   Ambush
        Raiders of Tomahawk
        Creek
1954   Battle of Rogue River
        Massacre Canyon
1955   Apache Ambush
1956   Giant
        The Last Frontier
        Reprisal!
        The White Squaw
1959   Gunmen from Laredo

Hale, Bob same as **Hale, Bobby**
1939   Charlie Chan in Reno
        Mr. Moto Takes a
        Vacation
1940   Escape to Glory
1948   Jiggs and Maggie in Court

Hale, Creighton
1924   The Mine with the Iron
        Door
1936   Custer's Last Stand
1937   Charlie Chan on
        Broadway
1939   Daughters Courageous
1940   East of the River
        Knute Rockne—All
        American
        Santa Fe Trail
1942   All Through the Night
        Wings for the Eagle
1943   Action in the North
        Atlantic
        Yankee Doodle Dandy
1944   Mr. Skeffington
1947   Humoresque

1949   The Girl from Jones
        Beach
        The Story of Seabiscuit
1956   Serenade

Hale, Fiona
1955   Shotgun

Hale, Georgia
1928   The Rawhide Kid

Hale, Gladys
1934   Broadway Bill

Hale, John d. 1947
1935   A Night at the Ritz

Hale, Jonathan d. 1966
1935   A Night at the Opera
1936   After the Thin Man
        Charlie Chan at the Race
        Track
        Charlie Chan's Secret
1937   Charlie Chan at the
        Olympics
        Man of the People
1938   Breaking the Ice
        Road Demon
1939   Stand Up and Fight
1943   The Amazing Mrs.
        Holliday
        Jack London
1944   Since You Went Away
1947   Black Gold
1948   Call Northside 777
        Rocky
        Tap Roots
1949   Rose of the Yukon
1950   The Baron of Arizona
1951   The Tall Target
1953   The Glory Brigade
        Taxi
1955   Headline Hunters

Hale, Karen
1951   Westward the Women

Hale, Louise Closser
1930   Big Boy
1932   The Son-Daughter

Hale, Monte
1945   Colorado Pioneers
1946   California Gold Rush
        Sun Valley Cyclone
1949   Ranger of Cherokee Strip
1950   The Missourians
1956   Giant

Hale, Nancy
1944   Something for the Boys
1956   The White Squaw

Hale, Rex
1937   Nation Aflame

Hale, Richard
1944   Knickerbocker Holiday
1953   San Antone
1954   Drum Beat
        Passion
1956   Pillars of the Sky

Hale, Teddy same as **Hall, Teddy**
1939   Lying Lips
        Straight to Heaven

Haley, Aileen
1941   Louisiana Purchase
1942   Three Hearts for Julia

Haley, Earl
1933   King of the Wild Horses

Haley, W. P.
1950   Intruder in the Dust

Halferty, James
1960   Cimarron

Hall, Adelyn
1934   Broadway Bill

Hall, Alexander same as **Hall, Alex**
1918   Doing Their Bit
1934   Limehouse Blues

Hall, Alfred
1941   You're Out of Luck
1942   Sunday Punch
        We Were Dancing

Hall, Ben
1935   Naughty Marietta
1936   After the Thin Man
1944   An American Romance
1948   My Girl Tisa

Hall, Betty
1949   Knock on Any Door

Hall, Bill see **Hall, William "Bill"**

Hall, Charles same as **Hall, Charlie**
1929   Why Bring That Up?
1931   Los calaveras
        Los calaveras (foreign
        version)
        Delicious
        Noche de duendes
        Politiquerías
1940   Mexican Spitfire Out
        West
1943   His Butler's Sister
1944   Hi, Beautiful
1946   Abie's Irish Rose
        Without Reservations

Hall, David
1944   Tomorrow the World!

Hall, Donald
1919?   The Chosen Path
1920   The Great Shadow
1920?   The Greatest Love

Hall, Donna
1951   Westward the Women

Hall, Earl
1940   While Thousands Cheer
1941   Four Shall Die

Hall, Eddie
1943   Good Luck, Mr. Yates
1944   Since You Went Away

Hall, Edmund
1957   Satchmo the Great

Hall, Ella
1916   The Love Girl
1917   A Jewel in Pawn

Hall, Frank G.
1919   The Other Man's Wife

Hall, Gordon
1940   The Ramparts We Watch

Hall, Henry
1934   Our Daily Bread
1935   Circle of Death
1936   General Spanky
1940   Santa Fe Trail
1943   Ladies' Day
1944   Sonora Stagecoach
1945   The Jade Mask
        Phantom of the Plains
1946   The Sailor Takes a Wife

Hall, Howard
1917   The Barrier

Hall, Huntz
1942   Let's Get Tough!
1944   Block Busters
1947   Bowery Buckaroos

Hall, Iris
1919   The Homesteader
1920   The Symbol of the
        Unconquered

Hall, J. Albert
1915   Children of the Ghetto
        The Girl I Left Behind Me

Hall, James
1926   The Campus Flirt
1929   Smiling Irish Eyes
        This Is Heaven
1930   Galas de la Paramount

Hall, Jon same as **Locher, Charles**
1935   Charlie Chan in Shanghai
1940   Kit Carson
1947   Last of the Redmen
1951   Hurricane Island
        When the Redskins Rode
1952   Brave Warrior

Hall, Juanita
1948   Miracle in Harlem

The Juanita Hall Choir
1948   Miracle in Harlem same
        as **The Juanita Hall
        Singers**
1940   Paradise in Harlem

Hall, Lillian
1920   The Last of the Mohicans

Hall, Lindsay J.
1914   When Broadway Was a
        Trail
1921   The Sport of the Gods

Hall, Lois
1950   Cherokee Uprising
1951   Cuban Fireball
        Slaughter Trail

Hall, Maie
1917   A Jewel in Pawn
Hall, Marian
1942   Secret Enemies
Hall, Milton
1939   Reform School
Hall, Newton
1920   Dinty
Hall, Norman S. *same as* **Hall, Norman Shannon**
1944   The San Antonio Kid
        Sheriff of Las Vegas
        Vigilantes of Dodge City
1949   Rose of the Yukon
1950   Indian Territory
1952   Apache Country
1959   The Young Land
Hall, Porter
1937   The Plainsman
        Souls at Sea
1938   Dangerous to Know
1941   Sullivan's Travels
1944   Going My Way
1948   Unconquered
1950   Intruder in the Dust
1952   The Half-Breed
Hall, Richard
1944   An American Romance
        Three Men in White
Hall, Robert
1954   Go Man Go
Hall, Ruth
1932   The Heart of New York
1933   Man from Monterey
1934   Beloved
Hall, Sherry
1934   Charlie Chan's Courage
        Coming Out Party
        Operator 13
        Straight Is the Way
1935   Rendezvous
        The Winning Ticket
1936   After the Thin Man
        Mad Holiday
1937   Charlie Chan on
        Broadway
        Man of the People
1938   Charlie Chan at Monte
        Carlo
        Mr. Moto's Gamble
1945   Betrayal from the East
1946   Canyon Passage
1948   Big City
1950   Mystery Street
1951   Gambling House
        The Magnificent Yankee
        The Tall Target
        The Well
1952   It's a Big Country: An
        American Anthology
Hall, Stewart
1944   Lake Placid Serenade
Hall, Teddy *see* **Hale, Teddy**
Hall, Thurston
1918   An Alien Enemy
        The Midnight Patrol
        The Squaw Man
1919   The Unpainted Woman
        Who Will Marry Me?
1920?   The Scarlet Dragon
1922   Fair Lady
1938   Little Miss Roughneck
1941   Accent on Love
        Where Did You Get That
        Girl?
1942   Twin Beds
        We Were Dancing
1943   Crash Dive
1944   Something for the Boys
1945   The Gay Senorita
1946   Saratoga Trunk
        Without Reservations
1947   Black Gold
        The Farmer's Daughter
        It Had To Be You
1948   Up in Central Park
1949   Stagecoach Kid
1950   Bandit Queen
        Belle of Old Mexico
Hall, Virginia
1953   Old Overland Trail

Hall, William "Bill" *same as* **Hall, Bill; Hall, William** *not the same as* **Hall, Willie**
1947   California
1948   Unconquered
1950   Annie Get Your Gun
1951   Show Boat
Hall, Willie
1930   King of Jazz
Hall, Winter
1917   The Bronze Bride
1918   The Bravest Way
        The City of Dim Faces
        The Squaw Man
1919   The Right to Happiness
1920   The Third Woman
1922   East Is West
        Saturday Night
1934   Judge Priest
1935   Rendezvous
1937   Slave Ship
1940   Escape
Hallacher, Harold
1918   The Unbeliever
Hallaran, Pat
1950   Damien
Hallard, C. M.
1920?   Her Story
Haller, Magda
1940   Perfidia
Hallett, Al
1925   The Gold Hunters
Halliday, Jack
1932   Parigi affascina; ovvero,
        Malavita
Halliday, John
1929   East Side Sadie
1940   Escape to Glory
Halligan, William
1941   Accent on Love
        Playmates
1942   Foreign Agent
        Tales of Manhattan
1943   Dixie
        The Leopard Man
Hallor, Edith
1937   Maid of Salem
Hallor, Ethel
1922   The Cub Reporter
Hallor, Ray
1929   In Old California
1932   Hidden Valley
Halloran, John
1947   The Last Round-Up
1951   Only the Valiant
1952   Bugles in the Afternoon
1953   San Antone
1957   The Deerslayer
        The Halliday Brand
Halloway, Carol *same as* **Holloway, Carol**
1917   The Tenderfoot
1927   Jake the Plumber
1937   Maid of Salem
Halls, Ethel May *same as* **Halls, Ethyl May**
1940   The Way of All Flesh
1945   A Tree Grows in Brooklyn
1946   Slightly Scandalous
1948   Old Los Angeles
Hallward, Joy
1949   Knock on Any Door
1951   Apache Drums
1953   So Big
Hallward, M.
1918   The Squaw Man
Halmay, Tibor von
1931   La pura verdad (*foreign
        version*)
Halop, Billy
1946   Gas House Kids
Halperin, Edward
1937   Nation Aflame
Halperin, Victor
1937   Nation Aflame
Halpern, Riesa
1938   The Singing Blacksmith
Halpin, Eugene, C.P.O.
1953   Beneath the 12-Mile Reef

Halsey, Brett
1958   Gunman's Walk
Halsey, Forrest
1920   White Youth
1931   La dama atrevida
Halsey, Mary
1942   Cat People
1943   Ladies' Day
        Mexican Spitfire's Blessed
        Event
1945   Betrayal from the East
Halsey, Mildred
1916   A Man of Sorrow
Halston, Howard
1920   It's a Great Life
Halton, Charles
1937   Black Legion
1939   Charlie Chan at Treasure
        Island
1940   Behind the News
        Little Nellie Kelly
1942   Across the Pacific
        Whispering Ghosts
1944   Address Unknown
1945   Rhapsody in Blue
        A Tree Grows in Brooklyn
1946   Singin' in the Corn
1949   The Daring Caballero
        3 Godfathers
1950   The Traveling
        Saleswoman
Hamada, Harry
1951   Go for Broke!
Hamaji, James
1951   Go for Broke!
Hamblen, Roland
1935   The Little Colonel
Hamel, William
1949   Streets of Laredo
1953   Dream Wife
1955   Seven Angry Men
Hamer, Gerald
1944   Hi, Beautiful
Hamer, Rusty
1953   Fort Ti
Hamerick, Burwell *see* **Hamrick, Burwell**
Hamilton, Bernie *same as* **Hamilton, Bernard**
1950   The Jackie Robinson Story
1951   The Harlem Globetrotters
1952   Bright Victory
Hamilton, Betty
1933   Victims of Persecution
Hamilton, Bret
1950   A Lady Without Passport
        Young Daniel Boone
1951   The Magnificent Yankee
Hamilton, Charles *same as* **Hamilton, Chuck**
1937   The Plainsman
1938   Little Miss Roughneck
1941   The Face Behind the
        Mask
        Mystery Ship
1944   The Racket Man
1945   Escape in the Fog
1947   Buck Privates Come
        Home
        Easy Come, Easy Go
        It Had To Be You
        The Last Round-Up
1948   Unconquered
1949   Knock on Any Door
1952   Anything Can Happen
        Indian Uprising
1953   The Man from the Alamo
Hamilton, Curtis
1957   Band of Angels
Hamilton, Donna
1949   House of Strangers
Hamilton, G. P., Jr.
1917   The Slacker (Metro
        Pictures Corp.)
Hamilton, George
1948   Tap Roots
1951   The Well
1960   All the Fine Young
        Cannibals

Hamilton, Gilbert P.
1914?   The Lust of the Red Man
Hamilton, Hale
1925   The Manicure Girl
1932   Call Her Savage
Hamilton, J. Frank
1943   The Amazing Mrs.
        Holliday
Hamilton, James Shelley
1924   North of 36
Hamilton, John *could be same as* **Hamilton, John R.** *not the same as* **Hamilton, John F.**
1937   It Could Happen to You
1938   Mr. Moto's Gamble
        Mr. Wong, Detective
1939   Confessions of a Nazi Spy
        Forged Passport
        Waterfront
1940   The Fatal Hour
1941   Hold Back the Dawn
1942   Across the Pacific
        In This Our Life
        Syncopation
        They Died With Their
        Boots On
        Wings for the Eagle
1943   Good Luck, Mr. Yates
        Yankee Doodle Dandy
1944   Hi, Beautiful
        Lake Placid Serenade
        Sheriff of Las Vegas
1945   Johnny Angel
1946   Shadows Over Chinatown
1947   The Foxes of Harrow
1950   Annie Get Your Gun
        Davy Crockett, Indian
        Scout
        The Missourians
        Right Cross
1951   The Great Caruso
1953   Jack McCall Desperado
1954   Sitting Bull
Hamilton, John F. *could be same as* **Hamilton, John R.** *not the same as* **Hamilton, John**
1939   Allegheny Uprising
1949   The Undercover Man
Hamilton, John R. *could be same as* **Hamilton, John** *or* **Hamilton, John F.**
1951   The Magnificent Yankee
Hamilton, Joseph H. *same as* **Hamilton, Joseph**
1958   Gunman's Walk
        The Rawhide Trail
1960   The Plunderers
Hamilton, Kim
1959   Odds Against Tomorrow
Hamilton, Kipp
1955   Good Morning, Miss Dove
1960   The Unforgiven
Hamilton, Lloyd
1924   His Darker Self
Hamilton, Mahlon
1917   The Red Woman
1921   That Girl Montana
1923   Little Old New York
1937   Big City
Hamilton, Marc *not the same as* **Hamilton, Mark**
1955   Headline Hunters
1956   Giant
        Man from Del Rio
Hamilton, Margaret
1934   Broadway Bill
1938   The Adventures of Tom
        Sawyer
        Breaking the Ice
1942   Twin Beds
1943   The Ox-Bow Incident
1948   Reaching from Heaven
Hamilton, Mark *not the same as* **Hamilton, Marc**
1927   Aflame in the Sky
1928   Heart Trouble
Hamilton, Maxwell
1948   The Miracle of the Bells
Hamilton, Murray
1952   Bright Victory
1958   Houseboat
1959   The FBI Story

Hamilton, Neil
1926   Desert Gold
1928   Mother Machree
1930   Anybody's War
        The Kibitzer
1944   Since You Went Away
1955   Murder in Villa Capri

Hamilton, Reed
1918   Love's Law

Hamilton, Robert
1945   Where Do We Go From
        Here?

Hamilton, Shorty
1918   Denny from Ireland
        The Ranger
1918?   The Snail
1922   Cross Roads

Hamm, Harry
1916   The Grip of Jealousy

Hammer, Alvin
1948   The Lady from Shanghai
1949   The Girl from Jones
        Beach
        Lust for Gold
1951   The Tall Target

Hammer, E. N. "Dick"
1949   Stallion Canyon

Hammer, Mike
1950   Catskill Honeymoon

Hammerstein, Oscar, II
1936   Show Boat

Hammett, Dashiell
1936   After the Thin Man

Hammond, Billy
1947   West to Glory
1949   Ride, Ryder, Ride!
        Stallion Canyon
1950   Riders of the Pony
        Express

Hammond, C. Norman *same as*
   Hammond, Charles
1916   Hop, the Devil's Brew
1918   An Alien Enemy
1921   Through the Back Door
1925   Irish Luck

Hammond, Frank *same as*
   Hammond, Frank H.
1934   Our Daily Bread
1935   The Little Colonel
1937   Maid of Salem

Hammond, Gilmore
1916   The Gilded Spider

Hammond, Harriet
1921   Bits of Life

Hammond, Kay (*American
   actress*), d. 1982
1930   Abraham Lincoln

Hammond, Kay (*British actress*), d.
   1980
1933   Racetrack

Hammond, Len
1941   Belle Starr

Hammond, Victor
1945   South of the Rio Grande

Hammond, Virginia
1934   Behold My Wife!
        Charlie Chan's Courage

Hammons, E. W.
1932   Hypnotized

Hampden, Walter
1942   They Died With Their
        Boots On

Hampton, Benjamin B.
1917   The Barrier
1919   Desert Gold
        The Westerners

Hampton, Grayce *same as*
   Hampton, Grace
1937   Souls at Sea
1946   Without Reservations
1949   Anna Lucasta
        The Girl from Jones
        Beach

Hampton, James
1960   Wild River

Hampton, Jesse D.
1920   Uncharted Channels
1921   That Girl Montana

Hampton, Lionel
1956   The Benny Goodman
        Story

Hampton, Orville *same as*
   Hampton, Orville H.
1950   Bandit Queen
        Train to Tombstone
1951   Mask of the Dragon
1952   Red Snow
1959   Inside the Mafia
1960   Oklahoma Territory

Hampton, Raye
1925   Quicker'n Lightnin'

Hampton University Choral Choir
1938   Hits and Bits of 1938

Hamrick, Burwell *same as*
   Hamerick, Burwell
1917   John Ermine of the
        Yellowstone
1918   How Could You, Jean?

Hanalis, Blanche
1960   Weddings and Babies

Hancharyk, S.
1939   Cossacks in Exile

Hancock, Elinor *same as* **Hancock,
   Eleanor**
1920   The Cup of Fury
        A Tokio Siren
1921   The Cave Girl
1922   Come On Over

Hand, Charles
1953   The Man from the Alamo

Handforth, Maude
1918   Little Red Decides

Handley, Tom
1948   Gentleman's Agreement

Handyside, Clarence *same as*
   Handysides, Clarence;
   Handysides, J. Clarence
1914   The Jungle
1916   Silks and Satins
1918   A Woman of Impulse

Hanemann, H. W.
1933   Rafter Romance
1943   Tahiti Honey

Hanford, Ray
1937   Maid of Salem
1938   The Buccaneer

Hanft, Jules
1925   Friendly Enemies

Hankin, Lieut.
1919   Injustice

Hankinson, Hank
1936   Klondike Annie

Hanlon, Alma
1916   Gold and the Woman

Hanlon, Bert
1932   The Golden West
        Me and My Gal
1936   Klondike Annie
1942   Gentleman Jim
1949   The Story of Seabiscuit
1950   The Daughter of Rosie
        O'Grady

Hanlon, Tom
1941   Where Did You Get That
        Girl?
1942   Sunday Punch
1949   The Undercover Man
1950   Right Cross
1951   The Harlem Globetrotters

Hanly, Tom
1949   Call of the Forest

Hanna, David
1935   Lem Hawkins' Confession

Hanna, Franklyn
1918   Doing Their Bit

Hannan, Chick *see* **Hannon, Chick**

Hannes, Art
1953   Taxi

Hannessy, April
1958   Seven Hills of Rome

Hannon, Betty
1948   The Paleface

Hannon, Chick *same as* **Hannan,
   Chick**
1940   Arizona Frontier
        Rhythm of the Rio
        Grande
1941   The Pioneers

1948   The Paleface
1953   Arrowhead

Hansell, Howell
1918   The Million Dollar
        Mystery

Hansen, Carl
1947   The Farmer's Daughter

Hansen, Earl
1955   The Lonesome Trail

Hansen, Else-Marie
1930   Un hombre de suerte
        (*foreign version*)

Hansen, Hans
1945   The House on 92nd St.

Hansen, Howard
1951   Saturday's Hero

Hansen, Myrna
1957   Raintree County

Hansen, Nina
1947   Northwest Outpost

Hansen, Peter *see* **Hanson, Peter**

Hansen, William
1949   Pinky
1953   The Member of the
        Wedding

Hanson, Einar
1926   Into Her Kingdom

Hanson, Erick
1945   Betrayal from the East

Hanson, Gladys
1914   The Straight Road

Hanson, Peter *same as* **Hansen,
   Peter**
1951   The Last Outpost
        Molly
1952   The Savage
1954   Drum Beat

Hanson, Ray
1936   Charlie Chan at the Race
        Track

Happy, Edith
1951   Westward the Women

Harakas, James
1953   Beneath the 12-Mile Reef

Haramis, Peter
1953   The Glory Brigade

Haran, Theo
1956   Full of Life

Harari, Robert
1931   Echec au roi
1937   Music for Madame
1941   Ice-Capades
        Sun Valley Serenade

Harasymyk, Jean
1939   Cossacks in Exile

Harbacher, Karl
1931   Chérie (*foreign version*)

Harbaugh, Carl *same as*
   Harbough, Carl
1916   Arms and the Woman
1919   The Other Man's Wife
1920   The North Wind's Malice
1921   Little Miss Hawkshaw
1936   Klondike Annie
1938   The Texans
1942   Gentleman Jim
        They Died With Their
        Boots On
1949   Colorado Territory
1950   The Daughter of Rosie
        O'Grady
1951   Distant Drums
1957   Band of Angels

Harber, Paul
1956   Man from Del Rio

Harbin, Suzette
1941   Up Jumped the Devil
1947   The Foxes of Harrow
1949   Lookout Sister
        The Sky Dragon

Harbon, John W.
1918   The Prussian Cur

Harbough, Carl *see* **Harbaugh,
   Carl**

Hardeman, Reather
1941?   The Blood of Jesus

Harden, Ray
1953   The Glory Brigade

Hardie, Russell
1934   As the Earth Turns
        Operator 13
1936   Down to the Sea

Hardin, Ira *see* **The Four Tones**

Hardin, Neil
1917   Sunshine and Gold

Hardin, Rellie
1939   The Bronze Buckaroo

Hardin, Ty
1959   Last Train from Gun Hill

Harding, Ann
1951   The Magnificent Yankee

Harding, Daisy
1930   A Daughter of the Congo

Harding, Halley
1938   The Duke Is Tops
1940   Mystery in Swing

Harding, John (*actor*)
1959   Night of the Quarter
        Moon

Harding, John Briard (*writer*)
1949   The Kissing Bandit

Harding, Kay
1945   The Mummy's Curse

Harding, Margaret
1933   It's Great to Be Alive
1934   Stand Up and Cheer!

Harding, Pat
1955   The Long Gray Line

Hardman, Ric
1958   Gunman's Walk

Hardt, Harry
1931   La pura verdad (*foreign
        version*)

Hardwicke, Cedric *same as*
   Hardwicke, Sir Cedric
1942   Valley of the Sun
1948   I Remember Mama

Hardwicke, Clarke
1947   Dark Delusion

Hardy, Frank (*actor circa 1940s*)
   not the same as **Hardy, Frank**
   (*silent film actor*)
1948   Louisiana Story

Hardy, Frank (*silent film actor*)
   not the same as **Hardy, Frank**
   (*actor circa 1940s*)
1914   The Great Diamond
        Robbery

Hardy, Glenn
1953   Taxi

Hardy, Oliver
1931   Los calaveras
        Los calaveras (*foreign
        version*)
        Noche de duendes
        Pardon Us
        Pardon Us (*foreign
        version*)
        Politiquerías
1949   The Fighting Kentuckian

Hardy, Paul
1954   Go Man Go

Hardy, Sam
1923   Little Old New York
1928   Diamond Handcuffs
        The Night Bird

Hare, Lumsden
1916   Arms and the Woman
1931   Charlie Chan Carries On
1936   The Last of the Mohicans
1940   Northwest Passage (Book
        I—Rogers' Rangers)
1943   Jack London
1945   The Valley of Decision

Hare, Marilyn
1944   Since You Went Away

Haretakis, John
1953   The Glory Brigade

Harford, Alec
1944   Hi, Beautiful
1948   Unconquered

Hargrave, Clarence
1940?   Mr. Washington Goes to
        Town
1942   Professor Creeps

Hargrave, Ron
1954   Drum Beat
1956   The Burning Hills

Bobby Hargreaves Orchestra
1937   Underworld
Hargreaves, William
1931   Delicious
Harker, Charmienne
1947   The Chinese Ring
1948   The Paleface
        Unconquered
1955   Foxfire
Harker, Jane
1947   Humoresque
Harkness, Carter B.
1916   Gold and the Woman
1918   The Birth of a Race
Harlam, Macey *same as* **Harlan, Macey**
1916   The Romantic Journey
1919   Toby's Bow
1922   Fair Lady
Harlan, Miss
1914   At the Cross Roads
Harlan, Kenneth *same as* **Harlan, Ken**
1918   The Wine Girl
1921   The Barricade
1923   April Showers
1924   Two Shall Be Born
1926   The Fighting Edge
1928   United States Smith
1940   Doomed to Die
        Prairie Schooners
1942   Foreign Agent
        Juke Girl
        Wings for the Eagle
1943   The Law Rides Again
Harlan, Macey *see* **Harlam, Macey**
Harlan, Otis
1923   The Spider and the Rose
        The Victor
1924   Welcome Stranger
1929   Show Boat
1930   Take the Heir
1931   Aloha
1933   The Telegraph Trail
1935   Chinatown Squad
1938   The Texans
Harlan, Richard
1930   El valiente
1931   Del infierno al cielo
1939   El otro soy yo
        Papá soltero
        El trovador de la radio
1940   Cuando canta la Ley
Harlash, Nicholas
1939   Cossacks in Exile
Harlemania Orchestra
1938   The Duke Is Tops
Harlemaniacs
1947   Boy! What a Girl!
Harlem's Apache Chorus
1937   Underworld
Harley, Eileen
1959   Anna Lucasta
Harling, W. Franke
1931   Chérie *(foreign version)*
Harmen, Lillian *could be same as* **Harmer, Lillian**
1927   A Harp in Hock
Harmer, Lillian *could be same as* **Harmen, Lillian**
1931   Huckleberry Finn
1935   Romance in Manhattan
1936   Rainbow on the River
1938   The Buccaneer
        Gateway
Harmon, David P.
1956   Reprisal!
Harmon, John
1939   The Escape
1940   The Way of All Flesh
1946   Dangerous Money
1948   Moonrise
        Unconquered
Harmon, Marie
1946   The Sailor Takes a Wife
1948   Jiggs and Maggie in Court
Harmon, Pat *not the same as* **Harmon, Patricia**
1926   The Barrier
        The Fighting Edge
1928   The Broken Mask

Harmon, Patricia *not the same as* **Harmon, Pat**
1947   Easy Come, Easy Go
Harmon, Sidney
1959   Anna Lucasta
Harolde, Ralf *same as* **Harold, Ralf; Harolde, Ralfe**
1930   Check and Double Check
1931   Smart Money
1934   He Was Her Man
1936   Human Cargo
1937   One Mile from Heaven
1947   Desperate
Harp, Kenneth B.
1956   Mohawk
Harper, Ann
1946   Rendezvous 24
Harper, Betty
1949   Jigsaw
Harper, Irene
1947   Going to Glory, Come to Jesus
Harper, Janet
1934   Broadway Bill
Leonard Harper and His Chorines
1931   The Exile
Harper, Rand
1958   Home Before Dark
1959   The FBI Story
Harper, Sally
1942   Young America
1943   Crash Dive
Harptones
1956   Rockin' the Blues
Harr, Silver
1947   Marshal of Cripple Creek
Harrell, Dean
1927   The Way of All Flesh
Harrigan, Nedda *same as* **Harrington, Nedda**
1937   Charlie Chan at the Opera
        Thank You, Mr. Moto
Harrigan, William
1935   His Family Tree
1938   Hawaii Calls
1947   Citizen Saint
        The Farmer's Daughter
Harrington, Buck
1948   Call Northside 777
Harrington, Hamtree
1939   The Devil's Daughter
        Keep Punching
Harrington, James
1949   The Red Menace
Harrington, Joy
1945   The Valley of Decision
Harrington, Kate
1943   Wintertime
1945   Rhapsody in Blue
Harrington, Mary Lou
1945   A Tree Grows in Brooklyn
Harrington, Nedda *see* **Harrigan, Nedda**
Harris and Scott
1949   Souls of Sin
Harris, Alan *same as* **Harris, Al**
1939   Tevya
1952   Anything Can Happen
Harris, Aranelle *same as* **Harris, Avanelle**
1941   Up Jumped the Devil
1942   Lucky Ghost
Harris, Arlene
1944   Hi, Beautiful
Harris, Blaney
1940   Kit Carson
Harris, Bud
1935   The Winning Ticket
1939   Moon over Harlem
1940   While Thousands Cheer
Harris, Burtt
1959   Odds Against Tomorrow
Harris, Caroline
1916   Gold and the Woman
Harris, Charles K.
1915   Hearts of Men
1916?   Should a Baby Die?

Harris, Clarence J., Rev
1917   The Little Samaritan
Harris, Clifford
1921   Hearts of the Woods
Harris, Connie *could be same as* **Harris, Consuelo**
1937   Harlem on the Prairie
Harris, Consuelo *could be same as* **Harris, Connie**
1938   God's Step Children
Harris, Darleen Marie
1957   All Mine to Give
Harris, Dorothy
1942   Song of the Islands
Harris, Eddie
1926   Buffalo Bill on the U. P. Trail
1927   Jake the Plumber
Harris, Edna Mae *same as* **Harris, Edna M.**
1936   The Green Pastures
1938   Spirit of Youth
1939   Lying Lips
1940   The Notorious Elinor Lee
        Paradise in Harlem
1941   Murder on Lenox Avenue
        Sunday Sinners
1946?   Harlem on Parade
Harris, Elmer
1921   All Souls' Eve
1928   Ransom
Harris, George *(actor)*
1925   Lights of Old Broadway
Harris, George F. *(prod)*
1938   Zamboanga
Harris, Gloria Elaine
1957   All Mine to Give
Harris, Gordon
1949   Border Incident
Harris, Harriet
1921   A Modern Cain
Harris, Harry *not the same as* **Harris, Henry**
1953   The Jazz Singer
Harris, Henry *not the same as* **Harris, Harry**
1922   Foolish Lives
Harris, Howard
1947   Copacabana
Harris, Jack
1957   Burden of Truth
1959   Al Capone
Harris, James
1917   Rosie O'Grady
Harris, Joseph
1923   Crashin' Thru
Harris, Judy
1960   Wild River
Harris, Julie
1953   The Member of the Wedding
Harris, June
1948   Unconquered
Harris, Louise
1917   The Trouble Buster
Harris, Lucretia
1917   A Kentucky Cinderella
Harris, Marcia
1917   The Little Boy Scout
1931   Aloha
Harris, Marilyn
1936   Show Boat
Harris, Mildred
1917   A Love Sublime
1930   The Melody Man
1935   Te quiero con locura
Harris, Mitchell
1932   Hypnotized
1933   Victims of Persecution
Harris, Phil
1945   I Love a Bandleader
Harris, Ray *(writer)*
1927   The Gay Defender
1936   Dancing Pirate
Harris, Raymond *(actor)*
1946   Mantan Messes Up
Harris, Rhina
1946   That Man of Mine

Harris, Richard
1959   Shake Hands with the Devil
Harris, Robin
1937   One Mile from Heaven
1938   Passport Husband
Harris, Ronnie
1944   The Sullivans
Harris, Roy *see* **Hill, Riley**
Harris, Sam, Major *same as* **Harris, Sam**
1939   Mr. Moto Takes a Vacation
1947   The Farmer's Daughter
1958   The Last Hurrah
Harris, Sherman A.
1958   The Lone Ranger and the Lost City of Gold
Harris, Stacy S. *same as* **Harris, Stacey**
1953   The Great Sioux Uprising
1956   Comanche
1957   Raintree County
Harris, Steve
1960   Ice Palace
Harris, Theresa
1937   Bargain with Bullets
        Charlie Chan at the Olympics
1938   Passport Husband
        The Toy Wife
1940   Santa Fe Trail
1942   Cat People
1943   What's Buzzin' Cousin?
1945   The Dolly Sisters
Harris, Toni
1956   Rockin' the Blues
Harris, Virginia
1921   Cheated Love
Harris, Vivian
1948?   Boarding House Blues
1955   Brevities of 1955
Harris, Wadsworth
1916   The Love Girl
Harris, Winifred
1940   New Moon
1942   Gentleman Jim
        Woman of the Year
1947   My Wild Irish Rose
Harrison, Bertram
1930   The Big Pond
Harrison, Bud
1946   Three Wise Fools
Harrison, Carey
1938   The Buccaneer
1942   Woman of the Year
1949   The Girl from Jones Beach
Harrison, Charles
1936   Ramona
Harrison, Doane
1959   The Jayhawkers!
Harrison, Irma
1919   The Red Viper
Harrison, Jack
1928   The Midnight Ace
Harrison, James *same as* **Harrison, James H.; Harrison, Jimmy**
1921   The Barricade
1941   The Mexican Spitfire's Baby
1947   King of the Bandits
1948   Fury at Furnace Creek
1950   Ambush
        Annie Get Your Gun
1951   The Tall Target
1953   Ride, Vaquero!
        San Antone
Harrison, Jan
1958   Fort Bowie
Harrison, Jester
1942   In This Our Life
Harrison, Jimmy *see* **Harrison, James**
Harrison, Joan
1944   Dark Waters
1947   Ride the Pink Horse
Harrison, June
1946   Bringing Up Father
1947   Citizen Saint
        Jiggs and Maggie in Society

1948 Jiggs and Maggie in Court
1949 Jiggs and Maggie in Jackpot Jitters
1950 Jiggs and Maggie Out West

Harrison, Lesley
1955 The View from Pompey's Head

Harrison, Lottie
1946 Romance of the West

Harrison, Mark
1933 Circle Canyon

Harrison, P. S.
1943 Deerslayer

Harrison, Rex
1947 The Foxes of Harrow

Harrison, Richard B.
1930 Easy Street

Harrison, Robert
1951 Jim Thorpe—All-American

Harrison, Stafford B.
1957 Journey to Freedom

Harrison, Stephen S. *same as* **Harrison, Stephen**
1950 The Baron of Arizona
   Young Daniel Boone

Harrison, Susan
1960 Key Witness

Harrison, W. F.
1915? The Beachcomber

Harrison, William
1918 The Prussian Cur

Harrod, Frances
1939 Moon over Harlem

Harron, John *same as* **Harron, Johnny**
1921 Through the Back Door
1922 The Five Dollar Baby
1926 The Little Irish Girl
   Rose of the Tenements
1930 Big Boy
1931 Law of the Tong
1937 Prairie Thunder
1938 The Beloved Brat
1939 Daughters Courageous

Harron, Robert d. 1920
1918 The Greatest Thing in Life

Harrower, Elizabeth
1954 Thunder Pass
1958 Marjorie Morningstar
1959 Al Capone
   The FBI Story
1960 I Passed for White

Harsányi, Zsolt
1930 El secreto del doctor *(foreign version)*

Hart, Adriana
1958 Seven Hills of Rome

Hart, Al
1921 Cotton and Cattle
   Diane of Star Hollow
1922 Cross Roads

Hart, Bertha
1938 The Power of Life
1939 Kol Nidre
   Motel the Operator

Hart, Dolores
1958 Wild Is the Wind
1960 The Plunderers

Hart, Eddie *same as* **Hart, Ed**
1935 Charlie Chan in Shanghai
1936 Charlie Chan at the Race Track
1937 The Devil's Playground
1938 Gateway
   Mr. Moto's Gamble
   Passport Husband
   Speed to Burn
1942 Syncopation
1945 Johnny Angel
   Nob Hill

Hart, Florence
1920 A Tokio Siren

Hart, Fred
1923 His Great Chance
1929 In Old California

Hart, Gordon
1938 The Beloved Brat
1941 Secret of the Wastelands
1942 Syncopation

Hart, Gypsy *see* **Harte, Gypsy**

Hart, Jean
1955 The Rose Tattoo

Hart, John
1938 Dangerous to Know
   Daughter of Shanghai
1949 The Cowboy and the Prizefighter
1951 Warpath
1959 Inside the Mafia

Hart, Lew
1918 The Unbeliever

Hart, Mary *see* **Roberts, Lynne**

Hart, Moss
1932 Flesh
1948 Gentleman's Agreement

Hart, Neal
1919? When the Desert Smiles
1923 The Secret of the Pueblo
1938 The Renegade Ranger

Hart, Neila
1943 Good Luck, Mr. Yates
1944 Since You Went Away

Hart, Stuart
1958 Seven Hills of Rome

Hart, Teddy
1933 Diplomaniacs
1936 After the Thin Man

Hart, Tommy
1953 Tumbleweed

Hart, Walter
1951 Molly

Hart, William S.
1916 The Aryan
1917 The Gun Fighter

Harte, Gypsy *same as* **Hart, Gypsy**
1917 The Flower of Doom
   The Pulse of Life

Hartelle, Jean
1950 Black Hand
1953 Thunder Bay

Hartford, David M.
1917 The Bride of Hate

Hartigan, P. C. *same as* **Hartigan, Pat; Hartigan, Pat J.**
1918 The Prussian Cur
1919 A Fallen Idol
1924 Welcome Stranger
1925 The Thundering Herd
1926 The Fighting Edge
1929 In Old Arizona
1934 Coming Out Party
   Judge Priest
1936 Human Cargo

Hartley, John
1940 The Way of All Flesh

Hartman, Beth
1935 Rescue Squad
1937 Souls at Sea

Hartman, Don
1935 Romance in Manhattan
1937 Waikiki Wedding
1947 It Had To Be You
1952 It's a Big Country: An American Anthology

Hartman, Joe
1938 Happy Landing
1950 No Way Out

Hartman, Karen D.
1957 All Mine to Give

Hartman, Vicki L.
1957 All Mine to Give

Hartmann, Edmund
1946 The Face of Marble
1948 The Paleface

Hartmann, John
1951 Across the Wide Missouri

Hartnell, William
1959 Shake Hands with the Devil

Hartsfield, Ann
1950 Intruder in the Dust

Hartsfield, Kathleen
1943 Cabin in the Sky

Hartwell, Oliver
1955 A Man Called Peter

Hartwig, Eva Brigitte
1930 Doña mentiras *(foreign version)*

Harty, Veola
1919 Lasca

Harvey, Charles
1952 Buffalo Bill in Tomahawk Territory

Harvey, Don C. *same as* **Harvey, Don**
1950 The Girl from San Lorenzo
1951 Hurricane Island
1952 Indian Uprising
1954 They Rode West
1955 Apache Ambush
   Headline Hunters
   Seven Angry Men
1959 Gunmen from Laredo

Harvey, Edward *same as* **Harvey, Ed**
1945 Rhapsody in Blue
1947 Humoresque
   It Had To Be You

Harvey, Fletcher
1915 The Melting Pot

Harvey, Forrester
1932 Mystery Ranch
1934 Broadway Bill
   Limehouse Blues
1937 Souls at Sea
1940 Little Nellie Kelly

Harvey, Georgette
1934 Chloe: Love Is Calling You

Harvey, Harry, Jr.
1940 Knute Rockne—All American
1942 Wings for the Eagle
1944 Chip Off the Old Block
1945 A Tree Grows in Brooklyn
1955 Shotgun

Harvey, Harry, Sr. *same as* **Harvey, Harry**
1916 The Twin Triangle
1939 Daughter of the Tong
1941 Hurry, Charlie, Hurry
1942 Mexican Spitfire's Elephant
1944 Lady, Let's Dance!
1945 Nob Hill
1946 Sunset Pass
1947 Crossfire
   Thunder Mountain
   Under the Tonto Rim
1948 The Arizona Ranger
   Fighting Father Dunne
   Gun Smugglers
   The Paleface
1949 Arctic Manhunt
   Stagecoach Kid
1950 Emergency Wedding
   Rio Grande Patrol
1952 High Noon
1953 The Jazz Singer
   Last of the Comanches
   Old Overland Trail
   Tumbleweed
1955 Bad Day at Black Rock
1957 Man in the Shadow

Harvey, J.
1915? The Beachcomber

Harvey, Jean G.
1957 Band of Angels

Harvey, John Joseph
1918 The Kaiser's Finish

Harvey, Ken
1949 The Undercover Man
1952 Bright Victory

Harvey, Lew
1922 The Half Breed
1926 The Fighting Edge
1930 Big Boy
1936 After the Thin Man
   Robin Hood of El Dorado
   Star for a Night
1937 Big City
   One Mile from Heaven
1940 If I Had My Way
1942 Gentleman Jim
1943 Good Luck, Mr. Yates
1949 The Story of Seabiscuit

Harvey, Mabelle *see* **Havey, Maie B.**

Harvey, Michael
1940 Knute Rockne—All American

Harvey, Paul
1934 Broadway Bill
   Charlie Chan's Courage
   She Was a Lady
1936 Rose of the Rancho
1937 Big City
   Black Legion
   The Plainsman
1939 Charlie Chan in Honolulu
   Mr. Moto in Danger Island
1940 Behind the News
1941 Ride on Vaquero
1948 Call Northside 777
1949 The Girl from Jones Beach
1950 The Lawless
   A Ticket to Tomahawk
1951 The Great Caruso

Harvey, Phil
1958 Touch of Evil

Harvey, William
1925 The Midnight Girl

Hasbrouck, Olive
1926 The Cohens and Kellys
1927 The Shamrock and the Rose

Hasenclever, Walter
1930 Anna Christie *(foreign version)*

Hashim, Edmund *same as* **Hashim, Ed**
1956 Ghost Town
   Quincannon, Frontier Scout
1960 I Passed for White

Haskell, Albert
1949 Border Incident

Haskett, Ed
1953 The Eddie Cantor Story

Haskin, Byron
1927 Irish Hearts
1951 Warpath

Haskins, Edith
1933 It's Great to Be Alive
1942 Song of the Islands

Hassell, George
1937 Think Fast, Mr. Moto

Hasso, Signe
1945 The House on 92nd St.
   Johnny Angel

Hastings, Carey
1917 Under False Colors

Hastings, Harry *not the same as* **Hastings, Henry**
1935 Black Fury

Hastings, Henry *not the same as* **Hastings, Harry**
1939 Stand Up and Fight
1940? Mr. Washington Goes to Town
1942 Lucky Ghost
1946 Without Reservations

Hastings, Seymour
1917 The Pulse of Life

Haswell, Ara
1934 Broadway Bill
   She Was a Lady

Hatch, Helene
1950 The Breaking Point

Hatch, Riley *same as* **Hatch, William R.**
1915 Children of the Ghetto
1923 Little Old New York

Hatchett, Inez
1941 Sullivan's Travels

Hatfield, Byron Ulric, Reverend
1940 The Ramparts We Watch

Hatfield, Harold *same as* **Hatfield, Hal**
1951 Saturday's Hero
1952 It's a Big Country: An American Anthology

Hatfield, Hurd
1950 Chinatown at Midnight

Hatfield, Jack
1935 Rendezvous
1936 It Had to Happen

Hathaway, Henry
1932	Wild Horse Mesa
1933	Thundering Herd
1937	Souls at Sea
1938	Spawn of the North
1945	The House on 92nd St.
	Nob Hill
1948	Call Northside 777

Hathaway, James
| 1918 | The Prussian Cur |

Hathaway, Rhody
| 1925 | A Daughter of the Sioux |

Hatswell, Don
| 1952 | The Quiet Man |

Hattie, Hilo
| 1944 | Tahiti Nights |

Hatton, Brad
| 1950 | Mystery Street |

Hatton, Dick *see* **Hatton, Richard**

Hatton, Fanny
1921	The Land of Hope
	Little Italy
1922	Peacock Alley
1925	The Manicure Girl
1928	The Night Bird
1929	Mister Antonio

Hatton, Frederick *same as* **Hatton, Frederic**
1921	The Land of Hope
	Little Italy
1922	Peacock Alley
1925	The Manicure Girl
1928	Kit Carson
	The Night Bird
1929	Mister Antonio

Hatton, James
| 1916 | Unprotected |

Hatton, Raymond
1915	Chimmie Fadden
	Chimmie Fadden Out West
	The Immigrant
	The Kindling
1916	The Honorable Friend
1917	Hashimura Togo
	The Little American
	The Secret Game
	The Squaw Man's Son
1918	One More American
	Sandy
	The Source
1922	Head over Heels
1924	The Mine with the Iron Door
1925	A Son of His Father
	The Thundering Herd
1931	The Squaw Man
1932	The Vanishing Frontier
1933	Thundering Herd
1934	Lazy River
	Straight Is the Way
	Wagon Wheels
1936	Desert Gold
	Laughing Irish Eyes
	Mad Holiday
1938	The Texans
1940	Covered Wagon Days
	Hi-Yo Silver
	Kit Carson
1942	Below the Border
1945	The Navajo Trail
	Sunbonnet Sue
1946	Border Bandits
1947	Black Gold
1948	Unconquered
1952	Trail of the Arrow
1954	Thunder Pass
1957	Pawnee

Hatton, Richard *same as* **Hatton, Dick**
| 1923 | The Sting of the Scorpion |
| 1925 | Warrior Gap |

Hatton, Rondo
| 1938 | In Old Chicago |
| 1943 | The Ox-Bow Incident |

Hatton, Temple
| 1960 | I Passed for White |

Hauer, Jerry
| 1954 | Go Man Go |

Haugan, Alf
| 1945 | Johnny Angel |

Haupt, Ullrich *same as* **Haupt, Ulrich**
| 1929 | Frozen Justice |
| 1931 | La gran jornada (*foreign version*) |

Haupt, Whitey
| 1953 | The Eddie Cantor Story |
| 1956 | The Benny Goodman Story |

Hauser, Philo
| 1950 | Give Us This Day |

Hausman, Ernst *could be same as* **Hausserman, Ernst**
| 1942 | Secret Enemies |

Hausserman, Ernst *could be same as* **Hausman, Ernst**
| 1943 | Action in the North Atlantic |

Havard, Joan
| 1937 | It Could Happen to You |

Haven, Shirle
| 1958 | Gunman's Walk |

Havens, Rusty
| 1959 | Last Train from Gun Hill |

Haver, June
1943	The Gang's All Here
1945	The Dolly Sisters
	Where Do We Go From Here?
1950	The Daughter of Rosie O'Grady

Haver, Phyllis
| 1924 | So Big |
| 1927 | The Way of All Flesh |

Haverly, Ned
| 1951 | Yes Sir, Mr. Bones |

Havey, Maie B. *same as* **Harvey, Mabelle**
| 1917 | A Jewel in Pawn |
| 1918 | How Could You, Jean? |

Havez, Jean
| 1924 | Racing Luck |

Havier, J. Alex
| 1943 | Bataan |

Havilland, Olivia de *see* **De Havilland, Olivia**

Havoc, June
| 1948 | Gentleman's Agreement |

Hawaiian Girls Glee Club
| 1934 | Song of the Islands |

Hawes, William
| 1949 | The Fighting Kentuckian |

Hawkey, Rock *see* **Hill, Robert**

Hawkins, Alfred
| 1946 | Dirty Gertie from Harlem, U.S.A. |

Hawkins, Charles *same as* **Hawkins, Charlie**
1938	The Duke Is Tops
1939	Double Deal
1940	Gang War
1940?	Mr. Washington Goes to Town
1942	Professor Creeps

Hawkins, Coleman
| 1943 | Stormy Weather |

Hawkins, Dolores
| 1960 | The Adventures of Huckleberry Finn |

Hawkins, Flo
| 1946 | That Man of Mine |

Hawkins, Georgia
| 1941 | Doomed Caravan |

Hawkins, Jimmie
1948	Moonrise
1949	The Red Menace
1950	Winchester '73
1951	Jim Thorpe—All-American

Hawkins, Mary Ann
| 1948 | The Golden Eye |

Hawkins, Timmy *same as* **Hawkins, Tim; Hawkins, Timmie**
1945	The Bells of St. Mary's
	The Valley of Decision
1947	Little Mister Jim
1948	Fighting Father Dunne
	Moonrise
1950	Winchester '73
1951	Jim Thorpe—All-American

Hawkins, Tuffy
| 1939 | Straight to Heaven |

Hawks, Howard
1932	La foule hurle
	Scarface
	Tiger Shark
1943	Air Force
	The Outlaw
1948	Red River
1952	The Big Sky

Hawks, J. G.
1917	The Bride of Hate
1920	Dangerous Days
1927	Clancy's Kosher Wedding
1931	Aloha

Hawks, John Kay
| 1954 | Taza, Son of Cochise |

Hawks, Kenneth
| 1929 | Masked Emotions |

Hawks, William B.
| 1956 | The Last Wagon |

Hawley, Helene
| 1956 | Serenade |

Hawley, Lowell S.
| 1960 | The Sign of Zorro |

Hawley, Monte *same as* **Hawley, Monty**
1924	A Son of Satan
1938	The Duke Is Tops
	Life Goes On
1939	Double Deal
	Gang Smashers
	One Dark Night
	Reform School
1940	Am I Guilty?
	Gang War
	Mystery in Swing
	While Thousands Cheer
1940?	Mr. Washington Goes to Town
1942	Lucky Ghost
	Take My Life
1946	Mantan Messes Up
	Tall, Tan and Terrific
1947?	What a Guy
1948	Miracle in Harlem
1949	Lookout Sister

Hawley, Ormi
1916	The Social Highwayman
1917	Runaway Romany
1918	The Ordeal of Rosetta

Hawley, Wanda
1918	The Gypsy Trail
1919	Told in the Hills
1923	Thirty Days

Haworth, Joe *same as* **Haworth, Joseph**
1944	The Sullivans
1945	Salome, Where She Danced
	Where Do We Go From Here?
1946	Without Reservations
1948	Gentleman's Agreement
1951	Go for Broke!
	Jim Thorpe—All-American
1958	The Badlanders
1959	The Wonderful Country

Haworth, Vinton *see* **Arnold, Jack**

Hay, Ned
| 1918 | Fields of Honor |
| 1919 | The Other Man's Wife |

Hayakawa, Sessue
1915	After Five
	The Cheat
	The Secret Sin
1916	Alien Souls
	The Honorable Friend
	The Soul of Kura-San
1917	The Bottle Imp
	The Call of the East
	Forbidden Paths
	Hashimura Togo
	The Secret Game
1918	The Bravest Way
	The City of Dim Faces
	Hidden Pearls
	His Birthright
	The Honor of His House
	The Temple of Dusk
1919	The Courageous Coward
	The Gray Horizon
	A Heart in Pawn
	His Debt
	The Tong Man

1920	The Devil's Claim
	Li Ting Lang
1921	Black Roses
	The First Born
	The Swamp
	Where Lights Are Low
1960	Hell to Eternity

Hayakawa, Tsuru Aoki *see* **Aoki, Tsuru**

Hayashi, Thomas
| 1930 | Chijiku wo mawasuru chikara |

Hayden, Barbara
| 1959 | The Crimson Kimono |

Hayden, Harry
1937	Black Legion
1939	Charlie Chan in Reno
	The Cisco Kid and the Lady
1940	Knute Rockne—All American
1941	Sullivan's Travels
1942	Tales of Manhattan
	Valley of the Sun
	We Were Dancing
	Whispering Ghosts
1943	The Meanest Man in the World
	Yankee Doodle Dandy
1944	Since You Went Away
1945	A Medal for Benny
1946	Notorious
	The Sailor Takes a Wife
	Till the End of Time
	Without Reservations
1947	California
	Easy Come, Easy Go
1948	Docks of New Orleans
	The Dude Goes West
	Fighting Father Dunne
1950	Intruder in the Dust
	The Traveling Saleswoman
1953	Tonight We Sing

Hayden, Nora
| 1925 | Friendly Enemies |

Hayden, Russell
1937	Hills of Old Wyoming
1941	Doomed Caravan
1942	Lawless Plainsmen
1949	Apache Chief

Hayden, Sarah
| 1952 | Wagons West |

Hayden, Sterling *same as* **Hayden, Stirling**
1941	Virginia
1951	Flaming Feather
1953	So Big
1954	Arrow in the Dust
1955	The Last Command
	Shotgun
1957	Gun Battle at Monterey
1958	Terror in a Texas Town

Haydn, Richard
| 1947 | The Foxes of Harrow |

Haydon, J. Charles
| 1914 | John Barleycorn |

Haydon, Julie
1932	Symphony of Six Million
	Thirteen Women
1933	Song of the Eagle
1947	Citizen Saint

Hayes, Alfred
| 1951 | Teresa |

Hayes, Allison
| 1956 | Mohawk |

Hayes, Bernadene
1935	Rendezvous
1939	King of Chinatown
1942	Nazi Agent

Hayes, Chester
| 1951 | Jim Thorpe—All-American |
| 1959 | The Wonderful Country |

Hayes, Frank
| 1918 | The Yellow Dog |

Hayes, George *same as* **Hayes, George "Gabby"; Hayes, George F.**
1929	Smiling Irish Eyes
1931	Cavalier of the West
1932	Border Devils
	Hidden Valley
	Riders of the Desert
	Wild Horse Mesa

1934   'Neath the Arizona Skies
     The Star Packer
1935   Texas Terror
1937   Hills of Old Wyoming
     The Plainsman
1939   In Old Caliente
     Let Freedom Ring
     Man of Conquest
1940   Young Buffalo Bill
1943   In Old Oklahoma
     Wagon Tracks West
1944   Marshal of Reno
     Tucson Raiders
1950   The Cariboo Trail

Hayes, Gordon
1943   Action in the North
     Atlantic

Hayes, Grace
1930   King of Jazz

Hayes, Harry
1944   Address Unknown

Hayes, Helen
1932   The Son-Daughter

Hayes, Herbert see **Heyes, Herbert**

Hayes, Ira H., Pfc.
1950   Sands of Iwo Jima

Hayes, J. William
1958   The Rawhide Trail

Hayes, Jimmy
1956   The Benny Goodman
     Story

Hayes, John Michael
1952   Red Ball Express
1953   Thunder Bay
1954   War Arrow

Hayes, Lind see **Hayes, Peter Lind**

Hayes, Linda
1939   The Girl from Mexico
1940   Mexican Spitfire
     Mexican Spitfire Out
     West

Hayes, Margaret
1941   Louisiana Purchase
     New York Town
     Sullivan's Travels
1955   Blackboard Jungle
     Violent Saturday

Hayes, Marvin
1954   Carmen Jones

Hayes, Patricia
1940   Knute Rockne—All
     American

Hayes, Peter Lind same as **Hayes, Lind**
1938   Outside of Paradise
1941   Playmates

Hayes, Raphael
1956   Reprisal!

Hayes, Ron
1959   Gunmen from Laredo

Hayes, Rosalind
1957   Raintree County

Hayes, Sam
1934   Stand Up and Cheer!
1936   Charlie Chan at the Race
     Track
1937   Song of the City
1939   Mr. Moto Takes a
     Vacation
1943   The Meanest Man in the
     World
1949   Jiggs and Maggie in
     Jackpot Jitters
1951   Jim Thorpe—All-American

Hayes, Sydney
1919   Diane of the Green Van

Hayle, Grace
1934   Laughing Boy
     Straight Is the Way
1937   It Could Happen to You
     Music for Madame
1939   Mr. Moto in Danger
     Island
1941   Birth of the Blues
     New York Town
1954   Dangerous Mission
1955   Foxfire

Haymes, Dick
1948   Up in Central Park

Haynes, Betty
1946   That Man of Mine

Haynes, Daniel L. same as **Haynes, Daniel**
1929   Hallelujah
1935   So Red the Rose

Haynes, Dick
1959   Last Train from Gun Hill

Haynes, Hilda
1953   Taxi
1960   Key Witness

Haynes, Len
1925   Warrior Gap

Haynes, Marques
1951   The Harlem Globetrotters
1954   Go Man Go

Haynes, Roberta
1949   Knock on Any Door
     We Were Strangers
1952   The Fighter
1953   The Nebraskan

Hays, Youda
1940   Mexican Spitfire Out
     West

Haysel, A. R.
1934   Broadway Bill

Hayward, Betty
1942   We Were Dancing

Hayward, Chuck
1951   Apache Drums
     Slaughter Trail
1952   Fort Osage
1953   San Antone
     The Sun Shines Bright
1957   Run of the Arrow
1960   Sergeant Rutledge

Hayward, Helen
1936   Show Boat

Hayward, Jim same as **Hayward, James**
1949   The Red Menace
1950   Mystery Street
     Mystery Submarine
     Right Cross
1952   The Big Sky
     My Man and I
     The Savage
1953   Ride, Vaquero!
1957   Band of Angels

Hayward, Leland
1927   For the Love of Mike

Hayward, Lillian (actress)
1916   At Piney Ridge
1917   The Hidden Children

Hayward, Lillie (writer)
1930   On the Border
1939   King of Chinatown
1943   Margin for Error
1944   My Pal Wolf
     Tahiti Nights
1952   The Raiders
1955   Santa Fe Passage
1958   Tonka

Hayward, Louis
1938   The Rage of Paris

Hayward, Susan
1941   Adam Had Four Sons
1943   Jack London
1946   Canyon Passage
1948   Tap Roots
1949   House of Strangers
     Tulsa
1959   Thunder in the Sun

Haywood, George
1940   Knute Rockne—All
     American
     Santa Fe Trail

Hayworth, Rita same as **Cansino, Rita** see also **Cansino Family**
1935   Charlie Chan in Egypt
     Piernas de seda
1936   Human Cargo
     Paddy O'Day
     Rebellion
1937   Old Louisiana
1938   The Renegade Ranger
1940   Music in My Heart
1942   Tales of Manhattan
1948   The Lady from Shanghai

Hazard, Jayne same as **Hazard, Jane**
1943   Let's Have Fun
1945   Nob Hill

Haze, Jonathan
1955   Apache Woman
1957   Bayou

Hazel, George
1933   Circle Canyon

Hazelton, Marie
1917   The Plow Woman

Hazlett, Boone
1941   Western Union

Hazlett, William see **Many Treaties, Chief**

Head, Hubert
1940   Little Nellie Kelly

Head, J. Manley
1938   The Texans

Headrick, Richard
1923   The Miracle Makers
     The Spider and the Rose

Healey, Michael
1958   Escape from Red Rock

Healey, Myron same as **Healy, Myron**
1947   Buck Privates Come
     Home
     It Had To Be You
1949   Knock on Any Door
     Laramie
1950   Emergency Wedding
     I Killed Geronimo
1951   Slaughter Trail
1952   Apache War Smoke
     Fort Osage
1954   Cattle Queen of Montana
     They Rode West
1956   The White Squaw
1958   Apache Territory

Healy, Jim
1959   Al Capone

Healy, Myron see **Healey, Myron**

Healy, Ted
1934   Lazy River
     Operator 13
1935   The Winning Ticket
1936   Mad Holiday
1937   Man of the People

Heard, Charles
1957   Band of Angels
1958   Gunman's Walk
1959   The Young Land

Heard, Cliff
1949   Knock on Any Door

Heard, "Crip"
1948?   Boarding House Blues

Heard, Janet
1953   Bright Road

Heard, Paul F.
1949   Prejudice

Hearn, Chick
1957   Burden of Truth

Hearn, Edward same as **Hearn, Ed; Hearn, Eddie; Hearn, Guy Edward**
1919   The Last of His People
1925   One of the Bravest
1927   Winners of the
     Wilderness
1931   The Avenger
     Smart Money
1932   The Rainbow Trail
1934   The Fighting Hero
     Fighting Through
     Laughing Boy
1937   The Devil's Playground
1939   Stand Up and Fight
1940   Little Nellie Kelly
     New Moon
     Santa Fe Trail
1941   Sullivan's Travels
1942   Mokey
     Nazi Agent
     The Vanishing Virginian
1944   An American Romance
1952   My Man and I
1953   Conquest of Cochise
     The Man Behind the Gun

Hearn, Fred G.
1918   The Kaiser's Finish

Hearn, Guy Edward see **Hearn, Edward**

Hearn, Lew
1929   Die Königsloge
1940   The Notorious Elinor Lee
1954   Go Man Go

Heasley, Bob
1938   My Lucky Star

Heasley, Jack
1938   My Lucky Star

Heath, Ariel
1943   Hitler's Children
     Ladies' Day
     The Leopard Man
     Mr. Lucky

Heath, Earlene
1934   Stand Up and Cheer!

Heath, Hy
1949   Stallion Canyon

Heath, John
1955   Murder in Villa Capri

Heath, Percy
1919   Lasca
1923   The Huntress
1930   Amor audaz

Heather, Jean
1944   Going My Way
1947   The Last Round-Up

The Heavenly Choir
1946?   Go Down, Death!

Hebbard, Mrs. Jessie
1922   The Pride of Palomar

Hebert, Henry same as **Herbert, Henry J.**
1916   A Man of Sorrow
1917   The Hidden Children
1920   The Cyclone
1921   Black Roses
1924   So Big

Hebert, Leo
1950   Panic in the Streets

Hecht, Ben
1930   Le spectre vert
1932   Scarface
1939   Gone With the Wind
     Let Freedom Ring
1942   Tales of Manhattan
1946   Notorious
1947   Ride the Pink Horse
1948   The Miracle of the Bells
1955   The Indian Fighter

Hecht, Harold
1954   Apache
1955   Marty

Hecht, Ted
1947   Riding the California
     Trail
     Spoilers of the North
1949   Apache Chief
     We Were Strangers

Heck, Bobby
1927   A Harp in Hock

Heck, Stanton
1920   Dangerous Days
1925   Old Clothes

Hector, Louis
1940   Northwest Passage (Book
     I—Rogers' Rangers)

Hedin, June
1940   The Way of All Flesh
1948   I Remember Mama
1952   It's a Big Country: An
     American Anthology
1953   The Member of the
     Wedding

Hedin, Margaret
1953   Dream Wife

Hedlund, Guy
1947   Last of the Redmen

Hedqvist, Ivan
1930   Doña mentiras (foreign
     version)
     Toda una vida (foreign
     version)

Heerin
1941   Z Dymem Pożarów

Heerman, Victor
1921   A Divorce of Convenience
1922   My Boy
1925   Irish Luck
1930   Galas de la Paramount
1934   Imitation of Life

Heermance, Richard
1952   Hiawatha
1957   The Oklahoman

Heffron, Thomas N. *same as* **Heffron, T. N.**
1916   Peck O' Pickles
1917   The Sudden Gentleman
1918   The Price of Applause
      Tony America

Heflin, Van
1940   Santa Fe Trail
1942   Seven Sweethearts
1948   Tap Roots
1951   Tomahawk
1958   Gunman's Walk

Hegedus, Rosalie
1936   Human Cargo

Hegedüs, Tibor
1930   El secreto del doctor
      (foreign version)

Heggie, O. P.
1930   The Bad Man
1936   The Prisoner of Shark Island

Heidloff, William
1915   Under Southern Skies

Heifetz, Jascha
1947   Carnegie Hall

Heifetz, L. E.
1937   Shadows of the Orient

Heigh, Helene
1950   Young Man with a Horn

Heilbron, Adelaide
1924   So Big
1931   Personal Maid
1942   Friendly Enemies

Heilbronne, Hans
1943   Action in the North Atlantic

Heimel, Otto
1936   Klondike Annie

Heimo, G.
1940   Americaner Schadchen

Heineman, William Joseph
1950   The Jackie Robinson Story

Heinz, Gerard
1960   I Aim at the Stars: the Wernher von Braun Story

Heisler, Stuart
1944   The Negro Soldier
1949   Tulsa
1956   The Burning Hills
      The Lone Ranger

Helbling, Jeanne
1931   Buster se marie
      La gran jornada *(foreign version)*
      Nuit d'Espagne
      Le père célibataire
      El proceso de Mary Dugan *(foreign version)*

Hellen, Marjorie
1955   A Man Called Peter

Heller, Cindy
1956   Singing in the Dark

Heller, Robert
1941   They Dare Not Love

Hellinger, Mark
1934   Broadway Bill

Hellman, George S.
1920   Pagan Love

Hellman, Les
1959   The FBI Story

Hellman, Marcoreta
1953   The Eddie Cantor Story
      The Jazz Singer
      The Sun Shines Bright

Hellman, Sam
1937   Slave Ship
1947   Pirates of Monterey

Hellum, Barney
1932   Hypnotized

Helm, Fay
1937   Song of the City
1942   Wings for the Eagle

Helm, Frances
1957   Revolt at Fort Laramie

Helmers, Peter
1944   Address Unknown

Helton, Percy
1948   Call Northside 777
1949   Harbor of Missing Men
      Lust for Gold
      Thieves' Highway
1951   The Tall Target
1953   Ambush at Tomahawk Gap
      Ride, Vaquero!
1955   Trial

Heming, Richard
1934   Broadway Bill

Hemingway, Frank
1949   The Prairie

Hemming, J. W. *see* **Hemmings, J. W.**

Hemming, Myra J. *see* **Hemmings, Myra**

Hemmings, J. W. *same as* **Hemming, J. W.; Hemmings, John**
1943   Marching On!
1945   Of One Blood
1946?   Beale Street Mama
1949?   Girl in Room 20

Hemmings, John *see* **Hemmings, J. W.**

Hemmings, Myra *same as* **Hemming, Myra J.; Hemmings, Myra D.**
1943   Marching On!
1946?   Go Down, Death!
1949?   Girl in Room 20

Hemphill, George T.
1950   Intruder in the Dust

Hempstead, David
1938   Happy Landing
1943   Mr. Lucky
1944   Tender Comrade
1949   Portrait of Jennie

Hemsley, Estelle
1957   Edge of the City
1960   Take a Giant Step

Hemstreet, David
1952?   Call of the Navajo

Henabery, Joseph
1915   The Birth of a Nation
1924   Tongues of Flame
1925   Cobra
1926   Meet the Prince
1928   United States Smith

Henderson, Bert
1928   Wyoming

Henderson, Bill
1944   Chip Off the Old Block

Henderson, Brenda
1941   They Dare Not Love

Henderson, Dell *same as* **Henderson, Del**
1918   The Golden Wall
      Hitting the Trail
1928   Riley the Cop
1930   Sins of the Children
1931   Noche de duendes
1935   Ruggles of Red Gap
1940   If I Had My Way
1941   Hurry, Charlie, Hurry
1943   Dixie
1944   An American Romance
1947   The Mighty McGurk

Henderson, Grace
1918   Thirty a Week

Henderson, Harry
1924   Smiling Hate
1926   A Prince of His Race
1926?   Ten Nights in a Barroom
1927   Children of Fate
      The Scar of Shame

Henderson, Jack *same as* **Henderson, Jack E.**
1948   Strange Victory
1953   So Big

1958   The Last Hurrah
1959   The FBI Story

Henderson, Lars, Jr.
1959   Last Train from Gun Hill

Henderson, Lucius
1915   Under Southern Skies

Henderson, Marcia
1953   Thunder Bay

Henderson, Mary
1948   The Miracle of the Bells

Hendrian, Dutch *same as* **Hendrian, Oscar G.; Hendrian. O. G.**
1933   Olsen's Big Moment
1934   Broadway Bill
1937   Charlie Chan at the Olympics
1938   Little Miss Roughneck
      The Texans
1939   Mr. Moto in Danger Island
      Waterfront
      Winner Take All
1940   Knute Rockne—All American
1942   All Through the Night
      Holiday Inn
      Valley of Hunted Men
1951   Saturday's Hero

Hendricks, Arch
1940   East of the River

Hendricks, Ben *same as* **Hendricks, Ben F.; Hendricks, Ben, Jr.**
1918   The Birth of a Race
1921   The Land of Hope
1930   Ladies Love Brutes
1934   Lazy River
1936   It Had to Happen
      Sins of Man
1937   Charlie Chan at the Olympics
      The Plainsman
1938   The Buccaneer
      Happy Landing
      Road Demon

Hendricks, Ray
1937   Think Fast, Mr. Moto

Hendricks, Sebie
1934   Imitation of Life

Hendrickson, Evelyn
1957   Bayou

Hendrix, Darlene
1960   Studs Lonigan

Hendrix, Wanda
1947   Ride the Pink Horse
1954   The Black Dakotas

Hendry, Len
1947   California
1948   The Paleface
      Unconquered
1950   The Breaking Point
1951   Show Boat
1953   The Stars Are Singing
1957   Beau James
1959   Last Train from Gun Hill

Hendryx, James B.
1923   Snowdrift

Hengen, Butch
1960   The Dark at the Top of the Stairs

Henie, Sonja
1938   Happy Landing
      My Lucky Star
1941   Sun Valley Serenade
1943   Wintertime

Henig, M.
1940   Americaner Schadchen

Henigson, Henry
1934   Imitation of Life

Henley, Hobart
1916   A Child of Mystery
      The Sign of the Poppy
1918   Laughing Bill Hyde
1921   Society Snobs
1922   The Scrapper
1930   The Big Pond
      The Big Pond *(foreign version)*

Henley, Jacques
1931   Die Dreigroschenoper *(foreign version)*

Henley, Rosina
1917   The Adventures of Carol
1918   Wanted, a Mother

Hennecke, Clarence
1926   The Strong Man
1927   Lost at the Front
1928   Heart Trouble
1948   Big City
      The Miracle of the Bells
1949   Prejudice
1951   The Tall Target

Hennerty, Ed
1944   An American Romance

Hennessy, Tom
1955   The Long Gray Line

Henning, Ann
1940   Taku

Henning, Uno
1930   Un hombre de suerte *(foreign version)*

Henreid, Paul
1950   Last of the Buccaneers
      So Young, So Bad

Henry, Bill *see* **Henry, William**

Henry, Buzz *see* **Henry, Robert Buzz**

Henry, Carol
1949   Roll Thunder Roll!
1950   Ambush
      Annie Get Your Gun
      Winchester '73
1952   Fort Osage
1957   The Deerslayer

Henry, Charlotte *same as* **Henry, Charlotte V.**
1931   Huckleberry Finn
1937   Charlie Chan at the Opera

Henry, Edwin T.
1945   Of One Blood

Henry, Frank *same as* **Henry, F. Patrick**
1943   Mr. Lucky
1952   The Raiders

Henry, George
1916?   Should a Baby Die?
1918   The Ordeal of Rosetta
1919   The Gray Towers Mystery

Henry, John
1924   Yankee Speed

Henry, Louise
1937   Charlie Chan on Broadway
1939   Charlie Chan in Reno

Henry, Marion
1916   Britton of the Seventh

Henry, Melton
1923   Deceit

Henry, Robert Buzz *same as* **Henry, Buzz; Henry, Buzzy; Henry, Robert "Buzzy"**
1946   Wild Beauty
      Wild West
1947   Last of the Redmen
1948   Moonrise
1950   Rocky Mountain
1955   The Indian Fighter
1957   The Lawless Eighties
1958   Tonka

Henry, Thomas B. *same as* **Henry, Thomas Browne; Henry, Tom Brown**
1949   House of Strangers
1951   Saturday's Hero
1952   Red Ball Express
1954   Sitting Bull
1960   I Passed for White

Henry, William *same as* **Henry, Bill**
1934   Operator 13
1940   Geronimo
      Jennie
      The Way of All Flesh
1942   Rubber Racketeers
1944   Going My Way
1946   G. I. War Brides
1958   The Last Hurrah
      The Lone Ranger and the Lost City of Gold

1960   Sergeant Rutledge

Hensel, O.
1958   Tonka

Hensley, E.
1947?   Return of Mandy's Husband

Hensley, John
1955   Good Morning, Miss Dove

Hepburn, Audrey
1960   The Unforgiven

Hepburn, Katharine
1942   Woman of the Year

Hepburn, Philip
1953   Bright Road

Herbers, Jean
1946   Abie's Irish Rose

Herbert, Alexander
1919   As a Man Thinks

Herbert, Charles
1955   The View from Pompey's Head
1958   Houseboat
1959   The Last Angry Man

Herbert, F. Hugh (*writer*)
1937   Music for Madame
1940   Three Faces West

Herbert, Fred
1931   Delicious

Herbert, Hans
1944   Lake Placid Serenade
       Mr. Skeffington
1947   Desperate

Herbert, Henry J. *see* **Hebert, Henry**

Herbert, Holmes
1934   Beloved
1936   Charlie Chan at the Race Track
1937   Slave Ship
1938   The Buccaneer
1939   Mr. Moto's Last Warning
       The Mystery of Mr. Wong
1945   The Mummy's Curse
1951   The Magnificent Yankee

Herbert, Hugh (*actor*)
1933   Diplomaniacs

Herbert, Jack
1918   How Could You, Jean?
       The Squaw Man
1919   Told in the Hills

Herbert, Joseph
1918   Laughing Bill Hyde

Herbert, Tom
1934   The Cat's-Paw
1937   Think Fast, Mr. Moto
1938   Rascals
1943   Dixie
1944   Block Busters

Herblin, David
1919   The Scar

Herdman, John
1922   The Power of Love

Hereford, Kathryn
1960   All the Fine Young Cannibals
       Key Witness

Hergesheimer, Joseph
1925   Flower of Night

Herlein, Lillian
1922   Solomon in Society

Herlinger, Carl
1929   Show Boat

Herman, Ace
1948   Rocky
1949   Tuna Clipper
1952   Desert Pursuit

Herman, Al (*actor*)
1935   Harmony Lane
1937   Man of the People
       Manhattan Merry-Go-Round
1940   East of the River
1943   Let's Have Fun
       Redhead from Manhattan
       Yankee Doodle Dandy

Herman, Al (*dir*)
1940   Arizona Frontier
       Rhythm of the Rio Grande
1941   The Pioneers

Herman, Gil
1950   No Way Out
       Sands of Iwo Jima
1953   Old Overland Trail

Herman, Kid
1935   So Red the Rose

Herman, Tommy *same as* **Herman, Tom**
1938   Mr. Moto's Gamble
1951   Saturday's Hero

Woody Herman and His Orchestra
1943   Wintertime
1947   New Orleans

Hermstad, James A.
1951   Tomahawk

Hern, Pepe
1949   Knock on Any Door
1950   Bandit Queen
       The Furies
1952   Bugles in the Afternoon
       The Ring
1953   San Antone
1955   The Last Command
1957   The Brothers Rico

Hern, Tom
1950   A Lady Without Passport

Hernán, Josita
1933   Melodía de arrabal

Hernandez, George
1915   The Rosary
1919   The Courageous Coward
1920   The Third Woman

Hernandez, Mrs. George
1920   Darling Mine
1922   The Pride of Palomar

Hernández, Joe *could be same as* **Hernández, José**
1949   Jiggs and Maggie in Jackpot Jitters
       The Story of Seabiscuit

Hernández, José *could be same as* **Hernández, Joe**
1938   Di que me quieres

Hernández, Juan
1950   The Breaking Point

Hernandez, Juano *not the same as* **Hernandez, Juan**
1939   Lying Lips
1940   The Notorious Elinor Lee
1950   The Breaking Point
       Intruder in the Dust
       Stars in My Crown
       Young Man with a Horn
1955   Trial
1958   Machete
       St. Louis Blues
1960   Sergeant Rutledge

Hernandez, Tom
1955   The Last Command

Herndon, Cleo
1937   Dark Manhattan

Herrera, George
1937   Waikiki Wedding

Herrera, Samuel
1949   Border Incident

Herrero, Goyita
1931   La pura verdad
1933   Espérame

Herrick, Fred
1959   Odds Against Tomorrow

Herrick, Jack
1930   The Arizona Kid

Herrick, Virginia
1950   I Killed Geronimo

Herrin, John
1955   The Long Gray Line
1956   The Benny Goodman Story

Herrin, William
1960   Flaming Star

Herring, Aggie
1919   The Lord Loves the Irish
       A Yankee Princess
1926   The Frontier Trail
       Kosher Kitty Kelly
       Laddie
       Sweet Daddies
1927   Finnegan's Ball
       McFadden's Flats
       The Princess from Hoboken

Herman, Tommy *same as* **Herman, Tom**

1929   Smiling Irish Eyes
1930   Kathleen Mavourneen
1934   Stand Up and Cheer!
1936   Daniel Boone
1939   The Escape

Herron, Robert D. actor circa 1950s *same as* **Herron, Bob**
1954   Saskatchewan
1955   The Far Horizons
1956   The Burning Hills
       Pillars of the Sky

Hersh, David L.
1947   Copacabana

Hershman, Mordechai, Cantor
1931   The Voice of Israel

Hersholt, Jean
1918   Little Red Decides
1924   So Big
1925   Don Q, Son of Zorro
1928   The Secret Hour
1929   Abie's Irish Rose
       The Younger Generation
1932   Flesh
       Hearts of Humanity
       Unashamed
1933   Song of the Eagle
1936   Sins of Man
1938   Happy Landing
1939   Mr. Moto in Danger Island

Hershon, Genie
1950   No Way Out

Hertz, James
1930   The Last Dance

Hervey, Irene
1935   Charlie Chan in Shanghai
       The Winning Ticket
1940   Three Cheers for the Irish
1942   Unseen Enemy

Herzbrun, Henry
1936   Klondike Annie

Herzig, Sig
1945   Where Do We Go From Here?

Hess, Hilda
1934   Dos más uno, dos

Hesterberg, Trude
1931   La pura verdad (*foreign version*)

Hestia, Lise
1931   Su noche de bodas (*foreign version*)

Heston, Charlton
1952   The Savage
1953   Arrowhead
1955   The Far Horizons
1958   Touch of Evil

Hewitt, Lee J.
1955   Kentucky Rifle

Hewitt, Sanford
1928   Hold 'Em Yale

Hewston, Alfred
1925   Warrior Gap

Heyburn, Weldon
1932   Call Her Savage
1942   They Died With Their Boots On
1944   The Chinese Cat

Heydt, Louis Jean
1939   Charlie Chan at Treasure Island
       Gone With the Wind
       Let Freedom Ring
1940   Santa Fe Trail
1942   Tortilla Flat
1945   Betrayal from the East
       Our Vines Have Tender Grapes
1946   Abie's Irish Rose
1947   Spoilers of the North
1950   The Furies
1951   Warpath
1956   Wetbacks
1957   Raiders of Old California
1959   Inside the Mafia

Heyes, Douglas
1954   Battle of Rogue River

Heyes, Herbert
1919   Deliverance
1921   Wolves of the North
1951   Only the Valiant

1955   The Far Horizons

Heyl, Nancy
1949   Lost Boundaries

Heyward, Du Bose
1933   The Emperor Jones

Don Heywood and His Band
1931   The Exile

Heywood, Donald (*writer*)
1932   The Black King

Heywood, Herbert
1935   Black Fury
       The Irish in Us
1936   It Had to Happen
       Sins of Man
1937   Slave Ship
1939   The Return of the Cisco Kid
1942   Gentleman Jim
       In This Our Life
       They Died With Their Boots On
1943   Yankee Doodle Dandy
1945   The Mummy's Curse
1948   Fury at Furnace Creek
1949   Arctic Manhunt
1950   A Ticket to Tomahawk

Heywood, W.
1922   The Son of the Wolf

Hi-Yo Silver
1940   Hi-Yo Silver

Hiatt, Joyce
1950   Panic in the Streets

Hiatt, Ruth
1934   Broadway Bill

Hibbs, Jesse
1940   Knute Rockne—All American
1942   Juke Girl
1950   Winchester '73
1951   Tomahawk
1953   The Great Sioux Uprising
       The Stand at Apache River
1956   Walk the Proud Land
1958   Ride a Crooked Trail

Hickman, Alfred
1916   The Flames of Johannis
1919   Erstwhile Susan

Hickman, Bill
1958   Houseboat

Hickman, Charles
1921   Shadows of the West

Hickman, Cordell
1942   Mokey
       Tales of Manhattan
1944   Buffalo Bill

Hickman, Darryl
1940   The Way of All Flesh
1942   Young America
1945   Rhapsody in Blue
1947   Black Gold
1948   Fighting Father Dunne

Hickman, Dwayne
1948   The Boy with Green Hair

Hickman, George
1946   Bringing Up Father
1949   Knock on Any Door

Hickman, Howard
1935   Rendezvous
1937   Charlie Chan at the Olympics
       One Mile from Heaven
1938   The Rage of Paris
       Rascals
1939   Gone With the Wind
1941   Belle Starr
1942   Three Hearts for Julia
       The Vanishing Virginian

Hickox, Sid
1930   Los que danzan (*foreign version*)

Hicks, Bert
1942   Three Hearts for Julia

Hicks, Chuck *same as* **Hicks, Charles**
1958   Gunfire at Indian Gap
       Home Before Dark
       The Last Hurrah
1960   Ice Palace

Hicks, Don
1950   No Way Out
1952   Red Ball Express
Hicks, Lew *same as* **Hicks, Lou**
1935   De la sartén al fuego
1936   Charlie Chan at the Race
          Track
1939   Verbena trágica
1948   I Remember Mama
Hicks, Maxine Elliott
1919   The Right to Happiness
1925   The Thundering Herd
Hicks, Russell
1935   Charlie Chan in Shanghai
1936   Laughing Irish Eyes
          Mad Holiday
          Sea Spoilers
1938   Gateway
          In Old Chicago
1940   East of the River
          Santa Fe Trail
1941   Western Union
1942   They Died With Their
          Boots On
          Three Hearts for Julia
          We Were Dancing
          Wings for the Eagle
1943   His Butler's Sister
1945   The Valley of Decision
1946   Dark Alibi
          G. I. War Brides
1947   Buck Privates Come
          Home
          Dark Delusion
1948   Jiggs and Maggie in Court
          Shanghai Chest
1950   The Big Hangover
1956   7th Cavalry
Hidalgo, Adela
1932   Amor y vida
Hidey, Val
1960   Studs Lonigan
Hiers, Walter
1919   Spotlight Sadie
Hiestand, John
1937   Black Legion
1938   Happy Landing
1940   The Man I Married
1941   Louisiana Purchase
1943   The Meanest Man in the
          World
          Riding High
1955   Good Morning, Miss Dove
Higbee, Mary Jane
1914   Where the Trail Divides
Higbee, William
1931   Street Scene
Higby, Wilbur
1916   Mixed Blood
          The Sign of the Poppy
1925   Lights of Old Broadway
Higgin, Howard
1923   Fashion Row
Higgins, John C.
1949   Border Incident
1955   Seven Cities of Gold
1956   The Broken Star
          Quincannon, Frontier
          Scout
Higgins, Rose
1943   The Leopard Man
1948   Unconquered
1950   North of the Great Divide
High, Freeman
1945   Nob Hill
High Eagle
1936   Custer's Last Stand
Hightower, Bryan
1951   Flaming Feather
          Fort Defiance
1953   Arrowhead
Hightower, Slim
1937   The Plainsman
1938   The Texans
1946   Sunset Pass
Hilbere, Philippa
1935   Piernas de seda
Hilbun, Ben J.
1950   Intruder in the Dust

Hildebrand, Rodney
1928   Mother Machree
1935   Harmony Lane
1937   It Could Happen to You
Hill, Al *same as* **Hill, Al M.; Hill,
  Al, Sr.** *not the same as* **Hill,
  Alex**
1934   Straight Is the Way
1935   The Winning Ticket
1939   The Escape
1941   The Face Behind the
          Mask
1942   Apache Trail
          Sunday Punch
1943   Good Luck, Mr. Yates
          In Old Oklahoma
1947   The Mighty McGurk
1948   Fury at Furnace Creek
          The Paleface
1949   Knock on Any Door
1950   A Lady Without Passport
          Right Cross
1951   The Girl on the Bridge
1952   The Half-Breed
1954   Broken Lance
Hill, Alex *not the same as* **Hill, Al**
1935   So Red the Rose
1938   The Buccaneer
Hill, Betty (*actress*)
1947   Easy Come, Easy Go
1950   Jolson Sings Again
Hill, Billy
1948   Singin' Spurs
Hill, Bob *see* **Hill, Robert**
Hill, Bonnie
1920   Billions
Hill, Craig
1954   Siege at Red River
Hill, Doris
1930   Song of the Caballero
1934   The Battling Buckaroo
Hill, Elizabeth (*writer*)
1934   Our Daily Bread
1940   Northwest Passage (Book
          I—Rogers' Rangers)
1949   Streets of Laredo
Hill, Ethel
1943   In Old Oklahoma
Hill, George
1926   The Barrier
1927   The Callahans and the
          Murphys
Hill, Hallene
1942   Syncopation
1943   The Gang's All Here
          Let's Have Fun
1948   Gentleman's Agreement
1949   Colorado Territory
Hill, Jack
1958   The Light in the Forest
Hill, James
1959   Thunder in the Sun
1960   The Unforgiven
Hill, Josephine
1919   Love and the Law
Hill, Maude
1922   Breaking Home Ties
Hill, Nelle *same as* **Hill, Nellie**
194-   Mistaken Identity
1948   Killer Diller
Hill, Paula
1947   Buffalo Bill Rides Again
Hill, Phyllis
1956   Singing in the Dark
Hill, Ramsay *same as* **Hill, Ramsey**
1935   L'homme des Folies
          Bergère
1937   Old Louisiana
1952   Battles of Chief Pontiac
          The Iron Mistress
Hill, Riley *same as* **Harris, Roy**
1942   North to the Klondike
1945   The Navajo Trail
1946   Border Bandits
1948   Jiggs and Maggie in Court
1950   Jiggs and Maggie Out
          West
1952   The Raiders
          Wagons West

Hill, Robert *same as* **Hawkey,
  Rock; Hill, Bob**
1918   The Reckoning Day
1935   Cowboy Holiday
          The Cyclone Ranger
1936   West of Nevada
1937   Law and Lead
1938   Wild Horse Canyon
1939   Drifting Westward
1943   Good Luck, Mr. Yates
          Redhead from Manhattan
1952   Arctic Flight
1956   Raw Edge
Hill, Robert Lee
1916   Man and His Angel
1922   Pals of the West
Hill, Steven
1950   A Lady Without Passport
Hill, W.
1927   The Broken Violin
Hillard, Leon
1954   Go Man Go
Hillebrand, Fred
1945   The House on 92nd St.
1949   House of Strangers
Hilliard, Ernest
1926   The Frontier Trail
1936   Sea Spoilers
          Show Boat
1943   Let's Have Fun
1947   Ride the Pink Horse
Hilliard, Harry
1916   Gold and the Woman
1918   Set Free
1919   The Sneak
Hilliard, Jacqueline Dalya *see*
  Dalya, Jacqueline
Hilliard, Joseph
1946   Beware
Hillias, Peg
1951   A Streetcar Named Desire
Hillie, Verna
1934   The Star Packer
1935   Rescue Squad
Hillier, Claire
1915   The Alien
Hilliker, Katherine
1921   The Cave Girl
1924   Welcome Stranger
1925   Kivalina of the Ice Lands
          The Prairie Wife
1928   Mother Machree
Hillyer, Lambert
1923   Scars of Jealousy
1932   White Eagle
1933   The California Trail
1941   Thunder Over the Prairie
1945   South of the Rio Grande
1946   Border Bandits
Hilo Hattie
1942   Song of the Islands
Hilton, Helen
1915   How Molly Malone Made
          Good
Hilton, Paul
1945   A Tree Grows in Brooklyn
Hilton, Robert
1950   Indian Territory
Himm, Michael *see* **Hinn, Michael**
Hinckley, William L.
1917   The Secret of Eve
Hinds, Samuel S. *same as* **Hinds,
  Samuel** *not the same as* **Hines,
  Samuel E.**
1934   The Cat's-Paw
          Massacre
          Operator 13
          She Was a Lady
1935   Black Fury
          Rendezvous
1937   Black Legion
1938   The Rage of Paris
1941   Road Agent
1944   Chip Off the Old Block
1948   The Boy with Green Hair
          Call Northside 777
Hines, Charles
1924   Conductor 1492
1928   Chinatown Charlie

Hines, Harry
1956   The Catered Affair
1960   Key Witness
Hines, John
1918   The Golden Wall
1924   Conductor 1492
1928   Chinatown Charlie
Hines, Samuel E. *not the same as*
  Hinds, Samuel S.
1934   He Was Her Man
Hing, Tom
1917   The War of the Tongs
Hingert, Maureen
1956   Pillars of the Sky
Hingle, Pat
1960   Wild River
Hinkle, Robert *same as* **Hinkle,
  Bob**
1956   Dakota Incident
1957   The Oklahoman
Hinn, Michael *same as* **Himm,
  Michael**
1957   The Halliday Brand
1958   Gun Fever
Hinsdell, Oliver
1946   Till the End of Time
Hinton, Ed *same as* **Hinton, Edgar**
1948   Harpoon
1955   Apache Ambush
          Seminole Uprising
1956   Walk the Proud Land
1958   Escape from Red Rock
          Fort Bowie
The Hip Paraders
1949?   Harlem Follies
Hipp, Dorothy
1920   A Tokio Siren
Hipp, Young
1920   Dinty
Hirai, Tommy T.
1951   Go for Broke!
Hirliman, George A.
1935   De la sartén al fuego
1936   Daniel Boone
1937   El capitán Tormenta
          El carnaval del diablo
Hirsch, Richard
1944   An American Romance
Hirsh, Nathan
1923   Purple Dawn
1931   Zein Weib's Lubovnick
Hirshbein, Omus
1940   Overture to Glory
Hirshbein, Peretz
1937   Green Fields
Hirshfeld, Alex
1936   Dimples
Hirst, Herb
1958   Tonka
Hitch, William
1949   The Red Menace
Hitchcock, Alfred
1944   Lifeboat
1946   Notorious
Hitchcock, Walter
1914   Uncle Tom's Cabin
1915   The Girl I Left Behind Me
Hittleman, Carl K.
1948   Shep Comes Home
1950   The Baron of Arizona
1951   Little Big Horn
1955   Kentucky Rifle
1957   Gun Battle at Monterey
Hively, George
1918   Wild Women
1924   The Broken Law
Hix, Tommy
1946   Beware
Hlaca, Rajner
1932   Ljubav i strast
Hoagland, George
1950   The Breaking Point
1953   The Jazz Singer
Hobart, Rose
1942   Dr. Gillespie's New
          Assistant
1946   Canyon Passage
1947   The Farmer's Daughter

Hobbes, Halliwell
1934   She Was a Lady
1935   Charlie Chan in Shanghai
1937   Maid of Salem
1943   His Butler's Sister
1944   Mr. Skeffington
1946   Canyon Passage

Hobbs, Peter
1949   Lost Boundaries

The Hobnobbers
1951   Yes Sir, Mr. Bones

Hobson, Valerie
1934   Strange Wives
1935   Chinatown Squad

Hoddison, Patricia
1953   Bright Road

Hodge, Noel
1950   Intruder in the Dust

Hodge, Rex
1919   The Sleeping Lion

Hodges, Eddie
1960   The Adventures of
         Huckleberry Finn

Hodges, Maxine
1914   The Jungle

Hodges, Ralph
1950   No Way Out
         Stars in My Crown

Hodgins, Earle *same as* **Hodgins,
Earl**
1935   The Cyclone Ranger
         Harmony Lane
1936   Aces and Eights
1937   Hills of Old Wyoming
         Nation Aflame
1942   Shut My Big Mouth
         Syncopation
1943   Gangway for Tomorrow
         Ladies' Day
1944   An American Romance
         The San Antonio Kid
1945   Nob Hill
         Phantom of the Plains
1947   Calendar Girl
         Oregon Trail Scouts
         The Return of Rin Tin Tin
         Vigilantes of Boomtown
1948   Jiggs and Maggie in Court
         Old Los Angeles
         The Paleface
         Unconquered
1949   Jiggs and Maggie in
         Jackpot Jitters
1951   Show Boat
         Slaughter Trail
         Westward the Women
1957   The Oklahoman

Hodgson, Leyland *same as*
Hodgson, Leland
1938   The Buccaneer
1939   Daughters Courageous
         Mr. Moto Takes a
         Vacation
         Mr. Moto's Last Warning
1940   The Man I Married
         Murder over New York
1941   Road Agent
1943   The Gang's All Here
1945   Johnny Angel
1946   Rendezvous 24
1948   Unconquered

Hodiak, John
1944   Lifeboat
1950   Ambush
         Battleground
         A Lady Without Passport
1951   Across the Wide Missouri
1953   Ambush at Tomahawk
         Gap
         Conquest of Cochise
1955   Trial

Hodnutt, Lois
1942   The Vanishing Virginian

Höcker, Oscar
1931   Die Dreigroschenoper

Hoerl, Arthur
1929   In Old California
         The Peacock Fan
1934   Drums O' Voodoo
1938   California Frontier
         Spirit of Youth
1939   Double Deal

Hoey, Dennis
1943   They Came to Blow Up
         America
1947   The Foxes of Harrow

Hoey, George
1938   Little Miss Roughneck

Hoffenstein, Samuel
1942   Tales of Manhattan
1943   His Butler's Sister

Hoffman, Aaron
1917   The Secret of Eve

Hoffman, Adolph
1956   Singing in the Dark

Hoffman, Anetta
1938   Two Sisters

Hoffman, Bern
1955   Murder in Villa Capri

Hoffman, Bob
1940   Lucky Cisco Kid
1948   Moonrise

Hoffman, Charles
1952   The Half-Breed

Hoffman, Gertrude W. *same as*
Hoffman, Gertrude
1934   The Cat's-Paw
1943   Dr. Gillespie's Criminal
         Case
1947   California

Hoffman, Herman
1955   Bad Day at Black Rock

Hoffman, Howard
1955   Headline Hunters

Hoffman, Jerry
1938   Road Demon
         Speed to Burn
1939   Winner Take All

Hoffman, John
1950   I Killed Geronimo

Hoffman, Joseph
1936   Charlie Chan at the Race
         Track
         Charlie Chan's Secret
1943   Redhead from Manhattan
1950   Buccaneer's Girl

Hoffman, Leonard
1939   Heaven with a Barbed
         Wire Fence
1948   Call Northside 777

Hoffman, Max, Jr.
1942   They Died With Their
         Boots On

Hoffman, Otto
1919   Behind the Door
1920   It's a Great Life
1922   The Five Dollar Baby
1926   Millionaires
1929   Is Everybody Happy?
1930   Abraham Lincoln
1931   The Avenger
         Cimarron
1934   Behold My Wife!
         Beloved
1939   Heaven with a Barbed
         Wire Fence
1940   Lucky Cisco Kid

Hoffman, Paul
1950   Mystery Submarine
1952   Bright Victory
1955   Blackboard Jungle
1959   Odds Against Tomorrow

Hoffman, Renaud
1925   One of the Bravest
1927   A Harp in Hock
1930   Sombras de gloria

Hoffman, Ruby
1915   Children of the Ghetto
         The Danger Signal
1916   A Woman's Honor
1918   Uncle Tom's Cabin

Hoffman, Stan
1956   Singing in the Dark

Hogaboom, Winfield
1916   The Daughter of the Don

Hogan, Carl
1946   Beware

Hogan, Dick
1939   Charlie Chan in Reno
1940   Mexican Spitfire Out
         West
1942   Rubber Racketeers
1943   Action in the North
         Atlantic
         They Came to Blow Up
         America

Hogan, Jack
1956   Man from Del Rio

Hogan, James *same as* **Hogan,
James P.**
1927   Finnegan's Ball
1928   The Broken Mask
1936   Desert Gold
1938   The Texans

Hogan, Michael
1941   Lady from Louisiana

Hogan, Pat
1953   Arrowhead
         The Nebraskan
1954   Overland Pacific
1955   Chief Crazy Horse
         Davy Crockett, King of
         the Wild Frontier
         Kiss of Fire
         Smoke Signal
1956   The Last Frontier
         Pillars of the Sky
         Secret of Treasure
         Mountain
         7th Cavalry
1960   Flaming Star

Hogen, Virginia
1942   Song of the Islands

Hogue, Eades
1956   Baby Doll

Hohl, Arthur
1934   As the Earth Turns
         Massacre
1935   Romance in Manhattan
1936   It Had to Happen
         Show Boat
1937   Slave Ship
1941   Ride on Vaquero
1942   Whispering Ghosts
1945   Our Vines Have Tender
         Grapes
         Salome, Where She
         Danced

Hohu, Martha
1950   Damien
1954   Hell's Half Acre

Hokanson, Mary Alan
1951   Jim Thorpe—All-American
         Westward the Women
1953   So Big
1958   Home Before Dark
1960   All the Fine Young
         Cannibals
         Key Witness

Holbrook, Allen
1933   Circle Canyon

Holbrook, James
1950   Right Cross

Holbrook, Vic
1947   Calendar Girl

Holcomb, Thomas, Maj.
1918   The Unbeliever

Holden, Fay
1937   Souls at Sea
1939   Judge Hardy and Son
1944   Andy Hardy's Blonde
         Trouble
1946   Canyon Passage
1950   The Big Hangover

Holden, Gloria
1938   Hawaii Calls
1942   Apache Trail
1953   Dream Wife

Holden, Harry
1919   A Bachelor's Wife
1927   The Gay Defender
1929   Show Boat
1931   Cimarron

Holden, James
1950   Sands of Iwo Jima

Holden, Tex
1951   Across the Wide Missouri
1957   Run of the Arrow

Holden, William
1931   Charlie Chan Carries On
1949   Streets of Laredo

Holder, Roland
1931   The Exile

Holding, Thomas
1916   Silks and Satins
1923   Ruggles of Red Gap

Holdren, Judd
1950   Mystery Submarine
1959   The FBI Story
1960   Ice Palace

Holeby, Walter
1921   A Giant of His Race
1923   A Shot in the Night

Holiday, Billie
1947   New Orleans

Hollacher, Harold
1916   Hulda from Holland

Holland, Cecil C.
1917   His Sweetheart

Holland, Clifford
1939   Reform School
1942   The Vanishing Virginian

Holland, Edna *same as* **Holland,
Edna M.**
1939   Judge Hardy and Son
1942   They Died With Their
         Boots On
1943   Dr. Gillespie's Criminal
         Case
1945   Between Two Women
         Sunbonnet Sue
1946   Dark Alibi
1948   Gentleman's Agreement
         Shep Comes Home
1949   The Prairie
         The Sky Dragon
1958   Home Before Dark
1959   The Last Angry Man

Holland, Eugene *same as* **Holland,
Gene**
1946   Song of the South
1948   Fighting Father Dunne
         I Remember Mama

Holland, Frank
1914   Springtime

Holland, Gene *see* **Holland,
Eugene**

Holland, Gladys
1951   Go for Broke!

Holland, Harold
1918   The Midnight Patrol
         Tony America
1921   Black Roses
         Where Lights Are Low
1922   Come On Over

Holland, John
1940   Phantom of Chinatown
1942   Submarine Raider
         We Were Dancing
1949   Massacre River
1950   Rio Grande Patrol
         Rock Island Trail

Holland, Leza
1947   Desperate

Holland, Willard
1948   Open Secret

Hollander, Hannah
1937   I Want to Be a Mother
1941   Mazel Tov Yidden

Holliday, Frank *(actor)*
1934   Broadway Bill

Holliday, J. Frank *(writer)*
1926   The Strong Man

Holliday, Judy
1956   Full of Life

Holliday, Marjorie
1949   House of Strangers

Holliman, Earl
1954   Broken Lance
1956   The Burning Hills
         Giant
1957   Trooper Hook
1959   Last Train from Gun Hill

Hollingshead, Gordon
1927   Irish Hearts
1928   The Jazz Singer
1937   Prairie Thunder

Hollingsworth, Alfred *same as* **Hollingsworth, A.**
1915   The Gambler of the West
1917   The Sudden Gentleman
1919   Diane of the Green Van
        The Red Viper
        The Sneak
1920   White Youth
Hollingsworth, Harry
1934   Coming Out Party
1938   Little Miss Roughneck
Hollister, Flora
1921   Across the Divide
Hollmann, Werner
1931   Tropennächte
Holloway, Carol *see* **Halloway, Carol**
Holloway, John
1921   Across the Divide
Holloway, Sterling
1934   Operator 13
1935   Rendezvous
1937   Maid of Salem
1955   Kentucky Rifle
1960   The Adventures of Huckleberry Finn
Holly, Ellen
1960   Take a Giant Step
Holly, Ruth
1942   Friendly Enemies
Hollywood, Edwin L.
1916   The Thousand Dollar Husband
1923   Jamestown
Holm, Bert
1945   Johnny Angel
Holm, Celeste
1948   Gentleman's Agreement
Holm, Fred
1950   Two Flags West
Holman, Harry
1932   So Big
1934   Broadway Bill
1937   Nation Aflame
1938   The Texans
1942   Mexican Spitfire at Sea
1945   Where Do We Go From Here?
1946   Without Reservations
Holmes, Ben
1942   Holiday Inn
Holmes, Dennis
1960   Key Witness
Holmes, George
1943   Crash Dive
1946   Dark Alibi
Holmes, Gerda
1918   Wanted, a Mother
Holmes, Gilbert
1933   Robbers' Roost
Holmes, Helen
1937   The Californian
Holmes, Herbert
1945   Jealousy
Holmes, J. Merrill
1941   Gauchos of Eldorado
Holmes, Leon
1926   April Fool
1927   Frisco Sally Levy
        The Shamrock and the Rose
Holmes, Mabel
1921   A Giant of His Race
Holmes, Maynard
1941   New York Town
1947   The Foxes of Harrow
1948   Big City
        The Lady from Shanghai
Holmes, Milton
1928   A Ship Comes In
1943   Mr. Lucky
Holmes, Phillips
1930   Galas de la Paramount
1936   General Spanky
Holmes, Rubber Neck
1938   The Duke Is Tops
1940   The Notorious Elinor Lee
Holmes, Stuart
1914   Life's Shop Window
1915   The Clemenceau Case
        The Girl I Left Behind Me

1917   The Wild Girl
1919   The Other Man's Wife
1920   Lifting Shadows
1921   No Woman Knows
1925   Friendly Enemies
1928   The Cavalier
        The Hawk's Nest
1942   All Through the Night
        Secret Enemies
1947   The Farmer's Daughter
        The Mighty McGurk
1948   Up in Central Park
1950   The Big Hangover
1951   The Great Caruso
1953   Ride, Vaquero!
1958   The Last Hurrah
Holmes, Taylor
1918   Ruggles of Red Gap
Holmes, Thor
1953   So Big
Holmes, Wendell
1949   Lost Boundaries
Holmquist, Sigrid
1924   Two Shall Be Born
Holt, Andrew
1946   Strange Voyage
Holt, Betty
1937   It Could Happen to You
Holt, Charity
1950   Two Flags West
Holt, David *same as* **Holt, David Jack**
1934   The Cat's-Paw
1938   The Adventures of Tom Sawyer
1950   Battleground
Holt, Edwin
1916   The Pretenders
Holt, George
1914   The Little Angel of Canyon Creek
Holt, Jack
1917   The Call of the East
        The Little American
        The Secret Game
1918   Hidden Pearls
        The Honor of His House
        One More American
        The Squaw Man
1921   All Souls' Eve
1924   North of 36
1925   The Thundering Herd
1935   The Littlest Rebel
1942   Cat People
1946   Renegade Girl
1948   The Arizona Ranger
1951   Across the Wide Missouri
Holt, Jennifer
1944   Outlaw Trail
1945   The Navajo Trail
1947   Buffalo Bill Rides Again
Holt, Nat
1950   The Cariboo Trail
1951   Flaming Feather
        Warpath
1953   Arrowhead
Holt, Tim
1938   The Renegade Ranger
1943   Hitler's Children
1947   Thunder Mountain
        Under the Tonto Rim
        Wild Horse Mesa
1948   The Arizona Ranger
        Gun Smugglers
        Guns of Hate
        Indian Agent
        Western Heritage
1949   Brothers in the Saddle
        Masked Raiders
        The Mysterious Desperado
        Riders of the Range
        Rustlers
        Stagecoach Kid
1950   Border Treasure
        Rio Grande Patrol
        Storm Over Wyoming
Holtz, Tenen
1927   Frisco Sally Levy
1930   The Kibitzer
        The Melody Man
1931   Gentleman's Fate

1939   Let Freedom Ring
Holtzman, Bernard
1932   The Unfortunate Bride
1933   The Eternal Jew
Holubar, Allen
1919   The Right to Happiness
Homans, Robert *same as* **Homans, Robert E.**
1927   The Princess from Hoboken
1929   Smiling Irish Eyes
1930   Check and Double Check
        Son of the Gods
1931   The Black Camel
1934   Straight Is the Way
1936   Below the Deadline
        Charlie Chan at the Race Track
        Laughing Irish Eyes
        The Prisoner of Shark Island
        Ride, Ranger, Ride
        Rose of the Rancho
1937   Black Legion
        Song of the City
1938   Outside of Paradise
1939   King of Chinatown
1940   East of the River
        Little Nellie Kelly
1941   The Gang's All Here
1942   Holiday Inn
        Nazi Agent
        North to the Klondike
1943   The Amazing Mrs. Holliday
        Jack London
1944   Buffalo Bill
1945   A Medal for Benny
        The Scarlet Clue
Homeier, Skip *same as* **Homeier, Skippy**
1944   Tomorrow the World!
1956   The Burning Hills
        Dakota Incident
Homer, Pete
1934   The Cat's-Paw
Homes, Geoffrey *see* **Mainwaring, Daniel**
Homolka, Oscar
1948   I Remember Mama
1949   Anna Lucasta
Homs, Juan de
1930   Estrellados
        Olimpia
        El presidio
1931   La fruta amarga
        La llama sagrada
        El príncipe gondolero
Hong, Ging
1939?   A Chinese Gains a Fortune in America
Honigman, Irving
1937   The Cantor's Son
Hoo, Hugh
1945   Betrayal from the East
Hoobvner, Luther
1935   A Night at the Opera
Hood, Ann
1956   Singing in the Dark
Hood, Danny
1945   Nob Hill
Hood, Foster
1959   Yellowstone Kelly
1960   Flaming Star
Hood, Janice
1945   A Tree Grows in Brooklyn
Hood, Jim
1945   The Navajo Trail
Hooker, Brian
1936   Rose of the Rancho
Hooker, E. L.
1950   Intruder in the Dust
Hooker, Hugh
1950   Bandit Queen
1951   Fort Defiance
Hooker, Ken
1958   Wild Is the Wind
Hoops, Arthur
1914   The Straight Road
1915   The Danger Signal
1917   The Secret of Eve

Hoose, Fred
1943   The Law Rides Again
1951   The Great Caruso
The Hoosier Hot Shots
1948   Singin' Spurs
Hope, Anna
1942   Foreign Agent
Hope, Bob
1941   Louisiana Purchase
1948   The Paleface
1957   Beau James
Hope, Boots
1927   The Broken Violin
Hope, Edward
1955   The Long Gray Line
Hope, Gloria
1918   Free and Equal
1920   The Third Woman
Hope, James *same as* **Hope, James E.**
1959   The Jayhawkers!
1960   Ice Palace
Hopf, Hans
1946   Three Wise Fools
Hopkins, George
1918   The Hell Cat
Hopkins, Jack
1917   Queen X
1922   For His Mother's Sake
Hopkins, Linda
1956   Rockin' the Blues
Hopkins, May
1921   Diane of Star Hollow
Hopkins, Peggy
1918   Woman and the Law
Hopkins, Robert *same as* **Hopkins, Robert E.**
1925   Old Clothes
1931   Buster se marie
Hopper, Bill *see* **Hopper, William**
Hopper, De Wolf *see* **Hopper, William**
Hopper, Dennis
1956   Giant
1959   The Young Land
1960   Key Witness
Hopper, E. Mason
1918   Her American Husband
        Mystic Faces
1920   It's a Great Life
1921   Hold Your Horses
1922   Hungry Hearts
Hopper, Hedda
1938   Dangerous to Know
Hopper, Jerry
1955   Smoke Signal
Hopper, Wesley
1937   The Devil's Playground
1947   California
1948   Fighting Father Dunne
1949   Knock on Any Door
Hopper, William *same as* **Hopper, Bill; Hopper, De Wolf; Hopper, De Wolfe**
1939   Daughters Courageous
1940   The Fighting 69th
        Knute Rockne—All American
        Santa Fe Trail
1942   Across the Pacific
        All Through the Night
        Gentleman Jim
        Juke Girl
        Secret Enemies
        They Died With Their Boots On
1943   Action in the North Atlantic
        Air Force
        Yankee Doodle Dandy
1954   Sitting Bull
Hopton, Russell
1931   Street Scene
1934   He Was Her Man
1935   Charlie Chan in Shanghai
1936   Below the Deadline
        Rose of the Rancho
        Sutter's Gold
1937   Big City
        One Mile from Heaven
1945   Betrayal from the East
        Johnny Angel

Horace, Johnny
1943   Stormy Weather
Horan, James
1960   The Adventures of
        Huckleberry Finn
Horan, John
1950   A Ticket to Tomahawk
Horkheimer, E. D.
1917   Sold at Auction
Horkheimer, H. M.
1917   Sold at Auction
Horman, Arthur T. *same as*
    Horman, Arthur
1936   Ellis Island
1943   Air Force
1944   Dark Waters
Horn, Camilla
1929   Die Königsloge
1931   La fiesta del diablo
        (*foreign version*)
Hornblow, Arthur, Jr.
1934   Limehouse Blues
1935   Ruggles of Red Gap
1937   Waikiki Wedding
1941   Hold Back the Dawn
Hornbostell, E.
1920   The Great Shadow
Hornbuckle, Benjamin
1955   Davy Crockett, King of
        the Wild Frontier
Horne, David
1959   The Sheriff of Fractured
        Jaw
Horne, James (*actor*)
1948   Unconquered
1950   Battleground
1951   The Magnificent Yankee
Horne, James W. (*dir*)
1926   Kosher Kitty Kelly
1930   Una cana al aire
        Locuras de amor
        El príncipe del dólar
        El príncipe del dólar
        (*foreign version*)
1931   Los calaveras
        Los calaveras (*foreign
        version*)
        Politiquerías
Horne, Joyce
1943   Yankee Doodle Dandy
1944   Since You Went Away
Horne, Lena
1938   The Duke Is Tops
1943   Cabin in the Sky
        Stormy Weather
1946   Mantan Messes Up
1946?   Harlem on Parade
Horne, Marilyn
1954   Carmen Jones
Horne, Victoria
1951   Cuban Fireball
Horne, William *same as* **Horne, W.
T.**
1916   The Social Buccaneer
1923   Purple Dawn
Hornemann, Anna Marie
1945   The House on 92nd St.
Horner, Harry
1956   Man from Del Rio
Horsley, David *same as* **Alison,
    David; Horsley, John David**
1934   Charlie Chan's Courage
1937   Charlie Chan at the
        Olympics
1940   New Moon
1943   Air Force
        Good Luck, Mr. Yates
        Margin for Error
1950   Jolson Sings Again
Horton, Clara
1917   The Plow Woman
1918   Huck and Tom; or, the
        Further Adventures of
        Tom Sawyer
        The Yellow Dog
1920   It's a Great Life
1927   Sailor Izzy Murphy
Horton, Edward Everett
1923   Ruggles of Red Gap
1930   Take the Heir
1943   The Gang's All Here

Horton, Robert
1952   Apache War Smoke
1953   Bright Road
Horvath, Charles
1949   Colorado Territory
1951   Jim Thorpe—All-American
        Saturday's Hero
        Snake River Desperadoes
1953   The Man Behind the Gun
1954   Taza, Son of Cochise
1955   Chief Crazy Horse
        Kiss of Fire
1956   Dakota Incident
        Pillars of the Sky
1957   Band of Angels
        The Guns of Fort
        Petticoat
        Man in the Shadow
        Pawnee
1959   Gunmen from Laredo
        Night of the Quarter
        Moon
Horváth, Eva
1930   El secreto del doctor
        (*foreign version*)
Horwin, Jerry
1943   Stormy Weather
Hosay, Professor
1924   A Son of Satan
Hoschelle, Marjorie
1943   Air Force
1946   The Red Dragon
Hostetler, Paul
1950   Panic in the Streets
Houck, Clyde
1955   Kentucky Rifle
Houck, Doris
1946   The Gentleman
        Misbehaves
Houck, Joy
1955   Kentucky Rifle
Hough, Bert
1957   Burden of Truth
Hough, E. Morton
1928   The House of Scandal
Houghton, Jean
1936   Star for a Night
Houghton, Shepherd *same as*
    Houghton, Shep
1948   Tap Roots
1959   Imitation of Life
Hould, Ra *see* **Sinclair, Ronald**
Houry, Henry
1918   Find the Woman
House, Allan
1943   The Meanest Man in the
        World
House, Billy
1931   Smart Money
1959   Imitation of Life
House, Carroll
1959   The FBI Story
House, Donald *same as* **House,
    Don**
1943   The Ox-Bow Incident
1944   Buffalo Bill
1951   Across the Wide Missouri
        Westward the Women
House, Jack
1944   Buffalo Bill
House, Lucille
1933   It's Great to Be Alive
1951   Westward the Women
Houser, Lionel
1937   Border Cafe
1939   The Girl from Mexico
1942   Three Hearts for Julia
Houser, Richard
1952   Bright Victory
Housman, Arthur
1919   Toby's Bow
1925   Braveheart
1928   Sins of the Fathers
1936   After the Thin Man
        Show Boat
Housner, Jerry
1942   Syncopation
Houston, Eddye L.
1946?   Go Down, Death!

Houston, George
1936   Let's Sing Again
Houston, Mark
1960   All the Fine Young
        Cannibals
Houston, Norman
1939   In Old Caliente
1940   Young Buffalo Bill
1945   Wanderer of the
        Wasteland
1946   Sunset Pass
1947   Thunder Mountain
        Under the Tonto Rim
        Wild Horse Mesa
1948   The Arizona Ranger
        Gun Smugglers
        Guns of Hate
        Indian Agent
        Western Heritage
1949   Brothers in the Saddle
        Masked Raiders
        The Mysterious
        Desperado
        Riders of the Range
        Stagecoach Kid
1950   Border Treasure
        Rio Grande Patrol
Houston, Wayne
1958   Tonka
Houten, Glympia
1934   Laughing Boy
Hoven, Adrian
1960   I Aim at the Stars: the
        Wernher von Braun
        Story
Hovey, Ann
1936   The Glory Trail
Hovey, Eugene
1945   Where Do We Go From
        Here?
Hovey, Tamara
1949   That Midnight Kiss
Hovick, Louise *see* **Lee, Gypsy
Rose**
Howard, Anne
1934   She Was a Lady
Howard, Art *same as* **Howard,
    Arthur**
1947   The Farmer's Daughter
1950   Emergency Wedding
Howard, Bert
1944   An American Romance
1949   Rustlers
Howard, Betty *same as* **Howard,
    Betsy**
1944   Since You Went Away
1956   The Benny Goodman
        Story
Howard, Bob
1946   Stars on Parade
1948?   Junction 88
1949?   The Joint Is Jumpin'
Howard, Boothe
1936   Charlie Chan at the
        Circus
        Charlie Chan at the Race
        Track
        Robin Hood of El Dorado
Howard, Catherine
1955   Good Morning, Miss Dove
Howard, Chuck
1958   The Last Hurrah
Howard, Clifford
1919   The Gray Horizon
        Lasca
Howard, Constance
1928   Mother Machree
1935   The Wedding Night
Howard, David
1930   Cuando el amor ríe
        Del mismo barro
        El último de los Vargas
1931   Charlie Chan Carries On
        (*foreign version*)
        ¿Conoces a tu mujer?
        Cuerpo y alma
        Esclavas de la moda
        La gran jornada
1932   The Golden West
        Mystery Ranch
        The Rainbow Trail

Howard, Willie (actor)
1936   Daniel Boone
1938   The Renegade Ranger
1939   The Fighting Gringo
Howard, Edward M.
1944   Tucson Raiders
Howard, Esther
1932   The Cohens and Kellys in
        Hollywood
1933   Grand Slam
1936   Klondike Annie
1938   The Texans
1941   Sullivan's Travels
1942   Tales of Manhattan
1946   Without Reservations
1952   Rose of Cimarron
Howard, Frederic *same as*
    **Howard, Fred; Howard,
    Frederick**
1931   The Guilty Generation
1934   Coming Out Party
1945   Great Stagecoach Robbery
1946   Till the End of Time
1947   The Jolson Story
Howard, Gertrude
1928   Uncle Tom's Cabin
1929   Hearts in Dixie
        Show Boat
Howard, Gloria
1955   Brevities of 1955
Howard, Harold (*actor*)
1937   Maid of Salem
Howard, Harry (*prod*)
1950   The Cariboo Trail
Howard, John
1942   Submarine Raider
1949   The Fighting Kentuckian
Howard, Judy
1960   Studs Lonigan
Howard, Kathleen
1943   Crash Dive
1948   Cry of the City
Howard, Laura
1922   Blazing Arrows
Howard, Leslie
1939   Gone With the Wind
Howard, Leta
1932   Hypnotized
Howard, Lewis
1942   Seven Sweethearts
Howard, Linda *see* **Perry, Susan**
Howard, Paul
1930   King of Jazz
Howard, Rance
1956   Frontier Woman
Howard, Richard
1926   Desert Gold
        The Vanishing American
Howard, Shemp
1940   Murder over New York
1946   The Gentleman
        Misbehaves
Howard, Shingzie
1922   The Dungeon
        Uncle Jasper's Will
        The Virgin of Seminole
1924   The House Behind the
        Cedars
        A Son of Satan
1926   A Prince of His Race
1927   Children of Fate
Howard, Sidney
1930   A Lady to Love
        A Lady to Love (*foreign
        version*)
1939   Gone With the Wind
1940   Northwest Passage (Book
        I—Rogers' Rangers)
Howard, Vance
1958   The Rawhide Trail
Howard, William K. (*dir*)
1922   Captain Fly-by-Night
1924   East of Broadway
1925   The Thundering Herd
1927   White Gold
1928   A Ship Comes In
1929   Love, Live and Laugh
1935   Rendezvous
Howard, Willie (*actor*)
1936   Rose of the Rancho

Howarth, James
1919   Deliverance
Howarth, Lillian
1919?   The Brand of Judas
1921   When the Clock Struck Nine
Howat, Clark
1951   Gambling House
Only the Valiant
Saturday's Hero
1952   The Fabulous Senorita
Red Ball Express
Howatt, William
1925   The Greatest Love of All
Howdy, Clyde
1959   Yellowstone Kelly
Howe, Betty
1919   As a Man Thinks
1922   Breaking Home Ties
Howe, Harlan
1951   Only the Valiant
Howe, James Wong
1930   Chijlku wo mawasuru chikara
1954   Go Man Go
Howe, Jimmy
1932   White Eagle
Howe, Wally
1934   Operator 13
1936   Tundra
Howell, Dorothy
1927   Sally in Our Alley
1928   Ransom
1932   Hombres en mi vida
Howell, Hazel
1926   Buffalo Bill on the U. P. Trail
A Trip to Chinatown
Howell, Jean
1955   Apache Woman
Howell, Kenneth
1941   Hurry, Charlie, Hurry
Howell, Lottice
1930   Estrellados
Howell, Virginia
1933   Ever in My Heart
Howes, Reed
1934   Chloe: Love Is Calling You
1936   Custer's Last Stand
1940   Covered Wagon Days
1941   Western Union
1950   Ambush
1952   Indian Uprising
The Iron Mistress
1953   The Man Behind the Gun
1957   The Guns of Fort Petticoat
1958   Sierra Baron
Howland, Jobyna
1933   The Cohens and Kellys in Trouble
Howland, Olin same as **Howlin, Olin**
1932   So Big
1934   Behold My Wife!
Wagon Wheels
1938   The Adventures of Tom Sawyer
Mr. Moto's Gamble
1939   Gone With the Wind
1941   Belle Starr
1943   Dixie
Jack London
1946   Three Wise Fools
1947   Easy Come, Easy Go
1948   The Dude Goes West
The Paleface
1949   Anna Lucasta
Massacre River
Top O' the Morning
1950   Rock Island Trail
A Ticket to Tomahawk
1952   The Fabulous Senorita
Howlett, Lloyd
1947   Going to Glory, Come to Jesus
Howlin, Olin see **Howland, Olin**
Howling Wolf
1934   Behold My Wife!
1936   Custer's Last Stand

Hoxie, Hart
1919   Told in the Hills
Hoxie, Jack
1915   Captain Courtesy
1921   The Double O
1922   The Crow's Nest
1925   The Red Rider
1926   The Last Frontier
1932   Law and Lawless
Hoy, Danny
1921   No Woman Knows
Hoy, Robert
1950   Ambush
1953   The Man from the Alamo
1954   Taza, Son of Cochise
1955   Kiss of Fire
The Long Gray Line
1956   Raw Edge
Hoyos, Rodolfo
1930   Revista Hispano-Americana
1931   Carne de cabaret
1934   Un capitán de cosacos
1935   A Night at the Opera
Piernas de seda
1949   We Were Strangers
1956   Secret of Treasure Mountain
1957   Gun Battle at Monterey
Hoyos, Rodolfo, Jr.
1950   A Lady Without Passport
1952   The Fighter
Hoyt, Arthur
1918   The Yellow Dog
1923   The White Flower
1932   Call Her Savage
1933   The Cohens and Kellys in Trouble
1934   The Cat's-Paw
1935   Chinatown Squad
A Night at the Ritz
1938   The Rage of Paris
1941   Sullivan's Travels
1942   Apache Trail
Hoyt, Clegg
1956   Mohawk
1958   Gun Fever
1959   Al Capone
1960   Cimarron
Hoyt, Harry O.
1918   Hitting the Trail
I Want to Forget
1926   Sweet Rosie O'Grady
1927   Bitter Apples
Hoyt, John
1950   The Lawless
1951   New Mexico
1955   Blackboard Jungle
Trial
1956   Death of a Scoundrel
Mohawk
Wetbacks
Hoyt, Russell
1942   The Navy Comes Through
1943   The Gang's All Here
Ladies' Day
1944   Since You Went Away
Something for the Boys
Hoyt, Susan
1949   The Kissing Bandit
Hruba, Rudy see **Ralston, Rudy**
Hruby, Delphine
1951   Gambling House
The Hubba Hubba Girls
1947   Jivin' in Be-Bop
Hubbard, John same as **Hubbard, Jack**
1938   The Buccaneer
1943   What's Buzzin' Cousin?
Hubbard, Lucien
1919   Mandarin's Gold
1920   Outside the Law
1921   Cheated Love
1925   The Thundering Herd
1926   Desert Gold
The Vanishing American
1931   Smart Money
The Squaw Man
1934   Lazy River
Operator 13
Straight Is the Way
1937   Man of the People
Song of the City

Hubbard, Ralph
1946   Without Reservations
Hubbard, T. Elbert
1952   Buffalo Bill in Tomahawk Territory
Hubbard, Tom same as **Hubbard, Thomas G.**
1946   Without Reservations
1952   Buffalo Bill in Tomahawk Territory
Red Snow
1954   Thunder Pass
1956   Daniel Boone, Trail Blazer
Secret of Treasure Mountain
1957   Raiders of Old California
Huber, Harold
1932   The Match King
1934   He Was Her Man
1935   Naughty Marietta
1936   Kelly the Second
Klondike Annie
Muss 'Em Up
1937   Charlie Chan on Broadway
1938   Charlie Chan at Monte Carlo
Mr. Moto's Gamble
Passport Husband
1939   City in Darkness
1940   Kit Carson
1941   Charlie Chan in Rio
1942   Little Tokyo, U.S.A.
Huber, Jacqueline
1945   Nob Hill
Hubert, René
1931   El proceso de Mary Dugan (foreign version)
Hudkins, Clyde, Jr.
1950   Colt .45
Hudkins, Dick
1950   Colt .45
Hudman, Wesley same as **Hudman, Wes**
1949   Satan's Cradle
1950   The Girl from San Lorenzo
I Killed Geronimo
Indian Territory
1951   Fort Defiance
1954   Battle of Rogue River
Hudson, Bill see **Hudson, William**
Hudson, Daral
1946   Canyon Passage
Hudson, Earl
1924   So Big
1925   Scarlet Saint
Hudson, Ethel
1940   The Ramparts We Watch
Hudson, John
1952   The Battle at Apache Pass
Bright Victory
Red Ball Express
1955   Fort Yuma
1956   Mohawk
Hudson, Larry
1952   The Raiders
Hudson, Rochelle
1934   Imitation of Life
Judge Priest
1937   That I May Live
1938   Mr. Moto Takes a Chance
Rascals
1942   Rubber Racketeers
Hudson, Rock
1950   Winchester '73
1951   Tomahawk
1952   Bright Victory
1953   Seminole
1954   Taza, Son of Cochise
1956   Giant
Hudson, Virginia Tyler
1918   Wanted, a Mother
Hudson, Wilbur
1915   An American Gentleman
Hudson, William same as **Hudson, Bill**
1949   The Red Menace
1950   Sands of Iwo Jima
1957   Band of Angels

Huey, Richard
1934   Chloe: Love Is Calling You
Huff, Carrie
1934   Drums O' Voodoo
Huff, Louise
1915   Marse Covington
1918   Sandy
Huffaker, Clair
1960   Flaming Star
Hug, Wallace Lee
1958   Tonka
Huggins, Bob
1917   The Tell-Tale Step
Hugh, R. John
1957   Naked in the Sun
Hughes, Andrew
1960   The Last Voyage
Hughes, Bill see **Hughes, William**
Hughes, Carol
1941   Under Fiesta Stars
1943   What's Buzzin' Cousin?
1946   The Red Dragon
1949   Stagecoach Kid
Hughes, Charles Anthony
1958   The Last Hurrah
Hughes, Charlie
1949   Call of the Forest
1952   Buffalo Bill in Tomahawk Territory
Hughes, David H.
1952   The Quiet Man
Hughes, Gareth
1919   The Red Viper
1925   The Midnight Girl
1927   The Auctioneer
Heroes in Blue
1929   Mister Antonio
Hughes, Howard
1928   The Mating Call
1932   Scarface
1943   The Outlaw
Hughes, J. Anthony same as **Hughes, Tony**
1936   It Had to Happen
1938   Gateway
In Old Chicago
Speed to Burn
1939   The Cisco Kid and the Lady
1942   Young America
1950   The Cariboo Trail
Hughes, John B.
1945   Rhapsody in Blue
Hughes, Kay
1936   Ride, Ranger, Ride
Robin Hood of El Dorado
Hughes, Langston
1939   Way Down South
Hughes, Llewellyn
1933   El rey de los gitanos
Hughes, Lloyd
1920   Dangerous Hours
1923   The Huntress
Scars of Jealousy
1924   The Heritage of the Desert
Untamed Youth
Welcome Stranger
1925   Scarlet Saint
1926   Irene
1930   Big Boy
1935   Harmony Lane
Hughes, Mary Beth
1940   Lucky Cisco Kid
1941   Charlie Chan in Rio
Ride on Vaquero
1943   The Ox-Bow Incident
1950   Young Man with a Horn
1957   Gun Battle at Monterey
Hughes, Michael
1946   G. I. War Brides
Hughes, Randolph
1945   Where Do We Go From Here?
Hughes, Rupert
1922   Come On Over
1923   Look Your Best

Hughes, Russell S.
1956 The Last Frontier
Hughes, Tony *see* **Hughes, J. Anthony**
Hughes, William *same as* **Hughes, Bill**
1955 Good Morning, Miss Dove
1957 Band of Angels
Burden of Truth
Hugo, Mauritz
1943 Crime Smasher
1945 Jealousy
1948 Fury at Furnace Creek
Gentleman's Agreement
Renegades of Sonora
1949 The Golden Stallion
1950 A Ticket to Tomahawk
1957 Gun Battle at Monterey
War Drums
1959 Al Capone
Hukalo, A.
1939 Cossacks in Exile
Hulett, Otto
1951 Saturday's Hero
1953 Ambush at Tomahawk Gap
1956 Reprisal!
Hulette, Gladys
1922 Fair Lady
Huling, Lorraine
1914 The Straight Road
1916 The Fall of a Nation
Hull, Arthur Stuart
1934 Stand Up and Cheer!
1935 The Little Colonel
1936 Dangerous Intrigue
1937 The Devil's Playground
Hull, George C.
1920 The Secret Gift
White Youth
1929 The Overland Telegraph
Sioux Blood
Hull, Henry
1939 Judge Hardy and Son
The Return of the Cisco Kid
1944 Lifeboat
1949 Colorado Territory
Portrait of Jennie
1955 Kentucky Rifle
1959 The Oregon Trail
The Sheriff of Fractured Jaw
Hull, Warren
1938 Hawaii Calls
Humberstone, H. Bruce *same as* **Humberstone, Bruce; Humberstone, H. B.; Humberstone, Lucky**
1930 Whoopee
1931 Street Scene
1936 Charlie Chan at the Race Track
1937 Charlie Chan at the Olympics
Charlie Chan at the Opera
1938 Rascals
1939 Charlie Chan in Honolulu
1940 Lucky Cisco Kid
1941 Sun Valley Serenade
1948 Fury at Furnace Creek
Humbert, George
1918 Woman and the Law
1925 The Greatest Love of All
1931 Street Scene
1932 Hearts of Humanity
1933 The California Trail
1934 Coming Out Party
1936 It Had to Happen
Sea Spoilers
Winterset
1938 City Streets
The Toy Wife
1939 Daughters Courageous
Fisherman's Wharf
Miracle on Main Street
Mr. Moto's Last Warning
1940 East of the River
Music in My Heart
1946 Saratoga Trunk
1947 The Mighty McGurk

1950 The Toast of New Orleans
1952 Anything Can Happen
1955 The Rose Tattoo
Hume, Austin
1922 Cardigan
Hume, Benita
1936 Rainbow on the River
Hume, Cyril
1934 Limehouse Blues
1950 A Lady Without Passport
Hume, Douglas
1960 This Rebel Breed
Hume, Fred
1934 The Cactus Kid
Hume, Harry
1934 Broadway Bill
Hume, Ilean
1916 Her Debt of Honor
The Pretenders
1936 Klondike Annie
Hume, Maude
1948 The Miracle of the Bells
Humes, Helen
1947 Jivin' in Be-Bop
Hummel, Wilson
1921 The First Born
1922 The Cub Reporter
Humming Bird
1936 Custer's Last Stand
Humphrey, Orral
1920 Huckleberry Finn
1929 In Old California
Humphrey, Tom *same as* **Humphreys, Tom**
1936 Ramona
1950 Annie Get Your Gun
Humphrey, William *same as* **Humphreys, William**
1925 The Gold Hunters
1927 Aflame in the Sky
Humphreys, Cecil
1925 Irish Luck
Humphreys, Dick
1941 This Woman Is Mine
Humphreys, Peter *same as* **Humphries, Peter**
1958 Flaming Frontier
1960 Walk Like a Dragon
Humphreys, Tom *see* **Humphrey, Tom**
Humphreys, William *see* **Humphrey, William**
Humphries, Peter *see* **Humphreys, Peter**
Hun, Chu Yut
1941 Golden Gate Girl
Hundley, George K.
1950 Two Flags West
Hundt, Charles J.
1916 The Pretenders
Hunnicutt, Arthur
1943 Frontier Fury
1944 Riding West
1949 Border Incident
Lust for Gold
Pinky
1950 Broken Arrow
The Furies
Stars in My Crown
A Ticket to Tomahawk
Two Flags West
1951 Distant Drums
1952 The Big Sky
1955 The Last Command
Hunt, Brook *same as* **Hunt, Brooks**
1945 Nob Hill
1946 Without Reservations
Hunt, Clara
1934 Laughing Boy
Hunt, Eleanor
1930 Whoopee
1936 Yellow Cargo
Hunt, Helen
1934 Wagon Wheels
Hunt, Irene
1915 The Penitentes
1922 Pawn Ticket 210
Hunt, Mrs. J.
1917 The Bride of Hate

Hunt, Jay
1924 Yankee Speed
1927 The Overland Stage
Hunt, Jerry
1947 It Had To Be You
Hunt, Jimmy
1949 Top O' the Morning
1950 Rock Island Trail
Hunt, Leslie
1919 Erstwhile Susan
Hunt, Madge
1928 Heart Trouble
Hunt, Marsha
1936 Desert Gold
1942 Seven Sweethearts
1945 The Valley of Decision
1947 Carnegie Hall
1949 Jigsaw
1960 The Plunderers
Hunter, Arthur
1913 Traffic in Souls
Hunter, Bill *same as* **Hunter, William**
1943 Action in the North Atlantic
Air Force
1945 Nob Hill
1947 California
1948 Unconquered
Hunter, C. Roy
1930 East Is West (*foreign version*)
1931 Don Juan diplomático (*foreign version*)
Hunter, Dick
1932 The Rainbow Trail
1933 Robbers' Roost
Hunter, Henry
1960 I Passed for White
Hunter, Ian (*actor*)
1941 Come Live with Me
Hunter, Ian (*writer*)
1939 Fisherman's Wharf
Hunter, Jeffrey
1955 Seven Angry Men
Seven Cities of Gold
White Feather
1956 The Searchers
1958 The Last Hurrah
1960 Hell to Eternity
Key Witness
Sergeant Rutledge
Hunter, Jerry
1948 The Paleface
1952 It's a Big Country: An American Anthology
Hunter, John
1930 El valiente
Hunter, Kenneth
1941 New York Town
Hunter, Kim
1944 Tender Comrade
1951 A Streetcar Named Desire
1952 Anything Can Happen
Hunter, Lynne
1959 Imitation of Life
Hunter, Mabel
1955 Brevities of 1955
Hunter, Nita
1948 Rocky
1950 The Men
Hunter, Patsy
1941 Up Jumped the Devil
Hunter, Robert
1952 The Big Sky
Hunter, Ross
1950 The Jackie Robinson Story
1952 The Battle at Apache Pass
1953 Tumbleweed
1954 Taza, Son of Cochise
1959 Imitation of Life
Hunter, Rudolph *see* **The Four Tones**
Hunter, T. Hayes
1919 Desert Gold
1920 The Cup of Fury
Hunter, Tab
1950 The Lawless
1956 The Burning Hills
1958 Gunman's Walk

Hunter, Tony
1957 Naked in the Sun
Hunter, William *see* **Hunter, Bill**
Hunter, Willie, Jr.
1955 Chief Crazy Horse
Hunting, Gardner *same as* **Hunting, Gardiner**
1916 The Scarlet Oath
1917 Her Own People
Lost in Transit
The Trouble Buster
Huntley, Chet
1949 Arctic Manhunt
1954 Barefoot Battalion
Huntley, Fred *same as* **Huntly, Fred**
1915 The Rosary
1916 A Man of Sorrow
1917 A Roadside Impresario
1918 Johanna Enlists
The Only Road
1919 The Heart of Wetona
1922 The Man with Two Mothers
Huntley, G. P., Jr. *same as* **Huntley, George P., Jr.**
1934 Imitation of Life
1936 Charlie Chan at the Race Track
1939 Mr. Moto Takes a Vacation
1942 They Died With Their Boots On
Huntley, Hugh
1920? The Greatest Love
1923 Backbone
1938 The Rage of Paris
Huntley, Laura
1913 Traffic in Souls
Huntly, Fred *see* **Huntley, Fred**
Hupalowa, K.
1938 Marusia
Hupp, George
1917 The Plow Woman
Hupp, Jack
1957 War Drums
Hurlbut, Gladys
1955 A Man Called Peter
Hurlbut, William
1921 Made in Heaven
1934 Imitation of Life
1936 Rainbow on the River
1938 Daughter of Shanghai
1941 Adam Had Four Sons
Hurley, Arthur
1929 Die Königsloge
Hurley, Harold
1933 Thundering Herd
1934 Wagon Wheels
1936 Desert Gold
Hurley, Julia
1914 The Jungle
1915 The Melting Pot
1916 Gold and the Woman
Hurley, Sharon
1945 Where Do We Go From Here?
Hurlic, Dolores
1941 Belle Starr
1942 The Vanishing Virginian
Hurlic, Phillip *same as* **Hurlic, Philip**
1936 The Green Pastures
1938 The Adventures of Tom Sawyer
1942 Tales of Manhattan
Hurni, Arthur
1931 Echec au roi
1932 L'athlète incomplet
Hurrell, Clancy
1956 Westward Ho the Wagons!
Hurricanes (*musical group*)
1956 Rockin' the Blues
Hurst, Brandon
1937 Maid of Salem
1940 If I Had My Way
1941 Birth of the Blues
1943 Dixie
The Leopard Man
1947 My Wild Irish Rose

Hurst, Fannie
1932   Symphony of Six Million
Hurst, Paul
1921   Shadows of the West
1922   The Crow's Nest
1925   The Gold Hunters
1926   Shadows of Chinatown
1927   The Devil's Saddle
      The Overland Stage
      The Red Raiders
1932   Men Are Such Fools
1934   Charlie Chan's Courage
1936   It Had to Happen
      Robin Hood of El Dorado
1937   Slave Ship
      Song of the City
1938   In Old Chicago
      Josette
      My Lucky Star
1939   Bad Lands
      Gone With the Wind
      Heaven with a Barbed
        Wire Fence
1941   This Woman Is Mine
      Virginia
1943   Jack London
      The Ox-Bow Incident
1944   Something for the Boys
1945   The Dolly Sisters
      Nob Hill
1948   The Arizona Ranger
      Gun Smugglers
1949   Ranger of Cherokee Strip
1950   The Missourians
1953   The Sun Shines Bright
Hurtado, Alfredo "Pitusín"
1931   Sombras del circo
Hurtado, Juan José
1955   Seven Cities of Gold
Hurwitz, Leo
1948   Strange Victory
Hussey, Ruth *same as* **March, Ruth**
1937   Big City
1940   Northwest Passage (Book
      I—Rogers' Rangers)
1944   Tender Comrade
Huston, John
1942   Across the Pacific
      In This Our Life
1948   Key Largo
1949   We Were Strangers
1960   The Unforgiven
Huston, Paul
1941   Mutiny in the Arctic
Huston, Walter
1930   Abraham Lincoln
      The Bad Man
1942   In This Our Life
1943   The Outlaw
      Yankee Doodle Dandy
1947   Duel in the Sun
1950   The Furies
Hutcherson, Le Vern
1954   Carmen Jones
Hutchin, George L.
1917   The Spirit of '76
Hutchinson, Charles *same as*
Hutchison, Charles
1914   The Little Angel of
      Canyon Creek
1935   Riddle Ranch
Hutchinson, Jack
1937   Big City
Hutchinson, Jody
1953   Seminole
Hutchinson, Josephine
1960   The Adventures of
      Huckleberry Finn
      Walk Like a Dragon
Hutchinson, Louise
1918   Sandy
Hutchison, Charles *see*
Hutchinson, Charles
Hutson, Mimi
1955   A Man Called Peter
Hutton, Betty
1950   Annie Get Your Gun
Hutton, Beulah
1937   Charlie Chan on
      Broadway

Hutton, Brian
1959   Last Train from Gun Hill
Hutton, F. Laws
1919   Diane of the Green Van
Hutton, Robert
1951   New Mexico
      Slaughter Trail
      The Steel Helmet
Huxley, Sophie
1946   Saratoga Trunk
Hyams, John
1936   It Had to Happen
1941   Virginia
Hyams, Leila
1930   Sins of the Children
1931   Gentleman's Fate
1935   Ruggles of Red Gap
Hyans, Edward
1945   Where Do We Go From
      Here?
Hyatt, Bobby
1952   It's a Big Country: An
      American Anthology
Hyde, Jack
1952   Red Ball Express
Hydell, Dorothy
1917   The Slacker (Metro
      Pictures Corp.)
Hyer, Martha
1947   Thunder Mountain
1948   Gun Smugglers
1949   The Clay Pigeon
      Rustlers
1950   The Lawless
1953   So Big
1954   Battle of Rogue River
1955   Kiss of Fire
1958   Houseboat
1960   Ice Palace
Hyke, Ray
1947   It Had To Be You
1948   Fort Apache
      Red River
1949   She Wore a Yellow
      Ribbon
1950   The Cariboo Trail
      The Lawless
      No Way Out
1951   Go for Broke!
1952   The Big Sky
Hyland, Dick Irving
1944   Hi, Beautiful
      Lake Placid Serenade
1947   New Orleans
Hyland, Frances
1928   The House of Scandal
1930   Kathleen Mavourneen
1936   Star for a Night
1939   Charlie Chan in Reno
      The Cisco Kid and the
       Lady
      Winner Take All
1940   Viva Cisco Kid
Hyland, Gus
1936   Star for a Night
Hyland, James
1957   Beau James
      The Midnight Story
Hylton, Richard
1949   Lost Boundaries
Hyman, Arthur S.
1932   Huddle
Hymer, Warren
1929   Frozen Justice
1931   Charlie Chan Carries On
1933   A Lady's Profession
1934   The Cat's-Paw
1936   Laughing Irish Eyes
1938   Gateway
1939   Mr. Moto in Danger
      Island
1941   Birth of the Blues
1943   Gangway for Tomorrow
1944   Since You Went Away
Hyson, Roberta
1930   Georgia Rose
Hytten, Olaf *same as* **Hytton, Olaf**
1934   Strange Wives
1936   The Last of the Mohicans
1937   Souls at Sea
1939   Allegheny Uprising

1940   Escape to Glory
1943   The Amazing Mrs.
      Holliday
1948   Shanghai Chest
      Unconquered
Hyun, Peter Lee
1934   White Heat
Ibargüen, Luis de
1930   Las campanas de
      Capistrano
Iblings, Henry
1949   The Girl from Jones
      Beach
Iglesias, Gene *same as* **Iglesias,
Eugene**
1952   California Conquest
      Hiawatha
      Indian Uprising
1953   Jack McCall Desperado
      Tumbleweed
1954   Taza, Son of Cochise
      They Rode West
1956   Walk the Proud Land
1960   Key Witness
Ignation, Tamara
1938   Gateway
Igor and Yvette
1946   Cuban Pete
Ikanikoff, Maj. Gen.
1926   Into Her Kingdom
Ike, Ukelele *see* **Edwards, Cliff**
Ilak, the Wolf Dog
1925   Justice of the Far North
Ilbagi, Mohamed
1953   Dream Wife
Ilikini, James
1944   Tahiti Nights
Iller, Robert
1960   Man on a String
Illington, Louise
1950   Jolson Sings Again
Illington, Martha
1915   An American Gentleman
Imhof, Marcelle *same as* **Imhoff,
Marcelle**
1947   Jiggs and Maggie in
      Society
1948   Jiggs and Maggie in Court
1949   Jiggs and Maggie in
      Jackpot Jitters
Imhof, Roger *same as* **Imhoff,
Roger**
1933   Charlie Chan's Greatest
      Case
1934   Judge Priest
1939   The Adventures of
      Huckleberry Finn
      Drums Along the Mohawk
1940   The Way of All Flesh
1941   Mystery Ship
Immella, Allesandro
1931   Così è la vita
Imoto, Tad
1951   Go for Broke!
Impolito, Millie
1921   Wolves of the North
Ince, John
1934   Broadway Bill
      The Cat's-Paw
1935   Circle of Death
      The Little Colonel
      Texas Terror
1939   The Adventures of
      Huckleberry Finn
      Stand Up and Fight
Ince, Ralph *same as* **Ince, Ralph
W.**
1918   Fields of Honor
1930   La fuerza del querer
1931   Gentleman's Fate
      Little Caesar
1932   The Hatchet Man
Ince, Thomas H. *same as* **Ince,
Thomas**
1915   The Alien
      The Italian
1916   The Aryan
      Civilization's Child
      The Criminal
      Three of Many
1917   The Bride of Hate
      The Gun Fighter

1918   The Midnight Patrol
1919   Behind the Door
1920   Dangerous Hours
      The Dark Mirror
1923   Anna Christie
      Scars of Jealousy
1925   Custer's Last Fight
1931   Aloha
Inclán, Miguel
1948   Fort Apache
1952   Indian Uprising
1955   Seven Cities of Gold
Indian Minnie
1923   Suzanna
The Indian Players
1913?   Hiawatha
Indrisano, John *same as*
Indrisano, Johnny
1935   The Winning Ticket
1936   Laughing Irish Eyes
1945   Johnny Angel
1947   Body and Soul
1949   Knock on Any Door
1952   My Man and I
1956   Hot Blood
1959   The Black Orchid
1960   I Passed for White
Inescort, Frieda
1943   The Amazing Mrs.
      Holliday
1955   Foxfire
Infanta, Alberto *see* "Don
Alberto"
Infante, Jorge
1931   Chérie (*foreign version*)
      Las luces de Buenos Aires
Infuhr, Teddy
1943   The Amazing Mrs.
      Holliday
1945   A Tree Grows in Brooklyn
1946   Three Wise Fools
      Till the End of Time
1947   Desperate
1948   The Boy with Green Hair
1950   The Traveling
      Saleswoman
1955   Blackboard Jungle
Ingersoll, Bob
1940   Little Nellie Kelly
Ingersoll, Thomas
1948   Cry of the City
1950   No Way Out
Ingham, Geoffrey
1944   Lake Placid Serenade
Ingram, Frank L.
1927   Red Clay
      Roarin' Broncs
Ingleton, Mrs. E. M.
1916   Broken Chains
Ingleton, E. Magnus
1917   The Pulse of Life
1918   Her American Husband
      Mystic Faces
      Who Is to Blame?
1920   The Dark Mirror
Ingoldsby, Leonard
1955   Good Morning, Miss Dove
Ingraham, Amo
1933   It's Great to Be Alive
Ingraham, Jack *see* **Ingram, Jack**
Ingraham, Lloyd
1915   The Sable Lorcha
1918?   Rosemary Climbs the
      Heights
1922   Second Hand Rose
1924   The Lightning Rider
1927   Don Mike
1928   Kit Carson
1930   A Lady to Love
      Take the Heir
1932   Hollywood, ciudad de
      ensueño
      Thirteen Women
1934   Our Daily Bread
1935   So Red the Rose
      Texas Terror
1942   Mexican Spitfire's
      Elephant
      Valley of the Sun
1943   Mr. Lucky

Ingraham, Mitchell
1935   Black Fury
1941   Hold Back the Dawn
Ingraham, Vi
1953   The Pathfinder
1956   Walk the Proud Land
        The White Squaw
Ingram, Clifford *same as* **Ingram, Cliff**
1928   Tenderfeet
1929   Hearts in Dixie
Ingram, Ed
1947   The Adventures of Don Coyote
Ingram, Jack *see* **Ingraham, Jack**
1936   Rebellion
1941   The Gang's All Here
        Prairie Pioneers
1943   Wagon Tracks West
1945   The Jade Mask
1946   Canyon Passage
1949   Illegal Entry
1950   Bandit Queen
1952   The Battle at Apache Pass
1953   Column South
        The Great Sioux Uprising
Ingram, Lawaune
1943   Cabin in the Sky
Ingram, Rex
1916   Broken Fetters
1917   The Flower of Doom
        The Pulse of Life
1936   The Green Pastures
1939   The Adventures of Huckleberry Finn
1943   Cabin in the Sky
1944   Dark Waters
1948   Moonrise
1959   Anna Lucasta
Ingrata
1934   Cuesta abajo
Ingster, Boris
1936   Dancing Pirate
1938   Happy Landing
1939   Miracle on Main Street
        Miracle on Main Street (*foreign version*)
1943   The Amazing Mrs. Holliday
1947   California
Íñigo, Enrique
1958   Sierra Baron
Inness, Jean
1942   Wings for the Eagle
1943   Yankee Doodle Dandy
1949   Pinky
1955   Good Morning, Miss Dove
1958   Gun Fever
Interlenghi, Franco
1951   Teresa
The International Jitterbugs
1947   Boy! What a Girl!
The International Sweethearts of Rhythm
1946   That Man of Mine
Interranti, Guiseppe
1931   Pagliacci
Intlekafer, John
1955   A Man Called Peter
Ireland, John
1948   Open Secret
        Red River
1949   Anna Lucasta
1951   Little Big Horn
Ireland, Mary
1937   Old Louisiana
Irene, Lilyan
1941   New York Town
Iris and Pierre
1945   Club Havana
Irish, Ann
1947   Citizen Saint
Irish, Tom
1951   Show Boat
1954   Hondo
1955   Seven Angry Men
Iron Eyes *see* **Cody, Iron Eyes**
1932   Texas Pioneers
1936   Custer's Last Stand
1951   Fort Defiance

Irvin, Victor
1928   The Cavalier
Irving, Bill
1934   Broadway Bill
1938   Little Miss Roughneck
Irving, George *same as* **Irving, George Henry**
1914   Dan
        The Jungle
1916   The Woman in 47
1919   As a Man Thinks
        The Volcano
1924   North of 36
1926   Desert Gold
1927   Drums of the Desert
1929   Thunderbolt
1930   Son of the Gods
1932   The Vanishing Frontier
1935   Charlie Chan in Egypt
        A Night at the Opera
1936   Charlie Chan at the Race Track
        It Had to Happen
        Sea Spoilers
        Sutter's Gold
1937   Border Cafe
1940   Knute Rockne—All American
        New Moon
1942   The Vanishing Virginian
1943   Dr. Gillespie's Criminal Case
Irving, Margaret
1937   Charlie Chan at the Opera
1938   Little Miss Roughneck
        The Toy Wife
1939   Mr. Moto's Last Warning
Irving, Mary Jane
1918   An Alien Enemy
        The Temple of Dusk
1919   Desert Gold
        The Gray Horizon
        The Westerners
1930   Tom Sawyer
Irving, Paul
1934   Broadway Bill
Irving, Richard
1947   Jiggs and Maggie in Society
1950   Battleground
1952   Woman in the Dark
Irving, Roland
1930   A Daughter of the Congo
Irving, William *same as* **Irving, William C.; Irving, William J.**
1920   Billions
1927   Ham and Eggs at the Front
1930   On the Border
        Song of the Caballero
1933   Diplomaniacs
1934   The Cat's-Paw
Irwin, Boyd *same as* **Irwin, Boyd, Sr.**
1936   Dangerous Intrigue
1938   City Streets
1942   Foreign Agent
1946   Rendezvous 24
1947   King of the Bandits
1948   Docks of New Orleans
        Gentleman's Agreement
        Unconquered
Irwin, Charles
1930   King of Jazz
1937   Think Fast, Mr. Moto
1940   The Man I Married
1943   Wintertime
        Yankee Doodle Dandy
1944   An American Romance
1947   The Foxes of Harrow
        My Wild Irish Rose
1948   The Luck of the Irish
1957   Beau James
1959   The Sheriff of Fractured Jaw
1960   Walk Like a Dragon
Irwin, Coulter
1947   The Jolson Story
Irwin, John
1934   Broadway Bill

Isaac, John
1936   Ramona
Isabelita *same as* **Baron, Lita**
1945   Club Havana
        The Gay Senorita
1946   Don Ricardo Returns
        Slightly Scandalous
1949   Border Incident
1956   The Broken Star
Isaura, Amalia de
1931   La pura verdad
Isbert, José
1931   La pura verdad
1932   ¿Cuándo te suicidas?
Ismond, Marie
1958   Kings Go Forth
Isnard, Loute
1931   Su noche de bodas (*foreign version*)
Ito, Michio
1938   Spawn of the North
Iturbi, Amparo
1949   That Midnight Kiss
Iturbi, José
1949   That Midnight Kiss
Iturbi, Maria
1936   Ramona
Iura, Toru
1951   Go for Broke!
Ivan, Rosalind
1916   Arms and the Woman
Ivans, Elaine
1914   The Littlest Rebel
Ivans, John
1936   Yellow Cargo
Ivans, Perry
1948   The Miracle of the Bells
1952   The Half-Breed
Ivens, Bryna
1941   Murder on Lenox Avenue
Ivers, Julia Crawford *same as* **Ivers, J. C.**
1916   A Son of Erin
1917   Her Own People
        Lost in Transit
1918   The Gypsy Trail
        Huck and Tom; or, the Further Adventures of Tom Sawyer
1920   Huckleberry Finn
1923   The White Flower
Ivins, Beth
1918   Doing Their Bit
Ivins, Perry
1934   Charlie Chan in London
1935   Charlie Chan in Paris
1938   Dangerous to Know
1947   The Foxes of Harrow
1948   Call Northside 777
1949   Streets of Laredo
1950   The Missourians
        Mystery Street
Ivo, Tommy
1948   I Remember Mama
        Moonrise
1949   Laramie
        Prejudice
1951   Snake River Desperadoes
1955   Blackboard Jungle
Iwanaga, Frank
1951   Go for Broke!
Izenhall, Aaron
1946   Beware
1949   Lookout Sister
Jaccard, Jacques
1922   The Great Alone
1924   California in '49
        Unseen Hands
1936   The Phantom of Santa Fe
Jack, Roland
1949   Tulsa
Jackie, a lion
1932   Hypnotized
Jackman, Fred
1926   The Devil Horse
Jacks, Robert L.
1955   White Feather
1956   Man from Del Rio

Jacks, S. T.
1920   Within Our Gates
1927   The Millionaire
Jackson and Lynam
1941   Ice-Capades
Jackson, Lieut.
1919   Injustice
Jackson, Alonzo *see* **Jackson, Al**
1927   Children of Fate
1947   Boy! What a Girl!
Jackson, Anne
1950   So Young, So Bad
Jackson, Avonne
1935   The Little Colonel
Jackson, Brad
1954   Taza, Son of Cochise
        War Arrow
Jackson, Bull Moose
1948?   Boarding House Blues
Jackson, Calvin
1960   I Passed for White
Jackson, Carolyn Ann
1953   Bright Road
Jackson, Clifford
1953   Bright Road
Jackson, Columbus
1938   Birthright
        God's Step Children
        Swing!
1940   The Notorious Elinor Lee
Jackson, Curtis
1948   The Boy with Green Hair
Jackson, Danny
1940   Knute Rockne—All American
1944   They Live in Fear
1946   Canyon Passage
Jackson, E. M.
1927?   You Can't Win
Jackson, Earl
1959   Porgy and Bess
Jackson, Edna
1945   A Tree Grows in Brooklyn
Jackson, Emmet
1943   Marching On!
Jackson, Ethel
1936   After the Thin Man
Jackson, Eugene
1929   Hearts in Dixie
1931   Cimarron
1938   The Buccaneer
1939   Reform School
1942   Take My Life
1943   What's Buzzin' Cousin?
1949   The Story of Seabiscuit
Jackson, Felix
1938   The Rage of Paris
1943   His Butler's Sister
Jackson, Francis
1931   Yankee Don
Jackson, Fred (*child actor, circa 1926*)
1926   The Devil Horse
Jackson, Freddie (*African-American actor*)
1937   Boy of the Streets
1939   Double Deal
        Reform School
1942   In This Our Life
Jackson, Frederick (*writer*)
1939   Miracle on Main Street
        Miracle on Main Street (*foreign version*)
1941   This Woman Is Mine
1943   Stormy Weather
1945   Club Havana
Jackson, Gary *same as* **Jackson, Gary Lee**
1950   A Lady Without Passport
        Winchester '73
1951   Molly
        Yes Sir, Mr. Bones
1952   Hiawatha
Jackson, George
1934   La veuve joyeuse
1940   The Ramparts We Watch
1943   Gangway for Tomorrow
Jackson, Ginny
1949   The Kissing Bandit

Jackson, Hal
1956   Rockin' the Blues
Jackson, Harry
1958   Gun Fever
Jackson, Herb
1936   Custer's Last Stand
Jackson, Horace
1931   Beyond Victory
Jackson, Inman
1951   The Harlem Globetrotters
Jackson, James *same as* **Jackson, James P.; Jackson, Jimmy**
1936   Show Boat
1949   Lookout Sister
1953   The Sun Shines Bright
Jackson, Jonathan
1953   Beneath the 12-Mile Reef
Jackson, Joseph
1929   Is Everybody Happy?
1930   Los que danzan
1931   Smart Money
Jackson, Joshua W.
1946   Beware
Jackson, Joy
1953   Bright Road
Jackson, Julia
1917   Castles for Two
Jackson, Louise
1949   Souls of Sin
Jackson, Mahalia
1958   St. Louis Blues
1959   Imitation of Life
Jackson, Marion
1924   North of Nevada
1925   The Wild Bull's Lair
1927   The Devil's Saddle
        The Overland Stage
        The Red Raiders
1928   The Canyon of Adventure
        The Glorious Trail
1931   La fruta amarga
1939   The Return of the Cisco
        Kid
Jackson, Marjorie
1951   The Tall Target
Jackson, Mary
1952   Anything Can Happen
Jackson, Mike *same as* **Jackson, Michael**
1932   The Black King
1953   Bright Road
Jackson, Milt
1947   Jivin' in Be-Bop
Jackson, Peaches
1917   His Sweetheart
1918   The Greatest Thing in
        Life
1920   Rio Grande
1921   Through the Back Door
1933   It's Great to Be Alive
Jackson, Selmer
1921?   The Supreme Passion
1929   Why Bring That Up?
1933   Let's Fall in Love
1934   Stand Up and Cheer!
1935   A Night at the Opera
1936   Charlie Chan at the Race
        Track
        It Had to Happen
        Paddy O'Day
        Show Boat
1937   Charlie Chan at the
        Olympics
        Man of the People
        Manhattan
        Merry-Go-Round
1938   Gateway
1939   Confessions of a Nazi Spy
        The Escape
        Stand Up and Fight
1940   Elsa Maxwell's Public
        Deb No. 1
        If I Had My Way
        Santa Fe Trail
1942   They Died With Their
        Boots On
1943   Margin for Error
1944   Sheriff of Las Vegas
        The Sullivans
1946   Dangerous Money
1951   The Magnificent Yankee
1952   Indian Uprising

1953   Jack McCall Desperado
1955   Seven Angry Men
Jackson, Sherry
1950   The Breaking Point
1951   Apache Drums
        The Great Caruso
1960   The Adventures of
        Huckleberry Finn
Jackson, Theron
1943   Gangway for Tomorrow
1953   Bright Road
Jackson, Thomas *same as* **Jackson, Thomas E.; Jackson, Tommy**
1931   Little Caesar
1932   Unashamed
1935   The Irish in Us
1936   Below the Deadline
        It Had to Happen
1939   The Escape
1940   Girl from God's Country
1943   Yankee Doodle Dandy
1946   The Face of Marble
1948   Up in Central Park
1952   Indian Uprising
1958   The Last Hurrah
Jackson, Warren
1940   Mexican Spitfire Out
        West
1942   Mexican Spitfire at Sea
1943   Dixie
1946   Notorious
        Till the End of Time
Jackson, Wilfred (*actor*)
1949   Pinky
1951   The Tall Target
Jackson, Wilfred (*cartoon dir*)
1946   Song of the South
Jacobini, Maria
1930   Doña mentiras (*foreign
        version*)
Jacobs, Angela
1933   Counsellor at Law
Jacobs, Betty
1938   Two Sisters
Jacobs, Billy
1917   Unconquered
Jacobs, Burdell
1916   Peck O' Pickles
Jacobs, Earl
1944   Since You Went Away
Jacobs, Harrison
1937   The Barrier
1940   Young Buffalo Bill
Jacobs, John R.
1950   Panic in the Streets
Jacobs, William
1936   Treachery Rides the
        Range
1947   My Wild Irish Rose
1949   The Story of Seabiscuit
1950   The Daughter of Rosie
        O'Grady
        Rocky Mountain
Jacobs, Wilma
1955   The View from Pompey's
        Head
Jacobson, Glenn
1959   Night of the Quarter
        Moon
Jacobson, Henrietta
1950   Catskill Honeymoon
Jacobson, Hymie
1933   Live and Laugh
1937   The Jester (Der
        Purimspieler)
Jacobson, Irving
1940   Eli Eli
        The Great Advisor
Jacobson, Joel
1950   Catskill Honeymoon
Jacobus, Eylla
1950   Intruder in the Dust
Jacoby, Hans
1953   Taxi
Jacoby, John
1943   The Amazing Mrs.
        Holliday
Jacoby, Michel
1940   Doomed to Die
1943   They Came to Blow Up
        America

1946   The Face of Marble
Jacoves, Felix
1945   Rhapsody in Blue
Jacques, Ted
1943   Action in the North
        Atlantic
1960   Flaming Star
Jacquet, Frank
1945   In Old New Mexico
1949   House of Strangers
Jade, Ben
1945   Nob Hill
Jadi, Chabon
1952   Hiawatha
1955   Foxfire
1956   Mohawk
Jaeckel, Richard
1950   Battleground
        Sands of Iwo Jima
1955   Apache Ambush
1960   Flaming Star
Jaeger, Casse
1951   Show Boat
Jaffe, Allen
1959   Al Capone
Jaffe, Carl
1960   Man on a String
Jaffe, Louis N.
1926   Broken Hearts
Jaffe, Sam
1933   Diplomaniacs
1944   The Sullivans
1948   Gentleman's Agreement
Jagger, Dean *same as* **Dean, Jeffrey**
1934   Behold My Wife!
1936   Star for a Night
1937   Song of the City
1941   Western Union
1942   Valley of the Sun
1949   C-Man
1951   Warpath
1955   Bad Day at Black Rock
Jahries, Jack
1949   Knock on Any Door
Jaillet, Lorraine
1930   The Big Pond (*foreign
        version*)
Jakubczak, Genia
1941   Wiejskie Wesele
Jallings, Johnnie
1950   No Way Out
James, Alan *same as* **Neitz, Alvin; Neitz, Alvin J.**
1923   The Secret of the Pueblo
1924   Down by the Rio Grande
1925   Warrior Gap
1934   Wheels of Destiny
1943   The Law Rides Again
1944   Outlaw Trail
James, Alfred P. *same as* **James, Alfred**
1934   Broadway Bill
1938   The Rage of Paris
James, Claire
1951   Only the Valiant
James, Edward
1941   Lady from Louisiana
James, Gardner
1928   The Mating Call
1931   The Great Meadow
James, Gladden
1917   Runaway Romany
1919   The Heart of Wetona
        Who's Your Brother?
1929   The Peacock Fan
1935   Charlie Chan in Shanghai
1936   It Had to Happen
1937   Big City
1938   Mr. Moto's Gamble
1943   The Meanest Man in the
        World
James, Harry
1942   Syncopation
1947   Carnegie Hall
1956   The Benny Goodman
        Story
James, Ida
1939   The Devil's Daughter
1947   Hi De Ho

James, Irene
1960   Cimarron
James, Ivor
1950   Young Man with a Horn
James, Jerry
1943   Dixie
1948   The Paleface
        Unconquered
James, John *same as* **James, John A.**
1944   Since You Went Away
1945   Great Stagecoach Robbery
1948   Tap Roots
        Unconquered
1949   The Valiant Hombre
James, Kyle
1953   Arrowhead
James, Leon "Poke"
1943   Cabin in the Sky
James, Marijo
1943   Yankee Doodle Dandy
James, Olga
1954   Carmen Jones
James, Polly
1952   The Raiders
James, Rian
1933   Best of Enemies
1934   Stand Up and Cheer!
James, Rich (*writer*)
1939   The Return of the Cisco
        Kid
James, Richard (*actor*)
1956   Raw Edge
James, Samuel H.
1946?   Go Down, Death!
James, Sidney
1950   Give Us This Day
1959   The Sheriff of Fractured
        Jaw
James, Walter
1922   Fair Lady
1924   Two Shall Be Born
1931   Street Scene
1936   Custer's Last Stand
Jameson, Joyce
1951   Show Boat
Jamieson, Bud *see* **Jamison, Bud**
Jamieson, Hazel Barnes *same as* **Jamieson, Hazel**
1939   Gang Smashers
        Reform School
Jamison, Bud *same as* **Jamieson, Bud**
1927   Jake the Plumber
1928   Heart Trouble
1930   The Grand Parade
1938   Little Miss Roughneck
1942   Holiday Inn
Jane, Baby *see* **Quigley, Juanita**
Janis, Bob
1958   Sierra Baron
Janis, Dorothy
1928   Kit Carson
1929   The Overland Telegraph
Janis, Elsie
1930   Galas de la Paramount
1931   The Squaw Man
Janney, Leon
1931   Die Maske Fällt
Janney, William *same as* **Janney, William Preston**
1931   Cimarron
1933   King of the Wild Horses
1934   As the Earth Turns
1936   Sutter's Gold
Jannings, Emil
1927   The Way of All Flesh
1928   Sins of the Fathers
Jans, Harry
1936   Charlie Chan at the Race
        Track
1937   That Girl from Paris
Janssen, David
1955   Chief Crazy Horse
1960   Hell to Eternity
Janssen, Eilene
1944   Since You Went Away
1946   Rendezvous 24
1948   The Boy with Green Hair
1958   Escape from Red Rock

Janssen, Else *same as* **Janssen, Elsa**
1937   It Could Happen to You
1943   His Butler's Sister
       Hitler's Children
       They Came to Blow Up America
1945   The Dolly Sisters

Janssen, Jill
1953   So Big

Janssen, William
1949   House of Strangers
1953   Seminole
1958   The Last Hurrah
1959   Al Capone

Jaques, Peggy
1958   Tonka

Jaques, Renee
1958   Tonka

Jaquet, Frank
1938   My Lucky Star
1939   Stand Up and Fight
1942   Tales of Manhattan
1943   The Meanest Man in the World
1944   Black Magic
1945   Colorado Pioneers
1949   The Daring Caballero
       Pinky
1950   No Way Out
       Rock Island Trail

Jara, Maurice
1950   The Lawless
1951   Apache Drums
1953   The Nebraskan
1954   Drum Beat
       They Rode West
1956   Giant
       Walk the Proud Land
1958   The Lone Ranger and the Lost City of Gold

Jaramillo, Jacinto
1930   El valiente
1931   La cautivadora

Jardiel Poncela, Enrique
1933   La melodía prohibida
       Primavera en otoño
       El rey de los gitanos
       Una viuda romántica
1934   Nada más que una mujer
1935   Angelina o el honor de un brigadier
       ¡Asegure a su mujer!

Jarman, Claude, Jr.
1950   Intruder in the Dust
       Rio Grande

Jarmuth, Jack
1927   Old San Francisco
1928   The Jazz Singer

Jarmyn, Jil
1957   War Drums

Jarrett, Arthur (*actor, singer*) *same as* **Jarrett, Arthur, Jr.**
1933   Let's Fall in Love
1938   My Lucky Star

Jarrett, Daniel (*actor*)
1917   The Slacker (Metro Pictures Corp.)

Jarrett, Daniel (*writer*) *same as* **Jarrett, Dan** (*writer*)
1936   Daniel Boone
       Let's Sing Again
1938   Hawaii Calls
1951   Tomahawk

Jarrett, Monte
1918   The Hell Cat

Jarrico, Paul
1941   The Face Behind the Mask
1954   Salt of the Earth

Jarvis, Dolly
1942   Syncopation

Jarvis, Sidney
1934   She Was a Lady

Jarwood, Arthur
1949?   Harlem Follies

Jasmine, Arthur
1919   Lasca
1920   A Tokio Siren
1922   The Son of the Wolf
1925   Justice of the Far North

Jason, Leigh
1928   Anybody Here Seen Kelly?
1937   That Girl from Paris

Jason, Rick
1958   Sierra Baron

Jason, Will
1944   Tahiti Nights
1946   Slightly Scandalous
1948   Music Man
1951   The Harlem Globetrotters

Jauregui, Edward
1944   Buffalo Bill
1959   The Young Land

Javor, Paul
1951   The Great Caruso

Jaxon, Budd
1952   Kid Monk Baroni

Jay, Griffin
1944   Cry of the Werewolf

Jay, Helen
1955   The Lonesome Trail
1958   The Badlanders

Jay, Steven
1959   The Black Orchid

Jaynes, Betty
1942   Dr. Gillespie's New Assistant

Jean, a dog
1928   Ramona

Jean, Annette
1923   Snowdrift

Jean, Gloria
1940   If I Had My Way
1947   Copacabana

Jeanette, Joe
1922   Square Joe

Jeansonne, Francis
1950   Panic in the Streets

Jeffers, Mike
1949   Pinky
1958   The Last Hurrah

Jefferson, L. V.
1919   His Debt
1935   Riddle Ranch

Jefferson, Thomas
1915   The Sable Lorcha
1916   A Child of Mystery
1919   Deliverance
1920   White Youth
1922   The Son of the Wolf

Jefferson, William Winter
1917   Her Own People

Jeffrey, Herbert *see* **Jeffries, Herb**

Jeffrey, Hugh
1916   The Pretenders
1917   The Call of Her People

Jeffrey, William
1935   A Night at the Ritz
1937   Charlie Chan on Broadway

Jeffreys, Anne
1943   Wagon Tracks West

Jeffries, Herb *same as* **Jeffrey, Herbert**
1937   Harlem on the Prairie
1938   Two Gun Man from Harlem
1939   The Bronze Buckaroo
       Harlem Rides the Range

Jeffries, James J.
1937   Big City

Jeffries, W. A.
1918   Her American Husband

Jellison, Robert
1950   Belle of Old Mexico

Jelly, W. Herbert
1938   Birthright

Jencks, Clinton
1954   Salt of the Earth

Jencks, Virginia
1954   Salt of the Earth

Jenkins, Allen
1935   The Irish in Us
       A Night at the Ritz
1936   Sins of Man
1942   Tortilla Flat
1946   Singin' in the Corn
1947   Easy Come, Easy Go

Jenkins, J. Wesley *same as* **Jenkins, J. W.**
1920   The Good-Bad Wife
1925   Scarlet Saint

Jenkins, Jackie "Butch" *same as* **Jenkins, Butch**
1944   An American Romance
1945   Our Vines Have Tender Grapes
1947   Little Mister Jim
1948   Big City

Jenkins, Margaret
1932   Harlem Is Heaven

Jenkins, Verda
1944   Chip Off the Old Block

Jenks, Frank
1937   That Girl from Paris
1940   Three Cheers for the Irish
1942   The Navy Comes Through
       Syncopation
1943   His Butler's Sister
1948   Shep Comes Home
1955   Not As a Stranger

Jenks, George Elwood
1922   The Cub Reporter

Jenks, Si
1931   Oklahoma Jim
1934   Charlie Chan's Courage
       Operator 13
       Stand Up and Cheer!
1936   Desert Gold
1937   The Devil's Playground
1938   Rascals
1939   Drums Along the Mohawk
1940   Girl from God's Country
1941   Gauchos of Eldorado
1942   Gentleman Jim
1946   Singin' in the Corn
1947   California
1948   The Dude Goes West
       Fury at Furnace Creek
       Unconquered
1949   Lust for Gold

Jennings, Al
1936   Song of the Gringo

Jennings, Al (*actor, dir*)
1917   The Captain of the Gray Horse Troop
1936   Song of the Gringo

Jennings, De Witt *same as* **Jennings, De Witt C.**
1917   The Little American
1922   Flesh and Blood
1927   McFadden's Flats
1928   The Crash
1931   The Squaw Man
1932   The Match King
1933   Grand Slam
       A Lady's Profession
1934   The Cat's-Paw
       Charlie Chan's Courage
       Massacre
       Operator 13
1936   Kelly the Second
       Sins of Man
1937   Slave Ship
       That I May Live

Jennings, Gordon
1948   The Paleface

Jennings, Jane
1918   I Want to Forget
1919   As a Man Thinks

Jennings, John
1947   Easy Come, Easy Go

Jennings, Maxine
1936   Muss 'Em Up
1938   Mr. Wong, Detective
1946   G. I. War Brides

Jennings, Ruth
1933   It's Great to Be Alive
1934   Stand Up and Cheer!

Jennings, Talbot
1938   Spawn of the North
1940   Northwest Passage (Book I—Rogers' Rangers)
1951   Across the Wide Missouri

Jennings, Virginia
1938   The Texans

Jenny, Jack
1942   Syncopation

Jack Jenny and His Orchestra
1937   Manhattan Merry-Go-Round

Jensen, Dick
1941   Mystery Ship
1944   Address Unknown
       The Racket Man
1945   Escape in the Fog

Jensen, Eulalie
1916   Britton of the Seventh
1917   I Will Repay
1925   Flower of Night
       The Thundering Herd
1926   Laddie
1928   Mother Machree
       Uncle Tom's Cabin
1931   Smart Money
1932   So Big

Jensen, Renaldo
1948   The Fight Never Ends

Jenson, Roy
1954   Broken Lance
1958   The Last Hurrah
1959   Al Capone
1960   Flaming Star

Jerado
1960   Pay or Die

Jergens, Adele
1943   The Gang's All Here
1950   The Traveling Saleswoman
1951   Show Boat
1954   Overland Pacific
1955   The Lonesome Trail

Jergens, Diane
1956   The Benny Goodman Story
1959   The FBI Story

Jerome, Edwin
1945   The House on 92nd St.
1949   Tale of the Navajos
1958   Home Before Dark

Jerome, Jerry
1934   Charlie Chan's Courage
       Coming Out Party
1936   Charlie Chan at the Race Track
1939   The Escape
1943   Dr. Gillespie's Criminal Case
1946   Romance of the West
1948   Key Largo
       The Miracle of the Bells

Jessel, George
1919   The Other Man's Wife
1926   Private Izzy Murphy
1927   Sailor Izzy Murphy
1928   George Washington Cohen
1929   Love, Live and Laugh
       Lucky Boy
1945   The Dolly Sisters
1953   Tonight We Sing
1957   Beau James

Jeter, Gloria
1947   The Peanut Man

Jeter, Irma
1944   Chip Off the Old Block

Jevne, Jack
1927   McFadden's Flats
1936   Kelly the Second
1943   Wintertime

Jewel, Austin
1927   Wild Geese

Jewell, Hollis
1937   Boy of the Streets
1942   Syncopation
1948   The Luck of the Irish

Jewell, Isabel
1933   Counsellor at Law
1939   Gone With the Wind
1940   Northwest Passage (Book I—Rogers' Rangers)
1943   The Leopard Man
1954   Drum Beat

Jewell, Kay
1946   Abie's Irish Rose

Jewkes, J. Delos *same as* **Jewkes, J. D.**
1935   Naughty Marietta
1942   Rio Rita

Jiang Wai-kwong
Yu Luh Shen Ping
1946? Yee Sio Bo Laan Sin
1947? Hai Jeow Chin Yuan
Luan Feng Heh Ming

Jillson, Willard see **Dunhill, Steve**

Jim, Tennesse
1951 Westward the Women

Jiménez, Carmen
1931 Chérie (foreign version)
Mamá
Sombras del circo

Jiménez, Soledad same as **Jiménez, Solidad; Jiminez, Soledad**
1929 In Old Arizona
Romance of the Rio Grande
1930 The Arizona Kid
La voluntad del muerto
1931 Carne de cabaret
Resurrección
1933 La melodía prohibida
1934 La cruz y la espada
Tres amores
1935 Bordertown
The Cyclone Ranger
Julieta compra un hijo
1936 The Bold Caballero
Robin Hood of El Dorado
The Traitor
La última cita
1937 Law and Lead
Man of the People
1938 California Frontier
1939 The Return of the Cisco Kid
1941 Hold Back the Dawn
1945 South of the Rio Grande
1948 Angel in Exile
1953 Seminole

Jimeno, Alvaro
1931 La llama sagrada

Jiminez, David
1956 Giant

Jimmie Davis and his Singing Buckaroos
1943 Frontier Fury

Jimmy, the Crow
1942 Whispering Ghosts
1949 Call of the Forest

Jinkins, Bo
1946 Mantan Messes Up

The Jitterbug Johnnies
1947 Juke Joint

Job, Thomas
1947 The Foxes of Harrow

Jobson, Edward
1919 The Delicious Little Devil
1922 The Scrapper

Joby, Hans
1937 It Could Happen to You
1938 Happy Landing
1940 Escape
1942 All Through the Night

Jochim, Anthony
1949 The Girl from Jones Beach
1951 The Girl on the Bridge
1952 The Big Sky
1953 The Jazz Singer
So Big
1957 Joe Dakota

Johann, Zita
1932 Tiger Shark
1933 The Man Who Dared: An Imaginative Biography

Johansson, Ingemar
1960 All the Young Men

John, H. W.
1960 I Aim at the Stars: the Wernher von Braun Story

Johnny and Henny
1947 Jivin' in Be-Bop

Johns, Glynis
1957 All Mine to Give
1959 Shake Hands with the Devil

Johns, Larry
1950 Rio Grande Patrol
1951 Queen for a Day

Johns, Ralph
1946 The Gay Cavalier

Johnson, Adrian
1917 Unknown 274
1918 The Firebrand

Johnson, Alice
1921 The Lure of a Woman

Johnson, Ben
1949 She Wore a Yellow Ribbon
3 Godfathers
1950 Rio Grande
1951 Fort Defiance
1957 War Drums
1958 Fort Bowie

Johnson, Bobby
1943 Cabin in the Sky
1949 The Story of Seabiscuit
1950 Emergency Wedding
1955 Bad Day at Black Rock
1958 St. Louis Blues
1960 Sergeant Rutledge

Johnson, Bubber
1952 Red Ball Express

Johnson, Carmencita
1927 The Way of All Flesh
1938 The Beloved Brat
1942 Young America

Johnson, Casey
1941 Gauchos of Eldorado

Ceepee Johnson and His Orchestra
1940 Mystery in Swing

Johnson, Charles
1946 Beware

Johnson, Chubby
1950 Rocky Mountain
1951 The Raging Tide
Westward the Women
1952 Apache War Smoke
1953 Last of the Comanches
1954 Cattle Queen of Montana
Overland Pacific
1955 Headline Hunters
1958 Gunfire at Indian Gap

Johnson, Clint
1950 Young Daniel Boone

Johnson, Copper
1951 Apache Drums

Johnson, Dick Winslow
1929 Love, Live and Laugh

Johnson, Donald H.
1955 Indian American

Johnson, Dora Dean
1930 Georgia Rose

Johnson, Dots same as **Johnson, Dotts**
1946 Tall, Tan and Terrific
1947 Reet, Petite and Gone
1950 No Way Out
1953 The Joe Louis Story

Johnson, Emory
1916 The Morals of Hilda
A Yoke of Gold
1917 A Kentucky Cinderella
1918 Johanna Enlists
1919 The Tiger Lily

Johnson, Erskine
1959 Al Capone

Johnson, Eva
1919 A Man's Duty

Johnson, Frederick
1947 Hi De Ho

Johnson, George P.
1921 By Right of Birth

Johnson, Gladys
1931 Call of the Rockies

The Hall Johnson Choir
1936 Dimples
The Green Pastures
Rainbow on the River
1939 Way Down South
1942 Syncopation
Tales of Manhattan
1943 Cabin in the Sky
1947 The Peanut Man

Johnson, Henry same as **Johnson, Hank**
1932 Hypnotized
1933 Olsen's Big Moment

Johnson, Howard
1945 Betrayal from the East

Johnson, J. Lewis same as **Johnson, J. Louis**
1942 Syncopation
1944 My Pal Wolf
1946 Saratoga Trunk
Without Reservations
1947 Reet, Petite and Gone
1950 No Way Out

Johnson, J. Rosamund
1939 Keep Punching

Johnson, Jack
1921 As the World Rolls On
1922 For His Mother's Sake

Johnson, James
1960 Sergeant Rutledge

Johnson, Jean
1925 His People

Johnson, Jessie
1948 The Betrayal

Johnson, John Lester
1922 Square Joe
1923 Flames of Wrath
1936 The Glory Trail
Klondike Annie
The Prisoner of Shark Island
1937 Bargain with Bullets
One Mile from Heaven
1940 Mystery in Swing
1940? Mr. Washington Goes to Town
1942 Lucky Ghost
Professor Creeps

Johnson, Julian
1920 Who's Your Servant?
1927 The Way of All Flesh
1928 The Secret Hour
Sins of the Fathers
1929 Abie's Irish Rose
Chinatown Nights
Redskin
Wolf Song
1930 The Silent Enemy
1940 Lucky Cisco Kid

Johnson, Junior
1931 Cimarron

Johnson, Kathy
1960 Studs Lonigan

Johnson, Kay
1932 Thirteen Women
1943 Mr. Lucky

Johnson, Lamont
1953 The Glory Brigade
1957 The Brothers Rico

Johnson, Laurence E.
1931 Le père célibataire
1932 Le plombier amoureux

Johnson, LeRoy
1948 The Paleface
1950 Colt .45
1953 Arrowhead
1955 The Far Horizons
1958 Tonka

Johnson, Lillian
1925 Body and Soul

Johnson, Mae E.
1939 Keep Punching
1943 Stormy Weather

Johnson, Marilyn
1944 The Racket Man
1945 I Love a Bandleader

Johnson, Max
1920 Our Christianity and Nobody's Child

Johnson, Myra
1932 Harlem Is Heaven

Johnson, Noble
1925 The Gold Hunters
1926 The Flaming Frontier
1927 Red Clay
Topsy and Eva
1929 Redskin
1932 Mystery Ranch
1936 My American Wife
1937 The Plainsman
1941 Hurry, Charlie, Hurry
1942 Shut My Big Mouth
1948 Unconquered
1949 She Wore a Yellow Ribbon

Johnson, Nunnally
1936 Dimples
The Prisoner of Shark Island
1937 Slave Ship
1960 Flaming Star

Johnson, Orine not the same as **Johnson, Orrin**
1928 Eleven P.M.

Johnson, Orrin
1915 The Penitentes
1916 Light at Dusk

Johnson, Paul
1934 Drums O' Voodoo

Johnson, Payne
1941 Birth of the Blues

Johnson, Pete
1946? Harlem on Parade

Johnson, Rafer
1960 Sergeant Rutledge

Johnson, Ralph
1920 Within Our Gates

Johnson, Ray (actor)
1943 Let's Have Fun
1949 Knock on Any Door

Johnson, Raymond K. (dir)
1931 Call of the Rockies
1939 Daughter of the Tong

Johnson, Rita
1948 Sleep, My Love
1957 All Mine to Give

Johnson, Robert
1940 Gang War
1944 Since You Went Away
1945 Rhapsody in Blue
1955 The View from Pompey's Head

Johnson, Robert Lee
1932 Huddle
1936 Down to the Sea
1940 Girl from God's Country
Prairie Schooners

Johnson, Russell
1953 Column South
Seminole
The Stand at Apache River
Tumbleweed

Johnson, Sol
1937 Underworld

Johnson, Stan
1946 Till the End of Time
1950 No Way Out

Johnson, Tim
1955 Good Morning, Miss Dove

Johnson, Tor
1943 The Meanest Man in the World
1957 Journey to Freedom

Johnson, Van
1940 Too Many Girls
1942 Dr. Gillespie's New Assistant
1943 Dr. Gillespie's Criminal Case
1944 Three Men in White
1945 Between Two Women
1950 Battleground
The Big Hangover
1951 Go for Broke!
1952 It's a Big Country: An American Anthology
1954 Siege at Red River

Johnson, Wallace
1922 The Schemers

Johnson, Walter
1934 Charlie Chan in London

Johnson, William
1926? Ten Nights in a Barroom

Johnston, Agnes Christine
1944 Andy Hardy's Blonde Trouble
1947 Black Gold

Johnston, Clint
1949 The Sky Dragon
1950 Young Daniel Boone

Johnston, Cullen
1940　The Way of All Flesh

Johnston, J. W. *same as* **Johnston, Jack**
1914　Rose of the Rancho
　　　　Where the Trail Divides
1915　Sealed Valley
1916?　Should a Baby Die?
1918　Uncle Tom's Cabin
1922　Cardigan
1923　Backbone
1925　The Greatest Love of All
1935　Ruggles of Red Gap

Johnston, Julianne
1929　Smiling Irish Eyes
　　　　The Younger Generation

Johnston, Maxine
1948　The Miracle of the Bells

Johnston, Norman *see* **Johnstone, Norman**

Johnston, Patty Kate
1949　That Midnight Kiss

Johnston, Rosemary
1956　The Last Hunt

Johnston, Stuart
1934　Imitation of Life

Johnston, W. Ray
1927　Heroes in Blue

Johnston, William Allen
1935　Charlie Chan in Paris

Johnstone, Calder
1916　A Yoke of Gold

Johnstone, Harold
1918　The Midnight Patrol

Johnstone, Lamar
1919　Diane of the Green Van

Johnstone, Norman *same as* **Johnston, Norman**
1923　Deceit
1927　The Scar of Shame

Johnstone, William *could be same as* **Johnstone, Wm. Llewellyn**
1951　The Magnificent Yankee

Johnstone, Wm. Llewellyn *could be same as* **Johnstone, William**
1953　Beneath the 12-Mile Reef

Joiner, Patricia
1950　The Men

Jolivet, Rita
1917　One Law for Both

Jolley, I. Stanford *same as* **Jolley, Stan; Jolley, Stanford**
1940　The Fatal Hour
1943　Frontier Fury
1944　The Chinese Cat
1945　The Scarlet Clue
1949　Roll Thunder Roll!
1950　The Baron of Arizona
　　　　Rock Island Trail
　　　　Sands of Iwo Jima
1951　Westward the Women
1952　Fort Osage
　　　　The Raiders
　　　　Wagons West
1953　Tumbleweed
1955　Kentucky Rifle
　　　　Seven Angry Men
1956　Wetbacks
　　　　The Wild Dakotas
1957　Gun Battle at Monterey
　　　　The Halliday Brand
　　　　The Oklahoman
1960　Ice Palace

Jolley, Norman
1957　Joe Dakota

Jolley, Stanford *see* **Jolley, I. Stanford**

Jolley, Sue
1943　Crash Dive

Jolly, Luce
1930　Toda una vida (*foreign version*)

Joloff, Friedrich
1960　Man on a String

Jolson, Al
1928　The Jazz Singer
1930　Big Boy
1945　Rhapsody in Blue

Jonay, Roberta
1943　Riding High

Jones, Alida *same as* **Jones, Alida D.**
1918　Her Moment
1920　White Youth

Jones, Allan (*actor*)
1935　A Night at the Opera
1936　Show Boat

Jones, Annabelle
1942　They Died With Their Boots On

Jones, Arthur Vernon *same as* **Jones, Arthur V.**
1936　Kelly the Second
1939　Papá soltero
　　　　El trovador de la radio

Jones, Beulah Hall
1934　Judge Priest
1936　The Prisoner of Shark Island
1938　The Toy Wife
1939　Drums Along the Mohawk

Jones, Beverly *not the same as* **Jons, Beverly**
1940　The Ramparts We Watch

Jones, Billy
1938　Daughter of Shanghai
1949　She Wore a Yellow Ribbon
1952　The Quiet Man

Jones, Buck
1923　Snowdrift
1927　Whispering Sage
1931　The Avenger
1932　White Eagle
1933　The California Trail
1936　For the Service
1938　California Frontier
1942　Below the Border

Jones, Burton
1947　Calendar Girl

Jones, Carolyn
1958　Marjorie Morningstar
1959　Last Train from Gun Hill
1960　Ice Palace

Jones, Chester
1951　Gambling House
　　　　A Streetcar Named Desire
1952　Bright Victory
1954　Dangerous Mission
1955　The Long Gray Line

Jones, Clem
1957　Beau James

Jones, Clifford
1933　The Man Who Dared: An Imaginative Biography
1934　Coming Out Party
1935　His Family Tree
1936　For the Service

Jones, Dan
1956　Frontier Woman

Jones, Darby
1940　Broken Strings
1941　Virginia
1944　Black Magic
1947　California

Jones, David
1948　The Betrayal

Jones, Dean
1959　Night of the Quarter Moon

Jones, Dickie *same as* **Jones, Dick**
1934　Strange Wives
1936　Daniel Boone
1937　Black Legion
1940　Knute Rockne—All American
1942　The Vanishing Virginian
1950　Battleground
　　　　Rocky Mountain
　　　　Sands of Iwo Jima
1956　The Wild Dakotas

Jones, Dolly
1946?　Go Down, Death!

Jones, Dorothy
1936　Ramona

Jones, Earl
1939　Lying Lips

Jones, Edmund
1937　Life Begins in College

Jones, Edna Mae
1938　In Old Chicago
1945　Nob Hill

Jones, Edward
1918　Wild Women

Jones, Elizabeth
1934　Imitation of Life
1939　Drums Along the Mohawk

Jones, F. Richard
1923　Suzanna

Jones, Fenton
1951　Slaughter Trail

Jones, Fred *same as* **Jones, Fred C.** *could be same as* **Jones, Fred T.**
1916　The Flower of No Man's Land
1917　Threads of Fate
　　　　A Wife by Proxy
1918　Love's Law
1919?　The Chosen Path

Jones, Fred T. *could be same as* **Jones, Fred**
1922　Solomon in Society

Jones, Gordon
1944　Buffalo Bill
1945　Wanderer of the Wasteland
1950　Belle of Old Mexico
　　　　North of the Great Divide
　　　　The Palomino
　　　　Sunset in the West
1955　Smoke Signal

Jones, Grover
1927　The Gay Defender
1930　Tom Sawyer
1931　Huckleberry Finn
　　　　Tropennächte
1934　Behold My Wife!
　　　　Limehouse Blues
1937　The Plainsman
　　　　Souls at Sea
1938　The Buccaneer

Jones, Harmon
1958　Bullwhip

Jones, Harry
1919　Injustice

Jones, Haywood
1948　Docks of New Orleans

Jones, Henry
1953　Taxi

Jones, Howard
1940　Knute Rockne—All American

Jones, Idwal
1934　Limehouse Blues

Jones, Ike
1959　Night of the Quarter Moon
1960　This Rebel Breed

Jones, Isaac
1953　The Joe Louis Story
1955　Blackboard Jungle
1959　Anna Lucasta

Jones, J. Parks
1916　Alien Souls
1918　Sandy
1929　Hawk of the Hills

Jones, J. Richardson
1943　Fighting Americans

Jones, Jack
1934　Fighting Through

Jones, Jane
1937　Slave Ship
1945　Nob Hill

Jones, Jas. B.
1941?　The Blood of Jesus

Jones, Jennifer
1944　Since You Went Away
1947　Duel in the Sun
1949　Portrait of Jennie
　　　　We Were Strangers
1954　Indiscretion of an American Wife
1955　Good Morning, Miss Dove

Jones, John Paul
1933　The California Trail

Jones, July
1946　Dirty Gertie from Harlem, U.S.A.
1946?　Beale Street Mama
1947　Juke Joint
1949?　Girl in Room 20

Jones, L. Q.
1958　The Young Lions
1960　Cimarron
　　　　Flaming Star

Jones, Lee
1960　The Pusher

Jones, Leonore
1921　The Lure of a Woman

Jones, Lu Ann
1944　Chip Off the Old Block

Jones, Marcia Mae *same as* **Jones, Marsha**
1931　Street Scene
1938　The Adventures of Tom Sawyer
1941　The Gang's All Here
1950　The Daughter of Rosie O'Grady

Jones, Matthew *see* **Jones, "Tia Juana" Matthew**

Jones, Melford
1951　Show Boat

Jones, Morgan
1954　They Rode West
1955　Apache Woman
1960　Key Witness

Jones, Olive
1935　A Night at the Ritz

Jones, Ora
1922　The Good Provider

Jones, Owen
1917　The Conqueror

Jones, Parke
1919　Deliverance

Jones, Paul
1941　Sullivan's Travels
1943　Dixie
1945　A Medal for Benny

Jones, Robert Earl *same as* **Jones, Robert**
1940　The Notorious Elinor Lee
1959　Odds Against Tomorrow
1960　Wild River

Jones, Roland *same as* **Jones, Rolland**
1951　Gambling House
1958　The Last Hurrah

Jones, Rozene
1949　Border Incident

Jones, Stan
1950　Rio Grande

Jones, Thaddeus
1938　The Buccaneer
1952　Bright Victory

Jones, "Tia Juana" Matthew *same as* **Jones, Matthew**
1936　Show Boat
1940　Am I Guilty?

Jones, Tiny
1938　The Buccaneer
1948　The Lady from Shanghai
1952　The Quiet Man

Jones, Wallace
1925　Red Love

Jones, Winston
1959　Thunder in the Sun

Jons, Beverly *not the same as* **Jones, Beverly**
1948　The Feathered Serpent
1949　The Gay Amigo
1951　The Well

Jordan, Lt.
1919　The Lost Battalion

Jordan, Beatrice
1920　The Good-Bad Wife

Jordan, Beverly
1949　Pinky

Jordan, Bobby
1942　Let's Get Tough!
1947　Bowery Buckaroos

Jordan, Charles *same as* **Jordan, Charlie**
1942　Cat People
1943　Crime Smasher
　　　　In Old Oklahoma

Jordan, Charles
1944   Black Magic
     Mr. Skeffington
1945   Escape in the Fog
1946   Cuban Pete
     Shadows Over Chinatown
1947   The Jolson Story
1948   Docks of New Orleans
     My Girl Tisa
1957   Edge of the City

Jordan, Dorothy
1931   Young Sinners
1953   The Sun Shines Bright
1956   The Searchers

Jordan, Dulcy
1953   Taxi

Jordan, Egon von *same as* **Von Jordan, Egon**
1931   Buster se marie *(foreign version)*
     El proceso de Mary Dugan *(foreign version)*

Jordan, Geraldine *same as* **Jordan, Jeraldine; Jordan, Jeri**
1943   Tahiti Honey
1949   House of Strangers
     Pinky
1951   The House on Telegraph Hill

Jordan, Jeri *same as* **Jordan, Jeraldine**

Jordan, Jewel
1940   New Moon

Jordan, Jimmy
1945   Wanderer of the Wasteland

Jordan, Judi
1957   Raintree County

Jordan, Kate
1916   Poor Little Peppina

Jordan, Lorna *same as* **Jordan, Llorna**
1948   The Paleface
     Unconquered
1950   Young Man with a Horn
1957   Beau James

Louis Jordan and His Tympany Band *same as* **Louis Jordan and His Tympany Five**
1946   Beware
1947   Reet, Petite and Gone
1949   Lookout Sister

Jordan, Mel
1946   Slightly Scandalous

Jordan, Michael
1951   The Great Caruso

Jordan, Miriam
1933   Let's Fall in Love

Jordan, Robert
1953   The Eddie Cantor Story

Jordan, Ruth
1943   Crash Dive

Jordan, Sam
1926   The Flying Ace

Jordan, Sid
1919   Fighting for Gold
1922   Sky High
1931   Young Sinners
1936   Charlie Chan's Secret
1940   Lucky Cisco Kid
1941   Western Union

Jordan, Ted
1949   The Undercover Man
1950   Emergency Wedding
1952   Bright Victory

Jordon, Charlie
1949   The Sky Dragon

Jory, Victor
1934   He Was Her Man
1938   The Adventures of Tom Sawyer
1939   Gone With the Wind
     Man of Conquest
1941   Charlie Chan in Rio
1942   Shut My Big Mouth
1950   The Cariboo Trail
1951   Flaming Feather
1953   The Man from the Alamo
1956   Death of a Scoundrel

José, Edward
1915   Children of the Ghetto
1918   My Cousin
     A Woman of Impulse
1920   The Riddle: Woman

Josefsberg, Milt
1941   Ice-Capades

Joseph, Edmund
1929   Die Königsloge
1943   Mr. Lucky
     Yankee Doodle Dandy

Joseph, Robert L.
1948   Open Secret

Josephine Beach, a rat
1942   Whispering Ghosts

Josephson, Julien
1918   The Midnight Patrol
1922   Head over Heels
     Hungry Hearts
     The Man with Two Mothers
1928   A Ship Comes In

Josephson, Sam
1938   The Power of Life

Josephson, Saul
1938   The Power of Life

Joslin, Howard
1959   The Black Orchid
     The Jayhawkers!

Joslyn, Allyn
1940   If I Had My Way
1948   Moonrise
1953   The Jazz Singer

Jou-Jerville, Jacques
1930   Amor audaz *(foreign version)*
1931   Echec au roi
     La gran jornada *(foreign version)*
     Le petit café
     El proceso de Mary Dugan *(foreign version)*
     Quand on est belle
1932   Le bluffeur

Jourdan, Robert
1950   Panic in the Streets

Journet, Marcel
1947   The Foxes of Harrow
1951   Adventures of Captain Fabian

Jowitt, Anthony
1932   Call Her Savage
1946   Canyon Passage
1950   Two Flags West
1951   The House on Telegraph Hill
1953   So Big

Joy, Ernest
1915   After Five
     Chimmie Fadden
     Chimmie Fadden Out West
     The Immigrant
1916   Pudd'nhead Wilson
     Unprotected
1917   The Call of the East
     Forbidden Paths
     Hashimura Togo
     The Squaw Man's Son
1918   One More American

Joy, Leatrice
1918   The City of Tears
1921   A Tale of Two Worlds
1922   Saturday Night

Joy, Nicholas
1948   Gentleman's Agreement
1951   Native Son

Joyce, Adrian
1922   For His Mother's Sake

Joyce, Alice
1918   Find the Woman

Joyce, Brenda
1940   Elsa Maxwell's Public Deb No. 1
1942   Little Tokyo, U.S.A.
     Whispering Ghosts

Joyce, Jean
1938   In Old Chicago

Joyce, John J., Jr.
1953   Taxi

Joyce, Marty
1936   Custer's Last Stand
1937   The Plainsman

Joyce, Mary
1940   Taku

Joyce, Natalie
1927   Whispering Sage

Joyce, William F.
1953   The Joe Louis Story

Joyeux, Odette
1930   El secreto del doctor *(foreign version)*

Joyita y Maravilla
1938   Di que me quieres

Joyner, Frank
1934   Chloe: Love Is Calling You
1953   Beneath the 12-Mile Reef

Joyner, Henry
1955   Davy Crockett, King of the Wild Frontier

Joyzelle
1929   Sombras habaneras
1930   Song of the Caballero
1932   The Vanishing Frontier

Juaregui, Ed
1951   Westward the Women

The Jubilaires
1949?   The Joint Is Jumpin'

The Jubilee Singers
1929   Show Boat

Judd, Forrest
1948   16 Fathoms Deep

Judd, Larry
1932   Hypnotized

Judels, Charles
1923   Little Old New York
1929   Frozen Justice
1937   The Plainsman
     Song of the City
1938   Passport Husband
1940   Elsa Maxwell's Public Deb No. 1
     Viva Cisco Kid
1941   This Woman Is Mine
1942   Tortilla Flat
1945   Sunbonnet Sue
1947   The Mighty McGurk

Judge, Arline
1936   It Had to Happen
     Star for a Night

Judson, Harold
1919   Deliverance

Jugo, Jenny
1931   La pura verdad *(foreign version)*

Julian, Hubert Fauntleroy
1940   The Notorious Elinor Lee

Julian, Rupert
1917   A Kentucky Cinderella
1919   The Sleeping Lion

Julio, Don
1938   Di que me quieres

Juncos, Victor
1955   Seven Cities of Gold

June, Ray
1933   It's Great to Be Alive *(foreign version)*

Jung, Allen
1942   Submarine Raider

Jung, Shia
1936   Charlie Chan at the Circus

Jungmeyer, Jack, Jr. *same as* **Jungmeyer, Jack**
1925   Scarlet Saint
1933   The Cohens and Kellys in Trouble
1939   Mr. Moto in Danger Island

Jungquist, Yvonne
1941   Birth of the Blues

Junior, Herbert
1948?   Junction 88

Junior, the monkey
1946   Strange Voyage

Junkermann, Hans
1930   Anna Christie *(foreign version)*
     Olimpia *(foreign version)*
1931   Don Juan diplomático *(foreign version)*

Jurado, Arthur
1950   The Men

Jurado, Katy
1952   High Noon
1953   Arrowhead
     San Antone
1954   Broken Lance
1955   Trial
1956   Man from Del Rio
1957   Dragoon Wells Massacre
1958   The Badlanders

Juran, Nathan
1953   Tumbleweed
1954   Drums Across the River

Jurgens, Curt
1960   I Aim at the Stars: the Wernher von Braun Story

Jurow, Martin
1959   The Hanging Tree

Justin, George
1957   Twelve Angry Men

Justman, Joseph
1951   New Mexico

Juston, Nikki
1951   The Great Caruso
     The Tall Target
1955   Blackboard Jungle

Jutte, William B.
1929   Chinatown Nights

Kabibble, Ish
1941   Playmates

Kabierske, Henry
1916   The Daughter of the Don

Kac, Zish
1939   Kol Nidre

Kacier, Johnny *see* **Kascier, John**

Kadish, Ben *same as* **Kadish, Benjamin**
1944   The Racket Man
1945   Jealousy
1949   The Prairie
1955   The Indian Fighter

Kadison, Harry
1940   The Notorious Elinor Lee

Kadler, Karen
1955   Kiss of Fire

Kafka, John
1960   Man on a String

Kahaleva, John
1954   Hell's Half Acre

Kahamkahi, David
1950   Damien

Kahanamoku, Sargeant *could be same as* **Kahanamoku, Duke**
1950   Damien

Kahn, Gordon
1942   Apache Trail

Kahn, Richard C.
1930   Las campanas de Capistrano
1935   Un hombre peligroso
1938   Two Gun Man from Harlem
1939   The Bronze Buckaroo
     Harlem Rides the Range
1940   Son of Ingagi

Kaiser, Augustus, Lt.
1919   The Lost Battalion

Kaito, Maui
1923   The White Flower

Kalich, Jacob *same as* **Kalish, Jacob**
1932   Mazel Tov

Kalili, Manuella
1937   Waikiki Wedding

Kalish, Jacob *see* **Kalich, Jacob**

Kalish, Mel
1937   Slave Ship

Kaliz, Armand
1927   The Love Mart
1930   Amor audaz *(foreign version)*

1931 Little Caesar
1934 Caravane
1935 Ruggles of Red Gap
1938 Josette

Kalmanovitch, Harry *see*
Kalmonowitz, H.

Kalmanowitz, Harry *see*
Kalmonowitz, H.

Kalmar, Bert
1930 Check and Double Check

Kalmonowitz, H. *same as*
Kalmanovitch, Harry;
Kalmanowitz, Harry
1930 Eternal Fools (Ewige
Naranim)

Kalser, Erwin
1940 Escape
Escape to Glory
1941 They Dare Not Love
1944 Address Unknown
They Live in Fear

Kaluna, George
1937 Waikiki Wedding

Kamai, Kolimau
1934 White Heat

Kamakaiwi, James
1934 Song of the Islands

Kamakau, Joe
1934 Song of the Islands

Joe Kamakau Singers
1934 Song of the Islands

Kamb, Karl
1947 Carnegie Hall

Kamber, Stan
1958 The Young Lions

Kami, Virginia
1937 Souls at Sea

Kaminska, Ester-Rokhl
1934 The Rabbi's Power

Kaminska, Ida
1934 The Rabbi's Power

Kamuca, Richie
1958 Kings Go Forth

Kandel, Aben
1939 Fisherman's Wharf
1943 What's Buzzin' Cousin?
1948 Big City
1952 The Fighter
Kid Monk Baroni
1956 Singing in the Dark

Kandel, Stephen
1956 Singing in the Dark
1958 Frontier Gun

Kane, Babe *see* Kane, Marjorie

Kane, Byron
1948 The Lady from Shanghai

Kane, Eddie *same as* Kane,
Edward
1929 Why Bring That Up?
1930 The Kibitzer
1931 The Cohens and Kellys in
Africa
Smart Money
1934 Broadway Bill
1937 Manhattan
Merry-Go-Round
1940 Music in My Heart
1941 Sun Valley Serenade
1943 Let's Have Fun
Redhead from Manhattan
Tahiti Honey
1944 Lake Placid Serenade
Minstrel Man
1945 The Dolly Sisters
1947 The Jolson Story
My Wild Irish Rose
1949 Jiggs and Maggie in
Jackpot Jitters

Kane, Gail
1914 Dan
The Great Diamond
Robbery
The Jungle
1916 The Scarlet Oath
1917 The Red Woman
Southern Pride
1918 Love's Law
1920? The Scarlet Dragon

Kane, Irving
1951 Apache Drums

Kane, Joe *see* Kane, Joseph

Kane, Joel
1957 The Tin Star

Kane, Joseph *same as* Kane, Joe
1935 Melody Trail
1936 Ride, Ranger, Ride
1937 Boots and Saddles
1939 In Old Caliente
1940 Young Buffalo Bill
1943 In Old Oklahoma
1948 Old Los Angeles
1950 Rock Island Trail
1951 Oh! Susanna
1953 San Antone
1955 The Vanishing American
1957 The Lawless Eighties
1958 Gunfire at Indian Gap

Kane, Louise
1950 Emergency Wedding
1951 Oh! Susanna

Kane, Marjorie *same as* Kane,
Babe; Kane, Marjorie Babe
1930 Sunny Skies
1943 Gangway for Tomorrow

Kane, Pat
1949 Pinky

Kane, Robert T. *same as* Kane,
Robert
1927 For the Love of Mike
1929 Mother's Boy
1930 Un hombre de suerte
Un hombre de suerte
(*foreign version*)
1934 Caravane
1944 The Sullivans

Kane, Sid
1948 Music Man
1950 Young Man with a Horn
1959 The FBI Story

Kane, William J.
1915 The Alien

Kanealii, Roger
1950 Damien

Kanin, Fay
1942 Sunday Punch

Kanin, Garson
1940 They Knew What They
Wanted

Kanin, Michael
1942 Sunday Punch
Woman of the Year

Kann, George E. *same as* Kann,
George
1930 ¡De frente, marchen!
Estrellados
Monsieur le Fox
Wu Li Chang
1931 Su última noche
1937 Boy of the Streets

Kanner, Michael
1953 The Eddie Cantor Story

Kano, Eddie
1943 Yankee Doodle Dandy

Kanter, Hal
1955 The Rose Tattoo

Kaplan, Marvin
1952 The Fabulous Senorita

Kaplan, Zelda
1950? Three Daughters

Kapp, Richard
1956 The Benny Goodman
Story

Kapps, Kendall
1950 The Daughter of Rosie
O'Grady

Kapu, Sam
1934 Song of the Islands

Karabanova, Zoia
1947 Northwest Outpost
1953 Tonight We Sing

Karen, Lillian
1932 The Unfortunate Bride

Karger, Maxwell
1918 Toys of Fate

Karlan, Richard
1952 Bright Victory
1959 Inside the Mafia

Karlo, Sergio de
1939 Verbena trágica

Karloff, Boris
1921 The Cave Girl
1925 The Prairie Wife
1927 The Love Mart
The Princess from
Hoboken
1931 The Guilty Generation
Smart Money
1932 The Cohens and Kellys in
Hollywood
Scarface
1937 Charlie Chan at the
Opera
1938 Mr. Wong, Detective
1939 Mr. Wong in Chinatown
The Mystery of Mr. Wong
1940 Doomed to Die
The Fatal Hour
1948 Tap Roots
Unconquered

Karlson, Phil *same as* Karlstein,
Phil
1934 Strange Wives
1941 Where Did You Get That
Girl?
1945 The Shanghai Cobra
1946 Dark Alibi
1947 Black Gold
1948 Rocky
1950 The Iroquois Trail
1954 They Rode West
1957 The Brothers Rico
1958 Gunman's Walk
1960 Hell to Eternity
Key Witness

Karlweis, Oscar *same as* Karlweis,
Oskar; Karlweiss, Oscar
1931 La pura verdad (*foreign
version*)
1952 Anything Can Happen
1953 Tonight We Sing

Karnes, Robert
1948 Call Northside 777
Cry of the City
Gentleman's Agreement
The Luck of the Irish
1952 Red Ball Express
1953 Seminole

Karns, Roscoe
1928 The Jazz Singer
1933 Grand Slam
A Lady's Profession
1938 Dangerous to Know
1939 King of Chinatown
1942 Woman of the Year
1943 His Butler's Sister
Riding High
1944 Minstrel Man
1947 Vigilantes of Boomtown

Karns, Todd
1951 The Magnificent Yankee

Karpe, Curt
1919 Love and the Law

Karr, Craig
1957 Burden of Truth
1958 The Young Lions

Karr, Darwin
1916 Britton of the Seventh
1918 The Unbeliever

Karr, H. S.
1922 Big Stakes

Karr, Norman, Dr.
1950 The Men

Kascier, John *same as* Kacier,
Johnny
1932 Hypnotized
1934 The Cat's-Paw
1940 Escape to Glory
1950 Emergency Wedding

Kasday, David
1956 The Benny Goodman
Story

Kashfi, Anna
1959 Night of the Quarter
Moon

Kashinskya, Dora
1934 The Youth of Russia

Kashner, Dave
1936 Ramona
1947 California
1955 Kiss of Fire

Kass, Lee
1947 The Farmer's Daughter

Kassler, Peter E.
1939 The Light Ahead
Moon over Harlem

Kasznar, Kurt
1952 Anything Can Happen
1953 Ride, Vaquero!

Katch, Kurt
1943 They Came to Blow Up
America
1945 The Mummy's Curse
Salome, Where She
Danced
1946 Rendezvous 24
1958 The Young Lions

Katcher, Aram
1953 Dream Wife

Katcher, Leo
1954 Barefoot Battalion
They Rode West

Katcher, Robert
1943 Jack London

Katchko, Adolph, Cantor
1931 The Voice of Israel

Katscher, Rudolph
1931 Tropennächte

Katsiotes, Nico
1954 Barefoot Battalion

Katterjohn, Monte M. *same as*
Katterjohn, Monte
1917 The Bride of Hate
The Gun Fighter
1918 An Alien Enemy
The Source
1919 The Lord Loves the Irish

Katz, Ben-Zion
1932 Uncle Moses

Katz, Lee
1939 Waterfront

Katz, Sidney
1960 The Pusher

Katz, Zishe
1939 The Light Ahead

Katzman, Sam
1933 Obey the Law
1939 Trigger Fingers
1942 Let's Get Tough!
1944 Block Busters
1947 Last of the Redmen
1950 Chinatown at Midnight
Last of the Buccaneers
1951 Hurricane Island
When the Redskins Rode
1952 Brave Warrior
California Conquest
1953 Conquest of Cochise
Fort Ti
Jack McCall Desperado
The Pathfinder
1954 Battle of Rogue River
1955 Duel on the Mississippi
The Gun That Won the
West
Seminole Uprising

Kauffin, Ida Belle
1940 While Thousands Cheer

Kaufman, Edward
1935 McFadden's Flats
Romance in Manhattan
1939 Charlie Chan at Treasure
Island

Kaufman, Ethel
1915 Children of the Ghetto

Kaufman, George S.
1935 A Night at the Opera

Kaufman, Millard
1952 My Man and I
1955 Bad Day at Black Rock
1957 Raintree County

Kaufman, Will *same as* Kaufman,
William; Kaufman, Willy
1939 Confessions of a Nazi Spy
1940 The Man I Married
1945 Where Do We Go From
Here?
1946 Canyon Passage
1949 Illegal Entry
1952 Anything Can Happen

Kaumakapili Choir
1954　Hell's Half Acre
Kavanaugh, Frances
1943　The Law Rides Again
1944　Outlaw Trail
　　　Sonora Stagecoach
1946　Romance of the West
　　　Wild West
1949　The Daring Caballero
Kavanaugh, Katharine *same as*
　Kavanaugh, Katherine
1918　The Liar
Kawai, Gosuke
1930　Chijlku wo mawasuru
　　　chikara
Kawaye
1930　Chijlku wo mawasuru
　　　chikara
Kay, Albert
1939　Winner Take All
Kay, Don
1947　The Last Round-Up
Kay, Edward J.
1948　Music Man
Kay, Gordon
1948　Renegades of Sonora
Kay, Jack
1949　Lust for Gold
Kay, Joyce
1934　As the Earth Turns
1935　Rosa de Francia
1936　The Prisoner of Shark
　　　Island
Kay, Karol
1934　She Was a Lady
Kay, Mary Ellen
1951　The Well
1954　Thunder Pass
Kay, Ormonde de
1949　Lost Boundaries
Kay, Richard
1950　Riders of the Pony
　　　Express
Kay, Steven
1956　Giant
Kaye, Adelaide
1938　In Old Chicago
Kaye, Frances
1919　Come Out of the Kitchen
Kaye, Gail
1934　Charlie Chan's Courage
Kaye, Leo
1948　Fighting Father Dunne
　　　Gentleman's Agreement
　　　Open Secret
Kaye, Louis S.
1941　Louisiana Purchase
Kaye, Stubby
1953　Taxi
Kazan, Elia
1945　A Tree Grows in Brooklyn
1948　Gentleman's Agreement
1949　Pinky
1950　Panic in the Streets
1951　A Streetcar Named Desire
1956　Baby Doll
1960　Wild River
Keach, Stacy (*actor, dial dir*), b.
　1914
1942　Secret Enemies
1944　Hi, Beautiful
1959　The FBI Story
Kean, Betty
1944　Slightly Terrific
Kean, Richard 1881–1959
1950　Storm Over Wyoming
Keane, Charles
1947　Untamed Fury
1955　A Man Called Peter
1957　Beau James
Keane, Constance *see* Lake,
　Veronica
Keane, Edward *same as* Keane, Ed;
　Keene, Edward
1921?　The Supreme Passion
1934　Broadway Bill
1935　The Irish in Us
　　　Naughty Marietta
　　　A Night at the Opera
1936　For the Service
　　　It Had to Happen

1937　Charlie Chan at the
　　　Olympics
1938　Josette
　　　Speed to Burn
　　　The Toy Wife
1939　Confessions of a Nazi Spy
　　　The Escape
　　　Mr. Moto in Danger
　　　Island
　　　Stand Up and Fight
1940　Charlie Chan in Panama
1942　They Died With Their
　　　Boots On
1943　Dr. Gillespie's Criminal
　　　Case
　　　Let's Have Fun
　　　Yankee Doodle Dandy
1945　Nob Hill
1947　Calendar Girl
　　　The Jolson Story
　　　On the Old Spanish Trail
1949　The Story of Seabiscuit
1950　The Baron of Arizona
1951　Show Boat
Keane, James
1918　The Spreading Evil
Keane, Mike
1956　Crowded Paradise
Keane, Raymond
1926　April Fool
Keane, Robert Emmett *same as*
　Keane, Robert E.
1937　Man of the People
1939　The Adventures of
　　　Huckleberry Finn
　　　Confessions of a Nazi Spy
1940　Little Nellie Kelly
1942　Young America
1943　The Meanest Man in the
　　　World
1944　Slightly Terrific
1946　The Red Dragon
1947　The Foxes of Harrow
1948　Big City
1950　Jolson Sings Again
　　　The Toast of New Orleans
Kearney, Muriel
1945　Where Do We Go From
　　　Here?
Keate, Crystal
1934　Stand Up and Cheer!
1938　In Old Chicago
Keating, Alice
1941　Birth of the Blues
　　　New York Town
Keating, F. Serrano
1925　Red Love
Keating, Larry
1950　Right Cross
1952　Bright Victory
Keaton, Buster
1928　The Cameraman
1930　¡De frente, marchen!
　　　Estrellados
1931　Buster se marie
　　　Buster se marie (*foreign
　　　version*)
1932　Le plombier amoureux
1940　New Moon
1960　The Adventures of
　　　Huckleberry Finn
Keaton, Harry
1934　Broadway Bill
Keckley, Jane
1918　Huck and Tom; or, the
　　　Further Adventures of
　　　Tom Sawyer
1927　Aflame in the Sky
1933　Dance Hall Hostess
1935　Ruggles of Red Gap
1936　Paddy O'Day
　　　Show Boat
1937　The Plainsman
　　　Souls at Sea
　　　That I May Live
1938　The Buccaneer
　　　Road Demon
Kedrowsky, Vladimir
1938　Marusia
Keedwell, Norval
1923　Little Old New York

Keefe, Cornelius
1929　The Cohens and Kellys in
　　　Atlantic City
1932　Thirteen Steps
1933　Charlie Chan's Greatest
　　　Case
1941　Saddlemates
Keefe, Zena
1923　None So Blind
1924　The Lure of Love
Keefer, Phil
1934　'Neath the Arizona Skies
Keel, Howard
1950　Annie Get Your Gun
1951　Across the Wide Missouri
　　　Show Boat
1953　Ride, Vaquero!
Keel, John M.
1950　Intruder in the Dust
Keeler, Betty
1933　It's Great to Be Alive
Keeler, Leonarde
1948　Call Northside 777
Keenan, Frank
1917　The Bride of Hate
1923　Scars of Jealousy
Keene, Dick *see* Keene, Richard
　1899–1971
Keene, Edward *see* Keane, Edward
Keene, Naomi
1945　Nob Hill
Keene, Richard 1899–1971 *same
　as* Keene, Dick
1940　Charlie Chan's Murder
　　　Cruise
　　　If I Had My Way
1941　Birth of the Blues
1949　Top O' the Morning
1957　Beau James
1958　The Last Hurrah
Keene, Tom *same as* Duryea,
　George; Powers, Richard
1929　In Old California
1934　Our Daily Bread
1936　Desert Gold
　　　The Glory Trail
　　　Rebellion
1937　Drums of Destiny
　　　Old Louisiana
1947　Crossfire
　　　Thunder Mountain
　　　Under the Tonto Rim
　　　Wild Horse Mesa
1948　Indian Agent
　　　Western Heritage
1949　Brothers in the Saddle
1950　Storm Over Wyoming
1956　Wetbacks
Keene, William
1960　Key Witness
Keener, Hazel
1924　North of Nevada
1927　Whispering Sage
1938　Gateway
1947　The Farmer's Daughter
Keeno, Gordo
1917　The Flower of Doom
Kehoe, Charles
1958　Flaming Frontier
Keighley, William
1932　The Match King
1936　The Green Pastures
1940　The Fighting 69th
1950　Rocky Mountain
Keir, Andrew
1960　The Day They Robbed the
　　　Bank of England
Keiser, Howard
1948　I Remember Mama
**"Shootsie" Keith and the
　Savannah Club Chorus**
1949?　Harlem Follies
Keith, Brian
1953　Arrowhead
1957　Run of the Arrow
1958　Sierra Baron
Keith, Byron
1951　Queen for a Day
Keith, Donald
1927　The Way of All Flesh
　　　Wild Geese

Keith, Ian
1925　My Son
1930　Abraham Lincoln
1938　The Buccaneer
1944　The Chinese Cat
1945　Phantom of the Plains
1955　Duel on the Mississippi
Keith, Robert
1954　Drum Beat
1960　Cimarron
Keithley, Jane
1930　Whoopee
Kellar, Gertrude
1915　The Immigrant
1916　For the Defense
　　　Pudd'nhead Wilson
Kellard, Robert
1938　Gateway
　　　Josette
　　　My Lucky Star
1940　Phantom of Chinatown
1941　Prairie Pioneers
Kellard, Thomas
1937　Life Begins in College
Kellaway, Cecil
1940　Mexican Spitfire
　　　Mexican Spitfire Out
　　　West
1941　Birth of the Blues
　　　New York Town
1948　The Luck of the Irish
　　　Unconquered
1949　Portrait of Jennie
Keller, Harry
1952　Rose of Cimarron
Keller, Helen
1919　Deliverance
Keller, Mrs. Kate Adams
1919　Deliverance
Keller, Nell Clark
1918　Out of a Clear Sky
Keller, Phillips Brooks
1919　Deliverance
Keller, Sam
1956　Frontier Woman
Kellett, Pete
1956　Reprisal!
　　　Westward Ho the
　　　Wagons!
Kelley, Barry *same as* Kelly, Barry
1949　Knock on Any Door
　　　The Undercover Man
1950　Black Hand
　　　Right Cross
1951　The Well
1955　Trial
1958　Gunfire at Indian Gap
1960　Ice Palace
Kelley, De Forest
1953　Taxi
1955　The View from Pompey's
　　　Head
1957　Raintree County
Kelley, Walter *same as* Kelly,
　Walter *not the same as* Kelly,
　Walter C.
1951　The Well
1955　Marty
Kellin, Mike
1959　The Wonderful Country
Kellogg, Bruce *same as* Kellogg,
　William
1943　Deerslayer
1946　Shadows Over Chinatown
1948　The Golden Eye
Kellogg, Cecil
1937　The Plainsman
1940　Geronimo
1941　Western Union
Kellogg, Gayle
1952　The Iron Mistress
1955　Seven Angry Men
Kellogg, John
1946　Without Reservations
1949　House of Strangers
1952　The Raiders
1957　Edge of the City
Kellogg, Ray
1957　Apache Warrior
1960　I Passed for White

Kellogg, William *see* **Kellogg, Bruce**

Kelly, Al
1956   Singing in the Dark

Kelly, Ann
1956   Frontier Woman

Kelly, Anthony Paul *same as* **Kelly, Anthony P.**
1916   Light at Dusk
1917   The Bar Sinister
1918   The Birth of a Race
1925   The Scarlet West

Kelly, Barry *see* **Kelley, Barry**

Kelly, Carol
1956   Daniel Boone, Trail Blazer
1958   Terror in a Texas Town

Kelly, Claire
1958   The Badlanders

Kelly, Colin, Capt. *same as* **Kelly, Colin**
1937   Maid of Salem
1944   The Negro Soldier

Kelly, Craig
1950   The Furies

Kelly, Daniel
1920   Hidden Charms
1921?   The Supreme Passion

Kelly, Dorothy
1943   Yankee Doodle Dandy

Kelly, Gene
1950   Black Hand
1952   It's a Big Country: An American Anthology
1958   Marjorie Morningstar

Kelly, George F., Jr.
1953   Thunder Bay

Kelly, Georgia
1943   Marching On!

Kelly, Grace
1952   High Noon

Kelly, Jack
1951   New Mexico
1952   Red Ball Express
1953   Column South
          The Stand at Apache River
1954   They Rode West

Kelly, James A. *not the same as* **Kelly, Tiny Jimmie**
1957   Twelve Angry Men

Kelly, Jeanne *see* **Brooks, Jean**
name assumed by actress **Jeanne Kelly** in 1943

Kelly, Jimmie *see* **Kelly, Tiny Jimmie**

Kelly, Jimmy *(skater)*
1941   Sun Valley Serenade

Kelly, John
1936   After the Thin Man
          It Had to Happen
1940   East of the River
1942   Tales of Manhattan
1943   Jack London
1945   Nob Hill
1947   The Mighty McGurk

Kelly, Karolee
1953   San Antone

Kelly, Kitty
1934   She Was a Lady
1940   Geronimo
1941   Hold Back the Dawn
1942   Holiday Inn

Kelly, Lew
1936   Ellis Island
          Rainbow on the River
          Rose of the Rancho
1939   The Adventures of Huckleberry Finn
1940   Lucky Cisco Kid
1941   Road Agent
1942   Shut My Big Mouth
1943   Action in the North Atlantic

Kelly, Mabel
1928   The Midnight Ace
          Thirty Years Later

Kelly, Nancy
1942   Friendly Enemies
1945   Betrayal from the East
1956   Crowded Paradise

Kelly, P. J. *same as* **Kelly, Patrick J.**
1946   The Gentleman Misbehaves
1947   The Jolson Story

Kelly, Patsy
1936   Kelly the Second
1941   Playmates
1943   Ladies' Day

Kelly, Paul
1939   Forged Passport
1941   Mystery Ship
1947   Crossfire
          Spoilers of the North

Kelly, Paula
1941   Sun Valley Serenade

Kelly, Ted
1946   Notorious

Kelly, Tiny Jimmie *same as* **Kelly, Jimmie** *not the same as* **Kelly, James A.**
1948   Moonrise
1949   Harbor of Missing Men

Kelly, Tommy
1938   The Adventures of Tom Sawyer
1950   Battleground
1951   The Magnificent Yankee

Kelly, Toni
1947   Copacabana

Kelly, Walter *see* **Kelley, Walter**

Kelly, Walter C. *not the same as* **Kelley, Walter**
1935   McFadden's Flats
1936   Laughing Irish Eyes

Kelman, Rickey
1959   The FBI Story
          Last Train from Gun Hill

Kelsay, Joe
1960   This Rebel Breed

Kelsey, Fred
1918   The Yellow Dog
1921   Puppets of Fate
1922   Captain Fly-by-Night
1925   Friendly Enemies
1929   Smiling Irish Eyes
1930   She Got What She Wanted
1934   Beloved
1936   Dimples
          Star for a Night
1937   One Mile from Heaven
          Slave Ship
          That I May Live
1938   Happy Landing
          Josette
          Mr. Moto's Gamble
          My Lucky Star
          Speed to Burn
1939   Charlie Chan in Reno
          Heaven with a Barbed Wire Fence
          Winner Take All
1940   Mexican Spitfire Out West
1942   Gentleman Jim
          In This Our Life
          Juke Girl
          Secret Enemies
          They Died With Their Boots On
          Wings for the Eagle
1943   Riding High
          Yankee Doodle Dandy
1946   Bringing Up Father
1949   Colorado Territory
1950   The Daughter of Rosie O'Grady

Kelso, Edmond *same as* **Kelso, Edmund**
1941   The Gang's All Here
          King of the Zombies
          You're Out of Luck

Kelso, James
1938   The Texans

Kelso, Mayme *same as* **Kelso, Maym**
1916   Man and His Angel
1917   Castles for Two
          The Secret Game
1918   His Birthright
          The Honor of His House

Kelson, Anna
1923   Flames of Wrath

Kelton, Dorrit
1955   The Rose Tattoo

Kelton, Pert
1935   Annie Oakley
1936   Kelly the Second

Kemble, Diana
1947   Citizen Saint

Kemble-Cooper, Lillian *same as* **Kemble Cooper, Lily; Kemble-Cooper, L.**
1939   Gone With the Wind
1953   So Big

Kemp, Jack
1937   Underworld
1948   Miracle in Harlem

Kemp, Mae
1921   The Call of His People

Kemp, Paul
1931   Die Dreigroschenoper

Kemper, Charles
1948   Fighting Father Dunne
          Fury at Furnace Creek
1950   Intruder in the Dust
          Stars in My Crown
          A Ticket to Tomahawk

Kemper, Doris
1934   Our Daily Bread
1947   Buck Privates Come Home
1948   Big City
1949   Tuna Clipper
1950   No Way Out
1957   The Oklahoman

Kemper, Rozene
1954   Passion

Kempler, Kurt
1933   The Telegraph Trail

Kenaston, Bob
1957   The Tin Star

Kendall, Cy *same as* **Kendall, Cyrus W.**
1936   Sea Spoilers
1937   It Could Happen to You
1938   Breaking the Ice
          Hawaii Calls
1939   Stand Up and Fight
1941   Mystery Ship
          They Dare Not Love
1942   Sunday Punch
1944   The Chinese Cat
          Outlaw Trail
          Tahiti Nights
1945   The Cisco Kid Returns
1946   Without Reservations
1947   The Farmer's Daughter
1948   Call Northside 777

Kendall, Harry
1923   Jamestown

Kendall, Messmore
1922   Cardigan

Kendall, Victor
1940   New Moon
1943   Action in the North Atlantic

Kendrick, Richard
1960   Man on a String

Kenig, M.
1936   Love and Sacrifice

Kenley, Jacqueline
1952   It's a Big Country: An American Anthology

Kennedy, Ann *same as* **Kennedy, Anne**
1924   Smiling Hate
1927   The Scar of Shame

Kennedy, Arthur
1942   They Died With Their Boots On
1943   Air Force
1952   Bright Victory
1955   Trial

Kennedy, Bill
1943   Air Force
1944   Mr. Skeffington
1945   Rhapsody in Blue
1950   Storm Over Wyoming

Kennedy, Burt
1959   Yellowstone Kelly

Kennedy, Charles circa 1923
1923   Little Old New York

Kennedy, Charles circa 1950
1950   Panic in the Streets

Kennedy, Daun *(actress)*
1945   Salome, Where She Danced
1946   Bringing Up Father

Kennedy, Don *(actor)*
1955   The Last Command
          Seven Angry Men
1960   Pay or Die
          Walk Like a Dragon

Kennedy, Dorothy
1953   Dream Wife

Kennedy, Douglas
1940   The Way of All Flesh
1949   Ranger of Cherokee Strip
1950   The Cariboo Trail
1951   Oh! Susanna
1952   Fort Osage
          Indian Uprising
1953   Jack McCall Desperado
          San Antone
          War Paint
1954   Massacre Canyon
          Sitting Bull
1956   The Last Wagon
1958   The Lone Ranger and the Lost City of Gold

Kennedy, Ed *could be same as* **Kennedy, Edgar**
1927   The Chinese Parrot

Kennedy, Edgar *could be same as* **Kennedy, Ed**
1925   His People
1933   Diplomaniacs
1936   Mad Holiday
          Robin Hood of El Dorado
1943   Crime Smasher
          The Girl from Monterrey

Kennedy, Edith *same as* **Kennedy, Edith M.**
1918   The Bravest Way
          Sandy

Kennedy, Edward circa 1950
1950   Panic in the Streets

Kennedy, Edward early 1920s
1921   Puppets of Fate

Kennedy, Elizabeth
1919   Who's Your Brother?

Kennedy, Estelle
1924   Smiling Hate

Kennedy, Florence
1926?   Ten Nights in a Barroom

Kennedy, Fred
1944   Buffalo Bill
1949   She Wore a Yellow Ribbon
1950   Rio Grande
1953   The Charge at Feather River
1958   The Last Hurrah

Kennedy, Jack
1931   Skyline
1934   The Cat's-Paw
1939   The Mystery of Mr. Wong
1940   Doomed to Die
          The Fatal Hour

Kennedy, Joe *(announcer)*
1949   The Story of Seabiscuit

Kennedy, Joseph P. *(prod)*
1926   Kosher Kitty Kelly
          Laddie
          Rose of the Tenements
1927   Aflame in the Sky
          Clancy's Kosher Wedding
          Don Mike
          The Fighting Hombre
          Jake the Plumber

Kennedy, Kathleen
1949   Top O' the Morning

Kennedy, Lyn Crost
1952   The Raiders

Kennedy, Madge
1919   Daughter of Mine
1956   The Catered Affair
1958   Houseboat

Kennedy, Mary
1923   Little Old New York

Kennedy, Merna
1930   King of Jazz
Kennedy, Phyllis
1943   Yankee Doodle Dandy
1944   An American Romance
1951   Molly
1952   The Half-Breed
Kennedy, Tom
1925   The Fearless Lover
1928   Hold 'Em Yale
1929   The Cohens and Kellys in Atlantic City
1931   El tenorio del harem
1932   Huddle
1937   Slave Ship
1940   Mexican Spitfire Out West
1941   The Mexican Spitfire's Baby
1942   Mexican Spitfire's Elephant
1943   Dixie
          Ladies' Day
          Riding High
1946   Bringing Up Father
1947   The Burning Cross
          The Mighty McGurk
1948   Jiggs and Maggie in Court
          The Paleface
1949   Jiggs and Maggie in Jackpot Jitters
1960   Walk Like a Dragon
Kenneth, Keith
1934   Limehouse Blues
1936   Daniel Boone
Kenney, Jack *same as* **Kenny, Jack**
1934   Broadway Bill
1937   It Could Happen to You
1941   The Gang's All Here
1943   In Old Oklahoma
1950   I Killed Geronimo
1956   The Catered Affair
1957   The Tin Star
1959   Inside the Mafia
          The Last Angry Man
Kenny, Colin
1919   Toby's Bow
1920   Darling Mine
1934   Limehouse Blues
1935   Charlie Chan in Shanghai
1936   Charlie Chan at the Race Track
1937   Souls at Sea
1948   Big City
          Unconquered
1951   The Great Caruso
Kenny, Jack *see* **Kenney, Jack**
Kensel, Frederick, U.S.M.C., Lieut.
1918   The Unbeliever
Kent, Arnold
1942   Mexican Spitfire's Elephant
Kent, Barbara
1929   Welcome Danger
1931   Chinatown After Dark
Kent, Carl
1944   My Pal Wolf
1945   Johnny Angel
1947   Desperate
          The Farmer's Daughter
Kent, Charles
1916   Britton of the Seventh
Kent, Crauford *same as* **Kent, Craufurd; Kent, Crawford**
1918   The Ordeal of Rosetta
1919   Come Out of the Kitchen
1930   Ladies Love Brutes
1936   Daniel Boone
1937   Souls at Sea
1945   The Dolly Sisters
1948   Unconquered
Kent, Douglas *see* **Montgomery, Douglass**
Kent, Earl
1943   Action in the North Atlantic
Kent, Julia
1940   The Ramparts We Watch
1947   Riding the California Trail

Kent, Larry
1927   McFadden's Flats
1930   Around the Corner
1936   Treachery Rides the Range
1955   A Man Called Peter
Kent, Leon
1918   Her Moment
1927   With Sitting Bull at the Spirit Lake Massacre
Kent, Marshall
1960   The Last Voyage
Kent, Mary
1950   The Cariboo Trail
Kent, Norman
1950   Winchester '73
Kent, Robert *(actor)* same as **Blackley, Douglas**
1936   Dimples
1937   That I May Live
1938   Charlie Chan at Monte Carlo
          Mr. Moto Takes a Chance
1943   Action in the North Atlantic
Kent, Robert E. *(prod, writer)*
1939   Charlie Chan in Reno
1950   Last of the Buccaneers
1951   When the Redskins Rode
1952   Brave Warrior
          California Conquest
1953   Fort Ti
          The Pathfinder
1955   Seminole Uprising
1959   Inside the Mafia
1960   Oklahoma Territory
Kent, Stapleton
1914   The Great Diamond Robbery
1951   The Magnificent Yankee
          The Tall Target
Kent, Travis
1947   Robin Hood of Monterey
Kent, William
1930   King of Jazz
Kent, Willis
1931   The Hurricane Horseman
1934   The Battling Buckaroo
1935   Circle of Death
Kenton, Erle C.
1937   The Devil's Playground
1942   North to the Klondike
Kenton, James B. "Pop"
1934   Wagon Wheels
Kenworthy, Charles
1947   Humoresque
Keny, Kitty
1954   Barefoot Battalion
Kenyon, Albert G. *same as* **Kenyon, Albert**
1918   The Girl in the Dark
1926   Pals in Paradise
Kenyon, Charles
1919   Fighting for Gold
1920   Dangerous Days
1926   The Flaming Frontier
1928   The Crash
1929   Show Boat
1937   Think Fast, Mr. Moto
1945   Phantom of the Plains
Kenyon, Curtis
1942   Twin Beds
1949   Tulsa
1950   Two Flags West
Kenyon, Doris
1928   The Hawk's Nest
1933   Counsellor at Law
Kenyon, Gwen
1938   Daughter of Shanghai
1939   King of Chinatown
1942   Lawless Plainsmen
1943   Crime Smasher
          Riding High
          Wintertime
1944   Charlie Chan in the Secret Service
1945   In Old New Mexico
Kenyon, Sandy
1959   Al Capone

Keon, Barbara
1938   The Adventures of Tom Sawyer
1939   Gone With the Wind
Kepich, Werner
1931   La fiesta del diablo *(foreign version)*
Ker, Paul
1919   Love and the Law
Kerbert, Alice
1948   I Remember Mama
Kerbert, Peggy
1948   I Remember Mama
Kerekes, Gabriel
1940   The Ramparts We Watch
Kerman, David
1938   Outside of Paradise
Kern, Cecil
1919   The Gray Towers Mystery
Kern, Donald
1946   The Face of Marble
Kern, Grace
1937   Maid of Salem
Kern, Hal C.
1958   Houseboat
Kern, James V.
1940   If I Had My Way
1941   Playmates
Kernan, Sarah
1917   His Sweetheart
1919   Hearts of Men
Kernell, William
1931   Hay que casar al príncipe
          La ley del harem
1932   El caballero de la noche
1933   It's Great to Be Alive
          It's Great to Be Alive *(foreign version)*
          La melodía prohibida
1934   Granaderos del amor
Kerns, Hubie *same as* **Kerns, Hubert**
1951   Jim Thorpe—All-American
          Saturday's Hero
1955   The Long Gray Line
1958   The Young Lions
Kerr, Deborah
1953   Dream Wife
Kerr, Donald *same as* **Kerr, Don**
1941   Birth of the Blues
          Louisiana Purchase
          The Mexican Spitfire's Baby
1942   Mexican Spitfire's Elephant
1943   Dixie
          Gangway for Tomorrow
          Ladies' Day
          Redhead from Manhattan
1946   Notorious
1947   Buck Privates Come Home
          Desperate
          My Wild Irish Rose
          Ride the Pink Horse
1948   The Miracle of the Bells
          The Time of Your Life
1949   Knock on Any Door
1951   Flaming Feather
Kerr, Geoffrey
1931   Women Love Once
Kerr, Jane
1935   Ruggles of Red Gap
Kerr, Joseph
1951   Jim Thorpe—All-American
Kerr, Laura
1947   The Farmer's Daughter
Kerr, Lon
1942   Cat People
Kerr, Robert P.
1926   A Trip to Chinatown
Kerrigan, J. M.
1923   Little Old New York
1931   The Black Camel
1932   The Rainbow Trail
1936   Laughing Irish Eyes
          The Prisoner of Shark Island
1937   The Barrier
1939   Gone With the Wind
1940   Three Cheers for the Irish

Kerrigan, J. Warren
1916   The Social Buccaneer
1919   The Lord Loves the Irish
Kerrigan, Kathleen
1923   None So Blind
Kerrigan, Marian
1945   Where Do We Go From Here?
Kerry, Daniel
1946   Strange Voyage
Kerry, Norman
1918   Amarilly of Clothes-Line Alley
1921   Little Italy
1926   The Barrier
1936   The Phantom of Santa Fe
Kertész, Dezsö
1930   El secreto del doctor *(foreign version)*
Kesler, Henry S. same as **Kessler, Henry**
1943   Dixie
1949   Knock on Any Door
Kessler, J.
1931   Delicious
Kessler, Sandra
1948   Jiggs and Maggie in Court
Kester, Karen
1950   The Baron of Arizona
Ketchum, Cliff
1959   The Young Land
Key, Kathleen
1926   The Flaming Frontier
1927   Irish Hearts
1936   Klondike Annie
1951   Queen for a Day
Keyes, Evelyn
1938   The Buccaneer
1939   Gone With the Wind
1941   The Face Behind the Mask
1947   The Jolson Story
1950   Jolson Sings Again
1954   Hell's Half Acre
Keymas, George
1954   The Black Dakotas
          They Rode West
1955   Apache Ambush
          Kentucky Rifle
          Santa Fe Passage
          The Vanishing American
1956   Walk the Proud Land
          The White Squaw
1957   Apache Warrior
1958   Gunfire at Indian Gap
          The Light in the Forest
1960   Studs Lonigan
Keys, Robert
1953   San Antone
1956   Wetbacks
1957   Revolt at Fort Laramie
Kezas, George
1942   Woman of the Year
Khoury, George
1959   The FBI Story
Khyyam, Hassan
1953   Dream Wife
Kibbee, Guy
1932   So Big
1939   Let Freedom Ring
1942   Sunday Punch
1948   Fort Apache
1949   3 Godfathers
Kibbee, Milt *same as* **Kibbee, Milton**
1936   Treachery Rides the Range
1937   Black Legion
1939   The Escape
1940   Little Nellie Kelly
          Lucky Cisco Kid
1941   New York Town

Keon, Barbara column continues:
1942   The Vanishing Virginian
1943   Action in the North Atlantic
          Mr. Lucky
1944   An American Romance
1945   The Great John L.
1946   Abie's Irish Rose
1948   Call Northside 777
          The Luck of the Irish

1942　Gentleman Jim
　　　Juke Girl
1943　Dr. Gillespie's Criminal
　　　Case
　　　The Meanest Man in the
　　　World
1945　The Scarlet Clue
1946　The Gentleman
　　　Misbehaves
1947　Body and Soul
　　　Buck Privates Come
　　　Home
　　　Desperate
1948　The Lady from Shanghai
1949　Daughter of the West
1951　When the Redskins Rode

Kibrick, Leonard
1936　Dimples
1937　It Could Happen to You
1939　Fisherman's Wharf

Kieffer, Philip, Major same as
　Kieffer, Philip
1948　Fort Apache
1949　Pinky
1953　The Sun Shines Bright
1955　The Long Gray Line
1956　Pillars of the Sky

Kier, H. W. (prod)
1943　Marching On!
1945　Of One Blood

Kier, Harvey (actor)
1938　Two Sisters

Kiesel, William
1950　Panic in the Streets

Kikevitch, V., General
1939　Cossacks in Exile

Kikume, Al
1936　Charlie Chan at the Race
　　　Track
1937　Charlie Chan at the
　　　Olympics
1938　Mr. Moto Takes a Chance
1939　Charlie Chan in Reno
　　　Mr. Moto in Danger
　　　Island
1940　Kit Carson
1944　Tahiti Nights

Kilbride, Percy
1944　Knickerbocker Holiday

Kilburn, Terry
1951　Only the Valiant

Kildaire, Dorothy
1937　Nation Aflame

Kiley, Richard
1955　Blackboard Jungle

Kilgannon, James
1938　The Texans
1939　Stand Up and Fight
1940　Escape to Glory

Kilgour, Joseph
1917　Runaway Romany

Kilian, Mike (actor, writer) same
　as **Kilian, Victor Mike; Kilian,
　Victor, Jr.**
1938　Passport Husband
1943　Action in the North
　　　Atlantic
1944　The Sullivans
1948　Unconquered

Kilian, Victor (actor) same as
　**Kilian, Victor, Sr.; Killian,
　Victor**
1936　Ramona
1938　The Adventures of Tom
　　　Sawyer
1939　The Adventures of
　　　Huckleberry Finn
　　　The Return of the Cisco
　　　Kid
1940　The Mark of Zorro
　　　Santa Fe Trail
　　　They Knew What They
　　　Wanted
1941　Western Union
1943　The Ox-Bow Incident
1947　Duel in the Sun
1948　Gentleman's Agreement
1949　Colorado Territory
1950　Bandit Queen
　　　No Way Out
　　　Stars in My Crown
1951　The Tall Target

Killens, John O.
1959　Odds Against Tomorrow

The Killer, a horse
1926　The Devil Horse

Killgore, Reed
1949　Pinky
1956　Giant

Killian, Victor see **Kilian, Victor**

Killmond, Frank
1960　Take a Giant Step

Killy, Edward same as **Killy, Ed**
1933　Diplomaniacs
1942　The Navy Comes Through
1945　Wanderer of the
　　　Wasteland

Kilpatrick, Reid
1942　In This Our Life
1945　The Scarlet Clue
1946　Without Reservations

Kilpatrick, Tom
1950　The Palomino

Kilroy, Edward
1950　Annie Get Your Gun

Kim, Arlene
1950　Damien

Kim, Joseph
1945　Samurai

Kimball, Bob
1942　All Through the Night
1943　Action in the North
　　　Atlantic

Kimball, Charles E.
1917　How Uncle Sam Prepares

Kimball, Edward M. same as
　Kimball, Edward
1916　The Yellow Passport
1920　For the Soul of Rafael

Kimball, Mrs. Edward M. same as
　Kimball, Pauline Garrett
1916　The Yellow Passport

Kimbell, Anne
1952　Fort Osage
　　　Wagons West

Kimbell, Helen
1950　Annie Get Your Gun
1951　Show Boat

Kimber, Peggy
1949　Lost Boundaries

Kimberly, Eve
1934　Stand Up and Cheer!

Kimble, Lawrence
1938　The Beloved Brat
1943　Tahiti Honey

Kimbley, Billy
1948　Shep Comes Home
　　　Up in Central Park
1949　Prejudice
1950　Raiders of Tomahawk
　　　Creek

Kimbrell, Lois
1955　Trial

Kimbrough, Baby Ruth
1921　By Right of Birth

Kimmell, Leslie
1951　The Tall Target
1957　The Oklahoman

Kimmons, W. G.
1950　Intruder in the Dust

Kinch, Myra
1929　Redskin

Kindermann, Helmo
1960　I Aim at the Stars: the
　　　Wernher von Braun
　　　Story

The King Sisters
1946　Cuban Pete

King, Andrea
1947　My Wild Irish Rose
　　　Ride the Pink Horse
1950　Buccaneer's Girl
1951　The Mark of the
　　　Renegade
1957　Band of Angels

King, Anita
1915　Chimmie Fadden
1917　The Squaw Man's Son

King, Bert
1950　Belle of Old Mexico

King, Brad (actor)
1941　Secret of the Wastelands

King, Bradley (writer) same as
　Wray, Bradley King
1923　Anna Christie
1928　Diamond Handcuffs
1930　The Lash
　　　Son of the Gods
1931　Die Maske Fällt
1937　Maid of Salem

King, Brett
1950　Battleground
　　　The Big Hangover

King, Burton
1916　Man and His Angel
1919　The Lost Battalion
1923　None So Blind
1929　In Old California
1932　The Forty-Niners

King, Cammie
1939　Gone With the Wind

King, Carlton
1929　The Peacock Fan

King, Charles 1895—1957 not the
　same as **King, Charles A.**
　(actor, writer)
1934　The Prescott Kid
1935　The Singing Vagabond
1937　Man of the People
1938　Wild Horse Canyon
1939　Frontiers of '49
1942　Below the Border
1943　Land of Hunted Men
1944　Outlaw Trail
　　　Sonora Stagecoach
1945　The Navajo Trail

King, Charles A. (actor, writer)
　same as **King, Charles** (actor,
　writer) not the same as **King,
　Charles** 1895—1957
1914　The Indian Wars
1917　The Adventures of Buffalo
　　　Bill

King, Claude
1925　Irish Luck
1930　Son of the Gods
1931　Women Love Once
1933　Charlie Chan's Greatest
　　　Case
1934　Charlie Chan in London
　　　Coming Out Party
1936　The Last of the Mohicans
1940　New Moon

King, Dennis
1930　Galas de la Paramount

King, Emmett
1920　Billions

King, F. (actor)
1916　The Colored American
　　　Winning His Suit

King, Frank (prod) same as **King,
　Franklin**
1942　Rubber Racketeers
1948　The Dude Goes West
1952　The Ring

King, George
1918　The City of Dim Faces

King, Georgia
1944　Mr. Skeffington

King, Gerald
1955　Blackboard Jungle

King, Henry
1917　Southern Pride
　　　Sunshine and Gold
1920　Uncharted Channels
1936　Ramona
1938　In Old Chicago

King, J. A.
1919　The Lost Battalion

King, Jean not the same as **King,
　Jean Paul**
1942　Foreign Agent

King, Jean Paul not the same as
　King, Jean
1960　The Dark at the Top of
　　　the Stairs

King, Jewel
1950　Panic in the Streets

King, Joe see **King, Joseph**

King, John b. 1909 same as **King,
　John "Dusty"** not the same as
　King, John (African-American
　actor)
1936　Sutter's Gold
1938　Breaking the Ice
1939　Charlie Chan in Honolulu
　　　Mr. Moto Takes a
　　　Vacation
1946　Renegade Girl

King, John (African-American
　actor) not the same as **King,
　John** b. 1909
1946　Dirty Gertie from
　　　Harlem, U.S.A.

King, Joseph same as **King, Joe**
1918　The Price of Applause
　　　Shifting Sands
1919　False Evidence
1920　The North Wind's Malice
1921　Anne of Little Smoky
1937　Big City
1938　City Streets
　　　Gateway
　　　In Old Chicago
1940　Charlie Chan at the Wax
　　　Museum
　　　If I Had My Way
　　　Three Cheers for the Irish
1942　Gentleman Jim
　　　They Died With Their
　　　Boots On
1943　The Amazing Mrs.
　　　Holliday
　　　His Butler's Sister

King, Judith
1939　King of Chinatown

King, Lew (actor) not the same as
　King, Louis (dir, actor)
1938　City Streets

King, Lewis see **King, Louis** (dir,
　actor)

King, Lily
1939　King of Chinatown

King, Louis (dir, actor) same as
　King, Lew; King, Lewis not the
　same as **King, Lew** (actor)
1918?　Rosemary Climbs the
　　　Heights
1928　Orphan of the Sage
1931　Die Maske Fällt
1933　Robbers' Roost
　　　Una viuda romántica
1934　La ciudad de cartón
1935　Angelina o el honor de
　　　un brigadier
　　　Charlie Chan in Egypt
　　　Julieta compra un hijo
1940　The Way of All Flesh
1942　Young America
1954　Dangerous Mission

King, Marie
1945　Nob Hill

King, Maurice
1942　Rubber Racketeers
1948　The Dude Goes West
1952　The Ring

King, Max M.
1942　Foreign Agent

King, Nicholas
1958　The Young Lions

King, Owen
1940　Knute Rockne—All
　　　American

King, Ruth
1920　For the Soul of Rafael
1921　Fifty Candles

King, Stanley
1937　It Could Happen to You

King, Walter Woolf same as **King,
　Walter**
1935　A Night at the Opera
1953　Taxi
　　　Tonight We Sing

King, Webb
1919　A Man's Duty
1920?　Reformation
1921　By Right of Birth
1930　Georgia Rose

King, William
1951　Teresa

King, Wright
1951 A Streetcar Named Desire
Kingdon, Edith
1936 After the Thin Man
Kingsbury, Jacob
1919 The Volcano
Kingsford, Guy
1946 G. I. War Brides
1948 Night Wind
Kingsford, Walter
1935 Naughty Marietta
1936 Mad Holiday
1937 It Could Happen to You
1938 The Toy Wife
1942 Dr. Gillespie's New
Assistant
1943 Dr. Gillespie's Criminal
Case
Mr. Lucky
1944 Mr. Skeffington
Three Men in White
1945 Between Two Women
1953 The Pathfinder
Kingsley, Dorothy
1952 It's a Big Country: An
American Anthology
Kingsley, Paul
1944 The Racket Man
Kingston, Muriel
1932 Parigi affascina; ovvero,
Malavita
Kingston, Natalie
1927 Lost at the Front
Kingston, Susan
1945 Club Havana
Kingston, Thomas
1951 Saturday's Hero
Kingston, Winifred
1914 The Squaw Man
Where the Trail Divides
1915 Captain Courtesy
1916 A Son of Erin
Kinnell, Murray
1931 The Black Camel
The Guilty Generation
1932 The Match King
1934 Charlie Chan in London
Charlie Chan's Courage
1935 Charlie Chan in Paris
Rendezvous
1937 Think Fast, Mr. Moto
Kinney, Charles W.
1925 Red Love
Kinney, Ray
1937 Waikiki Wedding
Ray Kinney and his Hawaiians
1934 Song of the Islands
Kino, Goro *same as* **Kino; Kino, G.**
1916 The Honorable Friend
1918 The Bravest Way
Little Red Decides
The Midnight Patrol
1920 The Purple Cipher
A Tokio Siren
1921 The First Born
Lotus Blossom
A Tale of Two Worlds
Where Lights Are Low
Kino, Robert
1959 The Crimson Kimono
Kinsella, Frank
1957 Burden of Truth
Kinskey, Leonid *same as* **Kinsky,
Leonid**
1934 Straight Is the Way
1938 Outside of Paradise
1940 Tengo fe en ti
1943 Let's Have Fun
Kinsley, Marilyn
1951 Show Boat
Kinsolving, Lee
1960 All the Young Men
The Dark at the Top of
the Stairs
Kipling, Richard *same as* **Kipling,
Dick**
1934 Broadway Bill
1935 Charlie Chan in Paris
1937 Man of the People
1940 Santa Fe Trail
1941 Louisiana Purchase

1942 Gentleman Jim
1944 Mr. Skeffington
1948 My Girl Tisa
Up in Central Park
1950 The Furies
1952 Anything Can Happen
Bugles in the Afternoon
Kiraly, Erno
1944 Lake Placid Serenade
Kirby, Bill
1959 Shake Hands with the
Devil
Kirby, David *same as* **Kirby,
"Red"**
1921 Shame
1926 The Fighting Edge
Kirby, Frank G.
1927 The Broken Violin
Kirby, George
1943 Action in the North
Atlantic
His Butler's Sister
1948 Unconquered
Kirby, Jay
1943 Border Patrol
1944 Marshal of Reno
Sheriff of Las Vegas
John Kirby's Band
1947 Sepia Cinderella
Kirby, June
1958 The Last Hurrah
Kirby, Michael
1946 Three Wise Fools
1947 Dark Delusion
Kirby, "Red" *see* **Kirby, David**
Kirby, Robert H.
1950 Panic in the Streets
Kirby, Stoddard
1960 The Dark at the Top of
the Stairs
Kirchhoffer, Hugo
1945 Rhapsody in Blue
Andy Kirk and His Orchestra
1948 Killer Diller
Kirk, Jack
1931 Riders of the Rio
1934 Fighting Through
1938 Outlaw Express
1941 Prairie Pioneers
Saddlemates
Under Fiesta Stars
1942 Valley of Hunted Men
1943 Frontier Fury
In Old Oklahoma
1944 Marshal of Reno
The San Antonio Kid
Sheriff of Las Vegas
1945 Colorado Pioneers
Phantom of the Plains
1946 California Gold Rush
Sheriff of Redwood Valley
Sun Valley Cyclone
1947 Oregon Trail Scouts
Kirk, Joseph *same as* **Kirk, Joe**
1943 Margin for Error
1947 Buck Privates Come
Home
Kirk, Mildred
1949? The Joint Is Jumpin'
Kirk, Phyllis
1952 The Iron Mistress
Kirke, Donald
1938 Hawaii Calls
Kirkham, Kathleen
1917 His Sweetheart
1922 One Eighth Apache
Kirkland, Alexander
1932 Charlie Chan's Chance
Kirkland, Jack
1936 Sutter's Gold
Kirkpatrick, Jess
1951 The Well
Kirksey, Iris
1944 Chip Off the Old Block
Kirkwood, Jack
1947 The Foxes of Harrow
Kirkwood, James (*African-
American actor*)
1950 Intruder in the Dust

Kirkwood, James (*dir, actor*)
1918 I Want to Forget
1920 The Luck of the Irish
1931 Young Sinners
1932 Charlie Chan's Chance
The Rainbow Trail
1953 The Sun Shines Bright
1954 Passion
Kirkwood, Katherine
1918 The Wine Girl
Kirkwood, Ray
1935 The Cyclone Ranger
Kirnan, Bey
1920 Frontier Days
Kirnan, Tommy
1920 Frontier Days
Kirsten, Dorothy
1951 The Great Caruso
Kishii, Fujii
1929 The Peacock Fan
Kissel, William
1951 Only the Valiant
Kissinger, Miriam
1946 Dangerous Money
The Trap
Kist, Andrei
1938 Marusia
Kit and Kit
1947 Juke Joint
Kitchen, Dorothy *same as* **Drexel,
Nancy**
Kitson, May
1919 Come Out of the Kitchen
1920? The Scarlet Dragon
Kitt, Eartha
1958 St. Louis Blues
1959 Anna Lucasta
Kitzmiller, Florence
1933 It's Great to Be Alive
Kivalina
1925 Kivalina of the Ice Lands
Kjellin, Alf
1952 The Iron Mistress
Klary, Léo
1931 Jenny Lind
Klauber, Marcel
1952 Red Ball Express
Klauber, Marcy
1939 Keep Punching
Tevya
Klein, Adelaide
1949 C-Man
Klein, Dick
1937 Life Begins in College
Klein, J. Herbert
1956 Death of a Scoundrel
Klein, Philip
1931 The Black Camel
Charlie Chan Carries On
Charlie Chan Carries On
(*foreign version*)
1932 Charlie Chan's Chance
Me and My Gal
The Rainbow Trail
1934 Stand Up and Cheer!
Klein, Robert
1917 Southern Pride
Klein, Wally
1938 The Beloved Brat
1942 They Died With Their
Boots On
Klein, William R.
1950 No Way Out
Kleine, George
1918 The Unbeliever
Kleiner, Harry
1954 Carmen Jones
1959 Cry Tough
1960 Ice Palace
Kleinerman, Morris
1931 Zein Weib's Lubovnick
Kleinschmidt, Frank E., Capt.
same as **Kleinschmidt, Frank E.**
1912 The Alaska-Siberian
Expedition
1914 Captain F. E.
Kleinschmidt's Arctic
Hunt
1927 Primitive Love

Kleint, Karl
1958 Tonka
Klemperer, Werner
1956 Death of a Scoundrel
1958 Houseboat
Kletter, Max
1935 Shir Hashirim
Klewer, Dorothy
1959 The Hanging Tree
Klida, Paula
1934 What a Mother-in-Law!
1940 The Jewish Melody
Kline, Herbert
1949 Illegal Entry
1952 The Fighter
Kline, Marvin
1933 Counsellor at Law
Kline, Tiny
1945 Nob Hill
Kling, Sazon
1922 The Mohican's Daughter
Klinger, Werner *same as* **Klingler,
Werner**
1930 Los que danzan (*foreign
version*)
Klingler, Werner
1931 Don Juan diplomático
(*foreign version*)
Klink, Clem
1958 Tonka
Kluge, George
1947 Citizen Saint
Klugman, Jack
1957 Twelve Angry Men
Klum, Eugene H.
1920 Billions
Klune, Tom
1937 Charlie Chan at the
Olympics
Knaggs, Skelton
1948 The Paleface
Knapp, Evalyn *same as* **Knapp,
Evelyn**
1931 Smart Money
1932 The Vanishing Frontier
1936 Laughing Irish Eyes
Knapp, Margaret
1931 El proceso de Mary
Dugan (*foreign
version*)
Knapp, Robert
1955 The Long Gray Line
1957 Revolt at Fort Laramie
Tomahawk Trail
1958 The Rawhide Trail
1959 Gunmen from Laredo
Kneeland, Frank
1931 Delicious
Kneubuhl, John
1950 Damien
Knickerbocker, Bob
1931 Delicious
Knife, Andrew
1951 Across the Wide Missouri
Knight, Charles
1946 Rendezvous 24
Knight, Christopher
1960 Studs Lonigan
Knight, Fuzzy
1934 Behold My Wife!
The Cat's-Paw
Operator 13
1936 Sea Spoilers
Song of the Gringo
1937 The Plainsman
1938 Spawn of the North
1941 New York Town
1942 Apache Trail
Juke Girl
1949 Apache Chief
1951 Show Boat
Knight, Glen
1947 Desperate
Knight, H. E.
1938 Birthright
Knight, Karen
1945 The Shanghai Cobra
Knight, Shirley
1960 The Dark at the Top of
the Stairs
Ice Palace

Knight, Ted
1960   Key Witness
Knight, Terry
1947?   Return of Mandy's
         Husband
Knoche, Jack
1938   Dangerous to Know
Knoles, Harley
1917   The Adventures of Carol
1918   Wanted, a Mother
1920   The Great Shadow
Knopf, Edwin H. *same as* **Knopf,
    Edwin**
1930   Galas de la Paramount
1935   The Wedding Night
1942   The Vanishing Virginian
1945   The Valley of Decision
1946   The Sailor Takes a Wife
Knopf, Verna
1944   Since You Went Away
Knott, Lydia
1917   Crime and Punishment
1918   Free and Equal
         In Judgment Of
1919   A Bachelor's Wife
         The Little Diplomat
1925   The Fearless Lover
1928   The House of Scandal
Knowland, Alice
1915   The Secret Sin
Knowlden, Marilyn *same as*
    Knowlder, Marilyn
1931   The Cisco Kid
         Women Love Once
1932   Call Her Savage
1934   As the Earth Turns
         Imitation of Life
1936   Rainbow on the River
         Show Boat
1937   Slave Ship
1940   The Way of All Flesh
Knowles, Carl
1939   Allegheny Uprising
1947   It Had To Be You
Knowles, Harry
1914   Northern Lights
Knowles, Patric
1944   Chip Off the Old Block
1957   Band of Angels
Knox, Alexander
1951   Saturday's Hero
Knox, Elyse
1947   Black Gold
Knox, Foster
1914   The Squaw Man
Knox, Mickey
1949   Knock on Any Door
1951   Saturday's Hero
1956   Singing in the Dark
Knox, Mona
1952   Kid Monk Baroni
Knox, Patricia
1941   New York Town
1960   I Passed for White
Knox, Walter
1940?   Mr. Washington Goes to
         Town
Knudsen, Peggy *same as* **Knudson,
    Peggy**
1947   Humoresque
         My Wild Irish Rose
1948   Half Past Midnight
1955   Good Morning, Miss Dove
Knudson, Barbara
1959   The Jayhawkers!
Knudson, Peggy *see* **Knudsen,
    Peggy**
Knutsen, Kelly
1931   Delicious
Kobayashi, Tak
1951   Go for Broke!
Kober, Arthur
1932   Me and My Gal
1933   It's Great to Be Alive
1943   Wintertime
Kobi, Michi
1960   Hell to Eternity
Kobliansky, Nicholas
1934   Strange Wives
1938   Gateway
1947   Northwest Outpost

Kobzar, Teklia
1938   Marusia
Koch, Elaine
1930   The Big Pond
Koch, Howard (*writer*)
1942   In This Our Life
1945   Rhapsody in Blue
Koch, Howard W. (*prod, dir*) *same
    as* **Koch, Howard** (*prod, dir*)
1949   Border Incident
         Tulsa
1951   Across the Wide Missouri
1953   War Paint
1954   The Yellow Tomahawk
1955   Fort Yuma
1956   The Broken Star
         Ghost Town
         Quincannon, Frontier
           Scout
1957   Revolt at Fort Laramie
         Tomahawk Trail
         War Drums
1958   Fort Bowie
Koch, Hugh B.
1916   A Son of Erin
Kodama, George
1930   Chijku wo mawasuru
         chikara
Kodison, L.
1934   The Rabbi's Power
Koechig, Terry
1942   Seven Sweethearts
Koehler, Jean
1946   Without Reservations
Koehler, Ted
1943   Stormy Weather
Kökert, Alexander
1931   La pura verdad (*foreign
         version*)
Koenig, Mabelle
1949   The Fighting Kentuckian
Koford, Helen *see* **Moore, Terry**
Kohler, Don
1950   No Way Out
1951   The House on Telegraph
         Hill
         Saturday's Hero
Kohler, Fred, Sr. *same as* **Kohler,
    Fred, Sr.**
1922   The Scrapper
         The Son of the Wolf
1923   Anna Christie
1925   The Thundering Herd
1927   The Gay Defender
         Open Range
         The Way of All Flesh
1928   Chinatown Charlie
1929   Thunderbolt
1930   The Lash
1931   Fighting Caravans
1932   Call Her Savage
         Wild Horse Mesa
1936   Dangerous Intrigue
         For the Service
1937   The Plainsman
1938   The Buccaneer
         Daughter of Shanghai
Kohler, Fred, Jr. *sometimes also
    known as* **Fred Kohler**
1936   The Prisoner of Shark
         Island
         Sins of Man
1937   Life Begins in College
1948   Unconquered
1949   The Gay Amigo
1950   The Baron of Arizona
1956   Daniel Boone, Trail
         Blazer
1957   Journey to Freedom
1958   Terror in a Texas Town
1960   The Adventures of
         Huckleberry Finn
Kohlmar, Fred
1943   Riding High
1948   Fury at Furnace Creek
         The Luck of the Irish
1956   Full of Life
1958   Gunman's Walk
1959   The Last Angry Man
Kohlmar, Lee
1920   The Secret Gift
1922   Breaking Home Ties

1923   Potash and Perlmutter
1930   The Kibitzer
         The Melody Man
         Sins of the Children
1935   McFadden's Flats
         Rendezvous
         Ruggles of Red Gap
1936   Ramona
Kohn, Ben Grauman
1929   Chinatown Nights
1939   Heaven with a Barbed
         Wire Fence
1942   American Empire
Kohn, Gabriel
1960   Weddings and Babies
Kohner, Frederick
1936   Sins of Man
1943   Tahiti Honey
1944   Lake Placid Serenade
Kohner, Paul
1930   East Is West (*foreign
         version*)
         La voluntad del muerto
1931   Don Juan diplomático
         Don Juan diplomático
         (*foreign version*)
         Drácula
         Resurrección
         El tenorio del harem
1935   Alas sobre el Chaco
Kohner, Susan
1956   The Last Wagon
1957   Trooper Hook
1959   Imitation of Life
1960   All the Fine Young
         Cannibals
Koko, a horse
1953   Old Overland Trail
Kolb, C. William
1916   Peck O' Pickles
Kolb, Clarence
1936   After the Thin Man
1937   Maid of Salem
1944   Something for the Boys
Kolb, John
1927   Lost at the Front
Kolker, Henry
1915   How Molly Malone Made
         Good
1920?   The Greatest Love
1929   Love, Live and Laugh
1930   East Is West
1934   Imitation of Life
         Massacre
1935   Charlie Chan in Paris
1937   Maid of Salem
Kollin, Jack
1940   The Notorious Elinor Lee
Kollin, John *same as* **Kollin, Jack**
1939   Lying Lips
Komai, Tetsu
1929   Chinatown Nights
1930   East Is West
         East Is West (*foreign
         version*)
1931   La mujer X
1932   Border Devils
         The Secrets of Wu Sin
1952   Japanese War Bride
Komshi, H. *could be same as*
    Konishi, Horin
1917   The Bottle Imp
Konishi, Horin *could be same as*
    Komshi, H.
1917   Hashimura Togo
Konjoian, George
1945   Anoush
Konnella, Sam
1920   White Youth
Konopka, Kenneth
1945   The House on 92nd St.
Konorez, John
1944   Buffalo Bill
1953   So Big
Konstant, Anna
1931   Street Scene
Konstantin, Madame
1946   Notorious
Kopp, Jacqueline
1938   In Old Chicago

Kopp, Mary Louise
1938   In Old Chicago
Koppel, Irving D.
1951   Fort Defiance
Korff, Arnold
1930   Olimpia (*foreign
         version*)
1931   Don Juan diplomático
         (*foreign version*)
         La gran jornada (*foreign
         version*)
         El proceso de Mary
         Dugan (*foreign
         version*)
1934   Behold My Wife!
Korlin, Boris
1916   The Scarlet Oath
Kornelia, Irma
1926   The Campus Flirt
Kornstein, Malka
1933   Counsellor at Law
Kortman, Bob
1932   White Eagle
1948   The Paleface
         Unconquered
1949   Streets of Laredo
1951   Flaming Feather
Kortman, Robert *same as*
    Kortman, Bob
1926   The Devil Horse
1934   The Lone Defender
1936   Rose of the Rancho
1938   The Renegade Ranger
Korvin, Charles
1953   Sangaree
Kory, Maureen
1946   Abie's Irish Rose
Kory, Patricia
1946   Abie's Irish Rose
Koser, H. E.
1918   Good-Bye, Bill
Koshetz, Marina
1951   The Great Caruso
Koshetz, Nina
1956   Hot Blood
Kosik, Marguerite
1924   Defying the Law
Kosleck, Martin *same as* **Yoshkin,
    Niccolai**
1939   Confessions of a Nazi Spy
1942   All Through the Night
         Nazi Agent
1945   The Mummy's Curse
1948   Half Past Midnight
Kosslyn, Jack
1959   Night of the Quarter
         Moon
Andre Kostelanetz and his band
1940   Music in My Heart
Koster, Henry *same as* **Kosterlitz,
    Hermann**
1930   Doña mentiras (*foreign
         version*)
1931   La carta (*foreign
         version*)
1938   The Rage of Paris
1948   The Luck of the Irish
1955   Good Morning, Miss Dove
         A Man Called Peter
Kostrick, Michael
1946   Till the End of Time
1949   The Kissing Bandit
         That Midnight Kiss
1950   The Toast of New Orleans
Kotowych, F.
1938   Marusia
Kottke, Otto
1931   Dämon des Meeres
Koury, Kay
1956   Hot Blood
Koutnik, Ken
1951   Slaughter Trail
Kova, Frank de *see* **De Kova,
    Frank**
Koval, Mary
1958   Home Before Dark
Kowal, Mitchell
1959   Al Capone
         The Jayhawkers!
         John Paul Jones

Kozlenko, William
1956   Raw Edge
Krafft, John W. *same as* **Krafft, John**
1925   Scarlet Saint
1927   Turkish Delight
        White Gold
1928   Hold 'Em Yale
        A Ship Comes In
1942   Foreign Agent
1943   Deerslayer
Kraft, H. S.
1943   Stormy Weather
Kraft, Marilyn Criss
1949   The Red Menace
Krah, Marc
1950   Black Hand
1953   Beneath the 12-Mile Reef
Kraike, Michel
1945   I Love a Bandleader
1947   Desperate
Kraly, Hans
1930   A Lady to Love (*foreign version*)
1931   Jenny Lind
1937   Music for Madame
Kramer, Al
1957   The Oklahoman
Kramer, Cecile
1944   Buffalo Bill
Kramer, Don
1943   Mexican Spitfire's Blessed Event
Kramer, Glen
1956   Pillars of the Sky
Kramer, Ida
1929   Abie's Irish Rose
Kramer, Louis
1936   Love and Sacrifice
1941   Mazel Tov Yidden
Kramer, Marc *see* **Cramer, Marc**
Kramer, Stanley
1949   Home of the Brave
1950   The Men
1955   Not As a Stranger
1958   The Defiant Ones
Kranjcina, Slavko
1932   Ljubav i strast
Krasna, Norman
1935   Romance in Manhattan
1936   It Had to Happen
1937   Big City
1950   The Big Hangover
Krasne, Philip N.
1944   Black Magic
        Charlie Chan in the Secret Service
        The Chinese Cat
1945   The Cisco Kid Returns
        In Old New Mexico
1949   The Daring Caballero
        The Gay Amigo
        Satan's Cradle
        The Valiant Hombre
1950   The Girl from San Lorenzo
1957   Pawnee
Krassowska, Danusi
1941   Z Dymem Pożarów
Krause, Gertrude *same as* **Krause, Gertie**
1930   Eternal Fools (Ewige Naranim)
1932   Mazel Tov
1939   Motel the Operator
        Mothers of Today
Krause, Solomon
1932   Mazel Tov
1939   The Light Ahead
Kravitz, Sam
1936   Love and Sacrifice
Kray, Walter
1958   Fort Massacre
Kreglicki, Edmund
1941   Wiejskie Wesele
Kreibich, Paul
1949   Knock on Any Door
Kreig, Frank
1945   The House on 92nd St.
1949   Thieves' Highway
1952   The Fabulous Senorita

1953   So Big
1957   Raintree County
Kress, Carl
1955   Blackboard Jungle
Kress, Harold
1952   Apache War Smoke
Kressyn, Miriam
1933   Live and Laugh
1937   The Jester (Der Purimspieler)
Kreuger, Kurt
1943   Action in the North Atlantic
Krims, Milton
1935   Harmony Lane
1939   Confessions of a Nazi Spy
1956   Mohawk
Krimsky, John
1933   The Emperor Jones
Krizman, Serge
1945   The Dolly Sisters
Kroeger, Berry
1948   Cry of the City
1952   Battles of Chief Pontiac
Kroenke, Carl
1948   Call Northside 777
Krohner, Maurice *same as* **Kroner, Maurice**
1935   The Yiddish King Lear
1939   Motel the Operator
1940   Overture to Glory
Krohner, Sara *same as* **Krohner, S.; Krohner, Sarah**
1939   Mirele Efros
1940   Americaner Schadchen
1951   Molly
Kroll, Alix
1921   The Gunsaulus Mystery
Kromarm, Anne *same as* **Kroman, Anne**
1918   Marked Cards
Krone, Fred
1956   Reprisal!
1958   Apache Territory
Kroner, Maurice *see* **Krohner, Maurice**
Krotoshinsky, Abraham, Pvt.
1919   The Lost Battalion
Krozos, Stavros
1954   Barefoot Battalion
Krueger, Carl
1956   Comanche
Krueger, Lorraine
1944   Slightly Terrific
Kruger, Alma
1938   The Toy Wife
1942   Dr. Gillespie's New Assistant
1943   Dr. Gillespie's Criminal Case
1944   Three Men in White
1945   Between Two Women
1947   Dark Delusion
Kruger, Faith
1942   Seven Sweethearts
1947   My Wild Irish Rose
Kruger, Otto
1933   Ever in My Heart
1937   The Barrier
1940   The Man I Married
1942   Friendly Enemies
1943   Hitler's Children
1944   Knickerbocker Holiday
        They Live in Fear
1945   Escape in the Fog
        The Great John L.
1947   Duel in the Sun
1952   High Noon
1955   The Last Command
Kruger, Paul
1936   Klondike Annie
        The Prisoner of Shark Island
1937   That I May Live
1938   Passport Husband
1939   Heaven with a Barbed Wire Fence
1940   Murder over New York
        Viva Cisco Kid
1941   Ride on Vaquero
1942   Castle in the Desert
        They Died With Their Boots On

1944   Address Unknown
1946   Rendezvous 24
1949   Colorado Territory
1952   The Raiders
1954   Broken Lance
1956   Giant
Kruger, Stubby
1946   Till the End of Time
Krugman, Lou
1955   Headline Hunters
Krumgold, Joseph
1938   Speed to Burn
Krumschmidt, Eberhard
1946   Notorious
Krupa, Gene
1942   Syncopation
1947   Boy! What a Girl!
1956   The Benny Goodman Story
Krusada, Carl *same as* **Cleveland, Val**
1922   Solomon in Society
1934   The Cactus Kid
        The Fighting Hero
1935   North of Arizona
        Wolf Riders
1940   Broken Strings
Kruschen, Jack
1951   Cuban Fireball
        Gambling House
1956   The Benny Goodman Story
1959   The Jayhawkers!
1960   The Last Voyage
        Studs Lonigan
Kruse, Lottie *same as* **Cruez, Lottie**
1917   The Spirit of '76
1918   The City of Tears
Kubiatowski, Helena
1941   Z Dymem Pożarów
Kugel, Lee
1915   How Molly Malone Made Good
Kuhn, Mickey
1939   Gone With the Wind
1945   A Tree Grows in Brooklyn
1948   Red River
1950   Broken Arrow
1951   A Streetcar Named Desire
1956   The Last Frontier
Kuindós
1931   Un caballero de frac
        Las luces de Buenos Aires
Kulky, Henry *same as* **Kulkavich, Bomber**
1947   Northwest Outpost
1948   Call Northside 777
1950   Jiggs and Maggie Out West
1953   The Charge at Feather River
        The Glory Brigade
1957   All Mine to Give
Kuller, Richie
1951   Slaughter Trail
Kuller, Sid
1951   Slaughter Trail
Kullers, John "Red"
1949   House of Strangers
1953   Taxi
Kuluva, Will
1959   Odds Against Tomorrow
Kulyk, Anton
1938   Marusia
Kulz, Frederic
1916   The Scarlet Oath
Kum, William
1935   Charlie Chan in Shanghai
Kunde, Al
1943   Gangway for Tomorrow
1946   Without Reservations
1950   Broken Arrow
        Stars in My Crown
Kunde, Anne
1943   Gangway for Tomorrow
1960   The Adventures of Huckleberry Finn
Kuney, Clark
1946   The Face of Marble

Kuney, Eva Lee
1944   Hi, Beautiful
1945   A Tree Grows in Brooklyn
Kunkel, George
1919   A Fighting Colleen
Kupfer, Kurt
1947   Citizen Saint
Kupperman, Joel
1944   Chip Off the Old Block
Kurahara, Tom *see* **Kurihara, Thomas**
Kurasch, Katharine
1950   Young Man with a Horn
Kurc, A.
1936   Yiddle with His Fiddle
Kurihara, Thomas *same as* **Kurahara, Tom**
1916   The Soul of Kura-San
1918   The Bravest Way
        Her American Husband
        The Honor of His House
Kurlan, David
1953   The Joe Louis Story
Kurnitz, Harry
1953   Tonight We Sing
Kurschen, Jack
1950   Young Man with a Horn
Kurt, Mortimer
1937   Boy of the Streets
Kurtis, Ken
1952   The Quiet Man
Kusell, Harold
1937   That Girl from Paris
Kushabsky, Peter
1937   Natalka Poltavka
Kuszewski, Hedda
1916   Light at Dusk
Kuter, Kay
1954   Drum Beat
1958   The Light in the Forest
1959   The FBI Story
Kuthlee, Geronimo, Chief
1954   Broken Lance
1957   The Guns of Fort Petticoat
Kutler, Benjamin S.
1914   The Jungle
Kutner, Nanette
1948   Big City
Kuwa, George *same as* **Kuwa, George K.**
1916   The Soul of Kura-San
1917   The Bottle Imp
1919   Toby's Bow
1922   The Half Breed
1925   A Son of His Father
1926   A Trip to Chinatown
1927   The Chinese Parrot
1928   Chinatown Charlie
        The Secret Hour
Kuwuhara (full name unknown)
1917   Hashimura Togo
Kuznetzoff, Adia
1938   Spawn of the North
1939   Let Freedom Ring
1940   Elsa Maxwell's Public Deb No. 1
1943   Good Luck, Mr. Yates
Kyatuk
1932   Igloo
Kyle, Billy
1957   Satchmo the Great
Kyne, Peter B.
1926   War Paint
1927   California
1928   The Rawhide Kid
1936   Robin Hood of El Dorado
Kyser, Kay
1941   Playmates
Kay Kyser's Band
1941   Playmates
Kyson, Charles
1936   West of Nevada
La Badie, Florence
1918   The Million Dollar Mystery
La Barr, Dona
1942   Song of the Islands
1945   Where Do We Go From Here?

La Bissoniere, Erin
1937   Souls at Sea
Labrador, Sam
1937   Think Fast, Mr. Moto
La Cava, Gregory
1927   The Gay Defender
1932   Symphony of Six Million
La Cava, Joseph *same as* **La Cava, Joe**
1950   Right Cross
1960   Pay or Die
LaCentra, Peg
1947   Humoresque
1960   The Dark at the Top of the Stairs
Lachman, Harry
1934   Nada más que una mujer
1936   Charlie Chan at the Circus
1940   Murder over New York
1941   Charlie Chan in Rio
        Dead Men Tell
1942   Castle in the Desert
Lackaye, Ruth
1916   The Twin Triangle
Lackaye, Wilton
1915   Children of the Ghetto
Lackey, William T. *same as* **Lackey, William**
1936   Desert Gold
1938   Mr. Wong, Detective
1939   Mr. Wong in Chinatown
        The Mystery of Mr. Wong
1940   The Fatal Hour
Lackteen, Frank
1926   Desert Gold
        The Last Frontier
1929   Hawk of the Hills
1931   Cimarron
        Law of the Tong
1932   Texas Pioneers
1935   Rendezvous
1936   Rose of the Rancho
1940   The Gay Caballero
        Lucky Cisco Kid
1946   Singin' in the Corn
1947   Oregon Trail Scouts
1949   The Cowboy and the Indians
        The Mysterious Desperado
1950   Indian Territory
        North of the Great Divide
1951   Flaming Feather
1952   The Big Sky
        Desert Pursuit
La Croix, Emile *same as* **La Croix, L. Emile**
1918   Love's Law
1923   Backbone
Lacy, Alva
1953   Jack McCall Desperado
Lacy, Jean
1932   Hypnotized
Lacy, Paul
1943   Gangway for Tomorrow
1948   The Miracle of the Bells
Ladd, Alan
1952   The Iron Mistress
1954   Drum Beat
        Saskatchewan
1958   The Badlanders
1960   All the Young Men
Ladd, Bernice
1920   Within Our Gates
Ladd, Schuyler
1921   The Land of Hope
Ladd, Tom
1945   Where Do We Go From Here?
Ladrón de Guevara, María
1931   Cheri-Bibi
        La mujer X
        El proceso de Mary Dugan
Lady, a horse
1926   The Devil Horse
1933   King of the Wild Horses
Laemmle, Beth
1930   King of Jazz

Laemmle, Carl
1919   The Delicious Little Devil
1920   Outside the Law
        White Youth
1921   No Woman Knows
1922   The Guttersnipe
        The Scrapper
        Second Hand Rose
        The Top O' the Morning
1924   Fools' Highway
1925   His People
1927   The Chinese Parrot
        Red Clay
1928   The Cohens and the Kellys in Paris
        The Rawhide Kid
        Uncle Tom's Cabin
1929   Señor Americano
        Show Boat
1930   The Cohens and the Kellys in Scotland
        East Is West
        King of Jazz
        Song of the Caballero
        La voluntad del muerto
1931   The Cohens and Kellys in Africa
        Drácula
        El tenorio del harem
1932   The Cohens and Kellys in Hollywood
        Igloo
1933   The Cohens and Kellys in Trouble
        Counsellor at Law
1934   Beloved
        Strange Wives
1935   Chinatown Squad
1936   For the Service
        Show Boat
        Sutter's Gold
Laemmle, Carl, Jr.
1928   We Americans
1930   King of Jazz
        La voluntad del muerto
1931   The Cohens and Kellys in Africa
        Drácula
1932   The Cohens and Kellys in Hollywood
1933   The Cohens and Kellys in Trouble
        Counsellor at Law
1934   Beloved
        Imitation of Life
1936   Show Boat
Laemmle, Edward
1922   The Top O' the Morning
1923   The Victor
1925   The Man in Blue
Laemmle, Ernst
1927   Red Clay
1941   Sullivan's Travels
La Farge, Oliver
1934   Behold My Wife!
Lafayette, Jeanne
1951   Go for Broke!
Lafayette, Nenette
1936   My American Wife
La Fayette, Ruby
1918   The Yellow Dog
1919   Toby's Bow
Laffe, John
1918   Woman and the Law
Laffey, J. P.
1918   A Daughter of the Old South
LaFranconi, Terry
1935   El cantante de Nápoles
Lagano, James *same as* **Lagano, Jimmy**
1947   The Foxes of Harrow
1950   Black Hand
Lago, Alicia del
1958   Sierra Baron
La Grange, Webster
1958   The Last Hurrah
La Hogue, Leonore
1933   It's Great to Be Alive
Lahr, Bert
1938   Josette

Lai Yee
1946?   Yee Sio Bo Laan Sin
1948?   Too Yien Fen Fong
Laidlaw, Ethan
1928   The Riding Renegade
1931   Cimarron
1936   Ramona
        Sea Spoilers
        Silly Billies
1939   Allegheny Uprising
        The Return of the Cisco Kid
1940   The Gay Caballero
        Lucky Cisco Kid
1942   Valley of the Sun
1943   The Outlaw
1944   An American Romance
1945   Wanderer of the Wasteland
1946   Singin' in the Corn
1947   California
        Spoilers of the North
1948   The Paleface
1950   The Traveling Saleswoman
        Winchester '73
1951   Flaming Feather
        The Mark of the Renegade
1952   Indian Uprising
        The Raiders
1953   The Man from the Alamo
1956   Hot Blood
Laidlaw, Roy
1917   The Gun Fighter
1918   An Alien Enemy
Laigre, Odette
1931   Su noche de bodas (*foreign version*)
Laird, Effie
1947   Jiggs and Maggie in Society
1952   Wagons West
Laird, John
1940   The Way of All Flesh
Laire, Judson
1959   John Paul Jones
Lake, Alice
1923   The Spider and the Rose
1929   Frozen Justice
1934   Broadway Bill
Lake, Annette
1936   Star for a Night
Lake, Arthur
1948   16 Fathoms Deep
Lake, Florence
1943   Crash Dive
1944   Hi, Beautiful
1950   Ambush
Lake, Janet
1957   Raintree County
Lake, Stuart N.
1950   Winchester '73
Lake, Veronica *same as* **Keane, Constance**
1941   Hold Back the Dawn
        Sullivan's Travels
Lally, Bill *same as* **Lally, William J.**
1938   City Streets
        Little Miss Roughneck
1941   The Face Behind the Mask
        Mystery Ship
1942   Syncopation
        Three Hearts for Julia
1943   Good Luck, Mr. Yates
1949   The Red Menace
Lally, Mike
1943   In Old Oklahoma
1945   I Love a Bandleader
1947   The Farmer's Daughter
        The Jolson Story
1948   Unconquered
        Up in Central Park
1949   Streets of Laredo
1950   Emergency Wedding
1953   So Big
1954   Dangerous Mission
Lally, William J. *see* **Lally, Bill**
LaMal, Isabelle *same as* **La Mal, Isabel**
1934   Straight Is the Way

Lamarr, Hedy (continued, see right column)
1935   Ruggles of Red Gap
1936   Show Boat
1937   Think Fast, Mr. Moto
1938   The Beloved Brat
1939   Mr. Moto Takes a Vacation
1944   Mr. Skeffington
1945   Betrayal from the East
Lamar, Adriana
1935   No matarás
1936   El crimen de media noche
Lamar, Monina
1931   Cheri-Bibi
Lamarr, Hedy
1941   Come Live with Me
1942   Tortilla Flat
1950   A Lady Without Passport
LaMarr, Lawrence
1949   The Story of Seabiscuit
LaMarr, Lucille *same as* **Lamarr, Lucille**
1936   Star for a Night
1944   Mr. Skeffington
La Marr, Moses
1959   Porgy and Bess
LaMarr, Richard
1950   Emergency Wedding
1951   The Great Caruso
LaMarr, Sam
1949   The Undercover Man
Lamas, Fernando
1953   Sangaree
Lamb, Gil
1943   Riding High
1958   Terror in a Texas Town
Lamb, Harold
1937   The Plainsman
1938   The Buccaneer
Lambert, Jack
1947   New Orleans
1948   Reaching from Heaven
1949   Border Incident
1950   North of the Great Divide
        Stars in My Crown
Lambert, Marc
1958   Sierra Baron
Lambert, Mel
1953   The Great Sioux Uprising
Lamont, B. Wayne
1930   Las campanas de Capistrano
Lamont, Charles
1936   Below the Deadline
1939   Verbena trágica
1941   Road Agent
1944   Chip Off the Old Block
1945   Salome, Where She Danced
Lamont, Harry
1934   La veuve joyeuse
1936   Rose of the Rancho
1942   Valley of the Sun
1947   The Mighty McGurk
LaMont, Jack
1950   Catskill Honeymoon
Lamont, Marten
1940   Music in My Heart
1942   Mexican Spitfire at Sea
        Mexican Spitfire Sees a Ghost
        Mexican Spitfire's Elephant
        The Navy Comes Through
1943   Ladies' Day
1944   Waterfront
Lamont, Molly
1936   Muss 'Em Up
1944   Minstrel Man
        Mr. Skeffington
Lamont, Syl
1952   Red Ball Express
LaMore, Isabelle
1936   My American Wife
La Morte, Anthony
1951   Go for Broke!
Lamothe, Julian Louis
1917   Southern Pride

Lamour, Dorothy
1938 Spawn of the North
1943 Dixie
Riding High
1945 A Medal for Benny
Lampe, Marie
1950 No Way Out
Lampell, Millard
1951 Saturday's Hero
Lampert, Zohra
1959 Odds Against Tomorrow
1960 Pay or Die
Lampkin, Charles
1951 Five
Lamson, David
1937 That I May Live
Lamy, Charles
1930 Un hombre de suerte
(*foreign version*)
Lanak
1932 Igloo
Lancaster, Burt
1951 Jim Thorpe—All-American
1954 Apache
1955 The Rose Tattoo
1960 The Unforgiven
Lancaster, Pearl
1941 Sullivan's Travels
Lance, Lia
1934 Operator 13
Lanchester, Elsa
1935 Naughty Marietta
1942 Tales of Manhattan
1947 Northwest Outpost
1950 Buccaneer's Girl
Mystery Street
1954 Hell's Half Acre
Landa, Juan de
1930 ¡De frente, marchen!
El presidio
El último de los Vargas
El valiente
1931 En cada puerto un amor
La fruta amarga
El proceso de Mary
Dugan
Su última noche
Landau, Mrs. *same as* **Landau, Mrs.**
David
1916 The Yellow Passport
Landau, Arthur M.
1944 Dark Waters
Landau, David
1931 Street Scene
1934 As the Earth Turns
Judge Priest
Landau, Samuel *same as* **Landau,**
S.
1936 Yiddle with His Fiddle
1937 The Jester (Der
Purimspieler)
1939 A Brivele der Mamen
Landeros, Elena
1931 En cada puerto un amor
El príncipe gondolero
1932 Hollywood, ciudad de
ensueño
Landers, Harry
1949 C-Man
1955 The Indian Fighter
Landers, Lew
1937 Border Cafe
1939 Bad Lands
1941 Mystery Ship
1942 Submarine Raider
1943 Deerslayer
Doughboys in Ireland
Redhead from Manhattan
1947 Thunder Mountain
Under the Tonto Rim
1949 Stagecoach Kid
1950 Davy Crockett, Indian
Scout
Last of the Buccaneers
1951 Hurricane Island
When the Redskins Rode
1952 Arctic Flight
California Conquest
1953 Captain John Smith and
Pocahontas

Landers, Robert
1915 The Rosary
Landers, Scott
1949 House of Strangers
Landi, Elissa
1934 The Great Flirtation
1936 After the Thin Man
Mad Holiday
Landi, Linda
1928 A Ship Comes In
Landin, Hope
1941 Where Did You Get That
Girl?
1943 Dixie
Gangway for Tomorrow
1944 Three Men in White
1945 The Great John L.
Where Do We Go From
Here?
1946 Gas House Kids
1948 I Remember Mama
Unconquered
Landis, Carole
1943 Wintertime
Landis, Cullen
1920 It's a Great Life
1922 The Man with Two
Mothers
1923 Crashin' Thru
1926 Buffalo Bill on the U. P.
Trail
Sweet Rosie O'Grady
1927 Finnegan's Ball
1928 The Broken Mask
Landis, Margaret
1918 Amarilly of Clothes-Line
Alley
Landon, Hal
1951 Oh! Susanna
Landon, Harold F. *same as*
Landon, Harold
1941 Hold Back the Dawn
1944 An American Romance
1949 The Clay Pigeon
Landon, John
1947 The Farmer's Daughter
Landon, Judy
1950 Annie Get Your Gun
1951 Show Boat
Landres, Morris
1949 Call of the Forest
Landres, Paul
1958 Frontier Gun
Oregon Passage
Landry, Margaret
1943 Gangway for Tomorrow
The Leopard Man
Mexican Spitfire's Blessed
Event
Landy, Ludwig
1937 Green Fields
1938 The Singing Blacksmith
1940 Overture to Glory
Lane, Al *could be same as* **Lane,**
Allan "Rocky"
1932 The Galloping Kid
Lane, Allan "Rocky" *same as*
Lane, Allan *could be same as*
Lane, Al
1937 Charlie Chan at the
Olympics
1943 Air Force
1946 Santa Fe Uprising
1947 Marshal of Cripple Creek
Oregon Trail Scouts
Rustlers of Devil's
Canyon
Vigilantes of Boomtown
1948 Renegades of Sonora
Lane, Billie
1944 Something for the Boys
Lane, Charles *same as* **Lane,**
Charles D.; Levinson, Charles
1918 Ruggles of Red Gap
1931 Smart Money
1933 Grand Slam
1934 Broadway Bill
1936 It Had to Happen
1937 One Mile from Heaven
1938 In Old Chicago
The Rage of Paris
1941 Birth of the Blues
New York Town

1942 Friendly Enemies
1947 The Farmer's Daughter
1948 The Boy with Green Hair
Call Northside 777
Moonrise
Lane, Howard
1942 The Navy Comes Through
Lane, Johnny
1946 The Sailor Takes a Wife
Lane, Laurie
1938 The Texans
Lane, Leela
1922 The Half Breed
Lane, Lenita
1934 Imitation of Life
1941 Dead Men Tell
1942 Castle in the Desert
Lane, Lillian
1931 Cimarron
Lane, Lola
1939 Daughters Courageous
1941 Mystery Ship
Lane, Lovey
1942 Take My Life
Lane, Magda
1920 Locked Lips
Lane, Morgan
1957 Journey to Freedom
1959 The FBI Story
Lane, Nora
1928 Kit Carson
1929 The Cohens and Kellys in
Atlantic City
Masked Emotions
1931 The Cisco Kid
Young Sinners
1934 Stand Up and Cheer!
1944 Lake Placid Serenade
Lane, Pat
1947 The Jolson Story
1949 Streets of Laredo
Top O' the Morning
The Undercover Man
Lane, Paul
1920? The Scarlet Dragon
Lane, Priscilla
1939 Daughters Courageous
1940 Three Cheers for the Irish
1943 The Meanest Man in the
World
Lane, Richard
1939 Charlie Chan in Honolulu
The Escape
Mr. Moto in Danger
Island
1943 Air Force
1944 Slightly Terrific
1949 Boston Blackie's Chinese
Venture
That Midnight Kiss
1950 The Jackie Robinson Story
Lane, Rosemary
1939 Daughters Courageous
Lane, Rusty
1945 The House on 92nd St.
1958 The Rawhide Trail
Lane, Vicky
1945 The Cisco Kid Returns
Lane, Wade
1937 Maid of Salem
Lane, Ward
1937 Maid of Salem
Lane, Warren
1945 Where Do We Go From
Here?
Lanfield, Sidney
1943 The Meanest Man in the
World
Lang, Charles
1941 Where Did You Get That
Girl?
1942 Gentleman Jim
Secret Enemies
1943 Air Force
1948 Night Wind
Lang, Cora
1938 The Toy Wife
1941 Sullivan's Travels

Lang, David
1951 The Last Outpost
1953 Ambush at Tomahawk
Gap
The Nebraskan
1954 Massacre Canyon
1955 Apache Ambush
1956 Secret of Treasure
Mountain
1957 Gun Battle at Monterey
Lang, Fritz
1941 Western Union
Lang, Harry
1950 A Lady Without Passport
Lang, Howard
1922 Peacock Alley
1936 Klondike Annie
1940 Escape
Lang, Jeanie
1930 King of Jazz
Lang, Jimmy
1945 Salome, Where She
Danced
Lang, June *same as* **Vlasek, June**
1933 The Man Who Dared: An
Imaginative Biography
1939 Forged Passport
Lang, Melvin
1940 Doomed to Die
Lang, Otto
1948 Call Northside 777
Lang, Vicki
1945 Nob Hill
Lang, Walter
1927 Sally in Our Alley
1933 Racetrack
1942 Song of the Islands
Langan, Glenn *same as* **Langan,**
Glen
1943 Riding High
1944 Something for the Boys
1948 Fury at Furnace Creek
1950 The Iroquois Trail
Langdon, Harry
1926 The Strong Man
1928 Heart Trouble
1944 Block Busters
Langdon, Lillian
1915 The Kindling
The Lamb
1918 Marked Cards
Shifting Sands
Who Is to Blame?
1921 The Swamp
1925 Cobra
Langdon, Mae Clarke *see* **Clarke,**
Mae
Langdon, Rose
1942 Mokey
Lange, Elaine
1946 Dangerous Money
Lange, Hope
1958 The Young Lions
Lange, Michele
1951 Go for Broke!
Langford, Edward
1919 The Volcano
Langford, Frances
1940 Too Many Girls
1943 Yankee Doodle Dandy
Langford, Sam
1920 The Brute
Langley, Bruce
1946 G. I. War Brides
Langley, Noel
1940 Northwest Passage (Book
I—Rogers' Rangers)
Langsner, Clara
1931 Personal Maid
1933 Counsellor at Law
Langton, Paul
1959 The Last Angry Man
Lani, Lei, Prince
1937 Waikiki Wedding
Lani, Pua
1938 Hawaii Calls
1939 Fisherman's Wharf
Lania, Leo
1931 Die Dreigroschenoper

La Niece, Ed
1921   The Double O
Lanning, Frank
1917   A Kentucky Cinderella
        The Squaw Man's Son
1918   The Goddess of Lost Lake
        Huck and Tom; or, the
            Further Adventures of
            Tom Sawyer
1919   Desert Gold
1920   Huckleberry Finn
        The Third Woman
1921   That Girl Montana
1922   East Is West
1925   The Red Rider
1934   The Lone Defender
Lanoe, Jiquel *same as* **Lanoe, J. J.**
1920   The Tiger's Coat
1921   The Kiss
La Nore, Dee
1948   The Paleface
Lanphier, Mary-Madeleine
1960   Weddings and Babies
Lansbury, Angela
1960   The Dark at the Top of
            the Stairs
Lansing, Joi
1949   The Girl from Jones
            Beach
1958   Touch of Evil
Lansing, Robert
1960   The Pusher
Lantz, Louis
1951   Fort Defiance
Lanza, Dina
1932   Genoveffa
Lanza, Mario
1949   That Midnight Kiss
1950   The Toast of New Orleans
1951   The Great Caruso
1956   Serenade
1958   Seven Hills of Rome
Lanzo, Rocco
1946   Gas House Kids
Lapan, Richard
1922   Little Miss Smiles
Lapenieks, Vilis
1957   Beau James
LaPlanche, Louise
1941   Louisiana Purchase
1942   Holiday Inn
La Planche, Rosemary
1943   Mexican Spitfire's Blessed
            Event
1945   Betrayal from the East
        Johnny Angel
La Plante, Laura
1929   Show Boat
1930   King of Jazz
1947   Little Mister Jim
LaPlante, Loulette
1938   The Buccaneer
Lappas, Anthony
1952   It's a Big Country: An
            American Anthology
Lara, Antonio de
1931   La fruta amarga
Larabee, Louise
1936   Star for a Night
Larch, John
1956   Man from Del Rio
1957   Man in the Shadow
1960   Hell to Eternity
Lardner, Ring, Jr.
1942   Woman of the Year
1944   Tomorrow the World!
La Reno, Dick *same as* **Loreno, Dick**
1914   Rose of the Rancho
        The Squaw Man
1918   Tony America
1922   One Eighth Apache
1926   Buffalo Bill on the U. P.
            Trail
La Reno, Utahna
1915   The Rosary
Largay, Raymond *same as* **Largay, Ray**
1948   Four Faces West
        Gentleman's Agreement
1950   Emergency Wedding

1953   Tonight We Sing
La Ricos, Ricky
1953   The Glory Brigade
Larios, Alfonso de
1931   La cautivadora
1936   Ramona
Larkin, George *same as* **Larkin, George Alan**
1917   The Primitive Call
1918   The Border Raiders
1924   The Pell Street Mystery
Larkin, Jacqueline
1945   A Tree Grows in Brooklyn
Larkin, John (*actor*)
1931   Smart Money
1934   Lazy River
        Operator 13
1935   So Red the Rose
1936   The Green Pastures
Larkin, John (*writer*)
1939   Charlie Chan at Treasure
            Island
1940   Charlie Chan at the Wax
            Museum
        Charlie Chan in Panama
        The Gay Caballero
1941   Accent on Love
        Dead Men Tell
1942   Castle in the Desert
1944   Buffalo Bill
1945   The Dolly Sisters
Ellis Larkins Trio
1953   The Joe Louis Story
Larna, Leo
1931   Die Dreigroschenoper
            (*foreign version*)
La Roche, Mary
1950   Catskill Honeymoon
La Roche, Norma
1955   The Long Gray Line
La Roche, Pete
1956   Wetbacks
La Rocque, Rod
1918   Ruggles of Red Gap
1925   Braveheart
1928   Hold 'Em Yale
Larosa, Viola
1931   La regina di Sparta
La Roux, Carmen *same as* **Le Roux, Carmen**
1927   Don Mike
1928   El Robin Hood de México
1930   Las campanas de
            Capistrano
1931   Cavalier of the West
1933   The California Trail
1935   Un hombre peligroso
1936   Ramona
1938   Daughter of Shanghai
Laroy, Guisseppi
1931   La regina di Sparta
La Roy, Rita
1930   Check and Double Check
1932   So Big
1938   Dangerous to Know
Larrabeiti, Carmen
1930   Doña mentiras
        Toda una vida
1931   La carta
        ¿Conoces a tu mujer?
        Esclavas de la moda
        La fiesta del diablo
        La ley del harem
Larrell, Steve
1950   Winchester '73
Larrimore, Rosalie
1946?   Beale Street Mama
Larry, Dene
1941   Murder on Lenox Avenue
Larsen, Bobby
1944   An American Romance
Larsen, Keith
1952   Hiawatha
1953   War Paint
1954   Arrow in the Dust
1955   Chief Crazy Horse
1957   Apache Warrior
Larsen, L. H.
1949   Stallion Canyon

Larsen, Tambi
1950   Damien
Larson, Ben
1952   The Big Sky
Larson, Bob *same as* **Larson, Bobby**
Larson, Bobby
1942   Woman of the Year
1943   Good Luck, Mr. Yates
1944   My Pal Wolf
        The Sullivans
1950   Emergency Wedding
Larson, Charles
1948   Angel in Exile
Larson, Christine *same as* **Cook, Christine Larson**
1948   Silver Trails
1951   The Well
1952   Brave Warrior
Larson, Elsie
1933   The Man Who Dared: An
            Imaginative Biography
1935   ¡Asegure a su mujer!
Larson, Jack
1952   Kid Monk Baroni
LaRue, Al "Lash" *same as* **LaRue, Al**
1946   Wild West
LaRue, Don
1936   Laughing Irish Eyes
La Rue, Emily
1960   Pay or Die
La Rue, Fontaine
1924   Unseen Hands
LaRue, Frank *same as* **LaRue, Frank H.**
1934   The Cat's-Paw
1935   The Singing Vagabond
1936   General Spanky
1937   Man of the People
1940   Arizona Frontier
1942   Lawless Plainsmen
1943   Frontier Fury
1946   Border Bandits
        The Gay Cavalier
La Rue, Grace
1940   If I Had My Way
LaRue, Jack
1934   Straight Is the Way
1936   Dancing Pirate
        Ellis Island
        Yellow Cargo
1937   That I May Live
1939   In Old Caliente
1940   Charlie Chan in Panama
        East of the River
1942   American Empire
1943   The Girl from Monterrey
        The Law Rides Again
1946   Santa Fe Uprising
1947   Robin Hood of Monterey
La Rue, John (*African-American actor*)
1926   Reckless Money
LaRue, "Lash" *see* **LaRue, Al "Lash"**
La Rue, Reese
1956   Rockin' the Blues
La Rue, Walter
1958   Gunman's Walk
1950   Ambush
La Salle, Katherine
1914   Northern Lights
Lascoe, Jerry, Jr.
1949   That Midnight Kiss
Lash, Harry
1937   Man of the People
Lash, Isidor
1937   I Want to Be a Mother
Lashley, Ella Mae
1942   Tales of Manhattan
Lasker, Edward
1949   Tulsa
1952   The Big Sky
Laskey, Charles
1941   Louisiana Purchase
Lasky, Jesse L. *same as* **Lasky, Jesse**
1915   After Five
        The Cheat
        Chimmie Fadden
        Chimmie Fadden Out
            West

        The Immigrant
        The Kindling
1916   Alien Souls
        The Soul of Kura-San
        Unprotected
1917   Castles for Two
1918   The Bravest Way
        The City of Dim Faces
        The Gypsy Trail
        Hidden Pearls
        Huck and Tom; or, the
            Further Adventures of
            Tom Sawyer
        One More American
        Sandy
        The Source
        The Squaw Man
1919   Told in the Hills
1920   Huckleberry Finn
1922   Saturday Night
1923   Ruggles of Red Gap
        Thirty Days
1924   The Heritage of the
            Desert
        North of 36
        Peter Pan
        Tongues of Flame
1925   Flower of Night
        Irish Luck
        The Manicure Girl
        Salome of the Tenements
        A Son of His Father
        The Thundering Herd
1926   The Campus Flirt
        Desert Gold
        The Vanishing American
1927   Blind Alleys
        Drums of the Desert
        The Gay Defender
        Open Range
        The Way of All Flesh
1928   The Secret Hour
1930   El cuerpo del delito
1934   Coming Out Party
1945   Rhapsody in Blue
1946   Without Reservations
1948   The Miracle of the Bells
1951   The Great Caruso
Lasky, Jesse, Jr. *same as* **Lasky, Jesse L., Jr.**
1934   Coming Out Party
1941   Land of Liberty
1948   Unconquered
1956   Hot Blood
1959   John Paul Jones
Lassick, Sidney
1959   Al Capone
Lassie Bronte, a dog *not the same as* **Lassie M-G-M dog star**
1925   The Beautiful City
Last Star, Theodore
1952   The Big Sky
Laster, Gwendolyn
1951   The Well
Laszlo, Aladar
1943   Gangway for Tomorrow
Laszlo, Miklos
1948   Big City
Latell, Lyle
1942   Foreign Agent
        The Navy Comes Through
1946   Shadows Over Chinatown
1947   Buck Privates Come
            Home
        Ride the Pink Horse
1949   The Sky Dragon
1951   A Streetcar Named Desire
1956   Mohawk
Latham, Jack
1936   Show Boat
Latham, Red
1943   Doughboys in Ireland
Lathrop, William Addison
1915   Under Southern Skies
1917   I Will Repay
        The Tell-Tale Step
1918   A Little Sister of
            Everybody
The Lathrops
1937   Manhattan
        Merry-Go-Round

Latimer, Carl Rocky
1953   The Joe Louis Story
Latimore, Frank
1945   The Dolly Sisters
1959   John Paul Jones
La Torre, Charles *same as* **Latorre, Charles**
1939   Lying Lips
1940   The Notorious Elinor Lee
1941   Louisiana Purchase
1942   Three Hearts for Julia
1943   Dixie
1949   Harbor of Missing Men
1950   Sunset in the West
1960   Pay or Die
Latorre, Don
1937   Boy of the Streets
La Tour, Donna
1949   House of Strangers
La Tour, Jack
1946   The Gay Cavalier
Latowich, Carl
1939   Mamele
Latta, Dorothy
1949   Roll Thunder Roll!
Lattimer, Dwain
1950   Panic in the Streets
Lattimore, Jacquelyn
1957   Burden of Truth
Laub, William B.
1920?   Her Story
Lauder, Harry
1931   Delicious
Laughlin, Anna
1914   Northern Lights
Laughton, Charles
1935   Ruggles of Red Gap
1940   They Knew What They Wanted
1942   Tales of Manhattan
Laughton, Eddie
1938   City Streets
        Little Miss Roughneck
1941   Mystery Ship
        Thunder Over the Prairie
1942   Lawless Plainsmen
        Submarine Raider
1944   The Racket Man
1952   Anything Can Happen
Launders, Perc
1941   Sullivan's Travels
1945   Johnny Angel
1947   California
        Desperate
        Easy Come, Easy Go
1948   Fighting Father Dunne
        Western Heritage
Launer, S. John
1960   Ice Palace
Laurel and Hardy *see* **Laurel, Stan; Hardy, Oliver**
Laurel, Stan
1931   Los calaveras
        Los calaveras (*foreign version*)
        Noche de duendes
        Pardon Us
        Pardon Us (*foreign version*)
        Politiquerías
Laurell, Kay
1921   Lonely Heart
Laurent, Tony
1947   The Foxes of Harrow
Laurents, Arthur
1949   Anna Lucasta
Laurents, Nancy
1950   Bandit Queen
Laurenz, John
1945   In Old New Mexico
1946   Sunset Pass
Laurie, Piper
1954   Dangerous Mission
1955   Smoke Signal
Laurier, Richard
1960   This Rebel Breed
Lauro, Giuseppe
1932   Amor y vida

Lauro, Luisa Bonancini de
1932   Amor y vida
Lauter, Harry
1948   Moonrise
1950   No Way Out
1952   Apache Country
        Bugles in the Afternoon
        Red Ball Express
1954   They Rode West
1955   Apache Ambush
1957   The Oklahoman
        Raiders of Old California
1958   The Last Hurrah
1960   Key Witness
Lavalle, León
1933   Espérame
La Varney, Lucille *see* **La Verne, Lucille**
La Varnie, Laura *same as* **Lavarnie, Laura**
1919   The Unpainted Woman
1922   The Man with Two Mothers
La Varr, Mert *see* **Merton, John**
Lavassor, Vera
1919   Injustice
1920?   Reformation
Lavelle, Miriam
1943   The Gang's All Here
Laven, Arnold
1959   Anna Lucasta
Lavenda, Pincus
1933   Live and Laugh
La Verne, Jane
1928   George Washington Cohen
1929   Show Boat
La Verne, Lucille *same as* **La Varney, Lucille**
1916   The Thousand Dollar Husband
1924   His Darker Self
1930   Abraham Lincoln
1931   The Great Meadow
        Little Caesar
1932   Hearts of Humanity
        Wild Horse Mesa
1934   Beloved
La Verre, Mort *see* **Merton, John**
Lavery, Emmet
1943   Hitler's Children
1951   The Magnificent Yankee
1953   Bright Road
La Vett, Gladys
1921   By Right of Birth
Lavryk, Maria
1937   Natalka Poltavka
Law, Burton
1919   Who Will Marry Me?
Law, Maria
1922   The Great Alone
Law, Mildred
1944   Tahiti Nights
Law, Walter
1922   The Great Alone
1930   Whoopee
Law, William
1936   After the Thin Man
1937   Think Fast, Mr. Moto
Lawford, Ernest
1925   Irish Luck
1931   Personal Maid
Lawler, Anderson
1930   A Lady to Love
1933   Let's Fall in Love
1934   Beloved
Lawler, Mimi
1937   Man of the People
Lawler, Robert
1916   Little Meena's Romance
Lawless, Kevin
1952   The Quiet Man
Lawless, Pat
1954   Drum Beat
1958   The Badlanders
Lawrance, Jody *same as* **Lawrence, Jody**
1953   Captain John Smith and Pocahontas

Lawrence, Ann (*actress beginning circa early 1940s*)
1946   Cuban Pete
Lawrence, Ann (*child actress*)
1947   Humoresque
Lawrence, Babe *see* **Lawrence, William E. "Babe"**
Lawrence, Barbara
1949   Thieves' Highway
1957   Joe Dakota
        Man in the Shadow
Lawrence, Bert
1941   Birth of the Blues
1942   Holiday Inn
Lawrence, Bob
1951   The Great Caruso
Lawrence, Charlotte
1955   Trial
Lawrence, Craig
1944   Lake Placid Serenade
Lawrence, Del
1941   The Pioneers
Lawrence, Edmund *same as* **Lawrence, Edward**
1915   Cohen's Luck
1918   The Firebrand
        The Liar
Lawrence, Edna
1936   Ramona
1937   Drums of Destiny
Lawrence, Edward *see* **Lawrence, Edmund**
Lawrence, Estelle
1957   The Brothers Rico
Lawrence, Helen
1935   Lem Hawkins' Confession
Lawrence, Hugh
1959   The Black Orchid
Lawrence, Jack
1945   A Tree Grows in Brooklyn
Lawrence, Jay
1950   A Lady Without Passport
1953   Cry of the Hunted
1957   The Halliday Brand
Lawrence, Jody *see* **Lawrance, Jody**
Lawrence, Lillian
1919   A Fallen Idol
1922   East Is West
1937   That I May Live
Lawrence, Marc
1936   Robin Hood of El Dorado
1937   Charlie Chan on Broadway
1939   Charlie Chan in Honolulu
1940   Charlie Chan at the Wax Museum
1942   Nazi Agent
1943   The Ox-Bow Incident
1945   Club Havana
1948   Key Largo
        Unconquered
1949   Jigsaw
1950   Black Hand
1951   Hurricane Island
Lawrence, Mary
1953   Dream Wife
Lawrence, Richard
1948   The Betrayal
Lawrence, Rosina
1936   Charlie Chan's Secret
        General Spanky
Lawrence, Sandy
1950   The Toast of New Orleans
Lawrence, Sheldon
1959   The Sheriff of Fractured Jaw
Lawrence, Terry
1957   Trooper Hook
Lawrence, Vincent
1931   Le petit café
1934   Behold My Wife!
1942   Gentleman Jim
Lawrence, W. E. *see* **Lawrence, William E. "Babe"**
Lawrence, Walter onscreen 1931—
1932   Hypnotized
1949   House of Strangers
1953   The Man from the Alamo

Lawrence, Walter M. circa late 1910s
1918   The Prussian Cur
Lawrence, William E. "Babe" *same as* **Lawrence, Babe; Lawrence, W. E.; Lawrence, William; Lawrence, William E.**
1917   The Slacker (Metro Pictures Corp.)
        The Spirit of '76
1921   The Kiss
1933   Best of Enemies
1934   Broadway Bill
        Coming Out Party
1938   The Rage of Paris
Lawson, Bob
1942   Mokey
Lawson, Eleanor
1917   The Renaissance at Charleroi
1925   Lights of Old Broadway
George Lawson and His Band
1949?   The Joint Is Jumpin'
Lawson, John Howard
1943   Action in the North Atlantic
Lawson, Kate Drain *same as* **Lawson, Kate**
1940   Girl from God's Country
1941   New York Town
1943   The Leopard Man
1950   Rock Island Trail
Lawson, Larry
1944   Buffalo Bill
1948   Unconquered
Lawson, Priscilla
1936   Sutter's Gold
1938   The Toy Wife
Lawson, Wilfrid
1939   Allegheny Uprising
Lax, Abraham *same as* **Lax, Abe**
1938   The Power of Life
1940   Americaner Schadchen
1950   Catskill Honeymoon
Lay, Eugene
1946   G. I. War Brides
Layne, Bill
1959   Night of the Quarter Moon
Layne, Tracy
1935   Melody Trail
Layng, Tony
1952   Rose of Cimarron
Layton, Frank
1937   The Plainsman
Lazarus, Erna
1946   Slightly Scandalous
Lazarus, Sidney
1928   Flying Romeos
1930   ¡De frente, marchen!
Lazelle, Perk
1936   Star for a Night
1945   Where Do We Go From Here?
1956   Serenade
Lazer, Joan
1949   The Undercover Man
Lea, Jenny
1957   The Oklahoman
Lea, Tom
1959   The Wonderful Country
Lea, William, Jr.
1950   The Men
Leacock, Philip
1960   Take a Giant Step
Leacock, Richard
1948   Louisiana Story
Leader, Anton M.
1954   Go Man Go
Leahy, Agnes Brand
1931   Fighting Caravans
Leal, Fernando Luis
1935   No matarás
Leão, Ester
1930   Toda una vida (*foreign version*)
Learn, Bessie *same as* **Lern, Bessie**
1919   The Lost Battalion

Leary, Nolan
1944 An American Romance
1946 California Gold Rush
1947 The Last Round-Up
1949 The Cowboy and the Indians
Laramie
1950 Annie Get Your Gun
Colt .45
The Furies
1952 Anything Can Happen
The Big Sky
High Noon
1953 Cry of the Hunted

Lease, Rex
1927 Clancy's Kosher Wedding
1929 The Younger Generation
1930 Sunny Skies
1931 Chinatown After Dark
1935 Cyclone of the Saddle
1936 Aces and Eights
Custer's Last Stand
1946 Canyon Passage
Sun Valley Cyclone
1947 Buck Privates Come Home
California
Easy Come, Easy Go
1949 Rose of the Yukon
1953 The Man Behind the Gun
Ride, Vaquero!

Leasure, C. B.
1922 Come On Over

Léaud, Pierre
1931 Die Dreigroschenoper (foreign version)

Leavitt, B. J.
1947 Bells of San Fernando

Leavitt, Douglas
1943 Good Luck, Mr. Yates
Redhead from Manhattan

Leavitt, Norman
1948 The Luck of the Irish
Music Man
1951 Show Boat
1953 Ride, Vaquero!

LeBaron, Bert
1931 Delicious
1944 Address Unknown
1951 Across the Wide Missouri
Westward the Women

Le Baron, Eddie same as **Le Baron, Edward**
1938 Castillos en el aire
1947 The Foxes of Harrow
1950 A Lady Without Passport

Eddie Le Baron Orchestra
1944 Lady, Let's Dance!

LeBaron, William
1927 Blind Alleys
1930 Check and Double Check
1931 Cimarron
Echec au roi
Three Who Loved
1936 Klondike Annie
My American Wife
Rose of the Rancho
1937 Maid of Salem
The Plainsman
Souls at Sea
Waikiki Wedding
1938 Dangerous to Know
Daughter of Shanghai
The Texans
1939 King of Chinatown
1940 Geronimo
The Way of All Flesh
1941 New York Town
Virginia
1942 Song of the Islands
1943 The Gang's All Here
Stormy Weather
Wintertime
1947 Carnegie Hall

LeBeau, Madeleine
1941 Hold Back the Dawn
1942 Gentleman Jim

Lebedeff, Ivan
1931 Echec au roi
1934 Strange Wives
1939 The Mystery of Mr. Wong
1940 Elsa Maxwell's Public Deb No. 1

1942 Foreign Agent
1945 Rhapsody in Blue
1952 California Conquest

Leberman, Joseph
1958 Never Love a Stranger

Le Blanc, Clifford
1950 Panic in the Streets

LeBlanc, Lionel
1948 Louisiana Story

LeBorg, Reginald
1947 The Adventures of Don Coyote
1950 Young Daniel Boone
1957 War Drums

Le Brandt, Gertrude
1918 Doing Their Bit

Lechner, Billy
1944 An American Romance
1950 Battleground
Sands of Iwo Jima

Lechonia, Jana
1930 Toda una vida (foreign version)

Lechuga, Raúl
1930 Monsieur le Fox
La rosa de fuego
El valiente
1931 ¿Conoces a tu mujer?
1936 El crimen de media noche
1939 El otro soy yo
Papá soltero
1940 Cuando canta la Ley

Ledbetter, Bertha
1948 The Miracle of the Bells

Ledebour, Leopold von
1931 La fiesta del diablo (foreign version)

Ledebur, Frederick
1946 Notorious
1948 My Girl Tisa

Lederer, Charles
1947 Ride the Pink Horse

Lederer, Francis
1935 Romance in Manhattan
1936 My American Wife
1939 Confessions of a Nazi Spy
1940 The Man I Married

Lederer, George W.
1917 Runaway Romany

Lederer, Gretchen
1916 The Morals of Hilda
A Yoke of Gold
1917 A Kentucky Cinderella
1918 The Red, Red Heart

Lederer, Otto
1914 The Little Angel of Canyon Creek
1917 The Captain of the Gray Horse Troop
1922 Hungry Hearts
1926 Sweet Rosie O'Grady
1927 Sailor Izzy Murphy
The Shamrock and the Rose
1928 The Jazz Singer
1929 Smiling Irish Eyes

Lederman, D. Ross same as **Lederman, Ross**
1925 Hogan's Alley
1927 Bitter Apples
Ham and Eggs at the Front
1944 The Racket Man

Lederman, David
1939 Kol Nidre

Lederman, Ross see **Lederman, D. Ross**

Ledoux, Fernand
1935 L'homme des Folies Bergère

Lee
1934 Blossom Time

Lee, Alberta
1916 Little Meena's Romance
A Sister of Six
1917 The Sudden Gentleman
1918 Real Folks
1919 The Red Viper

Lee, Alice
1919 Mandarin's Gold

Lee, Allen same as **Lee, Allan**
1938 Birthright
1945 Wanderer of the Wasteland
1947 Thunder Mountain

Lee, Ann not the same as **Lee, Anna**
1931 Cimarron
1955 Trial

Lee, Anna not the same as **Lee, Ann**
1946 G. I. War Brides
1948 Fort Apache
1958 The Last Hurrah
1959 The Crimson Kimono

Lee, Barbara
1948 The Betrayal

Lee, Betsy
1928 The Night Bird

Lee, Billie not the same as **Lee, Billy**
1938 In Old Chicago

Lee, Billy not the same as **Lee, Billie**
1934 Behold My Wife!
Wagon Wheels
1941 Hold Back the Dawn

Lee, Canada
1939 Keep Punching
1944 Lifeboat
1947 Body and Soul
1949 Lost Boundaries

Lee, Carolyn
1941 Birth of the Blues
Virginia

Lee, Catherine see **Lee, Katherine**

Lee, Mrs. Chan
1936 Klondike Annie

Lee, Charles
1915 The Sable Lorcha
1939 King of Chinatown

Lee, Ching Wah
1938 Daughter of Shanghai
1947 Little Mister Jim

Lee, Curry could be same as **Calmer, Lee** or **Calmes, Curry Lee**
1934 Imitation of Life

Lee, Daisy
1942 Little Tokyo, U.S.A.

Lee, Dick
1918 The Birth of a Race
1922 Cardigan
For His Mother's Sake

Lee, Dixie
1931 Young Sinners

Lee, Donald W.
1933 It's Great to Be Alive

Lee, Dorothy
1936 Silly Billies

Lee, Duke same as **Lee, Duke R.**
1925 The Red Rider
1934 Judge Priest
1936 The Prisoner of Shark Island
1937 The Plainsman

Lee, Earl
1951 Five
1952 My Man and I
1953 The Jazz Singer

Lee, Eddie
1935 Charlie Chan in Shanghai
1942 Across the Pacific
Submarine Raider
1943 Jack London
1945 Nob Hill
1948 Half Past Midnight
1949 Boston Blackie's Chinese Venture
The Clay Pigeon
1951 Mask of the Dragon

Lee, Eldridge
1919 Injustice

Lee, Etta
1921 A Tale of Two Worlds
1927 The Chinese Parrot

Lee, Eugene "Porky"
1936 General Spanky

Lee, Flo not the same as **Lee, Florence D.**
1941 Murder on Lenox Avenue

Lee, Florence D. not the same as **Lee, Flo**
1922 The Top O' the Morning

Lee, Frankie (child actor)
1917 The Bronze Bride
1919 The Westerners
1921 Shame
The Swamp
1922 The Scrapper

Lee, Frederick
1926 Twin Triggers

Lee, George T. same as **Lee, George** not the same as **Leigh, George**
1942 Submarine Raider
1945 Betrayal from the East
Nob Hill
1949 Boston Blackie's Chinese Venture

Lee, Glen
1947 Body and Soul

Lee, Gwen
1928 Diamond Handcuffs
1929 Lucky Boy
1930 Estrellados

Lee, Gypsy Rose same as **Hovick, Louise**
1938 My Lucky Star

Lee, Harry
1917 The Little Boy Scout
1918 Uncle Tom's Cabin

Lee, Ila
1934 Broadway Bill

Lee, Jack
1946 Till the End of Time
1948 Unconquered
1950 Broken Arrow
Two Flags West

Lee, James
1960 The Adventures of Huckleberry Finn

Lee, Jane same as **Lee, Little Jane**
1915 The Clemenceau Case
1918 Doing Their Bit
1949 Knock on Any Door

Lee, Jennie
1915 The Birth of a Nation
1918 Sandy
1920 The Secret Gift
1921 One Man in a Million

Lee, Jesse M.
1914 The Indian Wars
1917 The Adventures of Buffalo Bill

Lee, Jocelyn
1926 The Campus Flirt
1928 The Night Bird

Lee, Johnny same as **Lee, John D., Jr.**
1943 Stormy Weather
1946 Song of the South
1947 Mantan Runs for Mayor
1947? Return of Mandy's Husband
1948? Boarding House Blues
1949? Come On, Cowboy!
She's Too Mean for Me

Lee, Joseph
1919 Mandarin's Gold

Lee, Katherine same as **Lee, Catherine**
1915 The Last of the Mafia
1918 Doing Their Bit

Lee, Lester
1932 Men Are Such Fools
Symphony of Six Million
1934 Beloved

Lee, Lila
1925 The Midnight Girl
1926 Broken Hearts
1928 United States Smith
1929 Love, Live and Laugh
1932 The Unfortunate Bride
1934 Stand Up and Cheer!
1937 Nation Aflame

Lee, Lora
1942   Holiday Inn

Lee, Luana
1957   Raintree County

Lee, Mabel
1947   Reet, Petite and Gone
1947?   Swanee Showboat

Lee, May
1955   The Rose Tattoo

Lee, Moe
1920   The Good-Bad Wife

Lee, Palmer *see* **Palmer, Gregg**

Lee, Patricia *not the same as* **Lee, Patsy**
1938   In Old Chicago

Lee, Patsy *not the same as* **Lee, Patricia**
1933   It's Great to Be Alive
1938   In Old Chicago

Lee, Peggy
1953   The Jazz Singer

Lee, Phyllis
1933   Broken Dreams

Lee, Preston
1948   The Lady from Shanghai

Lee, Rae M.
1959   The Hanging Tree

Lee, Raymond
1921   No Woman Knows

Lee, Robert N.
1931   Little Caesar

Lee, Rowland V. *same as* **Lee, Rowland** *not the same as* **Leigh, Rowland**
1920   Dangerous Days
1928   The Secret Hour
1930   Galas de la Paramount
        Ladies Love Brutes
1931   The Guilty Generation

Lee, Rudy
1951   Queen for a Day

Lee, Ruta
1958   Marjorie Morningstar

Lee, Ruth
1943   Mexican Spitfire's Blessed Event
1944   Hi, Beautiful
        Tucson Raiders
1946   Cuban Pete
1947   Dark Delusion
1958   Wild Is the Wind

Lee, Scott
1953   San Antone
        Seminole

Lee, Sung
1945   Samurai

Lee, Veronica
1919   Mandarin's Gold

Lee, Virginia
1950   The Daughter of Rosie O'Grady

Lee, William A.
1957   Edge of the City

Lee Thompson, J.
1960   I Aim at the Stars: the Wernher von Braun Story

Leeds, Andrea *same as* **Lees, Antoinette**
1935   ¡Asegure a su mujer!
1937   It Could Happen to You

Leeds, Herbert I.
1939   The Cisco Kid and the Lady
        City in Darkness
        Mr. Moto in Danger Island
        The Return of the Cisco Kid
1941   Ride on Vaquero
        Romance of the Rio Grande

Leeds, Lila
1948   Moonrise

Leeds, Meredith
1950   Annie Get Your Gun
1951   Show Boat

Leeds, Peter
1943   Crash Dive
1952   My Man and I

Leedy, Glenn
1946   Song of the South

Lees, Antoinette *see* **Leeds, Andrea**

Lees, Paul
1951   Warpath

Lees, Robert
1947   Buck Privates Come Home

Leewood, Jack
1950   Bandit Queen
        Train to Tombstone

LeFevre, Ned
1956   The Benny Goodman Story

Leff, Abraham
1933   The Eternal Jew
1937   Where Is My Child?

Leffingwell, Tom
1947   Buffalo Bill Rides Again

Lefton, Abe
1935   Melody Trail

Leftwich, Alexander
1937   Waikiki Wedding
1938   The Buccaneer

Leftwich, William
1948   The Fight Never Ends

LeGon, Jeni
1939   Double Deal
1940   While Thousands Cheer
1941   Birth of the Blues
1942   Take My Life
1943   Stormy Weather
1947   Hi De Ho
1953   Bright Road

Le Guere, George
1918   The Birth of a Race

Lehman, Gladys
1934   Behold My Wife!
1937   Slave Ship
1942   Rio Rita

Lehman, John
1953   Beneath the 12-Mile Reef

Lehmann, Lotte
1948   Big City

Lehr, Anna
1916   Civilization's Child
        Ramona
1918   The Birth of a Race
        Laughing Bill Hyde
1923   Ruggles of Red Gap
1948   Unconquered

Lehrer, Shifra
1950   God, Man and Devil

Lehrman, Henry
1926   The Fighting Edge
1927   Sailor Izzy Murphy

Leiber, Fritz
1917   The Primitive Call
1936   Down to the Sea
        Sins of Man
1938   Gateway
1940   The Way of All Flesh
1944   Cry of the Werewolf
1945   The Cisco Kid Returns
1947   Dangerous Venture
        Humoresque
1950   Devil's Doorway

Leibfreed, Edwin
1919   Deliverance

Leibgold, Leon
1941   Mazel Tov Yidden

Leicester, William F.
1950   Battleground
        Mystery Street

Leichter, Mitchell
1935   Riddle Ranch

Leigh, Frank
1919   The Sleeping Lion
1920   The Cup of Fury
        Dangerous Days
1935   Rescue Squad

Leigh, George *not the same as* **Lee, George T.**
1945   Nob Hill
        Salome, Where She Danced
1948   Gentleman's Agreement
1953   Fort Ti

Leigh, Janet
1952   It's a Big Country: An American Anthology
1958   Touch of Evil

Leigh, Julian *same as* **Leigh, Julien**
1937   The Cantor's Son
        The Jester (Der Purimspieler)
1939   A Brivele der Mamen
        The Light Ahead
        Mamele
        Mirele Efros
1940   Overture to Glory

Leigh, Nelson
1946   The Sailor Takes a Wife
1950   Jolson Sings Again
1951   Hurricane Island
1952   Bugles in the Afternoon
1959   Imitation of Life
1960   The Dark at the Top of the Stairs

Leigh, Rowland *not the same as* **Lee, Rowland V.**
1944   Knickerbocker Holiday

Leigh, Vivien
1939   Gone With the Wind
1951   A Streetcar Named Desire

Leighton, Frank
1934   Operator 13

Leighton, Fred
1916   The Colored American Winning His Suit

Leighton, Jean
1949   The Red Menace

Leighton, Lillian *same as* **Leighton, Lillianne**
1916   Witchcraft
1917   Castles for Two
        The Little American
1921   The Girl from God's Country
1922   Saturday Night
1923   Ruggles of Red Gap
1925   The Thundering Herd
1927   California
        The Frontiersman
1930   The Grand Parade
        The Last Dance
1933   Man from Monterey
1934   Behold My Wife!

Leighton, Winifred
1918   The Golden Wall

Leisen, Mitchell *same as* **Leisen, "Mitele"**
1931   The Squaw Man
1934   Behold My Wife!
1941   Hold Back the Dawn
1953   Tonight We Sing

Leith, Virginia
1955   Violent Saturday
        White Feather

Leitzbach, Adeline
1929   The Peacock Fan

Leland, Harry
1933   Circle Canyon

Lem, Grace
1939   King of Chinatown
1945   Betrayal from the East
1948   The Lady from Shanghai

LeMay, Alan
1948   Tap Roots
1950   Rocky Mountain
1955   The Vanishing American

Le Mesurier, John
1959   Shake Hands with the Devil
1960   The Day They Robbed the Bank of England

Lemons, Eddie
1940   The Notorious Elinor Lee

Le Moyne, Charles
1923   Crashin' Thru

Lemport, Fay
1920   Huckleberry Finn

Lemuels, William
1935   His Family Tree

Lenard, Grace
1941   Playmates
1951   Queen for a Day
1955   Foxfire

Lengyel, Melchior
1934   Caravane

Leni, Paul
1927   The Chinese Parrot

Lenihan, Winifred
1949   Jigsaw

Lennart, Isobel
1949   The Kissing Bandit
1952   It's a Big Country: An American Anthology

Lennick, Ben
1958   Flaming Frontier

Lennon, Thomas *same as* **Lennon, Thomas Lloyd**
1932   Men Are Such Fools
1936   Silly Billies
1944   Knickerbocker Holiday

Lenny, Ben
1942   Woman of the Year

Lenoir, Leon
1947   The Foxes of Harrow
        Ride the Pink Horse

Le Noire, Rosetta
1959   Anna Lucasta

Lenox, Frank
1918   Love's Law

Lenrow, Bernard
1945   The House on 92nd St.

Lent, Jill
1956   Giant

Lent, Judy
1956   Giant

Lenya, Lotte
1931   Die Dreigroschenoper

Leon, Connie
1941   Where Did You Get That Girl?
1942   Cat People
        Tales of Manhattan
1944   Going My Way

Leon, Jimmy
1935   Captured in Chinatown

Leon, Peggy
1934   Broadway Bill
1944   They Live in Fear
1945   Jealousy
1946   Cuban Pete
1951   The Great Caruso

Leonard, Ada
1937   Music for Madame

Leonard, Arthur
1939   The Devil's Daughter
        Straight to Heaven
194-   Mistaken Identity
1947   Boy! What a Girl!
        Sepia Cinderella

Leonard, Barbara
1930   Monsieur le Fox (*foreign version*)
        Son of the Gods
1932   L'athlète incomplet
        Le plombier amoureux
1934   La veuve joyeuse
1935   ¡Asegure a su mujer!
        L'homme des Folies Bergère
        Julieta compra un hijo
        Señora casada necesita marido
1939   City in Darkness

Leonard, Betty
1945   Where Do We Go From Here?

Leonard, David
1933   Victims of Persecution
1946   Don Ricardo Returns
        Rendezvous 24
1947   Bells of San Fernando
1948   Big City
1949   The Daring Caballero
1950   Border Treasure
1953   The Jazz Singer
1955   Trial

Leonard, Eddie
1940   If I Had My Way

Leonard, Gus
1931   Smart Money

Leonard, Herbert
1953   Conquest of Cochise

Leonard, J. N. *not the same as*
Leonard, Jack
1917　His Sweetheart
Leonard, Jack *not the same as*
Leonard, J. N.
1931　Cimarron
1936　The Glory Trail
1952　My Man and I
1953　Cry of the Hunted
1957　Gun Battle at Monterey
Leonard, M. *(prod)*
1923　Fashion Row
Leonard, Murray *(actor)*
1950　Young Man with a Horn
Leonard, Queenie
1960　All the Fine Young
　　　Cannibals
Leonard, Robert Z.
1916　The Love Girl
1919　The Delicious Little Devil
1922　Peacock Alley
1923　Fashion Row
1932　The Son-Daughter
1940　New Moon
1942　We Were Dancing
Leonard, Sheldon
1942　Tortilla Flat
1946　The Gentleman
　　　Misbehaves
1948　Open Secret
　　　Shep Comes Home
1950　The Iroquois Trail
Leonardo & Zola
1947　Sepia Cinderella
Leone, Danny
1945　The House on 92nd St.
Leone, Henry *same as* **Leone,**
Henri
1915　Cohen's Luck
　　　The Melting Pot
1918　My Cousin
　　　The Ordeal of Rosetta
1922　Fair Lady
Leone, Johnny
1958　The Last Hurrah
Leong, James B. *same as* **Leong,**
James
1921　Lotus Blossom
1923　Purple Dawn
1924　Defying the Law
1928　Ransom
1934　The Cat's-Paw
1935　Charlie Chan in Shanghai
1937　Shadows of the Orient
1942　Across the Pacific
　　　Submarine Raider
1946　Shadows Over Chinatown
1949　Boston Blackie's Chinese
　　　Venture
Leontovich, Eugenie
1952　Anything Can Happen
Leopold, Ethelreda
1947　Calendar Girl
Leovalli, Emilia
1934　La buenaventura
　　　Tres amores
1935　El cantante de Nápoles
　　　Te quiero con locura
1938　Castillos en el aire
　　　Mis dos amores
1939　Los hijos mandan
1940　Tengo fe en ti
Le Pera, Alfredo
1933　Espérame
　　　Melodía de arrabal
1934　Cuesta abajo
　　　El tango en Broadway
1935　El día que me quieras
　　　Tango Bar
Lepere, Paul
1940　They Knew What They
　　　Wanted
Lerch, Georgia
1930　Whoopee
Lerch, Theodore
1920　The Last of the Mohicans
Lern, Bessie *see* **Learn, Bessie**
Lerna, Irma
1925　Salome of the Tenements

Lerner, Irving
1959　Anna Lucasta
1960　Studs Lonigan
Lerner, Joseph *same as* **Lerner,**
Joe
1948　The Fight Never Ends
1949　C-Man
Lerner, M. *not the same as* **Lerner,**
Murray
1940　Americaner Schadchen
Lerner, Murray *not the same as*
Lerner, M.
1950　Bandit Queen
　　　The Baron of Arizona
　　　Train to Tombstone
Le Roux, Carmen *see* **La Roux,**
Carmen
Leroy, Dickie
1953　The Eddie Cantor Story
LeRoy, Hal
1940　Too Many Girls
LeRoy, Mervyn
1926　Irene
1928　Flying Romeos
1931　Gentleman's Fate
　　　Little Caesar
1932　The Heart of New York
1939　Stand Up and Fight
1940　Escape
1946　Without Reservations
1958　Home Before Dark
1959　The FBI Story
Lert, Richard
1956　Serenade
Les Hite and His Cotton Club
Orchestra
1937　Bargain with Bullets
Le Saint, Edward J. *same as* **Le**
Saint, E. J.; Le Saint, Ed; Le
Saint, Edward
1916　The Honorable Friend
　　　The Soul of Kura-San
1917　The Squaw Man's Son
1919　Fighting for Gold
　　　The Sneak
1920　The Girl of My Heart
1932　Thirteen Women
1933　Broken Dreams
　　　The Cohens and Kellys in
　　　Trouble
1935　Chinatown Squad
　　　A Night at the Ritz
　　　Ruggles of Red Gap
1936　Below the Deadline
　　　Dangerous Intrigue
　　　Dimples
1937　Man of the People
1938　My Lucky Star
　　　The Texans
Le Saint, Stella
1937　Maid of Salem
1949　The Undercover Man
Lesberg, Jack
1957　Satchmo the Great
LeSeur, Hal
1938　The Toy Wife
Lesli, Kym
1959　Last Train from Gun Hill
Leslie, Edith
1947　Jiggs and Maggie in
　　　Society
Leslie, Frank
1930　King of Jazz
Leslie, Gladys
1916　Betrayed
1918　The Little Runaway
1919　The Gray Towers Mystery
Leslie, Joan
1943　Yankee Doodle Dandy
1945　Rhapsody in Blue
　　　Where Do We Go From
　　　Here?
Leslie, Kay
1941　Where Did You Get That
　　　Girl?
Leslie, Lawrence
1929　Why Bring That Up?
Leslie, Lila
1923　The Huntress

Leslie, Marguerite
1919?　The Chosen Path
Leslie, Maxine
1940　Doomed to Die
1941　Caught in the Act
1943　Crime Smasher
Leslie, Nan
1945　Wanderer of the
　　　Wasteland
1946　Sunset Pass
1947　Under the Tonto Rim
　　　Wild Horse Mesa
1948　The Arizona Ranger
　　　Guns of Hate
　　　Indian Agent
　　　Western Heritage
1950　Train to Tombstone
Leslie, William
1954　Taza, Son of Cochise
1955　The Long Gray Line
1956　7th Cavalry
　　　The White Squaw
1958　The Last Hurrah
Lesser, Budd
1950　Bandit Queen
Lesser, Julian
1949　Massacre River
Lesser, Sol
1922　My Boy
1936　Let's Sing Again
　　　Rainbow on the River
1937　The Californian
1938　Breaking the Ice
　　　Hawaii Calls
1939　Fisherman's Wharf
　　　Way Down South
Lesser, Ted
1937　Souls at Sea
Lessey, George
1921　A Divorce of
　　　Convenience
1938　Birthright
1944　Buffalo Bill
　　　Charlie Chan in the
　　　Secret Service
Lessing, Marion
1931　Buster se marie *(foreign*
　　　version)
　　　La gran jornada *(foreign*
　　　version)
Lessy, Ben
1947　Dark Delusion
1950　The Jackie Robinson Story
Lester, Bill *not the same as* **Lester,**
William
1950　The Girl from San
　　　Lorenzo
Lester, Bruce
1953　The Pathfinder
Lester, Elliott
1929　Frozen Justice
Lester, Ezella
1955　Brevities of 1955
Lester, Jack
1959　The Sheriff of Fractured
　　　Jaw
Lester, Kate
1917　The Adventures of Carol
1918　Broken Ties
　　　Doing Their Bit
　　　The Golden Wall
　　　The Unbeliever
1920　The Cup of Fury
　　　The Paliser Case
1921　Made in Heaven
Lester, Louise
1918　The Reckoning Day
1920　The Luck of the Irish
Lester, Susan
1945　A Tree Grows in Brooklyn
Lester, Vicki
1941　You're Out of Luck
Lester, Vonne
1946　Sunset Pass
1949　The Girl from Jones
　　　Beach
Lester, William *not the same as*
Lester, Bill
1921　The Double O
1922　The Crow's Nest
1925　Galloping Vengeance

Lestina, Adolphe *same as* **Lestina,**
Adolph
1916　The Yellow Passport
1918　The Greatest Thing in
　　　Life
　　　The Hun Within
1919　Scarlet Days
L'Estrange, Dick *same as* **Le**
Strange, Dick; Lestrange, Dick
1914　The Squaw Man
1942　Professor Creeps
1945　The Cisco Kid Returns
　　　In Old New Mexico
Letondal, Henri
1947　The Foxes of Harrow
1951　Across the Wide Missouri
1952　The Big Sky
Lettieri, Louis
1951　Cyclone Fury
1959　The Last Angry Man
Letuli, Fred
1954　They Rode West
Letz, George *see* **Montgomery,**
George
Leung, Mae
1939　Mr. Moto Takes a
　　　Vacation
Levant, Oscar
1945　Rhapsody in Blue
1947　Humoresque
Levee, M. C.
1923　Jealous Husbands
1926　Sweet Daddies
Levene, Sam
1936　After the Thin Man
1942　Sunday Punch
1943　Action in the North
　　　Atlantic
1947　Crossfire
Levenstein, Fannie
1935　The Yiddish King Lear
Leverett, Lew
1948　Gentleman's Agreement
Levering, Joseph
1917　The Little Samaritan
1931　La cautivadora
1939　Frontiers of '49
Levette, Harry
1942　Lucky Ghost
　　　Take My Life
Levey, Jules
1947　New Orleans
Levien, Sonya
1919　Who Will Marry Me?
1921　Cheated Love
1925　Salome of the Tenements
1927　A Harp in Hock
　　　The Princess from
　　　Hoboken
1928　A Ship Comes In
　　　A Ship Comes In *(foreign*
　　　version)
1929　Frozen Justice
　　　The Younger Generation
1931　Delicious
1936　Ramona
1938　In Old Chicago
1939　Drums Along the Mohawk
1943　The Amazing Mrs.
　　　Holliday
1945　Rhapsody in Blue
　　　The Valley of Decision
1951　The Great Caruso
Levigne, Maurice
1920　Humoresque
Levin, Chana
1939　A Brivele der Mamen
Levin, Henry
1944　Cry of the Werewolf
1950　Jolson Sings Again
Levin, Irving H.
1960　Hell to Eternity
Levin, Lucy *see* **Levine, Lucy**
Levin, Meyer, Sgt.
1944　The Negro Soldier
Levin, Robert
1958　The Last Hurrah
Levine, Anna
1938　Two Sisters

Levine, Helen
1927   Frisco Sally Levy
Levine, Isaac Don
1943   Jack London
Levine, Joe
1943   Yankee Doodle Dandy
Levine, Lucy *same as* **Levin, Lucy**
1931   Zein Weib's Lubovnick
1937   The Holy Oath
Levine, Nat
1934   The Lone Defender
1935   Harmony Lane
        The Singing Vagabond
1936   Down to the Sea
        Laughing Irish Eyes
        Ride, Ranger, Ride
1937   The Riders of the
        Whistling Skull
Levine, Saul
1937   Green Fields
Leviness, Carl
1917   The Spirit of '76
1938   The Buccaneer
1942   Sunday Punch
Le Vino, Albert Shelby
1918   The Only Road
1924   The Heritage of the
        Desert
1927   Turkish Delight
Levinson, Arthur
1941   The Face Behind the
        Mask
Levinson, Charles *see* **Lane, Charles**
Levinson, Joseph
1949   Shamrock Hill
Levinson, Morris M.
1932   The Black King
Levinson, Selvyn
1947   The Burning Cross
Levitan, Gertrude
1932   Joseph in the Land of
        Egypt
Levitt, Alfred Lewis
1948   The Boy with Green Hair
1953   Dream Wife
Levitt, Helen
1949   The Quiet One
Levitt, Paul
1951   The Mark of the
        Renegade
1959   Imitation of Life
Levitt, Saul
1948   Strange Victory
Levitt, William
1949   The Quiet One
Levoy, Albert E.
1936   The Bold Caballero
Levy, Melvin
1936   Robin Hood of El Dorado
1952   Trail of the Arrow
1953   The Great Sioux Uprising
Levy, P. H.
1934   Broadway Bill
Levy, Robert
1921   The Sport of the Gods
Levy, Weaver
1945   Betrayal from the East
1947   Little Mister Jim
1948   Half Past Midnight
1952   Japanese War Bride
Lew, Shirley
1943   The Amazing Mrs.
        Holliday
1947   Little Mister Jim
Lewandowski, Manfried
1940   Overture to Glory
Lewin, A. *(actress)*
1936   Yiddle with His Fiddle
Lewin, Albert *(prod, writer) not the same as* **Lewis, Albert** *(prod)*
1926   Blarney
1938   Spawn of the North
Lewis and White
1948?   Boarding House Blues
Lewis, Ada
1917   Her Own People

Lewis, Albert *(prod) not the same as* **Lewin, Albert** *(prod, wrt)*
1943   Cabin in the Sky
Lewis, Allan
1958   Sierra Baron
Lewis, Arthur
1953   Conquest of Cochise
Lewis, Ben
1916   A Sister of Six
1917   The Spirit of '76
1918   Marked Cards
Lewis, Bill *(writer)*
1940   Northwest Passage (Book
        I—Rogers' Rangers)
Lewis, Blaney
1943   His Butler's Sister
Lewis, Carlo
1950   The Men
Lewis, Catherine
1940   Little Nellie Kelly
1942   Wings for the Eagle
Lewis, Danny
1959   The Black Orchid
Lewis, David
1942   In This Our Life
1957   Raintree County
Lewis, Diana
1942   Seven Sweethearts
Lewis, Dorothy
1941   Ice-Capades
Lewis, Ed "Strangler" *(actor)*, d. 1966
1942   Gentleman Jim
Lewis, Eddie *(African-American actor)*
1945   Johnny Angel
Lewis, Edgar *(dir)*, d. 1938
1914   The Littlest Rebel
        Northern Lights
1915   The Nigger
1916   The Flames of Johannis
        Light at Dusk
1917   The Bar Sinister
        The Barrier
1919   Love and the Law
1925   Red Love
Lewis, Edward *(writer)*, circa 1959
1959   Last Train from Gun Hill
Lewis, Elliott
1951   Saturday's Hero
Lewis, Eugene B.
1920   Uncharted Channels
Lewis, Ferdie
1932   Harlem Is Heaven
Lewis, Forrest
1953   The Stand at Apache
        River
1955   Apache Ambush
1957   Man in the Shadow
Lewis, Franklin
1929   Mister Antonio
Lewis, Gene
1951   Flaming Feather
Lewis, George *same as* **Lewis, George J.; Lewis, Jorge** *not the same as* **Lewis, George "Beetlepuss"**
1925   His People
1928   We Americans
1930   El último de los Vargas
1931   Cuerpo y alma
        La gran jornada
1932   Marido y mujer
1933   No dejes la puerta abierta
1934   Lazy River
1935   Alas sobre el Chaco
1936   Ride, Ranger, Ride
1937   El capitán Tormenta
        El carnaval del diablo
1938   Di que me quieres
1941   Road Agent
1944   Charlie Chan in the
        Secret Service
1945   The Gay Senorita
        South of the Rio Grande
1946   Beauty and the Bandit
        South of Monterey
1947   Pirates of Monterey
1948   Docks of New Orleans
        The Feathered Serpent
        Renegades of Sonora
        Silver Trails
        Tap Roots

1949   The Dalton Gang
1952   The Iron Mistress
        The Raiders
1954   Drum Beat
        Saskatchewan
1957   The Brothers Rico
1958   Gunman's Walk
1960   The Sign of Zorro
Lewis, George "Beetlepuss" *not the same as* **Lewis, George**
1948   Half Past Midnight
Lewis, H. Clyde *(writer)*
1939   Fisherman's Wharf
Lewis, Harrison *(actor) not the same as* **Lewis, Harry** *(actor)*
1959   The Crimson Kimono
Lewis, Harry *(actor) not the same as* **Lewis, Harrison** *(actor)*
1942   Secret Enemies
        They Died With Their
        Boots On
1943   Air Force
1948   Key Largo
Lewis, Ida
1915   The Alien
Lewis, Jacqueline
1938   God's Step Children
Lewis, Jarma
1957   Raintree County
Lewis, Jean Ann
1957   Journey to Freedom
Lewis, Jeanetta
1953   So Big
Lewis, Jeffrys
1922   Peacock Alley
Lewis, Jessie
1916   Broken Chains
Lewis, Jimmy
1960   Cimarron
Lewis, John *(musician)*
1947   Jivin' in Be-Bop
Lewis, John E. *(actor)*
1950   Panic in the Streets
Lewis, Jorge *see* **Lewis, George**
Lewis, Joseph H.
1944   Minstrel Man
1947   The Jolson Story
1949   The Undercover Man
1950   A Lady Without Passport
1953   Cry of the Hunted
1956   7th Cavalry
1957   The Halliday Brand
1958   Terror in a Texas Town
Lewis, Joy
1917   Her Own People
Lewis, L. E.
1946   Dirty Gertie from
        Harlem, U.S.A.
Lewis, Mae Evlyn
1922   The Greatest Sin
Lewis, Meade Lux
1943   Cabin in the Sky
1947   New Orleans
Lewis, Mel
1958   Kings Go Forth
Lewis, Mildred
1933   It's Great to Be Alive
Lewis, Mitchell
1916   The Flower of No Man's
        Land
1917   The Bar Sinister
        The Barrier
1918   The Million Dollar
        Mystery
1919   The Last of His People
1923   The Miracle Makers
1924   The Mine with the Iron
        Door
1926   The Last Frontier
1928   The Hawk's Nest
1931   The Squaw Man
1936   Dancing Pirate
        Sutter's Gold
1937   Big City
        Waikiki Wedding
1939   Let Freedom Ring
        Stand Up and Fight
1942   Apache Trail
        Rio Rita
1944   An American Romance
1947   The Mighty McGurk

1949   Border Incident
        The Kissing Bandit
1950   The Toast of New Orleans
1953   The Sun Shines Bright
1955   Trial
Lewis, Ralph d. 1937
1915   The Birth of a Nation
1916   Gretchen, the Greenhorn
        A Sister of Six
1920   Outside the Law
1922   The Five Dollar Baby
        Flesh and Blood
1924   East of Broadway
        Untamed Youth
1925   One of the Bravest
1930   Abraham Lincoln
1934   The Fighting Hero
1937   Maid of Salem
1938   The Buccaneer
Lewis, Ralph circa mid-1940s
1945   The Jade Mask
Lewis, Raymond B.
1932   Amor in montagna
Lewis, Richard
1924   Yankee Speed
Lewis, Sandy
1954   Carmen Jones
Lewis, Sheldon
1916   The King's Game
1926   Buffalo Bill on the U. P.
        Trail
1927   The Overland Stage
1931   Riders of the Rio
1932   Thirteen Steps
Lewis, Sinclair
1919   The Unpainted Woman
Lewis, Sybil *same as* **Lewis, Sybyl**
1940   Am I Guilty?
        Broken Strings
        Mystery in Swing
1944   Going My Way
1947   Boy! What a Girl!
1948   Miracle in Harlem
Lewis, Ted
1929   Is Everybody Happy?
Ted Lewis and His Orchestra
1920?   The Scarlet Dragon
1937   Manhattan
        Merry-Go-Round
Lewis, Tom d. 1927 *not the same as* **Lewis, Tommy**
1927   The Callahans and the
        Murphys
Lewis, Tommy *not the same as* **Lewis, Tom** d. 1927
1951   Teresa
Lewis, Vera
1917   Lost in Transit
        The Trouble Buster
1919   Yvonne from Paris
1928   Ramona
1936   Dancing Pirate
        Paddy O'Day
1937   Maid of Salem
1942   All Through the Night
        They Died With Their
        Boots On
1943   Yankee Doodle Dandy
1944   Mr. Skeffington
1947   It Had To Be You
Lewis, Walter *same as* **Lewis, Walter P.**
1915   The Gambler of the West
1918   Out of a Clear Sky
        Uncle Tom's Cabin
1930   The Arizona Kid
1931   Cimarron
Lewis, Will
1950   Intruder in the Dust
Lewton, Val
1942   Cat People
1943   The Leopard Man
1951   Apache Drums
Leyba, Claire
1946?   Fight That Ghost
1959   Anna Lucasta
Leytes, Josef
1954   Passion
Leyton, Drue
1934   Charlie Chan in London
        Charlie Chan's Courage
1936   Charlie Chan at the
        Circus

Leyva, Dora
1943   The Leopard Man
Leyva, Frank
1936   Ramona
1948   The Feathered Serpent
Lezard, Cecile
1951   Native Son
Libby, Fred
1948   Fury at Furnace Creek
1949   The Fighting Kentuckian
    She Wore a Yellow
      Ribbon
    3 Godfathers
1950   The Cariboo Trail
1960   Sergeant Rutledge
Liberty, Bryson G.
1956   Pillars of the Sky
Libott, Robert
1949   Arctic Fury
1950   Chinatown at Midnight
Lichter, Baron *same as* **Lichter, B.**
1935   So Red the Rose
1936   Daniel Boone
1938   The Buccaneer
1948   Jiggs and Maggie in Court
1950   The Daughter of Rosie
      O'Grady
    The Furies
    Stars in My Crown
1959   The Hanging Tree
    Last Train from Gun Hill
Lichtman, Al
1958   The Young Lions
Liddell, Jane
1956   Westward Ho the
      Wagons!
Lieb, Herman
1924   Two Shall Be Born
Liebgold, Leon *same as* **Liebgold, L.**
1936   Yiddle with His Fiddle
1939   Kol Nidre
    Tevya
Liebmann, Robert
1934   Caravane
Ligero, Miguel
1930   Doña mentiras
1931   Charlie Chan Carries On
      (foreign version)
    Chérie *(foreign version)*
    ¿Conoces a tu mujer?
    La fiesta del diablo
    Hay que casar al príncipe
    La ley del harem
    Sombras del circo
    Su noche de bodas
1938   La vida bohemia
Liggett, Amelia
1946   Saratoga Trunk
Lighton, Louis D. *same as* **Lighton, Louis Duryea**
1922   Flesh and Blood
1923   April Showers
1924   The Mine with the Iron
      Door
1945   A Tree Grows in Brooklyn
Liguoro, Countess Rina de *see* **De Liguoro, Rina**
Likes, Don *same as* **Lykes, Don**
1918   Sandy
Lilburn, James
1952   The Quiet Man
1953   San Antone
    The Sun Shines Bright
1955   Fort Yuma
    The Long Gray Line
1956   Mohawk
Liliana, Lili
1939   Kol Nidre
1941   Mazel Tov Yidden
Lilien, Kurt
1931   Chérie *(foreign version)*
Lillard, Joe
1947   Reet, Petite and Gone
Lillian, Anna
1937   Where Is My Child?
Lillian, Isadore
1930   My Yiddishe Mama
Lilly, Dolores Mae
1936   The Green Pastures

Lim, Jim
1945   Escape in the Fog
Lima, Alberto de
1930   Revista
      Hispano-Americana
Linaker, Kay
1938   Charlie Chan at Monte
      Carlo
1939   Charlie Chan in Reno
    Drums Along the Mohawk
    Heaven with a Barbed
      Wire Fence
1940   Charlie Chan's Murder
      Cruise
1941   Charlie Chan in Rio
    They Dare Not Love
1943   Wintertime
Liñán, Filomena
1935   Julieta compra un hijo
Liñán, Matilde
1930   La jaula de los leones
1939   La Inmaculada
Lince, John
1918   Untamed
1921   Guile of Women
1923   The Huntress
Lincer, William
1947   Carnegie Hall
Lincoln, Caryl
1934   Charlie Chan's Courage
Lincoln, E. K.
1914   The Littlest Rebel
1919   Desert Gold
Lincoln, Elmo
1915   The Birth of a Nation
1918   The Greatest Thing in
      Life
1919   Deliverance
1923   Fashion Row
1943   Frontier Fury
1945   Escape in the Fog
1948   Tap Roots
Lincoln, Rose Lee *same as* **Lincoln, Rosa Lee**
1928   Absent
1938   Two Gun Man from
      Harlem
Lind, Charles
1941   Adam Had Four Sons
1949   The Story of Seabiscuit
Lind, Christina
1951   Show Boat
Lind, Jenny
1919   Deliverance
Lind, Sarah
1919   Deliverance
Lindan, Tove
1935   Circle of Death
Lindau, Rolf *same as* **Lindau, Rudolf**
1942   Secret Enemies
1943   Action in the North
      Atlantic
1945   The Dolly Sisters
Lindbom, Carl
1938   The Buccaneer
Linden, Eric
1936   Robin Hood of El Dorado
1939   Gone With the Wind
Linden, Marta
1942   Three Hearts for Julia
1944   Andy Hardy's Blonde
      Trouble
Linden, Virginia
1954   Dangerous Mission
Linder, Alfred
1945   The House on 92nd St.
1950   Black Hand
1957   Trooper Hook
Linder, Cecil
1958   Flaming Frontier
Lindfors, Viveca
1952   The Raiders
1957   The Halliday Brand
1960   Weddings and Babies
Lindgren, Alex
1941   Sun Valley Serenade
Lindgren, Orley
1943   Hitler's Children
1950   Young Man with a Horn
1952   Japanese War Bride
    The Savage

Lindley, Bert
1922   The Crow's Nest
1936   After the Thin Man
Lindquist, Jack
1944   Chip Off the Old Block
1948   The Miracle of the Bells
Lindroth, Helen
1916   The Innocent Lie
Lindsay, Margaret
1935   Bordertown
1937   Song of the City
1943   Let's Have Fun
1945   Club Havana
Lindsay, Powell *same as* **Lindsey, Powell**
1946   That Man of Mine
1947   Jivin' in Be-Bop
1949   Souls of Sin
Lindsey, Ben B., Judge
1937   One Mile from Heaven
Lindsey, Marilyn
1951   Westward the Women
Lindsey, Powell *see* **Lindsay, Powell**
Lindsley, Frederick
1937   Black Legion
Lindstrand, Fred
1931   Delicious
Linehan, Tony
1951   Saturday's Hero
Liney, Jack
1937   Dark Manhattan
Ling, Bo
1935   Captured in Chinatown
Ling, Eugene
1949   Lost Boundaries
Lingham, Thomas *same as* **Lingham, Thomas G.; Lingham, Tom**
1922   The Crow's Nest
1924   The Lightning Rider
1927   With Sitting Bull at the
      Spirit Lake Massacre
1928   Orphan of the Sage
    The Rawhide Kid
1929   The Invaders
1934   The Star Packer
Link, John F.
1949   Call of the Forest
Linn, Frank
1946   Sheriff of Redwood Valley
Linn, Ralph
1944   Address Unknown
1947   The Jolson Story
Linow, Ivan
1929   In Old Arizona
1934   The Cat's-Paw
Linton, Shorty
1953   The Joe Louis Story
Lion, Margo
1931   Die Dreigroschenoper
      (foreign version)
Lipman, Clara
1930   Sins of the Children
Lipman, Harry
1927   Lost at the Front
Lipman, William R. *same as* **Lipman, William**
1934   Behold My Wife!
1938   Dangerous to Know
1946   Bad Bascomb
1947   The Mighty McGurk
Lippe, Edouard, Dr.
1935   Naughty Marietta
Lippert, Robert L.
1946   Renegade Girl
1949   Apache Chief
    The Dalton Gang
1950   Bandit Queen
    The Baron of Arizona
    Train to Tombstone
1951   Little Big Horn
    The Steel Helmet
Lipson, Tiny
1946   Bringing Up Father
Lipton, Albert
1939   Mirele Efros
Lipton, Lew
1927   Frisco Sally Levy
1928   The Cameraman

Lindley, Bert

Lishman, Harold
1942   Song of the Islands
Lisle, Betsy Ann
1927   The Way of All Flesh
Liswood, Mary
1950   Panic in the Streets
Lisz, Hazel
1938   Birthright
Liszt, Margie
1953   Dream Wife
Litel, John *same as* **Litel, John B.**
1930   On the Border
1937   Black Legion
1940   The Fighting 69th
    Knute Rockne—All
      American
    Santa Fe Trail
1942   They Died With Their
      Boots On
1944   Lake Placid Serenade
1945   Salome, Where She
      Danced
1947   Easy Come, Easy Go
1949   Shamrock Hill
    The Valiant Hombre
1951   Cuban Fireball
1954   Sitting Bull
1956   Comanche
    The Wild Dakotas
1958   Houseboat
Litman, Moshe
1934   The Rabbi's Power
Liton, Eni
1937   The Jester (Der
      Purimspieler)
"Little Brown Jug" *see* **Reynolds, Don**
Little, Ann
1918   The Source
    The Squaw Man
1919   Told in the Hills
Little, Arthur, Jr.
1948   Gentleman's Agreement
1950   The Iroquois Trail
Little, Eddie *see* **Little Sky, Eddie**
Little, Herbert, Jr.
1957   Trooper Hook
Little, James
1949   House of Strangers
1953   Taxi
Little, Mickey
1949   The Daring Caballero
1952   It's a Big Country: An
      American Anthology
1955   Bad Day at Black Rock
    Blackboard Jungle
Little Angelo *see* **Rossitto, Angelo**
Little Bear
1917   The Conqueror
Little Eagle
1936   Custer's Last Stand
Little Pine
1932   The Rainbow Trail
Little Sky, Dawn
1960   Cimarron
Little Sky, Eddie *same as* **Little, Eddie**
1956   Westward Ho the
      Wagons!
1957   Apache Warrior
    Revolt at Fort Laramie
    Tomahawk Trail
1958   Gun Fever
    The Light in the Forest
    Ride a Crooked Trail
    Tonka
1959   The FBI Story
1960   Cimarron
Littlefield, Lucien
1917   The Squaw Man's Son
1928   A Ship Comes In
    Uncle Tom's Cabin
1929   This Is Heaven
1930   Tom Sawyer
1934   Stand Up and Cheer!
1935   Ruggles of Red Gap
1936   Let's Sing Again
1937   Souls at Sea
1942   Castle in the Desert

Lindsay, Margaret

Lindsay, Powell

Lindsey, Ben B., Judge

Lindsey, Marilyn

1944 Lady, Let's Dance!
Littrell, Helen
1938 The Buccaneer
Litvak, Anatole
1939 Confessions of a Nazi Spy
Litwina, Berta
1937 The Jester (Der Purimspieler)
Liu, Lotus
1937 Waikiki Wedding
Liu, Maurice
1937 Waikiki Wedding
1938 Daughter of Shanghai
Lively, Bob
1936 Custer's Last Stand
Lively, William
1937 Nation Aflame
1943 Wagon Tracks West
Livingston, Jack
1916 A Son of Erin
1918 The Price of Applause
   Who Is to Blame?
1920 A Tokio Siren
Livingston, Margaret
1926 A Trip to Chinatown
1928 Wheel of Chance
1931 Smart Money
1932 Call Her Savage
Livingston, Patricia
1957 The Guns of Fort Petticoat
Livingston, Robert *same as* **Livingstone, Robert**
1936 The Bold Caballero
1937 The Riders of the Whistling Skull
1940 Covered Wagon Days
1941 Prairie Pioneers
   Saddlemates
1944 Lake Placid Serenade
1948 The Feathered Serpent
1949 The Mysterious Desperado
Livingston, Sandy
1958 Marjorie Morningstar
Livingstone, Robert *see* **Livingston, Robert**
Llaneza, Luis
1930 Olimpia
   El presidio
1931 Un caballero de frac
   Los calaveras
   Gente alegre
   Monerías
   La mujer X
   El príncipe gondolero
1932 El hombre que asesinó
Llewelyn, Russ
1951 Jim Thorpe—All-American
Llorens Vidal, Luis
1931 Chérie (*foreign version*)
Lloyd, Al *not the same as* **Lloyd, Albert S.**
1939 Waterfront
1940 East of the River
1943 Yankee Doodle Dandy
1953 So Big
Lloyd, Albert S. *not the same as* **Lloyd, Al**
1922 The Half Breed
Lloyd, Charles *not the same as* **Lloyd-Pack, Charles**
1934 Operator 13
Lloyd, Doris
1927 The Auctioneer
1933 Robbers' Roost
1934 She Was a Lady
   Strange Wives
1946 G. I. War Brides
1955 A Man Called Peter
Lloyd, Frank
1921 A Tale of Two Worlds
1930 The Lash
   Son of the Gods
1937 Maid of Salem
1941 This Woman Is Mine
1955 The Last Command
Lloyd, George
1936 Dangerous Intrigue
   Sutter's Gold
1937 Souls at Sea

1938 Little Miss Roughneck
   Mr. Wong, Detective
1939 Waterfront
1940 East of the River
   New Moon
1941 Where Did You Get That Girl?
1942 Gentleman Jim
   Mokey
   Valley of the Sun
1943 The Ox-Bow Incident
1944 Since You Went Away
1945 Nob Hill
1947 California
   Vigilantes of Boomtown
1949 Boston Blackie's Chinese Venture
   Laramie
1954 Drum Beat
Lloyd, Gerrit
1930 Abraham Lincoln
Lloyd, Gladys
1931 Smart Money
1932 The Hatchet Man
Lloyd, Harold
1929 Welcome Danger
1934 The Cat's-Paw
Lloyd, J. Peter
1955 Trial
Lloyd, Jimmy
1945 I Love a Bandleader
1946 The Gentleman Misbehaves
1947 The Jolson Story
1954 Battle of Rogue River
Lloyd, Josie
1960 Studs Lonigan
Lloyd, Norman
1950 Buccaneer's Girl
Lloyd, Patricia
1959 Night of the Quarter Moon
Lloyd, Rollo
1937 Souls at Sea
1938 Spawn of the North
Lloyd-Pack, Charles *not the same as* **Lloyd, Charles**
1960 The Day They Robbed the Bank of England
Loback, Marvin
1934 Broadway Bill
Locher, Charles *see* **Hall, Jon**
Locher, Felix
1959 Thunder in the Sun
1960 Walk Tall
Lock, Lillian
1936 Star for a Night
Locke, Joe
1955 Trial
Locke, Jon
1956 Westward Ho the Wagons!
Lockhart, Gene
1940 Geronimo
1942 Juke Girl
   They Died With Their Boots On
1944 Going My Way
1945 The House on 92nd St.
1947 The Foxes of Harrow
1950 The Big Hangover
1952 Apache War Smoke
1955 The Vanishing American
Lockhart, June
1941 Adam Had Four Sons
Lockhart, Kathleen
1939 Man of Conquest
1948 Gentleman's Agreement
1950 The Big Hangover
Lockhart, Laura
1926 Twin Triggers
Lockhart, Louis
1950 Panic in the Streets
Lockney, J. P.
1916 Civilization's Child
1917 The Bride of Hate
   The Gun Fighter
1919 Behind the Door
1920 Uncharted Channels
1921 The Kiss

Lockwood, Alexander
1949 Jigsaw
Lockwood, Harold
1917 The Hidden Children
Loden, Barbara
1960 Wild River
Loder, John
1929 Love, Live and Laugh
1942 Gentleman Jim
1945 Jealousy
Lodge, John
1935 The Little Colonel
Lodijensky, General
1926 Into Her Kingdom
Loeb, Anne
1936 Love and Sacrifice
Loeb, Janice
1949 The Quiet One
Loeb, Lee
1939 Forged Passport
1940 Lucky Cisco Kid
1947 Calendar Girl
Loeb, Philip
1951 Molly
Loeffler, George
1922 Cardigan
Loeffler, Louis
1931 La gran jornada (*foreign version*)
Loew, Arthur M. (*prod*)
1951 Teresa
Loew, Arthur, Jr. (*actor*)
1950 Ambush
   A Lady Without Passport
   Mystery Street
1951 New Mexico
Loew, Evan
1953 The Man from the Alamo
   So Big
Loff, Jeanette
1928 Hold 'Em Yale
1930 King of Jazz
Loft, Arthur
1934 Stand Up and Cheer!
1936 The Prisoner of Shark Island
1937 The Devil's Playground
1938 City Streets
1941 Hold Back the Dawn
1942 They Died With Their Boots On
   Young America
1943 Dr. Gillespie's Criminal Case
   In Old Oklahoma
   Jack London
   The Meanest Man in the World
   The Outlaw
   Redhead from Manhattan
   Wintertime
1944 Buffalo Bill
   Charlie Chan in the Secret Service
   Chip Off the Old Block
1945 Nob Hill
   The Shanghai Cobra
1946 Sheriff of Redwood Valley
   Till the End of Time
1947 The Jolson Story
Loft-Lynn, Jay
1958 St. Louis Blues
Loftus, Cecilia
1931 Young Sinners
Logan, Gwendolen
1940 Northwest Passage (Book I—Rogers' Rangers)
Logan, Helen
1935 ¡Asegure a su mujer!
   Charlie Chan in Egypt
   Rosa de Francia
1936 Charlie Chan at the Circus
   Charlie Chan at the Race Track
   Charlie Chan's Secret
1937 Charlie Chan at the Olympics
   Charlie Chan on Broadway
   That I May Live

Lockwood, Alexander
1938 Charlie Chan at Monte Carlo
   Rascals
   Road Demon
   Speed to Burn
1939 City in Darkness
   The Escape
1940 Lucky Cisco Kid
1941 Sun Valley Serenade
1942 Song of the Islands
1944 Something for the Boys
Logan, Jacqueline
1929 Sombras habaneras
Logan, James
1946 Notorious
   Till the End of Time
Logan, John
1953 The Man Behind the Gun
   So Big
Logan, Ruby
1939 One Dark Night
Logan, Stanley
1940 Escape to Glory
1942 Twin Beds
1944 Knickerbocker Holiday
1950 Young Daniel Boone
Logian, Satig
1945 Anoush
Logue, Charles *same as* **Logue, Charles A.**
1917 A Wife by Proxy
1919 The Lost Battalion
1927 McFadden's Flats
   Red Clay
1934 Wagon Wheels
Loizeaux, Mayo
1957 Band of Angels
Lollier, George
1931 Cimarron
1942 Three Hearts for Julia
Lom, Herbert
1960 I Aim at the Stars: the Wernher von Braun Story
Lomas, Jack
1945 Where Do We Go From Here?
1949 The Story of Seabiscuit
1950 The Daughter of Rosie O'Grady
1955 Seven Angry Men
1956 The Benny Goodman Story
   Giant
   Reprisal!
   Walk the Proud Land
1959 Last Train from Gun Hill
Lombard, Carole *same as* **Lombard, Carol**
1930 The Arizona Kid
1940 They Knew What They Wanted
Lombard, Linda
1948 Moonrise
Lombardi, Carlo
1930 Toda una vida (*foreign version*)
1931 La carta (*foreign version*)
   Tropennächte (*foreign version*)
Lo Medico, Saverio
1959 The Black Orchid
1960 Pay or Die
Lomma, John
1959 Al Capone
1960 Pay or Die
Lomond, Britt
1958 Tonka
1960 The Sign of Zorro
Lon, Yong Sin
1934 Blossom Time
London, Babe *see* **London, Jean "Babe"**
London, Dirk
1958 Ambush at Cimarron Pass
London, Jean "Babe" *same as* **London, Babe**
1927 The Princess from Hoboken
1948 The Paleface

1949   Anna Lucasta

London, Julie
1948   Tap Roots
1959   Night of the Quarter
        Moon
        The Wonderful Country

London, Samuel H.
1913   The Inside of the White
        Slave Traffic
1918   Her Moment

London, Tom
1933   Thundering Herd
1934   The Cactus Kid
        The Fighting Hero
        The Prescott Kid
1936   Ramona
1938   The Renegade Ranger
1940   Covered Wagon Days
        The Gay Caballero
        Hi-Yo Silver
        Northwest Passage (Book
        I—Rogers' Rangers)
        Viva Cisco Kid
1941   Romance of the Rio
        Grande
        Western Union
1942   Valley of the Sun
1943   In Old Oklahoma
        The Ox-Bow Incident
        Wagon Tracks West
1944   Marshal of Reno
        Riding West
        The San Antonio Kid
        Vigilantes of Dodge City
1945   Colorado Pioneers
        Phantom of the Plains
1946   California Gold Rush
        Santa Fe Uprising
        Sheriff of Redwood Valley
        Sun Valley Cyclone
1947   Marshal of Cripple Creek
        Rustlers of Devil's
        Canyon
1952   Apache Country
        High Noon

Londregan, W. J.
1940   The Ramparts We Watch

Lone Pine
1936   Custer's Last Stand

Lone Star
1936   Custer's Last Stand

Lonegan, Lenore
1951   Westward the Women

Lonehill, Ed
1956   The Last Hunt

Lonergan, Lloyd
1917   Under False Colors
1918   The Million Dollar
        Mystery

Lonergan, Philip
1916   Betrayed
1919   Mandarin's Gold
1926   Private Izzy Murphy

Lonergan, Tim
1931   Cimarron

Long, Audrey
1943   Yankee Doodle Dandy
1945   Wanderer of the
        Wasteland
1947   Desperate
1951   Cavalry Scout
1952   Indian Uprising

Long, Benny
1950   The Breaking Point

Long, Hal
1935   L'homme des Folies
        Bergère
1940   Viva Cisco Kid

Long, Lotus *same as Lotus*
1929   The Peacock Fan
1934   Eskimo
1936   Sea Spoilers
1937   Think Fast, Mr. Moto
1939   Mr. Wong in Chinatown
        The Mystery of Mr. Wong
1940   Phantom of Chinatown
1949   Rose of the Yukon

Long, Louise
1926   The Campus Flirt

Long, Nicholas
1917   The Adventures of Carol

Long, Nicholas, Jr.
1915   Hearts of Men

Long, Richard
1948   Tap Roots
1954   Saskatchewan

Long, Sally
1924   His Darker Self

Long, Tommy
1952   Red Ball Express

Long, Walter
1915   The Birth of a Nation
1916   Sold for Marriage
        Unprotected
1917   Hashimura Togo
        The Little American
1919   Desert Gold
        Scarlet Days
1920   The Third Woman
1922   Shadows
1923   The Huntress
1931   Pardon Us
        Pardon Us (*foreign
        version*)
1932   Call Her Savage
1934   Lazy River
        Operator 13
1936   The Bold Caballero
        The Glory Trail
        Sutter's Gold
1938   Wild Horse Canyon

Long, Walter (*African-American
actor*) *not the same as* **Long,
Walter**
1921   A Giant of His Race
1923   The Devil's Match
        His Great Chance
        A Shot in the Night

Long Lance, Chief
1930   The Silent Enemy

Longacre, Frank
1915   Hearts of Men

Longstreet, Stephen
1947   The Jolson Story

Lono, James
1936   Ramona

Lonsdale, Harry *same as*
Lounsdale, H.
1915   The Rosary
1919   Fighting for Gold
        The Last of His People
1925   Brand of Cowardice

Loo, Bessie
1939   Mr. Wong in Chinatown

Loo, Richard
1932   The Secrets of Wu Sin
1936   After the Thin Man
        Mad Holiday
1939   Daughter of the Tong
        Mr. Wong in Chinatown
1940   Doomed to Die
        The Fatal Hour
1941   Secret of the Wastelands
1942   Across the Pacific
        Little Tokyo, U.S.A.
        Submarine Raider
1943   The Amazing Mrs.
        Holliday
        Jack London
1945   Betrayal from the East
1948   Half Past Midnight
1949   The Clay Pigeon
1951   The Steel Helmet

Loomis, Madge
1914   At the Cross Roads

Loomis, Margaret
1917   The Call of the East
        Hashimura Togo
1918   Hidden Pearls
1919   Told in the Hills
1922   The Hands of Nara

Loos, Anita
1918   Good-Bye, Bill
1945   A Tree Grows in Brooklyn

Loos, Anna
1943   Hitler's Children

Loos, Mary
1937   Man of the People
1947   Calendar Girl
1948   The Dude Goes West
1950   A Ticket to Tomahawk

Lopez, Augustina
1922   The Crow's Nest
1929   Redskin
        Wolf Song

López, Eva
1939   La Inmaculada

Lopez, Juan
1952   The Iron Mistress

Lopez, Manuel
1936   Ramona
1943   Action in the North
        Atlantic
1945   Betrayal from the East
1949   Border Incident

Lopez, Mary
1936   Ramona

Lopez, Paul
1936   Ramona

Lopez, Perry
1954   Drum Beat
1956   The Lone Ranger
1959   Cry Tough
1960   Flaming Star

Lopez, Primo
1952   The Iron Mistress

Lopez, Raymond
1931   Charlie Chan Carries On
        (*foreign version*)

Lopez, Richard
1946   The Red Dragon

Lopez, Rose Marie
1946   Without Reservations
1947   Ride the Pink Horse
1948   Angel in Exile

López Rubio, José
1931   Charlie Chan Carries On
        (*foreign version*)
        La fruta amarga
        Mamá
        Mi último amor
        La mujer X
        El proceso de Mary
        Dugan
1932   El caballero de la noche
        Marido y mujer
1933   It's Great to Be Alive
        (*foreign version*)
        No dejes la puerta abierta
        Primavera en otoño
        El rey de los gitanos
        Una viuda romántica
        Yo, tú y ella
1934   Un capitán de cosacos
        La ciudad de cartón
        Dos más uno, dos
        Granaderos del amor
1935   Julieta compra un hijo
        Piernas de seda
        Rosa de Francia
        Señora casada necesita
        marido
        Te quiero con locura
1938   La vida bohemia
1940   Tengo fe en ti

Loraine, Oscar
1945   Rhapsody in Blue

Loraine, Robert
1934   Limehouse Blues

Lorch, Theodore
1927   Sailor Izzy Murphy
1928   The Canyon of Adventure
1929   Show Boat
1936   Rebellion
        Show Boat
1939   Stand Up and Fight

Lord, Del
1927   Lost at the Front
        Topsy and Eva
1945   I Love a Bandleader
1946   Singin' in the Corn

Lord, Jack
1960   Walk Like a Dragon

Lord, Marjorie
1937   Border Cafe
1947   New Orleans
1949   Masked Raiders

Lord, Mary
1945   The Valley of Decision
1946   The Sailor Takes a Wife

Lord, Philip
1948   Call Northside 777

Lord, Robert
1932   So Big
1934   As the Earth Turns
        He Was Her Man
1935   Black Fury
        Bordertown
1937   Black Legion
1939   Confessions of a Nazi Spy
1942   Wings for the Eagle
1949   Knock on Any Door

Loredo, Linda
1931   Los calaveras
        Politiquerías

Loredo, Paul
1936   Ramona

Loren, Sophia
1958   Houseboat
1959   The Black Orchid

Loreno, Dick *see* **La Reno, Dick**

Lorenz, Jack
1943   They Came to Blow Up
        America
1958   The Light in the Forest

Loretz, Ralph
1949   The Red Menace

Lorimer, Elsa
1914   The Good-for-Nothing

Lorimer, Louise
1940   Elsa Maxwell's Public
        Deb No. 1
1948   Gentleman's Agreement
        The Luck of the Irish
1950   The Big Hangover
        Mystery Street
1952   Japanese War Bride
1956   The Benny Goodman
        Story

Loring, Ann
1936   Robin Hood of El Dorado

Loring, Hope
1922   Shadows
1923   April Showers
1924   The Mine with the Iron
        Door
1929   This Is Heaven

Loring, Teala
1946   Dark Alibi
        Gas House Kids
1947   Riding the California
        Trail

Lorraine, Betty
1937   Souls at Sea

Lorraine, Bob Locke
1942   Holiday Inn

Lorraine, Harry
1920   The Last of the Mohicans

Lorraine, Leota
1918   Her American Husband
1935   Ruggles of Red Gap
1946   Notorious
1959   Imitation of Life

Lorraine, Louise
1927   The Frontiersman
        Winners of the
        Wilderness
1928   Chinatown Charlie

Lorraine, Mary
1938   In Old Chicago

Lorre, Peter
1937   Thank You, Mr. Moto
        Think Fast, Mr. Moto
1938   Mr. Moto Takes a Chance
        Mr. Moto's Gamble
1939   Mr. Moto in Danger
        Island
        Mr. Moto Takes a
        Vacation
        Mr. Moto's Last Warning
1941   The Face Behind the
        Mask
1942   All Through the Night

Lorriea, John
1949   Thieves' Highway

Lorring, Lotte
1930   Doña mentiras (*foreign
        version*)

Lory, Jacques
1934   La veuve joyeuse
1935   L'homme des Folies
        Bergère

Lory, Jacques
1939   Mr. Moto's Last Warning
1943   Gangway for Tomorrow
        The Leopard Man
1945   Rhapsody in Blue
Los de Lima
1935   No matarás
Losby, Donald
1957   Raintree County
Losch, Tilly
1947   Duel in the Sun
Losee, Frank
1916   Hulda from Holland
        The Innocent Lie
1918   Uncle Tom's Cabin
1919   His Parisian Wife
1920   The Riddle: Woman
Losey, Joseph
1948   The Boy with Green Hair
1950   The Lawless
Losey, Michael
1948   The Boy with Green Hair
Lotta, Dorothy
1948   My Girl Tisa
Lotus see **Long, Lotus**
Louden, Thomas
1941   Virginia
Louie, Billy
1948   The Lady from Shanghai
Louie, Ducky
1947   Black Gold
Louis, Alyce
1948   Harpoon
Louis, Joe
1938   Spirit of Youth
1944   The Negro Soldier
1948   The Fight Never Ends
1953   The Joe Louis Story
Louis, Willard
1916   A Man of Sorrow
1919   The Unpainted Woman
1925   Hogan's Alley
Louise, Anita
1931   The Great Meadow
1934   Judge Priest
Lounsdale, H. see **Lonsdale, Harry**
Louvigny, Jacques
1935   L'homme des Folies
        Bergère
Love, Bessie
1916   The Aryan
        A Sister of Six
1918   A Little Sister of
        Everybody
1919   A Fighting Colleen
        A Yankee Princess
1921   The Swamp
1923   Purple Dawn
1924   Tongues of Flame
1925   A Son of His Father
1926   Meet the Prince
1927   A Harp in Hock
1928   Anybody Here Seen Kelly?
Love, Eula
1934   Stand Up and Cheer!
Love, Mary
1952   Anything Can Happen
Love, Montagu same as **Love, Montague**
1916   The Scarlet Oath
1918   Broken Ties
1920   The Riddle: Woman
1927   Rose of the Golden West
1928   The Hawk's Nest
1934   Limehouse Blues
1936   Sutter's Gold
1938   The Buccaneer
1940   The Mark of Zorro
        Northwest Passage (Book
        I—Rogers' Rangers)
Lovejoy, Alec same as **Lovejoy, Alex**
1935   Lem Hawkins' Confession
1938   Birthright
        God's Step Children
        Swing!
1939   Moon over Harlem
1940   Paradise in Harlem
1941   Murder on Lenox Avenue
        Sunday Sinners

Lovejoy, Arthur
1956   The Benny Goodman
        Story
        Full of Life
        Reprisal!
Lovejoy, Frank
1949   Home of the Brave
1953   The Charge at Feather
        River
Lovelady, Ann
1951   Apache Drums
Loveless, Henrietta
1927   The Spider's Web
1935   Lem Hawkins' Confession
Lovely, Louise
1916   The Gilded Spider
        The Grip of Jealousy
        The Social Buccaneer
1920   The Third Woman
Lovett, Helen
1931   Street Scene
Lovett, William
1959   The FBI Story
Lovsky, Celia
1947   The Foxes of Harrow
1955   Duel on the Mississippi
        Foxfire
1956   Death of a Scoundrel
1957   Trooper Hook
Low, Jack same as **Lowe, Jack**
1937   Slave Ship
1938   Little Miss Roughneck
1952   Indian Uprising
1954   Broken Lance
Low, Robert M.
1933   El rey de los gitanos
Lowdermilk, Romaine
1940   Arizona Frontier
Lowe, E. P.
1950   Intruder in the Dust
Lowe, Mrs. E. P.
1950   Intruder in the Dust
Lowe, E. T., Jr.
1922   The Scrapper
1927   Sailor Izzy Murphy
Lowe, Edmund (actor), 1890–1971
1922   Peacock Alley
1923   The White Flower
1929   In Old Arizona
1931   The Cisco Kid
1933   Let's Fall in Love
1936   Mad Holiday
1958   The Last Hurrah
Lowe, Edmund (child actor)
1950   Intruder in the Dust
Lowe, Edward T. same as **Lowe, Edward T., Jr.**
1919   Toby's Bow
1920   It's a Great Life
1926   The Fighting Edge
1930   King of Jazz
1932   Hearts of Humanity
        Igloo
1934   Stand Up and Cheer!
1935   Charlie Chan in Egypt
        Charlie Chan in Paris
        Charlie Chan in Shanghai
1936   Charlie Chan at the Race
        Track
1938   Dangerous to Know
        Daughter of Shanghai
1947   Pirates of Monterey
Lowe, Ellen
1936   Dancing Pirate
1938   The Beloved Brat
1941   Saddlemates
1948   Open Secret
Lowe, Ephraim
1950   Intruder in the Dust
Lowe, Jack see **Low, Jack**
Lowe, James
1928   Uncle Tom's Cabin
Lowe, Sherman
1935   Melody Trail
1940   Am I Guilty?
1941   Road Agent
1942   King of the Stallions
Lowe, Sun
1954   Hell's Half Acre

Lowell, Bob see **Lowell, Robert**
Lowell, Grace
1915   An American Gentleman
Lowell, John
1925   Red Love
Lowell, Mark
1959   Night of the Quarter
        Moon
Lowell, Martin
1950   Battleground
Lowell, Monte
1948   Moonrise
Lowell, Robert same as **Lowell, Bob**
1944   An American Romance
        The Racket Man
1946   Till the End of Time
1947   My Wild Irish Rose
1948   Jiggs and Maggie in Court
Lowenwirth, Anna
1933   Victims of Persecution
Lowery, Robert
1937   Life Begins in College
1938   Gateway
        Happy Landing
        Josette
        Passport Husband
1939   Charlie Chan in Reno
        Drums Along the Mohawk
        The Escape
        Mr. Moto in Danger
        Island
1940   Charlie Chan's Murder
        Cruise
        The Mark of Zorro
        Murder over New York
1941   Ride on Vaquero
1946   Gas House Kids
1948   Shep Comes Home
1949   Call of the Forest
        The Dalton Gang
1950   Train to Tombstone
Lowery, William A. same as **Lowery, William; Lowery, William E.**
1915   The Lamb
1916   Sold for Marriage
1918   Her Moment
1922   Pals of the West
1925   A Daughter of the Sioux
Lowry, Emily
1934   As the Earth Turns
Lowry, Ludwig
1918   Her American Husband
        Tony America
Lowry, Scooter
1928   Chinatown Charlie
Lox, Abraham
1940   The Great Advisor
Loxle, D. A.
1946   Bad Bascomb
Loy, Loo
1936   It Had to Happen
Loy, Myrna
1927   Bitter Apples
        Ham and Eggs at the
        Front
1928   The Jazz Singer
1931   Skyline
1932   Thirteen Women
1934   Broadway Bill
1936   After the Thin Man
Lozano, Ada
1933   Primavera en otoño
        El rey de los gitanos
Lozano, Berta
1932   Amor y vida
Lozano, Carmen
1932   Amor y vida
Lubelska, Paula same as **Lubelski, Paula**
1939   Mothers of Today
        Tevya
1940   Eli Eli
Luber, Bernard
1939   El trovador de la radio
Lubetty, Madeleine
1922   Cardigan
Lubin, Arthur
1925   His People
1926   Millionaires

Lubin, Lou
1944   Hi, Beautiful
1947   Easy Come, Easy Go
Lubitch, Louis
1938   Charlie Chan at Monte
        Carlo
Lubitsch, Ernst
1930   Galas de la Paramount
1932   Une heure près de toi
1934   La veuve joyeuse
1943   The Meanest Man in the
        World
Luboff, V.
1940   Americaner Schadchen
Lubow, Vera
1939   Mothers of Today
Lubritsky, Dave same as **Lubritzky, Dave**
1937   I Want to Be a Mother
1940   Her Second Mother
        The Jewish Melody
1941   Mazel Tov Yidden
Luby, S. Roy
1935   Range Warfare
1936   Border Phantom
1943   Land of Hunted Men
Lucanti, Carlos
1930   Charros, gauchos y
        manolas
Lucas, Charles D.
1919   The Homesteader
1920   Within Our Gates
Lucas, Clara
1917   The Hidden Children
Lucas, Eugene, Lieut.
1919   Injustice
Lucas, George
1923   Deceit
Lucas, Jimmie
1941   Birth of the Blues
Lucas, Jimmy
1936   After the Thin Man
Lucas, John Meredyth
1953   Tumbleweed
1960   The Sign of Zorro
Lucas, Marcelle
1931   Su noche de bodas
        (foreign version)
Lucas, Sam
1914   Uncle Tom's Cabin
Lucas, Sharon
1951   Westward the Women
1957   The Guns of Fort
        Petticoat
Lucas, Shirley
1951   Westward the Women
Lucas, Wilfred same as **Lucas, Wilfrid**
1917   A Love Sublime
1918   The Red, Red Heart
1919   The Westerners
1921   Through the Back Door
1922   Flesh and Blood
1924   North of Nevada
1930   The Arizona Kid
1931   Pardon Us
1932   Igloo
1933   Racetrack
1934   Operator 13
1935   Charlie Chan in Paris
1936   Dimples
        Human Cargo
        The Prisoner of Shark
        Island
1937   Black Legion
        Prairie Thunder
1938   Rascals
        Speed to Burn
1939   Daughters Courageous
1940   Santa Fe Trail
Lucca, Dino di
1930   Toda una vida (foreign
        version)
Lucero, Enrique
1958   Sierra Baron

Lucey, E. C.
1940   The Ramparts We Watch
Luck, Robert M.
1954   Hell's Half Acre
Lucke, Max
1943   Hitler's Children
Lucy, Arnold
1922   Fair Lady
1931   Young Sinners
Luddy, Edward I. see **Ludwig, Edward**
Luden, Jack
1927   Aflame in the Sky
1928   Sins of the Fathers
1929   Why Bring That Up?
1946   The Sailor Takes a Wife
Ludwig, Edward same as **Luddy, Edward; Luddy, Edward I.**
1927   Jake the Plumber
1931   The Cohens and Kellys in Africa
1943   Crash Dive
        They Came to Blow Up America
1952   The Half-Breed
1953   Sangaree
Ludwig, Salem
1958   Never Love a Stranger
Ludwig, William
1944   An American Romance
        Andy Hardy's Blonde Trouble
1951   The Great Caruso
1952   It's a Big Country: An American Anthology
Lufkin, Sam
1936   Rose of the Rancho
1945   Wanderer of the Wasteland
1948   The Miracle of the Bells
Luget, Andre see **Luguet, André**
Lugo, Bob
1950   Young Daniel Boone
1953   Dream Wife
Lugosi, Bela
1925   The Midnight Girl
1931   The Black Camel
Luguet, André same as **Luget, Andre**
1930   Olimpia (foreign version)
        Le spectre vert
1931   Buster se marie
        Jenny Lind
        Le père célibataire
        Quand on est belle
1932   Le bluffeur
Luis, Herman
1950   Damien
Luján, Paloma
1931   Chérie (foreign version)
Lukas, Aristides
1931   Such Is Life
Lukas, Paul
1930   Behind the Make-Up
1931   Women Love Once
1933   Grand Slam
1939   Confessions of a Nazi Spy
1941   They Dare Not Love
1944   Address Unknown
Lukather, Paul
1956   Mohawk
Lukats, Nick
1937   Waikiki Wedding
1940   Knute Rockne—All American
Luke, Edwin
1945   The Jade Mask
Luke, Keye
1935   Charlie Chan in Paris
        Charlie Chan in Shanghai
1936   Charlie Chan at the Circus
        Charlie Chan at the Race Track
1937   Charlie Chan at the Olympics
        Charlie Chan at the Opera
        Charlie Chan on Broadway

1938   Charlie Chan at Monte Carlo
        Mr. Moto's Gamble
1940   Phantom of Chinatown
1941   The Gang's All Here
1942   Across the Pacific
        Dr. Gillespie's New Assistant
        Mexican Spitfire's Elephant
        North to the Klondike
        Submarine Raider
1943   Dr. Gillespie's Criminal Case
1944   Andy Hardy's Blonde Trouble
        Three Men in White
1945   Between Two Women
1947   Dark Delusion
1948   The Feathered Serpent
        Sleep, My Love
1949   The Sky Dragon
1950   Young Man with a Horn
1954   Hell's Half Acre
Luke, Lucas C.
1920   White Youth
Luke, Sherrill
1942   Syncopation
Lumet, Sidney
1957   Twelve Angry Men
Lummis, Dayton
1955   A Man Called Peter
        The View from Pompey's Head
Luna, Away
1956   The Searchers
Luna, Barbara
1959   Cry Tough
Luna, Marguerito
1959   The Wonderful Country
Luna, Rita
1935   No matarás
Lund, John
1952   The Battle at Apache Pass
1955   Chief Crazy Horse
        White Feather
1956   Dakota Incident
Lund, Lucille
1934   Fighting Through
1935   Range Warfare
Lund, O. A. C.
1914   When Broadway Was a Trail
1915   Just Jim
Lund, Richard
1930   Toda una vida (foreign version)
Lundigan, William
1940   East of the River
        The Fighting 69th
        Santa Fe Trail
        Three Cheers for the Irish
1942   Apache Trail
        Sunday Punch
1943   Dr. Gillespie's Criminal Case
1949   Pinky
1951   The House on Telegraph Hill
Lundy, Kenneth
1941   Where Did You Get That Girl?
Lundy, William
1945   Where Do We Go From Here?
Lung, Charles
1943   Jack London
        The Leopard Man
Lung, Clarence
1960   Walk Like a Dragon
Lung, Jung Quai
1934   Blossom Time
Lunn, Nina
1948   Up in Central Park
Lunt, Alfred
1923   Backbone
Lupino, Ida
1949   Lust for Gold
Lupton, John
1955   Seven Angry Men
1958   Gun Fever

Lusiardo, Tito
1935   El día que me quieras
        Tango Bar
Lusk, Freeman
1951   Go for Broke!
        The Magnificent Yankee
1953   The Stars Are Singing
Lussier, Dane
1943   Ladies' Day
        Mexican Spitfire's Blessed Event
Luster, Marvin
1960   Sergeant Rutledge
Luster, Mary
1938   The Toy Wife
Luther, Anna
1918   Her Moment
Luther, Lester
1949   The Red Menace
Luxford, Nola
1920   The Tiger's Coat
Lyall, Archie
1959   John Paul Jones
Lyden, Pierce
1943   Border Patrol
1946   Wild Beauty
1947   The Adventures of Don Coyote
        Rustlers of Devil's Canyon
1948   Silver Trails
1949   Illegal Entry
1958   Gunman's Walk
Lyden, Robert
1950   Emergency Wedding
1956   The Searchers
Lydon, James
1948   The Time of Your Life
1951   The Magnificent Yankee
        Oh! Susanna
1960   I Passed for White
Lydon, Richard
1945   Colorado Pioneers
Lykes, Don see **Likes, Don**
Lyle, Bessie
1934   Imitation of Life
1935   The Littlest Rebel
Lyle, Edythe
1919   Deliverance
Lyle, Warren E.
1916   The Folly of Revenge
Abe Lyman and His Band
1930   Galas de la Paramount
Lyman, Lila
1940   The Ramparts We Watch
Lyman, Louis
1926   Broken Hearts
Lynch, Don
1948   Unconquered
1949   The Prairie
Lynch, Edward
1918   Fields of Honor
1930   The Bad Man
Lynch, Helen
1924   In High Gear
1926   General Custer at Little Big Horn
1929   In Old Arizona
        Why Bring That Up?
Lynch, John
1917   The Bride of Hate
1920   Darling Mine
        It's a Great Life
1922   The Good Provider
        The Pride of Palomar
Lynch, Ken
1960   The Dark at the Top of the Stairs
Lynch, Walter
1923   Scars of Jealousy
Lynden, Virginia
1945   Nob Hill
Lyndon, Barre
1945   The House on 92nd St.
Lynley, Carol
1958   The Light in the Forest
Lynn, Barbara
1942   Tales of Manhattan

Lynn, Diana
1947   Easy Come, Easy Go
Lynn, Eddie
1939   Reform School
1942   Take My Life
Lynn, Emmett
1941   Road Agent
1943   The Law Rides Again
1945   The Cisco Kid Returns
1946   Romance of the West
        Santa Fe Uprising
1947   Oregon Trail Scouts
        Rustlers of Devil's Canyon
1948   Western Heritage
1949   The Cowboy and the Prizefighter
        Ride, Ryder, Ride!
        Roll Thunder Roll!
1950   Rock Island Trail
        The Traveling Saleswoman
1951   Slaughter Trail
        The Tall Target
1952   Apache War Smoke
        Desert Pursuit
1955   A Man Called Peter
Lynn, George not the same as **Lynn, Peter George**
1938   Charlie Chan at Monte Carlo
1943   Dr. Gillespie's Criminal Case
        They Came to Blow Up America
1944   The Sullivans
1946   Notorious
1951   Apache Drums
        Show Boat
1952   My Man and I
1957   Beau James
        The Halliday Brand
Lynn, Henry
1932   The Unfortunate Bride
1934   The Youth of Russia
1935   Bar-Mitzvah
        Shir Hashirim
1937   The Holy Oath
        Where Is My Child?
1938   The Power of Life
1939   Mothers of Today
Lynn, Jeffrey
1939   Daughters Courageous
1940   The Fighting 69th
Lynn, Jennie
1959   The FBI Story
Lynn, Lee
1956   Rockin' the Blues
Lynn, Leni
1939   The Adventures of Huckleberry Finn
Lynn, Mara
1959   Last Train from Gun Hill
Lynn, Mauri (African-American actress)
1954   Carmen Jones
Lynn, Peter George same as **Lynn, Peter George** not the same as **Lynn, George**
1939   Mr. Wong in Chinatown
1940   Kit Carson
        Northwest Passage (Book I—Rogers' Rangers)
1941   Saddlemates
Lynn, Rita
1948   Western Heritage
1957   Joe Dakota
Lynn, Robert
1955   Good Morning, Miss Dove
        A Man Called Peter
Lynn, Robert, Jr.
1955   A Man Called Peter
Lynn, Sharon
1927   Aflame in the Sky
        Clancy's Kosher Wedding
        Jake the Plumber
Lynne, Andrea
1915   The Alien
Lynne, Bernice
1944   Something for the Boys

Lynton, Chris
1915   A Yankee from the West
Lynwood, Burt
1937   Shadows of the Orient
Lyon, Ben
1923   Potash and Perlmutter
1924   So Big
1927   For the Love of Mike
1931   Aloha
        Call of the Rockies
1936   Down to the Sea
Lyon, Earle
1955   The Lonesome Trail
1958   The Rawhide Trail
Lyon, Francis D. *same as Lyon, Francis; Lyon, Frank not the same as Lyon, Frank A.*
1930   The Big Pond
1932   Hypnotized
1957   The Oklahoman
Lyon, Frank A. *not the same as Lyon, Francis D.*
1915   Cohen's Luck
Lyon, Nanci
1936   Star for a Night
Lyon, Priscilla
1938   The Beloved Brat
Lyon, Richard (*child actor*)
1941   They Dare Not Love
1948   The Boy with Green Hair
Lyon, Wanda
1925   The Greatest Love of All
Lyons, Cliff
1932   The Rainbow Trail
1943   Wagon Tracks West
1949   The Fighting Kentuckian
        She Wore a Yellow
        Ribbon
1950   Rio Grande
1953   The Sun Shines Bright
1954   Drums Across the River
1956   The Searchers
1959   The Young Land
1960   Sergeant Rutledge
Lyons, Collette
1945   The Dolly Sisters
Lyons, Leonard
1949   Jigsaw
Lyons, Lurline
1916   Ramona
Lyons, Richard E. (*prod*)
1958   Frontier Gun
Lys, Lya
1931   Buster se marie
        Soyons gais
1934   La veuve joyeuse
1939   Confessions of a Nazi Spy
Lyston, Mrs. Hudson
1913   Traffic in Souls
Lytess, Natasha
1951   The House on Telegraph
        Hill
1952   Anything Can Happen
Lytton, Herbert
1950   No Way Out
1953   The Stars Are Singing
Maaski, Roberta
1940   The Ramparts We Watch
Maazel, Marvine
1931   Delicious
Mabley, Jackie "Moms" *same as Mabley, Jackie*
1933   The Emperor Jones
1948   Killer Diller
1948?   Boarding House Blues
Mabry, Anna
1955   The View from Pompey's
        Head
Mac and Ace
1947   Juke Joint
Mac, Jenny
1942   Rio Rita
Mac, Nila
1918   Toys of Fate
MacAfee, Florence
1958   Houseboat
McAlinney, Patrick
1959   Shake Hands with the
        Devil

McAllister, Helen
1947   Calendar Girl
McAllister, Mary
1925   The Red Rider
McAllister, Paul
1923   Jamestown
1929   Evangeline
1934   Judge Priest
1936   The Prisoner of Shark
        Island
McAnally, Ray
1959   Shake Hands with the
        Devil
McArt, Don
1957   Journey to Freedom
MacArthur, Charles
1930   King of Jazz
1931   En cada puerto un amor
MacArthur, James
1958   The Light in the Forest
McAtee, Clyde
1936   Charlie Chan at the Race
        Track
Macateer, Alan
1949   Jigsaw
Macaulay, Richard
1940   Three Cheers for the Irish
1942   Across the Pacific
        Wings for the Eagle
McAvoy, Charles
1937   It Could Happen to You
        Maid of Salem
1940   Little Nellie Kelly
1945   Salome, Where She
        Danced
1950   No Way Out
McAvoy, May
1927   Irish Hearts
1928   The Jazz Singer
1950   Mystery Street
McAvoy, Mickey
1939   Winner Take All
McBain, Diane
1960   Ice Palace
McBan, Mickey
1924   Untamed Youth
1927   The Way of All Flesh
MacBeth's Calypso Band
1946?   House-Rent Party
MacBride, Donald *same as McBride, Donald*
1939   Charlie Chan at Treasure
        Island
        The Girl from Mexico
1940   Murder over New York
        Northwest Passage (Book
        I—Rogers' Rangers)
1941   Louisiana Purchase
1942   Juke Girl
        Mexican Spitfire Sees a
        Ghost
1947   Buck Privates Come
        Home
1949   The Story of Seabiscuit
1951   Cuban Fireball
MacBride, Edith
1915   The Alien
McBride, Sue
1948   The Betrayal
McCabe, Frank
1940   The Ramparts We Watch
McCabe, James
1915   The Spender
McCabe, May
1914   The Jungle
McCall, Angelita
1951   Distant Drums
McCall, Castle
1946   Rendezvous 24
1947   Little Mister Jim
McCall, Jack
1960   All the Young Men
McCall, Mary, Jr.
1938   Breaking the Ice
1944   The Sullivans
McCall, William
1925   The Red Rider
McCalla, Vernon *same as McCallum, Vernon*
1938   The Duke Is Tops

1939   Double Deal
        Gang Smashers
        Reform School
1940   Am I Guilty?
1940?   Mr. Washington Goes to
        Town
1941   Four Shall Die
1942   Lucky Ghost
McCallion, James
1958   The Badlanders
McCallister, Lon *same as McCallister, Bud*
1942   Gentleman Jim
1943   The Meanest Man in the
        World
        Yankee Doodle Dandy
1949   The Story of Seabiscuit
McCallum, Vernon *see McCalla, Vernon*
McCambridge, Mercedes
1956   Giant
1958   Touch of Evil
1960   Cimarron
McCandless, Velma
1936   Ramona
McCann, Celia
1935   The Singing Vagabond
McCann, Doreen
1948   Moonrise
McCardle, Mickey
1950   The Big Hangover
        Sands of Iwo Jima
1951   Saturday's Hero
1958   Tonka
McCarey, Leo
1920   Outside the Law
1921   No Woman Knows
1930   Locuras de amor
1935   Ruggles of Red Gap
1944   Going My Way
1945   The Bells of St. Mary's
McCarey, Ray
1940   Too Many Girls
1941   Accent on Love
McCarroll, Frank *same as McCarrol, Frank*
1934   Fighting Through
1936   West of Nevada
1943   Land of Hunted Men
1944   Buffalo Bill
        Sheriff of Las Vegas
1946   Sheriff of Redwood Valley
1947   The Adventures of Don
        Coyote
        Buffalo Bill Rides Again
1948   Fury at Furnace Creek
McCarron, Ritchie
1936   Laughing Irish Eyes
McCarter, William
1950   Two Flags West
McCarthy, Anelle
1942   The Vanishing Virginian
McCarthy, Clem
1949   The Story of Seabiscuit
McCarthy, Glen
1946   Sunset Pass
1952   Fort Osage
McCarthy, Henry *same as McCarty, Henry*
1922   Blazing Arrows
        Silver Spurs
1925   One of the Bravest
1929   Señor Americano
1930   Sombras de gloria
McCarthy, John P. *same as McCarthy, John*
1925   Brand of Cowardice
1927   His Foreign Wife
1928   Diamond Handcuffs
1931   Cavalier of the West
1932   The Forty-Niners
1936   Song of the Gringo
1945   The Cisco Kid Returns
McCarthy, Mack
1950   Panic in the Streets
McCarthy, Myles *same as McCarthy, Miles*
1919   Auction of Souls
1920   The Tiger's Coat

McCarthy, Nobu
1960   Walk Like a Dragon
McCarthy, Red
1941   Ice-Capades
McCarty, Dorothy
1955   Brevities of 1955
McCarty, Henry *see McCarthy, Henry*
McCarty, Mary
1937   That I May Live
1944   The Sullivans
McCarty, Walter G.
1949   Jiggs and Maggie in
        Jackpot Jitters
McCaskill, Roddy
1951   The Great Caruso
McCauley, Jack
1915   Hearts of Men
McClain, Billy
1935   So Red the Rose
1936   Dimples
1937   Bargain with Bullets
        One Mile from Heaven
        The Plainsman
1938   The Toy Wife
1939   Gone With the Wind
McClane, Lorenzo
1935   Lem Hawkins' Confession
McClary, Clyde
1926   Twin Triggers
1933   Circle Canyon
McClelland, Charles
1949   House of Strangers
1952   Anything Can Happen
McClennan, Frank H.
1941?   The Blood of Jesus
McClory, Eileen
1944   They Live in Fear
McClory, Sean
1950   The Daughter of Rosie
        O'Grady
1952   The Quiet Man
1955   The Long Gray Line
1957   The Guns of Fort
        Petticoat
McCloskey, Lawrence
1916   Pasquale
1917   His Sweetheart
McClure, Doug
1960   The Unforgiven
McClure, Frank
1947   It Had To Be You
1950   Jolson Sings Again
McClure, Gaylen
1959   The Black Orchid
McClure, Greg
1945   The Great John L.
1949   The Dalton Gang
        The Golden Stallion
1950   Emergency Wedding
McClure, Jean
1944   Something for the Boys
McCollough, Philo *see McCullough, Philo*
McCollum, Hugh
1958   The Lone Ranger and the
        Lost City of Gold
McColm, Ralph
1945   Rhapsody in Blue
McConnell, Fred
1940   Taku
McConnell, Gladys
1926   A Trip to Chinatown
1928   The Glorious Trail
McConnell, Mollie *same as McConnell, Molly*
1916   The Twin Triangle
1918   Set Free
McConnor, Vincent
1949   Jigsaw
McConville, Bernard
1916   Gretchen, the Greenhorn
        A Sister of Six
1918?   Rosemary Climbs the
        Heights
1919   The Sleeping Lion
        A Yankee Princess
1921   Shame
1928   Vamping Venus
1936   Ride, Ranger, Ride

McCoo, Arthur *(continued)*
1937   The Riders of the
            Whistling Skull
1941   Saddlemates

McCoo, Arthur
1948   The Betrayal

McCord, Mrs. Lewis
1915   Chimmie Fadden
            Chimmie Fadden Out
            West
            The Immigrant
            The Kindling
1916   Unprotected

McCord, Vera
1920   The Good-Bad Wife

McCormack, Merrill *see*
    McCormick, Merrill

McCormack, Patty
1957   All Mine to Give
1960   The Adventures of
            Huckleberry Finn

McCormick, John
1926   Irene
1927   Lost at the Front
1929   Smiling Irish Eyes

McCormick, Merrill *same as*
    McCormack, Merrill;
    McCormick, William;
    McCormick, Wm. Merrill
1929   Romance of the Rio
            Grande
1932   Border Devils
1934   Call of the Coyote
1936   The Prisoner of Shark
            Island
            Rebellion
            Rose of the Rancho
            Tundra
1937   Boots and Saddles
1939   In Old Caliente
1942   Below the Border
1949   Arctic Fury
1951   Oh! Susanna
1953   Dream Wife

McCormick, Montyne
1946?   Beale Street Mama

McCormick, Myron
1936   Winterset
1949   Jigsaw
1950   Jolson Sings Again
1955   Not As a Stranger

McCormick, Pearl
1927   The Scar of Shame

McCormick, Thomas Patrick
1950   Emergency Wedding

McCormick, William *see*
    McCormick, Merrill

McCosh, Rufus
1928   The Crash

McCown, Frank *see* **Calhoun, Rory**

McCoy, Dewey
1950   Intruder in the Dust

McCoy, Dickie
1942   The Vanishing Virginian

McCoy, Harry
1932   Hypnotized

McCoy, Horace
1935   Rendezvous
1938   Dangerous to Know
1941   Western Union
1942   Gentleman Jim
            Valley of the Sun
1954   Dangerous Mission

McCoy, Kay
1934   Broadway Bill

McCoy, Kid
1923   April Showers

McCoy, Tim *same as* **McCoy, Tim**
    J., Col.; McCoy, Tim, Col.
1925   The Thundering Herd
1926   War Paint
1927   California
            The Frontiersman
            Spoilers of the West
            Winners of the
            Wilderness
1928   Wyoming
1929   The Desert Rider
            The Overland Telegraph
            Sioux Blood
1934   The Prescott Kid
1936   Aces and Eights
            The Traitor

McCoy, Tim *(continued)*
1939   Trigger Fingers
1942   Below the Border
1957   Run of the Arrow

McCoy, Wayne
1942   Mexican Spitfire at Sea
1943   Ladies' Day

McCoy, William M.
1919   Hearts of Men

McCracken, Don
1946   Dangerous Money

McCracken, Richard
1940   The Ramparts We Watch

McCrea, Joel
1941   Sullivan's Travels
1944   Buffalo Bill
1948   Four Faces West
1949   Colorado Territory
1950   Stars in My Crown
1957   The Oklahoman
            Trooper Hook
1958   Fort Massacre

McCready, Jack
1917   The Spirit of '76
1918   Me Und Gott

McCrillis, Harry
1936   Dimples

McCulley, Johnston
1936   The Bold Caballero
1941   Doomed Caravan
1945   South of the Rio Grande
1946   Don Ricardo Returns
1951   The Mark of the
            Renegade

McCullough, Philo *same as*
    McCollough, Philo;
    McCullough, P. M.
1915   The Adventures of a
            Madcap
1919   Spotlight Sadie
1930   On the Border
1934   Broadway Bill
            The Cactus Kid
            Wheels of Destiny
1935   Captured in Chinatown
1937   The Plainsman
1938   The Buccaneer
1939   Let Freedom Ring
1941   They Dare Not Love
1947   My Wild Irish Rose
1949   The Girl from Jones
            Beach
1950   The Big Hangover
            Devil's Doorway
            Stars in My Crown
1951   The Great Caruso
1952   The Raiders
1953   The Great Sioux Uprising

McCullough, Ralph *same as*
    McCullough, Ralph Fee
1921   Across the Divide
            The Swamp
1922   The Top O' the Morning
1925   Galloping Vengeance
            Speed Wild
1938   Little Miss Roughneck

McCune, Hank
1956   Wetbacks

McCurdy, Anna Marie
1960   The Crowning
            Experience

McCurdy, George
1960   The Crowning
            Experience

McCusker, Buford
1943   Wintertime

McCutcheon, Beryl
1953   Dream Wife

McDaniel, Etta
1936   The Glory Trail
            The Prisoner of Shark
            Island
1942   American Empire
            Mokey
1943   They Came to Blow Up
            America

McDaniel, George *same as*
    MacDaniel, George; McDaniels,
    George
1917   The Hidden Children
1922   The Scrapper

McDaniel, Hattie *same as*
    McDaniels, Hattie
1932   The Golden West
            Hypnotized
1934   Imitation of Life
            Judge Priest
            Operator 13
1935   Harmony Lane
            The Little Colonel
1936   Show Boat
            Star for a Night
1939   Gone With the Wind
1942   In This Our Life
            They Died With Their
            Boots On
1944   Hi, Beautiful
            Since You Went Away
1946   Song of the South

McDaniel, Sam *same as* **McDaniel,**
    Samuel R.; McDaniels,
    "Deacon"; McDaniels, Sam
1932   The Vanishing Frontier
1934   Charlie Chan's Courage
            Operator 13
            Wagon Wheels
1935   Rendezvous
1936   After the Thin Man
1937   Bargain with Bullets
            Dark Manhattan
1940   Am I Guilty?
1941   Birth of the Blues
            Louisiana Purchase
            New York Town
            Virginia
1942   All Through the Night
            In This Our Life
            Mokey
            They Died With Their
            Boots On
1943   Gangway for Tomorrow
1944   Andy Hardy's Blonde
            Trouble
            Three Men in White
1946   Without Reservations
1947   The Foxes of Harrow
1955   Good Morning, Miss Dove
            A Man Called Peter
1958   St. Louis Blues
1960   The Adventures of
            Huckleberry Finn
            Ice Palace

McDaniels, George *see* **McDaniel,**
    George

McDaniels, Hattie *see* **McDaniel,**
    Hattie

McDaniels, Sam *see* **McDaniel, Sam**

McDermott, John
1920   Dinty
1923   The Spider and the Rose
1928   Flying Romeos
1930   The Cohens and the
            Kellys in Scotland
1946   Three Wise Fools

MacDermott, Marc
1927   California

MacDonald, Archer
1952   Kid Monk Baroni
1953   The Glory Brigade

McDonald, Charles *could be same*
    as **MacDonald, Charles**

MacDonald, Charles *could be same*
    as **McDonald, Charles**
1917   The Little Samaritan

McDonald, Charles
1925   Irish Luck

McDonald, David J.
1957   Burden of Truth

MacDonald, Donald
1923   Crashin' Thru

MacDonald, Edmund
1940   The Gay Caballero
1942   Castle in the Desert
            Whispering Ghosts

MacDonald, Farrell *see*
    MacDonald, J. Farrell

MacDonald, Flora
1916   The Fall of a Nation

McDonald, Francis *(actor) same as*
    MacDonald, Francis;
    McDonald, Francis J.
1918   Real Folks
            Tony America

McDonald, Francis *(continued)*
1919   The Courageous Coward
            His Debt
1921   Puppets of Fate
1922   Captain Fly-by-Night
1923   Look Your Best
1924   East of Broadway
            Racing Luck
1926   Puppets
1932   Hidden Valley
1934   Operator 13
1936   Dimples
            The Prisoner of Shark
            Island
            Robin Hood of El Dorado
1937   The Devil's Playground
            The Plainsman
1938   The Buccaneer
1939   Bad Lands
1942   Valley of the Sun
1945   Great Stagecoach Robbery
            South of the Rio Grande
1946   Canyon Passage
            Notorious
1947   Dangerous Venture
            Duel in the Sun
            Spoilers of the North
1948   The Paleface
            Unconquered
1949   Apache Chief
            Brothers in the Saddle
            Rose of the Yukon
            Rustlers
1951   Oh! Susanna
1952   Fort Osage
            The Raiders
1953   San Antone
1955   Bad Day at Black Rock
            Shotgun
            The Vanishing American
1956   Raw Edge
            Walk the Proud Land
1957   The Guns of Fort
            Petticoat
            Pawnee
1958   Fort Massacre

McDonald, Frank *(dir)*
1935   Black Fury
            A Night at the Ritz
1936   Treachery Rides the
            Range
1941   Under Fiesta Stars
1948   Gun Smugglers
1949   Apache Chief
1954   Thunder Pass

McDonald, George
1946   Three Wise Fools
1947   California
1948   Fighting Father Dunne
            Four Faces West
1950   The Traveling
            Saleswoman
1952   It's a Big Country: An
            American Anthology

MacDonald, Ian
1941   Secret of the Wastelands
1942   They Died With Their
            Boots On
1948   My Girl Tisa
            16 Fathoms Deep
1950   Battleground
            Colt .45
            Comanche Territory
            The Lawless
1951   Flaming Feather
            New Mexico
            Show Boat
1952   Hiawatha
            High Noon
            The Savage
1954   Apache
            Taza, Son of Cochise
1955   The Lonesome Trail

MacDonald, J. Farrell *same as*
    MacDonald, Farrell; McDonald,
    J. Farrell
1921   Little Miss Hawkshaw
1922   Come On Over
            Sky High
1926   A Trip to Chinatown
1928   The Cohens and the
            Kellys in Paris
            Riley the Cop
1929   Abie's Irish Rose
            In Old Arizona
            Masked Emotions

MacDonald, J. Farrell

1931	The Squaw Man
1932	Hearts of Humanity
	Me and My Gal
	Men Are Such Fools
	The Vanishing Frontier
1934	The Cat's-Paw
1935	The Irish in Us
	Romance in Manhattan
1936	Show Boat
1937	Maid of Salem
	Shadows of the Orient
	Slave Ship
1941	Sullivan's Travels
1942	Little Tokyo, U.S.A.
1945	The Dolly Sisters
	Johnny Angel
	Nob Hill
	A Tree Grows in Brooklyn
1948	Fury at Furnace Creek
	Shep Comes Home
1949	The Dalton Gang

McDonald, Jack *same as* **McDonald, Jack F.**

1915	The Rosary
1920	The Last of the Mohicans
1922	A California Romance
1925	Don Q, Son of Zorro
1929	Show Boat

MacDonald, Jeanette

1932	Une heure près de toi
1934	La veuve joyeuse
1935	Naughty Marietta
1940	New Moon

McDonald, Joseph

| 1941 | Romance of the Rio Grande |

MacDonald, Katherine

| 1918 | The Squaw Man |

MacDonald, Kenneth *same as* **MacDonald, Ken; McDonald, Ken; McDonald, Kenneth**

1924	In High Gear
	Yankee Speed
1926	Shadows of Chinatown
1941	Mystery Ship
	Prairie Pioneers
1944	The Racket Man
1947	Crossfire
1949	The Gay Amigo
	The Mysterious Desperado
	Stagecoach Kid
1950	Border Treasure
	Storm Over Wyoming
1952	Arctic Flight
	Rose of Cimarron
1953	The Man from the Alamo
1955	The Gun That Won the West
	Seminole Uprising
	Seven Angry Men
1959	The Jayhawkers!

MacDonald, Philip

1934	Charlie Chan in London
	Limehouse Blues
1935	Charlie Chan in Paris
1939	Mr. Moto Takes a Vacation
	Mr. Moto's Last Warning
1942	Whispering Ghosts

McDonald, Ray

| 1949 | Shamrock Hill |

McDonald, Sandy

| 1940 | The Notorious Elinor Lee |

MacDonald, Sherwood

| 1917 | Sold at Auction |

MacDonald, Wallace

1918	Marked Cards
1919	Spotlight Sadie
1927	Drums of the Desert
	His Foreign Wife
1931	Smart Money
1932	The Vanishing Frontier
1933	King of the Wild Horses
1938	City Streets
	Little Miss Roughneck
1941	The Face Behind the Mask
1942	Submarine Raider
1943	Redhead from Manhattan
1944	Cry of the Werewolf
	The Racket Man
1945	Escape in the Fog

1953	Ambush at Tomahawk Gap
	The Nebraskan
1954	The Black Dakotas
	Massacre Canyon
1955	Apache Ambush
1956	Secret of Treasure Mountain
	The White Squaw
1959	Gunmen from Laredo

McDonald, Wilfred

| 1916 | A Son of Erin |

MacDonell, Duncan

| 1948 | The Miracle of the Bells |

MacDonnell, Kyle

| 1953 | Taxi |

McDonough, J. R.

| 1942 | Mexican Spitfire at Sea |

McDonough, Tom

| 1951 | The House on Telegraph Hill |

McDougal, Fred

| 1950 | Ambush |

McDougall, John

| 1950 | Panic in the Streets |

MacDougall, Kenneth

| 1915 | The Grandee's Ring |

MacDougall, Ranald

| 1950 | The Breaking Point |
| 1959 | The World, the Flesh and the Devil |

MacDougall, Rex

| 1918 | A Daughter of the Old South |

McDowall, Roddy

| 1948 | Rocky |
| 1949 | Tuna Clipper |

McDowell, Allen

| 1940 | George Washington Carver |

McDowell, Candy

| 1951 | Saturday's Hero |

McDowell, Claire

1916	Mixed Blood
1917	The Bronze Bride
1918	The Man Above the Law
1920	The Mark of Zorro
1925	One of the Bravest
1927	The Auctioneer
1934	Imitation of Life
1935	Black Fury
1939	Stand Up and Fight
1943	Gangway for Tomorrow
1944	Andy Hardy's Blonde Trouble

MacDowell, Melbourne

| 1920 | Outside the Law |

McDowell, Nelson

1920	The Last of the Mohicans
1926	The Frontier Trail
1928	Heart Trouble
	Kit Carson
	Uncle Tom's Cabin
1934	The Fighting Hero
	Fighting Through
	Wheels of Destiny
1936	Rose of the Rancho
1937	The Plainsman

McDowell, Violet

| 1938 | The Toy Wife |

MacDuff, Tyler

1955	Headline Hunters
	The Last Command
1956	The Burning Hills

Mace, Borden

| 1949 | Lost Boundaries |

Mace, Patsy *same as* **Mace, Patricia**

| 1941 | Louisiana Purchase |
| 1943 | Riding High |

Mace, Tut

| 1934 | She Was a Lady |

Mace, Warren

1943	Air Force
1949	Pinky
1950	Emergency Wedding
1951	Saturday's Hero

Mace, Wynn

| 1922 | Sky High |

McEachern, Murray

| 1956 | The Benny Goodman Story |

McElarney, Thomas

| 1940 | The Ramparts We Watch |

McElhern, James

| 1922 | Captain Fly-by-Night |

McElrath, Joyce

| 1946? | Beale Street Mama |

McEnany, Florence

| 1944 | Slightly Terrific |

McEvoy, Earl

| 1949 | Lust for Gold |

McEvoy, Renny

| 1942 | Wings for the Eagle |
| 1952 | Red Snow |

McEwen, Walter *(actor) not the same as* **MacEwen, Walter** *(prod)*

| 1918 | The Prussian Cur |
| 1920 | The Face at Your Window |

MacEwen, Walter *(prod) not the same as* **McEwen, Walter** *(actor)*

| 1946 | Without Reservations |
| 1948 | The Miracle of the Bells |

Macey, Carleton *see* **Macy, Carleton**

Macey, Cora

| 1926 | Irene |

MacFadden, Hamilton

1931	The Black Camel
	Charlie Chan Carries On
1933	Charlie Chan's Greatest Case
	The Man Who Dared: An Imaginative Biography
1934	She Was a Lady
	Stand Up and Cheer!
1935	Charlie Chan in Paris
1936	Human Cargo
1939	Charlie Chan in Reno
1941	Charlie Chan in Rio
1942	Young America

McFadden, Ivor *same as* **McFadden, Ivar**

| 1919 | The Delicious Little Devil |
| 1937 | Man of the People |

McFadden, Patricia

| 1945 | A Tree Grows in Brooklyn |

McFarland, Frank

1948	Up in Central Park
1950	Rock Island Trail
1951	Jim Thorpe—All-American

McFarland, Spanky *same as* **McFarland, George** *not the same as* **MacFarlane, George**

| 1936 | General Spanky |

MacFarlane, Bruce

| 1939 | Forged Passport |

MacFarlane, George *not the same as* **McFarland, George "Spanky"**

| 1929 | Frozen Justice |
| 1932 | The Heart of New York |

MacFarlane, Peter Clark

| 1921 | Guile of Women |

McGaffey, Elizabeth

| 1916 | The Honorable Friend |

McGann, William

1930	The Bad Man *(foreign version)*
	Los que danzan
	On the Border
1931	La dama atrevida
	La llama sagrada
1934	La buenaventura
1935	A Night at the Ritz
1942	American Empire

McGarrity, Everett

| 1929 | Hallelujah |

McGarry, William

| 1948 | Red River |

McGaugh, Wilbur

1922	One Eighth Apache
1924	California in '49
1934	The Prescott Kid
1947	The Jolson Story
1949	The Undercover Man
1950	Indian Territory
1951	When the Redskins Rode
1952	Japanese War Bride
1953	Captain John Smith and Pocahontas

| 1954 | The Black Dakotas |

McGavin, Darren

| 1951 | Queen for a Day |
| 1957 | Beau James |

McGee, Pat R.

| 1946 | Border Bandits |

McGee, Roger

1939	The Escape
1950	Battleground
	Sands of Iwo Jima
1951	The House on Telegraph Hill
1952	Red Ball Express

McGill, Dock

| 1947 | California |

McGill, Lawrence B.

1915	How Molly Malone Made Good
	Sealed Valley
1917	Crime and Punishment

Macgill, Moyna

| 1946 | The Sailor Takes a Wife |

McGinnis, Joel

| 1948 | Moonrise |

MacGinnis, Niall

| 1959 | Shake Hands with the Devil |

McGinnis, Terry

| 1950 | Jiggs and Maggie Out West |

McGinty, Artie Belle

| 1948? | Junction 88 |

McGiveney, Owen

1951	Show Boat
1957	Raintree County
1960	The Adventures of Huckleberry Finn
	Key Witness

McGlynn, Frank *see* **McGlynn, Frank, Sr.**

McGlynn, Frank, Jr.

1926	Rose of the Tenements
1934	Operator 13
1936	Custer's Last Stand
1937	That I May Live
1938	Mr. Moto's Gamble

McGlynn, Frank, Sr. *same as* **McGlynn, Frank**

1931	Huckleberry Finn
1933	Charlie Chan's Greatest Case
1934	Massacre
1935	The Littlest Rebel
1936	For the Service
	The Last of the Mohicans
	The Prisoner of Shark Island
1937	The Plainsman
	That I May Live
1938	The Adventures of Tom Sawyer
1940	Hi-Yo Silver
1942	Syncopation
1946	Slightly Scandalous

McGovern, John

| 1956 | The Benny Goodman Story |

McGovern, Merry

| 1950 | Emergency Wedding |

McGowan and Mack

| 1944 | Lake Placid Serenade |

McGowan, Billy

| 1936 | Klondike Annie |

McGowan, Dorrell

| 1936 | Ride, Ranger, Ride |
| | Sea Spoilers |

McGowan, Edward

| 1922 | For His Mother's Sake |

McGowan, Ira O.

| 1923 | Deceit |

McGowan, J. P. *same as* **McGowan, Jack; McGowan, John** *not the same as* **MacGowran, Jack**

1927	Aflame in the Sky
	The Red Raiders
	The Slaver
1929	The Invaders
	Señor Americano
1931	La pura verdad
1934	The Fighting Hero
	Wagon Wheels

1936   The Prisoner of Shark Island
      Robin Hood of El Dorado
1937   Prairie Thunder
      Slave Ship
1938   The Buccaneer
1940   Little Nellie Kelly

McGowan, Jo Ann
1944   Lake Placid Serenade

McGowan, John see **McGowan, J. P.**

Macgowan, Kenneth
1933   Rafter Romance
1936   Sins of Man
1938   In Old Chicago
1939   The Return of the Cisco Kid
1941   Belle Starr
1944   Lifeboat
1947   Easy Come, Easy Go

McGowan, Stuart same as **McGowan, Stuart E.**
1936   Ride, Ranger, Ride
      Sea Spoilers

MacGowran, Jack same as **McGowran, Jack** not the same as **McGowan, J. P.**
1952   The Quiet Man

McGrail, Walter
1918   Find the Woman
1920   Darling Mine
1923   Suzanna
1925   The Scarlet West
      A Son of His Father
1930   Anybody's War
1933   Robbers' Roost
1937   The Plainsman

McGranary, Al
1959   The FBI Story

McGrath, Frank
1932   The Rainbow Trail
1933   Robbers' Roost
1941   Western Union
1943   The Ox-Bow Incident
1948   Half Past Midnight
1949   She Wore a Yellow Ribbon
1951   Slaughter Trail
      Westward the Women
1953   Ride, Vaquero!
1957   The Tin Star

MacGrath, Harold
1918   The Million Dollar Mystery

McGrath, Larry
1930   The Arizona Kid
1931   Smart Money
1934   Broadway Bill
1938   Mr. Moto's Gamble
1939   King of Chinatown
1940   If I Had My Way
1942   Gentleman Jim
1943   Good Luck, Mr. Yates
1947   The Mighty McGurk
1950   The Jackie Robinson Story
1951   Flaming Feather

McGrath, Paul
1941   Dead Men Tell

McGrath, Tom
1916   The Woman in 47

McGrath, William J.
1932   The Secrets of Wu Sin

McGraw, Bill
1958   Blood Arrow

McGraw, Charles
1943   They Came to Blow Up America
1947   The Farmer's Daughter
      On the Old Spanish Trail
1949   Border Incident
1953   War Paint
1957   Joe Dakota
1958   The Defiant Ones
1959   The Wonderful Country
1960   Cimarron

McGraw, Martha
1921   The Land of Hope

MacGregor, Casey
1946   Canyon Passage
1947   Calendar Girl
      West to Glory
1948   Moonrise

1956   The Last Hunt
1960   Studs Lonigan

McGregor, Cathy
1948   Strange Victory

McGregor, James
1951   Saturday's Hero

MacGregor, Lee
1948   Gentleman's Agreement
      The Luck of the Irish
1950   A Ticket to Tomahawk
      Two Flags West
1952   The Half-Breed

McGregor, Malcolm
1926   The Vanishing American

MacGregor, Norval same as **McGregor, Norval**
1917   The Spirit of '76

MacGregor, Warren
1950   Annie Get Your Gun
1951   Distant Drums

McGuin, Marguerite
1947   The Peanut Man

McGuinn, Joe
1941   Mystery Ship
      Thunder Over the Prairie
1942   Shut My Big Mouth
1950   The Missourians
1953   Jack McCall Desperado
1955   Trial
1958   The Last Hurrah

McGuinness, James Kevin
1935   A Night at the Opera
1936   Robin Hood of El Dorado
1950   Rio Grande

McGuinness, Joe
1944   Chip Off the Old Block
      They Live in Fear

McGuire, Don
1945   Pride of the Marines
1947   Humoresque
      My Wild Irish Rose
1949   Boston Blackie's Chinese Venture
1955   Bad Day at Black Rock

McGuire, Dorothy
1945   A Tree Grows in Brooklyn
1946   Till the End of Time
1948   Gentleman's Agreement
1955   Trial
1960   The Dark at the Top of the Stairs

McGuire, John
1936   Charlie Chan at the Circus
      Human Cargo
      The Prisoner of Shark Island
1949   Border Incident
1950   Black Hand
      Sands of Iwo Jima

McGuire, Kathryn
1925   The Gold Hunters
      Tearing Through
1926   Buffalo Bill on the U. P. Trail

McGuire, Laurence
1921   Hearts of the Woods

McGuire, Mickey onscreen 1944— not the same as **Rooney, Mickey**
1945   A Tree Grows in Brooklyn
1947   Easy Come, Easy Go

McGuire, Paul
1950   The Breaking Point
      Raiders of Tomahawk Creek
1954   Thunder Pass
1955   Seminole Uprising
1956   Reprisal!
      Secret of Treasure Mountain
      Walk the Proud Land
1957   Band of Angels
1959   The Jayhawkers!
1960   Pay or Die

McGuire, Tom
1922   The Five Dollar Baby
1923   April Showers
      The Victor
1927   Pleasure Before Business
1932   Hearts of Humanity
      No Greater Love

1937   Charlie Chan at the Opera
      One Mile from Heaven
1938   Speed to Burn

McGuire, Tucker
1959   The Sheriff of Fractured Jaw

McGuire, Wm. Anthony
1931   Skyline

McGuirk, Charles J.
1918   Ruggles of Red Gap

Machado, Alonso
1929   Hambre

Machaty, Gustav
1945   Jealousy

Machin, Will
1918   The Yellow Dog

Machtenberg, Meyer
1931   The Voice of Israel
1933   Live and Laugh

McHugh, Charles
1925   Brand of Cowardice
      Lights of Old Broadway
1927   Finnegan's Ball
      The Princess from Hoboken
1929   Smiling Irish Eyes

McHugh, Frances
1947   Juke Joint

McHugh, Frank
1933   Grand Slam
      The Telegraph Trail
1935   The Irish in Us
1939   Daughters Courageous
1940   The Fighting 69th
1942   All Through the Night
1944   Going My Way
1945   A Medal for Benny
1947   Carnegie Hall
      Easy Come, Easy Go
1958   The Last Hurrah

McHugh, Jack
1929   Chinatown Nights
1935   The Irish in Us

McHugh, Kitty
1952   Apache Country

McHugh, Matt
1931   Street Scene
1932   Hypnotized
1933   The Man Who Dared: An Imaginative Biography
1934   Behold My Wife!
      The Cat's-Paw
      Judge Priest
1936   It Had to Happen
1937   Big City
1938   Happy Landing
      My Lucky Star
      The Rage of Paris
1939   The Escape
1942   Sunday Punch
1943   Riding High
1944   Mr. Skeffington
1945   The Bells of St. Mary's
      Salome, Where She Danced
1947   Easy Come, Easy Go

McHugh, Merle
1947   Copacabana

Macías, Gaby
1940   Perfidia

Macías, Jesús
1934   Las fronteras del amor

McIntire, John
1948   Call Northside 777
1949   Top O' the Morning
1950   Ambush
      Winchester '73
1951   The Raging Tide
      Westward the Women
1954   Apache
      War Arrow
1957   The Tin Star
1958   The Light in the Forest
1960   Flaming Star

McIntyre, Leila
1935   A Night at the Ritz
1936   The Prisoner of Shark Island
1941   Accent on Love
1943   Crash Dive
      Wintertime

1945   Nob Hill

McIntyre, Peggy
1942   Syncopation
1948   I Remember Mama

McIntyre, Robert B.
1920   The North Wind's Malice

McIvor, Mary
1917   The Sudden Gentleman

Mack, Betty
1932   The Forty-Niners
1936   Hair-Trigger Casey

Mack, Bobby
1929   Evangeline

Mack, Cactus same as **McPeters, Cactus**
1936   Custer's Last Stand
1939   The Fighting Gringo
1949   The Dalton Gang
1959   The Hanging Tree

Mack, Mrs. Charles
1927   A Harp in Hock

Mack, Charles E. (actor), 1887— 1934
1929   Why Bring That Up?
1930   Anybody's War
1932   Hypnotized

Mack, Charles Emmett (actor), 1900—1927
1927   Old San Francisco

Mack, Charles W. (prod)
1922   Blazing Arrows
      Silver Spurs

Mack, E. J. could be same as **Mack, Ed**
1920   It's a Great Life

Mack, Ed could be same as **Mack, E. J.**
1917   A Wife by Proxy

Mack, Hayward
1916   The Gilded Spider
      The Grip of Jealousy
      The Social Buccaneer
1918   The Goddess of Lost Lake

Mack, Helen
1933   The California Trail

Mack, James T. same as **Mack, James** could be same as **Mack, James, Sr.**
1927   Wild Geese
1930   Anna Christie
1934   The Cat's-Paw
1936   Charlie Chan's Secret
      Star for a Night
1937   The Devil's Playground
1938   The Texans
1941   Birth of the Blues

Mack, James, Sr. could be same as **Mack, James T.**
1939   The Escape

Mack, Joseph P.
1946   Canyon Passage

Mack, Marion
1925   One of the Bravest

Mack, Milton
1945   Rhapsody in Blue

Mack, Stanley
1934   Broadway Bill
1938   Mr. Moto's Gamble

Mack, Tommy
1945   The Dolly Sisters

Mack, Wilbur
1934   Stand Up and Cheer!
1935   A Night at the Opera
      The Winning Ticket
1936   Charlie Chan at the Race Track
      Mad Holiday
1937   The Plainsman
1938   Mr. Moto's Gamble
      Mr. Wong, Detective
1939   The Mystery of Mr. Wong
1940   Doomed to Die
1942   Nazi Agent
1943   Dixie
1946   Abie's Irish Rose
      Slightly Scandalous
1958   The Last Hurrah

Mack, Willard
1916   A Child of Mystery
      Mixed Blood
1918   The Hell Cat
      Laughing Bill Hyde

Mack, Willard
1924 Welcome Stranger
1925 Old Clothes
1927 The Dove
1930 Monsieur le Fox
Monsieur le Fox (foreign version)
Olimpia
Olimpia (foreign version)
1931 La mujer X
1933 Song of the Eagle

Mack, William B.
1923 Backbone

Mackaill, Dorothy
1921 Bits of Life
1924 The Mine with the Iron Door

McKay, Ann
1927 Roarin' Broncs

Mackay, Charles
1921 Diane of Star Hollow

McKay, Doreen
1936 Star for a Night

MacKay, Edward
1916 Man and His Angel

McKay, Gene
1934 Broadway Bill

McKay, George
1937 The Devil's Playground
1938 Little Miss Roughneck
1940 Little Nellie Kelly
1941 The Face Behind the Mask
Hurry, Charlie, Hurry
Playmates
1944 Going My Way

MacKay, Norman
1947 Untamed Fury
1948 Call Northside 777

McKay, Scott
1947 Duel in the Sun

McKay, Wanda
1940 The Way of All Flesh
1941 New York Town
The Pioneers
Virginia
1943 Deerslayer
1947 Jiggs and Maggie in Society
1948 The Golden Eye

MacKaye, Fred same as **McKaye, Fred**
1915 Time Lock Number 776
1934 Wheels of Destiny
1937 Black Legion

Mackaye, Marshall
1917 A Jewel in Pawn

McKee, Georgette
1940 The Ramparts We Watch

McKee, Harry
1937 One Mile from Heaven
1943 Action in the North Atlantic

McKee, John
1945 The House on 92nd St.
1950 Indian Territory
1951 Across the Wide Missouri
1952 The Big Sky
My Man and I
1953 The Man from the Alamo
1954 Siege at Red River
1955 Trial

McKee, Lafe same as **McKee, Lafayette**
1922 Blazing Arrows
1923 The Lone Wagon
1925 Warrior Gap
1926 Twin Triggers
1927 Roarin' Broncs
1928 The Riding Renegade
1931 The Hurricane Horseman
1933 Man from Monterey
The Telegraph Trail
1934 The Battling Buckaroo
The Lone Defender
1935 Range Warfare
Wolf Riders
1936 Custer's Last Stand
Silly Billies
1940 Santa Fe Trail

McKee, Pat
1939 Winner Take All
1942 Gentleman Jim

McKee, Raymond same as **McKee, Ray**
1917 The Little Chevalier
1918 The Unbeliever
1920 The Girl of My Heart
1921 Wing Toy

McKee, Scott
1921 Wing Toy
1926 Rose of the Tenements

McKee, Tom
1955 Blackboard Jungle

McKeen, Marie
1916 The Daughter of the Don

MacKellar, Helen
1940 Northwest Passage (Book I—Rogers' Rangers)
Three Faces West

McKelway, St. Clair
1948 Sleep, My Love

McKenna, Flicka
1960 This Rebel Breed

McKenny, Morris
1934 Drums O' Voodoo

MacKenzie, Aeneas
1942 The Navy Comes Through
They Died With Their Boots On
1944 Buffalo Bill

McKenzie, Barbara
1953 Taxi

McKenzie, Bill
1950 Winchester '73

McKenzie, Bob see **McKenzie, Robert**

MacKenzie, Donald same as **McKenzie, Donald**
1915 The Spender
1931 Fighting Caravans

MacKenzie, Joyce
1950 Broken Arrow
A Ticket to Tomahawk

MacKenzie, Lewis
1951 Native Son

MacKenzie, Phil
1938 The Rage of Paris

McKenzie, Randolph
1959 John Paul Jones

McKenzie, Robert same as **McKenzie, Bob**
1931 Cimarron
1935 Naughty Marietta
1936 Desert Gold
Rebellion
1937 Big City
Souls at Sea
1938 The Adventures of Tom Sawyer
1941 Where Did You Get That Girl?
1942 Syncopation
1946 Romance of the West
1947 Duel in the Sun

McKenzie, Tandy
1935 A Night at the Opera

McKeogh, Arthur F., Lt.
1919 The Lost Battalion

Mackey, Gerald
1943 The Meanest Man in the World
1944 Buffalo Bill
The Sullivans
1945 Nob Hill
A Tree Grows in Brooklyn
The Valley of Decision
1948 Fighting Father Dunne

McKim, Harry
1943 Good Luck, Mr. Yates
Hitler's Children
The Meanest Man in the World
1945 Wanderer of the Wasteland
1955 The Long Gray Line

McKim, Peggy
1948 I Remember Mama

McKim, Robert
1919 The Westerners
1920 The Mark of Zorro

1923 The Spider and the Rose
1926 The Strong Man
1927 Aflame in the Sky

McKim, Sammy
1940 Hi-Yo Silver
1947 Dark Delusion
1951 Saturday's Hero

Mackin, Harry
1949 The Cowboy and the Indians
1950 Battleground

Mackin, Laurie
1917 The Secret of Eve

McKinley, J. Edward
1960 Cimarron

McKinney, Betty
1943 Crash Dive

McKinney, Florine
1933 It's Great to Be Alive
1936 Muss 'Em Up
1940 Escape

McKinney, Mira same as **McKinney, Myra**
1937 Music for Madame
1940 Santa Fe Trail
1942 All Through the Night
1946 Shadows Over Chinatown
1949 Prejudice
1952 Rose of Cimarron
1953 The Eddie Cantor Story

McKinney, Nina Mae
1929 Hallelujah
1939 The Devil's Daughter
Gang Smashers
Straight to Heaven
1944 Dark Waters
1946 Mantan Messes Up
1947? Swanee Showboat
1949 Pinky

Mackintosh, Estella
1921 The Syrian Immigrant

Mackintosh, Louise
1931 The Black Camel

McLaglen, Andrew
1944 Since You Went Away

McLaglen, Victor
1928 Mother Machree
1936 Klondike Annie
1939 Let Freedom Ring
1947 Calendar Girl
The Foxes of Harrow
1948 Fort Apache
1949 She Wore a Yellow Ribbon
1950 Rio Grande
1952 The Quiet Man

MacLain, Barbara
1939 Charlie Chan in Reno

MacLane, Barton
1933 Thundering Herd
1935 Black Fury
1939 Stand Up and Fight
1941 Come Live with Me
Western Union
1942 All Through the Night
1944 Cry of the Werewolf
1946 Santa Fe Uprising
1948 Angel in Exile
The Dude Goes West
1950 Bandit Queen
1952 Bugles in the Afternoon
The Half-Breed
1955 Foxfire
1956 Wetbacks
1957 Naked in the Sun
1958 Frontier Gun

McLane, Lorenzo
1927 The Spider's Web

MacLane, Willa
1939 The Devil's Daughter

MacLaren, Ian
1936 The Last of the Mohicans

MacLaren, Mary same as **McLaren, Mary**
1917 The Plow Woman
1919 Bonnie, Bonnie Lassie
The Unpainted Woman
1934 Charlie Chan's Courage
1935 Harmony Lane
1941 Prairie Pioneers
1943 The Leopard Man
1945 The Navajo Trail

McLarin, Jimmy
1937 Big City

McLaughlin, Betty see **Ryan, Sheila**

McLaughlin, J. W. (dir)
1918 Hell's End

McLaughlin, James (actor)
1952 Red Ball Express
1953 Beneath the 12-Mile Reef

McLaughlin, Leon C.
1951 Saturday's Hero
1955 The Long Gray Line

McLaughlin, Robert
1920 Hidden Charms
1921? The Supreme Passion

McLean, Barbara
1955 Seven Cities of Gold

McLean, Billy
1956 Serenade

MacLean, Bob
1950 The Breaking Point

MacLean, Douglas
1918 The Hun Within
Johanna Enlists
1935 So Red the Rose

McLean, Eddie
1950 Riders of the Pony Express

McLean, Jack
1919 The Lost Battalion
1921 Society Snobs

McLean, Owen
1931 Riders of the Rio

McLeod, Catherine
1948 Old Los Angeles
1950 So Young, So Bad

MacLeod, Janet
1928 Vamping Venus

McLeod, Mary
1943 Bataan
1944 An American Romance
1946 G. I. War Brides

McLeod, Norman Z. same as **McLeod, Norman**
1933 A Lady's Profession
1948 The Paleface

McLeod, Victor
1941 Mutiny in the Arctic

McMackin, Archer
1917 The Winged Mystery

MacMahon, Aline
1932 The Heart of New York
1947 The Mighty McGurk
1953 The Eddie Cantor Story
1960 Cimarron

McMahon, David same as **McMahon, Dave**
1948 The Miracle of the Bells
1950 The Breaking Point
Mystery Street
1951 The Magnificent Yankee
1952 The Iron Mistress
1953 So Big
1956 The Burning Hills
Full of Life
1958 Gunman's Walk
1959 The Crimson Kimono
The FBI Story
1960 Ice Palace

MacMahon, Horace same as **McMahon, Horace**
1941 Birth of the Blues
Come Live with Me
1943 Good Luck, Mr. Yates
1955 Blackboard Jungle
1957 Beau James

MacMahon, J. G. same as **McMahon, J. G.**
1938 Little Miss Roughneck
1948 Up in Central Park

McMahon, Leo
1937 Hills of Old Wyoming
1950 Colt .45
Storm Over Wyoming
1952 The Raiders

MacManus, Edward A.
1919 The Lost Battalion

McManus, George
1946 Bringing Up Father
1948 Jiggs and Maggie in Court
1949 Jiggs and Maggie in Jackpot Jitters

1950   Jiggs and Maggie Out West

McManus, Sharon
1947   Little Mister Jim
1948   The Boy with Green Hair
          The Paleface
1949   Prejudice
1952   It's a Big Country: An American Anthology

McMillion, Walter
1946?   Go Down, Death!

McMinn, Fraser
1949   Illegal Entry

McMurphy, Charles
1933   Thundering Herd
1937   Big City

MacMurray, Fred
1937   Maid of Salem
1941   New York Town
          Virginia
1945   Where Do We Go From Here?
1948   The Miracle of the Bells
1955   The Far Horizons
1959   The Oregon Trail

McMurtry, George, Major
1919   The Lost Battalion

McNally, Edward "Skipper"
1950   Panic in the Streets
1958   The Last Hurrah
1959   The Last Angry Man

McNally, Horace *see* McNally, Stephen

McNally, James
1940   Rhythm of the Rio Grande

McNally, James E.
1957   Beau James

McNally, Stephen *same as* McNally, Horace
1942   Dr. Gillespie's New Assistant
1944   An American Romance
1950   No Way Out
          Winchester '73
1951   Apache Drums
          The Raging Tide
1953   The Stand at Apache River
1955   Violent Saturday

McNamara, Edward
1941   New York Town
1943   Margin for Error

MacNamara, James H., Major
1941   Lady from Louisiana

McNamara, John
1959   Imitation of Life

McNamara, Richard
1951   Teresa

McNamara, Ted
1928   Mother Machree

McNamara, Tom
1921   Little Italy

MacNamara, Walter
1913   Traffic in Souls

McNaughton, Charles
1932   Charlie Chan's Chance

McNear, Howard
1954   Drums Across the River

McNeely, Howard *same as* MacNeely, Howard Louis
1950   The Jackie Robinson Story
1953   Bright Road

McNeely, James
1946?   House-Rent Party

McNeely, Robert
1953   Bright Road

McNeil, Claudia
1959   The Last Angry Man

McNellis, Frank
1953   Taxi

McNulty, Dorothy *see* Singleton, Penny

McNulty, Harold
1959   The FBI Story

McNulty, John
1947   Easy Come, Easy Go

McNutt, Patterson
1930   Around the Corner
1941   Come Live with Me

McNutt, William Slavens
1930   Tom Sawyer
1931   Huckleberry Finn
          Tropennächte
1935   Ruggles of Red Gap
1936   My American Wife

McPeek, Lowell
1944   Chip Off the Old Block

McPeters, Cactus *see* Mack, Cactus

McPhail, Addie
1928   Anybody Here Seen Kelly?
1931   Aloha
1940   Northwest Passage (Book I—Rogers' Rangers)

McPhail, Douglas
1938   The Toy Wife
1940   Little Nellie Kelly

MacPherson, Donald
1920   The Dark Mirror

Macpherson, Jeanie *same as* MacPherson, Jeanie; McPherson, Jeanie
1914   Rose of the Rancho
1915   The Cheat
          Chimmie Fadden Out West
1917   The Little American
1922   Saturday Night
1937   The Plainsman
1938   The Buccaneer
1941   Land of Liberty
1948   Unconquered

McPortland, Percy
1936   General Spanky

McQuade, Arlene
1951   Molly
1958   Touch of Evil

MacQuarrie, Albert *same as* MacQuarrie, Al; McQuarrie, Albert
1917   The Pulse of Life
1919   The Little Diplomat
1920   The Mark of Zorro
1922   The Scrapper
1925   Don Q, Son of Zorro

MacQuarrie, Frank
1918   Little Red Decides

MacQuarrie, George
1917   The Adventures of Carol
1918   The Golden Wall
          Hitting the Trail
          Wanted, a Mother
1919   Mandarin's Gold
1923   Backbone
1930   Abraham Lincoln
1934   The Cat's-Paw
1936   Klondike Annie
          Robin Hood of El Dorado
1937   The Plainsman
          Souls at Sea

MacQuarrie, Murdock *same as* McQuarrie, Murdock
1918   Her Moment
1919   The Little Diplomat
1934   The Fighting Hero
1935   North of Arizona
1936   Pinto Rustlers
          The Prisoner of Shark Island
1939   Stand Up and Fight
1941   Thunder Over the Prairie
1942   Cat People
          Woman of the Year

McQueen, Butterfly
1939   Gone With the Wind
1943   Cabin in the Sky
1947   Duel in the Sun
1948   Killer Diller

McQueen, Steve
1958   Never Love a Stranger

Macrae, Arthur
1935   Ruggles of Red Gap

Macrae, Charlie
1949   Souls of Sin

McRae, Duncan
1915   Cohen's Luck
1916   The Flower of No Man's Land

MacRae, Gordon
1950   The Daughter of Rosie O'Grady

McRae, Henry *same as* MacRae, Henry
1917   The Bronze Bride
1925   The Fearless Lover

Macready, George
1949   Knock on Any Door
1950   A Lady Without Passport
1958   Gunfire at Indian Gap

McReynolds, Dexter
1925   Red Love

McSparron, Cozy
1952   Navajo

McSwain, Bill
1934   Laughing Boy

MacSweeney, John
1928   Mother Machree

McSweyn, Alexander
1949   We Were Strangers

McTaggart, Bud *same as* McTaggart, Malcolm
1939   Trigger Fingers
1943   Crash Dive
          Ladies' Day
          Margin for Error

McTurk, Joe
1949   Anna Lucasta
1957   Beau James
1958   Houseboat

McVeagh, Eve
1952   High Noon
1955   Not As a Stranger
1956   Reprisal!

McVey, Pat *same as* McVeigh, Pat
1942   In This Our Life
          Juke Girl
          They Died With Their Boots On
          Wings for the Eagle
1943   Let's Have Fun
1947   Easy Come, Easy Go

McVey, Paul
1934   Charlie Chan's Courage
          Coming Out Party
          Judge Priest
          Stand Up and Cheer!
1935   Charlie Chan in Paris
1936   Human Cargo
          The Prisoner of Shark Island
          Sins of Man
1937   One Mile from Heaven
          That I May Live
1938   Josette
          Passport Husband
          Speed to Burn
1939   Drums Along the Mohawk
1940   Phantom of Chinatown
1941   New York Town
1942   Dr. Gillespie's New Assistant
1943   Dixie

McVey, Tyler
1952   My Man and I
1953   Column South
1955   Santa Fe Passage
1956   Walk the Proud Land
1958   Terror in a Texas Town

MacVicar, Archie N.
1951   Tomahawk

MacVicar, Martha *see* Vickers, Martha

McWade, Edward *same as* McWade, Eddie
1920   Dangerous Days
1921   Wing Toy
1943   Crash Dive
          Yankee Doodle Dandy

McWade, M. *not the same as* McWade, Margaret
1922   Pals of the West

McWade, Margaret *not the same as* McWade, M.
1920   Darling Mine
1921   A Tale of Two Worlds
1938   The Texans
1943   The Meanest Man in the World

McWade, Robert
1930   Sins of the Children
1931   Cimarron
          Skyline
1932   The Match King

1934   Operator 13

McWalters, Raymond A.
1959   Last Train from Gun Hill

Macy, Mrs. Anne Sullivan *same as* Sullivan, Anne
1919   Deliverance

Macy, Carleton *same as* Macey, Carleton
1916   Gold and the Woman
          The Scarlet Oath
1918   The Firebrand

Macy, Mike
1944   Lake Placid Serenade
1949   House of Strangers

McZekkashing, Estrica
1943   Marching On!

Maddow, Ben
1950   Intruder in the Dust
1960   The Unforgiven

Maddox, Muriel
1950   Emergency Wedding
1952   Red Snow

Maddux, E. Jane
1959   The Hanging Tree

Maddux, Jim
1955   Davy Crockett, King of the Wild Frontier

Madison, Cleo
1924   Unseen Hands

Madison, Gloria
1951   Native Son

Madison, Guy
1944   Since You Went Away
1946   Till the End of Time
1949   Massacre River
1952   Red Snow
          Trail of the Arrow
1953   The Charge at Feather River
1956   The Last Frontier
          Reprisal!
1958   Bullwhip

Madison, James
1926   April Fool
1927   The Shamrock and the Rose

Madison, Julian
1934   Wagon Wheels

Madison, Mae
1931   Smart Money
1932   So Big
1934   Coming Out Party

Madison, Noel
1932   The Hatchet Man
          Me and My Gal
          Symphony of Six Million
1934   The Cat's-Paw
1936   Muss 'Em Up
1937   Man of the People
          Nation Aflame
1939   City in Darkness

Madrid, Francisco
1930   ¡De frente, marchen!
          Monsieur le Fox
1938   Di que me quieres

Madrid, Roberto de la
1959   The Young Land

Madrigal, Elena
1935   Un hombre peligroso
1939   La Inmaculada

Madson, Ronnee
1931   Personal Maid

Mae, Neola *see* Neola May, Princess

Maechivinko
1929   East Side Sadie

Maehen, Yvonne
1948   The Betrayal

Maga, Mickey
1957   Raintree County

Magaña, Delia
1930   Así es la vida
          The Bad Man (*foreign version*)
          Cascarrabias
          Charros, gauchos y manolas
1931   La dama atrevida
          Gente alegre
          El proceso de Mary Dugan

Maggert, Del
1931   The Cisco Kid
Magill, James
1944   Buffalo Bill
Magnani, Anna
1955   The Rose Tattoo
1958   Wild Is the Wind
Magnus, Annabelle
1928   Orphan of the Sage
Magrill, George
1924   North of Nevada
1927   Roarin' Broncs
1929   Hawk of the Hills
1934   Charlie Chan's Courage
1935   The Wedding Night
1936   Charlie Chan at the Race
        Track
        Star for a Night
1937   It Could Happen to You
        Maid of Salem
1938   Mr. Moto's Gamble
        Passport Husband
        Road Demon
1939   King of Chinatown
        Mr. Moto in Danger
        Island
        Winner Take All
1940   The Gay Caballero
        New Moon
1941   Mystery Ship
1942   Nazi Agent
        Tortilla Flat
1943   Gangway for Tomorrow
        Good Luck, Mr. Yates
1944   An American Romance
        The Racket Man
1945   Johnny Angel
1946   Without Reservations
1947   California
        The Jolson Story
        Pirates of Monterey
        Under the Tonto Rim
1948   Unconquered
1949   House of Strangers
        Masked Raiders
Magrin, Frank
1958   The Last Hurrah
Maguire, Hugh
1944   Going My Way
1945   Nob Hill
Maguire, John
1942   Mexican Spitfire at Sea
        Mexican Spitfire Sees a
        Ghost
        The Navy Comes Through
Maguire, Kathleen
1957   Edge of the City
Mahaffey, Blanche see **Mehaffey,
        Blanche**
Maher, Wally
1935   Rendezvous
        The Winning Ticket
1950   Mystery Street
        Right Cross
Mahin, John Lee
1932   Scarface
1934   Eskimo
        Laughing Boy
1935   Naughty Marietta
1942   Tortilla Flat
        Woman of the Year
1950   Panic in the Streets
1951   Show Boat
Mahlen, William
1931   Law of the Tong
Mahon, Carl
1931   The Exile
1932   Ten Minutes to Live
1932?   The Girl from Chicago
Mahoney, Ernestine
1930   Whoopee
Mahoney, Francis X.
1936   Show Boat
Mahoney, Jock same as
        O'Mahoney, Jock
1950   Jolson Sings Again
1954   Overland Pacific
1957   Joe Dakota
Mahoney, Mike
1953   The Stars Are Singing
1957   Beau James
1959   The Jayhawkers!

Mahoney, P. B.
1935?   The Irish Gringo
Mahoney, Wilkie
1941   Birth of the Blues
1943   The Meanest Man in the
        World
Maibaum, Richard
1941   Hold Back the Dawn
1960   The Day They Robbed the
        Bank of England
Maier, Carolyn
1957   Burden of Truth
Maier, Patricia
1941   Accent on Love
Maigne, Charles
1917   The Bottle Imp
        The Squaw Man's Son
1918   Out of a Clear Sky
1926   War Paint
Mailes, Charles Hill same as
        Mailes, Charles
1914   The Woman in Black
1917   The Bronze Bride
        The Winged Mystery
1920   The Mark of Zorro
1923   Crashin' Thru
1926   The Frontier Trail
1927   Bitter Apples
Main, Marjorie
1935   Naughty Marietta
1937   Boy of the Streets
1942   We Were Dancing
1946   Bad Bascomb
1952   It's a Big Country: An
        American Anthology
Mainwaring, Daniel same as
        Homes, Geoffrey
1946   Swamp Fire
1950   The Lawless
1951   The Last Outpost
        The Tall Target
1952   Bugles in the Afternoon
1960   Walk Like a Dragon
Mainz, Friedrich
1960   I Aim at the Stars: the
        Wernher von Braun
        Story
Maiori, Mrs. A.
1916   Poor Little Peppina
Maiori, Antonio
1916   Poor Little Peppina
Maisell, Lewis
1931?   La porta del destino
Maison, Alma
1949   The Undercover Man
Maizani, Azucena
1938   Di que me quieres
Maize, Andrew
194-   Mistaken Identity
Majalca, Anna Maria
1956   Giant
Majeroni, George
1921   Diane of Star Hollow
Majeroni, Mario
1914   The Nightingale
Majors, Eddie
1946   The Gay Cavalier
Makar, Zita
1927   The Fighting Hombre
1931   Zein Weib's Lubovnick
Makarenko, Dan
1937   The Cantor's Son
Makarenko, David
1939   Tevya
Mako, Gene
1938   Happy Landing
Mala, Ray same as **Chee-ak; Mala**
1932   Igloo
1934   Eskimo
1940   Girl from God's Country
1941   Hold Back the Dawn
1952   Red Snow
Malan, William
1927   The Overland Stage
Malatesta, Fred same as **Malatesta,
        Fred M.**
1918   The Border Raiders
1922   The Woman He Loved
1924   The Night Hawk
1929   The Peacock Fan
1930   El precio de un beso

1931   La mujer X
1933   L'amour guide
1934   Granaderos del amor
        La veuve joyeuse
1935   A Night at the Opera
1940   The Mark of Zorro
Malavsky, Sergei
1953   Tonight We Sing
Malcolm, Robert
1945   A Tree Grows in Brooklyn
1949   Lust for Gold
        The Undercover Man
        We Were Strangers
1950   Annie Get Your Gun
        Black Hand
1951   The Magnificent Yankee
        The Tall Target
1952   Bugles in the Afternoon
1956   The Lone Ranger
1957   The Brothers Rico
1958   Gunman's Walk
Maldanado, Bertha
1936   Tundra
Malde, Otto
1938   Happy Landing
Malden, Karl
1940   They Knew What They
        Wanted
1951   A Streetcar Named Desire
1956   Baby Doll
1959   The Hanging Tree
Maldonado, Ruben
1938   Hawaii Calls
Malena, Lena
1928   Diamond Handcuffs
Malendez, Harold A.
1941   Western Union
Maley, Peggy same as **Maley,
        Peggy June**
1944   Since You Went Away
1955   Not As a Stranger
1957   The Brothers Rico
        The Guns of Fort
        Petticoat
        The Midnight Story
Malinowski
1941   Z Dymem Pożarów
Malis, Cy
1943   Ladies' Day
1946   The Gentleman
        Misbehaves
1947   It Had To Be You
1949   The Story of Seabiscuit
        The Undercover Man
Malkin, Raymond
1950   Black Hand
Mallah, Vivian
1950   Young Man with a Horn
Malleson, Miles
1960   The Day They Robbed the
        Bank of England
Mallinson, Rory
1945   Pride of the Marines
1947   King of the Bandits
1948   Docks of New Orleans
        Open Secret
1951   Cavalry Scout
        Oh! Susanna
1952   The Big Sky
        Brave Warrior
        Trail of the Arrow
1953   The Man Behind the Gun
1955   Kentucky Rifle
        Seminole Uprising
        Shotgun
Mallon, John
1948   Unconquered
Ozzy Mallon's Jitterbugs
1946?   House-Rent Party
Mallory, Chad
1952   Kid Monk Baroni
Mallory, Wayne
1956   Reprisal!
1958   Bullwhip
Malloy, Doris
1936   Human Cargo
Malo, Frank
1937   Boy of the Streets
Malone, Dorothy
1949   Colorado Territory
1956   Pillars of the Sky

1960   The Last Voyage
Malone, J. (actor)
1931   Delicious
Malone, Joel (writer)
1946   Slightly Scandalous
1949   Arctic Manhunt
        Illegal Entry
Malone, Martin
1934   Behold My Wife!
Malone, Molly
1917   The Pulse of Life
1918   Wild Women
1920   It's a Great Life
1921   Made in Heaven
Malone, Ralph
1937   The Plainsman
Malone, Ray
1944   Slightly Terrific
Malone, Tom
1930   The Grand Parade
Malone, Violet
1914   The Little Angel of
        Canyon Creek
1916   Alien Souls
Maloney, Esther
1960   The Last Voyage
Maloney, Mike
1959   Last Train from Gun Hill
Malouf, Nefru
1956   Hot Blood
Maltz, Albert
1945   Pride of the Marines
1950   Broken Arrow
Malvern, Paul
1936   Sea Spoilers
1938   Outlaw Express
1940   Doomed to Die
        Phantom of Chinatown
1942   North to the Klondike
1947   Pirates of Monterey
1950   Rock Island Trail
Maly, Gero
1949   The Kissing Bandit
Maly, Walter
1927   The Fighting Hombre
Malyon, Eily
1934   Limehouse Blues
1935   Romance in Manhattan
1937   That I May Live
1939   Confessions of a Nazi Spy
1944   Going My Way
Mamakos, Peter
1949   House of Strangers
        Tuna Clipper
1951   The Mark of the
        Renegade
1953   The Glory Brigade
1956   Quincannon, Frontier
        Scout
1958   Fort Bowie
Mamet, Henry
1950   Panic in the Streets
Mamo see **Clark, Mamo**
Mamoulian, Rouben
1940   The Mark of Zorro
Man, Tso Yee
1941   Golden Gate Girl
Mandel, Israel
1939   The Light Ahead
Mandell, Harry L.
1960   Hell to Eternity
Mandelstamm, Valentin
1932   L'athlète incomplet
Mander, Miles
1937   Slave Ship
1942   Apache Trail
Mandeville, William
1917   The Call of Her People
Mandryka, N.
1939   Cossacks in Exile
Mandy, Jerry
1927   The Gay Defender
1928   Hold 'Em Yale
1929   Love, Live and Laugh
1938   Hawaii Calls
        Rascals
1940   East of the River
1942   Wings for the Eagle

Manfredi, Antonio
1935   Rosa de Francia
1936   El crimen de media
        noche
Mangean, Teddy *same as* **Manjean,**
    Teddy
1932   Hypnotized
1940   Mexican Spitfire Out
        West
1943   Ladies' Day
Manger, I.
1937   The Jester (Der
        Purimspieler)
Mangum, Joe
1944   Going My Way
Manheimer, E. S.
1922   Breaking Home Ties
Mankiewicz, Don M.
1955   Trial
Mankiewicz, Herman J. *same as*
    Mankiewicz, Herman
1927   The Gay Defender
1928   The Mating Call
1929   Abie's Irish Rose
        Thunderbolt
1930   Ladies Love Brutes
1931   Chérie (*foreign version*)
1935   Rendezvous
Mankiewicz, Joseph L. *same as*
    Mankiewicz, Joseph
1929   Thunderbolt
1930   Amor audaz
1933   Diplomaniacs
1934   Our Daily Bread
1939   The Adventures of
        Huckleberry Finn
1942   Woman of the Year
1949   House of Strangers
1950   No Way Out
Mankins, Roxie
1923   Flames of Wrath
Mann, Anthony
1947   Desperate
1949   Border Incident
1950   Devil's Doorway
        The Furies
        Winchester '73
1951   The Tall Target
1953   Thunder Bay
1956   The Last Frontier
        Serenade
1957   The Tin Star
1960   Cimarron
Mann, Arthur
1950   The Jackie Robinson Story
Mann, Daniel
1955   The Rose Tattoo
1959   The Last Angry Man
Mann, Delbert
1955   Marty
1960   The Dark at the Top of
        the Stairs
Mann, Dolores
1953   Tonight We Sing
Mann, Dorothy
1944   Since You Went Away
Mann, George
1945   Where Do We Go From
        Here?
Mann, Gerda
1931   Buster se marie (*foreign version*)
Mann, Hank
1930   The Arizona Kid
1932   Me and My Gal
1937   Man of the People
1938   Josette
1939   Charlie Chan in Reno
        Mr. Moto Takes a
        Vacation
1942   Juke Girl
1943   Yankee Doodle Dandy
1948   Big City
1949   Jiggs and Maggie in
        Jackpot Jitters
1950   Ambush
1958   The Last Hurrah
1959   Last Train from Gun Hill
Mann, Helen
1935   L'homme des Folies
        Bergère

Mann, Larry
1958   Flaming Frontier
Mann, Louis
1930   Sins of the Children
Mann, Margaret
1919   The Right to Happiness
1934   Beloved
        Charlie Chan in London
        Judge Priest
Mann, Virginia
1913   The Inside of the White
        Slave Traffic
Manners, David
1934   The Great Flirtation
Manners, Dorothy
1921   Across the Divide
1922   Pawn Ticket 210
1923   Snowdrift
        The Victor
Manners, Marjorie
1942   Rubber Racketeers
1947   The Burning Cross
Manners, Nikki
1945   Where Do We Go From
        Here?
Mannick, Jack
1948   Call Northside 777
Manning, Aileen
1922   The Power of Love
1928   Uncle Tom's Cabin
1931   Huckleberry Finn
Manning, Bruce
1938   The Rage of Paris
1943   The Amazing Mrs.
        Holliday
1949   That Midnight Kiss
Manning, Irene
1943   Yankee Doodle Dandy
Manning, Knox
1942   Wings for the Eagle
1944   The Sullivans
1947   Buck Privates Come
        Home
Manning, Martha
1936   Star for a Night
Manning, Mildred
1919   The Westerners
Manning, Paul
1952   Anything Can Happen
Manning, Philipp, Dr. *same as*
    Manning, Philipp
1930   Doña mentiras (*foreign version*)
1931   La carta (*foreign version*)
Manning, Robert
1946   Till the End of Time
Manning, T. H.
1931   Street Scene
1933   Counsellor at Law
Manning, Thelma
1938   In Old Chicago
Mannon, Alfred T.
1932   Soñadores de la gloria
1935   Fighting Pioneers
Mannors, Sheila *see* **Bromley,**
    Sheila
Manolas, Jack
1949   The Kissing Bandit
Manon, Marcia
1922   The Woman He Loved
1925   Justice of the Far North
1929   Love, Live and Laugh
Manrique, Aurelio
1931   La gran jornada
Mansfield, Alma
1953   The Member of the
        Wedding
Mansfield, Jayne
1959   The Sheriff of Fractured
        Jaw
Mansfield, John
1950   Battleground
1951   Warpath
1955   Duel on the Mississippi
        Kiss of Fire
Mansfield, Kay
1949   The Girl from Jones
        Beach

Mansfield, Martha
1923   Potash and Perlmutter
Mansfield, Rankin
1954   The Black Dakotas
1956   Dakota Incident
        Walk the Proud Land
1957   The Brothers Rico
        The Oklahoman
Manson, Helena
1932   Le cas du docteur
        Brenner
1951   Adventures of Captain
        Fabian
Manson, Maurice
1959   Porgy and Bess
Manstad, Margit
1930   Doña mentiras (*foreign version*)
        Toda una vida (*foreign version*)
Mantell, Arthur
1929   This Is Heaven
Mantell, Joe
1949   The Undercover Man
1955   Marty
1957   Beau James
Mantle, Burns
1915   How Molly Malone Made
        Good
Manuel, Eddie
1950   Panic in the Streets
Many Mules, Bob
1956   The Searchers
Many Mules Son
1956   The Searchers
Many Treaties, Chief *same as*
    Hazlett, William
1937   Drums of Destiny
1941   The Pioneers
1943   Deerslayer
        The Law Rides Again
1944   Buffalo Bill
1947   Buffalo Bill Rides Again
Manzey, Edward
1950   Panic in the Streets
Manzione, Frank
1932   Amor in montagna
Mapes, Ted
1942   Below the Border
1943   Frontier Fury
        Land of Hunted Men
1944   The Racket Man
        Riding West
1948   Fury at Furnace Creek
        The Paleface
        Unconquered
1950   Winchester '73
1953   Thunder Bay
Maple, Christine
1930   Whoopee
Maple, John E.
1920   Before the White Man
        Came
Mara, Adele
1942   Shut My Big Mouth
1943   Good Luck, Mr. Yates
        Redhead from Manhattan
1948   Angel in Exile
1950   Rock Island Trail
        Sands of Iwo Jima
Marable, Lawrence
1952   The Iron Mistress
Maracci, Livia
1932   Tormento
Maran, Donna
1960   The Pusher
Marán, Francisco *same as* **Marán,**
    Francesco
1930   Monsieur le Fox (*foreign version*)
        Sombras de gloria
1934   La buenaventura
        La ciudad de cartón
        Granaderos del amor
1935   Alas sobre el Chaco
        El cantante de Nápoles
        No matarás
1936   Down to the Sea
1940   The Mark of Zorro
1941   Hold Back the Dawn
1942   Syncopation

Marba, Joe Smith
1934   Stand Up and Cheer!
Marburgh, Bertram
1920?   The Greatest Love
1925   His People
1930   The Melody Man
Marc, Agnes
1959   The Black Orchid
Marc, Alice
1914   The Jungle
Marc, Ted
1955   Good Morning, Miss Dove
Marc-Hély
1931   Chérie
Marcel, Inez
1917   Unknown 274
Marcelle, Lou
1947   Jiggs and Maggie in
        Society
1950   Riders of the Pony
        Express
Marcelle, Sonia
1916?   Should a Baby Die?
1921   Diane of Star Hollow
Marcellino, Freddie
1952   Bright Victory
March, David
1952   Japanese War Bride
March, Eve
1950   Rio Grande
1953   The Sun Shines Bright
1958   The Last Hurrah
March, Fredric
1930   Ladies Love Brutes
1938   The Buccaneer
1944   Tomorrow the World!
1952   It's a Big Country: An
        American Anthology
March, Hal
1953   The Eddie Cantor Story
March, Joseph Moncure
1940   Three Faces West
March, Ruth *see* **Hussey, Ruth**
Marchal, Arlette
1931   Don Juan diplomático
        (*foreign version*)
Marchand, Léopold
1932   Une heure près de toi
Marchat, Jean
1932   Le cas du docteur
        Brenner
Marche, Gazelle
1916?   Should a Baby Die?
Marchetti, Milo, Jr.
1939   Fisherman's Wharf
Marcin, Max
1920   The Face at Your Window
Marco, Henry
1950   Devil's Doorway
Marco, Marya
1949   Boston Blackie's Chinese
        Venture
        The Clay Pigeon
Marcus, Bernie
1949   The Red Menace
Marcus, Betty
1939   Tevya
Marcus, James *same as* **Marcus, J.**
    A.; Marcus, James A.; Marcus,
    Jim
1917   The Conqueror
1918   The Prussian Cur
1919   Evangeline
1922   Come On Over
1928   The Broken Mask
1929   Evangeline
        In Old Arizona
1931   Fighting Caravans
        The Great Meadow
1934   Operator 13
        Wagon Wheels
1936   The Prisoner of Shark
        Island
        Rose of the Rancho
1937   Maid of Salem
Marcus, Lee
1936   Silly Billies
1939   The Fighting Gringo
        The Girl from Mexico
1940   Mexican Spitfire
        Mexican Spitfire Out
        West

1943   Crash Dive
       They Came to Blow Up America

Marcus, Morris
1934   The Youth of Russia

Marcus, Vicky same as **Marcus, Vicki**
1937   The Cantor's Son
1939   Tevya

Mardelli, George
1941   Louisiana Purchase

Marden, Adrienne
1936   Star for a Night
1948   Gentleman's Agreement
1956   Man from Del Rio
1960   This Rebel Breed

Mardiganian, Aurora
1919   Auction of Souls

Maren, Jerry
1946   Three Wise Fools

Margo
1936   Robin Hood of El Dorado
       Winterset
1939   Miracle on Main Street
       Miracle on Main Street (foreign version)
1943   Gangway for Tomorrow
       The Leopard Man

Margot, Herta
1940   Mexican Spitfire Out West

Mari, George same as **Mari, Jorge**
1939   Verbena trágica
1956   Comanche

Mari, John
1941   Hold Back the Dawn

Mari, Jorge see **Mari, George**

The Mariachis Los Reyes De Chapala
1959   The Young Land

Maricle, Leona
1939   Judge Hardy and Son
1944   My Pal Wolf
1946   Without Reservations

Baby Marie see **Osborne, Marie**

Marie, Norma
1927   Don Mike

Marier, Victor, Captain see **Taylor, S. E. V.**

Marievsky, Joseph
1940   Elsa Maxwell's Public Deb No. 1

Marigold, Todhunter, Col.
1920   The Cyclone

Marihugh, Tammy
1960   The Last Voyage

Marin, Albert
1948   Key Largo

Marin, Edwin L.
1937   Man of the People
1945   Johnny Angel
1950   The Cariboo Trail
       Colt .45

Marion, Beth
1936   For the Service

Marion, Charles R.
1952   The Fabulous Senorita
1958   Apache Territory

Marion, Don
1923   Jealous Husbands
1938   Passport Husband

Marion, Frances
1916   The Social Highwayman
       The Yellow Passport
1918   Amarilly of Clothes-Line Alley
       The City of Dim Faces
       How Could You, Jean?
       Johanna Enlists
       The Temple of Dusk
1920   Humoresque
1922   East Is West
1923   Potash and Perlmutter
1924   In Hollywood With Potash and Perlmutter
1927   The Callahans and the Murphys
1930   Anna Christie
       Anna Christie (foreign version)
       El presidio
       Wu Li Chang

1931   La fruta amarga
       Soyons gais
1940   Northwest Passage (Book I—Rogers' Rangers)

Marion, George F. (actor) see **Marion, George, Sr.** (actor)

Marion, George, Jr. (writer)
1926   Irene
       Sweet Daddies
1927   The Gay Defender
1929   This Is Heaven
       Why Bring That Up?

Marion, George, Sr. (actor) same as **Marion, George F.** (actor)
1923   Anna Christie
1929   Evangeline
1930   Anna Christie

Marion, Oskar
1931   La fiesta del diablo (foreign version)

Marion, Paul
1939   In Old Caliente
1940   Covered Wagon Days
1949   Border Incident
       Harbor of Missing Men
       The Undercover Man
       We Were Strangers
1950   Bandit Queen
       Last of the Buccaneers
       Raiders of Tomahawk Creek
1952   The Fighter
1953   Arrowhead
1955   Kiss of Fire
       Shotgun

Marion, Sid same as **Marion, Sidney**
1948   Jiggs and Maggie in Court
1949   Illegal Entry
       Jiggs and Maggie in Jackpot Jitters
1957   Beau James

Marion, William
1923   The Huntress

Maris, Mona
1929   Romance of the Rio Grande
1930   The Arizona Kid
       Cuando el amor ríe
       Del mismo barro
       El precio de un beso
1932   El caballero de la noche
1933   La melodía prohibida
       No dejes la puerta abierta
       Una viuda romántica
       Yo, tú y ella
1934   Un capitán de cosacos
       Cuesta abajo
       Tres amores
       White Heat
1935   ¡Asegure a su mujer!
       El cantante de Nápoles

Mariscal, Alberto
1958   Sierra Baron

Maritza, Sari
1933   A Lady's Profession

Maritza Dancers
1944   Slightly Terrific

Mark, Mel
1950   The Girl from San Lorenzo

Mark, Michael
1945   Jealousy
1947   Northwest Outpost

Russell Markert Girls
1930   King of Jazz

Markey, Gene
1929   Mother's Boy
1938   Josette
1940   Elsa Maxwell's Public Deb No. 1

Markham, Alice
1951   Show Boat
       Westward the Women

Markham, Dewey "Pigmeat" same as **Markham, "Pigmeat"; Markham, Pigmeat "Alamo"**
1940   Am I Guilty?
1946?   Fight That Ghost
       House-Rent Party
1947?   Swanee Showboat
1948?   Junction 88

1955   Brevities of 1955

Markle, Fletcher
1949   Jigsaw

Markopoulos, Vasilios, Rev.
1952   Anything Can Happen

Marks, Clarence
1936   Rainbow on the River
1952   Hiawatha
       The Ring

Marks, Herman
1934   Broadway Bill
1941   Mystery Ship

Marks, Joe E.
1938   Outside of Paradise

Marks, Patsy
1922   My Boy

Marks, Willis
1936   Desert Gold

Markson, Ben same as **Markson, Benjamin**
1929   Masked Emotions
1937   That I May Live

Markwell, Norman
1955   The Rose Tattoo

Marley, Jay
1919   A Fighting Colleen

Marley, John
1953   The Joe Louis Story
1960   Pay or Die

Marlin, John
1950   Black Hand

Marlin, Rena
1949   House of Strangers

Marlow, Nancy
1946   Slightly Scandalous

Marlowe, Anthony
1943   Action in the North Atlantic

Marlowe, Don
1957   Journey to Freedom
       The Oklahoman

Marlowe, Frank same as **Marlo, Frank**
1934   Operator 13
1936   My American Wife
1937   The Devil's Playground
       Man of the People
1941   Where Did You Get That Girl?
1942   Nazi Agent
1943   Air Force
1946   Bringing Up Father
       Dark Alibi
       Notorious
1947   Buck Privates Come Home
       King of the Bandits
       Riding the California Trail
1949   Knock on Any Door
1957   All Mine to Give
1958   Escape from Red Rock
       The Last Hurrah

Marlowe, Fred
1950   Broken Arrow

Marlowe, Gene
1955   Apache Woman

Marlowe, Gloria
1952   Anything Can Happen

Marlowe, Hugh
1952   Bugles in the Afternoon
1953   The Stand at Apache River

Marlowe, Jo Ann
1943   Yankee Doodle Dandy

Marlowe, John
1959   Imitation of Life

Marlowe, June
1931   Pardon Us
       Pardon Us (foreign version)
1934   The Lone Defender
1935   Riddle Ranch

Marlowe, Katharine
1950   No Way Out

Marlowe, Sam, Jr.
1950   No Way Out

Marly, Michele
1959   Thunder in the Sun

Marqués, María Elena
1951   Across the Wide Missouri
1953   Ambush at Tomahawk Gap

Marquis, a horse
1933   King of the Wild Horses

Marr, Eddie same as **Marr, Edward**
1938   Dangerous to Know
       Gateway
       Mr. Moto's Gamble
       Road Demon
       Spawn of the North
1939   Judge Hardy and Son
       King of Chinatown
       Mr. Moto in Danger Island
       Waterfront
1940   Charlie Chan at the Wax Museum
1945   Rhapsody in Blue

Marriott, John
1953   The Joe Louis Story

Mars, Roland
1931   Echec au roi

Marsac, Maurice
1947   The Foxes of Harrow
1953   Tonight We Sing
1957   Band of Angels

Marsaudon, Andre P. same as **Marsaudon, Andre**
1938   Dangerous to Know
       Daughter of Shanghai
1947   The Foxes of Harrow

Marsh, "Mother"
1918   Fields of Honor

Marsh, Anthony same as **Marsh, Tony**
1942   We Were Dancing
1943   Action in the North Atlantic
1946   Till the End of Time
1954   Broken Lance

Marsh, Charles
1942   Gentleman Jim
1943   Gangway for Tomorrow
1944   Mr. Skeffington
1945   A Tree Grows in Brooklyn
1947   The Jolson Story
       My Wild Irish Rose
1948   Angel in Exile
1949   The Story of Seabiscuit
1951   The Harlem Globetrotters

Marsh, Earle
1928   United States Smith

Marsh, Joan same as **Rosher, Dorothy**
1918   How Could You, Jean?
1933   It's Great to Be Alive
       The Man Who Dared: An Imaginative Biography
1937   Charlie Chan on Broadway
       Life Begins in College

Marsh, Judy
1959   The Wonderful Country

Marsh, Mae
1915   The Birth of a Nation
1918   Fields of Honor
1919   Spotlight Sadie
1935   Black Fury
1939   Drums Along the Mohawk
1941   Belle Starr
1942   Tales of Manhattan
1943   The Meanest Man in the World
1944   The Sullivans
1945   The Dolly Sisters
       A Tree Grows in Brooklyn
1948   Fort Apache
1949   The Fighting Kentuckian
       3 Godfathers
1952   The Quiet Man
1953   The Sun Shines Bright
1955   Good Morning, Miss Dove
1960   Sergeant Rutledge

Marsh, Marguerite same as **Marsh, Margaret**
1914   Threads of Destiny
1916   Little Meena's Romance
1918   Fields of Honor

Marsh, Marian *same as* **Morgan, Marilyn**
1930   Whoopee
Marsh, Myra
1936   Paddy O'Day
1938   Rascals
1942   Young America
1953   The Man from the Alamo
Marsh, Tani
1942   Song of the Islands
Marsh, Tiger Joe
1949   Pinky
1950   Panic in the Streets
1954   Hell's Half Acre
Marsh, Tony *see* **Marsh, Anthony**
Marshall, Alan
1936   After the Thin Man
Marshall, Arthur
1959   Night of the Quarter
          Moon
Marshall, Brenda
1940   East of the River
1950   The Iroquois Trail
Marshall, Chet
1954   Dangerous Mission
Marshall, Clark
1937   Man of the People
Marshall, E. G.
1945   The House on 92nd St.
1947   Untamed Fury
1948   Call Northside 777
1952   Anything Can Happen
1954   Broken Lance
1957   Twelve Angry Men
Marshall, George *same as*
Marshall, George E.
1926   A Trip to Chinatown
1933   Olsen's Big Moment
1942   Valley of the Sun
1943   Riding High
1948   Tap Roots
1952   The Savage
1956   Pillars of the Sky
1957   The Guns of Fort
          Petticoat
Marshall, Gregory
1952   Fort Osage
Marshall, Helene
1959   Night of the Quarter
          Moon
Marshall, Herbert
1944   Andy Hardy's Blonde
          Trouble
1947   Duel in the Sun
Marshall, Jack *could be same as*
Marshall, John
1946   Slightly Scandalous
Marshall, Jean
1947   Easy Come, Easy Go
Marshall, John *could be same as*
Marshall, Jack
1956   Reprisal!
Marshall, Loraine
1933   It's Great to Be Alive
Marshall, Marion
1948   Gentleman's Agreement
          The Luck of the Irish
1950   A Ticket to Tomahawk
Marshall, Mary
1949   Prejudice
Marshall, Mort
1954   Go Man Go
Marshall, Ruth
1941   Playmates
Marshall, Stacey
1958   Home Before Dark
Marshall, Tina
1934   Stand Up and Cheer!
1936   Dangerous Intrigue
Marshall, Trudy
1943   Crash Dive
1944   The Sullivans
1945   The Dolly Sisters
1949   Shamrock Hill
1956   Full of Life
Marshall, Tully
1915   The Sable Lorcha
1917   Unconquered
1918   The Squaw Man
1919   Daughter of Mine
1921   Lotus Blossom

1929   Redskin
          Thunderbolt
1930   Tom Sawyer
1931   Fighting Caravans
1932   The Hatchet Man
          Scarface
1934   Massacre
1935   Black Fury
1937   Souls at Sea
Marshall, William
1940   East of the River
          Knute Rockne—All
          American
          Santa Fe Trail
1947   Calendar Girl
1951   Adventures of Captain
          Fabian
Marshbanks, Julia S.
1950   Intruder in the Dust
Marshe, Vera
1946   Abie's Irish Rose
1950   Davy Crockett, Indian
          Scout
Marshman, D. M., Jr.
1953   Taxi
Marstini, Rosita
1918?   Rosemary Climbs the
          Heights
1919   The Tiger Lily
1928   We Americans
Marston, Joel
1949   Jiggs and Maggie in
          Jackpot Jitters
          The Sky Dragon
1958   Home Before Dark
1960   The Last Voyage
Marston, John
1934   Wagon Wheels
1936   Sins of Man
1949   The Girl from Jones
          Beach
1950   Broken Arrow
Marston, Lawrence
1914   The Woman in Black
Marston, Mrs. Lawrence
1914   The Woman in Black
Martan, Nita
1927   Lost at the Front
Martel, Alphonse *see* **Martell,**
Alphonse
Martel, William
1949   The Red Menace
Martell, Alphonse *same as* **Martel,**
Alphonse
1928   The Night Bird
1935   The Wedding Night
1936   Human Cargo
1938   Charlie Chan at Monte
          Carlo
1945   The Dolly Sisters
          Nob Hill
1946   The Gentleman
          Misbehaves
1951   Show Boat
1953   Dream Wife
Martell, Donna
1949   Illegal Entry
Martell, Gregg
1949   The Red Menace
1950   Winchester '73
1953   The Glory Brigade
          Tonight We Sing
1958   Tonka
Martell, Saul Z.
1949   Thieves' Highway
Martelli, Tony
1934   Broadway Bill
1939   Mr. Moto in Danger
          Island
Martens, Charlotte
1931   Chérie
Martens, Fred
1933   No dejes la puerta abierta
Marti, Alberto
1940   Perfidia
Martiánez, Antonio
1931   Un caballero de frac
1932   El hombre que asesinó
Martin and Williams
1939   Straight to Heaven

Martin, Master
1914   At the Cross Roads
Martin, Al *(actor)*
1924   Racing Luck
Martin, Al *(writer)*
1941   Caught in the Act
Martin, Alma
1915   The Spender
Martin, Andra
1959   Yellowstone Kelly
Martin, Bill *could be same as*
Martin, William
1951   Saturday's Hero
Martin, Buzz
1959   The FBI Story
1960   Cimarron
Martin, Carla
1951   Mask of the Dragon
Martin, Charles
1956   Death of a Scoundrel
Martin, Chris-Pin *same as* **Martin,**
Chris; Martin, Chris King;
Martin, Chris Pin; Martin,
Chrispin
1931   The Cisco Kid
          The Squaw Man
1933   The California Trail
          Man from Monterey
1934   Lazy River
1936   The Bold Caballero
1937   Boots and Saddles
1938   The Renegade Ranger
          The Texans
1939   The Cisco Kid and the
          Lady
          The Fighting Gringo
          The Return of the Cisco
          Kid
1940   Charlie Chan in Panama
          The Gay Caballero
          Lucky Cisco Kid
          The Mark of Zorro
          Viva Cisco Kid
1941   Ride on Vaquero
          Romance of the Rio
          Grande
1942   American Empire
1943   The Ox-Bow Incident
1947   King of the Bandits
          Pirates of Monterey
          Robin Hood of Monterey
1948   Old Los Angeles
1953   San Antone
Martin, Daisy
1922   Spitfire
Martin, Dean
1958   The Young Lions
Martin, Dewey
1949   Knock on Any Door
1950   Battleground
1952   The Big Sky
Martin, Don
1954   Arrow in the Dust
1956   Quincannon, Frontier
          Scout
Martin, Duke
1928   Flying Romeos
1929   In Old Arizona
Martin, Dwight
1949   That Midnight Kiss
Martin, Edgar
1947   Hi De Ho
1948   Killer Diller
1948?   Boarding House Blues
Martin, Eugene
1958   Terror in a Texas Town
1960   This Rebel Breed
Martin, Euline
1944   Tender Comrade
Martin, Francis *same as* **Martin,**
Francis J.
1931   El tenorio del harem
1937   Waikiki Wedding
1942   Shut My Big Mouth
Freddy Martin and His Orchestra
1943   What's Buzzin' Cousin?
Martin, George M., Jr.
1957   Segregation and the South
Martin, Henry
1941   Where Did You Get That
          Girl?

Martin, Hugh *could be same as*
Martin, Hugo
1943   Marching On!
Martin, Hugo *could be same as*
Martin, Hugh
1945   Of One Blood
Martin, Irene
1949   The Undercover Man
Martin, Jack
1942   The Navy Comes Through
Martin, James *same as* **Martin,**
Jim; Martin, Jimmy
1946   Renegade Girl
1947   West to Glory
1948   Harpoon
1950   Battleground
Martin, Janet *same as* **Terry, Valya**
1944   Lake Placid Serenade
1947   Calendar Girl
Martin, Jerry
1956   The Last Hunt
1960   Pay or Die
Martin, Jill
1939   Trigger Fingers
Martin, Jim *see* **Martin, James**
Martin, Jimmy *see* **Martin, James**
Martin, John Stuart
1945   The House on 92nd St.
Martin, Kewpie
1936   After the Thin Man
Martin, Lewis
1953   Arrowhead
Martin, Loraine Mae
1947   Citizen Saint
Martin, Marcella
1939   Gone With the Wind
Martin, Marguerite *same as*
Martin, Margaret
1938   The Buccaneer
1940   Viva Cisco Kid
1944   Buffalo Bill
1949   The Kissing Bandit
          Streets of Laredo
1950   The Men
1955   The Far Horizons
Martin, Marion
1941   The Mexican Spitfire's
          Baby
1942   Mexican Spitfire at Sea
          Mexican Spitfire's
          Elephant
          Tales of Manhattan
Martin, Mary
1941   Birth of the Blues
          New York Town
Martin, Mickey
1937   It Could Happen to You
1951   The Tall Target
1952   It's a Big Country: An
          American Anthology
Martin, Muriel
1922   The Good Provider
Martin, Orlando A.
1940   Elsa Maxwell's Public
          Deb No. 1
Martin, Ray
1936   The Green Pastures
1937   Bargain with Bullets
1938   The Duke Is Tops
Martin, Richard
1942   Mexican Spitfire at Sea
          Mexican Spitfire Sees a
          Ghost
1943   Gangway for Tomorrow
          Hitler's Children
          Ladies' Day
          The Leopard Man
1944   Tender Comrade
1945   Wanderer of the
          Wasteland
1947   The Adventures of Don
          Coyote
          Thunder Mountain
          Under the Tonto Rim
          Wild Horse Mesa
1948   The Arizona Ranger
          Gun Smugglers
          Guns of Hate
          Indian Agent
          Western Heritage
1949   Brothers in the Saddle
          Masked Raiders
          The Mysterious
          Desperado

Riders of the Range
Rustlers
Stagecoach Kid
1950   Border Treasure
Rio Grande Patrol
Storm Over Wyoming
1952   The Raiders

Martin, Robert
1960   The Last Voyage

Martin, Sally
1937   The Barrier

Martin, Salvador
1930   El valiente

Martin, Scoop
1938   The Texans

Martin, Shirley Vance
1922   My Boy

Martin, Slim
1938   Josette

Martin, Spear
1948   The Boy with Green Hair

Martin, Strother
1954   Drum Beat

Martin, Thomas F. *same as* **Martin, Tom**
1944   An American Romance
1950   Emergency Wedding

Martin, Tony
1937   Life Begins in College
1939   Winner Take All
1940   Music in My Heart
1956   Quincannon, Frontier Scout

Martin, Townsend
1924   Tongues of Flame
1925   The Manicure Girl

Martin, Valentine
1936   Ramona

Martin, Vivian
1917   Forbidden Paths
The Trouble Buster

Martin, William *could be same as* **Martin, Bill**
1952   Red Ball Express

Martindel, Edward
1923   The White Flower
1928   We Americans
1930   Check and Double Check

Martinelli, Elsa
1955   The Indian Fighter

Martinelli, Enrico
1935   A Night at the Opera

Martínez, Elena
1939   El trovador de la radio

Martínez, Emanuel
1930   La rosa de fuego

Martínez, Santiago
1949   We Were Strangers

Martínez, Tony
1952   The Ring

Martínez Baena, Carlos *same as* **Baena, Carlos**
1931   Un caballero de frac
Las luces de Buenos Aires
1932   ¿Cuándo te suicidas?

Martínez Plá, Juan
1931   Cheri-Bibi
La fruta amarga
La mujer X
1933   Dos noches
La melodía prohibida
Primavera en otoño
Una viuda romántica
1934   Las fronteras del amor

Martínez Sierra, Gregorio
1931   Mamá
El proceso de Mary Dugan
1933   Primavera en otoño
Una viuda romántica
Yo, tú y ella
1934   La ciudad de cartón
1935   Julieta compra un hijo
Señora casada necesita marido

Martini, Lou
1959   Odds Against Tomorrow

Martini, Mortimer
1918   The Unbeliever

Martini, Nino
1930   Galas de la Paramount
1937   Music for Madame

Martino, Giovanni
1930   El presidio
1931   Jenny Lind

Martufi, Guido
1951   Westward the Women

Marty, Lita
1938   The Buccaneer

Marvak, Eleanor
1950   Jolson Sings Again

Marvelle, Rene
1931   The Cohens and Kellys in Africa

Marvin, Alice
1918   Huck and Tom; or, the Further Adventures of Tom Sawyer

Marvin, Frankie *same as* **Marvin, Frank**
1937   Boots and Saddles
1947   The Last Round-Up
1950   Indian Territory

Marvin, Grace
1916   The Love Girl
1921   No Woman Knows

Marvin, Lee
1953   The Glory Brigade
Seminole
1955   Bad Day at Black Rock
Not As a Stranger
Violent Saturday
1956   Pillars of the Sky
1957   Raintree County

Marvis, Kay *see* **Gorcey, Kay**

Marx, Bob
1958   Tonka

Marx, Chico
1935   A Night at the Opera

Marx, Groucho
1935   A Night at the Opera
1947   Copacabana

Marx, Harpo
1935   A Night at the Opera

Marx, Max
1940   New Moon

Marx, Neyle
1944   Since You Went Away
1945   The Cisco Kid Returns

Marx, Samuel *same as* **Marx, Sam**
1942   Apache Trail
1950   A Lady Without Passport
1955   Kiss of Fire

Mary, Faithful
1938   Two Gun Man from Harlem

Mascari, Mickey
1945   Nob Hill

Maslow, Sophie
1948   Strange Victory

Mason, Ann
1919   Deliverance

Mason, Bernice
1934   Las fronteras del amor
1935   Te quiero con locura

Mason, C. E. *see* **Mason, Charles E.**

Mason, Cain
1957   Revolt at Fort Laramie

Mason, Charles E. *same as* **Mason, C. E.**
1920   Li Ting Lang
1922   Come On Over

Mason, Dan
1917   Unknown 274
1918   Laughing Bill Hyde
1924   Conductor 1492
1927   The Chinese Parrot

Mason, Hugh
1921   A Modern Cain

Mason, James (*American actor*), 1890–1959 *same as* **Mason, Jim**
1918   The Squaw Man
1923   Scars of Jealousy
1924   The Heritage of the Desert
1925   Old Clothes
1931   Call of the Rockies
1934   Laughing Boy

Mason, John
1932   Harlem Is Heaven
1948?   Boarding House Blues
1949?   The Joint Is Jumpin'

Mason, Laura
1956   Serenade

Mason, LeRoy
1932   Texas Pioneers
1935   Texas Terror
1938   Outlaw Express
1939   The Fighting Gringo
1940   The Gay Caballero
New Moon
Viva Cisco Kid
1943   In Old Oklahoma
1944   Marshal of Reno
The San Antonio Kid
Tucson Raiders
Vigilantes of Dodge City

Mason, Lesley *same as* **Mason, Leslie**
1929   Señor Americano
1930   Song of the Caballero
1931   Aloha
1933   Man from Monterey

Mason, Lewis *not the same as* **Mason, Louis**
1922   The Cub Reporter

Mason, Louis *not the same as* **Mason, Lewis**
1934   Judge Priest
1943   What's Buzzin' Cousin?
Yankee Doodle Dandy
1947   California
1949   Lust for Gold
1950   The Traveling Saleswoman
1953   The Sun Shines Bright

Mason, Noel
1931   Yankee Don

Mason, Reginald
1934   Charlie Chan's Courage

Mason, Ruby
1921   The Sport of the Gods

Mason, Ruth
1949?   Harlem Follies

Mason, Sarah Y.
1921   A Divorce of Convenience
1934   Imitation of Life

Mason, Shirley
1917   The Little Chevalier
The Tell-Tale Step
1918   Good-Bye, Bill
1920   The Girl of My Heart
1921   Wing Toy
1922   Little Miss Smiles
Pawn Ticket 210
1926   Desert Gold
Rose of the Tenements
Sweet Rosie O'Grady
1927   Sally in Our Alley

Mason, Sidney d. 1923
1917   The Peddler
1918   The Prussian Cur
1919   A Fallen Idol
1920   The Good-Bad Wife

Mason, Spike
1939   Winner Take All

Mason, Sully
1941   Playmates

Mason, Sydney d. 1976
1950   Emergency Wedding
1951   The Harlem Globetrotters
1952   Apache Country
Bright Victory
The Raiders
1953   Column South
1958   Frontier Gun

Mason, Vivian
1950   Emergency Wedding
1953   The Charge at Feather River

Massen, Osa
1941   Accent on Love
1943   Jack London
1944   Cry of the Werewolf
1946   The Gentleman Misbehaves

Massey, Daria
1952   The Iron Mistress

Massey, Ilona
1947   Northwest Outpost

Massey, Raymond
1940   Santa Fe Trail
1943   Action in the North Atlantic
1955   Seven Angry Men

Masters, Daryl
1958   Flaming Frontier

Masters, Margaret
1951   The House on Telegraph Hill

Masters, Natalie
1955   Trial

Mastroly, Frank R.
1945   The Great John L.

Mastrony, D. J.
1948?   Junction 88

Matachieri, Michele
1932   Amore e morte

Matania, Clelia
1958   Seven Hills of Rome

Mate, Jeno
1960   The Pusher

Maté, Rudolph
1947   It Had To Be You
1954   Siege at Red River
1955   The Far Horizons

Matha, Lucy de
1931   Die Dreigroschenoper (*foreign version*)

Mather, Aubrey
1947   The Mighty McGurk

Mather, Jack
1941   You're Out of Luck
1954   Broken Lance
1955   The View from Pompey's Head
1956   Walk the Proud Land

Mathews, Allen
1938   Mr. Moto's Gamble
1943   Action in the North Atlantic
1948   16 Fathoms Deep
1949   The Undercover Man
1951   New Mexico
The Well

Mathews, Carl
1936   Custer's Last Stand
1942   Lawless Plainsmen
1945   The Cisco Kid Returns
1947   Buffalo Bill Rides Again
West to Glory
1948   Unconquered
1952   Fort Osage
1956   Westward Ho the Wagons!

Mathews, Carole
1944   Tahiti Nights
1949   Massacre River
1952   Red Snow

Mathews, David
1946   Slightly Scandalous
1951   Hurricane Island

Mathews, Dorothy
1930   Son of the Gods

Mathews, George *see* **Matthews, George**

Mathews, Harriet
1933   It's Great to Be Alive

Mathews, Joyce
1938   Dangerous to Know
Daughter of Shanghai
1939   King of Chinatown
1940   The Way of All Flesh

Mathews, June
1933   Circle Canyon

Mathews, Kerwin
1960   Man on a String

Mathews, Lester *see* **Matthews, Lester**

Mathews, Mathew
1939   Moon over Harlem

Mathews, Nita
1949   Lust for Gold

Mathews, Ruth Moore
1950   Panic in the Streets

Mathis, June
1917　A ife By Proxy
　　　　The Call of Her People
　　　　Threads of Fate
　　　　A Wife by Proxy
1918　Toys of Fate
1926　Irene

Matlock, Harvey
1953　The Great Sioux Uprising

Matson, Rumena
1948?　Junction 88

Matsuda, Don Sugai
1937　Big City

Matsui, George
1960　Hell to Eternity

Matsumato, M.
1916　The Honorable Friend

Matsumoto, Susie
1952　Japanese War Bride

Matsumoto, Taruyo "Jack"
1930　Chijiku wo mawasuru
　　　　chikara

Matsumoto, Wakaba
1930　Chijiku wo mawasuru
　　　　chikara

Matsushige, Harris
1951　Go for Broke!

Matsuura, Thomas
1951　Go for Broke!

Matthau, Walter
1955　The Indian Fighter
1958　Ride a Crooked Trail

Matthews, Lieut.
1919　Injustice

Matthews, Arthur
1918　Broken Ties

Matthews, Babe
1940　Paradise in Harlem

Matthews, Forrest
1948　Docks of New Orleans

Matthews, George *same as*
　　Mathews, George
1945　The Great John L.
1953　Last of the Comanches
1956　The Last Wagon

Matthews, Junius
1946　Without Reservations
1955　Good Morning, Miss Dove

Matthews, Lester *same as*
　　Mathews, Lester
1940　Northwest Passage (Book
　　　　I—Rogers' Rangers)
1942　Across the Pacific
　　　　Sunday Punch
1947　Dark Delusion
1948　Fighting Father Dunne
1953　Fort Ti
　　　　Sangaree
1955　The Far Horizons
1960　Walk Like a Dragon

Mattison, Frank S.
1923　The Lone Wagon
1926　Buffalo Bill on the U. P.
　　　　Trail

Mattison, Matty
1923　The Lone Wagon

Mattoe, Most
1922　The Pride of Palomar

Mattox, Martha
1918　Wild Women
1920　The Girl of My Heart
　　　　Huckleberry Finn
1922　The Hands of Nara
　　　　The Top O' the Morning
1923　Look Your Best
1925　The Man in Blue
1932　No Greater Love
　　　　So Big

Mattox, Matt
1953　The Glory Brigade

Mattraw, Scotty
1938　In Old Chicago

Matts, Frank
1952　Apache Country

Mature, Victor
1942　Song of the Islands
1948　Cry of the City
　　　　Fury at Furnace Creek
1951　Gambling House
1953　The Glory Brigade
1954　Dangerous Mission

1955　Chief Crazy Horse
　　　　Violent Saturday
1956　The Last Frontier

Matzen, Madeline
1927　The Fighting Hombre

Mauclair, Anne
1930　Olimpia (*foreign
　　　　version*)

Maude, Arthur
1916　Lord Loveland Discovers
　　　　America
1917　A Jewel in Pawn

Mauldin, Bill
1951　Teresa

Mauloy, Georges *same as* **Mauloy,**
　　George
1930　Olimpia (*foreign
　　　　version*)
1931　Jenny Lind
　　　　Le père célibataire
　　　　El proceso de Mary
　　　　Dugan (*foreign
　　　　version*)

Maumetz, Frederick
1951　Saturday's Hero

Mauprey, André
1931　Die Dreigroschenoper
　　　　(*foreign version*)

Maura, Honorio
1931　Un caballero de frac

Maurey, Nicole
1959　The Jayhawkers!

Maurice, Marjorie
1922　The Five Dollar Baby

Maurice, Mary
1917　I Will Repay
1918　The Little Runaway

Maurice, Richard D. *same as*
　　Maurice, Richard
1920　Our Christianity and
　　　　Nobody's Child
1928　Eleven P.M.

Maurice, Vivian
1920　Our Christianity and
　　　　Nobody's Child

Maurice, Wanda
1928　Eleven P.M.

Maurier, Serge
1960　Ice Palace

Maus, Marion P.
1914　The Indian Wars
1917　The Adventures of Buffalo
　　　　Bill

Mauu, Charles
1950　Annie Get Your Gun
　　　　The Toast of New Orleans
1951　The Great Caruso

Max, Edwin *same as* **Max, Ed**
1949　Border Incident
　　　　Ride, Ryder, Ride!
　　　　Thieves' Highway
　　　　The Undercover Man
1951　Jim Thorpe—All-American
　　　　The Well

Maxell, Lucien
1940　Prairie Schooners

Maxey, Paul
1941　You're Out of Luck
1947　The Foxes of Harrow
　　　　Ride the Pink Horse
1949　Harbor of Missing Men
　　　　The Sky Dragon
1952　Kid Monk Baroni
1960　Walk Like a Dragon

Maxmillian, Robert
1922　Breaking Home Ties

Maxudian, Max
1930　El secreto del doctor
　　　　(*foreign version*)

Maxwell, Edwin
1932　The Cohens and Kellys in
　　　　Hollywood
　　　　Scarface
1934　The Cat's-Paw
1937　The Plainsman
　　　　Slave Ship
1938　The Buccaneer
　　　　The Rage of Paris
1939　Drums Along the Mohawk
　　　　Way Down South
1940　Kit Carson
　　　　New Moon

1941　Ride on Vaquero
1944　Since You Went Away
　　　　Waterfront
1946　Swamp Fire
1947　The Jolson Story

Maxwell, Elsa
1940　Elsa Maxwell's Public
　　　　Deb No. 1

Maxwell, John
1942　Gentleman Jim
　　　　Seven Sweethearts
　　　　Wings for the Eagle
1948　The Paleface
1950　Devil's Doorway
　　　　Mystery Street
　　　　Right Cross
1953　So Big
1955　Trial

Maxwell, M. C.
1923　Regeneration

Maxwell, Marilyn
1943　Dr. Gillespie's Criminal
　　　　Case
1944　Three Men in White
1945　Between Two Women
1951　New Mexico

Maxwell, Paisley
1958　Flaming Frontier

May, Ann
1922　The Half Breed

May, Betty
1934　Broadway Bill
1936　Dangerous Intrigue

May, Doris
1924　Conductor 1492

May, Joe
1934　Limehouse Blues
1950　Buccaneer's Girl

May, Karlyn
1935?　The Irish Gringo

May, Marc
1959　Odds Against Tomorrow

May, Neola *see* **Neola May,**
　　Princess

May, Patsy
1945　Great Stagecoach Robbery

Mayall, Herschel
1916　The Aryan
1919　The Sleeping Lion
1923　Thirty Days

Mayeda, Teruo
1930　Chijiku wo mawasuru
　　　　chikara

Mayeda, Tuki
1927　[Japanese-American Film]

Mayer, Edwin Justus
1927　The Love Mart
1930　Le spectre vert
1931　Cheri-Bibi
1935　So Red the Rose
1938　The Buccaneer
1947　The Foxes of Harrow

Mayer, Gerald
1953　Bright Road

Mayer, Greta *see* **Meyer, Greta**

Mayer, Ken *same as* **Mayer,**
　　Kenneth
1958　Ambush at Cimarron Pass
1959　The FBI Story

Mayer, Ray
1935　His Family Tree
1939　King of Chinatown

Mayer, Richard
1950　Mystery Submarine

Mayer, Turben *see* **Meyer, Torben**

Mayes, Norman
1941　Hurry, Charlie, Hurry
1943　Ladies' Day

Mayes, Wendell
1959　The Hanging Tree

Mayfield, Dora
1934　Limehouse Blues

Mayhew, Kate
1924　Tongues of Flame

Maylia
1949　Boston Blackie's Chinese
　　　　Venture
1950　Chinatown at Midnight

Maynard, Geraldine
1945　Of One Blood

Maynard, Ken
1927　The Devil's Saddle
　　　　The Overland Stage
　　　　The Red Raiders
1928　The Canyon of Adventure
　　　　The Glorious Trail
1929　Señor Americano
1930　Song of the Caballero
1934　Wheels of Destiny
1943　The Law Rides Again

Maynard, Kermit
1941　Western Union
1942　Lawless Plainsmen
　　　　Valley of Hunted Men
1944　Buffalo Bill
1948　Fury at Furnace Creek
　　　　The Paleface
1949　Lust for Gold
　　　　Massacre River
1953　Column South
　　　　The Eddie Cantor Story
　　　　The Great Sioux Uprising
1954　War Arrow

Mayne, Eric
1919　The Scar
1921　Little Miss Hawkshaw
1923　Suzanna
1928　The Canyon of Adventure

Mayo, Archie *same as* **Mayo,**
　　Archie L.
1929　Is Everybody Happy?
1933　Ever in My Heart
1935　Bordertown
1937　Black Legion
1943　Crash Dive
　　　　Wintertime

Mayo, Frank
1915　The Adventures of a
　　　　Madcap
1917　The Bronze Bride
　　　　Sold at Auction
1919　Lasca
1931　Chinatown After Dark
1936　Desert Gold
　　　　The Phantom of Santa Fe
　　　　Show Boat
1937　Think Fast, Mr. Moto
1939　Confessions of a Nazi Spy
　　　　Waterfront
1940　East of the River
　　　　Knute Rockne—All
　　　　American
　　　　Santa Fe Trail
1942　Across the Pacific
　　　　Gentleman Jim
　　　　In This Our Life
　　　　Juke Girl
　　　　Secret Enemies
　　　　They Died With Their
　　　　Boots On
　　　　Wings for the Eagle
1943　Action in the North
　　　　Atlantic
　　　　Yankee Doodle Dandy
1944　Lake Placid Serenade
1945　Escape in the Fog
1946　Shadows Over Chinatown
1947　Buck Privates Come
　　　　Home
　　　　The Mighty McGurk
1948　Big City
1949　The Undercover Man

Mayo, Rose
1918　Ruggles of Red Gap

Mayo, Stella
1923　Regeneration

Mayo, Virginia
1943　Jack London
1949　Colorado Territory
　　　　The Girl from Jones
　　　　Beach
1952　The Iron Mistress

Mayon, Charles
1943　Dixie

Mayon, Fred
1936　Star for a Night

Mayon, Helen
1955　Violent Saturday

Mayring, Lothar
1930   Los que danzan (*foreign version*)
1931   Dämon des Meeres
Mays, Betti
1947   Boy! What a Girl!
Mazola, Anthony
1951   The Great Caruso
        Jim Thorpe—All-American
Mazola, Richard
1951   Jim Thorpe—All-American
Mazurki, Mike
1942   Gentleman Jim
1945   Nob Hill
1948   Unconquered
1955   Davy Crockett, King of the Wild Frontier
1956   Comanche
Mazursky, Paul
1955   Blackboard Jungle
Mazzola, Al
1932   Hypnotized
Mazzola, Eugene
1953   Cry of the Hunted
1956   Walk the Proud Land
Mazzola, Frank
1956   Hot Blood
Mazzoti, Pat
1953   The Eddie Cantor Story
Mazzuca, Joseph
1949   House of Strangers
Mead, Edward
1939   Keep Punching
Meade, Claire *same as* **Mead, Claire**
1950   Belle of Old Mexico
Meader, Bill *see* **Meader, William**
Meader, George
1944   An American Romance
1945   A Tree Grows in Brooklyn
1947   Crossfire
1948   Half Past Midnight
1949   That Midnight Kiss
1950   Emergency Wedding
        The Toast of New Orleans
1958   The Young Lions
Meader, William *same as* **Meader, Bill**
1948   The Paleface
        Unconquered
1957   Beau James
Meadow, Herb
1956   The Lone Ranger
Meadows, Denny *see* **Moore, Dennis**
Meadows, Jayne
1947   Dark Delusion
1948   The Luck of the Irish
Meadows, Joyce
1958   Frontier Gun
1960   Walk Tall
Meagher, Edward
1929   The Overland Telegraph
Meakin, Charles
1936   Dangerous Intrigue
1948   The Lady from Shanghai
        Up in Central Park
Means, Grant
1948   Harpoon
        16 Fathoms Deep
Medbury, John P.
1943   What's Buzzin' Cousin?
Medford, Kay
1942   Three Hearts for Julia
1944   An American Romance
1948   Tap Roots
1949   The Undercover Man
1956   Singing in the Dark
Medford, Marjorie
1935?   The Irish Gringo
Medina, José
1931   Un caballero de frac
Medina, Patricia
1947   The Foxes of Harrow
1953   Sangaree
1955   Duel on the Mississippi
Meehan, Elizabeth
1931   Nuit d'Espagne
1935   Harmony Lane
1940   Girl from God's Country

1947   Northwest Outpost
Meehan, James Leo *same as* **Meehan, Leo**
1922   Silver Spurs
1926   Laddie
Meehan, Jeanette Porter
1926   Laddie
Meehan, John
1930   Doña mentiras
1931   Jenny Lind
1945   The Valley of Decision
Meehan, John, Jr.
1942   Nazi Agent
Meehan, Leo *see* **Meehan, James Leo**
Meehan, Lew
1921   By Right of Birth
1922   Blazing Arrows
1931   Cavalier of the West
        Mr. Lemon of Orange
Meek, Carmelita
1938   The Buccaneer
Meek, Donald
1931   Personal Maid
1935   Romance in Manhattan
1937   Maid of Salem
1938   The Adventures of Tom Sawyer
1941   Come Live with Me
1942   Seven Sweethearts
        Tortilla Flat
Meek, John
1953   Tonight We Sing
Meeker, George
1932   The Match King
1933   Song of the Eagle
1934   Broadway Bill
1935   The Wedding Night
1939   Gone With the Wind
1942   All Through the Night
        Secret Enemies
        Wings for the Eagle
1943   The Ox-Bow Incident
        Yankee Doodle Dandy
1946   The Red Dragon
1948   The Dude Goes West
        Silver Trails
1949   Ranger of Cherokee Strip
Meeker, Ralph
1951   Teresa
1957   Run of the Arrow
Meekins, Willie
1924   Smiling Hate
Megennis, Maggie
1956   Full of Life
Megowan, Debbie
1960   All the Fine Young Cannibals
Megowan, Don
1955   Davy Crockett, King of the Wild Frontier
1959   The Jayhawkers!
Mehaffey, Blanche *same as* **Mahaffey, Blanche; Morgan, Janet**
1925   His People
1927   Finnegan's Ball
        The Princess from Hoboken
1935   North of Arizona
Mehlberg, Luana
1952   It's a Big Country: An American Anthology
Mehra, Lal Chand
1939   Mr. Moto's Last Warning
1940   Murder over New York
1942   Submarine Raider
Meighan, Thomas
1915   The Immigrant
        The Kindling
        The Secret Sin
1916   Pudd'nhead Wilson
1918   Out of a Clear Sky
1919   The Heart of Wetona
1924   Tongues of Flame
1925   Irish Luck
1927   Blind Alleys
1928   The Mating Call
1931   Skyline
        Young Sinners

Meins, Gus
1936   Kelly the Second
1937   The Californian
Meiser, Edith
1951   Queen for a Day
Meissner, Alfred
1957   Band of Angels
Mejia, Al
1951   Jim Thorpe—All-American
Melchior, Lauritz
1953   The Stars Are Singing
Meléndez del Valle, F.
1930   La jaula de los leones
Melendez, Consuelo
1934   La buenaventura
Melford, Frank
1932   Ljubav i strast
        Uncle Moses
1936   Rebellion
1937   Old Louisiana
1949   Massacre River
1951   Fort Defiance
Melford, George *same as* **Melford, George H.**
1915   The Immigrant
1917   The Call of the East
1918   The Bravest Way
        The City of Dim Faces
        Hidden Pearls
        Sandy
        The Source
1919   Told in the Hills
1925   Friendly Enemies
1930   East Is West (*foreign version*)
        La voluntad del muerto
1931   Don Juan diplomático
        Drácula
1938   Dangerous to Know
1939   Heaven with a Barbed Wire Fence
1941   Belle Starr
        Virginia
1942   The Navy Comes Through
        Valley of the Sun
1943   Gangway for Tomorrow
1945   A Tree Grows in Brooklyn
1947   California
1948   Call Northside 777
        Cry of the City
        The Luck of the Irish
1950   A Ticket to Tomahawk
Mell, Joseph *same as* **Mell, Joe**
1952   Kid Monk Baroni
        My Man and I
1959   Imitation of Life
Meller, Harro
1943   Gangway for Tomorrow
1945   The House on 92nd St.
Mellinger, Max
1960   I Passed for White
Mellinger, Michael
1960   Man on a String
Mellinino, Ardita *see* **Mellonino, Ardita**
Mellish, Fuller
1921   Diane of Star Hollow
        The Land of Hope
1924   Two Shall Be Born
Mellonino, Ardita *same as* **Mellinino, Ardita**
1919   Deliverance
Mellville, Jose *see* **Melville, Jose**
Melnyk, Stephania
1938   Marusia
Melton, Frank
1934   Judge Priest
        Stand Up and Cheer!
1936   The Glory Trail
        The Traitor
1937   Life Begins in College
1938   The Buccaneer
        Dangerous to Know
Melton, Sid *same as* **Melton, Sidney**
1941   New York Town
1949   Knock on Any Door
1951   Mask of the Dragon
        The Steel Helmet
1957   Beau James

Melton, Troy
1956   Davy Crockett and the River Pirates
        Mohawk
Meltzer, Isadore
1930   Eternal Fools (Ewige Naranim)
Meltzer, Lewis
1941   New York Town
1950   Comanche Territory
1953   The Jazz Singer
1957   The Brothers Rico
Melville, George *same as* **Melville, George D.**
1916   The Woman in 47
1917   A Wife by Proxy
Melville, Jose *same as* **Mellville, Jose; Meville, Josie**
1917   A Roadside Impresario
Mena, Jesús
1934   La cruz y la espada
Menard, Jim
1960   Wild River
Menard, Tina
1934   The Cactus Kid
        Tres amores
1935   Julieta compra un hijo
1936   The Traitor
1937   The Devil's Playground
1938   Daughter of Shanghai
        La vida bohemia
1946   Notorious
1949   We Were Strangers
1950   Sunset in the West
1956   The Burning Hills
        Giant
1958   Escape from Red Rock
Mendelson, Herbert E.
1958   Ambush at Cimarron Pass
Mendelssohn, Eleonora
1950   Black Hand
Mendes, Lothar
1930   Galas de la Paramount
1931   Personal Maid
1942   Nazi Agent
Méndez, Lolita
1930   ¡De frente, marchen!
Mendina, Rudolfo
1936   Ramona
Mendl, Sir Charles
1946   Notorious
Mendoza, Alberto
1930   Alma de gaucho
Mendoza, George
1936   Ramona
Mendoza, Harry
1953   The Eddie Cantor Story
Mendoza, Victor
1959   The Wonderful Country
Mendoza López, Luis
1930   La jaula de los leones
Mendoza López, Manuel
1931   Don Juan diplomático
Menéndez, Nilo
1930   Revista Hispano-Americana
Ménessier, Henri *same as* **Ménessier, Henry**
1931   La pura verdad (*foreign version*)
Menjou, Adolphe *same as* **Menjou, Adolph**
1916   Man and His Angel
1921   Through the Back Door
1922   Head over Heels
1930   Amor audaz
        Amor audaz (*foreign version*)
1931   Soyons gais
1934   The Great Flirtation
1942   Syncopation
1951   Across the Wide Missouri
        The Tall Target
Menjou, Henri *same as* **Menjou, Henry**
1927   Pleasure Before Business
Menken, Shepard
1949   The Red Menace
1951   The Great Caruso
1953   Captain John Smith and Pocahontas

1956   The Benny Goodman
        Story
Menson, Mark
1960   Wild River
Mentkowska, Stefania
1941   Wiejskie Wesele
Menzer, Dawn
1959   The FBI Story
Menzies, James
1947   Calendar Girl
Menzies, Tommie
1947   Jiggs and Maggie in
        Society
Menzies, William Cameron *same as* **Menzies, William C.**
1939   Gone With the Wind
1944   Address Unknown
1947   Duel in the Sun
Mercanton, Jean
1930   Toda una vida (*foreign
        version*)
1931   Su noche de bodas
        (*foreign version*)
Mercanton, Louis
1931   Chérie
        Su noche de bodas
        Su noche de bodas
        (*foreign version*)
Mercer, Beryl
1928   We Americans
1929   Mother's Boy
1932   No Greater Love
1933   Broken Dreams
Mercer, Fred
1944   Tender Comrade
Mercer, Jane
1931   Street Scene
1934   Beloved
1935   Naughty Marietta
Mercer, Marilyn
1948   Guns of Hate
Mercier, Louis
1931   La gran jornada (*foreign
        version*)
1935   Naughty Marietta
1938   Charlie Chan at Monte
        Carlo
1939   City in Darkness
        Mr. Moto in Danger
        Island
1940   If I Had My Way
1941   This Woman Is Mine
1945   Johnny Angel
1946   Saratoga Trunk
1951   Go for Broke!
        Show Boat
Mercur, Florence
1955   Murder in Villa Capri
Mercur, William *same as* **Mercur, W.; Mercur, Wolf**
1939   The Light Ahead
1940   Americaner Schadchen
Meredith, Bess *see* **Merdyth, Bess**
Meredith, Burgess
1936   Winterset
1949   Jigsaw
Meredith, Charles
1921   The Cave Girl
1924   In Hollywood With
        Potash and Perlmutter
1948   The Boy with Green Hair
        The Miracle of the Bells
1956   Giant
        The Lone Ranger
1957   Beau James
        The Guns of Fort
        Petticoat
Meredith, Frank
1936   It Had to Happen
1937   Slave Ship
Meredith, Iris *same as* **Shunn, Iris**
1938   Little Miss Roughneck
1941   Caught in the Act
        Louisiana Purchase
Meredith, Jane
1935   The Winning Ticket
Meredith, Jill
1947   Copacabana
Meredith, Lois
1914   Dan
1917   Sold at Auction

Meredith, Madge
1953   Tumbleweed
1957   The Guns of Fort
        Petticoat
Meredyth, Bess *same as* **Meredith, Bess**
1916   The Twin Triangle
1918   The Red, Red Heart
1927   Irish Hearts
        Rose of the Golden West
1931   Cheri-Bibi
1935   L'homme des Folies
        Bergère
1937   Charlie Chan at the
        Opera
1939   Drums Along the Mohawk
1940   The Mark of Zorro
Merighi, Augusta
1931   Così è la vita
1955   The Rose Tattoo
1956   The Catered Affair
1958   Never Love a Stranger
Merin, Eda Reis *same as* **Merin, Eda Reiss**
1949   Knock on Any Door
1950   No Way Out
1953   Tonight We Sing
Merjanian, Charles
1945   Anoush
Merkel, Una
1930   Abraham Lincoln
1932   Huddle
        Men Are Such Fools
1934   The Cat's-Paw
1942   Twin Beds
1950   Emergency Wedding
Merkyl, John
1936   Desert Gold
1942   Gentleman Jim
Merlin, Joanna
1960   The Pusher
        Weddings and Babies
Merlo, Tony *same as* **Merlo, Anthony**
1919   Mandarin's Gold
1934   Coming Out Party
1937   Charlie Chan at the
        Olympics
1949   House of Strangers
Merman, Ethel
1938   Happy Landing
Merman, L. B.
1946   Swamp Fire
Merminod, Marcel
1931   Die Dreigroschenoper
        (*foreign version*)
Merriam, Charlotte
1924   So Big
1933   Broken Dreams
Merrick, George M. *same as* **Merrick, Geo. M.; Merrick, George**
1931   Cavalier of the West
1932   Border Devils
1935   Cyclone of the Saddle
1936   Custer's Last Stand
1940   Taku
Merrick, John
1957   Ride Out for Revenge
1958   Ambush at Cimarron Pass
Merrick, Lynn *same as* **Merrick, Marilyn**
1943   Doughboys in Ireland
Merrihugh, Mal
1943   Ladies' Day
Merrill, Anthony *see* **Merrill, Walter Anthony**
Merrill, Gary
1948   Strange Victory
1949   The Quiet One
1954   The Black Dakotas
1959   The Wonderful Country
Merrill, Lou *same as* **Merrill, Lew; Merrill, Louis**
1940   Kit Carson
1948   The Lady from Shanghai
1953   Fort Ti
1955   Duel on the Mississippi
Merrill, Walter Anthony *same as* **Merrill, Tony; Merrill, Anthony; Merrill, Walter; Merrill, Walter "Tony"**

1938   Little Miss Roughneck
1941   The Face Behind the
        Mask
1947   Buck Privates Come
        Home
1949   The Girl from Jones
        Beach
1951   Gambling House
        The Magnificent Yankee
1955   Trial
1959   Last Train from Gun Hill
1960   The Adventures of
        Huckleberry Finn
        Cimarron
Merrit, Joe
1956   Hot Blood
Merritt, Alan
1939   Daughter of the Tong
Merritt, Arnold
1960   The Unforgiven
Merritt, Bruce
1946   Abie's Irish Rose
Merritt, Paula
1920   For the Soul of Rafael
Merritt, Sybil
1952   Japanese War Bride
The Merry Meisters
1944   Lake Placid Serenade
Merry, Carla
1957   Band of Angels
Mers, Harold
1948   The Betrayal
Mersch, Mary
1917   Her Own People
        The Trouble Buster
1936   Star for a Night
Mersereau, Violet
1916   Broken Fetters
Merski, Richard
1941   Mystery Ship
Merton, John *same as* **La Varr, Mert; La Verre, Mort**
1934   Broadway Bill
1936   Aces and Eights
1937   Drums of Destiny
1938   The Buccaneer
1940   Arizona Frontier
        Covered Wagon Days
        Hi-Yo Silver
        Northwest Passage (Book
        I—Rogers' Rangers)
1941   Gauchos of Eldorado
        Mystery Ship
        Under Fiesta Stars
1943   Hitler's Children
        The Law Rides Again
1944   Address Unknown
        An American Romance
1946   Border Bandits
        The Gay Cavalier
1948   The Golden Eye
        Unconquered
1950   Bandit Queen
        A Ticket to Tomahawk
Merton, Roger
1942   King of the Stallions
Meskill, Katherine
1951   The House on Telegraph
        Hill
Mesreau, Charlotte
1919   Deliverance
Messenger, Frank
1934   Eskimo
Messenger, Buddy *same as* **Messenger, Buddy**
1922   Shadows
1941   Hold Back the Dawn
        The Mexican Spitfire's
        Baby
1950   Devil's Doorway
Messinger, Gertrude *same as* **Messenger, Gertrude; Messinger, Gertie**
1920   The Luck of the Irish
1932   Hidden Valley
        Riders of the Desert
1935   Melody Trail
1942   Syncopation
1943   Redhead from Manhattan

Mestas, Edward
1936   Ramona
Mestel, Jacob *same as* **Mestel, J.**
1932   A Daughter of Her People
        Uncle Moses
        Yiskor
1933   The Wandering Jew
1934   The Rabbi's Power
        What a Mother-in-Law!
1939   Mirele Efros
1940   Americaner Schadchen
Metcalfe, Earl *same as* **Mercalf, Earl; Metcalfe, Edward**
1920   The Face at Your Window
1923   The Lone Wagon
        Look Your Best
1926   Buffalo Bill on the U. P.
        Trail
1927   The Devil's Saddle
Metcalfe, James *same as* **Metcalf, James**
1943   Crash Dive
1945   The Dolly Sisters
Meter, Harry von *see* **Von Meter, Harry**
Methot, Mayo
1933   Counsellor at Law
Metz, Blaine
1950   Stars in My Crown
Metz, George
1932   The Rainbow Trail
Metz, Victor *see* **Metzetti, Victor**
Metzetti, Otto
1934   The Lone Defender
Metzetti, Victor *same as* **Metz, Victor**
1934   The Lone Defender
1939   Mr. Moto's Last Warning
Meyer, Emile
1950   Panic in the Streets
1954   Drums Across the River
1955   Blackboard Jungle
        White Feather
1956   Raw Edge
Meyer, Greta *same as* **Mayer, Greta; Meyers, Greta**
1929   Die Königsloge
1932   Flesh
        The Match King
1933   Let's Fall in Love
1934   Strange Wives
1935   Naughty Marietta
1936   Dimples
1940   The Man I Married
1941   Come Live with Me
1942   Friendly Enemies
1944   An American Romance
Meyer, Herbert, Dr. *could be same as* **Myers, Herbert**
1940   Son of Ingagi
Meyer, Hy
1934   Judge Priest
Meyer, John
1940   Santa Fe Trail
Meyer, Pet
1942   Song of the Islands
Meyer, Torben *same as* **Mayer, Turben**
1932   Le bluffeur
1935   Charlie Chan in Shanghai
1936   It Had to Happen
        Star for a Night
1940   The Way of All Flesh
1941   Sullivan's Travels
1943   Jack London
        They Came to Blow Up
        America
1947   The Mighty McGurk
Meyerinck, Hubert von
1931   La llama sagrada (*foreign
        version*)
Meyers Sisters
1929   Frozen Justice
Meyers, "Doc" George
1950   Ambush
Meyers, Bumps
1950   Young Man with a Horn
Meyers, Chief
1934   Laughing Boy

Meyers, Daniel
1949   The Undercover Man
1950   No Way Out
Meyers, Dickie
1943   Good Luck, Mr. Yates
Meyers, Greta see **Meyer, Greta**
Meyers, Pauline see **Myers, Pauline**
Meyers, Rosemarie
1959   The Black Orchid
Meyers, Sidney
1949   The Quiet One
Miceli, María
1930   Sombras de gloria
Michael, Gene
1951   Native Son
Michael, Gertrude
1932   Unashamed
1942   Prisoner of Japan
1945   Club Havana
1952   Bugles in the Afternoon
Michael, Paul
1940   Escape to Glory
Michael, Peter
1943   Action in the North
           Atlantic
           They Came to Blow Up
           America
1946   Without Reservations
1950   Battleground
           Mystery Submarine
1952   Red Ball Express
1957   All Mine to Give
Michaelides, George
1953   The Glory Brigade
Michaels, Beverly
1951   The Girl on the Bridge
Michaels, Dan
1932   The Black King
1933   Victims of Persecution
1946   Stars on Parade
Michaels, Dorothy
1946   The Gay Cavalier
Michaels, Edward
1945   The House on 92nd St.
Michaels, Johnny same as
    Michaels, John
1943   Deerslayer
1947   Buck Privates Come
           Home
Michaels, Pat
1946   Santa Fe Uprising
Michaels, Sidney
1960   Key Witness
Michaels, Sol
1934   Las fronteras del amor
1937   Charlie Chan at the
           Opera
           Think Fast, Mr. Moto
Michaelson, Esther
1947   Humoresque
Michalesko, Michal same as
    Michalesko, Michel
1938   The Power of Life
1950   Catskill Honeymoon
           God, Man and Devil
           Monticello, Here We
           Come!
Micheal, Peter
1945   Nob Hill
Micheaux, Oscar
1919   The Homesteader
1920   The Brute
           The Symbol of the
           Unconquered
           Within Our Gates
1921   The Gunsaulus Mystery
1922   The Dungeon
           The Virgin of Seminole
1923   Deceit
1924   Birthright
           The House Behind the
           Cedars
           A Son of Satan
1925   Body and Soul
           The Devil's Disciple
1927   The Broken Violin
           The Millionaire
           The Spider's Web
1928   Thirty Years Later
           The Wages of Sin

1929   When Men Betray
1930   A Daughter of the Congo
           Easy Street
1931   The Exile
1932   Ten Minutes to Live
           Veiled Aristocrats
1932?   The Girl from Chicago
1934?   Harlem After Midnight
1935   Lem Hawkins' Confession
1936   Temptation
1937   Underworld
1938   Birthright
           God's Step Children
           Swing!
1939   Lying Lips
1940   The Notorious Elinor Lee
1948   The Betrayal
Micheaux, Swan E., Jr.
1928   The Midnight Ace
Michelena, Beatriz
1919   Just Squaw
Michelena, Teresa
1914   Uncle Tom's Cabin
Michelsen, Jerry see **Mickelsen,
    Jerry**
Michelson, Esther
1935   McFadden's Flats
1941   Sullivan's Travels
1942   We Were Dancing
1945   Rhapsody in Blue
Michelson, Jerry see **Mickelsen,
    Jerry**
Michon, Pat
1960   I Passed for White
Mickelby, Roxanna
1926?   Ten Nights in a Barroom
Mickelsen, Jerry same as
    **Mickelson, Jerry; Michelson,
    Jerry**
1944   My Pal Wolf
1948   Big City
1950   Emergency Wedding
1955   Blackboard Jungle
Mickelsen, Richard
1948   The Miracle of the Bells
1951   Saturday's Hero
Mickelson, Jerry see **Mickelsen,
    Jerry**
Mickey, Arline
1924   Smiling Hate
1926   A Prince of His Race
1926?   Ten Nights in a Barroom
1927   Children of Fate
Middlemass, Robert same as
    Middlemas, Robert
1936   Dangerous Intrigue
           General Spanky
           Muss 'Em Up
1937   Charlie Chan on
           Broadway
1938   Spawn of the North
1939   Stand Up and Fight
1944   An American Romance
1945   The Dolly Sisters
Middleton, Charles same as
    Middleton, Charles B.
1929   Welcome Danger
1930   East Is West
1932   The Hatchet Man
           Mystery Ranch
1934   Behold My Wife!
           Broadway Bill
           Massacre
1936   Ramona
           Rose of the Rancho
           Show Boat
1937   Slave Ship
           Souls at Sea
1938   Rascals
1939   Allegheny Uprising
           Way Down South
1940   Charlie Chan's Murder
           Cruise
           Santa Fe Trail
1941   Belle Starr
           Western Union
1945   Our Vines Have Tender
           Grapes
1948   Jiggs and Maggie in Court
           My Girl Tisa
           Unconquered

Middleton, George (writer, actor)
    could be same as **Middleton,
    George E.** (dir) or **Middleton,
    George W.** (actor)
Middleton, George E. (dir) could
    be same as **Middleton, George**
    (writer, actor) or **Middleton,
    George W.** (actor)
1919   Just Squaw
Middleton, George W. (actor)
    could be same as **Middleton,
    George** (writer, actor) or
    Middleton, George E. (dir)
1915   An American Gentleman
Middleton, Ray
1941   Lady from Louisiana
Middleton, Robert
1955   Trial
Middleton, Velma
1957   Satchmo the Great
Midgley, Dorese
1946   Slightly Scandalous
Midgley, Fanny same as **Midgeley,
    Fannie; Midgley, Fannie;
    Midgley, Miss**
1915   The Alien
1918   How Could You, Jean?
1921   All Souls' Eve
1926   Laddie
Miele, Donald
1952   Bright Victory
Mieneke, Harry
1936   Show Boat
Miguel Angel, Amparo
1931   Chérie (foreign version)
Mikeler, Eugene
1944   Lady, Let's Dance!
Miki, George
1951   Go for Broke!
Mila', Renato de
1932   Parigi affascina; ovvero,
           Malavita
Milan, Lita
1957   Bayou
           Naked in the Sun
           The Ride Back
1958   Never Love a Stranger
Milana, T. R.
1932   Parigi affascina; ovvero,
           Malavita
Milani, Chef
1944   Mr. Skeffington
1946   Without Reservations
Milar, Adolph same as **Milar,
    Adolf** could be same as **Millard,
    Adolph** or **Miller, Adolph**
1923   Backbone
1928   Uncle Tom's Cabin
1931   Dämon des Meeres
1937   It Could Happen to You
1938   Gateway
           Happy Landing
1940   Escape
Mildred y Maurice
1938   Di que me quieres
Miles, Art
1937   Charlie Chan on
           Broadway
1946   Without Reservations
1947   Desperate
1950   Colt .45
Miles, Betty
1943   The Law Rides Again
1944   Sonora Stagecoach
Miles, Jennings
1950   Winchester '73
1953   So Big
           Tumbleweed
Miles, John
1945   Pride of the Marines
Miles, Leah
1924   Smiling Hate
Miles, Nelson Appleton
1914   The Indian Wars
1917   The Adventures of Buffalo
           Bill

Miles, Norbert see **Myles, Norbert**
Miles, Robert J.
1953   Arrowhead
Miles, Vera
1953   The Charge at Feather
           River
           So Big
1956   The Searchers
1957   Beau James
1959   The FBI Story
Miles, Viola
1923   Deceit
Milewicz, Stach
1941   Z Dymem Pożarów
Miley, Jerry
1936   Charlie Chan's Secret
1947   The Foxes of Harrow
1948   Fury at Furnace Creek
1950   Rock Island Trail
Milford, Gene same as **Milford,
    Eugene**
1960   The Pusher
Milford, Mary Beth
1925   Galloping Vengeance
Milhauser, Bertram see
    Millhauser, Bertram
1933   Ever in My Heart
Milhauser, James see **Mulhauser,
    James**
Miljan, John
1927   Old San Francisco
           Sailor Izzy Murphy
           The Slaver
1930   Estrellados
1931   Gentleman's Fate
           The Great Meadow
1932   Flesh
           Unashamed
1935   Charlie Chan in Paris
1936   Sutter's Gold
1937   The Plainsman
1940   New Moon
1948   Unconquered
1952   Anything Can Happen
           The Savage
1956   The Wild Dakotas
1957   Apache Warrior
1958   The Lone Ranger and the
           Lost City of Gold
Millan, Arthu
1953   The Man Behind the Gun
Millan, Arthur same as **Millan, Art**
1949   The Red Menace
Millan, Victor
1952   The Ring
1954   Drum Beat
1955   Apache Ambush
1956   Giant
           Walk the Proud Land
1957   The Ride Back
1958   Terror in a Texas Town
           Touch of Evil
1959   The FBI Story
Milland, Ray same as **Milland,
    Raymond**
1934   Charlie Chan in London
1947   California
1952   Bugles in the Afternoon
Millar, Adelqui
1930   Doña mentiras
           El secreto del doctor
           Toda una vida
1931   La carta
           La fiesta del diablo
           Las luces de Buenos Aires
           Sombras del circo
Millar, Wilson
1953   Tonight We Sing
Millard, Gerald
1956   The Last Hunt
Millard, Helene
1934   Broadway Bill
1936   My American Wife
1942   We Were Dancing
Millarde, Harry same as **Millard,
    Harry**
1917   Unknown 274
Millarde, June
1942   We Were Dancing
           Wings for the Eagle
1943   Yankee Doodle Dandy

Mille, Beatrice C. de *see* **de Mille, Beatrice**

Mille, Cecil B. de *see* **DeMille, Cecil B.**

Mille, Katherine de *see* **DeMille, Katherine**

Mille, William C. de *see* **de Mille, William C.**

Millen, Harold
1959   The Hanging Tree

Miller Bros. & Lois
1947   Hi De Ho

Miller Sisters
1956   Rockin' the Blues

Miller, Adolph *could be same as* **Milar, Adolph**
1930   Los que danzan (*foreign version*)

Miller, Alice Duer
1922   The Man with Two Mothers

Miller, Ann
1940   Too Many Girls
1943   What's Buzzin' Cousin?
1949   The Kissing Bandit

Miller, Arthur (*actor*)
1932   Hidden Valley

Miller, Ashley
1916   The King's Game

Miller, Beatrice
1930   Eternal Fools (Ewige Naranim)

Miller, Billy
1957   Run of the Arrow

Miller, Carl
1923   Jealous Husbands
1927   Whispering Sage

Miller, Charles B. circa 1930s and 1940s *same as* **Miller, Charles** circa 1930s and 1940s
1940   Phantom of Chinatown
1941   Caught in the Act
1943   Jack London
      Wagon Tracks West
1946   Rendezvous 24
1948   Call Northside 777
      Fighting Father Dunne
      The Miracle of the Bells
      Up in Central Park
1949   Colorado Territory

Miller, Colleen
1957   Man in the Shadow

Miller, David (*actor*) *same as* **Miller, David H.** (*actor*)
1951   Tomahawk
1952   The Savage
1955   Chief Crazy Horse

Miller, David (*dir*)
1942   Sunday Punch
1949   Top O' the Morning
1951   Saturday's Hero

Miller, Dean
1953   Dream Wife

Miller, Dick
1955   Apache Woman

Miller, Dolly
1944   Slightly Terrific

Miller, Dorie, Sgt.
1944   The Negro Soldier

Miller, Drew
1947   The Farmer's Daughter

Miller, Ella
1924   North of 36

Miller, Emmett
1951   Yes Sir, Mr. Bones

Miller, Eugene
1920   The Mark of Zorro

Miller, Eva
1933   Live and Laugh

Miller, Eve
1949   Arctic Fury

Miller, F. E. *see* **Miller, Flournoy E.**

Miller, Fay
1932   Out of the Crimson Fog

Miller, Flournoy E. *same as* **Miller, F. E.**
1937   Harlem on the Prairie

1939   The Bronze Buckaroo
      Double Deal
      Harlem Rides the Range
1940   Mystery in Swing
1940?   Mr. Washington Goes to Town
1942   Lucky Ghost
      Professor Creeps
1943   Stormy Weather
1947   Mantan Runs for Mayor
1947?   Return of Mandy's Husband
1949?   Come On, Cowboy!
      She's Too Mean for Me
1951   Yes Sir, Mr. Bones
1956   Rockin' the Blues

Miller, Frances
1917   The Adventures of Carol
1918   Broken Ties

Miller, Francis Trevelyan, Dr.
1919   Deliverance

Miller, Fred (*circa 1920s*)
1922   Square Joe

Miller, Fred (*circa 1930s–1940s*)
1948   Docks of New Orleans

Glenn Miller and His Orchestra
1941   Sun Valley Serenade

Miller, Harlan
1944   Since You Went Away
1948   Unconquered

Miller, Harold *not the same as* **Miller, Harry**
1947   Dark Delusion
1950   The Big Hangover
1951   The Great Caruso

Miller, Harriette B.
1949   Souls of Sin

Miller, Harry *not the same as* **Miller, Harold**
1934   The Youth of Russia
1958   Tonka

Miller, Hugh
1927   Blind Alleys

Miller, Irvin C.
1956   Rockin' the Blues

Miller, Mrs. Irvin C.
1923   Deceit

Miller, Ivan *same as* **Miller, Ivan "Dusty"**
1936   Charlie Chan at the Race Track
      Charlie Chan's Secret
      Human Cargo
      Robin Hood of El Dorado
1937   One Mile from Heaven
      That I May Live
1938   The Buccaneer
      Dangerous to Know
      Little Miss Roughneck
      Rascals
      Speed to Burn
1939   The Cisco Kid and the Lady
      The Escape
      Forged Passport
      King of Chinatown
1940   Geronimo
1941   Under Fiesta Stars
1944   An American Romance

Miller, J. Clarkson
1918   Love's Law
      Thirty a Week
1920?   The Scarlet Dragon
1927   For the Love of Mike

Miller, Joan
1948   Cry of the City

Miller, John "Skins" *same as* **Miller, "Skins"; Miller, John**
1934   Stand Up and Cheer!
1941   Birth of the Blues
      Sun Valley Serenade
1943   Dixie
      Yankee Doodle Dandy
1948   The Paleface
      The Time of Your Life
1949   Top O' the Morning
1950   The Men
1951   The Raging Tide

Miller, Kenny *same as* **Miller, Ken**
1958   Touch of Evil
1960   This Rebel Breed

Miller, Kristine
1950   Young Daniel Boone

Miller, Lorraine
1943   Riding High
1945   Between Two Women

Miller, Lucille
1933   It's Great to Be Alive
1934   Charlie Chan's Courage
      Stand Up and Cheer!
1935   Piernas de seda
1936   Charlie Chan at the Race Track
      Ramona

Miller, Marvin
1945   Johnny Angel
1946   Without Reservations

Miller, Mary Louise
1926   Into Her Kingdom

Miller, Merle
1958   Kings Go Forth

Miller, Olivette
1949?   The Joint Is Jumpin'

Miller, Palmer
1934   Song of the Islands

Miller, Patricia
1950   Stars in My Crown

Miller, Patsy Ruth
1925   Hogan's Alley
1926   The Fighting Edge
      Private Izzy Murphy
1928   We Americans

Miller, Peggy
1943   Gangway for Tomorrow

Miller, Peter
1955   Blackboard Jungle

Miller, Seton I.
1931   El código penal
1932   Scarface
1934   Charlie Chan's Courage
1941   This Woman Is Mine
1947   California
1951   Queen for a Day

Miller, Sidney
1933   Rafter Romance
1934   Our Daily Bread
1940   Little Nellie Kelly
1942   Syncopation
1944   Chip Off the Old Block

Miller, "Skins" *see* **Miller, John "Skins"**

Miller, Susan
1939   Miracle on Main Street

Miller, Taps
1943   Stormy Weather

Miller, Tom (*child actor*)
1943   Action in the North Atlantic

Miller, Veronica
1921   The Lure of a Woman

Miller, Virgil E. *same as* **Miller, Virgil**
1952   Navajo

Miller, Walk
1926   The Fighting Deacon

Miller, Walter *could be same as* **Miller, W.** *or* **Miller, Wallace**
1917   The Slacker (Metro Pictures Corp.)
1929   Hawk of the Hills
1930   On the Border
1931   The Hurricane Horseman
      Street Scene
1934   The Lone Defender
1936   Desert Gold
1937   Border Cafe
      Song of the City
1940   Three Cheers for the Irish

Miller, Watson B.
1949   Illegal Entry

Miller, Winston
1948   Fury at Furnace Creek
1950   Rocky Mountain
1951   The Last Outpost
1955   The Far Horizons

Millet, Arthur *same as*

Milletaire, Carl
1950   Black Hand
      A Lady Without Passport
1951   The Great Caruso
1959   Inside the Mafia

Millett, Arthur
1918   Her American Husband
      Shifting Sands
1936   The Prisoner of Shark Island

Millhauser, Bertram *same as* **Milhauser, Bertram**
1930   Check and Double Check
1931   Three Who Loved
1933   Ever in My Heart
1938   The Texans
1960   Pay or Die

Millican, James *same as* **Millican, James A.; Millican, Jim**
1942   Nazi Agent
1943   Air Force
      Riding High
1947   Spoilers of the North
1949   The Dalton Gang
1950   Devil's Doorway
      Winchester '73
1951   Cavalry Scout
      Warpath
1952   Bugles in the Afternoon
      High Noon
1955   Chief Crazy Horse
      The Vanishing American

Millie and Bubbles *see also* **Sublett, John W. "Bubbles"**
1939   Straight to Heaven

Lucky Millinder and his Orchestra
1933?   Scandal
1940   Paradise in Harlem
1946?   Harlem on Parade
1948?   Boarding House Blues

Millman, Barrie
1943   Ladies' Day

Millner, Marietta
1927   Drums of the Desert

The Mills Brothers
1934   Operator 13
1948   The Fight Never Ends

Mills, Edith
1950   Annie Get Your Gun
      Cherokee Uprising
1951   Across the Wide Missouri
      Westward the Women

Mills, Edwin
1943   Action in the North Atlantic
1944   The Racket Man

Mills, Evelyn
1928   A Ship Comes In

Mills, Frank 1891–1973
1934   Charlie Chan's Courage
1936   Star for a Night
1941   Sullivan's Travels
      Western Union
1942   Syncopation
      Woman of the Year
1943   Ladies' Day
      Mr. Lucky

Mills, Frank 1893–1973
1934   Broadway Bill
1943   Action in the North Atlantic

Mills, Gordon
1956   Daniel Boone, Trail Blazer

Mills, Irving
1943   Stormy Weather

Mills, Jerry
1919   The Homesteader

Mills, Marie
1917   Castles for Two

Mills, Mort
1955   Trial
1956   Davy Crockett and the River Pirates
1957   Man in the Shadow
1958   Ride a Crooked Trail
      Touch of Evil

Mills, Noel
1948   Gentleman's Agreement

Mills, Shirley
1944   Chip Off the Old Block

Mills, Thomas R. *same as* **Mills, Thom; Mills, Tom**
1917   A Night in New Arabia
      The Renaissance at Charleroi

Milne, Peter
1921   Little Italy
1939   Mr. Moto in Danger Island
1944   Lady, Let's Dance!
1947   My Wild Irish Rose
1950   The Daughter of Rosie O'Grady

Milner, Martin *same as* **Milner, Marty**
1950   Sands of Iwo Jima
1953   Last of the Comanches
1955   The Long Gray Line
1956   Pillars of the Sky
1958   Marjorie Morningstar

Milo, Ruth
1934   Broadway Bill

Milsfield Children
1934   Our Daily Bread

Miltern, John
1920   On with the Dance
1922   The Hands of Nara
1924   Tongues of Flame
1936   Sins of Man

Milton, Josh
1943   Gangway for Tomorrow

Milton, Robert
1921   The Land of Hope
1930   Behind the Make-Up

Milton, William
1924   Smiling Hate
1926?   Ten Nights in a Barroom

Mims, Bill
1960   Walk Tall

Minardos, Nico
1953   The Glory Brigade

Minciotti, Esther
1949   House of Strangers
        The Undercover Man
1955   Marty
1956   Full of Life

Minciotti, Silvio
1949   The Undercover Man
1950   Deported
1956   Full of Life
        Serenade

Mindenburg, Ben
1945   Samurai

Mineau, Charlotte
1918?   Rosemary Climbs the Heights

Mineo, Sal
1956   Giant
1958   Tonka

Miner, Allen
1956   Ghost Town
1957   The Ride Back

Miner, Allen H. *same as* **Miner, Allen**

Mines, Callie
1924   Birthright

Minevitch, Borrah
1938   Rascals

Borrah Minevitch and His Gang
1938   Rascals

Ming, Moy
1935   Charlie Chan in Shanghai
1948   The Time of Your Life

Miniciotti, Esther
1955   Murder in Villa Capri

Minjir, Harold
1934   Coming Out Party
1942   We Were Dancing
1943   The Amazing Mrs. Holliday
        Jack London
        The Meanest Man in the World

Minnelli, Vincente
1943   Cabin in the Sky

Minor, Frank
1934   Our Daily Bread

Minotis, Alexis *same as* **Minotis, Alex**
1946   Notorious
1950   Panic in the Streets

Minter, Mary Miles
1918?   Rosemary Climbs the Heights

1919   A Bachelor's Wife
        Yvonne from Paris
1921   All Souls' Eve

Mintz, Eli
1951   Molly

Mintz, Robert
1934   Drums O' Voodoo

Mintz, Sam
1927   The Gay Defender
1930   The Kibitzer
        Tom Sawyer
1933   Best of Enemies
        Rafter Romance
1948   Music Man

Minuti, Baldo
1950   Black Hand

Mio, Amleio
1931   Riders of the Rio

Mir, David
1928   The Cavalier

Miranda, Carmen
1943   The Gang's All Here
1944   Something for the Boys
1947   Copacabana

Miranda, José Antonio
1938   Mis dos amores

Miranda, Tom
1927   The Frontiersman

Mirande, Jacques
1930   El secreto del doctor (*foreign version*)

Mirande, Janine
1931   Su noche de bodas (*foreign version*)

Mirande, Yves
1930   Olimpia (*foreign version*)
        Le spectre vert
1931   Le père célibataire

Mireille
1931   Buster se marie
        El proceso de Mary Dugan (*foreign version*)

Mirelez, Henry
1946   Without Reservations
1948   Angel in Exile
1949   The Kissing Bandit

Mirelez, Yolanda
1951   The Great Caruso

Mirisch, Marvin
1954   Arrow in the Dust

Mirisch, Walter *same as* **Mirisch, Walter M.**
1951   Cavalry Scout
1952   Fort Osage
        Hiawatha
1955   Seven Angry Men
1957   The Oklahoman
1958   Fort Massacre

Miró, Carmen de
1939   Miracle on Main Street (*foreign version*)

Miró, Cesar
1939   Miracle on Main Street (*foreign version*)

Mirora, Myra
1931   Such Is Life

Mirsch, Marion
1931   Cimarron

Mishens, Ernest
1946   Till the End of Time

Mister Barker, a dog
1923   Ruggles of Red Gap

Mita, Edo
1959   The Crimson Kimono

Mita, Ura
1930   Wu Li Chang

Mitchel, Florence
1955   The View from Pompey's Head

Mitchell Boychoir *see* **Mitchell, Robert, Boychoir**

Mitchell, Aaron
1920   Dinty

Mitchell, Abbie *same as* **Mitchell, Abbey**
1920   Eyes of Youth
1948?   Junction 88

Mitchell, Allen
1950   Panic in the Streets

Mitchell, Belle
1928   Flying Romeos
1937   Man of the People
        Souls at Sea
1940   The Mark of Zorro
1943   The Leopard Man
1948   Unconquered
1949   Prejudice
1952   Hiawatha
1953   Tumbleweed
1954   Passion
1958   The Lone Ranger and the Lost City of Gold

Mitchell, Billy (*African-American actor*) *same as* **Mitchell, Frank "Billy"**
1942   In This Our Life
        Professor Creeps
1947   The Foxes of Harrow
        On the Old Spanish Trail
1950   Rock Island Trail
1951   The Tall Target

Bob Mitchell's Boys Choir *see* **Robert Mitchell and his St. Brendan's Boys Choir**

Mitchell, Bruce
1936   Charlie Chan at the Race Track
1938   The Adventures of Tom Sawyer
1939   The Escape

Mitchell, Cameron
1947   The Mighty McGurk
1952   Japanese War Bride
1955   The View from Pompey's Head
1957   All Mine to Give
1959   Inside the Mafia

Mitchell, Carlyle
1955   A Man Called Peter

Mitchell, Claude
1918   The Bravest Way
        The City of Dim Faces
        Hidden Pearls
        Sandy
        The Source

Mitchell, Dodson
1918   Toys of Fate

Mitchell, Dora
1921   By Right of Birth

Mitchell, Ewing
1951   The Last Outpost
1954   Drums Across the River
1957   Band of Angels
1958   Gunman's Walk

Mitchell, Frank
1920   Humoresque
1934   Stand Up and Cheer!
1940   Rhythm of the Rio Grande
1941   Where Did You Get That Girl?
1948   The Luck of the Irish
1949   The Story of Seabiscuit
1957   All Mine to Give

Mitchell, Frank "Billy" *see* **Mitchell, Billy** (*African-American actor*)

Mitchell, Geneva
1930   Son of the Gods

Mitchell, Grant
1934   The Cat's-Paw
1936   My American Wife
1937   Music for Madame
1940   New Moon
1943   The Amazing Mrs. Holliday
        Dixie
1945   A Medal for Benny

Mitchell, Horace
1949   Lost Boundaries

Mitchell, Howard *same as* **Mitchell, Howard M.**
1916   Betrayed
1921   Wing Toy
1940   East of the River
        Little Nellie Kelly
        The Way of All Flesh

Mitchell, Irving
1941   The Gang's All Here
1958   Gunman's Walk

Mitchell, James *same as* **Mitchell, Jim**
1942   Valley of Hunted Men
1949   Border Incident
        Colorado Territory
1950   Devil's Doorway
        Stars in My Crown
        The Toast of New Orleans

Mitchell, John circa 1950s
1952   Navajo

Mitchell, Johnny d. 1951 *same as* **Drake, Douglass**
1943   Good Luck, Mr. Yates
        Redhead from Manhattan
1944   Mr. Skeffington

Mitchell, Knolly
1932   The Black King

Mitchell, Laurie
1957   The Oklahoman

Mitchell, Millard
1942   Little Tokyo, U.S.A.
1949   Thieves' Highway
1950   Winchester '73

Mitchell, Nellie G.
1916   The Flower of No Man's Land

Mitchell, Pat
1951   The Well

Mitchell, Patsy (*child actress*)
1938   The Beloved Brat

Mitchell, Ray
1950   The Men

Mitchell, Rhea
1919   The Sleeping Lion
1920   The Devil's Claim
1934   Behold My Wife!
1947   The Mighty McGurk
1950   Annie Get Your Gun
        Stars in My Crown
1952   It's a Big Country: An American Anthology
1953   The Member of the Wedding

Mitchell, Robert (*actor*)
1956   Full of Life

Robert Mitchell and his St. Brendan's Boys Choir *same as* **Bob Mitchell's Boys Choir; Mitchell Boychoir**
1942   Tortilla Flat
1943   Good Luck, Mr. Yates
1944   Going My Way
1947   The Jolson Story

Mitchell, Sidney D. *same as* **Mitchell, Sidney**
1932   The Golden West

Mitchell, Steve
1958   Terror in a Texas Town

Mitchell, Thomas
1937   Man of the People
1939   Gone With the Wind
1940   Three Cheers for the Irish
1942   Song of the Islands
        Tales of Manhattan
1943   Bataan
        The Outlaw
1944   Buffalo Bill
        Dark Waters
        The Sullivans
1946   Three Wise Fools
1952   High Noon

Mitchell, Tressie
1932   Ten Minutes to Live

Within Our Gates (right column header, 1941 entries):
1941   Sullivan's Travels
1942   Gentleman Jim
        Mokey
1943   Action in the North Atlantic
1944   An American Romance
1945   Colorado Pioneers
1946   Notorious
1947   Easy Come, Easy Go
1949   House of Strangers
1950   No Way Out
        Stars in My Crown

Mitchell, Walter
1941   Sun Valley Serenade
Mitchell, Yvette
1917   The Flower of Doom
1919   The Last of His People
Mitchum, Bob *see* **Mitchum, Robert**
Mitchum, John *same as* **Mitchum, Jack**
1949   Knock on Any Door
       The Prairie
1950   Right Cross
1959   Al Capone
Mitchum, Robert *same as* **Mitchum, Bob**
1943   Border Patrol
       Doughboys in Ireland
1946   Till the End of Time
1947   Crossfire
1955   Not As a Stranger
1959   The Wonderful Country
Mitrovitch, Marta *same as* **Mitrovich, Martha**
1950   Ambush
       A Lady Without Passport
1952   Rose of Cimarron
Mitsoras, D. *same as* **Mitsoras, D. J.; Mitsoras, Demitrios J.**
1919   Just Squaw
1924   Racing Luck
1925   The Man in Blue
1953   Beneath the 12-Mile Reef
Mittler, Leo
1931   Chérie *(foreign version)*
       La fiesta del diablo *(foreign version)*
       La incorregible
       Tropennächte
Miwa, Ken
1951   Go for Broke!
Mix, Art some of the films listed below may be for one or more persons, one of whom may be **Denver Dixon**
1932   Border Devils
1933   King of the Wild Horses
1935   Cyclone of the Saddle
1942   Shut My Big Mouth
Mix, Emmet *see* **Mixx, Emmet**
Mix, Ruth
1935   Fighting Pioneers
1936   Custer's Last Stand
Mix, Tom
1914   In the Days of the Thundering Herd
1919   Fighting for Gold
1920   The Cyclone
1922   Sky High
1932   The Cohens and Kellys in Hollywood
Mixx, Emmet *same as* **Mix, Emmet**
1917   The Woman and the Beast
Mizer, Tom
1940   The Man I Married
Moad, Rex
1950   Panic in the Streets
Moats, Alice-Leone
1934   Coming Out Party
Mobley, James
1947   Jiggs and Maggie in Society
Moctezuma, Carlos López
1940   Perfidia
Modot, Gaston
1931   Die Dreigroschenoper *(foreign version)*
Modotti, Tina
1920   The Tiger's Coat
Moebus, Hans
1943   Action in the North Atlantic
       Crash Dive
1959   The Black Orchid
Moehring, "Kansas"
1950   The Cariboo Trail
       Colt .45
Moffat, Charles
1950   Give Us This Day
Moffat, Ivan
1956   Giant

Moffett, Sharyn
1944   My Pal Wolf
Moffitt, Jeff
1932   Hypnotized
1936   Kelly the Second
Mogilov, Lev
1934   The Rabbi's Power
Moh, Lee
1939?   A Chinese Gains a Fortune in America
Mohr, Gerald
1943   Redhead from Manhattan
1952   The Ring
1953   The Eddie Cantor Story
1960   This Rebel Breed
Moissi, Alexander
1929   Die Königsloge
Mojean, Olga
1920   White Youth
Mojica, José
1930   Cuando el amor ríe
       El precio de un beso
1931   Hay que casar al príncipe
       La ley del harem
       Mi último amor
1932   El caballero de la noche
1933   La melodía prohibida
       El rey de los gitanos
1934   Un capitán de cosacos
       La cruz y la espada
       Las fronteras del amor
Mokimana, Pualani *same as* **Mossoman, Pualani**
1934   Song of the Islands
Moler, Helaine
1938   Daughter of Shanghai
       The Texans
1939   King of Chinatown
Molieri, Lillian
1945   South of the Rio Grande
1950   A Lady Without Passport
1952   My Man and I
       The Ring
1956   Serenade
Molina, Carlos
1930   Sombras de gloria
1945   Club Havana
1950   Belle of Old Mexico
Molina, Joe *same as* **Molina, Joe E.**
1937   Waikiki Wedding
1941   Western Union
1950   Young Daniel Boone
Molinare, Nicanor
1932   Hollywood, ciudad de ensueño
Molinari, Ernest
1959   Al Capone
1960   Pay or Die
Molino, Magdalena
1935   Angelina o el honor de un brigadier
Moll, Elick
1951   The House on Telegraph Hill
Mollineaux, Constance *same as* **Molineaux, Constance**
1914   The Redemption of David Corson
Molnar, Ferenc
1942   Tales of Manhattan
Molnar, Julius *could be same as* **Molnar, Julius, Jr.**
1934   Imitation of Life
Moloney, Jim
1955   The Long Gray Line
       Seminole Uprising
Mom, Arturo S.
1931   La cautivadora
Monaco, Tepe
1932   Hypnotized
Monagas, Lionel *same as* **Monagos, Lionel; Monogas, Lionel**
1927   The Millionaire
1934   Drums O' Voodoo
1935   Lem Hawkins' Confession
1939   Keep Punching
       Straight to Heaven
1940   Paradise in Harlem
Monahan, Richard
1951   The Steel Helmet

Monda, Richard
1951   Go for Broke!
1953   The Eddie Cantor Story
1957   The Midnight Story
Mondshine, Baby
1937   That I May Live
Monet, M.
1914   The Nightingale
Monet, Robert
1953   Thunder Bay
Mong, William V. *same as* **Mong, W. V.; Mong, William; Mong, Wm. V.**
1919   The Delicious Little Devil
1921   Shame
1922   The Woman He Loved
1924   Welcome Stranger
1926   The Strong Man
1928   The Broken Mask
       Ransom
1934   Massacre
1936   Dancing Pirate
       The Last of the Mohicans
Monique
1949?   Harlem Follies
Monjardin, Antonio
1931   Un caballero de frac
       Su noche de bodas
Monk, Marilyn
1948   Gentleman's Agreement
Monk, Thomas
1940   Escape
Monks, John, Jr.
1945   The House on 92nd St.
1949   Knock on Any Door
Monogas, Lionel *see* **Monagas, Lionel**
The Monroe Singers
1930   Big Boy
Monroe, Buck
1952   Bugles in the Afternoon
Monroe, Clark
1949?   Harlem Follies
Monroe, Ellen Hope *same as* **Monroe, Hope**
1957   The Ride Back
1959   The Black Orchid
Monroe, Marilyn
1950   Right Cross
       A Ticket to Tomahawk
Monroe, Michael
1959   Inside the Mafia
Monroe, Millie
1941   Up Jumped the Devil
1942   Lucky Ghost
Monroe, Tom
1950   Border Treasure
       The Cariboo Trail
1951   The Tall Target
       Westward the Women
1952   The Half-Breed
       Rose of Cimarron
1953   San Antone
1955   The Far Horizons
       Santa Fe Passage
1956   Giant
1957   War Drums
1959   The FBI Story
Vaughn Monroe and His Orchestra
1947   Carnegie Hall
Monsour, Nira
1959   Cry Tough
Monta, Carlotta *see* **Monti, Carlotta**
Montagne, Edward J. *same as* **Montague, Edward J.**
1920?   The Greatest Love
1926   The Flaming Frontier
1928   Uncle Tom's Cabin
1929   Show Boat
Montague, Fred *same as* **Montague, Frederick; Montague, Mr.**
1914   The Squaw Man
       Where the Trail Divides
1917   The Winged Mystery
1919   His Debt
Montague, Monte *same as* **Montague, Monty**
1923   The Secret of the Pueblo

1936   Show Boat
       Treachery Rides the Range
1937   The Californian
1938   The Buccaneer
       The Renegade Ranger
1939   Allegheny Uprising
1942   The Navy Comes Through
1948   Gun Smugglers
       Moonrise
       Tap Roots
       Western Heritage
1949   Brothers in the Saddle
       Rustlers
1950   Rock Island Trail
       Sunset in the West
       Winchester '73
1951   Apache Drums
       Oh! Susanna
1952   The Raiders
1953   Column South
       The Great Sioux Uprising
       The Man from the Alamo
Montalbán, Carlos *same as* **Montalban, Carlos**
1934   Un capitán de cosacos
       La cruz y la espada
       Dos más uno, dos
       Tres amores
1935   Rosa de Francia
1936   El crimen de media noche
1937   El carnaval del diablo
1939   El otro soy yo
       Papá soltero
1940   Cuando canta la Ley
1956   Crowded Paradise
Montalban, Ricardo
1949   Border Incident
       The Kissing Bandit
1950   Battleground
       Mystery Street
       Right Cross
1951   Across the Wide Missouri
       The Mark of the Renegade
1952   My Man and I
Montalván, Celia
1931   Don Juan diplomático
       El proceso de Mary Dugan
Montana, Bull
1923   Breaking into Society
       Jealous Husbands
1925   The Gold Hunters
1937   Big City
Montana, Joy
1919   Deliverance
Montana, Monte
1935   Circle of Death
Monte, Alberto
1960   Walk Tall
Monte, Paul
1949   We Were Strangers
Monte, Phil
1947   Easy Come, Easy Go
Montell, Lisa
1956   The Wild Dakotas
1957   Tomahawk Trail
1958   The Lone Ranger and the Lost City of Gold
Montenegro, Conchita
1930   ¡De frente, marchen!
       Sevilla de mis amores
1931   The Cisco Kid
       En cada puerto un amor
       Hay que casar al príncipe
       Su última noche
1932   Marido y mujer
1933   Dos noches
       La melodía prohibida
1934   Caravane
       Granaderos del amor
1935   ¡Asegure a su mujer!
Montero, Lola
1934   Las fronteras del amor
Montes, Corazón *could be same as* **Montes, Cora**
1930   Las campanas de Capistrano
1935   De la sartén al fuego
1936   Contra la corriente

Montes, Lola
1945   The Gay Senorita
Montes, Luis *could be same as* **Montes, Lewis**
1932   Soñadores de la gloria
Montes, Monna
1938   Di que me quieres
Montes, Rodolfo
1929   Sombras habaneras
1930   Charros, gauchos y manolas
Montevecchi, Liliane
1958   The Young Lions
Montez, Christina
1940   Escape
Montez, Maria
1947   Pirates of Monterey
Montgomery, Douglass *same as* **Kent, Douglas; Kent, Douglass**
1935   Harmony Lane
Montgomery, Frank
1916   Her Debt of Honor
1917   The Call of Her People
        The Spirit of '76
1922   Cardigan
1925   Red Love
Montgomery, George *same as* **Letz, George**
1939   The Cisco Kid and the Lady
1940   Hi-Yo Silver
        Jennie
1941   Accent on Love
1950   Davy Crockett, Indian Scout
        The Iroquois Trail
1952   Indian Uprising
1953   Fort Ti
        Jack McCall Desperado
        The Pathfinder
1954   Battle of Rogue River
1955   Seminole Uprising
1957   Pawnee
Montgomery, Goodee
1931   Charlie Chan Carries On
Montgomery, Jack
1949   Colorado Territory
Montgomery, Peggy *same as* **Peggy, Baby**
1926   April Fool
1937   Souls at Sea
Montgomery, Ralph
1947   Calendar Girl
        Ride the Pink Horse
1950   Mystery Street
1951   Jim Thorpe—All-American
1953   The Member of the Wedding
1956   The Benny Goodman Story
1960   All the Fine Young Cannibals
Montgomery, Ray *same as* **Montgomery, Raymond**
1942   All Through the Night
        Wings for the Eagle
1943   Action in the North Atlantic
        Air Force
1949   The Girl from Jones Beach
1951   Tomahawk
1952   Bugles in the Afternoon
1953   Column South
1959   The FBI Story
Montgomery, Robert
1930   Sins of the Children
1947   Ride the Pink Horse
Monti, Carlotta *same as* **Monta, Carlotta; Monti, Carlotte**
1929   In Old California
1936   Robin Hood of El Dorado
Montiel, Sarita
1956   Serenade
1957   Run of the Arrow
Montis, Rene
1932   Le cas du docteur Brenner
Montor, Max
1931   Street Scene

Montoya, Alex *same as* **Montoya, Alex P.**
1946   Beauty and the Bandit
        The Gay Cavalier
1947   The Last Round-Up
        Riding the California Trail
        Robin Hood of Monterey
        West to Glory
1948   Old Los Angeles
1949   Illegal Entry
        The Kissing Bandit
        Streets of Laredo
        We Were Strangers
1950   Border Treasure
1951   Hurricane Island
        The Mark of the Renegade
1952   California Conquest
1953   Conquest of Cochise
        San Antone
1954   Passion
1955   Apache Ambush
        The Last Command
1957   War Drums
Montoya, Connie
1941   Hurry, Charlie, Hurry
Montoya, Felipe
1940   Perfidia
Montoya, Julia
1939   La Inmaculada
1948   Angel in Exile
1950   A Lady Without Passport
1952   The Ring
1953   The Great Sioux Uprising
1954   They Rode West
1955   The Far Horizons
1956   Raw Edge
1960   Key Witness
Montoya, María Teresa
1940   Perfidia
Montrose, Helene *same as* **Montrose, Helen**
1918   Out of a Clear Sky
Montt, Christina
1927   Rose of the Golden West
1930   Alma de gaucho
        El último de los Vargas
1931   Cavalier of the West
Moody, Harry
1926   Under Fire
Moody, Ralph
1950   Rock Island Trail
1952   Wagons West
1953   Column South
        Seminole
        Tumbleweed
1955   The Far Horizons
1956   The Last Hunt
        Reprisal!
1957   Pawnee
1958   The Lone Ranger and the Lost City of Gold
Moody, Ruth
1933   It's Great to Be Alive
Mooers, De Sacia
1923   Potash and Perlmutter
1930   The Arizona Kid
Mook, Beverly
1950   The Breaking Point
Mooney, Martin
1942   Foreign Agent
1944   Minstrel Man
        Waterfront
1945   Club Havana
1949   Daughter of the West
Mooney, Tex
1947   Calendar Girl
Moore & Allen
1935   Charlie Chan in Paris
Moore, Alvy
1953   The Glory Brigade
Moore, Archie
1960   The Adventures of Huckleberry Finn
Moore, Bette Gene
1941   Sun Valley Serenade
Moore, Bill *see* **Potter, Peter**
Moore, Brenda
1922   Solomon in Society

Moore, Buddy
1945   Where Do We Go From Here?
Moore, Carl
1956   Giant
Moore, Carlyle, Jr. *same as* **Moore, Carlisle, Jr.**
1934   Coming Out Party
1936   Treachery Rides the Range
1937   Black Legion
1938   Outlaw Express
1940   Knute Rockne—All American
Moore, Charles *same as* **Moore, Charles R.; Moore, Charlie**
1919   The Homesteader
1931   The Exile
1938   God's Step Children
1941   Sullivan's Travels
        Virginia
1942   Syncopation
1943   Dixie
        Riding High
1946   Without Reservations
Moore, Clayton
1940   Kit Carson
1949   The Cowboy and the Indians
        The Gay Amigo
        Masked Raiders
1951   Cyclone Fury
1952   Buffalo Bill in Tomahawk Territory
        The Raiders
1954   The Black Dakotas
1955   Apache Ambush
1956   The Lone Ranger
1958   The Lone Ranger and the Lost City of Gold
Moore, Cleo
1950   Rio Grande Patrol
1951   Gambling House
Moore, Clifford
1946   Rendezvous 24
Moore, Colleen
1920   The Cyclone
        The Devil's Claim
        Dinty
1922   Come On Over
1923   April Showers
        The Huntress
        Look Your Best
1924   So Big
1926   Irene
1929   Smiling Irish Eyes
Moore, Daniel *same as* **Moore, Dan**
1936   The Last of the Mohicans
1949   Illegal Entry
Moore, Daphne
1943   Mr. Lucky
Moore, Dauphine *(African-American actress)*
1947   Juke Joint
Moore, Dennie *not the same as* **Moore, Dennis**
1949   Anna Lucasta
Moore, Dennis *same as* **Meadows, Dennie; Meadows, Denny; Moore, Denny** *not the same as* **Moore, Dennie**
1936   Hair-Trigger Casey
1937   Black Legion
1938   Wild Horse Canyon
1942   Below the Border
1943   Action in the North Atlantic
        Land of Hunted Men
1945   The Mummy's Curse
1950   I Killed Geronimo
1951   Fort Defiance
1956   The White Squaw
Moore, Dickie *same as* **Moore, Dick; Moore, Dickey**
1930   Son of the Gods
1931   Aloha
        The Squaw Man
        Three Who Loved
1932   No Greater Love
        So Big
1933   Obey the Law
1935   So Red the Rose

Moore, Donna
1947   Citizen Saint
Moore, Ducky *(African-American actor)*
1954   Go Man Go
Moore, Edward
1926?   Ten Nights in a Barroom
Moore, Eleanor
1951   The House on Telegraph Hill
Moore, Mrs. Eugene L.
1922   Square Joe
Moore, Eunice *same as* **Murdock, Eunice; Van Moore, Eunice**
1920   Huckleberry Finn
Moore, Florence
1917   The Secret of Eve
Moore, Mrs. Fred R.
1922   Square Joe
Moore, Gar
1949   Illegal Entry
Moore, George *(African-American actor) not the same as* **Marriott, Moore** *(British actor), also known as* **Moore, George**
1954   Go Man Go
Moore, Gertrude
1923   His Great Chance
Moore, Gloria
1953   So Big
1955   Trial
Moore, Grace
1931   Jenny Lind
Moore, Hal
1949   The Story of Seabiscuit
Moore, Ida
1944   Hi, Beautiful
1947   Easy Come, Easy Go
1951   Show Boat
Moore, Jack
1938   The Texans
Moore, Joanna
1958   Ride a Crooked Trail
        Touch of Evil
1959   The Last Angry Man
Moore, Joyce
1916   The Twin Triangle
Moore, Juanita
1949   Pinky
1952   The Iron Mistress
1957   Band of Angels
1959   Imitation of Life
Moore, Katherine *same as* **Moore, Kathrine**
1946   Dirty Gertie from Harlem, U.S.A.
1947   Juke Joint
1949?   Girl in Room 20
Moore, Kieron
1960   The Day They Robbed the Bank of England
Moore, Larry
1945   Samurai
Moore, Lawrence
1952   Red Snow
Moore, Louis F. *same as* **Moore, Louis**
1938   Rascals
Moore, Marcia
1916   The Grip of Jealousy
Moore, Margery
1949?   Girl in Room 20
Moore, Marion
1922   Square Joe
Moore, Mary *circa 1914–1917*
1915   Under Southern Skies
Moore, Mary *circa 1940s*
1945   The Shanghai Cobra
Moore, Matt
1913   Traffic in Souls
1917   Runaway Romany
1942   Mokey
        The Vanishing Virginian
1943   Dr. Gillespie's Criminal Case
1950   The Big Hangover
        Mystery Street

1951   The Great Caruso
Moore, McElbert
1949   Shamrock Hill
Moore, Melvin H.
1950   Mystery Street
Moore, Mickey *same as* **Moore, Master Micky; Moore, Micky**
1919   The Unpainted Woman
1921   All Souls' Eve
            Shame
Moore, Monette
1951   Yes Sir, Mr. Bones
Moore, Nora
1916   The King's Game
Moore, Owen
1916   Little Meena's Romance
1917   The Little Boy Scout
1921   A Divorce of
            Convenience
1924   East of Broadway
Moore, Pat *same as* **Moore, Master Pat**
1918   The Squaw Man
1919   The Sleeping Lion
1926   April Fool
Moore, Pauline
1937   Charlie Chan at the
            Olympics
1938   Passport Husband
1939   Charlie Chan at Treasure
            Island
            Charlie Chan in Reno
1940   Young Buffalo Bill
Moore, Petrina
1939   Moon over Harlem
Moore, Phil
1946   Stars on Parade
Phil Moore and His Orchestra
1939   Gang Smashers
The Phil Moore Four
1946   Stars on Parade
1949?   The Joint Is Jumpin'
Moore, Roger *not the same as* **Moore, Roger** *(English actor)*, 1927—
1942   Nazi Agent
1949   House of Strangers
1951   Go for Broke!
            The Great Caruso
            The Tall Target
1952   It's a Big Country: An
            American Anthology
Moore, Ruth
1947   Citizen Saint
Moore, Scott
1945   The House on 92nd St.
Moore, Sue
1936   After the Thin Man
1945   A Tree Grows in Brooklyn
Moore, Terry *same as* **Koford, Helen**
1944   Since You Went Away
1951   Gambling House
1953   Beneath the 12-Mile Reef
Moore, Thomas Allen *not the same as* **Moore, Thomas; Moore, Tom** *or* **Moore, Tommie**
1938   Di que me quieres
Moore, Tim *circa 1920s*
1923   His Great Chance
Moore, Tim *(African-American actor)*
1947   Boy! What a Girl!
Moore, Tom *not the same as* **Moore, Thomas; Moore, Thomas Allen** *or* **Moore, Tommie**
1917   The Wild Girl
1918   Thirty a Week
1919   Toby's Bow
1921   Hold Your Horses
            Made in Heaven
1928   Anybody Here Seen Kelly?
1932   Men Are Such Fools
1936   Robin Hood of El Dorado
1948   Cry of the City
Moore, Tomiwatta *could be same as* **Moore, Tommie**
1943   Stormy Weather

Moore, Tommie *could be same as* **Moore, Tomiwatta** *not the same as* **Moore, Thomas; Moore, Thomas Allen** *or* **Moore, Tom**
1940   Mystery in Swing
1946   That Man of Mine
1957   Band of Angels
Moore, Tommiwatta
1940   Broken Strings
Moore, Vernetties
1948   The Betrayal
Moore, Vernol
1920?   Reformation
Moore, Victor
1915   Chimmie Fadden
            Chimmie Fadden Out
            West
1941   Louisiana Purchase
1943   Riding High
Moore, Vin
1931   The Cohens and Kellys in
            Africa
Moore, William *see* **Potter, Peter**
Moorehead, Agnes
1944   Since You Went Away
            Tomorrow the World!
1945   Our Vines Have Tender
            Grapes
1951   Adventures of Captain
            Fabian
            Show Boat
1957   Raintree County
1959   Night of the Quarter
            Moon
Moorehouse, Bert *see* **Moorhouse, Bert**
Moorhead, Jean
1955   The Long Gray Line
1959   Gunmen from Laredo
Moorhead, Natalie
1933   Dance Hall Hostess
1938   The Beloved Brat
Moorhouse, Bert *same as* **Moorehouse, Bert; Morehouse, Bert**
1934   Broadway Bill
1935   Rendezvous
1938   Little Miss Roughneck
1943   Gangway for Tomorrow
1944   Lake Placid Serenade
            My Pal Wolf
1948   Unconquered
            Up in Central Park
1950   The Big Hangover
            Right Cross
1951   Gambling House
1953   Dream Wife
1954   Dangerous Mission
Moorten, F.
1931   Delicious
Mora, Bradley
1950   Annie Get Your Gun
Mora, Carmen
1939   Los hijos mandan
            Miracle on Main Street
            (foreign version)
Mora, Emma
1930   Alma de gaucho
Mora, Hipólito
1930   El último de los Vargas
1931   ¿Conoces a tu mujer?
1932   Soñadores de la gloria
Mora, Julieta
1930   La rosa de fuego
Moraine, Lyle
1952   Anything Can Happen
1957   Beau James
Morales, Carmen
1943   Ladies' Day
Morales, Joe T.
1954   Salt of the Earth
Morales, Maria *(actress)*
1936   Ramona
Morales, María Luz *(writer)*
1930   Doña mentiras
Morales, Richard
1950   Panic in the Streets
Morales, Sofía
1932   Amor y vida

Moran, Dolores
1946   Without Reservations
Moran, E. Edwin
1942   Twin Beds
1943   Wintertime
Morán, Fernando
1931   Su última noche
Moran, Frank *same as* **Moran, Frank C.**
1932   Me and My Gal
1934   Coming Out Party
            Judge Priest
1935   The Winning Ticket
1936   It Had to Happen
1938   Passport Husband
1941   Sullivan's Travels
1942   Gentleman Jim
1948   Unconquered
Moran, George
1929   Why Bring That Up?
1930   Anybody's War
1932   Hypnotized
Moran, Jackie
1938   The Adventures of Tom
            Sawyer
1939   Gone With the Wind
1941   The Gang's All Here
1944   Andy Hardy's Blonde
            Trouble
            Since You Went Away
Moran, Lee
1926   The Little Irish Girl
1933   Grand Slam
            Racetrack
Morán, Luz F.
1936   Contra la corriente
Moran, Neil
1918   Fields of Honor
Moran, Pat *not the same as* **Moran, Patsy**
1957   Beau James
1958   Houseboat
Moran, Patsy *not the same as* **Moran, Pat**
1942   Foreign Agent
Moran, Peggy
1942   Seven Sweethearts
Moran, Polly
1927   The Callahans and the
            Murphys
1932   Le plombier amoureux
Moran, William
1922   The Top O' the Morning
Morange, Edward A.
1914   The Great Diamond
            Robbery
Morante, Milburn *same as* **Morante, Milt; Moranti, Milburn**
1926   Buffalo Bill on the U. P.
            Trail
1935   Cyclone of the Saddle
1935?   The Irish Gringo
1936   Custer's Last Stand
Moray, Antonio
1931   La regina di Sparta
Mordant, Edwin
1916   Poor Little Peppina
1935   A Night at the Ritz
1937   Maid of Salem
Moré de la Torre, Francisco
1930   Cuando el amor ríe
            Del mismo barro
            El precio de un beso
            El último de los Vargas
            El valiente
1931   ¿Conoces a tu mujer?
            Del infierno al cielo
            Esclavas de la moda
            La gran jornada
More, Kenneth
1959   The Sheriff of Fractured
            Jaw
The Moreau Choir of Notre Dame
1940   Knute Rockne—All
            American
Morehead, Dick
1939   The Mystery of Mr. Wong
Morehouse, Bert *see* **Moorhouse, Bert**

Morehouse, Clarence
1940?   Mr. Washington Goes to
            Town
Moreland, Betsy Jones
1956   Full of Life
1957   The Brothers Rico
Moreland, Craig
1954   Dangerous Mission
Moreland, Mantan *same as* **Moreland, Manton**
1937   Harlem on the Prairie
1938   Spirit of Youth
            Two Gun Man from
            Harlem
1939   Gang Smashers
            One Dark Night
1940   Viva Cisco Kid
            While Thousands Cheer
1940?   Mr. Washington Goes to
            Town
1941   Accent on Love
            Birth of the Blues
            Four Shall Die
            The Gang's All Here
            King of the Zombies
            Up Jumped the Devil
            You're Out of Luck
1942   Lucky Ghost
            Mexican Spitfire Sees a
            Ghost
            Professor Creeps
1943   Cabin in the Sky
            Crime Smasher
1944   Black Magic
            Charlie Chan in the
            Secret Service
            The Chinese Cat
            Chip Off the Old Block
1945   The Jade Mask
            The Scarlet Clue
            The Shanghai Cobra
1946   Dark Alibi
            Mantan Messes Up
            Shadows Over Chinatown
            Tall, Tan and Terrific
            The Trap
1947   The Chinese Ring
            Mantan Runs for Mayor
1947?   Return of Mandy's
            Husband
            What a Guy
1948   Docks of New Orleans
            The Feathered Serpent
            The Golden Eye
            Shanghai Chest
1949   The Sky Dragon
1949?   Come On, Cowboy!
            She's Too Mean for Me
1956   Rockin' the Blues
Moreland, Marcella
1940   Am I Guilty?
1942   Mokey
            The Vanishing Virginian
Moreland, Sherry
1951   When the Redskins Rode
Morella, Tony
1956   Giant
Morelle, Gaby
1931   La pura verdad
Morelli, Ernesto *same as* **Morrelli, Ernest**
1937   Man of the People
1938   The Buccaneer
1949   House of Strangers
1950   Black Hand
            Mystery Street
            The Toast of New Orleans
1951   Go for Broke!
            The Great Caruso
1957   The Brothers Rico
Morelli, Mike
1956   Hot Blood
Morelli, Naldo
1924   Defying the Law
Moreno, Antonio
1917   The Captain of the Gray
            Horse Troop
1923   Look Your Best
1929   Romance of the Rio
            Grande
1930   The Bad Man *(foreign
            version)*
            El cuerpo del delito
            Los que danzan
            El precio de un beso

	La voluntad del muerto
1933	Primavera en otoño
1934	La ciudad de cartón
1935	Alas sobre el Chaco
	¡Asegure a su mujer!
	Rosa de Francia
	Señora casada necesita marido
1942	Valley of the Sun
1946	Notorious
1949	Lust for Gold
1951	The Mark of the Renegade
1953	Thunder Bay
1954	Saskatchewan
1956	The Searchers

Moreno, Ascension
| 1940 | Tengo fe en ti |

Moreno, David
| 1956 | Comanche |

Moreno, Eduard
| 1950 | The Toast of New Orleans |

Moreno, Guillermo
| 1934 | El tango en Broadway |

Moreno, Hilda
1932	Law and Lawless
1933	It's Great to Be Alive (foreign version)
	Primavera en otoño

Moreno, Jorge
| 1958 | The Badlanders |

Moreno, Marguerite
1930	Un hombre de suerte (foreign version)
1931	Chérie
	Lo mejor es reír
	Su noche de bodas (foreign version)

Moreno, Mayo
| 1931 | La fiesta del diablo (foreign version) |

Moreno, Paco
1930	Amor audaz
	Cascarrabias
	El dios del mar
1931	La dama atrevida
	Esclavas de la moda
	Hay que casar al príncipe
	La ley del harem
	Mi último amor
	El proceso de Mary Dugan
1932	Hombres en mi vida
1933	El rey de los gitanos
	Una viuda romántica
1934	Un capitán de cosacos
	La cruz y la espada
	Granaderos del amor
	Tres amores
1935	Alas sobre el Chaco
	Angelina o el honor de un brigadier
	Piernas de seda
1937	El capitán Tormenta
1939	La Inmaculada
	Papá soltero
	El trovador de la radio
1940	The Mark of Zorro
	Tengo fe en ti
1941	Ride on Vaquero

Moreno, Rita 1931— *not the same as* **Moreno, Rosita** 1908—1993
1950	So Young, So Bad
	The Toast of New Orleans
1952	The Fabulous Senorita
	The Ring
1954	The Yellow Tomahawk
1955	Seven Cities of Gold
1957	The Deerslayer
1960	This Rebel Breed

Moreno, Rosita 1908—1993 *not the same as* **Moreno, Rita** 1931—
1930	Amor audaz
	El dios del mar
	Galas de la Paramount
1931	Gente alegre
	El príncipe gondolero
1932	El hombre que asesinó
1933	It's Great to Be Alive (foreign version)
	No dejes la puerta abierta
	El rey de los gitanos
	Yo, tú y ella

1934	Un capitán de cosacos
	Dos más uno, dos
	Las fronteras del amor
1935	De la sartén al fuego
	El día que me quieras
	Piernas de seda
	Tango Bar
	Te quiero con locura
1940	Tengo fe en ti
1945	A Medal for Benny

Morfis, Costas
| 1952 | It's a Big Country: An American Anthology |
| 1953 | The Glory Brigade |

Morgan, Ainsworth
| 1934 | Behold My Wife! |

Morgan, Bob
| 1955 | Shotgun |

Morgan, Boyd *same as* **Morgan, Boyd "Red"**
1940	Lucky Cisco Kid
1951	Saturday's Hero
	Snake River Desperadoes
1952	The Raiders
1953	Column South
	The Great Sioux Uprising
	The Nebraskan
1955	Violent Saturday
1959	The Jayhawkers!

Morgan, Bruce
| 1950 | Mystery Submarine |

Morgan, Buck
| 1935 | The Cyclone Ranger |

Morgan, Byron
| 1942 | Wings for the Eagle |

Morgan, Claudia
| 1939 | Stand Up and Fight |

Morgan, Cleo
| 1946 | Cuban Pete |

Morgan, Clive
1937	Maid of Salem
1939	Allegheny Uprising
1941	Hurry, Charlie, Hurry
1958	The Young Lions

Morgan, Dennis *same as* **Morner, Stanley; Stanley, Richard**
1937	Song of the City
1939	Waterfront
1940	The Fighting 69th
	Three Cheers for the Irish
1942	In This Our Life
	Wings for the Eagle
1947	My Wild Irish Rose
1955	The Gun That Won the West

Morgan, Eula
| 1951 | Jim Thorpe—All-American |
| 1952 | Hiawatha |

Morgan, Frank
1919	The Gray Towers Mystery
1925	Scarlet Saint
1933	Best of Enemies
1935	Naughty Marietta
1936	Dancing Pirate
	Dimples
1942	Tortilla Flat
	The Vanishing Virginian

Morgan, Gene *same as* **Morgan, Gene, Jr.**
1933	Song of the Eagle
1936	Dangerous Intrigue
1937	The Devil's Playground
1939	Winner Take All
1940	Girl from God's Country

Morgan, George
| 1931 | The Avenger |
| 1935 | Rescue Squad |

Morgan, H. A. *see* **Morgan, "Kewpie"**

Morgan, Harry Hays
| 1946 | Abie's Irish Rose |
| 1947 | It Had To Be You |

Morgan, Helen
| 1929 | Show Boat |
| 1936 | Show Boat |

Morgan, Henry "Harry"
1943	Crash Dive
	The Ox-Bow Incident
1948	Moonrise
1951	The Well
1952	Apache War Smoke
	High Noon

1953	Thunder Bay
1955	Not As a Stranger
1960	Cimarron

Morgan, Jackie
| 1925 | The Man in Blue |

Morgan, Janet *see* **Mehaffey, Blanche**

Morgan, Jeanne
| 1930 | Whoopee |

Morgan, Jim
| 1951 | Queen for a Day |

Morgan, John
| 1950 | The Breaking Point |
| | Intruder in the Dust |

Morgan, Kewpie *same as* **Morgan, H. A.**
| 1920 | The Cup of Fury |
| 1927 | Finnegan's Ball |

Morgan, Lee
1949	Roll Thunder Roll!
1950	Raiders of Tomahawk Creek
1952	The Raiders
1953	The Man Behind the Gun
1954	Drums Across the River
1956	Daniel Boone, Trail Blazer
1958	Sierra Baron

Morgan, Leota
| 1923 | None So Blind |
| 1927 | Heroes in Blue |

Morgan, Margaret
| 1934 | Broadway Bill |
| 1936 | Ramona |

Morgan, Marilyn *see* **Marsh, Marian**

Morgan, Marion
| 1936 | Klondike Annie |

Morgan, Michael
| 1955 | The Gun That Won the West |

Morgan, Oscar
| 1928 | Tenderfeet |

Morgan, Paul
| 1931 | Buster se marie |
| | Buster se marie (foreign version) |

Morgan, Ralph
1932	Charlie Chan's Chance
	The Son-Daughter
1934	She Was a Lady
	Stand Up and Cheer!
1936	General Spanky
	Human Cargo
	Muss 'Em Up
1939	Man of Conquest
	Way Down South
1940	Geronimo
1943	Jack London
1947	The Last Round-Up
1948	Sleep, My Love

Morgan, Red
| 1957 | War Drums |

Morgan, Robin
| 1947 | Citizen Saint |

Morgan, Sandra
| 1946 | Notorious |

Morgan, Will
| 1937 | Old Louisiana |
| 1942 | Across the Pacific |

Morgenthau, Henry
| 1919 | Auction of Souls |

Morhart, Hans von *see* **Von Morhart, Hans**

Mori, George
| 1938 | Little Miss Roughneck |

Mori, Torau
| 1959 | The Crimson Kimono |

Mori, Toshia *could be same as* **Jung, Toshia Mori** *or* **Mori, Toni**
1932	The Hatchet Man
	The Secrets of Wu Sin
1935	Chinatown Squad
1937	Charlie Chan on Broadway

Moriarity, Marcus
| 1916 | The Flower of No Man's Land |

Moriarity, Pat *same as* **Moriarity, Patrick**
1934	Broadway Bill
1935	Black Fury
	His Family Tree
	McFadden's Flats
1937	Man of the People
	The Plainsman
1940	Little Nellie Kelly
1942	Gentleman Jim
	Valley of the Sun
1950	Ambush

Moriarty, Bernard A.
1936	The Glory Trail
	Rebellion
1937	Drums of Destiny
	Old Louisiana

Moriche, José
| 1930 | Revista Hispano-Americana |
| 1934 | El tango en Broadway |

Morin, Albert *same as* **Morin, Alberto**
1938	The Toy Wife
1939	Gone With the Wind
1940	Charlie Chan in Panama
1947	The Foxes of Harrow
1948	The Luck of the Irish
1949	The Fighting Kentuckian
	The Kissing Bandit
	We Were Strangers
1950	Rio Grande
1951	The Mark of the Renegade
1952	The Iron Mistress
1953	The Glory Brigade
	The Man Behind the Gun
	The Man from the Alamo
1955	The Last Command
1956	Pillars of the Sky
1958	The Young Lions

Morison, Patricia
| 1941 | Romance of the Rio Grande |

Morita, Miki *same as* **Morita, Mike**
1934	Behold My Wife!
1936	Border Phantom
1937	The Devil's Playground

Moritarty, Pat *see* **Moriarity, Pat**

Moriyama, Rollin
| 1951 | Go for Broke! |
| 1959 | The Crimson Kimono |

Morla, Elvira
1930	Olimpia
1931	La fruta amarga
	La llama sagrada
	Mi último amor
	El proceso de Mary Dugan

Morley, Jay *same as* **Morley, J.**
1918	An Alien Enemy
1926	Buffalo Bill on the U. P. Trail
1927	With Sitting Bull at the Spirit Lake Massacre

Morley, Karen
1932	Flesh
	Scarface
1934	Our Daily Bread
	Straight Is the Way
1935	Black Fury
	The Littlest Rebel
1945	Jealousy

Morley, Robert
| 1959 | The Sheriff of Fractured Jaw |

Morner, Stanley *see* **Morgan, Dennis**

Moro and Yaconelli *see also* **Moro, Nick; Yaconelli, Frank**
| 1946 | Slightly Scandalous |

Moro, Nick *see also* **Moro and Yaconelli**
| 1956 | Serenade |

Morongo, Harold
| 1936 | Ramona |

Morosco, Oliver
| 1917 | His Sweetheart |
| 1922 | The Half Breed |

Morosco, Walter
| 1940 | Charlie Chan at the Wax Museum |
| | The Gay Caballero |

1941   Accent on Love
          Dead Men Tell
Moroz, Ben
1945   Rhapsody in Blue
Morrell, George
1917   The Secret of Eve
1934   Broadway Bill
1935   Circle of Death
          Cyclone of the Saddle
1936   Custer's Last Stand
1945   Salome, Where She
          Danced
1949   Lust for Gold
          The Prairie
Morrell, Stanley
1931   The Exile
Morrelli, Ernest see **Morelli, Ernesto**
Morris, Adrian same as **Morris, Michael**
1932   Me and My Gal
1936   My American Wife
1938   Mr. Moto's Gamble
1939   The Cisco Kid and the
          Lady
          Gone With the Wind
          The Return of the Cisco
          Kid
1940   Elsa Maxwell's Public
          Deb No. 1
          Lucky Cisco Kid
1941   Belle Starr
Morris, Charles
1935   So Red the Rose
1936   Rose of the Rancho
Morris, Chester
1937   The Devil's Playground
1940   Girl from God's Country
1949   Boston Blackie's Chinese
          Venture
Morris, Clara
1918   Mystic Faces
Morris, Corbet same as **Morris, Corbett**
1937   The Devil's Playground
1938   The Rage of Paris
Morris, Dave
1925   Tearing Through
1939   Heaven with a Barbed
          Wire Fence
1940   The Gay Caballero
1943   The Meanest Man in the
          World
Morris, Dick see **Morris, Richard**
Morris, Dorothy
1942   Dr. Gillespie's New
          Assistant
          Seven Sweethearts
          We Were Dancing
1945   Club Havana
          Our Vines Have Tender
          Grapes
Morris, Earl same as **Morris, Earl J.**
1939   The Bronze Buckaroo
1940   Broken Strings
          Mystery in Swing
          Son of Ingagi
1941   Up Jumped the Devil
Morris, Eileen
1946   The Sailor Takes a Wife
Morris, Frances same as **Morris, Francis**
1934   Stand Up and Cheer!
1936   Dangerous Intrigue
1938   Little Miss Roughneck
1941   New York Town
1946   Abie's Irish Rose
1947   California
1948   My Girl Tisa
1958   Wild Is the Wind
Morris, Gouverneur
1921   A Tale of Two Worlds
Morris, Henry
1942   Valley of Hunted Men
Morris, Johnnie same as **Morris, Johnny**
1937   Boy of the Streets
1947   My Wild Irish Rose
1948   Jiggs and Maggie in Court

Morris, Lea
1935   Lem Hawkins' Confession
Morris, Michael see **Morris, Adrian**
Morris, Mildred
1934   Stand Up and Cheer!
Morris, Philip same as **Morris, Phillip**
1936   Desert Gold
1937   Charlie Chan at the
          Olympics
          Charlie Chan on
          Broadway
1938   The Buccaneer
          Passport Husband
          The Texans
1939   Waterfront
1940   Charlie Chan in Panama
1945   Johnny Angel
1947   Crossfire
1948   Fighting Father Dunne
          The Lady from Shanghai
1949   Knock on Any Door
Morris, Phyllis
1950   Black Hand
Morris, Richard same as **Morris, Dick**
1916   The Morals of Hilda
          A Yoke of Gold
Morris, Stephen see **Ankrum, Morris**
Morris, Tony
1957   Naked in the Sun
Morris, Wayne
1948   The Time of Your Life
1952   Arctic Flight
          Desert Pursuit
1955   The Lonesome Trail
Morrisey, Joseph
1954   Drums Across the River
Morrison, Albert
1919   Just Squaw
1920   Who's Your Servant?
Morrison, Ann
1949   House of Strangers
          Thieves' Highway
1950   No Way Out
1955   Violent Saturday
Morrison, Arthur
1914   At the Cross Roads
1919   Desert Gold
1923   The Sting of the Scorpion
1934   The Lone Defender
Morrison, Barbara
1948   Unconquered
1955   A Man Called Peter
Morrison, Chuck same as **Morrison, Charles**
1935   Fighting Pioneers
1941   Road Agent
Morrison, Dorothy
1929   Hearts in Dixie
Morrison, James
1917   One Law for Both
Morrison, Louis same as **Morrison, Lew; Morrison, Lou**
1918   Denny from Ireland
1920   Dangerous Hours
1929   Frozen Justice
Morrison, Pete
1929   Chinatown Nights
Morrison, Mrs. Priestley
1918   Uncle Tom's Cabin
Morrison, Sunshine Sammy same as **Morrisson, Sunshine Sammy; Sunshine Sammy**
1942   In This Our Life
          Let's Get Tough!
Morrison, Walter
1951   The Well
Morrissey, Grace
1917   The Tell-Tale Step
Morrissey, Tommy
1917   The Flower of Doom
Morrissey, Will
1949   Lookout Sister
Morros, Boris
1942   Tales of Manhattan
1947   Carnegie Hall

Morrow, Brad
1951   The Tall Target
Morrow, Byron
1960   This Rebel Breed
Morrow, Clarence
1936   Ramona
Morrow, Douglas
1951   Jim Thorpe—All-American
Morrow, Gladys
1926   The Devil Horse
Morrow, Guernsey
1938   The Duke Is Tops
1939   One Dark Night
1940   Am I Guilty?
1941   Four Shall Die
1942   Take My Life
Morrow, Jeff
1954   Siege at Red River
Morrow, Neyle
1947   Dangerous Venture
          Pirates of Monterey
          Spoilers of the North
1949   Harbor of Missing Men
          Ranger of Cherokee Strip
1951   The Steel Helmet
1952   The Raiders
          Trail of the Arrow
1956   The White Squaw
1957   Run of the Arrow
1959   The Crimson Kimono
Morrow, Philip
1915   The Nigger
Morrow, Susan
1952   The Savage
Morrow, Vic
1955   Blackboard Jungle
1960   Cimarron
Morsbach, Louis
1952   Bright Victory
Morse, Eddie
1948   Unconquered
Morse, Freeman
1954   Battle of Rogue River
Morse, Laura
1934   Stand Up and Cheer!
Morse, Myrtle
1922   The Mohican's Daughter
Morse, N. Brewster same as **Morse, Brewster**
1938   Breaking the Ice
Morse, Robin
1955   Marty
Morse, Terry same as **Morse, T. O.**
1939   Waterfront
1946   Dangerous Money
          Don Ricardo Returns
          Shadows Over Chinatown
1947   Bells of San Fernando
Morsell, H. Tudor
1915   The Grandee's Ring
Mortensen, Inez
1934   Stand Up and Cheer!
1936   Star for a Night
Mortimer, Ed same as **Mortimer, Edmund; Mortimer, Edward**
1934   Behold My Wife!
1936   Dangerous Intrigue
1944   An American Romance
Mortimer, Henry same as **Mortimer, Harry**
1930   The Big Pond (foreign
          version)
Mortimer, William
1920   Hidden Charms
1921?   The Supreme Passion
Morton, Charles same as **Morton, Charles S.**
1930   Check and Double Check
1947   Calendar Girl
          Spoilers of the North
1950   Rock Island Trail
1953   The Eddie Cantor Story
1955   Shotgun
Morton, Clive
1959   Shake Hands with the
          Devil
Morton, Edna
1921   The Burden of Race
          The Call of His People
          The Secret Sorrow
1922   Easy Money
          The Schemers
          Spitfire

1924   A Son of Satan
Morton, Jack
1936   Star for a Night
Morton, James C. same as **Morton, James**
1934   Operator 13
1935   Naughty Marietta
1936   It Had to Happen
1937   Slave Ship
1938   City Streets
          Josette
          Speed to Burn
1941   Lady from Louisiana
1943   Let's Have Fun
Morton, John
1943   Land of Hunted Men
Morton, John Henry (child actor)
1945   Rhapsody in Blue
Morton, Tom
1953   The Stars Are Singing
Morton, Walter
1916   The Folly of Revenge
Morville, Guy
1916   Broken Fetters
Moscona, Nicola
1951   The Great Caruso
Mosconi, Louis
1945   Where Do We Go From
          Here?
Moscovitch, Maurice same as **Moscovich, Maurcie**
1936   Winterset
1938   Gateway
Moscow, Robert M
1946?   Go Down, Death!
Moseley, Thomas
1932   Harlem Is Heaven
          Out of the Crimson Fog
1939   Straight to Heaven
Moselle, Ben
1948   Big City
Moses, Ethel
1936   Temptation
1937   Underworld
1938   God's Step Children
Moses, Harry
1938   Birthright
Moses, Lucia Lynn
1927   The Scar of Shame
Moses, S. O.
1938   Birthright
Moskov, George same as **Moskov, George G.**
1932   Ljubav i strast
1937   Green Fields
1942   Foreign Agent
1944   Charlie Chan in the
          Secret Service
1945   Jealousy
1947   The Burning Cross
1949   The Prairie
Moskowitz, Jennie
1929   Mother's Boy
Mosley, Thomas M.
1916   The Colored American
          Winning His Suit
Mosner, Marianne
1940   Escape
Moss, Arnold
1949   Border Incident
Moss, Carleton same as **Moss, Carlton**
1926?   The House on Cedar Hill
1944   The Negro Soldier
Moss, Frank
1953   Sangaree
1958   Apache Territory
Moss, Jimmy
1947   The Foxes of Harrow
1950   Davy Crockett, Indian
          Scout
          Stars in My Crown
1951   Jim Thorpe—All-American
1953   Dream Wife
          The Eddie Cantor Story
Mossakowski, Marian
1941   Wiejskie Wesele
Mossoman, Pualani see **Mokimana, Pualani**

Mostel, Zero
1950   Panic in the Streets
Mostovoy, Leo *same as* **Mostovoy, Leonide**
1943   His Butler's Sister
1944   Since You Went Away
1949   The Kissing Bandit
1951   The Great Caruso
1953   Tonight We Sing
1956   Serenade
Mostowy, S.
1939   Cossacks in Exile
Moto, Mr.
1951   Mask of the Dragon
Motyleff, Ilya
1937   The Cantor's Son
Moulton, Lucille
1921   By Right of Birth
Moultrie, Fred
1953   Bright Road
Moultrie, James
1953   Bright Road
Moustafa, Amira
1946   Dangerous Money
Movarry, Medea de
1932   Soñadores de la gloria
Movita *same as* **Castaneda, Mawita; Castaneda, Movita; Casteneda, Movita**
1934   Tres amores
1935   Señora casada necesita marido
1936   El diablo del mar
1937   El capitán Tormenta
1948   Fort Apache
1949   The Mysterious Desperado
1950   The Furies
        A Lady Without Passport
1953   Dream Wife
        Ride, Vaquero!
1955   Apache Ambush
Mowbray, Alan
1934   Charlie Chan in London
1936   Muss 'Em Up
        Rainbow on the River
1937   Music for Madame
1939   Way Down South
1940   Music in My Heart
1941   Ice-Capades
1942   We Were Dancing
1943   His Butler's Sister
1945   Sunbonnet Sue
        Where Do We Go From Here?
Mowbray, Henry
1935   Rendezvous
1937   Souls at Sea
1948   Gentleman's Agreement
        Unconquered
Mower, Jack
1921   Cotton and Cattle
1922   Saturday Night
1928   Uncle Tom's Cabin
1932   Law and Lawless
1936   The Phantom of Santa Fe
1937   Black Legion
        Prairie Thunder
1938   The Beloved Brat
1939   Confessions of a Nazi Spy
        Daughters Courageous
        Waterfront
1940   East of the River
        Santa Fe Trail
1942   Across the Pacific
        Gentleman Jim
        In This Our Life
        Juke Girl
        Secret Enemies
        They Died With Their Boots On
        Wings for the Eagle
1943   Action in the North Atlantic
        Yankee Doodle Dandy
1946   Shadows Over Chinatown
1947   The Chinese Ring
        Jiggs and Maggie in Society
        My Wild Irish Rose
1948   My Girl Tisa
1949   The Girl from Jones Beach

1953   The Sun Shines Bright
1955   The Long Gray Line
        Seven Cities of Gold
Mowery, Helen
1948   Tap Roots
1949   Knock on Any Door
1950   Jolson Sings Again
1951   Queen for a Day
Moxzer, Jieno
1943   Cabin in the Sky
Moya, Billy
1942   Prisoner of Japan
Moya, Manuel de
1934   El tango en Broadway
1938   Di que me quieres
Mozelle, Nona
1932   Hypnotized
Mozin, Guate
1935   Fighting Pioneers
Mruwka, Gunther
1960   I Aim at the Stars: the Wernher von Braun Story
M'so, Tom
1958   Fort Massacre
Mucaulay, Richard
1947   Buck Privates Come Home
Mudie, Leonard
1935   Rendezvous
1938   The Rage of Paris
1940   Charlie Chan's Murder Cruise
1945   The Scarlet Clue
Muell, Faye
1956   Hot Blood
Mueller, Sally
1940   New Moon
Muhs, Jack
1958   Tonka
Muir, Esther
1938   The Toy Wife
Muir, Gavin
1936   Charlie Chan at the Race Track
1943   Hitler's Children
1945   Salome, Where She Danced
1947   California
1948   Unconquered
Muir, Jean
1934   As the Earth Turns
Mulder, Peter
1950   Panic in the Streets
Mulhall, Evelyn
1938   The Beloved Brat
Mulhall, Jack
1922   Flesh and Blood
1925   Friendly Enemies
1926   Sweet Daddies
1934   Behold My Wife!
        Broadway Bill
1935   Chinatown Squad
1936   Charlie Chan at the Race Track
        Custer's Last Stand
        Show Boat
1937   Music for Madame
1939   Judge Hardy and Son
1942   Foreign Agent
1943   The Amazing Mrs. Holliday
1944   An American Romance
Mulhauser, James *same as* **Milhauser, James; Mulhauser, J.**
1931   El tenorio del harem
1932   The Cohens and Kellys in Hollywood
1934   Strange Wives
Mullahey, Tom
1950   Damien
Mullally, Jode
1915   After Five
Mullaney, Frank
1954   Hell's Half Acre
Mullaney, Jack
1960   All the Fine Young Cannibals

Mullen, Gordon
1920   Dangerous Hours
Mullen, Virginia
1948   Moonrise
1949   Lust for Gold
1950   Jolson Sings Again
        Mystery Street
        Winchester '73
1952   Bright Victory
        The Raiders
1953   Dream Wife
        The Great Sioux Uprising
Muller, Raymond
1950   Panic in the Streets
Muller, Steven
1941   Adam Had Four Sons
Mulliner, Arthur
1940   Escape to Glory
Mulqueen, Kathleen
1952   Japanese War Bride
Mummert, Danny
1941   Thunder Over the Prairie
1943   Good Luck, Mr. Yates
1953   The Member of the Wedding
Mundin, Herbert
1933   It's Great to Be Alive
1936   Charlie Chan's Secret
Mundy, Ed *same as* **Mundy, Edward**
1947   The Foxes of Harrow
1948   Fury at Furnace Creek
1955   Good Morning, Miss Dove
        A Man Called Peter
Muni, Paul
1932   Scarface
1935   Black Fury
        Bordertown
1959   The Last Angry Man
Munier, Ferdinand
1918   Ruggles of Red Gap
1934   Behold My Wife!
        Laughing Boy
1935   Harmony Lane
        His Family Tree
1936   The Bold Caballero
1940   Northwest Passage (Book I—Rogers' Rangers)
1944   Lake Placid Serenade
1945   Where Do We Go From Here?
Muñoz Seca, Pedro
1931   Lo mejor es reír
        La pura verdad
Muñoz, Albert
1954   Salt of the Earth
Muñoz, Amelia
1930   Un hombre de suerte
1931   La fiesta del diablo
        Sombras del circo
Muñoz, Carmen
1931   La incorregible
Muñoz, Ramón
1930   La jaula de los leones
1931   Regeneración
1934   Tres amores
1935   Te quiero con locura
1936   El crimen de media noche
        El diablo del mar
Muñoz Seca, Pedro
1930   Un hombre de suerte
Munro, Mona
1933   It's Great to Be Alive
Munshin, Jules
1949   That Midnight Kiss
Munson, Chris
1951   Jim Thorpe—All-American
Munson, Ona
1939   Gone With the Wind
1941   Lady from Louisiana
Munz, Jack Mylong *see* **Mylong, John**
Mura, Corinna
1942   Prisoner of Japan
1945   The Gay Senorita
Murat, Jean
1930   Un hombre de suerte (*foreign version*)

Muratore, Lucien
1918   A Woman of Impulse
Murdoch, Tim
1946   Three Wise Fools
Murdock, Eunice *see* **Moore, Eunice**
Murdock, Perry
1936   Border Phantom
Murfin, Jane
1926   Meet the Prince
1935   Romance in Manhattan
1937   That Girl from Paris
1939   Stand Up and Fight
1940   Northwest Passage (Book I—Rogers' Rangers)
Muriel, Elisa
1935   De la sartén al fuego
        No matarás
Muriel, Roel
1927   Rose of the Golden West
Murillo, Mary
1916   Gold and the Woman
1919   The Heart of Wetona
        The Other Man's Wife
Murkland, Ted
1948   Open Secret
Murphy, Al
1943   The Gang's All Here
        Mr. Lucky
1945   The Dolly Sisters
        Johnny Angel
1946   Till the End of Time
1947   Buck Privates Come Home
1948   The Boy with Green Hair
        The Miracle of the Bells
        Unconquered
        Up in Central Park
1949   The Fighting Kentuckian
        Illegal Entry
        The Undercover Man
1950   No Way Out
        Sands of Iwo Jima
1951   Gambling House
        Oh! Susanna
1952   The Quiet Man
Murphy, Alma
1959   The Last Angry Man
Murphy, Althea
1947   Untamed Fury
Murphy, Audie
1953   Column South
        Tumbleweed
1954   Drums Across the River
1956   Walk the Proud Land
1957   The Guns of Fort Petticoat
1958   Ride a Crooked Trail
1960   The Unforgiven
Murphy, Bill "Red" *same as* **Murphy, Bill; Murphy, William "Red"**
1944   Something for the Boys
1945   Nob Hill
1946   Till the End of Time
1947   On the Old Spanish Trail
1948   Unconquered
1949   The Prairie
1950   Battleground
        Sands of Iwo Jima
1958   The Rawhide Trail
Murphy, Bob *see* **Murphy, Robert**
Murphy, Donald
1955   The Long Gray Line
        Seven Angry Men
Murphy, Dudley
1933   The Emperor Jones
Murphy, Edna
1920   The North Wind's Malice
1927   His Foreign Wife
        McFadden's Flats
Murphy, George (*actor*) *could be same as* **Murphy, George** (*football player*) *not the same as* **Murphy, George** (*actor, dancer*), 1902—1992
1942   They Died With Their Boots On
Murphy, George (*actor, dancer*), 1902—1992 *not the same as* **Murphy, George** (*actor*) *or* **Murphy, George** (*football player*)

1940   Elsa Maxwell's Public
       Deb No. 1
       Little Nellie Kelly
1942   The Navy Comes Through
1943   Bataan
1948   Big City
1949   Border Incident
1950   Battleground
1952   It's a Big Country: An
       American Anthology

Murphy, George (football player)
could be same as **Murphy,
George** (actor) *not the same as*
Murphy, George (actor,
dancer), 1902—1992
1951   Saturday's Hero

Murphy, Horace
1936   Border Phantom

Murphy, Jack
1924   Peter Pan
1932   Hypnotized
1947   Easy Come, Easy Go

Murphy, Jimmy *same as* **Murphy,
Jim**
1955   Blackboard Jungle
       A Man Called Peter
1958   The Last Hurrah

Murphy, Mary
1951   Westward the Women
1954   Sitting Bull

Murphy, Maurice
1936   Down to the Sea
       The Prisoner of Shark
       Island
1939   Forged Passport
1943   Action in the North
       Atlantic
       Air Force

Murphy, Ralph
1933   Song of the Eagle
1934   The Great Flirtation
1935   McFadden's Flats
1945   Sunbonnet Sue

Murphy, Richard
1948   Cry of the City
1950   Panic in the Streets
1951   The House on Telegraph
       Hill
1954   Broken Lance
1959   The Last Angry Man

Murphy, Robert *same as* **Murphy,
Bob**
1936   After the Thin Man
       Dimples
1937   It Could Happen to You
       Life Begins in College
       One Mile from Heaven
1938   The Adventures of Tom
       Sawyer
       In Old Chicago

Murphy, Steve
1924   Fools' Highway
1925   Justice of the Far North

Murphy, William "Red" *see*
Murphy, Bill "Red"

Murray, Al
1950   Catskill Honeymoon

Murray, Arthur
1947   Jiggs and Maggie in
       Society

Murray, Charles, Jr. *same as*
Murray, Chas., Jr. *not the same
as* **Murray, Charlie**
1943   The Law Rides Again
1944   Block Busters
       Outlaw Trail
       Sonora Stagecoach

Murray, Charlie *same as* **Murray,
Charles** *not the same as*
Murray, Charles, Jr.
1924   Fools' Highway
       The Mine with the Iron
       Door
1925   My Son
1926   The Cohens and Kellys
       Irene
       Sweet Daddies
1927   Lost at the Front
       McFadden's Flats
1928   The Cohens and the
       Kellys in Paris
       Flying Romeos
       Vamping Venus

1930   Around the Corner
       The Cohens and the
       Kellys in Scotland
1931   The Cohens and Kellys in
       Africa
1932   The Cohens and Kellys in
       Hollywood
       Hypnotized
1933   The Cohens and Kellys in
       Trouble
1938   Breaking the Ice

Murray, Don
1959   Shake Hands with the
       Devil

Murray, Edgar
1957   Beau James

Murray, Elizabeth
1923   Little Old New York

Murray, Forbes
1937   Souls at Sea
1940   New Moon
1941   Saddlemates
       Sun Valley Serenade
1942   Tales of Manhattan
1943   Tahiti Honey
       They Came to Blow Up
       America
1944   Hi, Beautiful
1945   Nob Hill
1946   Romance of the West
1947   My Wild Irish Rose
1949   The Story of Seabiscuit
1953   Dream Wife
1957   Band of Angels
1959   Imitation of Life

Murray, Gary
1956   Ghost Town
1958   Escape from Red Rock

Murray, Gordon
1943   Action in the North
       Atlantic

Murray, Harry
1928   The House of Scandal

Murray, Hugh
1950   Young Man with a Horn

Murray, Ian
1951   Apache Drums

Murray, Jack
1915   Time Lock Number 776
1916   Her Debt of Honor

Murray, Jerry
1959   Night of the Quarter
       Moon

Murray, John Rastus
1946? Fight That Ghost
       House-Rent Party

Murray, John T.
1931   Charlie Chan Carries On
1936   After the Thin Man
1941   Accent on Love
1943   Let's Have Fun

Murray, Lee
1942   Rio Rita

Murray, Mae
1919   The Delicious Little Devil
1920   On with the Dance
1922   Peacock Alley
1923   Fashion Row

Murray, Natalia
1955   The Rose Tattoo

Murray, Rickey
1955   Violent Saturday
1960   The Adventures of
       Huckleberry Finn

Murray, Roseanne
1946   Cuban Pete

Murray, Ross
1942   Holiday Inn

Murray, Thomas (prod)
1957   Burden of Truth

Murray, Tom (actor), 1875—1935
1926   Into Her Kingdom
       Private Izzy Murphy

Murray, Tom (actor), circa 1942—
1942   Mokey
1951   The Tall Target

Murray, Zon
1947   West to Glory
1951   Hurricane Island
1953   Old Overland Trail
1954   Passion

1956   The Lone Ranger
1957   Band of Angels
1958   Escape from Red Rock

Murrow, Edward R.
1957   Satchmo the Great

Muse, Clarence
1929   Hearts in Dixie
1931   Huckleberry Finn
1934   Broadway Bill
       Massacre
1935   Harmony Lane
       So Red the Rose
1936   Daniel Boone
       Laughing Irish Eyes
       Muss 'Em Up
       Show Boat
1938   Spirit of Youth
       The Toy Wife
1939   Way Down South
1940   Broken Strings
       Murder over New York
1941   Adam Had Four Sons
       Belle Starr
1942   Tales of Manhattan
1944   The Racket Man
1947   The Peanut Man
1948   Unconquered
1951   Apache Drums
1953   The Sun Shines Bright
1959   Porgy and Bess

Musgrave, William *same as*
**Musgrave, Billy; Musgrave, W.
F.**
1918   The Midnight Patrol

Mushinsky, Anna
1939   Cossacks in Exile

Mussalli, Hassan
1917   One Law for Both

Musselman, M. M.
1941   Playmates
1943   Mr. Lucky

Mussey, Francine
1932   La foule hurle

Mustin, Burt
1957   Raintree County
1959   The FBI Story
1960   The Adventures of
       Huckleberry Finn

Mutt, a dog
1933   L'amour guide

Múzquiz, Carlos
1955   Seven Cities of Gold
1956   Comanche
1958   Sierra Baron

Myers, Zion
1926   April Fool

Myers, Billie *not the same as*
Myers, Billy
1942   Take My Life

Myers, Billy *not the same as*
Myers, Billie
1939   One Dark Night

Myers, Carmel
1917   A Love Sublime
1918   A Broadway Scandal
       The City of Tears
       The Girl in the Dark
       The Wine Girl
1919   Who Will Marry Me?
1921   Cheated Love
       The Kiss
1931   Chinatown After Dark

Myers, Charles
1952   It's a Big Country: An
       American Anthology

Myers, Harry (actor)
1922   The Top O' the Morning
1927   The Dove
1938   Dangerous to Know

Myers, Henry (writer)
1931   Gente alegre
       El príncipe gondolero
       Su noche de bodas
1933   Diplomaniacs

Myers, Kathleen
1926   Kosher Kitty Kelly

Myers, Pauline *same as* **Meyers,
Pauline; Myers, Paulene**
1960   All the Fine Young
       Cannibals
       Take a Giant Step

Myers, Peter
1960   The Day They Robbed the
       Bank of England

Myers, Robert
1952   Bright Victory

Myers, Stevie
1951   Westward the Women

Myers, Zion *same as* **Myers, Z.**
1942   Holiday Inn

Myhers, John
1960   Weddings and Babies

Myles, Norbert *same as* **Miles,
Norbert**
1920   The Daughter of Dawn
1926   Under Fire

Mylong, John *same as* **Munz, Jack
Mylong**
1940   Overture to Glory
1943   Crash Dive
       They Came to Blow Up
       America
1948   Unconquered
1949   The Girl from Jones
       Beach
1950   Annie Get Your Gun
       Battleground
       Young Daniel Boone

Myrtil, Odette *same as* **Myrtle,
Odette**
1943   Yankee Doodle Dandy
1944   Dark Waters
1945   Rhapsody in Blue
1949   The Fighting Kentuckian

Myset, Rudolf *see* **Myzet, Rudolf**

Myton, Fred *same as* **Myton, Fred
Kennedy**
1916   The Social Buccaneer
1917   Follow the Girl
1919   Desert Gold
       Who Will Marry Me?
1921   The Land of Hope
1923   Jealous Husbands
1932   White Eagle
1933   King of the Wild Horses
1936   Border Phantom
1937   Harlem on the Prairie
1940   Prairie Schooners

Myzet, Rudolf *same as* **Myset,
Rudolf; Myzet, Rudolph**
1938   Dangerous to Know
       Gateway
1943   Action in the North
       Atlantic
1944   An American Romance

Nablo, James Benson
1956   Raw Edge

Nace, Anthony
1942   Holiday Inn

Nadel, Joseph H.
1928   Ransom
1933   The Emperor Jones
1943   Jack London
1950   The Jackie Robinson Story

Nadi, Aldo
1945   The Dolly Sisters

Nagafuchi, Somita
1951   Go for Broke!

Nagel, Anne *not the same as*
Neagle, Anna
1932   Hypnotized
1934   Coming Out Party
       Stand Up and Cheer!
1941   Mutiny in the Arctic
       Road Agent
1946   The Trap
1949   Prejudice

Nagel, Conrad
1922   Saturday Night
1925   Lights of Old Broadway
1928   Diamond Handcuffs
1931   Three Who Loved
1936   Yellow Cargo

Nagel, Curtis F.
1934   Song of the Islands

Nagel, Don
1953   Tumbleweed

Nagel, George
1932   Harlem Is Heaven

Nagoshiner, Saul
1939   The Light Ahead

Nagy, Alix
1959   The Black Orchid
Nahshook
1932   Igloo
Naish, Elaine
1951   Across the Wide Missouri
Naish, Herbert
1950   Young Daniel Boone
Naish, J. Carrol *same as* **Naish, Carrol; Naish, J. Carroll**
1932   The Hatchet Man
         Tiger Shark
1935   Black Fury
1936   Charlie Chan at the Circus
         Ramona
         Robin Hood of El Dorado
1937   Border Cafe
         Song of the City
         Think Fast, Mr. Moto
1938   Daughter of Shanghai
1939   King of Chinatown
1941   Accent on Love
         Birth of the Blues
1942   Sunday Punch
         Tales of Manhattan
1944   Waterfront
1945   A Medal for Benny
1946   Bad Bascomb
1947   Humoresque
1949   The Kissing Bandit
         That Midnight Kiss
1950   Annie Get Your Gun
         Black Hand
         Rio Grande
         The Toast of New Orleans
1951   Across the Wide Missouri
         The Mark of the Renegade
1953   Beneath the 12-Mile Reef
1954   Saskatchewan
         Sitting Bull
1955   The Last Command
         Violent Saturday
Najarian, Don
1944   Since You Went Away
Najarian, Jon
1944   Since You Went Away
Nakamura, Henry
1951   Go for Broke!
         Westward the Women
Nakamura, Tsutomu Paul
1951   Go for Broke!
Nakano, Lane
1951   Go for Broke!
1952   Japanese War Bride
Nakashima, George
1951   Go for Broke!
Nalder, Reggie
1951   Adventures of Captain Fabian
Naldi, Nita
1921   A Divorce of Convenience
1922   Anna Ascends
1925   Cobra
Naldi, Rino
1932   Tormento
Nanook
1922   Nanook of the North
Naomi, Leah
1935   Bar-Mitzvah
Napier, Alan
1942   Cat People
         We Were Dancing
1944   Dark Waters
1948   Unconquered
1951   Across the Wide Missouri
         The Great Caruso
Napier, Elmer
1945   The Cisco Kid Returns
1951   Across the Wide Missouri
         Westward the Women
Napoleon, a dog
1922   Peacock Alley
Napolino, Tina
1932   Amore e morte
Narcha, Agnes
1934   Massacre

Narcha, P.
1931   Cavalier of the West
Narciso, Grazia
1948   Music Man
         The Time of Your Life
1950   Black Hand
1959   The Black Orchid
Narcisse, Joe
1957   Band of Angels
Nardelli, George
1934   La veuve joyeuse
1950   The Toast of New Orleans
Nardi, Dino
1950   Deported
Nasboro, John *same as* **Nasboro, Jack; Nasoborough, John**
1936   Rose of the Rancho
Nasca, Charles P.
1932   The Black King
Nash, Florence
1914   Springtime
Nash, George
1914   The Jungle
1933   Broken Dreams
Nash, J. E.
1921   A Tale of Two Worlds
Nash, Johnny
1960   Key Witness
         Take a Giant Step
Nash, Mary
1916   Arms and the Woman
1940   Charlie Chan in Panama
Nash, N. Richard
1951   Molly
1959   Porgy and Bess
Nash, Noreen
1950   Storm Over Wyoming
1956   Giant
1958   The Lone Ranger and the Lost City of Gold
Nash, Robert
1957   Pawnee
Nashulik
1925   Kivalina of the Ice Lands
Nasser, James
1944   Dark Waters
Natale, Anthony
1935   The Cyclone Ranger
Natan, S. *same as* **Natan, Saul**
1932   Mazel Tov
1936   Yiddle with His Fiddle
Nathan, Paul
1958   Wild Is the Wind
1959   Last Train from Gun Hill
Nathanson, Charles
1926   Broken Hearts
1932   The Unfortunate Bride
Nathanson, George
1951   Native Son
Natheaux, Louis
1927   A Harp in Hock
         Turkish Delight
1928   A Ship Comes In
1931   Street Scene
1934   Broadway Bill
1935   Charlie Chan in Paris
         A Night at the Ritz
1936   After the Thin Man
1937   Charlie Chan at the Olympics
         Man of the People
         The Plainsman
1938   The Buccaneer
Natoni, Donald
1952?   Call of the Navajo
Natteford, Jack *same as* **Natteford, J. Francis; Natteford, John F.; Natteford, John Francis**
1933   The California Trail
1937   Boots and Saddles
1940   Cuando canta la Ley
1949   Rustlers
Natwick, Mildred
1949   The Kissing Bandit
         She Wore a Yellow Ribbon
         3 Godfathers
1952   The Quiet Man

Naumu, Nohili
1934   White Heat
Navarro, Anna
1958   The Badlanders
Navarro, Aurora
1937   Drums of Destiny
1950   Colt .45
Navarro, Gabriel
1930   Las campanas de Capistrano
1939   La Inmaculada
         El otro soy yo
         Papá soltero
         El trovador de la radio
1940   Cuando canta la Ley
Navarro, George
1947   Pirates of Monterey
         Robin Hood of Monterey
1951   Gambling House
1955   The Last Command
Navarro, Manuel Sanchez
1940   Perfidia
Navarro, Mary
1914   When Broadway Was a Trail
Navarro, Ralph *same as* **Navarro, Rafael**
1930   El cuerpo del delito
         Monsieur le Fox
         El valiente
1931   Carne de cabaret
         Charlie Chan Carries On (*foreign version*)
         Del infierno al cielo
         Don Juan diplomático
         Esclavas de la moda
         La ley del harem
         Mamá
         La melodía prohibida
1933   No dejes la puerta abierta
1934   La buenaventura
         La ciudad de cartón
         Tres amores
Navascués, Carmen
1932   ¿Cuándo te suicidas?
Naxboro, John
1938   The Buccaneer
Nayfack, Nicholas
1949   Border Incident
1950   Devil's Doorway
Nazarr, Norman
1959   Al Capone
1960   Pay or Die
Nazarro, Cliff
1938   Outside of Paradise
1939   Forged Passport
1941   New York Town
Nazarro, Ray *same as* **Nazarro, Raymond**
1939   Daughter of the Tong
1944   Tahiti Nights
1948   Singin' Spurs
1949   Laramie
1950   The Palomino
1951   Cyclone Fury
1952   Indian Uprising
1954   The Black Dakotas
1956   The White Squaw
1958   Apache Territory
Nazimova, Alla *same as* **Nazimova; Nazimova, Mme.**
1918   Toys of Fate
1920   Billions
1925   My Son
1940   Escape
1944   Since You Went Away
Neal, Ella
1941   Hold Back the Dawn
         New York Town
Neal, Erwin
1955   The Long Gray Line
1958   The Badlanders
Neal, Joseph H.
1957   Burden of Truth
Neal, Lex
1924   Racing Luck
1929   Welcome Danger
1940?   Mr. Washington Goes to Town
1942   Lucky Ghost

Neal, Lloyd
1934   As the Earth Turns
Neal, Mavis
1960   Studs Lonigan
Neal, Patricia
1950   The Breaking Point
Neal, Tom
1943   Air Force
         Good Luck, Mr. Yates
1944   The Racket Man
1945   Club Havana
1949   Apache Chief
1950   Train to Tombstone
Nearing, Margaret
1933   It's Great to Be Alive
Neary, Peggy Lou
1942   Song of the Islands
1944   Something for the Boys
Nebenzal, Seymour
1942   Prisoner of Japan
Nedd, Stuart
1953   The Glory Brigade
Nedell, Bernard
1938   Mr. Moto's Gamble
Needham, James *see* Crisp, Donald
Neel, Germaine de *same as* **De Neel, Germaine; Néel, Germaine de**
1931   Los calaveras (*foreign version*)
1933   L'amour guide
1934   La buenaventura
         Coming Out Party
1935   Rosa de Francia
Neeland, Walter *could be same as* **Nealand, Walter D.**
1920   The Dark Mirror
Neely, Lawrence "Pepper"
1943   Marching On!
Neeman, Robinson
1935   The Singing Vagabond
Neff, Bill *same as* **Neff, William**
1947   King of the Bandits
1948   Tap Roots
1958   The Last Hurrah
Neff, Mr.
1916   The Grip of Jealousy
Neff, Ralph
1956   The Benny Goodman Story
Neff, William *see* Neff, Bill
Neft, Else
1953   The Glass Wall
Negley, Howard *same as* **Negley, Howard J.**
1945   The Dolly Sisters
1946   Notorious
         Till the End of Time
         The Trap
1947   Ride the Pink Horse
1948   Docks of New Orleans
         Fury at Furnace Creek
         Gentleman's Agreement
1949   Arctic Manhunt
         The Clay Pigeon
         Lust for Gold
1950   Colt .45
         The Lawless
         The Missourians
         Mystery Submarine
1952   Red Ball Express
         The Savage
1953   The Man from the Alamo
         The Member of the Wedding
1955   The Gun That Won the West
         Santa Fe Passage
Negri, Pola
1925   Flower of Night
1928   The Secret Hour
Negulesco, Jean
1938   The Beloved Brat
1947   Humoresque
Neher, Carola
1931   Die Dreigroschenoper
Nehli-Kalini, Thais
1919   Injustice
Neil, Bill
1953   Taxi

Neil, James see Neill, James
Neil, Robert
1950   The Missourians
Neilan, Marshall same as Neilan, Marshal; Neilan, Marshall A.
1917   The Bottle Imp
1918   Amarilly of Clothes-Line Alley
        Out of a Clear Sky
1920   Dinty
1921   Bits of Life
1934   Chloe: Love Is Calling You
1938   The Adventures of Tom Sawyer
Neill, James same as Neil, James
1914   Rose of the Rancho
        Where the Trail Divides
1915   The Cheat
1916   For the Defense
        The Thousand Dollar Husband
1917   The Bottle Imp
        Forbidden Paths
        The Little American
        The Trouble Buster
1918   Sandy
1920   The Paliser Case
1921   Bits of Life
1922   Saturday Night
1923   Scars of Jealousy
Neill, Noel
1948   Music Man
1949   The Sky Dragon
Neill, R. William see Neill, Roy William
Neill, Richard R. same as Neal, Richard; Neill Richard; Neill, R. R.
1917   Unknown 274
1918   Doing Their Bit
1924   The Heritage of the Desert
1936   General Spanky
1948   Jiggs and Maggie in Court
Neill, Roy William same as Neill, R. William
1918   Free and Equal
1930   The Melody Man
1931   The Avenger
Neilsen, Agnes same as Neilson, Agnes; Nielson, Agnes
1918   Woman and the Law
Neilson, Eric see Nielsen, Erik
Neilson, Lester
1933   Obey the Law
Neise, George same as Neise, George N.
1942   Valley of Hunted Men
1943   Action in the North Atlantic
        Air Force
1957   Tomahawk Trail
1958   Fort Massacre
Neissen, Rhea
1936   Star for a Night
Neitz, Alvin J. see James, Alan
Nello, Tommy
1948   Cry of the City
Nelson, Babs
1937   Maid of Salem
Nelson, Barry
1942   Rio Rita
1943   Bataan
Nelson, Bek
1958   Gunman's Walk
Nelson, Billy same as Nelson, Bill
1944   Waterfront
1949   The Undercover Man
1950   Emergency Wedding
1957   Twelve Angry Men
Nelson, Bobby ((child actor)) same as Nelson, Bobbie
1935   Black Fury
        Captured in Chinatown
        Cyclone of the Saddle
1936   Custer's Last Stand
Nelson, Burt
1958   Bullwhip

Nelson, Clear, Jr.
1947   The Foxes of Harrow
Nelson, Dick same as Nelson, Richard
1957   Beau James
1958   Houseboat
Nelson, Edna
1947   Jiggs and Maggie in Society
Nelson, Edwin
1957   Bayou
Nelson, Evelyn
1921   The Double O
1922   The Crow's Nest
Nelson, Felix
1953   Sangaree
Nelson, Frank
1929   In Old Arizona
1937   Black Legion
Nelson, Gene
1948   Gentleman's Agreement
1950   The Daughter of Rosie O'Grady
Nelson, Gordon
1949   Knock on Any Door
1950   The Lawless
1952   The Iron Mistress
Nelson, Harold
1936   Show Boat
1937   Maid of Salem
Nelson, Henry
1948?   Junction 88
Nelson, Howard
1920   Our Christianity and Nobody's Child
Nelson, Jack (actor)
1915   The Alien
1916   Pasquale
1919   Fighting for Gold
1927   The Fighting Hombre
        The Shamrock and the Rose
Nelson, John
1944   They Live in Fear
Nelson, Lori
1953   Tumbleweed
1956   Mohawk
Nelson, Merlyn
1941   Western Union
1944   Buffalo Bill
1949   Colorado Territory
Nelson, Norma same as Nelson, Norma Gene
1940   The Way of All Flesh
Nelson, Richard see Nelson, Dick
Nelson, Ruth
1945   A Tree Grows in Brooklyn
1946   Till the End of Time
1947   Humoresque
Nelson, Sam
1928   Breed of the Sunsets
1930   The Melody Man
1940   Prairie Schooners
1942   Friendly Enemies
1943   Jack London
        The Outlaw
1947   It Had To Be You
1948   The Lady from Shanghai
1953   Conquest of Cochise
        The Member of the Wedding
1954   They Rode West
1956   The Last Frontier
        Reprisal!
        The White Squaw
1958   Gunman's Walk
        The Last Hurrah
Nelson, Terry
1956   The Benny Goodman Story
        Pillars of the Sky
Nelson, Tim
1948   The Paleface
Neola May, Princess same as Mae, Neola; May, Neola; Neola, Princess
1917   The Captain of the Gray Horse Troop
1918   The Red, Red Heart
1926   The Barrier

Neong, Lin
1917   The War of the Tongs
Neptune, Vincent
1952   Anything Can Happen
Nero, Curtis
1937   The Plainsman
Nervig, Conrad A.
1930   A Lady to Love (foreign version)
1931   El proceso de Mary Dugan (foreign version)
Nesbit, Evelyn same as Nesbit-Thaw, Evelyn; Thaw, Evelyn Nesbit
1914   Threads of Destiny
1918   I Want to Forget
1919   A Fallen Idol
Nesbit, Norman
1944   An American Romance
Nesbit, Pinna
1918   Broken Ties
Nesbitt, John
1944   The Sullivans
Nesmith, Ottola same as Nesmith, Tola
1938   The Beloved Brat
        The Buccaneer
1939   Miracle on Main Street
1942   We Were Dancing
1943   The Leopard Man
1947   Buck Privates Come Home
1948   Unconquered
1949   Boston Blackie's Chinese Venture
Nestell, Bill same as Nestell, William
1933   Robbers' Roost
1943   Wagon Tracks West
1947   Dangerous Venture
Nestor, Harry
1931   La pura verdad (foreign version)
Nestor, René
1929   Sombras habaneras
Netto, Hadrian Maria
1930   Doña mentiras (foreign version)
Neubert, Carl
1945   Rhapsody in Blue
Neufeld, Eugen
1932   Mazel Tov
Neufeld, Samuel see Newfield, Sam
Neufeld, Sigmund same as Neufeld, Sig
1936   The Traitor
1946   Gas House Kids
1951   Mask of the Dragon
1956   The Wild Dakotas
Neufeld, Stanley
1946   Gas House Kids
1951   Mask of the Dragon
Neuman, J. M.
1939   A Brivele der Mamen
Neuman, Sam same as Newman, Sam
1948   Shanghai Chest
1950   I Killed Geronimo
1952   Buffalo Bill in Tomahawk Territory
Neumann, Dorothy
1948   The Luck of the Irish
        The Miracle of the Bells
1952   The Fabulous Senorita
1955   Blackboard Jungle
        A Man Called Peter
1957   The Oklahoman
1959   The FBI Story
Neumann, Elisabeth
1945   The House on 92nd St.
Neumann, Kurt same as Newman, Kurt
1931   El tenorio del harem
1936   Let's Sing Again
        Rainbow on the River
1943   Action in the North Atlantic
1948   The Dude Goes West
1952   Hiawatha
        The Ring

1956   Mohawk
1957   Apache Warrior
        The Deerslayer
1958   Machete
Neville, Edgar
1930   El presidio
1931   En cada puerto un amor
Neville, George
1925   Scarlet Saint
Neville, Grace
1936   Dangerous Intrigue
1938   Little Miss Roughneck
Neville, Harry
1916   The Pretenders
Neville, John Thomas same as Neville, Jack; Neville, John; Neville, John T.
1927   Spoilers of the West
1933   Dos noches
1936   El crimen de media noche
        The Glory Trail
        Rebellion
        Robin Hood of El Dorado
        The Traitor
1937   Drums of Destiny
        Old Louisiana
Neville, Julia
1921   Diane of Star Hollow
Nevitt, Don
1950   Two Flags West
Newberry, Eunice
1950   The Men
Newcom, James E. same as Newcomb, James E.
1955   Trial
Newcombe, Jessamine
1942   We Were Dancing
Newell, Billy see Newell, William
Newell, David same as Newell, Dave
1930   The Kibitzer
1934   White Heat
1935   A Night at the Ritz
        So Red the Rose
1937   Waikiki Wedding
1938   Dangerous to Know
        Mr. Moto's Gamble
1939   The Escape
1943   Gangway for Tomorrow
1948   My Girl Tisa
        Up in Central Park
1950   Jolson Sings Again
1953   The Eddie Cantor Story
Newell, Gordon same as Powell, Charles Arthur
1937   The Californian
Newell, Inez
1946   Dirty Gertie from Harlem, U.S.A.
1947   Juke Joint
Newell, William same as Newell, Billy
1938   Speed to Burn
1940   Elsa Maxwell's Public Deb No. 1
1941   Caught in the Act
1943   The Meanest Man in the World
1946   Till the End of Time
1948   Up in Central Park
1950   The Traveling Saleswoman
1951   Only the Valiant
1952   Bright Victory
        High Noon
1955   Seven Angry Men
1959   Last Train from Gun Hill
Newfield, Sam same as Neufeld, Sam; Neufeld, Samuel; Newfield, Samuel; Scott, Sherman; Stewart, Peter
1936   Aces and Eights
        The Traitor
1937   Harlem on the Prairie
1939   Trigger Fingers
1940   Am I Guilty?
1946   Gas House Kids
1946?   Fight That Ghost
        House-Rent Party
1951   Mask of the Dragon
1956   The Wild Dakotas

1958   Flaming Frontier
Newhall, Mayo
1947   The Foxes of Harrow
Newhard, Joyce
1955   Violent Saturday
Newlan, Paul "Tiny" *see* **Newland, Paul**
Newland, Douglass
1942   Rio Rita
     Sunday Punch
     The Vanishing Virginian
Newland, John
1948   Gentleman's Agreement
Newland, Paul *same as* **Newlan, Paul; Newlan, Paul "Tiny"; Newlan, Tiny; Newland, P. E. "Tiny"; Newland, Tiny**
1937   Man of the People
     The Plainsman
1941   Sullivan's Travels
1945   The Shanghai Cobra
1946   Don Ricardo Returns
1947   Bells of San Fernando
1948   Fury at Furnace Creek
1950   Colt .45
1952   The Raiders
1956   Davy Crockett and the River Pirates
1957   Trooper Hook
Newman, Charlene
1943   Jack London
Newman, John K.
1925   The Greatest Love of All
Newman, Joseph M.
1955   Kiss of Fire
1958   Fort Massacre
Newman, Laura
1919   The Other Man's Wife
Newman, Pascal
1950   Panic in the Streets
Newman, Paul (actor) birthdate unknown *not the same as* **Newman, Paul** (actor) 26 Jan 1925—
1937   Big City
Newman, Sam *see* **Neuman, Sam**
Newman, Sidney
1938   The Buccaneer
Newmar, Julie *same as* **Newmeyer, Julie**
1953   The Eddie Cantor Story
Newmark, Lucille *same as* **Newmark, Lucile**
1929   Sioux Blood
1931   Soyons gais
Newmeyer, Fred
1928   The Night Bird
1930   The Grand Parade
1936   General Spanky
Newmeyer, Julie *see* **Newmar, Julie**
Newmeyer, Peter
1944   Address Unknown
Newsom, J. D.
1935   De la sartén al fuego
Newsome, Carman
1938   Birthright
     God's Step Children
     Swing!
1939   Lying Lips
1940   The Notorious Elinor Lee
Newsome, Nora
1931   The Exile
Newton, Charles
1916   Lord Loveland Discovers America
1917   My Fighting Gentleman
Newton, Jack circa 1920s *not the same as* **Newton, John** circa 1960
1922   For His Mother's Sake
     The Mohican's Daughter
Newton, John circa 1960 *not the same as* **Newton, Jack** circa 1920s
1960   This Rebel Breed
Newton, Marie
1914   The Woman in Black
1919   A Fallen Idol

Newton, Mary
1944   Tomorrow the World!
1945   Escape in the Fog
1946   Canyon Passage
     G. I. War Brides
1947   The Farmer's Daughter
1948   The Lady from Shanghai
1950   Emergency Wedding
1951   Oh! Susanna
Newton, Richard
1954   Dangerous Mission
Nez, Flora
1950   Ambush
Nez, Ted, Chief
1956   Ghost Town
Ng Kam-ha
1949?   Lang Hu Bee Yuh
Niako, Lea
1931   La carta
Niblack, Sam *same as* **Niblack, Samuel**
1917?   Barnaby Lee
Nibley, Sloan
1947   On the Old Spanish Trail
1949   The Golden Stallion
Niblo, Fred
1920   Dangerous Hours
     The Mark of Zorro
1930   Estrellados
Niblo, Fred, Jr.
1931   El código penal
1938   City Streets
     Little Miss Roughneck
1939   Waterfront
1940   East of the River
     The Fighting 69th
Niccodemi, Antonio
1930   El secreto del doctor (foreign version)
Niccolls, Herbert F.
1957   Journey to Freedom
Nicholas Brothers *same as* **Nicholas, Fayard; Nicholas, Harold**
1941   Sun Valley Serenade
1943   Stormy Weather
Nicholls, George, Jr. (dir) *not the same as* **Nichols, George** (actor)
1939   Man of Conquest
Nichols, Major
1930   The Melody Man
Nichols, Anne
1929   Abie's Irish Rose
1946   Abie's Irish Rose
Nichols, Dudley
1930   El precio de un beso
1931   The Black Camel
     Skyline
1933   The Man Who Dared: An Imaginative Biography
     Robbers' Roost
1934   Judge Priest
1935   Señora casada necesita marido
1943   Air Force
     Mr. Lucky
1945   The Bells of St. Mary's
1949   Pinky
1952   The Big Sky
1957   The Tin Star
Nichols, Eddie
1944   Buffalo Bill
     The Sullivans
1945   Nob Hill
Nichols, George (actor) *not the same as* **Nicholls, George, Jr.** (dir)
1921   Shame
1922   The Pride of Palomar
1923   The Miracle Makers
     Suzanna
1924   East of Broadway
1927   White Gold
Nichols, Lonnie
1942   Tales of Manhattan
Nichols, Marguerite *same as* **Nichols, Margaret**
1917   Sold at Auction

Nichols, Nellie V. *same as* **Nichols, Nellie**
1934   Our Daily Bread
1936   Dangerous Intrigue
1937   Manhattan Merry-Go-Round
1945   Rhapsody in Blue
Nichols, Robert *same as* **Nichols, Robert E.**
1953   Dream Wife
1956   Giant
Nicholson, Calvin
1924?   The Flaming Crisis
Nicholson, Carol
1960   Ice Palace
Nicholson, Jack
1960   Studs Lonigan
Nicholson, James
1949   Anna Lucasta
     Boston Blackie's Chinese Venture
     Lust for Gold
1953   Ambush at Tomahawk Gap
     Last of the Comanches
Nicholson, Kenyon *same as* **Nicholson, John Kenyon**
1931   Skyline
Nicholson, Lillian
1936   Ramona
1937   Big City
Nicholson, Paul
1931   Women Love Once
Nickols, Tom
1952   It's a Big Country: An American Anthology
Nicodemus *see* **Stewart, Nicodemus**
Nicol, Alex
1951   The Raging Tide
     Tomahawk
1952   Red Ball Express
Nicoletti, Louis
1950   Black Hand
1951   Across the Wide Missouri
Nicolle, André
1931   Don Juan diplomático (foreign version)
     Soyons gais
Nicova, Leda
1942   Cat People
Nielsen, Erik *same as* **Neilson, Eric**
1951   Slaughter Trail
1953   The Man from the Alamo
Nielson, Norman
1940   Little Nellie Kelly
Niemeyer, Bernard
1917   The Little Samaritan
Nieto, José
1931   Charlie Chan Carries On (foreign version)
     Cuerpo y alma
     Mamá
1932   Marido y mujer
1935   Tango Bar
1939   Miracle on Main Street (foreign version)
Nieto, Luciel
1955   Seven Cities of Gold
Nieto, Pepe
1959   John Paul Jones
Nieves, María
1939   El otro soy yo
Nigh, Jane
1948   Cry of the City
     Unconquered
1950   Border Treasure
     Rio Grande Patrol
1952   Fort Osage
Nigh, William
1916   Her Debt of Honor
1918   The Kaiser's Finish
1932   Border Devils
     Men Are Such Fools
1937   Boy of the Streets
1938   Mr. Wong, Detective
1939   Mr. Wong in Chinatown
     The Mystery of Mr. Wong
1940   Doomed to Die
     The Fatal Hour
1946   Beauty and the Bandit
     The Gay Cavalier
     South of Monterey

1947   Riding the California Trail
Night Hawk (actor)
1934   Laughing Boy
Nigi, Pierre
1931   Così è la vita
Nigro, Bea *same as* **Nigro, Bee**
1940   New Moon
Nikcevich, John
1951   Saturday's Hero
Niles, Denny
1955   The Long Gray Line
Niles, Wendell *same as* **Niles, Wen**
1940   Three Faces West
1942   Wings for the Eagle
Nilsen, Hazel
1949   Apache Chief
Nilsson, Anna Q.
1918   In Judgment Of
1919   Auction of Souls
1920   The Luck of the Irish
1942   They Died With Their Boots On
1945   The Valley of Decision
1946   The Sailor Takes a Wife
1947   The Farmer's Daughter
     It Had To Be You
1948   The Boy with Green Hair
     Fighting Father Dunne
1950   The Big Hangover
1951   Show Boat
Nimoy, Leonard
1951   Queen for a Day
1952   Kid Monk Baroni
1953   Old Overland Trail
Ninchi, Ave
1951   Teresa
Nind, Bill *see* **Nind, William**
1943   Action in the North Atlantic
1947   Crossfire
1951   The Great Caruso
Nissen, Greta
1927   Blind Alleys
1933   Best of Enemies
Niven, David
1950   The Toast of New Orleans
Nivón, Marcela
1930   Así es la vida
     Del mismo barro
     East Is West (foreign version)
     Wu Li Chang
1934   La buenaventura
Nix, Victor
1922   The Greatest Sin
Nixon, Alan *same as* **Nixon, Allan**
1943   Margin for Error
1957   Apache Warrior
Nixon, Joan
1953   Captain John Smith and Pocahontas
Nixon, Marian *same as* **Nixon, Marion**
1927   The Auctioneer
     The Chinese Parrot
1930   The Lash
1932   Charlie Chan's Chance
1933   Best of Enemies
Noa, Manfred S.
1931   La regina di Sparta
Noakes, George
1945   The Bells of St. Mary's
Noble, John W.
1917   The Call of Her People
1918   The Birth of a Race
1919   The Gray Towers Mystery
1922   Cardigan
1924   His Darker Self
Noble, Leighton
1955   Seven Angry Men
Noble, Lucille
1946   Abie's Irish Rose
Noble, Martin
1945   Rhapsody in Blue
Ray Noble and Orchestra
1944   Lake Placid Serenade
Nocki
1926   The Vanishing American

Nodell, Sonia
1923   None So Blind
1925   Salome of the Tenements
Noe, Ivan
1931   Buster se marie
Noe, Robert
1949   Jigsaw
Noel, "Fats"
1949?   Harlem Follies
Noemi, Lea
1937   Green Fields
1938   The Singing Blacksmith
Noie, Marles
1948   Big City
Noisette, Katherine same as
    Noisette, Kathleen
1929   When Men Betray
1930   A Daughter of the Congo
1931   The Exile
Noisom, George
1941   Hurry, Charlie, Hurry
1942   Nazi Agent
1943   Ladies' Day
Nokes, George
1944   Buffalo Bill
        Going My Way
1946   Song of the South
1949   The Cowboy and the
        Indians
Nolan, Bob
1947   On the Old Spanish Trail
Nolan, James same as **Nolan, Jim**
1946   Abie's Irish Rose
1947   Dark Delusion
1948   The Arizona Ranger
        Fighting Father Dunne
        Guns of Hate
        The Miracle of the Bells
        Unconquered
1949   The Clay Pigeon
        Illegal Entry
        Thieves' Highway
Nolan, Jeanette
1956   7th Cavalry
1957   The Guns of Fort
        Petticoat
        The Halliday Brand
Nolan, Jim see **Nolan, James**
Nolan, Lloyd
1938   Dangerous to Know
1940   Behind the News
        The Man I Married
1942   Apache Trail
1943   Bataan
1945   The House on 92nd St.
        A Tree Grows in Brooklyn
1956   The Last Hunt
Nolan, O'Neill
1940   East of the River
Nolte, Bill see **Nolte, William**
Nolte, Charles
1953   War Paint
Nolte, William same as **Nolte, Bill;
    Nolte, William L.**
1932   The Forty-Niners
1934   The Cactus Kid
1935   Wolf Riders
1936   Hair-Trigger Casey
        Sum Hun
1937   Bargain with Bullets
        Dark Manhattan
1938   The Duke Is Tops
        Life Goes On
1943   Land of Hunted Men
1946   Romance of the West
Nom, Liu
1941   Golden Gate Girl
Nomar, Ramon
1946   Notorious
Noonan, Tommy same as **Noonan,
    Tom**
1948   Open Secret
1950   Battleground
1955   Violent Saturday
Jimmie Noone and his orchestra
1944   Block Busters
Nora, Winona
1934   Laughing Boy
Norbeck, Jack
1931   Delicious

Norcha, Agnes
1934   Laughing Boy
Norcrum, Alfred
1923   Regeneration
Norden, Eric
1957   Apache Warrior
Nordquist, Pete
1918   The Hell Cat
Nordyke, Kenneth
1918   The Ranger
Noriega, Eduardo
1955   The Far Horizons
        Seven Cities of Gold
1956   Daniel Boone, Trail
        Blazer
        Serenade
Noriega, Manuel
1933   Dos noches
        No dejes la puerta abierta
Noriega, Nenette
1935   Te quiero con locura
1939   El trovador de la radio
Noriego, Felix
1954   Drum Beat
1956   Pillars of the Sky
Norin, Gus
1958   Tonka
Norman, Al
1930   King of Jazz
Norman, Amber
1931   La cautivadora
1942   Woman of the Year
Norman, B. G.
1950   The Traveling
        Saleswoman
Norman, Eris
1934   Broadway Bill
Norman, Gene
1953   The Stars Are Singing
Norman, Gertrude
1918   The Unbeliever
1921   Little Italy
Norman, Jack
1946   G. I. War Brides
1947   Black Gold
        Bowery Buckaroos
Lee Norman's Orchestra
1939   Keep Punching
Lee Norman Trio
1948?   Boarding House Blues
Norman, Loulie Jean
1950   The Big Hangover
Norman, Maidie same as **Norman,
    Madie**
1947   The Burning Cross
        The Peanut Man
1951   The Well
1953   Bright Road
Norman, Noralee
1953   So Big
1958   The Light in the Forest
Norman, Rolla
1931   Buster se marie
        El proceso de Mary
        Dugan (foreign
        version)
        Quand on est belle
Normand, Mabel
1922   Head over Heels
1923   Suzanna
Juggling Normans
1948   My Girl Tisa
Normond, Rod
1951   The Mark of the
        Renegade
Norris, Edward same as **Norris, Ed**
1934   Coming Out Party
1935   Naughty Marietta
1937   Song of the City
1939   The Escape
1949   The Mysterious
        Desperado
1953   The Man from the Alamo
Norris, Jay
1947   Crossfire
        Desperate
        Under the Tonto Rim
Norris, Karen
1959   The Hanging Tree

Norris, Richard
1946   Abie's Irish Rose
1959   Al Capone
1960   The Last Voyage
Norris, Trusse R.
1960   Sergeant Rutledge
North, Edmund H. same as **North,
    Edmund**
1949   Colorado Territory
1950   Young Man with a Horn
1951   Only the Valiant
1955   The Far Horizons
1959   Last Train from Gun Hill
North, Joe same as **North, Joseph**
1941   Hurry, Charlie, Hurry
North, Michael see **North, Ted**
North, Robert (prod)
1936   Dangerous Intrigue
1940   Behind the News
1941   Ice-Capades
1943   In Old Oklahoma
North, Robert G. (writer)
1948   Night Wind
North, Ted same as **North, Michael**
1940   The Mark of Zorro
1941   Charlie Chan in Rio
1942   Syncopation
1943   Margin for Error
        The Ox-Bow Incident
North, Wilfred same as **North,
    Wilfrid**
1923   The Huntress
1932   Unashamed
North, Mrs. Wilfred same as
    North, Mrs. Wilfrid
1941   Hold Back the Dawn
Northpole, John
1936   Dangerous Intrigue
1939   Winner Take All
1948   Unconquered
Northrop, Patricia
1949   The Girl from Jones
        Beach
Northrup, Ethel
1917   The Renaissance at
        Charleroi
Northrup, Harry S. same as
    Northrup, Harry
1916   Britton of the Seventh
1918   In Judgment Of
1920   The Luck of the Irish
1921   Wing Toy
1931   The Squaw Man
1934   Stand Up and Cheer!
Norton, Barry
1928   Sins of the Fathers
1930   Amor audaz
        Cascarrabias
        El cuerpo del delito
        East Is West (foreign
        version)
        Galas de la Paramount
1931   El código penal
        El comediante
        Drácula
        El pasado acusa
1934   Imitation of Life
1935   Alas sobre el Chaco
1936   El diablo del mar
1937   El capitán Tormenta
1938   The Buccaneer
1939   Papá soltero
        El trovador de la radio
Norton, Edgar
1930   East Is West
1933   A Lady's Profession
1934   Imitation of Life
Norton, Frances
1936   Ramona
Norton, Harold
1941   Sunday Sinners
1947   Sepia Cinderella
Norton, Jack
1935   Ruggles of Red Gap
1936   After the Thin Man
        Rose of the Rancho
1940   The Way of All Flesh
1941   Louisiana Purchase
        Ride on Vaquero
1944   The Chinese Cat
        Going My Way
1945   The Scarlet Clue

1946   Bringing Up Father
        Shadows Over Chinatown
Norton, Pearlie May same as
    Norton, Perlie May
1942   Song of the Islands
Norton, Samuel P.
1955   The Indian Fighter
Norton, Stuart
1945   Where Do We Go From
        Here?
Norton, Thelma
1941   Sunday Sinners
Norvo, Red
1958   Kings Go Forth
Nosseck, Max
1940   Overture to Glory
1947   The Return of Rin Tin Tin
1956   Singing in the Dark
Nossen, Bram
1954   Go Man Go
Notarro, Jimmy same as **Notaro,
    James**
1936   Star for a Night
Nourie, A. A.
1940   The Ramparts We Watch
Nourse, Allen
1959   Odds Against Tomorrow
Nourse, Neysa
1934   Beloved
Nova, Hedda
1917   The Bar Sinister
1921   Shadows of the West
1925   The Gold Hunters
Nova, Lou
1947   Calendar Girl
1949   The Cowboy and the
        Prizefighter
1951   The Tall Target
        Westward the Women
Novak, Eva
1921   Wolves of the North
1922   Sky High
1925   The Fearless Lover
1926   Irene
1936   Dangerous Intrigue
1945   The Bells of St. Mary's
1948   Four Faces West
1950   Sunset in the West
1953   The Eddie Cantor Story
1956   Dakota Incident
1960   Sergeant Rutledge
Novak, Jane
1917   The Spirit of '76
1918   The Temple of Dusk
1919   Behind the Door
        His Debt
1923   Jealous Husbands
1924   Two Shall Be Born
1929   Redskin
1950   The Furies
Novak, Joe
1943   Let's Have Fun
Novak, Mykola
1937   Natalka Poltavka
1938   Marusia
Novarro, Ramón
1930   Sevilla de mis amores
1932   Huddle
        The Son-Daughter
1934   Laughing Boy
1936   Contra la corriente
1949   We Were Strangers
Novella, Alba
1931   Pagliacci
Novello, Jay
1945   Rhapsody in Blue
1952   The Big Sky
        The Iron Mistress
1953   Beneath the 12-Mile Reef
1959   The Wonderful Country
1960   This Rebel Breed
Novello, Leon
1938   The Buccaneer
Nover, Virgil B.
1937   Charlie Chan at the
        Olympics
Novinsky, Alex same as **Novinsky,
    Alexander**
1938   Happy Landing

Novis, Donald same as **Novis, Don**
1944   Slightly Terrific
Novis, Julietta
1940   Music in My Heart
Novotna, Jarmila
1951   The Great Caruso
Nowell, Wedgwood same as **Nowell, Wedgewood**
1917   The Flower of Doom
        The Pulse of Life
1919   Diane of the Green Van
        The Lord Loves the Irish
1923   Jealous Husbands
1942   Gentleman Jim
1943   Let's Have Fun
1945   The Dolly Sisters
Nowina-Przybylski, Jan same as **Przybylski, Jan Nowina**
1936   Yiddle with His Fiddle
1937   The Jester (Der Purimspieler)
Nowland, Eugene
1917   Threads of Fate
Nowlin, Herman
1932   The Rainbow Trail
1941   Western Union
1948   The Arizona Ranger
1949   Rustlers
1951   Flaming Feather
1952   The Half-Breed
Noy, Wilfred
1925   The Midnight Girl
Noyes, Skeets
1947   The Mighty McGurk
1948   Big City
Nuell, Fay
1958   Marjorie Morningstar
Nuetzman, Delmar
1945   The House on 92nd St.
Nugent, Carol
1947   It Had To Be You
        Little Mister Jim
1952   It's a Big Country: An American Anthology
1954   Drum Beat
1958   The Badlanders
1959   The Crimson Kimono
        Inside the Mafia
Nugent, Eddie same as **Nugent, Edward; Nugent, Edward J.**
1931   Young Sinners
1932   Men Are Such Fools
1933   Dance Hall Hostess
1937   Man of the People
Nugent, Elliott
1930   Sins of the Children
1948   My Girl Tisa
Nugent, Frank S. same as **Nugent, Frank**
1948   Fort Apache
1949   She Wore a Yellow Ribbon
        3 Godfathers
        Tulsa
1950   Two Flags West
1952   The Quiet Man
1954   They Rode West
1956   The Searchers
1958   Gunman's Walk
        The Last Hurrah
Nugent, J. C.
1937   Life Begins in College
Nugent, Judy
1947   It Had To Be You
Nugent, Lee
1949   Lost Boundaries
Numkena, Anthony
1956   Westward Ho the Wagons!
Nunes, A. Robert
1954   Thunder Pass
Nuñez, Daniel
1955   Seven Cities of Gold
Núñez, Tomasita
1930   Revista Hispano-Americana
Nunn, Larry
1947   Desperate
Nurmi, Maila
1960   I Passed for White

Nurney, Fred
1943   They Came to Blow Up America
1946   Notorious
1948   Sleep, My Love
1950   Mystery Submarine
Nussbaum, Ruth
1944   They Live in Fear
Nusser, James
1956   Mohawk
Nutter, Earl
1949   Thieves' Highway
Nuwak
1925   Kivalina of the Ice Lands
Nye, Carroll
1926   Kosher Kitty Kelly
1939   Gone With the Wind
Nye, G. Raymond
1923   Snowdrift
Nye, William
1945   The Dolly Sisters
        Where Do We Go From Here?
Nyla
1922   Nanook of the North
Oaker, John
1919   The Sneak
Oakie, Jack
1929   Chinatown Nights
1930   Galas de la Paramount
1937   That Girl from Paris
1942   Song of the Islands
1943   Wintertime
1949   Thieves' Highway
1950   Last of the Buccaneers
1951   Tomahawk
1959   The Wonderful Country
Oakland, Dagmar
1934   Stand Up and Cheer!
1944   Mr. Skeffington
Oakland, Ethelmary
1915   Hearts of Men
Oakland, Vivian
1928   Uncle Tom's Cabin
Oakley, Bill same as **Oakley, Billie**
1936   Charlie Chan at the Race Track
1943   Gangway for Tomorrow
Oakley, Patricia
1940   They Knew What They Wanted
Oakman, Wheeler
1914   In the Days of the Thundering Herd
1915   The Rosary
1919   False Evidence
1920   Outside the Law
1922   The Half Breed
        The Son of the Wolf
1928   The Broken Mask
1934   Operator 13
1936   Aces and Eights
1938   The Texans
1943   The Girl from Monterrey
1944   Riding West
Oates, Warren
1959   Yellowstone Kelly
O'Beck, Fred
1928   Vamping Venus
Ober, Dillon
1936   Ramona
Ober, Philip
1934   Chloe: Love Is Calling You
1951   The Magnificent Yankee
1954   Broken Lance
Oberon, Merle
1944   Dark Waters
Oboler, Arch
1940   Escape
1943   Gangway for Tomorrow
1951   Five
Obregon, Antonio
1960   The Pusher
O'Brian, Hugh
1951   Little Big Horn
1952   The Battle at Apache Pass
        The Raiders
        Red Ball Express
1953   The Man from the Alamo
        Seminole
        The Stand at Apache River

1954   Broken Lance
        Drums Across the River
        Saskatchewan
1955   White Feather
O'Brien, Bill could be same as **O'Brien, Billy**
1953   The Eddie Cantor Story
        So Big
O'Brien, Billy could be same as **O'Brien, Bill**
1937   Charlie Chan on Broadway
O'Brien, Charles
1951   Jim Thorpe—All-American
O'Brien, Chris
1955   The Gun That Won the West
O'Brien, Cubby
1956   Westward Ho the Wagons!
O'Brien, Dave same as **O'Brien, David**
1939   Daughter of the Tong
        Drifting Westward
1942   King of the Stallions
        Prisoner of Japan
1944   Tahiti Nights
1935   The Little Colonel
O'Brien, Edmond
1943   The Amazing Mrs. Holliday
1951   Warpath
1960   The Last Voyage
O'Brien, Emmett
1936   Star for a Night
O'Brien, Erin not the same as **O'Brien-Moore, Erin**
1959   John Paul Jones
O'Brien, Eugene
1916   Poor Little Peppina
1919   Come Out of the Kitchen
O'Brien, Florence
1939   Double Deal
1940   While Thousands Cheer
1940?   Mr. Washington Goes to Town
1942   Lucky Ghost
        Professor Creeps
1943   Stormy Weather
O'Brien, George
1929   Masked Emotions
1932   The Golden West
        Mystery Ranch
        The Rainbow Trail
1933   Robbers' Roost
1936   Daniel Boone
1938   The Renegade Ranger
1939   The Fighting Gringo
1947   My Wild Irish Rose
1948   Fort Apache
1949   She Wore a Yellow Ribbon
O'Brien, Gypsy
1923   Little Old New York
O'Brien, Jimmy
1948   Jiggs and Maggie in Court
        The Luck of the Irish
1949   Top O' the Morning
1951   Yes Sir, Mr. Bones
O'Brien, John (child actor)
1949   Top O' the Morning
O'Brien, John B. (dir) could be same as **O'Brien, John J.** (dir)
1916   Hulda from Holland
1917   Queen X
1921   Lonely Heart
O'Brien, John J. (dir) could be same as **O'Brien, John B.** (dir)
1917   The Buffalo Bill Show
O'Brien, Liam
1953   The Stars Are Singing
O'Brien, Margaret
1943   Dr. Gillespie's Criminal Case
1945   Our Vines Have Tender Grapes
1946   Bad Bascomb
        Three Wise Fools
1948   Big City

O'Brien, Marissa
1946   Three Wise Fools
O'Brien, Oscar
1947   My Wild Irish Rose
O'Brien, Pat 1899–1983
1931   Personal Maid
1935   The Irish in Us
1940   Escape to Glory
        The Fighting 69th
        Knute Rockne—All American
1942   The Navy Comes Through
1943   His Butler's Sister
1948   The Boy with Green Hair
        Fighting Father Dunne
1958   The Last Hurrah
O'Brien, Pat J. (western actor) same as **O'Brien, Pat, Lt.** not the same as **O'Brien, Pat** 1899–1983
1921   Shadows of the West
1941   Doomed Caravan
O'Brien, Steve
1941   Western Union
O'Brien, Tom
1924   Fools' Highway
        Untamed Youth
1927   The Frontiersman
        Winners of the Wilderness
1928   Anybody Here Seen Kelly?
1929   The Peacock Fan
        Smiling Irish Eyes
1936   The Phantom of Santa Fe
O'Brien, W. J. same as **O'Brien, William J.**
1931   The Guilty Generation
1942   Syncopation
1943   Gangway for Tomorrow
1951   Gambling House
O'Brien, William H.
1946   Slightly Scandalous
1948   Up in Central Park
1958   The Last Hurrah
O'Brien-Moore, Erin not the same as **O'Brien, Erin**
1937   Black Legion
1955   The Long Gray Line
O'Byrne, Maggie
1957   The Brothers Rico
O'Byrne, Patsy
1935   Ruggles of Red Gap
1948   The Miracle of the Bells
        The Paleface
1950   Stars in My Crown
O'Casey, Ronan
1950   Give Us This Day
Ochoa, Goldie
1932   Amor y vida
Ocko, Daniel
1959   The Last Angry Man
O'Connell, Arthur
1948   Open Secret
1960   Cimarron
O'Connell, Hugh
1931   Personal Maid
1934   Strange Wives
1935   Chinatown Squad
O'Connell, Marion
1935   The Singing Vagabond
O'Connell, Robert
1958   Never Love a Stranger
O'Connor, Blueboy
1933   The Emperor Jones
O'Connor, Bob same as **O'Connor, Robert; O'Conor, Bob** not the same as **O'Connor, Robert Emmet**
1931   Noche de duendes
1937   Big City
        Waikiki Wedding
1942   Tortilla Flat
1943   The Leopard Man
1946   Cuban Pete
O'Connor, Donald
1944   Chip Off the Old Block
O'Connor, Frank
1925   One of the Bravest
1934   Broadway Bill
        Straight Is the Way
1935   The Little Colonel
        Ruggles of Red Gap

1938   The Adventures of Tom
        Sawyer
1940   Little Nellie Kelly
1942   Syncopation
1943   Frontier Fury
        Gangway for Tomorrow
        Good Luck, Mr. Yates
1945   Escape in the Fog
1946   Sun Valley Cyclone
        Sunset Pass
1947   Buffalo Bill Rides Again
        Desperate
        Marshal of Cripple Creek
        Rustlers of Devil's
        Canyon
1950   Sands of Iwo Jima
1951   Cyclone Fury
1952   The Half-Breed
        The Raiders
1957   Run of the Arrow

O'Connor, Jack (actor), d. 1955
not the same as **O'Connor,
John** (actor), circa 1917–1921
1943   Ladies' Day

O'Connor, John (actor), circa
1917–1921 *same as* **O'Connor,
Jack** *not the same as* **O'Connor,
Jack** (actor), d. 1955
1921   The Barricade

O'Connor, Kathleen
1922   Come On Over

O'Connor, Louis J.
1921   Diane of Star Hollow

O'Connor, Mary H. *same as*
O'Connor, Mary
1915   The Penitentes
        A Yankee from the West

O'Connor, Maureen
1937   Boy of the Streets

O'Connor, Robert Emmet *same as*
**O'Connor, Robert; O'Connor,
Robert E.** *not the same as*
O'Connor, Bob
1929   Smiling Irish Eyes
1931   Three Who Loved
1935   A Night at the Opera
1936   It Had to Happen
        Kelly the Second
1937   Boy of the Streets
1943   Dr. Gillespie's Criminal
        Case
1944   An American Romance
1946   Three Wise Fools
1947   The Mighty McGurk

O'Connor, Una
1944   My Pal Wolf
1945   The Bells of St. Mary's
1948   Fighting Father Dunne

O'Conor, Bob *see* **O'Connor, Bob**

O'Davoren, Vesey
1934   Coming Out Party
1947   Dark Delusion

O'Day, Dawn *see* **Shirley, Anne**

O'Day, Kerry
1950   Annie Get Your Gun

O'Day, Mary
1927   The Fighting Hombre

O'Day, Molly
1934   Chloe: Love Is Calling
        You

O'Day, Nell
1930   King of Jazz

O'Dea, John
1953   Jack McCall Desperado

O'Dea, Joseph
1952   The Quiet Man

O'Dea, Sunnie
1936   Show Boat

Odell, David
1958   Machete

O'Dell, Doye
1941   The Pioneers

O'Dell, Georgia
1936   Show Boat
        West of Nevada

Odell, Jack H.
1958   Machete

O'Dell, Janette
1938   Spirit of Youth

Odets, Clifford
1945   Rhapsody in Blue
1947   Humoresque

Odin, Susan
1950   Annie Get Your Gun
1953   The Eddie Cantor Story

Odom, Jack
1950   Intruder in the Dust

O'Donnell, Cathy
1957   The Deerslayer

O'Donnell, Gene
1941   You're Out of Luck
1943   Action in the North
        Atlantic
        The Amazing Mrs.
        Holliday

O'Donnell, Jack
1931   Skyline
1932   Hypnotized
1944   Tucson Raiders

O'Donnell, Jean
1943   The Gang's All Here

O'Donnell, Joseph *same as*
O'Donnell, Joe
1936   Aces and Eights
        The Traitor
1939   Reform School
1940   While Thousands Cheer

O'Donnell, Paddy
1952   The Quiet Man

O'Donnell, Spec *same as*
O'Donnell, Walter "Spec"
1926   Private Izzy Murphy
1928   Vamping Venus
1930   The Grand Parade
1932   Hypnotized
1934   Broadway Bill
1937   Life Begins in College
1941   Sun Valley Serenade
1942   Syncopation
1947   Calendar Girl
1950   The Daughter of Rosie
        O'Grady
1951   The Great Caruso
1953   So Big

O'Donohue, James T.
1928   The Hawk's Nest

O'Dowd, Dan
1957   Journey to Freedom

O'Dowd, Michael
1958   Never Love a Stranger

O'Driscoll, Martha
1939   Judge Hardy and Son
1944   Hi, Beautiful
1947   Carnegie Hall

Oemler, Marie Conway
1924   Two Shall Be Born

Oestreich, Newell
1951   Saturday's Hero

Oettel, Wally
1929   Hawk of the Hills

O'Farrell, Broderick
1927   The Princess from
        Hoboken
1936   Dangerous Intrigue
1945   Rhapsody in Blue
1948   Fighting Father Dunne
1949   The Girl from Jones
        Beach

O'Farrill, Alberto
1935   No matarás

Offerman, George, Jr. *same as*
Offerman, George
1935   Black Fury
1938   Happy Landing
1942   Sunday Punch
        Whispering Ghosts
1943   Action in the North
        Atlantic
        Air Force
1944   The Sullivans
1950   Battleground
1951   Go for Broke!
1957   Burden of Truth

Offley, Hilda *see* **Thompson, Hilda
Offley**

O'Flaherty, Liam
1937   The Devil's Playground

O'Flynn, Damian *same as* **Ford,
Damon**
1948   Half Past Midnight

1950   Mystery Submarine
        Young Daniel Boone
1951   Gambling House
1952   The Half-Breed
1956   Daniel Boone, Trail
        Blazer
1957   Apache Warrior

O'Flynn, Paddy
1930   The Kibitzer
1937   Charlie Chan on
        Broadway

O'Gatty, Jimmy *same as* **O'Gatty,
James**
1936   Laughing Irish Eyes
1937   Man of the People
1939   Winner Take All
1940   East of the River
1945   Johnny Angel
1950   Emergency Wedding
        Right Cross

Ogden, Daphne
1942   Young America

Ogg, Jimmy *could be same as* **Ogg,
Sammy**
1951   Jim Thorpe—All-American

Ogg, Sammy *could be same as* **Ogg,
Jimmy**
1955   Violent Saturday
1958   Frontier Gun

Ogilvie, Kathleen
1933   It's Great to Be Alive

Ogle, Charles
1915   Under Southern Skies
1917   The Secret Game
1918   The Source
        The Squaw Man
1919   Told in the Hills
1923   Ruggles of Red Gap
        Thirty Days
1925   The Thundering Herd

Ogletree, Luther E.
1956   Reprisal!

O'Grady, Monty
1927   The Callahans and the
        Murphys

O'Grady, Tom
1936   Human Cargo
1939   Mr. Moto Takes a
        Vacation
1942   Tales of Manhattan

O'Hanlon, George
1943   Action in the North
        Atlantic
        Ladies' Day

O'Hanlon, James
1946   Three Wise Fools

O'Hara, Barry
1957   Journey to Freedom

O'Hara, Brian
1943   Good Luck, Mr. Yates
1944   The Racket Man
1947   The Last Round-Up
1949   The Undercover Man
1958   The Last Hurrah
1959   The Crimson Kimono
1960   Studs Lonigan

O'Hara, George
1945   The Dolly Sisters

O'Hara, Helen
1945   Nob Hill
1946   Slightly Scandalous
1947   The Jolson Story

O'Hara, Henry
1942   Gentleman Jim

O'Hara, Mary
1925   Braveheart

O'Hara, Maureen
1944   Buffalo Bill
1947   The Foxes of Harrow
1950   Comanche Territory
        Rio Grande
1952   The Quiet Man
1954   War Arrow
1955   The Long Gray Line

O'Hara, Patricia Quinn *not the
same as* **O'Hara, Pat** (actor) *or*
O'Hara, Quinn
1949   Lost Boundaries

O'Hara, Shirley (actress), circa
mid-1940s *not the same as*
O'Hara, Shirley (actress), circa
mid-1920s

1946   Cuban Pete
1947   Bells of San Fernando

O'Hearn, Eileen
1941   Thunder Over the Prairie
1942   Submarine Raider

O'Herlihy, Dan
1950   The Iroquois Trail
1958   Home Before Dark
1959   Imitation of Life
        The Young Land

Ohira, Ted
1951   Go for Broke!

Ohme, H. C. "Dutch"
1950   Panic in the Streets

Ojala, Arvo
1959   The Oregon Trail

Ok-Ba-Ok
1927   Primitive Love

Okada, Frank
1951   Go for Broke!

Okamoto, Ken K.
1951   Go for Broke!

Okamura, George
1959   The Crimson Kimono

Okawa, Henry
1930   Chijlku wo mawasuru
        chikara

Okazaki, Robert *same as* **Okazaki,
Bob**
1959   The Crimson Kimono
1960   Hell to Eternity

O'Keefe, Dennis *same as* **Flanagan,
Bud; Flanagan, Edward James**
1934   Broadway Bill
1937   Big City
        The Plainsman
1943   The Leopard Man
        Tahiti Honey
1957   Dragoon Wells Massacre

O'Keefe, Mary
1931   Carne de cabaret

Ola, Juan
1934   Nada más que una mujer

Oland, Warner
1915?   Sin
1919   Mandarin's Gold
1922   East Is West
        The Pride of Palomar
1925   Don Q, Son of Zorro
        Flower of Night
1927   Old San Francisco
        Sailor Izzy Murphy
1928   The Jazz Singer
        Wheel of Chance
1929   Chinatown Nights
1931   The Black Camel
        Charlie Chan Carries On
1932   Charlie Chan's Chance
        The Son-Daughter
1933   Charlie Chan's Greatest
        Case
1934   Charlie Chan in London
        Charlie Chan's Courage
1935   Charlie Chan in Egypt
        Charlie Chan in Paris
        Charlie Chan in Shanghai
1936   Charlie Chan at the
        Circus
        Charlie Chan at the Race
        Track
        Charlie Chan's Secret
1937   Charlie Chan at the
        Olympics
        Charlie Chan at the
        Opera
        Charlie Chan on
        Broadway
1938   Charlie Chan at Monte
        Carlo

Olcott, Sidney
1916   The Innocent Lie
        Poor Little Peppina
1923   Little Old New York
1925   Salome of the Tenements

Oldstead, Remy
1937   Slave Ship

O'Leary, William *same as* **O'Leary,
Bill**
1945   The Valley of Decision
1946   Without Reservations
1949   Top O' the Morning

Oliva, Gilda
1949   House of Strangers
1952   Anything Can Happen
1958   Houseboat

Oliver, Clarence
1918   Laughing Bill Hyde

Oliver, David
1938   The Rage of Paris
1941   The Face Behind the Mask
      They Dare Not Love
1942   Rio Rita

Oliver, Edna May
1931   Cimarron
1933   It's Great to Be Alive
1939   Drums Along the Mohawk

Oliver, Gene
1944   Charlie Chan in the Secret Service

Oliver, George
194-   Mistaken Identity

Oliver, Gordon
1944   Since You Went Away

Oliver, Guy
1917   The Bottle Imp
      The Call of the East
      The Little American
1918   The Bravest Way
      The Squaw Man
1919   Told in the Hills
1923   Ruggles of Red Gap
1924   North of 36
1926   The Vanishing American
1927   Drums of the Desert
      Open Range
1930   The Kibitzer
1931   Huckleberry Finn

Oliver, Marjorie
194-   Mistaken Identity

Oliver, Shirling
1933   Victims of Persecution

Oliver, Ted
1933   Robbers' Roost
1936   Klondike Annie
      Rose of the Rancho
1937   The Plainsman
      Souls at Sea
1939   Stand Up and Fight
1940   Geronimo
      New Moon
      Northwest Passage (Book I—Rogers' Rangers)
1942   Wings for the Eagle

Ollestad, Norman *same as* **Ollestad, Norman, Jr.**
1945   The Valley of Decision
1950   Stars in My Crown
      Winchester '73
1957   All Mine to Give

Olmstead, Gertrude *same as* **Olmsted, Gertrude**
1922   The Scrapper
1925   Cobra
1926   Puppets
1927   The Callahans and the Murphys

Olmstead, Stanley
1918   Find the Woman

O'Locklin, Allen
1950   Mystery Street
1953   Dream Wife

Olsen, Donald
1948   My Girl Tisa

George Olsen and His Orchestra
1930   Whoopee

Olsen, Larry *same as* **Olsen, Larry Joe**
1944   Address Unknown
      My Pal Wolf
1950   Winchester '73

Olsen, Moroni
1935   Annie Oakley
1937   Manhattan Merry-Go-Round
1939   Allegheny Uprising
1940   East of the River
      If I Had My Way
      Santa Fe Trail
1942   Nazi Agent
1943   Air Force
1944   Buffalo Bill
1945   Pride of the Marines
      The Valley of Decision

1946   Notorious
1947   Black Gold
1948   Call Northside 777
      Up in Central Park

Olsen, Ole *same as* **Olsen** *of* Olsen and Johnson
1939   Winner Take All

Olsen, Steve
1946   Abie's Irish Rose

Olshansky, Murray
1952   Red Ball Express

Olson, Nancy
1953   So Big

Olsza, Tadeusz
1930   Toda una vida (*foreign version*)

O'Mahoney, Jock *see* **Mahoney, Jock**

O'Malley, Charles
1931   Smart Money

O'Malley, Jack
1941   Mystery Ship

O'Malley, Kathleen
1945   Salome, Where She Danced
1948   Singin' Spurs
1950   Emergency Wedding
1951   Westward the Women

O'Malley, Pat (*actor*), 1891—1966 *same as* **O'Malley, Patrick** *not the same as* **O'Malley, J. Pat** (*actor*), d. 1985
1917   The Tell-Tale Step
1918   The Prussian Cur
1919   False Evidence
1920   Dinty
1924   Fools' Highway
      The Mine with the Iron Door
1927   Pleasure Before Business
      The Slaver
1928   The House of Scandal
1931   Die Maske Fällt
1934   Behold My Wife!
      Broadway Bill
1935   Charlie Chan in Shanghai
1936   Charlie Chan at the Race Track
      Paddy O'Day
1938   Speed to Burn
1939   The Escape
      Mr. Moto Takes a Vacation
1940   East of the River
      Little Nellie Kelly
      Lucky Cisco Kid
1942   Gentleman Jim
1943   Redhead from Manhattan
1944   An American Romance
      The Racket Man
1946   Singin' in the Corn
1949   Boston Blackie's Chinese Venture
1950   Ambush
1952   The Quiet Man
1955   The Long Gray Line

O'Malley, Rex
1953   Taxi

O'Malley, Tom
1924   His Darker Self

O'Malley, Walter
1931   Delicious

O'Moore, Patrick
1946   G. I. War Brides
      Rendezvous 24
1957   Pawnee
      Trooper Hook
1958   Blood Arrow

On, Lim Yah
1934   Blossom Time

O'Neal, Anne
1934   Strange Wives
1937   Maid of Salem
1939   The Adventures of Huckleberry Finn
1943   In Old Oklahoma
      Mexican Spitfire's Blessed Event
1946   Slightly Scandalous
1948   Fighting Father Dunne
      Open Secret
1949   Lust for Gold
      That Midnight Kiss

1950   Annie Get Your Gun
      Belle of Old Mexico

O'Neal, Charles
1944   Cry of the Werewolf

O'Neal, Frederick
1949   Pinky
1959   Anna Lucasta
1960   Take a Giant Step

O'Neal, William
1956   Walk the Proud Land

O'Neil, Barbara
1938   The Toy Wife
1939   Gone With the Wind
1948   I Remember Mama

O'Neil, George
1934   Beloved
1936   Sutter's Gold

O'Neil, Henry *see* **O'Neill, Henry**

O'Neil, James (*actor*), born U.S. circa 1870 *not the same as* **O'Neil, James** (*actor*), born Ireland, 1847
1915   After Five
1927   With Sitting Bull at the Spirit Lake Massacre

O'Neil, Jerry
1944   An American Romance

O'Neil, Jim (*western actor*) *see* **O'Neill, Jim** (*western actor*)

O'Neil, Kitty
1950   No Way Out

O'Neil, Nance
1915   Kreutzer Sonata
1916   The Flames of Johannis
1931   Cimarron

O'Neil, Robert *same as* **O'Neill, Robert**
1948   Tap Roots
1949   The Girl from Jones Beach
1950   The Baron of Arizona
      Young Man with a Horn
1951   The Raging Tide

O'Neil, Sally
1927   The Callahans and the Murphys
      Frisco Sally Levy
1930   Kathleen Mavourneen

O'Neil, Tex
1932   Riders of the Desert

O'Neill, Ed
1931   Delicious
1940   New Moon
1944   An American Romance

O'Neill, Frank
1930   Amor audaz (*foreign version*)
1931   Echec au roi
      La gran jornada (*foreign version*)
      Quand on est belle
1932   La foule hurle

O'Neill, Henry *same as* **O'Neil, Henry**
1934   Massacre
1935   Black Fury
      Bordertown
1936   Rainbow on the River
1939   Confessions of a Nazi Spy
1940   The Fighting 69th
      Knute Rockne—All American
      Santa Fe Trail
1942   Tortilla Flat
1943   Dr. Gillespie's Criminal Case
1945   Between Two Women
1946   Bad Bascomb
      Three Wise Fools
1947   Little Mister Jim
1953   The Sun Shines Bright

O'Neill, James Joseph
1957   Beau James

O'Neill, Jim (*western actor*) *same as* **O'Neil, Jim** (*western actor*)
1922   Blazing Arrows

Ong, Dana
1915   The Cheat

Onofri, Guglielmo
1932   Amore e morte

O'Pace, Les
1951   The House on Telegraph Hill
1953   Tonight We Sing

Opatoshu, David
1939   The Light Ahead
1949   Thieves' Highway
1951   Molly
1956   Crowded Paradise
1960   Cimarron

Opel, Richard von
1950   Broken Arrow

Oppenheim, Menasha *same as* **Oppenheim, Menashe**
1939   Kol Nidre
      Mamele
1941   Mazel Tov Yidden

Oppenheimer, George
1935   Rendezvous
1952   Anything Can Happen
1953   Tonight We Sing

Opunui, Charles
1944   Tahiti Nights

Orchard, Thomas
1940   The Ramparts We Watch

Ordyński, Ryszard
1930   Toda una vida (*foreign version*)

O'Rear, James
1959   The Last Angry Man

Oreck, Don
1955   The Long Gray Line

Original New Orleans Ragtime Band
1947   New Orleans

Origo, Casare
1931   La regina di Sparta

Orkow, B. Harrison *same as* **Orkow, B. H.**
1942   Wings for the Eagle

Orla, Nina
1941   Where Did You Get That Girl?

Orlamond, William
1923   Look Your Best
1931   Cimarron

Orlandi, Felice
1958   Never Love a Stranger
1960   The Pusher

Orlando, Don
1935?   The Irish Gringo
1950   Black Hand
1955   Trial
1957   The Brothers Rico
      Run of the Arrow
1959   The Black Orchid

Orlean, Will
1952   Anything Can Happen

Orlebeck, Lester *same as* **Orlebeck, Les**
1941   Gauchos of Eldorado
      Prairie Pioneers
      Saddlemates

Orlenco, Helen
1939   Cossacks in Exile

Orlob, Harold
1947   Citizen Saint

Orloff, Arthur E.
1950   The Missourians

Orloff, Count John
1922   The Hands of Nara

Ormond, Ron
1948   Shep Comes Home
1949   The Dalton Gang
1951   Yes Sir, Mr. Bones
1956   Frontier Woman

Ormont, David
1952   Anything Can Happen

Ornelas, Adolfo
1950   The Baron of Arizona

Ornitz, Samuel *same as* **Ornitz, Sam**
1930   Sins of the Children
1932   Thirteen Women
1934   Imitation of Life
1937   It Could Happen to You
1939   Miracle on Main Street
      Miracle on Main Street (*foreign version*)
1940   Three Faces West
1944   They Live in Fear

Orosco, Henry see **Orozco, Henry**
Orosco, Tom
1943   The Leopard Man
O'Rourke, Carlyle
1937   Souls at Sea
O'Rourke, Baby Jean
1921   The Hunger of the Blood
Orozco, Henry same as **Orosco, Henry**
1936   Ramona
1946   Strange Voyage
Orozco, Lewis
1936   Ramona
Orquesta Puertorriqueña Sanabria
1930   Revista Hispano-Americana
Orr, Gertrude
1928   Mother Machree
Orr, Michael
1945   The Bells of St. Mary's
Orr, Robert
1945   Of One Blood
Orrison, Jack
1959   Al Capone
Orsatti, Frank
1935   The Irish in Us
Orsatti, Victor M. same as **Orsatti, Victor**
1957   Ride Out for Revenge
1958   Apache Territory
Orta, Sergio
1942   Woman of the Year
Ortega, Eva
1938   Di que me quieres
Ortega, Santos
1956   Crowded Paradise
Ortego, Artie
1934   The Prescott Kid
        The Star Packer
1935   North of Arizona
1936   Custer's Last Stand
1946   The Gay Cavalier
        Sunset Pass
1949   Colorado Territory
1950   Colt .45
Orth, Betty Jean
1945   Where Do We Go From Here?
Orth, Frank
1937   Prairie Thunder
1939   Winner Take All
1940   Mexican Spitfire Out West
1941   Come Live with Me
        Ride on Vaquero
1942   Dr. Gillespie's New Assistant
        Little Tokyo, U.S.A.
        Tales of Manhattan
        They Died With Their Boots On
1943   The Meanest Man in the World
1944   Buffalo Bill
1945   The Dolly Sisters
        Nob Hill
1947   It Had To Be You
1948   Fury at Furnace Creek
1955   Not As a Stranger
Orth, Marion
1927   White Gold
1929   Romance of the Rio Grande
1933   Charlie Chan's Greatest Case
Ortiz, Juan
1943   The Leopard Man
Ortiz, Marina
1930   Charros, gauchos y manolas
        Sombras de gloria
1936   Contra la corriente
Ortiz, Peter
1950   Rio Grande
1953   San Antone
1955   The Long Gray Line
1956   7th Cavalry
1957   The Halliday Brand

Ory, Kid same as **Ory, Edward "Kid"**
1947   New Orleans
1956   The Benny Goodman Story
Orzazewski, Kasia
1948   Call Northside 777
1949   Thieves' Highway
1951   Queen for a Day
Osato, Sono
1949   The Kissing Bandit
Osborn, Bud see **Osborne, Bud**
Osborn, Paul
1949   Portrait of Jennie
1960   Wild River
Osborn, Ted
1940   Charlie Chan at the Wax Museum
Osborne, Bud same as **Osborn, Bud**
1929   The Invaders
1934   The Prescott Kid
1936   Pinto Rustlers
        Treachery Rides the Range
1937   Boots and Saddles
        The Californian
        The Plainsman
1939   Allegheny Uprising
1940   Viva Cisco Kid
1942   Below the Border
        Valley of the Sun
1944   Outlaw Trail
        Sonora Stagecoach
1945   The Cisco Kid Returns
        The Navajo Trail
        Salome, Where She Danced
1946   Border Bandits
        California Gold Rush
        Wild West
1947   Bowery Buckaroos
        The Last Round-Up
        Under the Tonto Rim
1948   Indian Agent
        Western Heritage
1949   The Cowboy and the Prizefighter
        The Gay Amigo
1950   The Missourians
        Winchester '73
1952   Bugles in the Afternoon
        Indian Uprising
1953   Last of the Comanches
        So Big
Osborne, Frances
1953   So Big
Osborne, Marie same as **Osborne, Baby Marie**
1917   Sunshine and Gold
1919   The Little Diplomat
1943   His Butler's Sister
Osborne, Virgil
1955   The Rose Tattoo
Osborne, Vivienne
1922   The Good Provider
1932   Men Are Such Fools
1936   Let's Sing Again
Oscar, John
1949?   The Joint Is Jumpin'
Oser, Wendy
1948   The Boy with Green Hair
O'Shea, Jack
1944   The San Antonio Kid
1946   Romance of the West
1947   Bowery Buckaroos
        King of the Bandits
        Vigilantes of Boomtown
1949   Ride, Ryder, Ride!
        Roll Thunder Roll!
1955   The Last Command
O'Shea, James
1916   Little Meena's Romance
1917   A Love Sublime
O'Shea, Michael
1943   Jack London
1944   Something for the Boys
1947   Last of the Redmen
O'Shea, Oscar
1937   Big City
1941   Accent on Love
        Mutiny in the Arctic

1942   Three Hearts for Julia
1946   Abie's Irish Rose
        Without Reservations
1947   It Had To Be You
1948   Fury at Furnace Creek
1950   The Daughter of Rosie O'Grady
O'Shea, Ted
1941   The Mexican Spitfire's Baby
1943   Ladies' Day
Osherowitz, Mendel
1939   A Brivele der Mamen
O'Shiel, Fiona
1951   Westward the Women
Osmond, Kenneth
1953   So Big
1955   Good Morning, Miss Dove
Osmun, James
1916   Unprotected
Osmun, Leighton
1917   Castles for Two
        Forbidden Paths
        Unconquered
Ossetynski, Leonidas
1951   Gambling House
Osterloh, Robert
1949   Harbor of Missing Men
        Illegal Entry
        Pinky
        The Undercover Man
1950   A Lady Without Passport
        The Palomino
1951   New Mexico
        The Well
1952   The Ring
1955   Seven Angry Men
        Violent Saturday
1958   Fort Massacre
Ostriche, Muriel
1918   Hitting the Trail
Ostrow, Lou same as **Ostrow, L. L.**
1927   Wild Geese
1939   Judge Hardy and Son
1942   Cat People
1943   The Leopard Man
O'Sullivan, Lawrence
1931   Delicious
O'Sullivan, Maureen
1931   Skyline
1933   The Cohens and Kellys in Trouble
        Robbers' Roost
O'Sullivan, William J.
1944   The San Antonio Kid
        Sheriff of Las Vegas
        Vigilantes of Dodge City
1945   Great Stagecoach Robbery
        Phantom of the Plains
1955   Headline Hunters
Otho, Henry
1936   Treachery Rides the Range
1937   Charlie Chan on Broadway
        Prairie Thunder
1938   Gateway
Otis, Elita Proctor
1914   The Great Diamond Robbery
Otnott, Henry
1950   Panic in the Streets
Otoi, Robert
1951   Go for Broke!
O'Toole, Ollie
1959   The Oregon Trail
O'Toole, Peter
1960   The Day They Robbed the Bank of England
Otten, Alice Morton
1916   Ramona
Ottiano, Rafaela
1936   Mad Holiday
1937   That Girl from Paris
1938   The Toy Wife
Ottinger, Leonora von
1917   The Tell-Tale Step
Ottmar, Carl
1942   All Through the Night

Otto, Frank
1936   After the Thin Man
Otto, Henry
1930   Alma de gaucho
Ottum, Darlene
1945   Nob Hill
Ouhayou, Meyer
1921   Cheated Love
Ouspenskaya, Maria
1939   Judge Hardy and Son
1940   The Man I Married
Outlaw, Martha
1944   Since You Went Away
Overdorff, I. C.
1935?   The Irish Gringo
Overlander, Web
1952   The Quiet Man
Overman, Jack
1945   Johnny Angel
1947   The Mighty McGurk
1948   Unconquered
Overman, Lynne
1934   Broadway Bill
        The Great Flirtation
1938   Spawn of the North
1941   New York Town
1943   Dixie
Overstreet, Artie
1941   Sullivan's Travels
Overstreet, Tommy
1918   The Hell Cat
Overstreet, Tonya
1949   Pinky
Overton, Frank
1950   Mystery Street
        No Way Out
1960   The Dark at the Top of the Stairs
        Wild River
Ovey, George
1938   City Streets
1939   Daughters Courageous
        Stand Up and Fight
1942   Woman of the Year
1943   Yankee Doodle Dandy
Owen, Carroll
1922   The Sign of the Rose
Owen, Cecil same as **Owens, Cecil**
1920   Hidden Charms
1921?   The Supreme Passion
Owen, Eugene
1918   Her Moment
Owen, Garry
1937   The Devil's Playground
1938   Dangerous to Know
1943   Yankee Doodle Dandy
1944   Andy Hardy's Blonde Trouble
        Something for the Boys
1946   Notorious
        Three Wise Fools
1947   It Had To Be You
1948   My Girl Tisa
1949   Knock on Any Door
Owen, Milton
1935   The Winning Ticket
Owen, Myrtle
1920   The Third Woman
Owen, Reginald
1933   Robbers' Roost
1942   Three Hearts for Julia
        We Were Dancing
        Woman of the Year
1945   The Valley of Decision
1946   The Sailor Takes a Wife
Owen, Seena
1915   The Lamb
        The Penitentes
1935   McFadden's Flats
1947   Carnegie Hall
Owen, Tony
1950   The Traveling Saleswoman
Owen, Tudor
1948   Up in Central Park
1949   Top O' the Morning
1954   Arrow in the Dust
Owen, Virginia
1947   Thunder Mountain

Owens, Cecil *see* **Owen, Cecil**
Owens, Charles
1931   Delicious
Harry Owens and His Royal Hawaiians *same as* **Harry Owens and His Royal Hawaiian Orchestra**
1934   Song of the Islands
1942   Song of the Islands
1944   Lake Placid Serenade
Owens, Luella
1955   Brevities of 1955
Owens, Patricia
1960   Hell to Eternity
Owens, Robert C.
1919   Injustice
Owens, Robert F.
1939   Mr. Moto's Last Warning
Owens, Virgil
1928   Absent
Owens, Mrs. Wilhelmina
1919   Injustice
Owin, Rita
1937   Maid of Salem
        That I May Live
1938   The Buccaneer
1940   Mexican Spitfire Out West
Ownbey, Ina
1945   Salome, Where She Danced
Owsley, Monroe
1932   Call Her Savage
        Unashamed
1934   Behold My Wife!
        She Was a Lady
Oyama, Aya
1959   The Crimson Kimono
Oyasato, Henry
1951   Go for Broke!
Oysher, Moishe
1937   The Cantor's Son
1938   The Singing Blacksmith
1940   Overture to Glory
1956   Singing in the Dark
Pablo, Juan J. *same as* **Chang, Li Ho**
1930   Revista Hispano-Americana
Pabst, G. W.
1931   Die Dreigroschenoper
        Die Dreigroschenoper (*foreign version*)
Jose Pacheco and his Continental Orchestra
1936   Song of the Gringo
Pacino, Helen
1933   It's Great to Be Alive
Packer, Netta
1940   Prairie Schooners
1943   Crash Dive
        Let's Have Fun
1947   Desperate
1949   Knock on Any Door
Packer, Peter
1956   7th Cavalry
Padden, Sarah
1931   The Great Meadow
1934   As the Earth Turns
        He Was Her Man
1939   The Adventures of Huckleberry Finn
        Let Freedom Ring
1942   Dr. Gillespie's New Assistant
1943   Jack London
1946   Wild West
1948   The Dude Goes West
1950   The Missourians
1951   Oh! Susanna
Paddock, Charles
1926   The Campus Flirt
Padilla, Margarita
1952   The Fighter
Padilla, Miguel
1954   Passion
Padovani, Lea
1950   Give Us This Day

Padula, Vicente *same as* **Padula, Vincent**
1929   Hambre
1930   Amor audaz
        Charros, gauchos y manolas
        El cuerpo del delito
        Del mismo barro
        La fuerza del querer
        Monsieur le Fox
        El presidio
        El último de los Vargas
1931   Gente alegre
        Las luces de Buenos Aires
1933   Melodía de arrabal
1934   Cuesta abajo
        El tango en Broadway
1955   The Last Command
1956   Serenade
Pagan, William
1940   Lucky Cisco Kid
Pagano, Ernest
1933   Racetrack
Page, Anita
1931   Gentleman's Fate
Page, Bradley
1933   Broken Dreams
1934   He Was Her Man
1935   Chinatown Squad
1936   Ellis Island
1937   Music for Madame
1943   What's Buzzin' Cousin?
Page, David
1950   Catskill Honeymoon
Page, Don *see* **Alvarado, Don**
Page, Dorothy
1950   Catskill Honeymoon
Page, Gale
1939   Daughters Courageous
1940   Knute Rockne—All American
1948   The Time of Your Life
1949   Anna Lucasta
Page, Geraldine
1953   Taxi
1954   Hondo
Page, Joy
1953   Conquest of Cochise
1958   Tonka
Page, Rita
1940   Little Nellie Kelly
Pagel, Raoul
1937   Old Louisiana
1944   Knickerbocker Holiday
Paget, Alfred
1915   The Gambler of the West
        The Lamb
Paget, Debra
1948   Cry of the City
1949   House of Strangers
1950   Broken Arrow
1955   Seven Angry Men
        White Feather
1956   The Last Hunt
Pagett, Gary
1955   Good Morning, Miss Dove
Paige, Al
1959   The FBI Story
Paige, Jean
1918   Find the Woman
Paige, Lillian
1916   The Scarlet Oath
Paige, Mabel
1948   Half Past Midnight
Paige, Marvin
1951   Molly
Paige, Raymond
1938   Hawaii Calls
Paige, Ronald
1939   Fisherman's Wharf
Paige, "Satchel"
1959   The Wonderful Country
Paint, a horse
1942   King of the Stallions
Paisley, James
1951   Warpath
Paiva, Nestor
1940   Santa Fe Trail
1941   Hold Back the Dawn
1945   A Medal for Benny
        Nob Hill
        Salome, Where She Danced

1947   Humoresque
        Robin Hood of Monterey
1948   The Paleface
1950   Young Man with a Horn
1951   The Great Caruso
        Jim Thorpe—All-American
1952   The Fabulous Senorita
1954   Thunder Pass
1956   Comanche
1957   The Guns of Fort Petticoat
Pal, a dog
1954   Passion
Palacios, Isaac
1955   Blackboard Jungle
Palance, Jack *same as* **Palance, Walter Jack**
1950   Panic in the Streets
1953   Arrowhead
1955   Kiss of Fire
Palange, Inez *same as* **Palange, Ines**
1930   Sei tu l'amore
1932   Scarface
1935   A Night at the Opera
1936   It Had to Happen
        Robin Hood of El Dorado
1937   Man of the People
        Song of the City
1938   Little Miss Roughneck
        Road Demon
        Speed to Burn
1939   Winner Take All
1940   Viva Cisco Kid
1941   Caught in the Act
        Romance of the Rio Grande
        Under Fiesta Stars
1948   Unconquered
1953   Cry of the Hunted
1956   Hot Blood
Palasthy, Alex
1938   City Streets
        Happy Landing
        Road Demon
Palca, Alfred
1951   The Harlem Globetrotters
Palencia, Ceferino
1930   Toda una vida
Palermi, Amleto
1930   Doña mentiras (*foreign version*)
Paley, Natalie
1935   L'homme des Folies Bergère
Palfi, Lotte *could be same as* **Brooks, Jean**
1940   Escape
Palfy, Lou
1945   Wanderer of the Wasteland
Pall, Gloria
1959   The Crimson Kimono
Pallais, Carmen
1947   Ride the Pink Horse
1952   The Iron Mistress
Pallais, Dorita
1952   The Iron Mistress
Pallette, Eugene
1916   Gretchen, the Greenhorn
1917   The Bond Between
1926   The Fighting Edge
1930   The Kibitzer
1931   Fighting Caravans
        Huckleberry Finn
1935   Bordertown
1940   The Mark of Zorro
1942   Tales of Manhattan
1943   The Gang's All Here
1944   Lake Placid Serenade
Palma, Andrea
1936   La última cita
1939   La Inmaculada
Palma, Joseph
1938   City Streets
1941   Mystery Ship
1944   The Racket Man
1945   The Bells of St. Mary's
        Escape in the Fog
        I Love a Bandleader
1947   It Had To Be You
        The Jolson Story

1948   The Lady from Shanghai
1949   Knock on Any Door
        The Undercover Man
1950   Emergency Wedding
1956   Hot Blood
Palmer, Betsy
1955   The Long Gray Line
1957   The Tin Star
1959   The Last Angry Man
Palmer, Byron
1953   Tonight We Sing
Palmer, Charles
1948   Reaching from Heaven
1949   Lost Boundaries
Palmer, Corliss
1928   George Washington Cohen
        The Night Bird
Palmer, Devore
1916   A Woman's Honor
Fred Palmer's Orchestra
1940   The Notorious Elinor Lee
Palmer, Gregg *same as* **Lee, Palmer**
1952   The Battle at Apache Pass
        The Raiders
        Red Ball Express
1953   Column South
1954   Taza, Son of Cochise
1957   Revolt at Fort Laramie
Palmer, Jasper L.
1945   The Navajo Trail
        Salome, Where She Danced
1946   Bringing Up Father
1947   King of the Bandits
1948   Unconquered
Palmer, Jimmie
1949   Tale of the Navajos
Palmer, Lilli
1947   Body and Soul
1948   My Girl Tisa
Palmer, Maria
1946   Rendezvous 24
Palmer, May
1918   One More American
Palmer, Maybelle
1936   Dimples
1938   The Beloved Brat
Palmer, Shirley
1927   With Sitting Bull at the Spirit Lake Massacre
Palmese, Emma
1949   House of Strangers
1958   The Last Hurrah
Palsa, Nani
1934   White Heat
Panama, Norman
1947   It Had To Be You
1959   The Jayhawkers!
Pancho and Dolores *same as* **Brown, Dolores** (*African-American singer*); **Hagood, Kenny "Pancho"**
1947   Jivin' in Be-Bop
Pangborn, Franklin
1934   Imitation of Life
1940   Elsa Maxwell's Public Deb No. 1
1941   Sullivan's Travels
        Where Did You Get That Girl?
1946   The Sailor Takes a Wife
1947   Calendar Girl
Panzer, Paul *not the same as* **Panzer, Paul W.**
1915   The Spender
        Under Southern Skies
1916   Broken Fetters
1919   Who's Your Brother?
1922   The Mohican's Daughter
1927   Sally in Our Alley
1928   George Washington Cohen
1929   Hawk of the Hills
        Redskin
1930   Los que danzan (*foreign version*)
1931   Cavalier of the West

Panzer, Paul W. *not the same as*
Panzer, Paul
1937   Charlie Chan at the
        Olympics
        Prairie Thunder
1938   Happy Landing
1940   East of the River
1942   Juke Girl
1943   Action in the North
        Atlantic
1947   Humoresque
Paoli, Raoul
1928   Kit Carson
1931   La gran jornada (*foreign
        version*)
Papadopoulos, Elias
1954   Barefoot Battalion
Papana, Alex
1943   Gangway for Tomorrow
Papas, Lola
1931   Such Is Life
Papashvily, George
1952   Anything Can Happen
Pape, Lionel
1937   Slave Ship
1938   Outside of Paradise
        The Rage of Paris
1939   Drums Along the Mohawk
1942   We Were Dancing
Pappas, Alma
1942   Song of the Islands
Pappas, Jack
1953   Beneath the 12-Mile Reef
Pappas, Michael
1953   Beneath the 12-Mile Reef
Paquin, Robert
1939   Lying Lips
1940   The Notorious Elinor Lee
Paralupi, Benjamin Ingénito *see*
        Ellis, Paul
Paramore, Edward E., Jr. *same as*
        Paramore, Edward, Jr.
1931   Fighting Caravans
1939   Man of Conquest
Pardee, Ada
1932   Parigi affascina; ovvero,
        Malavita
Parera, Valentín
1930   Un hombre de suerte
1933   Yo, tú y ella
1934   Dos más uno, dos
        Granaderos del amor
1935   Señora casada necesita
        marido
Parillo, Lauretta
1937   Man of the People
Paris, George
1947   Northwest Outpost
Paris, Jerry
1950   Battleground
1952   Bright Victory
1953   The Glass Wall
1955   Good Morning, Miss Dove
        Marty
        Not As a Stranger
        The View from Pompey's
        Head
Paris, Jonni
1955   Seminole Uprising
Paris, Manuel *same as* **Conesa,**
        Manuel; París, Manuel
1929   Sombras habaneras
1930   The Bad Man (*foreign
        version*)
        Charros, gauchos y
        manolas
        El cuerpo del delito
        Estrellados
        La fuerza del querer
        Monsieur le Fox
        El valiente
1931   Cheri-Bibi
        El proceso de Mary
        Dugan
1932   El caballero de la noche
1933   Espérame
        Melodía de arrabal
1935   Piernas de seda
        Rosa de Francia
1936   El diablo del mar
1938   Charlie Chan at Monte
        Carlo

1943   The Leopard Man
1945   Betrayal from the East
1947   The Foxes of Harrow
1951   Across the Wide Missouri
        Cuban Fireball
        The Great Caruso
1955   Blackboard Jungle
1956   Hot Blood
Paris, Yvonne
1918   Tony America
Park, Ida May
1916   The Gilded Spider
        The Grip of Jealousy
Park, Post
1941   The Pioneers
1949   She Wore a Yellow
        Ribbon
1954   Massacre Canyon
Parke, Eddie
1947   Dark Delusion
Parke, Macdonald
1959   John Paul Jones
Parke, William
1920   The Paliser Case
Parker, Albert
1918   Shifting Sands
Parker, Barnett
1940   If I Had My Way
Parker, Ben
1940   George Washington
        Carver
        Overture to Glory
Parker, Carol
1938   Dangerous to Know
Parker, Cecilia
1932   Mystery Ranch
        The Rainbow Trail
1935   Naughty Marietta
1936   Below the Deadline
1939   Judge Hardy and Son
1942   Seven Sweethearts
Parker, Dolores
1949   House of Strangers
Parker, Ed *same as* **Parker, Eddie;**
        Parker, Edwin
1931   Delicious
1934   The Star Packer
1940   Northwest Passage (Book
        I—Rogers' Rangers)
1942   They Died With Their
        Boots On
1945   Escape in the Fog
1947   The Adventures of Don
        Coyote
        My Wild Irish Rose
1949   Knock on Any Door
1952   Apache Country
        The Raiders
1953   The Man from the Alamo
1956   Reprisal!
1959   Imitation of Life
Parker, Eleanor
1945   Pride of the Marines
Parker, Fess
1955   Davy Crockett, King of
        the Wild Frontier
1956   Davy Crockett and the
        River Pirates
        Westward Ho the
        Wagons!
1958   The Light in the Forest
1959   The Jayhawkers!
Parker, Franklin
1934   Operator 13
1937   Charlie Chan on
        Broadway
1938   Mr. Moto's Gamble
1944   Slightly Terrific
1945   The Dolly Sisters
1949   The Undercover Man
1952   Bugles in the Afternoon
Parker, Fred
1931   Riders of the Rio
1932   The Galloping Kid
Parker, Jack
1946   Till the End of Time
        Without Reservations
1953   The Man Behind the Gun
1956   7th Cavalry

Parker, Jean
1934   Lazy River
        Limehouse Blues
        Operator 13
1937   The Barrier
1943   Deerslayer
Parker, Jefferson
1936   Human Cargo
Parker, Jetsy
1941   Louisiana Purchase
Parker, John
1947   Bells of San Fernando
Parker, Linda
1935   Naughty Marietta
Parker, Loti
1945   South of the Rio Grande
Parker, Murray
1959   The Black Orchid
Parker, Norton S.
1927   Roarin' Broncs
1936   Tundra
1938   Outlaw Express
1949   Arctic Fury
Parker, Obie
1950   The Men
Parker, Penny
1960   The Dark at the Top of
        the Stairs
Parker, Thelma
1919   A Fallen Idol
Parker, Willard
1950   Bandit Queen
        Emergency Wedding
1951   Apache Drums
1953   Sangaree
1960   Walk Tall
Parker, William
1917   The Winged Mystery
1921   The Cave Girl
Parkhill, Forbes
1939   Stand Up and Fight
Parkington, Beulah
1936   Ramona
1949   Knock on Any Door
Parkinson, Cliff
1943   Border Patrol
1944   Buffalo Bill
        The San Antonio Kid
1951   Apache Drums
Parks, Eddie
1946   Abie's Irish Rose
        Cuban Pete
1947   Desperate
1948   Cry of the City
        The Luck of the Irish
1949   The Sky Dragon
1951   Cuban Fireball
        Slaughter Trail
Parks, George
1916   The King's Game
Parks, Larry
1941   Mystery Ship
1942   Submarine Raider
1943   Deerslayer
        Redhead from Manhattan
1944   The Racket Man
1947   The Jolson Story
1950   Emergency Wedding
        Jolson Sings Again
Parks, Nanette
1948   The Time of Your Life
Parlo, Dita
1931   Kismet
        La llama sagrada (*foreign
        version*)
        Tropennächte
Parma, Tula
1943   The Leopard Man
Parmenter, Margaret
1950   Panic in the Streets
Parnell, Effie
1942   Syncopation
Parnell, Emory
1939   Let Freedom Ring
1940   If I Had My Way
1941   Louisiana Purchase
        Sullivan's Travels
1942   All Through the Night
        Apache Trail
        Gentleman Jim
        Little Tokyo, U.S.A.
        Syncopation
        Wings for the Eagle

1943   Mr. Lucky
        The Outlaw
1944   Address Unknown
        Andy Hardy's Blonde
        Trouble
1946   Abie's Irish Rose
1947   Calendar Girl
1949   Massacre River
        Rose of the Yukon
1950   Rock Island Trail
1951   Show Boat
1954   Battle of Rogue River
Parnell, James *same as* **Parnell,**
        Jimmie
1951   Apache Drums
1952   Anything Can Happen
1953   War Paint
1955   Shotgun
1957   War Drums
Parola, Danièle
1934   La veuve joyeuse
Parr, Charles T.
1918   The Kaiser's Finish
Parra, Josephine
1951   Apache Drums
Parrish, Edna
1954   Taza, Son of Cochise
Parrish, Helen
1931   Cimarron
1941   Where Did You Get That
        Girl?
Parrish, Imboden
1938   Gateway
1939   Charlie Chan in Reno
Parrish, John
1948   Four Faces West
1952   Hiawatha
        Wagons West
Parrish, Pat
1944   They Live in Fear
Parrish, Patty
1938   In Old Chicago
Parrish, Robert
1928   Mother Machree
1937   It Could Happen to You
1959   The Wonderful Country
Parro, Molly
1921   Puppets of Fate
Parrott, James
1931   Monerías
        Noche de duendes
        Pardon Us
        Pardon Us (*foreign
        version*)
Parry, Barbara
1957   War Drums
1958   Fort Bowie
Parry, Harvey *same as* **Perry,**
        Harvey
1935   The Irish in Us
1936   After the Thin Man
1938   Happy Landing
1939   Winner Take All
1943   Good Luck, Mr. Yates
1952   The Iron Mistress
1958   The Last Hurrah
Parry, Ivan
1948   Red River
Parry, Paul
1935   So Red the Rose
Parsons, Harriet
1948   I Remember Mama
Parsons, Lindsley
1936   Song of the Gringo
1941   The Gang's All Here
        King of the Zombies
        You're Out of Luck
1943   Crime Smasher
1945   South of the Rio Grande
1949   Tuna Clipper
1952   Arctic Flight
        Desert Pursuit
1957   Dragoon Wells Massacre
1958   Oregon Passage
Parsons, Louella
1946   Without Reservations
Parsons, Milton
1939   Judge Hardy and Son
1940   Behind the News
1941   Dead Men Tell
1942   Castle in the Desert
        Mokey
        Whispering Ghosts

1944 Cry of the Werewolf
1946 Dark Alibi
1947 The Mighty McGurk
1948 Shanghai Chest
1953 Last of the Comanches
Parsons, Patsy Lee
1943 Yankee Doodle Dandy
Partington, Dorothy
1960 Ice Palace
Parton, Reg
1955 Chief Crazy Horse
1956 The Last Frontier
1958 Apache Territory
Partos, Frank
1936 Rose of the Rancho
1951 The House on Telegraph
Hill
Partos, Gus *same as* **Pártos,
Gusztáv**
1928 Vamping Venus
1930 El secreto del doctor
(*foreign version*)
Pascal, Eddie
1935 The Yiddish King Lear
Pascal, Ernest
1930 El último de los Vargas
1934 As the Earth Turns
1943 Jack London
1946 Canyon Passage
Pascal, Vicente X.
1932 Amor y vida
Pasch, Reginald
1931 Dämon des Meeres
El proceso de Mary
Dugan (*foreign
version*)
1960 Man on a String
Paseler, Myrtle
1940 The Ramparts We Watch
Pasetto, Angelo
1960 The Crowning
Experience
Pasha, Kalla
1923 Breaking into Society
Ruggles of Red Gap
Thirty Days
1926 Rose of the Tenements
1927 The Dove
Paskewich, Jeannette
1935 The Yiddish King Lear
Pasley, Fred
1932 Scarface
Pasque, Ernst
1922 The Five Dollar Baby
Pasquero, Margherita
1955 The Rose Tattoo
Pasques, Christian
1958 The Young Lions
Pastellides, Nino
1950 Give Us This Day
Pasternak, Joe *same as* **Pasternak,
Joseph**
1942 Seven Sweethearts
1948 Big City
1949 The Kissing Bandit
That Midnight Kiss
1950 The Toast of New Orleans
1951 The Great Caruso
Pataki, Michael
1958 The Young Lions
Pataky, Veronica
1948 The Miracle of the Bells
Pate, Michael
1954 Hondo
1956 Reprisal!
7th Cavalry
1957 The Oklahoman
1960 Walk Like a Dragon
Paterson, Pat
1935 Charlie Chan in Egypt
Paton, Stuart
1918 The Border Raiders
The Girl in the Dark
The Wine Girl
1919 The Little Diplomat
1924 The Night Hawk
1931 Chinatown After Dark
Paton, Tony
1942 North to the Klondike
1947 California
The Peanut Man

Patorno, Anthony
1938 The Buccaneer
Patric, Gil
1947 Buffalo Bill Rides Again
Patrick, Cynthia
1956 The Benny Goodman
Story
Patrick, Dorothy *same as* **Davis,
Dorothy Patrick**
1947 The Mighty McGurk
New Orleans
1950 Belle of Old Mexico
1954 Thunder Pass
1955 The View from Pompey's
Head
Violent Saturday
Patrick, Edward
1939 Reform School
Patrick, Gail
1934 Wagon Wheels
1938 Dangerous to Know
1939 Man of Conquest
1942 Tales of Manhattan
We Were Dancing
1947 Calendar Girl
Patrick, Jack *not the same as*
Patrick, John (*actor*)
1956 Daniel Boone, Trail
Blazer
Patrick, John (*writer*)
1937 One Mile from Heaven
1938 Mr. Moto Takes a Chance
Patrick, John (*actor*) *not the same
as* **Patrick, Jack**
1955 Santa Fe Passage
Patrick, Lee
1937 Border Cafe
Music for Madame
1939 Fisherman's Wharf
1942 In This Our Life
1948 Singin' Spurs
1950 The Lawless
Patrick, Mil
1951 Westward the Women
1957 Raintree County
Patrick, Nigel
1957 Raintree County
Patrick, Robert
1958 Tonka
Patricola, Tom *same as* **Patricola,
Tomas**
1929 Frozen Justice
1930 El precio de un beso
1941 Louisiana Purchase
1945 Rhapsody in Blue
Patrinakos, Father
1953 The Glory Brigade
Patten, Jane
1941 The Mexican Spitfire's
Baby
1942 Syncopation
Patten, Luana
1946 Song of the South
1947 Little Mister Jim
1957 Joe Dakota
Patten, Minerva
1934 Song of the Islands
Patten, William
1925 Warrior Gap
Patter Poe
1936 Custer's Last Stand
Patterson & Jackson
1948 Killer Diller
Patterson, Bob
1958 Tonka
Patterson, Elizabeth
1932 So Big
1933 Ever in My Heart
1935 So Red the Rose
1941 Belle Starr
1942 The Vanishing Virginian
1950 Intruder in the Dust
1959 The Oregon Trail
Patterson, Frances Taylor
1926 Broken Hearts
Patterson, Hank
1946 Santa Fe Uprising
Wild Beauty
1949 The Cowboy and the
Indians
1952 California Conquest
Indian Uprising
Rose of Cimarron

1958 Escape from Red Rock
Terror in a Texas Town
1959 Gunmen from Laredo
Patterson, Isabel
1916 Broken Fetters
Patterson, J. Patrick
1949? The Joint Is Jumpin'
Patterson, Jack
1922 Pals of the West
Patterson, Jessie
1947 The Peanut Man
Patterson, John
1938 The Buccaneer
Daughter of Shanghai
Patterson, Kenneth
1948 The Boy with Green Hair
1959 Night of the Quarter
Moon
1960 The Plunderers
Patterson, Mary
1947 It Had To Be You
Patterson, Neva
1953 Taxi
Patterson, Patsy (*child actress*)
1944 Hi, Beautiful
Patterson, Patti
1936 Show Boat
Patterson, Sam
1938 God's Step Children
Patterson, Shirley
1943 Good Luck, Mr. Yates
Let's Have Fun
Redhead from Manhattan
1944 Riding West
1945 Between Two Women
Patterson, Starke
1921 Wolves of the North
Patterson, Tilford
1947 Juke Joint
Patterson, Warren
1947 Boy! What a Girl!
Pattison, Ronnie
1945 Nob Hill
A Tree Grows in Brooklyn
Patton, Bill
1926 Under Fire
1928 Orphan of the Sage
1934 The Battling Buckaroo
Fighting Through
Patton, Doris
1951 Oh! Susanna
Patton, Freddie B.
1950 Intruder in the Dust
Patton, Jonella
1922 Foolish Lives
Patton, Marguerite
1922 Foolish Lives
Patton, Mary
1960 The Dark at the Top of
the Stairs
Patton, Virginia
1946 Canyon Passage
1947 The Burning Cross
Paul, Adolph
1930 El precio de un beso
Paul, Elliot *same as* **Paul, Elliott**
1945 Rhapsody in Blue
1947 New Orleans
Paul, Eugenia
1957 Apache Warrior
1960 The Sign of Zorro
Paul, Ike
1927 The Broken Violin
Paul, Logan
1916 Britton of the Seventh
Paul, "Manhattan"
1949? Harlem Follies
Paul, Pat
1951 Westward the Women
Paul, Rene
1949 C-Man
Paul, Val
1918 The Red, Red Heart
1923 Crashin' Thru
Paul, Victor
1950 Battleground
1951 Gambling House

Pavan, Marisa
1954 Drum Beat
1955 The Rose Tattoo
1957 The Midnight Story
1959 John Paul Jones
Pavanelli, Livio
1930 Doña mentiras (*foreign
version*)
Pavelec, Teddy
1950 Right Cross
Paver, Chaver
1939 The Light Ahead
Pavis, Marie
1921 The First Born
Pawl, Nick
1960 Pay or Die
Pawley, Edward
1932 Thirteen Women
1933 Olsen's Big Moment
1938 Dangerous to Know
Pawley, William
1933 Robbers' Roost
1937 That I May Live
1940 East of the River
Elsa Maxwell's Public
Deb No. 1
Pawley, William, Jr.
1960 The Crowning
Experience
Pawn, Doris
1917 The Spirit of '76
1918 The City of Dim Faces
1919 Toby's Bow
1920 Li Ting Lang
1921 Guile of Women
Shame
Paxton, Dick *see* **Paxton, Richard**
Paxton, John
1944 My Pal Wolf
1947 Crossfire
Paxton, Richard *same as* **Paxton,
Dick**
1942 Syncopation
1947 Dark Delusion
1950 No Way Out
1951 Little Big Horn
Mask of the Dragon
1952 The Iron Mistress
1953 Arrowhead
1955 Seven Angry Men
Paxton, Sidney
1925 The Midnight Girl
Payetta, Lou
1944 Chip Off the Old Block
Payne, Clarence
1920 Who's Your Servant?
Payne, Herbert
1915 The Pageant of San
Francisco
Payne, John
1939 Bad Lands
1941 Sun Valley Serenade
1945 The Dolly Sisters
1955 Santa Fe Passage
Payne, Louis *same as* **Payne, Lou**
1929 Evangeline
1946 Saratoga Trunk
Payne, Sally
1941 Playmates
Payne, Sidney
1920 The Devil's Claim
1936 Below the Deadline
Payson, Blanche
1937 That I May Live
Payton, Barbara
1951 Only the Valiant
Payton, Claude
1935 A Night at the Opera
Payton, Gloria
1921 Where Lights Are Low
Paz, Carlos de la
1936 El crimen de media
noche
Peacocke, Capt. Leslie T.
1919 Injustice
1920? Reformation
Pearce, Betty
1918 Little Red Decides
Real Folks

Pearce, George *same as* **Pierce, George**
1915 The Gambler of the West
The Sable Lorcha
1916 Little Meena's Romance
1917 A Jewel in Pawn
1918 Little Red Decides
Real Folks
1919 A Yankee Princess
1938 Little Miss Roughneck

Pearce, Peggy
1919 False Evidence
1920 A Tokio Siren

Pearce, Perce
1946 Song of the South

Pearl, Lillian
1936 Rose of the Rancho

Pearl, Lloyd
1916 A Sister of Six

Pearlman, Max
1939 Mamele

Pearse, Tom *could be same as* **Persse, Thomas H.**
1920 It's a Great Life

Pearson, Beatrice
1949 Lost Boundaries

Pearson, Charles
1923 Flames of Wrath

Pearson, Drew
1945 Betrayal from the East

Pearson, Eva
1948 Up in Central Park

Pearson, Fort
1951 Queen for a Day

Pearson, Humphrey
1934 The Great Flirtation
1935 Ruggles of Red Gap

Pearson, Josephine
1939 One Dark Night

Pearson, Virginia
1918 The Firebrand
The Liar

Pearson, W. B.
1917 The Bronze Bride

Peary, Harold
1956 Wetbacks

Peck, Charles K., Jr.
1953 Seminole

Peck, Gladys
1915 Hearts of Men

Peck, Gregory
1945 The Valley of Decision
1947 Duel in the Sun
1948 Gentleman's Agreement
1951 Only the Valiant

Peck, Steven
1948 Moonrise

Peckre, Maurice
1920 Humoresque

Pedi, Tom
1948 Up in Central Park

Pedlar, Gertrude
1920 White Youth
1936 Ramona

Pedraza, Samuel
1930 Charros, gauchos y manolas
1932 Hollywood, ciudad de ensueño

Pedrini, John
1949 House of Strangers
1960 Ice Palace

Pedrini, Rene
1943 The Leopard Man

Pedroza, Alfonso
1930 Una cana al aire
La jaula de los leones
Locuras de amor
1931 Noche de duendes
Pardon Us (*foreign version*)
1934 La buenaventura
1935 El cantante de Nápoles
1937 Waikiki Wedding
1938 Di que me quieres
1949 We Were Strangers

Peed, William
1946 Song of the South

Peerce, Jan
1947 Carnegie Hall
1953 Tonight We Sing

Peers, Joan
1930 Anybody's War
Around the Corner

Pegg, Vester
1918 Wild Women
1934 Judge Priest
1935 The Little Colonel
1936 The Prisoner of Shark Island

Peggy, Baby *see* **Montgomery, Peggy**

Peil, Edward, Jr. *same as* **Peil, Ed**
1940 Santa Fe Trail
1948 Call Northside 777
The Lady from Shanghai

Peil, Edward, Sr. *same as* **Peil, Edward; Piel, Eddie**
1916 At Piney Ridge
1918 The Greatest Thing in Life
1921 That Girl Montana
1923 Purple Dawn
1929 Masked Emotions
1931 The Avenger
1932 Charlie Chan's Chance
The Hatchet Man
1934 Our Daily Bread
1936 Dangerous Intrigue
Show Boat
1940 Geronimo
1942 Foreign Agent
Juke Girl
Shut My Big Mouth
Unseen Enemy
1947 The Last Round-Up
1948 The Miracle of the Bells
Up in Central Park
1950 Colt .45

Pelletier, Yvonne
1931 Young Sinners
1938 The Buccaneer

Pellicana
1934 Laughing Boy

Peltz, Paul
1950 The Men

Peluffo, Manuel
1934 Cuesta abajo
El tango en Broadway
1935 El día que me quieras
Piernas de seda
Tango Bar
Te quiero con locura

Pemberton, Marjorie
1950 Young Man with a Horn

Pembroke, George
1948 Call Northside 777
1952 Red Snow
1959 The FBI Story

Pembroke, Scott
1930 The Last Dance

Pena, Andrew
1940 Northwest Passage (Book I—Rogers' Rangers)

Peña, Carmela
1939 Miracle on Main Street (*foreign version*)

Peña, Julio
1930 Doña mentiras
1931 Esclavas de la moda
La fruta amarga
Mamá
La mujer X
1933 Primavera en otoño
Una viuda romántica
Yo, tú y ella
1934 Un capitán de cosacos
La ciudad de cartón
1935 Alas sobre el Chaco
Angelina o el honor de un brigadier
Julieta compra un hijo
Rosa de Francia

Peña Illescas, Luis
1930 Toda una vida

Peña Sánchez, Luis
1931 La carta

Peña "Pepet", José
1930 Charros, gauchos y manolas
El dios del mar
La jaula de los leones
1931 El comediante
La mujer X
El príncipe gondolero
El tenorio del harem
1932 Soñadores de la gloria
1933 No dejes la puerta abierta
Yo, tú y ella
1934 La ciudad de cartón
Granaderos del amor
1935 Angelina o el honor de un brigadier
¡Asegure a su mujer!
Julieta compra un hijo
No matarás
Piernas de seda
Rosa de Francia
Señora casada necesita marido
1936 Contra la corriente
El crimen de media noche
1937 El capitán Tormenta
1938 Castillos en el aire
Mis dos amores
La vida bohemia
1939 Los hijos mandan
La Inmaculada
El otro soy yo
Papá soltero
El trovador de la radio
1940 Cuando canta la Ley
Tengo fe en ti

Penalver, Clarence
1928 The Midnight Ace

Pendleton, Gaylord *same as* **Carson, Jack** (*western actor*); **Pendleton, Steve**
1931 Young Sinners
1935 Circle of Death
1940 Geronimo
Knute Rockne—All American
Young Buffalo Bill
1942 Sunday Punch
1947 The Return of Rin Tin Tin
Untamed Fury
1949 Ride, Ryder, Ride!
Roll Thunder Roll!
The Sky Dragon
1950 Battleground
A Lady Without Passport
Rio Grande
Sunset in the West
1952 Indian Uprising
Trail of the Arrow

Pendleton, Karen
1956 Westward Ho the Wagons!

Pendleton, Nat
1930 The Big Pond
1931 Mr. Lemon of Orange
1932 Flesh
1934 The Cat's-Paw
Lazy River
Straight Is the Way
1937 Life Begins in College
Song of the City
1940 New Moon
Northwest Passage (Book I—Rogers' Rangers)
1942 Dr. Gillespie's New Assistant
1943 Dr. Gillespie's Criminal Case
1947 Buck Privates Come Home

Penn, John
1950 Give Us This Day

Penn, Leo *not the same as* **Penn, Leonard**
1949 The Undercover Man

Penn, Leonard *not the same as* **Penn, Leo**
1938 The Toy Wife
1940 The Way of All Flesh
1950 The Girl from San Lorenzo
1954 Drum Beat

Penna, Big Eagle
1936 Ramona

Pennachi
1958 Seven Hills of Rome

Pennario, Leonard
1937 Song of the City

Pennell, Larry
1955 The Far Horizons
Seven Angry Men
1959 The FBI Story

Penney, Edmund
1955 Fort Yuma

Pennick, Jack *same as* **Pennick, J. Ronald; Pennick, Ronald J.**
1936 The Prisoner of Shark Island
1937 Big City
The Devil's Playground
1939 Drums Along the Mohawk
1941 Lady from Louisiana
1948 Fort Apache
Unconquered
1949 The Fighting Kentuckian
She Wore a Yellow Ribbon
3 Godfathers
1950 Rio Grande
Rock Island Trail
1953 The Sun Shines Bright
1955 The Long Gray Line
1956 The Last Frontier
1958 The Last Hurrah
1960 Sergeant Rutledge

Pennington, Ann
1917 The Little Boy Scout
1929 Is Everybody Happy?

Penny, Frank
1942 Rio Rita
1945 The Dolly Sisters

Pentzer, Kate
1935 Rescue Squad

Peón, Ramón
1931 El código penal
Del infierno al cielo

Peoples, Bob
1952 Fort Osage
1953 Arrowhead
1959 The FBI Story

Peoples, Neva
1938 The Duke Is Tops
1946 Mantan Messes Up

Pepitone, Nino
1942 Submarine Raider

Pepper, Barbara
1934 Our Daily Bread
1935 The Singing Vagabond
1936 Show Boat
Winterset
1937 Music for Madame
1941 Birth of the Blues
1944 An American Romance
Since You Went Away
1950 No Way Out
1953 The Eddie Cantor Story

Pepper, Bob
1946 Without Reservations

Pepper, Dave
1936 General Spanky

Pepper, Florence
1946 Sunset Pass

Pepper, Jack
1957 Beau James

Peralta, Gabriel
1952 The Iron Mistress

Percival, Walter
1931 The Avenger
Smart Money

Percy, Eileen
1919 Desert Gold
The Gray Horizon
Told in the Hills
1920 The Man Who Dared
1921 Little Miss Hawkshaw
1924 Tongues of Flame
1925 Cobra
1932 The Cohens and Kellys in Hollywood

Perdrière, Hélène
1932 La foule hurle

Perdue, Derelys
1924   Untamed Youth
Pereda, Ramón
1930   Amor audaz
       Cascarrabias
       El cuerpo del delito
       El dios del mar
       Galas de la Paramount
1931   Carne de cabaret
       La dama atrevida
       Gente alegre
       El proceso de Mary
         Dugan
1932   Hombres en mi vida
1935   No matarás
1936   El crimen de media
         noche
       El diablo del mar
Pereira, William L.
1945   Johnny Angel
Perez (*dancer*)
1936   Robin Hood of El Dorado
Perez, Giuseppe
1932   Amore e morte
Pérez, John *could be same as*
   Perez, José
1936   Contra la corriente
Perez, José *could be same as* **Pérez,**
   John
1938   California Frontier
1939   El otro soy yo
1949   We Were Strangers
Perez, Olga
1947   Ride the Pink Horse
Perez, Paul
1928   Chinatown Charlie
1930   El valiente
1931   Del infierno al cielo
       Hay que casar al príncipe
       La ley del harem
1932   El caballero de la noche
1933   It's Great to Be Alive
       It's Great to Be Alive
         (*foreign version*)
       La melodía prohibida
       No dejes la puerta abierta
       El rey de los gitanos
       Una viuda romántica
1935   Piernas de seda
       Te quiero con locura
1936   The Last of the Mohicans
1939   La Inmaculada
Perez, Pepito
1945   A Medal for Benny
1947   California
1951   The Raging Tide
Perez, Pia
1932   Amore e morte
Periolat, George
1917   Southern Pride
1918? Rosemary Climbs the
         Heights
1919   The Tiger Lily
1920   The Mark of Zorro
1921   The Kiss
1928   The Secret Hour
Perkins, Alberta
1934   Drums O' Voodoo
1941   Murder on Lenox Avenue
       Sunday Sinners
Perkins, Anthony
1957   The Tin Star
Perkins, G. William
1952   Red Snow
Perkins, Gilbert V. *same as*
   Perkins, Gil
1951   Show Boat
1952   Brave Warrior
1953   The Member of the
         Wedding
1959   Gunmen from Laredo
Perkins, Osgood
1929   Mother's Boy
1932   Scarface
Perkins, Valentine
1950   Rock Island Trail
Perkins, Voltaire
1953   Sangaree
1955   The Far Horizons
       A Man Called Peter
1958   The Young Lions

Perkins, War
1941   Sullivan's Travels
Perl, Alan
1938   The Toy Wife
Perlberg, William
1943   The Meanest Man in the
         World
1945   Where Do We Go From
         Here?
1952   Anything Can Happen
1957   The Tin Star
Perley, Charles
1915   The Gambler of the West
Perna, Billy
1953   The Eddie Cantor Story
Perojo, Benito
1930   Un hombre de suerte
1931   Mamá
Perrault, Serge
1953   Tonight We Sing
Perreau, Gerald
1944   Hi, Beautiful
Perreau, Gigi *same as* **Perreau,**
   Ghislaine; Perreau, Gillian
1944   Dark Waters
       Mr. Skeffington
Perreau, Janine
1950   Battleground
Perret, Léonce
1920   Lifting Shadows
1921   The Money Maniac
Perrin, Dolly
1945   Where Do We Go From
         Here?
Perrin, Jack
1922   The Guttersnipe
1934   The Cactus Kid
1935   North of Arizona
       Wolf Riders
1936   Hair-Trigger Casey
1938   The Texans
1940   New Moon
1950   Bandit Queen
1951   Jim Thorpe—All-American
1955   Apache Ambush
Perrin, Nat
1936   Dimples
       Rose of the Rancho
1947   The Mighty McGurk
1950   Emergency Wedding
Perrin, Patsy
1938   In Old Chicago
1942   Song of the Islands
Perrin, Victor
1952   The Iron Mistress
Perrott, Ruth
1960   All the Fine Young
         Cannibals
Perry, Augusta
1918   Love's Law
Perry, Barbara
1933   Counsellor at Law
1944   Hi, Beautiful
Perry, Ben L.
1957   The Brothers Rico
1958   Terror in a Texas Town
Perry, Bob *same as* **Perry, Robert**
1925   The Thundering Herd
1927   White Gold
1935   Rendezvous
1936   Robin Hood of El Dorado
1937   Manhattan
         Merry-Go-Round
1938   Mr. Moto's Gamble
1941   Mystery Ship
1942   All Through the Night
       They Died With Their
         Boots On
       Woman of the Year
1943   Good Luck, Mr. Yates
1944   Buffalo Bill
1950   Right Cross
1958   The Last Hurrah
Perry, Charles
1947   It Had To Be You
1950   Jolson Sings Again
1953   The Member of the
         Wedding
Perry, David
1948   The Miracle of the Bells

Perry, Fayette
1916   Silks and Satins
Perry, Fred
1932   Le plombier amoureux
Perry, Harvey *see* **Parry, Harvey**
Perry, Ida
1931   Chérie (*foreign version*)
Perry, Jack
1936   Rose of the Rancho
1939   Charlie Chan in Reno
       Mr. Moto's Last Warning
1945   Where Do We Go From
         Here?
1949   Knock on Any Door
Perry, Jean
1931   El proceso de Mary
         Dugan (*foreign
         version*)
1934   La veuve joyeuse
1938   Charlie Chan at Monte
         Carlo
Perry, Jessie
1934   Stand Up and Cheer!
Perry, Joan
1936   Dangerous Intrigue
Perry, Katherine
1921   A Divorce of
         Convenience
1932   Call Her Savage
Perry, Naomi
1956   Full of Life
Perry, Patricia
1960   Wild River
Perry, Robert *see* **Perry, Bob**
Perry, Roger L.
1948   The Boy with Green Hair
1956   Reprisal!
Perry, Stevie
1960   This Rebel Breed
Perry, Susan *same as* **Howard,**
   Linda
1949   The Kissing Bandit
       Knock on Any Door
Perry, Vincent
1955   Good Morning, Miss Dove
Perry, Walter
1917   The Sudden Gentleman
1918   Little Red Decides
1922   The Guttersnipe
       The Scrapper
       Second Hand Rose
1927   Irish Hearts
1930   Kathleen Mavourneen
Perry, Wanda
1948   Call Northside 777
1950   Jolson Sings Again
Perryman, Lloyd
1950   Rio Grande
Pershing, Frank
1951   The Great Caruso
Persoff, Nehemiah
1958   The Badlanders
1959   Al Capone
Person, Tiny
1940   Too Many Girls
Persse, Thomas H. *could be same
   as* **Pearse, Tom**
1920   Uncharted Channels
Persson, Eugene
1948   The Paleface
Perugini, Frank
1927   The Scar of Shame
Peters Sisters
1947   Hi De Ho
Peters, Brock
1954   Carmen Jones
1959   Porgy and Bess
Peters, Casey
1960   All the Fine Young
         Cannibals
Peters, Frank
1953   The Jazz Singer
Peters, Grant
1937   Life Begins in College
Peters, Hattie *could be same as*
   Peters, Mattie
1920   White Youth
Peters, House, Jr.
1948   Renegades of Sonora
1949   Rose of the Yukon

Peters, Jean
1954   Apache
       Broken Lance
1955   A Man Called Peter
Peters, John *same as* **Peters, John**
   S.
1927   The Frontiersman
1936   Border Phantom
1937   Charlie Chan at the
         Olympics
1947   Northwest Outpost
1951   Tomahawk
1952   The Savage
1953   Arrowhead
1955   Chief Crazy Horse
Peters, Mattie *could be same as*
   Peters, Hattie
1923   Scars of Jealousy
1927   The Love Mart
Peters, Moneta
1953   Bright Road
Peters, Page
1916   Pasquale
Peters, Patricia
1944   Since You Went Away
Peters, Ralph
1939   Trigger Fingers
1941   The Face Behind the
         Mask
       New York Town
       You're Out of Luck
1942   Shut My Big Mouth
1944   Black Magic
       Slightly Terrific
1945   Nob Hill
1946   Bringing Up Father
       Canyon Passage
1947   It Had To Be You
1948   My Girl Tisa
1949   The Valiant Hombre
1951   Slaughter Trail
Peters, Robert (*actor*)
1948   Old Los Angeles
Peters, Robert (*writer*)
1952   Red Snow
Peters, Roberta
1953   Tonight We Sing
Peters, Scott
1959   The FBI Story
Peters, Susan *same as* **Carnahan,**
   Suzanne
1940   Santa Fe Trail
1942   Dr. Gillespie's New
         Assistant
Peters, Thomas J.
1916? Fate's Chessboard
Peters, Volney
1951   Saturday's Hero
Petersalia, Patrick
1935? The Irish Gringo
Petersen, Bob
1959   The FBI Story
Petersen, Paul
1958   Houseboat
Peterson, Arthur
1948   Call Northside 777
Peterson, Bernice
1954   Carmen Jones
Peterson, Caleb
1946   Till the End of Time
Peterson, Dorothy
1931   Skyline
1932   Call Her Savage
       So Big
1934   As the Earth Turns
       Beloved
1938   Breaking the Ice
1943   Air Force
1944   Mr. Skeffington
1946   Canyon Passage
Peterson, Eleanor *not the same as*
   Peterson, Elinor O.
1942   Song of the Islands
1945   Where Do We Go From
         Here?
Peterson, Elinor O. *not the same as*
   Peterson, Eleanor
1913   The Inside of the White
         Slave Traffic

Peterson, Elmer
1914   At the Cross Roads
Peterson, Elsa
1944   The Sullivans
1947   The Farmer's Daughter
1950   The Big Hangover
          Emergency Wedding
Peterson, Gene
1952   Hiawatha
Peterson, Harry
1951   Tomahawk
Peterson, Helen
1934   Coming Out Party
Peterson, Lenka
1949   Answer for Anne
1950   Panic in the Streets
Peterson, Louis S.
1960   Take a Giant Step
Peterson, Preston
1944   An American Romance
Peterson, Ruth
1935   Charlie Chan in Paris
1938   Josette
Peterson, Toddy
1934   Stand Up and Cheer!
Petit, Albert
1931   Echec au roi
          Soyons gais
1934   La veuve joyeuse
1935   L'homme des Folies
          Bergère
          Ruggles of Red Gap
1938   The Buccaneer
1945   The Dolly Sisters
Petracca, Joseph
1955   Seven Cities of Gold
1959   The Jayhawkers!
Petrie, Howard
1950   Rocky Mountain
1952   Red Ball Express
1953   Fort Ti
1957   The Tin Star
Petroff, Boris L.
1936   Klondike Annie
1949   Arctic Fury
1952   Red Snow
Petroff, Gloria
1944   Minstrel Man
1949   Arctic Fury
Petroff, Hamil
1959   Night of the Quarter
          Moon
Petrova, Madame Olga
1917   The Secret of Eve
Petrovich, Ivan
1931   Don Juan diplomático
          (foreign version)
Petterson, William
1923   Deceit
Petti, Carl
1950   Stars in My Crown
Pettie, Graham
1918   Untamed
1919   The Westerners
Pettit, Albert
1951   Across the Wide Missouri
Pettit, Rosemary
1950   The Furies
Pettitt, Wilfrid
1944   They Live in Fear
Pettus, William E.
1927   The Scar of Shame
Petway, Bruce
1921   As the World Rolls On
Pevney, Joseph
1947   Body and Soul
1949   Thieves' Highway
1955   Foxfire
1957   The Midnight Story
1960   The Plunderers
Peyton, Larry
1918   How Could You, Jean?
Peyton, Robert
1950   Border Treasure
1952   Red Snow
Pezet, A. W.
1930   El cuerpo del delito
Pflug, Eva
1960   Man on a String

Pharr, Frank
1942   Juke Girl
1945   Rhapsody in Blue
1946   Wild West
          Without Reservations
1947   The Mighty McGurk
1948   The Miracle of the Bells
1949   Knock on Any Door
1950   Stars in My Crown
1951   Jim Thorpe—All-American
Phelan, Pat
1944   Chip Off the Old Block
Phelps, Buster
1933   Broken Dreams
1934   Strange Wives
Phelps, Lee
1918   Marked Cards
          The Reckoning Day
1930   Anna Christie
1935   The Winning Ticket
1936   After the Thin Man
          Human Cargo
          Robin Hood of El Dorado
          Show Boat
1937   Big City
          Black Legion
          Man of the People
          Nation Aflame
          One Mile from Heaven
          Souls at Sea
          Think Fast, Mr. Moto
1939   Gone With the Wind
          Mr. Moto Takes a
          Vacation
          Waterfront
1940   Knute Rockne—All
          American
          Little Nellie Kelly
          Murder over New York
1941   Dead Men Tell
          The Face Behind the
          Mask
1942   All Through the Night
          Gentleman Jim
          In This Our Life
          North to the Klondike
          Wings for the Eagle
1943   Action in the North
          Atlantic
          Dr. Gillespie's Criminal
          Case
1944   An American Romance
1945   Betrayal from the East
          The Valley of Decision
1946   Three Wise Fools
1947   California
          The Mighty McGurk
1948   Unconquered
1949   Knock on Any Door
          The Sky Dragon
          That Midnight Kiss
1950   Devil's Doorway
          The Girl from San
          Lorenzo
1951   Fort Defiance
1952   My Man and I
Phelps, Marilee
1953   The Eddie Cantor Story
Phelps, W.
1931   Delicious
Phethean, David
1959   John Paul Jones
Phil and Audrey *(dancers)*
1947   Jivin' in Be-Bop
Philbin, Mary
1924   Fools' Highway
Philbrick, William H.
1930   Whoopee
**Philharmonic Symphony
Orchestra of New York**
1947   Carnegie Hall
Philips, John *could be same as
Phillips, John*
1951   The Well
Philips, Lily
1923   The White Flower
Phillips, Arnold
1945   Jealousy
1951   The Girl on the Bridge
Phillips, Arthur
1934   Limehouse Blues
1941   Playmates

1943   Dixie
          Riding High
Phillips, Augustus
1917   Threads of Fate
1919   Toby's Bow
Phillips, Bill *see* **Phillips, William
"Bill"**
Phillips, Carmen
1917   Forbidden Paths
1921   All Souls' Eve
1922   The Guttersnipe
1923   Thirty Days
Phillips, Dorothy
1919   The Right to Happiness
1955   Violent Saturday
Phillips, Eddie *same as* **Phillips,
Edward**
1922   The Good Provider
1926   April Fool
1928   We Americans
1930   Big Boy
1932   Symphony of Six Million
1952   Buffalo Bill in Tomahawk
          Territory
Phillips, Edna
1918   Ruggles of Red Gap
Phillips, Eleanor
1940   Taku
Phillips, Frank
1936   Star for a Night
Phillips, Gerald
1955   Blackboard Jungle
Phillips, Gwen
1934   Coming Out Party
Phillips, Jean
1941   Hold Back the Dawn
          Louisiana Purchase
          New York Town
Phillips, Jimmy
1935   Charlie Chan in Shanghai
1937   The Plainsman
Phillips, Joe
1936   After the Thin Man
Phillips, John *could be same as*
Philips, John
1948   Key Largo
1953   The Man from the Alamo
          Seminole
1959   John Paul Jones
Phillips, Marcella
1943   Riding High
Phillips, Marilyn
1942   Gentleman Jim
Phillips, Michael J.
1945   Salome, Where She
          Danced
Phillips, Minna
1950   Bandit Queen
          Train to Tombstone
1951   Queen for a Day
Phillips, Norman
1951   Jim Thorpe—All-American
Phillips, William "Bill" *same as*
Phillips, Bill; Phillips, William
1942   Juke Girl
1943   Action in the North
          Atlantic
1949   Border Incident
1950   Devil's Doorway
1951   Cavalry Scout
          Only the Valiant
1952   Bugles in the Afternoon
          High Noon
1955   Fort Yuma
1956   The Broken Star
          Ghost Town
          The Last Hunt
1957   Revolt at Fort Laramie
Phillis, Chris
1930   Alma de gaucho
Phipps, William *same as* **Phipps,
Bill**
1947   Crossfire
1948   The Arizona Ranger
1951   Five
1952   Fort Osage
          Rose of Cimarron
1955   The Far Horizons
          The Indian Fighter
          Smoke Signal
1957   The Brothers Rico

1958   Escape from Red Rock
1959   The FBI Story
Piatigorsky, Gregor
1947   Carnegie Hall
Piazza, Ben
1959   The Hanging Tree
Piazza, Dario
1945   A Medal for Benny
1947   Easy Come, Easy Go
1951   The Great Caruso
1952   Anything Can Happen
1953   The Stars Are Singing
Piazza, Lida
1957   All Mine to Give
Picasso, Lamberto
1930   El secreto del doctor
          (foreign version)
1931   La carta *(foreign
          version)*
Picerni, Paul
1950   A Lady Without Passport
1957   The Brothers Rico
1958   Marjorie Morningstar
Pichel, Irving
1934   She Was a Lady
1936   Down to the Sea
          General Spanky
1940   The Man I Married
1945   A Medal for Benny
1948   The Miracle of the Bells
Pickard, John
1951   Little Big Horn
          Oh! Susanna
          Snake River Desperadoes
1952   Bugles in the Afternoon
1953   Arrowhead
          The Charge at Feather
          River
1954   Arrow in the Dust
          Massacre Canyon
1955   Kentucky Rifle
          Seminole Uprising
          Seven Angry Men
          Shotgun
1956   The Broken Star
          The Lone Ranger
          Walk the Proud Land
1957   The Oklahoman
          War Drums
1959   The FBI Story
1960   Cimarron
Pickens, Slim
1950   Rocky Mountain
1953   Old Overland Trail
          The Sun Shines Bright
1955   The Last Command
          Santa Fe Passage
1958   Tonka
Picker, Leonard S.
1949   Apache Chief
Picker, Sidney
1945   Colorado Pioneers
1946   California Gold Rush
          Santa Fe Uprising
          Sheriff of Redwood Valley
          Sun Valley Cyclone
1947   Marshal of Cripple Creek
          Oregon Trail Scouts
          Rustlers of Devil's
          Canyon
          Vigilantes of Boomtown
1949   Harbor of Missing Men
1951   Cuban Fireball
1952   The Fabulous Senorita
1955   Santa Fe Passage
Pickerell, June Terry *see* **Pickrell,
June**
Pickett, Bill
1922   The Bull-Dogger
          The Crimson Skull
Pickett, Elizabeth
1929   Redskin
Pickford, Jack
1916   Poor Little Peppina
1918   Huck and Tom; or, the
          Further Adventures of
          Tom Sawyer
          Sandy
1921   Through the Back Door
1925   My Son

Pickford, Lottie *same as* **Forrest, Lottie Pickford**
1925   Don Q, Son of Zorro
Pickford, Mary
1916   Hulda from Holland
         Poor Little Peppina
1917   The Little American
1918   Amarilly of Clothes-Line Alley
         How Could You, Jean?
         Johanna Enlists
1921   Through the Back Door
1948   Sleep, My Love
Pickrell, June *same as* **Pickerell, June Terry**
1941   Hold Back the Dawn
1943   In Old Oklahoma
1944   An American Romance
Picon, Molly
1932   Mazel Tov
1936   Yiddle with His Fiddle
1939   Mamele
Picorri, John
1936   Dangerous Intrigue
         Down to the Sea
1938   Charlie Chan at Monte Carlo
Pidgeon, Walter
1953   Dream Wife
Piedra, Ernesto
1930   Así es la vida
         Sombras de gloria
Piel, Eddie *see* **Peil, Edward, Sr.**
Piel, Edward *see* **Peil, Edward, Sr.**
Piel, Paul
1956   Frontier Woman
Pierce, Evelyn
1934   Broadway Bill
Pierce, George *see* **Pearce, George**
Pierce, Gerald
1941   They Dare Not Love
1943   Gangway for Tomorrow
1948   The Lady from Shanghai
1951   The Magnificent Yankee
Pierce, Jim *same as* **Pierce, James**
1937   Life Begins in College
1940   Arizona Frontier
         The Gay Caballero
1947   The Farmer's Daughter
1948   The Miracle of the Bells
1950   Black Hand
         Right Cross
         Stars in My Crown
1951   Saturday's Hero
         Show Boat
Pierce, Marion
1943   His Butler's Sister
Pierce, Mary
1958   The Young Lions
Pierce, Michael
1953   The Eddie Cantor Story
         So Big
Pierlot, Francis
1940   Escape to Glory
1943   Yankee Doodle Dandy
1945   Our Vines Have Tender Grapes
         A Tree Grows in Brooklyn
1946   G. I. War Brides
1948   The Dude Goes West
Pierre, Lora
1947   Sepia Cinderella
Pierson, Arthur
1932   The Golden West
Pierson, Carl
1935   The Singing Vagabond
Pierson, Carol Dawn
1948   Up in Central Park
Pierson, E. D., Jr.
1921   Hearts of the Woods
Pierson, F. M.
1916   Little Meena's Romance
Pierson, George
1919   Hearts of Men
Pierson, Leo
1916   At Piney Ridge
1918   The Spreading Evil
Pietila, Walter
1943   Riding High

Pietro, Don
1948   The Boy with Green Hair
Piffle, John
1942   Cat People
         Friendly Enemies
         We Were Dancing
1943   The Leopard Man
1950   The Toast of New Orleans
1951   The Great Caruso
Pigmeat *see* **Markham, Dewey "Pigmeat"**
Pigott, Tempe
1934   Limehouse Blues
1938   The Rage of Paris
Pike, Anita
1934   Broadway Bill
         La veuve joyeuse
Pike, Samuel M.
1928   Anybody Here Seen Kelly?
Pike, William *same as* **Swift, Cecil** *see also* **The Three Swifts**
1919   Just Squaw
1922   Cardigan
Pilcher, Roy
1916   Betrayed
Pilkerton, Paul
1914   The Littlest Rebel
Pilkington, Tom
1946   Slightly Scandalous
1947   The Mighty McGurk
Pilot, Bernice
1929   Hearts in Dixie
1938   The Beloved Brat
1940   Santa Fe Trail
Pilotto, Camillo
1931   La fiesta del diablo (*foreign version*)
         Tropennächte (*foreign version*)
Pimley, John
1949   The Red Menace
Pinchon, Edgecumb
1936   Daniel Boone
Pine, Howard
1958   Ride a Crooked Trail
Pine, Phillip
1946   The Sailor Takes a Wife
1950   Battleground
Pine, William H.
1938   The Buccaneer
1946   Swamp Fire
1950   The Lawless
1951   The Last Outpost
1953   Sangaree
1955   The Far Horizons
Ping, Su
1939?   A Chinese Gains a Fortune in America
Ping, Yip Quon
1934   Blossom Time
Pingree, Earl
1937   Souls at Sea
Pini, Davide
1932   Amor in montagna
Pinkerton, W. W.
1940   The Ramparts We Watch
Pinner, Richard
1951   The Girl on the Bridge
1952   Red Snow
Pino, Rosario
1930   Un hombre de suerte
Pinski, David
1938   The Singing Blacksmith
Pinson, Allen
1953   Thunder Bay
1956   The Burning Hills
         The Last Frontier
1958   Gunman's Walk
Pinto, Effingham
1922   Fair Lady
Pinza, Ezio
1947   Carnegie Hall
1953   Tonight We Sing
Piper, Frederick
1960   The Day They Robbed the Bank of England
Pipitone, Nino
1942   Little Tokyo, U.S.A.
1950   Annie Get Your Gun
         The Toast of New Orleans

1951   The Great Caruso
Pires, Antonio J.
1945   The House on 92nd St.
Pironne, Johnny, Jr. *see* **Pirrone, Johnnie, Jr.**
Pirosh, Robert
1935   The Winning Ticket
1942   Song of the Islands
1950   Battleground
1951   Go for Broke!
Pirrin, Chevo *see* **"Don Catarino"**
Pirrone, Johnnie, Jr. *same as* **Pironne, Johnny, Jr.; Pirrone, Johnnie**
1938   Road Demon
         Speed to Burn
1939   Winner Take All
Pitkin, Waldo
1950   Panic in the Streets
Pitti, Carl
1949   The Kissing Bandit
1950   Bandit Queen
1951   Westward the Women
Pittman, Thomas
1958   Apache Territory
Pitts, ZaSu
1918   How Could You, Jean?
1928   Sins of the Fathers
1931   Beyond Victory
1932   The Vanishing Frontier
1935   Ruggles of Red Gap
1936   Mad Holiday
1941   The Mexican Spitfire's Baby
1942   Mexican Spitfire at Sea
Pitusín *see* **Hurtado, Alfredo**
Pivar, Ben
1931   El código penal
1933   King of the Wild Horses
1941   Mutiny in the Arctic
         Road Agent
1945   The Mummy's Curse
Pivar, Maurice
1931   Don Juan diplomático (*foreign version*)
1935   Alas sobre el Chaco
         Chinatown Squad
Pizor, William M.
1934   Call of the Coyote
Place, Lou
1955   Apache Woman
Planta, Carl de
1918   Good-Bye, Bill
The Plantation Choir
1938   Spirit of Youth
Plater, Harry
1920   The Brute
Platt, Edward
1956   Reprisal!
         Serenade
1958   Gunman's Walk
         Oregon Passage
1959   Inside the Mafia
Platt, George Foster
1919   Deliverance
Platt, Louise
1938   Spawn of the North
Platt, William
1928   Mother Machree
Platts, Harlod
1926   The Flying Ace
Plauzoles, Pierre
1951   Go for Broke!
Plauzoles, Therese
1951   Go for Broke!
Playter, Wellington
1919   Spotlight Sadie
Plaza Hotel (N.Y.) Jazz Orquestra
1930   Revista Hispano-Americana
Pleasant, Harry
1921   Ties of Blood
Plemic, Ivan
1932   Ljubav i strast
Pleschkoff, Maj. Gen. Michael N.
1926   Into Her Kingdom
Pliego, Eduardo González
1955   Seven Cities of Gold

Ploski, Joe *same as* **Ploski, Joseph**
1943   Action in the North Atlantic
1948   Call Northside 777
1949   Anna Lucasta
         Illegal Entry
1953   The Stars Are Singing
Plowright, Hilda
1943   Mr. Lucky
Plues, George
1941   Western Union
1943   Mexican Spitfire's Blessed Event
         The Ox-Bow Incident
1946   Sunset Pass
Plumer, Rose
1943   Jack London
1949   Knock on Any Door
         The Undercover Man
Plummer, Lincoln
1924   Fools' Highway
Plympton, George H.
1917   The Tenderfoot
1918   The Little Runaway
1921   That Girl Montana
1925   Galloping Vengeance
1939   Daughter of the Tong
1947   Last of the Redmen
Po, Lee
1941   Golden Gate Girl
Pocock, Roger
1925   Brand of Cowardice
Poe, James
1959   Last Train from Gun Hill
Poff, Lon
1920   The Man Who Dared
1923   Suzanna
1930   Tom Sawyer
1931   Noche de duendes
1938   The Texans
Pohlenz, Peter
1943   Action in the North Atlantic
Pohlmann, Eric
1959   John Paul Jones
Poindexter, Ina
1956   Giant
Pointner, Anton
1930   Los que danzan (*foreign version*)
1931   Daemon des Meeres
         Kismet
         La llama sagrada (*foreign version*)
         Die Maske Fällt
Poitier, Sidney
1950   No Way Out
1952   Red Ball Express
1954   Go Man Go
1955   Blackboard Jungle
1957   Band of Angels
         Edge of the City
1958   The Defiant Ones
1959   Porgy and Bess
1960   All the Young Men
Polan, Rusty
1960   All the Fine Young Cannibals
Poland, Joseph Franklin
1918   Love's Law
         Set Free
1919   A Bachelor's Wife
         The Tiger Lily
         Yvonne from Paris
1924   The Night Hawk
1928   Anybody Here Seen Kelly?
         The Cohens and the Kellys in Paris
Poleri, David
1960   Pay or Die
Polk, Oscar *same as* **Polk, O. W.**
1936   The Green Pastures
1937   Underworld
1939   Gone With the Wind
1940   The Notorious Elinor Lee
1943   Cabin in the Sky
Pollack, Ben
1956   The Benny Goodman Story

Pollack, Dee see **Pollock, Dee**
Pollack, Nancy R.
1959   The Last Angry Man
Pollard, Alex
1939   King of Chinatown
1942   Song of the Islands
       Tales of Manhattan
       We Were Dancing
Pollard, Bud
1932   The Black King
       O festino o la legge
1933   Victims of Persecution
1946   Beware
       Tall, Tan and Terrific
1949   Lookout Sister
Pollard, Fritz
1956   Rockin' the Blues
Pollard, Harry
1926   The Cohens and Kellys
1928   Uncle Tom's Cabin
1929   Show Boat
Pollard, Jack
1934   Call of the Coyote
Pollard, Laura
1921   Cheated Love
Pollard, Snub same as **Pollard, Snubby**
1937   Nation Aflame
1943   Riding High
1944   An American Romance
1947   Calendar Girl
1948   The Miracle of the Bells
1950   Stars in My Crown
1960   Studs Lonigan
Pollard, William
1918   Doing Their Bit
Pollay, Louis
1957   Burden of Truth
Pollet, Albert
1931   Buster se marie
1934   La veuve joyeuse
1938   Charlie Chan at Monte Carlo
1939   Winner Take All
1941   Louisiana Purchase
1945   The Dolly Sisters
1948   The Miracle of the Bells
1950   Battleground
1951   Across the Wide Missouri
Pollexfen, Jack
1953   Captain John Smith and Pocahontas
Pollock, Channing
1916   The Pretenders
Pollock, Dee same as **Pollack, Dee**
1960   The Plunderers
       Take a Giant Step
Pollycutt, Ferguson
1950   Two Flags West
Polo, Eddie
1917   The Bronze Bride
       A Kentucky Cinderella
       The Plow Woman
Polonsky, Abraham
1947   Body and Soul
Polonsky, David
1945   Nob Hill
1947   It Had To Be You
Pom Pom, the dog
1947   The Peanut Man
Pomés, Félix de
1930   Doña mentiras
       El secreto del doctor
       Toda una vida
1931   Cuerpo y alma
       Esclavas de la moda
       La fiesta del diablo
       Mamá
       Sombras del circo
1959   John Paul Jones
Pommer, Erich
1940   They Knew What They Wanted
Ponchartrain Billy, an alligator
1946   Swamp Fire
Ponedel, Dorothy
1925   Galloping Vengeance
Pons, Beatrice
1960   The Pusher

Pons, Lily
1937   That Girl from Paris
1947   Carnegie Hall
Ponti, Carlo
1959   The Black Orchid
Ponti, Sal
1960   Ice Palace
Ponto, Erich
1931   La carta (foreign version)
Pool, John
1940   Taku
Poole, Leonard
1932   Amor y vida
Poore, Dan
1951   Apache Drums
1953   The Man from the Alamo
The Pope Sisters
1937   Underworld
Pope, Alexander same as **Pope, Alex**
1946   Till the End of Time
1947   The Burning Cross
Pope, Bud
1935   The Cyclone Ranger
Pope, Leo
1928   Eleven P.M.
Popkin, Harry M.
1937   Bargain with Bullets
1938   The Duke Is Tops
       Life Goes On
1939   Gang Smashers
       One Dark Night
       Reform School
       Straight to Heaven
1940   Gang War
       While Thousands Cheer
1941   Four Shall Die
1942   Take My Life
1951   The Well
Popkin, Leo C.
1937   Bargain with Bullets
1938   The Duke Is Tops
       Life Goes On
1939   Gang Smashers
       One Dark Night
       Reform School
1940   Gang War
       While Thousands Cheer
1941   Four Shall Die
1942   Take My Life
1951   The Well
Porcasi, Paul same as **Porcasi, Paolo**
1930   Monsieur le Fox (foreign version)
1931   Gentleman's Fate
       Jenny Lind
       El pasado acusa
       Smart Money
1932   Men Are Such Fools
1933   Grand Slam
1934   Coming Out Party
       The Great Flirtation
       Imitation of Life
1935   Charlie Chan in Egypt
       A Night at the Ritz
1936   Down to the Sea
       Muss 'Em Up
1937   That I May Live
1942   We Were Dancing
1944   An American Romance
Porcett, Lucille
1933   It's Great to Be Alive
1936   Ramona
Porcheur, Eugene
1951   The House on Telegraph Hill
Porchon, Tao
1951   Show Boat
Porcupine, Jim
1959   The FBI Story
Porta, James
1959   The FBI Story
Portanova, Paul
1935   Rosa de Francia
Portavella, Ramón
1931   La pura verdad
Porter, Arthur Gould
1948   Unconquered

Porter, Don same as **Porter, Donald**
1946   Cuban Pete
       Wild Beauty
1947   Buck Privates Come Home
1952   The Savage
Porter, Ed could be same as **Porter, Edward**
1935   Range Warfare
Porter, Edward could be same as **Porter, Ed**
1925   Friendly Enemies
Porter, Hoit
1935   Piernas de seda
Porter, Hugh
1958   Tonka
Porter, Jean
1944   Andy Hardy's Blonde Trouble
1946   Till the End of Time
Porter, Lawrence
1940   Northwest Passage (Book I—Rogers' Rangers)
Porter, Lillian
1938   Josette
1940   Elsa Maxwell's Public Deb No. 1
       The Man I Married
1941   Sun Valley Serenade
1942   Song of the Islands
Porter, Reed
1942   Holiday Inn
Porter, Robert N.
1950   Battleground
Porter, Thomas
1951   The Tall Target
Portney, Charlotte
1956   Full of Life
Portugal, Jose
1943   The Leopard Man
1951   The Great Caruso
Post, Charles "Buddy" same as **Post, Buddy**
1919   The Courageous Coward
1924   Defying the Law
Post, Guy Bates
1937   Maid of Salem
1938   Daughter of Shanghai
Post, Rex
1940   Escape to Glory
Post, William, Jr.
1931   The Black Camel
1942   Nazi Agent
1945   The House on 92nd St.
1948   Call Northside 777
Postal, Charles
1957   Gun Battle at Monterey
1959   The FBI Story
Potel, Victor
1914   The Good-for-Nothing
1920   Billions
1923   Anna Christie
1930   ¡De frente, marchen!
1931   The Squaw Man
1935   Ruggles of Red Gap
1936   Down to the Sea
1939   Heaven with a Barbed Wire Fence
       Let Freedom Ring
       Stand Up and Fight
1940   Girl from God's Country
       Birth of the Blues
       Ride on Vaquero
       Sullivan's Travels
1945   A Medal for Benny
1947   Calendar Girl
       The Farmer's Daughter
Potter, H. C.
1943   Mr. Lucky
1947   The Farmer's Daughter
1948   The Time of Your Life
Potter, Jim
1954   Dangerous Mission
Potter, Peter same as **Moore, Bill; Moore, William**
1935   The Cyclone Ranger
       Naughty Marietta
1937   Life Begins in College
1941   Mutiny in the Arctic
1953   The Stars Are Singing

Potts, Hank
1950   Two Flags West
Potts, Nyanza
1935   The Little Colonel
Poule, Ezelle
1949   The Story of Seabiscuit
1953   The Jazz Singer
       Tumbleweed
1954   War Arrow
Poulos, Angi O.
1948   Jiggs and Maggie in Court
1949   The Girl from Jones Beach
1950   Black Hand
1953   The Jazz Singer
Pourchot, Ray
1951   Saturday's Hero
Powell, A. Van Buren
1917   The Captain of the Gray Horse Troop
Powell, Bill not the same as **Powell, William**
1938   Daughter of Shanghai
Powell, Clara Bell
1937   Underworld
Powell, David
1919   His Parisian Wife
1920   On with the Dance
1922   Anna Ascends
Powell, Dick not the same as **Powell, Richard**
1943   Riding High
1950   Right Cross
1951   The Tall Target
Powell, Emory
1952   The Fabulous Senorita
Powell, Frank
1915   Children of the Ghetto
1916   The Scarlet Oath
Powell, Lee
1940   Hi-Yo Silver
1942   Secret Enemies
Powell, Lillian
1937   Bargain with Bullets
Powell, Paul
1916   Little Meena's Romance
1918?   Indian Life
1919   Who Will Marry Me?
1928   Kit Carson
Powell, Richard not the same as **Powell, Dick**
1931   Street Scene
1934   Operator 13
1935   Naughty Marietta
       Rendezvous
       The Wedding Night
1936   After the Thin Man
       Paddy O'Day
       Sins of Man
Powell, Robert Lawrence
1944   Address Unknown
Powell, Russ same as **Powell, Russell**
1922   Head over Heels
1928   Riley the Cop
       Vamping Venus
1930   Check and Double Check
       The Grand Parade
1932   Mystery Ranch
1935   A Night at the Ritz
1936   Rose of the Rancho
       Sutter's Gold
1937   Man of the People
1943   Action in the North Atlantic
Powell, Violet E.
1925   The Beautiful City
Powell, William not the same as **Powell, Bill**
1925   The Beautiful City
1926   Desert Gold
1930   Behind the Make-Up
1935   Rendezvous
1936   After the Thin Man
1952   It's a Big Country: An American Anthology
Power, John could be same as **Powers, John**
1937   Maid of Salem
1940   Little Nellie Kelly

Power, Max
1958   Wild Is the Wind
1959   The Jayhawkers!
1960   Walk Like a Dragon
Power, Paul
1932   The Cohens and Kellys in Hollywood
1941   They Dare Not Love
1956   The Lone Ranger
Power, Tyrone
1938   In Old Chicago
1940   The Mark of Zorro
1943   Crash Dive
1948   The Luck of the Irish
1955   The Long Gray Line
Power, Mrs. Tyrone
1915   A Texas Steer
Power, Tyrone, Sr. 1869—1931
1915   A Texas Steer
1920   The Great Shadow
1925   Braveheart
Powers, John *could be same as* **Power, John**
1937   Hills of Old Wyoming
Powers, Len
1937   Slave Ship
Powers, Mala
1952   Rose of Cimarron
1958   Sierra Baron
Powers, Margot
1950   Sands of Iwo Jima
Powers, Richard *see* **Keene, Tom**
Powers, Tom
1947   The Farmer's Daughter
1948   Angel in Exile
        The Time of Your Life
        Up in Central Park
1950   Chinatown at Midnight
        Right Cross
1951   The Tall Target
        The Well
1952   The Fabulous Senorita
Powers, William
1913   Traffic in Souls
Poynter, Beulah
1915   Hearts of Men
Poza, Blanca
1938   La vida bohemia
Pozzi, Gina
1932   Parigi affascina; ovvero, Malavita
Prades, James
1951   Native Son
Praskins, Leonard
1931   Gentleman's Fate
        Su última noche
1932   Flesh
1944   My Pal Wolf
Prather, Lee
1938   The Buccaneer
1941   The Face Behind the Mask
        New York Town
Prather, Nick
1936   General Spanky
Pratt, Aurora
1917   A Kentucky Cinderella
Pratt, Gilbert
1927   Clancy's Kosher Wedding
Pratt, Jack *see* **Pratt, John H.**
Pratt, James
1958   Tonka
Pratt, John H. *same as* **Pratt, Jack**
1914   Dan
        The Jungle
1925   The Red Rider
1929   Hawk of the Hills
Pratt, Judson
1960   Sergeant Rutledge
Pratt, Purnell B.
1914   The Great Diamond Robbery
1929   Is Everybody Happy?
1932   Scarface
1934   Lazy River
1935   Black Fury
        The Winning Ticket
1937   The Plainsman

Pray, Léonie
1933   L'amour guide
Preble, Ed
1959   Odds Against Tomorrow
Preer, Evelyn
1919   The Homesteader
1920   The Brute
        Within Our Gates
1921   The Gunsaulus Mystery
1923   Deceit
1924   Birthright
1925   The Devil's Disciple
1926   The Conjure Woman
1927   The Spider's Web
1930   Georgia Rose
Preisser, June
1939   Judge Hardy and Son
1948   Music Man
Préjean, Albert
1931   Die Dreigroschenoper (*foreign version*)
Prelle, Micheline
1951   Adventures of Captain Fabian
Preminger, Otto
1943   Margin for Error
1945   Where Do We Go From Here?
1954   Carmen Jones
1959   Porgy and Bess
Prentis, Jean
1918   Johanna Enlists
Prentis, June
1918   Johanna Enlists
Prentiss, Ed
1958   Home Before Dark
1959   The FBI Story
1960   Man on a String
Prentiss, Eleanor
1938   In Old Chicago
Prescott, Ellen
1940   The Ramparts We Watch
Prescott, Elsie
1932   Thirteen Women
1934   Limehouse Blues
1937   Maid of Salem
Prescott, Guy
1955   Shotgun
1958   Fort Massacre
Presley, Elvis
1960   Flaming Star
Presnell, Robert, Sr.
1930   The Big Pond
1933   Ever in My Heart
1946   Cuban Pete
Press, Gloria
1938   God's Step Children
Press, Marvin
1947   Northwest Outpost
1952   The Raiders
Pressburger, Fred
1956   Crowded Paradise
Pressel, Frederick
1944   Block Busters
Pressley, Louis "Babe"
1951   The Harlem Globetrotters
Preston, Billy
1958   St. Louis Blues
Preston, Robert
1941   New York Town
1948   Big City
1949   Tulsa
1956   The Last Frontier
1960   The Dark at the Top of the Stairs
Pretal, Camillus
1929   Abie's Irish Rose
Pretty, Arline
1923   The White Flower
Prevore, S.
1952   Anything Can Happen
Prevost, Marie
1931   Call of the Rockies
        Gentleman's Fate
Price, Alonzo
1936   Human Cargo
1937   Big City
        Black Legion
        Man of the People
        Souls at Sea

1939   The Adventures of Huckleberry Finn
1942   Mokey
1948   The Miracle of the Bells
Price, Edward *not the same as* **Price, Peter Edward**
1937   That Girl from Paris
Price, Hal
1938   Wild Horse Canyon
1939   Stand Up and Fight
1940   Arizona Frontier
1941   Secret of the Wastelands
1942   Valley of Hunted Men
1943   Wagon Tracks West
1944   Marshal of Reno
        Outlaw Trail
1946   Sun Valley Cyclone
Price, Kate
1918   Amarilly of Clothes-Line Alley
1920   Dinty
1921   That Girl Montana
1922   Come On Over
        Flesh and Blood
        The Guttersnipe
1924   Fools' Highway
1925   His People
1926   The Cohens and Kellys Irene
1927   Frisco Sally Levy
1928   Anybody Here Seen Kelly?
        The Cohens and the Kellys in Paris
1929   The Cohens and Kellys in Atlantic City
1930   The Cohens and the Kellys in Scotland
1931   The Cohens and Kellys in Africa
1934   Behold My Wife!
Price, Louise
1936   The Green Pastures
Price, Nanci
1928   The Broken Mask
Price, Naomi
1932   Harlem Is Heaven
Price, Paul
1920   The Good-Bad Wife
Price, Peter Edward *same as* **Price, Peter** *not the same as* **Price, Edward**
1951   The Great Caruso
        New Mexico
Price, Stanley
1940   The Way of All Flesh
1943   Riding High
1946   Romance of the West
1947   Easy Come, Easy Go
1950   Cherokee Uprising
1951   Gambling House
1952   Fort Osage
Price, Vincent
1948   Up in Central Park
1950   The Baron of Arizona
1951   Adventures of Captain Fabian
1954   Dangerous Mission
1956   Serenade
Prickett, Maudie *same as* **Prickett, Maude**
1949   Colorado Territory
        The Cowboy and the Indians
        Lust for Gold
1950   No Way Out
1955   Good Morning, Miss Dove
Prickett, Oliver *see* **Blake, Oliver**
Priddy, James
1956   The Benny Goodman Story
Prim, Frances
1925   The Prairie Wife
Louis Prima and His Band
1937   Manhattan Merry-Go-Round
Prince, Hugh
1949?   Harlem Follies
Prince, John T.
1924   Defying the Law
1925   The Gold Hunters
1928   Ramona
1929   Hawk of the Hills

Prince, Maurice
1947   It Had To Be You
Prince, William
1947   Carnegie Hall
1949   Lust for Gold
1956   Secret of Treasure Mountain
Pringle, Aileen
1942   They Died With Their Boots On
1943   Dr. Gillespie's Criminal Case
1944   Since You Went Away
Pringle, Jessie
1936   Paddy O'Day
Pringle, Norman
1931   Delicious
Printzlau, Olga
1918   The City of Tears
        One More American
1932   Hearts of Humanity
1933   Broken Dreams
Prinz, LeRoy
1936   Show Boat
Prior, Herbert *same as* **Pryor, Herbert**
1921   Made in Heaven
1922   The Half Breed
1925   Tearing Through
        The Wild Bull's Lair
1934   Stand Up and Cheer!
Prisco, Albert
1922   The Power of Love
1927   Don Mike
Pritchard, Dick
1934   Broadway Bill
Pritchard, Owen
1953   The Eddie Cantor Story
Prival, Lucien
1926   Puppets
1929   The Peacock Fan
1931   Young Sinners
1933   Grand Slam
1938   Mr. Wong, Detective
1939   Confessions of a Nazi Spy
1952   High Noon
Probert, George
1915   The Spender
1916   The King's Game
Proctor, John
1959   Anna Lucasta
Lynn Proctor Trio
1948   Miracle in Harlem
Proper, Alec
1940   Santa Fe Trail
Prosperi, Giorgio
1954   Indiscretion of an American Wife
1958   Seven Hills of Rome
Prosser, Hugh
1943   Action in the North Atlantic
        They Came to Blow Up America
1948   Unconquered
1953   The Man from the Alamo
Prouse, Peter
1949   Illegal Entry
1950   Ambush
Prouty, Jed
1925   Scarlet Saint
1937   Life Begins in College
1947   Citizen Saint
Provendie, Zina
1960   All the Fine Young Cannibals
Provincia, Anne
1951   Go for Broke!
Provost, Jon
1953   So Big
1957   All Mine to Give
Provost, Minnie
1921   By Right of Birth
Pruden, A. Sears *could be same as* **Sears, A. D.**
1915   The Grandee's Ring
Prudhomme, Cameron
1930   Abraham Lincoln

Pryne, Alberta
1946?   Fight That Ghost
      House-Rent Party
Pryor, Ainslie
1956   The Last Hunt
      Walk the Proud Land
1957   The Guns of Fort
      Petticoat
Pryor, H. L.
1922   Easy Money
Pryor, Herbert see **Prior, Herbert**
Pryor, Roger
1934   Strange Wives
1945   The Cisco Kid Returns
Przybylski, Jan Nowina see **Nowina-Przybylski, Jan**
Przybyla, W.
1941   Z Dymem Pożarów
Puailoa, Satini
1944   Tahiti Nights
Pucci, Ralph
1951   Saturday's Hero
Puente, Laura
1936   Ramona
1939   La Inmaculada
Puerta, Juan
1930   El valiente
Püttjer, Gustav
1931   Die Dreigroschenoper
Puga, Ricardo
1932   El hombre que asesinó
Pugh, Ei
1935   Lem Hawkins' Confession
Puglia, Frank same as **Puglia, Franco**
1925   The Beautiful City
1931   La gran jornada (foreign version)
1937   Song of the City
1938   Rascals
      Spawn of the North
1939   Forged Passport
      In Old Caliente
1940   Behind the News
      Charlie Chan in Panama
      The Fatal Hour
      The Mark of Zorro
      Tengo fe en ti
1943   Action in the North Atlantic
1946   Without Reservations
1947   Easy Come, Easy Go
1949   Colorado Territory
1950   Black Hand
1956   The Burning Hills
      Serenade
1959   The Black Orchid
      Cry Tough
Puig, Eva
1941   Hold Back the Dawn
      Ride on Vaquero
      Romance of the Rio Grande
1942   Below the Border
      Rio Rita
1945   The Cisco Kid Returns
      A Medal for Benny
1946   Wild Beauty
Puig, Lupe
1945   A Medal for Benny
Pulido, Juan
1930   Galas de la Paramount
Pulkaradse, Alexander
1952   Anything Can Happen
Pullen, William
1950   No Way Out
1953   War Paint
Pulliam, Ed
1950   Two Flags West
Pully, B. S. same as **Pulley, B. S.**
1945   Nob Hill
      A Tree Grows in Brooklyn
1953   Taxi
Pulver, Enid
1950   So Young, So Bad
Pumau, John
1944   Tahiti Nights
Punay, Rito
1946   Dangerous Money

Purcell, Gertrude
1934   She Was a Lady
1937   Music for Madame
Purcell, Irene
1932   Le plombier amoureux
Purcell, Noel
1959   Shake Hands with the Devil
Purcell, Richard same as **Purcell, Dick**
1940   New Moon
1941   King of the Zombies
Purcell, Robert
1949   The Red Menace
Purdy, Constance
1936   Star for a Night
1944   Going My Way
1945   Rhapsody in Blue
      A Tree Grows in Brooklyn
1947   Jiggs and Maggie in Society
1948   I Remember Mama
      Unconquered
Putnam, Nina Wilcox
1933   A Lady's Profession
Pyke, Wallace
1916   A Son of Erin
Pyle, Denver
1953   Column South
1954   Drum Beat
1956   7th Cavalry
1958   Fort Massacre
Pyper, George W.
1921   The Kiss
1925   A Daughter of the Sioux
      Warrior Gap
1927   Heroes in Blue
Qualen, John same as **Qualen, John M.**
1931   Street Scene
1933   Counsellor at Law
      Let's Fall in Love
1934   He Was Her Man
      Our Daily Bread
      Straight Is the Way
1935   Black Fury
      Charlie Chan in Paris
1938   The Texans
1939   Stand Up and Fight
1940   Knute Rockne—All American
1942   Tortilla Flat
1944   An American Romance
      Dark Waters
1948   My Girl Tisa
      Reaching from Heaven
      16 Fathoms Deep
1950   Buccaneer's Girl
1953   Ambush at Tomahawk Gap
1954   Passion
1956   The Searchers
Quan, Moon
1941   Golden Gate Girl
Quarles, Vivian
1921   A Modern Cain
Quartaro, Nena same as **Quartero, Nina**
1933   Man from Monterey
1935   The Cyclone Ranger
1936   The Phantom of Santa Fe
Quartucci, Pedro
1931   Las luces de Buenos Aires
Queant, Gilles
1951   Adventures of Captain Fabian
Quianna
1949   Arctic Manhunt
Quick, Dallas
1958   Tonka
Quigley, Charles
1936   Charlie Chan's Secret
1940   Mexican Spitfire Out West
1949   The Cowboy and the Indians
Quigley, George P.
194-   Mistaken Identity
1948?   Junction 88

Quigley, Juanita same as **Jane, Baby**
1934   Imitation of Life
1938   Hawaii Calls
1942   The Vanishing Virginian
1950   Mystery Street
Quigley, Rita
1940   Jennie
1942   The Vanishing Virginian
1946   The Trap
Quijada, John
1959   The FBI Story
      The Young Land
Quilan, William
1932   Law and Lawless
Quillan, Diane
1945   The Shanghai Cobra
      South of the Rio Grande
Quillan, Eddie
1937   Big City
1939   Allegheny Uprising
1941   Where Did You Get That Girl?
1944   Slightly Terrific
Quillan, Marie
1931   The Hurricane Horseman
1935   Melody Trail
      The Singing Vagabond
Quimby, Margaret
1929   Lucky Boy
1930   Ladies Love Brutes
Quince, Louis
1947   Humoresque
Quinchette, Paul
1949   Lookout Sister
Quine, Richard
1933   Counsellor at Law
1942   Dr. Gillespie's New Assistant
1949   The Clay Pigeon
1956   Full of Life
Quinlivan, Charles
1960   All the Young Men
Quinn, Anthony
1937   The Plainsman
      Waikiki Wedding
1938   The Buccaneer
      Dangerous to Know
      Daughter of Shanghai
1939   King of Chinatown
1942   They Died With Their Boots On
1943   The Ox-Bow Incident
1944   Buffalo Bill
1945   Where Do We Go From Here?
1947   Black Gold
      California
1953   Ride, Vaquero!
      Seminole
1955   Seven Cities of Gold
1956   Man from Del Rio
1957   The Ride Back
1958   Wild Is the Wind
1959   The Black Orchid
      Last Train from Gun Hill
Quinn, Fred
1916   The Colored American Winning His Suit
Quinn, Jack
1947   Dangerous Venture
Quinn, James
1937   Man of the People
Quinn, Louis
1959   Al Capone
Quinn, Regina
1919   The Other Man's Wife
Quinn, Tom same as **Quinn, Thomas; Quinn, Tommy**
1942   Syncopation
1944   Mr. Skeffington
1945   The Navajo Trail
1946   Border Bandits
1951   The Great Caruso
Quinn, William
1959   The Last Angry Man
Quiñones, Jaime González
1955   Seven Cities of Gold
Quintero, Rafaela
1930   La rosa de fuego

Quirk, Josephine
1925   Friendly Enemies
Quock, Andrew
1949   Thieves' Highway
Quon, Gong
1939?   A Chinese Gains a Fortune in America
Quon, Marianne
1943   Dr. Gillespie's Criminal Case
1944   Charlie Chan in the Secret Service
Qvale, Ragnar
1940   The Man I Married
Raaf, Vicki
1953   The Man Behind the Gun
1955   Foxfire
Rabagliati, Alberto
1930   Sei tu l'amore
Rabin, Jack
1950   I Killed Geronimo
Rabinowitz, Tillie
1939   The Light Ahead
Raboch, Al
1939   Fisherman's Wharf
1942   Sunday Punch
1943   Dr. Gillespie's Criminal Case
1944   Three Men in White
1945   Between Two Women
Ra-Chell, Shin
1931   Zein Weib's Lubovnick
Rachmil, Lewis J.
1941   Secret of the Wastelands
1942   American Empire
1943   Border Patrol
1947   Dangerous Venture
1954   They Rode West
1956   Reprisal!
1957   The Brothers Rico
Rackin, Martin
1947   Desperate
1948   Fighting Father Dunne
1951   Distant Drums
Radcliffe, E. J. same as **Ratcliffe, E. J.**
1918   Out of a Clear Sky
1930   The Cohens and the Kellys in Scotland
Radcliffe, Violet
1916   Gretchen, the Greenhorn
      A Sister of Six
Rader, Gordon
1945   A Tree Grows in Brooklyn
Radford, Mazie
1916   Little Meena's Romance
Radisse, Lucienne
1932   Le bluffeur
Radom, Bernice
1921   No Woman Knows
Radovich, William
1947   Calendar Girl
Rae, Alice
1917   A Love Sublime
Rae, Bud
1934   Our Daily Bread
1951   New Mexico
Rae, Rada
1927   Wild Geese
Rae, Sheila
1942   Song of the Islands
Rae, Stella
1948   Gentleman's Agreement
Rae, Zoe
1917   A Kentucky Cinderella
Raeburn, Frances
1942   Seven Sweethearts
Raetz, Baby Alice
1934   Stand Up and Cheer!
Rafferty, Frances
1942   Seven Sweethearts
1943   Dr. Gillespie's Criminal Case
1946   Bad Bascomb
1947   The Adventures of Don Coyote
Raffetto, Michael
1945   Sunbonnet Sue
1947   Pirates of Monterey
1948   The Miracle of the Bells

Raft, George
1932   Scarface
1934   Limehouse Blues
1936   It Had to Happen
1937   Souls at Sea
1938   Spawn of the North
1945   Johnny Angel
         Nob Hill

Ragan, Mike *could be same as*
Bane, Hollis
1951   Jim Thorpe—All-American
1953   Arrowhead
1955   Headline Hunters
1958   Frontier Gun

Ragland, "Rags"
1942   Sunday Punch
1944   Three Men in White

Rags, a dog
1923   Breaking into Society
1948   Rocky

Raguse, Elmer
1930   El príncipe del dólar
         (*foreign version*)
1931   Los calaveras (*foreign
         version*)
         Pardon Us (*foreign
         version*)

Rahawanaku, Mr.
1915?   The Beachcomber

Rahm, Whitney de
1934   White Heat

Raht, Carlysle Graham
1924   The Night Hawk

Raimondo, Toni
1946   The Red Dragon

Raine, Jack
1955   Not As a Stranger

Raine, Norman Reilly
1940   The Fighting 69th
1945   Nob Hill

Rainer, Luise
1937   Big City
1938   The Toy Wife

Raines, Steve
1954   Broken Lance
         Drums Across the River
1956   Reprisal!

Rainey, Ford
1958   The Badlanders
1959   John Paul Jones
1960   Flaming Star

Rainey, Norman
1950   Rock Island Trail

Rainey, Pat
1947   Reet, Petite and Gone

Rainnie, Hedley
1949   Jigsaw

Rains, Claude
1939   Daughters Courageous
1944   Mr. Skeffington
1946   Notorious

Rains, N.
1948   Unconquered

Rairden, Wallace
1940   The Way of All Flesh
1941   New York Town

Raisbeck, Kenneth
1927   The Gay Defender

Raison, Milton
1938   Mis dos amores
1947   Spoilers of the North
1953   Old Overland Trail

Raitt, John
1940   Little Nellie Kelly
1942   Sunday Punch
1944   Minstrel Man

Rajnglas, Jakub
1937   The Jester (Der
         Purimspieler)

Raker, Lorin
1929   Mother's Boy
1933   Let's Fall in Love
1941   Where Did You Get That
         Girl?
1943   Dr. Gillespie's Criminal
         Case
1946   Without Reservations
1947   Easy Come, Easy Go

Raleigh, Mrs. Cecil
1915   The Clemenceau Case
1916   A Woman's Honor

Rall, Tommy
1956   Walk the Proud Land

Ralph, Jessie
1934   Coming Out Party
1936   After the Thin Man
1939   Drums Along the Mohawk

Ralph, Ronnie
1949   The Undercover Man

Ralston, David
1948   Unconquered

Ralston, Esther
1920   Huckleberry Finn
1922   Pals of the West
1923   The Victor
1924   Peter Pan
1934   Strange Wives
1937   Shadows of the Orient

Ralston, Jobyna
1926   Sweet Daddies

Ralston, Marcia
1942   Sunday Punch

Ralston, Rudy *same as* **Hruba,
Rudy**
1957   The Lawless Eighties
1958   Gunfire at Indian Gap

Ralston, Vera Hruba *same as*
Ralston, Vera
1941   Ice-Capades
1944   Lake Placid Serenade
1949   The Fighting Kentuckian
1958   Gunfire at Indian Gap

Rama, Rudy
1949   Harbor of Missing Men
1953   Dream Wife
         Tonight We Sing

Rambeau, Marjorie
1939   Heaven with a Barbed
         Wire Fence
1940   East of the River
1943   In Old Oklahoma
1945   Salome, Where She
         Danced
1955   A Man Called Peter
         The View from Pompey's
         Head

Rambeau, Regina
1935   Charlie Chan in Shanghai

Rambula, Catalina
1934   Laughing Boy

Rameau, Emil
1948   Cry of the City

Rameau, Hans
1942   We Were Dancing

Ramírez, Ana M. de
1927?   El que a hierro mata

Ramírez, Antonio M.
1927?   El que a hierro mata

Ramirez, Carlos
1945   Where Do We Go From
         Here?

Ramirez, Ram *not the same as*
Ramírez, Ramon
1947   Boy! What a Girl!

Ramirez, Ramon *not the same as*
Ramirez, Ram
1956   Giant

Ramona, the mule
1915   Chimmie Fadden Out
         West

Ramos, Carlos
1930   The Bad Man (*foreign
         version*)

Ramos, Josefina
1931   La cautivadora

Ramos, Trini
1934   El tango en Broadway

Ramos Cobián, Rafael
1938   Mis dos amores
1939   Los hijos mandan

Ramsay, Alicia
1918   A Daughter of the Old
         South

Ramsey, Ed
1946   G. I. War Brides

Ramsey, George
1950   A Lady Without Passport
1956   The Benny Goodman
         Story

Rand, Edwin *same as* **Rand, Ed**
1950   Broken Arrow
1951   Oh! Susanna
1953   Column South
         The Great Sioux Uprising
1954   Siege at Red River

Rand, Hal
1943   Dixie

Rand, Jess
1960   The Plunderers

Rand, John
1938   City Streets

Rand, Lucia
1945   Where Do We Go From
         Here?

Rand, Sally
1925   Braveheart
1927   Heroes in Blue

Rand, Theodore *same as* **Rand,
Ted**
1945   Johnny Angel
1947   Easy Come, Easy Go
1949   Harbor of Missing Men

Randall Sisters
1934   Stand Up and Cheer!

Randall, Addison
1935   His Family Tree

Randall, Chris
1955   Blackboard Jungle

Randall, Jack
1938   Wild Horse Canyon
1939   Drifting Westward

Randall, Leon
1936   The Green Pastures

Randall, Margaret
1938   Dangerous to Know

Randall, Martha
1956   Giant

Randall, Rebel
1943   In Old Oklahoma

Randall, Robert
1930   Sunny Skies

Randall, Stuart
1951   Tomahawk
1952   Bugles in the Afternoon
         The Half-Breed
         Hiawatha
         Kid Monk Baroni
1953   Captain John Smith and
         Pocahontas
         The Man from the Alamo
1954   They Rode West
1955   Chief Crazy Horse
         Headline Hunters
1957   Run of the Arrow

Randall, Tony
1960   The Adventures of
         Huckleberry Finn

Randell, Ron
1947   It Had To Be You
1956   Quincannon, Frontier
         Scout

Randle, Karen
1945   Salome, Where She
         Danced
1949   The Cowboy and the
         Prizefighter
1951   Hurricane Island

Randol, George
1931   The Exile
1936   The Green Pastures
1937   Dark Manhattan
         Harlem on the Prairie
1940   Midnight Shadow

Randolf, Anders *see* **Randolph,
Anders**

Randolph, Amanda
1939   Lying Lips
1940   The Notorious Elinor Lee
1950   No Way Out
1952   The Iron Mistress
1955   A Man Called Peter
1956   Full of Life

Randolph, Anders *same as*
Randolf, Anders
1917   One Law for Both
1919   Erstwhile Susan
1922   Peacock Alley
1923   None So Blind
1924   In Hollywood With
         Potash and Perlmutter

1927   Old San Francisco
1928   The Jazz Singer
1930   Son of the Gods
1931   Call of the Rockies

Randolph, Charles
1936   Laughing Irish Eyes
1946   Singin' in the Corn

Randolph, Clay
1957   Revolt at Fort Laramie

Randolph, Donald
1951   Gambling House
1953   Dream Wife
1955   Chief Crazy Horse

Randolph, Ed *same as* **Randolph,
Eddie**
1947   California
1949   Illegal Entry
         Knock on Any Door
         The Undercover Man

Randolph, Isabel
1943   Dixie
1951   Oh! Susanna

Randolph, Jane
1942   Cat People
1945   Jealousy
1948   Open Secret

Randolph, Lillian
1938   Life Goes On
1940   Am I Guilty?
1942   Mexican Spitfire Sees a
         Ghost
1948   Sleep, My Love

Randolph, Mandy
1938   Swing!

Randolph, Marion
1951   Oh! Susanna

Randolph, Mrs. T.
1918   A Daughter of the Old
         South

Range Ranglers Band
1935   Cyclone of the Saddle

Ranger, a dog
1927   Aflame in the Sky

Rankin, Arthur
1922   The Five Dollar Baby
         Little Miss Smiles
1925   The Fearless Lover
         Tearing Through
1934   Broadway Bill
1936   Dangerous Intrigue
1938   Happy Landing
         My Lucky Star
         Road Demon
1939   Charlie Chan in Reno
         The Cisco Kid and the
         Lady
1940   Elsa Maxwell's Public
         Deb No. 1

Rankin, Caroline "Spike" *same as*
Rankin, Caroline
1924   Untamed Youth
1937   Charlie Chan at the
         Olympics

Rankin, Gilman
1956   Ghost Town

Rankin, Peter
1950   Battleground

Rankin, William
1943   Dixie
1944   Hi, Beautiful
1948   Fighting Father Dunne

Ranous, William V.
1914   The Little Angel of
         Canyon Creek

Ransom, Ernie
1941   Murder on Lenox Avenue
         Sunday Sinners

Ransome, Jean
1948   The Miracle of the Bells

Ransome, Vivian
1921   Little Miss Hawkshaw

Rantz, Louis
1935   De la sartén al fuego
1937   El capitán Tormenta
         El carnaval del diablo

Rapée, Ernö
1930   Los que danzan (*foreign
         version*)

Rapelye, Robert
1940   The Ramparts We Watch

Rapf, Harry
1920?   The Greatest Love
1931   Gentleman's Fate
1936   Mad Holiday
1939   Let Freedom Ring
Rapf, Maurice
1940   Jennie
1946   Song of the South
Raphaelson, Samson
1934   Caravane
        La veuve joyeuse
Rappel, Malvina
1939   Motel the Operator
Rapper, Irving
1939   Daughters Courageous
1945   Rhapsody in Blue
1949   Anna Lucasta
1958   Marjorie Morningstar
Rapport, Fred
1942   Three Hearts for Julia
1943   Mr. Lucky
1952   The Iron Mistress
1953   The Jazz Singer
1958   Marjorie Morningstar
Rapport, Lawrence
1958   Machete
Raquello, Edward
1938   Charlie Chan at Monte
        Carlo
1939   The Girl from Mexico
Rascel, Renato
1958   Seven Hills of Rome
Rasch, Albertina
1930   Galas de la Paramount
The Albertina Rasch Dancers
1930   Galas de la Paramount
Rasch, Pete
1931   Delicious
1938   The Buccaneer
Raskin, Sherman
1960   Take a Giant Step
Rasp, Fritz
1931   Die Dreigroschenoper
        Tropennächte
Rasumny, Mikhail
1941   Hold Back the Dawn
1945   A Medal for Benny
1947   Pirates of Monterey
1949   The Kissing Bandit
1952   Anything Can Happen
1953   The Stars Are Singing
        Tonight We Sing
1956   Hot Blood
Ratcliff, Carl
1960   Ice Palace
Ratcliffe, E. J. *see* **Radcliffe, E. J.**
Rathbone, Basil
1940   The Mark of Zorro
1958   The Last Hurrah
Rathmell, John
1937   The Riders of the
        Whistling Skull
Ratliff, Doris
1949?   The Joint Is Jumpin'
Ratner, Herbert
1948   Gentleman's Agreement
1953   The Joe Louis Story
Ratoff, Gregory
1932   Symphony of Six Million
1933   Let's Fall in Love
1934   The Great Flirtation
1936   Sins of Man
1938   Gateway
1940   Elsa Maxwell's Public
        Deb No. 1
1941   Adam Had Four Sons
1945   Where Do We Go From
        Here?
1953   Taxi
Rattenbury, Harry
1919   The Delicious Little Devil
        Hearts of Men
1920   Huckleberry Finn
Raucourt, Jules
1930   Le spectre vert
1931   Echec au roi
        La gran jornada (*foreign
        version*)
1934   Caravane
        La veuve joyeuse
1935   L'homme des Folies
        Bergère

Rauh, Stanley
1936   Laughing Irish Eyes
1939   The Cisco Kid and the
        Lady
Ravara, Mr.
1927?   You Can't Win
Ravel, Sandra
1930   Amor audaz (*foreign
        version*)
Ravel, Stelita
1948   Moonrise
Raven, a horse
1931   The Hurricane Horseman
Raven, Harry
1954   Drums Across the River
Raven, John
1951   The Great Caruso
1956   Hot Blood
Ravenel, Florence
1955   Violent Saturday
Ravenne, Arthur de
1934   La veuve joyeuse
Raver, Harry
1919   As a Man Thinks
        The Volcano
Ravetch, Irving
1960   The Dark at the Top of
        the Stairs
Ravoli, Amos
1958   Seven Hills of Rome
Rawles, Carrie E.
1926   General Custer at Little
        Big Horn
Rawlings, John (*actor*)
1941   Secret of the Wastelands
Rawlins, David
1951   Fort Defiance
Rawlins, John (*dir*)
1941   Mutiny in the Arctic
1942   Unseen Enemy
1948   The Arizona Ranger
1949   Massacre River
1951   Fort Defiance
Rawlins, Phil
1959   Al Capone
Rawlinson, Herbert
1922   The Scrapper
1923   The Victor
1925   The Man in Blue
        The Prairie Wife
1936   Mad Holiday
1938   Hawaii Calls
1941   Mystery Ship
1942   Foreign Agent
        We Were Dancing
1943   Crime Smasher
        Doughboys in Ireland
1944   Hi, Beautiful
        Marshal of Reno
Rawlinson, Sally
1948   Unconquered
Rawls, Frank
1950   Mystery Submarine
Ray, Adele
1914   Springtime
Ray, Albert
1930   Kathleen Mavourneen
1939   Charlie Chan in Reno
1943   Good Luck, Mr. Yates
1947   California
1948   Fighting Father Dunne
Ray, Aldo *same as* **DaRe, Aldo**
1951   Saturday's Hero
1960   The Day They Robbed the
        Bank of England
Ray, Allan *same as* **Ray, Allen**
1943   Dixie
1946   The Face of Marble
1947   Crossfire
1948   Unconquered
1949   Illegal Entry
1951   The Great Caruso
        Show Boat
1952   The Half-Breed
Ray, Allene
1929   Hawk of the Hills
Ray, Anita
1936   Ramona

Ray, Ann
1941   Sun Valley Serenade
Ray, Arthur
1921   The Burden of Race
        Ties of Blood
1938   The Duke Is Tops
1939   Double Deal
        One Dark Night
1940   Am I Guilty?
        Son of Ingagi
1940?   Mr. Washington Goes to
        Town
1942   Lucky Ghost
        Professor Creeps
        Take My Life
Ray, Bernard B. *same as* **Ray, B. B.**
1934   The Cactus Kid
        The Fighting Hero
1935   North of Arizona
        Wolf Riders
1936   El crimen de media
        noche
        Pinto Rustlers
        La última cita
1940   Broken Strings
1947   Buffalo Bill Rides Again
1952   Buffalo Bill in Tomahawk
        Territory
Ray, Billy
1941   Adam Had Four Sons
Ray, Bobby *same as* **Ray, Robert**
1936   Yellow Cargo
1942   Take My Life
1944   Black Magic
        The Chinese Cat
1945   The Navajo Trail
        Sunbonnet Sue
Ray, Charles
1941   Hurry, Charlie, Hurry
1949?   The Joint Is Jumpin'
Ray, Daphne
1939   Moon over Harlem
Ray, Dorothy
1931   Cimarron
Ray, Emma
1932   So Big
Ray, Jane
1938   In Old Chicago
Ray, Jimmy
1943   Dixie
Ray, Joe *not the same as* **Ray, Joey**
1914   John Barleycorn
1920   The Man Who Dared
1936   Sins of Man
Ray, Joey *not the same as* **Ray, Joe**
1940   Music in My Heart
1941   Caught in the Act
1942   The Navy Comes Through
1943   Hitler's Children
1945   Johnny Angel
1947   California
        Easy Come, Easy Go
1953   Ride, Vaquero!
Ray, Leah
1938   Happy Landing
Ray, Maria
1940   Escape
Ray, Michel
1957   The Tin Star
Ray, Mona
1928   Uncle Tom's Cabin
Ray, Nicholas
1945   A Tree Grows in Brooklyn
1949   Knock on Any Door
1956   Hot Blood
Ray, Robert *see* **Ray, Bobby**
Ray, Roland *could be same as* **Ray,
Rolin**
1958   Tonka
Ray, Rolin *could be same as* **Ray,
Roland**
1934   Stand Up and Cheer!
Ray, Terry
1938   Dangerous to Know
1939   The Escape
Ray, Virginia
1936   Star for a Night
Rayas, José de
1930   La rosa de fuego

Raye, Martha
1937   Waikiki Wedding
Rayford, Alma
1932   Law and Lawless
Raymaker, Herman C.
1924   Racing Luck
1926   Millionaires
Raymond, Dean
1917   The Wild Girl
Raymond, Earle
1915   The Sable Lorcha
Raymond, Eddie
1952?   Call of the Navajo
Raymond, Frances
1920   Li Ting Lang
1922   Shadows
1927   The Gay Defender
Raymond, Gene
1931   Personal Maid
1934   Behold My Wife!
        Coming Out Party
1937   That Girl from Paris
Raymond, Guy
1958   Marjorie Morningstar
Raymond, Helen
1921   Through the Back Door
1923   The Huntress
Raymond, Jack
1925   Scarlet Saint
1927   Pleasure Before Business
1929   The Younger Generation
1933   The Cohens and Kellys in
        Trouble
1936   After the Thin Man
1942   Foreign Agent
        Woman of the Year
1943   Gangway for Tomorrow
        In Old Oklahoma
Raymond, Paula
1950   Devil's Doorway
1951   The Tall Target
1955   The Gun That Won the
        West
Raymond, Robin
1942   Sunday Punch
1943   His Butler's Sister
1953   The Glass Wall
Raymond, Royal
1949   The Red Menace
Raymond, Sid
1952   Anything Can Happen
Raymond, William
1916   The Woman in 47
Rayo, Myra
1932   Hollywood, ciudad de
        ensueño
Rea, Daniel F.
1930   The Bad Man (*foreign
        version*)
        East Is West (*foreign
        version*)
1935   Un hombre peligroso
1936   El diablo del mar
1939   La Inmaculada
        Papá soltero
1941   Hold Back the Dawn
Reachi, Manuel
1934   La buenaventura
1935   El cantante de Nápoles
1941   Hold Back the Dawn
Read, Barbara
1942   Rubber Racketeers
Reagan, Martin
1914   The Littlest Rebel
Reagan, Neil
1943   Doughboys in Ireland
        Good Luck, Mr. Yates
Reagan, Ronald
1940   Knute Rockne—All
        American
        Santa Fe Trail
1942   Juke Girl
1949   The Girl from Jones
        Beach
1951   The Last Outpost
1954   Cattle Queen of Montana
Real, Alma
1930   El presidio
1931   La fruta amarga
        Mamá
        Yankee Don

1934	Las fronteras del amor
	Tres amores
1935	Alas sobre el Chaco
1936	Contra la corriente
	Dancing Pirate

Real, Aurora del
1931	Carne de cabaret

Reardon, "Beans"
1936	Klondike Annie

Reardon, Don
1960	I Passed for White

Reason, Rex *same as* **Roberts, Bart**
1954	Taza, Son of Cochise
1955	Kiss of Fire
	Smoke Signal
1956	Raw Edge
1957	Band of Angels
1958	The Rawhide Trail

Reason, Rhodes
1959	Yellowstone Kelly

Rebel, a horse
1934	Fighting Through
1935	Range Warfare

Rebush, Roman
1937	Green Fields
1938	The Singing Blacksmith
1939	Mirele Efros

Recht, Joe
1947	Desperate
1948	The Lady from Shanghai

Rechtzeit, Seymour
1930	Eternal Fools (Ewige Naranim)
1933	Live and Laugh
1935	Shir Hashirim
1939	Motel the Operator
1940	Her Second Mother
	The Jewish Melody
1941	Mazel Tov Yidden
1950	Monticello, Here We Come!

Reckwart, Wacklaw
1944	An American Romance

Red Dust, a dog
1953	The Stars Are Singing

Red Fox, Elmo
1936	Ramona

Red Wing *same as* **Red Wing, Princess; St. Cyr, Lillian Red Wing, Princess**
1914	In the Days of the Thundering Herd
	The Squaw Man
1916	Ramona

Redaelli, Guito
1931	La regina di Sparta

Redd, Frances
1940	Midnight Shadow

Redgrave, Michael
1959	Shake Hands with the Devil

Redlich, Ernst E., Dr.
1931	Don Juan diplomático (*foreign version*)

Redwing, Rod *same as* **Redwing, Rodd; Redwing, Roderic**
1946	Singin' in the Corn
1947	The Last Round-Up
1948	Key Largo
	Singin' Spurs
	Unconquered
1949	Apache Chief
	Laramie
	We Were Strangers
1950	Riders of the Pony Express
1951	Little Big Horn
1952	Buffalo Bill in Tomahawk Territory
	Trail of the Arrow
1953	Conquest of Cochise
	Last of the Comanches
	The Pathfinder
1954	Cattle Queen of Montana
1960	Flaming Star

Reed, Alan *same as* **Reed, Alan, Sr.**
1945	Nob Hill
1950	Emergency Wedding
1955	The Far Horizons
	Kiss of Fire
1958	Marjorie Morningstar

Reed, Billy *same as* **Reed, Billy Edward**
1942	Syncopation
1943	Mexican Spitfire's Blessed Event

Reed, Clarence
1930	A Daughter of the Congo

Reed, Cora
1919	Injustice

Reed, Mrs. Crystal
1919	Injustice

Reed, David
1946	G. I. War Brides
	Gas House Kids

Reed, Donald
1929	Evangeline
1931	Aloha
1932	Hollywood, ciudad de ensueño
1933	Man from Monterey
1935	The Cyclone Ranger
1936	Ramona
1937	Law and Lead

Reed, Donna
1942	Apache Trail
	Mokey
1943	Dr. Gillespie's Criminal Case
1951	Saturday's Hero
1954	They Rode West
1955	The Far Horizons
1956	The Benny Goodman Story

Reed, Emma
1935	So Red the Rose

Reed, George *same as* **Reed, George H.**
1920	Huckleberry Finn
1923	Scars of Jealousy
1928	Absent
1934	Judge Priest
1936	After the Thin Man
	The Green Pastures
	Show Boat
1937	One Mile from Heaven
1938	The Buccaneer
	Josette
	The Toy Wife
1941	Belle Starr
1942	Dr. Gillespie's New Assistant
	In This Our Life
	Tales of Manhattan
	They Died With Their Boots On
	We Were Dancing
1943	Dixie
	His Butler's Sister
1944	Chip Off the Old Block
	Three Men in White
1945	Between Two Women
	Nob Hill
1946	Saratoga Trunk
1947	Dark Delusion

Reed, Gus
1936	The Prisoner of Shark Island
1941	New York Town
	Sullivan's Travels

Reed, Ione
1935	Melody Trail
1938	The Buccaneer
1940	Escape to Glory

Reed, Katherine
1917	The Renaissance at Charleroi

Reed, Luther
1919	Behind the Door
1923	Little Old New York
1934	Tres amores

Reed, Lydia
1955	Good Morning, Miss Dove

Reed, Marshall
1944	Marshal of Reno
	Tucson Raiders
1947	On the Old Spanish Trail
	Spoilers of the North
1948	Renegades of Sonora
1949	The Cowboy and the Prizefighter
	The Dalton Gang
1950	Cherokee Uprising
	Rock Island Trail

Reed, Mary
1951	Hurricane Island
	Oh! Susanna
1952	Fort Osage
1953	Old Overland Trail
	San Antone

Reed, Mary
1941	Sullivan's Travels

Reed, Nat
1938	Swing!

Reed, Philip *same as* **Reed, Phillip**
1936	Klondike Annie
	The Last of the Mohicans
1947	Pirates of Monterey
1949	Daughter of the West
1950	Bandit Queen
	Davy Crockett, Indian Scout

Reed, Ralph
1944	Since You Went Away
1952	High Noon
1960	Cimarron

Reed, Richard
1945	Where Do We Go From Here?

Reed, Robert Ralston
1916	Witchcraft

Reed, Theodore
1920	The Mark of Zorro

Reed, Tom
1928	The Rawhide Kid
1929	Show Boat
1930	East Is West
1931	Don Juan diplomático
	Don Juan diplomático (*foreign version*)

Reed, Violet
1915	The Gambler of the West

Reed, Vivian *see* **Reid, Vivian**

Reed, Walter
1942	Mexican Spitfire's Elephant
1943	Mexican Spitfire's Blessed Event
1948	Western Heritage
1950	The Lawless
	Young Man with a Horn
1951	Go for Broke!
1952	Red Ball Express
1953	The Man from the Alamo
	Seminole
	War Paint
1954	Dangerous Mission
	The Yellow Tomahawk
1955	The Far Horizons
	The Last Command
1957	The Lawless Eighties
1960	Sergeant Rutledge

Reedor, Anna
1916	A Woman's Honor

Reeds, Robert A.
1958	Ambush at Cimarron Pass

Reedy, John
1915	How Molly Malone Made Good

Rees, Ed
1948	Moonrise

Rees, Lanny
1948	The Time of Your Life

Rees, Sonny
1948	Fighting Father Dunne

Reese, George
1948	Unconquered

Reese, John *same as* **Reese, Johnny**
1944	Buffalo Bill
1945	Where Do We Go From Here?

Reese, Tom
1960	Flaming Star

Reeves, Alice
1920	The Face at Your Window

Reeves, Bob
1931	Delicious
1934	Our Daily Bread

Reeves, Ellanora
1952	Rose of Cimarron

Reeves, George
1939	Gone With the Wind
1940	Knute Rockne—All American
1941	Dead Men Tell

Reeves, J. Harold
1931	Delicious

Reeves, Martha
1933	It's Great to Be Alive

Reeves, McKinley
1947?	Return of Mandy's Husband

Reeves, Myrtle
1917	A Kentucky Cinderella
1919	A Bachelor's Wife

Reeves, Richard
1948	Unconquered
1953	The Glass Wall

Regan, Barry
1950	Colt .45
1951	Jim Thorpe—All-American
1953	The Sun Shines Bright
1955	The Long Gray Line

Regan, Charles
1944	An American Romance
1950	Annie Get Your Gun
	Jolson Sings Again
1951	Show Boat
1952	The Big Sky

Regan, Jayne
1934	The Cactus Kid
1937	Thank You, Mr. Moto
1938	Josette
	Mr. Moto's Gamble

Regan, Phil
1936	Laughing Irish Eyes
1937	Manhattan Merry-Go-Round
1938	Outside of Paradise
1945	Sunbonnet Sue

Regan, Tony
1959	The Jayhawkers!

Regas, George *same as* **Rigas, George**
1926	Desert Gold
1929	Redskin
	Wolf Song
1930	Alma de gaucho
	La rosa de fuego
1932	The Golden West
1935	Bordertown
1936	Daniel Boone
	Robin Hood of El Dorado
1937	The Californian
	Charlie Chan on Broadway
	Waikiki Wedding
1938	Mr. Moto Takes a Chance
	The Toy Wife
1940	The Mark of Zorro

Regas, Manoles
1954	Barefoot Battalion

Regas, Pedro
1935	Black Fury
1936	Sutter's Gold
	The Traitor
1937	Waikiki Wedding
1943	Action in the North Atlantic
1945	South of the Rio Grande
1947	California
1949	The Kissing Bandit
1953	Ride, Vaquero!
	Tonight We Sing

Regnier, Roy
1953	Tonight We Sing

Reh, Philo
1943	The Meanest Man in the World

Rehfelt, Curt
1916	Sold for Marriage

Rei, Miri
1937	Waikiki Wedding

Reiber, Hilda
1932	Mazel Tov

Reicher, Frank
1915	The Secret Sin
1916	Alien Souls
	For the Defense
	Pudd'nhead Wilson
	Witchcraft
1917	Castles for Two
	The Trouble Buster
	Unconquered

1918　　The Only Road
1920?　The Scarlet Dragon
1928　　A Ship Comes In (*foreign version*)
　　　　Sins of the Fathers
1929　　Mister Antonio
1930　　Anna Christie (*foreign version*)
　　　　The Grand Parade
　　　　A Lady to Love (*foreign version*)
1931　　Beyond Victory
　　　　Gentleman's Fate
1933　　Ever in My Heart
1935　　Rendezvous
1936　　Star for a Night
　　　　Sutter's Gold
1937　　Man of the People
1938　　City Streets
　　　　Rascals
1939　　The Escape
1940　　The Man I Married
1941　　The Face Behind the Mask
　　　　They Dare Not Love
1942　　Nazi Agent
　　　　Secret Enemies
1944　　Address Unknown
1945　　The Jade Mask
　　　　A Medal for Benny
　　　　Rhapsody in Blue

Reicher, Hedwiga *same as* **Sibelius, Celia**
1931　　Beyond Victory
　　　　El proceso de Mary Dugan (*foreign version*)
1937　　It Could Happen to You
1939　　Confessions of a Nazi Spy

Reichert, Kittens
1916　　Broken Fetters
1917　　The Peddler
　　　　The Primitive Call
　　　　Unknown 274

Reichle, Art
1958　　The Young Lions

Reichow, Otto
1942　　All Through the Night
1943　　Action in the North Atlantic
　　　　Crash Dive
　　　　They Came to Blow Up America
1944　　Address Unknown
1945　　Nob Hill
1946　　Rendezvous 24
1950　　Battleground
1958　　The Young Lions

Reid, Carl Benton
1951　　The Great Caruso
1952　　Indian Uprising
1954　　Broken Lance
1956　　The Last Wagon

Reid, Cliff
1935　　Annie Oakley
　　　　His Family Tree
1940　　Mexican Spitfire
　　　　Mexican Spitfire Out West
1941　　The Mexican Spitfire's Baby
1942　　Mexican Spitfire at Sea
　　　　Mexican Spitfire Sees a Ghost
1947　　Crossfire
1958　　The Light in the Forest

Reid, Elliott
1940　　The Ramparts We Watch

Reid, Hal
1914　　Dan
1915　　Time Lock Number 776

Reid, Jane
1930　　Sins of the Children

Reid, Marita
1956　　Crowded Paradise

Reid, Max
1950　　Young Daniel Boone

Reid, Vivian *same as* **Reed, Vivian**
1916　　At Piney Ridge
1933　　The Man Who Dared: An Imaginative Biography

Reid, Wallace
1915　　The Birth of a Nation
　　　　A Yankee from the West
1917　　The Squaw Man's Son
1918　　The Source
1923　　Thirty Days

Reilly, Frank
1917　　The Bar Sinister

Reilly, Gina
1920　　The Face at Your Window

Reilly, Hugh
1952　　Bright Victory

Reilly, Jack
1951　　Go for Broke!

Reimer, Lorraine
1945　　Where Do We Go From Here?

Reineck, Willard *same as* **Reineck, Willard M.**
1958　　The Lone Ranger and the Lost City of Gold
1959　　Thunder in the Sun

Reiner, Fritz
1947　　Carnegie Hall

Reiner, Maxine
1936　　Charlie Chan at the Circus
　　　　It Had to Happen
　　　　Sins of Man

Reinhardt, Betty *same as* **Reinhardt, Elizabeth**
1934　　La buenaventura
1935　　Angelina o el honor de un brigadier
　　　　El cantante de Nápoles
1943　　His Butler's Sister

Reinhardt, John
1918　　The Birth of a Race
1929　　Love, Live and Laugh
1930　　Los que danzan (*foreign version*)
1933　　Primavera en otoño
　　　　Yo, tú y ella
1934　　Un capitán de cosacos
　　　　La ciudad de cartón
　　　　Dos más uno, dos
　　　　Granaderos del amor
　　　　Nada más que una mujer
1935　　De la sartén al fuego
　　　　El día que me quieras
　　　　Tango Bar
1937　　El capitán Tormenta
1938　　Rascals
1939　　Mr. Moto in Danger Island
1940　　Tengo fe en ti
1948　　Open Secret

Reinhardt, Wolfgang
1954　　Indiscretion of an American Wife

Reinicke, William
1951　　Snake River Desperadoes

Reis, Irving
1939　　King of Chinatown
1943　　Hitler's Children
1951　　New Mexico

Reisch, Walter
1938　　Gateway
1942　　Seven Sweethearts

Reisenberg, Nadia
1947　　Carnegie Hall

Leo Reisman and His Band
1946?　Harlem on Parade

Reisner, Allen
1957　　All Mine to Give
1958　　St. Louis Blues

Reisner, Chuck
1923　　Breaking into Society
1925　　Justice of the Far North

Reiter, William
1936　　Sutter's Gold

Reitzen, Jack
1951　　Mask of the Dragon

Rekwart, Waclaw
1952　　Anything Can Happen

Relampago, a horse
1958　　Sierra Baron

Remich, William R. *could be same as* **Remick, Bill**
1958　　Houseboat

Remick, Bill *could be same as* **Remich, William R.**
1960　　Cimarron

Remick, Lee
1960　　Wild River

Remley, Ralph
1934　　Behold My Wife!
1936　　Robin Hood of El Dorado
1937　　Waikiki Wedding
1938　　Outside of Paradise

Remmels, Morton
1958　　Tonka

Remsden, Frank
1940　　New Moon
1953　　The Jazz Singer

Rémy, Maurice
1932　　Le cas du docteur Brenner

Renaldo, Duncan
1936　　Rebellion
1938　　Spawn of the North
1940　　Covered Wagon Days
1941　　Gauchos of Eldorado
1942　　We Were Dancing
1943　　Border Patrol
1944　　The San Antonio Kid
1945　　The Cisco Kid Returns
　　　　In Old New Mexico
　　　　South of the Rio Grande
1949　　The Daring Caballero
　　　　The Gay Amigo
　　　　Satan's Cradle
　　　　The Valiant Hombre
1950　　The Girl from San Lorenzo

Renaldo, Tito
1936　　Ramona
1942　　Apache Trail
　　　　Sunday Punch
　　　　Tortilla Flat
1945　　South of the Rio Grande
1946　　Till the End of Time
1947　　Ride the Pink Horse
1948　　Old Los Angeles
1949　　We Were Strangers
1952　　California Conquest
　　　　The Fabulous Senorita
　　　　Trail of the Arrow

Renard, Carlo
1932　　Cuore d'emigrante

Renard, H.
1926　　Under Fire

Renard, Ken
194-　　Mistaken Identity
1948　　Killer Diller

Renault, George
1934　　La veuve joyeuse

Renavent, Georges *same as* **Renavent, George**
1919　　Erstwhile Susan
1930　　Le spectre vert
1932　　Le bluffeur
1933　　L'amour guide
1934　　La veuve joyeuse
1935　　L'homme des Folies Bergère
1938　　Charlie Chan at Monte Carlo
1939　　Mr. Moto's Last Warning
1941　　Sullivan's Travels
　　　　They Dare Not Love
1943　　Wintertime
1945　　Rhapsody in Blue
1946　　Saratoga Trunk
1947　　The Foxes of Harrow

Renay, Paul
1942　　Tales of Manhattan

Rene, Alex *same as* **Rene, Alexander**
1917?　Barnaby Lee
1920?　Broken Hearts

Rene, Joel
1949　　We Were Strangers

Renick, Ruth
1924　　Conductor 1492

Renner, María Teresa *same as* **Renner, Teresa**
1930　　El cuerpo del delito
　　　　Los que danzan
　　　　El último de los Vargas

Rennie, James
1930　　The Bad Man
　　　　The Lash
1942　　Tales of Manhattan

Rennie, Michael
1955　　Seven Cities of Gold

Renno, Vincent
1950　　Black Hand
1951　　The Great Caruso

Reno, Paul
1931　　La carta (*foreign version*)
　　　　La fiesta del diablo (*foreign version*)

Renoir, Jean
1943　　The Amazing Mrs. Holliday

Rentschler, Mickey
1935　　Black Fury
1936　　Sins of Man
1938　　The Adventures of Tom Sawyer
1939　　The Adventures of Huckleberry Finn
1942　　Valley of Hunted Men
1943　　Redhead from Manhattan

Repp, Ed Earl
1937　　Prairie Thunder
1948　　Guns of Hate
1950　　Storm Over Wyoming
1951　　Cyclone Fury

Repp, Stafford
1959　　The Crimson Kimono

The Republic Rhythm Riders
1953　　Old Overland Trail

Resner, Lawrence
1957　　Gun Battle at Monterey

Resnick, Sam
1950　　Battleground

Ressler, B.
1940　　Americaner Schadchen

Restivo, Carmella *same as* **Restivo, Carmela**
1950　　The Toast of New Orleans
1951　　Go for Broke!

Restivo, George
1950　　Black Hand
1951　　The Great Caruso

Retchin, Norman
1957　　Ride Out for Revenge

Rettig, Earl
1931　　The Cisco Kid

Rettig, Tommy
1950　　Panic in the Streets
1953　　So Big
1956　　The Last Wagon

Reuben, Alma
1916　　The Half-Breed

Reuss, Allan
1956　　The Benny Goodman Story

Reutemann, William
1931　　Così è la vita

Reve, Betty
1932　　Yiskor

Revel, Harry
1944　　Minstrel Man

Revell, Jerry
1944　　Since You Went Away

Revere, Anne
1943　　The Meanest Man in the World
1947　　Body and Soul
1948　　Gentleman's Agreement

Revier, Dorothy
1924　　Down by the Rio Grande
1930　　The Bad Man
1931　　The Avenger
　　　　The Black Camel
1932　　The Secrets of Wu Sin

Revier, Harry
1927　　The Slaver

Revueltas, Rosaura
1954　　Salt of the Earth

Rex, a horse
1926　　The Devil Horse
1933　　King of the Wild Horses

Rey, Alvino
1942　　Syncopation

Rey, Araceli
1932　Soñadores de la gloria
Rey, Florián
1931　Lo mejor es reír
　　　La pura verdad
　　　Su noche de bodas
1933　Espérame
　　　Melodía de arrabal
Rey, Frances
1946　Singin' in the Corn
1947　The Last Round-Up
Rey, Rita
1930　El príncipe del dólar
1931　Aloha
Rey, Roberto
1930　Un hombre de suerte
1931　Un caballero de frac
　　　Chérie (foreign version)
　　　Gente alegre
　　　El príncipe gondolero
Rey, Rosa
1934　La buenaventura
　　　Tres amores
1935　El cantante de Nápoles
　　　Julieta compra un hijo
　　　Rosa de Francia
1936　El crimen de media
　　　　noche
　　　Song of the Gringo
1937　El capitán Tormenta
1946　The Face of Marble
1955　The Rose Tattoo
Reyburn, Noel
1950　The Lawless
1951　Saturday's Hero
Reyes, Conchita
1948　Angel in Exile
Reyes, Delores
1936　Ramona
Reyes, Helen
1951　The Great Caruso
Reyes, Paul & Eva
1947　Copacabana
Reyes, Reva
1930　Revista
　　　Hispano-Americana
Reyes, Stanley J.
1950　Panic in the Streets
Reyher, Ferdinand
1959　The World, the Flesh and
　　　the Devil
Reymond, Dalton
1946　Song of the South
Reynolds, Adeline de Walt same
　　as Reynolds, Adeline deWalt
1941　Come Live with Me
1942　Tales of Manhattan
1944　Going My Way
　　　Since You Went Away
1945　A Tree Grows in Brooklyn
1950　Stars in My Crown
Reynolds, Alan
1958　Gunman's Walk
Reynolds, Audrey
1937　Maid of Salem
Reynolds, Blake
1956　The Benny Goodman
　　　Story
Reynolds, Charles
1918　The Prussian Cur
Reynolds, Clark E.
1955　Shotgun
1959　Gunmen from Laredo
Reynolds, Craig
1936　Treachery Rides the
　　　Range
1939　The Mystery of Mr. Wong
1940　The Fatal Hour
Reynolds, Debbie
1950　The Daughter of Rosie
　　　O'Grady
1956　The Catered Affair
Reynolds, Don same as "Little
　　Brown Jug"; Reynolds, Don
　　"Little Brown Jug"
1946　Romance of the West
1949　The Cowboy and the
　　　Prizefighter
　　　Ride, Ryder, Ride!
　　　Roll Thunder Roll!
1951　Snake River Desperadoes

Reynolds, Eve
1935　¡Asegure a su mujer!
1936　Star for a Night
Reynolds, Gene
1936　Sins of Man
1937　The Californian
1938　In Old Chicago
1940　Santa Fe Trail
Reynolds, George
1939　Lying Lips
Reynolds, Helene
1942　Tales of Manhattan
1943　The Meanest Man in the
　　　World
　　　Wintertime
Reynolds, Jack
1958　Bullwhip
Reynolds, Joan
1956　Hot Blood
Reynolds, Joyce
1943　Yankee Doodle Dandy
Reynolds, Lynn
1922　Sky High
1923　The Huntress
Reynolds, Marjorie
1939　Mr. Wong in Chinatown
1940　Doomed to Die
　　　The Fatal Hour
1942　Holiday Inn
1943　Dixie
1949　That Midnight Kiss
Reynolds, Peter
1959　Shake Hands with the
　　　Devil
Reynolds, Quentin
1948　Call Northside 777
　　　The Miracle of the Bells
Reynolds, Randall
1931　Delicious
Reynolds, Red
1958　Tonka
Reynolds, Reginald
1940　The Ramparts We Watch
Reynolds, Steve
1921　The Green-Eyed Monster
1922　The Bull-Dogger
　　　The Crimson Skull
1923　Regeneration
1926　The Flying Ace
1928　Black Gold
Reynolds, Vera
1930　The Last Dance
Reynolds, William
1952　The Battle at Apache Pass
　　　The Raiders
Rhein, Al
1938　Little Miss Roughneck
1940　East of the River
1941　The Face Behind the
　　　Mask
　　　Mystery Ship
1943　Mr. Lucky
1945　Johnny Angel
1950　Annie Get Your Gun
1951　Show Boat
Rhein, George
1950　Annie Get Your Gun
1951　Show Boat
1952　My Man and I
1953　Bright Road
Rheiner, Sam
1942　Tales of Manhattan
Rhett, Alicia
1939　Gone With the Wind
Rhetta, Jo
1946　Mantan Messes Up
1947?　What a Guy
Rhinehart, William
1949　The Undercover Man
1955　Blackboard Jungle
Rhinelander, Gregg
1950　The Breaking Point
Rhodes, Christopher
1959　John Paul Jones
　　　Shake Hands with the
　　　Devil
Rhodes, Don
1956　Reprisal!

Rhodes, Dusty
1946　The Gay Cavalier
Rhodes, Erik
1935　Charlie Chan in Paris
　　　A Night at the Ritz
1937　Music for Madame
Rhodes, Georgette
1930　El príncipe del dólar
　　　(foreign version)
1931　Buster se marie
　　　The Cohens and Kellys in
　　　Africa
　　　Quand on est belle
1934　La veuve joyeuse
Rhodes, Grandon
1943　Action in the North
　　　Atlantic
1944　The Sullivans
1945　Nob Hill
1947　Ride the Pink Horse
1949　The Clay Pigeon
　　　Streets of Laredo
1952　Indian Uprising
1953　So Big
1955　Headline Hunters
　　　Trial
1959　The FBI Story
1960　Oklahoma Territory
Rhodes, Hari
1957　Burden of Truth
1960　This Rebel Breed
Rhodes, Stanley
1959　The Hanging Tree
Rhubarb, a cat
1957　Beau James
The Rhythm Boys
1930　King of Jazz
Riano, John
1948?　Boarding House Blues
Riano, Renie
1938　Outside of Paradise
1939　Mr. Moto in Danger
　　　Island
1940　Kit Carson
1941　Adam Had Four Sons
　　　Ice-Capades
1942　They Died With Their
　　　Boots On
　　　Whispering Ghosts
1945　Club Havana
1946　Bad Bascomb
　　　Bringing Up Father
1947　Jiggs and Maggie in
　　　Society
1948　Jiggs and Maggie in Court
　　　The Time of Your Life
1949　Jiggs and Maggie in
　　　Jackpot Jitters
1950　Jiggs and Maggie Out
　　　West
Ribic, Captain
1932　Ljubav i strast
Ribio, John
1932　Ljubav i strast
Ricardi, Enrico
1936　Ramona
Ricciardi, Joseph
1918　My Cousin
Ricciardi, William
1926　Puppets
1932　Tiger Shark
1937　Man of the People
Riccioni, Enzo
1931　La fiesta del diablo
　　　(foreign version)
Rice, Andy
1935　McFadden's Flats
Rice, Arthur W.
1914?　The Chinese Lily
Rice, Elmer
1931　Street Scene
1933　Counsellor at Law
1942　Holiday Inn
Rice, Florence
1937　Man of the People
1939　Stand Up and Fight
1942　Let's Get Tough!
Rice, Frank
1928　Orphan of the Sage
1929　The Overland Telegraph
1930　Song of the Caballero

Rice, Jack
1941　New York Town
1943　Good Luck, Mr. Yates
1944　Hi, Beautiful
　　　Lady, Let's Dance!
1947　Dark Delusion
　　　It Had To Be You
Rice, John Wiley
1959　The Jayhawkers!
Rice, Roy
1935　Riddle Ranch
Rice, Sam
1935　A Night at the Ritz
1938　City Streets
Rice, Versia
1921　As the World Rolls On
Rice and Cady
1938　In Old Chicago
Rich, Bob could be same as Rich,
　　Bobby
1951　The Tall Target
Rich, Bobby could be same as
　　Rich, Bob
1944　An American Romance
Rich, Dick
1937　Big City
　　　Souls at Sea
1939　Let Freedom Ring
1940　Elsa Maxwell's Public
　　　Deb No. 1
　　　Escape to Glory
　　　Lucky Cisco Kid
1941　Accent on Love
　　　Belle Starr
　　　Ride on Vaquero
　　　Western Union
1942　Rio Rita
　　　Rubber Racketeers
　　　Three Hearts for Julia
1943　In Old Oklahoma
　　　The Ox-Bow Incident
1947　The Burning Cross
1948　Fury at Furnace Creek
1952　Bugles in the Afternoon
　　　Trail of the Arrow
1953　Dream Wife
1954　Overland Pacific
1956　The Last Hunt
Rich, Irene
1919　Diane of the Green Van
　　　The Sneak
1921　One Man in a Million
　　　A Tale of Two Worlds
1923　Snowdrift
1930　Check and Double Check
1947　Calendar Girl
　　　New Orleans
1948　Fort Apache
Rich, Lillian
1925　Braveheart
1936　Dangerous Intrigue
Rich, Mila
1943　The Amazing Mrs.
　　　Holliday
Rich, Vernon
1953　Dream Wife
1955　The Far Horizons
Rich, Vido
1943　The Amazing Mrs.
　　　Holliday
Rich, Vivian
1923　The Lone Wagon
Richard, Belle
1942　Song of the Islands
Richard, Ed
1943　The Ox-Bow Incident
Richards, Addison
1934　Our Daily Bread
1935　Black Fury
1936　Sutter's Gold
1937　The Barrier
　　　Black Legion
1938　Gateway
1939　Bad Lands
1940　Charlie Chan in Panama
　　　Elsa Maxwell's Public
　　　Deb No. 1
　　　Geronimo

Little Nellie Kelly
Northwest Passage (Book I—Rogers' Rangers)
Santa Fe Trail
1941 Mutiny in the Arctic
   Western Union
1942 Friendly Enemies
   Mokey
   Secret Enemies
   They Died With Their Boots On
1943 Air Force
   Deerslayer
1944 Since You Went Away
   The Sullivans
   Three Men in White
1945 Betrayal from the East
   The Mummy's Curse
   The Shanghai Cobra
1948 Call Northside 777
   Reaching from Heaven
1949 Rustlers
1950 Davy Crockett, Indian Scout
1955 Fort Yuma
1956 The Broken Star
   Reprisal!
   Walk the Proud Land
1960 All the Fine Young Cannibals
   The Dark at the Top of the Stairs

Richards, Ann
1942 Dr. Gillespie's New Assistant
   Three Hearts for Julia
1944 An American Romance

Richards, Beah
1960 Take a Giant Step

Richards, Claire
1945 The Dolly Sisters

Richards, Cully
1936 It Had to Happen
   Robin Hood of El Dorado
1938 My Lucky Star

Richards, Dorothy
1921 The Barricade

Richards, Frank
1942 Sunday Punch
1943 Redhead from Manhattan
1945 The House on 92nd St.
1949 The Cowboy and the Indians
1950 Black Hand
   No Way Out
1951 Across the Wide Missouri
1952 The Savage
1956 Davy Crockett and the River Pirates
   Man from Del Rio
1957 Gun Battle at Monterey
1958 Escape from Red Rock
1959 The Black Orchid

Richards, Gordon
1948 Unconquered
1950 The Big Hangover
1953 Dream Wife

Richards, Grant
1959 Inside the Mafia
1960 Oklahoma Territory

Richards, Harry
1953 The Member of the Wedding

Richards, Jeff
1951 The Tall Target

Richards, Keith
1941 Birth of the Blues
   New York Town
   Secret of the Wastelands
1942 Holiday Inn
1947 Calendar Girl
1948 Tap Roots
1950 Mystery Submarine
   North of the Great Divide
1958 Ambush at Cimarron Pass

Richards, Lloyd
1943 Gangway for Tomorrow
1946 Without Reservations
1950 The Men
1951 Gambling House

Richards, Paul
1953 War Paint
1958 Blood Arrow
1960 All the Young Men

Richards, Robert L.
1940 The Ramparts We Watch
1950 Winchester '73

Richards, Sandra Lee
1939 The Escape

Richards, Silvia
1951 Tomahawk

Richards, Stephen *see* **Stevens, Mark**

Richards, Toby
1960 Sergeant Rutledge

Richards, Tom
1952 Arctic Flight

Richards, Verne
1946 Without Reservations

Richardson, Anna Steese
1918 Hell's End

Richardson, Daisy
1947 Jivin' in Be-Bop

Richardson, Emory
1946 Beware
1947 Sepia Cinderella
1948? Boarding House Blues
1949 Lost Boundaries
   Souls of Sin

Richardson, Frank
1918 How Could You, Jean?
   Johanna Enlists
1925 Don Q, Son of Zorro

Richardson, Jack *same as* **Richardson, Jack H.**
1917 The Sudden Gentleman
1918 Free and Equal
   The Man Above the Law
   The Reckoning Day
1919 The She Wolf
1920 Dangerous Hours
1924 Down by the Rio Grande
1934 Stand Up and Cheer!
1937 Maid of Salem
1945 The Shanghai Cobra
1946 Romance of the West
1956 The Benny Goodman Story

Richardson, Virgil
1948 The Fight Never Ends
   Strange Victory

Richardson, Walter
1939 Moon over Harlem

Richard-Willm, Pierre
1930 Toda una vida (*foreign version*)

Richey, Alice
1949 Stallion Canyon
1950 Stars in My Crown
1952 Bright Victory

Richey, Grace
1952 Bright Victory

Richkova, Vera
1943 Action in the North Atlantic

Richman, Arthur
1931 Jenny Lind
1934 Imitation of Life

Richman, Charles
1938 The Adventures of Tom Sawyer

Richman, Mark *same as* **Richman, Peter Mark**
1959 The Black Orchid

Richmond, Felice
1953 The Man from the Alamo

Richmond, June
1947 Reet, Petite and Gone

Richmond, Kane
1931 Cavalier of the West
1932 Huddle
1933 Let's Fall in Love
1939 Charlie Chan in Reno
   The Escape
   The Return of the Cisco Kid
   Winner Take All
1940 Charlie Chan in Panama
   Knute Rockne—All American
   Murder over New York

1943 Action in the North Atlantic
1947 Black Gold

Richmond, Ted *same as* **Richmond, T. H.**
1941 Caught in the Act
1946 Singin' in the Corn
1953 Column South

Richmond, Warner *same as* **Richmond, Warner P.**
1914 Springtime
1919 The Gray Towers Mystery
1927 Irish Hearts
1931 Huckleberry Finn
1935 The Singing Vagabond
   So Red the Rose
1936 Below the Deadline
   Song of the Gringo
1938 Wild Horse Canyon
1940 Rhythm of the Rio Grande
1944 Outlaw Trail
1946 Wild West

Richonne, Richard
1950 Black Hand

Richter, Conrad
1940 Northwest Passage (Book I—Rogers' Rangers)

Rickaby, Ruth
1945 A Tree Grows in Brooklyn
1949 Pinky
1952 Anything Can Happen

Rickard, Ed
1958 The Young Lions

Rickards, Joseph E. *same as* **Rickards, Joe**
1945 The House on 92nd St.
1948 Call Northside 777
1949 Thieves' Highway
1950 A Ticket to Tomahawk
1953 Beneath the 12-Mile Reef
1955 Violent Saturday
1956 Giant
   The Last Wagon
1960 Flaming Star

Rickert, Shirley Jean
1934 'Neath the Arizona Skies

Ricketson, F. H., Jr.
1960 For the Love of Mike

Ricketts, Tom *same as* **Ricketts, Thomas**
1920 The Paliser Case
1921 Puppets of Fate
1934 Broadway Bill
1936 After the Thin Man
   Daniel Boone
   Human Cargo
   Show Boat
1937 Maid of Salem
1938 Gateway

Ricks, Archie
1925 A Daughter of the Sioux

Rickson, Joe *same as* **Rickson, Joseph**
1927 Whispering Sage
1934 The Prescott Kid
1953 The Sun Shines Bright

Rico, Benjamin
1938 Di que me quieres

Rico, Mona
1930 Alma de gaucho
   Sombras de gloria

Rideout, Ransom
1929 Hallelujah

The Riders of the Purple Sage
1949 The Golden Stallion
1950 North of the Great Divide
   Sunset in the West

Ridgely, John
1939 Confessions of a Nazi Spy
   Waterfront
1940 Knute Rockne—All American
1942 Secret Enemies
   They Died With Their Boots On
   Wings for the Eagle
1943 Air Force
1945 Pride of the Marines
1948 Night Wind
1949 Border Incident
1951 The Last Outpost
   When the Redskins Rode

1952 Fort Osage

Ridges, Stanley
1936 Winterset
1942 They Died With Their Boots On
1943 Air Force
1946 Canyon Passage
1949 Streets of Laredo
1950 No Way Out

Ridgeway, Darla
1952 The Quiet Man
1954 War Arrow

Ridgeway, Freddie
1952 The Quiet Man

Ridgeway, Fritzi *same as* **Ridgway, Fritzie**
1918 Real Folks
1919 The Unpainted Woman
1923 Ruggles of Red Gap
1928 Flying Romeos
1929 This Is Heaven

Ridgeway, John *see* **Ridgway, John**

Ridgley, Cleo
1948 I Remember Mama

Ridgway, Fritzie *see* **Ridgeway, Fritzi**

Ridgway, Inez A.
1925 Custer's Last Fight

Ridgway, John *same as* **Ridgway, John; Ridgway, Jack**
1915 Under Southern Skies
1917? Barnaby Lee
1921 Little Italy

Ridgway, Suzanne
1938 Dangerous to Know
1949 The Kissing Bandit

Rieger, Jack
1935 The Yiddish King Lear

Riehl, Kay
1949 The Red Menace
1953 Dream Wife

Riemann, Johannes
1931 Don Juan diplomático (*foreign version*)

Ries, Margarete
1944 Address Unknown

Riesner, Charles F.
1935 The Winning Ticket
1937 Manhattan Merry-Go-Round
1950 The Traveling Saleswoman

Riesner, Dean *same as* **"Dinky Dean"**
1950 The Traveling Saleswoman
   Young Man with a Horn

Rietty, Robert
1950 Give Us This Day

Riffel, John
1950 Battleground

Riga, Pedro
1928 The Riding Renegade

Rigas, George *see* **Regas, George**

Rigaud, George
1951 Native Son
1959 John Paul Jones

Rigby, Gordon
1932 The Golden West

Rigby, L. G.
1927 The Auctioneer
   The Frontiersman

Riggio, Jerry
1949 Border Incident

Riggs, Darrel
1951 Saturday's Hero

Riggs, Lynn
1937 The Plainsman

Riggs, Ralph
1949 Lost Boundaries

Rigny, Louise de
1918 The Golden Wall

Riley, Elaine
1943 Gangway for Tomorrow

Riley, George
1945 Rhapsody in Blue
1947 It Had To Be You
1959 Al Capone

Riley, Juanita
1941?   The Blood of Jesus

Riley, Ruth
1942   Song of the Islands

Riley, Tom
1957   Burden of Truth

Rilling, Margaret
1933   It's Great to Be Alive

Rimmer, Shane
1958   Flaming Frontier

Rin Tin Tin, a dog
1930   On the Border
1934   The Lone Defender

Rin Tin Tin, III, a dog
1947   The Return of Rin Tin Tin

Rinaldo, Ben
1937   Dark Manhattan

Rinaldo, Frederic I.
1947   Buck Privates Come Home

Rincón, Guillermo del
1931   La llama sagrada

Rinehart, Mary Roberts
1920   Dangerous Days
1927   Aflame in the Sky

Ring, Blanche
1940   If I Had My Way

Ring, Cyril *same as* **Ring, Cy**
1924   Tongues of Flame
1934   Behold My Wife!
1935   Rendezvous
1938   Dangerous to Know
        Little Miss Roughneck
1941   Accent on Love
        Mystery Ship
1942   The Navy Comes Through
        Woman of the Year
1943   Dixie
1944   Mr. Skeffington
1945   Where Do We Go From Here?
1947   Body and Soul

Ringer, Arthur C.
1941   Four Shall Die

Ringer, George D.
1939   Gang Smashers
1940   Gang War
        While Thousands Cheer
1941   Four Shall Die

Ringheim, Viking
1930   Un hombre de suerte (*foreign version*)

Rini, Philip
1953   The Jazz Singer

Rinker, Al
1930   King of Jazz

Río, Carmen
1935   El cantante de Nápoles

Rio, Eddie
1947   The Jolson Story
1948   Music Man

Rio, Joanne
1955   Seminole Uprising

Rio, Larry
1950   Young Man with a Horn

Riordan, Marjorie
1944   Mr. Skeffington
1946   South of Monterey

Riordan, Robert
1947   It Had To Be You

Rios, Edward C.
1951   The Mark of the Renegade

Rios, Lalo
1950   Bandit Queen
        The Lawless
1952   The Ring
1958   Touch of Evil

Ríos, Raquel
1934   La buenaventura
1935   Angelina o el honor de un brigadier

Ríos, Rosita
1938   Di que me quieres

Ripley, Arthur
1926   The Strong Man
1928   Heart Trouble
1932   Hypnotized
1939   Waterfront
1942   Prisoner of Japan

Ripley, Clements
1944   Buffalo Bill
1948   Old Los Angeles

Ripple, a deer
1949   Call of the Forest

Ripps, M. A.
1957   Bayou

Rische, Henry, The Reverend
1948   Reaching from Heaven

Risdon, Elisabeth *same as* **Risdon, Elizabeth**
1939   The Adventures of Huckleberry Finn
        The Girl from Mexico
1940   Mexican Spitfire
        Mexican Spitfire Out West
1941   The Mexican Spitfire's Baby
1942   Mexican Spitfire at Sea
        Mexican Spitfire Sees a Ghost
        Mexican Spitfire's Elephant
1943   The Amazing Mrs. Holliday
        Mexican Spitfire's Blessed Event
1952   It's a Big Country: An American Anthology

Riselle, Miriam
1938   The Singing Blacksmith
1939   Tevya

Riskin, Robert
1932   Hombres en mi vida
1934   Broadway Bill

Riss, Dan
1949   Arctic Fury
        Pinky
1950   Panic in the Streets
1951   Go for Broke!
        Only the Valiant
1954   The Yellow Tomahawk
1959   Al Capone

Risser, Margaret
1914   Threads of Destiny

Rissien, Edward L.
1958   Gun Fever

Riste, Tommy
1958   Sierra Baron

Rita and Rubin
1935   A Night at the Opera

Ritch, Steve *same as* **Ritch, Steven**
1953   Conquest of Cochise
1954   Battle of Rogue River
        Massacre Canyon
1955   Apache Ambush
        Seminole Uprising
1960   Studs Lonigan

Ritchey, J. V.
1914   Uncle Tom's Cabin

Ritchey, Will M.
1917   Sunshine and Gold
1919   Told in the Hills
1926   The Last Frontier
        Pals in Paradise

Ritchie, Ethel
1921   The Hunger of the Blood

Ritchie, Louise
1943   Cabin in the Sky

Ritt, Martin
1957   Edge of the City
1959   The Black Orchid

Ritter, Fred
1932   The Forty-Niners

Ritter, Tex
1936   Song of the Gringo
1940   Arizona Frontier
        Rhythm of the Rio Grande
1941   The Pioneers
1955   Apache Ambush

The Ritz Brothers *same as* **Ritz, Al; Ritz, Harry; Ritz, Jimmy**
1937   Life Begins in College

Ritzau, Erich von
1925   The Prairie Wife

Rivas, Carlos
1957   The Deerslayer
1958   Machete
1960   The Unforgiven

Rivas, Gabry *same as* **Rivas, Gabriel**
1930   ¡De frente, marchen!
        Olimpia
        El presidio
1931   El comediante

Rivas, Linda
1942   Mexican Spitfire Sees a Ghost

Rivas, Modesto
1930   Doña mentiras

Rivelles, Rafael
1931   ¿Conoces a tu mujer?
        Mamá
        La mujer X
        El proceso de Mary Dugan

River, W. L.
1931   En cada puerto un amor

Rivera, Beverly K.
1954   Hell's Half Acre

Rivera, Carlos *see* **Rivero, Carlos**

Rivera, Emilia
1951   Gambling House

Rivero, Carlos *same as* **Rivera, Carlos**
1952   The Raiders
1960   Key Witness

Rivero, Charles
1949   Arctic Manhunt
        Border Incident
1950   Border Treasure

Rivero, Julian
1930   Así es la vida
        El presidio
1931   La cautivadora
        La mujer X
        Yankee Don
1932   Law and Lawless
1934   La cruz y la espada
        Nada más que una mujer
1935   Cowboy Holiday
        Riddle Ranch
1936   Amor que vuelve
        Dancing Pirate
1938   Outlaw Express
1939   Drifting Westward
1940   Young Buffalo Bill
1942   Rio Rita
        Woman of the Year
1943   The Outlaw
1945   A Medal for Benny
1947   Ride the Pink Horse
        Robin Hood of Monterey
1948   Old Los Angeles
1949   The Kissing Bandit
        Streets of Laredo
        We Were Strangers
1950   Belle of Old Mexico
        Border Treasure
        Broken Arrow
1951   Cuban Fireball
1954   Broken Lance
1955   The Vanishing American
1956   The Burning Hills
        Giant
1958   Houseboat

Rivero, Lorraine
1929   Redskin

Rivers, Fletcher "Moke"
1943   Cabin in the Sky

Rivers, Joe
1937   Big City

Rivers, Wayne
1939   Mr. Moto's Last Warning

Riviere, Jorge
1959   John Paul Jones

Rivkin, Allen
1936   It Had to Happen
        Sins of Man
1940   Behind the News
1942   Sunday Punch
1946   Till the End of Time
1947   The Farmer's Daughter
1951   Gambling House
1952   It's a Big Country: An American Anthology

Rizzi, Gene
1943   Crash Dive
        The Outlaw

Rizzo, Carlo
1950   Deported
1958   Seven Hills of Rome

Roach, Bert
1929   The Desert Rider
1932   Call Her Savage
1937   Think Fast, Mr. Moto
1938   Rascals
1939   Mr. Moto's Last Warning
1941   Birth of the Blues
1945   Where Do We Go From Here?
1946   Bringing Up Father
        Rendezvous 24
1951   The Great Caruso
        Show Boat
        The Tall Target

Roach, Bryan
1920   Frontier Days

Roach, Dephine
1948?   Junction 88

Roach, Hal
1926   The Devil Horse
1930   Una cana al aire
        Locuras de amor
        Monsieur le Fox
        Monsieur le Fox (*foreign version*)
        El príncipe del dólar
        El príncipe del dólar (*foreign version*)
1931   Monerías
        Noche de duendes
        Pardon Us
        Pardon Us (*foreign version*)
        Politiquerías
1936   General Spanky

Roach, Joseph Anthony *same as* **Roach, J. Anthony; Roach, Joseph**
1917   The Sudden Gentleman
1920   The Cyclone
1951   Show Boat

Roach, Marjean *could be same as* **Rogers, Marjean**
1934   Stand Up and Cheer!

Road, Michael
1944   Tender Comrade

Roadman, Betty
1942   Cat People
1943   Hitler's Children
        The Leopard Man
        Wintertime
1947   The Burning Cross

Roan, Vinegar
1932   The Rainbow Trail
1933   Robbers' Roost
1941   Mystery Ship

Roark, Aidan
1936   It Had to Happen

Roark, Bob
1953   The Charge at Feather River

Roark, C. F.
1925   The Man in Blue

Roark, Robert
1955   The Long Gray Line

Robards, Jason *same as* **Robards, Jason, Sr.**
1921   The Land of Hope
1927   Irish Hearts
        Wild Geese
1930   Abraham Lincoln
        The Last Dance
1931   Charlie Chan Carries On
        Law of the Tong
1932   White Eagle
1933   Dance Hall Hostess
1934   Broadway Bill
1936   Robin Hood of El Dorado
1938   The Rage of Paris
1940   The Fatal Hour
1941   Hurry, Charlie, Hurry
1945   Betrayal from the East
        Johnny Angel
        Wanderer of the Wasteland
1947   Desperate
        The Farmer's Daughter
        Thunder Mountain
        Under the Tonto Rim
        Wild Horse Mesa

1948 Fighting Father Dunne
Guns of Hate
Western Heritage
1949 Masked Raiders
Robbins, Gale
1948 My Girl Tisa
Robbins, Harold
1958 Never Love a Stranger
1960 The Pusher
Robbins, Jeanne
1919 Yvonne from Paris
Robbins, Marc
1916 The Social Buccaneer
1919 The Tong Man
1920 Li Ting Lang
Robbins, Marty
1957 Raiders of Old California
Robbins, Patty
1948 Gentleman's Agreement
Robbins, Walter same as **Robbins, Walt**
1943 The Ox-Bow Incident
1944 Buffalo Bill
1945 A Tree Grows in Brooklyn
Robel, David
1936 Ramona
Rober, Richard
1948 Call Northside 777
1949 Illegal Entry
1950 Deported
1951 The Tall Target
The Well
1952 Kid Monk Baroni
The Savage
Roberson, Chuck
1947 Calendar Girl
1950 Bandit Queen
Rio Grande
Winchester '73
1952 Indian Uprising
1957 Run of the Arrow
1959 The Wonderful Country
1960 Sergeant Rutledge
Robert, Alan could be same as **Roberts, Al** not the same as **Roberts, Alan** (child actor)
1943 Action in the North Atlantic
Robert, Alfredo
1930 El secreto del doctor (foreign version)
Toda una vida (foreign version)
1931 La fiesta del diablo (foreign version)
Roberti, Alberto
1932 Parigi affascina; ovvero, Malavita
Roberti, Diana
1959 The Black Orchid
Roberti, Manya
1931 Delicious
Roberto, Frederic
1959 The Black Orchid
Roberts, Adele
1947 The Jolson Story
Roberts, Al could be same as **Robert, Alan** not the same as **Roberts, Alan** (child actor)
1942 Syncopation
Roberts, Alan (child actor) not the same as **Robert, Alan** or **Roberts, Al**
1959 Last Train from Gun Hill
Roberts, Allene
1949 Knock on Any Door
1952 Kid Monk Baroni
1953 The Sun Shines Bright
Roberts, Ann
1951 Westward the Women
Roberts, Bart see **Reason, Rex**
Roberts, Beatrice same as **Roberts, Bea**
1944 Hi, Beautiful
1947 Ride the Pink Horse
Roberts, Ben
1949 Prejudice
1956 Serenade
1957 Band of Angels
1959 Shake Hands with the Devil

Roberts, Bill same as **Roberts, William**
1934 Strange Wives
1938 The Texans
1942 Seven Sweethearts
Roberts, Bob
1947 Body and Soul
Roberts, Byron
1956 Wetbacks
Roberts, Charles not the same as **Roberts, Charles E.**
1925 Quicker'n Lightnin'
Roberts, Charles E. same as **Roberts, C. E.; Roberts, Chuck** not the same as **Roberts, Charles**
1934 The Fighting Hero
1935 Fighting Pioneers
1940 Mexican Spitfire
Mexican Spitfire Out West
1941 Hurry, Charlie, Hurry
The Mexican Spitfire's Baby
1942 Mexican Spitfire at Sea
Mexican Spitfire Sees a Ghost
Mexican Spitfire's Elephant
1943 Ladies' Day
Mexican Spitfire's Blessed Event
1951 Cuban Fireball
1952 The Fabulous Senorita
Roberts, Clete
1958 The Last Hurrah
Roberts, Connie
1944 Chip Off the Old Block
Roberts, Davis
1960 All the Fine Young Cannibals
Roberts, Desmond
1931 The Squaw Man
1934 Limehouse Blues
Roberts, Don
1934 Broadway Bill
Roberts, Dorothy
1940 Elsa Maxwell's Public Deb No. 1
Roberts, Edith
1918 Set Free
1919 Lasca
1920 White Youth
1922 Flesh and Blood
Saturday Night
The Son of the Wolf
1923 Backbone
Roberts, Elyce
1956 Rockin' the Blues
Roberts, Eric
1948 Fighting Father Dunne
Roberts, Flayette
1936 General Spanky
Roberts, Florence
1933 Ever in My Heart
1935 Harmony Lane
Roberts, Henry
1940 Gang War
1943 Cabin in the Sky
Roberts, Jack
1938 The Adventures of Tom Sawyer
Roberts, Jeanie
1935 Rendezvous
1936 After the Thin Man
Roberts, John S.
1946 Till the End of Time
1947 Calendar Girl
Roberts, Lee
1946 Romance of the West
Wild West
1948 Harpoon
1949 The Cowboy and the Indians
The Dalton Gang
1950 Cherokee Uprising
1951 Distant Drums
1952 Fort Osage
1953 Tumbleweed
1954 Battle of Rogue River
1955 Fort Yuma

1956 The Lone Ranger
Roberts, Leona
1937 Border Cafe
1939 The Escape
Gone With the Wind
Roberts, Lynne same as **Hart, Mary**
1939 In Old Caliente
1940 Hi-Yo Silver
1941 Ride on Vaquero
Romance of the Rio Grande
Sun Valley Serenade
1942 Young America
Roberts, Marguerite
1940 Escape
1950 Ambush
1952 My Man and I
Roberts, Mark
1953 Taxi
Roberts, Morgan
1958 St. Louis Blues
1960 All the Young Men
Roberts, Ned
1951 Go for Broke!
Roberts, Roy
1944 The Sullivans
1947 The Foxes of Harrow
1948 Fury at Furnace Creek
Gentleman's Agreement
1950 The Palomino
1952 Battles of Chief Pontiac
1953 The Glory Brigade
The Man Behind the Gun
San Antone
Tumbleweed
1954 They Rode West
1955 The Last Command
1956 The White Squaw
Roberts, Ruth
1946 Notorious
1951 Native Son
Roberts, Shepard
1947 Hi De Ho
Roberts, Stephen (dir)
1935 Romance in Manhattan
Roberts, Steve (actor, beginning 1940s)
1959 Inside the Mafia
Roberts, Steve (African-American actor)
1955 Blackboard Jungle
Roberts, Steve (African-American child actor)
1951 The Harlem Globetrotters
Roberts, Thayer
1947 The Chinese Ring
Jiggs and Maggie in Society
1948 The Miracle of the Bells
1957 Burden of Truth
Roberts, Theodore
1914 Where the Trail Divides
1915 After Five
The Immigrant
1916 Pudd'nhead Wilson
The Thousand Dollar Husband
Unprotected
1918 Hidden Pearls
The Source
The Squaw Man
1922 Saturday Night
Roberts, Tracey
1951 Fort Defiance
Queen for a Day
Roberts, Walter
1915 A Texas Steer
Roberts, William see **Roberts, Bill**
Robertson, Charles
1919 The She Wolf
Robertson, Dale same as **Robertson, Dayle**
1948 The Boy with Green Hair
1949 The Girl from Jones Beach
1950 The Cariboo Trail
Two Flags West
1954 Sitting Bull
1956 Dakota Incident

Robertson, Edward
1938 Life Goes On
Robertson, Jack, Capt. same as **Robertson, John; Robertson, John S.**
1919 Come Out of the Kitchen
Erstwhile Susan
1925 The True North
1930 The Break Up
1931 Beyond Victory
Robertson, Margaret
1931 Street Scene
Robertson, R. L., Rev.
1941? The Blood of Jesus
Robertson, Wilbur
1951 Saturday's Hero
Robertson, Willard
1931 The Cisco Kid
1932 Call Her Savage
So Big
1933 Ever in My Heart
1934 Operator 13
1935 Black Fury
1936 The Last of the Mohicans
Winterset
1937 That Girl from Paris
1940 Lucky Cisco Kid
1941 Sullivan's Travels
1942 Juke Girl
1943 Air Force
The Ox-Bow Incident
1948 Fury at Furnace Creek
Robeson, Andrew
1920 Who's Your Servant?
Robeson, Paul
1925 Body and Soul
1933 The Emperor Jones
1936 Show Boat
1942 Tales of Manhattan
Robichaux, Cynthia
1948 The Boy with Green Hair
Robie, Earl
1955 Santa Fe Passage
Robins, Edward H.
1937 Music for Madame
Robinson, Madame
1922 Spitfire
1925 Body and Soul
Robinson, Ann
1953 The Glass Wall
1959 Imitation of Life
Robinson, Arthur
1922 Spitfire
Robinson, Bill same as **Robinson, Bill "Bojangles"**
1932 Harlem Is Heaven
1935 The Little Colonel
The Littlest Rebel
1937 One Mile from Heaven
1938 Road Demon
1943 Stormy Weather
Robinson, Bob
1948 The Miracle of the Bells
1952 The Half-Breed
Robinson, Casey
1928 The Hawk's Nest
1933 Song of the Eagle
1935 McFadden's Flats
1944 The Racket Man
1946 Saratoga Trunk
1950 Two Flags West
Robinson, Dewey
1933 Diplomaniacs
A Lady's Profession
1934 Behold My Wife!
The Cat's-Paw
1937 Big City
Slave Ship
1938 The Rage of Paris
1939 Forged Passport
1941 Sullivan's Travels
1942 Juke Girl
Rubber Racketeers
Syncopation
Tales of Manhattan
1943 Redhead from Manhattan
1944 The Chinese Cat
1945 The Bells of St. Mary's
1946 Slightly Scandalous
1947 The Mighty McGurk
1949 That Midnight Kiss
1950 Buccaneer's Girl
The Jackie Robinson Story
Right Cross

Robinson, Dewey
1951 Jim Thorpe—All-American
Robinson, Edward G.
1930 East Is West
 A Lady to Love
 A Lady to Love (foreign version)
1931 Little Caesar
 Smart Money
1932 The Hatchet Man
 Tiger Shark
1939 Confessions of a Nazi Spy
1942 Tales of Manhattan
1945 Our Vines Have Tender Grapes
1948 Key Largo
1949 House of Strangers
Robinson, Ermer
1951 The Harlem Globetrotters
1954 Go Man Go
Robinson, Frances
1938 The Rage of Paris
Robinson, Fred J.
1921 All Souls' Eve
Robinson, Freddie
1939 Moon over Harlem
1948 Killer Diller
1948? Boarding House Blues
Robinson, Gail
1953 Ambush at Tomahawk Gap
Robinson, George
1930 East Is West (foreign version)
Robinson, Gertrude
1915 The Gambler of the West
1918 A Woman of Impulse
Robinson, Hayes
1934 Imitation of Life
Robinson, Jackie
1950 The Jackie Robinson Story
Robinson, James
1928 Tenderfeet
Robinson, John M. same as **Robinson, John**
1952 Bright Victory
1957 The Midnight Story
Robinson, Ky
1934 Broadway Bill
1938 Speed to Burn
Robinson, Larry
1951 Molly
Robinson, Louise
1938 The Toy Wife
Robinson, Nancy June
1944 The Sullivans
1945 A Tree Grows in Brooklyn
Robinson, Ollie Ann
1940 Midnight Shadow
Robinson, Paul
1952 Bright Victory
Robinson, Rex
1932 Hypnotized
Robinson, Rocky
1950 Young Man with a Horn
Robinson, Ruth
1936 Sins of Man
1938 The Buccaneer
1940 Covered Wagon Days
 Knute Rockne—All American
1943 Yankee Doodle Dandy
Robinson, Sam
1917 The Little Samaritan
Robinson, Seymour B.
1943 Stormy Weather
Robinson, Shari
1951 Molly
Robinson, Walter
1939 Keep Punching
Robison, Arthur
1931 Jenny Lind
 El proceso de Mary Dugan (foreign version)
 Quand on est belle
 Soyons gais
Robles, Richard
1937 The Plainsman

Robles, Rudy
1942 Across the Pacific
 Song of the Islands
 Submarine Raider
Robotham, George
1957 The Deerslayer
Robson, Andrew
1918 A Broadway Scandal
1919 The Gray Horizon
 Just Squaw
1921 Black Roses
Robson, Flora
1946 Saratoga Trunk
Robson, Mark
1949 Home of the Brave
1952 Bright Victory
1955 Trial
Robson, May
1915 How Molly Malone Made Good
1926 Pals in Paradise
1927 A Harp in Hock
 Turkish Delight
1934 Straight Is the Way
1936 Rainbow on the River
1938 The Adventures of Tom Sawyer
 The Texans
1939 Daughters Courageous
1941 Playmates
Robson, Mrs. Stuart same as **Waldron, May**
1914 At the Cross Roads
1919 The Lost Battalion
Roc, Patricia
1946 Canyon Passage
Rocca, Joe
1949 That Midnight Kiss
Roccardi, Albert
1918 The Liar
1929 Romance of the Rio Grande
Rocco, José
1935 No matarás
Rocha, Miguel Faust
1931 Don Juan diplomático
 Resurrección
Rochay, Joe
1929 Frozen Justice
Roche, Aurora
1945 In Old New Mexico
Roche, Betty
1936 Show Boat
Roche, John
1922 The Good Provider
1928 Diamond Handcuffs
 Uncle Tom's Cabin
1932 The Cohens and Kellys in Hollywood
1942 Sunday Punch
 We Were Dancing
1945 Where Do We Go From Here?
Rochefort, Charles de
1930 El secreto del doctor (foreign version)
Rochelle, Claire
1936 After the Thin Man
1940 New Moon
1941 The Face Behind the Mask
1944 Waterfront
1945 Nob Hill
Rochelle, Edwin
1949 We Were Strangers
"Rochester" see **Anderson, Eddie**
Rochin, P.
1952 Anything Can Happen
Rock, Warren
1940 New Moon
Rockett, Al
1934 She Was a Lady
Rockwell, E. A.
1954 Salt of the Earth
Rockwell, Jack
1934 'Neath the Arizona Skies
 The Prescott Kid
 Wheels of Destiny
1936 The Traitor
1941 Road Agent
 Secret of the Wastelands
 Thunder Over the Prairie

1943 Frontier Fury
 Wagon Tracks West
1945 Colorado Pioneers
 Phantom of the Plains
1946 Canyon Passage
Rockwell, Robert
1949 The Red Menace
1950 Belle of Old Mexico
Rockwell, William
1954 Salt of the Earth
Rockwood, Roy
1931 Delicious
Rocquemore, Henry see **Roquemore, Henry**
Rodann, Ziva
1959 Last Train from Gun Hill
Roddy, Drew
1944 An American Romance
Roddy, Jean
1946? Go Down, Death!
Rode, Walter
1943 Action in the North Atlantic
Roden, Edward
1956 The Lone Ranger
Roden, Molly
1958 The Last Hurrah
Roder, Eugene
1931 Così è la vita
Rodgers, Dorothy
1938 The Buccaneer
Rodgers, Douglas F. same as **Rodgers, Douglas**
1958 Never Love a Stranger
1960 The Pusher
Rodgers, Marshall
1925 Body and Soul
1927 The Spider's Web
Rodgers, Sondra
1948 Tap Roots
Rodgers, Walter same as **Rodgers, Walter L.**
1917 The Tenderfoot
1926 The Flaming Frontier
1927 Irish Hearts
Rodin, Merrill same as **Rodin, Merrill Guy**
1942 American Empire
1944 Buffalo Bill
 The Sullivans
Rodman, Nancy
1956 Daniel Boone, Trail Blazer
Rodman, Nick
1950 Indian Territory
1951 Jim Thorpe—All-American
Rodney, Earl (actor) could be same as **Rodney, Earle** (writer)
1918 The City of Tears
Rodney, Earle (writer) could be same as **Rodney, Earl** (actor)
1928 Heart Trouble
1932 Hypnotized
Rodney, John
1948 Key Largo
Rodríguez, Carmen
1930 Cuando el amor ríe
 Olimpia
 Revista Hispano-Americana
 El último de los Vargas
1931 Charlie Chan Carries On (foreign version)
 Del infierno al cielo
 Gente alegre
 La llama sagrada
 Mi último amor
 La mujer X
1932 El caballero de la noche
1933 It's Great to Be Alive (foreign version)
 La melodía prohibida
1934 La cruz y la espada
 Dos más uno, dos
 Nada más que una mujer
1935 Tango Bar
Rodriguez, Estelita same as **Estelita**
1947 On the Old Spanish Trail
1948 Old Los Angeles
1949 The Golden Stallion

1950 Belle of Old Mexico
 Sunset in the West
1951 Cuban Fireball
1952 The Fabulous Senorita
Genaro Rodriguez and His Orchestra
1932 Amor y vida
Rodriguez, Ismael
1956 Daniel Boone, Trail Blazer
Rodriguez, Lillian
1950 Panic in the Streets
Rodriguez, Miguel A.
1956 Crowded Paradise
Rodriguez, Mike J.
1940 Rhythm of the Rio Grande
1946 The Gay Cavalier
Rodriguez, Orlando
1956 Pillars of the Sky
Rodriguez, Raymond
1958 Touch of Evil
Rodríguez de la Vega, Cecilio
1931 La carta
Rodzinski, Artur
1947 Carnegie Hall
Roeburt, John
1949 Jigsaw
Roeca, Sam
1957 Raiders of Old California
Roehn, Franz
1948 The Miracle of the Bells
1949 Knock on Any Door
1956 Hot Blood
Roellinghoff, Charles
1931 Chérie (foreign version)
Rogan, Barney
1930 The Big Pond (foreign version)
1939 Miracle on Main Street (foreign version)
Rogato, Joseph
1951 Gambling House
Rogell, Albert S. same as **Rogell, Albert**
1924 North of Nevada
1927 The Devil's Saddle
 The Overland Stage
 The Red Raiders
1928 The Canyon of Adventure
 The Glorious Trail
1931 Aloha
1938 City Streets
1943 In Old Oklahoma
Rogell, Sid
1933 Man from Monterey
 The Telegraph Trail
1944 My Pal Wolf
1945 Betrayal from the East
 Wanderer of the Wasteland
1946 Sunset Pass
1948 Western Heritage
1951 Gambling House
Rogers, Buddy (actor) see **Rogers, Charles "Buddy"** (actor)
Rogers, Cameron
1941 Belle Starr
Rogers, Charles (actor) see **Rogers, Charles "Buddy"** (actor)
Rogers, Charles (prod) see **Rogers, Charles R.** (prod)
Rogers, Charles "Buddy" (actor) same as **Rogers, Buddy** (actor); **Rogers, Charles** (actor)
1929 Abie's Irish Rose
1930 Galas de la Paramount
1933 Best of Enemies
1941 The Mexican Spitfire's Baby
1942 Mexican Spitfire at Sea
 Mexican Spitfire Sees a Ghost
1947 The Adventures of Don Coyote
1948 Sleep, My Love
Rogers, Charles R. (prod)
1926 The Frontier Trail
1927 The Devil's Saddle
 The Overland Stage
 The Red Raiders

1928   The Glorious Trail
1935   McFadden's Flats
Rogers, Dorothy
1943   Mexican Spitfire's Blessed
        Event
Rogers, George
1943   Mexican Spitfire's Blessed
        Event
Rogers, Ginger
1933   Rafter Romance
1935   Romance in Manhattan
1942   Tales of Manhattan
1944   Tender Comrade
1947   It Had To Be You
Rogers, Hilda
1936   Temptation
Rogers, Howard Emmett
1935   Rendezvous
1936   Robin Hood of El Dorado
Rogers, Jean
1939   Heaven with a Barbed
        Wire Fence
1940   Charlie Chan in Panama
        Viva Cisco Kid
1942   Sunday Punch
Rogers, John (*actor*)
1931   Charlie Chan Carries On
1934   Charlie Chan in London
        Limehouse Blues
1936   Charlie Chan at the Race
        Track
        Human Cargo
        Klondike Annie
1937   Think Fast, Mr. Moto
1938   The Buccaneer
        Gateway
1941   Mutiny in the Arctic
        They Dare Not Love
Rogers, John W. (*prod*)
1950   Buccaneer's Girl
1951   The Raging Tide
1954   War Arrow
Rogers, Kent
1937   Boy of the Streets
1940   Northwest Passage (Book
        I—Rogers' Rangers)
Rogers, Lambert
1931   Street Scene
Rogers, Leonard
1947   Hi De Ho
Rogers, Marjean *could be same as*
    Roach, Marjean
1934   Stand Up and Cheer!
Rogers, Mildred
1932   The Forty-Niners
Rogers, Rock
1956   Crowded Paradise
Rogers, Roy
1939   In Old Caliente
1940   Young Buffalo Bill
1944   Lake Placid Serenade
1947   On the Old Spanish Trail
1949   The Golden Stallion
1950   North of the Great Divide
        Sunset in the West
Rogers, Ruth
1938   Dangerous to Know
Shorty Rogers and His Band
1953   The Glass Wall
Rogers, Wayne
1959   Odds Against Tomorrow
Rogers, Will
1918   Laughing Bill Hyde
1921   Guile of Women
1934   Judge Priest
        Stand Up and Cheer!
Rogers, Will, Jr.
1953   The Eddie Cantor Story
Rogulski, Stefek
1930   Toda una vida (*foreign
        version*)
Roitman, David, Cantor
1931   The Voice of Israel
Rojas, Luis
1939   La Inmaculada
Roland, George *could be same as*
    Rolands, George K.
1932   A Daughter of Her People
        Joseph in the Land of
        Egypt
        Yiskor

1933   The Eternal Jew
        The Wandering Jew
1934   The Rabbi's Power
1936   Love and Sacrifice
1937   I Want to Be a Mother
Roland, Gilbert
1926   The Campus Flirt
1927   The Dove
        The Love Mart
        Rose of the Golden West
1930   Monsieur le Fox
1931   Resurrección
1932   Call Her Savage
        Hombres en mi vida
1933   Una viuda romántica
        Yo, tú y ella
1935   Julieta compra un hijo
1938   Gateway
        La vida bohemia
1946   Beauty and the Bandit
        The Gay Cavalier
        South of Monterey
1947   King of the Bandits
        Pirates of Monterey
        Riding the California
        Trail
        Robin Hood of Monterey
1948   The Dude Goes West
1949   We Were Strangers
1950   The Furies
1951   The Mark of the
        Renegade
1952   Apache War Smoke
1953   Beneath the 12-Mile Reef
        Thunder Bay
1957   The Midnight Story
Rolands, George K. *could be same*
    as **Roland, George**
1922   Breaking Home Ties
Roldán, Emma
1931   ¿Conoces a tu mujer?
        El impostor
1932   Soñadores de la gloria
Rolf, Erik
1946   Song of the South
1950   Davy Crockett, Indian
        Scout
Rolfe, Sam
1956   Pillars of the Sky
Rollens, Jacques
1928   Mother Machree
Rollins, David
1928   Riley the Cop
1929   Love, Live and Laugh
1931   Young Sinners
Rollins, Jack
1924   Unseen Hands
Rollow, Preston
1917   The Bar Sinister
Rolph, Alice
1955   Kentucky Rifle
Rolson, Robert E.
1917   His Sweetheart
Romain, George E.
1921   Diane of Star Hollow
Romaine, Jean
1951   Show Boat
Roman, Lawrence
1954   Drums Across the River
Roman, Nina *not the same as*
    Romano, Nina
1959   The Crimson Kimono
Roman, Peter
1948   Big City
1951   Jim Thorpe—All-American
Roman, Ric
1951   Slaughter Trail
1953   Last of the Comanches
Roman, Ruth
1944   Since You Went Away
1946   Without Reservations
1950   Colt .45
Romano, Felix
1950   Black Hand
1959   The Black Orchid
Romano, Michael
1936   It Had to Happen
1957   Bayou
Romano, Nina *not the same as*
    Roman, Nina
1927   Lost at the Front

Romanoff, Constantine
1929   Wolf Song
1934   The Cat's-Paw
        Judge Priest
1936   After the Thin Man
1937   Man of the People
1939   Let Freedom Ring
1947   Northwest Outpost
Romanówna, Janina
1930   Toda una vida (*foreign
        version*)
Romantini, Joseph
1938   Charlie Chan at Monte
        Carlo
Romay, Lina
1953   The Man Behind the Gun
Rombouts, Ben
1958   Fort Massacre
Rome, Tina
1950   The Baron of Arizona
Romeo, Adolpho
1950   Black Hand
Romeo, Carmelina
1932   Amore e morte
Romeo, Rosario
1932   Amore e morte
Romero, Carlos
1959   The Young Land
Romero, Cesar
1934   Strange Wives
1935   Rendezvous
1938   Happy Landing
        My Lucky Star
1939   Charlie Chan at Treasure
        Island
        The Cisco Kid and the
        Lady
        The Return of the Cisco
        Kid
1940   The Gay Caballero
        Lucky Cisco Kid
        Viva Cisco Kid
1941   Ride on Vaquero
        Romance of the Rio
        Grande
1942   Tales of Manhattan
1943   Wintertime
Romero, Johnny
1945   South of the Rio Grande
Romero, Manuel
1931   Las luces de Buenos Aires
        La pura verdad
1932   ¿Cuándo te suicidas?
Romeu, Pepe
1931   Su noche de bodas
Romheld, Heinz
1930   East Is West (*foreign
        version*)
1931   Don Juan diplomático
        (*foreign version*)
Romito, Victor
1947   Pirates of Monterey
1956   Serenade
1958   The Last Hurrah
1959   The Black Orchid
Romoff, Nicco
1947   Northwest Outpost
Rondell, Ronnie
1942   Holiday Inn
        Mexican Spitfire's
        Elephant
1944   Mr. Skeffington
1950   Deported
1955   Foxfire
Ronn, Gale
1934   Stand Up and Cheer!
Rooney, Anne
1944   Slightly Terrific
Rooney, Bert
1916   The Woman in 47
Rooney, Mickey
1934   Beloved
1935   Rendezvous
1937   Slave Ship
1939   The Adventures of
        Huckleberry Finn
        Judge Hardy and Son
1944   Andy Hardy's Blonde
        Trouble

Roope, Fay
1952   Indian Uprising
1953   The Charge at Feather
        River
        Seminole
1954   The Black Dakotas
1959   The FBI Story
Roos, Alford
1954   Salt of the Earth
Roos, George
1951   Native Son
Roosevelt, Buddy
1926   Twin Triggers
1932   Wild Horse Mesa
1933   Circle Canyon
1934   Operator 13
1936   General Spanky
1937   The Devil's Playground
1938   The Buccaneer
1947   Buck Privates Come
        Home
1948   Fighting Father Dunne
        Unconquered
1949   The Girl from Jones
        Beach
1950   Annie Get Your Gun
        Colt .45
        Stars in My Crown
1951   Apache Drums
1952   The Raiders
1953   The Great Sioux Uprising
Root, George, Jr.
1943   The Gang's All Here
Root, Jerry
1950   The Cariboo Trail
Root, Wells
1932   Tiger Shark
1933   Racetrack
1936   The Bold Caballero
1939   Man of Conquest
1942   Mokey
Roper, Eugene
1950   Intruder in the Dust
Roper, Jack
1941   Mutiny in the Arctic
1942   Gentleman Jim
1943   Jack London
1952   The Quiet Man
Ropes, Bradford
1945   Sunbonnet Sue
1947   Buck Privates Come
        Home
        Pirates of Monterey
1950   Belle of Old Mexico
Roque, Joe
1955   The Rose Tattoo
Roquemore, Henry *same as*
    Rocquemore, Henry
1930   The Last Dance
1931   Cimarron
1935   Naughty Marietta
        Ruggles of Red Gap
        The Singing Vagabond
        Texas Terror
1936   After the Thin Man
        My American Wife
1937   Waikiki Wedding
1938   The Toy Wife
1940   Lucky Cisco Kid
        The Way of All Flesh
1941   Hold Back the Dawn
1942   We Were Dancing
        Woman of the Year
1943   Dixie
Rork, Sam E.
1932   Call Her Savage
Rorke, Hayden
1949   Lust for Gold
1951   The Magnificent Yankee
1953   The Stars Are Singing
1954   Drum Beat
1960   I Aim at the Stars: the
        Wernher von Braun
        Story
Rorke, J. F., Lieut.
1918   The Unbeliever
Ros, Ramon
1936   Ramona
1947   Humoresque
Rosa, Ria
1938?   I due gemelli

Rosalean and Seville
1937   Manhattan
        Merry-Go-Round
Rosamond, Marion
1943   The Gang's All Here
Rosanova, Rosa *same as* **Rosanova, Madame Rosa**
1922   Hungry Hearts
1923   Fashion Row
1925   Cobra
        His People
1927   Jake the Plumber
        Pleasure Before Business
        The Shamrock and the Rose
1929   Abie's Irish Rose
        Lucky Boy
        The Younger Generation
1934   The Fighting Hero
Rosanska, Countess
1947   Northwest Outpost
Rosario, Rosa del
1946   Border Bandits
Rosas, Alejandro
1932   Amor y vida
Rosas, Enrique de
1932   ¿Cuándo te suicidas?
1935   Angelina o el honor de un brigadier
        Piernas de seda
        Rosa de Francia
        Tango Bar
        Te quiero con locura
1937   El carnaval del diablo
Rosay, Françoise
1930   Olimpia (*foreign version*)
1931   Buster se marie
        Buster se marie (*foreign version*)
        Echec au roi
        Jenny Lind
        Le petit café
        El proceso de Mary Dugan (*foreign version*)
        Quand on est belle
        Soyons gais
Roschig, Kraft
1931   Die Dreigroschenoper
Roscoe, Alan
1928   The Mating Call
Roscoe, Albert
1919   Evangeline
1920   The Last of the Mohicans
        The Paliser Case
Rose, Don
1930   King of Jazz
Rose, Jack
1948   The Paleface
1950   The Daughter of Rosie O'Grady
1957   Beau James
1958   Houseboat
Rose, Jewel
1951   The Great Caruso
Rose, Leonard *same as* **Rose, Leo**
1947   Carnegie Hall
1948   Open Secret
Rose, Max
1948   The Boy with Green Hair
Rose, Norman
1953   The Joe Louis Story
Rose, Reginald
1957   Twelve Angry Men
Rose, Virginia
1960   The Adventures of Huckleberry Finn
Rose, Wally
1947   It Had To Be You
1949   The Undercover Man
Rosebrook, Rod
1958   Tonka
Roseleigh, Jack
1921   That Girl Montana
Roselle, Mario
1950   Black Hand
Roseman, Edward *same as* **Roseman, Ed F.; Roseman, Edward F.**
1914   Springtime
        When Broadway Was a Trail

1917   The Barrier
        The Red Woman
        The Secret of Eve
1918   The Liar
1920   The Face at Your Window
1921   Anne of Little Smoky
Rosemond, Bertha
1953   Tonight We Sing
Rosemond, Clinton
1931   Smart Money
1936   The Green Pastures
1938   The Toy Wife
1939   Stand Up and Fight
1940   Midnight Shadow
        Santa Fe Trail
1941   Belle Starr
1942   Syncopation
        The Vanishing Virginian
1943   Yankee Doodle Dandy
1947   The Burning Cross
1949   The Story of Seabiscuit
1953   Tonight We Sing
Rosen, Al
1946   Without Reservations
Rosen, Herman *same as* **Rosen, H.**
1936   Love and Sacrifice
1939   Motel the Operator
        My Son
1940   Eli Eli
        The Great Advisor
        Her Second Mother
        The Jewish Melody
Rosen, Phil *same as* **Rosen, Philip E.**
1926   Rose of the Tenements
1929   The Peacock Fan
1931   El código penal
1932   The Vanishing Frontier
1936   Ellis Island
1937   It Could Happen to You
1940   Phantom of Chinatown
1944   Black Magic
        Charlie Chan in the Secret Service
        The Chinese Cat
1945   In Old New Mexico
        The Jade Mask
        The Scarlet Clue
1946   The Red Dragon
Rosen, Sam
1932   Mazel Tov
Rosenberg, Aaron
1935   Charlie Chan in Shanghai
1936   Charlie Chan at the Race Track
        Paddy O'Day
1937   That I May Live
1940   Lucky Cisco Kid
1943   The Meanest Man in the World
1948   Tap Roots
1950   Winchester '73
1951   The Raging Tide
1952   Red Ball Express
1953   The Man from the Alamo
        Thunder Bay
1954   Saskatchewan
1955   Foxfire
1956   The Benny Goodman Story
        Walk the Proud Land
1958   The Badlanders
Rosenberg, Jerry
1939   Mirele Efros
        My Son
Rosenberg, Michael *same as* **Rosenberg, Michel**
1931   Zein Weib's Lubovnick
1932   A Daughter of Her People
        Uncle Moses
        The Unfortunate Bride
1937   The Cantor's Son
1938   Two Sisters
1939   Mirele Efros
1941   Mazel Tov Yidden
1950   Monticello, Here We Come!
1950?   Three Daughters
Rosenberg, Ruby
1939   Papá soltero
1940   They Knew What They Wanted
1942   Mexican Spitfire's Elephant

1943   Ladies' Day
1946   Till the End of Time
Rosenberger, Jim
1947   California
Rosenblatt, Josef, Cantor *same as* **Rosenblatt, Joseph, Cantor**
1928   The Jazz Singer
1931   The Voice of Israel
1933   Live and Laugh
Rosenblatt, Max
1939   Mothers of Today
Rosenbloom, Maxie *same as* **Rosenbloom, "Slapsie" Maxie; Rosenbloom, Max**
1936   Kelly the Second
        Muss 'Em Up
1937   Big City
1938   Mr. Moto's Gamble
1940   Elsa Maxwell's Public Deb No. 1
1941   Louisiana Purchase
Rosenblum, Arthur
1956   Rockin' the Blues
Rosenblum, Ralph
1960   The Pusher
Rosener, George *same as* **Rosener, George M.**
1917   The Wild Girl
1930   She Got What She Wanted
1936   Ellis Island
1939   Confessions of a Nazi Spy
Rosenker, Michael
1947   Carnegie Hall
Rosensohn, Leopold
1930   Toda una vida (*foreign version*)
Rosenthal, Boris
1920   The Face at Your Window
1929   East Side Sadie
1933   Live and Laugh
Rosenthal, Harry
1941   Birth of the Blues
        Sullivan's Travels
Rosher, Dorothy *see* **Marsh, Joan**
Rosing, Bodil
1925   Lights of Old Broadway
1927   Wild Geese
1928   Wheel of Chance
1931   Three Who Loved
1932   The Match King
1935   A Night at the Ritz
1939   Confessions of a Nazi Spy
1941   They Dare Not Love
Rosito, Angelo *see* **Rossitto, Angelo**
Roskam, Edward M.
1914   Springtime
Rosley, Adrian
1934   The Great Flirtation
        Straight Is the Way
1936   Mad Holiday
        Sins of Man
Ross, Allan
1945   Where Do We Go From Here?
Ross, Alma
1936   Show Boat
1938   Daughter of Shanghai
Ross, Ann
1932   Texas Pioneers
Ross, Anthony
1953   Taxi
Ross, Arthur
1953   The Stand at Apache River
Ross, Charles J.
1914   The Great Diamond Robbery
1915   How Molly Malone Made Good
Ross, Churchill
1930   King of Jazz
Ross, Claudette
1948   Cry of the City
Ross, Clinton, Lieut.
1919   Injustice
Ross, Dennis
1952   The Raiders

Ross, Earle
1937   The Riders of the Whistling Skull
Ross, Etna, Little
1919   Deliverance
Ross, Frances
1924   The Lightning Rider
Ross, Frank
1958   Kings Go Forth
Ross, George
1954   Drum Beat
1956   The Last Wagon
        Westward Ho the Wagons!
1957   Run of the Arrow
Ross, H. Milton
1920   Dangerous Days
Ross, Hal
1953   The Jazz Singer
Ross, Jack
1945   Where Do We Go From Here?
Ross, Leonard Q. *see* **Rosten, Leo**
Ross, Michael
1949   The Fighting Kentuckian
1950   The Daughter of Rosie O'Grady
1951   The Well
1960   Walk Like a Dragon
Ross, Milton
1917   The Gun Fighter
1924   Down by the Rio Grande
1948   The Feathered Serpent
Ross, Nat
1926   April Fool
Ross, Richard
1958   Kings Go Forth
Ross, Rita
1934   Broadway Bill
Ross, Robert
1929   Show Boat
1930   King of Jazz
Ross, Robert C.
1956   The White Squaw
Ross, Shelly
1946   Dirty Gertie from Harlem, U.S.A.
Ross, Shirley
1937   Waikiki Wedding
Ross, Terry Ann
1957   All Mine to Give
Ross, Thomas W.
1943   Yankee Doodle Dandy
Ross, Virginia
1919   False Evidence
Ross-MacKenzie, Kenneth
1947   Ride the Pink Horse
Rosse, Herman
1930   East Is West (*foreign version*)
1931   Don Juan diplomático (*foreign version*)
Rossen, Robert
1934   The Unknown Soldier Speaks
1945   Rhapsody in Blue
1947   Body and Soul
Rosser, John
1950   The Big Hangover
1955   Trial
Rosser, Susanne
1945   Nob Hill
1947   My Wild Irish Rose
Rosset, Barnet L., Jr.
1948   Strange Victory
Rossi, Beatrice
1933   It's Great to Be Alive
Rossitto, Angelo *same as* **Angie; Little Angelo; Rosito, Angelo**
1927   Old San Francisco
1939   Mr. Wong in Chinatown
1950   Bandit Queen
        The Baron of Arizona
Rossman, Earl
1925   Kivalina of the Ice Lands
1932   Dangers of the Arctic
Rosson, Arthur *same as* **Rosson, Arthur H.**
1925   Tearing Through
1937   The Plainsman

1938	The Buccaneer
1940	Kit Carson
1943	The Outlaw
1948	Red River
	Unconquered
1950	The Cariboo Trail
1952	The Big Sky
1958	Wild Is the Wind
1959	The Jayhawkers!

Rosson, Helene
| 1923 | The Sting of the Scorpion |

Rosson, Richard
1932	Scarface
	Tiger Shark
1939	Stand Up and Fight
1942	Apache Trail

Rosten, Leo *same as* **Ross, Leonard Q.**
| 1942 | All Through the Night |
| 1948 | Sleep, My Love |

Roth, Carl
| 1943 | Action in the North Atlantic |

Roth, Cy
| 1951 | Slaughter Trail |

Roth, Gene *same as* **Roth, Eugene; Stutenroth, Gene**
1944	Charlie Chan in the Secret Service
1945	The Shanghai Cobra
1946	Canyon Passage
1947	Marshal of Cripple Creek
1948	Reaching from Heaven
1949	The Valiant Hombre
1950	The Baron of Arizona
1951	Oh! Susanna
	Westward the Women
1952	Red Snow
1953	Jack McCall Desperado
1956	Wetbacks
1958	The Young Lions

Roth, Johannes
| 1932 | Mazel Tov |

Roth, Lillian
| 1930 | Galas de la Paramount |

Roth, Mickey
| 1945 | Rhapsody in Blue |
| 1955 | The Long Gray Line |

Roth, Murray
1926	The Strong Man
1929	Die Königsloge
1935	Chinatown Squad

Roth, Noreen
| 1944 | An American Romance |

Roth, Sandy
1926	The Fighting Edge
	The Little Irish Girl
	Private Izzy Murphy
1932	Unashamed

Roth, Seymour
| 1945 | In Old New Mexico |

Rothblum, Isaak
| 1939 | The Light Ahead |

Rothe, Elliott
| 1931 | The Guilty Generation |

Rothenberg, Cal
| 1944 | Chip Off the Old Block |

Rotoli, Francesca
| 1936 | Sins of Man |

Rotsten, Herman
| 1944 | Cry of the Werewolf |

Roubert, Matty
1914	John Barleycorn
1934	Broadway Bill
1936	Star for a Night
1937	Big City
1938	Mr. Moto's Gamble
1945	South of the Rio Grande
1946	Romance of the West
	Wild West

Roulien, Raúl
1931	Charlie Chan Carries On (*foreign version*)
	Delicious
1933	It's Great to Be Alive
	It's Great to Be Alive (*foreign version*)
	No dejes la puerta abierta
	Primavera en otoño
1934	Granaderos del amor
1935	¡Asegure a su mujer!
	Piernas de seda
	Te quiero con locura

Rounds, Steve
| 1917 | A Kentucky Cinderella |

Rouse, Russell
| 1951 | The Well |
| 1959 | Thunder in the Sun |

Rousseau, May
| 1934 | Judge Priest |

Rousseroy, Margot
| 1931 | La gran jornada (*foreign version*) |

Rout, Maria
| 1955 | Brevities of 1955 |

Rouverol, Jean
| 1950 | So Young, So Bad |

Roux, Tony *same as* **Roux, Antonio**
1930	Las campanas de Capistrano
1941	Gauchos de Eldorado
	Hold Back the Dawn
1950	A Lady Without Passport
	Sunset in the West

Rovner, Seidel, Cantor
| 1931 | The Voice of Israel |

Rowan, Don
1937	Charlie Chan on Broadway
	The Devil's Playground
	The Plainsman
	Souls at Sea

Rowe, Preston
| 1950 | Panic in the Streets |

Rowell, Ross E., Maj.
| 1918 | The Unbeliever |

Rowland, George
| 1944 | Chip Off the Old Block |

Rowland, Henry
1940	Escape
1946	Rendezvous 24
1950	Battleground
1951	The House on Telegraph Hill
1953	Captain John Smith and Pocahontas
1955	Kiss of Fire
1956	The White Squaw
1958	The Young Lions

Rowland, Richard A.
1926	The Strong Man
1927	The Love Mart
	Rose of the Golden West
1928	The Crash
	The Hawk's Nest
	Vamping Venus
	Wheel of Chance

Rowland, Roy
1945	Our Vines Have Tender Grapes
1952	Bugles in the Afternoon
1958	Seven Hills of Rome

Rowland, Steve
| 1954 | Dangerous Mission |

Rowland, William
1938	Di que me quieres
1940	Perfidia
1960	This Rebel Breed

Rowlands, Art
| 1936 | My American Wife |

Rowley, Kenneth
| 1931 | Delicious |

Roy, Billy *same as* **Roy, William**
1943	Gangway for Tomorrow
	Good Luck, Mr. Yates
1950	Young Daniel Boone

Roy, Gloria
1933	Charlie Chan's Greatest Case
	It's Great to Be Alive
1935	¡Asegure a su mujer!
	Charlie Chan in Egypt
	Charlie Chan in Paris
1936	Charlie Chan at the Race Track
	Charlie Chan's Secret
1937	Charlie Chan on Broadway
	That I May Live
1938	Mr. Moto Takes a Chance
	Mr. Moto's Gamble
	Rascals
	Speed to Burn

Roy, John
1939	Mr. Moto in Danger Island
1940	Charlie Chan in Panama
	Lucky Cisco Kid

Roy, John
| 1938 | In Old Chicago |
| 1948 | The Luck of the Irish |

Royal, Charles Francis *same as* **Royal, Charles; Royal, Charles F.**
1936	The Phantom of Santa Fe Tundra
1937	Shadows of the Orient
1949	Arctic Fury

Royal, Lloyd
| 1956 | Frontier Woman |

Royal, Michael
| 1949 | Ranger of Cherokee Strip |

Royal, Tom
| 1953 | So Big |

Royal, William H., Captain *see* **Royle, William**

The Royal Gospel Choir
| 1947 | Going to Glory, Come to Jesus |

Royce, Frosty
1944	Riding West
1949	Colorado Territory
1954	Broken Lance
	They Rode West
1958	Escape from Red Rock

Royce, John
1943	Action in the North Atlantic
1950	Battleground
1951	The Great Caruso

Royce, Lionel *same as* **Royce, Lyonel**
1939	Confessions of a Nazi Spy
	Let Freedom Ring
1940	Charlie Chan in Panama
	The Man I Married
1942	Unseen Enemy
1943	Crash Dive

Royce, Riza
| 1957 | Band of Angels |

Royce, Ruth
1924	California in '49
1925	Tonio, Son of the Sierras
	Warrior Gap

Royle, Selena
1944	The Sullivans
1946	Till the End of Time
1948	Moonrise
1950	The Big Hangover

Royle, William *same as* **Royal, William H., Captain; Royle, William H.**
1936	The Glory Trail
	Rebellion
1937	The Plainsman
1938	The Renegade Ranger
1939	The Cisco Kid and the Lady
	The Fighting Gringo
	Mr. Wong in Chinatown
1940	Lucky Cisco Kid

Royo, Rita
| 1930 | La fuerza del querer |

Rozan, Gerta
| 1940 | Escape |

Rozelle, Elouise
| 1936 | Star for a Night |

Rozelle, Rita
| 1931 | The Black Camel |

Rub, Christian
1932	Le bluffeur
1935	Black Fury
1936	Sins of Man
	Star for a Night
1937	It Could Happen to You
1939	Forged Passport
1942	Nazi Agent
	Tales of Manhattan
1945	Rhapsody in Blue

Ruben, J. Walter
1927	Open Range
1930	Check and Double Check
1931	Echec au roi
1932	Symphony of Six Million
1933	Racetrack

Ruben, José
| 1925 | Salome of the Tenements |

Rubens, Alma
1919	Diane of the Green Van
1920	Humoresque
1929	Show Boat

Rubin, Benny
| 1930 | Sunny Skies |
| 1956 | The Benny Goodman Story |

Rubin, Stanley *same as* **Rubin, Stanley Crea**
1941	Where Did You Get That Girl?
1942	Unseen Enemy
1946	Slightly Scandalous

Rubina, Fania
| 1939 | My Son |

Rubino, Joe
| 1949 | House of Strangers |

Rubinstein, Artur
| 1947 | Carnegie Hall |

Rubinstein, S.
| 1940 | Americaner Schadchen |

Rubio, José
1934	La ciudad de cartón
1935	Alas sobre el Chaco
1936	Sutter's Gold

Ruby, Harry
| 1930 | Check and Double Check |

Ruby, Mary
| 1916 | A Man of Sorrow |

Rucker, Clarence
| 1923 | Regeneration |

Rudd, Anthony H.
| 1923 | Scars of Jealousy |

Rudd, Enid
| 1956 | Crowded Paradise |

Rudd, Sam
| 1943 | Good Luck, Mr. Yates |

Rudie, Evelyn
| 1955 | The Last Command |
| | The View from Pompey's Head |

Rudin, Herman
| 1959 | The FBI Story |

Ruditsky, Barney
| 1943 | Margin for Error |

Rudley, Herbert
1945	Rhapsody in Blue
1956	Raw Edge
1958	Tonka
	The Young Lions
1959	The Jayhawkers!

Rudolph, Oscar
1937	The Plainsman
1942	Holiday Inn
1945	A Medal for Benny
1947	Easy Come, Easy Go
1949	Top O' the Morning
1950	The Furies
1951	Molly
1952	The Savage

Rue, Greta von
| 1927 | His Foreign Wife |

Ruffin, James D.
| 1920 | Within Our Gates |

Ruffino, Carlos
1939	Papá soltero
	Verbena trágica
1940	Cuando canta la Ley

Ruffino, Mercedes
| 1942 | Rio Rita |
| | Tortilla Flat |

Ruggiero, Ada
| 1932 | Amore e morte |

Ruggiero, Gloria
| 1960 | Pay or Die |

Ruggiero, Nino
| 1932 | Amore e morte |

Ruggiero, Robert
| 1960 | Pay or Die |

Ruggles, Charlie *same as* **Ruggles, Charles**
1935	Ruggles of Red Gap
1938	Breaking the Ice
1940	Elsa Maxwell's Public Deb No. 1

Ruggles, Charlie
1942   Friendly Enemies
Ruggles, Wesley
1931   Cimarron
Ruhl, William *same as* **Ruhl, Bill**
1936   Sutter's Gold
1941   Gauchos of Eldorado
          Road Agent
1942   North to the Klondike
          Unseen Enemy
1945   The Shanghai Cobra
1946   Dark Alibi
1947   Ride the Pink Horse
1948   Rocky
          Shanghai Chest
Ruick, Barbara
1952   Apache War Smoke
Ruick, Mel *same as* **Ruick, Melville**
1938   The Buccaneer
1941   Sun Valley Serenade
1942   Holiday Inn
          Little Tokyo, U.S.A.
1953   Taxi
Ruiz, Adolf
1936   Ramona
Ruiz, Maclovia
1936   Ramona
Ruiz, Nick
1930   La voluntad del muerto
Ruiz, Virginia
1930   Wu Li Chang
1931   Del infierno al cielo
1932   Hombres en mi vida
Ruiz Moragas, Carmen
1930   Doña mentiras
Ruman, Sam
1938   The Renegade Ranger
1939   Bad Lands
          The Girl from Mexico
1943   Hitler's Children
1945   Betrayal from the East
          Johnny Angel
          Wanderer of the
          Wasteland
1949   Stagecoach Kid
Rumann, Sig *same as* **Ruman, Sig; Rumann, Siegfried**
1929   Die Königsloge
1935   A Night at the Opera
          The Wedding Night
1936   The Bold Caballero
1937   Thank You, Mr. Moto
          Think Fast, Mr. Moto
1939   Confessions of a Nazi Spy
1941   This Woman Is Mine
1943   They Came to Blow Up
          America
1945   The Dolly Sisters
1949   Border Incident
Rummage, J. Reid
1957   Burden of Truth
Rundt, Arthur, Dr.
1929   Die Königsloge
Ruscio, Al
1959   Al Capone
Rush, Barbara
1951   Flaming Feather
          Molly
1954   Taza, Son of Cochise
1955   Kiss of Fire
1958   The Young Lions
Rush, Celeste
1929   The Invaders
Rush, Dick
1930   The Kibitzer
1933   Thundering Herd
1936   After the Thin Man
1937   Big City
1938   Little Miss Roughneck
          Mr. Moto's Gamble
          Speed to Burn
1941   The Mexican Spitfire's
          Baby
1943   Gangway for Tomorrow
          Let's Have Fun
          Mr. Lucky
1947   The Farmer's Daughter
1948   Western Heritage
Rush, Ford
1949   House of Strangers

Rush, Geneva
1956   Frontier Woman
Rushkin, Shimen *see* **Ruskin, Shimen**
Ruskin, Harry
1930   King of Jazz
1942   Dr. Gillespie's New
          Assistant
1943   Dr. Gillespie's Criminal
          Case
1944   Andy Hardy's Blonde
          Trouble
          Three Men in White
1945   Between Two Women
1947   Dark Delusion
Rusoff, Lou
1955   Apache Woman
Russel, George *not the same as* **Russell, George**
1921   The Gunsaulus Mystery
Russell, A. Burton *same as* **Russell, Burton**
1929   When Men Betray
1932   Ten Minutes to Live
1932?   The Girl from Chicago
1935   Lem Hawkins' Confession
1938   Birthright
          Swing!
Russell, Alice B.
1927   The Broken Violin
1930   Easy Street
1932?   The Girl from Chicago
1935   Lem Hawkins' Confession
1938   Birthright
          God's Step Children
1948   The Betrayal
Russell, Andy
1947   Copacabana
Russell, Autumn
1956   Serenade
Russell, Bernard D.
1924   The Broken Law
Russell, Bing
1957   Beau James
1959   Last Train from Gun Hill
Russell, Buck
1958   The Last Hurrah
Russell, Burton *see* **Russell, A. Burton**
Russell, Charles
1943   Ladies' Day
1948   Night Wind
1950   Chinatown at Midnight
Russell, Dixie
1932   Hypnotized
1934   Broadway Bill
Russell, Elizabeth
1942   Cat People
1945   Our Vines Have Tender
          Grapes
1953   So Big
Russell, Evangeline
1925   Red Love
1929   Hawk of the Hills
Russell, Gail
1948   Moonrise
1950   The Lawless
Russell, George *not the same as* **Russel, George**
1943   Frontier Fury
1946   Without Reservations
1947   Marshal of Cripple Creek
1952   Apache Country
Russell, Gilbert
1951   The Great Caruso
Russell, Henry
1919   Deliverance
Russell, Howard
1931   Street Scene
Russell, J. Gordon
1925   Quicker'n Lightnin'
1928   Uncle Tom's Cabin

Russell, Jackie (*actress*)
1960   I Passed for White
Russell, Jamie
1956   Hot Blood
1958   Terror in a Texas Town
Russell, Jane
1943   The Outlaw
1948   The Paleface
1955   Foxfire
1956   Hot Blood
Russell, Jean
1944   They Live in Fear
Russell, John (*actor*) *same as* **Russell, Johnny**
1940   The Man I Married
1953   The Sun Shines Bright
1955   The Last Command
1958   Fort Massacre
1959   Yellowstone Kelly
Russell, John (*writer*)
1930   El dios del mar
Russell, Julia Theresa
1925   Body and Soul
Russell, L. Case
1925   Red Love
Russell, Lewis L.
1951   When the Redskins Rode
1953   Sangaree
Russell, Manuel
1931   La fiesta del diablo
          Lo mejor es reír
          La pura verdad
          Su noche de bodas
1932   ¿Cuándo te suicidas?
Russell, Mary
1935   Black Fury
          A Night at the Ritz
1937   The Riders of the
          Whistling Skull
Russell, Mavis
1946   Dangerous Money
Russell, Reb
1934   Fighting Through
1935   Range Warfare
Russell, Rosalind
1935   Rendezvous
1936   It Had to Happen
Russell, Sally
1922   The Top O' the Morning
Russell, Sam
1923   His Great Chance
Russell, Wally
1956   Hot Blood
Russell, William *not the same as* **Russell, William D.**
1914   The Straight Road
1916   Lone Star
1917   My Fighting Gentleman
1920   The Man Who Dared
1923   Anna Christie
Russell, William D. *not the same as* **Russell, William**
1941   Virginia
Russin, Babe
1956   The Benny Goodman
          Story
Russo, Emanuel
1953   Thunder Bay
Russo, Mario
1958   Seven Hills of Rome
Russo, Tony
1959   Last Train from Gun Hill
1960   The Sign of Zorro
Rust, Henri
1931   Die Dreigroschenoper
          (*foreign version*)
Rust, Richard
1960   This Rebel Breed
Rusty, the Wonder Horse
1939   Drifting Westward
Ruth, Frances
1950   No Way Out
Ruth, Marshall
1941   New York Town
1945   Nob Hill
1947   Desperate
1952   The Iron Mistress
Ruth, Phyllis
1941   Louisiana Purchase

Ruth, Wally
1947   My Wild Irish Rose
Rutherford, Ann
1935   Melody Trail
          The Singing Vagabond
1936   Down to the Sea
1939   Gone With the Wind
          Judge Hardy and Son
Rutherford, Douglas
1945   The House on 92nd St.
1947   Citizen Saint
Rutherford, John *same as* **Rutherford, Jack**
1920   The Great Shadow
1930   Whoopee
1931   Mr. Lemon of Orange
1938   The Buccaneer
1947   Untamed Fury
1956   Mohawk
Rutherford, Tom
1938   The Toy Wife
1941   Virginia
Ruthven, Madeleine
1927   The Frontiersman
          Spoilers of the West
1928   Wyoming
1930   Wu Li Chang
Ruwe, Jeanne
1934   Coming Out Party
Ruwe, John
1934   Coming Out Party
Ruysdael, Basil
1949   Colorado Territory
          Pinky
1950   Broken Arrow
1951   Gambling House
1955   Blackboard Jungle
          Davy Crockett, King of
          the Wild Frontier
1958   The Last Hurrah
R'Wanda, Princess
1949?   Harlem Follies
Ryan, Ben
1935   Chinatown Squad
1936   Laughing Irish Eyes
Ryan, Bob *not the same as* **Ryan, Robert**
1934   Broadway Bill
1938   Mr. Moto's Gamble
1942   Sunday Punch
1947   It Had To Be You
Ryan, Dick
1946   Bringing Up Father
1947   Jiggs and Maggie in
          Society
1948   Call Northside 777
          Jiggs and Maggie in Court
1949   House of Strangers
          Jiggs and Maggie in
          Jackpot Jitters
          Top O' the Morning
1950   A Ticket to Tomahawk
1956   The Benny Goodman
          Story
1957   Beau James
1958   The Last Hurrah
          Wild Is the Wind
Ryan, Don
1927   The Red Raiders
1928   The Glorious Trail
1939   Waterfront
Ryan, Edmon
1950   Battleground
          The Breaking Point
          Mystery Street
1954   Go Man Go
Ryan, Edward
1944   The Sullivans
Ryan, Frank
1943   The Amazing Mrs.
          Holliday
Ryan, Gertrude
1915   The Rosary
1923   Snowdrift
Ryan, Jerry
1947   It Had To Be You
Ryan, Joe
1917   The Tenderfoot
1926   The Vanishing American

Ryan, Kathleen
1950   Give Us This Day
Ryan, Mike
1945   The Valley of Decision
Ryan, Pat
1945   The Valley of Decision
Ryan, Peggy
1944   Chip Off the Old Block
1949   Shamrock Hill
Ryan, Phil L.
1948   Fighting Father Dunne
Ryan, Robert *not the same as*
  Ryan, Bob
1943   Gangway for Tomorrow
1944   Tender Comrade
1947   Crossfire
1948   The Boy with Green Hair
1955   Bad Day at Black Rock
1959   Odds Against Tomorrow
1960   Ice Palace
Ryan, Sam *same as* **Ryan, Sam J.**
1915   The Spender
1923   Backbone
Ryan, Sheila *same as* **McLaughlin,**
  Betty
1940   The Gay Caballero
        The Way of All Flesh
1941   Dead Men Tell
        Sun Valley Serenade
1943   The Gang's All Here
1944   Something for the Boys
1946   Slightly Scandalous
1949   The Cowboy and the
        Indians
1951   Mask of the Dragon
Ryan, Ted
1952   Red Ball Express
Ryan, Tim
1941   Dead Men Tell
        Ice-Capades
        Where Did You Get That
        Girl?
1942   Nazi Agent
        Tortilla Flat
1943   Redhead from Manhattan
        Riding High
1944   Hi, Beautiful
1946   Bringing Up Father
        Dark Alibi
        Till the End of Time
1947   Body and Soul
        Bowery Buckaroos
        Jiggs and Maggie in
        Society
1948   The Golden Eye
        Half Past Midnight
        Jiggs and Maggie in Court
        The Luck of the Irish
        Rocky
        Shanghai Chest
1949   Jiggs and Maggie in
        Jackpot Jitters
        Shamrock Hill
        The Sky Dragon
1950   Jiggs and Maggie Out
        West
1951   Cuban Fireball
1957   Beau James
Ryan, Tommy
1947   Calendar Girl
Ryan, William
1942   Rio Rita
Ryder, Edward
1958   Kings Go Forth
Ryen, Richard
1943   Gangway for Tomorrow
1944   An American Romance
1945   Salome, Where She
        Danced
Ryerson, Florence
1936   Mad Holiday
Ryland, Bob, Cpl.
1918   The Unbeliever
Ryley, Phil
1918   Uncle Tom's Cabin
Rymer, Luba
1938   The Singing Blacksmith
Rynd, Sol C.
1950   God, Man and Devil

Ryskind, Morrie
1935   A Night at the Opera
1943   The Meanest Man in the
        World
1945   Where Do We Go From
        Here?
Saa Silva, Roberto
1930   Las campanas de
        Capistrano
        Monsieur le Fox
        El presidio
        Sombras de gloria
Saavedra, Rafael A.
1940   Perfidia
Sabanieeva, Thalia
1937   Natalka Poltavka
Sabato, Alfredo *same as* **Sabato,**
  Alfred; Sabato, Alfredo, Dr.
1930   Sei tu l'amore
1933   No dejes la puerta abierta
1934   La ciudad de cartón
1945   The Gay Senorita
Sabbatini, Marcella
1930   Doña mentiras (*foreign*
        version)
Sabello, Julio
1924   Down by the Rio Grande
Sabenie, Eva
1933   It's Great to Be Alive
Sabin, Ruth
1920   Humoresque
Sablon, Loulette
1950   The Toast of New Orleans
Sabor, Timmy
1945   Where Do We Go From
        Here?
Sachs, Walter
1956   Crowded Paradise
Sack, Alfred N.
1937   Underworld
1939   Lying Lips
1940   The Notorious Elinor Lee
1946   Dirty Gertie from
        Harlem, U.S.A.
1946?   Beale Street Mama
        Go Down, Death!
1947   Juke Joint
Sackett, Theodore T.
1949   The Red Menace
Sackheim, William
1953   Column South
Sackin, Moe
1934   Tres amores
1936   El crimen de media
        noche
        La última cita
Sackville, Gordon
1914   An Odyssey of the North
Saddoris, Sarah
1927   Red Clay
Sadio, Jan
1955   Indian American
Sadler, Sam
1926?   Ten Nights in a Barroom
Sadovsky, Felix
1944   Lake Placid Serenade
Saeger, Roy
1931   Delicious
Saenz, Armando
1958   Sierra Baron
Saenz, Edward
1949   House of Strangers
1951   Saturday's Hero
Saenz, Ignacio
1941   This Woman Is Mine
Safley, Gard
1958   Tonka
Sage, Byron
1924   Conductor 1492
1926   Into Her Kingdom
Sage, Frances
1944   Mr. Skeffington
Sage, Sally
1939   Waterfront
Sage, Willard
1955   Blackboard Jungle
Saggau, Charles
1943   The Gang's All Here

Sagor, Frederica
1935   Piernas de seda
Sahey, Myrna
1958   The Light in the Forest
Sahji
1947   Jivin' in Be-Bop
Sahl, Mort
1960   All the Young Men
Sainpolis, John *see* **St. Polis, John**
Saint, Eva Marie
1957   Raintree County
St. Angel, Michael
1943   Gangway for Tomorrow
St. Angelo, Robert *same as* **St.**
  Angelo, Bob
1937   Slave Ship
1938   The Buccaneer
1940   Northwest Passage (Book
        I—Rogers' Rangers)
1944   Tahiti Nights
1945   Where Do We Go From
        Here?
1949   House of Strangers
1951   Gambling House
1955   Chief Crazy Horse
1956   The Last Frontier
St. Clair, Ana
1960   All the Young Men
St. Clair, Lydia
1945   The House on 92nd St.
St. Clair, Malcolm
1933   Olsen's Big Moment
1941   Sun Valley Serenade
St. Clair, Maurice
1944   Lady, Let's Dance!
1949   The Girl from Jones
        Beach
St. Claire, Arthur
1941   Road Agent
1942   King of the Stallions
1949   The Prairie
St. Cyr, Lillian Red Wing, Princess
  see **Red Wing**
St. Cyr, Vince
1959   The FBI Story
        Yellowstone Kelly
St. George, Ernest
1940   George Washington
        Carver
St. John, Al
1931   Aloha
1932   Riders of the Desert
1936   Pinto Rustlers
        West of Nevada
1942   Valley of the Sun
St. John, Betta
1953   Dream Wife
1954   Dangerous Mission
St. John, Howard
1949   The Undercover Man
1950   The Men
1951   Saturday's Hero
St. John, William
1960   All the Young Men
        I Passed for White
St. Johns, Adela Rogers
1918   Marked Cards
St. Leo, Leonard
1943   Riding High
St. Leonard, Florence
1917   The Bar Sinister
St. Luke's Choristers *same as*
  Dorr's St. Luke's Choristers
1936   Rainbow on the River
1937   Song of the City
1939   Fisherman's Wharf
1951   The Great Caruso
St. Maur, Adele
1933   Broken Dreams
1953   The Pathfinder
St. Polis, John *same as* **Sainpolis,**
  John; Sainpolis, John M.
1916   The Social Highwayman
        The Yellow Passport
1918   Laughing Bill Hyde
1922   Shadows
1930   The Melody Man
1932   Symphony of Six Million
1936   Below the Deadline
1938   Mr. Wong, Detective

St. Rayner, Helen
1953   The Member of the
        Wedding
Saint-Granier
1931   Un caballero de frac
        Chérie
        Su noche de bodas
        (*foreign version*)
1932   ¿Cuándo te suicidas?
Sais, Marin
1918   The City of Dim Faces
        His Birthright
1925   The Red Rider
1935   Circle of Death
1941   Saddlemates
1946   Rendezvous 24
1949   The Cowboy and the
        Prizefighter
        Ride, Ryder, Ride!
        Roll Thunder Roll!
Sakaguchi, Bo
1951   Go for Broke!
Sakall, S. Z. *same as* **Sakall,**
  Cuddles
1942   Seven Sweethearts
1943   Wintertime
        Yankee Doodle Dandy
1945   The Dolly Sisters
1950   The Daughter of Rosie
        O'Grady
1952   It's a Big Country: An
        American Anthology
Sakayan, Vram
1937   Arshin Mal Alan
Salado, José Luis
1931   La incorregible
Salamonic, Yucca
1932   Ljubav i strast
Sale, Fred, Jr.
1934   Wheels of Destiny
Sale, Richard
1947   Calendar Girl
        Northwest Outpost
        Spoilers of the North
1948   The Dude Goes West
1950   A Ticket to Tomahawk
Sale, Virginia
1929   The Cohens and Kellys in
        Atlantic City
1937   Think Fast, Mr. Moto
1939   Charlie Chan in Reno
1942   They Died With Their
        Boots On
1943   The Gang's All Here
1944   Hi, Beautiful
1945   Rhapsody in Blue
Salerno, Cindy Ames
1959   Al Capone
Salerno, Signor N.
1925   The Midnight Girl
Sales, Clifford
1947   Citizen Saint
Salisbury, Monroe
1914   Rose of the Rancho
        The Squaw Man
1915   After Five
        The Lamb
1916   Ramona
1918   The Red, Red Heart
1919   The Sleeping Lion
1922   The Great Alone
Salkow, Sidney
1940   Girl from God's Country
1953   Jack McCall Desperado
        The Pathfinder
1954   Sitting Bull
Salle, Michael
1950   Riders of the Pony
        Express
Salling, Jackie
1939   Fisherman's Wharf
1943   Yankee Doodle Dandy
Salmi, Albert
1960   The Unforgiven
        Wild River
Salt, Waldo
1939   The Adventures of
        Huckleberry Finn
Salter, Hal
1927   The Red Raiders
1928   The Canyon of Adventure

Salter, Lou
1919   Spotlight Sadie
Salter, Thelma
1915   The Alien
1920   Huckleberry Finn
Salters, Dottie
1937   Underworld
Saltus, Edgar
1920   The Paliser Case
Saluskin, Ed
1958   Tonka
Salvador, Jaime
1938   Castillos en el aire
Salvaneschi, Lillian
1945   Nob Hill
Salvaneschi, Mario
1945   Nob Hill
Salvatori, Jack
1930   El secreto del doctor
        (*foreign version*)
        Toda una vida (*foreign*
        version)
1931   La carta (*foreign*
        version)
        La fiesta del diablo
        (*foreign version*)
Salvi, Delia
1960   Pay or Die
Salvi, Lola
1929   Hambre
Salvini, Sandro *same as* **Salvini,
  Alessandro**
1930   Toda una vida (*foreign*
        version)
1931   La fiesta del diablo
        (*foreign version*)
Salzman, Esta
1934   The Youth of Russia
1936   Love and Sacrifice
1937   I Want to Be a Mother
1940   Her Second Mother
        The Jewish Melody
1941   Mazel Tov Yidden
1950   God, Man and Devil
        Monticello, Here We
        Come!
1950?   Three Daughters
Samaniego, Carmen
1936   Contra la corriente
Samaniego, L. G. de, Sra.
1930   Sevilla de mis amores
Samberg, Ajzyk
1937   The Jester (Der
        Purimspieler)
Sambo, Little
1919   The Little Diplomat
Sambola, Louis
1950   Panic in the Streets
Sampson, Chet
1958   The Rawhide Trail
Sampson, Teddy
1918   Her American Husband
1919   Fighting for Gold
1921   Bits of Life
Samrich, Bobby
1938   Gateway
Samuel, Price
1945   Where Do We Go From
        Here?
Samuels, Henri
1936   Pinto Rustlers
Samuels, Lesser
1950   No Way Out
Samuels, Maurice
1949   House of Strangers
        Thieves' Highway
1950   Black Hand
        Mystery Street
1951   The Great Caruso
Samuelson, G. B.
1920?   Her Story
Samuylow, M. B. *same as*
  Samuylow, Morris B.
1933   The Eternal Jew
        The Wandering Jew
1938   The Power of Life
San, Wahneta
1941   Murder on Lenox Avenue

**The San Carlo Grand Opera
  Company**
1931   Pagliacci
San Carlo Symphony Orchestra
1931   Pagliacci
San Marco, Maria
1948   Sleep, My Love
San Marco, Rossana
1955   The Rose Tattoo
San Martín, Carlos
1930   Un hombre de suerte
1931   Un caballero de frac
        Lo mejor es reír
1932   El hombre que asesinó
Sanborn, Charles
1950   Panic in the Streets
Sanchez, Angela
1954   Salt of the Earth
Sanchez, Elvira
1932   Law and Lawless
Sánchez García, José María
1934   Un capitán de cosacos
        Granaderos del amor
1935   El cantante de Nápoles
Sanci, Francesco
1932   Amore e morte
Sande, Serena
1956   Ghost Town
Sande, Walter
1941   Mystery Ship
1942   Tortilla Flat
        Wings for the Eagle
1943   Air Force
        They Came to Blow Up
        America
1948   Half Past Midnight
1951   Warpath
1953   The Great Sioux Uprising
1954   Apache
        Overland Pacific
1955   Bad Day at Black Rock
1959   Last Train from Gun Hill
1960   Oklahoma Territory
Sandefure, Ben
1955   Blackboard Jungle
Sanders, Barbara Ann
1953   Bright Road
Sanders, Elsie
1959   The Hanging Tree
Sanders, George
1937   Slave Ship
1939   Allegheny Uprising
        Confessions of a Nazi Spy
        Mr. Moto's Last Warning
1942   Tales of Manhattan
1943   They Came to Blow Up
        America
1956   Death of a Scoundrel
1960   The Last Voyage
Sanders, Hugh
1951   The Magnificent Yankee
        Only the Valiant
1952   The Fighter
        Indian Uprising
1953   Last of the Comanches
1955   The Last Command
1957   The Guns of Fort
        Petticoat
Sanders, Sandy
1947   The Last Round-Up
1950   Indian Territory
1956   Westward Ho the
        Wagons!
Sanders, Sherman
1947   Bowery Buckaroos
1952   The Big Sky
Sanders, W. H.
1919   A Man's Duty
Sandfier, F.
1923   Deceit
Sandford, Tiny *same as* **Sandford,
  Stanley; Sandford, Stanley J.;
  Sanford, Tiny**
1923   Breaking into Society
1931   Noche de duendes
        Pardon Us
        Pardon Us (*foreign
        version*)
1936   Show Boat

Sandler, Mike
1948   The Miracle of the Bells
Sandoval, Chico
1945   A Medal for Benny
Sandoval, Nena
1936   Contra la corriente
Sandrich, Mark
1942   Holiday Inn
Sandrino, Oreste
1932   O festino o la legge
Sands, Eddie
1953   The Eddie Cantor Story
Sands, Johnny *same as* **Sands,
  John**
1946   Till the End of Time
1949   Massacre River
1950   The Lawless
        Two Flags West
Sanford, Erskine
1944   Mr. Skeffington
1945   A Tree Grows in Brooklyn
1946   Without Reservations
1948   The Lady from Shanghai
Sanford, Frances
1948   Unconquered
Sanford, Joseph G.
1941   Where Did You Get That
        Girl?
Sanford, Ralph
1940   East of the River
1941   Sun Valley Serenade
1943   Ladies' Day
1945   Nob Hill
        Where Do We Go From
        Here?
1947   Copacabana
1951   Fort Defiance
1955   Shotgun
1957   All Mine to Give
1958   St. Louis Blues
1959   The Oregon Trail
Sanford, Tiny *see* **Sandford, Tiny**
Sanforth, Clifford
1940   Gang War
        While Thousands Cheer
1941   Four Shall Die
1942   Take My Life
Sano, Marcel de *see* **De Sano,
  Marcel**
Sansom, Lester A.
1960   Hell to Eternity
Santee, Amalia
1931   Charlie Chan Carries On
        (*foreign version*)
Santell, Alfred
1926   Sweet Daddies
1928   Wheel of Chance
1929   Romance of the Rio
        Grande
        This Is Heaven
1930   The Arizona Kid
1936   Winterset
1943   Jack London
Santillo, Norma
1951   Westward the Women
Santley, Fred *same as* **Santley,
  Freddie; Santley, Fredric;
  Santly, Fredric**
1931   Three Who Loved
1936   After the Thin Man
1942   We Were Dancing
1943   Dixie
        Yankee Doodle Dandy
1947   California
1950   Mystery Street
1952   It's a Big Country: An
        American Anthology
1953   Cry of the Hunted
Santley, Joseph
1935   Harmony Lane
1936   Laughing Irish Eyes
1940   Behind the News
        Music in My Heart
1941   Ice-Capades
Santly, Fredric *see* **Santley, Fred**
Santon, Penny
1956   Full of Life
1959   Cry Tough
Santoro, Jack
1956   Serenade

Santoro, Tony
1945   The Mummy's Curse
        A Tree Grows in Brooklyn
Santos, Emily
1941   Murder on Lenox Avenue
Santos, Jack
1936   Tundra
Santos, Lita
1932   El caballero de la noche
1933   Dos noches
        It's Great to Be Alive
        (*foreign version*)
1934   La buenaventura
        Granaderos del amor
1938   Di que me quieres
Santschi, Tom
1918   The Hell Cat
1920   The North Wind's Malice
1927   The Overland Stage
1929   In Old Arizona
Saper, Jack
1942   Across the Pacific
        Juke Girl
Saraydar, Louise
1948   Unconquered
Sardegna, Nicky
1951   Jim Thorpe—All-American
Sardo, Cosmo
1947   It Had To Be You
1950   The Big Hangover
        Emergency Wedding
1956   The Benny Goodman
        Story
1958   The Last Hurrah
Sarecky, Barney *same as* **Sarecky,
  Barney A.**
1942   Let's Get Tough!
1944   Block Busters
1947   Buffalo Bill Rides Again
Sarecky, Louis *same as* **Sarecky,
  Lou**
1931   Cimarron
1942   North to the Klondike
Sargent, Brent
1938   The Toy Wife
Sargent, Joseph D.
1959   Al Capone
1960   Pay or Die
Sargent, Lewis
1920   Huckleberry Finn
Sargent, Michael
1958   Touch of Evil
Saris, George
1953   The Glory Brigade
Saris, Marilyn
1957   The Lawless Eighties
Sarno, Hector *same as* **Sarno,
  Hector V.**
1914   The Woman in Black
1917   The Plow Woman
1918   A Little Sister of
        Everybody
1919   The Right to Happiness
1920   Rio Grande
1925   Cobra
1936   Human Cargo
1937   Man of the People
1940   East of the River
        The Mark of Zorro
1941   Accent on Love
        Mystery Ship
        Ride on Vaquero
Sarno, James
1937   It Could Happen to You
Sarver, Charles
1916   The Soul of Kura-San
1917   The Little Boy Scout
1918   A Little Sister of
        Everybody
Sarvis, David
1954   Salt of the Earth
Sasso, Peter
1945   The Bells of St. Mary's
Sassone, Felipe
1933   Melodía de arrabal
Satenstein, Frank
1948   Open Secret
Satherwaite, Lillian
1918   Woman and the Law

Sato, Chieko
1952   Japanese War Bride
Sato, Reiko
1960   Hell to Eternity
Satow, Kiyosho
1921   Where Lights Are Low
Sattaneo, William
1959   The Black Orchid
Satz, Ludwig
1931   Zein Weib's Lubovnick
1934   What a Mother-in-Law!
Sauber, Harry
1933   Obey the Law
1937   Manhattan
       Merry-Go-Round
1938   City Streets
       Outside of Paradise
1943   Let's Have Fun
       What's Buzzin' Cousin?
Saucedo, Frank
1945   The Gay Senorita
Sauers, Joseph see **Sawyer, Joe**
Saul, Beverly Jean see **Tyler, Beverly**
Saul, Oscar
1951   A Streetcar Named Desire
Saum, Cliff same as **Saum, Clifford P.**
1918   The Kaiser's Finish
1935   A Night at the Ritz
1938   The Beloved Brat
1939   Waterfront
1940   East of the River
1942   Juke Girl
1943   Action in the North Atlantic
Saunders, Gertrude
1938   The Toy Wife
1947   Sepia Cinderella
1949? The Joint Is Jumpin'
Saunders, Gloria
1952   Red Snow
Saunders, Jackie
1915   The Adventures of a Madcap
1916   The Twin Triangle
1921   Puppets of Fate
Saunders, Lloyd
1937   The Plainsman
Saunders, Nancy
1947   It Had To Be You
Saunders, Rai
1949   Lost Boundaries
Saunders, Russ
1954   Saskatchewan
Sautter, Paul
1931   Delicious
Savage, Ann
1946   Renegade Girl
1949   Satan's Cradle
Savage, Archie
1942   Tales of Manhattan
Savage, Carol
1946   G. I. War Brides
Savage, Cary
1955   Good Morning, Miss Dove
1956   Full of Life
Savage, Les, Jr.
1956   The White Squaw
Savage, Margaret
1943   Redhead from Manhattan
Savage, Paul
1947   Untamed Fury
Savage, Steve
1947   Under the Tonto Rim
1948   Gun Smugglers
       Indian Agent
Savage, Turner
1927   The Callahans and the Murphys
       Frisco Sally Levy
Savanarola, Elena
1952   It's a Big Country: An American Anthology
Savidan, George
1931   Quand on est belle
Savidan, Willy
1931   Quand on est belle

Savilla, Margarita
1947   Ride the Pink Horse
Savin, Lillian
1930   Monsieur le Fox
       Monsieur le Fox (foreign version)
Savini, R. M.
1946   Beware
       Tall, Tan and Terrific
1947   Reet, Petite and Gone
1949   Lookout Sister
Savitsky, Sam same as **Savitsky, General**
1937   Man of the People
1945   Rhapsody in Blue
1947   Northwest Outpost
Savoca, John
1957   Twelve Angry Men
Savoi, Celeste
1949   Boston Blackie's Chinese Venture
Savonarola, Elena
1948   Cry of the City
Sawaya, Joe
1949   We Were Strangers
Sawyer, Bob
1932   Harlem Is Heaven
Sawyer, Geneva
1933   It's Great to Be Alive
Sawyer, Joe same as **Sauers, Joe; Sauers, Joseph; Sawyer, Joseph**
1932   Huddle
1933   Olsen's Big Moment
1934   Behold My Wife!
       Eskimo
       The Prescott Kid
1937   Black Legion
1938   Passport Husband
1939   Confessions of a Nazi Spy
1940   Lucky Cisco Kid
       Santa Fe Trail
1941   Belle Starr
1942   They Died With Their Boots On
1943   The Outlaw
1946   G. I. War Brides
1948   Fighting Father Dunne
       Half Past Midnight
1949   The Gay Amigo
       Stagecoach Kid
1950   The Traveling Saleswoman
1952   Indian Uprising
1954   Taza, Son of Cochise
Sax, Carrol
1958   Terror in a Texas Town
Sax, Samuel same as **Sax, Sam**
1925   One of the Bravest
1928   United States Smith
Saxe, Carl same as **Saxe, Carl H.**
1947   Desperate
1948   The Boy with Green Hair
       Unconquered
1950   Battleground
1951   Jim Thorpe—All-American
1959   Last Train from Gun Hill
Saxon, Aaron
1958   Gun Fever
Saxon, Hugh
1922   The Guttersnipe
Saxon, John
1959   Cry Tough
1960   The Plunderers
       The Unforgiven
Sayers, Jo Ann
1939   The Adventures of Huckleberry Finn
Sayles, Francis
1937   Black Legion
       The Plainsman
1939   Man of Conquest
1941   Thunder Over the Prairie
1942   Unseen Enemy
Sayles, Olive
1955   Brevities of 1955
Saylor, Syd
1936   Kelly the Second
1938   Happy Landing
       Mr. Moto's Gamble
       Passport Husband

1939   Let Freedom Ring
       Stand Up and Fight
       Winner Take All
1940   Geronimo
       Lucky Cisco Kid
1942   Gentleman Jim
       Sunday Punch
1943   Action in the North Atlantic
       Doughboys in Ireland
       Yankee Doodle Dandy
1944   Buffalo Bill
       Slightly Terrific
1945   Nob Hill
1947   Easy Come, Easy Go
1948   The Miracle of the Bells
       The Paleface
       Sleep, My Love
       Unconquered
1951   The Raging Tide
Sayne, Robert
1945   Rhapsody in Blue
Sayre, George Wallace same as **Sayre, George**
1940   Am I Guilty?
1942   Unseen Enemy
1945   The Shanghai Cobra
1948   Rocky
Sayre, Jeffrey
1936   General Spanky
1940   Knute Rockne—All American
1951   The House on Telegraph Hill
1958   The Young Lions
Sayre, Joel
1935   Annie Oakley
       His Family Tree
Sbragia, Vincent
1949   Thieves' Highway
Scaduto, Joe
1924   Racing Luck
Scaffa, Francesca di
1953   Captain John Smith and Pocahontas
Scala, Gia
1958   Ride a Crooked Trail
1960   I Aim at the Stars: the Wernher von Braun Story
Scales, Earldon
1957   Burden of Truth
Scales, William
1923   A Shot in the Night
Scallon, Billy
1948   My Girl Tisa
Scanlan, George
1951   Distant Drums
Scanlon, Vivian
1950   Panic in the Streets
Scannell, Frank
1952   Rose of Cimarron
1958   The Last Hurrah
Scar, Sam
1959   Al Capone
Scarborough, George
1917   Unknown 274
1919   The Heart of Wetona
Scardon, Paul
1914   Uncle Tom's Cabin
1941   Lady from Louisiana
1943   His Butler's Sister
1948   Shanghai Chest
1950   Belle of Old Mexico
Scarpa, Eddie
1948   Up in Central Park
1959   The Black Orchid
Scarpa, Joseph
1949   Thieves' Highway
Scarpitta, Guy
1936   Ramona
Schable, Robert
1920   On with the Dance
Schacter, Leon same as **Shachter, Leon**
1939   The Light Ahead
1950   God, Man and Devil
1950? Three Daughters
Schade, Betty
1915   After Five
1916   The Love Girl

1917   The Bronze Bride
1918   The Girl in the Dark
1919   Deliverance
       Spotlight Sadie
       Who Will Marry Me?
1920   Darling Mine
1921   Wing Toy
Schaefer, Anne same as **Schaefer, Ann; Schaeffer, Ann**
1918   Her Moment
       Johanna Enlists
1919   A Fighting Colleen
1924   The Heritage of the Desert
1927   With Sitting Bull at the Spirit Lake Massacre
1928   Wheel of Chance
1929   Smiling Irish Eyes
Schaefer, Armand same as **Schaeffer, Armand**
1931   The Hurricane Horseman
1932   Law and Lawless
1935   Melody Trail
       The Singing Vagabond
1936   Down to the Sea
       Ride, Ranger, Ride
1940   Girl from God's Country
1946   G. I. War Brides
1947   The Last Round-Up
1949   The Cowboy and the Indians
1950   Indian Territory
1952   Apache Country
Schaefer, Ed
1931   Delicious
1937   It Could Happen to You
       The Plainsman
Schaefer, Robert
1950   Raiders of Tomahawk Creek
1958   The Lone Ranger and the Lost City of Gold
Schaeffer, Ann see **Schaefer, Anne**
Schaeffer, Armand see **Schaefer, Armand**
Schafer, Natalie
1948   The Time of Your Life
Schaffer, Doris
1944   Something for the Boys
Schaffer, Henry B.
1922   Breaking Home Ties
Schaffer, Rube
1941   Playmates
1943   Ladies' Day
1955   Seminole Uprising
1956   Full of Life
Schaller, Ramon
1943   Riding High
Schallert, William same as **Schallert, Bill**
1947   The Foxes of Harrow
1952   Rose of Cimarron
1953   The Jazz Singer
1955   Smoke Signal
1956   The Lone Ranger
       Raw Edge
1957   Band of Angels
       Man in the Shadow
Schanzer, Karl
1957   Burden of Truth
Scharff, Herman
1955   The Far Horizons
Scharff, Lester
1940   The Way of All Flesh
Schary, Dore
1935   Chinatown Squad
1937   Big City
1940   Behind the News
1947   Crossfire
1948   I Remember Mama
1950   Battleground
1951   Go for Broke!
       Westward the Women
1952   It's a Big Country: An American Anthology
1953   Dream Wife
1955   Bad Day at Black Rock
1956   The Last Hunt
Schatz, Edwin
1938   Hawaii Calls

Schayer, Richard *same as* **Schayer, E. Richard; Shayer, Richard**
1919 The Tong Man
      The Westerners
1920 The Cup of Fury
      Li Ting Lang
1921 Black Roses
1923 The Victor
1925 The Man in Blue
1926 The Frontier Trail
1928 The Cameraman
1929 Hallelujah
1930 ¡De frente, marchen!
      Estrellados
      Monsieur le Fox
      Monsieur le Fox (*foreign version*)
1931 Buster se marie
      Buster se marie (*foreign version*)
1932 The Cohens and Kellys in Hollywood
1935 The Winning Ticket
1940 Northwest Passage (Book I—Rogers' Rangers)
1950 Davy Crockett, Indian Scout
      The Iroquois Trail
1952 Indian Uprising
Schechtman, Benjamin *same as* **Schechtman, Barney; Schechtman, Bennie**
1932 Mazel Tov
1933 The Eternal Jew
1935 Bar-Mitzvah
Schechtman, Frank *same as* **Schechtman, Frankie**
1932 Mazel Tov
1938 The Power of Life
Schechtman, Simon
1932 Mazel Tov
Scheck, Muriel
1938 In Old Chicago
Schectman, Leo
1937 Where Is My Child?
Schee, Tamara
1951 The House on Telegraph Hill
Scheerer, Bobby
1944 Chip Off the Old Block
Schell, Maria
1959 The Hanging Tree
1960 Cimarron
Schell, Maximilian
1958 The Young Lions
Scheller, George
1931 Delicious
Schenck, Aubrey
1953 War Paint
1954 The Yellow Tomahawk
1955 Fort Yuma
1956 The Broken Star
      Ghost Town
      Quincannon, Frontier Scout
1957 Revolt at Fort Laramie
      Tomahawk Trail
      War Drums
1958 Fort Bowie
Schenck, Earl
1918 The Kaiser's Finish
      The Unbeliever
1921 No Woman Knows
Schenck, Joseph M.
1919 The Heart of Wetona
1922 East Is West
1927 The Dove
1930 Abraham Lincoln
1935 L'homme des Folies Bergère
1936 The Prisoner of Shark Island
      Sins of Man
Schenck, Walter
1958 Tonka
Schenz, Judy K.
1947 Jiggs and Maggie in Society
Scher, Harry *could be same as* **Scherr, Harry**
1949 The Red Menace

Schermer, Jules
1944 The Sullivans
1949 Illegal Entry
Scherr, Harry *could be same as* **Scher, Harry**
1915 Cohen's Luck
Schertzer, Hymie
1956 The Benny Goodman Story
Schertzinger, Victor
1921 Made in Heaven
1922 Head over Heels
1929 Redskin
1930 Galas de la Paramount
1934 Beloved
1941 Birth of the Blues
Scheue, Mary
1948 The Miracle of the Bells
Schiffman, Frank
1931 The Exile
Schildkraut, Joseph
1926 Meet the Prince
1929 Show Boat
1930 A Lady to Love (*foreign version*)
1937 Slave Ship
      Souls at Sea
1939 Mr. Moto Takes a Vacation
1947 Northwest Outpost
1948 Old Los Angeles
Schildkraut, Rudolph *same as* **Schildkraut, Rudolf**
1925 His People
1926 Pals in Paradise
1927 A Harp in Hock
      Turkish Delight
1928 A Ship Comes In
      A Ship Comes In (*foreign version*)
Schilleci, John
1950 Panic in the Streets
Schiller, Carl *see* **Von Schiller, Carl**
Schiller, Fanny
1956 Comanche
Schiller, Joseph
1934 What a Mother-in-Law!
Schiller, Norbert
1940 Escape to Glory
1949 Thieves' Highway
1958 The Young Lions
Schiller, Paul
1931 La pura verdad (*foreign version*)
Schilling, Erich von
1948 Up in Central Park
Schilling, Gus
1940 Mexican Spitfire Out West
1941 Ice-Capades
1943 The Amazing Mrs. Holliday
1947 Calendar Girl
1948 The Lady from Shanghai
Schindell, Cy *same as* **Schindel, Cy; Shindell, Cy**
1938 The Buccaneer
      Little Miss Roughneck
1946 The Gentleman Misbehaves
1947 The Foxes of Harrow
      My Wild Irish Rose
Schipa, Carlo
1927 The Fighting Hombre
1949 Harbor of Missing Men
1950 Black Hand
Schlank, Morris R.
1928 The Broken Mask
Schlesinger, Leon
1933 Man from Monterey
      The Telegraph Trail
Schlettow, Hans Adalbert
1931 La pura verdad (*foreign version*)
Schlom, Herman
1945 Betrayal from the East
      Wanderer of the Wasteland
1946 Sunset Pass
1947 Thunder Mountain
      Under the Tonto Rim
      Wild Horse Mesa

1948 The Arizona Ranger
      Gun Smugglers
      Guns of Hate
      Indian Agent
      Western Heritage
1949 Brothers in the Saddle
      The Clay Pigeon
      Masked Raiders
      The Mysterious Desperado
      Riders of the Range
      Rustlers
      Stagecoach Kid
1950 Border Treasure
      Rio Grande Patrol
      Storm Over Wyoming
1952 The Half-Breed
Schlossberg, Lucile
1952 It's a Big Country: An American Anthology
Schmidt, Michael
1958 Sierra Baron
Schmidt, Milton
1950 Panic in the Streets
Schmidt, Walter Roeber
1960 Hell to Eternity
Schnabel, Stefan
1956 Crowded Paradise
Schnee, Charles *not the same as* **Schneer, Charles H.**
1948 Red River
1950 The Furies
      Right Cross
1951 Westward the Women
1955 Trial
Schneer, Charles H. *not the same as* **Schnee, Charles**
1960 I Aim at the Stars: the Wernher von Braun Story
Schneider, Joe
1957 Man in the Shadow
Schneider, Leonard
1952 Red Ball Express
Schneider, Milton
1953 Thunder Bay
1957 Bayou
Schneier, Ray *same as* **Schnier, Ray**
1936 Love and Sacrifice
1938 The Singing Blacksmith
Schnitzer, Henrietta
1926 Broken Hearts
1932 The Unfortunate Bride
Schnitzer, Joseph I.
1932 Men Are Such Fools
Schoeller, William F.
1929 Die Königsloge
Schoenfeld, Mae *same as* **Schoenfeld, May**
1940 Eli Eli
      The Great Advisor
      The Jewish Melody
Schoenfeld, Margaret
1940 Her Second Mother
Schoengold, Joseph *same as* **Sheongold, Joseph**
1939 Kol Nidre
      Motel the Operator
Schofield, Paul (*not the same as* **Scofield, Paul**)
1924 East of Broadway
1934 La cruz y la espada
Scholl, Olga Linek
1919 The Right to Happiness
Schomer, Abraham S.
1916 The Yellow Passport
Schonberg, Alex
1938 Happy Landing
Schooler, Lewis *same as* **Schooler, Louis**
1920 The Brute
1923 Deceit
Schor, Sally
1932 Uncle Moses
Schorr, Moishe
1939 Mirele Efros
Schorr, William
1955 The Indian Fighter

Schottland, Millie
1922 Hungry Hearts
Schram, Violet
1919 Toby's Bow
Schrank, Joseph
1942 Song of the Islands
1943 Cabin in the Sky
      Riding High
Schrier, Harold G., U.S.M.C., Capt.
1950 Sands of Iwo Jima
Schriftzecer, Lew
1939 Mamele
Schrindel, George William
1959 The Hanging Tree
Schrock, Raymond L. *same as* **Schrock, Raymond**
1919 The She Wolf
1920 The Third Woman
1926 The Flaming Frontier
      Millionaires
      Private Izzy Murphy
1942 Secret Enemies
1944 Minstrel Man
1945 Club Havana
1946 Gas House Kids
      Shadows Over Chinatown
1949 Daughter of the West
Schroeder, Doris
1917 My Fighting Gentleman
1918 The Price of Applause
      Tony America
1920 A Tokio Siren
1921 Cheated Love
1947 Dangerous Venture
1949 The Gay Amigo
Schryver, Red
1958 The Rawhide Trail
Schubert, Bernard
1932 Symphony of Six Million
1934 Straight Is the Way
1937 The Barrier
1938 Breaking the Ice
1939 Fisherman's Wharf
1945 The Mummy's Curse
Schubert, Mel
1944 The Racket Man
      The Sullivans
Schulberg, B. P.
1922 Shadows
1923 April Showers
1926 Desert Gold
1929 Abie's Irish Rose
1930 El cuerpo del delito
Schulman, Arnold
1958 Wild Is the Wind
1960 Cimarron
Schultz, Harry *same as* **Schultz, Henry**
1928 Riley the Cop
1932 Hypnotized
Schultz, Samuel
1946 Cuban Pete
Schumacher, Phil
1943 Bataan
1944 Buffalo Bill
1950 Ambush
1951 The Tall Target
1957 The Deerslayer
Schumann-Heink, Ferdinand
1928 Riley the Cop
1936 Treachery Rides the Range
1937 Charlie Chan at the Olympics
1939 Confessions of a Nazi Spy
1943 Action in the North Atlantic
Schumberg, Alex
1934 Our Daily Bread
Schumm, Hans
1940 Escape
      Escape to Glory
      The Man I Married
1941 They Dare Not Love
1942 All Through the Night
      Foreign Agent
      The Navy Comes Through
1943 Action in the North Atlantic
      Margin for Error
1953 The Stars Are Singing
1960 I Aim at the Stars: the Wernher von Braun Story

Schünzel, Reinhold
1931   Die Dreigroschenoper
1946   Notorious
Schuster, Harold
1952   Kid Monk Baroni
1957   Dragoon Wells Massacre
1960   The Crowning
          Experience
Schutzman, Harold
1935   The Yiddish King Lear
Schwartsberg, Josef *same as*
    Schwartzberg, Joseph
1932   Joseph in the Land of
          Egypt
          Yiskor
Schwartz, Abraham
1919   Daughter of Mine
Schwartz, M. *could be same as*
    Schwartz, Maurice
1940   Americaner Schadchen
Schwartz, Maurice *could be same*
    as **Schwartz, M.**
1926   Broken Hearts
1932   Uncle Moses
          The Unfortunate Bride
          Yiskor
1939   Tevya
Schwartz, Samuel
1952   Anything Can Happen
Schwartz, Willie
1936   Love and Sacrifice
Schwartzberg, Joseph *see*
    Schwartsberg, Josef
Schwartzberg, Rose
1935   The Yiddish King Lear
1939   My Son
Schwarz, Jack
1943   The Girl from Monterrey
1947   Buffalo Bill Rides Again
1950   I Killed Geronimo
Schwarzwald, Milton
1944   Chip Off the Old Block
Schwed, Blanche
1915   The Alien
Schweid, Mark
1929   East Side Sadie
1932   Uncle Moses
          Yiskor
1937   The Cantor's Son
Schwieller, Fred
1959   Night of the Quarter
          Moon
Scola, Kathryn
1931   La dama atrevida
1936   It Had to Happen
Scollay, Fred J.
1959   Odds Against Tomorrow
Scooler, Zvee
1932   Uncle Moses
The Scots Guards
1960   The Day They Robbed the
          Bank of England
Scott, Adrian
1943   Mr. Lucky
1944   My Pal Wolf
1947   Crossfire
Scott, Allan
1941   Sun Valley Serenade
1959   Imitation of Life
Scott, Anthony
1938   Spirit of Youth
Scott, Ashmead
1951   The House on Telegraph
          Hill
Scott, Audrey
1944   Buffalo Bill
Scott, Bert
1936   After the Thin Man
Scott, Billy *see* **Scott, William**
Scott, Bob (*African-American*
    actor)
1949   Lookout Sister
Scott, Bud
1947   New Orleans
Scott, Cyril
1915   How Molly Malone Made
          Good
Scott, De Vallon
1953   Conquest of Cochise
1954   The Black Dakotas
          They Rode West

Scott, Dick
1944   Lake Placid Serenade
Scott, Douglas
1931   Cimarron
1937   Slave Ship
Scott, Eileen
1945   Where Do We Go From
          Here?
Scott, Ernest
1933   Circle Canyon
Scott, Ewing
1932   Igloo
1947   Untamed Fury
1948   Harpoon
1949   Arctic Manhunt
1952   Arctic Flight
          Red Snow
Scott, Fred
1920?   Reformation
1930   The Grand Parade
1931   Beyond Victory
Scott, George C.
1959   The Hanging Tree
Scott, Grant
1959   The FBI Story
Scott, Harrison
1945   The House on 92nd St.
Scott, Hazel
1945   Rhapsody in Blue
Scott, Henry
1959   Anna Lucasta
Scott, Ivy
1940   Too Many Girls
Scott, Jacques
1957   Journey to Freedom
Scott, Jesse
1936   Dimples
Scott, Joey
1960   All the Fine Young
          Cannibals
Scott, Katharine
1959   Night of the Quarter
          Moon
Scott, Leslie
1959   Porgy and Bess
Scott, Lester F., Jr.
1925   Quicker'n Lightnin'
1926   Twin Triggers
1927   Roarin' Broncs
1933   Dance Hall Hostess
1939   Daughter of the Tong
Scott, Louis
1932   Le cas du docteur
          Brenner
Scott, Mabel Julienne
1917   The Barrier
1921   No Woman Knows
1926   The Frontier Trail
Scott, Martha
1941   They Dare Not Love
1943   In Old Oklahoma
Scott, Mary
1952   Apache Country
Scott, Miriam
1950   Panic in the Streets
Scott, Morton
1942   Rio Rita
Scott, Nelson
1950   Battleground
Scott, Ovid
1919   Injustice
Scott, Patricia
1934   Coming Out Party
Scott, Pippa
1956   The Searchers
Scott, Randolph
1932   Wild Horse Mesa
1933   Broken Dreams
          Thundering Herd
1934   Wagon Wheels
1935   So Red the Rose
1936   The Last of the Mohicans
1938   The Texans
1941   Belle Starr
          Western Union
1950   The Cariboo Trail
          Colt .45
1953   The Man Behind the Gun
1956   7th Cavalry

Raymond Scott Quintet
1938   Happy Landing
Scott, Reginald
1931   Cimarron
Scott, Robert (*actor, beginning*
    circa early 1940s) same as
    Scott, Bob; Scott, Bobby
1947   Calendar Girl
1958   Houseboat
1959   Last Train from Gun Hill
Scott, Robert (*child actor*)
1939   The Escape
Scott, Susan
1945   Nob Hill
Scott, Wallace *same as* **Scott,**
    Wally
1946   Canyon Passage
          Without Reservations
1947   The Foxes of Harrow
1948   Gentleman's Agreement
Scott, William *same as* **Scott, Billy**
1916   At Piney Ridge
          A Man of Sorrow
1918   Amarilly of Clothes-Line
          Alley
1919   The Sneak
1920   Who's Your Servant?
1927   Aflame in the Sky
Scott, Zachary
1950   Colt .45
1955   Shotgun
Scotti, Vito
1948   Cry of the City
1949   Illegal Entry
1952   The Fabulous Senorita
1959   The Black Orchid
1960   Pay or Die
Scotto, Aubrey
1932   Uncle Moses
1934   Tres amores
1938   Little Miss Roughneck
Scourby, Alexander
1953   The Glory Brigade
1956   Giant
1960   Man on a String
Scroggy, Jack
1960   Cimarron
Scully, Mary Alice
1924   The Mine with the Iron
          Door
Scully, William (*actor*)
1951   Saturday's Hero
Scully, William J. (*dir*)
1921   Bits of Life
1927   Turkish Delight
1930   Cuando el amor ríe
Seabrook, Gay
1934   Imitation of Life
Seabrook, Harold
1934   Eskimo
Seabury, Forrest
1918   The Honor of His House
Seabury, Ynez
1927   Red Clay
Seacombe, Belle
1918   The Birth of a Race
Seager, Gwen
1933   It's Great to Be Alive
1943   Let's Have Fun
Seager, Mrs. James B.
1919   Injustice
Seal, Peter
1945   Salome, Where She
          Danced
1946   Cuban Pete
1947   Northwest Outpost
1948   Call Northside 777
Sealy, Lewis
1917   The Primitive Call
Seaman, Earl
1935   A Night at the Opera
1937   Man of the People
Seamans, Dorothy
1949   Lookout Sister
Seamon, Helen
1936   Star for a Night
Searl, Jack *same as* **Searl, Jackie;**
    Searle, Jackie
1930   Tom Sawyer
1931   Huckleberry Finn

1932   Hearts of Humanity
1933   A Lady's Profession
1934   She Was a Lady
1948   The Paleface
Sears, A. D. *could be same as*
    Pruden, A. Sears *not the same as*
    as **Sears, Allan**
1915   The Penitentes
1916   A Sister of Six
          Sold for Marriage
Sears, Allan *not the same as* **Sears,**
    A. D.
1915   The Birth of a Nation
1918   The Red, Red Heart
1920   Rio Grande
1926   Into Her Kingdom
1935   The Singing Vagabond
Sears, Barbara
1945   Nob Hill
Sears, Fred F. *same as* **Sears, Fred**
1947   It Had To Be You
          The Jolson Story
1948   Singin' Spurs
1949   Boston Blackie's Chinese
          Venture
          Laramie
          Lust for Gold
1950   Raiders of Tomahawk
          Creek
1951   Cyclone Fury
          Saturday's Hero
          Snake River Desperadoes
1953   Ambush at Tomahawk
          Gap
          The Nebraskan
1954   Massacre Canyon
          Overland Pacific
1955   Apache Ambush
Sears, James
1955   The Long Gray Line
Sears, Zelda
1934   Operator 13
Seastrom, Victor
1930   A Lady to Love
          A Lady to Love (*foreign*
          version)
Seaton, George
1935   The Winning Ticket
1943   The Meanest Man in the
          World
1945   Where Do We Go From
          Here?
1952   Anything Can Happen
1957   The Tin Star
Seaton, Scott
1935   Ruggles of Red Gap
Seaton, Violet
1932   Thirteen Women
Seavey, Marjorie
1933   It's Great to Be Alive
Seay, James
1940   The Way of All Flesh
1941   The Face Behind the
          Mask
1942   They Died With Their
          Boots On
1949   Prejudice
1951   When the Redskins Rode
1952   Brave Warrior
1953   Captain John Smith and
          Pocahontas
          Fort Ti
          Jack McCall Desperado
Sebastian, A. H.
1925   Friendly Enemies
Sebastian, Dorothy
1927   California
1928   The House of Scandal
          Wyoming
1948   The Miracle of the Bells
Sebastian, John
1959   Cry Tough
Sebby, Sam
1951   Oh! Susanna
Sebell, Bert E.
1931   Mamá
1932   Marido y mujer
Sebor, Sonia
1931   Le petit café

Seckler, Harry
1932   Yiskor
Sedan, Rolfe
1928   Uncle Tom's Cabin
1932   Unashamed
1934   La veuve joyeuse
1935   Charlie Chan in Paris
        A Night at the Opera
        Ruggles of Red Gap
1937   Souls at Sea
Seddon, Margaret
1926   Blarney
1943   The Meanest Man in the
        World
Sedgwick, Edward *same as*
Sedgwick, Eduardo
1920   The Face at Your Window
1926   The Flaming Frontier
1928   The Cameraman
1930   ¡De frente, marchen!
        Estrellados
Sedgwick, Josie
1918   Hell's End
        The Man Above the Law
1919   The She Wolf
Seeger, Hal
1947   Hi De Ho
1948   Killer Diller
1948?   Boarding House Blues
1949?   The Joint Is Jumpin'
Seel, Charles *same as* **Seel, Charles
F.**
1960   Cimarron
        The Dark at the Top of
        the Stairs
        Sergeant Rutledge
Seeley, Perry E.
1937   Charlie Chan at the
        Olympics
Seeling, Charles R.
1923   Purple Dawn
Seese, Dorothy Ann
1943   Let's Have Fun
1955   The Long Gray Line
Seff, Manuel
1935   A Night at the Ritz
1938   Breaking the Ice
Segal, Samuel M.
1937   The Cantor's Son
Segar, Stilman
1958   Sierra Baron
Segarra, Estela
1935   No matarás
Seger, Lucia Backus
1929   East Side Sadie
Segovia, Jesús
1930   La jaula de los leones
Segovia, Juan
1932   Amor y vida
Segovia, Luz
1931   Su última noche
1933   It's Great to Be Alive
        (*foreign version*)
1939   El trovador de la radio
Segrera, Carolina
1938   Mis dos amores
Segurola, Andrés de
1930   The Bad Man (*foreign
        version*)
        Cascarrabias
        El cuerpo del delito
        La fuerza del querer
        La voluntad del muerto
1931   Mamá
        Mi último amor
        El príncipe gondolero
1932   El caballero de la noche
1934   Un capitán de cosacos
        La ciudad de cartón
        Dos más uno, dos
        Granaderos del amor
        Tres amores
1935   Angelina o el honor de
        un brigadier
1938   Castillos en el aire
Seidel, Louise
1935   A Night at the Ritz
1938   In Old Chicago
Seidel, Tom *same as* **Seidel,
Tommy**
1942   Prisoner of Japan

1943   Margin for Error
        Tahiti Honey
Seidemann, Conrad
1930   A Lady to Love (*foreign
        version*)
Seiden, Joseph *same as* **Seiden,
Josef**
1930   My Yiddishe Mama
1935   The Yiddish King Lear
1936   Love and Sacrifice
1937   I Want to Be a Mother
1939   Kol Nidre
        Motel the Operator
        My Son
1940   Eli Eli
        The Great Advisor
        Her Second Mother
        The Jewish Melody
        Paradise in Harlem
1941   Mazel Tov Yidden
1946   Stars on Parade
1950   Monticello, Here We
        Come!
Seidenberg, Leon
1932   Uncle Moses
1939   The Light Ahead
        Mothers of Today
Seidl, Lea
1960   I Aim at the Stars: the
        Wernher von Braun
        Story
Seidner, Irene
1942   All Through the Night
1948   Big City
1950   Battleground
        The Daughter of Rosie
        O'Grady
1959   The Black Orchid
Seiler, Lewis *same as* **Seiler, Lou;
Seiler, Louis**
1931   La gran jornada (*foreign
        version*)
        Hay que casar al príncipe
        El impostor
        La ley del harem
        Mi último amor
1932   No Greater Love
1933   No dejes la puerta abierta
1935   ¡Asegure a su mujer!
        Charlie Chan in Paris
1936   Paddy O'Day
        Star for a Night
1944   Something for the Boys
Seiling, Kenneth
1931   Street Scene
Seiter, William A. *same as* **Seiter,
William**
1929   Smiling Irish Eyes
1933   Diplomaniacs
        Rafter Romance
1936   Dimples
1937   Life Begins in College
1939   Allegheny Uprising
1948   Up in Central Park
Seith Webb, Mrs.
1919   Injustice
Seitz, Chris
1960   All the Young Men
Seitz, George B. *same as* **Seitz,
George Brackett**
1915   The Spender
1916   The King's Game
1926   Desert Gold
        The Last Frontier
        Pals in Paradise
        The Vanishing American
1928   Ransom
1933   King of the Wild Horses
1934   Lazy River
1936   The Last of the Mohicans
        Mad Holiday
1937   Big City
1939   Judge Hardy and Son
1940   Kit Carson
1944   Andy Hardy's Blonde
        Trouble
Seke, M.
1918   Mystic Faces
Sekely, Steve *same as* **Sekely,
Steven**
1939   Miracle on Main Street
        Miracle on Main Street
        (*foreign version*)

1944   Lake Placid Serenade
        Waterfront
Seki, Frank M. *same as* **Seki, Frank**
could be same as **Seki, Misao**
1920   The Purple Cipher
1921   The First Born
Seki, Misao *could be same as* **Seki,
Frank**
1918   Her American Husband
1921   Where Lights Are Low
Sekino, Nori
1951   Go for Broke!
Selander, Lesley *same as* **Selander,
Les; Selander, Leslie**
1934   Laughing Boy
1935   A Night at the Opera
1936   For the Service
1937   The Barrier
1941   Doomed Caravan
1943   Border Patrol
1944   Sheriff of Las Vegas
1945   Great Stagecoach Robbery
        Phantom of the Plains
1948   Guns of Hate
        Indian Agent
1949   Brothers in the Saddle
        Masked Raiders
        The Mysterious
        Desperado
        Riders of the Range
        Rustlers
        The Sky Dragon
1950   Rio Grande Patrol
        Storm Over Wyoming
1951   Cavalry Scout
1952   Fort Osage
        The Raiders
1953   War Paint
1954   Arrow in the Dust
        The Yellow Tomahawk
1955   Fort Yuma
        Shotgun
1956   The Broken Star
        Quincannon, Frontier
        Scout
1957   Revolt at Fort Laramie
        Tomahawk Trail
1958   The Lone Ranger and the
        Lost City of Gold
Selbie, Evelyn
1914   The Good-for-Nothing
1917   The Flower of Doom
1920   Uncharted Channels
1922   The Half Breed
1923   Snowdrift
1926   Into Her Kingdom
        Rose of the Tenements
1927   Wild Geese
1932   The Hatchet Man
1934   Behold My Wife!
1936   Paddy O'Day
        Ramona
        Rose of the Rancho
1937   Song of the City
Selby, Gertrude
1916   A Child of Mystery
        The Sign of the Poppy
Selby, Sarah
1951   Jim Thorpe—All-American
1952   The Iron Mistress
1955   Good Morning, Miss Dove
1958   Gunfire at Indian Gap
Selden, Tom
1955   Indian American
        A Man Called Peter
1957   Burden of Truth
Seldes, Marian
1958   The Light in the Forest
Self, William *same as* **Self, Bill**
1947   Marshal of Cripple Creek
1948   Red River
1950   Battleground
        Sands of Iwo Jima
        A Ticket to Tomahawk
1952   The Big Sky
Selig, William N. *same as* **Selig,
William N., Col.**
1919   Auction of Souls
1921   The Hunger of the Blood
Selk, George
1953   Cry of the Hunted
        So Big
1958   Gun Fever

1959   The FBI Story
        The Last Angry Man
1960   All the Fine Young
        Cannibals
Sell, Bernie *same as* **Sell, Bernard**
1944   The Sullivans
1949   The Undercover Man
Sell, Henry G.
1921   The Money Maniac
Sellars, Elizabeth
1960   The Day They Robbed the
        Bank of England
Sellers, Oliver L.
1921   Diane of Star Hollow
Selling, William
1939   Gone With the Wind
Sellon, Charles
1930   Tom Sawyer
1934   The Cat's-Paw
Selman, David
1930   Around the Corner
1931   El código penal
        El pasado acusa
1932   Hombres en mi vida
1934   The Prescott Kid
1936   Dangerous Intrigue
Seltzer, Frank N.
1922   Breaking Home Ties
1958   Terror in a Texas Town
Seltzer, Walter
1959   Shake Hands with the
        Devil
Selwynne, Clarissa *same as*
Selwyn, Clarissa
1919   Bonnie, Bonnie Lassie
1920   The Cup of Fury
        Dangerous Days
Selznick, David O. *same as*
Selznick, David
1929   Chinatown Nights
1932   Symphony of Six Million
        Thirteen Women
1938   The Adventures of Tom
        Sawyer
1939   Gone With the Wind
1944   Since You Went Away
1947   Duel in the Sun
1949   Portrait of Jennie
1954   Indiscretion of an
        American Wife
Selznick, Lewis J.
1920   Darling Mine
1920?   The Greatest Love
1921   Society Snobs
Selznick, Myron
1927   Topsy and Eva
Semaskay, Benjamin
1940   The Ramparts We Watch
Semels, Harry
1919   A Fallen Idol
1929   Hawk of the Hills
1930   The Bad Man
1933   King of the Wild Horses
1934   Our Daily Bread
1935   The Wedding Night
1936   Human Cargo
        Rose of the Rancho
1937   Big City
        It Could Happen to You
1940   Kit Carson
1942   Woman of the Year
1944   An American Romance
Semenoff, Simon
1945   The Great John L.
Semple, Elmer Jack
1943   Margin for Error
Senisterra, Amelia
1931   Drácula
        Resurrección
Sennett, Mack
1923   Suzanna
1932   Hypnotized
Sepulveda, Carl
1940   Geronimo
1942   Valley of the Sun
1948   Up in Central Park
1950   Annie Get Your Gun
Seragnoli, Oreste
1959   The Black Orchid
1960   Pay or Die

Serda, Julia
1930   Olimpia *(foreign version)*
1931   El proceso de Mary Dugan *(foreign version)*

Serebroff, Muni *see* Seroff, Muni
Serino, Josef de
1919   Deliverance
Serjius
1932   La foule hurle
Seroff, Muni *same as* Serebroff, Muni
1937   I Want to Be a Mother
1938   Two Sisters
1940   Eli Eli
        The Great Advisor
        Her Second Mother
1943   Doughboys in Ireland
        Wintertime
1944   Charlie Chan in the Secret Service
1947   Northwest Outpost
Serotsky, Herman
1932   Joseph in the Land of Egypt
Serrano, Enriqueta
1931   La incorregible
        La pura verdad
Serrano, Luis
1946   Notorious
Serrano, Maria
1956   Serenade
Serrano, Vincent
1917   One Law for Both
Servaes, Dagny
1932   Yiskor
Servet, Mercedes
1930   Doña mentiras
        El secreto del doctor
1931   La carta
        La fiesta del diablo
Servis, Helen
1945   Where Do We Go From Here?
1947   The Burning Cross
1949   Daughter of the West
        The Gay Amigo
Servoss, Mary
1942   All Through the Night
        In This Our Life
Sessions, Almira
1940   Jennie
        Little Nellie Kelly
1941   Sullivan's Travels
        Sun Valley Serenade
1943   The Ox-Bow Incident
1945   Nob Hill
1950   Black Hand
1951   Oh! Susanna
1952   Wagons West
1953   Ride, Vaquero!
        The Sun Shines Bright
1958   The Badlanders
Seton, Bruce
1959   John Paul Jones
Seveck, Chester
1960   Ice Palace
Seveck, Helen
1960   Ice Palace
Severn, Christopher
1943   The Amazing Mrs. Holliday
Severn, Clifford
1944   They Live in Fear
Severn, Maida
1958   Marjorie Morningstar
1959   Imitation of Life
Severn, Margaret
1922   The Good Provider
Severn, Yvonne
1943   The Amazing Mrs. Holliday
Sevilla, Raphael J.
1956   7th Cavalry
1958   Sierra Baron
Sewall, Allen D.
1937   Maid of Salem

Sewall, Alma
1924   Birthright
Sewall, Olivia
1924   A Son of Satan
Seward, Billie
1939   Charlie Chan at Treasure Island
1943   The Gang's All Here
Seward, Edmond
1947   Bowery Buckaroos
Sexton, Patrick Joseph
1954   The Yellow Tomahawk
Seyffertitz, Gustav von *same as* Clonblough, G. Butler
1918   Hidden Pearls
        The Source
1925   Flower of Night
1926   Private Izzy Murphy
1927   Rose of the Golden West
1928   Vamping Venus
1936   Mad Holiday
1938   In Old Chicago
Seymour, Al
1941   The Face Behind the Mask
        Mystery Ship
1942   Lawless Plainsmen
        Woman of the Year
Seymour, Anne
1960   All the Fine Young Cannibals
Seymour, Clarine
1919   Scarlet Days
Seymour, Dan
1943   Tahiti Honey
1948   Key Largo
1950   Young Man with a Horn
Seymour, Harry
1935   The Irish in Us
1941   Sullivan's Travels
1943   Action in the North Atlantic
        Yankee Doodle Dandy
1945   The Dolly Sisters
        Rhapsody in Blue
        A Tree Grows in Brooklyn
1948   Cry of the City
        My Girl Tisa
1950   A Ticket to Tomahawk
1951   Show Boat
1955   Violent Saturday
1958   Marjorie Morningstar
Seymour, James
1932   Symphony of Six Million
Seymour, Larry
1937   Underworld
1938   Swing!
Shaan, Morgan
1957   Band of Angels
Shachter, Leon *see* Schacter, Leon
Shack, Sammy *same as* Shack, Sam
1942   Sunday Punch
1945   Wanderer of the Wasteland
1954   Dangerous Mission
1956   The Catered Affair
Shackelford, Floyd
1928   Absent
1941   Louisiana Purchase
1942   Sunday Punch
1943   Crash Dive
Shade, Jameson
1947   The Burning Cross
Shade, Pat
1951   Cuban Fireball
Shafer, Charles
1931   The Hurricane Horseman
Shaff, Monroe
1938   California Frontier
Shah, Lord A.
1935   Melody Trail
Shahan, Rocky
1949   Roll Thunder Roll!
1952   Fort Osage
1957   The Deerslayer
1958   Blood Arrow
Shairp, Mordaunt
1937   The Barrier
Shaklett, Gwendolyn
1955   Brevities of 1955

Shaler, Virginia
1949   Lost Boundaries
1960   Man on a String
Shall, Theo
1930   Anna Christie *(foreign version)*
        Olimpia *(foreign version)*
1931   La gran jornada *(foreign version)*
Shamburger, Lucille
1950   Emergency Wedding
1952   Bugles in the Afternoon
The Shamrock Cowboys
1948   Singin' Spurs
Shanberg, Edward
1938   Spirit of Youth
Shane, Francis C.
1957   Burden of Truth
Shane, Jerry
1944   An American Romance
Shane, Maxwell
1953   The Glass Wall
Shane, Ted
1929   The Desert Rider
Shane, Thomas
1957   Burden of Truth
Shannon, Alex K. *same as* Shannon, Alexander
1917   Unknown 274
1922   Easy Money
Shannon, Bill
1946   Without Reservations
Shannon, Cora
1945   The Bells of St. Mary's
Shannon, Elene
1933   It's Great to Be Alive
Shannon, Ethel
1922   The Top O' the Morning
1925   Speed Wild
Shannon, Frank
1936   The Prisoner of Shark Island
Shannon, Harry
1940   Too Many Girls
1941   Hold Back the Dawn
1943   Doughboys in Ireland
        In Old Oklahoma
1944   The Sullivans
1945   Nob Hill
1946   Canyon Passage
1947   The Farmer's Daughter
        The Jolson Story
1948   Fighting Father Dunne
        The Lady from Shanghai
        My Girl Tisa
1949   Rustlers
        Tulsa
1950   The Jackie Robinson Story
        Right Cross
1952   High Noon
1953   Cry of the Hunted
1955   Not As a Stranger
1958   Touch of Evil
1959   Yellowstone Kelly
Shannon, Jack
1944   Buffalo Bill
Shannon, Peggy
1936   Ellis Island
Shannon, Richard
1953   Arrowhead
1957   Beau James
        Ride Out for Revenge
        The Tin Star
        Trooper Hook
1959   The Jayhawkers!
Shannon, Robert T.
1935   A Night at the Ritz
Shannon, Sue
1958   The Last Hurrah
Shannon, Warren
1948   The Boy with Green Hair
Shanock, R.
1938   The Singing Blacksmith
Shapiro, Anne
1931   Zein Weib's Lubovnick
Shapiro, Joseph, Cantor
1931   The Voice of Israel

Shapiro, Lionel
1950   Deported
Shapiro, William D.
1944   Lady, Let's Dance!
Sharbutt, Del
1946   Cuban Pete
Shargel, Jack
1933   Live and Laugh
1939   Mothers of Today
Sharon, William
1947   Citizen Saint
Sharp, Alex *same as* Sharpe, Alex
1948   Harpoon
1950   Rocky Mountain
1951   Apache Drums
        Jim Thorpe—All-American
1953   Seminole
Sharp, Clint
1932   The Rainbow Trail
1933   Robbers' Roost
1941   Western Union
1943   The Ox-Bow Incident
1944   Buffalo Bill
1951   Westward the Women
1954   Broken Lance
Sharp, Roland
1915   The Rosary
Sharpe, Albert
1948   Up in Central Park
1949   Portrait of Jennie
1960   The Day They Robbed the Bank of England
Sharpe, Alex *see* Sharp, Alex
Sharpe, David *same as* Sharpe, Dave
1929   Masked Emotions
1937   Drums of Destiny
1941   Mutiny in the Arctic
        Thunder Over the Prairie
1950   The Girl from San Lorenzo
1951   Tomahawk
1952   Trail of the Arrow
Sharpe, Henry
1956   Singing in the Dark
Sharpe, Lester
1936   Rose of the Rancho
1948   Call Northside 777
1949   Illegal Entry
1950   Mystery Submarine
1953   Tonight We Sing
Shauer, Melville
1940   Tengo fe en ti
Shaughnessy, Mickey
1953   Last of the Comanches
1958   Gunman's Walk
1960   The Adventures of Huckleberry Finn
Shavelson, Melville *same as* Shavelson, Mel
1941   Ice-Capades
1948   The Paleface
1950   The Daughter of Rosie O'Grady
1957   Beau James
1958   Houseboat
Shaw, Arvell
1957   Satchmo the Great
Shaw, Brinsley
1927   The Dove
Shaw, Buddy *see* Shaw, Robert "Buddy"
Shaw, C. Montague *same as* Shaw, Montague
1934   Beloved
        Charlie Chan in London
1935   The Winning Ticket
1936   My American Wife
1937   Nation Aflame
        The Riders of the Whistling Skull
1938   Gateway
1939   Mr. Moto's Last Warning
1940   Charlie Chan's Murder Cruise
        The Gay Caballero
1948   Unconquered
Shaw, Danny
1945   Nob Hill
        A Tree Grows in Brooklyn

Shaw, Frank
1943   The Amazing Mrs.
       Holliday
       His Butler's Sister

Freida Shaw's Etudes
1936   General Spanky

Shaw, Freita
1960   I Passed for White

Shaw, Janet
1940   Escape
1941   You're Out of Luck
1945   The Scarlet Clue
1946   Dark Alibi

Shaw, Lloyd
1947   Duel in the Sun

Shaw, Montague see **Shaw, C. Montague**

Shaw, Peggy
1924   In Hollywood With
       Potash and Perlmutter

Shaw, Reta
1957   All Mine to Give

Shaw, Robert "Buddy" same as
Shaw, Buddy
1940   Elsa Maxwell's Public
       Deb No. 1
1941   Adam Had Four Sons
       Ride on Vaquero
1951   Jim Thorpe—All-American
1960   Ice Palace

Shaw, Victoria
1959   The Crimson Kimono
1960   I Aim at the Stars: the
       Wernher von Braun
       Story

Shaw, William
1952   Red Snow

The Shaw Negro Choir
1935   Harmony Lane

Shawaway, Alba
1958   Tonka

Shawaway, Nettie
1958   Tonka

Shawlee, Joan same as **Fulton, Joan**
1946   Cuban Pete
1947   Buck Privates Come
       Home

Shawn, Shirley
1957   Burden of Truth

Shay, John same as **Shay, Jack**
1942   Submarine Raider
1948   Shanghai Chest

Shay, William E.
1915   The Clemenceau Case
       Kreutzer Sonata
1915?   Sin

Shayer, Richard see **Schayer, Richard**

Shayne, Edith
1916   Poor Little Peppina

Shayne, Konstantin
1945   Escape in the Fog
1948   Cry of the City
       Night Wind

Shayne, Robert
1944   Mr. Skeffington
1946   The Face of Marble
1952   Indian Uprising
       The Ring

Shayne, Tamara
1947   The Jolson Story
       Northwest Outpost
       Pirates of Monterey
1949   Thieves' Highway
1950   Jolson Sings Again
1953   Tonight We Sing

Shea, Gloria
1936   Dangerous Intrigue

Shea, Jack
1943   Ladies' Day
1947   Calendar Girl
       Easy Come, Easy Go
1950   Mystery Street
       Young Man with a Horn
1951   Gambling House
1953   San Antone

Shean, Al
1937   It Could Happen to You

Shearer, Norma
1940   Escape
1942   We Were Dancing

Shearing, Renee
1931   Street Scene

Shearon, Lillian Nicholson
1915?   Sam Davis, the Hero of
       Tennessee

Sheehan, Howard
1945   Jealousy

Sheehan, James
1916   Gold and the Woman

Sheehan, John
1933   Grand Slam
1936   It Had to Happen
       Laughing Irish Eyes
1938   Rascals
1939   Winner Take All
1940   East of the River
       Mexican Spitfire Out
       West
1942   Woman of the Year
1943   Gangway for Tomorrow
       Ladies' Day
       Yankee Doodle Dandy
1944   An American Romance
1946   Three Wise Fools
1947   Buck Privates Come
       Home
       California
       Easy Come, Easy Go
1949   Top O' the Morning

Sheehan, Perry
1953   Dream Wife

Sheehan, Winfield R. same as
Sheehan, Winfield
1934   Charlie Chan's Courage
       Coming Out Party
       She Was a Lady
       Stand Up and Cheer!

Sheekman, Arthur
1936   Dimples
       Rose of the Rancho

Sheffield, Billy
1940   Knute Rockne—All
       American
1948   The Boy with Green Hair

Sheffield, John
1940   Knute Rockne—All
       American
       Lucky Cisco Kid
1951   The Great Caruso

Sheffield, Maceo B. same as
Sheffield, Maceo
1937   Harlem on the Prairie
1939   Double Deal
       Reform School
1940   Gang War
1940?   Mr. Washington Goes to
       Town
1941   Up Jumped the Devil
1942   Lucky Ghost
       Professor Creeps
1949   Lookout Sister

Sheffield, Phillip
1914   The Great Diamond
       Robbery

Sheffield, Reginald
1934   Charlie Chan in London
1938   The Buccaneer
1956   Secret of Treasure
       Mountain
1958   Marjorie Morningstar

Sheik, a horse
1947   California

Shelby, Margaret
1918?   Rosemary Climbs the
       Heights
1919   A Bachelor's Wife

Sheldon, Anita
1934   Laughing Boy

Sheldon, Ann
1940   Escape

Sheldon, E. Lloyd
1918   The Firebrand
1919   A Fallen Idol
1928   Sins of the Fathers

Sheldon, Gene
1945   The Dolly Sisters
       Where Do We Go From
       Here?
1960   The Sign of Zorro

Sheldon, Jerry
1950   No Way Out
       A Ticket to Tomahawk
1955   Smoke Signal

Sheldon, Kathryn same as
Sheldon, Katherine
1934   Laughing Boy
1936   Below the Deadline
       Ramona
       Star for a Night
1937   Maid of Salem
1940   Elsa Maxwell's Public
       Deb No. 1
1947   California
1950   No Way Out
       Rock Island Trail

Sheldon, Marion same as **Shelton, Marion**
1934   Stand Up and Cheer!
1936   After the Thin Man

Sheldon, Sheila
1941   Sullivan's Travels

Sheldon, Sidney
1950   Annie Get Your Gun
1953   Dream Wife

Shellac, Fred
1950   The Big Hangover
1955   Violent Saturday

Shelley, George
1937   Music for Madame

Shelley, Jordan
1958   The Last Hurrah

Shelton, Don
1950   Mystery Street
1951   Queen for a Day
1958   Bullwhip

Shelton, George
1945   The House on 92nd St.

Shelton, John
1942   Foreign Agent
       Whispering Ghosts

Shelton, Marion see **Sheldon, Marion**

Shelton, Marla
1937   Song of the City

Shelton, Yvonne
1920?   The Greatest Love

Sheongold, Joseph see
Schoengold, Joseph

Shepard, Courtland
1950   Right Cross
1958   Escape from Red Rock
       Wild Is the Wind
1959   The Black Orchid
       The Jayhawkers!
       Last Train from Gun Hill

Shepard, Iva
1914   Northern Lights
       The Straight Road

Shepard, Jan
1957   Burden of Truth

Shepard, Miles
1951   Slaughter Trail
1957   Journey to Freedom

Shepherd, Elaine
1935   The Singing Vagabond

Shepherd, Norma
1948   Miracle in Harlem

Shepherd, Richard
1959   The Hanging Tree

Shepherd, Wallace
1934   Call of the Coyote

Shepodd, Jon
1955   Indian American
1957   Dragoon Wells Massacre
1958   Oregon Passage

Shepperd, John
1941   Belle Starr

Sher, Jack
1956   Walk the Proud Land

Sherdeman, Ted
1949   Lust for Gold
1953   The Eddie Cantor Story
1958   St. Louis Blues
1960   Hell to Eternity

Sheridan, Ann same as **Sheridan, Anne; Sheridan, Clara Lou; Sheridan, Gail**
1927   The Way of All Flesh
1934   Behold My Wife!

1937   Black Legion
       Hills of Old Wyoming
       The Plainsman
1942   Juke Girl
       Wings for the Eagle

Sheridan, Dan
1958   Bullwhip

Sheridan, Frank
1921   Anne of Little Smoky
1924   Two Shall Be Born
1933   The Man Who Dared: An
       Imaginative Biography
1934   The Cat's-Paw
       Stand Up and Cheer!
1938   City Streets

Sheridan, Gail see **Sheridan, Ann**

Sheridan, James
1936   Custer's Last Stand
1939   Drifting Westward

Sheridan, John
1945   Pride of the Marines

Sheridan, Michael
1948   Cry of the City

The Sheriff's Boys Band
1943   Good Luck, Mr. Yates

Sherin, Leo
1943   Dixie

Sherk, Gretl
1940   Escape

Sherlock, Charles
1938   The Rage of Paris
1939   Confessions of a Nazi Spy
1940   Charlie Chan in Panama
       East of the River
1942   All Through the Night
       Nazi Agent
1943   The Amazing Mrs.
       Holliday
1944   Hi, Beautiful
1945   The Scarlet Clue
1950   Colt .45
       The Daughter of Rosie
       O'Grady

Sherman, Evelyn
1923   Suzanna
1930   Song of the Caballero
1933   The California Trail

Sherman, Fred same as **Sherman, Fred E.**
1950   Mystery Street
1957   Gun Battle at Monterey
       War Drums

Sherman, George
1932   Hypnotized
1935   Melody Trail
1936   Daniel Boone
       Rainbow on the River
1937   Manhattan
       Merry-Go-Round
1940   Covered Wagon Days
1946   The Gentleman
       Misbehaves
1947   Last of the Redmen
1950   Comanche Territory
1951   The Raging Tide
       Tomahawk
1952   The Battle at Apache Pass
1954   War Arrow
1955   Chief Crazy Horse
1956   Comanche
       Reprisal!
1960   For the Love of Mike

Sherman, Harry same as **Sherman, Harry A.**
1937   The Barrier
1941   Doomed Caravan
       Secret of the Wastelands
1942   American Empire
1943   Border Patrol
1944   Buffalo Bill
1948   Four Faces West

Sherman, Kathryn
1924?   The Flaming Crisis

Sherman, Lewis
1940   Gang War

Sherman, Ransom same as
Sherman, Ransom M.
1947   Dark Delusion
1948   Gentleman's Agreement

Sherman, Reed
1956   Comanche
Sherman, Teddi
1948   Four Faces West
Sherman, Vincent
1933   Counsellor at Law
1942   Across the Pacific
          All Through the Night
1944   Mr. Skeffington
1960   Ice Palace
Shero, Terry
1939   Gone With the Wind
Sheron, Molio
1944   An American Romance
1947   Northwest Outpost
Sherrill, Jack
1916   The Woman in 47
Sherrill, Martha
1949   Call of the Forest
Sherrill, William L.
1919   The She Wolf
Sherris, Kay
1934   Broadway Bill
Sherry, J. Barney *same as* **Sherry, Barney**
1916   Civilization's Child
1918   Real Folks
          The Reckoning Day
1919   The Tiger Lily
          Yvonne from Paris
1920   Darling Mine
          Dinty
Sherwood, Billy *see* **Sherwood, William**
Sherwood, C. L. *same as* **Sherwood, Clarence L.**
1935   Ruggles of Red Gap
1938   City Streets
Sherwood, Gale
1948   Rocky
Sherwood, George
1942   Gentleman Jim
1943   Action in the North Atlantic
          The Leopard Man
1944   An American Romance
          Buffalo Bill
1945   Salome, Where She Danced
          The Valley of Decision
1947   Buffalo Bill Rides Again
1948   My Girl Tisa
1950   Mystery Street
          Right Cross
1951   Queen for a Day
          Show Boat
1954   Dangerous Mission
Sherwood, John *same as* **Sherwood, John F.**
1938   Hawaii Calls
1939   Fisherman's Wharf
          Gone With the Wind
          Way Down South
1941   Secret of the Wastelands
1944   Address Unknown
1947   Ride the Pink Horse
1949   Arctic Manhunt
1950   Comanche Territory
1952   Bright Victory
          Red Ball Express
1953   Thunder Bay
          Tumbleweed
1956   Raw Edge
Sherwood, Robert *(actor)*
1951   The Great Caruso
          Little Big Horn
          The Magnificent Yankee
Sherwood, Robert E. *(writer, prod)*
1940   Northwest Passage (Book I—Rogers' Rangers)
1941   Adam Had Four Sons
Sherwood, William *same as* **Sherwood, Billy**
1915   The Danger Signal
1916   Broken Chains
Sheva, Bas
1950   Catskill Honeymoon
Shibata, George
1960   Hell to Eternity

Shield, Ernest *same as* **Shields, Ernest**
1920   The Purple Cipher
1934   Judge Priest
1937   The Devil's Playground
Shield, Robert
1954   Hell's Half Acre
Shields, Arthur
1939   Drums Along the Mohawk
1940   Little Nellie Kelly
1942   Dr. Gillespie's New Assistant
          Gentleman Jim
1945   The Valley of Decision
1947   Easy Come, Easy Go
1948   Fighting Father Dunne
          Tap Roots
1949   She Wore a Yellow Ribbon
1951   Apache Drums
1952   The Quiet Man
1959   Night of the Quarter Moon
1960   For the Love of Mike
Shields, Ernest *see* **Shield, Ernest**
Shields, Sidney
1915   The Clemenceau Case
Shigeta, James
1959   The Crimson Kimono
1960   Walk Like a Dragon
Shillal, Francis
1953   The Great Sioux Uprising
Shilling, Marion
1931   Beyond Victory
1935   Captured in Chinatown
Shilling, S. K.
1918   A Broadway Scandal
Shillingford, Margaret
1917   The Sudden Gentleman
Shimada, Teru
1934   Charlie Chan's Courage
1939   Mr. Moto's Last Warning
1950   Emergency Wedding
Shimizu, George
1951   Go for Broke!
Shindell, Cy *see* **Schindell, Cy**
Shipman, Barry
1940   Hi-Yo Silver
1941   Prairie Pioneers
1948   Singin' Spurs
1949   Laramie
1950   Raiders of Tomahawk Creek
1951   Cyclone Fury
          Snake River Desperadoes
1958   Gunfire at Indian Gap
Shipman, Helen
1935   Naughty Marietta
Shipman, Nell
1917   My Fighting Gentleman
1921   The Girl from God's Country
Shipman, Nina
1959   The Oregon Trail
Shipp, J. Raymond
1952   Bright Victory
Shirley, Anne *same as* **Dawn O'Day**
1927   The Callahans and the Murphys
1928   Sins of the Fathers
1932   So Big
Shirley, Arthur
1916   The Fall of a Nation
Shirley, Florence
1940   New Moon
1942   We Were Dancing
Shirley, Peg
1959   Imitation of Life
Shlifko, Ola
1939   Mamele
Shlisky, Joseph, Cantor
1931   The Voice of Israel
Shneyer, Chaim
1932   A Daughter of Her People
Shoemaker, Ann
1936   Sins of Man
Shoemaker, Ida
1943   Gangway for Tomorrow

Shoenfeld, Ben-Zion
1939   The Light Ahead
Sholem, Lee
1939   Way Down South
1953   The Stand at Apache River
Shoor, Salcia
1950?   Three Daughters
Shooting Star *same as* **Shooting Star, Percy**
1947   Buffalo Bill Rides Again
1948   Singin' Spurs
1949   The Cowboy and the Indians
          Laramie
1950   Annie Get Your Gun
          A Ticket to Tomahawk
1952   Buffalo Bill in Tomahawk Territory
1954   The Black Dakotas
1955   Kiss of Fire
1956   The Searchers
Shope, Hedi
1935   The Wedding Night
Shore, Byron *(African-American actor) not the same as* **Shores, Byron**
1935   Lem Hawkins' Confession
Shore, Jean
1954   Go Man Go
Shore, Michael
1954   Go Man Go
Shore, Viola Brothers
1928   The House of Scandal
1929   Lucky Boy
1930   The Kibitzer
1932   Men Are Such Fools
Shores, Byron
1940   Too Many Girls
Shores, Lynn
1936   The Glory Trail
          Rebellion
1940   Charlie Chan at the Wax Museum
          The Mark of Zorro
1941   Western Union
Shorr, Morris
1939   The Light Ahead
Short, Antrim *same as* **Short, A., Master**
1914   John Barleycorn
          Where the Trail Divides
1915   The Gambler of the West
1917   A Jewel in Pawn
1918   Amarilly of Clothes-Line Alley
          Huck and Tom; or, the Further Adventures of Tom Sawyer
          The Yellow Dog
Short, Doris *could be same as* **Short, Dorothy**
1931   Huckleberry Finn
Short, Dorothy *could be same as* **Short, Doris**
1938   Wild Horse Canyon
1939   Daughter of the Tong
Short, Edward
1943   Cabin in the Sky
Short, Florence
1922   Cardigan
Short, Gertrude
1914   The Little Angel of Canyon Creek
1918   Amarilly of Clothes-Line Alley
          The Only Road
1923   Breaking into Society
1929   In Old California
1930   The Last Dance
Short, Jimmy
1949?   The Joint Is Jumpin'
Short, Luke
1941   Hurry, Charlie, Hurry
Short, Robin
1944   Something for the Boys
1945   I Love a Bandleader
1946   Without Reservations
1950   Ambush
          The Baron of Arizona
1957   The Halliday Brand

Short Bull *same as* **Short Bull, Chief**
1914   The Indian Wars
1917   The Adventures of Buffalo Bill
Shotwell, Marie
1915   Under Southern Skies
1917   The Woman and the Beast
1925   The Manicure Girl
Shoup, D. M.
1950   Sands of Iwo Jima
Shrum, Cal
1944   Riding West
Cal Shrum and His Rhythm Rangers
1941   Thunder Over the Prairie
Shryer, Art
1932   Mazel Tov
Shubert, Albert
1955   Blackboard Jungle
Shubert, Eddie
1935   Black Fury
1937   Man of the People
Shuford, Andy
1931   The Great Meadow
          Oklahoma Jim
1932   Texas Pioneers
Shulman, Irving
1952   The Ring
Shuman, Paul
1941   Sun Valley Serenade
Shumate, Harold
1926   Meet the Prince
1927   Whispering Sage
1928   United States Smith
1932   Wild Horse Mesa
1936   Dangerous Intrigue
1939   Man of Conquest
1950   Buccaneer's Girl
1951   Little Big Horn
1952   The Half-Breed
Shumpert, James
1955   Blackboard Jungle
Shumway, Cora
1937   The Plainsman
Shumway, Lee *same as* **Shumway, L. C.**
1917   The Plow Woman
1923   Snowdrift
1927   His Foreign Wife
1928   The House of Scandal
1929   Evangeline
1934   Lazy River
          The Lone Defender
1936   Robin Hood of El Dorado
1937   Charlie Chan at the Olympics
          Charlie Chan on Broadway
          Nation Aflame
          Souls at Sea
1938   City Streets
          Daughter of Shanghai
          Gateway
          Mr. Moto's Gamble
          Passport Husband
          Spawn of the North
1939   Mr. Moto in Danger Island
          The Return of the Cisco Kid
1940   Elsa Maxwell's Public Deb No. 1
          The Gay Caballero
          Geronimo
1941   The Face Behind the Mask
          Prairie Pioneers
          Ride on Vaquero
1947   Buck Privates Come Home
          Buffalo Bill Rides Again
1953   Old Overland Trail
          San Antone
Shumway, Walter
1938   The Buccaneer
1941   Mystery Ship
Shun, Chan Ligh
1941   Golden Gate Girl
Shunn, Iris *see* **Meredith, Iris**

Shurlock, Geoffrey
1930   Amor audaz
        Cascarrabias
        El cuerpo del delito
        El dios del mar
        Galas de la Paramount
1931   Gente alegre
        El príncipe gondolero
Shurr, Robert
1940   George Washington
        Carver
Shurtz, Sewall
1944   Lake Placid Serenade
Shutan, Harry
1927   The Red Raiders
Shutan, Shelah
1947   Calendar Girl
Shute, James L.
1940   The Ramparts We Watch
Shutta, Ethel
1930   Whoopee
Shutta, Jack
1947   The Burning Cross
1948   Tap Roots
Shvetz, Michael
1937   Natalka Poltavka
1939   Cossacks in Exile
Sibelius, Celia *see* **Reicher, Hedwiga**
Sibley, Dorothy
1921   Fifty Candles
Sibole, Douglas
1915   An American Gentleman
Sickles, H. G.
1914   The Indian Wars
1917   The Adventures of Buffalo
        Bill
Sidney, George *(actor)*
1924   In Hollywood With
        Potash and Perlmutter
1926   The Cohens and Kellys
        Millionaires
        Sweet Daddies
1927   The Auctioneer
        Clancy's Kosher Wedding
        For the Love of Mike
        Lost at the Front
1928   The Cohens and the
        Kellys in Paris
        Flying Romeos
        We Americans
1929   The Cohens and Kellys in
        Atlantic City
1930   Around the Corner
        The Cohens and the
        Kellys in Scotland
        King of Jazz
1931   The Cohens and Kellys in
        Africa
1932   The Cohens and Kellys in
        Hollywood
        The Heart of New York
1933   The Cohens and Kellys in
        Trouble
        Rafter Romance
Sidney, George *(dir)*
1950   Annie Get Your Gun
1951   Show Boat
Sidney, P. Jay
1953   The Joe Louis Story
Sidney, Scott
1917   Her Own People
Sidney, Suzanne
1960   Studs Lonigan
Sidney, Sylvia
1931   Street Scene
1934   Behold My Wife!
1955   Violent Saturday
Siebert, William
1916   Sold for Marriage
Sieg, Edward
1952   The Ring
Siegel, Bernard
1914   Threads of Destiny
1923   None So Blind
1926   Desert Gold
        The Vanishing American
1927   Drums of the Desert
        Open Range
1929   Redskin
1935   The Wedding Night

1938   Happy Landing
Siegel, Chris *see* **Tabori, Kristoffer**
Siegel, Don
1960   Flaming Star
Siegel, Joseph
1941   Louisiana Purchase
Siegel, Sol C.
1937   Boots and Saddles
        The Riders of the
        Whistling Skull
1939   Man of Conquest
1940   Hi-Yo Silver
        Three Faces West
1948   Cry of the City
1949   House of Strangers
1950   Panic in the Streets
1954   Broken Lance
Siegler, Allen
1919   The Unpainted Woman
Siegmann, George
1915   The Birth of a Nation
        A Yankee from the West
1921   Shame
1922   A California Romance
        Hungry Hearts
1923   Anna Christie
        Jealous Husbands
1928   Uncle Tom's Cabin
Sierra, María Luisa
1935   Rosa de Francia
Sierra, Milissa
1939   La Inmaculada
Sierra de Luna, José
1931   La fiesta del diablo
        La pura verdad
Sigaloff, Eugene
1939   Mirele Efros
1946   The Sailor Takes a Wife
1947   Northwest Outpost
1949   Rose of the Yukon
Sigismondi, Anstide
1955   Murder in Villa Capri
Sigueiros, Placido
1941   Hold Back the Dawn
Sikawitt, Mortimer D.
1932   Joseph in the Land of
        Egypt
Silberber, Wolf
1932   Yiskor
Silberkasten, Morris
1937   Where Is My Child?
Silbert, Liza
1926   Broken Hearts
1932   The Unfortunate Bride
Silbert, Theodore
1926   Broken Hearts
1932   The Unfortunate Bride
Silczer, Meyer
1934   The Youth of Russia
Siletti, Mario
1949   House of Strangers
        Thieves' Highway
1950   Black Hand
        A Lady Without Passport
1951   Go for Broke!
        The Great Caruso
        The House on Telegraph
        Hill
1953   Taxi
        Thunder Bay
1956   Serenade
1957   Man in the Shadow
1960   Pay or Die
Silliphant, Stirling
1953   The Joe Louis Story
Sills, Milton
1915   Under Southern Skies
1918   The Hell Cat
1926   Puppets
1928   The Crash
        The Hawk's Nest
Silva, Aura de
1935   Angelina o el honor de
        un brigadier
        Rosa de Francia
1936   El crimen de media
        noche
        Sutter's Gold
Silva, Fred
1936   Dimples

Silva, Henry
1956   Crowded Paradise
1958   Ride a Crooked Trail
1959   The Jayhawkers!
Silva, José Vasques
1955   Seven Cities of Gold
Silva, Miguel
1930   La rosa de fuego
Silva, Petra
1946   G. I. War Brides
1949   House of Strangers
1950   North of the Great Divide
Silva, Uilani
1938   Hawaii Calls
Silvani, Aldo
1951   Teresa
1959   Al Capone
Silveira, Mario
1951   The Mark of the
        Renegade
Silver, a horse circa 1930s
1932   White Eagle
Silver, a horse circa 1940s
1942   Below the Border
Silver, Daniel
1950   God, Man and Devil
Silver, Marcel
1931   En cada puerto un amor
Silver King, a horse
1924   North of Nevada
1925   The Wild Bull's Lair
1927   Don Mike
Silvera, Carl
1924   The Pell Street Mystery
Silvera, Frank
1952   The Fighter
1956   Crowded Paradise
1960   Key Witness
Silverheels, Jay *same as* **Smith, Harry "Silverheels"; Smith, Silverheels**
1941   Western Union
1944   Tahiti Nights
1946   Singin' in the Corn
1947   The Last Round-Up
        Northwest Outpost
1948   The Feathered Serpent
        Fury at Furnace Creek
        Key Largo
        Singin' Spurs
        Unconquered
1949   The Cowboy and the
        Indians
        Laramie
        Lust for Gold
        The Prairie
1950   Broken Arrow
1951   Cyclone Fury
1952   The Battle at Apache Pass
        Brave Warrior
1953   Jack McCall Desperado
        Last of the Comanches
        The Nebraskan
        The Pathfinder
1954   The Black Dakotas
        Drums Across the River
        Saskatchewan
        War Arrow
1955   The Vanishing American
1956   The Lone Ranger
        Walk the Proud Land
1958   The Lone Ranger and the
        Lost City of Gold
Silverman, Stanley H.
1958   Gun Fever
Silvers, Phil
1941   Ice-Capades
1942   All Through the Night
1944   Something for the Boys
Silverstein, David
1941   Mystery Ship
Silverstein, Moishe *same as* **Zilberstein, Moishe**
1934   The Youth of Russia
1940   The Great Advisor
Silvestre, Armando
1951   Apache Drums
        The Mark of the
        Renegade
1952   Hiawatha
1960   For the Love of Mike

Silvestri, Antone
1949   Thieves' Highway
Siméon, André
1931   Su noche de bodas
        (foreign version)
Simetti, Otto
1955   Murder in Villa Capri
Similuk, Peter
1950   Mystery Submarine
Simmonds, Charles
1951   Native Son
Simmonds, Leslie
1936   Aces and Eights
        The Traitor
Simmons, Beverly
1946   Cuban Pete
1947   Buck Privates Come
        Home
Simmons, Bobby
1939   One Dark Night
        Reform School
Simmons, Dan
1958   Frontier Gun
Simmons, Dick *(actor)*
1942   Dr. Gillespie's New
        Assistant
        Seven Sweethearts
1951   The Well
Simmons, Earl
1916   Broken Fetters
Simmons, Floyd
1956   Pillars of the Sky
Simmons, Georgia
1955   The Rose Tattoo
Simmons, H. C.
1918   Untamed
1926   Into Her Kingdom
Simmons, James
1949   The Story of Seabiscuit
Simmons, Jean
1958   Home Before Dark
Simmons, Maude
1948?   Junction 88
1949   Portrait of Jennie
1950   No Way Out
Simmons, Michael L. *same as* **Simmons, Michael**
1938   Little Miss Roughneck
1943   Crime Smasher
1944   They Live in Fear
Simmons, Richard Alan *(writer)*
1953   War Paint
1954   The Yellow Tomahawk
Simmons, Sada
1937   It Could Happen to You
Simms, Dorothy
1931   Cimarron
Simms, Eddie Lou *same as* **Simms, Eddie**
1942   Sunday Punch
        Woman of the Year
1947   Vigilantes of Boomtown
1950   Right Cross
Simms, Ginny
1941   Playmates
Simms, Hank
1957   Burden of Truth
Simms, Hilda
1953   The Joe Louis Story
Simms, J. M.
1921   The Lure of a Woman
Simms, Sylvia
1951   Molly
Simon, Abe
1940   The Notorious Elinor Lee
1956   Singing in the Dark
1958   Never Love a Stranger
Simon, Mae
1930   My Yiddishe Mama
1933   Live and Laugh
Simon, Pete
1950   The Men
Simon, Robert F. *same as* **Simon, Robert**
1952   Bright Victory
1954   The Black Dakotas
1955   Chief Crazy Horse
        Foxfire
        Seven Angry Men
1956   The Benny Goodman
        Story
        The Catered Affair

1957	Edge of the City
1958	Gunman's Walk
1959	The Last Angry Man
1960	Pay or Die

Simon, S. S. (actor)
| 1936 | Rose of the Rancho |

Simon, S. Sylvan (dir, prod)
1942	Rio Rita
1946	Bad Bascomb
1949	Lust for Gold

Simon, Simone
1938	Josette
1942	Cat People
1943	Tahiti Honey

Simone, Pat de
| 1959 | The Last Angry Man |

Simone, Ralph
| 1947 | Citizen Saint |

Simoneaux, Ernest
| 1950 | Panic in the Streets |

Simpkins, Jesse
| 1946 | Beware |

Simpson, Gertrude
| 1936 | Desert Gold |
| 1938 | The Buccaneer |

Simpson, Ivan
1933	Charlie Chan's Greatest Case
1937	Maid of Salem
1940	New Moon
1942	Nazi Agent
1948	My Girl Tisa

Simpson, Jessie
| 1920? | The Greatest Love |

Simpson, Lanny
| 1949 | Shamrock Hill |

Simpson, Mickey
1942	Syncopation
1947	Calendar Girl
1948	Angel in Exile
	Half Past Midnight
1949	The Fighting Kentuckian
	She Wore a Yellow Ribbon
1952	Apache Country
1953	The Eddie Cantor Story
	The Sun Shines Bright
1955	The Long Gray Line
	Seven Angry Men
1956	Giant
	The Lone Ranger

Simpson, Napoleon
1940	Am I Guilty?
	Midnight Shadow
	Santa Fe Trail
1942	In This Our Life
1943	Yankee Doodle Dandy
1945	The Mummy's Curse
1947	The Foxes of Harrow
1949	The Red Menace

Simpson, Reginald
1934	Broadway Bill
	Stand Up and Cheer!
1937	The Devil's Playground
1943	Let's Have Fun

Simpson, Robert same as **Simpson, Bob** could be same as **Simpson, Robert J. T.**
| 1951 | Jim Thorpe—All-American |
| | Saturday's Hero |

Simpson, Robert J. T. could be same as **Simpson, Robert**
| 1951 | Tomahawk |

Simpson, Russell
1917	The Barrier
1919	Desert Gold
1923	The Huntress
1927	The Frontiersman
	Wild Geese
1930	Abraham Lincoln
1931	Call of the Rockies
	The Great Meadow
1932	Call Her Savage
1936	Paddy O'Day
	Ramona
1937	Maid of Salem
	That I May Live
1939	Drums Along the Mohawk
1940	Geronimo
	Santa Fe Trail
	Three Faces West
1942	Nazi Agent
	Shut My Big Mouth

1943	Border Patrol
	Riding High
1946	Bad Bascomb
	California Gold Rush
1947	Bowery Buckaroos
1948	Tap Roots
1949	Tuna Clipper
1951	Across the Wide Missouri
1953	The Sun Shines Bright
1954	Broken Lance
1955	The Last Command
1956	The Lone Ranger
1957	The Tin Star

Simpson, Sloan
| 1960 | The Pusher |

Simpson, Walter
| 1921 | As the World Rolls On |

Artie Sims and His Band
| 1948 | The Fight Never Ends |

Sinatra, Dick
| 1949 | Knock on Any Door |

Sinatra, Frank
1948	The Miracle of the Bells
1949	The Kissing Bandit
1955	Not As a Stranger
1958	Kings Go Forth

Sinclair, Carol
| 1954 | Go Man Go |

Sinclair, Eric
| 1944 | Since You Went Away |
| 1945 | Club Havana |

Sinclair, John
| 1942 | All Through the Night |

Sinclair, Mary
| 1953 | Arrowhead |

Sinclair, Neal
| 1945 | Where Do We Go From Here? |

Sinclair, Ronald same as **Hould, Ra**
| 1937 | Boots and Saddles |

Sincoff, Abe same as **Sinkoff, Abe**
| 1929 | East Side Sadie |
| 1932 | Uncle Moses |

Sindle, W. D.
| 1921 | The Gunsaulus Mystery |

Sing, Hop
| 1919 | Hearts of Men |

Sing, Jessie Tai
| 1944 | Chip Off the Old Block |

Sing, Su Yu
| 1939? | A Chinese Gains a Fortune in America |

Singer, Jack
| 1940 | Northwest Passage (Book I—Rogers' Rangers) |

Singer, Jerry
| 1944 | Chip Off the Old Block |

Singer, Ray (actor)
| 1951 | Mask of the Dragon |

Singer, Ray (writer)
| 1942 | Whispering Ghosts |

Singer, Simon "Stuffy"
| 1950 | Emergency Wedding |

Singerman, Berta
| 1934 | Nada más que una mujer |

The Singing Indian Braves
| 1946 | Singin' in the Corn |

Singleton, Jack
| 1928 | The House of Scandal |

Singleton, Joseph E. same as **Singleton, Joseph**
| 1914 | The Squaw Man |
| 1920 | The Last of the Mohicans |

Singleton, Penny same as **McNulty, Dorothy**
| 1936 | After the Thin Man |
| 1938 | Outside of Paradise |

Singleton, Zutty
1943	Stormy Weather
1947	New Orleans
1950	Young Man with a Horn

Singley, Arthur
| 1937 | Nation Aflame |
| | The Plainsman |

Sinko, Gayoush
| 1937 | Arshin Mal Alan |

Sinkoff, Abe see **Sincoff, Abe**

Sinnerella, Nickelas
| 1914 | The Jungle |

Sino, Rafael
| 1936 | Ramona |

Siodmak, Robert
| 1948 | Cry of the City |
| 1950 | Deported |

Sipple, Crete
| 1940 | Escape to Glory |

Sirk, Douglas
1948	Sleep, My Love
1950	Mystery Submarine
1954	Taza, Son of Cochise
1959	Imitation of Life

Sisk, Robert
1935	Annie Oakley
1937	Border Cafe
1939	Bad Lands
	The Girl from Mexico
1945	Our Vines Have Tender Grapes
1951	Across the Wide Missouri
1952	It's a Big Country: An American Anthology
1953	The Man Behind the Gun

Sissel, Noble
| 1948? | Junction 88 |

The Sisters G
| 1930 | King of Jazz |

Sistrom, William
| 1931 | The Black Camel |

Sitka, Emil
1950	Emergency Wedding
	Rock Island Trail
1955	Blackboard Jungle
1956	The White Squaw

Sitting Bull, Chief not the same as **Sitting Bull, John**
| 1917 | The Adventures of Buffalo Bill |

Sitting Bull, John not the same as **Sitting Bull, Chief**
| 1952 | The Savage |

Siu, Ronald
| 1945 | Samurai |

6-Harlem Beauties-6
| 1946 | Dirty Gertie from Harlem, U.S.A. |

Six Hits and a Miss
| 1940 | If I Had My Way |

The Six Sizzlers
| 1937 | Underworld |

Sjöström, Victor see **Seastrom, Victor**

Skarstedt, Vance
| 1960 | Pay or Die |

Skelly, Hal
| 1930 | Behind the Make-Up |

Sketchley, Leslie same as **Sketchley, Les**
| 1936 | Charlie Chan at the Race Track |
| 1948 | Up in Central Park |

Skewis, Ski
| 1953 | Beneath the 12-Mile Reef |

Skinner, Edna
| 1949 | The Kissing Bandit |

Skinner, Harold
| 1916 | A Yoke of Gold |

Skinner, Herbert
| 1939 | One Dark Night |
| 1942 | Take My Life |

Skinner, Marion same as **Skinner, Marian**
1918	Real Folks
1919	The Sleeping Lion
	Who Will Marry Me?
1920	Billions

Skinner, Mary
| 1950 | Panic in the Streets |

Skinner, Thomas M.
| 1947 | Buck Privates Come Home |

Skipper, William
| 1948 | Up in Central Park |

Skippy, a dog see **Asta, a dog**

Skipworth, Alison
| 1933 | A Lady's Profession |
| 1934 | Coming Out Party |

Skirball, Jack H. same as **Skirball, Jack**
| 1939 | Miracle on Main Street |
| | Miracle on Main Street (foreign version) |

| 1941 | This Woman Is Mine |

Sklover, Carl
1950	Annie Get Your Gun
1951	Gambling House
	Show Boat
1958	Marjorie Morningstar

Skolsky, Sidney
| 1947 | The Jolson Story |
| 1953 | The Eddie Cantor Story |

Skorobohach, Michael
| 1937 | Natalka Poltavka |
| 1938 | Marusia |

Skouras, Edith
| 1939 | Mr. Moto in Danger Island |

Skouras, Plato A. same as **Skouras, Plato**
| 1957 | Apache Warrior |
| 1958 | Sierra Baron |

Skubowa, Maria
| 1938 | Marusia |

Skulnick, Menashe
| 1933 | Live and Laugh |
| 1950 | Monticello, Here We Come! |

Skultesky, George
| 1937 | Big City |

Skurkoy, Mary
| 1925 | The Greatest Love of All |

Sky Eagle, Dorothy
| 1950 | Annie Get Your Gun |
| 1959 | The FBI Story |

Sky Eagle, George same as **Sky Eagle, Chief**
| 1949 | She Wore a Yellow Ribbon |
| 1950 | Devil's Doorway |

Sky Eagle, Helen
| 1936 | Ramona |

Slabe, Betty
| 1945 | Where Do We Go From Here? |

Slate, Henry
| 1953 | The Jazz Singer |

Slaten, Max
| 1959 | The Wonderful Country |

Slater, Barbara
| 1941 | Louisiana Purchase |
| 1942 | Holiday Inn |

Slater, Barney
| 1957 | The Tin Star |

Slater, Bob
1922	The Schemers
	Spitfire
	Square Joe

Slater, Lee
| 1946 | Till the End of Time |

Slater, Mark
| 1923 | His Great Chance |

Slattery, Desmond
| 1958 | Ambush at Cimarron Pass |
| | Blood Arrow |

Slattery, Nellie
| 1915 | Under Southern Skies |

Slattery, Richard
| 1946 | Till the End of Time |

Slaughter, Frank G.
| 1957 | Naked in the Sun |

Slaughter, Vernon
| 1960 | The Crowning Experience |

Slaven, Brad
| 1947 | Calendar Girl |

Slavin, George F.
1950	Mystery Submarine
1953	Thunder Bay
1955	Smoke Signal
1957	The Halliday Brand

Sleeman, Phil
| 1927 | The Slaver |

Sleeper, Martha
1932	Huddle
1933	Broken Dreams
1945	The Bells of St. Mary's

Slesinger, Tess
| 1945 | A Tree Grows in Brooklyn |

Slezak, Walter
| 1944 | Lifeboat |
| 1945 | Salome, Where She Danced |

Slick and Slack
1949?   The Joint Is Jumpin'
Slicker, a seal
1938   Spawn of the North
1939   Fisherman's Wharf
Slifer, Elizabeth
1952   The Fabulous Senorita
1953   The Glass Wall
        The Sun Shines Bright
Slip and Slide
1955   Brevities of 1955
Sloane, Everett
1948   The Lady from Shanghai
1950   The Men
1958   Marjorie Morningstar
Sloane, Paul H. *same as* **Sloane, Paul**
1927   Turkish Delight
1929   Hearts in Dixie
1934   Straight Is the Way
1938   The Texans
1940   Geronimo
Sloca Bruna
1927   Primitive Love
Sloman, Edward
1916   Lone Star
1917   My Fighting Gentleman
1919   The Westerners
1922   The Woman He Loved
1923   Backbone
1925   His People
1928   We Americans
1930   The Kibitzer
Slosser, John
1959   The Oregon Trail
Slough, C. E.
1950   Intruder in the Dust
Small, Bernard
1950   Davy Crockett, Indian Scout
        The Iroquois Trail
1952   Indian Uprising
Small, Edward
1927   McFadden's Flats
1932   Igloo
1940   Kit Carson
1942   Friendly Enemies
        Twin Beds
1950   Davy Crockett, Indian Scout
        The Iroquois Trail
1953   Captain John Smith and Pocahontas
1954   Overland Pacific
Smalley, Phillips *same as* **Smalley, Phil**
1915   Captain Courtesy
1916   Hop, the Devil's Brew
1934   Behold My Wife!
1935   A Night at the Opera
1936   Dangerous Intrigue
        My American Wife
1937   Man of the People
        Souls at Sea
1938   Rascals
        Speed to Burn
Smallwood, Mildred
1924   A Son of Satan
Smallwood, Ray C.
1920   Billions
Smaney, Mabel
1948   The Lady from Shanghai
1949   Knock on Any Door
1952   Anything Can Happen
Smart, Bobby
1923   The Devil's Match
        His Great Chance
        A Shot in the Night
Smart, Patricia
1946   Notorious
Smead, Walt
1958   Tonka
Smeraldo, Ida
1959   The Black Orchid
1960   Pay or Die
Smiley, Bob
1953   The Man from the Alamo
Smiley, Charles A.
1921   Guile of Women

Smiley, Joseph *same as* **Smiley, Joseph W.**
1914   Threads of Destiny
1918   Hitting the Trail
1919   As a Man Thinks
Smiley, Ralph
1952   The Iron Mistress
Smirnova, Dina
1937   It Could Happen to You
1938   Gateway
1947   Northwest Outpost
Smith, Al *(actor)*, 1894—1939 *see* **Smith, Albert J.** *(actor)*, 1894—1939
Smith, Albert *(African-American actor)*
1947   Juke Joint
Smith, Albert E. *(prod) not the same as* **Smith, Albert I.** *(prod)*
1918   Find the Woman
1920   The Purple Cipher
Smith, Albert I. *(prod) not the same as* **Smith, Albert E.** *(prod)*
1926   Under Fire
Smith, Albert J. *(actor)*, 1894—1939 *same as* **Smith, Al**
1927   Red Clay
        Whispering Sage
1931   Delicious
1932   Border Devils
1933   The Telegraph Trail
1934   The Prescott Kid
1936   Sutter's Gold
1937   Prairie Thunder
Smith, Alexis
1942   Gentleman Jim
1945   Rhapsody in Blue
1957   Beau James
Smith, Alfred E. *(actor) not the same as* **Smith, Alfred E., Governor**
1960   Wild River
Smith, Alfred E., Governor *not the same as* **Smith, Alfred E.** *(actor)*
1919   The Volcano
Smith, Alice H.
1936   After the Thin Man
Smith, Alma
1932   Harlem Is Heaven
Smith, Archie
1948   The Fight Never Ends
Smith, Art
1945   A Tree Grows in Brooklyn
1947   Body and Soul
        Ride the Pink Horse
1948   Angel in Exile
1952   Rose of Cimarron
Smith, Augustus *same as* **Smith, Gus; Smith, J. Augustus**
1934   Chloe: Love Is Calling You
        Drums O' Voodoo
1941   Murder on Lenox Avenue
        Sunday Sinners
1947   Hi De Ho
1948   Killer Diller
1948?   Boarding House Blues
        Junction 88
Smith, Augustus, Jr.
1948?   Junction 88
Smith, Barbara
1946   Without Reservations
1950   A Ticket to Tomahawk
Smith, Bernard
1934   The Battling Buckaroo
Smith, Bobby Lee
1960   Sergeant Rutledge
Smith, C. Aubrey
1948   Unconquered
Smith, Cecil *(actor)*
1950   Devil's Doorway
Smith, Charles *same as* **Smith, Charles B.**
1943   Yankee Doodle Dandy
1949   That Midnight Kiss
1950   Battleground
Smith, Clifford S. *same as* **Smith, Cliff**
1918   Untamed
1919   The She Wolf

1920   The Cyclone
1925   The Red Rider
1927   Open Range
Smith, Constance
1953   Taxi
Smith, Darr
1951   The Girl on the Bridge
Smith, David
1919   A Fighting Colleen
        A Yankee Princess
Smith, Dudley
1918   The Hell Cat
Smith, Elwood
1947   Boy! What a Girl!
1948   The Fight Never Ends
Smith, Emmett
1949   The Story of Seabiscuit
1950   The Jackie Robinson Story
        No Way Out
1952   Red Ball Express
Smith, Ervin
1941   Sullivan's Travels
Smith, Ethel *(African-American actress)*
1924   Smiling Hate
1926   A Prince of His Race
1926?   Ten Nights in a Barroom
1927   The Broken Violin
Smith, Ethel *(organist)*
1946   Cuban Pete
Smith, Frank
1916   Broken Fetters
Smith, Fred
1949   Arctic Fury
Smith, Garland
1942   Across the Pacific
        They Died With Their Boots On
Smith, Georgann
1946   Slightly Scandalous
Smith, Gerald Oliver
1938   Gateway
1945   Sunbonnet Sue
1946   The Sailor Takes a Wife
1950   Belle of Old Mexico
Smith, Gil
1959   The FBI Story
Smith, Grace *same as* **Smythe, Grace**
1927   The Millionaire
        The Spider's Web
1932?   The Girl from Chicago
Smith, Gus *see* **Smith, Augustus**
Smith, Hal *(actor) could be same as* **Smith, Harold** *(actor)*
1955   Santa Fe Passage
Smith, Hal *(writer) not the same as* **Smith, Harold Jacob** *(writer)*
1943   Good Luck, Mr. Yates
Smith, Hamilton
1918   I Want to Forget
1919   The Scar
Smith, Harold *(actor) could be same as* **Smith, Hal** *(actor)*
1948   Fighting Father Dunne
Smith, Harold Jacob *(writer) not the same as* **Smith, Hal** *(writer)*
1958   The Defiant Ones
Smith, Harry "Silverheels" *see* **Silverheels, Jay**
Smith, Holland M., Ret., Lt. Gen.
1950   Sands of Iwo Jima
Smith, Howard *(actor)*
1948   Call Northside 777
Smith, Howard Ellis *(writer)*
1936   It Had to Happen
1937   Think Fast, Mr. Moto
Smith, Inez
1919   The Homesteader
Smith, Irving
1951   The Tall Target
Smith, J. Augustus *see* **Smith, Augustus**
Smith, Jack C. *not the same as* **Smith, John**
1941   The Pioneers
Smith, James Ellis *could be same as* **Smith, Jim**
1953   Bright Road

Smith, Jewel
1938   Spirit of Youth
Smith, Jili
1932   Harlem Is Heaven
1939   Straight to Heaven
Smith, Jim *could be same as* **Smith, James Ellis**
1958   Tonka
Jimmy Smith and His Orchestra
1937   The Devil's Playground
Smith, Joanne
1936   Sutter's Gold
Smith, Jody
1951   Westward the Women
Smith, Joe *(actor)*, 1884—1981
1932   The Heart of New York
1945   Nob Hill
Smith, Joe P. *(actor, beginning circa early 1940s) same as* **Smith, Joe** *not the same as* **Smith, Joe** *(actor, 1884—1981)*
1941   Western Union
1944   Buffalo Bill
1947   Humoresque
1948   Key Largo
1949   The Story of Seabiscuit
Smith, Joel
1953   The Eddie Cantor Story
1957   Beau James
Smith, John *not the same as* **Smith, Jack C.**
1955   Seven Angry Men
1956   Ghost Town
        Quincannon, Frontier Scout
1957   The Lawless Eighties
        Tomahawk Trail
Smith, Justin
1953   The Jazz Singer
Smith, Kay
1940   Escape to Glory
Smith, Ken
1949   Jigsaw
1954   Drum Beat
1955   Bad Day at Black Rock
Smith, Kent
1942   Cat People
1943   Hitler's Children
1956   Comanche
1958   The Badlanders
Smith, L. K.
1943   Marching On!
1945   Of One Blood
1956   Full of Life
Smith, Lenny
1958   The Last Hurrah
Smith, Lew
1947   The Mighty McGurk
1950   The Big Hangover
Smith, Loring
1947   Citizen Saint
Smith, Mamie
1940   Paradise in Harlem
1941   Murder on Lenox Avenue
        Sunday Sinners
Smith, Martin
1957   Band of Angels
Smith, Mary Jane
1950   Mystery Street
Smith, Merritt
1940   Paradise in Harlem
Smith, Michael *not the same as* **Smith, Mike**
1958   The Young Lions
Smith, Mike *not the same as* **Smith, Michael**
1959   The FBI Story
Smith, Mildred Joanne *(African-American actress) not the same as* **Smith, Joanne**
1950   No Way Out
Smith, Minnie
1916   The Colored American Winning His Suit
Smith, Muriel
1948   Strange Victory
1960   The Crowning Experience

Smith, Oscar
1935   So Red the Rose
1938   The Texans
1940   The Way of All Flesh
Smith, Paul (*actor*) *could be same as* **Smith, Paul F.** (*actor*)
1946   Till the End of Time
1952   The Battle at Apache Pass
1956   Pillars of the Sky
1959   The FBI Story
Smith, Paul F. (*actor*) *could be same as* **Smith, Paul** (*actor*)
1953   Dream Wife
Smith, Paul Gerard (*writer*)
1929   Welcome Danger
1940   Tengo fe en ti
1941   Hurry, Charlie, Hurry
1944   Lady, Let's Dance!
1945   Sunbonnet Sue
1947   Untamed Fury
1948   Harpoon
Smith, Pete
1928   The Midnight Ace
Smith, Queenie
1936   Show Boat
1948   Sleep, My Love
1949   Massacre River
1950   Emergency Wedding
Smith, R. Cecil (*writer*)
1917   The Sudden Gentleman
1918   Free and Equal
Smith, Ray
1956   Full of Life
Smith, Robert (*actor, beginning circa 1940*)
1950   Panic in the Streets
Smith, Robert (*actor, prod mgr*)
1931   The Hurricane Horseman
Smith, Robert (*writer, prod*)
1958   St. Louis Blues
Smith, Roberta
1944   Block Busters
Smith, Sharon
1945   The Cisco Kid Returns
Smith, Sidney *not the same as* **Smith, Sydney**
1915   The Rosary
Smith, Silverheels *see* **Silverheels, Jay**
Smith, Stanley
1930   King of Jazz
Smith, Sydney *not the same as* **Smith, Sidney**
1958   Tonka
Smith, Tom
1929   The Invaders
Smith, Trixie
1932   The Black King
1934   Drums O' Voodoo
1938   Birthright
         God's Step Children
         Swing!
Smith, Verner L., Captain
1932   Hidden Valley
Smith, Vernon
1927   Frisco Sally Levy
1933   The Cohens and Kellys in Trouble
1942   Lucky Ghost
Smith, Veronica
1919   Injustice
Smith, Vic
1958   Gun Fever
Smith, Vivian
1929   Hearts in Dixie
Smith, W. M.
1921   Cotton and Cattle
Smith, W. S., Rev.
1916   The Colored American Winning His Suit
Smith, Wallace
1927   The Dove
1935   Bordertown
Smith, Walter
1957   Band of Angels
Smith, Walton Hall
1932   Huddle
Smith, Warren
1946   Till the End of Time
         Without Reservations

Smith, William
1920   Within Our Gates
1924   Smiling Hate
Smoke, the Wonder Horse
1937   Prairie Thunder
Smythe, Grace *see* **Smith, Grace**
Smythe, Vanita
1947   Reet, Petite and Gone
Snapp, Edna
1960   Wild River
Snead, Mrs. E.
1916   The Colored American Winning His Suit
Snead, Edgar
1916   The Colored American Winning His Suit
Snead, Florence
1916   The Colored American Winning His Suit
Sneed, Edwin
1950   No Way Out
Sneed, Ray
1947   Jivin' in Be-Bop
Sneed, William
1943   Stormy Weather
Snegoff, Leonid
1926   Broken Hearts
1932   The Unfortunate Bride
1933   The Man Who Dared: An Imaginative Biography
1934   Strange Wives
1935   Rendezvous
         The Wedding Night
1936   Paddy O'Day
1938   Spawn of the North
Snell, Earle *same as* **Snell, Earl**
1919   Just Squaw
1928   Anybody Here Seen Kelly?
         The Night Bird
1929   The Cohens and Kellys in Atlantic City
1930   Sunny Skies
1936   Rainbow on the River
1940   Am I Guilty?
         Covered Wagon Days
1941   Gauchos of Eldorado
1945   Colorado Pioneers
         Phantom of the Plains
1946   Santa Fe Uprising
         Sheriff of Redwood Valley
         Sun Valley Cyclone
1947   The Last Round-Up
         Marshal of Cripple Creek
         Oregon Trail Scouts
         Rustlers of Devil's Canyon
         Vigilantes of Boomtown
1949   Ranger of Cherokee Strip
Snelson, Gertrude
1927   The Broken Violin
1928   Thirty Years Later
Snez, Nakai
1950   Rocky Mountain
Snitzer, Miriam
1947   Easy Come, Easy Go
Snody, Robert
1934   Cuesta abajo
         El tango en Broadway
1935   El día que me quieras
1938   Di que me quieres
Snow, H. A.
1928   The Great White North
Snow, Marc
1950   Black Hand
Snow, Marguerite
1918   The Million Dollar Mystery
1921?   The Slave Market
Snow, Mortimer
1922   The Mohican's Daughter
Snow, Sydney
1928   The Great White North
Snowflake *see* **Toones, Fred "Snowflake"**
Snyder, Billy
1941   You're Out of Luck
Snyder, Clarence
1918   The Hell Cat

Snyder, Gladys
1940   Gang War
Snyder, Jackson
1936   Klondike Annie
Soames, Arthur
1921   A Tale of Two Worlds
Soble, Ron
1959   Al Capone
1960   Walk Tall
Sobol, Louie
1947   Copacabana
Sobral, Mara del
1930   Wu Li Chang
Sochor, Judy
1950   Sands of Iwo Jima
Soderling, Walter
1937   Maid of Salem
         Man of the People
1939   Stand Up and Fight
1940   Santa Fe Trail
1941   The Face Behind the Mask
1942   Mokey
1943   Action in the North Atlantic
         What's Buzzin' Cousin?
1945   The Dolly Sisters
         Rhapsody in Blue
1946   Abie's Irish Rose
1948   Fury at Furnace Creek
Sogabe, Ryosho S., Reverend
1959   The Crimson Kimono
Sojin *same as* **Sojin, K.**
1927   The Chinese Parrot
         Old San Francisco
1928   Chinatown Charlie
         The Hawk's Nest
Sojin, Jr.
1937   Waikiki Wedding
Sokil, Maria
1939   Cossacks in Exile
Sokoloff, Vladimir *same as* **Sokoloff, Wladimir**
1931   Die Dreigroschenoper
         Die Dreigroschenoper (*foreign version*)
         Kismet
         La llama sagrada (*foreign version*)
1938   Spawn of the North
1943   Mr. Lucky
1950   The Baron of Arizona
1960   Cimarron
         Man on a String
Sokolskaya, Myra
1947   Northwest Outpost
Sokouroglou, Christos
1954   Barefoot Battalion
Soldani, Charles *same as* **Soldani, Chief**
1941   The Pioneers
1943   Riding High
1944   Tahiti Nights
1949   Apache Chief
         Rose of the Yukon
1950   Broken Arrow
         A Ticket to Tomahawk
         Young Daniel Boone
1951   The Mark of the Renegade
1955   Foxfire
1959   The FBI Story
Soldi, Stephen
1939   Winner Take All
1949   House of Strangers
1958   The Last Hurrah
Soler, Domingo
1940   Perfidia
Soler, Enriqueta
1931   Chérie (*foreign version*)
         ¿Conoces a tu mujer?
         Cuerpo y alma
         Esclavas de la moda
         Mamá
Soler, Fernando
1932   ¿Cuándo te suicidas?
1939   Los hijos mandan
         Verbena trágica
Soler, Julián
1939   Los hijos mandan

Solomon, Elimelech
1959   The Last Angry Man
Solomon, Louis
1951   The Mark of the Renegade
Solomon, M.
1922   The Sign of the Rose
Solomon, Phil
1948   The Miracle of the Bells
Solt, Andrew
1946   Without Reservations
1947   The Jolson Story
Solway, Larry
1958   Flaming Frontier
Somers, Captain *see* **Somers, Fred**
Somers, Esther
1949   Portrait of Jennie
1950   The Iroquois Trail
1955   Violent Saturday
Somers, Fred *same as* **Somers, Captain**
1943   Dr. Gillespie's Criminal Case
1950   Ambush
1959   Imitation of Life
Somerset, Pat
1925   One of the Bravest
1928   Mother Machree
1935   Charlie Chan in Shanghai
1936   Dangerous Intrigue
Somerville, Roy
1918   Hitting the Trail
Somlay, Arthur
1930   El secreto del doctor (*foreign version*)
Sommers, John
1940   The Ramparts We Watch
Sondergaard, Gale
1937   Maid of Salem
1940   The Mark of Zorro
1947   Pirates of Monterey
Sondergaard, Hester
1949   Jigsaw
Sondfield, Eugene
1957   Bayou
Sonessa, Joseph
1960   Take a Giant Step
Sonfield, Eugene
1950   Panic in the Streets
Song, Alfred
1945   Betrayal from the East
Sonnenberg, Gus
1937   Big City
The Sons of the Pioneers
1947   On the Old Spanish Trail
Soo Hoo, Edward
1942   Little Tokyo, U.S.A.
1943   Air Force
Soo Hoo, Eleanor
1943   The Amazing Mrs. Holliday
Soo Hoo, Walter
1943   Air Force
Soon-goot
1913?   Hiawatha
Sorel, George
1938   Charlie Chan at Monte Carlo
1940   The Mark of Zorro
1943   Action in the North Atlantic
1944   They Live in Fear
1946   Rendezvous 24
         The Sailor Takes a Wife
1947   Northwest Outpost
Sorel, Sonia
1945   Club Havana
Sorelle, William J. *same as* **Sorrell, William F.**
1914   The Littlest Rebel
Sorenson, Harriet
1917   Castles for Two
Soria, Gabriel
1939   Los hijos mandan
Soria, José
1931   La pura verdad
Soriano Viosca, José *same as* **Soriano Viosca**
1930   East Is West (*foreign version*)
         Los que danzan
         El presidio

Sevilla de mis amores
Wu Li Chang
1931   Cheri-Bibi
El código penal
El comediante
Drácula
El proceso de Mary
     Dugan

Sorin, Louis
1929   Mother's Boy

Sorrell, William F. *see* **Sorelle, William J.**

Sorelle, William J.
1914   Northern Lights

Sosso, Pietro
1917   Lost in Transit
1941   Adam Had Four Sons
1947   Dark Delusion

Sotello, Dimas
1945   South of the Rio Grande
1946   Beauty and the Bandit
1948   Angel in Exile
1950   Young Daniel Boone

Sothern, Ann
1933   Let's Fall in Love
1936   My American Wife
1942   Three Hearts for Julia

Sothern, Hugh
1938   The Buccaneer
     Dangerous to Know
1940   Northwest Passage (Book I—Rogers' Rangers)
     Young Buffalo Bill
1942   They Died With Their Boots On

Soto, Manuel
1930   El secreto del doctor

Sotoff, Paul
1936   Rose of the Rancho

Sotomayor, José Ignacio
1930   Las campanas de Capistrano

Soubier, Clifford
1937   Black Legion

Souers, Glenn
1951   Saturday's Hero

Soule, Larry
1936   General Spanky

Soule, Olan
1951   Cuban Fireball

Sourabian, Masha
1937   Arshin Mal Alan

Sourabian, Setrag
1937   Arshin Mal Alan

South, Eddie
1946   Stars on Parade
1949?   The Joint Is Jumpin'

Southard, Bennett
1922   Second Hand Rose

Southern, Eve
1927   Wild Geese
1931   Fighting Caravans

Southern, Tom *same as* **Southern, Thomas; Southern, Tommy**
1938   Spirit of Youth
     Two Gun Man from Harlem
1939   Double Deal
     Harlem Rides the Range
1940   Mystery in Swing
1949   Lookout Sister

Sovern, Whitey
1937   The Plainsman
1938   The Texans

Space, Arthur *not the same as* **Space, Charles Arthur**
1942   Rio Rita
     Tortilla Flat
1943   They Came to Blow Up America
1945   Our Vines Have Tender Grapes
1946   Bad Bascomb
1947   Rustlers of Devil's Canyon
1948   The Paleface
     Tap Roots
1949   House of Strangers
     Lust for Gold
1951   Tomahawk
1952   Red Ball Express

1953   The Eddie Cantor Story
     The Man from the Alamo
1954   Drum Beat
1955   Foxfire

Space, Charles Arthur *not the same as* **Space, Arthur**
1958   St. Louis Blues

Spacey, John
1937   Maid of Salem

Spagnoli, Genaro
1935   Ruggles of Red Gap
1937   Man of the People

Spain, Fay
1959   Al Capone

Spainard, Earl
1942   American Empire
1953   Seminole
1958   Houseboat

Spalding, George
1951   Jim Thorpe—All-American

Spalding, Sherry
1959   The Oregon Trail

Spalla, Ermino
1950   Deported

Spangler, Jean
1948   The Miracle of the Bells

Sparks, Floyd
1951   Tomahawk

Sparks, George
1937   One Mile from Heaven
     The Plainsman

Sparks, Jack
1946   Sun Valley Cyclone
1947   Marshal of Cripple Creek
     Oregon Trail Scouts
1949   The Golden Stallion

Sparks, Katherine
1949   Pinky

Sparks, Ned
1934   Imitation of Life
1938   Hawaii Calls

Sparks, Robert
1942   Shut My Big Mouth

Sparling, Elliott
1922   The Power of Love

Sparlis, Al
1947   The Foxes of Harrow

Sparrow, Anitra
1948   My Girl Tisa

Spaulding, George *same as* **Spaulding, George L.**
1947   The Chinese Ring
1948   Call Northside 777
     Up in Central Park
1949   House of Strangers
     Pinky
1950   Mystery Submarine
1951   The Magnificent Yankee
1953   The Eddie Cantor Story
1958   The Last Hurrah

Spaulding, William "Bill"
1940   Knute Rockne—All American
1950   The Jackie Robinson Story

Spaventa, Carlos
1934   Cuesta abajo
     El tango en Broadway

Speaks, John
1936   Dancing Pirate

Spear, Rita
1919   Come Out of the Kitchen

Spears, Basil
1947   Boy! What a Girl!

Spears, Jack
1940   While Thousands Cheer

Spence, Ralph
1924   His Darker Self
1926   The Campus Flirt
1927   The Callahans and the Murphys
     Lost at the Front
1928   Vamping Venus
1934   Stand Up and Cheer!
1935   The Winning Ticket

Spence, Sandra
1950   Annie Get Your Gun

Spencer, Arnold
1950   Damien

Spencer, Dean
1939   Drifting Westward

Spencer, Douglas
1941   Hurry, Charlie, Hurry
1951   Molly
     Warpath
1953   The Glass Wall
1955   Smoke Signal
1956   Man from Del Rio

Spencer, J. *could be same as* **Spencer, Jimmy**
1936   Custer's Last Stand

Spencer, James *(actor),* 1877–1929 *not the same as* **Spencer, James I.** *or* **Spencer, Jimmy**
1929   Frozen Justice

Spencer, James I. *not the same as* **Spencer, James** *(actor),* 1877–1929 *or* **Spencer, Jimmy**
1941   Western Union

Spencer, Jimmy *could be same as* **Spencer, J.** *not the same as* **Spencer, James** *(actor),* 1877–1929 *or* **Spencer, James I.**
1950   Two Flags West

Spencer, Katherine
1921   The Barricade

Spencer, Kenneth
1943   Bataan
     Cabin in the Sky

Spencer, Richard V.
1925   Custer's Last Fight

Spencer, Robert
1951   Go for Broke!
     The Tall Target

Spencer, Sarah
1951   Oh! Susanna

Spencer, Titus
1948   The Paleface
1950   Devil's Doorway

Spencer, Tom
1916   Gretchen, the Greenhorn

Sper, Norman
1930   Song of the Caballero

Spere, Charles
1919   A Bachelor's Wife
     A Fighting Colleen
1920   The Tiger's Coat

Sperl, Edna May
1924   His Darker Self

Sperling, Milton
1938   Happy Landing
1939   The Return of the Cisco Kid
1941   Sun Valley Serenade
1943   Crash Dive
1948   My Girl Tisa
1951   Distant Drums
1958   Marjorie Morningstar

Spewack, Bella
1935   Rendezvous

Spewack, Samuel
1935   Rendezvous

Spiegel, Sam *same as* **Eagle, S. P.**
1942   Tales of Manhattan
1949   We Were Strangers

Spigelgass, Leonard
1942   All Through the Night
1950   Mystery Street

Spiker, Ray
1934   Our Daily Bread
1943   Riding High
1948   Unconquered
1953   The Man Behind the Gun

Spindola, Robert
1936   Ramona
1938   The Toy Wife
1943   The Leopard Man

Spitz, Henry L.
1956   Comanche

Spitzer, Marian
1945   The Dolly Sisters

Spivey, Victoria
1929   Hallelujah

Spivy, Mme.
1960   Studs Lonigan

Spotted Elk
1930   The Silent Enemy

Spottswood, James
1929   Thunderbolt

Sprager, Hart
1958   Home Before Dark
1960   Pay or Die

Sprague, Chandler
1939   Charlie Chan in Honolulu

Sprague, Milton
1940   George Washington Carver

Spring, Helen
1950   Emergency Wedding
1956   The Benny Goodman Story

Springer, Louise
1939   Stand Up and Fight

Springer, Norman
1937   The Devil's Playground

Springler, Harry
1914   Northern Lights

Springsteen, R. G.
1936   Pinto Rustlers
1945   Colorado Pioneers
     Phantom of the Plains
1946   California Gold Rush
     Santa Fe Uprising
     Sheriff of Redwood Valley
     Sun Valley Cyclone
1947   Marshal of Cripple Creek
     Oregon Trail Scouts
     Rustlers of Devil's Canyon
     Vigilantes of Boomtown
1948   Renegades of Sonora
1949   Harbor of Missing Men
     The Red Menace
1950   Belle of Old Mexico
1952   The Fabulous Senorita

Sprotte, Bert
1921   Guile of Women
1922   Hungry Hearts
1923   Purple Dawn
     Snowdrift
1927   The Fighting Hombre
     Wild Geese
1931   Dämon des Meeres
1933   Song of the Eagle
1937   It Could Happen to You
1938   Happy Landing

Squier, Lucita
1921   Bits of Life

Squire, Katherine
1960   Studs Lonigan

Squire, Louise
1943   Let's Have Fun

Squire, Ronald
1959   The Sheriff of Fractured Jaw

Stabenau, Tony
1931   Delicious

Stabler, Robert
1957   Trooper Hook
1958   Blood Arrow

Stacey, Patricia
1941   King of the Zombies

Stack, Robert
1953   Conquest of Cochise
     War Paint
1955   Good Morning, Miss Dove
1959   John Paul Jones
1960   The Last Voyage

Stack, William
1933   Charlie Chan's Greatest Case
1935   Rendezvous
     The Winning Ticket
1936   The Last of the Mohicans
1937   Souls at Sea

Stader, Paul
1946   Till the End of Time

Stafford, Grace
1939   Confessions of a Nazi Spy
1940   Santa Fe Trail

Stafford, Harry B.
1937   Man of the People
1942   Nazi Agent

Stafford, Jo *see* **Six Hits and a Miss**

Stagg, Alonzo
1940   Knute Rockne—All American

Stahl, John M.
1934 Imitation of Life
1947 The Foxes of Harrow
Stahl, Walter O. *same as* **Stahl, Walter**
1938 Little Miss Roughneck
1941 They Dare Not Love
1942 Woman of the Year
1943 They Came to Blow Up America
Stahl-Nachbaur, Ernst
1931 La carta (*foreign version*)
Stajica, Obren
1932 Ljubav i strast
Stallings, George
1946 Song of the South
Stallings, Laurence
1931 En cada puerto un amor
1935 So Red the Rose
1939 Stand Up and Fight
1940 Northwest Passage (Book I—Rogers' Rangers)
1945 Salome, Where She Danced
1949 She Wore a Yellow Ribbon
3 Godfathers
1953 The Sun Shines Bright
Stallmaster, Lynn
1951 The Steel Helmet
Stamford, Henry
1918 Uncle Tom's Cabin
Stammers, Frank
1916 Peck O' Pickles
Stamper, George
1933 The Emperor Jones
Stanbridge, Ed
1945 Where Do We Go From Here?
Stander, Lionel
1943 Tahiti Honey
1948 Call Northside 777
Standing, Herbert
1915 Captain Courtesy
1918 Amarilly of Clothes-Line Alley
How Could You, Jean?
In Judgment Of
The Squaw Man
1920 The Cup of Fury
Standing, Jack
1916 Civilization's Child
Standing, Joan
1926 The Campus Flirt
1934 Behold My Wife!
Broadway Bill
Standing, Percy
1914 The Great Diamond Robbery
1916 The Fall of a Nation
1918 The Kaiser's Finish
Standing, Wyndham
1920 Lifting Shadows
1934 Imitation of Life
Limehouse Blues
1940 Escape to Glory
Standing Bear, Chief *same as* **Standing Bear**
1916 Ramona
1932 Texas Pioneers
1934 Laughing Boy
1935 Circle of Death
Cyclone of the Saddle
Fighting Pioneers
Standish, Joseph
1914 Threads of Destiny
Stanfield, Ned
1943 Stormy Weather
Stanford, Victor
1931 Yankee Don
Stange, Hugh
1931 The Black Camel
Stanhope, Ted
1942 Tales of Manhattan
1947 The Burning Cross
It Had To Be You
Jiggs and Maggie in Society
The Jolson Story
1950 Emergency Wedding

1951 Saturday's Hero
1952 High Noon
1958 The Last Hurrah
Terror in a Texas Town
Stanislavsky, Andrew
1937 Natalka Poltavka
Stanley, Al
1929 East Side Sadie
Stanley, Barbara
1949 Harbor of Missing Men
1950 Train to Tombstone
Stanley, Clifford
1933 Robbers' Roost
Stanley, Dick
1946 Singin' in the Corn
Stanley, Edwin *same as* **Stanley, Ed**
1933 Let's Fall in Love
1935 A Night at the Ritz
1936 My American Wife
1937 Charlie Chan on Broadway
1938 The Buccaneer
Mr. Moto's Gamble
Road Demon
Speed to Burn
1939 Charlie Chan in Reno
Confessions of a Nazi Spy
Mr. Moto in Danger Island
1940 Charlie Chan in Panama
East of the River
Knute Rockne—All American
1941 The Face Behind the Mask
Hurry, Charlie, Hurry
Where Did You Get That Girl?
1942 Gentleman Jim
Syncopation
1943 Air Force
1944 Buffalo Bill
The Racket Man
Stanley, Eric
1938 The Buccaneer
Stanley, Forrest
1922 The Pride of Palomar
1936 Show Boat
Stanley, Fred
1928 Riley the Cop
Stanley, George
1914 The Little Angel of Canyon Creek
Stanley, Gil
1943 Crime Smasher
Stanley, Helene
1955 Davy Crockett, King of the Wild Frontier
Stanley, Maxfield
1915 The Birth of a Nation
Stanley, Paul
1959 Cry Tough
Stanley, Ralph
1953 The Joe Louis Story
Stanlow, Frank
1959 Al Capone
Stanton, Dean *see* **Stanton, Harry Dean**
Stanton, Edward
1920 Humoresque
Stanton, Edwin M.
1917 Queen X
Stanton, Ernie
1939 Mr. Wong in Chinatown
1943 Yankee Doodle Dandy
Stanton, Fred
1922 The Son of the Wolf
Stanton, Harry *not the same as* **Stanton, Harry Dean**
1950 Right Cross
1952 It's a Big Country: An American Anthology
1953 Dream Wife
Stanton, Harry Dean *same as* **Stanton, Dean** *not the same as* **Stanton, Harry**
1957 Revolt at Fort Laramie
Tomahawk Trail
1959 The Jayhawkers!
1960 The Adventures of Huckleberry Finn

Stanton, Myra
1948 The Betrayal
Stanton, Paul
1934 She Was a Lady
Stand Up and Cheer!
1936 Charlie Chan at the Circus
Dimples
It Had to Happen
The Prisoner of Shark Island
Sins of Man
Star for a Night
1937 Black Legion
It Could Happen to You
Man of the People
Souls at Sea
1938 My Lucky Star
Rascals
1940 Elsa Maxwell's Public Deb No. 1
1942 Across the Pacific
1943 Crash Dive
Stanton, Phil
1947 My Wild Irish Rose
Stanton, Richard
1920 The Face at Your Window
Stanton, Robert
1946 The Gentleman Misbehaves
Stanton, Ronald
1944 Chip Off the Old Block
1945 Where Do We Go From Here?
Stanton, Will
1932 Me and My Gal
1935 The Irish in Us
1936 The Last of the Mohicans
1937 Big City
1944 Mr. Skeffington
1945 Nob Hill
Stanwyck, Barbara
1932 So Big
1933 Ever in My Heart
1935 Annie Oakley
1947 California
1950 The Furies
1954 Cattle Queen of Montana
1957 Trooper Hook
Stapler, Maurice
1919 Injustice
Stapp, Marjorie *same as* **Stapp, Margie**
1950 Emergency Wedding
Jolson Sings Again
Star, Dixie
1932 Law and Lawless
Stardusk, a horse
1939 Harlem Rides the Range
The Stardusters
1944 Slightly Terrific
Stark, Bud
1941 Sun Valley Serenade
1952 Indian Uprising
Stark, Georgia
1942 Tortilla Flat
Stark, Jack *not the same as* **Stark, John**
1917 Her Own People
Stark, John *not the same as* **Stark, Jack**
1940 The Man I Married
1942 All Through the Night
Stark, Juanita
1943 Yankee Doodle Dandy
Stark, Michael
1948 Cry of the City
1949 House of Strangers
Starke, Pauline
1920 Dangerous Days
1926 War Paint
Starkey, Bert
1920 The Dark Mirror
1927 Wild Geese
1932 Scarface
1934 Broadway Bill
1938 Little Miss Roughneck
Starkey, John
1915 Time Lock Number 776

Starkman, David
1927 The Scar of Shame
Starks, William
1920 Within Our Gates
Starlight, a horse
1934 The Cactus Kid
1935 Wolf Riders
1936 Hair-Trigger Casey
Starling, Lynn
1930 Cuando el amor ríe
1931 ¿Conoces a tu mujer?
1936 Robin Hood of El Dorado
1937 Music for Madame
1943 Wintertime
Starr, Dave
1956 Singing in the Dark
Starr, Frederick
1918 The Yellow Dog
Starr, Henry
1924 A Debtor to the Law
Starr, Irving
1940 Music in My Heart
1942 Sunday Punch
1943 Bataan
1944 Something for the Boys
1952 Battles of Chief Pontiac
The Half-Breed
Starr, James A. (*writer*)
1927 Ham and Eggs at the Front
1929 Is Everybody Happy?
Starr, Jane
1921 Guile of Women
Starr, Jimmy (*actor*)
1942 Foreign Agent
Starrett, Charles
1935 So Red the Rose
1941 Thunder Over the Prairie
1942 Lawless Plainsmen
1943 Frontier Fury
1944 Riding West
1949 Laramie
1950 Raiders of Tomahawk Creek
1951 Cyclone Fury
Snake River Desperadoes
Statter, Arthur *same as* **Statter, Arthur F.**
1921 Made in Heaven
1924 The Mine with the Iron Door
1928 The Rawhide Kid
Stattler, Marion
1930 King of Jazz
Staunton, Ann
1942 Prisoner of Japan
1948 Call Northside 777
1957 Band of Angels
Steadman, Vera
1926 Meet the Prince
1937 That I May Live
1938 The Texans
Steakley, James
1960 Wild River
Stearns, Louis *see* **Stern, Louis**
Stebbins, Bobby *same as* **Stebbins, Robert**
1942 Mokey
Syncopation
1951 Show Boat
Steckler, Michael
1960 For the Love of Mike
Stedman, Mr. *same as* **Stedman, Marshall**
1915? The Beachcomber
Stedman, Myrtle
1916 Pasquale
The Soul of Kura-San
1920 The Tiger's Coat
1921 Black Roses
1922 The Hands of Nara
1923 Crashin' Thru
Steel, Varick
1935 Rosa de Francia
Steel, Vernon *see* **Steele, Vernon**
Steele, Agnes
1939 The Escape
Steele, Bill *see* **Steele, William**

Steele, Bob *same as* **Bradbury, Bob, Jr.**
1927 With Sitting Bull at the Spirit Lake Massacre
1928 Breed of the Sunsets
The Riding Renegade
1929 The Invaders
1932 Hidden Valley
Riders of the Desert
1933 The California Trail
1936 Border Phantom
1941 Gauchos of Eldorado
Prairie Pioneers
Saddlemates
1942 Valley of Hunted Men
1944 Outlaw Trail
Sonora Stagecoach
1946 Sheriff of Redwood Valley
1952 Bugles in the Afternoon
Rose of Cimarron
1953 Column South
San Antone
1954 Drums Across the River
1957 Band of Angels

Steele, Elbert
1955 The Long Gray Line

Steele, Freddie *same as* **Steele, Fred**
1943 Air Force
1944 Hi, Beautiful
1947 Desperate
1948 Call Northside 777

Steele, Geraldine
1920? Reformation

Steele, Karen
1955 Marty

Steele, Lou
1950 The Furies

Steele, Olivia
1941 New York Town

Steele, Roy
1941 Gauchos of Eldorado

Steele, Tom *not the same as* **Steele, Tommy**
1944 Marshal of Reno
Tucson Raiders
1952 Rose of Cimarron
Trail of the Arrow
1954 Cattle Queen of Montana

Steele, Vernon *same as* **Steel, Vernon**
1916 Silks and Satins
1918 Fields of Honor
1922 The Hands of Nara
1934 The Great Flirtation
1935 No matarás
Te quiero con locura

Steele, William *same as* **Gettinger, William; Goettinger, Bill; Steele, Bill; Steele, William A.**
1917 Her Own People
1926 The Flaming Frontier
1927 Whispering Sage
1934 Laughing Boy
1949 She Wore a Yellow Ribbon
1950 Colt .45
1956 The Searchers

Steers, Larry *same as* **Steers, Lawrence**
1918 The City of Dim Faces
Mystic Faces
1923 The Huntress
1929 In Old California
Redskin
1935 The Winning Ticket
1936 Paddy O'Day
1938 Dangerous to Know
1946 The Gay Cavalier
1947 The Farmer's Daughter
1948 Docks of New Orleans
1950 Rock Island Trail

Stefano, Joseph
1959 The Black Orchid

Stefanson, Vilhjalmur
1928 The Great White North

Steffen, Geary
1943 Wintertime

Stehli, Edgar
1954 Drum Beat

Stehnitzky, Nicholas
1938 Marusia

Steiger, O. M.
1945 Johnny Angel

Steiger, Rod
1951 Teresa
1957 Run of the Arrow
1959 Al Capone

Stein, Alexander
1939 A Brivele der Mamen

Stein, Anna *not the same as* **Sten, Anna**
1958 The Last Hurrah
1960 Pay or Die

Stein, Gita
1950 Catskill Honeymoon

Stein, Lotte
1948 Big City
1953 So Big

Stein, Phil
1959 Odds Against Tomorrow

Stein, Ralph
1948 The Miracle of the Bells

Stein, Sammy
1940 Mexican Spitfire Out West
Prairie Schooners
1942 Gentleman Jim
Syncopation

Stein, Sheila
1949 That Midnight Kiss

Steinart, Alex
1953 Tonight We Sing

Steinbeck, John
1944 Lifeboat
1945 A Medal for Benny

Steinbeck, Rudolf
1942 Secret Enemies

Steinberg, Solomon
1937 Where Is My Child?

Steindorff, Ulrich
1931 Dämon des Meeres
Kismet
Die Maske Fällt

Steiner, William
1915 How Molly Malone Made Good

Steinhoff, Ninon
1931 Die Dreigroschenoper (*foreign version*)

Steinke, Hans
1938 The Buccaneer

Stelling, William
1940 Doomed to Die
1948 Night Wind

Sten, Anna
1935 The Wedding Night
1940 The Man I Married
1943 They Came to Blow Up America

Stengel, Leni
1929 Die Königsloge
1931 Buster se marie (*foreign version*)

Stepanek, Karel
1950 Give Us This Day
1960 I Aim at the Stars: the Wernher von Braun Story

Stepanian, Roupen
1937 Arshin Mal Alan

Stephan, Steve *could be same as* **Stephens, Steve**
1953 So Big

Stephens, Charles *see* **Stevens, Charles**

Stephens, Frank
1948 Docks of New Orleans

Stephens, Harvey *not the same as* **Stevens, Harvey**
1936 Robin Hood of El Dorado
1937 Maid of Salem
1938 Dangerous to Know
The Texans
1940 The Fighting 69th
1958 Oregon Passage
The Young Lions
1960 The Plunderers

Stephens, J. M.
1928 Eleven P.M.

Stephens, Marvin
1936 Star for a Night
1938 Speed to Burn
1942 Whispering Ghosts

Stephens, Miles
1960 The Adventures of Huckleberry Finn

Stephens, Steve *same as* **Stevens, Steve** *could be same as* **Stephan, Steve**
1946 Sunset Pass
1949 Colorado Territory

Stephens, William
1947 The Return of Rin Tin Tin

Stephenson, Bob *see* **Stephenson, Robert**

Stephenson, Henry
1935 Rendezvous
1941 Lady from Louisiana
1943 Mr. Lucky
1947 Dark Delusion

Stephenson, James
1939 Confessions of a Nazi Spy

Stephenson, Maureen
1954 Dangerous Mission

Stephenson, Robert (*actor*), 1901—1970; *some of the films listed below may actually be credits of Robert Stevenson, 1915—1975 same as* **Stephenson, Bob; Stephenson, Robert R.** *not the same as* **Stephenson, Robert L.**
1943 They Came to Blow Up America
1945 Where Do We Go From Here?
1947 California
Easy Come, Easy Go
1950 Right Cross
1951 The Tall Target
1953 The Eddie Cantor Story
Ride, Vaquero!
So Big
1956 The Catered Affair
1958 Wild Is the Wind

Stephenson, Robert L. *could be same as* **Stevenson, Robert Louis, II** (*actor, writer*) *not the same as* **Stephenson, Robert** (*actor*), 1901—1970
1944 Address Unknown

Steppling, John
1918 Johanna Enlists
1920 Billions

Steptean, Zerita
1939 Moon over Harlem
1940? Mr. Washington Goes to Town

Sterett, Thomas, Capt.
1918 The Unbeliever

Sterler, Hermine
1935 Te quiero con locura
1940 Jennie
1942 Nazi Agent
1944 They Live in Fear
1945 Betrayal from the East

Sterling, Ford
1924 So Big
1927 Drums of the Desert
For the Love of Mike

Sterling, Jack
1951 Across the Wide Missouri
The Tall Target

Sterling, Jan
1950 Mystery Street

Sterling, Leigh
1942 Dr. Gillespie's New Assistant
Three Hearts for Julia

Sterling, Lynne
1945 Where Do We Go From Here?

Sterling, Richard
1916 Ramona

Sterling, Robert
1940 The Gay Caballero
1951 Show Boat
1953 Column South

Stern, Bill
1954 Go Man Go

Stern, Ernest
1929 The Witching Eyes

Stern, Isaac
1953 Tonight We Sing

Stern, Leonard
1953 The Jazz Singer

Stern, Louis *same as* **Stearns, Louis**
1916 Gold and the Woman
1919 Love and the Law
1920 The Great Shadow
Humoresque
The Riddle: Woman
1929 In Old California

Stern, Stewart
1951 Teresa
1959 Thunder in the Sun

Sternbach, Bert
1935 Captured in Chinatown
1937 Harlem on the Prairie

Sternberg, Josef von
1929 Thunderbolt

Sterns, Joseph
1921 No Woman Knows

Sterret, Walter
1929 The Invaders

Steuart, Eldine
1916 The Flower of No Man's Land

Steuermann, Salka
1930 Anna Christie (*foreign version*)
1931 La llama sagrada (*foreign version*)
Die Maske Fällt

Stevans, Norman
1959 Imitation of Life

Steven, James
1921 The Call of His People

The Stevens Sisters
1940 Broken Strings

Stevens, Aline
1950 Panic in the Streets

Stevens, Angela
1953 Jack McCall Desperado

Stevens, Anita
1953 The Jazz Singer

Stevens, Bee
1933 It's Great to Be Alive

Stevens, Bert
1953 The Jazz Singer

Stevens, Bob *see* **Stevens, Robert**

Stevens, Cedric
1945 The Cisco Kid Returns
1948 Fighting Father Dunne

Stevens, Charles *same as* **Stephens, Charles; Stevens, Charley**
1916 A Sister of Six
1920 The Mark of Zorro
1922 Captain Fly-by-Night
1925 Don Q, Son of Zorro
A Son of His Father
1926 The Vanishing American
1928 Diamond Handcuffs
1930 Tom Sawyer
1931 The Cisco Kid
La gran jornada
1932 Mystery Ranch
1933 The California Trail
1934 Behold My Wife!
Call of the Coyote
1936 Aces and Eights
The Bold Caballero
Robin Hood of El Dorado
Rose of the Rancho
1938 The Renegade Ranger
1940 Behind the News
Charlie Chan in Panama
Geronimo
Kit Carson
The Mark of Zorro
1945 A Medal for Benny
The Mummy's Curse
South of the Rio Grande
1946 Border Bandits
1947 Buffalo Bill Rides Again
Ride the Pink Horse
1948 The Feathered Serpent
Fury at Furnace Creek

1949   The Cowboy and the
            Indians
        Roll Thunder Roll!
1950   Ambush
        Indian Territory
        A Ticket to Tomahawk
1951   Oh! Susanna
        Warpath
1952   Rose of Cimarron
        Wagons West
1953   Ride, Vaquero!
        San Antone
1955   Indian American
        The Last Command
        The Vanishing American
1959   Last Train from Gun Hill

Stevens, Clarke
1947   Buffalo Bill Rides Again
Stevens, Craig
1942   Secret Enemies
1944   Since You Went Away
1947   Humoresque
1955   Duel on the Mississippi
Stevens, Dick
1931   Delicious
Stevens, Edwin
1918   The Squaw Man
1922   The Hands of Nara
1923   The Spider and the Rose
Stevens, Eileene
1957   Raintree County
1958   Escape from Red Rock
Stevens, Emily
1917   The Slacker (Metro
            Pictures Corp.)
Stevens, George (*actor*)
1916   The Pretenders
1919   Come Out of the Kitchen
Stevens, George (*dir*)
1933   The Cohens and Kellys in
            Trouble
1935   Annie Oakley
1942   Woman of the Year
1948   I Remember Mama
1953   The Eddie Cantor Story
1956   Giant
Stevens, Gösta
1930   Un hombre de suerte
            (*foreign version*)
Stevens, Harmon
1950   Rock Island Trail
Stevens, Harvey *not the same as*
    Stephens, Harvey
1949   Answer for Anne
Stevens, Inger
1959   The World, the Flesh and
            the Devil
Stevens, Jessie
1915   Cohen's Luck
1917   The Tell-Tale Step
1917?   Barnaby Lee
1918   Find the Woman
        The Little Runaway
Stevens, K. T.
1944   Address Unknown
1953   Tumbleweed
Stevens, Landers
1929   Frozen Justice
1931   Little Caesar
1932   The Rainbow Trail
1935   Charlie Chan in Paris
1936   Charlie Chan's Secret
1937   Big City
        Slave Ship
        That Girl from Paris
1938   Mr. Moto's Gamble
Stevens, Leith
1942   Syncopation
Stevens, Louis
1928   United States Smith
1949   Massacre River
        Streets of Laredo
1958   Flaming Frontier
Stevens, Mark *same as* **Richards,**
    Stephen
1945   Pride of the Marines
1958   Gun Fever
Stevens, Mary Louise
1946?   Beale Street Mama

Stevens, Morton
1949   Lost Boundaries
Stevens, Naomi
1959   The Black Orchid
Stevens, Onslow
1932   The Golden West
1933   Counsellor at Law
1946   Canyon Passage
1953   The Charge at Feather
            River
1954   They Rode West
1960   All the Fine Young
            Cannibals
Stevens, Paul
1952   Hiawatha
Stevens, Randie
1959   The Black Orchid
Stevens, Ray
1957   Run of the Arrow
Stevens, Risë
1944   Going My Way
1947   Carnegie Hall
Stevens, Robert *same as* **Stevens,**
    Bob
1947   The Jolson Story
1958   Never Love a Stranger
Stevens, Ruthelma
1933   Grand Slam
1951   Apache Drums
Stevens, Steve *see* **Stephens, Steve**
Stevens, Sue
1934   Broadway Bill
Stevens, Warren
1955   Duel on the Mississippi
Stevenson, Anglo
1932   The Cohens and Kellys in
            Hollywood
Stevenson, Bob *see* **Stevenson,**
    Robert (*actor*), 1915—1975
Stevenson, Charles A.
1914   The Nightingale
1927   Aflame in the Sky
Stevenson, Hayden
1937   Maid of Salem
1941   Birth of the Blues
Stevenson, Houseley
1946   Without Reservations
1947   Easy Come, Easy Go
1948   Four Faces West
        Moonrise
        The Paleface
1949   Colorado Territory
        Knock on Any Door
        Masked Raiders
Stevenson, Robert (*actor*), 1915—
    1975; *some of the films listed*
    below may actually be credits of
    Stephenson, Robert,
    1901—1970 *same as* **Stevenson,**
    Bob
1934   Operator 13
        White Heat
1942   The Navy Comes Through
        Secret Enemies
        Valley of Hunted Men
1943   Action in the North
            Atlantic
1958   Gun Fever
Stevenson, Robert (*dir*)
1951   Gambling House
Stevenson, Robert Louis, II (*actor,*
    writer) *could be same as*
    Stephenson, Robert L.
1935   The Wedding Night
Stevenson, Roberta
1947   Calendar Girl
Stevenson, Tom
1942   Across the Pacific
        Nazi Agent
1944   Mr. Skeffington
1945   Rhapsody in Blue
1947   My Wild Irish Rose
1948   The Luck of the Irish
        The Miracle of the Bells
Stevenson, Venetia
1960   Studs Lonigan
Steward, Henry
1937   The Holy Oath
Stewart, Al
1937   Maid of Salem
1938   City Streets

Stewart, Anita
1927   Wild Geese
Stewart, Anna Marie
1942   Valley of Hunted Men
Stewart, Bobby
1914   The Nightingale
Stewart, Cecil
1942   Seven Sweethearts
1945   Wanderer of the
            Wasteland
Stewart, Christopher
1957   Burden of Truth
Stewart, Diane
1946   Slightly Scandalous
Stewart, Dick
1955   Good Morning, Miss Dove
Stewart, Dink
1921   The Sport of the Gods
1924   A Son of Satan
Stewart, Donald (*actor*)
1959   The Sheriff of Fractured
            Jaw
Stewart, Donald Ogden (*writer*)
1942   Tales of Manhattan
Stewart, Dorothy
1932   Hypnotized
Stewart, Eleanor
1941   Louisiana Purchase
Stewart, Freddie
1948   Music Man
Stewart, Gary
1953   The Eddie Cantor Story
Stewart, Iva
1939   Mr. Moto Takes a
            Vacation
Stewart, Jack *not the same as*
    Stewart, Johnny
1942   Syncopation
1943   Ladies' Day
Stewart, James
1936   After the Thin Man
1941   Come Live with Me
1948   Call Northside 777
1950   Broken Arrow
        Winchester '73
1953   Thunder Bay
1959   The FBI Story
Stewart, Janet
1955   A Man Called Peter
Stewart, Johnny *not the same as*
    Stewart, Jack
1953   Last of the Comanches
Stewart, Julia *could be same as*
    Stuart, Julia
1920   The North Wind's Malice
Stewart, Larry
1943   In Old Oklahoma
1951   Little Big Horn
Stewart, Leonora
1918   The Prussian Cur
Stewart, Lucille Lee
1925   Friendly Enemies
Stewart, Margie
1943   Mexican Spitfire's Blessed
            Event
1945   Betrayal from the East
Stewart, Marianne
1950   Right Cross
Stewart, Mary *see* **Stuart, Mary**
Stewart, Mil
1959   Odds Against Tomorrow
Stewart, Nicodemus *same as*
    Nicodemus; Stewart, Nick
1937   Dark Manhattan
1943   Cabin in the Sky
        The Meanest Man in the
            World
        Stormy Weather
1944   Andy Hardy's Blonde
            Trouble
1945   I Love a Bandleader
1946   Song of the South
1954   Carmen Jones
1958   St. Louis Blues
Stewart, Paul
1943   Mr. Lucky
1949   Illegal Entry
1953   The Joe Louis Story

Stewart, Peggy
1944   Sheriff of Las Vegas
        Tucson Raiders
1946   California Gold Rush
        Sheriff of Redwood Valley
1947   Rustlers of Devil's
            Canyon
        Vigilantes of Boomtown
1949   Ride, Ryder, Ride!
Stewart, Rex
1942   Syncopation
Stewart, Ronnie
1959   Odds Against Tomorrow
Stewart, Roy
1916   Mixed Blood
1917   Follow the Girl
1918   Untamed
1919   Deliverance
        The Westerners
1922   One Eighth Apache
1926   Buffalo Bill on the U. P.
            Trail
        General Custer at Little
            Big Horn
1929   In Old Arizona
1931   Fighting Caravans
1932   Mystery Ranch
Stewart, S. S.
1929   Thunderbolt
Stewart, Victor A.
1918   Find the Woman
Slam Stewart Trio
1947   Boy! What a Girl!
Stickney, Dorothy
1956   The Catered Affair
Stidder, Edward F.
1956   7th Cavalry
Stille, Per
1930   Doña mentiras (*foreign*
            version)
        Toda una vida (*foreign*
            version)
Stillman, Robert
1942   Tales of Manhattan
1949   Home of the Brave
1951   Queen for a Day
Stillson, Charles
1924   Untamed Youth
Stine, Jan
1960   Sergeant Rutledge
Stinson, Bessie
1920   The Good-Bad Wife
Stinson, Mortimer E.
1921   Hold Your Horses
Stirling, Brand
1956   Westward Ho the
            Wagons!
Stirling, Linda
1944   The San Antonio Kid
        Vigilantes of Dodge City
Stockbridge, Robert Bronson
1919   Who's Your Brother?
Stockdale, Carl
1914   The Good-for-Nothing
1918?   Rosemary Climbs the
            Heights
1919   The Unpainted Woman
1922   The Half Breed
1923   Suzanna
1925   A Son of His Father
1930   Abraham Lincoln
1931   Cimarron
1932   Call Her Savage
1934   Charlie Chan's Courage
        Laughing Boy
        Stand Up and Cheer!
1937   Nation Aflame
        That I May Live
Stockman, Boyd
1946   Sunset Pass
1950   Indian Territory
1952   The Raiders
1956   Secret of Treasure
            Mountain
Stockton, Betty
1930   Whoopee
Stockton, Edith
1919   Who's Your Brother?
Stockton, John
1943   Hitler's Children

Stockton, Sadie
1949   The Quiet One
Stockwell, Dean
1945   The Valley of Decision
1947   The Mighty McGurk
1948   The Boy with Green Hair
        Gentleman's Agreement
1950   Stars in My Crown
Stockwell, Guy
1947   The Mighty McGurk
Stoddard, Betsy
1946   The Sailor Takes a Wife
        Three Wise Fools
Stoker, Catherine
1935   Rescue Squad
Stokes, Al
1936   The Green Pastures
Stokes, Vera
1951   Gambling House
Stokowski, Leopold
1947   Carnegie Hall
Stoll, Frieda
1946   Rendezvous 24
1958   Home Before Dark
Stollery, David
1956   Westward Ho the
        Wagons!
Stoloff, Benjamin *same as* **Stoloff, Ben**
1932   No Greater Love
1933   Obey the Law
1942   Secret Enemies
Stoloff, Morris
1950   Jolson Sings Again
Stombs, Alice
1932   Hypnotized
Stone, Andrew L. *same as* **Stone, Andrew**
1930   Sombras de gloria
1943   Stormy Weather
1960   The Last Voyage
Stone, Arthur
1929   Frozen Justice
1930   The Arizona Kid
        The Bad Man
        The Lash
1932   So Big
1935   Bordertown
        Charlie Chan in Egypt
Stone, Bobby
1942   Let's Get Tough!
        Song of the Islands
Stone, Doris
1934   Charlie Chan in London
Stone, E.
1915   The Gambler of the West
Stone, Fred
1936   My American Wife
1937   Life Begins in College
Stone, Gene
1938   City Streets
        Little Miss Roughneck
1947   Easy Come, Easy Go
Stone, George E.
1931   Cimarron
        Little Caesar
1933   Song of the Eagle
1938   Mr. Moto's Gamble
1941   The Face Behind the
        Mask
1942   Little Tokyo, U.S.A.
1946   Abie's Irish Rose
1953   Tonight We Sing
1954   Broken Lance
1959   Night of the Quarter
        Moon
Stone, Georgie (*child actor*)
1916   Gretchen, the Greenhorn
        A Sister of Six
1917   The Gun Fighter
1918   The Gypsy Trail
1920   Rio Grande
Stone, Hilda
1938   Passport Husband
1944   They Live in Fear
Stone, James F.
1953   So Big
1954   Broken Lance
Stone, John
1927   The Auctioneer
        Drums of the Desert
        Open Range

1930   Cuando el amor ríe
        Del mismo barro
        El precio de un beso
        El valiente
1931   Mi último amor
1933   It's Great to Be Alive
        La melodía prohibida
        Primavera en otoño
        El rey de los gitanos
        Una viuda romántica
        Yo, tú y ella
1934   Charlie Chan in London
        Charlie Chan's Courage
        La ciudad de cartón
        La cruz y la espada
        Dos más uno, dos
        Las fronteras del amor
        Granaderos del amor
        Nada más que una mujer
1935   Angelina o el honor de
        un brigadier
        ¡Asegure a su mujer!
        Charlie Chan in Paris
        Charlie Chan in Shanghai
        Julieta compra un hijo
        Piernas de seda
        Rosa de Francia
        Te quiero con locura
1936   Charlie Chan at the
        Circus
        Charlie Chan at the Race
        Track
        Charlie Chan's Secret
        Ramona
1937   Charlie Chan at the
        Olympics
        Charlie Chan at the
        Opera
        Charlie Chan on
        Broadway
1938   Charlie Chan at Monte
        Carlo
        Mr. Moto's Gamble
        Rascals
1939   Charlie Chan in Honolulu
        Charlie Chan in Reno
        The Cisco Kid and the
        Lady
        City in Darkness
        Mr. Moto in Danger
        Island
1940   Charlie Chan's Murder
        Cruise
        Lucky Cisco Kid
1944   The Racket Man
Stone, Lewis
1932   The Son-Daughter
        Unashamed
1939   Judge Hardy and Son
1944   Andy Hardy's Blonde
        Trouble
1946   Three Wise Fools
1950   Stars in My Crown
1952   It's a Big Country: An
        American Anthology
Stone, Milburn
1937   Music for Madame
1938   California Frontier
1940   Elsa Maxwell's Public
        Deb No. 1
1942   Rubber Racketeers
1947   Buck Privates Come
        Home
1949   The Sky Dragon
1952   The Savage
1953   Arrowhead
        The Sun Shines Bright
1954   Siege at Red River
1955   The Long Gray Line
        Smoke Signal
        White Feather
Stone, Paula
1936   Treachery Rides the
        Range
Stone, Phil
1927   Wild Geese
Stonehouse, Ruth
1917   Follow the Girl
1919   The Red Viper
1925   The Scarlet West
Stoney, Jack
1937   Slave Ship
1938   Gateway
        Mr. Moto's Gamble

1939   Mr. Moto in Danger
        Island
1940   The Gay Caballero
1948   The Miracle of the Bells
1951   Gambling House
Stopher, Harry C.
1940   The Ramparts We Watch
Storch, Larry
1958   Gun Fever
Storey, Edith
1917   The Captain of the Gray
        Horse Troop
Storey, June
1938   Happy Landing
        In Old Chicago
1948   Cry of the City
Storm, Gale
1941   Saddlemates
1942   Foreign Agent
1943   Crime Smasher
1945   Sunbonnet Sue
1948   The Dude Goes West
Storm, Jerry *same as* **Storm, Jerome**
1917   The Bride of Hate
1922   A California Romance
1938   Speed to Burn
Storm, Rafael
1934   Behold My Wife!
        Dos más uno, dos
1935   Ruggles of Red Gap
1936   La última cita
1940   Mexican Spitfire Out
        West
        New Moon
Storper, Bernard
1960   The Pusher
Storrer, Arnold
1919   Love and the Law
Stossel, Ludwig
1940   Jennie
        The Man I Married
1942   All Through the Night
        Woman of the Year
1943   Action in the North
        Atlantic
        They Came to Blow Up
        America
1944   Lake Placid Serenade
1953   The Sun Shines Bright
Stoul, Frank
1958   Tonka
Stout, George W.
1936   Tundra
Stowe, Leslie
1920   The Good-Bad Wife
1923   Jamestown
1924   Tongues of Flame
1929   Mother's Boy
Stowell, C. W.
1940   The Ramparts We Watch
Stowell, Dan
1946   The Gentleman
        Misbehaves
1947   The Jolson Story
Stowell, William
1919   The Right to Happiness
Stowers, Frederick *same as* **Stowers, Fred**
1921   The First Born
1925   Tearing Through
Stradella, Dante Charles
1959   Last Train from Gun Hill
Straight, Clarence
1946   G. I. War Brides
1947   Buck Privates Come
        Home
1948   Up in Central Park
1949   The Golden Stallion
1950   A Ticket to Tomahawk
1959   Gunmen from Laredo
        The Hanging Tree
1960   Ice Palace
        Sergeant Rutledge
Strand, Jimmy
1944   Block Busters
Strand, Le Roy
1953   The Eddie Cantor Story
Strand, Margaret
1935   ¡Asegure a su mujer!

Strang, Harry
1930   Around the Corner
1935   Charlie Chan in Shanghai
        The Little Colonel
1936   General Spanky
        The Prisoner of Shark
        Island
1937   Charlie Chan on
        Broadway
1938   Daughter of Shanghai
        Little Miss Roughneck
        Mr. Moto's Gamble
        Road Demon
1939   The Cisco Kid and the
        Lady
        Heaven with a Barbed
        Wire Fence
        Mr. Moto in Danger
        Island
        Mr. Moto Takes a
        Vacation
        The Return of the Cisco
        Kid
        Stand Up and Fight
1940   The Fatal Hour
        Kit Carson
        Lucky Cisco Kid
        New Moon
        Santa Fe Trail
1941   The Face Behind the
        Mask
        Mutiny in the Arctic
        Road Agent
        Western Union
1942   Dr. Gillespie's New
        Assistant
        They Died With Their
        Boots On
        Tortilla Flat
1944   The Sullivans
1945   Nob Hill
        The Valley of Decision
1946   Without Reservations
1948   The Lady from Shanghai
1949   Boston Blackie's Chinese
        Venture
        Colorado Territory
1952   Wagons West
1955   Apache Ambush
1956   The White Squaw
1958   The Last Hurrah
Strange, Glenn *same as* **Strange, Glen**
1938   California Frontier
1939   The Fighting Gringo
1940   Rhythm of the Rio
        Grande
1941   Saddlemates
1942   Juke Girl
1943   Action in the North
        Atlantic
1944   The San Antonio Kid
        Sonora Stagecoach
1946   Saratoga Trunk
1948   Red River
1949   Roll Thunder Roll!
1950   Comanche Territory
1952   Wagons West
1953   The Great Sioux Uprising
1955   The Vanishing American
1957   The Halliday Brand
1958   Gunfire at Indian Gap
1959   The Jayhawkers!
        Last Train from Gun Hill
Strange, Henry
1936   Yellow Cargo
Strange, Mary
1919   Injustice
Strange, Robert
1943   Mr. Lucky
1945   A Tree Grows in Brooklyn
1948   Silver Trails
Stranger, Lotte
1932   Yiskor
Stranges, Judy
1957   Dragoon Wells Massacre
1960   Pay or Die
Strassberg, Morris
1926   Broken Hearts
1932   The Unfortunate Bride
        Yiskor
1934   The Youth of Russia
1935   Bar-Mitzvah

1937   The Holy Oath
        Where Is My Child?
1938   The Power of Life
1939   Tevya
1951   Molly
Strasser, Ben
1921   A Giant of His Race
1923   The Devil's Match
        His Great Chance
        A Shot in the Night
Strassny, Fritz
1932   Yiskor
Stratton, Bob
1955   Trial
Stratton, Gene
1926   Laddie
Stratton, Gil, Jr.
1948   Half Past Midnight
Stratton, William
1929   The Invaders
Strauch, Joseph, Jr.
1941   Under Fiesta Stars
Straugh, Leslie
1951   Native Son
Strauss, Alfred
1954   Sitting Bull
Strauss, Robert
1958   Frontier Gun
1959   Inside the Mafia
Strauss, Theodore
1947   California
Strauss, William H. same as
    Strauss, William
1920   The North Wind's Malice
1921   The Barricade
1922   Solomon in Society
1926   Millionaires
        Private Izzy Murphy
1927   Sally in Our Alley
        The Shamrock and the
        Rose
1928   The Rawhide Kid
1929   Lucky Boy
        Smiling Irish Eyes
1934   Beloved
        Broadway Bill
Strawn, Arthur
1941   Road Agent
1952   Hiawatha
Strayer, Frank R. same as **Strayer,
Frank**
1926   Sweet Rosie O'Grady
1927   Pleasure Before Business
1933   La melodía prohibida
        El rey de los gitanos
1934   La cruz y la espada
        Las fronteras del amor
1936   Sea Spoilers
1948   Reaching from Heaven
Streaton, Anne
1914   The Little Angel of
        Canyon Creek
Streaton, George
1914   The Little Angel of
        Canyon Creek
Street, David
1948   Moonrise
Streimer, Charles H.
1914   At the Cross Roads
Strengell, Sara
1945   The House on 92nd St.
Strichevsky, Vladimir
1952   Anything Can Happen
Strickland, Helen
1917   Threads of Fate
Strickland, Hugh
1920   Frontier Days
Strickland, Mabel
1936   Custer's Last Stand
Stricklyn, Ray
1956   The Catered Affair
        The Last Wagon
1960   The Plunderers
Stride, April
1956   Serenade
Striker, Joseph
1927   A Harp in Hock
Strine, Leroy
1943   Gangway for Tomorrow

Stringbeans
1937   Underworld
Stringer, Arthur
1925   The Prairie Wife
Stroback, Ted
1931   La cautivadora
1932   Hypnotized
Strode, Woody
1960   The Last Voyage
        Sergeant Rutledge
Stroele, H. W.
1939   Mr. Moto's Last Warning
Stroheim, Erich von same as
    Stroheim, Eric von
1918   The Hun Within
        The Unbeliever
Stromberg, Hunt
1923   Breaking into Society
1924   The Lightning Rider
        The Night Hawk
1934   Eskimo
        Laughing Boy
1935   Naughty Marietta
1936   After the Thin Man
1940   Northwest Passage (Book
        I—Rogers' Rangers)
Strong, Barbara
1944   Chip Off the Old Block
Strong, Jay
1918   Doing Their Bit
Strong, Leonard
1942   Little Tokyo, U.S.A.
1943   Jack London
1949   We Were Strangers
1954   Hell's Half Acre
Strong, M. David
1935   Un hombre peligroso
Strong, Mark
1937   The Plainsman
Strong, Robert
1947   The Farmer's Daughter
1950   Mystery Street
1951   The Tall Target
1952   The Iron Mistress
1957   Beau James
Strong, Ted
1951   The Harlem Globetrotters
Strongheart, Nipo T.
1950   Young Daniel Boone
1951   Across the Wide Missouri
Stroschein, Breck
1951   Saturday's Hero
Stroud, Claude
1950   Train to Tombstone
Stroud, Leonard
1920   Frontier Days
Strudwick, Shepperd see
    Shepperd, John
Strumwasser, Jack
1922   Little Miss Smiles
1923   Snowdrift
Stuart, Angela
1947   Northwest Outpost
Stuart, Gloria
1932   The Cohens and Kellys in
        Hollywood
1933   It's Great to Be Alive
1934   Beloved
1936   The Prisoner of Shark
        Island
1937   Life Begins in College
1939   Winner Take All
Stuart, Henry
1938   The Power of Life
Stuart, Jane
1940   The Ramparts We Watch
Stuart, Julia could be same as
    Stewart, Julia
1914   When Broadway Was a
        Trail
1919   Injustice
Stuart, Kathryne
1919   Erstwhile Susan
Stuart, Leslie
1925   The Prairie Wife
Stuart, Louise
1937   The Plainsman
Stuart, Mary same as **Stewart,
Mary**
1942   Mexican Spitfire Sees a
        Ghost
        Mexican Spitfire's
        Elephant

        Song of the Islands
1943   Hitler's Children
        Ladies' Day
        Mr. Lucky
1944   Something for the Boys
1947   Dark Delusion
1949   The Girl from Jones
        Beach
1950   The Cariboo Trail
Stuart, Nicholas
1959   The Sheriff of Fractured
        Jaw
Stuart, Randy
1947   The Foxes of Harrow
Stubbs, Billy
1949   The Undercover Man
Stubbs, Harry
1930   Abraham Lincoln
1936   It Had to Happen
        Sutter's Gold
1937   Waikiki Wedding
1938   In Old Chicago
Stuckmann, Eugene
1945   The House on 92nd St.
Stufflebeam, Pamela
1955   The View from Pompey's
        Head
Stump & Stumpy
1948?   Boarding House Blues
Sturdy, John Rhodes
1950   The Cariboo Trail
Sturgeon, Edna
1950   Emergency Wedding
Sturgeon, Rollin S.
1914   The Little Angel of
        Canyon Creek
Sturges, John
1950   Mystery Street
        Right Cross
1951   The Magnificent Yankee
1952   It's a Big Country: An
        American Anthology
1955   Bad Day at Black Rock
1959   Last Train from Gun Hill
Sturges, Preston
1930   The Big Pond
1934   Imitation of Life
1941   Sullivan's Travels
Sturgis, Eddie same as **Sturgis,
Edwin**
1918   Doing Their Bit
1934   Broadway Bill
Stutchkof, Mischa
1937   Where Is My Child?
Stutenroth, Gene see Roth, Gene
Stymie see Beard, Stymie
Suárez, Juan
1932   Amor y vida
Suathojame, Manley
1955   Foxfire
Sublett, John W. "Bubbles" see
    also Buck and Bubbles; Millie
    and Bubbles
1943   Cabin in the Sky
Sudlow, Joan
1951   Queen for a Day
Sues, Leonard
1941   Where Did You Get That
        Girl?
Suey, Chan
1939   Mr. Moto Takes a
        Vacation
Suk, Lok
1939?   A Chinese Gains a
        Fortune in America
Sullavan, Margaret
1935   So Red the Rose
Sullivan, Anne see Macy, Mrs.
    Anne Sullivan
Sullivan, Barry
1953   Cry of the Hunted
1957   Dragoon Wells Massacre
Sullivan, Billy
1927   Red Clay
Sullivan, Brick
1942   Nazi Agent
1948   Big City
        The Boy with Green Hair
        Up in Central Park
1949   Knock on Any Door

1954   Drums Across the River
Sullivan, C. Gardner
1915   The Italian
1916   The Aryan
        Civilization's Child
        The Criminal
        Three of Many
1920   Dangerous Hours
1927   Turkish Delight
        White Gold
1932   Huddle
1936   Robin Hood of El Dorado
1938   The Buccaneer
Sullivan, Carolyn
1956   Crowded Paradise
Sullivan, Charles same as **Sullivan,
Charlie**
1925   His People
1939   Waterfront
        Winner Take All
1941   Mutiny in the Arctic
1942   All Through the Night
        Syncopation
        Unseen Enemy
        We Were Dancing
        Wings for the Eagle
        Woman of the Year
1943   Action in the North
        Atlantic
        Air Force
1944   Marshal of Reno
1945   Johnny Angel
1946   G. I. War Brides
1947   Buck Privates Come
        Home
        Easy Come, Easy Go
1948   Big City
        Shanghai Chest
        Unconquered
1949   Knock on Any Door
1952   The Fabulous Senorita
        Woman in the Dark
1953   Dream Wife
1958   The Last Hurrah
Sullivan, Danny
1919   The Other Man's Wife
Sullivan, Edward
1915   How Molly Malone Made
        Good
        Time Lock Number 776
Sullivan, Elliott same as **Sullivan,
Elliot**
1939   Waterfront
1941   Where Did You Get That
        Girl?
1942   In This Our Life
1943   Action in the North
        Atlantic
        Yankee Doodle Dandy
1944   An American Romance
1953   Taxi
1956   Crowded Paradise
Sullivan, Francis L.
1934   Strange Wives
1953   Sangaree
Sullivan, Fred
1930   Around the Corner
Sullivan, Gil
1948   Unconquered
Sullivan, Helene
1920   For the Soul of Rafael
        The Tiger's Coat
1922   The Sign of the Rose
Sullivan, J. M. see **Sullivan, John
M.**
Sullivan, Joe same as **Sullivan,
Joseph**
1945   Rhapsody in Blue
1959   The Last Angry Man
Sullivan, John M. same as
    Sullivan, J. M.
1934   The Cat's-Paw
1937   Souls at Sea
1938   The Buccaneer
1940   Geronimo
Sullivan, Lee
1945   The Great John L.
Sullivan, Paddy
1916   Broken Fetters
Sullivan, Peter
1941   Where Did You Get That
        Girl?

Sullivan, Tim
1957   The Tin Star
Sullivan, Wallace
1936   Laughing Irish Eyes
Sully, Frank
1937   Black Legion
         Life Begins in College
1938   Daughter of Shanghai
1940   Escape to Glory
1942   All Through the Night
1943   Good Luck, Mr. Yates
         Yankee Doodle Dandy
1945   I Love a Bandleader
1946   The Gentleman
         Misbehaves
1948   Gun Smugglers
1949   Boston Blackie's Chinese
         Venture
1951   The Tall Target
1954   Battle of Rogue River
         Massacre Canyon
1955   Apache Ambush
1958   The Last Hurrah
Sully, Thomas
1949   Knock on Any Door
Sul-te-wan, Madame
1924   The Lightning Rider
1934   Imitation of Life
1937   Maid of Salem
1938   In Old Chicago
         The Toy Wife
1941   King of the Zombies
         Sullivan's Travels
1942   Mokey
1949   The Story of Seabiscuit
1957   Band of Angels
Sumida, Sumi
1934   La ciudad de cartón
Summer, Minnie
1922   Square Joe
Summers, Ann
1942   Mexican Spitfire's
         Elephant
1943   Hitler's Children
         Ladies' Day
         Mexican Spitfire's Blessed
         Event
Summers, Don
1949   She Wore a Yellow
         Ribbon
         3 Godfathers
1950   Rock Island Trail
Summers, Jerry
1957   The Brothers Rico
Summers, Tommy
1947   Easy Come, Easy Go
Summerville, Slim
1927   The Chinese Parrot
1930   King of Jazz
1931   El tenorio del harem
1939   Charlie Chan in Reno
         Winner Take All
1941   Western Union
Sumner, Dick
1934   Broadway Bill
Sunasky, Irving
1960   Weddings and Babies
Sunday, a horse
1936   Custer's Last Stand
Sundberg, Clinton
1947   The Mighty McGurk
1949   The Kissing Bandit
1950   Annie Get Your Gun
         The Toast of New Orleans
Sunderland, John
1918   The Kaiser's Finish
Sunderland, Nan
1948   Unconquered
Sundholm, Bill
1946   Without Reservations
1948   Unconquered
1951   The Tall Target
Sundstrom, Florence
1955   The Rose Tattoo
The Sunkissed Brown Skin Chorus
1941   Sunday Sinners
Sunn, Joseph
1934   Blossom Time
1940   Hua Chio Juh Guang
1941   Min Jok Jay Hung Sing
1943   Gin Guo Chin Yuan

1944   Chin Hai In Siong
         Kuan Fong Lang Tyeh
1947?   Gin Fen Nee Shaan
         Jia O Tien Chen
         Sing Yun Sin Nian
1948?   Kuang Feng Juu Yien Fay
1949?   Shuang Feng Cheo Huang
Sunrise, Riley
1949   Border Incident
1950   Annie Get Your Gun
The Sunshine Boys
1947   West to Glory
Sunshine Sammy *see* **Morrison,
  Sunshine Sammy**
Sunshine, Bunny
1944   Mr. Skeffington
Supplee, Cuyler
1925   Brand of Cowardice
Suratt, Valeska
1915   The Immigrant
Sureau, Amy
1934   Stand Up and Cheer!
Surette, Al
1941   Ice-Capades
Suso, Amelia
1931   El pasado acusa
Susskind, David
1957   Edge of the City
Sussman, Lester P.
1938   Mis dos amores
Sutch, Herbert *same as* **Sutch, Bert**
1918   The Hun Within
1919   Scarlet Days
Sutherland, A. Edward
1930   Galas de la Paramount
1942   The Navy Comes Through
1943   Dixie
1946   Abie's Irish Rose
Sutherland, A. Mackay
1915   The Pageant of San
         Francisco
Sutherland, Dick
1924   Defying the Law
1928   Uncle Tom's Cabin
Sutherland, Eddie
1920   The Paliser Case
1922   Second Hand Rose
         The Woman He Loved
Sutherland, Hope
1923   Potash and Perlmutter
Sutherland, Hugh
1918   Tongues of Flame
Sutherland, Mitzi
1956   Giant
Sutherland, Sidney
1932   The Match King
1936   Laughing Irish Eyes
1945   Sunbonnet Sue
1946   The Gay Cavalier
Sutherland, Tom
1946   Till the End of Time
Sutherland, Victor
1916   The Flames of Johannis
1917   The Bar Sinister
         The Barrier
1918   The Firebrand
         The Liar
1945   The House on 92nd St.
Sutton, Charles
1917   The Tell-Tale Step
Sutton, Ellen
1951   Yes Sir, Mr. Bones
Sutton, Frank
1955   Marty
Sutton, George T. *same as* **Sutton,
  G. T.; Sutton, George**
1943   Marching On!
1946?   Beale Street Mama
1949?   Girl in Room 20
Sutton, Grady
1937   Waikiki Wedding
1941   Hurry, Charlie, Hurry
1942   Whispering Ghosts
1944   Hi, Beautiful
         Since You Went Away
1947   My Wild Irish Rose
1948   Jiggs and Maggie in Court
Sutton, John
1940   Murder over New York
1953   Sangaree

1956   Death of a Scoundrel
Sutton, Kay
1941   You're Out of Luck
Sutton, Paul
1939   The Cisco Kid and the
         Lady
1940   The Mark of Zorro
         Viva Cisco Kid
1941   Ride on Vaquero
Sutton, Susie
1920   The Brute
1928   The Midnight Ace
Swain, Charles
1959   Anna Lucasta
Swain, Mack
1927   Finnegan's Ball
         The Shamrock and the
         Rose
1929   The Cohens and Kellys in
         Atlantic City
Swallow (full name unknown)
1916   The Aryan
Swan, Bob
1957   The Lawless Eighties
Swan, Buddy
1944   The Sullivans
1949   Prejudice
Swan, Tex
1948   Fighting Father Dunne
1949   Knock on Any Door
Swann, Francis
1942   Holiday Inn
1950   Belle of Old Mexico
Swanson, Audrey
1956   Full of Life
Swanson, Gloria
1918   Shifting Sands
Swanson, Ken
1951   Jim Thorpe—All-American
Swanson, Ruth
1941   Louisiana Purchase
1953   So Big
Swanström, Karin
1930   Un hombre de suerte
         (foreign version)
Swapp, D. C.
1949   Stallion Canyon
Swarthout, Gladys
1936   Rose of the Rancho
Swartz, Howard B.
1953   The Great Sioux Uprising
Swarz, Lou
1946   Stars on Parade
         Tall, Tan and Terrific
1946?   House-Rent Party
Swayne, Marian
1917   The Little Samaritan
Sweeney, Bob
1958   The Last Hurrah
Sweeney, Fred
1942   The Navy Comes Through
Sweeney, Joseph
1957   Twelve Angry Men
Sweeny, Edward
1959   The Young Land
1960   Sergeant Rutledge
Sweet, Blanche
1915   The Secret Sin
1916   The Thousand Dollar
         Husband
         Unprotected
1921   That Girl Montana
1923   Anna Christie
Sweet, Katie
1959   The Crimson Kimono
1960   All the Fine Young
         Cannibals
Swenson, Karl
1958   The Badlanders
         Kings Go Forth
1959   The Hanging Tree
1960   Flaming Star
         Ice Palace
Swerdlov, Itzak
1934   The Youth of Russia
Swerling, Jo
1930   Around the Corner
1931   Carne de cabaret
         El pasado acusa
1939   Gone With the Wind

1941   New York Town
1943   Crash Dive
1944   Lifeboat
         The Negro Soldier
Swickard, Charles
1916   Mixed Blood
         The Sign of the Poppy
1917   The Plow Woman
1920   The Devil's Claim
         Li Ting Lang
         The Third Woman
Swickard, Josef *same as* **Swickard,
  Joseph**
1919   The Last of His People
1921   No Woman Knows
1924   Defying the Law
         North of Nevada
         Untamed Youth
1926   Desert Gold
1927   Old San Francisco
1930   Song of the Caballero
1934   Beloved
         The Lone Defender
1935?   The Irish Gringo
1936   Custer's Last Stand
Swift, Don
1936   Let's Sing Again
Swift Eagle, I. R.
1936   Custer's Last Stand
         Ramona
Swingley, Bill
1948   The Luck of the Irish
Switlick, Michael
1959   The FBI Story
Switzer, Carl "Alfalfa" *same as*
  Switzer, Carl
1936   General Spanky
         Kelly the Second
1943   Dixie
1944   Going My Way
1946   Gas House Kids
1955   Not As a Stranger
1958   The Defiant Ones
Switzer, Harold
1936   General Spanky
Swor, Bert
1929   Why Bring That Up?
Swor, John
1931   Charlie Chan Carries On
Swor, Mabel
1927   For the Love of Mike
Swystun, Theodore
1937   Natalka Poltavka
Sydes, Anthony
1952   Trail of the Arrow
Sydes, Carol
1955   Good Morning, Miss Dove
Sydney, Basil
1959   John Paul Jones
Sydney, Steffi
1953   The Eddie Cantor Story
Sydnor, Earl
1941   Murder on Lenox Avenue
         Sunday Sinners
Sykes, Ethel
1934   Broadway Bill
         Imitation of Life
Sylber, Charles, Jr.
1946   Slightly Scandalous
Sylva, Fred
1936   Star for a Night
Sylva, Marguerita
1941   They Dare Not Love
1943   The Leopard Man
1945   The Gay Senorita
Sylvester, Hannah
1946?   House-Rent Party
Sylvester, Henry
1935   Riddle Ranch
1946   Three Wise Fools
1950   Emergency Wedding
1952   It's a Big Country: An
         American Anthology
1953   The Member of the
         Wedding
Sylvester, John
1946   Saratoga Trunk
Sylvester, Robert
1953   The Joe Louis Story

Sylvester, William
1950   Give Us This Day
Symon, Burk
1950   Black Hand
        Young Man with a Horn
Szafnicki, Marian
1941   Wiejskie Wesele
Szemere, Paul Peter
1948   Up in Central Park
Szold, Bernard
1951   Queen for a Day
Szombathelyi, Blanke
1930   El secreto del doctor
        (*foreign version*)
Ta-wah-yi
1954   Apache
Tabori, Kristoffer *same as* **Chris;**
    Siegel, Chris
1960   Weddings and Babies
Tackney, Stanley
1945   The House on 92nd St.
Tafoya, Sam
1950   Two Flags West
Taft, Lucille
1917   Queen X
Taft, Sara
1952   Bright Victory
1953   So Big
1956   The Benny Goodman
        Story
Tafur, Robert
1944   Going My Way
1949   We Were Strangers
Tagawa, Yoshita
1945   The House on 92nd St.
Taggart, Ben
1931   Smart Money
1936   It Had to Happen
        Robin Hood of El Dorado
1937   Souls at Sea
1939   King of Chinatown
1941   The Face Behind the
        Mask
Taggart, Errol *same as* **Taggart,**
    Earl
1937   Song of the City
Taggart, Hal
1945   Where Do We Go From
        Here?
1948   Up in Central Park
1958   Gunman's Walk
        Home Before Dark
        St. Louis Blues
Taillon, Gus
1949   Top O' the Morning
Tait, Edward
1938   Zamboanga
Tait, Robert
1945   A Tree Grows in Brooklyn
Tait, Walter
1929   Hallelujah
Taka, Martha
1918   Mystic Faces
Taka, Miiko
1960   Hell to Eternity
Takasugi, May
1952   Japanese War Bride
Takei, George
1960   Hell to Eternity
        Ice Palace
Talata, Gelal
1933   It's Great to Be Alive
Talbert, Wen
1946?   Fight That Ghost
Talbird, Audrey
1939   Moon over Harlem
Talbot, Gloria *see* **Talbott, Gloria**
Talbot, Lyle
1935   Chinatown Squad
1938   Gateway
1939   Forged Passport
        Miracle on Main Street
1942   Mexican Spitfire's
        Elephant
1943   The Meanest Man in the
        World
1948   Shep Comes Home
1949   The Sky Dragon
1950   Cherokee Uprising
1951   Hurricane Island
        Mask of the Dragon

1953   Tumbleweed
Talbot, Monroe *same as* **Talbot,**
    Munro
1936   Hair-Trigger Casey
Talbot, Slim
1938   The Texans
1956   Giant
1959   The Hanging Tree
Talbott, Gloria *same as* **Talbot,**
    Gloria
1952   Desert Pursuit
1957   The Oklahoman
1959   The Oregon Trail
1960   Oklahoma Territory
Talevera, Frank
1954   Salt of the Earth
Taliaferro, Edith
1919   Who's Your Brother?
Taliaferro, Hal *same as* **Wales,**
    Wally
1932   Law and Lawless
1934   The Cactus Kid
        Fighting Through
        Range Warfare
1935   Range Warfare
1936   Hair-Trigger Casey
        The Traitor
1937   Law and Lead
1939   Daughter of the Tong
        Frontiers of '49
1940   Hi-Yo Silver
1942   American Empire
1944   Vigilantes of Dodge City
1948   Red River
1950   Colt .45
Taliaferro, Mabel
1917   A Wife by Proxy
Tall Bull, Chief
1917   The Adventures of Buffalo
        Bill
Tall Man's Boy
1934   Laughing Boy
Tall Tree
1936   Custer's Last Stand
Tallant, Jane
1936   After the Thin Man
Tallas, Gregg G. *see* **Tallas, Gregg**
1954   Barefoot Battalion
Tallman, Chester *same as* **Tallman,**
    Chet
1941   The Mexican Spitfire's
        Baby
Tally, Josephine
1924   Smiling Hate
Talma, Zola circa 1920s *could be*
    same as **Talma, Zolya** circa
    1950s
1920   On with the Dance
Talma, Zolya circa 1950s *could be*
    same as **Talma, Zola** circa 1920s
1955   The Rose Tattoo
1959   The Black Orchid
Talmadge, Constance
1922   East Is West
1924   In Hollywood With
        Potash and Perlmutter
Talmadge, Norma
1919   The Heart of Wetona
1924   In Hollywood With
        Potash and Perlmutter
1927   The Dove
Talmadge, Richard
1922   The Cub Reporter
1925   Tearing Through
1928   The Cavalier
1931   Yankee Don
1937   Souls at Sea
1938   Spawn of the North
1943   Redhead from Manhattan
1950   Two Flags West
1960   Flaming Star
Talman, William
1955   Smoke Signal
1957   Joe Dakota
Talton, Alice
1949   Ranger of Cherokee Strip
Tamaki, Ray
1951   Go for Broke!
Tamara *could be same as* **Geva,**
    Tamara *not the same as* **Tamara**
    d. 1943
1933   Live and Laugh

Tamato, P.
1917   Queen X
Tamayo, Fernando C.
1930   Sombras de gloria
1931   La cautivadora
Tamayo, Marina
1940   Perfidia
Tamblyn, Eddie
1936   Star for a Night
Tamblyn, Russ *same as* **Tamblyn,**
    Rusty
1948   The Boy with Green Hair
1956   The Last Hunt
1960   Cimarron
Tamiroff, Akim
1934   The Great Flirtation
        La veuve joyeuse
1935   Black Fury
        Naughty Marietta
        The Winning Ticket
1938   The Buccaneer
        Dangerous to Know
        Spawn of the North
1939   King of Chinatown
1940   The Way of All Flesh
1941   New York Town
1942   Tortilla Flat
1943   His Butler's Sister
1948   My Girl Tisa
1958   Touch of Evil
Tana
1939   La Inmaculada
        Miracle on Main Street
        (*foreign version*)
        El otro soy yo
        Papá soltero
        El trovador de la radio
1940   Cuando canta la Ley
Tanaguchi, George
1951   Go for Broke!
Tanchuck, Nat
1950   I Killed Geronimo
1952   Buffalo Bill in Tomahawk
        Territory
Tandy, Jessica
1945   The Valley of Decision
1958   The Light in the Forest
Tang, Charles
1916   Broken Fetters
Tang, Frank
1936   Sum Hun
Tanguay, Eva
1917   The Wild Girl
Tannen, Charles
1936   Dimples
        Sins of Man
1937   Think Fast, Mr. Moto
1938   Gateway
        Happy Landing
        My Lucky Star
1939   Drums Along the Mohawk
        The Return of the Cisco
        Kid
1940   Elsa Maxwell's Public
        Deb No. 1
        Jennie
        Lucky Cisco Kid
1941   Dead Men Tell
1942   Little Tokyo, U.S.A.
        Tales of Manhattan
        Young America
1943   Crash Dive
        They Came to Blow Up
        America
1948   Cry of the City
1955   Trial
1956   The Benny Goodman
        Story
Tannen, Julius
1936   Dimples
        Sins of Man
1941   Sullivan's Travels
1945   The Dolly Sisters
        Nob Hill
1958   The Last Hurrah
1959   Last Train from Gun Hill
Tannen, William *same as* **Tannen,**
    William J.
1939   Judge Hardy and Son
        Stand Up and Fight
1940   New Moon
1942   Nazi Agent
        Rio Rita
        Three Hearts for Julia
        Woman of the Year

Tarshis, Harold
1944   An American Romance
1946   Three Wise Fools
1947   Dark Delusion
        Little Mister Jim
1949   Lust for Gold
        The Mysterious
        Desperado
        Riders of the Range
1950   Annie Get Your Gun
        Sunset in the West
1951   New Mexico
        Show Boat
1953   Jack McCall Desperado
1954   Sitting Bull
Tanner, Gordon
1959   The Sheriff of Fractured
        Jaw
Tansey, John *same as* **Tansy, John**
1916   Broken Chains
1917?   Barnaby Lee
1931   Riders of the Rio
1932   Thirteen Steps
Tansey, Robert Emmett *same as*
    Tansey, Bob; Tansey, Robert
1932   The Galloping Kid
1936   Pinto Rustlers
        Song of the Gringo
1938   Wild Horse Canyon
1939   Drifting Westward
1940   Arizona Frontier
        Rhythm of the Rio
        Grande
1943   The Law Rides Again
1944   Outlaw Trail
        Sonora Stagecoach
1946   Romance of the West
        Wild West
Tansey, Sherry
1924   Fools' Highway
1931   Riders of the Rio
1934   Operator 13
1936   Pinto Rustlers
Tansill, Bob *could be same as*
    Tanzel, Bobby
1934   Broadway Bill
Tansler, Hans *see* **Tanzler, Hans**
Tansy, John *see* **Tansey, John**
Tanzel, Bobby *could be same as*
    Tansill, Bob
1936   Charlie Chan at the Race
        Track
Tanzler, Hans *same as* **Tansler,**
    Hans
1938   Happy Landing
1946   Rendezvous 24
Tanzler, Hilda
1944   Address Unknown
Tapia, Cesar
1936   Ramona
Tapia, Miguel
1946   Without Reservations
1947   Ride the Pink Horse
Tapley, Colin
1934   Limehouse Blues
        Wagon Wheels
1937   Maid of Salem
        Souls at Sea
Tapley, Rose *same as* **Tapley, Rose**
    E.
1916   Britton of the Seventh
Taradash, Daniel
1949   Knock on Any Door
Tarallo, Frank
1951   Go for Broke!
Tarallo, Lucia
1951   Go for Broke!
Taranda, Anya
1940   Escape
Tarler, Harriette
1959   Last Train from Gun Hill
Tarleton, W. A., Dr.
1919   Injustice
Tarlofsky, Morris *same as*
    Tarlowsky, Morris
1935   Bar-Mitzvah
        The Yiddish King Lear
Tarpenning, Norman
1941   Sun Valley Serenade
Tarshis, Harold
1947   The Adventures of Don
        Coyote

Tarver, Leonard
1955   The Lonesome Trail
Tarzan, a horse
1927   The Devil's Saddle
1928   The Canyon of Adventure
1929   Señor Americano
1930   Song of the Caballero
1934   Wheels of Destiny
Tarzan, The Police Dog
1935   Captured in Chinatown
Tashlin, Frank
1948   The Paleface
Tashman, Lilyan
1922   Head over Heels
Tassell, Reba
1955   Good Morning, Miss Dove
Tatara, Leo
1951   Go for Broke!
Tate, Cullen
1917   The Little American
1927   Rose of the Golden West
1941   Hold Back the Dawn
Tate, Patricia
1947   Dangerous Venture
Tatelman, Harry
1956   Hot Blood
Tattersall, Viva
1937   Souls at Sea
Tatum, Dee
1951   Mask of the Dragon
Tatum, E. G.
1920   The Brute
        The Symbol of the
          Unconquered
        Within Our Gates
1921   The Gunsaulus Mystery
1924   Birthright
        A Son of Satan
1927   The Millionaire
Tatum, Reece "Goose"
1951   The Harlem Globetrotters
1954   Go Man Go
Tatums, L. B.
1928   Black Gold
Taub, Sam
1940   The Notorious Elinor Lee
Taube, Mathias
1930   Toda una vida (foreign
          version)
Tauber, Chaim same as **Tauber, C.;**
Tauber, Chiam
1933   Live and Laugh
1939   Kol Nidre
        Motel the Operator
1940   The Great Advisor
        The Jewish Melody
1941   Mazel Tov Yidden
Taurog, Norman
1929   Lucky Boy
1930   Sunny Skies
1931   Huckleberry Finn
1933   L'amour guide
1938   The Adventures of Tom
          Sawyer
1940   Little Nellie Kelly
1948   Big City
1949   That Midnight Kiss
1950   The Toast of New Orleans
1953   The Stars Are Singing
Taute, Gus
1948   Unconquered
Tavares, Arthur same as **Tavares,**
Arturo
1916   Ramona
1930   East Is West (foreign
          version)
Tavares, Maria same as **Tavares,**
Maria J.
1948   The Paleface
        Unconquered
Taylor, Al (Western actor)
1932   Law and Lawless
1944   Marshal of Reno
Taylor, Beth
1948   The Miracle of the Bells
1949   The Prairie
Taylor, Betty not the same as
leader of the Betty Taylor
Taylorettes
1949   Knock on Any Door

The Betty Taylor Taylorettes
1955   Brevities of 1955
Taylor, Blanche
1943   The Gang's All Here
1945   Where Do We Go From
        Here?
Taylor, Bobby (child actor)
1951   Jim Thorpe—All-American
Taylor, "Cannonball" see **Taylor,**
Dub
Taylor, Carlie
1934   Charlie Chan in London
Taylor, Charles A. same as **Taylor,**
Charles
1917   Crime and Punishment
1922   The Half Breed
Taylor, Cliff (African-American
actor)
1951   Yes Sir, Mr. Bones
Taylor, Cliff (Western actor)
1949   The Dalton Gang
Taylor, Dick see **Taylor, Richard**
(actor)
Taylor, Don not the same as
Taylor, Donald Dexter
1950   Ambush
        Battleground
1952   Japanese War Bride
Taylor, Donald Dexter not the
same as **Taylor, Don**
1946   The Red Dragon
Taylor, Dub same as **Taylor,**
"Cannonball"; Taylor, Dub
"Cannonball"
1940   Prairie Schooners
1943   What's Buzzin' Cousin?
1948   Silver Trails
1953   The Charge at Feather
        River
Taylor, Dwight
1947   The Foxes of Harrow
Taylor, Eileen
1932   Hypnotized
Taylor, Elizabeth
1950   The Big Hangover
1956   Giant
1957   Raintree County
Taylor, Elsie
1932   Hypnotized
Taylor, Emily
1950   Damien
Taylor, Eric
1950   North of the Great Divide
Taylor, Estelle
1922   A California Romance
1931   Cimarron
        Street Scene
1932   Call Her Savage
Taylor, Ferris
1939   Man of Conquest
1940   Mexican Spitfire Out
        West
1942   Mexican Spitfire at Sea
1946   Bringing Up Father
        Rendezvous 24
1948   Docks of New Orleans
1950   Two Flags West
1952   Trail of the Arrow
1954   Siege at Red River
Taylor, Forrest same as **Taylor,**
Forest
1936   Song of the Gringo
        West of Nevada
1938   California Frontier
        Outlaw Express
1939   Stand Up and Fight
        Trigger Fingers
1940   Rhythm of the Rio
        Grande
1942   Juke Girl
        King of the Stallions
        Lawless Plainsmen
1943   Land of Hunted Men
1944   Sonora Stagecoach
1946   Romance of the West
        Santa Fe Uprising
        Strange Voyage
1947   Rustlers of Devil's
        Canyon
1948   Four Faces West
        The Golden Eye
        Unconquered

1949   The Cowboy and the
        Prizefighter
        Stallion Canyon
1950   Cherokee Uprising
        Winchester '73
1952   Wagons West
1959   The FBI Story
Taylor, Frank E.
1950   Mystery Street
Taylor, Fred
1955   The Rose Tattoo
Taylor, George same as **Taylor,**
George R.
1936   After the Thin Man
1938   Swing!
1949   The Red Menace
1950   Rock Island Trail
1953   The Great Sioux Uprising
Taylor, Henrietta
1949   The Girl from Jones
        Beach
Taylor, Hope
1938   In Old Chicago
Taylor, Jackie infant, circa 1939
1939   Miracle on Main Street
Taylor, Jean
1915   Just Jim
Taylor, Joan
1952   The Savage
1953   War Paint
1955   Apache Woman
        Fort Yuma
1957   War Drums
Taylor, Johnny same as **Taylor,**
Johnnie
1938   The Duke Is Tops
1940?   Mr. Washington Goes to
        Town
1947   Jivin' in Be-Bop
Taylor, Joyce
1959   The FBI Story
Taylor, Kent
1933   A Lady's Profession
1934   Limehouse Blues
1936   Ramona
1948   Half Past Midnight
1956   Ghost Town
1958   Fort Bowie
1960   Walk Tall
Taylor, Lance
1946?   House-Rent Party
Taylor, Larry (actor)
1959   The Sheriff of Fractured
        Jaw
Taylor, Lawrence (writer)
1950   The Jackie Robinson Story
        A Lady Without Passport
Taylor, LeRoy
1945   Escape in the Fog
1947   California
Taylor, Libby
1934   Imitation of Life
1935   Ruggles of Red Gap
1938   The Toy Wife
1940   Santa Fe Trail
1946   Saratoga Trunk
1947   The Foxes of Harrow
1953   Bright Road
Taylor, Lillian
1941   Sullivan's Travels
Taylor, Marian
1952?   Call of the Navajo
Taylor, Megan
1941   Ice-Capades
Taylor, Phil
1941   Ice-Capades
        They Dare Not Love
Taylor, Ray
1937   Drums of Destiny
1947   West to Glory
Taylor, Rex
1918   Set Free
1922   The Five Dollar Baby
1926   Irene
1927   McFadden's Flats
1930   Big Boy
1943   Redhead from Manhattan
Taylor, Richard (actor) same as
Taylor, Dick
1949   The Girl from Jones
        Beach

1954   Saskatchewan
Taylor, Richard G. (writer)
1958   Ambush at Cimarron Pass
Taylor, Robert
1939   Stand Up and Fight
1940   Escape
1943   Bataan
1950   Ambush
        Devil's Doorway
1951   Westward the Women
1953   Ride, Vaquero!
1956   The Last Hunt
Taylor, Roberto (African-American
actor)
1921   The Lure of a Woman
Taylor, Rod same as **Taylor,**
Rodney
1956   The Catered Affair
        Giant
1957   Raintree County
Taylor, S. E. V. same as **Marier,**
Victor, Captain
1918   The Greatest Thing in
        Life
        The Hun Within
1919   Scarlet Days
1922   The Mohican's Daughter
1928   Breed of the Sunsets
Taylor, Sam
1919   The Gray Towers Mystery
1931   Skyline
1934   The Cat's-Paw
Taylor, Scott Clarke (child actor)
same as **Taylor, Scott**
1947   Jiggs and Maggie in
        Society
1948   Jiggs and Maggie in Court
Taylor, Stan (dir) same as **Taylor,**
Stanley Earl
1952?   Call of the Navajo
Taylor, Stanley (actor)
1926   Kosher Kitty Kelly
1940   Elsa Maxwell's Public
        Deb No. 1
Taylor, Steve
1946   Till the End of Time
Taylor, Tony
1950   Annie Get Your Gun
        Winchester '73
1952   It's a Big Country: An
        American Anthology
Taylor, Vaughn
1958   The Young Lions
1960   The Plunderers
Taylor, Wayne
1953   The Charge at Feather
        River
1958   Touch of Evil
Taylor, Wilfred could be same as
Taylor, Wilton
1918   Wild Women
Taylor, William Desmond same as
Taylor, William D.
1916   Pasquale
1918   How Could You, Jean?
        Huck and Tom; or, the
        Further Adventures of
        Tom Sawyer
        Johanna Enlists
1920   Huckleberry Finn
Taylor, Wilton could be same as
Taylor, Wilfred
1920   Outside the Law
1921   The Cave Girl
Tayo, Lyle
1948   The Miracle of the Bells
Tazil, Zara
1935   The Cyclone Ranger
Tcherkasshy, Alexis same as
Tcherkassky, Alexis
1939   Cossacks in Exile
1940   Elsa Maxwell's Public
        Deb No. 1
Tchkowski, Ivan
1919   Deliverance
Tead, Phil
1931   The Guilty Generation
1934   Behold My Wife!
        The Cat's-Paw
        Stand Up and Cheer!
1935   Charlie Chan in Shanghai

1940   Music in My Heart
1945   The Dolly Sisters
1947   California
1951   Jim Thorpe—All-American
1952   Arctic Flight
1953   So Big

Teagarden, Jack
1941   Birth of the Blues
1953   The Glass Wall

Teague, Guy same as **Teague, A. Guy**
1947   King of the Bandits
1952   Battles of Chief Pontiac
       Indian Uprising
1953   Arrowhead
       The Nebraskan
1955   Apache Ambush
1956   Giant
       The White Squaw
1959   The FBI Story

Teal, Ray
1940   New Moon
       Northwest Passage (Book I—Rogers' Rangers)
       Prairie Schooners
       Viva Cisco Kid
1942   Apache Trail
       Juke Girl
       Nazi Agent
       Secret Enemies
       They Died With Their Boots On
       Woman of the Year
1944   An American Romance
1946   Canyon Passage
       Strange Voyage
       Three Wise Fools
1947   Northwest Outpost
       The Peanut Man
1948   Fury at Furnace Creek
       The Miracle of the Bells
       Unconquered
1949   Harbor of Missing Men
       Streets of Laredo
1950   Ambush
       Davy Crockett, Indian Scout
       The Men
       No Way Out
       Winchester '73
1951   Distant Drums
       Flaming Feather
       Oh! Susanna
1953   Ambush at Tomahawk Gap
1955   Apache Ambush
       The Indian Fighter
1956   The Burning Hills
1957   Band of Angels
       The Guns of Fort Petticoat
       The Oklahoman
1958   Gunman's Walk

Tearle, Conway
1914   The Nightingale
1921   Society Snobs
1936   Klondike Annie

Tearle, Godfrey
1925   Salome of the Tenements

Teasdale, Verree
1941   Come Live with Me

Tedford, Charles
1942   Valley of Hunted Men

Tedrow, Irene
1943   Dr. Gillespie's Criminal Case
1949   Thieves' Highway
1955   Santa Fe Passage
1960   All the Fine Young Cannibals

Tegström, Rickard
1960   The Crowning Experience

Teitelbaum, Abraham
1933   The Wandering Jew
1938   Two Sisters

Tell, Alma
1920   On with the Dance
1934   Imitation of Life

Tell, Olive
1931   Delicious

Tellegan, Mike see **Tellegen, Mike**

Tellegen, Lou
1927   The Princess from Hoboken
1934   Caravane

Tellegen, Mike same as **Tellegan, Mike; Tellegen, Michael**
1936   Down to the Sea
1947   The Mighty McGurk
1950   The Toast of New Orleans
1960   Pay or Die

Teller, Eloise
1952   Navajo

Teller, Francis Key
1952   Navajo

Teller, Mrs. Kee
1952   Navajo

Teller, Linda
1952   Navajo

Téllez, Cristina
1938   Castillos en el aire

Tello, Lisbeth
1956   Comanche

Tellou, Basil
1949   Harbor of Missing Men

Temoff, Serge
1928   Tyrant of Red Gulch

Temple, Shirley
1934   Stand Up and Cheer!
1935   The Little Colonel
       The Littlest Rebel
1936   Dimples
1944   Since You Went Away
1948   Fort Apache
1949   The Story of Seabiscuit

Templeton, Bob
1953   Arrowhead

Templeton, George "Dink" same as **Templeton, "Dink"**
1936   Klondike Annie

Templeton, Harry
1940   Geronimo

Tenbrook, Harry
1934   Judge Priest
1938   Little Miss Roughneck
1941   Mystery Ship
1942   Woman of the Year
1943   Gangway for Tomorrow
1949   Pinky
1952   The Quiet Man
1958   The Last Hurrah

Tenenholtz, Elihu
1925   Salome of the Tenements

Tennant, Barbara
1914   When Broadway Was a Trail
1921   Wolves of the North

Tennant, Dorothy
1936   My American Wife

Tennes, Gloria
1960   This Rebel Breed

Tennessee Jim
1951   Go for Broke!

The Tennessee Ramblers
1936   Ride, Ranger, Ride

Terán, Elisa
1932   Amor y vida

Terhune, Max same as **Terhune, Max "Alibi"**
1936   Ride, Ranger, Ride
1937   Manhattan Merry-Go-Round
       The Riders of the Whistling Skull
1939   Man of Conquest
1943   Land of Hunted Men
1951   Jim Thorpe—All-American
1956   Giant

Terhune, William
1936   Kelly the Second

Terr, Al
1958   Bullwhip

Terranova, Dan
1955   Blackboard Jungle

Terrell, Kenneth same as **Terrell, Ken**
1942   Syncopation
1944   Marshal of Reno
1945   In Old New Mexico
1948   The Miracle of the Bells

1949   The Clay Pigeon
1954   Drums Across the River
1956   Reprisal!

Terrell, Lynne
1948   The Miracle of the Bells

Terrell, Terry
1952   Bright Victory

Terrill, Evelyn
1916   Light at Dusk

Terriss, Tom
1918   Find the Woman

Terry, Barbara
1956   Full of Life

Terry, Bob same as **Terry, Robert**
1938   The Buccaneer
       California Frontier

Terry, Dick see **Terry, Richard**

Terry, Don
1941   Mutiny in the Arctic
1942   Unseen Enemy
       Valley of the Sun

Terry, Edwin
1927   California

Terry, Ellen
1918   Denny from Ireland

Terry, Griffen Trixie
1955   Brevities of 1955

Terry, James
1958   The Rawhide Trail

Terry, June
1938   In Old Chicago

Terry, Peggy
1934   Beloved

Terry, Phillip
1943   Bataan

Terry, Richard same as **Terry, Dick**
1937   Waikiki Wedding
1940   Phantom of Chinatown
1941   Caught in the Act

Terry, Robert see **Terry, Bob**

Terry, Ruth
1944   Lake Placid Serenade

Terry, Sheila
1934   'Neath the Arizona Skies
1935   Rescue Squad

Terry, Tex
1942   Valley of Hunted Men
1947   Spoilers of the North
1948   Old Los Angeles
1950   Rock Island Trail
       Stars in My Crown
1951   Oh! Susanna
1952   Rose of Cimarron
1958   The Badlanders
1959   The Oregon Trail

Terry, Tony
1956   The Burning Hills

Terry, Valya see **Martin, Janet**

Terry, William
1943   Gangway for Tomorrow

Terwilliger, George W. same as **Terwilliger, George**
1921   Little Italy
1939   The Devil's Daughter

Tesler, Jack
1953   Thunder Bay
1959   The FBI Story

Testa, Alfred
1922   Little Miss Smiles

Testa, Theresa
1949   House of Strangers
1950   Black Hand
1960   Pay or Die

Tettemer, John
1942   Syncopation
1943   The Leopard Man

Tetzel, Joan
1947   Duel in the Sun

Tetzlaff, Ted
1948   Fighting Father Dunne
1951   Gambling House
1959   The Young Land

The Texas Rangers
1947   The Last Round-Up

Texas, a horse
1922   Spitfire

Teycer, B. L.
1921?   [Unidentified Film]

Thalasso, Arthur
1922   The Sign of the Rose
1926   The Strong Man
1945   Nob Hill

Thalberg, Irving
1935   A Night at the Opera

Thane, Dirk
1937   It Could Happen to You
1939   Daughter of the Tong
1956   Reprisal!

Thanhouser, Edwin
1916   Betrayed

Thatcher, Heather
1942   We Were Dancing

Thatcher, Torin
1957   Band of Angels

Thaw, Evelyn Nesbit see **Nesbit, Evelyn**

Thaw, Russell same as **Thaw, Russell William**
1914   Threads of Destiny
1918   I Want to Forget

Thaxter, Phyllis
1950   The Breaking Point
1951   Jim Thorpe—All-American

Thayler, Carl
1956   Man from Del Rio

Thayler, Helen
1959   The Black Orchid

Thebom, Blanche
1951   The Great Caruso

Theby, Rosemary
1917   The Winged Mystery
1918   The Midnight Patrol
1919   Yvonne from Paris
1920   Rio Grande
1921   Across the Divide
       Shame
1924   So Big
1929   The Peacock Fan

Theodore, Paul
1946   Till the End of Time

Theriot, Al
1950   Panic in the Streets

Thew, Harvey same as **Thew, Harvey F.**
1919   The Delicious Little Devil
       Hearts of Men
       The She Wolf
1928   Uncle Tom's Cabin
1931   La llama sagrada
1934   Operator 13

Thi-The, Hoang
1931   La carta (foreign version)

Thiele, Walter
1937   It Could Happen to You
1943   Action in the North Atlantic

Thiele, William
1946   The Face of Marble

Thigpen, Helen
1959   Porgy and Bess

Thimig, Herman
1931   Die Dreigroschenoper
       Die Dreigroschenoper (foreign version)

Thinnes, Roy
1959   The FBI Story

Thireaux, Jack
1931   Delicious

Thoeren, Robert
1931   La carta (foreign version)
       Tropennächte

Thom, Bob (actor)
1943   Action in the North Atlantic
       Gangway for Tomorrow
1944   An American Romance
1948   The Miracle of the Bells

Thom, Robert (writer)
1960   All the Fine Young Cannibals

Thomajan, Guy
1949   House of Strangers
1950   The Breaking Point
       Panic in the Streets

Thomas, Mr. (*African-American actor*)
1921   The Gunsaulus Mystery
Thomas, Augustus
1914   The Jungle
        The Nightingale
1919   As a Man Thinks
        The Volcano
Thomas, Billie "Buckwheat" *see*
    Thomas, William "Buckwheat"
Thomas, D. Ireland
1919   A Man's Duty
Thomas, Danny
1948   Big City
1953   The Jazz Singer
Thomas, Edna
1951   A Streetcar Named Desire
Thomas, Evan (*actor*)
1938   The Buccaneer
1946   Rendezvous 24
Thomas, Evon (*child actress*)
1945   The Dolly Sisters
Thomas, Frank M. (*actor*) *same as*
    Thomas, Frank, Sr. *not the*
    same as **Thomas, Frankie**
1938   The Renegade Ranger
1940   Geronimo
1942   Apache Trail
Thomas, Henry
1938   The Toy Wife
Thomas, "Hot Shot"
1941   Sullivan's Travels
Thomas, "Jackie"
1945   Of One Blood
Thomas, Jameson
1935   Charlie Chan in Egypt
1937   Souls at Sea
Thomas, Jane
1920   The North Wind's Malice
1922   Breaking Home Ties
Thomas, Janet
1947   California
Thomas, Jean
1913   The Inside of the White
        Slave Traffic
Thomas, Jerry
1947   West to Glory
1949   The Cowboy and the
        Prizefighter
        Ride, Ryder, Ride!
        Roll Thunder Roll!
Thomas, John *same as* **Thomas,**
    Johnny
1939   Harlem Rides the Range
        One Dark Night
1940   Gang War
        While Thousands Cheer
1941   Four Shall Die
1943   Cabin in the Sky
Thomas, Lyn
1950   The Missourians
1958   Frontier Gun
Thomas, Maggie
1941   Sullivan's Travels
Thomas, Mary
1941   Birth of the Blues
Thomas, Nona
1915   The Alien
1917   The Bride of Hate
Thomas, Olive
1920   Darling Mine
Thomas, Peggy
1949   Lookout Sister
Thomas, Ray
1951   Westward the Women
Thomas, Reed
1921   As the World Rolls On
Thomas, Ruth
1943   Crash Dive
Thomas, Ted
1939   Confessions of a Nazi Spy
Thomas, Walter
1921   The Sport of the Gods
1922   The Schemers
Thomas, William "Buckwheat"
    same as **Buckwheat; Thomas,**
    "Buckwheat"; Thomas, Billie
1936   General Spanky
1942   Mokey
1945   Colorado Pioneers

Thomas, William C. (*prod*)
1946   Swamp Fire
1950   The Lawless
1951   The Last Outpost
1953   Sangaree
1955   The Far Horizons
Thomas, William J. (*actor*)
1959   The FBI Story
Thomashefsky, Anna *same as*
    Thomashefsky, Annie
1936   Love and Sacrifice
1941   Mazel Tov Yidden
Thomashefsky, Boris
1915?   The Jewish Crown
        The Period of the Jew
1935   Bar-Mitzvah
Thomashefsky, Harry
1935   The Yiddish King Lear
Thomason, Ike
1956   Reprisal!
Thompson, Al
1924   Racing Luck
1936   Below the Deadline
1948   Fury at Furnace Creek
1949   That Midnight Kiss
Thompson, Anita
1919   A Man's Duty
1921   By Right of Birth
1935   Piernas de seda
Thompson, Art
1948   Up in Central Park
1950   No Way Out
Thompson, Blanche
1921   As the World Rolls On
1922   The Dungeon
1924   A Son of Satan
Thompson, Carl
1952   Woman in the Dark
Thompson, Charles
1938   God's Step Children
Thompson, Creighton
1948   Miracle in Harlem
Thompson, D. J.
1957   Trooper Hook
Thompson, David H.
1916   Her Debt of Honor
Thompson, Davies
1919   Deliverance
Thompson, Donald
1949   The Quiet One
Thompson, Dorothy
1934   Stand Up and Cheer!
Thompson, Duane
1926   April Fool
Thompson, Edward *same as*
    Thompson, Eddie *not the same*
    as **Thompson, Edward L.**
1927   The Spider's Web
1930   Georgia Rose
1937   Bargain with Bullets
1938   The Duke Is Tops
        Life Goes On
1939   Double Deal
        Gang Smashers
        Reform School
1940   Am I Guilty?
        Broken Strings
        Mystery in Swing
        While Thousands Cheer
1941   Four Shall Die
1942   Lucky Ghost
Thompson, Edward L. *not the*
    same as **Thompson, Edward**
1950   Panic in the Streets
Thompson, Eugene
1948?   Junction 88
Thompson, Frank
1916   Peck O' Pickles
Thompson, Garfield
1914   Uncle Tom's Cabin
Thompson, George
1929   Why Bring That Up?
Thompson, Glenn *same as*
    Thompson, Glen
1949   Colorado Territory
        Knock on Any Door
        The Undercover Man
1951   Saturday's Hero
1953   The Nebraskan
1954   They Rode West

Thompson, Grace
1916   The Grip of Jealousy
Thompson, Harlan
1935   Ruggles of Red Gap
1936   Rose of the Rancho
1940   East of the River
Thompson, Harrison
1941   Sun Valley Serenade
Thompson, Henry
1950   Damien
Thompson, Hilda Offley *same as*
    Offley, Hilda
1939   Keep Punching
1947   Sepia Cinderella
1948   Miracle in Harlem
Thompson, Hugh
1917   Queen X
1917?   Barnaby Lee
1922   The Half Breed
        Head over Heels
Thompson, Irene
1932   Hypnotized
Thompson, J. Lee *see* **Lee**
    Thompson, J.
Thompson, Jack (*American actor*)
1942   Syncopation
Thompson, Jeff
1955   Davy Crockett, King of
        the Wild Frontier
Thompson, Jim (*African-American*
    actor) *see* **Thompson, Slim**
Thompson, June
1935   The Singing Vagabond
Thompson, Junice
1935   The Singing Vagabond
Kay Thompson and Her Radio
    Choir
1937   Manhattan
        Merry-Go-Round
Thompson, Keene
1929   Wolf Song
1931   Fighting Caravans
Thompson, Ken *see* **Thomson,**
    Kenneth
Thompson, Larry
1943   Doughboys in Ireland
1944   Something for the Boys
        The Sullivans
1945   The Dolly Sisters
        Where Do We Go From
        Here?
1948   Unconquered
Thompson, Leland
1958   Tonka
Thompson, Lucky
1947   New Orleans
Thompson, Marian
1959   Shake Hands with the
        Devil
Thompson, Marshall
1945   The Valley of Decision
1946   Bad Bascomb
1950   Battleground
        Devil's Doorway
        Mystery Street
        Stars in My Crown
1951   The Tall Target
1955   Good Morning, Miss Dove
Thompson, Mary
1931   Riders of the Rio
Thompson, Natalie
1942   The Vanishing Virginian
Thompson, Nick
1922   The Mohican's Daughter
1924   Tongues of Flame
1926   Puppets
1928   The Riding Renegade
1936   Rose of the Rancho
1937   Big City
        Song of the City
1942   Lawless Plainsmen
1944   Buffalo Bill
1946   Renegade Girl
        Singin' in the Corn
1949   The Girl from Jones
        Beach
        The Kissing Bandit
1950   The Toast of New Orleans
        The Traveling
        Saleswoman
1953   The Nebraskan

Thompson, Grace
1916   The Grip of Jealousy
1956   The White Squaw
1957   Apache Warrior
Thompson, Patsy Ann
1944   Tomorrow the World!
Thompson, Peter
1947   Buck Privates Come
        Home
1950   The Big Hangover
        Mystery Street
1951   The Harlem Globetrotters
        Saturday's Hero
1952   Indian Uprising
Thompson, Rex
1957   All Mine to Give
Thompson, Riley
1944   Something for the Boys
Thompson, Slim (*African-American*
    actor) *same as* **Thompson, Jim**
1936   The Green Pastures
1939   Lying Lips
        Moon over Harlem
Thompson, Ted
1939   Let Freedom Ring
Thompson, Tom (*dancer*)
1936   Star for a Night
Thompson, True T.
1946   Dirty Gertie from
        Harlem, U.S.A.
1947   Juke Joint
Thompson, Walker
1920   The Symbol of the
        Unconquered
Thompson, Wanda Lee
1956   Giant
Thompson, William C. (*prod, dir,*
    writer)
1935?   The Irish Gringo
Thompson, William H. (*actor*)
    same as **Thompson, William**
1916   Civilization's Child
1922   The Mohican's Daughter
Thomson, Fred
1924   North of Nevada
1925   The Wild Bull's Lair
1927   Don Mike
1928   Kit Carson
Thomson, Kenneth *same as*
    Thompson, Ken; Thomson,
    Ken
1927   Turkish Delight
        White Gold
1928   The Secret Hour
1932   Thirteen Women
1934   Behold My Wife!
        Call of the Coyote
Thomson, Norman
1948   The Lady from Shanghai
Thomson, Polly
1919   Deliverance
Thor, Larry
1959   Gunmen from Laredo
Thorgersen, Ed
1937   Life Begins in College
Thorn, Bert
1953   Taxi
Thornby, Robert
1916   Broken Chains
1917   Forbidden Paths
1918   A Little Sister of
        Everybody
1921   That Girl Montana
Thorndike, Oliver
1948   Unconquered
Thorndike, Sybil
1959   Shake Hands with the
        Devil
Thorne, Edward
1914   At the Cross Roads
Thorne, Lois
1959   Odds Against Tomorrow
Thorne, W. L.
1929   Thunderbolt
1930   Abraham Lincoln
1932   The Rainbow Trail
Thornhill, Alan
1960   The Crowning
        Experience
Thornton, Cherokee
1932?   The Girl from Chicago
1939   Lying Lips

Thornton, Cyril
1936   The Prisoner of Shark
        Island
Thornton, E. J.
1935   Riddle Ranch
Thornton, Fannie
1955   Brevities of 1955
Thorpe, Phil
1940   Knute Rockne—All
        American
Thorpe, Ed
1936   Desert Gold
Thorpe, Gordon
1927   The Way of All Flesh
1930   Abraham Lincoln
Thorpe, James *see* **Thorpe, Jim**
Thorpe, Jim *same as* **Thorpe,
    James**
1932   White Eagle
        Wild Horse Mesa
1934   Behold My Wife!
1936   Klondike Annie
        Sutter's Gold
        Treachery Rides the
        Range
1937   Big City
1940   Arizona Frontier
        Prairie Schooners
1944   Outlaw Trail
1951   Jim Thorpe—All-American
Thorpe, Norman
1916   The Romantic Journey
Thorpe, Richard
1925   Quicker'n Lightnin'
1926   Twin Triggers
1927   Roarin' Broncs
1932   The Secrets of Wu Sin
1934   The Lone Defender
        Strange Wives
1938   The Toy Wife
1939   The Adventures of
        Huckleberry Finn
1942   Apache Trail
        Three Hearts for Julia
1950   Black Hand
1951   The Great Caruso
1952   It's a Big Country: An
        American Anthology
Thorpe, Ted
1959   Imitation of Life
Thorsen, Duane
1953   Seminole
Thorson, Russell *same as* **Thorsen,
    Russell**
1954   Dangerous Mission
1958   Gun Fever
        Gunman's Walk
Threatt, Elizabeth
1952   The Big Sky
The Three Dunhills
1947   My Wild Irish Rose
The Three Peppers
1939   Straight to Heaven
The Three Swifts *see also* **Pike,
    William**
1945   Nob Hill
Thrower, Maxie
1951   A Streetcar Named Desire
1952   Anything Can Happen
Thunder, a horse
1942   King of the Stallions
1946   Sun Valley Cyclone
Thunder Cloud, Chief *same as*
    **Daniels, Victor; Thundercloud,
    Chief**
1935   Cyclone of the Saddle
        Fighting Pioneers
        The Singing Vagabond
1936   Custer's Last Stand
        For the Service
        Ramona
        Ride, Ranger, Ride
1937   The Plainsman
        The Riders of the
        Whistling Skull
1940   Geronimo
        Hi-Yo Silver
        Young Buffalo Bill
1941   Western Union
1942   King of the Stallions
        Shut My Big Mouth
1943   The Law Rides Again

1944   Buffalo Bill
        Outlaw Trail
        Sonora Stagecoach
1945   Nob Hill
1946   Renegade Girl
        Romance of the West
1948   Unconquered
1949   Call of the Forest
        The Prairie
1950   Ambush
        Colt .45
        Davy Crockett, Indian
        Scout
        I Killed Geronimo
        Indian Territory
        A Ticket to Tomahawk
        The Traveling
        Saleswoman
1952   Buffalo Bill in Tomahawk
        Territory
        The Half-Breed
Thunder Sky, Chief
1950   Indian Territory
Thunderbird, Chief
1934   Laughing Boy
1935   Annie Oakley
1936   Silly Billies
1940   Geronimo
Thunderbred, a horse
1949   Stallion Canyon
Thurber, Kent
1942   Prisoner of Japan
Thurman, Mary
1919   Spotlight Sadie
Thurn-Taxis, Alexis
1944   Slightly Terrific
1946   The Gentleman
        Misbehaves
Thursby, David *same as* **Thursby,
    Dave**
1929   Smiling Irish Eyes
1936   Charlie Chan at the Race
        Track
        Dimples
1938   Speed to Burn
1943   Gangway for Tomorrow
Thurston, Carol
1946   Swamp Fire
1947   The Last Round-Up
1949   Apache Chief
        Arctic Manhunt
1951   Flaming Feather
1952   Arctic Flight
1953   Conquest of Cochise
Thurston, Charles
1927   Spoilers of the West
Thurston, Helen
1957   The Guns of Fort
        Petticoat
The Tico Tico Guitars
1945   The Gay Senorita
Tidbury, Eldred
1934   Wagon Wheels
Tiernan, Patricia
1952   Apache War Smoke
1953   Dream Wife
Tierney, Gene
1941   Belle Starr
Tierney, Lawrence
1956   Singing in the Dark
Tighe, Gertrude
1950   No Way Out
Tihmar, David
1941   Where Did You Get That
        Girl?
1942   Holiday Inn
Tilbury, Zeffie
1931   Charlie Chan Carries On
1936   After the Thin Man
1937   Maid of Salem
Tiller Girls
1923   Potash and Perlmutter
Tillman, Harrel
1948   The Fight Never Ends
Tilton, Edward Booth *same as*
    Tilton, E. B.
1914   Hearts United
1922   The Cub Reporter
        Hungry Hearts

Tilton, Martha
1956   The Benny Goodman
        Story
Timbrell, Tiny
1952   Anything Can Happen
Timmons, Lee
1932   Parigi affascina; ovvero,
        Malavita
Tin, Lee
1934   La veuve joyeuse
Tin Horn, Jack
1956   The Searchers
Tindall, Loren
1946   Till the End of Time
Tiner, Tom
1959   The Young Land
Tinling, James
1930   El precio de un beso
1932   El caballero de la noche
1933   It's Great to Be Alive
        (foreign version)
1935   Charlie Chan in Shanghai
        Señora casada necesita
        marido
1938   Mr. Moto's Gamble
        Passport Husband
1943   Crime Smasher
        The Ox-Bow Incident
1946   Rendezvous 24
1948   Night Wind
Tirado, Romualdo
1930   Charros, gauchos y
        manolas
        ¡De frente, marchen!
        La jaula de los leones
        El presidio
1931   En cada puerto un amor
        El proceso de Mary
        Dugan
        Su última noche
1932   El caballero de la noche
1933   Dos noches
        It's Great to Be Alive
        (foreign version)
        La melodía prohibida
        No dejes la puerta abierta
        Primavera en otoño
        El rey de los gitanos
        Una viuda romántica
        Yo, tú y ella
1934   Granaderos del amor
1935   Alas sobre el Chaco
        Angelina o el honor de
        un brigadier
        De la sartén al fuego
        Piernas de seda
        Señora casada necesita
        marido
        Te quiero con locura
1936   La última cita
1937   El capitán Tormenta
        El carnaval del diablo
1938   Mis dos amores
        La vida bohemia
1939   Miracle on Main Street
        (foreign version)
        Verbena trágica
1940   Tengo fe en ti
Tishman and O'Neal
1932   Harlem Is Heaven
Tissot, Alice
1930   El secreto del doctor
        (foreign version)
Titheradge, Dion
1920?   Her Story
Titheradge, Madge
1920?   Her Story
Titus, Lydia Yeamans
1919   The Unpainted Woman
        A Yankee Princess
1926   Irene
1927   Heroes in Blue
Toback, Hannah
1935   Shir Hashirim
Tobey, Dan *same as* **Toby, Dan**
1938   Mr. Moto's Gamble
1942   Gentleman Jim
1947   Body and Soul
Tobey, Kenneth *same as* **Tobey,
    Ken**
1947   Dangerous Venture
1949   Illegal Entry

1950   Right Cross
1955   Davy Crockett, King of
        the Wild Frontier
1956   Davy Crockett and the
        River Pirates
Tobey, Ruth
1948   I Remember Mama
Tobias, George
1934   What a Mother-in-Law!
1940   East of the River
        Music in My Heart
1942   Juke Girl
        Wings for the Eagle
1943   Air Force
        Yankee Doodle Dandy
1947   My Wild Irish Rose
1951   The Mark of the
        Renegade
1952   Desert Pursuit
1958   Marjorie Morningstar
Tobias, Nettie
1925   Salome of the Tenements
Tobin, Dan
1942   Woman of the Year
1951   The Magnificent Yankee
        Queen for a Day
1953   Dream Wife
1956   The Catered Affair
1959   The Last Angry Man
Tobin, Genevieve
1932   The Cohens and Kellys in
        Hollywood
Tobin, Vivian
1935   Bordertown
Toby, Dan *see* **Tobey, Dan**
Toby, Ruth
1940   Knute Rockne—All
        American
Todd, Ann b. 1932 *not the same as*
    Todd, Ann (English actress),
    1909–1993
1945   Pride of the Marines
1947   The Jolson Story
Todd, Harry
1925   Quicker'n Lightnin'
1926   The Flaming Frontier
1927   Roarin' Broncs
1928   The Rawhide Kid
1930   The Last Dance
1934   Broadway Bill
        The Prescott Kid
Todd, James
1932   Charlie Chan's Chance
1948   The Luck of the Irish
1955   Trial
Todd, Lola
1927   Red Clay
Todd, Richard
1955   A Man Called Peter
Todd, Ruth
1927   Red Clay
Todd, Sally
1959   Al Capone
Todd, Sherman
1944   Tender Comrade
Todd, Thelma
1927   The Gay Defender
1928   The Crash
        Vamping Venus
1931   Aloha
1932   Call Her Savage
1933   Counsellor at Law
Toddles, a dog
1921   One Man in a Million
Toddy, Ted
1943   Fighting Americans
1946   Mantan Messes Up
1946?   Fight That Ghost
        House-Rent Party
1947?   Return of Mandy's
        Husband
1949?   Come On, Cowboy!
        She's Too Mean for Me
Togawa, Paul
1951   Go for Broke!
1960   Hell to Eternity
Tokanaga, Frank *see* **Tokunaga,
    Frank**
Tokatoo
1925   Kivalina of the Ice Lands

Tokunaga, Frank *same as*
Tokanaga, Frank
- 1917   The Flower of Doom
- 1918   The Girl in the Dark

Tolan, Michael
- 1952   Hiawatha
-          The Savage

Toledo, Fernando de *same as*
Toledo, Fernando G.
- 1933   Dos noches
-          Una viuda romántica

Tolenski, Mary
- 1919   Deliverance

Toler, Hooper
- 1920   The Girl of My Heart

Toler, Sidney
- 1934   Massacre
-          Operator 13
- 1935   Romance in Manhattan
- 1939   Charlie Chan at Treasure
-          Island
-          Charlie Chan in Honolulu
-          Charlie Chan in Reno
-          City in Darkness
-          King of Chinatown
- 1940   Charlie Chan at the Wax
-          Museum
-          Charlie Chan in Panama
-          Charlie Chan's Murder
-          Cruise
-          Murder over New York
- 1941   Charlie Chan in Rio
-          Dead Men Tell
- 1942   Castle in the Desert
- 1944   Black Magic
-          Charlie Chan in the
-          Secret Service
-          The Chinese Cat
- 1945   The Jade Mask
-          The Scarlet Clue
-          The Shanghai Cobra
- 1946   Dangerous Money
-          Dark Alibi
-          The Red Dragon
-          Shadows Over Chinatown
-          The Trap

Tollaire, Auguste *same as* **Tollaire,**
August
- 1934   La veuve joyeuse
- 1935   Charlie Chan in Paris
-          The Wedding Night

Tolliver Brothers
- 1923   A Shot in the Night

Tom, Konrad
- 1936   Yiddle with His Fiddle
- 1939   Mamele

Tom, Layne, Jr.
- 1937   Charlie Chan at the
-          Olympics
- 1938   Daughter of Shanghai
- 1939   Charlie Chan in Honolulu
- 1940   Charlie Chan's Murder
-          Cruise

Tomack, David *same as* **Tomack,**
Dave
- 1955   The Lonesome Trail
- 1959   Imitation of Life

Tomack, Sid
- 1948   My Girl Tisa
- 1949   Boston Blackie's Chinese
-          Venture
-          House of Strangers
-          Knock on Any Door
- 1950   Black Hand
- 1959   Last Train from Gun Hill

Tomarchio, Ludovico
- 1935   A Night at the Opera

Tombes, Andrew *same as* **Tombes,**
Andrew J.
- 1936   It Had to Happen
- 1937   Big City
-          Charlie Chan at the
-          Olympics
- 1941   Louisiana Purchase
- 1943   His Butler's Sister
-          The Meanest Man in the
-          World
-          Riding High
- 1944   Lake Placid Serenade
-          Something for the Boys
- 1945   Rhapsody in Blue
- 1947   My Wild Irish Rose

Tombragel, Maurice
- 1941   Mutiny in the Arctic
-          Road Agent
- 1949   Boston Blackie's Chinese
-          Venture
- 1952   Trail of the Arrow
- 1958   Fort Bowie

Tomei, Louis
- 1952   The Iron Mistress
- 1953   The Charge at Feather
-          River

Tomelty, Joseph
- 1960   The Day They Robbed the
-          Bank of England

Tomita, Yoshi
- 1955   Blackboard Jungle

Tomlin, Pinky
- 1936   Paddy O'Day

Tomlinson, Frank
- 1952   The Half-Breed

Toncray, Kate
- 1915   The Lamb
- 1916   Little Meena's Romance

Tondaleyo
- 1947   Sepia Cinderella

Tone, Franchot
- 1934   Straight Is the Way
- 1941   This Woman Is Mine
- 1943   His Butler's Sister
- 1944   Dark Waters
- 1949   Jigsaw

Toney, Jim
- 1936   My American Wife
- 1943   Yankee Doodle Dandy
- 1947   The Foxes of Harrow
- 1949   Pinky
- 1950   No Way Out
-          A Ticket to Tomahawk

Tong, Arthur
- 1950   Panic in the Streets

Tong, Kam
- 1942   Across the Pacific
-          Rubber Racketeers
- 1960   Walk Like a Dragon

Tong, Sam
- 1935   Charlie Chan in Shanghai
- 1937   Think Fast, Mr. Moto

Tonkle, Al *same as* **Tonkel, Alfred**
- 1958   The Young Lions
- 1959   The FBI Story

Tony, Edward
- 1939   Reform School

Tooker, Armin
- 1914   Springtime

Tooker, William H. *same as*
Tooker, William
- 1914   Northern Lights
-          Springtime
- 1915   How Molly Malone Made
-          Good
- 1919   The Lost Battalion
- 1920?   The Greatest Love
- 1922   Peacock Alley
- 1927   Jake the Plumber

Toombs, Rudolph *same as*
Toombs, Rudy
- 1946   Tall, Tan and Terrific
- 1946?   Fight That Ghost
-          House-Rent Party
- 1947   Reet, Petite and Gone

Toomey, Regis
- 1937   Big City
-          Shadows of the Orient
- 1938   Passport Husband
- 1940   Northwest Passage (Book
-          I—Rogers' Rangers)
- 1941   New York Town
- 1942   They Died With Their
-          Boots On
- 1943   Jack London
- 1945   Betrayal from the East
- 1948   The Boy with Green Hair
-          Reaching from Heaven
- 1951   Show Boat
-          The Tall Target
- 1952   The Battle at Apache Pass
- 1953   The Nebraskan
- 1954   Drums Across the River
- 1956   Dakota Incident

Toones, Fred "Snowflake" *same as*
Snowflake
- 1933   Robbers' Roost
- 1934   Imitation of Life
- 1935   A Night at the Ritz
-          Riddle Ranch
- 1936   The Green Pastures
-          Hair-Trigger Casey
- 1941   Sun Valley Serenade
- 1943   Land of Hunted Men
- 1946   G. I. War Brides

Toones, Ray
- 1948   The Miracle of the Bells

Topaz, Norma
- 1950   A Lady Without Passport

Topete, Jesús
- 1934   Tres amores
- 1936   El crimen de media
-          noche
- 1939   La Inmaculada
- 1941   Hold Back the Dawn

Topete, Luisa
- 1932   Amor y vida

Topham, Louis
- 1953   Thunder Bay

Topper, Bert
- 1952   Hiawatha

Tor, Michael
- 1950   Deported

Tor, Sigurd
- 1942   The Navy Comes Through
- 1943   Action in the North
-          Atlantic
-          Crash Dive
-          They Came to Blow Up
-          America

Torá, Lia
- 1931   Charlie Chan Carries On
-          (*foreign version*)
-          Don Juan diplomático
- 1932   Hollywood, ciudad de
-          ensueño
-          Soñadores de la gloria

Toren, Marta
- 1949   Illegal Entry
- 1950   Deported
-          Mystery Submarine

Torena, Juan
- 1929   Sombras habaneras
- 1930   The Bad Man (*foreign
-          version*)
-          Del mismo barro
-          El precio de un beso
-          Sombras de gloria
-          El valiente
- 1931   Charlie Chan Carries On
-          (*foreign version*)
-          Del infierno al cielo
-          El impostor
- 1933   Una viuda romántica
- 1934   La cruz y la espada
-          Nada más que una mujer
- 1935   Alas sobre el Chaco
-          Angelina o el honor de
-          un brigadier
-          De la sartén al fuego
-          Te quiero con locura
- 1936   El crimen de media
-          noche
- 1937   El capitán Tormenta
-          El carnaval del diablo
- 1938   Mis dos amores
-          La vida bohemia
- 1939   Verbena trágica
- 1952   My Man and I

Torey, Hal
- 1959   Inside the Mafia

Torgerson, Skip
- 1955   Blackboard Jungle

Tormé, Mel
- 1960   Walk Like a Dragon

Torneck, Jack
- 1954   War Arrow

Torre, Claudio de la
- 1932   ¿Cuándo te suicidas?

Torrence, David
- 1926   Laddie
- 1928   The Cavalier
- 1934   Charlie Chan in London
- 1935   Charlie Chan in Shanghai
-          Harmony Lane

Torrence, Ernest
- 1923   Ruggles of Red Gap
- 1924   The Heritage of the
-          Desert
-          North of 36
-          Peter Pan
- 1931   Fighting Caravans
- 1932   Hypnotized

Torrence, Lena
- 1943   Stormy Weather
- 1947   The Foxes of Harrow

Torrence, Walter
- 1960   Sergeant Rutledge

Torrés, Henry
- 1931   El proceso de Mary
-          Dugan (*foreign
-          version*)

Torres, Nancy
- 1930   King of Jazz
- 1931   Carne de cabaret
-          Mi último amor

Torres, Raquel
- 1929   The Desert Rider
- 1930   Estrellados
- 1931   Aloha

Torres, Renée
- 1930   Estrellados
-          La rosa de fuego
- 1931   La gran jornada
- 1936   Amor que vuelve
- 1939   El otro soy yo

Torres, Victor
- 1954   Salt of the Earth

Torrey, Roger
- 1960   The Plunderers

Torrientti
- 1921   As the World Rolls On

Tors, Ivan
- 1953   The Glass Wall

Torti, Ernesto
- 1916   Poor Little Peppina

Tortosa, José Luis
- 1935   De la sartén al fuego
-          El día que me quieras
-          No matarás
-          Tango Bar
- 1936   El crimen de media
-          noche
- 1937   El capitán Tormenta
- 1939   Miracle on Main Street
-          (*foreign version*)
-          El otro soy yo
- 1940   Cuando canta la Ley
-          Tengo fe en ti
- 1941   Doomed Caravan

Torvay, José
- 1949   Border Incident
- 1952   My Man and I
- 1956   Serenade

Tosi, Charles
- 1936   Ramona

Toth, Andre de *see* **De Toth,**
Andre

Totheroh, Dan
- 1936   Robin Hood of El Dorado

Totman, Wellyn *same as* **Totman,**
W.
- 1931   Aloha
- 1932   Hidden Valley
-          Riders of the Desert
-          Texas Pioneers
- 1936   Down to the Sea

Toto, a dog
- 1942   Twin Beds

Toto, Chiyo
- 1959   The Crimson Kimono

Totten, Robert
- 1958   The Badlanders

Totter, Audrey
- 1946   The Sailor Takes a Wife
- 1954   Massacre Canyon
- 1955   The Vanishing American

Touber, Chiam
- 1939   My Son

Toumanova, Tamara
- 1953   Tonight We Sing

Tourneur, Jacques
- 1942   Cat People
- 1943   The Leopard Man
- 1946   Canyon Passage
- 1950   Stars in My Crown

Tourneur, Maurice
1920   The Last of the Mohicans
1923   Jealous Husbands
Tovar, Lupita
1930   La voluntad del muerto
1931   Carne de cabaret
        Drácula
        El tenorio del harem
        Yankee Don
1935   Alas sobre el Chaco
1937   El capitán Tormenta
1939   The Fighting Gringo
Tovar Avalos, Enrique
1930   East Is West (*foreign
        version*)
        La voluntad del muerto
1931   Don Juan diplomático
        Drácula
1935   Alas sobre el Chaco
Tovey, Arthur
1955   A Man Called Peter
Towers, Constance
1960   Sergeant Rutledge
Towers, Don
1960   All the Fine Young
        Cannibals
Towers, Louis
1957   The Ride Back
Towne, Alice
1933   It's Great to Be Alive
Towne, Aline
1949   Harbor of Missing Men
Towne, Gene
1928   Flying Romeos
1933   Song of the Eagle
Towne, Michael
1947   It Had To Be You
Townes, Harry
1959   Cry Tough
Townley, Jack
1926   Twin Triggers
1929   The Cohens and Kellys in
        Atlantic City
1930   The Last Dance
1931   The Avenger
1936   Silly Billies
1940   Mexican Spitfire Out
        West
1941   Ice-Capades
1947   The Last Round-Up
1951   Cuban Fireball
1952   The Fabulous Senorita
Townsend, Leo
1942   Seven Sweethearts
1943   The Amazing Mrs.
        Holliday
1944   Chip Off the Old Block
1950   Black Hand
1955   White Feather
Townsend, Mary
1924   Smiling Hate
Townsend, Vince *same as*
Townsend, Vince M.;
Townsend, Vince M., Jr.
1955   Duel on the Mississippi
        Trial
1959   Porgy and Bess
Toxton, Candy
1948   Moonrise
Toy, Teri
1945   Nob Hill
Toyuk
1932   Igloo
Tozer, Joseph
1937   Maid of Salem
Tozere, Fred
1939   Confessions of a Nazi Spy
Tracey, Doreen
1956   Westward Ho the
        Wagons!
Trach, N.
1939   Cossacks in Exile
Tracy, Clyde
1921   Wolves of the North
Tracy, Lee
1930   She Got What She Wanted
1936   Sutter's Gold
1945   Betrayal from the East

Tracy, Spencer
1932   Me and My Gal
1937   Big City
1940   Northwest Passage (Book
        I—Rogers' Rangers)
1942   Tortilla Flat
        Woman of the Year
1954   Broken Lance
1955   Bad Day at Black Rock
1958   The Last Hurrah
Tracy, William
1942   Young America
Trado, Mae
1915   Time Lock Number 776
Traeger, Louis
1947   The Jolson Story
Trainor, Jack
1934   Coming Out Party
Trainor, Leonard
1936   My American Wife
The Tramp Band
1943   Stormy Weather
Trask, Helen
1931   Cimarron
Traube, Shepard
1940   The Ramparts We Watch
Travell, George
1936   Ramona
1942   Foreign Agent
Travers, Celia
1944   Three Men in White
1947   Little Mister Jim
        The Mighty McGurk
Travers, Henry
1945   The Bells of St. Mary's
1949   The Girl from Jones
        Beach
Travers, Tony
1949   The Fighting Kentuckian
Travers, Victor
1941   The Face Behind the
        Mask
1944   Tahiti Nights
1945   Escape in the Fog
1946   The Gentleman
        Misbehaves
1947   It Had To Be You
Travis, Charles
1914   Springtime
**Merle Travis and his Brunco
Busters**
1951   Cyclone Fury
Travis, Richard
1951   Mask of the Dragon
Traxler, Colleen
1936   Ramona
Traxler, Valerie
1918   How Could You, Jean?
1936   Star for a Night
1938   In Old Chicago
1942   Song of the Islands
1944   Something for the Boys
Traylor, William
1956   The Last Frontier
Treacher, Arthur
1938   My Lucky Star
1943   The Amazing Mrs.
        Holliday
1944   Chip Off the Old Block
1949   That Midnight Kiss
Treacy, Emerson
1960   All the Fine Young
        Cannibals
        The Dark at the Top of
        the Stairs
Treadville, Betty
1939   One Dark Night
Treadway, Charlotte
1941   Where Did You Get That
        Girl?
1942   Gentleman Jim
Treadwell, Dorothy
1927   The Spider's Web
Treadwell, Laura
1936   Klondike Annie
1937   That I May Live
1946   Bringing Up Father
1947   King of the Bandits
1948   Gentleman's Agreement

Trebaol, Francis
1923   Breaking into Society
Tredway, Wayn
1948   Up in Central Park
Tree, Dorothy
1935   A Night at the Ritz
1939   City in Darkness
        Confessions of a Nazi Spy
        The Mystery of Mr. Wong
1940   Knute Rockne—All
        American
1942   Nazi Agent
1950   The Men
Treen, Mary
1935   A Night at the Ritz
1937   Maid of Salem
1938   Rascals
1944   Tahiti Nights
1950   Young Daniel Boone
Trell, Max
1948   16 Fathoms Deep
1951   New Mexico
Trelvar, Norma
1937   Nation Aflame
Tremaine, Trevor
1947   The Mighty McGurk
Tremayne, Les
1953   Dream Wife
1955   A Man Called Peter
Trent, Jack
1927   The Chinese Parrot
1942   American Empire
1950   Annie Get Your Gun
Trent, Jean
1945   Salome, Where She
        Danced
Trent, Russell
1951   The Well
Trento, Guido
1931   La gran jornada (*foreign
        version*)
Trevino, George *could be same as*
    Treviño, Jorge
1957   The Ride Back
Treviño, Jorge *could be same as*
    Trevino, George
1955   Seven Cities of Gold
Trevor, Claire
1936   Human Cargo
        Star for a Night
1937   One Mile from Heaven
1939   Allegheny Uprising
1943   Good Luck, Mr. Yates
1945   Johnny Angel
1948   Key Largo
1952   My Man and I
1958   Marjorie Morningstar
Trevor, Edward
1936   Charlie Chan's Secret
Trevor, Olive
1919   The Other Man's Wife
1924   Down by the Rio Grande
Triana, Antonio
1945   The Gay Senorita
1956   Serenade
Triana, Luisita *same as* **Triana,
Luisa**
1945   The Gay Senorita
1947   Bells of San Fernando
Tricoli, Carlo
1949   House of Strangers
1950   Black Hand
        A Lady Without Passport
1952   The Iron Mistress
1960   Pay or Die
Triesault, Ivan
1944   Cry of the Werewolf
1945   Escape in the Fog
1946   Notorious
1950   Battleground
1958   The Young Lions
1960   Cimarron
Trigger
1939   In Old Caliente
1947   On the Old Spanish Trail
1949   The Golden Stallion
1950   North of the Great Divide
        Sunset in the West
Trimble, Laurence
1919   Spotlight Sadie
1920   Darling Mine

Triola, Anne
1946   Without Reservations
1948   Sleep, My Love
Trivers, Barry
1934   Coming Out Party
        Strange Wives
1936   Human Cargo
Trivers, Edith
1936   After the Thin Man
Troitzka, Halia
1938   Marusia
Trolle, Elsa af
1930   Doña mentiras (*foreign
        version*)
Trop, J. D.
1934   Chloe: Love Is Calling
        You
Trosper, Guy
1950   Devil's Doorway
1959   Thunder in the Sun
Trotti, Lamar
1933   The Man Who Dared: An
        Imaginative Biography
1934   Judge Priest
1936   Ramona
        Star for a Night
1937   Slave Ship
1938   Gateway
        In Old Chicago
1939   Drums Along the Mohawk
1941   Belle Starr
1942   Tales of Manhattan
1943   The Ox-Bow Incident
Troubetzkoy, Youcca
1925   Flower of Night
Trout, Dink
1945   A Tree Grows in Brooklyn
1946   Notorious
Trout, Tom
1945   Between Two Women
1950   The Palomino
Trowbridge, Charles
1935   Rendezvous
1936   Mad Holiday
        Robin Hood of El Dorado
1937   Man of the People
1938   The Buccaneer
1939   Confessions of a Nazi Spy
        King of Chinatown
        Waterfront
1940   The Fatal Hour
        The Fighting 69th
        Knute Rockne—All
        American
1941   Belle Starr
1943   Action in the North
        Atlantic
        The Amazing Mrs.
        Holliday
        Wintertime
1946   The Red Dragon
1947   Black Gold
        Buck Privates Come
        Home
1948   The Paleface
1958   The Last Hurrah
Trowbridge, Fred
1941   Playmates
Trowe, José
1958   Sierra Baron
Troy, Helen
1936   Human Cargo
1937   Big City
1948   Cry of the City
Troyan, Halia
1938   Marusia
Truax, John
1959   The FBI Story
True, Alice
1929   The Peacock Fan
Truel, John
1944   Chip Off the Old Block
Truesdell, Howard
1915   Marse Covington
1916   The Pretenders
Truex, Barry
1956   The Benny Goodman
        Story
Truex, Ernest
1918   Good-Bye, Bill
1942   Twin Beds

1944	Chip Off the Old Block
1945	Club Havana
	Salome, Where She Danced
1957	All Mine to Give

Trujillo, Margaret
| 1956 | Giant |

Trumbo, Dalton
1937	The Devil's Playground
1939	Heaven with a Barbed Wire Fence
1941	Accent on Love
1944	Tender Comrade
1945	Jealousy
	Our Vines Have Tender Grapes
1950	Emergency Wedding
1958	Terror in a Texas Town

Trundy, Natalie
| 1960 | Walk Like a Dragon |

Tryden, Doreen
| 1945 | Salome, Where She Danced |

Tryon, Glenn
| 1930 | King of Jazz |
| 1933 | Rafter Romance |

Tschechova, Olga
| 1931 | Don Juan diplomático (foreign version) |

Tsen Mei, Lady
| 1921 | Lotus Blossom |

Tsiang, H. T.
1947	Black Gold
	Little Mister Jim
1950	Panic in the Streets

Tsien, Maria
| 1960 | All the Young Men |

Tsourakis, George
| 1953 | Beneath the 12-Mile Reef |

Tsuchiya, Yuriko
| 1930 | Chijlku wo mawasuru chikara |

Tubau, María
| 1931 | Cheri-Bibi |

Ernest Tubb and His Singing Cowboys
| 1944 | Riding West |

Tuchock, Wanda
1929	Hallelujah
1938	Hawaii Calls
1945	Nob Hill
1947	The Foxes of Harrow

Tucker, Alonzo
| 1929 | When Men Betray |
| 1939 | Straight to Heaven |

Tucker, Edward
| 1934 | Broadway Bill |

Tucker, Forrest
1942	Shut My Big Mouth
	Submarine Raider
1950	Rock Island Trail
	Sands of Iwo Jima
1951	Flaming Feather
	Oh! Susanna
	Warpath
1952	Bugles in the Afternoon
1953	San Antone
1955	The Vanishing American
1957	The Deerslayer
1958	Fort Massacre

Tucker, George Loane
| 1913 | Traffic in Souls |

Tucker, Harland same as Tucker, Harlan
| 1921 | The Swamp |
| 1936 | Charlie Chan at the Race Track |

Tucker, Jay
| 1941 | Hold Back the Dawn |

Tucker, Jerry
| 1936 | General Spanky |

Tucker, Joyce
| 1945 | A Tree Grows in Brooklyn |

Tucker, Lillian
| 1921 | The Cave Girl |

Tucker, Lorenzo
1928	The Wages of Sin
1930	Easy Street
1932	The Black King
	Ten Minutes to Live
	Veiled Aristocrats

1936	Temptation
1937	Underworld
1947	Boy! What a Girl!
	Reet, Petite and Gone

Tucker, Loretta
| 1930 | A Daughter of the Congo |

Tucker, Melville
1949	Ranger of Cherokee Strip
1950	The Missourians
1954	Drums Across the River

Tucker, Richard
1917	The Little Chevalier
	Threads of Fate
1920	Darling Mine
1928	The Jazz Singer
1929	Lucky Boy
	This Is Heaven
1931	The Black Camel
1934	Operator 13
1937	Big City
1938	The Texans

Tucker, Robert
| 1937 | Boy of the Streets |

Tucker, Tommy same as Tucker, Tom
| 1942 | Little Tokyo, U.S.A. |
| 1947 | California |

Tuff, Jimmy
| 1918 | The Hell Cat |

Tufts, Sonny
| 1947 | Easy Come, Easy Go |

Tugend, Harry
1935	The Littlest Rebel
1938	My Lucky Star
1941	Birth of the Blues

Tuima, Kuka
| 1948 | The Paleface |

Tuller, Joseph
| 1955 | Brevities of 1955 |

Tullis, Edward
| 1951 | Tomahawk |

Tully, Ethel
| 1916 | The Flames of Johannis |

Tully, Phil same as Tully, Phillip Milton
1949	House of Strangers
	Illegal Entry
	Lust for Gold
1950	No Way Out
1953	The Stars Are Singing
1958	The Last Hurrah

Tully, Tom
1946	Till the End of Time
1949	Illegal Entry
1951	Tomahawk
1953	The Jazz Singer
1954	Arrow in the Dust

Tunberg, Karl
1937	Life Begins in College
1938	My Lucky Star
1940	Elsa Maxwell's Public Deb No. 1
1943	Dixie
1948	Up in Central Park

Tunberg, William
| 1953 | War Paint |

Tung, Henry
| 1936 | Sum Hun |

Tung-Foo, Lee see Foo, Lee Tong

Turham, Francis
| 1937 | Bargain with Bullets |

Turich, Arturo
| 1930 | Locuras de amor |
| | Monsieur le Fox |

Turich, Felipe same as Turick, Phillipe
1935	Un hombre peligroso
1938	Little Miss Roughneck
1939	La Inmaculada
1946	Beauty and the Bandit
1947	Bells of San Fernando
	Robin Hood of Monterey
1949	We Were Strangers
1950	Bandit Queen
	A Lady Without Passport
	The Lawless
1951	The Mark of the Renegade
1953	Tumbleweed
1956	Giant
1957	Gun Battle at Monterey

Turich, Leonor	
1939	Verbena trágica
Turich, Raquel	
1939	La Inmaculada
Turich, Rosa	
1939	Drifting Westward
	Papá soltero
1946	South of Monterey
1947	Bowery Buckaroos
	Riding the California Trail
1948	Old Los Angeles
1949	Arctic Manhunt
	Illegal Entry
1950	Belle of Old Mexico
1951	Cuban Fireball
1954	Passion

Turick, Phillipe see Turich, Felipe

Turkel, Joseph
| 1953 | The Glass Wall |
| 1957 | Beau James |

Turkles, Brinton
| 1950 | Two Flags West |

Turkow, Ruth
| 1939 | Mamele |

Turkow, Zygmunt
| 1934 | The Rabbi's Power |
| 1937 | The Jester (Der Purimspieler) |

Turnbowe, Guy
| 1950 | Intruder in the Dust |

Turnbull, Glen
| 1950 | The Breaking Point |
| | The Daughter of Rosie O'Grady |

Turnbull, Hector
1915	The Cheat
1916	Alien Souls
	For the Defense
1926	Desert Gold
1929	Why Bring That Up?
1930	Anybody's War

Turnbull, Margaret
1915	The Secret Sin
1916	Alien Souls
	For the Defense
	Pudd'nhead Wilson
	The Thousand Dollar Husband
	Witchcraft
1918	A Daughter of the Old South
	My Cousin
1922	Anna Ascends

Turnell, Dee
| 1947 | Copacabana |

Turner, Anita
| 1956 | Rockin' the Blues |

Turner, Clyde, Sgt.
| 1944 | The Negro Soldier |

Turner, D. H.
| 1944 | An American Romance |

Turner, Don
1940	East of the River
1942	All Through the Night
	Juke Girl
1947	Humoresque
1956	Serenade

Turner, Doreen
| 1921 | Through the Back Door |
| 1922 | The Top O' the Morning |

Turner, F. A. same as Turner, Fred; Turner, Fred A.
1915	The Penitentes
1916	Little Meena's Romance
1917	A Love Sublime
1919	Bonnie, Bonnie Lassie
	The Heart of Wetona

Turner, Florence
1927	The Chinese Parrot
	The Overland Stage
	Sally in Our Alley

Turner, Fred see Turner, F. A.

Turner, George (actor)
1947	Crossfire
	Vigilantes of Boomtown
1948	Call Northside 777

Turner, George Kibbe (writer)
| 1930 | Los que danzan |

Turner, John	
1928	Tenderfeet
Turner, Lana	
1959	Imitation of Life
Turner, Mae (African-American actress)	
1938	Life Goes On
	Spirit of Youth
	Two Gun Man from Harlem
1940	Am I Guilty?
Turner, Maidel	
1933	Olsen's Big Moment
1936	Klondike Annie
	Show Boat
Turner, Martin	
1934	Imitation of Life
	Operator 13
1936	Dimples
1937	Life Begins in College
1942	We Were Dancing
Turner, Raymond	
1925	Speed Wild
1927	The Love Mart
1928	Kit Carson
1934	Behold My Wife!
1936	It Had to Happen
	The Prisoner of Shark Island
1938	Josette
Turner, Smoke	
1921	Cheated Love
Turner, William H. same as Turner, William	
1913	Traffic in Souls
1935	Black Fury
1936	Dimples
Turney, Catherine	
1952	Japanese War Bride
Turnour, Dayse	
1927?	You Can't Win
Turpin, Ben same as Turpin, Bennie	
1922	The Bull-Dogger
1925	Hogan's Alley
Tuskegee Choir	
1940	George Washington Carver
Tutt, J. Homer	
1924	Birthright
1927	The Broken Violin
Tuttle, B. R. same as Tuttle, Burl	
1933	Circle Canyon
1934	'Neath the Arizona Skies
Tuttle, Frank	
1925	The Manicure Girl
1927	Blind Alleys
1930	Galas de la Paramount
1937	Waikiki Wedding
1945	The Great John L.
Tuttle, Lurene	
1934	Stand Up and Cheer!
Tuttle, Wes	
1944	Riding West
Twardowski, Hans von same as Twardowski, Hans Heinrich von; Twardowsky, Hans von	
1931	La llama sagrada (foreign version)
1935	Alas sobre el Chaco
1939	Confessions of a Nazi Spy
1942	The Navy Comes Through
1943	Margin for Error
Twelvetrees, Helen	
1930	The Grand Parade
1932	Unashamed
1934	She Was a Lady
Twerp, Joe	
1938	In Old Chicago
Twiddell, Frank	
1949	The Undercover Man
Twist, John	
1935	Annie Oakley
	His Family Tree
1940	Too Many Girls
1942	The Navy Comes Through
1949	Colorado Territory
1953	The Man Behind the Gun
	So Big
1956	Serenade
1957	Band of Angels

1959   The FBI Story
Twitchell, Archie *see* **Branden, Michael**
The Two Fat Men
1946   Tall, Tan and Terrific
The Tyler Twins
1938   God's Step Children
        Swing!
Tyler, Beverly *same as* **Saul, Beverly Jean**
1950   The Palomino
1952   The Battle at Apache Pass
Tyler, Dickie *same as* **Tyler, Richard**
1945   The Bells of St. Mary's
1946   Till the End of Time
1955   Trial
Tyler, Harry *same as* **Tyler, Harry O.**
1935   Black Fury
        Naughty Marietta
        A Night at the Opera
1936   After the Thin Man
1937   Waikiki Wedding
1940   Behind the News
        Jennie
1941   Sullivan's Travels
1942   Mexican Spitfire Sees a
        Ghost
        Mokey
1943   Dixie
        What's Buzzin' Cousin?
1944   Buffalo Bill
1946   The Sailor Takes a Wife
        Slightly Scandalous
1947   The Mighty McGurk
1950   The Traveling
        Saleswoman
1951   Cuban Fireball
1952   The Quiet Man
        Wagons West
1954   Cattle Queen of Montana
1956   Mohawk
1958   The Last Hurrah
Tyler, Lelah
1944   Charlie Chan in the
        Secret Service
        Mr. Skeffington
Tyler, Leon
1944   The Sullivans
1945   Great Stagecoach Robbery
Tyler, Richard *see* **Tyler, Dickie**
Tyler, Tom
1928   Tyrant of Red Gulch
1932   The Forty-Niners
1934   The Fighting Hero
1936   Pinto Rustlers
1939   Gone With the Wind
1941   Gauchos of Eldorado
1942   Valley of Hunted Men
        Valley of the Sun
1943   Wagon Tracks West
1948   The Dude Goes West
        Red River
1949   Lust for Gold
        Masked Raiders
        Riders of the Range
        She Wore a Yellow
        Ribbon
1950   Rio Grande Patrol
Tynan, James *same as* **Tynan, James J.**
1925   One of the Bravest
1927   Jake the Plumber
1933   Olsen's Big Moment
Tyne, George *same as* **Yarus, Buddy**
1943   Doughboys in Ireland
1944   The Racket Man
1948   Call Northside 777
        Open Secret
1949   Thieves' Highway
1950   No Way Out
        Sands of Iwo Jima
Tynes, Gwendolyn
1948   The Fight Never Ends
Tyrell, Ann *see* **Tyrrell, Ann**
Tyrol, Jacques
1919   The Red Viper
Tyrone, Madge
1920   Rio Grande

Tyrrell, Ann *same as* **Tyrell, Ann**
1950   Emergency Wedding
        No Way Out
1955   Good Morning, Miss Dove
        Seven Angry Men
Tyrrell, John
1936   Dangerous Intrigue
1941   The Face Behind the
        Mask
        Mystery Ship
        Thunder Over the Prairie
1942   Shut My Big Mouth
        Submarine Raider
1943   Let's Have Fun
        What's Buzzin' Cousin?
1944   Cry of the Werewolf
        The Racket Man
1945   Escape in the Fog
        I Love a Bandleader
1947   The Jolson Story
Tyson, Cicely
1959   The Last Angry Man
        Odds Against Tomorrow
Udell, Bill
1946   Without Reservations
Udell, Harvey
1951   Only the Valiant
Uehlein, Mitzi
1951   Show Boat
Ugarte, Eduardo
1931   La mujer X
        El proceso de Mary
        Dugan
        Su última noche
Uhthoff, Enrique
1939   Miracle on Main Street
        (foreign version)
        El otro soy yo
        Papá soltero
1940   Cuando canta la Ley
Ukelele Ike *see* **Edwards, Cliff**
Uller, Lurline
1938   In Old Chicago
Ullman, Carl *same as* **Ulman, Carl**
1920   The Secret Gift
Ullman, Daniel B. *same as* **Ullman, Dan; Ullman, Daniel**
1948   Guns of Hate
1950   Cherokee Uprising
1951   Cavalry Scout
1952   Fort Osage
        Hiawatha
        Wagons West
1955   Seven Angry Men
1957   The Oklahoman
Ullman, Elwood
1946   Singin' in the Corn
Ulman, Carl *see* **Ullman, Carl**
Ulman, William A., Jr.
1936   Down to the Sea
Ulmer, A.
1940   Americaner Schadchen
Ulmer, Edgar G. *same as* **Warner, John**
1931   Aloha
1937   Green Fields
        Natalka Poltavka
1938   The Singing Blacksmith
1939   Cossacks in Exile
        The Light Ahead
        Moon over Harlem
1940   Americaner Schadchen
1942   Prisoner of Japan
1945   Club Havana
1947   Carnegie Hall
Ulmer, Shirley *same as* **Castle, S.; Castle, Sherle; Ulmer, Sherle**
1939   The Light Ahead
        Moon over Harlem
1940   Americaner Schadchen
Ulric, Lenore *same as* **Ulrich, Lenore**
1917   Her Own People
1929   Frozen Justice
1947   Northwest Outpost
Underhill, Bruce
1955   A Man Called Peter
Underwood, Betty
1949   The Girl from Jones
        Beach
1950   Storm Over Wyoming

1951   Gambling House
Underwood, Evelyn
1949   Knock on Any Door
Underwood, Loyal
1948   The Paleface
Ung, Richard
1938   Spawn of the North
Ung, Tom
1937   Think Fast, Mr. Moto
Unger, Gladys
1934   Coming Out Party
        Strange Wives
1938   Daughter of Shanghai
1939   King of Chinatown
Unger, Paula
1943   Riding High
Unsell, Eve *same as* **Blankfield, Eve**
1916   The Honorable Friend
1917   Forbidden Paths
1918   A Woman of Impulse
1919   His Parisian Wife
1922   Captain Fly-by-Night
        Shadows
1933   La melodía prohibida
Updyke, Randall, III
1950   The Men
Urbach, Leslie
1945   Wanderer of the
        Wasteland
Urchel, Tony
1937   Waikiki Wedding
1941   Western Union
1950   Young Daniel Boone
Urecal, Minerva
1934   Straight Is the Way
1937   Charlie Chan at the
        Olympics
1938   City Streets
1941   Accent on Love
1942   They Died With Their
        Boots On
1943   Wagon Tracks West
1944   Block Busters
        Mr. Skeffington
1945   The Bells of St. Mary's
        A Medal for Benny
        Wanderer of the
        Wasteland
1946   Dark Alibi
        The Trap
        Without Reservations
1947   Bowery Buckaroos
        California
1948   Fury at Furnace Creek
1950   The Traveling
        Saleswoman
1951   The Great Caruso
        The Raging Tide
1952   Anything Can Happen
1960   The Adventures of
        Huckleberry Finn
Urueta, Chano
1928   El Robin Hood de México
Urueta, Jesús
1928   El Robin Hood de México
Usher, Guy
1934   Straight Is the Way
1935   Charlie Chan in Shanghai
        Naughty Marietta
        Rendezvous
1936   After the Thin Man
1937   Boots and Saddles
        Boy of the Streets
        Charlie Chan at the
        Opera
1938   City Streets
        Little Miss Roughneck
        The Renegade Ranger
        Spawn of the North
1939   King of Chinatown
        Mr. Wong in Chinatown
1940   Doomed to Die
1941   King of the Zombies
Uzzell, Corrine *same as* **Uzzell, Corene**
1918   A Woman of Impulse
Uzzo, Ignazio
1932   Amore e morte
Vaccari, Lee
1953   Thunder Bay

Vachon, Jean
1958   Marjorie Morningstar
Vacio, Natividad
1956   Giant
        Walk the Proud Land
1958   Escape from Red Rock
Vadnai, Laslo *same as* **Vadnai, L.**
1942   Tales of Manhattan
Vadnay, Laslo
1947   Copacabana
The Vagabonds
1944   Tahiti Nights
Vague, Vera *same as* **Allen, Barbara Jo**
1941   Ice-Capades
1944   Lake Placid Serenade
1956   Mohawk
Vahar, Harry
1936   Dangerous Intrigue
Vaiches, Peter G.
1959   Night of the Quarter
        Moon
Vajda, Ernest
1934   La veuve joyeuse
1941   They Dare Not Love
Vajda, Ladislaus
1931   Die Dreigroschenoper
        Die Dreigroschenoper
        (foreign version)
Val, Jean del *see* **Del Val, Jean**
Valadez, Enrique
1947   Ride the Pink Horse
1952   The Iron Mistress
Valde, Leona
1938   Little Miss Roughneck
Valdemar, Thais
1925   Flower of Night
Valdengo, Giuseppe
1951   The Great Caruso
Valdez, Carlos de *see* **De Valdez, Carlos**
Valdez, Enrique
1952   The Raiders
Valdez, Fernando
1936   The Phantom of Santa Fe
Valdivieso, Pedro
1931   La pura verdad
Vale, Travers
1916   The Scarlet Oath
Vale, Vola
1917   The Bond Between
1919   A Heart in Pawn
1920   The Purple Cipher
1923   Crashin' Thru
Valencia, E.
1916   Ramona
Valente, Danilo
1949   Border Incident
1951   The Great Caruso
Valentine, John
1948   Up in Central Park
1950   The Big Hangover
Valentine, Nancy
1949   The Girl from Jones
        Beach
Valentine, Paul
1949   House of Strangers
Valentini, Vincent
1940   Paradise in Harlem
1941   Murder on Lenox Avenue
        Sunday Sinners
1946   Stars on Parade
1947   Boy! What a Girl!
        Sepia Cinderella
1948   Miracle in Harlem
Valentino, Rudolph
1948   The Paleface
Valentino, Rudolph 1895—1926
1919   The Delicious Little Devil
1925   Cobra
Valentinova, Valie
1934   The Youth of Russia
Valenty, Lili
1958   Wild Is the Wind
1959   The Black Orchid
Valenzuela, Pedro
1928   El Robin Hood de México
1930   Las campanas de
        Capistrano

Valenzuela, Rose Marie
1951   The Girl on the Bridge
Valerie, Gertrude
1948   Unconquered
Valerie, Joan
1938   Road Demon
1940   Charlie Chan at the Wax
          Museum
          Jennie
          Murder over New York
1942   Rio Rita
1951   Westward the Women
Valerio, Albano
1951   The Great Caruso
Valéry, Olga
1931   Su noche de bodas
Valez, Kippee
1949   The Daring Caballero
Vallarino, Ramón
1940   Perfidia
Valle, Mario
1931   Pagliacci
Vallée, Marcel
1933   L'amour guide
1934   Caravane
          La veuve joyeuse
Vallee, Rudy
1948   I Remember Mama
Vallée, Yvonne
1931   Le petit café
Vallejo, Victor
1916   Ramona
Valles, Mary Alice
1950   Belle of Old Mexico
Valletty, Bruno
1932   Tormento
Valli same as **Valli, Alida**
1948   The Miracle of the Bells
Valli, Valli
1916   Her Debt of Honor
Valli, Virginia
1918   Ruggles of Red Gap
1929   Mister Antonio
Vallin, Rick same as **Vallin, Ric**
1942   King of the Stallions
1943   Wagon Tracks West
1946   Dangerous Money
1947   Last of the Redmen
          Northwest Outpost
1949   Shamrock Hill
          Tuna Clipper
1950   Comanche Territory
          Rio Grande Patrol
1951   Hurricane Island
          When the Redskins Rode
1952   Woman in the Dark
1954   Thunder Pass
1957   Raiders of Old California
1958   Bullwhip
          Escape from Red Rock
Vallon, Michael
1949   Tuna Clipper
1950   Black Hand
1957   Gun Battle at Monterey
Vallon, Nanette
1946   Gas House Kids
          Without Reservations
1948   Unconquered
Valmy, Ruth
1944   Since You Went Away
Valverde, Rafael
1930   Cuando el amor ríe
          Del mismo barro
          La fuerza del querer
1932   Soñadores de la gloria
Van, Beatrice
1919   The Tiger Lily
1923   Crashin' Thru
1926   A Trip to Chinatown
1930   Take the Heir
Van, Connie
1950   Stars in My Crown
Van, Frankie
1949   Illegal Entry
1952   The Ring
Van, Jean
1947   Little Mister Jim
Van, Vannette
1931   Così è la vita

Vana, Lidia
1960   Pay or Die
Vanaire, Jacques same as **Vanaire;
Venaire, Jacques**
1930   Behind the Make-Up
1931   La gran jornada (foreign
          version)
1934   La veuve joyeuse
1941   Playmates
1942   Holiday Inn
          We Were Dancing
Van Antwerp, Albert
1943   Jack London
Van Auker, Cecil same as **Van
Auker, C. K.**
1920   The Girl of My Heart
1921   The Girl from God's
          Country
Van Beaver, E.
1918   Wild Women
Van Brocklin, Norman
1955   The Long Gray Line
Van Buren, A. H.
1929   Hearts in Dixie
Van Buren, Catherine
1919   The Last of His People
Van Buren, Mabel
1916   Ramona
1917   Hashimura Togo
          The Squaw Man's Son
          Unconquered
1919   Hearts of Men
Vance, Charles
1947   My Wild Irish Rose
Vance, Lucille
1958   Gunman's Walk
Vance, Peggy
1924   Smiling Hate
Van Cleef, Lee
1952   High Noon
1953   The Nebraskan
          Tumbleweed
1954   Arrow in the Dust
          The Yellow Tomahawk
1955   The Vanishing American
1957   Gun Battle at Monterey
          Joe Dakota
          Raiders of Old California
          The Tin Star
1958   Machete
          The Young Lions
Vandergrift, Monte same as
Vandegrift, Monty
1935   Rendezvous
1936   After the Thin Man
          Ellis Island
1937   Charlie Chan on
          Broadway
1938   The Beloved Brat
Vanderveen, Joyce
1958   The Light in the Forest
Vanderveer, Elinor
1926   Into Her Kingdom
Van Derzee, Stella
1947   Going to Glory, Come to
          Jesus
Van de Water, M.
1918   The Goddess of Lost Lake
Vandiveer, Jimmy
1936   My American Wife
Vando, Poppy del
1953   Conquest of Cochise
Van Dolsen, Foy
1938   The Buccaneer
Van Dongen, Helen
1948   Louisiana Story
Van Dorn, Mildred
1930   Son of the Gods
Van Dusen, Ricki
1945   The Dolly Sisters
Van Dyke, Truman
1950   Riders of the Pony
          Express
Van Dyke, W. S. same as **Van
Dyke, W. S., II**
1916   Unprotected
1923   The Miracle Makers
1926   War Paint
1927   California
          Spoilers of the West
          Winners of the
          Wilderness

1928   Wyoming
1934   Eskimo
          Laughing Boy
1935   Naughty Marietta
1936   After the Thin Man
1939   Stand Up and Fight
1940   New Moon
Vane, Myrtle
1923   April Showers
Van Engle, Dorothy
1935   Lem Hawkins' Confession
1938   Swing!
Van Every, Billee same as **Van
Every, Billie**
1934   Broadway Bill
Van Every, Dale
1937   Souls at Sea
1938   Spawn of the North
Van Eyck, Goetz see **Van Eyck,
Peter**
Van Eyck, John
1942   Three Hearts for Julia
Van Eyck, Peter same as **Van Eyck,
Goetz**
1943   Action in the North
          Atlantic
          Hitler's Children
1944   Address Unknown
Van Fleet, Jo
1955   The Rose Tattoo
1960   Wild River
Van Haden, Anders
1931   Die Maske Fällt
1933   Best of Enemies
1936   Desert Gold
Van Horn, James same as **Van
Horn, Jim**
1950   Ambush
1952   The Raiders
          The Savage
1953   The Great Sioux Uprising
1954   Taza, Son of Cochise
Vaniver, Patricia
1948   Big City
Van Keuren, S. S.
1936   General Spanky
Van Loan, H. H.
1925   Speed Wild
Van Loan, Philip
1918   The Birth of a Race
          The Kaiser's Finish
Van Marter, George
1954   Thunder Pass
Van Moore, Eunice see **Moore,
Eunice**
Vann, Polly see **Bailey, Polly**
Vann, Vickie
1949   House of Strangers
Vann, Virginia
1946   The Gentleman
          Misbehaves
Vanni, Renata
1948   Music Man
1951   Westward the Women
1959   The Jayhawkers!
1960   Pay or Die
Van Nostrand, A.
1936   Ramona
Vanoni, César
1930   Así es la vida
          El presidio
          Sombras de gloria
1932   Hollywood, ciudad de
          ensueño
          Tormento
1938   The Buccaneer
Van Pelt, John
1937   The Riders of the
          Whistling Skull
Van Ronkel, Rip
1946   Abie's Irish Rose
Van Rooten, Luis same as **Van
Rooten, Louis**
1949   Boston Blackie's Chinese
          Venture
Van Sickel, Dale same as **Van
Sickle, Dale**
1937   Slave Ship
1948   Renegades of Sonora
1949   The Golden Stallion
          Ranger of Cherokee Strip

1951   Jim Thorpe—All-American
1952   Arctic Flight
1953   Thunder Bay
1956   The Burning Hills
Van Sloan, Edward
1933   It's Great to Be Alive
1936   Sins of Man
1937   Souls at Sea
1938   The Toy Wife
1941   Virginia
1942   Valley of Hunted Men
1943   Hitler's Children
Van Slyke, Arthur
1938   Outlaw Express
Vanstone, Bob
1958   Flaming Frontier
Van Tassell, Marie
1916   Peck O' Pickles
1918   The Only Road
Van Tuyle, Bert
1921   The Girl from God's
          Country
Van Upp, Virginia
1936   My American Wife
1941   Come Live with Me
          Virginia
Van Vleck, Bill same as **Van Vleck,
Will; Van Vleck, William**
1948   The Miracle of the Bells
Van Zandt, Philip same as **Van
Zandt, Phil**
1941   New York Town
          They Dare Not Love
          Where Did You Get That
          Girl?
1942   All Through the Night
          Nazi Agent
1943   Deerslayer
1944   They Live in Fear
1945   I Love a Bandleader
1947   California
          Easy Come, Easy Go
1948   The Lady from Shanghai
          Shanghai Chest
1950   Indian Territory
1953   Captain John Smith and
          Pocahontas
          Ride, Vaquero!
1957   Beau James
Varconi, Victor
1931   The Black Camel
1936   Dancing Pirate
1937   Big City
          The Plainsman
1939   Mr. Moto Takes a
          Vacation
1947   Pirates of Monterey
1948   Unconquered
Varden, Arlyne
1941   Louisiana Purchase
Varden, Evelyn
1949   Pinky
Varden, Norma
1942   We Were Dancing
1943   Dixie
Varela, Amanda
1939   El otro soy yo
          Papá soltero
Varela, Gloria
1948   Angel in Exile
1952   The Iron Mistress
Varela, Nina
1959   The Black Orchid
Varela, Trini same as **Varela, Trina**
1948   Angel in Exile
1950   Bandit Queen
Varella, Ann
1958   Terror in a Texas Town
Varella, Rosa Rita
1943   The Leopard Man
Varietiettes Dancing Girls
1948   Killer Diller
Varney, Peter
1946   Till the End of Time
Varno, Roland
1936   Sins of Man
1940   Three Faces West
1942   Nazi Agent
          Valley of Hunted Men
1943   Action in the North
          Atlantic
          Hitler's Children

1945   Betrayal from the East
1950   Battleground

Varnum, John
1959   The FBI Story

Varro, Juan see **Verros, John**

Vartian, Setrag same as **V. T., Setrag**
1937   Arshin Mal Alan
1945   Anoush

Vasilaki, Lambi
1931   Such Is Life

Vath, Richard
1952   Red Snow

Vaughan, Dorothy same as **Vaughn, Dorothy**
1936   After the Thin Man
1937   Black Legion
1942   Dr. Gillespie's New Assistant
        Gentleman Jim
        Wings for the Eagle
1943   The Amazing Mrs. Holliday
        Doughboys in Ireland
1948   The Lady from Shanghai
1950   Emergency Wedding
1951   The Great Caruso

Vaughan, William born Wilhelm von Brincken see **Von Brincken, William**

Vaughan, William circa late 1950s see **Vaughn, William** circa late 1950s

Vaughn, Alberta
1933   Dance Hall Hostess

Vaughn, Dorothy see **Vaughan, Dorothy**

Vaughn, Hilda
1935   The Wedding Night
1940   Charlie Chan at the Wax Museum

Vaughn, Jimmy
1939   King of Chinatown

Vaughn, Kerry
1945   Salome, Where She Danced

Vaughn, Laura
1942   Tales of Manhattan

Vaughn, Robert
1917   Under False Colors

Vaughn, Tyra
1946   Shadows Over Chinatown

Vaughn, Walter
1949   C-Man
        Jigsaw

Vaughn, William born Wilhelm von Brincken see **Von Brincken, William**

Vaughn, William circa 1910s
1914   The Redemption of David Corson

Vaughn, William circa late 1950s same as **Vaughan, William** circa late 1950s
1958   Ambush at Cimarron Pass
1959   Night of the Quarter Moon

Vautier, Elmire
1930   Toda una vida (foreign version)

Vaux, Vincent
1945   Where Do We Go From Here?

Vaux, William
1945   Where Do We Go From Here?

Vaverka, Anton
1930   The Melody Man

Vavitch, Michael
1927   The Dove
1929   Wolf Song
1930   Sevilla de mis amores

Veater, Clark
1949   Stallion Canyon

Veazie, Carol
1956   The Catered Affair

Vedder, William
1949   The Undercover Man
1953   Dream Wife
1955   Not As a Stranger

Vega, Carmen de la
1932   Amor y vida

Vega, Gloria de la
1934   Las fronteras del amor

Vega, Nila de la
1932   Amor y vida

Vehr, Nick same as **Vehr, Nicholas**
1942   The Navy Comes Through
        Three Hearts for Julia
1943   Crash Dive
        Hitler's Children

Veidt, Conrad
1940   Escape
1942   All Through the Night
        Nazi Agent

Veiller, Anthony
1933   El rey de los gitanos
1936   Winterset
1941   New York Town
1949   Colorado Territory

Veiller, Bayard
1932   Unashamed

Veitch, John
1954   Drum Beat

Vejar, Chico
1957   The Midnight Story

Vejar, Harry same as **Vejar, Harry J.**
1932   Scarface
1937   Waikiki Wedding
1947   Ride the Pink Horse
        West to Glory
1949   We Were Strangers
1951   Cuban Fireball

Vekroff, Perry N. same as **Vekroff, Perry**
1915   Hearts of Men
1916?   Should a Baby Die?
1917   The Secret of Eve
1930   Big Boy

Velasco, Armando
1940   Perfidia

Velasco, Fred same as **Velasco, Federico**
1931   La carta
1936   Ramona

Velasquez, Ernest
1954   Salt of the Earth

Vélez, Lupe
1929   Wolf Song
1930   East Is West
        East Is West (foreign version)
1931   Resurrección
        The Squaw Man
1932   Hombres en mi vida
1934   Laughing Boy
1939   The Girl from Mexico
1940   Mexican Spitfire
        Mexican Spitfire Out West
1941   The Mexican Spitfire's Baby
        Playmates
1942   Mexican Spitfire at Sea
        Mexican Spitfire Sees a Ghost
        Mexican Spitfire's Elephant
1943   Ladies' Day
        Mexican Spitfire's Blessed Event
        Redhead from Manhattan

Venable, Evelyn
1935   Harmony Lane
        The Little Colonel
1936   Star for a Night
1940   Lucky Cisco Kid

Vendetta, Bill
1948   Call Northside 777

Vendrell, Lolita
1930   Así es la vida

Ventre, Lou
1952   Hiawatha

Ventrella, Michele
1950   Black Hand

Ventura, Marcel
1934   La veuve joyeuse
1936   Klondike Annie

Venturi, Augusta
1951   Teresa

Venturini, Eduardo same as **Venturini, E. D.**
1930   El dios del mar
        Galas de la Paramount
1931   Gente alegre
        El príncipe gondolero

Venuta, Benay
1950   Annie Get Your Gun

Venuti, Joe
1942   Syncopation
1950   Belle of Old Mexico

Vepruk, h.
1939   Cossacks in Exile

Vera, Carlos
1952   Apache War Smoke

Vera, Connie
1952   Apache War Smoke

Vera, Robert
1952   The Half-Breed

Verdaine, Robert
1948   Up in Central Park

Verdugo, Elena
1946   Strange Voyage
1949   The Sky Dragon
        Tuna Clipper
1953   The Pathfinder

Verebes, Erno
1947   Easy Come, Easy Go
        Northwest Outpost
1951   Molly

Ver Halen, C. J.
1956   Daniel Boone, Trail Blazer

Vermilyea, Harold same as **Vermilye, Harold**
1914   The Jungle
1948   Gentleman's Agreement
        The Miracle of the Bells

Verne, Kaaren
1942   All Through the Night

Verner, Lois
1936   Show Boat

Verney, Richard
1958   Machete

Vernon, Charles E.
1916   Hulda from Holland

Vernon, Dorothy same as **Burns, Dorothy**
1924   Conductor 1492
1940   Geronimo
1944   Address Unknown
1949   Knock on Any Door
        Lust for Gold

Vernon, Frank de see **De Vernon, Frank**

Vernon, Glen
1950   Sands of Iwo Jima
1953   The Stars Are Singing

Vernon, Howard
1951   Adventures of Captain Fabian

Vernon, Lou
1931   The Exile
1948   The Betrayal

Vernon, Wally
1938   Happy Landing
1939   Charlie Chan at Treasure Island
1943   Tahiti Honey
1950   Train to Tombstone
1956   The White Squaw

Vernot, Henry
1921   The Sport of the Gods

Verrier, André
1934   La veuve joyeuse

Verros, John same as **Varro, Juan**
1942   Submarine Raider
1943   Action in the North Atlantic
        Mr. Lucky
1947   The Foxes of Harrow
1953   The Glory Brigade

Verwayen, Percy same as **Verwayne, Percy**
1921   The Burden of Race
        The Call of His People
        The Secret Sorrow
1922   Easy Money
1925   The Devil's Disciple

1926   The Conjure Woman
1939   Straight to Heaven
1940   Paradise in Harlem
1941   Sunday Sinners
1946?   Fight That Ghost
1947   Sepia Cinderella

Vespermann, Kurt
1931   Chérie (foreign version)

Vialar, Paul
1932   Le cas du docteur Brenner

Vicas, Victor
194-   Mistaken Identity

Vickers, Martha same as **MacVicar, Martha**
1949   Daughter of the West

Vickers, Sunny
1951   Saturday's Hero

Vickery, James
1959   The FBI Story

Vico, Manuel
1931   La fiesta del diablo
        La pura verdad
1932   ¿Cuándo te suicidas?

Victor and Shirley
1941   Mazel Tov Yidden

Victor, Charles
1948   Unconquered
1957   Band of Angels

Victor, David
1957   Trooper Hook

Victor, Gloria
1958   Gunman's Walk

Victor, Henry
1925   Braveheart
1927   Topsy and Eva
1939   Confessions of a Nazi Spy
1940   Escape
1941   King of the Zombies
1942   All Through the Night
1945   Betrayal from the East

Victor, Joseph
1937   The Jester (Der Purimspieler)

Vidacovich, Irving
1950   Panic in the Streets

Vidal, Antonio
1930   El presidio
1931   Charlie Chan Carries On (foreign version)
        El comediante
        La dama atrevida
        El impostor
        La llama sagrada
        La mujer X
1933   It's Great to Be Alive (foreign version)
        La melodía prohibida
        El rey de los gitanos
        Una viuda romántica
1934   La buenaventura
1935   Angelina o el honor de un brigadier
        El cantante de Nápoles
        Julieta compra un hijo
        Piernas de seda
        Rosa de Francia
1939   Papá soltero

Vidal, Gore
1956   The Catered Affair

Vidor, Charles
1932   Me and My Gal
1935   His Family Tree
1936   Muss 'Em Up
1941   New York Town
        They Dare Not Love
1952   It's a Big Country: An American Anthology

Vidor, Florence
1917   Hashimura Togo
        The Secret Game
1918   The Bravest Way
        Hidden Pearls
        The Honor of His House
1924   Welcome Stranger
1929   Chinatown Nights

Vidor, King
1929   Hallelujah
1931   Street Scene
1934   Our Daily Bread
1935   So Red the Rose
        The Wedding Night

Vidor, King
1940 Northwest Passage (Book I—Rogers' Rangers)
1944 An American Romance
1947 Duel in the Sun
1952 Japanese War Bride

Vierro, Paul
1950 The Breaking Point

Viertel, Berthold
1931 La llama sagrada (foreign version)

Viertel, Peter
1949 We Were Strangers

Vieweg, Brita
1930 Doña mentiras (foreign version)

Vignola, Robert G. same as Vignola, Robert
1933 Broken Dreams

Vigny, Benno
1931 Lo mejor es reír

Vigran, Herbert same as Vigran, Herb
1941 New York Town
1943 Dr. Gillespie's Criminal Case
1949 House of Strangers
1953 So Big
1957 The Midnight Story

Vigren, Herb
1955 Good Morning, Miss Dove

Vigue, Pete
1952 The Big Sky

Vilches, Ernesto
1930 Cascarrabias
      Galas de la Paramount
      Wu Li Chang
1931 Cheri-Bibi
      El comediante
      Su última noche

Vildo, Roland
1955 The Rose Tattoo

Villa, Celia
1935 El día que me quieras

Villalobos, Francisco
1956 Giant
1960 Pay or Die

Villar, Carlos see Villarías, Carlos

Villard, Joseph
1940 The Mark of Zorro

Villarías, Carlos same as Villar, Carlos
1930 Amor audaz
      The Bad Man (foreign version)
      Cuando el amor ríe
      El cuerpo del delito
      Del mismo barro
      Estrellados
      El precio de un beso
      El último de los Vargas
      El valiente
1931 El código penal
      Cuerpo y alma
      Del infierno al cielo
      Drácula
      La gran jornada
      Hay que casar al príncipe
      El impostor
      El pasado acusa
1932 Hombres en mi vida
1933 The California Trail
      Dos noches
      No dejes la puerta abierta
1934 La ciudad de cartón
      Dos más uno, dos
      Granaderos del amor
      Tres amores
1935 ¡Asegure a su mujer!
      Señora casada necesita marido
      Te quiero con locura
1936 El diablo del mar
1938 California Frontier
      Mis dos amores
      La vida bohemia
1939 Frontiers of '49
      Los hijos mandan
      La Inmaculada
      Miracle on Main Street (foreign version)
      El otro soy yo
      Papá soltero
      El trovador de la radio
      Verbena trágica

1940 Tengo fe en ti
1941 Hold Back the Dawn

Villarreal, Julio
1930 Del mismo barro
      El dios del mar
      El valiente
1931 Charlie Chan Carries On (foreign version)
      El código penal
      Don Juan diplomático
      La gran jornada
      El impostor
      La ley del harem
      El pasado acusa
      El proceso de Mary Dugan
1933 El rey de los gitanos
1955 Seven Cities of Gold

Villasainte, Albert
1959 Thunder in the Sun

Villasana, Juan
1950 Panic in the Streets

Villaseñor, Salvador
1930 Las campanas de Capistrano

Villavicenio, Adolfo
1930 Las campanas de Capistrano

Villegas, Lucio
1930 East Is West (foreign version)
      La voluntad del muerto
1931 Del infierno al cielo
      La fruta amarga
      La gran jornada
      La mujer X
      El proceso de Mary Dugan
1934 La cruz y la espada
      Dos más uno, dos
      Granaderos del amor
      Nada más que una mujer
1935 Alas sobre el Chaco
      Julieta compra un hijo
      No matarás
      Rosa de Francia
      Te quiero con locura
1936 El crimen de media noche
1938 The Renegade Ranger
1939 The Fighting Gringo
      Papá soltero
      El trovador de la radio
1940 The Mark of Zorro
1946 Border Bandits
      The Red Dragon
1947 Pirates of Monterey
1948 Old Los Angeles

Villiers, Patrick
1959 John Paul Jones

Viñas, Pedro
1939 Verbena trágica

Vincenot, Louis
1934 Limehouse Blues

Vincent, Allen
1929 Mother's Boy
1936 Sutter's Gold
1941 The Face Behind the Mask

Vincent, Bernice
1939 Straight to Heaven

Vincent, Billy see Vincent, Sailor

Vincent, Elmore
1955 Good Morning, Miss Dove
1956 The Lone Ranger
1959 The FBI Story

Vincent, James
1915 The Melting Pot
1916 Gold and the Woman
1931 Such Is Life

Vincent, Romo
1937 Music for Madame
1950 The Toast of New Orleans
1951 Hurricane Island

Vincent, Russ
1947 The Last Round-Up
1949 The Prairie
1951 Cuban Fireball

Vincent, Sailor same as Vincent, Billy; Vincent, Sailor Billy
1935 The Irish in Us
1943 Yankee Doodle Dandy

1944 The San Antonio Kid
1946 Bringing Up Father
1947 The Mighty McGurk
1948 Big City
1953 The Man Behind the Gun
      So Big

Vincent, Virginia
1953 Taxi
1959 The Black Orchid

Vinci, Eddie
1949 Thieves' Highway

Vines, Notable
1941 Sullivan's Travels

Vining, Laurie J.
1953 Thunder Bay

Vinna, Padre Francisca de la
1914 Rose of the Rancho

Vinson, Gary
1959 Yellowstone Kelly

Vinson, Helen
1933 Grand Slam
1934 Broadway Bill
1935 The Wedding Night
1944 Chip Off the Old Block

Vinton, Arthur
1934 Stand Up and Cheer!

Vinton, Horace
1917 A Night in New Arabia

Virgo, Peter
1947 Body and Soul
1949 Knock on Any Door
      The Undercover Man
      We Were Strangers
1951 The Harlem Globetrotters
      Saturday's Hero

Virzie, Eleanor
1936 Rose of the Rancho
1938 Road Demon
      Speed to Burn
1939 Winner Take All

Visaroff, Michael
1928 The Night Bird
      Ramona
      We Americans
1931 Chinatown After Dark
1933 Let's Fall in Love
1934 The Cat's-Paw
      Wagon Wheels
1936 Paddy O'Day
1940 Charlie Chan at the Wax Museum
1942 Woman of the Year
1944 An American Romance
1946 Don Ricardo Returns
1947 Desperate
      Northwest Outpost

Visaroff, Nina
1936 Paddy O'Day

Vischer, Blanca
1932 El caballero de la noche
1933 It's Great to Be Alive (foreign version)
      No dejes la puerta abierta
1934 La ciudad de cartón
      El tango en Broadway
1935 ¡Asegure a su mujer!
1937 El carnaval del diablo
      The Devil's Playground
1938 Dangerous to Know
      Daughter of Shanghai
1946 Without Reservations

Vital, Geymond same as Vital
1931 Nuit d'Espagne
      Le père célibataire

Vitale, Joseph
1948 The Paleface
1949 Illegal Entry
1956 Serenade
1957 The Deerslayer
1958 Wild Is the Wind

Vitch, Eddie
1935 Charlie Chan in Paris

Vitek, Lorelei
1960 Studs Lonigan

Vitina, Dolores
1958 Never Love a Stranger

Vittes, Louis
1957 Pawnee
1959 The Oregon Trail

Vitti, Ralph
1957 Raintree County

Viva, Sim
1935 L'homme des Folies Bergère

Vivian, Robert
1918 Out of a Clear Sky

Vivyan, John
1959 Imitation of Life

Vlasek, June same as Lang, June

Vodiany, Mathew
1937 Natalka Poltavka

Vodnoy, Max
1937 Green Fields
1938 The Singing Blacksmith

Vogan, Emmett same as Vogan, Emmet
1935 The Irish in Us
1936 It Had to Happen
      Star for a Night
1937 Black Legion
      Charlie Chan at the Olympics
1938 The Beloved Brat
      Mr. Moto's Gamble
      Speed to Burn
1939 Confessions of a Nazi Spy
1940 Geronimo
      Santa Fe Trail
1942 Gentleman Jim
      Little Tokyo, U.S.A.
      Tortilla Flat
      We Were Dancing
      Wings for the Eagle
1943 Crime Smasher
      In Old Oklahoma
      Margin for Error
1944 An American Romance
      Andy Hardy's Blonde Trouble
      Lady, Let's Dance!
1945 Colorado Pioneers
      Escape in the Fog
1946 Dangerous Money
      Notorious
      Rendezvous 24
      Three Wise Fools
1947 The Jolson Story
      Last of the Redmen
      My Wild Irish Rose
1948 Docks of New Orleans
      Fighting Father Dunne
1949 Brothers in the Saddle
      The Sky Dragon
1953 Ride, Vaquero!

Vogeding, Frederik same as Vogeding, Fred; Vogeding, Frederick
1935 Charlie Chan in Shanghai
1936 Dangerous Intrigue
      Human Cargo
1937 Charlie Chan at the Olympics
      Think Fast, Mr. Moto
1938 Happy Landing
      Mr. Moto Takes a Chance
1939 City in Darkness
      Confessions of a Nazi Spy
1940 Escape
      Knute Rockne—All American
      The Man I Married
      They Dare Not Love
      Three Faces West
1942 All Through the Night

Vogel, Eleanore same as Vogel, Eleanor
1947 The Farmer's Daughter
1955 Good Morning, Miss Dove

Vohs, Joan
1949 The Girl from Jones Beach
1953 Fort Ti
1955 Fort Yuma

Voigt, John (not the same as Voight, Jon) see Zilzer, Wolfgang

Volkie, Ralph
1940 East of the River
1947 It Had To Be You
1949 Knock on Any Door
      The Story of Seabiscuit
      The Undercover Man

1951 New Mexico
Slaughter Trail
1953 The Eddie Cantor Story
So Big
1954 Dangerous Mission
1956 Serenade
1959 Al Capone

Volusia, Eros
1942 Rio Rita

Von Seyffertitz, Gustav *see* **Seyffertitz, Gustav von**

Von Sternberg, Josef *see* **Sternberg, Josef von**

Von Stroheim, Erich *see* **Stroheim, Erich von**

Von Altenberger, Franz
1940 Escape to Glory

Von Boden, Lucy
1944 Address Unknown

Von Brincken, William *same as* **Beckwith, Roger; Brincken, Wilhelm von; Vaughan, William; Vaughn, William**
1937 Charlie Chan at the Olympics
Thank You, Mr. Moto
1939 Confessions of a Nazi Spy
1942 The Navy Comes Through
1943 Action in the North Atlantic

Von Eltz, Theodore *same as* **Von Eltz, Theodor**
1926 Laddie
1930 The Arizona Kid
1931 Beyond Victory
1936 Below the Deadline
1943 Air Force
1944 Since You Went Away
1945 Rhapsody in Blue
1946 Saratoga Trunk

Vonic, Gloria
1931 Cimarron

Von Jordan, Egon *see* **Jordan, Egon von**

Von Meter, Harry *same as* **Meter, Harry von**
1916 Lone Star
1917 My Fighting Gentleman
1918 His Birthright
1919 Diane of the Green Van

Von Morhart, Hans *same as* **Morhart, Hans von; Morhart, Herbert**
1930 ¡De frente, marchen!
1937 It Could Happen to You
1940 Escape to Glory
The Man I Married
1942 Submarine Raider
Three Hearts for Julia
1943 Action in the North Atlantic
Crash Dive
1945 Where Do We Go From Here?

Vonn, Viola
1952 The Big Sky

Von Pelt, Chester
1958 Tonka

Von Pelt, Levi
1958 Tonka

Von Schiller, Carl *same as* **Schiller, Carl**
1915 Captain Courtesy

von Twardowski, Hans *see* **Twardowski, Hans**

Von Zell, Harry
1946 Till the End of Time
1950 Two Flags West

Von Zerneck, Peter
1946 Notorious

Voorhees, Bill
1945 Where Do We Go From Here?

Vorhaus, Bernard
1939 Fisherman's Wharf
Way Down South
1940 Three Faces West
1941 Lady from Louisiana
1950 So Young, So Bad

Vosburgh, Jack *could be same as* **Vosburgh, John**
1917 My Fighting Gentleman
Southern Pride

Vosburgh, John *could be same as* **Vosburgh, Jack**
1932 Hearts of Humanity

Voskovec, George
1952 Anything Can Happen
The Iron Mistress
1957 Twelve Angry Men

Vosper, John
1944 Mr. Skeffington
1946 Notorious

Voss, Carl
1936 General Spanky

Vosselli, Judith
1934 The Great Flirtation

Votrian, Peter
1955 A Man Called Peter
1957 The Oklahoman

Votrian, Ralph J.
1956 Pillars of the Sky

Voulgaris, Antonios
1954 Barefoot Battalion

Vroom, Frederick
1918 Little Red Decides
1920 A Tokio Siren

Vroom, Henry
1946 Without Reservations
1948 Tap Roots

Vuolo, Tito
1948 Cry of the City
The Luck of the Irish
1949 House of Strangers
1950 Deported
1951 The Great Caruso
The Raging Tide
Saturday's Hero
1957 The Midnight Story

Vye, Murvyn
1959 Al Capone

Vynnychok, M.
1939 Cossacks in Exile

Waagenaar, Sam
1943 Action in the North Atlantic

Wade, Bessie *same as* **Wade, Besse**
1938 The Buccaneer
1941 Birth of the Blues
The Face Behind the Mask
1943 Hitler's Children
The Meanest Man in the World
1948 Unconquered
1949 Pinky

Wade, Boots
1959 Night of the Quarter Moon

Wade, David
1940 Knute Rockne—All American

Wade, Ernestine
1957 The Guns of Fort Petticoat

Wade, John H.
1928 The Midnight Ace

Wade, Lindy
1942 Syncopation

Wade, Roy
1932 Hypnotized

Wade, Russell
1943 Ladies' Day
The Leopard Man
1946 Renegade Girl

Wade, Vanita
1942 Song of the Islands

Wadelow, Diane
1948 Unconquered

Wadsworth, Henry
1934 Operator 13

Wadsworth, Sally
1942 Mexican Spitfire Sees a Ghost
1943 Ladies' Day

Wadsworth, William
1915 Cohen's Luck
1917 The Little Chevalier
1917? Barnaby Lee

Wafford, a pig
1937 Waikiki Wedding

Wagenheim, Charles
1940 Charlie Chan at the Wax Museum
1941 They Dare Not Love
1944 An American Romance
1945 The House on 92nd St.
Salome, Where She Danced
1947 Pirates of Monterey
1948 Cry of the City
The Miracle of the Bells
1950 A Lady Without Passport
Mystery Street
1951 The House on Telegraph Hill
Jim Thorpe—All-American
Molly
A Streetcar Named Desire
The Tall Target
1953 Beneath the 12-Mile Reef

Waggner, George *same as* **Waggoner, George; West, Joseph**
1922 The Great Alone
1936 Sea Spoilers
1938 Outlaw Express
1940 The Fatal Hour
Phantom of Chinatown
1949 The Fighting Kentuckian
1957 Pawnee

Waggner, Shy
1949 The Fighting Kentuckian

Waggoner, George *see* **Waggner, George**

Wagner, Billie
1918 The Kaiser's Finish

Wagner, Carlyn
1918 The Spreading Evil

Wagner, Ed
1959 The FBI Story

Wagner, Fernando
1955 Seven Cities of Gold
1958 Sierra Baron

Wagner, Jack
1926 The Fighting Edge
1927 McFadden's Flats
1936 Dancing Pirate
1945 A Medal for Benny

Wagner, Lawrence
1931 Street Scene

Wagner, Max *same as* **Barón, Max**
1930 El último de los Vargas
El valiente
1931 Cuerpo y alma
El pasado acusa
1935 Charlie Chan in Shanghai
1936 Charlie Chan at the Race Track
Dancing Pirate
Show Boat
1937 Black Legion
Border Cafe
1938 Mr. Moto's Gamble
Passport Husband
1939 Mr. Moto in Danger Island
The Return of the Cisco Kid
Waterfront
1940 Charlie Chan in Panama
1941 The Mexican Spitfire's Baby
Ride on Vaquero
1942 Mexican Spitfire's Elephant
Syncopation
1944 Hi, Beautiful
1945 A Medal for Benny
Where Do We Go From Here?
1948 Half Past Midnight
The Miracle of the Bells
1951 Jim Thorpe—All-American
1952 The Big Sky
The Raiders
1956 Westward Ho the Wagons!

Wagner, Pauline
1941 Hold Back the Dawn
New York Town

Wagner, Rob *(writer) same as* **Wagner, Robert** *(writer)*
1916 A Yoke of Gold
1928 Anybody Here Seen Kelly?

Wagner, Robert *(actor)*
1953 Beneath the 12-Mile Reef
1954 Broken Lance
1955 White Feather
1960 All the Fine Young Cannibals

Wagner, Sid
1948 Fighting Father Dunne

Wagner, William
1936 My American Wife
1937 Maid of Salem
1938 Gateway
Happy Landing

Wah, Tso Dak
1941 Min Jok Jay Hung Sing

Wahl, Adiel F.
1951 Tomahawk

Wahlbom, Nils
1930 Un hombre de suerte (foreign version)

Waid, Dan
1915? The Beachcomber

Wain, Dick
1919 Behind the Door

Waipahu, Lehua
1917 The Bottle Imp

Waite, Malcolm
1926 Blarney
1942 The Navy Comes Through

Waites, Hunter
1950 Panic in the Streets

Waizman, Max
1942 The Navy Comes Through

Wakefield, Marjory
1921 By Right of Birth

Wakely, Jimmy
1948 Silver Trails
1954 Arrow in the Dust

Waki, George
1951 Go for Broke!

Walberg, Bobby
1941 Adam Had Four Sons

Walburn, Freddie *same as* **Walburn, Fred**
1938 Gateway
1939 The Escape
1943 The Gang's All Here
The Meanest Man in the World

Walburn, Raymond
1934 Broadway Bill
The Great Flirtation
1938 Gateway
1939 Heaven with a Barbed Wire Fence
Let Freedom Ring
1941 Louisiana Purchase
1943 Dixie

Walcamp, Marie
1916 Hop, the Devil's Brew
1918 Tongues of Flame

Walcott, George
1940 Murder over New York
1942 Submarine Raider

Walcott, William
1923 Backbone

Wald, Jerry
1940 Three Cheers for the Irish
1942 Across the Pacific
All Through the Night
Juke Girl
1943 Action in the North Atlantic
1945 Pride of the Marines
1947 Humoresque
1948 Key Largo
1950 The Breaking Point
Young Man with a Horn

Wald, John
1940 Elsa Maxwell's Public Deb No. 1
1942 Little Tokyo, U.S.A.
1943 Gangway for Tomorrow
Margin for Error

Wald, Malvin
1949 The Undercover Man
1959 Al Capone

Walden, Barbara
1959   Night of the Quarter Moon

Waldis, Otto
1948   Call Northside 777
1949   Border Incident
1952   Anything Can Happen
1953   The Stars Are Singing
1956   Man from Del Rio

Waldman, Leibele *same as* **Waldman, Leibele, Cantor; Waldman, Leible; Waldman, Louis, Cantor**
1931   The Voice of Israel
1933   The Eternal Jew
1936   Love and Sacrifice
1937   I Want to Be a Mother
1939   Kol Nidre
1940   The Great Advisor
1941   Mazel Tov Yidden
1950   Monticello, Here We Come!

Waldo, Janet
1940   If I Had My Way
        The Way of All Flesh

Waldridge, Harold
1932   The Heart of New York
1936   Dancing Pirate
        Show Boat

Waldron, Andrew
1922   When East Comes West
1924   Down by the Rio Grande

Waldron, Charles
1936   Ramona
1940   Three Faces West
1945   Rhapsody in Blue

Waldron, Charles, Jr.
1948   Open Secret

Waldron, Jackee
1950   Annie Get Your Gun

Waldron, John A.
1932   Hypnotized

Waldron, May *see* **Robson, Mrs. Stuart**

Waldron, Wendy
1952   Trail of the Arrow

Wales, Ethel
1930   Tom Sawyer
1933   Ever in My Heart
1939   In Old Caliente
1948   Unconquered

Wales, Wally *see* **Taliaferro, Hal**

Walker, Algernon G.
1957   Burden of Truth

Walker, Mrs. Allan *same as* **Walker, Mrs. Allen**
1917   The Call of Her People
        The Little Samaritan

Walker, Arthur
1943   Cabin in the Sky

Walker, Betty
1951   Molly

Walker, Bill (*African-American actor*) *same as* **Walker, William "Bill"**
1947   The Foxes of Harrow
1950   No Way Out
        Young Man with a Horn
1951   The Harlem Globetrotters
        The Well
1953   Bright Road
        Sangaree
1955   The Far Horizons
        Good Morning, Miss Dove
        A Man Called Peter
        The View from Pompey's Head
1957   Raintree County
1958   Ride a Crooked Trail
1959   Porgy and Bess
1960   Take a Giant Step

Walker, Bob *see* **Walker, Robert 1888–1954**

Walker, Charlotte
1915   The Kindling
1925   The Manicure Girl
        The Midnight Girl

Walker, Cheryl
1948   Reaching from Heaven

Walker, Clint
1959   Yellowstone Kelly

Walker, Elaine
1960   Studs Lonigan

Walker, Francis
1942   Lawless Plainsmen

Walker, Gene
1959   Night of the Quarter Moon

Walker, George
1929   Redskin
1950   Panic in the Streets

Walker, H. M.
1930   Una cana al aire
        Locuras de amor
        El príncipe del dólar
        El príncipe del dólar (*foreign version*)
1931   Los calaveras
        Los calaveras (*foreign version*)
        Monerías
        Noche de duendes
        Pardon Us
        Pardon Us (*foreign version*)
        Politiquerías

Walker, Harry
1933   Song of the Eagle

Walker, Helen
1948   Call Northside 777

Walker, Jessie
1949   Souls of Sin

Walker, Jimmy
1954   Hell's Half Acre

Walker, Johnnie (*prod*)
1935   The Yiddish King Lear

Walker, Johnny (*actor*) *same as* **Walker, John; Walker, Johnnie**
1915   Cohen's Luck
1922   Captain Fly-by-Night
1925   The Scarlet West
1930   The Melody Man

Walker, June
1960   The Unforgiven

Walker, Ken
1960   All the Fine Young Cannibals

Walker, Lillian
1950   Panic in the Streets

Walker, Nella
1933   Ever in My Heart
1934   Behold My Wife!
1935   Bordertown
        McFadden's Flats
1936   Klondike Annie
1938   The Rage of Paris
1942   We Were Dancing
1943   Wintertime

Walker, Pax
1946   G. I. War Brides

Walker, Ray
1936   Laughing Irish Eyes
1937   Big City
        One Mile from Heaven
1939   Mr. Moto in Danger Island
1940   New Moon
1943   The Amazing Mrs. Holliday
1946   Dark Alibi
1948   Fighting Father Dunne
1950   Chinatown at Midnight
1951   The Harlem Globetrotters
        The Raging Tide

Walker, Robert 1888–1954 *same as* **Walker, Bob**
1917   A Wife by Proxy
1925   A Daughter of the Sioux
        Tonio, Son of the Sierras
        Warrior Gap
1935   Captured in Chinatown
1936   Custer's Last Stand
        Hair-Trigger Casey

Walker, Robert 1918–1951
1943   Bataan
1944   Since You Went Away
1946   The Sailor Takes a Wife

Walker, Stuart
1939   King of Chinatown

Walker, Tommy
1950   Battleground

Walker, Virginia
1945   Nob Hill

Walker, Wally
1941   Playmates
1948   Docks of New Orleans
1958   Houseboat

Walker, Walter
1934   Imitation of Life
        Strange Wives

Walker, William "Bill" (*African-American actor*) *see* **Walker, Bill** (*African-American actor*)

Walker, William, Sr.
1950   Panic in the Streets

Walks Alone
1934   Laughing Boy

Wall, Boots
1914   Uncle Tom's Cabin

Wall, David
1914   Northern Lights
1915   Time Lock Number 776
1918   The Birth of a Race

Wall, Fay
1942   Foreign Agent
1945   Betrayal from the East

Wall, Geraldine
1944   Black Magic
1945   The Valley of Decision
1947   Dark Delusion
1948   Unconquered

Wall, Margaret
1915   Under Southern Skies

Wallace, Alice
1949   The Girl from Jones Beach
1950   Annie Get Your Gun

Wallace, Babe *see* **Wallace, Emmett "Babe"**

Wallace, Beryl
1938   The Rage of Paris
1943   Let's Have Fun

Wallace, Bill
1947   Desperate
1948   The Miracle of the Bells
        Unconquered
1954   Broken Lance

Wallace, Bob
1946   Without Reservations

Wallace, Catherine
1919   Toby's Bow
1934   Broadway Bill

Wallace, Coley
1953   The Joe Louis Story

Wallace, Dick
1932   Hearts of Humanity

Wallace, Emmett "Babe" *same as* **Wallace, Babe**
1939   The Devil's Daughter
1943   Stormy Weather
1948   The Fight Never Ends

Wallace, Fred
1936   Dimples
        Star for a Night

Wallace, George
1952   The Big Sky
        Japanese War Bride
1954   Drums Across the River

Wallace, Harry
1931   Street Scene

Wallace, Helen *could be same as* **Wallace, Helene**
1947   Marshal of Cripple Creek
1948   Moonrise
1949   The Undercover Man
1955   The Far Horizons
1957   The Midnight Story
1960   The Dark at the Top of the Stairs

Wallace, Helene *could be same as* **Wallace, Helen**
1915   The Grandee's Ring

Wallace, Irene
1913   Traffic in Souls

Wallace, Irving
1956   The Burning Hills

Wallace, Jack
1936   Klondike Annie

Wallace, Jean
1941   Louisiana Purchase
1949   Jigsaw
1951   Native Son

Wallace, Joe
1949   The Red Menace

Wallace, John
1937   Slave Ship
1941   Dead Men Tell

Wallace, King
1939   El otro soy yo
        Papá soltero

Wallace, Morgan
1931   Smart Money
1935   Rendezvous
1936   Human Cargo
        Sutter's Gold
1937   The Californian
        Charlie Chan at the Olympics
1939   Mr. Moto Takes a Vacation
        The Mystery of Mr. Wong

Wallace, Ramsey
1918   Woman and the Law

Wallace, Raymond
1918   The Hell Cat

Wallace, Regina
1942   All Through the Night
1944   Mr. Skeffington
1948   The Miracle of the Bells

Wallace, Richard
1927   McFadden's Flats
1930   Anybody's War

Wallace, Royce
1960   Take a Giant Step

Wallach, Eli
1956   Baby Doll

Waller, Mrs. Allan
1915   The Clemenceau Case

Waller, Eddy *same as* **Waller, Eddie; Waller, Eddy C.**
1939   Allegheny Uprising
        The Cisco Kid and the Lady
        The Return of the Cisco Kid
        Stand Up and Fight
1940   Geronimo
        Santa Fe Trail
        Viva Cisco Kid
1941   Road Agent
        Western Union
1942   Juke Girl
        Shut My Big Mouth
        Wings for the Eagle
1944   An American Romance
1946   Sun Valley Cyclone
1948   Renegades of Sonora
1949   Lust for Gold
        Massacre River
1950   The Furies
        The Traveling Saleswoman
1951   Cavalry Scout
1952   Indian Uprising
1955   Foxfire

Waller, Fats
1943   Stormy Weather

Wallerstein, Rose
1934   The Youth of Russia
1937   The Cantor's Son

Wallick, Ann
1920   Humoresque

Walling, William *same as* **Walling, Will; Walling, Will R.**
1927   The Devil's Saddle
        The Princess from Hoboken
        Winners of the Wilderness
1928   The Jazz Singer
        The Mating Call
1929   Welcome Danger

Wallis, Hal B.
1933   Ever in My Heart
1935   Black Fury
        Bordertown
        A Night at the Ritz
1936   The Green Pastures
1937   Black Legion
        Prairie Thunder

1938	The Beloved Brat
1939	Confessions of a Nazi Spy
	Daughters Courageous
	Waterfront
1940	East of the River
	The Fighting 69th
	Knute Rockne—All American
	Santa Fe Trail
	Three Cheers for the Irish
1942	All Through the Night
	In This Our Life
	Juke Girl
	They Died With Their Boots On
1943	Air Force
	Yankee Doodle Dandy
1950	The Furies
1955	The Rose Tattoo
1958	Wild Is the Wind
1959	Last Train from Gun Hill

Wallis, Samuel
1942   King of the Stallions

Waln, Nora
1919   Auction of Souls

Walorz, John
1950   Panic in the Streets

Walper, Cicely
1960   Walk Like a Dragon

Walpole, Stanley
1921   The Sport of the Gods

Walron, Helen
1923   The Huntress

Walsh, Arthur
1948   Big City
1949   Ranger of Cherokee Strip
1950   Battleground
1952   The Fabulous Senorita
1958   The Last Hurrah

Walsh, Bill (*actor*)
1958   Flaming Frontier

Walsh, Bill (*prod*)
1955   Davy Crockett, King of the Wild Frontier
1956   Davy Crockett and the River Pirates
       Westward Ho the Wagons!

Walsh, George
1923   The Miracle Makers
1932   Me and My Gal
1936   Klondike Annie
       Pinto Rustlers

Walsh, Gordon
1952   Red Ball Express

Walsh, John D.
1925   The Midnight Girl

Walsh, Johnny *same as* **Walsh, John**
1939   The Adventures of Huckleberry Finn
1944   An American Romance
1947   Humoresque

Walsh, Judy
1952   The Half-Breed
       Hiawatha

Walsh, Raoul *same as* **Walsh, R. A.; Walsh, Raoul A.**
1915   The Birth of a Nation
1917   The Conqueror
1918   The Prussian Cur
       Woman and the Law
1919   Evangeline
1929   In Old Arizona
1931   Del infierno al cielo
1932   Me and My Gal
1936   Klondike Annie
1942   Gentleman Jim
       They Died With Their Boots On
1949   Colorado Territory
1951   Distant Drums
1954   Saskatchewan
1957   Band of Angels
1959   The Sheriff of Fractured Jaw

Walsh, Richard
1947   Humoresque

Walsh, Ronald
1959   Shake Hands with the Devil

Walsh, Tom
1915   The Danger Signal

Walshe, Pat
1949   Pinky
1950   Panic in the Streets

Walski, Gene, Lieut.
1926   Into Her Kingdom

Walter, Bruno
1947   Carnegie Hall

Walter, Paula
1939   Mirele Efros

Walters, Albert
1953   The Eddie Cantor Story

Walters, Dickie
1936   Star for a Night

Walters, Esther
1942   Tales of Manhattan

Walters, Floyd
1948   The Time of Your Life

Walters, Glen
1934   Stand Up and Cheer!
1951   The House on Telegraph Hill

Walters, Jack
1937   The Plainsman
1939   Frontiers of '49

Walters, Luana
1936   Aces and Eights
1937   Souls at Sea
1938   The Buccaneer
1939   King of Chinatown
1941   Road Agent
1942   Lawless Plainsmen

Walters, Polly
1931   Smart Money

Walters, Selene
1959   The FBI Story

Walthall, Henry B.
1915   The Birth of a Nation
1926   The Barrier
1929   In Old California
1930   Abraham Lincoln
1932   Me and My Gal
1934   Judge Priest

Walton, Douglas
1934   Charlie Chan in London
1937   Nation Aflame
1939   Bad Lands
1940   Northwest Passage (Book I—Rogers' Rangers)
       Too Many Girls
1941   Hurry, Charlie, Hurry

Walton, Fred
1930   The Last Dance
1934   Broadway Bill
       The Cat's-Paw
1936   Dangerous Intrigue

Walton, Gladys
1920   The Secret Gift
1922   The Guttersnipe
       Second Hand Rose
       The Top O' the Morning

Walton, Paul
1937   Souls at Sea

Wan, Ging
1939?   A Chinese Gains a Fortune in America

Wanamaker, Sam
1948   My Girl Tisa
1950   Give Us This Day

Wanderers
1956   Rockin' the Blues

Wang, James *same as* **Wang, Jim**
1918   The City of Dim Faces
1921   Lotus Blossom
1922   East Is West
1929   Welcome Danger
1932   Charlie Chan's Chance
       The Secrets of Wu Sin
1934   Charlie Chan's Courage

Wang, Richard
1947   The Chinese Ring

Wanger, David
1959   The Last Angry Man

Wanger, Walter
1945   Salome, Where She Danced
1946   Canyon Passage
1948   Tap Roots
1949   Tulsa

Wangoman, Bryan
1918   The Hell Cat

War Eagle, John *same as* **War Eagle**
1950   Annie Get Your Gun
       Broken Arrow
       A Ticket to Tomahawk
       Winchester '73
1951   Apache Drums
       The Last Outpost
       Tomahawk
       Westward the Women
1952   Bugles in the Afternoon
1953   Ambush at Tomahawk Gap
       The Great Sioux Uprising
       Last of the Comanches
1954   The Black Dakotas
       They Rode West
1956   Westward Ho the Wagons!
1957   Dragoon Wells Massacre
1958   Tonka

Waram, Percy
1947   It Had To Be You
1950   The Big Hangover

Warburton, Cotton
1937   Big City

Warburton, John
1933   Charlie Chan's Greatest Case
1945   The Valley of Decision
1946   Saratoga Trunk
1955   Headline Hunters

Warcloud, Suni
1951   Jim Thorpe—All-American

Ward, Alan
1944   My Pal Wolf
1945   Betrayal from the East
1946   Notorious
       Till the End of Time

Ward, Alice
1931   Skyline
1932   The Rainbow Trail

Ward, Amelita
1943   Gangway for Tomorrow

Ward, Anthony *see* **Warde, Anthony**

Ward, Baby Ivy
1917   The Slacker (Metro Pictures Corp.)

Ward, Barney
1950?   Three Daughters

Ward, Bill *could be same as* **Ward, Billy**
1954   War Arrow

Ward, Billy (*child actor*), mid-1940s
1943   The Amazing Mrs. Holliday

Ward, Blackjack
1937   The Plainsman
1942   Shut My Big Mouth

Ward, Bobby
1919   As a Man Thinks

Ward, Carrie Clark *same as* **Ward, Carrie Clarke; Ward, Carrie Lee**
1917   The Conqueror
1920   The Paliser Case
1921   Black Roses
1923   Breaking into Society
1925   The Man in Blue

Ward, Colleen
1936   Star for a Night

Ward, Dorothy
1932   The Golden West

Ward, Fannie
1915   The Cheat
1916   For the Defense
       Witchcraft
1917   Unconquered

Ward, Frank
1942   Mokey

Ward, Jackie
1939   Straight to Heaven

Ward, Jay
1933   The Man Who Dared: An Imaginative Biography

Ward, John
1937   Boots and Saddles
       The Riders of the Whistling Skull
1938   Birthright

Ward, Katherine Clare
1935   Black Fury
1936   Klondike Annie

Ward, Lewis
1951   Saturday's Hero

Ward, Luci
1942   Lawless Plainsmen
1944   Riding West
1949   Rustlers

Ward, Lucille
1917   My Fighting Gentleman
1918   How Could You, Jean?
1922   The Woman He Loved
1935   The Little Colonel
1937   The Devil's Playground

Ward, Norman
1921   A Modern Cain

Ward, Tony *see* **Warde, Anthony**

Warde, Anthony *same as* **Ward, Anthony; Ward, Tony; Warde, Tony**
1939   Mr. Moto Takes a Vacation
1942   Three Hearts for Julia
1944   The Chinese Cat
1945   The Cisco Kid Returns
1946   Dark Alibi
       Don Ricardo Returns
1947   Bells of San Fernando
       King of the Bandits
1953   The Stars Are Singing
1959   Inside the Mafia

Warde, Ernest C.
1917   The Woman and the Beast
1919   The Lord Loves the Irish

Warde, Frederick
1917   Under False Colors

Warde, Harlan
1947   Buck Privates Come Home
       It Had To Be You
1948   Night Wind
1949   The Undercover Man
1951   The Magnificent Yankee
1957   Beau James

Warde, Shirley
1940   Murder over New York
1942   Dr. Gillespie's New Assistant
       Tortilla Flat

Warde, "Sonny Boy"
1921   The First Born

Warde, Tony *see* **Warde, Anthony**

Warden, Jack
1957   Edge of the City
       Twelve Angry Men

Ware, Ann
1953   Tonight We Sing

Ware, Darrell
1940   Elsa Maxwell's Public Deb No. 1
1943   Dixie

Ware, Eroy C.
1927?   You Can't Win

Ware, Harlan
1937   Maid of Salem

Ware, Helen
1930   Abraham Lincoln
1935   Romance in Manhattan

Ware, Juliet
1934   Massacre

Ware, Virginia
1947   Ride the Pink Horse

Warfield, Irene
1915   The Girl I Left Behind Me

Warfield, James
1919   Deliverance

Warfield, Natalie
1925   The Red Rider

Warfield, William
1951   Show Boat

Warga, Robin L. *same as* **Warga, Robin**
1959   Last Train from Gun Hill
1960   The Dark at the Top of the Stairs

Warick, Rick
1957   Gun Battle at Monterey
Waring, Joseph
1953   Conquest of Cochise
1955   Kiss of Fire
Waring, Richard
1944   Mr. Skeffington
Wark, Robert
1957   Naked in the Sun
Warnack, Henry Christeen same
    as **Warnack, H. C.**
1916   The Morals of Hilda
1917   The Conqueror
Warner, A. (prod)
1918   The Kaiser's Finish
Warner, Adele
1922   Sky High
Warner, Eltinge F.
1919   Desert Gold
Warner, Frank
1957   Run of the Arrow
Warner, Glenn "Pop"
1940   Knute Rockne—All
        American
Warner, H. B.
1920   Uncharted Channels
1932   Charlie Chan's Chance
        The Son-Daughter
1934   Behold My Wife!
1936   Rose of the Rancho
1938   The Toy Wife
1939   Let Freedom Ring
1940   New Moon
1943   Hitler's Children
Warner, Hansel
1945   Where Do We Go From
        Here?
Warner, J. B.
1922   Big Stakes
Warner, J. Wesley
1916   Ramona
1919   Scarlet Days
Warner, Jack L.
1935   Black Fury
        Bordertown
        A Night at the Ritz
1936   The Green Pastures
1937   Black Legion
        Prairie Thunder
1938   The Beloved Brat
1939   Confessions of a Nazi Spy
        Waterfront
1943   Action in the North
        Atlantic
        Air Force
        Yankee Doodle Dandy
1944   Mr. Skeffington
1945   Pride of the Marines
        Rhapsody in Blue
1946   Saratoga Trunk
1947   Humoresque
        My Wild Irish Rose
Warner, Jerry
1946   Bringing Up Father
        Slightly Scandalous
1947   Bowery Buckaroos
Warner, John see **Ulmer, Edgar G.**
Warner, Larry
1932   The Galloping Kid
Warner, Marguerite
1933   It's Great to Be Alive
1936   Show Boat
Warner, Pop see **Warner, Glenn
    "Pop"**
Warner, S. L.
1918   The Kaiser's Finish
Warren, Anne
1951   Little Big Horn
        Oh! Susanna
Warren, Bruce
1934   Imitation of Life
1937   One Mile from Heaven
        The Plainsman
1943   They Came to Blow Up
        America
1944   Mr. Skeffington
Warren, Charles Marquis
1949   Streets of Laredo
1951   Little Big Horn
        Oh! Susanna
1953   Arrowhead

1955   Seven Angry Men
1957   Trooper Hook
1958   Blood Arrow
Warren, E. Alyn same as **Warren,
    E. A.; Warren, E. Allyn;
    Warren, E. Alyn "Fred"** not the
    same as **Warren, Fred**
1918   The Wine Girl
1919   The Tiger Lily
        Yvonne from Paris
1920   Outside the Law
1921   No Woman Knows
        A Tale of Two Worlds
1922   East Is West
        Hungry Hearts
1926   Sweet Rosie O'Grady
1930   Abraham Lincoln
        East Is West
        Son of the Gods
1931   Fighting Caravans
1932   The Hatchet Man
1934   Limehouse Blues
        Wagon Wheels
1935   Chinatown Squad
1939   The Adventures of
        Huckleberry Finn
Warren, Ed
1941   Western Union
Warren, Elena
1947   Desperate
Warren, Fred not the same as
    Warren, E. Alyn
1920   The Man Who Dared
1922   Pawn Ticket 210
1927   California
        With Sitting Bull at the
        Spirit Lake Massacre
1928   The Crash
1929   In Old Arizona
1930   Abraham Lincoln
1932   Hypnotized
1934   The Cat's-Paw
        Operator 13
Warren, Gil
1949   The Story of Seabiscuit
1952   The Big Sky
Warren, Giles R.
1915   A Texas Steer
Warren, Gloria
1946   Dangerous Money
1947   Bells of San Fernando
Warren, Hamilton
1948   The Miracle of the Bells
Warren, James
1942   Seven Sweethearts
        Three Hearts for Julia
1945   Wanderer of the
        Wasteland
1946   Sunset Pass
Warren, Janet
1945   The Jade Mask
        The Shanghai Cobra
Warren, Jeannette
1936   Star for a Night
Warren, Jerry
1945   Where Do We Go From
        Here?
Warren, Jill
1944   Since You Went Away
Warren, Julie
1942   Mexican Spitfire at Sea
        Mexican Spitfire Sees a
        Ghost
Warren, Katharine
1950   Mystery Submarine
1951   The Tall Target
1952   Battles of Chief Pontiac
1953   The Man Behind the Gun
Warren, Mary
1921   Guile of Women
1922   Come On Over
Warren, Phillip
1940   Geronimo
Warren, Richard
1957   Gun Battle at Monterey
1958   The Rawhide Trail
Warren, Ruth same as **Warren,
    Ruth O.**
1931   The Guilty Generation
        Mr. Lemon of Orange
1933   Let's Fall in Love
1938   Passport Husband

1939   The Cisco Kid and the
        Lady
1944   Lake Placid Serenade
1950   Emergency Wedding
        No Way Out
1958   The Last Hurrah
Warren, Sam
1940?   Mr. Washington Goes to
        Town
Warren, Steve
1958   Gunfire at Indian Gap
Warrenton, Lule
1916   The Gilded Spider
Warrick, Ruth
1946   Song of the South
Warrocks, Andrew
1944   An American Romance
Warwick, Granville
1918   The Hun Within
Warwick, Helen
1930   Chijiku wo mawasuru
        chikara
Warwick, James
1930   Chijiku wo mawasuru
        chikara
Warwick, John
1916   The Woman in 47
Warwick, Leon
1944   An American Romance
Warwick, Robert
1919   Told in the Hills
1932   The Secrets of Wu Sin
        So Big
        Unashamed
1933   Charlie Chan's Greatest
        Case
1935   The Little Colonel
1936   The Bold Caballero
        Charlie Chan at the Race
        Track
        Sutter's Gold
1937   Souls at Sea
1940   New Moon
1941   Louisiana Purchase
        Sullivan's Travels
1942   Secret Enemies
1943   Deerslayer
        Dixie
        In Old Oklahoma
1947   Pirates of Monterey
1948   Fury at Furnace Creek
        Gentleman's Agreement
        Gun Smugglers
        Unconquered
1951   The Mark of the
        Renegade
1954   Passion
1955   Chief Crazy Horse
1956   Walk the Proud Land
1959   Night of the Quarter
        Moon
Washbrook, Don
1958   The Light in the Forest
Washburn, Beverly
1956   The Lone Ranger
Washburn, Bryant same as
    Washburn, Bryant, Sr.
1918   The Gypsy Trail
1922   Hungry Hearts
1926   Meet the Prince
1927   With Sitting Bull at the
        Spirit Lake Massacre
1935?   The Irish Gringo
1936   Ellis Island
        Sutter's Gold
1942   We Were Dancing
1943   The Girl from Monterrey
        The Law Rides Again
        Wagon Tracks West
1944   My Pal Wolf
1945   Betrayal from the East
        Johnny Angel
Washburn, Conway same as
    Washburne, Conway
1931   Street Scene
1933   Counsellor at Law
Washburn, Hazel
1918   The Ordeal of Rosetta
1922   The Mohican's Daughter
Washburn, Jack
1959   The Black Orchid

Washington, Benevenita
1936   The Green Pastures
Washington, Mrs. Bennie could be
    same as **Washington,
    Benevenita**
1953   The Sun Shines Bright
Washington, Billy
1956   Rockin' the Blues
Washington, Blue same as
    Washington, Edgar
1928   Ransom
        Wyoming
1937   Charlie Chan on
        Broadway
        The Plainsman
1939   Gone With the Wind
1949   Pinky
Washington, Booker T., III
1940   George Washington
        Carver
Washington, Charlie
1946?   Go Down, Death!
Washington, David
1960   Sergeant Rutledge
Washington, Edgar see
    Washington, Blue
Washington, Fannie
1938   The Toy Wife
Washington, Flora
1928   Tenderfeet
Washington, Ford L. "Buck"
1943   Cabin in the Sky
Washington, Frank
1951   The Harlem Globetrotters
Washington, Frederica (actress),
    circa 1922 could be same as
    Washington, Fredi (actress),
    mid-1930s
1922   Square Joe
Washington, Fredi (actress), mid-
    1930s could be same as
    Washington, Frederica
    (actress), circa 1922
1933   The Emperor Jones
1934   Imitation of Life
1937   One Mile from Heaven
Washington, George (actor)
1919   Come Out of the Kitchen
Washington, George (musician)
1950   Young Man with a Horn
1958   St. Louis Blues
Washington, Hannah
1935   The Littlest Rebel
Washington, Henry
1936   The Prisoner of Shark
        Island
Washington, Howard
1949   The Story of Seabiscuit
Washington, Kenny same as
    Washington, Kenneth
1940   While Thousands Cheer
1947   The Foxes of Harrow
1949   Pinky
1950   The Jackie Robinson Story
Washington, Mildred
1928   Tenderfeet
1929   Hearts in Dixie
Washington, William
1940   Broken Strings
1950   No Way Out
Washizu, Ruth
1930   Chijiku wo mawasuru
        chikara
Wassem, Rebecca see **Darcy,
    Sheila**
Waterman, Ida
1918   Amarilly of Clothes-Line
        Alley
        A Woman of Impulse
1920   On with the Dance
Waterman, Willard
1950   Mystery Street
Waters, Bunny
1948   Up in Central Park
1950   Annie Get Your Gun
1958   Home Before Dark
Waters, Dennis
1946   Sunset Pass

Waters, Ella Mae
1940   The Notorious Elinor Lee
Waters, Ethel
1943   Cabin in the Sky
1949   Pinky
1953   The Member of the Wedding
Waters, James
1957   The Brothers Rico
Waters, John
1927   Drums of the Desert
1929   The Overland Telegraph
        Sioux Blood
1947   The Mighty McGurk
Watkin, Lawrence Edward
1958   The Light in the Forest
Watkin, Pierre same as **Watkins, Pierre**
1936   It Had to Happen
1937   The Californian
        The Devil's Playground
        Waikiki Wedding
1938   Dangerous to Know
        Daughter of Shanghai
        Mr. Moto's Gamble
1939   King of Chinatown
1940   Geronimo
        Knute Rockne—All American
1942   Nazi Agent
        We Were Dancing
1943   Good Luck, Mr. Yates
        Jack London
        Riding High
        They Came to Blow Up America
1945   I Love a Bandleader
1946   G. I. War Brides
        Swamp Fire
1947   The Jolson Story
1948   Shanghai Chest
1949   Knock on Any Door
        The Story of Seabiscuit
        Tulsa
1950   The Big Hangover
        Emergency Wedding
        Last of the Buccaneers
        Rock Island Trail
        Sunset in the West
1958   Marjorie Morningstar
Watkins, Cornelius
1923   Deceit
Watkins, Edith
1944   Slightly Terrific
Watkins, George, Capt.
1953   Ride, Vaquero!
Watkins, Linda
1932   Charlie Chan's Chance
Watkins, Mary could be same as **Watkins, Mary Jane**
1923   Deceit
Watkins, Mary Jane could be same as **Watkins, Mary**
1932   The Black King
Watkins, Pierre see **Watkin, Pierre**
Watson, Adele
1927   A Harp in Hock
1931   Street Scene
Watson, Allan
1931   Delicious
Watson, Ben
1943   Gangway for Tomorrow
        The Ox-Bow Incident
1950   Stars in My Crown
1951   Across the Wide Missouri
Watson, Billy
1935   The Winning Ticket
1936   Show Boat
1938   In Old Chicago
1939   The Adventures of Huckleberry Finn
Watson, Bobby (actor) not the same as **Watson, Bobs** (child actor)
1936   After the Thin Man
1937   Song of the City
Watson, Bobs (child actor) not the same as **Watson, Bobby** (actor)
1936   Show Boat
1938   In Old Chicago

Watson, Coy, Jr.
1927   The Shamrock and the Rose
Deek Watson and The Brown Dots
1947   Boy! What a Girl!
        Sepia Cinderella
Watson, Delmar
1934   Straight Is the Way
1935   Annie Oakley
1936   Show Boat
        Silly Billies
1938   Breaking the Ice
1939   The Adventures of Huckleberry Finn
1941   New York Town
Watson, Duke
1948   Call Northside 777
1950   No Way Out
Watson, Frank
1937   The Plainsman
Watson, Gary
1940   Knute Rockne—All American
Watson, Harry
1923   Little Old New York
1936   Paddy O'Day
        Show Boat
1939   The Adventures of Huckleberry Finn
Watson, Hugh
1946   Dirty Gertie from Harlem, U.S.A.
Watson, Justice
1956   Death of a Scoundrel
Watson, Lane
1947   Buck Privates Come Home
Watson, Lucile
1946   Song of the South
Watson, Minor
1935   Charlie Chan in Paris
1936   Rose of the Rancho
1939   The Adventures of Huckleberry Finn
        Stand Up and Fight
1940   Viva Cisco Kid
1941   Birth of the Blues
        Western Union
1942   Gentleman Jim
        They Died With Their Boots On
        Woman of the Year
1943   Action in the North Atlantic
        Crash Dive
        Yankee Doodle Dandy
1946   Saratoga Trunk
1950   The Jackie Robinson Story
1952   Bright Victory
Watson, Robert
1948   The Paleface
Watson, Sheila
1951   Queen for a Day
Watt, Jack
1950   Colt .45
Watt, Nate
1921   The Hunger of the Blood
1937   Hills of Old Wyoming
Watters, George Manker
1930   Behind the Make-Up
Watts, Charles not the same as **Watts, Charles "Cotton"** or **Watts, Chick**
1953   The Jazz Singer
1955   The View from Pompey's Head
1956   Giant
1957   Raintree County
1958   The Lone Ranger and the Lost City of Gold
1960   Cimarron
Watts, Chick same as **Watts, Charles "Cotton"** not the same as **Watts, Charles**
1951   Yes Sir, Mr. Bones
Watts, Ethel
1921   The Gunsaulus Mystery
Watts, George
1940   Little Nellie Kelly
1941   Hurry, Charlie, Hurry
1942   Apache Trail

Watts, John
1947   Going to Glory, Come to Jesus
Watts, Jonas
1914   Dan
Watts, Peggy
1934   Stand Up and Cheer!
Watts, Twinkle
1944   Lake Placid Serenade
Watts, W. E.
1949   Thieves' Highway
Way, Guy
1955   The Long Gray Line
1960   Flaming Star
Waycoff, Leon see **Ames, Leon**
Wayne, Billy same as **Wayne, William**
1936   Charlie Chan at the Race Track
1937   Charlie Chan at the Olympics
        Charlie Chan on Broadway
1938   Happy Landing
        Passport Husband
        Rascals
1939   Heaven with a Barbed Wire Fence
        Winner Take All
1940   Elsa Maxwell's Public Deb No. 1
1941   Belle Starr
1942   All Through the Night
        In This Our Life
1948   The Miracle of the Bells
1949   The Girl from Jones Beach
1950   The Jackie Robinson Story
1951   Jim Thorpe—All-American
Wayne, Bob
1946   G. I. War Brides
Wayne, Carter
1936   Custer's Last Stand
Wayne, David
1949   Portrait of Jennie
1953   Tonight We Sing
1959   The Last Angry Man
Wayne, Frank
1937   It Could Happen to You
Wayne, Harte
1950   I Killed Geronimo
1951   Apache Drums
1953   The Man from the Alamo
Wayne, John
1933   Man from Monterey
        The Telegraph Trail
1934   'Neath the Arizona Skies
        The Star Packer
1935   Texas Terror
1936   Sea Spoilers
1939   Allegheny Uprising
1940   Three Faces West
1941   Lady from Louisiana
1943   In Old Oklahoma
1946   Without Reservations
1948   Fort Apache
        Red River
1949   The Fighting Kentuckian
        She Wore a Yellow Ribbon
        3 Godfathers
1950   Rio Grande
        Sands of Iwo Jima
1952   The Quiet Man
1954   Hondo
1956   The Searchers
Wayne, Maude
1918   Who Is to Blame?
Wayne, Patrick same as **Wayne, Pat**
1950   Rio Grande
1955   The Long Gray Line
1956   The Searchers
1959   The Young Land
Wayne, Robert
1916   A Man of Sorrow
Wayne, Stephen
1944   Since You Went Away
Wayne, Steve
1950   Sands of Iwo Jima
1953   The Charge at Feather River

Wayne, William see **Wayne, Billy**
1937   Black Legion
Wead, Frank (writer)
1935   Alas sobre el Chaco
Weatherwax, Jack
1948   Unconquered
Weatherwax, Rudd same as **Weatherwax, Ruddell**
1922   The Crow's Nest
Weaver, Charles
1949?   The Joint Is Jumpin'
Weaver, Dennis
1952   The Raiders
1953   Column South
        The Man from the Alamo
        The Nebraskan
1954   Dangerous Mission
        War Arrow
1955   Chief Crazy Horse
        Seven Angry Men
1958   Touch of Evil
Weaver, Doodles
1936   My American Wife
1944   Since You Went Away
1958   Frontier Gun
Weaver, Garland
1939   The Escape
Weaver, John V. A.
1938   The Adventures of Tom Sawyer
Weaver, Lee
1959   Al Capone
Weaver, Marjorie
1937   The Californian
        Life Begins in College
1939   The Cisco Kid and the Lady
1940   Charlie Chan's Murder Cruise
        Murder over New York
Weaver, Mattie
1949?   The Joint Is Jumpin'
Weaver, Merle L.
1945   Where Do We Go From Here?
Webb, Blanche
1943   Gangway for Tomorrow
Webb, Dorothy
1944   Chip Off the Old Block
Webb, George
1916   The Soul of Kura-San
1921   Fifty Candles
Webb, Harry S. same as **Webb, Henry S.**
1934   The Cactus Kid
        The Fighting Hero
1935   North of Arizona
        Wolf Riders
1936   El crimen de media noche
        Pinto Rustlers
1939   Daughter of the Tong
Webb, Ira S. same as **Webb, Ira**
1948   Shep Comes Home
1949   The Dalton Gang
1955   Kentucky Rifle
Webb, Jack
1950   The Men
Webb, James R. same as **Webb, James**
1939   Forged Passport
1952   The Iron Mistress
1953   The Charge at Feather River
1954   Apache
Webb, Kenneth
1922   Fair Lady
1925   The Beautiful City
Webb, Percy
1918   The Unbeliever
Webb, Richard
1941   Hold Back the Dawn
        Sullivan's Travels
1942   American Empire
1950   Sands of Iwo Jima
1951   Distant Drums
1953   The Nebraskan
1954   The Black Dakotas
Webb, Robert (African-American actor)
1940   Mystery in Swing

1942　　Take My Life
Webb, Robert D. (*dir*) *same as*
　Webb, Robert (*dir*)
1953　　Beneath the 12-Mile Reef
　　　　　The Glory Brigade
1955　　Seven Cities of Gold
　　　　　White Feather
Webber, Robert
1957　　Twelve Angry Men
Webber, Zelda
1934　　Stand Up and Cheer!
Weber, Ethel
1916　　Hop, the Devil's Brew
Weber, Harry
1917　　The Wild Girl
Weber, Joe
1925　　Friendly Enemies
Weber, Lois
1915　　Captain Courtesy
1916　　Hop, the Devil's Brew
1927　　Topsy and Eva
1934　　White Heat
Webster, Bob
1940　　Taku
Webster, Charles
1955　　Good Morning, Miss Dove
Webster, M. Coates
1946　　Cuban Pete
1948　　Renegades of Sonora
Webster, Mary
1957　　The Tin Star
Webster, Pete
1940　　Broken Strings
　　　　　Midnight Shadow
　　　　　While Thousands Cheer
1941　　Four Shall Die
Wechter, Julius
1950　　Young Man with a Horn
Wee, Gee
1947　　Little Mister Jim
Weed, Frank (*actor*)
1915　　A Texas Steer
1920　　The Tiger's Coat
Weeks, Barbara
1932　　White Eagle
1933　　Olsen's Big Moment
1934　　She Was a Lady
Weeks, George W.
1930　　Así es la vida
　　　　　Sombras de gloria
1933　　Dance Hall Hostess
Weems, Walter
1929　　Hearts in Dixie
1930　　Anybody's War
1940?　　Mr. Washington Goes to
　　　　　Town
Wehlen, Emmy
1916　　The Pretenders
1920　　Lifting Shadows
Wehling, Bob
1960　　The Sign of Zorro
Weible, Jimmy
1958　　Kings Go Forth
Weidenaar, Clair
1954　　Hell's Half Acre
Weidhaas, Oscar
1949　　The Red Menace
Weidler, George
1936　　Dimples
Weidler, Virginia
1937　　Maid of Salem
　　　　　Souls at Sea
Weidler, Walter
1936　　Dimples
Weidler, Warner
1936　　Dimples
Weidman, Jerome
1953　　The Eddie Cantor Story
Weigel, Paul *same as* **Weigle, Paul**
1916　　Witchcraft
1917　　The Bond Between
　　　　　Forbidden Paths
1918　　Me Und Gott
　　　　　The Only Road
1919　　Evangeline
1931　　Don Juan diplomático
　　　　　(*foreign version*)
　　　　　Die Maske Fällt
1936　　Sutter's Gold
1945　　A Tree Grows in Brooklyn
　　　　　Where Do We Go From
　　　　　Here?

Weil, Elvira
1917　　The Bride of Hate
1918　　Untamed
Weil, Harry
1931　　Delicious
Weil, Jeri
1955　　Violent Saturday
Weil, Patricia
1953　　The Man from the Alamo
1955　　Violent Saturday
Weil, Richard
1946　　The Gentleman
　　　　　Misbehaves
　　　　　Singin' in the Corn
Weiler, Lorraine
1922　　The Guttersnipe
Weinberg, Benjamin J. *same as*
　Weinberg, Bernard J.
1939　　A Brivele der Mamen
　　　　　Mamele
Weingarten, Lawrence
1935　　Rendezvous
1940　　Escape
Weinthal, Sylvia
1932　　Mazel Tov
Weintraub, Mrs.
1925　　Salome of the Tenements
Weintraub, Rebecca
1922　　Breaking Home Ties
1932　　Uncle Moses
1938　　Two Sisters
1939　　Tevya
Weir, Jane
1937　　Souls at Sea
Weirman, Marie
1915　　Under Southern Skies
Weis, Don
1952　　It's a Big Country: An
　　　　　American Anthology
Weisbart, David
1953　　The Charge at Feather
　　　　　River
1960　　Flaming Star
Weisberg, Louis
1939　　The Light Ahead
　　　　　Tevya
Weisman, Morris
1935　　The Yiddish King Lear
Weiss, Florence
1937　　The Cantor's Son
1938　　The Singing Blacksmith
1940　　Overture to Glory
Weiss, John
1915?　　The Beachcomber
Weiss, Louis
1932　　Border Devils
　　　　　Uncle Moses
1934　　Drums O' Voodoo
1935　　Cyclone of the Saddle
1936　　Custer's Last Stand
Weissman, Anna
1937　　The Holy Oath
Weissman, Dora
1935　　Shir Hashirim
1940　　The Great Advisor
Weissmuller, Johnny
1946　　Swamp Fire
Welch, Charles
1956　　Crowded Paradise
Welch, Harry
1958　　Tonka
Welch, James *same as* **Welch, Jim**
　could be same as **Welch, James**
　T. (*actor*), *circa 1918*
1925　　Tonio, Son of the Sierras
　　　　　Warrior Gap
1935　　Ruggles of Red Gap
Welch, James T. (*actor*), *circa*
　1918 could be same as **Welch,**
　James
1918　　Me Und Gott
Welch, Joe
1915　　Time Lock Number 776
1917　　The Peddler
Welch, Lester
1958　　Seven Hills of Rome
Welch, Nelson
1953　　Tonight We Sing

Welch, Niles
1932　　Border Devils
　　　　　The Rainbow Trail
1933　　Let's Fall in Love
1935　　The Singing Vagabond
Welch, Robert L.
1948　　The Paleface
1949　　Top O' the Morning
Welch, Winfield Scott
1951　　The Harlem Globetrotters
Welden, Ben *same as* **Weldon, Ben**
1938　　Gateway
　　　　　Happy Landing
1939　　Stand Up and Fight
1942　　All Through the Night
1948　　The Dude Goes West
1950　　Buccaneer's Girl
　　　　　The Jackie Robinson Story
1953　　Thunder Bay
1956　　The Benny Goodman
　　　　　Story
Weldon, Jasper
1947　　The Foxes of Harrow
1949　　Pinky
1950　　No Way Out
Weldon, Joan
1958　　Home Before Dark
Weldon, Marion
1932　　Hypnotized
1938　　In Old Chicago
Weldon, Robert
1941　　Dead Men Tell
Well, Conrad
1958　　Tonka
Weller, Alfred
1920　　The Girl of My Heart
Weller, Calvin
1920　　The Girl of My Heart
Welles, Halsted
1959　　The Hanging Tree
Welles, Mel
1954　　Massacre Canyon
1955　　Duel on the Mississippi
Welles, Orson
1948　　The Lady from Shanghai
1957　　Man in the Shadow
1958　　Touch of Evil
Welling, Hal
1943　　Air Force
Wellman, Bill, Jr.
1960　　Sergeant Rutledge
Wellman, William A. *same as*
　Wellman, William
1920　　It's a Great Life
1929　　Chinatown Nights
1932　　The Hatchet Man
　　　　　So Big
1936　　Robin Hood of El Dorado
1938　　The Adventures of Tom
　　　　　Sawyer
1943　　The Ox-Bow Incident
1944　　Buffalo Bill
1950　　Battleground
1951　　Across the Wide Missouri
　　　　　Westward the Women
1952　　It's a Big Country: An
　　　　　American Anthology
　　　　　My Man and I
Wells, Alan
1949　　Apache Chief
Wells, Alexander J.
1958　　The Rawhide Trail
Wells, Betty
1942　　Tortilla Flat
Wells, Eleanor
1933　　It's Great to Be Alive
Wells, Evelyn
1940　　Kit Carson
Wells, Florence
1932　　The Forty-Niners
Wells, George
1950　　The Toast of New Orleans
1952　　It's a Big Country: An
　　　　　American Anthology
Wells, Gladys
1934　　Judge Priest
Wells, Jacqueline *see* **Bishop, Julie**
Wells, L. M.
1920　　Huckleberry Finn
1921　　The Girl from God's
　　　　　Country

Wells, Margaret
1946　　Till the End of Time
1948　　The Luck of the Irish
1951　　The Well
Wells, Marie
1936　　Klondike Annie
Wells, Maurice
1959　　The FBI Story
1960　　Ice Palace
Wells, Raymond
1915　　The Sable Lorcha
1918　　The Man Above the Law
1919?　　In the Land of the Setting
　　　　　Sun; or, Martyrs of
　　　　　Yesterday
Wells, Robert
1952　　The Fighter
Wells, Roxene
1959　　The Oregon Trail
Wells, Ted
1940　　Geronimo
Wells, William K.
1930　　Big Boy
1931　　The Cohens and Kellys in
　　　　　Africa
Welsch, Howard
1946　　Cuban Pete
1956　　Hot Blood
Welsh, Bill (*TV announcer*) *same*
　as **Welsh, William H.** *not the*
　same as **Welsh, William** (*actor*)
1951　　The Harlem Globetrotters
1952　　It's a Big Country: An
　　　　　American Anthology
Welsh, Harry "Zoop"
1935　　A Night at the Opera
　　　　　Rendezvous
Welsh, Scott
1921　　Bits of Life
Welsh, William (*actor*) *not the*
　same as **Welsh, Bill** (*TV*
　announcer)
1913　　Traffic in Souls
1919　　The Little Diplomat
1922　　The Scrapper
　　　　　The Top O' the Morning
1925　　The Red Rider
1935　　Ruggles of Red Gap
Welton, Myron
1950　　Emergency Wedding
Wendell, Howard
1954　　The Black Dakotas
1955　　The View from Pompey's
　　　　　Head
Wendell, William G.
1949　　Lost Boundaries
Wendorff, Laiola
1950　　No Way Out
Wendorff, Ruben *same as*
　Wendorf, Ruben; Wendorff,
　Rubin; Wendroff, R.;
　Wendroff, Rubin
1933　　The Eternal Jew
1935　　Shir Hashirim
1937　　Where Is My Child?
1938　　The Singing Blacksmith
1939　　Mirele Efros
1949　　Illegal Entry
1950　　No Way Out
Wenga
1927　　Primitive Love
Wengren, Dave
1935　　The Wedding Night
1941　　Mutiny in the Arctic
Wentworth, Martha
1945　　A Tree Grows in Brooklyn
1946　　Santa Fe Uprising
1947　　Marshal of Cripple Creek
　　　　　Oregon Trail Scouts
　　　　　Rustlers of Devil's
　　　　　Canyon
　　　　　Vigilantes of Boomtown
1952　　My Man and I
1955　　Blackboard Jungle
　　　　　Good Morning, Miss Dove
Wenzel, Art
1944　　Riding West
Wenzel, J. A.
1955　　The Lonesome Trail

Werbowetzka, Donia Stephania
1938 Marusia

Werckenthien, William
1940 Mystery in Swing

Werker, Alfred *same as* **Werker, Al; Werker, Alfred L.**
1925 The Wild Bull's Lair
1928 Kit Carson
1933 It's Great to Be Alive
1938 Gateway
1942 Whispering Ghosts
1944 My Pal Wolf
1947 Pirates of Monterey
1949 Lost Boundaries

Werner, Christine
1956 Giant

Werner, Leon
1937 It Could Happen to You

Wernicke, Otto
1931 La pura verdad (*foreign version*)

Wescoatt, Rusty
1950 Last of the Buccaneers
Sunset in the West
1951 Hurricane Island
When the Redskins Rode
1952 Brave Warrior
1954 Drums Across the River
1958 Touch of Evil

Wescott, H. G.
1940 The Ramparts We Watch

Wesley, Jay
1945 The House on 92nd St.

Wesley, John
1948 My Girl Tisa

Wesoly, Luba
1938 The Singing Blacksmith
1940 Overture to Glory

Wessel, Dick
1942 Gentleman Jim
Sunday Punch
They Died With Their Boots On
Three Hearts for Julia
Wings for the Eagle
1943 Action in the North Atlantic
Yankee Doodle Dandy
1944 An American Romance
1947 California
1949 Thieves' Highway
1950 The Jackie Robinson Story
Sands of Iwo Jima

Wessel, Jessie
1930 Toda una vida (*foreign version*)

Wessel, John
1918 Fields of Honor

Wesselhoeft, Eleanor
1931 Street Scene
1935 The Wedding Night
1940 The Man I Married

Wessell, Henri
1932 Harlem Is Heaven

Wesslen, Al
1939 Mr. Moto's Last Warning

Wessner, Lillian
1936 Yellow Cargo

Wesson, Dick
1951 Jim Thorpe—All-American
1953 The Charge at Feather River
The Man Behind the Gun

West, Charles *same as* **West, Charles H.**
1915 The Gambler of the West
1917 The Trouble Buster
1918 The Source

West, Claudine
1931 Jenny Lind
1932 The Son-Daughter
1942 We Were Dancing

West, Ed
1914 The Nightingale

West, Evelyn
1941 Birth of the Blues

West, Ford
1931 Cimarron
1933 King of the Wild Horses
1935 The Little Colonel

West, Hank (*African-American actor*)
1922 For His Mother's Sake

West, Henry
1916 Broken Chains
1920 The North Wind's Malice

West, James
1940 The Way of All Flesh

West, Joseph *see* **Waggner, George**

West, Lillian
1917 The Hidden Children
1918 Who Is to Blame?
1919 Auction of Souls
1931 Cimarron
1934 Broadway Bill
Stand Up and Cheer!
1935 The Little Colonel
1940 If I Had My Way
The Man I Married
1941 Louisiana Purchase
1942 Syncopation
1946 Notorious
1958 Home Before Dark

West, Mae
1936 Klondike Annie

West, Nathanael
1937 It Could Happen to You

West, Pat (*actor*)
1936 Sins of Man
1938 The Texans
1939 King of Chinatown
1940 Geronimo
1941 Birth of the Blues
Sullivan's Travels
1942 Mokey
Sunday Punch
1943 Air Force

West, Patricia
1947 Easy Come, Easy Go

West, Paul
1918 The Little Runaway
The Ordeal of Rosetta

West, Roland
1916 A Woman's Honor
1927 The Dove

West, Victor
1950 Bandit Queen
Train to Tombstone

West, Wally
1936 The Traitor
1940 Rhythm of the Rio Grande

Westberg, Margaret
1945 Where Do We Go From Here?

Westcott, Gordon
1935 A Night at the Ritz

Westcott, Helen
1949 The Girl from Jones Beach
1952 Battles of Chief Pontiac
1953 The Charge at Feather River
1956 Hot Blood
1958 The Last Hurrah
1960 Cimarron
Studs Lonigan

Wester, Carl
1946 The Face of Marble

Westerfield, James
1944 Since You Went Away
1955 Chief Crazy Horse
1960 The Plunderers
Wild River

Western, Johnny
1958 Fort Bowie

Westervelt, John
1931 Delicious

Westfall, Michael
1943 Wintertime

Westfall, Zenda
1948 Angel in Exile

Westley, Helen
1936 Dimples
Show Boat
1941 Adam Had Four Sons
Lady from Louisiana

Westmore, Jean
1959 Imitation of Life

Weston, Cecil
1931 Huckleberry Finn
1934 Behold My Wife!
1936 Dangerous Intrigue
The Prisoner of Shark Island
Ramona
1941 Accent on Love
1943 Crash Dive
1944 Buffalo Bill
Going My Way
1945 A Tree Grows in Brooklyn
1950 Bandit Queen
1952 The Iron Mistress

Weston, Garnett
1933 Robbers' Roost
1935 Ruggles of Red Gap
1938 Daughter of Shanghai

Weston, Jack
1959 Imitation of Life

Weston, Joe
1946 Bringing Up Father

Weston, Rosina
1936 The Green Pastures

Weston, Sam
1958 Gun Fever

Weston, William
1914 The Little Angel of Canyon Creek

Westover, Winifred
1921 Anne of Little Smoky

Westrate, Edwin V.
1946 Renegade Girl

Wetherby, J. Carlton
1919 A Yankee Princess

Wever, Ned
1958 Ride a Crooked Trail

Wexler, Jack
1938 Two Sisters

Wexler, Jacob
1936 Love and Sacrifice

Wexler, Paul
1954 Drum Beat

Wexley, John
1939 Confessions of a Nazi Spy

Whale, James
1936 Show Boat
1941 They Dare Not Love

Whalen, Michael
1938 Speed to Burn
1943 Tahiti Honey
1948 Shep Comes Home
1951 Mask of the Dragon
1955 Indian American

Whaley, Roy
1954 War Arrow

Wharton, Theodore
1914 The Indian Wars

Whately, Roger
1935 De la sartén al fuego
1937 Drums of Destiny

Wheat, Larry *same as* **Wheat, Laurence**
1921 The Land of Hope
1926 Irene
1937 Big City
1945 Wanderer of the Wasteland
1946 Abie's Irish Rose

Wheatcroft, Stanhope
1916 Broken Chains
1919 The Right to Happiness
1920 Locked Lips
1922 The Sign of the Rose
1923 Breaking into Society

Wheeler, Bert
1922 Captain Fly-by-Night
1933 Diplomaniacs
1936 Silly Billies

Wheeler, Cliff
1929 Sombras habaneras

Wheeler, Dorothy
1920 The North Wind's Malice

Wheeler, George F.
1918 The Birth of a Race

Wheeler, Sam
1954 Go Man Go

Wheeler, Thomas
1916 The Colored American Winning His Suit

Wheelock, Charles
1917 The Tenderfoot

Whelan, Arleen
1938 Gateway
1942 Castle in the Desert
1951 Flaming Feather
1953 San Antone
The Sun Shines Bright
1957 Raiders of Old California

Whelan, Tim
1926 The Strong Man
1942 Twin Beds

Whipper, Leigh
1920 The Symbol of the Unconquered
1941 King of the Zombies
Virginia
1942 The Vanishing Virginian
1943 The Ox-Bow Incident
1947 Untamed Fury
1949 Lost Boundaries

Whistler, Rudy
1948 Fighting Father Dunne

Whitaker, Charles *same as* **Whitaker, Charles "Slim"; Whittaker, Charles; Whittaker, Chas.; Whittaker, Slim; Wittaker, Charles**
1926 Twin Triggers
1928 The Canyon of Adventure
1933 Man from Monterey
1934 The Cactus Kid
Fighting Through
The Prescott Kid
1935 Circle of Death
Range Warfare
Wolf Riders
1936 The Bold Caballero
Pinto Rustlers
1937 Prairie Thunder
1939 The Fighting Gringo
Frontiers of '49
1943 In Old Oklahoma

Whitcomb, Daniel F. *same as* **Whitcomb, Daniel**
1917 Sold at Auction
1918? Rosemary Climbs the Heights
1923 The Sting of the Scorpion

Whitcomb, Dennis
1960 The Dark at the Top of the Stairs

White Bird
1937 Maid of Salem

White Dove
1934 Laughing Boy

White Eagle
1919 The Heart of Wetona

White Flash, a horse
1936 Song of the Gringo
1940 Arizona Frontier
Rhythm of the Rio Grande
1941 The Pioneers

White Flower
1934 Laughing Boy

White Sheep, Smile
1956 The Searchers

White, Alan
1959 Shake Hands with the Devil

White, Alice
1937 Big City

White, Baron
1948 The Boy with Green Hair

White, Beverly
1948 Killer Diller

White, Bill, Jr. *could be same as* **White, Billy**
1954 Dangerous Mission
1957 Run of the Arrow

White, Billy *could be same as* **White, Bill Jr.**
1948 The Boy with Green Hair

White, Bob
1917 Lost in Transit

White, Bremond
1950 Panic in the Streets

White, Carl
1930 Big Boy

White, Carolina
1918   My Cousin
White, Charles
1932   Out of the Crimson Fog
White, Crystal
1949   The Fighting Kentuckian
White, Dan *same as* **White, Daniel**
1947   Duel in the Sun
1948   Four Faces West
        Red River
1950   Intruder in the Dust
        A Lady Without Passport
1951   Distant Drums
        Oh! Susanna
        The Tall Target
1954   Taza, Son of Cochise
1956   Giant
        The Last Hunt
1957   Band of Angels
1958   Escape from Red Rock
        Frontier Gun
        Gunfire at Indian Gap
1959   Gunmen from Laredo
White, Delia
1946   Mantan Messes Up
White, Dorothy *could be same as*
White, Dorothy Ann
1934   Stand Up and Cheer!
1938   In Old Chicago
1939   King of Chinatown
White, Dorothy Ann *could be
same as* **White, Dorothy**
1950   Sunset in the West
White, Edward J. *same as* **White,
Eddy**
1944   Tucson Raiders
1947   On the Old Spanish Trail
1949   The Golden Stallion
1950   Belle of Old Mexico
        North of the Great Divide
        Sunset in the West
1953   Old Overland Trail
White, Fleet
1946   Till the End of Time
        Without Reservations
White, Frank
1948   Tap Roots
White, Frank (*African-American
actor*)
1919   A Man's Duty
White, George
1945   Rhapsody in Blue
White, Glenn *same as* **White, Glen**
1919   Love and the Law
1921   Love's Plaything
White, Gloria Ann
1939   The Cisco Kid and the
        Lady
White, J. Francis
1955   Kentucky Rifle
White, Jack
1930   King of Jazz
White, Jacqueline
1942   Dr. Gillespie's New
        Assistant
        Three Hearts for Julia
1947   Crossfire
1949   Riders of the Range
White, Jane
1949   Pinky
White, Jesse
1948   Gentleman's Agreement
1954   Hell's Half Acre
1955   Not As a Stranger
1958   Marjorie Morningstar
White, John J.
1946   Slightly Scandalous
White, Johnstone
1956   Serenade
1958   Home Before Dark
White, Journee, Lieut.
1919   Injustice
White, Lee "Lasses" *same as*
White, Lee
1940   If I Had My Way
1944   Minstrel Man
1945   In Old New Mexico
1948   The Dude Goes West
        The Golden Eye
        Indian Agent
1949   The Valiant Hombre

White, Leo
1923   Breaking into Society
1927   McFadden's Flats
        The Slaver
1928   Breed of the Sunsets
1931   Die Maske Fällt
        El proceso de Mary
        Dugan (*foreign
        version*)
1935   A Night at the Opera
        A Night at the Ritz
1938   Charlie Chan at Monte
        Carlo
1942   All Through the Night
        Gentleman Jim
White, Marjorie
1931   The Black Camel
        Charlie Chan Carries On
1933   Diplomaniacs
White, Meredith
1938   The Beloved Brat
White, Murray
1937   The Holy Oath
White, Patricia
1947   Humoresque
1948   Singin' Spurs
1949   The Undercover Man
White, Paul
1937   Boy of the Streets
1942   Take My Life
White, Pearl
1916   The King's Game
White, Priscilla
1945   Nob Hill
White, Robertson
1940   Charlie Chan's Murder
        Cruise
White, Ruth
1957   Edge of the City
White, Sammy *same as* **White, Sam**
1936   Show Boat
1944   Tahiti Nights
1952   The Half-Breed
White, Stewart Edward
1919   The Westerners
White, Talford
1924?   The Flaming Crisis
White, Thelma
1942   Syncopation
White, Tom
1930   La rosa de fuego
White, Walter
1945   Rhapsody in Blue
White, Will J.
1957   The Lawless Eighties
1959   The FBI Story
1960   Key Witness
White, Yolanda
1957   All Mine to Give
Tony Whitecloud's Jemez Indians
1952   Apache Country
Whitefeather, Felix
1926   Buffalo Bill on the U. P.
        Trail
1927   Red Clay
Whiteford, Blackie *same as*
Whiteford, J. P. "Blackie"
1944   Riding West
1949   Knock on Any Door
Whitehead, Hubert
1916   Ramona
Whitehead, Joe
1940   If I Had My Way
1941   Ride on Vaquero
1944   Black Magic
1945   The Jade Mask
1947   California
1948   Tap Roots
        Unconquered
1949   The Sky Dragon
Whitehead, Kay
1938   The Texans
Whitehead, O. Z.
1958   The Last Hurrah
Whitehead, Peter
1945   Colorado Pioneers
Whitehead, V. O.
1916   The Daughter of the Don

Whitehorse, Chief
1926   War Paint
1929   Hawk of the Hills
Whitell, Josephine
1950   Chinatown at Midnight
Whiteman, Paul
1945   Rhapsody in Blue
Paul Whiteman and His Band
1930   King of Jazz
Whiteman, Russ
1946   Without Reservations
1959   Al Capone
Whiteside, Walker
1915   The Melting Pot
Whitespear, Greg *same as*
        Whitespear, Chief
1931   The Great Meadow
1932   Riders of the Desert
1934   Behold My Wife!
1937   The Plainsman
Whitetree, Ray
1955   Davy Crockett, King of
        the Wild Frontier
Whitey's Savoy Lindy Hoppers
1939   Keep Punching
Whitfield, Geraldine
1940?   Mr. Washington Goes to
        Town
Whitfield, Jordan "Smoki" *same
as* **Whitfield, Smokey;
Whitfield, Smoki**
1950   Right Cross
1953   The Man from the Alamo
1955   Seven Angry Men
1956   The Benny Goodman
        Story
1959   The Last Angry Man
Whiting, Napoleon *same as*
        Whiting, Nappie
1942   Lucky Ghost
        Professor Creeps
1943   Riding High
1950   Mystery Street
1951   The Tall Target
1956   Giant
1959   Imitation of Life
Whitley, Crane
1943   Hitler's Children
1944   Black Magic
        Mr. Skeffington
1947   California
        Easy Come, Easy Go
1948   Unconquered
1951   Oh! Susanna
1952   The Big Sky
Whitley, June
1950   Right Cross
1952   Bright Victory
Whitley, Ray
1938   The Renegade Ranger
1956   Giant
Whitlock, Lloyd
1919   Lasca
1921   One Man in a Million
1930   The Cohens and the
        Kellys in Scotland
1931   Chinatown After Dark
        The Cohens and Kellys in
        Africa
1936   It Had to Happen
        The Prisoner of Shark
        Island
        Ride, Ranger, Ride
        Show Boat
1948   Unconquered
Whitman, Al
1918   Tongues of Flame
Whitman, Ernest
1936   The Green Pastures
        The Prisoner of Shark
        Island
1938   Daughter of Shanghai
1939   Gone With the Wind
1940   Santa Fe Trail
1941   Birth of the Blues
1943   Cabin in the Sky
        Stormy Weather
1953   The Sun Shines Bright
Whitman, Gayne
1929   Lucky Boy
1931   Yankee Don
1934   Stand Up and Cheer!

1940   New Moon
1950   The Big Hangover
1951   The Magnificent Yankee
1952   Indian Uprising
1953   Dream Wife
        The Jazz Singer
Whitman, Peggy
1958   Gunman's Walk
Whitman, Stuart
1953   The Man from the Alamo
1954   Passion
1957   War Drums
Whitman, Velma
1917   The Primitive Call
Whitman, Walt
1916   The Criminal
1918   The Price of Applause
1920   Dangerous Hours
        Darling Mine
        The Mark of Zorro
1921   The Girl from God's
        Country
Whitmore, James
1949   The Undercover Man
1950   Battleground
1951   Across the Wide Missouri
1952   It's a Big Country: An
        American Anthology
1956   The Last Frontier
Whitney, C. V.
1959   The Young Land
Whitney, Claire
1914   Life's Shop Window
1915   The Girl I Left Behind Me
        The Nigger
1918   The Kaiser's Finish
1943   Wintertime
1944   Tender Comrade
1948   Rocky
Whitney, Eve
1942   Three Hearts for Julia
1947   Riding the California
        Trail
1949   The Girl from Jones
        Beach
Whitney, John
1943   Action in the North
        Atlantic
1944   The Sullivans
        Tucson Raiders
1950   No Way Out
        Sands of Iwo Jima
Whitney, Lynn
1948   The Boy with Green Hair
1949   Border Incident
        The Undercover Man
Whitney, Peter
1942   Rio Rita
        Valley of the Sun
1943   Action in the North
        Atlantic
1944   Mr. Skeffington
1946   Canyon Passage
1947   Northwest Outpost
1953   The Great Sioux Uprising
1954   The Black Dakotas
1956   The Last Frontier
        Man from Del Rio
Whitney, Renee
1936   Show Boat
Whitney, Salem Tutt
1924   Birthright
1925   Marcus Garland
Whitney, Shirley
1950   Emergency Wedding
Whitney, William
1955   Headline Hunters
Whitson, Frank
1916   Gold and the Woman
        The Morals of Hilda
1936   Show Boat
Whittaker, Charles E.
1920   Billions
        For the Soul of Rafael
1923   Backbone
1925   His People
Whittell, Josephine
1932   Symphony of Six Million
1943   Dixie
1951   Molly

Whitten, Marguerite *same as* **Whitten, Margaret**
1938   Spirit of Youth
        The Toy Wife
        Two Gun Man from Harlem
1939   Way Down South
1940   Mystery in Swing
1940?   Mr. Washington Goes to Town
1941   King of the Zombies
1942   Professor Creeps

Whittier, Robert
1916   Betrayed
1917   The Call of Her People
        Threads of Fate

Whittington, Dick, a dog
1944   Since You Went Away

Whittington, Gene
1955   The Long Gray Line

Whittlesey, Lt. Col. Charles W.
1919   The Lost Battalion

Whitty, Dame May
1943   Crash Dive

Whorf, Richard
1942   Juke Girl
1943   Yankee Doodle Dandy
1946   The Sailor Takes a Wife
1956   The Burning Hills

Whynemah, Princess
1943   Deerslayer

Whyte, Gilbert
1948   The Fight Never Ends

Whyte, Patrick
1959   The FBI Story
1960   The Adventures of Huckleberry Finn

Whytock, Grant
1950   Davy Crockett, Indian Scout

Wick, Bruno
1945   The House on 92nd St.
1953   Taxi

Wickes, Mary
1949   Anna Lucasta
1955   Good Morning, Miss Dove
1960   Cimarron

Wicki, Norbert *same as* **Wicke, Norbert**
1917?   Barnaby Lee
1920?   The Scarlet Dragon

Wickland, Josephine
1942   Lucky Ghost

Wicks, Elsie
1937   Man of the People

Widder, Lincoln A.
1949   Roll Thunder Roll!
        Shamrock Hill

Widmark, Richard
1950   No Way Out
        Panic in the Streets
1954   Broken Lance
1956   The Last Wagon

Wiedell, Conrad
1944   They Live in Fear

Wiesenthal, Sam
1957   All Mine to Give

Wiggam, Lionel
1948   Tap Roots

Wigton, Anne
1946   Abie's Irish Rose

Wilber, Robert
1937   The Plainsman
1938   Little Miss Roughneck

Wilbur, Crane
1936   Yellow Cargo
1937   El capitán Tormenta
        El carnaval del diablo

Wilbur, James
1946?   House-Rent Party

Wilbur, Robert
1945   Rhapsody in Blue

Wilcox, Art
1940   Arizona Frontier

Wilcox, Frank
1940   The Fighting 69th
        Santa Fe Trail
1942   Across the Pacific
        Juke Girl
        Secret Enemies
        They Died With Their Boots On
        Wings for the Eagle

1944   Chip Off the Old Block
        The Sullivans
1946   Notorious
1948   Gentleman's Agreement
        The Miracle of the Bells
        Unconquered
1949   The Clay Pigeon
        House of Strangers
        Masked Raiders
        The Mysterious Desperado
1950   Annie Get Your Gun
1951   Cavalry Scout
        Go for Broke!
        Show Boat
1952   The Half-Breed
        The Raiders
1953   The Man from the Alamo
1954   The Black Dakotas
        Dangerous Mission
1955   Trial
1956   7th Cavalry
1959   The Jayhawkers!

Wilcox, Fred M.
1960   I Passed for White

Wilcox, Izinetta
1939   Moon over Harlem

Wilcox, James *same as* **Wilcox, Jimmy**
1929   The Peacock Fan
1930   Sunny Skies
1931   The Guilty Generation

Wilcox, Robert
1938   Rascals
1946   Wild Beauty

Wilcoxon, Henry
1936   The Last of the Mohicans
1937   Souls at Sea
1948   Unconquered

Wild, Anna
1919   The She Wolf

Wild, Poppy
1941   They Dare Not Love

Wild Beauty, a horse
1946   Wild Beauty

Wilde, Brandon de *see* **de Wilde, Brandon**

Wilde, Cornel
1943   Wintertime
1947   It Had To Be You
1950   Two Flags West
1952   California Conquest
1954   Passion
1956   Hot Blood

Wilde, J. P.
1918   Tongues of Flame

Wilde, Lee
1944   Andy Hardy's Blonde Trouble

Wilde, Lyn
1944   Andy Hardy's Blonde Trouble
1951   Show Boat

Wilde, Percival
1922   The Guttersnipe

Wilde, Sonya
1960   I Passed for White

Wilder, Billy
1941   Hold Back the Dawn

Wilder, Leslie F.
1930   Sins of the Children

Wilder, Marc
1958   Houseboat

Wilder, Margaret Buell
1944   Since You Went Away
1947   Pirates of Monterey

Wilder, Patricia
1937   That Girl from Paris
1938   My Lucky Star

Wilens, Jack
1956   Death of a Scoundrel

Wilensky, Mike
1938   The Power of Life

Wiles, Buster
1944   Buffalo Bill

Wiles, Gordon
1935   Rosa de Francia
1936   Charlie Chan's Secret

Wiles, Mabel
1916   A Son of Erin

Wiley, Jan
1945   The Cisco Kid Returns
1946   Without Reservations

Wiley, John
1956   Giant

Wiley, Kay
1951   Queen for a Day

Wilk, Max
1948   Open Secret

Wilke, Robert *same as* **Wilke, Bob; Wilke, Robert J.**
1944   Marshal of Reno
        The San Antonio Kid
        Sheriff of Las Vegas
        Vigilantes of Dodge City
1947   Buck Privates Come Home
1949   Laramie
1950   The Traveling Saleswoman
1951   Cyclone Fury
1952   High Noon
        Indian Uprising
1953   Arrowhead
        War Paint
1955   Shotgun
        Smoke Signal
1956   The Lone Ranger
        Raw Edge

Wilkerson, Bill *same as* **Wilkerson, Billy; Wilkerson, W. P.; Wilkerson, William; Wilkerson, William P.**
1942   King of the Stallions
1943   Frontier Fury
1944   Riding West
1947   Bowery Buckaroos
        The Last Round-Up
1948   Singin' Spurs
1949   Apache Chief
1950   Annie Get Your Gun
        Broken Arrow
        Davy Crockett, Indian Scout
        Rock Island Trail
        The Traveling Saleswoman
1952   Brave Warrior
        California Conquest
        Desert Pursuit
1954   The Black Dakotas
        They Rode West
        Thunder Pass
1955   Foxfire

Wilkerson, Guy
1941   Birth of the Blues
1942   Juke Girl
1947   California
1948   Fury at Furnace Creek
        Unconquered
1949   The Girl from Jones Beach
1950   A Ticket to Tomahawk
        Winchester '73
1952   The Big Sky
1953   The Man from the Alamo
1955   Foxfire
1957   Band of Angels
1959   The FBI Story
        The Hanging Tree

Wilkes, Mattie
1920   The Symbol of the Unconquered
1921   The Gunsaulus Mystery
1922   For His Mother's Sake

Wilkins, June
1937   Song of the City
1941   Hold Back the Dawn

Wilkins, Lester
1937   Life Begins in College

Wilkins, Martin
1951   The Harlem Globetrotters

Willa, Susanne
1916   Arms and the Woman

Willard, Mrs. Charles
1920   Hidden Charms
1921?   The Supreme Passion

Willard, John
1933   Victims of Persecution

Willard, Lee
1914   The Good-for-Nothing
1916   A Son of Erin
1934   Broadway Bill

Willat, Irvin *same as* **Willat, Irvin V.**
1918   The Midnight Patrol
1919   Behind the Door
1921   Fifty Candles
1924   The Heritage of the Desert
        North of 36
1928   The Cavalier
1937   Old Louisiana

Willenz, Max
1940   Overture to Glory
1942   Three Hearts for Julia
1947   Northwest Outpost

Willes, Jean
1950   Chinatown at Midnight
        Emergency Wedding
1959   The FBI Story

Willets, Gilson
1914   In the Days of the Thundering Herd
1916   At Piney Ridge

William, Jimmy
1940   Won Lee Shuen Fu

William, Warren
1932   The Match King
1934   Imitation of Life

Williams, Adam
1951   Queen for a Day
1954   The Yellow Tomahawk
1957   The Oklahoman
1958   The Badlanders

Williams, Judge Arthur H.
1915   The Cheat

Williams, Augusta
1920   In the Depths of Our Hearts

Williams, Bill 1916—1992 *not the same as* **Williams, Billy**
1945   Johnny Angel
1946   Till the End of Time
1949   The Clay Pigeon
1950   The Cariboo Trail
1951   The Last Outpost
1952   Rose of Cimarron
1955   Apache Ambush
        Chief Crazy Horse
1956   The Broken Star
        The Wild Dakotas
1957   The Halliday Brand
        Pawnee
1960   Hell to Eternity
        Oklahoma Territory

Williams, Billy *not the same as* **Williams, Bill 1916—1992**
1952   Indian Uprising

Williams, Billy Dee
1959   The Last Angry Man

Williams, Bob *(actor)*
1949   Boston Blackie's Chinese Venture
1950   The Breaking Point
1951   Jim Thorpe—All-American
1953   The Stars Are Singing
1956   The Lone Ranger

Williams, Bob *(writer)*
1946   California Gold Rush
1947   The Adventures of Don Coyote
1949   Ranger of Cherokee Strip

Williams, Cara
1944   Something for the Boys
1949   Knock on Any Door
1958   The Defiant Ones

Williams, Chalky
1952   The Half-Breed
1953   So Big

Williams, Charles
1932   Flesh
1934   The Cat's-Paw
1936   Charlie Chan at the Race Track
1937   Charlie Chan on Broadway
1938   Gateway
        Mr. Moto's Gamble
1942   Tales of Manhattan
1943   The Girl from Monterey

1944 Lake Placid Serenade
Since You Went Away
1946 Without Reservations
1947 My Wild Irish Rose
1948 The Dude Goes West
Half Past Midnight
1950 The Missourians

Williams, Chili
1945 Johnny Angel
1947 Copacabana

Williams, Clara
1915 The Italian
1916 The Criminal
Three of Many

Williams, Clarence
1918 The Hell Cat
1928 Absent

Williams, Clark
1947 Citizen Saint

Williams, Cora
1919 His Parisian Wife

Williams, Cristola
1941 Murder on Lenox Avenue
Sunday Sinners

Williams, Don
1946 Romance of the West

Williams, Doug
1950 Black Hand
1960 I Passed for White
Pay or Die

Williams, Duke
1946 Stars on Parade
1947 Boy! What a Girl!
1949 The Red Menace

Williams, Earle
1920 The Purple Cipher
1923 Jealous Husbands

Williams, Ed
1922 Spitfire

Williams, Elizabeth
1921 The Burden of Race

Williams, Elmo
1957 Apache Warrior

Williams, Estha
1914 At the Cross Roads

Williams, Ethel
1921 The Gunsaulus Mystery

Williams, Eugene
1928 Eleven P.M.

Williams, Frances *same as* **Williams, Frances E.**
1939 Lying Lips
1951 Queen for a Day
Show Boat

Williams, Fred (*African-American actor*)
1921 A Modern Cain

Williams, Fred C.
1919 A Fallen Idol

Williams, Fred Tomago
1943 Stormy Weather

Williams, G. B.
1918 The Spreading Evil

Williams, Geneva
1935 The Little Colonel
1938 The Toy Wife
1946 Saratoga Trunk

Williams, George 1854—1936
1922 Little Miss Smiles

Williams, George (*African-American actor*)
1932 Ten Minutes to Live
1939 Straight to Heaven
1940 Paradise in Harlem
1941 Murder on Lenox Avenue
Sunday Sinners
1947 Sepia Cinderella

Williams, George B. 1866—1931
1921 Cheated Love
One Man in a Million
1922 Second Hand Rose

Williams, Gladys
1939 Lying Lips
1940 The Notorious Elinor Lee
1948 The Betrayal

Williams, Gloria
1937 Souls at Sea
Waikiki Wedding
1938 The Buccaneer
1939 King of Chinatown
1940 Geronimo
1941 New York Town

Williams, Guinn "Big Boy" *same as* **Williams, Big Boy; Williams, Guinn**
1928 Vamping Venus
1930 The Bad Man
1931 The Great Meadow
1933 Rafter Romance
1935 Cowboy Holiday
The Littlest Rebel
Romance in Manhattan
1936 Kelly the Second
Muss 'Em Up
1937 Big City
1939 Bad Lands
1940 The Fighting 69th
Santa Fe Trail
1942 American Empire
1946 Singin' in the Corn
1950 Rocky Mountain
1954 Massacre Canyon
1956 Man from Del Rio

Williams, Guy
1953 The Man from the Alamo
1955 Seven Angry Men
1956 The Last Frontier
1960 The Sign of Zorro

Williams, H. Marion
1928 Eleven P.M.

Williams, Henrietta
1954 Salt of the Earth

Williams, Herb
1936 Rose of the Rancho

Williams, Herberta
1951 Apache Drums

Williams, Irene
1947 Going to Glory, Come to Jesus

Williams, Ivory
1936 The Green Pastures

Williams, Jack (*African-American actor*)
1937 Harlem on the Prairie
1956 The Burning Hills
1957 Band of Angels

Williams, Jan
1945 Salome, Where She Danced

Williams, Jeff
1919 Just Squaw

Williams, John "Buddy" *same as* **Williams, John B.**
1942 We Were Dancing
1951 A Streetcar Named Desire

Williams, John J.
1915 Marse Covington

Williams, Kathlyn
1915 The Rosary
1917 Lost in Transit
1927 Sally in Our Alley
1928 We Americans

Williams, Ken
1953 The Sun Shines Bright

Williams, Larry
1939 Waterfront
1945 Nob Hill
1951 The Great Caruso
1954 Drums Across the River

Williams, Leon
1921 The Sport of the Gods

Williams, Lottie
1921 All Souls' Eve
1938 The Beloved Brat
1942 All Through the Night
1944 Mr. Skeffington

Williams, Lyman
1934 Coming Out Party

Williams, Mack
1950 No Way Out
1951 The Harlem Globetrotters
1955 Violent Saturday

Williams, Maria P.
1923 Flames of Wrath

Williams, Maston
1931 Cavalier of the West
1932 Border Devils
1938 The Buccaneer
1940 Hi-Yo Silver

Williams, Mervin
1951 Saturday's Hero
1954 Salt of the Earth

Williams, Milton
1948 Miracle in Harlem

Williams, Osborne
1922 Spitfire

Williams, Percy
1922 The Pride of Palomar

Williams, Pinky
194- Mistaken Identity

Williams, R. S.
1950 Intruder in the Dust

Williams, Rex
1942 Secret Enemies
1943 They Came to Blow Up America

Williams, Rhoda
1945 Our Vines Have Tender Grapes
1949 House of Strangers

Williams, Rhys
1942 Gentleman Jim
1945 The Bells of St. Mary's
1947 Easy Come, Easy Go
The Farmer's Daughter
1950 Devil's Doorway
1956 Mohawk
1957 Raintree County

Williams, Robert B. *same as* **Williams, Robert**
1944 Cry of the Werewolf
The Racket Man
1945 Escape in the Fog
I Love a Bandleader
1948 Call Northside 777
1949 The Mysterious Desperado
Stagecoach Kid
1950 The Lawless
1953 The Nebraskan
1954 Massacre Canyon
1955 Apache Ambush
1960 Cimarron

Williams, Roger
1935 Fighting Pioneers
Range Warfare
1936 Pinto Rustlers
The Traitor
1937 Law and Lead
Nation Aflame
The Riders of the Whistling Skull
1945 Colorado Pioneers

Williams, Rush
1950 Rocky Mountain
1952 The Raiders
1953 Beneath the 12-Mile Reef
1956 Giant
The Lone Ranger
1957 Trooper Hook
1958 Bullwhip

Williams, Skippy
194- Mistaken Identity

Williams, Slim
1951 Yes Sir, Mr. Bones

Williams, Sonny Boy
1941 Hold Back the Dawn

Williams, Spencer, Jr. *same as* **Williams, Spencer**
1928 Tenderfeet
1930 Georgia Rose
1937 Harlem on the Prairie
1938 Two Gun Man from Harlem
1939 The Bronze Buckaroo
Harlem Rides the Range
1940 Son of Ingagi
1941? The Blood of Jesus
1943 Marching On!
1945 Of One Blood
1946 Dirty Gertie from Harlem, U.S.A.
1946? Beale Street Mama
Go Down, Death!
1947 Juke Joint
1949? Girl in Room 20

Williams, Sumner
1949 Knock on Any Door

Williams, Ted
1949 The Story of Seabiscuit

Williams, Tennessee
1951 A Streetcar Named Desire
1955 The Rose Tattoo
1956 Baby Doll

Williams, Theodore
1921 A Modern Cain

Williams, Tom
1919 Love and the Law

Williams, Tudor
1942 Rio Rita

Williams, Virgil
1920 The Brute
In the Depths of Our Hearts

Williams, Voyt
1941 This Woman Is Mine

Williams, William A. *same as* **Williams, W. A.; Williams, William**
1915 How Molly Malone Made Good
1916 Silks and Satins
1917 The Bar Sinister
1930 The Big Pond (*foreign version*)

Williams, Zack
1929 Hearts in Dixie
1940 Son of Ingagi
1942 Professor Creeps

Williamson, Bob
1933 Circle Canyon

Williamson, Earl
1960 Wild River

Williamson, Noah
1956 Baby Doll

Willing, Foy
1949 The Golden Stallion
1950 North of the Great Divide
Sunset in the West

Willingham, Ralph
1948 The Paleface

Willingham, Willard
1952 The Savage
1953 Arrowhead
1957 The Guns of Fort Petticoat

Willis, Austin
1960 I Aim at the Stars: the Wernher von Braun Story

Willis, Enid
1916 The Criminal

Willis, F. McGrew
1932 The Forty-Niners

Willis, Jimmy
1946 Stars on Parade

Willis, Leo
1931 Cimarron

Willis, Matt
1946 Strange Voyage
1947 The Burning Cross
1948 Shep Comes Home
1951 Jim Thorpe—All-American

Willis, Norman
1936 After the Thin Man
Charlie Chan at the Race Track
1937 Life Begins in College
1938 Happy Landing
1941 Belle Starr
Gauchos of Eldorado
1945 In Old New Mexico
1954 Drum Beat

Willis, Paul
1916 The Fall of a Nation
1917 The Trouble Buster

Willis, Ross B.
1940 East of the River

Willis, Susanne
1918 Uncle Tom's Cabin

Willis, William
1922 Cardigan

Willmering, William
1940 Doomed to Die

Willock, Dave *same as* **Willock, David**
1941 Louisiana Purchase
Playmates
1942 Sunday Punch
Wings for the Eagle
1943 Action in the North Atlantic
The Gang's All Here

Yankee Doodle Dandy
1945   Pride of the Marines
1950   Belle of Old Mexico

Willoughby, Lewis
1918   The Temple of Dusk

Willow Bird, Chris *same as* **Willow Bird**
1942   Valley of the Sun
1944   Tahiti Nights
1949   Daughter of the West
1950   Broken Arrow

Wills, Alice
1951   Westward the Women

Wills, Chill
1939   Allegheny Uprising
1941   Belle Starr
        Western Union
1942   Apache Trail
1949   Tulsa
1950   Rio Grande
        Rock Island Trail
1951   Oh! Susanna
1953   The Man from the Alamo
        Tumbleweed
1955   Kentucky Rifle
1956   Giant

Wills, Henry
1944   Buffalo Bill
1951   Westward the Women
1952   The Raiders
        The Savage
1953   Arrowhead
        Ride, Vaquero!
1954   Saskatchewan
1955   Chief Crazy Horse
1959   Last Train from Gun Hill

Wills, Lou, Jr.
1947   My Wild Irish Rose

Wills, Ross B.
1927   The Frontiersman
        Spoilers of the West
1928   Wyoming

Wills, Si
1937   Nation Aflame

Wills, William
1940   Jennie

Wilma, Dana
1939   El otro soy yo
        Papá soltero

Wilner, Max
1933   Live and Laugh
1934   What a Mother-in-Law!
1950   Monticello, Here We Come!
1950?   Three Daughters

Wilsey, Jay *same as* **Buffalo Bill, Jr.**
1925   Quicker'n Lightnin'
1927   Roarin' Broncs
1934   'Neath the Arizona Skies
        Riding Speed
        Wheels of Destiny
1935   Texas Terror

Wilson, Arthur "Dooky"
1939   Keep Punching

Wilson, Ben *same as* **Wilson, Ben D.**
1921   The Man from Texas
1922   One Eighth Apache
1925   A Daughter of the Sioux
        Tonio, Son of the Sierras
        Warrior Gap

Wilson, Bill *could be same as* **Wilson, Billy**
1960   The Last Voyage

Wilson, Billy *could be same as* **Wilson, Bill**
1949   We Were Strangers

Wilson, Boyd L.
1957   Burden of Truth

Wilson, Carey
1925   Lights of Old Broadway
1926   Into Her Kingdom
1928   Diamond Handcuffs
1939   Judge Hardy and Son
1944   Andy Hardy's Blonde Trouble
        Three Men in White
1945   Between Two Women
1947   Dark Delusion

Wilson, Charles *(actor) same as* **Wilson, Charles C.** *(actor)*
1934   Behold My Wife!
        Broadway Bill
1935   Black Fury
        The Little Colonel
        Rendezvous
1936   Show Boat
1937   Life Begins in College
        One Mile from Heaven
1938   Daughter of Shanghai
        Gateway
1940   Elsa Maxwell's Public Deb No. 1
        Knute Rockne—All American
1941   The Face Behind the Mask
1942   All Through the Night
        Gentleman Jim
        Young America
1946   Bringing Up Father
        Gas House Kids

Wilson, Charles C. *(dir)*
1929   Lucky Boy

Wilson, Charles J., Jr.
1918   Hell's End
1919   Spotlight Sadie

Wilson, Clarence *(African-American actor)*
1951   The Harlem Globetrotters
1954   Go Man Go

Wilson, Clarence H. *same as* **Wilson, Clarence; Wilson, Clarence Hummel**
1934   Imitation of Life
        Operator 13
1935   Ruggles of Red Gap
        The Winning Ticket
1936   Paddy O'Day
        Rainbow on the River
        Sutter's Gold
1937   Man of the People
1938   In Old Chicago
        The Texans
1939   Drums Along the Mohawk

Wilson, Don *(African-American actor)*
1946   Dirty Gertie from Harlem, U.S.A.

Wilson, Don *(Radio/TV announcer)*
1953   The Stars Are Singing

Wilson, Dooley
1943   Stormy Weather
1949   Knock on Any Door

Wilson, Douglas
1957   Naked in the Sun

Wilson, Earl
1947   Copacabana

Wilson, Ed
1926   The Flaming Frontier

Wilson, Edna May
1916   The Fall of a Nation

Wilson, Edna Morton
1921   The Sport of the Gods

Wilson, Elsie Jane
1917   A Kentucky Cinderella
1918   The City of Tears

Wilson, Ernest
1938   The Toy Wife
1949   The Story of Seabiscuit

Wilson, Eunice
1935   Lem Hawkins' Confession

Wilson, Everdinne
1959   Porgy and Bess

Wilson, Frank *not the same as* **Wilson, Frank C.**
1932?   The Girl from Chicago
1933   The Emperor Jones
1936   The Green Pastures
1940   Paradise in Harlem
1941   Murder on Lenox Avenue
        Sunday Sinners
1946   Beware

Wilson, Frank C. *not the same as* **Wilson, Frank**
1938   Little Miss Roughneck

Wilson, Fred L.
1921   Little Miss Hawkshaw

Wilson, Gilbert
1948   Unconquered

Wilson, Hal *(actor), d. 1933*
1915   The Sable Lorcha
1920   Dinty

Wilson, Harold *(prod)*
1937   Life Begins in College
1941   Louisiana Purchase

Wilson, Harry *(actor)*
1934   Judge Priest
1949   Knock on Any Door
        Thieves' Highway

Wilson, Howard
1934   Wagon Wheels
1935   McFadden's Flats
1937   Think Fast, Mr. Moto

Wilson, Irene
1930   Georgia Rose

Wilson, Janice
1921   The Swamp

Wilson, Jerome N. *same as* **Wilson, Jerome**
1916   The Pretenders
1917   A Wife by Proxy

Wilson, John
1954   Go Man Go

Wilson, Johnny
1932   Hypnotized

Wilson, Kathleen
1943   Hitler's Children

Wilson, Lewis
1943   Good Luck, Mr. Yates
        Redhead from Manhattan
1944   The Racket Man

Wilson, Lois
1916   The Morals of Hilda
1920   Who's Your Servant?
1923   Ruggles of Red Gap
1924   North of 36
1925   Irish Luck
        The Thundering Herd
1926   The Vanishing American
1928   Ransom
1932   The Secrets of Wu Sin
1933   Obey the Law
1949   The Girl from Jones Beach

Wilson, M. K.
1917   The Flower of Doom

Wilson, Marcellus
1948?   Boarding House Blues

Wilson, Margery
1917   The Bride of Hate
        The Gun Fighter
1918   Marked Cards
1919   Desert Gold

Wilson, Marie
1939   Waterfront
1941   Virginia

Wilson, Marriott
1945   The House on 92nd St.

Wilson, Michael
1943   Border Patrol
1954   Salt of the Earth

Wilson, Millard K.
1917   The Pulse of Life

Wilson, Richard
1948   The Lady from Shanghai
1959   Al Capone
1960   Pay or Die

Wilson, Sox
1947   Going to Glory, Come to Jesus

Wilson, Teddy
1956   The Benny Goodman Story

Teddy Wilson and His Band
1946?   Harlem on Parade

Wilson, Terry
1951   Westward the Women
1952   Bugles in the Afternoon
1953   Ride, Vaquero!
1956   The Last Frontier
        The Last Hunt
        Pillars of the Sky

Wilson, Tom *same as* **Wilson, Thomas**
1915   The Birth of a Nation
        A Yankee from the West
1916   The Half-Breed
1918   Amarilly of Clothes-Line Alley

Wilson, Gilbert — *(continued top right)*

1920   Dinty
1924   His Darker Self
1927   Ham and Eggs at the Front
1928   Riley the Cop
1930   Big Boy
1935   A Night at the Ritz
1936   Treachery Rides the Range
1940   East of the River
1944   Mr. Skeffington
1955   The View from Pompey's Head

Wilson, Violette
1944   Three Men in White

Wilson, Virginia
1943   The Gang's All Here

Wilson, Warren
1942   Shut My Big Mouth

Wilson, Whip
1948   Silver Trails
1950   Cherokee Uprising

Wilson, William
1948   The Fight Never Ends
1954   Go Man Go

Wilton, Eric
1935   Rendezvous
1936   After the Thin Man
1937   Big City
        One Mile from Heaven
1939   Mr. Moto's Last Warning
1942   Castle in the Desert
        Tales of Manhattan
1948   Docks of New Orleans
1950   Emergency Wedding
        Jolson Sings Again
1951   The Great Caruso

Wiltshire, George *same as* **Wilshire, George**
1939   Keep Punching
1946?   Fight That Ghost
1947   Hi De Ho
1948   Killer Diller
1948?   Junction 88
1955   Brevities of 1955

Teacho Wiltshire Hot Band
1956   Rockin' the Blues

Winans, Robert
1950   Winchester '73

Winburn, Anna Mae
1946   That Man of Mine

Winch, Frank
1944   Buffalo Bill

Winchell, Walter
1957   Beau James

Winckler, Robert
1939   Mr. Moto Takes a Vacation

Windbeil, Morgan
1959   Al Capone

Windham, E. H.
1950   Intruder in the Dust

Windheim, Marek
1940   Escape
1942   Holiday Inn
        Three Hearts for Julia
1946   The Sailor Takes a Wife

Windom, Lawrence C.
1918   Ruggles of Red Gap
1922   Solomon in Society

Windrow, Stellan
1930   Toda una vida (*foreign version*)

Windsor, Adele
1929   Frozen Justice

Windsor, Claire
1927   The Frontiersman

Windsor, Joy
1950   Sands of Iwo Jima

Windsor, Kay
1959   Night of the Quarter Moon

Windsor, Marie
1942   Three Hearts for Julia
1949   The Fighting Kentuckian
1951   Hurricane Island
        Little Big Horn
1952   Japanese War Bride
1953   The Eddie Cantor Story
1954   Hell's Half Acre

Wineglass, Dewey
1946?   House-Rent Party
Winehouse, Irwin
1947   Reet, Petite and Gone
Winfield, Joan
1942   Gentleman Jim
1943   Yankee Doodle Dandy
1944   Mr. Skeffington
1945   Rhapsody in Blue
1951   Queen for a Day
1953   The Jazz Singer
Wing, Ah
1919   The She Wolf
1921   A Tale of Two Worlds
Wing, Pat
1932   Hypnotized
Wing, Ward
1929   The Overland Telegraph
1930   El presidio
Wing, William E.
1916   Sold for Marriage
1920   Before the White Man Came
1921   The Hunger of the Blood
Winkelman, Michael
1955   The Indian Fighter
1957   Ride Out for Revenge
Winkler, Baby
1940   Overture to Glory
Winkler, Robert same as **Winkler, Bobby**
1940   Knute Rockne—All American
1941   Sullivan's Travels
1942   Wings for the Eagle
1944   An American Romance
Winn, Jack
1931   The Great Meadow
Winn, John
1920   The Mark of Zorro
Winninger, Charles
1931   Fighting Caravans
1936   Show Boat
1940   If I Had My Way
       Little Nellie Kelly
1942   Friendly Enemies
1953   The Sun Shines Bright
Winogradoff, Anatol
1950?   Three Daughters
1954   Go Man Go
1959   The Last Angry Man
Winslow, Dick
1930   Tom Sawyer
1932   So Big
1935   A Night at the Ritz
1936   General Spanky
1956   The Benny Goodman Story
1960   All the Fine Young Cannibals
Winslow, Herbert Hall
1914   The Great Diamond Robbery
Winslow, Jack
1941   Sullivan's Travels
Winslow, Lutra
1937   The Devil's Playground
Winston, Ellen
1927   Whispering Sage
Winston, Helen
1950   The Men
1953   Cry of the Hunted
Winston, Laura
1919   Desert Gold
Winston, Lloyd
1960   Sergeant Rutledge
Winston, Steve
1945   Betrayal from the East
Winston, Vivian
1934   Stand Up and Cheer!
Winter, George
1950   Intruder in the Dust
Winter, Larry
1950   Mystery Submarine
1951   Go for Broke!
1952   Bright Victory
Winter, Laska
1925   Justice of the Far North
1929   Frozen Justice
1931   Chinatown After Dark
1932   The Rainbow Trail

Winter, Lee
1958   The Young Lions
Winter, Shelley see **Winters, Shelley**
Winter, Val
1950   Panic in the Streets
Winters, Al
1943   Action in the North Atlantic
Winters, Arthur same as **Winters, A.**
1936   Love and Sacrifice
1939   Mothers of Today
1940   Americaner Schadchen
Winters, David
1959   The Last Angry Man
Winters, Gloria
1950   The Lawless
1951   Gambling House
Winters, Howard
1950   Intruder in the Dust
Winters, Roland
1947   The Chinese Ring
1948   Cry of the City
       Docks of New Orleans
       The Feathered Serpent
       The Golden Eye
       Shanghai Chest
1949   The Sky Dragon
       Tuna Clipper
1953   So Big
Winters, Sally
1929   The Invaders
Winters, Shelley same as **Winter, Shelley**
1944   Knickerbocker Holiday
1945   Escape in the Fog
1948   Cry of the City
       Red River
1950   Winchester '73
1951   The Raging Tide
1952   My Man and I
1954   Saskatchewan
1959   Odds Against Tomorrow
Winters, Shirley
1946   Abie's Irish Rose
Winters, Verne
1920   The Secret Gift
Wintner, Nancy
1943   The Gang's All Here
Winton, Jane
1926   Millionaires
Winwood, Estelle
1960   Sergeant Rutledge
Wippler, Joe
1955   Murder in Villa Capri
Wirard, Joyce
1928   Mother Machree
Wisbar, Frank
1949   The Prairie
Wisberg, Aubrey
1942   Submarine Raider
1943   They Came to Blow Up America
1945   Betrayal from the East
       Escape in the Fog
1946   Rendezvous 24
1947   The Burning Cross
1953   Captain John Smith and Pocahontas
Wisberg, Claude
1946   Rendezvous 24
Wise, Charles
1959   John Paul Jones
Wise, Jack
1935   A Night at the Ritz
1940   East of the River
1942   Gentleman Jim
Wise, Robert
1950   Two Flags West
1951   The House on Telegraph Hill
1953   So Big
1959   Odds Against Tomorrow
Wiseman, Joseph
1960   The Unforgiven
Wiser, Bud
1938   Speed to Burn

Wiso, Jack
1943   Yankee Doodle Dandy
Wiss, Doris
1958   The Young Lions
Wissler, Jerry
1948   My Girl Tisa
Wissler, Rudy
1943   Good Luck, Mr. Yates
1944   Tomorrow the World!
1945   Nob Hill
1948   My Girl Tisa
Wissner, Willard
1955   Blackboard Jungle
Wit, Jacqueline de
1943   The Leopard Man
1944   Black Magic
1946   Cuban Pete
       Saratoga Trunk
       Wild Beauty
1950   Chinatown at Midnight
Withers, Edward
1924   The Lightning Rider
Withers, Grant
1932   The Secrets of Wu Sin
1936   Let's Sing Again
1938   Mr. Wong, Detective
1939   Daughter of the Tong
       Mr. Wong in Chinatown
       The Mystery of Mr. Wong
1940   Doomed to Die
       The Fatal Hour
       Mexican Spitfire Out West
       Phantom of Chinatown
1942   Apache Trail
       Woman of the Year
1943   Dr. Gillespie's Criminal Case
       In Old Oklahoma
1948   Angel in Exile
       Fort Apache
       Old Los Angeles
1949   The Fighting Kentuckian
1950   Rio Grande
       Rock Island Trail
1953   The Sun Shines Bright
1956   The White Squaw
Withers, Isabel
1943   Mr. Lucky
1944   Tahiti Nights
1945   The Gay Senorita
1946   Wild Beauty
1953   Tonight We Sing
Withers, Jane
1936   Paddy O'Day
1938   Rascals
1942   Young America
1956   Giant
Witherspoon, Cora
1940   Charlie Chan's Murder Cruise
Witherspoon, Eloise
1938   Life Goes On
Withey, Chet
1918   The Hun Within
Withrow, Ed
1936   Custer's Last Stand
Witney, William
1940   Hi-Yo Silver
1947   On the Old Spanish Trail
1949   The Golden Stallion
1950   North of the Great Divide
       Sunset in the West
1953   Old Overland Trail
1955   Santa Fe Passage
Wittaker, Charles see **Whitaker, Charles**
Witting, A. E.
1916   The Fall of a Nation
Witting, Mrs.
1917   Follow the Girl
Wix, Florence
1936   My American Wife
1939   King of Chinatown
1942   We Were Dancing
1947   The Farmer's Daughter
Wixon, Mel
1947   The Farmer's Daughter
1948   The Miracle of the Bells

Wolbert, Dorothea
1928   Anybody Here Seen Kelly?
1956   Hot Blood
Wolbert, William
1917   The Captain of the Gray Horse Troop
Wolcott, Helen
1915?   The Beachcomber
Wolcott, William
1917   Queen X
Wold, David
1947   Easy Come, Easy Go
Wolf, Barney
1928   The Great White North
Wolf, Ed
1932   Hypnotized
Wolf, Ian see **Wolfe, Ian**
Wolf, Jane see **Wolfe, Jane**
Wolf, Rennold
1916   The Pretenders
Wolf, Simon
1939   Mothers of Today
Wolfe, Bill
1947   The Mighty McGurk
Wolfe, Bonnadene
1943   Riding High
1945   Nob Hill
Wolfe, David
1949   House of Strangers
       The Undercover Man
1950   Right Cross
1951   The Mark of the Renegade
1952   The Iron Mistress
1954   Salt of the Earth
Wolfe, Ian same as **Wolf, Ian**
1936   The Bold Caballero
1939   Allegheny Uprising
1946   Without Reservations
1947   California
1948   Angel in Exile
       The Miracle of the Bells
1949   Colorado Territory
1950   Emergency Wedding
       No Way Out
1951   The Great Caruso
       The Magnificent Yankee
Wolfe, James
1935   A Night at the Opera
Wolfe, Jane same as **Wolf, Jane; Wolff, Jane**
1915   The Immigrant
1916   Pudd'nhead Wilson
       Unprotected
1917   The Call of the East
       Castles for Two
       Unconquered
1918   The Bravest Way
Wolfe, Marion
1953   Cry of the Hunted
Wolfe, Sam
1950   I Killed Geronimo
1953   The Jazz Singer
Wolff, Efraim
1958   Marjorie Morningstar
Wolff, Fred
1940   Escape
       Escape to Glory
1941   They Dare Not Love
1943   Action in the North Atlantic
Wolff, Jane see **Wolfe, Jane**
Wolff, Lothar
1949   Lost Boundaries
1960   Man on a String
Wolff, Peter
1930   Doña mentiras (foreign version)
Wolford, Bertha
1944   The Negro Soldier
Wolfson, David
1955   Seven Angry Men
Wolfson, P. J.
1935   Rendezvous
1937   That Girl from Paris
1939   Allegheny Uprising
1940   Escape to Glory
Wolheim, Dan
1938   The Adventures of Tom Sawyer

Wolheim, Louis
1923   Little Old New York
1929   Frozen Justice
       Wolf Song
1931   Gentleman's Fate
Wolk, E.
1939   Cossacks in Exile
Wollis, Harriet
1958   The Last Hurrah
Wollis, Helaine
1958   The Last Hurrah
Woloshin, Alex
1938   Daughter of Shanghai
       Spawn of the North
Wolter, U.
1960   I Aim at the Stars: the
       Wernher von Braun
       Story
Womack, Clay
1945   Rhapsody in Blue
Wonacott, Edna *same as*
    Wonacott, Edna May
1944   Hi, Beautiful
1945   The Bells of St. Mary's
Wonder, Leo
1947   Humoresque
Wong, Anna May
1921   Bits of Life
       Shame
1924   Peter Pan
1926   A Trip to Chinatown
1927   The Chinese Parrot
       Old San Francisco
1928   Chinatown Charlie
1934   Limehouse Blues
1938   Dangerous to Know
       Daughter of Shanghai
1939   King of Chinatown
Wong, Barbara Jean
1946   The Trap
1950   Chinatown at Midnight
Wong, Beal
1936   Sum Hun
1942   Across the Pacific
       Little Tokyo, U.S.A.
       Prisoner of Japan
       Submarine Raider
1943   Bataan
1945   Nob Hill
       Samurai
Wong, Bruce
1936   Sum Hun
1937   The Devil's Playground
1938   Daughter of Shanghai
1939   The Mystery of Mr. Wong
1942   Song of the Islands
       Submarine Raider
1943   The Amazing Mrs.
       Holliday
       Bataan
       Crash Dive
       Jack London
1945   Nob Hill
Wong, Frank
1945   Samurai
Wong, Iris
1939   Charlie Chan in Reno
       Mr. Moto Takes a
       Vacation
1941   Charlie Chan in Rio
1943   The Amazing Mrs.
       Holliday
Wong, Jadine
1939   Mr. Moto Takes a
       Vacation
Wong, Jean
1945   Betrayal from the East
       Nob Hill
1946   The Red Dragon
       Without Reservations
1947   The Chinese Ring
1948   Half Past Midnight
       The Lady from Shanghai
1955   Trial
Wong, Jehim
1935   Charlie Chan in Shanghai
Wong, Joe
1949   The Story of Seabiscuit
Wong, Victor
1936   Hair-Trigger Casey
1937   Waikiki Wedding
1938   The Beloved Brat

1939   Mr. Moto Takes a
       Vacation
1940   Phantom of Chinatown
1945   Betrayal from the East
Wong, Walter
1935   Charlie Chan in Shanghai
Wong, Willie
1935   Charlie Chan in Shanghai
Wong Foo
1929   The Peacock Fan
Wong Hok-sing
1941   Golden Gate Girl
1943   Gin Guo Chin Yuan
1944   Chin Hai In Siong
       Guon Min Guh Lu
       Kuan Fong Lang Tyeh
1946?   Yee Sio Bo Laan Sin
1947?   Gin Fen Nee Shaan
       Hoon Si Gway Lai
1948?   Jeng Yien Doe Lee
1949?   Yein Dow
Wong Wing, Mrs.
1929   Chinatown Nights
1936   Klondike Annie
1938   Daughter of Shanghai
Woo, Thomas Quon
1949   We Were Strangers
Wood, Allen
1937   Charlie Chan on
       Broadway
1943   Ladies' Day
Wood, Britt
1946   Santa Fe Uprising
1953   Column South
1959   The FBI Story
Wood, Charles B.
1939   King of Chinatown
Wood, Constance
1943   Doughboys in Ireland
Wood, Cyrus, Jr.
1939   Straight to Heaven
Wood, Donald *see* **Woods, Donald**
Wood, Douglas
1935   A Night at the Ritz
       The Wedding Night
1936   The Prisoner of Shark
       Island
1938   The Beloved Brat
1940   Elsa Maxwell's Public
       Deb No. 1
1942   We Were Dancing
1943   The Amazing Mrs.
       Holliday
1944   They Live in Fear
1947   It Had To Be You
       My Wild Irish Rose
1949   Shamrock Hill
Wood, Ernest
1934   The Cat's-Paw
1938   Little Miss Roughneck
Wood, Freeman
1921   Diane of Star Hollow
       Made in Heaven
1923   Fashion Row
1927   McFadden's Flats
1929   Chinatown Nights
       Why Bring That Up?
Wood, Gordon *see* **De Main,**
    Gordon
Wood, Grace
1938   Mr. Wong, Detective
Wood, Harley
1936   Border Phantom
1937   Law and Lead
Wood, Harry
1936   Human Cargo
Wood, Helen
1936   Charlie Chan at the Race
       Track
Wood, Jeane circa 1930
1930   Sins of the Children
Wood, Jeane mid-1950s
1957   Burden of Truth
       Joe Dakota
1958   Wild Is the Wind
1960   Cimarron
Wood, Jiggs
1951   Queen for a Day
Wood, Judith
1931   Women Love Once

Wood, Lana
1956   The Searchers
1958   Marjorie Morningstar
Wood, Leonard
1947   Marshal of Cripple Creek
Wood, Marjorie
1950   Annie Get Your Gun
1951   Show Boat
Wood, Milton *see* **Woods, Milton**
Wood, Natalie
1956   The Burning Hills
       The Searchers
1958   Kings Go Forth
       Marjorie Morningstar
1960   All the Fine Young
       Cannibals
Wood, Richard C.
1944   Since You Went Away
Wood, Robert Ward (actor) *could*
   be same as **Woods, Robert W.**
   (writer) *or* **Wood, Ward**
1950   Battleground
1951   Go for Broke!
1952   Bugles in the Afternoon
Wood, Sam
1924   The Mine with the Iron
       Door
1930   Sins of the Children
1932   Huddle
1935   A Night at the Opera
       Rendezvous
1939   Gone With the Wind
1946   Saratoga Trunk
1950   Ambush
Wood, Ward *could be same as*
   Wood, Robert Ward
1943   Air Force
1955   Shotgun
Wood, Wilson
1948   Big City
       The Luck of the Irish
1949   The Kissing Bandit
       That Midnight Kiss
1950   Stars in My Crown
       Young Man with a Horn
1951   The Magnificent Yankee
       The Tall Target
1953   Ride, Vaquero!
1955   Trial
1960   Cimarron
Woodbury, Joan
1936   Song of the Gringo
1937   Charlie Chan on
       Broadway
1938   Passport Husband
1941   King of the Zombies
       Ride on Vaquero
1942   Shut My Big Mouth
1944   The Chinese Cat
1949   Boston Blackie's Chinese
       Venture
Henri Woode and His Sextet
1946   That Man of Mine
Woodell, Barbara *same as*
    Wooddell, Barbara
1944   Lady, Let's Dance!
1945   Samurai
1948   Gentleman's Agreement
1950   The Baron of Arizona
1951   Little Big Horn
1952   Fort Osage
1955   Seven Angry Men
1956   Westward Ho the
       Wagons!
1958   Bullwhip
Woodford, Helen
1948   Music Man
Woodruff, Bert
1917   A Love Sublime
1924   The Mine with the Iron
       Door
1926   The Barrier
       The Vanishing American
Woodruff, Deanna
1948   Night Wind
Woodruff, Eleanor
1916   Britton of the Seventh
Woodruff, Frank
1944   Lady, Let's Dance!

Woodruff, Richard
1943   Action in the North
       Atlantic
Woods, Adelaide
1917   Her Own People
Woods, Bobbie
1936   Star for a Night
Woods, Buck *see* **Woods, Ira Buck**
Woods, Clarise
1933   Circle Canyon
Woods, Craig
1943   Doughboys in Ireland
       What's Buzzin' Cousin?
1951   Fort Defiance
Woods, Donald *same as* **Wood,**
   Donald
1934   As the Earth Turns
       Charlie Chan's Courage
       She Was a Lady
1937   Charlie Chan on
       Broadway
1939   The Girl from Mexico
1940   If I Had My Way
       Mexican Spitfire
       Mexican Spitfire Out
       West
1947   Bells of San Fernando
       The Return of Rin Tin Tin
1949   Daughter of the West
Woods, Edward
1934   Beloved
Woods, Frank E.
1915   The Birth of a Nation
Woods, Harry
1926   A Trip to Chinatown
1928   Tyrant of Red Gulch
1929   The Desert Rider
1936   It Had to Happen
       Robin Hood of El Dorado
       Rose of the Rancho
       Silly Billies
1937   Big City
       The Plainsman
1938   The Buccaneer
       The Texans
1939   In Old Caliente
       Mr. Moto in Danger
       Island
1943   In Old Oklahoma
1944   Slightly Terrific
1945   Wanderer of the
       Wasteland
1946   South of Monterey
       Sunset Pass
1947   Thunder Mountain
       Wild Horse Mesa
1948   Indian Agent
       Western Heritage
1949   Colorado Territory
       Masked Raiders
       She Wore a Yellow
       Ribbon
1950   The Traveling
       Saleswoman
1955   The Last Command
Woods, Ira Buck *same as* **Woods,**
   Buck
1939   Double Deal
1940   Broken Strings
       Midnight Shadow
       Mystery in Swing
1942   In This Our Life
       Lucky Ghost
1951   A Streetcar Named Desire
1958   St. Louis Blues
Woods, Lotta
1925   Don Q, Son of Zorro
Woods, Madeline
1946   Stars on Parade
Woods, Milton *same as* **Wood,**
   Milton
1946   Beware
       Stars on Parade
       Tall, Tan and Terrific
1946?   Fight That Ghost
1947   Boy! What a Girl!
       Reet, Petite and Gone
1948   The Fight Never Ends
Woods, Pearl
1956   Rockin' the Blues

Woods, Robert W. (*writer*) *could be same as* **Wood, Robert Ward** (*actor*)
1958   Ambush at Cimarron Pass
Woods, Trevy
1919   The Homesteader
Woods, Walter
1923   Ruggles of Red Gap
        Thirty Days
1928   The Mating Call
1930   La fuerza del querer
1936   Sutter's Gold
Woodward, Bob
1941   Mystery Ship
1948   Silver Trails
1958   Apache Territory
Woodward, Henry *same as* **Woodward, Henry F.**
1918   Hidden Pearls
1920   The Last of the Mohicans
Woodward, Morgan
1956   Westward Ho the Wagons!
Woodward, Sunshine
1931   Chérie
Woodward, William
1939   Moon over Harlem
Woodworth, Jane
1940   Mexican Spitfire Out West
1941   The Mexican Spitfire's Baby
1942   Mexican Spitfire Sees a Ghost
Woody, Jack
1953   Last of the Comanches
Woody, Lois
1933   It's Great to Be Alive
Wooley, Sheb
1950   Rocky Mountain
1951   Apache Drums
        Distant Drums
        Little Big Horn
1952   Bugles in the Afternoon
        High Noon
1955   Trial
1956   Giant
1957   The Oklahoman
        Trooper Hook
1958   Terror in a Texas Town
Woolf, Edgar Allan
1932   Flesh
1936   Mad Holiday
Woolford, Bertha
1946   Saratoga Trunk
Woolley, Monty
1944   Since You Went Away
Woolsey, Robert
1933   Diplomaniacs
1936   Silly Billies
Wooten, Red
1958   Kings Go Forth
Wooton, Rodney
1951   The Tall Target
Wooton, Sarita
1939   Papá soltero
        El trovador de la radio
Wootton, Stephen
1957   All Mine to Give
Worden, Hank *same as* **Snow, Heber**
1940   Northwest Passage (Book I—Rogers' Rangers)
        Viva Cisco Kid
1948   Fort Apache
        Red River
        Tap Roots
1949   The Fighting Kentuckian
        Streets of Laredo
        3 Godfathers
1952   Apache War Smoke
        The Big Sky
        The Quiet Man
1955   The Indian Fighter
        The Vanishing American
1956   Davy Crockett and the River Pirates
        The Searchers
1957   Dragoon Wells Massacre
1958   Bullwhip
1960   Sergeant Rutledge

Worlock, Frederick
1940   Little Nellie Kelly
        Murder over New York
        Northwest Passage (Book I—Rogers' Rangers)
1947   Last of the Redmen
Wormser, Richard
1949   Tulsa
1952   The Half-Breed
Worne, Duke
1915   Just Jim
1917   John Ermine of the Yellowstone
1927   Heroes in Blue
Worsley, Wallace
1918   An Alien Enemy
        The Goddess of Lost Lake
1919   Diane of the Green Van
Worth, Cedric R.
1940   The Ramparts We Watch
Worth, Constance
1943   Let's Have Fun
Worth, David
1935   Riddle Ranch
1936   Charlie Chan at the Race Track
        General Spanky
Worth, Harry
1936   Sea Spoilers
1938   Dangerous to Know
1940   The Mark of Zorro
Worth, Jack
1947   Ride the Pink Horse
1948   Big City
        Tap Roots
Worth, Lillian
1937   Big City
Worth, Mary
1946   Till the End of Time
1948   Gentleman's Agreement
Worth, Thelma
1921   By Right of Birth
Worthen, Ken
1956   Reprisal!
Worthing, Helen Lee
1925   Flower of Night
Worthington, William *same as* **Worthington, William J.**
1918   His Birthright
1919   The Courageous Coward
        The Gray Horizon
        A Heart in Pawn
        His Debt
        The Tong Man
1935   A Night at the Ritz
1936   Dangerous Intrigue
1937   The Devil's Playground
        Man of the People
1938   The Beloved Brat
Worthley, Althea
1918   How Could You, Jean?
Wottitz, Gertrude
1945   The House on 92nd St.
Wragge, Edward
1940   The Ramparts We Watch
Wray, Ardel
1943   The Leopard Man
Wray, Bradley King *see* **King, Bradley** (*writer*)
Wray, C. C. L.
1960   Wild River
Wray, Fay
1929   Thunderbolt
1930   Behind the Make-Up
        Galas de la Paramount
1941   Adam Had Four Sons
Wray, Joe
1920   The Devil's Claim
Wray, John
1932   The Match King
1934   The Cat's-Paw
1938   Spawn of the North
Wray, John Griffith
1923   Anna Christie
Wray, Willow
1933   It's Great to Be Alive
Wren, Chris
1943   Hitler's Children
1945   Great Stagecoach Robbery

Wren, Ginny
1945   Great Stagecoach Robbery
Wren, Sam
1943   Action in the North Atlantic
        They Came to Blow Up America
Wright, Armand "Curly"
1937   That I May Live
1940   East of the River
Wright, Barbara Bell
1958   Home Before Dark
Wright, Ben
1955   A Man Called Peter
Wright, Bertha
1936   The Green Pastures
Wright, Cobina, Jr.
1941   Accent on Love
        Charlie Chan in Rio
Wright, Dave
1958   Flaming Frontier
Wright, Dora
1960   The Day They Robbed the Bank of England
Wright, Ed
1959   The Oregon Trail
Wright, Ellsworth
1954   Go Man Go
Wright, Gilbert
1937   The Californian
Wright, Glen
1958   Tonka
Wright, Harold Bell
1937   The Californian
Wright, Howard
1955   The Gun That Won the West
        Headline Hunters
        Seminole Uprising
Wright, Jimmy
1949   Souls of Sin
Wright, John Wayne
1946   Sheriff of Redwood Valley
Wright, Lydia
1950   Damien
Wright, Mack V. *same as* **Wright, Mack**
1917   The Bar Sinister
1933   Man from Monterey
1937   The Riders of the Whistling Skull
Wright, Marbeth
1933   It's Great to Be Alive
Wright, Milton B.
1953   Beneath the 12-Mile Reef
Wright, Nanine
1916   A Child of Mystery
1918?   Rosemary Climbs the Heights
Wright, Norman
1950   Damien
Wright, Ralph
1946   Song of the South
Wright, Richard
1951   Native Son
Wright, Tenny
1933   The Telegraph Trail
Wright, Teresa
1950   The Men
1952   California Conquest
Wright, Wen
1946   California Gold Rush
Wright, Will
1942   Shut My Big Mouth
        Tales of Manhattan
1943   In Old Oklahoma
        The Meanest Man in the World
1945   Rhapsody in Blue
        Salome, Where She Danced
1946   Without Reservations
1947   California
        The Jolson Story
1949   Lust for Gold
1950   No Way Out
        Sunset in the West
        A Ticket to Tomahawk
1951   The Tall Target
1955   Not As a Stranger

1958   Gunman's Walk
Wright, William 1912—1949
1941   Louisiana Purchase
1945   Escape in the Fog
1949   Rose of the Yukon
Wright, William (*musician*)
1951   Slaughter Trail
Wright, William H. *not the same as* **Wright, William** 1912—1949
1946   Three Wise Fools
1950   Black Hand
        Stars in My Crown
Wrixon, Maris
1939   Daughters Courageous
1940   Knute Rockne—All American
        Santa Fe Trail
1944   Waterfront
1946   The Face of Marble
Wroński, Tadeusz
1941   Z Dymem Pożarów
Wu, Honorable
1939   Mr. Moto Takes a Vacation
Wu, Michael
1938   Daughter of Shanghai
Wui, Ng
1941   Min Jok Jay Hung Sing
Wunder, Thelma
1937   Manhattan Merry-Go-Round
Wunderley, Frank
1921   A Divorce of Convenience
Wurtzel, Lillian
1936   Ramona
Wurtzel, Sol M.
1933   Charlie Chan's Greatest Case
        The Man Who Dared: An Imaginative Biography
1934   Judge Priest
1935   ¡Asegure a su mujer!
        Charlie Chan in Paris
1936   Human Cargo
        Paddy O'Day
        Ramona
        Star for a Night
1937   One Mile from Heaven
        Thank You, Mr. Moto
        That I May Live
        Think Fast, Mr. Moto
1938   Mr. Moto Takes a Chance
        Mr. Moto's Gamble
        Passport Husband
1939   Charlie Chan at Treasure Island
        Charlie Chan in Honolulu
        The Cisco Kid and the Lady
        City in Darkness
        The Escape
        Heaven with a Barbed Wire Fence
        Mr. Moto Takes a Vacation
        Mr. Moto's Last Warning
1940   Charlie Chan in Panama
        Charlie Chan's Murder Cruise
        Jennie
        Lucky Cisco Kid
        Murder over New York
        Viva Cisco Kid
1941   Charlie Chan in Rio
        Ride on Vaquero
        Romance of the Rio Grande
1942   Whispering Ghosts
        Young America
1948   Half Past Midnight
        Night Wind
Wyatt, Al *same as* **Wyatt, Alan**
1953   The Great Sioux Uprising
1954   Sitting Bull
1955   The Far Horizons
        Seven Angry Men
        Shotgun
1956   7th Cavalry
1957   The Guns of Fort Petticoat
1958   The Rawhide Trail
        Tonka

1959   The Jayhawkers!
Wyatt, David
1952   It's a Big Country: An
        American Anthology
Wyatt, Jane
1940   Girl from God's Country
1942   The Navy Comes Through
1948   Gentleman's Agreement
Wycherly, Margaret
1945   Johnny Angel
Wyenn, Than
1955   Good Morning, Miss Dove
1959   Imitation of Life
1960   The Sign of Zorro
Wykoff, Frank
1937   Big City
Wykoff, Leon see **Ames, Leon**
Wyler, Jorie
1960   Cimarron
Wyler, Robert
1946   The Gentleman
        Misbehaves
Wyler, Trude
1958   Wild Is the Wind
Wyler, William
1928   Anybody Here Seen Kelly?
1933   Counsellor at Law
Wylie, Irene
1918   The Spreading Evil
Wylie, Philip
1939   Charlie Chan in Reno
Wyman, Jane
1953   So Big
Wyman, Steve
1954   War Arrow
Wymore, Patrice
1950   Rocky Mountain
1953   The Man Behind the Gun
Wynant, H. M.
1957   Run of the Arrow
1958   Oregon Passage
        Tonka
Wyndham, Bruce
1933   L'amour guide
Wyndham, Herbert
1946   Notorious
Wynn, Ed
1958   Marjorie Morningstar
Wynn, Gordon see **Wynne,**
  Gordon
Wynn, Keenan
1944   Since You Went Away
1945   Between Two Women
1949   That Midnight Kiss
1950   Annie Get Your Gun
1952   It's a Big Country: An
        American Anthology
1958   Touch of Evil
Wynn, Mary
1922   The Woman He Loved
Wynn, May
1954   They Rode West
1956   The White Squaw
Wynn, Nan
1943   Good Luck, Mr. Yates
Wynne, Gordon same as **Wynn,**
  Gordon
1944   Something for the Boys
1947   Calendar Girl
1951   Gambling House
        Little Big Horn
1954   Thunder Pass
1957   Beau James
1958   Houseboat
Wynne, Jerry
1955   Blackboard Jungle
Wynter, Dana
1955   The View from Pompey's
        Head
1959   Shake Hands with the
        Devil
Wynters, Charlotte
1931   Personal Maid
1955   Foxfire
Wyss, Alfredo U.
1940   The Ramparts We Watch
Xazexrestou, Lola
1954   Barefoot Battalion

Xydias, Anthony J.
1922   The Crow's Nest
1924   Yankee Speed
1926   Buffalo Bill on the U. P.
        Trail
        General Custer at Little
        Big Horn
1927   With Sitting Bull at the
        Spirit Lake Massacre
Yaconelli, Frank see also **Moro**
  and Yaconelli
1929   Señor Americano
1934   Broadway Bill
1936   Down to the Sea
        Robin Hood of El Dorado
1937   It Could Happen to You
1938   Wild Horse Canyon
1939   Drifting Westward
1940   The Mark of Zorro
1941   Hurry, Charlie, Hurry
1946   Beauty and the Bandit
        South of Monterey
1947   Riding the California
        Trail
        Wild Horse Mesa
1948   The Dude Goes West
1956   Serenade
1959   The Black Orchid
Yaconelli, Lou
1936   Robin Hood of El Dorado
Yaconelli, Zachary same as
  Yaconelli, Z.
1950   The Baron of Arizona
1951   The Great Caruso
        Westward the Women
Yacyna, William
1939   Cossacks in Exile
Yaen, Chai
1934   The Youth of Russia
Yama, Togo could be same as
  Yamamatto or **Yamamoto,**
  Togo
1918   The City of Dim Faces
Yamaguchi, Shirley
1952   Japanese War Bride
Yamamatto could be same as
  Yama, Togo or **Yamamoto,**
  Togo
1918   The Midnight Patrol
Yamamoto, Togo could be same as
  Yama, Togo or **Yamamatto**
1920   Pagan Love
1921   A Tale of Two Worlds
        Where Lights Are Low
1922   Flesh and Blood
Yamaoka, Iris
1937   Waikiki Wedding
Yamaoka, Josephine
1930   Chijlku wo mawasuru
        chikara
Yamaoka, Otto
1931   The Black Camel
1932   The Hatchet Man
1934   Limehouse Blues
1935   The Wedding Night
1937   Song of the City
Yamin, Robert H.
1960   This Rebel Breed
Yance, Luis
1930   Galas de la Paramount
Yankee, Dolly
1945   Where Do We Go From
        Here?
Yanover, David
1940   Eli Eli
Yap, Barry
1950   Damien
Yaray, Hans
1947   Carnegie Hall
Yarbo, Lillian
1936   Rainbow on the River
1939   Way Down South
1940   Lucky Cisco Kid
1943   The Gang's All Here
        Redhead from Manhattan
1946   The Sailor Takes a Wife
        Saratoga Trunk
Yarborough, Barton
1946   The Red Dragon

Yarbrough, Jean same as
  Yarbrough, Gene
1932   Hypnotized
1936   Silly Billies
1941   Caught in the Act
        The Gang's All Here
        King of the Zombies
1946   Cuban Pete
Yarnell, Sally
1949   House of Strangers
1954   War Arrow
Yarson, Lilo
1947   Pirates of Monterey
Yarus, Buddy see **Tyne, George**
Yates, George Worthing
1940   Hi-Yo Silver
1951   The Last Outpost
        The Tall Target
Yates, Hal (*writer*)
1936   General Spanky
Yates, Herbert J. (*prod*)
1949   The Red Menace
1950   Rio Grande
        Rock Island Trail
        Sands of Iwo Jima
1951   Adventures of Captain
        Fabian
        Cuban Fireball
        Oh! Susanna
1952   The Fabulous Senorita
        The Quiet Man
1953   The Sun Shines Bright
1954   Hell's Half Acre
1955   The Last Command
        Santa Fe Passage
        The Vanishing American
1956   Dakota Incident
Yates, Irving
1932   Harlem Is Heaven
Yates, John
1956   The Benny Goodman
        Story
Yawitz, Paul
1944   The Racket Man
1945   I Love a Bandleader
Yazloff, Thomas Alan
1944   Buffalo Bill
Ybarra, Roque same as **Ybarra,**
  Rocky
1942   Tortilla Flat
1949   Arctic Manhunt
        Border Incident
1952   Indian Uprising
        The Iron Mistress
1959   The FBI Story
Ybarra, Roque, Jr.
1947   Ride the Pink Horse
Yea, Uwane, Princess
1919   The Heart of Wetona
Yeargan, Arthur
1924?   The Flaming Crisis
Yearsley, Ralph
1923   Anna Christie
1926   Desert Gold
1929   Show Boat
Yeats, Murray F.
1949   Top O' the Morning
Yellen, Jack
1938   My Lucky Star
Yellow, Billy
1956   The Searchers
Yellow Hand, Chief
1917   The Adventures of Buffalo
        Bill
Yellow Robe, Chief
1930   The Silent Enemy
Yellowhorse, Ki
1934   Laughing Boy
Yeoman, Art
1943   Mr. Lucky
Yeomans, W. C.
1958   Tonka
Yetter, William could be same as
  Yetter, William, Jr.
1940   Escape
        The Man I Married
1943   Action in the North
        Atlantic
        Crash Dive
        They Came to Blow Up
        America

1949   The Girl from Jones
        Beach
1951   Go for Broke!
Yetter, William, Jr. could be same
  as **Yetter, William**
1944   Lifeboat
        They Live in Fear
1951   The Great Caruso
Ying, Jow Sil
1934   Blossom Time
Ying, Jung
1941   Min Jok Jay Hung Sing
Ying, Wu Dip could be same as
  Dip-Ying, Wu
1934   Blossom Time
Yip, William
1945   Escape in the Fog
1949   Boston Blackie's Chinese
        Venture
1960   Ice Palace
Yohalem, George
1921   Lotus Blossom
        No Woman Knows
1930   Cascarrabias
1931   Gente alegre
Yokei, Harris
1951   Go for Broke!
Yokota, William
1952   Japanese War Bride
Yonemura, Hitoshi
1930   Chijlku wo mawasuru
        chikara
Yong, Soo
1936   Klondike Annie
        Mad Holiday
1937   Think Fast, Mr. Moto
1941   Secret of the Wastelands
Yonover, David
1940   The Great Advisor
Yorba, Charles
1917   His Sweetheart
Yordan, Philip
1942   Syncopation
1949   Anna Lucasta
        House of Strangers
1950   No Way Out
        Panic in the Streets
1954   Broken Lance
1956   The Last Frontier
1959   Anna Lucasta
1960   Studs Lonigan
Yorga, Viola
1924   Yankee Speed
York, Catherine
1945   I Love a Bandleader
York, Duke same as **Yorke, Duke**
1935   So Red the Rose
1942   Nazi Agent
        Sunday Punch
        Woman of the Year
1944   An American Romance
1948   The Paleface
1950   Winchester '73
1951   Fort Defiance
        Oh! Susanna
        Snake River Desperadoes
York, Jeff
1942   Nazi Agent
1948   The Paleface
        Unconquered
1949   Knock on Any Door
1956   Davy Crockett and the
        River Pirates
        Westward Ho the
        Wagons!
York, Mary
1933   It's Great to Be Alive
York, Melanie
1951   Queen for a Day
Yorke, Duke see **York, Duke**
Yorke, Edith
1923   The Miracle Makers
Yoshinaga, George
1959   The Crimson Kimono
Yoshkin, Niccolai see **Kosleck,**
  Martin
1939   Confessions of a Nazi Spy
Yost, Dorothy
1920   For the Soul of Rafael
1921   One Man in a Million
1922   Little Miss Smiles

1937	That Girl from Paris
1949	The Cowboy and the Indians

Yost, Robert
1936	Desert Gold
1939	King of Chinatown
1940	Young Buffalo Bill

Youling, Tschang
1931	La carta (foreign version)

Young, Miss
1921	A Giant of His Race

Young, Al
1941	Sunday Sinners
1947	Sepia Cinderella
1948?	Junction 88

Young, Arthur H. not the same as **Young, Artie** (African-American actor)
1925	The True North

Young, Artie (African-American actor) not the same as **Young, Arthur H.**
1939	The Bronze Buckaroo
	Harlem Rides the Range

Young, Billy
1938	Outside of Paradise

Young, Boas same as **Young, Boaz**
1934	The Youth of Russia
1939	Tevya

Young, Buck
1959	Night of the Quarter Moon

Young, Carleton not the same as **Young, Carleton G.**
1937	It Could Happen to You
1938	Outlaw Express
1939	Trigger Fingers
1942	Valley of the Sun
1953	The Glory Brigade
	Last of the Comanches
1954	Arrow in the Dust
1955	Seven Angry Men
1957	Run of the Arrow
1958	The Last Hurrah
1960	Sergeant Rutledge

Young, Carleton G. not the same as **Young, Carleton**
1949	The Kissing Bandit

Young, Carroll
1957	Apache Warrior
	The Deerslayer
1958	Machete

Young, Chow
1921	Lotus Blossom
	A Tale of Two Worlds

Young, Clara Kimball
1916	The Yellow Passport
1920	For the Soul of Rafael
1922	The Hands of Nara
1937	Hills of Old Wyoming

Young, Clarence Upson same as **Young, Clarence**
1939	Bad Lands
1942	North to the Klondike
1947	Riding the California Trail

Young, Clifton
1947	My Wild Irish Rose
1949	Illegal Entry

Young, Clint
1959	Odds Against Tomorrow

Young, Collier
1957	The Halliday Brand

Young, Delores
1936	Ramona

Young, Ernest "Tex"
1947	Oregon Trail Scouts

Young, Evelyn
1940	Prairie Schooners

Young, Faron
1956	Daniel Boone, Trail Blazer
1957	Raiders of Old California

Young, Felix
1933	Let's Fall in Love

Young, Frank H.
1945	The Navajo Trail
1946	Border Bandits

Young, Gig same as **Barr, Byron**
1942	They Died With Their Boots On
1943	Air Force
1949	Lust for Gold
1951	Only the Valiant
	Slaughter Trail

Young, Gordon
1937	El capitán Tormenta

Young, Grace
1949	The Girl from Jones Beach

Young, Harold
1936	My American Wife
1942	Rubber Racketeers
1947	Citizen Saint

Young, Jack, Capt.
1943	Yankee Doodle Dandy

Young, Jackie
1932	Harlem Is Heaven

Young, James
1916	The Thousand Dollar Husband
	Unprotected
1918	The Temple of Dusk
1924	Welcome Stranger

Young, Lee
1958	St. Louis Blues

Young, Lon
1929	The Peacock Fan

Young, Loretta
1932	The Hatchet Man
1933	Grand Slam
1936	Ramona
1947	The Farmer's Daughter

Young, Lucille
1919	Fighting for Gold
1925	Quicker'n Lightnin'

Young, Mabel
1920?	Broken Hearts
1921	The Burden of Race
	The Gunsaulus Mystery
1922	Spitfire
1923	Deceit

Young, Mari
1951	The House on Telegraph Hill

Young, Marie
1939	Moon over Harlem

Young, Mary
1942	The Navy Comes Through
1944	Address Unknown

Young, Nedrick same as **Douglas, Nathan E.; Young, Ned**
1943	Ladies' Day
1949	Border Incident
1950	A Lady Without Passport
1952	The Iron Mistress
1953	The Eddie Cantor Story
1958	The Defiant Ones
	Terror in a Texas Town

Young, Noah
1927	Don Mike
	Ham and Eggs at the Front
1929	Welcome Danger
1934	The Cat's-Paw

Young, Norma
1951	Westward the Women

Young, Robert
1931	The Black Camel
	The Guilty Generation
1932	Unashamed
1934	La ciudad de cartón
	Lazy River
1938	Josette
	The Toy Wife
1940	Northwest Passage (Book I—Rogers' Rangers)
1941	Western Union
1947	Crossfire
1952	The Half-Breed

Young, Robert Lee
1950	Intruder in the Dust

Young, Roland
1931	The Squaw Man
1933	A Lady's Profession
1935	Ruggles of Red Gap
1942	Tales of Manhattan

Young, Sen see **Yung, Victor Sen**

Young, Tammany
1921	Bits of Life
1927	Blind Alleys

Young, Tarza
1955	Brevities of 1955

Young, Tony
1960	Walk Like a Dragon

Young, Trummy
1957	Satchmo the Great

Young, Victor Sen see **Yung, Victor Sen**

Young, Waldemar
1919	Bonnie, Bonnie Lassie
	The Unpainted Woman
1930	Ladies Love Brutes
1937	The Plainsman

Young, Z. Y.
1921	A Modern Cain

Young, Zella
1939	Reform School

Youngblood, Hal
1955	Davy Crockett, King of the Wild Frontier

Younger, A. P.
1921	The Kiss
1922	Second Hand Rose
1927	Wild Geese
1930	Sunny Skies

Younger, Jack
1957	Burden of Truth
1960	The Adventures of Huckleberry Finn

Yount, C. R.
1958	Tonka

Yowlache, Chief not the same as **Yowlachie, Chief**
1925	Tonio, Son of the Sierras
1926	War Paint
1927	The Red Raiders
	With Sitting Bull at the Spirit Lake Massacre
1928	The Glorious Trail
1929	Hawk of the Hills
	The Invaders

Yowlachie, Chief same as **Yowlachi, Chief** not the same as **Yowlache, Chief**
1941	This Woman Is Mine
1942	King of the Stallions
1943	Frontier Fury
1946	Canyon Passage
	Wild West
1947	Bowery Buckaroos
1948	The Dude Goes West
	The Paleface
	Red River
1949	The Cowboy and the Indians
	The Prairie
1950	Annie Get Your Gun
	Cherokee Uprising
	Indian Territory
	A Ticket to Tomahawk
	The Traveling Saleswoman
	Winchester '73
	Young Daniel Boone
1951	Warpath
1952	Buffalo Bill in Tomahawk Territory
	The Half-Breed
1953	The Pathfinder
1954	Drums Across the River
1959	The FBI Story
	Yellowstone Kelly

Yrigoyen, Joe
1953	Old Overland Trail
1958	Gunfire at Indian Gap

Yuck, Tong
1939?	A Chinese Gains a Fortune in America

Yuen, Tom
1943	Bataan

Yuk, Yip Foot
1939?	A Chinese Gains a Fortune in America

Yule, Joe
1939	Judge Hardy and Son
1940	New Moon
1942	Nazi Agent
	Three Hearts for Julia

Yung, Far Sui
1941	Golden Gate Girl

Yung, Victor Sen same as **Young, Sen; Young, Victor Sen; Yung, Sen**
1939	Charlie Chan at Treasure Island
	Charlie Chan in Honolulu
	Charlie Chan in Reno
1940	Charlie Chan at the Wax Museum
	Charlie Chan in Panama
	Charlie Chan's Murder Cruise
	Murder over New York
1941	Charlie Chan in Rio
	Dead Men Tell
1942	Across the Pacific
	Castle in the Desert
	Little Tokyo, U.S.A.
1945	Betrayal from the East
1946	Dangerous Money
	G. I. War Brides
	Shadows Over Chinatown
	The Trap
1947	The Chinese Ring
1948	Docks of New Orleans
	The Feathered Serpent
	The Golden Eye
	Half Past Midnight
	Shanghai Chest
1949	Boston Blackie's Chinese Venture
1950	The Breaking Point
	Chinatown at Midnight
	A Ticket to Tomahawk

Yurka, Blanche
1940	Escape
1944	Cry of the Werewolf
1950	The Furies
1953	Taxi
1959	Thunder in the Sun

Yvonne, Mimi
1914	The Littlest Rebel
1915	Kreutzer Sonata

Żabczyński, Aleksander
1930	Toda una vida (foreign version)

Zaccone, Michael
1951	The Mark of the Renegade

Zachary, Mark
1958	Sierra Baron

Zajic, Haldane
1960	The Adventures of Huckleberry Finn

Zak, John
1945	The House on 92nd St.

Zakin, Alexander
1953	Tonight We Sing

Zambrano, Ernesto
1930	Las campanas de Capistrano
1956	The Burning Hills

Zamudio, Victor
1956	Reprisal!

Zandt, Philip van see **Van Zandt, Philip**

Zane, a horse
1950	Riders of the Pony Express

Zaner, Jimmy
1943	Hitler's Children
1944	They Live in Fear

Zanette, Guy same as **Zanett, Guy**
1943	The Girl from Monterrey
1945	Betrayal from the East
1951	Gambling House

Zanger, Jacob
1939	Motel the Operator
	My Son
1940	The Great Advisor
	Her Second Mother
	The Jewish Melody

1941   Mazel Tov Yidden
Zangrilli, O.
1925   The Greatest Love of All
Zanuck, Darryl F. *same as*
    Crossman, Melville
1925   Hogan's Alley
1926   The Little Irish Girl
1927   Ham and Eggs at the
        Front
        Irish Hearts
        Old San Francisco
1940   Elsa Maxwell's Public
        Deb No. 1
        The Man I Married
        The Mark of Zorro
1941   Sun Valley Serenade
        Western Union
1942   Song of the Islands
1943   Crash Dive
        Wintertime
1944   Buffalo Bill
        Lifeboat
1945   The Dolly Sisters
        The House on 92nd St.
1947   The Foxes of Harrow
1948   Call Northside 777
        Cry of the City
        Fury at Furnace Creek
        Gentleman's Agreement
        The Luck of the Irish
1949   House of Strangers
        Pinky
        Thieves' Highway
1950   No Way Out
        A Ticket to Tomahawk
1953   Beneath the 12-Mile Reef
1954   Broken Lance
1955   Good Morning, Miss Dove
        A Man Called Peter
        Seven Cities of Gold
        The View from Pompey's
        Head
Zanville, Bernard *see* **Clark, Dane**
Zaranova, Erika
1940   Overture to Glory
Zarco, Estelita
1940   Young Buffalo Bill
Zaremba, John
1955   Apache Ambush
1956   Reprisal!
1960   Key Witness
Zárraga, Miguel de, Jr.
1938   Castillos en el aire
Zárraga, Miguel de, Sr.
1930   Olimpia
1931   Cheri-Bibi
1932   Hollywood, ciudad de
        ensueño
1933   Dos noches
1934   La buenaventura
        La cruz y la espada
        Nada más que una mujer
1935   No matarás
1939   Verbena trágica
Zavattini, Cesare
1954   Indiscretion of an
        American Wife
Zavian, Mary
1945   Nob Hill
1953   Cry of the Hunted
Zaxarias, Nikos
1954   Barefoot Battalion
Zayenda, Edmund
1939   A Brivele der Mamen
        Mamele
Zazi, Siru
1931   Zein Weib's Lubovnick
ZeBrack, Raymond
1945   Great Stagecoach Robbery
Zeer, E. L.
1927   [Japanese-American Film]
Zeiden, Joseph *same as* **Zeiden,**
    Josef
1950   God, Man and Devil
1950?   Three Daughters
Zeidman, B. F. *same as* **Zeidman,**
    Bernard F.
1934   Beloved
Zeisler, Alfred
1945   The House on 92nd St.

Zeitlin, Esther
1949   The Undercover Man
1950   A Lady Without Passport
1951   The Great Caruso
1952   Anything Can Happen
Zekley, Gary
1947   Jiggs and Maggie in
        Society
Zelaya, Don
1940   Girl from God's Country
Zelazo, Shirley
1932   Uncle Moses
Zeldis, Joshua
1950   God, Man and Devil
Zeliff, Seymour *same as* **Zeliff,**
    Skipper
1921   Shadows of the West
1922   The Guttersnipe
1928   Uncle Tom's Cabin
Zelinka, Sydney P.
1947   Copacabana
Zelitsky, Vladimir
1937   Natalka Poltavka
1939   Cossacks in Exile
Zellner, Lois
1916   The Innocent Lie
Zendar, Fred
1948   Unconquered
1950   Battleground
Zenor, Olivia
1930   Revista
        Hispano-Americana
Zepeda, Elsa Lorraine
1948   Angel in Exile
Zeuthen, Durwood von
1931   Delicious
Ziegfeld, Florenz
1929   Show Boat
1930   Whoopee
Zieliński, Stefan
1941   Ten Ostatni
Zierler, Samuel
1930   She Got What She Wanted
1932   Men Are Such Fools
1933   Racetrack
Ziffren, Lester
1938   Passport Husband
1940   Charlie Chan in Panama
        Charlie Chan's Murder
        Cruise
        Murder over New York
1941   Charlie Chan in Rio
Zilberstein, Moishe *see* **Silverstein,**
    Moishe
Zilly, John "Jack"
1951   Saturday's Hero
Zilzer, Wolfgang *same as* **Andor,**
    Paul; Voigt, John
1931   Buster se marie *(foreign*
        version)
1939   Confessions of a Nazi Spy
1940   Escape
        Three Faces West
1942   All Through the Night
1943   Margin for Error
        They Came to Blow Up
        America
1944   They Live in Fear
1956   Singing in the Dark
Zimbalist, Efrem, Jr.
1949   House of Strangers
1957   Band of Angels
1958   Home Before Dark
Zimbalist, Sam
1942   Tortilla Flat
1956   The Catered Affair
Zimina, Valentina
1925   A Son of His Father
1926   Rose of the Tenements
Zimmer, Bernard
1934   Caravane
Zimmer, Norma
1956   Serenade
Zimmerman, Pierre
1930   Toda una vida *(foreign*
        version)
Zimmerman, Victor
1942   Gentleman Jim
        Juke Girl
        Secret Enemies
        They Died With Their
        Boots On
        Wings for the Eagle

1943   Air Force
        Yankee Doodle Dandy
Zinnemann, Fred
1947   Little Mister Jim
1950   The Men
1951   Teresa
1952   High Noon
1953   The Member of the
        Wedding
Zinser, Leo
1950   Panic in the Streets
Zirato, Bruno
1918   My Cousin
Ziskin, Henry
1939   Tevya
Zizold, Carlos
1929   Die Königsloge
Zoppetti, Cesare
1930   Toda una vida *(foreign*
        version)
1931   La fiesta del diablo
        (foreign version)
Zorina, Vera
1941   Louisiana Purchase
Zucco, George
1936   After the Thin Man
1937   Souls at Sea
1939   Charlie Chan in Honolulu
1940   New Moon
1949   Harbor of Missing Men
Zuckerberg, Regina
1935   Bar-Mitzvah
Zuckerberg, Sigmund
1932   Joseph in the Land of
        Egypt
Zuckerman, George
1949   Border Incident
1954   Taza, Son of Cochise
Zuckert, William
1959   Odds Against Tomorrow
Zuckmann, Eric
1960   I Aim at the Stars: the
        Wernher von Braun
        Story
Zúffoli, Eugenia
1930   El secreto del doctor
Zugsmith, Albert
1956   Raw Edge
1957   Man in the Shadow
1958   Touch of Evil
Zukor, Adolph
1918   Amarilly of Clothes-Line
        Alley
        A Daughter of the Old
        South
        Good-Bye, Bill
        My Cousin
        Out of a Clear Sky
        Uncle Tom's Cabin
        A Woman of Impulse
1919   Come Out of the Kitchen
        His Parisian Wife
1920   On with the Dance
1922   Anna Ascends
1923   The White Flower
1924   The Heritage of the
        Desert
        North of 36
        Peter Pan
        Tongues of Flame
1925   Flower of Night
        Irish Luck
        The Manicure Girl
        Salome of the Tenements
        A Son of His Father
        The Thundering Herd
1926   The Campus Flirt
        Desert Gold
        The Vanishing American
1927   Blind Alleys
        Drums of the Desert
        The Gay Defender
        Open Range
        The Way of All Flesh
1928   The Secret Hour
1930   El cuerpo del delito
1934   Behold My Wife!
        Limehouse Blues
        Wagon Wheels
1935   McFadden's Flats
        Ruggles of Red Gap
        So Red the Rose

1936   Desert Gold
        Klondike Annie
        Rose of the Rancho
1937   The Barrier
        Hills of Old Wyoming
        Maid of Salem
        The Plainsman
        Souls at Sea
        Waikiki Wedding
1938   The Buccaneer
        Dangerous to Know
        Daughter of Shanghai
        Spawn of the North
        The Texans
Zukor, Eugene J.
1940   The Way of All Flesh
Zwerling, Yetta
1937   I Want to Be a Mother
1939   Kol Nidre
        Motel the Operator
1940   The Great Advisor
        Her Second Mother
        The Jewish Melody
1941   Mazel Tov Yidden
1950   Monticello, Here We
        Come!

SUBJECT INDEX

★The Subject Index is arranged alphabetically by subject terms. Film entries are subdividied chronologically, then alphabetically, beneath the headings. A unique aspect of the Subject Index, however, is that the film titles are entered in two different type styles: Roman type to indicate major subjects, and italic type to indicate minor subjects.

Most of the entries in the Subject Index correspond to the most recent edition of the Library of Congress Subject Headings. Following the philosophy of the Library of Congress to create a dynamic rather than static thesaurus, we have added a large number of entries reflective of persons, places and themes that are uniquely suited to this book.

In the index, the reader will notice several headings which, despite efforts at paring, are enormous. Marriage and its various sub-divisions, Impersonation and imposture and Murder are each cited hundreds of times. Yet the reason why these categories are so vast is that they have been extremely popular motifs in the motion pictures. To increase the value of seemingly overwhelming numbers of films under specific headings, a scheme of "major" and "minor" headings was devised to divide each category. Thus, the user will find that the titles in Roman type under specific headings represent important themes within that film. Usually, entries for individual films will list five to six major headings. Titles listed in italics indicate less importance within the film entries, which characteristically contain ten to twenty minor headings. It is hoped that this devision, which was established in the *AFI Catalog of Feature Films, 1911-1920*, will increase the value of the index, both as a listing of important subjects and also as a motif or "key word" index for those scholars interested in knowning all films which included particular themes, locations, or persons.

In addition to general themes, actual historical persons, events and geographic locations are listed in the Subject Index. Literary works and fictional characters are also included if they were significant to the plots of individual films.

SUBJECT INDEX

4-F
1943 *Good Luck, Mr. Yates*
1944 *The Racket Man*
1945 *Where Do We Go From Here?*

4-H clubs
1942 Young America

4th of July
use **Fourth of July**

A-Bomb
use **Atomic bomb**

Abdication
1933 *Victims of Persecution*

Abduction
1913 Traffic in Souls
1913? The Call of the Blood
1914 Hearts United
In the Land of the Head Hunters
An Odyssey of the North
1915 The Lamb
1917 *The Call of the East*
Follow the Girl
The Gun Fighter
John Ermine of the Yellowstone
The Primitive Call
Unconquered
1918 The Gypsy Trail
The Hell Cat
The Midnight Patrol
Mystic Faces
The Red, Red Heart
The Source
1919 *The She Wolf*
1920 *Before the White Man Came*
The Cyclone
The Daughter of Dawn
Dinty
The Girl of My Heart
Huckleberry Finn
The Mark of Zorro
1923 A Shot in the Night
1924 Two Shall Be Born
1925 The Gold Hunters
Justice of the Far North
Quicker'n Lightnin'
1928 Breed of the Sunsets
1929 Sioux Blood
1931 *The Cohens and Kellys in Africa*
Del infierno al cielo
1932 *The Golden West*
White Eagle
1933 *A Lady's Profession*
El rey de los gitanos
1934 La buenaventura
Charlie Chan's Courage
The Fighting Hero
Nada más que una mujer
Wagon Wheels
1935 *Charlie Chan in Shanghai*
His Family Tree
1936 *Border Phantom*
Desert Gold
El diablo del mar
1937 *Think Fast, Mr. Moto*
1938 *Dangerous to Know*
The Rage of Paris
1939 *The Cisco Kid and the Lady*
Confessions of a Nazi Spy
Straight to Heaven
1940 Am I Guilty?
Mexican Spitfire Out West
While Thousands Cheer
1942 Prisoner of Japan
1943 Ladies' Day
Three Hearts for Julia

1945 *The Cisco Kid Returns*
In Old New Mexico
South of the Rio Grande
1947 *Vigilantes of Boomtown*
1950 Ambush
Jiggs and Maggie Out West
1951 *Cavalry Scout*
1952 *The Big Sky*
The Fighter
1953 *The Charge at Feather River*
Conquest of Cochise
1954 *Apache*
Passion
1956 *Reprisal!*
Westward Ho the Wagons!
1958 Oregon Passage
1960 *Comanche Station*

Abilene (KS)
1924 North of 36
1938 *The Texans*
1948 *Red River*

Abnormalities, Human
1924 Smiling Hate

Abolitionists
1915 The Birth of a Nation
1918 *Free and Equal*
1930 Abraham Lincoln
1937 Souls at Sea
1951 The Tall Target
1955 Seven Angry Men
1957 *Raintree County*
1959 *The Jayhawkers!*

Abraham (Biblical character)
1930 My Yiddishe Mama

Abused children
use **Battered children**

Abused women
use **Battered women**

Acadia (LA)
1929 Evangeline

Acadia (Nova Scotia)
1919 Evangeline
1929 Evangeline

Acapulco (Mexico)
1948 *The Lady from Shanghai*

Accidental death
1918 The Squaw Man
1919 *The Last of His People*
Told in the Hills
1921 *The First Born*
1927 *The Broken Violin*
1931 *Smart Money*
The Squaw Man
1933 *Melodía de arrabal*
La melodía prohibida
1934 Eskimo
Laughing Boy
1936 *The Last of the Mohicans*
Robin Hood of El Dorado
Sins of Man
1937 Underworld
1938 *Mis dos amores*
1939 *Gone With the Wind*
Waterfront
Way Down South
1940 *The Gay Caballero*
1941 *Sullivan's Travels*
1941? The Blood of Jesus
1942 *American Empire*
Mokey
Rubber Racketeers
1945 *Of One Blood*
1946 *Swamp Fire*
1947 *The Foxes of Harrow*
1948 *Old Los Angeles*

1949 *Arctic Manhunt*
We Were Strangers
1950 Give Us This Day
God, Man and Devil
1951 Native Son
Westward the Women
1954 *Barefoot Battalion*
Dangerous Mission
1955 *The Rose Tattoo*
Seven Cities of Gold
1956 *Death of a Scoundrel*
1957 *Bayou*
The Midnight Story
1959 *Cry Tough*
Porgy and Bess
Thunder in the Sun
1960 *This Rebel Breed*

Accidents
1915 After Five
The Danger Signal
Just Jim
1916 *Lone Star*
1920 *The Great Shadow*
Hidden Charms
1921 Hold Your Horses
1931 La llama sagrada
Riders of the Rio
1938 *Spirit of Youth*
1942 *Tortilla Flat*
1946 *The Gentleman Misbehaves*
The Sailor Takes a Wife
1947 *Carnegie Hall*
1948 *Reaching from Heaven*
1949 *The Story of Seabiscuit*
1951 *The Well*
1952 *It's a Big Country: An American Anthology*
1955 *The Far Horizons*

Accountants
1950? *Three Daughters*
1955 *Marty*
1957 *The Brothers Rico*

Acoma
1951 New Mexico

Acoma Indians
New Mexico

Acquittals
1931 *Such Is Life*
1951 *The Girl on the Bridge*
1960 *Sergeant Rutledge*

Acrobats
1922 Head over Heels
1923 Look Your Best
1928 Chinatown Charlie
1933 *Grand Slam*
1941? *The Blood of Jesus*
1950 *The Daughter of Rosie O'Grady*

Acting—Study and teaching
1947 Juke Joint

Actors and actresses
1915 How Molly Malone Made Good
1916 *Lord Loveland Discovers America*
1920 *Darling Mine*
Huckleberry Finn
1921 Cheated Love
1922 Solomon in Society
1923 Deceit
Fashion Row
The Victor
1924 In Hollywood With Potash and Perlmutter
1926 Sweet Daddies
1929 Die Königsloge
1930 *Behind the Make-Up*
El cuerpo del delito

Galas de la Paramount
1931 El comediante
Die Maske Fällt
Pagliacci
Regeneración
Su noche de bodas
1932 Harlem Is Heaven
The Match King
Ten Minutes to Live
1934 Blossom Time
Granaderos del amor
Granaderos del amor
The Great Flirtation
Operator 13
1936 Dimples
Sum Hun
1937 The Jester (Der Purimspieler)
Shadows of the Orient
1939 *The Adventures of Huckleberry Finn*
My Son
1940 *Escape*
Murder over New York
Paradise in Harlem
Perfidia
1941 Playmates
1942 *Mexican Spitfire at Sea*
Tales of Manhattan
Whispering Ghosts
1943 *Dixie*
Let's Have Fun
Yankee Doodle Dandy
1944 *Address Unknown*
Chip Off the Old Block
1945 *The Cisco Kid Returns*
The Great John L.
Rhapsody in Blue
The Scarlet Clue
1946 The Gentleman Misbehaves
That Man of Mine
1947 The Jolson Story
1949? *She's Too Mean for Me*
1951 Show Boat
1956 *Death of a Scoundrel*
1958 *Marjorie Morningstar*
1959 *Imitation of Life*

Adirondack Mountains
1931 Young Sinners
1942 *Secret Enemies*
1958 *Marjorie Morningstar*

Adolescence
1935 *Angelina o el honor de un brigadier*
1945 *A Tree Grows in Brooklyn*
1959 *Imitation of Life*
1960 Take a Giant Step

Adolescents
1934? *Harlem After Midnight*
1936 *Paddy O'Day*
1938 Rascals
1939 The Adventures of Huckleberry Finn
1942 Young America
1943 *Good Luck, Mr. Yates*
1944 *Minstrel Man*
Since You Went Away
1947 *The Adventures of Don Coyote*
Black Gold
1948 *I Remember Mama*
Rocky
1949 *Portrait of Jennie*
1950 *Intruder in the Dust*
1953 The Member of the Wedding
So Big
1955 *The Rose Tattoo*

1956 The Last Wagon
1958 *Never Love a Stranger*
Tonka
1959 Yellowstone Kelly
1960 The Dark at the Top of the
Stairs
This Rebel Breed

Adoption
1913? *Hiawatha*
The Lure of New York
1914 *Where the Trail Divides*
1915 The Adventures of a Madcap
1916 *The Criminal*
The Flames of Johannis
The Morals of Hilda
The Scarlet Oath
1917 *John Ermine of the
Yellowstone*
A Roadside Impresario
Unknown 274
1918 *The Hun Within*
Little Red Decides
Sandy
A Woman of Impulse
1919 The Little Diplomat
The Right to Happiness
The Sleeping Lion
1920 Dinty
The Girl of My Heart
Huckleberry Finn
The Riddle: Woman
1920? Broken Hearts
1921 *Love's Plaything*
One Man in a Million
The Secret Sorrow
1922 The Woman He Loved
1925 Lights of Old Broadway
1927 The Auctioneer
The Callahans and the
Murphys
A Harp in Hock
1930 *Sombras de gloria*
Toda una vida
1931 *Oklahoma Jim*
1932 Hearts of Humanity
No Greater Love
1933 *Racetrack*
1934 Tres amores
1936 *General Spanky*
Let's Sing Again
La última cita
1938 City Streets
God's Step Children
1939 The Escape
Fisherman's Wharf
Miracle on Main Street
Motel the Operator
1940 *East of the River*
Tengo fe en ti
1941 *The Mexican Spitfire's Baby*
1942 *Woman of the Year*
1945 Samurai
Wanderer of the Wasteland
1946 *Three Wise Fools*
1947 Black Gold
Buck Privates Come Home
Dark Delusion
Oregon Trail Scouts
1948 Big City
1950 *Annie Get Your Gun*
Belle of Old Mexico
1952 *The Savage*
1953 *Arrowhead*
1956 *Ghost Town*
1957 *The Brothers Rico*
Run of the Arrow
1960 *Hell to Eternity*

S.S. *Adriatic*
1915 *How Molly Malone Made
Good*

Adultery
use **Infidelity**

Adventurers
1919 Diane of the Green Van
1927 Turkish Delight
1930 El dios del mar
1932 El caballero de la noche
1943 Jack London
1953 *Captain John Smith and
Pocahontas*
1955 Davy Crockett, King of the
Wild Frontier
1956 Davy Crockett and the River
Pirates
Secret of Treasure Mountain

1960 *Cimarron*
Adventures
1937 Waikiki Wedding
Adventuresses
1916 Gold and the Woman
1917 A Wife by Proxy
1918 His Birthright
1919 The Scar
1924 California in '49
1927 The Way of All Flesh
1928 Sins of the Fathers
1930 Behind the Make-Up
Advertisements
1918 *Wanted, a Mother*
1935 *Señora casada necesita
marido*
1937 *Shadows of the Orient*
1948 *Call Northside 777*
1949 *Jigsaw*
Portrait of Jennie
Advertising
1915 Chimmie Fadden Out West
1931 *Quand on est belle*
1935 *Piernas de seda*
1937 *Waikiki Wedding*
1939 The Girl from Mexico
1941 *The Mexican Spitfire's Baby*
1946 *The Sailor Takes a Wife*
Advertising agencies
1943 *Let's Have Fun*
1946 Cuban Pete
1958 *Marjorie Morningstar*
1960 *I Passed for White*
Aerial bombardment
use **Bombing, Aerial**
Aerial combat
1931 *Cuerpo y alma*
1934 *The Unknown Soldier
Speaks*
1935 *Alas sobre el Chaco*
1942 *Wings for the Eagle*
1943 Air Force
1944 *The Negro Soldier*
Aerialists
1923 Look Your Best
1931 Sombras del circo
1932 *Thirteen Women*
1936 *Let's Sing Again*
Aeronautics
1921 The Girl from God's
Country
1936 *Sins of Man*
Aeronautics—Accidents
use **Airplane accidents**
Affidavits
1958 Bullwhip
Africa
1921 A Giant of His Race
1927 The Slaver
1930 King of Jazz
1931 The Cohens and Kellys in
Africa
1932 *The Black King*
1937 *Slave Ship*
1940 *Son of Ingagi*
1957 Satchmo the Great
Africa, North
1932 Soñadores de la gloria
1934 *The Unknown Soldier
Speaks*
1952 *Bright Victory*
1958 *The Young Lions*
African Americans
1914 At the Cross Roads
John Barleycorn
The Littlest Rebel
1915 The Birth of a Nation
Marse Covington
A Texas Steer
Under Southern Skies
1915? *The Life of Sam Davis: A
Confederate Hero of the
Sixties*
*Sam Davis, the Hero of
Tennessee*
1916 *At Piney Ridge*
Broken Chains
The Colored American
Winning His Suit
Unprotected
1917 The Bar Sinister
The Bride of Hate
How Uncle Sam Prepares

I Will Repay
A Kentucky Cinderella
The Little Samaritan
My Fighting Gentleman
The Slacker
Unconquered
1918 Free and Equal
The Greatest Thing in Life
The Liar
1919 *Come Out of the Kitchen*
The Homesteader
Injustice
The Little Diplomat
A Man's Duty
Toby's Bow
1920 The Brute
Eyes of Youth
In the Depths of Our Hearts
Our Christianity and
Nobody's Child
The Symbol of the
Unconquered
Within Our Gates
1920? Reformation
1921 As the World Rolls On
The Burden of Race
By Right of Birth
The Call of His People
A Child in Pawn
Cotton and Cattle
A Fool's Promise
A Giant of His Race
The Green-Eyed Monster
The Gunsaulus Mystery
Hearts of the Woods
The Hypocrite
The Lure of a Woman
The Man from Texas
A Modern Cain
The Negro of Today
The Secret Sorrow
The Shadow
The Sport of the Gods
Ties of Blood
1921? [Unidentified Film]
1922 The Bull-Dogger
The Crimson Skull
The Dungeon
Easy Money
Foolish Lives
For His Mother's Sake
The Greatest Sin
The Perfect Dreamer
The Schemers
Spitfire
Square Joe
Uncle Jasper's Will
Undisputed Evidence
The Virgin of Seminole
You Can't Keep a Good Man
Down
1923 Deceit
The Devil's Match
Flames of Wrath
His Great Chance
Regeneration
A Shot in the Night
Tuskegee Finds the Way Out
1924 Birthright
A Debtor to the Law
His Darker Self
The House Behind the
Cedars
Smiling Hate
A Son of Satan
1924? The Flaming Crisis
1925 The Black Boomerang
Body and Soul
The Devil's Disciple
Marcus Garland
1926 The Conjure Woman
The Fighting Deacon
The Flying Ace
A Prince of His Race
Reckless Money
1926? The House on Cedar Hill
Ten Nights in a Barroom
1927 The Broken Violin
Children of Fate
Ham and Eggs at the Front
The Love Mart
The Millionaire
Poro College in Moving
Pictures
The Scar of Shame

The Slaver
The Spider's Web
Topsy and Eva
1927? You Can't Win
1928 Absent
Black Gold
Diamond Handcuffs
Eleven P.M.
The Midnight Ace
Tenderfeet
Thirty Years Later
Uncle Tom's Cabin
The Wages of Sin
1929 Hallelujah
Hearts in Dixie
Show Boat
Thunderbolt
When Men Betray
The Witching Eyes
1930 Anybody's War
Big Boy
Check and Double Check
A Daughter of the Congo
Easy Street
Georgia Rose
1931 *Cherie*
Cimarron
The Exile
The White Renegade
1932 The Black King
Harlem Is Heaven
Hypnotized
Out of the Crimson Fog
Veiled Aristocrats
1932? The Girl from Chicago
1933 The Emperor Jones
Victims of Persecution
1934 *Broadway Bill*
Chloe: Love Is Calling You
Judge Priest
Massacre
Stand Up and Cheer!
The Unknown Soldier
Speaks
The Youth of Russia
1934? Harlem After Midnight
1935 *Charlie Chan in Egypt*
Harmony Lane
Lem Hawkins' Confession
The Little Colonel
The Littlest Rebel
Riddle Ranch
So Red the Rose
1936 *Charlie Chan at the Race
Track*
General Spanky
The Green Pastures
Muss 'Em Up
*The Prisoner of Shark
Island*
Rainbow on the River
Show Boat
Temptation
1937 Bargain with Bullets
Boy of the Streets
Dark Manhattan
Harlem on the Prairie
Maid of Salem
One Mile from Heaven
Souls at Sea
A Study of Negro Artists
Underworld
We Work Again
1938 *The Beloved Brat*
Birthright
The Duke Is Tops
Gone Harlem
Hits and Bits of 1938
Life Goes On
Policy Man
Spirit of Youth
Sugar Hill Baby
Two Gun Man from Harlem
1939 *The Adventures of
Huckleberry Finn*
The Bronze Buckaroo
The Devil's Daughter
Double Deal
Gang Smashers
Gone With the Wind
Harlem Rides the Range
Keep Punching
Lying Lips
Moon over Harlem
One Dark Night

Reform School
Straight to Heaven
194- Mistaken Identity
1940 Am I Guilty?
Gang War
George Washington Carver
Midnight Shadow
Mystery in Swing
The Notorious Elinor Lee
Paradise in Harlem
Son of Ingagi
While Thousands Cheer
1940? Mr. Washington Goes to
Town
1941 Belle Starr
Birth of the Blues
Four Shall Die
The Gang's All Here
King of the Zombies
Lady from Louisiana
Land of Liberty
Louisiana Purchase
Murder on Lenox Avenue
Ride on Vaquero
Sullivan's Travels
Sun Valley Serenade
Sunday Sinners
Up Jumped the Devil
Virginia
You're Out of Luck
1942 Holiday Inn
In This Our Life
Lucky Ghost
Mokey
Professor Creeps
Syncopation
Take My Life
Tales of Manhattan
The Vanishing Virginian
Whispering Ghosts
Young America
1943 Bataan
Cabin in the Sky
Crash Dive
Crime Smasher
Fighting Americans
Jack London
Land of Hunted Men
Marching On!
The Meanest Man in the
World
The Ox-Bow Incident
Redhead from Manhattan
Stormy Weather
What's Buzzin' Cousin?
1944 Black Magic
The Chinese Cat
Hi, Beautiful
Lake Placid Serenade
Lifeboat
The Negro Soldier
The Racket Man
Since You Went Away
We've Come a Long, Long
Way
1945 Colorado Pioneers
I Love a Bandleader
The Jade Mask
The Mummy's Curse
Of One Blood
Rhapsody in Blue
The Scarlet Clue
The Shanghai Cobra
1946 Beware
Dangerous Money
Dirty Gertie from Harlem,
U.S.A.
The Red Dragon
The Sailor Takes a Wife
Shadows Over Chinatown
Song of the South
Stars on Parade
Tall, Tan and Terrific
That Man of Mine
The Trap
1946? Beale Street Mama
Fight That Ghost
House-Rent Party
1947 Body and Soul
Boy! What a Girl!
The Burning Cross
The Foxes of Harrow
Going to Glory, Come to
Jesus
Hi De Ho

Jivin' in Be-Bop
Juke Joint
Mantan Runs for Mayor
New Orleans
The Peanut Man
Sepia Cinderella
Untamed Fury
1947? What a Guy
1948 The Betrayal
Docks of New Orleans
The Fight Never Ends
The Golden Eye
Half Past Midnight
Miracle in Harlem
Moonrise
Shanghai Chest
Strange Victory
Tap Roots
1948? Boarding House Blues
Junction 88
1949 Home of the Brave
Knock on Any Door
Lookout Sister
Lost Boundaries
Pinky
Portrait of Jennie
Prejudice
The Quiet One
The Sky Dragon
Souls of Sin
1949? Come On, Cowboy!
Girl in Room 20
Harlem Follies
The Joint Is Jumpin'
1950 The Breaking Point
Intruder in the Dust
The Jackie Robinson Story
No Way Out
Stars in My Crown
Young Man with a Horn
1951 Five
The Harlem Globetrotters
Native Son
Queen for a Day
Show Boat
The Steel Helmet
The Tall Target
The Well
Yes Sir, Mr. Bones
1952 Bright Victory
It's a Big Country: An
American Anthology
Red Ball Express
1953 Bright Road
The Member of the Wedding
Sangaree
The Sun Shines Bright
Taxi
1954 Carmen Jones
Go Man Go
Sitting Bull
1955 Blackboard Jungle
Brevities of 1955
Duel on the Mississippi
Seven Angry Men
Trial
The View from Pompey's
Head
1956 Baby Doll
The Benny Goodman Story
Rockin' the Blues
1957 Band of Angels
Burden of Truth
Edge of the City
The Guns of Fort Petticoat
Naked in the Sun
Raintree County
Satchmo the Great
Segregation and the South
1958 The Defiant Ones
St. Louis Blues
1959 Anna Lucasta
Anna Lucasta
Gunmen from Laredo
Imitation of Life
John Paul Jones
The Last Angry Man
Night of the Quarter Moon
Odds Against Tomorrow
Porgy and Bess
The Wonderful Country
The World, the Flesh and
the Devil
1960 All the Fine Young
Cannibals

All the Young Men
The Crowning Experience
I Passed for White
Key Witness
The Last Voyage
Sergeant Rutledge
Take a Giant Step
This Rebel Breed
Wild River

African Americans—Mixed blood
1915 The Birth of a Nation
The Nigger
1916 At Piney Ridge
Pudd'nhead Wilson
1917 The Bar Sinister
The Renaissance at
Charleroi
Sold at Auction
1918 Broken Ties
Free and Equal
A Woman of Impulse
1920 Within Our Gates
1920? Broken Hearts
1924 The House Behind the
Cedars
1928 Eleven P.M.
Thirty Years Later
Uncle Tom's Cabin
1930 A Daughter of the Congo
1931 The Exile
1938 The Adventures of Tom
Sawyer
God's Step Children
1946 Saratoga Trunk
1948 The Betrayal
1951 Show Boat
1955 The View from Pompey's
Head
1957 Band of Angels
1958 Kings Go Forth
1959 Night of the Quarter Moon

African-American leadership
1960 The Crowning Experience

African-American universities
and colleges
1940 George Washington Carver
1941? Hampton Institute: Its
Program of Education for
Life
1951 The Harlem Globetrotters

Africans
1930 A Daughter of the Congo

Afterlife
1920 Pagan Love
1943 Cabin in the Sky

Age difference
use Romance—Age difference

Aged men
1930 Easy Street
1931 Zein Weib's Lubovnick
1934 Eskimo
1941 Secret of the Wastelands
1951 Flaming Feather
The Raging Tide
1953 Ambush at Tomahawk Gap
The Sun Shines Bright
1957 Twelve Angry Men
1959 The Last Angry Man

Aged persons
1918 How Could You, Jean?
1932 Igloo
1940 Eli Eli
1949 Lust for Gold
1951 The Magnificent Yankee

Aged women
1932 Mazel Tov
1934 Tres amores
1941 Dead Men Tell
1943 The Meanest Man in the
World
1948 Cry of the City
Half Past Midnight
Miracle in Harlem
1949 Top O' the Morning
1950 Intruder in the Dust
1952 It's a Big Country: An
American Anthology
1953 Cry of the Hunted
1960 Weddings and Babies
Wild River

Agents
use Specific types of agents

Aging
1942 The Vanishing Virginian
1955 The Long Gray Line

Agriculture
1940 George Washington Carver
1947 The Peanut Man
1954 Apache
1956 Serenade

Agriculture, Cooperative
1934 Our Daily Bread

Air lines
1949 Illegal Entry

Air pilots
1926 The Flying Ace
1927 Aflame in the Sky
1928 Flying Romeos
1931 Cuerpo y alma
La llama sagrada
Le père célibataire
1935 Alas sobre el Chaco
A Night at the Opera
1936 Sea Spoilers
Sum Hun
1937 Shadows of the Orient
1940 Phantom of Chinatown
1941 King of the Zombies
1941? Hampton Institute: Its
Program of Education
for Life
1942 Across the Pacific
1949 Illegal Entry
The Sky Dragon
1952 Arctic Flight
Red Snow
1954 Barefoot Battalion

Air pilots, Military
1941 Adam Had Four Sons
1942 Submarine Raider
Wings for the Eagle
1943 Bataan
Fighting Americans

Air raids
use Bombing, Aerial

Aircraft carriers
1942 Submarine Raider

Aircraft industry
1940 Murder over New York
1942 Wings for the Eagle
1943 Gangway for Tomorrow
1944 An American Romance

Airplane accidents
1931 Le père célibataire
1933 It's Great to Be Alive
1936 Sins of Man
Sum Hun
Tundra
1937 Shadows of the Orient
1940 Knute Rockne—All
American
Murder over New York
1941 King of the Zombies
Mutiny in the Arctic
1949 Arctic Fury
1950 A Lady Without Passport
1960 Ice Palace

Airplanes
1915 How Molly Malone Made
Good
1922 Sky High
1928 Flying Romeos
1932 Hidden Valley
1935 Alas sobre el Chaco
Te quiero con locura
1937 Charlie Chan at the
Olympics
1938 Happy Landing
1940 Murder over New York
Taku
1942 Tales of Manhattan
Young America
1943 Action in the North
Atlantic
Air Force
Bataan
1947 The Chinese Ring
1948 Sleep, My Love
1949 C-Man
The Sky Dragon
1952 Red Snow
1960 I Passed for White

Airports
1939 *Charlie Chan at Treasure Island*
1947 *Buck Privates Come Home*
1949 *Illegal Entry*
1954 *Hell's Half Acre*
1958 *Wild Is the Wind*
1959 Inside the Mafia
1960 *Man on a String*

Alabama
1923 Scars of Jealousy
1934 *Lazy River*
1949 The Fighting Kentuckian

Alamo (San Antonio, TX)
1916 *Following the Flag in Mexico*
1939 *Man of Conquest*
1953 The Man from the Alamo
1955 *Davy Crockett, King of the Wild Frontier*
    The Last Command

Alamogordo (NM)
1948 *Four Faces West*

Alaska
19?? *A Trip Through the Arctic with Uncle Sam*
1912 *The Alaska-Siberian Expedition*
    Atop of the World in Motion
1914 *In the Land of the Head Hunters*
    An Odyssey of the North
1917 Alaska Wonders in Motion
    The Barrier
1918 Laughing Bill Hyde
1919? Alaska
1920 The North Wind's Malice
1921 Shame
    Wolves of the North
1922 *The Dungeon*
1925 The True North
1926 The Barrier
1927 Primitive Love
1930 The Break Up
1932 Dangers of the Arctic
1936 *Klondike Annie*
    Sea Spoilers
    Tundra
1937 *The Barrier*
1938 Spawn of the North
1940 Girl from God's Country
    Taku
1942 North to the Klondike
1947 Spoilers of the North
1948 Harpoon
1949 *Arctic Fury*
    Arctic Manhunt
    Rose of the Yukon
1952 *Red Snow*
1960 Ice Palace

Albany (NY)
1937 *Bargain with Bullets*
1950 *The Iroquois Trail*
1953 *Fort Ti*

Albuquerque (NM)
1946 *Without Reservations*
1950 *Train to Tombstone*

Alcatraz Federal Penitentiary
1959 *Al Capone*

Alcohol
    use **Liquor**

Alcoholics
1915 *The Rosary*
1916 *The Flames of Johannis Pasquale*
1917 I Will Repay
    The Secret of Eve
1918 The Honor of His House
    Sandy
    The Source
1919 *The She Wolf*
    The Unpainted Woman
1926? Ten Nights in a Barroom
1927 *The Scar of Shame*
1928 Eleven P.M.
1931 *Huckleberry Finn*
    Regeneración
    Skyline
1932 *Me and My Gal*
1933 Dance Hall Hostess
    Olsen's Big Moment
    Rafter Romance

1936 *Show Boat*
1937 *Border Cafe*
1938 *Spirit of Youth*
1939 *The Adventures of Huckleberry Finn*
    My Son
1940 *Paradise in Harlem*
1942 *Mokey*
1945 The Great John L.
    Jealousy
    A Tree Grows in Brooklyn
1947 *Humoresque*
    Little Mister Jim
    Thunder Mountain
1948 *Fighting Father Dunne*
    I Remember Mama
    Key Largo
    Open Secret
1948? *Boarding House Blues*
1949 *Knock on Any Door*
1950 *Ambush*
1951 *Oh! Susanna*
    Show Boat
1952 *The Big Sky*
    My Man and I
1953 *The Stars Are Singing*
1954 *Apache*
    They Rode West
1955 *Bad Day at Black Rock*
    Foxfire
    The Gun That Won the West
    Not As a Stranger
    White Feather
1956 *The Burning Hills*
    Crowded Paradise
    Man from Del Rio
1957 *Raiders of Old California*
    Ride Out for Revenge
1958 *Frontier Gun*
    Home Before Dark
    Oregon Passage
    Touch of Evil
1959 *The Crimson Kimono*
1960 *The Adventures of Huckleberry Finn*
    All the Fine Young Cannibals
    The Plunderers

Alcoholism
1914 John Barleycorn
1919 *A Heart in Pawn*
1920 Darling Mine
1927 The Broken Violin
1928 Wheel of Chance
1930 The Grand Parade
1931 Del infierno al cielo
1932 *La foule hurle*
1935 Harmony Lane
1946 *Bringing Up Father*
1948 *Fury at Furnace Creek*
1949 *Daughter of the West*
1950 The Big Hangover
    Cherokee Uprising
    The Furies
1951 *Jim Thorpe—All-American*
1954 *Cattle Queen of Montana*
1959 *Anna Lucasta*

Aldermen
1919 *The Lord Loves the Irish*
1926 Kosher Kitty Kelly

Alexander Mitchell Palmer
1919 *The Volcano*

Aliases
1930 El valiente
1941 *Road Agent*
1943 *Bataan*
1944 *Marshal of Reno*
1945 *Phantom of the Plains*
    The Shanghai Cobra
1948 *Docks of New Orleans*
    Fury at Furnace Creek
    Half Past Midnight
1948? Junction 88
1949 *C-Man*
1950 *Black Hand*
    Riders of the Pony Express
1951 *Warpath*
1952 *Brave Warrior*
1957 *Edge of the City*

Alibi
1931 *El pasado acusa*
1937 *Man of the People*
1946 *Dark Alibi*
1948 *Old Los Angeles*

1949 *Knock on Any Door*
1952 *Woman in the Dark*
1957 *The Midnight Story*

Aliens, Illegal
1932 *The Secrets of Wu Sin*
1936 Human Cargo
    Paddy O'Day
    Yellow Cargo
1938 *Daughter of Shanghai*
1946 *G. I. War Brides*
    The Gentleman Misbehaves
1947 *Buck Privates Come Home*
1949 *Border Incident*
    C-Man
    Illegal Entry
1950 *A Lady Without Passport*
    Panic in the Streets
1956 Wetbacks
1959 *Cry Tough*

Alimony
1933 *The Cohens and Kellys in Trouble*

Allegory
1941 *Z Dymem Pożarów*
1946 *Song of the South*

Allergy
1942 *Sunday Punch*
1949 *Jiggs and Maggie in Jackpot Jitters*
1950 *The Big Hangover*

Alliances
    use **Political alliances**

Alligators
1934 *Chloe: Love Is Calling You*
1946 *Swamp Fire*
1947 *Untamed Fury*
1948 *Louisiana Story*
1951 *Distant Drums*
1953 *Cry of the Hunted*

Allowances
1916 *Her Debt of Honor*

Alps
1936 Sins of Man
1958 *Kings Go Forth*

Alumni
    use **Universities and colleges—Alumni**

Juan Bautista Alvarado
1920 *The Mark of Zorro*
1936 *Sutter's Gold*

Amateur detectives
1921 *By Right of Birth*
1930 El cuerpo del delito
1936 Mad Holiday
1937 Think Fast, Mr. Moto
1941 You're Out of Luck
1942 Whispering Ghosts
1943 Crime Smasher
1944 *Charlie Chan in the Secret Service*
1946? House-Rent Party
1949 Boston Blackie's Chinese Venture
1950 *Raiders of Tomahawk Creek*

Amateur shows
1944 *Chip Off the Old Block*

Ambassadors
1917 *Forbidden Paths*
1919 *Auction of Souls*
1929 Die Königsloge
1939 *Man of Conquest*

Ambition
1915 The Danger Signal
1917 The Spirit of '76
1921 A Giant of His Race
1930 *Locuras de amor*
    She Got What She Wanted
1931 Little Caesar
    Skyline
1932 Ten Minutes to Live
1934 Beloved
1937 Dark Manhattan
1938 Dangerous to Know
1943 Doughboys in Ireland
    In Old Oklahoma
1944 An American Romance
1945 *The Dolly Sisters*
1947 The Foxes of Harrow
    Humoresque
1948 *Fort Apache*
    The Miracle of the Bells

1951 Saturday's Hero
1952 *California Conquest*
1953 The Eddie Cantor Story
    Tonight We Sing
1955 Not As a Stranger
1957 *Beau James*
1959 *Al Capone*
    Imitation of Life
    John Paul Jones
    The Last Angry Man
    Yellowstone Kelly

Ambulance chasing
1943 *The Meanest Man in the World*

Ambulance drivers
1944 *Three Men in White*

Ambulances
1940 *While Thousands Cheer*
1941 *Mystery Ship*
1949 *C-Man*

Ambushes
1934 *Nada más que una mujer*
1937 *Hills of Old Wyoming*
1941 *Belle Starr*
    Saddlemates
    This Woman Is Mine
    Under Fiesta Stars
1942 *King of the Stallions*
1943 *The Law Rides Again*
1946 *California Gold Rush*
    Wild West
1947 *Rustlers of Devil's Canyon*
1948 *Renegades of Sonora*
1950 Ambush
    Broken Arrow
    Colt .45
    Davy Crockett, Indian Scout
    Train to Tombstone
1951 *Cavalry Scout*
    The Steel Helmet
1952 *The Battle at Apache Pass*
    Battles of Chief Pontiac
    Buffalo Bill in Tomahawk Territory
    Fort Osage
    The Half-Breed
    Indian Uprising
    The Savage
1953 *Ambush at Tomahawk Gap*
    Conquest of Cochise
    Fort Ti
    Jack McCall Desperado
    The Man from the Alamo
    Old Overland Trail
    War Paint
1954 *The Black Dakotas*
    Taza, Son of Cochise
    Thunder Pass
1955 *Apache Woman*
    The Far Horizons
    Shotgun
1956 *The Burning Hills*
    The Last Wagon
    Quincannon, Frontier Scout
    Reprisal!
    Walk the Proud Land
1957 Apache Warrior
    Dragoon Wells Massacre
    Run of the Arrow
    War Drums
1958 *The Light in the Forest*
1959 *The Jayhawkers!*
    Shake Hands with the Devil
    Thunder in the Sun
1960 *Comanche Station*
    Flaming Star

American Civil Liberties Union
1926 *The Passaic Textile Strike*

American Expeditionary Force
1919 The Lost Battalion
1928 *Anybody Here Seen Kelly?*

American Federation of Labor
1926 *The Passaic Textile Strike*

American Legion
1920 *The Face at Your Window*
1921 *Shadows of the West*
1928 Absent

American loyalists
1939 *Drums Along the Mohawk*

Americans in foreign countries
1916 *The Gilded Spider*
1917 The Call of the East
The Little American
The Red Woman
Rosie O'Grady
The Spirit of '76
Under False Colors
1918 The Firebrand
Her American Husband
The Temple of Dusk
A Woman of Impulse
1918? *The Snail*
1919 *Auction of Souls*
His Parisian Wife
The Right to Happiness
The Scar
1920 *The Good-Bad Wife*
The Luck of the Irish
A Tokio Siren
1930 *Amor audaz*
East Is West
1931 *Aloha*
The Cohens and Kellys in Africa
Cuerpo y alma
Monerías
El príncipe gondolero
1932 *Flesh*
Hombres en mi vida
Parigi affascina; ovvero, Malavita
1933 *L'amour guide*
Dos noches
1934 Charlie Chan in London
Nada más que una mujer
1935 Charlie Chan in Paris
De la sartén al fuego
Ruggles of Red Gap
Tango Bar
1936 *Laughing Irish Eyes*
The Phantom of Santa Fe
1937 *El carnaval del diablo*
Thank You, Mr. Moto
1938 Outside of Paradise
Zamboanga
1939 *City in Darkness*
Forged Passport
1940 Escape
Escape to Glory
1941 Hold Back the Dawn
King of the Zombies
1942 *Prisoner of Japan*
1943 *The Amazing Mrs. Holliday*
Hitler's Children
Hitler's Children
Jack London
Tahiti Honey
1944 *Lake Placid Serenade*
1945 *The Great John L.*
Salome, Where She Danced
Samurai
1946 *Cuban Pete*
Rendezvous 24
1947 Pirates of Monterey
1948 *The Luck of the Irish*
1950 *Belle of Old Mexico*
Deported
1951 Go for Broke!
1952 *The Fabulous Senorita*
The Quiet Man
Red Ball Express
1953 *Dream Wife*
1954 *Barefoot Battalion*
Indiscretion of an American Wife
1956 *Wetbacks*
1958 The Young Lions
1959 Shake Hands with the Devil

Jeffrey Amherst
1952 *Battles of Chief Pontiac*
1953 *Fort Ti*

Amish
1955 Violent Saturday

Ammunition
1933 *Diplomaniacs*
1935 *The Singing Vagabond*
1936 *The Glory Trail*
Ride, Ranger, Ride
1937 *Drums of Destiny*

Amnesia
1916 The Innocent Lie
The Sign of the Poppy
1921 A Modern Cain

1928 Absent
Ramona
1934 La ciudad de cartón
The Lone Defender
1936 Dangerous Intrigue
1937 *Charlie Chan at the Opera*
1938 Rascals
1940 *Her Second Mother*
The Way of All Flesh
1942 Dr. Gillespie's New Assistant
1943 *Marching On!*
1945 I Love a Bandleader
The Mummy's Curse
1949 *The Clay Pigeon*
The Cowboy and the Prizefighter
1956 Singing in the Dark

Amputation
1950 *The Breaking Point*
1960 *All the Young Men*

Amputees
1919 *The Volcano*
1943 Dr. Gillespie's Criminal Case
1946 *Till the End of Time*
1948? *Boarding House Blues*
1950 *The Cariboo Trail*
1958 *Kings Go Forth*

Amusement parks
1930 *Anna Christie*
1944 *Hi, Beautiful*
1948 *The Lady from Shanghai*
1949 *The Red Menace*
1951 *Native Son*

Anarchists
1916 *Arms and the Woman*
1918 *A Little Sister of Everybody*
1919 The Red Viper
1920 *The Great Shadow*

Angels
1933 *The Eternal Jew*
1941? *The Blood of Jesus*

Anger
use **Temper**

Animal culture
1949 *The Golden Stallion*

Animal trainers
1932 *Hypnotized*
1936 *Charlie Chan at the Circus*
1949 *The Golden Stallion*
Stallion Canyon
1950 *Riders of the Pony Express*

Animal traps
1917 *The Bronze Bride*
1947 *Buffalo Bill Rides Again*
1948 The Arizona Ranger
Night Wind
1956 *The Last Frontier*

Annapolis
use **United States Naval Academy**

"Annie Laurie" (Song)
1945 *A Tree Grows in Brooklyn*

Anniversaries
use **Wedding anniversaries**

Annulment
use **Marriage—Annulment**

Antenuptial contracts
1925 Scarlet Saint

Anthropologists
1914 *Hearts United*

Antique dealers
1916 The Romantic Journey
1917 Southern Pride
1925 Cobra
1929 *The Younger Generation*
1932 *Hearts of Humanity*
1934 *The Cat's-Paw*
1935 *Rescue Squad*
1937 *Thank You, Mr. Moto*
1938 Breaking the Ice
1939 *Mr. Moto's Last Warning*

Antique shops
1934 *The Cat's-Paw*
1938 *Breaking the Ice*

Antiques
1919 The Little Diplomat
1948 *The Feathered Serpent*
1950 *Chinatown at Midnight*

Antisemitism
1914? A Boy and the Law
1916 The Yellow Passport
1919 *As a Man Thinks*
Who's Your Brother?
1932 Yiskor
1933 Victims of Persecution
The Wandering Jew
1939 Tevya
1943 *Margin for Error*
1944 Address Unknown
Tomorrow the World!
1947 *The Burning Cross*
Crossfire
1948 Gentleman's Agreement
Open Secret
Strange Victory
1949 Prejudice
1951 *The Magnificent Yankee*
1952 It's a Big Country: An American Anthology
1958 *Home Before Dark*
The Young Lions
1960 The Dark at the Top of the Stairs

Ants
1942 *Valley of the Sun*

Apache dancers
1919 *Yvonne from Paris*
1930 Galas de la Paramount
1935 *Charlie Chan in Paris*

Apache Indians
1922 One Eighth Apache
1925 Tonio, Son of the Sierras
⚡32 *Mystery Ranch*
Riders of the Desert
1939 Bad Lands
1940 Geronimo
1942 Apache Trail
1948 Fort Apache
Fury at Furnace Creek
Red River
1949 Apache Chief
Lust for Gold
1950 Ambush
Broken Arrow
I Killed Geronimo
1951 *Apache Drums*
The Last Outpost
Only the Valiant
1952 *Apache Country*
Apache War Smoke
The Battle at Apache Pass
The Half-Breed
Indian Uprising
1953 Ambush at Tomahawk Gap
Arrowhead
Conquest of Cochise
Old Overland Trail
San Antone
The Stand at Apache River
1954 *Apache*
Arrow in the Dust
Hondo
Massacre Canyon
Taza, Son of Cochise
1955 *Apache Ambush*
Apache Woman
Fort Yuma
Foxfire
The Lonesome Trail
Shotgun
Smoke Signal
The Vanishing American
1956 *The Broken Star*
The Last Wagon
Secret of Treasure Mountain
Walk the Proud Land
1957 Apache Warrior
Dragoon Wells Massacre
The Ride Back
Tomahawk Trail
Trooper Hook
War Drums
1958 Ambush at Cimarron Pass
Apache Territory
Escape from Red Rock
Fort Bowie
Fort Massacre
1959 Gunmen from Laredo
The Wonderful Country
1960 *Sergeant Rutledge*

Apaches—Paris
1928 The Cohens and the Kellys in Paris
1933 *Dos noches*

Apartment managers
1941 *You're Out of Luck*

Apartments
1920 *Outside the Law*
1933 Olsen's Big Moment
1938 *Passport Husband*
1940 *Mystery in Swing*
1941 *New York Town*
1942 *Nazi Agent*
Twin Beds
1943 *The Meanest Man in the World*
1947 *Crossfire*
1949 *C-Man*
1950 *No Way Out*
1956 *The Catered Affair*
Crowded Paradise

Apemen
1940 Son of Ingagi

Apes
1936 *Charlie Chan at the Circus*

Appendicitis
1932 *Huddle*
1940 *The Man I Married*

Apple growers
1949 Thieves' Highway

Appomattox Campaign, 1865
1957 *Run of the Arrow*

Aqueducts
1947 *The Last Round-Up*

Arab countries
1931 El tenorio del harem

Arabs
1930 A Daughter of the Congo
1931 La ley del harem
1935 *De la sartén al fuego*
1937 *The Holy Oath*
1952 Desert Pursuit

Arapaho Indians
1926 War Paint
1949 *She Wore a Yellow Ribbon*
1950 A Ticket to Tomahawk
1955 *White Feather*
1956 Quincannon, Frontier Scout
The Wild Dakotas
1959 *The Oregon Trail*
Yellowstone Kelly

Archaeologists
1934 *Dos más uno, dos*
1935 Charlie Chan in Egypt
1937 The Riders of the Whistling Skull
1938 *Mr. Moto Takes a Chance*
1939 *Mr. Moto Takes a Vacation*
1940 Phantom of Chinatown
1941 Secret of the Wastelands
1945 The Mummy's Curse
1947 Dangerous Venture
1948 The Feathered Serpent

Architects
1916 Her Debt of Honor
1920 *On with the Dance*
1920? The Greatest Love
1921 Black Roses
1924 So Big
1931 *The Guilty Generation*
1932 *So Big*
1942 *Syncopation*
1945 *The Gay Senorita*
1948 *Sleep, My Love*
1953 *So Big*
1954 *The Yellow Tomahawk*
1957 *Bayou*
Twelve Angry Men

Arctic regions
1912 The Alaska-Siberian Expedition
Atop of the World in Motion
1914 Captain F. E. Kleinschmidt's Arctic Hunt
1922 Nanook of the North
1925 Justice of the Far North
1927 Primitive Love
1928 The Great White North
1932 Dangers of the Arctic
Igloo
1934 Eskimo
1936 *Tundra*

Arctic regions
1941 Mutiny in the Arctic
1949 Arctic Fury
1952 Arctic Flight
     Red Snow
Argentina
1927 The Millionaire
1930 Alma de gaucho
     Charros, gauchos y manolas
1931 Las luces de Buenos Aires
1959 *The FBI Story*
Argentines
1928 The Broken Mask
     Hold 'Em Yale
1936 Contra la corriente
Argonne Forest (France)
1919 The Lost Battalion
Argonne, Battle of the, 1918
1940 *The Fighting 69th*
Aristocracy
1933 A Lady's Profession
1936 *The Bold Caballero*
Aristocrats
1915 The Grandee's Ring
1916 A Yoke of Gold
1917 The Renaissance at
     Charleroi
1919 Come Out of the Kitchen
     Toby's Bow
1920 The Mark of Zorro
1925 Irish Luck
1926 Irene
1928 The Mating Call
1931 Chérie
1932 *Hombres en mi vida*
1933 Dos noches
1934 *Beloved*
     She Was a Lady
1936 *Daniel Boone*
1947 *The Foxes of Harrow*
1960 *The Sign of Zorro*
Arizona
1914 *Life's Shop Window*
1915 *The Immigrant*
     The Lamb
1917 *The Gun Fighter*
1918 Denny from Ireland
     Her Moment
     The Red, Red Heart
     Ruggles of Red Gap
1919 Hearts of Men
1920 The Third Woman
1923 The Secret of the Pueblo
1924 Unseen Hands
     Yankee Speed
1927 Drums of the Desert
     White Gold
1929 In Old Arizona
1931 *The Squaw Man*
1932 *Mystery Ranch*
     Riders of the Desert
1933 *King of the Wild Horses*
     Robbers' Roost
1934 *Call of the Coyote*
     The Prescott Kid
1936 *Desert Gold*
     My American Wife
1939 Bad Lands
     The Cisco Kid and the Lady
     Harlem Rides the Range
     *Heaven with a Barbed Wire
      Fence*
     The Return of the Cisco Kid
1940 Geronimo
     Lucky Cisco Kid
1941 *The Face Behind the Mask*
     Ride on Vaquero
     Romance of the Rio Grande
1942 *Valley of the Sun*
1943 *The Law Rides Again*
     Marching On!
     *Mexican Spitfire's Blessed
      Event*
     Riding High
1945 *Wanderer of the Wasteland*
1946 *Sun Valley Cyclone*
     Sunset Pass
     Wild Beauty
1947 *King of the Bandits*
     Thunder Mountain
     Under the Tonto Rim
1948 The Arizona Ranger
     Fort Apache
     The Golden Eye
     Guns of Hate

     Western Heritage
1949 *Brothers in the Saddle*
     Daughter of the West
     The Gay Amigo
     The Mysterious Desperado
     The Red Menace
     Riders of the Range
     Stagecoach Kid
     3 Godfathers
1950 *Ambush*
     The Baron of Arizona
     Rio Grande Patrol
1951 *Cyclone Fury*
     Flaming Feather
     Fort Defiance
     Slaughter Trail
1952 The Half-Breed
     Indian Uprising
1953 *Ambush at Tomahawk Gap*
     Conquest of Cochise
1954 *Taza, Son of Cochise*
1955 *Apache Woman*
     Bad Day at Black Rock
     Foxfire
1956 *The Broken Star*
     The Last Wagon
1957 *The Brothers Rico*
     Dragoon Wells Massacre
     Trooper Hook
1958 Apache Territory
     The Badlanders
     Gunfire at Indian Gap
     *The Lone Ranger and the
      Lost City of Gold*
1960 Sergeant Rutledge
Armenian Americans
1950 *Panic in the Streets*
Armenians
1919 Auction of Souls
     Who's Your Brother?
1945 Anoush
1952 *Anything Can Happen*
Arms
     use **Munitions**
Arms and armor
1942 *Castle in the Desert*
Army Bases
     use **Military bases;
      Military posts**
Arrests
1926 *The Passaic Textile Strike*
1944 *Block Busters*
1947 *The Adventures of Don
      Coyote*
     Marshal of Cripple Creek
1948 *Old Los Angeles*
     Renegades of Sonora
1949 The Dalton Gang
     Daughter of the West
     Ride, Ryder, Ride!
     Satan's Cradle
     The Sky Dragon
1950 *The Girl from San Lorenzo*
     North of the Great Divide
1951 *Gambling House*
1954 *Indiscretion of an
      American Wife*
     They Rode West
1955 *The Gun That Won the
      West*
1959 The FBI Story
1960 *Key Witness*
Arson
1914 *The Littlest Rebel*
1915 *The Spender*
1918 *The Hell Cat*
1919 *The Unpainted Woman*
1935 *So Red the Rose*
1937 *Boots and Saddles*
1939 *Drums Along the Mohawk*
     Let Freedom Ring
     The Return of the Cisco Kid
1941 Western Union
1945 Colorado Pioneers
1947 *The Burning Cross*
     Rustlers of Devil's Canyon
1950 *North of the Great Divide*
     Rock Island Trail
     So Young, So Bad
1951 *Oh! Susanna*
1952 *The Big Sky*
     Brave Warrior
1953 *Arrowhead*
     *Captain John Smith and
      Pocahontas*

     Ride, Vaquero!
1954 *Passion*
1956 *Baby Doll*
1957 *Band of Angels*
1958 *Machete*
     Terror in a Texas Town
1959 *Last Train from Gun Hill*
Art—Collectors and collecting
1939 The Mystery of Mr. Wong
Art dealers
1917 *The Bond Between*
1944 *Address Unknown*
1949 *Portrait of Jennie*
Art galleries
1917 *The Trouble Buster*
Art objects
1949 *The Quiet One*
1951 *Mask of the Dragon*
Art patronage
1918 Love's Law
1931 *Women Love Once*
1935 El cantante de Nápoles
1947 *Humoresque*
1949 *That Midnight Kiss*
1951 *The Great Caruso*
Art students
1917 *The Bond Between*
Arthritis
1944 *Three Men in White*
Artificial limbs
     use **Prostheses and artificial
      limbs**
Artists
1915 The Clemenceau Case
1916 Broken Fetters
     The Gilded Spider
     Hulda from Holland
     The Soul of Kura-San
     The Twin Triangle
     Unprotected
1917 *The Pulse of Life*
1918 The City of Tears
     Shifting Sands
1918? Rosemary Climbs the
      Heights
1920 *Locked Lips*
1924 Smiling Hate
1928 The Cohens and the Kellys
      in Paris
1930 Charros, gauchos y manolas
1931 *The Black Camel*
     Women Love Once
1932 So Big
1933 *Rafter Romance*
1935 *Charlie Chan in Paris*
     Rescue Squad
1940 Northwest Passage (Book
      I—Rogers' Rangers)
     *Northwest Passage (Book
      I—Rogers' Rangers)*
1941 New York Town
1941? *Hampton Institute: Its
      Program of Education
      for Life*
1942 *Apache Trail*
1946 *The Red Dragon*
1953 *The Charge at Feather
      River*
     So Big
1956 *Mohawk*
1959 *The Crimson Kimono*
Asia, Southeastern
1938 Mr. Moto Takes a Chance
Asparagus
1932 *So Big*
1953 *So Big*
Asphalt industry
1917 *The Squaw Man's Son*
Asphyxia
1915 *Time Lock Number 776*
1930 *Un hombre de suerte*
1946 *The Face of Marble*
Assassination
1915 *The Birth of a Nation*
1916 *The King's Game*
     The Morals of Hilda
1918 *The Firebrand*
     The Kaiser's Finish
1919 *The Red Viper*
     The Tong Man
     The Volcano
1925 Don Q, Son of Zorro

1931 Kismet
1933 The Man Who Dared: An
      Imaginative Biography
1936 *The Prisoner of Shark
      Island*
1937 Nation Aflame
1949 *We Were Strangers*
1951 The Tall Target
     When the Redskins Rode
Assassins
1954 Dangerous Mission
Assayers
1936 *Desert Gold*
1948 *The Golden Eye*
     Guns of Hate
Assimilation (Sociology)
1929 The Younger Generation
1932 Cuore d'emigrante
1933 The Wandering Jew
1939 Kol Nidre
1942 Friendly Enemies
1943 *Redhead from Manhattan*
1944 *An American Romance*
     Block Busters
1945 *Samurai*
1947 *The Return of Rin Tin Tin*
1948 *Up in Central Park*
1950 *Right Cross*
1951 Saturday's Hero
1952 Japanese War Bride
     The Ring
1954 *Apache*
1955 *Good Morning, Miss Dove*
1956 *Hot Blood*
     Pillars of the Sky
1960 *Pay or Die*
     The Pusher
John Jacob Astor
1923 Little Old New York
1941 *This Woman Is Mine*
Astrologers
1942 *Castle in the Desert*
Astrology
1932 Thirteen Women
Astronomers
1942 *Prisoner of Japan*
Asylums
     use **Insane asylums;
      Sanitariums**
Atheists
1918 The Unbeliever
Athens (Greece)
1931 Such Is Life
Athletes
1921 *By Right of Birth*
1924 Yankee Speed
1932 *L'athlète incomplet*
1936 *Contra la corriente*
1937 *Big City*
1949 *Tulsa*
Athletic coaches
1926 The Campus Flirt
1932 *L'athlète incomplet*
1940 Knute Rockne—All American
1951 The Harlem Globetrotters
1954 *Go Man Go*
1960 *Hell to Eternity*
Athletics
     use **Physical education and
      training**
Atlanta (GA)
1915 *The Birth of a Nation*
1925 *Body and Soul*
1939 *Gone With the Wind*
1955 *A Man Called Peter*
1957 *Raintree County*
Atlantic City (NJ)
1929 The Cohens and Kellys in
      Atlantic City
Atlantic Ocean
1943 *Action in the North
      Atlantic*
1944 *Lifeboat*
Atomic bomb
1945 The House on 92nd St.
1946 Rendezvous 24
1951 Five
Attempted murder
1915 *The Gambler of the West*
     Under Southern Skies
1916 The Folly of Revenge
     The Sign of the Poppy

1917 His Sweetheart
1918 A Little Sister of Everybody
       Sandy
       Untamed
1919 His Debt
1920 The Girl of My Heart
       The Third Woman
1921 A Modern Cain
1926 General Custer at Little Big
       Horn
1928 The Midnight Ace
1931 Little Caesar
       Women Love Once
1932 Amore e morte
       Charlie Chan's Chance
1933 Victims of Persecution
1935 Alas sobre el Chaco
       Charlie Chan in Egypt
1936 Border Phantom
       Ride, Ranger, Ride
       Robin Hood of El Dorado
1937 El carnaval del diablo
       Thank You, Mr. Moto
1939 Kol Nidre
       Mr. Moto's Last Warning
       Mothers of Today
1940 The Way of All Flesh
1941 King of the Zombies
       Murder on Lenox Avenue
       Sunday Sinners
1942 Submarine Raider
1946 Sheriff of Redwood Valley
       Swamp Fire
       Wild Beauty
1947 Hi De Ho
       Untamed Fury
1949 The Clay Pigeon
       House of Strangers
       The Mysterious Desperado
       Stagecoach Kid
1950 No Way Out
       The Palomino
       Rio Grande Patrol
1951 Cavalry Scout
       The House on Telegraph
       Hill
       Only the Valiant
       Warpath
1952 Bugles in the Afternoon
       Fort Osage
       The Iron Mistress
1953 Conquest of Cochise
1954 Barefoot Battalion
       Hondo
       Thunder Pass
1955 Bad Day at Black Rock
       Smoke Signal
1956 The Searchers
1958 Bullwhip
       The Defiant Ones
1959 The Crimson Kimono
1960 Pay or Die

Attempted rape
1913? The Lure of New York
1914 Dan
       The Littlest Rebel
1916 Her Debt of Honor
       The Soul of Kura-San
       Three of Many
       The Twin Triangle
       The Yellow Passport
1917 The Woman and the Beast
1918 The Border Raiders
       The Bravest Way
       The Goddess of Lost Lake
       The Little Runaway
       The Only Road
1919 Just Squaw
1920 Within Our Gates
1920? Her Story
1927 The Scar of Shame
1931 Such Is Life
1932 Call Her Savage
       The Rainbow Trail
1933 Robbers' Roost
1934 Un capitán de cosacos
1938 Daughter of Shanghai
1945 Samurai
1949 Pinky
       Souls of Sin
       Streets of Laredo
1953 Ambush at Tomahawk Gap
1955 Blackboard Jungle
1956 Crowded Paradise
       Raw Edge

1957 Band of Angels
       Bayou
       Joe Dakota
       Tomahawk Trail
1959 The Hanging Tree
1960 All the Young Men
       Studs Lonigan

Attempted suicide
1914 The Jungle
1916 Alien Souls
       For the Defense
       Gold and the Woman
       A Man of Sorrow
       The Morals of Hilda
1918 A Daughter of the Old
       South
       Toys of Fate
1919 A Fallen Idol
1920 The Girl of My Heart
       The Riddle: Woman
1930 Sei tu l'amore
1931 La cautivadora
       Smart Money
1932 The Secrets of Wu Sin
1933 Counsellor at Law
       Olsen's Big Moment
1935 Alas sobre el Chaco
1937 Where Is My Child?
1938 The Power of Life
       Two Sisters
1939 Kol Nidre
1941 Adam Had Four Sons
1945 Club Havana
       Jealousy
1946? Fight That Ghost
1948 Miracle in Harlem
1949 The Girl from Jones Beach
1952 Bright Victory
       My Man and I
1958 Kings Go Forth
       The Light in the Forest
1960 All the Fine Young
       Cannibals
       The Last Voyage

Attics
1932 Me and My Gal

Attorneys
   use Lawyers

Auctions
1927 The Auctioneer
1930 East Is West
1932 The Son-Daughter
1933 Dos noches
       It's Great to Be Alive
       No dejes la puerta abierta
1934 Lazy River
       Our Daily Bread
1937 Slave Ship
1938 Speed to Burn
1939 Frontiers of '49
1942 All Through the Night
1948 16 Fathoms Deep
1949 The Golden Stallion
1953 So Big

Auditions
1934 Stand Up and Cheer!
1938 Swing!
1939 The Girl from Mexico
194- Mistaken Identity
1941 Golden Gate Girl
       Sun Valley Serenade
1942 Tales of Manhattan
1943 His Butler's Sister
1946 Mantan Messes Up
       Slightly Scandalous
       Stars on Parade
       That Man of Mine
1947 Hi De Ho
       Reet, Petite and Gone
1948 Up in Central Park
1949 That Midnight Kiss
1953 The Jazz Singer
1956 Serenade

John James Audubon
1952 The Iron Mistress

Aunts
1915 After Five
1916 The Innocent Lie
       The Love Girl
       Sold for Marriage
1917 A Kentucky Cinderella
       The Little Boy Scout
1918 Amarilly of Clothes-Line
       Alley

The Little Runaway
       Sandy
       Set Free
1919 Who Will Marry Me?
       Yvonne from Paris
1920 The Brute
       Darling Mine
       The Secret Gift
1921? The Slave Market
1927 Sally in Our Alley
1928 Riley the Cop
1930 Tom Sawyer
1931 Resurrección
1932 Le plombier amoureux
1933 Broken Dreams
1934 La cruz y la espada
       Dos más uno, dos
1935 Un hombre peligroso
       Julieta compra un hijo
       The Singing Vagabond
       Te quiero con locura
1936 Dimples
       Paddy O'Day
       Rainbow on the River
1937 Arshin Mal Alan
       I Want to Be a Mother
1938 The Adventures of Tom
       Sawyer
       God's Step Children
       The Rage of Paris
       The Singing Blacksmith
       Two Sisters
1939 The Girl from Mexico
       Lying Lips
       El otro soy yo
       Stand Up and Fight
1940 The Gay Caballero
       Mexican Spitfire
       Mexican Spitfire Out West
       New Moon
1941 Saddlemates
1942 Mexican Spitfire at Sea
       Sunday Punch
       We Were Dancing
       Woman of the Year
1943 The Outlaw
1944 Dark Waters
       Marshal of Reno
       The San Antonio Kid
       Sheriff of Las Vegas
       Tomorrow the World!
       Tucson Raiders
       Vigilantes of Dodge City
1945 Colorado Pioneers
       The Gay Senorita
       Great Stagecoach Robbery
       Phantom of the Plains
       Sunbonnet Sue
1946 California Gold Rush
       Santa Fe Uprising
       Sheriff of Redwood Valley
       Sun Valley Cyclone
1946? Go Down, Death!
1947 Desperate
       Oregon Trail Scouts
       Vigilantes of Boomtown
1949 Knock on Any Door
       Roll Thunder Roll!
1950 Belle of Old Mexico
       The Big Hangover
1951 Adventures of Captain
       Fabian
       The House on Telegraph
       Hill
1952 Anything Can Happen
1955 Marty
1956 Mohawk
1958 Houseboat
       St. Louis Blues

Stephen Austin
1939 Man of Conquest
1955 The Last Command

Australians
1931 The Black Camel
1942 Dr. Gillespie's New
       Assistant

Austria
1930 Olimpia
1932 Le cas du docteur Brenner
1936 Star for a Night
1941 They Dare Not Love

Austria—History
1932 A Daughter of Her People
1934 Beloved
Austria. Army
1916 Three of Many
Austrian Americans
1918 I Want to Forget
1930 The Melody Man
1934 Beloved
1936 Sins of Man
       Star for a Night
1940 The Ramparts We Watch
       Three Faces West
1942 We Were Dancing
1950 Indian Territory
Austrians
1916 Three of Many
1936 Star for a Night
1941 Come Live with Me
       Louisiana Purchase
       They Dare Not Love
1942 The Navy Comes Through
1945 Salome, Where She Danced
Authors
1914 The Jungle
1916 The Criminal
1917 I Will Repay
1918 The Ordeal of Rosetta
1919 His Parisian Wife
1922 Silver Spurs
1924 His Darker Self
1926 Broken Hearts
1928 Eleven P.M.
1930 She Got What She Wanted
1932 Mazel Tov
       Soñadores de la gloria
1933 Grand Slam
1935 Lem Hawkins' Confession
1936 Mad Holiday
1945 Jealousy
1947 Untamed Fury
1948 I Remember Mama
1949 Souls of Sin
1953 Taxi
1955 The View from Pompey's
       Head
1956 Full of Life

Auto camps
1937 That I May Live

Autographs
1946 Tall, Tan and Terrific

Automobile accidents
1913? The Lure of New York
1915 The Alien
       An American Gentleman
       How Molly Malone Made
       Good
1916 Hulda from Holland
       Pasquale
1917 A Love Sublime
1919 Who's Your Brother?
1927 The Broken Violin
1928 The House of Scandal
       The Secret Hour
1930 Locuras de amor
       El secreto del doctor
1931 Buster se marie
       Mi último amor
       Women Love Once
1932 Le cas du docteur Brenner
       La foule hurle
1933 Dance Hall Hostess
1934 Behold My Wife!
       Dos más uno, dos
       Riding Speed
1935 Julieta compra un hijo
       Rescue Squad
1936 Kelly the Second
       Muss 'Em Up
1937 Boy of the Streets
       It Could Happen to You
       One Mile from Heaven
       Underworld
1938 The Beloved Brat
       Charlie Chan at Monte
       Carlo
       Road Demon
       Speed to Burn
1939 A Brivele der Mamen
       Kol Nidre
       Papá soltero
1940 Broken Strings
1941 Hold Back the Dawn

1942 *In This Our Life*
Rubber Racketeers
Take My Life
1943 *Gangway for Tomorrow*
1944 *Three Men in White*
1945 *The Dolly Sisters*
The House on 92nd St.
1946 *Gas House Kids*
Rendezvous 24
1947 *Desperate*
Easy Come, Easy Go
New Orleans
1948 *The Lady from Shanghai*
Singin' Spurs
1949? *She's Too Mean for Me*
1950 *Emergency Wedding*
The Lawless
The Men
Young Man with a Horn
1951 *The House on Telegraph
Hill*
1953 *The Member of the
Wedding*
1957 *Man in the Shadow*
1960 *The Dark at the Top of the
Stairs*

Automobile chases
1934 *Massacre*
1936 *Yellow Cargo*
1939 *City in Darkness*
1940 *Gang War*
1941 *Hold Back the Dawn*
1942 *In This Our Life*
Take My Life
1950 *Belle of Old Mexico*
1955 *Bad Day at Black Rock*

Automobile industry and trade
1944 *An American Romance*

Automobile racing
1918 *Thirty a Week*
1924 *Racing Luck*
1927? *You Can't Win*
1932 *La foule hurle*
1944 *An American Romance*
1947 *Buck Privates Come Home*

Automobile theft
1942 *Mokey*
1950 *Mystery Street*

Automobiles
1918 *A Broadway Scandal*
1930 *Así es la vida*
Check and Double Check
Whoopee
1931 *La incorregible*
1935 *Texas Terror*
1936 *Laughing Irish Eyes*
1938 *Swing!*
1942 *Rio Rita*
1943 *Marching On!*
1946 *Without Reservations*
1947 *On the Old Spanish Trail*
1959 *The World, the Flesh and
the Devil*

Automobiles, Antique
1942 *The Vanishing Virginian*

Automobiles, Electric
1946 *Rendezvous 24*

Automobiles—Service stations
use **Gas stations**

Autopsy
1935 *Charlie Chan in Egypt*
1950 *No Way Out*

Avalanches
1921 *Wolves of the North*
1925 *The Gold Hunters*
1930 *Monsieur le Fox*
1937 *The Riders of the Whistling
Skull*
1938 *Spawn of the North*
1950 *Davy Crockett, Indian
Scout*
1952 *Red Snow*
1954 *Dangerous Mission*

Avarice
use **Greed**

Aviation
use **Aeronautics**

Aviators
use **Air pilots**

Awards
1942 *Woman of the Year*
1945 *Pride of the Marines*

1947 *Calendar Girl*
AWOL
1958 *The Young Lions*
Axes
1936 *Hair-Trigger Casey*
1957 *Bayou*
1958 *Fort Bowie*
Aztec Indians
1928 The Cavalier
1948 *The Feathered Serpent*
Azusa (CA)
1952 *Anything Can Happen*
Babel, Tower of
1931 *The Voice of Israel*
Babies
use **Infants**
Baby showers
use **Showers (Parties)**
Baby sitters
1934 *What a Mother-in-Law!*
1944 *They Live in Fear*
Babylon
1933 *The Eternal Jew*
Bachelor parties
1918 *The Spreading Evil*
1942 *Tales of Manhattan*
Bachelors
1928 The Secret Hour
1930 *Charros, gauchos y
manolas*
1931 *¿Conoces a tu mujer?*
1934 *Strange Wives*
1940 *Americaner Schadchen*
1946 Three Wise Fools
1953 *Taxi*
1955 *Marty*
Bagpipes
1941 *This Woman Is Mine*
1959 *John Paul Jones*
Bail
1948 *Indian Agent*
1950 *The Lawless*
Bailiffs
1929 *Die Königsloge*
Josephine Baker
1930 *Charros, gauchos y
manolas*
Bakers and bakeries
1919? *America Was Right*
1928 Riley the Cop
1949 *Lust for Gold*
1952 *Woman in the Dark*
1960 *Pay or Die*
Balconies
1949 *Satan's Cradle*
Baldness
1951 *The Steel Helmet*
Balkan Peninsula
1919 Diane of the Green Van
Ballerinas
1933 Dos noches
1938 *Outside of Paradise*
1940 *Tengo fe en ti*
1945 Salome, Where She Danced
Ballet
1941 *Louisiana Purchase*
1953 *Tonight We Sing*
Balloons (Hot air)
1927 *Ham and Eggs at the Front*
1931 *Cuerpo y alma*
Balloons (Toy)
1930 *Una cana al aire*
Balls (Parties)
1914 *Rose of the Rancho*
1916 *A Child of Mystery*
1917 *The Little Chevalier*
Southern Pride
1920 *Rio Grande*
1931 *Echec au roi*
Mamá
La pura verdad
Women Love Once
1932 *A Daughter of Her People*
1934 *La veuve joyeuse*
1935 *Naughty Marietta*
1938 *The Buccaneer*
1939 *Gone With the Wind*
Man of Conquest
Waterfront
1940 *Little Nellie Kelly*
1942 *Gentleman Jim*

1943 *His Butler's Sister*
1944 *Knickerbocker Holiday*
1945 *Salome, Where She Danced*
1948 *Unconquered*
1953 *The Pathfinder*
The Sun Shines Bright
Baltimore (MD)
1951 *The Tall Target*
Baltimore State College
The Harlem Globetrotters
Bananas
1936 *Kelly the Second*
1943 *The Gang's All Here*
Band leaders
1934 *Coming Out Party*
1938 *Happy Landing*
1941 *Murder on Lenox Avenue*
Playmates
Sun Valley Serenade
*Where Did You Get That
Girl?*
1943 *Doughboys in Ireland*
The Gang's All Here
What's Buzzin' Cousin?
1944 *Lady, Let's Dance!*
Slightly Terrific
Tahiti Nights
1945 *The Gay Senorita*
I Love a Bandleader
1946 *Beware*
Cuban Pete
1947 *New Orleans*
Sepia Cinderella
1956 The Benny Goodman Story
Bandits
1915 Captain Courtesy
The Grandee's Ring
1916 The Aryan
1917 *The Red Woman*
1919 *Desert Gold*
Scarlet Days
1920 *For the Soul of Rafael*
1922 A California Romance
1924 The Lightning Rider
The Mine with the Iron
Door
1925 Brand of Cowardice
Galloping Vengeance
The Thundering Herd
1927 Whispering Sage
1928 The Riding Renegade
1929 The Desert Rider
In Old Arizona
In Old California
1930 The Arizona Kid
The Bad Man
The Lash
Song of the Caballero
El último de los Vargas
1931 The Hurricane Horseman
La ley del harem
1932 Border Devils
The Vanishing Frontier
1933 *The California Trail*
1934 The Battling Buckaroo
La cruz y la espada
The Lone Defender
1935 Cowboy Holiday
The Cyclone Ranger
Wolf Riders
1936 Robin Hood of El Dorado
1937 The Californian
El carnaval del diablo
Law and Lead
1938 Outlaw Express
1939 The Cisco Kid and the Lady
In Old Caliente
The Return of the Cisco Kid
1940 The Gay Caballero
Rhythm of the Rio Grande
Viva Cisco Kid
1941 Belle Starr
Doomed Caravan
Ride on Vaquero
Romance of the Rio Grande
1943 Frontier Fury
1944 Marshal of Reno
1945 The Cisco Kid Returns
In Old New Mexico
Salome, Where She Danced
South of the Rio Grande
1946 Bad Bascomb
Beauty and the Bandit
The Gay Cavalier

1947 King of the Bandits
Riding the California Trail
1948 The Dude Goes West
1949 *Border Incident*
*The Cowboy and the
Prizefighter*
The Gay Amigo
The Kissing Bandit
Ride, Ryder, Ride!
1950 Bandit Queen
Colt .45
1951 *Slaughter Trail*
1952 Apache War Smoke
California Conquest
1953 *The Man Behind the Gun*
Ride, Vaquero!
1956 *Davy Crockett and the
River Pirates*
1957 Gun Battle at Monterey
1958 Gunfire at Indian Gap
Bands (Music)
1930 King of Jazz
1938 *Outside of Paradise*
194- *Mistaken Identity*
1941 *Playmates*
*Where Did You Get That
Girl?*
1944 *Tahiti Nights*
1945 *Club Havana*
1946 *Cuban Pete*
That Man of Mine
1946? *Beale Street Mama*
1947 *Boy! What a Girl!*
1948 *Music Man*
1949 *Lookout Sister*
1949? *Girl in Room 20*
1956 The Benny Goodman Story
1958 *St. Louis Blues*
Banjos
1936 *The Green Pastures*
Rainbow on the River
1940 *Broken Strings*
Bank clerks
1922 *The Top O' the Morning*
1929 *Thunderbolt*
1935 *Charlie Chan in Paris*
1938 *Castillos en el aire*
1940 The Way of All Flesh
1956 *Dakota Incident*
1957 *Twelve Angry Men*
Bank examiners
1948 *Moonrise*
Bank failures
1949 *House of Strangers*
1955 *Good Morning, Miss Dove*
Bank of England
1960 The Day They Robbed the
Bank of England
Bank presidents
1919 *The Lord Loves the Irish*
1935 *Charlie Chan in Paris*
1939 *Mr. Wong in Chinatown*
1944 *Sheriff of Las Vegas*
1945 *The Shanghai Cobra*
1955 *Good Morning, Miss Dove*
Bank robberies
1918 *Set Free*
1931 *The Cisco Kid*
1932 *Me and My Gal*
1936 Ellis Island
1937 *That I May Live*
1939 The Return of the Cisco Kid
1941 *Gauchos of Eldorado*
1944 *Sheriff of Las Vegas*
1945 *Great Stagecoach Robbery*
1946 *Bad Bascomb*
Dark Alibi
1948 *The Dude Goes West*
Four Faces West
Shep Comes Home
1949 *The Cowboy and the
Prizefighter*
The Daring Caballero
Masked Raiders
3 Godfathers
1950 *Winchester '73*
1951 *Cyclone Fury*
1953 *Ride, Vaquero!*
1955 Violent Saturday
1956 *Dakota Incident*
1958 Ride a Crooked Trail
1959 Odds Against Tomorrow
1960 *Cimarron*
The Day They Robbed the
Bank of England

Bank tellers
1931 *Three Who Loved*
1933 *Charlie Chan's Greatest Case*
1942 *Gentleman Jim*

Bankers
1914 *The Great Diamond Robbery*
       The Nightingale
1916 *At Piney Ridge*
       The Colored American Winning His Suit
1922 *Easy Money*
1923 *Deceit*
1927 *The Way of All Flesh*
1928 *George Washington Cohen*
1930 *Locuras de amor*
1931 *The Cisco Kid*
       Die Dreigroschenoper
       El pasado acusa
       La pura verdad
1935 *L'homme des Folies Bergère*
       The Winning Ticket
1936 *My American Wife*
       West of Nevada
       West of Nevada
1938 *Birthright*
1940 *If I Had My Way*
1941 *Gauchos of Eldorado*
       Ride on Vaquero
       Road Agent
1942 *Friendly Enemies*
1944 *Outlaw Trail*
       Sonora Stagecoach
       Tucson Raiders
       Vigilantes of Dodge City
1946 *Border Bandits*
       Canyon Passage
       Sunset Pass
       Three Wise Fools
1947 *Calendar Girl*
       The Chinese Ring
1948 *Four Faces West*
1949 *House of Strangers*
       Masked Raiders
1950 *Comanche Territory*
       The Furies
       The Traveling Saleswoman
1952 *The Fabulous Senorita*
1955 *Violent Saturday*
1958 *The Last Hurrah*
1960 *Man on a String*

Bankruptcy
1914 *The Good-for-Nothing*
1919 *A Yankee Princess*
1922 *The Good Provider*
1927 *Bitter Apples*
1932 *Hombres en mi vida*
       The Match King
1933 *A Lady's Profession*
1935 *L'homme des Folies Bergère*
1939 *La Inmaculada*
1948 *Music Man*
1953 *Tonight We Sing*

Banks
1932 *Cuore d'emigrante*
1945 *The Shanghai Cobra*
1947 *Buck Privates Come Home*
1949 *We Were Strangers*
1951 *Five*
1952 *My Man and I*
1957 *The Brothers Rico*

Banquets
1927 *For the Love of Mike*
1931 *Gentleman's Fate*
       Little Caesar
1933 *The Eternal Jew*
1935 *Charlie Chan in Shanghai*
1937 *Big City*
1942 *Woman of the Year*
1944 *Buffalo Bill*
1957 *Beau James*

Baptism
1935 *The Little Colonel*
1941? *The Blood of Jesus*

Bar mitzvah
1935 Bar-Mitzvah
1939 *Mirele Efros*
1958 *Marjorie Morningstar*

Barataria Bay (LA)
1938 The Buccaneer

Barbeques
1939 *Gone With the Wind*
1946 *Till the End of Time*

Barbers and barbershops
1921 Bits of Life
       Puppets of Fate
1923 Breaking into Society
1927 McFadden's Flats
1928 Flying Romeos
1930 Sins of the Children
1931 Smart Money
1932 Scarface
1933 Diplomaniacs
       No dejes la puerta abierta
       Obey the Law
1934 Judge Priest
1935 *McFadden's Flats*
       The Winning Ticket
1946? House-Rent Party
1947 *The Adventures of Don Coyote*
1948 *The Boy with Green Hair*
1948? Junction 88
1949 Roll Thunder Roll!
1950 Emergency Wedding
       Intruder in the Dust
1957 Man in the Shadow
1959 Inside the Mafia

Barcelona (Spain)
1935 *Tango Bar*

Barges
1923 Anna Christie
1930 *Anna Christie*
1931 *Skyline*

Barkers (Carnival)
1938 *The Duke Is Tops*
1945 *Betrayal from the East*

Barmaids
1932 *El caballero de la noche*
1948 *Unconquered*
1956 *Mohawk*
1959 *Shake Hands with the Devil*

Barns
1934 *Broadway Bill*
1945 *Our Vines Have Tender Grapes*

P. T. Barnum
1931 *Jenny Lind*

Barrels
1952 *Bright Victory*

Bars
1930 *Anna Christie*
1931 *Aloha*
1933 *The Cohens and Kellys in Trouble*
       La melodía prohibida
1936 *It Had to Happen*
1940 *Three Cheers for the Irish*
1942 *Woman of the Year*
1943 *Three Hearts for Julia*
1946 *Till the End of Time*
1947 *The Burning Cross*
1948 *Call Northside 777*
       Open Secret
1949 *Anna Lucasta*
       House of Strangers
       Portrait of Jennie
       The Red Menace
       Roll Thunder Roll!
       Souls of Sin
       Thieves' Highway
1950 *Give Us This Day*
       The Men
1952 *My Man and I*
       The Ring
1953 *The Member of the Wedding*
       Thunder Bay
1956 *Crowded Paradise*
1957 *Burden of Truth*
1958 *Gun Fever*
       The Young Lions
1959 *Anna Lucasta*
1960 *Hell to Eternity*
       The Pusher
       Take a Giant Step

Bartenders
1918 *Amarilly of Clothes-Line Alley*
1927 Lost at the Front
1931 Die Maske Fällt
1932 *Parigi affascina; ovvero, Malavita*

1936 *Rose of the Rancho*
1938 *Charlie Chan at Monte Carlo*
1940 *Elsa Maxwell's Public Deb No. 1*
1942 *Foreign Agent*
       Woman of the Year
1943 *The Ox-Bow Incident*
1948 *Jiggs and Maggie in Court*
       The Time of Your Life
1949 *Anna Lucasta*
       Illegal Entry
       Knock on Any Door
1949? *Come On, Cowboy!*
       Harlem Follies
1950 *Black Hand*
       Comanche Territory
1955 *Headline Hunters*
1956 *Wetbacks*
1959 *Anna Lucasta*

Baseball
1915 *The Grandee's Ring*
       The Grandee's Ring
1921 *As the World Rolls On*
1939 *The Girl from Mexico*
1942 *Woman of the Year*
1943 Ladies' Day
1944 Block Busters
       Going My Way
1947 *It Had To Be You*
1950 *The Jackie Robinson Story*
1951 *Jim Thorpe–All-American*
1957 *Beau James*

Baseball—Umpires
1944 *Block Busters*

Basketball
1951 The Harlem Globetrotters
1954 Go Man Go

Basketwork
1938 *Zamboanga*

Basque Americans
1927 *Whispering Sage*
1958 *Wild Is the Wind*
1959 *Thunder in the Sun*

Basques
1931 *Mi último amor*

Bastogne (Belgium)
1950 *Battleground*

Bataan (Philippines)
1943 *Bataan*

Bathing suits
1929 *The Cohens and Kellys in Atlantic City*
1949 *The Girl from Jones Beach*

Bathrooms
1947 *Crossfire*
1957 *The Brothers Rico*

Baths
1918 Johanna Enlists
1940 *Lucky Cisco Kid*

Bats
1931 *Drácula*
       Noche de duendes

Battered children
1915 *Kreutzer Sonata*
1917 *A Kentucky Cinderella*
1927 *The Broken Violin*
       The Scar of Shame
1931 *Huckleberry Finn*
1934 *Limehouse Blues*
1939 *The Adventures of Huckleberry Finn*
1942 *Little Tokyo, U.S.A.*
       Mokey
1945 *Our Vines Have Tender Grapes*
1948 *Fighting Father Dunne*
1958 Escape from Red Rock

Battered wives
       use Battered women

Battered women
1916 Pasquale
       Witchcraft
1917 I Will Repay
1918 Her Moment
       The Prussian Cur
1919? *When the Desert Smiles*
1920 The Brute
1927 *The Broken Violin*
1931 *Skyline*
1932 Flesh
       The Forty-Niners

1933 *L'amour guide*
1935 *The Wedding Night*
1937 *The Barrier*
1948 *The Arizona Ranger*
1950 *Ambush*
1951 A Streetcar Named Desire
1952 *My Man and I*
1954 *Apache*
1958 *Flaming Frontier*

Battle of the sexes
1931 *¿Conoces a tu mujer?*
1932 Call Her Savage
1933 *Robbers' Roost*
1934 What a Mother-in-Law!
1942 Woman of the Year
1947 The Foxes of Harrow
1953 Dream Wife
1955 Duel on the Mississippi

Battles
1925 Custer's Last Fight
1926 General Custer at Little Big Horn
1933 *The Eternal Jew*
1937 *Drums of Destiny*
1939 *Cossacks in Exile*
1942 *Submarine Raider*
1943 *Crash Dive*
1944 Buffalo Bill
1947? Swanee Showboat
1950 *Battleground*
1951 *Apache Drums*
       Go for Broke!
       Hurricane Island
       The Last Outpost
       New Mexico
       The Steel Helmet
       Warpath
1952 *Battles of Chief Pontiac*
       Bugles in the Afternoon
       The Savage
       Wagons West
1953 *Captain John Smith and Pocahontas*
       The Charge at Feather River
       Column South
       Jack McCall Desperado
       Last of the Comanches
       The Pathfinder
1954 *Sitting Bull*
       Taza, Son of Cochise
       They Rode West
       War Arrow
       The Yellow Tomahawk
1955 *Davy Crockett, King of the Wild Frontier*
       The Far Horizons
       The Indian Fighter
       Kentucky Rifle
       Seminole Uprising
       Seven Cities of Gold
       The Vanishing American
1956 Comanche
       Daniel Boone, Trail Blazer
       The Last Frontier
       Mohawk
       Pillars of the Sky
       The Searchers
1957 The Guns of Fort Petticoat
       Naked in the Sun
       Raiders of Old California
       Raintree County
       Trooper Hook
       War Drums
1958 *Flaming Frontier*
       Fort Massacre
       Oregon Passage
1959 *The Oregon Trail*
       Thunder in the Sun
       The Wonderful Country
1960 *All the Young Men*
       Hell to Eternity
       Sergeant Rutledge
       The Unforgiven

Battleships
1934 *The Unknown Soldier Speaks*

Bauxite
1941 *Gauchos of Eldorado*

Bavaria (Germany)
1913? *The Lure of New York*

Bayonets
1950 *Sands of Iwo Jima*
Bayous
1952 *The Iron Mistress*
1955 *Duel on the Mississippi*
Bayous (LA)
1946 Swamp Fire
1950 *The Toast of New Orleans*
1953 Cry of the Hunted
1957 Bayou
Bazaars
1929 This Is Heaven
Beachcombing
1915? *The Beachcomber*
1931 *The Black Camel*
1933 *Charlie Chan's Greatest Case*
Beaches
1931 *Young Sinners*
       Zein Weib's Lubovnick
1934 *Dos más uno, dos*
1944 *Hi, Beautiful*
1949 *Home of the Brave*
1950 *Mystery Submarine*
Beale Street (Memphis, TN)
1958 *St. Louis Blues*
Beards
1937 *Man of the People*
1942 *Nazi Agent*
Bears
1917 A Roadside Impresario
1919 *Fighting for Gold*
1925 The True North
1928 Kit Carson
1932 *Yiskor*
1940 Tundra
       Taku
1945 *Where Do We Go From Here?*
1946 *Song of the South*
1949 *Arctic Fury*
       Rose of the Yukon
1955 *Davy Crockett, King of the Wild Frontier*
1960 *Ice Palace*
Beauty contests
1929 *The Cohens and Kellys in Atlantic City*
1930 *Estrellados*
1939 *Keep Punching*
1943 *Gangway for Tomorrow*
1947 *Juke Joint*
1954 *Go Man Go*
Beauty operators
1937 *Underworld*
Beauty shops
1925 *The Manicure Girl*
1945 *Betrayal from the East*
1958 *Home Before Dark*
1960 *The Dark at the Top of the Stairs*
Beauty, Personal
1934 *Stand Up and Cheer!*
1941 *Ice-Capades*
1944 Mr. Skeffington
1951 Queen for a Day
Beer
1914 *John Barleycorn*
1933 *Best of Enemies*
Beer gardens
1928 Sins of the Fathers
1932 *Le cas du docteur Brenner*
Bees
1936 *Ellis Island*
1953 *Bright Road*
Beggars
1917 *Lost in Transit*
1931 Die Dreigroschenoper
       Kismet
1934 *The Rabbi's Power*
1935 *The Yiddish King Lear*
1939 *The Light Ahead*
Belgian Americans
1918 Out of a Clear Sky
1921 Through the Back Door
1926 The Strong Man
Belgians
1921 One Man in a Million
Belgium
1918 *The Unbeliever*
1921 Through the Back Door
1940 *The Ramparts We Watch*

Alexander Graham Bell
1941 *Land of Liberty*
Bell towers
1936 *Charlie Chan's Secret*
Bellboys
1931 *Buster se marie*
1937 *Charlie Chan on Broadway*
1940? *Mr. Washington Goes to Town*
1941 *Min Jok Jay Hung Sing*
1943 *What's Buzzin' Cousin?*
1947 *Ride the Pink Horse*
1948 *Half Past Midnight*
Bellevue Hospital (New York City)
1951 *Teresa*
Bells
1921 Lotus Blossom
1936 *Sins of Man*
1947 Bells of San Fernando
1948 *The Miracle of the Bells*
Belts
       Renegades of Sonora
Bends (Medicine)
     use Decompression sickness
Benefactors
1936 *Sum Hun*
1939 *King of Chinatown*
1951 Saturday's Hero
1953 *Sangaree*
Benefit performances
1941 *Golden Gate Girl*
1942 *Mexican Spitfire's Elephant*
1943 *Stormy Weather*
1946 *Beware*
1950 *Jolson Sings Again*
1951 *The Great Caruso*
Bergen-Belsen (Germany: Concentration camps)
       The House on Telegraph Hill
Bering Sea
1912 *Atop of the World in Motion*
1925 The True North
1930 The Break Up
1943 *Jack London*
1952 *Arctic Flight*
Berlin (Germany)
1918 Good-Bye, Bill
       The Spreading Evil
1937 *Charlie Chan at the Olympics*
1939 *Confessions of a Nazi Spy*
1940 *The Man I Married*
1945 *Salome, Where She Danced*
1958 *The Young Lions*
1960 *Man on a String*
Mary McLeod Bethune
       The Crowning Experience
Betrayal
1915 Hearts of Men
       The Rosary
       A Yankee from the West
1918? *The Snail*
1919? *The Brand of Judas*
1928 *The Wages of Sin*
1931 *Die Dreigroschenoper*
       Three Who Loved
1932 *The Forty-Niners*
       O festino o la legge
       The Vanishing Frontier
1934 *Call of the Coyote*
       Eskimo
       The Fighting Hero
       'Neath the Arizona Skies
1935 *Riddle Ranch*
       The Singing Vagabond
1937 *The Californian*
1938 *The Renegade Ranger*
1939 *The Fighting Gringo*
1940 *Escape to Glory*
       The Man I Married
       Viva Cisco Kid
1941 They Dare Not Love
1944 Address Unknown
1945 *Phantom of the Plains*
1946 *Strange Voyage*
1947 *Bells of San Fernando*
       Body and Soul
1948 *Angel in Exile*
       Fury at Furnace Creek
       Guns of Hate

       Tap Roots
1949 The Clay Pigeon
       Colorado Territory
       The Daring Caballero
       The Sky Dragon
       Stagecoach Kid
       Streets of Laredo
       The Undercover Man
1950 *Border Treasure*
       Last of the Buccaneers
1952 *The Savage*
1953 Tumbleweed
1954 Apache
       The Black Dakotas
       Massacre Canyon
       They Rode West
1955 *Apache Woman*
       Chief Crazy Horse
       Seven Cities of Gold
1957 *The Guns of Fort Petticoat*
       Journey to Freedom
1958 *The Defiant Ones*
       Touch of Evil
       Wild Is the Wind
1959 The Jayhawkers!
1960 *Take a Giant Step*
Bets and betting
     use Wagers
Beverly Hills (CA)
1932 *Thirteen Women*
1952 *The Ring*
1960 *Man on a String*
Biarritz (France)
1935 *Julieta compra un hijo*
Bible
1919 *Spotlight Sadie*
1919? In the Land of the Setting Sun; or, Martyrs of Yesterday
1936 The Green Pastures
1938 *The Adventures of Tom Sawyer*
1949 *Call of the Forest*
       3 Godfathers
1950 *Stars in My Crown*
1955 *The Lonesome Trail*
1956 *Pillars of the Sky*
       Walk the Proud Land
Bible. Old Testament. Book of Exodus
1931 *The Voice of Israel*
Bible. Old Testament. Book of Job
1936 *Sins of Man*
Biblical characters
1918 *The Birth of a Race*
1931 Shulamith
       The Voice of Israel
1932 Joseph in the Land of Egypt
1933 The Eternal Jew
       The Wandering Jew
1934 The Rabbi's Power
1936 The Green Pastures
1943 *Cabin in the Sky*
Bicycle racing
1939 *The Girl from Mexico*
Bicycles
1944 *Block Busters*
1949 *Prejudice*
1952 *Red Ball Express*
Chief Big Foot
1914 *The Indian Wars*
Big Tujunga Creek (Los Angeles, CA)
1948 *Old Los Angeles*
Bigamy
1915 Cohen's Luck
1916 The Flower of No Man's Land
       Light at Dusk
1918 *The Border Raiders*
       Free and Equal
1919 A Heart in Pawn
1920 The Good-Bad Wife
       Locked Lips
1921 A Divorce of Convenience
       Puppets of Fate
       The Sport of the Gods
1924 Unseen Hands
1926 Broken Hearts
1932 The Unfortunate Bride
1938 *Charlie Chan at Monte Carlo*
1949? *She's Too Mean for Me*

Bigotry
1922 *Pals of the West*
       The Woman He Loved
1924 *Birthright*
       Welcome Stranger
1926 *Private Izzy Murphy*
1927 His Foreign Wife
       Wild Geese
1929 Abie's Irish Rose
1933 *Ever in My Heart*
1936 *It Had to Happen*
       My American Wife
1941 *Birth of the Blues*
1942 *Dr. Gillespie's New Assistant*
       Let's Get Tough!
       Mokey
1946 *Till the End of Time*
1947 The Burning Cross
1948 Strange Victory
1949 *Prejudice*
1950 Devil's Doorway
       Right Cross
1951 *The Great Caruso*
       Oh! Susanna
       When the Redskins Rode
1952 *Battles of Chief Pontiac*
       It's a Big Country: An American Anthology
       My Man and I
       The Ring
1953 *Arrowhead*
       Column South
       The Glory Brigade
       The Stand at Apache River
1954 *Broken Lance*
       Saskatchewan
1955 Bad Day at Black Rock
       Good Morning, Miss Dove
       Santa Fe Passage
1956 Crowded Paradise
       Ghost Town
       Man from Del Rio
1957 Twelve Angry Men
1958 *Ambush at Cimarron Pass*
       Flaming Frontier
       The Last Hurrah
       Never Love a Stranger
       The Young Lions
1959 *The Wonderful Country*
       The Young Land
1960 *The Dark at the Top of the Stairs*
       Take a Giant Step
       Walk Like a Dragon
Bill collectors
1938 *Sugar Hill Baby*
1942 *Professor Creeps*
1946? *House-Rent Party*
Billboards
1919 *Bonnie, Bonnie Lassie*
Billiards and billiard parlors
1931 *Quand on est belle*
1937 *Dark Manhattan*
1939 *Daughters Courageous*
Billings (MT)
1948 *Angel in Exile*
Bills, Legislative
1949 *We Were Strangers*
Billy the Kid
1943 The Outlaw
Biological warfare
1952 Battles of Chief Pontiac
Birds
1928 The Great White North
1936 *Paddy O'Day*
1943 *Margin for Error*
1950 *Sunset in the West*
Birmingham (AL)
1938 *Spirit of Youth*
       Swing!
Birthdays
1917 *Sunshine and Gold*
1930 *Check and Double Check*
1931 *Cavalier of the West*
       Così è la vita
       Three Who Loved
1932 *Amore e morte*
       Cuore d'emigrante
1933 *Broken Dreams*
1935 *The Littlest Rebel*
1936 *The Bold Caballero*
       Rainbow on the River
       Song of the Gringo

1937 *Big City*
Where Is My Child?
1938 *The Beloved Brat*
Spawn of the North
1939 *Daughters Courageous*
1940 *Eli Eli*
1943 *His Butler's Sister*
1944 *Minstrel Man*
Since You Went Away
1946 *The Sailor Takes a Wife*
Song of the South
1947 *Little Mister Jim*
1948 *Gun Smugglers*
1950 *The Big Hangover*
Give Us This Day
1950? *Three Daughters*
1953 *The Jazz Singer*
1957 *The Oklahoman*
1958 *Wild Is the Wind*
1959 *The Young Land*
1960 *Flaming Star*
Man on a String

Birthmarks
1914 *Northern Lights*
1917 *Queen X*
Runaway Romany

Bishops
1943 *Hitler's Children*
1944 *Going My Way*

Otto Eduard Leopold von Bismarck
1945 *Salome, Where She Danced*

Bismarck (ND)
1951 *Warpath*
1952 *Bugles in the Afternoon*

Bison, American
1914 *In the Days of the Thundering Herd*
1925 *The Thundering Herd*
The Wild Bull's Lair
1926 *Buffalo Bill on the U. P. Trail*
The Last Frontier
1931 *La gran jornada*
1932 *The Forty-Niners*
The Golden West
1933 *Thundering Herd*
1936 *Treachery Rides the Range*
1944 *Buffalo Bill*
1946 *Wild West*
1949 *The Prairie*
She Wore a Yellow Ribbon
1956 *The Last Hunt*
Westward Ho the Wagons!

Black Dragon Society
1942 *Little Tokyo, U.S.A.*

Black Hand (United States)
1912 *The Adventures of Lieutenant Petrosino*
1914 *The Nightingale*
1915 *After Five*
The Alien
1916 *A Child of Mystery*
1917 *The Tell-Tale Step*
1921 *Diane of Star Hollow*
1950 *Black Hand*
1960 *Pay or Die*

Black Hills (SD and WY)
1914? *Sitting Bull—The Hostile Sioux Indian Chief*
1925 *Custer's Last Fight*
1936 *Custer's Last Stand*
1937 *The Plainsman*
1942 *They Died With Their Boots On*
1951 *Oh! Susanna*
1952 *The Savage*
1954 *Sitting Bull*
1955 *Chief Crazy Horse*
1957 *Ride Out for Revenge*
1960 *Walk Tall*

Black market
1944 *The Racket Man*
1950 *Deported*
1954 *Barefoot Battalion*

Black Sea
1959 *John Paul Jones*

Blackfoot Indians
use **Siksika Indians**

Blackmail
1912 *The Adventures of Lieutenant Petrosino*
1914 *The Woman in Black*

1915 *The Nigger*
Under Southern Skies
A Yankee from the West
1916 *Pasquale*
Witchcraft
1918 *I Want to Forget*
In Judgment Of
The Liar
Shifting Sands
1918? *The Snail*
1920 *The Riddle: Woman*
Within Our Gates
1922 *The Five Dollar Baby*
Shadows
1923 *Jealous Husbands*
1925 *Salome of the Tenements*
1929 *Sombras habaneras*
1931 *The Black Camel*
La carta
La dama atrevida
La mujer X
Nuit d'Espagne
Politiquerías
Quand on est belle
Smart Money
1932 *Hombres en mi vida*
1933 *Charlie Chan's Greatest Case*
Counsellor at Law
1934 *Drums O' Voodoo*
Straight Is the Way
1934? *Harlem After Midnight*
1935 *Un hombre peligroso*
Rendezvous
1937 *Charlie Chan on Broadway*
It Could Happen to You
1938 *Charlie Chan at Monte Carlo*
1939 *Charlie Chan at Treasure Island*
Charlie Chan in Reno
Judge Hardy and Son
Motel the Operator
1940 *The Notorious Elinor Lee*
While Thousands Cheer
1941 *Louisiana Purchase*
1942 *Lucky Ghost*
1943 *Margin for Error*
1944 *Black Magic*
1946 *Beware*
Dangerous Money
Saratoga Trunk
The Trap
1947 *It Had To Be You*
The Mighty McGurk
Ride the Pink Horse
Wild Horse Mesa
1948 *Half Past Midnight*
Miracle in Harlem
1949 *Illegal Entry*
1949? *She's Too Mean for Me*
1950 *Mystery Street*
So Young, So Bad
1951 *Adventures of Captain Fabian*
Cuban Fireball
The Girl on the Bridge
The Mark of the Renegade
1952 *The Fabulous Senorita*
1953 *Sangaree*
1954 *Drums Across the River*
Hell's Half Acre
1955 *The View from Pompey's Head*
1957 *Edge of the City*
1958 *The Last Hurrah*
Touch of Evil

Blacks
use **African Americans**

Blacksmiths
1915 *The Danger Signal*
1917 *The Sudden Gentleman*
1922 *Easy Money*
1934 *Judge Priest*
1935 *El cantante de Nápoles*
1936 *Laughing Irish Eyes*
1938 *The Singing Blacksmith*
1947 *Bells of San Fernando*
1949 *The Gay Amigo*
1951 *Apache Drums*
1952 *The Iron Mistress*
1953 *The Great Sioux Uprising*

Bladensburg, Battle of, 1814
1938 *The Buccaneer*

The Blarney Stone
1949 Top O' the Morning

Blind dates
1960 *The Dark at the Top of the Stairs*

Blind—Rehabilitation
1952 Bright Victory

Blindness
1914 *The Redemption of David Corson*
1917 *The Secret of Eve*
The Tell-Tale Step
The Trouble Buster
1918 *The Little Runaway*
1919 Deliverance
1920 Pagan Love
The Secret Gift
1922 Little Miss Smiles
1926 The Strong Man
1928 Sins of the Fathers
1929 Love, Live and Laugh
1930 *La jaula de los leones*
1931 Jenny Lind
1932 *Symphony of Six Million*
1934 *Drums O' Voodoo*
The Lone Defender
1935 *The Cyclone Ranger*
Shir Hashirim
1939 The Light Ahead
Mothers of Today
My Son
1941 *The Face Behind the Mask*
1944 *Mr. Skeffington*
1945 Pride of the Marines
1947 *Citizen Saint*
1951 Fort Defiance
Native Son
1952? *Call of the Navajo*
1955 *Smoke Signal*
The View from Pompey's Head
1956 *Crowded Paradise*
1958 *Blood Arrow*

Blindness—Temporary
1934 *Nada más que una mujer*
1935 *The Yiddish King Lear*
1936 Star for a Night
1940 *Girl from God's Country*
1958 *St. Louis Blues*
1959 *The Hanging Tree*

Blizzards
1919 *The Homesteader*
1931 *La gran jornada*
1932 *Igloo*
1938 *The Texans*
1940 *Taku*
1956 *The Last Hunt*

Blockades
1939 *Gone With the Wind*

Blood
1944 *Black Magic*
1947 *Body and Soul*

Blood brotherhood
1952 *Battles of Chief Pontiac*
1954 *Hondo*
1957 *The Deerslayer*
1959 *The Sheriff of Fractured Jaw*

Blood tests
use **Blood—Examinations**

Blood—Transfusion
1918 *The Honor of His House*
1930 *Sunny Skies*
1931 *Beyond Victory*
1940 *Perfidia*
1960 *All the Young Men*

Blowguns
1938 *Mr. Moto Takes a Chance*

Blueprints
1944 *Chip Off the Old Block*

Blues music
1943 *Stormy Weather*
1956 *Rockin' the Blues*
1958 *The Defiant Ones*
St. Louis Blues
1960 All the Fine Young Cannibals

Boarders
use **Lodgers**

Boarding schools
1917 *Her Own People*
A Jewel in Pawn
1918 *The Million Dollar Mystery*
1920 *It's a Great Life*
1927 *McFadden's Flats*
1928 *Mother Machree*
1935 *McFadden's Flats*
1950 *Belle of Old Mexico*
1953 *So Big*

Boardinghouse mistresses
1948? *Boarding House Blues*
1950 *Mystery Street*
1957 *Ride Out for Revenge*
1958 *Never Love a Stranger*

Boardinghouses
1916 Hulda from Holland
The Thousand Dollar Husband
Three of Many
1917 *The Bond Between*
1927 *The Scar of Shame*
1930 *The Big Pond*
1931 *Los calaveras*
Three Who Loved
1932 *Harlem Is Heaven*
1932? *The Girl from Chicago*
1933 *Grand Slam*
1933? *Scandal*
1934 *Beloved*
The Cat's-Paw
1941 *Where Did You Get That Girl?*
1942 *Sunday Punch*
1943 *Dixie*
Good Luck, Mr. Yates
1944 *Andy Hardy's Blonde Trouble*
Waterfront
1946 *Dark Alibi*
1947 *Calendar Girl*
Easy Come, Easy Go
Juke Joint
1948 *My Girl Tisa*
Reaching from Heaven
1948? *Boarding House Blues*
1949 *Portrait of Jennie*
Souls of Sin
1952 *Anything Can Happen*
1954 *Carmen Jones*

Boards of trade
use **Chambers of Commerce**

Boating accidents
1933 *The Cohens and Kellys in Trouble*
1944 *Dark Waters*
1946 *Swamp Fire*

Boatracing
1928 The Cameraman
1934 *Dos más uno, dos*
1956 Davy Crockett and the River Pirates

Boats
1919 *Yvonne from Paris*
1920 *The Luck of the Irish*
1932 *The Vanishing Frontier*
1933 The Cohens and Kellys in Trouble
1936 *Klondike Annie*
1939 *Fisherman's Wharf*
Mr. Moto in Danger Island
1940 *Taku*
1942 *All Through the Night*
Whispering Ghosts
1948 *Harpoon*
Key Largo
16 Fathoms Deep
1949 *Home of the Brave*
Portrait of Jennie
Tuna Clipper
1950 *A Lady Without Passport*
Sunset in the West
1952 *Brave Warrior*
1954 *Barefoot Battalion*
1955 *Smoke Signal*
1957 *All Mine to Give*
1959 *The World, the Flesh and the Devil*
1960 *Man on a String*

Boatswains
1921 The First Born
1935 *His Family Tree*

Bodyguards
1931   *The Guilty Generation*
1932   *The Hatchet Man*
1936   *Muss 'Em Up*
1940   *Too Many Girls*
1943   *Margin for Error*
1945   *I Love a Bandleader*
1952   *Desert Pursuit*
1957   *Trooper Hook*
1959   *Al Capone*

Bohemians and bohemianism
1918? Rosemary Climbs the
       Heights
1919   *The Last of His People*
       Toby's Bow
1930   *Charros, gauchos y manolas*
1931   *Su última noche*
       Women Love Once
1933   *L'amour guide*
1936   *La última cita*
1938   *La vida bohemia*
1958   *Marjorie Morningstar*
       Seven Hills of Rome

Bolivia—History—1879-1938
1935   *Alas sobre el Chaco*

Bolshevists and Bolshevism
1919   *The Volcano*
1920   *Dangerous Hours*
       The Face at Your Window
       The Great Shadow
       Uncharted Channels
1926   *Into Her Kingdom*
       Rose of the Tenements
1934   *Strange Wives*

Bombing, Aerial
1935   *Alas sobre el Chaco*
1941   *Ten Ostatni*
1943   *Air Force*
       Bataan
1954   *Barefoot Battalion*
1958   *Kings Go Forth*
       The Young Lions
1960   *I Aim at the Stars: the
       Wernher von Braun Story*

Bombings
1950   *Black Hand*
1959   *The FBI Story*
1960   *Pay or Die*

Bombs
1914   *The Nightingale*
1915   *The Last of the Mafia*
1918   *The Hun Within*
1920   *Lifting Shadows*
1928   *A Ship Comes In*
1933   *Diplomaniacs*
       Victims of Persecution
1935   *De la sartén al fuego*
1937   *Song of the City*
1939   *Forged Passport*
       King of Chinatown
1941   *The Face Behind the Mask*
       Murder on Lenox Avenue
       Mystery Ship
1942   *Submarine Raider*
1943   *Action in the North
       Atlantic*
       *They Came to Blow Up
       America*
1946   *The Red Dragon*
1947   *Buck Privates Come Home*
1952   *Red Snow*

Bonds
1935   *Charlie Chan in Paris*
1938   *Charlie Chan at Monte Carlo*
       Dangerous to Know
1940   *Cuando canta la Ley*

Boogie-woogie music
1948   *Docks of New Orleans*

Book burning
1933   *The Wandering Jew*

Bookies
       Racetrack
1934   *Broadway Bill*
1937   *It Could Happen to You*
1938   *Mr. Moto's Gamble*
1940   *Three Cheers for the Irish*
       While Thousands Cheer
1947   *Easy Come, Easy Go*
1949   *Tuna Clipper*

Bookishness
1960   *The Sign of Zorro*

Bookkeepers
1938   The Power of Life
1939   *Mirele Efros*
1940   *Her Second Mother*
1949   The Undercover Man

Books
1919   *Toby's Bow*
1935   *Lem Hawkins' Confession*
1937   *I Want to Be a Mother*
1944   *The Chinese Cat*
1948   *The Dude Goes West*
1956   *Westward Ho the Wagons!*

Booksellers and bookselling
1916   *Man and His Angel*
1919   *The Volcano*
1930   *El presidio*
       She Got What She Wanted
1932   *L'athlète incomplet*
1939   The Light Ahead
1942   *Nazi Agent*
1945   *The House on 92nd St.*

Boom towns
1943   *In Old Oklahoma*

Daniel Boone
1931   *The Great Meadow*
1936   *Daniel Boone*
1950   *Young Daniel Boone*
1956   *Daniel Boone, Trail Blazer*

Boonesboro (KY)
1936   *Daniel Boone*
1956   *Daniel Boone, Trail Blazer*

Bootblacks
1915   *The Italian*
       The Last of the Mafia
1936   *General Spanky*
1945   *Of One Blood*

John Wilkes Booth
1930   Abraham Lincoln
1936   *The Prisoner of Shark
       Island*

Bootleggers
1924   *His Darker Self*
1926   *The Strong Man*
       Sweet Daddies
1927   The Callahans and the
       Murphys
1928   Sins of the Fathers
1931   Gentleman's Fate
       The Guilty Generation
       Mr. Lemon of Orange
       Pardon Us
1932   *Hombres en mi vida*
       Scarface
1933   The Cohens and Kellys in
       Trouble
       Dance Hall Hostess
       A Lady's Profession
       Song of the Eagle
1935   *No matarás*
1944   *Mr. Skeffington*
1945   Of One Blood

Boots
1949   *Laramie*

Border patrols
1927   Aflame in the Sky
       Roarin' Broncs
1930   On the Border
1934   *The Lone Defender*
       Riding Speed
1936   *Hair-Trigger Casey*
1941   *Hold Back the Dawn*
1943   Border Patrol
1949   *Border Incident*
1950   Rio Grande Patrol

Borders
       use **Boundaries**

Borgia family
1942   Castle in the Desert

Boris Godunov (Opera)
1953   *Tonight We Sing*

Borneo
1934   Nada más que una mujer

Boston (MA)
1918   The Liar
1920   *Within Our Gates*
1936   *Dancing Pirate*
1937   *Border Cafe*
1945   *The Great John L.*
1948   *Sleep, My Love*
1950   *Mystery Street*
1952   *It's a Big Country: An
       American Anthology*

1958   *Home Before Dark*

Bostonians
1918   The Source
1956   *Mohawk*

Botanists
1929   Welcome Danger
1932   *L'athlète incomplet*

Bouncers
1947   *The Mighty McGurk*

Boundaries
1936   *Human Cargo*
1937   Drums of Destiny
1949   *Ranger of Cherokee Strip*
1952   *Red Snow*
1958   *Escape from Red Rock*
1959   *The Oregon Trail*

Bounty hunters
1944   *Riding West*
1948   *Four Faces West*
1952   *Rose of Cimarron*
1955   *Shotgun*
1956   *Comanche*
       Daniel Boone, Trail Blazer
1957   *Apache Warrior*
       The Deerslayer
       The Tin Star
1960   *The Adventures of
       Huckleberry Finn*
       Comanche Station
       Walk Tall

Henry Bouquet
1958   *The Light in the Forest*

Bow and arrow
1950   *Cherokee Uprising*
       Rio Grande
1952   *Hiawatha*
       Indian Uprising
1955   *Kentucky Rifle*
       The Lonesome Trail
1956   *Westward Ho the Wagons!*

James Bowie
1939   *Man of Conquest*
1950   Comanche Territory
1952   The Iron Mistress
1955   *Davy Crockett, King of the
       Wild Frontier*
       The Last Command

Bowling and bowling alleys
1945   *Pride of the Marines*
1951   *A Streetcar Named Desire*

Boxers
1917   Rosie O'Grady
1918   One More American
1920   *The Brute*
1921   The Secret Sorrow
1922   *The Dungeon*
       For His Mother's Sake
       Little Miss Smiles
1923   April Showers
       The Victor
1925   His People
1926   Blarney
       The Fighting Deacon
1927   Clancy's Kosher Wedding
1928   The Night Bird
1930   Around the Corner
1934   *The Cactus Kid*
1935   *The Irish in Us*
1936   Kelly the Second
       Laughing Irish Eyes
1938   Spirit of Youth
1939   *Keep Punching*
       Verbena trágica
       Winner Take All
1941   *Lady from Louisiana*
1942   Gentleman Jim
       Sunday Punch
1943   The Girl from Monterrey
       Good Luck, Mr. Yates
1945   The Great John L.
1946   *Till the End of Time*
1947   Body and Soul
       The Mighty McGurk
1948   *The Fight Never Ends*
1949   *House of Strangers*
1950   Right Cross
1951   Native Son
1952   The Fighter
       Kid Monk Baroni
       The Quiet Man
       The Ring
1954   *Carmen Jones*
1956   *Serenade*

Boxing
1920   The Brute
1921   As the World Rolls On
1922   *Square Joe*
1925   Hogan's Alley
1928   *Eleven P.M.*
       United States Smith
1930   La fuerza del querer
1932   *Marido y mujer*
       Mazel Tov
1935   *The Irish in Us*
1936   *Below the Deadline*
1938   Mr. Moto's Gamble
1939   *King of Chinatown*
       Winner Take All
1940   The Notorious Elinor Lee
1945   *The Great John L.*
1946   *Gas House Kids*
1947   Vigilantes of Boomtown
1953   The Joe Louis Story
1955   *The Long Gray Line*
1958   *Never Love a Stranger*

Boxing managers
1926   The Fighting Deacon
1928   The Night Bird
1930   *La fuerza del querer*
1936   *Laughing Irish Eyes*
1938   *Spirit of Youth*
1939   *Keep Punching*
1940   *The Notorious Elinor Lee*
1943   *The Girl from Monterrey*
1945   *The Great John L.*
1947   Body and Soul
1952   *Kid Monk Baroni*
       The Ring
1953   The Joe Louis Story

Boxing trainers
1947   *Body and Soul*
1950   *Right Cross*
1952   *The Ring*
1953   *The Joe Louis Story*

Boy Scouts
1917   *The Little Boy Scout*
1939   *The Escape*

Boys schools
1955   *Blackboard Jungle*

Bozeman Trail (MT)
1936   *The Glory Trail*
1951   Tomahawk
1955   *The Gun That Won the
       West*

Bracelets
1932   *The Hatchet Man*
1934   *Laughing Boy*
1944   *Lifeboat*
1948   *Red River*
       Sleep, My Love
1958   *Seven Hills of Rome*

Edward Braddock
1927   Winners of the Wilderness

Braggarts
1925   *Custer's Last Fight*
1932   *L'athlète incomplet*
1940   The Fighting 69th
1956   *Davy Crockett and the
       River Pirates*

Braille Institute for the Blind
1932   *Symphony of Six Million*

Brain surgery
1946   *The Face of Marble*
1947   *Dark Delusion*
1959   *The Last Angry Man*

Louis Brandeis
1951   *The Magnificent Yankee*

Branding
1915   The Cheat
1931   *La ley del harem*
1937   *The Riders of the Whistling
       Skull*
1939   *The Bronze Buckaroo*
1948   *Red River*
1951   *The Mark of the Renegade*

Brassieres
1955   *Brevities of 1955*

Brats
1936   *Rainbow on the River*
1938   The Beloved Brat

Wernher von Braun
1960   I Aim at the Stars: the
       Wernher von Braun Story

Brazil
1920   *Within Our Gates*
Brazilian Americans
1943   *The Gang's All Here*
1944   Something for the Boys
Brazilians
1933   *Primavera en otoño*
1938   *Mis dos amores*
Breach of promise
1930   The Last Dance
1931   *Shulamith*
1933   *Counsellor at Law*
1937   *Natalka Poltavka*
1938   *The Rage of Paris*
Bread lines
1939   *A Brivele der Mamen*
Brest (France)
1959   *John Paul Jones*
Brewers and breweries
1933   *Best of Enemies*
      Song of the Eagle
1942   *Friendly Enemies*
Bribery
1914   *The Redemption of David
      Corson*
1917   *The Renaissance at
      Charleroi*
1918   *One More American*
      Sandy
1919   *Lasca*
1921   *The Call of His People*
1931   *Regeneración*
1934   Stand Up and Cheer!
1936   *Amor que vuelve*
1937   *Charlie Chan on Broadway*
1940   *Behind the News*
      The Man I Married
1941   *Lady from Louisiana*
1942   *Rio Rita*
1944   *Riding West*
1947   *The Mighty McGurk*
      Northwest Outpost
      Robin Hood of Monterey
1948   *Up in Central Park*
1949   *House of Strangers*
      Jigsaw
      The Undercover Man
1957   *Trooper Hook*
1958   Bullwhip
      Gunman's Walk
1959   *Al Capone*
Brick layers
1935   McFadden's Flats
1950   Give Us This Day
Brides
1930   *King of Jazz*
1936   Border Phantom
      The Glory Trail
1937   *Manhattan
      Merry-Go-Round*
Bridge (Game)
1919   *Mandarin's Gold*
1933   Grand Slam
Bridges
1943   *Bataan*
1949   *Daughter of the West*
      The Valiant Hombre
1950   *Rock Island Trail*
      A Ticket to Tomahawk
1951   *The Girl on the Bridge*
1953   *The Glory Brigade*
British Columbia (Canada)
1914   *In the Land of the Head
      Hunters*
British Columbia (Canada)
1950   The Cariboo Trail
Broken limbs
1951   *The Mark of the Renegade*
Brokers
1915   *Time Lock Number 776*
1927   The Auctioneer
1931   *Esclavas de la moda*
      Lo mejor es reír
      Die Maske Fällt
Brokers (Marriage)
      use **Matchmakers**
Brooklyn Bridge (New York City)
1936   *Winterset*
**Brooklyn Dodgers (Baseball
team)**
1950   The Jackie Robinson Story

Brothels
1913   The Inside of the White
      Slave Traffic
1918   *Free and Equal*
1919   *A Man's Duty*
1920   *The Luck of the Irish*
1931   *Die Dreigroschenoper*
1934   *Drums O' Voodoo*
1949?   *Girl in Room 20*
1953   *The Sun Shines Bright*
1958   *Touch of Evil*
1959   *Last Train from Gun Hill*
1960   *Cimarron*
Brothers
1914   The Good-for-Nothing
1915   *The Alien*
      The Birth of a Nation
      Chimmie Fadden
1916   *Broken Chains*
      The Grip of Jealousy
      The Sign of the Poppy
1917   *Hashimura Togo*
      A Kentucky Cinderella
      The Winged Mystery
1917?   *Barnaby Lee*
1918   *Ruggles of Red Gap*
1919   Told in the Hills
1920   *Dangerous Days*
      The Good-Bad Wife
1921   Across the Divide
      A Modern Cain
      The Secret Sorrow
1922   For His Mother's Sake
      The Sign of the Rose
1923   *Flames of Wrath*
      His Great Chance
1924   Untamed Youth
1925   Red Love
1926   Twin Triggers
1927   His Foreign Wife
      Old San Francisco
      *With Sitting Bull at the
      Spirit Lake Massacre*
1928   The House of Scandal
      The Wages of Sin
      Wheel of Chance
1929   Hallelujah
      Masked Emotions
      Sioux Blood
1931   *The Avenger*
      The Black Camel
      La cautivadora
      Cavalier of the West
      La fiesta del diablo
      Gentleman's Fate
      Hay que casar al príncipe
      La llama sagrada
1932   La foule hurle
      Joseph in the Land of Egypt
      Mazel Tov
      Wild Horse Mesa
1933   *Charlie Chan's Greatest
      Case*
1935   The Irish in Us
      No matarás
      Shir Hashirim
1936   *Charlie Chan at the Circus*
      Desert Gold
      Hair-Trigger Casey
      Pinto Rustlers
1937   Drums of Destiny
      Life Begins in College
1938   The Adventures of Tom
      Sawyer
      In Old Chicago
      Josette
      Life Goes On
1939   *Charlie Chan in Honolulu*
      Double Deal
      Drifting Westward
      The Escape
      Waterfront
1940   *Covered Wagon Days*
      East of the River
      Son of Ingagi
1941   Adam Had Four Sons
      Thunder Over the Prairie
      Under Fiesta Stars
      You're Out of Luck
1942   Apache Trail
      Let's Get Tough!
      *Mexican Spitfire Sees a
      Ghost*
      Submarine Raider
      Take My Life

1943   *Gangway for Tomorrow*
1944   *The Chinese Cat*
      Slightly Terrific
      Sonora Stagecoach
      The Sullivans
1945   *Johnny Angel*
      Of One Blood
      Rhapsody in Blue
1946   Slightly Scandalous
1947   *Desperate*
      Duel in the Sun
      Humoresque
      Pirates of Monterey
      Spoilers of the North
      Thunder Mountain
1948   *Angel in Exile*
      Cry of the City
      Fury at Furnace Creek
      Gun Smugglers
      Key Largo
      Music Man
      Old Los Angeles
      Renegades of Sonora
      Shanghai Chest
1949   Brothers in the Saddle
      The Dalton Gang
      House of Strangers
      Lust for Gold
      The Prairie
1950   *The Girl from San Lorenzo*
      Intruder in the Dust
      The Jackie Robinson Story
      The Missourians
      Mystery Submarine
      No Way Out
      *Raiders of Tomahawk
      Creek*
      Winchester '73
1951   Fort Defiance
      The Last Outpost
      Saturday's Hero
      Teresa
1952   *The Battle at Apache Pass*
      The Ring
      Woman in the Dark
1953   *Ambush at Tomahawk Gap*
      Conquest of Cochise
      Old Overland Trail
      Tumbleweed
1954   Taza, Son of Cochise
1956   *Death of a Scoundrel*
      Hot Blood
      Raw Edge
      The White Squaw
1957   The Brothers Rico
      The Halliday Brand
      Joe Dakota
      The Oklahoman
1958   Escape from Red Rock
      Flaming Frontier
      Gunman's Walk
      Wild Is the Wind
1959   Night of the Quarter Moon
      The Wonderful Country
1960   *This Rebel Breed*
Brothers and sisters
1913?   *The Call of the Blood*
1914   *Dan*
1915   *The Birth of a Nation*
      The Gambler of the West
1915?   *The Beachcomber*
1916   *Arms and the Woman*
      Betrayed
1917   The Call of the East
      Castles for Two
      One Law for Both
      The Pulse of Life
      The Renaissance at
      Charleroi
      Rosie O'Grady
      The Spirit of '76
1918   *The Birth of a Race*
      Fields of Honor
      The Golden Wall
      The Kaiser's Finish
1919   The Gray Horizon
      Just Squaw
      Lasca
      The Last of His People
      The Volcano
1920   Our Christianity and
      Nobody's Child
      Rio Grande
1921   Anne of Little Smoky
      The Call of His People

      No Woman Knows
1922   Anna Ascends
      Little Miss Smiles
      The Top O' the Morning
1923   April Showers
      Jealous Husbands
1924   The Lure of Love
1925   The Fearless Lover
      Galloping Vengeance
      A Son of His Father
      Speed Wild
      Tearing Through
1927   Bitter Apples
      The Fighting Hombre
      [*Japanese-American Film*]
1928   The Night Bird
      The Wages of Sin
1929   East Side Sadie
      In Old California
      The Invaders
      Sombras habaneras
1930   Doña mentiras
      La fuerza del querer
      Los que danzan
      El presidio
      Sevilla de mis amores
      El valiente
1931   Aloha
      Così è la vita
      Mr. Lemon of Orange
      Nuit d'Espagne
      El proceso de Mary Dugan
1932   *Amor in montagna*
      Flesh
      The Galloping Kid
      Hidden Valley
      Huddle
      Igloo
      Marido y mujer
      The Rainbow Trail
      Scarface
      Unashamed
      The Vanishing Frontier
      Veiled Aristocrats
      White Eagle
1933   *Dance Hall Hostess*
      Olsen's Big Moment
      Robbers' Roost
      Una viuda romántica
1934   Un capitán de cosacos
      Charlie Chan in London
      'Neath the Arizona Skies
      Wheels of Destiny
1935   Circle of Death
      Cyclone of the Saddle
      Lem Hawkins' Confession
      Romance in Manhattan
1936   *Muss 'Em Up*
      Paddy O'Day
      The Traitor
      Winterset
1937   Big City
      I Want to Be a Mother
1938   God's Step Children
      Road Demon
      *Two Gun Man from
      Harlem*
      Wild Horse Canyon
1939   *The Bronze Buckaroo*
      Daughter of the Tong
      The Escape
      The Fighting Gringo
      Mothers of Today
1940   *Americaner Schadchen*
      Son of Ingagi
1941   *Belle Starr*
      Mutiny in the Arctic
      Thunder Over the Prairie
      Western Union
1942   *The Navy Comes Through*
      North to the Klondike
      Rubber Racketeers
1943   *Air Force*
      The Amazing Mrs. Holliday
      The Girl from Monterey
      His Butler's Sister
1944   *Charlie Chan in the Secret
      Service*
      Chip Off the Old Block
      Mr. Skeffington
      The Racket Man
      Slightly Terrific
1945   Anoush
      Great Stagecoach Robbery
      The Jade Mask

South of the Rio Grande
Wanderer of the Wasteland
1946 *Gas House Kids*
Renegade Girl
Slightly Scandalous
Song of the South
South of Monterey
Stars on Parade
Sunset Pass
1947 *The Adventures of Don Coyote*
Dangerous Venture
King of the Bandits
Last of the Redmen
Thunder Mountain
Under the Tonto Rim
1948 *The Feathered Serpent*
The Fight Never Ends
1949 *Arctic Manhunt*
The Cowboy and the Prizefighter
Harbor of Missing Men
Illegal Entry
Jigsaw
Lookout Sister
Masked Raiders
Massacre River
Riders of the Range
Rose of the Yukon
Tale of the Navajos
We Were Strangers
1950 *Belle of Old Mexico*
Comanche Territory
Right Cross
Young Man with a Horn
1951 *The Tall Target*
1952 *The Iron Mistress*
The Quiet Man
The Raiders
Wagons West
1953 *Arrowhead*
Column South
Fort Ti
San Antone
1954 *Drum Beat*
1955 *Apache Ambush*
Apache Woman
Fort Yuma
White Feather
1956 *The Benny Goodman Story*
Westward Ho the Wagons!
1957 *All Mine to Give*
Ride Out for Revenge
War Drums
1958 *Gunman's Walk*
Sierra Baron
1959 *Cry Tough*
1960 *I Passed for White*
The Unforgiven

Brothers-in-law
1919 *Spotlight Sadie*
1920 The North Wind's Malice
1931 *Mr. Lemon of Orange*
1935 *The Winning Ticket*
1948 *Fighting Father Dunne*
1953 Conquest of Cochise
1957 *The Brothers Rico*

Willis Brown
1914? A Boy and the Law

John Brown
1930 Abraham Lincoln
1940 Santa Fe Trail
1955 Seven Angry Men

Brownsville (TX)
1949 *The Valiant Hombre*
1953 Ride, Vaquero!

Budapest (Hungary)
1929 Is Everybody Happy?
1934 *The Great Flirtation*
1935 *Señora casada necesita marido*
1940 *Tengo fe en ti*

Buddhism
1932 *The Hatchet Man*
1951 *The Steel Helmet*
1959 *The Crimson Kimono*

Buenos Aires (Argentina)
1931 *Las luces de Buenos Aires*
1933 Espérame
Melodía de arrabal
1934 *Cuesta abajo*
1935 *El día que me quieras*

Buffalo
use **Bison, American;**
Water buffalo

Buffalo (NY)
1931 *Call of the Rockies*
1934 *Wheels of Destiny*
1935 *Fighting Pioneers*
1939 *Mothers of Today*

Bulgarians
1957 Journey to Freedom

Bulge, Battle of the, 1944-1945
1950 *Battleground*

Bull Run, Battle of, 1862
1934 *Operator 13*

Bulldozers
1953 *The Glory Brigade*

Bullets
1933 *The Emperor Jones*
1947 *Robin Hood of Monterey*
1949 *Harbor of Missing Men*
Stallion Canyon
1950 *Intruder in the Dust*
1956 *The Lone Ranger*

Bullfighters and bullfighting
1923 Suzanna
1930 *Charros, gauchos y manolas*
Galas de la Paramount
1932 *Soñadores de la gloria*
1936 *The Bold Caballero*
1941 *Hold Back the Dawn*
Playmates
1956 *Serenade*

Bullies
1915 *Chimmie Fadden*
1924 Birthright
1939 *The Bronze Buckaroo*
1940 The Fighting 69th
Jennie
1943 *The Ox-Bow Incident*
1946 *Song of the South*
1949 *Tuna Clipper*
1957 *Bayou*
The Tin Star
1958 *Never Love a Stranger*
1959 *Porgy and Bess*
1960 The Plunderers

Bulls
1925 The Wild Bull's Lair
1942 *The Vanishing Virginian*
1947 *Bowery Buckaroos*

Bumblers
1928 Hold 'Em Yale
1930 Estrellados
1931 *Buster se marie*
Los calaveras
Mr. Lemon of Orange
Noche de duendes
Pardon Us
Politiquerías
1934 What a Mother-in-Law!
1937 The Jester (Der Purimspieler)
1938 Passport Husband
1940 *Midnight Shadow*
Son of Ingagi
1946? Fight That Ghost
1960 *The Sign of Zorro*

Bums (Tramps)
use **Beggars;**
Hoboes;
Tramps;
Vagabonds

Ned Buntline
1944 *Buffalo Bill*

Burglars
1915 *The Kindling*
1919 *The Lost Battalion*
1941 *Where Did You Get That Girl?*
1948 *Shanghai Chest*

Burgos (Spain)
1935 *Julieta compra un hijo*

Burial
1943 *Bataan*
The Outlaw
1949 *Arctic Fury*
1954 *Drum Beat*
Drums Across the River
Siege at Red River
Sitting Bull
1955 *Kentucky Rifle*

1956 *7th Cavalry*
1958 *Gun Fever*
1959 *Porgy and Bess*

Burial grounds
1947 *Dangerous Venture*

Buried treasure
1915 *An American Gentleman*
1923 Regeneration
1932 *Hidden Valley*
1946 Strange Voyage
1956 Secret of Treasure Mountain

Burlesque
1930 The Grand Parade
1943 *Riding High*
1947 *The Jolson Story*
1953 *The Eddie Cantor Story*
1955 Brevities of 1955

Burlesque dancers
1946 Dirty Gertie from Harlem, U.S.A.
1948 *The Time of Your Life*
1953 *The Glass Wall*

Burns
1941 The Face Behind the Mask

Burros
use **Donkeys**

Bus drivers
1944 *Hi, Beautiful*

Busboys
1938 Passport Husband

Buses
1937 *Music for Madame*
1946 *Shadows Over Chinatown*
1947 *Desperate*
1948 *Half Past Midnight*
16 Fathoms Deep

Bushido
1945 Samurai

Bushy Run, Battle of
1948 *Unconquered*

Business competition
1915 *The Immigrant*
1921 *The Call of His People*
1931 La cautivadora
1935 *Piernas de seda*
1938 *Charlie Chan at Monte Carlo*
Di que me quieres
1939 *El otro soy yo*
Stand Up and Fight
1940 *Doomed to Die*
Mexican Spitfire Out West
1942 *Mexican Spitfire at Sea*
1943 Mexican Spitfire's Blessed Event
1946 Tall, Tan and Terrific
1948 Miracle in Harlem
1950 A Ticket to Tomahawk
1951 *The Raging Tide*
1952 The Big Sky
1958 Bullwhip

Business ethics
1930 *Una cana al aire*
1941 Sunday Sinners
1944 *Buffalo Bill*
1948 *Reaching from Heaven*
1950 The Big Hangover
God, Man and Devil

Business managers
1921 The Call of His People
1930 The Big Pond
1940 *Broken Strings*
1945 *The Cisco Kid Returns*

Business partners
use **Partnership**

Business rivals
1941 *The Gang's All Here*
1947 *Hi De Ho*
1948 *Reaching from Heaven*
1950 *Right Cross*
1952 *The Iron Mistress*
1956 Baby Doll

Businessmen
1915 *The Sable Lorcha*
1916 *Broken Fetters*
1917 *The Primitive Call*
1920 The Secret Gift
1921 The Burden of Race
1925 Braveheart
1927 Bitter Apples
1928 The Cohens and the Kellys in Paris

1929 The Cohens and Kellys in Atlantic City
1930 Una cana al aire
1931 Nuit d'Espagne
La pura verdad
1932 *So Big*
1933 *Best of Enemies*
The Cohens and Kellys in Trouble
A Lady's Profession
1934 *Broadway Bill*
Stand Up and Cheer!
1935 *El día que me quieras*
Harmony Lane
1937 *Waikiki Wedding*
1941 *Min Jok Jay Hung Sing*
Murder on Lenox Avenue
1941? *Hampton Institute: Its Program of Education for Life*
1942 *Nazi Agent*
Song of the Islands
1943 *The Gang's All Here*
1944 *Buffalo Bill*
1945 *The Bells of St. Mary's*
The Gay Senorita
1946 *Slightly Scandalous*
1947 *Buffalo Bill Rides Again*
Wild Horse Mesa
1948 *Fighting Father Dunne*
1950 *A Ticket to Tomahawk*
1950? *Three Daughters*
1953 *So Big*
1956 *Giant*
1957 *Twelve Angry Men*

Businesswomen
use **Women in business**

Butchers
1918 *Tony America*
1938 *Two Sisters*
1955 Marty

Benjamin Butler
1957 *Band of Angels*

Butlers
1916 *For the Defense*
1917 *Hashimura Togo*
1918 *Amarilly of Clothes-Line Alley*
Me Und Gott
1919 *The Other Man's Wife*
1926 Meet the Prince
1930 *Así es la vida*
El cuerpo del delito
1931 *The Black Camel*
La dama atrevida
1932 *The Cohens and Kellys in Hollywood*
1934 *Coming Out Party*
Granaderos del amor
1936 *Love and Sacrifice*
Rainbow on the River
1937 *Thank You, Mr. Moto*
1938 *The Beloved Brat*
The Rage of Paris
1939 *City in Darkness*
The Mystery of Mr. Wong
1940 *Elsa Maxwell's Public Deb No. 1*
Mexican Spitfire Out West
Murder over New York
Music in My Heart
Phantom of Chinatown
1941 *Charlie Chan in Rio*
New York Town
Sullivan's Travels
1942 *Nazi Agent*
1943 *The Amazing Mrs. Holliday*
His Butler's Sister
1944 *Chip Off the Old Block*
My Pal Wolf
1945 *The Jade Mask*
1946 *The Face of Marble*
Notorious
1947 *The Chinese Ring*
The Farmer's Daughter
1948 *Shanghai Chest*
1949 *The Fighting Kentuckian*
1950 *Belle of Old Mexico*

Butterflies
1953 *Bright Road*

Buttons
1935 *Piernas de seda*
1943 *Tahiti Honey*

Cabaret performers
1920   On with the Dance
1921?   *The Slave Market*
1934   *Nada más que una mujer*
1935   *De la sartén al fuego*
1937   *The Cantor's Son*
      Music for Madame
1938   *My Lucky Star*
1939   *Gang Smashers*
1940   *Charlie Chan in Panama*

Cabarets
1918   Wild Women
1919   The Delicious Little Devil
      Yvonne from Paris
1921   The Sport of the Gods
1921?   *The Slave Market*
1928   Eleven P.M.
      The Wages of Sin
1929   Mother's Boy
      Sombras habaneras
1930   Georgia Rose
1931   *Such Is Life*
1933   *Yo, tú y ella*
1934   *Blossom Time*
      La buenaventura
      Drums O' Voodoo
      La veuve joyeuse
1935   *Shir Hashirim*
      Te quiero con locura
1936   *La última cita*
1938   *God's Step Children*
1939   *Gang Smashers*
1940   *Charlie Chan in Panama*
      The Notorious Elinor Lee
      Paradise in Harlem

Cabin boys
1921   *Love's Plaything*
1937   Slave Ship
1945   *Betrayal from the East*

Cabinet officers
1944   *My Pal Wolf*

Cabins
1925   *Body and Soul*
      Tonio, Son of the Sierras
1931   *The Great Meadow*
      Young Sinners
1934   *Las fronteras del amor*
1946   *Rendezvous 24*
1947   *Oregon Trail Scouts*
1949   *The Fighting Kentuckian*
      Roll Thunder Roll!
      Rose of the Yukon
1950   *The Iroquois Trail*
      The Missourians
1957   *All Mine to Give*
1959   *The Hanging Tree*

Frances Xavier Cabrini, Saint
1947   *Citizen Saint*

Cactus
1932   *L'athlète incomplet*
1942   *Rio Rita*

Cadets
1944   Chip Off the Old Block
1955   *The Long Gray Line*

Cads
1914   The Woman in Black
1916   The Gilded Spider
1919   *The Heart of Wetona*
      The Other Man's Wife
1920   The Paliser Case
1927   Frisco Sally Levy
1933   *Broken Dreams*
1934   *Coming Out Party*
1935   *A Night at the Opera*
1939   *Stand Up and Fight*

Café owners
1942   *Valley of the Sun*
1945   *The Cisco Kid Returns*
1949   *Illegal Entry*

Cafés
1917   *The Pulse of Life*
1918   *My Cousin*
1922   Anna Ascends
1928   The Hawk's Nest
1930   *El precio de un beso*
      Sevilla de mis amores
1931   *The Cisco Kid*
      Delicious
      Die Maske Fällt
1932   *Law and Lawless*
      Men Are Such Fools
1933   *The Man Who Dared: An
      Imaginative Biography*
      Melodía de arrabal

      Yo, tú y ella
1934   *Cuesta abajo*
1935   *El cantante de Nápoles*
      Charlie Chan in Paris
      Chinatown Squad
1936   *Paddy O'Day*
1937   *Border Cafe*
      *The Jester (Der
      Purimspieler)*
1938   *Josette*
1940   *While Thousands Cheer*
1941   *Birth of the Blues*
1942   *Submarine Raider*
      Unseen Enemy
1945   *The Mummy's Curse*
1947   *Ride the Pink Horse*
1949   *The Valiant Hombre*
1950   *Mystery Street*

Cafeterias
1953   *The Glass Wall*

Cajuns
1919   Evangeline
1923   Scars of Jealousy
1929   Evangeline
1934   Lazy River
1945   *The Mummy's Curse*
1946   Swamp Fire
1948   Louisiana Story
1950   The Toast of New Orleans
1953   Cry of the Hunted
      Thunder Bay
1957   Bayou

Cake
1930   *Check and Double Check*
1945   *Phantom of the Plains*

Calamity Jane
1937   The Plainsman
1948   The Paleface

Calendars
1947   *Calendar Girl*

California
1914   In the Days of the
      Thundering Herd
      John Barleycorn
      Rose of the Rancho
1916   *The Honorable Friend*
1918   *Fields of Honor*
      The Only Road
      Real Folks
      Tongues of Flame
      Who Is to Blame?
      The Wine Girl
1919   False Evidence
1920   For the Soul of Rafael
1921   *By Right of Birth*
      The Girl from God's
      Country
      Shadows of the West
1922   Captain Fly-by-Night
      The Power of Love
      The Pride of Palomar
      Silver Spurs
      The Woman He Loved
1923   Suzanna
1924   California in '49
1925   Don Q, Son of Zorro
      Flower of Night
1926   Pals in Paradise
1927   Don Mike
      The Gay Defender
1928   The Canyon of Adventure
1929   In Old California
      Señor Americano
      Wolf Song
1930   *Cuando el amor ríe*
      A Lady to Love
      The Lash
1931   Yankee Don
1932   *The Forty-Niners*
1936   *Aces and Eights*
1942   *Castle in the Desert*
1945   A Medal for Benny
      Wanderer of the Wasteland
1946   *Beauty and the Bandit*
1947   Riding the California Trail
      Robin Hood of Monterey
1948   *Angel in Exile*
      Silver Trails
1949   Border Incident
      *Jiggs and Maggie in
      Jackpot Jitters*
      The Mysterious Desperado
      The Story of Seabiscuit

1950   The Lawless
      Rocky Mountain
      Sunset in the West
      Young Man with a Horn
1954   Drum Beat
1956   The Benny Goodman Story
      Serenade
1957   *The Brothers Rico*
      Joe Dakota
1959   *Thunder in the Sun*

California—History
1915   The Pageant of San
      Francisco
1916   Ramona
      A Sister of Six
1940   Kit Carson
1946   Don Ricardo Returns
      South of Monterey
1947   Bells of San Fernando
      Northwest Outpost
1948   *Old Los Angeles*
1952   *Desert Pursuit*

California—History—1846-1850
1916   The Daughter of the Don
1919   Scarlet Days
1931   The Avenger
1932   The Vanishing Frontier
1933   Man from Monterey
1936   Ramona
      Rebellion
      Robin Hood of El Dorado
      Rose of the Rancho
      Sutter's Gold
1937   The Californian
1938   California Frontier
      Outlaw Express
1939   Frontiers of '49
1946   The Gay Cavalier
1947   California
1950   Bandit Queen
1952   The Raiders
1953   The Man Behind the Gun
1957   Raiders of Old California
1958   Sierra Baron
1959   The Young Land

California—History—1850-1950
1941   *Prairie Pioneers*

California—History—To 1846
1915   Captain Courtesy
1916   A Yoke of Gold
1920   The Mark of Zorro
1921   The Kiss
1922   A California Romance
1923   The Spider and the Rose
1927   Rose of the Golden West
1928   The Cavalier
1930   *Lás campanas de Capistrano*
      Song of the Caballero
1933   *The California Trail*
1934   *La cruz y la espada*
1936   The Bold Caballero
      Dancing Pirate
1939   In Old Caliente
1940   The Mark of Zorro
1947   Pirates of Monterey
1949   The Kissing Bandit
1951   The Mark of the Renegade
1952   California Conquest
1954   Passion
1955   Kiss of Fire
      Seven Cities of Gold
1960   The Sign of Zorro

California. University (Berkeley)
1943   *Jack London*

California. University (Los Angeles)
1950   *The Jackie Robinson Story*

***Call of the Wild* (Novel)**
1943   *Jack London*

Camels
1937   *Thank You, Mr. Moto*
1952   Desert Pursuit

Cameramen
   use **Motion picture
      cameramen;
      Newsreel cameramen;
      Photographers**

Cameras
1948   *Open Secret*

Camp Manzanar (CA)
1960   *Hell to Eternity*

Camp Paekakariki (New Zealand)
1950   *Sands of Iwo Jima*

Campaigns (Political)
   use **Political campaigns**

Camping
1916   *The Twin Triangle*

Camps
1947   *Vigilantes of Boomtown*
1949   *The Prairie*
      Satan's Cradle
1950   *Davy Crockett, Indian
      Scout*
1952   *Desert Pursuit*
1953   *The Eddie Cantor Story*
1955   *The Indian Fighter*
1958   *Marjorie Morningstar*

Can-can (Dance)
1934   *La veuve joyeuse*

Canada
1917   The Bronze Bride
1919   The Last of His People
1922   The Virgin of Seminole
1929   Wolf Song
1936   *Human Cargo*
      Sutter's Gold
1937   *The Barrier*
1943   *Mexican Spitfire's Blessed
      Event*
      Wintertime
1956   *Death of a Scoundrel*

Canada. Army
1919?   *America Was Right*

Canadian Northwest
1930   *Monsieur le Fox*
      The Silent Enemy

Canadian-American border region
1916   Her Debt of Honor
1920   The Cyclone
1942   *Unseen Enemy*
1950   *North of the Great Divide*
1954   *Saskatchewan*

Canadians
1919?   In the Land of the Setting
      Sun; or, Martyrs of
      Yesterday
1942   Unseen Enemy
1954   Saskatchewan
1957   *Beau James*

Canaries
1942   *Nazi Agent*

Candlesticks
      Tortilla Flat

Candy
1934   *Judge Priest*
1937   *It Could Happen to You*
1944   *Three Men in White*
1948   Miracle in Harlem
      The Time of Your Life

Canneries
1938   *Josette*
1942   *Tortilla Flat*
1943   *Jack London*
1947   Spoilers of the North
1950   North of the Great Divide
1960   *Ice Palace*

Cannibalism
1930   *El dios del mar*
1931   *The Cohens and Kellys in
      Africa*

Cannons
1952   *The Battle at Apache Pass
      Brave Warrior*

Canoes and canoeing
1914   *In the Land of the Head
      Hunters*
1932   *Parigi affascina; ovvero,
      Malavita*
1936   *The Last of the Mohicans*
1941   *This Woman Is Mine*
1942   *North to the Klondike*
1947   *Last of the Redmen*
1954   *Saskatchewan*
1955   *The Far Horizons*
1957   *Bayou*

**Canteens (War-time, emergency,
   etc.)**
1924   *Smiling Hate*
1930   *¡De frente, marchen!*
1943   *The Gang's All Here*
1946   *The Sailor Takes a Wife*
1955   *A Man Called Peter*

Cantinas
1930 *Cuando el amor ríe*
1931 *Riders of the Rio*
1936 *The Phantom of Santa Fe*
1945 *The Cisco Kid Returns*
1946 *Don Ricardo Returns*
1947 *Ride the Pink Horse*
1949 *The Gay Amigo*
1950 *Sunset in the West*
1959 *The Young Land*

Eddie Cantor
1953 The Eddie Cantor Story

Cantors, Jewish
1926 *Broken Hearts*
1928 *The Jazz Singer*
1931 *The Voice of Israel*
1932 *Mazel Tov*
     The Unfortunate Bride
1935 *Bar-Mitzvah*
1937 *The Cantor's Son*
1939 *Mothers of Today*
1940 *The Great Advisor*
     The Jewish Melody
     Overture to Glory
1947 *The Jolson Story*
1948 *Big City*
1950 *Catskill Honeymoon*
     Jolson Sings Again
     Monticello, Here We Come!
1953 The Jazz Singer
1956 *Singing in the Dark*

Canyon de Chelly (AZ)
1929 *Redskin*
1949 *Tale of the Navajos*

Canyons
     The Golden Stallion
1955 *Smoke Signal*

Cape Canaveral (FL)
1960 *I Aim at the Stars: the
     Wernher von Braun Story*

Cape Cod (MA)
1949 *Portrait of Jennie*
1950 *Mystery Street*
     Mystery Submarine
1955 *A Man Called Peter*

Capital punishment
1914 *The Little Angel of Canyon
     Creek*
1924 *His Darker Self*
1926 *The Frontier Trail*
1929 *Thunderbolt*
1930 *El valiente*
1942 *Take My Life*

Capitalists and financiers
1932 *Charlie Chan's Chance*
1936 *Yellow Cargo*

Al Capone
1959 Al Capone

Capri (Italy)
1917 *The Pulse of Life*

Caravans
1931 *La ley del harem*
1937 *Thank You, Mr. Moto*
1938 *Rascals*
1946 *Bad Bascomb*
1954 *Thunder Pass*

Carbon monoxide
1935 *Bordertown*

Cards
1914 *The Little Angel of Canyon
     Creek*
1914? *The Mysterious Mr. Wu
     Chung Foo*
1917 *The Bride of Hate*
1918 *The Border Raiders*
1933 *Robbers' Roost*
1934 *The Fighting Hero*
     Fighting Through
1939 *Bad Lands*
     The Bronze Buckaroo
1940 *Mystery in Swing*
1944 *Lifeboat*
1945 *The Dolly Sisters*
1947 *Little Mister Jim*
     Marshal of Cripple Creek
1947? *What a Guy*
1950 *Riders of the Pony Express*
1951 *Slaughter Trail*
     A Streetcar Named Desire

Cardsharping
1921 *That Girl Montana*
1931 *La mujer X*

1933 *Melodía de arrabal*
1935 *Circle of Death*
1936 *Aces and Eights*
1947 *Bowery Buckaroos*
     The Foxes of Harrow

Caretakers
1925 The Prairie Wife
1938 *The Rage of Paris*
1944 *Hi, Beautiful*
1953 *Ambush at Tomahawk Gap*

Caribou
1925 The True North
1930 The Silent Enemy

**Carlisle (PA). United States Indian
School**
1925 Red Love
1951 Jim Thorpe—All-American

Carnegie Hall (New York City)
1947 *Carnegie Hall*
1956 *The Benny Goodman Story*

**Carnegie Museum (New York
City)**
1912 *The Alaska-Siberian
     Expedition*

Carnivals
1931 *El príncipe gondolero*
1939 Miracle on Main Street
1957 *Bayou*
1958 *Houseboat*

Carpathian Mountains
1940 *The Tragedy of
     Carpatho-Ukraine*

Carpetbaggers
1915 The Birth of a Nation
1917 *My Fighting Gentleman*
1941 *Belle Starr*

Carpools
1943 *Gangway for Tomorrow*

Venustiano Carranza
1916 Following the Flag in
     Mexico

Carriages and carts
1917 *Lost in Transit*
1947 *Vigilantes of Boomtown*

Carrier pigeons
1942 *Castle in the Desert*

Col. Henry Carrington
1955 *The Gun That Won the
     West*

Kit Carson
1927 California
1928 *Kit Carson*
1936 *Sutter's Gold*
1940 *Kit Carson*
1942 *Lawless Plainsmen*

Carson City (NV)
1947 *Vigilantes of Boomtown*

Cartographers
1949 *The Prairie*

Cartoonists
1947 *Jiggs and Maggie in Society*
1948 Jiggs and Maggie in Court
1949 *Jiggs and Maggie in
     Jackpot Jitters*
1950 *Jiggs and Maggie Out West*

Enrico Caruso
1951 *The Great Caruso*
1960 *Pay or Die*

George Washington Carver
1940 George Washington Carver
1941 *Land of Liberty*
1944 *The Negro Soldier*
     *We've Come a Long, Long
     Way*
1947 The Peanut Man

Cashiers
1940 *Jennie*

Casino owners
1936 *Custer's Last Stand*
1939 *Papá soltero*

Casinos
1931 *Hay que casar al príncipe*
1933 *Dos noches*
1934 *Nada más que una mujer*
1939 *Papá soltero*
1942 *Lucky Ghost*
1943 *Cabin in the Sky*
1953 *Ride, Vaquero!*

Castaways
1915? The Beachcomber
1918 *The Honor of His House*
     Wild Women

1921 *Love's Plaything*
1930 *El dios del mar*

Castles
     Un hombre de suerte
1931 *Drácula*
1932 *El caballero de la noche
     Genoveffa*
1933 *Dos noches*
1934 Granaderos del amor
1938 *Outside of Paradise*
1942 Castle in the Desert
1949 *Top O' the Morning*
1950 *The Baron of Arizona
     Last of the Buccaneers*
1954 *Barefoot Battalion*

**Catherine I, Empress of Russia,
1684-1727**
1939 *Cossacks in Exile*

**Catherine II, Empress of Russia,
1729-1796**
1959 *John Paul Jones*

Catholic Church
1915 *The Penitentes*
1932 *No Greater Love*
1935 *Bordertown*
1947 Citizen Saint
1948 *Fighting Father Dunne
     The Miracle of the Bells*
1953 *Taxi*
1955 *Marty
     The Rose Tattoo
     Seven Cities of Gold*
1956 *Full of Life*
1957 *Beau James*
1958 *The Last Hurrah*
1960 *The Dark at the Top of the
     Stairs*

Catholics
1930 *Anna Christie*
1944 *The Sullivans*
1946 Abie's Irish Rose
1948 *Big City
     Call Northside 777
     Strange Victory*
1958 *Never Love a Stranger*
1960 *For the Love of Mike*

Cats
1924 A Son of Satan
1932 *Charlie Chan's Chance*
1936 *Paddy O'Day*
1938 *The Duke Is Tops
     Mr. Moto's Gamble*
1942 *Cat People*
1943 *Action in the North
     Atlantic*
1944 *Cry of the Werewolf
     Hi, Beautiful*
1946 *Santa Fe Uprising*
1948 *I Remember Mama*
1952 *My Man and I*

Catskill Mountains (NY)
1932 *Amor in montagna*

Cattle
1919? *When the Desert Smiles*
1924 North of 36
1925 The Wild Bull's Lair
1931 *Riders of the Rio*
1933 *Robbers' Roost*
1934 *As the Earth Turns
     Circle of Death
     Melody Trail*
1938 *In Old Chicago*
1942 *Young America*
1946 *Santa Fe Uprising*
1947 *The Last Round-Up
     Rustlers of Devil's Canyon*
1948 *Four Faces West*
1949 *The Prairie
     Ranger of Cherokee Strip
     Tulsa*
1950 *The Furies
     The Palomino*
1955 *Apache Ambush*
1956 *The Broken Star
     Giant
     Reprisal!*
1957 *Raiders of Old California*
1959 *Gunmen from Laredo*

Cattle drives
1942 *Lawless Plainsmen*
1944 *Outlaw Trail*
1945 *Colorado Pioneers*
1948 Red River

1950 The Cariboo Trail
1958 *Ride a Crooked Trail*

Cattlemen
1915 *A Texas Steer*
1917 The Captain of the Gray
     Horse Troop
1919 *Lasca*
1938 *The Texans*
1942 Song of the Islands
1943 *The Ox-Bow Incident*
1947 The Last Round-Up
     West to Glory
1948 *Four Faces West*
1950 *The Palomino*
1953 San Antone
1954 *Passion*
1955 *Apache Ambush*
1956 *The White Squaw*
1959 *Gunmen from Laredo
     Last Train from Gun Hill*

Cattlemen's associations
1932 *Border Devils*
1937 *Border Cafe
     Law and Lead*

Caucasus Mountains
1945 Anoush

Cavalry
     use United States. Army.
     Cavalry

Caves
1915 *Sealed Valley*
1918 *Huck and Tom; or, the
     Further Adventures of
     Tom Sawyer*
1919 *Just Squaw*
1931 *Huckleberry Finn
     The White Renegade*
1932 *Genoveffa
     Yiskor*
1933 *La melodía prohibida*
1934 *La cruz y la espada*
1936 *General Spanky*
1937 *Harlem on the Prairie
     The Riders of the Whistling
     Skull*
1938 The Adventures of Tom
     Sawyer
1939 *In Old Caliente*
1943 *Wagon Tracks West*
1944 *The San Antonio Kid
     Vigilantes of Dodge City*
1946 *Santa Fe Uprising*
1947 *Last of the Redmen
     Rustlers of Devil's Canyon*
1950 *The Girl from San Lorenzo*
1953 *Fort Ti*
1954 *Barefoot Battalion
     The Black Dakotas*
1956 *Davy Crockett and the
     River Pirates
     Secret of Treasure
     Mountain*
1957 *Pawnee*
1959 *Gunmen from Laredo
     Yellowstone Kelly*

Cayuga Indians
1922 Cardigan

Cayuse Indians
1919? In the Land of the Setting
     Sun; or, Martyrs of
     Yesterday

Cellars
1940 *Son of Ingagi*
1949 *The Daring Caballero*

Cement
1950 *Give Us This Day*

Cemeteries
1918 *Huck and Tom; or, the
     Further Adventures of
     Tom Sawyer*
1932 *Yiskor*
1936 *Ellis Island*
1938 *The Adventures of Tom
     Sawyer*
1939 *The Light Ahead*
1941 *King of the Zombies
     Road Agent*
1941? *The Blood of Jesus*
1943 *The Leopard Man*
1948 *Shanghai Chest*
1949 *Arctic Manhunt
     We Were Strangers*
1953 *Ambush at Tomahawk Gap
     Cry of the Hunted*

1958 *Sierra Baron*
1960 *Weddings and Babies*
Censorship
1923 *Deceit*
1944 *Address Unknown*
Census
1952 *It's a Big Country: An American Anthology*
Central America
1938 *Daughter of Shanghai*
A Century of Progress International Exposition, 1933-1934 (Chicago, IL)
1934 *Massacre*
Chaco War, 1932-1935
1935 *Alas sobre el Chaco*
Chain gangs
1924 *Birthright*
1929 *Hallelujah*
1933 *The Emperor Jones*
1941 *Sullivan's Travels*
1947 *Northwest Outpost*
1958 *The Defiant Ones*
Feodor Chaliapin
1953 *Tonight We Sing*
Chalmette (LA)
1938 The Buccaneer
Chambers of Commerce
1930 *Estrellados*
1936 *Sum Hun*
Champagne
1948 *The Time of Your Life*
1949 *The Valiant Hombre*
Chaperons
1947 *Riding the California Trail*
Chaplains
1946 *Abie's Irish Rose*
1947 *Little Mister Jim*
1955 *A Man Called Peter*
Character tests
use Tests of character
Toussiaint Charbonneau
The Far Horizons
Charities
1917 *A Night in New Arabia*
1918 *The Reckoning Day*
1939 *Winner Take All*
1948 Fighting Father Dunne
1951 *Gambling House*
1952 *Kid Monk Baroni*
1953 *The Eddie Cantor Story*
Charity
1914 *The Redemption of David Corson*
1919 *His Debt*
1920 *Billions*
1925 Abie's Imported Bride
1930 *Sei tu l'amore*
1936 *Down to the Sea*
1945 *Our Vines Have Tender Grapes*
Charity balls
1943 *The Amazing Mrs. Holliday*
Mr. Lucky
Charity bazaars
1941 *Up Jumped the Devil*
Charity workers
1915 *Chimmie Fadden*
1932 *No Greater Love*
Charlatans
The Black King
1936 *Charlie Chan's Secret*
1937 Where Is My Child?
1939 Charlie Chan at Treasure Island
1940 Midnight Shadow
Charleston (SC)
1942 *We Were Dancing*
Charwomen and cleaners
1920 *Dinty*
1927 A Harp in Hock
Chases
1913 *Traffic in Souls*
1914 *In the Land of the Head Hunters*
Uncle Tom's Cabin
1915? *Sam Davis, the Hero of Tennessee*
1916 *Arms and the Woman*
1918 *The Hell Cat*
1926 The Campus Flirt
The Flying Ace

1928 *The Midnight Ace*
1930 *Monsieur le Fox*
1931 *The Cohens and Kellys in Africa*
Delicious
The Hurricane Horseman
1932 *El caballero de la noche*
The Galloping Kid
Hypnotized
Mystery Ranch
The Rainbow Trail
Ten Minutes to Live
1933 *The Cohens and Kellys in Trouble*
Dos noches
It's Great to Be Alive
1934 *Eskimo*
'Neath the Arizona Skies
The Star Packer
1935 *Fighting Pioneers*
Te quiero con locura
1936 *Ellis Island*
Paddy O'Day
The Phantom of Santa Fe
1938 *Hawaii Calls*
1939 *Daughter of the Tong*
Forged Passport
1940 *Lucky Cisco Kid*
1941? *The Blood of Jesus*
1942 *Unseen Enemy*
Valley of Hunted Men
1943 *The Outlaw*
1944 *Marshal of Reno*
Tucson Raiders
Vigilantes of Dodge City
1945 *The Cisco Kid Returns*
Great Stagecoach Robbery
In Old New Mexico
The Mummy's Curse
Phantom of the Plains
Salome, Where She Danced
The Shanghai Cobra
1946 *Sheriff of Redwood Valley*
Sun Valley Cyclone
1947 *The Adventures of Don Coyote*
Buck Privates Come Home
Dark Delusion
1948 *Half Past Midnight*
Singin' Spurs
1949 *Lookout Sister*
Masked Raiders
Massacre River
Roll Thunder Roll!
Rustlers
1950 *Chinatown at Midnight*
Comanche Territory
The Lawless
Mystery Street
Panic in the Streets
Rock Island Trail
Storm Over Wyoming
Winchester '73
1951 *Across the Wide Missouri*
Native Son
1952 *Desert Pursuit*
Fort Osage
1953 *Cry of the Hunted*
The Glass Wall
The Man Behind the Gun
The Man from the Alamo
Ride, Vaquero!
1954 *Saskatchewan*
1956 The Burning Hills
Daniel Boone, Trail Blazer
The Last Hunt
Wetbacks
The White Squaw
1957 *Raiders of Old California*
1958 *The Lone Ranger and the Lost City of Gold*
1959 *The Crimson Kimono*
Cry Tough
The FBI Story
1960 *The Adventures of Huckleberry Finn*
Key Witness
The Pusher
The Unforgiven
Chauffeurs
1914 Hearts United
1916 *Lord Loveland Discovers America*
1917 *Sunshine and Gold*

1918 *The Ordeal of Rosetta*
Thirty a Week
The Unbeliever
1921 *By Right of Birth*
1922 Saturday Night
1926 *The Passaic Textile Strike*
1929 This Is Heaven
1930 *Así es la vida*
¡De frente, marchen!
Un hombre de suerte
1931 *El código penal*
Personal Maid
1932 *Le plombier amoureux*
1935 *Charlie Chan in Shanghai*
1936 *Contra la corriente*
Love and Sacrifice
Muss 'Em Up
1938 *Daughter of Shanghai*
1940 *Doomed to Die*
The Jewish Melody
1942 *Lucky Ghost*
Nazi Agent
1944 *Charlie Chan in the Secret Service*
1945 The Jade Mask
The Scarlet Clue
The Shanghai Cobra
1946 *Dark Alibi*
Rendezvous 24
1947 *Dark Delusion*
1948 *The Golden Eye*
Shanghai Chest
1949 *The Sky Dragon*
1949? *She's Too Mean for Me*
1951 *Native Son*
Cheating
1917 *The War of the Tongs*
1931 *Smart Money*
1945 *Wanderer of the Wasteland*
1949 *Brothers in the Saddle*
1955 *Davy Crockett, King of the Wild Frontier*
1956 *Davy Crockett and the River Pirates*
Checkers (Game)
1931 *Echec au roi*
Checks
1943 *Mr. Lucky*
1947 *Ride the Pink Horse*
Cheesecake
1942 *All Through the Night*
Chefs
1952 *Anything Can Happen*
Chemical formulas
1932 *Le bluffeur*
1942 Valley of Hunted Men
1948 Docks of New Orleans
Chemistry
1947 *The Peanut Man*
Chemists
1918 The Spreading Evil
1922 The Schemers
1928 Ransom
1932 *Charlie Chan's Chance*
1935 *Charlie Chan in Egypt*
1939 *Straight to Heaven*
1940 *Knute Rockne—All American*
Murder over New York
1947 The Peanut Man
Cherokee Indians
1917 The Conqueror
1931 *Cimarron*
1939 *Man of Conquest*
1949 *Ranger of Cherokee Strip*
1950 *Cherokee Uprising*
1951 *Tomahawk*
1952 Rose of Cimarron
1954 *Apache*
1956 *Daniel Boone, Trail Blazer*
1960 Oklahoma Territory
Cherry Valley Massacre, 1778
1917 *The Spirit of '76*
Chess
1934 *Un capitán de cosacos*
1939 *Mr. Moto Takes a Vacation*
1941 *This Woman Is Mine*
Chewing gum
1923 The Victor
1930 The Big Pond
1931 Pardon Us
1948 *The Time of Your Life*

Cheyenne (WY)
1918 *The Hell Cat*
Cheyenne Indians
1918? Indian Life
1925 *Custer's Last Fight*
1926 General Custer at Little Big Horn
1934 Cheyenne Sun Dance
1936 Custer's Last Stand
Treachery Rides the Range
1937 The Plainsman
1944 Buffalo Bill
1949 *She Wore a Yellow Ribbon*
1951 Cavalry Scout
1952 Wagons West
1953 The Charge at Feather River
1954 The Yellow Tomahawk
1955 *The Gun That Won the West*
White Feather
1956 Dakota Incident
Ghost Town
1957 *The Guns of Fort Petticoat*
Ride Out for Revenge
Chicago (IL)
1914 The Jungle
1917 *The Sudden Gentleman*
1919 *The Gray Towers Mystery*
1921 No Woman Knows
1923 Anna Christie
1924 So Big
1927 *The Way of All Flesh*
1928 *The Jazz Singer*
The Wages of Sin
1929 Show Boat
When Men Betray
1931 *The Exile*
The Guilty Generation
1932 *The Black King*
Call Her Savage
The Match King
Scarface
So Big
1933 The Man Who Dared: An Imaginative Biography
1936 *Show Boat*
1937 Underworld
1939 *My Son*
1940 *Knute Rockne—All American*
1942 *Syncopation*
1944 *An American Romance*
1945 *Colorado Pioneers*
1946 *Without Reservations*
1947 *Citizen Saint*
New Orleans
1948 *The Betrayal*
Call Northside 777
1949 *Lost Boundaries*
1951 *The Harlem Globetrotters*
Native Son
Show Boat
1953 *So Big*
1954 *Carmen Jones*
Go Man Go
1956 The Benny Goodman Story
1959 Al Capone
1960 *Studs Lonigan*
Chicago (IL)—History
1938 In Old Chicago
Chicago American Giants (Baseball team)
1921 As the World Rolls On
Chicago and Rock Island Railroad
1950 *Rock Island Trail*
Chickasaw Indians
1956 *Davy Crockett and the River Pirates*
Chilcotin Valley (Canada)
1950 The Cariboo Trail
Child actors and actresses
1953 *The Eddie Cantor Story*
Child custody
1916 *Civilization's Child*
1917 Unconquered
1918 Tony America
Woman and the Law
1931 *The Squaw Man*
1933 Broken Dreams
1934 *Wagon Wheels*
1937 One Mile from Heaven
1939 *Miracle on Main Street*
1945 *Colorado Pioneers*

1947   *The Mighty McGurk*
1948   *Big City*
Child prodigies
   use **Prodigies**
Child selling
1916   *The Flames of Johannis*
1917   Unknown 274
1918   Her Moment
1918? The Snail
1937   *Where Is My Child?*
Childbirth
1913? *The Call of the Blood*
1914   Northern Lights
1918   Out of a Clear Sky
1931   *The Great Meadow*
       Street Scene
1932   *Marido y mujer*
       Uncle Moses
1933   *The Eternal Jew*
       *The Man Who Dared: An
         Imaginative Biography*
1934   *Our Daily Bread*
1937   *Big City*
1938   *The Singing Blacksmith*
1939   Gone With the Wind
1940   Girl from God's Country
       Little Nellie Kelly
       Three Cheers for the Irish
1941   *Golden Gate Girl*
1944   *Buffalo Bill*
1945   *A Tree Grows in Brooklyn*
1949   *3 Godfathers*
1951   *Five*
       Westward the Women
1952   *The Battle at Apache Pass*
1953   *The Eddie Cantor Story*
1954   *Apache*
       Salt of the Earth
1955   *Kentucky Rifle*
1956   *Giant*
1957   *War Drums*
1958   *Terror in a Texas Town*
1960   *Cimarron*
       Ice Palace
Childhood sweethearts
1921   The Call of His People
1927   Children of Fate
1931   *Huckleberry Finn*
1937   The Cantor's Son
1938   Spirit of Youth
1947   *The Burning Cross*
       It Had To Be You
       The Jolson Story
1951   *When the Redskins Rode*
1955   *The View from Pompey's
         Head*
Childlessness
1950   *God, Man and Devil*
Children
1914   *The Squaw Man*
1915   An American Gentleman
       Hearts of Men
1916   *The Aryan*
       Gretchen, the Greenhorn
1917   The Adventures of Carol
       His Sweetheart
       The Secret of Eve
       Sunshine and Gold
       Unconquered
       The Woman and the Beast
1918   Doing Their Bit
       Little Red Decides
       Uncle Tom's Cabin
       Untamed
       Wanted, a Mother
1918? *Rosemary Climbs the
         Heights*
1920   *The Great Shadow*
       Humoresque
       Outside the Law
1922   Winning of the West
1923   Jealous Husbands
       A Shot in the Night
1924   Peter Pan
1926   Laddie
1927   Topsy and Eva
1929   Hearts in Dixie
1930   *Cuando el amor ríe*
       Eternal Fools (Ewige
         Naranim)
       Ladies Love Brutes
       Tom Sawyer
1931   *The Cisco Kid*
       Riders of the Rio

       Soyons gais
       Three Who Loved
1932   *Mazel Tov*
       So Big
1933   Broken Dreams
       Dance Hall Hostess
       The Eternal Jew
       Obey the Law
1934   *Call of the Coyote*
       Stand Up and Cheer!
1935   The Little Colonel
1935? The Irish Gringo
1936   *Charlie Chan at the Circus*
       Daniel Boone
       General Spanky
       The Green Pastures
       Silly Billies
1937   *The Holy Oath*
1938   The Adventures of Tom
         Sawyer
       Breaking the Ice
       The Toy Wife
1939   *Lying Lips*
1941   *Birth of the Blues*
       Gauchos of Eldorado
       Hold Back the Dawn
       Virginia
1942   *American Empire*
       Holiday Inn
       Mokey
1943   *Dr. Gillespie's Criminal
         Case*
       The Leopard Man
       *The Meanest Man in the
         World*
1944   Hi, Beautiful
       My Pal Wolf
       Three Men in White
       Tomorrow the World!
1945   *The Cisco Kid Returns*
       Colorado Pioneers
       Nob Hill
       Our Vines Have Tender
         Grapes
1946   Bad Bascomb
       Cuban Pete
       G. I. War Brides
       Song of the South
1947   The Foxes of Harrow
       Jiggs and Maggie in Society
       Little Mister Jim
       The Peanut Man
       Untamed Fury
1948   The Boy with Green Hair
       Gun Smugglers
       Louisiana Story
       Night Wind
1949   *The Cowboy and the
         Indians*
       Masked Raiders
       Prejudice
       Shamrock Hill
1950   Annie Get Your Gun
       Stars in My Crown
       The Traveling Saleswoman
1951   Cyclone Fury
       Queen for a Day
       Show Boat
       Snake River Desperadoes
       The Steel Helmet
       The Well
       Yes Sir, Mr. Bones
1953   Bright Road
       Fort Ti
       Last of the Comanches
       *The Member of the
         Wedding*
       So Big
1954   Barefoot Battalion
       *Indiscretion of an
         American Wife*
1955   Good Morning, Miss Dove
       The Indian Fighter
       Violent Saturday
1956   *Daniel Boone, Trail Blazer*
       The Last Wagon
       Walk the Proud Land
       Westward Ho the Wagons!
       Wetbacks
1957   *Raintree County*
1958   *The Defiant Ones*
       Terror in a Texas Town
1959   *The Jayhawkers!*
1960   The Adventures of
         Huckleberry Finn

       *The Dark at the Top of the
         Stairs*
Chimney sweeps
1930   *Galas de la Paramount*
Chimpanzees
1933   *Broken Dreams*
1948   *Up in Central Park*
China
1916   *Broken Fetters*
       The Social Buccaneer
1918? *The Snail*
1919   *Mandarin's Gold*
1920   Li Ting Lang
       Pagan Love
1921   The First Born
       Lotus Blossom
1930   *Wu Li Chang*
1931   *Charlie Chan Carries On*
       Del infierno al cielo
1934   *The Cat's-Paw*
1936   *Sum Hun*
1939? *A Chinese Gains a Fortune
         in America*
1945   *Samurai*
China—History
1932   *The Son-Daughter*
1936   *Sum Hun*
**China—History—Boxer Rebellion,
   1899-1901**
1921   A Tale of Two Worlds
**China—History—Civil War,
   1945-1949**
1947   *The Chinese Ring*
**China—History—Sino-Japanese
   Conflict, 1937-1945**
   use **Sino-Japanese Conflict,
       1937-1945**
1943   *The Amazing Mrs. Holliday*
China. Army
       The Amazing Mrs. Holliday
China clipper (Airplane)
1939   *Charlie Chan at Treasure
         Island*
Chinatowns
1915   The Secret Sin
1915? Chinatown Pictures
1916   *The Sign of the Poppy*
1917   The Flower of Doom
1918   The Midnight Patrol
1919   The Courageous Coward
1920   *The Cyclone*
1924   In High Gear
       The Pell Street Mystery
1925   Tearing Through
1926   Shadows of Chinatown
1928   The Cameraman
1929   Chinatown Nights
1935   Captured in Chinatown
1936   *Hair-Trigger Casey*
       Klondike Annie
1937   *Shadows of the Orient*
1939   King of Chinatown
       Mr. Wong in Chinatown
1940   *Doomed to Die*
1948   *The Lady from Shanghai*
1949   Boston Blackie's Chinese
         Venture
1951   *Mask of the Dragon*
Chinese
1916   Broken Fetters
       The Social Buccaneer
1918   The City of Dim Faces
1920   The Cyclone
       Li Ting Lang
       Pagan Love
1921   Bits of Life
       The First Born
       Shame
1930   Wu Li Chang
1931   La carta
1934   *Fighting Through*
       Riding Speed
       The Youth of Russia
1936   Charlie Chan at the Race
         Track
       Hair-Trigger Casey
       Yellow Cargo
1941   Min Jok Jay Hung Sing
1942   *Let's Get Tough!*
1947   *The Chinese Ring*
       Little Mister Jim
1948   *The Time of Your Life*
1950   *The Breaking Point*
       A Ticket to Tomahawk

1960   *All the Young Men*
Chinese Americans
1914   *The Yellow Traffic*
1914? The Chinese Lily
       The Mysterious Mr. Wu
         Chung Foo
1915   *Just Jim*
       The Sable Lorcha
1915? Chinatown Pictures
1916   Broken Fetters
       Hop, the Devil's Brew
       The Sign of the Poppy
       The Social Buccaneer
1917   The Flower of Doom
       Queen X
       The War of the Tongs
1918   The Border Raiders
       The City of Dim Faces
       The Girl in the Dark
       Little Red Decides
       The Midnight Patrol
1918? The Snail
1919   *The Lost Battalion*
       Mandarin's Gold
       She Wolf
       The Tong Man
1920   Dinty
       Outside the Law
       The Purple Cipher
1921   Bits of Life
       Fifty Candles
       The First Born
       Shame
       The Swamp
       A Tale of Two Worlds
       Where Lights Are Low
       Wing Toy
1922   The Cub Reporter
       East Is West
       Flesh and Blood
       Pals of the West
       Shadows
       Sky High
       When East Comes West
1923   The Miracle Makers
       Purple Dawn
1924   Defying the Law
       In High Gear
       The Pell Street Mystery
1925   Speed Wild
       Tearing Through
1926   Shadows of Chinatown
       A Trip to Chinatown
       Twin Triggers
1927   The Chinese Parrot
       Old San Francisco
       Roarin' Broncs
1928   The Cameraman
       Chinatown Charlie
       The Hawk's Nest
       Ransom
1929   Chinatown Nights
       Masked Emotions
       The Peacock Fan
       Welcome Danger
1930   East Is West
       On the Border
       Son of the Gods
1931   The Black Camel
       Charlie Chan Carries On
       Chinatown After Dark
       Law of the Tong
1932   *Border Devils*
       Charlie Chan's Chance
       The Hatchet Man
       The Secrets of Wu Sin
       The Son-Daughter
       Thirteen Steps
1933   Charlie Chan's Greatest Case
1934   Blossom Time
       The Cat's-Paw
       Charlie Chan in London
       Charlie Chan's Courage
       Lazy River
       Limehouse Blues
1935   Captured in Chinatown
       Charlie Chan in Egypt
       Charlie Chan in Paris
       Charlie Chan in Shanghai
       Chinatown Squad
1936   *After the Thin Man*
       Border Phantom
       Charlie Chan at the Circus
       Charlie Chan's Secret
       Klondike Annie

Mad Holiday
Sum Hun
1937 Charlie Chan at the
Olympics
Charlie Chan at the Opera
Charlie Chan on Broadway
Shadows of the Orient
1938 *Charlie Chan at Monte Carlo*
Dangerous to Know
Daughter of Shanghai
Mr. Moto's Gamble
Mr. Wong, Detective
1939 *Charlie Chan at Treasure
Island*
Charlie Chan in Honolulu
Charlie Chan in Reno
City in Darkness
Daughter of the Tong
King of Chinatown
Mr. Wong in Chinatown
The Mystery of Mr. Wong
1939? A Chinese Gains a Fortune
in America
1940 *Charlie Chan at the Wax
Museum*
Charlie Chan in Panama
*Charlie Chan's Murder
Cruise*
Doomed to Die
The Fatal Hour
Murder over New York
Phantom of Chinatown
1941 *Charlie Chan in Rio*
Dead Men Tell
The Gang's All Here
Golden Gate Girl
Secret of the Wastelands
Sunday Sinners
1942 *Castle in the Desert*
*Dr. Gillespie's New
Assistant*
North to the Klondike
Rubber Racketeers
1943 *Dr. Gillespie's Criminal
Case*
1944 *Andy Hardy's Blonde
Trouble*
Black Magic
*Charlie Chan in the Secret
Service*
The Chinese Cat
Three Men in White
1945 *Between Two Women*
Escape in the Fog
The Jade Mask
Nob Hill
Salome, Where She Danced
The Scarlet Clue
The Shanghai Cobra
1946 *Dangerous Money*
Dark Alibi
The Red Dragon
Shadows Over Chinatown
The Trap
1946? *House-Rent Party*
1947 *Black Gold*
The Chinese Ring
Dark Delusion
1947? *What a Guy*
1948 *Docks of New Orleans*
The Feathered Serpent
The Golden Eye
Half Past Midnight
The Miracle of the Bells
Shanghai Chest
Sleep, My Love
1949 *Boston Blackie's Chinese
Venture*
The Sky Dragon
1950 *The Big Hangover*
The Cariboo Trail
Chinatown at Midnight
1951 *The House on Telegraph
Hill*
Mask of the Dragon
1954 *Hell's Half Acre*
1960 *Ice Palace*
Walk Like a Dragon

Chinese New Year
1919 *The Courageous Coward*
1935 *Chinatown Squad*
1937 *Think Fast, Mr. Moto*

Chinese restaurants
1934 *Blossom Time*
1948 *The Miracle of the Bells*
Chippewa Indians
1930 The Silent Enemy
1952 Hiawatha
1958 *Flaming Frontier*
Chiricahua Indians
use **Apache Indians**
Chiropractors
1923 *Breaking into Society*
Chisholm Trail
1948 Red River
Chloroform
1936 *Silly Billies*
Choctaw Indians
1948 *Tap Roots*
Choirs (Music)
1936 *The Green Pastures*
1939 *Moon over Harlem*
1944 *Chip Off the Old Block*
Going My Way
1947 *The Jolson Story*
1958 *St. Louis Blues*
Cholera
1939 The Light Ahead
Chorus girls
1921 *No Woman Knows*
1929 Why Bring That Up?
1931 Die Maske Fällt
1932 *Ten Minutes to Live*
1933? *Scandal*
1935 Romance in Manhattan
1936 Star for a Night
1943 *Stormy Weather*
1948 *The Miracle of the Bells*
1950 *Rio Grande Patrol*
1955 *Brevities of 1955*
1959 *Imitation of Life*
Christian ethics
1948 Reaching from Heaven
Christianity
1913? Hiawatha
1915? *The Beachcomber*
1918 *The City of Dim Faces*
1919 Auction of Souls
1919? *In the Land of the Setting
Sun; or, Martyrs of
Yesterday*
1920 *The Man Who Dared*
1936 Ramona
1941 *Z Dymem Pożarów*
1949 Prejudice
1952? Call of the Navajo
1955 Indian American
1956 *The Last Wagon*
Pillars of the Sky
Christmas
1920 *The Girl of My Heart*
1922 *The Sign of the Rose*
1923 His Great Chance
1927 The Way of All Flesh
1929 Is Everybody Happy?
1930 *Sins of the Children*
Sombras de gloria
1931 *Quand on est belle*
1939 *Gone With the Wind*
Miracle on Main Street
1940 *Three Cheers for the Irish*
The Way of All Flesh
1945 *Our Vines Have Tender
Grapes*
1946 *Abie's Irish Rose*
1950 *The Daughter of Rosie
O'Grady*
1951 *Across the Wide Missouri*
The Great Caruso
Saturday's Hero
1952 *Desert Pursuit*
1953 *Bright Road*
1955 *The Long Gray Line*
1956 *Giant*
1957 *All Mine to Give*
Christmas Eve
1942 *Holiday Inn*
Tales of Manhattan
1944 *Lake Placid Serenade*
Since You Went Away
1945 *Pride of the Marines*
A Tree Grows in Brooklyn
1948 *The Miracle of the Bells*

Churches
1915 *The Rosary*
1915? *Sin*
1917 *The Little American*
The Little Samaritan
1921? [Unidentified Film]
1932 *The Black King*
So Big
1934 *Drums O' Voodoo*
1936 *Sins of Man*
1939 *Keep Punching*
Miracle on Main Street
1941 *Sullivan's Travels*
1941? *The Blood of Jesus*
1942 *Seven Sweethearts*
1943 *Cabin in the Sky*
1944 *Going My Way*
The Negro Soldier
1945 *The Bells of St. Mary's*
Nob Hill
1946 *The Gay Cavalier*
Saratoga Trunk
1947 *Going to Glory, Come to
Jesus*
1948 *Cry of the City*
The Miracle of the Bells
Silver Trails
1948? Junction 88
1949 *Arctic Manhunt*
Prejudice
The Red Menace
Satan's Cradle
1950 *The Missourians*
Rio Grande
Stars in My Crown
Young Man with a Horn
1951 *Apache Drums*
New Mexico
1952 *High Noon*
Kid Monk Baroni
1956 *Serenade*
1958 *Frontier Gun*
St. Louis Blues
1959 *The Black Orchid*
1960 *For the Love of Mike*
Cibola, Seven Cities of
1958 The Lone Ranger and the
Lost City of Gold
Cigar and cigarette manufacturers
1951 *Cuban Fireball*
Cigar stores
use **Tobacconists**
Cigarette cases
1933 *No dejes la puerta abierta*
Cigarette girls
1918 Amarilly of Clothes-Line
Alley
1934 *The Cat's-Paw*
1941 *Sunday Sinners*
1943 *Tahiti Honey*
Cigarette lighters
1960 *Man on a String*
Cigarettes
1941 *Charlie Chan in Rio*
1942 *The Vanishing Virginian*
1943 *Crash Dive*
1945 *The Scarlet Clue*
1948 *Docks of New Orleans*
Cigars
1927 Pleasure Before Business
1940 *Viva Cisco Kid*
1944 *Lifeboat*
1947 *Boy! What a Girl!*
Mantan Runs for Mayor
1951 *The Last Outpost*
Le Cigne (Ballet)
1953 *Tonight We Sing*
Cincinnati (OH)
1935 *Annie Oakley*
1950 *Annie Get Your Gun*
1957 *Band of Angels*
Cinderella (Fictional character)
1944 *Lake Placid Serenade*
1947 Sepia Cinderella
Circumstantial evidence
1917 *The Pulse of Life*
1918 *In Judgment Of*
1924? *The Flaming Crisis*
1941 *Dead Men Tell*
1943 *The Ox-Bow Incident*
1944 *Sheriff of Las Vegas*
1945 *Great Stagecoach Robbery*
1946 Sheriff of Redwood Valley

1960 *Sergeant Rutledge*
Circus owners
1932 *Hypnotized*
1936 Charlie Chan at the Circus
1951 *Queen for a Day*
Circus performers
1930 *La jaula de los leones*
1931 *Sombras del circo*
1932 *Hypnotized*
1933 *L'amour guide*
1936 Charlie Chan at the Circus
1937 *The Jester (Der
Purimspieler)*
1951 *Queen for a Day*
Circuses
1917 *The Woman and the Beast*
1930 La jaula de los leones
1931 Sombras del circo
1932 *Thirteen Women*
1933 *Let's Fall in Love*
1934 *She Was a Lady*
1937 *The Jester (Der
Purimspieler)*
1942 *Professor Creeps*
1945 *Our Vines Have Tender
Grapes*
1960 *The Adventures of
Huckleberry Finn*
Cities and towns
use **Small town life;
Urban life**
**Cities and towns, ruined, extinct,
etc.**
1939 *Charlie Chan in Reno*
1951 Five
Citizenship
1917 Follow the Girl
1918 One More American
Ruggles of Red Gap
1928 A Ship Comes In
1931 *Cimarron*
1933 *Obey the Law*
1935 Romance in Manhattan
1940 *Little Nellie Kelly*
1941 *Accent on Love*
New York Town
1942 *Nazi Agent*
Wings for the Eagle
1944 *An American Romance*
1946 The Gentleman Misbehaves
1948 *My Girl Tisa*
1951 *Gambling House*
1952 Anything Can Happen
My Man and I
1955 *Bad Day at Black Rock*
1957 *Journey to Freedom*
City life
use **Urban life**
City slickers
1931 *Call of the Rockies*
City-country contrast
1915 The Adventures of a Madcap
A Texas Steer
1919 The Lord Loves the Irish
Toby's Bow
1923 His Great Chance
1931 The Exile
Las luces de Buenos Aires
1932 *Le cas du docteur Brenner
Hollywood, ciudad de
ensueño*
1934 *As the Earth Turns
Blossom Time*
1935 *Ruggles of Red Gap*
1936 *Yiddle with His Fiddle*
1937 *The Cantor's Son
Green Fields*
Underworld
1938 *The Duke Is Tops*
1940 *Eli Eli*
1941 *Virginia*
1942 *Young America*
1945 *Our Vines Have Tender
Grapes*
1947 *The Farmer's Daughter
Untamed Fury*
1949? *Come On, Cowboy!
Girl in Room 20*
1950 Jiggs and Maggie Out West
The Toast of New Orleans
1951 Five

Civil defense
1928   Heart Trouble
Civil War veterans
1934   Judge Priest
1935   The Little Colonel
1950   *Devil's Doorway*
1951   Fort Defiance
1953   *The Charge at Feather
         River*
         The Sun Shines Bright
1954   *Overland Pacific*
1957   *Run of the Arrow*
1960   The Plunderers
William Charles Coles Claiborne
1938   *The Buccaneer*
Claim jumpers
1914   Rose of the Rancho
1917   *A Kentucky Cinderella*
1922   *The Dungeon*
1936   Desert Gold
         West of Nevada
1941   *Secret of the Wastelands*
1949   Call of the Forest
Clairvoyants
1928   Chinatown Charlie
1939   *Charlie Chan at Treasure
         Island*
Clams
1948   *16 Fathoms Deep*
Clarinets
1956   *The Benny Goodman Story*
George Rogers Clark
1919? *In the Land of the Setting
         Sun; or, Martyrs of
         Yesterday*
William Clark
1955   The Far Horizons
Class conflict
1927   *The Scar of Shame*
1932   Amor in montagna
1959   John Paul Jones
Class distinction
1914   The Straight Road
1916   The Thousand Dollar
         Husband
         A Yoke of Gold
1916? Should a Baby Die?
1917   *A Kentucky Cinderella*
1918   Amarilly of Clothes-Line
         Alley
         The Unbeliever
1919   Erstwhile Susan
         The Last of His People
         The Other Man's Wife
         The Tiger Lily
         Who Will Marry Me?
1921   The Barricade
1922   Saturday Night
1924   Birthright
1930   Alma de gaucho
         Así es la vida
         Cuando el amor ríe
         Del mismo barro
         Doña mentiras
         Olimpia
         El secreto del doctor
1931   El comediante
         Così è la vita
         Delicious
         Hay que casar al príncipe
         Personal Maid
         Women Love Once
1932   Huddle
         Ljubav i strast
         Marido y mujer
         Unashamed
1933   Broken Dreams
         Counsellor at Law
         Dance Hall Hostess
         A Lady's Profession
         El rey de los gitanos
         Robbers' Roost
1934   Behold My Wife!
         La buenaventura
         Caravane
         Coming Out Party
         Las fronteras del amor
         She Was a Lady
1935   Bordertown
         El cantante de Nápoles
         McFadden's Flats
         Ruggles of Red Gap
         The Winning Ticket

1936   Amor que vuelve
         Contra la corriente
         Down to the Sea
         It Had to Happen
         Rainbow on the River
         Robin Hood of El Dorado
1937   Green Fields
         Man of the People
         Natalka Poltavka
1938   *The Buccaneer*
         Dangerous to Know
         Gateway
         The Singing Blacksmith
1939   *Mirele Efros*
1943   *His Butler's Sister*
         Mr. Lucky
1944   Block Busters
         Lifeboat
1945   Nob Hill
         The Valley of Decision
1946   *Song of the South*
1947   The Foxes of Harrow
         New Orleans
1948   *Fort Apache*
1949   *House of Strangers*
1950   *Annie Get Your Gun*
         Belle of Old Mexico
         The Toast of New Orleans
1950? *Three Daughters*
1951   Adventures of Captain
         Fabian
         The Great Caruso
         *The House on Telegraph
         Hill*
         Oh! Susanna
         Saturday's Hero
1952   The Iron Mistress
         Woman in the Dark
1953   San Antone
1955   Duel on the Mississippi
         The View from Pompey's
         Head
1956   *The Catered Affair*
         Crowded Paradise
         Death of a Scoundrel
1957   *Twelve Angry Men*
1958   The Last Hurrah
1959   Night of the Quarter Moon
1960   I Passed for White
         Take a Giant Step
Classified advertisements
1917   *Lost in Transit*
1941   *The Gang's All Here*
Cleaners
         use **Dry cleaning;
                 Laundries**
**Cleopatra VII, Queen of Egypt,
69-30 B.C.**
1948   *Jiggs and Maggie in Court*
Clergy
1914   *At the Cross Roads*
         *The Little Angel of Canyon
         Creek*
         The Redemption of David
         Corson
1917   The Little Samaritan
         Southern Pride
1918   *Hitting the Trail*
         Little Red Decides
         Tongues of Flame
1919   *The She Wolf*
         Spotlight Sadie
1920   *Within Our Gates*
1922   The Power of Love
         Shadows
         The Son of the Wolf
1923   Deceit
1930   Georgia Rose
1931   Dämon des Meeres
1937   *That Girl from Paris*
1938   *Two Gun Man from
         Harlem*
1939   *Drums Along the Mohawk*
1942   *The Vanishing Virginian*
1943   *Cabin in the Sky*
1944   We've Come a Long, Long
         Way
1946? Go Down, Death!
1948   *Reaching from Heaven*
1952   The Quiet Man
1955   A Man Called Peter
1958   *The Last Hurrah*
         Never Love a Stranger

Clerks
1917   *The Renaissance at
         Charleroi*
1919   *Hearts of Men*
1947? *What a Guy*
1948   *Angel in Exile*
1949   *The Mysterious Desperado*
1959   *John Paul Jones*
Cleveland (OH)
1935   *A Night at the Ritz*
Cliff-dwellings
1951   *Flaming Feather*
1958   *Fort Massacre*
Clinics
1940   Am I Guilty?
Clock and watch makers
1920   The Secret Gift
1951   *The Girl on the Bridge*
Clocks
1921   Lotus Blossom
1945   *Escape in the Fog*
1952   *High Noon*
Clothes
1915   *The Cheat*
1931   *Los calaveras*
1934   *The Cactus Kid*
1938   My Lucky Star
         The Rage of Paris
1939   *Gone With the Wind*
         One Dark Night
1942   Tales of Manhattan
1947   *The Adventures of Don
         Coyote*
1948   Open Secret
1949   *The Gay Amigo*
1950   *Rock Island Trail*
Clothing industry
1915   *Cohen's Luck*
1917   The Peddler
1923   Potash and Perlmutter
1924   Fools' Highway
1927   Clancy's Kosher Wedding
         Jake the Plumber
1930   The Cohens and the Kellys
         in Scotland
1932   Uncle Moses
1951   *Molly*
Clubhouses
1944   *Block Busters*
Clubs
1914? *The Mysterious Mr. Wu
         Chung Foo*
1918   *The Yellow Dog*
1920   *The Paliser Case*
1931   *Hay que casar al príncipe*
1932   *Charlie Chan's Chance*
1937   *Dark Manhattan*
1939   *Waterfront*
         Winner Take All
1949   Jigsaw
1953   *The Member of the
         Wedding*
1958   *The Last Hurrah*
1960   *The Crowning Experience*
John Philip Clum
1956   Walk the Proud Land
Coaches
         use **Athletic coaches;
                 Specific types of coaches**
Coal
1930   *Anna Christie*
Coal miners
1916   *A Woman's Honor*
1917   Threads of Fate
1933   *The Man Who Dared: An
         Imaginative Biography*
1935   Black Fury
1948   *The Miracle of the Bells*
Coal mines
1917   *Threads of Fate*
Coats
1932   *Joseph in the Land of Egypt*
1938   *Mr. Moto's Gamble*
1948   Night Wind
Cobblers
         use **Shoemakers**
Cocaine
1959   *Porgy and Bess*
Cochise
1942   *Valley of the Sun*
1950   Broken Arrow
1952   The Battle at Apache Pass

1953   Conquest of Cochise
1954   *Taza, Son of Cochise*
Cochise
1948   *Fort Apache*
Cock-fighting
1934   *La cruz y la espada*
1939   *The Devil's Daughter*
**The Cocoanut Grove (Los Angeles,
CA)**
1932   *The Cohens and Kellys in
         Hollywood*
Codes
1942   *Rio Rita*
1944   Waterfront
1952   *Red Snow*
Buffalo Bill Cody
1917   The Adventures of Buffalo
         Bill
1926   Buffalo Bill on the U. P.
         Trail
         The Last Frontier
1928   Wyoming
1935   Annie Oakley
1937   The Plainsman
1940   Young Buffalo Bill
1944   Buffalo Bill
1947   Buffalo Bill Rides Again
1950   Annie Get Your Gun
Coeur d'Alene War, 1858
1956   Pillars of the Sky
Coffee
1921   The Call of His People
1937   *El carnaval del diablo*
1941   *Charlie Chan in Rio*
1949   *The Sky Dragon*
1952   *It's a Big Country: An
         American Anthology*
Coffee shops
1938   *Life Goes On*
1945   *The Shanghai Cobra*
Coffins
1931   *Drácula*
1950   *Damien*
1951   *Cyclone Fury*
George M. Cohan
1943   Yankee Doodle Dandy
Coins
         Frontier Fury
         Mr. Lucky
1948   *The Luck of the Irish*
Colds
         use **Head colds**
Collection agents
1918   The Little Runaway
Collective farms
         use **Agriculture, Cooperative**
Collectors and collecting
1919   The Little Diplomat
1929   The Peacock Fan
1937   *Shadows of the Orient*
College deans
         Life Begins in College
1944   *Andy Hardy's Blonde
         Trouble*
1946   *Beware*
College life
1915   The Grandee's Ring
1916   *Betrayed*
1920   *Li Ting Lang*
1921   The Burden of Race
1925   *Braveheart*
1926   The Campus Flirt
1927   For the Love of Mike
1928   Hold 'Em Yale
1930   Sunny Skies
1932   *L'athlète incomplet*
         Huddle
1934   *Cuesta abajo*
1937   Life Begins in College
1938   My Lucky Star
1940   Knute Rockne—All
         American
         Too Many Girls
         While Thousands Cheer
1944   Andy Hardy's Blonde
         Trouble
1951   Jim Thorpe—All-American
1958   *Home Before Dark*
College presidents
1950   Belle of Old Mexico

College sports
1940   Knute Rockne—All American
1950   *The Jackie Robinson Story*
1951   *Saturday's Hero*
1960   *The Crowning Experience*
College students
1916   *The Innocent Lie*
     The Thousand Dollar
     Husband
1917   *Crime and Punishment*
1918   *The City of Dim Faces*
     Real Folks
1937   Life Begins in College
     Underworld
1940   George Washington Carver
     Too Many Girls
1943   *Jack London*
1944   Andy Hardy's Blonde
     Trouble
     The Chinese Cat
1946   *Till the End of Time*
1955   *A Man Called Peter*
1957   *Burden of Truth*
1958   *Wild Is the Wind*
Colleges
1939   *Keep Punching*
1946   Beware
1960   The Crowning Experience
Colonies
1914   When Broadway Was a Trail
1915   *The Pageant of San
     Francisco*
1917   *The Hidden Children*
1921   Shadows of the West
1922   *The Pride of Palomar*
1929   Evangeline
1935   *Naughty Marietta*
1936   *Sutter's Gold*
1949   *The Kissing Bandit*
1951   *Hurricane Island*
Colorado
1931   *Quand on est belle*
1940   *Prairie Schooners*
1945   *Colorado Pioneers*
1949   Colorado Territory
1950   A Ticket to Tomahawk
1953   The Charge at Feather River
1954   *Drums Across the River*
Colorado River (CO—Mexico)
1955   Smoke Signal
Columbia River
     The Far Horizons
Columbia University
1922   Blazing Arrows
Christopher Columbus
1931   *Street Scene*
1945   *Where Do We Go From
     Here?*
Columbus (NM)
1916   *Following the Flag in
     Mexico*
Columbus Day
1939   *Verbena trágica*
Columnists
1942   Woman of the Year
Coma
1933   *Broken Dreams*
1949   *The Clay Pigeon*
Comanche Indians
1920   The Daughter of Dawn
1924   North of 36
1938   *The Texans*
1940   *Young Buffalo Bill*
1948   *Red River*
1950   Comanche Territory
1952   *Rose of Cimarron*
1953   Conquest of Cochise
     Last of the Comanches
1954   Overland Pacific
     They Rode West
     Thunder Pass
1955   Kentucky Rifle
     Kiss of Fire
1956   Comanche
     The Last Wagon
     The Searchers
1957   *Raiders of Old California*
1958   The Rawhide Trail
1960   Comanche Station
Combat
1915   *The Birth of a Nation*
1916   *The Daughter of the Don
     Peck O' Pickles*

1918   The Unbeliever
1919   The Lost Battalion
1931   Beyond Victory
1934   *The Unknown Soldier
     Speaks*
1936   *Hair-Trigger Casey*
1943   Bataan
1944   *The Negro Soldier*
1949   Home of the Brave
1950   Sands of Iwo Jima
1951   *Teresa*
Comedians
1930   Galas de la Paramount
1935   *Melody Trail*
1940   *Paradise in Harlem*
1943   *The Gang's All Here*
1946   Tall, Tan and Terrific
1947   *Jivin' in Be-Bop*
1948   *The Time of Your Life*
1949?   *The Joint Is Jumpin'*
     She's Too Mean for Me
1950   Monticello, Here We Come!
1951   Yes Sir, Mr. Bones
1953   The Jazz Singer
1955   Brevities of 1955
1956   *Singing in the Dark*
Commercial artists
1949   The Girl from Jones Beach
Committees
1951   *The Well*
Communal living
1941   *Min Jok Jay Hung Sing*
Communism
1940   Elsa Maxwell's Public Deb
     No. 1
1949   The Red Menace
1959   *The FBI Story*
1960   The Crowning Experience
Communists
1933   *Counsellor at Law*
1934   *The Youth of Russia*
1935   *Chinatown Squad*
1951   *The Steel Helmet*
1952   *Red Snow*
1955   Trial
1957   Journey to Freedom
Compasses
1944   *Lifeboat*
Composers
1915   *The Melting Pot*
1919   *A Fallen Idol*
1927   *The Scar of Shame*
1930   The Melody Man
1931   Jenny Lind
     Regeneración
     Su noche de bodas
1932   Men Are Such Fools
1933   *L'amour guide*
1934   *Beloved*
     Caravane
1935   Harmony Lane
     Shir Hashirim
1937   Music for Madame
1938?   *Amore che non torna*
1940   *Overture to Glory*
1942   Tales of Manhattan
1943   Dixie
     His Butler's Sister
1945   Rhapsody in Blue
1947   *Carnegie Hall*
1948?   Junction 88
1949   *Lost Boundaries*
1950?   *Three Daughters*
1953   *So Big*
Compulsive gamblers
1943   Cabin in the Sky
Concentration camps
1940   *The Man I Married*
1943   *They Came to Blow Up
     America*
1948   *Strange Victory*
1949   *Answer for Anne*
1956   *Singing in the Dark*
1958   *The Young Lions*
Concerts
1928   *The Jazz Singer*
1933   *Melodía de arrabal*
1934   *Las fronteras del amor*
1936   *Let's Sing Again*
     Sins of Man
1939   *A Brivele der Mamen*
1940   *The Way of All Flesh*
1946   *Beware*

1947   *Humoresque*
     Jivin' in Be-Bop
1948   *The Fight Never Ends*
1949   *That Midnight Kiss*
1958   *Houseboat*
Concord (MA)
1922   Cardigan
Concubinage
1931   *La ley del harem*
Conductors (Music)
1925   The Midnight Girl
1929   Is Everybody Happy?
1932   *Men Are Such Fools*
1937   *Music for Madame*
1942   *Tales of Manhattan*
1943   *Three Hearts for Julia*
1947   Carnegie Hall
1949   That Midnight Kiss
1958   Houseboat
Conductors (Train)
     use Train conductors
**Confectioners and
confectionaries**
1913   *Traffic in Souls*
1952   *It's a Big Country: An
     American Anthology*
**Confederate States of America.
Army**
1936   The Glory Trail
1939   Gone With the Wind
1948   Tap Roots
1950   Rocky Mountain
     Two Flags West
1951   The Last Outpost
1953   Column South
1954   Siege at Red River
1958   *Ambush at Cimarron Pass*
Confession
1915   *The Penitentes*
     The Rosary
1917   *The Bar Sinister*
     Lost in Transit
1918   *The Reckoning Day*
1919   *The Gray Horizon*
     Just Squaw
     Mandarin's Gold
1931   *Così è la vita*
     Nuit d'Espagne
     La pura verdad
1932   *Amore e morte*
1933   *Yo, tú y ella*
1934   *Behold My Wife!*
     The Great Flirtation
     Limehouse Blues
1935   *Wolf Riders*
1936   *Love and Sacrifice*
1937   *Think Fast, Mr. Moto*
1938   *Road Demon*
1939   *The Devil's Daughter*
     King of Chinatown
     Mothers of Today
     Reform School
1940   *Eli Eli*
     The Notorious Elinor Lee
1943   *Bataan*
1946   *Sunset Pass*
1948   *The Time of Your Life*
1949   *Rose of the Yukon*
1952   *Rose of Cimarron*
1954   *Drums Across the River*
Confession (Law)
1914   *The Squaw Man*
1915   *Chimmie Fadden*
     The Clemenceau Case
     A Yankee from the West
1916   *Broken Chains*
     For the Defense
1917   *His Sweetheart*
     My Fighting Gentleman
     The Pulse of Life
     Runaway Romany
1918   *Broken Ties*
     Hitting the Trail
     In Judgment Of
     The Liar
     Sandy
     The Squaw Man
     A Woman of Impulse
1918?   *Rosemary Climbs the
     Heights*
1919   *The Courageous Coward*
1920   *The Good-Bad Wife*
     The Man Who Dared
     The Paliser Case

1930   *Sombras de gloria*
1931   *The Black Camel*
     Cheri-Bibi
     El código penal
     Three Who Loved
1932   *Border Devils*
     Harlem Is Heaven
     El hombre que asesinó
1932?   *The Girl from Chicago*
1934   *The Cactus Kid*
     The Cat's-Paw
1935   *Cowboy Holiday*
     North of Arizona
1936   *Muss 'Em Up*
1937   *Big City*
     Maid of Salem
     That I May Live
1938   *The Beloved Brat*
     Life Goes On
     The Renegade Ranger
     Sugar Hill Baby
1939   *The Fighting Gringo*
     Forged Passport
     Lying Lips
1940   *Covered Wagon Days*
     Doomed to Die
     Paradise in Harlem
1941   *Charlie Chan in Rio*
     Thunder Over the Prairie
1942   *Castle in the Desert*
     Take My Life
1943   *Margin for Error*
1944   *Outlaw Trail*
     Sheriff of Las Vegas
     Sonora Stagecoach
1945   *In Old New Mexico*
     The Navajo Trail
     Wanderer of the Wasteland
1946   *Singin' in the Corn*
     Tall, Tan and Terrific
1947   *Bowery Buckaroos*
     The Burning Cross
     King of the Bandits
     Robin Hood of Monterey
1948   *Cry of the City*
     Fury at Furnace Creek
     The Lady from Shanghai
     Miracle in Harlem
1949   *C-Man*
     The Dalton Gang
     Daughter of the West
     The Mysterious Desperado
     Rustlers
1950   *The Missourians*
1951   *The Raging Tide*
1952   *The Half-Breed*
     Indian Uprising
     My Man and I
1953   *Seminole*
1954   *Passion*
1957   *The Midnight Story*
1958   *Gunfire at Indian Gap*
Confession (Religion)
1960   *The Crowning Experience*
Confidence games
1914   The Little Jewess
1935   Bar-Mitzvah
1947   Jiggs and Maggie in Society
Confidence men
1925   One of the Bravest
1926   The Little Irish Girl
1931   Call of the Rockies
     Huckleberry Finn
1932   *Le bluffeur*
     The Match King
1934   *She Was a Lady*
1935   *A Night at the Ritz*
1936   *Dimples*
1937   *Man of the People*
     Nation Aflame
     Underworld
1938   *The Duke Is Tops*
1939   The Adventures of
     Huckleberry Finn
     The Devil's Daughter
1940   The Great Advisor
1943   Mr. Lucky
1945   Phantom of the Plains
1947   Oregon Trail Scouts
1956   Rockin' the Blues
1959   *Anna Lucasta*
1960   The Adventures of
     Huckleberry Finn

Confucianism
1920   Outside the Law
Congressional Medal of Honor
1943   *Yankee Doodle Dandy*
1944   *Buffalo Bill*
1950   *Devil's Doorway*
Congressmen
1940   *The Ramparts We Watch*
1947   The Farmer's Daughter
1949   *The Cowboy and the Indians*
Connecticut
1915   *Kreutzer Sonata*
       The Sable Lorcha
1935   *The Wedding Night*
1936   *Let's Sing Again*
1942   *Woman of the Year*
1948   *Gentleman's Agreement*
Conquering Bear (Sioux chieftan)
1955   *Chief Crazy Horse*
Conscience
1915   *The Italian*
       A Yankee from the West
1917   Crime and Punishment
       A Night in New Arabia
1931   Three Who Loved
1938   *Road Demon*
1943   The Ox-Bow Incident
1944   *Minstrel Man*
1945   *Club Havana*
1950   Give Us This Day
1951   The Girl on the Bridge
1952   *My Man and I*
1955   Violent Saturday
1960   I Aim at the Stars: the Wernher von Braun Story
Conservation of natural resources
     use **Nature conservation**
Conspiracy
1916   The Fall of a Nation
1917   *His Sweetheart*
       A Wife by Proxy
1918   *The Source*
       The Yellow Dog
1920   The Purple Cipher
1927   Rose of the Golden West
1933   Diplomaniacs
       Dos noches
1936   Muss 'Em Up
1949   *The Daring Caballero*
       Daughter of the West
       Satan's Cradle
1951   The Mark of the Renegade
1955   Bad Day at Black Rock
Constables
1922   Easy Money
1924   *Birthright*
1926   *The Flying Ace*
1947   *On the Old Spanish Trail*
1951   *Adventures of Captain Fabian*
Construction foremen
1935   *McFadden's Flats*
1936   *It Had to Happen*
1941   Caught in the Act
Construction industry
1951   *The Well*
Construction workers
1931   Skyline
1939   *Let Freedom Ring*
1941   *Western Union*
1947   *Untamed Fury*
1950   *Rock Island Trail*
1953   *Fort Ti*
Consuls
1942   Nazi Agent
1943   Margin for Error
1947   *Buck Privates Come Home*
Contests
1919   Daughter of Mine
1925   Irish Luck
1930   Charros, gauchos y manolas
1932   *Hearts of Humanity*
1933   Grand Slam
1934   *Laughing Boy*
1935   *Annie Oakley*
1936   *Laughing Irish Eyes*
1937   *Man of the People*
       Waikiki Wedding
1939   *Judge Hardy and Son*
1940   *Broken Strings*
1941   *In the Land of the Navajo*
       New York Town

1942   *Young America*
1944   Hi, Beautiful
1947   *Calendar Girl*
       Sepia Cinderella
1949   *The Fighting Kentuckian*
       Jiggs and Maggie in Jackpot Jitters
1950   *Winchester '73*
1953   *The Stars Are Singing*
Contortionists
1936   *Charlie Chan at the Circus*
Contractors
1915   The Immigrant
1919   *A Yankee Princess*
1920   *Hidden Charms*
1920?   *The Greatest Love*
1922   The Scrapper
       Second Hand Rose
1927   McFadden's Flats
1930   Ladies Love Brutes
1948   *Reaching from Heaven*
Contracts
1918   Untamed
1932   *The Cohens and Kellys in Hollywood*
1933   *Let's Fall in Love*
1935   Julieta compra un hijo
1938   *The Duke Is Tops*
1939   *El otro soy yo*
       Winner Take All
1940   Mexican Spitfire
       Too Many Girls
1941   *Come Live with Me*
       Playmates
1942   Mexican Spitfire at Sea
       Mexican Spitfire Sees a Ghost
1943   *In Old Oklahoma*
       Mexican Spitfire's Blessed Event
1944   *Lake Placid Serenade*
1948   *Jiggs and Maggie in Court*
1950   *Right Cross*
       Rock Island Trail
       A Ticket to Tomahawk
1951   *The Harlem Globetrotters*
1955   *The Lonesome Trail*
Convalescence
1918   *The Red, Red Heart*
1931   *Cavalier of the West*
1939   *Gang Smashers*
1949   *Lookout Sister*
Conventions (Gatherings)
1935   *A Night at the Ritz*
1942   *Young America*
Convents
1914   *Threads of Destiny*
1917   *The Conqueror*
1918   *The Only Road*
1919?   *The Chosen Path*
1920   For the Soul of Rafael
1930   *Sevilla de mis amores*
1938   *God's Step Children*
1938?   *Amore che non torna*
1946   *Three Wise Fools*
1949   *Portrait of Jennie*
Conversion (Religious)
1933   The Wandering Jew
1936   Klondike Annie
1956   *Pillars of the Sky*
Convicts
1916   Unprotected
1918   Laughing Bill Hyde
1920?   Her Story
1930   El presidio
1936   Love and Sacrifice
1939   *Gone With the Wind*
1950   *Rock Island Trail*
1957   Dragoon Wells Massacre
Cooks
1917   *Southern Pride*
1918   *How Could You, Jean?*
       Little Red Decides
       The Wine Girl
1919   Come Out of the Kitchen
1922   When East Comes West
1925   Justice of the Far North
1926   The Fighting Edge
1929   This Is Heaven
1930   Whoopee
1932   *The Heart of New York*
1933   *Victims of Persecution*
1934   *Charlie Chan's Courage*
       'Neath the Arizona Skies

1935   *The Little Colonel*
       Melody Trail
       A Night at the Ritz
1936   *Down to the Sea*
       The Green Pastures
       Hair-Trigger Casey
1937   *Slave Ship*
1938   *Swing!*
1939   *Harlem Rides the Range*
       Moon over Harlem
1941   *Golden Gate Girl*
       Mutiny in the Arctic
       Secret of the Wastelands
       Western Union
1942   *Apache Trail*
1943   *Bataan*
       Fighting Americans
       His Butler's Sister
1946   *The Sailor Takes a Wife*
1948   *Red River*
       Rocky
       The Time of Your Life
1950   *The Cariboo Trail*
       Indian Territory
1951   *Yes Sir, Mr. Bones*
1952   *The Big Sky*
1953   *The Great Sioux Uprising*
Cooperatives
1941   *Under Fiesta Stars*
1950   *God, Man and Devil*
Copacabana Nightclub (New York City)
1947   Copacabana
Copper mines
1954   *Broken Lance*
Copper River (AK)
1917   Alaska Wonders in Motion
Coral Sea, Battle of, 1942
1943   *Air Force*
James J. Corbett
1942   Gentleman Jim
1947   Vigilantes of Boomtown
Cork County (Ireland)
1936   *Laughing Irish Eyes*
Corn
1934   *Our Daily Bread*
1954   *Apache*
Cornets
1958   *St. Louis Blues*
Charles Cornwallis
1917   *The Spirit of '76*
Coronations
1931   *Die Dreigroschenoper*
Coroners
1940   *Charlie Chan's Murder Cruise*
1944   *Black Magic*
1945   *The Jade Mask*
1948   *Moonrise*
1950   *No Way Out*
       Panic in the Streets
1956   *The Broken Star*
1957   *Man in the Shadow*
1959   *Porgy and Bess*
Corpses
1918   *The Price of Applause*
1931   *Drácula*
       Such Is Life
1934   *Chloe: Love Is Calling You*
1936   *Mad Holiday*
1937   *Hills of Old Wyoming*
1947   *Oregon Trail Scouts*
1949   *The Gay Amigo*
       The Prairie
1950   *Damien*
       Panic in the Streets
       Sands of Iwo Jima
1956   *The Searchers*
Correspondence schools and courses
1941   *Mutiny in the Arctic*
Corruption
1930   Las campanas de Capistrano
1933   Racetrack
1941   Thunder Over the Prairie
1943   *Margin for Error*
1950   Give Us This Day
       So Young, So Bad
1951   *Adventures of Captain Fabian*
       Saturday's Hero
1956   The Broken Star

1957   Man in the Shadow
Cosmetics
1945   *The House on 92nd St.*
Cossacks
1916   *Civilization's Child*
1919   *The Right to Happiness*
       Who's Your Brother?
1932   *The Unfortunate Bride*
1934   *Un capitán de cosacos*
1939   *Cossacks in Exile*
Costume parties
1940   Elsa Maxwell's Public Deb No. 1
Costumes
1933   *Una viuda romántica*
1948?   *Boarding House Blues*
Cottages
1942   *We Were Dancing*
Cotton
1921   Cotton and Cattle
1929   Hallelujah
1930   Georgia Rose
1931   *Pardon Us*
1952   *The Iron Mistress*
1956   *Baby Doll*
Cougars
     use **Pumas**
Counterfeiters and counterfeiting
1915   Time Lock Number 776
1916   Gretchen, the Greenhorn
       Poor Little Peppina
1919   The Gray Horizon
       The Lord Loves the Irish
1922   The Guttersnipe
1943   Riding High
1946?   *Beale Street Mama*
1949   The Clay Pigeon
Country boys
1914   *John Barleycorn*
1915   *The Adventures of a Madcap*
1918   Huck and Tom; or, the Further Adventures of Tom Sawyer
1920   Huckleberry Finn
1931   Huckleberry Finn
Country clubs
1960   *The Dark at the Top of the Stairs*
Country girls
1915?   Sin
1918?   Rosemary Climbs the Heights
1939   *La Inmaculada*
1950   *Annie Get Your Gun*
Country life
     use **Rural life**
Coups d'état
1916   The Fall of a Nation
1933   *Dos noches*
Courage
1918   The Greatest Thing in Life
1919   The Red Viper
1920   *The Daughter of Dawn*
1932   *Igloo*
1940   Escape
1942   The Navy Comes Through
1950   Broken Arrow
1952   High Noon
1953   *Last of the Comanches*
       The Sun Shines Bright
1955   *White Feather*
1957   *The Guns of Fort Petticoat*
1958   *Oregon Passage*
       Terror in a Texas Town
1959   *The Young Land*
1960   Key Witness
Couriers
1915?   *The Life of Sam Davis: A Confederate Hero of the Sixties*
       Sam Davis, the Hero of Tennessee
1948   *Renegades of Sonora*
Courtrooms
     use **Trials**
Courts-martial and courts of inquiry
1918   Johanna Enlists
1926   The Frontier Trail
       Under Fire
1932   *Texas Pioneers*

1934 Operator 13
La veuve joyeuse
1935 The Littlest Rebel
1936 General Spanky
The Last of the Mobicans
Ride, Ranger, Ride
1940 The Fighting 69th
1942 Across the Pacific
1947 King of the Bandits
1948 Fury at Furnace Creek
Unconquered
1953 Seminole
1954 Sitting Bull
1957 The Guns of Fort Petticoat
1960 Sergeant Rutledge

Courtship
1921 When the Clock Struck Nine
1922 Second Hand Rose
The Son of the Wolf
1926 The Campus Flirt
Kosher Kitty Kelly
Laddie
Pals in Paradise
Private Izzy Murphy
A Trip to Chinatown
1927 The Auctioneer
Bitter Apples
California
Don Mike
Finnegan's Ball
Frisco Sally Levy
Irish Hearts
Turkish Delight
Whispering Sage
1929 Evangeline
Die Königsloge
Love, Live and Laugh
This Is Heaven
1930 Abraham Lincoln
Alma de gaucho
Anybody's War
The Arizona Kid
Around the Corner
Big Boy
The Big Pond
Doña mentiras
The Grand Parade
Kathleen Mavourneen
Ladies Love Brutes
The Melody Man
Sevilla de mis amores
Son of the Gods
Song of the Caballero
Sunny Skies
Tom Sawyer
Whoopee
1931 Chérie
Dämon des Meeres
En cada puerto un amor
La fruta amarga
La gran jornada
La incorrigible
Jenny Lind
Le petit café
Su noche de bodas
Su última noche
1932 Igloo
1934 Judge Priest
1938 The Adventures of Tom
Sawyer
My Lucky Star
1939 Judge Hardy and Son
1940 Too Many Girls
1945 The Gay Senorita
A Tree Grows in Brooklyn
1948 Silver Trails
1951 Teresa
1952 Battles of Chief Pontiac
The Quiet Man
1955 The Long Gray Line
Marty
The Rose Tattoo

Cousins
1914 Springtime
Threads of Destiny
1916 The Innocent Lie
Silks and Satins
1917 The Sudden Gentleman
A Wife by Proxy
The Wild Girl
1918 Doing Their Bit
My Cousin
Ruggles of Red Gap
The Squaw Man

1919 A Bachelor's Wife
Diane of the Green Van
False Evidence
The Gray Towers Mystery
1931 Mi último amor
The Squaw Man
1932 El hombre que asesinó
1933 Charlie Chan's Greatest
Case
The Eternal Jew
1935 Julieta compra un hijo
So Red the Rose
1936 Love and Sacrifice
Rainbow on the River
1938 Two Sisters
1939 The Escape
La Inmaculada
Lying Lips
El otro soy yo
1940 The Great Advisor
The Jewish Melody
1941 Adam Had Four Sons
1942 Song of the Islands
1943 Marching On!
Redhead from Manhattan
1944 An American Romance
Lake Placid Serenade
Mr. Skeffington
Something for the Boys
Tomorrow the World!
1945 Our Vines Have Tender
Grapes
1946 Don Ricardo Returns
1948 My Girl Tisa
1949 Masked Raiders
The Mysterious Desperado
Pinky
Top O' the Morning
Tulsa
1949? Harlem Follies
1951 Cuban Fireball
The Girl on the Bridge
Queen for a Day
1952 My Man and I
1953 Jack McCall Desperado
The Member of the
Wedding
1955 Marty
1956 The Broken Star
Comanche
Crowded Paradise
Serenade
1957 War Drums
1958 Machete
Seven Hills of Rome
Tonka
1959 Night of the Quarter Moon

Couturiers
1917 Unknown 274
1922 Solomon in Society
1925 Salome of the Tenements
1926 Irene
1930 The Cohens and the Kellys
in Scotland
1931 Esclavas de la moda
1939 Miracle on Main Street
1942 Dr. Gillespie's New
Assistant
Nazi Agent

Covered wagons
1914? Sitting Bull—The Hostile
Sioux Indian Chief
1931 Call of the Rockies
1936 My American Wife
1938 In Old Chicago

Cowardice
1914 Northern Lights
1915 The Danger Signal
The Girl I Left Behind Me
The Lamb
1917 The Slacker
1918 The Price of Applause
1919 The Heart of Wetona
1925 Custer's Last Fight
1928 The Wages of Sin
1932 Scarface
1935 So Red the Rose
1936 For the Service
It Had to Happen
1940 The Fighting 69th
1943 The Ox-Bow Incident
1950 Winchester '73
1951 Only the Valiant
1953 The Glory Brigade
The Man from the Alamo

1955 Kentucky Rifle
Shotgun
1956 Daniel Boone, Trail Blazer
7th Cavalry
1957 Ride Out for Revenge
1958 Apache Territory

Cowboys
1915 Where Cowboy Is King
1916 The Flower of No Man's
Land
A Sister of Six
1918 The Border Raiders
Little Red Decides
The Squaw Man
Untamed
Wild Women
1919 The Sleeping Lion
1919? When the Desert Smiles
1920 Frontier Days
1921 Cotton and Cattle
The Hunger of the Blood
Shadows of the West
1922 Big Stakes
The Bull-Dogger
The Crimson Skull
1923 The Secret of the Pueblo
1924 The Broken Law
1927 The Fighting Hombre
Open Range
Roarin' Broncs
1928 Breed of the Sunsets
1931 Cavalier of the West
1933 Circle Canyon
Robbers' Roost
1934 The Cactus Kid
Fighting Through
'Neath the Arizona Skies
1935 Annie Oakley
Ruggles of Red Gap
1935? The Irish Gringo
1936 Song of the Gringo
1937 Boots and Saddles
Border Cafe
Harlem on the Prairie
Harlem on the Prairie
Hills of Old Wyoming
Manhattan
Merry-Go-Round
The Riders of the Whistling
Skull
1938 The Renegade Ranger
Two Gun Man from Harlem
Wild Horse Canyon
1939 The Bronze Buckaroo
Harlem Rides the Range
Winner Take All
1940 Covered Wagon Days
Rhythm of the Rio Grande
1940? Mr. Washington Goes to
Town
1941 Gauchos of Eldorado
Prairie Pioneers
Road Agent
Under Fiesta Stars
1942 Lawless Plainsmen
1943 Wagon Tracks West
1944 Marshal of Reno
The San Antonio Kid
Sheriff of Las Vegas
Tucson Raiders
1945 Phantom of the Plains
1946 California Gold Rush
Till the End of Time
Wild Beauty
1947 The Adventures of Don
Coyote
On the Old Spanish Trail
Wild Horse Mesa
1948 Gun Smugglers
Guns of Hate
Red River
Renegades of Sonora
The Time of Your Life
1949 Brothers in the Saddle
The Daring Caballero
Lookout Sister
Ride, Ryder, Ride!
Riders of the Range
Rustlers
Satan's Cradle
The Valiant Hombre
1949? Come On, Cowboy!
1950 Annie Get Your Gun
Border Treasure
The Girl from San Lorenzo

Riders of the Pony Express
Storm Over Wyoming
1956 Giant
1957 Trooper Hook
1958 Sierra Baron
1960 The Plunderers
The Unforgiven

Cowgirls
1915 Where Cowboy Is King
1935 Melody Trail

Coyotes
1949 Tale of the Navajos

Craps (Game)
1941 Up Jumped the Devil
1942 Lucky Ghost
1946? House-Rent Party
1947 Mantan Runs for Mayor
1959 Porgy and Bess

Chief Crazy Horse
1914? Sitting Bull—The Hostile
Sioux Indian Chief
1936 Custer's Last Stand
1942 They Died With Their Boots
On
1944 Buffalo Bill
1954 Saskatchewan
1955 Chief Crazy Horse

Creation
1937 The Holy Oath

Cree Indians
Drums of Destiny
1954 Saskatchewan

Creek Indians
1927 The Frontiersman

Creek War, 1813—1814
1955 Davy Crockett, King of the
Wild Frontier

Creoles
1914 Springtime
1917 Southern Pride
1918 A Daughter of the Old South
A Woman of Impulse
1930 Charros, gauchos y
manolas
1935 El día que me quieras
1938 The Buccaneer
1942 American Empire
1947 The Foxes of Harrow
1951 Adventures of Captain
Fabian
1952 The Big Sky
1955 Duel on the Mississippi
1958 Ride a Crooked Trail

Crime
1920? The Scarlet Dragon
1931 Little Caesar
1938 Life Goes On
1939 Frontiers of '49
1946? Go Down, Death!

Criminal investigations
use Investigations

Criminals
1913? The Lure of New York
1916 The Thousand Dollar
Husband
1917 The Tell-Tale Step
1918 The Midnight Patrol
Set Free
The Wine Girl
1920 The Luck of the Irish
1932 White Eagle
1932? The Girl from Chicago
1933 Dos noches
1934 The Cat's-Paw
1939 Mamele
1940 Charlie Chan at the Wax
Museum
1945 Colorado Pioneers
1946 Gas House Kids
1948 Cry of the City
1949 Thieves' Highway
1950 Chinatown at Midnight

Criminals—Rehabilitation
1914? A Boy and the Law
1915 Captain Courtesy
Just Jim
1916 A Yoke of Gold
1918 Hell's End
Hitting the Trail
The Ranger
1920 Outside the Law
1924 The Night Hawk

Criminals—Rehabilitation (continued)

1926 The Little Irish Girl
1927 The Millionaire
1928 Wheel of Chance
1929 Thunderbolt
1930 Amor audaz
     El presidio
1931 El impostor
1934 Lazy River
     Straight Is the Way
1935 No matarás
1937 *Harlem on the Prairie*
1939 Miracle on Main Street
1940 East of the River
1941 Western Union
1945 Great Stagecoach Robbery
     Salome, Where She Danced
1946 Bad Bascomb
     Sunset Pass
1949 *Arctic Manhunt*
     Colorado Territory
     Knock on Any Door
     Streets of Laredo
1954 Hell's Half Acre
1959 Cry Tough

Criminologists
1916 Pudd'nhead Wilson
1930 Cascarrabias
1936 El crimen de media noche
1938 Mr. Moto's Gamble
1940 Charlie Chan at the Wax
     Museum
1944 *The Chinese Cat*

Cripple Creek (WY)
1947 *Marshal of Cripple Creek*

Cripples
     use **Handicapped**

Critics
1918 *Find the Woman*
1919 *As a Man Thinks*
1943 *His Butler's Sister*

Davy Crockett
1939 *Man of Conquest*
1955 Davy Crockett, King of the
     Wild Frontier
     The Last Command
1956 Davy Crockett and the River
     Pirates
     Frontier Woman

Crocodiles
1935 *Alas sobre el Chaco*

George Crook
1954 *Taza, Son of Cochise*
1955 *Chief Crazy Horse*

Crop dusters
1942 *Valley of Hunted Men*

Croquet (Game)
1934 *Judge Priest*

Crow Indians
1917 John Ermine of the
     Yellowstone
1918? Indian Life
1935 Fighting Pioneers
1951 *Little Big Horn*
1952 *The Savage*
1955 *White Feather*

Crucifixes
1930 *Anna Christie*
1936 *The Phantom of Santa Fe*
1941? *The Blood of Jesus*
1949 *Daughter of the West*
     Harbor of Missing Men

Crucifixion
1915 *The Penitentes*

Cruelty to animals
1934 *Charlie Chan in London*
1945 *Phantom of the Plains*
1946 *The Face of Marble*
     Sun Valley Cyclone
1947 The Return of Rin Tin Tin
     Wild Horse Mesa
1956 *The Last Hunt*
1958 *Tonka*

Cruises
1940 Charlie Chan's Murder
     Cruise
1942 Mexican Spitfire at Sea

Crusades
1933 *The Wandering Jew*

Crutches
1926 *The Flying Ace*
1949 *Lookout Sister*

Crypts
1941 *Virginia*

Crystal balls
1920 *Eyes of Youth*
1931 *The Black Camel*

Cuba
1946 *Cuban Pete*
1949 We Were Strangers
1951 *Hurricane Island*

Cuban Americans
1927 Blind Alleys
1949 We Were Strangers
1959 *Cry Tough*

Cubans
1927 The Spider's Web
1929 Sombras habaneras
1932? *The Girl from Chicago*
1942 *The Navy Comes Through*
1946 Cuban Pete
1951 Cuban Fireball
1952 The Fabulous Senorita

Cults
1915 The Penitentes
1937 The Riders of the Whistling
     Skull

Cultural conflict
1914 When Broadway Was a Trail
1916 *Alien Souls*
     The Morals of Hilda
1916? Should a Baby Die?
1917 The Bronze Bride
     Her Own People
     John Ermine of the
       Yellowstone
1919 The Courageous Coward
1929 The Younger Generation
1931 Aloha
     La ley del harem
     Mi último amor
1932 Cuore d'emigrante
     The Golden West
     The Hatchet Man
     Mazel Tov
1933 La melodía prohibida
1934 Behold My Wife!
     Eskimo
     Laughing Boy
     Limehouse Blues
     Massacre
     White Heat
     The Youth of Russia
1937 Old Louisiana
1940 Overture to Glory
1941 Birth of the Blues
     Doomed Caravan
     Virginia
1945 *The Gay Senorita*
1950 Two Flags West
1951 New Mexico
1953 Dream Wife
     The Glory Brigade
     Thunder Bay
1955 Foxfire
     Kiss of Fire
1956 *The Benny Goodman Story*
     The Last Hunt
     Westward Ho the Wagons!
1957 *Bayou*
1959 The Sheriff of Fractured Jaw
     Thunder in the Sun
     The Wonderful Country

Cultural elitism
1943 *Three Hearts for Julia*
1956 *The Benny Goodman Story*

Cumberland Mountains
1936 *Daniel Boone*

Curators
1943 *The Leopard Man*
1944 *Cry of the Werewolf*

Cures
1917 *The Tell-Tale Step*
     The Trouble Buster
1918 *Huck and Tom; or, the
       Further Adventures of
       Tom Sawyer*
1920 Humoresque
     Pagan Love
     The Secret Gift
1938 *The Adventures of Tom
       Sawyer*
1947 *The Peanut Man*
1948 *Angel in Exile*
     Tap Roots

Curio dealers
1915 *The Cheat*
1916 *The Honorable Friend*
1937 *Think Fast, Mr. Moto*
1942 *Let's Get Tough!*
1948 *The Golden Eye*
1951 Mask of the Dragon

Curses
1923 The White Flower
1932 Amore e morte
     Igloo
1934 *Drums O' Voodoo*
1935 Charlie Chan in Egypt
     Rescue Squad
1937 Slave Ship
1940 *Phantom of Chinatown*
1942 Tales of Manhattan
1945 *Anoush*

Curtains
1939 *Gone With the Wind*
1942 *Mokey*

General George Armstrong Custer
1916 *Britton of the Seventh*
1925 Custer's Last Fight
     The Scarlet West
1926 The Flaming Frontier
     General Custer at Little Big
       Horn
     The Last Frontier
1927 Spoilers of the West
1936 Custer's Last Stand
1937 The Plainsman
1940 Santa Fe Trail
1942 They Died With Their Boots
       On
1951 *Warpath*
1952 *Bugles in the Afternoon*
1954 *Sitting Bull*
1955 *Chief Crazy Horse*
1956 *7th Cavalry*
1958 Tonka

Customs officials
1916 Hop, the Devil's Brew
1928 Anybody Here Seen Kelly?
1949 *C-Man*

Cynics
1935 Alas sobre el Chaco
1938 *Rascals*
1944 *Lifeboat*
1955 *Blackboard Jungle*
     Headline Hunters
1958 Blood Arrow

Czechoslovakia
1940 *The Tragedy of
       Carpatho-Ukraine*
1944 *Lake Placid Serenade*

Czechoslovakian Americans
1933 The Man Who Dared: An
       Imaginative Biography
1935 Romance in Manhattan
1944 *An American Romance*
     Lake Placid Serenade
     Lifeboat
1947 *Desperate*
1949 *The Girl from Jones Beach*
1956 Death of a Scoundrel

Czechs
1940 *The Man I Married*
1944 *Slightly Terrific*

Dade's Battle, 1835
1957 *Naked in the Sun*

Daggers
1931 Chinatown After Dark

Dairy farms
1918 *Johanna Enlists*

Dakota Indians
1914 The Indian Wars
1914? Sitting Bull—The Hostile
       Sioux Indian Chief
1918? Indian Life
1925 Custer's Last Fight
     A Daughter of the Sioux
     Red Love
     Warrior Gap
1926 The Frontier Trail
     General Custer at Little Big
       Horn
     The Last Frontier
1927 The Overland Stage
     The Red Raiders
     With Sitting Bull at the
       Spirit Lake Massacre

1950 *Train to Tombstone*
1951 *Hurricane Island*

1929 Sioux Blood
1934 Massacre
1936 Custer's Last Stand
     The Glory Trail
1937 The Plainsman
1940 Prairie Schooners
1941 Western Union
1942 *They Died With Their Boots
       On*
1944 *Buffalo Bill*
1949 *The Prairie*
1951 Cavalry Scout
     Little Big Horn
     Oh! Susanna
     Tomahawk
     Warpath
1952 Buffalo Bill in Tomahawk
       Territory
     Bugles in the Afternoon
     Hiawatha
     The Savage
1953 The Great Sioux Uprising
     Jack McCall Desperado
     The Nebraskan
1954 The Black Dakotas
     Saskatchewan
     Sitting Bull
1955 Chief Crazy Horse
     The Gun That Won the West
     The Indian Fighter
     White Feather
1956 The Last Frontier
     The Last Hunt
     7th Cavalry
     Westward Ho the Wagons!
     The White Squaw
1957 The Lawless Eighties
     Revolt at Fort Laramie
     Run of the Arrow
1958 Flaming Frontier
     Gunman's Walk
     Tonka
1959 Yellowstone Kelly

Dakota Territory
1927 The Overland Stage
1956 The Last Hunt

Thomas Dale
1923 Jamestown

Walter Johannes Damrosch
1947 *Carnegie Hall*

Dams
1915 *The Immigrant*
1918 *The Source*
1925 *Galloping Vengeance*
1941 *Thunder Over the Prairie*
1948 Old Los Angeles

Dance contests
1941 *Sunday Sinners*

Dance hall girls
1916 The Aryan
1918 Tongues of Flame
1919 Scarlet Days
     The Westerners
1921 Across the Divide
1922 The Son of the Wolf
1925 Flower of Night
1927 The Dove
     White Gold
1931 Carne de cabaret
     Law of the Tong
1933 Dance Hall Hostess
1935 Señora casada necesita
       marido
1939 *The Cisco Kid and the Lady*
1943 *Jack London*
1945 *In Old New Mexico*
1947 *Riding the California Trail*
     Thunder Mountain
1948 *Guns of Hate*
1949 *Brothers in the Saddle*
1950 *Winchester '73*
1951 *Apache Drums*
     Fort Defiance
     New Mexico
1953 *The Nebraskan*
1955 *Shotgun*
1956 *The Last Hunt*
1957 *The Guns of Fort Petticoat*
1958 *Ride a Crooked Trail*
1959 *The Sheriff of Fractured
       Jaw*

Dance hall owners
1919 *Scarlet Days*
Dance halls
1924 *His Darker Self*
1936 *Klondike Annie*
1948 *Moonrise*
1950 *Sands of Iwo Jima*
1952 *My Man and I*
1953 *The Man Behind the Gun*
1955 Marty
Dance parties
1939 *Gone With the Wind*
1942 *Shut My Big Mouth*
1949 *She Wore a Yellow Ribbon*
Dance teachers
1936 *Dancing Pirate*
1939 *A Brivele der Mamen*
1940 Tengo fe en ti
1947 *Jiggs and Maggie in Society*
Dancers
1916 *The Twin Triangle*
1917 *The Flower of Doom*
The Pulse of Life
1918 A Broadway Scandal
Wild Women
1919 The Delicious Little Devil
Yvonne from Paris
1920 The Good-Bad Wife
On with the Dance
The Tiger's Coat
1921 The Land of Hope
1922 Peacock Alley
1923 His Great Chance
Look Your Best
1925 Lights of Old Broadway
The Midnight Girl
1928 The Broken Mask
Diamond Handcuffs
The Hawk's Nest
The Jazz Singer
Kit Carson
1929 *Sombras habaneras*
1930 *Charros, gauchos y manolas*
Galas de la Paramount
El precio de un beso
1931 *La cautivadora*
The Exile
Gente alegre
Little Caesar
Las luces de Buenos Aires
Le père célibataire
La pura verdad
1933 *Una viuda romántica*
1934 *Blossom Time*
Strange Wives
La veuve joyeuse
1934? *Harlem After Midnight*
1935 *El día que me quieras*
Tango Bar
1936 *Dancing Pirate*
The Green Pastures
Human Cargo
La última cita
1937 *Charlie Chan on Broadway*
The Devil's Playground
That Girl from Paris
1938 The Duke Is Tops
Mis dos amores
Outside of Paradise
Passport Husband
1939 *Forged Passport*
Miracle on Main Street
One Dark Night
1940 Tengo fe en ti
1941 *Hold Back the Dawn*
Playmates
Prairie Pioneers
Ride on Vaquero
Sun Valley Serenade
1941? *Hampton Institute: Its Program of Education for Life*
1942 Holiday Inn
Mexican Spitfire's Elephant
1943 The Gang's All Here
The Leopard Man
Stormy Weather
What's Buzzin' Cousin?
Yankee Doodle Dandy
1944 *Chip Off the Old Block*
Lady, Let's Dance!
Slightly Terrific
1945 *Club Havana*
Rhapsody in Blue

1946 *Mantan Messes Up*
Tall, Tan and Terrific
1946? *Beale Street Mama*
1947 *Hi De Ho*
Jivin' in Be-Bop
The Jolson Story
Juke Joint
1948 *Half Past Midnight*
The Time of Your Life
Up in Central Park
1948? *Boarding House Blues*
1949 *The Kissing Bandit*
1949? Harlem Follies
1950 *Catskill Honeymoon*
A Lady Without Passport
1951 *Show Boat*
Yes Sir, Mr. Bones
1952 *The Fabulous Senorita*
1953 *Dream Wife*
The Stars Are Singing
1955 *Brevities of 1955*
1956 *Hot Blood*
1960 *The Pusher*
Dances
1919 *False Evidence*
1926 *General Custer at Little Big Horn*
1932 *Mazel Tov*
1934 *As the Earth Turns*
Cheyenne Sun Dance
Granaderos del amor
1935 *His Family Tree*
The Irish in Us
Texas Terror
1936 *Dangerous Intrigue*
Ramona
1937 *Life Begins in College*
Natalka Poltavka
1938 *Happy Landing*
Spawn of the North
1940 *Broken Strings*
The Man I Married
1944 *Since You Went Away*
1945 *A Medal for Benny*
1946 *Swamp Fire*
1947 *Boy! What a Girl!*
Untamed Fury
1948 *Fort Apache*
1950 *The Lawless*
1951 *Apache Drums*
The Mark of the Renegade
Molly
Oh! Susanna
Snake River Desperadoes
1952 *Bright Victory*
The Savage
1953 *Arrowhead*
1955 *The Indian Fighter*
1956 *Man from Del Rio*
Walk the Proud Land
Westward Ho the Wagons!
1957 *Bayou*
The Lawless Eighties
1958 *Home Before Dark*
Houseboat
The Light in the Forest
1959 *Thunder in the Sun*
1960 *Man on a String*
Dancing
1918 *Amarilly of Clothes-Line Alley*
1925 *Custer's Last Fight*
1928 *Eleven P.M.*
1931 *Aloha*
The Hurricane Horseman
1933 *La melodía prohibida*
1934 *The Rabbi's Power*
1935 *The Littlest Rebel*
1936 *Contra la corriente*
Rose of the Rancho
1938 *The Singing Blacksmith*
1940 *The Ramparts We Watch*
1941 *Wiejskie Wesele*
1942 *Syncopation*
We Were Dancing
1945 *Salome, Where She Danced*
1946 *Slightly Scandalous*
1947 *Pirates of Monterey*
1956 *Rockin' the Blues*
1960 *I Passed for White*
Key Witness
Dandies
1916 *Silks and Satins*
1920 The Mark of Zorro

1947 *The Foxes of Harrow*
Danish Americans
1920 The Riddle: Woman
1931 *Street Scene*
1958 *Flaming Frontier*
Danube River
1939 *Cossacks in Exile*
Daredevils
1922 The Cub Reporter
1953 *The Glory Brigade*
Darts (Game)
1936 *Charlie Chan at the Race Track*
El crimen de media noche
Dating
use **Romance**
Daughters and fathers
use **Fathers and daughters**
Daughters and mothers
use **Mothers and daughters**
Daughters-in-law
1939 *Los hijos mandan*
Mirele Efros
1940 *Jennie*
Sam Davis
1915? The Life of Sam Davis: A Confederate Hero of the Sixties
Deacons
1926 The Fighting Deacon
1932 *The Black King*
Deadwood (SD)
1937 *The Plainsman*
Deaf-mutes
1919 Deliverance
1945 *Of One Blood*
1947 *The Chinese Ring*
1948 *Moonrise*
1950 *No Way Out*
Deafness
1921 Bits of Life
1936 *Sins of Man*
1947 *Ride the Pink Horse*
Deans (in schools)
1949 *The Girl from Jones Beach*
Death and dying
1926? Ten Nights in a Barroom
1928 *The Jazz Singer*
1929 *The Younger Generation*
1931 Drácula
Die Maske Fällt
1935 *Angelina o el honor de un brigadier*
The Littlest Rebel
1936 *Klondike Annie*
Sum Hun
1938 *La vida bohemia*
1939 *Gone With the Wind*
Tevya
1941 *Virginia*
1941? The Blood of Jesus
1943 Cabin in the Sky
Marching On!
1945 A Tree Grows in Brooklyn
The Valley of Decision
1946 *The Face of Marble*
1946? *Go Down, Death!*
1947 *Hi De Ho*
Little Mister Jim
Reet, Petite and Gone
1948 *I Remember Mama*
Miracle in Harlem
1949 *House of Strangers*
3 Godfathers
1950 *Battleground*
Broken Arrow
Devil's Doorway
Stars in My Crown
1951 *The Great Caruso*
Jim Thorpe—All-American
The Steel Helmet
1952 *Anything Can Happen*
Battles of Chief Pontiac
1953 *Beneath the 12-Mile Reef*
Bright Road
The Member of the Wedding
Sangaree
1955 *The Long Gray Line*
1958 *Houseboat*
1959 *Anna Lucasta*
The Last Angry Man

1960 *Flaming Star*
Death by animals
1930 *La jaula de los leones*
1931 *Call of the Rockies*
1933 King of the Wild Horses
1938 *In Old Chicago*
1942 *Cat People*
1957 *Raiders of Old California*
1960 *Ice Palace*
Death by shock
1916 *The Gilded Spider*
1917 *A Roadside Impresario*
1928 *Eleven P.M.*
1934 *Imitation of Life*
1955 *Trial*
Death in childbirth
1933 *Broken Dreams*
1936 *Sins of Man*
1940 *Her Second Mother*
1947 *Little Mister Jim*
1957 *Pawnee*
1960 *Ice Palace*
Death Valley (CA)
1915 *Chimmie Fadden Out West*
1948 *Flight to the Sun*
1952 *Desert Pursuit*
Debates
1942 *Friendly Enemies*
1960 *I Aim at the Stars: the Wernher von Braun Story*
Debt
1913? The Lure of New York
1914 *The Jungle*
The Yellow Traffic
1916 *Her Debt of Honor*
Lord Loveland Discovers America
The Thousand Dollar Husband
1918 *Tony America*
1919 *His Debt*
Mandarin's Gold
1920 *The Man Who Dared*
1923 *Crashin' Thru*
1929 *Die Königsloge*
Sombras habaneras
1930 *La fuerza del querer*
Un hombre de suerte
1931 *Carne de cabaret*
Esclavas de la moda
Mamá
1932 *Law and Lawless*
The Match King
1933 *Espérame*
1934 Broadway Bill
The Prescott Kid
1935 *Circle of Death*
McFadden's Flats
The Wedding Night
1936 *Aces and Eights*
Charlie Chan at the Circus
1937 *Boots and Saddles*
1939 *Forged Passport*
Judge Hardy and Son
1940 *Prairie Schooners*
1943 *The Meanest Man in the World*
1944 *The San Antonio Kid*
Something for the Boys
1946 *Slightly Scandalous*
Tall, Tan and Terrific
1946? *House-Rent Party*
1947 *Easy Come, Easy Go*
The Last Round-Up
On the Old Spanish Trail
Thunder Mountain
1948? Boarding House Blues
1949 *The Cowboy and the Prizefighter*
Masked Raiders
Riders of the Range
Stallion Canyon
Tuna Clipper
1950 The Breaking Point
Indian Territory
1951 *Flaming Feather*
1952 *The Iron Mistress*
1953 *Beneath the 12-Mile Reef*
The Joe Louis Story
1955 *Duel on the Mississippi*
Good Morning, Miss Dove
Violent Saturday
1957 *Pawnee*

1958　*Never Love a Stranger*
Debutantes
1918　*In Judgment Of*
1934　*Coming Out Party*
1947　*New Orleans*
1950　*Annie Get Your Gun*
Decapitation
1931　*La ley del barem*
1942　*Little Tokyo, U.S.A.*
Decatur (GA)
1955　*A Man Called Peter*
Deception
1922　Easy Money
1924　The House Behind the
　　　　Cedars
1927　With Sitting Bull at the
　　　　Spirit Lake Massacre
1928　The Midnight Ace
1929　When Men Betray
1931　Los calaveras
　　　　La cautivadora
　　　　The Cisco Kid
　　　　El comediante
　　　　The Hurricane Horseman
　　　　Oklahoma Jim
　　　　Politiquerías
　　　　The White Renegade
1932　*Amore e morte*
　　　　Flesh
　　　　Une heure près de toi
　　　　Joseph in the Land of Egypt
　　　　Law and Lawless
　　　　Senza mamma e'nnamurato
　　　　Texas Pioneers
1933　*Best of Enemies*
　　　　Let's Fall in Love
　　　　The Telegraph Trail
1934　Blossom Time
　　　　Caravane
　　　　The Rabbi's Power
　　　　Strange Wives
　　　　Tres amores
1935　L'homme des Folies Bergère
　　　　The Little Colonel
　　　　Te quiero con locura
1936　Amor que vuelve
　　　　Charlie Chan at the Race
　　　　　Track
　　　　Star for a Night
1937　Charlie Chan at the
　　　　　Olympics
　　　　I Want to Be a Mother
　　　　One Mile from Heaven
　　　　Slave Ship
　　　　Where Is My Child?
1938　Charlie Chan at Monte Carlo
　　　　Passport Husband
　　　　Spawn of the North
　　　　Speed to Burn
　　　　The Texans
　　　　La vida bohemia
1939　*Moon over Harlem*
1940　*Behind the News*
　　　　Her Second Mother
　　　　The Man I Married
1941　Hold Back the Dawn
　　　　Mutiny in the Arctic
　　　　This Woman Is Mine
1942　Dr. Gillespie's New Assistant
　　　　Holiday Inn
　　　　Mokey
1943　*The Amazing Mrs. Holliday*
　　　　The Gang's All Here
　　　　Good Luck, Mr. Yates
　　　　Tahiti Honey
　　　　Wintertime
1946　*Without Reservations*
1947　Copacabana
　　　　Dark Delusion
1947?　*Return of Mandy's
　　　　　Husband*
1949　*The Girl from Jones Beach*
　　　　The Golden Stallion
1950　*Comanche Territory*
　　　　Deported
　　　　Mystery Submarine
1951　Oh! Susanna
　　　　Slaughter Trail
　　　　Snake River Desperadoes
　　　　A Streetcar Named Desire
1953　Fort Ti
　　　　The Great Sioux Uprising
　　　　Seminole
　　　　Taxi
　　　　Tonight We Sing

The Declaration of Independence
1917　*The Spirit of '76*
1959　*John Paul Jones*
Decompression sickness
1949　*Harbor of Missing Men*
1953　*Beneath the 12-Mile Reef*
Decorators
　　　use **Interior decorators**
Deeds
1915　*Marse Covington*
1917　*The Primitive Call*
1924　*Birthright*
1930　Check and Double Check
1935　*The Little Colonel*
1938　*Birthright*
1939　The Return of the Cisco Kid
1940　Midnight Shadow
1945　*The Gay Senorita*
1946　Three Wise Fools
1948　Old Los Angeles
1949　*Massacre River*
1957　*Raiders of Old California*
Defectors
1952　*Red Snow*
Defense plant workers
1942　Rubber Racketeers
1943　Gangway for Tomorrow
1954　*Carmen Jones*
Defense—National
　　　use **United States—Defenses**
Delaware Indians
1920　*The Last of the Mohicans*
1950　*The Iroquois Trail*
1951　When the Redskins Rode
1958　The Light in the Forest
Delgado (Mexico)
1956　Wetbacks
Delicatessens
1918　*The City of Tears*
1921　Guile of Women
1926　Kosher Kitty Kelly
　　　　Private Izzy Murphy
1927　*For the Love of Mike*
1932　*No Greater Love*
　　　　Unashamed
1933　*Rafter Romance*
1938　*Road Demon*
　　　　Speed to Burn
1939　Winner Take All
Delivery boys
1917　*A Night in New Arabia*
1918　*Mystic Faces*
Loenzo Delmonico
1923　Little Old New York
Democracy
1918　The Birth of a Race
1939　*Let Freedom Ring*
1944　Knickerbocker Holiday
　　　　Tender Comrade
　　　　They Live in Fear
1950　*The Jackie Robinson Story*
Democratic Party
1957　*Beau James*
Denmark
1920　*The Riddle: Woman*
Dentists
1921　Bits of Life
1926　*The Flying Ace*
1931　*Pardon Us*
1936　*Desert Gold*
　　　　Silly Billies
1937　*Waikiki Wedding*
1948　*The Paleface*
Dentures
1950　Battleground
Denver (CO)
1913　*The Inside of the White
　　　　　Slave Traffic*
Department store clerks
　　　use **Salesclerks;
　　　　Salesmen**
Department store owners
1931　*Cimarron*
1938　*My Lucky Star*
1951　*Molly*
Department stores
1920?　*Her Story*
1921　*No Woman Knows*
1931　*Quand on est belle*
1938　My Lucky Star
1948　*Jiggs and Maggie in Court*

Deportation
1918?　*The Snail*
1921　Fifty Candles
1928　Anybody Here Seen Kelly?
1931　Delicious
1935　*A Night at the Opera*
1936　Ellis Island
1937　Big City
　　　　That Girl from Paris
1938　Gateway
　　　　Passport Husband
1940　Music in My Heart
1941　*Come Live with Me*
　　　　Ice-Capades
　　　　Mystery Ship
1946　*G. I. War Brides*
1948　*My Girl Tisa*
1949　*The Red Menace*
1950　Deported
1951　*Gambling House*
1953　*Captain John Smith and
　　　　　Pocahontas*
　　　　The Glass Wall
The Depression, 1929
1933　A Lady's Profession
1934　Stand Up and Cheer!
1937　*Nation Aflame*
1947　*Humoresque*
1950　*Give Us This Day*
1960　*Hell to Eternity*
Depression, Mental
1930　*La jaula de los leones*
1932　*Men Are Such Fools*
1933　*Counsellor at Law*
1943　*Dr. Gillespie's Criminal
　　　　　Case*
1946　*Till the End of Time*
1950　*The Men*
1951　*Jim Thorpe—All-American*
1953　*The Eddie Cantor Story*
1960　*Take a Giant Step*
Deputies
1931　*Cavalier of the West*
1932　*The Galloping Kid*
1935　*Cowboy Holiday*
1936　Pinto Rustlers
1939　Trigger Fingers
1940　*The Gay Caballero*
1941　Road Agent
1943　*Land of Hunted Men*
　　　　The Ox-Bow Incident
1944　*Outlaw Trail*
　　　　Tucson Raiders
1946　*Santa Fe Uprising*
1947　Marshal of Cripple Creek
　　　　Vigilantes of Boomtown
1949　*Lust for Gold*
　　　　The Valiant Hombre
1950　*Border Treasure*
　　　　Cherokee Uprising
　　　　The Girl from San Lorenzo
　　　　North of the Great Divide
　　　　Sunset in the West
1952　High Noon
1954　*Broken Lance*
1955　Shotgun
1956　*The Broken Star*
1957　*Man in the Shadow*
　　　　The Ride Back
1958　*Gunman's Walk*
1959　*The Young Land*
Desert survival
1949　3 Godfathers
1953　War Paint
1955　*Seminole Uprising*
Desertion (Marital)
1914　At the Cross Roads
　　　　The Woman in Black
1917　The Bronze Bride
　　　　The Pulse of Life
　　　　Rosie O'Grady
　　　　Threads of Fate
1918　An Alien Enemy
　　　　Toys of Fate
1918?　Rosemary Climbs the
　　　　　Heights
1919　A Bachelor's Wife
　　　　The Gray Horizon
1920　The Devil's Claim
　　　　Locked Lips
1922　Pals of the West
1929　Frozen Justice
　　　　Show Boat
　　　　When Men Betray

1930　*Toda una vida*
1931　*Lo mejor es reír*
　　　　La mujer X
　　　　Women Love Once
1932　*Hombres en mi vida*
1936　*Let's Sing Again*
　　　　Show Boat
　　　　Sutter's Gold
1938　*God's Step Children*
1939　Daughters Courageous
　　　　One Dark Night
1948　The Betrayal
1951　Show Boat
1952　*The Quiet Man*
1954　Hondo
1960　*Cimarron*
Desertion, Military
1914　Northern Lights
1915　*Under Southern Skies*
1934　*Granaderos del amor*
1943　Marching On!
1947　*California*
1949　Rose of the Yukon
1951　*Little Big Horn*
　　　　Warpath
1954　Arrow in the Dust
　　　　Carmen Jones
1955　Smoke Signal
1957　*Edge of the City*
　　　　The Guns of Fort Petticoat
1958　*The Young Lions*
Deserts
1916　*The Aryan*
　　　　A Yoke of Gold
1918　The Red, Red Heart
1919　Desert Gold
1924　The Heritage of the Desert
1926　Desert Gold
1927　Aflame in the Sky
1929　Redskin
1931　La ley del harem
　　　　The Squaw Man
1932　Hidden Valley
　　　　Wild Horse Mesa
1933　*King of the Wild Horses*
1934　*The Lone Defender*
1935　*Riddle Ranch*
1936　*Border Phantom*
1937　*The Riders of the Whistling
　　　　　Skull*
1939　Bad Lands
　　　　One Dark Night
1941　*The Face Behind the Mask*
　　　　Secret of the Wastelands
1942　*Rio Rita*
　　　　Valley of the Sun
1943　*Marching On!*
　　　　The Outlaw
1946　Strange Voyage
1947　*Under the Tonto Rim*
1948　*The Dude Goes West*
　　　　Four Faces West
1949　*She Wore a Yellow Ribbon*
　　　　Stagecoach Kid
1950　*Riders of the Pony Express*
1951　*Apache Drums*
　　　　New Mexico
1952　*Desert Pursuit*
1953　Last of the Comanches
　　　　Tumbleweed
1955　*Bad Day at Black Rock*
　　　　Fort Yuma
　　　　Foxfire
　　　　Seven Cities of Gold
1958　*Apache Territory*
　　　　Sierra Baron
　　　　The Young Lions
1959　*Gunmen from Laredo*
　　　　Thunder in the Sun
Designers
　　　use **Specific types of
　　　　designers**
Despair
1941　*The Face Behind the Mask*
1944　Lifeboat
Desperation
　　　use **Despair**
Despotism
1940　The Mark of Zorro
1960　The Sign of Zorro
Despots
　　　use **Dictators**

Detective and mystery stories
1936　Mad Holiday
1946?　*House-Rent Party*

Detectives
1912　The Adventures of
　　　Lieutenant Petrosino
1914　The Little Jewess
1914?　The Mysterious Mr. Wu
　　　Chung Foo
1915　The Last of the Mafia
1916　*The Colored American
　　　Winning His Suit*
1917　A Night in New Arabia
　　　The Secret Game
　　　The Winged Mystery
1918　Denny from Ireland
1920　*Lifting Shadows*
　　　The Purple Cipher
　　　Within Our Gates
1921　Little Miss Hawkshaw
　　　When the Clock Struck Nine
1922　The Schemers
1926　*The Strong Man*
1927　The Chinese Parrot
1928　Hold 'Em Yale
　　　The Midnight Ace
1930　Le spectre vert
1931　The Black Camel
　　　Charlie Chan Carries On
　　　El impostor
　　　Noche de duendes
　　　El pasado acusa
1932　Charlie Chan's Chance
　　　Une heure près de toi
　　　Me and My Gal
　　　Men Are Such Fools
　　　The Secrets of Wu Sin
1933　Charlie Chan's Greatest Case
　　　Counsellor at Law
　　　Grand Slam
1934　Charlie Chan in London
　　　Charlie Chan's Courage
　　　Fighting Through
1935　Charlie Chan in Egypt
　　　Charlie Chan in Paris
　　　Charlie Chan in Shanghai
1936　After the Thin Man
　　　Charlie Chan at the Circus
　　　Charlie Chan at the Race
　　　　Track
　　　Charlie Chan's Secret
　　　El crimen de media noche
　　　Love and Sacrifice
1937　*Big City*
　　　Charlie Chan at the
　　　　Olympics
　　　Charlie Chan at the Opera
　　　Charlie Chan on Broadway
　　　Thank You, Mr. Moto
　　　Underworld
1938　Charlie Chan at Monte Carlo
　　　Daughter of Shanghai
　　　Mr. Moto's Gamble
　　　Mr. Wong, Detective
1939　Charlie Chan at Treasure
　　　　Island
　　　Charlie Chan in Honolulu
　　　Charlie Chan in Reno
　　　City in Darkness
　　　Lying Lips
　　　Mr. Moto in Danger Island
　　　Mr. Moto Takes a Vacation
　　　Mr. Wong in Chinatown
　　　My Son
　　　The Mystery of Mr. Wong
1940　Charlie Chan at the Wax
　　　　Museum
　　　Charlie Chan in Panama
　　　Charlie Chan's Murder
　　　　Cruise
　　　Doomed to Die
　　　The Fatal Hour
　　　Murder over New York
　　　Phantom of Chinatown
1941　Charlie Chan in Rio
　　　Dead Men Tell
1942　Castle in the Desert
1943　Ladies' Day
1944　Black Magic
　　　Charlie Chan in the Secret
　　　　Service
　　　The Chinese Cat
1946　Dangerous Money
　　　The Red Dragon

1946?　Beale Street Mama
1947　The Chinese Ring
1948　The Feathered Serpent
1950　*Black Hand*
1953　*The Stars Are Singing*
1959　*The Crimson Kimono*

Detroit (MI)
1930　The Grand Parade
1938　*Happy Landing
　　　Spirit of Youth*
1944　An American Romance
1953　*The Joe Louis Story*

Detroit Stars (Baseball team)
1921　As the World Rolls On

The Devil
1920　The Devil's Claim
1937　Maid of Salem
1941?　The Blood of Jesus
1943　Cabin in the Sky
1946?　*Go Down, Death!*
1947　Going to Glory, Come to
　　　　Jesus
1950　God, Man and Devil

Diamonds
1914　The Great Diamond Robbery
　　　The Little Jewess
1923　*Flames of Wrath*
1928　Diamond Handcuffs
1930　*Una cana al aire
　　　Cascarrabias*
1935　*Tango Bar*
1936　*Below the Deadline*
　　　Mad Holiday
1938　Passport Husband
1939　Mr. Moto in Danger Island
　　　Mothers of Today
1942　Mexican Spitfire's Elephant
1944　*The Chinese Cat*
1947　West to Glory
1949　Boston Blackie's Chinese
　　　　Venture
　　　The Golden Stallion

Diaries
1916　Silks and Satins
1933　*Charlie Chan's Greatest
　　　　Case*
1934　Wagon Wheels
1935　*Charlie Chan in Paris*
1936　*Charlie Chan's Secret
　　　Tundra*
1937　Charlie Chan on Broadway
1960　*Oklahoma Territory*

Porfirio Díaz
1952　The Fighter

Dice
1933　*The Emperor Jones*
1934　*Broadway Bill*
1942　*Lucky Ghost*
1943　*Cabin in the Sky
　　　What's Buzzin' Cousin?*

Dictating machines
1945　*The Jade Mask*

Dictators
1927　Rose of the Golden West
1928　Tyrant of Red Gulch
1933　*The Emperor Jones*
1936　*The Bold Caballero*
1952　*The Fighter*
1956　Raw Edge
1959　The Jayhawkers!

Dictograph
1949　*Top O' the Morning*

Diegueño Indians
1955　Seven Cities of Gold

Diets
1923　Look Your Best
1944　*Three Men in White*

Charles Dillingham
1953　*Tonight We Sing*

Diners (Restaurants)
1941　Come Live with Me
　　　Sullivan's Travels
1942　*Wings for the Eagle*

Dinners and dining
1944　*Mr. Skeffington*
1948　*Fighting Father Dunne*
1949　*Shamrock Hill*
1951　*Molly*

Robert Dinwiddie
1927　Winners of the Wilderness
1951　*When the Redskins Rode*

Diomede Islands
1952　*Arctic Flight*

Diphtheria
1944　*Mr. Skeffington*
1948　Four Faces West
1957　All Mine to Give

Diplomats
1917　*The Little American*
1931　*La dama atrevida*
　　　Don Juan diplomático
1933　Diplomaniacs
　　　Primavera en otoño
1934　*La veuve joyeuse*
1937　*Charlie Chan at the
　　　　Olympics*
1942　*Woman of the Year*
1953　*Dream Wife*
1955　*The Far Horizons*

Directors
　　　use **Motion picture directors;
　　　Theatrical directors**

Disabled persons
　　　use **Handicapped**

Disasters
1960　The Last Voyage

Disc jockeys
1953　*The Jazz Singer
　　　The Stars Are Singing*
1956　*Rockin' the Blues*

Discrimination in employment
　　　Crowded Paradise
1958　*Home Before Dark*
1960　I Passed for White

Discrimination in housing
1956　Crowded Paradise
1959　*Night of the Quarter Moon*

Disease
1918　*The Temple of Dusk*
　　　Uncle Tom's Cabin
1932　*Une heure près de toi*
1935　*El día que me quieras*
1939　*The Light Ahead*
1943　*Dr. Gillespie's Criminal
　　　　Case
　　　They Came to Blow Up
　　　　America*
1944　*Block Busters*
1951　*Only the Valiant*
1955　Seven Cities of Gold
1956　*Serenade*

Disfiguration
1920　*Hidden Charms*
1928　The Broken Mask
1941　The Face Behind the Mask

Disguise
1914　Dan
　　　*The Great Diamond
　　　　Robbery*
1915　*Captain Courtesy*
1918　*Mystic Faces*
1919　*Auction of Souls*
1920　The Mark of Zorro
　　　On with the Dance
1921　Black Roses
1924　His Darker Self
　　　In High Gear
　　　The Lightning Rider
1925　Scarlet Saint
1927　The Overland Stage
1928　The Cavalier
1931　*The Avenger*
　　　Kismet
1932　*Hypnotized
　　　Mazel Tov
　　　White Eagle*
1933　*The California Trail
　　　Circle Canyon
　　　Thundering Herd*
1934　*The Cactus Kid
　　　The Lone Defender*
1935　*Angelina o el honor de un
　　　　brigadier*
　　　Charlie Chan in Paris
　　　*Chinatown Squad
　　　Cowboy Holiday
　　　Cyclone of the Saddle
　　　Rosa de Francia
　　　Te quiero con locura*
1936　Charlie Chan at the Circus
　　　Hair-Trigger Casey
　　　The Last of the Mohicans
　　　Rose of the Rancho
1937　The Californian
　　　Charlie Chan at the Opera

　　　Law and Lead
　　　Prairie Thunder
1938　Two Gun Man from Harlem
1939　*Charlie Chan at Treasure
　　　　Island
　　　Heaven with a Barbed Wire
　　　　Fence*
1940　*Music in My Heart*
　　　Santa Fe Trail
1941　*Dead Men Tell
　　　Prairie Pioneers*
1942　Mexican Spitfire at Sea
　　　Professor Creeps
1945　*The Jade Mask*
1946　Sheriff of Redwood Valley
　　　Sun Valley Cyclone
1946?　*House-Rent Party*
1947　*Buck Privates Come Home
　　　Riding the California Trail*
1947?　Return of Mandy's Husband
1949　*Border Incident
　　　The Gay Amigo*
　　　Laramie
1950　*Raiders of Tomahawk
　　　　Creek*
1951　Cuban Fireball
　　　Hurricane Island
1952　*Buffalo Bill in Tomahawk
　　　　Territory
　　　Trail of the Arrow*
1953　*The Man from the Alamo*
1956　*Quincannon, Frontier
　　　　Scout*
1959　The Oregon Trail

Dishwashing
1928　*Eleven P.M.*
1932　*The Heart of New York*
1937　*That I May Live*
1956　*Crowded Paradise*

Disillusionment
1917　The Red Woman
1931　*Personal Maid*
1932　Hollywood, ciudad de
　　　　ensueño
　　　Symphony of Six Million
1940　Behind the News
1941　*Accent on Love
　　　Belle Starr*
　　　The Face Behind the Mask
1944　*Buffalo Bill
1945　Nob Hill*
　　　A Tree Grows in Brooklyn
1946　Three Wise Fools
1947　*The Burning Cross*
1948　Key Largo
1950　*The Lawless*
1951　*The Harlem Globetrotters*
1952　High Noon
1954　Go Man Go
1955　Smoke Signal
1957　Run of the Arrow
1958　*The Young Lions*

Disinheritance
1914　*The Good-for-Nothing*
1915　The Spender
1917　The Adventures of Carol
　　　A Jewel in Pawn
1918　*Real Folks*
1920　Uncharted Channels
1924　Two Shall Be Born
1944　*Sheriff of Las Vegas*

Dismissal (Employment)
1913　*Traffic in Souls*
1915　*Chimmie Fadden*
1918　*The City of Tears
　　　Thirty a Week
　　　Who Is to Blame?*
1919　*The Delicious Little Devil
　　　Love and the Law
　　　The Volcano*
1923　Flames of Wrath
1926　*The Passaic Textile Strike*
1928　*Eleven P.M.
　　　The Wages of Sin*
1931　*Mr. Lemon of Orange*
1932　*Cuore d'emigrante
　　　Harlem Is Heaven
　　　Men Are Such Fools
　　　Senza mamma
　　　　e'nnamurato*
1933　*Olsen's Big Moment
　　　The Wandering Jew*
1934　*Chloe: Love Is Calling You
　　　Limehouse Blues*

1935 *Piernas de seda*
1938 *Little Miss Roughneck*
    Passport Husband
    The Renegade Ranger
    Spirit of Youth
1939 *Forged Passport*
    Mothers of Today
1939? *A Chinese Gains a Fortune*
    in America
1940 *The Jewish Melody*
    Son of Ingagi
1941 *Sunday Sinners*
    Thunder Over the Prairie
1942 *Wings for the Eagle*
1943 *His Butler's Sister*
    Stormy Weather
1944 *Lady, Let's Dance!*
1946 *Mantan Messes Up*
1947 *Body and Soul*
    Dark Delusion
    Humoresque
    Thunder Mountain
    Wild Horse Mesa
1948 *The Miracle of the Bells*
    Up in Central Park
1949 *Anna Lucasta*
    The Girl from Jones Beach
    Masked Raiders
1950 *So Young, So Bad*
1951 *The Harlem Globetrotters*
    The House on Telegraph
    Hill
1953 *Tonight We Sing*
1958 *Seven Hills of Rome*

Dissipation
1916 *Gold and the Woman*
    Her Debt of Honor
1919 *A Man's Duty*
1931 *Del infierno al cielo*
    Resurrección
    Young Sinners
1938 *Spirit of Youth*
1947 *Little Mister Jim*
1950 *The Cariboo Trail*
1959 *Al Capone*

Distillers
1915 *The Nigger*
1940 Mexican Spitfire Out West

District attorneys
1916 Poor Little Peppina
1917 *His Sweetheart*
    Queen X
1918 *The Reckoning Day*
1919 The Courageous Coward
    A Fighting Colleen
1921 The Secret Sorrow
1923 Flames of Wrath
    A Shot in the Night
1925 Tearing Through
1928 Wheel of Chance
1930 *El cuerpo del delito*
    Sombras de gloria
1931 *La incorregible*
    El proceso de Mary Dugan
    Smart Money
1932 *Harlem Is Heaven*
    Unashamed
1934 *The Cat's-Paw*
1936 Human Cargo
    It Had to Happen
1937 *Big City*
    Dark Manhattan
    Man of the People
    Music for Madame
    Nation Aflame
1938 *Mis dos amores*
1939 *King of Chinatown*
1940 *Behind the News*
    Escape to Glory
    Her Second Mother
1942 The Vanishing Virginian
1948 *Shanghai Chest*
1949 *Jigsaw*
    Knock on Any Door
1955 *Headline Hunters*
    Trial
1957 *The Brothers Rico*
1958 *Touch of Evil*
1960 Oklahoma Territory

Ditch diggers
1915 *The Alien*
1941 *Thunder Over the Prairie*

Divers and diving
1930 El dios del mar
1936 Down to the Sea
1937 The Devil's Playground
1947 *Easy Come, Easy Go*
1948 16 Fathoms Deep
1949 *Harbor of Missing Men*
    Lookout Sister
1951 Queen for a Day
1953 Beneath the 12-Mile Reef

Divorce
1914 Where the Trail Divides
1915 *Children of the Ghetto*
1916 *Civilization's Child*
1917 *The Squaw Man's Son*
    Unconquered
1918 *Tony America*
    Woman and the Law
1919 As a Man Thinks
1921 A Divorce of Convenience
    The Swamp
1922 Saturday Night
    Solomon in Society
1928 George Washington Cohen
1931 *Un caballero de frac*
    Los calaveras
    Carne de cabaret
    Soyons gais
    Women Love Once
1932 *Une heure près de toi*
    Uncle Moses
1933 *Yo, tú y ella*
1934 *Lazy River*
1934? *Harlem After Midnight*
1935 Señora casada necesita
    marido
1936 *Contra la corriente*
    It Had to Happen
    Yiddle with His Fiddle
1938 My Lucky Star
1939 *Charlie Chan in Honolulu*
    Charlie Chan in Reno
    Man of Conquest
1940 *Mexican Spitfire*
    Mexican Spitfire Out West
1941 *Accent on Love*
    Come Live with Me
    The Mexican Spitfire's Baby
1942 *We Were Dancing*
1943 Three Hearts for Julia
1944 *Mr. Skeffington*
1945 *Club Havana*
    The Dolly Sisters
1947 *Humoresque*
1948 *Call Northside 777*
1950 *God, Man and Devil*
    Jolson Sings Again
1953 *The Joe Louis Story*
1957 *Beau James*
1958 Home Before Dark

Dock workers
1944 *Waterfront*
1957 Edge of the City

Docks
1939 *Waterfront*
1941 *This Woman Is Mine*
1945 *The Scarlet Clue*
1948 *Docks of New Orleans*
1955 *A Man Called Peter*

Doctors
    use **Physicians**

Dodge City (KS)
1950 *Winchester '73*

Dog-catchers
1921 One Man in a Million
1930 Anybody's War

Dogs
1914 *An Odyssey of the North*
    Uncle Tom's Cabin
1918 *Mystic Faces*
1921 One Man in a Million
1922 Peacock Alley
1923 Breaking into Society
    Ruggles of Red Gap
1924 The Broken Law
1925 The Beautiful City
    Justice of the Far North
1927 Aflame in the Sky
    Ham and Eggs at the Front
1928 *Eleven P.M.*
    Ramona
1930 Anybody's War
    The Break Up
    On the Border

1931 Los calaveras
    The Great Meadow
    Pardon Us
1932 *Igloo*
    Me and My Gal
1933 *L'amour guide*
    Broken Dreams
    Ever in My Heart
    Olsen's Big Moment
1934 *Un capitán de cosacos*
    Granaderos del amor
    The Lone Defender
1935 *Angelina o el honor de un*
    brigadier
    Captured in Chinatown
    Melody Trail
    Tango Bar
1936 *After the Thin Man*
    General Spanky
    Paddy O'Day
    Tundra
1937 *Law and Lead*
    Slave Ship
1938 *The Beloved Brat*
    City Streets
1940 *Girl from God's Country*
1941 *Mutiny in the Arctic*
    New York Town
1942 *Rio Rita*
    Tortilla Flat
1943 *Action in the North*
    Atlantic
    Air Force
1944 *Hi, Beautiful*
    Since You Went Away
    The Sullivans
1945 *Nob Hill*
    Rhapsody in Blue
1946 *The Face of Marble*
    Song of the South
    Wild Beauty
1947 *Little Mister Jim*
    The Return of Rin Tin Tin
1948 *Gun Smugglers*
    Moonrise
    Rocky
1949 *Arctic Fury*
    The Valiant Hombre
1950 *The Big Hangover*
    Mystery Submarine
    Rocky Mountain
    Sunset in the West
1951 *Oh! Susanna*
    The Well
1952 *My Man and I*
    Red Snow
    Wagons West
1953 *The Stars Are Singing*
1954 *Hondo*
1955 *A Man Called Peter*
1958 *The Defiant Ones*
    Wild Is the Wind
1960 *For the Love of Mike*

Dogs, War use of
1944 My Pal Wolf
1948 *Night Wind*
    Shep Comes Home

Dogsledding
1912 *Atop of the World in*
    Motion
1934 *Eskimo*
1940 *Girl from God's Country*
    Taku
1949 *Arctic Manhunt*
    Rose of the Yukon
1952 *Arctic Flight*
1960 *Ice Palace*

Dolls
1918? *Rosemary Climbs the*
    Heights
1944 *Lake Placid Serenade*

Jenny Dolly
1945 The Dolly Sisters

Rosie Dolly
    The Dolly Sisters

Domesticity
1948 *Rocky*

Donkeys
1942 *Rio Rita*

Doormen
1953 *Tonight We Sing*

Walter Dornberger
1960 *I Aim at the Stars: the*
    Wernher von Braun Story

Doubles
1914 *Hearts United*
1916 The King's Game
    A Man of Sorrow
    The Scarlet Oath
    The Sign of the Poppy
1925 Irish Luck
1931 Mr. Lemon of Orange
1934 Charlie Chan's Courage
1935 *L'homme des Folies Bergère*
1941 Romance of the Rio Grande
1943 *Redhead from Manhattan*
1946 *Rendezvous 24*

Doughnuts
1936 *Charlie Chan at the Circus*
1943 *The Gang's All Here*

Stephen Douglas
1930 *Abraham Lincoln*

Frederick Douglass
1926? The House on Cedar Hill

Dowagers
1913? *The Lure of New York*
1957 *The Guns of Fort Petticoat*

Dowry
1917 *The War of the Tongs*
1927 Pleasure Before Business
1932 *The Son-Daughter*
1933 *King of the Wild Horses*
1952 *The Quiet Man*
1953 *Dream Wife*

Draft dodgers
    use **Military service,**
      Compulsory

Drama
    use **Plays**

Dreams
1915 The Grandee's Ring
1916 Peck O' Pickles
1917 Rosie O'Grady
1918 The Ordeal of Rosetta
    Wanted, a Mother
    Wild Women
1919 Mandarin's Gold
1920 The Dark Mirror
    Within Our Gates
1921 Bits of Life
    When the Clock Struck Nine
1922 *The Dungeon*
1925 Body and Soul
1926 Meet the Prince
1928 Eleven P.M.
    Vamping Venus
1930 *Charros, gauchos y*
    manolas
    Sei tu l'amore
·1931 *Delicious*
    Noche de duendes
1932 Joseph in the Land of Egypt
    Parigi affascina; ovvero,
    Malavita
    Uncle Moses
1933 *The Wandering Jew*
1934 *The Rabbi's Power*
1935 *Bar-Mitzvah*
1936 *Yiddle with His Fiddle*
1940? Mr. Washington Goes to
    Town
1942 Professor Creeps
1947 *Bowery Buckaroos*
    It Had To Be You
    King of the Bandits
1949 Lookout Sister
1951 *Native Son*

Dred Scott Decision, 1857
1928 Uncle Tom's Cabin

Dresden (Germany)
1921 *No Woman Knows*

Dressmakers
1930 *Sei tu l'amore*
1931 *Women Love Once*
1938 *The Power of Life*
    The Singing Blacksmith
1958 *Home Before Dark*
    Seven Hills of Rome

Drifters
    use **Hoboes;**
      Tramps;
      Vagabonds

Droughts
1927　White Gold
1934　Our Daily Bread
1940　Prairie Schooners
1941　Thunder Over the Prairie
1949　Tale of the Navajos
1952?　Call of the Navajo

Drowning
1914　In the Land of the Head
　　　　Hunters
1916　A Man of Sorrow
1918　A Daughter of the Old
　　　　South
1919　A Heart in Pawn
　　　　The Scar
1920　The Dark Mirror
1932　A Daughter of Her People
1936　Down to the Sea
1937　Slave Ship
　　　　Souls at Sea
1939　Daughters Courageous
　　　　Mr. Moto's Last Warning
1944　Dark Waters
1945　Of One Blood
1946　Singin' in the Corn
1948　16 Fathoms Deep
1949　Portrait of Jennie
1951　The Raging Tide
1953　Ride, Vaquero!
　　　　Thunder Bay
1957　Raintree County
1960　The Last Voyage

Drudges
1917　The Plow Woman
　　　　Sold at Auction
1918　The Wine Girl
1919　Erstwhile Susan
1930　The Grand Parade
1939　Mamele

Drug addicts
1915　The Secret Sin
1916　Hop, the Devil's Brew
　　　　The Sign of the Poppy
1917　Queen X
　　　　The Squaw Man's Son
1920　Lifting Shadows
　　　　Our Christianity and
　　　　Nobody's Child
1920?　The Scarlet Dragon
1921　A Modern Cain
1925　Tearing Through
1931　Del infierno al cielo
1932　The Hatchet Man
1934?　Harlem After Midnight
1959　Porgy and Bess
1960　The Pusher

Drug dealers
1917　Queen X
1919　The Tong Man
1958　Touch of Evil
1959　Porgy and Bess
1960　The Pusher
　　　　This Rebel Breed

Drugging
1913　The Inside of the White
　　　　Slave Traffic
1919　The Little Diplomat
1922　The Dungeon
1926　The Flying Ace
1930　La fuerza del querer
1932　Border Devils
1934　Chloe: Love Is Calling You
1935　Charlie Chan in Egypt
1937　Underworld
1939　Keep Punching
1940　Elsa Maxwell's Public Deb
　　　　No. 1
　　　　Midnight Shadow
1941　Charlie Chan in Rio
1945　The House on 92nd St.
1947　Boy! What a Girl!
1948　Sleep, My Love
1956　The Burning Hills
1959　Night of the Quarter Moon

Drugs
1915　The Sable Lorcha
　　　　The Secret Sin
1920　Li Ting Lang
1921　A Modern Cain
1922　The Schemers
1923　Purple Dawn
1929　Welcome Danger
1931　Del infierno al cielo

1936　The Traitor
1940　Girl from God's Country
1949　Home of the Brave
1958　Touch of Evil
1960　Key Witness

Drugstores
1944　Chip Off the Old Block
1949　Answer for Anne
1951　Native Son
1958　The Young Lions
1960　The Dark at the Top of the
　　　　Stairs

Drunk driving
1939　Kol Nidre

Drunkenness
1914　The Nightingale
　　　　The Redemption of David
　　　　Corson
　　　　The Straight Road
1915　Children of the Ghetto
　　　　A Texas Steer
　　　　A Yankee from the West
1916　Peck O' Pickles
　　　　The Pretenders
1918　Doing Their Bit
　　　　The Man Above the Law
　　　　Marked Cards
　　　　Toys of Fate
　　　　Wild Women
1919　His Parisian Wife
　　　　A Man's Duty
　　　　Who Will Marry Me?
1920　Lifting Shadows
　　　　A Son of Satan
1924　The Strong Man
1926　The Strong Man
　　　　Sweet Daddies
1927　For the Love of Mike
1928　The Crash
　　　　Uncle Tom's Cabin
1929　Chinatown Nights
1930　Anna Christie
　　　　Charros, gauchos y
　　　　manolas
　　　　King of Jazz
　　　　Take the Heir
1931　El código penal
　　　　Gentleman's Fate
　　　　Personal Maid
　　　　Resurrección
　　　　The Squaw Man
　　　　Street Scene
　　　　Young Sinners
1932　L'athlète incomplet
　　　　Le bluffeur
　　　　El caballero de la noche
　　　　Call Her Savage
　　　　Le cas du docteur Brenner
　　　　Flesh
　　　　The Forty-Niners
　　　　The Golden West
　　　　Harlem Is Heaven
　　　　Huddle
　　　　O festino o la legge
1933　L'amour guide
　　　　The Cohens and Kellys in
　　　　Trouble
　　　　Diplomaniacs
　　　　It's Great to Be Alive
　　　　A Lady's Profession
　　　　La melodía prohibida
　　　　No dejes la puerta abierta
1933?　Scandal
1934　Behold My Wife!
　　　　The Cactus Kid
　　　　Un capitán de cosacos
　　　　The Cat's-Paw
　　　　Coming Out Party
　　　　Eskimo
　　　　Laughing Boy
　　　　She Was a Lady
　　　　La veuve joyeuse
　　　　What a Mother-in-Law!
1935　His Family Tree
　　　　The Irish in Us
　　　　Lem Hawkins' Confession
　　　　Ruggles of Red Gap
　　　　The Yiddish King Lear
1936　Custer's Last Stand
　　　　Down to the Sea
　　　　Ellis Island
　　　　Laughing Irish Eyes
　　　　Mad Holiday
　　　　Silly Billies
1937　Black Legion
　　　　Natalka Poltavka

　　　　Nation Aflame
　　　　Think Fast, Mr. Moto
1938　Josette
　　　　Road Demon
　　　　The Singing Blacksmith
　　　　Swing!
　　　　The Texans
　　　　Two Sisters
1939　The Cisco Kid and the Lady
　　　　Drums Along the Mohawk
　　　　Gone With the Wind
　　　　Mamele
　　　　El otro soy yo
　　　　Verbena trágica
　　　　Waterfront
　　　　Winner Take All
1940　Am I Guilty?
　　　　Behind the News
　　　　The Jewish Melody
　　　　Lucky Cisco Kid
　　　　Mexican Spitfire Out West
　　　　Mystery in Swing
　　　　Northwest Passage (Book
　　　　I—Rogers' Rangers)
　　　　The Way of All Flesh
1941　Adam Had Four Sons
　　　　Charlie Chan in Rio
　　　　Louisiana Purchase
　　　　New York Town
　　　　Virginia
　　　　Western Union
1942　Gentleman Jim
　　　　Holiday Inn
　　　　Juke Girl
　　　　North to the Klondike
　　　　Twin Beds
　　　　Woman of the Year
1943　The Girl from Monterrey
　　　　Jack London
　　　　Let's Have Fun
　　　　The Meanest Man in the
　　　　World
　　　　Tahiti Honey
　　　　Three Hearts for Julia
1945　The Great John L.
　　　　Nob Hill
　　　　The Valley of Decision
1946　Dirty Gertie from Harlem,
　　　　U.S.A.
　　　　The Gentleman Misbehaves
　　　　Notorious
　　　　The Sailor Takes a Wife
　　　　Three Wise Fools
　　　　Till the End of Time
　　　　Without Reservations
1947　The Burning Cross
　　　　Carnegie Hall
　　　　The Farmer's Daughter
　　　　The Foxes of Harrow
　　　　Mantan Runs for Mayor
　　　　Marshal of Cripple Creek
　　　　New Orleans
　　　　Ride the Pink Horse
1948　The Lady from Shanghai
　　　　The Time of Your Life
　　　　Up in Central Park
1949　Illegal Entry
　　　　Tulsa
　　　　The Valiant Hombre
1949?　The Joint Is Jumpin'
1950　The Daughter of Rosie
　　　　O'Grady
　　　　Emergency Wedding
　　　　Give Us This Day
　　　　Mystery Street
　　　　No Way Out
　　　　The Palomino
　　　　Right Cross
　　　　The Traveling Saleswoman
　　　　Young Man with a Horn
1950?　Three Daughters
1951　Across the Wide Missouri
　　　　Native Son
　　　　Only the Valiant
　　　　The Raging Tide
　　　　A Streetcar Named Desire
1952　The Quiet Man
1953　Arrowhead
　　　　Dream Wife
　　　　The Man from the Alamo
　　　　The Member of the
　　　　Wedding
　　　　Old Overland Trail
　　　　Ride, Vaquero!

1954　Battle of Rogue River
　　　　Massacre Canyon
　　　　Siege at Red River
1955　Headline Hunters
　　　　Santa Fe Passage
　　　　Violent Saturday
1956　Davy Crockett and the
　　　　River Pirates
　　　　Giant
　　　　The Last Frontier
　　　　The Last Hunt
　　　　Man from Del Rio
　　　　Pillars of the Sky
　　　　Quincannon, Frontier
　　　　Scout
1957　Joe Dakota
　　　　Man in the Shadow
1958　Flaming Frontier
　　　　Machete
　　　　Ride a Crooked Trail
　　　　Wild Is the Wind
1959　The Hanging Tree
　　　　The Sheriff of Fractured
　　　　Jaw
　　　　The Wonderful Country
1960　All the Young Men
　　　　The Dark at the Top of the
　　　　Stairs
　　　　Studs Lonigan

Dry cleaning
1937　Life Begins in College
1950　Chinatown at Midnight

Dry Tortugas (FL)
1936　The Prisoner of Shark Island

Dublin (Ireland)
1920　Hidden Charms
1925　Irish Luck
1936　Laughing Irish Eyes
1959　Shake Hands with the Devil

Dubuque (IA)
1954　Go Man Go

Bluford "Blue" Duck
1941　Belle Starr

Dude ranches
1934　She Was a Lady
1943　Mexican Spitfire's Blessed
　　　　Event
　　　　Riding High
1947?　Swanee Showboat
1948　The Golden Eye
　　　　The Golden Eye
　　　　Singin' Spurs

Dudes
1917　The Tenderfoot

Duels
1915　The Clemenceau Case
1917　The Little Chevalier
　　　　The Tenderfoot
1919　The Scar
　　　　The Sneak
1920　White Youth
1924　California in '49
1925　Scarlet Saint
1927　The Gay Defender
1931　Le petit café
　　　　El príncipe gondolero
1932　Parigi affascina; ovvero,
　　　　Malavita
1933　El rey de los gitanos
1935　Angelina o el honor de un
　　　　brigadier
1936　Custer's Last Stand
　　　　La última cita
1937　The Californian
1938　The Toy Wife
1941　The Mexican Spitfire's Baby
1943　The Outlaw
1946　Don Ricardo Returns
1947　The Foxes of Harrow
　　　　King of the Bandits
1948　The Paleface
1949　Ride, Ryder, Ride!
1950　Rock Island Trail
1951　The Mark of the Renegade
1952　California Conquest
　　　　The Iron Mistress
1953　Sangaree
1955　Duel on the Mississippi
　　　　Shotgun
1959　Gunmen from Laredo

Father Francis Duffy
1940　The Fighting 69th

Dumb-waiters
1939 *Verbena trágica*
Dungeons
1922 The Dungeon
1932 *Yiskor*
Father Peter J. Dunne
1948 Fighting Father Dunne
Duplicity
1915 *The Girl I Left Behind Me*
1916 *The Daughter of the Don*
    Gold and the Woman
    Gretchen, the Greenhorn
    The Honorable Friend
    Witchcraft
1917 The Call of Her People
    Hashimura Togo
    The Primitive Call
1919 *As a Man Thinks*
    Hearts of Men
    Who Will Marry Me?
1920 *The Paliser Case*
1932 *Le cas du docteur Brenner*
    The Forty-Niners
    Wild Horse Mesa
1933 Man from Monterey
1934 *Nada más que una mujer*
    The Prescott Kid
    Wheels of Destiny
1936 *The Bold Caballero*
    Custer's Last Stand
    Hair-Trigger Casey
    Laughing Irish Eyes
    Pinto Rustlers
    Ride, Ranger, Ride
    Song of the Gringo
1937 Prairie Thunder
    Underworld
1938 *Breaking the Ice*
1939 The Cisco Kid and the Lady
    Forged Passport
1940 Lucky Cisco Kid
    Music in My Heart
    Young Buffalo Bill
1941 The Pioneers
    Ride on Vaquero
    Saddlemates
1942 Lawless Plainsmen
    Tales of Manhattan
    Valley of the Sun
1943 Land of Hunted Men
1944 *Marshal of Reno*
    The San Antonio Kid
    Tucson Raiders
    Vigilantes of Dodge City
1945 Colorado Pioneers
1946 Don Ricardo Returns
    Singin' in the Corn
1947 The Adventures of Don
    Coyote
    Buffalo Bill Rides Again
    The Farmer's Daughter
    The Last Round-Up
    Riding the California Trail
    Riding the California Trail
    Spoilers of the North
1948 *Fort Apache*
    Indian Agent
    The Paleface
1949 Lust for Gold
1950 *The Big Hangover*
1951 *Tomahawk*
1952 *The Battle at Apache Pass*
1953 *Seminole*
1954 *Arrow in the Dust*
    Battle of Rogue River
    The Yellow Tomahawk
1955 *Duel on the Mississippi*
    The Indian Fighter
    Trial
1956 Death of a Scoundrel
1957 *Dragoon Wells Massacre*
    Naked in the Sun
1958 The Badlanders
    Fort Bowie
    Ride a Crooked Trail
1959 Night of the Quarter Moon
Dust storms
1940 Three Faces West
1958 *Apache Territory*
Dutch
1914 When Broadway Was a Trail
1924 So Big
1949 *C-Man*

Dutch Americans
1916 Gretchen, the Greenhorn
    Hulda from Holland
1918? Rosemary Climbs the
    Heights
1920 The Secret Gift
1932 *So Big*
1938 The Buccaneer
1942 Seven Sweethearts
1944 *Knickerbocker Holiday*
1945 *Where Do We Go From
    Here?*
1953 So Big
Duty
1934 *La veuve joyeuse*
1936 The Last of the Mohicans
1943 *Bataan*
1944 *My Pal Wolf*
1952 *High Noon*
1955 *Smoke Signal*
1958 *The Young Lions*
1960 *Sergeant Rutledge*
Dwarfs
1927 Old San Francisco
1936 *Charlie Chan at the Circus*
1942 *Wings for the Eagle*
1946 *Saratoga Trunk*
    Three Wise Fools
1948 *Jiggs and Maggie in Court*
1950 *Bandit Queen*
Dwellings—Remodeling
1943 *What's Buzzin' Cousin?*
Dynamite
1915 *The Danger Signal*
    The Immigrant
1932 *Border Devils*
1936 *Desert Gold*
1939 *Drifting Westward*
1940 *Viva Cisco Kid*
1943 *Redhead from Manhattan*
1948 *The Paleface*
1949 *Satan's Cradle*
    We Were Strangers
1950 *A Ticket to Tomahawk*
1953 *Thunder Bay*
1954 *Massacre Canyon*
1955 *Apache Ambush*
1956 *The Lone Ranger*
1958 *Touch of Evil*
Eagles
1949 *Tale of the Navajos*
Wyatt Earp
1950 *Winchester '73*
Ears
1943 *Good Luck, Mr. Yates*
Earthquakes
1915 *The Pageant of San
    Francisco*
1918 *The Ordeal of Rosetta*
1945 *Samurai*
1949 *Lust for Gold*
1950 *Border Treasure*
1953 *Dream Wife*
East Indians
1916 The Love Girl
    The Romantic Journey
1932 Thirteen Women
1935 Rescue Squad
East Indies
1931 La carta
Easter
1915 *The Melting Pot*
1942 *Holiday Inn*
Easterners
1931 *Oklahoma Jim*
1941 *Under Fiesta Stars*
1943 *In Old Oklahoma*
1944 *Buffalo Bill*
1946 *Wild Beauty*
1948 *The Dude Goes West*
1955 *Fort Yuma*
1957 *Tomahawk Trail*
Eavesdropping
1927 *With Sitting Bull at the
    Spirit Lake Massacre*
1930 *Una cana al aire*
194- *Mistaken Identity*
1941 *The Gang's All Here*
1944 *Chip Off the Old Block*
1949 *Daughter of the West*
    The Fighting Kentuckian
    The Gay Amigo
    Jigsaw

    Massacre River
    The Red Menace
    Satan's Cradle
    The Sky Dragon
1952 *Brave Warrior*
1953 *The Great Sioux Uprising*
1960 *Man on a String*
Eavesdropping (Electronic)
    use **Surveillance devices;
    Wire-tapping**
Eccentrics
1935 A Night at the Ritz
1940 Music in My Heart
1942 *Castle in the Desert*
1946 *Cuban Pete*
1954 *Hell's Half Acre*
William Eckstein
1914? A Boy and the Law
Eclipses, Solar
1938 *Zamboanga*
Economics
1934 *La veuve joyeuse*
The Ed Sullivan Show (Television
    program)
1955 *Marty*
Eden
1936 *The Green Pastures*
Thomas Alva Edison
1925 Lights of Old Broadway
1941 *Land of Liberty*
Editors
1915 *How Molly Malone Made
    Good*
1917 *I Will Repay*
    The Wild Girl
1918 *The Ranger*
1931 *Cimarron*
1932 *The Black King*
    The Secrets of Wu Sin
1935 *Captured in Chinatown*
1936 *Human Cargo*
1937 *Charlie Chan on Broadway*
    One Mile from Heaven
194- *Mistaken Identity*
1940 *Behind the News*
    Mystery in Swing
1945 *Our Vines Have Tender
    Grapes*
1946 *Three Wise Fools*
1948 *Call Northside 777*
    Gentleman's Agreement
    Indian Agent
    The Luck of the Irish
    Tap Roots
1949 *Answer for Anne*
    The Dalton Gang
    The Gay Amigo
    Ride, Ryder, Ride!
1952 *It's a Big Country: An
    American Anthology*
1955 Headline Hunters
1959 *The Last Angry Man*
1960 *Cimarron*
    Oklahoma Territory
Education
1916 *The Twin Triangle*
1919 Deliverance
1929 East Side Sadie
1938 *Birthright*
    Life Goes On
1939 *Moon over Harlem*
1940 George Washington Carver
1941 *Min Jok Jay Hung Sing*
1943 *Hitler's Children*
1945 *A Tree Grows in Brooklyn*
1947 *The Farmer's Daughter*
    Untamed Fury
1957 *All Mine to Give*
    Segregation and the South
**Edward VII, King of England,
    1841-1910**
1945 *The Great John L.*
Effeminacy
1924 North of Nevada
Egotists
1919 *The Homesteader*
1931 Little Caesar
1934 The Great Flirtation
1942 Gentleman Jim
1951 The Harlem Globetrotters

Egypt
1921 *The Syrian Immigrant*
1931 *Charlie Chan Carries On*
1935 Charlie Chan in Egypt
Egypt—History
1931 *The Voice of Israel*
1932 *Joseph in the Land of Egypt*
1933 *The Wandering Jew*
Egyptians
    The Eternal Jew
1945 The Mummy's Curse
Dwight David Eisenhower
1953 *The Stars Are Singing*
1955 *The Long Gray Line*
El Paso (TX)
1952 *The Fighter*
Elections
1915 *Cohen's Luck*
    The Nigger
1917 My Fighting Gentleman
1919 *Erstwhile Susan*
1922 The Dungeon
1926? *Ten Nights in a Barroom*
1930 Abraham Lincoln
1931 *El código penal*
1937 *Man of the People*
    Nation Aflame
1938 *In Old Chicago*
1939 *Man of Conquest*
1940 *Three Cheers for the Irish*
    The Tragedy of
    Carpatho-Ukraine
1941 *Road Agent*
1942 *The Vanishing Virginian*
1945 *Nob Hill*
    Sunbonnet Sue
1947 The Farmer's Daughter
1948 *Up in Central Park*
1950 Sunset in the West
1953 The Sun Shines Bright
1958 *The Last Hurrah*
Electric chair
1939 *Mothers of Today*
1948 *Miracle in Harlem*
Electricians
1925 The Manicure Girl
Electricity
1924 Welcome Stranger
1925 Lights of Old Broadway
1948 *Singin' Spurs*
Electrocardiography
1959 *The Last Angry Man*
Electrocution
1940 *Charlie Chan at the Wax
    Museum*
1944 *Charlie Chan in the Secret
    Service*
1946 *The Face of Marble*
Elephants
1932 *Hypnotized*
1942 *Mexican Spitfire's Elephant*
1945 *Our Vines Have Tender
    Grapes*
1953 *Tonight We Sing*
Elevator operators
1941 You're Out of Luck
1950 *No Way Out*
Elevators
1916 *Lone Star*
1935 *Rescue Squad*
1942 *Seven Sweethearts*
1945 *The Scarlet Clue*
1946 *The Sailor Takes a Wife*
1951 *Native Son*
Elks Club
1921 As the World Rolls On
Ellis Island (New York City)
    use **New York City—Ellis
    Island**
Elopement
1914 *Life's Shop Window*
    *The Redemption of David
    Corson*
1916 *Alien Souls*
    Silks and Satins
1917 *A Night in New Arabia*
1918 *Sandy*
1919 *Hearts of Men*
    The Sleeping Lion
1920 *For the Soul of Rafael*
    White Youth
1929 Wolf Song

1930 Whoopee
1931 *Buster se marie*
Echec au roi
The Guilty Generation
La ley del harem
Su noche de bodas
1933 *A Lady's Profession*
1934 *Coming Out Party*
1935 Angelina o el honor de un
brigadier
The Little Colonel
Naughty Marietta
Rescue Squad
1937 *Shadows of the Orient*
1939 *Daughters Courageous*
Kol Nidre
Mothers of Today
1941 Hurry, Charlie, Hurry
Murder on Lenox Avenue
1942 We Were Dancing
1943 *Wintertime*
1947 *My Wild Irish Rose*
1948 *Tap Roots*
1949 *Massacre River*
1952 The Fabulous Senorita
1953 *Thunder Bay*
1960 *Ice Palace*

Emancipation Proclamation
1930 Abraham Lincoln

Embassies
1934 *La veuve joyeuse*

Embezzlement
1914 The Squaw Man
1915 The Cheat
1916 *At Piney Ridge*
1918 *The Squaw Man*
1923 Backbone
1928 Riley the Cop
1931 The Squaw Man
1933 *The Emperor Jones*
1936 *West of Nevada*
1938 *The Power of Life*
1939 El trovador de la radio
1940 *Her Second Mother*
1944 *Mr. Skeffington*
Sonora Stagecoach
Tucson Raiders
1945 The Cisco Kid Returns
1946 *Beware*
Canyon Passage
1948 *Singin' Spurs*
1949 Stagecoach Kid
1952 The Half-Breed
1955 *Good Morning, Miss Dove*
*The View from Pompey's
Head*
1956 Death of a Scoundrel

Daniel Decatur Emmett
1943 Dixie

Emperors
1933 The Emperor Jones

**Empire State Building (New York
City)**
1939 *Heaven with a Barbed Wire
Fence*

Employer-employee relations
1914 The Jungle
1916 Light at Dusk
1917 The Secret of Eve
1918 A Little Sister of Everybody
Love's Law
Tony America
1920 *The Face at Your Window*
The Great Shadow
Uncharted Channels
1921 *The Call of His People*
1926 The Passaic Textile Strike
1931 Quand on est belle
1932 *Harlem Is Heaven*
Ljubav i strast
Uncle Moses
1934 *Chloe: Love Is Calling You*
1939 *Let Freedom Ring*
Motel the Operator
Winner Take All
1941 *Golden Gate Girl*
Ice-Capades
Min Jok Jay Hung Sing
1943 *His Butler's Sister*
1944 *An American Romance*
Hi, Beautiful
1946 *The Sailor Takes a Wife*
1949 *Prejudice*
Shamrock Hill

1950 The Big Hangover
1950? *Three Daughters*
1951 Cuban Fireball
1959 *The Last Angry Man*

Employment
1920 In the Depths of Our Hearts
1936 *Contra la corriente*
1937 We Work Again
1950 *The Baron of Arizona*
1957 Burden of Truth

Employment agencies
1956 *Crowded Paradise*

Encino (CA)
1950 *Jolson Sings Again*

Engagements
1914 *In the Days of the
Thundering Herd*
1916 *The Honorable Friend*
1918 Marked Cards
The Reckoning Day
1919 Evangeline
The Lord Loves the Irish
The She Wolf
A Yankee Princess
1920 *Within Our Gates*
1924 Birthright
Smiling Hate
1929 *Sombras habaneras*
1930 Una cana al aire
Cuando el amor ríe
1931 *The Black Camel*
Così è la vita
Delicious
Drácula
Gentleman's Fate
Le père célibataire
Personal Maid
Three Who Loved
Young Sinners
1932 *El caballero de la noche*
Hombres en mi vida
The Secrets of Wu Sin
Senza mamma e'nnamurato
The Son-Daughter
Soñadores de la gloria
Wild Horse Mesa
1933 *Espérame*
It's Great to Be Alive
Let's Fall in Love
Olsen's Big Moment
El rey de los gitanos
Thundering Herd
1934 *La buenaventura*
Charlie Chan in London
Las fronteras del amor
Granaderos del amor
Imitation of Life
The Rabbi's Power
1935 *Charlie Chan in Paris*
Harmony Lane
His Family Tree
Te quiero con locura
1936 *El crimen de media noche*
Dangerous Intrigue
Dimples
Ellis Island
For the Service
Robin Hood of El Dorado
Rose of the Rancho
1937 *Green Fields*
Natalka Poltavka
Waikiki Wedding
1938 *Gateway*
Marusia
Sugar Hill Baby
The Texans
1939 *A Brivele der Mamen*
Daughters Courageous
The Escape
The Girl from Mexico
Verbena trágica
1940 *Americaner Schadchen*
Behind the News
Geronimo
Music in My Heart
*Northwest Passage (Book
I—Rogers' Rangers)*
Three Faces West
1941 *Charlie Chan in Rio*
1942 *Holiday Inn*
Secret Enemies
Seven Sweethearts
Tales of Manhattan
We Were Dancing

1943 *Crash Dive*
Crime Smasher
Dixie
*Dr. Gillespie's Criminal
Case*
Jack London
Marching On!
The Meanest Man in the
World
1944 *Knickerbocker Holiday*
Since You Went Away
Tomorrow the World!
Waterfront
1945 Of One Blood
Phantom of the Plains
Pride of the Marines
1946 *Canyon Passage*
Don Ricardo Returns
The Face of Marble
Gas House Kids
Slightly Scandalous
Swamp Fire
That Man of Mine
1946? *Go Down, Death!*
1947 *The Burning Cross*
Duel in the Sun
Easy Come, Easy Go
It Had To Be You
The Peanut Man
Pirates of Monterey
Robin Hood of Monterey
Sepia Cinderella
Spoilers of the North
1948 *The Feathered Serpent*
Gentleman's Agreement
I Remember Mama
Killer Diller
The Luck of the Irish
Moonrise
Old Los Angeles
Tap Roots
1948? *Boarding House Blues*
1949 *Brothers in the Saddle*
C-Man
The Fighting Kentuckian
House of Strangers
Jigsaw
The Red Menace
Ride, Ryder, Ride!
Roll Thunder Roll!
Rose of the Yukon
That Midnight Kiss
Thieves' Highway
1949? *Harlem Follies*
She's Too Mean for Me
1950 *Belle of Old Mexico*
Buccaneer's Girl
The Girl from San Lorenzo
God, Man and Devil
The Men
Rio Grande Patrol
Rock Island Trail
Train to Tombstone
Winchester '73
1951 *The Mark of the Renegade*
Molly
A Streetcar Named Desire
1952 Bright Victory
*Buffalo Bill in Tomahawk
Territory*
The Fabulous Senorita
The Fighter
Woman in the Dark
1953 *The Charge at Feather
River*
Dream Wife
Sangaree
1954 *Sitting Bull*
The Yellow Tomahawk
1956 Crowded Paradise
Ghost Town
7th Cavalry
1957 *Dragoon Wells Massacre*
The Midnight Story
Pawnee
1958 *Apache Territory*
The Rawhide Trail
Seven Hills of Rome
1959 *The Black Orchid*
Cry Tough
1960 *The Pusher*

Engineers
1923 Snowdrift
1930 *Sei tu l'amore*

1931 *Die Maske Fällt*
1936 *Desert Gold*
Sins of Man
1941 *Western Union*
1942 North to the Klondike
1943 *Bataan*
1949 *Shamrock Hill*
1955 *Foxfire*
1958 *The Badlanders*

Engineers—Civil
1915 The Immigrant
1922 The Scrapper
1931 Skyline
1932 *The Golden West*
1947 Untamed Fury
1959 *The World, the Flesh and
the Devil*

England
1914 *Life's Shop Window*
The Squaw Man
1917 *The Spirit of '76*
The Squaw Man's Son
1921 The Money Maniac
1931 Drácula
Nuit d'Espagne
Le père célibataire
The Squaw Man
1934 Charlie Chan in London
Dos más uno, dos
She Was a Lady

English
1914? The Mysterious Mr. Wu
Chung Foo
1915 The Spender
The Spender
1916 *The Daughter of the Don*
Lord Loveland Discovers
America
The Pretenders
The Social Highwayman
1918 Ruggles of Red Gap
Shifting Sands
The Squaw Man
1919 Evangeline
Fighting for Gold
1920 On with the Dance
1923 The Victor
1925 *The Prairie Wife*
1926 Laddie
1930 Take the Heir
Wu Li Chang
1932 *El hombre que asesinó*
Mystery Ranch
1933 *The Emperor Jones*
No dejes la puerta abierta
Robbers' Roost
1934 She Was a Lady
1936 *The Last of the Mohicans*
1937 Boots and Saddles
Slave Ship
1938 *Outside of Paradise*
1939 *Bad Lands*
1940 The Gay Caballero
Mexican Spitfire Out West
Music in My Heart
1941 *The Mexican Spitfire's Baby*
1944 Lifeboat
1945 *Phantom of the Plains*
1947 *The Mighty McGurk*
1951 *Across the Wide Missouri*
1952 Battles of Chief Pontiac
1953 Captain John Smith and
Pocahontas
Fort Ti
1954 *Saskatchewan*
1956 *Secret of Treasure
Mountain*
1959 John Paul Jones

English Derby
1915 *The Danger Signal*

English in foreign countries
1923 Ruggles of Red Gap
1931 Nuit d'Espagne
The Squaw Man
1933 A Lady's Profession
1935 Ruggles of Red Gap
1940 Northwest Passage (Book
I—Rogers' Rangers)
1942 *Valley of the Sun*
1946 *Canyon Passage*
G. I. War Brides
1953 *The Pathfinder*
1956 *Daniel Boone, Trail Blazer*
1959 The Sheriff of Fractured Jaw

English language
1944 *An American Romance*
1947 *The Adventures of Don Coyote*

Engravers
1915 Time Lock Number 776
1916 Gretchen, the Greenhorn

Entertainers
1929 Abie's Irish Rose
1930 Revista Hispano-Americana
Sombras de gloria
1934 Stand Up and Cheer!
1935 *L'homme des Folies Bergère*
1939 Double Deal
1940 Paradise in Harlem
1944 Minstrel Man
Something for the Boys
1945 The Dolly Sisters
I Love a Bandleader
1946 *Dirty Gertie from Harlem, U.S.A.*
The Trap
1947 On the Old Spanish Trail
1948 *The Time of Your Life*
1950 Jolson Sings Again
1951 *The Harlem Globetrotters*
1954 Go Man Go
1957 *Dragoon Wells Massacre*

Entomologists
1936 *Border Phantom*

Entrepreneurs
1932 The Match King
1943 *Wintertime*
1946 Canyon Passage
1947 *The Peanut Man*
1948 16 Fathoms Deep
1951 *Saturday's Hero*
1952 *The Iron Mistress*
1960 Ice Palace

Envy
1932 *Hollywood, ciudad de ensueño*
1934 *The Great Flirtation*
1937 *Green Fields*
1950 Annie Get Your Gun
1953 *Jack McCall Desperado*
1958 *Tonka*

Epidemics
1918 *Love's Law*
1919? *In the Land of the Setting Sun; or, Martyrs of Yesterday*
1933 It's Great to Be Alive
1936 *The Prisoner of Shark Island*
1950 Panic in the Streets

Leif Ericsson
1931 *Street Scene*

Escapes
1913? *The Lure of New York*
1914 *In the Days of the Thundering Herd*
Threads of Destiny
Uncle Tom's Cabin
1914? *A Boy and the Law*
1915 *A Yankee from the West*
1916 *For the Defense*
1917 *The Little American*
The Little Boy Scout
Sunshine and Gold
1917? *Barnaby Lee*
1918 *The Golden Wall*
Huck and Tom; or, the Further Adventures of Tom Sawyer
The Only Road
The Price of Applause
Uncle Tom's Cabin
1919 *Auction of Souls*
Daughter of Mine
A Heart in Pawn
1925 *Body and Soul*
1931 Cheri-Bibi
The Cisco Kid
La ley del harem
Oklahoma Jim
Pagliacci
1932 *Border Devils*
El caballero de la noche
The Vanishing Frontier
Yiskor
1933 *It's Great to Be Alive*
El rey de los gitanos

1934 *Eskimo*
Granaderos del amor
The Lone Defender
Operator 13
Wheels of Destiny
1935 *Charlie Chan in Shanghai*
North of Arizona
1936 *Below the Deadline*
The Bold Caballero
Dancing Pirate
Daniel Boone
Ellis Island
Human Cargo
Let's Sing Again
Muss 'Em Up
Paddy O'Day
Silly Billies
1937 *Big City*
Prairie Thunder
Shadows of the Orient
1938 *Charlie Chan at Monte Carlo*
Gateway
Wild Horse Canyon
1939 *The Adventures of Huckleberry Finn*
Daughter of the Tong
Forged Passport
Mr. Moto in Danger Island
Mr. Moto's Last Warning
Reform School
The Return of the Cisco Kid
1940 Escape
The Fighting 69th
1941 *Prairie Pioneers*
Ride on Vaquero
Z Dymem Pożarów
1942 *Mokey*
Rio Rita
Unseen Enemy
Valley of Hunted Men
Valley of the Sun
1943 *Action in the North Atlantic*
They Came to Blow Up America
1944 *Marshal of Reno*
Tahiti Nights
1945 *The Cisco Kid Returns*
In Old New Mexico
The Mummy's Curse
Salome, Where She Danced
The Shanghai Cobra
South of the Rio Grande
1946 *Renegade Girl*
1947 *Bells of San Fernando*
Buck Privates Come Home
Oregon Trail Scouts
Pirates of Monterey
Ride the Pink Horse
Robin Hood of Monterey
1948 *The Lady from Shanghai*
Old Los Angeles
Renegades of Sonora
Unconquered
1949 *Apache Chief*
Brothers in the Saddle
Call of the Forest
The Dalton Gang
The Fighting Kentuckian
The Gay Amigo
Jigsaw
Masked Raiders
The Red Menace
Rose of the Yukon
The Valiant Hombre
1950 *Bandit Queen*
The Baron of Arizona
Buccaneer's Girl
Cherokee Uprising
Comanche Territory
The Girl from San Lorenzo
I Killed Geronimo
The Iroquois Trail
A Lady Without Passport
The Missourians
No Way Out
Riders of the Pony Express
Rio Grande
So Young, So Bad
Storm Over Wyoming
1951 *Across the Wide Missouri*
The Mark of the Renegade
Warpath

1952 *Battles of Chief Pontiac*
Brave Warrior
Bugles in the Afternoon
Navajo
1953 *Captain John Smith and Pocahontas*
The Glass Wall
The Great Sioux Uprising
1954 Apache
Carmen Jones
Hell's Half Acre
Sitting Bull
Taza, Son of Cochise
1955 *Duel on the Mississippi*
Santa Fe Passage
Seminole Uprising
Smoke Signal
The Vanishing American
1956 *The Burning Hills*
Daniel Boone, Trail Blazer
Mohawk
Pillars of the Sky
Westward Ho the Wagons!
Wetbacks
1957 *Band of Angels*
The Brothers Rico
1958 The Badlanders
The Rawhide Trail
1959 *The FBI Story*
1960 *The Adventures of Huckleberry Finn*
Sergeant Rutledge

Escort services
1930 *Una cana al aire*

Eskimos
use **Native Alaskans**

Espionage
1915? The Life of Sam Davis: A Confederate Hero of the Sixties
Sam Davis, the Hero of Tennessee
1917 The Secret Game
1918 An Alien Enemy
The Greatest Thing in Life
1920 The Cup of Fury
Dangerous Days
Who's Your Servant?
1931 *Cuerpo y alma*
1935 *Rendezvous*
1938 Hawaii Calls
1939 Confessions of a Nazi Spy
1940 Murder over New York
1943 They Came to Blow Up America
1945 Betrayal from the East
The House on 92nd St.
Salome, Where She Danced
Samurai
Where Do We Go From Here?
1946 Rendezvous 24
1950 *Cherokee Uprising*
I Killed Geronimo
The Iroquois Trail
1951 Mask of the Dragon
1952 *Arctic Flight*
1953 Fort Ti
The Pathfinder
1954 Siege at Red River
1959 *The FBI Story*
1960 Man on a String

Estates
1930 *Cascarrabias*
1939 *Straight to Heaven*
1950 *Rock Island Trail*

Ethics
1933 Counsellor at Law
1939 Let Freedom Ring
1940 Am I Guilty?
1943 The Meanest Man in the World
1955 Good Morning, Miss Dove
1959 The Last Angry Man

Ethiopians
1931 *The Exile*

Etiquette
1915 *The Danger Signal*
1918 *Ruggles of Red Gap*
1920 Huckleberry Finn
1927 Sally in Our Alley
1932 *Hombres en mi vida*
1950 *The Toast of New Orleans*

Eunuchs
1931 *La ley del harem*

Europe
1919 Injustice
1935 *Annie Oakley*
1937 *The Cantor's Son*
1938 *Castillos en el aire*
1957 *Satchmo the Great*

Euthanasia
1940 *Girl from God's Country*
1957 *Run of the Arrow*

Evacuations
1919 *Auction of Souls*
1948 *Renegades of Sonora*
1950 *Rio Grande*
1953 *The Man from the Alamo*
1954 *Thunder Pass*

Evangelists
1938 *Birthright*

Everglades (FL)
1919 Diane of the Green Van
1934 *Chloe: Love Is Calling You*
1950 *A Lady Without Passport*
1951 *Distant Drums*
1953 *Seminole*
1957 *Naked in the Sun*

Eviction
1918 *Denny from Ireland*
The Little Runaway
1919 *The Red Viper*
1929 *The Younger Generation*
1931 *Street Scene*
1932 *The Heart of New York*
1938 *La vida bohemia*
1942 *Song of the Islands*
1943 *The Meanest Man in the World*
1948 Western Heritage
1950 *The Baron of Arizona*
The Big Hangover

Evidence
1918 Marked Cards
1919 *A Fighting Colleen*
The Gray Horizon
1922 *Square Joe*
1924 *Smiling Hate*
1931 *The Black Camel*
1932 *El hombre que asesinó*
1933 *Melodía de arrabal*
1936 *Border Phantom*
1937 *The Californian*
Hills of Old Wyoming
It Could Happen to You
1939 *Charlie Chan in Reno*
1941 *Charlie Chan in Rio*
The Pioneers
1946 *Don Ricardo Returns*
Santa Fe Uprising
1951 *Adventures of Captain Fabian*
1956 *The Broken Star*
The Burning Hills
1959 *Al Capone*
1960 *Oklahoma Territory*

Ex-convicts
1915 Just Jim
1918 Hitting the Trail
1932 *Flesh*
1934 *Lazy River*
1934? Harlem After Midnight
1936 *Rose of the Rancho*
1937 *One Mile from Heaven*
That I May Live
1938 *The Power of Life*
1940 *The Notorious Elinor Lee*
1942 Rubber Racketeers
1943 The Law Rides Again
1946 Dark Alibi
1947 *Riding the California Trail*
1948 *Angel in Exile*
The Time of Your Life
1949 Arctic Manhunt
1953 *Ambush at Tomahawk Gap*
1954 *Broken Lance*
1956 *Crowded Paradise*
1958 *The Badlanders*
The Defiant Ones
1959 *Cry Tough*

Ex-spouses
1931 *The Black Camel*
¿Conoces a tu mujer?
1933 *The Cohens and Kellys in Trouble*

1940 *Murder over New York*
1942 *Lawless Plainsmen*
Examinations
    use **Examinations, Academic**
Examinations, Academic
1960 *Pay or Die*
Excommunication
1934 *Behold My Wife!*
Executions
1914 *Dan*
1915? *The Beachcomber*
        *The Life of Sam Davis: A
          Confederate Hero of the
          Sixties*
        *Sam Davis, the Hero of
          Tennessee*
1917 *The Hidden Children*
1918 *The Unbeliever*
1919? *In the Land of the Setting
          Sun; or, Martyrs of
          Yesterday*
1920 *The Man Who Dared*
        Our Christianity and
          Nobody's Child
1932 *Genoveffa*
        The Vanishing Frontier
1933 *The California Trail*
        The Emperor Jones
1934 *The Cat's-Paw*
        Operator 13
1936 *The Bold Caballero*
        El crimen de media noche
        Dancing Pirate
        The Glory Trail
1937 *Bargain with Bullets*
        Maid of Salem
1938 *Mr. Moto Takes a Chance*
1943 *Gangway for Tomorrow*
1947 *Citizen Saint*
1948 *Fighting Father Dunne*
1955 *The Indian Fighter*
1959 *Shake Hands with the Devil*
Executors
1914 The Squaw Man
1939 *Papá soltero*
Exercise
1950 *The Men*
Exhibitions
1939 *Charlie Chan at Treasure
          Island*
Exhumation
1950 *Intruder in the Dust*
1951 *Adventures of Captain
          Fabian*
1953 *The Man Behind the Gun*
Exile
1914 *Threads of Destiny*
1916 The Yellow Passport
1923 *Backbone*
1924 The Lure of Love
1926 *Laddie*
1936 *The Green Pastures*
1950 *Damien*
Exiles
1916 *Man and His Angel*
        The Scarlet Oath
1917 *Crime and Punishment*
        Under False Colors
1917? Barnaby Lee
1919 *Evangeline*
1931 *Resurrección*
1934 *Un capitán de cosacos*
1936 Robin Hood of El Dorado
1945 *A Medal for Benny*
1954 *Broken Lance*
Exodus, Book of
    use **Bible. Old Testament.
          Book of Exodus**
Expatriates
1947 Northwest Outpost
1952 The Fighter
1959 The Wonderful Country
Expeditions
1912 The Alaska-Siberian
          Expedition
        Atop of the World in Motion
1914 Captain F. E. Kleinschmidt's
          Arctic Hunt
1939 *Mr. Moto Takes a Vacation*
1940 *Phantom of Chinatown*
1941 Secret of the Wastelands
        This Woman Is Mine

1947 Dangerous Venture
1948 The Feathered Serpent
1950 Ambush
1951 *Hurricane Island*
1952 The Big Sky
1955 Kiss of Fire
        Seven Cities of Gold
Experiments
1918 *Amarilly of Clothes-Line
          Alley*
Experiments, Human
1931 *Such Is Life*
1946 The Face of Marble
Explorer (Artificial satellite)
1960 *I Aim at the Stars: the
          Wernher von Braun Story*
Explorers
1912 The Alaska-Siberian
          Expedition
1914 *John Barleycorn*
1915 *The Pageant of San
          Francisco*
1925 Justice of the Far North
1928 The Great White North
1932 Dangers of the Arctic
1940 Northwest Passage (Book
          I—Rogers' Rangers)
1941 Mutiny in the Arctic
1951 *Five*
        Hurricane Island
1955 The Far Horizons
Explosions
1918 *The Kaiser's Finish*
        The Prussian Cur
1920 *Dangerous Days*
        Dangerous Hours
        Lifting Shadows
1921 *Cheated Love*
1933 *The Cohens and Kellys in
          Trouble*
1937 *Bargain with Bullets*
        Souls at Sea
1938 *In Old Chicago*
1939 *Gang Smashers*
1940 *Covered Wagon Days*
        Escape to Glory
        Son of Ingagi
1941 *Thunder Over the Prairie*
        Under Fiesta Stars
1942 *All Through the Night*
        Rio Rita
1943 *Action in the North
          Atlantic*
        Air Force
        Bataan
        In Old Oklahoma
        Redhead from Manhattan
        *They Came to Blow Up
          America*
1944 *Tucson Raiders*
1945 *Colorado Pioneers*
1946? *Fight That Ghost*
1947 *The Adventures of Don
          Coyote*
        Duel in the Sun
1948 *The Paleface*
        Reaching from Heaven
1949 *Ranger of Cherokee Strip*
        Tulsa
1950 *Rock Island Trail*
1951 *Adventures of Captain
          Fabian*
        Distant Drums
        New Mexico
        Only the Valiant
1952 *California Conquest*
1953 *Ambush at Tomahawk Gap*
        The Glory Brigade
        The Man Behind the Gun
        The Pathfinder
        Sangaree
1954 *Cattle Queen of Montana*
        Dangerous Mission
1955 *Violent Saturday*
1956 *Quincannon, Frontier
          Scout*
        *Secret of Treasure
          Mountain*
        The White Squaw
1959 *The FBI Story*
        Odds Against Tomorrow
        Shake Hands with the Devil
1960 *The Last Voyage*

Explosives
1917 *His Sweetheart*
1919? America Was Right
1938 *Mr. Moto Takes a Chance*
1939 *Mr. Moto's Last Warning*
1942 *Mexican Spitfire Sees a
          Ghost*
1950 *Davy Crockett, Indian
          Scout*
        Sands of Iwo Jima
1951 *Hurricane Island*
1958 *Apache Territory*
        The Badlanders
Expulsion
1931 *Personal Maid*
1935 *Angelina o el honor de un
          brigadier*
1938 *Life Goes On*
1940 *Santa Fe Trail*
1960 *Take a Giant Step*
Extortion
1915 Time Lock Number 776
1917 *The Little Chevalier*
1918 The Wine Girl
1920 *Dangerous Hours*
        The Purple Cipher
1933 *Olsen's Big Moment*
1934 Lazy River
        Straight Is the Way
1936 *Human Cargo*
1939 The Bronze Buckaroo
        Frontiers of '49
        King of Chinatown
        Miracle on Main Street
1942 *Nazi Agent*
        Secret Enemies
        Sunday Punch
1947 The Burning Cross
1948 Angel in Exile
1949 *Streets of Laredo*
1956 *The Broken Star*
1957 *Raiders of Old California*
1959 *Al Capone*
1960 Pay or Die
Extradition
1928 *Uncle Tom's Cabin*
Extrasensory perception
1918 In Judgment Of
1920 The Dark Mirror
Extravagance
1915 The Cheat
Eye surgery
1929 Love, Live and Laugh
Eyeglasses
1948 *Sleep, My Love*
1952 *It's a Big Country: An
          American Anthology*
Eyes
1935 *Annie Oakley*
F.B.I.
    use **United States. Federal
          Bureau of Investigation**
Factories
1915 *Hearts of Men*
1918 *Good-Bye, Bill*
1919 *The Right to Happiness*
1920 The Face at Your Window
1934 *Chloe: Love Is Calling You*
1937 *The Holy Oath*
1946 *Till the End of Time*
1952 *Bright Victory*
Factory management
1921 The Gunsaulus Mystery
1949 *Prejudice*
Factory owners
1918 *Hitting the Trail*
        A Little Sister of Everybody
1920 The Face at Your Window
1931 *El príncipe gondolero*
1951 *Molly*
Factory workers
1915 *The Spender*
1918 *Doing Their Bit*
        Hitting the Trail
        A Little Sister of Everybody
        Love's Law
1919 *The Unpainted Woman*
1920 *Uncharted Channels*
1932 *Senza mamma
          e'nnamurato*
1937 Black Legion
1941 *Min Jok Jay Hung Sing*

Fainting
1947 *Rustlers of Devil's Canyon*
Fairies
1917 *Castles for Two*
1918 *Wanted, a Mother*
1946 Three Wise Fools
Fairs
1918? Indian Life
1925 Red Love
1933 *The Man Who Dared: An
          Imaginative Biography*
        El rey de los gitanos
1936 *Laughing Irish Eyes*
1942 *Young America*
1944 *Knickerbocker Holiday*
1948 *Moonrise*
        Singin' Spurs
Faith
1914? The Lust of the Red Man
1920 *The Girl of My Heart*
1931 The Voice of Israel
1936 *The Green Pastures*
1940 The Fighting 69th
1945 The Bells of St. Mary's
1947 *The Peanut Man*
        The Return of Rin Tin Tin
        The Return of Rin Tin Tin
1948 The Miracle of the Bells
1950 Stars in My Crown
1952? Call of the Navajo
1953 Taxi
1955 *A Man Called Peter*
        Seven Cities of Gold
Faith healers
    use **Healers;
          Spiritual healing**
Fakirs
1931 *El tenorio del harem*
Falkland Islands
1941 *This Woman Is Mine*
Falls from heights
1913 Traffic in Souls
1915 An American Gentleman
        The Birth of a Nation
1918 *In Judgment Of*
        Wanted, a Mother
1919 *Desert Gold*
        The Gray Horizon
        The Gray Towers Mystery
        The Last of His People
        The Westerners
1921 *As the World Rolls On*
        The First Born
        A Modern Cain
1928 *The Midnight Ace*
1931 *Skyline*
1932 *Mystery Ranch*
        Thirteen Women
        Wild Horse Mesa
1934 *'Neath the Arizona Skies*
        Straight Is the Way
1936 *Charlie Chan at the Circus*
        Desert Gold
        The Last of the Mohicans
1937 One Mile from Heaven
1938 *The Adventures of Tom
          Sawyer*
        Marusia
        Speed to Burn
1940 *If I Had My Way*
        *They Knew What They
          Wanted*
1941 *King of the Zombies*
1944 *Black Magic*
1947 *Buck Privates Come Home*
1948 *Moonrise*
        Sleep, My Love
1949 *Jigsaw*
        Lust for Gold
        The Valiant Hombre
1951 *The House on Telegraph
          Hill*
1954 *Barefoot Battalion*
1955 *Apache Woman*
        Seven Cities of Gold
1956 *The Last Frontier*
1959 *Cry Tough*
False accusations
1914 *The Little Angel of Canyon
          Creek*
1915 *The Secret Sin*
1916 *Broken Chains*
        The Half-Breed
        Witchcraft

False accusations

1917 Crime and Punishment
The Little Samaritan
The Secret of Eve
1918 *I Want to Forget*
Marked Cards
The Only Road
The Ranger
Sandy
1919 Fighting for Gold
The Heart of Wetona
The Tong Man
1930 Los que danzan
Monsieur le Fox
1931 *La cautivadora*
Delicious
The Exile
La llama sagrada
Mamá
Yankee Don
Young Sinners
1932 *Une heure près de toi*
Marido y mujer
Senza mamma e'nnamurato
White Eagle
1933 *It's Great to Be Alive*
1934 *The Cactus Kid*
La cruz y la espada
Fighting Through
Judge Priest
The Lone Defender
1935 *Captured in Chinatown*
Cowboy Holiday
Fighting Pioneers
North of Arizona
Range Warfare
Señora casada necesita marido
Texas Terror
1936 *Aces and Eights*
Below the Deadline
Ellis Island
It Had to Happen
The Phantom of Santa Fe
Pinto Rustlers
Robin Hood of El Dorado
Sutter's Gold
The Traitor
West of Nevada
1937 The Barrier
Black Legion
Charlie Chan at the Olympics
Maid of Salem
Manhattan Merry-Go-Round
Old Louisiana
Underworld
1938 The Adventures of Tom Sawyer
Breaking the Ice
The Buccaneer
Little Miss Roughneck
Mis dos amores
Mr. Moto Takes a Chance
Road Demon
La vida bohemia
1939 The Adventures of Huckleberry Finn
Charlie Chan in Reno
Double Deal
The Light Ahead
The Mystery of Mr. Wong
1940 Arizona Frontier
Doomed to Die
Eli Eli
Girl from God's Country
Mystery in Swing
Perfidia
Rhythm of the Rio Grande
Son of Ingagi
1941 *The Mexican Spitfire's Baby*
Road Agent
Western Union
1942 All Through the Night
In This Our Life
Lawless Plainsmen
The Navy Comes Through
Tortilla Flat
1943 Good Luck, Mr. Yates
The Outlaw
The Ox-Bow Incident
Redhead from Manhattan
They Came to Blow Up America
1944 *The Chinese Cat*
Marshal of Reno

Riding West
1945 The Cisco Kid Returns
In Old New Mexico
Wanderer of the Wasteland
1946 *California Gold Rush*
Gas House Kids
Song of the South
1947 *California*
Desperate
Hi De Ho
Jiggs and Maggie in Society
The Last Round-Up
Robin Hood of Monterey
1948 *The Betrayal*
1949 The Clay Pigeon
The Mysterious Desperado
The Prairie
Riders of the Range
1950 *Ambush*
Border Treasure
Broken Arrow
Davy Crockett, Indian Scout
The Lawless
Mystery Submarine
No Way Out
Raiders of Tomahawk Creek
Riders of the Pony Express
Sunset in the West
1951 *Adventures of Captain Fabian*
Flaming Feather
The Girl on the Bridge
Only the Valiant
The Well
1952 Apache War Smoke
The Fabulous Senorita
Japanese War Bride
Red Ball Express
1952? Call of the Navajo
1953 *Captain John Smith and Pocahontas*
Column South
Fort Ti
Jack McCall Desperado
The Man from the Alamo
The Nebraskan
Old Overland Trail
Tumbleweed
1954 Saskatchewan
1956 *The Broken Star*
Dakota Incident
The Last Wagon
Raw Edge
Reprisal!
7th Cavalry
1957 Apache Warrior
Gun Battle at Monterey
The Halliday Brand
The Lawless Eighties
The Oklahoman
Pawnee
Revolt at Fort Laramie
1958 Bullwhip
Escape from Red Rock
Gunfire at Indian Gap
The Rawhide Trail
1959 *The Crimson Kimono*
John Paul Jones

False arrests

1915 Chimmie Fadden
Just Jim
1916 *Broken Chains*
The Criminal
Pudd'nhead Wilson
1917 His Sweetheart
1918 Broken Ties
The City of Tears
Hitting the Trail
Huck and Tom; or, the Further Adventures of Tom Sawyer
In Judgment Of
Set Free
A Woman of Impulse
1918? Rosemary Climbs the Heights
1919 A Fallen Idol
The Gray Towers Mystery
Scarlet Days
Told in the Hills
1920 *The Face at Your Window*
1920? *The Greatest Love*
1921 The Gunsaulus Mystery

1922 Square Joe
1926 *The Flying Ace*
1928 *A Ship Comes In*
1931 *Cheri-Bibi*
La ley del barem
Three Who Loved
1932 Hidden Valley
Joseph in the Land of Egypt
Ljubav i strast
The Vanishing Frontier
Yiskor
1932? The Girl from Chicago
1933 *Dance Hall Hostess*
El rey de los gitanos
1934 *Behold My Wife!*
Charlie Chan in London
Massacre
The Prescott Kid
1935 *Charlie Chan in Paris*
Charlie Chan in Shanghai
North of Arizona
The Singing Vagabond
1936 *Border Phantom*
Custer's Last Stand
The Last of the Mohicans
The Prisoner of Shark Island
Ride, Ranger, Ride
The Traitor
1938 *Happy Landing*
Mr. Moto's Gamble
1939 *Harlem Rides the Range*
Papá soltero
1941 Caught in the Act
Ride on Vaquero
Sunday Sinners
1943 Frontier Fury
1944 Tucson Raiders
Waterfront
1945 *The Shanghai Cobra*
South of the Rio Grande
1946 Tall, Tan and Terrific
1947 *Buck Privates Come Home*
Easy Come, Easy Go
Jiggs and Maggie in Society
King of the Bandits
1948 Call Northside 777
Indian Agent
Unconquered
1949 Brothers in the Saddle
The Daring Caballero
The Gay Amigo
Roll Thunder Roll!
The Valiant Hombre
1950 *Colt .45*
Mystery Street
1952 *My Man and I*
1953 *The Sun Shines Bright*
1958 *Touch of Evil*
1959 *Gunmen from Laredo*
1960 Sergeant Rutledge

Fame

1931 *Las luces de Buenos Aires*
1936 *La última cita*
1944 *Buffalo Bill*
1951 *The Great Caruso*
1953 *The Eddie Cantor Story*
1956 Serenade
1958 *St. Louis Blues*

Family honor

1914 The Good-for-Nothing
The Squaw Man
1916 The Grip of Jealousy
1917 Castles for Two
The Pulse of Life
The Renaissance at Charleroi
1931 *El príncipe gondolero*
1935 His Family Tree
1937 *Manhattan Merry-Go-Round*
Thank You, Mr. Moto
1939 *Mirele Efros*
1941 Adam Had Four Sons
1951 Adventures of Captain Fabian
1952 *Woman in the Dark*
1955 *Duel on the Mississippi*
The View from Pompey's Head
1956 The Searchers
1957 *The Midnight Story*
1959 Cry Tough
1960 *The Unforgiven*

Family life

1916 *A Sister of Six*
1917 *The Bar Sinister*
Southern Pride
1918 *Johanna Enlists*
The Man Above the Law
1919 Come Out of the Kitchen
Erstwhile Susan
The Other Man's Wife
Toby's Bow
1922 Little Miss Smiles
1924 Peter Pan
1925 The Beautiful City
His People
1926 Laddie
Millionaires
1927 The Broken Violin
The Callahans and the Murphys
Finnegan's Ball
Frisco Sally Levy
Jake the Plumber
The Way of All Flesh
Wild Geese
1928 A Ship Comes In
1929 Is Everybody Happy?
Mother's Boy
The Younger Generation
1930 Eternal Fools (Ewige Naranim)
Sins of the Children
1931 The Great Meadow
Le père célibataire
Quand on est belle
1932 The Cohens and Kellys in Hollywood
Cuore d'emigrante
The Heart of New York
Uncle Moses
1933 *The Man Who Dared: An Imaginative Biography*
Song of the Eagle
1934 As the Earth Turns
Beloved
1935 *Angelina o el honor de un brigadier*
The Irish in Us
Shir Hashirim
The Winning Ticket
1938 In Old Chicago
The Power of Life
1939 A Brivele der Mamen
Daughters Courageous
Judge Hardy and Son
Mamele
Mirele Efros
My Son
One Dark Night
Winner Take All
1940 Jennie
Knute Rockne—All American
The Way of All Flesh
1942 The Vanishing Virginian
1943 Doughboys in Ireland
1944 Since You Went Away
The Sullivans
1945 *Of One Blood*
Our Vines Have Tender Grapes
A Tree Grows in Brooklyn
The Valley of Decision
1947 Juke Joint
1948 I Remember Mama
1948? *Junction 88*
1950 *No Way Out*
1950? *Three Daughters*
1951 *Native Son*
1953 *The Eddie Cantor Story*
1957 All Mine to Give
1959 Anna Lucasta
1960 The Dark at the Top of the Stairs
Hell to Eternity
Key Witness

Family relationships

1914 The Good-for-Nothing
The Nightingale
1915 Kreutzer Sonata
1917 The Bronze Bride
1918 A Broadway Scandal
The Ranger
The Reckoning Day
1919 The Delicious Little Devil

1919? America Was Right
1921 Little Italy
No Woman Knows
The Sport of the Gods
1922 The Man with Two Mothers
1923 His Great Chance
Scars of Jealousy
1925 Abie's Imported Bride
The Greatest Love of All
1926 Irene
The Passaic Textile Strike
A Prince of His Race
Sweet Daddies
1927 The Devil's Saddle
Jake the Plumber
[Japanese-American Film]
White Gold
1928 The Riding Renegade
Uncle Tom's Cabin
1929 Lucky Boy
Mother's Boy
Romance of the Rio Grande
1930 Eternal Fools (Ewige
Naranim)
The Melody Man
My Yiddishe Mama
La rosa de fuego
Song of the Caballero
1931 Cimarron
Del infierno al cielo
The Guilty Generation
Kismet
Mamá
Le père célibataire
Personal Maid
Riders of the Rio
Street Scene
Su última noche
1932 Call Her Savage
The Golden West
Huddle
Me and My Gal
Symphony of Six Million
Unashamed
Uncle Moses
Wild Horse Mesa
1933 Broken Dreams
The California Trail
Dos noches
Obey the Law
1934 Behold My Wife!
Beloved
Coming Out Party
Massacre
The Rabbi's Power
1934? Harlem After Midnight
1935 Charlie Chan in Egypt
El día que me quieras
His Family Tree
Shir Hashirim
1936 After the Thin Man
Love and Sacrifice
My American Wife
Show Boat
Star for a Night
1937 The Cantor's Son
Green Fields
The Jester (Der
Purimspieler)
1938 The Beloved Brat
The Singing Blacksmith
1939 Kol Nidre
Mothers of Today
Straight to Heaven
Verbena trágica
1940 Broken Strings
Doomed to Die
Eli Eli
Her Second Mother
The Jewish Melody
Little Nellie Kelly
Midnight Shadow
1941 Min Jok Jay Hung Sing
Prairie Pioneers
Sunday Sinners
1942 Gentleman Jim
Valley of Hunted Men
1943 Deerslayer
Yankee Doodle Dandy
1944 An American Romance
Tomorrow the World!
1945 The Great John L.
Rhapsody in Blue
Samurai

1946 Canyon Passage
Till the End of Time
1947 The Burning Cross
Untamed Fury
1948 Cry of the City
Moonrise
Tap Roots
1949 Anna Lucasta
Answer for Anne
Apache Chief
Daughter of the West
The Girl from Jones Beach
Lost Boundaries
The Prairie
Prejudice
The Quiet One
Ride, Ryder, Ride!
Shamrock Hill
Tuna Clipper
1950 Davy Crockett, Indian
Scout
God, Man and Devil
The Iroquois Trail
The Lawless
Panic in the Streets
1951 Molly
Queen for a Day
Show Boat
The Well
1952 Brave Warrior
Bright Victory
The Savage
Woman in the Dark
1952? Call of the Navajo
1954 Salt of the Earth
1956 The Benny Goodman Story
The Burning Hills
The Catered Affair
Daniel Boone, Trail Blazer
Giant
Hot Blood
The Searchers
1957 All Mine to Give
The Midnight Story
1958 Houseboat
The Light in the Forest
Marjorie Morningstar
1959 The Black Orchid
The FBI Story
Night of the Quarter Moon
Odds Against Tomorrow
1960 All the Fine Young
Cannibals
Cimarron
Flaming Star
Ice Palace
The Last Voyage
Take a Giant Step
This Rebel Breed
The Unforgiven
Wild River

Famines
1913? Hiawatha
1925 Abie's Imported Bride
1930 The Silent Enemy
1932 Joseph in the Land of Egypt

Fanatics
1916 The Morals of Hilda
1934 The Youth of Russia
1955 Seven Angry Men

Fans (Clothing accessory)
1929 Die Königsloge

Fans (Sports, motion pictures,
etc.)
use Specific type of fans

Farm hands
1932 Amore e morte
The Hatchet Man
1942 Juke Girl
1946 Song of the South
1950 The Lawless
1952 My Man and I

Farm life
1914 Life's Shop Window
1939 Tevya

Farmers
1914 The Indian Wars
1915 A Yankee from the West
1916 At Piney Ridge
The Colored American
Winning His Suit
The Flames of Johannis
1918? Indian Life

1919 The Lord Loves the Irish
The Unpainted Woman
1921 Cotton and Cattle
1924 So Big
1927 [Japanese-American Film]
Wild Geese
1928 The Mating Call
1929 Evangeline
Hearts in Dixie
1931 Beyond Victory
The Exile
La fiesta del diablo
Sombras del circo
1932 Amor in montagna
Amore e morte
Le cas du docteur Brenner
So Big
1934 As the Earth Turns
Blossom Time
1935 The Wedding Night
The Wedding Night
1936 Border Phantom
1937 Green Fields
1938 God's Step Children
1939 Drums Along the Mohawk
1939? A Chinese Gains a Fortune
in America
1940 Jennie
Prairie Schooners
They Knew What They
Wanted
Three Faces West
1941 Z Dymem Pozarów
1942 Holiday Inn
Juke Girl
Mokey
1943 The Meanest Man in the
World
1945 Our Vines Have Tender
Grapes
1946 Beauty and the Bandit
1947 The Burning Cross
California
Desperate
The Farmer's Daughter
1949 Anna Lucasta
1952 Japanese War Bride
My Man and I
1953 So Big
1955 Violent Saturday
1956 Westward Ho the Wagons!
1957 Raiders of Old California
1958 Terror in a Texas Town
1959 John Paul Jones
The Wonderful Country

Farms
1914 John Barleycorn
1914? A Boy and the Law
1915 Kreutzer Sonata
1916 The Pretenders
1918 Johanna Enlists
Real Folks
1919 Love and the Law
1920 In the Depths of Our Hearts
1932 Amore e morte
1934 Our Daily Bread
1936 Ellis Island
Kelly the Second
1937 The Holy Oath
1938 Breaking the Ice
1940 Eli Eli
1941 Come Live with Me
1942 The Vanishing Virginian
1943 Land of Hunted Men
1945 Our Vines Have Tender
Grapes
1946 Gas House Kids
Rendezvous 24
1948 The Betrayal
1949 The Undercover Man
1953 Fort Ti
1957 The Brothers Rico

Faro (Game)
1916 Mixed Blood

Fascism
1940 The Man I Married
1948 Open Secret

Fashion designers
use Couturiers;
Dressmakers

Fashion shows
1926 Irene
1938 My Lucky Star
1958 Seven Hills of Rome

Fatherhood
1921 Across the Divide
That Girl Montana
1922 Flesh and Blood
1923 Jealous Husbands
1924 Defying the Law
Yankee Speed
1927 Rose of the Golden West
The Way of All Flesh
1928 Sins of the Fathers
1930 Doña mentiras
Eternal Fools (Ewige
Naranim)
Sins of the Children
1931 La dama atrevida
1935 Julieta compra un hijo
1939 One Dark Night
1958 Houseboat

Fathers and daughters
1913 The Inside of the White
Slave Traffic
1914 The Little Jewess
The Littlest Rebel
Springtime
Threads of Destiny
The Yellow Traffic
1915 The Alien
The Birth of a Nation
Children of the Ghetto
Cohen's Luck
The Girl I Left Behind Me
1916 At Piney Ridge
The Flower of No Man's
Land
The Folly of Revenge
The Gilded Spider
Gretchen, the Greenborn
The Honorable Friend
Lone Star
The Scarlet Oath
The Soul of Kura-San
1917 The Barrier
A Night in New Arabia
The Plow Woman
Unknown 274
1918 The Greatest Thing in Life
The Million Dollar Mystery
Thirty a Week
Wanted, a Mother
1919 Daughter of Mine
Evangeline
False Evidence
The Homesteader
The Right to Happiness
The Sneak
The Tong Man
Who's Your Brother?
1920 Outside the Law
The Paliser Case
Rio Grande
The Secret Gift
1922 The Crimson Skull
1924 Smiling Hate
1925 Tonio, Son of the Sierras
1926? Ten Nights in a Barroom
1927 The Scar of Shame
1928 Eleven P.M.
1930 Anna Christie
Cuando el amor ríe
Locuras de amor
Monsieur le Fox
Wu Li Chang
1931 The Avenger
Cheri-Bibi
El código penal
El comediante
Echec au roi
The Exile
La ley del harem
Le père célibataire
La pura verdad
Quand on est belle
Regeneración
Shulamith
El tenorio del harem
Yankee Don
1932 Amore e morte
The Forty-Niners
Igloo
The Secrets of Wu Sin
Senza mamma
e'nnamurato
The Son-Daughter
Thirteen Steps
The Unfortunate Bride

Yiskor
1933 Best of Enemies
     *Charlie Chan's Greatest
          Case*
     *The Cohens and Kellys in
          Trouble*
     Victims of Persecution
1934 *The Battling Buckaroo*
     Broadway Bill
     Chloe: Love Is Calling You
     Judge Priest
     Limehouse Blues
     The Lone Defender
     She Was a Lady
     Song of the Islands
     Stand Up and Cheer!
     The Youth of Russia
1935 *Fighting Pioneers*
     Harmony Lane
     The Littlest Rebel
     McFadden's Flats
     Melody Trail
     Piernas de seda
     So Red the Rose
     The Wedding Night
     The Yiddish King Lear
1936 *Amor que vuelve*
     The Bold Caballero
     Contra la corriente
     El crimen de media noche
     Custer's Last Stand
     Down to the Sea
     Laughing Irish Eyes
     Robin Hood of El Dorado
     Rose of the Rancho
     Song of the Gringo
     Yiddle with His Fiddle
1937 *The Barrier*
     Charlie Chan at the Opera
     Drums of Destiny
     Harlem on the Prairie
     Law and Lead
     Life Begins in College
     Natalka Poltavka
     Nation Aflame
     Old Louisiana
     *The Riders of the Whistling
          Skull*
     Thank You, Mr. Moto
1938 *Happy Landing*
     Mis dos amores
     The Power of Life
     Wild Horse Canyon
1939 *Allegheny Uprising*
     Daughters Courageous
     Drifting Westward
     The Fighting Gringo
     Harlem Rides the Range
     Los hijos mandan
     In Old Caliente
     King of Chinatown
     Tevya
     Trigger Fingers
1940 Am I Guilty?
     The Gay Caballero
     Hi-Yo Silver
     Jennie
     Mystery in Swing
     Taku
     Three Cheers for the Irish
     Three Faces West
     Too Many Girls
     Viva Cisco Kid
1941 *Caught in the Act*
     The Gang's All Here
     Golden Gate Girl
     Hurry, Charlie, Hurry
     Lady from Louisiana
     Murder on Lenox Avenue
     Road Agent
     They Dare Not Love
     Virginia
1942 Across the Pacific
     All Through the Night
     King of the Stallions
     Lawless Plainsmen
     Seven Sweethearts
     Shut My Big Mouth
     Song of the Islands
     Syncopation
     Woman of the Year
1943 Border Patrol
     Dixie
     The Gang's All Here
     Land of Hunted Men

     Let's Have Fun
     Riding High
1944 *Address Unknown*
     Black Magic
     *Charlie Chan in the Secret
          Service*
     Knickerbocker Holiday
     Minstrel Man
     Mr. Skeffington
     Outlaw Trail
     Riding West
     Tomorrow the World!
1945 *The Cisco Kid Returns*
     Great Stagecoach Robbery
     *Our Vines Have Tender
          Grapes*
     The Shanghai Cobra
     Sunbonnet Sue
     A Tree Grows in Brooklyn
     The Valley of Decision
1946 *Abie's Irish Rose*
     Beauty and the Bandit
     California Gold Rush
     Dark Alibi
     The Gay Cavalier
     Notorious
     Slightly Scandalous
     Stars on Parade
     Strange Voyage
1947 *Boy! What a Girl!*
     Buffalo Bill Rides Again
     Calendar Girl
     Dark Delusion
     Duel in the Sun
     Easy Come, Easy Go
     The Farmer's Daughter
     The Foxes of Harrow
     *Going to Glory, Come to
          Jesus*
     The Mighty McGurk
     My Wild Irish Rose
     Vigilantes of Boomtown
     Wild Horse Mesa
1948 *The Betrayal*
     Fort Apache
     The Golden Eye
     Gun Smugglers
     Reaching from Heaven
     Silver Trails
     Up in Central Park
1949 Anna Lucasta
     Colorado Territory
     The Fighting Kentuckian
     The Kissing Bandit
     Massacre River
     Rustlers
     Stagecoach Kid
     Top O' the Morning
     Tulsa
     The Undercover Man
1950 *The Big Hangover*
     The Daughter of Rosie
          O'Grady
     The Furies
     Indian Territory
     Right Cross
     Rock Island Trail
     The Traveling Saleswoman
     Young Daniel Boone
     Young Man with a Horn
1950? Three Daughters
1951 *The Great Caruso*
     The Mark of the Renegade
     Slaughter Trail
     Warpath
1952 *Apache Country*
     California Conquest
     The Fabulous Senorita
     Fort Osage
     It's a Big Country: An
          American Anthology
     *It's a Big Country: An
          American Anthology*
     The Raiders
1953 *Captain John Smith and
          Pocahontas*
     Dream Wife
     *The Member of the
          Wedding*
     San Antone
     Thunder Bay
1954 *Apache*
     Battle of Rogue River
     The Black Dakotas
     Cattle Queen of Montana

     Dangerous Mission
     Taza, Son of Cochise
     War Arrow
1955 *Duel on the Mississippi*
     Good Morning, Miss Dove
     The Lonesome Trail
     Murder in Villa Capri
     Seminole Uprising
     Smoke Signal
     White Feather
1956 *Crowded Paradise*
     Frontier Woman
     The Lone Ranger
     *Secret of Treasure
          Mountain*
     7th Cavalry
     The White Squaw
1957 *Apache Warrior*
     Bayou
     The Deerslayer
     The Halliday Brand
     Man in the Shadow
     The Oklahoman
     Tomahawk Trail
1958 *Escape from Red Rock*
     Houseboat
     The Light in the Forest
     The Young Lions
1959 Anna Lucasta
     The Black Orchid
     Inside the Mafia
     The Oregon Trail
     The Young Land
1960 *The Dark at the Top of the
          Stairs*
     Oklahoma Territory
     The Plunderers
     The Pusher

Fathers and sons
1914 At the Cross Roads
1915 Children of the Ghetto
1916 *Broken Fetters*
1917 The Bond Between
     The Call of Her People
     The Peddler
     The Red Woman
1917? *Barnaby Lee*
1918 His Birthright
     The Hun Within
     In Judgment Of
     Real Folks
     The Spreading Evil
     Woman and the Law
1919 *Bonnie, Bonnie Lassie*
     Hearts of Men
1920 *Huckleberry Finn*
     Uncharted Channels
1924 *Smiling Hate*
1925 Tonio, Son of the Sierras
1928 The Jazz Singer
1929 Sombras habaneras
1930 Chijiku wo mawasuru
          chikara
     Del mismo barro
     Locuras de amor
     Sombras de gloria
1931 Del infierno al cielo
     Gentleman's Fate
     Hay que casar al príncipe
     Huckleberry Finn
     Skyline
     Young Sinners
1932 *Amor in montagna*
     Hearts of Humanity
     Joseph in the Land of Egypt
1933 Best of Enemies
     Song of the Eagle
     Victims of Persecution
     The Wandering Jew
1934 *She Was a Lady*
1935 *El cantante de Nápoles*
     Charlie Chan in Paris
     Charlie Chan in Shanghai
1936 For the Service
     Sins of Man
     Winterset
1937 *Arshin Mal Alan*
     Border Cafe
     Boy of the Streets
     The Californian
     Charlie Chan at the
          Olympics
     Charlie Chan at the Opera
     Charlie Chan on Broadway
     Think Fast, Mr. Moto

1938 *Charlie Chan at Monte
          Carlo*
     Josette
     My Lucky Star
     Road Demon
1938? *Amore che non torna*
1939 *The Adventures of
          Huckleberry Finn*
     *Charlie Chan at Treasure
          Island*
     Charlie Chan in Honolulu
     Charlie Chan in Reno
     Fisherman's Wharf
     Los hijos mandan
     Judge Hardy and Son
     Let Freedom Ring
     Motel the Operator
     Reform School
1939? A Chinese Gains a Fortune
          in America
1940 Broken Strings
     Charlie Chan in Panama
     *Charlie Chan's Murder
          Cruise*
     The Fatal Hour
     Geronimo
     The Man I Married
     The Mark of Zorro
     Murder over New York
     Overture to Glory
     Santa Fe Trail
     The Way of All Flesh
     Young Buffalo Bill
1941 Adam Had Four Sons
     Birth of the Blues
     Charlie Chan in Rio
     Dead Men Tell
     Four Shall Die
     Thunder Over the Prairie
1942 *Castle in the Desert*
     Friendly Enemies
     Lawless Plainsmen
     Let's Get Tough!
     Mokey
     North to the Klondike
     Song of the Islands
     Submarine Raider
     Wings for the Eagle
1943 *Air Force*
     The Gang's All Here
     Marching On!
     The Ox-Bow Incident
     *They Came to Blow Up
          America*
1944 *Address Unknown*
     Andy Hardy's Blonde
          Trouble
     *Charlie Chan in the Secret
          Service*
     The Chinese Cat
     Chip Off the Old Block
     Cry of the Werewolf
     Going My Way
     Sheriff of Las Vegas
1945 *Great Stagecoach Robbery*
     The Jade Mask
     Johnny Angel
     A Medal for Benny
     The Scarlet Clue
     The Shanghai Cobra
     The Valley of Decision
1946 *Abie's Irish Rose*
     Dangerous Money
     Dark Alibi
     The Red Dragon
     Santa Fe Uprising
     Shadows Over Chinatown
     The Trap
     Wild West
1947 *The Chinese Ring*
     Duel in the Sun
     The Foxes of Harrow
     Humoresque
     The Jolson Story
     The Last Round-Up
     Little Mister Jim
     Marshal of Cripple Creek
     Reet, Petite and Gone
     Robin Hood of Monterey
     Untamed Fury
1948 The Arizona Ranger
     Cry of the City
     Docks of New Orleans
     The Feathered Serpent
     Fighting Father Dunne

Fury at Furnace Creek
Gentleman's Agreement
The Golden Eye
Harpoon
Louisiana Story
Miracle in Harlem
Rocky
Shanghai Chest
16 Fathoms Deep
1949   Call of the Forest
     The Cowboy and the
       Prizefighter
     Harbor of Missing Men
     House of Strangers
     Laramie
     The Sky Dragon
     That Midnight Kiss
1950   *Black Hand*
     Broken Arrow
     Comanche Territory
     Devil's Doorway
     The Furies
     Intruder in the Dust
     Jolson Sings Again
     The Lawless
     North of the Great Divide
     Rio Grande
     Sands of Iwo Jima
     Stars in My Crown
1951   *Across the Wide Missouri*
     Cuban Fireball
     Distant Drums
     Jim Thorpe—All-American
     New Mexico
     The Raging Tide
     Saturday's Hero
     Teresa
1952   Apache War Smoke
     Buffalo Bill in Tomahawk
       Territory
     Hiawatha
     Indian Uprising
     It's a Big Country: An
       American Anthology
     The Ring
     The Savage
1953   *Arrowhead*
     Beneath the 12-Mile Reef
     Cry of the Hunted
     The Jazz Singer
     The Nebraskan
     San Antone
     Seminole
     Tumbleweed
1954   Broken Lance
     Cattle Queen of Montana
     Drums Across the River
1955   *Apache Ambush*
     Not As a Stranger
     Seven Angry Men
     Violent Saturday
1956   Full of Life
     Raw Edge
     Westward Ho the Wagons!
     The White Squaw
1957   *Burden of Truth*
     The Halliday Brand
     The Lawless Eighties
     The Oklahoman
     Twelve Angry Men
1958   Frontier Gun
     Gun Fever
     Gunman's Walk
     Houseboat
     The Last Hurrah
     St. Louis Blues
1959   Cry Tough
     Gunmen from Laredo
     Last Train from Gun Hill
     Shake Hands with the Devil
1960   *The Adventures of*
       Huckleberry Finn
     Man on a String
     Oklahoma Territory
     The Sign of Zorro
     Studs Lonigan

Fathers-in-law
1915   *The Spender*
1919   The Homesteader
1933   Victims of Persecution
1934   *What a Mother-in-Law!*
1935   Rosa de Francia
1940   *Overture to Glory*
1941   *Accent on Love*
     Z Dymem Pożarów

1942   *They Died With Their Boots*
     On
1948   Key Largo
1956   Full of Life
Faust (Opera)
1918   *Find the Woman*
1953   *Tonight We Sing*
Fear
1918   *The Liar*
1930   La voluntad del muerto
1933   *The Emperor Jones*
1953   *Last of the Comanches*
1955   *Bad Day at Black Rock*
1956   *The Burning Hills*
1959   *Odds Against Tomorrow*
1960   *All the Young Men*
     Key Witness
     The Last Voyage
     Pay or Die
Feathers
1949   *Tale of the Navajos*
Feats of strength
1936   *Tundra*
1954   *Apache*
Federal Bureau of Investigation
   use   **United States. Federal**
       Bureau of Investigation
Federal Reserve bank
1936   *Ellis Island*
Female impersonation
1932   *Hypnotized*
1939   *The Adventures of*
       Huckleberry Finn
1941   Up Jumped the Devil
1942   Shut My Big Mouth
1944   *Slightly Terrific*
1946   *Dangerous Money*
1947   Boy! What a Girl!
1948   *Jiggs and Maggie in Court*
1950   *Belle of Old Mexico*
1952   *Buffalo Bill in Tomahawk*
       Territory
1953   *The Man Behind the Gun*
1960   *The Adventures of*
       Huckleberry Finn
Feminism
1920   *Uncharted Channels*
1942   Woman of the Year
Femmes fatales
     Tales of Manhattan
1946   Dirty Gertie from Harlem,
       U.S.A.
1948   The Lady from Shanghai
     Sleep, My Love
1955   *Not As a Stranger*
Fences (Criminal)
1930   *Cascarrabias*
1942   *Below the Border*
Francis Ferdinand, Archduke of
     Austria, 1863-1914
1934   *The Unknown Soldier*
     Speaks
Ferris wheels
1922   Saturday Night
1948   *Moonrise*
Ferryboats
1932   *O festino o la legge*
1933   *Robbers' Roost*
1935   *Chinatown Squad*
1937   *Old Louisiana*
1953   *The Stand at Apache River*
Festivals
1915?   *Sin*
1931   *Hay que casar al príncipe*
1932   *Amore e morte*
1934   *Un capitán de cosacos*
1935   *Alas sobre el Chaco*
     El cantante de Nápoles
1936   *Rebellion*
1939   *The Fighting Gringo*
1942   *Seven Sweethearts*
1947   *Pirates of Monterey*
1949   *Daughter of the West*
1950   *The Toast of New Orleans*
1956   *Wetbacks*
1958   *The Badlanders*
1960   *Pay or Die*
Fetishes
1936   *Yellow Cargo*
William Judd Fetterman
     The Glory Trail
1955   *Chief Crazy Horse*

Fetterman Fight, 1866
1936   The Glory Trail
Feuds
1917   The Little Chevalier
1921   Little Italy
1927   Finnegan's Ball
     The Shamrock and the Rose
1931   The Guilty Generation
1932   *Border Devils*
     The Golden West
1933   Best of Enemies
1935   Captured in Chinatown
1937   *Green Fields*
1938   Outside of Paradise
1943   Doughboys in Ireland
1945   *Great Stagecoach Robbery*
     The Valley of Decision
1947   Thunder Mountain
1948   Music Man
1950   *Jiggs and Maggie Out West*
1951   *The Magnificent Yankee*
1952   *Red Ball Express*
1954   Broken Lance
1955   *The Far Horizons*
1960   Ice Palace
Fever
1943   *Bataan*
     Dr. Gillespie's Criminal
       Case
     Wagon Tracks West
1950   *Jolson Sings Again*
1953   *Cry of the Hunted*
1955   *The Far Horizons*
Fidelity
1915?   *Sin*
1916   Alien Souls
     Mixed Blood
1918   The Honor of His House
1919   As a Man Thinks
     Evangeline
     Lasca
1920   For the Soul of Rafael
1933   *It's Great to Be Alive*
1935   *Alas sobre el Chaco*
1937   *Manhattan*
       Merry-Go-Round
Lew Fields
1925   Lights of Old Broadway
Fiestas
1930   *Alma de gaucho*
1934   *La cruz y la espada*
1939   *Miracle on Main Street*
1941   *Prairie Pioneers*
     Under Fiesta Stars
1947   *Bells of San Fernando*
     Ride the Pink Horse
1949   *The Kissing Bandit*
1951   *The Mark of the Renegade*
1952   *The Fighter*
1956   *Serenade*
Fights
1914   *The Straight Road*
1915   *Captain Courtesy*
     Children of the Ghetto
     Chimmie Fadden
     The Danger Signal
     The Gambler of the West
1917   *A Love Sublime*
     Rosie O'Grady
     The Secret of Eve
     The Sudden Gentleman
     The Tenderfoot
     The Wild Girl
     The Winged Mystery
1918   *The Girl in the Dark*
     Hell's End
     The Hun Within
     In Judgment Of
     The Liar
     Real Folks
     The Red, Red Heart
     The Source
     Tongues of Flame
     The Yellow Dog
1919   *A Fallen Idol*
     Fighting for Gold
     The Gray Horizon
     A Man's Duty
     The Tiger Lily
     The Unpainted Woman
1919?   *The Brand of Judas*
1920   *Locked Lips*
     On with the Dance
     Outside the Law

     The Riddle: Woman
1921   As the World Rolls On
1921?   *The Slave Market*
1923   Regeneration
1924   Smiling Hate
1926   *The Flying Ace*
     The Strong Man
1928   Eleven P.M.
1931   Skyline
1932   Call Her Savage
     Law and Lawless
     Me and My Gal
     Men Are Such Fools
     Le plombier amoureux
     Wild Horse Mesa
1933   *L'amour guide*
     Melodía de arrabal
     Olsen's Big Moment
     Rafter Romance
     El rey de los gitanos
     Song of the Eagle
1934   *The Cactus Kid*
     Charlie Chan's Courage
     La cruz y la espada
     Fighting Through
     Lazy River
     The Lone Defender
     Nada más que una mujer
     'Neath the Arizona Skies
     Riding Speed
     She Was a Lady
     Straight Is the Way
     Wheels of Destiny
1935   Bar-Mitzvah
     Un hombre peligroso
1935?   *The Irish Gringo*
1936   Daniel Boone
     Down to the Sea
     It Had to Happen
     Song of the Gringo
1937   *Boy of the Streets*
     Charlie Chan at the
       Olympics
     Old Louisiana
     Slave Ship
     Thank You, Mr. Moto
     Think Fast, Mr. Moto
1938   *Happy Landing*
     Mis dos amores
     Mr. Moto Takes a Chance
     Rascals
     Spirit of Youth
     Two Gun Man from
       Harlem
     Zamboanga
1939   *Double Deal*
     Moon over Harlem
     Tevya
     Trigger Fingers
     Waterfront
1939?   *A Chinese Gains a Fortune*
       in America
1940   *Mexican Spitfire*
     Three Cheers for the Irish
1941   *Caught in the Act*
     Mutiny in the Arctic
     Road Agent
     This Woman Is Mine
1942   Across the Pacific
     Let's Get Tough!
1943   *Marching On!*
1944   *Block Busters*
     The Racket Man
1945   *Great Stagecoach Robbery*
     In Old New Mexico
     The Mummy's Curse
     Nob Hill
     Sunbonnet Sue
1946   *Canyon Passage*
     Don Ricardo Returns
     Sheriff of Redwood Valley
     South of Monterey
     Sun Valley Cyclone
     Swamp Fire
     Till the End of Time
     Wild Beauty
1947   *The Adventures of Don*
       Coyote
     Boy! What a Girl!
     Buck Privates Come Home
     Buffalo Bill Rides Again
     The Burning Cross
     California
     The Farmer's Daughter
     Oregon Trail Scouts

Untamed Fury
Wild Horse Mesa
1948 *Fighting Father Dunne*
Gun Smugglers
Open Secret
16 Fathoms Deep
Western Heritage
1949 *Arctic Manhunt*
Brothers in the Saddle
Illegal Entry
Masked Raiders
The Mysterious Desperado
Riders of the Range
Rustlers
Stagecoach Kid
Thieves' Highway
1950 *Buccaneer's Girl*
Comanche Territory
The Jackie Robinson Story
Riders of the Pony Express
Storm Over Wyoming
Winchester '73
1951 *Go for Broke!*
1952 *Arctic Flight*
The Battle at Apache Pass
Wagons West
1953 *Bright Road*
Cry of the Hunted
1954 *Siege at Red River*
1955 *Apache Ambush*
Duel on the Mississippi
Fort Yuma
Kentucky Rifle
Santa Fe Passage
1956 *Frontier Woman*
Hot Blood
1957 *Bayou*
Dragoon Wells Massacre
Man in the Shadow
1958 *Apache Territory*
Flaming Frontier
Seven Hills of Rome
Terror in a Texas Town
1959 *John Paul Jones*
Porgy and Bess
1960 *This Rebel Breed*

Fights (Boxing matches)
use **Boxing**

Filial relations
use **Family relationships**

Filibusters
1941 *Louisiana Purchase*

Filipinos
1942 *Across the Pacific*
1943 *Bataan*

Finance—Personal
1922 Hungry Hearts
The Power of Love
1923 The Victor
1931 *Mi último amor*
El proceso de Mary Dugan
1932 The Cohens and Kellys in
Hollywood
1935 *Romance in Manhattan*
1937 *Song of the City*
1939? A Chinese Gains a Fortune
in America
1940 *Jennie*
1946? House-Rent Party
1947 Easy Come, Easy Go
1948 *I Remember Mama*

Financial crisis
1930 *Check and Double Check*
1939 *The Adventures of
Huckleberry Finn*
1941 Adam Had Four Sons
Come Live with Me
1943 Let's Have Fun
Wintertime
1944 Andy Hardy's Blonde
Trouble
1946 *Beware*
The Gentleman Misbehaves
1947 *The Foxes of Harrow*
1949? Harlem Follies
1952 *The Fighter*
1955 Not As a Stranger
1956 The Catered Affair
1960 *The Dark at the Top of the
Stairs*

Fingerprints
1937 *It Could Happen to You*
1939 *Trigger Fingers*

1944 *Cry of the Werewolf*
1946 Dark Alibi
Rendezvous 24
1948 *Shanghai Chest*

Finishing schools
1918 *Marked Cards*
1919 *A Yankee Princess*
1932 *Call Her Savage*
1957 *Band of Angels*

Fire departments
1921 Made in Heaven
1947 *Calendar Girl*

Fire-engines
1933 *La melodía probibida*

Fire-escapes
1939 *Verbena trágica*

Firearms
1918? *Rosemary Climbs the
Heights*
1919 *The Gray Towers Mystery*
1929 *Sombras babaneras*
1931 *The Hurricane Horseman*
Pardon Us
1932 *Le plombier amoureux*
Wild Horse Mesa
1934 *Straight Is the Way*
1935 *Annie Oakley*
1936 *The Green Pastures*
The Last of the Mobicans
Muss 'Em Up
1937 *Prairie Thunder*
1939 *Charlie Chan in Honolulu*
1942 *Apache Trail*
Valley of Hunted Men
1943 *Dr. Gillespie's Criminal
Case*
1944 *Sheriff of Las Vegas*
Waterfront
1945 *Jealousy*
1946 *Tall, Tan and Terrific*
1947 *Marshal of Cripple Creek*
On the Old Spanish Trail
Robin Hood of Monterey
Thunder Mountain
Wild Horse Mesa
1948 *The Dude Goes West*
Gun Smugglers
Key Largo
Old Los Angeles
Shanghai Chest
The Time of Your Life
1949 *Harbor of Missing Men*
Laramie
The Prairie
Ride, Ryder, Ride!
Rose of the Yukon
1950 *Bandit Queen*
The Breaking Point
Colt .45
I Killed Geronimo
North of the Great Divide
Sands of Iwo Jima
1951 *Hurricane Island*
Tomahawk
1952 *Brave Warrior*
California Conquest
My Man and I
1953 *Old Overland Trail*
1954 Massacre Canyon
Overland Pacific
1956 *Frontier Woman*
1958 *Gunman's Walk*
1959 The Sheriff of Fractured Jaw

Fireflies
1941 *Come Live with Me*

Firemen
1925 One of the Bravest
1927 Heroes in Blue
1935 *The Irish in Us*
1947 *Calendar Girl*
It Had To Be You

Fires
1915 *The Pageant of San
Francisco*
1916 *The Half-Breed*
1920 *The North Wind's Malice*
1923 *Regeneration*
1924 Tongues of Flame
1926 *The Flying Ace*
Puppets
1929 *The Younger Generation*
1932 *Call Her Savage*
Hypnotized
Law and Lawless

1934 *As the Earth Turns*
The Lone Defender
She Was a Lady
Wheels of Destiny
White Heat
1935 *Rescue Squad*
1936 *Charlie Chan at the Race
Track*
The Last of the Mohicans
*The Phantom of Santa Fe
Tundra*
1937 *Boots and Saddles*
Song of the City
Souls at Sea
1938 *The Duke Is Tops*
In Old Chicago
Passport Husband
1939 *Gone With the Wind*
1940 *Am I Guilty?*
Lucky Cisco Kid
Son of Ingagi
1941 *Belle Starr*
The Face Behind the Mask
1942 *Shut My Big Mouth*
Tortilla Flat
1943 *Action in the North
Atlantic*
Crash Dive
Dixie
1944 *Going My Way*
The San Antonio Kid
1945 *Our Vines Have Tender
Grapes*
1946 *Swamp Fire*
1947 *Dangerous Venture*
Dark Delusion
Pirates of Monterey
Rustlers of Devil's Canyon
1948 *Four Faces West*
1949 *Arctic Fury*
Call of the Forest
Ranger of Cherokee Strip
Rustlers
Tulsa
1950 *Indian Territory*
1951 *Distant Drums*
The Magnificent Yankee
1953 *Beneath the 12-Mile Reef*
The Stand at Apache River
1955 *Bad Day at Black Rock*
Santa Fe Passage
Seminole Uprising
1956 *The White Squaw*
1957 *The Lawless Eighties*
1958 *Machete*
1959 *John Paul Jones*
Thunder in the Sun
1960 *The Last Voyage*

Fireworks
1958 *The Badlanders*

Firing squads
1916 *Following the Flag in
Mexico*
1917 *The Little American*
1937 *Drums of Destiny*
1939 *The Return of the Cisco Kid*
1945 *South of the Rio Grande*
1947 *Robin Hood of Monterey*
1953 *The Pathfinder*

Fish
1934 *Song of the Islands*
1937 *Man of the People*

Fishermen
1914 John Barleycorn
1917 *The Bottle Imp*
The Pulse of Life
1924 Defying the Law
1931 La fruta amarga
1932 Tiger Shark
1934 He Was Her Man
1936 El diablo del mar
Sea Spoilers
1937 *Song of the City*
1938 Spawn of the North
1939 Fisherman's Wharf
1943 *Jack London*
Redbead from Manhattan
1945 *A Medal for Benny*
1949 Tuna Clipper
1950 *The Breaking Point*
The Toast of New Orleans
1951 The Raging Tide
1953 Beneath the 12-Mile Reef
1960 *Ice Palace*

Fishing
1921 *By Right of Birth*
1922 Nanook of the North
1931 *Noche de duendes*
1932 Dangers of the Arctic
1940 *Taku*
1941 *Hurry, Charlie, Hurry*
1948 *Louisiana Story*
Rocky
1950 *Stars in My Crown*
1956 *Wetbacks*
1959 *The Last Angry Man*

Fishing boats
1923 *Regeneration*
1939 *Daughters Courageous*
1949 *Harbor of Missing Men*
1950 The Breaking Point
1953 *Beneath the 12-Mile Reef*
Thunder Bay

Fishing rights
1925 *Braveheart*
1947 *Spoilers of the North*

Fishing villages
1925 My Son
1934 Lazy River
1939 *Daughters Courageous*
1953 *Beneath the 12-Mile Reef*
Thunder Bay
1959 *Night of the Quarter Moon*
Porgy and Bess
1960 *Ice Palace*

Fishmongers
1932 *Senza mamma
e'nnamurato*

Fistfights
1915 *A Yankee from the West*
1918 *Untamed*
1920 *Our Christianity and
Nobody's Child*
1931 *The Hurricane Horseman*
Young Sinners
1932 *Huddle*
White Eagle
1933 *Robbers' Roost*
Thundering Herd
1934 *The Prescott Kid*
White Heat
1935 *Charlie Chan in Shanghai*
Rendezvous
1936 *Contra la corriente*
Kelly the Second
My American Wife
Rebellion
1937 *Big City*
El capitán Tormenta
That I May Live
1938 *California Frontier*
Life Goes On
The Renegade Ranger
Swing!
1939 *Frontiers of '49*
Harlem Rides the Range
1940 *The Great Advisor*
Mystery in Swing
While Thousands Cheer
1941 *Birth of the Blues*
Murder on Lenox Avenue
New York Town
Saddlemates
Sunday Sinners
1942 *Foreign Agent*
Juke Girl
Lucky Ghost
North to the Klondike
Valley of the Sun
1943 *Cabin in the Sky*
In Old Oklahoma
Land of Hunted Men
The Ox-Bow Incident
1944 *The San Antonio Kid*
The Sullivans
Vigilantes of Dodge City
1945 *Phantom of the Plains*
1946 *Santa Fe Uprising*
Saratoga Trunk
Sunset Pass
Wild West
1947 *Little Mister Jim*
The Mighty McGurk
Thunder Mountain
1948 *The Arizona Ranger*
The Dude Goes West
The Fight Never Ends
Guns of Hate
Harpoon

The Lady from Shanghai
The Luck of the Irish
Miracle in Harlem
Red River
Silver Trails
The Time of Your Life
1949 *Border Incident*
The Kissing Bandit
Knock on Any Door
Lookout Sister
The Quiet One
Rose of the Yukon
Souls of Sin
1949? *Girl in Room 20*
The Joint Is Jumpin'
1950 *Ambush*
Border Treasure
Indian Territory
The Lawless
Raiders of Tomahawk
  Creek
Rio Grande
Sands of Iwo Jima
Sunset in the West
1951 *Across the Wide Missouri*
Little Big Horn
The Raging Tide
Show Boat
A Streetcar Named Desire
1952 *The Big Sky*
Buffalo Bill in Tomahawk
  Territory
Bugles in the Afternoon
The Fabulous Senorita
High Noon
Indian Uprising
Japanese War Bride
The Quiet Man
Red Ball Express
Rose of Cimarron
Woman in the Dark
1953 *Ambush at Tomahawk Gap*
Arrowhead
Beneath the 12-Mile Reef
The Charge at Feather
  River
Column South
The Man Behind the Gun
The Man from the Alamo
Old Overland Trail
San Antone
Sangaree
1954 *Battle of Rogue River*
Broken Lance
Carmen Jones
Drums Across the River
Hondo
1955 *Blackboard Jungle*
Davy Crockett, King of the
  Wild Frontier
The Far Horizons
Violent Saturday
1956 *The Broken Star*
The Burning Hills
Davy Crockett and the
  River Pirates
The Last Hunt
Man from Del Rio
Raw Edge
The Searchers
The White Squaw
1957 *All Mine to Give*
Edge of the City
Joe Dakota
1958 *The Light in the Forest*
Never Love a Stranger
The Young Lions
1959 *The Jayhawkers!*
Thunder in the Sun
Yellowstone Kelly
The Young Land
1960 *Flaming Star*
I Passed for White
Bob Fitzsimmons
1947 *Vigilantes of Boomtown*
Fixed fights
1920 *The Brute*
1932 *Flesh*
1936 *Laughing Irish Eyes*
1939 *Winner Take All*
1943 *The Girl from Monterrey*
1947 *Body and Soul*
1949 *The Cowboy and the*
  Prizefighter

1952 *The Ring*
Fixed horse races
1918 *Sandy*
1934 *Broadway Bill*
1935 *Riddle Ranch*
1936 *Charlie Chan at the Race*
  Track
Flagellation
   use **Whips and whippings**
Flags
1917 *The Slacker*
1918 *Tony America*
1919 *The Volcano*
1936 *It Had to Happen*
1950 *Sands of Iwo Jima*
Flags of truce
1951 *Slaughter Trail*
Flamenco dancers
1960 *The Sign of Zorro*
Flappers
1925 My Son
1927 *Irish Hearts*
1928 *Riley the Cop*
Flattery
1926 *Blarney*
Flax
1939 *Mirele Efros*
Flight crews, Military
1943 Air Force
Flight instructors
   use **Flight training**
Flight training
1936 *Sum Hun*
Flirtation
1919 *As a Man Thinks*
   Lasca
   Mandarin's Gold
1931 *The Cisco Kid*
   The Cohens and Kellys in
    Africa
   ¿Conoces a tu mujer?
   Soyons gais
1932 *Marido y mujer*
1933 *Yo, tú y ella*
1934 *As the Earth Turns*
   Straight Is the Way
   La veuve joyeuse
1935 *L'homme des Folies Bergère*
   Rosa de Francia
   So Red the Rose
1940 *The Mark of Zorro*
1947 *Mantan Runs for Mayor*
   Sepia Cinderella
1954 *They Rode West*
1956 *Baby Doll*
1959 *Odds Against Tomorrow*
Flirts
1919 *False Evidence*
   The Last of His People
1920? *Reformation*
1926 *The Campus Flirt*
1930 *Alma de gaucho*
   Una cana al aire
1931 *Street Scene*
   The White Renegade
1933 *It's Great to Be Alive*
1938 The Toy Wife
1939 *Gone With the Wind*
1943 *Let's Have Fun*
1944 *Andy Hardy's Blonde*
   Trouble
   Mr. Skeffington
1945 *Where Do We Go From*
   Here?
1946 *Mantan Messes Up*
1946? *Go Down, Death!*
1960 *Key Witness*
Flogging
1941 *This Woman Is Mine*
1943 *Hitler's Children*
Floods
1915 *The Immigrant*
1925 Galloping Vengeance
1931 Die Maske Fällt
1936 *The Green Pastures*
1941 *Lady from Louisiana*
1945 *Of One Blood*
   Our Vines Have Tender
    Grapes
1960 *Wild River*

Florida
1917 Unconquered
1926 *The Flying Ace*
   Sweet Daddies
1928 The Mating Call
1931 *The Guilty Generation*
   Young Sinners
1934 Chloe: Love Is Calling You
1936 *Down to the Sea*
1937 *Maid of Salem*
1942 *Juke Girl*
1948 16 Fathoms Deep
1950 *The Jackie Robinson Story*
1952 *Bright Victory*
1953 Beneath the 12-Mile Reef
   Seminole
1957 *The Brothers Rico*
   Naked in the Sun
Florida—History
1937 *Drums of Destiny*
1951 *Hurricane Island*
Florists
1915 *The Alien*
1918 Real Folks
1925 *The Man in Blue*
1929 Mister Antonio
1942 *Holiday Inn*
Flower vendors
1915 *The Adventures of a*
   Madcap
1919 *Hearts of Men*
1921 *Puppets of Fate*
1925 *The Beautiful City*
1939 *Motel the Operator*
Theodore Flowers
1926 The Fighting Deacon
Flowers
   Rose of the Tenements
1932 *The Forty-Niners*
1934 *Song of the Islands*
1948 *Jiggs and Maggie in Court*
1951 *Queen for a Day*
1959 *The Black Orchid*
Flutes
1950 *Young Daniel Boone*
1960 *The Unforgiven*
Fog
1930 *Anna Christie*
1942 *The Navy Comes Through*
   Whispering Ghosts
1945 *Escape in the Fog*
1946 *Swamp Fire*
1949 *Harbor of Missing Men*
1950 *Battleground*
Folies Bergère
1935 L'homme des Folies Bergère
Folk dancing
1914 *The Indian Wars*
1920 *Frontier Days*
1934 *La cruz y la espada*
Folk songs
1951 *Slaughter Trail*
1952 *Anything Can Happen*
Food
1934 *Our Daily Bread*
1942 *Rio Rita*
Food fights
1948 *Jiggs and Maggie in Court*
Food, Canned
1939 Straight to Heaven
Football
1922 The Great Alone
1925 *Braveheart*
1927 Red Clay
1928 Hold 'Em Yale
1930 Sunny Skies
1932 Huddle
1937 *Life Begins in College*
1940 Knute Rockne—All American
   While Thousands Cheer
1949 *Prejudice*
1951 Jim Thorpe—All-American
1955 *The Long Gray Line*
Football coaches
1937 *Life Begins in College*
1940 *While Thousands Cheer*
1951 *Jim Thorpe—All-American*
   Saturday's Hero
Football players
1933 *La melodía probibida*
1934 *Fighting Through*
1940 Knute Rockne—All American
   Too Many Girls

   Too Many Girls
   While Thousands Cheer
1951 *Saturday's Hero*
Fops
1931 *Echec au roi*
1936 *The Bold Caballero*
1940 *The Mark of Zorro*
Ford's Theatre (Washington, DC)
1930 Abraham Lincoln
1936 *The Prisoner of Shark*
   Island
Foreclosure
1917 *The Little Samaritan*
1938 *Two Gun Man from*
   Harlem
1947 *The Last Round-Up*
Foreign agents
1917 Follow the Girl
   The Secret Game
1919? *America Was Right*
1938 *The Buccaneer*
   Hawaii Calls
1939 *City in Darkness*
   Mr. Moto's Last Warning
1941 *Mystery Ship*
1942 Little Tokyo, U.S.A.
   Valley of Hunted Men
1944 *Charlie Chan in the Secret*
   Service
1945 The House on 92nd St.
1948 Docks of New Orleans
Foreign correspondents
1943 *Three Hearts for Julia*
Foreign Legion
   use **France. Army. Foreign**
    Legion
Foremen
1919 *The Right to Happiness*
1934 *Chloe: Love Is Calling You*
1948 *Reaching from Heaven*
1950 *Give Us This Day*
   North of the Great Divide
1957 *Man in the Shadow*
Forensic pathology
1950 Mystery Street
Forensics
1946 *The Red Dragon*
1951 *Mask of the Dragon*
1959 *The FBI Story*
Forest fires
1918 *Tongues of Flame*
1923 Scars of Jealousy
1934 *The Rabbi's Power*
1954 *Dangerous Mission*
Forest rangers
1921 Anne of Little Smoky
Forests
1914 *When Broadway Was a*
   Trail
1916 *The Half-Breed*
1917 *The Woman and the Beast*
1932 *Genoveffa*
1935 *Shir Hashirim*
1936 *Tundra*
1947 *The Return of Rin Tin Tin*
1948 *The Boy with Green Hair*
   The Luck of the Irish
1949 *Top O' the Morning*
Forgers and forgery
1918 *The Liar*
1920 *The Man Who Dared*
1921 *By Right of Birth*
1922 Peacock Alley
1929 *Sombras habaneras*
1930 Big Boy
1932 *The Match King*
1933 *Diplomaniacs*
   Dos noches
1935 Charlie Chan in Paris
1939 *City in Darkness*
   Mr. Wong in Chinatown
1940 *East of the River*
1942 *Young America*
1946 *Dangerous Money*
   Dark Alibi
1947 *Northwest Outpost*
   Riding the California Trail
1948 *Western Heritage*
1949 *The Red Menace*
   Satan's Cradle
1950 The Baron of Arizona
1957 *Joe Dakota*

Forgiveness
1925 Body and Soul
1932 *O festino o la legge*
1948 *Reaching from Heaven*
1950 Give Us This Day
1958 *Wild Is the Wind*
1959 Anna Lucasta

Formulas
use Chemical formulas;
  Secret formulas

Fort Abraham Lincoln (ND)
1957 *Run of the Arrow*

Fort Apache Indian Reservation (AZ)
1954 *Taza, Son of Cochise*

Fort Bliss (TX)
1916 *Following the Flag in Mexico*

Fort Clark (TX)
1953 *Arrowhead*

Fort Detroit (IL)
1952 Battles of Chief Pontiac

Fort Harrod (KY)
1931 *The Great Meadow*

Fort Laramie (WY)
1932 *The Forty-Niners*
1955 *Chief Crazy Horse*
  The Gun That Won the West
  White Feather
1956 *Westward Ho the Wagons!*
1957 Revolt at Fort Laramie
1959 *The Oregon Trail*

Fort Le Boeuf (PA)
1951 *When the Redskins Rode*

Fort Leavenworth (KS)
1940 *Santa Fe Trail*

Fort Lincoln (NE)
1958 *Tonka*

Fort McHenry (MD)
1943 *Three Hearts for Julia*

Fort Osage (MO)
1952 *Fort Osage*

Fort Phil Kearny (WY)
1936 *The Glory Trail*
1951 Tomahawk
1955 *Chief Crazy Horse*

Fort Pitt (PA)
1948 Unconquered

Fort Ross (CA)
1947 Northwest Outpost
1952 *California Conquest*

Fort Sumter (SC)
1915 *Under Southern Skies*

Fort William Henry (NY)
1936 *The Last of the Mohicans*
1947 *Last of the Redmen*

Fortresses
1950 *Devil's Doorway*

Forts
1914 *Northern Lights*
1915 *The Girl I Left Behind Me*
1917 *The Plow Woman*
1925 A Daughter of the Sioux
  Tonio, Son of the Sierras
1926 The Devil Horse
  The Frontier Trail
  Under Fire
  War Paint
1932 *Texas Pioneers*
1933 *The California Trail*
1935 *Cyclone of the Saddle*
  Fighting Pioneers
1937 *Boots and Saddles*
1939 *Allegheny Uprising*
  Drums Along the Mohawk
1940 *Geronimo*
  Hi-Yo Silver
  Northwest Passage (Book I—Rogers' Rangers)
1941 *This Woman Is Mine*
1947 Northwest Outpost
1948 Fort Apache
  Fury at Furnace Creek
  The Paleface
1949 *Daughter of the West*
  Laramie
  Massacre River
  She Wore a Yellow Ribbon
1950 *Ambush*
  Davy Crockett, Indian Scout

I Killed Geronimo
The Iroquois Trail
Rio Grande
Young Daniel Boone
1951 *Distant Drums*
  Fort Defiance
  The Last Outpost
  New Mexico
  Only the Valiant
  Slaughter Trail
  Warpath
1952 *The Battle at Apache Pass*
  Bugles in the Afternoon
  Indian Uprising
  The Savage
1953 *The Charge at Feather River*
  Column South
  The Great Sioux Uprising
  The Nebraskan
  The Pathfinder
  Seminole
1954 *Arrow in the Dust*
  Battle of Rogue River
  Drum Beat
  Saskatchewan
  Siege at Red River
  They Rode West
  War Arrow
  The Yellow Tomahawk
1955 Fort Yuma
  The Indian Fighter
  Seminole Uprising
  Smoke Signal
1956 *Daniel Boone, Trail Blazer*
  The Last Frontier
  Mohawk
  Quincannon, Frontier Scout
  7th Cavalry
1957 *The Deerslayer*
  Dragoon Wells Massacre
  Naked in the Sun
  Pawnee
  Tomahawk Trail
1958 Fort Bowie
  Oregon Passage
1959 *The Wonderful Country*

Fortune hunters
1915 The Spender
1916 Alien Souls
  Lord Loveland Discovers America
  The Thousand Dollar Husband
1917 Castles for Two
  Forbidden Paths
1930 The Big Pond
  El príncipe del dólar
1931 *Lo mejor es reír*
1932 *Unashamed*
1933 *Olsen's Big Moment*
1935 A Night at the Opera
  The Singing Vagabond
1936 Rainbow on the River
  Robin Hood of El Dorado
1938 *Rascals*
1939 Fisherman's Wharf
1940 *Lucky Cisco Kid*
  Midnight Shadow
  Music in My Heart
1943 *Wintertime*
1948 Singin' Spurs
1951 *Cuban Fireball*

Fortune-tellers
1921 The Swamp
1933 *The Eternal Jew*
  Man from Monterey
1934 *La buenaventura*
1935 *Un hombre peligroso*
  Melody Trail
1938 *My Lucky Star*
  Rascals
1939 *Trigger Fingers*
1941 Up Jumped the Devil
1943 *The Leopard Man*
1945 *Anoush*
1946 *Dirty Gertie from Harlem, U.S.A.*
  Singin' in the Corn
1947 *Sepia Cinderella*
1948? *Boarding House Blues*
1956 *Hot Blood*

Stephen Collins Foster
1935 *Harmony Lane*

Foster children
1917 *The Peddler*
1919 The Little Diplomat
1920 Rio Grande
1932 *Le cas du docteur Brenner*
  White Eagle
1933 Circle Canyon
1934 'Neath the Arizona Skies
1948 *Miracle in Harlem*
1953 Ride, Vaquero!
  Sangaree

Foster parents
1914? *The Mysterious Mr. Wu Chung Foo*
1915 *The Adventures of a Madcap*
1916 *Broken Fetters*
  The Flames of Johannis
  The Flower of No Man's Land
1916? Should a Baby Die?
1917 *A Jewel in Pawn*
  A Kentucky Cinderella
  The Secret of Eve
  Threads of Fate
1918 *An Alien Enemy*
  Broken Ties
  The Temple of Dusk
1920 *The Cup of Fury*
  Huckleberry Finn
1921 By Right of Birth
1927 Sally in Our Alley
1932 *Le cas du docteur Brenner*
1934 *La buenaventura*
1936 Rainbow on the River
1937 *It Could Happen to You*
  Where Is My Child?
1939 *The Adventures of Huckleberry Finn*
1940 Her Second Mother
  Tengo fe en ti
1941 *Under Fiesta Stars*
1948 Big City
  The Boy with Green Hair
1952 *Rose of Cimarron*
1957 *Burden of Truth*

Foundlings
1916 The Criminal
1917 The Hidden Children
  Lost in Transit
1927 For the Love of Mike
1930 Around the Corner
1936 General Spanky
1948 Big City
1952 Rose of Cimarron
1960 *The Unforgiven*

Foundries
1938 *Spirit of Youth*
1940 *Son of Ingagi*

Fourth of July
1934 *Laughing Boy*
1939 *Judge Hardy and Son*
1941 *Western Union*
1942 Holiday Inn
1943 *Yankee Doodle Dandy*
1944 *An American Romance*
1950 Winchester '73
1957 *Raintree County*

Fox hunts
1931 *The Squaw Man*
1936 *Kelly the Second*

Foxes
1925 Kivalina of the Ice Lands
1946 *Song of the South*

Frame-ups
1914 The Great Diamond Robbery
  The Littlest Rebel
1915 The Alien
1915? *The Beachcomber*
1916 The Colored American Winning His Suit
  For the Defense
  A Son of Erin
1917 My Fighting Gentleman
  The Sudden Gentleman
  Unconquered
1918 The Reckoning Day
  Shifting Sands
1919 *Spotlight Sadie*
1919? *The Brand of Judas*
1920 The Man Who Dared
  Outside the Law

1921 *As the World Rolls On*
1923 Flames of Wrath
1924 *His Darker Self*
1925 Tonio, Son of the Sierras
1927 The Dove
  The Gay Defender
1928 The Hawk's Nest
  Orphan of the Sage
1930 *Los que danzan*
1931 *Cavalier of the West*
  Gentleman's Fate
  Oklahoma Jim
  Riders of the Rio
  Smart Money
1932 *Border Devils*
  Harlem Is Heaven
  Hidden Valley
  El hombre que asesinó
  Wild Horse Mesa
1934 The Cat's-Paw
  The Fighting Hero
  He Was Her Man
1935 *¡Asegure a su mujer!*
  Lem Hawkins' Confession
  Wolf Riders
1935? *The Irish Gringo*
1936 After the Thin Man
  Below the Deadline
  The Bold Caballero
  The Glory Trail
  Song of the Gringo
1937 Hills of Old Wyoming
  Law and Lead
  Music for Madame
  That I May Live
1938 The Adventures of Tom Sawyer
  Life Goes On
  The Renegade Ranger
  Two Gun Man from Harlem
1939 *Allegheny Uprising*
  The Cisco Kid and the Lady
  The Fighting Gringo
  Harlem Rides the Range
  In Old Caliente
  Lying Lips
  Mothers of Today
  Reform School
  Straight to Heaven
  Trigger Fingers
194- *Mistaken Identity*
1940 Behind the News
  Broken Strings
  Covered Wagon Days
  East of the River
  The Fatal Hour
  The Gay Caballero
  Her Second Mother
  Lucky Cisco Kid
  The Notorious Elinor Lee
  Rhythm of the Rio Grande
1941 Louisiana Purchase
  The Pioneers
  Prairie Pioneers
  Thunder Over the Prairie
1942 Castle in the Desert
  Juke Girl
  King of the Stallions
  Little Tokyo, U.S.A.
  Lucky Ghost
  Take My Life
1943 The Leopard Man
  Margin for Error
  Wagon Tracks West
1944 Address Unknown
  Sheriff of Las Vegas
  Sonora Stagecoach
  Vigilantes of Dodge City
1945 Great Stagecoach Robbery
  Jealousy
1946 Dark Alibi
  Sheriff of Redwood Valley
  Sun Valley Cyclone
  Sunset Pass
  The Trap
1946? Go Down, Death!
1947 Bowery Buckaroos
  Buffalo Bill Rides Again
  On the Old Spanish Trail
  Robin Hood of Monterey
  Thunder Mountain
  Wild Horse Mesa
1948 Fury at Furnace Creek
  Fury at Furnace Creek
  The Lady from Shanghai

Shanghai Chest
The Time of Your Life
1949 *The Cowboy and the
        Indians*
      The Dalton Gang
      The Daring Caballero
      Lookout Sister
      Roll Thunder Roll!
      Rustlers
      Stallion Canyon
1950 *Belle of Old Mexico*
      The Girl from San Lorenzo
      Intruder in the Dust
      The Missourians
      So Young, So Bad
      Storm Over Wyoming
1951 *Native Son*
      The Raging Tide
1952 *The Battle at Apache Pass*
      Indian Uprising
      Trail of the Arrow
1953 *Ambush at Tomahawk Gap*
      *Captain John Smith and
        Pocahontas*
      The Great Sioux Uprising
1954 *Drums Across the River*
1955 Headline Hunters
1956 The Lone Ranger
1957 Joe Dakota
      Journey to Freedom
1958 Touch of Evil
1960 Oklahoma Territory
      This Rebel Breed

France
1917 The Little American
      The Little Chevalier
1918 Fields of Honor
      The Greatest Thing in Life
      The Price of Applause
1919 The Lost Battalion
1920 Humoresque
1921 The Money Maniac
1927 Ham and Eggs at the Front
      Red Clay
1928 Anybody Here Seen Kelly?
1930 *Amor audaz*
      Anybody's War
      ¡De frente, marchen!
1931 *Beyond Victory*
      La mujer X
      Su noche de bodas
1934 *La buenaventura*
1939 *City in Darkness*
      Mr. Moto's Last Warning
1940 *The Fighting 69th*
1947? Swanee Showboat
1952 *Red Ball Express*
1957 *Journey to Freedom*
1958 The Young Lions
**France—German occupation,
  1940-1945**
      Kings Go Forth
France—History—1789-1815
1916 Silks and Satins
France—History—19th century
1935 Naughty Marietta
**France—History—Revolution,
  1789-1799**
1919? The Brand of Judas
1940 New Moon
France. Army. Foreign Legion
1935 *De la sartén al fuego*
**Francis Joseph I, Emperor of
  Austria, 1830-1916**
1929 *Is Everybody Happy?*
1930 *The Melody Man*
Franciscans
1934 *La cruz y la espada*
1951 *The Mark of the Renegade*
Benjamin Franklin
1940 *Elsa Maxwell's Public Deb
        No. 1*
1959 *John Paul Jones*
Fraternities
1937 *Life Begins in College*
      Think Fast, Mr. Moto
Fratricide
1921 A Modern Cain
1942 Nazi Agent
1954 *Saskatchewan*
1956 *Dakota Incident*

Fraud
1914 Rose of the Rancho
1915 *Chimmie Fadden Out West*
      Marse Covington
1918 *Laughing Bill Hyde*
      The Reckoning Day
1922 Silver Spurs
1931 *Nuit d'Espagne*
1932 The Black King
      Le bluffeur
      The Match King
      White Eagle
1933 *Espérame*
1936 Charlie Chan at the Circus
      Silly Billies
1938 *The Duke Is Tops*
1940 The Gay Caballero
1943 The Law Rides Again
1947 Reet, Petite and Gone
1949 *Daughter of the West*
      The Red Menace
      Satan's Cradle
1956 *Crowded Paradise*
      Death of a Scoundrel
Fredericksburg (VA)
1959 *John Paul Jones*
Freemasons
1932 *The Black King*
Freezers
1944 *The Racket Man*
Freight lines
1941 *Doomed Caravan*
1944 *Vigilantes of Dodge City*
1948 Indian Agent
1954 *Drums Across the River*
1958 *Blood Arrow*
Freighters
1939 Charlie Chan in Honolulu
1940 Escape to Glory
1956 *Wetbacks*
John Fremont
1940 *Kit Carson*
1952 *California Conquest*
French
1915 The Clemenceau Case
1916 For the Defense
      Silks and Satins
1920 The Good-Bad Wife
      The Last of the Mobicans
1930 The Big Pond
1931 La ley del harem
      Monerías
1934 *Granaderos del amor*
1935 Rosa de Francia
1936 *The Last of the Mobicans*
1937 That Girl from Paris
1938 *Charlie Chan at Monte
        Carlo*
      The Rage of Paris
1940 New Moon
1941 *Lady from Louisiana*
      The Mexican Spitfire's Baby
1943 *Gangway for Tomorrow*
      Tabiti Honey
1945 *Johnny Angel*
1946 The Gentleman Misbehaves
1947 *Boy! What a Girl!*
      Buck Privates Come Home
      Copacabana
1950 *Battleground*
      Young Daniel Boone
1951 When the Redskins Rode
1953 *Fort Ti*
      The Pathfinder
      Sangaree
French Americans
1915 *Chimmie Fadden*
      The Clemenceau Case
1916 Silks and Satins
1917 The Bond Between
      The Little Chevalier
      A Love Sublime
      The Renaissance at
        Charleroi
1918 A Broadway Scandal
      Fields of Honor
      Find the Woman
      The Golden Wall
      The Greatest Thing in Life
1919 His Parisian Wife
      Yvonne from Paris
1920 The Good-Bad Wife
      White Youth

1921 Love's Plaything
1922 Peacock Alley
1923 Backbone
1925 Scarlet Saint
1928 Anybody Here Seen Kelly?
1938 The Toy Wife
1944 Block Busters
1949 The Fighting Kentuckian
      Ride, Ryder, Ride!
1950 *The Iroquois Trail*
1951 *Westward the Women*
1952 *The Iron Mistress*
1956 *Westward Ho the Wagons!*
1957 *Revolt at Fort Laramie*
1958 *Flaming Frontier*
1959 *The Jayhawkers!*
      Thunder in the Sun
1960 *Cimarron*
French Canadians
1930 Monsieur le Fox
1941 This Woman Is Mine
1951 *Across the Wide Missouri*
1953 *Fort Ti*
1954 *Saskatchewan*
1955 *The Far Horizons*
Fresno (CA)
1934 *La ciudad de cartón*
1949 *Thieves' Highway*
Friendship
1914 Northern Lights
      *The Redemption of David
        Corson*
1915 The Birth of a Nation
      The Clemenceau Case
      Hearts of Men
1916 *Betrayed*
      Three of Many
1917 The Trouble Buster
1918 Laughing Bill Hyde
      The Unbeliever
1919 The Gray Horizon
      Hearts of Men
      His Parisian Wife
1920 Huckleberry Finn
      Li Ting Lang
1922 Pals of the West
1925 Cobra
1927 Lost at the Front
1928 Tyrant of Red Gulch
1931 *Los calaveras*
      Carne de cabaret
      *The Cohens and Kellys in
        Africa*
      Huckleberry Finn
      Little Caesar
      El pasado acusa
1932 The Cohens and Kellys in
        Hollywood
      ¿Cuándo te suicidas?
      La foule burle
      The Hatchet Man
      Une beure près de toi
      El hombre que asesinó
      Huddle
      So Big
      Soñadores de la gloria
      Texas Pioneers
1933 The Cohens and Kellys in
        Trouble
      Song of the Eagle
      Broadway Bill
1934 *Un capitán de cosacos*
      Wagon Wheels
1935 Alas sobre el Chaco
      McFadden's Flats
      Ruggles of Red Gap
1936 *Show Boat*
      Star for a Night
      Sutter's Gold
1937 *Arshin Mal Alan*
      Bargain with Bullets
      The Devil's Playground
      Natalka Poltavka
      The Plainsman
      Slave Ship
1938 *Marusia*
      The Rage of Paris
      The Renegade Ranger
      Spawn of the North
1939 The Adventures of
        Huckleberry Finn
      The Bronze Buckaroo
      Double Deal
      Keep Punching
      Waterfront

1940 *If I Had My Way*
      *Northwest Passage (Book
        I—Rogers' Rangers)*
      Viva Cisco Kid
1941 *Accent on Love*
1942 *Gentleman Jim*
      Juke Girl
      Sunday Punch
      Tortilla Flat
      Wings for the Eagle
      Young America
1943 Crash Dive
      The Outlaw
1944 *The San Antonio Kid*
1945 *The Navajo Trail*
      The Valley of Decision
1946 *Bad Bascomb*
      Canyon Passage
      Don Ricardo Returns
      Gas House Kids
      Song of the South
1947 Pirates of Monterey
1948 Four Faces West
      Gentleman's Agreement
      Red River
      Shep Comes Home
      The Time of Your Life
1949 *Colorado Territory*
      Home of the Brave
      Massacre River
      Pinky
      Streets of Laredo
      Tale of the Navajos
1949? Girl in Room 20
1950 The Cariboo Trail
      *The Daughter of Rosie
        O'Grady*
      Give Us This Day
      Intruder in the Dust
      Young Man with a Horn
1951 *The House on Telegraph
        Hill*
      Show Boat
1952 *Bright Victory*
      High Noon
      *It's a Big Country: An
        American Anthology*
      The Raiders
      The Savage
1953 *The Great Sioux Uprising*
      The Pathfinder
      Seminole
      So Big
      The Sun Shines Bright
      Thunder Bay
1954 *Cattle Queen of Montana*
      Go Man Go
      The Yellow Tomahawk
1955 *Davy Crockett, King of the
        Wild Frontier*
      The Far Horizons
      The Gun That Won the West
      The Long Gray Line
      Marty
      White Feather
1956 The Broken Star
      The Catered Affair
      Dakota Incident
      *Davy Crockett and the
        River Pirates*
      Pillars of the Sky
1957 Burden of Truth
      The Midnight Story
      Naked in the Sun
      Raintree County
      War Drums
1958 Flaming Frontier
      Kings Go Forth
      The Light in the Forest
      Marjorie Morningstar
      Never Love a Stranger
      Touch of Evil
      The Young Lions
1959 The Crimson Kimono
      Imitation of Life
      The Jayhawkers!
      *The World, the Flesh and
        the Devil*
      Yellowstone Kelly
1960 The Adventures of
        Huckleberry Finn
      Cimarron
      Hell to Eternity
      I Passed for White
      Take a Giant Step

Frogs
1946   *Song of the South*
Frontier and pioneer life
1913?   The Call of the Blood
1916   Ramona
1919   The Westerners
1920   The Last of the Mohicans
1923   The Lone Wagon
1926   War Paint
1927   Don Mike
        The Red Raiders
1928   The Glorious Trail
        Wyoming
Frontier scouts
    use Scouts (Frontier)
Fruit
1918   *Tony America*
Fugitives
1916   The Half-Breed
1917   The Woman and the Beast
1918   Huck and Tom; or, the
        Further Adventures of
        Tom Sawyer
1919   Just Squaw
1920   Outside the Law
1924   The Mine with the Iron
        Door
1924?   The Flaming Crisis
1930   The Melody Man
        El último de los Vargas
1931   *Cheri-Bibi*
1934   *Un capitán de cosacos*
        The Fighting Hero
        Our Daily Bread
1935   *Un hombre peligroso*
        Naughty Marietta
1936   *Love and Sacrifice*
        Yellow Cargo
1937   *Maid of Salem*
        That I May Live
1938   *Birthright*
1939   Heaven with a Barbed Wire
        Fence
        Waterfront
1940   *Escape to Glory*
        Girl from God's Country
        The Man I Married
        Music in My Heart
1941   *Thunder Over the Prairie*
        Western Union
1943   The Outlaw
        Redhead from Manhattan
1946   Bad Bascomb
1947   Desperate
        Juke Joint
        On the Old Spanish Trail
        Robin Hood of Monterey
1948   Four Faces West
        Half Past Midnight
1949   Brothers in the Saddle
        Illegal Entry
        Lust for Gold
        The Prairie
        Ranger of Cherokee Strip
        Stallion Canyon
1950   *The Lawless*
        The Missourians
        Riders of the Pony Express
        Rio Grande
1951   Fort Defiance
        The Raging Tide
1953   Cry of the Hunted
        *The Member of the
        Wedding*
        The Nebraskan
1954   *Dangerous Mission*
        Saskatchewan
1956   Secret of Treasure Mountain
1957   The Ride Back
1958   Escape from Red Rock
Sarah Fuller
1919   *Deliverance*
Robert Fulton
1923   Little Old New York
Fun houses
1944   *The Chinese Cat*
Fund-raising
1945   *Between Two Women*
1948   *Singin' Spurs*
Funerals
1916   *Following the Flag in
        Mexico*
1928   *The Wages of Sin*

1930   Tom Sawyer
1931   *Un caballero de frac*
        Little Caesar
1932   *The Hatchet Man*
1934   *Broadway Bill*
        Imitation of Life
        Massacre
1936   *Ramona*
1937   *Big City*
1938   The Adventures of Tom
        Sawyer
1939   *Moon over Harlem*
1942   *The Vanishing Virginian*
1946?   *Go Down, Death!*
1947   *Duel in the Sun*
        The Last Round-Up
1947?   What a Guy
1948   The Miracle of the Bells
1949   *Arctic Manhunt*
        Daughter of the West
        Knock on Any Door
1950   *Devil's Doorway*
        Young Man with a Horn
1951   *Across the Wide Missouri*
1953   *The Sun Shines Bright*
1954   *Broken Lance*
1955   *Trial*
1956   *Giant*
1957   *Band of Angels*
        Bayou
1959   *The Black Orchid*
        Cry Tough
        Imitation of Life
1960   *All the Fine Young
        Cannibals*
Fur
1935   Wolf Riders
1937   *Bargain with Bullets*
Fur coats
1946   *The Gentleman Misbehaves*
1949   *Rose of the Yukon*
Fur industry
1919?   Alaska
Fur traders
1917   *The Barrier*
1932   The Forty-Niners
1933   Thundering Herd
1934   *Eskimo*
        Wagon Wheels
1937   Old Louisiana
1940   Prairie Schooners
1941   This Woman Is Mine
1951   Tomahawk
1952   *Brave Warrior*
1955   *Smoke Signal*
1958   Bullwhip
Fur trappers
1947   Oregon Trail Scouts
1952   The Big Sky
1956   *Davy Crockett and the
        River Pirates*
        The Last Frontier
Furniture
1942   *We Were Dancing*
G-men
1937   Shadows of the Orient
Guy Gabaldon
1960   Hell to Eternity
Galicia
1932   Mazel Tov
1937   The Jester (Der
        Purimspieler)
Gall (Sioux chieftain)
1959   Yellowstone Kelly
Galveston (TX)
1950   Last of the Buccaneers
Gamblers
1914   *Hearts United*
1915   The Gambler of the West
1919   His Debt
        The Sleeping Lion
1920   *The Brute*
1921   When the Clock Struck Nine
1927   Children of Fate
        For the Love of Mike
        The Overland Stage
        The Scar of Shame
1929   Hallelujah
        In Old California
        Show Boat
1930   *El cuerpo del delito*
        She Got What She Wanted
1931   Carne de cabaret
        Oklahoma Jim

        Smart Money
1934   *Broadway Bill*
1936   Charlie Chan at the Race
        Track
        Muss 'Em Up
1938   *Birthright*
        Di que me quieres
        In Old Chicago
        Spirit of Youth
1939   *Winner Take All*
1940   While Thousands Cheer
1942   All Through the Night
1943   *His Butler's Sister*
        Mr. Lucky
1944   *Marshal of Reno*
        Riding West
1945   *Club Havana*
1946   Saratoga Trunk
1947   *California*
1948   Four Faces West
1949   *Souls of Sin*
1951   *Apache Drums*
        Flaming Feather
        Gambling House
        The Harlem Globetrotters
        The Mark of the Renegade
        Show Boat
1952   *Apache War Smoke*
        The Half-Breed
        The Iron Mistress
1953   *The Nebraskan*
1955   *Davy Crockett, King of the
        Wild Frontier*
1956   *Raw Edge*
        The Wild Dakotas
1958   *Blood Arrow*
1959   Odds Against Tomorrow
Gambling
1915   *Marse Covington*
1916   *Peck O' Pickles*
        *The Thousand Dollar
        Husband*
1918   *Marked Cards*
1919   *Mandarin's Gold*
1920?   *Reformation*
1923   Snowdrift
1925   *A Son of His Father*
1927   The Dove
        The Spider's Web
1928   The Rawhide Kid
1929   Hallelujah
        Sombras habaneras
1930   *La fuerza del querer*
1931   *Cavalier of the West*
        The Exile
        Mamá
        Tropennächte
1932   *Call Her Savage*
1933   The Emperor Jones
        Espérame
1934   *The Fighting Hero*
        Fighting Through
        Lazy River
1935   *Circle of Death*
1936   *The Green Pastures*
1937   *That Girl from Paris*
1938   *Life Goes On*
        Mr. Moto's Gamble
        Swing!
1939   *Double Deal*
        Los hijos mandan
        Moon over Harlem
1940   *East of the River*
        Young Buffalo Bill
1941   *You're Out of Luck*
1942   *Gentleman Jim*
        Lawless Plainsmen
        Lucky Ghost
1943   *Dixie*
1944   *Something for the Boys*
1945   *The Dolly Sisters*
        Wanderer of the Wasteland
1946   *Canyon Passage*
        Tall, Tan and Terrific
1946?   *Beale Street Mama*
        Go Down, Death!
1947   Easy Come, Easy Go
        The Foxes of Harrow
        Marshal of Cripple Creek
        Vigilantes of Boomtown
        Vigilantes of Boomtown
1948   *The Time of Your Life*
1949   *Riders of the Range*
        Tuna Clipper

1950   *Comanche Territory*
1956   *Singing in the Dark*
1959   *Al Capone*
        The Hanging Tree
1960   *For the Love of Mike*
Gambling houses
1917   *The War of the Tongs*
1918   *Her Moment*
        Mystic Faces
1919   *His Debt*
        The Scar
1922   *Square Joe*
1931   *Cimarron*
        The White Renegade
1933   *Obey the Law*
1934   *She Was a Lady*
1937   *Shadows of the Orient*
        Think Fast, Mr. Moto
1947   *New Orleans*
1951   *Gambling House*
1957   Gun Battle at Monterey
1959   *Gunmen from Laredo*
Gambling ships
1943   *Mr. Lucky*
1955   Duel on the Mississippi
Game-preserves
1921   Anne of Little Smoky
Games
1944   *Block Busters*
Gang wars
1917   The War of the Tongs
1932   *The Hatchet Man*
1937   *Dark Manhattan*
Gangs
1914   The Yellow Traffic
1914?   *The Mysterious Mr. Wu
        Chung Foo*
1916   Hop, the Devil's Brew
        The Sign of the Poppy
1917   The War of the Tongs
1918   The Border Raiders
        The Girl in the Dark
1921   Black Roses
1923   Purple Dawn
        A Shot in the Night
1924   Fools' Highway
        The Night Hawk
1925   A Son of His Father
1926   Kosher Kitty Kelly
        Shadows of Chinatown
1928   *Eleven P.M.*
        The Midnight Ace
        Ransom
1929   Hawk of the Hills
1930   *Amor audaz*
        El último de los Vargas
1933   *King of the Wild Horses*
1935   North of Arizona
1936   *West of Nevada*
1937   Boy of the Streets
        That I May Live
1939   *Mothers of Today*
1940   *Lucky Cisco Kid*
1941   *Gauchos of Eldorado*
1942   Take My Life
1944   Block Busters
1948   *Old Los Angeles*
1950   *Bandit Queen*
1952   The Raiders
1953   *The Eddie Cantor Story*
1955   *Blackboard Jungle*
1958   *Touch of Evil*
1960   Key Witness
        The Pusher
        Studs Lonigan
        This Rebel Breed
        Walk Tall
Gangsters
1917   A Love Sublime
1918   Hell's End
        Hitting the Trail
1920   *The Brute*
        The Dark Mirror
        Outside the Law
        Within Our Gates
1920?   The Scarlet Dragon
1921   The Secret Sorrow
        Where Lights Are Low
1922   Little Miss Smiles
1924   Racing Luck
1925   The Beautiful City
1928   Diamond Handcuffs
        The Hawk's Nest

1929 Thunderbolt
      Welcome Danger
1930 Easy Street
      La fuerza del querer
      Ladies Love Brutes
      Los que danzan
1931 *Chinatown After Dark*
      The Guilty Generation
      Little Caesar
      Mr. Lemon of Orange
      El pasado acusa
      Smart Money
1932 *Harlem Is Heaven*
      The Hatchet Man
      Me and My Gal
      Scarface
      Uncle Moses
1933 *Dos noches*
      A Lady's Profession
      Olsen's Big Moment
1934 He Was Her Man
      Straight Is the Way
1934? Harlem After Midnight
1935 De la sartén al fuego
1936 Below the Deadline
      Kelly the Second
      Winterset
1937 Bargain with Bullets
      Border Cafe
      Charlie Chan on Broadway
      Dark Manhattan
      Manhattan Merry-Go-Round
      Shadows of the Orient
1938 Dangerous to Know
      Life Goes On
      Passport Husband
1939 *Daughter of the Tong*
      The Escape
      Motel the Operator
1940 Am I Guilty?
      East of the River
      Escape to Glory
      Gang War
      The Notorious Elinor Lee
      Paradise in Harlem
      The Way of All Flesh
      While Thousands Cheer
1941 *Birth of the Blues*
      You're Out of Luck
1942 Mexican Spitfire Sees a
          Ghost
      Syncopation
      Take My Life
1943 *Crime Smasher*
1945 *The Shanghai Cobra*
1946 *The Gentleman Misbehaves*
1947 *The Mighty McGurk*
      Ride the Pink Horse
1947? *Return of Mandy's
          Husband*
      What a Guy
1948 *The Betrayal*
      Key Largo
1949 Illegal Entry
      Souls of Sin
      The Undercover Man
1950 The Breaking Point
      Deported
1951 Gambling House
1952 Woman in the Dark
1953 *The Eddie Cantor Story*
1956 *Singing in the Dark*
1957 The Brothers Rico
1959 Al Capone
      The Black Orchid
      Cry Tough
      The FBI Story
      Inside the Mafia
      Odds Against Tomorrow
1960 *Studs Lonigan*

Garages
1930 The Kibitzer
1934 *Straight Is the Way*
1942 *Rio Rita*
1944 *Slightly Terrific*
1947 *Buck Privates Come Home*
1949 *The Sky Dragon*
1960 *Key Witness*

Gardeners
1918 *The Bravest Way*
      Wanted, a Mother
1921 Black Roses
1931 Così è la vita

Gardens
1935 *Angelina o el honor de un
          brigadier*
1949 Shamrock Hill

Pat Garrett
1943 The Outlaw
1948 *Four Faces West*

David Garrick
1939 *The Adventures of
          Huckleberry Finn*

Gary (IN)
1932 *Huddle*

Gas masks
1926 *The Passaic Textile Strike*
1943 *Fighting Americans*

Gas stations
1939 *Forged Passport*
1947 *The Burning Cross*
1949 *The Red Menace*
1955 *Bad Day at Black Rock*

**Gases, Asphyxiating and
      poisonous**
1926 *The Passaic Textile Strike*
1928 *The Midnight Ace*
      Ransom
1930 Sombras de gloria
1932 *Charlie Chan's Chance*
1938 *Mr. Wong, Detective*
1940 *Murder over New York*
1942 *Secret Enemies*
1945 *The Jade Mask*
      The Scarlet Clue
1948 Docks of New Orleans

Gasoline
1921 The Girl from God's
          Country
1922 The Schemers

Gatling guns
1951 Cavalry Scout
1954 Siege at Red River

Gauchos
1930 Alma de gaucho

Geishas
1919 A Heart in Pawn

Gems
1940 *The Fatal Hour*
1946 Border Bandits

Genealogy
1926 Irene
1947 *Jiggs and Maggie in Society*

General stores
1925 My Son
1926 The Cohens and Kellys
1932 *Wild Horse Mesa*
1935 *North of Arizona*
1940 *Jennie*
1945 *Of One Blood*
1946 *Canyon Passage*
1955 *Apache Ambush*

Generals
1932 *Le plombier amoureux*
1936 *General Spanky*
1944 *Vigilantes of Dodge City*
1947 *Little Mister Jim*
1948 *Fury at Furnace Creek*
1956 *Walk the Proud Land*
1959 *The Wonderful Country*

Generation gap
1934 *Imitation of Life*
1941 *Golden Gate Girl*

Generosity
1918 *Thirty a Week*
1945 *Of One Blood*

Geneva (Switzerland)
1933 *Diplomaniacs*

Genies
1917 The Bottle Imp
1945 Where Do We Go From
          Here?

Genocide
1919 Auction of Souls

**George II, King of England,
      1683-1760**
1936 *The Last of the Mohicans*

**George III, King of England,
      1738-1820**
1917 The Spirit of '76
1948 *Unconquered*

**George IV, King of England,
      1820-1830**
1929 Die Königsloge

Georgia
1925 *Body and Soul*
1930 Georgia Rose
1939 Gone With the Wind
1944 *Something for the Boys*
1946 Song of the South
1949 *Lost Boundaries*
1953 *The Member of the
          Wedding*
      Sangaree

German Americans
1913? The Lure of New York
1915 Hearts of Men
      The Kindling
1916 Little Meena's Romance
      Peck O' Pickles
1917 *The Little American*
      The Secret Game
      The Winged Mystery
1918 An Alien Enemy
      The Birth of a Race
      Good-Bye, Bill
      The Hun Within
      The Kaiser's Finish
      Me Und Gott
      The Price of Applause
      The Prussian Cur
      The Ranger
      The Reckoning Day
      Shifting Sands
      The Spreading Evil
      The Yellow Dog
1919 Behind the Door
      Love and the Law
1919? America Was Right
      When the Desert Smiles
1920 The Cup of Fury
      Dangerous Days
1925 Friendly Enemies
1926 The Strong Man
1927 For the Love of Mike
      His Foreign Wife
      Lost at the Front
      The Way of All Flesh
1928 Heart Trouble
      Riley the Cop
      Sins of the Fathers
      We Americans
1930 Sins of the Children
1931 *Beyond Victory*
      Street Scene
1932 *Flesh*
      Unashamed
1933 *Best of Enemies*
      Broken Dreams
      Ever in My Heart
      Song of the Eagle
1935 Rendezvous
1939 Confessions of a Nazi Spy
1940 Escape
      Escape to Glory
      Jennie
      The Man I Married
      The Ramparts We Watch
1942 *All Through the Night*
      Foreign Agent
      Friendly Enemies
      Little Tokyo, U.S.A.
      Nazi Agent
1943 *Good Luck, Mr. Yates*
      Hitler's Children
      They Came to Blow Up
          America
1944 *Chip Off the Old Block*
      Lifeboat
1945 *The House on 92nd St.*
1946 *Rendezvous 24*
1947 *The Foxes of Harrow*
1949 Illegal Entry
      Jigsaw
      Lust for Gold
1950 Mystery Submarine
1952 *Woman in the Dark*
1953 *The Sun Shines Bright*
1959 *The Wonderful Country*
1960 I Aim at the Stars: the
          Wernher von Braun Story

German shepherd dogs
1943 *Jack London*
1948 Night Wind

Germans
1916 *Arms and the Woman*
1917 *The Secret Game*
      The Slacker
      The Winged Mystery

1918 An Alien Enemy
      Doing Their Bit
      Fields of Honor
      His Birthright
      The Hun Within
      I Want to Forget
      Mystic Faces
      The Price of Applause
      The Prussian Cur
      The Reckoning Day
      The Source
      The Spreading Evil
      Tony America
      The Yellow Dog
1919 Behind the Door
1920 The Cup of Fury
      Dangerous Days
1927 His Foreign Wife
1928 Riley the Cop
1930 *¡De frente, marchen!*
      Sombras de gloria
1931 *Drácula*
1933 Best of Enemies
1934 *The Rabbi's Power*
1940 *The Notorious Elinor Lee*
1942 *Friendly Enemies*
      Valley of Hunted Men
1943 Margin for Error
1944 Address Unknown
      Lifeboat
      Tender Comrade
      They Live in Fear
      Tomorrow the World!
      Waterfront
1945 The House on 92nd St.
1946 *Notorious*
1948 Night Wind
1950 *Mystery Submarine*
1953 *The Joe Louis Story*

Germany
1915 *Hearts of Men*
1917 *The Winged Mystery*
1918 *The Firebrand*
      The Kaiser's Finish
1920 *The Cup of Fury*
1928 Riley the Cop
1932 Flesh
1933 Best of Enemies
      Ever in My Heart
      The Wandering Jew
1940 Escape
      The Man I Married
1941 *They Dare Not Love*
1943 Hitler's Children
      *They Came to Blow Up
          America*
1944 *Address Unknown*
      They Live in Fear
1946 *Rendezvous 24*
1951 *The House on Telegraph
          Hill*
1958 The Young Lions

Germany—History
1960 I Aim at the Stars: the
          Wernher von Braun Story

Germany. Army
1917 *The Little American*
      The Winged Mystery
1918 *The Birth of a Race*
      Good-Bye, Bill
      The Greatest Thing in Life
      Me Und Gott
      The Unbeliever
1919 *The Lost Battalion*
1919? America Was Right
1931 *Beyond Victory*
1934 *The Unknown Soldier
          Speaks*
1944 *The Negro Soldier*
1960 I Aim at the Stars: the
          Wernher von Braun Story

Germany. Intelligence Service
1943 *They Came to Blow Up
          America*

Germany. Navy
1939 Confessions of a Nazi Spy
1940 *Escape to Glory*
1942 *The Navy Comes Through*
1943 Action in the North
          Atlantic
      Crash Dive

Geronimo
1940 Geronimo
1942 *Valley of the Sun*
1948 *Fort Apache*
1950 *Broken Arrow*
 I Killed Geronimo
1951 *The Last Outpost*
1952 *Apache War Smoke*
 The Battle at Apache Pass
 Indian Uprising
1954 *Apache*
 Taza, Son of Cochise
1956 Walk the Proud Land
1957 *Apache Warrior*
George Gershwin
1945 Rhapsody in Blue
Ira Gershwin
 Rhapsody in Blue
Gestapo
1940 *The Man I Married*
1941 *They Dare Not Love*
1942 *Nazi Agent*
1943 *Hitler's Children*
 They Came to Blow Up America
1945 *The House on 92nd St.*
Get-rich-quick schemes
1941 *Sunday Sinners*
1947? Return of Mandy's Husband
The Gettysburg Address
1935 *Ruggles of Red Gap*
Gettysburg, Battle of, 1863
1916 *Peck O' Pickles*
Ghana
1957 Satchmo the Great
Ghost towns
1943 *What's Buzzin' Cousin?*
1949 *Colorado Territory*
1950 *Jiggs and Maggie Out West*
1953 Ambush at Tomahawk Gap
1956 Ghost Town
Ghosts
1920 *The Man Who Dared*
1924 A Son of Satan
 Unseen Hands
1934 *Beloved*
1935 *Angelina o el honor de un brigadier*
1939 *Mr. Moto in Danger Island*
1941 Four Shall Die
1942 Lucky Ghost
 Mexican Spitfire Sees a Ghost
1943 *Cabin in the Sky*
1946 *Singin' in the Corn*
1946? *Fight That Ghost*
 Go Down, Death!
1947? *Return of Mandy's Husband*
1948 *Angel in Exile*
1949 *Portrait of Jennie*
1950 Jiggs and Maggie Out West
Giants
1947 *Bells of San Fernando*
Gifts
1917 *The Tenderfoot*
1919? *In the Land of the Setting Sun; or, Martyrs of Yesterday*
1920 The Secret Gift
1935 *The Yiddish King Lear*
1944 *Lake Placid Serenade*
1947 *Little Mister Jim*
1948 *I Remember Mama*
1949 *Call of the Forest*
 Shamrock Hill
1952 *Desert Pursuit*
Gigolos
1941 Hold Back the Dawn
Girls' schools
1935 *Angelina o el honor de un brigadier*
1938 *The Beloved Brat*
1943 *Crash Dive*
1950 So Young, So Bad
Simon Girty
1936 Daniel Boone
1956 *Daniel Boone, Trail Blazer*
Christopher Gist
1951 *When the Redskins Rode*

Glacier Bay National Park and Preserve (AK)
1929 The Overland Telegraph
Glacier National Park (MT)
1954 Dangerous Mission
Glaciers
1917 Alaska Wonders in Motion
1936 *Tundra*
1954 *Dangerous Mission*
 Passion
Glasgow (Scotland)
1955 *A Man Called Peter*
Glass
1938 *Mr. Wong, Detective*
1948 *Docks of New Orleans*
Glasses (Eye)
 use Eyeglasses
Gluttony
1937 *Man of the People*
Goat ranchers
1934 *Laughing Boy*
Goats
1953 *Dream Wife*
1959 *Porgy and Bess*
Gobi Desert (Mongolia and China)
1937 *Thank You, Mr. Moto*
Godparents
1918 *Real Folks*
1932 *Ten Minutes to Live*
1941 *Golden Gate Girl*
1944 *Lake Placid Serenade*
1948 *Fort Apache*
Gods
1930 *El dios del mar*
1935 *Charlie Chan in Egypt*
1951 *Hurricane Island*
Joseph Paul Goebbels
1939 *Confessions of a Nazi Spy*
1940 *The Man I Married*
Gold
1915 *Captain Courtesy*
 Sealed Valley
1917 *A Kentucky Cinderella*
1918 *Find the Woman*
 The Goddess of Lost Lake
 Laughing Bill Hyde
1921 The Hunger of the Blood
1931 *Cavalier of the West*
1932 *El caballero de la noche*
1933 *The California Trail*
1934 *The Fighting Hero*
1935 *Circle of Death*
 The Little Colonel
 North of Arizona
1936 *Silly Billies*
1937 *Harlem on the Prairie*
 Man of the People
1939 *The Bronze Buckaroo*
1940 *Son of Ingagi*
1941 *Secret of the Wastelands*
1942 *They Died With Their Boots On*
1946 *Bad Bascomb*
 California Gold Rush
1947 Bells of San Fernando
 Bowery Buckaroos
1948 The Golden Eye
 Renegades of Sonora
1949 *The Gay Amigo*
 Lust for Gold
 The Valiant Hombre
1950 The Cariboo Trail
 Train to Tombstone
1951 Hurricane Island
1952 *Apache War Smoke*
 Buffalo Bill in Tomahawk Territory
 Desert Pursuit
 The Half-Breed
 The Raiders
1953 *Captain John Smith and Pocahontas*
 Jack McCall Desperado
1954 *The Black Dakotas*
 Sitting Bull
1955 *The Indian Fighter*
1957 *Revolt at Fort Laramie*
 Ride Out for Revenge
1958 *Apache Territory*
 The Lone Ranger and the Lost City of Gold

1959 *The Hanging Tree*
1960 *The Day They Robbed the Bank of England*
Gold diggers
1917 The Red Woman
1918 The Wine Girl
1930 *El príncipe del dólar*
1931 Le petit café
 Politiquerías
 Quand on est belle
1933 The Cohens and Kellys in Trouble
1934 *Lazy River*
 Strange Wives
 Tres amores
1938 Josette
 The Rage of Paris
1941 *Hold Back the Dawn*
1942 *Holiday Inn*
 Sunday Punch
1946? Beale Street Mama
1947 *Body and Soul*
1952 *Kid Monk Baroni*
Gold miners
1916 The Aryan
1930 Monsieur le Fox
1934 Wheels of Destiny
1942 North to the Klondike
1949 *The Valiant Hombre*
1952 Indian Uprising
1954 Drums Across the River
1955 *Chief Crazy Horse*
 Foxfire
 White Feather
1956 Ghost Town
1957 *War Drums*
1958 The Badlanders
 Gun Fever
 Sierra Baron
1959 The Hanging Tree
Gold mines
1912 *Atop of the World in Motion*
1915 *Chimmie Fadden Out West*
1918 Laughing Bill Hyde
1919 *Desert Gold*
 Fighting for Gold
1919? When the Desert Smiles
1923 The Sting of the Scorpion
1924 The Mine with the Iron Door
 Smiling Hate
1932 *The Forty-Niners*
 The Galloping Kid
1934 The Battling Buckaroo
 Call of the Coyote
 La cruz y la espada
 The Lone Defender
1935 *Cowboy Holiday*
1936 Desert Gold
 Song of the Gringo
 West of Nevada
1939 The Cisco Kid and the Lady
1940 *Rhythm of the Rio Grande*
 Taku
1947 *Marshal of Cripple Creek*
 Vigilantes of Boomtown
1948 Angel in Exile
 The Dude Goes West
 The Golden Eye
 Guns of Hate
 Old Los Angeles
1949 *Rose of the Yukon*
1950 *Bandit Queen*
 Jiggs and Maggie Out West
 The Missourians
1952 *The Raiders*
1953 *War Paint*
1955 Foxfire
1958 *The Badlanders*
 Blood Arrow
Gold rushes
1914 In the Days of the Thundering Herd
1915 *The Pageant of San Francisco*
1931 *The Avenger*
1936 *Robin Hood of El Dorado*
 Silly Billies
1937 *The Barrier*
1941 *Land of Liberty*
1943 *Jack London*
 What's Buzzin' Cousin?
1947 California

1950 *Bandit Queen*
 Jiggs and Maggie Out West
1951 Oh! Susanna
1952 *Fort Osage*
Golden Gate Bridge (San Francisco, CA)
1936 *Sum Hun*
1940 *If I Had My Way*
Goldsmiths
1918 Find the Woman
Golf
1917 *His Sweetheart*
1927 *Pleasure Before Business*
1930 *Alma de gaucho*
 The Cohens and the Kellys in Scotland
1944 *Going My Way*
1953 *The Joe Louis Story*
1955 *Violent Saturday*
Golf, miniature
1931 *The Cohens and Kellys in Africa*
Gondolas and gondoliers
1915 *The Italian*
1931 *La ley del harem*
 El príncipe gondolero
Gone With the Wind (Novel)
1941 *Louisiana Purchase*
Good Friday
1915 *The Penitentes*
1950 *Give Us This Day*
Good Samaritans
1918 *Wild Women*
1919 Deliverance
1921 Bits of Life
1933 Obey the Law
1935? The Irish Gringo
1937 *Boy of the Streets*
1938 *Di que me quieres*
1943 *Dr. Gillespie's Criminal Case*
1948 Reaching from Heaven
 The Time of Your Life
1949 3 Godfathers
Benny Goodman
1956 The Benny Goodman Story
Gorillas
1940? *Mr. Washington Goes to Town*
1942 *Professor Creeps*
Hermann Göring
1939 *Confessions of a Nazi Spy*
Maxim Gorky
 Tevya
Gossip
1918 Find the Woman
1931 Street Scene
1932 *The Unfortunate Bride*
 Veiled Aristocrats
1933 *Dance Hall Hostess*
1938 *Swing!*
1939 *La Inmaculada*
1940 *The Ramparts We Watch*
1941 *Caught in the Act*
1945 *Between Two Women*
 A Tree Grows in Brooklyn
1949 *Pinky*
1949? *Girl in Room 20*
1957 *The Oklahoman*
1960 *The Dark at the Top of the Stairs*
 The Unforgiven
Gossip columnists
1931 *Buster se marie*
Governesses
1918 *The Firebrand*
 Wanted, a Mother
1920? Her Story
1922 The Top O' the Morning
1931 *Aloha*
1934 Call of the Coyote
1938 *The Beloved Brat*
1941 Adam Had Four Sons
1944 My Pal Wolf
1950 *The Baron of Arizona*
1951 *The House on Telegraph Hill*
Government agents
1915 *Chimmie Fadden Out West*
1916 Broken Chains
1918 *The Border Raiders*
1919 *The Heart of Wetona*
 The Red Viper

1922 Captain Fly-by-Night
1926 The Fighting Edge
1927 The Spider's Web
1929 Hawk of the Hills
1935 Range Warfare
1936 *Ellis Island*
Robin Hood of El Dorado
Rose of the Rancho
1938 California Frontier
1939 Daughter of the Tong
Trigger Fingers
1940 *Cuando canta la Ley*
1941 Mystery Ship
1942 *Secret Enemies*
Submarine Raider
Unseen Enemy
Young America
1944 *The Racket Man*
1945 The Jade Mask
The Scarlet Clue
The Shanghai Cobra
1946 Notorious
1947 West to Glory
1949 Illegal Entry
Laramie
1950 Comanche Territory
1951 Cyclone Fury
1952 Brave Warrior
1953 Ambush at Tomahawk Gap
1956 *The Lone Ranger*
1958 The Rawhide Trail

Government officials
1924 North of 36
1927 The Gay Defender
1928 The Canyon of Adventure
1936 It Had to Happen
1939 Forged Passport
1944 *My Pal Wolf*
1945 South of the Rio Grande
1950 *North of the Great Divide*
1951 *The Last Outpost*
1952 It's a Big Country: An
American Anthology
1953 *Taxi*
1956 *Comanche*

Governors
1915 *Just Jim*
The Nigger
1916 The Morals of Hilda
Unprotected
1917 The Conqueror
1917? *Barnaby Lee*
1919 *Auction of Souls*
Erstwhile Susan
Love and the Law
1920 *The Mark of Zorro*
1924 His Darker Self
1930 *Las campanas de Capistrano*
1931 *El código penal*
1933 The California Trail
1934 *Un capitán de cosacos*
1935 *Naughty Marietta*
1937 *Maid of Salem*
Man of the People
Nation Aflame
Old Louisiana
1938 *Wild Horse Canyon*
1939 *Man of Conquest*
1941 *Doomed Caravan*
1944 Knickerbocker Holiday
1945 *Sunbonnet Sue*
1946 *Bad Bascomb*
1947 Bells of San Fernando
Vigilantes of Boomtown
1948 *Fighting Father Dunne*
The Paleface
Up in Central Park
1949 *The Kissing Bandit*
Tulsa
1950 Last of the Buccaneers
1951 Jim Thorpe—All-American
1952 *Brave Warrior*
The Iron Mistress
1953 *Fort Ti*
1954 *Broken Lance*
1956 *The Lone Ranger*
Walk the Proud Land
1959 *The Wonderful Country*
1960 *The Sign of Zorro*

Graduations
1932 *Le cas du docteur Brenner*
Huddle
1944 *An American Romance*
Since You Went Away

1945 *The Bells of St. Mary's*
A Tree Grows in Brooklyn
1950 *The Big Hangover*

Graft
1916 *A Son of Erin*
1918 The Midnight Patrol
One More American
1919 *A Fighting Colleen*
1936 *El crimen de media noche*
1938 The Renegade Ranger
1941 *Louisiana Purchase*
1958 *The Last Hurrah*

Edith Graham
1919 Auction of Souls

Grand Canyon (AZ)
1941 *Land of Liberty*
1948 Flight to the Sun
1952 *Navajo*

Grand Central Station (New York City)
1946 *Without Reservations*

Grand juries
1936 *It Had to Happen*

Granddaughters
1916 A Child of Mystery
1930 *La jaula de los leones*
1931 *El príncipe gondolero*
1940 *Young Buffalo Bill*
1946 *Singin' in the Corn*
1949 *That Midnight Kiss*
1960 *Ice Palace*

Grandfathers
1916 *Britton of the Seventh*
1917 A Jewel in Pawn
Sunshine and Gold
1918 *A Little Sister of Everybody*
1920 White Youth
1921 *Love's Plaything*
Shame
1923 None So Blind
1925 *The Gold Hunters*
1927 Aflame in the Sky
1929 *Romance of the Rio Grande*
1930 Cascarrabias
1931 *Aloha*
Personal Maid
1932 *The Unfortunate Bride*
1934 *La buenaventura*
1935 *Shir Hashirim*
1935? *The Irish Gringo*
1936 *Dimples*
My American Wife
1939 *Charlie Chan in Honolulu*
1940 *Young Buffalo Bill*
1941 *Golden Gate Girl*
1943 Marching On!
Mr. Lucky
1946 *Border Bandits*
1947 *Dangerous Venture*
1948 *The Betrayal*
1949 *The Cowboy and the
Indians*
Tale of the Navajos
1950 *A Ticket to Tomahawk*
1952 *Japanese War Bride*
1956 *Reprisal!*
1958 *Fort Massacre*

Grandmothers
1917 *The Little Samaritan*
1918 *A Daughter of the Old
South*
The Gypsy Trail
The Little Runaway
1919 *Toby's Bow*
1921 *By Right of Birth*
Love's Plaything
1922 My Boy
1926 *The Little Irish Girl*
1931 *Mi último amor*
Soyons gais
1932 *No Greater Love*
1933 *Una viuda romántica*
1936 Rainbow on the River
1938 *City Streets*
1939 *Los hijos mandan*
1941 *Come Live with Me*
1942 *Young America*
1943 *Crash Dive*
1944 *Chip Off the Old Block*
1945 *A Tree Grows in Brooklyn*
1946 *Shadows Over Chinatown*
Song of the South
1949 *Pinky*
The Undercover Man

1952 *Anything Can Happen*
Hiawatha
1953 *The Eddie Cantor Story*
1959 *The Oregon Trail*
1960 *I Passed for White*
Take a Giant Step

Grandparents
1942 *The Vanishing Virginian*
1946 *Swamp Fire*

Grandsons
1917 *A Night in New Arabia*
1931 *El príncipe gondolero*
1934 *Beloved*
1936 *Custer's Last Stand*
1939 *Mirele Efros*
1943 The Amazing Mrs. Holliday
1944 *Since You Went Away*
1947 *Oregon Trail Scouts*
1949 *Lust for Gold*

Ulysses Simpson Grant
1914 *The Littlest Rebel*
1915 *The Birth of a Nation*
1926 The Flaming Frontier
1930 Abraham Lincoln
1954 *Drum Beat*
Sitting Bull

Gratitude
1931 *The Squaw Man*
1939 *Mamele*
1940 *Girl from God's Country*
1941 *Sun Valley Serenade*
1950 *Rio Grande*
1951 *Flaming Feather*
1955 *Good Morning, Miss Dove*
1960 *Sergeant Rutledge*

Grauman's Chinese Theatre (Los Angeles, CA)
1930 *Estrellados*

Grave robbers
1918 *Huck and Tom; or, the
Further Adventures of
Tom Sawyer*

Graves
1917 *The Squaw Man's Son*
1932 *A Daughter of Her People*
1934 *Chloe: Love Is Calling You*
The Rabbi's Power
1936 *Ellis Island*
1940 *The Gay Caballero*
The Way of All Flesh
1943 *Bataan*
1946 *The Gay Cavalier*
1949 *She Wore a Yellow Ribbon*
1950 *The Baron of Arizona*
I Killed Geronimo
1951 *Distant Drums*
1957 *Joe Dakota*

Great Britain—History
1932 El caballero de la noche

Great Britain—History—17th century
1917? Barnaby Lee

Great Britain—History—19th century
1929 Die Königsloge

Great Britain—History—Social life and customs
Die Königsloge

Great Britain. Air Force
1931 Cuerpo y alma

Great Britain. Army
1917 The Hidden Children
The Spirit of '76
1930 *Le spectre vert*
1931 El impostor
1947 Last of the Redmen
1948 *Unconquered*

Great Britain. Intelligence Service
1937 *Souls at Sea*
1938 Mr. Moto Takes a Chance

Great Britain. Navy
1937 *Souls at Sea*
1938 The Buccaneer
1939 Mr. Moto's Last Warning

Great Britain. Parliament
1959 *John Paul Jones*

Great Lakes
1953 *The Pathfinder*

Great Plains
1928 The Glorious Trail

Harry Greb
1926 The Fighting Deacon

Greece—History
1928 Vamping Venus
1931 La regina di Sparta
1954 Barefoot Battalion

Greed
1915 *The Gambler of the West*
1916 *Light at Dusk*
1917 *Under False Colors*
1918 The Spreading Evil
Tony America
1920 Huckleberry Finn
1921 A Modern Cain
1935 *The Yiddish King Lear*
1936 *Song of the Gringo*
1938 *Breaking the Ice*
1939 *Way Down South*
1941 *Sunday Sinners*
1942 American Empire
1945 Johnny Angel
1946 *Three Wise Fools*
1947 Bells of San Fernando
Riding the California Trail
1948 *Guns of Hate*
The Miracle of the Bells
1949 *Anna Lucasta*
Arctic Manhunt
1952 *Fort Osage*
The Quiet Man
1953 Old Overland Trail
War Paint
1954 *The Yellow Tomahawk*
1955 The Indian Fighter
Seven Cities of Gold
1956 The Burning Hills
Death of a Scoundrel
Mohawk
1957 *Joe Dakota*
1958 Flaming Frontier
The Lone Ranger and the
Lost City of Gold
1959 *The Black Orchid*
Odds Against Tomorrow
1960 Ice Palace

Greek Americans
1917 *A Love Sublime*
1931 Smart Money
1936 Down to the Sea
1942 *Juke Girl*
1943 *Good Luck, Mr. Yates*
Mr. Lucky
1948 16 Fathoms Deep
1950 *Panic in the Streets*
Sands of Iwo Jima
1952 It's a Big Country: An
American Anthology
1953 Beneath the 12-Mile Reef
The Glory Brigade

Greek letter societies
use **Fraternities**

Greeks
1942 *Woman of the Year*
1954 Barefoot Battalion

Green Mountains
1918 *The Source*

Grenades
1949 *Rose of the Yukon*
1953 *The Glory Brigade*
1956 *Crowded Paradise*
1959 *Shake Hands with the Devil*

Grief
1915 *The Italian*
1934 *Eskimo*
1944 *An American Romance*
Minstrel Man
The Sullivans
1945 *Our Vines Have Tender
Grapes*
A Tree Grows in Brooklyn
The Valley of Decision
1946 *Till the End of Time*
1947 Little Mister Jim
1948 *Red River*
1950 *Mystery Street*
1953 *Beneath the 12-Mile Reef*
The Joe Louis Story
1955 *The Long Gray Line*
The Rose Tattoo
1957 *Ride Out for Revenge*
1958 Houseboat
1959 *The FBI Story*
Imitation of Life

1960 Take a Giant Step
The Unforgiven

Grocers
1916 Pasquale
1918 My Cousin
1921 Cheated Love
1947 Humoresque

Grocery stores
1916 Pasquale
1947 Body and Soul
1960 Key Witness

Guadalcanal Island (Solomon Islands), Battle of, 1942-1943
1944 The Sullivans
1945 Pride of the Marines

Guardians
use Wards and guardians

Guards
1930 Estrellados
1932 El caballero de la noche
1939 Reform School
1947 Bells of San Fernando
1949 Portrait of Jennie
1950 The Girl from San Lorenzo
1960 The Day They Robbed the Bank of England

Guerrilla warfare
1941 Min Jok Jay Hung Sing
1952 The Fighter

Guides
1919 Told in the Hills
1920 The Purple Cipher
1923 The Lone Wagon
1924 California in '49
1928 Chinatown Charlie
1930 The Big Pond
1931 Young Sinners
1932 The Forty-Niners
1937 The Riders of the Whistling Skull
1950 Davy Crockett, Indian Scout
The Iroquois Trail
1952 Navajo
1953 Tumbleweed
War Paint
1955 The Far Horizons
Kiss of Fire

Guillotine
1919? The Brand of Judas

Guilt
1915? Sin
1916 Her Debt of Honor
Man and His Angel
1917 Crime and Punishment
A Night in New Arabia
1918 Hidden Pearls
In Judgment Of
1919 Mandarin's Gold
1931 Huckleberry Finn
Le père célibataire
1932 La foule burle
Hearts of Humanity
1935 McFadden's Flats
1936 Winterset
1945 Between Two Women
1946? Go Down, Death!
1947 The Burning Cross
1948 Moonrise
1949 Home of the Brave
The Prairie
1955 Bad Day at Black Rock
Murder in Villa Capri
1956 The Catered Affair
The Last Hunt
1957 The Brothers Rico
Edge of the City
The Midnight Story
Raintree County
1959 Al Capone
The Black Orchid
1960 I Aim at the Stars: the Wernher von Braun Story

Guitars
1935 The Winning Ticket
1942 Tortilla Flat
1950 Riders of the Pony Express

Gulf of Mexico
1938 The Buccaneer
1946 Swamp Fire
1949 Harbor of Missing Men
1953 Thunder Bay

Gullibility
1939 The Bronze Buckaroo

Gun accidents
1919 The Scar
1942 The Navy Comes Through
1955 Murder in Villa Capri

Gun battles
use Gunfights

Gun powder
1950 Young Daniel Boone
1952 California Conquest
1953 Ambush at Tomahawk Gap

Gunfighters
1917 The Gun Fighter
1919 The She Wolf
1932 Law and Lawless
1939 The Fighting Gringo
1953 The Man Behind the Gun
1956 Man from Del Rio
Raw Edge
1958 Blood Arrow
Bullwhip
Frontier Gun
Terror in a Texas Town
1960 Oklahoma Territory
Walk Like a Dragon

Gunfights
1916 Arms and the Woman
1917 The Gun Fighter
1919 The She Wolf
1921 Diane of Star Hollow
1922 The Virgin of Seminole
1930 El presidio
1931 Call of the Rockies
Cavalier of the West
Cimarron
1932 Scarface
1933 Circle Canyon
1934 Call of the Coyote
1935 Range Warfare
The Singing Vagabond
Texas Terror
1936 Desert Gold
Hair-Trigger Casey
Pinto Rustlers
Rebellion
The Traitor
1937 Border Cafe
Prairie Thunder
That I May Live
1938 California Frontier
Daughter of Shanghai
The Renegade Ranger
1939 Drifting Westward
Drums Along the Mohawk
The Fighting Gringo
Gang Smashers
Harlem Rides the Range
1940 The Gay Caballero
1941 Doomed Caravan
Murder on Lenox Avenue
Prairie Pioneers
Road Agent
Under Fiesta Stars
Western Union
1942 All Through the Night
American Empire
Apache Trail
Nazi Agent
Unseen Enemy
1943 Air Force
Border Patrol
Crime Smasher
The Law Rides Again
The Outlaw
Wagon Tracks West
1944 Sonora Stagecoach
1945 The Valley of Decision
1946 Bad Bascomb
Rendezvous 24
Renegade Girl
Wild West
1947 The Adventures of Don Coyote
Dangerous Venture
Desperate
Hi De Ho
Last of the Redmen
The Last Round-Up
Thunder Mountain
Under the Tonto Rim
West to Glory
Wild Horse Mesa
1948 The Arizona Ranger
The Dude Goes West

The Golden Eye
Gun Smugglers
Guns of Hate
The Lady from Shanghai
Red River
Silver Trails
Western Heritage
1949 Border Incident
The Cowboy and the Indians
The Dalton Gang
Riders of the Range
Rustlers
Stagecoach Kid
Streets of Laredo
The Valiant Hombre
1950 Ambush
Border Treasure
The Breaking Point
Colt .45
Devil's Doorway
Jiggs and Maggie Out West
Rio Grande Patrol
Sunset in the West
The Traveling Saleswoman
1951 Across the Wide Missouri
Cavalry Scout
Flaming Feather
Fort Defiance
Gambling House
Snake River Desperadoes
Warpath
1952 Apache War Smoke
The Battle at Apache Pass
Buffalo Bill in Tomahawk Territory
Bugles in the Afternoon
Desert Pursuit
Fort Osage
High Noon
Indian Uprising
Rose of Cimarron
1953 Ambush at Tomahawk Gap
Arrowhead
Ride, Vaquero!
War Paint
1954 The Black Dakotas
Overland Pacific
Passion
Thunder Pass
1955 Fort Yuma
The Lonesome Trail
1956 The Broken Star
The Burning Hills
Dakota Incident
Frontier Woman
The Last Hunt
Quincannon, Frontier Scout
Raw Edge
Reprisal!
1957 Apache Warrior
Gun Battle at Monterey
The Oklahoman
Raiders of Old California
Ride Out for Revenge
The Tin Star
War Drums
1958 Gunfire at Indian Gap
Gunman's Walk
Never Love a Stranger
Ride a Crooked Trail
Sierra Baron
1959 Inside the Mafia
The Jayhawkers!
The Sheriff of Fractured Jaw
1960 The Plunderers
Walk Like a Dragon

Gunrunners
1922 When East Comes West
1932 Texas Pioneers
1935 Cyclone of the Saddle
Fighting Pioneers
1937 Drums of Destiny
Old Louisiana
1938 The Texans
1947 Pirates of Monterey
1948 Gun Smugglers
Unconquered
1950 Indian Territory
Rio Grande Patrol
Sunset in the West
Winchester '73

1952 The Fighter
Wagons West
1953 Last of the Comanches
The Man Behind the Gun
1954 Cattle Queen of Montana
Drum Beat
Thunder Pass
1955 Apache Ambush
Santa Fe Passage
Shotgun
1956 Ghost Town
1958 Ambush at Cimarron Pass

Guns
use Firearms

Gunshot wounds
1915 The Cheat
1918 A Broadway Scandal
The Firebrand
The Temple of Dusk
1919 The Gray Towers Mystery
His Debt
The Red Viper
The Sleeping Lion
1920 Huckleberry Finn
1927 The Scar of Shame
1931 Cavalier of the West
Charlie Chan Carries On
1932 The Forty-Niners
Scarface
The Secrets of Wu Sin
The Vanishing Frontier
1933 Circle Canyon
Obey the Law
1934 Behold My Wife!
Limehouse Blues
Massacre
'Neath the Arizona Skies
The Prescott Kid
Tres amores
1935 The Singing Vagabond
1936 Charlie Chan at the Race Track
The Traitor
West of Nevada
1937 Boy of the Streets
Dark Manhattan
Law and Lead
Think Fast, Mr. Moto
1938 Spawn of the North
1939 Double Deal
The Escape
Let Freedom Ring
The Return of the Cisco Kid
1940 Gang War
1941 Romance of the Rio Grande
1942 Below the Border
Take My Life
Tales of Manhattan
Unseen Enemy
1943 Cabin in the Sky
Land of Hunted Men
Margin for Error
The Outlaw
1944 Cry of the Werewolf
1945 Great Stagecoach Robbery
The Navajo Trail
1946 Bad Bascomb
Border Bandits
Sheriff of Redwood Valley
South of Monterey
Sunset Pass
Wild Beauty
Wild West
1947 Desperate
Marshal of Cripple Creek
Pirates of Monterey
Robin Hood of Monterey
Rustlers of Devil's Canyon
Under the Tonto Rim
1948 The Arizona Ranger
The Betrayal
Cry of the City
The Dude Goes West
Fury at Furnace Creek
Gun Smugglers
Indian Agent
Silver Trails
Sleep, My Love
1949 Apache Chief
Call of the Forest
The Dalton Gang
The Fighting Kentuckian
The Gay Amigo
Home of the Brave
Masked Raiders

Massacre River
The Prairie
Rose of the Yukon
Souls of Sin
Streets of Laredo
3 Godfathers
1949? *Girl in Room 20*
1950 *The Breaking Point*
Cherokee Uprising
Colt .45
Comanche Territory
Devil's Doorway
I Killed Geronimo
The Iroquois Trail
The Missourians
No Way Out
Rio Grande Patrol
Winchester '73
1951 *Gambling House*
The Steel Helmet
1952 *The Fighter*
The Half-Breed
My Man and I
1953 *Ambush at Tomahawk Gap*
The Man from the Alamo
Old Overland Trail
Tumbleweed
War Paint
1954 *Drums Across the River*
Thunder Pass
1955 *Violent Saturday*
1956 *The Burning Hills*
Death of a Scoundrel
Man from Del Rio
Quincannon, Frontier Scout
Raw Edge
The White Squaw
1957 *The Lawless Eighties*
1959 *Yellowstone Kelly*
1960 *Flaming Star*
Walk Tall

Gunsmiths
1931 *The Hurricane Horseman*
1948 *The Dude Goes West*
1950 *I Killed Geronimo*
1955 *Kentucky Rifle*

Gurus
1938 *Mr. Moto Takes a Chance*
1941 *Playmates*

Gymnasiums
1936 *Below the Deadline*
Laughing Irish Eyes
1951 *The Harlem Globetrotters*
1954 *Carmen Jones*
Go Man Go

Gypsies
1914 *The Redemption of David Corson*
The Woman in Black
1915 *The Adventures of a Madcap*
An American Gentleman
Hearts of Men
1916 *The Flames of Johannis*
The Folly of Revenge
A Man of Sorrow
The Twin Triangle
1917 The Call of Her People
Runaway Romany
The Secret of Eve
Sunshine and Gold
The Wild Girl
1918 *The Gypsy Trail*
In Judgment Of
Set Free
Toys of Fate
1919 The Sneak
1920 *The Dark Mirror*
1920? Broken Hearts
1921 Anne of Little Smoky
1923 Jealous Husbands
1924 Untamed Youth
1931 Call of the Rockies
1932 Hypnotized
1933 El rey de los gitanos
1934 La buenaventura
Caravane
1935 *Un hombre peligroso*
Melody Trail
1938 *Happy Landing*
Rascals
1939 Trigger Fingers
1944 Cry of the Werewolf
Slightly Terrific

1947 On the Old Spanish Trail
1950 *The Baron of Arizona*
1956 Hot Blood

Haciendas
1936 *Aces and Eights*
The Phantom of Santa Fe
1945 *South of the Rio Grande*
1946 *The Gay Cavalier*
1947 *Riding the California Trail*
West to Glory
1948 *Silver Trails*
1949 *The Kissing Bandit*
1953 *Conquest of Cochise*
1954 *Passion*
1957 *Raiders of Old California*
1958 *Sierra Baron*

Hair
1932 *Harlem Is Heaven*
1934 *Call of the Coyote*
1946? *House-Rent Party*
1948 The Boy with Green Hair
1956 *Westward Ho the Wagons!*

Hairdressers
1939 *Confessions of a Nazi Spy*

Haiti
1929 The Witching Eyes

Half brothers
1916 Pudd'nhead Wilson
1936 *El crimen de media noche*
1940 *Young Buffalo Bill*
1950 *Jiggs and Maggie Out West*
1954 Broken Lance

Half sisters
1939 The Devil's Daughter
1956 *The Last Wagon*
The White Squaw

Half-breeds
use **Half-castes;**
Indians of North America—Mixed blood

Half-castes
1918 The City of Dim Faces
Hidden Pearls
His Birthright
1921 *Bits of Life*
Shame
1922 Pals of the West
1927 Old San Francisco
1932 *Thirteen Women*

Fitz-Greene Halleck
1923 Little Old New York

Halloween
1931 *Such Is Life*
1934 *As the Earth Turns*
1937 *Boy of the Streets*

Hallucinations
1931 *Such Is Life*
1940 *Eli Eli*
1944 *Lifeboat*
Mr. Skeffington
1946 *Dirty Gertie from Harlem, U.S.A.*
1947 *California*
It Had To Be You
1949 *The Prairie*
1950 *The Big Hangover*
1951 *The Girl on the Bridge*
1953 *Cry of the Hunted*

Hamburgers
1938 *Outside of Paradise*

Henry Hamilton
1956 *Daniel Boone, Trail Blazer*

Hamlet (Play)
1929 *Die Königsloge*

Oscar Hammerstein
1945 *The Dolly Sisters*
1947 *The Jolson Story*

Hampton Institute
1941? Hampton Institute: Its Program of Education for Life

John Hancock
1922 Cardigan

Handcuffs
1944 *Sheriff of Las Vegas*
1952 *My Man and I*

Handicapped
1914 *The Straight Road*
1920 *Humoresque*
The Paliser Case
1922 *The Crimson Skull*
Flesh and Blood

1925 Scarlet Saint
1926 *The Flying Ace*
1929 Welcome Danger
1932 *Igloo*
No Greater Love
Symphony of Six Million
1935 *Rescue Squad*
1936 *Down to the Sea*
1938 City Streets
1939 The Light Ahead
1941 *New York Town*
1944 *Charlie Chan in the Secret Service*
Three Men in White
1945 *Between Two Women*
Pride of the Marines
The Valley of Decision
1946 Gas House Kids
Till the End of Time
1947 *Duel in the Sun*
The Foxes of Harrow
1948 *I Remember Mama*
Key Largo
The Lady from Shanghai
1950 *Right Cross*
1955 *Bad Day at Black Rock*
1959 Porgy and Bess
1960 The Plunderers

Handkerchiefs
1940 *Lucky Cisco Kid*
1942 *The Vanishing Virginian*

Handy, W. C.
1958 St. Louis Blues

Handymen
1944 *My Pal Wolf*

Hanging
1932 *El caballero de la noche*
1934 *Un capitán de cosacos*
1948 *Harpoon*
Moonrise
1949 *Illegal Entry*
The Mysterious Desperado
1950 *The Furies*
God, Man and Devil
Last of the Buccaneers
1952 *The Battle at Apache Pass*
1954 *The Black Dakotas*
1955 *Seven Angry Men*

Hangovers
1941 *Ice-Capades*
1942 *Twin Beds*

Hansom cabs
1940 *Little Nellie Kelly*

Hanukkah
1950 *God, Man and Devil*

Hapsburg Family
1945 *Salome, Where She Danced*

Hara-kiri
1915 *After Five*
1920 *Who's Your Servant?*
1937 *Thank You, Mr. Moto*
1942 *Submarine Raider*
1945 *Samurai*
1960 *Hell to Eternity*

Harbors
1942 *Song of the Islands*

Hardware stores
1953 *Tonight We Sing*

Harems
1927 Turkish Delight
1931 *The Cohens and Kellys in Africa*
Kismet
La ley del harem
1938 *Mr. Moto Takes a Chance*
1939 *Cossacks in Exile*

Harlem Globetrotters (Basketball team)
1951 The Harlem Globetrotters
1954 Go Man Go

Harmonicas
1931 *Mr. Lemon of Orange*
1934 *The Cactus Kid*
1944 *Hi, Beautiful*
1946 *California Gold Rush*
1958 *Houseboat*

Harper's Ferry (WV)
1940 Santa Fe Trail
1955 *Seven Angry Men*

Harpoons
1948 *Harpoon*
1958 *Terror in a Texas Town*

Harps and Harpists
1932 *Hearts of Humanity*

Harvard University
1924 *Birthright*
1938 *Birthright*
1950 *Mystery Street*

Harvest festivals
1931 *Mi último amor*

Hat check girls
1919 *The Delicious Little Devil*
1932 *Men Are Such Fools*
1945 *I Love a Bandleader*
1951 *The Raging Tide*

Hatchets
1932 *The Hatchet Man*

Hate
1954 Taza, Son of Cochise
1956 *Comanche*
The White Squaw
1957 *Naked in the Sun*
1960 The Unforgiven

Hats
1933 *Una viuda romántica*
1936 *Rose of the Rancho*
1942 *We Were Dancing*
Woman of the Year
1952 *My Man and I*
1959 *The Wonderful Country*

Haunted houses
1918 *Huck and Tom; or, the Further Adventures of Tom Sawyer*
1924 A Son of Satan
1930 *La voluntad del muerto*
1931 *Noche de duendes*
1939 *Lying Lips*
1946? Fight That Ghost

Havana (Cuba)
1944 *Minstrel Man*
1949 *Harbor of Missing Men*
1950 *A Lady Without Passport*

Hawaii
1915? The Beachcomber
1918 *Hidden Pearls*
Wild Women
1920 *Locked Lips*
1921 Fifty Candles
1923 The White Flower
1927 The Chinese Parrot
1934 White Heat
1937 *Charlie Chan at the Olympics*
Waikiki Wedding
1938 Hawaii Calls
1940 Hawaii
1942 Song of the Islands
1944 *Tahiti Nights*

Hawaiians
1917 The Bottle Imp
1918 Hidden Pearls
1919 A Fallen Idol
1923 The White Flower
1931 *The Black Camel*
1934 Song of the Islands
1937 *Waikiki Wedding*
1938 *Hawaii Calls*
1942 Song of the Islands
1950 Damien
1954 Hell's Half Acre

John Hay
1930 Abraham Lincoln
1935 *The Littlest Rebel*

Head colds
1942 *Seven Sweethearts*
1949 *Ride, Ryder, Ride!*

Headhunters
1914 In the Land of the Head Hunters

Healers
1941 *In the Land of the Navajo*
1950 *Stars in My Crown*

Health
1927 Children of Fate

Health officials
1950 *Damien*
Panic in the Streets

Hearst News Service
1928 The Cameraman

Heart disease
1914 *Hearts United*
1919 *Scarlet Days*
1920 *The Paliser Case*

1921 *As the World Rolls On*
1934 *Straight Is the Way*
1936 *Sum Hun*
1937 *Dark Manhattan*
1938 *The Toy Wife*
1940 *Escape*
      Jennie
1942 *The Vanishing Virginian*
1943 *Crash Dive*
1945 *The Bells of St. Mary's*
      The Valley of Decision
1947 *Dark Delusion*
1952 *Anything Can Happen*
1953 *The Eddie Cantor Story*
1955 *A Man Called Peter*
1958 *The Last Hurrah*
      Marjorie Morningstar
1959 *The Last Angry Man*
1960 *Ice Palace*

Heaven
1918 *Uncle Tom's Cabin*
1936 *The Green Pastures*
1941? *The Blood of Jesus*
1943 *Cabin in the Sky*
1945 *Of One Blood*
1946? *Go Down, Death!*

Hebrew Immigrant Aid Society
1939 *A Brivele der Mamen*

Heiresses
1916 Lord Loveland Discovers
      America
1917 Castles for Two
      Her Own People
1918 *Woman and the Law*
1919 Diane of the Green Van
1919? *The Brand of Judas*
1921 Little Miss Hawkshaw
1930 La voluntad del muerto
1935 *El día que me quieras*
      Rescue Squad
      The Singing Vagabond
1936 *Human Cargo*
1937 *Song of the City*
1940 Elsa Maxwell's Public Deb
      No. 1
      Too Many Girls
1942 *Professor Creeps*

Heirs
1915 *The Grandee's Ring*
1916 *Pudd'nhead Wilson*
1917 Lost in Transit
1918 The Greatest Thing in Life
1919 *Fighting for Gold*
      A Yankee Princess
1930 *Le spectre vert*
1936 Charlie Chan's Secret
1941 Four Shall Die
1949 *Tulsa*

Helen of Troy
1931 La regina di Sparta

Helicopters
1958 *Seven Hills of Rome*

Hell
1946? Go Down, Death!

Henpecked husbands
1934 *What a Mother-in-Law!*
1935 *Ruggles of Red Gap*
1936 *Rainbow on the River*
1947 *Juke Joint*
1947? *Return of Mandy's
      Husband*
1948 Jiggs and Maggie in Court
1949? She's Too Mean for Me
1960 *The Dark at the Top of the
      Stairs*

Patrick Henry
1922 Cardigan
1941 *Land of Liberty*
1959 *John Paul Jones*

Herald Island
1928 The Great White North

Heraldry
1931 El príncipe gondolero

Hereditary tendencies
1914 Northern Lights
1916 *Gold and the Woman*
      The Social Highwayman
1918 In Judgment Of
1919 A Heart in Pawn
1932 Call Her Savage
1936 *El crimen de media noche*
1937 *Maid of Salem*
1948 Moonrise

Heredity
1916 Silks and Satins
1919 *A Yankee Princess*
1921 Love's Plaything

Hermits
1917 *John Ermine of the
      Yellowstone*
1920 *The Girl of My Heart*
1933 *Diplomaniacs*
1952 *Anything Can Happen*

Hero worship
1943 Good Luck, Mr. Yates
1944 *Buffalo Bill*
1945 *Colorado Pioneers*

Heroes
1930 *¡De frente, marchen!*
1936 *The Bold Caballero*
1938 *The Adventures of Tom
      Sawyer*
1939 Let Freedom Ring
1946 *Bad Bascomb*
1949 *3 Godfathers*

Heroin
1960 The Pusher

Heroism
1915 *The Girl I Left Behind Me*
      The Lamb
      The Spender
1917 The Little American
      The Slacker
      The Woman and the Beast
1918 The Price of Applause
      The Source
1920 The Mark of Zorro
1925 Custer's Last Fight
1926 *General Custer at Little Big
      Horn*
1931 *Cuerpo y alma*
1932 The Rainbow Trail
1940 *The Fighting 69th*
1943 *Marching On!*
1944 *The Sullivans*
1951 *Warpath*
1952 Red Ball Express
1953 *The Great Sioux Uprising*
1954 Massacre Canyon
1955 *Davy Crockett, King of the
      Wild Frontier*
      *The Gun That Won the
      West*
      Violent Saturday
      White Feather
1956 *The Last Frontier*
      Pillars of the Sky
      Walk the Proud Land
1958 *Kings Go Forth*
1959 *The FBI Story*
1960 The Last Voyage
      Pay or Die
      Sergeant Rutledge

David Herold
1936 *The Prisoner of Shark
      Island*

Theodor Herzl
1933 *The Wandering Jew*
1937 *The Holy Oath*

Hessians
1950 *Young Daniel Boone*
1952 Battles of Chief Pontiac

Wild Bill Hickok
1926 The Last Frontier
1936 *Aces and Eights*
1937 The Plainsman
1940 *Prairie Schooners*
1953 Jack McCall Desperado

Hidatsa Indians
1955 *The Far Horizons*

Hideouts
1933 *Robbers' Roost*
1934 *Un capitán de cosacos*
1936 *West of Nevada*
1937 *Harlem on the Prairie*
1939 *In Old Caliente*
      Mr. Moto in Danger Island
1940 *Am I Guilty?*
      Hi-Yo Silver
      Phantom of Chinatown
      Santa Fe Trail
      While Thousands Cheer
1941 *Belle Starr*
1944 *The Chinese Cat*
      Vigilantes of Dodge City
1945 *Of One Blood*

1946 *South of Monterey*
1946? *Fight That Ghost*
1947 *The Adventures of Don
      Coyote*
      Buffalo Bill Rides Again
      Oregon Trail Scouts
      Robin Hood of Monterey
      Rustlers of Devil's Canyon
      Under the Tonto Rim
      Vigilantes of Boomtown
1947? *Return of Mandy's
      Husband*
1948 *Gun Smugglers*
1949 *Apache Chief*
      Brothers in the Saddle
      Colorado Territory
      The Daring Caballero
      Satan's Cradle
      The Valiant Hombre
1950 *Border Treasure*
      Cherokee Uprising
      The Girl from San Lorenzo
      Riders of the Pony Express
      Rio Grande Patrol
      Sunset in the West
      Winchester '73
1954 *The Black Dakotas*
1957 *The Tin Star*
1959 *Shake Hands with the Devil*

High school students
1944 They Live in Fear

High schools
1919 Erstwhile Susan
1921? [Unidentified Film]
1955 Blackboard Jungle
1960 *This Rebel Breed*

High society
1923 Breaking into Society
1931 *Such Is Life*
1936 *Contra la corriente*
1947 *It Had To Be You*
1948 Jiggs and Maggie in Court
1949 *Jiggs and Maggie in Jackpot
      Jitters*

Highwaymen
1922 Captain Fly-by-Night

Hijackers
1937 *Charlie Chan at the
      Olympics*
1947 *Marshal of Cripple Creek*
1950 *Deported*
      Sunset in the West

Hillbillies
1934 *Stand Up and Cheer!*
1943 *What's Buzzin' Cousin?*

Heinrich Himmler
1960 *I Aim at the Stars: the
      Wernher von Braun Story*

Hindenburg (Airship)
1937 *Charlie Chan at the
      Olympics*

Hindus
1919 *The Little Diplomat*
1920 *The Devil's Claim*

Hippodrome (New York City)
1953 *Tonight We Sing*

Hired hands
1918 How Could You, Jean?
1954 *Passion*

Hired killers
1918 *Untamed*
1919 The Tong Man
1920 *The Girl of My Heart*
1932 *Scarface*
      The Secrets of Wu Sin
1936 Song of the Gringo
1939 *Daughter of the Tong*
      Drifting Westward
      King of Chinatown
1940 *Gang War*
1945 *Club Havana*
1947 *Hi De Ho*
1948 *The Lady from Shanghai*
      Silver Trails
1951 *Mask of the Dragon*
1957 *Gun Battle at Monterey*
1958 *Never Love a Stranger*
      Sierra Baron
1959 *Inside the Mafia*
      The Wonderful Country

Hispanic Americans
      use Latino

Hitchhiking
1931 *Buster se marie*
1937 *That Girl from Paris*
      That I May Live
1938 *Two Gun Man from
      Harlem*
1939 *Heaven with a Barbed Wire
      Fence*
1941 *Sullivan's Travels*
      Up Jumped the Devil
1942 *Valley of Hunted Men*

Adolf Hitler
1939 *Confessions of a Nazi Spy*
1940 *The Man I Married*
      The Ramparts We Watch
1943 *Margin for Error*
1944 *The Negro Soldier*
1948 *Strange Victory*

Hoaxes
1915 Chimmie Fadden Out West
1918 *One More American*
      The Price of Applause
1931 Buster se marie
      Hay que casar al príncipe
1934 *The Cat's-Paw*
1937 *Manhattan
      Merry-Go-Round*
      Waikiki Wedding
1938 Little Miss Roughneck
1940 *Elsa Maxwell's Public Deb
      No. 1*
1941 Four Shall Die
1946 *Three Wise Fools*
1948 *Music Man*
1950 *The Traveling Saleswoman*

Hoboes
1930 *Así es la vida*
1932 *La foule hurle*
1939 Heaven with a Barbed Wire
      Fence
1940 The Way of All Flesh
1941 Sullivan's Travels
1943 *Gangway for Tomorrow*
1948 *The Time of Your Life*

Hoboken (NJ)
1927 The Princess from Hoboken
1932 *Hypnotized*

Holidays
1936 *Rose of the Rancho*
1941 *Hold Back the Dawn*
1942 *Holiday Inn*
1945 *Anoush*

Holland
1918 *The Spreading Evil*

Doc Holliday
1943 The Outlaw

Hollywood (CA)
1924 In Hollywood With Potash
      and Perlmutter
1932 Hollywood, ciudad de
      ensueño
1933 Let's Fall in Love
1934 La ciudad de cartón
1936 Yellow Cargo
1938 *Castillos en el aire*
      Little Miss Roughneck
1940 *Tengo fe en ti*
1942 *Foreign Agent*
      We Were Dancing
1945 *Jealousy*
1947 *The Jolson Story*

**The Hollywood Bowl (Los
Angeles, CA)**
1937 *Music for Madame*
1945 *Rhapsody in Blue*

Burton Holmes
1940 *Hawaii*

Oliver Wendell Holmes
1951 The Magnificent Yankee

Homelessness
1938 *In Old Chicago*
1942 Tales of Manhattan
      Tales of Manhattan

Homesickness
1932 *O festino o la legge*
1940 *Overture to Glory*
1960 *All the Young Men*

Homesteaders
1925 The Prairie Wife
1932 *Law and Lawless
      Mystery Ranch*

1933 Circle Canyon
1935 Cyclone of the Saddle
1947 Rustlers of Devil's Canyon
1948 The Betrayal
1949 The Prairie
1950 *Davy Crockett, Indian Scout*
     Devil's Doorway
1953 Ride, Vaquero!
1955 *Davy Crockett, King of the Wild Frontier*
1957 All Mine to Give
1960 Cimarron

Homosexuality
1959 *Odds Against Tomorrow*

Honesty
1937 *Waikiki Wedding*

Honeymoons
1915 *The Birth of a Nation*
1931 *Zein Weib's Lubovnick*
1933 *Yo, tú y ella*
1934 *Dos más uno, dos*
1935 *Julieta compra un hijo*
1936 *Contra la corriente*
1938 *Birthright*
1941 *Hold Back the Dawn*
1942 *Seven Sweethearts*
1950 *Broken Arrow*
     Give Us This Day
1951 *Show Boat*
1952 *The Quiet Man*
1953 *Tonight We Sing*
1959 *Night of the Quarter Moon*

Hong Kong
1931 *Charlie Chan Carries On*
1941 Min Jok Jay Hung Sing

Honolulu (HI)
1918 *Hidden Pearls*
1931 The Black Camel
     Charlie Chan Carries On
     Del infierno al cielo
1933 Charlie Chan's Greatest Case
1934 Song of the Islands
1936 *Charlie Chan at the Race Track*
1937 *Think Fast, Mr. Moto*
1939 *Charlie Chan in Honolulu*
1940 *Charlie Chan's Murder Cruise*
1950 *Sands of Iwo Jima*
1954 *Hell's Half Acre*
1960 *Hell to Eternity*

Honor
1921 The Kiss
1934 Eskimo
1935 Angelina o el honor de un brigadier
     The Littlest Rebel
1938 *The Buccaneer*
1939 Los hijos mandan
     Reform School
1947 *The Adventures of Don Coyote*
1950 *Rock Island Trail*
1951 *Saturday's Hero*
1952 *Bugles in the Afternoon*
     The Iron Mistress
1955 *The Long Gray Line*
1960 *For the Love of Mike*
     Hell to Eternity

Hoodlums
     use **Criminals;**
          Juvenile delinquents

Herbert Hoover
1940 *The Ramparts We Watch*

J. Edgar Hoover
1959 *The FBI Story*

Hopi Indians
1927 *The Devil's Saddle*

Horse owners
1936 *Charlie Chan at the Race Track*
1947 *Black Gold*
1950 The Palomino
1952 Apache War Smoke
1955 Not As a Stranger
1958 *Gunman's Walk*

Horse thieves
1915 *An American Gentleman*
1922 Spitfire
1935 *Cyclone of the Saddle*
     The Singing Vagabond
1936 Ramona

1938 Wild Horse Canyon
1941 *Belle Starr*
1945 The Navajo Trail
1949 *Ranger of Cherokee Strip*
1950 The Palomino
1951 Cyclone Fury
     Slaughter Trail
1952 *Rose of Cimarron*
1953 The Great Sioux Uprising
1957 *War Drums*
1958 *Ambush at Cimarron Pass*

Horse traders
1947 *Wild Horse Mesa*

Horse trading
1953 *The Great Sioux Uprising*
1958 *Tonka*

Horse trainers
1930 Big Boy
     Cuando el amor ríe
1947 *Black Gold*
1949 The Story of Seabiscuit
1960 *For the Love of Mike*

Horseback riding
     use **Riding**

Horseracing
1915 *Marse Covington*
     Where Cowboy Is King
1927 Jake the Plumber
     Pleasure Before Business
1928 *The Rawhide Kid*
1930 Big Boy
     The Kibitzer
1933 Racetrack
1934 Broadway Bill
     Laughing Bill
1935 The Winning Ticket
1936 It Had to Happen
     Ramona
1937 *Boots and Saddles*
1938 *Speed to Burn*
1941 *Virginia*
1947 Black Gold
1948 *The Time of Your Life*
1949 Jiggs and Maggie in Jackpot Jitters
     Stallion Canyon
     The Story of Seabiscuit
     Tuna Clipper
1950 *North of the Great Divide*
1952 *The Iron Mistress*
     The Quiet Man
1960 *For the Love of Mike*

Horses
1915 *The Danger Signal*
     Where Cowboy Is King
1917 *The Tenderfoot*
1921 *By Right of Birth*
     Hold Your Horses
     The Swamp
1925 Old Clothes
     The Wild Bull's Lair
1926 The Devil Horse
1927 Don Mike
     Pleasure Before Business
1928 The Canyon of Adventure
1930 Big Boy
     Check and Double Check
     Song of the Caballero
1931 Call of the Rockies
     Delicious
     The Hurricane Horseman
1932 Amore e morte
     Law and Lawless
     Wild Horse Mesa
1933 Circle Canyon
     King of the Wild Horses
     A Lady's Profession
     Racetrack
     The Telegraph Trail
1934 The Battling Buckaroo
     Broadway Bill
     The Cactus Kid
     Charlie Chan in London
     The Lone Defender
     'Neath the Arizona Skies
     The Prescott Kid
     Wheels of Destiny
1935 Cyclone of the Saddle
     Range Warfare
     Riddle Ranch
1936 Charlie Chan at the Race Track
     Desert Gold
     Pinto Rustlers

     The Traitor
1937 Boots and Saddles
1938 Speed to Burn
1939 Bad Lands
     Drifting Westward
     Gone With the Wind
     Tevya
1940 George Washington Carver
1941 Thunder Over the Prairie
     Under Fiesta Stars
1942 King of the Stallions
     Young America
1943 The Outlaw
1944 Marshal of Reno
     Vigilantes of Dodge City
1945 Colorado Pioneers
     Great Stagecoach Robbery
1946 Sun Valley Cyclone
     Sunset Pass
     Wild Beauty
1947 Black Gold
     Buffalo Bill Rides Again
     Duel in the Sun
     Rustlers of Devil's Canyon
1948 Fighting Father Dunne
     Gun Smugglers
1949 Brothers in the Saddle
     The Golden Stallion
     Jiggs and Maggie in Jackpot Jitters
     The Prairie
1949? Come On, Cowboy!
     Come On, Cowboy!
1950 Riders of the Pony Express
     Rio Grande Patrol
1951 Cyclone Fury
     Queen for a Day
1952 Navajo
     Rose of Cimarron
1953 Tumbleweed
1955 Santa Fe Passage
     White Feather
1956 Giant
     7th Cavalry
     Westward Ho the Wagons!
1958 Gunman's Walk
     Tonka
1959 The Wonderful Country
1960 For the Love of Mike
     The Unforgiven

Horseshoe Bend National Military Park (AL)
1927 The Frontiersman

Horseshoes
1946 The Gentleman Misbehaves
1949 The Golden Stallion

Horticulturalists
1942 Shut My Big Mouth

Hosiery
1933 Dance Hall Hostess
1935 Piernas de seda

Hospitals
1915 The Birth of a Nation
1917 The Little American
     A Love Sublime
1918 The Birth of a Race
     A Broadway Scandal
     Fields of Honor
     Hell's End
     Wanted, a Mother
1919 Deliverance
1928 Eleven P.M.
1930 Toda una vida
1931 Beyond Victory
1932 Marido y mujer
     Symphony of Six Million
1934 Broadway Bill
1935 Alas sobre el Chaco
1936 Dangerous Intrigue
1939 Charlie Chan in Honolulu
     Gang Smashers
     Gone With the Wind
     Heaven with a Barbed Wire Fence
     Mirele Efros
     Mr. Moto in Danger Island
     El trovador de la radio
1940 Paradise in Harlem
     Phantom of Chinatown
1942 Dr. Gillespie's New Assistant
     Take My Life
1943 Dr. Gillespie's Criminal Case
     Doughboys in Ireland

1944 Dark Waters
     Tender Comrade
     Three Men in White
1945 Between Two Women
1946 Gas House Kids
     Swamp Fire
     Till the End of Time
1947 Citizen Saint
     Dark Delusion
     Desperate
     Rustlers of Devil's Canyon
1948 Cry of the City
     The Fight Never Ends
     I Remember Mama
1949 The Clay Pigeon
     Home of the Brave
     Lookout Sister
     Lost Boundaries
1949? She's Too Mean for Me
1950 Emergency Wedding
     Jolson Sings Again
     The Men
     Mystery Submarine
     No Way Out
     Young Man with a Horn
1952 Bright Victory
     My Man and I
1955 Not As a Stranger
1957 Journey to Freedom

Hostages
1922 The Cub Reporter
1931 Mr. Lemon of Orange
1932 Yiskor
1933 Circle Canyon
1934 'Neath the Arizona Skies
     The Star Packer
1936 Border Phantom
     Pinto Rustlers
     Treachery Rides the Range
1937 Shadows of the Orient
1939 Daughter of the Tong
     Frontiers of '49
1940 Prairie Schooners
1941 Doomed Caravan
1942 Nazi Agent
1943 Dr. Gillespie's Criminal Case
1944 Waterfront
1948 The Feathered Serpent
     The Paleface
1949 Brothers in the Saddle
     Ranger of Cherokee Strip
     Stagecoach Kid
1950 A Lady Without Passport
     Young Daniel Boone
1952 Fort Osage
     Indian Uprising
1953 The Man Behind the Gun
1954 Battle of Rogue River
     Drums Across the River
1955 Seminole Uprising
     Seven Angry Men
1956 The Lone Ranger
1958 Fort Massacre
1959 Shake Hands with the Devil
1960 The Sign of Zorro

Hostesses
1942 Lucky Ghost
1951 Oh! Susanna

Hot-water bottles
1949 Harbor of Missing Men

Hotel bellmen
     use **Use Bellboys**

Hotel clerks
1946 California Gold Rush
1952 High Noon
1956 Singing in the Dark

Hotel managers
1941 The Mexican Spitfire's Baby
1946 The Gentleman Misbehaves

Hotel owners
1935 Wolf Riders
1942 Secret Enemies
1947 On the Old Spanish Trail
1949 Massacre River
     Ride, Ryder, Ride!
1950 Annie Get Your Gun
1958 Frontier Gun

Hotelkeepers
1931 La fruta amarga
1949 The Golden Stallion
1950 Black Hand
1959 The Sheriff of Fractured Jaw

1960 *Ice Palace*
Hotels
1916 The Woman in 47
1917 *I Will Repay*
1925 The Manicure Girl
1926 The Little Irish Girl
1930 *Una cana al aire*
      El príncipe del dólar
1931 *Buster se marie*
      Charlie Chan Carries On
      Mi último amor
      Personal Maid
      Tropennächte
1932 *El caballero de la noche*
      Flesh
      Thirteen Steps
      Unashamed
1933 *Charlie Chan's Greatest*
      Case
      Dos noches
      Yo, tú y ella
1934 *The Rabbi's Power*
      She Was a Lady
      Wheels of Destiny
1935 *¡Asegure a su mujer!*
      A Night at the Ritz
      Señora casada necesita
      marido
1936 *Laughing Irish Eyes*
1937 *Charlie Chan on Broadway*
      Thank You, Mr. Moto
1938 The Rage of Paris
      The Rage of Paris
      Spawn of the North
1939 *Charlie Chan in Reno*
      Confessions of a Nazi Spy
      Mr. Moto Takes a Vacation
      Verbena trágica
1940 *Charlie Chan's Murder*
      Cruise
      Elsa Maxwell's Public Deb
      No. 1
      Escape
      Mexican Spitfire Out West
      Northwest Passage (Book
      1—Rogers' Rangers)
1940? Mr. Washington Goes to
      Town
1941 *The Face Behind the Mask*
      The Mexican Spitfire's Baby
      Sun Valley Serenade
1942 *Mexican Spitfire's Elephant*
      Secret Enemies
      Seven Sweethearts
1943 *In Old Oklahoma*
      What's Buzzin' Cousin?
      Wintertime
1944 *Lady, Let's Dance!*
      Slightly Terrific
1945 *Escape in the Fog*
      The Jade Mask
1946 *Dirty Gertie from Harlem,*
      U.S.A.
      The Gentleman Misbehaves
      Shadows Over Chinatown
      Without Reservations
1947 *Copacabana*
      Crossfire
      On the Old Spanish Trail
      Ride the Pink Horse
1948 *Key Largo*
1949 *Arctic Manhunt*
      C-Man
      The Dalton Gang
      Illegal Entry
      Tulsa
      The Valiant Hombre
1949? *Girl in Room 20*
1950 *Chinatown at Midnight*
1951 *Cuban Fireball*
      Cyclone Fury
1952 *Brave Warrior*
1955 *Bad Day at Black Rock*
1957 *The Brothers Rico*
1958 *Terror in a Texas Town*
1959 *Last Train from Gun Hill*
1960 *Man on a String*
      The Plunderers
House detectives
1942 Rio Rita
House guests
      use **Houseguests**

House painters
1945 *I Love a Bandleader*
1948 Rocky
1960 *Studs Lonigan*
Houseboats
1943 *Deerslayer*
1958 Houseboat
Houseboys
1932 *Charlie Chan's Chance*
1933 *Charlie Chan's Greatest*
      Case
1951 *The House on Telegraph*
      Hill
1960 *Ice Palace*
Houseguests
1942 We Were Dancing
1943 *Three Hearts for Julia*
Housekeepers
1917 *The Peddler*
1928 Mother Machree
1934 *White Heat*
1939 *Fisherman's Wharf*
1941 *The Pioneers*
1942 *Holiday Inn*
1943 *The Amazing Mrs. Holliday*
      Jack London
1944 *Charlie Chan in the Secret*
      Service
      Going My Way
      My Pal Wolf
      Since You Went Away
      Tender Comrade
      Tomorrow the World!
1951 *The Girl on the Bridge*
1956 *Secret of Treasure*
      Mountain
1959 *Imitation of Life*
Houses
1937 *The Devil's Playground*
1948 *Gentleman's Agreement*
1950 Give Us This Day
1956 *Full of Life*
Housewarmings
1948 *Reaching from Heaven*
Housing shortages
1944 Since You Went Away
Sam Houston
1917 The Conqueror
1939 Man of Conquest
1953 *The Man from the Alamo*
1955 *The Last Command*
Charles S. Howard
1949 *The Story of Seabiscuit*
General Oliver Otis Howard
1950 *Broken Arrow*
Howard University
1944 *The Negro Soldier*
Hudson River (NY)
1917? *Barnaby Lee*
Huguenots
1916 *Witchcraft*
Hula (Dance)
1934 *Song of the Islands*
1936 *The Green Pastures*
1942 *Song of the Islands*
Human experimentation
      use **Experiments, Human**
Human sacrifice
1915 The Penitentes
1917 Unconquered
1921 Lotus Blossom
1925 *Quicker'n Lightnin'*
      The Red Rider
1930 *El dios del mar*
      Wu Li Chang
1933 *The Eternal Jew*
1937 *The Riders of the Whistling*
      Skull
1947 *Dangerous Venture*
Humanitarianism
1919 *Who's Your Brother?*
1958 *The Defiant Ones*
Hunchbacks
1916 Man and His Angel
1932 *Yiskor*
1938 Marusia
1939 *The Light Ahead*
1941 *Murder on Lenox Avenue*
Hungarian Americans
1916 Arms and the Woman
1929 This Is Heaven
1931 *Women Love Once*

1934 The Great Flirtation
1935 *A Night at the Ritz*
1940 The Way of All Flesh
1941 *The Face Behind the Mask*
1945 *The Dolly Sisters*
1952 It's a Big Country: An
      American Anthology
Hungarians
1929 Is Everybody Happy?
      Die Königsloge
1932 *Hypnotized*
1935 *Señora casada necesita*
      marido
1950 *A Lady Without Passport*
Hungary
1934 Caravane
Hunger
1921 The Cave Girl
1932 Igloo
1934 *Eskimo*
      Lazy River
      Our Daily Bread
1936 *Sutter's Gold*
      Tundra
1939 *Gone With the Wind*
1951 *Go for Broke!*
      Teresa
1954 *Apache*
Hunger strikes
1959 *Shake Hands with the Devil*
Hunters
1913? *Hiawatha*
1914 *In the Days of the*
      Thundering Herd
      John Barleycorn
      An Odyssey of the North
1917 *Alaska Wonders in Motion*
      The Bronze Bride
1925 The Gold Hunters
1930 *The Silent Enemy*
1932 Igloo
      Yiskor
1936 *Treachery Rides the Range*
1942 *Tales of Manhattan*
1947 *Buffalo Bill Rides Again*
1948 *Night Wind*
      Rocky
1949 *Massacre River*
Hunting
1912 *Atop of the World in*
      Motion
1918 *The Goddess of Lost Lake*
1919 *The Last of His People*
1921 *The Girl from God's*
      Country
1934 *Charlie Chan in London*
      Eskimo
1947 *Untamed Fury*
1948 *Louisiana Story*
1949 *Arctic Manhunt*
1952 *Arctic Flight*
      Hiawatha
1956 *The Last Hunt*
Hurdy-gurdies
1929 Love, Live and Laugh
      Mister Antonio
1936 *Kelly the Second*
      Winterset
Sol Hurok
1953 Tonight We Sing
Huron Indians
1920 The Last of the Mohicans
1943 Deerslayer
1950 *The Iroquois Trail*
1951 *When the Redskins Rode*
1957 The Deerslayer
Hurricanes
1948 *Key Largo*
1951 *Hurricane Island*
1953 *Thunder Bay*
1957 *Bayou*
1959 *Porgy and Bess*
Hyannis (MA)
1950 *Mystery Street*
Hydraulic mining
1941 *Prairie Pioneers*
Hymns
1950 *Stars in My Crown*
1958 *St. Louis Blues*
Hypnotism
1916 The Love Girl
      The Romantic Journey

1922 The Dungeon
1931 *Drácula*
1932 Thirteen Women
1941 King of the Zombies
1947 *Buck Privates Come Home*
      Dark Delusion
1948 Sleep, My Love
1956 *Singing in the Dark*
Hypnotists
1916 The Love Girl
      The Romantic Journey
1932 *Hypnotized*
1944 Black Magic
Hypochondria
1926 A Trip to Chinatown
1932 *Symphony of Six Million*
Hypocrisy
1915 The Kindling
1921 The Hypocrite
1930 Del mismo barro
1931 *Young Sinners*
1933 *Best of Enemies*
1952 *Fort Osage*
      High Noon
1957 *Burden of Truth*
Hypodermic needles
1949 *C-Man*
Hypothermia
1956 *The Last Hunt*
Hysteria (Social psychology)
1937 Maid of Salem
Ice cream
1927 The Shamrock and the Rose
Ice cream parlors
1948 *My Girl Tisa*
Ice floes
1912 *Atop of the World in*
      Motion
1926 The Barrier
1932 *Igloo*
1934 *Eskimo*
1940 *Taku*
1952 *Red Snow*
Ice shows
1944 Lake Placid Serenade
Ice skaters and ice skating
1938 *Breaking the Ice*
      Happy Landing
      My Lucky Star
1940 *Escape*
1941 *Ice-Capades*
      Sun Valley Serenade
1943 *Wintertime*
1944 Lady, Let's Dance!
      Lake Placid Serenade
1946 *Till the End of Time*
1947 *The Farmer's Daughter*
Icebergs
1941 *Mutiny in the Arctic*
1949 *Arctic Fury*
Icemen
1917 *His Sweetheart*
1925 The Greatest Love of All
Ichthyologists
1934 *Imitation of Life*
1946 *Dangerous Money*
Idaho
1951 *Snake River Desperadoes*
Idealism
1932 So Big
      Symphony of Six Million
1953 *So Big*
1955 Not As a Stranger
1960 *Wild River*
Idealists
1915 The Melting Pot
1931 *Street Scene*
1941 Belle Starr
1942 *Song of the Islands*
1945 A Tree Grows in Brooklyn
1950 *The Big Hangover*
1953 *Thunder Bay*
1954 *Cattle Queen of Montana*
1957 Raintree County
1960 *Cimarron*
Idle rich
1930 Sei tu l'amore
1933 *A Lady's Profession*
1935 *Rescue Squad*
1951 *Adventures of Captain*
      Fabian
1953 *So Big*

1958 *The Last Hurrah*
1960 *All the Fine Young
        Cannibals*

Idlers
1946? House-Rent Party
1947 Juke Joint

Idolatry
1917 Rosie O'Grady
1933 *The Eternal Jew*

Igloos
1932 *Igloo*
1949 *Arctic Fury*
1952 *Red Snow*

Illegal immigration
    use Aliens, Illegal;
        Immigrants;
        United States. Dept. of
        Immigration

Illegitimacy
1916 *At Piney Ridge*
        The Criminal
        Man and His Angel
        The Morals of Hilda
1918 The Kaiser's Finish
1919 A Man's Duty
1919? *America Was Right*
1927 *Wild Geese*
1930 *Del mismo barro*
1931 *Così è la vita*
        La dama atrevida
1932 *Call Her Savage*
1937 I Want to Be a Mother
1946 *Saratoga Trunk*
1947 *The Foxes of Harrow*
1948 *Tap Roots*
1950? *Three Daughters*
1953 *The Sun Shines Bright*
1955 *Good Morning, Miss Dove*

Illinois
1924 So Big
1930 Abraham Lincoln
1950 *Rock Island Trail*

Illinois Indians
1952 *Hiawatha*

Illiteracy
    use Literacy

Illness
    use Disease

Illustrators
1942 *Cat People*

Imaginary lands
1919 Diane of the Green Van
1927 Turkish Delight
1931 Don Juan diplomático
1933 El rey de los gitanos
        Victims of Persecution
1938 Mr. Moto Takes a Chance

Immigrants
1913 The Inside of the White
        Slave Traffic
        Traffic in Souls
1913? The Lure of New York
1914 The Jungle
        Life's Shop Window
        *The Little Angel of Canyon
        Creek*
        The Little Jewess
        Threads of Destiny
1914? A Boy and the Law
1915 *Hearts of Men*
        How Molly Malone Made
        Good
        The Immigrant
        The Italian
        Kreutzer Sonata
1916 Arms and the Woman
        Civilization's Child
        The Criminal
        The Fall of a Nation
        The Gilded Spider
        Gretchen, the Greenhorn
        Hulda from Holland
        Light at Dusk
        Man and His Angel
        The Morals of Hilda
        Pasquale
        Sold for Marriage
        A Son of Erin
        The Woman in 47
        A Woman's Honor
1917 *Hashimura Togo*
        His Sweetheart
        A Roadside Impresario
        The Tell-Tale Step

        The Trouble Buster
        Unknown 274
        The Woman and the Beast
1918 *The Bravest Way*
        Denny from Ireland
        Fields of Honor
        The Golden Wall
        Her Moment
        A Little Sister of Everybody
        The Million Dollar Mystery
        One More American
        The Ordeal of Rosetta
        Out of a Clear Sky
        Sandy
        Tony America
1919 *Deliverance*
        The Lord Loves the Irish
        Who's Your Brother?
        A Yankee Princess
        Yvonne from Paris
1920 The Cup of Fury
        Darling Mine
        Dinty
        The Face at Your Window
        Hidden Charms
        Lifting Shadows
        The Riddle: Woman
        The Secret Gift
1920? The Greatest Love
1921 All Souls' Eve
        Cheated Love
        Hold Your Horses
        The Land of Hope
        Made in Heaven
        The Money Maniac
        One Man in a Million
        Puppets of Fate
        The Syrian Immigrant
1921? The Slave Market
        The Supreme Passion
1922 Anna Ascends
        Come On Over
        The Good Provider
        Hungry Hearts
        My Boy
        The Woman He Loved
1923 Little Old New York
        The Miracle Makers
1924 Conductor 1492
        The Lure of Love
1925 Friendly Enemies
        The Greatest Love of All
        A Son of His Father
1926 Blarney
        Broken Hearts
        Into Her Kingdom
        Meet the Prince
        The Passaic Textile Strike
        Private Izzy Murphy
1927 Finnegan's Ball
        Irish Hearts
        [Japanese-American Film]
1928 Anybody Here Seen Kelly?
        Heart Trouble
        The House of Scandal
        The Mating Call
        Mother Machree
        A Ship Comes In
        We Americans
        Wheel of Chance
1929 Love, Live and Laugh
        Smiling Irish Eyes
        This Is Heaven
1930 Ladies Love Brutes
1931 Delicious
        Street Scene
        Three Who Loved
1932 Cuore d'emigrante
        Flesh
        The Match King
        O festino o la legge
1933 *The Man Who Dared: An
        Imaginative Biography*
        Obey the Law
1934 *Beloved*
        Strange Wives
1935 Black Fury
        His Family Tree
        Romance in Manhattan
        The Winning Ticket
1936 It Had to Happen
        My American Wife
        Paddy O'Day
        Sins of Man
        Sum Hun

1937 Big City
        Black Legion
        The Cantor's Son
        It Could Happen to You
        Music for Madame
        Shadows of the Orient
        That Girl from Paris
1938 Daughter of Shanghai
        Gateway
        In Old Chicago
1939 *A Brivele der Mamen*
        Forged Passport
        *Heaven with a Barbed Wire
        Fence*
        Judge Hardy and Son
        Let Freedom Ring
1939? *A Chinese Gains a Fortune
        in America*
1940 *Knute Rockne—All
        American*
        Little Nellie Kelly
1941 Come Live with Me
        The Face Behind the Mask
        Golden Gate Girl
        Hold Back the Dawn
        Louisiana Purchase
        Murder on Lenox Avenue
        New York Town
1942 From Across the Border
        Wings for the Eagle
1943 Wintertime
1944 An American Romance
        Since You Went Away
1945 *Nob Hill*
        The Valley of Decision
1946 *Canyon Passage*
        G. I. War Brides
1948 My Girl Tisa
        Reaching from Heaven
        Shep Comes Home
        Up in Central Park
1949 Answer for Anne
        The Girl from Jones Beach
1950 *Black Hand*
        Emergency Wedding
        Give Us This Day
        Mystery Submarine
        Panic in the Streets
        Right Cross
1951 Gambling House
        Saturday's Hero
1952 Anything Can Happen
        It's a Big Country: An
        American Anthology
1953 The Glass Wall
        Taxi
        Tonight We Sing
1955 *A Man Called Peter*
        Marty
1956 Crowded Paradise
        Death of a Scoundrel
        Singing in the Dark
        Wetbacks
1957 All Mine to Give
        Twelve Angry Men
1958 Wild Is the Wind
1959 *The Black Orchid*
        Cry Tough
        The Hanging Tree
        The Jayhawkers!
        Thunder in the Sun
        The Wonderful Country
1960 *Pay or Die*
        The Pusher
        Walk Like a Dragon

Imperialism
1936 *The Bold Caballero*

Impersonation and imposture
1914 Hearts United
        The Little Jewess
        The Littlest Rebel
        The Woman in Black
1915 An American Gentleman
        The Spender
1915? *The Life of Sam Davis: A
        Confederate Hero of the
        Sixties*
        Sam Davis, the Hero of
        Tennessee
1916 For the Defense
        A Man of Sorrow
        The Pretenders
        The Scarlet Oath
        The Sign of the Poppy
        The Yellow Passport

1917 The Bride of Hate
        Castles for Two
        A Night in New Arabia
        Runaway Romany
        Threads of Fate
        Under False Colors
1918 *Free and Equal*
        The Goddess of Lost Lake
        How Could You, Jean?
        A Little Sister of Everybody
        The Ranger
        Set Free
        Shifting Sands
        Who Is to Blame?
1919 A Bachelor's Wife
        Come Out of the Kitchen
        The Delicious Little Devil
        Fighting for Gold
        Toby's Bow
        A Yankee Princess
        Yvonne from Paris
1920 Billions
        Huckleberry Finn
        The Mark of Zorro
1921 Across the Divide
        By Right of Birth
        Little Miss Hawkshaw
        Society Snobs
1923 Fashion Row
        Little Old New York
1924 Smiling Hate
1925 Body and Soul
        Irish Luck
1926 The Fighting Edge
        The Flying Ace
        Meet the Prince
        Shadows of Chinatown
        The Strong Man
1927 The Princess from Hoboken
1928 *Eleven P.M.*
1929 This Is Heaven
1930 Amor audaz
        Así es la vida
        *Charros, gauchos y
        manolas*
        Un hombre de suerte
        Los que danzan
        Take the Heir
1931 *The Avenger*
        The Black Camel
        Cavalier of the West
        Cheri-Bibi
        Chérie
        Del infierno al cielo
        Hay que casar al príncipe
        Huckleberry Finn
        El impostor
        Mr. Lemon of Orange
        El príncipe gondolero
        Su noche de bodas
        Zein Weib's Lubovnick
1932 Border Devils
        El caballero de la noche
        Call Her Savage
        Le cas du docteur Brenner
        Charlie Chan's Chance
        *Parigi affascina; ovvero,
        Malavita*
        Le plombier amoureux
        The Rainbow Trail
        The Vanishing Frontier
1933 *The Cohens and Kellys in
        Trouble*
        King of the Wild Horses
        Let's Fall in Love
        No dejes la puerta abierta
        Olsen's Big Moment
1934 Charlie Chan's Courage
        Dos más uno, dos
        Las fronteras del amor
        Granaderos del amor
        The Great Flirtation
        The Lone Defender
        The Rabbi's Power
        The Star Packer
        Strange Wives
1935 Bar-Mitzvah
        Charlie Chan in Shanghai
        Cowboy Holiday
        Cyclone of the Saddle
        The Cyclone Ranger
        L'homme des Folies Bergère
        The Littlest Rebel
        Naughty Marietta
        North of Arizona

Piernas de seda
The Singing Vagabond
1936 Below the Deadline
The Bold Caballero
Ellis Island
Hair-Trigger Casey
Human Cargo
Klondike Annie
The Last of the Mobicans
Laughing Irish Eyes
Love and Sacrifice
Mad Holiday
The Phantom of Santa Fe
Pinto Rustlers
Song of the Gringo
Yellow Cargo
1937 Arshin Mal Alan
Big City
Boots and Saddles
Law and Lead
Music for Madame
Shadows of the Orient
That I May Live
Think Fast, Mr. Moto
1938 Castillos en el aire
Josette
Mr. Moto Takes a Chance
Outside of Paradise
The Rage of Paris
The Renegade Ranger
Swing!
Two Gun Man from Harlem
1939 *Allegbeny Uprising*
Charlie Chan in Honolulu
Cossacks in Exile
Daughter of the Tong
Drifting Westward
Frontiers of '49
Gang Smashers
Judge Hardy and Son
Let Freedom Ring
Mr. Moto in Danger Island
Mr. Moto Takes a Vacation
Mr. Moto's Last Warning
Motel the Operator
El otro soy yo
Trigger Fingers
1940 Americaner Schadchen
*Charlie Chan at the Wax
Museum*
Charlie Chan in Panama
Charlie Chan's Murder
Cruise
Cuando canta la Ley
Hi-Yo Silver
Lucky Cisco Kid
The Mark of Zorro
Mexican Spitfire
Mexican Spitfire Out West
Midnight Shadow
Murder over New York
New Moon
They Knew What They
Wanted
The Way of All Flesh
1941 *Doomed Caravan*
Hurry, Charlie, Hurry
Louisiana Purchase
The Mexican Spitfire's Baby
Mystery Ship
Romance of the Rio Grande
Saddlemates
Sullivan's Travels
They Dare Not Love
*Where Did You Get That
Girl?*
You're Out of Luck
1942 *Friendly Enemies*
Mexican Spitfire at Sea
Mexican Spitfire Sees a
Ghost
Mexican Spitfire's Elephant
Nazi Agent
Secret Enemies
Unseen Enemy
Valley of Hunted Men
Whispering Ghosts
1943 The Amazing Mrs. Holliday
Crime Smasher
Frontier Fury
Mexican Spitfire's Blessed
Event
Mr. Lucky
Redhead from Manhattan
They Came to Blow Up
America

1944 *Andy Hardy's Blonde
Trouble*
Black Magic
*Charlie Chan in the Secret
Service*
Chip Off the Old Block
Dark Waters
Riding West
Slightly Terrific
1945 *Betrayal from the East*
The Cisco Kid Returns
The Gay Senorita
In Old New Mexico
The Jade Mask
The Scarlet Clue
South of the Rio Grande
1946 California Gold Rush
Don Ricardo Returns
G. I. War Brides
Rendezvous 24
Shadows Over Chinatown
Singin' in the Corn
Slightly Scandalous
Without Reservations
1947 *Bowery Buckaroos*
Copacabana
Jiggs and Maggie in Society
Juke Joint
King of the Bandits
Riding the California Trail
Robin Hood of Monterey
Under the Tonto Rim
1948 *The Feathered Serpent*
Gentleman's Agreement
Half Past Midnight
The Luck of the Irish
Music Man
The Paleface
Renegades of Sonora
Sleep, My Love
The Time of Your Life
1949 *Arctic Manhunt*
The Daring Caballero
The Fighting Kentuckian
The Kissing Bandit
Ranger of Cherokee Strip
Roll Thunder Roll!
The Sky Dragon
Top O' the Morning
1949? The Joint Is Jumpin'
1950 Bandit Queen
The Baron of Arizona
Buccaneer's Girl
Cherokee Uprising
*The Daughter of Rosie
O'Grady*
The Girl from San Lorenzo
I Killed Geronimo
A Lady Without Passport
Mystery Submarine
Train to Tombstone
1951 Cuban Fireball
The House on Telegraph
Hill
The Last Outpost
The Mark of the Renegade
Mask of the Dragon
Ob! Susanna
Queen for a Day
Snake River Desperadoes
The Tall Target
When the Redskins Rode
1952 Apache War Smoke
California Conquest
The Fabulous Senorita
*It's a Big Country: An
American Antbology*
Trail of the Arrow
1953 *Fort Ti*
The Man Behind the Gun
The Nebraskan
Sangaree
1954 Arrow in the Dust
The Black Dakotas
Cattle Queen of Montana
Dangerous Mission
Hell's Half Acre
Massacre Canyon
Siege at Red River
Thunder Pass
1955 Fort Yuma
Violent Saturday
1956 *Davy Crockett and the
River Pirates*
The Lone Ranger

Wetbacks
1957 Gun Battle at Monterey
Joe Dakota
The Midnight Story
1958 *Home Before Dark*
Houseboat
Ride a Crooked Trail
1960 The Adventures of
Huckleberry Finn
*The Day They Robbed the
Bank of England*
The Sign of Zorro

Impersonations (Comic)
1930 *Galas de la Paramount*
1947? *What a Guy*
1948 *Killer Diller*
1950 *Catskill Honeymoon
Monticello, Here We Come!*

Importers
1916 *Alien Souls*
The Social Buccaneer
1918 *Her American Husband*
1937 *Thank You, Mr. Moto*
Think Fast, Mr. Moto
1951 *When the Redskins Rode*

Impresarios
1916 *The Yellow Passport*
1925 *The Midnight Girl*
1931 *Las luces de Buenos Aires*
1933 *Melodía de arrabal*
1937 *The Cantor's Son*
1944 *Lake Placid Serenade*
1947 *New Orleans*
1953 *Tonight We Sing*

Imprisonment
1914 *An Odyssey of the North*
1914? The Mysterious Mr. Wu
Chung Foo
1915 *The Italian*
The Melting Pot
The Sable Lorcha
1916 *The Honorable Friend*
1917 *A Roadside Impresario*
The Wild Girl
1918 *The Border Raiders*
The Firebrand
Good-Bye, Bill
The Hun Within
Shifting Sands
1932 *Genoveffa*
1934 *The Battling Buckaroo
Eskimo*
Tres amores
1936 *The Bold Caballero*
Dancing Pirate
1939 *Verbena trágica*
1944 *Tahiti Nights*
1952 *Battles of Chief Pontiac*
1954 *Carmen Jones*

In-laws
1931 *El pasado acusa*
1934 *Broadway Bill*
Laughing Boy
Strange Wives
1935 *Ruggles of Red Gap*
1939 One Dark Night
1955 *Foxfire*
1956 *The Catered Affair*

Incest
1917 *The Spirit of '76*
1933 *Thundering Herd*
1937 *I Want to Be a Mother*

Income tax
use Taxation

Incurable diseases
1916 *Her Debt of Honor*
1940 *Knute Rockne—All
American*
1956 *Hot Blood*

Indentured servants
1921 Fifty Candles
1948 *My Girl Tisa*
Unconquered
1953 Sangaree
1958 *The Light in the Forest*
1959 *The Hanging Tree*

Independence (MO)
Thunder in the Sun

Indian agents
1917 *The Squaw Man's Son*
1926 The Flaming Frontier
The Vanishing American
1929 Hawk of the Hills

1934 *Massacre*
'Neath the Arizona Skies
1935 *Wolf Riders*
1937 Hills of Old Wyoming
1942 Valley of the Sun
1943 Frontier Fury
The Law Rides Again
Wagon Tracks West
1946 Romance of the West
1947 Oregon Trail Scouts
1948 Fort Apache
Indian Agent
Renegades of Sonora
1949 *Daughter of the West*
She Wore a Yellow Ribbon
1950 *Cherokee Uprising*
*Davy Crockett, Indian
Scout*
North of the Great Divide
Raiders of Tomahawk Creek
1951 *New Mexico*
1952 Apache Country
The Battle at Apache Pass
The Half-Breed
Trail of the Arrow
1954 *Sitting Bull*
1955 *Apache Woman*
The Vanishing American
1956 *The Broken Star*
Walk the Proud Land
The White Squaw
1957 *The Lawless Eighties*
Naked in the Sun
1960 *Oklahoma Territory*

Indian reservations
use **Indians of North
America—Reservations**

Indiana
1952 *Brave Warrior*
1957 Raintree County

Indianapolis (IN)
1932 *La foule burle*
1944 *An American Romance*

Indians (Native American)
use **Indians of Central
America;
Indians of North
America;
Specific Indian tribes**

Indians (Persons from India)
use **East Indians**

Indians of Central America
1915 The Penitentes

Indians of North America
1913? *The Call of the Blood*
Hiawatha
1914 *The Good-for-Nothing*
Hearts United
In the Days of the
Thundering Herd
In the Land of the Head
Hunters
The Indian Wars
Life's Shop Window
The Little Angel of Canyon
Creek
Northern Lights
The Squaw Man
Where the Trail Divides
1914? The Lust of the Red Man
Sitting Bull—The Hostile
Sioux Indian Chief
1915 The Gambler of the West
The Lure of Woman
Sealed Valley
Where Cowboy Is King
1915? Life of American Indian [sic]
1916 *The Aryan*
Betrayed
Britton of the Seventh
The Flower of No Man's
Land
Gold and the Woman
The Half-Breed
Her Debt of Honor
Lone Star
Ramona
Witchcraft
1917 The Adventures of Buffalo
Bill
The Barrier
The Bronze Bride
The Buffalo Bill Show
The Captain of the Gray
Horse Troop

Her Own People
The Plow Woman
The Primitive Call
The Red Woman
The Squaw Man's Son
The Tenderfoot
1918 The Goddess of Lost Lake
The Hell Cat
Laughing Bill Hyde
The Man Above the Law
The Red, Red Heart
The Squaw Man
Tongues of Flame
1918? Indian Life
1919 The Heart of Wetona
The Last of His People
Told in the Hills
1919? In the Land of the Setting
Sun; or, Martyrs of
Yesterday
1920 Before the White Man Came
For the Soul of Rafael
Frontier Days
The Girl of My Heart
The Third Woman
1921 Across the Divide
Anne of Little Smoky
By Right of Birth
The Hunger of the Blood
Lonely Heart
That Girl Montana
1922 Blazing Arrows
The Crow's Nest
The Great Alone
The Half Breed
The Son of the Wolf
Winning of the West
1923 The Huntress
Jamestown
The Lone Wagon
The Sting of the Scorpion
1924 The Broken Law
The Heritage of the Desert
The Mine with the Iron
Door
North of Nevada
Peter Pan
Tongues of Flame
Unseen Hands
1925 Braveheart
Custer's Last Fight
Galloping Vengeance
The Gold Hunters
Quicker'n Lightnin'
The Red Rider
The Scarlet West
The Thundering Herd
Warrior Gap
The Wild Bull's Lair
1926 Buffalo Bill on the U. P.
Trail
The Devil Horse
The Flaming Frontier
Under Fire
The Vanishing American
1927 The Fighting Hombre
Open Range
Red Clay
Spoilers of the West
With Sitting Bull at the
Spirit Lake Massacre
1928 The Glorious Trail
Orphan of the Sage
Ramona
The Riding Renegade
Wyoming
1929 Hawk of the Hills
The Invaders
The Overland Telegraph
Wolf Song
1930 Whoopee
1931 Call of the Rockies
Cavalier of the West
Fighting Caravans
La gran jornada
Oklahoma Jim
The Squaw Man
The White Renegade
1932 Call Her Savage
The Forty-Niners
The Golden West
Hidden Valley
The Rainbow Trail
Riders of the Desert
Texas Pioneers

White Eagle
Wild Horse Mesa
1933 Diplomaniacs
The Telegraph Trail
Thundering Herd
1934 Behold My Wife!
Fighting Through
The Star Packer
Wagon Wheels
Wheels of Destiny
1935 Annie Oakley
Circle of Death
Cyclone of the Saddle
North of Arizona
Range Warfare
The Singing Vagabond
Texas Terror
Wolf Riders
1936 The Bold Caballero
Custer's Last Stand
Dancing Pirate
Daniel Boone
Desert Gold
For the Service
Ramona
Ride, Ranger, Ride
Silly Billies
West of Nevada
1937 The Barrier
Hills of Old Wyoming
Life Begins in College
The Riders of the Whistling
Skull
1938 The Adventures of Tom
Sawyer
Outlaw Express
Spawn of the North
The Texans
1939 Allegheny Uprising
Drifting Westward
Drums Along the Mohawk
Man of Conquest
1940 Arizona Frontier
Geronimo
Hi-Yo Silver
Kit Carson
Northwest Passage (Book
I—Rogers' Rangers)
1941 Hurry, Charlie, Hurry
Land of Liberty
The Pioneers
Saddlemates
This Woman Is Mine
Thunder Over the Prairie
1942 King of the Stallions
Lawless Plainsmen
Shut My Big Mouth
They Died With Their Boots
On
Valley of the Sun
1943 Frontier Fury
In Old Oklahoma
The Law Rides Again
The Leopard Man
The Outlaw
1944 Knickerbocker Holiday
Marshal of Reno
Outlaw Trail
Riding West
The San Antonio Kid
Sheriff of Las Vegas
Sonora Stagecoach
Tucson Raiders
Vigilantes of Dodge City
1945 Colorado Pioneers
Great Stagecoach Robbery
Phantom of the Plains
Where Do We Go From
Here?
1946 Bad Bascomb
California Gold Rush
Canyon Passage
Renegade Girl
Romance of the West
Santa Fe Uprising
Sheriff of Redwood Valley
Singin' in the Corn
South of Monterey
Sun Valley Cyclone
Wild Beauty
Wild West
1947 Bells of San Fernando
Black Gold
Bowery Buckaroos
Buffalo Bill Rides Again

Dangerous Venture
It Had To Be You
The Last Round-Up
Northwest Outpost
Oregon Trail Scouts
1948 Flight to the Sun
Indian Agent
The Paleface
Renegades of Sonora
Singin' Spurs
Unconquered
1949 Call of the Forest
Colorado Territory
The Cowboy and the Indians
Laramie
Massacre River
Ride, Ryder, Ride!
Roll Thunder Roll!
She Wore a Yellow Ribbon
Stallion Canyon
Tulsa
1950 Ambush
Annie Get Your Gun
The Cariboo Trail
Colt .45
Davy Crockett, Indian Scout
Indian Territory
North of the Great Divide
Raiders of Tomahawk Creek
Rock Island Trail
Rocky Mountain
Train to Tombstone
The Traveling Saleswoman
Winchester '73
1951 Cyclone Fury
Distant Drums
Hurricane Island
Jim Thorpe—All-American
The Last Outpost
New Mexico
Snake River Desperadoes
Warpath
Westward the Women
1952 Anything Can Happen
The Big Sky
Bugles in the Afternoon
Desert Pursuit
Indian Uprising
The Savage
1953 Captain John Smith and
Pocahontas
Fort Ti
The Great Sioux Uprising
Last of the Comanches
War Paint
1954 Arrow in the Dust
Broken Lance
Dangerous Mission
Taza, Son of Cochise
1955 Apache Woman
Davy Crockett, King of the
Wild Frontier
The Far Horizons
Indian American
The Indian Fighter
Kentucky Rifle
Kiss of Fire
Seven Cities of Gold
1956 Davy Crockett and the
River Pirates
Frontier Woman
The Last Frontier
The Lone Ranger
Mohawk
Pillars of the Sky
Raw Edge
Reprisal!
1957 The Guns of Fort Petticoat
Joe Dakota
Naked in the Sun
The Oklahoman
Run of the Arrow
The Tin Star
1958 Blood Arrow
Bullwhip
Gun Fever
The Lone Ranger and the
Lost City of Gold
1959 The FBI Story
Last Train from Gun Hill
The Oregon Trail
The Sheriff of Fractured
Jaw
Thunder in the Sun

1960 Cimarron
For the Love of Mike
The Unforgiven

Indians of North America—Mixed blood

1914 Where the Trail Divides
1916 The Half-Breed
Ramona
1917 The Barrier
The Gun Fighter
Her Own People
The Plow Woman
The Spirit of '76
The Squaw Man's Son
1918 Huck and Tom; or, the
Further Adventures of
Tom Sawyer
Laughing Bill Hyde
The Squaw Man
Tongues of Flame
1919 The Gray Towers Mystery
The Heart of Wetona
Just Squaw
The Westerners
1919? In the Land of the Setting
Sun; or, Martyrs of
Yesterday
1920 The Third Woman
1921 Across the Divide
The Cave Girl
The Girl from God's
Country
The Hunger of the Blood
1922 The Great Alone
The Half Breed
The Mohican's Daughter
Silver Spurs
1923 Crashin' Thru
Snowdrift
1924 The Heritage of the Desert
1925 Justice of the Far North
Red Love
1926 The Barrier
The Fighting Edge
1928 Ramona
1929 Frozen Justice
Hawk of the Hills
1930 Tom Sawyer
1932 Call Her Savage
1933 Circle Canyon
1934 The Cactus Kid
'Neath the Arizona Skies
Wagon Wheels
1936 Ramona
1937 The Barrier
The Riders of the Whistling
Skull
1941 Saddlemates
1943 In Old Oklahoma
1947 Duel in the Sun
Spoilers of the North
1949 Colorado Territory
The Cowboy and the
Indians
1950 Indian Territory
Riders of the Pony Express
1951 Distant Drums
Oh! Susanna
1952 The Big Sky
The Half-Breed
1953 Arrowhead
Seminole
1954 Broken Lance
Hondo
The Yellow Tomahawk
1955 Apache Woman
Foxfire
The Lonesome Trail
Santa Fe Passage
Seminole Uprising
1956 The Burning Hills
Comanche
The Last Hunt
The Last Wagon
Reprisal!
The Searchers
Secret of Treasure Mountain
The White Squaw
1957 The Halliday Brand
Revolt at Fort Laramie
The Tin Star
Trooper Hook
War Drums
1958 Apache Territory
Bullwhip

Flaming Frontier
Frontier Gun
Gun Fever
Gunman's Walk
Oregon Passage
1959 *The Oregon Trail*
1960 *Flaming Star*
Ice Palace

**Indians of North
America—Reservations**
1917 The Squaw Man's Son
1918? Indian Life
1933 *Diplomaniacs*
King of the Wild Horses
1934 Massacre
Wheels of Destiny
1935 Range Warfare
1937 Hills of Old Wyoming
1941 In the Land of the Navajo
1945 El Navajo
1946 *Wild Beauty*
1948 *Fort Apache*
Indian Agent
1949 *The Cowboy and the
Indians*
The Dalton Gang
Daughter of the West
1950 *Devil's Doorway*
North of the Great Divide
1951 Jim Thorpe—All-American
1952 *The Battle at Apache Pass*
Indian Uprising
Indian Uprising
Trail of the Arrow
1952? *Call of the Navajo*
1953 *Seminole*
1954 *Drum Beat*
Taza, Son of Cochise
They Rode West
1955 *Chief Crazy Horse*
Foxfire
The Vanishing American
White Feather
1956 *The Last Hunt*
The Lone Ranger
Walk the Proud Land
The White Squaw
1957 *Apache Warrior*
The Guns of Fort Petticoat
War Drums
1960 *Oklahoma Territory*
**Indians of North America—Social
life and customs**
1926 *General Custer at Little Big
Horn*
1952 Navajo
1958 Oregon Passage
Indigestion
1935 *A Night at the Ritz*
Industrial accidents
1931 *Cimarron*
1936 *Dangerous Intrigue*
Industrialists
1944 *Lifeboat*
Industry
use **Specific industries**
Infant death
1951 *Five*
1955 *Chief Crazy Horse*
The Long Gray Line
Infants
1914 Uncle Tom's Cabin
1915 The Italian
1916 *Poor Little Peppina*
1916? *Should a Baby Die?*
1917 *The Plow Woman*
Sold at Auction
The Wild Girl
1919? *The Brand of Judas*
1920 The Riddle: Woman
1931 *El pasado acusa*
El tenorio del harem
1932 *Flesh*
Genoveffa
1934 *What a Mother-in-Law!*
1935 *Melody Trail*
The Winning Ticket
1937 *That I May Live*
1939 The Cisco Kid and the Lady
Miracle on Main Street
1942 *Tortilla Flat*
1943 Mexican Spitfire's Blessed
Event

1944 *Tender Comrade*
1945 *A Tree Grows in Brooklyn*
1946 *Abie's Irish Rose*
1947 *Desperate*
1948 *Indian Agent*
1949 *3 Godfathers*
1951 *Across the Wide Missouri*
The Girl on the Bridge
Queen for a Day
Teresa
1953 *Taxi*
1954 *Passion*
1956 *The Last Hunt*
1957 *The Brothers Rico*
1958 *Escape from Red Rock*
*The Lone Ranger and the
Lost City of Gold*
1959 *Porgy and Bess*
Infants (Premature)
1955 *Blackboard Jungle*
Infatuation
1914 Life's Shop Window
The Redemption of David
Corson
1917 *The Flower of Doom*
1931 *La cautivadora*
Skyline
1933 *Rafter Romance*
1936 *La última cita*
Yiddle with His Fiddle
1937 *Green Fields*
Life Begins in College
1938 Happy Landing
Passport Husband
1940 Overture to Glory
1941 *This Woman Is Mine*
1944 *Andy Hardy's Blonde
Trouble*
Since You Went Away
1948 *Killer Diller*
1952 *Arctic Flight*
The Iron Mistress
1953 *The Member of the
Wedding*
1956 *Daniel Boone, Trail Blazer*
1959 *Imitation of Life*
Inferiority complexes
1932 L'athlète incomplet
1955 *Violent Saturday*
Infertility
1951 *The Magnificent Yankee*
Infidelity
1914 The Straight Road
Where the Trail Divides
1915 The Clemenceau Case
Kreutzer Sonata
1916 *Britton of the Seventh*
Civilization's Child
Gold and the Woman
A Man of Sorrow
The Woman in 47
1917 *Sold at Auction*
1918 Broken Ties
The Golden Wall
The Temple of Dusk
Tony America
Woman and the Law
1919 As a Man Thinks
1919? *The Brand of Judas*
1920 *For the Soul of Rafael*
On with the Dance
1923 Jealous Husbands
1925 *Cobra*
Scarlet Saint
1926 Under Fire
1928 George Washington Cohen
The Midnight Ace
Sins of the Fathers
1929 Die Königsloge
The Peacock Fan
1930 El secreto del doctor
1931 *Buster se marie*
Un caballero de frac
Carne de cabaret
La carta
Così è la vita
Gente alegre
La llama sagrada
Nuit d'Espagne
Pagliacci
La pura verdad
The Squaw Man
Street Scene
Su última noche
Women Love Once

Zein Weib's Lubovnick
1932 *Amore e morte*
Call Her Savage
Genoveffa
The Hatchet Man
Une heure près de toi
El hombre que asesinó
Men Are Such Fools
So Big
1933 *L'amour guide*
Counsellor at Law
Grand Slam
Yo, tú y ella
1934 *Behold My Wife!*
The Great Flirtation
Laughing Boy
Our Daily Bread
Strange Wives
La veuve joyeuse
White Heat
1935 Angelina o el honor de un
brigadier
¡Asegure a su mujer!
Te quiero con locura
The Wedding Night
1936 *After the Thin Man*
La última cita
1937 Charlie Chan at the Opera
The Devil's Playground
Underworld
1938 *The Singing Blacksmith*
The Toy Wife
*Two Gun Man from
Harlem*
1939 *Confessions of a Nazi Spy*
Gone With the Wind
La Inmaculada
Kol Nidre
Moon over Harlem
Verbena trágica
1940 *Perfidia*
*They Knew What They
Wanted*
1941 Adam Had Four Sons
The Mexican Spitfire's Baby
Sunday Sinners
1942 *In This Our Life*
Take My Life
Tales of Manhattan
Twin Beds
1943 *Cabin in the Sky*
Dixie
1944 *Black Magic*
Mr. Skeffington
Tender Comrade
1945 Johnny Angel
1948 Sleep, My Love
1949? *Girl in Room 20*
1950 *Ambush*
Give Us This Day
1950? Three Daughters
1951 *Little Big Horn*
1952 *The Iron Mistress*
1953 *Ride, Vaquero!*
1954 Indiscretion of an American
Wife
1955 The Rose Tattoo
*The View from Pompey's
Head*
Violent Saturday
1956 Baby Doll
Pillars of the Sky
1957 Beau James
The Midnight Story
Raintree County
1958 Home Before Dark
Machete
Oregon Passage
Wild Is the Wind
The Young Lions
1959 *Odds Against Tomorrow*
The Wonderful Country
1960 *Man on a String*
Information, Please (Radio
program)
1942 *Woman of the Year*
Informers
1918 *The Ranger*
1924 *Birthright*
1930 Las campanas de Capistrano
El presidio
1931 *El pasado acusa*
1934 *Limehouse Blues*
1934? Harlem After Midnight

1937 *Shadows of the Orient*
1939 *Confessions of a Nazi Spy*
1948 *The Time of Your Life*
1956 *Death of a Scoundrel*
Ingenues
1917 Rosie O'Grady
1929 *Die Königsloge*
Ingratitude
use **Gratitude**
Inheritance
1914 *The Good-for-Nothing*
1915 *The Alien*
The Clemenceau Case
The Gambler of the West
1916 *Gold and the Woman*
Little Meena's Romance
The Thousand Dollar
Husband
1917 *The Little Boy Scout*
The Peddler
The Sudden Gentleman
Threads of Fate
A Wife by Proxy
The Wild Girl
1918 *The Goddess of Lost Lake*
The Wine Girl
1919 A Bachelor's Wife
The Gray Towers Mystery
1920 *Billions*
The Luck of the Irish
*The Symbol of the
Unconquered*
1922 The Crow's Nest
The Man with Two Mothers
1923 Little Old New York
1924 North of Nevada
Yankee Speed
1925 Irish Luck
1926 The Cohens and Kellys
1927 Finnegan's Ball
1930 El príncipe del dólar
Take the Heir
La voluntad del muerto
1931 *Un caballero de frac*
Los calaveras
Gentleman's Fate
Noche de duendes
Le petit café
1932 *Call Her Savage*
¿Cuándo te suicidas?
1933 *Espérame*
1934 *Call of the Coyote*
'Neath the Arizona Skies
1936 *My American Wife*
1937 *Boy of the Streets*
*The Jester (Der
Purimspieler)*
1938 Outside of Paradise
1939 Papá soltero
Way Down South
1940 *Eli Eli*
1940? Mr. Washington Goes to
Town
1941 Under Fiesta Stars
Virginia
1942 *Castle in the Desert*
Professor Creeps
Tortilla Flat
Whispering Ghosts
1944 Dark Waters
Something for the Boys
1945 *The Valley of Decision*
1946 *Santa Fe Uprising*
1946? Fight That Ghost
1947 Riding the California Trail
1948 *Singin' Spurs*
1949 *Massacre River*
The Mysterious Desperado
1950 Jiggs and Maggie Out West
1951 Cuban Fireball
The House on Telegraph
Hill
1953 *Sangaree*
1955 *The Vanishing American*
Injuries
use **Specific injuries or
wounds;
Wounds and injuries**
Injustice
1921 The Sport of the Gods
1924 His Darker Self
The Mine with the Iron
Door
1924? The Flaming Crisis

1925 The Greatest Love of All
1928 Riley the Cop
1936 Winterset
1937 *Maid of Salem*
1943 The Ox-Bow Incident

Ink
1942 *The Vanishing Virginian*

Innkeepers
1917 *The Sudden Gentleman*
1918 *Find the Woman*
1932 *Amore e morte*
1935 *Angelina o el honor de un brigadier*
1946 *Rendezvous 24*
1949 *The Kissing Bandit*

Innocence
1927 *The Scar of Shame*
1938? *Amore che non torna*

Innocents
1921? The Slave Market
1931 *Cuerpo y alma*
Nuit d'Espagne
1933 *La melodía prohibida*
1934 The Cat's-Paw
1938 Passport Husband
1940 The Way of All Flesh
1941 Hold Back the Dawn
Sun Valley Serenade
1953 Taxi

Innovations
1941 *Western Union*
1944 *An American Romance*

Inns
1918 *The Ordeal of Rosetta*
1919 The Tiger Lily
1931 *Mi último amor*
1932 *Hombres en mi vida*
Yiskor
1934 *Caravane*
1937 *Natalka Poltavka*
1938 *The Singing Blacksmith*
1942 *Holiday Inn*
We Were Dancing
1946 *Rendezvous 24*
1947? What a Guy
1948 *Gentleman's Agreement*
The Luck of the Irish
1949 *The Kissing Bandit*
1951 *When the Redskins Rode*

Inquisition—Spain
1933 *The Wandering Jew*

Insane asylums
1930 *Locuras de amor*
1934 What a Mother-in-Law!
1937 *Where Is My Child?*

Insanity
1913 *Traffic in Souls*
1915? *Sin*
1916 *The Morals of Hilda*
1918 *The City of Dim Faces*
1919 *The Homesteader*
The Scar
1930 *La voluntad del muerto*
1932 *Amore e morte*
Le bluffeur
1934 *The Lone Defender*
The Youth of Russia
1935 *Bordertown*
Te quiero con locura
1936 *Winterset*
1937 *Charlie Chan at the Opera*
1939 *Bad Lands*
1940 *Northwest Passage (Book I—Rogers' Rangers)*
1942 *Castle in the Desert*
1943 *Dr. Gillespie's Criminal Case*
1951 *A Streetcar Named Desire*
1956 *The Last Hunt*
1957 *Raintree County*
Tomahawk Trail
1959 *Anna Lucasta*
1960 *The Unforgiven*

Inscription Rock (NM)
use **El Morro National Monument (NM)**

Installment plans
1940 *Jennie*
1950 *Give Us This Day*

Insubordination
1954 *They Rode West*
1958 *Oregon Passage*
1960 *All the Young Men*

Insurance
1935 *¡Asegure a su mujer!*
1939 *Charlie Chan at Treasure Island*
Lying Lips
1944 *Vigilantes of Dodge City*
Waterfront
1949 *C-Man*
Tuna Clipper

Insurance—Agents
1935 *The Winning Ticket*
1936 *Below the Deadline*
1945 *A Tree Grows in Brooklyn*
1946 Slightly Scandalous

Insurance—Investigators
1939 *Mr. Moto Takes a Vacation*
1941 *The Gang's All Here*
1949 *Arctic Manhunt*
The Sky Dragon
Top O' the Morning

Insurance fraud
1941 The Gang's All Here

Insurgency
1953 The Man Behind the Gun

Intellect
1927 Old San Francisco

Intelligence (Espionage)
use **Espionage;**
Military intelligence;
Secret agents;
Spies;
Undercover operations

Intelligence (Mental capacity)
use **Intellect**

Interior decorators
1935 *McFadden's Flats*
1942 *In This Our Life*
We Were Dancing
1950 *Chinatown at Midnight*

Internment
1953 *Arrowhead*

Interns (Medicine)
1926 *Kosher Kitty Kelly*
1950 *Emergency Wedding*

Interpreters
use **Translators**

Interrogation
1931 *La cautivadora*
1935 *Charlie Chan in Shanghai*
1936 *Ellis Island*
Human Cargo
1939 *Confessions of a Nazi Spy*
1940 *The Man I Married*
1954 *Barefoot Battalion*
1959 *The FBI Story*
Night of the Quarter Moon

Interviews
1915 How Molly Malone Made Good

Intolerance
1931 *Cimarron*
1946 *Abie's Irish Rose*
1948 The Boy with Green Hair
I Remember Mama

Invalids
1917 *I Will Repay*
1919 *A Bachelor's Wife*
Bonnie, Bonnie Lassie
1923 Crashin' Thru
1927 Pleasure Before Business
1930 *Whoopee*
1931 *La llama sagrada*
1932 *Soñadores de la gloria*
1944 *Three Men in White*
1960 For the Love of Mike
Take a Giant Step

Invasions
1941 *Ten Ostatni*
Z Dymem Pożarów
1952 *California Conquest*

Inventions
1915 Time Lock Number 776
1918 Good-Bye, Bill
1932 *Le bluffeur*
The Match King
1934 *Charlie Chan in London*
1937 Charlie Chan at the Olympics
1942 Foreign Agent

Inventors
1921 The Girl from God's Country
Lotus Blossom
1932 The Heart of New York
1937 *Charlie Chan at the Olympics*
1938 The Power of Life
1944 Charlie Chan in the Secret Service
Something for the Boys
1953 *The Charge at Feather River*

Investigations
1929 *Señor Americano*
Sombras habaneras
1930 *Amor audaz*
Cascarrabias
La voluntad del muerto
1931 Noche de duendes
1937 *Bargain with Bullets*
1939 Confessions of a Nazi Spy
1941 Louisiana Purchase
1942 Whispering Ghosts
1943 Frontier Fury
1944 *Cry of the Werewolf*
1947 *The Burning Cross*
Crossfire
1948 Call Northside 777
Cry of the City
Moonrise
Shanghai Chest
1949 C-Man
Jigsaw
Rose of the Yukon
1950 *Bandit Queen*
Cherokee Uprising
Mystery Street
Sunset in the West
1957 *The Midnight Story*
1958 Touch of Evil
1959 The FBI Story
1960 *The Pusher*

Investments
1934 El tango en Broadway
1938 *The Rage of Paris*
1943 *Wintertime*

Investors
1919 *A Yankee Princess*
1930 *El cuerpo del delito*
1937 Song of the City
1943 *Riding High*
1948 *Music Man*

Iowa
1927 A Harp in Hock
1944 *The Sullivans*
1947 *On the Old Spanish Trail*

Ireland
1915 The Rosary
1916 A Son of Erin
1917 Castles for Two
The Sudden Gentleman
1918 Denny from Ireland
The Little Runaway
1919 The Lord Loves the Irish
A Yankee Princess
1921? The Supreme Passion
1925 Irish Luck
1928 Mother Machree
1929 Smiling Irish Eyes
1938 Outside of Paradise
1943 Doughboys in Ireland
1948 The Luck of the Irish
1949 Top O' the Morning
1952 The Quiet Man
The Quiet Man
1959 Shake Hands with the Devil

Irish
1915 How Molly Malone Made Good
1916 The Innocent Lie
Mixed Blood
A Son of Erin
1917 Castles for Two
The Sudden Gentleman
A Wife by Proxy
1918 Denny from Ireland
Doing Their Bit
The Little Runaway
1919 A Bachelor's Wife
1920 Darling Mine
Pagan Love
1921 The Barricade

1921? The Supreme Passion
1922 The Five Dollar Baby
The Scrapper
Second Hand Rose
1923 Little Old New York
1924 Fools' Highway
1925 His People
Hogan's Alley
One of the Bravest
1926 Kosher Kitty Kelly
Private Izzy Murphy
Sweet Daddies
Sweet Rosie O'Grady
1927 Clancy's Kosher Wedding
Frisco Sally Levy
A Harp in Hock
Jake the Plumber
Pleasure Before Business
The Shamrock and the Rose
1928 Flying Romeos
Mother Machree
The Rawhide Kid
Vamping Venus
1929 Abie's Irish Rose
Smiling Irish Eyes
1930 *Anna Christie*
Around the Corner
1935 The Winning Ticket
1936 Laughing Irish Eyes
1944 *Going My Way*
1945 Nob Hill
1946 *Three Wise Fools*
1947 Last of the Redmen
1948 *The Lady from Shanghai*
1949 *The Story of Seabiscuit*
1953 Taxi
1959 *Night of the Quarter Moon*
1960 The Day They Robbed the Bank of England

Irish Americans
1914 *The Straight Road*
1915 Chimmie Fadden
Chimmie Fadden Out West
The Danger Signal
The Rosary
The Spender
1917 Castles for Two
Rosie O'Grady
1918 Amarilly of Clothes-Line Alley
The Gypsy Trail
The Hell Cat
Hell's End
Hitting the Trail
Marked Cards
Real Folks
Thirty a Week
1919 *The Delicious Little Devil*
A Fighting Colleen
The Lord Loves the Irish
Spotlight Sadie
A Yankee Princess
1920 Dinty
Hidden Charms
The Luck of the Irish
1921 All Souls' Eve
Hold Your Horses
Little Miss Hawkshaw
Made in Heaven
When the Clock Struck Nine
1921? The Supreme Passion
1922 Come On Over
The Guttersnipe
The Man with Two Mothers
Saturday Night
The Top O' the Morning
1923 April Showers
Breaking into Society
Little Old New York
1924 Conductor 1492
East of Broadway
1925 The Beautiful City
The Fearless Lover
Irish Luck
Lights of Old Broadway
The Man in Blue
Old Clothes
A Son of His Father
1926 Blarney
The Cohens and Kellys
Irene
The Little Irish Girl
1927 The Callahans and the Murphys
Finnegan's Ball

For the Love of Mike
Heroes in Blue
Irish Hearts
Lost at the Front
McFadden's Flats
1928 Anybody Here Seen Kelly?
The Cohens and the Kellys
in Paris
The Crash
The House of Scandal
Mother Machree
Riley the Cop
Vamping Venus
1929 The Cohens and Kellys in
Atlantic City
East Side Sadie
Mother's Boy
Smiling Irish Eyes
1930 The Cohens and the Kellys
in Scotland
Kathleen Mavourneen
The Last Dance
1931 The Cohens and Kellys in
Africa
Personal Maid
Skyline
Young Sinners
1932 The Cohens and Kellys in
Hollywood
The Golden West
Hearts of Humanity
Me and My Gal
No Greater Love
1933 The Cohens and Kellys in
Trouble
Dance Hall Hostess
1935 His Family Tree
The Irish in Us
McFadden's Flats
1935? The Irish Gringo
1936 *Below the Deadline*
Kelly the Second
Laughing Irish Eyes
Paddy O'Day
1937 Boy of the Streets
Man of the People
1938 *City Streets*
Gateway
In Old Chicago
Outside of Paradise
Speed to Burn
1939 *Let Freedom Ring*
Waterfront
1940 The Fighting 69th
Little Nellie Kelly
Three Cheers for the Irish
1942 *Gentleman Jim*
Song of the Islands
1943 *The Amazing Mrs. Holliday*
Doughboys in Ireland
Yankee Doodle Dandy
1944 *The Racket Man*
The Sullivans
1945 *The Bells of St. Mary's*
The Great John L.
Sunbonnet Sue
A Tree Grows in Brooklyn
The Valley of Decision
1946 Abie's Irish Rose
Bringing Up Father
Gas House Kids
Three Wise Fools
1947 *Bells of San Fernando*
Calendar Girl
California
Carnegie Hall
Easy Come, Easy Go
The Foxes of Harrow
Jiggs and Maggie in Society
My Wild Irish Rose
1948 *Big City*
The Boy with Green Hair
Fighting Father Dunne
Fort Apache
The Luck of the Irish
The Time of Your Life
Up in Central Park
Western Heritage
1949 *Portrait of Jennie*
Shamrock Hill
Top O' the Morning
1950 *The Daughter of Rosie
O'Grady*
Jiggs and Maggie Out West
Right Cross

Sands of Iwo Jima
1952 *Bugles in the Afternoon*
Indian Uprising
It's a Big Country: An
American Anthology
The Quiet Man
1953 *Taxi*
1954 *They Rode West*
1955 *Blackboard Jungle*
The Long Gray Line
1956 *The Catered Affair*
Ghost Town
1957 *All Mine to Give*
Beau James
The Guns of Fort Petticoat
Run of the Arrow
1958 *Fort Massacre*
The Last Hurrah
1959 *Al Capone*
Shake Hands with the Devil
1960 The Day They Robbed the
Bank of England
Ice Palace
Studs Lonigan
"The Irish Washerwoman" (Song)
1936 *Kelly the Second*
Iron mines
1944 *An American Romance*
Iroquois Indians
1917 The Hidden Children
1947 Last of the Redmen
1950 *The Iroquois Trail*
Young Daniel Boone
1956 Mohawk
Irresponsibility
1931 Del infierno al cielo
Women Love Once
1937 Border Cafe
1948? *Boarding House Blues*
Irrigation
1918 *The Red, Red Heart*
1941 *Thunder Over the Prairie*
1943 *Wagon Tracks West*
Washington Irving
1923 Little Old New York
Isaac (Biblical character)
1930 My Yiddishe Mama
Islands
1918 *The Honor of His House*
1923 Regeneration
1931 Aloha
1933 *The Emperor Jones*
It's Great to Be Alive
1936 El diablo del mar
The Prisoner of Shark Island
Sea Spoilers
Yellow Cargo
1940 *New Moon*
1941 *King of the Zombies*
1946 Dirty Gertie from Harlem,
U.S.A.
Swamp Fire
1947 *Last of the Redmen*
1949 *Home of the Brave*
1950 *Last of the Buccaneers*
Sands of Iwo Jima
1951 *Distant Drums*
1953 *The Charge at Feather
River*
1959 *Porgy and Bess*
Isolationism
1949 *Answer for Anne*
Istanbul (Turkey)
1932 El hombre que asesinó
Italian Americans
1912 *The Adventures of
Lieutenant Petrosino*
1914 The Nightingale
1915 The Alien
1916 A Child of Mystery
The Criminal
Gretchen, the Greenhorn
Pasquale
The Social Highwayman
1917 His Sweetheart
Lost in Transit
The Pulse of Life
A Roadside Impresario
1918 The City of Tears
Hitting the Trail
My Cousin
One More American
The Ordeal of Rosetta
The Wine Girl

1919 Hearts of Men
The Sleeping Lion
The Tiger Lily
Who Will Marry Me?
1919? *The Chosen Path*
1920 *The Man Who Dared*
1921 Diane of Star Hollow
Little Italy
One Man in a Million
Puppets of Fate
Society Snobs
When the Clock Struck Nine
1921? The Slave Market
1922 Fair Lady
Head over Heels
The Sign of the Rose
1923 Look Your Best
Thirty Days
1924 Defying the Law
Racing Luck
1925 The Beautiful City
Cobra
The Greatest Love of All
The Man in Blue
The Manicure Girl
1926 Puppets
Rose of the Tenements
1927 Bitter Apples
For the Love of Mike
Sally in Our Alley
1928 The Night Bird
The Secret Hour
We Americans
1929 East Side Sadie
Love, Live and Laugh
Mister Antonio
1930 Behind the Make-Up
Ladies Love Brutes
A Lady to Love
Sombras de gloria
1931 *Gentleman's Fate*
The Guilty Generation
Little Caesar
El pasado acusa
Street Scene
1932 Amor in montagna
Cuore d'emigrante
Huddle
Men Are Such Fools
O festino o la legge
Scarface
Senza mamma e'nnamurato
1933 Obey the Law
Racetrack
1934 *Our Daily Bread*
1935 *A Night at the Opera*
The Winning Ticket
1936 It Had to Happen
Let's Sing Again
Winterset
1937 Man of the People
Manhattan Merry-Go-Round
Music for Madame
Nation Aflame
Song of the City
1938 City Streets
Road Demon
Speed to Burn
1938? Amore che non torna
I due gemelli
1939 The Escape
Fisherman's Wharf
Judge Hardy and Son
Winner Take All
1940 East of the River
They Knew What They
Wanted
1941 *Caught in the Act*
1942 *Unseen Enemy*
1944 *The Racket Man*
1945 *Sunbonnet Sue*
1946 *Gas House Kids*
1947 *The Burning Cross*
Citizen Saint
1948 Cry of the City
Music Man
1949 House of Strangers
Jigsaw
Knock on Any Door
That Midnight Kiss
The Undercover Man
1950 Black Hand
Deported
Give Us This Day
The Jackie Robinson Story

Sands of Iwo Jima
1951 *The Great Caruso*
Teresa
Westward the Women
1952 It's a Big Country: An
American Anthology
Kid Monk Baroni
Woman in the Dark
1953 *Taxi*
1954 Indiscretion of an American
Wife
1955 *Blackboard Jungle*
Marty
Murder in Villa Capri
The Rose Tattoo
1956 Baby Doll
Full of Life
Serenade
1957 The Brothers Rico
Joe Dakota
The Midnight Story
1958 *Houseboat*
Never Love a Stranger
Seven Hills of Rome
Wild Is the Wind
1959 Al Capone
The Black Orchid
Inside the Mafia
Odds Against Tomorrow
1960 Pay or Die
Weddings and Babies
Italians
1915 The Italian
The Last of the Mafia
1915? Sin
1916 The Gilded Spider
Poor Little Peppina
The Social Highwayman
Three of Many
The Woman in 47
A Woman's Honor
1917 *The Adventures of Carol*
The Pulse of Life
The Tell-Tale Step
Threads of Fate
The Woman and the Beast
1918 Tony America
Wanted, a Mother
A Woman of Impulse
1919 *The Tiger Lily*
1920 *It's a Great Life*
1920? The Greatest Love
1922 Fair Lady
1930 *Charros, gauchos y
manolas*
1931 *Le père célibataire*
1931? La porta del destino
1932 Tormento
1936 *Sins of Man*
1938? I due gemelli
1939 *Lying Lips*
1940 *The Jewish Melody*
1951 *Gambling House*
Teresa
1958 Houseboat
Seven Hills of Rome
Italy
1915? Sin
1916 *The Gilded Spider*
Poor Little Peppina
The Woman in 47
A Woman's Honor
1917 *A Roadside Impresario*
1930 Sei tu l'amore
1931 Pagliacci
1935 El cantante de Nápoles
1947 *Citizen Saint*
1950 *Black Hand*
Deported
1951 Teresa
Italy. Army
1916 *Pasquale*
Three of Many
1929 Love, Live and Laugh
1934 *The Unknown Soldier
Speaks*
Ivory
1931 The Cohens and Kellys in
Africa
Iwo Jima (Japan)
1950 Sands of Iwo Jima

Andrew Jackson
1914 *Springtime*
1927 The Frontiersman
1938 The Buccaneer
1939 *Man of Conquest*
1955 *Davy Crockett, King of the Wild Frontier*

General Thomas Jonathan Jackson
1914 *Dan*

Jade
1935 *Captured in Chinatown*

Jailbreaks
1925 *Tonio, Son of the Sierras*
1931 *The Avenger*
Cavalier of the West
Die Dreigroschenoper
1932 *The Galloping Kid*
Law and Lawless
1934 *Massacre*
1935 *The Singing Vagabond*
1936 *Border Phantom*
Ride, Ranger, Ride
1937 *Prairie Thunder*
1938 *Birthright*
The Renegade Ranger
1939 *The Cisco Kid and the Lady*
Harlem Rides the Range
The Return of the Cisco Kid
Waterfront
1940 *The Gay Caballero*
Hi-Yo Silver
Rhythm of the Rio Grande
1941 *Belle Starr*
1942 *Valley of the Sun*
1944 *Knickerbocker Holiday*
Sonora Stagecoach
1946 *Border Bandits*
South of Monterey
1947 *Buffalo Bill Rides Again*
Under the Tonto Rim
Wild Horse Mesa
1948 *Guns of Hate*
Renegades of Sonora
Western Heritage
1949 *Colorado Territory*
The Dalton Gang
The Daring Caballero
Laramie
Roll Thunder Roll!
Rustlers
Stagecoach Kid
The Valiant Hombre
1950 *Border Treasure*
Buccaneer's Girl
1952 *The Fighter*
My Man and I
1953 *Jack McCall Desperado*
The Man from the Alamo
The Nebraskan
Tumbleweed
1954 *War Arrow*
1955 *Good Morning, Miss Dove*
1958 *Gunman's Walk*

Jails
1918 *The Prussian Cur*
The Ranger
1919 *The Gray Towers Mystery*
1923 *Thirty Days*
1926 *A Prince of His Race*
1930 *El precio de un beso*
1931 *Die Dreigroschenoper*
1932 *Border Devils*
1933 *Racetrack*
1934 *La veuve joyeuse*
1935 *The Winning Ticket*
1936 *Contra la corriente*
1939 *Lying Lips*
194- *Mistaken Identity*
1940 *Am I Guilty?*
Her Second Mother
1940? *Mr. Washington Goes to Town*
1941 *Caught in the Act*
Road Agent
1942 *Apache Trail*
Mokey
Tortilla Flat
1946 *Tall, Tan and Terrific*
Without Reservations
1946? *Beale Street Mama*
1947 *Hi De Ho*
On the Old Spanish Trail
1948 *Indian Agent*
Shanghai Chest

1949 *The Fighting Kentuckian*
The Golden Stallion
Ranger of Cherokee Strip
Stallion Canyon
1949? *She's Too Mean for Me*
1950 *The Girl from San Lorenzo*
Intruder in the Dust
The Iroquois Trail
The Missourians
Mystery Street
Sunset in the West
1952 *The Big Sky*
Rose of Cimarron
1954 *Salt of the Earth*
1956 *Reprisal!*
1958 *The Rawhide Trail*
1959 *The Young Land*
1960 *The Sign of Zorro*

Jamaica
1933 *The Emperor Jones*
1937 *Slave Ship*
1939 *The Devil's Daughter*

James Butler
use **Wild Bill Hickok**

Jamestown (VA)
1923 *Jamestown*
1953 *Captain John Smith and Pocahontas*

Janitors
1915 *A Texas Steer*
1921 *The Gunsaulus Mystery*
1926 *The Campus Flirt*
1928 *A Ship Comes In*
1933 *Olsen's Big Moment*
1942 *Sunday Punch*
1944 *Cry of the Werewolf*
1946 *The Sailor Takes a Wife*
1947 *Mantan Runs for Mayor*

Japan
1916 *The Soul of Kura-San*
1917 *The Call of the East*
Hashimura Togo
1918 *Her American Husband*
His Birthright
The Temple of Dusk
1920 *A Tokio Siren*
1945 *Samurai*

Japan. Air Force
1943 *Air Force*

Japan. Army
1942 *Prisoner of Japan*
1943 *Bataan*
1944 *The Negro Soldier*
1945 *Pride of the Marines*
Samurai
1950 *Sands of Iwo Jima*

Japan. Navy
1942 *Submarine Raider*
1943 *Air Force*

Japanese
1915 *After Five*
1916 *The Soul of Kura-San*
1917 *The Call of the East*
Hashimura Togo
The Secret Game
1918 *The Bravest Way*
Her American Husband
His Birthright
The Temple of Dusk
Who Is to Blame?
1919 *The Courageous Coward*
A Heart in Pawn
1920 *A Tokio Siren*
1930 *Chijiku wo mawasuru chikara*
1942 *Across the Pacific*
Let's Get Tough!
Professor Creeps
1943 *Jack London*
Marching On!
1945 *Betrayal from the East*
1949 *The Clay Pigeon*

Japanese Americans
1915 *The Cheat*
1916 *Alien Souls*
The Honorable Friend
The Soul of Kura-San
1917 *The Call of the East*
Forbidden Paths
1918 *The Bravest Way*
Her American Husband
His Birthright
The Honor of His House
The Temple of Dusk

1919 *The Courageous Coward*
The Gray Horizon
A Heart in Pawn
His Debt
1920 *Locked Lips*
A Tokio Siren
Who's Your Servant?
1921 *Black Roses*
Shadows of the West
1922 *The Pride of Palomar*
1927 *[Japanese-American Film]*
1931 *The Black Camel*
1935 *The Wedding Night*
1937 *Thank You, Mr. Moto*
Think Fast, Mr. Moto
1938 *Mr. Moto Takes a Chance*
Mr. Moto's Gamble
1939 *Mr. Moto in Danger Island*
Mr. Moto Takes a Vacation
Mr. Moto's Last Warning
1942 *Little Tokyo, U.S.A.*
Prisoner of Japan
1945 *Samurai*
1951 *The Steel Helmet*
Westward the Women
1952 *Japanese War Bride*
1955 *Bad Day at Black Rock*
1959 *The Crimson Kimono*
1960 *Hell to Eternity*

Japanese Americans—Evacuation and relocation, 1942-1945
1942 *Little Tokyo, U.S.A.*
1951 *Go for Broke!*
1952 *Japanese War Bride*
1955 *Bad Day at Black Rock*
1960 *Hell to Eternity*

Jazz music
1928 *The Jazz Singer*
1929 *Is Everybody Happy?*
1930 *King of Jazz*
The Melody Man
1933 *Best of Enemies*
La melodía prohibida
194- *Mistaken Identity*
1940 *Broken Strings*
Mystery in Swing
1941 *Birth of the Blues*
Murder on Lenox Avenue
1941? *The Blood of Jesus*
1942 *Lucky Ghost*
Syncopation
1944 *Slightly Terrific*
1946 *Beware*
Stars on Parade
Tall, Tan and Terrific
1946? *Beale Street Mama*
1947 *Carnegie Hall*
Hi De Ho
Jivin' in Be-Bop
New Orleans
Reet, Petite and Gone
1949? *Harlem Follies*
The Joint Is Jumpin'
1950 *Young Man with a Horn*
1953 *The Jazz Singer*
1956 *The Benny Goodman Story*
1957 *Satchmo the Great*
1958 *Kings Go Forth*
1959 *Night of the Quarter Moon*
1960 *All the Fine Young Cannibals*
I Passed for White

Jealousy
1915 *The Lure of Woman*
The Rosary
The Secret Sin
1916 *The Twin Triangle*
1917 *The Little Chevalier*
The Wild Girl
The Woman and the Beast
1918 *Hell's End*
Hitting the Trail
In Judgment Of
The Little Runaway
Tongues of Flame
A Woman of Impulse
1918? *Rosemary Climbs the Heights*
1919 *Erstwhile Susan*
The Gray Towers Mystery
Lasca
The Sneak
Spotlight Sadie
The Unpainted Woman

1920 *Within Our Gates*
1921 *The First Born*
The Green-Eyed Monster
1923 *Jealous Husbands*
Thirty Days
1924 *Peter Pan*
1925 *The Prairie Wife*
1926 *A Trip to Chinatown*
1927 *White Gold*
1928 *The Crash*
United States Smith
1930 *Behind the Make-Up*
Check and Double Check
1931 *Buster se marie*
Carne de cabaret
Cavalier of the West
Così è la vita
The Exile
Mi último amor
La pura verdad
Regeneración
Sombras del circo
1932 *L'athlète incomplet*
Hollywood, ciudad de ensueño
Joseph in the Land of Egypt
Men Are Such Fools
Le plombier amoureux
Scarface
Yiskor
1933 *Dance Hall Hostess*
Grand Slam
Let's Fall in Love
Man from Monterey
No dejes la puerta abierta
Primavera en otoño
Thundering Herd
1933? *Scandal*
1934 *Blossom Time*
La buenaventura
Caravane
La cruz y la espada
Limehouse Blues
La veuve joyeuse
White Heat
1935 *Alas sobre el Chaco*
Angelina o el honor de un brigadier
Bordertown
A Night at the Ritz
North of Arizona
Rendezvous
Señora casada necesita marido
1935? *The Irish Gringo*
1936 *Kelly the Second*
Laughing Irish Eyes
My American Wife
Ramona
Sum Hun
Yiddle with His Fiddle
1937 *El carnaval del diablo*
Charlie Chan at the Opera
The Devil's Playground
Green Fields
I Want to Be a Mother
It Could Happen to You
Life Begins in College
That Girl from Paris
1938 *God's Step Children*
Mis dos amores
My Lucky Star
Outside of Paradise
The Rage of Paris
Swing!
La vida bohemia
1939 *Charlie Chan at Treasure Island*
The Cisco Kid and the Lady
Cossacks in Exile
Double Deal
The Girl from Mexico
Let Freedom Ring
El otro soy yo
The Return of the Cisco Kid
Verbena trágica
194- *Mistaken Identity*
1940 *Broken Strings*
The Fatal Hour
Mexican Spitfire Out West
Mystery in Swing
1941 *Murder on Lenox Avenue*
New York Town
Romance of the Rio Grande
Sun Valley Serenade

1942   Cat People
        Lucky Ghost
        Rio Rita
        Tales of Manhattan
        The Vanishing Virginian
        We Were Dancing
        Wings for the Eagle
1943   *Cabin in the Sky*
        Good Luck, Mr. Yates
        Stormy Weather
        Tahiti Honey
        Wintertime
1944   *Andy Hardy's Blonde
            Trouble*
        Buffalo Bill
        Cry of the Werewolf
        Lake Placid Serenade
        Something for the Boys
        Tucson Raiders
1945   *Between Two Women*
        The Cisco Kid Returns
        The Dolly Sisters
        Jealousy
        Nob Hill
        Salome, Where She Danced
        South of the Rio Grande
        The Valley of Decision
        Wanderer of the Wasteland
1946   *Beware*
        Notorious
        The Sailor Takes a Wife
        Slightly Scandalous
        Till the End of Time
        Without Reservations
1946?   *Beale Street Mama*
1947   *Bells of San Fernando*
        Buck Privates Come Home
        Duel in the Sun
        Hi De Ho
        It Had To Be You
        On the Old Spanish Trail
        Robin Hood of Monterey
        Untamed Fury
1948   *Harpoon*
        The Lady from Shanghai
        The Paleface
        Rocky
        Tap Roots
1949   Anna Lucasta
        House of Strangers
        Illegal Entry
        Jigsaw
        The Quiet One
        Shamrock Hill
        Souls of Sin
        That Midnight Kiss
1950   *Belle of Old Mexico*
        The Breaking Point
        Buccaneer's Girl
        Emergency Wedding
        Last of the Buccaneers
1951   *Flaming Feather*
        *The House on Telegraph
            Hill*
        The Last Outpost
        Native Son
1952   *Japanese War Bride*
        The Quiet Man
1953   *Captain John Smith and
            Pocahontas*
        Dream Wife
        The Eddie Cantor Story
        Fort Ti
        The Man Behind the Gun
        San Antone
        Sangaree
        Seminole
        So Big
        Thunder Bay
1954   Carmen Jones
        Cattle Queen of Montana
        War Arrow
1955   *Blackboard Jungle*
        Foxfire
        Santa Fe Passage
1956   *Crowded Paradise*
        Frontier Woman
        Hot Blood
        Mohawk
        Reprisal!
        *Secret of Treasure
            Mountain*
        Serenade
1957   *Band of Angels*
        Man in the Shadow

        Ride Out for Revenge
1958   Fort Bowie
        Houseboat
        Oregon Passage
        St. Louis Blues
        Seven Hills of Rome
1959   *Anna Lucasta*
        The Crimson Kimono
1960   All the Fine Young
            Cannibals
        Cimarron
        The Unforgiven
        Weddings and Babies

Thomas Jefferson
1937   *Old Louisiana*
1941   *Land of Liberty*
1955   *The Far Horizons*

Thomas Jeffords
1950   Broken Arrow

Jericho
1936   *The Green Pastures*

Jersey City (NJ)
1929   *Abie's Irish Rose*
1931   *Gentleman's Fate*

Jerusalem (Palestine)
        Shulamith
1935   *The Yiddish King Lear*
1937   *The Holy Oath*

Jerusalem—Siege, 586 B.C.
1933   *The Wandering Jew*

Jesus Christ
1915   *The Birth of a Nation*
1916   *Light at Dusk*
1918   *The Unbeliever*
1920   *The Man Who Dared*
1941?   *The Blood of Jesus*

Jewel thieves
1929   *The Younger Generation*
1930   *Amor audaz*
1936   *Mad Holiday*
1937   Music for Madame
1939   Mr. Moto Takes a Vacation
        The Mystery of Mr. Wong
1941   Up Jumped the Devil
1944   The Chinese Cat
1946?   House-Rent Party
1947   *Jiggs and Maggie in Society*
1948   *Cry of the City*
1949   Boston Blackie's Chinese
            Venture
        C-Man
        Souls of Sin
1952   *Woman in the Dark*

Jewelers
1928   The House of Scandal
1929   Lucky Boy
1936   *Sum Hun*
1940   *The Fatal Hour*
1946   *Slightly Scandalous*
1953   *Tonight We Sing*

Jewelry
1915   *The Birth of a Nation*
1915?   *Sin*
1916   *The Colored American
            Winning His Suit*
        The Social Buccaneer
1917   Southern Pride
1918   Find the Woman
        The Girl in the Dark
1920   *Outside the Law*
1921   *Love's Plaything*
1927   The Chinese Parrot
1930   *El cuerpo del delito*
1931   *Chinatown After Dark*
1933   *Charlie Chan's Greatest
            Case*
        El rey de los gitanos
1934   *The Rabbi's Power*
1935   *Chinatown Squad*
1937   *Think Fast, Mr. Moto*
1939   *Double Deal*
1941   *Charlie Chan in Rio*
1942   *Below the Border*
1947   *Northwest Outpost*
1948   *I Remember Mama*
1949   *Harbor of Missing Men*
        Rose of the Yukon
        Tale of the Navajos
1950   *The Men*
1951   *Slaughter Trail*
1955   *The Lonesome Trail*

Jewelry stores
1951   *The Girl on the Bridge*
1952   *Woman in the Dark*

Jews
1914   The Little Jewess
        Threads of Destiny
1914?   A Boy and the Law
1915   Children of the Ghetto
        Cohen's Luck
        Kreutzer Sonata
        The Melting Pot
        Time Lock Number 776
1915?   The Jewish Crown
        The Period of the Jew
1916   Civilization's Child
        Civilization's Child
        The Social Buccaneer
        The Yellow Passport
1916?   Should a Baby Die?
1917   *A Jewel in Pawn*
        A Night in New Arabia
        The Peddler
1918   *Hitting the Trail*
1919   As a Man Thinks
        Daughter of Mine
        The Other Man's Wife
        The Right to Happiness
        The Volcano
        Who's Your Brother?
1920   Humoresque
        The North Wind's Malice
        Pagan Love
1921   The Barricade
        Cheated Love
        No Woman Knows
1922   Breaking Home Ties
        The Five Dollar Baby
        The Good Provider
        Hungry Hearts
        Little Miss Smiles
        Pawn Ticket 210
        Second Hand Rose
        Solomon in Society
        The Woman He Loved
1923   None So Blind
        Potash and Perlmutter
1924   Fools' Highway
        In Hollywood With Potash
            and Perlmutter
        Welcome Stranger
1925   Abie's Imported Bride
        His People
        Hogan's Alley
        Old Clothes
        One of the Bravest
        Salome of the Tenements
1926   April Fool
        Broken Hearts
        The Cohens and Kellys
        Kosher Kitty Kelly
        Millionaires
        Pals in Paradise
        Private Izzy Murphy
        Rose of the Tenements
        Sweet Daddies
        Sweet Rosie O'Grady
1927   The Auctioneer
        Clancy's Kosher Wedding
        For the Love of Mike
        Frisco Sally Levy
        A Harp in Hock
        Jake the Plumber
        Pleasure Before Business
        Sailor Izzy Murphy
        Sally in Our Alley
        The Shamrock and the Rose
1928   The Cohens and the Kellys
            in Paris
        Flying Romeos
        George Washington Cohen
        The Jazz Singer
        The Rawhide Kid
        We Americans
1929   Abie's Irish Rose
        The Cohens and Kellys in
            Atlantic City
        East Side Sadie
        Lucky Boy
        The Younger Generation
1930   Around the Corner
        The Cohens and the Kellys
            in Scotland
        Eternal Fools (Ewige
            Naranim)
        The Kibitzer

        My Yiddishe Mama
        Sunny Skies
1931   Cimarron
        The Cohens and Kellys in
            Africa
        Shulamith
        Street Scene
        The Voice of Israel
        Zein Weib's Lubovnick
1932   The Cohens and Kellys in
            Hollywood
        The Golden West
        The Heart of New York
        Hearts of Humanity
        Mazel Tov
        No Greater Love
        Symphony of Six Million
        Uncle Moses
        The Unfortunate Bride
        Yiskor
1933   The Cohens and Kellys in
            Trouble
        Counsellor at Law
        Live and Laugh
        Rafter Romance
        Victims of Persecution
        The Wandering Jew
1934   *Coming Out Party*
        Our Daily Bread
        The Rabbi's Power
        Straight Is the Way
        What a Mother-in-Law!
        The Youth of Russia
1934?   *Harlem After Midnight*
1935   Bar-Mitzvah
        Lem Hawkins' Confession
        Shir Hashirim
        The Yiddish King Lear
1936   *The Green Pastures*
        Love and Sacrifice
        Yiddle with His Fiddle
1937   The Cantor's Son
        Green Fields
        I Want to Be a Mother
        The Jester (Der
            Purimspieler)
        Man of the People
        That I May Live
        Where Is My Child?
1938   The Power of Life
        The Singing Blacksmith
        Two Sisters
1939   A Brivele der Mamen
        Kol Nidre
        The Light Ahead
        Mamele
        Mirele Efros
        Motel the Operator
        Mothers of Today
        My Son
        Tevya
1940   Americaner Schadchen
        Eli Eli
        The Great Advisor
        Her Second Mother
        The Jewish Melody
        The Man I Married
        Overture to Glory
1941   Mazel Tov Yidden
1943   *Bataan*
        Margin for Error
1944   *Address Unknown*
        Mr. Skeffington
        Tomorrow the World!
1945   *Pride of the Marines*
        Rhapsody in Blue
1946   Abie's Irish Rose
        Gas House Kids
1947   *Body and Soul*
        The Jolson Story
1948   *Big City*
        Gentleman's Agreement
        Strange Victory
1949   The Prairie
        Prejudice
1950   Catskill Honeymoon
        God, Man and Devil
        Jolson Sings Again
        Monticello, Here We Come!
        Sands of Iwo Jima
1950?   Three Daughters
1951   *The Girl on the Bridge*
        Molly
1952   It's a Big Country: An
            American Anthology

1953 *The Eddie Cantor Story*
 The Jazz Singer
 Tonight We Sing
1954 *Go Man Go*
1955 *Blackboard Jungle*
 Good Morning, Miss Dove
 Not As a Stranger
1956 *The Benny Goodman Story*
 Singing in the Dark
1958 *Home Before Dark*
 The Last Hurrah
 Marjorie Morningstar
 Never Love a Stranger
 The Young Lions
1959 *The Last Angry Man*
1960 *Cimarron*
 The Dark at the Top of the
 Stairs

Jews—History
1931 *The Voice of Israel*
1932 *A Daughter of Her People*
 Joseph in the Land of Egypt
1933 *The Eternal Jew*
 The Wandering Jew
1937 *The Holy Oath*

Jiu-jitsu
1939 *Mr. Moto in Danger Island*

Joan, of Arc, Saint, 1412-1431
1948 *The Miracle of the Bells*

Job, Book of
 use **Bible. Old Testament.
 Book of Job**

Jockeys
1918 *Sandy*
1930 *Big Boy*
1934 *Broadway Bill*
1936 *Charlie Chan at the Race
 Track*
1938 *Speed to Burn*
1947 *Black Gold*
1949 *The Story of Seabiscuit*
 Tuna Clipper

Sir William Johnson
1922 *Cardigan*

Ben Johnson
1944 *The Negro Soldier*

Johnstown (NY)
1922 *Cardigan*

Al Jolson
1947 *The Jolson Story*
1950 *Jolson Sings Again*

John Paul Jones
1955 *A Man Called Peter*
1959 *John Paul Jones*

Journalistic ethics
1948 *The Luck of the Irish*

Journalists
 use **Reporters**

Juarez (Mexico)
1916 *Following the Flag in
 Mexico*

Judges
1914? *A Boy and the Law*
1916 *A Child of Mystery*
 Civilization's Child
1917 *I Will Repay*
1918 *Fields of Honor*
 Free and Equal
 In Judgment Of
 Sandy
1919 *The Red Viper*
1920 *Dinty*
1928 *A Ship Comes In*
1929 *Sombras habaneras*
1930 *Del mismo barro*
 El valiente
1931 *Delicious*
 Skyline
1932 *The Black King*
 O festino o la legge
 Unashamed
1933 *Broken Dreams*
 Victims of Persecution
1934 *Judge Priest*
1935 *Romance in Manhattan*
 The Singing Vagabond
 Te quiero con locura
1936 *Kelly the Second*
 *The Prisoner of Shark
 Island*
 Winterset
1937 *Man of the People*
 One Mile from Heaven

 Shadows of the Orient
1939 *Daughters Courageous*
 Judge Hardy and Son
 Way Down South
1940 *Elsa Maxwell's Public Deb
 No. 1*
 Her Second Mother
 Lucky Cisco Kid
1941 *Lady from Louisiana*
1942 *Mokey*
 We Were Dancing
1943 *Border Patrol*
 *The Meanest Man in the
 World*
 The Ox-Bow Incident
1944 *Andy Hardy's Blonde
 Trouble*
 Block Busters
 Marshal of Reno
 Sheriff of Las Vegas
1945 *Colorado Pioneers*
1946 *Gas House Kids*
 Three Wise Fools
 Wild West
1947 *Mantan Runs for Mayor*
 Vigilantes of Boomtown
1948 *Big City*
 Fury at Furnace Creek
 Night Wind
 Shanghai Chest
 Western Heritage
1949 *Brothers in the Saddle*
 The Dalton Gang
 The Daring Caballero
 Pinky
 Ride, Ryder, Ride!
 Shamrock Hill
 3 Godfathers
 Tulsa
1950 *Cherokee Uprising*
1951 *Gambling House*
 The Magnificent Yankee
 New Mexico
1952 *High Noon*
1953 The Sun Shines Bright
1954 *The Black Dakotas*
 *Indiscretion of an
 American Wife*
1955 *Headline Hunters*
 Trial
1956 *The Last Wagon*
 Reprisal!
1957 *Raiders of Old California*
1958 *Ambush at Cimarron Pass*
 Bullwhip
 Gunman's Walk
1959 *Gunmen from Laredo*
 The Young Land

Judo
1951 *Mask of the Dragon*
1955 *Bad Day at Black Rock*

Jukeboxes
1940 *Gang War*
1945 *The Shanghai Cobra*
1947 *Juke Joint*

Jumps from heights
1919 *The Tong Man*
1932 *Mystery Ranch*
1934 *Behold My Wife!*
1937 *It Could Happen to You*
1949 *Daughter of the West*

Jungles
1930 *King of Jazz*
1931 *The Cohens and Kellys in
 Africa*
1933 *The Emperor Jones*
1935 *Alas sobre el Chaco*
1939 *The Devil's Daughter*
1943 *Bataan*
1959 *The FBI Story*

Junk trade
1917 *Lost in Transit*
1922 *The Man with Two Mothers*
1925 *Old Clothes*
1959 *Anna Lucasta*

Junks
1915 *The Sable Lorcha*
1937 *Thank You, Mr. Moto*

Juries
1916 *Pudd'nhead Wilson*
1930 *Sombras de gloria*
1949 *The Daring Caballero*
 House of Strangers
 Knock on Any Door

 The Undercover Man
1955 *Trial*
1956 *Reprisal!*
1957 *Twelve Angry Men*
1959 *The Young Land*

Justice
1936 *The Traitor*
1937 *The Barrier*
1951 *The Magnificent Yankee*
1954 *Passion*
1955 *The Indian Fighter*
1956 *The Burning Hills*
1959 *The Young Land*
1960 *Walk Tall*

Justices of the peace
1939 *The Cisco Kid and the Lady*
1942 *Valley of the Sun*
1949 *The Sky Dragon*

Justifiable homicide
1916 *Broken Fetters*
1931 *Such Is Life*
1933 *Song of the Eagle*
1951 *The Girl on the Bridge*
1956 *The Last Wagon*
1959 *The Wonderful Country*

Juvenile delinquency
1948 *The Fight Never Ends*
1960 *Studs Lonigan*

Juvenile delinquents
1914? *A Boy and the Law*
1937 *Boy of the Streets*
1938 *The Beloved Brat*
 Life Goes On
1939 *Daughters Courageous*
 The Escape
 Reform School
1942 *Let's Get Tough!*
 Mokey
 Take My Life
1944 *Going My Way*
1949 *Knock on Any Door*
1950 *So Young, So Bad*
1952 *Kid Monk Baroni*
1955 *Blackboard Jungle*
1959 *The Black Orchid*
 The Last Angry Man

K.P. duty
1947 *Buck Privates Come Home*

Kamiakin
1956 *Pillars of the Sky*

Kangaroos
1932 *Hypnotized*

Kansas
1925 *The Thundering Herd*
1930 *Estrellados*
1940 *Prairie Schooners*
1943 *In Old Oklahoma*
1949 *Ranger of Cherokee Strip*
1955 *Seven Angry Men*
1959 *The Jayhawkers!*

Kansas City (KS)
1943 *Ladies' Day*

**Kansas City Monarchs (Baseball
team)**
1921 *As the World Rolls On*

Karate
1959 *The Crimson Kimono*

Edmund Kean
1929 *Die Königsloge*

Stephen Watts Kearny
1915 *Captain Courtesy*
1927 *California*

Laura Keene
1936 *The Prisoner of Shark
 Island*

Helen Keller
1919 *Deliverance*

Luther Sage Kelly
1959 *Yellowstone Kelly*

Kendo
 The Crimson Kimono

Kenosha (WI)
1954 *Go Man Go*

Kentucky
1917 *A Kentucky Cinderella*
1918 *Sandy*
 Uncle Tom's Cabin
1919 *Told in the Hills*
1928 *Uncle Tom's Cabin*
1929 *Wolf Song*
1932 *The Golden West*

1934 *Judge Priest*
1935 *Harmony Lane*
 The Little Colonel
1936 *Daniel Boone*
1949 *The Story of Seabiscuit*
1950 *Young Daniel Boone*
1953 *The Sun Shines Bright*
1957 *Band of Angels*

Kentucky Derby
1918 *Sandy*
1930 *Big Boy*
1947 *Black Gold*

Kerry County (Ireland)
1935 *His Family Tree*

Key Largo (FL)
1948 *Key Largo*

Key West (FL)
1949 *Harbor of Missing Men*
1953 *Beneath the 12-Mile Reef*

Keys
1937 *Charlie Chan on Broadway*
1946 *Notorious*
1949 *The Sky Dragon*
 The Valiant Hombre

Kidnapping
1914 *The Great Diamond
 Robbery*
1915 *The Alien*
 The Gambler of the West
 The Grandee's Ring
 Hearts of Men
 Just Jim
 The Last of the Mafia
 The Sable Lorcha
 Time Lock Number 776
1916 *A Child of Mystery*
 The Daughter of the Don
 The Folly of Revenge
 For the Defense
 The Gilded Spider
 Gretchen, the Greenhorn
 The Love Girl
 Poor Little Peppina
 The Sign of the Poppy
 The Twin Triangle
1917 *The Bar Sinister*
 Sunshine and Gold
 Unknown 274
 The Winged Mystery
1918 *The Girl in the Dark*
 Little Red Decides
 The Million Dollar Mystery
 Wild Women
1919 *The Westerners*
1920 *Li Ting Lang*
 The Luck of the Irish
 *Our Christianity and
 Nobody's Child*
 The Purple Cipher
1921 *The Double O*
 The Money Maniac
 Shadows of the West
1922 *The Crimson Skull*
 East Is West
 The Schemers
 The Sign of the Rose
 Winning of the West
1924 *Defying the Law*
 In High Gear
 *The Mine with the Iron
 Door*
 Peter Pan
1925 *Galloping Vengeance*
 The Man in Blue
1927 *Blind Alleys*
 The Chinese Parrot
 *With Sitting Bull at the
 Spirit Lake Massacre*
1928 *Ransom*
1929 *Masked Emotions*
 The Witching Eyes
1930 *East Is West*
 Ladies Love Brutes
 El último de los Vargas
1931 *Chinatown After Dark*
 Huckleberry Finn
 The Hurricane Horseman
1932 *The Forty-Niners*
 The Galloping Kid
 Hypnotized
 The Rainbow Trail
 Riders of the Desert
 Thirteen Steps

1933 *Man from Monterey*
    Thundering Herd
1934 *The Battling Buckaroo*
    Call of the Coyote
    Un capitán de cosacos
    La cruz y la espada
    Fighting Through
    Lazy River
    Massacre
1934? *Harlem After Midnight*
1935 *Cyclone of the Saddle*
    The Cyclone Ranger
    De la sartén al fuego
    Un hombre peligroso
    Melody Trail
    A Night at the Ritz
    So Red the Rose
1936 *Dancing Pirate*
    Ellis Island
    The Last of the Mohicans
    Muss 'Em Up
    Rebellion
    Sea Spoilers
1937 *The Barrier*
    Border Cafe
    The Californian
    El carnaval del diablo
    Harlem on the Prairie
    Manhattan
      Merry-Go-Round
    *The Riders of the Whistling
      Skull*
1938 Little Miss Roughneck
    Speed to Burn
    *Two Gun Man from
      Harlem*
1939 The Bronze Buckaroo
    Drifting Westward
    The Escape
1940 *Arizona Frontier*
    *Elsa Maxwell's Public Deb
      No. 1*
    George Washington Carver
    Taku
1941 The Gang's All Here
    Gauchos of Eldorado
    Ride on Vaquero
1942 *Foreign Agent*
    Shut My Big Mouth
1943 Border Patrol
    Crime Smasher
    Deerslayer
1944 *Outlaw Trail*
1945 *Of One Blood*
1946 *California Gold Rush*
    Gas House Kids
    Santa Fe Uprising
1947 *Boy! What a Girl!*
    Buffalo Bill Rides Again
    The Chinese Ring
    Last of the Redmen
    On the Old Spanish Trail
    Oregon Trail Scouts
1948 *Old Los Angeles*
    Singin' Spurs
1949 *Apache Chief*
    *Boston Blackie's Chinese
      Venture*
    The Fighting Kentuckian
    Harbor of Missing Men
    The Prairie
    Roll Thunder Roll!
    The Valiant Hombre
1950 *Black Hand*
    Cherokee Uprising
    The Girl from San Lorenzo
    The Iroquois Trail
    Mystery Submarine
    North of the Great Divide
    Sunset in the West
1951 *Flaming Feather*
1952 *The Battle at Apache Pass*
1953 Ambush at Tomahawk Gap
    Fort Ti
    The Great Sioux Uprising
1955 *Violent Saturday*
1956 The Searchers
1957 *The Deerslayer*
    The Lawless Eighties
    Naked in the Sun
    War Drums
1958 *Never Love a Stranger*
1959 *Shake Hands with the Devil*
1960 *Key Witness*
    The Unforgiven

Kiev (Ukraine)
1916 *Civilization's Child*
    The King's Game
Joyce Kilmer
1940 The Fighting 69th
King Lear (Play)
1935 The Yiddish King Lear
Kings
1933 *The Eternal Jew*
1936 *The Green Pastures*
1953 *Captain John Smith and
      Pocahontas*
1956 *Hot Blood*
Kings and rulers
    use **Kings**
Kiowa Indians
1920 The Daughter of Dawn
1937 *Prairie Thunder*
1950 *Davy Crockett, Indian
      Scout*
    Two Flags West
1954 *They Rode West*
    Thunder Pass
    War Arrow
1955 *Santa Fe Passage*
1960 *Flaming Star*
    The Unforgiven
Kishinev (Russia)
1915 *The Melting Pot*
1931 *The Voice of Israel*
Kisses
1919 *False Evidence*
1926 *The Flying Ace*
1930 *El precio de un beso*
1931 *¿Conoces a tu mujer?*
1933 *El rey de los gitanos*
    Robbers' Roost
1937 *Green Fields*
1943 *The Outlaw*
1948 *Old Los Angeles*
1949 *Daughter of the West*
    Jigsaw
    The Kissing Bandit
    Tulsa
1957 *Pawnee*
1958 *The Light in the Forest*
Kitchens
1928 *Eleven P.M.*
Frank E. Kleinschmidt
1912 The Alaska-Siberian
      Expedition
1914 Captain F. E. Kleinschmidt's
      Arctic Hunt
Kleptomania
1938 *Mr. Moto's Gamble*
1947 *Dark Delusion*
Knife fighting
1919 *The Last of His People*
1934 *Nada más que una mujer*
1937 *Dark Manhattan*
1951 *Only the Valiant*
1952 *California Conquest*
    The Iron Mistress
1953 *Old Overland Trail*
    The Pathfinder
    San Antone
    War Paint
1954 *Hondo*
    Passion
    Sitting Bull
    Taza, Son of Cochise
    Thunder Pass
1955 *Apache Woman*
    Blackboard Jungle
    The Last Command
1957 *Ride Out for Revenge*
1958 *Fort Massacre*
1959 *Cry Tough*
    Gunmen from Laredo
Knife throwing
1946 *Dangerous Money*
1952 *The Iron Mistress*
1957 *Apache Warrior*
Knife wounds
1916 The Twin Triangle
1917 *A Love Sublime*
1919 *False Evidence*
    Lasca
    The Sneak
1920 *The Face at Your Window*
1934 *The Cactus Kid*
    Judge Priest

1935 *The Cyclone Ranger*
1950 *I Killed Geronimo*
Knives
1948 *Moonrise*
1950 *Comanche Territory*
1952 *The Iron Mistress*
1957 *Twelve Angry Men*
1960 *The Plunderers*
Ted Knowles
1949 *The Story of Seabiscuit*
Kodiak Island (AK)
1917 Alaska Wonders in Motion
**Korea—History—Japanese
    occupation, 1910-1945**
1943 *Jack London*
Korean Americans
1959 *The Crimson Kimono*
Korean War, 1950-1953
1951 The Steel Helmet
1952 *It's a Big Country: An
      American Anthology*
    Japanese War Bride
1953 The Glory Brigade
    The Jazz Singer
1960 All the Young Men
    *I Aim at the Stars: the
      Wernher von Braun Story*
Koreans
1951 The Steel Helmet
1960 *All the Young Men*
Kremlin (Moscow)
    Man on a String
Ku Klux Klan
1915 The Birth of a Nation
1920 The Symbol of the
      Unconquered
1928 The Mating Call
1938 *The Texans*
1939 *Gone With the Wind*
1947 The Burning Cross
1959 *The FBI Story*
Kurds
1919 Auction of Souls
La Paz (Bolivia)
1935 *Alas sobre el Chaco*
Labor
    use **Employment;
    Specific industries or
    trades**
Labor agitators
1917 *Threads of Fate*
1920 Dangerous Hours
    The Face at Your Window
    Uncharted Channels
1923 Potash and Perlmutter
1932 *Uncle Moses*
1937 *Big City*
Labor camps
1941 *Sullivan's Travels*
1943 *Hitler's Children*
Labor leaders
1920 *The Face at Your Window*
    The Great Shadow
1926 The Passaic Textile Strike
Labor unions
    use **Trade unions**
Labor violence
1915 *The Spender*
1919 The Right to Happiness
1932 *Uncle Moses*
1935 *Black Fury*
Laboratories
1922 The Schemers
1935 *Lem Hawkins' Confession*
1944 *Charlie Chan in the Secret
      Service*
1945 *The Scarlet Clue*
Laborers
1915 *The Kindling*
1918 Wanted, a Mother
    The Wine Girl
1941 *Min Jok Jay Hung Sing*
1951 *Saturday's Hero*
1957 Man in the Shadow
1958 *The Badlanders*
Jean Lafitte
1938 The Buccaneer
1950 Last of the Buccaneers
Lagoons
1949 *Harbor of Missing Men*

Lakes
1918 *Wanted, a Mother*
1920 *The Dark Mirror*
1947 *The Farmer's Daughter*
    Last of the Redmen
1948 *Rocky*
1951 *Distant Drums*
1954 *Saskatchewan*
Land barons
1922 The Pride of Palomar
1924 North of 36
1927 The Gay Defender
1942 American Empire
1952 *The Raiders*
1956 *The Broken Star*
    Raw Edge
Land claims
1924 Down by the Rio Grande
1925 The Red Rider
1926 Buffalo Bill on the U. P.
      Trail
1930 *La rosa de fuego*
1931 *The Avenger*
1933 Man from Monterey
1936 *Daniel Boone*
    Robin Hood of El Dorado
1941 Secret of the Wastelands
1946 Singin' in the Corn
1948 *The Betrayal*
    Old Los Angeles
    Red River
    Western Heritage
1949 The Fighting Kentuckian
    The Mysterious Desperado
1950 Devil's Doorway
1952 *The Half-Breed*
    The Raiders
1953 *The Charge at Feather
      River*
    Conquest of Cochise
1954 Cattle Queen of Montana
    Drums Across the River
    Passion
Land companies
1952 *The Raiders*
Land developers
1940 *Midnight Shadow*
    Rhythm of the Rio Grande
1943 *What's Buzzin' Cousin?*
1945 The Gay Senorita
1949 *The Mysterious Desperado*
Land grants
1930 *The Lash*
1957 Raiders of Old California
1958 Sierra Baron
Land rights
1914 Rose of the Rancho
1916 Gold and the Woman
1917 *The Captain of the Gray
      Horse Troop*
    The Primitive Call
1919 The Gray Towers Mystery
1919? When the Desert Smiles
1921 Anne of Little Smoky
1922 The Half Breed
1924 Tongues of Flame
    Unseen Hands
1927 Don Mike
    Drums of the Desert
    The Gay Defender
    Old San Francisco
    Whispering Sage
1928 The Canyon of Adventure
1929 The Desert Rider
    Señor Americano
1931 Yankee Don
1932 *Mystery Ranch*
    The Vanishing Frontier
1935 *The Little Colonel*
1936 *Ramona*
    Rebellion
    Rose of the Rancho
1937 The Californian
    Natalka Poltavka
1938 *Birthright*
    California Frontier
    Outlaw Express
1939 *The Bronze Buckaroo*
    Drums Along the Mohawk
    The Fighting Gringo
    Frontiers of '49
    Let Freedom Ring
    The Return of the Cisco Kid

1940 Young Buffalo Bill
1941 *The Pioneers*
     Prairie Pioneers
1943 In Old Oklahoma
1946 Beauty and the Bandit
     Sheriff of Redwood Valley
     South of Monterey
     Swamp Fire
1947 The Adventures of Don
     Coyote
1948 Silver Trails
     Silver Trails
1949 The Dalton Gang
     Daughter of the West
1950 The Baron of Arizona
     Comanche Territory
1955 *Davy Crockett, King of the
      · Wild Frontier*
     The Vanishing American
1956 *The Wild Dakotas*
1957 Joe Dakota
     Raiders of Old California
1958 Terror in a Texas Town

Land rushes
1931 *Cimarron*
1960 Cimarron

Land sales
1916 Hulda from Holland
1919 Hearts of Men
1931 *The Squaw Man*
1942 *American Empire*
1944 *The San Antonio Kid*
1947 Buffalo Bill Rides Again
     Thunder Mountain
1952 *Brave Warrior*

Landladies
1918 *Tony America*
1930 The Big Pond
1938 *Passport Husband*
     The Rage of Paris
1939 *Miracle on Main Street*
1940 *Tengo fe en ti*
1941 *Ice-Capades*
1944 *Andy Hardy's Blonde
      Trouble*
1946 *Dark Alibi*
1947 *Mantan Runs for Mayor*
     Sepia Cinderella
1948 *Open Secret*
     Shanghai Chest
1949 *Souls of Sin*
1952 *My Man and I*
1953 *The Glass Wall*
1956 *The Broken Star*
     Crowded Paradise

Landlords
1916 Lone Star
1917 The War of the Tongs
1918 *Denny from Ireland*
     The Little Runaway
1921 *By Right of Birth*
1922 Hungry Hearts
1931 *Los calaveras*
1932 *The Heart of New York*
1942 *Twin Beds*
1946 *Gas House Kids*
1946? *Fight That Ghost*
1947 *Boy! What a Girl!*
1948? Boarding House Blues
1951 *Native Son*

Landslides
1945 *Colorado Pioneers*

Language and languages
1943 *Dr. Gillespie's Criminal
      Case*
1950 *Chinatown at Midnight*
1953 *Dream Wife*
1960 *Hell to Eternity*

Laramie (WY)
1956 *Dakota Incident*

Laredo (TX)
1949 *Streets of Laredo*
1959 *Gunmen from Laredo*

**Las Flores Canyon (Los Angeles,
CA)**
1948 *Old Los Angeles*

Las Vegas (NV)
1944 *Sheriff of Las Vegas*

Lassoes
1947 *Vigilantes of Boomtown*
1949 *Call of the Forest*
     The Golden Stallion

Latin Americans
1936 *Human Cargo*
     Yellow Cargo
1943 Redhead from Manhattan
1945 *Club Havana*
1947 Copacabana

Latino
1914 Rose of the Rancho
1915 The Grandee's Ring
1920 For the Soul of Rafael
1922 Captain Fly-by-Night
     The Power of Love
     The Pride of Palomar
1923 Jealous Husbands
1925 Tonio, Son of the Sierras
1926 Desert Gold
1928 Breed of the Sunsets
1930 Cuando el amor ríe
     Estrellados
     El último de los Vargas
1932 The Vanishing Frontier
1933 Man from Monterey
1936 Aces and Eights
     Dancing Pirate
1938 Mis dos amores
     Outlaw Express
     Passport Husband
1939 Heaven with a Barbed Wire
     Fence
     Verbena trágica
1940 Too Many Girls
1941 Romance of the Rio Grande
1943 Bataan
1944 *The San Antonio Kid*
1950 *Mystery Street*
1952 *The Iron Mistress*
1957 *Trooper Hook*
1958 Sierra Baron
1959 *Cry Tough*
1960 Key Witness
     The Pusher

Laundresses
1918 *Amarilly of Clothes-Line
      Alley*
1922 Saturday Night
     Solomon in Society
1925 The Greatest Love of All
1949 *Pinky*
1958 *Fort Bowie*

Laundries
1921 Wing Toy
1938 *In Old Chicago*
1939? *A Chinese Gains a Fortune
       in America*
1941 *Golden Gate Girl*
     Sunday Sinners
1942 *Rio Rita*
1945 *The Shanghai Cobra*
1946? *House-Rent Party*
1949 *Boston Blackie's Chinese
      Venture*
1957 *The Brothers Rico*
1959 *Cry Tough*
1960 *Walk Like a Dragon*

Law (Concept)
1927 The Devil's Saddle
1947 *Vigilantes of Boomtown*
1951 *The Magnificent Yankee*
1955 *Trial*
1957 Twelve Angry Men

Law and order
1934 *The Prescott Kid*
1936 *Rose of the Rancho*
1938 *California Frontier*
1939 *Reform School*
1948 The Arizona Ranger
1956 *The Broken Star*
1958 *Ride a Crooked Trail*

Law students
1919 *The Courageous Coward*
1921 *By Right of Birth*
1935 *Lem Hawkins' Confession*
1936 *Winterset*
1950 *The Big Hangover*
1951 *The Magnificent Yankee*

Lawsuits
1917 *The Squaw Man's Son*
1941 *Ice-Capades*
1954 *Broken Lance*
1955 *The View from Pompey's
      Head*

Lawyers
1915 *Marse Covington*
1916 The Colored American
     Winning His Suit
     Pudd'nhead Wilson
     A Woman's Honor
1917 *A Wife by Proxy*
1918 *Broken Ties*
     Thirty a Week
1919 His Parisian Wife
1920 Lifting Shadows
1921 By Right of Birth
     The Gunsaulus Mystery
1922 Breaking Home Ties
     The Dungeon
     Hungry Hearts
     Solomon in Society
1923 Flames of Wrath
     Potash and Perlmutter
1925 Braveheart
1927 Old San Francisco
     The Scar of Shame
1928 Uncle Tom's Cabin
1930 Abraham Lincoln
     Cascarrabias
     Del mismo barro
     Doña mentiras
     Ladies Love Brutes
     My Yiddishe Mama
     Sombras de gloria
     Toda una vida
     La voluntad del muerto
1931 *Charlie Chan Carries On*
     Cimarron
     ¿Conoces a tu mujer?
     La incorregible
     Die Maske Fällt
     Le père célibataire
     El proceso de Mary Dugan
     Three Who Loved
1932 *The Black King*
     Le bluffeur
     The Heart of New York
     Hombres en mi vida
     Ljubav i strast
     Veiled Aristocrats
1933 *Charlie Chan's Greatest
      Case*
     Counsellor at Law
     Racetrack
1934 *Charlie Chan in London*
     Judge Priest
     Lazy River
     Massacre
     Our Daily Bread
     Tres amores
1935 *Bordertown*
     Lem Hawkins' Confession
     Romance in Manhattan
     *Señora casada necesita
      marido*
     The Winning Ticket
1937 *Boots and Saddles*
     It Could Happen to You
     Man of the People
     Souls at Sea
1938 *Life Goes On*
     Outside of Paradise
     Passport Husband
     The Power of Life
1939 Confessions of a Nazi Spy
     King of Chinatown
     Let Freedom Ring
     Motel the Operator
     The Mystery of Mr. Wong
     Papá soltero
     Straight to Heaven
     Way Down South
1940 *Am I Guilty?*
     Americaner Schadchen
     Doomed to Die
     Son of Ingagi
1941 *Caught in the Act*
     Lady from Louisiana
     New York Town
     Secret of the Wastelands
     Sunday Sinners
     Under Fiesta Stars
1942 *Castle in the Desert*
     In This Our Life
     In This Our Life
     Secret Enemies
     Tales of Manhattan
     The Vanishing Virginian
     We Were Dancing

1943 The Meanest Man in the
     World
     What's Buzzin' Cousin?
1945 Of One Blood
1946 Sheriff of Redwood Valley
1947 *Reet, Petite and Gone*
     Thunder Mountain
1948 *Call Northside 777*
     Cry of the City
     The Dude Goes West
     Fighting Father Dunne
     The Lady from Shanghai
     Shanghai Chest
1949 House of Strangers
     Knock on Any Door
     Ride, Ryder, Ride!
     Satan's Cradle
     Shamrock Hill
     The Undercover Man
1950 Bandit Queen
     Belle of Old Mexico
     The Big Hangover
     Black Hand
     The Breaking Point
     Devil's Doorway
     Intruder in the Dust
     The Missourians
     Mystery Submarine
     Right Cross
     Sunset in the West
1951 *Gambling House*
     *The House on Telegraph
      Hill*
     Native Son
1952 *Bright Victory*
     Woman in the Dark
1954 *Broken Lance*
1955 *Not As a Stranger*
     Trial
     The View from Pompey's
     Head
1956 *Death of a Scoundrel*
     Giant
1957 *Journey to Freedom*
1958 *Houseboat*
     Never Love a Stranger
1959 *The FBI Story*
     Night of the Quarter Moon
     Porgy and Bess
1960 *Ice Palace*
     Sergeant Rutledge
     The Sign of Zorro

Laziness
1932 *The Heart of New York*
1939 One Dark Night
1942 *Holiday Inn*
1956 *The Burning Hills*

Lechery
1917 *Rosie O'Grady*
1918 Hitting the Trail
     I Want to Forget
     Shifting Sands
1920 The Luck of the Irish
1927 *The Scar of Shame*
     The Spider's Web
1932 Genoveffa
1934 *Chloe: Love Is Calling You*
1947 Duel in the Sun
     The Farmer's Daughter
1949 *Apache Chief*
1954 *Saskatchewan*
1955 *Duel on the Mississippi*
1956 *Crowded Paradise*
1959 The Hanging Tree

Lectures
1936 *El crimen de media noche*
1940 *Phantom of Chinatown*

Robert E. Lee
1915 *The Birth of a Nation*
1930 Abraham Lincoln
1945 *Salome, Where She Danced*
1955 *Seminole Uprising*

Legendary characters
1949 *The Kissing Bandit*
1954 Apache

Legends
1929 *The Peacock Fan*
1932 *A Daughter of Her People*
1941 *Virginia*
1942 Cat People
1944 *Cry of the Werewolf*
1949 *Tale of the Navajos*
     Top O' the Morning

1956 Secret of Treasure Mountain
1957 Raintree County
1958 *The Lone Ranger and the
       Lost City of Gold*
Legislation
    use Bills, Legislative
Leopards
1943 The Leopard Man
     The Leopard Man
Leprechauns
1946 *Three Wise Fools*
1948 The Luck of the Irish
1949 Shamrock Hill
Leprosy
1917 *The Bottle Imp*
1950 Damien
Letters
1913? The Lure of New York
1914 *The Great Diamond
       Robbery
     Threads of Destiny*
1916 Britton of the Seventh
1918 *The Ranger*
1920 *The Riddle: Woman
     Who's Your Servant?*
1926 *The Strong Man*
1929 Smiling Irish Eyes
1930 *Anna Christie
     El secreto del doctor*
1931 *Charlie Chan Carries On
     Cuerpo y alma
     Nuit d'Espagne
     Zein Weib's Lubovnick*
1932 *L'athlète incomplet
     Genoveffa
     Ten Minutes to Live
     Thirteen Women*
1933 *Let's Fall in Love
     The Telegraph Trail*
1934 *As the Earth Turns*
1935 *Charlie Chan in Paris
     Chinatown Squad*
1936 *Sins of Man
     The Traitor
     West of Nevada*
1937 *Think Fast, Mr. Moto*
1939 *Mamele*
1940 *They Knew What They
       Wanted*
1941 *Accent on Love*
1942 *Nazi Agent
     Tales of Manhattan*
1943 *Bataan
     Dr. Gillespie's Criminal
       Case
     Doughboys in Ireland
     Good Luck, Mr. Yates
     Mr. Lucky
     The Ox-Bow Incident
     Tabiti Honey*
1944 Address Unknown
     *Andy Hardy's Blonde
       Trouble
     The Negro Soldier
     Outlaw Trail
     They Live in Fear*
1945 *The Cisco Kid Returns
     In Old New Mexico*
1946 *The Trap*
1947 *My Wild Irish Rose
     Reet, Petite and Gone*
1948 *The Boy with Green Hair
     Shanghai Chest*
1949 *Anna Lucasta*
1950 *Riders of the Pony Express
     Sands of Iwo Jima*
1951 *Queen for a Day*
1952 *It's a Big Country: An
       American Anthology
     Japanese War Bride
     My Man and I*
1953 *The Member of the
       Wedding*
1955 *The Far Horizons*
1956 *The Searchers*
1960 *For the Love of Mike*
Leukemia
1945 *Rhapsody in Blue*
Levees
1941 *Lady from Louisiana*
Levitation
1939 *Charlie Chan at Treasure
       Island*

Meriwether Lewis
1955 The Far Horizons
**Lewis and Clark Expedition,
   1803—1806**
     The Far Horizons
Lexington, Battle of, 1775
1917 *The Spirit of '76*
1922 Cardigan
Liars
1916 At Piney Ridge
1942 In This Our Life
1948 *The Time of Your Life*
1950 *The Iroquois Trail*
1960 *The Adventures of
       Huckleberry Finn*
Libel and slander
1916 *The Yellow Passport*
1918 *Fields of Honor*
1937 *One Mile from Heaven*
Liberia
1930 *A Daughter of the Congo*
Libertines
    use Cads;
        Lechery
Libraries and librarians
1922 Spitfire
1937 A Study of Negro Artists
1950 *The Baron of Arizona*
1959 *The Crimson Kimono
     The FBI Story*
1960 *This Rebel Breed*
Lice
1939 *Gone With the Wind*
Lie detectors and detection
1948 *Call Northside* 777
Life (Magazine)
1938 *My Lucky Star*
Life insurance
1915 After Five
1939 *Moon over Harlem*
1946 *Shadows Over Chinatown*
Lifeboats
1917 *Under False Colors*
1942 *Submarine Raider*
1943 *Action in the North
       Atlantic
     The Amazing Mrs. Holliday*
1944 Lifeboat
1960 *The Last Voyage*
Lighthouses
1949 *Portrait of Jennie*
Lightning
1918 *Out of a Clear Sky*
1919? The Brand of Judas
1932 *Amore e morte*
1934 *As the Earth Turns
     Drums O' Voodoo*
Limousines
1935 *¡Asegure a su mujer!*
Abraham Lincoln
1915 *The Birth of a Nation*
1930 Abraham Lincoln
1935 *The Littlest Rebel*
1936 *The Prisoner of Shark
       Island*
1937 *The Plainsman*
1940 *Elsa Maxwell's Public Deb
       No. 1
     Hi-Yo Silver*
1941 *Land of Liberty*
1951 *New Mexico*
     The Tall Target
1955 *Apache Ambush*
1958 *Flaming Frontier*
Mary Todd Lincoln
1930 Abraham Lincoln
Jenny Lind
1931 Jenny Lind
Lion tamers
1930 La jaula de los leones
Lions
1917 The Woman and the Beast
1930 La jaula de los leones
1932 *Hypnotized*
1939 *Charlie Chan in Honolulu*
Liquor
1920 *The Girl of My Heart*
1931 *Oklahoma Jim*
1934 *Laughing Boy*
1936 *Custer's Last Stand
     For the Service*

1955 *The Indian Fighter*
1956 *Quincannon, Frontier
       Scout
     Singing in the Dark*
Literacy
1915 *The Birth of a Nation*
1948 *Up in Central Park*
1949 *Pinky*
1950 *Annie Get Your Gun*
1960 *Pay or Die*
Lithuanian Americans
1914 The Jungle
Little Big Horn, Battle of the, 1876
1916 *Britton of the Seventh*
1917 The Buffalo Bill Show
1925 Custer's Last Fight
1926 The Flaming Frontier
     General Custer at Little Big
       Horn
1936 Custer's Last Stand
1937 The Plainsman
1941 *Land of Liberty*
1942 *They Died With Their Boots
       On*
1951 *Little Big Horn
     Warpath*
1952 *Bugles in the Afternoon*
1954 *Sitting Bull*
1956 7th Cavalry
1958 Tonka
Little Wolf (Cheyenne Indian)
1957 Ride Out for Revenge
Live burial
1916 *The Romantic Journey*
1932 *Yiskor*
1950 *Give Us This Day*
Liverpool (England)
1940 *Escape to Glory*
Lloyd's of London (England)
1959 *John Paul Jones*
Loan sharks
1938 Sugar Hill Baby
Loans
1917 *A Jewel in Pawn
     Under False Colors*
1931 *Carne de cabaret*
1932 *The Match King*
1934 *La ciudad de cartón*
1935 *L'homme des Folies Bergère
     McFadden's Flats*
1938 *Two Gun Man from
       Harlem*
1940 *If I Had My Way*
1947 *The Adventures of Don
       Coyote*
1949 *House of Strangers*
1950 *The Furies*
1952 *The Fabulous Senorita*
1953 *Taxi*
1960 *Cimarron*
Lobsters
1958 *Home Before Dark*
Lockets
1945 *Salome, Where She Danced*
1947 *King of the Bandits*
**Lockheed Aircraft Plant
   (Burbank, CA)**
1942 *Wings for the Eagle*
Locks
1915 *Time Lock Number 776*
Locksmiths
1939 *City in Darkness*
Lodgers
1918 *How Could You, Jean?*
1934 *He Was Her Man*
1944 *Since You Went Away*
1948 *I Remember Mama*
1949 *Tuna Clipper*
1958 *Home Before Dark*
Lodges
1937 Nation Aflame
1943 *Mexican Spitfire's Blessed
       Event*
1959 *Inside the Mafia*
Lodges (Fraternal organizations)
1930 Check and Double Check
1931 *Los calaveras*
Lodz (Poland)
1939 Mamele

Jack London
1943 Jack London
London (England)
1929 *Die Königsloge*
1930 *Cascarrabias*
     Le spectre vert
1931 *Charlie Chan Carries On
     Drácula
     Die Dreigroschenoper
     El impostor*
1934 Limehouse Blues
1940 *The Ramparts We Watch*
1945 *The Great John L.*
1946 Abie's Irish Rose
1948 *Unconquered*
1958 *The Young Lions*
1960 *The Day They Robbed the
       Bank of England*
Loneliness
1915 *Children of the Ghetto*
1931 *Le père célibataire*
1936 *Tundra*
1938 *Dangerous to Know*
1948 *The Time of Your Life*
1953 *The Member of the
       Wedding*
1955 *The Rose Tattoo*
1958 *The Defiant Ones
     Wild Is the Wind*
1959 *The Black Orchid*
1960 *Ice Palace*
     Take a Giant Step
Long Beach (CA)
1949 *The Clay Pigeon*
Long Island (NY)
1915 *The Cheat
     Chimmie Fadden*
1917 The Winged Mystery
1918 *Real Folks*
1937 *Manhattan
     Merry-Go-Round*
1943 *Svenkst I Och Omkring
       New York
     They Came to Blow Up
       America*
Long-lost relatives
1913? The Call of the Blood
1916 The Sign of the Poppy
1917 Runaway Romany
1918 The City of Tears
     The Girl in the Dark
     In Judgment Of
     The Only Road
     The Ordeal of Rosetta
     The Ranger
1919 Diane of the Green Van
     The Right to Happiness
1921 By Right of Birth
     The Secret Sorrow
1930 *El valiente*
1931 Skyline
1932 *Amor in montaña*
1933 Racetrack
1934 *Chloe: Love Is Calling You*
1935 Bar-Mitzvah
1936 Let's Sing Again
     Love and Sacrifice
     Sins of Man
1937 *Charlie Chan at the Opera*
1939 *A Brivele der Mamen
     Motel the Operator
     Papá soltero*
1940 *The Jewish Melody*
1941 *Gauchos of Eldorado*
1943 Marching On!
1956 *The Searchers*
1958 *The Lone Ranger and the
       Lost City of Gold*
Longshoremen
1939 Waterfront
Los Angeles (CA)
1916 *The Daughter of the Don*
1930 *Las campanas de
       Capistrano*
1934 *Las fronteras del amor*
1935 *Bordertown*
1936 *Charlie Chan at the Race
       Track*
     Contra la corriente
1937 *Music for Madame*
1938 *Mis dos amores*
1939 *Miracle on Main Street
     El trovador de la radio*

1941 *The Gang's All Here*
1945 *Betrayal from the East*
Rhapsody in Blue
1946 *G. I. War Brides*
Till the End of Time
1948 *Half Past Midnight*
1949 *Illegal Entry*
1951 *Cuban Fireball*
The Mark of the Renegade
Mask of the Dragon
1952 *California Conquest*
My Man and I
1953 *The Man Behind the Gun*
1956 *Full of Life*
Hot Blood
1959 *Anna Lucasta*
1960 *I Passed for White*
Key Witness
Man on a String

Los Angeles (CA)—Chinatown
1948 *Half Past Midnight*
1949 *The Clay Pigeon*

Los Angeles (CA)—Little Tokyo
1942 Little Tokyo, U.S.A.
1959 *The Crimson Kimono*

Los Angeles (CA)—Olvera Street
1952 *The Ring*

The Lost Battalion
1919 The Lost Battalion

Lost cities
use **Cities and towns, Ruins, extinct, etc.; Ghost towns**

Lotteries
1915 Cohen's Luck
1916 Peck O' Pickles
1921 Where Lights Are Low
1940 *The Great Advisor*
1941 Lady from Louisiana
1950 *God, Man and Devil*

Joe Louis
1944 *The Negro Soldier*
1948 *The Fight Never Ends*
1953 *The Joe Louis Story*

Louis XV, King of France, 1710-1774
1923 Backbone
1935 *Naughty Marietta*

Louis XVI, King of France, 1754-1793
1959 *John Paul Jones*

Louisiana
1917 The Bride of Hate
1919 Evangeline
1934 Lazy River
1936 *The Green Pastures*
1941 Louisiana Purchase
1943 *Fighting Americans*
1944 Dark Waters
1945 *The Mummy's Curse*
1946 Swamp Fire
1948 Louisiana Story
1953 *Thunder Bay*
1954 *Carmen Jones*
1955 Duel on the Mississippi
The Far Horizons
1957 *Band of Angels*

Louisiana Purchase
1937 Old Louisiana
1949 The Prairie
1955 *The Far Horizons*

Love
1931 *Street Scene*
1932 *Une heure près de toi*
No Greater Love
The Son-Daughter
1937 *Natalka Poltavka*
1944 Hi, Beautiful
1945 *The Mummy's Curse*
1949 *Arctic Manhunt*
Portrait of Jennie
1950 *Deported*
1954 Carmen Jones
1955 *The Long Gray Line*
1957 *Band of Angels*
1958 *St. Louis Blues*
1959 The Black Orchid

Love affairs
1925 The Devil's Disciple
1931 *Little Caesar*
Such Is Life
1932 *Amore e morte*
La foule hurle

Une heure près de toi
Scarface
So Big
1934 Straight Is the Way
1935 *Rescue Squad*
Shir Hashirim
1936 *Muss 'Em Up*
1943 *Jack London*
1945 Jealousy
1955 *Trial*
1956 *Death of a Scoundrel*
1958 *The Defiant Ones*
Marjorie Morningstar
1960 *All the Fine Young Cannibals*
I Aim at the Stars: the Wernher von Braun Story
Weddings and Babies
Wild River

Love letters
1949? *She's Too Mean for Me*

Love tests
1917 Her Own People
1937 *Manhattan Merry-Go-Round*

Lowell (MA)
1917 *The Little Boy Scout*

Loyalty
1914 Dan
1916 The Daughter of the Don
1918 The Birth of a Race
Good-Bye, Bill
The Hun Within
1931 *Little Caesar*
1932 *Border Devils*
Scarface
1934 *Beloved*
1936 *The Last of the Mohicans*
Sutter's Gold
1939 *The Bronze Buckaroo*
Keep Punching
Waterfront
1941 Western Union
1943 *In Old Oklahoma*
1945 The Dolly Sisters
A Medal for Benny
Pride of the Marines
Samurai
1946 *The Face of Marble*
Tall, Tan and Terrific
1948 *The Time of Your Life*
1949 Streets of Laredo
1950 Two Flags West
1951 *The Great Caruso*
The Harlem Globetrotters
The Last Outpost
The Raging Tide
1952 High Noon
The Savage
1953 *Last of the Comanches*
The Sun Shines Bright
1954 Go Man Go
Siege at Red River
Taza, Son of Cochise
1955 *Apache Woman*
The Last Command
The Rose Tattoo
Smoke Signal
1957 *The Guns of Fort Petticoat*
Raintree County
Revolt at Fort Laramie
1958 *The Badlanders*
Gunman's Walk
The Last Hurrah
Never Love a Stranger
St. Louis Blues
Touch of Evil
1959 The Jayhawkers!
Shake Hands with the Devil
1960 *Flaming Star*
Man on a String
Sergeant Rutledge
The Unforgiven

Luaus
1938 *Hawaii Calls*
1942 *Song of the Islands*

Luck
1931 *Smart Money*

Luggage
1949 *Massacre River*

Lumber camp foremen
1918 *The Source*
1957 *All Mine to Give*

Lumber camps
1918 The Source

Lumber industry
1923 Backbone

Lumber mills
1921 Hearts of the Woods
1939 *Gone With the Wind*

Lumberjacks
1914 *The Redemption of David Corson*
1918 *The Source*
1950 *Intruder in the Dust*
1957 *All Mine to Give*

Lunatics
1921 All Souls' Eve
1927 Sailor Izzy Murphy

Lunch stands
1932 *La foule hurle*

Lungs—Diseases
1948 *The Miracle of the Bells*
1950 *Jolson Sings Again*

Lure of riches
1931 Personal Maid
1932 *So Big*
1939 Gone With the Wind
1946 *Strange Voyage*
1949 Lust for Gold
1950 God, Man and Devil
1953 *So Big*

Lure of the city
1918? Rosemary Climbs the Heights
1919? *The Chosen Path*
1923 His Great Chance
1929 When Men Betray
1931 Skyline
1938 *Di que me quieres*
Life Goes On
1939 *Keep Punching*

Lure of the country
1932 *Le cas du docteur Brenner*
1939 *Waterfront*
1942 *Holiday Inn*

Lure of the primitive
1921 The Cave Girl

S.S. Lusitania
1918 *The Price of Applause*
1933 *Ever in My Heart*
1940 *The Ramparts We Watch*

Lust
use **Lechery**

Lutheran Church
1930 *Anna Christie*
1948 Reaching from Heaven
1949 Answer for Anne

Lynchburg (VA)
1942 The Vanishing Virginian

Lynching
1914 *The Good-for-Nothing*
1915 The Birth of a Nation
1917 The Captain of the Gray Horse Troop
My Fighting Gentleman
1919 False Evidence
Just Squaw
The Unpainted Woman
1920 Within Our Gates
1923 Scars of Jealousy
1934 *Fighting Through*
The Prescott Kid
1936 *Rose of the Rancho*
Silly Billies
The Traitor
1937 *The Barrier*
It Could Happen to You
1940 *Covered Wagon Days*
Prairie Schooners
Viva Cisco Kid
1942 *Juke Girl*
1943 The Ox-Bow Incident
1947 *King of the Bandits*
1948 *The Dude Goes West*
Silver Trails
1949 *The Prairie*
1950 *Bandit Queen*
Broken Arrow
The Lawless
Stars in My Crown
Storm Over Wyoming
1951 *Adventures of Captain Fabian*
1953 *Conquest of Cochise*
The Great Sioux Uprising

The Man Behind the Gun
The Man from the Alamo
The Sun Shines Bright
1956 *Raw Edge*
Reprisal!
1957 *Gun Battle at Monterey*
The Halliday Brand
The Lawless Eighties
1958 *The Defiant Ones*
1959 *The Hanging Tree*
1960 *Cimarron*
The Unforgiven

Gerardo Machado y Morales
1949 *We Were Strangers*

Machine-guns
1931 *Little Caesar*
1934 *The Star Packer*
1950 *Rio Grande Patrol*
1951 *Only the Valiant*

Mackinac Island (MI)
1960 *The Crowning Experience*

Mad scientists
1942 *Professor Creeps*
1946 *The Face of Marble*

Madame Butterfly (Opera)
1950 *The Toast of New Orleans*

Madams
1949? *Girl in Room 20*

James Madison
1937 *Old Louisiana*

Dolly Madison
1938 *The Buccaneer*

Madison Square Garden (New York City)
1936 *Laughing Irish Eyes*
1953 *The Joe Louis Story*

Madrid (Spain)
1930 *Un hombre de suerte*
Sevilla de mis amores
1931 *Mamá*
1933 *Primavera en otoño*
Yo, tú y ella
1935 *Angelina o el honor de un brigadier*
1950 *The Baron of Arizona*

Mafia
1915 The Last of the Mafia
1915? *Sin*
1916 Poor Little Peppina
1922 Fair Lady
1936 *Muss 'Em Up*
1950 Black Hand
1959 Inside the Mafia
1960 Pay or Die

Magazines
1917 I Will Repay
1922 *The Guttersnipe*
1930 *Charros, gauchos y manolas*
1942 *Seven Sweethearts*
1948 *Gentleman's Agreement*

Magic
1917 The Bottle Imp
1936 *Custer's Last Stand*
1948 *The Dude Goes West*

Magic lamps
1945 *Where Do We Go From Here?*

Magic lanterns
1930 *King of Jazz*

Magicians
1926 The Conjure Woman
1930 *Revista Hispano-Americana*
1931 *Cheri-Bibi*
1936 *The Green Pastures*
1939 *Charlie Chan at Treasure Island*
1940? *Mr. Washington Goes to Town*
1944 Black Magic
1948 Killer Diller

Magnates (Tycoons)
use **Businessmen; Industrialists; Specific types of magnates; Tycoons**

Magnesium
1942 *Let's Get Tough!*

Mahican Indians
  use **Mohegan Indians**
Maids
1914   *The Great Diamond Robbery*
1915   *Chimmie Fadden*
      Chimmie Fadden Out West
      The Immigrant
1916   *For the Defense*
1919   *The Little Diplomat*
1920?   *Broken Hearts*
1921   Through the Back Door
1928   Diamond Handcuffs
1930   *Del mismo barro*
      Take the Heir
1931   *The Black Camel*
      Drácula
      The Exile
      Personal Maid
      Regeneración
1932   *Genoveffa*
      Hypnotized
      Unashamed
1933   *Dos noches*
      The Eternal Jew
      El rey de los gitanos
1934   *Imitation of Life*
1935   *Naughty Marietta*
      A Night at the Opera
1936   *Mad Holiday*
1938   *Birthright*
1939   *The Mystery of Mr. Wong*
1940?   *Mr. Washington Goes to Town*
1941   *Charlie Chan in Rio*
1942   *Seven Sweethearts*
      Shut My Big Mouth
      Syncopation
      They Died With Their Boots On
      Twin Beds
1943   *His Butler's Sister*
1944   *Chip Off the Old Block*
      Hi, Beautiful
      Tomorrow the World!
1945   *The Cisco Kid Returns*
      Club Havana
      The Valley of Decision
1946   *Saratoga Trunk*
1947   *The Chinese Ring*
      The Farmer's Daughter
      New Orleans
1950   *Emergency Wedding*
      No Way Out
1951   *Cuban Fireball*
      Molly
      Queen for a Day
1953   *Sangaree*
      Tonight We Sing
1958   *Houseboat*
1960   *I Passed for White*
      Take a Giant Step
Mail order brides
1951   *Westward the Women*
Mail service
  use **Post offices; Postal workers**
Mailmen
  use **Postal workers**
Maine
1919   *Behind the Door*
1923   Backbone
1934   *As the Earth Turns*
1947   *It Had To Be You*
Makeup
  use **Cosmetics**
Malaria
1943   *Bataan*
1950   *Chinatown at Midnight*
1954   *They Rode West*
1955   *Duel on the Mississippi*
Male impersonation
1916   The Daughter of the Don
      Poor Little Peppina
1917   *The Little Boy Scout*
      The Little Chevalier
      The Trouble Buster
      The Wild Girl
1934   *The Cactus Kid*
1936   Rose of the Rancho
      Yiddle with His Fiddle
1938   *Daughter of Shanghai*
1945   *The House on 92nd St.*

1946   *Beauty and the Bandit*
1947   *Buck Privates Come Home*
1949   *Masked Raiders*
      Stagecoach Kid
1950   *Buccaneer's Girl*
Malibu (CA)
1946   *The Trap*
Man-haters
1919   The She Wolf
1931   La fiesta del diablo
Managers
  use **Specific types of managers**
Managers (Entertainment)
1930   *Estrellados*
1936   *Sum Hun*
1954   *Carmen Jones*
Mangas Coloradas
1955   Fort Yuma
1957   War Drums
Manhood
1915   *The Lamb*
1921   As the World Rolls On
1933   *King of the Wild Horses*
1936   Contra la corriente
1937   *Slave Ship*
1938   The Singing Blacksmith
1946   *Swamp Fire*
1951   Saturday's Hero
1958   Tonka
1959   *Odds Against Tomorrow*
Manicurists
1921   Puppets of Fate
1925   The Manicure Girl
1928   Flying Romeos
1931   La fiesta del diablo
      Smart Money
1935   A Night at the Ritz
Manila (Philippines)
1943   *Air Force*
Mannequins (Figures)
1959   *The World, the Flesh and the Devil*
Manors
1931   *Le père célibataire*
1934   *She Was a Lady*
1940   Son of Ingagi
1944   *Something for the Boys*
Mansions
1915   *Chimmie Fadden*
1917   *The Renaissance at Charleroi*
1919   Come Out of the Kitchen
      The Right to Happiness
1930   *Así es la vida*
1932   *The Heart of New York*
1934   *Un capitán de cosacos*
1938   *Birthright*
1939   *Charlie Chan at Treasure Island*
1941   *King of the Zombies*
1943   *The Amazing Mrs. Holliday*
1945   *The Jade Mask*
1949   *Shamrock Hill*
      Tulsa
1950   *The Baron of Arizona*
1955   *The View from Pompey's Head*
Manslaughter
1918   *Free and Equal*
      Woman and the Law
1926   A Prince of His Race
1930   *El presidio*
1931   La fruta amarga
      La incorregible
      Smart Money
1933   *The Emperor Jones*
1939   *Verbena trágica*
1942   *In This Our Life*
1949   *Ride, Ryder, Ride!*
1959   *Odds Against Tomorrow*
Manuscripts
1939   *Charlie Chan at Treasure Island*
1944   *Cry of the Werewolf*
Maps
1914   *An Odyssey of the North*
1915   *An American Gentleman*
1923   *Regeneration*
1930   *Un hombre de suerte*
1932   *The Forty-Niners*
      The Galloping Kid
      Hidden Valley

1934   Call of the Coyote
      Wheels of Destiny
1935?   *The Irish Gringo*
1937   *The Riders of the Whistling Skull*
      Thank You, Mr. Moto
1938   *Mr. Moto Takes a Chance*
1939   *The Cisco Kid and the Lady*
      Drifting Westward
1940   *Northwest Passage (Book I—Rogers' Rangers)*
1941   *Dead Men Tell*
      The Pioneers
1948   *The Dude Goes West*
1949   *Call of the Forest*
      Home of the Brave
      Rose of the Yukon
1955   *The Far Horizons*
Marbles (Game)
1948   *The Time of Your Life*
Marching bands
1955   *The Long Gray Line*
Mardi Gras
1921   Love's Plaything
1925   Scarlet Saint
1941   *Lady from Louisiana*
      Louisiana Purchase
Marie Antoinette, Queen, consort of Louis XVI, King of France, 1755-1793
1948   *Jiggs and Maggie in Court*
1959   *John Paul Jones*
Marihuana
1934?   *Harlem After Midnight*
1960   *This Rebel Breed*
Marin County (CA)
1937   *Song of the City*
Mark Hopkins Hotel (San Francisco, CA)
1956   *Serenade*
Marksmen
  use **Sharpshooters**
Marne River (France)
1918   *The Greatest Thing in Life*
Marriage
1914   *Dan*
      John Barleycorn
      The Jungle
      The Redemption of David Corson
      Springtime
      The Squaw Man
1915   The Cheat
1916   The Honorable Friend
      The Morals of Hilda
      Pasquale
1917   *The Barrier*
      The Bottle Imp
      The Little Boy Scout
      One Law for Both
      Unconquered
      The Woman and the Beast
1918   *An Alien Enemy*
      The City of Dim Faces
      The Prussian Cur
      Thirty a Week
1919   A Bachelor's Wife
      His Parisian Wife
      The Homesteader
      Mandarin's Gold
      The Scar
      The Sneak
      The Unpainted Woman
1920   The North Wind's Malice
      On with the Dance
      The Riddle: Woman
1921   As the World Rolls On
      Society Snobs
1921?   The Supreme Passion
1922   One Eighth Apache
      Peacock Alley
      Saturday Night
1923   The Miracle Makers
1925   The Manicure Girl
1926   The Cohens and Kellys
1927   The Scar of Shame
      White Gold
      Wild Geese
1928   The Crash
      The Secret Hour
      Uncle Tom's Cabin
1930   Behind the Make-Up
      Cuando el amor ríe
      The Grand Parade

A Lady to Love
El secreto del doctor
She Got What She Wanted
Sombras de gloria
1931   Aloha
      The Avenger
      Buster se marie
      Un caballero de frac
      Carne de cabaret
      La carta
      Cimarron
      The Cohens and Kellys in Africa
      ¿Conoces a tu mujer?
      The Exile
      La fiesta del diablo
      Fighting Caravans
      The Great Meadow
      La ley del harem
      Lo mejor es reír
      Mamá
      Nuit d'Espagne
      El pasado acusa
      La pura verdad
      Regeneración
      Shulamith
      Soyons gais
      Su última noche
      El tenorio del harem
      The White Renegade
      Zein Weib's Lubovnick
1932   *Call Her Savage*
      Cuore d'emigrante
      The Golden West
      Une heure près de toi
      Hombres en mi vida
      Marido y mujer
      Mazel Tov
      Scarface
      Ten Minutes to Live
      Tiger Shark
      Veiled Aristocrats
1933   *Dance Hall Hostess*
      The Eternal Jew
      Ever in My Heart
      Grand Slam
      Live and Laugh
      The Man Who Dared: An Imaginative Biography
      No dejes la puerta abierta
      Yo, tú y ella
1934   *As the Earth Turns*
      Behold My Wife!
      Beloved
      Broadway Bill
      La ciudad de cartón
      The Great Flirtation
      Laughing Boy
      Strange Wives
      El tango en Broadway
      What a Mother-in-Law!
      White Heat
      The Youth of Russia
1934?   Harlem After Midnight
1935   Alas sobre el Chaco
      ¡Asegure a su mujer!
      Bar-Mitzvah
      El día que me quieras
      Harmony Lane
      L'homme des Folies Bergère
      Romance in Manhattan
      Señora casada necesita marido
      Shir Hashirim
      The Wedding Night
1936   After the Thin Man
      Contra la corriente
      Ellis Island
      Love and Sacrifice
      Ramona
      Ride, Ranger, Ride
      La última cita
1937   Big City
      The Devil's Playground
      Slave Ship
      That I May Live
1938   *Birthright*
      Charlie Chan at Monte Carlo
      God's Step Children
      In Old Chicago
      The Singing Blacksmith
      The Toy Wife
1938?   *I due gemelli*

1939 Cossacks in Exile
     La Inmaculada
     My Son
     The Mystery of Mr. Wong
     Waterfront
1940 Jennie
     The Man I Married
     Mexican Spitfire
     Mystery in Swing
     Overture to Glory
     While Thousands Cheer
1941 Hold Back the Dawn
     The Mexican Spitfire's Baby
     Sunday Sinners
     Z Dymem Pozarów
1942 American Empire
     Cat People
     Mexican Spitfire Sees a
       Ghost
     Mexican Spitfire's Elephant
     *They Died With Their Boots
       On*
     Twin Beds
     We Were Dancing
     Woman of the Year
1943 Cabin in the Sky
     Dixie
1944 An American Romance
     Buffalo Bill
     Mr. Skeffington
     Tender Comrade
1945 *The Great John L.*
     Jealousy
     A Tree Grows in Brooklyn
1946 Bringing Up Father
     The Face of Marble
     Mantan Messes Up
     Notorious
     The Sailor Takes a Wife
1946? *House-Rent Party*
1947 *Black Gold*
     Body and Soul
     Carnegie Hall
     The Foxes of Harrow
     The Jolson Story
     Spoilers of the North
1947? *What a Guy*
1948 The Betrayal
     The Betrayal
     Big City
     I Remember Mama
     Jiggs and Maggie in Court
     The Time of Your Life
     Unconquered
1948? *Junction 88*
1949 *Arctic Fury*
     The Fighting Kentuckian
     Knock on Any Door
     The Undercover Man
1949? *She's Too Mean for Me*
1950 *The Baron of Arizona*
     The Breaking Point
     Colt .45
     Emergency Wedding
     Give Us This Day
     The Jackie Robinson Story
     Jolson Sings Again
     The Men
     No Way Out
     Panic in the Streets
     So Young, So Bad
     Young Man with a Horn
1951 *The Great Caruso*
     The Harlem Globetrotters
     Jim Thorpe—All-American
     The Magnificent Yankee
     Show Boat
1952 *The Battle at Apache Pass*
     The Big Sky
     High Noon
     The Iron Mistress
     Japanese War Bride
     My Man and I
     The Quiet Man
1953 *Conquest of Cochise*
     The Eddie Cantor Story
     The Stand at Apache River
     Tonight We Sing
1954 *Go Man Go*
     Indiscretion of an
       American Wife
     Salt of the Earth
     Taza, Son of Cochise
1955 Blackboard Jungle
     Chief Crazy Horse

     The Gun That Won the West
     The Long Gray Line
     A Man Called Peter
     Marty
     *The View from Pompey's
       Head*
     Violent Saturday
1956 Baby Doll
     The Catered Affair
     Serenade
     Walk the Proud Land
1957 *Beau James*
     The Brothers Rico
     Burden of Truth
     Naked in the Sun
     Trooper Hook
1958 Fort Bowie
     Home Before Dark
     Machete
     Terror in a Texas Town
     Wild Is the Wind
1959 The FBI Story
1960 All the Fine Young
       Cannibals
     Cimarron
     The Crowning Experience
     The Dark at the Top of the
       Stairs
     Weddings and Babies

Marriage—Annulment
1915 Cohen's Luck
1917 The Call of Her People
1918 *Thirty a Week*
1928 The Mating Call
1934 *Caravane*
     Coming Out Party
1938 *Passport Husband*
1956 *Hot Blood*
1959 *Night of the Quarter Moon*

Marriage—Arranged
1914 Springtime
1915 *Kreutzer Sonata*
1916 The Flames of Johannis
     The Woman in 47
1917 *The Little Boy Scout*
1918 *A Daughter of the Old
       South*
     Her American Husband
1918? The Snail
1919 Bonnie, Bonnie Lassie
     False Evidence
1920 For the Soul of Rafael
     A Tokio Siren
     White Youth
1921 Wing Toy
1928 The Canyon of Adventure
     The Cavalier
1930 *Wu Li Chang*
1931 *Cheri-Bibi*
     Echec au roi
1932 *The Hatchet Man*
1933 *L'amour guide*
     *The Cohens and Kellys in
       Trouble*
1935 Naughty Marietta
     Rosa de Francia
     The Singing Vagabond
1936 *Dancing Pirate*
     Yiddle with His Fiddle
1937 Arshin Mal Alan
     That Girl from Paris
1939 Los hijos mandan
     La Inmaculada
1940 The Jewish Melody
1941 *Murder on Lenox Avenue*
1943 *Deerslayer*
1944 Tahiti Nights
1946 The Gay Cavalier
1947 Reet, Petite and Gone
     Riding the California Trail
1951 *Across the Wide Missouri*
1952 *The Fabulous Senorita*
1953 *Sangaree*
     Thunder Bay
1956 *Hot Blood*
1959 *Thunder in the Sun*
1960 *Ice Palace*

Marriage—Fake
1913 *The Inside of the White
       Slave Traffic*
1915 *Children of the Ghetto*
1917 *Rosie O'Grady*
1920 The Paliser Case
1920? Her Story

1921 Hearts of the Woods
     Made in Heaven
1928 *Eleven P.M.*
1931 *Oklahoma Jim*
1932 *A Daughter of Her People*

Marriage—Forced
1915 *The Birth of a Nation*
     Under Southern Skies
1916 Gold and the Woman
     The Grip of Jealousy
     The Romantic Journey
     Silks and Satins
     Sold for Marriage
     Witchcraft
1917 Hashimura Togo
     The Wild Girl
1918 The Only Road
     Out of a Clear Sky
1919 The Heart of Wetona
1919? The Chosen Path
1920 The Brute
     The Good-Bad Wife
1921 The First Born
     Love's Plaything
1922 The Dungeon
1932 *Mystery Ranch*
1933 *Man from Monterey*
1934 *Beloved*
     Tres amores
1936 Border Phantom
     The Phantom of Santa Fe
1938 *Dangerous to Know*
     God's Step Children
1939 *The Cisco Kid and the Lady*
1943 *The Meanest Man in the
       World*
1945 *Where Do We Go From
       Here?*
1946 *Beware*
     South of Monterey
1948 Singin' Spurs
1951 *Adventures of Captain
       Fabian*
1954 *Hondo*
1956 Raw Edge

**Marriage—Forced by
circumstances**
1914 The Woman in Black
1917 Castles for Two
     Forbidden Paths
1918 The Bravest Way
1919 Told in the Hills
     Who Will Marry Me?
1931 *Mi último amor*
1932 The Son-Daughter
1933 Olsen's Big Moment
1934 *The Prescott Kid*
1935 *Un hombre peligroso*
1937 Natalka Poltavka
1938 Passport Husband
     *Two Gun Man from
       Harlem*
1939 Heaven with a Barbed Wire
       Fence
     The Light Ahead
1943 *Margin for Error*
1948 *Big City*
     The Lady from Shanghai
     The Paleface
1950? Three Daughters
1952 *Battles of Chief Pontiac*
1955 *The Lonesome Trail*
1957 *Raintree County*
1958 Bullwhip
1959 *Cry Tough*

Marriage—Mixed
1915 *Kreutzer Sonata*
1916 *Gold and the Woman*
1917 *Her Own People*
1918 Free and Equal
     The Squaw Man
1919 Daughter of Mine
     The Other Man's Wife
1922 The Woman He Loved
1929 Abie's Irish Rose
1932 A Daughter of Her People
1933 *Counsellor at Law*
1939 *Tevya*
1940 *The Jewish Melody*
1946 *Abie's Irish Rose*
1951 *Tomahawk*
1952 Hiawatha
1953 *Beneath the 12-Mile Reef*
     The Pathfinder

1954 *They Rode West*
1955 The Far Horizons
     Foxfire
1956 Giant
1957 *Run of the Arrow*
     War Drums
1958 *Flaming Frontier*
     Touch of Evil
1959 Night of the Quarter Moon
1960 *Cimarron*
     I Passed for White

Marriage—Secret
1914 *Life's Shop Window*
1917 The Plow Woman
1919 *Behind the Door*
1931 *Gente alegre*
     The Guilty Generation
1939 The Escape
     Kol Nidre
1940 Three Cheers for the Irish
1942 *Secret Enemies*
1943 *The Outlaw*
     Redhead from Manhattan
1944 *Going My Way*
1945 *The Jade Mask*
     The Valley of Decision
1946 *Abie's Irish Rose*
1950 *The Daughter of Rosie
       O'Grady*
1952 *The Fabulous Senorita*
     It's a Big Country: An
       American Anthology

Marriage brokers
     use Matchmakers
Marriage by Proxy
1917 A Wife by Proxy
Marriage licenses
1919 *A Bachelor's Wife*
     Desert Gold

Marriage of convenience
1917 The Conqueror
1918 Tony America
1920 A Tokio Siren
1921 Made in Heaven
1928 The Mating Call
1932 Uncle Moses
1935 Julieta compra un hijo
1940 They Knew What They
       Wanted
1941 Come Live with Me
     Ice-Capades
1946 The Gentleman Misbehaves
1950 *Buccaneer's Girl*
1951 The House on Telegraph
       Hill
1955 Not As a Stranger

James Marshall
1936 *Sutter's Gold*

Peter Marshall
1955 A Man Called Peter

Marshals
1942 *Shut My Big Mouth*
1943 Land of Hunted Men
     The Law Rides Again
1946 Santa Fe Uprising
1947 *Wild Horse Mesa*
1948 *Old Los Angeles*
1949 *Masked Raiders*
     Roll Thunder Roll!
1950 *Cherokee Uprising*
     The Missourians
     The Missourians
     Train to Tombstone
1952 High Noon
     Rose of Cimarron
1953 *Jack McCall Desperado*
1954 *The Black Dakotas*
1955 *Shotgun*
1957 *Dragoon Wells Massacre*
     The Oklahoman
     Ride Out for Revenge
1958 *The Badlanders*
1960 *Oklahoma Territory*

Martha Jane Canary
     use Calamity Jane

Martial law
1926 *The Passaic Textile Strike*
1931 *Cavalier of the West*

Martyrs
     The Voice of Israel
1932 Yiskor

Mary, Blessed Virgin, Saint
1938 *California Frontier*
Maryland
1917? Barnaby Lee
1919? The Brand of Judas
1922 Spitfire
1936 *The Prisoner of Shark Island*
1943 *Mr. Lucky*
Masked balls
1930 *Sei tu l'amore*
1932 *The Golden West*
The Vanishing Frontier
1933 Espérame
No dejes la puerta abierta
Una viuda romántica
1934 *Dos más uno, dos*
1935 *Julieta compra un hijo*
1937 *The Holy Oath*
1947 *The Foxes of Harrow*
Masked bandits
1932 El caballero de la noche
1936 The Bold Caballero
1940 The Mark of Zorro
1942 Shut My Big Mouth
1949 Masked Raiders
1951 Cyclone Fury
Flaming Feather
1958 The Lone Ranger and the Lost City of Gold
Masks
1940 Hi-Yo Silver
1941 *The Face Behind the Mask*
1945 *The Jade Mask*
1956 *The Lone Ranger*
Massachusetts
1949 *Lost Boundaries*
1958 Home Before Dark
Massacres
1914 In the Days of the Thundering Herd
1914? Sitting Bull—The Hostile Sioux Indian Chief
1915 *The Gambler of the West*
The Melting Pot
The Penitentes
1916 *Britton of the Seventh*
Civilization's Child
1919 Who's Your Brother?
1919? *In the Land of the Setting Sun; or, Martyrs of Yesterday*
1920 The Last of the Mohicans
1925 *Custer's Last Fight*
1926 *General Custer at Little Big Horn*
1934 *Wheels of Destiny*
1935 *Circle of Death*
1936 *Daniel Boone*
For the Service
Silly Billies
1940 *Geronimo*
Northwest Passage (Book I—Rogers' Rangers)
1948 *Fury at Furnace Creek*
Unconquered
1950 *Two Flags West*
1951 *Apache Drums*
Oh! Susanna
The Steel Helmet
Tomahawk
Warpath
1952 *Bugles in the Afternoon*
The Fighter
Fort Osage
Indian Uprising
The Savage
1953 *The Charge at Feather River*
The Glory Brigade
Last of the Comanches
The Man from the Alamo
The Pathfinder
1954 *Drum Beat*
Massacre Canyon
Sitting Bull
Taza, Son of Cochise
The Yellow Tomahawk
1955 *Santa Fe Passage*
1956 Comanche
Frontier Woman
Pillars of the Sky
The Searchers

1957 *Dragoon Wells Massacre*
Pawnee
Run of the Arrow
Tomahawk Trail
1958 Fort Bowie
Fort Massacre
The Light in the Forest
1960 *Flaming Star*
Massai
1954 Apache
Masseurs
1948 *Cry of the City*
Bat Masterson
1950 *Winchester '73*
Match industry
1932 The Match King
Matchmakers
1918 *The City of Dim Faces*
1925 Abie's Imported Bride
1929 East Side Sadie
1932 *The Heart of New York*
1934 *The Rabbi's Power*
Straight Is the Way
1937 *Natalka Poltavka*
1938 *The Singing Blacksmith*
1939 *Mamele*
1940 Americaner Schadchen
The Great Advisor
1952 *The Quiet Man*
Materialism
1932 Symphony of Six Million
1947 *Going to Glory, Come to Jesus*
Matricide
use **Parricide**
Maturation
1934 *Imitation of Life*
1936 *My American Wife*
1937 *Boots and Saddles*
Boy of the Streets
1944 *Andy Hardy's Blonde Trouble*
The Sullivans
1945 *Colorado Pioneers*
A Tree Grows in Brooklyn
1946 Song of the South
1948 *I Remember Mama*
1952 Kid Monk Baroni
1956 *Baby Doll*
1958 Marjorie Morningstar
1959 *Imitation of Life*
1960 Studs Lonigan
Take a Giant Step
Maximilian, Emperor of Mexico, 1832-1867
1938 *The Texans*
Mayors
1919 *A Fighting Colleen*
1920? The Scarlet Dragon
1924 Welcome Stranger
1926? *Ten Nights in a Barroom*
1927 Don Mike
1929 Mister Antonio
1933 The California Trail
The Man Who Dared: An Imaginative Biography
1934 The Cat's-Paw
1936 *Dancing Pirate*
It Had to Happen
Rose of the Rancho
1937 *Big City*
1938 *Dangerous to Know*
Gateway
In Old Chicago
1940 *The Mark of Zorro*
1941 *Ten Ostatni*
Z Dymem Pożarów
1943 *Border Patrol*
Margin for Error
1947 *Calendar Girl*
Robin Hood of Monterey
1948 *Up in Central Park*
1949 *Answer for Anne*
The Daring Caballero
1950 *The Missourians*
Panic in the Streets
A Ticket to Tomahawk
1951 *Apache Drums*
The Well
1952 *High Noon*
1957 Beau James
1958 The Last Hurrah
The Young Lions

1959 *The Sheriff of Fractured Jaw*
1960 *Wild River*
Mazes
1944 *The Chinese Cat*
Jack McCall
1953 Jack McCall Desperado
John McGraw
1951 *Jim Thorpe—All-American*
William McKinley
1933 *The Man Who Dared: An Imaginative Biography*
McKinley, Mount (AK)
1925 The True North
1930 The Break Up
1932 Dangers of the Arctic
Measles
1919? *In the Land of the Setting Sun; or, Martyrs of Yesterday*
1939 *Gone With the Wind*
Meatpackers and meatpacking
1914 The Jungle
Mechanics
1922 *Easy Money*
1934 *Straight Is the Way*
1935 *Bordertown*
1941 *The Gang's All Here*
Hold Back the Dawn
1943 *Bataan*
Fighting Americans
1944 *Slightly Terrific*
1950 *Rock Island Trail*
1951 *The House on Telegraph Hill*
1956 *Crowded Paradise*
Medals
use **Awards;**
Specific medals or awards
John Medariss
1960 *I Aim at the Stars: the Wernher von Braun Story*
Medical clinics
1930 Un hombre de suerte
1949 *Lost Boundaries*
Medical colleges
1943 *Wagon Tracks West*
1949 *Lost Boundaries*
1955 *Not As a Stranger*
Medical ethics
1954 *They Rode West*
Medical students
1916 Lone Star
1932 *Le cas du docteur Brenner*
Symphony of Six Million
1938 *Mis dos amores*
1942 *Sunday Punch*
1955 *Not As a Stranger*
1959 *Shake Hands with the Devil*
Medicine
1916 Lone Star
1918 The Spreading Evil
1919? *In the Land of the Setting Sun; or, Martyrs of Yesterday*
1922 The Mohican's Daughter
1932 *Call Her Savage*
1940 *Son of Ingagi*
1946 *Sheriff of Redwood Valley*
1958 Blood Arrow
Medicine Bow (WY)
1950 *Devil's Doorway*
Medicine men
1919 *Diane of the Green Van*
1920 *Before the White Man Came*
1922 The Mohican's Daughter
1925 *Custer's Last Fight*
1926 *General Custer at Little Big Horn*
War Paint
1930 *The Silent Enemy*
1932 *Igloo*
1936 *Custer's Last Stand*
1940 *Young Buffalo Bill*
1948 *Tap Roots*
Unconquered
1949 *Apache Chief*
1952 *Brave Warrior*
Navajo
1954 *They Rode West*
1956 *Westward Ho the Wagons!*
1957 *War Drums*

Medicine shows
1914 *The Redemption of David Corson*
1931 *The White Renegade*
1934 *Operator 13*
1937 *Harlem on the Prairie*
1938 *The Duke Is Tops*
1943 *Frontier Fury*
1947 *Oregon Trail Scouts*
1950 *Stars in My Crown*
1952 *Apache Country*
1954 *Siege at Red River*
Mediterranean Sea
1958 *Kings Go Forth*
Mediums
1920 *Eyes of Youth*
1936 *Charlie Chan's Secret*
1939 Charlie Chan at Treasure Island
1941 *Charlie Chan in Rio*
1947? Return of Mandy's Husband
Meetings
1935 *His Family Tree*
1939 *The Light Ahead*
Tevya
1944 *An American Romance*
1945 *Of One Blood*
1947 *The Burning Cross*
Rustlers of Devil's Canyon
1949 *The Red Menace*
1958 *Terror in a Texas Town*
1960 *The Crowning Experience*
Megalomania
1932 *Mystery Ranch*
1947 *California*
1951 The Mark of the Renegade
1956 *Man from Del Rio*
1957 *Raiders of Old California*
1958 *Flaming Frontier*
Frontier Gun
Mein Kampf (Book)
1944 *The Negro Soldier*
Melanesia
1930 *El dios del mar*
Melbourne (Australia)
1936 *Charlie Chan at the Race Track*
Memory
Hair-Trigger Casey
1945 *The House on 92nd St.*
1956 *Singing in the Dark*
Memphis (TN)
1943 *Stormy Weather*
1946? Beale Street Mama
1958 *St. Louis Blues*
Felix Mendelssohn
1942 *Nazi Agent*
Meningitis
1950 *The Men*
Mennonites
1938 Breaking the Ice
Mental illness
1931 *Regeneración*
1944 Dark Waters
1945 *Our Vines Have Tender Grapes*
1947 Dark Delusion
1955 *Seven Angry Men*
1956 *The Last Frontier*
1958 Home Before Dark
1959 *The Black Orchid*
Night of the Quarter Moon
Mentally handicapped persons
1927 [Japanese-American Film]
1930 *Locuras de amor*
1948 *Moonrise*
Merchant Marine
1927 *Blind Alleys*
1942 *The Navy Comes Through*
1943 Action in the North Atlantic
1944 *Lifeboat*
Merchants
1914 The Little Jewess
The Yellow Traffic
1914? The Mysterious Mr. Wu Chung Foo
1915 *The Last of the Mafia*
1916 *The Social Buccaneer*
1918 *The Bravest Way*
1921 The First Born
1923 Flames of Wrath
1926 The Cohens and Kellys

1932 *The Golden West*
    Joseph in the Land of Egypt
1937 *Arsbin Mal Alan*
1939 *King of Chinatown*
1960 *Cimarron*

Merry-go-rounds
1947 *Ride the Pink Horse*
1948 *Up in Central Park*

Mesabi Range (MN)
1944 *An American Romance*

Mescalero Indians
1951 Apache Drums
1955 Foxfire

Messengers
1950 *Davy Crockett, Indian Scout*
1951 *Cyclone Fury*
1957 *Revolt at Fort Laramie*

Metamorphosis
1931 *Drácula*

Metropolitan Opera (New York City)
1914 *The Nightingale*
1951 The Great Caruso
1956 *Serenade*
1960 *Pay or Die*

Mexican Americans
1917 The Little Boy Scout
1918 The Only Road
    Untamed
1919 Lasca
1921 *By Right of Birth*
    The Double O
1922 Big Stakes
1924 California in '49
    The Night Hawk
    Yankee Speed
1925 Brand of Cowardice
1926 The Fighting Edge
1927 Aflame in the Sky
    White Gold
1929 Romance of the Rio Grande
1930 The Arizona Kid
    On the Border
1931 The Cisco Kid
    The Hurricane Horseman
    Riders of the Rio
    Yankee Don
1932 Amor y vida
    The Galloping Kid
1934 The Battling Buckaroo
    The Lone Defender
    The Prescott Kid
1935 Bordertown
    Cowboy Holiday
    The Cyclone Ranger
    Riddle Ranch
1935? The Irish Gringo
1936 Ramona
    Rebellion
    The Traitor
1937 *Border Cafe*
    The Devil's Playground
1938 *Little Miss Roughneck*
    The Renegade Ranger
1939 Drifting Westward
    The Fighting Gringo
    Miracle on Main Street
1940 *Behind the News*
    Covered Wagon Days
    The Gay Caballero
    Mexican Spitfire
    Mexican Spitfire Out West
    Young Buffalo Bill
1941 *Land of Liberty*
    Road Agent
1942 From Across the Border
    Mexican Spitfire's Elephant
    Rio Rita
    Tortilla Flat
1943 Border Patrol
    The Leopard Man
    The Outlaw
1945 The Cisco Kid Returns
    The Gay Senorita
    A Medal for Benny
    Wanderer of the Wasteland
1946 *Border Bandits*
    Sunset Pass
    Without Reservations
1947 Ride the Pink Horse
    Robin Hood of Monterey
    Thunder Mountain
    Under the Tonto Rim

    Wild Horse Mesa
1948 *The Arizona Ranger*
    Four Faces West
    Gun Smugglers
    Guns of Hate
    Indian Agent
    Silver Trails
    Western Heritage
1949 *Brothers in the Saddle*
    The Daring Caballero
    The Gay Amigo
    The Golden Stallion
    Illegal Entry
    Masked Raiders
    The Mysterious Desperado
    Riders of the Range
    Roll Thunder Roll!
    Rustlers
    Satan's Cradle
    Stagecoach Kid
    3 Godfathers
    The Valiant Hombre
1950 *The Baron of Arizona*
    Battleground
    Border Treasure
    The Furies
    The Girl from San Lorenzo
    The Lawless
    The Men
    The Palomino
    Right Cross
    Rio Grande Patrol
    Storm Over Wyoming
    Sunset in the West
    Two Flags West
1951 *Apache Drums*
1952 Apache War Smoke
    California Conquest
    High Noon
    My Man and I
    The Ring
1953 Conquest of Cochise
    The Man Behind the Gun
    San Antone
1954 Salt of the Earth
1955 *Apache Ambush*
    Headline Hunters
    Santa Fe Passage
    Trial
1956 The Broken Star
    The Burning Hills
    Giant
    Man from Del Rio
    The Searchers
    Wetbacks
1957 *Gun Battle at Monterey*
    Man in the Shadow
    Raiders of Old California
    The Ride Back
1958 Ambush at Cimarron Pass
    The Badlanders
    Escape from Red Rock
    Gunfire at Indian Gap
    Terror in a Texas Town
    Touch of Evil
1959 The Young Land
1960 *Hell to Eternity*
    This Rebel Breed

Mexican-American border region
1915 *The Grandee's Ring*
1917 *The Little Boy Scout*
1918 *Untamed*
1920 Rio Grande
1921 The Double O
1922 Sky High
1924 The Lightning Rider
1926 Desert Gold
    The Fighting Edge
1927 Roarin' Broncs
1930 On the Border
1931 The Cisco Kid
1932 *Border Devils*
1934 *Call of the Coyote*
    The Lone Defender
    Riding Speed
1935 *The Cyclone Ranger*
1936 *Border Phantom*
    Hair-Trigger Casey
1937 *Border Cafe*
    Shadows of the Orient
1939 Forged Passport
    The Return of the Cisco Kid
1940 Covered Wagon Days
    Rhythm of the Rio Grande

1941 *Doomed Caravan*
    Hold Back the Dawn
1942 *Below the Border*
1943 Border Patrol
1947 *The Adventures of Don Coyote*
    Black Gold
1948 *The Golden Eye*
    Shep Comes Home
1949 Border Incident
    The Gay Amigo
    The Golden Stallion
1950 *Border Treasure*
    Rio Grande Patrol
1953 *San Antone*
1955 Apache Ambush
1956 *Comanche*
    Wetbacks
1957 *The Ride Back*
1958 Touch of Evil
1959 The Wonderful Country
1960 *Man on a String*

Mexicans
1915 Captain Courtesy
1916 *The Aryan*
    Gold and the Woman
    A Sister of Six
1917 *The Conqueror*
1918 *The Man Above the Law*
    Untamed
1919 *Desert Gold*
    Scarlet Days
1920 Rio Grande
    The Tiger's Coat
1921 The Double O
1922 A California Romance
    Cross Roads
1927 California
    The Dove
1929 The Desert Rider
    In Old Arizona
    Señor Americano
1930 The Bad Man
    King of Jazz
    The Lash
    Song of the Caballero
1931 *The Avenger*
1932 Law and Lawless
1934 Call of the Coyote
    The Fighting Hero
1935 The Cyclone Ranger
1936 *The Bold Caballero*
    Hair-Trigger Casey
    Pinto Rustlers
    Robin Hood of El Dorado
    Song of the Gringo
    Sutter's Gold
1937 *Law and Lead*
1938 California Frontier
    Wild Horse Canyon
1939 The Cisco Kid and the Lady
    Forged Passport
    The Girl from Mexico
    The Return of the Cisco Kid
1940 *Cuando canta la Ley*
    Kit Carson
    Lucky Cisco Kid
    Rhythm of the Rio Grande
    Viva Cisco Kid
1941 *Doomed Caravan*
    Ride on Vaquero
    Under Fiesta Stars
1942 *Shut My Big Mouth*
1943 The Girl from Monterrey
    The Ox-Bow Incident
1945 In Old New Mexico
    South of the Rio Grande
1946 *Singin' in the Corn*
    Slightly Scandalous
1947 The Adventures of Don Coyote
    California
    King of the Bandits
    On the Old Spanish Trail
    Pirates of Monterey
    Under the Tonto Rim
    West to Glory
1948 Angel in Exile
    Red River
    Shep Comes Home
1949 Border Incident
    Lust for Gold
1950 Belle of Old Mexico
    Mystery Submarine
    The Palomino

    Rio Grande Patrol
1951 The Mark of the Renegade
1952 California Conquest
    The Fighter
    My Man and I
    The Raiders
1953 *Arrowhead*
    The Man from the Alamo
    Ride, Vaquero!
1954 Passion
    The Yellow Tomahawk
1955 Apache Ambush
    Headline Hunters
    The Last Command
1956 *Comanche*
    Wetbacks
1957 *The Guns of Fort Petticoat*
    Raiders of Old California
    War Drums
1958 *Gun Fever*
    Touch of Evil
1959 Gunmen from Laredo
    The Wonderful Country
1960 *The Plunderers*

Mexico
1915 *The Lamb*
1916 Following the Flag in Mexico
1917 Forbidden Paths
    The Little Boy Scout
1918 *The Ranger*
1920 Rio Grande
1922 For His Mother's Sake
1927 California
1929 Romance of the Rio Grande
1930 Charros, gauchos y manolas
1931 *Riders of the Rio*
1934 Las fronteras del amor
1935 *Rendezvous*
1939 *The Girl from Mexico*
1940 *Mexican Spitfire*
1941 Hold Back the Dawn
1943 *The Girl from Monterrey*
1945 *South of the Rio Grande*
1946 *Strange Voyage*
1948 The Feathered Serpent
    Fort Apache
1949 *Border Incident*
    Brothers in the Saddle
    Illegal Entry
1950 *The Breaking Point*
    Mystery Submarine
1956 Serenade
1957 *Raiders of Old California*
    The Ride Back
1959 *Night of the Quarter Moon*

Mexico—History
1930 Las campanas de Capistrano
1948 *The Feathered Serpent*
1952 The Fighter
1953 San Antone

Mexico—History—1867-1910
1956 *Comanche*
1959 The Wonderful Country

Mexico. Army
1916 Following the Flag in Mexico
1939 *The Return of the Cisco Kid*
1940 *Kit Carson*
1947 *Pirates of Monterey*

Mexico. Secret Service
1948 *The Feathered Serpent*

Mexico City (Mexico)
1916 *Following the Flag in Mexico*
1939 *La Inmaculada*
1946 The Red Dragon
1955 *The Last Command*
1956 *Serenade*

Miami (FL)
1933 *The Man Who Dared: An Imaginative Biography*
1938 *Happy Landing*
1943 *Tahiti Honey*
1945 *Club Havana*
1946 *Notorious*
1957 *The Brothers Rico*

Miami Indians
1951 *When the Redskins Rode*

Mice
1926 The Campus Flirt
1936 *Rainbow on the River*
1943 *Three Hearts for Julia*

Michigan
1942 *Seven Sweethearts*
They Died With Their Boots On

Mickey Mouse (Cartoon character)
1941 *Sullivan's Travels*

Adam Mickiewicz
Z Dymem Pożarów

Microfilm
1945 *The House on 92nd St.*
1952 *Arctic Flight*

Middle Ages
1932 Genoveffa
1942 *Castle in the Desert*

Middle East
1953 *Dream Wife*

Midgets
use **Dwarfs**

Midwives
1928 Wheel of Chance
1945 *Of One Blood*
1950 *Give Us This Day*
1957 *All Mine to Give*

Migrant workers
1942 *Juke Girl*
1949 Border Incident
1956 *Giant*

Milan (Italy)
1935 *El cantante de Nápoles*
A Night at the Opera

General Nelson Miles
1956 *Comanche*

Military bases
1939 *Confessions of a Nazi Spy*
1943 *Fighting Americans*
1950 *Sands of Iwo Jima*
1951 *Go for Broke!*
1958 *The Young Lions*

Military camps
use **Military bases;**
Military posts

Military discharge
1946 *The Sailor Takes a Wife*

Military discipline
1948 *Fort Apache*
1951 *Go for Broke!*
1953 *Last of the Comanches*
1954 *Battle of Rogue River*
They Rode West

Military education
1943 *Fighting Americans*
1950 *Young Daniel Boone*
1957 *The Guns of Fort Petticoat*

Military enlistment
use **Military service, Voluntary**

Military government
1932 The Vanishing Frontier

Military intelligence
1948 *Night Wind*
1950 *I Killed Geronimo*

Military invasion
1918 *Me Und Gott*
1934 *The Unknown Soldier Speaks*
1950 Battleground

Military leave
Battleground
Sands of Iwo Jima

Military life
1940 *The Fighting 69th*
1943 *Fighting Americans*
1944 *The Racket Man*
Something for the Boys
1947 Little Mister Jim
1948 Fury at Furnace Creek
1950 Battleground
1951 *Little Big Horn*
Warpath
1952 *Bugles in the Afternoon*
1955 The Long Gray Line

Military occupation
1927 *His Foreign Wife*
1955 Seven Cities of Gold

Military offenses
use **Courts-martial and courts of inquiry;**
Military discharge;
Military discipline

Military officers
use **Officers (Military)**

Military police
use **United States. Army. Military Police**

Military posts
1915 *The Girl I Left Behind Me*
The Lure of Woman
1917 *John Ermine of the Yellowstone*
1937 *Drums of Destiny*
1943 *Doughboys in Ireland*
Marching On!
Three Hearts for Julia
1944 *The Negro Soldier*
1950 *Two Flags West*

Military schools
1915? *The Life of Sam Davis: A Confederate Hero of the Sixties*
1943 *Good Luck, Mr. Yates*
1944 *Chip Off the Old Block*
1955 *The Long Gray Line*
1960 *The Dark at the Top of the Stairs*

Military service, Compulsory
1916 *Pasquale*
1918 *The Yellow Dog*
1919 *The Lost Battalion*
1930 *¡De frente, marchen!*
1933 *Diplomaniacs*
1940 *The Ramparts We Watch*
1941 *Charlie Chan in Rio*
1942 *Friendly Enemies*
Young America
1943 *Marching On!*
Mr. Lucky
1944 *The Racket Man*
1947? Swanee Showboat
1950 *The Jackie Robinson Story*
1958 *The Young Lions*

Military service, Voluntary
1915 *The Birth of a Nation*
1917 *How Uncle Sam Prepares*
1918 *Doing Their Bit*
Good-Bye, Bill
The Kaiser's Finish
The Unbeliever
1919 *The Other Man's Wife*
1931 *Beyond Victory*
1940 *The Ramparts We Watch*
The Tragedy of Carpatho-Ukraine
1942 *Take My Life*
1943 *Good Luck, Mr. Yates*
Tahiti Honey
1944 *The Negro Soldier*
The Sullivans
1945 *The Dolly Sisters*
Where Do We Go From Here?
1947? Swanee Showboat
1953 *The Great Sioux Uprising*
The Joe Louis Story

Military training
use **Military education**

Militia
1922 Cardigan
1954 *Battle of Rogue River*

Milk
1915 *The Italian*
1918 Johanna Enlists

Milk trucks
1934 *Straight Is the Way*

Milkmen
1931 *Street Scene*
1939 Tevya
1948 *The Boy with Green Hair*
Music Man
1958 *The Young Lions*

Mill owners
1918 *The Birth of a Race*

Milliners
1917 *The Gun Fighter*

Millinery shops
1940 *Charlie Chan in Panama*

Millionaires
1916 *The Fall of a Nation*
1917 A Night in New Arabia
The Red Woman
Unknown 274
1918 The Golden Wall
Hell's End

How Could You, Jean?
Love's Law
1919 *Spotlight Sadie*
1921 *The Girl from God's Country*
Made in Heaven
1922 *The Top O' the Morning*
1923 Fashion Row
1924 *The House Behind the Cedars*
1926 Millionaires
A Trip to Chinatown
1927 *The Millionaire*
Sailor Izzy Murphy
1929 This Is Heaven
1930 La voluntad del muerto
1931 *Cheri-Bibi*
El comediante
Del infierno al cielo
Noche de duendes
Le père célibataire
El príncipe gondolero
Quand on est belle
1932 *Call Her Savage*
The Secrets of Wu Sin
Unashamed
1933 *Victims of Persecution*
1934 *Charlie Chan's Courage*
1935 *Ruggles of Red Gap*
1938 *Castillos en el aire*
The Rage of Paris
1939 *La Inmaculada*
1940 The Jewish Melody
1951 *Saturday's Hero*
1960 *Man on a String*

Mills
1925 Abie's Imported Bride
1955 *A Man Called Peter*

Milwaukee (WI)
1927 The Way of All Flesh

Mind-reading
1942 *Mexican Spitfire's Elephant*
1946? *House-Rent Party*

Mine accidents
1954 *Salt of the Earth*
1955 *Foxfire*
1958 *The Badlanders*
1959 *The World, the Flesh and the Devil*

Mine foremen
1918 *Laughing Bill Hyde*
1955 *Foxfire*
Violent Saturday

Mine owners
1917 The Red Woman
Runaway Romany
1948 *The Golden Eye*
1951 *Flaming Feather*
1955 *Foxfire*
1958 The Badlanders

Miners
1914 *An Odyssey of the North*
1915 *Sealed Valley*
1918 *Laughing Bill Hyde*
1923 *Snowdrift*
1924 *Unseen Hands*
1928 *Absent*
1930 *The Arizona Kid*
1936 *Song of the Gringo*
1938 *Two Gun Man from Harlem*
1940 *Girl from God's Country*
1943 *Jack London*
Riding High
1944 *An American Romance*
1945 *Salome, Where She Danced*
1946 *Canyon Passage*
1948 *The Golden Eye*
1951 *Apache Drums*
1954 Salt of the Earth

Mines
1914 *The Good-for-Nothing*
1916 A Sister of Six
1917 *Her Own People*
Runaway Romany
1919 *Told in the Hills*
1920 *The Symbol of the Unconquered*
1925 *Flower of Night*
1931 *The Avenger*
1934 *Charlie Chan's Courage*
1935 *L'homme des Folies Bergère*
1939 *The Bronze Buckaroo*
Charlie Chan in Reno

1941 *Gauchos of Eldorado*
Secret of the Wastelands
Under Fiesta Stars
1943 *Border Patrol*
Land of Hunted Men
1948 *Fury at Furnace Creek*
1949 Call of the Forest
Satan's Cradle
1950 *Raiders of Tomahawk Creek*
Stars in My Crown
1956 *The Broken Star*
The Burning Hills

Mines and mineral resources
1935? The Irish Gringo
1939 *Harlem Rides the Range*
1940 *Viva Cisco Kid*
1942 *North to the Klondike*

Mines, Military
1936 *Sea Spoilers*
1958 *Kings Go Forth*
The Young Lions
1960 *All the Young Men*

Mingo Indians
1953 *The Pathfinder*

Miniature golf
use **Golf, Miniature**

Miniconjou Indians
1952 The Savage

Mining claims
1916 A Sister of Six
1926 Pals in Paradise
1934 *The Lone Defender*

Mining towns
1918 *Her Moment*
1919 *The She Wolf*
1922 Pals of the West
1928 *Tyrant of Red Gulch*
1936 *Desert Gold*
1937 *The Barrier*
1951 *Apache Drums*
1959 *The Hanging Tree*
1960 *Walk Like a Dragon*
Walk Tall

Ministers
1923 *The Devil's Match*
1932 *The Black King*
So Big
1940 *They Knew What They Wanted*
1942 *From Across the Border*
1944 *The Negro Soldier*
1949 Prejudice
1951 *Apache Drums*
1952 It's a Big Country: An American Anthology
1956 *The Searchers*
1957 *Band of Angels*
1958 St. Louis Blues

Minnesota
1927 Wild Geese
1958 *Flaming Frontier*

Minstrel shows
1930 The Grand Parade
1935 Harmony Lane
The Singing Vagabond
1936 *Dimples*
1937 *Harlem on the Prairie*
1943 Dixie
1944 Minstrel Man
1947 *My Wild Irish Rose*
1947? *Swanee Showboat*
1951 Yes Sir, Mr. Bones

Miracles
1920 *The Man Who Dared*
1924 Untamed Youth
1927 Topsy and Eva
1947 Citizen Saint
1948 *Angel in Exile*
The Miracle of the Bells
1949 *Harbor of Missing Men*
1955 *Seven Cities of Gold*

Mirages
1956 *Dakota Incident*

Mirrors
1938 *Happy Landing*
1948 *The Lady from Shanghai*

Miscarriage
1939 *Drums Along the Mohawk*
1955 *Foxfire*
1959 *The FBI Story*
1960 *I Passed for White*

Miscegenation
- 1915 The Birth of a Nation
- 1916 Betrayed
  - Lone Star
- 1917 The Bronze Bride
  - The Red Woman
  - *The Renaissance at Charleroi*
  - *The Tenderfoot*
- 1918 The Red, Red Heart
- 1919 The Homesteader
- 1920 Li Ting Lang
  - Pagan Love
- 1921 Wing Toy
- 1924 Unseen Hands
- 1927 [Japanese-American Film]
- 1928 Thirty Years Later
- 1931 Aloha
  - The Exile
  - *Oklahoma Jim*
  - The Squaw Man
- 1932 *The Forty-Niners*
- 1934 Behold My Wife!
  - Chloe: Love Is Calling You
  - White Heat
- 1935 *Rescue Squad*
- 1936 *The Last of the Mohicans*
  - Show Boat
- 1938 God's Step Children
- 1948 The Betrayal
  - *Unconquered*
- 1949 Pinky
- 1950 *Right Cross*
- 1951 Across the Wide Missouri
  - *The Last Outpost*
  - Show Boat
- 1952 *The Big Sky*
  - Japanese War Bride
- 1953 Captain John Smith and Pocahontas
  - *Fort Ti*
- 1954 Broken Lance
- 1955 Seminole Uprising
  - The View from Pompey's Head
- 1956 *Raw Edge*
  - *The Searchers*
- 1957 Band of Angels
  - *Ride Out for Revenge*
- 1958 *Gun Fever*
  - Kings Go Forth
- 1959 The World, the Flesh and the Devil
  - Yellowstone Kelly

Misers
- 1916 *Witchcraft*
- 1935 *McFadden's Flats*
- 1952 *Anything Can Happen*

Misogyny
- 1927 Turkish Delight
- 1931 *¿Conoces a tu mujer?*
  - *Zein Weib's Lubovnick*
- 1937 *Maid of Salem*
- 1941 *Ice-Capades*
- 1959 *Shake Hands with the Devil*

Miss America Beauty Pageant
- 1943 *Gangway for Tomorrow*

Missing persons
- 1915 The Gambler of the West
- 1917 *The Hidden Children*
  - Lost in Transit
  - The Renaissance at Charleroi
- 1920? The Scarlet Dragon
- 1926 *The Flying Ace*
- 1930 El valiente
- 1936 El diablo del mar
- 1940 Taku
- 1941 *King of the Zombies*
  - Secret of the Wastelands
- 1942 Professor Creeps
- 1943 *Border Patrol*
  - Good Luck, Mr. Yates
- 1946 Shadows Over Chinatown
- 1947 *Jiggs and Maggie in Society*
- 1949 Arctic Fury
- 1953 The Stars Are Singing

Missing persons, Assumed dead
- 1917 A Roadside Impresario
- 1917? *Barnaby Lee*
- 1918 The Price of Applause
- 1919 The Other Man's Wife
- 1920 The Purple Cipher
- 1921 A Modern Cain

- 1931 *Cheri-Bibi*
- 1932 *Genoveffa*
  - *Soñadores de la gloria*
- 1933 It's Great to Be Alive
- 1935 Bar-Mitzvah
- 1936 *Below the Deadline*
  - *Sins of Man*
- 1937 One Mile from Heaven
- 1938 *The Adventures of Tom Sawyer*
- 1939 *Daughters Courageous*
  - *Harlem Rides the Range*
  - One Dark Night
- 1940 Her Second Mother
  - *Phantom of Chinatown*
  - Three Faces West
  - The Way of All Flesh
- 1943 *The Amazing Mrs. Holliday*
- 1944 *Minstrel Man*
- 1945 *Johnny Angel*
  - Of One Blood
- 1954 *Hell's Half Acre*
  - *War Arrow*

Mission San Diego de Alcala
- 1955 Seven Cities of Gold

Mission, Battle of the, 1890
- 1914 *The Indian Wars*

Missionaries
- 1918 *The Temple of Dusk*
- 1919? In the Land of the Setting Sun; or, Martyrs of Yesterday
- 1934 The Cat's-Paw
- 1936 *Klondike Annie*
- 1940 *Son of Ingagi*
- 1943 *The Amazing Mrs. Holliday*
- 1945 *Samurai*
- 1946 *Bad Bascomb*
  - Dirty Gertie from Harlem, U.S.A.
- 1948 *Harpoon*
- 1949 *Arctic Manhunt*
- 1952? Call of the Navajo
- 1955 *Fort Yuma*
  - Indian American
  - *Seven Cities of Gold*
- 1956 Pillars of the Sky
- 1957 The Lawless Eighties

Missions
- 1918 *Hitting the Trail*
- 1919 *Auction of Souls*
  - *The Gray Horizon*
  - *Who Will Marry Me?*
- 1919? In the Land of the Setting Sun; or, Martyrs of Yesterday
- 1930 A Daughter of the Congo
- 1934 *La cruz y la espada*
- 1936 *The Phantom of Santa Fe*
- 1942 *Tales of Manhattan*
- 1945 *The Cisco Kid Returns*
  - In Old New Mexico
  - El Navajo
- 1946 *Don Ricardo Returns*
  - Romance of the West
- 1947 *Bells of San Fernando*
  - The Return of Rin Tin Tin
- 1949 *The Daring Caballero*
  - *Daughter of the West*
  - *The Mysterious Desperado*
- 1950 *Bandit Queen*
  - *Border Treasure*
- 1952 Desert Pursuit
  - *Navajo*
- 1953 Last of the Comanches
- 1955 Seven Cities of Gold
- 1956 *Pillars of the Sky*
- 1957 *The Guns of Fort Petticoat*
- 1958 *The Lone Ranger and the Lost City of Gold*

Mississippi
- 1927 The Spider's Web
- 1931 La gran jornada
- 1932 *The Black King*
- 1935 So Red the Rose
- 1948 *Tap Roots*
- 1956 Baby Doll

Mississippi—History
- 1937 Drums of Destiny
- 1955 *Davy Crockett, King of the Wild Frontier*

Mississippi River
- 1918 Uncle Tom's Cabin
- 1920 Huckleberry Finn
- 1929 Show Boat
- 1930 Tom Sawyer
- 1931 *Huckleberry Finn*
  - Die Maske Fällt
- 1936 *Show Boat*
- 1937 Old Louisiana
- 1938 *The Adventures of Tom Sawyer*
- 1939 The Adventures of Huckleberry Finn
- 1946 Swamp Fire
- 1947 *The Foxes of Harrow*
- 1951 *Show Boat*
  - Yes Sir, Mr. Bones
- 1955 Duel on the Mississippi
- 1956 *Davy Crockett and the River Pirates*
- 1960 The Adventures of Huckleberry Finn

Missouri
- 1930 Tom Sawyer
- 1941 *Belle Starr*
- 1946 Renegade Girl
- 1952 *Fort Osage*
- 1960 *The Adventures of Huckleberry Finn*

Missouri River
- 1955 *The Far Horizons*

Mistaken identity
- 1915 The Sable Lorcha
- 1916 The Folly of Revenge
  - The Innocent Lie
  - The King's Game
- 1917 The Barrier
  - Castles for Two
- 1918 Ruggles of Red Gap
  - Set Free
- 1919 Yvonne from Paris
- 1924 Racing Luck
- 1928 The House of Scandal
  - The Secret Hour
- 1930 *Una cana al aire*
  - The Last Dance
  - *Locuras de amor*
  - *El príncipe del dólar*
- 1931 Buster se marie
  - *Un caballero de frac*
  - *Cuerpo y alma*
  - *Delicious*
  - Mr. Lemon of Orange
  - *Pardon Us*
- 1933 *The Cohens and Kellys in Trouble*
  - *A Lady's Profession*
  - *Man from Monterey*
  - *Olsen's Big Moment*
- 1934 *Caravane*
  - *La ciudad de cartón*
  - The Prescott Kid
  - *La veuve joyeuse*
- 1935 The Cyclone Ranger
  - *Lem Hawkins' Confession*
  - *Rosa de Francia*
  - Ruggles of Red Gap
  - *Señora casada necesita marido*
  - *The Singing Vagabond*
- 1935? *The Irish Gringo*
- 1936 Dancing Pirate
  - *Laughing Irish Eyes*
- 1937 *Maid of Salem*
- 1938 *Castillos en el aire*
  - Josette
- 1939 The Cisco Kid and the Lady
- 194- *Mistaken Identity*
- 1940 Arizona Frontier
  - *The Gay Caballero*
  - Mexican Spitfire
  - Mexican Spitfire Out West
  - New Moon
- 1941 Gauchos of Eldorado
  - Ice-Capades
  - The Mexican Spitfire's Baby
  - Sullivan's Travels
- 1942 Mexican Spitfire at Sea
  - Mexican Spitfire Sees a Ghost
  - Mexican Spitfire's Elephant
- 1943 *His Butler's Sister*
  - *Mexican Spitfire's Blessed Event*

- 1944 *Slightly Terrific*
  - *Tahiti Nights*
- 1946 *Slightly Scandalous*
- 1947 *It Had To Be You*
- 1949 Arctic Manhunt
  - *The Gay Amigo*
- 1949? She's Too Mean for Me
- 1952 *Apache War Smoke*
- 1953 *Dream Wife*
- 1954 Hondo

Mistresses
- 1914 At the Cross Roads
  - *Threads of Destiny*
- 1915 The Immigrant
- 1916 *Unprotected*
- 1917 The Call of the East
  - The Spirit of '76
  - *Unconquered*
- 1918 Her Moment
  - *The Temple of Dusk*
- 1931 *The Black Camel*
  - *Cuerpo y alma*
  - El pasado acusa
  - El proceso de Mary Dugan
  - Quand on est belle
- 1932 *Amore e morte*
  - Call Her Savage
  - *La foule hurle*
- 1933 *Charlie Chan's Greatest Case*
  - *The Emperor Jones*
- 1934 *La buenaventura*
  - *Un capitán de cosacos*
  - Laughing Boy
- 1934? *Harlem After Midnight*
- 1935 *¡Asegure a su mujer!*
  - *Rendezvous*
- 1936 Klondike Annie
  - *Sutter's Gold*
- 1938 Dangerous to Know
- 1939 *Way Down South*
- 1947 *The Foxes of Harrow*
- 1948 *Key Largo*
- 1950 *Mystery Street*
- 1958 *The Badlanders*
  - *Frontier Gun*
- 1959 *Last Train from Gun Hill*

Mixed blood
  use Indians of North America—Mixed blood

Moats
- 1936 *The Prisoner of Shark Island*

Mobs
- 1915 The Cheat
  - *The Spender*
- 1915? *Sin*
- 1917 *The Captain of the Gray Horse Troop*
  - *My Fighting Gentleman*
- 1919 *The Right to Happiness*
- 1920 Dangerous Hours
  - The Face at Your Window
  - The Great Shadow
  - *Within Our Gates*
- 1933 *Victims of Persecution*
  - *The Wandering Jew*
- 1937 *It Could Happen to You*
  - *Natalka Poltavka*
  - Nation Aflame
- 1938 *In Old Chicago*
  - *Little Miss Roughneck*
- 1940 *Covered Wagon Days*
- 1943 The Ox-Bow Incident
- 1944 *Address Unknown*
  - Knickerbocker Holiday
  - *Sheriff of Las Vegas*
- 1946 Santa Fe Uprising
- 1950 *The Baron of Arizona*
  - Broken Arrow
  - Intruder in the Dust
  - *The Lawless*
  - *The Missourians*
  - Stars in My Crown
- 1951 Adventures of Captain Fabian
  - *The Last Outpost*
- 1953 The Sun Shines Bright
  - *Thunder Bay*
- 1954 *The Black Dakotas*
- 1955 *Apache Woman*
  - Bad Day at Black Rock
  - Trial
- 1957 *Burden of Truth*
  - *The Tin Star*

1959 *The Hanging Tree*
Mobsters
   use **Gangsters**
Mobulidae
1936 *El diablo del mar*
Mock trials
1942 *Tales of Manhattan*
1943 Border Patrol
Model houses
1944 Hi, Beautiful
Models
1915 The Clemenceau Case
1916 *Broken Fetters*
   The Soul of Kura-San
1917 *The Pulse of Life*
1918 The City of Tears
   The Spreading Evil
1919 *As a Man Thinks*
   The Sneak
1926 Irene
1928 The Cohens and the Kellys
   in Paris
1931 *Quand on est belle*
1932 *Marido y mujer*
1935 *Rescue Squad*
1938 *The Rage of Paris*
1941 Louisiana Purchase
1945 *Club Havana*
1949 The Girl from Jones Beach
1950 *Right Cross*
Modernity
1931 *Fighting Caravans*
Modoc Indians
1954 Drum Beat
Mohawk Valley (NY)
1956 *Mohawk*
Mohegan Indians
1917 *The Hidden Children*
1920 The Last of the Mohicans
1922 *The Mohican's Daughter*
1936 The Last of the Mohicans
1943 Deerslayer
1947 Last of the Redmen
1953 The Pathfinder
1957 The Deerslayer
Mojave Desert
1942 *Castle in the Desert*
Molasses
1926 Sweet Daddies
Molls
1931 *Gentleman's Fate*
1932 *Scarface*
1933 *Olsen's Big Moment*
1934 *Straight Is the Way*
1937 *Bargain with Bullets*
1938 *Sugar Hill Baby*
1940 *East of the River*
   The Fatal Hour
   The Way of All Flesh
Molokai (HI)
1950 Damien
Monasteries
1936 *Sins of Man*
1945 *The Mummy's Curse*
Money
1918 Huck and Tom; or, the
   Further Adventures of
   Tom Sawyer
1931 *Such Is Life*
1933 *Diplomaniacs*
1934 *The Cactus Kid*
1936 Muss 'Em Up
1938 *Breaking the Ice*
1939 *Charlie Chan in Honolulu*
1939? *A Chinese Gains a Fortune*
   in America
1941 *You're Out of Luck*
1942 *Tales of Manhattan*
1943 *Land of Hunted Men*
1946 *Dangerous Money*
   Sunset Pass
1947 *Easy Come, Easy Go*
1949 *Anna Lucasta*
   Arctic Manhunt
   Colorado Territory
   Masked Raiders
   Riders of the Range
   Rustlers
   The Sky Dragon
1950 *The Missourians*
1953 Ambush at Tomahawk Gap
1956 *Quincannon, Frontier*
   Scout

1958 *Gunfire at Indian Gap*
Moneylenders
1923 None So Blind
Mongols
1937 *Thank You, Mr. Moto*
Stanislaw Moniuszko
1940 *Overture to Glory*
Monkeys
1928 Hold 'Em Yale
1931 *Monerías*
1935 *Angelina o el honor de un*
   brigadier
1939 *Charlie Chan in Honolulu*
1944 *Tahiti Nights*
1946 *Strange Voyage*
Monks
1915 *The Penitentes*
1916 *A Yoke of Gold*
1949 *Colorado Territory*
1950 *The Baron of Arizona*
James Monroe
1941 *Land of Liberty*
Montana
1914? *Sitting Bull—The Hostile*
   Sioux Indian Chief
1918? *Indian Life*
1919 Told in the Hills
1925 *Custer's Last Fight*
1926 The Devil Horse
   General Custer at Little Big
   Horn
1934 *She Was a Lady*
1951 *Little Big Horn*
1952 *The Big Sky*
1954 Cattle Queen of Montana
1958 Tonka
Monte Carlo (Monaco)
1933 Dos noches
1935 *Señora casada necesita*
   marido
1938 Charlie Chan at Monte Carlo
Monterey (CA)
1927 Rose of the Golden West
1940 *Kit Carson*
1942 Tortilla Flat
1947 *Bells of San Fernando*
   California
   Robin Hood of Monterey
1952 *California Conquest*
1955 *Kiss of Fire*
1957 *Gun Battle at Monterey*
Monticello (NY)
1950 Monticello, Here We Come!
Montreal (Canada)
1931 *Gentleman's Fate*
1950 *The Jackie Robinson Story*
Monument Valley (AZ and UT)
1949 *Tale of the Navajos*
Moonshiners
1916 *Broken Chains*
Moose
1925 The True North
Moral corruption
1913 The Inside of the White
   Slave Traffic
   Traffic in Souls
1915 The Gambler of the West
1925 The Devil's Disciple
1926? Ten Nights in a Barroom
1931 Die Dreigroschenoper
   Resurrección
1932 The Match King
1933 The Emperor Jones
1938 *Sugar Hill Baby*
1939 Keep Punching
1949 Brothers in the Saddle
1950 God, Man and Devil
1956 Death of a Scoundrel
1958 Never Love a Stranger
1959 *Cry Tough*
Moral rearmament
1960 The Crowning Experience
Moral reformation
1914 The Good-for-Nothing
   The Straight Road
1916 Light at Dusk
1917 The Peddler
   The Secret Game
   The Slacker
1918 *Denny from Ireland*
   The Price of Applause
1919 *Deliverance*
   A Man's Duty

1920 Uncharted Channels
1921? The Slave Market
1926 *General Custer at Little Big*
   Horn
1931 *Del infierno al cielo*
1932 *Cuore d'emigrante*
   Hearts of Humanity
1934 *Limehouse Blues*
   Nada más que una mujer
1935 Bordertown
   The Cyclone Ranger
   Tango Bar
1936 Custer's Last Stand
   Song of the Gringo
   The Traitor
1937 Boy of the Streets
1938 *Life Goes On*
   The Power of Life
   Speed to Burn
   Spirit of Youth
   Swing!
1939 *Keep Punching*
   King of Chinatown
1940 *Eli Eli*
1941 *Hold Back the Dawn*
   Romance of the Rio Grande
1942 *American Empire*
   Take My Life
1943 Cabin in the Sky
   Mr. Lucky
1944 The Racket Man
   Sheriff of Las Vegas
1946 *Beauty and the Bandit*
1948 *The Fight Never Ends*
   Gun Smugglers
1951 Apache Drums
   Gambling House
   The Girl on the Bridge
   The Raging Tide
   Slaughter Trail
1952 Fort Osage
   My Man and I
1955 Bad Day at Black Rock
   The Gun That Won the West
   Seven Cities of Gold
1956 Dakota Incident
1957 *Gun Battle at Monterey*
1958 Ride a Crooked Trail
1959 The Last Angry Man
Henry Morgenthau
1919 *Auction of Souls*
Morgues
1941 *Four Shall Die*
1942 *Little Tokyo, U.S.A.*
1954 *Hell's Half Acre*
Mormons
1946 Bad Bascomb
   Canyon Passage
1958 Blood Arrow
Morocco
1935 De la sartén al fuego
Morphine
1917 *The Squaw Man's Son*
1931 *Del infierno al cielo*
**El Morro National Monument
(NM)**
1948 *Four Faces West*
Boris Morros
1960 Man on a String
Morse code
1932 *Me and My Gal*
1944 *Something for the Boys*
1945 *The Shanghai Cobra*
Mortgages
1915 *Marse Covington*
1917 *The Little Samaritan*
1919 *Toby's Bow*
1921 Cotton and Cattle
1934 *Our Daily Bread*
1939 *Harlem Rides the Range*
1940 *Eli Eli*
1940? *Mr. Washington Goes to*
   Town
1941 *Gauchos of Eldorado*
Morticians
   use **Undertakers and
   undertaking**
Mory's Tavern (New Haven, CT)
1932 *Huddle*
Moscow (Russia)
1960 *Man on a String*

Moses
1936 *The Green Pastures*
Motels
1952 *My Man and I*
1958 *Touch of Evil*
Motherhood
1914 Life's Shop Window
1917 Unconquered
1921 The Swamp
1924 So Big
1925 The Greatest Love of All
   My Son
1928 Mother Machree
1930 My Yiddishe Mama
1931 Esclavas de la moda
   La fruta amarga
   The Great Meadow
   La mujer X
1932 Veiled Aristocrats
1935 A Night at the Ritz
1936 Star for a Night
1939 Mothers of Today
1946 *Wild West*
1948 I Remember Mama
1960 *The Pusher*
Mothers and daughters
1913? The Lure of New York
1914 *When Broadway Was a*
   Trail
   The Woman in Black
1917 The Hidden Children
   A Jewel in Pawn
1919 *Injustice*
   Scarlet Days
1919? The Chosen Path
1920 *In the Depths of Our Hearts*
1921 By Right of Birth
1925 Body and Soul
1930 *Así es la vida*
   Cuando el amor ríe
   Estrellados
   Olimpia
1931 *Delicious*
   Women Love Once
   Young Sinners
1932 Parigi affascina; ovvero,
   Malavita
   Scarface
   Senza mamma e'nnamurato
   The Unfortunate Bride
1933 *Olsen's Big Moment*
   Primavera en otoño
1934 Imitation of Life
1935 *Señora casada necesita*
   marido
1936 *Charlie Chan's Secret*
   El crimen de media noche
   My American Wife
1937 *Charlie Chan at the Opera*
   I Want to Be a Mother
   Man of the People
   Natalka Poltavka
   One Mile from Heaven
1938 God's Step Children
   Little Miss Roughneck
   Mis dos amores
   Sugar Hill Baby
   Two Sisters
1939 Daughters Courageous
   Judge Hardy and Son
   Moon over Harlem
   Tevya
1940 Perfidia
   Taku
1941 *Hurry, Charlie, Hurry*
1942 *Apache Trail*
1944 Chip Off the Old Block
   Mr. Skeffington
   Three Men in White
   Waterfront
1945 *The Bells of St. Mary's*
   Our Vines Have Tender
   Grapes
   A Tree Grows in Brooklyn
1946 *Saratoga Trunk*
1947 *Bowery Buckaroos*
   King of the Bandits
   New Orleans
   Reet, Petite and Gone
1949 *The Red Menace*
1955 *Foxfire*
   The Rose Tattoo
   Santa Fe Passage
1956 *The Lone Ranger*

1957 *The Oklaboman*
1958 *Kings Go Forth*
     The Young Lions
1959 *Imitation of Life*
1960 The Crowning Experience
Mothers and sons
1915 *The Birth of a Nation*
1916 *The Aryan*
     The Morals of Hilda
1917 His Sweetheart
1918 *The City of Dim Faces*
     Denny from Ireland
     Doing Their Bit
     Marked Cards
     Woman and the Law
1919 Hearts of Men
     The Tiger Lily
1920 *Dangerous Days*
     Dinty
     Humoresque
     In the Depths of Our Hearts
1920? *The Greatest Love*
1921 No Woman Knows
1922 For His Mother's Sake
1924 *Birthright*
1928 The Jazz Singer
1930 *Toda una vida*
     El último de los Vargas
     El valiente
     Wu Li Chang
1931 Aloha
     Beyond Victory
     The Guilty Generation
     Little Caesar
     La llama sagrada
     Skyline
1932 *Amor in montagna*
     Le cas du docteur Brenner
     Genoveffa
     El hombre que asesinó
     O festino o la legge
     Scarface
     So Big
     Thirteen Women
1933 *Counsellor at Law*
     Obey the Law
     Racetrack
1934 *Blossom Time*
     Straight Is the Way
     Tres amores
1935 Bar-Mitzvah
     Bordertown
     El cantante de Nápoles
     Cowboy Holiday
     The Cyclone Ranger
     The Irish in Us
1936 El diablo del mar
     Robin Hood of El Dorado
1937 *Law and Lead*
     Manhattan
        Merry-Go-Round
     Thank You, Mr. Moto
     Where Is My Child?
1938 *Birthright*
     Life Goes On
     Spirit of Youth
1939 Los hijos mandan
     Mirele Efros
1939? *A Chinese Gains a Fortune*
        in America
1940 *Americaner Schadchen*
     East of the River
     Escape
     Mexican Spitfire Out West
     The Notorious Elinor Lee
1941 Gauchos of Eldorado
1942 *All Through the Night*
     From Across the Border
     Syncopation
1943 *Marching On!*
1944 *Going My Way*
     Tahiti Nights
1946 *Gas House Kids*
     Notorious
     Saratoga Trunk
     Song of the South
1947 *Body and Soul*
     Carnegie Hall
     The Farmer's Daughter
     Humoresque
     My Wild Irish Rose
1948 *Big City*
     Call Northside 777
     Cry of the City
     Music Man

1950 *The Jackie Robinson Story*
     Jolson Sings Again
     The Missourians
1951 *The Great Caruso*
     Teresa
     Yes Sir, Mr. Bones
1952 It's a Big Country: An
        American Anthology
     Navajo
1953 *The Jazz Singer*
     The Joe Louis Story
     So Big
     Taxi
     Tumbleweed
1954 *Hell's Half Acre*
     Hondo
1955 *Marty*
     Trial
1956 The Benny Goodman Story
     Death of a Scoundrel
     Frontier Woman
     Westward Ho the Wagons!
1957 The Brothers Rico
     The Tin Star
     Trooper Hook
1959 The Black Orchid
1960 *The Dark at the Top of the*
        Stairs
     Key Witness
     Studs Lonigan
     Walk Like a Dragon
     Weddings and Babies
Mothers-in-law
1934 What a Mother-in-Law!
1935 Rosa de Francia
1939 *My Son*
1955 *Marty*
Motion picture actors and
   actresses
1930 Estrellados
1931 The Black Camel
     Un caballero de frac
1932 *The Cohens and Kellys in*
        Hollywood
     Hollywood, ciudad de
        ensueño
1933 Let's Fall in Love
1934 La ciudad de cartón
1936 Mad Holiday
     Yellow Cargo
1937 El carnaval del diablo
     Music for Madame
1940 *Tengo fe en ti*
1941 *Sullivan's Travels*
1942 *Foreign Agent*
1943 *Ladies' Day*
1946 *Without Reservations*
1948 The Miracle of the Bells
Motion picture cameramen
1940 *Phantom of Chinatown*
Motion picture crews
1930 Estrellados
1934 *Charlie Chan's Courage*
Motion picture directors
1930 Estrellados
1933 Let's Fall in Love
1936 *Yellow Cargo*
1937 *Music for Madame*
1940 *Tengo fe en ti*
1941 *Hold Back the Dawn*
     Sullivan's Travels
1946 That Man of Mine
Motion picture premieres
1930 Estrellados
Motion picture producers
1923 Deceit
1928 The Wages of Sin
1932 The Cohens and Kellys in
        Hollywood
     Harlem Is Heaven
     Hollywood, ciudad de
        ensueño
1933 *Let's Fall in Love*
1936 *Yellow Cargo*
1941 *Sullivan's Travels*
1942 *Holiday Inn*
1946 That Man of Mine
     Without Reservations
1947 *Copacabana*
     The Peanut Man
1948 *The Miracle of the Bells*
1950 *Jolson Sings Again*
1960 *Man on a String*

Motion picture studios
1930 Estrellados
1934 *La ciudad de cartón*
1935 *El día que me quieras*
1936 Yellow Cargo
1938 *Little Miss Roughneck*
1941 *Hold Back the Dawn*
1942 *Holiday Inn*
1960 *Man on a String*
Motion picture stuntmen and
   stand-ins
1934 *La ciudad de cartón*
Motion picture theaters
1933 *Yo, tú y ella*
1941 *Birth of the Blues*
     Sullivan's Travels
1947 *Buck Privates Come Home*
     Crossfire
1949 *Boston Blackie's Chinese*
        Venture
1951 *Native Son*
Motion pictures
1922 Head over Heels
     Solomon in Society
1924 In Hollywood With Potash
        and Perlmutter
1930 Big Boy
1931 Su noche de bodas
1932 Hollywood, ciudad de
        ensueño
1938 *Little Miss Roughneck*
1941 Land of Liberty
1945 *The House on 92nd St.*
1946 That Man of Mine
1948 *The Fight Never Ends*
1949 *The Girl from Jones Beach*
1950 *Jolson Sings Again*
Motion pictures—History
1947 *The Jolson Story*
Motorboats
1956 *Wetbacks*
Motorcycle racing
1944 *The Sullivans*
Motorcycles
1927 Roarin' Broncs
1958 *The Young Lions*
Mount Suribachi (Iwo Jima,
   Japan)
1950 *Sands of Iwo Jima*
Mountain life
1918 The Goddess of Lost Lake
Mountaineering
1921 Anne of Little Smoky
Mountains
1933 *Robbers' Roost*
1935 *Shir Hashirim*
1936 *Desert Gold*
1940 *Hi-Yo Silver*
1949 *Satan's Cradle*
     Stallion Canyon
1950 *Davy Crockett, Indian*
        Scout
     The Girl from San Lorenzo
     The Palomino
1954 *Passion*
1959 *Thunder in the Sun*
1960 *All the Young Men*
Mounties
   use **North West Mounted**
      Police
Mr. Smith Goes to Washington
   (Motion picture)
1941 *Louisiana Purchase*
Dr. Samuel Mudd
1936 The Prisoner of Shark Island
Mugs
   use **Ruffians**
Mulattoes
   use **African**
      Americans—Mixed
      blood
Mule trains
1946 *Canyon Passage*
1950 *A Ticket to Tomahawk*
Mules
1929 Hearts in Dixie
1939 *The Bronze Buckaroo*
1945 *Of One Blood*
Mummies
1935 *Charlie Chan in Egypt*
1945 *The Mummy's Curse*
     Nob Hill

Mumps
1938 *Rascals*
1944 *Since You Went Away*
Munich (Germany)
1928 Riley the Cop
1932 *Le cas du docteur Brenner*
Munich agreement, 1938
1939 *City in Darkness*
Munitions
1932 *The Son-Daughter*
1938 *Mr. Moto Takes a Chance*
1939 *City in Darkness*
1947 *The Chinese Ring*
1952 *California Conquest*
1953 *The Glory Brigade*
1958 *Kings Go Forth*
Munitions dealers
1937 *Charlie Chan at the*
        Olympics
1959 *The Wonderful Country*
Munitions factories
1916 Arms and the Woman
1918 Doing Their Bit
Murder
1912 The Adventures of
        Lieutenant Petrosino
1914 At the Cross Roads
     The Great Diamond Robbery
     The Jungle
     The Little Angel of Canyon
        Creek
     The Nightingale
     The Squaw Man
     Threads of Destiny
1915 *An American Gentleman*
     The Clemenceau Case
     Kreutzer Sonata
     The Last of the Mafia
     Marse Covington
1916 Arms and the Woman
     The Aryan
     At Piney Ridge
     Broken Chains
     Broken Fetters
     Civilization's Child
     The Flower of No Man's
        Land
     For the Defense
     The Honorable Friend
     Pudd'nhead Wilson
     Ramona
     The Romantic Journey
     The Scarlet Oath
     The Sign of the Poppy
     Unprotected
     The Yellow Passport
1917 *The Call of Her People*
     The Captain of the Gray
        Horse Troop
     Crime and Punishment
     A Kentucky Cinderella
     My Fighting Gentleman
     The Pulse of Life
     The Secret of Eve
     The Woman and the Beast
1918 *An Alien Enemy*
     The Bravest Way
     Broken Ties
     Denny from Ireland
     Her American Husband
     Her Moment
     Hitting the Trail
     Huck and Tom; or, the
        Further Adventures of
        Tom Sawyer
     Marked Cards
     The Midnight Patrol
     The Prussian Cur
     The Reckoning Day
     The Temple of Dusk
     Tongues of Flame
     Untamed
     A Woman of Impulse
1918? Rosemary Climbs the
        Heights
1919 *Behind the Door*
     The Gray Horizon
     The Gray Towers Mystery
     A Heart in Pawn
     Just Squaw
     Mandarin's Gold
     The Westerners
     Who Will Marry Me?

1920 *The Dark Mirror*
The Good-Bad Wife
On with the Dance
The Paliser Case
The Riddle: Woman
Within Our Gates
1920? The Greatest Love
1921 Black Roses
Fifty Candles
The First Born
The Gunsaulus Mystery
The Secret Sorrow
1922 Anna Ascends
Blazing Arrows
The Dungeon
One Eighth Apache
The Power of Love
Square Joe
1923 Crashin' Thru
Flames of Wrath
A Shot in the Night
1924 His Darker Self
The Pell Street Mystery
1924? The Flaming Crisis
1925 *Body and Soul*
Custer's Last Fight
The Man in Blue
Quicker'n Lightnin'
Tonio, Son of the Sierras
1927 The Devil's Saddle
Don Mike
The Dove
The Fighting Hombre
The Gay Defender
Heroes in Blue
The Spider's Web
1928 Ramona
A Ship Comes In
Wyoming
1929 The Peacock Fan
Sombras habaneras
1930 *Amor audaz*
The Bad Man
El cuerpo del delito
Kathleen Mavourneen
The Lash
Los que danzan
The Melody Man
She Got What She Wanted
Sombras de gloria
Le spectre vert
Tom Sawyer
El último de los Vargas
El valiente
La voluntad del muerto
Wu Li Chang
1931 The Black Camel
La carta
Cavalier of the West
Charlie Chan Carries On
Cheri-Bibi
Chinatown After Dark
Cimarron
El código penal
Drácula
The Exile
Gentleman's Fate
The Great Meadow
The Guilty Generation
Little Caesar
La mujer X
Nuit d'Espagne
Pagliacci
El pasado acusa
El proceso de Mary Dugan
Sombras del circo
The Squaw Man
Street Scene
Tropennächte
1932 Border Devils
Charlie Chan's Chance
The Galloping Kid
The Hatchet Man
Hidden Valley
El hombre que asesinó
Hombres en mi vida
Law and Lawless
The Match King
Men Are Such Fools
Mystery Ranch
O festino o la legge
Riders of the Desert
Scarface
The Son-Daughter
Ten Minutes to Live

Thirteen Steps
Thirteen Women
Unashamed
1932? The Girl from Chicago
1933 Charlie Chan's Greatest Case
Circle Canyon
The Eternal Jew
Obey the Law
Robbers' Roost
Song of the Eagle
The Telegraph Trail
Thundering Herd
1934 *Behold My Wife!*
The Cactus Kid
Call of the Coyote
Charlie Chan in London
Charlie Chan's Courage
Eskimo
The Fighting Hero
Fighting Through
He Was Her Man
Lazy River
Limehouse Blues
The Lone Defender
'Neath the Arizona Skies
The Star Packer
Wagon Wheels
1935 *Bordertown*
Captured in Chinatown
Charlie Chan in Egypt
Charlie Chan in Paris
Chinatown Squad
Cowboy Holiday
Lem Hawkins' Confession
Rendezvous
Wolf Riders
1935? *The Irish Gringo*
1936 Aces and Eights
After the Thin Man
The Bold Caballero
Border Phantom
Charlie Chan at the Circus
Charlie Chan at the Race
Track
Charlie Chan's Secret
El crimen de media noche
Custer's Last Stand
Daniel Boone
Down to the Sea
Hair-Trigger Casey
Klondike Annie
Love and Sacrifice
Mad Holiday
Muss 'Em Up
Pinto Rustlers
Ramona
Rebellion
Robin Hood of El Dorado
Sea Spoilers
Silly Billies
Song of the Gringo
Sutter's Gold
Treachery Rides the Range
Winterset
1937 Bargain with Bullets
The Barrier
Black Legion
The Californian
*Charlie Chan at the
Olympics*
Charlie Chan at the Opera
Charlie Chan on Broadway
Hills of Old Wyoming
It Could Happen to You
Maid of Salem
The Plainsman
The Riders of the Whistling
Skull
Shadows of the Orient
Thank You, Mr. Moto
Think Fast, Mr. Moto
Underworld
1938 The Adventures of Tom
Sawyer
Birthright
California Frontier
Charlie Chan at Monte Carlo
Daughter of Shanghai
Life Goes On
Mis dos amores
Mr. Moto Takes a Chance
Mr. Moto's Gamble
Mr. Wong, Detective
Outlaw Express
The Renegade Ranger

Spawn of the North
Two Gun Man from Harlem
Wild Horse Canyon
1939 The Adventures of
Huckleberry Finn
Allegheny Uprising
Bad Lands
Charlie Chan at Treasure
Island
Charlie Chan in Honolulu
Charlie Chan in Reno
The Cisco Kid and the Lady
City in Darkness
Daughter of the Tong
Double Deal
The Escape
The Fighting Gringo
Forged Passport
Frontiers of '49
Gang Smashers
Harlem Rides the Range
In Old Caliente
Keep Punching
King of Chinatown
Lying Lips
Mr. Moto in Danger Island
Mr. Moto Takes a Vacation
Mr. Wong in Chinatown
Moon over Harlem
The Mystery of Mr. Wong
194- Mistaken Identity
1940 *Behind the News*
Charlie Chan at the Wax
Museum
Charlie Chan in Panama
Charlie Chan's Murder
Cruise
Covered Wagon Days
Doomed to Die
Escape to Glory
The Fatal Hour
Hi-Yo Silver
Midnight Shadow
Murder over New York
Mystery in Swing
Paradise in Harlem
Phantom of Chinatown
Rhythm of the Rio Grande
Son of Ingagi
Viva Cisco Kid
1941 *Birth of the Blues*
Charlie Chan in Rio
Dead Men Tell
Four Shall Die
The Gang's All Here
Lady from Louisiana
Mutiny in the Arctic
The Pioneers
Prairie Pioneers
Road Agent
Romance of the Rio Grande
Saddlemates
Secret of the Wastelands
You're Out of Luck
1942 All Through the Night
Below the Border
Cat People
Juke Girl
King of the Stallions
Lawless Plainsmen
Let's Get Tough!
Little Tokyo, U.S.A.
North to the Klondike
Prisoner of Japan
Rio Rita
Rubber Racketeers
Take My Life
Valley of Hunted Men
Whispering Ghosts
1943 *Border Patrol*
Crime Smasher
Deerslayer
*Dr. Gillespie's Criminal
Case*
Frontier Fury
The Law Rides Again
The Leopard Man
Margin for Error
*They Came to Blow Up
America*
1944 *Address Unknown*
Black Magic
Charlie Chan in the Secret
Service
The Chinese Cat

Cry of the Werewolf
Dark Waters
Marshal of Reno
Outlaw Trail
The Racket Man
Riding West
Sheriff of Las Vegas
Sonora Stagecoach
Tucson Raiders
Waterfront
1945 *Anoush*
Betrayal from the East
The Cisco Kid Returns
Club Havana
Great Stagecoach Robbery
The House on 92nd St.
In Old New Mexico
The Jade Mask
Jealousy
Johnny Angel
The Mummy's Curse
The Navajo Trail
Samurai
The Scarlet Clue
The Shanghai Cobra
South of the Rio Grande
Wanderer of the Wasteland
1946 *Bad Bascomb*
Beauty and the Bandit
Border Bandits
California Gold Rush
Canyon Passage
Dangerous Money
Dark Alibi
The Face of Marble
Gas House Kids
The Red Dragon
Romance of the West
Santa Fe Uprising
Shadows Over Chinatown
Tall, Tan and Terrific
The Trap
1946? Go Down, Death!
1947 *Bells of San Fernando*
Black Gold
Bowery Buckaroos
Buffalo Bill Rides Again
The Burning Cross
California
The Chinese Ring
Crossfire
Desperate
Duel in the Sun
The Last Round-Up
Pirates of Monterey
Ride the Pink Horse
Robin Hood of Monterey
Spoilers of the North
Thunder Mountain
Under the Tonto Rim
West to Glory
Wild Horse Mesa
1948 *The Betrayal*
Call Northside 777
Cry of the City
Cry of the City
Docks of New Orleans
The Dude Goes West
The Feathered Serpent
Fighting Father Dunne
Fury at Furnace Creek
The Golden Eye
The Golden Eye
Guns of Hate
Half Past Midnight
Indian Agent
Key Largo
The Lady from Shanghai
Miracle in Harlem
Moonrise
Old Los Angeles
Open Secret
Shanghai Chest
Silver Trails
Sleep, My Love
Western Heritage
1949 *Apache Chief*
Border Incident
Boston Blackie's Chinese
Venture
Brothers in the Saddle
C-Man
Call of the Forest
Colorado Territory
*The Cowboy and the
Indians*

The Cowboy and the
    Prizefighter
The Dalton Gang
Illegal Entry
Jigsaw
Knock on Any Door
Laramie
Lust for Gold
The Red Menace
Rustlers
The Sky Dragon
Souls of Sin
Stallion Canyon
Streets of Laredo
Top O' the Morning
The Undercover Man
We Were Strangers
1950 Bandit Queen
      Black Hand
      The Breaking Point
      Broken Arrow
      Chinatown at Midnight
      Colt .45
      The Furies
      Indian Territory
      Intruder in the Dust
      A Lady Without Passport
      Mystery Street
      Mystery Submarine
      North of the Great Divide
      Raiders of Tomahawk Creek
      Storm Over Wyoming
      The Traveling Saleswoman
      Two Flags West
      Winchester '73
1951 Across the Wide Missouri
      Adventures of Captain
          Fabian
      Five
      Flaming Feather
      Fort Defiance
      The Last Outpost
      Mask of the Dragon
      Native Son
      New Mexico
      The Raging Tide
      Slaughter Trail
      The Steel Helmet
      The Tall Target
1952 California Conquest
      Fort Osage
      The Half-Breed
      Hiawatha
      The Raiders
      Rose of Cimarron
      Trail of the Arrow
      Woman in the Dark
1953 Arrowhead
      Captain John Smith and
          Pocahontas
      Column South
      Conquest of Cochise
      The Great Sioux Uprising
      Jack McCall Desperado
      The Nebraskan
      Old Overland Trail
      Sangaree
      Seminole
      The Stand at Apache River
      War Paint
1954 The Black Dakotas
      Carmen Jones
      Cattle Queen of Montana
      Dangerous Mission
      Hell's Half Acre
      Overland Pacific
      Passion
      Siege at Red River
1955 Apache Woman
      Bad Day at Black Rock
      Chief Crazy Horse
      Duel on the Mississippi
      Headline Hunters
      The Indian Fighter
      Murder in Villa Capri
      Seminole Uprising
      Seven Angry Men
      Shotgun
      Trial
      Violent Saturday
      White Feather
1956 The Broken Star
      The Burning Hills
      Daniel Boone, Trail Blazer
      The Last Hunt

      The Lone Ranger
      Quincannon, Frontier
          Scout
      Secret of Treasure Mountain
      Secret of Treasure
          Mountain
      The White Squaw
1957 The Brothers Rico
      Edge of the City
      The Guns of Fort Petticoat
      The Halliday Brand
      Journey to Freedom
      The Lawless Eighties
      Man in the Shadow
      The Midnight Story
      Raiders of Old California
      Ride Out for Revenge
      The Tin Star
      Twelve Angry Men
1958 Ambush at Cimarron Pass
      Escape from Red Rock
      Gun Fever
      Gunfire at Indian Gap
      Gunman's Walk
      The Light in the Forest
      The Lone Ranger and the
          Lost City of Gold
      Never Love a Stranger
      Terror in a Texas Town
      Touch of Evil
1959 Al Capone
      The Black Orchid
      The Crimson Kimono
      The Crimson Kimono
      The FBI Story
      Gunmen from Laredo
      Inside the Mafia
      Last Train from Gun Hill
      Porgy and Bess
      The Wonderful Country
1960 Flaming Star
      Key Witness
      Oklahoma Territory
      Pay or Die
      The Pusher
      Sergeant Rutledge
      The Unforgiven
      Walk Tall

Joaquin Murieta
1931 The Avenger
1953 The Man Behind the Gun
Murphy beds
1935 Annie Oakley
Museums
1917 The Bond Between
1937 A Study of Negro Artists
1938 Breaking the Ice
1939 Mr. Moto Takes a Vacation
1943 The Leopard Man
1944 Cry of the Werewolf
1945 The Mummy's Curse
1946 Dangerous Money
1949 Jigsaw
1960 The Day They Robbed the
          Bank of England
Music
1915 The Melting Pot
1936 Sins of Man
1938 Dangerous to Know
1940 Broken Strings
1953 The Glory Brigade
Music boxes
1932 The Golden West
1944 Lake Placid Serenade
      Since You Went Away
Music halls
1926 The Strong Man
Music publishers and publishing
1943 Dixie
1945 Rhapsody in Blue
1948 Music Man
Music schools
1933 Best of Enemies
1947 Humoresque
Music stores
1954 Hell's Half Acre
Music students
1916 The Yellow Passport
1933 Best of Enemies
1940 The Jewish Melody

Music teachers
1917 Unknown 274
1927 The Scar of Shame
1934 Beloved
1935 El cantante de Nápoles
1938? Amore che non torna
1940 The Jewish Melody
      Overture to Glory
1945 Rhapsody in Blue
      Salome, Where She Danced
1951 Molly
1953 Tonight We Sing
1956 The Benny Goodman Story
Musical instruments
1941 Where Did You Get That
          Girl?
Musical revues
1919 Spotlight Sadie
1929 Mother's Boy
      Why Bring That Up?
1930 King of Jazz
1941 Louisiana Purchase
      Mazel Tov Yidden
1943 The Gang's All Here
      Riding High
1944 Chip Off the Old Block
      Slightly Terrific
      Something for the Boys
1950 Catskill Honeymoon
      Monticello, Here We Come!
1953 The Eddie Cantor Story
1956 Rockin' the Blues
1958 Marjorie Morningstar
Musicians
1916 Civilization's Child
1917 The Woman and the Beast
1918 Love's Law
1922 Breaking Home Ties
1929 Is Everybody Happy?
      Smiling Irish Eyes
1930 Check and Double Check
      The Last Dance
      The Melody Man
      Revista Hispano-Americana
1931 Such Is Life
1932 Harlem Is Heaven
      Men Are Such Fools
1933 Yo, tú y ella
1934 Coming Out Party
1935 El día que me quieras
      Harmony Lane
      Naughty Marietta
1936 Yiddle with His Fiddle
1937 That Girl from Paris
1940 Mystery in Swing
      Paradise in Harlem
1941 Birth of the Blues
      Sun Valley Serenade
1942 Seven Sweethearts
      Syncopation
1943 Bataan
      Dixie
      Doughboys in Ireland
      Redhead from Manhattan
      Tahiti Honey
      Three Hearts for Julia
1945 South of the Rio Grande
1946 Beware
      Dirty Gertie from Harlem,
          U.S.A.
      Singin' in the Corn
      Slightly Scandalous
1946? House-Rent Party
1947 Calendar Girl
      Jivin' in Be-Bop
      New Orleans
1948 Moonrise
      Music Man
      Singin' Spurs
1948? Junction 88
1949 Lookout Sister
      Souls of Sin
1950 Young Man with a Horn
1950? Three Daughters
1953 The Glass Wall
      The Member of the
          Wedding
1956 The Benny Goodman Story
1958 St. Louis Blues
1960 All the Fine Young
          Cannibals
      I Passed for White

Musk oxen
1936 Tundra
Muslims
1919 Auction of Souls
1953 Dream Wife
Benito Mussolini
1934 The Unknown Soldier
          Speaks
Mutes
1932 Mystery Ranch
1939 El trovador de la radio
1940 Overture to Glory
1945 The Jade Mask
1957 The Ride Back
      Run of the Arrow
      Trooper Hook
1958 Blood Arrow
Mutiny
1916 Unprotected
1918 Wild Women
1936 Sutter's Gold
1937 Slave Ship
1941 Mutiny in the Arctic
      This Woman Is Mine
1945 Johnny Angel
      Where Do We Go From
          Here?
1953 War Paint
1954 Saskatchewan
1959 John Paul Jones
Mysticism
1932 Thirteen Women
1937 Maid of Salem
Mystics
1931 The Black Camel
Mythical characters
1917 The Bottle Imp
1928 Vamping Venus
1949 Tale of the Navajos
Mythical lands
1931 Echec au roi
      Hay que casar al príncipe
1933 Dos noches
1934 La veuve joyeuse
Nannies
1953 The Member of the Wedding
Napa Valley (CA)
1940 They Knew What They
          Wanted
Naples (Italy)
1916 A Woman's Honor
1922 Head over Heels
1925 Cobra
1931 Così è la vita
1932 Cuore d'emigrante
1935 El cantante de Nápoles
1936 Let's Sing Again
1950 Black Hand
      Deported
1951 Go for Broke!
      The Great Caruso
Napoleon I, Emperor of the
    French, 1769-1821
1938 Dangerous to Know
1941 Land of Liberty
Narcotics
    use Drugs
Nashville (TN)
1915? The Life of Sam Davis: A
          Confederate Hero of the
          Sixties
1917 I Will Repay
National Socialism
    use Nazism
Nationalism
1940 The Ramparts We Watch
      The Tragedy of
          Carpatho-Ukraine
1941 Min Jok Jay Hung Sing
1944 We've Come a Long, Long
          Way
Native Alaskans
19?? A Trip Through the Arctic
          with Uncle Sam
1912 The Alaska-Siberian
          Expedition
      Atop of the World in
          Motion
1914 Captain F. E. Kleinschmidt's
          Arctic Hunt
      An Odyssey of the North
1917 Alaska Wonders in Motion

Native Alaskans

1919? Alaska
1921 Wolves of the North
1922 Nanook of the North
1925 Justice of the Far North
Kivalina of the Ice Lands
The True North
1927 Primitive Love
1929 Frozen Justice
1930 The Break Up
1932 Dangers of the Arctic
Igloo
1934 Eskimo
1936 *Sea Spoilers*
Tundra
1940 Girl from God's Country
1941 *Mutiny in the Arctic*
1947 *Spoilers of the North*
1948 *Harpoon*
1949 Arctic Fury
Arctic Manhunt
1952 Arctic Flight
Red Snow
1960 *Ice Palace*

Native Americans
use **Indians of Central
America;
Indians of North
America;
Specific Indian tribes**

Nature conservation
1949 Tulsa

Navajo Indians
1926 The Vanishing American
1927 Drums of the Desert
1929 Redskin
1933 King of the Wild Horses
1934 Laughing Boy
1941 In the Land of the Navajo
1945 El Navajo
The Navajo Trail
1949 The Dalton Gang
Daughter of the West
Tale of the Navajos
1950 *Rio Grande*
1951 *Fort Defiance*
Slaughter Trail
1952 Navajo
1952? Call of the Navajo
1953 *Ambush at Tomahawk Gap*
Column South
1955 Day of Decision
The Vanishing American
1960 *All the Young Men*

Naval bases
use **Military bases;
Military posts**

Naval maneuvers
1959 John Paul Jones

Nazism
use **Nazism**

Nazis
1941 King of the Zombies
Ten Ostatni
They Dare Not Love
Z Dymem Pozarów
1942 *Foreign Agent*
Let's Get Tough!
Nazi Agent
Rio Rita
Secret Enemies
Unseen Enemy
1943 *Gangway for Tomorrow*
Hitler's Children
They Came to Blow Up
America
1944 Address Unknown
They Live in Fear
Tomorrow the World!
1946 Notorious
The Red Dragon
1950 Battleground
1954 Barefoot Battalion
1960 I Aim at the Stars: the
Wernher von Braun Story

Nazism
1933 The Wandering Jew
1934 *The Unknown Soldier
Speaks*
1939 Confessions of a Nazi Spy
1940 Escape
The Man I Married
Three Faces West
1944 We've Come a Long, Long
Way

1958 The Young Lions
Ne'er-do-wells
1914 The Good-for-Nothing
1918 The Little Runaway
1928 The Wages of Sin
1934 *Strange Wives*
1941 *Min Jok Jay Hung Sing*
1941? *The Blood of Jesus*
1942 Lucky Ghost
1945 *A Medal for Benny*
1947 Mantan Runs for Mayor
1948 *Miracle in Harlem*
1949 *Pinky*
Souls of Sin
1951 *Five*
1952 Woman in the Dark
1954 *Hondo*

Nebraska
1953 *The Nebraskan*

Necklaces
1931 *La cautivadora*
1934 Charlie Chan's Courage
1935 *Captured in Chinatown*
1940 *The Jewish Melody*
1941 *Up Jumped the Devil*
1948 Killer Diller
1949 *The Cowboy and the
Indians*
1950 *Border Treasure*
1952 *The Raiders*
1960 *This Rebel Breed*

Needlework
1941 *Come Live with Me*

Neglected children
1918 Wanted, a Mother
1931 *Young Sinners*
1938 The Beloved Brat
1939 *Mothers of Today*
1944 My Pal Wolf
1949 The Quiet One
1959 Imitation of Life
1960 *Ice Palace*

Neglected husbands
1939 *Mothers of Today*
1944 *Mr. Skeffington*

Neglected wives
1916 *The Flower of No Man's
Land*
1918 Her American Husband
1919 *The Other Man's Wife*
1931 *La dama atrevida*
Mamá
1932 *Amore e morte*
Call Her Savage
El hombre que asesinó
1940 *Mexican Spitfire Out West*
1952 *My Man and I*
1953 The Joe Louis Story
1958 *The Defiant Ones*
Home Before Dark
1960 *Ice Palace*

Neighbors
1914 *Springtime*
1916 *The Love Girl*
1929 *The Younger Generation*
1931 Street Scene
1934 *Straight Is the Way*
1935 *Lem Hawkins' Confession*
McFadden's Flats
1937 Green Fields
1939 *Mamele*
1940 Eli Eli
1945 *A Tree Grows in Brooklyn*
1948 Open Secret
1949 *Call of the Forest*
Prejudice
1950 *God, Man and Devil*
1951 *The Girl on the Bridge*
Molly
1953 *So Big*
1955 *The Rose Tattoo*
1956 *The Catered Affair*
1957 *All Mine to Give*
The Midnight Story
1959 *The Black Orchid*
1960 *Flaming Star*

Nephews
1914 *Where the Trail Divides*
1915 *Just Jim*
1917 *Runaway Romany*
1919 *The Little Diplomat*
1919? *When the Desert Smiles*
1932 *Uncle Moses*

1933 *Circle Canyon*
1934 *Judge Priest*
1937 *Law and Lead*
1940 *Charlie Chan's Murder
Cruise*
Mexican Spitfire Out West
Paradise in Harlem
1944 *Tomorrow the World!*
1945 *The Gay Senorita*
1947 *Vigilantes of Boomtown*
1948 *Shanghai Chest*
Silver Trails
1951 *The Well*
1952 *Wagons West*
1954 *Indiscretion of an
American Wife*
1957 *Ride Out for Revenge*
1958 *The Last Hurrah*
1959 *The Last Angry Man*
The Wonderful Country
Yellowstone Kelly

Nervous breakdown
1914 *Springtime*
1934 *Coming Out Party*
1937 *Underworld*
1940 *The Jewish Melody*
Overture to Glory
1949 *We Were Strangers*
1950 *Young Man with a Horn*

Nevada
1924 North of Nevada
1943 *The Ox-Bow Incident*
1948 The Dude Goes West
1958 *Wild Is the Wind*

New Bedford (MA)
1931 Dämon des Meeres

New Deal, 1933-1939
1960 Wild River

New England
1914 The Yellow Traffic
1915 The Grandee's Ring
1916 *A Sister of Six*
Witchcraft
1919 *His Parisian Wife*
1924 Welcome Stranger
1925 My Son
1933 *Ever in My Heart*
1958 The Last Hurrah

New Englanders
1919 *The Westerners*
1941 *Lady from Louisiana*
1959 *The Young Land*
1960 *I Passed for White*

New Jersey
1926 Into Her Kingdom
1940 *Eli Eli*
1942 *Whispering Ghosts*
1943 *Svenskt I Och Omkring
New York*
1946 *Gas House Kids*
1951 *Saturday's Hero*

New London (CT)
1943 Crash Dive

New Mexico
1915 The Penitentes
1917 The Red Woman
1918 *The Man Above the Law*
1927 Aflame in the Sky
1932 *Hidden Valley*
1940 *Too Many Girls*
Young Buffalo Bill
1943 The Leopard Man
The Outlaw
1945 *In Old New Mexico*
1946 *Santa Fe Uprising*
Without Reservations
1947 *Bowery Buckaroos*
Ride the Pink Horse
1948 Four Faces West
1950 *The Furies*
Two Flags West
1951 *Apache Drums*
Only the Valiant
Slaughter Trail
1952 Apache War Smoke
The Battle at Apache Pass
1953 Column South
1954 *Apache*
Salt of the Earth
1955 *The Vanishing American*
1958 *Fort Massacre*
1959 *Gunmen from Laredo*
1960 *For the Love of Mike*
*I Aim at the Stars: the
Wernher von Braun Story*

New Orleans (LA)
1913 *The Inside of the White
Slave Traffic*
1917 The Little Chevalier
Southern Pride
1918 *Find the Woman*
Uncle Tom's Cabin
1921 Love's Plaything
1922 Fair Lady
1925 Scarlet Saint
1928 The Broken Mask
Uncle Tom's Cabin
1930 Behind the Make-Up
1931 *Beyond Victory*
La cautivadora
1932 *Call Her Savage*
1935 *Naughty Marietta*
1936 *Rainbow on the River*
1938 The Buccaneer
Josette
The Toy Wife
1939 *Gone With the Wind*
1940 *New Moon*
1941 Birth of the Blues
Lady from Louisiana
Louisiana Purchase
1942 *Syncopation*
1943 *Dixie*
Tahiti Honey
1944 *Cry of the Werewolf*
1945 *Johnny Angel*
1946 *Saratoga Trunk*
1947 *The Foxes of Harrow*
1950 *Buccaneer's Girl*
Last of the Buccaneers
Panic in the Streets
The Toast of New Orleans
1951 Adventures of Captain
Fabian
A Streetcar Named Desire
1952 *The Iron Mistress*
1955 *Duel on the Mississippi*
1956 *Davy Crockett and the
River Pirates*
1957 *Band of Angels*
Bayou
Raintree County

New Orleans (LA)—Storyville
1947 New Orleans

New Orleans, Battle of, 1815
1938 The Buccaneer

New Rochelle (NY)
1918 *Her American Husband*

New Year's Eve
1931 *Little Caesar*
1933 *Yo, tú y ella*
1936 *After the Thin Man*
1942 *Holiday Inn*
1951 *Show Boat*
1958 *The Young Lions*
1960 *Studs Lonigan*

New York (State)
1915 *How Molly Malone Made
Good*
1936 *Winterset*
1939 *Confessions of a Nazi Spy*
Drums Along the Mohawk
1943 *The Meanest Man in the
World*
1955 *The Long Gray Line*
1956 *Mohawk*
1959 *Odds Against Tomorrow*

**New York Celtics (Basketball
team)**
1951 *The Harlem Globetrotters*

New York City
1913 *The Inside of the White
Slave Traffic*
1914 *The Little Angel of Canyon
Creek*
The Little Jewess
*When Broadway Was a
Trail*
Where the Trail Divides
1915 The Italian
Kreutzer Sonata
The Lamb
The Last of the Mafia
Marse Covington
1915? *Sin*
1916 Broken Fetters
For the Defense
The King's Game
Little Meena's Romance

Man and His Angel
Poor Little Peppina
The Pretenders
A Son of Erin
The Twin Triangle
A Woman's Honor
1917 *The Bond Between*
The Pulse of Life
Unknown 274
The Winged Mystery
1918 *A Broadway Scandal*
The Greatest Thing in Life
Hell's End
Her Moment
The Little Runaway
The Ordeal of Rosetta
Sandy
Set Free
Shifting Sands
The Spreading Evil
Tony America
The Unbeliever
Woman and the Law
1918? *Rosemary Climbs the Heights*
1919 *As a Man Thinks*
A Bachelor's Wife
The Lost Battalion
The Other Man's Wife
Spotlight Sadie
A Yankee Princess
1920 Humoresque
On with the Dance
Pagan Love
The Riddle: Woman
The Third Woman
1920? *The Greatest Love*
Her Story
The Scarlet Dragon
1921 *The Secret Sorrow*
The Sport of the Gods
When the Clock Struck Nine
1921? *The Slave Market*
1922 Come On Over
The Good Provider
The Guttersnipe
Little Miss Smiles
Peacock Alley
Silver Spurs
1923 Anna Christie
Little Old New York
1924 The Night Hawk
Racing Luck
Two Shall Be Born
1925 The Beautiful City
The Greatest Love of All
Salome of the Tenements
1926 Blarney
Broken Hearts
Irene
Private Izzy Murphy
1927 *Blind Alleys*
A Harp in Hock
The Millionaire
Turkish Delight
1928 *Diamond Handcuffs*
1929 *Is Everybody Happy?*
This Is Heaven
When Men Betray
1930 *Anna Christie*
Kathleen Mavourneen
Ladies Love Brutes
Los que danzan
The Melody Man
She Got What She Wanted
Toda una vida
1931 *Beyond Victory*
Carne de cabaret
Delicious
Esclavas de la moda
Le père célibataire
Skyline
Street Scene
Women Love Once
Yankee Don
Zein Weib's Lubovnick
1932 *Call Her Savage*
Charlie Chan's Chance
Cuore d'emigrante
Hombres en mi vida
Mazel Tov
Me and My Gal
O festino o la legge
Symphony of Six Million
Thirteen Women

Unashamed
The Unfortunate Bride
1933 *Counsellor at Law*
Victims of Persecution
1934 *Cuesta abajo*
The Great Flirtation
She Was a Lady
El tango en Broadway
What a Mother-in-Law!
1935 *The Irish in Us*
A Night at the Opera
No matarás
Romance in Manhattan
Shir Hashirim
Te quiero con locura
The Wedding Night
The Winning Ticket
1936 Below the Deadline
Dangerous Intrigue
It Had to Happen
Kelly the Second
Let's Sing Again
Love and Sacrifice
Rainbow on the River
Sins of Man
Star for a Night
La última cita
1937 Big City
Charlie Chan on Broadway
That Girl from Paris
Where Is My Child?
1938 *Castillos en el aire*
City Streets
Di que me quieres
Happy Landing
Josette
Outside of Paradise
The Rage of Paris
Two Sisters
1939 *The Girl from Mexico*
Heaven with a Barbed Wire Fence
Keep Punching
Mothers of Today
My Son
Verbena trágica
Waterfront
1940 *Eli Eli*
If I Had My Way
The Jewish Melody
Little Nellie Kelly
Mexican Spitfire
Murder over New York
The Way of All Flesh
1941 *Come Live with Me*
The Face Behind the Mask
New York Town
They Dare Not Love
This Woman Is Mine
Thunder Over the Prairie
1942 *All Through the Night*
Dr. Gillespie's New Assistant
Friendly Enemies
Holiday Inn
Let's Get Tough!
Mexican Spitfire's Elephant
Secret Enemies
Seven Sweethearts
Sunday Punch
Syncopation
Tales of Manhattan
We Were Dancing
Whispering Ghosts
Woman of the Year
1943 *Dr. Gillespie's Criminal Case*
Doughboys in Ireland
The Girl from Monterrey
His Butler's Sister
Margin for Error
The Meanest Man in the World
Mr. Lucky
Svenkst I Och Omkring New York
Three Hearts for Julia
1944 *An American Romance*
Block Busters
Chip Off the Old Block
Going My Way
Mr. Skeffington
1945 *Between Two Women*
The Great John L.
The House on 92nd St.

The Shanghai Cobra
Where Do We Go From Here?
1946 *Cuban Pete*
1947 *Buck Privates Come Home*
Citizen Saint
Dark Delusion
Easy Come, Easy Go
Humoresque
It Had To Be You
My Wild Irish Rose
New Orleans
Reet, Petite and Gone
1948 Cry of the City
Gentleman's Agreement
The Lady from Shanghai
The Luck of the Irish
Music Man
My Girl Tisa
Sleep, My Love
1949 *C-Man*
The Quiet One
Top O' the Morning
1949? *Come On, Cowboy!*
Girl in Room 20
1950 *Annie Get Your Gun*
The Daughter of Rosie O'Grady
Deported
Give Us This Day
Jolson Sings Again
Young Man with a Horn
1950? *Three Daughters*
1951 *Gambling House*
1952 *Anything Can Happen*
1953 The Glass Wall
The Jazz Singer
The Stars Are Singing
Taxi
Tonight We Sing
1954 *Dangerous Mission*
1955 *Blackboard Jungle*
Trial
The View from Pompey's Head
1956 *The Benny Goodman Story*
Crowded Paradise
Death of a Scoundrel
Rockin' the Blues
1957 Beau James
The Brothers Rico
Edge of the City
Satchmo the Great
1958 *Marjorie Morningstar*
The Young Lions
1959 *The FBI Story*
Inside the Mafia
Odds Against Tomorrow
The World, the Flesh and the Devil
1960 *All the Fine Young Cannibals*
I Passed for White
Man on a String
Weddings and Babies
New York City—Bowery
1913? The Lure of New York
1915 *Chimmie Fadden*
1924 Fools' Highway
1934 *Beloved*
1942 *Tales of Manhattan*
1945 *Sunbonnet Sue*
1947 Bowery Buckaroos
The Mighty McGurk
New York City—Broadway
1925 Lights of Old Broadway
1928 The Jazz Singer
1929 Lucky Boy
Mother's Boy
Why Bring That Up?
1930 Behind the Make-Up
1938 *The Duke Is Tops*
Swing!
1940 *Music in My Heart*
1943 *The Gang's All Here*
Gangway for Tomorrow
Let's Have Fun
Redhead from Manhattan
Yankee Doodle Dandy
1944 Minstrel Man
1945 *I Love a Bandleader*
Rhapsody in Blue
1946 *The Gentleman Misbehaves*
1947 *The Jolson Story*

1953 *The Eddie Cantor Story*
1958 *Marjorie Morningstar*
1959 *Imitation of Life*
New York City—Bronx
1921 Little Italy
1929 Lucky Boy
1930 The Last Dance
1940 *Americaner Schadchen*
1943 *Svenkst I Och Omkring New York*
1951 Molly
1953 *Tonight We Sing*
1955 Marty
1956 The Catered Affair
New York City—Brooklyn
1943 *Svenkst I Och Omkring New York*
1945 A Tree Grows in Brooklyn
1948 *The Dude Goes West*
1949 *Anna Lucasta*
Jigsaw
1950 *Give Us This Day*
The Jackie Robinson Story
1959 *The Last Angry Man*
New York City—Central Park
1938 *Happy Landing*
1941 *Ice-Capades*
1948 *The Lady from Shanghai*
Up in Central Park
1949 *Portrait of Jennie*
1951 *Teresa*
1952 *Anything Can Happen*
New York City—Chinatown
1915 *The Sable Lorcha*
1916 *The Social Buccaneer*
1917 Queen X
1919 Mandarin's Gold
1920? *The Scarlet Dragon*
1921 Wing Toy
New York City—Coney Island
1922 Saturday Night
1940 *The Great Advisor*
1946 *Cuban Pete*
1948 *Big City*
1959 *Imitation of Life*
New York City—East Side
1915 *The Melting Pot*
Time Lock Number 776
1917 *Crime and Punishment*
Rosie O'Grady
1918 A Little Sister of Everybody
1919 The Red Viper
1920 Darling Mine
1921 The Barricade
Little Miss Hawkshaw
1922 Second Hand Rose
Solomon in Society
1924 East of Broadway
1925 Hogan's Alley
1926 The Cohens and Kellys
Kosher Kitty Kelly
Meet the Prince
Millionaires
Rose of the Tenements
1927 The Auctioneer
1929 East Side Sadie
1932 The Heart of New York
Ljubav i strast
Uncle Moses
1933 Obey the Law
1934 Straight Is the Way
1935 McFadden's Flats
1937 *It Could Happen to You*
1939 The Escape
Motel the Operator
1940 East of the River
1944 Block Busters
1946 *Gas House Kids*
1947 *Body and Soul*
1948 Big City
Music Man
1949 *House of Strangers*
1951 *Teresa*
1953 *The Eddie Cantor Story*
New York City—Ellis Island
1918 *One More American*
1922 *My Boy*
1927 A Harp in Hock
1928 The Mating Call
1929 This Is Heaven
1934 *Strange Wives*
1936 Ellis Island
Paddy O'Day

1938 Gateway
1941 *Sun Valley Serenade*
1944 *An American Romance*
1947 *The Mighty McGurk*
1948 *My Girl Tisa*
1951 *Gambling House*

New York City—Fifth Avenue
1922 Solomon in Society
1926 Millionaires
1928 Mother Machree
1929 The Younger Generation
1945 *Sunbonnet Sue*

New York City—Greenwich Village
1918 *The Price of Applause*
1919 Toby's Bow
    Yvonne from Paris
1920 The Devil's Claim
1933 *Rafter Romance*
1947 Calendar Girl

New York City—Harlem
1916 *Three of Many*
1925 The Devil's Disciple
1927 The Spider's Web
1929 Thunderbolt
1930 *Check and Double Check*
1932 *The Black King*
    Harlem Is Heaven
1932? *The Girl from Chicago*
1933? *Scandal*
1934? Harlem After Midnight
1937 *Bargain with Bullets*
    Dark Manhattan
    A Study of Negro Artists
1938 *Life Goes On*
    Sugar Hill Baby
    Swing!
    Two Gun Man from Harlem
1939 Gang Smashers
    Moon over Harlem
    Reform School
    Straight to Heaven
1940 Gang War
    Paradise in Harlem
1941 Murder on Lenox Avenue
1943 *Stormy Weather*
1946 *Dirty Gertie from Harlem, U.S.A.*
    Tall, Tan and Terrific
1946? Harlem on Parade
    House-Rent Party
1947 Boy! What a Girl!
1948 The Fight Never Ends
    Miracle in Harlem
1949 *Lost Boundaries*
    Souls of Sin

New York City—Hell's Kitchen
1927 For the Love of Mike

New York City—History
1914 When Broadway Was a Trail
1917? Barnaby Lee
1936 Dimples
1944 Knickerbocker Holiday

New York City—Jones Beach
1949 *The Girl from Jones Beach*
1951 *Teresa*

New York City—Little Italy
1916 A Child of Mystery
1918 *My Cousin*
    One More American
1919 The Tiger Lily
    Who Will Marry Me?
1921 Little Italy
1926 Puppets
1929 Love, Live and Laugh
1937 Man of the People
1950 Black Hand
1952 Kid Monk Baroni
1960 Pay or Die

New York City—Lower East Side
1915 Cohen's Luck
1916 *Arms and the Woman*
1918 *Hitting the Trail*
1919 Daughter of Mine
    The Volcano
1925 His People
1929 Mother's Boy
    The Younger Generation

New York City—Park Avenue
1946 Bringing Up Father
1947 *Jiggs and Maggie in Society*
1948 *Jiggs and Maggie in Court*

1949 *Jiggs and Maggie in Jackpot Jitters*
1950 *Jiggs and Maggie Out West*

New York City—Second Avenue
1937 *The Cantor's Son*

New York City—Spanish Harlem
1959 Cry Tough
1960 *The Pusher*

New York City—Staten Island
1943 *The Gang's All Here*
    Svenskt I Och Omkring New York

New York City—Times Square
1947 *Copacabana*

New York City—Wall Street
1915 The Rosary
1923 None So Blind
1928 George Washington Cohen

New York Stock Exchange
1930 *El cuerpo del delito*

The New York Times (Newspaper)
1948 *Up in Central Park*

New York Tribune (Newspaper)
1915 How Molly Malone Made Good

New York Yankees (Baseball team)
1942 *Woman of the Year*

New Zealand
1950 *Sands of Iwo Jima*

New Zealanders
1953 *The Glory Brigade*

Newfoundland (Canada)
1959 *John Paul Jones*

Newlyweds
1916 *The Sign of the Poppy*
1918 *Thirty a Week*
1925 *Body and Soul*
1932? *The Girl from Chicago*
1936 *My American Wife*
1937 *The Plainsman*
1940 *New Moon*
1941 *Dead Men Tell*
1942 *Dr. Gillespie's New Assistant*
1943 Ladies' Day
1944 *The Sullivans*
1946 *Canyon Passage*
    The Sailor Takes a Wife
1947 *Desperate*
1948 *Open Secret*
1956 *Hot Blood*
1958 *Touch of Evil*

Newport Beach (CA)
1950 *The Breaking Point*

News vendors
1917 *Rosie O'Grady*
1919 A Fighting Colleen
1921 Little Miss Hawkshaw
1935 *Romance in Manhattan*

Newsboys
1914 *John Barleycorn*
1914? *A Boy and the Law*
1915 *Chimmie Fadden*
1917 *The Trouble Buster*
1920 Dinty
1930 *Sombras de gloria*
1934 *The Cat's-Paw*
1935 *Captured in Chinatown*
1948 Fighting Father Dunne
    The Time of Your Life

Newspaper editors
    use **Editors**

Newspaper publishers
1944 Knickerbocker Holiday
    Marshal of Reno
1945 *Of One Blood*
1946 Santa Fe Uprising
1950 The Lawless
1958 *The Last Hurrah*
1959 *The Oregon Trail*

Newspaper women
    use **Women reporters**

Newspapermen
    use **Reporters**

Newspapers
1917 *A Jewel in Pawn*
    The Wild Girl
1918 The Ranger
1920 *The Dark Mirror*
    Pagan Love

1922 *The Dungeon*
1925 Salome of the Tenements
1931 Cimarron
    The Guilty Generation
1935 *Ruggles of Red Gap*
1936 *Star for a Night*
1937 *Nation Aflame*
1939 Let Freedom Ring
1940 *Gang War*
    Music in My Heart
    The Ramparts We Watch
1942 *Woman of the Year*
1948 *Indian Agent*
1949 *The Gay Amigo*
    Jigsaw
    Portrait of Jennie
    The Red Menace
    Ride, Ryder, Ride!
1950 *The Baron of Arizona*
    The Missourians
1960 *Cimarron*

Newsreel cameramen
1926 *The Passaic Textile Strike*
1928 *The Cameraman*
1938 *Mr. Moto Takes a Chance*
1941 Ice-Capades

Newsreels
1940 The Ramparts We Watch

Nice (France)
1931 *Charlie Chan Carries On*
1958 *Kings Go Forth*

Nicholas II, Czar of Russia, 1868-1918
1926 Into Her Kingdom

Nieces
1917 *The Bride of Hate*
1918 *The Wine Girl*
1930 *Un hombre de suerte*
1931 Oklahoma Jim
1933 *A Lady's Profession*
    The Telegraph Trail
1934 *Chloe: Love Is Calling You*
    Drums O' Voodoo
    The Star Packer
1935 *Charlie Chan in Shanghai*
1936 Ellis Island
1937 *Maid of Salem*
1939 *In Old Caliente*
    Stand Up and Fight
1940 *The Mark of Zorro*
1941 *King of the Zombies*
    Under Fiesta Stars
1942 *Whispering Ghosts*
1945 *The Gay Senorita*
    The Jade Mask
    The Mummy's Curse
    Wanderer of the Wasteland
1946 *Cuban Pete*
1946? *Go Down, Death!*
1948 *Docks of New Orleans*
    Guns of Hate
    Miracle in Harlem
    Western Heritage
1949 *Roll Thunder Roll!*
    She Wore a Yellow Ribbon
    Stallion Canyon
    The Story of Seabiscuit
    3 Godfathers
1950 God, Man and Devil
    Riders of the Pony Express
    Train to Tombstone
1954 *Drum Beat*
1960 *Studs Lonigan*

Night watchmen
    use **Watchmen**

Nightclub entertainers
1946 *Slightly Scandalous*
1947 Copacabana
1956 *Singing in the Dark*
1958 *St. Louis Blues*
1959 *Odds Against Tomorrow*

Nightclub owners
1931 *El pasado acusa*
1932 *Men Are Such Fools*
1937 *Underworld*
1938 *Josette*
    Mis dos amores
1939 *Double Deal*
    Lying Lips
194- Mistaken Identity
1941 Sunday Sinners
1945 *I Love a Bandleader*
    Johnny Angel

1946 Tall, Tan and Terrific
1947 *Copacabana*
    New Orleans
    Sepia Cinderella
1949? *Girl in Room 20*
1951 *Native Son*
1956 *Singing in the Dark*
1958 *St. Louis Blues*

Nightclubs
1927 *The Scar of Shame*
1929 Lucky Boy
1930 *Una cana al aire*
    Charros, gauchos y manolas
    Del mismo barro
    La fuerza del querer
1931 *La cautivadora*
    The Exile
    Gente alegre
1932 *Harlem Is Heaven*
    Men Are Such Fools
    Parigi affascina; ovvero, Malavita
    Scarface
    Ten Minutes to Live
    Veiled Aristocrats
1932? *The Girl from Chicago*
1933 *The Emperor Jones*
    Espérame
    A Lady's Profession
1934 *The Cat's-Paw*
    Limehouse Blues
    She Was a Lady
1935 *Bordertown*
    Lem Hawkins' Confession
    No matarás
    Tango Bar
1936 *After the Thin Man*
    Contra la corriente
1937 *Boy of the Streets*
    Charlie Chan on Broadway
    Think Fast, Mr. Moto
    Underworld
1938 *Birthright*
    Daughter of Shanghai
    Di que me quieres
    The Duke Is Tops
    Happy Landing
    Mis dos amores
    Outside of Paradise
    Passport Husband
    Spirit of Youth
    Swing!
1939 Double Deal
    Forged Passport
    Forged Passport
    The Girl from Mexico
    Keep Punching
    Lying Lips
    Mamele
    Miracle on Main Street
    Moon over Harlem
    One Dark Night
    Straight to Heaven
194- *Mistaken Identity*
1940 *Broken Strings*
    The Fatal Hour
    Gang War
    If I Had My Way
    Mystery in Swing
    The Notorious Elinor Lee
1941 *Charlie Chan in Rio*
    Murder on Lenox Avenue
1941? *The Blood of Jesus*
1942 Holiday Inn
    Mexican Spitfire's Elephant
1943 *Crime Smasher*
    The Gang's All Here
    The Girl from Monterrey
    The Leopard Man
    Redhead from Manhattan
    What's Buzzin' Cousin?
1944 *Andy Hardy's Blonde Trouble*
    Block Busters
    Minstrel Man
1945 *Betrayal from the East*
    Between Two Women
    Club Havana
    I Love a Bandleader
1946 *Cuban Pete*
    Tall, Tan and Terrific
1946? *Beale Street Mama*
1947 *Going to Glory, Come to Jesus*

Hi De Ho
The Jolson Story
Sepia Cinderella
1948 *Half Past Midnight*
Music Man
1949 *Boston Blackie's Chinese Venture*
Jigsaw
1949? Harlem Follies
1950 *Young Man with a Horn*
1952 *The Fabulous Senorita*
1953 *The Glass Wall*
The Jazz Singer
1954 *Carmen Jones*
Hell's Half Acre
1957 *Beau James*
Edge of the City
1958 *Kings Go Forth*
St. Louis Blues
Seven Hills of Rome
1959 *Cry Tough*
Night of the Quarter Moon
The World, the Flesh and the Devil
1960 *All the Fine Young Cannibals*
Man on a String
The Pusher

Nightmares
1945 *Escape in the Fog*

Nihilists
1916 *The King's Game*
The Scarlet Oath

Nobility
1914 *The Squaw Man*
1914? The Mysterious Mr. Wu Chung Foo
1915 *The Clemenceau Case*
Kreutzer Sonata
The Melting Pot
1916 *The Daughter of the Don*
The King's Game
Little Meena's Romance
Lord Loveland Discovers America
Man and His Angel
Poor Little Peppina
The Pretenders
The Social Highwayman
A Woman's Honor
1917 *The Little Chevalier*
The Squaw Man's Son
The Sudden Gentleman
Threads of Fate
Under False Colors
1918 *The Golden Wall*
The Honor of His House
The Little Runaway
The Million Dollar Mystery
Out of a Clear Sky
The Prussian Cur
Ruggles of Red Gap
Shifting Sands
The Squaw Man
A Woman of Impulse
1919 *The Delicious Little Devil*
Diane of the Green Van
Fighting for Gold
Injustice
A Yankee Princess
1919? The Brand of Judas
1920 *Billions*
On with the Dance
1921 *Love's Plaything*
1922 Anna Ascends
Fair Lady
1925 *Cobra*
Scarlet Saint
1928 *The Canyon of Adventure*
The Cavalier
1929 *Die Königsloge*
1930 Take the Heir
1931 *Un caballero de frac*
Cheri-Bibi
Così è la vita
Don Juan diplomático
Drácula
Hay que casar al príncipe
Mi último amor
Nuit d'Espagne
El príncipe gondolero
Young Sinners
1932 *Amor in montagna*
El caballero de la noche
¿Cuándo te suicidas?

A Daughter of Her People
Genoveffa
El hombre que asesinó
Joseph in the Land of Egypt
Parigi affascina; ovvero, Malavita
Yiskor
1934 *Caravane*
Granaderos del amor
La veuve joyeuse
1935 L'homme des Folies Bergère
Julieta compra un hijo
Rosa de Francia
Ruggles of Red Gap
1936 *My American Wife*
1937 *Boots and Saddles*
1938 *Happy Landing*
Mr. Wong, Detective
Rascals
La vida bohemia
1939 *Los hijos mandan*
1940 *Mexican Spitfire*
Mexican Spitfire Out West
New Moon
Overture to Glory
1941 *The Mexican Spitfire's Baby*
They Dare Not Love
1942 *Mexican Spitfire at Sea*
Mexican Spitfire Sees a Ghost
Mexican Spitfire's Elephant
Nazi Agent
We Were Dancing
1943 *Mexican Spitfire's Blessed Event*
1944 *Address Unknown*
1946 *Don Ricardo Returns*
1955 *Kiss of Fire*

Nomads
1922 Nanook of the North
1931 *La ley del harem*

Nome (AK)
1912 *Atop of the World in Motion*
1929 Frozen Justice
1949 *Arctic Manhunt*

Nonconformists
1939 Daughters Courageous

Norfolk (VA)
1937 *Slave Ship*

***Norma* (Opera)**
1931 Jenny Lind

North Carolina
1916 The Colored American Winning His Suit

North Dakota
1940 *Three Faces West*
1951 *Warpath*
1952 *Bugles in the Afternoon*

North West Mounted Police
1920 The Cyclone
1922 The Virgin of Seminole
1930 *Monsieur le Fox*
1934 *Eskimo*
1950 *North of the Great Divide*
1954 *Saskatchewan*

Northerners
1915 *Marse Covington*
1934 *Chloe: Love Is Calling You*
1936 Rainbow on the River
1957 *Bayou*
1960 *Wild River*

Norway
1938 *Happy Landing*

Norwegian Americans
1915 A Yankee from the West
1938 *My Lucky Star*
1945 Our Vines Have Tender Grapes
1948 I Remember Mama

Norwegians
1938 Happy Landing
1940 *Knute Rockne—All American*
1941 Sun Valley Serenade
1943 *Wintertime*

Notre Dame University
use University of Notre Dame

Nouveaux riches
1915 The Spender
1918 Real Folks
1919 A Yankee Princess

1923 Ruggles of Red Gap
1926 April Fool
Millionaires
1930 *Amor audaz*
1935 Ruggles of Red Gap
1937 *The Jester (Der Purimspieler)*
1939 *One Dark Night*
1942 *Lucky Ghost*

Novelists
1918 A Daughter of the Old South
1919 Daughter of Mine
Toby's Bow
1920 The Devil's Claim
1922 Anna Ascends
1930 Son of the Gods
1933 *No dejes la puerta abierta*
Una viuda romántica
1935 The Wedding Night
1939 *Charlie Chan at Treasure Island*
1941 Come Live with Me
1943 Jack London
1946 Without Reservations

Nuclear warfare
1959 The World, the Flesh and the Devil

Nuclear weapons
1952 *Red Snow*

Nudism
1931 *La pura verdad*

Nudity
La cautivadora
1959 *Night of the Quarter Moon*

Numbers racket
1927 The Spider's Web
1932? The Girl from Chicago
1937 Dark Manhattan

Nuns
1916 For the Defense
1927 Rose of the Golden West
1930 Sevilla de mis amores
1932 *O festino o la legge*
1935 *Angelina o el honor de un brigadier*
1945 The Bells of St. Mary's
1946 *Three Wise Fools*
1947 *Citizen Saint*
1958 *Sierra Baron*

Nuremberg (Germany)
1949 *Answer for Anne*

Nursemaids
1914 *John Barleycorn*
1917 *A Kentucky Cinderella*
1921 *Through the Back Door*

Nurses
1915 *The Birth of a Nation*
1916 Lone Star
Three of Many
1917 The Slacker
1918 *The Birth of a Race*
1919 *Evangeline*
His Debt
1919? *America Was Right*
1922 Fair Lady
1931 *La llama sagrada*
1936 *Dangerous Intrigue*
1937 *Song of the City*
1938 Two Sisters
1939 *Confessions of a Nazi Spy*
Gang Smashers
Heaven with a Barbed Wire Fence
King of Chinatown
El trovador de la radio
1940 *Am I Guilty?*
Girl from God's Country
1942 *Dr. Gillespie's New Assistant*
The Navy Comes Through
They Died With Their Boots On
1943 *Bataan*
Dr. Gillespie's Criminal Case
1944 *Lifeboat*
Since You Went Away
Three Men in White
1945 *Between Two Women*
Escape in the Fog
In Old New Mexico
Pride of the Marines
1947 Buck Privates Come Home

1948 *Cry of the City*
Four Faces West
The Golden Eye
1949 *Harbor of Missing Men*
Lookout Sister
Pinky
The Story of Seabiscuit
1950 *Emergency Wedding*
Jolson Sings Again
The Men
North of the Great Divide
1951 Queen for a Day
1952 *Arctic Flight*
Japanese War Bride
1952? Call of the Navajo
1954 Siege at Red River
1955 *Foxfire*
Good Morning, Miss Dove
Marty
Not As a Stranger
Violent Saturday
1957 *Journey to Freedom*

Nursing back to health
1914 The Nightingale
1915? The Beachcomber
1916 Her Debt of Honor
A Yoke of Gold
1917 *The Bronze Bride*
1918 *Amarilly of Clothes-Line Alley*
The Red, Red Heart
1919 *A Bachelor's Wife*
His Debt
The Red Viper
The She Wolf
1920 *The Dark Mirror*
1931 *The Cisco Kid*
1932 *The Golden West*
1933 *Broken Dreams*
1934 *Behold My Wife!*
Broadway Bill
Nada más que una mujer
1939 *Drums Along the Mohawk*
King of Chinatown
1943 *The Outlaw*
1945 *The Navajo Trail*
1946 *Sunset Pass*
1949 *The Clay Pigeon*
1950 *Young Man with a Horn*
1955 *The Lonesome Trail*
Seven Angry Men
1957 *Gun Battle at Monterey*
1958 *Flaming Frontier*
1959 *The Hanging Tree*
Porgy and Bess
Yellowstone Kelly

Nursing homes
1960 *Weddings and Babies*

Annie Oakley
1935 Annie Oakley
1947 *Thunder Mountain*
1950 Annie Get Your Gun

Oases
1958 Apache Territory

Oaths
1927 *With Sitting Bull at the Spirit Lake Massacre*
1928 *Eleven P.M.*
1930 *Anna Christie*
1947 *Dangerous Venture*
1953 *Conquest of Cochise*
1954 *Barefoot Battalion*
Thunder Pass

Obesity
1923 Look Your Best
1949 *That Midnight Kiss*

Obsession
1946 *The Face of Marble*
1948 *Red River*
1950 *Two Flags West*
1951 *Warpath*
1953 The Member of the Wedding
1954 *Apache*
Carmen Jones
1956 The Searchers
1957 *Naked in the Sun*
1958 Wild Is the Wind
1959 Shake Hands with the Devil

Obstinacy
1953 *Bright Road*

Ocean liners
1927 Bitter Apples
1931 *Charlie Chan Carries On*
En cada puerto un amor

Ocean liners
1932 Hypnotized
    Parigi affascina; ovvero, Malavita
1932? *The Girl from Chicago*
1933 Best of Enemies
    Charlie Chan's Greatest Case
    No dejes la puerta abierta
1934 *The Great Flirtation*
1935 *Julieta compra un hijo*
1936 *Charlie Chan at the Race Track*
    Yiddle with His Fiddle
1937 *Charlie Chan at the Olympics*
    Charlie Chan on Broadway
    That Girl from Paris
    Think Fast, Mr. Moto
1938 *Gateway*
    Hawaii Calls
1939 *Mr. Moto Takes a Vacation*
1953 *Tonight We Sing*
1960 The Last Voyage

Oceanside (CA)
1949 *The Clay Pigeon*

Octopi
1946 *Strange Voyage*
1953 *Beneath the 12-Mile Reef*

Octoroons and quadroons
  use **African Americans—Mixed blood**

Officers (Military)
1915 The Girl I Left Behind Me
    Marse Covington
1916 *At Piney Ridge*
    Britton of the Seventh
    The Daughter of the Don
    Gold and the Woman
1917 *The Adventures of Carol*
    The Hidden Children
    John Ermine of the Yellowstone
    The Little Boy Scout
    The Secret Game
1918 *His Birthright*
    I Want to Forget
    Johanna Enlists
    Little Red Decides
    The Unbeliever
1919 The Lost Battalion
    A Yankee Princess
1919? *The Brand of Judas*
1920 Li Ting Lang
1925 *Custer's Last Fight*
    Tonio, Son of the Sierras
1926 General Custer at Little Big Horn
1930 ¡De frente, marchen!
    Olimpia
1931 The Cisco Kid
    Echec au roi
    Hay que casar al príncipe
    Monerías
    El tenorio del harem
1932 *El caballero de la noche*
    El hombre que asesinó
1934 Caravane
    Granaderos del amor
    La veuve joyeuse
1935 *Alas sobre el Chaco*
    Angelina o el honor de un brigadier
1936 *The Bold Caballero*
    The Glory Trail
    Hair-Trigger Casey
    The Last of the Mohicans
    Rebellion
    Ride, Ranger, Ride
1937 *The Barrier*
    Boots and Saddles
    Drums of Destiny
    Thank You, Mr. Moto
1938 *Hawaii Calls*
1939 *Cossacks in Exile*
    Frontiers of '49
1940 *Kit Carson*
    Santa Fe Trail
1941 *Belle Starr*
    Saddlemates
1942 *Valley of Hunted Men*
1943 Crash Dive
    Tahiti Honey
1944 *Chip Off the Old Block*
    Since You Went Away

Something for the Boys
    The Sullivans
1945 *Salome, Where She Danced*
1946 *Till the End of Time*
    Without Reservations
1947 *Buck Privates Come Home*
    King of the Bandits
    Last of the Redmen
    Little Mister Jim
    Northwest Outpost
    Pirates of Monterey
1948 Fort Apache
    Gentleman's Agreement
    Tap Roots
1949 Apache Chief
    The Fighting Kentuckian
    The Gay Amigo
    Home of the Brave
    Massacre River
1950 *Ambush*
    Bandit Queen
    Battleground
    Broken Arrow
    Davy Crockett, Indian Scout
    I Killed Geronimo
    Indian Territory
    The Iroquois Trail
    North of the Great Divide
    Rio Grande
    Sands of Iwo Jima
    Train to Tombstone
    Young Daniel Boone
1951 *Cyclone Fury*
    Distant Drums
    Go for Broke!
    The House on Telegraph Hill
    The Last Outpost
    Little Big Horn
    Mask of the Dragon
    New Mexico
    Oh! Susanna
    Only the Valiant
    Slaughter Trail
    The Steel Helmet
    The Tall Target
    Teresa
1952 *The Battle at Apache Pass*
    Brave Warrior
    Bright Victory
    Bugles in the Afternoon
    Indian Uprising
    Red Ball Express
    The Savage
1953 *The Charge at Feather River*
    Column South
    The Glory Brigade
    The Man from the Alamo
    The Pathfinder
    Seminole
    The Stand at Apache River
    War Paint
1954 *Sitting Bull*
    Taza, Son of Cochise
    They Rode West
1955 *Apache Ambush*
    Chief Crazy Horse
    The Gun That Won the West
    The Indian Fighter
    The Long Gray Line
    Seminole Uprising
    Seven Cities of Gold
1956 Comanche
    The Last Wagon
    Pillars of the Sky
    Quincannon, Frontier Scout
1957 *Apache Warrior*
    Dragoon Wells Massacre
    The Guns of Fort Petticoat
    Naked in the Sun
    Raiders of Old California
    Ride Out for Revenge
    Tomahawk Trail
1958 *Ambush at Cimarron Pass*
    Flaming Frontier
    Fort Bowie
    Fort Massacre
    Kings Go Forth
    The Light in the Forest
    Oregon Passage
    Tonka

The Young Lions
1959 John Paul Jones
    The Wonderful Country
    Yellowstone Kelly
1960 *I Aim at the Stars: the Wernher von Braun Story*
    Sergeant Rutledge
    Walk Tall

Oglala Indians
1952 *The Savage*

Ohio
1926 Laddie
1935 *Annie Oakley*
1940 *Jennie*
1943 *Dixie*
1954 *Siege at Red River*

Ohio River
1918 *Uncle Tom's Cabin*
1956 *Davy Crockett and the River Pirates*
1958 *The Light in the Forest*

Oil
1914 *Where the Trail Divides*
1916 *The Pretenders*
1917 *The Peddler*
1918 *Real Folks*
1919 *Hearts of Men*
1920 *The Symbol of the Unconquered*
1921 *By Right of Birth*
    The Money Maniac
1927 Drums of the Desert [Japanese-American Film]
1929 *Redskin*
1930 The Bad Man
1931 *Cimarron*
1934 'Neath the Arizona Skies
1940 Phantom of Chinatown
1944 The San Antonio Kid
1947 *Buffalo Bill Rides Again*
1949 *Lookout Sister*
1953 *Dream Wife*
    Thunder Bay
1957 The Oklahoman
1958 Terror in a Texas Town

Oil companies
1947 *On the Old Spanish Trail*
1949 Tulsa
1956 *Death of a Scoundrel*

Oil fields
1921 Lonely Heart
1924 Yankee Speed
1940 *Midnight Shadow*

Oil magnates
1938? *Amore che non torna*
1953 *Dream Wife*
    Thunder Bay
1960 *Cimarron*

Oil prospectors
1928 Black Gold
1948 Louisiana Story
1953 Thunder Bay
1957 Joe Dakota

Oil wells
1924 Tongues of Flame
1947 *Black Gold*
1948 Louisiana Story
1949 *Tulsa*
1956 Giant
1957 Joe Dakota

Oilmen
1915 *The Secret Sin*
1943 In Old Oklahoma

Ojibwa Indians
  use **Chippewa Indians**

Okefenokee Swamp (FL)
1947 Untamed Fury

Oklahoma
1921 *By Right of Birth*
    Cotton and Cattle
1922 The Crimson Skull
1927 The Spider's Web
1931 *Cimarron*
1933 *Diplomaniacs*
1941 *Hurry, Charlie, Hurry*
1943 *In Old Oklahoma*
1947 *Black Gold*
1949 Tulsa
1951 *Jim Thorpe—All-American*
1952 *Rose of Cimarron*
1956 *Reprisal!*
1957 The Oklahoman

1959 *The FBI Story*
1960 Cimarron
    The Dark at the Top of the Stairs
    Oklahoma Territory

Chauncey Olcott
1947 My Wild Irish Rose

Old persons
  use **Aged men;**
        Aged persons;
        Aged women

Olympic games
1937 Charlie Chan at the Olympics
1951 *Jim Thorpe—All-American*

Olympic Games, Los Angeles, 1932
1936 Contra la corriente

Omaha (NE)
1941 *Western Union*

Ontario (Canada)
1930 The Silent Enemy

Open marriage
1941 Come Live with Me

Opera
1920 *The Paliser Case*
1925 *The Midnight Girl*
1930 Sevilla de mis amores
1931 *Drácula*
    Jenny Lind
1934 Blossom Time
    La buenaventura
1935 El cantante de Nápoles
    Shir Hashirim
1938 *The Rage of Paris*
1939 *Mamele*
1941 Golden Gate Girl
1946 *Saratoga Trunk*
1949 *House of Strangers*
1951 *The Great Caruso*
1960 *Pay or Die*

Opera houses
1948 *Up in Central Park*
1949 That Midnight Kiss

Opera singers
1914 The Nightingale
1915 *How Molly Malone Made Good*
1916 *The Flower of No Man's Land*
    The Yellow Passport
1918 *The City of Tears*
    Find the Woman
    My Cousin
    A Woman of Impulse
1918? Rosemary Climbs the Heights
1930 *Galas de la Paramount*
1933 *Primavera en otoño*
1934 Las fronteras del amor
1935 A Night at the Opera
1936 Let's Sing Again
1937 Charlie Chan at the Opera
    Manhattan Merry-Go-Round
    Music for Madame
    That Girl from Paris
1940 Overture to Glory
1944 Going My Way
1947 *Carnegie Hall*
    New Orleans
    New Orleans
1948 *Up in Central Park*
1949 That Midnight Kiss
1950 The Toast of New Orleans
1951 The Great Caruso
1953 The Stars Are Singing
    Tonight We Sing
1956 Serenade

Operations, Surgical
1916 Lone Star
1917 *A Love Sublime*
    The Tell-Tale Step
1918 *Wanted, a Mother*
1919 *Come Out of the Kitchen*
1920 *Pagan Love*
    The Secret Gift
1932 *Le cas du docteur Brenner*
    No Greater Love
    Symphony of Six Million
1932? *The Girl from Chicago*
1936 Dangerous Intrigue
1938 *City Streets*
    Spawn of the North

1940   *Girl from God's Country*
1941   *Adam Had Four Sons*
1943   *Dr. Gillespie's Criminal Case*
1944   *Lifeboat*
1945   *Between Two Women*
1948   *Cry of the City*
1949   *Harbor of Missing Men*
1955   *Good Morning, Miss Dove*
      Not As a Stranger
1956   *Westward Ho the Wagons!*

Opium
1916   Hop, the Devil's Brew
1917   *Queen X*
1918   The Border Raiders
      The Midnight Patrol
1919   *The Tong Man*
1920   *Dinty*
1920?   *The Scarlet Dragon*
1921   Bits of Life
      Shame
1925   Tearing Through
1932   *The Hatchet Man*
1935   Charlie Chan in Shanghai

Opium dens
1915   *The Secret Sin*
1917   The Flower of Doom
1931   *Del infierno al cielo*

Opportunists
1955   Not As a Stranger

Optimism
1934   Stand Up and Cheer!

Optometrists
1944   *Waterfront*

Orange groves
1952   *Anything Can Happen*

Orangemen
1925   Lights of Old Broadway

Oranges
1939   *Heaven with a Barbed Wire Fence*

Orchestras
1940   *Paradise in Harlem*
1943   Three Hearts for Julia
      What's Buzzin' Cousin?
1947   Carnegie Hall
      Jivin' in Be-Bop
1958   *St. Louis Blues*

Orchids
1951   *Native Son*

Orderlies (Hospital)
1917   *A Love Sublime*

Ordnance
1915   *The Lamb*
1918   *The Firebrand*
1920   Dangerous Days

Oregon
1919?   In the Land of the Setting Sun; or, Martyrs of Yesterday
1928   Orphan of the Sage
1931   La gran jornada
1934   Wagon Wheels
1940   *Three Faces West*
1941   *This Woman Is Mine*
1946   *Canyon Passage*
1954   Battle of Rogue River
      Drum Beat
1956   Raw Edge
1958   Oregon Passage

Oregon Trail
1931   La gran jornada
1940   Kit Carson
1956   Westward Ho the Wagons!
1959   The Oregon Trail

Organ grinders
1914   *The Nightingale*
1917   *The Adventures of Carol*

Organ transplants
     use **Transplantation of organs, tissues, etc.**

Organists
1942   *Mokey*
1946   *Cuban Pete*
1950   *Stars in My Crown*

Organs
1938   *Dangerous to Know*
1958   *St. Louis Blues*

Orgies
1947   *Going to Glory, Come to Jesus*

Ornithologists
1950   *Mystery Street*

Orphanages
1917   *Unknown 274*
1932   *No Greater Love*
1936   *Let's Sing Again*
1937   *Where Is My Child?*
1938   City Streets
1942   *Woman of the Year*
1947   *Citizen Saint*
1957   *The Midnight Story*
1958   *Never Love a Stranger*

Orphans
1914   The Little Angel of Canyon Creek
      Where the Trail Divides
1915   *Captain Courtesy*
1916   Broken Fetters
      Her Debt of Honor
1917   *Follow the Girl*
      A Jewel in Pawn
      A Kentucky Cinderella
      The Little Boy Scout
      The Little Samaritan
      The Trouble Buster
      A Wife by Proxy
1918   *An Alien Enemy*
      Little Red Decides
      The Unbeliever
1919   *The Gray Towers Mystery*
      The Little Diplomat
1920   The Girl of My Heart
      Our Christianity and Nobody's Child
      The Secret Gift
1920?   *Broken Hearts*
1921   A Modern Cain
      Through the Back Door
1922   My Boy
1923   The Huntress
      Regeneration
      Snowdrift
1925   Lights of Old Broadway
1926   Rose of the Tenements
      Sweet Rosie O'Grady
1927   A Harp in Hock
      Sally in Our Alley
1928   United States Smith
1930   *Sei tu l'amore*
1931   *Gentleman's Fate*
      Huckleberry Finn
1932   *Marido y mujer*
      No Greater Love
1933   Racetrack
1935   *Naughty Marietta*
      Romance in Manhattan
      Wolf Riders
1935?   *The Irish Gringo*
1936   Let's Sing Again
      Rainbow on the River
1937   *Green Fields*
      Natalka Poltavka
1938   Hawaii Calls
      The Singing Blacksmith
1939   The Escape
1940   If I Had My Way
      Tengo fe en ti
1943   The Amazing Mrs. Holliday
1944   *Tomorrow the World!*
1946   *Cuban Pete*
      Romance of the West
      Three Wise Fools
      Wild Beauty
1946?   *Go Down, Death!*
1947   Black Gold
      Black Gold
      Buck Privates Come Home
      The Mighty McGurk
      Oregon Trail Scouts
      The Return of Rin Tin Tin
1948   *The Boy with Green Hair*
      The Fight Never Ends
      Fighting Father Dunne
      Shep Comes Home
1950   *Stars in My Crown*
1951   *Cyclone Fury*
      The Steel Helmet
1953   *The Man from the Alamo*
1954   Barefoot Battalion
      Saskatchewan
1957   All Mine to Give
      The Ride Back
1958   *Kings Go Forth*
      The Light in the Forest
      The Lone Ranger and the Lost City of Gold

      Never Love a Stranger
      Ride a Crooked Trail
1960   For the Love of Mike

Orthodox Eastern Church
1953   *Beneath the 12-Mile Reef*

Osage Indians
1931   *Cimarron*
1952   Fort Osage
      Trail of the Arrow
1959   *The FBI Story*

Osceola, Seminole chief, 1804–1838
1953   Seminole
1957   Naked in the Sun

Ostracism
1914   When Broadway Was a Trail
1916   The Half-Breed
1917   *The Bride of Hate*
      Her Own People
      The Little Samaritan
      My Fighting Gentleman
      The Primitive Call
1919   The Courageous Coward
1920   Li Ting Lang
1931   Quand on est belle
1932   A Daughter of Her People
      Mazel Tov
1933   *The Eternal Jew*
1934   *Laughing Boy*
      She Was a Lady
1936   The Prisoner of Shark Island
      Show Boat
1939   Tevya
1940   *The Ramparts We Watch*
1941   *Birth of the Blues*
1942   *King of the Stallions*
      Young America
1947   California
      Going to Glory, Come to Jesus
1948   *Big City*
      The Boy with Green Hair
1951   *Show Boat*
1952   *Hiawatha*
1955   *Duel on the Mississippi*
1956   *Man from Del Rio*
1958   *Home Before Dark*
      The Light in the Forest
1960   *I Passed for White*

Othello (Opera)
1956   *Serenade*

Othello (Play)
1940   *Paradise in Harlem*

Ottawa Indians
1948   *Unconquered*
1951   *When the Redskins Rode*
1952   *Battles of Chief Pontiac*

Outlaws
1917   The Gun Fighter
1918   The Hell Cat
      The Squaw Man
1922   The Crimson Skull
1924?   The Flaming Crisis
1926   Desert Gold
1930   El precio de un beso
1931   Call of the Rockies
      Cavalier of the West
      Cimarron
      The Cisco Kid
      Tropennächte
      Yankee Don
1932   The Galloping Kid
      Law and Lawless
      The Rainbow Trail
      Riders of the Desert
1933   Circle Canyon
1934   The Cactus Kid
      Call of the Coyote
      The Fighting Hero
      'Neath the Arizona Skies
      The Star Packer
      Wheels of Destiny
1935   Cyclone of the Saddle
1935?   The Irish Gringo
1936   The Bold Caballero
      The Phantom of Santa Fe
      Rose of the Rancho
      Silly Billies
      Song of the Gringo
1937   *The Barrier*
      Harlem on the Prairie
1938   *The Buccaneer*
      Two Gun Man from Harlem
      Wild Horse Canyon

1939   Bad Lands
      Drifting Westward
      Frontiers of '49
1940   *Arizona Frontier*
      Hi-Yo Silver
      Lucky Cisco Kid
      Viva Cisco Kid
1941   Ride on Vaquero
      Road Agent
      Western Union
1943   *Border Patrol*
      Land of Hunted Men
1944   Outlaw Trail
      The San Antonio Kid
      Sonora Stagecoach
1945   Great Stagecoach Robbery
      Phantom of the Plains
1946   California Gold Rush
      Canyon Passage
      Renegade Girl
      Sunset Pass
1947   The Adventures of Don Coyote
      Buffalo Bill Rides Again
      King of the Bandits
      Marshal of Cripple Creek
      Oregon Trail Scouts
      Under the Tonto Rim
      Vigilantes of Boomtown
1948   The Paleface
1949   Colorado Territory
      The Dalton Gang
      The Golden Stallion
      Ranger of Cherokee Strip
      Roll Thunder Roll!
      Streets of Laredo
      3 Godfathers
1949?   Come On, Cowboy!
1950   Border Treasure
      Cherokee Uprising
      The Missourians
      Rocky Mountain
      Sunset in the West
      Winchester '73
1951   *Flaming Feather*
1952   Apache Country
      Brave Warrior
      High Noon
      The Raiders
      Rose of Cimarron
1953   *Ride, Vaquero!*
1955   *Apache Woman*
1957   The Guns of Fort Petticoat
      The Tin Star
1958   Escape from Red Rock
      Ride a Crooked Trail
1959   *The Young Land*
1960   *Cimarron*

Overland Pacific Railroad
1954   Overland Pacific

Overland Stage Co.
1927   The Overland Stage

Overseers
1917   *The Bride of Hate*
1939   *Gone With the Wind*
1944   *Dark Waters*
1946   *Don Ricardo Returns*
1947   Bells of San Fernando

Jesse Owens
1944   *The Negro Soldier*

Owls
1949   *Tale of the Navajos*

Oysters
1920   It's a Great Life

Pacific Ocean
1917   *The Secret Game*

Pacifism and pacifists
1916   *The Fall of a Nation*
1931   Beyond Victory
1935   So Red the Rose
1943   *Bataan*
1948   The Boy with Green Hair
1952   Hiawatha
      High Noon
1955   *Violent Saturday*
1957   The Lawless Eighties
1960   The Plunderers

Paddleboats
1936   *General Spanky*

Paganism
1924   *Untamed Youth*

I Pagliacci (Opera)
1935 *A Night at the Opera*
1942 *Twin Beds*
Painters (Of houses)
    use **Hopainters**
Painters (Of paintings)
1916 The Soul of Kura-San
1919 Bonnie, Bonnie Lassie
      The Gray Horizon
      The Last of His People
      The Sneak
1933 The Wandering Jew
1937 A Study of Negro Artists
1945 *Rhapsody in Blue*
1947 *Body and Soul*
      Calendar Girl
1949 *Jigsaw*
      Portrait of Jennie
1952 *The Iron Mistress*
Painters (Of signs)
    use **Sign painters and sign
      painting**
Paintings
1916 *The Soul of Kura-San*
1917 *The Bond Between*
1930 Charros, gauchos y manolas
1933 The Wandering Jew
1934 *Granaderos del amor*
1937 Thank You, Mr. Moto
1941 *In the Land of the Navajo*
1945 *Salome, Where She Danced*
      Samurai
1947 *Calendar Girl*
1949 Portrait of Jennie
Paiute Indians
1934 *Laughing Boy*
1948 The Dude Goes West
1955 *Kiss of Fire*
1958 *Fort Massacre*
Palaces
1918 *Good-Bye, Bill*
1930 *Wu Li Chang*
1931 *Hay que casar al príncipe*
      El príncipe gondolero
1933 *The Emperor Jones*
      El rey de los gitanos
Palermo (Sicily)
1912 *The Adventures of
      Lieutenant Petrosino*
1960 *Pay or Die*
Palestine
1921 *The Syrian Immigrant*
1931 *The Voice of Israel*
1933 *The Wandering Jew*
1937 The Holy Oath
1950 *Catskill Honeymoon*
Palomino horses
      The Palomino
Palouse Indians
1956 Pillars of the Sky
Pampas (Argentina)
1931 *Las luces de Buenos Aires*
Pamphleteers
1918 The Firebrand
Panama
1950 *The Jackie Robinson Story*
Panama Canal (Panama)
1940 *Charlie Chan in Panama*
1942 Across the Pacific
      Nazi Agent
1945 Betrayal from the East
**Panama-Pacific International
  Exposition**
1915 *Chimmie Fadden Out West*
      *The Pageant of San
      Francisco*
Pancakes, waffles, etc.
1942 *Woman of the Year*
Panic
1951 *Teresa*
1955 *The Indian Fighter*
1960 *The Last Voyage*
Panthers
1942 Cat People
Pants-pressers
1926 April Fool
Paperboys
    use **Newsboys**
Parachuting
1943 *Air Force*
1948 *Night Wind*

Parades
1919 *The Lost Battalion*
1921? [*Unidentified Film*]
1934 *Judge Priest*
      Stand Up and Cheer!
      La veuve joyeuse
1936 *The Prisoner of Shark
      Island*
1943 *Yankee Doodle Dandy*
1945 *Where Do We Go From
      Here?*
1947 *The Mighty McGurk*
      Ride the Pink Horse
1950 *The Daughter of Rosie
      O'Grady*
1955 *The Long Gray Line*
1956 *Giant*
1957 *Beau James*
1959 *The Crimson Kimono*
Paraguay
1935 *Alas sobre el Chaco*
Paralysis
1925 Scarlet Saint
1932 *Me and My Gal*
1936 *Down to the Sea*
1940 *Broken Strings*
1943 *Dixie*
1945 *Wanderer of the Wasteland*
1947 *The Burning Cross*
1948 *Tap Roots*
1960 *The Plunderers*
Paramount Pictures Corp.
1941 *Hold Back the Dawn*
Paranoia
1940 *The Ramparts We Watch*
1947 *It Had To Be You*
Paraplegics
1942 Dr. Gillespie's New Assistant
1943 Dr. Gillespie's Criminal
      Case
1950 The Men
      Train to Tombstone
Pardons
1914 *The Littlest Rebel*
1915 *The Birth of a Nation*
1916 *Unprotected*
1917 *The Gun Fighter*
1919 *Love and the Law*
1931 Pardon Us
1935 *The Littlest Rebel*
1938 *The Renegade Ranger*
1950 *Bandit Queen*
1952 *The Raiders*
Parentage
1914 At the Cross Roads
1915 Just Jim
      The Nigger
      The Penitentes
      Under Southern Skies
1916 *At Piney Ridge*
      The Flames of Johannis
      The Grip of Jealousy
      The Half-Breed
1916? Should a Baby Die?
1917 The Adventures of Carol
      The Bride of Hate
      The Call of Her People
      The Call of the East
      John Ermine of the
      Yellowstone
      The Little Samaritan
      Lost in Transit
      Runaway Romany
      Sold at Auction
      Sunshine and Gold
      Threads of Fate
1918 The Kaiser's Finish
      The Only Road
      The Ranger
      Tongues of Flame
      Tony America
1918? The Snail
1919 Desert Gold
      A Heart in Pawn
      Injustice
      Just Squaw
      The Last of His People
      A Man's Duty
1920 The Dark Mirror
      The Last of the Mobicans
      The Riddle: Woman
      Rio Grande
      The Third Woman

1920? Broken Hearts
1921 Across the Divide
      By Right of Birth
      The Girl from God's
      Country
      A Tale of Two Worlds
      Through the Back Door
1922 The Crow's Nest
      Pawn Ticket 210
      The Woman He Loved
1923 The Huntress
      Suzanna
1925 A Daughter of the Sioux
1926 The Barrier
1927 The Love Mart
1931 *Così è la vita*
      Gentleman's Fate
      Le père célibataire
      Skyline
1932 *Amor in montagna*
1933 *Circle Canyon*
1934 Chloe: Love Is Calling You
      Judge Priest
      'Neath the Arizona Skies
1936 Rainbow on the River
1937 I Want to Be a Mother
1939 *Fisherman's Wharf*
      Judge Hardy and Son
1940 Her Second Mother
1944 Minstrel Man
1950? *Three Daughters*
1957 *Band of Angels*
      The Deerslayer
1960 The Unforgiven
Parenthood
1933 Broken Dreams
1944 *My Pal Wolf*
1953 *The Joe Louis Story*
1955 *A Man Called Peter*
1960 *The Dark at the Top of the
      Stairs*
Paris (France)
1914 *The Nightingale*
1915 The Clemenceau Case
1917 *The Trouble Buster*
1918 *Ruggles of Red Gap*
      A Woman of Impulse
1919 *As a Man Thinks*
      His Parisian Wife
      Yvonne from Paris
1919? *The Brand of Judas*
1920 *The Good-Bad Wife*
1922 Peacock Alley
1928 The Cohens and the Kellys
      in Paris
      Riley the Cop
1930 *Charros, gauchos y
      manolas*
      Doña mentiras
1931 Un caballero de frac
      Cheri-Bibi
      Hay que casar al príncipe
      La ley del harem
      Nuit d'Espagne
      Le petit café
      Su noche de bodas
      Su última noche
1932 *Une heure près de toi*
      Hombres en mi vida
      Parigi affascina; ovvero,
      Malavita
      Le plombier amoureux
1933 L'amour guide
      Diplomaniacs
      Yo, tú y ella
1934 *Cuesta abajo*
      La veuve joyeuse
1935 Charlie Chan in Paris
      De la sartén al fuego
      L'homme des Folies Bergère
      Ruggles of Red Gap
1937 *That Girl from Paris*
1938 Happy Landing
1939 City in Darkness
1940 Perfidia
1945 *The Great John L.*
      Rhapsody in Blue
1949 *C-Man*
1953 *Tonight We Sing*
1958 *The Young Lions*
1959 *John Paul Jones*
Paris (France)—Latin Quarter
1931 *Women Love Once*

Quanah Parker
1956 Comanche
Parking garage attendants
1941 *You're Out of Luck*
Parks
1917 *A Love Sublime*
1921 *As the World Rolls On*
1930 *King of Jazz*
      Sombras de gloria
1931 *Mi último amor*
1935 *Rosa de Francia*
Parliaments
1940 The Tragedy of
      Carpatho-Ukraine
Parole
1919 *The Scar*
1932 *Men Are Such Fools*
1939 *Reform School*
1941 Up Jumped the Devil
1947? *What a Guy*
1949 *The Golden Stallion*
Parole boards
1948 *Call Northside 777*
Parricide
1919 *The Homesteader*
1952 *Hiawatha*
1956 *Raw Edge*
1958 *Gun Fever*
1959 *The FBI Story*
Parrots
1921 One Man in a Million
1927 *The Chinese Parrot*
1932 *Parigi affascina; ovvero,
      Malavita*
1934 *Charlie Chan's Courage*
1935 *Angelina o el honor de un
      brigadier*
1941 *Dead Men Tell*
1946 *Cuban Pete*
Parsons
1927 *With Sitting Bull at the
      Spirit Lake Massacre*
1950 Stars in My Crown
Parties
1916 *The Gilded Spider*
      Her Debt of Honor
1917 *The Bronze Bride*
      Sunshine and Gold
      The Winged Mystery
1918 *The Little Runaway*
1919 *The Delicious Little Devil*
      The Little Diplomat
1927 *For the Love of Mike*
      The Scar of Shame
1928 *The Wages of Sin*
1930 *Así es la vida*
      Check and Double Check
      Del mismo barro
1931 *Aloha*
      Charlie Chan Carries On
      Cheri-Bibi
      Delicious
      The Exile
      The Guilty Generation
      La ley del harem
      Nuit d'Espagne
      Politiquerías
      Young Sinners
1932 *Amor in montagna*
      Charlie Chan's Chance
      Une heure près de toi
      Mazel Tov
      Le plombier amoureux
      *Senza mamma
      e'nnamurato*
      Unashamed
1933 *Broken Dreams*
      Espérame
      Grand Slam
      Let's Fall in Love
1934 *Behold My Wife!*
      Las fronteras del amor
      Imitation of Life
      Lazy River
      The Rabbi's Power
      The Youth of Russia
1935 *Alas sobre el Chaco*
      *Angelina o el honor de un
      brigadier*
      McFadden's Flats
      Rescue Squad
1936 *After the Thin Man*
      Contra la corriente
      General Spanky

Rainbow on the River
1937 *Thank You, Mr. Moto*
Where Is My Child?
1938 *Dangerous to Know*
Sugar Hill Baby
1939 *Charlie Chan at Treasure Island*
Keep Punching
Lying Lips
Mothers of Today
The Mystery of Mr. Wong
194- *Mistaken Identity*
1940 *Charlie Chan's Murder Cruise*
Eli Eli
1941 *Doomed Caravan*
Hurry, Charlie, Hurry
New York Town
Road Agent
1942 *Lucky Ghost*
Mexican Spitfire at Sea
North to the Klondike
Twin Beds
We Were Dancing
Woman of the Year
1943 *The Gang's All Here*
1944 *Block Busters*
1945 *Sunbonnet Sue*
1946 *Notorious*
Tall, Tan and Terrific
1946? *Beale Street Mama*
House-Rent Party
1947 *Boy! What a Girl!*
Humoresque
Jiggs and Maggie in Society
Pirates of Monterey
Robin Hood of Monterey
Sepia Cinderella
1948 *Jiggs and Maggie in Court*
Sleep, My Love
1949 *Jigsaw*
Massacre River
Portrait of Jennie
Top O' the Morning
Tulsa
1949? *Girl in Room 20*
1950 *Bandit Queen*
The Baron of Arizona
Belle of Old Mexico
Comanche Territory
Rock Island Trail
1952 *Brave Warrior*
Japanese War Bride
The Ring
Woman in the Dark
1953 *The Man Behind the Gun*
1954 *Salt of the Earth*
1956 *Death of a Scoundrel*
1957 *The Midnight Story*
The Oklahoman
1958 *Bullwhip*
The Light in the Forest
Seven Hills of Rome
The Young Lions
1959 *The Wonderful Country*
1960 *The Dark at the Top of the Stairs*
Flaming Star
Take a Giant Step
This Rebel Breed

Partnership
1918 Untamed
1919 Fighting for Gold
1923 Potash and Perlmutter
1926 The Cohens and Kellys
Sweet Daddies
1927 Clancy's Kosher Wedding
Sailor Izzy Murphy
1928 The Cohens and the Kellys in Paris
1931 *The Cohens and Kellys in Africa*
1933 *The Emperor Jones*
1934 *The Cactus Kid*
1935 *McFadden's Flats*
1936 *Charlie Chan at the Circus*
Love and Sacrifice
Paddy O'Day
Song of the Gringo
Yiddle with His Fiddle
1937 *Shadows of the Orient*
1938 *Mr. Wong, Detective*
1939 The Cisco Kid and the Lady
Forged Passport
Harlem Rides the Range

1940 *Midnight Shadow*
1941 *Louisiana Purchase*
Sunday Sinners
1942 *American Empire*
Mexican Spitfire Sees a Ghost
1943 *Riding High*
1944 *Address Unknown*
An American Romance
The Chinese Cat
1947 *Buck Privates Come Home*
Mantan Runs for Mayor
1948 *Docks of New Orleans*
Old Los Angeles
1949 *Thieves' Highway*
Tulsa
1950 *The Cariboo Trail*
God, Man and Devil
Intruder in the Dust
1950? *Three Daughters*
1951 *Mask of the Dragon*
1952 *Fort Osage*
1955 *Duel on the Mississippi*
1956 *The Catered Affair*
1958 *Blood Arrow*
Gun Fever

Pasadena (CA)
1923 *Breaking into Society*
1950 *The Jackie Robinson Story*
1952 *Anything Can Happen*

Passaic (NJ)
1926 The Passaic Textile Strike

Passover
1915 Children of the Ghetto
1953 *The Jazz Singer*

Passports
1917 *The Winged Mystery*
1918 *The Kaiser's Finish*
1939 *City in Darkness*
1956 *Death of a Scoundrel*

Tony Pastor
1925 Lights of Old Broadway
1950 The Daughter of Rosie O'Grady

Paternity
1919 As a Man Thinks

Paterson (NJ)
1920 *Dangerous Hours*

Pathologists
1955 *Not As a Stranger*

Patricide
use **Parricide**

Patriotism
1917 The Little American
The Slacker
1918 *An Alien Enemy*
The Kaiser's Finish
Me Und Gott
The Yellow Dog
1919 The Red Viper
1920 The Cup of Fury
The Face at Your Window
1922 A California Romance
1925 Friendly Enemies
1928 Heart Trouble
A Ship Comes In
1933 *Ever in My Heart*
The Man Who Dared: An Imaginative Biography
Obey the Law
1935 *Rendezvous*
1937 *Nation Aflame*
1938 *The Buccaneer*
1939 *Confessions of a Nazi Spy*
Man of Conquest
1940 *Escape to Glory*
1941 *Accent on Love*
They Dare Not Love
1942 *Friendly Enemies*
The Navy Comes Through
Take My Life
Wings for the Eagle
1943 *Air Force*
Good Luck, Mr. Yates
Mr. Lucky
Yankee Doodle Dandy
1944 An American Romance
The Racket Man
Since You Went Away
Tender Comrade
They Live in Fear
1946 *Notorious*
Without Reservations

1951 *The Magnificent Yankee*
1959 The FBI Story
1960 Hell to Eternity

Patronage, Political
1920 Hidden Charms
1929 *Die Königsloge*

Anna Pavlova
1953 *Tonight We Sing*

Pawnbrokers
1915 *Time Lock Number 776*
1917 *Crime and Punishment*
A Jewel in Pawn
1922 The Five Dollar Baby
Pawn Ticket 210
Second Hand Rose
1923 None So Blind
1926 Sweet Rosie O'Grady
1927 The Auctioneer
A Harp in Hock
1930 Around the Corner
1937 *Underworld*
1941 Where Did You Get That Girl?
1942 *Tales of Manhattan*
1947 *Easy Come, Easy Go*

Pawnee Indians
1943 Wagon Tracks West
1949 *The Prairie*
1954 Arrow in the Dust
1956 *Westward Ho the Wagons!*
1957 Pawnee
1958 Fort Massacre

Pawnshops
1932 *Hearts of Humanity*
1942 *Tortilla Flat*
1947 *The Mighty McGurk*
1953 *Taxi*

Payrolls
1926 *The Flying Ace*
1943 *Land of Hunted Men*
1949 *The Cowboy and the Prizefighter*
1950 *I Killed Geronimo*
1958 *Ride a Crooked Trail*

Peace
1917 The Captain of the Gray Horse Troop
1924 Two Shall Be Born
1933 Diplomaniacs
1950 Broken Arrow
1954 *The Black Dakotas*
Drum Beat
1957 *War Drums*

Peace conferences
1933 *Diplomaniacs*
1935 *Captured in Chinatown*
1950 *Broken Arrow*
1952 *Battles of Chief Pontiac*
1953 *Captain John Smith and Pocahontas*
1954 Battle of Rogue River
Drum Beat
1955 *Fort Yuma*

Peace pipes
1950 *Comanche Territory*
1951 *Snake River Desperadoes*
1952 *Battles of Chief Pontiac*

Peanuts
1940 *George Washington Carver*
1947 *The Peanut Man*

Pearl diving
1930 El dios del mar
1938 *Zamboanga*

Pearl Harbor (HI), Attack on, 1941
1942 *Little Tokyo, U.S.A.*
Submarine Raider
Wings for the Eagle
1943 Air Force
Dr. Gillespie's Criminal Case
Tahiti Honey
1944 *The Negro Soldier*
The Sullivans
We've Come a Long, Long Way

Pearls
1918 Hidden Pearls
1920 It's a Great Life
1930 Amor audaz
El dios del mar
1937 *Music for Madame*
Waikiki Wedding

Peasantry
1916 *Light at Dusk*
Poor Little Peppina
The Social Highwayman
Sold for Marriage
1918 *Her Moment*
1920 On with the Dance
1923 Fashion Row
Suzanna
1931 *Nuit d'Espagne*
1932 Amor in montagna
1937 Natalka Poltavka
1940 *The Mark of Zorro*
1945 Anoush
1946 *Don Ricardo Returns*

Peddlers and peddling
1917 *The Peddler*
1918 Tony America
1921 The Swamp
1922 The Woman He Loved
1925 His People
1927 The Auctioneer
Clancy's Kosher Wedding
1928 The Rawhide Kid
1932 *No Greater Love*
1933 *The Man Who Dared: An Imaginative Biography*
1937 Arshin Mal Alan
That I May Live
1956 Rockin' the Blues

Peeping Toms
1955 *Violent Saturday*

Peking (China)
1937 *Thank You, Mr. Moto*

Penal colonies
1916 Unprotected

Pendleton (OR)
1915 Where Cowboy Is King

Penguins
1934 *Stand Up and Cheer!*

Penicillin
1956 *Death of a Scoundrel*

Penitentiaries
use Prisons;
Specific penitentiaries

Pennsylvania
1916 *The Flames of Johannis*
Little Meena's Romance
A Woman's Honor
1922 Peacock Alley
1938 Breaking the Ice
1939 Allegheny Uprising
1948 *The Miracle of the Bells*
1949 *Anna Lucasta*
1952 *Bright Victory*
1959 *The World, the Flesh and the Devil*

Pennsylvania Dutch
1916 Little Meena's Romance
1918 Johanna Enlists
1919 Erstwhile Susan

Perfume
1915 *Hearts of Men*
1927 Sailor Izzy Murphy
1946 *Cuban Pete*
1950 *Comanche Territory*

Perjury
1921 When the Clock Struck Nine
1928 George Washington Cohen
1952 *My Man and I*
1958 *Gunman's Walk*

John Joseph Pershing
1916 Following the Flag in Mexico

Persia
1937 Arshin Mal Alan

Persians
1920 The Devil's Claim
1937 Arshin Mal Alan

Personality change
1915 The Danger Signal
1943 Hitler's Children
1951 The Well
1952 *It's a Big Country: An American Anthology*
1953 *Fort Ti*
1955 Santa Fe Passage
1958 *Blood Arrow*
1959 *The Hanging Tree*
The Wonderful Country
Yellowstone Kelly

Peru
- 1931 Don Juan diplomático

Pet shops
- 1933 *Broken Dreams*
- 1934 *Limehouse Blues*
- 1942 *Rio Rita*

Petersburg (VA)
- 1915 *The Birth of a Nation*

Petitions
- 1944 *Tucson Raiders*
- 1946 *Bringing Up Father*

Joseph Petrosino
- 1912 *The Adventures of Lieutenant Petrosino*
- 1960 Pay or Die

Pharmacists
- 1936 *Kelly the Second*
- 1950 *Chinatown at Midnight*

Philadelphia (PA)
- 1929 Evangeline
- 1931 *El pasado acusa*
- 1937 *Souls at Sea*
- 1938 *Breaking the Ice*
- 1940 *Eli Eli*
- 1945 *Pride of the Marines*
- 1949 *That Midnight Kiss*
- 1952 *Bright Victory*
- 1953 *The Jazz Singer*
- 1956 *Singing in the Dark*

Philanderers
- 1916 At Piney Ridge
- 1921 Hearts of the Woods
- 1928 The Midnight Ace
- 1931 El tenorio del harem
        Three Who Loved
- 1932 Ten Minutes to Live
        Uncle Moses
- 1935 Alas sobre el Chaco
        Rescue Squad
- 1938 Happy Landing
        The Singing Blacksmith
        Swing!
- 1940 Mystery in Swing
- 1946 The Gentleman Misbehaves
- 1947 *Juke Joint*
- 1953 *The Charge at Feather River*
- 1958 Kings Go Forth
- 1959 *Thunder in the Sun*

Philanthropists
- 1913 *Traffic in Souls*
- 1917 *The Secret of Eve*
- 1918 *Shifting Sands*
        The Spreading Evil
- 1919 *Who's Your Brother?*
- 1921 The Land of Hope
- 1925 Salome of the Tenements
- 1931 *Such Is Life*
- 1939 *Mr. Moto Takes a Vacation*
- 1947 *Riding the California Trail*

Philanthropy
- *use* **Charity;**
        Philanthropists
- 1920 *Within Our Gates*

Philippines
- 1938 Zamboanga

Philosophers
- 1914 *Life's Shop Window*
- 1918 *A Little Sister of Everybody*
- 1921 Lotus Blossom
- 1947 *Little Mister Jim*

Phobias
- 1925 One of the Bravest
- 1931 *Skyline*
- 1936 *Sea Spoilers*
- 1960 *The Dark at the Top of the Stairs*

Phoenix (AZ)
- 1950 *The Baron of Arizona*

Phonograph records
- *use* **Recordings**

Phonographs
- 1913 *Traffic in Souls*

Photographers
- 1915 *How Molly Malone Made Good*
- 1931 *Charlie Chan Carries On*
- 1932 *Thirteen Steps*
- 1935 *¡Asegure a su mujer!*
- 1936 *Yellow Cargo*
- 1937 *A Study of Negro Artists*
- 1941 New York Town
        Sullivan's Travels

- 1943 *The Meanest Man in the World*
        Wintertime
- 1948 *16 Fathoms Deep*
        Sleep, My Love
- 1949 *The Girl from Jones Beach*
        Rose of the Yukon
- 1954 *Dangerous Mission*
- 1959 *Imitation of Life*
- 1960 Weddings and Babies

Photographs
- 1913? *The Call of the Blood*
- 1916 *The Honorable Friend*
- 1926 *The Strong Man*
- 1931 *The Black Camel*
        El pasado acusa
- 1932 *Cuore d'emigrante*
- 1933 *No dejes la puerta abierta*
- 1937 *Charlie Chan on Broadway*
        One Mile from Heaven
- 1939 *Charlie Chan in Honolulu*
        The Cisco Kid and the Lady
        Harlem Rides the Range
- 1940 *Charlie Chan's Murder Cruise*
        Mystery in Swing
- 1941 *Louisiana Purchase*
- 1942 *Sunday Punch*
- 1943 *The Gang's All Here*
- 1944 *Hi, Beautiful*
        Tender Comrade
- 1945 *The Dolly Sisters*
- 1946 *G. I. War Brides*
        Tall, Tan and Terrific
- 1947 *On the Old Spanish Trail*
- 1948 *Call Northside 777*
        Open Secret
- 1949 *Answer for Anne*
        Portrait of Jennie
        The Sky Dragon
- 1950 *Belle of Old Mexico*
        Give Us This Day
- 1952 *Arctic Flight*
- 1953 *The Glass Wall*
- 1954 *Hondo*

Physical education and training
- 1921 As the World Rolls On
- 1955 The Long Gray Line

Physical therapy
- 1950 *The Men*

Physicians
- 1914 Northern Lights
- 1915 *The Birth of a Nation*
        The Italian
        Sealed Valley
        The Secret Sin
- 1915? *The Life of Sam Davis: A Confederate Hero of the Sixties*
        Sam Davis, the Hero of Tennessee
- 1916 Lone Star
- 1917 The Bride of Hate
        Hashimura Togo
        A Love Sublime
        The Plow Woman
        The Squaw Man's Son
        Threads of Fate
- 1918 The Honor of His House
        In Judgment Of
        Laughing Bill Hyde
        Little Red Decides
        One More American
        The Spreading Evil
        Wanted, a Mother
        A Woman of Impulse
- 1919 *As a Man Thinks*
        Erstwhile Susan
- 1920 The Dark Mirror
        Pagan Love
        A Tokio Siren
- 1921 The Barricade
        Cheated Love
        A Modern Cain
        The Secret Sorrow
- 1922 The Hands of Nara
        Little Miss Smiles
- 1925 Hogan's Alley
- 1927 Pleasure Before Business
- 1929 Hearts in Dixie
        Welcome Danger
- 1930 Un hombre de suerte
        El secreto del doctor
        Sins of the Children

- 1931 *Cheri-Bibi*
        Drácula
        Le père célibataire
- 1932 *Une heure près de toi*
        Huddle
        Marido y mujer
        No Greater Love
        Le plombier amoureux
        So Big
        The Son-Daughter
- 1933 Broken Dreams
        Dance Hall Hostess
- 1934 *Massacre*
        Nada más que una mujer
        The Prescott Kid
- 1935 *Angelina o el honor de un brigadier*
        Charlie Chan in Egypt
        The Yiddish King Lear
- 1936 *Charlie Chan at the Circus*
        Dangerous Intrigue
        Desert Gold
        The Prisoner of Shark Island
        Ramona
        Sins of Man
        Tundra
- 1937 *Boy of the Streets*
        Dark Manhattan
        I Want to Be a Mother
        Where Is My Child?
- 1938 *City Streets*
        Rascals
        Two Sisters
- 1939 *Charlie Chan in Reno*
        Confessions of a Nazi Spy
        The Escape
        Gone With the Wind
        Judge Hardy and Son
        Miracle on Main Street
        My Son
- 1940 Am I Guilty?
        Americaner Schadchen
        Broken Strings
        Eli Eli
        Escape
        Escape to Glory
        Girl from God's Country
        Three Faces West
- 1941 *Adam Had Four Sons*
        The Face Behind the Mask
        Thunder Over the Prairie
- 1942 Castle in the Desert
        Dr. Gillespie's New Assistant
        In This Our Life
        North to the Klondike
        Take My Life
- 1943 Dr. Gillespie's Criminal Case
        Good Luck, Mr. Yates
        Mexican Spitfire's Blessed Event
        They Came to Blow Up America
        Wagon Tracks West
- 1944 *Andy Hardy's Blonde Trouble*
        Block Busters
        Dark Waters
        Three Men in White
- 1945 *The Bells of St. Mary's*
        Between Two Women
        Club Havana
        I Love a Bandleader
        In Old New Mexico
        Jealousy
        The Mummy's Curse
        Salome, Where She Danced
- 1946 Abie's Irish Rose
        Border Bandits
        Three Wise Fools
        The Trap
        Wild Beauty
        Wild West
- 1947 Dark Delusion
        Going to Glory, Come to Jesus
        Robin Hood of Monterey
        Rustlers of Devil's Canyon
- 1948 *The Boy with Green Hair*
        Cry of the City
        Fighting Father Dunne
        Gentleman's Agreement
        The Golden Eye
        I Remember Mama
        The Miracle of the Bells

        Moonrise
        Tap Roots
- 1949 *Arctic Fury*
        C-Man
        Home of the Brave
        Lost Boundaries
        Masked Raiders
        Pinky
        Rose of the Yukon
        She Wore a Yellow Ribbon
- 1949? *She's Too Mean for Me*
- 1950 *The Breaking Point*
        Emergency Wedding
        The Men
        Mystery Submarine
        No Way Out
        Right Cross
        Rio Grande
        Stars in My Crown
        Train to Tombstone
- 1951 *Flaming Feather*
        Gambling House
        Saturday's Hero
        The Well
- 1953 *The Eddie Cantor Story*
        The Great Sioux Uprising
        Sangaree
        The Sun Shines Bright
- 1954 They Rode West
- 1955 *Foxfire*
        Good Morning, Miss Dove
        A Man Called Peter
        Not As a Stranger
        Trial
- 1956 *Giant*
        Man from Del Rio
        Westward Ho the Wagons!
- 1957 *All Mine to Give*
        The Oklahoman
        The Tin Star
        War Drums
- 1958 *Gunman's Walk*
        The Lone Ranger and the Lost City of Gold
- 1959 The Hanging Tree
        The Last Angry Man
        Night of the Quarter Moon
        The Wonderful Country
- 1960 *For the Love of Mike*
        The Plunderers

Physicists
- 1948 *Gentleman's Agreement*

Pianists
- 1922 Solomon in Society
- 1931 *Lo mejor es reír*
- 1932 *Mystery Ranch*
- 1936 *Star for a Night*
- 194- *Mistaken Identity*
- 1945 *Club Havana*
        Rhapsody in Blue
- 1946 *Stars on Parade*
- 1946? Harlem on Parade
- 1947 Carnegie Hall
        Humoresque
- 1948 *The Time of Your Life*
- 1949 *That Midnight Kiss*
- 1958 *Seven Hills of Rome*

Piano makers
- 1931 *The Cohens and Kellys in Africa*

Pianos
- 1947 *Calendar Girl*
- 1958 *St. Louis Blues*
- 1960 *The Unforgiven*

Picketing
- 1954 Salt of the Earth

Pickpockets
- 1934 *Lazy River*
        Limehouse Blues
- 1941? *The Blood of Jesus*
- 1946 *Shadows Over Chinatown*
- 1948 *The Luck of the Irish*

Picnicking
- 1916 Peck O' Pickles
- 1918 *Huck and Tom; or, the Further Adventures of Tom Sawyer*
- 1919 *Fighting for Gold*
- 1933 *The Man Who Dared: An Imaginative Biography*
        Rafter Romance
- 1935 *Un hombre peligroso*
        Piernas de seda
        Rosa de Francia

The Winning Ticket
1941 *Under Fiesta Stars*
      Virginia
1943 *Hitler's Children*
1948 *Rocky*
1959 *Porgy and Bess*

Pio Pico
1916 *The Daughter of the Don*

Piedmont (SC)
1915 The Birth of a Nation

Piers
1932 Me and My Gal
1944 *The Chinese Cat*
      Waterfront

Piety
1953 The Jazz Singer

Pigeons
1917 The Winged Mystery
1938 *Mr. Moto Takes a Chance*
      Rascals
1943 *The Meanest Man in the*
      World

Pigs
1934 *Song of the Islands*
1937 *Waikiki Wedding*
1939 *The Devil's Daughter*
1941 *This Woman Is Mine*
1951 *Go for Broke!*

Pilgrims and pilgrimages
1931 *Shulamith*

Pilots
      use **Air pilots**

Pima Indians
1955 Day of Decision
1958 *Apache Territory*

Pimps
1913 The Inside of the White
      Slave Traffic
      Traffic in Souls
1934 Drums O' Voodoo
1934? *Harlem After Midnight*

Pinball machines
1938 *Passport Husband*
1948 *The Time of Your Life*

Pine Ridge Reservation (SD)
1918? Indian Life

Ping-pong (Game)
1938 *Happy Landing*

Pinochle (Game)
1930 The Kibitzer

Pioneers
1926 Laddie
1931 *La gran jornada*
1946 Canyon Passage
1951 Cavalry Scout
1952 Buffalo Bill in Tomahawk
      Territory

Pirates
1917? Barnaby Lee
1924 Peter Pan
1935 *Naughty Marietta*
1936 Dancing Pirate
1937 *El capitán Tormenta*
1938 The Buccaneer
1941 *Dead Men Tell*
1947 *Pirates of Monterey*
1950 Buccaneer's Girl
      Last of the Buccaneers
1951 Hurricane Island
      The Mark of the Renegade
1953 *Sangaree*

Pistols
1950 *Mystery Street*
1951 *The Mark of the Renegade*

William Pitt, the Elder, 1st Earl of
Chatham
1936 *The Last of the Mohicans*

Pittsburgh (PA)
1945 *The Valley of Decision*
1948 *Unconquered*
1958 *The Light in the Forest*

Placid, Lake (NY)
1944 Lake Placid Serenade

Plagiarism
1934 *Beloved*

Plague
1916 Mixed Blood
1919 *Evangeline*
1921 A Giant of His Race
1927 Children of Fate
1936 *Tundra*

1949 Arctic Fury
1950 Panic in the Streets
1953 *Sangaree*

Plant foremen
1920 *The Great Shadow*

Plantation owners
1917 *Southern Pride*
1918 *Uncle Tom's Cabin*
1920 Within Our Gates
1927 The Chinese Parrot
      The Spider's Web
1928 Uncle Tom's Cabin
1939 Way Down South
1953 *Jack McCall Desperado*
1957 Band of Angels

Plantations
1914 *The Littlest Rebel*
      Uncle Tom's Cabin
1915 *Under Southern Skies*
1915? *Sam Davis, the Hero of*
      Tennessee
1916 The Grip of Jealousy
1917 *The Adventures of Carol*
      The Bride of Hate
      My Fighting Gentleman
1918 *The Liar*
1920 *White Youth*
1921 Cotton and Cattle
1928 Uncle Tom's Cabin
1931 *La carta*
1934 *Nada más que una mujer*
      White Heat
1935 *The Littlest Rebel*
      So Red the Rose
1937 *El carnaval del diablo*
      Slave Ship
1939 *The Devil's Daughter*
      Gone With the Wind
      Way Down South
1940 *New Moon*
1942 *Across the Pacific*
1944 *Dark Waters*
1946 *Cuban Pete*
      Song of the South
1947 The Foxes of Harrow
1948 Tap Roots
1951 *Yes Sir, Mr. Bones*
1953 Sangaree
1955 Duel on the Mississippi
1957 *Band of Angels*
1958 Machete

Plastic surgeons
1941 *The Face Behind the Mask*

Plastic surgery
1928 The Broken Mask
      The Hawk's Nest
1931 *Cheri-Bibi*
      El impostor
1936 *Below the Deadline*
1940 Charlie Chan at the Wax
      Museum
1952 *Kid Monk Baroni*

Playboys
1918 Her American Husband
1920 *The Luck of the Irish*
1931 *Beyond Victory*
      Personal Maid
1933 It's Great to Be Alive
      No dejes la puerta abierta
1934 She Was a Lady
      La veuve joyeuse
1935 *Señora casada necesita*
      marido
1939 *La Inmaculada*
1940 *Charlie Chan's Murder*
      Cruise
      Perfidia
1942 *Tales of Manhattan*
1948 Half Past Midnight
1950 *Right Cross*
1958 *The Last Hurrah*

Plays
1939 *My Son*
1940 Paradise in Harlem
1942 *Mexican Spitfire at Sea*
1943 *Let's Have Fun*
1956 *Death of a Scoundrel*

Playwrights
1916 Lord Loveland Discovers
      America
1919 *Yvonne from Paris*
1920 Darling Mine
1934 *Granaderos del amor*
      The Great Flirtation

1935 *Señora casada necesita*
      marido
1938 La vida bohemia
1940 *The Fatal Hour*
      Perfidia
1943 Yankee Doodle Dandy
1955 *Good Morning, Miss Dove*
1958 *Marjorie Morningstar*
1959 *Imitation of Life*

Pledges
1914 Uncle Tom's Cabin
1917 Queen X
1918 The Golden Wall
      The Ordeal of Rosetta
      Uncle Tom's Cabin
1920 For the Soul of Rafael
1931 El comediante
      Shulamith
      Young Sinners
1932 The Hatchet Man
1934 The Rabbi's Power
      Wheels of Destiny
1937 The Holy Oath
      Natalka Poltavka
      Thank You, Mr. Moto
1938 Two Sisters
1939 *Waterfront*
1944 *An American Romance*
1947 *Robin Hood of Monterey*
      Spoilers of the North
1948 *Renegades of Sonora*
1949 *3 Godfathers*
1950 Rock Island Trail
1951 *The Magnificent Yankee*
1952 *Brave Warrior*
1954 *Arrow in the Dust*

Plumbers
1920 The Luck of the Irish
1925 Hogan's Alley
1927 Jake the Plumber
      Sally in Our Alley
1930 Kathleen Mavourneen
1932 *The Heart of New York*
      Le plombier amoureux

Pneumonia
1918 *Little Red Decides*
1932 *No Greater Love*
1938 *The Toy Wife*
1939 *Judge Hardy and Son*
1950 *Jolson Sings Again*

Poachers
1918 *Denny from Ireland*
1936 Down to the Sea
      Sea Spoilers

Pocahontas
1923 Jamestown
1953 Captain John Smith and
      Pocahontas

Pocketwatches
      use **Watches**

Poetry
1919 Evangeline
1936 *Contra la corriente*
1939 *The Bronze Buckaroo*
1941 *Come Live with Me*
1947 *On the Old Spanish Trail*

Poets
1915 *Children of the Ghetto*
1918 The Price of Applause
      The Temple of Dusk
1920 *Billions*
1929 The Witching Eyes
1931 *Women Love Once*
1935 *Angelina o el honor de un*
      brigadier
1947 *Calendar Girl*
1949 *The Red Menace*
1959 *Shake Hands with the Devil*

Pogroms
1914 Threads of Destiny
1919 *The Right to Happiness*
1931 *The Voice of Israel*
1933 *The Wandering Jew*

Poison
1930 *Wu Li Chang*
1931 *La cautivadora*
      Riders of the Rio
1936 *El crimen de media noche*
1938 *Mr. Moto Takes a Chance*
      Mr. Moto's Gamble
1939 *Charlie Chan at Treasure*
      Island
      Straight to Heaven
      El trovador de la radio

1940 *Charlie Chan at the Wax*
      Museum
1943 *Margin for Error*
1951 *Hurricane Island*

Poisoning
1914 *The Great Diamond*
      Robbery
1916 *The Folly of Revenge*
1917 *The Bride of Hate*
1918 *The Honor of His House*
      The Ranger
      Toys of Fate
1920 Locked Lips
      The Purple Cipher
1931 *Cuerpo y alma*
1932 *The Son-Daughter*
      Thirteen Women
      Yiskor
1938 Marusia
1939 *Charlie Chan in Reno*
1940 *Mystery in Swing*
      Phantom of Chinatown
1942 Castle in the Desert
1943 *Wagon Tracks West*
1945 *In Old New Mexico*
      The Shanghai Cobra
1946 Beauty and the Bandit
      Notorious
1948 *Miracle in Harlem*
1951 *The House on Telegraph*
      Hill
1956 *The White Squaw*
1958 *Flaming Frontier*

Poker (Game)
1916 *The Thousand Dollar*
      Husband
1917 *The Bride of Hate*
1918 *Little Red Decides*
      Ruggles of Red Gap
1919 *The She Wolf*
1923 Ruggles of Red Gap
1931 *Smart Money*
1932 *The Galloping Kid*
1935 *Ruggles of Red Gap*
      Tango Bar
1936 *Aces and Eights*
1937 *The Plainsman*
1939 *Double Deal*
1942 *Mexican Spitfire Sees a*
      Ghost
1943 *The Outlaw*
1944 *The San Antonio Kid*
1946 *Canyon Passage*
      Saratoga Trunk
1947 *California*
1949 *Brothers in the Saddle*
      Illegal Entry
1950 *Winchester '73*
1953 *Column South*

Poland
1932 Yiskor
1936 Yiddle with His Fiddle
1937 The Cantor's Son
1939 *Mirele Efros*
1940 *The Tragedy of*
      Carpatho-Ukraine
1941 *Wiejskie Wesele*
1951 *The House on Telegraph*
      Hill

Poland—History
1932 *A Daughter of Her People*
1941 Ten Ostatni
      Z Dymem Pożarów

Polar bears
1927 *Primitive Love*
1928 The Great White North
1932 *Igloo*
1941 *Mutiny in the Arctic*
1949 *Arctic Fury*
      Arctic Manhunt
1952 *Arctic Flight*

Poles
1924 Two Shall Be Born
1939 Mirele Efros
1940 *Overture to Glory*
1941 Ten Ostatni
1951 *Gambling House*

Police
1912 *The Adventures of*
      Lieutenant Petrosino
1913 Traffic in Souls
1915 *The Sable Lorcha*
      A Texas Steer
      A Yankee from the West

Police

1916 The Criminal
Gretchen, the Greenhorn
The King's Game
The Social Highwayman
A Son of Erin
1917 The Adventures of Carol
Lost in Transit
A Love Sublime
The Winged Mystery
1918 A Broadway Scandal
His Birthright
The Little Runaway
The Midnight Patrol
The Wine Girl
1919 The Lord Loves the Irish
Love and the Law
The Tiger Lily
1922 Square Joe
1923 April Showers
1924 East of Broadway
Fools' Highway
The Pell Street Mystery
Two Shall Be Born
1925 The Fearless Lover
Irish Luck
The Man in Blue
Red Love
Speed Wild
1926 The Cohens and Kellys
Kosher Kitty Kelly
Sweet Rosie O'Grady
1927 Frisco Sally Levy
Heroes in Blue
Lost at the Front
The Scar of Shame
Spoilers of the West
1928 Anybody Here Seen Kelly?
The House of Scandal
Riley the Cop
1929 Welcome Danger
1930 Amor audaz
Around the Corner
La fuerza del querer
Galas de la Paramount
King of Jazz
La voluntad del muerto
1931 Buster se marie
Die Dreigroschenoper
Kismet
Law of the Tong
El pasado acusa
Smart Money
Street Scene
1932 Harlem Is Heaven
El hombre que asesinó
Me and My Gal
Scarface
Thirteen Steps
1934 La buenaventura
He Was Her Man
Straight Is the Way
1935 Black Fury
Captured in Chinatown
Chinatown Squad
The Irish in Us
Lem Hawkins' Confession
Romance in Manhattan
1936 Charlie Chan at the Circus
Contra la corriente
El crimen de media noche
Kelly the Second
Let's Sing Again
Mad Holiday
Paddy O'Day
Winterset
Yellow Cargo
1937 Bargain with Bullets
Boy of the Streets
Charlie Chan at the
Olympics
Manhattan
Merry-Go-Round
One Mile from Heaven
That Girl from Paris
That I May Live
Think Fast, Mr. Moto
Waikiki Wedding
Where Is My Child?
1938 City Streets
Dangerous to Know
Hawaii Calls
Little Miss Roughneck
Mr. Moto's Gamble
Mr. Wong, Detective
Rascals

Speed to Burn
1939 Charlie Chan at Treasure
Island
Double Deal
The Escape
Gang Smashers
Mr. Moto in Danger Island
Mr. Moto Takes a Vacation
Mr. Wong in Chinatown
Straight to Heaven
Verbena trágica
Waterfront
194- Mistaken Identity
1940 Charlie Chan at the Wax
Museum
Doomed to Die
East of the River
The Fatal Hour
Gang War
Little Nellie Kelly
Mystery in Swing
Paradise in Harlem
Phantom of Chinatown
Three Cheers for the Irish
While Thousands Cheer
1941 Accent on Love
Caught in the Act
The Face Behind the Mask
Four Shall Die
The Gang's All Here
Murder on Lenox Avenue
Up Jumped the Devil
1942 All Through the Night
Gentleman Jim
Let's Get Tough!
Mokey
Nazi Agent
Rubber Racketeers
1943 Crime Smasher
Margin for Error
Redhead from Manhattan
They Came to Blow Up
America
1944 Cry of the Werewolf
Going My Way
Slightly Terrific
Three Men in White
Waterfront
1945 Club Havana
Escape in the Fog
The Jade Mask
Of One Blood
Samurai
The Scarlet Clue
Sunbonnet Sue
A Tree Grows in Brooklyn
1946 Abie's Irish Rose
Cuban Pete
Gas House Kids
Notorious
The Red Dragon
1946? House-Rent Party
1947 Buck Privates Come Home
The Burning Cross
Desperate
Easy Come, Easy Go
The Jolson Story
Spoilers of the North
1947? Return of Mandy's
Husband
What a Guy
1948 Big City
Docks of New Orleans
Fighting Father Dunne
The Golden Eye
Half Past Midnight
Key Largo
Killer Diller
Open Secret
Sleep, My Love
The Time of Your Life
1949 Answer for Anne
Boston Blackie's Chinese
Venture
The Clay Pigeon
Knock on Any Door
Lost Boundaries
The Red Menace
Shamrock Hill
The Sky Dragon
Thieves' Highway
Top O' the Morning
The Undercover Man
We Were Strangers

1950 Black Hand
Buccaneer's Girl
Chinatown at Midnight
The Daughter of Rosie
O'Grady
The Lawless
No Way Out
1951 Gambling House
Mask of the Dragon
The Tall Target
1952 My Man and I
The Ring
Woman in the Dark
1953 Cry of the Hunted
The Glass Wall
Taxi
1954 Barefoot Battalion
Hell's Half Acre
Passion
Salt of the Earth
1955 Good Morning, Miss Dove
Murder in Villa Capri
1956 Baby Doll
Rockin' the Blues
1957 Burden of Truth
The Midnight Story
1958 The Defiant Ones
1959 Al Capone
Inside the Mafia
1960 Key Witness
The Pusher

Police brutality
1926 The Passaic Textile Strike
1949 Pinky

Police chiefs
1918 The Girl in the Dark
1931 Cheri-Bibi
1932 El hombre que asesinó
1936 El crimen de media noche
1937 Bargain with Bullets
Shadows of the Orient
1939 Charlie Chan in Reno
Forged Passport
Gang Smashers
1950 Panic in the Streets

Police commissioners
1934 The Cat's-Paw
1943 Crime Smasher
1954 Indiscretion of an
American Wife
1960 Pay or Die

Police corruption
1946 South of Monterey
1948 Call Northside 777
1959 Odds Against Tomorrow

Police detectives
1931 Three Who Loved
1932 Thirteen Women
1937 Music for Madame
1939 The Mystery of Mr. Wong
1940 Midnight Shadow
Son of Ingagi
1941 Where Did You Get That
Girl?
You're Out of Luck
1942 Little Tokyo, U.S.A.
1944 The Chinese Cat
1947 Crossfire
1948 Cry of the City
The Fight Never Ends
Shanghai Chest
1950 Mystery Street
1951 Cuban Fireball
Native Son
The Raging Tide
1956 Crowded Paradise
1957 Edge of the City
1958 Touch of Evil
1959 Porgy and Bess
1960 Key Witness
Pay or Die

Police inspectors
1933 Melodía de arrabal
1934 Limehouse Blues
1936 Charlie Chan's Secret
Klondike Annie
Muss 'Em Up
1937 Charlie Chan at the Opera
Charlie Chan on Broadway
1938 Charlie Chan at Monte Carlo
1940 Charlie Chan's Murder
Cruise
1942 Whispering Ghosts

1945 The Shanghai Cobra
1946 The Face of Marble
1951 The House on Telegraph
Hill

Police raids
1915 The Secret Sin
1916 Hop, the Devil's Brew
1918 Her Moment
The Midnight Patrol
Mystic Faces
1919 Spotlight Sadie
1919? The Chosen Path
1922 Square Joe
1924 Birthright
1930 Del mismo barro
1931 La cautivadora
1933 A Lady's Profession
1937 Dark Manhattan
Shadows of the Orient
1938 Life Goes On
1939 Papá soltero
1941 Lady from Louisiana
You're Out of Luck

Policemen
use Police

Poliomyelitis
1947 Dark Delusion
The Peanut Man
1951 Queen for a Day

Polish Americans
1918 Love's Law
1921 The Land of Hope
1924 Two Shall Be Born
1926 The Passaic Textile Strike
1932 Uncle Moses
1934 As the Earth Turns
1935 The Wedding Night
1941 New York Town
Z Dymem Pożarów
1942 We Were Dancing
1943 Bataan
1948 Call Northside 777
The Miracle of the Bells
The Time of Your Life
1949 Anna Lucasta
Illegal Entry
1950 The Men
The Missourians
Sands of Iwo Jima
1951 The House on Telegraph
Hill
Queen for a Day
Saturday's Hero
A Streetcar Named Desire
1953 The Stars Are Singing
War Paint
1955 Good Morning, Miss Dove
1959 Al Capone
1960 Take a Giant Step

Political alliances
1917 My Fighting Gentleman
1926 General Custer at Little Big
Horn
1951 The Last Outpost
1953 The Pathfinder
1955 Davy Crockett, King of the
Wild Frontier
1956 Pillars of the Sky
1957 Beau James
Revolt at Fort Laramie

Political bosses
1915 The Danger Signal
The Immigrant
The Italian
The Nigger
A Texas Steer
1918 One More American
1930 Kathleen Mavourneen
1932? The Girl from Chicago
1933 The Man Who Dared: An
Imaginative Biography
Obey the Law
1934 The Cat's-Paw
1937 Boy of the Streets
Man of the People
1938 The Renegade Ranger
1948 Up in Central Park
1952 Woman in the Dark
1958 The Last Hurrah
1959 Cry Tough

Political campaigns
1929 Mister Antonio
1935 His Family Tree

1940 *Elsa Maxwell's Public Deb No. 1*
      Three Cheers for the Irish
1945 *Sunbonnet Sue*
1947 Mantan Runs for Mayor
1948 *The Luck of the Irish*
1953 *The Sun Shines Bright*
1955 *Davy Crockett, King of the Wild Frontier*
1957 *Beau James*
1958 The Last Hurrah

Political candidates
1914 *The Woman in Black*
1931 *Politiquerías*
1933 *Victims of Persecution*
1960 *Ice Palace*

Political corruption
1915 The Nigger
      The Pageant of San Francisco
      A Texas Steer
1916 *Hop, the Devil's Brew*
1917 *One Law for Both*
      A Roadside Impresario
1918 *Hell's End*
      The Midnight Patrol
      One More American
1920? The Scarlet Dragon
1921 The Secret Sorrow
1922 The Dungeon
1930 El precio de un beso
1931 *Cimarron*
      Die Dreigroschenoper
1934 The Cat's-Paw
      Massacre
1935 *His Family Tree*
1937 Man of the People
1938 *In Old Chicago*
1940 Behind the News
1941 *Lady from Louisiana*
1944 Knickerbocker Holiday
1945 South of the Rio Grande
1946 Romance of the West
1947 California
      The Farmer's Daughter
1948 *Call Northside 777*
      Up in Central Park
1949 *The Red Menace*
      We Were Strangers
1952 *Woman in the Dark*
1955 Headline Hunters
1957 *Beau James*
1958 *The Last Hurrah*
1959 *Al Capone*
1960 *Cimarron*
      Oklahoma Territory

Political prisoners
1940 *Escape*
      The Man I Married
1945 *Samurai*
1947 *Northwest Outpost*

Politicians
1916 Hop, the Devil's Brew
1918 *Hell's End*
1920 *Hidden Charms*
1921 Hold Your Horses
      The Secret Sorrow
1921? The Supreme Passion
1925 The Man in Blue
1927 Old San Francisco
1936 Daniel Boone
1939 *Keep Punching*
      Man of Conquest
      Moon over Harlem
1940 *Elsa Maxwell's Public Deb No. 1*
      The Tragedy of Carpatho-Ukraine
1944 *Charlie Chan in the Secret Service*
1947 *My Wild Irish Rose*
1948 *My Girl Tisa*
1952 *Indian Uprising*

Politics
1917 The Conqueror
1940 Elsa Maxwell's Public Deb No. 1
      The Man I Married
1947 The Farmer's Daughter
1952 The Fighter
1957 Beau James

James K. Polk
1959 *The Oregon Trail*

Polka (Dance)
1941 *Sun Valley Serenade*

Polo
1915 *The Danger Signal*
1931 *Delicious*
      The Squaw Man

Polygamy
1934 *Eskimo*
1938 *Zamboanga*

Polynesians
1931 Aloha
1946 *Dangerous Money*

Pomona (CA)
1952 *The Ring*

Madame de Pompadour
1948 *Jiggs and Maggie in Court*

Pontiac
1927 Winners of the Wilderness
1952 Battles of Chief Pontiac

Pontiac's Conspiracy, 1763-1765
1948 Unconquered

Pony Express
1917 *The Adventures of Buffalo Bill*
1926 The Flaming Frontier
1929 The Desert Rider
1932 White Eagle
1938 Outlaw Express
1944 Riding West
1950 Riders of the Pony Express
1957 *Revolt at Fort Laramie*

Poorhouses
1914 *The Good-for-Nothing*
1919 *Evangeline*

Porcupines
1936 *Tundra*

Poro College (St. Louis, MO)
1927 Poro College in Moving Pictures

Porters
1919 Injustice
1921 Puppets of Fate
1926 The Fighting Deacon
1932 Hypnotized
1933 *The Emperor Jones*
1935 *Piernas de seda*
1938 *God's Step Children*
1944 *Chip Off the Old Block*
1951 *Yes Sir, Mr. Bones*

Portland (OR)
1946 *Canyon Passage*

Portraits (Paintings)
1916 *The Gilded Spider*
      The Twin Triangle
1949 *House of Strangers*
1951 *The House on Telegraph Hill*
1952 *The Iron Mistress*

Portsmouth (NH)
1940 *Northwest Passage (Book I—Rogers' Rangers)*
1959 *John Paul Jones*

Portuguese Americans
1920 *The Paliser Case*
1925 My Son
1932 *Tiger Shark*
1934 *He Was Her Man*
1939 *Daughters Courageous*
1941 Accent on Love
      Ride on Vaquero
1942 *Tortilla Flat*
1949 *Tuna Clipper*

Posses
1917 *The Call of Her People*
1918 *The Hell Cat*
1919 *Just Squaw*
      Scarlet Days
1931 *The Hurricane Horseman*
1934 *The Battling Buckaroo*
      The Fighting Hero
1935 *The Cyclone Ranger*
1935? *The Irish Gringo*
1936 *Robin Hood of El Dorado*
1939 Bad Lands
      Trigger Fingers
1940 *Viva Cisco Kid*
1941 *Road Agent*
      Secret of the Wastelands
1942 *Shut My Big Mouth*
1944 *Marshal of Reno*

1945 *In Old New Mexico*
      Wanderer of the Wasteland
1946 Sunset Pass
1947 *Buffalo Bill Rides Again*
      Marshal of Cripple Creek
      Rustlers of Devil's Canyon
      Under the Tonto Rim
1948 *Four Faces West*
      Shep Comes Home
1949 *Colorado Territory*
      Masked Raiders
      The Mysterious Desperado
      Riders of the Range
      Roll Thunder Roll!
      Stallion Canyon
      3 Godfathers
1950 *Border Treasure*
      Devil's Doorway
      The Girl from San Lorenzo
      A Ticket to Tomahawk
      Winchester '73
1952 *Fort Osage*
1953 *Tumbleweed*
1956 *The Broken Star*
1957 *The Tin Star*
1958 *The Defiant Ones*
      Escape from Red Rock
      Gunfire at Indian Gap

Post offices
1945 *In Old New Mexico*

Post-traumatic stress disorder
      Escape in the Fog
1946 Swamp Fire
      Till the End of Time
1947 Crossfire

Post-war life
1946 Till the End of Time
1947 *The Return of Rin Tin Tin*

Postage-stamps—Collectors and collecting
1942 *Nazi Agent*

Postal service
1912 *Atop of the World in Motion*
1921 The Green-Eyed Monster
1939 *Confessions of a Nazi Spy*
1950 *Broken Arrow*
1951 *Slaughter Trail*

Postal workers
1937 *Where Is My Child?*
1949 *Daughter of the West*
1950 Riders of the Pony Express
1958 *The Young Lions*
1959 *Anna Lucasta*

Postmasters
1950 *The Missourians*

Potions
1956 *Hot Blood*

Potomac River
1958 *Houseboat*

Pottery
1919 *The Sleeping Lion*

Poverty
1915 The Kindling
      Marse Covington
1917 Crime and Punishment
      I Will Repay
1918 Hidden Pearls
      Love's Law
1919 Come Out of the Kitchen
      The Red Viper
1921 The Secret Sorrow
1926 Sweet Rosie O'Grady
1927 The Broken Violin
1930 La jaula de los leones
1931 Aloha
      Un caballero de frac
      Chérie
      Die Dreigroschenoper
      Personal Maid
      Quand on est belle
      Such Is Life
1932 Amore e morte
      Marido y mujer
      The Secrets of Wu Sin
1934 *Beloved*
      The Great Flirtation
1935 Bordertown
      El día que me quieras
      Romance in Manhattan
1936 *Show Boat*
1937 Natalka Poltavka
1938 City Streets
      The Rage of Paris

      La vida bohemia
1939 Gone With the Wind
      Judge Hardy and Son
      Motel the Operator
1940 *Am I Guilty?*
      George Washington Carver
1941 *Min Jok Jay Hung Sing*
      New York Town
      Sullivan's Travels
1942 *Tales of Manhattan*
1945 *A Medal for Benny*
      A Tree Grows in Brooklyn
1946 *Sheriff of Redwood Valley*
      Song of the South
1946? *Beale Street Mama*
1947 *Body and Soul*
1948 Fighting Father Dunne
      The Miracle of the Bells
1951 *Native Son*
      Show Boat
1953 *Bright Road*
1955 *Good Morning, Miss Dove*
1956 *Baby Doll*
      The Benny Goodman Story
      Giant
1957 *Twelve Angry Men*
1958 *The Badlanders*
1959 *The Last Angry Man*
      Porgy and Bess

Powhatan
1923 Jamestown

Practical jokes
1917 *Castles for Two*
      His Sweetheart
1933 *Rafter Romance*
1940 *Viva Cisco Kid*
1942 *Whispering Ghosts*
1948 *Jiggs and Maggie in Court*

Prairies
1934 *Wheels of Destiny*
1959 *Thunder in the Sun*

Prayer
1917 *The Tell-Tale Step*
1931 *Shulamith*
1932 *Amore e morte*
      Harlem Is Heaven
1934 *Limehouse Blues*
      Wheels of Destiny
1935 *Bar-Mitzvah*
1936 The Green Pastures
1937 *Natalka Poltavka*
1939 *Keep Punching*
      Mothers of Today
1940 *Overture to Glory*
1942 *Tales of Manhattan*
      Tortilla Flat
1943 *Bataan*
      Marching On!
      The Ox-Bow Incident
1944 *The Negro Soldier*
1947 *The Peanut Man*
1948 *Reaching from Heaven*
1949 *Answer for Anne*
      The Red Menace
1950 *God, Man and Devil*
      Stars in My Crown
1951 *The Raging Tide*
1953 *Taxi*
1955 *Kentucky Rifle*
      A Man Called Peter
1959 *Porgy and Bess*
1960 *The Crowning Experience*

Pre-nuptial contracts
    use Antenuptial contracts

Preachers
1919 *The Homesteader*
1929 Hallelujah
1931 Die Maske Fällt
1934 Drums O' Voodoo
1936 The Green Pastures
1940 *Viva Cisco Kid*
1941 *Sullivan's Travels*
1947 *Going to Glory, Come to Jesus*
1949 Satan's Cradle
1955 *Kentucky Rifle*
1956 Ghost Town

Predictions
1932 Thirteen Women
1934 *Drums O' Voodoo*
1941 *Four Shall Die*
1945 *Escape in the Fog*
1949 *Top O' the Morning*

Pregnancy
1915 *Kreutzer Sonata*
1917 *The Red Woman*
        The Slacker
1919 A Man's Duty
1920 The North Wind's Malice
1930 The Grand Parade
1931 *Resurrección*
1932 *Amore e morte*
        Marido y mujer
        The Vanishing Frontier
1934 As the Earth Turns
        Beloved
        Coming Out Party
1937 *The Plainsman*
1940 *Jennie*
        They Knew What They
            Wanted
1941 *Hold Back the Dawn*
1943 *Redhead from Manhattan*
1944 *Mr. Skeffington*
        The Sullivans
1946 *The Gentleman Misbehaves*
1947 *Desperate*
        Little Mister Jim
1949 Knock on Any Door
1950 *The Daughter of Rosie
            O'Grady*
1951 *Across the Wide Missouri*
        Five
        The Girl on the Bridge
        A Streetcar Named Desire
        Teresa
1952 *The Fabulous Senorita*
1954 *Indiscretion of an
            American Wife*
1955 *Blackboard Jungle*
        Good Morning, Miss Dove
        Not As a Stranger
1956 Full of Life
1957 *The Guns of Fort Petticoat*
1960 *All the Fine Young
            Cannibals*
        I Passed for White
        This Rebel Breed

Prejudice
    use **Bigotry;**
            Racism

Premarital sex
1932 *Senza mamma
            e'nnamurato*
1954 Carmen Jones
1957 *Raintree County*
1958 *Marjorie Morningstar*
1960 *All the Fine Young
            Cannibals*
        Take a Giant Step

Preparatory schools
1939 *Keep Punching*

Presbyterians
1955 A Man Called Peter

Prescott (AZ)
1946 *Wild West*
1958 *The Badlanders*

Presidents
1931 *Such Is Life*

Press agents
1917 *Runaway Romany*
1919 *Spotlight Sadie*
1922 Head over Heels
1929 Mother's Boy
1935 A Night at the Ritz
1936 *Mad Holiday*
1941 *Playmates*
1943 *The Leopard Man*
1944 *Lake Placid Serenade*
1946 *The Trap*
1947 *Sepia Cinderella*
1948 *The Miracle of the Bells*

Pride and vanity
1933 *The Emperor Jones*
        A Lady's Profession
1934 *Caravane*
1935 The Little Colonel
        McFadden's Flats
1937 *Waikiki Wedding*
1939 *Mirele Efros*
1940 Three Cheers for the Irish
        The Way of All Flesh
1947 *The Foxes of Harrow*
1951 Adventures of Captain
            Fabian
1952 The Iron Mistress

1956 Man from Del Rio
Priests
1913? *Hiawatha*
1915 The Rosary
1916 *The Woman in 47*
1917 *The Woman and the Beast*
1918 *Denny from Ireland*
1921 *No Woman Knows*
1929 Abie's Irish Rose
        Evangeline
1930 *Monsieur le Fox*
        Sevilla de mis amores
1931 *Die Dreigroschenoper*
1932 *No Greater Love*
1934 Cheyenne Sun Dance
1935 *Bordertown*
1936 *The Phantom of Santa Fe*
        Rainbow on the River
        Ramona
1938 *City Streets*
        Mr. Moto Takes a Chance
1939 *Tevya*
        Waterfront
1940 The Fighting 69th
        Hi-Yo Silver
1941 *Romance of the Rio Grande*
1942 *Gentleman Jim*
        Tortilla Flat
1943 *Mr. Lucky*
1944 *Going My Way*
        The Sullivans
1945 The Bells of St. Mary's
        The Cisco Kid Returns
        Colorado Pioneers
        The Great John L.
        In Old New Mexico
        The Mummy's Curse
        Samurai
        Sunbonnet Sue
1946 *Abie's Irish Rose*
        Don Ricardo Returns
        Romance of the West
1947 *Bells of San Fernando*
        Easy Come, Easy Go
        The Jolson Story
        The Return of Rin Tin Tin
1948 *Cry of the City*
        Fighting Father Dunne
        The Miracle of the Bells
1949 *The Daring Caballero*
        The Mysterious Desperado
        The Red Menace
1950 Bandit Queen
        Buccaneer's Girl
        Damien
        Give Us This Day
1951 *The Mark of the Renegade*
1952 Kid Monk Baroni
        The Quiet Man
        Woman in the Dark
1953 *Beneath the 12-Mile Reef*
        Ride, Vaquero!
1954 *Passion*
1955 *The Rose Tattoo*
        Santa Fe Passage
1956 *Full of Life*
1957 *The Midnight Story*
        Raiders of Old California
        The Ride Back
1958 *The Lone Ranger and the
            Lost City of Gold*
1960 For the Love of Mike
        Studs Lonigan

Primates
    use **Apes;**
            Specific types of apes

Princes
1918 The Firebrand
1919 Mandarin's Gold
1931 Hay que casar al príncipe
        La ley del harem
1932 *The Son-Daughter*
1933 *Dance Hall Hostess*
        Victims of Persecution
1934 Song of the Islands
1937 Thank You, Mr. Moto
1938 Castillos en el aire
1940 *Midnight Shadow*
1947 Northwest Outpost
1951 When the Redskins Rode

Princesses
1919 A Fallen Idol
1930 *Olimpia*
1933 El rey de los gitanos

1934 *Strange Wives*
1935 Naughty Marietta
1939 Mr. Wong in Chinatown
1947 *The Chinese Ring*
        Northwest Outpost
1953 *Captain John Smith and
            Pocahontas*
        Dream Wife
1955 *Kiss of Fire*

Princeton University
1928 Hold 'Em Yale

Printers
1931 *Cimarron*
1945 *In Old New Mexico*
1949 *Jigsaw*

Prison camps
1941 *Z Dymem Pożarów*

Prison escapees
1919 *A Heart in Pawn*
1927 *The Scar of Shame*
1930 El presidio
1931 *Three Who Loved*
1939 *Charlie Chan in Honolulu*
194- *Mistaken Identity*
1942 *Unseen Enemy*
1949 Ranger of Cherokee Strip
1953 *Cry of the Hunted*
1958 The Defiant Ones

Prison escapes
1918 *Good-Bye, Bill*
        Laughing Bill Hyde
        The Temple of Dusk
1919 *Told in the Hills*
1920 *Our Christianity and
            Nobody's Child*
1920? *Her Story*
1922 Flesh and Blood
1923 *Flames of Wrath*
1931 *El código penal*
        Pardon Us
        El pasado acusa
1932 Riders of the Desert
1933 *The Emperor Jones*
1934 *Lazy River*
1934? *Harlem After Midnight*
1936 *The Prisoner of Shark
            Island*
        Rebellion
1937 *One Mile from Heaven*
1943 *Dr. Gillespie's Criminal
            Case*
1946 *Sheriff of Redwood Valley*
1948 *Cry of the City*
1950 *Buccaneer's Girl*
1959 *Gunmen from Laredo*
        Shake Hands with the Devil

Prison guards
1930 El presidio

Prison life
1916 Unprotected
1919 *The Scar*
1931 Pardon Us
1932 *Men Are Such Fools*

Prison reform
1930 El presidio

Prison trustees
1941 *Sullivan's Travels*

Prison wardens
1930 El presidio
1931 *El código penal*
        Pardon Us
1932 *Men Are Such Fools*
1936 *Love and Sacrifice*
1937 *One Mile from Heaven*
1941 *Sullivan's Travels*
1943 *Dr. Gillespie's Criminal
            Case*
        Gangway for Tomorrow
        Call Northside 777
1948 *Angel in Exile*
1953 *Cry of the Hunted*

Prisoners
1934 *Un capitán de cosacos*
1935 *Fighting Pioneers*
1939 *The Bronze Buckaroo*
1940? Mr. Washington Goes to
            Town
1941 *Mystery Ship*
1944 *Sonora Stagecoach*
1949 *Border Incident*
        The Fighting Kentuckian
        House of Strangers
        Ranger of Cherokee Strip

1951 *Distant Drums*
1954 *Apache*
        Sitting Bull
1955 Smoke Signal
1957 *Tomahawk Trail*
        Trooper Hook
1958 *Ambush at Cimarron Pass*

Prisoners of war
1918 *The Price of Applause*
1920 *Rio Grande*
1926 *The Strong Man*
1929 Love, Live and Laugh
1941 *They Dare Not Love*
1942 *Unseen Enemy*
        Valley of Hunted Men
1943 *Jack London*
1950 *Battleground*
1951 *The Steel Helmet*
1952 *Battles of Chief Pontiac*
1953 San Antone
1958 *The Light in the Forest*

Prisons
1920 *The North Wind's Malice*
1930 El valiente
1931 El código penal
        La incorregible
        Kismet
        Resurrección
1932 *Le cas du docteur Brenner
            Hombres en mi vida
            Joseph in the Land of Egypt*
1936 *Love and Sacrifice*
        The Prisoner of Shark Island
1938 *The Power of Life*
1943 *Dr. Gillespie's Criminal
            Case*
1946 *Dark Alibi*
1947 *Marshal of Cripple Creek*
1948 *Call Northside 777*
        Cry of the City
1950 *The Baron of Arizona*
        Two Flags West
1953 *Cry of the Hunted*
1954 *Broken Lance*
1955 *Duel on the Mississippi*

Private detectives
1914 *The Great Diamond
            Robbery*
1936 *Muss 'Em Up*
1937 *Song of the City*
1940 *Midnight Shadow*
1941 *Four Shall Die*
1942 *Professor Creeps*
        Twin Beds
1945 *The Shanghai Cobra*
1946 Dark Alibi
        Shadows Over Chinatown
        The Trap
1947 *Desperate*
1948 Docks of New Orleans
        The Golden Eye
        The Lady from Shanghai
        Shanghai Chest
1951 Mask of the Dragon
1957 *The Midnight Story*

Privateering
1938 The Buccaneer
1953 *Captain John Smith and
            Pocahontas*

Prizes and trophies
1945 *Colorado Pioneers*
1950 *Annie Get Your Gun*
1953 *The Man Behind the Gun*

Probation
1939 *Reform School*
1942 *Mokey*
1951 *The Raging Tide*

Process servers
1937 *Boots and Saddles*

Prodigies
1927 The Broken Violin
1938 Little Miss Roughneck

Produce trade
1949 Thieves' Highway

Producers
    use **Motion picture
            producers;**
            Television producers;
            Theatrical producers

Professors
1914 Hearts United
1915 *The Grandee's Ring*
1918 *Good-Bye, Bill*
        The Ordeal of Rosetta

1919　The Westerners
1921　The Cave Girl
1932　Hidden Valley
1933　Ever in My Heart
1936　Charlie Chan's Secret
　　　Winterset
1939　Heaven with a Barbed Wire
　　　Fence
　　　Mr. Moto Takes a Vacation
1940　Charlie Chan's Murder
　　　Cruise
　　　Escape to Glory
1942　Nazi Agent
1943　Crime Smasher
　　　Jack London
1944　Riding West
1946　Beware
1951　The Harlem Globetrotters
　　　Saturday's Hero
　　　Teresa
1952　The Fabulous Senorita
　　　It's a Big Country: An
　　　American Anthology
1954　Indiscretion of an
　　　American Wife
1955　Trial
1958　Home Before Dark

Profiteering
1946　Wild West
1947　The Chinese Ring
　　　Ride the Pink Horse
1948　Unconquered
1952　Fort Osage

Progress
1947　Untamed Fury
1953　Thunder Bay
1960　Wild River

Prohibition
1915　The Nigger
1920?　Reformation
1930　Una cana al aire
1933　Best of Enemies
　　　The Cohens and Kellys in
　　　Trouble
　　　Dance Hall Hostess
　　　A Lady's Profession
　　　The Man Who Dared: An
　　　Imaginative Biography
　　　Song of the Eagle
1959　Al Capone

Promiscuity
1946　Notorious

Promises
　　use Oaths;
　　　Pledges

Promoters
1928　Eleven P.M.
1932　Le bluffeur
1933　La melodía probibida
1940　The Notorious Elinor Lee
1941　Mutiny in the Arctic
1942　Sunday Punch
1943　The Girl from Monterrey
1945　Club Havana
1949　The Cowboy and the
　　　Prizefighter
1950　Right Cross
1954　Go Man Go

Promotions
1941　Caught in the Act
1944　An American Romance

Propaganda
1918　The Ranger
1939　Confessions of a Nazi Spy
1942　Friendly Enemies
1946　The Red Dragon
1949　Jigsaw

Prophesies
　　use Revelation (Theology,
　　　inspiration)

Prophets
1913?　Hiawatha
1927　With Sitting Bull at the
　　　Spirit Lake Massacre
1932　Joseph in the Land of Egypt
1936　The Green Pastures

Proposals (Marital)
1918　The Gypsy Trail
　　　Ruggles of Red Gap
1925　Body and Soul
1926　The Flying Ace
1930　Estrellados
　　　Sei tu l'amore

1931　Cavalier of the West
　　　Delicious
　　　The Exile
　　　Women Love Once
1932　Amor in montagna
　　　Charlie Chan's Chance
　　　The Forty-Niners
　　　Ljubav i strast
　　　Ten Minutes to Live
1932?　The Girl from Chicago
1933　The Cohens and Kellys in
　　　Trouble
　　　A Lady's Profession
　　　Robbers' Roost
　　　Victims of Persecution
1933?　Scandal
1934　The Cat's-Paw
　　　Chloe: Love Is Calling You
　　　Dos más uno, dos
　　　Las fronteras del amor
　　　Granaderos del amor
　　　Nada más que una mujer
　　　Riding Speed
　　　She Was a Lady
　　　Wagon Wheels
1935　Shir Hashirim
　　　So Red the Rose
1936　Border Phantom
　　　Custer's Last Stand
　　　Hair-Trigger Casey
　　　Klondike Annie
1937　Manhattan
　　　Merry-Go-Round
　　　Natalka Poltavka
　　　That I May Live
　　　Waikiki Wedding
1938　The Buccaneer
　　　Daughter of Shanghai
　　　Happy Landing
　　　In Old Chicago
　　　Life Goes On
1939　The Devil's Daughter
　　　Gang Smashers
　　　La Inmaculada
　　　The Light Ahead
1940　The Great Advisor
　　　Santa Fe Trail
　　　They Knew What They
　　　Wanted
1941　New York Town
1942　Foreign Agent
　　　Holiday Inn
1943　Dixie
　　　Redhead from Manhattan
1944　Dark Waters
　　　Hi, Beautiful
1945　Club Havana
　　　The Great John L.
　　　Our Vines Have Tender
　　　Grapes
　　　Salome, Where She Danced
　　　The Valley of Decision
1946　Border Bandits
　　　Bringing Up Father
1947　The Farmer's Daughter
　　　The Jolson Story
1948　Fort Apache
1949　The Dalton Gang
　　　The Fighting Kentuckian
　　　Massacre River
　　　That Midnight Kiss
1950　Bandit Queen
　　　Give Us This Day
　　　The Toast of New Orleans
1950?　Three Daughters
1951　Only the Valiant
1952　The Quiet Man
1953　Dream Wife
　　　So Big
1955　Duel on the Mississippi
　　　Good Morning, Miss Dove
　　　Santa Fe Passage
1956　Death of a Scoundrel
1957　The Oklahoman
　　　Revolt at Fort Laramie
1958　The Light in the Forest
　　　Sierra Baron
1959　The Black Orchid
　　　The Sheriff of Fractured
　　　Jaw

Propriety
1920　The Good-Bad Wife
1943　The Gang's All Here
1949　The Girl from Jones Beach

Prospectors
1915　The Gambler of the West
1917　Her Own People
1918　The Goddess of Lost Lake
　　　Real Folks
1919　Scarlet Days
　　　Told in the Hills
1920　The North Wind's Malice
1923　The Huntress
1924　The Mine with the Iron
　　　Door
1926　Pals in Paradise
　　　Under Fire
1927　The Devil's Saddle
1929　Hawk of the Hills
　　　Redskin
1931　The Avenger
1932　Hidden Valley
1936　Custer's Last Stand
　　　Robin Hood of El Dorado
　　　Sutter's Gold
1937　The Barrier
1939　Bad Lands
1940　Taku
1948　Guns of Hate
1949　The Valiant Hombre
1950　The Cariboo Trail
1952　The Raiders
1953　Column South
1954　Sitting Bull
　　　Thunder Pass
　　　The Yellow Tomahawk
1956　The Lone Ranger
　　　Secret of Treasure
　　　Mountain
1960　Walk Tall

Prostheses and artificial limbs
1932　Tiger Shark
1944　Knickerbocker Holiday

Prostitutes
　　use Prostitution;
　　　White-slave traffic

Prostitution
1913　The Inside of the White
　　　Slave Traffic
1914　The Jungle
1916　Civilization's Child
1917　Sold at Auction
1918　The City of Dim Faces
　　　Fields of Honor
1923　Anna Christie
1928　Eleven P.M.
1930　Anna Christie
1931　Cimarron
　　　Die Dreigroschenoper
　　　Resurrección
1932　Call Her Savage
　　　So Big
　　　Ten Minutes to Live
1933　The Emperor Jones
1934　He Was Her Man
1939　The Escape
　　　Gone With the Wind
1948　The Time of Your Life
1951　Oh! Susanna
　　　Westward the Women
1958　The Badlanders
1959　Anna Lucasta
1960　Take a Giant Step
　　　Walk Like a Dragon

Protection racket
1941　Caught in the Act
　　　Lady from Louisiana

Protest marches
1926　Rose of the Tenements
1940　Americaner Schadchen

Protestantism
1921?　[Unidentified Film]
1929　Abie's Irish Rose
1948　Big City
1960　For the Love of Mike

Proverbs
1934　The Cat's-Paw

Prudes
1941　Louisiana Purchase
1959　The Hanging Tree

Prussians
1945　Salome, Where She Danced

Psychiatrists
1935　Te quiero con locura
1939　Charlie Chan in Honolulu
1940　Americaner Schadchen
1942　Cat People

1944　Mr. Skeffington
1948　Sleep, My Love
1949　The Quiet One
1950　So Young, So Bad
1956　Singing in the Dark

Psychics
　　use Mediums

Psychoanalysis
1932　L'athlète incomplet

Psychoanalysts
1941　Dead Men Tell
1950　The Big Hangover

Psychological torment
1944　Dark Waters
1946　The Face of Marble
1948　Key Largo
　　　Sleep, My Love
1950　The Men

Psychologists
　　　Belle of Old Mexico
1951　Teresa

Psychology
1947　Jiggs and Maggie in Society
1949　Home of the Brave

Psychosomatic illness
1945　Between Two Women
1949　Home of the Brave
1956　Serenade
1958　St. Louis Blues

Psycopaths
1950　No Way Out

Public defenders
1931　La mujer X
1950　The Big Hangover

Public works
　　use Public utilities

Publicists
1931　The Guilty Generation
1934　She Was a Lady
1941　Sun Valley Serenade

Publicity
1917　Runaway Romany
1929　The Cohens and Kellys in
　　　Atlantic City
1933　Let's Fall in Love
1934　Las fronteras del amor
1938　Happy Landing
　　　Little Miss Roughneck
1940　Americaner Schadchen
1945　A Medal for Benny

Publicity stunts
1934　Beloved
1937　Waikiki Wedding
1941　Playmates
1944　Lake Placid Serenade
1945　I Love a Bandleader
1948　The Miracle of the Bells
1949?　She's Too Mean for Me
1953　The Stars Are Singing

Publishers and publishing
1919　As a Man Thinks
　　　Daughter of Mine
　　　Toby's Bow
1922　Spitfire
1935　Harmony Lane
1937　Nation Aflame
1941　Come Live with Me
1943　Jack London
1944　Going My Way
1948　Call Northside 777
　　　The Luck of the Irish
1953　Taxi

Pubs
1935　His Family Tree
1952　The Quiet Man
1959　Shake Hands with the Devil

Pueblo Indians
1923　The Secret of the Pueblo

Pueblos
1951　New Mexico

Puerto Ricans
1955　Blackboard Jungle
1956　Crowded Paradise
1957　Twelve Angry Men
1958　Machete
1959　Cry Tough
1960　The Pusher

Puerto Rico
1918　The Liar
1939　Mr. Moto in Danger Island
1956　Crowded Paradise

Pulaski (TN)
1915? *Sam Davis, the Hero of Tennessee*

Pulp fiction
1922 Silver Spurs

Pumas
1960 *For the Love of Mike*

Puppeteers
1945 *The Jade Mask*

Puppets
1918 One More American
1921 Puppets of Fate
1926 Puppets
1933 *L'amour guide*
1935 *Naughty Marietta*

Purim
The Yiddish King Lear
1937 The Jester (Der Purimspieler)

Puritanism
1914 When Broadway Was a Trail

Puritans
1937 Maid of Salem

Pyromania
1927 Heroes in Blue

Quacks and quackery
1948 *The Paleface*

Quakers
1914 The Redemption of David Corson
1917 *The Secret of Eve*
1928 Uncle Tom's Cabin
1952 *High Noon*

Quanah
use **Quanah Parker**

Quarantine
1917 *The Bride of Hate*
1938 *Rascals*
1943 *Ladies' Day*
1950 *Stars in My Crown*
1957 *All Mine to Give*

Quarries and quarrying
1955 *A Man Called Peter*

Queens
1944 *Tahiti Nights*

Quicksand
1919 *Lasca*
1927 Wild Geese
1932 *Riders of the Desert*
1934 *Drums O' Voodoo*
1936 *Silly Billies*
1944 *Dark Waters*
1947 *Untamed Fury*
1949 *Border Incident*
1950 *Intruder in the Dust*
1953 *Cry of the Hunted*
Seminole

Quintuplets
1941 *New York Town*

Rabbis
1915 Children of the Ghetto
1921 *No Woman Knows*
1925 His People
1929 Abie's Irish Rose
1932 *A Daughter of Her People*
Mazel Tov
No Greater Love
Yiskor
1933 *The Eternal Jew*
1934 *The Rabbi's Power*
1939 *Kol Nidre*
Mothers of Today
1940 *Americaner Schadchen*
Overture to Glory
1946 *Abie's Irish Rose*
1958 *The Young Lions*

Rabbits
1940 *Viva Cisco Kid*
1946 *Song of the South*
1948? *Boarding House Blues*

Raccoons
1948 *Louisiana Story*
Moonrise

Race car drivers
1932 La foule hurle
1938 Road Demon
1943 *Gangway for Tomorrow*
1947 Buck Privates Come Home

Racehorse owners
1949 The Story of Seabiscuit

Racehorses
The Story of Seabiscuit

Racetracks
The Story of Seabiscuit
Tuna Clipper

Racial impersonation
1920 *The Symbol of the Unconquered*
1921 The Call of His People
1924 His Darker Self
The House Behind the Cedars
1928 *The Jazz Singer*
1929 Why Bring That Up?
1931 *Pardon Us*
1934 Imitation of Life
Operator 13
1935 *The Littlest Rebel*
1940 *Arizona Frontier*
1941 *Western Union*
1942 *Mokey*
The Vanishing Virginian
1943 *Dixie*
The Meanest Man in the World
Redhead from Manhattan
Wagon Tracks West
1945 *The Dolly Sisters*
1947 *The Jolson Story*
1949 Lost Boundaries
Pinky
1951 *Mask of the Dragon*
Yes Sir, Mr. Bones
1956 *Reprisal!*
1957 *Band of Angels*
1958 The Lone Ranger and the Lost City of Gold
1959 Imitation of Life
1960 I Passed for White
This Rebel Breed

Racing
1927 Open Range
1930 *El dios del mar*
1943 *Riding High*
1945 *Colorado Pioneers*
1950 *Rock Island Trail*
1957 *Bayou*
Raintree County
Run of the Arrow

Racism
1914 At the Cross Roads
1915 *The Cheat*
The Lure of Woman
Marse Covington
The Nigger
Sealed Valley
1916 Betrayed
The Half-Breed
Lone Star
Ramona
1917 *The Bar Sinister*
The Barrier
The Bride of Hate
The Captain of the Gray Horse Troop
Her Own People
John Ermine of the Yellowstone
The Primitive Call
1918 *Broken Ties*
The Goddess of Lost Lake
The Liar
Toys of Fate
The Unbeliever
1919 A Fallen Idol
His Debt
The Homesteader
Injustice
The Little Diplomat
1920 In the Depths of Our Hearts
Li Ting Lang
Pagan Love
Rio Grande
The Symbol of the Unconquered
The Third Woman
The Tiger's Coat
Within Our Gates
1920? Broken Hearts
1921 Shadows of the West
1922 Blazing Arrows
The Crow's Nest
The Great Alone
The Half Breed
Spitfire

1927 Red Clay
1930 Son of the Gods
Whoopee
1931 *Street Scene*
1932 Thirteen Women
Veiled Aristocrats
White Eagle
1933 Victims of Persecution
1934 *Behold My Wife!*
Imitation of Life
Massacre
1935 Bordertown
Circle of Death
1936 *For the Service*
Ramona
1937 *Charlie Chan at the Opera*
Life Begins in College
1938 Birthright
California Frontier
God's Step Children
1939 *Lying Lips*
1940 *The Notorious Elinor Lee*
1943 Wagon Tracks West
1944 Buffalo Bill
1947 Black Gold
The Farmer's Daughter
Little Mister Jim
1948 *The Betrayal*
Open Secret
Strange Victory
1949 Home of the Brave
Jigsaw
Lost Boundaries
Pinky
Prejudice
1950 *The Big Hangover*
Broken Arrow
Intruder in the Dust
The Jackie Robinson Story
The Lawless
No Way Out
1951 *Apache Drums*
Cyclone Fury
Five
Go for Broke!
Jim Thorpe—All-American
The Last Outpost
Native Son
New Mexico
Tomahawk
The Well
1952 *The Big Sky*
Bright Victory
Japanese War Bride
Red Ball Express
The Ring
1953 The Great Sioux Uprising
The Member of the Wedding
The Pathfinder
1954 *Apache*
Cattle Queen of Montana
Go Man Go
They Rode West
The Yellow Tomahawk
1955 *Apache Woman*
Blackboard Jungle
Chief Crazy Horse
Fort Yuma
Foxfire
The Indian Fighter
Seminole Uprising
Seven Angry Men
Seven Cities of Gold
Trial
The View from Pompey's Head
1956 *Comanche*
Giant
The Last Hunt
The Last Wagon
Reprisal!
The Searchers
The White Squaw
1957 Burden of Truth
Edge of the City
Naked in the Sun
The Oklahoman
Pawnee
Ride Out for Revenge
Run of the Arrow
Satchmo the Great
The Tin Star
Trooper Hook

1958 *The Badlanders*
The Defiant Ones
Fort Massacre
Gun Fever
Gunman's Walk
Kings Go Forth
The Light in the Forest
The Lone Ranger and the Lost City of Gold
Touch of Evil
1959 The Crimson Kimono
The Crimson Kimono
Imitation of Life
Last Train from Gun Hill
Night of the Quarter Moon
Odds Against Tomorrow
Yellowstone Kelly
1960 *All the Fine Young Cannibals*
All the Young Men
Cimarron
The Crowning Experience
Flaming Star
Hell to Eternity
I Passed for White
Ice Palace
Key Witness
Sergeant Rutledge
Take a Giant Step
This Rebel Breed
The Unforgiven
Walk Tall
Wild River

Racketeers
1931 *Charlie Chan Carries On*
Gentleman's Fate
1932 Harlem Is Heaven
Hombres en mi vida
1933 *Song of the Eagle*
1936 Human Cargo
1937 *Boy of the Streets*
Charlie Chan on Broadway
It Could Happen to You
1938 Sugar Hill Baby
1939 Gang Smashers
King of Chinatown
Moon over Harlem
Straight to Heaven
1940 *Behind the News*
1942 Rubber Racketeers
1944 The Racket Man
1947 Body and Soul
Hi De Ho
1948 The Fight Never Ends
Miracle in Harlem
1949 *The Sky Dragon*
1951 *The Raging Tide*
1954 Hell's Half Acre
1955 Murder in Villa Capri
1958 Never Love a Stranger

Radar
1945 *The Scarlet Clue*

Radiation
1951 Five

Radicalism
1936 *Winterset*
1951 *Native Son*

Radio, Short wave
1942 *The Navy Comes Through*
Prisoner of Japan
1945 *The House on 92nd St.*

Radio announcers
1942 *Little Tokyo, U.S.A.*
1947 *Jiggs and Maggie in Society*

Radio beams
1944 *Something for the Boys*

Radio broadcasting
1931 *Delicious*
Le père célibataire
1933 *La melodía prohibida*
Obey the Law
1934 *Las fronteras del amor*
Stand Up and Cheer!
What a Mother-in-Law!
1935 *His Family Tree*
Piernas de seda
1936 *Charlie Chan's Secret*
Laughing Irish Eyes
Sea Spoilers
1937 *Bargain with Bullets*
The Cantor's Son
Dark Manhattan
Manhattan Merry-Go-Round

Music for Madame
1938? I due gemelli
1939 The Girl from Mexico
El otro soy yo
Straight to Heaven
1940 Behind the News
Broken Strings
Charlie Chan at the Wax
Museum
The Fatal Hour
The Great Advisor
Music in My Heart
Three Faces West
1941 The Mexican Spitfire's Baby
1942 Little Tokyo, U.S.A.
1943 Marching On!
What's Buzzin' Cousin?
1951 The Harlem Globetrotters
1959 The World, the Flesh and
the Devil

Radio Free Europe
1957 Journey to Freedom

Radio operators
1927 Lost at the Front
1942 Prisoner of Japan
1958 Kings Go Forth

Radio performers
1930 She Got What She Wanted
1939 El trovador de la radio
1942 Foreign Agent
Whispering Ghosts
1945 The Scarlet Clue
1946 Stars on Parade

Radio programs
1941 New York Town
Where Did You Get That
Girl?
1942 Nazi Agent
Rio Rita
Woman of the Year
1943 Margin for Error
1945 The Scarlet Clue
1946 Cuban Pete
Slightly Scandalous
1947 Humoresque
1948 Docks of New Orleans
1949 That Midnight Kiss
1953 The Eddie Cantor Story
The Stars Are Singing
1956 The Benny Goodman Story

Radio sponsors
1939 The Girl from Mexico
1941 Playmates
Where Did You Get That
Girl?
1942 Whispering Ghosts
1944 Hi, Beautiful
1945 The Scarlet Clue
1946 Cuban Pete
Stars on Parade

Radio stations
Stars on Parade
1947 Reet, Petite and Gone

Radios
1925 The Manicure Girl
1941 King of the Zombies
1946 Till the End of Time
1948 Docks of New Orleans
1958 The Defiant Ones

Radium
1939 Harlem Rides the Range
One Dark Night
1945 The Shanghai Cobra

Raffles
1942 Tortilla Flat

Rafts
1920 Huckleberry Finn
1943 Redhead from Manhattan
1950 North of the Great Divide
1957 The Deerslayer
1960 The Adventures of
Huckleberry Finn

Ragpickers
1912 The Adventures of
Lieutenant Petrosino

Raids
1927 With Sitting Bull at the
Spirit Lake Massacre
1930 Las campanas de
Capistrano
1932 The Golden West
Texas Pioneers
1936 Custer's Last Stand
Rose of the Rancho

1937 The Californian
1942 Gentleman Jim
Lawless Plainsmen
1943 Deerslayer
1947 Easy Come, Easy Go
1951 Flaming Feather
The Last Outpost
Snake River Desperadoes
When the Redskins Rode
1952 Apache Country
Brave Warrior
California Conquest
1954 Arrow in the Dust
War Arrow
1955 Duel on the Mississippi
1956 Comanche
Daniel Boone, Trail Blazer
The Last Frontier
1957 The Deerslayer
The Ride Back
Ride Out for Revenge
Tomahawk Trail
1958 Fort Bowie
Gun Fever
1959 Al Capone
The Jayhawkers!
1960 Comanche Station
Sergeant Rutledge

Railroad agents
1926 The Flying Ace
1954 Overland Pacific
1959 The Wonderful Country
1960 Oklahoma Territory

Railroad companies
1939 Let Freedom Ring
1950 Rock Island Trail
A Ticket to Tomahawk

Railroad detectives
1926 The Flying Ace
1946 Sunset Pass

Railroad engineers
1950 Rock Island Trail
A Ticket to Tomahawk
Train to Tombstone

Railroad stations
1915 A Yankee from the West
1926 The Flying Ace
1928 The Jazz Singer
1950 A Ticket to Tomahawk

Railroad workers
1919 Hearts of Men
1926 The Flying Ace
1953 Old Overland Trail
1954 Overland Pacific

Railroads
1915 Chimmie Fadden Out West
1916 Hulda from Holland
1921 The Green-Eyed Monster
1926 Buffalo Bill on the U. P.
Trail
1929 Romance of the Rio Grande
1931 Fighting Caravans
1932 The Golden West
1935 The Little Colonel
1937 Prairie Thunder
1938 The Texans
1939 Let Freedom Ring
Stand Up and Fight
1940 Arizona Frontier
Santa Fe Trail
1941 Land of Liberty
1942 American Empire
1946 Saratoga Trunk
Sheriff of Redwood Valley
1947 Duel in the Sun
1948 Four Faces West
Red River
1953 The Charge at Feather
River
Old Overland Trail
1958 Ride a Crooked Trail

Railroads—Refrigerator cars
use **Trains—Refrigerator cars**

Rainstorms
1919 His Parisian Wife
1930 Check and Double Check
1931 Hay que casar al príncipe
Mi último amor
1933 Primavera en otoño
Rafter Romance
Una viuda romántica
1934 Our Daily Bread
White Heat

1935 The Littlest Rebel
1936 Daniel Boone
The Prisoner of Shark
Island
Winterset
1938 Outside of Paradise
1940 Her Second Mother
1941 Lady from Louisiana
1942 Seven Sweethearts
Song of the Islands
1945 The Shanghai Cobra
1946 Canyon Passage
1959 Gunmen from Laredo

Rallies
1935 His Family Tree
1940 The Man I Married
The Ramparts We Watch
1947 The Farmer's Daughter
Mantan Runs for Mayor
1955 Trial
1958 St. Louis Blues

Ranch foremen
1920 The Cyclone
1921 The Double O
The Kiss
1922 The Crimson Skull
When East Comes West
1924 The Broken Law
North of Nevada
North of 36
1927 Aflame in the Sky
The Fighting Hombre
1931 Cavalier of the West
1932 Law and Lawless
1933 Robbers' Roost
1934 The Battling Buckaroo
The Prescott Kid
Riding Speed
1935 Range Warfare
Texas Terror
1936 Hair-Trigger Casey
1937 Boots and Saddles
1938 Wild Horse Canyon
1939 Harlem Rides the Range
In Old Caliente
Trigger Fingers
1940 Cuando canta la Ley
The Gay Caballero
Young Buffalo Bill
1942 Song of the Islands
1944 The San Antonio Kid
Tucson Raiders
1945 Colorado Pioneers
Wanderer of the Wasteland
1946 Sun Valley Cyclone
1949 Stagecoach Kid
Stallion Canyon
1950 The Furies
Storm Over Wyoming
1954 Broken Lance
1956 The Lone Ranger

Ranchers
1917 Follow the Girl
1918 The Border Raiders
The Hell Cat
1918? Indian Life
1919? When the Desert Smiles
1921 Cotton and Cattle
The Double O
Shadows of the West
1922 The Crimson Skull
One Eighth Apache
The Virgin of Seminole
When East Comes West
1923 The Sting of the Scorpion
Suzanna
1924 The Heritage of the Desert
North of 36
1925 Brand of Cowardice
A Son of His Father
1927 The Fighting Hombre
Whispering Sage
White Gold
1929 In Old California
Romance of the Rio Grande
1930 On the Border
1931 Las luces de Buenos Aires
Riders of the Rio
1932 Border Devils
The Galloping Kid
Law and Lawless
Mystery Ranch
1933 Circle Canyon
Man from Monterey
Robbers' Roost

1934 The Battling Buckaroo
The Cactus Kid
La ciudad de cartón
Fighting Through
Las fronteras del amor
Laughing Boy
The Prescott Kid
Riding Speed
The Star Packer
1935 Circle of Death
Cowboy Holiday
Melody Trail
Range Warfare
1935? The Irish Gringo
1936 Aces and Eights
Amor que vuelve
Hair-Trigger Casey
Song of the Gringo
1937 Boots and Saddles
Border Cafe
The Californian
Law and Lead
1938 Outlaw Express
The Renegade Ranger
The Texans
Two Gun Man from
Harlem
Wild Horse Canyon
1939 The Fighting Gringo
Forged Passport
In Old Caliente
Let Freedom Ring
Miracle on Main Street
1940 Hi-Yo Silver
Rhythm of the Rio Grande
Young Buffalo Bill
1941 Doomed Caravan
Ride on Vaquero
Romance of the Rio Grande
Secret of the Wastelands
1942 American Empire
King of the Stallions
Valley of Hunted Men
1943 Wagon Tracks West
1944 Outlaw Trail
1945 South of the Rio Grande
Sun Valley Cyclone
1946 Sunset Pass
Without Reservations
1947 The Adventures of Don
Coyote
Dangerous Venture
Duel in the Sun
The Last Round-Up
Rustlers of Devil's Canyon
Thunder Mountain
Vigilantes of Boomtown
1948 Indian Agent
Rocky
Singin' Spurs
Western Heritage
1949 Border Incident
Brothers in the Saddle
Call of the Forest
The Cowboy and the Indians
The Cowboy and the
Prizefighter
The Golden Stallion
Masked Raiders
Riders of the Range
Rustlers
Stagecoach Kid
Stallion Canyon
Streets of Laredo
Tulsa
1950 Broken Arrow
Cherokee Uprising
The Furies
The Girl from San Lorenzo
Indian Territory
Storm Over Wyoming
Sunset in the West
1951 Cyclone Fury
Flaming Feather
Fort Defiance
Oh! Susanna
1952 California Conquest
Trail of the Arrow
1953 Tumbleweed
1954 Broken Lance
Cattle Queen of Montana
1956 The Burning Hills
The Lone Ranger
The Searchers

Ranchers
- 1957 *The Lawless Eighties*
  - Man in the Shadow
  - The Oklahoman
  - *Trooper Hook*
- 1958 Escape from Red Rock
  - *Gunman's Walk*
- 1960 *Flaming Star*
  - *The Unforgiven*

Ranches
- 1914 Rose of the Rancho
  - *The Squaw Man*
- 1915 *The Lure of Woman*
- 1918 The Border Raiders
  - *Denny from Ireland*
  - *The Hell Cat*
  - Little Red Decides
  - The Only Road
  - *The Squaw Man*
  - Untamed
  - *Wild Women*
- 1919 *Desert Gold*
  - The Gray Towers Mystery
- 1920 *The Cyclone*
- 1921 The Kiss
- 1924 Down by the Rio Grande
  - North of Nevada
- 1925 The Wild Bull's Lair
- 1930 *The Bad Man*
  - Cuando el amor ríe
  - La rosa de fuego
  - Song of the Caballero
  - *Whoopee*
- 1931 *The Avenger*
  - *Cavalier of the West*
  - *The Cisco Kid*
  - *The Squaw Man*
  - Yankee Don
- 1933 *Primavera en otoño*
- 1934 *Charlie Chan's Courage*
  - *Las fronteras del amor*
  - *She Was a Lady*
- 1935 *The Cyclone Ranger*
  - *Riddle Ranch*
  - Texas Terror
- 1936 *For the Service*
  - *My American Wife*
  - Rose of the Rancho
  - *The Traitor*
- 1937 *Manhattan*
  - *Merry-Go-Round*
- 1939 The Bronze Buckaroo
  - *Drifting Westward*
  - Harlem Rides the Range
  - Heaven with a Barbed Wire
  - Fence
  - *The Return of the Cisco Kid*
- 1940 *Cuando canta la Ley*
  - *Lucky Cisco Kid*
- 1942 *Below the Border*
  - Song of the Islands
- 1945 *Colorado Pioneers*
  - *The Navajo Trail*
- 1947 *Robin Hood of Monterey*
  - West to Glory
- 1948 *Four Faces West*
  - *Gun Smugglers*
  - *I Remember Mama*
  - Old Los Angeles
  - *Red River*
  - *Silver Trails*
- 1949 *Colorado Territory*
  - Lookout Sister
  - The Mysterious Desperado
  - *Roll Thunder Roll!*
  - *The Valiant Hombre*
- 1950 *I Killed Geronimo*
- 1954 *The Black Dakotas*
- 1956 Giant
  - *Raw Edge*
- 1957 *Man in the Shadow*
- 1960 *The Plunderers*

Ranchhands
- 1941 *Doomed Caravan*
- 1942 *American Empire*
- 1950 *Cherokee Uprising*

Range wars
- Storm Over Wyoming
- 1959 The Sheriff of Fractured Jaw

Rangers
- 1932 Mystery Ranch
  - Riders of the Desert
- 1936 The Traitor
- 1946 Wild West
- 1948 The Arizona Ranger

- 1949 Ranger of Cherokee Strip
- 1954 Dangerous Mission

Ransom
- 1915 *The Alien*
  - *The Last of the Mafia*
- 1916 *A Child of Mystery*
- 1917 *Sunshine and Gold*
  - The Winged Mystery
- 1921 The Double O
- 1931 *The Hurricane Horseman*
- 1934 *Un capitán de cosacos*
- 1937 *Harlem on the Prairie*
- 1941 *Ride on Vaquero*
- 1942 *Shut My Big Mouth*
- 1943 *Deerslayer*
- 1949 *Rustlers*
- 1951 *Native Son*
- 1953 *San Antone*
- 1956 *Quincannon, Frontier*
  - *Scout*

Rape
- 1914 *The Jungle*
- 1915 The Birth of a Nation
- 1916 *The Grip of Jealousy*
  - *Unprotected*
  - A Woman's Honor
- 1918 *The Birth of a Race*
- 1919 Auction of Souls
  - *Behind the Door*
  - A Fallen Idol
- 1919? *America Was Right*
- 1924 Smiling Hate
- 1925 *Body and Soul*
- 1931 Resurrección
- 1934 *Eskimo*
  - *Massacre*
- 1946 *Canyon Passage*
- 1947 *The Foxes of Harrow*
- 1950 *The Lawless*
- 1951 A Streetcar Named Desire
- 1953 *The Sun Shines Bright*
- 1956 *The Searchers*
- 1957 *Naked in the Sun*
- 1958 *Machete*
- 1959 Last Train from Gun Hill
- 1960 *Comanche Station*
  - *Sergeant Rutledge*

Rapids
- 1942 *North to the Klondike*
- 1958 *The Defiant Ones*

Rationing in wartime
- 1942 *Rubber Racketeers*
- 1944 Since You Went Away
  - *Tender Comrade*
- 1945 *Where Do We Go From*
  - *Here?*
- 1946 *Without Reservations*

Rats
- 1918 *The Midnight Patrol*
- 1951 *Native Son*

Rattlesnakes
- 1949 *Lust for Gold*
- 1955 *Shotgun*
- 1956 *The Last Wagon*

Maurice Ravel
- 1945 *Rhapsody in Blue*

Ravens
- 1949 *Tale of the Navajos*

Real estate
- 1922 *The Dungeon*

Real estate agents
- 1917 *Her Own People*
- 1940 *Jennie*
  - *The Jewish Melody*
- 1943 *What's Buzzin' Cousin?*
- 1944 *Hi, Beautiful*
- 1949 *The Clay Pigeon*
  - *The Red Menace*
- 1957 *Burden of Truth*
- 1958 Sierra Baron
- 1959 *The Last Angry Man*
- 1960 *Key Witness*

Real estate magnates
- 1946 Bringing Up Father

James Addison Reavis
- 1950 The Baron of Arizona

Receptionists
- 1942 *Dr. Gillespie's New*
  - *Assistant*
- 1948 *Shanghai Chest*

Recipes
- *I Remember Mama*

Recitals
- 1944 *Chip Off the Old Block*
- 1953 *Tonight We Sing*

Recluses
- 1919 The She Wolf
- 1936 Paddy O'Day
- 1942 *Tortilla Flat*
- 1951 *Distant Drums*
- 1955 *The View from Pompey's*
  - *Head*

Recognition
- 1914 *Threads of Destiny*
- 1916 *A Child of Mystery*
  - *The Gilded Spider*
- 1917 *A Roadside Impresario*
  - *Unknown 274*
- 1918 My Cousin
- 1932 *The Golden West*
- 1934 *He Was Her Man*
  - *The Lone Defender*
- 1937 *Music for Madame*
- 1939 *Motel the Operator*
- 1946 *Don Ricardo Returns*
- 1948 *Fury at Furnace Creek*
- 1950 *Chinatown at Midnight*
- 1957 *Edge of the City*
  - *Pawnee*

Reconciliation
- 1931 *Women Love Once*
- 1940 Little Nellie Kelly
- 1942 *The Navy Comes Through*
  - *Syncopation*
- 1944 *Lady, Let's Dance!*
- 1945 *The Bells of St. Mary's*
  - *A Tree Grows in Brooklyn*
- 1948 *Music Man*
- 1949 *House of Strangers*
- 1950 *Annie Get Your Gun*
- 1951 *The Last Outpost*
  - *New Mexico*
- 1953 *The Great Sioux Uprising*
  - *Tonight We Sing*
- 1955 *Headline Hunters*
- 1956 *The Searchers*
- 1958 *St. Louis Blues*
- 1960 *All the Fine Young*
  - *Cannibals*
  - *Cimarron*
  - *I Aim at the Stars: the*
  - *Wernher von Braun Story*

Reconstruction (1939-1951)
- *use* **Postwar reconstruction**

Recording industry
- 1941 Where Did You Get That
  - Girl?

Recordings
- 1935 *Captured in Chinatown*
- 1936 *Sins of Man*
- 1937 Manhattan Merry-Go-Round
- 1938 *Happy Landing*
- 1941 *Charlie Chan in Rio*
  - *Playmates*
- 1942 *Rio Rita*
- 1948 *Docks of New Orleans*
- 1949 *Top O' the Morning*

Recruiting and enlistment
- *use* **Military service,**
  - **Compulsory;**
  - **Military service,**
  - **Volunatry**

Red Cloud
- 1925 Warrior Gap
- 1951 *Tomahawk*
- 1953 The Great Sioux Uprising
- 1955 The Gun That Won the West
  - The Indian Fighter
- 1956 *The Last Frontier*

Red Cross
- 1915 The Cheat
- 1916 Following the Flag in
  - Mexico
- 1918 *Hell's End*
- 1945 *Of One Blood*
- 1954 *Barefoot Battalion*

Red Sea
- 1931 *La ley del harem*

Redwood forests
- 1918 Tongues of Flame

Major Walter Reed
- 1941 *Land of Liberty*

Reformatories
- 1914? *A Boy and the Law*
- 1918 *Her Moment*
- 1939 Reform School
- 1949 *Knock on Any Door*
- 1950 So Young, So Bad

Reformers
- 1915 The Nigger
- 1917 A Roadside Impresario
  - The Secret of Eve
- 1933 *Obey the Law*
- 1934 Massacre
- 1936 Klondike Annie
- 1937 *Boy of the Streets*
- 1938 In Old Chicago
  - Sugar Hill Baby
- 1941 Lady from Louisiana
  - Murder on Lenox Avenue
- 1944 Knickerbocker Holiday

Refugees, Political
- 1916 *Following the Flag in*
  - *Mexico*
- 1922 The Hands of Nara
- 1923 Fashion Row
- 1926 Into Her Kingdom
- 1932 The Unfortunate Bride
- 1934 *Lazy River*
- 1937 Where Is My Child?
- 1938 *Gateway*
- 1940 Three Faces West
- 1944 *Charlie Chan in the Secret*
  - *Service*
- 1950 *A Lady Without Passport*
- 1953 The Stars Are Singing
- 1957 Journey to Freedom

Regeneration
- 1914 John Barleycorn
- 1915 The Rosary
- 1916 The Aryan
  - *Hop, the Devil's Brew*
- 1917 The Gun Fighter
  - Queen X
- 1918 The Honor of His House
  - The Source
- 1923 Regeneration
- 1926? Ten Nights in a Barroom
- 1931 *Cavalier of the West*
  - Die Maske Fällt
  - Young Sinners
- 1932 *La foule hurle*
- 1937 Border Cafe
  - The Holy Oath
- 1941? *The Blood of Jesus*
- 1945 *The Great John L.*
- 1946 *Notorious*
  - *Three Wise Fools*
- 1947 Little Mister Jim
  - *The Mighty McGurk*
  - *Thunder Mountain*
- 1950 *Young Man with a Horn*

Rehearsals
- 1941 *Sun Valley Serenade*
- 1944 *Chip Off the Old Block*
  - *Slightly Terrific*
- 1945 *The Scarlet Clue*
- 1946 *Cuban Pete*
  - *Slightly Scandalous*
  - *That Man of Mine*
- 1947 *Carnegie Hall*

Reincarnation
- 1921 All Souls' Eve
- 1928 Eleven P.M.

Reindeer
- 1952 *Arctic Flight*

Rejuvenation
- 1931 *El pasado acusa*
- 1936 *Paddy O'Day*

Relay racing
- 1932 *L'athlète incomplet*

Relics and reliquaries
- 1947 *Dangerous Venture*

Religion
- 1915? The Beachcomber
  - Sin
- 1920 *Within Our Gates*
- 1920? *Reformation*
- 1924 Untamed Youth
- 1925 Quicker'n Lightnin'
- 1928 *Eleven P.M.*
- 1929 Hallelujah
- 1930 The Grand Parade
  - *Sevilla de mis amores*

The Silent Enemy
1933 The Eternal Jew
1936 Down to the Sea
Sins of Man
1940 The Jewish Melody
1941? The Blood of Jesus
1945 Of One Blood
1947 Little Mister Jim
1948 Big City
Reaching from Heaven
1949 Tale of the Navajos
1950 Stars in My Crown
1952 Desert Pursuit
1953 Bright Road
1955 A Man Called Peter
1956 Full of Life
7th Cavalry
Westward Ho the Wagons!
1960 The Crowning Experience

Religiosity
1931 The Voice of Israel
1933 The Eternal Jew
1934 La cruz y la espada
The Rabbi's Power
1937 Green Fields
Where Is My Child?
1939 Tevya
1943 Cabin in the Sky
Marching On!
1947 Going to Glory, Come to
Jesus
1949 Harbor of Missing Men
1950 God, Man and Devil
1951 Native Son
1955 Day of Decision
1958 Blood Arrow
1959 Porgy and Bess

Religious articles
1936 Custer's Last Stand
1950 God, Man and Devil
1955 Seven Cities of Gold
1957 The Brothers Rico

Religious conversion
1917 Crime and Punishment
1918 The Unbeliever
1919? In the Land of the Setting
Sun; or, Martyrs of
Yesterday
1920 The Man Who Dared
1922 Shadows
1952? Call of the Navajo
1960 The Crowning Experience

Religious cults
1932 The Black King

Religious persecution
1914? A Boy and the Law
1915 The Melting Pot
1916 Civilization's Child
Witchcraft
The Yellow Passport
1931 The Voice of Israel
1932 Yiskor
1933 The Wandering Jew
1937 The Holy Oath

Remarriage
1914 Where the Trail Divides
1933 Yo, tú y ella
1959 The Black Orchid

Remodeling (Of dwellings)
use Dwellings—Remodeling

Renegades
1915 Captain Courtesy
1931 Fighting Caravans
1932 Mystery Ranch
1934 Wagon Wheels
1935 The Singing Vagabond
1936 Dancing Pirate
Daniel Boone
For the Service
The Glory Trail
1938 The Renegade Ranger
1940 Geronimo
1948 The Paleface
1949 Apache Chief
1950 Broken Arrow
Riders of the Pony Express
1951 Flaming Feather
The Mark of the Renegade
1953 Last of the Comanches
The Man from the Alamo
The Nebraskan
The Pathfinder
1954 Drum Beat
They Rode West

1956 Comanche
1957 Apache Warrior
1958 Apache Territory
Reno (NV)
1939 Charlie Chan in Reno
1940 Mexican Spitfire Out West
1950 Emergency Wedding
Reporters
1915 How Molly Malone Made
Good
1917 The Flower of Doom
Hashimura Togo
A Jewel in Pawn
Sold at Auction
1918 The Gypsy Trail
The Million Dollar Mystery
One More American
The Ranger
1919 His Parisian Wife
1921 Wing Toy
1921? The Supreme Passion
1922 The Cub Reporter
1924 The Pell Street Mystery
1924? The Flaming Crisis
1925 Salome of the Tenements
1929 Sombras habaneras
1931 Mr. Lemon of Orange
El pasado acusa
Quand on est belle
1932 Scarface
The Secrets of Wu Sin
Thirteen Steps
The Unfortunate Bride
1933 The Wandering Jew
1934 The Cat's-Paw
1935 Captured in Chinatown
A Night at the Ritz
Rendezvous
The Winning Ticket
1936 After the Thin Man
Human Cargo
Yellow Cargo
1937 Charlie Chan on Broadway
1938 Gateway
Josette
Spawn of the North
1939 Charlie Chan at Treasure
Island
The Escape
Mr. Wong in Chinatown
Winner Take All
194- Mistaken Identity
1940 Behind the News
Doomed to Die
Elsa Maxwell's Public Deb
No. 1
The Man I Married
Mystery in Swing
The Way of All Flesh
1941 Caught in the Act
Four Shall Die
Mystery Ship
You're Out of Luck
1942 All Through the Night
Seven Sweethearts
Woman of the Year
1943 Action in the North
Atlantic
The Amazing Mrs. Holliday
Hitler's Children
Jack London
1944 Buffalo Bill
The Racket Man
1945 Betrayal from the East
I Love a Bandleader
Salome, Where She Danced
1946 G. I. War Brides
Without Reservations
1946? Beale Street Mama
1947 The Farmer's Daughter
1948 Call Northside 777
Fort Apache
Gentleman's Agreement
The Luck of the Irish
Up in Central Park
1949 The Cowboy and the
Indians
Jigsaw
The Red Menace
Rose of the Yukon
1950 Mystery Street
Panic in the Streets
1951 The Magnificent Yankee
Native Son
Saturday's Hero

1952 It's a Big Country: An
American Anthology
1953 Taxi
1954 Sitting Bull
1955 Headline Hunters
1957 Journey to Freedom
1958 The Last Hurrah
The Rawhide Trail
1959 Al Capone
The Last Angry Man
The Oregon Trail
1960 The Crowning Experience
I Aim at the Stars: the
Wernher von Braun Story

Reputation
1913 The Inside of the White
Slave Traffic
Traffic in Souls
1915 Under Southern Skies
1916 Britton of the Seventh
The Gilded Spider
Man and His Angel
A Son of Erin
1917 Hashimura Togo
One Law for Both
1918 A Broadway Scandal
Broken Ties
Fields of Honor
1919 Spotlight Sadie
1920? Her Story
1921 The Sport of the Gods
1929 Mister Antonio
1931 El pasado acusa
1932 Call Her Savage
Huddle
Unashamed
1933 A Lady's Profession
1936 Laughing Irish Eyes
1937 Black Legion
1938 The Singing Blacksmith
1943 The Outlaw
1945 Great Stagecoach Robbery
Sheriff of Redwood Valley
1946 Singin' in the Corn
1950 The Furies
1951 Jim Thorpe—All-American
1956 Dakota Incident
7th Cavalry

Rescues
1913 Traffic in Souls
1914 Dan
The Great Diamond
Robbery
Hearts United
In the Days of the
Thundering Herd
In the Land of the Head
Hunters
Uncle Tom's Cabin
1914? The Lust of the Red Man
Sitting Bull—The Hostile
Sioux Indian Chief
1915 The Birth of a Nation
Chimmie Fadden
The Gambler of the West
The Grandee's Ring
Hearts of Men
The Immigrant
The Last of the Mafia
Sealed Valley
1916 A Child of Mystery
The Daughter of the Don
The Half-Breed
Silks and Satins
1917 The Bronze Bride
The Conqueror
The Gun Fighter
The Hidden Children
The Plow Woman
A Roadside Impresario
Runaway Romany
Unconquered
The Wild Girl
1918 The Bravest Way
The Girl in the Dark
The Goddess of Lost Lake
His Birthright
Hitting the Trail
The Honor of His House
How Could You, Jean?
Huck and Tom; or, the
Further Adventures of
Tom Sawyer
The Hun Within
In Judgment Of

The Man Above the Law
The Million Dollar Mystery
Mystic Faces
The Only Road
The Only Road
The Squaw Man
Uncle Tom's Cabin
1919 Auction of Souls
Behind the Door
Desert Gold
A Fallen Idol
Fighting for Gold
Just Squaw
The She Wolf
The Sleeping Lion
Told in the Hills
The Tong Man
The Unpainted Woman
1920 Before the White Man Came
Dinty
The Luck of the Irish
The Purple Cipher
The Symbol of the
Unconquered
1921 As the World Rolls On
Shadows of the West
1921? The Slave Market
1922 The Dungeon
1925 Tonio, Son of the Sierras
1926 The Flying Ace
1930 Anna Christie
A Daughter of the Congo
El dios del mar
Un hombre de suerte
Monsieur le Fox
El último de los Vargas
1931 ¿Conoces a tu mujer?
The Hurricane Horseman
La ley del harem
Shulamith
1932 The Forty-Niners
Hidden Valley
Me and My Gal
Mystery Ranch
Parigi affascina; ovvero,
Malavita
The Rainbow Trail
Riders of the Desert
Thirteen Steps
White Eagle
1933 Robbers' Roost
1934 The Battling Buckaroo
Call of the Coyote
Charlie Chan's Courage
Chloe: Love Is Calling You
La cruz y la espada
Fighting Through
The Lone Defender
'Neath the Arizona Skies
Riding Speed
The Star Packer
White Heat
1935 Captured in Chinatown
Chinatown Squad
Cyclone of the Saddle
De la sartén al fuego
Fighting Pioneers
His Family Tree
Rescue Squad
The Singing Vagabond
Tango Bar
Texas Terror
1936 The Bold Caballero
Custer's Last Stand
Desert Gold
El diablo del mar
Down to the Sea
Hair-Trigger Casey
Sum Hun
Tundra
1937 Big City
El carnaval del diablo
Drums of Destiny
Maid of Salem
Old Louisiana
Prairie Thunder
The Riders of the Whistling
Skull
Shadows of the Orient
Song of the City
1938 The Renegade Ranger
Two Gun Man from
Harlem
Wild Horse Canyon

1939 *Bad Lands*
Drums Along the Mohawk
Frontiers of '49
Gone With the Wind
Mr. Wong in Chinatown
The Return of the Cisco Kid
1940 *Hi-Yo Silver*
Northwest Passage (Book
I—Rogers' Rangers)
Santa Fe Trail
Taku
Viva Cisco Kid
While Thousands Cheer
1941 *Doomed Caravan*
Gauchos of Eldorado
Mutiny in the Arctic
The Pioneers
This Woman Is Mine
1942 *Lawless Plainsmen*
The Navy Comes Through
1943 *Deerslayer*
Good Luck, Mr. Yates
*They Came to Blow Up
America*
1944 *Outlaw Trail*
The San Antonio Kid
1945 *The Jade Mask*
The Mummy's Curse
The Navajo Trail
*Our Vines Have Tender
Grapes*
The Shanghai Cobra
South of the Rio Grande
1946 *Bad Bascomb*
Swamp Fire
Wild Beauty
1947 *The Adventures of Don
Coyote*
Buffalo Bill Rides Again
Dangerous Venture
King of the Bandits
Last of the Redmen
The Return of Rin Tin Tin
Untamed Fury
1948 *The Arizona Ranger*
The Lady from Shanghai
The Paleface
Rocky
16 Fathoms Deep
Tap Roots
1949 *The Cowboy and the
Prizefighter*
The Fighting Kentuckian
Tulsa
Tuna Clipper
1950 *Ambush*
Battleground
Comanche Territory
*Davy Crockett, Indian
Scout*
A Lady Without Passport
Rock Island Trail
Rocky Mountain
Sands of Iwo Jima
1951 *Adventures of Captain
Fabian*
Apache Drums
Distant Drums
The Last Outpost
Little Big Horn
The Mark of the Renegade
New Mexico
Only the Valiant
The Raging Tide
Tomahawk
Warpath
The Well
When the Redskins Rode
1952 *The Big Sky*
The Half-Breed
Red Ball Express
Red Snow
The Savage
1953 *Beneath the 12-Mile Reef*
The Charge at Feather River
Conquest of Cochise
Fort Ti
The Glory Brigade
Last of the Comanches
The Man Behind the Gun
The Pathfinder
Ride, Vaquero!
Seminole
The Stand at Apache River

1954 *Saskatchewan*
1955 *Chief Crazy Horse*
*Davy Crockett, King of the
Wild Frontier*
Smoke Signal
1956 *Pillars of the Sky*
The Searchers
1957 *The Deerslayer*
The Lawless Eighties
Pawnee
Run of the Arrow
1958 *The Badlanders*
Houseboat
*The Lone Ranger and the
Lost City of Gold*
1959 *Yellowstone Kelly*
1960 *All the Young Men*
Cimarron
Comanche Station
Ice Palace
The Last Voyage
Sergeant Rutledge
The Sign of Zorro

Reservations (Indian)
use **Indians of North
America—Reservations**
Resistance movements
use **World War II—Resistance
movements**
Resorts
1920 Billions
1924 In High Gear
1931 *Zein Weib's Lubovnick*
1941 *The Mexican Spitfire's Baby*
1942 *Rio Rita*
1950 Catskill Honeymoon
1954 *Dangerous Mission*
1955 *Foxfire*
1958 *Kings Go Forth*
Marjorie Morningstar
Restaurants
1915 Cohen's Luck
1918 *A Broadway Scandal*
Ruggles of Red Gap
1919 *A Fighting Colleen*
1920 *In the Depths of Our Hearts*
1923 Ruggles of Red Gap
1929 This Is Heaven
1932 *Call Her Savage*
Uncle Moses
1933 *Best of Enemies*
Rafter Romance
Una viuda romántica
1935 *¡Asegure a su mujer!*
Piernas de seda
1937 *Man of the People*
That I May Live
1938 *Outside of Paradise*
1939 *Waterfront*
1940 *East of the River*
*Elsa Maxwell's Public Deb
No. 1*
If I Had My Way
1941 *Come Live with Me*
They Dare Not Love
1942 *Dr. Gillespie's New
Assistant*
Nazi Agent
1943 *His Butler's Sister*
1945 *The Dolly Sisters*
1946 *Dangerous Money*
Saratoga Trunk
1947 *Mantan Runs for Mayor*
1948 *Shep Comes Home*
Up in Central Park
1949? *The Joint Is Jumpin'*
1950 *The Toast of New Orleans*
1951 *The Great Caruso*
1952 *The Ring*
1953 *Taxi*
1955 *Headline Hunters*
Marty
Murder in Villa Capri
1956 *Serenade*
1958 *Kings Go Forth*
1960 *This Rebel Breed*
Restaurateurs
1924 Racing Luck
1927 The Princess from Hoboken
1928 Sins of the Fathers
1931 *Le petit café*
1932 *Senza mamma
e'nnamurato*
1934 *Cuesta abajo*
Imitation of Life

1935 *Ruggles of Red Gap*
1936 *Yiddle with His Fiddle*
1938 *Josette*
The Rage of Paris
1939 *Winner Take All*
1941 *Louisiana Purchase*
1950 *Panic in the Streets*
1957 *The Midnight Story*
Retirement
1940 *Three Cheers for the Irish*
1944 *An American Romance*
Buffalo Bill
1947 *The Jolson Story*
Vigilantes of Boomtown
1949 *She Wore a Yellow Ribbon*
1950 *Right Cross*
1951 *The Magnificent Yankee*
1955 *The Long Gray Line*
Retirement homes
1922 *Breaking Home Ties*
1934 *Tres amores*
1939 *My Son*
1940 *Eli Eli*
1951 *Yes Sir, Mr. Bones*
Reunions
1914 *In the Days of the
Thundering Herd*
The Little Jewess
1915 *An American Gentleman*
Children of the Ghetto
1917 *The Renaissance at
Charleroi*
1919 Evangeline
1932 *Genoveffa*
1936 *Let's Sing Again*
Show Boat
Sins of Man
Sum Hun
Sutter's Gold
1938 *Spawn of the North*
1941 *Golden Gate Girl*
1942 *Tales of Manhattan*
1943 *Stormy Weather*
1947 *Carnegie Hall*
1951 *Show Boat*
**Revelation (Theology,
inspiration)**
1932 *Joseph in the Land of Egypt*
1933 *The Eternal Jew*
1955 *Chief Crazy Horse*
Revenge
1914 *At the Cross Roads*
In the Land of the Head
Hunters
The Littlest Rebel
An Odyssey of the North
The Woman in Black
1915 An American Gentleman
Captain Courtesy
The Italian
The Sable Lorcha
A Yankee from the West
1916 At Piney Ridge
Civilization's Child
The Flower of No Man's
Land
The Folly of Revenge
The Honorable Friend
Poor Little Peppina
The Soul of Kura-San
The Twin Triangle
A Woman's Honor
The Yellow Passport
1917 The Bar Sinister
The Bride of Hate
The Call of the East
Forbidden Paths
His Sweetheart
Rosie O'Grady
1918 An Alien Enemy
A Daughter of the Old South
The Firebrand
The Ordeal of Rosetta
The Prussian Cur
1919 Behind the Door
His Debt
Lasca
The Scar
The Sleeping Lion
The Tiger Lily
The Westerners
1919? America Was Right
1920 *The Brute*
Dangerous Days
Dinty

The North Wind's Malice
1921 Black Roses
The First Born
When the Clock Struck Nine
1922 Fair Lady
Flesh and Blood
1925 Galloping Vengeance
1926 *General Custer at Little Big
Horn*
1927 Bitter Apples
The Gay Defender
Heroes in Blue
Old San Francisco
1930 The Lash
Song of the Caballero
El valiente
1931 The Avenger
Charlie Chan Carries On
El código penal
La fiesta del diablo
Gentleman's Fate
La gran jornada
The Great Meadow
The Guilty Generation
Kismet
Mr. Lemon of Orange
Nuit d'Espagne
Oklahoma Jim
Pagliacci
El pasado acusa
Regeneración
Smart Money
1932 *Amore e morte*
The Hatchet Man
Men Are Such Fools
O festino o la legge
Ten Minutes to Live
Thirteen Steps
Thirteen Women
The Unfortunate Bride
1933 *Charlie Chan's Greatest
Case*
Grand Slam
King of the Wild Horses
1934 *Behold My Wife!*
Call of the Coyote
Chloe: Love Is Calling You
He Was Her Man
Laughing Boy
Limehouse Blues
1934? Harlem After Midnight
1935 *Circle of Death*
Cyclone of the Saddle
His Family Tree
Piernas de seda
Shir Hashirim
Wolf Riders
1936 *The Bold Caballero*
Charlie Chan's Secret
Pinto Rustlers
Robin Hood of El Dorado
1937 *The Barrier*
The Californian
Maid of Salem
1938 *California Frontier*
Life Goes On
Life Goes On
Wild Horse Canyon
1939 *Bad Lands*
Forged Passport
Harlem Rides the Range
Miracle on Main Street
The Mystery of Mr. Wong
Waterfront
Winner Take All
1940 Charlie Chan at the Wax
Museum
Charlie Chan's Murder
Cruise
East of the River
Escape to Glory
Geronimo
Rhythm of the Rio Grande
1941 Charlie Chan in Rio
The Face Behind the Mask
Murder on Lenox Avenue
Western Union
1942 American Empire
Wings for the Eagle
1943 *The Outlaw*
1944 *Black Magic*
The Racket Man
1945 Anoush
Wanderer of the Wasteland

1946 *Beware*
Renegade Girl
Saratoga Trunk
Sheriff of Redwood Valley
1947 California
Desperate
Duel in the Sun
Last of the Redmen
Ride the Pink Horse
Under the Tonto Rim
Wild Horse Mesa
1948 *The Betrayal*
Harpoon
Miracle in Harlem
1949 *The Daring Caballero*
House of Strangers
Streets of Laredo
We Were Strangers
1950 Black Hand
Broken Arrow
Buccaneer's Girl
Colt .45
The Furies
Intruder in the Dust
Sunset in the West
Two Flags West
Winchester '73
1951 *Across the Wide Missouri*
Adventures of Captain
Fabian
Flaming Feather
Fort Defiance
The Last Outpost
Little Big Horn
New Mexico
Show Boat
Warpath
1952 *Apache War Smoke*
Battles of Chief Pontiac
Bugles in the Afternoon
California Conquest
The Fighter
The Half-Breed
High Noon
The Iron Mistress
The Quiet Man
The Raiders
Rose of Cimarron
The Savage
1953 *Beneath the 12-Mile Reef*
Conquest of Cochise
The Man from the Alamo
San Antone
The Stand at Apache River
1954 Apache
Hondo
Passion
The Yellow Tomahawk
1955 *Apache Woman*
Duel on the Mississippi
The Indian Fighter
Seminole Uprising
Seven Angry Men
Seven Cities of Gold
Shotgun
1956 *The Broken Star*
Comanche
Daniel Boone, Trail Blazer
Death of a Scoundrel
The Last Wagon
Man from Del Rio
Mohawk
Raw Edge
Raw Edge
Reprisal!
The Searchers
1957 *Apache Warrior*
Band of Angels
Gun Battle at Monterey
The Halliday Brand
Naked in the Sun
Ride Out for Revenge
The Tin Star
1958 The Badlanders
Gun Fever
The Light in the Forest
1959 *Al Capone*
Gunmen from Laredo
The Jayhawkers!
Last Train from Gun Hill
Shake Hands with the Devil
1960 *All the Fine Young
Cannibals*
The Crowning Experience
Flaming Star

Hell to Eternity
The Unforgiven
Walk Tall
Paul Revere
1922 Cardigan
Reverends
1925 Body and Soul
1934 *Judge Priest*
1939 *Lying Lips*
1941 Sunday Sinners
1942 *Tales of Manhattan*
1944 *Tucson Raiders*
1947 *Hi De Ho*
1948 *Miracle in Harlem*
Tap Roots
1948? *Junction 88*
1949 *Answer for Anne*
Lost Boundaries
1950 *The Jackie Robinson Story*
Train to Tombstone
1958 *Frontier Gun*
Revivals
1934 *Drums O' Voodoo*
Revivification
1931 *Such Is Life*
1934 *The Rabbi's Power*
1941? The Blood of Jesus
1945 *The Mummy's Curse*
1946 The Face of Marble
1947 *Citizen Saint*
Revolts
use **Revolutions;
Uprisings**
Revolutionaries
1916 Following the Flag in
Mexico
1917 Crime and Punishment
Under False Colors
1917? *Barnaby Lee*
1918 The Firebrand
1919 The Right to Happiness
1920 Lifting Shadows
Rio Grande
1928 *A Ship Comes In*
1931 *Echec au roi*
1932 The Vanishing Frontier
1934 *Strange Wives*
1940 New Moon
1949 We Were Strangers
1959 Shake Hands with the Devil
1960 *The Crowning Experience*
The Day They Robbed the
Bank of England
Revolutions
1920 Li Ting Lang
1923 The Spider and the Rose
Rewards
1914 *The Yellow Traffic*
1917 *Lost in Transit*
1918 *Mystic Faces*
The Ranger
1919 *A Fighting Colleen*
1931 *The Cisco Kid*
Mr. Lemon of Orange
1934 *Our Daily Bread*
1935 *Un bombre peligroso*
Naughty Marietta
North of Arizona
Riddle Ranch
1936 *The Bold Caballero*
The Phantom of Santa Fe
1937 *The Californian*
Maid of Salem
Music for Madame
1939 *Double Deal*
1940 *Lucky Cisco Kid*
1941 *Belle Starr*
The Face Behind the Mask
Gauchos of Eldorado
1946 *Gas House Kids*
1946? *House-Rent Party*
1949 *Colorado Territory*
Top O' the Morning
1952 *The Raiders*
Rhodes scholars
1937 *Song of the City*
Richmond (VA)
1936 *Daniel Boone*
Branch Rickey
1950 *The Jackie Robinson Story*

Rickshaw drivers
1918 Who Is to Blame?
Riding
1915 Where Cowboy Is King
1931 *¿Conoces a tu mujer?*
1934 *She Was a Lady*
1947 *Pirates of Monterey*
1948 Fort Apache
1949 *Lookout Sister*
1950 *Rio Grande*
Riding accidents
1921 *By Right of Birth*
1934 *Un capitán de cosacos*
Charlie Chan in London
1945 *Of One Blood*
1947 *Dark Delusion*
1951 *The Mark of the Renegade*
1956 *Westward Ho the Wagons!*
Rifles
1935 *Fighting Pioneers*
1937 *The Plainsman*
1942 *We Were Dancing*
1950 *Comanche Territory*
Train to Tombstone
Winchester '73
1951 *Ob! Susanna*
Snake River Desperadoes
1952 *My Man and I*
Wagons West
1954 *Arrow in the Dust*
War Arrow
1955 *Apache Ambush*
The Gun That Won the West
Kentucky Rifle
1956 *Quincannon, Frontier
Scout*
Walk the Proud Land
1958 *Ambush at Cimarron Pass*
Rings
1923 *Flames of Wrath*
1930 *Una cana al aire*
1931 *The Black Camel*
1942 *Foreign Agent*
1950 *Raiders of Tomahawk Creek*
Rio de Janeiro (Brazil)
1941 *Charlie Chan in Rio*
1946 *Notorious*
Rio Grande
1915 *The Grandee's Ring*
1916 *Following the Flag in
Mexico*
1924 *Down by the Rio Grande*
1950 *Rio Grande*
1959 *Gunmen from Laredo*
The Wonderful Country
Riots
1931 *Die Dreigroschenoper*
Pardon Us
1937 *The Holy Oath*
1938 *Gateway*
God's Step Children
1940 Elsa Maxwell's Public Deb
No. 1
1945 *The Valley of Decision*
1947 *The Mighty McGurk*
1949 *The Red Menace*
1950 *The Baron of Arizona*
No Way Out
1951 The Well
Rites and ceremonies
1912 *Atop of the World in
Motion*
1918? Indian Life
1919 *The Heart of Wetona*
1925 *Custer's Last Fight*
1926 *General Custer at Little Big
Horn*
1931 Aloba
1932 *A Daughter of Her People*
Igloo
Mazel Tov
Symphony of Six Million
Yiskor
1933 King of the Wild Horses
La melodía prohibida
1934 *Cheyenne Sun Dance*
Chloe: Love Is Calling You
Eskimo
Laughing Boy
Massacre
Song of the Islands
The Youth of Russia
1936 *The Phantom of Santa Fe*
Silly Billies

1937 *Natalka Poltavka*
Nation Aflame
Waikiki Wedding
1939 *The Devil's Daughter*
Mothers of Today
1941 In the Land of the Navajo
King of the Zombies
1944 *Tabiti Nights*
1947 *The Burning Cross*
Dangerous Venture
1948 *The Dude Goes West*
Indian Agent
16 Fathoms Deep
1949 *Tale of the Navajos*
1950 *Broken Arrow*
The Men
1951 *Apache Drums*
Warpath
1952 *Arctic Flight*
Navajo
Red Snow
The Savage
1954 *Apache*
1955 *White Feather*
1956 *7th Cavalry*
1957 Run of the Arrow
Run of the Arrow
1958 *The Lone Ranger and the
Lost City of Gold*
1959 *The Crimson Kimono*
Rivalry
1914 The Redemption of David
Corson
The Woman in Black
1915 The Girl I Left Behind Me
Marse Covington
Under Southern Skies
1915? Sin
1916 At Piney Ridge
Three of Many
1917 *A Kentucky Cinderella*
The Little American
Lost in Transit
1918 *The Ordeal of Rosetta*
1920 Before the White Man Came
The Daughter of Dawn
The Man Who Dared
1931 The Cisco Kid
Gentleman's Fate
The Guilty Generation
Little Caesar
1933 *The Man Who Dared: An
Imaginative Biography*
1935 Annie Oakley
Chinatown Squad
1936 Human Cargo
Sea Spoilers
Yiddle with His Fiddle
1937 *One Mile from Heaven*
1938 *Passport Husband*
1939 The Devil's Daughter
The Escape
King of Chinatown
1940 Gang War
Kit Carson
1942 Dr. Gillespie's New Assistant
Friendly Enemies
1943 Dr. Gillespie's Criminal
Case
The Outlaw
1944 *Block Busters*
Three Men in White
1946 Sun Valley Cyclone
1947 *Sepia Cinderella*
Untamed Fury
1948 Red River
1949 Apache Chief
Tuna Clipper
1950 *Annie Get Your Gun*
1951 *Molly*
1953 Beneath the 12-Mile Reef
1954 *Massacre Canyon*
1955 *The Last Command*
1957 *Bayou*
1958 Gunman's Walk
Never Love a Stranger
1959 Al Capone
The Black Orchid
Cry Tough
Jordan River
1937 *The Holy Oath*
River boats
1917 *The Bride of Hate*
1928 Uncle Tom's Cabin

1939 *Gone With the Wind*
1942 *American Empire*
1946 Swamp Fire
1949 *The Fighting Kentuckian*
1956 Davy Crockett and the River
     Pirates
1958 *Ride a Crooked Trail*
Rivers
1915 *Sealed Valley*
1918 *The Source*
1930 The Break Up
1932 *The Rainbow Trail*
1934 *'Neath the Arizona Skies*
     Our Daily Bread
     Wheels of Destiny
1936 *Yiddle with His Fiddle*
1937 *Thank You, Mr. Moto*
1938 *Marusia*
1939 *The Light Ahead*
1940 *Northwest Passage (Book
     I—Rogers' Rangers)*
1943 *Deerslayer*
1947 *On the Old Spanish Trail*
1948 *Red River*
1949 *The Prairie*
     She Wore a Yellow Ribbon
     Tulsa
     The Valiant Hombre
1952 *The Big Sky*
     Brave Warrior
1953 *The Glory Brigade*
1954 *Saskatchewan*
1955 *The Far Horizons*
1956 *The Burning Hills*
     Davy Crockett and the River
     Pirates
1957 *The Deerslayer*
1960 *Wild River*
Riviera (France)
1930 Son of the Gods
1958 *Kings Go Forth*
Roadhouses
1917 *A Roadside Impresario*
1919 *Spotlight Sadie*
1919? The Chosen Path
1934 *Coming Out Party*
1937 *That Girl from Paris*
1942 *Juke Girl*
1943 *Redhead from Manhattan*
1947 Juke Joint
1948 *Sleep, My Love*
Robbers
     use **Thieves**
Robbery
1914 The Great Diamond Robbery
     The Nightingale
1915 *The Alien*
     An American Gentleman
     Chimmie Fadden
     Coben's Luck
     Hearts of Men
     The Italian
     The Kindling
     A Yankee from the West
1915? Sin
1916 *The Colored American
     Winning His Suit*
     Gold and the Woman
     The Social Buccaneer
     A Yoke of Gold
1917 Crime and Punishment
     The Little Samaritan
     The Peddler
     Runaway Romany
     The Winged Mystery
1918 *A Broadway Scandal*
     Denny from Ireland
     Find the Woman
     The Girl in the Dark
     Hidden Pearls
     *Huck and Tom; or, the
     Further Adventures of
     Tom Sawyer*
     Laughing Bill Hyde
     The Little Runaway
1919 *A Fallen Idol*
     Fighting for Gold
     The Sneak
1920 *The Man Who Dared*
     The North Wind's Malice
     Outside the Law
     Who's Your Servant?
1921 *As the World Rolls On*
     When the Clock Struck Nine

1922 For His Mother's Sake
     The Power of Love
     The Top O' the Morning
1923 *Flames of Wrath*
1924 East of Broadway
1925 *Body and Soul*
     My Son
1926 April Fool
     The Flying Ace
1927 The Way of All Flesh
1928 *Eleven P.M.*
     The Midnight Ace
     The Wages of Sin
1929 In Old Arizona
     Mother's Boy
1930 *Cascarrabias*
     Los que danzan
     Monsieur le Fox
1931 *Gentleman's Fate*
1932 *El caballero de la noche*
     Wild Horse Mesa
1933 *The California Trail*
     *Charlie Chan's Greatest
     Case*
     Obey the Law
     Thundering Herd
1934 *The Fighting Hero*
     He Was Her Man
     'Neath the Arizona Skies
1935 Cowboy Holiday
     Cyclone of the Saddle
     North of Arizona
1936 Below the Deadline
1937 *Man of the People*
1938 *Two Gun Man from
     Harlem*
1939 *The Escape*
     Frontiers of '49
     In Old Caliente
1940 *Am I Guilty?*
     Arizona Frontier
     Rhythm of the Rio Grande
1941 *Golden Gate Girl*
     Sullivan's Travels
     Sunday Sinners
1942 *Apache Trail*
     Lawless Plainsmen
     Mokey
     Take My Life
     Tortilla Flat
1943 Frontier Fury
     The Law Rides Again
     Mr. Lucky
1944 *Outlaw Trail*
     Sonora Stagecoach
     Vigilantes of Dodge City
     Waterfront
1945 *Colorado Pioneers*
     Johnny Angel
     A Medal for Benny
1946 Border Bandits
     South of Monterey
1946? *Beale Street Mama*
     House-Rent Party
1947 Desperate
     Marshal of Cripple Creek
     On the Old Spanish Trail
     Wild Horse Mesa
1948 *Fighting Father Dunne*
     Guns of Hate
     The Lady from Shanghai
     Silver Trails
     Western Heritage
1949 *Anna Lucasta*
     Apache Chief
     The Fighting Kentuckian
     Harbor of Missing Men
     Knock on Any Door
     Riders of the Range
     Roll Thunder Roll!
     Thieves' Highway
1950 Border Treasure
     The Missourians
1951 *Gambling House*
1952 Woman in the Dark
1952? *Call of the Navajo*
1953 *Beneath the 12-Mile Reef*
     The Glass Wall
1954 Barefoot Battalion
1956 *The Broken Star*
1957 *The Deerslayer*
     Gun Battle at Monterey
1958 *Apache Territory*
     The Badlanders
     Escape from Red Rock

     Gun Fever
1959 *Cry Tough*
     Gunmen from Laredo
1960 *The Sign of Zorro*
**Robin Hood (Legendary
     character)**
1949 *Masked Raiders*
Jackie Robinson
1950 The Jackie Robinson Story
Rock Island (IL)
     Two Flags West
Rocketry
1960 I Aim at the Stars: the
     Wernher von Braun Story
Knute Rockne
1940 Knute Rockne—All American
Rocks
1947 *Rustlers of Devil's Canyon*
Rocky Mountains
1917 The Adventures of Buffalo
     Bill
1931 *Call of the Rockies*
     Fighting Caravans
1951 Across the Wide Missouri
Rodeos
1915 Where Cowboy Is King
1918 *Wild Women*
1920 Frontier Days
1922 The Bull-Dogger
1927 Open Range
1930 *Alma de gaucho*
1935 *Melody Trail*
Major Robert Rogers
1940 Northwest Passage (Book
     I—Rogers' Rangers)
1953 Fort Ti
**Rogue River Indian War,
     1855-1856**
1954 Battle of Rogue River
John Rolfe
1923 Jamestown
1953 *Captain John Smith and
     Pocahontas*
Roller-skating
1945 *Our Vines Have Tender
     Grapes*
Roman Catholics
     use **Catholic Church;
     Catholics**
Romance
1921 A Giant of His Race
     No Woman Knows
     The Secret Sorrow
1922 *The Crimson Skull*
     The Virgin of Seminole
1923 *His Great Chance*
     Regeneration
1924 *Smiling Hate*
1926 The Strong Man
1927 For the Love of Mike
     The Scar of Shame
     *With Sitting Bull at the
     Spirit Lake Massacre*
1929 *The Younger Generation*
1930 Alma de gaucho
     Anna Christie
     Así es la vida
     Cascarrabias
     *Charros, gauchos y
     manolas*
     Check and Double Check
     El dios del mar
     Doña mentiras
     Easy Street
     Estrellados
     Un hombre de suerte
     Locuras de amor
     Los que danzan
     Monsieur le Fox
     Olimpia
     El precio de un beso
     El presidio
     El príncipe del dólar
     La rosa de fuego
     El último de los Vargas
     Wu Li Chang
1931 *The Avenger*
     Call of the Rockies
     Charlie Chan Carries On
     El código penal
     El comediante
     Cuerpo y alma
     Delicious

     The Exile
     The Guilty Generation
     Hay que casar al príncipe
     La ley del harem
     Mi último amor
     Mr. Lemon of Orange
     Monerías
     Personal Maid
     Quand on est belle
     Resurrección
     Sombras del circo
     Yankee Don
     Young Sinners
     Zein Weib's Lubovnick
1932 *L'athlète incomplet*
     El caballero de la noche
     Cuore d'emigrante
     The Galloping Kid
     The Golden West
     Harlem Is Heaven
     The Hatchet Man
     Une heure près de toi
     El hombre que asesinó
     Huddle
     Hypnotized
     Law and Lawless
     Ljubav i strast
     The Match King
     Mazel Tov
     Me and My Gal
     The Unfortunate Bride
     The Vanishing Frontier
     White Eagle
1933 *L'amour guide*
     Best of Enemies
     Circle Canyon
     Dos noches
     Espérame
     Ever in My Heart
     Melodía de arrabal
     Olsen's Big Moment
     Rafter Romance
     Robbers' Roost
     The Telegraph Trail
     Una viuda romántica
1934 As the Earth Turns
     The Battling Buckaroo
     Broadway Bill
     La buenaventura
     The Cactus Kid
     Un capitán de cosacos
     The Cat's-Paw
     Coming Out Party
     Dos más uno, dos
     The Fighting Hero
     Las fronteras del amor
     Granaderos del amor
     He Was Her Man
     Laughing Boy
     Lazy River
     Limehouse Blues
     Nada más que una mujer
     'Neath the Arizona Skies
     Operator 13
     The Rabbi's Power
     Riding Speed
     She Was a Lady
     Song of the Islands
     Stand Up and Cheer!
     The Star Packer
     Tres amores
     La veuve joyeuse
     Wheels of Destiny
1935 *Alas sobre el Chaco*
     Annie Oakley
     ¡Asegure a su mujer!
     Black Fury
     El cantante de Nápoles
     Cyclone of the Saddle
     El día que me quieras
     A Night at the Opera
     No matarás
     Piernas de seda
     Rendezvous
     Riddle Ranch
     Te quiero con locura
1936 Amor que vuelve
     Below the Deadline
     The Bold Caballero
     General Spanky
     It Had to Happen
     Kelly the Second
     The Last of the Mohicans
     Mad Holiday
     Paddy O'Day

The Phantom of Santa Fe
Ramona
Rebellion
Robin Hood of El Dorado
Rose of the Rancho
Silly Billies
Sum Hun
La última cita
West of Nevada
Yiddle with His Fiddle
1937 Arshin Mal Alan
Drums of Destiny
Green Fields
Hills of Old Wyoming
Law and Lead
Maid of Salem
Man of the People
Music for Madame
Souls at Sea
That Girl from Paris
That I May Live
Think Fast, Mr. Moto
Think Fast, Mr. Moto
Waikiki Wedding
1938 Castillos en el aire
Di que me quieres
The Duke Is Tops
Gateway
Happy Landing
In Old Chicago
Josette
Outside of Paradise
Rascals
The Renegade Ranger
Road Demon
Spawn of the North
Speed to Burn
Two Gun Man from Harlem
La vida bohemia
Zamboanga
1939 The Cisco Kid and the Lady
Cossacks in Exile
The Devil's Daughter
Gang Smashers
Let Freedom Ring
Mamele
Man of Conquest
Moon over Harlem
Winner Take All
1939? A Chinese Gains a Fortune in America
1940 Am I Guilty?
Americaner Schadchen
Elsa Maxwell's Public Deb No. 1
Escape to Glory
Gang War
Girl from God's Country
The Mark of Zorro
Mystery in Swing
The Notorious Elinor Lee
Three Faces West
Too Many Girls
While Thousands Cheer
1941 Accent on Love
Belle Starr
Come Live with Me
Four Shall Die
The Gang's All Here
Golden Gate Girl
Ice-Capades
Lady from Louisiana
Louisiana Purchase
New York Town
Romance of the Rio Grande
Sun Valley Serenade
Under Fiesta Stars
Virginia
Where Did You Get That Girl?
1942 *Across the Pacific*
Foreign Agent
Gentleman Jim
Juke Girl
Nazi Agent
Prisoner of Japan
Rio Rita
Seven Sweethearts
Song of the Islands
Sunday Punch
Tales of Manhattan
Tortilla Flat
1943 *Dr. Gillespie's Criminal Case*

Doughboys in Ireland
The Gang's All Here
His Butler's Sister
Hitler's Children
Ladies' Day
Mr. Lucky
The Outlaw
Redhead from Manhattan
Riding High
Stormy Weather
Tahiti Honey
What's Buzzin' Cousin?
Wintertime
Yankee Doodle Dandy
1944 Andy Hardy's Blonde Trouble
Lake Placid Serenade
Lifeboat
Something for the Boys
Tahiti Nights
Three Men in White
1945 Anoush
Between Two Women
The Cisco Kid Returns
Club Havana
The Dolly Sisters
I Love a Bandleader
Nob Hill
Our Vines Have Tender Grapes
Pride of the Marines
Rhapsody in Blue
The Valley of Decision
Where Do We Go From Here?
1946 *Bad Bascomb*
Beware
Border Bandits
Cuban Pete
G. I. War Brides
Notorious
Renegade Girl
The Sailor Takes a Wife
Saratoga Trunk
South of Monterey
Stars on Parade
Strange Voyage
Sunset Pass
That Man of Mine
Till the End of Time
Wild West
Without Reservations
1946? Beale Street Mama
Harlem on Parade
1947 *The Adventures of Don Coyote*
Bells of San Fernando
Boy! What a Girl!
Buffalo Bill Rides Again
Calendar Girl
The Farmer's Daughter
It Had To Be You
The Jolson Story
Last of the Redmen
The Last Round-Up
The Mighty McGurk
New Orleans
Reet, Petite and Gone
Ride the Pink Horse
Sepia Cinderella
Untamed Fury
Wild Horse Mesa
1948 *The Arizona Ranger*
The Dude Goes West
Guns of Hate
Harpoon
The Lady from Shanghai
The Luck of the Irish
Miracle in Harlem
My Girl Tisa
Reaching from Heaven
Red River
Singin' Spurs
Western Heritage
1948? Boarding House Blues
1949 *The Clay Pigeon*
Colorado Territory
The Girl from Jones Beach
The Kissing Bandit
Lookout Sister
Lust for Gold
Rustlers
Souls of Sin
Stagecoach Kid
The Story of Seabiscuit

That Midnight Kiss
Thieves' Highway
Top O' the Morning
We Were Strangers
1949? *Girl in Room 20*
1950 *Ambush*
Annie Get Your Gun
The Big Hangover
Black Hand
Broken Arrow
The Daughter of Rosie O'Grady
The Furies
Indian Territory
A Lady Without Passport
Last of the Buccaneers
The Lawless
The Palomino
Right Cross
Rocky Mountain
So Young, So Bad
Stars in My Crown
The Toast of New Orleans
Young Daniel Boone
Young Man with a Horn
1950? Three Daughters
1951 *Apache Drums*
Cavalry Scout
Cuban Fireball
Distant Drums
Five
Fort Defiance
Gambling House
Jim Thorpe—All-American
The Magnificent Yankee
The Mark of the Renegade
Saturday's Hero
Warpath
Westward the Women
1952 Anything Can Happen
Apache War Smoke
Battles of Chief Pontiac
Bright Victory
California Conquest
Desert Pursuit
The Fighter
Fort Osage
Hiawatha
Kid Monk Baroni
My Man and I
The Quiet Man
The Raiders
Rose of Cimarron
1953 Beneath the 12-Mile Reef
Captain John Smith and Pocahontas
The Charge at Feather River
Column South
Conquest of Cochise
Fort Ti
The Great Sioux Uprising
Jack McCall Desperado
The Jazz Singer
The Man from the Alamo
The Nebraskan
The Pathfinder
San Antone
Sangaree
Seminole
So Big
The Stand at Apache River
The Sun Shines Bright
Taxi
Tumbleweed
1954 *Apache*
Arrow in the Dust
Broken Lance
Cattle Queen of Montana
Drum Beat
Drums Across the River
Hondo
Massacre Canyon
Saskatchewan
Siege at Red River
Thunder Pass
War Arrow
1955 *Apache Woman*
Duel on the Mississippi
Headline Hunters
The Indian Fighter
The Last Command
The Lonesome Trail
A Man Called Peter
Santa Fe Passage
Seminole Uprising

Seven Angry Men
Shotgun
The Vanishing American
1956 *The Burning Hills*
Dakota Incident
Man from Del Rio
Mohawk
Quincannon, Frontier Scout
Serenade
Westward Ho the Wagons!
Wetbacks
The White Squaw
1957 Bayou
Burden of Truth
Edge of the City
Gun Battle at Monterey
The Lawless Eighties
The Midnight Story
The Oklahoman
Pawnee
Ride Out for Revenge
Tomahawk Trail
Trooper Hook
1958 *Apache Territory*
Blood Arrow
Frontier Gun
Gun Fever
Gunfire at Indian Gap
Gunman's Walk
The Light in the Forest
Never Love a Stranger
Oregon Passage
St. Louis Blues
Seven Hills of Rome
The Young Lions
1959 Anna Lucasta
Gunmen from Laredo
Imitation of Life
The Oregon Trail
Porgy and Bess
Shake Hands with the Devil
Yellowstone Kelly
The Young Land
1960 I Passed for White
Studs Lonigan

Romance—Age difference
1938? Amore che non torna
1950 *Jolson Sings Again*
1951 The Girl on the Bridge
Molly
1958 *Machete*

Romania
1918 Her Moment

Romanian Americans
1917 The Trouble Buster
1918 Her Moment
1946 *The Sailor Takes a Wife*

Romanians
1941 *Hold Back the Dawn*

Romanov, House of
1926 Into Her Kingdom

Romantic obsession
1946 Dirty Gertie from Harlem, U.S.A.

Romantic rivalry
1919 A Man's Duty
The Sneak
The Unpainted Woman
Who's Your Brother?
1921 As the World Rolls On
The Green-Eyed Monster
1925 Tonio, Son of the Sierras
1926 *General Custer at Little Big Horn*
1930 *Charros, gauchos y manolas*
Cuando el amor ríe
Sei tu l'amore
1931 *Buster se marie*
Cavalier of the West
Cheri-Bibi
Così è la vita
Drácula
Gente alegre
La ley del harem
El príncipe gondolero
Riders of the Rio
Sombras del circo
El tenorio del circo
Three Who Loved
The White Renegade
Women Love Once

1932 *The Black King*
The Forty-Niners
Hombres en mi vida
Parigi affascina; ovvero,
  Malavita
Texas Pioneers
Tiger Shark
Wild Horse Mesa
1933 *L'amour guide*
Dos noches
Victims of Persecution
1934 Blossom Time
Chloe: Love Is Calling You
Cuesta abajo
The Great Flirtation
The Rabbi's Power
Strange Wives
El tango en Broadway
What a Mother-in-Law!
1935 Angelina o el honor de un
  brigadier
Un hombre peligroso
The Irish in Us
McFadden's Flats
The Singing Vagabond
Wolf Riders
1936 *Contra la corriente*
El crimen de media noche
Desert Gold
El diablo del mar
Down to the Sea
Laughing Irish Eyes
Ride, Ranger, Ride
Song of the Gringo
1937 *The Barrier*
El carnaval del diablo
It Could Happen to You
Manhattan
  Merry-Go-Round
Song of the City
1938 *Dangerous to Know*
Marusia
Mis dos amores
Mr. Moto's Gamble
The Rage of Paris
Two Sisters
1938? *Amore che non torna*
1939 *Double Deal*
The Girl from Mexico
Kol Nidre
The Mystery of Mr. Wong
1940 *Broken Strings*
The Fatal Hour
Lucky Cisco Kid
Mexican Spitfire
Midnight Shadow
Santa Fe Trail
1941 Birth of the Blues
Come Live with Me
Playmates
Romance of the Rio Grande
This Woman Is Mine
Western Union
1942 Holiday Inn
Twin Beds
Valley of the Sun
Wings for the Eagle
Young America
1943 Crash Dive
Deerslayer
His Butler's Sister
In Old Oklahoma
Land of Hunted Men
Three Hearts for Julia
1944 *Block Busters*
Chip Off the Old Block
Knickerbocker Holiday
The Racket Man
They Live in Fear
1945 A Medal for Benny
Salome, Where She Danced
1946 *Bringing Up Father*
Canyon Passage
The Face of Marble
The Gentleman Misbehaves
Renegade Girl
The Sailor Takes a Wife
Swamp Fire
1947 *Body and Soul*
Boy! What a Girl!
California
Copacabana
Easy Come, Easy Go
Pirates of Monterey
Riding the California Trail

Spoilers of the North
1948 Music Man
Rocky
Tap Roots
Unconquered
1948? *Junction 88*
1949 *Daughter of the West*
The Fighting Kentuckian
Jigsaw
Massacre River
The Prairie
She Wore a Yellow Ribbon
Streets of Laredo
1950 Buccaneer's Girl
Emergency Wedding
Rock Island Trail
1951 Apache Drums
Flaming Feather
Jim Thorpe—All-American
Little Big Horn
Oh! Susanna
Only the Valiant
The Raging Tide
1952 Bugles in the Afternoon
The Savage
1953 *The Eddie Cantor Story*
The Man Behind the Gun
1954 *Apache*
Overland Pacific
Taza, Son of Cochise
They Rode West
1955 The Far Horizons
Kentucky Rifle
Kiss of Fire
Santa Fe Passage
Seminole Uprising
Smoke Signal
White Feather
1956 *Baby Doll*
Hot Blood
The Last Frontier
The Last Hunt
Pillars of the Sky
Walk the Proud Land
The Wild Dakotas
1957 *Apache Warrior*
Dragoon Wells Massacre
The Guns of Fort Petticoat
Pawnee
Raintree County
War Drums
1958 Kings Go Forth
Ride a Crooked Trail
1959 The Crimson Kimono
Porgy and Bess
Thunder in the Sun
1960 All the Fine Young
  Cannibals
Flaming Star
Ice Palace
Pay or Die
Walk Like a Dragon
Wild River

Rome (Italy)
1951 *Teresa*
1954 Indiscretion of an American
  Wife
1958 Seven Hills of Rome
Romeo and Juliet (Play)
1939 *The Adventures of
  Huckleberry Finn*
1942 *Castle in the Desert*
Rooftops
1934 *Straight Is the Way*
1940 *Gang War*
1950 *Chinatown at Midnight*
Roommates
1915 *The Grandee's Ring*
1933 *Best of Enemies*
Rafter Romance
1937 *Music for Madame*
1938 *My Lucky Star*
1940 *Knute Rockne—All
  American*
1941 *New York Town*
1942 *Foreign Agent*
1949 *Souls of Sin*
1950 *Mystery Street*
1959 *Shake Hands with the Devil*
Franklin Delano Roosevelt
1933 *The Man Who Dared: An
  Imaginative Biography*
1941 *Land of Liberty*
1943 Air Force
Yankee Doodle Dandy

1951 *The Magnificent Yankee*
1952 It's a Big Country: An
  American Anthology
1957 *Beau James*
Theodore Roosevelt
1925 Lights of Old Broadway
1941 *Land of Liberty*
1943 *In Old Oklahoma*
Jack London
1946 *Sun Valley Cyclone*
1948 *My Girl Tisa*
Roosevelt (AK)
1917 Alaska Wonders in Motion
Rosh Hashanah
1940 *Overture to Glory*
1953 *The Jazz Singer*
Rough Riders
1931 *Cimarron*
1946 *Sun Valley Cyclone*
Roulette (Game)
1935 *Señora casada necesita
  marido*
1949 *Rustlers*
Roundups
1920 Frontier Days
1932 *Wild Horse Mesa*
1947 *Wild Horse Mesa*
1949 *Stallion Canyon*
Rowboats
1932 *Senza mamma
  e'nnamurato*
1933 *Rafter Romance*
1955 *A Man Called Peter*
Rowing
1927 *For the Love of Mike*
Royal Canadian Mounted Police
  use **North West Mounted
  Police**
Royalty
1915 *The Spender*
1917 *The Bottle Imp*
1918 *Hidden Pearls*
Who Is to Blame?
Wild Women
1919 *The Sneak*
1920 *The Last of the Mohicans*
1925 Don Q, Son of Zorro
1926 Into Her Kingdom
Meet the Prince
1927 The Princess from Hoboken
Turkish Delight
1929 *Die Königsloge*
1930 The Melody Man
Olimpia
1931 *Echec au roi*
Kismet
1934 *La veuve joyeuse*
1935 Rosa de Francia
1945 *Salome, Where She Danced*
1950 *Deported*
Rubber
1931 La carta
1932 *Le bluffeur*
1939 *El otro soy yo*
1942 Rubber Racketeers
Valley of Hunted Men
Ruffians
1921 As the World Rolls On
1937 *Music for Madame*
1941 *Sunday Sinners*
1955 Bad Day at Black Rock
1959 *Odds Against Tomorrow*
Rugs
1927 Turkish Delight
1937 *Think Fast, Mr. Moto*
1941 *In the Land of the Navajo*
Ruins
Secret of the Wastelands
1951 *Go for Broke!*
1960 *Man on a String*
Rum
1949 *The Fighting Kentuckian*
Rumania
  use **Romania**
Rumors
1915 *The Lure of Woman*
1916 Man and His Angel
1917 *The Sudden Gentleman*
1930 *Olimpia*
Sei tu l'amore
1938 *God's Step Children*
In Old Chicago
Outside of Paradise

1939 *A Brivele der Mamen*
1943 *Good Luck, Mr. Yates*
1944 *Vigilantes of Dodge City*
1950 *Sands of Iwo Jima*
1951 *The Girl on the Bridge*
Runaways
1915 *The Adventures of a Madcap*
1916 *The Social Highwayman*
1917 *Sold at Auction*
1919 Bonnie, Bonnie Lassie
Who Will Marry Me?
Yvonne from Paris
1920 *The Girl of My Heart*
Huckleberry Finn
1920? *Broken Hearts*
1931 Huckleberry Finn
1933 *L'amour guide*
1934 *Imitation of Life*
1935 *The Singing Vagabond*
1937 *The Cantor's Son*
*The Jester (Der
  Purimspieler)*
1938 The Adventures of Tom
  Sawyer
The Beloved Brat
1939 *Fisherman's Wharf*
1940 *Taku*
1944 *Going My Way*
1945 *Anoush*
1947 *The Jolson Story*
1948 *The Boy with Green Hair*
1952 Wagons West
1953 *The Member of the
  Wedding*
1958 Escape from Red Rock
Houseboat
1959 *The Black Orchid*
1960 The Adventures of
  Huckleberry Finn
For the Love of Mike
Take a Giant Step
Rural life
1930 Abraham Lincoln
1936 Yiddle with His Fiddle
1939 *Drums Along the Mohawk*
1945 Our Vines Have Tender
  Grapes
1957 All Mine to Give
1959 *Porgy and Bess*
1960 *The Adventures of
  Huckleberry Finn*
*All the Fine Young
  Cannibals*
Wild River
Ruses
1930 *Olimpia*
El precio de un beso
1931 Charlie Chan Carries On
1934 *Charlie Chan in London*
What a Mother-in-Law!
1935 *¡Asegure a su mujer!*
L'homme des Folies Bergère
The Littlest Rebel
Piernas de seda
1936 *Charlie Chan's Secret*
Love and Sacrifice
1937 *One Mile from Heaven*
Thank You, Mr. Moto
1940 *If I Had My Way*
1941 *Birth of the Blues*
1942 *Sunday Punch*
1943 *Ladies' Day*
Stormy Weather
1945 *I Love a Bandleader*
1946? *Fight That Ghost*
1948 Singin' Spurs
1949 *The Valiant Hombre*
1949? The Joint Is Jumpin'
1953 *Tumbleweed*
1956 *Daniel Boone, Trail Blazer*
*Davy Crockett and the
  River Pirates*
Hot Blood
1959 *The Oregon Trail*
1960 *The Sign of Zorro*
Lillian Russell
1947 *My Wild Irish Rose*
Russia
1914? *A Boy and the Law*
1915 *Kreutzer Sonata*
1916 *Man and His Angel*
The Scarlet Oath
Sold for Marriage
The Yellow Passport

1917 *One Law for Both*
1919 The Right to Happiness
1920? Her Story
1925 Abie's Imported Bride
1926 Broken Hearts
1927 Lost at the Front
Rose of the Golden West
1931 *Resurrección*
El tenorio del harem
1932 *The Unfortunate Bride*
1933 *The Wandering Jew*
1934 The Youth of Russia
1937 Green Fields
1939 *Tevya*
1960 Man on a String

Russia—History
1939 Cossacks in Exile

Russia—History—1904-1914
1934 *Un capitán de cosacos*

Russia—History—Revolution, 1917-1921
1917 Under False Colors
1918 The Firebrand
1920 *Billions*
Lifting Shadows
1923 Fashion Row
1926 Into Her Kingdom
Meet the Prince

Russia. Army
1916 *The King's Game*
1918 *The Firebrand*

Russia. Secret Police
1914 Threads of Destiny
1916 The Yellow Passport

Russia. Secret Service
1918 The Million Dollar Mystery

Russian Americans
1915 *The Clemenceau Case*
The Immigrant
1916 The King's Game
Light at Dusk
Man and His Angel
The Scarlet Oath
Sold for Marriage
1917 Crime and Punishment
One Law for Both
Under False Colors
1918 The Firebrand
The Million Dollar Mystery
1918? *Rosemary Climbs the Heights*
1919 The Red Viper
1920 Billions
The Face at Your Window
The Great Shadow
Lifting Shadows
On with the Dance
Uncharted Channels
1920? Her Story
1922 The Hands of Nara
1923 Fashion Row
1924 The Lure of Love
1925 The Midnight Girl
1926 Into Her Kingdom
Meet the Prince
1927 The Princess from Hoboken
1928 The Mating Call
Tyrant of Red Gulch
United States Smith
Wheel of Chance
1930 She Got What She Wanted
1933 Grand Slam
1934 Strange Wives
1936 *Paddy O'Day*
1937 Big City
1940 *Elsa Maxwell's Public Deb No. 1*
1943 *Good Luck, Mr. Yates*
His Butler's Sister
1952 Anything Can Happen
1953 Tonight We Sing
1960 Man on a String

Russians
1914 *An Odyssey of the North*
1915 *The Clemenceau Case*
Kreutzer Sonata
1916 Civilization's Child
The King's Game
The Scarlet Oath
Sold for Marriage
1918 The Firebrand
1920 Lifting Shadows
1922 Breaking Home Ties
Hungry Hearts

1924 The Lure of Love
1926 Broken Hearts
Into Her Kingdom
Meet the Prince
Private Izzy Murphy
1927 The Princess from Hoboken
1928 We Americans
Wheel of Chance
1930 King of Jazz
1931 Delicious
1936 Sutter's Gold
1937 *Think Fast, Mr. Moto*
1938 *Castillos en el aire*
Gateway
Outside of Paradise
Spawn of the North
1939 *The Mystery of Mr. Wong*
1942 Twin Beds
1943 *Action in the North Atlantic*
Jack London
Let's Have Fun
1945 *Salome, Where She Danced*
1947 Northwest Outpost
1949 *The Red Menace*
1952 Arctic Flight
California Conquest
Red Snow
Red Snow
1960 *Man on a String*

Russo-Japanese War, 1904-1905
1943 *Jack London*

Rustlers
1914 *The Indian Wars*
1921 The Double O
1923 Crashin' Thru
1924 *The Night Hawk*
1927 Open Range
1930 *El último de los Vargas*
1931 *Call of the Rockies*
The Cisco Kid
Riders of the Rio
1932 Law and Lawless
Wild Horse Mesa
1933 Robbers' Roost
1934 Fighting Through
The Prescott Kid
The Prescott Kid
1935 The Cyclone Ranger
Melody Trail
Range Warfare
Texas Terror
1936 *For the Service*
Pinto Rustlers
1937 *Border Cafe*
Hills of Old Wyoming
1939 Trigger Fingers
1942 American Empire
Below the Border
King of the Stallions
1943 *The Ox-Bow Incident*
1944 Vigilantes of Dodge City
1945 *South of the Rio Grande*
1946 Santa Fe Uprising
Sun Valley Cyclone
1947 Dangerous Venture
Rustlers of Devil's Canyon
Vigilantes of Boomtown
1948 The Arizona Ranger
Old Los Angeles
1949 Riders of the Range
Rustlers
Stallion Canyon
Streets of Laredo
1950 Storm Over Wyoming
1952 *The Raiders*
Trail of the Arrow
1954 *Broken Lance*
Cattle Queen of Montana
1956 *The Lone Ranger*
1957 The Lawless Eighties

Ann Rutledge
1930 Abraham Lincoln

Sabotage
1915 The Immigrant
1916 Arms and the Woman
1918 Good-Bye, Bill
The Hun Within
The Prussian Cur
The Yellow Dog
1919 *Love and the Law*
1920 The Cup of Fury
Dangerous Days
1925 Friendly Enemies

1934 *Charlie Chan in London*
1935 *Piernas de seda*
1938 *Spawn of the North*
1939 Mr. Moto's Last Warning
1940 Charlie Chan in Panama
Murder over New York
The Ramparts We Watch
1941 The Gang's All Here
Secret of the Wastelands
1942 All Through the Night
Friendly Enemies
Nazi Agent
Rio Rita
Valley of Hunted Men
1943 In Old Oklahoma
Margin for Error
They Came to Blow Up America
1945 Betrayal from the East
1948 16 Fathoms Deep
1949 *Thieves' Highway*
1950 North of the Great Divide
A Ticket to Tomahawk
Young Daniel Boone
1951 The House on Telegraph Hill
1952 The Big Sky
Red Snow
Rose of Cimarron
1953 *The Pathfinder*
War Paint
War Paint
1954 Overland Pacific
Thunder Pass
1957 *Man in the Shadow*

Sacajawea
1955 The Far Horizons

Sacramento (CA)
1914? The Mysterious Mr. Wu Chung Foo
1924 California in '49
1932 *The Hatchet Man*
1952 *My Man and I*

Sacramento Valley (CA)
1956 *Full of Life*

Sacrifice
use **Human sacrifice;**
Self-sacrifice

Saddlery
1946 *Sun Valley Cyclone*
1947 *King of the Bandits*
1960 *The Dark at the Top of the Stairs*

Sadism
1918 Uncle Tom's Cabin
1932 *Yiskor*
1936 *The Prisoner of Shark Island*
1950 So Young, So Bad
1956 The Last Hunt
1957 *The Guns of Fort Petticoat*
Raiders of Old California

Safe-deposit boxes
1949 *The Daring Caballero*

Safecrackers
1919 *The Little Diplomat*
1930 *Así es la vida*
1934 *Lazy River*
1936 *Pinto Rustlers*
1937 That I May Live
1938 *Life Goes On*

Safes
1918 *Find the Woman*
1932 *Charlie Chan's Chance*
1934 *The Star Packer*
1938 *Charlie Chan at Monte Carlo*
1939 *Double Deal*
1944 *Charlie Chan in the Secret Service*
1946? *Go Down, Death!*
1950 *The Girl from San Lorenzo*

Safety
Give Us This Day

Sailboats
1946 *Strange Voyage*

Sailors
1914 *An Odyssey of the North*
1915? The Beachcomber
1917 *How Uncle Sam Prepares*
1921 Guile of Women
1923 Anna Christie
Purple Dawn

1930 Anna Christie
Galas de la Paramount
1931 *Aloha*
En cada puerto un amor
Law of the Tong
1934 *Eskimo*
Limehouse Blues
1937 Souls at Sea
1941 This Woman Is Mine
1942 Whispering Ghosts
1943 Action in the North Atlantic
The Amazing Mrs. Holliday
Crash Dive
Jack London
1944 *Since You Went Away*
1946 *The Sailor Takes a Wife*
1948 Harpoon
Harpoon
The Lady from Shanghai
1949 *Anna Lucasta*
1950 The Breaking Point
Mystery Submarine
Panic in the Streets
1952 *My Man and I*
1955 *A Man Called Peter*
The Rose Tattoo
1956 *Davy Crockett and the River Pirates*
1958 *Terror in a Texas Town*
1959 *Anna Lucasta*

Sainthood
1947 Citizen Saint

Saipan
1960 *Hell to Eternity*

Salads
1933 *El rey de los gitanos*

Salem (MA)
1914 When Broadway Was a Trail
1937 *Maid of Salem*

Salem (MA)—History
Maid of Salem

Salesclerks
1917 The War of the Tongs
1920? Her Story
1930 Doña mentiras

Salesmen
1916 Little Meena's Romance
1929 *The Younger Generation*
1931 *The Cohens and Kellys in Africa*
1932 *Le bluffeur*
Marido y mujer
So Big
1935 Piernas de seda
1936 *Rose of the Rancho*
1947 Buck Privates Come Home
Desperate
1948 Jiggs and Maggie in Court
1949 *Ranger of Cherokee Strip*
Tuna Clipper
1949? *The Joint Is Jumpin'*
1951 *Slaughter Trail*
Teresa
1953 Dream Wife
So Big
1954 *Thunder Pass*
1956 *Quincannon, Frontier Scout*
1960 The Dark at the Top of the Stairs

Saleswomen
1913 Traffic in Souls
1922 The Guttersnipe
1931 *Quand on est belle*
1933 *Rafter Romance*
1934 *The Cactus Kid*
1935 Piernas de seda

Salina (KS)
1926 The Last Frontier

Salinas (CA)
1952 *Japanese War Bride*

Salmon
1925 The True North
1930 The Break Up
1938 *Spawn of the North*
1940 *Taku*
1947 Spoilers of the North
1950 North of the Great Divide
1960 Ice Palace

Saloon keepers
1919 *The Lord Loves the Irish*
The She Wolf
1923 The Sting of the Scorpion

1931 *Oklahoma Jim*
1934 *The Fighting Hero*
     Fighting Through
     The Lone Defender
1935 *Circle of Death*
1935? *The Irish Gringo*
1936 *Aces and Eights*
1939 *Heaven with a Barbed Wire*
     Fence
1941 *Ride on Vaquero*
     Road Agent
1942 *Below the Border*
1944 The San Antonio Kid
     Sheriff of Las Vegas
1945 *In Old New Mexico*
     Sunbonnet Sue
     A Tree Grows in Brooklyn
1946 *Bringing Up Father*
1947 *Bowery Buckaroos*
     California
     Thunder Mountain
1948 *The Dude Goes West*
     Guns of Hate
     The Time of Your Life
1949 *Brothers in the Saddle*
     The Cowboy and the
        Prizefighter
     Riders of the Range
     Rustlers
     Satan's Cradle
     The Valiant Hombre
1950 *Border Treasure*
     The Cariboo Trail
     Comanche Territory
     The Furies
     Rio Grande Patrol
     Winchester '73
1951 *Oh! Susanna*
1952 *Indian Uprising*
1955 *White Feather*
1956 Man from Del Rio
1957 *Joe Dakota*
1958 *Frontier Gun*
1960 *The Plunderers*

Saloons
1914 *The Straight Road*
1917 *The Tenderfoot*
1919 *The Unpainted Woman*
1919? *The Brand of Judas*
1926? Ten Nights in a Barroom
1927 *The Scar of Shame*
1929 Frozen Justice
1931 *The White Renegade*
1934 *Behold My Wife!*
     Beloved
     The Cactus Kid
     The Prescott Kid
     The Star Packer
1935 *North of Arizona*
     Range Warfare
     Ruggles of Red Gap
1936 *Custer's Last Stand*
     Rose of the Rancho
     The Traitor
1937 *Law and Lead*
1938 In Old Chicago
     The Renegade Ranger
1939 *The Bronze Buckaroo*
     The Cisco Kid and the Lady
1940 *Lucky Cisco Kid*
     Viva Cisco Kid
1941 *Road Agent*
1942 *Lawless Plainsmen*
     North to the Klondike
1943 *Jack London*
     Land of Hunted Men
     The Ox-Bow Incident
1944 *Marshal of Reno*
     Outlaw Trail
1945 *The Great John L.*
     Nob Hill
     Salome, Where She Danced
     South of the Rio Grande
1946 *Border Bandits*
     Bringing Up Father
     Sunset Pass
1947 *Marshal of Cripple Creek*
     The Mighty McGurk
     Robin Hood of Monterey
     West to Glory
1948 *The Dude Goes West*
     Four Faces West
     Harpoon
     Old Los Angeles
     The Paleface

     The Time of Your Life
     Western Heritage
1949 *Jiggs and Maggie in*
        Jackpot Jitters
     Masked Raiders
     Massacre River
     The Mysterious Desperado
     Ranger of Cherokee Strip
     Riders of the Range
     The Valiant Hombre
1950 *The Cariboo Trail*
     I Killed Geronimo
     The Iroquois Trail
     Jiggs and Maggie Out West
     Rio Grande
     Rock Island Trail
     Stars in My Crown
     Storm Over Wyoming
     The Traveling Saleswoman
1951 *Adventures of Captain*
        Fabian
     Flaming Feather
1952 *High Noon*
     The Raiders
     Rose of Cimarron
1953 *Ambush at Tomahawk Gap*
     Jack McCall Desperado
1954 *Overland Pacific*
1955 *Shotgun*
1956 *The Broken Star*
     Davy Crockett and the
        River Pirates
     Ghost Town
     Raw Edge
1957 *Raiders of Old California*
     Ride Out for Revenge
1958 *Gunman's Walk*
     Ride a Crooked Trail
     Terror in a Texas Town
1959 *The Sheriff of Fractured*
        Jaw
1960 *The Plunderers*

Salt
1939 *Straight to Heaven*
1952 *Brave Warrior*

Salt Lake City (UT)
1914? *A Boy and the Law*
1941 *Western Union*

Salvage operations
1937 *The Devil's Playground*

Salvation Army
1918 *How Could You, Jean?*
     Shifting Sands
1931 *Law of the Tong*
1934 *Limehouse Blues*
1947 The Mighty McGurk
1948 *The Time of Your Life*

Samoan Islands
1931 *Young Sinners*
1946 *Dangerous Money*

Samurai
1918 *The Temple of Dusk*
1945 *Samurai*

San Antonio (TX)
1916 *Following the Flag in*
        Mexico
1921? [Unidentified Film]
1955 *The Last Command*

San Bernardino (CA)
1952 *Desert Pursuit*

San Carlos Indian Reservation
(AZ)
1954 Taza, Son of Cochise

San Diego (CA)
1915 *The Pageant of San*
        Francisco
1932 *Tiger Shark*
1935 *Rendezvous*
1937 *The Devil's Playground*
1944 *An American Romance*
1946 *Without Reservations*
1949 *The Clay Pigeon*
1952 *The Ring*
1955 *Seven Cities of Gold*
1959 *Anna Lucasta*

San Fernando Mission (CA)
1915 Captain Courtesy

San Francisco (CA)
1914 *John Barleycorn*
1915 *Chimmie Fadden Out West*
     The Pageant of San
        Francisco
1916 Hop, the Devil's Brew

1918 *Wild Women*
1920 Dinty
     A Tokio Siren
1921 *Fifty Candles*
     The First Born
     Guile of Women
     Shame
1922 The Woman He Loved
1923 Purple Dawn
1925 Flower of Night
1926 The Little Irish Girl
1927 The Chinese Parrot
     Frisco Sally Levy
     Old San Francisco
1928 *The Jazz Singer*
1929 Lucky Boy
     Welcome Danger
1930 A Lady to Love
1931 *Aloha*
     Del infierno al cielo
1932 *Men Are Such Fools*
     La melodía prohibida
1933 *Charlie Chan's Greatest*
        Case
     La ciudad de cartón
     He Was Her Man
     White Heat
1936 After the Thin Man
     Klondike Annie
     Mad Holiday
1937 Song of the City
     That I May Live
1938 *Daughter of Shanghai*
     Mr. Wong, Detective
1938? *Amore che non torna*
1939 *Charlie Chan at Treasure*
        Island
     Fisherman's Wharf
1939? *A Chinese Gains a Fortune*
        in America
1940 *Charlie Chan's Murder*
        Cruise
     If I Had My Way
     They Knew What They
        Wanted
     Three Faces West
1941 *Mutiny in the Arctic*
1942 *Gentleman Jim*
     Unseen Enemy
1943 *The Amazing Mrs. Holliday*
     Jack London
     Tahiti Honey
1944 *Address Unknown*
     Minstrel Man
     Waterfront
1945 *Betrayal from the East*
     Salome, Where She Danced
     Samurai
1946 Shadows Over Chinatown
1947 *The Chinese Ring*
1948 I Remember Mama
     The Lady from Shanghai
     Shanghai Chest
     The Time of Your Life
1949 Thieves' Highway
1950 *The Furies*
1951 *The Raging Tide*
1952 *It's a Big Country: An*
        American Anthology
1956 *Serenade*
1959 *Night of the Quarter Moon*
1960 *Walk Like a Dragon*

San Francisco (CA)—Barbary
Coast
1945 Nob Hill

San Francisco (CA)—Chinatown
1915 *Just Jim*
1918 The City of Dim Faces
     Mystic Faces
1919 The Tong Man
1920 Dinty
     The Purple Cipher
1921 Bits of Life
     A Tale of Two Worlds
     Where Lights Are Low
1922 East Is West
1925 Speed Wild
1926 A Trip to Chinatown
1928 The Hawk's Nest
1930 East Is West
     Son of the Gods
1931 *Chinatown After Dark*
     Law of the Tong

1932 *The Hatchet Man*
     The Secrets of Wu Sin
     The Son-Daughter
1935 *Chinatown Squad*
1936 *After the Thin Man*
     Mad Holiday
     Sum Hun
1937 *Think Fast, Mr. Moto*
1939 Mr. Moto Takes a Vacation
     The Mystery of Mr. Wong
1940 The Fatal Hour
     Phantom of Chinatown
1941 Golden Gate Girl
1945 *Escape in the Fog*
     Nob Hill
1948 *The Golden Eye*
     The Lady from Shanghai
     Shanghai Chest
1950 *Chinatown at Midnight*

San Francisco (CA)—Golden Gate
Bridge
1945 *Escape in the Fog*

San Francisco (CA)—Nob Hill
     Nob Hill

San Francisco (CA)—North Beach
1957 *The Midnight Story*

San Francisco earthquake, 1906
1927 Old San Francisco
1941 *Land of Liberty*

San Juan Capistrano Mission (San
Juan Capistrano, CA)
1930 Las campanas de Capistrano
1949 *Daughter of the West*

San Pedro (CA)
1953 *The Man Behind the Gun*

San Quentin Federal Penitentiary
(CA)
1932 *Men Are Such Fools*
1940 *East of the River*

San Remo (Italy)
1931 *Charlie Chan Carries On*

San Vicente (CA)
1932 *The Vanishing Frontier*

Sand Creek Massacre, CO, 1864
1957 *The Guns of Fort Petticoat*

Sandstorms
1919 *Desert Gold*
1926 *Desert Gold*
1934 *The Lone Defender*
1949 *3 Godfathers*
1955 *Seven Cities of Gold*
1959 *Gunmen from Laredo*

Sanitariums
1930 Sins of the Children
1931 *Drácula*
1935 *Te quiero con locura*
1937 *Charlie Chan at the Opera*
1940 *Eli Eli*
1942 Lucky Ghost
1943 *They Came to Blow Up*
        America
1958 *Home Before Dark*

Santa Ana (CA)
1939 *Man of Conquest*

General Antonio López de Santa
Anna
1953 *The Man from the Alamo*
1955 The Last Command

Santa Barbara (CA)
1919 *A Fallen Idol*

Santa Fe (Mexico)
1955 *Santa Fe Passage*

Santa Fe (NM)
1936 The Phantom of Santa Fe
1950 *The Baron of Arizona*
1953 *Column South*
1955 *Kiss of Fire*

Santa Fe Trail
1951 *The Last Outpost*
1955 Santa Fe Passage

Santa Monica (CA)
1933 *Let's Fall in Love*

Santa Ynez Mission (CA)
1947 *The Return of Rin Tin Tin*

Abe Saperstein
1954 Go Man Go

Sarajevo (Yugoslavia)
1934 *The Unknown Soldier*
        Speaks

Saratoga (NY)
1946 *Saratoga Trunk*
Saskatchewan (Canada)
1954 Saskatchewan
Satan
use **The Devil**
Satank
1955 Santa Fe Passage
Savannah (GA)
1953 *Sangaree*
Saxophones
1929 Is Everybody Happy?
1930 The Last Dance
1943 *Redhead from Manhattan*
Scalping
1949 *Massacre River*
1951 *Cavalry Scout*
1953 *Column South*
1956 *Comanche*
Walk the Proud Land
1957 *The Deerslayer*
1958 *The Light in the Forest*
1960 *Walk Tall*
Scandal
1913 *Traffic in Souls*
1929 *The Younger Generation*
1930 Del mismo barro
1931 Del infierno al cielo
La pura verdad
Regeneración
Women Love Once
1934 *She Was a Lady*
1935 *Señora casada necesita marido*
1937 *Nation Aflame*
Shadows of the Orient
1938 *Gateway*
1939 *Man of Conquest*
1943 The Meanest Man in the World
1947 *The Farmer's Daughter*
1951 *Jim Thorpe—All-American*
1952 *The Fabulous Senorita*
Scandinavian Americans
1947 *Calendar Girl*
William Scanlon
My Wild Irish Rose
Scapegoats
1925 The Beautiful City
1949 *Prejudice*
1958 *The Young Lions*
Scarecrows
1942 *Tales of Manhattan*
Scars
Castle in the Desert
Nazi Agent
1946 *Don Ricardo Returns*
1958 *Gun Fever*
1959 *Al Capone*
Scarves
1937 *Natalka Poltavka*
1949 *Portrait of Jennie*
Max Schmeling
1944 *The Negro Soldier*
Al Schmid
1945 Pride of the Marines
Scholars
1942 *Castle in the Desert*
Scholarships
1940 *Behind the News*
1955 *Headline Hunters*
School attendance
1938 *God's Step Children*
School buses
1941 *Hold Back the Dawn*
School life
1955 *Blackboard Jungle*
School superintendents and principals
1916 The Colored American Winning His Suit
1939 *Reform School*
1944 *They Live in Fear*
1952 *Navajo*
1953 *Bright Road*
1955 *Blackboard Jungle*
Schools
1914 *The Indian Wars*
1915 Hearts of Men
1920 Within Our Gates
1931 *Huckleberry Finn*

1937 It Could Happen to You
1938 *The Adventures of Tom Sawyer*
Birthright
God's Step Children
1939 Reform School
1945 *The Bells of St. Mary's*
1947 *Citizen Saint*
1948 *Up in Central Park*
1949 *Answer for Anne*
Prejudice
Ranger of Cherokee Strip
1957 *Satchmo the Great*
Schoolteachers
1917 Runaway Romany
The Squaw Man's Son
1919 The Volcano
1920 *Locked Lips*
The Luck of the Irish
Rio Grande
1921 A Giant of His Race
1922 *Spitfire*
1923 *Deceit*
1924 So Big
1925 Red Love
1926 The Vanishing American
1927 Wild Geese
1931 *Street Scene*
1934 *Imitation of Life*
The Rabbi's Power
1936 *Silly Billies*
1939 *The Cisco Kid and the Lady*
1941 *Hold Back the Dawn*
1943 The Amazing Mrs. Holliday
Crash Dive
Good Luck, Mr. Yates
In Old Oklahoma
1944 *An American Romance*
Buffalo Bill
Sheriff of Las Vegas
1945 Great Stagecoach Robbery
Our Vines Have Tender Grapes
A Tree Grows in Brooklyn
1946 Wild Beauty
1947 *Black Gold*
The Last Round-Up
1948 *The Boy with Green Hair*
Moonrise
Up in Central Park
1949 The Girl from Jones Beach
1950 *Stars in My Crown*
1951 *Slaughter Trail*
1952 *Indian Uprising*
It's a Big Country: An American Anthology
1953 Bright Road
The Man Behind the Gun
So Big
1955 Good Morning, Miss Dove
Marty
1959 *Anna Lucasta*
1960 The Crowning Experience
Schooners
1912 *Atop of the World in Motion*
1930 El dios del mar
Science
use **Specific branches of science**
Scientific apparatus and instruments
1945 *The House on 92nd St.*
Scientists
1925 Justice of the Far North
1931 *Such Is Life*
1938 *Gateway*
Mr. Wong, Detective
1940 *Charlie Chan in Panama*
George Washington Carver
Son of Ingagi
1941 Four Shall Die
1942 *Valley of Hunted Men*
1944 *Charlie Chan in the Secret Service*
Cry of the Werewolf
1945 *The House on 92nd St.*
The Jade Mask
The Scarlet Clue
1946 Rendezvous 24
1948 *Night Wind*
1950 Mystery Submarine
1960 I Aim at the Stars: the Wernher von Braun Story

Scotland
1930 The Cohens and the Kellys in Scotland
1955 *A Man Called Peter*
1959 *John Paul Jones*
Scotland Yard (London, England)
1930 Le spectre vert
1931 Charlie Chan Carries On
El impostor
1932 *Charlie Chan's Chance*
Scots
1916 *Ramona*
1920 *The Tiger's Coat*
1927 Sally in Our Alley
1930 King of Jazz
1931 *Delicious*
1938 *The Buccaneer*
1948 *Harpoon*
Winfield Scott
1930 Abraham Lincoln
Scottish Americans
1917 *The Plow Woman*
1919 Bonnie, Bonnie Lassie
False Evidence
The Homesteader
1927 McFadden's Flats
1934 *Coming Out Party*
1935 McFadden's Flats
1940 *Three Cheers for the Irish*
1941 *This Woman Is Mine*
Where Did You Get That Girl?
1948 *Rocky*
1949 *Tuna Clipper*
1951 *Across the Wide Missouri*
1955 A Man Called Peter
1957 *All Mine to Give*
1959 John Paul Jones
1960 *Ice Palace*
Scouts (Frontier)
1916 Britton of the Seventh
1917 *The Hidden Children*
John Ermine of the Yellowstone
1919 The Westerners
1920 The Last of the Mohicans
1925 A Daughter of the Sioux
The Red Rider
Tonio, Son of the Sierras
1926 The Frontier Trail
The Last Frontier
1927 The Overland Stage
1928 Kit Carson
Orphan of the Sage
1929 Sioux Blood
1931 *Call of the Rockies*
Fighting Caravans
La gran jornada
1932 *Texas Pioneers*
1933 The Telegraph Trail
1934 Wagon Wheels
1935 *Fighting Pioneers*
1936 Custer's Last Stand
For the Service
The Last of the Mohicans
1937 The Plainsman
1940 *Geronimo*
Kit Carson
1941 The Pioneers
Western Union
1942 Valley of the Sun
1943 Deerslayer
1944 Buffalo Bill
1947 *Last of the Redmen*
1948 *Unconquered*
1949 *Laramie*
1950 Ambush
Young Daniel Boone
1951 *Apache Drums*
Slaughter Trail
Tomahawk
1952 Apache Country
The Battle at Apache Pass
Buffalo Bill in Tomahawk Territory
Fort Osage
The Savage
Wagons West
1953 Arrowhead
Column South
The Nebraskan
The Pathfinder
1954 *Arrow in the Dust*
Saskatchewan
Thunder Pass

1955 Apache Ambush
Davy Crockett, King of the Wild Frontier
Fort Yuma
The Gun That Won the West
The Indian Fighter
Santa Fe Passage
Seminole Uprising
1956 *The Burning Hills*
Comanche
The Last Frontier
Pillars of the Sky
Quincannon, Frontier Scout
Westward Ho the Wagons!
The Wild Dakotas
1957 *The Deerslayer*
Pawnee
Revolt at Fort Laramie
Run of the Arrow
Tomahawk Trail
1958 *Fort Massacre*
The Light in the Forest
1959 Thunder in the Sun
Scouts (Youth)
use **Boy Scouts**
Scranton (PA)
1936 *Dangerous Intrigue*
Scrubwomen
1945 *A Tree Grows in Brooklyn*
1947 *Carnegie Hall*
1948 *Call Northside 777*
Sculptors
1916 *The Folly of Revenge*
1918 *Amarilly of Clothes-Line Alley*
My Cousin
1920 *The Man Who Dared*
1921 All Souls' Eve
1922 The Hands of Nara
1927 Lost at the Front
1931 Lo mejor es reír
1932 *So Big*
1937 *A Study of Negro Artists*
1947 *It Had To Be You*
1956 *Serenade*
Sculpture
1917 The Trouble Buster
1920 The Man Who Dared
Sea battles
1944 *Lifeboat*
1950 *Buccaneer's Girl*
Sea captains
1914 The Yellow Traffic
1919 Behind the Door
1920? *Her Story*
1922 My Boy
1923 Anna Christie
Purple Dawn
Regeneration
1926 The Barrier
1927 Blind Alleys
The Slaver
1930 El dios del mar
1931 Dämon des Meeres
1933 *Diplomaniacs*
1934 *Eskimo*
1935 *Tango Bar*
1936 *Klondike Annie*
1937 *El capitán Tormenta*
1938 *Hawaii Calls*
Zamboanga
1939 *Confessions of a Nazi Spy*
Mr. Wong in Chinatown
1941 *Dead Men Tell*
Mutiny in the Arctic
Mystery Ship
This Woman Is Mine
1942 Submarine Raider
1943 *Action in the North Atlantic*
Mr. Lucky
1944 *Lifeboat*
1945 *Johnny Angel*
1946 *Swamp Fire*
1947 *The Chinese Ring*
1948 *Unconquered*
1949 *Harbor of Missing Men*
1950 *Buccaneer's Girl*
1951 *Adventures of Captain Fabian*
1956 Wetbacks
1960 *The Last Voyage*

Sea rescues
- 1914 *The Little Jewess*
- 1917 *The Little American*
- 1933 *The Cohens and Kellys in Trouble*
- 1934 *Lazy River*
- 1936 *Sea Spoilers*
- 1937 *Souls at Sea*
- 1938 *Spawn of the North*
- 1942 *Submarine Raider*
- 1944 *Lifeboat*

The Sea Wolf (Novel)
- 1943 *Jack London*

Seabiscuit (Horse)
- 1949 The Story of Seabiscuit

Seals (Animals)
- 1925 *Kivalina of the Ice Lands*
- 1932 *Igloo*
- 1936 *Sea Spoilers*
- 1938 *Spawn of the North*
- 1939 *Fisherman's Wharf*
- 1945 *The Dolly Sisters*
- 1946 *Slightly Scandalous*

Seamstresses
- 1915 *The Kindling*
- *The Secret Sin*
- 1924 *Fools' Highway*
- 1929 East Side Sadie
- 1937 *One Mile from Heaven*
- 1938 *Swing!*
- *La vida bohemia*
- 1939 *Miracle on Main Street*
- 1948 My Girl Tisa
- 1955 *The Rose Tattoo*

Séances
- 1936 Charlie Chan's Secret
- 1944 Black Magic
- 1947? Return of Mandy's Husband

Seaplanes
- 1926 Sweet Daddies
- 1938 *Daughter of Shanghai*
- 1941 *Mutiny in the Arctic*

Search and rescue operations
- 1949 Arctic Fury

Searches
- 1945 *The Mummy's Curse*
- 1946 *Santa Fe Uprising*
- 1948? *Junction 88*
- 1949 *Arctic Manhunt*
- *Call of the Forest*
- *The Fighting Kentuckian*
- 1950 *Cherokee Uprising*
- *Intruder in the Dust*
- 1953 *The Glass Wall*
- Taxi
- 1956 The Searchers
- 1957 *Raintree County*
- 1960 *For the Love of Mike*

Seasickness
- 1942 *Across the Pacific*

Seattle (WA)
- 1947 *Spoilers of the North*
- 1960 *Ice Palace*

Secession
- 1953 The Man Behind the Gun

Secret agents
- 1914 Rose of the Rancho
- 1917 The Bond Between
- 1918 The Kaiser's Finish
- 1920 *The Face at Your Window*
- 1935 *Charlie Chan in Shanghai*
- 1939 *Mr. Moto in Danger Island*
- 1943 They Came to Blow Up America

Secret codes
- 1935 Rendezvous
- 1936 *Sea Spoilers*
- 1944 *Tucson Raiders*
- 1952 *Apache Country*

Secret documents
- 1915 *Just Jim*
- 1915? *Sam Davis, the Hero of Tennessee*
- 1916 *Her Debt of Honor*
- 1917 Follow the Girl
- *The Little Chevalier*
- 1918 *The Birth of a Race*
- *The Firebrand*
- *His Birthright*
- I Want to Forget
- *Shifting Sands*
- 1924 North of 36
- Two Shall Be Born

- 1925 *The Gold Hunters*
- 1926 The Frontier Trail
- 1933 Dos noches
- 1937 *Souls at Sea*
- 1938 *Hawaii Calls*
- 1940 Phantom of Chinatown
- 1942 *Nazi Agent*
- 1945 Escape in the Fog
- 1948 *Shanghai Chest*

Secret formulas
- 1915 *Hearts of Men*
- 1922 The Schemers
- 1945 *The Jade Mask*
- 1946 The Red Dragon

Secret identities
- *use* **Impersonation and imposture**

Secret passageways
- 1934 *The Lone Defender*
- 1935 *Charlie Chan in Egypt*
- 1936 *Charlie Chan's Secret*
- 1943 *The Law Rides Again*
- 1944 *Cry of the Werewolf*
- 1945 *The Jade Mask*
- *The Shanghai Cobra*
- 1946 *The Trap*

Secret plans
- 1920 Who's Your Servant?
- 1936 Ride, Ranger, Ride
- 1944 Charlie Chan in the Secret Service

Secret Service
- 1914 *The Little Jewess*
- The Yellow Traffic
- 1915 *Time Lock Number* 776
- 1917 Follow the Girl
- 1918 *The Hun Within*
- I Want to Forget
- Shifting Sands
- 1919 *The Lord Loves the Irish*
- The Volcano
- 1919? *America Was Right*
- 1920? Reformation
- 1925 Friendly Enemies
- 1932? The Girl from Chicago
- 1935 Rendezvous
- 1941 *King of the Zombies*
- 1944 *Charlie Chan in the Secret Service*
- 1946 Rendezvous 24
- 1952 *It's a Big Country: An American Anthology*

Secret societies
- 1914? *A Boy and the Law*
- 1916 The Fall of a Nation
- 1918 The Girl in the Dark
- 1918? *The Snail*
- 1921 Diane of Star Hollow
- 1937 Black Legion
- Nation Aflame
- 1941 *Secret of the Wastelands*
- 1945 *Samurai*
- 1949 Jigsaw

Secretaries
- 1915 *A Texas Steer*
- 1917 *Castles for Two*
- *The Little Chevalier*
- The Secret Game
- *The Wild Girl*
- 1918 *Free and Equal*
- The Liar
- The Ordeal of Rosetta
- 1919 *Daughter of Mine*
- *The Lord Loves the Irish*
- 1921 The Call of His People
- Fifty Candles
- Shame
- 1922 The Schemers
- The Scrapper
- 1923 Deceit
- 1925 Salome of the Tenements
- 1928 The Cameraman
- George Washington Cohen
- 1932 *Le bluffeur*
- *Harlem Is Heaven*
- 1933 *Counsellor at Law*
- *Victims of Persecution*
- Una viuda romántica
- 1934 *Charlie Chan in London*
- *Charlie Chan's Courage*
- 1935 *¡Asegure a su mujer!*
- *Charlie Chan in Shanghai*
- *Chinatown Squad*

- 1936 *El crimen de media noche*
- *Muss 'Em Up*
- 1938 *The Beloved Brat*
- *Mr. Wong, Detective*
- Speed to Burn
- *Swing!*
- 1939 *Charlie Chan in Honolulu*
- *Mr. Moto Takes a Vacation*
- *The Mystery of Mr. Wong*
- *El otro soy yo*
- *El trovador de la radio*
- 194- *Mistaken Identity*
- 1940 *Broken Strings*
- *Charlie Chan's Murder Cruise*
- *Escape to Glory*
- *Mystery in Swing*
- 1941 *Charlie Chan in Rio*
- 1942 *Woman of the Year*
- 1943 *Doughboys in Ireland*
- *The Meanest Man in the World*
- 1944 *Waterfront*
- 1945 *Johnny Angel*
- *The Mummy's Curse*
- *The Shanghai Cobra*
- 1946 *Mantan Messes Up*
- *The Red Dragon*
- *Till the End of Time*
- 1947 *Copacabana*
- *Mantan Runs for Mayor*
- *Reet, Petite and Gone*
- *Ride the Pink Horse*
- *Spoilers of the North*
- 1948 *Gentleman's Agreement*
- *Killer Diller*
- *Music Man*
- *Reaching from Heaven*
- *Shanghai Chest*
- 1949 *Harbor of Missing Men*
- 1950 *Buccaneer's Girl*
- 1952 *Apache Country*
- 1955 *Trial*
- 1957 *Beau James*
- 1960 *I Passed for White*

Secrets
- 1931 Così è la vita
- 1937 I Want to Be a Mother
- 1942 *Friendly Enemies*
- 1948 The Betrayal
- *Rocky*
- *The Time of Your Life*
- 1950 *Give Us This Day*
- *Right Cross*
- 1950? Three Daughters
- 1952 Bugles in the Afternoon
- 1955 Santa Fe Passage
- 1959 *The Hanging Tree*

Seder (Jewish holiday)
- 1939 *A Brivele der Mamen*
- 1958 *Marjorie Morningstar*

Seduction
- 1914 The Nightingale
- *The Woman in Black*
- 1917 The Bride of Hate
- The Call of the East
- 1918 *The Ordeal of Rosetta*
- 1919 *The Last of His People*
- Told in the Hills
- 1920? The Greatest Love
- 1921 Hearts of the Woods
- 1926 *The Passaic Textile Strike*
- 1927 For the Love of Mike
- The Way of All Flesh
- 1930 *Cuando el amor ríe*
- Del mismo barro
- *Un hombre de suerte*
- 1931 Buster se marie
- *Call of the Rockies*
- *Così è la vita*
- *Mamá*
- *Mr. Lemon of Orange*
- Nuit d'Espagne
- Oklahoma Jim
- *Three Who Loved*
- Tropennächte
- *Young Sinners*
- 1932 *La foule hurle*
- *Harlem Is Heaven*
- *Joseph in the Land of Egypt*
- *Yiskor*
- 1932? *The Girl from Chicago*
- 1933 La melodía prohibida
- 1934 *Behold My Wife!*
- *Laughing Boy*

- 1935 *¡Asegure a su mujer!*
- *Lem Hawkins' Confession*
- 1936 *Love and Sacrifice*
- *La última cita*
- 1938 *Josette*
- *The Singing Blacksmith*
- 1939 *A Brivele der Mamen*
- *Mothers of Today*
- 1940 *Paradise in Harlem*
- *The Way of All Flesh*
- 1941 *Adam Had Four Sons*
- 1943 Let's Have Fun
- 1947 *Duel in the Sun*
- *Juke Joint*
- 1948 *Tap Roots*
- 1949 *Daughter of the West*
- *House of Strangers*
- *Massacre River*
- *Thieves' Highway*
- 1949? *Girl in Room 20*
- 1950 *The Breaking Point*
- 1951 A Streetcar Named Desire
- *When the Redskins Rode*
- 1952 *My Man and I*
- 1955 *Apache Ambush*
- *Seven Cities of Gold*
- 1956 *Baby Doll*
- *Hot Blood*
- *Serenade*
- 1958 *Machete*
- *The Young Lions*
- 1959 *Imitation of Life*
- 1960 *Hell to Eternity*

Seers
- 1917 *The Hidden Children*

Segregation
- 1922 The Dungeon
- 1924 Birthright
- 1938 *Birthright*
- 1943 Fighting Americans
- 1950 *The Jackie Robinson Story*
- 1957 Segregation and the South
- 1960 *Wild River*

Self-confidence
- 1915 The Danger Signal
- 1948 *Big City*
- 1949 *Prejudice*
- 1950 *No Way Out*
- 1957 The Ride Back
- 1960 *The Dark at the Top of the Stairs*

Self-defense
- 1916 *The Twin Triangle*
- 1918 *The Hell Cat*
- *In Judgment Of*
- 1920 Lifting Shadows
- *Who's Your Servant?*
- 1930 *El último de los Vargas*
- 1939 *Gone With the Wind*
- 1949 *Massacre River*
- *Satan's Cradle*
- 1950 *Cherokee Uprising*
- 1956 *The Last Frontier*
- 1957 *The Oklahoman*
- 1958 *Apache Territory*
- 1960 *Walk Like a Dragon*

Self-made men
- 1953 *So Big*

Self-mutilation
- 1958 *Flaming Frontier*

Self-reliance
- 1934 *Imitation of Life*
- 1944 Lifeboat

Self-respect
- 1955 Bad Day at Black Rock
- 1958 Marjorie Morningstar
- 1960 *Sergeant Rutledge*
- Take a Giant Step

Self-sacrifice
- 1914 Dan
- *The Jungle*
- The Little Angel of Canyon Creek
- The Squaw Man
- 1915 *The Cheat*
- Chimmie Fadden
- *The Kindling*
- *The Melting Pot*
- *The Nigger*
- Sealed Valley
- 1916 The Criminal
- The Flames of Johannis
- The Honorable Friend
- The Morals of Hilda

Unprotected
1917 The Barrier
The Bottle Imp
Forbidden Paths
The Gun Fighter
Hashimura Togo
John Ermine of the
Yellowstone
The Little American
The Little Samaritan
My Fighting Gentleman
One Law for Both
The Plow Woman
A Roadside Impresario
The Slacker
The Squaw Man's Son
Unconquered
1918 The Bravest Way
Broken Ties
The Hell Cat
Hitting the Trail
The Honor of His House
The Kaiser's Finish
The Price of Applause
The Ranger
The Squaw Man
The Temple of Dusk
The Unbeliever
Who Is to Blame?
1919 Daughter of Mine
False Evidence
A Heart in Pawn
Lasca
The Right to Happiness
Scarlet Days
The Volcano
Who Will Marry Me?
Who's Your Brother?
1920 The Paliser Case
1921 No Woman Knows
The Sport of the Gods
1922 For His Mother's Sake
1928 George Washington Cohen
1930 Eternal Fools (Ewige
Naranim)
Sins of the Children
Sombras de gloria
El valiente
Wu Li Chang
1931 The Black Camel
Carne de cabaret
Cavalier of the West
Cimarron
El comediante
La dama atrevida
Law of the Tong
The Squaw Man
Such Is Life
Three Who Loved
Women Love Once
1932 Call Her Savage
Le cas du docteur Brenner
Genoveffa
Harlem Is Heaven
Marido y mujer
The Son-Daughter
Soñadores de la gloria
Texas Pioneers
The Unfortunate Bride
Wild Horse Mesa
Yiskor
1933 L'amour guide
Obey the Law
Racetrack
Song of the Eagle
Victims of Persecution
1934 Behold My Wife!
Beloved
The Great Flirtation
He Was Her Man
Imitation of Life
Limehouse Blues
Our Daily Bread
Tres amores
1935 The Cyclone Ranger
The Irish in Us
McFadden's Flats
Shir Hashirim
1936 Dimples
Down to the Sea
For the Service
The Last of the Mobicans
Rebellion
Robin Hood of El Dorado
Show Boat

Sum Hun
The Traitor
1937 The Barrier
Souls at Sea
1938 The Adventures of Tom
Sawyer
The Buccaneer
City Streets
The Duke Is Tops
Life Goes On
Little Miss Roughneck
Two Sisters
La vida bohemia
1939 The Escape
Gone With the Wind
Los hijos mandan
La Inmaculada
Keep Punching
Mamele
Motel the Operator
My Son
1940 Escape
Escape to Glory
Girl from God's Country
Her Second Mother
Paradise in Harlem
1941 Adam Had Four Sons
The Face Behind the Mask
Murder on Lenox Avenue
1942 Apache Trail
Prisoner of Japan
Sunday Punch
They Died With Their Boots
On
1943 Bataan
Crash Dive
Dixie
Hitler's Children
1944 The Racket Man
Since You Went Away
The Sullivans
1945 Betrayal from the East
Of One Blood
1946 G. I. War Brides
1947 Bells of San Fernando
California
Hi De Ho
The Jolson Story
King of the Bandits
1948 The Betrayal
Big City
I Remember Mama
Tap Roots
Unconquered
1949 3 Godfathers
Tuna Clipper
1949? Girl in Room 20
1950 Damien
Emergency Wedding
Give Us This Day
Rocky Mountain
Two Flags West
1950? Three Daughters
1951 Fort Defiance
Gambling House
The Harlem Globetrotters
Little Big Horn
The Mark of the Renegade
New Mexico
Only the Valiant
Show Boat
Warpath
1952 Red Ball Express
1953 Captain John Smith and
Pocabontas
Last of the Comanches
The Member of the
Wedding
The Stars Are Singing
War Paint
1954 Barefoot Battalion
Broken Lance
Cattle Queen of Montana
Drum Beat
Hell's Half Acre
Taza, Son of Cochise
1955 Fort Yuma
Good Morning, Miss Dove
Santa Fe Passage
Seven Cities of Gold
1956 Ghost Town
Pillars of the Sky
1957 Run of the Arrow
1958 The Defiant Ones
The Light in the Forest

The Lone Ranger and the
Lost City of Gold
Tonka
1959 The Black Orchid
The FBI Story
The Last Angry Man
1960 All the Young Men

Seminaries
use **Theological seminaries**

Seminole Indians
1916? Fate's Chessboard
1919 Diane of the Green Van
1937 Drums of Destiny
1948 Key Largo
1951 Distant Drums
1953 Seminole
1954 War Arrow
1955 Seminole Uprising
1957 Naked in the Sun

Seminole War, 2d, 1835-1842
1951 Distant Drums
1957 Naked in the Sun

Seminole War, 3d, 1855-1858
1955 Seminole Uprising

Senators
1934 Judge Priest
1936 West of Nevada
1937 Border Cafe
1941 Louisiana Purchase
1944 Buffalo Bill
1953 The Man Behind the Gun
1955 A Man Called Peter
1956 Dakota Incident

Seneca Indians
1948 Unconquered

Senility
1960 Weddings and Babies

Separation (Marital)
1918 Who Is to Blame?
1919 Hearts of Men
His Parisian Wife
1919? The Chosen Path
1920 The North Wind's Malice
1931 Gente alegre
The White Renegade
1934 Cuesta abajo
1935 Señora casada necesita
marido
1936 My American Wife
1938 The Singing Blacksmith
1939 Kol Nidre
1940 Eli Eli
1942 Syncopation
Wings for the Eagle
Woman of the Year
1946 Song of the South
1947 Crossfire
1951 Jim Thorpe—All-American
The Last Outpost
Teresa
1953 Taxi
Tonight We Sing
1955 The Gun That Won the
West
Murder in Villa Capri
1959 The FBI Story
1960 The Crowning Experience

Serbian Americans
1942 Cat People

Sermons
1917 The Little Samaritan
1925 Body and Soul
1939 Kol Nidre
1941 Sunday Sinners
1944 Going My Way
1946? Go Down, Death!
1949 Prejudice
1952 It's a Big Country: An
American Anthology
1952? Call of the Navajo
1955 A Man Called Peter

Servants
1913? The Lure of New York
1914 Life's Shop Window
1915 The Birth of a Nation
Chimmie Fadden
Marse Covington
1916 The Thousand Dollar
Husband
Three of Many
1918 The Girl in the Dark
1919 Come Out of the Kitchen
Toby's Bow

1920 The Mark of Zorro
Who's Your Servant?
1931 Chérie
Cimarron
Echec au roi
Nuit d'Espagne
1932 Amore e morte
Mystery Ranch
1933 Broken Dreams
The Wandering Jew
1934 La buenaventura
Fighting Through
The Great Flirtation
1935 Charlie Chan in Egypt
The Cyclone Ranger
The Wedding Night
The Yiddish King Lear
1936 Charlie Chan's Secret
Paddy O'Day
The Phantom of Santa Fe
Ramona
The Traitor
1938 In Old Chicago
Mr. Wong, Detective
1939 Charlie Chan at Treasure
Island
Gone With the Wind
Mr. Moto Takes a Vacation
1940 The Gay Caballero
Girl from God's Country
Mystery in Swing
New Moon
1941 Belle Starr
King of the Zombies
Lady from Louisiana
Min Jok Jay Hung Sing
Up Jumped the Devil
1942 Across the Pacific
Mexican Spitfire Sees a
Ghost
Rubber Racketeers
Syncopation
Tales of Manhattan
The Vanishing Virginian
Young America
1944 Black Magic
1945 Nob Hill
1946 Border Bandits
Song of the South
Three Wise Fools
1947 Little Mister Jim
1948 The Lady from Shanghai
The Luck of the Irish
Tap Roots
1949 Ranger of Cherokee Strip
1953 Jack McCall Desperado
San Antone
1955 Duel on the Mississippi
1958 Machete
1960 The Sign of Zorro

Service stations
use **Gas stations**

Set-ups
1944 Block Busters
1948 Sleep, My Love
1949 Ride, Ryder, Ride!

Settlement workers
1914 The Straight Road
1915 The Kindling
1918 The Man Above the Law
The Midnight Patrol
1919 Mandarin's Gold
1921 Cheated Love

Settlers
1914? The Lust of the Red Man
Sitting Bull—The Hostile
Sioux Indian Chief
The Pageant of San
Francisco
1915
1916 The Aryan
Gold and the Woman
1917 John Ermine of the
Yellowstone
1919? When the Desert Smiles
1926 The Devil Horse
General Custer at Little Big
Horn
1927 The Overland Stage
With Sitting Bull at the
Spirit Lake Massacre
1928 The Glorious Trail
Orphan of the Sage
1931 Call of the Rockies
Cimarron
Fighting Caravans

The Great Meadow
1932 *Texas Pioneers*
1934 Wagon Wheels
1936 Custer's Last Stand
Daniel Boone
The Glory Trail
Klondike Annie
Ramona
Sutter's Gold
1937 Old Louisiana
1938 *Sugar Hill Baby*
1939 Allegheny Uprising
Drums Along the Mohawk
In Old Caliente
1941 Prairie Pioneers
1942 *Lawless Plainsmen*
North to the Klondike
1943 Deerslayer
1947 Buffalo Bill Rides Again
California
1948 Silver Trails
Unconquered
1951 *Apache Drums*
Warpath
1952 *Fort Osage*
The Raiders
1953 *The Great Sioux Uprising*
1954 *Battle of Rogue River*
Drum Beat
Thunder Pass
War Arrow
1955 The Indian Fighter
Kentucky Rifle
Seminole Uprising
1956 Daniel Boone, Trail Blazer
Frontier Woman
Mohawk
The White Squaw
1957 *Trooper Hook*
1958 *Flaming Frontier*
The Light in the Forest
Sierra Baron
1960 *Flaming Star*
The Unforgiven

Seville (Spain)
1930 *Sevilla de mis amores*
1932 *Soñadores de la gloria*

Samuel Sewall
1937 *Maid of Salem*

Sewers
1935 *Charlie Chan in Paris*
1945 *The Shanghai Cobra*
1960 *The Day They Robbed the Bank of England*

Sex
1932 Une heure près de toi
1956 Baby Doll
1960 The Dark at the Top of the Stairs

Sex (Premarital)
use Premarital sex

Sex crimes
1921 The Gunsaulus Mystery

Sexual equality
1954 Salt of the Earth

Sexual harassment
1916 *Civilization's Child*
1933 *Rafter Romance*
1935 *Circle of Death*
1948 *My Girl Tisa*
1949 *The Red Menace*
1958 *The Light in the Forest*
1959 *The World, the Flesh and the Devil*

William Shakespeare
1939 *Forged Passport*
1940 *Paradise in Harlem*
1941 *Playmates*
1947 *Juke Joint*

Shamrocks
1944 *The Racket Man*
1945 *Nob Hill*

Shanghai (China)
1921 Shame
1931 *Chinatown After Dark*
1935 Charlie Chan in Shanghai
1937 *Think Fast, Mr. Moto*

Shanghaiing
1927 The Slaver
1931 *Del infierno al cielo*
1948 *Harpoon*

Shantytowns
1941 *Sullivan's Travels*

Sharecroppers
1920 Within Our Gates
1940 *George Washington Carver*

Sharks
1932 Tiger Shark
1936 *Down to the Sea*
The Prisoner of Shark Island
1946 *Strange Voyage*

Sharpshooters
1935 Annie Oakley
1947 *Bowery Buckaroos*
Thunder Mountain
1948 The Paleface
1950 Annie Get Your Gun
Winchester '73
1952 *Apache Country*
1957 *The Lawless Eighties*

Shawnee Indians
1931 The Great Meadow
1950 *Young Daniel Boone*
1952 *Brave Warrior*
1956 Daniel Boone, Trail Blazer

Sheep
1948 *Rocky*
1949 *The Cowboy and the Indians*
1950 *Train to Tombstone*
1958 *Wild Is the Wind*

Sheep ranchers
1945 Wanderer of the Wasteland
1958 *Wild Is the Wind*

Sheepherders
1927 White Gold
1932 *Amor in montagna*
1949 *Tale of the Navajos*
1950 *Devil's Doorway*
Storm Over Wyoming
1952? *Call of the Navajo*
1956 *The Burning Hills*

Sheiks
1931 *The Cohens and Kellys in Africa*

Shell shock
1926 *Puppets*
1928 *Absent*
1944 *Lifeboat*

Shepherds
1919 *Auction of Souls*
1934 *Las fronteras del amor*
1936 *The Green Pastures*
1948 *Rocky*

General Philip Henry Sheridan
1930 Abraham Lincoln
1950 *Rio Grande*

Sheriffs
1916 *The Half-Breed*
Mixed Blood
1917? *Barnaby Lee*
1918 Denny from Ireland
The Hell Cat
Her Moment
The Only Road
Tongues of Flame
1919 The Gray Towers Mystery
Love and the Law
Scarlet Days
1920 The Man Who Dared
1922 *The Crimson Skull*
Cross Roads
When East Comes West
1924 The Broken Law
The Lightning Rider
The Night Hawk
1928 The Riding Renegade
1930 The Lash
Whoopee
1931 *Cavalier of the West*
The Cisco Kid
The Hurricane Horseman
Riders of the Rio
The Squaw Man
1932 *Hidden Valley*
Mystery Ranch
Wild Horse Mesa
1933 *Circle Canyon*
Dance Hall Hostess
1934 *The Battling Buckaroo*
The Cactus Kid
The Fighting Hero
Fighting Through
Lazy River

The Lone Defender
Our Daily Bread
The Prescott Kid
The Star Packer
1935 *Circle of Death*
Cowboy Holiday
The Cyclone Ranger
The Little Colonel
Range Warfare
Texas Terror
1935? *The Irish Gringo*
1936 *Aces and Eights*
Border Phantom
Pinto Rustlers
1937 *The Californian*
Harlem on the Prairie
The Riders of the Whistling Skull
1938 *The Duke Is Tops*
Two Gun Man from Harlem
1939 *Bad Lands*
Charlie Chan in Reno
Harlem Rides the Range
Heaven with a Barbed Wire Fence
The Return of the Cisco Kid
1940 *Rhythm of the Rio Grande*
1941 *Gauchos of Eldorado*
The Mexican Spitfire's Baby
The Pioneers
Ride on Vaquero
Road Agent
Secret of the Wastelands
1942 *Below the Border*
Lawless Plainsmen
1943 *Border Patrol*
Land of Hunted Men
The Law Rides Again
The Leopard Man
Mexican Spitfire's Blessed Event
The Outlaw
Wagon Tracks West
1944 *Marshal of Reno*
Outlaw Trail
Sheriff of Las Vegas
Sonora Stagecoach
Tucson Raiders
1945 *The Cisco Kid Returns*
In Old New Mexico
The Jade Mask
1946 *California Gold Rush*
Sheriff of Redwood Valley
Sun Valley Cyclone
1947 *The Adventures of Don Coyote*
Bowery Buckaroos
Buffalo Bill Rides Again
Desperate
On the Old Spanish Trail
Oregon Trail Scouts
Rustlers of Devil's Canyon
Thunder Mountain
Under the Tonto Rim
Vigilantes of Boomtown
1948 *Guns of Hate*
Moonrise
Night Wind
Renegades of Sonora
Shep Comes Home
Western Heritage
1949 *Brothers in the Saddle*
The Cowboy and the Indians
The Dalton Gang
The Fighting Kentuckian
The Golden Stallion
Lookout Sister
Lust for Gold
Massacre River
The Mysterious Desperado
Ranger of Cherokee Strip
The Red Menace
Riders of the Range
Rustlers
Stagecoach Kid
Stallion Canyon
Streets of Laredo
3 Godfathers
The Valiant Hombre
1949? *Come On, Cowboy!*
1950 *Border Treasure*
Colt .45
The Girl from San Lorenzo

North of the Great Divide
Raiders of Tomahawk Creek
Sunset in the West
A Ticket to Tomahawk
1951 *Show Boat*
The Well
1952 *The Half-Breed*
1953 *Cry of the Hunted*
Ride, Vaquero!
The Stand at Apache River
Thunder Bay
Tumbleweed
1954 *Salt of the Earth*
Siege at Red River
1955 *Apache Ambush*
Apache Woman
Bad Day at Black Rock
1956 *The Last Wagon*
The Lone Ranger
Man from Del Rio
Reprisal!
The White Squaw
1957 *Gun Battle at Monterey*
Man in the Shadow
The Tin Star
1958 *The Defiant Ones*
Escape from Red Rock
Gunfire at Indian Gap
Gunman's Walk
Terror in a Texas Town
1959 The Sheriff of Fractured Jaw
The Young Land
1960 *The Plunderers*

William Tecumseh Sherman
1915 *The Birth of a Nation*
1927 Spoilers of the West
1954 *Drum Beat*

The Sherman Anti-Trust Act of 1890
1951 *The Magnificent Yankee*

Ship builders
use Shipbuilders

Ship captains
use Sea captains

Ship crews
1918 *Wild Women*
1933 *No dejes la puerta abierta*
1936 *Down to the Sea*
1937 Slave Ship
1938 *Daughter of Shanghai*
1939 *Charlie Chan in Honolulu*
1944 *Waterfront*
1948 *16 Fathoms Deep*
1960 The Last Voyage

Ship fires
1937 *Slave Ship*
1938 *The Buccaneer*
1943 *Good Luck, Mr. Yates*

Ship owners
1918 *Wild Women*
1936 *Down to the Sea*
1937 Slave Ship
1945 *Johnny Angel*
1950 *Last of the Buccaneers*

Shipbuilders
1918 *The Yellow Dog*
1920 *The Cup of Fury*
1942 *Cat People*
1950 *Mystery Street*

Shipping
1940 Doomed to Die

Shipping magnates
1937 *Think Fast, Mr. Moto*
1943 *The Amazing Mrs. Holliday*

Ships
1913? *The Lure of New York*
1914 *An Odyssey of the North*
1917 *The Little American*
Runaway Romany
The Secret Game
Under False Colors
1917? Barnaby Lee
1918 *Fields of Honor*
The Hun Within
Sandy
Wild Women
1919 *The Tong Man*
1921 Guile of Women
1931 Delicious
Drácula
En cada puerto un amor
Monerías

1932? *The Girl from Chicago*
1933 *A Lady's Profession*
1934 *Eskimo*
1935 *Naughty Marietta*
 A Night at the Opera
 Rescue Squad
 Tango Bar
 The Winning Ticket
1936 *Dancing Pirate*
 Human Cargo
 Mad Holiday
1937 *Slave Ship*
 Souls at Sea
 Think Fast, Mr. Moto
 Waikiki Wedding
1938 *The Buccaneer*
 The Rage of Paris
1939 *Confessions of a Nazi Spy*
1940 *Charlie Chan's Murder Cruise*
 New Moon
1941 *Dead Men Tell*
 Mutiny in the Arctic
 Mystery Ship
 New York Town
 They Dare Not Love
1942 *Across the Pacific*
 Friendly Enemies
 Mexican Spitfire's Elephant
 The Navy Comes Through
 Nazi Agent
 Unseen Enemy
1943 Action in the North Atlantic
1944 *The Sullivans*
1945 *Betrayal from the East*
1946 Dangerous Money
 G. I. War Brides
1947 *Buck Privates Come Home*
 Northwest Outpost
1948 Unconquered
1950 *The Baron of Arizona*
 Last of the Buccaneers
 Panic in the Streets
1955 *Kiss of Fire*
 Seven Cities of Gold
1959 John Paul Jones

Shipwrecks
1914 *The Little Jewess*
1916 *The Morals of Hilda*
1920 *The Brute*
1923 *Regeneration*
1927 *Bitter Apples*
1929 *Frozen Justice*
1932 *Tiger Shark*
1935 *Bar-Mitzvah*
1936 *Charlie Chan's Secret*
 El diablo del mar
1937 *The Devil's Playground*
 Song of the City
1940 *New Moon*
1943 *The Amazing Mrs. Holliday*
 Redhead from Manhattan
1944 *Minstrel Man*
1950 *The Toast of New Orleans*
1960 The Last Voyage

Shipyards
1918 *The Yellow Dog*
1920 *The Cup of Fury*
 Dangerous Hours
 The Great Shadow
1927 *Irish Hearts*
1942 *All Through the Night*
1943 Good Luck, Mr. Yates

Ed Shirley
1941 *Belle Starr*

Shivarees
1957 Bayou

Shoe clerks
1940 *Jennie*

Shoe manufacturers
1939 El otro soy yo

Shoemakers
1916 *Peck O' Pickles*
1934 *The Youth of Russia*
1937 *The Jester (Der Purimspieler)*
1949 *Answer for Anne*
 Laramie

Shoes
1916 *Peck O' Pickles*
1936 *The Prisoner of Shark Island*
 Yellow Cargo

1944 *Three Men in White*
1947 *Sepia Cinderella*
Shoeshine boys
 use **Bootblacks**
Shootings
1934 *Nada más que una mujer*
1935 *Shir Hashirim*
1936 *Love and Sacrifice*
 The Phantom of Santa Fe
1938 *In Old Chicago*
1939 *Motel the Operator*
1940 *Paradise in Harlem*
1946 *Dirty Gertie from Harlem, U.S.A.*
1947 *Duel in the Sun*
1948 *Renegades of Sonora*
1949 *C-Man*
 The Daring Caballero
 Daughter of the West
 Jigsaw
 Massacre River
 Ride, Ryder, Ride!
 The Sky Dragon
 Stallion Canyon
1950 *The Baron of Arizona*
 Davy Crockett, Indian Scout
 The Girl from San Lorenzo
 Riders of the Pony Express
 Train to Tombstone
1954 *Hell's Half Acre*
1956 *The Last Frontier*
 The White Squaw
1959 *Al Capone*
1960 *Cimarron*
 The Pusher
Shootouts
1932 *Me and My Gal*
1933 *Robbers' Roost*
1935 *Charlie Chan in Shanghai*
1943 *Dr. Gillespie's Criminal Case*
1944 *The San Antonio Kid*
 Tucson Raiders
1945 *South of the Rio Grande*
1946 *Romance of the West*
 Sun Valley Cyclone
1947? *Return of Mandy's Husband*
1948 *Angel in Exile*
1949 *Satan's Cradle*
 We Were Strangers
1950 *Chinatown at Midnight*
 Raiders of Tomahawk Creek
 Winchester '73
1951 *Flaming Feather*
 Fort Defiance
 Native Son
1956 *Man from Del Rio*
1958 *Frontier Gun*
1959 *The FBI Story*
 Gunmen from Laredo
 Last Train from Gun Hill
 The World, the Flesh and the Devil
 The Young Land
Shopkeepers
 use **Storekeepers**
Shoplifting
1923 April Showers
1958 *Seven Hills of Rome*
Shops
 use **Specific types of shops or stores**
Short wave radios
 use **Radio, Short wave**
Shoshoni Indians
1950 Devil's Doorway
1955 *Chief Crazy Horse*
 The Far Horizons
1960 Walk Tall
Show business
1935 Annie Oakley
1938 *The Duke Is Tops*
1940 *Broken Strings*
1943 Stormy Weather
1947 *On the Old Spanish Trail*
1950 *Annie Get Your Gun*
1953 The Eddie Cantor Story
 The Jazz Singer
1956 *Singing in the Dark*

Show girls
1917 Runaway Romany
1919 Spotlight Sadie
1931 Esclavas de la moda
1935 *The Singing Vagabond*
1938 *The Duke Is Tops*
1950 *A Ticket to Tomahawk*
1956 *Rockin' the Blues*
Showboats
1929 Show Boat
1936 Show Boat
1951 Show Boat
 Yes Sir, Mr. Bones
Showers (Parties)
1938? *I due gemelli*
1959 *The Black Orchid*
Shreveport (LA)
1940 *Midnight Shadow*
Shrews
1935 Señora casada necesita marido
1949? *She's Too Mean for Me*
1951 *Show Boat*
Shrimpers (Persons)
1953 *Thunder Bay*
Shrines
1917 *The Call of the East*
1919 *Lasca*
Shyness
1936 *Contra la corriente*
1956 *The Benny Goodman Story*
1958 *Apache Territory*
Siberia
19?? A Trip Through the Arctic with Uncle Sam
1912 The Alaska-Siberian Expedition
 Atop of the World in Motion
1914 *An Odyssey of the North*
 Threads of Destiny
1925 The True North
1931 *Resurrección*
1934 Un capitán de cosacos
1952 *Red Snow*
Siblings
 use **Brothers;
 Brothers and sisters;
 Family relationships;
 Sisters**
Sicilians
1927 Bitter Apples
1932 Amore e morte
Sicily
1912 The Adventures of Lieutenant Petrosino
1918 *The Ordeal of Rosetta*
1922 *Fair Lady*
Mrs. Sarah Kemble Siddons
1939 *The Adventures of Huckleberry Finn*
Sideshows
1928 Mother Machree
1934 *El tango en Broadway*
1936 *Let's Sing Again*
1944 *Buffalo Bill*
1951 *Queen for a Day*
Sieges
1917 *John Ermine of the Yellowstone*
 The Plow Woman
1918 *Good-Bye, Bill*
1920 The Last of the Mohicans
1933 *Victims of Persecution*
1938 The Buccaneer
1939 *Drums Along the Mohawk*
1951 *Oh! Susanna*
1953 *Ride, Vaquero!*
 The Stand at Apache River
1955 The Last Command
 Smoke Signal
1956 *Ghost Town*
1958 Apache Territory
 The Rawhide Trail
Sierra Nevada Mountains (CA and NV)
1928 The Crash
1929 Wolf Song
1954 *Passion*
Sign language
1948 *The Dude Goes West*
1956 *Westward Ho the Wagons!*

Sign painters and sign painting
1931 *Buster se marie*
Signing
 use **Sign language**
Siksika Indians
1915 The Girl I Left Behind Me
1928 Kit Carson
1951 Across the Wide Missouri
1952 The Big Sky
1954 Cattle Queen of Montana
1958 Blood Arrow
 Flaming Frontier
Silver
1940 *Hi-Yo Silver*
1946 *Beauty and the Bandit*
 Romance of the West
1953 *Tumbleweed*
1956 *The Lone Ranger*
Silver mines
1939 *Bad Lands*
 Drifting Westward
1940 *Covered Wagon Days*
1950 *Comanche Territory*
Silversmiths
1934 *Laughing Boy*
Upton Sinclair
1914 The Jungle
Sing Sing Prison (NY)
1920? *Her Story*
1929 *Thunderbolt*
1931 *Three Who Loved*
1947 *Citizen Saint*
Singers
1916 *Arms and the Woman*
1918 The Bravest Way
1919 *The Courageous Coward*
1920 *The Paliser Case*
1920? *Reformation*
1921 The Sport of the Gods
1925 The Midnight Girl
1927 The Scar of Shame
1928 The Jazz Singer
1929 *Frozen Justice*
 Lucky Boy
 Mother's Boy
 Show Boat
 Why Bring That Up?
1930 *Galas de la Paramount*
 Georgia Rose
 Revista Hispano-Americana
 Sevilla de mis amores
 Toda una vida
1931 The Cisco Kid
 Del infierno al cielo
 Gente alegre
 Jenny Lind
 Las luces de Buenos Aires
 Regeneración
 The White Renegade
 Zein Weib's Lubovnick
1932 *Harlem Is Heaven*
 Men Are Such Fools
 Ten Minutes to Live
 Veiled Aristocrats
1932? *The Girl from Chicago*
1933 *Espérame*
 Melodía de arrabal
1934 *Blossom Time*
 La buenaventura
 The Cat's-Paw
1935 El cantante de Nápoles
 Harmony Lane
 Melody Trail
 A Night at the Ritz
 No matarás
 Piernas de seda
 The Singing Vagabond
 Tango Bar
1936 *General Spanky*
 Laughing Irish Eyes
 Rainbow on the River
 Rose of the Rancho
 Show Boat
 Sum Hun
 Yiddle with His Fiddle
1937 *Bargain with Bullets*
 The Barrier
 Border Cafe
 Boy of the Streets
 Dark Manhattan
 The Jester (Der Purimspieler)
 Manhattan Merry-Go-Round
 Song of the City

Think Fast, Mr. Moto
Underworld
1938 *Birthright*
Breaking the Ice
Di que me quieres
The Duke Is Tops
Happy Landing
Hawaii Calls
In Old Chicago
Josette
Mis dos amores
Outside of Paradise
Spirit of Youth
Swing!
1938? Amore che non torna
I due gemelli
1939 A Brivele der Mamen
The Devil's Daughter
Double Deal
The Girl from Mexico
Los hijos mandan
Lying Lips
Moon over Harlem
My Son
The Mystery of Mr. Wong
El otro soy yo
Papá soltero
Straight to Heaven
El trovador de la radio
194- Mistaken Identity
1940 *Gang War*
Lucky Cisco Kid
Music in My Heart
Mystery in Swing
Paradise in Harlem
1941 Birth of the Blues
Charlie Chan in Rio
Murder on Lenox Avenue
Playmates
Sun Valley Serenade
Sunday Sinners
This Woman Is Mine
Where Did You Get That Girl?
1942 *All Through the Night*
Foreign Agent
Holiday Inn
Lucky Ghost
Rio Rita
Secret Enemies
Seven Sweethearts
Sunday Punch
Unseen Enemy
The Vanishing Virginian
1943 *Cabin in the Sky*
Doughboys in Ireland
The Gang's All Here
Gangway for Tomorrow
The Girl from Monterrey
His Butler's Sister
Marching On!
Redhead from Manhattan
Stormy Weather
Tahiti Honey
What's Buzzin' Cousin?
Wintertime
1944 *Andy Hardy's Blonde Trouble*
Chip Off the Old Block
Slightly Terrific
1945 Between Two Women
Club Havana
The Great John L.
In Old New Mexico
The Mummy's Curse
Nob Hill
Rhapsody in Blue
South of the Rio Grande
Sunbonnet Sue
1946 *Cuban Pete*
Mantan Messes Up
The Red Dragon
Slightly Scandalous
South of Monterey
Stars on Parade
Sunset Pass
Tall, Tan and Terrific
That Man of Mine
1946? *Beale Street Mama*
Harlem on Parade
House-Rent Party
1947 *Carnegie Hall*
Citizen Saint
Copacabana
Going to Glory, Come to Jesus

Hi De Ho
Jivin' in Be-Bop
The Jolson Story
My Wild Irish Rose
New Orleans
Reet, Petite and Gone
Sepia Cinderella
1948 *Big City*
Docks of New Orleans
Harpoon
Music Man
The Paleface
The Time of Your Life
1948? Boarding House Blues
Junction 88
1949 *Jigsaw*
The Kissing Bandit
Lookout Sister
Rustlers
Souls of Sin
Top O' the Morning
1949? *Come On, Cowboy!*
Girl in Room 20
Harlem Follies
The Joint Is Jumpin'
1950 *Annie Get Your Gun*
Belle of Old Mexico
Border Treasure
Buccaneer's Girl
Catskill Honeymoon
Monticello, Here We Come!
Riders of the Pony Express
Rio Grande Patrol
Storm Over Wyoming
Sunset in the West
Young Man with a Horn
1951 Cuban Fireball
Flaming Feather
Mask of the Dragon
Native Son
Show Boat
1952 *The Fabulous Senorita*
1953 The Jazz Singer
The Joe Louis Story
The Man Behind the Gun
The Stars Are Singing
1955 Brevities of 1955
1956 *The Broken Star*
Dakota Incident
Singing in the Dark
1957 *Beau James*
1958 *Never Love a Stranger*
St. Louis Blues
Seven Hills of Rome
The Young Lions
1960 *All the Fine Young Cannibals*

Singing teachers
use **Vocal instructors**

Singing telegrams
1943 *Three Hearts for Julia*

Sino-Japanese Conflict, 1937-1945
1941 Min Jok Jay Hung Sing
1945 *Samurai*

Sioux Indians
use **Dakota Indians**

Sisterhoods
1929 Evangeline

Sisters
1913 Traffic in Souls
1915 *Kreutzer Sonata*
The Rosary
The Secret Sin
1916 *A Man of Sorrow*
The Scarlet Oath
1917 The Plow Woman
1918 Doing Their Bit
Fields of Honor
The Ordeal of Rosetta
Shifting Sands
A Woman of Impulse
1919 *Spotlight Sadie*
1920 The Dark Mirror
The Last of the Mobicans
1920? The Scarlet Dragon
1923 Fashion Row
1925 Lights of Old Broadway
1927 *With Sitting Bull at the Spirit Lake Massacre*
1931 *Buster se marie*
The Great Meadow
Huckleberry Finn
Las luces de Buenos Aires

1932 Me and My Gal
1932? *The Girl from Chicago*
1933 *Yo, tú y ella*
1934? Harlem After Midnight
1935 The Yiddish King Lear
1936 *Charlie Chan at the Circus*
1937 *The Jester (Der Purimspieler)*
1938 *Birthright*
The Buccaneer
Little Miss Roughneck
Spirit of Youth
The Toy Wife
Two Sisters
Wild Horse Canyon
1939 *My Son*
Papá soltero
Tevya
1940 *Music in My Heart*
Mystery in Swing
Three Cheers for the Irish
1941 *Sunday Sinners*
1942 In This Our Life
Mexican Spitfire Sees a Ghost
Seven Sweethearts
1943 *Deerslayer*
1944 *Andy Hardy's Blonde Trouble*
The Sullivans
1945 The Dolly Sisters
A Tree Grows in Brooklyn
1946 *Cuban Pete*
G. I. War Brides
The Gay Cavalier
Wild West
1948 *Gentleman's Agreement*
I Remember Mama
Rocky
1949 *The Sky Dragon*
1950 *Ambush*
The Daughter of Rosie O'Grady
1950? Three Daughters
1951 A Streetcar Named Desire
1952 *The Fabulous Senorita*
Wagons West
1953 *The Charge at Feather River*
The Member of the Wedding
Thunder Bay
Tumbleweed
1955 *Marty*
1960 *The Dark at the Top of the Stairs*

Sisters and brothers
use **Brothers and sisters**

Sisters-in-law
1939 Fisherman's Wharf
1950 *Two Flags West*
1951 *Tomahawk*
1952 *Japanese War Bride*
1958 *Wild Is the Wind*

Sitting Bull
1914? *Sitting Bull—The Hostile Sioux Indian Chief*
1925 Custer's Last Fight
1926 The Flaming Frontier
General Custer at Little Big Horn
1927 With Sitting Bull at the Spirit Lake Massacre
1935 *Annie Oakley*
1936 Custer's Last Stand
1937 The Plainsman
1942 *They Died With Their Boots On*
1950 Annie Get Your Gun
1954 *Saskatchewan*
Sitting Bull
1958 Tonka

Skating
use **Ice skating;**
Roller-skating

Skeletons
1939 *Bad Lands*
1942 *Lucky Ghost*
1950 *Mystery Street*
1951 *Five*

Skiing
1931 *Young Sinners*
1940 *Escape*

1941 *Sun Valley Serenade*
1943 *Wintertime*
1958 *The Young Lions*
Skitswish Indians
1956 *Pillars of the Sky*
Skunks
1936 *West of Nevada*
Skydivers
1932 *Hidden Valley*
1933 *It's Great to Be Alive*
1938 *Mr. Moto Takes a Chance*
Skyscrapers
1931 Skyline
1933 *Counsellor at Law*
Skywriting
1927 Aflame in the Sky
Slackers
1917 The Slacker
1943 Marching On!
Slang
1947 *The Return of Rin Tin Tin*
Slave traders
1918 *Uncle Tom's Cabin*
1930 *A Daughter of the Congo*
1936 *Sutter's Gold*
1937 Slave Ship
Souls at Sea
1939 Stand Up and Fight
1947 *California*
1957 Band of Angels
Naked in the Sun

Slavery
1914 Uncle Tom's Cabin
1915 *The Birth of a Nation*
Marse Covington
1919 Auction of Souls
1920 Huckleberry Finn
1921 A Giant of His Race
Where Lights Are Low
1926? The House on Cedar Hill
1927 The Slaver
Topsy and Eva
1931 Huckleberry Finn
1932 *Joseph in the Land of Egypt*
1933 *The Emperor Jones*
1934 *Operator 13*
1935 *The Littlest Rebel*
So Red the Rose
1936 *General Spanky*
The Green Pastures
1937 *Maid of Salem*
1939 *Gone With the Wind*
Way Down South
Way Down South
1940 *George Washington Carver*
Santa Fe Trail
1944 *We've Come a Long, Long Way*
1947 *The Foxes of Harrow*
1953 *The Man Behind the Gun*
1955 Seven Angry Men
1957 Band of Angels
Naked in the Sun
1959 *The Jayhawkers!*
1960 *Walk Like a Dragon*

Slavery—Emancipation
1916 *The Colored American Winning His Suit*
The Grip of Jealousy
1918 Uncle Tom's Cabin
1927 The Love Mart
1931 *The White Renegade*
1932 *Cuore d'emigrante*
1936 *The Bold Caballero*
Sutter's Gold
1937 *Slave Ship*
1939 Stand Up and Fight
1953 *Sangaree*
1957 *Raintree County*

Slaves
1914 Dan
The Littlest Rebel
1914? *The Mysterious Mr. Wu Chung Foo*
1917 The Bride of Hate
1918 Uncle Tom's Cabin
1919? The Brand of Judas
1920 Huckleberry Finn
1928 Uncle Tom's Cabin
1951 *The Tall Target*
1954 *Sitting Bull*
1957 *Band of Angels*
1959 *John Paul Jones*

1960 The Adventures of
     Huckleberry Finn
Slaves—Runaway
1926 Buffalo Bill on the U. P.
     Trail
1939 *The Adventures of*
     Huckleberry Finn
Slavic Americans
1936 *Dangerous Intrigue*
1950 *Give Us This Day*
     Panic in the Streets
Sleeping Beauty (Play)
1953 *Bright Road*
Sleeping potions
1931 *La llama sagrada*
1947 *Rustlers of Devil's Canyon*
1949 *The Sky Dragon*
Sleepwalking
     use Somnambulism
Slovakian Americans
1928 *A Ship Comes In*
Slumming
1948 *The Time of Your Life*
Slums
1914 The Straight Road
1915 *The Kindling*
1916 *Lone Star*
1917 A Jewel in Pawn
1918 Hell's End
1920 *The Dark Mirror*
1921 The Swamp
1932 *Symphony of Six Million*
1934 *Limehouse Blues*
1937 Boy of the Streets
1949 *Knock on Any Door*
1954 *Hell's Half Acre*
Small town life
1918 *The Only Road*
1921 *No Woman Knows*
1922 Easy Money
     The Good Provider
1923 *The Devil's Match*
1924 Birthright
     Welcome Stranger
1925 Body and Soul
1926 The Little Irish Girl
1926? Ten Nights in a Barroom
1928 The Rawhide Kid
1930 Tom Sawyer
1934 Judge Priest
1936 *Sins of Man*
1937 The Jester (Der
     Purimspieler)
     Maid of Salem
     That I May Live
1938 The Adventures of Tom
     Sawyer
     The Singing Blacksmith
1939 A Brivele der Mamen
     Keep Punching
     The Light Ahead
1940 Jennie
     Midnight Shadow
     The Ramparts We Watch
1942 *Mokey*
     Seven Sweethearts
1945 A Medal for Benny
1946 *Singin' in the Corn*
1947 Dark Delusion
1948 *The Boy with Green Hair*
     The Miracle of the Bells
     Shep Comes Home
1948? *Junction 88*
1949 Answer for Anne
     Answer for Anne
     Lost Boundaries
     Prejudice
1950 *Intruder in the Dust*
1951 The Well
1952 *High Noon*
1953 *The Member of the*
     Wedding
     So Big
     The Sun Shines Bright
1955 *Apache Woman*
     Bad Day at Black Rock
     Foxfire
     Good Morning, Miss Dove
     Not As a Stranger
     The View from Pompey's
     Head
     Violent Saturday
1956 Man from Del Rio

1957 *Joe Dakota*
     Man in the Shadow
     Raintree County
1958 Home Before Dark
1960 *Cimarron*
     The Dark at the Top of the
     Stairs
Smallpox
1914 *The Good-for-Nothing*
1952 *Battles of Chief Pontiac*
1958 *Blood Arrow*
Alfred E. Smith
1919 *The Volcano*
1957 *Beau James*
Captain John Smith
1953 Captain John Smith and
     Pocahontas
Smoking
1944 *The Sullivans*
Smuggling
1914 *The Yellow Traffic*
1915 *Just Jim*
     The Sable Lorcha
1916 Hop, the Devil's Brew
1917 The Bond Between
     Queen X
1918 The Border Raiders
     The Midnight Patrol
1919 *A Fallen Idol*
1920 *The Cyclone*
     Dinty
1922 Anna Ascends
     Sky High
1923 The Miracle Makers
     Purple Dawn
1924 Defying the Law
1925 A Son of His Father
     Speed Wild
     Tearing Through
1926 The Fighting Edge
     Twin Triggers
1927 Roarin' Broncs
1929 *Masked Emotions*
1930 On the Border
1931 La dama atrevida
1932 The Secrets of Wu Sin
1933 *The Cohens and Kellys in*
     Trouble
1934 Lazy River
     Limehouse Blues
     Riding Speed
1935 Charlie Chan in Shanghai
1936 Border Phantom
     Hair-Trigger Casey
     Human Cargo
     The Traitor
     Yellow Cargo
1937 Shadows of the Orient
     Think Fast, Mr. Moto
1938 Daughter of Shanghai
     Mr. Wong, Detective
1939 Daughter of the Tong
     Forged Passport
     Mr. Moto in Danger Island
1940 Covered Wagon Days
     Doomed to Die
     The Fatal Hour
1942 Mexican Spitfire's Elephant
1946 *The Red Dragon*
1948 *The Golden Eye*
1949 Border Incident
     The Golden Stallion
     Harbor of Missing Men
     Illegal Entry
1950 *The Breaking Point*
     Comanche Territory
     I Killed Geronimo
     A Lady Without Passport
     Panic in the Streets
1951 Cavalry Scout
     Mask of the Dragon
1955 *The Rose Tattoo*
1956 Wetbacks
Snake bites
1948 *Four Faces West*
1958 *Blood Arrow*
1960 *Walk Tall*
Snake River (NW United States)
1947 *Oregon Trail Scouts*
1951 *Snake River Desperadoes*
Snakes
1932 *Call Her Savage*
1936 *Charlie Chan at the Circus*
     The Green Pastures

1941? *The Blood of Jesus*
1950 *A Lady Without Passport*
1951 *Distant Drums*
1952 *The Big Sky*
1954 *Broken Lance*
Sneezing
1948 *Jiggs and Maggie in Court*
1952 *The Fabulous Senorita*
Snipers
1943 *Bataan*
1949 *Ranger of Cherokee Strip*
Snobs and snobbishness
1915 *A Texas Steer*
1917 *The Little Samaritan*
1918 The Greatest Thing in Life
     Marked Cards
1919 His Parisian Wife
     The Unpainted Woman
1921 Society Snobs
1926 The Campus Flirt
1927 Sally in Our Alley
1928 Riley the Cop
1931 *Mi último amor*
     Quand on est belle
     The Squaw Man
1932 The Cohens and Kellys in
     Hollywood
     Marido y mujer
1933 *Dance Hall Hostess*
1934 *Behold My Wife!*
1935 His Family Tree
     McFadden's Flats
1936 My American Wife
1937 *Boots and Saddles*
1940 *Mexican Spitfire*
1941 *Accent on Love*
     Hurry, Charlie, Hurry
1944 *Something for the Boys*
1945 *Sunbonnet Sue*
1946 Bringing Up Father
1950 *Buccaneer's Girl*
1951 *The Great Caruso*
     A Streetcar Named Desire
1952 *Woman in the Dark*
1953 *So Big*
1958 *Home Before Dark*
1960 *The Crowning Experience*
Snow
1930 *Monsieur le Fox*
1936 *Tundra*
1950 *Give Us This Day*
1951 *Across the Wide Missouri*
1960 *All the Young Men*
Snow storms
1917 *The Squaw Man's Son*
1931 *Young Sinners*
1939 *Stand Up and Fight*
1949 *Arctic Fury*
1954 *Passion*
1957 *All Mine to Give*
1960 *Ice Palace*
Snowshoe rabbits
1936 *Tundra*
Snuff boxes and bottles
1932 *El caballero de la noche*
John Soane
1960 *The Day They Robbed the*
     Bank of England
Soap
1950 The Traveling Saleswoman
Social climbers
1915 The Danger Signal
1916 *Light at Dusk*
     The Pretenders
1918 Real Folks
1923 Breaking into Society
1931 *The Guilty Generation*
1935 *His Family Tree*
     McFadden's Flats
     Ruggles of Red Gap
1936 My American Wife
1940 If I Had My Way
1941 *Playmates*
     They Dare Not Love
1942 *Mexican Spitfire at Sea*
     We Were Dancing
1946 Bringing Up Father
1947 *Jiggs and Maggie in Society*
1948 *Jiggs and Maggie in Court*
1949 *Jiggs and Maggie in Jackpot*
     Jitters
1950 Belle of Old Mexico
1951 Adventures of Captain
     Fabian

1952 The Iron Mistress
1953 *So Big*
1960 *Cimarron*
Social customs
1916 *The Honorable Friend*
1919 The Courageous Coward
     False Evidence
1955 *Santa Fe Passage*
Social reform
1916 The Social Buccaneer
     The Social Highwayman
1918 Hell's End
1948 Fighting Father Dunne
1960 The Crowning Experience
Social workers
1920 *The Devil's Claim*
1923 April Showers
1931 *Street Scene*
1936 *Love and Sacrifice*
1938 *City Streets*
1939 *The Escape*
     Kol Nidre
1949 *Knock on Any Door*
1950 *So Young, So Bad*
1951 *Gambling House*
1953 *The Eddie Cantor Story*
1957 *Edge of the City*
Socialism
1914 The Jungle
1918 *A Little Sister of Everybody*
1931 *Street Scene*
Socialites
1915 *The Cheat*
1917 The Primitive Call
     The Red Woman
1919 *A Fallen Idol*
     Injustice
     Mandarin's Gold
     A Man's Duty
     The Tiger Lily
1920 *Dangerous Days*
     Li Ting Lang
     The Paliser Case
     The Third Woman
1920? Reformation
1921 Hold Your Horses
1922 One Eighth Apache
     Saturday Night
1929 Chinatown Nights
1930 Amor audaz
     Around the Corner
     Ladies Love Brutes
1931 *La incorregible*
     Mamá
     Soyons gais
     Three Who Loved
1932 *Hombres en mi vida*
     Le plombier amoureux
1933 *Counsellor at Law*
     La melodía prohibida
1934 White Heat
1935 *Bordertown*
     Rendezvous
1936 Contra la corriente
     La última cita
1938 Dangerous to Know
     Daughter of Shanghai
     Outside of Paradise
     The Rage of Paris
1940 *Elsa Maxwell's Public Deb*
     No. 1
1941 *They Dare Not Love*
1942 *Mexican Spitfire's Elephant*
1943 *Crime Smasher*
     Dr. Gillespie's Criminal
     Case
     His Butler's Sister
     Mr. Lucky
1944 *The Chinese Cat*
     Three Men in White
1945 *Sunbonnet Sue*
1946 *Swamp Fire*
1947 *Humoresque*
     Jiggs and Maggie in Society
1949 *Jigsaw*
1950 Jiggs and Maggie Out West
1955 Foxfire
1956 *The Benny Goodman Story*
     Death of a Scoundrel
1958 *Seven Hills of Rome*
1959 *John Paul Jones*

Societies
   use **Names of specific societies**
Society
   use **High society**
Soda clerks
   1922   The Guttersnipe
Soda jerks
   use **Soda clerks**
Soldiers
   1914   The Littlest Rebel
   1914? *The Mysterious Mr. Wu Chung Foo*
          Sitting Bull—The Hostile Sioux Indian Chief
   1915   *The Birth of a Nation*
          Under Southern Skies
   1915? *Sam Davis, the Hero of Tennessee*
   1916   The Daughter of the Don
          The Fall of a Nation
   1917   The Captain of the Gray Horse Troop
          How Uncle Sam Prepares
   1918   The Birth of a Race
          Doing Their Bit
          The Firebrand
          The Greatest Thing in Life
          Johanna Enlists
          The Price of Applause
          The Prussian Cur
   1919   *Evangeline*
   1920   *Humoresque*
   1921   *Shadows of the West*
   1926   *The Strong Man*
   1929   Abie's Irish Rose
   1930   Anybody's War
          ¡De frente, marchen!
          Sombras de gloria
          Toda una vida
   1931   Beyond Victory
          Monerías
          Resurrección
          El tenorio del harem
   1932   *Genoveffa*
   1933   *The California Trail*
          The Emperor Jones
          The Eternal Jew
          Man from Monterey
          The Man Who Dared: An Imaginative Biography
          The Telegraph Trail
          Victims of Persecution
   1934   *Operator 13*
          The Unknown Soldier Speaks
   1935   *The Little Colonel*
          The Littlest Rebel
          Naughty Marietta
   1936   *Dancing Pirate*
          General Spanky
          The Phantom of Santa Fe
          The Prisoner of Shark Island
   1937   *Boots and Saddles*
          El carnaval del diablo
   1939   *Allegheny Uprising*
          The Cisco Kid and the Lady
          Drums Along the Mohawk
   1940   Geronimo
          Lucky Cisco Kid
          The Mark of Zorro
   1942   *Prisoner of Japan*
          They Died With Their Boots On
   1943   Bataan
          Dr. Gillespie's Criminal Case
          Doughboys in Ireland
          The Gang's All Here
          Marching On!
          Stormy Weather
   1944   Hi, Beautiful
          Since You Went Away
          Something for the Boys
   1947   Robin Hood of Monterey
   1949   Home of the Brave
          Rose of the Yukon
          She Wore a Yellow Ribbon
   1950   *Jolson Sings Again*
   1951   *Distant Drums*
          Little Big Horn
          Only the Valiant
          The Steel Helmet
          Teresa

   1953   *Column South*
          Jack McCall Desperado
          Last of the Comanches
          The Man from the Alamo
          The Member of the Wedding
          San Antone
          The Sun Shines Bright
          War Paint
   1954   *Carmen Jones*
   1955   *Kiss of Fire*
          A Man Called Peter
   1956   Quincannon, Frontier Scout
          7th Cavalry
   1957   *Band of Angels*
          Revolt at Fort Laramie
          Run of the Arrow
   1958   *Fort Massacre*
          Kings Go Forth
          The Rawhide Trail
          The Young Lions
   1959   The Oregon Trail
   1960   All the Young Men
          Sergeant Rutledge
          The Sign of Zorro
Soldiers of fortune
   1924   California in '49
   1927   The Millionaire
   1935   Alas sobre el Chaco
   1937   Thank You, Mr. Moto
   1940   Escape to Glory
   1947   Pirates of Monterey
   1950   Mystery Submarine
Solomon Islands
   1920   *It's a Great Life*
Somnambulism
   1918   *Wanted, a Mother*
   1943   *Marching On!*
Songs
   1932   *Cuore d'emigrante*
          No Greater Love
          Senza mamma e'nnamurato
   1933   La melodía prohibida
   1934   Caravane
   1935   Harmony Lane
          The Little Colonel
   1936   *Rose of the Rancho*
   1939   *Let Freedom Ring*
   1941   *Wiejskie Wesele*
   1943   *Doughboys in Ireland*
   1944   *Minstrel Man*
   1947   *Sepia Cinderella*
   1949   *Top O' the Morning*
   1951   *Apache Drums*
          Slaughter Trail
   1954   *Dangerous Mission*
          Hell's Half Acre
          Siege at Red River
   1957   *Beau James*
Songwriters
   1932   *The Cohens and Kellys in Hollywood*
   1933   Best of Enemies
   1935   Harmony Lane
   1936   *Paddy O'Day*
   1938   Di que me quieres
          Hawaii Calls
   1939   *A Brivele der Mamen*
   1941   Where Did You Get That Girl?
   1943   Yankee Doodle Dandy
   1944   *Going My Way*
   1945   *The Dolly Sisters*
   1947   Sepia Cinderella
   1948   Music Man
   1958   *Marjorie Morningstar*
          St. Louis Blues
Sonora (CA)
   1948   *Renegades of Sonora*
Sons and mothers
   use **Mothers and sons**
Sons-in-law
   1935   *The Yiddish King Lear*
Soothsayers
   use **Clairvoyants;**
          Fortune-tellers;
          Seers
Sorcerers
   1914   In the Land of the Head Hunters
   1923   The White Flower

Sound recordings
   use **Recordings**
Soup industry
   1940   *Elsa Maxwell's Public Deb No. 1*
South Africa
   1928   Diamond Handcuffs
South African War, 1899-1902
   1943   *Jack London*
South America
   1919   *The Scar*
   1927   The Millionaire
   1932   *Hollywood, ciudad de ensueño*
   1937   El carnaval del diablo
South Americans
   1914   *The Great Diamond Robbery*
   1918   *Woman and the Law*
   1938   *Castillos en el aire*
South Dakota
   1918? *Indian Life*
   1919   The Homesteader
   1931   *The Exile*
   1948   *The Betrayal*
South Sea islands
   1923   Regeneration
   1931   *Tropennächte*
   1933   La melodía prohibida
   1934   Nada más que una mujer
   1937   El capitán Tormenta
   1942   *Prisoner of Japan*
South Seas
   1931   *Aloha*
Southern belles
   1915   Under Southern Skies
   1935   So Red the Rose
   1953   *San Antone*
   1955   *The View from Pompey's Head*
Southerners
   1914   Dan
          The Littlest Rebel
   1915   The Birth of a Nation
          Marse Covington
   1917   The Bride of Hate
          How Uncle Sam Prepares
          My Fighting Gentleman
   1918   Uncle Tom's Cabin
   1919   Come Out of the Kitchen
   1920   The Good-Bad Wife
          On with the Dance
          The Symbol of the Unconquered
          White Youth
          Within Our Gates
   1921   Love's Plaything
   1934   *Beloved*
          Operator 13
   1935   The Little Colonel
          The Littlest Rebel
   1936   Rainbow on the River
   1939   The Return of the Cisco Kid
          Stand Up and Fight
          Way Down South
   1941   Belle Starr
          Lady from Louisiana
          Virginia
   1943   Dixie
   1944   *Something for the Boys*
   1946   Song of the South
   1949   *She Wore a Yellow Ribbon*
   1950   *Jolson Sings Again*
   1951   *Oh! Susanna*
   1952   Bright Victory
   1953   *The Charge at Feather River*
          Column South
          The Member of the Wedding
   1954   The Black Dakotas
   1955   Apache Ambush
   1957   *Revolt at Fort Laramie*
   1958   Ambush at Cimarron Pass
   1959   *Anna Lucasta*
Soviet Union
   use **Russia**
Spaghetti
   1949   *House of Strangers*
Spain
   1921   The Money Maniac
   1925   Don Q, Son of Zorro
   1930   Charros, gauchos y manolas

   1931   Mi último amor
          Nuit d'Espagne
   1935   Rosa de Francia
   1940   *The Mark of Zorro*
   1955   *Kiss of Fire*
Spaniards
   1915   *The Grandee's Ring*
          The Pageant of San Francisco
   1916   *The Daughter of the Don*
          Mixed Blood
   1917   *The Bride of Hate*
   1918   *A Daughter of the Old South*
          A Woman of Impulse
   1919   The Scar
   1921   A Divorce of Convenience
   1922   Silver Spurs
   1923   The Lone Wagon
   1924   Down by the Rio Grande
   1925   Flower of Night
   1927   Don Mike
          Old San Francisco
   1928   The Cavalier
          Ramona
   1929   Señor Americano
          Wolf Song
   1930   *Charros, gauchos y manolas*
   1932   Soñadores de la gloria
   1933   Primavera en otoño
          Yo, tú y ella
   1935   *Naughty Marietta*
   1936   Aces and Eights
          The Bold Caballero
   1937   *Drums of Destiny*
          Old Louisiana
   1939   Frontiers of '49
          In Old Caliente
   1941   Prairie Pioneers
   1946   *The Gay Cavalier*
          South of Monterey
   1947   *Pirates of Monterey*
   1949   *The Kissing Bandit*
   1951   Hurricane Island
   1955   Kiss of Fire
          Seven Cities of Gold
Spanish Americans
   1927   The Gay Defender
   1928   The Canyon of Adventure
   1935   No matarás
   1937   The Californian
   1942   *Apache Trail*
   1946   Don Ricardo Returns
   1947   Bells of San Fernando
          Riding the California Trail
   1949   The Kissing Bandit
   1952   *The Iron Mistress*
   1955   Kiss of Fire
Spanking
   1942   *Mokey*
   1947   *Thunder Mountain*
   1949   *Rustlers*
          Stagecoach Kid
   1951   *Across the Wide Missouri*
Speakeasies
   1931   *Mr. Lemon of Orange*
   1933   *It's Great to Be Alive*
          A Lady's Profession
          Olsen's Big Moment
   1948   *Call Northside 777*
Special agents
   1946   *Bad Bascomb*
Speculation
   1915   *The Cheat*
   1921   The Money Maniac
   1922   Easy Money
   1925   Old Clothes
   1930   The Kibitzer
   1931   *Three Who Loved*
   1943   *What's Buzzin' Cousin?*
   1956   *Westward Ho the Wagons!*
Speeches
   1935   *His Family Tree*
   1938   *Sugar Hill Baby*
   1939   *Let Freedom Ring*
   1940   *The Man I Married*
   1941   *Min Jok Jay Hung Sing*
   1944   *An American Romance*
          They Live in Fear
   1947   *The Farmer's Daughter*
          Mantan Runs for Mayor
   1948   *The Luck of the Irish*

1954 *Dangerous Mission*
1955 *Davy Crockett, King of the Wild Frontier*
1960 *The Crowning Experience*

Spells
1944 *Cry of the Werewolf*
1946 *The Face of Marble*
Three Wise Fools
1949 *Tale of the Navajos*

Spendthrifts
1915 *The Spender*
1917 *The Red Woman*
1920 *On with the Dance*
Uncharted Channels

Spies
1915? *Sam Davis, the Hero of Tennessee*
1916 *Arms and the Woman*
The Scarlet Oath
1917 *The Adventures of Carol*
The Secret Game
The Winged Mystery
1918 *An Alien Enemy*
The Birth of a Race
Doing Their Bit
His Birthright
The Hun Within
I Want to Forget
Mystic Faces
The Price of Applause
The Prussian Cur
The Ranger
The Reckoning Day
Shifting Sands
The Source
The Yellow Dog
1920 *The Cup of Fury*
Dangerous Days
1925 *A Daughter of the Sioux*
Friendly Enemies
1927 *Ham and Eggs at the Front*
1928 *Heart Trouble*
1930 *Anybody's War*
1931 *Del infierno al cielo*
1933 *Ever in My Heart*
1934 *Charlie Chan in London*
Operator 13
1935 *Te quiero con locura*
1936 *The Last of the Mohicans*
1938 *Mr. Moto Takes a Chance*
Mr. Wong, Detective
1939 *City in Darkness*
Cossacks in Exile
Mr. Moto's Last Warning
1940 *Charlie Chan in Panama*
Murder over New York
1942 *Across the Pacific*
All Through the Night
Foreign Agent
Let's Get Tough!
Nazi Agent
Prisoner of Japan
Rio Rita
Secret Enemies
Unseen Enemy
1944 *Waterfront*
1945 *Escape in the Fog*
The Scarlet Clue
1946 *Notorious*
The Red Dragon
1947 *Last of the Redmen*
1950 *Two Flags West*
1951 *Mask of the Dragon*
When the Redskins Rode
1952 *Arctic Flight*
1953 *Jack McCall Desperado*
The Pathfinder
1954 *Massacre Canyon*
1959 *The FBI Story*
1960 *I Aim at the Stars: the Wernher von Braun Story*

Mickey Spillane
1955 *Marty*

Spinsters
1917 *Castles for Two*
1918 *Little Red Decides*
1930 *Un hombre de suerte*
1931 *Nuit d'Espagne*
1934 *Tres amores*
1936 *Paddy O'Day*
1944 *Tomorrow the World!*
1946 *Bad Bascomb*
1948 *I Remember Mama*
1955 *Good Morning, Miss Dove*

Spirit Lake (IA)
1927 *With Sitting Bull at the Spirit Lake Massacre*

Spirits
use **Ghosts**

Spiritual healing
1922 *The Hands of Nara*

Spiritualism
1930 *Le spectre vert*
1949 *Tale of the Navajos*
1952 *Battles of Chief Pontiac*

Spiritualists
use **Clairvoyants**

Spirituals (Songs)
1929 *Show Boat*
1936 *Show Boat*
1955 *Blackboard Jungle*
1957 *Band of Angels*
1959 *Imitation of Life*

Spokan Indians
1956 *Pillars of the Sky*

Sponges
1936 *Down to the Sea*
1948 *16 Fathoms Deep*
1949 *Harbor of Missing Men*
1953 *Beneath the 12-Mile Reef*

Sponsors
use **Radio sponsors;**
Television sponsors

Sports
use **Specific types of sports**

Sports fans
1942 *Woman of the Year*

Sports reporters
1950 *Right Cross*
1951 *The Harlem Globetrotters*
1953 *The Joe Louis Story*
1954 *Go Man Go*

Sportsmanship
1940 *Knute Rockne—All American*

Spring
1932 *Une heure près de toi*

Springfield (IL)
1948 *Call Northside 777*

Springs
1934 *Operator 13*
1951 *New Mexico*

Square dances
1949 *The Golden Stallion*
1951 *Slaughter Trail*
1956 *The Broken Star*

Squatters
1922 *The Half Breed*
1927 *Spoilers of the West*
1950 *The Furies*

St. Helena
1937 *Slave Ship*

St. Lawrence River
1940 *Northwest Passage (Book I—Rogers' Rangers)*

St. Louis (MO)
1919? *In the Land of the Setting Sun; or, Martyrs of Yesterday*
1935 *The Singing Vagabond*
1937 *Old Louisiana*
The Plainsman
1942 *We Were Dancing*
1948 *Fighting Father Dunne*
1952 *The Big Sky*
1954 *Apache*

St. Patrick's Day
1940 *Little Nellie Kelly*
1942 *Song of the Islands*

St. Petersburg (Russia)
1935 *The Yiddish King Lear*
1953 *Tonight We Sing*
1959 *John Paul Jones*

St. Valentine's Day
1942 *Holiday Inn*

St. Valentine's Day Massacre, 1929
1932 *Scarface*
1959 *Al Capone*

Stabbings
1932 *El hombre que asesinó*
1934 *La cruz y la espada*
1937 *Charlie Chan at the Opera*
The Riders of the Whistling Skull
1947 *Ride the Pink Horse*

1948 *Cry of the City*
Renegades of Sonora
1949 *Apache Chief*
Ranger of Cherokee Strip
Rose of the Yukon
1953 *Fort Ti*
1957 *Edge of the City*
1960 *The Pusher*

Stableboys
1936 *Charlie Chan at the Race Track*
1950 *Davy Crockett, Indian Scout*

Stables
1932 *Amore e morte*
1949 *The Golden Stallion*
1953 *The Stand at Apache River*
1956 *Ghost Town*
1960 *The Plunderers*

Stage fright
1923 *His Great Chance*

Stagecoach drivers
1940 *Lucky Cisco Kid*
Viva Cisco Kid
1941 *Romance of the Rio Grande*
Western Union
1943 *Frontier Fury*
The Law Rides Again
1944 *Sonora Stagecoach*
1947 Under the Tonto Rim
1950 *Rocky Mountain*
1953 *Last of the Comanches*
1957 *Trooper Hook*

Stagecoach lines
1945 *Great Stagecoach Robbery*
1949 *Stagecoach Kid*
1950 A Ticket to Tomahawk
1952 Apache War Smoke
1958 Gunfire at Indian Gap
The Rawhide Trail

Stagecoach robberies
1925 *Tonio, Son of the Sierras*
1928 The Riding Renegade
1931 *Cavalier of the West*
Yankee Don
1932 *The Vanishing Frontier*
White Eagle
1934 *The Lone Defender*
The Prescott Kid
The Star Packer
1939 *The Fighting Gringo*
The Return of the Cisco Kid
1940 *The Gay Caballero*
Lucky Cisco Kid
Viva Cisco Kid
1941 *Road Agent*
1942 *Below the Border*
1943 *Land of Hunted Men*
1944 *Tucson Raiders*
1945 *Great Stagecoach Robbery*
In Old New Mexico
1946 California Gold Rush
The Gay Cavalier
1947 *King of the Bandits*
1949 *Brothers in the Saddle*
The Cowboy and the Prizefighter
The Gay Amigo
Stagecoach Kid
Streets of Laredo
1950 *Colt .45*
The Girl from San Lorenzo
1951 *Slaughter Trail*
1952 *Apache Country*
Apache War Smoke
The Raiders
1953 *Jack McCall Desperado*
Old Overland Trail
1954 The Black Dakotas
Drums Across the River
1955 Apache Woman
1958 *Gunfire at Indian Gap*
1959 *The Hanging Tree*

Stagecoaches
1915 *Just Jim*
Where Cowboy Is King
1932 *The Golden West*
1935 *Texas Terror*
1939 *Stand Up and Fight*
1940 *Young Buffalo Bill*
1942 Apache Trail
Valley of the Sun
1944 *Sonora Stagecoach*

1945 *Salome, Where She Danced*
1946 *Romance of the West*
Wild Beauty
1948 *The Arizona Ranger*
Old Los Angeles
1949 *The Dalton Gang*
Daughter of the West
Massacre River
Ride, Ryder, Ride!
She Wore a Yellow Ribbon
The Valiant Hombre
1950 *Broken Arrow*
I Killed Geronimo
Rock Island Trail
1951 *Fort Defiance*
New Mexico
Snake River Desperadoes
1952 *The Battle at Apache Pass*
1953 *Last of the Comanches*
The Stand at Apache River
1954 *Drum Beat*
Overland Pacific
1956 *Dakota Incident*
Ghost Town
1957 *Trooper Hook*
1959 *The Sheriff of Fractured Jaw*

Stairs
1939 *Gone With the Wind*

Stamp collectors
use **Postage-stamps—Collectors and collecting**

Stampedes
1914 *In the Days of the Thundering Herd*
1919 *Lasca*
1926 *Buffalo Bill on the U. P. Trail*
The Last Frontier
1927 *Open Range*
1930 *The Lash*
1931 *Call of the Rockies*
1932 *The Forty-Niners*
The Golden West
1933 *Robbers' Roost*
Thundering Herd
1934 *Wheels of Destiny*
1941 *Secret of the Wastelands*
Thunder Over the Prairie
1946 *Wild Beauty*
1947 *The Last Round-Up*
Rustlers of Devil's Canyon
Wild Horse Mesa
1948 *Red River*
1949 *Call of the Forest*
The Golden Stallion
Ranger of Cherokee Strip
1950 *The Cariboo Trail*
1954 *Cattle Queen of Montana*
1955 *Santa Fe Passage*
1956 *The Last Hunt*
1957 *The Lawless Eighties*
Raiders of Old California

Stamps
use **Postage-stamps**

Stanford University
1922 *The Great Alone*

Edwin McMasters Stanton
1930 *Abraham Lincoln*
1955 *The Gun That Won the West*

Belle Starr
1941 *Belle Starr*

Sam Starr
Belle Starr

Starvation
1914 *An Odyssey of the North*
1920 *Locked Lips*
1933 *The California Trail*
1940 *Northwest Passage (Book I—Rogers' Rangers)*
1942 *Rio Rita*
1945 *Between Two Women*
1948 *Indian Agent*
1949 *Arctic Fury*
The Cowboy and the Indians
1950 *North of the Great Divide*
1955 *Seven Cities of Gold*
1956 *The Last Hunt*

Stefan Starzynski
1941 *Ten Ostatni*
Z Dymem Pożarów

State governments
1936 *Rebellion*
1955 *Davy Crockett, King of the Wild Frontier*

Statehood (American politics)
1947 California
1949 *The Gay Amigo*
1950 *The Baron of Arizona*
1952 *The Raiders*
1954 *Battle of Rogue River*
1960 Ice Palace

Staterooms
1935 *A Night at the Opera*

Statue of Liberty National Monument (New York City)
1926 *The Passaic Textile Strike*
1942 *Nazi Agent*
1949 *Answer for Anne*

Statues
1918 *My Cousin*
1931 *Charlie Chan Carries On Cimarron*
1944 *The Chinese Cat*
1948 *The Miracle of the Bells*
1949 *The Story of Seabiscuit*
1953 *Taxi*

Stay of execution
1942 *Take My Life*

Steam rooms
1932 *Le bluffeur*

Steamboats
1916 *The Scarlet Oath*
1918 *Hidden Pearls*
1923 Little Old New York
1933 *Diplomaniacs*
1935 *Romance in Manhattan The Winning Ticket*
1937 *Big City*
1939 *The Adventures of Huckleberry Finn*
1941 *Lady from Louisiana*
1950 *Rock Island Trail*
1952 *The Iron Mistress*
1959 *Yellowstone Kelly*
1960 *The Adventures of Huckleberry Finn*

Steel
1944 *An American Romance*

Steel industry
1920 *Dangerous Days*
1924 *The Lure of Love*

Steel magnates
1916 Arms and the Woman Light at Dusk
1918 *Love's Law*
1920? *Her Story*
1945 *The Valley of Decision*

Steel mills
1918 *The Birth of a Race* Love's Law
1932 *Huddle*
1936 *Dangerous Intrigue*
1944 *An American Romance*
1945 The Valley of Decision
1957 *Burden of Truth*

Steel workers
1916 *Light at Dusk*
1945 *The Valley of Decision*

Stefanson Polar Expedition
1928 The Great White North

Stenographers
1923 *Flames of Wrath*
1932 *Ljubav i strast*
1934 *El tango en Broadway*
1934? *Harlem After Midnight*
1937 *Waikiki Wedding*
1940 *Her Second Mother*
1946 *The Sailor Takes a Wife*

Stepbrothers
1918 *In Judgment Of*
1942 *Castle in the Desert*

Stepchildren
1915 *The Gambler of the West*
1931 Call of the Rockies
1944 *The Chinese Cat*

Stepfathers
1920 Our Christianity and Nobody's Child
1925 The Thundering Herd
1927 *The Scar of Shame*
1931 Call of the Rockies
1933 Thundering Herd

1939 Moon over Harlem
1942 Unseen Enemy
1944 *The Chinese Cat*
1948 Night Wind

Stepmothers
1919 Erstwhile Susan
1922 The Top O' the Morning
1928 *Eleven P.M.*
1931 *Mi último amor*
1942 Mokey
1947 Robin Hood of Monterey
1958 *Home Before Dark*

Stepsisters
Home Before Dark

Sterilization
1943 *Hitler's Children*

Stewardesses
1949 *C-Man* The Sky Dragon

Stewards
1937 *Think Fast, Mr. Moto*

Stock market
1914 *The Good-for-Nothing*
1915 After Five Chimmie Fadden Out West
1931 *Carne de cabaret*
1947 *The Foxes of Harrow*

Stock market crash of 1929
1930 *El cuerpo del delito*
1932 *The Match King*
1950 *Give Us This Day*
1960 *Studs Lonigan*

Stockbrokers
1915 *After Five The Rosary*
1930 El cuerpo del delito
1934 *Strange Wives*
1938 *Charlie Chan at Monte Carlo*
1940 *Murder over New York*
1956 *Death of a Scoundrel*
1957 *Twelve Angry Men*

Stocks
1918 Find the Woman
1931 *La pura verdad*
1932 Le bluffeur
1956 Death of a Scoundrel

Stockyards
1938 *In Old Chicago*

Stonemasons
1956 Full of Life

Stonewall Jackson
use **General Thomas Jonathan Jackson**

Storekeepers
1920 *The North Wind's Malice*
1921 *No Woman Knows*
1932 Law and Lawless
1937 *Hills of Old Wyoming*
1938 *City Streets*
1939 *Mothers of Today*
1940 *Lucky Cisco Kid*
1943 *The Ox-Bow Incident*
1949 *Pinky*
1950 *The Missourians*
1951 *Warpath*
1953 *The Sun Shines Bright*
1954 *Drum Beat* Siege at Red River
1959 *The Hanging Tree*
1960 *The Plunderers*

Stores, Retail
1939 *Gone With the Wind*
1950 *The Traveling Saleswoman*

Storms
1915? *The Beachcomber*
1922 The Great Alone
1925 Kivalina of the Ice Lands
1930 *Anna Christie*
1931 *Drácula*
1932 *Amore e morte*
1934 *Wheels of Destiny*
1936 *The Green Pastures Song of the Gringo*
1940 *New Moon*
1944 *Lifeboat*
1949 *She Wore a Yellow Ribbon*
1950 *The Toast of New Orleans*
1951 *The Raging Tide*
1952? *Call of the Navajo*

Storytellers
1920 The Devil's Claim
1946 Song of the South
1949 Shamrock Hill Tale of the Navajos

Stowaways
1916 *The Morals of Hilda Poor Little Peppina*
1918 *Sandy*
1930 *El dios del mar*
1931 *Monerías*
1935 A Night at the Opera Tango Bar The Winning Ticket
1938 Hawaii Calls
1941 *Dead Men Tell Mystery Ship This Woman Is Mine*
1943 *The Amazing Mrs. Holliday*
1945 *Johnny Angel*
1946 *G. I. War Brides Strange Voyage*
1947 *Oregon Trail Scouts Pirates of Monterey*
1950 *Buccaneer's Girl Two Flags West*
1953 *The Glass Wall The Stars Are Singing*

Strangers
1919 Just Squaw The She Wolf
1922 Captain Fly-by-Night
1929 When Men Betray
1934 *The Prescott Kid* The Rabbi's Power
1947 *Juke Joint*
1951 The Well

Strangling
1917 *I Will Repay*
1918 *Her American Husband*
1932 *Flesh The Son-Daughter*
1939 *Charlie Chan in Reno*
1940 Charlie Chan's Murder Cruise
1945 *The Mummy's Curse*
1946 *The Trap*
1948 *Moonrise*

Street cleaners
1921 Hold Your Horses
1927 *For the Love of Mike*

Street entertainers
1917 *The Tell-Tale Step*
1928 Eleven P.M.
1929 Mister Antonio

Street vendors
1927 The Shamrock and the Rose
1937 *Arshin Mal Alan*

Streetcar conductors
1924 Conductor 1492

Streetcars
Conductor 1492
1936 *Sutter's Gold*
1950 *The Daughter of Rosie O'Grady*
1951 *A Streetcar Named Desire*

Strikebreakers
1935 *Black Fury*
1936 *Sutter's Gold*
1945 *The Valley of Decision*
1954 *Salt of the Earth*

Strikes
use **Hunger strikes; Strikes and lockouts**

Strikes and lockouts
1914 *The Jungle*
1915 *The Spender*
1917 *Threads of Fate*
1918 *Love's Law The Prussian Cur*
1920 Dangerous Hours The Face at Your Window The Great Shadow
1926 The Passaic Textile Strike
1932 *Uncle Moses*
1935 Black Fury
1939 *Motel the Operator*
1941 *Min Jok Jay Hung Sing*
1944 *An American Romance*
1945 *The Valley of Decision*
1947 *The Burning Cross*
1952 *My Man and I*
1954 Salt of the Earth

Strip-tease
1946 *Dirty Gertie from Harlem, U.S.A.*
1955 Brevities of 1955
1959 *The Crimson Kimono*
1960 Hell to Eternity

Stroke
1916 *Witchcraft*
1919 *Erstwhile Susan*
1934 *Beloved*
1939 *La Inmaculada Kol Nidre*
1948 *Gentleman's Agreement*
1954 *Broken Lance*
1957 *The Halliday Brand*

Strong men
1926 The Strong Man
1928 Vamping Venus

Jeb Stuart
1940 Santa Fe Trail

Students
1916 *Alien Souls Betrayed*
1918 *Her Moment*
1919 *A Heart in Pawn*
1920 It's a Great Life Li Ting Lang *Pagan Love*
1921 The Burden of Race
1922 Blazing Arrows
1930 *Doña mentiras* La rosa de fuego Son of the Gods Sunny Skies
1931 *La cautivadora* Esclavas de la moda *Skyline*
1932 Mazel Tov *The Son-Daughter*
1934 The Rabbi's Power
1935 *Lem Hawkins' Confession*
1937 *Green Fields*
1941? Hampton Institute: Its Program of Education for Life
1945 *The Bells of St. Mary's*
1949 Answer for Anne *We Were Strangers*
1952 *It's a Big Country: An American Anthology*

Stunt flying
1928 Flying Romeos

Stuttering
1944 *Hi, Beautiful*
1948? *Boarding House Blues*

Submarine boats
1918 *Doing Their Bit The Spreading Evil*
1919 Behind the Door
1920 *The Purple Cipher*
1937 The Devil's Playground
1940 Escape to Glory
1942 *The Navy Comes Through Secret Enemies* Submarine Raider
1943 Action in the North Atlantic
1950 Mystery Submarine

Submarine warfare
1943 Crash Dive

Subpoena
Three Hearts for Julia
1949 *Shamrock Hill The Undercover Man*
1955 *Trial*
1957 *Raiders of Old California*

Suburban life
1960 *Take a Giant Step*

Subways
1915 *The Danger Signal*
1917 *The Adventures of Carol*
1929 This Is Heaven
1948 *Cry of the City The Luck of the Irish*
1953 *The Glass Wall*

Suez Canal (Egypt)
1939 *Mr. Moto's Last Warning*

Suffocation
use **Asphyxia**

Suffragettes
1916 *The Fall of a Nation*

Sugar
1934   *White Heat*
1955   *Duel on the Mississippi*
1958   Machete

Suicide
1914   The Great Diamond Robbery
     The Squaw Man
1915   After Five
     The Birth of a Nation
     Kreutzer Sonata
1915?   *Sin*
1916   *Betrayed*
     The Folly of Revenge
     The Gilded Spider
     Hop, the Devil's Brew
     The Sign of the Poppy
     The Soul of Kura-San
     The Woman in 47
1917   *The Bride of Hate*
     The Secret Game
     The Squaw Man's Son
1918   *Broken Ties*
     Fields of Honor
     Her American Husband
     His Birthright
     The Ordeal of Rosetta
     The Ranger
     The Spreading Evil
     The Squaw Man
     Toys of Fate
1919   A Heart in Pawn
     The Homesteader
1920   *The Cup of Fury*
     The Dark Mirror
     The Daughter of Dawn
     The Man Who Dared
     Pagan Love
     The Riddle: Woman
1921   Diane of Star Hollow
1924   California in '49
1925   Don Q, Son of Zorro
     Flower of Night
     The Prairie Wife
1927   *Bitter Apples*
     The Scar of Shame
1928   The Mating Call
1931   *Aloha*
     Cuerpo y alma
     Lo mejor es reír
     Oklahoma Jim
     The Squaw Man
1932   *L'athlète incomplet*
     ¿Cuándo te suicidas?
     A Daughter of Her People
     The Match King
     Men Are Such Fools
     Mystery Ranch
     Senza mamma
       e'nnamurato
     The Son-Daughter
     Thirteen Women
     Yiskor
1933   *Dance Hall Hostess*
     Ever in My Heart
     Victims of Persecution
1934   *Behold My Wife!*
     Limehouse Blues
1935   *The Cyclone Ranger*
     Rendezvous
1937   *It Could Happen to You*
1938   Dangerous to Know
     God's Step Children
     Spawn of the North
1939   Charlie Chan at Treasure
       Island
     La Inmaculada
     Motel the Operator
1940   *Girl from God's Country*
1941   *Four Shall Die*
     Hold Back the Dawn
     Murder on Lenox Avenue
     New York Town
     They Dare Not Love
1942   *In This Our Life*
     Let's Get Tough!
1943   *The Ox-Bow Incident*
1944   *Black Magic*
     Lifeboat
1946   *The Face of Marble*
1947   *The Foxes of Harrow*
     Humoresque
1949   *Daughter of the West*
     Illegal Entry
     Knock on Any Door
     3 Godfathers

     The Undercover Man
1950   *God, Man and Devil*
     So Young, So Bad
1951   *The Girl on the Bridge*
1952   *Buffalo Bill in Tomahawk*
       Territory
1953   *Arrowhead*
     Fort Ti
     War Paint
1954   *Overland Pacific*
1955   *Chief Crazy Horse*
     Shotgun
1958   *The Young Lions*
1960   *The Dark at the Top of the*
       Stairs
     Hell to Eternity
     Pay or Die

Suicide notes
1916   *The Woman in 47*

Suitcases
1947   *On the Old Spanish Trail*

Sukkoth
1939   *Mamele*

Sullivan family
1944   The Sullivans

Anne Sullivan
1919   Deliverance

John L. Sullivan
1942   *Gentleman Jim*
1945   The Great John L.

Sultans
1939   Cossacks in Exile

Summit Springs, Battle of, 1869
1914   *The Indian Wars*
1917   The Adventures of Buffalo
       Bill

Summons
   use   **Subpoena**

Sun Valley (ID)
1941   Sun Valley Serenade

Superintendents
1938   *God's Step Children*
1948   *The Golden Eye*
1956   Crowded Paradise

Superstition
1922   Cross Roads
1924   A Son of Satan
1930   *Anna Christie*
1931   *Drácula*
1934   *The Cactus Kid*
1938   *Life Goes On*
1939   *The Devil's Daughter*
     The Light Ahead
1941   Dead Men Tell
1942   *They Died With Their Boots*
       On
1944   *Lake Placid Serenade*
1946   *Strange Voyage*
     Three Wise Fools
1948   *Louisiana Story*
1949   *Satan's Cradle*
1950   *Give Us This Day*
     The Palomino
     The Toast of New Orleans
     Young Daniel Boone
1957   *The Guns of Fort Petticoat*
1959   *Cry Tough*

Mary Suratt
1936   *The Prisoner of Shark*
       Island

Surgeons
1919   Who's Your Brother?
1928   The Broken Mask
1932   *Le cas du docteur Brenner*
     Symphony of Six Million
1936   *El crimen de media noche*
     Star for a Night
1940   *Charlie Chan at the Wax*
       Museum
1947   Dark Delusion
1955   Not As a Stranger
1959   *Shake Hands with the Devil*

Surgery
   use   **Operations, Surgical;**
      Specific types of surgery

Surveillance devices
1945   *Betrayal from the East*
     Escape in the Fog
     The House on 92nd St.
1946   *Notorious*

Surveyors
1925   A Daughter of the Sioux
1940   Young Buffalo Bill
1948   Silver Trails
1949   *The Fighting Kentuckian*
     Home of the Brave
1950   *The Baron of Arizona*
1955   *White Feather*

Survival skills
1932   Igloo
1949   Arctic Fury
1959   The World, the Flesh and
       the Devil

John Sutter
1924   California in '49
1936   Sutter's Gold
     Robin Hood of El Dorado
     Sutter's Gold

Sutter's Mill (CA)
     Robin Hood of El Dorado
     Sutter's Gold

Suwalki (Poland)
1937   *I Want to Be a Mother*

Swamps
1926   *The Flying Ace*
1933   *The Emperor Jones*
1934   *Chloe: Love Is Calling You*
1939   *Mr. Moto in Danger Island*
1941   *Sunday Sinners*
1944   *Dark Waters*
1945   *The Mummy's Curse*
1946   *Swamp Fire*
1947   *Untamed Fury*
1948   *Moonrise*
     Tap Roots
1951   *Distant Drums*
1953   *Cry of the Hunted*
1957   *The Oklahoman*
1958   *The Defiant Ones*

Sweatshops
1915   *Cohen's Luck*
1916   *Civilization's Child*
1919   *Deliverance*
1929   East Side Sadie
1932   Uncle Moses
     The Unfortunate Bride
1939   *Motel the Operator*

Sweden
1931   Jenny Lind
1932   The Match King

Swedes
1941   *Ice-Capades*

Swedish Americans
1916   The Thousand Dollar
       Husband
1917   Follow the Girl
1918   *How Could You, Jean?*
     The Source
1919   The Unpainted Woman
1921   Guile of Women
1922   The Scrapper
1923   Anna Christie
1925   The Prairie Wife
1926   The Campus Flirt
1927   Wild Geese
1930   Anna Christie
1931   *Delicious*
     Mr. Lemon of Orange
     Three Who Loved
1932   *The Match King*
1933   *Let's Fall in Love*
     Olsen's Big Moment
1934   *Coming Out Party*
     Our Daily Bread
1940   *If I Had My Way*
1942   *Sunday Punch*
1943   *His Butler's Sister*
     Svenkst I Och Omkring New
       York
1945   The Bells of St. Mary's
1947   *The Farmer's Daughter*
1949   Prejudice
1951   The Raging Tide
1953   *The Man Behind the Gun*
1955   *Not As a Stranger*
1956   *The Searchers*
     The White Squaw
1958   Terror in a Texas Town
1960   *All the Young Men*
     Weddings and Babies

Sweepstakes
1932   Hypnotized
1935   The Winning Ticket
1943   *Cabin in the Sky*
1949   *Rose of the Yukon*

Swimmers
1936   *Contra la corriente*
1937   *Charlie Chan at the*
       Olympics

Swimming
1933   *Yo, tú y ella*
1939   *The Light Ahead*
1942   *Cat People*
1955   *The Long Gray Line*
1959   *Night of the Quarter Moon*

Swindlers and swindling
1920   *Within Our Gates*
1925   *Body and Soul*
     Irish Luck
1930   *The Bad Man*
     Easy Street
1931   *Mamá*
1933   *The Man Who Dared: An*
       Imaginative Biography
1935   Chinatown Squad
1945   *Where Do We Go From*
       Here?
1947   *Black Gold*
     The Chinese Ring
1947?   Return of Mandy's Husband
     What a Guy
1948   *Miracle in Harlem*
1949   *The Cowboy and the*
       Indians
1953   *The Man Behind the Gun*
     Old Overland Trail
1956   *Hot Blood*
1958   *St. Louis Blues*
1959   *The FBI Story*
1960   *Cimarron*

Swing music
1941   *Where Did You Get That*
       Girl?
1946   Stars on Parade
1946?   Harlem on Parade
1948?   Junction 88
1949   Lookout Sister
1949?   The Joint Is Jumpin'
1956   The Benny Goodman Story

Swiss
1959   The Hanging Tree

Switzerland
1960   Man on a String

Sword fights
1917   *The Little Chevalier*
1933   *Man from Monterey*
1940   *The Mark of Zorro*
1945   *Salome, Where She Danced*
1946   Don Ricardo Returns
     The Gay Cavalier
1947   *Pirates of Monterey*
     Riding the California Trail
1950   *Buccaneer's Girl*
1951   *The Mark of the Renegade*
1952   *California Conquest*
1955   *Kiss of Fire*
1960   *The Sign of Zorro*

Swords
1934   *The Cat's-Paw*
1954   *War Arrow*

Synagogues
1932   *The Unfortunate Bride*
1937   *I Want to Be a Mother*
1939   *Kol Nidre*
1940   *Overture to Glory*
1948   *Big City*
1950   *God, Man and Devil*
1953   *The Jazz Singer*
1956   *Singing in the Dark*

Syndicates (Finance)
1948   *Fury at Furnace Creek*

Syphilis
1918   The Spreading Evil

Syria
1921   The Syrian Immigrant

Syrian Americans
1952   *Anything Can Happen*

Syrians
1921   The Syrian Immigrant
1922   Anna Ascends

Tahiti
1943   *Tahiti Honey*
1944   Tahiti Nights

Tailors
1922   Solomon in Society
1925   One of the Bravest
1926   Millionaires

Tailors
- 1927　*For the Love of Mike*
- 1934　*As the Earth Turns*
- 1939　*A Brivele der Mamen*
- 1942　*Tales of Manhattan*
　　　　They Died With Their Boots On
- 1946?　Fight That Ghost

Talent agents
- 1934　*La ciudad de cartón*
- 1937　*Music for Madame*
- 1938　*Little Miss Roughneck*
- 1941　*Where Did You Get That Girl?*
- 1946　*That Man of Mine*
- 1947　*Hi De Ho*
- 1949　The Girl from Jones Beach
- 1953　*The Jazz Singer*
　　　　The Stars Are Singing
- 1960　*All the Fine Young Cannibals*

Talent scouts
- 1933　*Melodía de arrabal*

Talismans
- 1916　*Witchcraft*
- 1921　Hold Your Horses
- 1927　*Irish Hearts*

Chief Tall Bull
- 1917　*The Adventures of Buffalo Bill*

Tango (Dance)
- 1930　*Una cana al aire*
- 1931　*Nuit d'Espagne*
- 1933　*Melodía de arrabal*
- 1935　Tango Bar

Tank warfare
- 1952　Red Ball Express

Tankers
- 1943　*Action in the North Atlantic*

Tanks (Military science)
- 1953　*The Glory Brigade*
- 1960　*All the Young Men*

Taos (NM)
- 1928　Kit Carson

Tap dancing
- 1938　*God's Step Children*
　　　　Swing!
- 194-　*Mistaken Identity*
- 1946　*That Man of Mine*
- 1946?　Harlem on Parade
- 1947　*Jivin' in Be-Bop*
- 1948　*The Time of Your Life*
- 1949?　*The Joint Is Jumpin'*
- 1953　*The Stars Are Singing*

Tar and feathering
- 1947　*The Burning Cross*

Tarantulas
- 1918　*The Red, Red Heart*

Tarawa (Kiribati)
- 1950　*Sands of Iwo Jima*

Tarpon Springs (FL)
- 1949　*Harbor of Missing Men*
- 1953　*Beneath the 12-Mile Reef*

Tarrant County (TX)
- 1920　Frontier Days

Tattoos
- 1937　*Life Begins in College*
　　　　Think Fast, Mr. Moto
- 1942　*Valley of Hunted Men*
- 1943　*Frontier Fury*
- 1944　*Lifeboat*
- 1955　*The Rose Tattoo*

Tax evasion
- 1949　*The Undercover Man*

Taxation
- 1930　El precio de un beso
- 1936　*The Bold Caballero*
- 1937　*The Californian*
　　　　Maid of Salem
- 1938　*The Renegade Ranger*
　　　　The Texans
- 1946　*South of Monterey*
- 1949　*The Kissing Bandit*

Taxi dancers
- 1930　The Last Dance
- 1947　*Crossfire*
- 1954　*Hell's Half Acre*

Taxicab drivers
- 1916　The Pretenders
- 1930　Check and Double Check
　　　　Locuras de amor

Taxicabs
- 1933　Dance Hall Hostess
　　　　Rafter Romance
- 1935　*Charlie Chan in Shanghai*
　　　　A Night at the Ritz
- 1936　*Below the Deadline*
　　　　Star for a Night
- 1937　Big City
- 1938　*Charlie Chan at Monte Carlo*
- 1942　All Through the Night
- 1944　The Chinese Cat
- 1945　*Jealousy*
　　　　Johnny Angel
- 1946　*The Gentleman Misbehaves*
　　　　Slightly Scandalous
- 1947　*Easy Come, Easy Go*
- 1949?　Girl in Room 20
- 1953　Taxi
- 1954　*Hell's Half Acre*
- 1956　*The Catered Affair*

Taxicabs
- 1940　*Music in My Heart*
- 1942　*Rio Rita*
- 1945　*Escape in the Fog*
- 1949　*C-Man*
- 1960　*Man on a String*

Taxidermy
- 1936　*West of Nevada*

Zachary Taylor
　　　　Rebellion
- 1951　*Distant Drums*
- 1953　*Seminole*

Peter Ilyich Tchaikowsky
- 1947　*Carnegie Hall*

Tea
- 1917　*The War of the Tongs*
- 1930　The Last Dance
　　　　Wu Li Chang
- 1944　*Block Busters*
- 1949　*Boston Blackie's Chinese Venture*

Teachers
- 1919　Deliverance
- 1931　Pardon Us
- 1932　So Big
- 1932?　*The Girl from Chicago*
- 1934　*The Great Flirtation*
- 1937　Green Fields
- 1938　*The Beloved Brat*
　　　　God's Step Children
- 1939　*The Escape*
- 1940　*Charlie Chan in Panama*
　　　　Knute Rockne—All American
- 1941　*Murder on Lenox Avenue*
- 1941?　Hampton Institute: Its Program of Education for Life
- 1943　*Hitler's Children*
- 1944　Tomorrow the World!
- 1948　Big City
- 1949　Answer for Anne
　　　　Daughter of the West
　　　　The Quiet One
　　　　The Red Menace
- 1950　So Young, So Bad
　　　　The Toast of New Orleans
- 1952　*Arctic Flight*
- 1953　*The Stars Are Singing*
- 1954　*Barefoot Battalion*
- 1955　Blackboard Jungle
　　　　Fort Yuma
- 1957　*Raintree County*
- 1960　*Studs Lonigan*

Tear gas
- 1945　*The House on 92nd St.*

Teche Bayou (LA)
- 1938　The Buccaneer

Technological innovations
　　　　use **Innovations**

Technology
- 1928　Vamping Venus

Teenagers
　　　　use **Adolescents**

Teeth
- 1943　*What's Buzzin' Cousin?*
- 1944　*Something for the Boys*

Teetotalers
- 1941　*Louisiana Purchase*

Tel Aviv (Palestine)
- 1937　*The Holy Oath*

Telegrams
- 1914　*The Yellow Traffic*
- 1916　*The Aryan*
- 1936　Muss 'Em Up
- 1938　*Passport Husband*
- 1939　*My Son*
- 1941　*Hurry, Charlie, Hurry*
- 1942　*Young America*
- 1943　*Mexican Spitfire's Blessed Event*
- 1944　*Black Magic*
　　　　Hi, Beautiful
　　　　Tender Comrade
- 1946　*Without Reservations*
- 1949　*Lookout Sister*
- 1950　*Storm Over Wyoming*
- 1954　*Siege at Red River*

Telegraph
- 1928　The Glorious Trail
- 1929　The Overland Telegraph
- 1933　The Telegraph Trail
- 1937　*Prairie Thunder*
- 1946　Wild West
- 1954　*Drum Beat*
　　　　Overland Pacific

Telephone
- 1917　*The Little American*
- 1918　*The Greatest Thing in Life*
- 1933　*Olsen's Big Moment*
- 1934　*The Cat's-Paw*
- 1940　*Gang War*
- 1942　*Nazi Agent*
- 1951　*The House on Telegraph Hill*

Telephone booths
- 1931　*Mr. Lemon of Orange*
- 1960　*Key Witness*

Telephone operators
- 1933　*Counsellor at Law*
- 1935　*Charlie Chan in Shanghai*
- 1941　*You're Out of Luck*
- 1945　Between Two Women
　　　　Club Havana
- 1950　Chinatown at Midnight

Telephone wire-tapping
　　　　use **Wire-tapping**

Television
- 1935　*Te quiero con locura*
- 1937　*Manhattan Merry-Go-Round*
- 1938　Hits and Bits of 1938
- 194-　*Mistaken Identity*
- 1947　*The Last Round-Up*
- 1949　*Shamrock Hill*
　　　　Souls of Sin
- 1949?　*The Joint Is Jumpin'*
- 1950　*The Lawless*
- 1951　Mask of the Dragon
- 1957　*Burden of Truth*
- 1958　*The Last Hurrah*
- 1959　*Inside the Mafia*

Television producers
　　　　The Last Angry Man

Television programs
- 1945　*The Scarlet Clue*
- 1946　Mantan Messes Up
　　　　Slightly Scandalous
- 1949　*The Girl from Jones Beach*
　　　　Jiggs and Maggie in Jackpot Jitters
- 1951　Queen for a Day
- 1953　Taxi
- 1958　*Seven Hills of Rome*
- 1960　*I Aim at the Stars: the Wernher von Braun Story*

Television sponsors
- 1946　Slightly Scandalous
- 1959　*The Last Angry Man*

Temper
- 1930　Cascarrabias
- 1936　Contra la corriente

Temperance
- 1916　*Peck O' Pickles*
- 1922　Come On Over
- 1945　*The Great John L.*
- 1955　*A Man Called Peter*

Temples
- 1938　*Mr. Moto Takes a Chance*
- 1948　*The Feathered Serpent*
- 1951　*The Steel Helmet*

Temptresses
- 1933　*The Man Who Dared: An Imaginative Biography*
- 1938　*The Singing Blacksmith*
- 1942　*Little Tokyo, U.S.A.*
- 1943　*Cabin in the Sky*
- 1954　Carmen Jones

Tenant farmers
- 1929　*Hallelujah*
- 1930　Georgia Rose

Tenderfoots
- 1936　*Desert Gold*
- 1941　*Western Union*
- 1944　Marshal of Reno
- 1948　The Dude Goes West
- 1957　The Tin Star

Tenement-houses
- 1915　*The Kindling*
- 1916　*The Criminal*
　　　　Gretchen, the Greenhorn
- 1917　*The Adventures of Carol*
- 1918　Amarilly of Clothes-Line Alley
　　　　Hell's End
　　　　A Little Sister of Everybody
- 1919　*A Fighting Colleen*
- 1920　*Darling Mine*
- 1922　Little Miss Smiles
- 1927　The Callahans and the Murphys
　　　　For the Love of Mike
　　　　Sally in Our Alley
- 1931　Street Scene
- 1932　*Marido y mujer*
　　　　No Greater Love
- 1933　Rafter Romance
- 1934　*Straight Is the Way*
- 1935　McFadden's Flats
- 1936　*Winterset*
- 1937　*Boy of the Streets*
- 1941　*Accent on Love*
- 1945　*A Tree Grows in Brooklyn*
- 1950　*Black Hand*
　　　　Give Us This Day
- 1951　*Molly*
- 1959　*Cry Tough*

Tennessee
- 1915?　The Life of Sam Davis: A Confederate Hero of the Sixties
　　　　Sam Davis, the Hero of Tennessee
- 1917　*The Conqueror*
- 1918　Out of a Clear Sky
- 1927　The Frontiersman
- 1930　Anybody's War
- 1939　*Man of Conquest*
- 1940　*Paradise in Harlem*
- 1955　*Davy Crockett, King of the Wild Frontier*
- 1956　*Frontier Woman*
- 1960　Wild River

Tents
- 1950　*Davy Crockett, Indian Scout*

Termites
- 1956　*Full of Life*

Territorial governors
- 1916　*Witchcraft*
- 1917　*The Little Chevalier*
- 1930　*El precio de un beso*
- 1936　The Bold Caballero
- 1937　*Drums of Destiny*
- 1940　*Kit Carson*
- 1944　Tucson Raiders
- 1951　*The Mark of the Renegade*

Terrorism
- 1921　Cotton and Cattle
- 1937　Black Legion
- 1959　*The FBI Story*
　　　　Shake Hands with the Devil

Tests of character
- 1915　Just Jim
- 1930　Check and Double Check
- 1931　*¿Conoces a tu mujer?*
　　　　Young Sinners
　　　　Zein Weib's Lubovnick
- 1932　*Call Her Savage*
- 1934　Dos más uno, dos
- 1936　Contra la corriente
- 1938　*The Singing Blacksmith*
- 1944　Three Men in White
- 1946　Swamp Fire

1950   *Broken Arrow*
       God, Man and Devil
1953   *The Great Sioux Uprising*
1956   *Daniel Boone, Trail Blazer*

Teton Indians
1952   *The Savage*

Texans
1915   *A Texas Steer*
1921   *The Man from Texas*
1930   *El último de los Vargas*
1942   *Song of the Islands*
1946   *Saratoga Trunk*
1949   *Illegal Entry*
1950   *Belle of Old Mexico*
1951   *Go for Broke!*
1952   It's a Big Country: An
       American Anthology
1953   *The Jazz Singer*
       San Antone
1955   *Apache Ambush*
       The Last Command
1957   *The Lawless Eighties*
1958   *Sierra Baron*
1959   *The Wonderful Country*

Texas
1917   *The Conqueror*
1924   *North of 36*
1932   *Call Her Savage*
1935   *Cowboy Holiday*
1936   *The Traitor*
1937   *Border Cafe*
1938   The Texans
1939   Man of Conquest
1940   Hi-Yo Silver
1942   *American Empire*
       From Across the Border
       Rio Rita
1943   *Marching On!*
1945   *The Navajo Trail*
1947   *Duel in the Sun*
1948   Red River
1949   *The Red Menace*
       Roll Thunder Roll!
       Streets of Laredo
1949? *Girl in Room 20*
1950   *Comanche Territory*
1951   *The Last Outpost*
1952   *The Iron Mistress*
1953   *Arrowhead*
1955   *Seminole Uprising*
1956   *Giant*
       The Searchers
1957   *The Guns of Fort Petticoat*
       The Ride Back
1958   *The Lone Ranger and the
       Lost City of Gold*
       The Rawhide Trail
1959   *The Wonderful Country*
1960   *All the Fine Young
       Cannibals*
       Flaming Star
       The Unforgiven

Texas—History
1953   *The Man from the Alamo*
       Ride, Vaquero!
1954   War Arrow
1955   *Davy Crockett, King of the
       Wild Frontier*
       The Last Command

Texas Rangers
1918   The Ranger
1920   Rio Grande
1925   Galloping Vengeance
1930   *El último de los Vargas*
1936   Ride, Ranger, Ride
1938   The Renegade Ranger
1940   Hi-Yo Silver
1941   Saddlemates
1942   *Rio Rita*
1943   Border Patrol
1945   *The Navajo Trail*
1949   Masked Raiders
       Streets of Laredo
1956   *The Searchers*
1958   The Lone Ranger and the
       Lost City of Gold
1959   *The Wonderful Country*

Textile mills
1920   *Dangerous Hours*
1924   In Hollywood With Potash
       and Perlmutter
1926   The Passaic Textile Strike

Thames River (England)
1960   *The Day They Robbed the
       Bank of England*

Thanksgiving Day
1936   *Star for a Night*
1941   *Adam Had Four Sons*
1942   *Holiday Inn*
1944   *Andy Hardy's Blonde
       Trouble*
1956   *Giant*

Theater
1916   The Twin Triangle
1921   Cheated Love
       The Land of Hope
1925   The Beautiful City
1926   Puppets
1929   Lucky Boy
       Smiling Irish Eyes
1959   *Imitation of Life*

Theater owners
1920? *The Greatest Love*

Theaters
1929   *Die Königsloge*
1930   *Sombras de gloria*
1932   *Harlem Is Heaven*
1936   *Mad Holiday*
1949   *The Sky Dragon*
1951   *Gambling House*
1956   *Rockin' the Blues*

Theatrical agents
1922   Head over Heels
1928   *The Jazz Singer*
1938   *The Duke Is Tops*
1942   *Holiday Inn*
1943   *His Butler's Sister*
       Let's Have Fun
1944   *Minstrel Man*
       Slightly Terrific
1945   *Between Two Women*
       I Love a Bandleader
1947   *Copacabana*
1948? *Junction 88*
1949   *Lookout Sister*
1959   *Imitation of Life*

Theatrical backers
1931   *Gente alegre*
1938   *The Duke Is Tops*
1940   *Perfidia*
1943   *Let's Have Fun*
1947   *Boy! What a Girl!*
       Sepia Cinderella
1949? *Harlem Follies*
1950   *Annie Get Your Gun*
1953   *The Jazz Singer*
1956   *Death of a Scoundrel*
1958   *Marjorie Morningstar*

Theatrical directors
1934   *Blossom Time*
1943   *Let's Have Fun*
1949? *Harlem Follies*

Theatrical managers
1923   *His Great Chance*
1929   *Lucky Boy*
1931   *Regeneración*
       Zein Weib's Lubovnick
1933? *Scandal*
1934   *Las fronteras del amor*
1936   *Yiddle with His Fiddle*
1937   *The Cantor's Son*
1938   *The Duke Is Tops*
       Happy Landing
1939   *Lying Lips*
       My Son
1943   *Redhead from Manhattan*
1947   *Hi De Ho*
       The Jolson Story
1948   Killer Diller
1949? *She's Too Mean for Me*

Theatrical producers
1919   *Yvonne from Paris*
1934   *Granaderos del amor*
1936   *Star for a Night*
1938   *The Duke Is Tops*
       Swing!
       La vida bohemia
1941   *Ice-Capades*
1943   *His Butler's Sister*
       Let's Have Fun
       Yankee Doodle Dandy
1944   *Chip Off the Old Block*
       Minstrel Man
1946   The Gentleman Misbehaves
1947   Boy! What a Girl!
       Copacabana

Reet, Petite and Gone
1948? *Boarding House Blues*
1950   Annie Get Your Gun
1951   *Show Boat*
1953   *The Eddie Cantor Story*
       The Jazz Singer
1957   *Beau James*

Theatrical troupes
1916   *Lord Loveland Discovers
       America*
1928   The Crash
       Vamping Venus
1931   *Regeneración*
1933? *Scandal*
1935   *The Singing Vagabond*
1936   Show Boat
1937   *The Cantor's Son*
1940   *Perfidia*
1944   *Slightly Terrific*
1947   *The Jolson Story*
1951   Show Boat

Theft
       use **Robbery**

Theological seminaries
1919? *The Brand of Judas*
1924   Untamed Youth
1955   *A Man Called Peter*

Thieves
1916   *The Pretenders*
       The Social Buccaneer
       The Social Highwayman
1917   The Bond Between
       The Trouble Buster
1918   *Denny from Ireland*
       In Judgment Of
       Laughing Bill Hyde
1924   Smiling Hate
1925   Brand of Cowardice
1927   Blind Alleys
1928   The House of Scandal
1931   Carne de cabaret
       La cautivadora
       Charlie Chan Carries On
       Die Dreigroschenoper
       Huckleberry Finn
       El impostor
       Kismet
       Personal Maid
       Three Who Loved
1932   *Amore e morte*
       The Forty-Niners
       Hearts of Humanity
       Hombres en mi vida
1933   *Circle Canyon*
       Diplomaniacs
       Racetrack
       Thundering Herd
1934   *The Battling Buckaroo*
       The Cactus Kid
       Call of the Coyote
       Lazy River
       The Lone Defender
       Wheels of Destiny
1935   Captured in Chinatown
       El día que me quieras
       Fighting Pioneers
       Melody Trail
       North of Arizona
       Tango Bar
       Texas Terror
       Wolf Riders
1936   *The Bold Caballero*
       Border Phantom
       El crimen de media noche
       Desert Gold
       Dimples
       Down to the Sea
       Ellis Island
       Muss 'Em Up
       The Phantom of Santa Fe
       Rebellion
1937   *Bargain with Bullets*
       Thank You, Mr. Moto
       Underworld
1938   *Birthright*
       Breaking the Ice
       Spawn of the North
1939   *City in Darkness*
       Double Deal
       Harlem Rides the Range
       Let Freedom Ring
       The Light Ahead
       Mothers of Today
       Reform School

1940   *Cuando canta la Ley*
       *Elsa Maxwell's Public Deb
       No. 1*
       Hi-Yo Silver
       Midnight Shadow
       Phantom of Chinatown
       The Way of All Flesh
1941   *The Face Behind the Mask*
1942   *Tales of Manhattan*
1946? *Fight That Ghost*
1947   *Dangerous Venture*
       West to Glory
1948   *Killer Diller*
       Moonrise
       Renegades of Sonora
1949   The Sky Dragon
1950   *The Men*
1951   *Little Big Horn*
1955   *Duel on the Mississippi*
1956   *Crowded Paradise*
       Secret of Treasure Mountain

Thirst
1927   *Aflame in the Sky*
1936   *Sutter's Gold*
1943   *The Outlaw*
1944   Lifeboat
1946   *Strange Voyage*
1949   *3 Godfathers*
1951   *New Mexico*
1953   Last of the Comanches
       War Paint
1955   *Seminole Uprising*
1956   *Dakota Incident*
1959   *Thunder in the Sun*

Henry David Thoreau
       The Last Angry Man

Jim Thorpe
1951   Jim Thorpe—All-American

Thought control
       use **Psychological torment**

Threats
1930   *La voluntad del muerto*
1931   *Monerías*
1932   *Harlem Is Heaven*
       The Rainbow Trail
       Ten Minutes to Live
1933   *It's Great to Be Alive*
       Victims of Persecution
1935   *Charlie Chan in Paris*
       The Little Colonel
1936   *Charlie Chan at the Race
       Track*
1937   *Charlie Chan at the Opera*
       That I May Live
1939   *Mamele*
1940   *Americaner Schadchen*
       The Jewish Melody
       Mystery in Swing
       The Notorious Elinor Lee
       Paradise in Harlem
1942   *Valley of Hunted Men*
1947   *Hi De Ho*
1948   *Old Los Angeles*
1949   *Massacre River*
       Ranger of Cherokee Strip
       Roll Thunder Roll!
       Tulsa
       The Valiant Hombre
1950   *Bandit Queen*
1952   *Woman in the Dark*
1953   *The Pathfinder*
1957   *Raiders of Old California*
       Trooper Hook
1958   *Flaming Frontier*
1959   *Odds Against Tomorrow*
1960   *Key Witness*
       Pay or Die

Tidal waves
1949   *Portrait of Jennie*

Tijuana (Mexico)
1939   *Forged Passport*

Time travel
1945   Where Do We Go From
       Here?

Timidity
1915   The Danger Signal
1918   The Gypsy Trail
1937   *Manhattan
       Merry-Go-Round*
1946   *Slightly Scandalous*
1948   *I Remember Mama*
       The Paleface

Tires, Rubber
1939   *El otro soy yo*
Tobacco
1935   *The Wedding Night*
Tobacconists
1918   The Greatest Thing in Life
1921   The Barricade
1930   The Kibitzer
Tokyo (Japan)
1943   *Jack London*
Tomatoes
1942   *Juke Girl*
Tomboys
1918   The Only Road
1932   Mazel Tov
1935   *McFadden's Flats*
1945   *Great Stagecoach Robbery*
1946   *Wild West*
1947   *The Adventures of Don Coyote*
Tombs
1935   *Charlie Chan in Egypt*
1937   Thank You, Mr. Moto
1940   *Phantom of Chinatown*
1944   *Cry of the Werewolf*
1948   *The Feathered Serpent*
Tombstone (AZ)
1950   *Train to Tombstone*
Tongs (Secret societies)
1917   The Flower of Doom
        The War of the Tongs
1919   *The Lost Battalion*
        The Tong Man
1922   The Cub Reporter
1923   Purple Dawn
1928   The Cameraman
1929   Chinatown Nights
1931   Law of the Tong
1932   The Hatchet Man
        The Secrets of Wu Sin
1935   Captured in Chinatown
1939   Mr. Wong in Chinatown
Toothache
1935   *The Irish in Us*
1936   Desert Gold
1954   *Thunder Pass*
Tornadoes
1943   *Cabin in the Sky*
Torpedoes
1917   *The Little American*
        Under False Colors
1918   *The Spreading Evil*
1942   *Submarine Raider*
1943   *Action in the North Atlantic*
        The Amazing Mrs. Holliday
1950   *Mystery Submarine*
Torrance (CA)
1951   *Queen for a Day*
Torréon (Mexico)
1916   *Following the Flag in Mexico*
Torture
1915   *The Sable Lorcha*
1919   *Mandarin's Gold*
1928   Ransom
1931   *La ley del harem*
        El príncipe gondolero
1932   *The Son-Daughter*
1933   *Dos noches*
1935   *Circle of Death*
1935? *The Irish Gringo*
1936   Desert Gold
1937   *The Riders of the Whistling Skull*
1940   *The Man I Married*
        Northwest Passage (Book I—Rogers' Rangers)
1947   *Pirates of Monterey*
1948   *Unconquered*
1949   *Border Incident*
        Streets of Laredo
1950   *Broken Arrow*
        North of the Great Divide
1952   *Indian Uprising*
1953   *Conquest of Cochise*
1957   *The Brothers Rico*
        Journey to Freedom
        Pawnee
        Run of the Arrow
1958   *Apache Territory*
1959   *Shake Hands with the Devil*

Tour guides
1933   L'amour guide
1947   *Untamed Fury*
1949   *Boston Blackie's Chinese Venture*
Tourists
1920   The Luck of the Irish
1928   Chinatown Charlie
1929   Chinatown Nights
1930   The Big Pond
1931   Charlie Chan Carries On
1932   Men Are Such Fools
1933   *La melodía prohibida*
1939   *Mr. Moto Takes a Vacation*
1947   *Untamed Fury*
1950   *Chinatown at Midnight*
Tournaments
1951   *The Harlem Globetrotters*
1954   *Go Man Go*
Towers
1918   *The Golden Wall*
Toxicologists
        The Honor of His House
Toy trains
1951   *Queen for a Day*
Toys
1931   *Mr. Lemon of Orange*
1948   *The Time of Your Life*
Track and field athletics
1926   The Campus Flirt
1951   Jim Thorpe—All-American
Trade unions
1915   *Coben's Luck*
1920   The Great Shadow
        Uncharted Channels
1926   The Passaic Textile Strike
1932   *Uncle Moses*
1935   Black Fury
        McFadden's Flats
1944   *An American Romance*
1945   *The Valley of Decision*
1954   Salt of the Earth
Traders
1918   The Man Above the Law
1926   The Barrier
        The Last Frontier
1927   The Overland Stage
1929   Frozen Justice
1930   *El dios del mar*
1932   Texas Pioneers
1933   The Emperor Jones
1935   *Fighting Pioneers*
1937   *Prairie Thunder*
1939   Allegheny Uprising
1941   *In the Land of the Navajo*
        Secret of the Wastelands
1946   *Dangerous Money*
1950   *Young Daniel Boone*
1956   *Frontier Woman*
        Westward Ho the Wagons!
1957   Dragoon Wells Massacre
1960   Comanche Station
Trading posts
1922   The Mohican's Daughter
1925   Justice of the Far North
1931   Oklahoma Jim
1937   The Barrier
        Hills of Old Wyoming
        The Riders of the Whistling Skull
1940   *Taku*
1946   *Wild Beauty*
1949   The Cowboy and the Indians
        Tale of the Navajos
1951   *Flaming Feather*
1952   *Navajo*
1952? *Call of the Navajo*
1953   *War Paint*
1955   *Chief Crazy Horse*
        The Vanishing American
1958   *Blood Arrow*
        Flaming Frontier
1959   *The Oregon Trail*
Traffic violations
1934   *Tres amores*
1941   *The Gang's All Here*
1944   *An American Romance*
Train conductors
1935   *Piernas de seda*
1944   *Chip Off the Old Block*
1950   *Train to Tombstone*
1951   *The Tall Target*

Train robberies
1946   Sunset Pass
1949   *Colorado Territory*
1950   Train to Tombstone
1952   *Apache Country*
        Rose of Cimarron
Train stations
1943   *The Amazing Mrs. Holliday*
1946   *Without Reservations*
1949   *Call of the Forest*
1950   *Mystery Street*
        Train to Tombstone
1952   *Bright Victory*
        High Noon
        The Quiet Man
1954   Indiscretion of an American Wife
1960   *Sergeant Rutledge*
Train wrecks
1915   *How Molly Malone Made Good*
1918   *I Want to Forget*
1925   Hogan's Alley
1928   The Crash
1934   *La ciudad de cartón*
1936   *Below the Deadline*
1946   *Saratoga Trunk*
1947   *Duel in the Sun*
1950   *Sunset in the West*
Trains
1914   *The Little Angel of Canyon Creek*
1915   *The Lamb*
1918   *Out of a Clear Sky*
1931   *Buster se marie*
        Noche de duendes
        Personal Maid
        Smart Money
        Sombras del circo
        Yankee Don
1932   *La foule hurle*
        Thirteen Women
1933   *The Emperor Jones*
1934   *Behold My Wife!*
        Un capitán de cosacos
1935   *Señora casada necesita marido*
1936   *After the Thin Man*
        Charlie Chan at the Circus
        Contra la corriente
1937   *Underworld*
1938   *Birthright*
        Little Miss Roughneck
1939   Heaven with a Barbed Wire Fence
1940   *The Man I Married*
        The Way of All Flesh
1941   *Sullivan's Travels*
1942   *Gentleman Jim*
        Mokey
        Twin Beds
1943   *Crash Dive*
        His Butler's Sister
        In Old Oklahoma
        Marching On!
1944   *Andy Hardy's Blonde Trouble*
        Chip Off the Old Block
1945   *Betrayal from the East*
        The Dolly Sisters
        Of One Blood
        Pride of the Marines
1946   *Without Reservations*
1947   *Desperate*
        It Had To Be You
1948   *The Dude Goes West*
        Sleep, My Love
1949   *The Clay Pigeon*
        Jiggs and Maggie in Jackpot Jitters
1950   *Sunset in the West*
        Train to Tombstone
1951   The Tall Target
1952   *It's a Big Country: An American Anthology*
        My Man and I
1953   *Cry of the Hunted*
        The Jazz Singer
1954   Apache
        Indiscretion of an American Wife
1955   *Bad Day at Black Rock*
1958   *The Defiant Ones*
        Seven Hills of Rome

1960   *Man on a String*
Trains—Pullman cars
1924   *Birthright*
1933   *The Emperor Jones*
Traitors
1918   *The Firebrand*
        Out of a Clear Sky
        The Prussian Cur
        The Reckoning Day
        The Source
1920   The Daughter of Dawn
1926   The Frontier Trail
1928   The Glorious Trail
1929   Hawk of the Hills
1935   Fighting Pioneers
1941   Min Jok Jay Hung Sing
1943   *Deerslayer*
1947   *Pirates of Monterey*
1948   Unconquered
1949   The Clay Pigeon
        Rose of the Yukon
1950   Young Daniel Boone
1952   Brave Warrior
        The Fighter
1953   Column South
1954   Battle of Rogue River
        War Arrow
1955   *Kiss of Fire*
        Santa Fe Passage
1957   Apache Warrior
1958   The Rawhide Trail
1960   Man on a String
Tramps
1917   *The Renaissance at Charleroi*
1918   *Huck and Tom; or, the Further Adventures of Tom Sawyer*
1919   The Unpainted Woman
1926   *The Flying Ace*
1927   The Way of All Flesh
1930   *La jaula de los leones*
        On the Border
1931   *Cimarron*
        Die Maske Fällt
1943   *Marching On!*
Trance
1921   The Hunger of the Blood
1925   *Custer's Last Fight*
1944   *Black Magic*
Transformation
1915   The Kindling
1916   The Thousand Dollar Husband
1919? America Was Right
1920   Hidden Charms
1931   Echec au roi
        Nuit d'Espagne
1932   *L'athlète incomplet*
        Mazel Tov
1933   The Wandering Jew
1934   *Behold My Wife!*
1937   *Natalka Poltavka*
1938   The Beloved Brat
        Gateway
        God's Step Children
        The Singing Blacksmith
1940   Behind the News
        The Fighting 69th
1941   Accent on Love
1942   Tales of Manhattan
1943   The Meanest Man in the World
1944   *Since You Went Away*
        Tender Comrade
        Tomorrow the World!
1945   The Bells of St. Mary's
1946   *Slightly Scandalous*
1947   *The Adventures of Don Coyote*
        Going to Glory, Come to Jesus
        The Return of Rin Tin Tin
1948   Gentleman's Agreement
        The Paleface
1949   *House of Strangers*
        Pinky
1950   The Toast of New Orleans
1951   *Five*
        Fort Defiance
        Go for Broke!
        The Harlem Globetrotters
1953   *So Big*
1954   *Arrow in the Dust*

1955 *Headline Hunters*
1956 *Full of Life*
  Hot Blood
1957 *Edge of the City*
  Ride Out for Revenge
  Run of the Arrow
  The Tin Star
1958 The Defiant Ones
  Houseboat
1959 Thunder in the Sun
1960 Man on a String
  Walk Like a Dragon

Translators
1915 *The Lure of Woman*
1936 *Ride, Ranger, Ride*
1940 *Behind the News*
1944 *An American Romance*
1949 *She Wore a Yellow Ribbon*
1953 *The Glory Brigade*
  The Pathfinder
1954 *Barefoot Battalion*
1955 *Headline Hunters*
  Kentucky Rifle

Transmutation
1942 Cat People
  Professor Creeps

**Transplantation of organs,
  tissues, etc.**
1931 *Such Is Life*

Transvestism
1933 *Man from Monterey*
1948 *Jiggs and Maggie in Court*

Transylvania (Romania)
1931 *Drácula*

Trapeze artists
  use **Aerialists**

Trappers
1917 *The Bronze Bride*
1927 Primitive Love
  Spoilers of the West
1929 Wolf Song
1930 Monsieur le Fox
1934 *Wheels of Destiny*
1936 *The Last of the Mohicans*
1946 *Swamp Fire*
1947 *Last of the Redmen*
1949 *Arctic Fury*
1951 *Across the Wide Missouri*
1955 *The Far Horizons*
1956 *Raw Edge*
1957 *The Deerslayer*
1958 *Blood Arrow*
1959 *The Oregon Trail*
  Yellowstone Kelly
1960 *Flaming Star*

Traps
1914 An Odyssey of the North
1915 *The Immigrant*
1918 *Hitting the Trail*
  The Reckoning Day
1932 *Thirteen Women*
1933 *King of the Wild Horses*
1934 *The Lone Defender*
1936 *The Bold Caballero*
1937 *The Californian*
1939 *Allegheny Uprising*
  Forged Passport
  In Old Caliente
  Mr. Moto in Danger Island
  Mr. Moto Takes a Vacation
  The Return of the Cisco Kid
1940 *East of the River*
  Mystery in Swing
  Phantom of Chinatown
1942 *Submarine Raider*
  Unseen Enemy
1945 *The Cisco Kid Returns*
  In Old New Mexico
  Salome, Where She Danced
  The Scarlet Clue
1946 *Rendezvous 24*
  Singin' in the Corn
  The Trap
1947 *Crossfire*
  Last of the Redmen
  Pirates of Monterey
1948 *Fort Apache*
  Gun Smugglers
  Miracle in Harlem
1949 *Border Incident*
  Illegal Entry
1950 *Bandit Queen*
  Cherokee Uprising
  Intruder in the Dust

  A Lady Without Passport
  The Palomino
  The Traveling Saleswoman
1953 *Arrowhead*
1954 *Massacre Canyon*
1955 *Bad Day at Black Rock*
  Duel on the Mississippi
1956 *Crowded Paradise*
1958 *Machete*
  Oregon Passage

Traps (Animal)
  use **Animal traps**

Travel
  use **Voyages and travel**

Traveling companions
1931 *Charlie Chan Carries On*
1938 *The Toy Wife*
1950 *Rock Island Trail*

Traveling salesmen
  A Ticket to Tomahawk
  Train to Tombstone
  The Traveling Saleswoman
1954 *Massacre Canyon*
1959 *The Sheriff of Fractured
  Jaw*

William Travis
1955 *The Last Command*

Treachery
1918 The Firebrand
1932 *Genoveffa*
1935 Charlie Chan in Egypt
1936 *Treachery Rides the Range*
1938 Marusia
1945 Samurai
1948 *16 Fathoms Deep*
1952 Indian Uprising
1954 *Drum Beat*
1955 *Kentucky Rifle*
  Seminole Uprising
  The Vanishing American
1956 Daniel Boone, Trail Blazer
  The Wild Dakotas
1957 Ride Out for Revenge

Treason
1914 Dan
  The Littlest Rebel
1917 The Secret Game
1918 The Hun Within
1919 Love and the Law
1920 *The Cup of Fury*
1934 *La veuve joyeuse*
1937 Old Louisiana
1939 Allegheny Uprising
1946 *Notorious*
1950 *The Iroquois Trail*
  Mystery Submarine
1953 Fort Ti
1954 *Sitting Bull*
1955 *Seven Angry Men*
1957 *Raiders of Old California*

Treasure
1921 *Love's Plaything*
1924 The Broken Law
1925 The Gold Hunters
1930 *Un hombre de suerte*
  Tom Sawyer
1931 *Huckleberry Finn*
1935 *Charlie Chan in Egypt*
1937 *El capitán Tormenta*
  Harlem on the Prairie
  *The Riders of the Whistling
  Skull*
  Thank You, Mr. Moto
1938 *The Adventures of Tom
  Sawyer*
1939 Drifting Westward
1940? *Mr. Washington Goes to
  Town*
1942 Whispering Ghosts
1946 Dangerous Money
1948 *The Feathered Serpent*
  The Luck of the Irish
1950 *Last of the Buccaneers*
1958 *The Lone Ranger and the
  Lost City of Gold*

Treasure hunts
1941 Dead Men Tell

Treasure Island (CA)
1939 *Charlie Chan at Treasure
  Island*

Treaties
1925 The Red Rider
1931 Don Juan diplomático
1933 *Diplomaniacs*
1935 *Cyclone of the Saddle*
1936 *Daniel Boone*
  Rebellion
  Treachery Rides the Range
1944 Buffalo Bill
1949 *Apache Chief*
  Massacre River
1950 Broken Arrow
  Comanche Territory
1951 *New Mexico*
  Oh! Susanna
  Snake River Desperadoes
  Tomahawk
  When the Redskins Rode
1952 *Battles of Chief Pontiac*
  Buffalo Bill in Tomahawk
  Territory
  Fort Osage
  Indian Uprising
  The Savage
1953 *Arrowhead*
  Conquest of Cochise
  Seminole
  War Paint
1954 The Black Dakotas
  Drums Across the River
  Taza, Son of Cochise
  Thunder Pass
  The Yellow Tomahawk
1955 *Chief Crazy Horse*
  *The Gun That Won the
  West*
  The Indian Fighter
  White Feather
1956 Pillars of the Sky
1957 *Naked in the Sun*
  Revolt at Fort Laramie
1958 *Blood Arrow*
  The Light in the Forest
1959 *Shake Hands with the Devil*
1960 *Walk Tall*

Trees
1918 *Tongues of Flame*
1919 False Evidence
1945 A Tree Grows in Brooklyn
1946 Three Wise Fools
1949 Shamrock Hill
1959 *The Oregon Trail*

Trench warfare
1918 *The Greatest Thing in Life*
1930 *Sombras de gloria*

Trials
1915 *The Cheat*
1915? *The Life of Sam Davis: A
  Confederate Hero of the
  Sixties*
  Sam Davis, the Hero of
  Tennessee
1916 Pudd'nhead Wilson
1917 Rosie O'Grady
1918 *Broken Ties*
  Free and Equal
  Huck and Tom; or, the
  Further Adventures of
  Tom Sawyer
  In Judgment Of
  Marked Cards
  Toys of Fate
  Woman and the Law
1919 Love and the Law
  Who Will Marry Me?
1920 *The Good-Bad Wife*
  On with the Dance
1921 As the World Rolls On
  The Gunsaulus Mystery
  The Secret Sorrow
1922 The Crimson Skull
1923 Flames of Wrath
1928 The Midnight Ace
1930 Monsieur le Fox
  Sombras de gloria
  El valiente
1931 La carta
  Cavalier of the West
  Cimarron
  Così è la vita
  La mujer X
  Oklahoma Jim
  El proceso de Mary Dugan
  Resurrección

1932 *Hidden Valley*
  Hombres en mi vida
  O festino o la legge
  Unashamed
  The Vanishing Frontier
1933 *Obey the Law*
1934 *The Fighting Hero*
  Judge Priest
  Massacre
1935 *Bordertown*
  Lem Hawkins' Confession
  The Singing Vagabond
  Te quiero con locura
1936 *The Traitor*
  Winterset
1937 *Black Legion*
  It Could Happen to You
  Maid of Salem
  Man of the People
  Slave Ship
  Souls at Sea
1938 *The Adventures of Tom
  Sawyer*
  Life Goes On
  Life Goes On
1939 *Allegheny Uprising*
  Confessions of a Nazi Spy
  Motel the Operator
1940 *Am I Guilty?*
  Behind the News
  Elsa Maxwell's Public Deb
  No. 1
1941 *Lady from Louisiana*
  Thunder Over the Prairie
1942 *Mokey*
  The Navy Comes Through
  The Vanishing Virginian
1943 Border Patrol
  Hitler's Children
  *The Meanest Man in the
  World*
1945 *Jealousy*
1948 Big City
  Jiggs and Maggie in Court
  The Lady from Shanghai
  My Girl Tisa
1949 *Brothers in the Saddle*
  The Daring Caballero
  The Girl from Jones Beach
  House of Strangers
  Knock on Any Door
  Pinky
  Ride, Ryder, Ride!
  Shamrock Hill
1950 *Black Hand*
  Emergency Wedding
1951 *Adventures of Captain
  Fabian*
  Gambling House
1952 *Anything Can Happen*
  The Fighter
  My Man and I
  The Raiders
1953 *Jack McCall Desperado*
1954 *The Black Dakotas*
  Broken Lance
1955 *Duel on the Mississippi*
  Trial
1956 *The Last Wagon*
  Reprisal!
1957 *Raiders of Old California*
  Twelve Angry Men
1959 *Gunmen from Laredo*
  Night of the Quarter Moon
  The Young Land
1960 *Key Witness*
  Oklahoma Territory
  The Sign of Zorro

Tribal chiefs
1917 *The Bronze Bride*
1919 *Auction of Souls*
  The Heart of Wetona
  Told in the Hills
1919? *In the Land of the Setting
  Sun; or, Martyrs of
  Yesterday*
1920 The Daughter of Dawn
1925 Tonio, Son of the Sierras
1926 *General Custer at Little Big
  Horn*
1927 The Slaver
1930 A Daughter of the Congo
1931 *Aloha*
1932 *Igloo*

1934 *Song of the Islands*
1935 Fighting Pioneers
1936 *Desert Gold*
        El diablo del mar
1938 *Mr. Moto Takes a Chance*
1940 *Prairie Schooners*
1944 *Tahiti Nights*
1948 *Renegades of Sonora*
        Unconquered
1949 Apache Chief
        *The Cowboy and the
            Indians*
        Laramie
        Massacre River
        Ranger of Cherokee Strip
        She Wore a Yellow Ribbon
1950 *Annie Get Your Gun*
        The Iroquois Trail
1951 *Across the Wide Missouri*
        Apache Drums
        The Last Outpost
        New Mexico
        Tomahawk
1952 *Desert Pursuit*
        Fort Osage
        Hiawatha
        The Savage
1953 *Arrowhead*
        *Captain John Smith and
            Pocahontas*
        *The Charge at Feather
            River*
        Column South
        Conquest of Cochise
        Last of the Comanches
        Seminole
        The Stand at Apache River
1954 *Apache*
        Battle of Rogue River
        The Black Dakotas
        Drum Beat
        Drums Across the River
        Siege at Red River
        Sitting Bull
        Taza, Son of Cochise
        They Rode West
        War Arrow
1955 *Apache Woman*
        The Far Horizons
        The Indian Fighter
        Kentucky Rifle
        Kiss of Fire
        White Feather
1956 *Comanche*
        *Davy Crockett and the
            River Pirates*
        Mohawk
        Pillars of the Sky
        Raw Edge
        Westward Ho the Wagons!
1957 The Lawless Eighties
        Naked in the Sun
        Pawnee
        Revolt at Fort Laramie
        Ride Out for Revenge
        Run of the Arrow
        Satchmo the Great
        Tomahawk Trail
1958 Blood Arrow
        Flaming Frontier
        The Light in the Forest
        *The Lone Ranger and the
            Lost City of Gold*
        Oregon Passage
1959 *Gunmen from Laredo*
1960 Flaming Star
        Walk Tall
Tribal life
1914 In the Land of the Head
            Hunters
1915? The Beachcomber
1917 *The Primitive Call*
1918 Hidden Pearls
1932 Igloo
1933 La melodía prohibida
1936 *El diablo del mar*
1949 *The Cowboy and the
            Indians*
        Tale of the Navajos
1952 Brave Warrior
        Hiawatha
        Red Snow
1956 *Mohawk*

Triplets
1946 *Slightly Scandalous*
Troilus and Cressida (Play)
1945 *A Tree Grows in Brooklyn*
Trojan War
1931 La regina di Sparta
Troop transports
1919 Love and the Law
1925 Friendly Enemies
Il Trovatore (Opera)
1935 *A Night at the Opera*
Truck accidents
1949 *Thieves' Highway*
1958 *The Defiant Ones*
Truck drivers
1938 *Birthright*
        Road Demon
1939 *Heaven with a Barbed Wire
            Fence*
1947 *Desperate*
1949 *That Midnight Kiss*
        Thieves' Highway
1952 Red Ball Express
1954 *Barefoot Battalion*
1955 *The Rose Tattoo*
Truck farmers
1921 Little Italy
1924 So Big
1953 So Big
Trucking
1941 The Gang's All Here
Trucks
1936 *Kelly the Second*
1937 *That I May Live*
1939 *Forged Passport*
1942 *Juke Girl*
1948 *Shep Comes Home*
Harry S. Truman
1951 *Go for Broke!*
Trumpets
1938 *Swing!*
1940 *Mystery in Swing*
1950 *Young Man with a Horn*
1960 *All the Fine Young
            Cannibals*
Trusts and trustees
1917 *The Squaw Man's Son*
1919 *Erstwhile Susan*
1936 *It Had to Happen*
1955 *A Man Called Peter*
Truth serums
1947 *Dark Delusion*
Tuberculosis
1918 *Fields of Honor*
1920 *Dinty*
        The Girl of My Heart
1928 Diamond Handcuffs
1937 *Boy of the Streets*
1945 *The Bells of St. Mary's*
1948 *The Miracle of the Bells*
1951 *Only the Valiant*
1955 *Chief Crazy Horse*
        A Man Called Peter
Tucson (AZ)
1942 *Lawless Plainsmen*
1948 *Western Heritage*
1950 *Broken Arrow*
1952 *Indian Uprising*
1953 *Conquest of Cochise*
1956 Walk the Proud Land
1958 *Fort Bowie*
Tug of war (Game)
1947 *Calendar Girl*
Tulips
1942 *Seven Sweethearts*
Tulsa (OK)
1932 *The Black King*
1949 Tulsa
        Tulsa
Tuna
1932 *Tiger Shark*
Tunnels
1934 *The Lone Defender*
1946 *Rendezvous 24*
1949 We Were Strangers
1951 *The Well*
1954 *Massacre Canyon*
1960 *The Day They Robbed the
            Bank of England*

Turkey
1919 Auction of Souls
        Who's Your Brother?
1957 *Journey to Freedom*
Turkey—History
1931 La regina di Sparta
1939 Cossacks in Exile
Turkeys
1944 *Going My Way*
Turkish Americans
1927 *Turkish Delight*
1952 *Anything Can Happen*
Turks
1919 Auction of Souls
1927 Turkish Delight
1939 *Charlie Chan at Treasure
            Island*
Turpentine industry and trade
1916 *Unprotected*
Turquoise
1949 *Tale of the Navajos*
Tuscarora Indians
1953 *The Pathfinder*
Tuskegee (AL)
1943 *Fighting Americans*
Tuskegee Institute
1918 *Free and Equal*
1923 Tuskegee Finds the Way Out
1940 George Washington Carver
1944 *The Negro Soldier*
1947 The Peanut Man
Tutors and tutoring
1918 *Her Moment*
1933 *Broken Dreams*
1944 *They Live in Fear*
1960 *Pay or Die*
Tututni Indians
1954 Battle of Rogue River
William Marcy "Boss" Tweed
1948 Up in Central Park
Twins
1915 The Sable Lorcha
        The Secret Sin
1916 The Scarlet Oath
        The Sign of the Poppy
1917 The Winged Mystery
1918 The Ordeal of Rosetta
1919 *Lasca*
        The Right to Happiness
1920 The Dark Mirror
1921 A Modern Cain
1925 Lights of Old Broadway
1926 Twin Triggers
1928 Wheel of Chance
1935 *Shir Hashirim*
1938? I due gemelli
1939 El otro soy yo
1942 Nazi Agent
1944 Andy Hardy's Blonde
            Trouble
        The Chinese Cat
        Slightly Terrific
1946 *Abie's Irish Rose*
        Slightly Scandalous
1956 *Giant*
1957 *The Ride Back*
Tycoons
1916 Hulda from Holland
1939 The Girl from Mexico
1940 *Too Many Girls*
1941 Accent on Love
        Hurry, Charlie, Hurry
1943 *Crime Smasher*
1946 Bringing Up Father
1947 Spoilers of the North
1949 *Shamrock Hill*
Typewriters
1946 The Red Dragon
Typhoid fever
1918 *Untamed*
1950 Stars in My Crown
1955 *Not As a Stranger*
1957 *All Mine to Give*
Typhus fever
1948 Angel in Exile
Typists
1938 Castillos en el aire
Tyrol (Austria)
1936 *Sins of Man*

**Tyrol
(Austria)—History—Uprising
of 1809**
1934 Granaderos del amor
U.S.O.
    use **United Service
            Organizations**
Ukraine
1937 Natalka Poltavka
1939 A Brivele der Mamen
1940 The Tragedy of
            Carpatho-Ukraine
1953 *Tonight We Sing*
Ukrainians
1938 Marusia
1939 Cossacks in Exile
Ultraviolet radiation
1936 *Charlie Chan's Secret*
Ulysses (Book)
1958 *The Young Lions*
Umbrellas
1926 April Fool
Umpires
    use **Baseball—Umpires**
Uncle Sam (Fictional character)
1940 *Elsa Maxwell's Public Deb
            No. 1*
Uncle Tom's Cabin (Novel)
1927 Topsy and Eva
1936 Dimples
Uncles
1916 *Civilization's Child*
        Hulda from Holland
        A Sister of Six
        Sold for Marriage
        Unprotected
        A Woman's Honor
        The Yellow Passport
1917 *The Little Boy Scout*
        The Wild Girl
1918 *Doing Their Bit*
        The Firebrand
        Mystic Faces
        Out of a Clear Sky
1919 *The Lord Loves the Irish*
        Love and the Law
1920 *In the Depths of Our Hearts*
1924 Racing Luck
1929 This Is Heaven
1930 *Alma de gaucho*
1931 *Delicious*
        Zein Weib's Lubovnick
1932 *El caballero de la noche*
        ¿Cuándo te suicidas?
        Mazel Tov
        Yiskor
1934 *Caravane*
        Dos más uno, dos
        Las fronteras del amor
        El tango en Broadway
        What a Mother-in-Law!
1935 *Naughty Marietta*
        Riddle Ranch
        *Señora casada necesita
            marido*
        Te quiero con locura
1936 *Border Phantom*
        Rainbow on the River
        Sum Hun
1938 *The Singing Blacksmith*
        Two Sisters
1939 *The Girl from Mexico*
        In Old Caliente
1939? *A Chinese Gains a Fortune
            in America*
1940 *Americaner Schadchen*
        Covered Wagon Days
        *Elsa Maxwell's Public Deb
            No. 1*
        The Great Advisor
        If I Had My Way
        Mexican Spitfire
        Mexican Spitfire Out West
        Music in My Heart
1940? *Mr. Washington Goes to
            Town*
1941 *Doomed Caravan*
1942 *In This Our Life*
        Mexican Spitfire at Sea
        Mexican Spitfire's Elephant
1943 *The Amazing Mrs. Holliday*
        Crash Dive
        *Mexican Spitfire's Blessed
            Event*

Wintertime
1944 *Dark Waters*
     Lake Placid Serenade
1945 *The Dolly Sisters*
     The Gay Senorita
     The Mummy's Curse
     Pride of the Marines
     Wanderer of the Wasteland
1946 *Border Bandits*
1947 *Desperate*
     The Mighty McGurk
     Riding the California Trail
1948 Four Faces West
     I Remember Mama
     Silver Trails
1949 *Masked Raiders*
     The Story of Seabiscuit
1950 *The Big Hangover*
     Deported
     Intruder in the Dust
     Last of the Buccaneers
     The Toast of New Orleans
1951 Adventures of Captain
     Fabian
     Fort Defiance
     Saturday's Hero
1952 *The Big Sky*
1953 *The Jazz Singer*
1955 *The Last Command*
1956 *The Catered Affair*
1957 *Pawnee*
1958 *Marjorie Morningstar*
1960 *Walk Like a Dragon*

Undercover agents
1930 *Así es la vida*
1931 *Law of the Tong*
1936 *The Traitor*
     West of Nevada
1937 Law and Lead
     Thank You, Mr. Moto
1938 Mr. Moto Takes a Chance
1941 *Road Agent*
1942 *Across the Pacific*
     Let's Get Tough!
1945 *Escape in the Fog*
     The Navajo Trail
     Of One Blood
1946 *The Red Dragon*
1947 *West to Glory*
1949 *Illegal Entry*
1950 Indian Territory
     A Lady Without Passport
     Mystery Submarine
1951 The Mark of the Renegade
     The Tall Target
1953 The Man Behind the Gun
1954 *Cattle Queen of Montana*
     Dangerous Mission
1957 Journey to Freedom
1959 *The Jayhawkers!*

Undercover operations
1934 *The Battling Buckaroo*
     The Fighting Hero
     Fighting Through
     Riding Speed
1936 *Sea Spoilers*
     Song of the Gringo
     Yellow Cargo
1937 Nation Aflame
1938 *California Frontier*
     Daughter of Shanghai
     Outlaw Express
     The Renegade Ranger
1939 *Gang Smashers*
     Straight to Heaven
     Trigger Fingers
1942 *Below the Border*
     Rio Rita
1944 *Marshal of Reno*
     Outlaw Trail
     The Racket Man
1945 The House on 92nd St.
1946 Border Bandits
     Rendezvous 24
1949 *Border Incident*
     The Dalton Gang
     Jigsaw
1950 I Killed Geronimo
1952 Apache Country
     Brave Warrior
1954 Overland Pacific
1956 *Crowded Paradise*
     Wetbacks
1960 *Pay or Die*
     This Rebel Breed

Understudies
1936 *Star for a Night*
Undertakers and undertaking
1948 *I Remember Mama*
     Shanghai Chest
1950 *Mystery Street*
     Storm Over Wyoming
1958 *The Last Hurrah*
1959 *Porgy and Bess*
     *The Sheriff of Fractured
     Jaw*

Unemployment
1919 *Deliverance*
1930 *La jaula de los leones*
     Sombras de gloria
1933 *Song of the Eagle*
1934 *Our Daily Bread*
1937 *The Cantor's Son*
     Nation Aflame
1938 *The Duke Is Tops*
1939 *Reform School*
     Winner Take All
1943 *Let's Have Fun*
1946 *Mantan Messes Up*
1947? *What a Guy*
1948 *The Time of Your Life*
1950? *Three Daughters*
1951 *Teresa*
1956 *The Catered Affair*
1957 *Edge of the City*
1960 *The Dark at the Top of the
     Stairs*
     Studs Lonigan

Uniforms
1932 *The Black King*
1933 *The Emperor Jones*

Union Pacific Railroad
1926 Buffalo Bill on the U. P.
     Trail

Unions
  use **Trade unions**

United Nations
1953 *The Glass Wall*
1959 *The World, the Flesh and
     the Devil*

United Service Organizations
1942 *Twin Beds*
1943 *Three Hearts for Julia*
1944 *Hi, Beautiful*
1945 *Where Do We Go From
     Here?*
1946 *Abie's Irish Rose*

United States—Defenses
1917 *How Uncle Sam Prepares*
1918 The Birth of a Race

United States—History
     The Birth of a Race
1939 *Man of Conquest*
     Way Down South
1940 Santa Fe Trail
1941 Land of Liberty
1944 *We've Come a Long, Long
     Way*
1945 Where Do We Go From
     Here?
1956 *Raw Edge*

United States—History—1815-1861
1950 Last of the Buccaneers
1951 The Tall Target

**United States—History—18th
  century**
1953 Sangaree

United States—History—1901-1909
1948 Fighting Father Dunne

United States—History—1909-1919
     I Remember Mama

**United States—History—19th
  century**
1931 Call of the Rockies
     Huckleberry Finn
1932 The Forty-Niners
1935 The Singing Vagabond
1936 Silly Billies
1937 *Old Louisiana*
     Souls at Sea
1939 Stand Up and Fight
1946 Song of the South
1947 Thunder Mountain
1948 The Arizona Ranger
1949 *The Prairie*
1950 The Baron of Arizona
1951 Across the Wide Missouri
     Cyclone Fury

1953 The Man from the Alamo
1955 Davy Crockett, King of the
     Wild Frontier
     Duel on the Mississippi
1956 *Mohawk*
1957 *All Mine to Give*
1959 *The Jayhawkers!*
1960 The Adventures of
     Huckleberry Finn

**United States—History—20th
  century**
1933 *The Man Who Dared: An
     Imaginative Biography*
1949 Tulsa

**United States—History—Civil War,
  1861-1865**
1914 Dan
     The Littlest Rebel
1915 The Birth of a Nation
     Marse Covington
     Under Southern Skies
1915? The Life of Sam Davis: A
     Confederate Hero of the
     Sixties
     Sam Davis, the Hero of
     Tennessee
1916 *Peck O' Pickles*
1926? The House on Cedar Hill
1929 The Overland Telegraph
1930 Abraham Lincoln
1934 *Beloved*
     Judge Priest
     Operator 13
1935 The Littlest Rebel
     So Red the Rose
1936 General Spanky
1937 The Plainsman
1939 Gone With the Wind
1941 *Land of Liberty*
     Western Union
1942 They Died With Their Boots
     On
1944 *The Negro Soldier*
1945 *Salome, Where She Danced*
1946 Renegade Girl
1948 Tap Roots
1950 Rocky Mountain
     Two Flags West
1951 The Last Outpost
1952 *The Battle at Apache Pass*
1953 Column South
     The Great Sioux Uprising
     Jack McCall Desperado
     San Antone
1954 The Black Dakotas
1957 Band of Angels
     The Guns of Fort Petticoat
     Raintree County
     Revolt at Fort Laramie
     Run of the Arrow
     War Drums
1958 *Flaming Frontier*

**United States—History—Colonial
  period, ca. 1600-1775**
1914 When Broadway Was a Trail
1916 Witchcraft
1917 The Hidden Children
     The Little Chevalier
1917? Barnaby Lee
1931 The Great Meadow
1936 Daniel Boone
1937 Maid of Salem
1939 Allegheny Uprising
1941 *Land of Liberty*
1943 Deerslayer
1944 Knickerbocker Holiday
1948 Unconquered
1950 Young Daniel Boone
1952 Battles of Chief Pontiac
1953 Captain John Smith and
     Pocahontas
1957 *The Deerslayer*
1958 The Light in the Forest

**United States—History—French
  and Indian War, 1755-1763**
1920 The Last of the Mohicans
1927 Winners of the Wilderness
1929 Evangeline
1936 The Last of the Mohicans
1940 Northwest Passage (Book
     I—Rogers' Rangers)
1947 Last of the Redmen
1950 The Iroquois Trail
     Young Daniel Boone

1951 When the Redskins Rode
1953 Fort Ti
     The Pathfinder

**United States—History—Indian
  campaigns**
1914 The Indian Wars
1917 The Adventures of Buffalo
     Bill
     The Buffalo Bill Show
1925 *Custer's Last Fight*
     Tonio, Son of the Sierras
1926 *General Custer at Little Big
     Horn*
1927 The Frontiersman
1940 Geronimo
1941 *Land of Liberty*
1950 Two Flags West
1951 Oh! Susanna
     Warpath
1952 The Battle at Apache Pass
     Bugles in the Afternoon
     Indian Uprising
1953 Arrowhead
     The Charge at Feather River
     Conquest of Cochise
     Seminole
1954 *Taza, Son of Cochise*
     They Rode West
     War Arrow
1955 Chief Crazy Horse
     The Gun That Won the West
     Seminole Uprising
1956 The Last Frontier
1957 Apache Warrior
     The Guns of Fort Petticoat
     The Lawless Eighties
     Trooper Hook
1958 Ambush at Cimarron Pass
     Gun Fever
     Oregon Passage
1959 Yellowstone Kelly

**United
  States—History—Reconstruction,
  1865-1898**
1915 The Birth of a Nation
1917 My Fighting Gentleman
1931 Cimarron
1935 *Circle of Death*
     The Little Colonel
1936 The Glory Trail
     The Prisoner of Shark Island
     Rainbow on the River
1938 The Texans
1939 Gone With the Wind
1940 *George Washington Carver*
     Hi-Yo Silver
1941 Belle Starr
     Land of Liberty
1942 American Empire
     They Died With Their Boots
     On
1948 Fort Apache
     Red River
1949 She Wore a Yellow Ribbon
1950 Indian Territory
     Rio Grande
1953 *Jack McCall Desperado*

**United
  States—History—Revolutionary
  War, 1776-1783**
1917 The Spirit of '76
1919 Evangeline
1922 Cardigan
1939 Drums Along the Mohawk
1941 *Land of Liberty*
1944 *The Negro Soldier*
1956 Daniel Boone, Trail Blazer
1959 John Paul Jones

**United States—History—Social life
  and customs**
1938 *The Toy Wife*
1939 *The Adventures of
     Huckleberry Finn*
1942 *Syncopation*
     The Vanishing Virginian
1944 An American Romance
1947 *Calendar Girl*
     Carnegie Hall
1948 Strange Victory
1950 *The Daughter of Rosie
     O'Grady*
     Rock Island Trail
1951 Westward the Women
1953 The Eddie Cantor Story

United States—History—Social life (cont.)
- 1955 The Long Gray Line
- 1960 Wild River

United States—History—War of 1812
- 1914 *Springtime*
- 1938 The Buccaneer
- 1941 *Land of Liberty*
- 1944 *The Negro Soldier*
- 1949 *The Fighting Kentuckian*
- 1950 *Last of the Buccaneers*

United States—History—War of 1898
- 1931 *Cimarron*
- 1933 *The Man Who Dared: An Imaginative Biography*
- 1934 *Beloved*
- 1941 *Land of Liberty*
- 1950 *The Daughter of Rosie O'Grady*

United States—History—War with Mexico, 1845-1848
- 1917 The Conqueror
- 1923 Jamestown
- 1927 California
- 1936 *Rebellion*
- 1939 Man of Conquest
- 1941 *Land of Liberty*
- 1957 *Raiders of Old California*

United States—Midwest
- 1919 Love and the Law
- 1930 Georgia Rose
- 1932 *So Big*
- 1934 *Wheels of Destiny*
- 1947 *The Farmer's Daughter*
- 1953 *So Big*

United States—Northwest
- 1914 *Hearts United*

United States—Senators
- use **Senators;**
  United States. Congress. Senate

United States—South
- At the Cross Roads
- 1915 The Nigger
- Under Southern Skies
- 1916 Broken Chains
- The Grip of Jealousy
- Pudd'nhead Wilson
- Unprotected
- 1917 *The Bar Sinister*
- The Bride of Hate
- My Fighting Gentleman
- The Renaissance at Charleroi
- 1919 Toby's Bow
- 1920 Within Our Gates
- 1922 Easy Money
- 1924 Birthright
- 1927 The Love Mart
- 1929 Hearts in Dixie
- Show Boat
- 1930 Georgia Rose
- 1935 *Harmony Lane*
- 1936 General Spanky
- Show Boat
- 1938 Birthright
- *Life Goes On*
- *The Toy Wife*
- 1939 Gone With the Wind
- 1940 *Paradise in Harlem*
- 1941 *Virginia*
- 1945 *Of One Blood*
- 1949 *Lost Boundaries*
- Pinky
- 1950 Intruder in the Dust
- *The Jackie Robinson Story*
- Stars in My Crown
- 1951 *Show Boat*
- 1953 *Jack McCall Desperado*
- The Sun Shines Bright
- 1954 *Carmen Jones*
- 1955 The View from Pompey's Head
- 1957 Segregation and the South
- 1958 The Defiant Ones
- 1959 *Porgy and Bess*
- 1960 *Wild River*

United States—Southwest
- 1949 She Wore a Yellow Ribbon
- 1952 *Apache Country*
- 1953 *Last of the Comanches*
- 1954 *Thunder Pass*

United States—West
- use **The West**

United States. Air Force
- 1952 Red Snow

United States. Army
- 1915 *Captain Courtesy*
- The Girl I Left Behind Me
- *The Lure of Woman*
- 1916 *The Daughter of the Don*
- Following the Flag in Mexico
- 1917 How Uncle Sam Prepares
- *John Ermine of the Yellowstone*
- *The Little Boy Scout*
- The Secret Game
- 1918 *The Birth of a Race*
- *The Greatest Thing in Life*
- 1926 The Fighting Edge
- War Paint
- 1927 Ham and Eggs at the Front
- 1928 United States Smith
- 1930 Anybody's War
- ¡De frente, marchen!
- 1931 *The Avenger*
- *Beyond Victory*
- 1934 Operator 13
- The Unknown Soldier Speaks
- 1936 *The Glory Trail*
- 1937 *The Barrier*
- Drums of Destiny
- 1940 *The Fighting 69th*
- 1941 *Land of Liberty*
- 1942 *They Died With Their Boots On*
- 1943 Bataan
- Fighting Americans
- 1944 Hi, Beautiful
- The Negro Soldier
- 1945 *A Medal for Benny*
- 1946 *Renegade Girl*
- Romance of the West
- 1947 *Buck Privates Come Home*
- Crossfire
- *King of the Bandits*
- 1948 *Old Los Angeles*
- 1949 *Laramie*
- Massacre River
- 1950 Battleground
- The Iroquois Trail
- Rocky Mountain
- 1951 *Cyclone Fury*
- Distant Drums
- *Mask of the Dragon*
- The Steel Helmet
- 1952 Red Ball Express
- 1953 *Seminole*
- 1954 Battle of Rogue River
- 1955 *Seven Angry Men*
- 1957 *Naked in the Sun*
- 1958 *Kings Go Forth*

United States. Army Air Corps
- 1943 Air Force

United States. Army. 442nd Regimental Combat Team
- 1951 Go for Broke!

United States. Army. 100th Infantry Battalion
- *Go for Broke!*

United States. Army. 36th Division
- *Go for Broke!*

United States. Army. Cavalry
- 1913? *The Call of the Blood*
- 1914 The Indian Wars
- *Northern Lights*
- 1914? The Lust of the Red Man
- 1915 *The Girl I Left Behind Me*
- The Lamb
- *The Penitentes*
- 1916 *Britton of the Seventh*
- *A Sister of Six*
- 1919 *Told in the Hills*
- 1922 Winning of the West
- 1925 *Custer's Last Fight*
- The Scarlet West
- A Son of His Father
- Warrior Gap
- 1926 *The Devil Horse*
- The Frontier Trail
- *General Custer at Little Big Horn*
- The Last Frontier

- Under Fire
- The Vanishing American
- 1927 Drums of the Desert
- The Red Raiders
- Spoilers of the West
- 1928 Orphan of the Sage
- Wyoming
- 1929 Hawk of the Hills
- In Old Arizona
- The Invaders
- 1930 A Daughter of the Congo
- 1931 Cavalier of the West
- 1932 *The Forty-Niners*
- Texas Pioneers
- *The Vanishing Frontier*
- *White Eagle*
- 1935 *Cyclone of the Saddle*
- Fighting Pioneers
- The Singing Vagabond
- 1936 Custer's Last Stand
- Ride, Ranger, Ride
- *Silly Billies*
- Treachery Rides the Range
- 1937 *The Plainsman*
- Prairie Thunder
- 1938 *Outlaw Express*
- *The Texans*
- 1939 *Bad Lands*
- 1940 *Arizona Frontier*
- Geronimo
- *Kit Carson*
- *Young Buffalo Bill*
- 1941 Saddlemates
- 1942 *Apache Trail*
- *Valley of the Sun*
- 1944 *Buffalo Bill*
- *Vigilantes of Dodge City*
- 1946 *Bad Bascomb*
- 1948 Fort Apache
- Fury at Furnace Creek
- Gun Smugglers
- 1949 *Apache Chief*
- The Gay Amigo
- She Wore a Yellow Ribbon
- 1950 Ambush
- Davy Crockett, Indian Scout
- *Devil's Doorway*
- I Killed Geronimo
- *Indian Territory*
- Rio Grande
- Two Flags West
- *Winchester '73*
- 1951 *Apache Drums*
- *Cavalry Scout*
- Flaming Feather
- *The Last Outpost*
- Little Big Horn
- Oh! Susanna
- Only the Valiant
- Slaughter Trail
- Tomahawk
- Warpath
- 1952 *Buffalo Bill in Tomahawk Territory*
- Bugles in the Afternoon
- *The Half-Breed*
- Indian Uprising
- The Savage
- 1953 Arrowhead
- The Charge at Feather River
- Column South
- Conquest of Cochise
- *The Great Sioux Uprising*
- Last of the Comanches
- *The Nebraskan*
- *Ride, Vaquero!*
- *The Stand at Apache River*
- War Paint
- 1954 *Apache*
- Arrow in the Dust
- *Cattle Queen of Montana*
- Drum Beat
- Hondo
- Massacre Canyon
- Sitting Bull
- *Taza, Son of Cochise*
- They Rode West
- Thunder Pass
- War Arrow
- The Yellow Tomahawk
- 1955 *Chief Crazy Horse*
- *Davy Crockett, King of the Wild Frontier*
- Fort Yuma
- The Gun That Won the West

- *The Indian Fighter*
- Seminole Uprising
- Smoke Signal
- White Feather
- 1956 *Comanche*
- The Last Frontier
- *The Last Wagon*
- *Pillars of the Sky*
- Quincannon, Frontier Scout
- *The Searchers*
- 7th Cavalry
- *Walk the Proud Land*
- *The Wild Dakotas*
- 1957 Apache Warrior
- *Dragoon Wells Massacre*
- *The Lawless Eighties*
- Pawnee
- Revolt at Fort Laramie
- Ride Out for Revenge
- *Run of the Arrow*
- Tomahawk Trail
- Trooper Hook
- War Drums
- 1958 Ambush at Cimarron Pass
- *Apache Territory*
- Fort Bowie
- Fort Massacre
- Oregon Passage
- *Tonka*
- 1959 *The Wonderful Country*
- 1960 Sergeant Rutledge
- *Walk Tall*

United States. Army. Corps of Engineers
- 1953 The Glory Brigade

United States. Army. Medical personnel
- 1943 *Bataan*

United States. Army. Military Police
- 1954 *Taza, Son of Cochise*

United States. Border Patrol
- 1948 *Shep Comes Home*

United States. Bureau of Indian Affairs
- 1934 *Massacre*
- 1951 *New Mexico*
- Snake River Desperadoes
- 1952 *Apache Country*
- 1953 Old Overland Trail

United States. Coast Guard
- 1914 The Yellow Traffic
- 1923 The Miracle Makers
- 1933 *The Cohens and Kellys in Trouble*
- 1934 *Lazy River*
- 1936 *Sea Spoilers*
- 1946 *Swamp Fire*
- 1956 *Wetbacks*

United States. Congress
- 1915 *The Birth of a Nation*
- A Texas Steer
- 1916 *The Fall of a Nation*
- 1921 A Divorce of Convenience
- *Shadows of the West*
- 1926 The Flaming Frontier
- 1927 Red Clay
- 1941 *Land of Liberty*

United States. Congress. House of Representatives
- 1931 *Cimarron*
- 1941 *Louisiana Purchase*
- 1947 *The Farmer's Daughter*
- 1950 *The Jackie Robinson Story*
- 1955 *Davy Crockett, King of the Wild Frontier*

United States. Congress. Senate
- 1918 *The Reckoning Day*
- Ruggles of Red Gap
- 1934 *Stand Up and Cheer!*
- 1955 A Man Called Peter

United States. Customs Service
- 1949 *C-Man*

United States. Dept. of Immigration
- 1922 Sky High
- 1936 *Yellow Cargo*
- 1941 *Come Live with Me*
- Ice-Capades
- 1946 G. I. War Brides
- 1947 *Buck Privates Come Home*
- 1949 Border Incident
- Illegal Entry

1950 A Lady Without Passport
1951 Gambling House
1953 The Stars Are Singing
1956 Wetbacks
United States. Dept. of Justice
1936 *Yellow Cargo*
United States. Dept. of State
1953 Dream Wife
United States. Diplomatic and Consular Service
1916 *Broken Fetters*
1917 *Rosie O'Grady*
United States. Federal Bureau of Investigation
1934 *The Lone Defender*
1939 Confessions of a Nazi Spy
    Daughter of the Tong
1942 *Nazi Agent*
1943 They Came to Blow Up America
1945 The House on 92nd St.
    Of One Blood
1946 *Rendezvous 24*
1947 Ride the Pink Horse
1959 The FBI Story
United States. Internal Revenue Service
1924 His Darker Self
United States. Marine Corps
1918 *The Unbeliever*
1919? *America Was Right*
1927 Rose of the Golden West
1928 United States Smith
1943 Air Force
1945 *Pride of the Marines*
1946 Shadows Over Chinatown
    Without Reservations
1950 Sands of Iwo Jima
1959 *The Young Land*
1960 All the Young Men
    Hell to Eternity
United States. Marshals
1925 Brand of Cowardice
1934 The Battling Buckaroo
    The Star Packer
1937 *The Californian*
1940 Girl from God's Country
1942 Below the Border
1944 Outlaw Trail
    Sonora Stagecoach
1945 The Navajo Trail
1946 Border Bandits
    Sun Valley Cyclone
1947 *Bowery Buckaroos*
    Marshal of Cripple Creek
    West to Glory
1948 Four Faces West
1949 The Dalton Gang
1950 Cherokee Uprising
    A Ticket to Tomahawk
    Winchester '73
1952 *The Raiders*
    Trail of the Arrow
    Wagons West
1954 *Saskatchewan*
1955 *The Vanishing American*
1956 The Broken Star
1957 *Raiders of Old California*
1958 Frontier Gun
    Ride a Crooked Trail
    Sierra Baron
1959 *Gunmen from Laredo*
    Last Train from Gun Hill
    The Young Land
United States. National Guard
1915 *The Birth of a Nation*
United States. Navy
1917 How Uncle Sam Prepares
1919 *Behind the Door*
1920 Who's Your Servant?
1926 Shadows of Chinatown
1927 Bitter Apples
1934 The Unknown Soldier
    Speaks
1937 *Boy of the Streets*
    The Devil's Playground
1938 *Hawaii Calls*
1939 *Confessions of a Nazi Spy*
1942 The Navy Comes Through
    Prisoner of Japan
    Submarine Raider
1943 Crash Dive
1944 *Chip Off the Old Block*
    The Sullivans

1949 *Lost Boundaries*
1950 *Mystery Submarine*
1959 *John Paul Jones*
United States. Presidents
1934 *Stand Up and Cheer!*
1936 *Rebellion*
1937 *Nation Aflame*
United States. Secret Service
    use **Secret Service**
United States. Supreme Court
1941 *Land of Liberty*
1951 The Magnificent Yankee
1957 Segregation and the South
United States. Treasury Department
1931 *La dama atrevida*
1949 The Undercover Man
United States. Vice Presidents
1941 *Hurry, Charlie, Hurry*
United States. War Department
1935 Rendezvous
1951 *The Tall Target*
United States. Women's Army Corps
1943 Fighting Americans
    Marching On!
1944 *The Negro Soldier*
1946 *G. I. War Brides*
1947 *Buck Privates Come Home*
United States. Work Projects Administration
1941 *Accent on Love*
United States Military Academy
1926 The Flaming Frontier
1940 *Santa Fe Trail*
1942 *They Died With Their Boots On*
1949 *Rose of the Yukon*
1950 *Rio Grande*
1955 The Long Gray Line
United States Naval Academy
    A Man Called Peter
Universities
1921 *By Right of Birth*
1931 Such Is Life
1941 *Thunder Over the Prairie*
1946 *Three Wise Fools*
1960 *Man on a String*
Universities and colleges—Alumni
1950 *The Big Hangover*
University of Notre Dame
1940 Knute Rockne—All American
University of Southern California
1926 The Campus Flirt
Unmarried mothers
1931 *Resurrección*
1951 *The Girl on the Bridge*
Unrequited love
1916 Alien Souls
    Britton of the Seventh
1918 The Hell Cat
    The Liar
    The Man Above the Law
    A Woman of Impulse
1919 His Debt
1921 The First Born
1930 *Estrellados*
    La jaula de los leones
1931 *Così è la vita*
    Regeneración
    Women Love Once
1932 The Golden West
    Yiskor
1933 *Counsellor at Law*
    Victims of Persecution
1934 Limehouse Blues
1935 *Shir Hashirim*
1935? *The Irish Gringo*
1937 *The Cantor's Son*
    The Jester (Der Purimspieler)
    Man of the People
    Natalka Poltavka
1938 *Mis dos amores*
1939 Gone With the Wind
1940 *Tengo fe en ti*
1942 Apache Trail
    Sunday Punch
    Woman of the Year
1943 *Doughboys in Ireland*
1945 *Between Two Women*
    Club Havana
    The Great John L.

1946 *Bringing Up Father*
    Till the End of Time
1947 *Bells of San Fernando*
    Mantan Runs for Mayor
1948 Tap Roots
1949 *Colorado Territory*
    The Prairie
1951 *Flaming Feather*
1952 *Woman in the Dark*
1953 *Fort Ti*
    So Big
1954 *Carmen Jones*
    Drum Beat
    The Yellow Tomahawk
1955 *Foxfire*
    The Gun That Won the West
1956 *Death of a Scoundrel*
    Frontier Woman
    Secret of Treasure Mountain
1957 *The Oklahoman*
1958 *Houseboat*
    Kings Go Forth
    Marjorie Morningstar
    Seven Hills of Rome
    Sierra Baron
1960 *All the Fine Young Cannibals*
Upper classes
1915 *The Adventures of a Madcap*
    The Kindling
    The Nigger
1917 Hashimura Togo
    A Jewel in Pawn
    A Kentucky Cinderella
    A Roadside Impresario
1918 Set Free
    A Woman of Impulse
1918? The Snail
1921 Hold Your Horses
    Society Snobs
1921? The Slave Market
1925 Old Clothes
1926 The Campus Flirt
    Millionaires
    Sweet Rosie O'Grady
1927 Sally in Our Alley
1928 We Americans
1930 Georgia Rose
    The Last Dance
    Sins of the Children
1931 Gentleman's Fate
1932 *Symphony of Six Million*
1934 Coming Out Party
    Las fronteras del amor
1941 *Up Jumped the Devil*
1946 *Saratoga Trunk*
1951 *The Great Caruso*
1955 *The View from Pompey's Head*
1958 *The Last Hurrah*
Uprisings
1914 *Where the Trail Divides*
1915 *The Girl I Left Behind Me*
    The Lure of Woman
1916 *Witchcraft*
1918 *The Source*
1930 *Las campanas de Capistrano*
1931 *Echec au roi*
1933 *The Emperor Jones*
1934 Un capitán de cosacos
1935 *So Red the Rose*
1936 *The Bold Caballero*
1937 *El carnaval del diablo*
1938 Mr. Moto Takes a Chance
1940 The Mark of Zorro
1941 *Doomed Caravan*
1946 *Don Ricardo Returns*
1949 Laramie
1950 *Colt .45*
    Two Flags West
1951 Apache Drums
1954 Thunder Pass
1955 Apache Ambush
    The Vanishing American
1959 Shake Hands with the Devil
Uranium
1946 *Notorious*
Uranium mines
1949 Rose of the Yukon

Urban life
1950 *Panic in the Streets*
1952 *Woman in the Dark*
1958 *The Last Hurrah*
1959 *The Black Orchid*
1960 *Take a Giant Step*
Usurpers
1919 *Diane of the Green Van*
1931 *Echec au roi*
1936 *Rebellion*
Usury
1925 *Salome of the Tenements*
Ute Indians
1951 *Flaming Feather*
1952 *Navajo*
1954 *Drums Across the River*
1955 *Smoke Signal*
1956 *The Burning Hills*
Vacations
1931 *La cautivadora*
1934 *Dos más uno, dos*
1935 *Shir Hashirim*
1936 *Charlie Chan at the Circus*
Vaccination
1949 *The Cowboy and the Indians*
Vacuum cleaners
1942 *Tortilla Flat*
Vagabonds
1924 Unseen Hands
1934 *Imitation of Life*
1939 El otro soy yo
1958 Apache Territory
    Never Love a Stranger
Valdez (AK)
1917 Alaska Wonders in Motion
Valets
1915 *After Five*
    The Spender
1916 Pudd'nhead Wilson
    The Yellow Passport
1918 Ruggles of Red Gap
    Who Is to Blame?
1923 Ruggles of Red Gap
1930 Take the Heir
1931 *Delicious*
1935 Ruggles of Red Gap
1936 *Hair-Trigger Casey*
    Mad Holiday
    My American Wife
1941 *Sullivan's Travels*
1942 *Whispering Ghosts*
1947 *Reet, Petite and Gone*
1948 *The Feathered Serpent*
1960 *The Sign of Zorro*
Valley Forge (PA)
1917 *The Spirit of '76*
1952 Bright Victory
1959 *John Paul Jones*
Vampires
1931 Drácula
Vamps
1915 The Clemenceau Case
1917 *Southern Pride*
1918 Who Is to Blame?
1924 In Hollywood With Potash and Perlmutter
1926 Blarney
1929 Hallelujah
1932 *Thirteen Steps*
1933 *Diplomaniacs*
1934 Cuesta abajo
1935 *¡Asegure a su mujer!*
    Lem Hawkins' Confession
1937 The Devil's Playground
1940 *Lucky Cisco Kid*
1941 *Murder on Lenox Avenue*
Vancouver (Canada)
1920 *The Cyclone*
Cornelius Vanderbilt, Jr.
1923 Little Old New York
Vatican City
1947 *Citizen Saint*
Vaudeville
1918? *Indian Life*
1926 The Strong Man
1929 Why Bring That Up?
1930 Behind the Make-Up
    Toda una vida
1933 Live and Laugh
1938 Little Miss Roughneck
    Swing!

1945 *Rhapsody in Blue*
1953 *The Eddie Cantor Story*

Vaudevillians
1931 *Beyond Victory*
1935 *Annie Oakley*
1940 *If I Had My Way*
1943 *Yankee Doodle Dandy*
1948 *The Boy with Green Hair*
     Killer Diller
1950 The Daughter of Rosie
     O'Grady
1951 *Tomahawk*

Vaults
1915 *Time Lock Number 776*
1945 *The Jade Mask*
     The Shanghai Cobra
1949 *The Daring Caballero*
1960 *The Day They Robbed the*
     Bank of England

Vegetarians
1936 *Paddy O'Day*

Vending machines
1952 *My Man and I*

Vendors
    use **Flower vendors;**
        News vendors;
        Salesclerks;
        Salesmen;
        Saleswomen;
        Street vendors;
        Traveling salesmen

Venice (Italy)
1915 *The Italian*
1921 *Puppets of Fate*
1930 *The Big Pond*
1931 *La ley del harem*
     El príncipe gondolero
1933 *Yo, tú y ella*
1940 *The Jewish Melody*

Ventriloquists and ventriloquism
1939 *The Bronze Buckaroo*
     Mr. Moto's Last Warning
1943 *Land of Hunted Men*
1945 *The Jade Mask*
1946 *Beauty and the Bandit*

Vermont
1958 *The Young Lions*

Versailles (France)
1959 *John Paul Jones*

Veterans
1917 *The Slacker*
1921 Anne of Little Smoky
1922 The Pride of Palomar
1924 *Birthright*
1926 *Puppets*
1928 Absent
     The Crash
     The Mating Call
     We Americans
1929 Abie's Irish Rose
1941 *New York Town*
1943 *Marching On!*
     Stormy Weather
1946 *Abie's Irish Rose*
     Gas House Kids
     Stars on Parade
     Swamp Fire
     Till the End of Time
1947 Buck Privates Come Home
     The Burning Cross
     Crossfire
     Desperate
     Easy Come, Easy Go
     Ride the Pink Horse
     Rustlers of Devil's Canyon
1948 *The Arizona Ranger*
     Key Largo
1949 The Clay Pigeon
     Illegal Entry
     The Red Menace
1950 *Belle of Old Mexico*
     The Big Hangover
     The Daughter of Rosie
     O'Grady
     The Lawless
     The Men
1951 *Cavalry Scout*
     Mask of the Dragon
     Teresa
1952 Bright Victory
     It's a Big Country: An
     American Anthology
     Japanese War Bride

1953 *The Glass Wall*
     The Jazz Singer
1955 *Bad Day at Black Rock*
     The Vanishing American
1957 *Joe Dakota*
1959 *Night of the Quarter Moon*

Veterinarians
1950 *Riders of the Pony Express*
     Sunset in the West
1953 *The Great Sioux Uprising*
1955 *Bad Day at Black Rock*
1956 *Ghost Town*

Joseph Damien de Veuster
1950 Damien

Vice raids
    use **Police raids**

Victoria, Queen of England,
1819-1901
     Annie Get Your Gun

Victorio (Chiricahua Apache)
1951 *Apache Drums*

Victory gardens
1943 *What's Buzzin' Cousin?*

Vienna (Austria)
1930 The Melody Man
1932 *Mazel Tov*
     Men Are Such Fools
1934 Granaderos del amor

Vigilantes
1917 The Captain of the Gray
     Horse Troop
1918 The Prussian Cur
     The Ranger
1925 Flower of Night
1931 The Avenger
1934 *The Prescott Kid*
1936 Robin Hood of El Dorado
     Rose of the Rancho
1938 *Spawn of the North*
1943 *Frontier Fury*
     Land of Hunted Men
1947 King of the Bandits
     Riding the California Trail
1948 *Shep Comes Home*
1958 *The Light in the Forest*

Francisco "Pancho" Villa
1916 Following the Flag in
     Mexico
1928 El Robin Hood de México

Village life
1918 *The Little Runaway*
1919 *Evangeline*
     False Evidence
1929 *Evangeline*
1934 *Eskimo*
1936 *Dancing Pirate*
1937 *The Cantor's Son*
     Natalka Poltavka
1938 *Happy Landing*
     Marusia
1939 *Tevya*
1941 *Ten Ostatni*
     Wiejskie Wesele
     Z Dymem Pożarów
1951 *Teresa*
1952 *The Quiet Man*

Villages
1948 Angel in Exile
     Angel in Exile
1949 *Apache Chief*
     The Prairie
1950 *The Iroquois Trail*

The Vilna Balabessel (Historical
person)
1940 Overture to Glory

Vilnius (Lithuania)
1934 The Rabbi's Power
1935 *The Yiddish King Lear*
1940 Overture to Glory

Vineyards
1918 *The Wine Girl*
1937 *The Holy Oath*
1947 *California*
1956 *Serenade*

Violinists
1915 *The Melting Pot*
1917 *The Tell-Tale Step*
     Unknown 274
1918 Love's Law
1919 *Deliverance*
     Yvonne from Paris
1920 Humoresque
     The Paliser Case

1921 No Woman Knows
1923 Potash and Perlmutter
1927 The Broken Violin
     The Way of All Flesh
1929 Is Everybody Happy?
     Smiling Irish Eyes
1931 *Tropennächte*
1932 *Hypnotized*
     Men Are Such Fools
1934 *As the Earth Turns*
     Beloved
     Caravane
     Strange Wives
1936 *La última cita*
1939 *Mamele*
1940 Broken Strings
     Jennie
     The Way of All Flesh
1942 *The Navy Comes Through*
1946 *Stars on Parade*
1947 Humoresque
1950 *God, Man and Devil*

Violins
1918 Love's Law
1935 *Charlie Chan in Egypt*

Virginia
1916 *The Colored American*
     Winning His Suit
1917 *My Fighting Gentleman*
     The Wild Girl
1919 Come Out of the Kitchen
1920 *The Good-Bad Wife*
1931 *Chérie*
     The Great Meadow
1932? *The Girl from Chicago*
1941 *Virginia*
1941? Hampton Institute: Its
     Program of Education for
     Life
1951 *Saturday's Hero*
     When the Redskins Rode
1953 Captain John Smith and
     Pocahontas
1958 *Houseboat*

Virginians
1921 The Sport of the Gods
1926 The Barrier
1937 *Maid of Salem*
1948 *Unconquered*
1959 *John Paul Jones*

Virginity
1919 The Heart of Wetona
     The She Wolf
1932 *Amore e morte*
1934 *Drums O' Voodoo*
1956 *Baby Doll*

Visions
1916 *Light at Dusk*
1917 *The Slacker*
1918 *Her American Husband*
     Uncle Tom's Cabin
1919 *Behind the Door*
1920 The Dark Mirror
1933 *The Emperor Jones*
1934 *La cruz y la espada*
     Eskimo
     Our Daily Bread
     The Rabbi's Power
1935 *Charlie Chan in Egypt*
     The Little Colonel
     So Red the Rose
1936 *Charlie Chan's Secret*
1943 *Marching On!*
1948 *The Boy with Green Hair*
1955 *Chief Crazy Horse*

Vocal instructors
1930 *Sevilla de mis amores*
1933 Melodía de arrabal
1956 *Serenade*

Vocational obsession
1933 The Man Who Dared: An
     Imaginative Biography
1939 My Son
1940 *Girl from God's Country*
1943 *Gangway for Tomorrow*
     Three Hearts for Julia
1948 Red River
1950 The Breaking Point
     Jolson Sings Again
1953 *The Eddie Cantor Story*
     Thunder Bay
1955 Foxfire
1957 The Ride Back

1959 *Imitation of Life*

Voice of America (Radio program)
1957 *Journey to Freedom*

Volcanoes
1923 The White Flower
1931 *Aloha*
1937 *Waikiki Wedding*

Voodoo
1917 Unconquered
1929 Hearts in Dixie
     The Witching Eyes
1934 Chloe: Love Is Calling You
     Drums O' Voodoo
1941 King of the Zombies
1946 The Face of Marble
1947 *The Foxes of Harrow*

Vows
    use **Oaths;**
        Pledges

Voyages and travel
1954 *Apache*

WACS
    use **Use United States.**
        Women's Army Corps

Wagers
1915 *Marse Covington*
1918 *The Wine Girl*
1919 The Last of His People
1927 Clancy's Kosher Wedding
     For the Love of Mike
     Pleasure Before Business
1930 *El dios del mar*
1931 *¿Conoces a tu mujer?*
     La pura verdad
     Zein Weib's Lubovnick
1932 Ljubav i strast
1932? *The Girl from Chicago*
1934 *Broadway Bill*
     Wheels of Destiny
1935 The Winning Ticket
1936 *Below the Deadline*
     Mad Holiday
1938 *Sugar Hill Baby*
1939 *King of Chinatown*
1941 *Saddlemates*
1943 *The Girl from Monterrey*
     Riding High
1947 *Body and Soul*
     Easy Come, Easy Go
1948 *The Time of Your Life*
1949 *The Cowboy and the*
     Prizefighter
     Jiggs and Maggie in
     Jackpot Jitters
     Rustlers
     Stallion Canyon
1950 *Broken Arrow*
1951 *Flaming Feather*
1952 *The Fighter*
     The Iron Mistress
     The Quiet Man
1953 *Tonight We Sing*

Wagon trains
1914 In the Days of the
     Thundering Herd
1917 *John Ermine of the*
     Yellowstone
1919 *The Westerners*
1924 California in '49
1925 The Red Rider
1926 Buffalo Bill on the U. P.
     Trail
     The Devil Horse
     The Last Frontier
1927 The Overland Stage
1928 Orphan of the Sage
     Wyoming
1929 The Invaders
1931 *Call of the Rockies*
     Fighting Caravans
     The Great Meadow
     The White Renegade
1932 *Call Her Savage*
     The Forty-Niners
     The Golden West
     Texas Pioneers
1933 *The California Trail*
     The Telegraph Trail
     Thundering Herd
1934 Wagon Wheels
     Wheels of Destiny
1935 *Circle of Death*
     Cyclone of the Saddle
     Fighting Pioneers

The Singing Vagabond
1936 *The Glory Trail*
The Phantom of Santa Fe
Silly Billies
1939 In Old Caliente
1940 Kit Carson
Prairie Schooners
1941 *Doomed Caravan*
The Pioneers
Saddlemates
1942 Lawless Plainsmen
They Died With Their Boots On
1946 Bad Bascomb
1947 California
1948 *The Paleface*
Red River
1949 *The Prairie*
1950 Broken Arrow
Cherokee Uprising
Davy Crockett, Indian Scout
Indian Territory
Rio Grande
Two Flags West
1951 Across the Wide Missouri
Warpath
Westward the Women
1952 Buffalo Bill in Tomahawk Territory
Fort Osage
Wagons West
1953 The Man from the Alamo
Old Overland Trail
1954 Arrow in the Dust
Massacre Canyon
1955 *Apache Ambush*
The Indian Fighter
Kentucky Rifle
Santa Fe Passage
1956 The Last Wagon
Westward Ho the Wagons!
The Wild Dakotas
1957 Dragoon Wells Massacre
Pawnee
1958 *Apache Territory*
Bullwhip
Sierra Baron
1959 The Oregon Trail
Thunder in the Sun

Wagons
1937 *Harlem on the Prairie*
1943 *Riding High*
1947 *Marshal of Cripple Creek*
1948 *The Dude Goes West*
Renegades of Sonora
1949 *Apache Chief*
1955 Kentucky Rifle
1959 *The Wonderful Country*

Waifs
1914 *The Little Angel of Canyon Creek*
1915 The Adventures of a Madcap
1916 *The Twin Triangle*
1919 The Sleeping Lion
1921 The Hunger of the Blood
One Man in a Million
Wing Toy
1922 The Five Dollar Baby
Pawn Ticket 210
1930 Tom Sawyer
1953 The Stars Are Singing

Waiters
1916 *Lord Loveland Discovers America*
1921 Society Snobs
1928 Sins of the Fathers
1929 *Sombras habaneras*
1930 *El precio de un beso*
1931 *Mr. Lemon of Orange*
Le petit café
1932 *Parigi affascina; ovvero, Malavita*
1933 *Grand Slam*
1938 The Rage of Paris
1939 *Winner Take All*
1940 Elsa Maxwell's Public Deb No. 1
1942 *Unseen Enemy*
1946 *Rendezvous 24*
1949 *The Daring Caballero*
Illegal Entry
1949? *The Joint Is Jumpin'*

Waitresses
1920 *In the Depths of Our Hearts*
1922 Big Stakes
1928 The Secret Hour
1930 Behind the Make-Up
A Lady to Love
1932 *Law and Lawless*
Me and My Gal
1936 *Kelly the Second*
1937 That I May Live
1938 *Speed to Burn*
1940 *They Knew What They Wanted*
1944 Lady, Let's Dance!
1949 *The Gay Amigo*
1950 *Mystery Street*
1952 *The Ring*

Wake Island, Battle of, 1941
1943 *Air Force*

Wakes
1958 *The Last Hurrah*

Waldorf-Astoria Hotel (New York City)
1942 *Tales of Manhattan*

Jimmy Walker
1957 *Beau James*

Walla Walla River (WA)
1919? *In the Land of the Setting Sun; or, Martyrs of Yesterday*

Wallpaper
1918 *Find the Woman*

Walruses
1912 *Atop of the World in Motion*
1927 Primitive Love
1928 The Great White North
1932 *Igloo*
1949 *Arctic Manhunt*

Wanderers
1917 Threads of Fate
1928 The Riding Renegade
1933 The Wandering Jew
1934 *The Rabbi's Power*
1935 *The Yiddish King Lear*
1937 Green Fields
The Jester (Der Purimspieler)
1940 *Overture to Glory*

War
1916 Three of Many
1920 *Before the White Man Came*
1931 Beyond Victory
1933 *Diplomaniacs*
1934 The Unknown Soldier Speaks
1935 *Alas sobre el Chaco*
1952 *Brave Warrior*

War atrocities
use War crimes

War bonds
1943 *The Gang's All Here*
Ladies' Day
1945 *Between Two Women*

War brides
1927 His Foreign Wife
1946 G. I. War Brides
1951 *Teresa*

War crimes
1956 *The Last Frontier*
1958 *The Young Lions*
1960 I Aim at the Stars: the Wernher von Braun Story

War criminals
use War crimes

War games
1943 *Fighting Americans*
1944 *Something for the Boys*

War heroes
1915? The Life of Sam Davis: A Confederate Hero of the Sixties
Sam Davis, the Hero of Tennessee
1919 The Lost Battalion
The Volcano
1926 *The Flying Ace*
1927 Red Clay
1933 *Song of the Eagle*
1934 Judge Priest
1936 *Sum Hun*
1945 A Medal for Benny
Pride of the Marines

1948 *Night Wind*
1950 Sands of Iwo Jima
1951 Go for Broke!
1955 *Bad Day at Black Rock*
1960 *All the Young Men*
Hell to Eternity

War injuries
1915 *The Birth of a Nation*
1916 *Pasquale*
1918 *The Unbeliever*
1920 *Humoresque*
1930 *Sombras de gloria*
Toda una vida
1931 *Beyond Victory*
1932 *Soñadores de la gloria*
1935 *So Red the Rose*
1943 *Bataan*
Doughboys in Ireland
1944 Lady, Let's Dance!
1945 *Pride of the Marines*
1946 *Gas House Kids*
1950 *Battleground*
1952 *Bright Victory*
1953 *The Glory Brigade*
1954 *Battle of Rogue River*
1955 *Apache Ambush*
Bad Day at Black Rock
1958 *Kings Go Forth*
The Young Lions

War materiels
use Munitions

War preparedness
1940 *The Ramparts We Watch*
1943 *Fighting Americans*
1944 *Tender Comrade*

War profiteering
use Profiteering

War refugees
1921 Through the Back Door
1941 *Come Live with Me*
Golden Gate Girl
Min Jok Jay Hung Sing
Sun Valley Serenade
They Dare Not Love
1942 *Seven Sweethearts*
Valley of Hunted Men
Woman of the Year
1943 The Amazing Mrs. Holliday
Gangway for Tomorrow
Three Hearts for Julia
1944 Lady, Let's Dance!
Since You Went Away
1945 *Jealousy*
1947 The Return of Rin Tin Tin
1949 *Answer for Anne*
1951 *The Girl on the Bridge*
The House on Telegraph Hill
1955 *Good Morning, Miss Dove*
1956 Singing in the Dark

War relief organizations
1943 *Mr. Lucky*

War veterans
use Veterans

War victims
1919 *Deliverance*
The Lost Battalion
Who's Your Brother?
1919? *America Was Right*
1941 Ten Ostatni
Z Dymem Pożarów
1951 *Go for Broke!*
1952 It's a Big Country: An American Anthology
1954 Barefoot Battalion
1958 *Kings Go Forth*
1960 *All the Young Men*
Hell to Eternity

Warbonnet Creek, Battle of, 1876
1914 *The Indian Wars*
1917 The Adventures of Buffalo Bill

Wardens
use Prison wardens

Wards and guardians
1914 Threads of Destiny
1915 *After Five*
Captain Courtesy
The Rosary
1916 *Gold and the Woman*
Witchcraft
1917 Forbidden Paths
The Sudden Gentleman

1918 *The Kaiser's Finish*
Love's Law
1919 *Told in the Hills*
1919? *The Brand of Judas*
When the Desert Smiles
1920 For the Soul of Rafael
The Tiger's Coat
1922 Head over Heels
Sky High
1928 George Washington Cohen
1929 *Die Königsloge*
1930 Around the Corner
1931 *Chinatown After Dark*
La fruta amarga
Le père célibataire
Resurrección
1932 *The Hatchet Man*
The Secrets of Wu Sin
1933 *L'amour guide*
1935 *The Cyclone Ranger*
Wolf Riders
1936 Dimples
Muss 'Em Up
Ramona
1937 One Mile from Heaven
1939 *Papá soltero*
1941 *Romance of the Rio Grande*
1942 *Mokey*
1944 *Marshal of Reno*
The San Antonio Kid
Sheriff of Las Vegas
Tucson Raiders
Vigilantes of Dodge City
1945 *Colorado Pioneers*
Great Stagecoach Robbery
Phantom of the Plains
1946 *California Gold Rush*
Santa Fe Uprising
Sheriff of Redwood Valley
Sun Valley Cyclone
Three Wise Fools
1947 *The Mighty McGurk*
1949 *Daughter of the West*
1950 *Stars in My Crown*
1951 *Saturday's Hero*
1953 *The Man from the Alamo*
1955 *Kiss of Fire*

Warehouses
1937 *Shadows of the Orient*
1939 *Forged Passport*
1942 *All Through the Night*
Rubber Racketeers
1945 *The Gay Senorita*
1946 *Dark Alibi*
1950 *Deported*
Panic in the Streets

Warrants
1949 *The Dalton Gang*
The Daring Caballero
Daughter of the West

Warsaw (Poland)
1935 *Bar-Mitzvah*
1936 *Yiddle with His Fiddle*
1940 *Overture to Glory*
1941 *Ten Ostatni*
Z Dymem Pożarów

Washerwomen
1919 *The Delicious Little Devil*

Booker T. Washington
1922 Spitfire
1923 Tuskegee Finds the Way Out
1940 *George Washington Carver*
1941 *Land of Liberty*
1944 *The Negro Soldier*

George Washington
1927 Winners of the Wilderness
1941 *Land of Liberty*
1945 *Where Do We Go From Here?*
1948 *Unconquered*
1951 When the Redskins Rode
1959 *John Paul Jones*

Kenny Washington
1940 While Thousands Cheer

Samuel Washington
1944 *The Negro Soldier*

Washington (D.C.)
1915 *The Birth of a Nation*
A Texas Steer
1916 *Peck O' Pickles*
1934 *Massacre*
Stand Up and Cheer!
1935 *Annie Oakley*

Washington (D.C.)
1936 *The Prisoner of Shark Island*
1938 *Breaking the Ice*
1939 *Man of Conquest*
1940 *Santa Fe Trail*
1943 *Crash Dive*
1944 *Buffalo Bill*
Charlie Chan in the Secret Service
My Pal Wolf
1945 *The House on 92nd St.*
1947 *Crossfire*
The Jolson Story
1950 *The Jackie Robinson Story*
1951 *The Magnificent Yankee*
1952 *Apache Country*
It's a Big Country: An American Anthology
1953 *The Stars Are Singing*
1954 *Drum Beat*
1955 *The Far Horizons*
The Gun That Won the West
A Man Called Peter
1958 *Houseboat*
1959 *The FBI Story*
1960 *The Crowning Experience*
Man on a String

Washington (State)
1935 *Ruggles of Red Gap*
1949 *Arctic Manhunt*

Washington's Expedition to the Ohio, 1st, 1753-1754
1951 *When the Redskins Rode*

Washington's Expedition to the Ohio, 2d, 1754
When the Redskins Rode

Watches
1933 *Charlie Chan's Greatest Case*
1934 *The Lone Defender*
1939 *Heaven with a Barbed Wire Fence*
1944 *Since You Went Away*
1945 *The House on 92nd St.*
South of the Rio Grande
1947 *My Wild Irish Rose*
1947? *What a Guy*
1949 *Apache Chief*
1955 *Good Morning, Miss Dove*
1958 *Fort Massacre*

Watchmakers
use Clock and watch makers

Watchmen
1921 *The Gunsaulus Mystery*
1930 *Los que danzan*
1935 *Lem Hawkins' Confession*
1937 *That I May Live*
1939 *Bad Lands*
1941 *Ride on Vaquero*
1949 *Jigsaw*

Water
1943 *Wagon Tracks West*
1949 *3 Godfathers*
1950 *Riders of the Pony Express*
1951 *Only the Valiant*
1953 *Last of the Comanches*
The Man Behind the Gun
Tumbleweed

Water-rights
1924 *The Heritage of the Desert*
North of Nevada
1947 *The Last Round-Up*
1954 *Broken Lance*
1956 *The Broken Star*

Waterfalls
1921 *The Cave Girl*
1925 *The Red Rider*
1941 *This Woman Is Mine*
1942 *North to the Klondike*
1948 *Unconquered*
1958 *The Light in the Forest*

Waterfronts
1930 *Anna Christie*
1931 *La fruta amarga*
1935 *Charlie Chan in Shanghai*
1941 *Dead Men Tell*
1942 *Unseen Enemy*
1950 *Panic in the Streets*

Stand Watie
1953 *The Great Sioux Uprising*

Wax museums
use Waxworks

Waxworks
1940 *Charlie Chan at the Wax Museum*

Wealth
1918 *The Golden Wall*
Out of a Clear Sky
1924 *In High Gear*
Smiling Hate
1925 *Lights of Old Broadway*
Old Clothes
1926 *Millionaires*
Sweet Rosie O'Grady
1927 *Finnegan's Ball*
McFadden's Flats
Pleasure Before Business
1929 *The Younger Generation*
1930 *¡De frente, marchen!*
The Last Dance
El príncipe del dólar
1931 *Aloha*
Delicious
El pasado acusa
Shulamith
1932 *Hypnotized*
1933 *The California Trail*
Dance Hall Hostess
1934 *Imitation of Life*
Tres amores
1938 *Birthright*
1939 *Judge Hardy and Son*
1943 *The Gang's All Here*
1945 *The Dolly Sisters*
1947 *Body and Soul*
Boy! What a Girl!
1949 *That Midnight Kiss*
1950 *Emergency Wedding*
1956 *Giant*

Joe Weber
1925 *Lights of Old Broadway*

Wedding anniversaries
1920 *The Riddle: Woman*
1933 *No dejes la puerta abierta*
1935 *Alas sobre el Chaco*
1947 *Desperate*
The Jolson Story
1950 *Catskill Honeymoon*
1953 *Tonight We Sing*

Weddings
1914 *In the Land of the Head Hunters*
An Odyssey of the North
Rose of the Rancho
The Woman in Black
1916 *The Flames of Johannis*
The Honorable Friend
Hulda from Holland
1917 *The Bride of Hate*
A Jewel in Pawn
A Kentucky Cinderella
1919 *Evangeline*
The Last of His People
The Volcano
Who Will Marry Me?
1920 *The Third Woman*
A Tokio Siren
1926 *A Prince of His Race*
1927 *Irish Hearts*
1929 *Abie's Irish Rose*
East Side Sadie
When Men Betray
1931 *Così è la vita*
Die Dreigroschenoper
Monerías
Oklahoma Jim
1932 *Hypnotized*
Mazel Tov
Me and My Gal
O festino o la legge
Senza mamma e'nnamurato
Soñadores de la gloria
Tiger Shark
Uncle Moses
The Unfortunate Bride
Yiskor
1933 *The Cohens and Kellys in Trouble*
Man from Monterey
La melodía prohibida
Olsen's Big Moment
1934 *La cruz y la espada*
Las fronteras del amor
He Was Her Man

The Rabbi's Power
Song of the Islands
1935 *Captured in Chinatown*
Julieta compra un hijo
Melody Trail
Rosa de Francia
The Wedding Night
The Yiddish King Lear
1935? *The Irish Gringo*
1936 *Contra la corriente*
Dancing Pirate
Desert Gold
The Glory Trail
Love and Sacrifice
The Phantom of Santa Fe
Yiddle with His Fiddle
1937 *Arshin Mal Alan*
The Californian
The Cantor's Son
I Want to Be a Mother
Manhattan Merry-Go-Round
Music for Madame
Natalka Poltavka
That Girl from Paris
That I May Live
1938 *In Old Chicago*
The Power of Life
Rascals
Two Sisters
1939 *The Cisco Kid and the Lady*
Daughters Courageous
Drums Along the Mohawk
Heaven with a Barbed Wire Fence
Mamele
Moon over Harlem
Tevya
1940 *Americaner Schadchen*
Covered Wagon Days
East of the River
The Jewish Melody
Mexican Spitfire
New Moon
Son of Ingagi
Viva Cisco Kid
1941 *Caught in the Act*
Hold Back the Dawn
In the Land of the Navajo
Min Jok Jay Hung Sing
Mystery Ship
Ten Ostatni
Virginia
Wiejskie Wesele
1942 *Friendly Enemies*
Tortilla Flat
Twin Beds
Valley of the Sun
Woman of the Year
1944 *Mr. Skeffington*
The Sullivans
Tahiti Nights
1945 *Anoush*
The Cisco Kid Returns
The Great John L.
1946 *Abie's Irish Rose*
Canyon Passage
1947 *Carnegie Hall*
Dark Delusion
Desperate
Hi De Ho
It Had To Be You
Sepia Cinderella
1948 *The Luck of the Irish*
Sleep, My Love
1949 *Anna Lucasta*
1950 *Bandit Queen*
The Furies
Give Us This Day
1951 *Across the Wide Missouri*
Flaming Feather
Hurricane Island
The Mark of the Renegade
Teresa
Westward the Women
1952 *My Man and I*
The Quiet Man
Red Snow
1953 *Dream Wife*
The Joe Louis Story
The Member of the Wedding
Tonight We Sing
1955 *Day of Decision*

1956 *The Catered Affair*
Crowded Paradise
Full of Life
Hot Blood
The Searchers
Walk the Proud Land
1957 *Bayou*
1958 *Houseboat*
Marjorie Morningstar
1959 *Anna Lucasta*
The Sheriff of Fractured Jaw

Welders
1944 *Since You Went Away*
1945 *Pride of the Marines*

Welfare fraud
1938 *Swing!*

Welfare workers
1939 *Miracle on Main Street*

Wells
1931 *Shulamith*
1937 *Natalka Poltavka*
1944 *My Pal Wolf*
1951 *The Well*
1953 *Last of the Comanches*

Wells Fargo & Co.
1934 *The Fighting Hero*
1941 *Road Agent*
1952 *Apache War Smoke*

Welsh Americans
1951 *Apache Drums*

Werewolves
1944 *Cry of the Werewolf*

The West
1914 *The Little Angel of Canyon Creek*
1916 *The Flower of No Man's Land*
1917 *The Buffalo Bill Show*
1919 *The Gray Towers Mystery*
1920 *The Symbol of the Unconquered*
The Third Woman
1931 *Cavalier of the West*
Yankee Don
1932 *The Golden West*
1933 *The Telegraph Trail*
1934 *Wheels of Destiny*
1935 *Ruggles of Red Gap*
1936 *My American Wife*
1941 *Western Union*
1942 *Shut My Big Mouth*
They Died With Their Boots On
1946 *Bad Bascomb*
1947 *Bowery Buckaroos*
1948 *Unconquered*
1949? *Come On, Cowboy!*
1950 *Jiggs and Maggie Out West*
The Traveling Saleswoman
1951 *Cavalry Scout*
Westward the Women
1952 *Buffalo Bill in Tomahawk Territory*
1953 *Jack McCall Desperado*
1955 *The Far Horizons*
Kentucky Rifle

West Hoboken (NJ)
1918 *Good-Bye, Bill*

West Indies
1959 *John Paul Jones*

West Point
use United States Military Academy

Western Union
1941 *Western Union*

Western Wall (Jerusalem)
1931 *The Voice of Israel*

Whales and whaling
1925 *Justice of the Far North*
1928 *The Great White North*
1931 *Dämon des Meeres*
En cada puerto un amor
1932 *Igloo*
1934 *Eskimo*
1946 *Strange Voyage*
1948 *Harpoon*
1949 *Arctic Manhunt*

Wharfs
1951 *The Raging Tide*

Wheat
1919 *The Unpainted Woman*
1931 *La fiesta del diablo*
Wheelchairs
1955 *The Lonesome Trail*
1960 *The Crowning Experience*
Whips and whippings
1928 The Broken Mask
The Midnight Ace
1930 Son of the Gods
1932 *Amore e morte*
Call Her Savage
Yiskor
1933 *Dos noches*
1936 *Desert Gold*
1947 *Bells of San Fernando*
California
1948 *Silver Trails*
1949 *Arctic Manhunt*
1950 *Cherokee Uprising*
North of the Great Divide
1952 *California Conquest*
1953 *Captain John Smith and*
Pocahontas
1955 *Kiss of Fire*
1956 *The Wild Dakotas*
1958 *Bullwhip*
Whistling
1942 *Tales of Manhattan*
1944 *The Sullivans*
Whitby (England)
1931 *Dracula*
White-slave traffic
1913 The Inside of the White
Slave Traffic
Traffic in Souls
1916 Broken Fetters
For the Defense
1919 *A Man's Duty*
1921? *The Slave Market*
Marcus Whitman
1919? In the Land of the Setting
Sun; or, Martyrs of
Yesterday
Wichita (KS)
1931 *Cimarron*
Widowers
1918 Wanted, a Mother
1921 *All Souls' Eve*
1922 The Top O' the Morning
1930 *Anna Christie*
Doña mentiras
Wu Li Chang
1932 *Cuore d'emigrante*
Hearts of Humanity
Unashamed
1933 *Broken Dreams*
The Cohens and Kellys in
Trouble
1934 *Judge Priest*
1936 Sins of Man
1939 *Mamele*
1940 *Little Nellie Kelly*
1941 *Adam Had Four Sons*
1942 *Mokey*
Seven Sweethearts
Tortilla Flat
1944 *Chip Off the Old Block*
Minstrel Man
Tomorrow the World!
1948 *Gentleman's Agreement*
1950 *The Daughter of Rosie*
O'Grady
1951 *Across the Wide Missouri*
Distant Drums
The Girl on the Bridge
1954 *Hondo*
1955 *Davy Crockett, King of the*
Wild Frontier
The Last Command
Smoke Signal
1957 *The Oklahoman*
1958 *Houseboat*
Wild Is the Wind
1959 *The Jayhawkers!*
Widows
1915 *The Lure of Woman*
1917 *A Jewel in Pawn*
A Kentucky Cinderella
The Sudden Gentleman
The Woman and the Beast
1918 *Little Red Decides*
Ruggles of Red Gap

1919 *A Fighting Colleen*
1920 *Huckleberry Finn*
1921 The Secret Sorrow
Through the Back Door
1926 A Trip to Chinatown
1927 Turkish Delight
1928 Mother Machree
Ransom
1930 *El cuerpo del delito*
My Yiddishe Mama
1931 *Chérie*
The Cisco Kid
Cuerpo y alma
Huckleberry Finn
1932 *¿Cuándo te suicidas?*
The Forty-Niners
So Big
1933 *Una viuda romántica*
1934 *Imitation of Life*
Lazy River
La veuve joyeuse
Wagon Wheels
1935 *His Family Tree*
Ruggles of Red Gap
1936 *Rainbow on the River*
1937 *Maid of Salem*
1938 *God's Step Children*
Life Goes On
1939 *Drums Along the Mohawk*
Fisherman's Wharf
Gone With the Wind
The Light Ahead
Moon over Harlem
1940 The Great Advisor
Lucky Cisco Kid
1941 *Sullivan's Travels*
1942 *Apache Trail*
1944 *Chip Off the Old Block*
Tender Comrade
1945 *The Valley of Decision*
1946 *Bad Bascomb*
Till the End of Time
1947 *Carnegie Hall*
The Peanut Man
The Return of Rin Tin Tin
1948 *Key Largo*
1949 *The Clay Pigeon*
House of Strangers
Illegal Entry
Satan's Cradle
1950 *The Cariboo Trail*
Deported
Mystery Submarine
Two Flags West
1951 *Molly*
A Streetcar Named Desire
Westward the Women
1952 *The Fighter*
My Man and I
The Quiet Man
The Raiders
1953 *The Member of the*
Wedding
So Big
1954 *War Arrow*
1955 *The Indian Fighter*
The Long Gray Line
Marty
Not As a Stranger
The Rose Tattoo
1956 Man from Del Rio
Raw Edge
1957 *The Oklahoman*
The Tin Star
1958 *The Last Hurrah*
1959 *Imitation of Life*
The Jayhawkers!
1960 *The Adventures of*
Huckleberry Finn
The Dark at the Top of the
Stairs
The Day They Robbed the
Bank of England
Wild River
Wigs
1930 *Una cana al aire*
1942 *Shut My Big Mouth*
1943 *Mexican Spitfire's Blessed*
Event
1959 *The Crimson Kimono*
Wild animals
1912 The Alaska-Siberian
Expedition
1931 The Cohens and Kellys in
Africa

1932 Dangers of the Arctic
1952 *Red Snow*
Wild horses
1930 Cuando el amor ríe
1932 *Mystery Ranch*
1947 Wild Horse Mesa
1949 Call of the Forest
Stallion Canyon
1958 *Wild Is the Wind*
Wild West shows
1944 *Buffalo Bill*
1950 Annie Get Your Gun
1955 *The Gun That Won the*
West
Wilderness areas
1952 Red Snow
1955 Davy Crockett, King of the
Wild Frontier
1956 *Davy Crockett and the*
River Pirates
Wilhelm II, German Emperor,
1859-1941
1918 *Good-Bye, Bill*
The Kaiser's Finish
The Prussian Cur
Wilhelm, Crown Prince of
Germany, 1882-1951
The Kaiser's Finish
William F. Cody
use **Buffalo Bill Cody**
William H. Bonney
use **Billy the Kid**
Williamsburg (VA)
1951 *When the Redskins Rode*
Wills
1916 The Thousand Dollar
Husband
1917 The Red Woman
A Wife by Proxy
1922 Uncle Jasper's Will
1924 Unseen Hands
1930 Le spectre vert
La voluntad del muerto
1931 *Cheri-Bibi*
1932 *The Hatchet Man*
1934 *Caravane*
1936 *Amor que vuelve*
Charlie Chan's Secret
1938 *Birthright*
1939 *The Mystery of Mr. Wong*
Papá soltero
1940 *Doomed to Die*
Mystery in Swing
Son of Ingagi
1945 *Wanderer of the Wasteland*
1946 Singin' in the Corn
1947 Reet, Petite and Gone
Riding the California Trail
1949 *Pinky*
1950 *Stars in My Crown*
1951 *The Magnificent Yankee*
1953 *Sangaree*
1956 *The White Squaw*
1958 *Bullwhip*
Thomas Wilson
1944 *The Negro Soldier*
Woodrow Wilson
1918 *The Prussian Cur*
1940 *The Ramparts We Watch*
1941 *Land of Liberty*
Wiltwyck School for Boys
1949 The Quiet One
Walter Winchell
1938 *Gateway*
Wind storms
1940 *Phantom of Chinatown*
1953 *Ambush at Tomahawk Gap*
1960 *The Unforgiven*
Windmills
1942 *Seven Sweethearts*
Window washers
1940 *Mexican Spitfire Out West*
Wine
use **Wine and wine making**
Wine and wine making
1930 A Lady to Love
1934 *Caravane*
1942 *Tortilla Flat*
1959 *Thunder in the Sun*

Wine cellars
1946 *Notorious*
Winnebago (WI)
1921 No Woman Knows
Winter
No Woman Knows
1949 *Portrait of Jennie*
Wire-tapping
1936 *Ellis Island*
1942 *Foreign Agent*
Wisconsin
1920 *In the Depths of Our Hearts*
1945 *Our Vines Have Tender*
Grapes
1957 *All Mine to Give*
Wishes
1917 The Bottle Imp
1945 *Where Do We Go From*
Here?
Witch doctors
1925 Kivalina of the Ice Lands
Witchcraft
1914 *When Broadway Was a*
Trail
1916 Witchcraft
1937 *Maid of Salem*
1939 *The Devil's Daughter*
Witnesses
1930 *Sombras de gloria*
1940 *Paradise in Harlem*
1945 *Johnny Angel*
1947 *The Burning Cross*
1949 *The Undercover Man*
1954 *Dangerous Mission*
1955 *Trial*
1956 *The Broken Star*
1959 *Porgy and Bess*
1960 Key Witness
Wives
1931 Los calaveras
Politiquerías
1935 *¡Asegure a su mujer!*
1938 *Swing!*
1939 *Charlie Chan at Treasure*
Island
1941 *Accent on Love*
Caught in the Act
King of the Zombies
1942 *Tales of Manhattan*
1943 *Ladies' Day*
1944 *Address Unknown*
Something for the Boys
1946 *The Trap*
1949 *She Wore a Yellow Ribbon*
1952 High Noon
1953 *Cry of the Hunted*
1959 *The Last Angry Man*
Wives—Employment
use **Working wives**
Thomas Wolfe
1951 *Gambling House*
Wolves
1934 *The Lone Defender*
Woman haters
use **Misogyny**
Womanizers
1931 *Gente alegre*
Nuit d'Espagne
1932 *Amore e morte*
1935 *Angelina o el honor de un*
brigadier
1943 *Crash Dive*
Tahiti Honey
1946 *The Gay Cavalier*
1957 *Beau James*
Women air pilots
1934 *Las fronteras del amor*
1937 *Shadows of the Orient*
1938 Mr. Moto Takes a Chance
1941 *Mutiny in the Arctic*
Women defense plant workers
1944 *Since You Went Away*
Something for the Boys
Tender Comrade
Women explorers
1941 *Mutiny in the Arctic*
Women gangsters
1933 *It's Great to Be Alive*
Women in business
1921 No Woman Knows
1930 Sei tu l'amore
1932 *Hollywood, ciudad de*
ensueño

Women in business
1934   Imitation of Life
1939   *Mirele Efros*
1941   *Doomed Caravan*
1950   *Comanche Territory*
         The Traveling Saleswoman
1958   Bullwhip
Women in politics
1916   The Fall of a Nation
1931   *Cimarron*
1953   Dream Wife
1960   The Crowning Experience
Women lawyers
1918   The Reckoning Day
1923   Flames of Wrath
1950   *Devil's Doorway*
Women military officers
1943   *Fighting Americans*
Women outlaws
1949   *Masked Raiders*
1951   *Slaughter Trail*
Women physicians
1933   It's Great to Be Alive
1945   *Jealousy*
1949   The Cowboy and the Indians
Women priests
1934   Drums O' Voodoo
Women prisoners
1931   *Such Is Life*
1951   *Hurricane Island*
Women ranchers
1940   The Gay Caballero
1943   *The Ox-Bow Incident*
1944   *Marshal of Reno*
         The San Antonio Kid
         Tucson Raiders
1945   Phantom of the Plains
1946   *Sheriff of Redwood Valley*
1949   *Stallion Canyon*
1950   The Palomino
1954   Hondo
Women reporters
1930   *King of Jazz*
1931   *Cimarron*
1936   Human Cargo
1937   One Mile from Heaven
1938   *Mr. Moto's Gamble*
1940   The Fatal Hour
1944   *Lifeboat*
1947   *The Chinese Ring*
Women sheriffs
1950   A Ticket to Tomahawk
Women soldiers
1957   The Guns of Fort Petticoat
Women's rights
1934   The Youth of Russia
1953   Dream Wife
Women's suffrage
1933   *The Man Who Dared: An
         Imaginative Biography*
1935   *Rendezvous*
1942   *The Vanishing Virginian*
Wooden shoes
    use **Clogs**
Woodsmen
1919   The Last of His People
Woodworkers
1918? Rosemary Climbs the
         Heights
Woolen mills
1925   Abie's Imported Bride
George Woolf
1949   *The Story of Seabiscuit*
Workaholics
    use **Vocational obsession**
Working wives
1933   No dejes la puerta abierta
1934   *Beloved*
Working women
1920   *Within Our Gates*
1942   *The Vanishing Virginian*
World Series (Baseball)
1943   *Ladies' Day*
World War I
1916   Arms and the Woman
         Three of Many
1917   How Uncle Sam Prepares
         The Little American
         The Slacker
1918   An Alien Enemy
         The Birth of a Race
         A Broadway Scandal
         Doing Their Bit

         Fields of Honor
         The Firebrand
         Good-Bye, Bill
         The Greatest Thing in Life
         His Birthright
         The Hun Within
         I Want to Forget
         Johanna Enlists
         The Kaiser's Finish
         Me Und Gott
         Mystic Faces
         Out of a Clear Sky
         The Price of Applause
         The Prussian Cur
         The Reckoning Day
         Shifting Sands
         The Source
         The Spreading Evil
         The Unbeliever
         The Yellow Dog
1919   Behind the Door
         Injustice
         The Lost Battalion
         Love and the Law
         The Other Man's Wife
1919? America Was Right
1920   The Cup of Fury
         Dangerous Days
         Humoresque
1921   *Shadows of the West*
         Through the Back Door
1923   The Miracle Makers
1925   *Friendly Enemies*
1926   The Fighting Deacon
         Private Izzy Murphy
         Puppets
         Rose of the Tenements
         The Strong Man
1927   Ham and Eggs at the Front
         His Foreign Wife
         Lost at the Front
         Red Clay
1928   Anybody Here Seen Kelly?
         Heart Trouble
         A Ship Comes In
         We Americans
1929   Abie's Irish Rose
         Love, Live and Laugh
1930   Anybody's War
         ¡De frente, marchen!
         King of Jazz
         Sombras de gloria
         Toda una vida
         El valiente
1931   Beyond Victory
         Cuerpo y alma
         El impostor
         Monerías
         El tenorio del harem
1933   *Ever in My Heart*
         *The Man Who Dared: An
         Imaginative Biography*
         Song of the Eagle
         The Wandering Jew
1934   *Beloved*
         The Rabbi's Power
         *The Unknown Soldier
         Speaks*
1935   Rendezvous
1936   *Hair-Trigger Casey*
         Sins of Man
1939   *A Brivele der Mamen*
1940   The Fighting 69th
         The Ramparts We Watch
1941   *Adam Had Four Sons*
         Land of Liberty
1942   *Friendly Enemies*
         Syncopation
1943   *Stormy Weather*
         Yankee Doodle Dandy
1944   *An American Romance*
         Mr. Skeffington
         The Negro Soldier
1945   *The Dolly Sisters*
1953   *Tonight We Sing*
1955   *The Long Gray Line*
World War II
1940   Escape to Glory
         The Ramparts We Watch
         Three Faces West
         The Tragedy of
         Carpatho-Ukraine
1941   *King of the Zombies*
         Ten Ostatni
         They Dare Not Love

         Z Dymem Požarów
1942   Across the Pacific
         Let's Get Tough!
         Little Tokyo, U.S.A.
         The Navy Comes Through
         Prisoner of Japan
         Valley of Hunted Men
         Wings for the Eagle
1943   Action in the North Atlantic
         Fighting Americans
         Hitler's Children
         Mr. Lucky
         Stormy Weather
         *They Came to Blow Up
         America*
1944   *An American Romance*
         Lifeboat
         Mr. Skeffington
         The Negro Soldier
         The Racket Man
         Since You Went Away
         The Sullivans
         We've Come a Long, Long
         Way
1945   *Escape in the Fog*
         The House on 92nd St.
         A Medal for Benny
         Pride of the Marines
         Samurai
1948   *Night Wind*
         Shep Comes Home
         Strange Victory
1949   *Answer for Anne*
         Home of the Brave
         Rose of the Yukon
1950   Battleground
         Jolson Sings Again
         Sands of Iwo Jima
1951   Go for Broke!
         *The House on Telegraph
         Hill*
1952   *Bright Victory*
         Red Ball Express
1954   *Carmen Jones*
1955   *Bad Day at Black Rock*
         The Long Gray Line
         A Man Called Peter
1956   *Giant*
         Singing in the Dark
1958   Kings Go Forth
         The Young Lions
1959   *The FBI Story*
1960   Hell to Eternity
World War II—Collaborators
1942   Foreign Agent
**World War II—Resistance
movements**
1943   *Gangway for Tomorrow*
1954   Barefoot Battalion
**Wounded Knee Creek, Battle of,
1890**
1914   *The Indian Wars*
1942   *They Died With Their Boots
         On*
Wounds and injuries
1917   The Woman and the Beast
1941   *Western Union*
1946   *Don Ricardo Returns*
         Song of the South
1947   *Spoilers of the North*
1948   *Cry of the City*
1949   *She Wore a Yellow Ribbon*
1950   *Sands of Iwo Jima*
1951   *Cyclone Fury*
         The Harlem Globetrotters
         Only the Valiant
         Saturday's Hero
1953   *Cry of the Hunted*
         The Glass Wall
1956   *Pillars of the Sky*
         Serenade
1957   *War Drums*
1958   *The Rawhide Trail*
1959   *The Wonderful Country*
Wreckers
1928   The Crash
Wrestlers and wrestling
1932   Flesh
1934   *Laughing Boy*
1939   *The Girl from Mexico*
         Mr. Moto in Danger Island
1945   *Anoush*
1950   *Jiggs and Maggie Out West*

1951   *When the Redskins Rode*
Writers
    use **Specific types of writers**
Wyandot Indians
    use **Huron Indians**
Wyoming
1914   *The Squaw Man*
1915   *The Gambler of the West*
1918   *The Squaw Man*
1918? *Indian Life*
1925   *Custer's Last Fight*
1932   *The Golden West*
1938   *Two Gun Man from
         Harlem*
1942   *Valley of Hunted Men*
1946   *Sun Valley Cyclone*
1947   *Marshal of Cripple Creek*
1954   *The Yellow Tomahawk*
1955   *The Indian Fighter*
1956   *The Last Frontier*
         The White Squaw
1958   *Blood Arrow*
         Bullwhip
         Gunman's Walk
X-rays
1945   *Between Two Women*
1951   *Five*
Xenophobia
1921   *Shadows of the West*
1922   Peacock Alley
1937   Black Legion
         Nation Aflame
1947   *The Burning Cross*
1949   *Answer for Anne*
Yachts and yachting
1915   *The Sable Lorcha*
1919   A Fallen Idol
1925   Speed Wild
1927   Sailor Izzy Murphy
1931   *Aloha*
         ¿Conoces a tu mujer?
         Mi último amor
         Women Love Once
1933   *La melodía prohibida*
1934   *Stand Up and Cheer!*
         White Heat
1938   *Josette*
1948   The Lady from Shanghai
1950   *Mystery Submarine*
1958   *Seven Hills of Rome*
Yadkin Riverh (NC)
1936   *Daniel Boone*
Yakima Indians
1956   *Raw Edge*
Yale University
1927   For the Love of Mike
1928   Hold 'Em Yale
1932   Huddle
Yaqui Indians
1915   *The Lamb*
1919   Desert Gold
1922   Cross Roads
1926   Desert Gold
1953   Tumbleweed
Yellow fever
1917   *The Bride of Hate*
1936   *The Prisoner of Shark
         Island*
Chief Yellow Hand
1917   *The Adventures of Buffalo
         Bill*
1937   *The Plainsman*
1944   *Buffalo Bill*
Yellowstone National Park (WY)
1917   *John Ermine of the
         Yellowstone*
1959   Yellowstone Kelly
YMCA
    use **Young Men's Christian
         Association**
Yom Kippur
1926   Broken Hearts
1928   The Jazz Singer
1932   *Mazel Tov*
1939   *Kol Nidre*
         Mothers of Today
1940   *Overture to Glory*
**Young Men's Christian
Association**
1930   Anybody's War
1951   *Teresa*

Youth
1924 Untamed Youth
1934 Tres amores
1941 Sunday Sinners
1944 Slightly Terrific
1946 Wild Beauty
1952 The Ring
1958 The Light in the Forest
1959 *Night of the Quarter Moon*
1960 Key Witness

Eugène Ysaye
1953 *Tonight We Sing*

Yugoslavian Americans
1932 Ljubav i strast

Yugoslavians
1942 *Woman of the Year*

Yukon River (Yukon and AK)
1925 The True North

Yukon Territory
1922 The Great Alone
　　　The Son of the Wolf
1923 Snowdrift
1930 The Break Up
1943 *Jack London*

Yuma (AZ)
1957 *Apache Warrior*
1958 *The Badlanders*

Ziegfeld Follies
1929 Is Everybody Happy?
1953 *The Eddie Cantor Story*

Florenz Ziegfeld, Jr.
　　　The Eddie Cantor Story

Zionism
1937 The Holy Oath

Zombies
1941 *King of the Zombies*

Zoos
1942 *Cat People*
1945 *The Great John L.*
1948 *Up in Central Park*

Zurich (Switzerland)
1935 *Señora casada necesita marido*

ETHNIC CATEGORY INDEX

★ This index contains listings arranged alphabetically by ethnic category, primarily ethnic groups, but also including the listings "Multi-ethnic," for some films in which no particular ethnic groups dominates, "Immigrants," in which the experiences of immigrants of unspecified ethnicity is presented and various language designations, referring to films made for foreign- language speaking audiences. Films listed for specific American Indian groups are also included under the heading "Native Americans." The term "Latino" has been used for a number of groups of Hispanic heritage, including Argentinian, Brazilian, Cuban, Mexican and Puerto Rican Americans.

ETHNIC CATEGORY INDEX

Acoma
1951 New Mexico

African Americans
1914 At the Cross Roads
      Dan
      John Barleycorn
      The Littlest Rebel
      Uncle Tom's Cabin
1915 The Birth of a Nation
      Marse Covington
      The Nigger
      A Texas Steer
      Under Southern Skies
1915? The Life of Sam Davis: A
        Confederate Hero of the
        Sixties
      Sam Davis, the Hero of
        Tennessee
1916 At Piney Ridge
      Broken Chains
      The Colored American
        Winning His Suit
      The Grip of Jealousy
      Pudd'nhead Wilson
      Unprotected
1917 The Bar Sinister
      The Bride of Hate
      How Uncle Sam Prepares
      I Will Repay
      A Kentucky Cinderella
      The Little Samaritan
      My Fighting Gentleman
      The Slacker
      Sold at Auction
      Unconquered
1918 The Birth of a Race
      Broken Ties
      Free and Equal
      The Greatest Thing in Life
      The Liar
      Uncle Tom's Cabin
      A Woman of Impulse
1919 Come Out of the Kitchen
      The Homesteader
      Injustice
      The Little Diplomat
      A Man's Duty
      Toby's Bow
1919? The Brand of Judas
1920 The Brute
      Eyes of Youth
      Huckleberry Finn
      In the Depths of Our Hearts
      Our Christianity and
        Nobody's Child
      The Symbol of the
        Unconquered
      Within Our Gates
1920? Broken Hearts
      Reformation
1921 As the World Rolls On
      The Burden of Race
      By Right of Birth
      The Call of His People
      A Child in Pawn
      Cotton and Cattle
      A Fool's Promise
      A Giant of His Race
      The Green-Eyed Monster
      The Gunsaulus Mystery
      Hearts of the Woods
      The Hypocrite
      The Lure of a Woman
      The Man from Texas

A Modern Cain
The Negro of Today
The Secret Sorrow
The Shadow
The Sport of the Gods
Ties of Blood
1921? [Unidentified Film]
1922 The Bull-Dogger
      The Crimson Skull
      The Dungeon
      Easy Money
      Foolish Lives
      For His Mother's Sake
      The Greatest Sin
      The Perfect Dreamer
      The Schemers
      Spitfire
      Square Joe
      Uncle Jasper's Will
      Undisputed Evidence
      The Virgin of Seminole
      You Can't Keep a Good Man
        Down
1923 Deceit
      The Devil's Match
      Flames of Wrath
      His Great Chance
      Regeneration
      A Shot in the Night
      Tuskegee Finds the Way Out
1924 Birthright
      A Debtor to the Law
      His Darker Self
      The House Behind the
        Cedars
      Smiling Hate
      A Son of Satan
1924? The Flaming Crisis
1925 The Black Boomerang
      Body and Soul
      The Devil's Disciple
      Marcus Garland
1926 The Conjure Woman
      The Fighting Deacon
      The Flying Ace
      A Prince of His Race
      Reckless Money
1926? The House on Cedar Hill
      Ten Nights in a Barroom
1927 The Broken Violin
      Children of Fate
      Ham and Eggs at the Front
      The Love Mart
      The Millionaire
      Poro College in Moving
        Pictures
      The Scar of Shame
      The Slaver
      The Spider's Web
      Topsy and Eva
1927? You Can't Win
1928 Absent
      Black Gold
      Diamond Handcuffs
      Eleven P.M.
      The Midnight Ace
      Tenderfeet
      Thirty Years Later
      Uncle Tom's Cabin
      The Wages of Sin
1929 Hallelujah
      Hearts in Dixie
      Show Boat
      Thunderbolt

When Men Betray
The Witching Eyes
1930 Abraham Lincoln
      Anybody's War
      Big Boy
      Check and Double Check
      A Daughter of the Congo
      Easy Street
      Georgia Rose
1931 The Exile
      Huckleberry Finn
      The White Renegade
1932 The Black King
      Harlem Is Heaven
      Hypnotized
      Out of the Crimson Fog
      Ten Minutes to Live
      Veiled Aristocrats
1932? The Girl from Chicago
1933 The Emperor Jones
      Victims of Persecution
1933? Scandal
1934 Broadway Bill
      Chloe: Love Is Calling You
      Drums O' Voodoo
      Imitation of Life
      Judge Priest
      Operator 13
      Stand Up and Cheer!
      The Unknown Soldier
        Speaks
1934? Harlem After Midnight
1935 Lem Hawkins' Confession
      The Little Colonel
      The Littlest Rebel
      So Red the Rose
1936 General Spanky
      The Green Pastures
      Muss 'Em Up
      The Prisoner of Shark Island
      Rainbow on the River
      Show Boat
      Temptation
1937 Bargain with Bullets
      Dark Manhattan
      Harlem on the Prairie
      Maid of Salem
      One Mile from Heaven
      Slave Ship
      Souls at Sea
      A Study of Negro Artists
      Underworld
      We Work Again
1938 The Beloved Brat
      Birthright
      The Duke Is Tops
      God's Step Children
      Gone Harlem
      Hits and Bits of 1938
      Life Goes On
      Policy Man
      Spirit of Youth
      Sugar Hill Baby
      Swing!
      Two Gun Man from Harlem
1939 The Adventures of
        Huckleberry Finn
      The Bronze Buckaroo
      The Devil's Daughter
      Double Deal
      Gang Smashers
      Gone With the Wind
      Harlem Rides the Range
      Keep Punching

Lying Lips
Moon over Harlem
One Dark Night
Reform School
Stand Up and Fight
Straight to Heaven
Way Down South
194- Mistaken Identity
1940 Am I Guilty?
      Broken Strings
      Gang War
      George Washington Carver
      Midnight Shadow
      Mystery in Swing
      The Notorious Elinor Lee
      Paradise in Harlem
      Santa Fe Trail
      Son of Ingagi
      While Thousands Cheer
1940? Mr. Washington Goes to
        Town
1941 Belle Starr
      Birth of the Blues
      Four Shall Die
      The Gang's All Here
      King of the Zombies
      Land of Liberty
      Murder on Lenox Avenue
      Sullivan's Travels
      Sunday Sinners
      Up Jumped the Devil
      Virginia
      You're Out of Luck
1941? The Blood of Jesus
      Hampton Institute: Its
        Program of Education for
        Life
1942 Holiday Inn
      In This Our Life
      Lucky Ghost
      Mokey
      Professor Creeps
      Syncopation
      Take My Life
      Tales of Manhattan
      The Vanishing Virginian
      Whispering Ghosts
      Young America
1943 Bataan
      Cabin in the Sky
      Crash Dive
      Crime Smasher
      Dixie
      Fighting Americans
      Jack London
      Land of Hunted Men
      Marching On!
      The Meanest Man in the
        World
      The Ox-Bow Incident
      Riding High
      Stormy Weather
      What's Buzzin' Cousin?
1944 Black Magic
      Dark Waters
      Hi, Beautiful
      Lifeboat
      The Negro Soldier
      Since You Went Away
      We've Come a Long, Long
        Way
1945 I Love a Bandleader
      Of One Blood
      The Scarlet Clue

1946 Beware
      Dirty Gertie from Harlem,
        U.S.A.
      Mantan Messes Up
      The Red Dragon
      The Sailor Takes a Wife
      Song of the South
      Stars on Parade
      Tall, Tan and Terrific
      That Man of Mine
      Till the End of Time
1946? Beale Street Mama
      Fight That Ghost
      Go Down, Death!
      Harlem on Parade
      House-Rent Party
1947 Body and Soul
      Boy! What a Girl!
      The Burning Cross
      The Foxes of Harrow
      Going to Glory, Come to
        Jesus
      Hi De Ho
      Jivin' in Be-Bop
      Juke Joint
      Mantan Runs for Mayor
      New Orleans
      The Peanut Man
      Reet, Petite and Gone
      Sepia Cinderella
      Untamed Fury
1947? Return of Mandy's Husband
      Swanee Showboat
      What a Guy
1948 The Betrayal
      The Fight Never Ends
      Killer Diller
      Miracle in Harlem
      Moonrise
      Strange Victory
      Tap Roots
      The Time of Your Life
1948? Boarding House Blues
      Junction 88
1949 Home of the Brave
      Jigsaw
      Knock on Any Door
      Lookout Sister
      Lost Boundaries
      Pinky
      The Quiet One
      The Red Menace
      Souls of Sin
1949? Come On, Cowboy!
      Girl in Room 20
      Harlem Follies
      The Joint Is Jumpin'
      She's Too Mean for Me
1950 The Breaking Point
      Intruder in the Dust
      The Jackie Robinson Story
      No Way Out
      Stars in My Crown
      Young Man with a Horn
1951 Apache Drums
      Five
      The Harlem Globetrotters
      Native Son
      Show Boat
      The Tall Target
      The Well
      Yes Sir, Mr. Bones
1952 Bright Victory
      It's a Big Country: An
        American Anthology
      Red Ball Express
1953 Bright Road
      The Joe Louis Story
      The Member of the Wedding
      Sangaree
      The Sun Shines Bright
1954 Carmen Jones
      Go Man Go
1955 Blackboard Jungle
      Brevities of 1955
      Seven Angry Men
      The View from Pompey's
        Head
1956 Baby Doll
      The Benny Goodman Story

      Rockin' the Blues
1957 Band of Angels
      Burden of Truth
      Edge of the City
      The Guns of Fort Petticoat
      Raintree County
      Satchmo the Great
      Segregation and the South
1958 The Defiant Ones
      Kings Go Forth
      St. Louis Blues
1959 Anna Lucasta
      Imitation of Life
      Night of the Quarter Moon
      Odds Against Tomorrow
      Porgy and Bess
      The Wonderful Country
      The World, the Flesh and
        the Devil
1960 The Adventures of
        Huckleberry Finn
      All the Fine Young
        Cannibals
      All the Young Men
      The Crowning Experience
      I Passed for White
      Key Witness
      The Last Voyage
      Sergeant Rutledge
      Take a Giant Step
      This Rebel Breed
      Wild River

Amish
1955 Violent Saturday
Apache
1922 One Eighth Apache
1925 Tonio, Son of the Sierras
1932 Mystery Ranch
      Riders of the Desert
1939 Bad Lands
1940 Geronimo
1942 Apache Trail
1948 Fort Apache
      Fury at Furnace Creek
      Red River
1949 Apache Chief
      Lust for Gold
1950 Ambush
      Broken Arrow
      I Killed Geronimo
      Rio Grande
      Two Flags West
1951 Apache Drums
      The Last Outpost
      Only the Valiant
1952 Apache Country
      Apache War Smoke
      The Battle at Apache Pass
      The Half-Breed
      Indian Uprising
1953 Ambush at Tomahawk Gap
      Arrowhead
      Conquest of Cochise
      Old Overland Trail
      The Stand at Apache River
1954 Apache
      Arrow in the Dust
      Hondo
      Massacre Canyon
      Taza, Son of Cochise
1955 Apache Ambush
      Apache Woman
      Foxfire
      The Lonesome Trail
      Shotgun
      Smoke Signal
      The Vanishing American
1956 The Broken Star
      The Last Wagon
      Secret of Treasure Mountain
      Walk the Proud Land
1957 Apache Warrior
      Dragoon Wells Massacre
      The Ride Back
      Tomahawk Trail
      Trooper Hook
      War Drums
1958 Ambush at Cimarron Pass
      Apache Territory
      Escape from Red Rock

      Fort Bowie
      Fort Massacre
1959 Gunmen from Laredo
      The Wonderful Country
Arab Americans
1948 The Time of Your Life
1952 Desert Pursuit
Arapaho
1926 War Paint
1949 She Wore a Yellow Ribbon
1950 A Ticket to Tomahawk
1955 White Feather
1956 Ghost Town
      Quincannon, Frontier Scout
      The Wild Dakotas
1959 The Oregon Trail
      Yellowstone Kelly
Armenian Americans
1919 Auction of Souls
Armenian language
1937 Arshin Mal Alan
1945 Anoush
Asian Americans
1955 Bad Day at Black Rock
Austrian Americans
1916 Three of Many
1918 I Want to Forget
1930 The Melody Man
1934 Beloved
1936 Sins of Man
      Star for a Night
1940 The Ramparts We Watch
      Three Faces West
1941 Come Live with Me
      Louisiana Purchase
      They Dare Not Love
1942 The Navy Comes Through
      We Were Dancing
1945 Salome, Where She Danced
1950 A Lady Without Passport
Aztec
1921 The Cave Girl
Basque Americans
1927 Whispering Sage
1958 Wild Is the Wind
1959 Thunder in the Sun
Belgian Americans
1918 Out of a Clear Sky
1921 Through the Back Door
1926 The Strong Man
Blackfoot
1915 The Girl I Left Behind Me
1919 The Heart of Wetona
1928 Kit Carson
1952 The Big Sky
1954 Cattle Queen of Montana
1958 Blood Arrow
Bulgarian Americans
1957 Journey to Freedom
Cajuns
1919 Evangeline
1923 Scars of Jealousy
1929 Evangeline
1934 Lazy River
1944 Dark Waters
1945 The Mummy's Curse
1946 Swamp Fire
1948 Louisiana Story
1953 Cry of the Hunted
      Thunder Bay
1957 Bayou
Cayuga
1922 Cardigan
Cayuse
1919? In the Land of the Setting
        Sun; or, Martyrs of
        Yesterday
Cherokee
1917 The Conqueror
1931 Cimarron
1939 Man of Conquest
1949 Ranger of Cherokee Strip
1950 Cherokee Uprising
1951 Tomahawk
1952 Rose of Cimarron
1954 Apache
1956 Daniel Boone, Trail Blazer
1960 Oklahoma Territory
Cheyenne
1918? Indian Life
1925 Custer's Last Fight

1926 General Custer at Little Big
        Horn
1934 Cheyenne Sun Dance
1936 Custer's Last Stand
      Treachery Rides the Range
1937 The Plainsman
1944 Buffalo Bill
1949 She Wore a Yellow Ribbon
1951 Cavalry Scout
1952 Wagons West
1953 The Charge at Feather River
      Last of the Comanches
1954 The Yellow Tomahawk
1955 White Feather
1956 Dakota Incident
      Ghost Town
1957 The Guns of Fort Petticoat
      Ride Out for Revenge
Chickasaw
1956 Davy Crockett and the River
        Pirates
Chinese Americans
1914 The Yellow Traffic
1914? The Chinese Lily
      The Mysterious Mr. Wu
        Chung Foo
1915 Just Jim
      The Sable Lorcha
      The Secret Sin
1915? Chinatown Pictures
1916 Broken Fetters
      Hop, the Devil's Brew
      The Sign of the Poppy
      The Social Buccaneer
1917 The Flower of Doom
      Queen X
      The War of the Tongs
1918 The Border Raiders
      The City of Dim Faces
      The Girl in the Dark
      Little Red Decides
      The Midnight Patrol
      Mystic Faces
1918? The Snail
1919 The Lost Battalion
      Mandarin's Gold
      The She Wolf
      The Tong Man
1920 The Cyclone
      Dinty
      Li Ting Lang
      Outside the Law
      Pagan Love
      The Purple Cipher
1920? The Scarlet Dragon
1921 Bits of Life
      Fifty Candles
      The First Born
      Lotus Blossom
      Shame
      The Swamp
      A Tale of Two Worlds
      Where Lights Are Low
      Wing Toy
1922 The Cub Reporter
      East Is West
      Flesh and Blood
      Pals of the West
      Shadows
      Sky High
      When East Comes West
1923 The Miracle Makers
      Purple Dawn
1924 Defying the Law
      In High Gear
      The Pell Street Mystery
1925 Speed Wild
      Tearing Through
1926 Shadows of Chinatown
      A Trip to Chinatown
      Twin Triggers
1927 The Chinese Parrot
      Old San Francisco
      Roarin' Broncs
1928 The Cameraman
      Chinatown Charlie
      The Hawk's Nest
      Ransom
1929 Chinatown Nights
      Masked Emotions
      The Peacock Fan

Welcome Danger
1930 East Is West
On the Border
Son of the Gods
1931 The Black Camel
Charlie Chan Carries On
Chinatown After Dark
Law of the Tong
1932 Border Devils
Charlie Chan's Chance
The Hatchet Man
The Secrets of Wu Sin
The Son-Daughter
Thirteen Steps
1933 Charlie Chan's Greatest Case
1934 Blossom Time
The Cat's-Paw
Charlie Chan in London
Charlie Chan's Courage
Lazy River
Limehouse Blues
Riding Speed
1935 Captured in Chinatown
Charlie Chan in Egypt
Charlie Chan in Paris
Charlie Chan in Shanghai
Chinatown Squad
1936 After the Thin Man
Border Phantom
Charlie Chan at the Circus
Charlie Chan at the Race
Track
Charlie Chan's Secret
Hair-Trigger Casey
Klondike Annie
Mad Holiday
Yellow Cargo
1937 Charlie Chan at the
Olympics
Charlie Chan at the Opera
Charlie Chan on Broadway
Shadows of the Orient
1938 Charlie Chan at Monte Carlo
Dangerous to Know
Daughter of Shanghai
Mr. Wong, Detective
1939 Charlie Chan at Treasure
Island
Charlie Chan in Honolulu
Charlie Chan in Reno
City in Darkness
Daughter of the Tong
King of Chinatown
Mr. Wong in Chinatown
The Mystery of Mr. Wong
1939? A Chinese Gains a Fortune
in America
1940 Charlie Chan at the Wax
Museum
Charlie Chan in Panama
Charlie Chan's Murder
Cruise
Doomed to Die
The Fatal Hour
Murder over New York
Phantom of Chinatown
1941 Charlie Chan in Rio
Dead Men Tell
Golden Gate Girl
Secret of the Wastelands
Sunday Sinners
1942 Castle in the Desert
Dr. Gillespie's New Assistant
Let's Get Tough!
North to the Klondike
Rubber Racketeers
1943 The Amazing Mrs. Holliday
Dr. Gillespie's Criminal
Case
1944 Andy Hardy's Blonde
Trouble
Black Magic
Charlie Chan in the Secret
Service
The Chinese Cat
Three Men in White
1945 Between Two Women
Escape in the Fog
The Jade Mask
The Scarlet Clue

The Shanghai Cobra
1946 Dangerous Money
Dark Alibi
The Red Dragon
Shadows Over Chinatown
The Trap
1946? House-Rent Party
1947 Black Gold
The Chinese Ring
Dark Delusion
Little Mister Jim
1947? What a Guy
1948 Docks of New Orleans
The Feathered Serpent
The Golden Eye
Half Past Midnight
The Lady from Shanghai
Shanghai Chest
Sleep, My Love
The Time of Your Life
1949 Boston Blackie's Chinese
Venture
The Sky Dragon
1950 The Big Hangover
The Breaking Point
The Cariboo Trail
Chinatown at Midnight
A Ticket to Tomahawk
1951 Mask of the Dragon
1954 Hell's Half Acre
1960 Walk Like a Dragon
Chinese language
1934 Blossom Time
1936 Sum Hun
1939? A Chinese Gains a Fortune
in America
1940 Hua Chio Juh Guang
Won Lee Shuen Fu
1941 Golden Gate Girl
Min Jok Jay Hung Sing
1943 Gin Guo Chin Yuan
1944 Chin Hai In Siong
Guon Min Guh Lu
Kuan Fong Lang Tyeh
1946? Yee Sio Bo Laan Sin
1947? Bow Yu Lee Hua
Gin Fen Nee Shaan
Hai Jeow Chin Yuan
Hong Yien Fei Bo Ming
Hoon Si Gway Lai
Jia O Tien Chen
Luan Feng Heh Ming
Sing Yun Sin Nian
Yu Luh Shen Ping
1948? Jeng Yien Doe Lee
Kuang Feng Juu Yien Fay
Too Yien Fen Fong
1949? Lang Hu Bee Yuh
Shuang Feng Cheo Huang
Yein Dow
1953? Tan Dow Jia Jen
1955? Yin Hua Chu Chu Kai
Chippewa
1930 The Silent Enemy
1952 Hiawatha
1958 Flaming Frontier
Chiricahua
1953 Arrowhead
Choctaw
1948 Tap Roots
Coeur d'Alene
1956 Pillars of the Sky
Comanche
1920 The Daughter of Dawn
1924 North of 36
1938 The Texans
1940 Young Buffalo Bill
1948 Red River
1950 Comanche Territory
1952 Rose of Cimarron
1953 Conquest of Cochise
Last of the Comanches
1954 Overland Pacific
They Rode West
Thunder Pass
1955 Kentucky Rifle
Kiss of Fire
1956 Comanche
The Last Wagon
The Searchers

1958 The Rawhide Trail
1960 Comanche Station
Cree
1937 Drums of Destiny
1954 Saskatchewan
Creek
1927 The Frontiersman
1955 Davy Crockett, King of the
Wild Frontier
Creoles
1914 Springtime
1917 Southern Pride
1918 A Daughter of the Old South
A Woman of Impulse
1938 The Buccaneer
1942 American Empire
1944 Dark Waters
1946 Saratoga Trunk
1947 The Foxes of Harrow
1951 Adventures of Captain
Fabian
1955 Duel on the Mississippi
1958 Ride a Crooked Trail
Croatian language
1932 Ljubav i strast
Crow
1917 John Ermine of the
Yellowstone
1918? Indian Life
1935 Fighting Pioneers
1955 White Feather
Czech Americans
1933 The Man Who Dared: An
Imaginative Biography
1935 Romance in Manhattan
1944 An American Romance
Lake Placid Serenade
Slightly Terrific
1947 Desperate
1956 Death of a Scoundrel
Dakota
1914 The Indian Wars
1914? Sitting Bull—The Hostile
Sioux Indian Chief
1918? Indian Life
1925 Custer's Last Fight
A Daughter of the Sioux
Red Love
Warrior Gap
1926 The Frontier Trail
General Custer at Little Big
Horn
The Last Frontier
1927 The Overland Stage
The Red Raiders
With Sitting Bull at the
Spirit Lake Massacre
1929 Sioux Blood
1934 Massacre
1936 Custer's Last Stand
The Glory Trail
1937 The Plainsman
1940 Prairie Schooners
1941 Western Union
1942 They Died With Their Boots
On
1949 The Prairie
1951 Cavalry Scout
Oh! Susanna
Tomahawk
Warpath
1952 Buffalo Bill in Tomahawk
Territory
Bugles in the Afternoon
Hiawatha
The Savage
1953 The Great Sioux Uprising
Jack McCall Desperado
The Nebraskan
1954 The Black Dakotas
Saskatchewan
Sitting Bull
1955 Chief Crazy Horse
The Gun That Won the West
The Indian Fighter
White Feather
1956 The Last Frontier
The Last Hunt
7th Cavalry
Westward Ho the Wagons!
The White Squaw

1957 The Lawless Eighties
Revolt at Fort Laramie
Run of the Arrow
1958 Flaming Frontier
Gun Fever
Gunman's Walk
Tonka
1959 Yellowstone Kelly
Danish Americans
1920 The Riddle: Woman
Delaware
1920 The Last of the Mohicans
1951 When the Redskins Rode
Diegueño
1955 Seven Cities of Gold
Dutch Americans
1914 When Broadway Was a Trail
1916 Gretchen, the Greenhorn
Hulda from Holland
1918? Rosemary Climbs the
Heights
1920 The Secret Gift
1924 So Big
1932 So Big
1938 The Buccaneer
1942 Seven Sweethearts
1944 Knickerbocker Holiday
1945 Where Do We Go From
Here?
1949 C-Man
1953 So Big
English Americans
1914 Life's Shop Window
The Squaw Man
1915 The Spender
1916 Lord Loveland Discovers
America
The Pretenders
1917 The Squaw Man's Son
1917? Barnaby Lee
1918 Ruggles of Red Gap
The Squaw Man
1919 Fighting for Gold
1923 Ruggles of Red Gap
The Victor
1926 Laddie
1930 Take the Heir
1931 The Squaw Man
1933 A Lady's Profession
Robbers' Roost
1934 She Was a Lady
1935 Ruggles of Red Gap
1937 Boots and Saddles
1946 G. I. War Brides
1947 The Mighty McGurk
1959 The Sheriff of Fractured Jaw
French Americans
1914 Springtime
1915 The Clemenceau Case
1916 For the Defense
Silks and Satins
Witchcraft
1917 The Bond Between
The Little Chevalier
A Love Sublime
The Renaissance at
Charleroi
1918 A Broadway Scandal
Fields of Honor
Find the Woman
The Golden Wall
The Greatest Thing in Life
1919 His Parisian Wife
Yvonne from Paris
1920 The Good-Bad Wife
White Youth
1921 Love's Plaything
1922 Peacock Alley
1923 Backbone
1925 Scarlet Saint
1928 Anybody Here Seen Kelly?
1930 Behind the Make-Up
The Big Pond
1935 Naughty Marietta
1937 That Girl from Paris
1938 Josette
The Rage of Paris
The Toy Wife
1940 New Moon
1941 Lady from Louisiana
1943 Gangway for Tomorrow
Tahiti Honey

1944 Block Busters
1945 Johnny Angel
1946 The Gentleman Misbehaves
       Saratoga Trunk
       Swamp Fire
1947 Buck Privates Come Home
1949 The Fighting Kentuckian
1950 Buccaneer's Girl
       Last of the Buccaneers
       The Toast of New Orleans
1951 Westward the Women
1952 The Iron Mistress
1953 The Pathfinder
1959 The Jayhawkers!
       Thunder in the Sun

French language
1930 Le spectre vert
1931 Buster se marie
       Chérie
       Echec au roi
       Jenny Lind
       Nuit d'Espagne
       Le père célibataire
       Le petit café
       Quand on est belle
       Soyons gais
1932 L'athlète incomplet
       Le bluffeur
       Le cas du docteur Brenner
       La foule hurle
       Une heure près de toi
       Le plombier amoureux
1933 L'amour guide
1934 Caravane
       La veuve joyeuse
1935 L'homme des Folies Bergère

German Americans
1913? The Lure of New York
1915 Hearts of Men
       The Kindling
1916 Little Meena's Romance
       Peck O' Pickles
1917 The Little American
       The Secret Game
       The Slacker
       The Winged Mystery
1918 An Alien Enemy
       The Birth of a Race
       Good-Bye, Bill
       The Hun Within
       Johanna Enlists
       The Kaiser's Finish
       Me Und Gott
       The Price of Applause
       The Prussian Cur
       The Ranger
       The Reckoning Day
       Shifting Sands
       The Spreading Evil
       The Unbeliever
       The Yellow Dog
1919 Behind the Door
       Erstwhile Susan
       Love and the Law
1919? America Was Right
       When the Desert Smiles
1920 The Cup of Fury
       Dangerous Days
1924 California in '49
1925 Friendly Enemies
1926 The Strong Man
1927 For the Love of Mike
       His Foreign Wife
       Lost at the Front
       The Way of All Flesh
1928 Heart Trouble
       Sins of the Fathers
       We Americans
1930 Sins of the Children
1931 Beyond Victory
1932 Flesh
       Unashamed
1933 Best of Enemies
       Broken Dreams
       Ever in My Heart
       Song of the Eagle
1935 Rendezvous
1936 Sutter's Gold
1939 Confessions of a Nazi Spy
1940 Escape
       Escape to Glory

       Jennie
       The Man I Married
       The Ramparts We Watch
1942 All Through the Night
       Foreign Agent
       Friendly Enemies
       Nazi Agent
       Secret Enemies
       Valley of Hunted Men
       Wings for the Eagle
1943 Good Luck, Mr. Yates
       Hitler's Children
       They Came to Blow Up
         America
1944 Address Unknown
       Chip Off the Old Block
       Tender Comrade
       They Live in Fear
       Tomorrow the World!
       Waterfront
1945 The House on 92nd St.
1946 Notorious
       Rendezvous 24
1948 Night Wind
1949 Lust for Gold
1950 Mystery Submarine
1952 Woman in the Dark
1953 The Sun Shines Bright
1959 The Wonderful Country
1960 I Aim at the Stars: the
         Wernher von Braun Story

German language
1929 Die Königsloge
1931 Dämon des Meeres
       Die Dreigroschenoper
       Kismet
       Die Maske Fällt
       Tropennächte

Greek Americans
1917 A Love Sublime
1931 Smart Money
1936 Down to the Sea
1942 Juke Girl
       Woman of the Year
1943 Good Luck, Mr. Yates
       Mr. Lucky
1948 16 Fathoms Deep
       The Time of Your Life
1949 Harbor of Missing Men
       Thieves' Highway
1950 Sands of Iwo Jima
1952 It's a Big Country: An
         American Anthology
1953 Beneath the 12-Mile Reef
       The Glory Brigade

Greek language
1931 Such Is Life
1954 Barefoot Battalion

Gypsies
1914 The Redemption of David
         Corson
       The Woman in Black
1915 The Adventures of a Madcap
       An American Gentleman
1916 The Flames of Johannis
       The Folly of Revenge
       A Man of Sorrow
       The Twin Triangle
1917 The Call of Her People
       Runaway Romany
       The Secret of Eve
       Sunshine and Gold
       The Wild Girl
1918 In Judgment Of
       Set Free
       Toys of Fate
1919 The Sneak
1920 The Dark Mirror
1920? Broken Hearts
1921 Anne of Little Smoky
1923 Jealous Husbands
1924 Untamed Youth
1931 Call of the Rockies
1935 Melody Trail
1938 Rascals
1939 Trigger Fingers
1944 Cry of the Werewolf
1947 On the Old Spanish Trail
1956 Hot Blood

Haitian Americans
1946 The Face of Marble
Hawaiians
1915? The Beachcomber
1917 The Bottle Imp
1918 Hidden Pearls
       Wild Women
1919 A Fallen Idol
1923 The White Flower
1934 Song of the Islands
       White Heat
1937 Waikiki Wedding
1938 Hawaii Calls
1940 Hawaii
1942 Song of the Islands
1950 Damien
1954 Hell's Half Acre
Hidatsa
1955 The Far Horizons
Hopi
1927 The Devil's Saddle
Hungarian Americans
1916 Arms and the Woman
1929 Is Everybody Happy?
       This Is Heaven
1931 Women Love Once
1934 The Great Flirtation
1935 A Night at the Ritz
1940 The Way of All Flesh
1941 The Face Behind the Mask
1945 The Dolly Sisters
1952 It's a Big Country: An
         American Anthology
Huron
1920 The Last of the Mohicans
1943 Deerslayer
1950 The Iroquois Trail
1951 When the Redskins Rode
1957 The Deerslayer
Illinois
1952 Hiawatha
Immigrants
1913 The Inside of the White
         Slave Traffic
       Traffic in Souls
1914 The Jungle
       The Little Angel of Canyon
         Creek
1916 The Fall of a Nation
       The Morals of Hilda
1917 Unknown 274
1918 A Little Sister of Everybody
1919 Deliverance
1921 The Money Maniac
       One Man in a Million
1922 My Boy
1935 Black Fury
1936 Ellis Island
       Human Cargo
       My American Wife
1937 Black Legion
       It Could Happen to You
1939 Forged Passport
       Let Freedom Ring
1940 Music in My Heart
1941 Adam Had Four Sons
       Hold Back the Dawn
       Ice-Capades
       Mystery Ship
1946 G. I. War Brides
       Three Wise Fools
1947 Buck Privates Come Home
1948 My Girl Tisa
       Reaching from Heaven
1949 Answer for Anne
       The Girl from Jones Beach
       Illegal Entry
1950 Emergency Wedding
       Panic in the Streets
Indo-Americans
1916 The Love Girl
       The Romantic Journey
1932 Thirteen Women
1935 Rescue Squad
Irish Americans
1914 The Straight Road
1915 Chimmie Fadden
       Chimmie Fadden Out West
       The Danger Signal
       How Molly Malone Made
         Good
       The Rosary

       The Spender
1916 The Innocent Lie
       Mixed Blood
       A Son of Erin
1917 Castles for Two
       Rosie O'Grady
       The Sudden Gentleman
       A Wife by Proxy
1918 Amarilly of Clothes-Line
         Alley
       Denny from Ireland
       Doing Their Bit
       The Gypsy Trail
       The Hell Cat
       Hell's End
       Hitting the Trail
       The Little Runaway
       Marked Cards
       Real Folks
       Sandy
       Thirty a Week
1919 A Bachelor's Wife
       The Delicious Little Devil
       A Fighting Colleen
       The Lord Loves the Irish
       Spotlight Sadie
       A Yankee Princess
1920 Darling Mine
       Dinty
       Hidden Charms
       The Luck of the Irish
       Pagan Love
1921 All Souls' Eve
       Hold Your Horses
       Little Miss Hawkshaw
       Made in Heaven
       When the Clock Struck Nine
1921? The Supreme Passion
1922 Come On Over
       The Guttersnipe
       The Man with Two Mothers
       Saturday Night
       The Top O' the Morning ·
1923 April Showers
       Breaking into Society
       Little Old New York
1924 Conductor 1492
       East of Broadway
1925 The Beautiful City
       The Fearless Lover
       Hogan's Alley
       Irish Luck
       Lights of Old Broadway
       The Man in Blue
       Old Clothes
       A Son of His Father
1926 Blarney
       The Cohens and Kellys
       Irene
       The Little Irish Girl
1927 The Callahans and the
         Murphys
       Finnegan's Ball
       For the Love of Mike
       Heroes in Blue
       Irish Hearts
       Lost at the Front
       McFadden's Flats
1928 Anybody Here Seen Kelly?
       The Cohens and the Kellys
         in Paris
       The Crash
       The House of Scandal
       Mother Machree
       Riley the Cop
       Vamping Venus
1929 The Cohens and Kellys in
         Atlantic City
       Mother's Boy
       Smiling Irish Eyes
1930 The Cohens and the Kellys
         in Scotland
       Kathleen Mavourneen
       The Last Dance
1931 The Cohens and Kellys in
         Africa
       Personal Maid
       Skyline
       Young Sinners

1932 The Cohens and Kellys in
      Hollywood
      The Golden West
      Hearts of Humanity
      Me and My Gal
      No Greater Love
1933 The Cohens and Kellys in
      Trouble
      Dance Hall Hostess
1935 His Family Tree
      The Irish in Us
      McFadden's Flats
1935? The Irish Gringo
1936 Below the Deadline
      Kelly the Second
      Laughing Irish Eyes
      Paddy O'Day
1937 Boy of the Streets
1938 City Streets
      Gateway
      In Old Chicago
      Outside of Paradise
      Speed to Burn
1939 Waterfront
1940 The Fighting 69th
      Little Nellie Kelly
      Three Cheers for the Irish
1942 Gentleman Jim
1943 Doughboys in Ireland
      The Girl from Monterrey
      Yankee Doodle Dandy
1944 An American Romance
      Going My Way
      The Sullivans
1945 The Bells of St. Mary's
      The Great John L.
      Nob Hill
      Sunbonnet Sue
      A Tree Grows in Brooklyn
      The Valley of Decision
1946 Abie's Irish Rose
      Bringing Up Father
      Gas House Kids
      Three Wise Fools
1947 Calendar Girl
      California
      Carnegie Hall
      Crossfire
      Easy Come, Easy Go
      The Foxes of Harrow
      Jiggs and Maggie in Society
      My Wild Irish Rose
1948 Big City
      The Boy with Green Hair
      Fighting Father Dunne
      Jiggs and Maggie in Court
      The Luck of the Irish
      The Time of Your Life
      Up in Central Park
1949 Jiggs and Maggie in Jackpot
      Jitters
      Portrait of Jennie
      Shamrock Hill
      The Story of Seabiscuit
      Top O' the Morning
1950 The Daughter of Rosie
      O'Grady
      Jiggs and Maggie Out West
      Right Cross
      Sands of Iwo Jima
1952 Bugles in the Afternoon
      It's a Big Country: An
      American Anthology
      The Quiet Man
1953 Taxi
1954 They Rode West
1955 The Long Gray Line
1956 The Catered Affair
1957 Beau James
      The Guns of Fort Petticoat
1958 The Last Hurrah
1959 Al Capone
      Shake Hands with the Devil
1960 The Day They Robbed the
      Bank of England
      Studs Lonigan

Iroquois
1917 The Hidden Children
1947 Last of the Redmen
1950 The Iroquois Trail
      Young Daniel Boone

1956 Mohawk
Italian Americans
1912 The Adventures of
      Lieutenant Petrosino
1914 The Nightingale
1915 The Alien
      The Italian
      The Last of the Mafia
1915? Sin
1916 A Child of Mystery
      The Criminal
      The Gilded Spider
      Gretchen, the Greenhorn
      Pasquale
      Poor Little Peppina
      The Social Highwayman
      Three of Many
      The Woman in 47
      A Woman's Honor
1917 The Adventures of Carol
      His Sweetheart
      Lost in Transit
      The Pulse of Life
      A Roadside Impresario
      The Tell-Tale Step
      Threads of Fate
      The Woman and the Beast
1918 The City of Tears
      Hitting the Trail
      My Cousin
      One More American
      The Ordeal of Rosetta
      Tony America
      Wanted, a Mother
      The Wine Girl
      A Woman of Impulse
1919 Hearts of Men
      The Sleeping Lion
      The Tiger Lily
      Who Will Marry Me?
1919? The Chosen Path
1920 It's a Great Life
      The Man Who Dared
1920? The Greatest Love
1921 Diane of Star Hollow
      Little Italy
      One Man in a Million
      Puppets of Fate
      Society Snobs
      When the Clock Struck Nine
1921? The Slave Market
1922 Fair Lady
      Head over Heels
      The Sign of the Rose
1923 Look Your Best
      Thirty Days
1924 Defying the Law
      Racing Luck
1925 The Beautiful City
      Cobra
      The Greatest Love of All
      The Man in Blue
      The Manicure Girl
1926 Puppets
      Rose of the Tenements
1927 Bitter Apples
      For the Love of Mike
      Sally in Our Alley
1928 The Night Bird
      The Secret Hour
      We Americans
1929 Love, Live and Laugh
      Mister Antonio
1930 Behind the Make-Up
      Ladies Love Brutes
      A Lady to Love
1931 Gentleman's Fate
      The Guilty Generation
      Little Caesar
1932 Amor in montagna
      Cuore d'emigrante
      Huddle
      Men Are Such Fools
      O festino o la legge
      Scarface
      Senza mamma e'nnamurato
1933 Obey the Law
      Racetrack
1934 Our Daily Bread
1935 A Night at the Opera
      The Winning Ticket

1936 It Had to Happen
      Let's Sing Again
      Muss 'Em Up
      Winterset
1937 Man of the People
      Manhattan Merry-Go-Round
      Music for Madame
      Nation Aflame
      Song of the City
1938 City Streets
      Road Demon
      Speed to Burn
1938? Amore che non torna
      I due gemelli
1939 The Escape
      Fisherman's Wharf
      Judge Hardy and Son
      Winner Take All
1940 East of the River
      They Knew What They
      Wanted
1941 Caught in the Act
1942 Foreign Agent
      Unseen Enemy
1944 The Racket Man
1946 Gas House Kids
1947 Citizen Saint
1948 Cry of the City
      Key Largo
      Music Man
      The Time of Your Life
1949 House of Strangers
      Knock on Any Door
      The Red Menace
      That Midnight Kiss
      Thieves' Highway
      The Undercover Man
1950 Black Hand
      Deported
      Give Us This Day
      Sands of Iwo Jima
1951 Gambling House
      The Great Caruso
      Teresa
      Westward the Women
1952 It's a Big Country: An
      American Anthology
      Kid Monk Baroni
      Woman in the Dark
1953 The Glass Wall
1954 Indiscretion of an American
      Wife
1955 Marty
      Murder in Villa Capri
      The Rose Tattoo
1956 Baby Doll
      Full of Life
      Serenade
1957 The Brothers Rico
      The Midnight Story
1958 Houseboat
      Seven Hills of Rome
      Wild Is the Wind
1959 Al Capone
      The Black Orchid
      Inside the Mafia
      Odds Against Tomorrow
1960 Pay or Die
      Weddings and Babies
Italian language
1930 Sei tu l'amore
1931 Così è la vita
      Pagliacci
      La regina di Sparta
1931? La porta del destino
1932 Amor in montagna
      Amore e morte
      Cuore d'emigrante
      Genoveffa
      O.festino o la legge
      Parigi affascina; ovvero,
      Malavita
      Senza mamma e'nnamurato
      Tormento
1938? Amore che non torna
      I due gemelli
Japanese Americans
1915 After Five
      The Cheat
1916 Alien Souls
      The Honorable Friend

      The Soul of Kura-San
1917 The Call of the East
      Forbidden Paths
      Hashimura Togo
1918 The Bravest Way
      Her American Husband
      His Birthright
      The Honor of His House
      The Temple of Dusk
      Who Is to Blame?
1919 The Courageous Coward
      The Gray Horizon
      A Heart in Pawn
      His Debt
1920 Locked Lips
      A Tokio Siren
      Who's Your Servant?
1921 Black Roses
      Shadows of the West
1922 The Pride of Palomar
1927 [Japanese-American Film]
1937 Thank You, Mr. Moto
      Think Fast, Mr. Moto
1938 Mr. Moto Takes a Chance
      Mr. Moto's Gamble
1939 Mr. Moto in Danger Island
      Mr. Moto Takes a Vacation
      Mr. Moto's Last Warning
1942 Across the Pacific
      Foreign Agent
      Let's Get Tough!
      Little Tokyo, U.S.A.
      Prisoner of Japan
      Submarine Raider
1943 Air Force
1945 Betrayal from the East
      Samurai
1949 The Clay Pigeon
1951 Go for Broke!
      The Steel Helmet
      Westward the Women
1952 Japanese War Bride
1955 Bad Day at Black Rock
1959 The Crimson Kimono
1960 Hell to Eternity
Japanese language
1927 [Japanese-American Film]
1930 Chijiku wo mawasuru
      chikara

Jewish Americans
1914 The Little Jewess
      Threads of Destiny
1914? A Boy and the Law
1915 Children of the Ghetto
      Cohen's Luck
      Kreutzer Sonata
      The Melting Pot
      Time Lock Number 776
1915? The Jewish Crown
      The Period of the Jew
1916 Civilization's Child
      The Social Buccaneer
      The Yellow Passport
1916? Should a Baby Die?
1917 A Jewel in Pawn
      A Night in New Arabia
      The Peddler
1919 As a Man Thinks
      Daughter of Mine
      The Other Man's Wife
      The Right to Happiness
      The Volcano
      Who's Your Brother?
1920 Humoresque
      The North Wind's Malice
      Pagan Love
1921 The Barricade
      Cheated Love
      No Woman Knows
1922 Breaking Home Ties
      The Five Dollar Baby
      The Good Provider
      Hungry Hearts
      Little Miss Smiles
      Pawn Ticket 210
      Second Hand Rose
      Solomon in Society
      The Woman He Loved
1923 None So Blind
      Potash and Perlmutter

1924 Fools' Highway
In Hollywood With Potash
  and Perlmutter
Welcome Stranger
1925 Abie's Imported Bride
His People
Hogan's Alley
Old Clothes
One of the Bravest
Salome of the Tenements
1926 April Fool
Broken Hearts
The Cohens and Kellys
Kosher Kitty Kelly
Millionaires
Pals in Paradise
Private Izzy Murphy
Rose of the Tenements
Sweet Daddies
Sweet Rosie O'Grady
1927 The Auctioneer
Clancy's Kosher Wedding
For the Love of Mike
Frisco Sally Levy
A Harp in Hock
Jake the Plumber
Pleasure Before Business
Sailor Izzy Murphy
Sally in Our Alley
The Shamrock and the Rose
1928 The Cohens and the Kellys
  in Paris
Flying Romeos
George Washington Cohen
The Jazz Singer
The Rawhide Kid
We Americans
1929 Abie's Irish Rose
The Cohens and Kellys in
  Atlantic City
East Side Sadie
Lucky Boy
The Younger Generation
1930 Around the Corner
The Cohens and the Kellys
  in Scotland
Eternal Fools (Ewige
  Naraim)
The Kibitzer
My Yiddishe Mama
Sunny Skies
1931 The Cohens and Kellys in
  Africa
1932 The Cohens and Kellys in
  Hollywood
The Golden West
The Heart of New York
Hearts of Humanity
No Greater Love
Symphony of Six Million
1933 The Cohens and Kellys in
  Trouble
Counsellor at Law
Rafter Romance
Victims of Persecution
1934 Our Daily Bread
Straight Is the Way
1937 The Cantor's Son
That I May Live
1939 A Brivele der Mamen
1940 Americaner Schadchen
1941 Mazel Tov Yidden
1943 Action in the North Atlantic
Bataan
Margin for Error
1944 Address Unknown
Mr. Skeffington
Tomorrow the World!
1945 Pride of the Marines
Rhapsody in Blue
1946 Abie's Irish Rose
1947 The Burning Cross
Crossfire
Humoresque
The Jolson Story
1948 Big City
Gentleman's Agreement
Open Secret
1949 Jigsaw
The Prairie

Prejudice
The Red Menace
1950 Battleground
Catskill Honeymoon
Jolson Sings Again
Monticello, Here We Come!
Sands of Iwo Jima
1950? Three Daughters
1951 The Magnificent Yankee
Molly
1952 It's a Big Country: An
  American Anthology
1953 The Eddie Cantor Story
The Jazz Singer
Tonight We Sing
1954 Go Man Go
1955 Good Morning, Miss Dove
Not As a Stranger
1956 The Benny Goodman Story
Singing in the Dark
1958 Home Before Dark
Marjorie Morningstar
Never Love a Stranger
The Young Lions
1959 The Last Angry Man
1960 The Dark at the Top of the
  Stairs

Kiowa
1920 The Daughter of Dawn
1937 Prairie Thunder
1950 Two Flags West
1953 Last of the Comanches
1954 They Rode West
Thunder Pass
War Arrow
1955 Santa Fe Passage
1960 Flaming Star
The Unforgiven

Latino
1914 The Great Diamond Robbery
Rose of the Rancho
1915 Captain Courtesy
The Grandee's Ring
The Pageant of San
  Francisco
The Penitentes
1916 The Aryan
The Daughter of the Don
Following the Flag in
  Mexico
Mixed Blood
Ramona
A Sister of Six
A Yoke of Gold
1917 The Little Boy Scout
1918 The Only Road
Untamed
Woman and the Law
A Woman of Impulse
1919 Desert Gold
Lasca
The Scar
Scarlet Days
1920 For the Soul of Rafael
The Mark of Zorro
Rio Grande
The Tiger's Coat
1921 By Right of Birth
A Divorce of Convenience
The Double O
The Kiss
1922 Big Stakes
A California Romance
Captain Fly-by-Night
Cross Roads
The Power of Love
The Pride of Palomar
Silver Spurs
1923 Jealous Husbands
The Spider and the Rose
Suzanna
1924 California in '49
Down by the Rio Grande
The Lightning Rider
The Night Hawk
Yankee Speed
1925 Brand of Cowardice
Don Q, Son of Zorro
Flower of Night
Tonio, Son of the Sierras

1926 Desert Gold
The Fighting Edge
1927 Aflame in the Sky
Blind Alleys
California
Don Mike
The Dove
The Gay Defender
Rose of the Golden West
White Gold
1927? El que a hierro mata
1928 Breed of the Sunsets
The Broken Mask
The Canyon of Adventure
The Cavalier
Hold 'Em Yale
1929 The Desert Rider
In Old Arizona
In Old California
Romance of the Rio Grande
Señor Americano
1930 The Arizona Kid
The Bad Man
Las campanas de Capistrano
Cuando el amor ríe
Estrellados
The Lash
On the Border
Song of the Caballero
Toda una vida
El último de los Vargas
1931 The Avenger
The Cisco Kid
The Hurricane Horseman
Riders of the Rio
Yankee Don
1932 Amor y vida
The Galloping Kid
Law and Lawless
The Vanishing Frontier
1933 The California Trail
It's Great to Be Alive
Man from Monterey
1934 The Battling Buckaroo
Call of the Coyote
The Fighting Hero
The Lone Defender
The Prescott Kid
1935 Bordertown
Cowboy Holiday
The Cyclone Ranger
Riddle Ranch
1935? The Irish Gringo
1936 Aces and Eights
The Bold Caballero
Dancing Pirate
The Phantom of Santa Fe
Pinto Rustlers
Ramona
Rebellion
Robin Hood of El Dorado
Rose of the Rancho
Song of the Gringo
Sutter's Gold
The Traitor
1937 Border Cafe
The Californian
The Devil's Playground
Law and Lead
Old Louisiana
1938 California Frontier
Little Miss Roughneck
Outlaw Express
Passport Husband
The Renegade Ranger
Wild Horse Canyon
1939 Bad Lands
The Cisco Kid and the Lady
Drifting Westward
The Fighting Gringo
Frontiers of '49
The Girl from Mexico
Heaven with a Barbed Wire
  Fence
In Old Caliente
Miracle on Main Street
The Return of the Cisco Kid
1940 Behind the News
Covered Wagon Days
The Gay Caballero

Kit Carson
Lucky Cisco Kid
The Mark of Zorro
Mexican Spitfire
Mexican Spitfire Out West
Rhythm of the Rio Grande
Too Many Girls
Viva Cisco Kid
Young Buffalo Bill
1941 Doomed Caravan
Gauchos of Eldorado
Land of Liberty
The Mexican Spitfire's Baby
Playmates
Prairie Pioneers
Ride on Vaquero
Road Agent
Romance of the Rio Grande
Under Fiesta Stars
1942 Below the Border
From Across the Border
Mexican Spitfire at Sea
Mexican Spitfire Sees a
  Ghost
Mexican Spitfire's Elephant
The Navy Comes Through
Rio Rita
Tortilla Flat
1943 Bataan
Border Patrol
The Gang's All Here
The Girl from Monterrey
Ladies' Day
The Leopard Man
Mexican Spitfire's Blessed
  Event
The Ox-Bow Incident
Redhead from Manhattan
1944 Something for the Boys
1945 The Cisco Kid Returns
Club Havana
The Gay Senorita
In Old New Mexico
A Medal for Benny
Pride of the Marines
South of the Rio Grande
Wanderer of the Wasteland
1946 Beauty and the Bandit
Border Bandits
Cuban Pete
Don Ricardo Returns
The Gay Cavalier
Slightly Scandalous
South of Monterey
Strange Voyage
Sunset Pass
Without Reservations
1947 The Adventures of Don
  Coyote
Bells of San Fernando
California
Copacabana
King of the Bandits
Pirates of Monterey
Ride the Pink Horse
Riding the California Trail
Robin Hood of Monterey
Thunder Mountain
Under the Tonto Rim
West to Glory
Wild Horse Mesa
1948 Angel in Exile
The Arizona Ranger
Four Faces West
Gun Smugglers
Guns of Hate
Half Past Midnight
Indian Agent
Old Los Angeles
Red River
Shep Comes Home
Silver Trails
Western Heritage
1949 Border Incident
Brothers in the Saddle
The Daring Caballero
The Gay Amigo
The Golden Stallion
The Kissing Bandit
Knock on Any Door

Lust for Gold
Masked Raiders
The Mysterious Desperado
Riders of the Range
Roll Thunder Roll!
Rustlers
Satan's Cradle
Stagecoach Kid
Streets of Laredo
3 Godfathers
The Valiant Hombre
We Were Strangers
1950 Bandit Queen
The Baron of Arizona
Battleground
Belle of Old Mexico
Border Treasure
The Furies
The Girl from San Lorenzo
The Lawless
The Men
Mystery Street
The Palomino
Right Cross
Rio Grande Patrol
So Young, So Bad
Storm Over Wyoming
Sunset in the West
1951 Apache Drums
Cuban Fireball
Hurricane Island
The Mark of the Renegade
1952 California Conquest
The Fabulous Senorita
The Fighter
High Noon
The Iron Mistress
My Man and I
The Raiders
The Ring
1953 The Man Behind the Gun
The Man from the Alamo
Ride, Vaquero!
San Antone
Sangaree
1954 Passion
Salt of the Earth
1955 Apache Ambush
Headline Hunters
Kiss of Fire
The Last Command
Seven Cities of Gold
Trial
1956 The Broken Star
The Burning Hills
Comanche
Crowded Paradise
Giant
Man from Del Rio
Wetbacks
1957 Gun Battle at Monterey
The Guns of Fort Petticoat
Man in the Shadow
Raiders of Old California
The Ride Back
Twelve Angry Men
War Drums
1958 Ambush at Cimarron Pass
The Badlanders
Escape from Red Rock
Gunfire at Indian Gap
Machete
Sierra Baron
Terror in a Texas Town
Touch of Evil
1959 Cry Tough
Gunmen from Laredo
The Young Land
1960 Key Witness
The Plunderers
The Pusher
The Sign of Zorro
This Rebel Breed
Lithuanian Americans
1914 The Jungle
Membreno Apache
1955 Fort Yuma

Mennonites
1938 Breaking the Ice
Mescalero
1951 Apache Drums
Miami
1951 When the Redskins Rode
Middle Eastern Americans
1953 Dream Wife
Mingo
1953 The Pathfinder
Modoc
1954 Drum Beat
Mohawk
1950 The Iroquois Trail
1956 Mohawk
Mohegan
1917 The Hidden Children
1920 The Last of the Mohicans
1922 The Mohican's Daughter
1936 The Last of the Mohicans
1943 Deerslayer
1953 The Pathfinder
1957 The Deerslayer
Multi-ethnic
1917 The Slacker
1918 Hitting the Trail
1919 The Lost Battalion
1930 King of Jazz
1931 Street Scene
1943 Action in the North Atlantic
        Air Force
        Bataan
1944 Lifeboat
1946 Gas House Kids
1947 Body and Soul
1950 Battleground
Native Alaskans
19?? A Trip Through the Arctic
        with Uncle Sam
1912 The Alaska-Siberian
        Expedition
        Atop of the World in Motion
1914 Captain F. E. Kleinschmidt's
        Arctic Hunt
        An Odyssey of the North
1917 Alaska Wonders in Motion
1919? Alaska
1921 Wolves of the North
1922 Nanook of the North
1925 Justice of the Far North
        Kivalina of the Ice Lands
        The True North
1927 Primitive Love
1928 The Great White North
1929 Frozen Justice
1930 The Break Up
1932 Dangers of the Arctic
        Igloo
1934 Eskimo
1936 Sea Spoilers
        Tundra
1937 The Barrier
1938 Spawn of the North
1940 Girl from God's Country
        Taku
1941 Mutiny in the Arctic
1947 Spoilers of the North
1948 Harpoon
1949 Arctic Fury
        Arctic Manhunt
        Rose of the Yukon
1952 Arctic Flight
        Red Snow
1960 Ice Palace
Native Americans *see also* **entries**
    under specific tribes
19?? A Trip Through the Arctic
        with Uncle Sam
1912 The Alaska-Siberian
        Expedition
        Atop of the World in Motion
1913? The Call of the Blood
        Hiawatha
1914 Captain F. E. Kleinschmidt's
        Arctic Hunt
        The Good-for-Nothing
        Hearts United
        In the Days of the
        Thundering Herd
        In the Land of the Head
        Hunters
        The Indian Wars

Life's Shop Window
The Little Angel of Canyon
    Creek
Northern Lights
An Odyssey of the North
The Squaw Man
Where the Trail Divides
1914? The Lust of the Red Man
        Sitting Bull—The Hostile
        Sioux Indian Chief
1915 The Gambler of the West
        The Girl I Left Behind Me
        The Lamb
        The Lure of Woman
        The Penitentes
        Sealed Valley
        Where Cowboy Is King
1915? Life of American Indian [sic]
1916 The Aryan
        Betrayed
        Britton of the Seventh
        The Flower of No Man's
        Land
        Gold and the Woman
        The Half-Breed
        Her Debt of Honor
        Lone Star
        Ramona
        Witchcraft
1916? Fate's Chessboard
1917 The Adventures of Buffalo
        Bill
        Alaska Wonders in Motion
        The Barrier
        The Bronze Bride
        The Buffalo Bill Show
        The Captain of the Gray
        Horse Troop
        The Conqueror
        The Gun Fighter
        Her Own People
        The Hidden Children
        John Ermine of the
        Yellowstone
        The Plow Woman
        The Primitive Call
        The Red Woman
        The Spirit of '76
        The Squaw Man's Son
        The Tenderfoot
1918 The Goddess of Lost Lake
        The Hell Cat
        Huck and Tom; or, the
        Further Adventures of
        Tom Sawyer
        Laughing Bill Hyde
        The Man Above the Law
        The Red, Red Heart
        The Squaw Man
        Tongues of Flame
1918? Indian Life
1919 Desert Gold
        Diane of the Green Van
        The Gray Towers Mystery
        The Heart of Wetona
        Just Squaw
        The Last of His People
        Told in the Hills
        The Westerners
1919? Alaska
        In the Land of the Setting
        Sun; or, Martyrs of
        Yesterday
1920 Before the White Man Came
        The Daughter of Dawn
        Frontier Days
        The Girl of My Heart
        The Last of the Mohicans
        The Third Woman
1921 Across the Divide
        By Right of Birth
        The Cave Girl
        The Girl from God's
        Country
        The Hunger of the Blood
        Lonely Heart
        That Girl Montana
        Wolves of the North
1922 Blazing Arrows
        Cardigan

Cross Roads
The Crow's Nest
The Great Alone
The Half Breed
The Mohican's Daughter
Nanook of the North
One Eighth Apache
The Son of the Wolf
Winning of the West
1923 Crashin' Thru
        The Huntress
        Jamestown
        The Lone Wagon
        The Secret of the Pueblo
        Snowdrift
        The Sting of the Scorpion
1924 The Broken Law
        The Heritage of the Desert
        The Mine with the Iron
        Door
        North of Nevada
        North of 36
        Peter Pan
        Tongues of Flame
        Unseen Hands
1925 Braveheart
        Custer's Last Fight
        A Daughter of the Sioux
        Galloping Vengeance
        The Gold Hunters
        Justice of the Far North
        Kivalina of the Ice Lands
        Quicker'n Lightnin'
        Red Love
        The Red Rider
        The Scarlet West
        The Thundering Herd
        Tonio, Son of the Sierras
        The True North
        Warrior Gap
        The Wild Bull's Lair
1926 The Barrier
        Buffalo Bill on the U. P.
        Trail
        Desert Gold
        The Devil Horse
        The Flaming Frontier
        The Frontier Trail
        General Custer at Little Big
        Horn
        The Last Frontier
        Under Fire
        The Vanishing American
        War Paint
1927 The Devil's Saddle
        Drums of the Desert
        The Fighting Hombre
        The Frontiersman
        Open Range
        The Overland Stage
        Primitive Love
        Red Clay
        The Red Raiders
        Spoilers of the West
        Winners of the Wilderness
        With Sitting Bull at the
        Spirit Lake Massacre
1928 The Glorious Trail
        The Great White North
        Kit Carson
        Orphan of the Sage
        Ramona
        The Riding Renegade
        Wyoming
1929 Frozen Justice
        Hawk of the Hills
        The Invaders
        The Overland Telegraph
        Redskin
        Sioux Blood
        Wolf Song
1930 The Break Up
        The Silent Enemy
        Tom Sawyer
        Whoopee
1931 Call of the Rockies
        Cavalier of the West
        Cimarron
        Fighting Caravans
        The Great Meadow

Oklahoma Jim
The Squaw Man
1932 Call Her Savage
Dangers of the Arctic
The Forty-Niners
The Golden West
Hidden Valley
Igloo
Mystery Ranch
The Rainbow Trail
Riders of the Desert
Texas Pioneers
White Eagle
Wild Horse Mesa
1933 Circle Canyon
Diplomaniacs
King of the Wild Horses
The Telegraph Trail
Thundering Herd
1934 Behold My Wife!
The Cactus Kid
Cheyenne Sun Dance
Eskimo
Fighting Through
Laughing Boy
Massacre
'Neath the Arizona Skies
The Star Packer
Wagon Wheels
Wheels of Destiny
1935 Annie Oakley
Circle of Death
Cyclone of the Saddle
Fighting Pioneers
North of Arizona
Range Warfare
The Singing Vagabond
Texas Terror
Wolf Riders
1936 Custer's Last Stand
Daniel Boone
Desert Gold
For the Service
The Glory Trail
The Last of the Mohicans
Ramona
Ride, Ranger, Ride
Sea Spoilers
Silly Billies
Treachery Rides the Range
Tundra
West of Nevada
1937 The Barrier
Drums of Destiny
Hills of Old Wyoming
Life Begins in College
The Plainsman
Prairie Thunder
The Riders of the Whistling
Skull
1938 The Adventures of Tom
Sawyer
Spawn of the North
The Texans
1939 Allegheny Uprising
Bad Lands
Drums Along the Mohawk
Man of Conquest
1940 Arizona Frontier
Geronimo
Girl from God's Country
Hi-Yo Silver
Kit Carson
Northwest Passage (Book
I—Rogers' Rangers)
Prairie Schooners
Taku
Young Buffalo Bill
1941 Hurry, Charlie, Hurry
In the Land of the Navajo
Land of Liberty
Mutiny in the Arctic
The Pioneers
Saddlemates
This Woman Is Mine
Thunder Over the Prairie
Western Union
1942 Apache Trail
King of the Stallions
Lawless Plainsmen

Shut My Big Mouth
They Died With Their Boots
On
Valley of the Sun
1943 Deerslayer
Frontier Fury
In Old Oklahoma
The Law Rides Again
The Outlaw
Wagon Tracks West
1944 Buffalo Bill
Marshal of Reno
Outlaw Trail
Riding West
The San Antonio Kid
Sheriff of Las Vegas
Sonora Stagecoach
Tucson Raiders
Vigilantes of Dodge City
1945 Colorado Pioneers
Great Stagecoach Robbery
El Navajo
The Navajo Trail
Phantom of the Plains
Where Do We Go From
Here?
1946 Bad Bascomb
California Gold Rush
Canyon Passage
Renegade Girl
Romance of the West
Santa Fe Uprising
Sheriff of Redwood Valley
Singin' in the Corn
Sun Valley Cyclone
Wild Beauty
Wild West
1947 Black Gold
Bowery Buckaroos
Buffalo Bill Rides Again
Dangerous Venture
Duel in the Sun
It Had To Be You
Last of the Redmen
The Last Round-Up
Marshal of Cripple Creek
Oregon Trail Scouts
Rustlers of Devil's Canyon
Spoilers of the North
Vigilantes of Boomtown
1948 The Dude Goes West
Flight to the Sun
Fort Apache
Fury at Furnace Creek
Harpoon
Indian Agent
Key Largo
The Paleface
Red River
Renegades of Sonora
Singin' Spurs
Tap Roots
Unconquered
1949 Apache Chief
Arctic Fury
Arctic Manhunt
Call of the Forest
Colorado Territory
The Cowboy and the Indians
The Cowboy and the
Prizefighter
The Dalton Gang
Daughter of the West
Laramie
Lust for Gold
Massacre River
The Prairie
Ranger of Cherokee Strip
Ride, Ryder, Ride!
Roll Thunder Roll!
Rose of the Yukon
She Wore a Yellow Ribbon
Stallion Canyon
Tale of the Navajos
Tulsa
1950 Ambush
Annie Get Your Gun
Broken Arrow
Cherokee Uprising
Colt .45

Comanche Territory
Davy Crockett, Indian Scout
Devil's Doorway
I Killed Geronimo
Indian Territory
The Iroquois Trail
North of the Great Divide
Raiders of Tomahawk Creek
Riders of the Pony Express
Rio Grande
Rock Island Trail
Rocky Mountain
A Ticket to Tomahawk
Train to Tombstone
The Traveling Saleswoman
Two Flags West
Winchester '73
Young Daniel Boone
1951 Across the Wide Missouri
Apache Drums
Cavalry Scout
Cyclone Fury
Distant Drums
Flaming Feather
Fort Defiance
Hurricane Island
Jim Thorpe—All-American
The Last Outpost
Little Big Horn
New Mexico
Oh! Susanna
Only the Valiant
Slaughter Trail
Snake River Desperadoes
Tomahawk
Warpath
When the Redskins Rode
1952 Apache Country
Apache War Smoke
Arctic Flight
The Battle at Apache Pass
Battles of Chief Pontiac
The Big Sky
Brave Warrior
Buffalo Bill in Tomahawk
Territory
Bugles in the Afternoon
Desert Pursuit
Fort Osage
The Half-Breed
Hiawatha
Indian Uprising
Navajo
Red Snow
Rose of Cimarron
The Savage
Trail of the Arrow
Wagons West
1952? Call of the Navajo
1953 Ambush at Tomahawk Gap
Arrowhead
Captain John Smith and
Pocahontas
The Charge at Feather River
Column South
Conquest of Cochise
Fort Ti
The Great Sioux Uprising
Jack McCall Desperado
Last of the Comanches
The Nebraskan
Old Overland Trail
The Pathfinder
Seminole
The Stand at Apache River
Tumbleweed
War Paint
1954 Apache
Arrow in the Dust
Battle of Rogue River
The Black Dakotas
Broken Lance
Cattle Queen of Montana
Dangerous Mission
Drum Beat
Drums Across the River
Hondo
Massacre Canyon
Overland Pacific

Saskatchewan
Siege at Red River
Sitting Bull
Taza, Son of Cochise
They Rode West
Thunder Pass
War Arrow
The Yellow Tomahawk
1955 Apache Ambush
Apache Woman
Chief Crazy Horse
Davy Crockett, King of the
Wild Frontier
Day of Decision
The Far Horizons
Fort Yuma
Foxfire
The Gun That Won the West
Indian American
The Indian Fighter
Kentucky Rifle
Kiss of Fire
The Lonesome Trail
Santa Fe Passage
Seminole Uprising
Seven Cities of Gold
Shotgun
Smoke Signal
The Vanishing American
White Feather
1956 The Broken Star
The Burning Hills
Comanche
Dakota Incident
Daniel Boone, Trail Blazer
Davy Crockett and the River
Pirates
Frontier Woman
Ghost Town
The Last Frontier
The Last Hunt
The Last Wagon
The Lone Ranger
Mohawk
Pillars of the Sky
Quincannon, Frontier Scout
Raw Edge
Reprisal!
The Searchers
Secret of Treasure Mountain
7th Cavalry
Walk the Proud Land
Westward Ho the Wagons!
The White Squaw
The Wild Dakotas
1957 Apache Warrior
The Deerslayer
Dragoon Wells Massacre
The Guns of Fort Petticoat
The Halliday Brand
Joe Dakota
The Lawless Eighties
Naked in the Sun
The Oklahoman
Pawnee
Revolt at Fort Laramie
The Ride Back
Ride Out for Revenge
Run of the Arrow
The Tin Star
Tomahawk Trail
Trooper Hook
War Drums
1958 Ambush at Cimarron Pass
Apache Territory
Blood Arrow
Bullwhip
Escape from Red Rock
Flaming Frontier
Fort Bowie
Fort Massacre
Frontier Gun
Gun Fever
Gunman's Walk
The Light in the Forest
The Lone Ranger and the
Lost City of Gold
Oregon Passage
The Rawhide Trail

Tonka
1959   The FBI Story
Gunmen from Laredo
Last Train from Gun Hill
The Oregon Trail
The Sheriff of Fractured Jaw
The Wonderful Country
Yellowstone Kelly
1960   All the Young Men
Cimarron
Comanche Station
Flaming Star
For the Love of Mike
Ice Palace
Oklahoma Territory
The Unforgiven
Walk Tall

Navajo
1918   The Man Above the Law
1925   Tonio, Son of the Sierras
1926   The Vanishing American
1927   Drums of the Desert
1929   Redskin
1933   King of the Wild Horses
1934   Laughing Boy
1941   In the Land of the Navajo
1945   El Navajo
The Navajo Trail
1949   The Dalton Gang
Daughter of the West
Tale of the Navajos
1951   Fort Defiance
Slaughter Trail
1952   Navajo
1952?   Call of the Navajo
1953   Ambush at Tomahawk Gap
Column South
1955   Day of Decision
The Vanishing American
1960   All the Young Men
Norwegian Americans
1915   A Yankee from the West
1938   Happy Landing
My Lucky Star
1940   Knute Rockne—All American
1941   Sun Valley Serenade
1943   Wintertime
1944   My Pal Wolf
1945   Our Vines Have Tender
Grapes
1948   I Remember Mama
Ojibway
1952   Hiawatha
Osage
1931   Cimarron
1952   Fort Osage
Trail of the Arrow
1959   The FBI Story
Ottawa
1948   Unconquered
1951   When the Redskins Rode
1952   Battles of Chief Pontiac
1953   Fort Ti
Paiute
1934   Laughing Boy
1948   The Dude Goes West
1955   Kiss of Fire
Palouse
1956   Pillars of the Sky
Pawnee
1943   Wagon Tracks West
1954   Arrow in the Dust
1956   Westward Ho the Wagons!
1957   Pawnee
1958   Fort Massacre
Persian Americans
1920   The Devil's Claim
Pima
1942   Lawless Plainsmen
1955   Day of Decision
1958   Apache Territory
Piute
1958   Fort Massacre
Polish Americans
1918   Love's Law
1921   The Land of Hope
1924   Two Shall Be Born
1926   The Passaic Textile Strike
1934   As the Earth Turns
1935   The Wedding Night
1941   New York Town

1942   We Were Dancing
1944   Since You Went Away
1948   Call Northside 777
The Miracle of the Bells
The Time of Your Life
1949   Anna Lucasta
1950   The Missourians
Sands of Iwo Jima
1951   Gambling House
The House on Telegraph
Hill
Queen for a Day
Saturday's Hero
A Streetcar Named Desire
1953   The Stars Are Singing
1955   Good Morning, Miss Dove
Polish language
1941   Ten Ostatni
Wiejskie Wesele
Z Dymem Pożarów
Polynesian Americans
1931   Aloha
1944   Tahiti Nights
Portuguese Americans
1920   The Paliser Case
1925   My Son
1932   Tiger Shark
1934   He Was Her Man
1939   Daughters Courageous
1941   Accent on Love
1942   Tortilla Flat
1949   Tuna Clipper
Pueblo
1923   The Secret of the Pueblo
Racial impersonation
1929   Why Bring That Up?
1930   The Grand Parade
1931   Pardon Us
1935   Harmony Lane
1936   Dimples
1944   Minstrel Man
Refugees
1916   Following the Flag in
Mexico
1941   New York Town
1942   Woman of the Year
1943   The Amazing Mrs. Holliday
Gangway for Tomorrow
Three Hearts for Julia
1944   Lady, Let's Dance!
1945   Jealousy
1946   The Gentleman Misbehaves
Rendezvous 24
1947   The Return of Rin Tin Tin
1950   A Lady Without Passport
1951   The Girl on the Bridge
Romanian Americans
1917   The Trouble Buster
1918   Her Moment
1946   The Sailor Takes a Wife
Russian Americans
1915   The Clemenceau Case
The Immigrant
The Melting Pot
1916   The King's Game
Light at Dusk
Man and His Angel
The Scarlet Oath
Sold for Marriage
1917   Crime and Punishment
One Law for Both
Under False Colors
1918   The Firebrand
The Million Dollar Mystery
1919   The Red Viper
1920   Billions
Dangerous Hours
The Face at Your Window
The Great Shadow
Lifting Shadows
On with the Dance
Uncharted Channels
1920?   Her Story
1922   The Hands of Nara
1923   Fashion Row
1924   The Lure of Love
1925   The Midnight Girl
1926   Into Her Kingdom
Meet the Prince
1927   The Princess from Hoboken
1928   The Mating Call
Tyrant of Red Gulch

United States Smith
Wheel of Chance
1930   She Got What She Wanted
1931   Delicious
1933   Grand Slam
1934   Strange Wives
1936   Paddy O'Day
1937   Big City
1939   The Mystery of Mr. Wong
1940   Elsa Maxwell's Public Deb
No. 1
1942   Twin Beds
1943   Good Luck, Mr. Yates
His Butler's Sister
Let's Have Fun
1945   Salome, Where She Danced
1947   Northwest Outpost
1952   Anything Can Happen
1953   Tonight We Sing
1960   Man on a String
Scandinavian Americans
1947   Calendar Girl
1956   The White Squaw
Scottish Americans
1916   Ramona
1917   The Plow Woman
1918   Sandy
1919   Bonnie, Bonnie Lassie
False Evidence
The Homesteader
1927   McFadden's Flats
1931   Delicious
1935   McFadden's Flats
1940   Three Cheers for the Irish
1941   This Woman Is Mine
Where Did You Get That
Girl?
1948   Rocky
1949   Tuna Clipper
1955   A Man Called Peter
1957   All Mine to Give
1959   John Paul Jones
Seminole
1916?   Fate's Chessboard
1919   Diane of the Green Van
1937   Drums of Destiny
1948   Key Largo
1951   Distant Drums
1953   Seminole
1954   War Arrow
1955   Seminole Uprising
1957   Naked in the Sun
Serbian Americans
1942   Cat People
Shawnee
1931   The Great Meadow
1950   Young Daniel Boone
1952   Brave Warrior
1956   Daniel Boone, Trail Blazer
Shoshoni
1940   Kit Carson
1950   Devil's Doorway
1955   Chief Crazy Horse
The Far Horizons
1958   Oregon Passage
1960   Walk Tall
Siksika
1915   The Girl I Left Behind Me
1928   Kit Carson
1951   Across the Wide Missouri
1952   The Big Sky
1954   Cattle Queen of Montana
1958   Blood Arrow
Flaming Frontier
Siwash
1924   Tongues of Flame
Skitswish
1956   Pillars of the Sky
Slavic Americans
1936   Dangerous Intrigue
1949   Knock on Any Door
Slovakian Americans
1928   A Ship Comes In
Spanish language
1928   El Robin Hood de México
1929   Hambre
Sombras habaneras
1930   Alma de gaucho
Amor audaz
Así es la vida
The Bad Man
Las campanas de Capistrano

Una cana al aire
Cascarrabias
Charros, gauchos y manolas
Cuando el amor ríe
El cuerpo del delito
¡De frente, marchen!
Del mismo barro
El dios del mar
Doña mentiras
Estrellados
La fuerza del querer
Galas de la Paramount
Un hombre de suerte
La jaula de los leones
Locuras de amor
Los que danzan
Monsieur le Fox
Olimpia
El precio de un beso
El presidio
El príncipe del dólar
Revista Hispano-Americana
La rosa de fuego
El secreto del doctor
Sevilla de mis amores
Sombras de gloria
Toda una vida
El último de los Vargas
El valiente
La voluntad del muerto
Wu Li Chang
1931   Un caballero de frac
Los calaveras
Carne de cabaret
La carta
La cautivadora
Cheri-Bibi
El código penal
El comediante
¿Conoces a tu mujer?
Cuerpo y alma
La dama atrevida
Del infierno al cielo
Don Juan diplomático
Drácula
En cada puerto un amor
Esclavas de la moda
La fiesta del diablo
La fruta amarga
Gente alegre
La gran jornada
Hay que casar al príncipe
El impostor
La incorregible
La ley del harem
La llama sagrada
Lo mejor es reír
Las luces de Buenos Aires
Mamá
Mi último amor
Monerías
La mujer X
Noche de duendes
El pasado acusa
Politiquerías
El príncipe gondolero
El proceso de Mary Dugan
La pura verdad
Regeneración
Resurrección
Sombras del circo
Su noche de bodas
Su última noche
El tenorio del harem
1932   El caballero de la noche
¿Cuándo te suicidas?
Hollywood, ciudad de
ensueño
El hombre que asesinó
Hombres en mi vida
Marido y mujer
Soñadores de la gloria
1933   Dos noches
Espérame
Melodía de arrabal
La melodía prohibida
No dejes la puerta abierta
Primavera en otoño
El rey de los gitanos

Una viuda romántica
Yo, tú y ella
1934 La buenaventura
Un capitán de cosacos
La ciudad de cartón
La cruz y la espada
Cuesta abajo
Dos más uno, dos
Las fronteras del amor
Granaderos del amor
Nada más que una mujer
El tango en Broadway
Tres amores
1935 Alas sobre el Chaco
Angelina o el honor de un
brigadier
¡Asegure a su mujer!
El cantante de Nápoles
De la sartén al fuego
El día que me quieras
Un hombre peligroso
Julieta compra un hijo
No matarás
Piernas de seda
Rosa de Francia
Señora casada necesita
marido
Tango Bar
Te quiero con locura
1936 Amor que vuelve
Contra la corriente
El crimen de media noche
El diablo del mar
La última cita
1937 El capitán Tormenta
El carnaval del diablo
1938 Castillos en el aire
Di que me quieres
Mis dos amores
La vida bohemia
1939 Los hijos mandan
La Inmaculada
Miracle on Main Street
El otro soy yo
Papá soltero
El trovador de la radio
Verbena trágica
1940 Cuando canta la Ley
Perfidia
Tengo fe en ti

Spokane
1956 Pillars of the Sky
Swedish Americans
1916 The Thousand Dollar
Husband
1917 Follow the Girl
1918 How Could You, Jean?
The Source
1919 The Unpainted Woman
1921 Guile of Women
1922 The Scrapper
1923 Anna Christie
1925 The Prairie Wife
1926 The Campus Flirt
1927 Wild Geese
1930 Anna Christie
1931 Mr. Lemon of Orange
Three Who Loved
1932 The Match King
1933 Let's Fall in Love
Olsen's Big Moment
1934 Coming Out Party
Our Daily Bread
1940 If I Had My Way
1941 Ice-Capades
1942 Sunday Punch
1943 His Butler's Sister
Svenkst I Och Omkring New
York
1947 The Burning Cross
The Farmer's Daughter
1949 Prejudice
1951 The Raging Tide
1955 Not As a Stranger
1956 The Searchers
1958 Terror in a Texas Town
1960 All the Young Men
Weddings and Babies

Swedish language
1943 Svenkst I Och Omkring New
York
Swiss Americans
1959 The Hanging Tree
Syrian Americans
1921 The Syrian Immigrant
1922 Anna Ascends
Tagalog language
1938 Zamboanga
Turkish Americans
1927 Turkish Delight
Tuscarora
1953 The Pathfinder
1956 Mohawk
Tututni
1954 Battle of Rogue River
Ukrainian Americans
1940 The Tragedy of
Carpatho-Ukraine
Ukrainian language
1937 Natalka Poltavka
1938 Marusia
1939 Cossacks in Exile
1940 The Tragedy of
Carpatho-Ukraine
Ute
1951 Flaming Feather
1952 Navajo
1954 Drums Across the River
1955 Smoke Signal
1956 The Burning Hills
Welsh Americans
1951 Apache Drums
Yakima
1956 Raw Edge
Yaqui
1915 The Lamb
1919 Desert Gold
1922 Cross Roads
1926 Desert Gold
1953 Tumbleweed
Yiddish language
1930 Eternal Fools (Ewige
Naranim)
My Yiddishe Mama
1931 Shulamith
The Voice of Israel
Zein Weib's Lubovnick
1932 A Daughter of Her People
Joseph in the Land of Egypt
Mazel Tov
Uncle Moses
The Unfortunate Bride
Yiskor
1933 The Eternal Jew
Live and Laugh
The Wandering Jew
1934 The Rabbi's Power
What a Mother-in-Law!
The Youth of Russia
1935 Bar-Mitzvah
Shir Hashirim
The Yiddish King Lear
1936 Love and Sacrifice
Yiddle with His Fiddle
1937 The Cantor's Son
Green Fields
The Holy Oath
I Want to Be a Mother
The Jester (Der
Purimspieler)
Where Is My Child?
1938 The Power of Life
The Singing Blacksmith
Two Sisters
1939 A Brivele der Mamen
Kol Nidre
The Light Ahead
Mamele
Mirele Efros
Motel the Operator
Mothers of Today
My Son
Tevya
1940 Americaner Schadchen
Eli Eli
The Great Advisor
Her Second Mother
The Jewish Melody
Overture to Glory

1941 Mazel Tov Yidden
1950 Catskill Honeymoon
God, Man and Devil
Monticello, Here We Come!
1950? Three Daughters
Yugoslavian Americans
1932 Ljubav i strast

FOREIGN LANGUAGE INDEX

★ The following index identifies films included in *Within Our Gates* that were produced either completely or partially in languages other than English. The index is arranged by language, and the film titles are listed chronologically, then alphabetically. Films that were made in more than one foreign language are listed separately under each language.

FOREIGN LANGUAGE INDEX

Armenian
1937   Arshin Mal Alan
1945   Anoush
Chinese
1934   Blossom Time
1936   Sum Hun
1939?   A Chinese Gains a
           Fortune in America
1940   Hua Chio Juh Guang
           Won Lee Shuen Fu
1941   Golden Gate Girl
           Min Jok Jay Hung Sing
1943   Gin Guo Chin Yuan
1944   Chin Hai In Siong
           Guon Min Guh Lu
           Kuan Fong Lang Tyeh
1946?   Yee Sio Bo Laan Sin
1947?   Bow Yu Lee Hua
           Gin Fen Nee Shaan
           Hai Jeow Chin Yuan
           Hong Yien Fei Bo Ming
           Hoon Si Gway Lai
           Jia O Tien Chen
           Luan Feng Heh Ming
           Sing Yun Sin Nian
           Yu Luh Shen Ping
1948?   Jeng Yien Doe Lee
           Kuang Feng Juu Yien Fay
           Too Yien Fen Fong
1949?   Lang Hu Bee Yuh
           Shuang Feng Cheo Huang
           Yein Dow
1953?   Tan Dow Jia Jen
1955?   Yin Hua Chu Chu Kai
Croatian
1932   Ljubav i strast
French
1930   Les chercheuses d'or
           L'énigmatique Monsieur
              Parkes
           La grande mare
           Le secret du docteur
           Si l'empereur savait ça!
           Le spectre vert
           Toute sa vie
           Un trou dans le mur
1931   Boudoir diplomatique
           Buster se marie
           Les carottiers
           Chérie
           Echec au roi
           Jenny Lind
           Marions-nous
           Nuit d'Espagne
           L'opera de quat' sous
           Le père célibataire
           Le petit café
           La piste des géants
           Le procès de Mary Dugan
           Quand on est belle
           Soyons gais
1932   L'athlète incomplet
           Le bluffeur
           Le cas du docteur
              Brenner
           La foule hurle
           Une heure près de toi
           Le plombier amoureux
1933   L'amour guide
1934   Caravane
           La veuve joyeuse
1935   L'homme des Folies
              Bergère

German
1928   Das Grosse Glueck
1929   Die Königsloge
1930   Anna Christie
           Olympia
           Die Sehnsucht Jeder Frau
           Seine Freundin Annette
           Der Tanz geht weiter
1931   Casanova wider Willen
           Dämon des Meeres
           Die Dreigroschenoper
           Die grosse Fahrt
           Die heilige Flamme
           Jede Frau hat etwas
           Kismet
           Liebe auf Befehl
           Die Maske Fällt
           Mordprozess Mary Dugan
           Die nackte Wahrheit
           Sonntag des Lebens
           Tropennächte
           Weib im Dschungel
Greek
1931   Such Is Life
1954   Barefoot Battalion
Hebrew
1950   Monticello, Here We
              Come!
Hungarian
1930   Az orvos titka
Italian
1930   Monsieur la Volpe
           Perché no?
           Il richiamo del cuore
           Il segreto del dottore
           Sei tu l'amore
1931   Così è la vita
           La donna bianca
           Il grande sentiero
           Pagliacci
           La regina di Sparta
           La riva dei bruti
           La vacanza del diavolo
1931?   La porta del destino
1932   Amor in montagna
           Amore e morte
           Cuore d'emigrante
           Genoveffa
           O festino o la legge
           Parigi affascina; ovvero,
              Malavita
           Senza mamma
              e'nnamurato
           Tormento
1938?   Amore che non torna
           I due gemelli
Japanese
1927   [Japanese-American Film]
1930   Chijiku wo mawasuru
              chikara
Polish
1930   Glos serca
1941   Ten Ostatni
           Wiejskie Wesele
           Z Dymem Pożarów
Portuguese
1930   A canção do berço
Spanish
1928   El Robin Hood de México
1929   Sombras habaneras
1930   Alma de gaucho
           Amor audaz
           Así es la vida
           Las campanas de
              Capistrano
           Una cana al aire

           Cascarrabias
           Charros, gauchos y
              manolas
           El cuerpo del delito
           ¡De frente, marchen!
           Del mismo barro
           El dios del mar
           Doña mentiras
           Estrellados
           La fuerza del querer
           Un hombre de suerte
           El hombre malo
           Locuras de amor
           Los que danzan
           Monsieur le Fox
           Olimpia
           Oriente y Occidente
           El precio de un beso
           El presidio
           El príncipe del dólar
           La rosa de fuego
           El secreto del doctor
           Sevilla de mis amores
           Sombras de gloria
           Toda una vida
           El último de los Vargas
           La voluntad del muerto
           Wu Li Chang
1931   Un caballero de frac
           Los calaveras
           Carne de cabaret
           La carta
           La cautivadora
           Cheri-Bibi
           El código penal
           El comediante
           ¿Conoces a tu mujer?
           Cuerpo y alma
           La dama atrevida
           De bote en bote
           Del infierno al cielo
           Don Juan diplomático
           Drácula
           En cada puerto un amor
           Eran trece
           Esclavas de la moda
           La fiesta del diablo
           La fruta amarga
           Gente alegre
           La gran jornada
           Hay que casar al príncipe
           El impostor
           La incorregible
           La ley del harem
           La llama sagrada
           Lo mejor es reír
           Las luces de Buenos Aires
           Mamá
           Mi último amor
           Monerías
           La mujer X
           Noche de duendes
           El pasado acusa
           Politiquerías
           El príncipe gondolero
           El proceso de Mary
              Dugan
           La pura verdad
           Regeneración
           Resurrección
           ¡Salga de la cocina!
           Sombras del circo
           Su noche de bodas
           Su última noche
           El tenorio del harem

1932   Amor y vida
           El caballero de la noche
           ¿Cuándo te suicidas?
           Hollywood, ciudad de
              ensueño
           El hombre que asesinó
           Hombres en mi vida
           Marido y mujer
           Soñadores de la gloria
1933   Dos noches
           Espérame
           Melodía de arrabal
           La melodía prohibida
           No dejes la puerta abierta
           Primavera en otoño
           El rey de los gitanos
           El último varón sobre la
              Tierra
           Una viuda romántica
           Yo, tú y ella
1934   La buenaventura
           Un capitán de cosacos
           La ciudad de cartón
           La cruz y la espada
           Cuesta abajo
           Dos más uno, dos
           Las fronteras del amor
           Granaderos del amor
           Nada más que una mujer
           El tango en Broadway
           Tres amores
1935   Alas sobre el Chaco
           Angelina o el honor de
              un brigadier
           ¡Asegure a su mujer!
           El cantante de Nápoles
           De la sartén al fuego
           El día que me quieras
           Un hombre peligroso
           Julieta compra un hijo
           No matarás
           Piernas de seda
           Rosa de Francia
           Señora casada necesita
              marido
           Tango Bar
           Te quiero con locura
1936   Amor que vuelve
           Contra la corriente
           El crimen de media
              noche
           El diablo del mar
           La última cita
1937   El capitán Tormenta
           El carnaval del diablo
1938   Castillos en el aire
           Di que me quieres
           Mis dos amores
           La vida bohemia
1939   Los hijos mandan
           La Inmaculada
           El milagro de la Calle
              Mayor
           El otro soy yo
           Papá soltero
           El trovador de la radio
           Verbena trágica
1940   Cuando canta la Ley
           Perfidia
           Tengo fe en ti
1956   Crowded Paradise
Swedish
1930   Hjärtats röst
           När rosorna slå ut
           Vi två

1943   Svenkst I Och Omkring
         New York

Tagalog
1938   Zamboanga

Ukrainian
1937   Natalka Poltavka
1938   Marusia
1939   Cossacks in Exile
1940   The Tragedy of
         Carpatho-Ukraine

Vietnamese
1955?   Yin Hua Chu Chu Kai

Yiddish
1930   Eternal Fools (Ewige
         Naranim)
       My Yiddishe Mama
1931   Shulamith
       The Voice of Israel
       Zein Weib's Lubovnick
1932   A Daughter of Her People
       Joseph in the Land of
         Egypt
       Mazel Tov
       Uncle Moses
       The Unfortunate Bride
       Yiskor
1933   The Eternal Jew
       Live and Laugh
       The Wandering Jew
1934   The Rabbi's Power
       What a Mother-in-Law!
       The Youth of Russia
1935   Bar-Mitzvah
       Shir Hashirim
       The Yiddish King Lear
1936   Love and Sacrifice
       Yiddle with His Fiddle
1937   The Cantor's Son
       Green Fields
       The Holy Oath
       I Want to Be a Mother
       The Jester (Der
         Purimspieler)
       Where Is My Child?
1938   The Power of Life
       The Singing Blacksmith
       Two Sisters
1939   A Brivele der Mamen
       Kol Nidre
       The Light Ahead
       Mamele
       Mirele Efros
       Motel the Operator
       Mothers of Today
       My Son
       Tevya
1940   Americaner Schadchen
       Eli Eli
       The Great Advisor
       Her Second Mother
       The Jewish Melody
       Overture to Glory
1941   Mazel Tov Yidden
1950   Catskill Honeymoon
       God, Man and Devil
       Monticello, Here We
         Come!
1950?   Three Daughters

SELECTED BIBLIOGRAPHY

American Folklore Films and Video Tapes. Compiled by Carolyn Lipson. Memphis: Center for Southern Folklore, 1976.

Bailey, Pearl. *The Raw Pearl*. New York: Harcourt, Brace & World, 1968.

Bataille, Gretchen M., and Charles L. P. Silet. *Images of American Indians on Film: An Annotated Bibliography*. New York: Garland Publishing, Inc., 1985.

Bataille, Gretchen M., and Charles L. P. Silet, ed. *The Pretend Indians: Images of Native Americans in the Movies*. Ames, IA: The Iowa State University Press, 1980.

Bernardi, Daniel, ed. *The Birth of Whiteness: Race and the Emergence of U.S. Cinema*. New Brunswick, NJ: Rutgers University Press, 1996.

Bogle, Donald. *Blacks in American Films and Television*. New York: Simon & Schuster, Inc.; A Fireside Book, 1988.

Bogle, Donald. *Brown Sugar: Eighty Years of America's Black Female Superstars*. New York: Harmony Books, 1980.

Bogle, Donald. *Toms, Coons, Mulattoes, Mammies, and Bucks: An Interpretive History of Blacks in American Films*. New expanded edition. New York: Continuum, A Frederick Ungar Book, 1989.

Brathovde, Jennifer, comp. *American Indians on Film and Video: Documentaries in the Library of Congress*. Washington: Library of Congress, 1992.

Brownlow, Kevin. *Behind the Mask of Innocence*. New York: Alfred A. Knopf, 1990.

Brownlow, Kevin. *The War, the West and the Wilderness*. New York: Alfred A. Knopf, 1979.

Buckley, Gail Lumet. *The Hornes: An American Family*. New York: Alfred A. Knopf, 1986.

Cardenas, Don, and Suzanne Schneider. *Chicano Images in Film*. Denver: Denver International Film Festival in conjunction with the Bilingual Communications Center, 1981.

Carson, Diane, and Lester D. Friedman, ed. *Shared Differences: Multicultural Media and Practical Pedagogy*. Urbana, IL and Chicago: University of Illinois Press, 1995.

Cripps, Thomas. *Black Film As Genre*. Bloomington, IN: Indiana University Press, 1978.

Cripps, Thomas. *Slow Fade to Black: The Negro in American Film, 1900-1942*. New York: Oxford University Press, 1977.

Cripps, Thomas. *Making Movies Black: The Hollywood Message Movie from World War II to the Civil Rights Era*. New York: Oxford University Press, 1993.

Cripps, Thomas, and David Culbert. *"The Negro Soldier" (1944): "Film Propaganda in Black and White." American Quarterly* (Winter 1979): 616-40.

Curran, Joseph M. *Hibernian Green on the Silver Screen: The Irish and American Movies*. Westport, CT: Greenwood Press, 1989.

Dandridge, Dorothy, and Earl Conrad. *Everything and Nothing: The Dorothy Dandridge Tragedy*. New York: Abelard-Schuman, 1970.

Davis, Leonard G. *A Paul Robeson Research Guide: A Selected Annotated Bibliography*. Westport, CT: Greenwood Press, 1982.

Davis, Sammy, Jr., and Jane and Burt Boyar. *Yes, I Can: The Story of Sammy Davis, Jr*. New York: Farrar, Straus and Giroux, 1965.

Desser, David, and Lester D. Friedman. *American-Jewish Filmmakers*. Urbana, IL and Chicago: University of Illinois Press, 1993.

Diawara, Manthia, ed. *Black American Cinema*. AFI Film Readers. New York: Routledge, 1993.

Duberman, Martin B. *Paul Robeson*. New York: Alfred A. Knopf, 1989.

Erens, Patricia. *The Jew in American Cinema*. Bloomington, IN: Indiana University Press, 1984.

Fox, Stuart, comp. *Jewish Films in the United States: A Comprehensive Survey and Descriptive Filmography*. Boston: G. K. Hall Co., 1976.

Friar, Ralph E., and Natasha A. Friar. *The Only Good Indian ... The Hollywood Gospel*. New York: Drama Book Specialists, 1972.

Friedman, Lester D. *Hollywood's Image of the Jew*. New York: Frederick Ungar Publishing Co., 1982.

Friedman, Lester D. *The Jewish Image in American Film*. Secaucus, NJ: Citadel Press, 1987.

Friedman, Lester D., ed. *Unspeakable Images: Ethnicity and the American Cinema*. Urbana, IL and Chicago: University of Illinois Press, 1991.

Gabler, Neal. *An Empire of Their Own: How the Jews Invented Hollywood*. New York: Crown Publishers, Inc., 1988.

Gilliam, Dorothy Butler. *Paul Robeson: All-American*. Washington: New Republic Book Co., Inc., 1976.

Goldberg, Judith N. *Laughter Through Tears: The Yiddish Cinema*. Rutherford, NJ: Fairleigh Dickinson University Press, 1983.

Goldman, Eric A. *Visions, Images and Dreams: Yiddish Film Past and Present*. Ann Arbor, MI: UMI Research Press, 1983.

Gray, John, comp. *Blacks in Film and Television: A Pan-African Bibliography of Film, Filmmakers, and Performers*. Bibliographies and Indexes in Afro-American and African Studies, Number 27. Westport, CT: Greenwood Press, 1990.

Gribben, Arthur, and Marsha Maguire, comp. *The Irish Cultural Directory for Southern California*. Los Angeles, CA: UCLA Folklore and Mythology Publications, 1985.

Grupenhoff, Richard. *The Black Valentino: The Stage and Screen Career of Lorenzo Tucker*. Metuchen, NJ: Scarecrow Press, 1988.

Guerrero, Ed. *Framing Blackness: The African American Image in Film*. Philadelphia: Temple University Press, 1993.

Guide to Films (16mm) about Negroes. Copyright by Daniel Sprecher. Alexandria, VA: Serina Press, 1970.

Ham, Debra Newman, ed. *The African-American Mosaic: A Library of Congress Resource Guide for the Study of Black History and Culture*. Washington: Library of Congress, 1993.

Hanke, Ken. *Charlie Chan at the Movies: History, Filmography, and Criticism*. Jefferson, NC: McFarland & Co., Inc., 1989.

Hayakawa, Sessue. *Zen Showed Me the Way*. Indianapolis: Bobbs-Merrill, 1961.

Heinink, Juan B., and Robert G. Dickson. *Cita en Hollywood: Antologìa de las películas norteamericanas habladas en ñespañol*. Bilbao, Spain: Ediciones Mensajero, 1990.

Hilger, Michael. *The American Indian in Film*. Metuchen, NJ: Scarecrow Press, 1986.

Hoberman, J. *Bridge of Light: Yiddish Film Between Two Worlds*. New York: The Museum of Modern Art; Schocken Books, 1991.

Hughes, Langston, and Milton Meltzer. *Black Magic: A Pictorial History of the Negro in American Entertainment*. Englewood Cliffs, NJ: Prentice-Hall, Inc., 1967.

Jarvie, I. C. *Window on Hong Kong: A Sociological Study of the Hong Kong Film Industry and Its Audience*. [Hong Kong]: Centre of Asian Studies, University of Hong Kong, 1977.

Jerome, V. J. *The Negro in Hollywood Films*. New York: Masses and Mainstream, 1950.

Jewish Film Directory: A Guide to More Than 1200 Films of Jewish Interest from 32 Countries over 85 Years. Westport, CT: Greenwood Press, 1992.

Jones, G. William. *Black Cinema Treasures, Lost and Found*. Denton, TX: University of North Texas Press, 1991.

Keller, Gary D. *Hispanics and United States Film: An Overview and Handbook*. Tempe, AZ: Bilingual Review/Press, 1994.

Keyser, Lester J., and Andre H. Ruszkowski. *The Cinema of Sidney Poitier: The Black Man's Changing Role on the American Screen*. San Diego: A. S. Barnes & Co., Inc., 1980.

Kisch, John, and Edward Mapp. *A Separate Cinema: Fifty Years of Black-Cast Posters*. New York: Farrar, Straus and Giroux, 1992.

Klotman, Phyllis Rauch. *Frame by Frame: A Black Filmography*. Bloomington, IN: Indiana University Press, 1979.

Leab, Daniel J. *From Sambo to Superspade: The Black Experience in Motion Pictures*. Boston: Houghton Mifflin Co., 1975.

Loukides, Paul, and Linda K. Fuller, ed. *Beyond the Stars: Stock Characters in American Popular Film*. Bowling Green, OH: Bowling Green State University Popular Press, 1990.

Lourdeaux, Lee. *Italian and Irish Filmmakers in America: Ford, Capra, Coppola, and Scorsese*. Philadelphia: Temple University Press, 1990.

Lund, Karen C., comp. *American Indians in Silent Film: Motion Pictures in the Library of Congress*. Washington: Library of Congress, 1992.

Mapp, Edward. *Dictionary of Blacks in the Performing Arts*. 2d ed. Metuchen, NJ: Scarecrow Press, 1990.

Marill, Alvin H. *The Films of Sidney Poitier*. Secaucus, NJ: The Citadel Press, 1978.

Martin, Michael T., ed. *Cinemas of the Black Diaspora: Diversity, Dependence, and Oppositionality*. Detroit: Wayne State University Press, 1995.

Meeker, David. *Jazz in the Movies*. New York: Da Capo Press, Inc., 1981.

Miller, Randall M., ed. *The Kaleidoscopic Lens: How Hollywood Views Ethnic Groups*. Englewood, NJ: Jerome S. Ozer, 1980.

Mills, Earl. *Dorothy Dandridge, a Portrait in Black*. Los Angeles: Holloway House Publishing Co., 1970.

Nestby, James R. *Black Images in American Films, 1896-1954: The Interplay Between Civil Rights and Film Culture*. Lanham, MD: University Press of America, 1982.

Noriega, Chon, ed. *Chicanos and Film: Essays on Chicano Representation and Resistance*. New York: Garland Publishing, Inc., 1992.

Null, Gary. *Black Hollywood: The Negro in Motion Pictures*. Secaucus, NJ: The Citadel Press, 1975.

Oshana, Maryann. *Women of Color: A Filmography of Minority and Third World Women*. New York: Garland Publishing, Inc., 1985.

Parish, James Robert. *Black Action Films: Plots, Critiques, Casts and Credits for 235 Theatrical and Made-for-Television Releases*. Jefferson, NC: McFarland & Co., Inc., 1989.

Poitier, Sidney. *This Life*. New York: Alfred A. Knopf, 1980.

Powers, Anne, comp. and ed. *Blacks in American Movies: A Selected Bibliography*. Metuchen, NJ: Scarecrow Press, 1974.

Reyes, Luis, and Peter Rubie. *Hispanics in Hollywood: An Encyclopedia of Film and Television*. New York: Garland Publishing, Inc., 1994.

Reyes, Luis, with contributions by Ed Rampell. *Made in Paradise: Hollywood's Films of Hawai'i and the South Seas*. Honolulu: Mutual Pub., 1995.

Richard, Alfred Charles, Jr. *Censorship and Hollywood's Hispanic Image: An Interpretive Filmography, 1936-1955*. Westport, CT: Greenwood Press, 1993.

Richard, Alfred Charles, Jr. *Contemporary Hollywood's Negative Hispanic Image: An Interpretive Filmography, 1956-1993*. Westport, CT: Greenwood Press, 1994.

Richard, Alfred Charles, Jr. *The Hispanic Image on the Silver Screen: An Interpretive Filmography from Silents into Sound, 1898-1935*. Westport, CT: Greenwood Press, 1992.

Sampson, Henry T. *Blacks in Black and White: A Source Book on Black Films*. Metuchen, NJ: Scarecrow Press, 1977.

Shaw, Arnold. *Belafonte: An Unauthorized Biography*. Philadelphia: Chilton Book Co., 1960.

Silk, Catherine, and John Silk. *Racism and Anti-Racism in American Popular Culture: Portrayals of African-Americans in Fiction and Film*. Manchester: Manchester University Press, 1990.

Stedman, Raymond William. *Shadows of the Indian: Stereotypes in American Culture*. Norman, OK: University of Oklahoma Press, 1982.

Thernstrom, Stephan, ed. *Harvard Encyclopedia of American Ethnic Groups*. Cambridge, MA: The Belknap Press of Harvard University Press, 1980.

Toplin, Robert Brent, ed. *Changing Views of 'Outsiders' and 'Enemies' in American Movies*. Contributions to the Study of Popular Culture, no. 38. Westport, CT: Greenwood Press, 1993.

Van Deburg, William L. *Slavery & Race in American Popular Culture*. Madison, WI: University of Wisconsin Press, 1984.

Waters, Ethel. *To Me It's Wonderful*. New York: Harper & Row, 1972.

Waters, Ethel, with Charles Samuels. *His Eye Is on the Sparrow*. Garden City, NY: Doubleday & Co., 1951.

Weatherford, Elizabeth, ed. *Native Americans on Film and Video*. New York: Museum of the American Indian/Heye Foundation, 1981.

Winquist, Sven G. *Swedish Sound Pictures 1929-1969 and Their Directors*. 2d ed. Stockholm: Swedish Film Institute, 1969.

Woll, Allen L. *The Latin Image in American Film*. Rev. ed. Los Angeles: UCLA Latin American Center Publications, University of California, 1980.

Woll, Allen L., and Randall M. Miller. *Ethnic and Racial Images in American Film and Television: Historical Essays and Bibliography*. New York: Garland Publishing, Inc., 1987.

Wynar, Lubomyr R., and Lois Buttlar. *Ethnic Film and Filmstrip Guide for Libraries and Media Centers: A Selective Filmography*. Littleton, CO: Libraries Unlimited, Inc., 1980.